ENGLISH

prəˈnaʊnt.sɪŋ

PRONOUNCING DICTIONARY

Daniel Jones

15th EDITION

Edited by
Peter Roach & James Hartman

Pronunciation Associate
Jane Setter

CAMBRIDGE
UNIVERSITY PRESS

PUBLISHED BY THE PRESS SYNDICATE OF THE UNIVERSITY OF CAMBRIDGE
The Pitt Building, Trumpington Street, Cambridge CB2 1RP, United Kingdom

CAMBRIDGE UNIVERSITY PRESS
The Edinburgh Buiding, Cambridge CB2 2RU, United Kingdom
40 West 20th Street, New York, NY 10011-4211, USA
10 Stamford Road, Oakleigh, Melbourne 3166, Australia

First published by J. M. Dent & Sons Ltd 1917

First published by Cambridge University Press 1991

Printed in the United Kingdom at the University Press, Cambridge

Typeset in Times Phonetic IPA 7/9 pt

A catalogue record for this book is available from the British Library

Library of Congress Cataloguing in Publication data applied for

ISBN 0 521 45272 4 hardback
ISBN 0 521 45903 6 paperback
ISBN 3 12 539682 4 Klett hardback
ISBN 3 12 539681 6 Klett paperback

Contents

Editors' preface to the 15th Edition

The *English Pronouncing Dictionary* was first published in 1917, perhaps the greatest work of the greatest of British phoneticians, Daniel Jones (born in 1881). Jones was Professor of Phonetics at University College London from 1921 until his retirement in 1949. He was still an occasional visitor to the Department in 1967 when Peter Roach went there as a postgraduate student of phonetics, though he died in December of that year. The dictionary was preceded by a now forgotten work by Michaelis and Jones (1913) in which the phonemic transcription was presented first and the corresponding spelling followed it. The last edition in which Jones was directly involved was the 12th, and the 13th was substantially revised by his successor as Professor of Phonetics at University College, A.C. Gimson. From the 13th edition, Gimson was assisted by Dr. Susan Ramsaran, and in her preface to the 14th edition she notes that they had been making plans for a 15th edition at the time of Gimson's death. After this, the publishing rights were acquired from the original publishers, J. M. Dent & Sons, by Cambridge University Press.

The *English Pronouncing Dictionary* has been in use for nearly 80 years, and during that time it has become established as a classic work of reference, both for native speakers of English wanting an authoritative guide to pronunciation and for users of English as a foreign or second language all over the world. Above all, the aim of the 15th edition has been to include information which is relevant to the needs of contemporary users and which is presented in the clearest possible way. This aim has informed both the choice of vocabulary covered and the range of pronunciations shown.

Over 18,000 new entries have been added to this edition of the dictionary to serve the interests and needs of today's users. For instance, large numbers of new words connected with science and technology are now included, as are hundreds of people and places which have acquired fame or notoriety in recent years. The more cosmopolitan nature of contemporary life is reflected in the increase of geographical names as well as a significant number of items of international cuisine. Personal names, both first names and family names, are now based on census reports and statistical analysis, and many subject areas such as literature and law, have been revised and updated. In addition to this, U.S. spellings and vocabulary items have been added.

With this 15th Edition, the *English Pronouncing Dictionary* has entered the computer age. The typeset text of the 14th Edition has been converted into a computer database, and the task of editing has been carried out by a team of phonetics experts who have worked by transferring the data of the developing new edition in electronic form between universities in Reading, Leeds, Kansas and Hong Kong, and the University Press in Cambridge. Despite the complexity of this operation, the process of updating and adding to the previous edition has been made more efficient, and will enable future revisions and new editions to be prepared much more rapidly. We expect that the dictionary will be useful not only as a conventional reference book but also as a database in computer-based research.

There are many people to whom we are grateful. Two people in particular have been indispensable. Jane Setter (Assistant Professor at Hong Kong Polytechnic University) has worked on the pronunciations since 1992; she has done an enormous amount of work on the transcriptions, combining phonetic expertise with skill in database technology and cheerfully keeping us from drifting into inconsistency. Liz Walter (Commissioning Editor, Cambridge University Press) has overseen the project since its beginning. She has made innumerable contributions to the work, suffered patiently when our work has been delayed, and always been ready to give us guidance. Other people who have worked on the pronunciations are Lee Hornbrook, Jonathan Rodgers, Karen Stromberg and Alison Tunley, while editorial contributions have been made by Ann Kennedy, Kerry Maxwell, Clea McEnery and Jane Walsh. We have often needed assistance with computing matters, and have been glad of the help provided by Simon Arnfield, Andrew Harley, Philip Makower and Robert Fleischman. Finally, we have often sought the advice of other phoneticians when we were in doubt over pronunciations. We would like to thank especially Jack Windsor Lewis, Mike MacMahon, Graham Pointon, Marion Shirt, Michael MT Henderson and Linda Shockey.

PETER ROACH, University of Reading
JAMES HARTMAN, University of Kansas

Introduction

It is strongly recommended that users of this dictionary read the introduction, since a full understanding of the information in it will ensure the most effective use of the dictionary.

(PART 1) **'What is the English Pronouncing Dictionary?'**: The intended use of the dictionary, the principles of its design and the accents of English represented in it.

(PART 2) **'Principles of Transcription'**: The main characteristics of the British and American accents.

(PART 3) **'Explanatory Notes'**: How to interpret the information provided with the individual words in the dictionary.

Part 1: Introduction to the English Pronouncing Dictionary

1.1 What is the English Pronouncing Dictionary?

This dictionary is designed to provide information on the current pronunciation of approximately 80,000 English words and phrases. For each entry, a British and an American pronunciation is shown (see Section 1.2 below). The pronunciation is given in modified phonemic transcription, and you need to understand the principles of phonemic transcription in order to be able to make proper use of this information (see Section 2.1 below).

The Pronouncing Dictionary provides much essential information that is not available in a general dictionary, such as the pronunciation of proper names, the pronunciation of all inflected forms of each word, and a larger amount of detail about variant pronunciations than is usual in a general dictionary.

1.2 Whose pronunciation is represented?

A pronouncing dictionary must base its recommendations on one or more *models.* A pronunciation model is a carefully chosen and defined accent of a language. In the first edition of this dictionary (1917), Daniel Jones described the type of pronunciation recorded as "that most usually heard in everyday speech in the families of Southern English persons whose menfolk have been educated at the great public boarding-schools". Accordingly, he felt able to refer to his model as "Public School Pronunciation" (PSP). In later editions, e.g. that of 1937, he added the remark that boys in boarding-schools tend to lose their markedly local peculiarities, whereas this is not the case for those in day-schools. He had by 1926, however, abandoned the term PSP in favour of "Received Pronunciation" (RP). The type of speech he had in mind had for centuries been regarded as a kind of standard, having its base in the educated pronunciation of London and the Home Counties (the counties surrounding London). Its use was not restricted to this region, however, being characteristic by the nineteenth century of upper-class speech throughout the country. The Editor of the 14th Edition of this dictionary, A. C. Gimson, commented in 1977 "Such a definition of RP is hardly tenable today", and went on "If I have retained the traditional, though imprecise, term 'received pronunciation', it is because the label has such wide currency in books on present-day English and because it is a convenient name for an accent which remains generally acceptable and intelligible within Britain".

For this edition a more broadly-based and accessible model accent for British English is represented, and pronunciations for one broadly-conceived accent of American English have been added. The time has come to abandon the archaic name *Received Pronunciation*. The model used for British English is what is referred to as *BBC English*; this is the pronunciation of professional speakers employed by the BBC as newsreaders and announcers on BBC1 and BBC2 television, the World Service and BBC Radio 3 and 4, as well as many commercial broadcasting organisations such as ITN. Of course, one finds differences between such speakers, but there is still a reasonable consensus on pronunciation in this group of professionals, and their speech does not carry for most people the connotations of high social class and privilege that PSP and RP have had in the past. An additional advantage in concentrating on the accent of broadcasters is that it is easy to gain access to examples, and the sound quality is usually of a very high standard.

For American English, the selection also follows what is frequently heard from professional voices on national network news and information programmes. It is similar to what has been termed "General American", which refers to a geographically (largely non-coastal) and socially based set of pronunciation features. It is important to note that no single dialect – regional or social – has been singled out as an American standard. Even national media (radio, television, movies, CD-ROM, etc.), with professionally trained voices have speakers with regionally mixed features. However, "Network English", in its most colourless form, can be described as a relatively homogeneous dialect that reflects the ongoing development of progressive American dialects (Canadian English has several notable differences). This "dialect" itself contains some variant forms. The variants included within this targeted accent involve vowels before /r/, possible differences in words like 'cot' and 'caught' and some vowels before /l/. It is fully rhotic. These differences largely pass unnoticed by the audiences for Network English, and are also reflective of age differences. What are thought to be the more progressive (used by educated, socially mobile, and younger speakers) variants are listed first in each entry. The intent is to list the variety of pronunciations with the least amount of regional or social marking, while still being sensitive to the traits of the individual word.

1.3 How are the pronunciations chosen?

It is important to remember that the pronunciation of English words is not governed by a strict set of rules; most words have more than one pronunciation, and the speaker's choice of which to use depends on a wide range of factors. These include the degree of formality, the amount of background noise, the speed of utterance, the speaker's perception of the listener and the frequency with which the speaker uses the word. For example, the two words 'virtuous' and 'virtuoso' are closely similar in spelling and share a common origin. However, the former is more common than the latter, and for British English /ˈvɜː.tʃu.əs/ is given as the first pronunciation of the former but /ˈvɜː.tju.əʊ.səʊ/ for the latter (which in general is typical of more careful speech). If such variation did not exist, most of the work of compiling a pronouncing dictionary could be done easily by means of one of the available computer programs that convert English spelling into a phonemic transcription. Ultimately, however, the decisions about which pronunciation to recommend, which pronunciations have dropped out of use, and so on, have been based on the editors' intuitions as professional phoneticians and observers of the pronunciation of English (particularly broadcast English) over many years. The opinion of many colleagues and acquaintances has also been a valuable source of advice.

In general, a pronunciation typical of a more casual, informal style of speaking is given for common words, and a more careful pronunciation for uncommon words. In real life, speakers tend to articulate most carefully when listeners are likely to have difficulty in recognising the words they hear. When more than one pronunciation of a word is given, the order of the alternatives is important. The first pronunciation given is believed to be the most usual one although the distance between the alternatives may vary, with some alternant forms rivalling the first-given in perceived frequency while others may be a more distant second.

1.4 Regional Accents

A pronouncing dictionary that systematically presented the pronunciations of a range of regional accents would be very valuable, but it would be very much bigger than the present volume and the job of ensuring an adequate coverage which treated all accents as equally important would have taken many years. In the case of place-names, information about local pronunciations has been retained or added as well as "official" broadcasting ones, but the other words are given only in the standard accents chosen for British and American English.

1.5 Pronunciation of foreign words

Many of the words in an English dictionary are of foreign origin, and in previous editions of this dictionary many such words have been given both in an Anglicised pronunciation used by most English speakers, and in a broad phonetic transcription of the "authentic" pronunciation in the original language. This edition does not give phonetic transcriptions of all the foreign words; the primary aim of this dictionary is to list pronunciations likely to be used by educated speakers of English, and an authentic pronunciation would in some circumstances be quite inappropriate (pronouncing 'Paris' as /pæˈriː/, for example). In some cases the information is unnecessary (very few English speakers would attempt, or even recognise, an authentic pronunciation of a word from a non-European language), while in other cases it is difficult to establish the authentic original (many African place-names, for example, have reached us after being adapted by British, French or Portuguese colonists; place-names in Spain may be pronounced in different ways according to their regional affiliation, so that the name of Barcelona might be given a Catalan or a Castilian Spanish pronunciation, while other Spanish names are different according to whether they originate in

Spain or South America). Words and names of foreign origin are therefore given in what is felt to be the pronunciation most likely to be used among educated speakers of English.

In some cases it is possible to identify an alternative pronunciation which represents an attempt to pronounce in a manner closer to the supposed original. This is marked by first indicating the language which the speaker would be aiming at, then giving the pronunciation, using where necessary additional phonetic symbols not required for the phonemic transcription of English. For example, the word 'bolognese' is widely used to refer to a sauce served with pasta. This is given as /ˌbɒl.əˈneɪz/ for British English and as /ˌboʊ.ləˈniːz/ for American; for speakers of both groups, a pronunciation aimed at being nearer to the Italian original would be /ˌbɒl.əˈnjeɪ.zeɪ/ (though this would still be different from the pronunciation that would be produced by an Italian speaker). To indicate that this last pronunciation is aimed at sounding Italian, it is marked in the entry as: *as if Italian:* ˌbɒl.əˈnjeɪ.zeɪ. In a few cases it has been necessary to mark separate British and American pronunciations within this field, as the degree of Anglicisation of any given word may vary between British and American English.

1.6 Usage notes

Usage notes are included with some words. In some cases these are needed so that users of the dictionary can understand how alternative pronunciations are to be used. In some cases the rules needed for correct pronunciation are quite complex, most noticeably in the case of the so-called "weak-form words" such as 'there', 'her'. Explanations with examples are given in such cases.

1.7 Syllable divisions

Earlier editions of this dictionary regularly marked the division between syllables. This practice was largely abandoned in the 14th Edition, but this new edition gives syllable divisions in all cases, since it is felt that foreign learners will find the information useful. Syllable division is marked with the symbol . recommended by the International Phonetic Association. The decision on where to place a syllable division is not always easy, and the rules used in this work are explained later in this Introduction (Section 2.6).

Part 2: Principles of transcription

2.1 The phoneme principle

The basic principle of the transcription used is, as in all previous editions, *phonemic*. This means that a small set of symbols is used to represent the sounds that can be shown to be distinctive in English, so that replacing one phoneme by another can change the identity of a word. We do not usually add phonetic detail such as the presence of glottal stops, aspiration or vowel devoicing. It is usual to put slant brackets before and after symbols representing phonemes (e.g. the word 'cat' would be represented phonemically as /kæt/). When non-phonemic symbols are used, the convention is to use square brackets (e.g. the glottal stop will be represented as [ʔ]). In entries in the dictionary itself, however, we do not use these brackets, in order to keep the information simple; only in explanatory notes do we use slant or square brackets. For an explanation of the principle of the phoneme and some of the problems associated with it, see Roach (1991), Chapters 5 and 13. The use of phonemic transcription in works on pronunciation (including this one) has remained in the "realist" tradition established by Jones, while approaches to the phoneme by theoretical phonologists have changed radically during recent decades and become much more abstract. There are a few exceptions to our general use of the phoneme principle that should be mentioned here, however. One is the use, in American pronunciations, of the [ˬ] diacritic to indicate the "flapping" of /t/ in words such as 'getting' /ˈget̬.ɪŋ/, and 'better' /ˈbet̬.ɚ/. This is an important feature of American pronunciation, but speakers of British English find it difficult to apply the rule which determines when phonemes are flapped. Another is the use of the symbols [i] and [u], the use of which is explained below (Section 2.9). Finally, it is necessary to use a number of special symbols which are not normally used for English phonemes. This set includes some nasalised vowels used particularly in some words taken from French, the [x] sound found in Scottish words such as 'loch', and some non-linguistic sounds used in certain exclamations and interjections (see Section 2.4).

2.2 Vowels and diphthongs

It is standard practice in phonetics to represent the quality of vowels and diphthongs by placing them on a four-sided figure usually known as the *Cardinal Vowel quadrilateral* (see Roach (1991), pp 11-14). This device is used in the vowel descriptions in the following section.

(a) British English

British English (BBC accent) is generally described as having short vowels, long vowels and diphthongs. There are said to be seven short vowels, five long ones and eight diphthongs. At the end of this section some attention is also given to triphthongs.

- Short vowels:

p**i**t	p**e**t	p**a**t	p**u**tt	p**o**t	p**u**t	**a**noth**er**
ɪ	e	æ	ʌ	ɒ	ʊ	ə ə

- Long vowels:

b**ea**n	b**ar**n	b**or**n	b**oo**n	b**ur**n
iː	ɑː	ɔː	uː	ɜː

- Diphthongs:

b**ay**	b**uy**	b**oy**	n**o**	n**ow**	p**eer**	p**air**	p**oor**
eɪ	aɪ	ɔɪ	əʊ	aʊ	ɪə	eə	ʊə

These vowels and diphthongs may be placed on the Cardinal Vowel quadrilateral as shown in Figs. 1 -3. It should be noted that though each vowel (or diphthong starting-point) is marked with a point (●), it is misleading to think of this as a precise target; the point represents the centre of an area within which the typical vowel pronunciation falls.

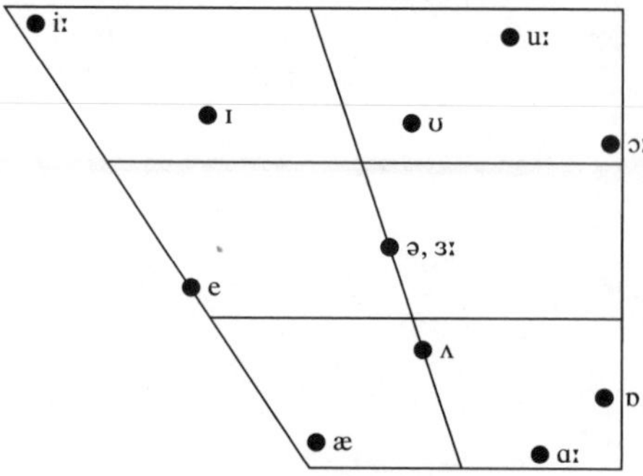

Fig. 1 BBC English pure vowels

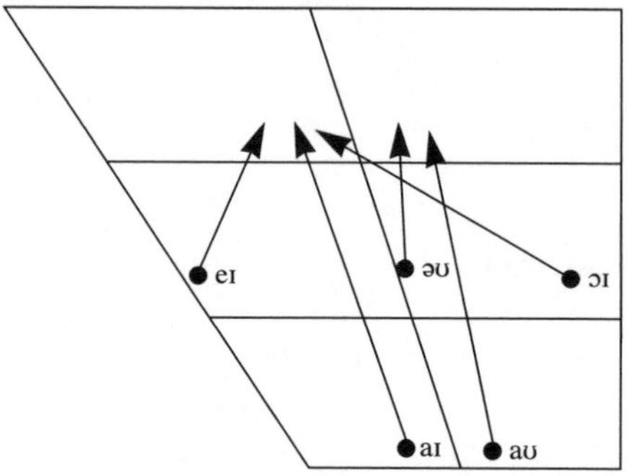

Fig. 2 BBC English closing diphthongs

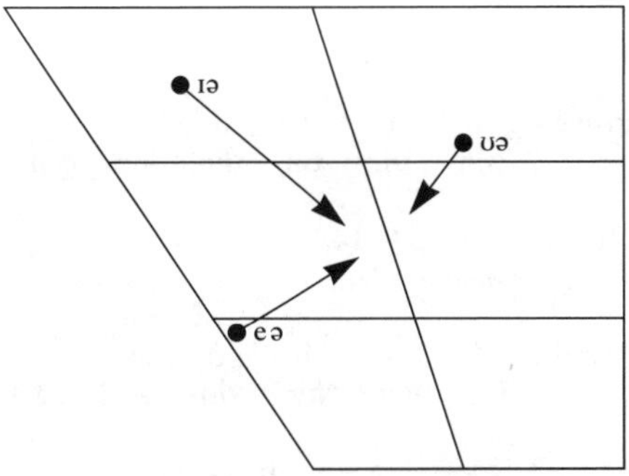

Fig. 3 BBC English centring diphthongs

A few comments on individual vowels and vowel symbols are needed. The pronunciation of any language is constantly changing, and a dictionary such as this one should reflect such changes. However, there is a general reluctance among users of phonemic transcription to change the symbols used too frequently, as this causes existing teaching materials and textbooks to become out of date. The following remarks apply chiefly to BBC pronunciation.

(a) The length of long vowels and diphthongs is very much reduced when they occur in syllables closed by the consonants / p, t, k, tʃ, f, θ, s, ʃ /. Thus /iː/ in 'beat' has only about half the length of /iː/ in 'bead' or 'bee'; similarly /eɪ/ in 'place' is much reduced in length compared with /eɪ/ in 'plays' or 'play'.

(b) The vowel /æ/, classified as a short vowel, is nevertheless generally lengthened before /b, d, g, dʒ, m , n/. Thus /æ/ in 'bag' is considerably longer than /æ/ in 'back'. The quality of this vowel is now more open than it used to be, and the symbol /a/ might one day be considered preferable. We have retained the /æ/ symbol partly because it is phonetically appropriate for the corresponding American vowel.

(c) The vowel /ʌ/ used to be a back vowel, and the symbol was chosen for this reason. This is no longer a back vowel, but a central one. Alternative symbols could be considered in the future.

(d) Among younger speakers, the /uː/ vowel has moved to a more front quality, with less lip-rounding, particularly when preceded by /j/ as in 'use'.

(e) Among the diphthongs, there seems to be a progressive decline in the use of /ʊə/, with /ɔː/ taking its place (e.g. the pronunciation of the word 'poor' as /pɔː/ is increasingly common).

(f) Triphthongs create some problems. These three-vowel sequences are generally held to be composed of one of the diphthongs /eɪ, aɪ, ɔɪ, əʊ, aʊ/ plus a schwa (e.g. 'layer' /leɪəʳ/; 'fire' /faɪəʳ/). In British English many of these triphthongs are pronounced with such slight movement in vowel quality that it is difficult for foreign learners to recognise them; for example, the name 'Ireland', which is generally transcribed /ˈaɪə.lənd/, frequently has an initial syllable which sounds virtually indistinguishable from /ɑː/. It seems reasonable in this case to treat these sounds as being monosyllabic (e.g. the word 'fire' is a single syllable), but in other words and names transcribed with the same symbols it seems necessary to insert a syllable division. This is usually done (i) when there is a morpheme boundary (e.g. 'buyer' /baɪ.əʳ/) and (ii) when the word is felt to be foreign (this includes many Biblical names originating from Hebrew, e.g. 'Messiah').

Another problem with triphthongs is that before an /r/ consonant at the beginning of a following syllable, the distinction between /aɪə/ and /aɪ/ seems to be neutralised – it seems to make no difference whether one represents 'Irish', 'irate' as /ˈaɪə.rɪʃ/, /aɪəˈreɪt/ or as /ˈaɪ.rɪʃ/ , /aɪˈreɪt/, since there is no regular distinction made in pronunciation. In general, the practice of this edition is to transcribe such cases as /aɪə- /.

(b) American English

American English is commonly described as having lax vowels, tense vowels, and wide diphthongs. Generally speaking, lax vowels are lower and made with less oral tension; they do not usually end syllables. Vowel length in American English is generally considered to be conditioned by phonological environment, so the long/short distinction described for BBC English is not usually present, though we have retained the length mark on the tense vowels /iː, ɑː, ɔː, ɜː/ in order to mark their relationship to the English long vowels. Since the diphthongal movement in /eɪ/ and /oʊ/ is small in American pronunciation, these are treated as tense vowels. Vowels preceding /r/ are notably influenced by rhotic colouring. Word spellings such as 'bird', 'word', 'curd', 'earth', 'jerk', which now rhyme with /ɜːr/ in American English, at one time in history had differing vowels. The retroflexed vowels /ɜːr/ and /ɚ/, stressed and unstressed, are among those features that noticeably distinguish

American English from BBC English. All vowels occurring before /r/ within a syllable are likely to become "r-coloured" to some extent.

- lax vowels: ɪ e æ ʊ ə
- tense vowels: iː ɑː ɔː ɜː eɪ oʊ
- wide diphthongs: aʊ aɪ ɔɪ
- retroflexed vowels ("r-coloured") ɚ ɜːr

There is an issue in the symbolization of the diphthong in the word "home". This has for many years been represented as /əʊ/, but in earlier editions of this and others of Jones' works the symbolization /ou/ indicated a rounded initial vowel. This is still the preferred transcription for the American English diphthong. In order to preserve compatibility with other works, we have chosen to use /əʊ/ for BBC English and /oʊ/ for American, though it can be argued that the latter symbolization would be suitable for both.

The American /æ/ vowel is somewhat closer than BBC /æ/, and seems to be evolving into an even closer vowel in many speakers. It is used in the same words as BBC /æ/ and also in most of the words which in BBC have /ɑː/ when there is no letter r in the spelling, e.g. 'pass', 'ask'. The quality of American /ɑː/ is similar to the BBC /ɑː/ vowel; it is used in some of the words which have /ɑː/ in BBC when there is no letter r in the spelling (e.g. 'father', 'calm'). It also replaces the BBC short /ɒ/ vowel in many words (e.g. 'hot', 'top', 'bother'): 'bother' rhymes with 'father'. American /ɔː/ is more open in quality than BBC /ɔː/. It is used where BBC has /ɔː/ (e.g. 'cause', 'walk'), and also replaces BBC short /ɒ/ in many words, e.g. 'long', 'dog'. American /uː/ is similar to BBC /uː/, but is also used where BBC has /juː/ after alveolar consonants (e.g. 'new', 'duty').

2.3 Consonants

(a) British English (BBC)

- Plosives: p b t d k g
  pin **b**in **t**in **d**in **k**in **g**um
- Affricates: tʃ dʒ
  chain **J**ane
- Fricatives: f v θ ð s z
  fine **v**ine **th**ink **th**is **s**eal **z**eal
  ʃ ʒ h
  sheep mea**s**ure **h**ow
- Nasals: m n ŋ
  su**m** su**n** su**ng**
- Approximants: l r w j
  light **r**ight **w**et **y**et

These consonants can be arranged in table form as shown below. The layout of the symbols follows the principle that, where there are two consonants which differ only in voicing, they are placed side by side with the voiceless one to the left.

(a) Certain types of consonant have a distinction such as that between /t/ and /d/; this is commonly classed as a distinction between voiceless and voiced consonants, but the distinction is in fact much more complex. Consonants usually classed as voiceless are /p, t, k, f, θ, s, ʃ, h, tʃ/, with voiced partners /b, d, g, v, ð, z, ʒ, dʒ/. Since the presence or absence of voicing is often less important than some other phonetic features, it has been suggested that instead the terms *fortis* (equivalent to voiceless) and *lenis* (equivalent to voiced) should be used. These terms imply that the main distinguishing factor is the amount of energy used in the articulation (fortis consonants being made with greater energy than lenis). These terms

Table of English Consonants

	Bilabial	*Labio-dental*	*Dental*	*Alveolar*	*Post-alveolar*	*Palatal*	*Velar*	*Glottal*
Plosive	p b			t d			k g	
Affricate					tʃ dʒ			
Fricative		f v	θ ð	s z	ʃ ʒ		(x)	h
Nasal	m			n			ŋ	
Lateral				l				
Approximant	w				r	j		

are not used in this dictionary, since the usefulness of this terminology is uncertain. Some of the characteristics of the two types of consonant are set out below.

(b) /p,t,k/ are typically accompanied by aspiration (i.e. an interval of breath before the following vowel onset), especially when initial in a stressed syllable. Thus, 'pin' is distinguished from 'bin' very largely by the aspiration accompanying /p/. However, in the syllable-initial sequences /sp-, st-, sk- /, /p, t, k/ lack such aspiration. When /l/ or /r/ immediately follow /p,t,k/, they are devoiced and are pronounced as fricatives. Another characteristic of /p,t,k/ that is not marked in transcriptions is glottalization; when one of these consonants is followed by another consonant it is now usual to find that a glottal closure precedes the /p/, /t/ or /k/, particularly if the syllable in which they occur is stressed. Thus the pronunciation of 'captain', 'rightful', 'Yorkshire', which are phonemically /ˈkæp.tɪn/, /ˈraɪt.fᵊl/, /ˈjɔːk.ʃəʳ/, could be shown (using the symbol [ʔ] for glottal closure) as [ˈkæʔp.tɪn], [ˈraɪʔt.fl̩], [ˈjɔːʔk.ʃəʳ]. Similarly, in American English 'mountain' has one pronunciation that could be represented as [maʊ̃.ʔn̩].

(c) Voiceless consonants have a shortening effect on sounds preceding them within a syllable. Thus in the words 'right' and 'ride' (/raɪt/ and /raɪd/) the diphthong is noticeably shorter in the first word than in the second; in the words 'bent' and 'bend' (/bent/ and /bend/), both the vowel /e/ and the nasal consonant /n/ are shorter in the first word. This length difference is not always easy to observe in connected speech.

(d) The consonant /l/ has two different allophones in BBC English, the so-called "clear" and "dark" allophones. The "clear" one (which has an /iː/-like quality) occurs before vowels, the "dark" one (which has an /uː/-like quality) before consonants or before a pause.

(e) The consonants /ʃ/, /ʒ/, /tʃ/, dʒ/, /r/ are usually accompanied by lip-rounding.

(b) American English

The consonants of the American English model, at the phonemic level, may be represented by the same broad scheme used for British English above. Similarly, many of the distinguishing phonetic traits discussed for British English hold for American English as well: initial /p,t,k/ are normally aspirated except when immediately preceded by /s/. Glottalization preceding and, at times, replacing the plosives occurs often in rapid speech. There are, of course, numerous phonetic and phonological differences between British and American English, as there are within regional and social varieties within the two political entities. Two differences receive sufficient attention and have attained sufficient generality within the two varieties that they are represented here. One is phonetic: the "flapped" medial /t/ (as in 'butter') is transcribed as /t̬/ (see Section 2.1 above); the other is phonological: the presence (in American English) of postvocalic /r/ (as in 'farmer' /ˈfɑːr.mɚ/). It should also be noted that the difference between "clear" and "dark" /l/ is much less marked in American than in the BBC accent, so that even prevocalic /l/ in American pronunciation sounds dark to English ears.

2.4 Non-English sounds

In addition to the phonemes of English described above, most English speakers are aware of, and often attempt to pronounce, some sounds of languages other than English. The number of such sounds is small, since most foreign words and names are Anglicised so that they are pronounced with English phonemes. We find the voiceless velar fricative [x] in the Gaelic languages of Scotland and Ireland in words such as 'loch' and names such as 'Strachan'. The same sound is often used by English speakers for the German sound which is written 'ch' (e.g. 'Bach' [bɑːx]) and the Spanish sound spelt 'j' (e.g. 'Badajoz' [ˌbæd.əˈxɒθ]), though these sounds are often not really velar fricatives. The voiceless lateral fricative [ɬ] is found (always represented in spelling with 'll') in Welsh words and names such as 'Llanberis'; we give the pronunciation of this sound as *h*l to indicate that it may be pronounced as a voiceless [ɬ] (as many British English speakers do), but alternatively as a voiced one: thus /*h*lænˈber.ɪs/. The dictionary lists a few names with more than one of these sounds (e.g. Llanelli). Most non-Welsh speakers are unlikely to pronounce more than one [ɬ] sound in a word, so we give the pronunciation as /θl/ for 'll' sounds after the initial one.

The other case which needs special attention is the pronunciation of French nasalised vowels. Many English speakers attempt to produce something similar to the French vowels /ɛ̃/, /ɑ̃/, /ɔ̃/, /œ̃/ in words such as '**vin** rouge', 'restaur**ant**', ' **bon** marché', 'Verd**un**'.

Although many speakers do not get close to the French vowels, the principle adopted here is to use symbols for English vowels, with added nasalisation. The equivalents are:

French	*English*
ɛ̃	æ̃
ɑ̃	ɑ̃ː
ɔ̃	ɔ̃ː
œ̃	ɜ̃ː

2.5 Stress

Stress patterns present one of the most difficult problems in a pronouncing dictionary. One reason for this is that many polysyllabic words have more than one possible stress pattern, and one must consider carefully which should be recommended. Secondly, the stress of many words changes in different contexts, and it is necessary to indicate how this happens. Thirdly, there is no straightforward way to decide on how many different levels of stress are recognisable.

(a) Where more than one stress pattern is possible, the preferred pronunciation is given first and then alternatives are listed. Many dictionaries use the convention of representing stress patterns using dashes to represent syllables: thus the two possible patterns for 'cigarette' (ˌciga'rette and 'cigarette) can be shown as ˌ--'- and '---. This convention, which is sometimes referred to (incorrectly) as "Morse Code", is used in this work for short words, since it is economical on space. However, in longer words users are likely to find it difficult to interpret. In the planning of this edition, an experiment was carried out to test this, and it was found that readers (both native speakers and non-native speakers of English) do indeed take less time to read word stress patterns when the whole word is given, rather than just a "dashes and dots" pattern (Stromberg and Roach, 1993). Consequently, words of more than three syllables are given in full when alternative stress patterns are being given.

(b) The most common case of variable stress placement caused by context is what is usually nowadays known as "stress-shift". As a general rule, when a word of several syllables has a stress near the end of the word, and is followed by another word with stress near its beginning, there is a tendency for the stress in the first word to move nearer the beginning if it contains a syllable that is capable of receiving stress. For example, the word 'academic' in isolation usually has the stress on the penultimate syllable /-dem-/. However, when the word 'year' follows, the stress is often found to move to the first syllable /æk-/. The whole phrase 'academic year' will have its primary stress on the word 'year', so the resulting stress pattern will be ˌacademic 'year (where ˌ represents secondary stress and ' represents primary stress). To make this process easier to understand, this dictionary now gives specific examples in each case where stress-shift is possible except where certain prefixes such as 'un-' produce hundreds of such cases. In general, this shift is not obligatory: it would not be a mispronunciation to say acaˌdemic 'year. However, it is undoubtedly widespread and in some cases is used almost without exception: for example, although the adjective 'compact' on its own is pronounced with the stress pattern -'- , in the phrase 'compact disc' it is virtually always pronounced with stress on the first syllable.

(c) It is necessary to decide how many levels of stress to mark. The minimum possible range is two: stressed and unstressed. This is inadequate for representing English words in a pronouncing dictionary: a word such as 'controversial' clearly has stress(es) on the first and third syllables, and equally clearly has stronger stress on the third syllable than on the first. It is therefore necessary to recognise an intermediate level of stress ("secondary"). The transcription of this word, therefore, is /ˌkɒn.trə'vɜː.ʃəl/. An argument can be made for recognising yet another level (tertiary stress): in a word such as 'indivisibility', for example, it can be claimed that the level of stress on the third syllable /vɪz/ is weaker than that on the first syllable /ɪn/, which has secondary stress (primary stress being placed on the penultimate syllable /bɪl/). However, introducing this extra level creates a degree of complexity that it is better to avoid. In EPD14 some long polysyllabic words were transcribed with two primary stress marks (e.g. 'cross-examination' was given as /'krɒsɪɡˌzæmɪ'neɪʃn/): for the present edition only one primary stress may occur in a word or compound.

(d) Secondary stresses have only limited occurrence after a primary stress: such a secondary stress is only marked in closed or hyphenated compound words where the second element is polysyllabic (e.g. **'fishˌmonger**).

(e) Stress assignment on prefixes:

(i) In words containing a prefix such as, for example, **con-**, **de-**, **im-**, **in-**, secondary stress is not applied to the prefix where the following (i.e., second) syllable is stressed. Examples include 'intoxicate' /ɪn'tɒk.sɪ.keɪt (US) -'tɑːk-/.

(ii) Where the prefix is separable, however, as in **impossible**, a variant showing secondary stress on the prefix is listed, as follows: /ɪm'pɒs.ə.bl̩ ,ˌɪm -/.

(iii) In all other cases, primary or secondary stress is applied to the prefix where appropriate.

2.6 Syllable divisions

The 14th Edition of EPD marked syllable division (using hyphens) only when it was important to distinguish between the affricate /tʃ/ and the phonemes /t/ and /ʃ/ at a syllable juncture (e.g. 'satchel' /'sætʃəl/ and 'nutshell' /'nʌt-ʃel/). However, although native speakers may well find no difficulty in dividing words into syllables, it seems that learners of English have trouble in doing so, and the divisions are therefore marked. Descriptions of stress and rhythm are usually expressed in terms of syllables, and so it is helpful to have polysyllabic words clearly broken up into their constituent syllables. The syllabified transcription of a polysyllabic word is easier to read and interpret than an undivided one. In addition, the dictionary is likely to be of interest to the field of speech and language technology, where syllable divisions can be useful in developing automatic speech and language analysis systems.

A dot . is used to divide syllables, in accordance with the current recommendations of the International Phonetic Association (these may be read in the *Journal of the International Phonetic Association*, Vol.19.2, (1989), pp.67-80, and in the forthcoming *IPA Handbook*). However, this is not used where a stress mark ' or ˌ occurs, as these are effectively also syllable division markers.

No completely satisfactory scheme of syllable division can be produced – all sets of rules will throw up some cases which cannot be dealt with properly. The principles used in this edition are set out below. This requires some discussion of *phonotactics*, the study of permissible phoneme sequences.

(a) As far as possible, syllables should not be divided in a way that violates what is known of English syllable structure. The 'Maximal Onsets Principle', which is widely recognised in contemporary phonology, is followed as far as possible. This means that, where possible, syllables should be divided in such a way that as many consonants as possible are assigned to the beginning of the syllable to the right (if one thinks in terms of how they are written in transcription), rather than to the end of the syllable to the left. However, when this would result in a syllable ending with a stressed /ɪ/, /e/, /æ/, /ʌ/, /ɒ/ or /ʊ/, it is considered that this would constitute a violation of English phonotactics, and the first (or only) intervocalic consonant is assigned to the preceding syllable; thus the word 'better' is divided /'bet.əʳ/, whereas 'beater' is divided /'biː.təʳ/. In the case of unstressed short vowels, /e/, /æ/, /ʌ/ and /ɒ/ are also prevented from appearing in syllable-final position; however, unstressed /ɪ/ and /ʊ/ are allowed the same "privilege of occurrence" as /ə/ when a consonant begins a following syllable, and may therefore occur in final position in unstressed syllables except pre-pausally. Thus in a word such as 'develop', the syllable division is /dɪ'vel.əp/.

(b) Notwithstanding the above, words in compounds should not be re-divided syllabically in a way that does not agree with perceived word boundaries. For example, 'hardware' could in theory be divided /'hɑː.dweəʳ/, but most readers would find this counter-intuitive and would prefer /'hɑːd.weəʳ/. This principle applies to open, closed and hyphenated compounds.

2.7 Assimilation

Assimilation is a process found in all languages which causes speech sounds to be modified in a way which makes them more similar to their neighbours. A well-known example is that of English alveolar consonants such as /t , d , n/, which, when they are followed by a consonant which does not have alveolar place of articulation, tend to adopt the place of articulation of the following consonant. Thus the /t/ at the end of 'foot' /fʊt/ changes to /p/ when followed by /b/ in the word 'football', giving the pronunciation /'fʊp.bɔːl/. A similar case is the assimilation of /s/ to a following /ʃ/ or /j/, resulting in the pronunciation of 'this ship' as /ðɪʃ'ʃɪp/ and 'this year' as /ðɪʃ'jɪəʳ/. This assimilation can be considered to be optional.

The assimilation of /n/ is a rather special case: many English words begin with the prefixes 'in-' and 'un-', and in a number of cases the /n/ of these prefixes is followed by a consonant which is not alveolar. In some cases it seems to be normal that the /n/ is regularly assimilated to the place of articulation of the following consonant (e.g. 'inquest' /ˈɪŋ.kwest/), while in others this assimilation is optional (e.g. 'incautious' may be /ɪnˈkɔː.ʃəs/ or /ɪŋˈkɔː.ʃəs/). Where it is clear that the prefix is attached to a word that exists independently, so that prefix and stem are easily separable, the assimilation is normally treated as optional. When it seems more like an integral part of the word, the assimilation is shown as obligatory. The occurrence of assimilation in British and American English may differ.

2.8 Treatment of /r/

The accent used for British English is classed as *non-rhotic* – the phoneme /r/ is not usually pronounced except when a vowel follows it. The American pronunciations, on the other hand, do show a rhotic accent, and in general in the accent described, /r/ is pronounced where the letter r is found in the spelling.

It is necessary to show, in British English entries, cases of *potential* pronunciation of /r/, mainly in word-final position; in other words, it is necessary to indicate, in a word such as 'car', that though the word when said in isolation does not have /r/ in the pronunciation (/kɑː/), there is a *potential* /r/ which is realised if a vowel follows (e.g. in 'car owner'). This is indicated by giving the transcription as /kɑː^{r}/, where the superscript /^{r}/ indicates the potential for pronunciation. This is traditionally known as 'linking r'. A controversial question is that of so-called 'intrusive r', where the phoneme /r/ is pronounced when no 'r' is seen in the spelling. For example, the phrase 'china and glass' will often be pronounced with /r/ at the end of the word 'china'; although this type of pronunciation is widespread in the speech of native speakers of the accent described, it is still safer not to recommend it to foreign learners, and it is therefore avoided in this dictionary.

2.9 Use of /i/ and /u/

There are many places in present-day British and American English where the distinction between /ɪ/ and /iː/ is neutralised. For example, the final vowel of 'city' and 'seedy' seems to belong neither to the /ɪ/ phoneme nor to /iː/. The symbol /i/ is used in this case (though it is not, strictly speaking, a phoneme symbol; there is no obvious way to choose suitable brackets for this symbol, but phoneme brackets // will be used for simplicity). A parallel argument can be made for the distinction between /ʊ/ and /uː/ (with a corresponding 'neutralised' symbol /u/), though this is needed much less frequently. This issue, and the issues which follow, are discussed in detail in Roach (1991), pp. 77-78.

(a) In word-final position, /ɪ/ and /ʊ/ do not occur. Word-final, close vowels are transcribed with /i/ and /u/ if unstressed. Word-final /iː/ and /uː/ are possible both with stress ('grandee', 'bamboo') and without ('Hindi', 'argue'), although in the unstressed case it is often not possible to draw a clear line between /iː/ and /i/ , or between /uː/ and /u/.

(b) In compounds such as 'busybody' and names such as 'Merryweather', /i/ is permitted to occur word-medially, e.g. 'busybody' is transcribed /ˈbɪz.iˌbɒd.i ⓤⓢ ˈbɪz.i.bɑː.di/) and 'Merry-weather' as /ˈmer.iˌweð.ə^{r} ⓤⓢ ˈmer.i.weð.ɚ/ . In all other cases word-medially, /ɪ/ is used when the vowel is unstressed, unless a vowel follows (see below).

(c) The vowel symbols /ɪ/ and /ʊ/ only occur in front of another vowel symbol if they form part of a composite (diphthong or triphthong) phoneme symbol (e.g. /ɪə, ʊə/). Otherwise /i/ or /u/ is used (e.g. 'scurrying' /ˈskʌr.i.ɪŋ/, 'influenza' /ˌɪn.fluˈen.zə/.

(d) A matter related to this decision concerns words ending in '-ier', '-eer', '-ia'. The usual transcription in the 14th Edition of the EPD was /ɪə/. However, 'reindeer' and 'windier' (comparative form of 'windy') do not have identical pronunciations in their final syllables in British English (BBC). In this edition, the alternative /-jə/ previously given for the latter type of word has been dropped; 'reindeer' is transcribed as /ˈreɪn.dɪə^{r}/ and 'windier' as /ˈwɪn.di.ə^{r}/. The latter transcription, which indicates a different (closer) vowel quality in the second syllable of 'windier', and implies a pronunciation with three rather than two syllables, is felt to be accurate in terms of contemporary pronunciation.

The long vowels /iː/ and /uː/ may also occur before other vowels, but only when in a stressed syllable (e.g. 'skiing' /ˈskiː.ɪŋ/, 'canoeing' /kəˈnuː.ɪŋ/).

2.10 Syllabic consonants

Syllabic consonants are frequently found in English pronunciation: these are cases where instead of an expected vowel-plus-consonant sequence, the consonant alone (usually one of /m, n, ŋ, l, r/) is pronounced with the rhythmical value of a syllable. (See Roach, 1991, pp.78-82). In EPD14, syllabic consonants were only marked where there is ambiguity in the pronunciation of a word; for example, in a word such as 'bottle', the transcription /ˈbɒtl/ is said to imply unambiguously that the /l/ is syllabic, whereas in the derived form 'bottling' there may be two pronunciations, one with and one without a syllabic /l/. In this instance the EPD14 preferred pronunciation was /ˈbɒtl̩ɪŋ/, with /ˈbɒtlɪŋ/ given as an alternative.

(a) The main problem here is how to deal with optional and obligatory syllabicity and the permissibility of vowels. The most frequently found case is where an item may have (i) a schwa vowel followed by a non-syllabic consonant, (ii) a syllabic consonant not preceded by schwa or (iii) a non-syllabic consonant not preceded by schwa. For example, 'lightening' may be (i) /ˈlaɪ.tə.nɪŋ/, (ii) /ˈlaɪt.n̩.ɪŋ/ or (iii) /ˈlaɪt.nɪŋ/. Such items are transcribed as /ˈlaɪ.tᵊn.ɪŋ/ and /ˈlaɪt.nɪŋ/, the first representing cases (i) and (ii), in which there are three syllables, and the second representing only the disyllabic pronunciation, (iii). The use of superscript schwa in words such as /ˈlaɪ.tᵊn.ɪŋ/ should be interpreted as meaning that the schwa may be pronounced, or may be omitted while giving its syllabic character to the following consonant.

(b) The problem remaining is that of /l/ corresponding to the '-le' spelling form, preceded by any plosive or homorganic fricative, as in 'bottle', 'wrestle'. It is not felt to be acceptable in BBC pronunciation to pronounce this with a vowel in the second syllable, and therefore the superscript schwa convention is not used in such cases: rather, the /l/ is marked as syllabic, i.e. /l̩/. The entry for 'bottle' is /ˈbɒt.l̩/, and for 'cycle', /ˈsaɪ.kl̩/.

(c) Where a word such as the above carries a suffix with an initial vowel, as in 'bottling', 'cycling', speakers' intuitions about the number of syllables are very divergent, so no single recommendation will be adequate. The entry for 'bottle' gives the syllabic /l̩/ (three-syllable) version of 'bottling' as the first recommendation, and it is therefore necessary to add for the -ing form the two-syllable alternative /ˈbɒt.lɪŋ/.

(d) Syllabic nasals are not usual where they would result in a nasal-plosive-syllabic consonant sequence (e.g. 'London', 'abandon' must contain a schwa vowel in the final syllable).

2.11 Optional sounds

The convention used in EPD14 of printing phoneme symbols in italics to indicate that they may be omitted is retained, though used more sparingly. It is not necessary to give alternative pronunciations that simply follow general rules of simplification that apply in rapid speech. For example, pointing out the possibility of omitting the [d] sound in 'engine' seems unnecessary, whereas it does seem worth recording the fact that some speakers pronounce words such as 'lunch' and 'French' with a final /ntʃ/ while others have final /nʃ/. There is a difference between the two cases: the former is a straightforward example of elision, and needs no special explanation that refers to a specific word or class of word, while the latter is a particular case of an insertion or deletion that is restricted to a particular phonological environment; speakers are usually consistent in using one or other of the alternative pronunciations in the latter case.

2.12 Elision

As mentioned in the preceding section, there are many cases where sounds which are produced in words pronounced on their own, or in slow, careful speech, are not found in a different style of speech. This is known as *elision*, and this dictionary normally does not show elisions in order to avoid adding a large number of additional pronunciations that are typical of casual speech. It is usual to explain elision in terms of the Principle of Least Effort – we try to avoid doing more work than is necessary. We find elision most commonly in the simplification of consonant clusters. A common example is the loss of /t/ and /d/ in combination with other consonants. Examples are:

> 'act badly' /ˌæktˈbæd.li/ (careful speech) /ˌækˈbæd.li/ (rapid speech)

> 'strange person' /ˌstreɪndʒˈpɜː.sᵊn Ⓤⓢ -ˈpɜːr.sᵊn/ (careful speech) /ˌstreɪnʒˈpɜː.sᵊn Ⓤⓢ -ˈpɜːr.sᵊn/ (rapid speech)

The fricative /θ/ is also frequently lost in clusters in rapid speech. Examples are:

> 'sixth place' /ˌsɪksθˈpleɪs/ (careful speech) /ˌsɪksˈpleɪs/ (rapid speech)

Elision of vowels is also found, and again this seems to be characteristic of rapid or casual speech. Examples are:

> 'philosophy' /fɪˈlɒs.ə.fi Ⓤⓢ -ˈlɑː.sə-/ (careful speech) /fəˈlɒs.fi Ⓤⓢ -ˈlɑːs.fi/ (rapid speech)

> 'persuade' /pəˈsweɪd Ⓤⓢ pɚˈ-/ (careful speech) /psweɪd/ (rapid speech)

Part 3: Explanatory notes

In order to explain the way in which the information in the dictionary is laid out, several entries are presented below with explanatory notes.

- Throughout the dictionary we use the convention of the cutback bar, a vertical line | which marks the place at which a word is divided so that alternative endings can be shown without having to print the entire word again.

- The brackets used for phonemic and phonetic transcriptions are not used in the entries in the dictionary, for the sake of clarity.

affectation ˌæf.ekˈteɪ.ʃᵊn,-ɪkˈ- **-s** -z

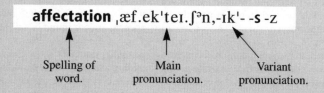

Spelling of word. — Main pronunciation. — Variant pronunciation.

afar əˈfɑːʳ (US) -ˈfɑːr

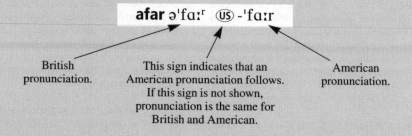

British pronunciation. — This sign indicates that an American pronunciation follows. If this sign is not shown, pronunciation is the same for British and American. — American pronunciation.

affected əˈfek.tɪd **-ly** -li **-ness** -nəs, -nɪs

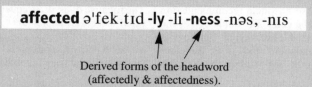

Derived forms of the headword (affectedly & affectedness).

addl|e ˈæd.l̩ **-es** -z **-ing** -ɪŋ, ˈæd.lɪŋ **-ed** -d

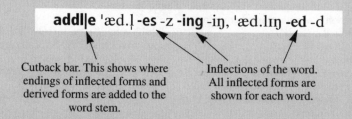

Cutback bar. This shows where endings of inflected forms and derived forms are added to the word stem. — Inflections of the word. All inflected forms are shown for each word.

Adam ˈæd.əm ˌ**Adam's** ˈ**apple** (US) ˈ**Adam's** ˌ**apple**

American stress pattern for compound word.

Stress pattern for compound word, British pronunciation.

Aden *in the Yemen:* ˈeɪ.dən (US) ˈɑː-, ˈeɪ- *in Grampian region:* ˈæd.ən

Glosses indicate where pronunciations differ according to meaning.

addict (*n.*) ˈæd.ɪkt **-s** -s
addict (*v.*) əˈdɪkt **-s** -s **-ing** -ɪŋ

Labels indicate where pronunciation differs according to part of speech.

Adriatic ˌeɪ.driˈæt.ɪk (US) -ˈæt̬ - *stress shift:* ˌAdriatic ˈSea

Example of stress shift when the word is used before a noun.

advent (A) ˈæd.vent, -vənt **-s** -s

This indicates that the word can be spelled with a capital letter in some contexts.

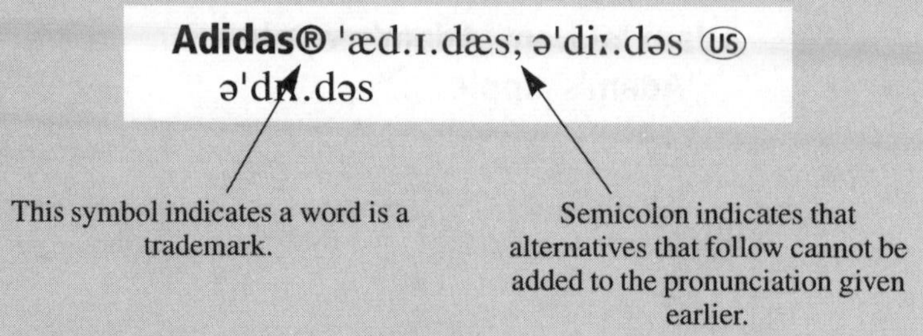

Adidas® 'æd.ɪ.dæs; ə'diː.dəs US
This symbol indicates a word is a trademark.
Semicolon indicates that alternatives that follow cannot be added to the pronunciation given earlier.

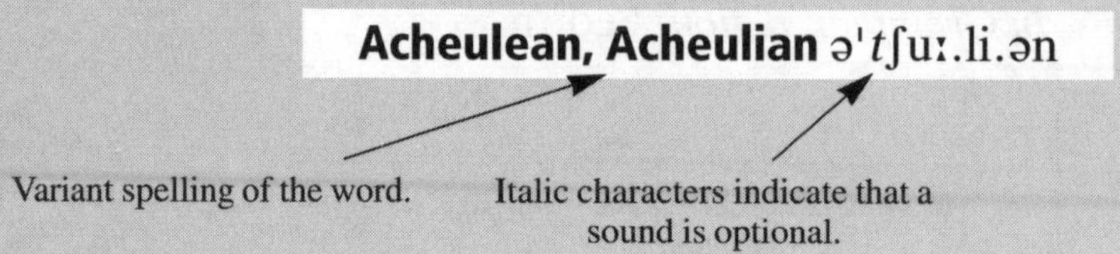

Variant spelling of the word.
Italic characters indicate that a sound is optional.

References in introduction

Roach, P. (1991) *English Phonetics and Phonology,* 2nd ed., Cambridge University Press.

Stromberg, K. and Roach, P. (1993) 'The representation of stress-patterns in pronunciation dictionaries: 'Morse-code' vs. orthographic marking', *Journal of the International Phonetic Association*, vol.23.3, pp. 55-58.

Michaelis, H., and Jones, D. (1913) *A Phonetic Dictionary of the English Language*, Carl Meyer (Gustav Prior), Hanover.

List of recommended reading

A. Works principally on British English

Brown, G. (1977) *Listening to Spoken English*, Longman.
An introductory book with many insights on connected speech.

Jones, D. (1960) *Outline of English Phonetics*, (9th ed.), Cambridge University Press.
The classic textbook written by the original author of the *English Pronouncing Dictionary*. First published in 1918, but still readable and informative.

Fudge, E. (1984) *English Word Stress*, Allen and Unwin.
A comprehensive and valuable treatment of stress.

Giegerich, H.J. (1992) *English Phonology*, Cambridge University Press.
A theoretical introduction to the phonology of English.

Gimson, A.C., revised by A.Cruttenden (1994) *The Pronunciation of English (5th Edition)*, Edward Arnold.
The best contemporary description of the phonetics of English, written by the person responsible for the 13th and 14th editions of the *English Pronouncing Dictionary*.

Knowles, G.O., (1987) *Patterns of Spoken English*, Longman.
An introductory textbook on the phonetics of English.

Kreidler, C.W. (1989) *The Pronunciation of English*, Blackwell.
A modern treatment of the phonetics and phonology of English, with coverage of American as well as British English.

Roach, P. (1991) *English Phonetics and Phonology*, Cambridge University Press.
An introductory textbook with practical exercises.

Roach. P. (1992) *Introducing Phonetics*, Penguin.
A small encyclopaedia-style book giving short explanations of the main concepts and terms in phonetics.

Wells, J.C (1982) *Accents of English*, Cambridge University Press (3 vols).
A very detailed and comprehensive account of the different accents of English throughout the world.

Wells, J.C. (1991) *Longman Pronunciation Dictionary*, Longman.
An alternative pronouncing dictionary to this one.

B. American English

Bronstein, A.J. (1960) *The Pronunciation of American English: An Introduction to Phonetics*, Appleton-Century-Crofts.
A solid introductory book with a good level of detail.

Cassidy, F.G (ed.) (1985) *Dictionary of American Regional English*, Belknap Press, Harvard.
An ongoing publication, each entry listing pronunciations in designated regions.

Kenyon, J.S and Knott, T.A. (1953) *A Pronouncing Dictionary of American English*, G.&C. Merrian & Co.
One of the earlier pronouncing dictionaries for American English.

Kurath, H. and McDavid, R.F. (1961) *The Pronunciation of English in the Atlantic States*, University of Michigan Press.
A basic field study of pronunciation variables on the East Coast.

Labov, W., Yaeger, M. and Steiner, R. (1972) *A Quantitative Study of Sound Change in Progress*, Philadelphia, University of Pennsylvania, U.S. Regional Survey.
Technically-based insights into the dynamics of American English pronunciation.

Thomas, C. (1958) *The Phonetics of American English* (2nd ed.), Romald Press, New York.
A helpful introductory overview of basic phonetic/phonemic traits.

Wolfram, W. (1991) *Dialect and American English*, Prentice Hall.
A good view of American English in its social and regional contexts

Van Riper, C. and Smith, D. (1992) *Introduction to General American Phonetics*, Waveland Press.
A practical workbook.

A

a *indefinite article: strong form:* eɪ *weak form:* ə
Note: Weak form word. The strong form /eɪ/ is used mainly for contrast (e.g. 'This is *a* solution, but not the only one.'). The weak form only occurs before consonants, and is usually pronounced /ə/. In rapid speech, when /ə/ is preceded by a consonant, it may combine with a following /l/, /n/ or /r/ to produce a syllabic consonant (e.g. 'got a light' /ˌgɒt.l̩ˈaɪt (US) ˌgɑːt̬.əˈlaɪt/; 'get another' /ˌget.n̩ˈʌð.əʳ (US) -ɚ/).
a (A) *the letter:* eɪ **-'s** -z
A-1 ˌeɪˈwʌn *stress shift:* ˌA-1 conˈdition
A4 ˌeɪˈfɔːʳ (US) -ˈfɔːr *stress shift:* ˌA4 ˈpaper
AA ˌeɪˈeɪ *stress shift:* ˌAA patˈrol
Aachen ˈɑː.kən
aah ɑː
Aalborg ˈɑːl.bɔːg (US) ˈɑːl.bɔːrg, ˈɔːl-
aardvark® ˈɑːd.vɑːk (US) ˈɑːrd.vɑːrk **-s** -s
aardwol|f ˈɑːd.wʊl|f (US) ˈɑːrd- **-ves** -vz
Aarhus ˈɑː.hʊs (US) ˈɑːr-, ˈɔːr-
Aaron ˈeə.rən (US) ˈer.ən, ˈær-
ab- æb-, əb-
Note: Prefix. Examples include **abnegate** /ˈæb.nɪ.geɪt/, in which it is stressed, and **abduct** /əbˈdʌkt/, where it is unstressed.
ab (A) æb
AB eɪˈbiː
aback əˈbæk
Abaco ˈæb.ə.kəʊ (US) -koʊ
abacus ˈæb.ə.kəs **-es** -ɪz
Abadan ˌæb.əˈdɑːn, -ˈdæn
Abaddon əˈbæd.ᵊn
abaft əˈbɑːft (US) -ˈbæft
abalone æb.əˈləʊ.ni (US) -ˈloʊ-
abandon əˈbæn.dən **-s** -z **-ing** -ɪŋ **-ed** -d **-ment** -mənt
à bas æˈbɑː
abas|e əˈbeɪs **-es** -ɪz **-ing** -ɪŋ **-ed** -t **-ement** -mənt
abash əˈbæʃ **-es** -ɪz **-ing** -ɪŋ **-ed** -t
abatab|le əˈbeɪ.tə.b|l̩ (US) -t̬ə- **-ly** -li
a|bate ə|ˈbeɪt **-bates** -ˈbeɪts **-bating** -ˈbeɪ.tɪŋ (US) -ˈbeɪ.t̬ɪŋ **-bated** -ˈbeɪ.tɪd (US) -ˈbeɪ.t̬ɪd **-batement/s** -ˈbeɪt.mənt/s
abat(t)is ˈæb.ə.tɪs, -tiː (US) -ə.t̬ɪs, əˈbæt̬.ɪs **-es** ˈæb.ə.tɪ.sɪz (US) -t̬ɪ-, əˈbæt̬.ɪ.sɪz *alternative plur.:* ˈæb.ə.tiːz (US) -t̬iːz, əˈbæt̬.iːz
abattoir ˈæb.ə.twɑːʳ (US) -twɑːr, -twɔːr **-s** -z
abaxial əˈbæk.si.əl, æbˈæk-
Abba ˈæb.ə
abbac|y ˈæb.ə.s|i **-ies** -iz
Abbado əˈbɑː.dəʊ (US) -oʊ
Abbas ˈæb.əs, əˈbæs
Abbassid, Abbasid əˈbæs.ɪd **-s** -z
abbé ˈæb.eɪ (US) ˈæb.eɪ, -ˈ- **-s** -z
abbess ˈæb.es, -ɪs (US) -əs **-es** -ɪz
Abbeville *in France:* ˈæb.viːl (US) ˌæbˈviːl *in US:* ˈæb.ɪ.vɪl
abbey (A) ˈæb.i **-s** -z
Abbie ˈæb.i
abbot (A) ˈæb.ət **-s** -s
Abbotsford ˈæb.əts.fəd (US) -fɚd
abbotship ˈæb.ət.ʃɪp **-s** -s
Abbott ˈæb.ət **-s** -s ˌAbbott and Cosˈtello
abbrevi|ate əˈbriː.vi|.eɪt **-ates** -eɪts **-ating** -eɪ.tɪŋ (US) -eɪ.t̬ɪŋ **-ated** -eɪ.tɪd (US) -eɪ.t̬ɪd **-ator/s** -eɪ.təʳ/z (US) -eɪ.t̬ɚ/z
abbreviation əˌbriː.viˈeɪ.ʃᵊn **-s** -z
abbreviatory əˈbriː.vi.ə.tri, əˌbriː.viˈeɪ.tᵊr.i (US) əˈbriː.vi.ə.tɔːr.i
Abbs æbz
Abby ˈæb.i
abc, ABC ˌeɪ.biːˈsiː **-'s** -z
Abdera æbˈdɪə.rə (US) -ˈdɪr.ə
abdicant ˈæb.dɪ.kənt **-s** -s
abdi|cate ˈæb.dɪ|.keɪt **-cates** -keɪts **-cating** -keɪ.tɪŋ (US) -keɪ.t̬ɪŋ **-cated** -keɪ.tɪd (US) -keɪ.t̬ɪd **-cator/s** -keɪ.təʳ/z (US) -keɪ.t̬ɚ/z
abdication ˌæb.dɪˈkeɪ.ʃᵊn **-s** -z
Abdiel ˈæb.dɪəl (US) -di.əl
abdomen ˈæb.də.mən, -men; æbˈdəʊ.mən (US) ˈæb.də.mən, æbˈdoʊ- **-s** -z
abdominal æbˈdɒm.ɪ.nᵊl, əb-, -ˈdəʊ.mɪ- (US) -ˈdɑː.mə- **-ly** -i
abducent əbˈdjuː.sᵊnt, æb- (US) -ˈduː-, -ˈdjuː-
abduct əbˈdʌkt, æb- **-s** -s **-ing** -ɪŋ **-ed** -ɪd **-or/s** -əʳ/z (US) -ɚ/z
abduction əbˈdʌk.ʃᵊn, æb- **-s** -z
Abdul ˈæb.dʊl
Abdulla(h) æbˈdʌl.ə, əb-, -ˈdʊl-
Abe eɪb
abeam əˈbiːm
abecedarian ˌeɪ.biː.siːˈdeə.ri.ən (US) -ˈder.i-
à Becket əˈbek.ɪt
abed əˈbed
Abednego ˌæb.edˈniː.gəʊ, əˈbed.nɪ.gəʊ (US) -goʊ
Abel ˈeɪ.bᵊl
Abelard ˈæb.ə.lɑːd, -ˈɪ- (US) -lɑːrd
Abelmeholah ˌeɪ.bᵊl.miˈhəʊ.lə, -məˈ- (US) -ˈhoʊ-
Abenaki ˌæb.əˈnæk.i (US) ˌɑː.bəˈnɑː.ki, ˌæb.əˈ-, -ˈnæk.i **-s** -z
Aberavon ˌæb.əˈræv.ᵊn (US) -ɚˈæv-
Abercanaid ˌæb.ə.kəˈnaɪd (US) ˌ-ɚ-
Abercarn ˌæb.əˈkɑːn (US) -ɚˈkɑːrn
Aberconway ˌæb.əˈkɒn.weɪ (US) -ɚˈkɑːn-
Aberconwy ˌæb.əˈkɒn.wi (US) -ɚˈkɑːn-
Abercorn ˈæb.ə.kɔːn (US) -ɚ.kɔːrn
Abercrombie, Abercromby ˈæb.ə.krɒm.bi, -krʌm-, ˌæb.əˈkrɒm.bi, -ˈkrʌm- (US) -ɚ.krɑːm-, -ɚˈkrɑːm-
Aberdare ˌæb.əˈdeəʳ (US) -ɚˈder
Aberdeen ˌæb.əˈdiːn (US) -ɚˈ- **-shire** -ʃəʳ, -ˌʃɪəʳ (US) -ʃɚ, -ˌʃɪr *stress shift:* ˌAberdeen ˈstation
Aberdonian ˌæb.əˈdəʊ.ni.ən (US) -ɚˈdoʊ- **-s** -z
Aberdour ˌæb.əˈdaʊəʳ (US) -ɚˈdaʊɚ
Aberdovey ˌæb.əˈdʌv.i (US) -ɚˈ-
Aberfan ˌæb.əˈvæn (US) -ɚˈ-
Abergavenny *place:* ˌæb.ə.gəˈven.i (US) -ɚˈ- *family name:* ˌæb.əˈgen.i (US) -ɚˈ-
Abergele ˌæb.əˈgel.i (US) -ɚˈ-
Aberkenfig ˌæb.əˈken.fɪg (US) -ɚˈ-
Abernathy ˌæb.əˈnæθ.i (US) ˈæb.ɚ.næθ-
Abernethy ˌæb.əˈneθ.i, -ˈniː.θi (US) ˈæb.ɚˈneθ.i
aberran|t æbˈer.ᵊn|t, əˈber-; ˈæb.ə.rᵊn|t **-ce** -*t*s **-cy** -*t*.si
aber|rate ˈæb.ə|.reɪt **-rates** -reɪts **-rating** -reɪ.tɪŋ (US) -reɪ.t̬ɪŋ **-rated** -reɪ.tɪd (US) -reɪ.t̬ɪd
aberration ˌæb.əˈreɪ.ʃᵊn **-s** -z
Abersychan ˌæb.əˈsɪk.ən (US) -ɚˈ-
Abert ˈeɪ.bɜːt, -bət (US) -bɜːrt, -bɚt
Abertillery ˌæb.ə.tɪˈleə.ri, -təˈ- (US) -ɚ.təˈler.i
Abertridwr ˌæb.əˈtrɪd.ʊəʳ (US) -ʊr
Aberystwyth ˌæb.əˈrɪs.*t*wɪθ
a|bet ə|ˈbet **-bets** -ˈbets **-betting** -ˈbet.ɪŋ (US) -ˈbet̬.ɪŋ **-betted** -ˈbet.ɪd (US) -ˈbet̬.ɪd **-bettor/s** -ˈbet.əʳ/z (US) -ˈbet̬.ɚ/z **-betment** -ˈbet.mənt
abeyance əˈbeɪ.ən*t*s
abhor əbˈhɔːʳ, əˈbɔːʳ (US) æbˈhɔːr, əb- **-s** -z **-ring** -ɪŋ **-red** -d **-rer/s** -əʳ/z (US) -ɚ/z
abhorren|ce əbˈhɒr.ᵊn|*t*s, əˈbɒr- (US) æbˈhɔːr-, əb- **-t** -t
Abia *biblical name:* əˈbaɪ.ə *city:* ˈæb.i.ə
Abiathar əˈbaɪ.ə.θəʳ (US) -θɚ
abid|e əˈbaɪd **-es** -z **-ing** -ɪŋ **-ed** -ɪd
abode əˈbəʊd (US) -ˈboʊd
Abidjan ˌæb.iːˈdʒɑːn, -ɪˈ-
abigail (A) ˈæb.ɪ.geɪl **-s** -z
Abilene *in Syria:* ˌæb.ɪˈliː.ni, -əˈ- *in US:* ˈæb.ə.liːn

abilit|y əˈbɪl.ə.t|i, -ɪ.t|i (US) -ə.t̬|i **-ies** -iz

-ability -əˈbɪl.ə.ti, -ɪ.ti (US) -ə.t̬i

Note: Suffix. Words containing **-ability** always exhibit primary stress as shown above, e.g. **capability** /ˌkeɪ.pəˈbɪl.ə.ti (US) -ə.t̬i/.

Abimelech əˈbɪm.ə.lek

Abingdon ˈæb.ɪŋ.dən

Abinger ˈæb.ɪn.dʒəʳ (US) -dʒɚ

Abington ˈæb.ɪŋ.tən

ab initio ˌæb.ɪˈnɪʃ.i.əʊ, -əˈ-, -ˈnɪs- (US) -oʊ

abiogenesis ˌeɪ.baɪ.əʊˈdʒen.ə.sɪs, ˈ-ɪ- (US) -oʊˈ-

abiotic ˌeɪ.baɪˈɒt.ɪk (US) -ˈɑː.t̬ɪk

abject ˈæb.dʒekt (US) ˈæb.dʒekt, -ˈ- **-ly** -li **-ness** -nəs, -nɪs

abjection æbˈdʒek.ʃᵊn

abjudi|cate æbˈdʒuː.dɪ|.keɪt, əb- (US) -də- **-cates** -keɪts **-cating** -keɪ.tɪŋ (US) -keɪ.t̬ɪŋ **-cated** -keɪ.tɪd (US) -keɪ.t̬ɪd

abjuration ˌæb.dʒʊˈreɪ.ʃᵊn, -dʒəˈ-, -dʒʊəˈ- (US) -dʒəˈ-, -dʒʊˈ- **-s** -z

abjur|e əbˈdʒʊəʳ, æb-, -ˈdʒɔːʳ (US) -ˈdʒʊr **-es** -z **-ing** -ɪŋ **-ed** -d **-er/s** -əʳ/z (US) -ɚ/z

ablat|e əˈbleɪt, æbˈleɪt, ˌæbˈleɪt **-es** -s **-ing** -ɪŋ (US) ˌæbˈleɪ.t̬ɪŋ **-ed** -ɪd (US) ˌæbˈleɪ.t̬ɪd

ablation əˈbleɪ.ʃᵊn, æbˈleɪ- (US) ˌæb-

ablatival ˌæb.ləˈtaɪ.vᵊl

ablative ˈæb.lə.tɪv (US) -t̬ɪv **-s** -z

ablaut ˈæb.laʊt **-s** -s

ablaze əˈbleɪz

ab|le ˈeɪ.b|l̩ **-ler** -l̩.əʳ, -ləʳ (US) -l̩.ɚ, -lɚ **-lest** -l̩.əst, -ləst, -l̩.ɪst, -lɪst **-ly** -l̩.i, -li

-able -ə.bl̩

Note: Suffix. Does not normally affect stress patterning, e.g. **knowledge** /ˈnɒl.ɪdʒ (US) ˈnɑː.lɪdʒ/, **knowledgeable** /ˈnɒl.ɪ.dʒə.bl̩ (US) ˈnɑː.lɪ-/; **rely** /rɪˈlaɪ/, **reliable** /rɪˈlaɪ.ə.bl̩/. In some cases, however, the stress patterning may change, e.g. **admire** /ədˈmaɪəʳ (US) -ˈmaɪɚ/, **admirable** /ˈæd.mᵊr.ə.bl̩/.

able-bodied ˌeɪ.bl̩ˈbɒd.ɪd (US) ˈeɪ.bl̩ˌbɑː.dɪd, ˌeɪ.bl̩ˈbɑː- *stress shift, British only:* ˌable-bodied ˈperson

Ablett ˈæb.lət, -lɪt

ablution əˈbluː.ʃᵊn **-s** -z

-ably -ə.bli

Note: Suffix. Behaves as **-able** above.

Abnaki æbˈnæk.i (US) -ˈnɑː.ki **-s** -z

abneg|ate ˈæb.nɪ.g|eɪt, -neg|.eɪt, -nə.g|eɪt **-ates** -eɪts **-ating** -eɪ.tɪŋ (US) -eɪ.t̬ɪŋ **-ated** -eɪ.tɪd (US) -eɪ.t̬ɪd

abnegation ˌæb.nɪˈgeɪ.ʃᵊn, -negˈeɪ-, -nəˈgeɪ- **-s** -z

Abner ˈæb.nəʳ (US) -nɚ

abnormal æbˈnɔː.mᵊl, əb- (US) -ˈnɔːr- **-ly** -i

abnormalit|y ˌæb.nɔːˈmæl.ə.t|i, -ɪ.t|i (US) -nɔːrˈmæl.ə.t̬|i **-ies** -iz

abnormit|y æbˈnɔː.mə.t|i, əb-, -mɪ- (US) -ˈnɔːr.mə.t̬|i **-ies** -iz

abo ˈæb.əʊ (US) -oʊ **-s** -z

ABO ˌeɪ.biːˈəʊ (US) -ˈoʊ

aboard əˈbɔːd (US) -ˈbɔːrd

abode əˈbəʊd (US) -ˈboʊd **-s** -z

abolish əˈbɒl.ɪʃ (US) -ˈbɑː.lɪʃ **-es** -ɪz **-ing** -ɪŋ **-ed** -t **-er/s** -əʳ/z (US) **-er/z** -ɚ/z

abolition ˌæb.əˈlɪʃ.ᵊn **-s** -z

abolition|ism ˌæb.əˈlɪʃ.ᵊn|.ɪ.zᵊm **-ist/s** -ɪst/s

abomas|um ˌæb.əʊˈmeɪ.s|ᵊm (US) -oʊˈ- **-a** -ə

A-bomb ˈeɪˌbɒm (US) -ˌbɑːm **-s** -z

abominab|le əˈbɒm.ɪ.nə.b|l̩, -ᵊn.ə- (US) -ˈbɑː.mɪ- **-ly** -li **-leness** -l̩.nəs, -nɪs

abomi|nate əˈbɒm.ɪ|.neɪt, ˈ-ə- (US) -ˈbɑː.mɪ- **-nates** -neɪts **-nating** -neɪ.tɪŋ (US) -neɪ.t̬ɪŋ **-nated** -neɪ.tɪd (US) -neɪ.t̬ɪd

abomination əˌbɒm.ɪˈneɪ.ʃᵊn, -əˈ- (US) -ˌbɑː.mɪˈ- **-s** -z

à bon marché æˌbɔ̃.mɑːˈʃeɪ, -ˌbɒn- (US) -ˌbõʊ*n*.mɑːrˈ-

aboriginal (A) ˌæb.əˈrɪdʒ.ᵊn.ᵊl, -ɪ.nᵊl **-s** -z **-ly** -i

aborigine (A) ˌæb.əˈrɪdʒ.ᵊn.i, -ɪ.ni **-s** -z

a|bort ə|ˈbɔːt (US) -ˈbɔrt **-borts** -ˈbɔːts (US) -ˈbɔːrts **-borting** -ˈbɔː.tɪŋ (US) -ˈbɔːr.t̬ɪŋ **-borted** -ˈbɔː.tɪd (US) -ˈbɔːr.t̬ɪd

aborticide əˈbɔː.tɪ.saɪd (US) -ˈbɔːr.t̬ə-

abortifacient əˌbɔː.tɪˈfeɪ.ʃi.ənt, -ʃᵊnt (US) -ˌbɔːr.t̬ə-

abortion əˈbɔː.ʃᵊn (US) -ˈbɔːr- **-s** -z **-ist/s** -ɪst/s

abortive əˈbɔː.tɪv (US) -ˈbɔːr.t̬ɪv **-ly** -li **-ness** -nəs, -nɪs

Aboukir ˌæb.uːˈkɪəʳ, -ʊˈ- (US) -ˈkɪr

abound əˈbaʊnd **-s** -z **-ing** -ɪŋ **-ed** -ɪd

about əˈbaʊt

about-fac|e əˌbaʊtˈfeɪs **-es** -ɪz **-ing** -ɪŋ **-ed** -d

about-turn əˌbaʊtˈtɜːn (US) -ˈtɜːrn **-s** -z

above əˈbʌv

above-board əˌbʌvˈbɔːd (US) əˈbʌv.bɔːrd

aboveground əˌbʌvˈgraʊnd (US) əˈbʌv.graʊnd

above-mentioned əˌbʌvˈmen.*t*ʃᵊnd (US) -ˈmen*t*.ʃᵊnd *stress shift:* aˌbove-mentioned ˈperson

ab ovo ˌæbˈəʊ.vəʊ (US) -ˈoʊ.voʊ

abracadabra ˌæb.rə.kəˈdæb.rə **-s** -z

abrad|e əˈbreɪd **-es** -z **-ing** -ɪŋ **-ed** -ɪd

Abraham ˈeɪ.brə.hæm, -həm *as a biblical name in Britain often also:* ˈɑː-

Abrahams ˈeɪ.brə.hæmz

Abram ˈeɪ.brəm, -bræm *as a biblical name in Britain often also:* ˈɑː-

abranchi|al eɪˈbræŋ.ki|.əl, əˈbræŋ-, æbˈræŋ- **-ate** -eɪt, -ət

abrasion əˈbreɪ.ʒᵊn **-s** -z

abrasive əˈbreɪ.sɪv, -zɪv **-ly** -li **-s** -z

abraxas əˈbræk.səs

abreact ˌæb.riˈækt **-s** -s **-ing** -ɪŋ **-ed** -ɪd

abreaction ˌæb.riˈæk.ʃᵊn

abreast əˈbrest

abridg|e əˈbrɪdʒ **-es** -ɪz **-ing** -ɪŋ **-ed** -d

abridg(e)ment əˈbrɪdʒ.mənt **-s** -s

abroad əˈbrɔːd (US) -ˈbrɑːd, -ˈbrɔːd

abro|gate ˈæb.rəʊ|.geɪt (US) -rə- **-gates** -geɪts **-gating** -geɪ.tɪŋ (US) -geɪ.t̬ɪŋ **-gated** -geɪ.tɪd (US) -geɪ.t̬ɪd

abrogation ˌæb.rəʊˈgeɪ.ʃᵊn (US) -rəˈ- **-s** -z

A'Brook əˈbrʊk

abrupt əˈbrʌpt **-er** -əʳ (US) -ɚ **-est** -əst, -ɪst **-ly** -li **-ness** -nəs, -nɪs

abruption əˈbrʌp.ʃᵊn

Abruzzi əˈbrʊt.si

Absalom ˈæb.sᵊl.əm

abscess ˈæb.ses, -sɪs **-es** -ɪz

abscis|e æbˈsaɪz, əb- **-es** -ɪz **-ing** -ɪŋ **-ed** -d

abscisin æbˈsɪs.ɪn

absciss|a æbˈsɪs|.ə, əb- **-ae** -i **-as** -əz

abscission æbˈsɪʃ.ᵊn, -ˈsɪʒ- **-s** -z

abscond əbˈskɒnd, æb- (US) -ˈskɑːnd **-s** -z **-ing** -ɪŋ **-ed** -ɪd **-er/s** -əʳ/z (US) -ɚ/z

Abse ˈæb.si, -zi

abseil ˈæb.seɪl, -saɪl **-s** -z **-ing** -ɪŋ **-ed** -d

absenc|e ˈæb.sᵊn*t*s **-es** -ɪz

absent (*adj.*) ˈæb.sᵊnt **-ly** -li **ˌabsent without ˈleave**

ab|sent (*v.*) æb|ˈsent, əb- **-sents** -ˈsents **-senting** -ˈsen.tɪŋ (US) -ˈsen.t̬ɪŋ **-sented** -ˈsen.tɪd (US) -ˈsen.t̬ɪd

absentee ˌæb.sᵊnˈtiː, -senˈ- **-s** -z **-ism** -ɪ.zᵊm *stress shift, see compounds:* **ˌabsentee ˈballot** ; **ˌabsentee ˈlandlord**

absentia æbˈsen.ti.ɑː, -ˈsen*t*.ʃi- (US) -ˈsen*t*.ʃə, ˈ-ʃi.ə

absent-minded ˌæb.sᵊntˈmaɪn.dɪd **-ly** -li **-ness** -nəs, -nɪs *stress shift:* ˌabsent-minded ˈperson

absinth(e) ˈæb.sæ̃θ, -sɪn*t*θ

absolut|e ˌæb.səˈluːt, -ljuːt, ˈæb.sᵊl.uːt, -juːt (US) ˌæb.səˈluːt, ˈ--- **-es** -s **-est** -əst, -ɪst **-ness** -nəs, -nɪs

absolutely ˌæb.səˈluːt.li, -ˈljuːt- (US) ˌæb.səˈluːt-, ˈæb.sə.luːt- *stress shift:* ˌabsolutely ˈfabulous

absolution ˌæb.səˈluː.ʃᵊn, -ˈljuː- (US) -ˈluː- **-s** -z

absolut|ism ˈæb.sᵊl.uː.t|ɪ.zᵊm, -juː- (US) -sə.luː.t̬|ɪ- **-ist/s** -ɪst/s

absolutive ˌæb.səˈluː.tɪv, -ˈljuː- (US) -ˈluː.t̬ɪv

absolv|e əb'zɒlv, -'sɒlv (US) -'zɑːlv, -'sɑːlv, -'zɔːlv, -'sɔːlv **-es** -z **-ing** -ɪŋ **-ed** -d **-er/s** -ər/z (US) -ɚ/z

absorb əb'zɔːb, -'sɔːb (US) -'sɔːrb, -'zɔːrb **-s** -z **-ed** -d **-edly** -ɪd.li, -əd.li **-able** -ə.bl̩

absorbency əb'zɔː.bənt.si, -'sɔː- (US) -'sɔːr-, -'zɔːr-

absorbent əb'zɔː.bənt, -'sɔː- (US) -'sɔːr-, -'zɔːr- **-ly** -li

absorbing əb'zɔː.bɪŋ, -'sɔː- (US) -'sɔːr-, -'zɔːr- **-ly** -li

absorbing əb'zɔː.bɪŋ, -'sɔː- (US) -'sɔːr-, -'zɔːr- **-ly** -li

absorption əb'zɔːp.ʃən, -'sɔːp- (US) -'sɔːrp-, -'zɔːrp-

absorptive əb'zɔːp.tɪv, -'sɔːp- (US) -'sɔːrp-, -'zɔːrp-

abstain əb'steɪn, æb- **-s** -z **-ing** -ɪŋ **-ed** -d **-er/s** -ər/z (US) -ɚ/z

abstemious æb'stiː.mi.əs, əb- **-ly** -li **-ness** -nəs, -nɪs

abstention əb'sten.tʃən, æb- (US) -'stent.ʃən **-s** -z

abstergent æb'stɜː.dʒənt, əb- (US) -'stɜːr- **-s** -s

abstinen|ce 'æb.stɪ.nən|ts, -stə- **-t** -t

abstract (*n. adj.*) 'æb.strækt **-s** -s

abstract (*v.*) æb'strækt, əb- **-s** -s **-ing** -ɪŋ **-ed/ly** -ɪd/li

abstraction æb'stræk.ʃən, əb- **-s** -z

abstraction|ism æb'stræk.ʃən|.ɪ.zəm, əb- **-ist/s** -ɪst/s

abstract|ly 'æb.strækt|.li, əb'strækt-, æb'- **-ness** -nəs, -nɪs

abstrict əb'strɪkt, æb- **-s** -s **-ing** -ɪŋ **-ed** -ɪd

abstriction əb'strɪk.ʃən, æb-

abstruse æb'struːs, əb- **-ly** -li **-ness** -nəs, -nɪs

absurd əb'zɜːd, -'sɜːd (US) -'sɜːrd, -'zɜːrd **-est** -ɪst, -əst **-ly** -li **-ness** -nəs, -nɪs

absurd|ism əb'zɜː.d|ɪ.zəm, -'sɜː- (US) -'sɜːr-, -'zɜːr- **-ist** -ɪst

absurdit|y əb'zɜː.də.t|i, -'sɜː-, -dɪ- (US) -'sɜːr.də.ţ|i, -'zɜːr- **-ies** -iz

ABTA 'æb.tə

Abu 'ɑː.buː, 'æb.uː

Abu Dhabi ˌæb.uː'dɑː.bi, ˌɑː.buː-, -'dæb.i (US) ˌɑː.buː'dɑː.bi

Abuja ə'buː.dʒə

abulia ə'buː.li.ə, eɪ-, -'bjuː-

abundance ə'bʌn.dənts

abundant ə'bʌn.dənt **-ly** -li

Abu Nidal ˌæb.uː.niː'dɑːl, ˌɑː.buː-, -'dæl (US) ˌɑː.buː-

Abury 'eɪ.bər.i (US) -ber-, -bɚ-

abus|e (*n.*) ə'bjuːs **-es** -ɪz

abus|e (*v.*) ə'bjuːz **-es** -ɪz **-ing** -ɪŋ **-ed** -d **-er/s** -ər/z (US) -ɚ/z

Abu Simbel ˌæb.uː'sɪm.bəl, -bel (US) ˌɑː.buː'-

abusive ə'bjuː.sɪv, -zɪv **-ly** -li **-ness** -nəs, -nɪs

a|but ə|'bʌt **-buts** -'bʌts **-butting** -'bʌt.ɪŋ (US) -'bʌţ.ɪŋ **-butted** -'bʌt.ɪd (US) -'bʌţ.ɪd **-buttal** -'bʌt.əl (US) -'bʌţ.əl

abutment ə'bʌt.mənt **-s** -s

abutilon ə'bjuː.tɪ.lən, -lɒn (US) -ţə.lɑːn, -lən **-s** -z

abutment ə'bʌt.mənt **-s** -s

abutter ə'bʌt.ər (US) -'bʌţ.ɚ **-s** -z

abuzz ə'bʌz

Abydos ə'baɪ.dɒs, -dəs; 'æb.ɪ.dɒs (US) ə'baɪ.dɑːs; 'æb.ɪ-

abysm ə'bɪz.əm **-s** -z

abysmal ə'bɪz.məl **-ly** -i

abyss ə'bɪs **-es** -ɪz

abyssal ə'bɪs.əl

Abyssini|a ˌæb.ɪ'sɪn.i|.ə, -ə'- **-an/s** -ən/z

AC, a/c (*US abbrev. for* **air conditioning**) ˌeɪ'siː

a/c (*abbrev. for* **account**) ə'kaʊnt

-ac -æk, -ək

Note: Suffix. Does not normally affect stress patterning, e.g. **mania** /'meɪ.ni.ə/, **maniac** /'meɪ.ni.æk/.

acacia ə'keɪ.ʃə, '-si.ə (US) '-ʃə **-s** -z

academe (A) 'æk.ə.diːm

academia ˌæk.ə'diː.mi.ə

academic ˌæk.ə'dem.ɪk *stress shift, see compound:* **ˌacademic 'year**

academic|al ˌæk.ə'dem.ɪ.k|əl **-als** -əlz **-ally** -əl.i, -li

academician əˌkæd.ə'mɪʃ.ən, ˌæk.ə.də'-, -dɪ'- (US) ˌæk.ə-, əˌkæd- **-s** -z

academicism ˌæk.ə'dem.ɪ.sɪ.zəm, '-ə-

academism ə'kæd.ə.mɪ.zəm

academ|y ə'kæd.ə.m|i **-ies** -iz **Aˌcademy A'ward**

Acadi|a ə'keɪ.di|.ə **-an/s** -ən/z

acajou 'æk.ə.ʒuː **-s** -z

acanth|oid ə'kænt.θ|ɔɪd **-ous** -əs

acanth|us ə'kænt.θ|əs **-i** -aɪ **-uses** -ə.sɪz **-ine** -aɪn

a cap(p)ella ˌæ.kə'pel.ə, -kæp'el- (US) ˌɑː.kə'pel-

Acapulco ˌæk.ə'pʊl.kəʊ (US) ˌæk.ə'puːl.koʊ, ˌɑː.kə'-, -'pʊl-

acarid 'æk.ər.ɪd **-s** -z

acarolog|y ˌæk.ə'rɒl.ə.dʒ|i (US) -'rɑː.lə- **-ist/s** -ɪst/s

acarpel(l)ous ˌeɪ'kɑː.pəl.əs (US) -'kɑːr-

acarpous ˌeɪ'kɑː.pəs (US) -'kɑːr-

ACAS 'eɪˌkæs

acatalectic ˌeɪ.kæt.ə'lek.tɪk, əˌkæt- (US) -kæţ.ə'- **-s** -s *stress shift:* ˌacatalectic 'verse, aˌcatalectic 'verse

acatalepsy ˌeɪ'kæt.ə.lep.si, ə'kæt- (US) -'kæţ.ə-

acataleptic ˌeɪ.kæt.ə'lep.tɪk, əˌkæt- (US) -kæţ.ə'-

Accad 'æk.æd

Accadi|a ə'keɪ.di|.ə, æk'eɪ- **-an/s** -ən/z

acced|e æk'siːd, ək- **-es** -z **-ing** -ɪŋ **-ed** -ɪd **-er/s** -ər/z (US) -ɚ/z

accelerando ækˌsel.ə'ræn.dəʊ, ək-, əˌtʃel- (US) -'rɑːn.doʊ

accelerant ək'sel.ə.rənt, æk- (US) -ɚ.ənt **-s** -s

accele|rate ək'sel.ə|.reɪt, æk- **-rates** -reɪts **-rating** -reɪ.tɪŋ (US) -reɪ.ţɪŋ **-rated** -reɪ.tɪd (US) -reɪ.ţɪd

acceleration əkˌsel.ə'reɪ.ʃən, æk- **-s** -z

accelerative ək'sel.ə.rə.tɪv, æk- (US) -ɚ.ə.ţɪv

accelerator ək'sel.ə.reɪ.tər, æk- (US) -ţɚ **-s** -z

accelerometer əkˌsel.ə'rɒm.ɪ.tər, æk-, '-ə- (US) -'rɑː.mə.ţɚ **-s** -z

accent (*n.*) 'æk.sənt (US) -sent **-s** -s

ac|cent (*v.*) ək|'sent, æk- (US) æk-, ək- **-cents** -'sents **-centing** -'sen.tɪŋ (US) -'sen.ţɪŋ **-cented** -'sen.tɪd (US) -'sen.ţɪd

accentual ək'sen.tʃu.əl, æk-, -tju- **-ly** -i

accentu|ate ək'sen.tʃu.eɪt, æk-, -tju- **-ates** -eɪts **-ating** -eɪ.tɪŋ (US) -eɪ.ţɪŋ **-ated** -eɪ.tɪd (US) -eɪ.ţɪd

accentuation əkˌsen.tʃu'eɪ.ʃən, æk-, -tju'- **-s** -z

accept ək'sept, æk- **-s** -s **-ing** -ɪŋ **-ed** -ɪd **-er/s** -ər/z (US) -ɚ/z **-or/s** -ər/z (US) -ɚ/z

acceptability əkˌsep.tə'bɪl.ə.ti, æk-, -ɪ.ti (US) -ə.ţi

acceptab|le ək'sep.tə.b|l̩, æk- **-ly** -li **-leness** -l̩.nəs, -nɪs

acceptanc|e ək'sep.tənts, æk- **-es** -ɪz

acceptant ək'sep.tənt, æk- **-s** -s

acceptation ˌæk.sep'teɪ.ʃən **-s** -z

access (A®) 'æk.ses **-es** -ɪz **-ing** -ɪŋ **-ed** -t

accessar|y ək'ses.ər|.i, æk- **-ies** -iz

accessibility əkˌses.ə'bɪl.ə.ti, æk-, -ɪ'-, -ɪ.ti (US) -ə.ţi

accessible ək'ses.ə.bl̩, æk-, '-ɪ-

accession ək'seʃ.ən, æk- **-s** -z

accessit æk'ses.ɪt, ək- **-s** -s

accessoriz|e, -is|e ək'ses.ər.aɪz (US) -ə.raɪz **-es** -ɪz **-ing** -ɪŋ **-ed** -d

accessor|y ək'ses.ər|.i, æk- **-ies** -iz

acciaccatur|a əˌtʃæk.ə'tʊə.r|ə (US) ɑːˌtʃɑː.kə'tʊr|.ə **-as** -əz **-e** -eɪ, -iː

accidence 'æk.sɪ.dənts, -sə-

accident 'æk.sɪ.dənt, -sə- **-s** -s **'accident-ˌprone**

accidental ˌæk.sɪ'den.təl, -sə'- (US) -ţəl **-ly** -i

accidia æk'sɪd.i.ə

accidie 'æk.sɪ.di, -sə-

accipiter æk'sɪp.ɪ.tər, ək-, -ə.tər (US) -ə.ţɚ **-s** -z

acclaim ə'kleɪm **-s** -z **-ing** -ɪŋ **-ed** -d

acclamation ˌæk.ləˈmeɪ.ʃᵊn **-s** -z

acclamatory əˈklæm.ə.tᵊr.i (US) -ə.tɔːr.i

acclimatation əˌklaɪ.məˈteɪ.ʃᵊn

acclima|te ˈæk.lɪ.meɪ|t, -lə-; əˈklaɪ.mə|t (US) ˈæk.lə.meɪ|t; əˈklaɪ.mə|t **-tes** -ts **-ting** -tɪŋ (US) -t̬ɪŋ **-ted** -tɪd (US) -t̬ɪd

acclimation ˌæk.lɪˈmeɪ.ʃᵊn

acclimatization, -isa- əˌklaɪ.mə.taɪˈzeɪ.ʃᵊn, -tɪˈ- (US) -t̬əˈ-

acclimatiz|e, -is|e əˈklaɪ.mə.taɪz, -mɪ- **-es** -ɪz **-ing** -ɪŋ **-ed** -d

acclivit|y əˈklɪv.ə.t|i, ækˈlɪv-, -ɪ.t|i (US) -t̬i **-ies** -iz

accolade ˈæk.ə.leɪd, ˌ--ˈ- **-s** -z

accommo|date əˈkɒm.ə|.deɪt (US) -ˈkɑː.mə- **-dates** -deɪts **-dated** -de.tɪd (US) -deɪ.t̬ɪd **-dator/s** -deɪ.təʳ/z (US) -deɪ.t̬ɚ/z **-dative/ly** -deɪ.tɪv/li (US) -deɪ.t̬ɪv/li

accommodating əˈkɒm.ə.deɪ.tɪŋ (US) əˈkɑː.mə.deɪ.t̬ɪŋ **-ly** -li

accommodation əˌkɒm.əˈdeɪ.ʃᵊn (US) əˌkɑː.məˈ- **-s** -z

accompaniment əˈkʌm.pᵊn.ɪ.mənt **-s** -s

accompanist əˈkʌm.pə.nɪst **-s** -s

accompan|y əˈkʌm.pə.n|i **-ies** -iz **-ying** -i.ɪŋ **-ied** -id **-yist/s** -i.ɪsts **-ier/s** -i.əʳ/z (US) -i.ɚ/z

accomplic|e əˈkʌm.plɪs, -ˈkɒm- (US) -ˈkɑːm-, -ˈkʌm- **-es** -ɪz

accomplish əˈkʌm.plɪʃ, -ˈkɒm- (US) -ˈkɑːm-, -ˈkʌm- **-es** -ɪz **-ing** -ɪŋ **-ed** -t

accomplishment əˈkʌm.plɪʃ.mənt, -ˈkɒm- (US) -ˈkɑːm-, -ˈkʌm- **-s** -s

accord əˈkɔːd (US) -ˈkɔːrd **-ed** -ɪd **-ing** -ɪŋ **-s** -z

accordan|ce əˈkɔː.dᵊn|*t*s (US) -ˈkɔːr- **-t** -t

according əˈkɔː.dɪŋ (US) -ˈkɔːr- **-ly** -li

accordion əˈkɔː.di.ən (US) -ˈkɔːr- **-s** -z

accost əˈkɒst (US) -ˈkɑːst **-s** -s **-ing** -ɪŋ **-ed** -ɪd

accouchement əˈkuːʃ.mɑ̃ː*ŋ* (US) -mɑːnt, ˌæk.uːʃˈmɑ̃ː

accoucheur ˌæk.uːˈʃɜːʳ, əˈkuː.ʃɜːʳ (US) ˌæk.uːˈʃɜːr **-s** -z

accoucheus|e ˌæk.uːˈʃɜːz, əˈkuː.ʃɜːz (US) ˌæk.uːˈʃɜːz **-es** -ɪz

ac|count ə|ˈkaʊnt **-counts** -ˈkaʊnts **-counting** -ˈkaʊn.tɪŋ (US) -ˈkaʊn.t̬ɪŋ **-counted** -ˈkaʊn.tɪd (US) -ˈkaʊn.t̬ɪd **aˈccount ˌbook**

accountability əˌkaʊn.təˈbɪl.ə.ti, -ɪ.ti (US) -t̬əˈbɪl.ə.t̬i

accountab|le əˈkaʊn.tə.bl̩ (US) -t̬ə- **-ly** -li **-leness** -l̩.nəs, -nɪs

accountancy əˈkaʊn.tən*t*.si (US) -t̬ᵊn*t*-

accountant əˈkaʊn.tənt **-s** -s

accout|er əˈkuː.t|əʳ (US) -t̬|ɚ **-ers** -əz (US) -ɚz **-ering** -ᵊr.ɪŋ **-ered** -əd (US) -ɚd **-erment/s** -ə.mənt/s (US) -ɚ-

accout|re əˈkuː.t|əʳ (US) əˈkuː.t̬|ɚ **-res** -əz **-ring** -ᵊr.ɪŋ **-red** -əd (US) -ɚd **-rement/s** -rə.mənt/s, -ə.mənt/s (US) -ɚ.mənt/s

Accra əˈkrɑː, ækˈrɑː

accred|it əˈkred|.ɪt **-its** -ɪts **-iting** -ɪ.tɪŋ (US) -ɪ.t̬ɪŋ **-ited** -ɪ.tɪd (US) -ɪ.t̬ɪd

accreditation əˌkred.ɪˈteɪ.ʃᵊn (US) -əˈ-

accre|te əˈkriː|t, ækˈriː|t **-tes** -ts **-ting** -tɪŋ (US) -t̬ɪŋ **-ted** -tɪd (US) -t̬ɪd

accretion əˈkriː.ʃᵊn, ækˈriː- **-s** -z

accretive əˈkriː.tɪv, ækˈriː- (US) əˈkriː.t̬ɪv

Accrington ˈæk.rɪŋ.tən

accrual əˈkruː.əl, -ˈkrʊəl (US) -ˈkruː.əl

accru|e əˈkruː **-es** -z **-ing** -ɪŋ **-ed** -d

accruement əˈkruː.mənt

accultur|ate əˈkʌl.tʃᵊr|.eɪt, ækˈʌl- (US) -tʃə.r|eɪt **-ates** -eɪts **-ating** -eɪ.tɪŋ (US) -eɪ.t̬ɪŋ **-ated** -eɪ.tɪd (US) -eɪ.t̬ɪd

acculturation əˌkʌl.tʃᵊrˈeɪ.ʃᵊn, ækˌʌl- (US) -tʃəˈreɪ-

accumben|t əˈkʌm.bən|t **-cy** -*t*.si

accumu|late əˈkjuː.mjə|.leɪt, -mjʊ- **-lates** -leɪts **-lating** -leɪ.tɪŋ (US) -leɪ.t̬ɪŋ **-lated** -leɪ.tɪd (US) -leɪ.t̬ɪd **-lator/s** -leɪ.təʳ/z (US) -leɪ.t̬ɚ/z

accumulation əˌkjuː.mjəˈleɪ.ʃᵊn, -mjʊˈ- **-s** -z

accumulative əˈkjuː.mjə.lə.tɪv, -mjʊ- (US) -t̬ɪv

accuracy ˈæk.jə.rə.si, -jʊ- (US) -jɚ.ə-, -jʊ.rə-

accurate ˈæk.jə.rət, -jʊ-, -rɪt (US) -jɚ.ət, -jʊ.rət, -rɪt **-ly** -li **-ness** -nəs, -nɪs

accursed əˈkɜː.sɪd, -ˈkɜːst (US) əˈkɜːrst, -ˈkɜːr.səd **-ly** -li

accusal əˈkjuː.zᵊl **-s** -z

accusation ˌæk.jʊˈzeɪ.ʃᵊn, -jəˈ- **-s** -z

accusatival əˌkjuː.zəˈtaɪ.vᵊl

accusative əˈkjuː.zə.tɪv (US) -t̬ɪv **-s** -z

accusativity əˌkjuː.zəˈtɪv.ə.ti, -ɪ.ti (US) -ə.t̬i

accusatory əˈkjuː.zə.tᵊr.i, ˌæk.jʊˈzeɪ-, -jəˈ-, -tri (US) əˈkjuː.zə.tɔːr.i

accus|e əˈkjuːz **-es** -ɪz **-ing/ly** -ɪŋ/li **-ed** -d **-er/s** -əʳ/z (US) -ɚ/z

accustom əˈkʌs.təm **-s** -z **-ing** -ɪŋ **-ed/ness** -d/nəs, -nɪs

AC/DC ˌeɪ.siːˈdiː.siː

ac|e eɪs **-es** -ɪz

acedia əˈsiː.di.ə

Aceldama əˈkel.də.mə, -ˈsel-; ˌæk.elˈdɑː- (US) əˈsel.də-

-aceous -ˈeɪ.ʃi.əs, -ˈeɪ.ʃəs

Note: Suffix. Words containing **-aceous** always exhibit primary stress as shown above, e.g. **herbaceous** /hɜːˈbeɪ.ʃəs (US) hɚ-/.

acephalous əˈsef.ᵊl.əs, ˌeɪ-, -ˈkef- (US) eɪˈsef-, ə-

acequia əˈseɪ.ki.ə, -ˈsiː- **-s** -z

acer|bate ˈæs.ə.|beɪt (US) ˈ-ɚ- **-bates** -beɪts **-bating** -beɪ.tɪŋ (US) -beɪ.t̬ɪŋ **-bated** -beɪ.tɪd (US) -beɪ.t̬ɪd

acerbic əˈsɜː.bɪk, æsˈɜː- (US) əˈsɜːr- **-ally** -ᵊl.i, -li

acerbity əˈsɜː.bə.ti, -bɪ- (US) əˈsɜːr.bə.t̬i

Acestes əˈses.tiːz, -ˈkes-

acetabul|um ˌæs.ɪˈtæb.jə.l|əm, -jʊ- **-ums** -əmz **-a** -ə **-ar** -əʳ (US) -ɚ

acetaldehyde ˌæs.ɪˈtæl.dɪ.haɪd, -də-

acetaminophen ˌæs.ɪ.təˈmɪn.ə.fən (US) ˌæs.ɪ.t̬əˈ-; əˌsiː.t̬əˈ-, -ˌset̬.əˈ-

acetate ˈæs.ɪ.teɪt, ˈ-ə- **-s** -s

acetic əˈsiː.tɪk, æsˈiː-, -ˈet.ɪk (US) əˈsiː.t̬ɪk **aˌcetic ˈacid**

acetif|y əˈsiː.tɪ.f|aɪ, æsˈiː-, -ˈset.ɪ- (US) -ˈset̬.ə- **-ies** -aɪz **-ying** -aɪ.ɪŋ **-ied** -aɪd

acetin ˈæs.ə.tɪn, ˈ-ɪ- (US) -t̬ɪn

acetone ˈæs.ɪ.təʊn, ˈ-ə- (US) -t̬oʊn

acetose ˈæs.ɪ.təʊs, ˈ-ə-, -təʊz (US) -toʊs

acetous ˈæs.ɪ.təs, ˈ-ə- (US) ˈæs.ɪ.t̬əs; əˈsiː-

acetum əˈsiː.təm (US) -t̬əm

acetyl ˈæs.ɪ.taɪl, ˈ-ə-, -tɪl; əˈsiː-, -taɪl (US) ˈæs.ə.t̬ᵊl, -t̬iːl; əˈsiː.t̬ᵊl

acetyl|ate əˈset.ɪ.l|eɪt, -ᵊl|.eɪt (US) -ˈset̬.ə.l|eɪt, -ˈsiː.t̬ə- **-ates** -eɪts **-ating** -eɪ.tɪŋ (US) -eɪ.t̬ɪŋ **-ated** -eɪ.tɪd (US) -eɪ.t̬ɪd

acetylation əˌset.ɪˈleɪ.ʃᵊn, -ᵊlˈeɪ- (US) -ˌset̬.əˈleɪ-

acetylcholine ˌæs.ɪ.taɪlˈkəʊ.liːn, ˌ-ə- (US) əˌsiː.t̬ᵊlˈkoʊ-, -ˌset̬.ᵊlˈ-; ˌæs.ə.t̬ᵊlˈ-

acetylene əˈset.ɪ.liːn, -ᵊl.iːn (US) -ˈset̬.ə.liːn

Achae|a əˈkiː|.ə **-an/s** -ən/z

Achaia əˈkaɪ.ə

Achates əˈkeɪ.tiːz, -ˈkɑː- (US) -t̬iːz

ach|e eɪk **-es** -s **-ing/ly** -ɪŋ/li **-ed** -t **-er/s** -əʳ/z (US) -ɚ/z

Achebe əˈtʃeɪ.bi

Achernar ˈeɪ.kə.nɑːʳ (US) -kɚ.nɑːr

Acheron ˈæk.ə.rɒn, -rᵊn (US) -rɑːn

Acheson ˈætʃ.ɪ.sᵊn, ˈ-ə-

Acheulean, Acheulian əˈtʃuː.li.ən

à cheval ˌæ.ʃəˈvæl

achiev|e əˈtʃiːv **-es** -z **-ing** -ɪŋ **-ed** -d **-able** -ə.bl̩ **-er/s** -əʳ/z (US) -ɚ/z

achievement əˈtʃiːv.mənt **-s** -s

Achil(l) ˈæk.ɪl

Achilles əˈkɪl.iːz **Aˌchilles ˈheel** (US) **Aˈchilles ˌheel**

Achille Serre ˌæʃ.ɪlˈseəʳ, -iːlˈ- (US) -ˈser

Achin əˈtʃiːn

Achish ˈeɪ.kɪʃ

achondro|plasia əˌkɒn.drəʊ|ˈpleɪ.zi.ə, -ʒə (US) -ˌkɑːn.drə|ˈpleɪ.ʒi.ə, ˌeɪ- **-plastic** -ˈplæs.tɪk
Achray əˈkreɪ, əˈxreɪ
achromatic ˌæk.rəʊˈmæt.ɪk, ˌeɪ.krəʊ- (US) ˌæk.rəˈmæt̬- **-ally** -əl.i *stress shift:* ˌachromatic ˈlens
achromatism əˈkrəʊ.mə.tɪ.zəm, ˌeɪ- (US) -ˈkroʊ-
achromatiz|e, -is|e əˈkrəʊ.mə.taɪz, ˌeɪ- (US) -ˈkroʊ- **-es** -ɪz **-ing** -ɪŋ **-ed** -d
achromatous əˈkrəʊ.mə.təs, ˌeɪ- (US) -ˈkroʊ.mə.t̬əs
achtung ˈɑːx.tʊŋ, ˈæx- (US) ˈɑːx-, ˈɑːk-
achy ˈeɪ.ki
acicul|a əˈsɪk.jʊ.l|ə, -jə- **-ae** -i **-ar** -ə
acid ˈæs.ɪd **-s** -z **-ly** -li **-ness** -nəs, -nɪs ˈ**acid** ˌ**drop** ; ˌ**acid** ˈ**rain** ; ˌ**acid** ˈ**test**, ˈ**acid** ˌ**test**
acidhead ˈæs.ɪd.hed **-s** -z
acidic əˈsɪd.ɪk
acidif|y əˈsɪd.ɪ.f|aɪ, æsˈɪd- **-ies** -aɪz **-ying** -aɪ.ɪŋ **-ied** -aɪd
acidity əˈsɪd.ə.ti, æsˈɪd-, -ɪ.ti (US) -ə.t̬i
acidiz|e, -is|e ˈæs.ɪ.daɪz **-es** -ɪz **-ing** -ɪŋ **-ed** -d
acidophilus ˌæs.ɪˈdɒf.ɪ.ləs, -əl.əs (US) -ˈdɑː.fəl-
acidosis ˌæs.ɪˈdəʊ.sɪs (US) -ˈdoʊ-
acidu|late əˈsɪd.jʊ|.leɪt, æsˈɪd-, -jə-, -ˈsɪdʒ.ʊ-, ˈ-ə- **-lates** -leɪts **-lating** -leɪ.tɪŋ (US) -leɪ.t̬ɪŋ **-lated** -leɪ.tɪd (US) -leɪ.t̬ɪd
acidulous əˈsɪd.jʊ.ləs, æsˈɪd-, -jə-, -ˈsɪdʒ.ʊ-, ˈ-ə-
acin|ose ˈæs.ɪ.n|əʊs, -n|əʊz (US) -n|oʊs, -n|oʊz **-ous** -əs
acin|us ˈæs.ɪ.n|əs **-i** -aɪ
Acis ˈeɪ.sɪs
ack-ack ˌækˈæk *stress shift:* ˈack-ack ˌgun
ackee ˈæk.i **-s** -z
Ackerley ˈæk.əl.i (US) -ɚ.li
Ackerman(n) ˈæk.ə.mən, -mæn (US) ˈ-ɚ-
Ackland ˈæk.lənd
acknowledg|e əkˈnɒl.ɪdʒ, æk- (US) -ˈnɑː.lɪdʒ **-es** -ɪz **-ing** -ɪŋ **-ed** -d **-eable** -ə.bl̩
acknowledg(e)ment əkˈnɒl.ɪdʒ.mənt, æk- (US) -ˈnɑː.lɪdʒ- **-s** -s
Ackroyd ˈæk.rɔɪd
Ackworth Moor Top ˌæk.wəθˌmɔːˈtɒp (US) -wɚθˌmʊrˈtɑːp
Acland ˈæk.lənd
ACLU ˌeɪ.siː.elˈjuː
acme ˈæk.mi **-s** -z
acne ˈæk.ni
acnode ˈæk.nəʊd (US) -noʊd **-s** -z
Acol *road in London, system of bridge playing:* ˈæk.əl *in Kent:* ˈeɪ.kɒl (US) -kɑːl

acolyte ˈæk.əl.aɪt (US) -ə.laɪt **-s** -s
Acomb ˈeɪ.kəm
Aconcagua ˌæk.ɒnˈkæg.wə, -ɒŋˈ- (US) ˌɑː.kənˈ-, -kəŋˈ-, -kɑː.gwə
aconite ˈæk.ə.naɪt **-s** -s
acorn ˈeɪ.kɔːn (US) -kɔrn **-s** -z ˈ**acorn** ˌ**squash**
acotyledon əˌkɒt.ɪˈliː.dən, ˌeɪ-, -əlˈiː- (US) -ˌkɑː.t̬əˈliː- **-s** -z
acouchi əˈkuː.ʃi (US) ɑːˈkuː.ʃi, ə-
acoustic əˈkuː.stɪk **-s** -s **-ally** -əl.i (US) -li
acoustician ˌæ.kuːˈstɪʃ.ən **-s** -z
acoustooptic əˌkuː.stəʊˈɒp.tɪk (US) -stoʊˈɑːp- **-s** -s **-al** -əl
ac|quaint ə|ˈkweɪnt **-quaints** -ˈkweɪnts **-quainting** -ˈkweɪn.tɪŋ (US) -ˈkweɪn.t̬ɪŋ **-quainted** -ˈkweɪn.tɪd (US) -ˈkweɪn.t̬ɪd
acquaintanc|e əˈkweɪn.tənts **-es** -ɪz
acquaintanceship əˈkweɪn.tənts.ʃɪp, -tənt.ʃɪp **-s** -s
acquest əˈkwest **-s** -s
acquiesc|e ˌæk.wiˈes **-es** -ɪz **-ing** -ɪŋ **-ed** -t **-ence** -ənts **-ent/ly** -ənt/li
acquir|e əˈkwaɪər (US) -ˈkwaɪɚ **-es** -z **-ing** -ɪŋ **-ed** -d **-ement/s** -mənt/s **-able** -ə.bl̩
acquisition ˌæk.wɪˈzɪʃ.ən **-s** -z
acquisitive əˈkwɪz.ɪ.tɪv, ˈ-ə- (US) -ə.t̬ɪv **-ly** -li **-ness** -nəs, -nɪs
acquit əˈkwɪt **-s** -s **-ting** -ɪŋ (US) əˈkwɪt̬.ɪŋ **-ted** -ɪd (US) əˈkwɪt̬.ɪd
acquittal əˈkwɪt.əl (US) -ˈkwɪt̬- **-s** -z
acquittance əˈkwɪt.ənts
acre (A) ˈeɪ.kər (US) -kɚ **-s** -z
acreag|e ˈeɪ.kər.ɪdʒ, ˈ-krɪdʒ **-es** -ɪz
acrid ˈæk.rɪd **-ly** -li **-ness** -nəs, -nɪs
acridine ˈæk.rɪ.diːn, -daɪn
acridity əˈkrɪd.ə.ti, ækˈrɪd-, -ɪ.ti (US) -ə.t̬i
Acrilan® ˈæk.rɪ.læn, -rə-
acrimonious ˌæk.rɪˈməʊ.ni.əs, -rəˈ- (US) -ˈmoʊ- **-ly** -li **-ness** -nəs, -nɪs
acrimon|y ˈæk.rɪ.mə.n|i, -rə- (US) -moʊ- **-ies** -iz
acritical ˌeɪˈkrɪt.ɪ.kəl, ˈ-ə- (US) -ˈkrɪt̬.ə-
acritude ˈæk.rɪ.tjuːd, -rə-, -tʃuːd (US) -tuːd, -tjuːd
acro- æk.rəʊ-; əˈkrɒ- (US) æk.rə-, -roʊ-; əˈkrɑː-
Note: Prefix. Either takes primary or secondary stress on the first syllable, e.g. **acrosome** /ˈæk.rəʊ.səʊm (US) -rə.soʊm/, **acrosomal** /ˌæk.rəʊˈsəʊ.məl (US) -rəˈsoʊ-/, or primary stress only on the second syllable, e.g. **acropolis** /əˈkrɒp.ə.lɪs (US) -ˈkrɑː.pə-/.
acrobat ˈæk.rə.bæt **-s** -s
acrobatic ˌæk.rəˈbæt.ɪk (US) -ˈbæt̬- **-s** -s **-ally** -əl.i, -li *stress shift:* ˌacrobatic ˈleap

acrobatism ˈæk.rə.bæt.ɪ.zəm, ˌæk.rəˈbæt- (US) ˈæk.rə.bæt̬-, ˌæk.rəˈbæt̬-
acrogen ˈæk.rəʊ.dʒən, -dʒen (US) -roʊ-, -rə- **-s** -z
acrolect ˈæk.rəʊ.lekt (US) -roʊ-, -rə- **-s** -s **-al** -əl
acrolith ˈæk.rəʊ.lɪθ (US) -roʊ-, -rə- **-s** -s
acromegalic ˌæk.rəʊ.mɪˈgæl.ɪk, -məˈ- (US) -roʊ-
acromegaly ˌæk.rəʊˈmeg.əl.i (US) -roʊˈ-
acromion əˈkrəʊ.mi.ən (US) -ˈkroʊ- **-s** -z
acronym ˈæk.rəʊ.nɪm (US) -rə- **-s** -z
acropetal əˈkrɒp.ɪ.təl (US) -ˈkrɑː.pə.t̬əl **-ly** -i
acrophob|ia ˌæk.rəʊˈfəʊ.b|i.ə (US) -rəˈfoʊ- **-ic** -ɪk
acropolis (A) əˈkrɒp.ə.lɪs (US) -ˈkrɑː.pə- **-es** -ɪz
acrosomal ˌæk.rəʊˈsəʊ.məl (US) -rəˈsoʊ-
acrosome ˈæk.rəʊ.səʊm (US) -rə.soʊm
across əˈkrɒs (US) -ˈkrɑːs
across-the-board əˌkrɒs.ðəˈbɔːd (US) -ˌkrɑːs.ðəˈbɔːrd
acrostic əˈkrɒs.tɪk (US) -ˈkrɑː.stɪk **-s** -s
Acrux ˈeɪ.krʌks
acrylic əˈkrɪl.ɪk, ækˈrɪl- **-s** -s
act ækt **-s** -s **-ing** -ɪŋ **-ed** -ɪd **get** ˌ**in on the** ˈ**act** ; ˌ**get one's** ˈ**act together**
ACT ˌeɪ.siːˈtiː
acta ˈæk.tə
Actaeon ˈæk.ti.ən (US) ækˈtiː-
ACTH ˌeɪ.siː.tiːˈeɪtʃ, ækθ
actinic ækˈtɪn.ɪk **-ly** -li
actinide ˈæk.tɪn.aɪd **-s** -z
actinism ˈæk.tɪn.ɪz.əm
actinium ækˈtɪn.i.əm
action ˈæk.ʃən **-s** -z **-ing** -ɪŋ **-ed** -d ˈ**action** ˌ**man** ; ˈ**action** ˌ**stations**
actionable ˈæk.ʃən.ə.bl̩
Actium ˈæk.ti.əm
activable ˈæk.tɪv.ə.bl̩
acti|vate ˈæk.tɪ|.veɪt **-vates** -veɪts **-vating** -veɪ.tɪŋ (US) -veɪ.t̬ɪŋ **-vated** -veɪ.tɪd (US) -veɪ.t̬ɪd **-vator/s** -veɪ.tər/z (US) -veɪ.t̬ɚ/z
activation ˌæk.tɪˈveɪ.ʃən
active ˈæk.tɪv **-ly** -li **-ness** -nəs, -nɪs
activ|ism ˈæk.tɪ.v|ɪ.zəm **-ist/s** -ɪst/s
activit|y ækˈtɪv.ə.t|i, -ɪ.t|i (US) -ə.t̬|i **-ies** -iz
activiz|e ˈæk.tɪ.vaɪz **-es** -ɪz **-ing** -ɪŋ **-ed** -d
Acton ˈæk.tən
actor ˈæk.tər (US) -tɚ **-s** -z
actress ˈæk.trəs, -trɪs **-es** -ɪz
Acts ækts
actual ˈæk.tʃu.əl, -tju-, -tʃəl, -tʃʊl (US) -tʃu.əl, -tʃəl, -tʃʊl **-ly** -i
actualit|y ˌæk.tʃuˈæl.ə.t|i, -tju-, -ɪ.t|i (US) -tʃuˈæl.ə.t̬|i **-ies** -iz

actualiz|e, -is|e 'æk.*t*ʃu.ə.laɪz, -tju-, -ʃu- US -*t*ʃu- **-es** -ɪz **-ing** -ɪŋ **-ed** -d

actuarial ˌæk.tʃu'eə.ri.əl, -tju- US -tʃu'er.i-

actuar|y 'æk.tʃu.ə.r|i, -tju- US -tʃu- **-ies** -iz

actu|ate 'æk.tʃu|.eɪt, -tju- US -tʃu- **-ates** -eɪts **-ating** -eɪ.tɪŋ US -eɪ.t̬ɪŋ **-ated** -eɪ.tɪd US -eɪ.t̬ɪd

actuation ˌæk.tʃu'eɪ.ʃᵊn, -tju'- US -tʃu'- **-s** -z

Act-Up ˌækt'ʌp

acuity ə'kjuː.ə.ti, -ɪt.i US -ə.t̬i

acumen 'æk.jʊ.mən, -jə-, -men US ə'kjuː.mən, 'æk.jə-

acupressure 'æk.jʊ.preʃ.əʳ, -jə- US -ɚ

acupunctur|e 'æk.jʊ.pʌŋ*k*.tʃəʳ, -jə- US -tʃɚ **-ist/s** -ɪst/s

a|cute ə|'kjuːt **-cuter** -'kjuː.təʳ US -'kjuː.t̬ɚ **-cutest** -'kjuː.tɪst, -təst US -'kjuː.t̬ɪst, -t̬əst **-cutely** -'kjuːt.li **-cuteness** -'kjuːt.nəs, -nɪs **aˌcute 'angle**

acyl 'æs.ɪl **-s** -z

ad- æd-, əd-

Note: Prefix. Examples include **adjective** /'ædʒ.ɪk.tɪv/, in which it is stressed, and **admonish** /əd'mɒn.ɪʃ US -'mɑː.nɪʃ/, where it is unstressed.

ad æd

AD (*abbrev. for* **Anno Domini**) ˌeɪ'diː, ˌæn.əʊ'dɒm.ɪ.naɪ US ˌeɪ'diː, ˌæn.oʊ'dɑː.mə.niː, -'doʊ-, -naɪ

ADA ˌeɪ.diː'eɪ

Ada, ADA *woman's name, trademark, US town:* 'eɪ.də

adactylous ˌeɪ'dæk.tɪ.ləs

adag|e 'æd.ɪdʒ **-es** -ɪz

adagio ə'dɑː.dʒi.əʊ, '-ʒi- US -'dɑː.*d*ʒoʊ, -*d*ʒi.oʊ **-s** -z

Adair ə'deəʳ US -'der

Adalbert 'æd.ᵊl.bɜːt US -bɜːrt

Adam 'æd.əm ˌ**Adam's 'apple** US **'Adam's ˌapple**

adamant 'æd.ə.mənt **-ly** -li

adamantine ˌæd.ə'mæn.taɪn US -tiːn, -taɪn, -tᵊn

adamite (A) 'æd.ə.maɪt **-s** -s

Adams 'æd.əmz

adamsite 'æd.əm.zaɪt

Adamson 'æd.əm.sᵊn

Adamthwaite 'æd.əm.θweɪt

Adana 'ɑː.də.nə; ə'dɑː-

Adapazari ˌɑː.də'pɑː.zᵊr.i US -ˌpɑː.zə'riː

adapt ə'dæpt **-s** -s **-ing** -ɪŋ **-ed** -ɪd **-ive** -ɪv

adaptability əˌdæp.tə'bɪl.ə.ti, -ɪt.i US -ə.t̬i

adaptable ə'dæp.tə.bl̩ **-ness** -nɪs, -nəs

adaptation ˌæd.æp'teɪ.ʃᵊn, -əp'- **-s** -z

adapter ə'dæp.təʳ US -tɚ **-s** -z

adaption ə'dæp.ʃən, æd'æp- **-s** -z

adaptive ə'dæp.tɪv, æd'æp- **-ly** -li

adaptor ə'dæp.təʳ US -tɚ **-s** -z

Adare ə'deəʳ US -'der

Adar Sheni ɑːˌdɑː'ʃeɪ.ni US -ˌdɑːr'-

ADC ˌeɪ.diː'siː

Adcock 'æd.kɒk US -kɑːk

add æd **-s** -z **-ing** -ɪŋ **-ed** -ɪd

Addams 'æd.əmz

addax 'æd.æks **-es** -ɪz

addend ə'dend, æd'end US 'æd.end; ə'dend **-s** -z

addend|um ə'den.d|əm, æd'en- **-a** -ə

adder 'æd.əʳ US -ɚ **-s** -z **'adder's ˌtongue**

adderwort 'æd.ə.wɜːt US -ɚ.wɜːrt, -wɔːrt

addict (*n.*) 'æd.ɪkt **-s** -s

addict (*v.*) ə'dɪkt **-s** -s **-ing** -ɪŋ **-ed/ness** -ɪd/nəs, -nɪs

addictive ə'dɪk.tɪv **-ly** -li **-ness** -nəs, -nɪs

addiction ə'dɪk.ʃᵊn **-s** -z

Addington 'æd.ɪŋ.tən

Addis 'æd.ɪs

Addis Ababa ˌæd.ɪs'æb.ə.bə, -'ɑːb-

Addiscombe 'æd.ɪ.skəm

Addison 'æd.ɪ.sən

addition ə'dɪʃ.ᵊn **-s** -z

additional ə'dɪʃ.ᵊn.ᵊl **-ly** -i

additive 'æd.ɪ.tɪv, '-ə- US -ə.t̬ɪv **-s** -z

addl|e 'æd.l̩ **-es** -z **-ing** -ɪŋ, 'æd.lɪŋ **-ed** -d

addleheaded ˌæd.l̩'hed.ɪd US 'æd.l̩ˌhed- *stress shift, British only:* ˌaddleheaded 'person

Addlestone 'æd.l̩.stən

add-on 'æd.ɒn US -ɑːn **-s** -z

address (*n.*) ə'dres US 'æd.res, ə'dres **-es** -ɪz **a'ddress ˌbook** US **'address ˌbook**

address (*v.*) ə'dres **-es** -ɪz **-ing** -ɪŋ **-ed** -t

addressable ə'dres.ə.bl̩

addressee ˌæd.res'iː **-s** -z

Addressograph® ə'dres.əʊ.grɑːf, -græf US -ə.græf **-s** -s

adduc|e ə'djuːs, æd'juːs US ə'duːs, -'djuːs **-es** -ɪz **-ing** -ɪŋ **-ed** -t **-er/s** -əʳ/z US -ɚ/z **-ible** -ə.bl̩, -ɪ.bl̩

adducent ə'djuː.sᵊnt US -'duː-, -'djuː-

adduct ə'dʌkt **-s** -s **-ing** -ɪŋ **-ed** -ɪd **-ive** -ɪv

adduction ə'dʌk.ʃᵊn

adductor ə'dʌk.təʳ US -tɚ **-s** -z

Ade eɪd

-ade -eɪd, -ɑːd

Note: Suffix. Generally carries primary stress, e.g. **lemonade** /ˌlem.ə'neɪd/, but see individual entries. For instance, **escapade** is also /'es.kə.peɪd/. In words derived from French it is often pronounced /-ɑːd/, e.g. **roulade** is /ruː'lɑːd/.

Adeane ə'diːn

Adel 'æd.ᵊl

Adela *English name:* 'æd.ɪ.lə, '-ə- *foreign name:* ə'deɪ.lə

Adelaide 'æd.ᵊl.eɪd, -ɪ.leɪd US -ə.leɪd

Adele ə'del

Adelina ˌæd.ɪ'liː.nə, -ᵊl'iː- US -ə'liː-

Adeline 'æd.ɪ.liːn, -ᵊl.iːn, -aɪn US -ə.laɪn, -liːn

Adelphi ə'del.fi

ademption ə'demp.ʃᵊn **-s** -z

Aden *in the Yemen:* 'eɪ.dᵊn US 'ɑː-, 'eɪ- *in Grampian region:* 'æd.ᵊn

Adenauer 'æd.ᵊn.aʊ.əʳ, 'ɑː.dᵊn- US -ɚ

adenoid 'æd.ɪ.nɔɪd, -ᵊn.ɔɪd US -ᵊn.ɔɪd; 'æd.nɔɪd **-s** -z

adenoidal ˌæd.ɪ'nɔɪ.dᵊl, -ᵊn'ɔɪ- US -ᵊn'ɔɪ-; æd'nɔɪ-

adenoidectom|y ˌæd.ɪ.nɔɪ'dek.tə.m|i, -ᵊn.ɔɪ'- US -ᵊn.ɔɪ'-; ˌæd.nɔɪ'- **-ies** -iz

adenoma ˌæd.ɪ'nəʊ.mə, -ə'- US -'noʊ- **-s** -z **-tous** -təs US -t̬əs

adenosine æd'en.*ə*ʊ.siːn, ə'den-; ˌæd.ɪ'nəʊ- US ə'den.ə.siːn, -sᵊn

adept (*n.*) 'æd.ept, ə'dept, æd'ept **-s** -s

adept (*adj.*) ə'dept, æd'ept; 'æd.ept US ə'dept **-ly** -li

adequacy 'æd.ɪ.kwə.si, '-ə-

adequate 'æd.ɪ.kwət, '-ə-, -kwɪt **-ly** -li **-ness** -nəs, -nɪs

adessive ə'des.ɪv, æd'es-

à deux æ'dɜː

adher|e əd'hɪəʳ, æd-; ə'dɪəʳ US əd'hɪr, æd- **-es** -z **-ing** -ɪŋ **-ed** -d **-er/s** -əʳ/z US -ɚ/z

adheren|ce əd'hɪə.rᵊn|*t*s, æd-, -'her.ᵊn|*t*s; ə'dɪə.rᵊn|*t*s US əd'hɪr.ᵊn|*t*s, æd- **-t/s** -t/s

adhesion əd'hiː.ʒən, æd-; ə'diː- **-s** -z

adhesive əd'hiː.sɪv, æd-, -zɪv; ə'diː.sɪv, -zɪv **-ly** -li **-ness** -nɪs, -nəs

ad hoc ˌæd'hɒk, -'həʊk US -'hɑːk, -'hoʊk

ad hominem ˌæd'hɒm.ɪ.nəm, '-ə-, -nem US -'hɑː.mə.nəm, -nem

adiabatic ˌeɪ.daɪə'bæt.ɪk, ˌæd.aɪə- US ˌæd.i.ə'bæt̬-; ˌeɪ.daɪə'- **-ally** -ᵊl.i, -li

Adidas® 'æd.ɪ.dæs; ə'diː.dəs US ə'diː.dəs

Adie 'eɪ.di

adieu ə'djuː *as if French:* æd'jɜː US ə'duː, -'djuː

adieus, adieux ə'djuː, -'djuːz *as if French:* æd'jɜː US ə'duːz, -'djuːz

Adige 'æd.ɪ.dʒeɪ US 'ɑː.di.eɪ, -ə

ad infinitum ˌæd.ɪn.fɪ'naɪ.təm US ˌæd.ɪn.fɪ'naɪ.t̬əm, ˌɑːd-

adios 'æd.i.ɒs, --'- ⓊⓈ ˌɑː.d.i'oʊs, ˌæ.di'-
adipocere ˌæd.ɪ.pəʊ'sɪəʳ ⓊⓈ 'æd.ə.poʊ.sɪr, -pə-
adipose 'æd.ɪ.pəʊs, -pəʊz ⓊⓈ -ə.poʊs
adiposity ˌæd.ɪ'pɒs.ə.ti, -ɪ.ti ⓊⓈ -ə'pɑː.sə.t̬i
Adirondack ˌæd.ɪ'rɒn.dæk, -ə'rɒn- ⓊⓈ -rɑːn- **-s** -s
adit 'æd.ɪt **-s** -s
adjacency ə'dʒeɪ.sᵊnt.si
adjacent ə'dʒeɪ.sᵊnt **-ly** -li
adjectival ˌædʒ.ɪk'taɪ.vᵊl, -ek'-, -ək'- **-ly** -i
adjective 'ædʒ.ɪk.tɪv, -ek-, -ək- **-s** -z
adjoin ə'dʒɔɪn **-s** -z **-ing** -ɪŋ **-ed** -d
adjourn ə'dʒɜːn ⓊⓈ -'dʒɜːrn **-s** -z **-ing** -ɪŋ **-ed** -d **-ment/s** -mənt/s
adjudg|e ə'dʒʌdʒ, ædʒ'ʌdʒ ⓊⓈ ə'dʒʌdʒ **-es** -ɪz **-ing** -ɪŋ **-ed** -d **-ment/s** -mənt/s
adjudi|cate ə'dʒuː.dɪ|.keɪt, -də- **-cates** -keɪts **-cating** -keɪ.tɪŋ ⓊⓈ -keɪ.t̬ɪŋ **-cated** -keɪ.tɪd ⓊⓈ -keɪ.t̬ɪd
adjudication əˌdʒuː.dɪ'keɪ.ʃᵊn, -də'- **-s** -z
adjudicator ə'dʒuː.dɪ.keɪ.təʳ, -də- ⓊⓈ -t̬ɚ **-s** -z
adjunct 'ædʒ.ʌŋ*k*t **-s** -s **-ly** -li; ə'dʒʌŋ*k*t.li
adjunction ə'dʒʌŋ*k*.ʃᵊn, ædʒ'ʌŋ*k*-
adjunctival ˌædʒ.ʌŋ*k*'taɪ.vᵊl
adjuration ˌædʒ.ə'reɪ.ʃᵊn, -ʊə'-, -ɔː'- ⓊⓈ -ə'- **-s** -z
adjuratory ə'dʒʊə.rə.tᵊr.i, -'dʒɔː- ⓊⓈ -'dʒʊr.ə.tɔːr-
adjur|e ə'dʒʊəʳ, -ɔːʳ ⓊⓈ -dʒʊr **-es** -z **-ing** -ɪŋ **-ed** -d
adjust ə'dʒʌst **-s** -s **-ing** -ɪŋ **-ed** -ɪd **-able** -ə.bl̩ **-er/s** -əʳ/z ⓊⓈ -ɚ/z
adjustment ə'dʒʌst.mənt **-s** -s
adjutage 'ædʒ.ʊ.tɪdʒ; ə'dʒuː-
adjutan|cy 'ædʒ.ʊ.tᵊn|*t*.si, '-ə- **-t/s** -t/s
Adkins 'æd.kɪnz
Adkinson 'æd.kɪn.sən
Adlai 'æd.leɪ
Adler 'æd.ləʳ, 'ɑːd.ləʳ ⓊⓈ -lɚ
ad-lib ˌæd'lɪb **-s** -z **-bing** -ɪŋ **-bed** -d
Adlington 'æd.lɪŋ.tən
ad|man 'æd.mæn, -mən **-men** -men, -mən
admass 'æd.mæs
admeasur|e æd'meʒ.əʳ, əd- ⓊⓈ -ɚ, -'meɪ.ʒɚ **-es** -z **-ing** -ɪŋ **-ed** -d **-ement/s** -mənt/s
Admetus æd'miː.təs ⓊⓈ -t̬əs
admin 'æd.mɪn
administer əd'mɪn.ɪ.stəʳ, '-ə- ⓊⓈ -ɚ, æd- **-s** -z **-ing** -ɪŋ **-ed** -d
administr|able əd'mɪn.ɪ.str|ə.bl̩, '-ə- ⓊⓈ əd-, æd- **-ant/s** -ᵊnt/s
admini|strate əd'mɪn.ɪ|.streɪt, '-ə- ⓊⓈ əd-, æd- **-strates** -streɪts **-strating** -streɪ.tɪŋ ⓊⓈ -streɪ.t̬ɪŋ **-strated** -streɪ.tɪd ⓊⓈ -streɪ.t̬ɪd
administration ədˌmɪn.ɪ'streɪ.ʃᵊn, -ə'- ⓊⓈ əd-, æd- **-s** -z
administrative əd'mɪn.ɪ.strə.tɪv, '-ə-, -streɪ- ⓊⓈ əd-, æd- **-ly** -li
administrator əd'mɪn.ɪ.streɪ.təʳ, '-ə- ⓊⓈ -t̬ɚ, æd- **-s** -z **-ship/s** -ʃɪp/s
administra|trix əd'mɪn.ɪ.streɪ|.trɪks, '-ə- ⓊⓈ əd-, æd- **-trixes** -trɪk.sɪz **-trices** -trɪ.siːz
admirab|le 'æd.mᵊr.ə.bl̩ **-ly** -li **-leness** -l̩.nəs, -nɪs
admiral 'æd.mᵊr.əl, -mɪ.rəl **-s** -z
admiralt|y (A) 'æd.mᵊr.əl.t|i, -mɪ.rəl- ⓊⓈ -t̬|i **-ies** -iz
admiration ˌæd.mə'reɪ.ʃᵊn, -mɪ'-
admir|e əd'maɪəʳ ⓊⓈ -'maɪɚ, æd- **-es** -z **-ing/ly** -ɪŋ/li **-ed** -d **-er/s** -əʳ/z ⓊⓈ **-er/z** -ɚ/z
admissibility ədˌmɪs.ə'bɪl.ə.ti, æd-, -ɪ'-, -ɪ.ti ⓊⓈ -ə.t̬i
admissibl|e əd'mɪs.ə.bl|̩, æd-, -ɪ.bl|̩ **-y** -i
admission əd'mɪʃ.ᵊn, æd- **-s** -z
ad|mit əd|'mɪt **-mits** -'mɪts **-mitting** -'mɪt.ɪŋ ⓊⓈ -'mɪt̬.ɪŋ **-mitted/ly** -'mɪt.ɪd/li ⓊⓈ -'mɪt̬.ɪd/li
admittanc|e əd'mɪt.ᵊn*t*s **-es** -ɪz
admix æd'mɪks, əd- **-es** -ɪz **-ing** -ɪŋ **-ed** -t
admixture əd'mɪks.tʃəʳ, æd- **-s** -z
admonish əd'mɒn.ɪʃ, æd- ⓊⓈ -'mɑː.nɪʃ **-es** -ɪz **-ing/ly** -ɪŋ **-ed** -t **-ment/s** -mənt/s
admonition ˌæd.mə'nɪʃ.ᵊn **-s** -z
admonitory əd'mɒn.ɪ.tᵊr.i, æd- ⓊⓈ -'mɑː.nə.tɔːr-
Adnams 'æd.nəmz
ad nauseam ˌæd'nɔː.zi.æm, -si-, -əm ⓊⓈ -'nɑː-, -'nɔː-
adnomial əd'nəʊ.mi.əl, æd'- ⓊⓈ -'noʊ- **-s** -z
ado ə'duː
adobe ə'dəʊ.bi, æd'əʊ- ⓊⓈ -'doʊ- **-s** -z
adolescence ˌæd.ᵊl'es.ᵊn*t*s, -əʊ'les- ⓊⓈ -ə'les-
adolescent ˌæd.ᵊl'es.ᵊnt, -əʊ'les- ⓊⓈ -ə'les- **-s** -s
Adolf 'æd.ɒlf ⓊⓈ 'eɪ.dɑːlf, 'æd.ɑːlf
Adolphus ə'dɒl.fəs ⓊⓈ -'dɑːl-
Adonai 'æd.əʊ.naɪ ⓊⓈ ˌɑː.də'naɪ, -doʊ'-, -'nɔɪ
Adonais ˌæd.əʊ'neɪ.ɪs ⓊⓈ -ə'-
Adonijah ˌæd.əʊ'naɪ.dʒə ⓊⓈ -ə'-
Adonis ə'dəʊ.nɪs, -'dɒn.ɪs ⓊⓈ -'dɑː.nɪs, -'doʊ-
adopt ə'dɒpt ⓊⓈ -'dɑːpt **-s** -s **-ing** -ɪŋ **-ed** -ɪd **-ive** -ɪv
adoption ə'dɒp.ʃᵊn ⓊⓈ -'dɑːp- **-s** -z
adoptionism ə'dɒp.ʃᵊn.ɪ.zᵊm ⓊⓈ -'dɑːp-
adorab|le ə'dɔː.rə.bl|̩ ⓊⓈ -'dɔːr.ə- **-ly** -li **-leness** -l̩.nəs, -nɪs
adoration ˌæd.ə'reɪ.ʃᵊn, -ɔː'- ⓊⓈ -ə'reɪ- **-s** -z
ador|e ə'dɔːʳ ⓊⓈ -'dɔːr **-es** -z **-ing/ly** -ɪŋ/li **-ed** -d **-er/s** -əʳ/z ⓊⓈ -ɚ/z
adorn ə'dɔːn ⓊⓈ -'dɔːrn **-s** -z **-ing** -ɪŋ **-ed** -d **-ment/s** -mənt/s
Adorno ə'dɔː.nəʊ ⓊⓈ -'dɔːr.noʊ
ADP ˌeɪ.diː'piː
Adrastus ə'dræs.təs
adrenal ə'driː.nᵊl **a'drenal ˌgland**
adrenalin ə'dren.ᵊl.ɪn ⓊⓈ -ə.lɪn
adrenocortical əˌdriː.nəʊ'kɔː.tɪ.kᵊl ⓊⓈ -noʊ'kɔːr.t̬ɪ-, -ˌdren.oʊ'-, -ə'-
adrenocorticotroph|ic əˌdriː.nəʊˌkɔː.tɪ.kəʊ'trɒf|.ɪk ⓊⓈ -noʊˌkɔːr.t̬ɪ.koʊ'troʊ.f|ɪk, -ˌdren.oʊˌ-, -əˌ-, -'trɑː- **-in** -ɪn
Adria 'eɪ.dri.ə
Adrian 'eɪ.dri.ən
Adriana ˌeɪ.dri'ɑː.nə
Adrianople ˌeɪ.dri.ə'nəʊ.pl̩, ˌæd.ri- ⓊⓈ -'noʊ-
Adrianopolis ˌeɪ.dri.ə'nɒp.ᵊl.ɪs, ˌæd.ri- ⓊⓈ -'nɑː.pᵊl-
Adriatic ˌeɪ.dri'æt.ɪk ⓊⓈ -'æt̬- *stress shift:* ˌAdriatic 'Sea
Adrienne ˌeɪ.dri'en, ˌæd.ri'-; 'eɪ.dri.ən, 'æd.ri-
adrift ə'drɪft
adroit ə'drɔɪt **-est** -əst, -ɪst **-ly** -li **-ness** -nəs, -nɪs
adsorb æd'zɔːb, əd-, -'sɔːb ⓊⓈ -'sɔːrb, -'zɔːrb **-s** -z **-ing** -ɪŋ **-ed** -d
adsorbent æd'zɔː.bᵊnt, əd'-, -'sɔː- ⓊⓈ -'sɔːr-, -'zɔːr-
adsorption æd'zɔːp.ʃᵊn, əd'-, -'sɔːp- ⓊⓈ -'sɔːrp-, -'zɔːrp-
adsorptive æd'zɔːp.tɪv, əd'-, -'sɔːp- ⓊⓈ -'sɔːrp-, -'zɔːrp-
adsum 'æd.sʌm, -sʊm, -səm
adularia ˌæd.jʊ'leə.ri.ə, -jə'-, ˌædʒ.ʊ'- ⓊⓈ ˌædʒ.ʊ'ler.i-, ˌæd.jə'-
adu|late 'æd.jʊ|.leɪt, -jə-, 'ædʒ.ʊ-, '-ə- ⓊⓈ 'ædʒ.ə-, 'æd.jə-, '-ə- **-lates** -leɪts **-lating** -leɪ.tɪŋ ⓊⓈ -leɪ.t̬ɪŋ **-lated** -leɪ.tɪd ⓊⓈ -leɪ.t̬ɪd
adulation ˌæd.jʊ'leɪ.ʃᵊn, -jə'-, ˌædʒ.ʊ'-, -ə'- ⓊⓈ ˌædʒ.ə'-, ˌæd.jə'-, -ə'- **-s** -z
adulatory ˌæd.jʊ'leɪ.tᵊr.i, -jə'-, ˌædʒ.ʊ'-, -ə'-; 'æd.jʊ.leɪ-, -jə-, 'ædʒ.ʊ-, '-ə-, -tᵊr.i ⓊⓈ 'ædʒ.ᵊl.ə.tɔːr-, 'æd.jᵊl-, -ᵊl-
Adullam ə'dʌl.əm **-ite/s** -aɪt/s
adult 'æd.ʌlt, ə'dʌlt ⓊⓈ ə'dʌlt, 'æd.ʌlt **-s** -s **ˌadult edu'cation**
adulterant ə'dʌl.tᵊr.ənt ⓊⓈ -t̬ɚ- **-s** -s

adulter|ate ə'dʌl.tᵊr|.eɪt US -t̬ə.r|eɪt **-ates** -eɪts **-ating** -eɪ.tɪŋ US -eɪ.t̬ɪŋ **-ated** -eɪ.tɪd US -eɪ.t̬ɪd **-ator/s** -eɪ.təʳ/z US -eɪ.t̬ɚ/z

adulteration ə,dʌl.tᵊr'eɪ.ʃᵊn US -t̬ə'reɪ- **-s** -z

adulterer ə'dʌl.tᵊr.əʳ US -t̬ɚ.ɚ **-s** -z

adulteress ə'dʌl.tᵊr.es, -ɪs, -əs US -t̬ɚ-, '-trɪs **-es** -ɪz

adulterous ə'dʌl.tᵊr.əs, '-trəs US '-t̬ɚ.əs, '-trəs **-ly** -li

adulter|y ə'dʌl.tᵊr|.i, '-tr|i US '-t̬ɚ.i '-tri **-ies** -iz

adulthood 'æd.ʌlt.hʊd, ə'dʌlt- US ə'dʌlt-

adum|brate 'æd.ʌm|.breɪt, -əm- **-brates** -breɪts **-brating** -breɪ.tɪŋ US -breɪ.t̬ɪŋ **-brated** -breɪ.tɪd US -breɪ.t̬ɪd

adumbration ,æd.ʌm'breɪ.ʃᵊn, -əm- **-s** -z

Adur 'eɪ.dəʳ US -dɚ

ad valorem ,æd.və'lɔː.rem, -væl'ɔː-, -rəm US -və'lɔːr.əm

advanc|e əd'vɑːn*t*s US -'væn*t*s, æd- **-es** -ɪz **-ing** -ɪŋ **-ed** -t **-ment/s** -mənt/s **ad,vance 'notice; ad,vance 'payment; Ad'vanced ,Level**

advantag|e əd'vɑːn.tɪdʒ US -'væn.t̬ɪdʒ, æd- **-es** -ɪz

advantageous ,æd.vən'teɪ.dʒəs, -vɑːn'-, -væn'- US -væn'-, -vən'- **-ly** -li **-ness** -nəs, -nɪs

adven|e æd'viːn, əd- **-es** -z **-ing** -ɪŋ **-ed** -d

advent (A) 'æd.vent, -vənt **-s** -s **'Advent ,calendar**

Adventism 'æd.ven.tɪ.zᵊm, -vən- US -vən-

Adventist 'æd.ven.tɪst, -vən- US -vən-; əd'ven-

adventitious ,æd.vᵊn'tɪʃ.əs, -ven- **-ly** -li

adventive æd'ven.tɪv US -t̬ɪv **-ly** -li

advent|ure əd'ven.tʃ|əʳ US -tʃ|ɚ, æd- **-ures** -əz, -ɚz **-uring** -ᵊr.ɪŋ **-ured** -əd, -ɚd **-urer/s** -ᵊr.əʳ/z US -ɚ.ɚ/z **-uress/es** -ᵊr.əs/ɪz, -ə.res/ɪz **ad,venture 'playground**

adventuresome əd'ven.tʃə.sᵊm US -tʃɚ-, æd-

adventurous əd'ven.tʃᵊr.əs US əd-, æd- **-ly** -li **-ness** -nəs, -nɪs

adverb 'æd.vɜːb US -vɜːrb **-s** -z

adverbial əd'vɜː.bi.əl, æd- US -'vɜːr- **-ly** -i

adversarial ,æd.və'seə.ri.əl, -vɜː'- US -vɚ'ser.i- **-ly** -i

adversar|y 'æd.və.sᵊr|.i, əd'vɜː- US 'æd.vɚ.ser- **-ies** -iz

adversative əd'vɜː.sə.tɪv, æd- US -'vɜːr.sə.t̬ɪv

adverse 'æd.vɜːs, -'-, əd- US æd'vɜːrs, '-- **-ly** -li

adversit|y əd'vɜː.sə.t|i, -sɪ- US -'vɜːr.sə.t̬|i, æd- **-ies** -iz

advert (*n.*) 'æd.vɜːt US -vɜːrt **-s** -s

ad|vert (*v.*) əd|'vɜːt, æd- US -'vɜːrt **-verts** -'vɜːts US -'vɜːrts **-verting** -'vɜː.tɪŋ US -'vɜːr.t̬ɪŋ **-verted** -'vɜː.tɪd US -'vɜːr.t̬ɪd

advertenc|e əd'vɜː.tᵊn*t*s US -'vɜːr-, æd- **-y** -i

advertent əd'vɜː.tᵊnt US -'vɜːr-, æd- **-ly** -li

advertis|e, -iz|e 'æd.və.taɪz US -vɚ- **-es** -ɪz **-ing** -ɪŋ **-ed** -d **-er/s** -əʳ/z US -ɚ/z

advertisement, -ize- əd'vɜː.tɪs.mənt, -tɪz-, -təs-, -təz- US ,æd.vɚ'taɪz.mənt; əd'vɜːr.t̬əs-, -t̬əz- **-s** -s

advertorial ,æd.və'tɔː.ri.əl US -vɚ'tɔːr.i-

advic|e əd'vaɪs US əd-, æd- **-es** -ɪz

advisability əd,vaɪ.zə'bɪl.ə.ti, '-ɪ- US -ə.t̬i, æd-

advisab|le əd'vaɪ.zə.b|l̩ US əd-, æd- **-ly** -li **-leness** -l̩.nəs, -nɪs

advis|e əd'vaɪz US əd-, æd- **-es** -ɪz **-ing** -ɪŋ **-ed** -d **-edly** -ɪd.li **-edness** -ɪd.nəs, -nɪs

adviser, advisor əd'vaɪ.zəʳ US -zɚ, æd- **-s** -z

advisor|y əd'vaɪ.zᵊr|.i US əd-, æd- **-ies** -iz **ad'visory ,body**

advocaat 'æd.vəʊ.kɑː, -kɑːt US -voʊ-

advocacy 'æd.və.kə.si

advocate (*n.*) 'æd.və.kət, -keɪt, -kɪt **-s** -s

advo|cate (*v.*) 'æd.və|.keɪt **-cates** -keɪts **-cating** -keɪ.tɪŋ US -keɪ.t̬ɪŋ **-cated** -keɪ.tɪd US -keɪ.t̬ɪd **-cator/s** -keɪ.təʳ/z US -keɪ.t̬ɚ/z

advocation ,æd.və'keɪ.ʃᵊn

advowson əd'vaʊ.zᵊn **-s** -z

Adwa 'ɑː.dwə

Adwick le Street ,æd.wɪk.lɪ'striːt

Adye 'eɪ.di

adynamia ,eɪ.daɪ'neɪ.mi.ə, ,æd.ɪ'-

adynamic ,eɪ.daɪ'næm.ɪk, ,æd.aɪ'-, -ɪ'-

adz|e, adz ædz **-es** -ɪz **-ing** -ɪŋ **-ed** -d

adzuki æd'zuː.ki **ad'zuki ,bean**

Aeacus 'iː.ə.kəs

aedile 'iː.daɪl **-s** -z **-ship/s** -ʃɪp/s

Aeetes iː'iː.tiːz

Aegean iː'dʒiː.ən, ɪ'-

Aegeus 'iː.dʒi.əs US 'iː.dʒi.əs, 'iː.dʒuːs

Aegina iː'dʒaɪ.nə, ɪ'dʒaɪ-

aegis 'iː.dʒɪs

Aegisthus iː'dʒɪs.θəs, ɪ'dʒɪs-

aegrotat 'aɪ.grəʊ.tæt, 'iː- US -groʊ- **-s** -s

Aegyptus iː'dʒɪp.təs

Aelfric 'æl.frɪk

Aemilius iː'mɪl.i.əs, ɪ'mɪl-

Aeneas iː'niː.əs, ɪ'niː-, -æs

Aeneid 'iː.ni.ɪd, iː'niː.ɪd, ɪ'- **-s** -z

Aeneus 'iː.ni.əs, iː'niː-, ɪ-

Aeoli|a iː'əʊ.li|.ə US -'oʊ- **-an/s** -ən/z

Aeolic iː'ɒl.ɪk, -'əʊ.lɪk US -'ɑː.lɪk

Aeolus 'iː.əʊ.ləs US '-ə-

aeon 'iː.ən, -ɒn US -ɑːn **-s** -z

aera|te eə'reɪ|t US er'eɪ|t **-tes** -ts **-ting** -tɪŋ US -t̬ɪŋ **-ted** -tɪd US -t̬ɪd **-tor/s** -təʳ/z US -t̬ɚ/z

aeration eə'reɪ.ʃᵊn US er'eɪ-

aerial 'eə.ri.əl US 'er.i- **-s** -z **-ly** -i

aerie 'ɪə.ri, 'eə- US 'er.i, 'ɪr-, 'eɪ.ri **-s** -z

aerif|y 'eə.rɪ.faɪ US 'er.ə- **-ies** -z **-ying** -ɪŋ **-ied** -aɪd

Aer Lingus® ,eə'lɪŋ.gəs US ,er-

aero- eə.rəʊ-; eə'rɒ- US er.oʊ-, er.ə-; er'ɑː-

Note: Prefix. Either takes primary or secondary stress on the first syllable, e.g. **aeronaut** /'eə.rə.nɔːt US 'er.ə.nɑːt/ **aeronautic** /,eə.rə'nɔː.tɪk US ,er.ə'nɑː.t̬ɪk/, or primary stress on the second syllable, e.g. **aerology** /eə'rɒl.ə.dʒi US er'ɑː.lə-/.

aero 'eə.rəʊ US 'er.oʊ

aeroballistics ,eə.rəʊ.bə'lɪs.tɪks US ,er.oʊ-

aerobatic ,eə.rəʊ'bæt.ɪk US ,er.oʊ'bæt̬- **-s** -s **-ally** -ᵊl.i, -li

aerobe 'eə.rəʊb US 'er.oʊb **-s** -z

aerobic eə'rəʊ.bɪk US er'oʊ- **-s** -s

aerodrome 'eə.rə.drəʊm US 'er.ə.droʊm **-s** -z

aerodynamic ,eə.rəʊ.daɪ'næm.ɪk, -dɪ'- US ,er.oʊ- **-s** -s **-ally** -ᵊl.i, -li *stress shift:* ,aerodynamic 'fairing

aerodyne 'eə.rəʊ.daɪn US 'er.ə- **-s** -z

Aeroflot® 'eə.rəʊ.flɒt US 'er.ə.floʊt, -flɑːt

aerofoil 'eə.rəʊ.fɔɪl US 'er.oʊ- **-s** -z

aerogram, aerogramme 'eə.rəʊ.græm US 'er.ə- **-s** -z

aerolite 'eə.rəʊ.laɪt US 'er.ə- **-s** -s

aerolith 'eə.rəʊ.lɪθ US 'er.ə- **-s** -s

aerological ,eə.rəʊ'lɒdʒ.ɪ.kᵊl US ,er.oʊ'lɑː.dʒɪ-

aerologist eə'rɒl.ə.dʒɪst US er'ɑːl.ə- **-s** -s

aerolog|y eə'rɒl.ə.dʒ|i US er'ɑː.lə- **-ist/s** -ɪst/s

aeronaut 'eə.rə.nɔːt US 'er.ə.nɑːt, -nɔːt **-s** -s

aeronautic ,eə.rə'nɔː.tɪk US ,er.ə'nɑː.t̬ɪk, -'nɔː- **-s** -s **-al** -ᵊl

aerophone 'eə.rə.fəʊn US 'er.ə.foʊn **-s** -z

aeroplane 'eə.rə.pleɪn US 'er- **-s** -z

aerosol 'eə.rə.sɒl (US) 'er.ə.sɑːl **-s** -z
aerospace 'eə.rəʊ.speɪs (US) 'er.oʊ-
aerostat 'eə.rəʊ.stæt (US) 'er.oʊ- **-s** -s
Aertex® 'eə.teks (US) 'er-
aer|y (*n.*) 'ɪə.r|i, 'eə- (US) 'er|.i, 'ɪr-, 'eɪ.r|i **-ies** -iz
aery (*adj.*) 'eə.ri (US) 'er|.i, 'eɪ.ə.ri
Aeschines 'iː.skɪ.niːz, -skə.niːz (US) 'es.kə-, 'iː.skə-
Aeschylus 'iː.skɪ.ləs, -skə.ləs (US) 'es.kə-, 'iː.skə-
Aesculapi|us ˌiː.skjʊ'leɪ.pi|.əs (US) ˌes.kjə'-, -kə'- **-an** -ən
Aesop 'iː.sɒp (US) -sɑːp, -səp
aesthete 'iːs.θiːt, 'es- (US) 'es- **-s** -s
aesthetic iːs'θet.ɪk, ɪs-, es- (US) es'θet̬-, ɪs- **-s** -s **-al** -əl **-ally** -əl.i, -li
aesthetic|ism iːs'θet.ɪ.s|ɪ.zəm, ɪs-, es- (US) es-, ɪs- **-ist/s** -ɪst/s
aestival iː'staɪ.vəl (US) 'es.tə-, es'taɪ-
Aethelstan 'æθ.əl.stən, -stæn
aether 'iː.θəʳ (US) -θɚ
aetiolog|y ˌiː.ti'ɒl.ə.dʒ|i (US) -t̬i'ɑː.lə- **-ist/s** -ɪst/s
Aetna 'et.nə
afar ə'fɑːʳ (US) -'fɑːr
afeard ə'fɪəd (US) -'fɪrd
affability ˌæf.ə'bɪl.ə.ti, -ɪ.ti (US) -ə.t̬i
affab|le 'æf.ə.b|l̩ **-ly** -li **-leness** -l̩.nəs, -nɪs
affair ə'feəʳ (US) -'fer **-s** -z
affect (*v.*) ə'fekt **-s** -s **-ing/ly** -ɪŋ/li **-ed** -ɪd
affect (*n.*) *in psychology:* 'æf.ekt **-s** -s
affectation ˌæf.ek'teɪ.ʃən, -ɪk'- **-s** -z
affected ə'fek.tɪd **-ly** -li **-ness** -nəs, -nɪs
affection ə'fek.ʃən **-s** -z
affectionate ə'fek.ʃən.ət, -ɪt **-ly** -li **-ness** -nəs, -nɪs
affective ə'fek.tɪv, æf'ek-
affenpinscher 'æf.ən,pɪn.*t*ʃəʳ (US) -ˌpɪn*t*.ʃɚ **-s** -z
afferent 'æf.ər.ənt
affettuoso əˌfet.ju'əʊ.səʊ, æfˌet-, -zəʊ (US) əˌfet.ju'oʊ.soʊ, æfˌet-, -ˌetʃ.u'-
affianc|e ə'faɪən*t*s **-es** -ɪz **-ing** -ɪŋ **-ed** -t
affiant ə'faɪənt **-s** -s
affich|e æf'iːʃ, ə'fiːʃ **-es** -ɪz
affidavit ˌæf.ɪ'deɪ.vɪt, -ə'- **-s** -s
affili|ate ə'fɪl.i|.eɪt **-ates** -eɪts **-ating** -eɪ.tɪŋ (US) -eɪ.t̬ɪŋ **-ated** -eɪ.tɪd (US) -eɪ.t̬ɪd
affiliation əˌfɪl.i'eɪ.ʃən **-s** -z
affinit|y ə'fɪn.ə.t|i, -ɪt|i (US) -ə.t̬|i **-ies** -iz
affirm ə'fɜːm (US) -'fɜːrm **-s** -z **-ing** -ɪŋ **-ed** -d **-able** -ə.bl̩
affirmation ˌæf.ə'meɪ.ʃən (US) -ɚ'- **-s** -z
affirmative ə'fɜː.mə.tɪv (US) -'fɜːr.mə.t̬ɪv **-ly** -li **afˌfirmative 'action**
affirmatory ə'fɜː.mə.tər.i (US) -'fɜːr.mə.tɔːr-
affix (*n.*) 'æf.ɪks **-es** -ɪz
affix (*v.*) ə'fɪks, 'æf.ɪks **-es** -ɪz **-ing** -ɪŋ **-ed** -d
affixation ˌæf.ɪk'seɪ.ʃən
affixture æf'ɪks.tʃəʳ (US) -tʃɚ, æf'ɪks-
afflatus ə'fleɪ.təs (US) -t̬əs
afflict ə'flɪkt **-s** -s **-ing** -ɪŋ **-ed** -ɪd **-ive** -ɪv
affliction ə'flɪk.ʃən **-s** -z
affluence 'æf.lu.ən*t*s
afflux 'æf.lʌks **-es** -ɪz
afford ə'fɔːd (US) -'fɔːrd **-s** -z **-ing** -ɪŋ **-ed** -ɪd
affordab|le ə'fɔː.də.b|l̩ (US) -'fɔːr- **-ly** -li
afforest ə'fɒr.ɪst, æf'ɒr- (US) ə'fɔːr.əst **-s** -s **-ing** -ɪŋ **-ed** -ɪd
afforestation æfˌɒr.ɪ'steɪ.ʃən, əˌfɒr-, -ə'- (US) əˌfɔːr.ə'- **-s** -z
affranchis|e ə'fræn.*t*ʃaɪz, æf'ræn- (US) ə'fræn.tʃaɪz **-es** -ɪz **-ing** -ɪŋ **-ed** -d
affray ə'freɪ **-s** -z
affricate 'æf.rɪ.kət, -rə-, -kɪt, -keɪt (US) -kɪt **-s** -s
affricated 'æf.rɪ.keɪ.tɪd, -rə- (US) -t̬ɪd
affrication ˌæf.rɪ'keɪ.ʃən, -rə'-
affricative æf'rɪk.ə.tɪv, ə'frɪk- (US) -t̬ɪv **-s** -z
af|fright ə|'fraɪt **-frights** -'fraɪts **-frighting** -'fraɪ.tɪŋ (US) -'fraɪ.t̬ɪŋ **-frighted/ly** -'fraɪ.tɪd/li (US) -'fraɪ.t̬ɪd/li
af|front ə|'frʌnt **-fronts** -'frʌnts **-fronting** -'frʌn.tɪŋ (US) -'frʌn.t̬ɪŋ **-fronted** -'frʌn.tɪd (US) -'frʌn.t̬ɪd
Afghan 'æf.gæn **-s** -z ˌ**Afghan 'hound**
afghani æf'gɑː.ni, -'gæn.i **-s** -z
Afghanistan æf'gæn.ɪ.stæn, '-ə-, -stɑːn, æfˌgæn.ɪ'stɑːn, -ə'-, -'stæn (US) æf'gæn.ə.stæn
aficionado əˌfɪʃ.i.ən'ɑː.dəʊ, -ˌfɪs- *as if Spanish:* æfˌɪθ.jə'nɑː.dəʊ (US) əˌfɪʃ.i.ə'nɑː.doʊ, -ˌfɪs-, -ˌfiː.si- **-s** -z
afield ə'fiːld
afire ə'faɪəʳ (US) -'faɪɚ
aflame ə'fleɪm
aflatoxin ˌæf.lə'tɒk.sɪn (US) -'tɑːk.sən
AFL-CIO eɪ.ef,el.siː.aɪ'əʊ (US) -'oʊ
afloat ə'fləʊt (US) -'floʊt
aflutter ə'flʌt.əʳ (US) -'flʌt̬.ɚ
afoot ə'fʊt
afore ə'fɔːʳ (US) -'fɔːr
aforementioned ə'fɔː.men.*t*ʃənd, əˌfɔː'men- (US) ə'fɔːr.men*t*.ʃənd
Note: In British English, the latter form is not used attributively.
aforesaid ə'fɔː.sed (US) -'fɔːr-
aforethought ə'fɔː.θɔːt (US) -'fɔːr.θɑːt, -θɔːt
aforetime ə'fɔː.taɪm (US) -'fɔːr-
a fortiori eɪˌfɔː.ti'ɔː.raɪ, ɑːˌ-, -ri (US) ˌeɪ.fɔːr.t̬i'ɔːr.i, -ʃi'-, -aɪ
afraid ə'freɪd
afreet 'æf.riːt, ə'friːt **-s** -s
afresh ə'freʃ
Afric 'æf.rɪk
Afric|a 'æf.rɪ.k|ə **-an/s** -ən/z
African-American ˌæf.rɪ.kən.ə'mer.ɪ.kən **-s** -z
Africander ˌæf.rɪ'kæn.dəʳ (US) -dɚ **-s** -z
Africanist 'æf.rɪ.kə.nɪst **-s** -s
Africanization, -isa- ˌæf.rɪ.kə.naɪ'zeɪ.ʃən, -rə-, -nɪ'- (US) -nɪ'-
Africaniz|e, -is|e 'æf.rɪ.kə.naɪz **-es** -ɪz **-ing** -ɪŋ **-ed** -d
Africanus ˌæf.rɪ'kɑː.nəs, -'keɪ-
Afridi æf'riː.di, ə'friː- **-s** -z
Afrikaans ˌæf.rɪ'kɑːn*t*s, -rə'kɑːn*t*s, -rɪk'ɑːnz, -rə'kɑːnz
Afrikaner ˌæf.rɪ'kɑː.nəʳ (US) -nɚ **-s** -z
afrit 'æf.riːt, ə'friːt **-s** -s
Afro- ˌæf.rəʊ- (US) ˌæf.roʊ-
Note: Prefix. Normally carries secondary stress on the first syllable, e.g. **Afro-American** /ˌæf.rəʊ.ə'mer.ɪ.kən (US) -roʊ-/.
Afro 'æf.rəʊ (US) -roʊ **-s** -z
Afro-American ˌæf.rəʊ.ə'mer.ɪ.kən (US) -roʊ- **-s** -z
Afro-Asian ˌæf.rəʊ'eɪ.ʃən, -ʒən (US) -roʊ'eɪ.ʒən, -ʃən **-s** -z
Afro-Asiatic ˌæf.rəʊ.eɪ.ʃi'æt.ɪk, -si'-, -ʒi'-, -zi'- (US) -roʊ.eɪ.ʒi'-, -ʃi'-
Afro-Caribbean ˌæf.rəʊ.kær.ɪ'biː.ən (US) -roʊ.ker-, -kær-; -kə'rɪb.i- **-s** -z
aft ɑːft (US) æft
after- 'ɑːf.tə- (US) 'æf.tɚ-
Note: Prefix. Words containing **after-** usually carry primary stress on the first syllable, e.g. **afterglow** /'ɑːf.tə.gləʊ (US) 'æf.tɚ.gloʊ/, but there are exceptions, including **afternoon** /ˌɑːf.tə'nuːn (US) ˌæf.tɚ-/.
after 'ɑːf.təʳ (US) 'æf.tɚ ˌ**after 'all** ; ˌ**After 'Eights®**
afterbirth 'ɑːf.tə.bɜːθ (US) 'æf.tɚ.bɜːrθ **-s** -s
after-burner 'ɑːf.təˌbɜː.nəʳ (US) 'æf.tɚˌbɜːr.nɚ **-s** -z
aftercare 'ɑːf.tə.keəʳ (US) 'æf.tɚ.ker
after-crop 'ɑːf.tə.krɒp (US) 'æf.tɚ.krɑːp **-s** -s
aftereffect 'ɑːf.tər.ɪˌfekt, -əˌfekt (US) 'æf.tɚ- **-s** -s
afterglow 'ɑːf.tə.gləʊ (US) 'æf.tɚ.gloʊ **-s** -z
after-hours ˌɑːf.tər'aʊəz (US) 'æf.tɚˌaʊɚz, ˌ--'-
afterli|fe 'ɑːf.tə.laɪ|f (US) 'æf.tɚ- **-ves** -vz

aftermath ˈɑːf.tə.mɑːθ, -mæθ (US) ˈæf.tɚ.mæθ **-s** -s

afternoon ˌɑːf.təˈnuːn (US) ˌæf.tɚˈ- **-s** -z *stress shift, see compounds:* ˌ**afternoon ˈtea; good ˌafterˈnoon**

afterpiec|e ˈɑːf.tə.piːs (US) ˈæf.tɚ- **-es** -ɪz

afters ˈɑːf.təz (US) ˈæf.tɚz

after-sales ˌɑːf.təˈseɪlz (US) ˌæf.tɚˈ- *stress shift:* ˌafter-sales ˈservice

aftershave ˈɑːf.tə.ʃeɪv (US) ˈæf.tɚ- **-s** -z

aftershock ˈɑːf.tə.ʃɒk (US) ˈæf.tɚ.ʃɑːk **-s** -s

aftertaste ˈɑːf.tə.teɪst (US) ˈæf.tɚ- **-s** -s

afterthought ˈɑːf.tə.θɔːt (US) ˈæf.tɚ.θɑːt, -θɔːt **-s** -s

afterward ˈɑːf.tə.wəd (US) ˈæf.tɚ.wɚd **-s** -z

AFTRA ˈæf.trə

Aga® ˈɑː.gə

Agadir ˌæg.əˈdɪə (US) ˌɑː.gəˈdɪr, ˌæg.əˈ-

Agag ˈeɪ.gæg

again əˈgen, -ˈgeɪn (US) -ˈgen

against əˈgen*t*st, ˈgeɪn*t*st (US) -ˈgentst

Agha Khan ˌɑː.gəˈkɑːn

Agamemnon ˌæg.əˈmem.nən, -nɒn (US) -nɑːn, -nən

agamete eɪˈgæm.iːt, əˈ- (US) ˌæg.əˈmiːt **-s** -s

Agana ɑːˈgɑː.nə, -njə (US) -njə

agape (*adj. adv.*) əˈgeɪp

agape (*n.*) ˈæg.ə.pi, -peɪ (US) ɑːˈgɑː.peɪ, ˈɑː.gə- **-s** -z

Agar *family name:* ˈeɪ.gəʳ, -gɑːʳ (US) -gɚ, -gɑːr

agar *jelly:* ˈeɪ.gɑːʳ, -əʳ (US) -gɑːr, ˈɑː-, -gɚ

agar-agar ˌeɪ.gəʳˈeɪ.gəʳ, -gɑːʳˈ-, -gɑːʳ (US) -gɚˈeɪ.gɚ, ˌɑː.gɚˈɑ-, -gɑːrˈ-, -gɑːr

agaric (*n.*) ˈæg.ə.rɪk; əˈgær.ɪk (US) ˈæg.ɚ.ɪk, əˈger-; -ˈgær- **-s** -s

agaric (*adj.*) ægˈær.ɪk, əˈgær-

Agassi ˈæg.ə.si

Agassiz ˌæg.əˈsiː (US) ˈæg.ə.si

Agassizhorn əˈgæs.ɪ.hɔːn (US) -hɔːrn

agate *stone:* ˈæg.ət, -gɪt **-s** -s

Agate *surname:* ˈeɪ.gət, ˈæg.ət

Agatha ˈæg.ə.θə

Agathocles əˈgæθ.əʊ.kliːz (US) ˈ-ə-

agave əˈgeɪ.vi, -ˈgɑː-, ˈæg.eɪ- (US) əˈgɑː- **-s** -z

agaze əˈgeɪz

ag|e eɪdʒ **-es** -ɪz **-(e)ing** -ɪŋ **-ed** -d ˌ**age of conˈsent**; ˈ**golden** ˌ**age**

-age -ɪdʒ, -ɑːʒ

Note: Suffix. Normally pronounced /-ɪdʒ/, e.g. **advantage** /ədˈvɑːn.tɪdʒ (US) -ˈvæn.t̬ɪdʒ/, which is unstressed, but in words of French origin it is often /-ɑːʒ/, which may be stress bearing; see for example, **corsage**, in which it has both stressed and unstressed variants.

aged (*adj.*) *old:* ˈeɪ.dʒɪd *of the age of:* eɪdʒd

agedness ˈeɪdʒ.ɪd.nəs, -nɪs

Agee ˈeɪ.dʒi

age|ism ˈeɪdʒ.|ɪ.zᵊm **-ist/s** -ɪst/s

ageless ˈeɪdʒ.ləs, -lɪs

agelong ˈeɪdʒ.lɒŋ (US) -lɑːŋ, -lɔːŋ

agenc|y ˈeɪ.dʒᵊn*t*.s|i **-ies** -iz

agenda əˈdʒen.də **-s** -z

agendum əˈdʒen.dəm **-s** -z

agene ˈeɪ.dʒiːn

agenesis ˌeɪˈdʒen.ə.sɪs, ˈ-ɪ-

agent ˈeɪ.dʒᵊnt **-s** -s ˌ**Agent ˈOrange**

agentival ˌeɪ.dʒᵊnˈtaɪ.vᵊl

agentive ˈeɪ.dʒᵊn.tɪv

agent(s) provocateur(s) ˌæʒ.ɑ̃ː.prəˌvɒk.əˈtɜːʳ, ˌæʒ.ɒŋ- (US) ˌɑːʒ.ɑ̃ː.proʊˌvɑː.kəˈtɜːr, -tʊr

age-old ˌeɪdʒˈəʊld (US) ˈeɪdʒ.oʊld *stress shift, British only:* ˌage-old ˈcity

-ageous -ˈeɪ.dʒəs

Note: Suffix. Words containing **-ageous** are normally stressed on the penultimate syllable, e.g. **advantageous** /ˌæd.vənˈteɪ.dʒəs (US) -vænˈ-/.

Ager ˈeɪ.dʒəʳ (US) -dʒɚ

Agesilaus əˌdʒes.ɪˈleɪ.əs, ædʒˌes- (US) -əˈ-

Agfa® ˈæg.fə

aggie (A) ˈæg.i **-s** -z

aggiornamento əˌdʒɔː.nəˈmen.təʊ (US) -ˌdʒɔːr.nəˈmen.toʊ

agglomerate (*n. adj.*) əˈglɒm.ᵊr.ət, -ɪt (US) -ˈglɑː.mɚ- **-s** -s

agglomer|ate (*v.*) əˈglɒm.ᵊr|.eɪt (US) -ˈglɑː.mə.r|eɪt **-ates** -eɪts **-ating** -eɪ.tɪŋ (US) -eɪ.t̬ɪŋ **-ated** -eɪ.tɪd (US) -eɪ.t̬ɪd

agglomeration əˌglɒm.əˈreɪ.ʃᵊn (US) -ˌglɑː.məˈ- **-s** -z

agglutinate (*adj.*) əˈgluː.tɪ.nət, -ɪt (US) -tᵊn.ət

agglutin|ate (*v.*) əˈgluː.tɪ.n|eɪt (US) -tᵊn|.eɪt **-ates** -eɪts **-ating** -eɪ.tɪŋ (US) -eɪ.t̬ɪŋ **-ated** -eɪ.tɪd (US) -eɪ.t̬ɪd

agglutination əˌgluː.tɪˈneɪ.ʃᵊn (US) -tᵊnˈeɪ- **-s** -z

agglutinative əˈgluː.tɪ.nə.tɪv, -eɪ.tɪv (US) -tᵊn.eɪ.t̬ɪv

agglutinin əˈgluː.tɪ.nɪn (US) -tᵊn.ɪn

agglutinogen ˌæg.lʊˈtɪn.ə.dʒᵊn (US) -luːˈ-

aggrandiz|e, -is|e əˈgræn.daɪz **-es** -ɪz **-ing** -ɪŋ **-ed** -d

aggrandizement, -ise- əˈgræn.dɪz.mənt (US) -dɪz-, -daɪz-

aggra|vate ˈæg.rə|.veɪt **-vates** -veɪts **-vating/ly** -veɪ.tɪŋ/li (US) -veɪ.t̬ɪŋ/li **-vated** -veɪ.tɪd (US) -veɪ.t̬ɪd

aggravation ˌæg.rəˈveɪ.ʃᵊn **-s** -z

aggregate (*n. adj.*) ˈæg.rɪ.gət, -rə.gət, -gɪt **-s** -s

aggre|gate (*v.*) ˈæg.rɪ|.geɪt, -rə- **-gates** -geɪts **-gating** -geɪ.tɪŋ (US) -geɪ.t̬ɪŋ **-gated** -geɪ.tɪd (US) -geɪ.t̬ɪd

aggregation ˌæg.rɪˈgeɪ.ʃᵊn, -rəˈ- **-s** -z

aggregative ˈæg.rɪ.gə.tɪv, -rə-

aggress əˈgres, ægˈres **-es** -ɪz **-ing** -ɪŋ **-ed** -t

aggression əˈgreʃ.ᵊn, ægˈreʃ- **-s** -z

aggressive əˈgres.ɪv, ægˈres- **-ly** -li **-ness** -nəs, -nɪs

aggressor əˈgres.əʳ, ægˈres- (US) -ɚ **-s** -z

aggriev|e əˈgriːv **-es** -z **-ing** -ɪŋ **-ed** -d

aggro ˈæg.rəʊ (US) -roʊ

aghast əˈgɑːst (US) -ˈgæst

agil|e ˈædʒ.aɪl (US) -ᵊl **-ist** -əst, -ɪst **-ely** -li

agility əˈdʒɪl.ə.ti, -ɪ.ti (US) -ə.t̬i

agin əˈgɪn

Agincourt ˈædʒ.ɪn.kɔːʳ, -kɔːt, -kʊəʳ (US) -kɔːrt

agiotage ˈædʒ.ə.tɪdʒ, ˈædʒ.i.əʊ-, -tɑːʒ (US) ˈædʒ.i.ə.tɪdʒ; ˌæʒ.əˈtɑːʒ

ag|ism ˈeɪ.dʒ|ɪ.zᵊm **-ist/s** -ɪst/s

agi|tate ˈædʒ.ɪ|.teɪt, ˈ-ə- **-tates** -teɪts **-tating** -teɪ.tɪŋ (US) -teɪ.t̬ɪŋ **-tated** -teɪ.tɪd (US) -teɪ.t̬ɪd **-tator/s** -teɪ.təʳ/z (US) -teɪ.t̬ɚ/z

agitation ˌædʒ.ɪˈteɪ.ʃᵊn, -əˈ- **-s** -z

agitato ˌædʒ.ɪˈtɑː.təʊ (US) -t̬oʊ

agitprop ˈædʒ.ɪt.prɒp (US) -prɑːp

Aglaia əˈglaɪ.ə, -ˈgleɪ-

aglow əˈgləʊ (US) -ˈgloʊ

AGM ˌeɪ.dʒiːˈem

agnail ˈæg.neɪl **-s** -z

agnate ˈæg.neɪt

agnation ægˈneɪ.ʃᵊn

Agnes ˈæg.nəs, -nɪs

Agnew ˈæg.njuː (US) -nuː, -njuː

Agni ˈæg.ni

agnomen ægˈnəʊ.men, -mən (US) -ˈnoʊ- **-s** -z

agnostic ægˈnɒs.tɪk, əg- (US) -ˈnɑː.stɪk **-s** -s

agnosticism ægˈnɒs.tɪ.sɪ.zᵊm, əg-, -tə- (US) -ˈnɑː.stɪ-, -stə-

Agnus Dei ˌæg.nəsˈdeɪ.i, -nʊs-, -ˈdiː.aɪ **-s** -z

ago əˈgəʊ (US) -ˈgoʊ

agog əˈgɒg (US) -ˈgɑːg, -ˈgɔːg

-agogic -əˈgɒdʒ.ɪk, -ˈgɒg-, -ˈgəʊ.dʒɪk (US) -əˈgɑː.dʒɪk, -ˈgoʊ-

Note: Suffix. Words containing **-agogic** are normally stressed on the penultimate syllable, e.g. **pedagogic** /ˌped.əˈgɒdʒ.ɪk (US) -ˈgɑː-/.

a go-go, à go-go əˈgəʊ.gəʊ (US) -ˈgoʊ.goʊ

-agogue -ə.gɒg (US) -ə.gɑːg, -ə.gɔːg

Note: Suffix. Normally unstressed, e.g. **pedagogue** /'ped.ə.gɒg ⓤⓢ -gɑːg/.
-agogy -ə.gɒdʒ.i, -gɒg-, -gəʊ.dʒi ⓤⓢ -ə.gɑː.dʒi, -goʊ.gi
Note: Suffix. Normally unstressed, e.g. **pedagogy** /'ped.ə.gɒdʒ.i ⓤⓢ -gɑː.dʒi/.
agone ə'gɒn ⓤⓢ -'gɑːn
agonist 'æg.ə.nɪst **-s** -s
Agonistes ˌæg.əʊ'nɪs.tiːz ⓤⓢ -ə'-
agonistic ˌæg.əʊ'nɪs.tɪk ⓤⓢ -ə'- **-s** -s **-ally** -əl.i
agoniz|e, -is|e 'æg.ə.naɪz **-es** -ɪz **-ing/ly** -ɪŋ/li **-ed** -d
agon|y 'æg.ə.n|i **-ies** -iz 'agony ˌaunt; 'agony ˌcolumn
agor|a 'æg.ə.r|ə, -ɒr.ə, ˌæg.ə'rɑː ⓤⓢ 'æg.ə.r|ə, -ɔːr.ə **-ae** -iː **-as** -əz
agoraphob|ia ˌæg.ər.ə'fəʊ.b|i.ə, -ɔː.rə'- ⓤⓢ -ɚ.ə'foʊ-; əˌgɔːr.ə'- **-ic/s** -ɪk
agouti ə'guː.ti ⓤⓢ -t̬i **-s** -z
Agra 'ɑː.grə, 'æg.rə
agrarian ə'greə.ri.ən ⓤⓢ -'grer.i- **-s** -z **-ism** -ɪ.zəm
agree ə'griː **-s** -z **-ing** -ɪŋ **-d** -d
agreeab|le ə'griː.ə.b|l̩ **-ly** -li **-leness** -l̩.nəs, -nɪs
agreement ə'griː.mənt **-s** -s
agribusiness 'æg.riˌbɪz.nɪs, -nəs **-es** -ɪz
Agricola ə'grɪk.əʊ.lə ⓤⓢ -əl.ə
agricultural ˌæg.rɪ'kʌl.tʃər.əl, -rə'- **-ist/s** -ɪst/s
agriculture 'æg.rɪ.kʌl.tʃər, -rə- ⓤⓢ -tʃɚ
agriculturist ˌæg.rɪ'kʌl.tʃər.ɪst, -rə'- **-s** -s
Agrigento ˌæg.rɪ'dʒen.təʊ ⓤⓢ -toʊ
agrimony 'æg.rɪ.mə.ni, -rə- ⓤⓢ -moʊ-
Agrippa ə'grɪp.ə
Agrippina ˌæg.rɪ'piː.nə, -rə'-
agro- æg.rəʊ-; ə'grɒ- ⓤⓢ æg.roʊ-, -rə-; ə'grɑː-
Note: Prefix. Either takes primary or secondary stress on the first syllable, e.g. **agronomics** /ˌæg.rə'nɒm.ɪks ⓤⓢ -'nɑː.mɪks/, or primary stress on the second syllable, e.g. **agronomy** /ə'grɒn.ə.mi ⓤⓢ -'grɑː.nə-/.
agrobiologic ˌæg.rəʊ.baɪə'lɒdʒ.ɪk ⓤⓢ -roʊ.baɪə'lɑː.dʒɪk **-al** -əl **-ally** -əl.i, -li
agrobiology ˌæg.rəʊ.baɪ'ɒl.ə.dʒi ⓤⓢ -roʊ.baɪ'ɑː.lə-
agrochemical ˌæg.rəʊ'kem.ɪ.kəl ⓤⓢ -roʊ'- **-s** -z
agrolog|y ə'grɒl.ə.dʒ|i, æg'- ⓤⓢ ə'grɑː.lə- **-ist/s** -ɪst/s
agronomics ˌæg.rə'nɒm.ɪks ⓤⓢ -'nɑː.mɪks
agronom|y ə'grɒn.ə.m|i ⓤⓢ -'grɑː.nə- **-ist/s** -ɪst/s
aground ə'graʊnd
Aguascalientes ˌæg.wɑːs.kæl.i'en.tes ⓤⓢ ˌɑː.gwɑːs.kæl'jen.tes, -i'en-
ague 'eɪg.juː **-s** -z
Aguecheek 'eɪg.juː.tʃiːk
Agulhas ə'gʌl.əs
Agutter 'æg.ə.tər; ə'gʌt.ər ⓤⓢ ə'gʌt̬.ɚ; 'æg.ə.t̬ɚ
ah ɑː
aha ɑː'hɑː, ə'hɑː
Ahab 'eɪ.hæb
Ahasuerus eɪˌhæz.ju'ɪə.rəs, əˌhæz- ⓤⓢ -'ɪr.əs
Ahaz 'eɪ.hæz
Ahaziah ˌeɪ.*h*ə'zaɪ.ə
ahead ə'hed
aheap ə'hiːp
ahem m'ʔm̥m, 'ʔm̥m, hm, ə'hem
Note: Interjection. The spelling attempts to represent a clearing of the throat to attract attention. The pronunciation /ə'hem/ represents the reading aloud of this word by someone who does not know what it stands for.
Ahenobarbus əˌhen.əʊ'bɑː.bəs ⓤⓢ -oʊ'bɑːr-, -ˌhiː.noʊ'-
A'Hern 'eɪ.hɜːn ⓤⓢ -hɜːrn
Aherne ə'hɜːn ⓤⓢ -'hɜːrn
Ahimsa ɑː'hɪm.sɑː ⓤⓢ ə-
ahistorical ˌeɪ.hɪ'stɒr.ɪ.kəl ⓤⓢ -'stɔːr-
Ahithophel ə'hɪθ.əʊ.fel ⓤⓢ '-ə-
Ahmadabad 'ɑː.mə.də.bæd ⓤⓢ -bɑːd
Ahmed 'ɑː.med
ahoy ə'hɔɪ
ahungered ə'hʌŋ.gəd ⓤⓢ -gɚd
AI ˌeɪ'aɪ
ai 'ɑː.i, aɪ
Aicken 'eɪ.kən
aid eɪd **-s** -z **-ing** -ɪŋ **-ed** -ɪd **-er/s** -ər/z ⓤⓢ -ɚ/z ˌ**aid and a'bet**
Aïda, Aida aɪ'iː.də, ɑː-
Aidan 'eɪ.dən
aide eɪd **-s** -z
aide(s)-de-camp ˌeɪd.də'kɑ̃ː ⓤⓢ -'kæmp
Aideed aɪ'diːd
aide(s)-mémoire ˌeɪd.mem'wɑː ⓤⓢ -'wɑːr
aid|-man 'eɪd|.mən, -mæn **-men** -men, -mən
AIDS, Aids eɪdz
aigrette 'eɪ.gret, eɪ'gret **-s** -s
aiguille ˌeɪ'gwiː, -'gwiːl ⓤⓢ ˌeɪ'gwiːl, '-- **-s** -z
Aiken 'eɪ.kən
aikido ˌaɪ'kiː.dəʊ, 'aɪ.kɪ- ⓤⓢ ˌaɪ'kiː.doʊ
Aikin 'eɪ.kɪn, -kən
Aikman 'eɪk.mən
ail eɪl **-s** -z **-ing** -ɪŋ **-ed** -d
ailanthus ˌaɪ'læn*t*.θəs **-es** -ɪz
Aileen 'eɪ.liːn ⓤⓢ aɪ'liːn
aileron 'eɪ.lər.ɒn ⓤⓢ -ə.rɑːn **-s** -z
Ailesbury 'eɪlz.bər.i ⓤⓢ -ber-
ailment 'eɪl.mənt **-s** -s
Ailred 'eɪl.red, 'aɪl-
Ailsa 'eɪl.sə
ailuro- aɪ'ljʊə.rəʊ-, eɪ-, 'aɪ.ljʊə.rəʊ- ⓤⓢ aɪ'lʊr.ə-
ailurophile aɪ'ljʊə.rəʊ.faɪl, eɪ- ⓤⓢ -'lʊr.ə- **-s** -z
ailurophobe aɪ'ljʊə.rəʊ.fəʊb, eɪ- ⓤⓢ -'lʊr.ə.foʊb **-s** -z
ailurophobia aɪˌljʊə.rəʊ'fəʊ.bi.ə, eɪ- ⓤⓢ -ˌlʊr.ə'foʊ-
aim eɪm **-s** -z **-ing** -ɪŋ **-ed** -d
aimless 'eɪm.ləs, -lɪs **-ly** -li **-ness** -nəs, -nɪs
Ainger 'eɪn.dʒər ⓤⓢ -dʒɚ
Ainsley, Ainslie 'eɪnz.li
Ainsworth 'eɪnz.wəθ, -wɜːθ ⓤⓢ -wɚθ, -wɜːrθ
ain't eɪnt
Aintree 'eɪn.triː
Ainu 'aɪ.nuː **-s** -z
aïoli, aioli aɪ'əʊ.li, eɪ'- ⓤⓢ -'oʊ-
air eər ⓤⓢ er **-s** -z **-ing/s** -ɪŋ/z **-ed** -d 'air ˌforce; 'air hoˌstess; 'air ˌletter; 'air ˌpocket; 'air ˌraid; 'air ˌrifle; 'air ˌroute; 'air ˌterminal; ˌair traffic con'trol; ˌair traffic con'troller; ˌclear the 'air
airbag 'eə.bæg ⓤⓢ 'er- **-s** -z
airbase 'eə.beɪs ⓤⓢ 'er- **-s** -ɪz
airbed 'eə.bed ⓤⓢ 'er- **-s** -z
air-boat 'eə.bəʊt ⓤⓢ 'er.boʊt **-s** -s
airborne 'eə.bɔːn ⓤⓢ 'er.bɔːrn
airbrake 'eə.breɪk ⓤⓢ 'er- **-s** -s
airbrush 'eə.brʌʃ ⓤⓢ 'er- **-es** -ɪz **-ing** -ɪŋ **-ed** -d
air-burst 'eə.bɜːst ⓤⓢ 'er.bɜːrst **-s** -s
airbus (A ®) 'eə.bʌs ⓤⓢ 'er- **-es** -ɪz
air-check 'eə.tʃek ⓤⓢ 'er- **-s** -s
air-condition 'eə.kənˌdɪʃ.ən, ˌeə.kən'dɪʃ- ⓤⓢ 'er.kənˌdɪʃ- **-s** -z **-ing** -ɪŋ **-ed** -d **-er/s** -ər/z ⓤⓢ -ɚ/z
air-cool 'eə.kuːl ⓤⓢ 'er- **-s** -z **-ing** -ɪŋ **-ed** -d
aircraft 'eə.krɑːft ⓤⓢ 'er.kræft
aircraft|man 'eə.krɑːft|.mən ⓤⓢ 'er.kræft- **-men** -mən
aircraft|woman 'eə.krɑːft|ˌwʊm.ən ⓤⓢ 'er.kræft- **-women** -ˌwɪm.ɪn
aircrew 'eə.kruː ⓤⓢ 'er- **-s** -z
Aird eəd ⓤⓢ erd
airdate 'eə.deɪt ⓤⓢ 'er- **-s** -s
Airdrie 'eə.dri ⓤⓢ 'er-
Airdrieonian ˌeə.dri'əʊ.ni.ən ⓤⓢ ˌer.dri'oʊ- **-s** -z
airdrome 'eə.drəʊm ⓤⓢ 'er.droʊm **-s** -z
air-drop 'eə.drɒp ⓤⓢ 'er.drɑːp **-s** -s **-ping** -ɪŋ **-ped** -t
air-dr|y 'eə.dr|aɪ ⓤⓢ 'er- **-ies** -z **-ing** -ɪŋ **-ied** -d

Aire eəʳ US er

Airedale 'eə.deɪl US 'er- **-s** -z

air-engine 'eəʳ.en.dʒɪn US 'er- **-s** -z

airer 'eə.rəʳ US 'er.ɚ **-s** -z

Airey 'eə.ri US 'er.i

airfare 'eə.feəʳ US 'er.fer **-s** -z

airfield 'eə.fiːld US 'er- **-s** -z

airfleet 'eə.fliːt US 'er-

airflow 'eə.fləʊ US 'er.floʊ **-s** -z

air-foil 'eə.fɔɪl US 'er- **-s** -z

airgraph 'eə.grɑːf, -græf US 'er.græf **-s** -s

airgun 'eə,gʌn US 'er- **-s** -z

airhead 'eə.hed US 'er- **-s** -z

airi|ly 'eə.rɪ|.li, -rᵊl|.i US 'er- **-ness** -nəs, -nɪs

airing 'eə.rɪŋ US 'er.ɪŋ **-s** -z **'airing ,cupboard**

airless 'eə.ləs, -lɪs US 'er-

Airlie 'eə.li US 'er-

airlift 'eə.lɪft US 'er- **-s** -s **-ing** -ɪŋ **-ed** -ɪd

airlin|e 'eə.laɪn US 'er- **-es** -z **-er/s** -əʳ/z US -ɚ/z

airlock 'eə.lɒk US 'er.lɑːk **-s** -s

airmail 'eə.meɪl US 'er- **-s** -z

air|man 'eə|.mən, -mæn US 'er- **-men** -mən, -men

airmarshal 'eə,mɑː.ʃᵊl US 'er,mɑːr-

airmobile 'eə.məʊ.biːl US 'er,moʊ.bᵊl

airplane 'eə.pleɪn US 'er- **-s** -z

airplay 'eə.pleɪ US 'er-

airport 'eə.pɔːt US 'er.pɔːrt **-s** -s

air-sea ,eə'siː US ,er- *stress shift, see compound:* **,air-sea 'rescue**

airship 'eə.ʃɪp US 'er- **-s** -s

airshow 'eə.ʃəʊ US 'er.ʃoʊ **-s** -z

airsick 'eə.sɪk US 'er- **-ness** -nəs, -nɪs

airspace 'eə.speɪs US 'er-

airspeed 'eə.spiːd US 'er- **-s** -z

airstream 'eə.striːm US 'er-

airstrike 'eə.straɪk US 'er- **-s** -s

airstrip 'eə.strɪp US 'er- **-s** -s

airtight 'eə.taɪt US 'er-

airtime 'eə.taɪm US 'er-

air-to-air ,eə.tu'eəʳ US ,er.t̬ə'er, -tu'- *stress shift:* ,air-to-air 'missile

air-to-surface ,eə.tə'sɜː.fɪs US ,er.t̬ə'sɜːr.fəs *stress shift:* ,air-to-surface 'missile

air traffic 'eə,træf.ɪk US 'er-

airwave 'eə.weɪv US 'er- **-s** -z

airway 'eə.weɪ US 'er- **-s** -z

air|woman 'eə|,wʊm.ən US 'er- **-women** -,wɪm.ɪn

airworth|y 'eə,wɜː.ðli US 'er,wɜːr- **-iness** -ɪ.nəs, -ɪ.nɪs

air|y (A) 'eə.r|i US 'er|.i **-ier** -i.əʳ US -i.ɚ **-iest** -i.əst, -i.ɪst **-ily** -ɪ.li, -ə.li **-iness** -ɪ.nəs, -ɪ.nɪs

airy-fairy ,eə.ri'feə.ri US ,er.i'fer.i *stress shift:* ,airy-fairy 'concept

Aisha aɪ'iː.ʃə

Aislaby 'eɪz.lə.bi *locally:* 'eɪ.zᵊl.bi

aisle aɪl **-s** -z **-d** -d

aitch eɪtʃ **-es** -ɪz

aitchbone 'eɪtʃ.bəʊn US -boʊn **-s** -z

Aitchison 'eɪ.tʃɪ.sᵊn

Aith eɪθ

Aitken 'eɪ*t*.kɪn, -kən

Aix eɪks, eks

Aix-en-Provence ,eɪks.ɑ̃ːm.prə'vɑ̃ːns, ,eks- US -ɑːn.proʊ'vɑ̃ːs

Aix-la-Chapelle ,eɪks.lɑː.ʃæp'el, ,eks-, -ʃə'pel US -ʃɑː'pel

Aix-les-Bains ,eɪks.leɪ'bæ̃ː, ,eks-, -'bæŋ

Ajaccio ə'jætʃ.i.əʊ, ə'dʒæs.i.əʊ US ɑː'jɑː.tʃoʊ, -tʃi.oʊ

ajar ə'dʒɑːʳ US -dʒɑːr

Ajax *cleaning substance ®:* 'eɪ.dʒæks *football team:* 'aɪ.æks

ajutage 'ædʒ.ʊ.tɪdʒ, ə'dʒuːt- US 'ædʒ.ə.t̬ɪdʒ, ə'dʒuː-

AKA, aka ,eɪ.keɪ'eɪ, 'æk.ə

Akaba 'æk.ə.bə

Akabusi ,æk.ə'buː.si

Akahito ,æk.ə'hiː.təʊ US ,ɑː.kə'hiː.toʊ

Akbar 'æk.bɑːʳ US -bɑːr

akela ɑː'keɪ.lə

Akenside 'eɪ.kən.saɪd, -kɪn-

Akerman 'æk.ə.mən US '-ɚ-

Akers 'eɪ.kəz US -kɚz

Akhmatova ək'mɑː.tə.və, ,ɑːk.mə'təʊ- US ʌk'mɑː.tə.və, ,ɑːk.mə'toʊ-

Akihito ,æk.i'hiː.təʊ US ,ɑː.ki'hiː.toʊ

akimbo ə'kɪm.bəʊ US -boʊ

akin ə'kɪn

Akkad 'æk.æd US 'æk.æd, 'ɑː.kɑːd

Akkadian ə'keɪ.di.ən US -'keɪ-, -'kɑː- **-s** -z

Akond of Swat *former title of the Wali of Swat territory in Pakistan:* ə,kuːnd.əv'swɒt US -'swɑːt *name in poem by Edward Lear:* ,æk.ənd.əv'swɒt US -'swɑːt

Akron 'æk.rɒn, -rən US -rən

Akrotiri 'æk.rəʊ'tɪə.ri US ,ɑːk.roʊ'tɪr.i

Akroyd 'æk.rɔɪd

al- əl-, æl-

Note: Prefix. Examples include **allocate** /'æl.ə.keɪt/, in which it is stressed, and **allure** /ə'ljʊəʳ US -'lʊr/, where it is unstressed.

AL ,eɪ'el

Al æl

-al -əl

Note: Suffix. When forming a noun, **-al** does not normally affect the stress pattern, e.g. **arouse** /ə'raʊz/, **arousal** /ə'raʊ.zᵊl/. In forming adjectives, however, the resulting item is usually either stressed one or two syllables before the suffix, e.g. **abdomen** becomes **abdominal** /æb'dɒm.ɪ.nᵊl US -'dɑː.mə-/, **adjective** becomes **adjectival** /,ædʒ.ɪk'taɪ.vᵊl/.

Ala. (*abbrev. for* **Alabama**) ,æl.ə'bæm.ə, -'bɑː.mə US -'bæm.ə

à la 'æl.ɑː, 'ɑː.lɑː US 'ɑː.lɑː, 'ɑː.lə, 'æl.ə

Alabama ,æl.ə'bæm.ə, -'bɑː.mə US -'bæm.ə

alabaster (A) ,æl.ə'bæs.təʳ, -'bɑː.stəʳ, 'æl.ə.bæs.təʳ, -bɑː.stəʳ US 'æl.ə.bæs.tɚ

à la carte ,æl.ə'kɑːt, ,ɑː.lɑː'- US ,ɑː.lə'kɑːrt, ,æl.ə'-

alack ə'læk

alackaday ə'læk.ə.deɪ, ə,læk.ə'deɪ

alacrity ə'læk.rə.ti, -rɪ.ti US -t̬i

Aladdin ə'læd.ɪn US -ᵊn **A,laddin's 'cave**

Alagoas ,æl.ə'gəʊ.əs US -'goʊ-

à la grecque ,æl.ə'grek, ,ɑː.lɑː'- US ,ɑː.lə'-, ,æl.ə'-

Alain *man's name:* æl'æ̃ US æl'ẽ*n* *woman's name:* ə'leɪn

Alain-Fournier æl,æ̃'fɔː.ni.eɪ *as if French:* -fʊə'njeɪ US -,ẽ*n*.fɔːr'njeɪ

Alameda æl.ə'miː.də, -'meɪ-

Alamein 'æl.ə.meɪn

Alamo 'æl.ə.məʊ US -moʊ

à la mode ,æl.ə'məʊd, ,ɑː.lɑː-, -'mɒd US ,ɑː.lə'moʊd, ,æl.ə'-

Alamogordo ,æl.ə.mə'gɔː.dəʊ US -'gɔːr.doʊ

Alan 'æl.ən

Alana ə'lɑː.nə, -'læn.ə

Aland *islands:* 'ɑː.lənd, 'ɔː-

aland (*adv.*) ə'lænd

à l'anglaise ,æl.ɑ̃ːŋ'gleɪz, ,ɑː.lɑ̃ːŋ'-, -'glez

alanine 'æl.ə.naɪn, -niːn

alar 'eɪ.ləʳ, -lɑːʳ US -lɚ

Alaric 'æl.ə.rɪk

alarm ə'lɑːm US -'lɑːrm **-s** -z **-ing/ly** -ɪŋ/li **-ed** -d **a'larm ,clock**

alarmist ə'lɑː.mɪst US -'lɑːr- **-s** -s

alarum ə'lær.əm, -'lɑː.rəm, -'leə- US -'ler.əm, -'lɑːr- **-s** -z

alas ə'læs, -'lɑːs US -'læs

Alasdair 'æl.ə.stəʳ, -steəʳ US -stɚ

Alask|a ə'læs.k|ə **-an/s** -ən/z

Alastair 'æl.ə.stəʳ, -steəʳ US -stɚ, -ster

Alastor ə'læs.tɔːʳ, æl'æs- US -tɔːr, -tɚ

alate 'eɪ.leɪt **-s** -s

alb ælb **-s** -z

Alba 'æl.bə

albacore 'æl.bə.kɔː US -kɔːr **-s** -z

Alba Longa ,æl.bə'lɒŋ.gə US -'lɑːŋ.gə, -'lɔːŋ-

Alban 'ɔːl.bən, 'ɒl- US 'ɑːl-

Albani æl'bɑː.ni US ɑːl-, ɔːl-

Albani|a æl'beɪ.ni|.ə, ɔːl- **-an/s** -ən/z
Albany *in London:* 'ɔːl.bə.ni, 'ɒl-, 'æl- US 'ɑːl-, 'ɔːl- *in Australia:* 'æl.bə.ni US 'ɑːl.bə-, 'ɔːl- *in US:* 'ɔːl.bə.ni, 'ɒl- US 'ɑːl-
Albarn 'ɔːl.bɑːn, 'ɒl- US 'ɑːl.bɑːrn
albatross 'æl.bə.trɒs US -trɑːs, -trɔːs **-es** -ɪz
albedo æl'biː.dəʊ US -doʊ **-(e)s** -z
Albee 'ɔːl.biː, 'æl- US 'ɑːl-, 'ɔːl-, 'æl-
albeit ɔːl'biː.ɪt US ɔːl-, ɑːl-
Albemarle 'æl.bə.mɑːl, -bɪ- US -mɑːrl
Alberic 'æl.bə.rɪk
Alberich 'æl.bə.rɪk, -rɪx US -rɪk
Albers 'æl.bɜːz, 'ɔːl.bəz US 'æl.bɜːrz, 'ɑːl.bɚz
albert (A) 'æl.bət US -bɚt **-s** -s ,**Albert 'Hall**
Alberta æl'bɜː.tə US -'bɜːr.t̬ə
albertite 'æl.bə.taɪt US -bɚ-
Alberton 'æl.bə.tən US -bɚ-
albescen|ce æl'bes.ᵊn|*t*s **-t** -t
Albi 'æl.bi
Albigenses ,æl.bɪ'gen*t*.siːz, -bɪ'dʒen*t*-
albinism 'æl.bɪ.nɪ.zᵊm
albino æl'biː.nəʊ US -'baɪ.noʊ **-s** -z
Albinoni ,æl.bɪ'nəʊ.ni US -'noʊ-
Albinus æl'biː.nəs
Albion 'æl.bi.ən
Albrecht 'æl.brekt, -brext US 'ɑːl.brekt
Albright 'ɔːl.braɪt, 'ɒl- US 'ɑːl-, 'ɔːl-
Albrighton 'ɔː.braɪ.tᵊn, 'ɔːl-, 'ɒl- US 'ɑːl-
Albrow 'ɔːl.braʊ US 'ɑːl-
Albufeira ,æl.bʊ'feə.rə US ,ɑːl.buː'feɪ.rə
Albula 'æl.bjʊ.lə US 'ɑːl.buː-, -bjuː-
album 'æl.bəm **-s** -z
albumen 'æl.bjʊ.mən, -men, -mɪn US æl'bjuː.mən
albumin 'æl.bjʊ.mɪn, -bjə.mɪn US æl'bjuː.mən
albuminoid æl'bjuː.mɪ.nɔɪd **-s** -z
albuminous æl'bjuː.mɪ.nəs
albuminuria ,æl.bjuː.mɪ'njʊə.ri.ə US -'nʊr.i-, -'njʊr-
Albuquerque ,æl.bə'kɜː.ki, 'æl.bə,kɜː- US 'æl.bə,kɜːr- *esp. for person:* ,--'--
alburnum æl'bɜː.nəm US -'bɜːr- **-s** -z
Albury 'ɔːl.bᵊr.i, 'ɒl- US 'ɔːl-, 'ɑːl-
Alcaeus æl'siː.əs
alcaic (A) æl'keɪ.ɪk **-s** -s
alcalde æl'kæl.deɪ, -di US -'kɑːl.di, -deɪ **-s** -z
Alcan® 'æl.kæn
Alcatraz 'æl.kə.træz, ,--'-
Alcazar *Spanish palace:* ,æl.kə'zɑː US 'æl.kə.zɑːr; æl'kæz.ɚ *music hall:* æl'kæz.əʳ US -ɚ
Alcester 'ɔːl.stəʳ, 'ɒl- US 'ɔːl.stɚ, 'ɑːl-
Alcestis æl'ses.tɪs
alchemic æl'kem.ɪk **-al** -ᵊl
alchemist 'æl.kə.mɪst, -kɪ- **-s** -s
alchemy 'æl.kə.mi, -kɪ-
Alcibiades ,æl.sɪ'baɪ.ə.diːz
Alcinous ,æl'sɪn.əʊ.əs US '-oʊ-
Alcmene ælk'miː.niː
Alcock 'æl.kɒk, 'ɔːl-, 'ɒl- US 'æl.kɑːk, 'ɑːl-, 'ɔːl-
alcohol 'æl.kə.hɒl US -hɑːl **-s** -z
alcoholic ,æl.kə'hɒl.ɪk US -'hɑː.lɪk **-s** -s *stress shift:* ,alcoholic 'drink
alcoholism 'æl.kə.hɒl.ɪ.zᵊm US -hɑː.lɪ-
Alconbury 'ɔːl.kən.bᵊr.i, 'ɔː-, 'ɒl-, -kəm-, -bri US 'ɔːl.kən.ber.i, 'ɑːl-, -bɚ-
Alcott 'ɔːl.kət, 'ɒl-, -kɒt US 'ɑːl.kɑːt, 'æl-, -kət
alcove 'æl.kəʊv, 'ɒl- US 'æl.koʊv **-s** -z **-d** -d
Alcuin 'æl.kwɪn, 'ɒl- US 'æl-
Alcyone æl'saɪə.ni
Aldborough 'ɔːl*d*.bᵊr.ə, 'ɒl- *locally:* 'ɔː.brə US 'ɔːld.bɚ.oʊ, 'ɑːld-
Aldbury 'ɔːld.bᵊr.i, 'ɒl- US 'ɔːld.ber-, 'ɑːld-, -bɚ-
Alde ɔːld US ɔːld, ɑːld
Aldebaran æl'deb.ə.rən, -ræn
Aldeburgh 'ɔːld.bᵊr.ə, 'ɒl- US 'ɔːld.bɚ.oʊ, 'ɑːld-
aldehyde 'æl.dɪ.haɪd, -də- **-s** -z
Alden 'ɔːl.dᵊn, 'ɒl- US 'ɔːl-, 'ɑːl-
Aldenham 'ɔːld.ᵊn.əm, 'ɒl- US 'ɔːl-, 'ɑːl-
al dente æl'den.teɪ, ɑːl-
alder (A) 'ɔːl.dəʳ, 'ɒl- US 'ɔːl.dɚ, 'ɑːl- **-s** -z
Alderley Edge ,ɔːl.də.li'edʒ, ,ɒl- US ,ɔːl.dɚ-, ,ɑːl-
alder|man (A) 'ɔːl.də|.mən, 'ɒl- US 'ɔːl.dɚ-, 'ɑːl- **-men** -mən, -men
aldermanic ,ɔːl.də'mæn.ɪk, ,ɒl- US ,ɔːl.dɚ'-, ,ɑːl-
Aldermaston 'ɔːl.də.mɑː.stən US 'ɔːl.dɚ-, 'ɑːl-
aldern 'ɔːl.dən, 'ɒl-, -dɜːn US 'ɔːl.dɚn, 'ɑːl-
Alderney 'ɔːl.də.ni, 'ɒl- US 'ɔːl.dɚ-, 'ɑːl-
Aldersgate 'ɔːl.dəz.geɪt, 'ɒl-, -gɪt US 'ɔːl.dɚz-, 'ɑːl-
Aldershot 'ɔːl.də.ʃɒt, 'ɒl- US 'ɔːl.dɚ.ʃɑːt, 'ɑːl-
Alderson 'ɔːl.də.sᵊn, 'ɒl- US 'ɔːl.dɚ-, 'ɑːl-
Alderton 'ɔːl.də.tᵊn, 'ɒl- US 'ɔːl.dɚ-, 'ɑːl-
Aldgate 'ɔːl*d*.geɪt, 'ɒl-, -gɪt US 'ɔːl*d*-, 'ɑːl*d*-
Aldhelm 'ɔːld.helm, 'ɒl- US 'ɔːld-, 'ɑːld-
Aldine 'ɔːl.daɪn, ɒl-, -diːn US 'ɔːl-, 'ɑːl-
Aldington 'ɔːl.dɪŋ.tən, 'ɒl- US 'ɔːl-, 'ɑːl-
Aldis(s) 'ɔːl.dɪs, 'ɒl- US 'ɔːl-, 'ɑːl-
Aldous 'ɔːl.dəs, 'ɒl- US 'ɔːl.dəs, 'ɑːl-, 'æl-
Aldred 'ɔːl.drɪd, 'ɒl-, -dred US 'ɔːl-, 'ɑːl-
Aldrich 'ɔːl.drɪtʃ, 'ɒl-, -drɪdʒ US 'ɔːl-, 'ɑːl-
Aldridge 'ɔːl.drɪdʒ, 'ɒl- US 'ɔːl-, 'ɑːl-
Aldrin 'ɔːl.drɪn, 'ɒl- US 'ɔːl-, 'ɑːl-
Aldsworth 'ɔːldz.wəθ, 'ɒl-, -wɜːθ US 'ɔːldz.wɚθ, 'ɑːldz-, -wɜːrθ
Aldus 'ɔːl.dəs, 'ɒl-, 'æl- US 'ɔːl-, 'ɑːl-
Aldwych 'ɔːld.wɪtʃ, 'ɒld- US 'ɔːld-, 'ɑːld-
ale (A) eɪl **-s** -z
aleatoric ,æl.i.ə'tɒr.ɪk, ,eɪ.li- US -'tɔːr-, -'tɑːr- **-ally** -ᵊl.i, -li
aleatory 'eɪ.li.ə.tᵊr.i, ,æl.i'eɪ.tᵊr.i US 'eɪ.li.ə.tɔːr-
Alec(k) 'æl.ɪk, -lek
Alecto ə'lek.təʊ US -toʊ
Aled 'æl.ed, -ɪd
alehou|se 'eɪl.haʊ|s **-ses** -zɪz
Alemannic ,æl.ɪ'mæn.ɪk, -ə'-
alembic ə'lem.bɪk **-s** -s
Alençon 'æl.æ̃n.sɔ̃ː*ŋ* US ə'len.sən; ,æl.ɑːn'soʊn
Aleppo ə'lep.əʊ, æl'ep- US -oʊ
a|lert ə|'lɜːt US -'lɜːrt **-lerts** -'lɜːts US -'lɜːrts **-lertest** -'lɜː.təst, -tɪst US -'lɜːr.t̬əst, -t̬ɪst **-lertly** -'lɜːt.li US -'lɜːrt- **-lertness** -'lɜːt.nəs, -nɪs US -'lɜːrt.nəs, -nɪs **-lerting** -'lɜː.tɪŋ US -'lɜːr.t̬ɪŋ **-lerted** -'lɜː.tɪd US -'lɜːr.t̬ɪd
Alessandria ,æl.ɪ'sæn.dri.ə, -es'- US ,ɑː.lə'sɑːn-, ,æl.ə'-, -'sæn-
Alethea ,æl.ə'θiː.ə; ə'liː.θi-; 'æl.ɪ.θi- US ,æl.ɪ'θiː.ə; ə'liː.θi-
alethic æl'iː.θɪk, ə'liː-
Aletsch 'æl.ɪtʃ, 'ɑː.lɪtʃ, -letʃ US 'ɑː.letʃ
Aleut ə'ljuːt, -luːt; 'æl.juːt, -uːt US ə'luːt; 'æl.juːt, -i.uːt **-s** -s
Aleutian ə'ljuː.ʃən, -'luː- US -'luː-
A-level 'eɪ.lev.ᵊl **-s** -z
alewi|fe 'eɪl.waɪ|f **-ves** -vz
Alex 'æl.ɪks
Alexander ,æl.ɪg'zɑːn.dəʳ, -eg'-, -'əg'-, -'zæn-, -ɪk'sɑːn- US -'zæn.dɚ **Alex'ander tech,nique**
Alexandra ,æl.ɪg'zɑːn.drə, -eg'-, -əg'-, -'zæn-, -ɪk'sɑːn- US -'zæn-
alexandrian ,æl.ɪg'zɑːn.dri.ən, -eg'-, -əg'-, -'zæn-, -ɪk'sɑːn- US -'zæn- **-s** -z
Alexandrina ,æl.ɪg.zæn'driː.nə, -eg-, -əg'-, -zɑːn-, -ɪk.sɑːn'-
alexandrine ,æl.ɪg'zæn.draɪn, -eg'-, -əg'-, -'zɑːn-, -ɪk'sɑːn US -'zæn.drɪn, -draɪn **-s** -z

alexia ˌeɪˈlek.si.ə, ə- (US) ə-
Alexis əˈlek.sɪs
Alf ælf
alfalfa ˌælˈfæl.fə
Alfa Romeo® ˌæl.fə.rəʊˈmeɪ.əʊ (US) -roʊˈmeɪ.oʊ
Alfie ˈæl.fi
Alfonso ælˈfɒn*t*.səʊ, -ˈfɒn.zəʊ (US) -ˈfɑːn*t*.soʊ, -ˈfɑːn.zoʊ
Alford ˈɔːl.fəd, ˈɒl- (US) ˈɔːl.fɚd, ˈɑːl-
Alfred ˈæl.frɪd, -frəd
Alfreda ælˈfriː.də
Alfredian ælˈfriː.di.ən
alfresco, al fresco ælˈfres.kəʊ (US) -koʊ
Alfreton ˈɔːl.frɪ.tᵊn, ˈɒl- (US) ˈɔːl.frɪ.tən, ˈɑːl-
Alfric ˈæl.frɪk
Alfriston ˈæl.frɪ.stən, ˈɔːl-
al|ga ˈæl.gə **-gae** -dʒiː, -dʒaɪ, -giː, -gaɪ
Algarve ælˈgɑːv, ˈæl.gɑːv (US) ɑːlˈgɑːr.və
algebra ˈæl.dʒɪ.brə, -dʒə- **-s** -z
algebraic ˌæl.dʒɪˈbreɪ.ɪk, -dʒəˈ- **-al** -ᵊl **-ally** -ᵊl.i, -li *stress shift:* ˌalgebraic ˈsum
algebraist ˌæl.dʒɪˈbreɪ.ɪst, -dʒəˈ- **-s** -s
Algeciras ˌæl.dʒɪˈsɪə.rəs, -dʒəˈ-, -dʒesˈɪə-, -ˈsɪr.əs (US) -ˈsɪr-
Alger ˈæl.dʒəʳ (US) -dʒɚ
Algeri|a ælˈdʒɪə.ri|.ə (US) -ˈdʒɪr.i- **-an/s** -ən/z
Algerine ˌæl.dʒəˈriːn
Algernon ˈæl.dʒə.nən, -nɒn (US) -dʒɚ.nɑːn, -nən
Algiers ælˈdʒɪəz (US) -ˈdʒɪrz
Algoa ælˈgəʊ.ə (US) -ˈgoʊ-
Algol, ALGOL ˈæl.gɒl (US) -gɑːl
Algonquian ælˈgɒŋ.kwi.ən, -ki.ən (US) -ˈgɑːŋ-, -ˈgɔːŋ-
Algonquin ælˈgɒŋ.kwɪn, -kɪn (US) -ˈgɑːn-, -ˈgɔːŋ-
algorism ˈæl.gᵊr.ɪ.zᵊm
algorithm ˈæl.gᵊr.ɪ.ðᵊm **-s** -z
algorithmic ˌæl.gəˈrɪð.mɪk *stress shift:* ˌalgorithmic deˈsign
Algren ˈɔːl.grɪn, ˈɒl- (US) ˈɔːl-, ˈɑːl-
Algy ˈæl.dʒi
Alhambra *in Spain:* ælˈhæm.brə, əl-; əˈlæm- *in California:* ælˈhæm.brə
Ali *female name:* ˈæl.i *male name or surname:* ˈɑː.li, ɑːˈli
alias ˈeɪ.li.əs, -æs **-es** -ɪz
Ali Baba ˌæl.iˈbɑː.bə, ˌɑː.li-, -bɑː
alibi ˈæl.ɪ.baɪ **-s** -z
Alicante ˌæl.ɪˈkæn.teɪ, -ti (US) -ti, -teɪ
Alice ˈæl.ɪs ˌ**Alice ˈSprings**; ˌ**Alice in ˈWonderland**
Alicia əˈlɪs.i.ə, -ˈlɪʃ.ə (US) -ˈlɪʃ.ə, -i.ə
Alick ˈæl.ɪk
alien ˈeɪ.li.ən **-s** -z **ing** -ɪŋ **-ed** -d **-age** -ɪdʒ
alienable ˈeɪ.li.ən.ə.bl̩
alie|nate ˈeɪ.li.ə|.neɪt **-nates** -neɪts **-nating** -neɪ.tɪŋ (US) -neɪ.t̬ɪŋ **-nated** -neɪ.tɪd (US) -neɪ.t̬ɪd **-nator/s** -neɪ.təʳ/z (US) -neɪ.t̬ɚ/z
alienation ˌeɪ.li.əˈneɪ.ʃᵊn **-s** -z
alien|ism ˈeɪ.li.ə.n|ɪ.zᵊm **-ist/s** -ɪst/s
a|light ə|ˈlaɪt **-lights** -ˈlaɪts **-lighting** -ˈlaɪ.tɪŋ (US) -ˈlaɪ.t̬ɪŋ **-lighted** -ˈlaɪ.tɪd (US) -ˈlaɪ.t̬ɪd
align əˈlaɪn **-s** -z **-ing** -ɪŋ **-ed** -d
alignment əˈlaɪn.mənt, -ˈlaɪm- (US) -ˈlaɪn- **-s** -s
alike əˈlaɪk
aliment ˈæl.ɪ.mənt **-s** -s
alimental ˌæl.ɪˈmen.tᵊl (US) -t̬ᵊl
alimentary ˌæl.ɪˈmen.tᵊr.i, ˈ-tri (US) -t̬ᵊr.i, ˈ-tri **aliˌmentary caˈnal** (US) **aliˈmentary caˌnal**
alimentation ˌæl.ɪ.menˈteɪ.ʃᵊn
alimon|y ˈæl.ɪ.mə.n|i (US) -moʊ- **-ies** -iz
A-line ˈeɪ.laɪn
Aline *woman's name:* ælˈiːn, əˈliːn; ˈæl.iːn
alin|e əˈlaɪn **-es** -z **-ing** -ɪŋ **-ed** -d
alineation əˌlɪn.iˈeɪ.ʃᵊn **-s** -z
Alington ˈæl.ɪŋ.tən
Ali Pasha ˌæl.iˈpɑː.ʃə, ˌɑː.li-, -ˈpæʃ.ə (US) ˌɑː.liˈpɑː.ʃɑː, ˌæl.iˈ-
aliqu|ant ˈæl.ɪ.kw|ənt **-ot** -ɒt (US) -ɑːt
Alisha əˈlɪʃ.ə
Alison ˈæl.ɪ.sᵊn
Alissa əˈlɪs.ə
Alistair, Alister ˈæl.ɪ.stəʳ (US) -stɚ
alit əˈlɪt
Alitalia® ˌæl.ɪˈtæl.i.ə, ˌɑː.liˈtɑː.li- (US) -jə
alive əˈlaɪv
Alix ˈæl.ɪks
alizarin əˈlɪz.ə.rɪn
alkahest ˈæl.kə.hest
alkalescen|ce ˌæl.kᵊlˈes.ᵊn|*t*s (US) -kəˈles- **-cy** -*t*.si **-t** -t
alkali ˈæl.kᵊl.aɪ (US) -kə.laɪ **-(e)s** -z
alkalic ˌælˈkæl.ɪk
alkalif|y ælˈkæl.ɪ.f|aɪ **-ies** -aɪz **-ying** -aɪ.ɪŋ **-ied** -aɪd
alkaline ˈæl.kᵊl.aɪn (US) -kə.laɪn
alkalinity ˌæl.kᵊlˈɪn.ə.ti, -ɪ.ti (US) -kəˈlɪn.ə.t̬i
alkalization, -isa- ˌæl.kᵊl.aɪˈzeɪ.ʃᵊn, -ɪˈ- (US) -ɪˈ-
alkaliz|e, -is|e ˈæl.kᵊl.aɪz (US) -kə.laɪz **-es** -ɪz **-ing** -ɪŋ **-ed** -d
alkaloid ˈæl.kᵊl.ɔɪd (US) -kə.lɔɪd **-s** -z **-al** -ᵊl
alkane ˈæl.keɪn **-s** -z
Alka Seltzer® ˌæl.kəˈselt.səʳ (US) ˈæl.kəˌselt.sɚ
alkene ˈæl.kiːn **-s** -z
Alkoran ˌæl.kɒrˈɑːn, -kɔːˈrɑːn, -kəˈrɑːn (US) -kɔːrˈɑːn, -kəˈrɑːn, -ˈræn
alkyl ˈæl.kɪl (US) -kᵊl **-s** -z
alkyne ˈæl.kaɪn **-s** -z
all ɔːl (US) ɔːl, ɑːl ˌ**all ˈfours**; ˌ**all ˈright**
alla breve ˌæl.əˈbreɪ.veɪ, -vi (US) ˌɑː.ləˈbreɪ.vi, -veɪ
Allah ˈæl.ə, -ɑː; əˈlɑː, ælˈɑː
Allahabad ˌæl.ə.həˈbɑːd, -ˈbæd
all-American ˌɔːl.əˈmer.ɪ.kᵊn (US) ˌɔːl-, ˌɑːl-
Allan ˈæl.ən
Allan-a-Dale ˌæl.ən.əˈdeɪl
Allandale ˈæl.ən.deɪl
allantois əˈlæn.təʊ.ɪs (US) -toʊ- **allantoides** əˌlænˈtəʊ.ɪ.diːz (US) ˌæl.ənˈtoʊ.ə-
Allard ˈæl.ɑːd, -əd (US) -ɑːrd, -ɚd
Allardice ˈæl.ə.daɪs (US) ˈ-ɚ-
allargando ˌæl.ɑːˈgæn.dəʊ (US) ˌɑː.lɑːrˈgɑːn.doʊ
allative ˈæl.ə.tɪv (US) -t̬ɪv
allay əˈleɪ **-s** -z **-ing** -ɪŋ **-ed** -d
All-Bran® ˈɔːl.bræn (US) ˈɔːl-, ˈɑːl-
Allbright ˈɔːl.braɪt, ˈɒl- (US) ˈɔːl-, ˈɑːl-
all-clear ˌɔːlˈklɪəʳ (US) ˌɔːlˈklɪr, ˌɑːl-
Allcock ˈɔːl.kɒk (US) ˈɔːl.kɑːk, ˈɑːl-
Allcroft ˈɔːl.krɒft, ˈɒl- (US) ˈɔːl.krɑːft, ˈɑːl-
allegation ˌæl.ɪˈgeɪ.ʃᵊn, -əˈ-, -egˈeɪ- **-s** -z
alleg|e əˈledʒ **-es** -ɪz **-ing** -ɪŋ **-ed** -d
allegedly əˈledʒ.ɪd.li, -əd-
Alleghany ˌæl.ɪˈgeɪ.ni, -əˈ- (US) -əˈ-
Allegheny ˈæl.ɪ.gen.i (US) ˌæl.əˈgeɪ.ni
allegian|ce əˈliː.dʒᵊn|*t*s **-t** -t
allegoric ˌæl.ɪˈgɒr.ɪk, -əˈgɒr- (US) -ˈgɔːr- **-al** -ᵊl **-ally** -ᵊl.i, -li
allegorist ˈæl.ɪ.gə.rɪst, ˈ-ə- (US) -gɔːr.ɪst **-s** -s
allegoriz|e, -is|e ˈæl.ɪ.gə.raɪz, ˈ-ə- (US) -gɔː-, -gə- **-es** -ɪz **-ing** -ɪŋ **-ed** -d
allegor|y ˈæl.ɪ.gə.r|i, ˈ-ə- (US) -gɔːr|.i **-ies** -iz
allegretto ˌæl.ɪˈgret.əʊ, -əˈ- (US) -ˈgret̬.oʊ **-s** -z
Allegri ælˈeg.ri, -ˈeɪ.gri
allegro əˈleg.rəʊ, ælˈeg-, -ˈeɪ.grəʊ (US) -ˈleg.roʊ, -ˈleɪ.groʊ **-s** -z
Allein(e) ˈæl.ɪn
allele əˈliːl **-s** -z
allelic əˈliː.lɪk
allelism əˈliː.li.zᵊm
alleluia (A) ˌæl.ɪˈluː.jə, -əˈ- **-s** -z
allemande ˈæl.ə.mɑːnd, -mænd, -mɒnd (US) -mænd, -mɑːnd, -mæn, -mən **-s** -z
all-embracing ˌɔːl.ɪmˈbreɪ.sɪŋ, -emˈ- (US) ˌɔːl.emˈ-, ˌɑːl-, -ɪmˈ- *stress shift:* ˌall-embracing ˈtheory
Allen ˈæl.ən, -ɪn ˈ**Allen ˌkey**; ˈ**Allen ˌwrench**
Allenby ˈæl.ən.bi
Allendale ˈæl.ən.deɪl, -ɪn-

Allende aɪ'end.i, -eɪ (US) ɑː'jen.deɪ, ɑːl-
Allentown 'æl.ən.taʊn, -ɪn-
allergen 'æl.ə.dʒen, -dʒən (US) '-ɚ- **-s** -z
allergenic ˌæl.ə'dʒen.ɪk (US) -ɚ'-
allergic ə'lɜː.dʒɪk (US) -'lɜːr-
allergist 'æl.ə.dʒɪst (US) '-ɚ- **-s** -s
allergly 'æl.ə.dʒli (US) '-ɚ- **-ies** -iz
Allerton 'æl.ə.tᵊn (US) '-ɚ.tən
alleviľate ə'liː.vi|.eɪt **-ates** -eɪts **-ating** -eɪ.tɪŋ (US) -eɪ.t̬ɪŋ **-ated** -eɪ.tɪd (US) -eɪ.t̬ɪd **-ator/s** -eɪ.təʳ/z (US) -eɪ.t̬ɚ/z
alleviation əˌliː.vi'eɪ.ʃᵊn
alley 'æl.i **-s** -z 'alley ˌcat
Alleyn 'æl.ɪn
Alleyne æl'iːn, 'æl.ɪn, æl'eɪn
Alleynian ə'leɪ.ni.ən, æl'eɪ- **-s** -z
alleyway 'æl.i.weɪ **-s** -z
All Fools' Day ˌɔːl'fuːlz.deɪ (US) ˌɔːl-, ˌɑːl- **-s** -z
Allhallows ˌɔːl'hæl.əʊz (US) -oʊz, ˌɑːl-
allianc|e ə'laɪ.ənts **-es** -ɪz
allicin 'æl.ə.sɪn, '-ɪ-
allied 'æl.aɪd
Allies 'æl.aɪz
alligator 'æl.ɪ.geɪ.təʳ (US) -t̬ɚ **-s** -z
all-in ˌɔːl'ɪn (US) ˌɔːl-, ˌɑːl- *stress shift:* ˌall-in 'wrestling
all-inclusive ˌɔːl.ɪŋ'kluː.sɪv (US) -ɪn'-, ˌɑːl-, -ɪŋ'-
allineation əˌlɪn.i'eɪ.ʃᵊn, ælˌɪn- **-s** -z
Allingham 'æl.ɪŋ.əm
all-in-one ˌɔːl.ɪn'wʌn (US) ˌɔːl-, ˌɑːl- *stress shift:* ˌall-in-one sham'poo
Allison 'æl.ɪ.sᵊn
alliter|ate ə'lɪt.ᵊr|.eɪt, æl'ɪt- (US) ə'lɪt̬.ə.r|eɪt **-ates** -eɪts **-ating** -eɪ.tɪŋ (US) -eɪ.t̬ɪŋ **-ated** -eɪ.tɪd (US) -eɪ.t̬ɪd
alliteration əˌlɪt.ə'reɪ.ʃᵊn, ælˌɪt- (US) əˌlɪt̬- **-s** -z
alliterative ə'lɪt.ᵊr.ə.tɪv, æl'ɪt-, -eɪ- (US) ə'lɪt̬.ᵊr.ə.t̬ɪv, -ə.reɪ.t̬ɪv
Allman 'ɔːl.mən (US) 'ɔːl-, 'ɑːl-
all-nighter ˌɔːl'naɪ.təʳ (US) -t̬ɚ, ˌɑːl- **-s** -z
Alloa 'æl.əʊə (US) -oʊə
Allobroges ə'lɒb.rə.dʒiːz, æl'ɒb-, -rəʊ- (US) ə'lɑː.broʊ-
allo|cate 'æl.ə|.keɪt **-cates** -keɪts **-cating** -keɪ.tɪŋ (US) -keɪ.t̬ɪŋ **-cated** -keɪ.tɪd (US) -keɪ.t̬ɪd
allocation ˌæl.ə.keɪ.ʃᵊn **-s** -z
allocution ˌæl.ə'kjuː.ʃᵊn **-s** -z
allodi|al ə'ləʊ.di|.əl (US) -'loʊ- **-um** -əm
allogeneic ˌæl.əʊ.dʒə'niː.ɪk, -'neɪ- (US) ˌ-ə-, ˌ-oʊ- **-ally** -ᵊl.i
allokine 'æl.əʊ.kaɪn (US) '-ə- **-s** -z
allomorph 'æl.əʊ.mɔːf (US) -ə.mɔːrf, -oʊ- **-s** -s
Allon 'æl.ən
allopath 'æl.əʊ.pæθ (US) '-ə-, '-oʊ- **-s** -s
allopathic ˌæl.əʊ'pæθ.ɪk (US) -ə'-, -oʊ'-
allopath|y ə'lɒp.ə.θ|i, æl'ɒp- (US) ə'lɑː.pə- **-ist/s** -ɪst/s
allophone 'æl.əʊ.fəʊn (US) -ə.foʊn, -oʊ- **-s** -z
allophonic ˌæl.əʊ'fɒn.ɪk (US) -ə'fɑː.nɪk *stress shift:* ˌallophonic 'variant
all-or-nothing ˌɔːl.ɔː'nʌθ.ɪŋ, -ə'- (US) -ɔːr'-, ˌɑːl-, -ɚ'- *stress shift:* ˌall-or-nothing 'gamble
alloseme 'æl.əʊ.siːm (US) '-ə- **-s** -z
al|lot ə|'lɒt (US) -|'lɑːt **-lots** -'lɒts (US) -'lɑːts **-lotting** -'lɒt.ɪŋ (US) -'lɑː.t̬ɪŋ **-lotted** -'lɒt.ɪd (US) -'lɑː.t̬ɪd
allotment ə'lɒt.mənt (US) -'lɑːt- **-s** -s
allotone 'æl.əʊ.təʊn (US) -ə.toʊn **-s** -z
allotrope 'æl.ə.trəʊp (US) -troʊp **-s** -s
allotropic ˌæl.ə'trɒp.ɪk (US) -'trɑː.pɪk
allotropy æl'ɒt.rə.pi, ə'lɒt- (US) ə'lɑː.trə-
all-out ˌɔːl'aʊt (US) ˌɔːl-, ˌɑːl- *stress shift:* ˌall-out 'effort
allow ə'laʊ **-s** -z **-ing** -ɪŋ **-ed** -d
allowab|le ə'laʊ.ə.b|l̩ **-ly** -li **-leness** -l̩.nəs, -nɪs
allowanc|e ə'laʊ.ənts **-es** -ɪz **-ing** -ɪŋ **-ed** -t
Alloway 'æl.ə.weɪ
allowedly ə'laʊ.ɪd.li, -əd-
alloy (*n.*) 'æl.ɔɪ **-s** -z
alloy (*v.*) ə'lɔɪ **-s** -z **-ing** -ɪŋ **-ed** -d
all-powerful ˌɔːl'paʊə.fᵊl, -fʊl (US) -'paʊɚ-, ˌɑːl- *stress shift:* ˌall-powerful 'monarch
all-purpose ˌɔːl'pɜː.pəs (US) ˌɔːl'pɜːr-, ˌɑːl- *stress shift:* ˌall-purpose 'knife
all-round ˌɔːl'raʊnd (US) ˌɔːl-, ˌɑːl- *stress shift:* ˌall-round 'athlete
all-rounder ˌɔːl'raʊn.dəʳ (US) -dɚ, ˌɑːl- **-s** -z
All Saints' Day ˌɔːl'seɪnts ˌdeɪ (US) ˌɔːl-, ˌɑːl- **-s** -z
Allsop(p) 'ɔːl.sɒp (US) 'ɔːl.sɑːp, 'ɑːl-
allsorts 'ɔːl.sɔːts (US) -sɔːrts, 'ɑːl-
All Souls' Day ˌɔːl'səʊlz ˌdeɪ (US) ˌɔːl'soʊlz-, ˌɑːl- **-s** -z
allspice 'ɔːl.spaɪs (US) 'ɔːl-, 'ɑːl-
all-star 'ɔːl.stɑːʳ (US) 'ɔːl.stɑːr, 'ɑːl-
all-time ˌɔːl'taɪm (US) 'ɔːl.taɪm, 'ɑːl- *stress shift, British only, see compound:* ˌall-time 'greats
allud|e ə'luːd, -'ljuːd (US) -'luːd **-es** -z **-ing** -ɪŋ **-ed** -ɪd
Allum 'æl.əm
allur|e ə'ljʊəʳ, -'lʊəʳ, -'ljɔːʳ (US) -'lʊr **-es** -z **-ing/ly** -ɪŋ/li **-ed** -d **-ement/s** -mənt/s
allusion ə'luː.ʒᵊn, ə'ljuː- (US) -'luː- **-s** -z
allusive ə'luː.sɪv, -'ljuː- (US) -'luː- **-ly** -li **-ness** -nəs, -nɪs
alluvi|al ə'luː.vi|.əl, -'ljuː- (US) -'luː- **-a** -ə
alluvion ə'luː.vi.ən, -'ljuː- (US) -'luː- **-s** -z
alluvi|um ə'luː.vi|.əm, -'ljuː- (US) -'luː- **-ums** -əmz **-a** -ə
Allworth 'ɔːl.wəθ, -wɜːθ (US) -wɚθ, 'ɑːl-, -wɜːrθ
Allworthy 'ɔːlˌwɜː.ði (US) -ˌwɜːr-, ɑːl-
all|y (*n.*) 'æl.aɪ, ə'laɪ **-ies** -z
all|y (*v.*) ə'l|aɪ, æl|'aɪ; 'æl|.aɪ **-ies** -aɪz **-ying** -aɪ.ɪŋ **-ied** -aɪd
Note: **Allied** is usually pronounced /'æl.aɪd/ when attributive.
Ally 'æl.i
-ally -əl.i, -li
Note: Suffix. Words containing **-ally** are stressed in the same manner as adjectives containing **-al**. Where the word ends **-ically**, two forms are possible, e.g. **musically** is either /'mjuː.zɪ.kᵊl.i/ or /'mjuː.zɪ.kli/.
Allyson 'æl.ɪ.sᵊn
Alma 'æl.mə
Alma-Ata ˌæl.mɑː.ə'tɑː, ælˌmɑː-, ˌɑːl.mə'ɑː.tə
Almack 'ɔːl.mæk, 'ɒl- (US) 'ɔːl-, 'ɑːl-
almagest 'æl.mə.dʒest **-s** -s
alma mater (A M) ˌæl.mə'mɑː.təʳ, -'meɪ.təʳ (US) -'mɑː.t̬ɚ, ˌɑːl- **-s** -z
almanac(k) 'ɔːl.mə.næk, 'ɒl-, 'æl- (US) 'ɔːl-, 'ɑːl-, 'æl- **-s** -s
almandine 'æl.mən.diːn, -dɪn **-s** -z
Almanzor æl'mæn.zɔːʳ, -zəʳ (US) -zɔːr, -zɚ
Alma-Tadema ˌæl.mə'tæd.ɪ.mə
Almería ˌæl.mə'ri.ə
Almesbury 'ɑːmz.bᵊr.i (US) -ber-, -bɚ-
almight|y (A) ɔːl'maɪ.t|i (US) -t̬|i, ɑːl- **-ily** -ɪ.li, -ᵊl.i **-iness** -ɪ.nəs, -ɪ.nɪs
Almon 'æl.mən
almond (A) 'ɑː.mənd (US) 'ɑː-, 'ɑːl-, 'æl- **-s** -z
Almondbury 'æl.mən*d*.bᵊr.i, 'ɑː-, 'ɔː- (US) 'æl.mən*d*.ber.i, 'ɑː-, 'ɑːl-, -bɚ-
Almondsbury 'ɑː.mən*dz*.bᵊr.i *locally also:* 'eɪmz.bᵊr.i (US) 'ɑː.mən*dz*.ber.i, 'ɑːl-, -bɚ-
almoner 'ɑː.mə.nəʳ, 'æl- (US) 'æl.mə.nɚ, 'ɑː-, 'ɑːl- **-s** -z
almonr|y 'ɑː.mən.r|i, 'æl- (US) 'æl-, 'ɑː-, 'ɑːl- **-ies** -iz
almost 'ɔːl.məʊst, -məst (US) 'ɔːl.moʊst, 'ɑːl-
alms ɑːmz
almsgiv|er 'ɑːmz.gɪ.v|əʳ (US) -v|ɚ **-ers** -əz (US) -ɚz **-ing** -ɪŋ
almshou|se 'ɑːmz.haʊ|s **-ses** -zɪz
Alne ɔːn
Alness 'ɔːl.nɪs, 'æl-
Alnmouth 'æln.maʊθ, 'eɪl-
Alnwick 'æn.ɪk

aloe 'æl.əʊ (US) -oʊ **-s** -z
aloe vera ˌæl.əʊ'vɪə.rə (US) -oʊ'vɪr.ə
aloft ə'lɒft (US) -'lɑːft
aloha ə'ləʊ.hə, æl'əʊ-, -hɑː, -ə (US) ə'loʊ-
alone ə'ləʊn (US) -'loʊn **-ness** -nəs, -nɪs
along ə'lɒŋ (US) -'lɑːŋ, -'lɔːŋ
alongside əˌlɒŋ'saɪd (US) ə'lɑːŋ.saɪd, -'lɔːŋ-, -ˌ-'-
Alonso ə'lɒn*t*.səʊ, -'lɒn.zəʊ (US) -'lɑːn*t*.soʊ, -'lɑːn.zoʊ
aloof ə'luːf **-ness** -nəs, -nɪs
alopecia ˌæl.əʊ'piː.ʃə, '-ʃi.ə (US) -ə'-, -oʊ'-
aloud ə'laʊd
Aloysius ˌæl.əʊ'ɪʃ.əs, -'ɪs.i.əs (US) ˌæl.oʊ'ɪʃ-, -'ɪs.i.əs, -ə'wɪʃ.əs, -i.əs
alp (A) ælp **-s** -s
alpaca æl'pæk.ə **-s** -z
Alpen® 'æl.pən
alpenglow 'æl.pən.gləʊ (US) -gloʊ
alpenhorn 'æl.pən.hɔːn, -pɪn- (US) -hɔːrn **-s** -z
alpenstock 'æl.pən.stɒk, -pɪn- (US) -stɑːk **-s** -s
Alperton 'æl.pə.tᵊn (US) -pɚ-
alpha 'æl.fə **-s** -z **'alpha ˌparticle** ; **'alpha ˌray** ; **'alpha ˌrhythm** ; **'alpha ˌwave**
alphabet 'æl.fə.bet, -bɪt **-s** -s
alphabetic ˌæl.fə'bet.ɪk (US) -'beṭ- *stress shift:* ˌalphabetic 'writing
alphabetic|al ˌæl.fə'bet.ɪ.k|ᵊl (US) **alphabeti|cal** -'beṭ- **-ally** -ᵊl.i, -li **ˌalphabetical 'order, alphaˌbetical 'order**
alphabeticiz|e, -is|e ˌæl.fə'bet.ɪ.saɪz (US) -'beṭ.ə- **-es** -ɪz **-ing** -ɪŋ **-ed** -d
alphabetization, -isa- ˌæl.fə.bet.aɪ'zeɪ.ʃᵊn (US) -beṭ.ɪ'-
alphabetiz|e, -is|e 'æl.fə.bet.aɪz, -bə.taɪz, -bɪ- (US) -bə.taɪz **-es** -ɪz **-ing** -ɪŋ **-ed** -d
Alpha Centauri ˌæl.fə.sen'tɔː.ri, -ken'-, -'taʊ- (US) -sen'tɔːr.i
Alphaeus æl'fiː.əs
alphanumeric ˌæl.fə.njuː'mer.ɪk (US) -nuː'-, -njuː'- **-al** -ᵊl **-ally** -ᵊl.i, -li *stress shift:* ˌalphanumeric 'code
Alphonse æl'fɒn*t*s, '-- (US) æl'fɑːn*t*s, -'fɔːn*t*s, '--
Alphonso æl'fɒn*t*.səʊ, -'fɒn.zəʊ (US) -'fɑːn*t*.soʊ, -'fɑːn.zoʊ
alpine (A) 'æl.paɪn
alpin|ism 'æl.pɪ.n|ɪ.zᵊm **-ist/s** -ɪst/s
Alps ælps
already ɔːl'red.i (US) ɔːl-, ɑːl- *stress shift:* ˌalready 'here
Alresford 'ɔːlz.fəd, 'ɔːls-, 'ɑːlz-, 'ɑːls- (US) -fɚd
alright ɔːl'raɪt (US) ɔːl-, ɑːl-
Alsace æl'sæs, -'zæs
Alsace-Lorraine ælˌsæs.lɒr'eɪn, -'zæs (US) -loʊ'reɪn, -ˌseɪs-, -lə'-
Alsager 'ɔːl.sɪ.dʒəʳ, -sə.dʒəʳ, ɔːl'seɪ.dʒəʳ (US) 'ɔːl.sə.dʒɚ, 'ɑːl-, ɔːl'seɪ.dʒɚ, ɑːl-
Alsatia æl'seɪ.ʃə, '-ʃi.ə
alsatian (A) æl'seɪ.ʃᵊn **-s** -z
also 'ɔːl.səʊ (US) 'ɔːl.soʊ, 'ɑːl-
Alsop(p) 'ɔːl.sɒp, 'ɒl-, -səp (US) 'ɔːl.sɑːp, 'ɑːl-
also-ran ˌɔːl.səʊ'ræn, '--ˌ- (US) 'ɔːl.soʊ.ræn, 'ɑːl- **-s** -z
Note: In British English, the latter form is used attributively.
Alston 'ɔːl.stən, 'ɒl- (US) 'ɔːl-, 'ɑːl-
alt ælt, ɔːlt (US) ælt, ɑːlt
Altai ɑːl'taɪ
Altaic æl'teɪ.ɪk
Altair 'æl.teəʳ, -'- (US) æl'ter, -'tær, -'taɪr
altar 'ɔːl.təʳ, 'ɒl- (US) 'ɔːl.ṭɚ, 'ɑːl- **-s** -z **'altar ˌboy** ; **'altar ˌrail**
altarpiec|e 'ɔːl.tə.piːs, 'ɒl- (US) 'ɔːl.ṭɚ-, 'ɑːl- **-es** -ɪz
altazimuth æl'tæz.ɪ.məθ **-s** -s
Altdorf 'ælt.dɔːf (US) 'ɑːlt.dɔːrf, 'ælt-
alter 'ɔːl.təʳ, 'ɒl- (US) 'ɔːl.ṭɚ, 'ɑːl- **-s** -z **-ing** -ɪŋ **-ed** -d **-able** -ə.bḷ **-ant/s** -ᵊnt/s
alteration ˌɔːl.tᵊr'eɪ.ʃᵊn, ˌɒl- (US) ˌɔːl.ṭə'reɪ-, ˌɑːl- **-s** -z
alterative 'ɔːl.tᵊr.ə.tɪv, 'ɒl-, -tᵊr.eɪ- (US) 'ɔːl.ṭə.reɪ.ṭɪv, 'ɑːl-, -ṭɚ.ə-
alter|cate 'ɔːl.tə|.keɪt, 'ɒl- (US) 'ɔːl.ṭɚ-, 'ɑːl- **-cates** -keɪts **-cating** -keɪ.tɪŋ (US) -keɪ.ṭɪŋ **-cated** -keɪ.tɪd (US) -keɪ.ṭɪd
altercation ˌɔːl.tə'keɪ.ʃᵊn, ˌɒl- (US) ˌɔːl.ṭɚ'-, ˌɑːl- **-s** -z
alter ego ˌɔːl.təʳ'iː.gəʊ, ˌɒl-, ˌæl-, -'eg.əʊ (US) ˌɔːl.ṭɚ'iː.goʊ, ˌɑːl- **-s** -z
alternanc|e ɔːl'tɜː.nən*t*s, 'ɒl- (US) ɔːl'tɜːr-, ɑːl- **-es** -ɪz
alternant ɔːl'tɜː.nənt, ɒl- (US) ɔːl'tɜːr-, ɑːl- **-s** -s
alternate (*adj.*) ɔːl'tɜː.nət, ɒl-, -nɪt (US) ɔːl'tɜːr-, ɑːl-; 'ɔːl.ṭɚ-, 'ɑːl- **-ly** -li **-ness** -nəs, -nɪs
alter|nate (*v.*) 'ɔːl.tə|.neɪt, 'ɒl- (US) 'ɔːl.ṭɚ-, 'ɑːl- **-nates** -neɪts **-nating** -neɪ.tɪŋ (US) -neɪ.ṭɪŋ **-nated** -neɪ.tɪd (US) -neɪ.ṭɪd
alternation ˌɔːl.tə'neɪ.ʃᵊn, ˌɒl- (US) ˌɔːl.ṭɚ'-, ˌɑːl- **-s** -z
alternative ɔːl'tɜː.nə.tɪv, ɒl- (US) ɔːl'tɜːr.nə.ṭɪv, ɑːl- **-s** -z **-ly** -li **alˌternative 'medicine**
alternator 'ɔːl.tə.neɪ.təʳ (US) 'ɔːl.tɚ.neɪ.ṭɚ, 'ɑːl-, 'æl- **-s** -z
Althea 'æl.θi.ə (US) æl'θiː-
Althorp 'ɔːl.θɔːp, 'ɒl-, -trəp (US) 'ɔːl.θɔːrp, 'ɑːl-
Note: Viscount Althorp pronounces /'ɔːl.trəp/.
although ɔːl'ðəʊ (US) ɔːl'ðoʊ, ɑːl-
Althusser ˌæl.tʊ'seə (US) ˌɑːl.tuː'ser
altimeter 'æl.tɪ.miː.təʳ, 'ɔːl-, 'ɒl-; æl'tɪm.ɪ- (US) æl'tɪm.ə.ṭɚ, 'æl.ṭə.miː- **-s** -z
altimetry æl'tɪm.ɪ.tri, ɔːl-, ɒl-, '-ə- (US) æl'tɪm.ə-
altissimo æl'tɪs.ɪ.məʊ (US) -moʊ, ɑːl-
altitude 'æl.tɪ.tjuːd, 'ɔːl-, 'ɒl-, -tʃuːd (US) 'æl.tə.tuːd, -tjuːd **-s** -z
Altman 'ɔːlt.mən (US) 'ɔːlt-, 'ɑːlt-
alto 'æl.təʊ, 'ɒl- (US) 'æl.toʊ **-s** -z
altogether ˌɔːl.tə'geð.əʳ (US) -ɚ, ˌɑːl- *stress shift:* ˌaltogether 'marvellous
Alton 'ɔːl.tᵊn, 'ɒl- (US) 'ɔːl-, 'ɑːl-
Altona 'æl.təʊ.nə (US) ɑːl'toʊ-
Altoona æl'təʊ.nə (US) -'tuː-
alto-relievo, alto-rilievo ˌæl.təʊ.rɪ'liː.vəʊ (US) -toʊ.rə'liː.voʊ, ˌɑːl-
Altrincham 'ɔːl.trɪŋ.əm, 'ɒl- (US) 'ɔːl-, 'ɑːl-
altru|ism 'æl.tru|.ɪ.zᵊm **-ist/s** -ɪst/s
altruistic ˌæl.tru'ɪs.tɪk **-ally** -ᵊl.i, -li *stress shift:* ˌaltruistic 'action
alum (A) 'æl.əm **-s** -z
alumina ə'luː.mɪ.nə, æl'uː-, -'ljuː- (US) ə'luː-
aluminium ˌæl.jə'mɪn.i.əm, -jʊ'-, -ə-, '-jəm *stress shift:* ˌaluminium 'foil
aluminiz|e, -is|e ə'ljuː.mɪ.naɪz, ə'luː- (US) -'luː- **-es** -ɪz **-ing** -ɪŋ **-ed** -d
aluminous ə'luː.mɪ.nəs, -'ljuː- (US) -'luː-
aluminum ə'luː.mɪ.nəm, -'ljuː- (US) -'luː-
alumn|a ə'lʌm.n|ə **-ae** -iː
alumn|us ə'lʌm.n|əs **-i** -aɪ
Alun 'æl.ɪn
Alva 'æl.və
Alvar 'æl.vɑːʳ, -vəʳ (US) -vɑːr, -vɚ
Alvarez æl'vɑː.rez; 'æl.və- (US) 'æl.və.rez; 'ɑːl.vɑː.reθ
Alvary 'æl.vᵊr.i
alveolar ˌæl.vi'əʊ.ləʳ; æl'viː.ə-; 'æl.vi- (US) æl'viː.ə.lɚ **-s** -z
alveolate æl'viː.ə.lət, -lɪt, -leɪt (US) -lɪt
alveole 'æl.vi.əʊl (US) -oʊl **-s** -z
alveol|us ˌæl.vi'əʊ.l|əs; æl'viː.ə-; 'æl.vi.ə- (US) æl'viː.ə- **-i** -aɪ, -iː
Alverstone 'ɔːl.və.stᵊn, 'ɒl- (US) 'ɔːl.vɚ-, 'ɑːl-
Alvescot 'æl.vɪ.skɒt, -skət *locally:* 'ɔːl.skət (US) -skɑːt
Alveston 'æl.vɪ.stən
Alvey 'æl.vi
Alvin 'æl.vɪn
alway 'ɔːl.weɪ, 'ɑːl-
always 'ɔːl.weɪz, -wəz, -wɪz (US) 'ɔːl-, 'ɑːl-

Alwyn 'æl.wɪn, 'ɔːl-
Alyn 'æl.ɪn, -ən
Alyson 'æl.ɪ.sən
Alyssa æl'ɪs.ə
alyssum 'æl.ɪ.səm
Alzheimer 'ælts.haɪ.məʳ ⓤⓢ 'ɑːlts.haɪ.mɚ, 'ælts- **'Alzheimer's di,sease**
a.m., AM ,eɪ'em
am *strong form:* æm *weak forms:* əm, m
Note: Weak form word. The strong form /æm/ is used for emphasis (e.g. 'I **am** going to leave.'), for contrast (e.g. 'I know what I **am** and am **not** capable of.') and in final position (e.g. 'That's who I am.'). The weak form is usually /əm/ (e.g. 'How am I going to pay?' /,haʊ.əm.aɪ,gəʊ.ɪŋ.tə'peɪ ⓤⓢ -goʊ.ɪŋ.t̬ə'-/) but after 'I'/aɪ/ it is frequently shortened to /m/ (e.g. 'I am (I'm) here' /aɪm 'hɪəʳ ⓤⓢ aɪm 'hɪr/).
AMA ,eɪ.em'eɪ
Amabel 'æm.ə.bel
Amadeus ,æm.ə'deɪ.əs ⓤⓢ ,ɑː.mə'deɪ.ʊs, -əs
Amadis 'æm.ə.dɪs
amadou 'æm.ə.duː
amah 'ɑː.mə, 'æm.ɑː ⓤⓢ 'ɑː.mɑː **-s** -z
Amahl 'æm.ɑːl ⓤⓢ ə'mɑːl
amain ə'meɪn
Amalekite ə'mæl.ə.kaɪt, '-ɪ- ⓤⓢ ,æm.ə'lek.aɪt; ə'mæl.ə.kaɪt **-s** -s
Amalfi ə'mæl.fi, æm'æl- ⓤⓢ ə'mæl-, -'mɑːl
amalgam ə'mæl.gəm **-s** -z
amalga|mate ə'mæl.gə|.meɪt **-mates** -meɪts **-mating** -meɪ.tɪŋ ⓤⓢ -meɪ.t̬ɪŋ **-mated** -meɪ.tɪd ⓤⓢ -meɪ.t̬ɪd
amalgamation ə,mæl.gə'meɪ.ʃᵊn **-s** -z
amalgamative ə'mæl.gə.mə.tɪv ⓤⓢ -t̬ɪv
Amalia ə'mɑː.li.ə, æm'ɑː- ⓤⓢ ə'meɪl.jə
Amalth(a)ea ,æm.əl'θiː.ə
Aman 'æm.ən ⓤⓢ 'eɪ.mən
Amanda ə'mæn.də
amandine ə'mæn.daɪn; ,ɑː.mən'diːn ⓤⓢ ,ɑː.mən'diːn, ,æm.ən'-
Amantia ə'mæn.ʃi.ə
amanuens|is ə,mæn.ju'en*t*.s|ɪs **-es** -iːz
Amara ə'mɑː.rə
amaranth 'æm.ᵊr.æn*t*θ ⓤⓢ -ə.ræn*t*θ **-s** -s
amaranthine ,æm.ᵊr'æn*t*.θaɪn ⓤⓢ -ə'ræn*t*.θɪn, -θiːn, -θaɪn
amaretto (A) ,æm.ᵊr'et.əʊ ⓤⓢ -ə'ret̬.oʊ
Amarillo ,æm.ᵊr'ɪl.əʊ ⓤⓢ -ə'rɪl.oʊ
amaryllis (A) ,æm.ᵊr'ɪl.ɪs ⓤⓢ -ə'rɪl- **-es** -ɪz
Amasis ə'meɪ.sɪs
amass ə'mæs **-es** -ɪz **-ing** -ɪŋ **-ed** -t
amateur 'æm.ə.təʳ, -tɜːʳ, -tjʊəʳ, -tjəʳ, -tʃəʳ; ,æm.ə'tɜːʳ ⓤⓢ 'æm.ə.tʃɚ, -tʃʊr, -t̬ɚ, -tɜːr **-s** -z ,**amateur dra'matics**
Note: The final British form is not used attributively.
amateurish 'æm.ə.tᵊr.ɪʃ, -tɜː.rɪʃ, -tjʊə-, -tjɔː-, -tjᵊr.ɪʃ, -tʃᵊr- ⓤⓢ ,æm.ə'tɜːr.ɪʃ, -'tʃʊr-, -'tjʊr- **-ly** -li **-ness** -nəs, -nɪs
amateurism 'æm.ə.tᵊr.ɪ.zᵊm, -tɜː.rɪ-, -tjʊə-, -tjɔː-, -tjᵊr.ɪ-, -tʃᵊr- ⓤⓢ 'æm.ə.tʃɚ.ɪ-, -tʃʊ.rɪ-, -t̬ɚ.ɪ-
Amati ə'mɑː.ti, æm'ɑː- ⓤⓢ -t̬i **-s** -z
amatol 'æm.ə.tɒl ⓤⓢ -tɑːl
amatory 'æm.ə.tᵊr.i ⓤⓢ -tɔːr-
amaurosis ,æm.ɔː'rəʊ.sɪs ⓤⓢ -'roʊ-
amaz|e ə'meɪz **-es** -ɪz **-ed** -d **-edly** -ɪd.li **-edness** -ɪd.nəs, -nɪs **-ement/s** -mənt/s
amazing ə'meɪ.zɪŋ **-ly** -li
amazon (A) 'æm.ə.zᵊn ⓤⓢ -zɑːn **-s** -z
Amazonia ,æm.ə'zəʊ.ni.ə ⓤⓢ -'zoʊ-
amazonian (A) ,æm.ə'zəʊ.ni.ən ⓤⓢ -'zoʊ-
amazonite 'æm.ə.zə.naɪt **-s** -s
ambassador æm'bæs.ə.dəʳ ⓤⓢ -dɚ **-s** -z
ambassadorial æm,bæs.ə'dɔː.ri.əl, ,æm.bæs-
ambassadress æm'bæs.ə.drəs, -drɪs, -dres ⓤⓢ -drəs **-es** -ɪz
Ambato ɑːm'bɑː.təʊ, æm- ⓤⓢ -toʊ
amber (A) 'æm.bəʳ ⓤⓢ -bɚ
ambergris 'æm.bə.griːs, -bɚ.grɪs
amberjack 'æm.bə.dʒæk ⓤⓢ -bɚ- **-s** -s
ambi- æm.bɪ-, æm.bi-, æm'bɪ-
Note: Prefix. Normally takes primary or secondary stress on the first syllable, e.g. **ambient** /'æm.bi.ənt/, **ambidextrous** /,æm.bɪ'dek.strəs/, or primary stress on the second syllable, e.g. **ambivalence** /æm'bɪv.ᵊlən*t*s/.
ambianc|e 'æm.bi.ən*t*s, -ɑ̃ːn*t*s ⓤⓢ 'æm.bi.ən*t*s, ,ɑːm.bi'ɑːn*t*s **-es** -ɪz
ambidexter ,æm.bɪ'dek.stəʳ ⓤⓢ -stɚ **-s** -z
ambidexterity ,æm.bɪ.dek'ster.ə.ti, -ɪ.ti ⓤⓢ -ə.t̬i
ambidextrous ,æm.bɪ'dek.strəs
ambienc|e 'æm.bi.ən*t*s, -ɑ̃ːn*t*s ⓤⓢ 'æm.bi.ən*t*s, ,ɑːm.bi'ɑːn*t*s **-es** -ɪz
ambient 'æm.bi.ənt
ambiguit|y ,æm.bɪ'gjuː.ə.t|i, -ɪ.t|i ⓤⓢ -bə'gjuː.ə.t̬|i **-ies** -iz
ambiguous æm'bɪg.ju.əs **-ly** -li **-ness** -nəs, -nɪs
Ambiorix æm'baɪ.ə.rɪks ⓤⓢ -ɚ.ɪks, -oʊ.rɪks
ambit 'æm.bɪt **-s** -s
ambition æm'bɪʃ.ᵊn **-s** -z
ambitious æm'bɪʃ.əs **-ly** -li **-ness** -nəs, -nɪs
ambivalen|ce æm'bɪv.ᵊl.ən|*t*s **-t/ly** -t/li
ambl|e (A) 'æm.bl̩ **-es** -z **-ing** -ɪŋ, 'æm.blɪŋ **-ed** -d **-er/s** -əʳ/z, '-bləʳ/z ⓤⓢ '-bl̩.ɚ/z, '-blɚ/z
Ambler 'æm.bləʳ, '-bl̩.əʳ ⓤⓢ '-blɚ, '-bl̩.ɚ
Ambleside 'æm.bl̩.saɪd
amboyna (A) æm'bɔɪ.nə
Ambree 'æm.bri
Ambridge 'æm.brɪdʒ
Ambrose 'æm.brəʊz, -brəʊs ⓤⓢ -broʊz
ambrosi|a æm'brəʊ.zi|.ə, -ʒ|ə ⓤⓢ -'broʊ.ʒ|ə **-al** -əl **-ally** -ᵊl.i **-an** -ən
Ambrosius æm'brəʊ.zi.əs, -ʒəs ⓤⓢ -'broʊ.ʒəs
ambsace 'eɪm.zeɪs, 'æm-
ambulance 'æm.bjə.lən*t*s, -bjʊ.lən*t*s, -bə- **-s** -ɪz **-man** -mæn **-men** -men **-woman** -,wʊm.ən **-women** -,wɪm.ɪn
ambulance-chaser 'æm.bjə.lən*t*s,tʃeɪ.səʳ, -bjʊ- ⓤⓢ -sɚ **-s** -z
ambulant 'æm.bjə.lənt, -bjʊ.lənt
ambu|late 'æm.bjə|.leɪt, -bjʊ- **-lates** -leɪts **-lating** -leɪ.tɪŋ ⓤⓢ -leɪ.t̬ɪŋ **-lated** -leɪ.tɪd ⓤⓢ -leɪ.t̬ɪd
ambulation ,æm.bjə'leɪ.ʃᵊn, -bjʊ'- **-s** -z
ambulator|y ,æm.bjə'leɪ.tᵊr|.i, -bjʊ-; 'æm.bjə.lə-, -bjʊ- ⓤⓢ 'æm.bjə.lə.tɔːr-, -bjʊ- **-ies** -iz
ambuscad|e ,æm.bə'skeɪd **-es** -z **-ing** -ɪŋ **-ed** -ɪd
ambush 'æm.bʊʃ **-es** -ɪz **-ing** -ɪŋ **-ed** -t
ameb|a ə'miː.b|ə **-as** -əz **-ae** -iː **-ic** -ɪk
Amelia ə'miː.li.ə ⓤⓢ -'miːl.jə, -'miː.li.ə
amelior|ate ə'miː.li.ᵊr|.eɪt ⓤⓢ -'miː.li.ə.r|eɪt, -'miːl.jə- **-ates** -eɪts **-ating** -eɪ.tɪŋ ⓤⓢ -eɪ.t̬ɪŋ **-ated** -eɪ.tɪd ⓤⓢ -eɪ.t̬ɪd
amelioration ə,miː.li.ᵊr'eɪ.ʃᵊn ⓤⓢ -,miː.li.ə'reɪ-, -,miːl.jə'- **-s** -z
ameliorative ə'miː.li.ᵊr.ə.tɪv, -eɪ- ⓤⓢ -'miː.li.ə.reɪ.t̬ɪv, -'miːl.jə-
amen ,ɑː'men, ,eɪ- **-s** -z
amenability ə,miː.nə'bɪl.ə.ti, -ɪ.ti ⓤⓢ -ə.t̬i
amenab|le ə'miː.nə.bl̩| ⓤⓢ -'miː.nə-, -'men.ə- **-ly** -li **-leness** -l̩.nəs, -nɪs
Amen Corner ,eɪ.men'kɔː.nəʳ ⓤⓢ -'kɔr.nɚ
amend ə'mend **-s** -z **-ing** -ɪŋ **-ed** -ɪd
amendatory ə'men.də.tᵊr.i ⓤⓢ -tɔː.ri
amendment ə'men*d*.mənt **-s** -s
amenit|y ə'miː.nə.t|i, -'men.ə-, -ɪ.t|i ⓤⓢ ə'men.ə.t̬|i **-ies** -iz
amenorrh(o)ea ,eɪ.men.ə'riː.ə, ,æm.en- ⓤⓢ ,eɪ.men-

Amerasian ˌæm.əˈreɪ.ʃᵊn, -ʒᵊn (US) -əˈreɪ.ʒᵊn, -ʃᵊn **-s** -z
amerc|e əˈmɜːs (US) -ˈmɜːrs **-es** -ɪz **-ing** -ɪŋ **-ed** -t **-ement/s** -mənt/s
America əˈmer.ɪ.kə
American əˈmer.ɪ.kən **-s** -z **-ist/s** -ɪst/s **Aˌmerican Exˈpress®**
Americana əˌmer.ɪˈkɑː.nə (US) -ˈkæn.ə, -ˈkɑː.nə
Americanese əˌmer.ɪ.kəˈniːz (US) -ˈniːz, -ˈniːs
american|ism (A) əˈmer.ɪ.kə.n|ɪ.zᵊm **-isms** -ɪ.zᵊmz **-ist/s** -ɪst/s
americanization, -isa- (A) əˌmer.ɪ.kə.naɪˈzeɪ.ʃᵊn, -nɪˈ- (US) -nɪˈ-
americaniz|e, -is|e (A) əˈmer.ɪ.kə.naɪz **-es** -ɪz **-ing** -ɪŋ **-ed** -d
americium ˌæm.əˈrɪs.i.əm, -ˈrɪʃ-
Amerindian ˌæm.əˈrɪn.di.ən **-s** -z
Amersham ˈæm.ə.ʃᵊm (US) -ɚ-
Amery ˈeɪ.mᵊr.i
Ames eɪmz
Amesbury ˈeɪmz.bᵊr.i (US) -ber.i
Ameslan ˈæm.ɪ.slæn
amethyst ˈæm.ə.θɪst, -ɪ.θɪst **-s** -s
amethystine ˌæm.əˈθɪs.taɪn, -ɪˈ- (US) -tᵊn, -taɪn, -tɪn, -tiːn
Amex ˈæm.eks
AMF ˌeɪ.emˈef
Amharic æmˈhær.ɪk (US) -ˈhær-, -ˈhɑːr-
Amherst ˈæm.əst, -hɜːst (US) -ɚst, -hɜːrst
amiability ˌeɪ.mi.əˈbɪl.ə.ti, -ɪ.ti (US) -ə.t̬i
amiab|le ˈeɪ.mi.ə.b|l̩ **-ly** -li **-leness** -l̩.nəs, -nɪs
amicability ˌæm.ɪ.kəˈbɪl.ə.ti, -ɪ.ti (US) -ə.t̬i
amicab|le ˈæm.ɪ.kə.b|l̩, əˈmɪk- **-ly** -li **-leness** -l̩.nəs, -nɪs
amic|e ˈæm.ɪs **-es** -ɪz
Amice ˈeɪ.mɪs
amid əˈmɪd
amide ˈæm.aɪd, ˈeɪ.maɪd (US) ˈæm.aɪd, -əd **-s** -z
amidships əˈmɪd.ʃɪps
amidst əˈmɪdst, -ˈmɪtst
Amiel ˈæm.i.əl, ˈeɪ.mi-
Amiens *French city:* ˈæm.jæ̃, -i.ɑ̃ː, -i.ɒŋ, -i.ənz *Shakespearean character:* ˈæm.i.ənz *street in Dublin:* ˈeɪ.mi.ənz
Amies ˈeɪ.miz
amiga (A®) əˈmiː.gə (US) əˈmiː.gə, ɑː- **-s** -z
amigo əˈmiː.gəʊ (US) -goʊ, ɑː- **-s** -z
Amin ɑːˈmiːn, æmˈiːn
amino əˈmiː.nəʊ, æmˈiː- (US) -noʊ **aˌmino ˈacid, aˈmino ˌacid**
amir əˈmɪəʳ (US) -ˈmɪr **-s** -z
Amis ˈeɪ.mɪs
Amish ˈɑː.mɪʃ, ˈæm.ɪʃ, ˈeɪ.mɪʃ (US) ˈɑː-, ˈæm-
amiss əˈmɪs
amitosis ˌæm.ɪˈtəʊ.sɪs (US) -ˈtoʊ-
amitotic ˌæm.ɪˈtəʊ.tɪk (US) -ˈtoʊ-
amity ˈæm.ɪ.ti, -ə.ti (US) -ə.t̬i
Amlwch ˈæm.lʊk, -lʊx
Amman əˈmɑːn (US) ɑːˈmɑːn
Ammanford ˈæm.ən.fəd (US) -fɚd
ammeter ˈæm.iː.təʳ, -ɪ.təʳ (US) -t̬ɚ **-s** -z
ammo ˈæm.əʊ (US) -oʊ
Ammon ˈæm.ən, -ɒn (US) -ən
ammonia əˈməʊ.ni.ə (US) -ˈmoʊ.njə
ammoniac əˈməʊ.ni.æk (US) -ˈmoʊ-
ammoniacal ˌæm.əʊˈnaɪ.ə.kᵊl, -əˈ-
ammoniated əˈməʊ.ni.eɪ.tɪd (US) -ˈmoʊ.ni.eɪ.t̬ɪd
ammonification əˌməʊ.nɪ.fɪˈkeɪ.ʃᵊn, -nə- (US) -mɑː-, -moʊ-
ammonif|y əˈməʊ.nɪ|.faɪ, -nə- (US) -ˈmɑː-, -ˈmoʊ- **-ies** -aɪz **-ying** -aɪ.ɪŋ **-ied** -aɪd **-ier/s** -aɪ.əʳ/z (US) -aɪ.ɚ/z
ammonite (A) ˈæm.ə.naɪt **-s** -s
ammonium əˈməʊ.ni.əm (US) -ˈmoʊ-
Ammons ˈæm.ənz
ammunition ˌæm.jəˈnɪʃ.ᵊn, -jʊˈ- (US) -jəˈ-
amnesia æmˈniː.zi.ə, -ʒə (US) -ʒə
amnesiac æmˈniː.zi.æk (US) -ʒi- **-s** -s
amnesic æmˈniː.zɪk, -sɪk **-s** -s
amnest|y ˈæm.nə.st|i, -nɪ- **-ies** -iz **ˌAmnesty Interˈnational**
amniocentesis ˌæm.ni.əʊ.senˈtiː.sɪs, -sənˈ- (US) -oʊ-
amniotic ˌæm.niˈɒt.ɪk (US) -ˈɑː.t̬ɪk *stress shift:* ˌamniotic ˈmembrane
Amoco® ˈæm.ə.kəʊ; əˈməʊ- (US) ˈæm.ə-
amoeb|a əˈmiː.b|ə **-ae** -iː **-as** -əz **-ic** -ɪk
amoebiasis ˌæm.iːˈbaɪə.sɪs, -ɪˈ-
amok əˈmɒk, -ˈmʌk (US) -ˈmʌk, -ˈmaːk
Amon ˈɑː.mən
among əˈmʌŋ
amongst əˈmʌŋst
Amon-Ra ˌɑː.mənˈrɑː
amontillado (A) əˌmɒn.tɪˈjɑː.dəʊ, -tɪˈlɑː- (US) -ˌmɑːn.təˈlɑː.doʊ **-s** -z
amoral ˌeɪˈmɒr.əl, æmˈɒr- (US) ˌeɪˈmɔːr- **-ly** -li
Amoretti ˌæm.əˈret.i (US) -ˈret̬-, ˌɑː.məˈ-
amorett|o ˌæm.əˈret|.əʊ (US) -ˈret̬|.oʊ, ˌɑː.məˈ- **-i** -i
amorist ˈæm.ᵊr.ɪst **-s** -s
Amorite ˈæm.ᵊr.aɪt (US) -ə.raɪt **-s** -s
amorous ˈæm.ᵊr.əs **-ly** -li **-ness** -nəs, -nɪs
amorph|ism əˈmɔː.f|ɪ.zᵊm (US) -ˈmɔːr- **-ous** -əs
amortizable, -isa- əˈmɔː.taɪ.zə.bl̩ (US) ˌæm.ɔːrˈtaɪ-
amortization, -isa- əˌmɔː.tɪˈzeɪ.ʃᵊn, -təˈ- (US) æmˌɔːr.t̬əˈ- **-s** -z
amortiz|e, -is|e əˈmɔː.taɪz (US) æmˈɔːr- **-es** -ɪz **-ing** -ɪŋ **-ed** -d
amortizement, -ise- əˈmɔː.tɪz.mənt (US) ˈæm.ɚˈtaɪz.mənt, əˈmɔːr.t̬ɪz.mənt
Amory ˈeɪ.mᵊr.i
Amos ˈeɪ.mɒs (US) -məs
a|mount ə|ˈmaʊnt **-mounts** -ˈmaʊnts **-mounting** -ˈmaʊn.tɪŋ (US) -ˈmaʊn.t̬ɪŋ **-mounted** -ˈmaʊn.tɪd (US) -ˈmaʊn.t̬ɪd
amour əˈmʊəʳ, æmˈʊəʳ, əˈmɔːʳ, æmˈɔːʳ (US) əˈmʊr, æmˈʊr **-s** -z
amour-propre ˌæm.ʊəˈprɒp.rə (US) ˌɑː.mʊrˈproʊ.prə, ˌæm.ʊrˈ-
Amoy əˈmɔɪ, æmˈɔɪ
amp æmp **-s** -s
ampelopsis ˌæm.pɪˈlɒp.sɪs (US) -ˈlɑːp-
amperage ˈæm.pᵊr.ɪdʒ, -per-, -peə.rɪdʒ (US) ˈæm.prɪdʒ, -pɪ.rɪdʒ
ampère, ampere (A) ˈæm.peəʳ (US) -pɪr, -per **-s** -z
ampersand ˈæm.pə.sænd (US) -pɚ- **-s** -z
amphetamine æmˈfet.ə.miːn, -mɪn (US) -fet̬- **-s** -z
amphi- æmp.fɪ-; æmˈfɪ- (US) æmp.fɪ-, -fə-; æmˈfɪ-
Note: Prefix. Either takes primary or secondary stress on the first syllable, e.g. **amphora** /ˈæmp.fᵊr.ə/, **amphibiotic** /ˌæmp.fɪ.baɪˈɒt.ɪk (US) -ˈɑː.t̬ɪk/, or primary stress on the second syllable, e.g. **amphibian** /æmˈfɪb.i.ən/.
amphibi|a æmˈfɪb.i|ə **-ous** -əs
amphibian æmˈfɪb.i.ən **-s** -z
amphibiotic ˌæmp.fɪ.baɪˈɒt.ɪk (US) -ˈɑː.t̬ɪk
amphibole ˈæmp.fɪ.bəʊl (US) -boʊl
amphibology ˌæmp.fɪˈbɒl.ə.dʒi (US) -ˈbɑː.lə-
amphiboll|y æmˈfɪb.ə.l|i **-ies** -iz
amphibrach ˈæmp.fɪ.bræk **-s** -s
Amphictyon æmˈfɪk.ti.ən **-s** -z
amphictyonic æmˌfɪk.tiˈɒn.ɪk (US) -ˈɑː.nɪk
amphimacer æmˈfɪm.ɪ.səʳ (US) -ə.sɚ
Amphion æmˈfaɪən
Amphipolis æmˈfɪp.ə.lɪs
amphitheatre, amphitheater ˈæmp.fɪˌθɪə.təʳ (US) -fəˌθiː.ə.t̬ɚ **-s** -z
Amphitrite ˌæmp.fɪˈtraɪ.ti (US) -t̬i
Amphitryon æmˈfɪt.ri.ən
amphor|a ˈæmp.fᵊr|.ə **-ae** -iː **-as** -əz
amphoric æmˈfɒr.ɪk (US) -ˈfɔːr-
amphoteric ˌæmp.fəʊˈter.ɪk (US) -fəˈ-
ampicillin ˌæm.pɪˈsɪl.ɪn (US) -pəˈ-
amp|le ˈæm.p|l̩ **-ler** -ləʳ (US) -lɚ **-lest** -ləst, -lɪst **-ly** -li **-leness** -l̩.nəs, -nɪs

amplification ˌæm.plɪ.fɪˈkeɪ.ʃᵊn, -plə- **-s** -z
amplificatory ˌæm.plɪ.fɪˈkeɪ.tᵊr.i, -plə-, ˈ-tri ⓤⓢ æmˈplɪf.ɪ.kə.tɔːr.i
amplifier ˈæm.plɪ.faɪ.əʳ ⓤⓢ -ɚ **-s** -z
amplif|y ˈæm.plɪ.f|aɪ **-ies** -aɪz **-ying** -aɪ.ɪŋ **-ied** -aɪd
amplitude ˈæm.plɪ.tjuːd, -tʃuːd ⓤⓢ -tuːd, -tjuːd **-s** -z
ampoule ˈæm.puːl **-s** -z
Amps æmps
Ampthill ˈæm*p*t.*h*ɪl
ampule ˈæm.pjuːl ⓤⓢ -pjuːl, -puːl **-s** -z
ampull|a æmˈpʊl|.ə **-ae** -iː
ampu|tate ˈæm.pjə|.teɪt, ˈæm.pjʊ- **-tates** -teɪts **-tating** -teɪ.tɪŋ ⓤⓢ -teɪ.t̬ɪŋ **-tated** -teɪ.tɪd ⓤⓢ -teɪ.t̬ɪd
amputation ˌæm.pjəˈteɪ.ʃᵊn, ˌæm.pjʊˈ- **-s** -z
amputee ˌæm.pjəˈtiː, -pjʊˈ- **-s** -z
Amram ˈæm.ræm
Amritsar æmˈrɪt.səʳ, -sɑːʳ ⓤⓢ -sɚ
Amsterdam ˌæm*p*.stəˈdæm, ˈ--ˌ- ⓤⓢ ˈæm*p*.stɚ.dæm
Note: In British English, the latter form is used when attributive.
Amstrad® ˈæm.stræd
Amtrak® ˈæm.træk
amuck əˈmʌk
amulet ˈæm.jʊ.lət, -jə-, -let, -lɪt **-s** -s
Amundsen ˈɑː.mən*d*.sᵊn, -mʊn*d*-
Amur əˈmʊəʳ, æmˈʊəʳ, ˈæm.ʊəʳ ⓤⓢ ɑːˈmʊr
amus|e əˈmjuːz **-es** -ɪz **-ing/ly** -ɪŋ/li **-ingness** -ɪŋ.nəs, -nɪs **-ed** -d
amusement əˈmjuːz.mənt **-s** -s aˈmusement arˌcade ; aˈmusement ˌpark
Amway® ˈæm.weɪ
Amy ˈeɪ.mi
Amyas ˈeɪ.mi.əs
amygdalin əˈmɪg.də.lɪn, æmˈɪg-
amygdaloid əˈmɪg.də.lɔɪd
amyl ˈæm.ɪl, -əl **-s** -z
amylase ˈæm.ɪ.leɪz, ˈ-ə-, -leɪs
amylic æmˈɪl.ɪk, əˈmɪl-
amylopsin ˌæm.ɪˈlɒp.sɪn ⓤⓢ -ˈlɑːp-
amytal ˈæm.ɪ.tæl ⓤⓢ -tɑːl
an- æn-, ən-
Note: Prefix. When used as a negative prefix, **an-** is normally /æn-/, e.g. **anaerobic** /ˌæn.əˈrəʊ.bɪk ⓤⓢ -erˈoʊ-/, but in some items it may be reduced, e.g. **anomaly** /əˈnɒm.ə.li ⓤⓢ -ˈnɑː.mə-/. Otherwise, it contains /æ/ when stressed, e.g. **annular** /ˈænj.ə.ləʳ ⓤⓢ -lɚ/, and /ə/ when unstressed, e.g. **annul** /əˈnʌl/.
an *strong form:* æn *weak form:* ᵊn
Note: Weak form word. The strong form /æn/ is used mainly for contrast (e.g. 'This is **an** ideal, but it's not **the** ideal.'). The weak form is usually /ən/ (e.g., 'make an excuse' /ˌmeɪk.ən.ɪkˈskjuːs/); in rapid speech, and particularly after an alveolar or palatoalveolar consonant, it may be pronounced as a syllabic /n̩/ (e.g. 'find an example' /ˌfaɪnd.n̩.ɪgˈzɑːm.pl̩ ⓤⓢ -ˈzæm-/).
ana- æn.ə-, əˈnæ-
Note: Prefix. Either takes primary or secondary stress on the first syllable, e.g. **anagram** /ˈæn.ə.græm/, **anatomic** /ˌæn.əˈtɒm.ɪk/, or primary stress on the second syllable, e.g. **anachronism** /əˈnæk.rə.nɪ.zᵊm/.
ana (A) ˈɑː.nə
Anabapt|ism ˌæn.əˈbæp.t|ɪ.zᵊm **-ist/s** -ɪst/s
anabas|is əˈnæb.ə.s|ɪs **-es** -iːz
anabi|osis ˌæn.ə.baɪ|ˈəʊ.sɪs ⓤⓢ -ˈoʊ- **-otic** -ˈɒt.ɪk ⓤⓢ -ˈɑː.t̬ɪk
anabolic ˌæn.əˈbɒl.ɪk ⓤⓢ -ˈbɑː.lɪk *stress shift, see compound:* ˌanabolic ˈsteroid
anabolism əˈnæb.əʊ.lɪ.zᵊm ⓤⓢ -ᵊl.ɪ-
anachronism əˈnæk.rə.nɪ.zᵊm **-s** -z
anachronistic əˌnæk.rəˈnɪs.tɪk **-ally** -ᵊl.i, -li
anachronous əˈnæk.rə.nəs **-ly** -li
Anacin® ˈæn.ə.sɪn
anacoluth|on ˌæn.ə.kəʊˈluː.θ|ɒn, -ˈljuː-, -θ|ᵊn ⓤⓢ -kəˈluː.θ|ᵊn **-a** -ə
anaconda ˌæn.əˈkɒn.də ⓤⓢ -ˈkɑːn- **-s** -z
Anacreon əˈnæk.ri.ən ⓤⓢ -ɑːn, -ən
anacrus|is ˌæn.əˈkruː.s|ɪs **-es** -iːz
Anadin® ˈæn.ə.dɪn
anadiplosis ˌæn.ə.dɪˈpləʊ.sɪs ⓤⓢ -ˈploʊ-
anaemia əˈniː.mi.ə
anaemic əˈniː.mɪk
anaerobe ˈæn.ə.rəʊb, ˈæn.ɪ- ⓤⓢ -roʊb **-s** -z
anaerobic ˌæn.əˈrəʊ.bɪk, -eəˈ- ⓤⓢ -erˈoʊ-, -əˈroʊ-
anaesthesia ˌæn.əsˈθiː.zi.ə, -ɪsˈ-, -iːsˈ-, -ʒi-, ˈ-ʒə ⓤⓢ ˌæn.əsˈθiː.ʒə
anaesthesiology ˌæn.əsˌθiː.ziˈɒl.ə.dʒi, -ɪsˌ-, -iːsˌ-, -ʒiˈ- ⓤⓢ -ziˈɑː.lə-
anaesthetic ˌæn.əsˈθet.ɪk, -ɪsˈ-, -iːsˈ- ⓤⓢ -ˈθet̬- **-s** -s **-ally** -ᵊl.i, -li *stress shift:* ˌanaesthetic ˈmask
anaesthetist əˈniːs.θə.tɪst, ænˈiːs-, -θɪ- ⓤⓢ əˈnes.θə.t̬ɪst **-s** -s
anaesthetiz|e, -is|e əˈniːs.θə.taɪz, ænˈiːs-, -θɪ- ⓤⓢ əˈnes- **-es** -ɪz **-ing** -ɪŋ **-ed** -d
anaglyph ˈæn.ə.glɪf **-s** -s
anagram ˈæn.ə.græm **-s** -z
anagrammatic ˌæn.ə.grəˈmæt.ɪk ⓤⓢ -ˈmæt̬- **-al** -ᵊl **-ally** -ᵊl.i
Anaheim ˈæn.ə.haɪm
Anaïs ˌæn.aɪˈiːs
anal ˈeɪ.nᵊl **-ly** -i
analects ˈæn.ə.lekts
analeptic ˌæn.əˈlep.tɪk
analgesia ˌæn.əlˈdʒiː.zi.ə, -ælˈ-, -si- ⓤⓢ ˈ-ʒə
analgesic ˌæn.əlˈdʒiː.zɪk, -ælˈ-, -sɪk
analog ˈæn.ə.lɒg ⓤⓢ -lɑːg, -lɔːg **-s** -z
analogic ˌæn.əˈlɒdʒ.ɪk ⓤⓢ -ˈlɑː.dʒɪk **-al** -ᵊl **-ally** -ᵊl.i, -li
analogist əˈnæl.ə.dʒɪst **-s** -s
analogous əˈnæl.ə.gəs **-ly** -li **-ness** -nəs, -nɪs
analogue ˈæn.ə.lɒg ⓤⓢ -lɑːg, -lɔːg **-s** -z
analog|y əˈnæl.ə.dʒ|i **-ies** -iz
analphabetic ˌæn.æl.fəˈbet.ɪk ⓤⓢ -ˈbet̬- **-al** -ᵊl **-ally** -ᵊl.i, -li
anal-retentive ˌeɪ.nᵊl.rɪˈten.tɪv ⓤⓢ -t̬ɪv
analysable ˌæn.ᵊlˈaɪ.zə.bl̩ ⓤⓢ -əˈlaɪ-, ˈæn.ə.laɪ-
analysand əˈnæl.ɪ.sænd, ˈ-ə- **-s** -z
analys|e, -yz|e ˈæn.ᵊl.aɪz, -ə.laɪz **-es** -ɪz **-ing** -ɪŋ **-ed** -d
analys|is əˈnæl.ə.s|ɪs, -ɪ.sɪs **-es** -iːz
analyst ˈæn.ᵊl.ɪst ⓤⓢ -ə.lɪst **-s** -s
analytic ˌæn.ᵊlˈɪt.ɪk ⓤⓢ -əˈlɪt̬- **-s** -s **-al** -ᵊl **-ally** -ᵊl.i, -li *stress shift:* ˌanalytic ˈmind
analyzable ˌæn.ᵊlˈaɪ.zə.bl̩ ⓤⓢ -əˈlaɪ-, ˈæn.ə.laɪ-
analyz|e, -ys|e ˈæn.ᵊl.aɪz, -ə.laɪz **-es** -ɪz **-ing** -ɪŋ **-ed** -d
anamorphosis ˌæn.əˈmɔː.fə.sɪs; -mɔːˈfəʊ- ⓤⓢ -ˈmɔːr.fə-; -mɔːrˈfoʊ-
Anand ˈɑː.nənd
Ananias ˌæn.əˈnaɪ.əs
anap(a)est ˈæn.ə.pest, -piːst ⓤⓢ -pest **-s** -s
anap(a)estic ˌæn.əˈpes.tɪk, -ˈpiː.stɪk ⓤⓢ -ˈpes.tɪk
anaphor ˈæn.ə.fɔːʳ, -fəʳ ⓤⓢ -fɔːr **-s** -z
anaphora əˈnæf.ᵊr.ə **-s** -z
anaphoric ˌæn.əˈfɒr.ɪk ⓤⓢ -ˈfɔːr- *stress shift:* ˌanaphoric ˈreference
anaphrodisiac ˌæn.æf.rəʊˈdɪz.i.æk ⓤⓢ -roʊˈ- **-s** -s
anaptyctic ˌæn.əpˈtɪk.tɪk, -æpˈ-
anaptyxis ˌæn.əpˈtɪk.sɪs, -æpˈ-
Anapurna ˌæn.əˈpɜː.nə, -ˈpʊə- ⓤⓢ -ˈpɜːr-, -ˈpʊr-
anarch ˈæn.ɑːk ⓤⓢ -ɑːrk **-s** -s
anarchic ænˈɑː.kɪk, əˈnɑː- ⓤⓢ ænˈɑːr-, əˈnɑːr- **-al** -ᵊl **-ally** -ᵊl.i, -li
anarchism ˈæn.ə.kɪ.zᵊm, -ɑː- ⓤⓢ -ɚ-, -ɑːr-
anarchist ˈæn.ə.kɪst, -ɑː- ⓤⓢ -ɚ-, -ɑːr- **-s** -s
anarchistic ˌæn.əˈkɪs.tɪk, -ɑːˈ- ⓤⓢ -ɚˈ-, -ɑːrˈ- *stress shift:* ˌanarchistic ˈviews
anarchy ˈæn.ə.ki, -ɑː- ⓤⓢ -ɚ-, -ɑːr-

Anastasia *English Christian name:* ˌæn.əˈsteɪ.zi.ə, ˈ-ʒə (US) ˈ-ʒə *foreign name:* ˌæn.əˈstɑː.zi.ə (US) ˈ-ʒə
Anastasius ˌæn.əˈstɑː.zi.əs, -ˈsteɪ- (US) ˈ-ʒəs
anastigmat əˈnæs.tɪg.mæt, ænˈæs-; ˌæn.əˈstɪg- (US) əˈnæs.tɪg-; ˌæn.əˈstɪg- **-s** -s
anastigmatic ˌæn.ə.stɪgˈmæt.ɪk; əˌnæs.tɪgˈ- (US) əˌnæs.tɪgˈmæt̬-; ˌæn.ə.stɪgˈmæt̬-
anastomosis ˌæn.ə.stəˈməʊ.sɪs (US) -ˈmoʊ-
anastrophe əˈnæs.trə.fi, ænˈæs- **-s** -z
anathema əˈnæθ.ə.mə, ænˈ-, ˈ-ɪ- **-s** -z
anathematization, -isa- əˌnæθ.ə.mə.taɪˈzeɪ.ʃᵊn, ænˈ-, ˌ-ɪ-, -tɪˈ- **-s** -z
anathematiz|e, -is|e əˈnæθ.ə.mə.taɪz, ænˈ-, ˈ-ɪ- **-es** -ɪz **-ing** -ɪŋ **-ed** -d
Anatole ˈæn.ə.təʊl (US) -toʊl
Anatoli|a ˌæn.əˈtəʊ.li|.ə (US) -ˈtoʊ- **-an/s** -ən/z
anatomic ˌæn.əˈtɒm.ɪk (US) -ˈtɑː.mɪk **-al** -ᵊl **-ally** -ᵊl.i, -li *stress shift:* ˌanatomic ˈdiagram
anatomist əˈnæt.ə.mɪst (US) -ˈnæt̬- **-s** -s
anatomiz|e, -is|e əˈnæt.ə.maɪz (US) -ˈnæt̬- **-es** -ɪz **-ing** -ɪŋ **-ed** -d
anatom|y əˈnæt.ə.m|i (US) -ˈnæt̬- **-ies** -iz
Anaxagoras ˌæn.ækˈsæg.ə.rəs, -ræs (US) -ɚ.əs
ANC ˌeɪ.enˈsiː
-ance -ən*t*s
Note: Suffix. When attached to a free stem, **-ance** does not change the stress pattern of the word, e.g. **admit** /ədˈmɪt/, **admittance** /ədˈmɪt.ᵊn*t*s/. In other cases, the stress may be on the penultimate or antepenultimate syllable, e.g. **reluctance** /rɪˈlʌk.tᵊn*t*s/, **brilliance** /ˈbrɪl.i.ən*t*s (US) ˈ-jən*t*s/. There are exceptions; see individual entries.
ancestor ˈæn.ses.təʳ, -sɪ.stəʳ, -sə- (US) -ses.tɚ **-s** -z
ancestral ænˈses.trᵊl
ancestress ˈæn.ses.trəs, -sɪ.strəs, -ses.trɪs (US) -ses.trɪs **-es** -ɪz
ancestr|y ˈæn.ses.tr|i, -sɪ.str|i, -sə- (US) -ses.tr|i **-ies** -iz
Anchises ænˈkaɪ.siːz, æŋˈ-
anch|or ˈæŋ.k|əʳ (US) -k|ɚ **-s** -əz (US) -ɚz **-ing** -ᵊr.ɪŋ **-ed** -əd (US) -ɚd
anchorag|e (A) ˈæŋ.kᵊr.ɪdʒ **-es** -ɪz
anchoress ˈæŋ.kᵊr.ɪs, -es, -əs **-es** -ɪz
anchoret ˈæŋ.kᵊr.et, -ɪt **-s** -s
anchorhold ˈæŋ.kə.həʊld (US) -kɚ.hoʊld **-s** -z
anchorite ˈæŋ.kᵊr.aɪt (US) -kə.raɪt **-s** -s
anchor|man ˈæŋ.kə|.mæn, -mən (US) -kɚ- **-men** -men, -mən
anchorperson ˈæŋ.kəˌpɜː.sᵊn (US) -kɚˌpɜːr-
anchor|woman ˈæŋ.kə|ˌwʊm.ən (US) -kɚˌ- **-women** -ˌwɪm.ɪn
anchov|y ˈæn.tʃə.v|i, ænˈtʃəʊ- (US) ˈæn.tʃoʊ-, -ˈ-- **-ies** -iz
ancien(s)-régime(s) ˌɑ̃ː*n*t.si.æ̃*n*.reɪˈʒiːm, ˌɑːn*t*-, ɒn*t*ˌsjæn- (US) ˌɑːn*t*.si.æn-
ancient ˈeɪn.*t*ʃᵊnt (US) ˈeɪn*t*.ʃᵊnt **-est** -əst, -ɪst **-ly** -li **-s** -s ˌ**ancient ˈGreek**; ˌ**ancient ˈhistory**
ancillar|y ænˈsɪl.ᵊr|.i (US) ˈæn*t*.sə.ler- **-ies** -iz
ancipit|al ænˈsɪp.ɪ.t|ᵊl (US) -t̬|ᵊl **-ous** -əs
Ancona æŋˈkəʊ.nə (US) -ˈkoʊ-, ænˈ-, ɑːnˈ-
Ancren Riwle ˌæŋ.krɪnˈri.ʊ.li, -krenˈ-, -krənˈ-, -lə
-ancy -ən*t*.si
Note: Suffix. Words containing **-ancy** are stressed in a similar way to those containing **-ance**; see above.
and *strong form:* ænd *weak forms:* ənd, ən, nd, n, m, ŋ
Note: Weak form word. The strong form /ænd/ is used for emphasis (e.g. 'The price included bed **and** breakfast.'), for contrast (e.g. 'It's not trick **and** treat, it's trick **or** treat.') or for citation (e.g. 'You should not begin a sentence with "and".'). There are several weak pronunciations. In slow, careful speech the pronunciation may be /ənd/, but is more often /ən/ (e.g. 'Come and see.' /ˌkʌm.ənˈsiː/). In more rapid speech, when it occurs between consonants, the pronunciation may be a syllabic nasal consonant with a place of articulation assimilated to the neighbouring consonants (e.g. 'cut and dried' /ˌkʌt.n̩ˈdraɪd/; 'thick and creamy' /ˌθɪk.ŋ̍ˈkriː.mi/; 'up and back' /ˌʌp.m̩ˈbæk/).
Andalusi|a ˌæn.dəˈluː.si|.ə, -zi-, -lʊˈsiː|.ə (US) -ˈluː.ʒ|ə, ˈ-ʒi|.ə, -ʃi- **-an** -ən
Andaman ˈæn.də.mæn, -mən
andante ænˈdæn.teɪ, -ti (US) ɑːnˈdɑːn.teɪ, ænˈdæn.t̬i **-s** -z
andantino ˌæn.dænˈtiː.nəʊ (US) ˌɑːn.dɑːnˈtiː.noʊ, ˌæn.dænˈ-
Andean ænˈdiː.ən, ˈæn.di.ən
Andersen, Anderson ˈæn.də.sᵊn (US) -dɚ-
Andes ˈæn.diːz
Andhra Pradesh ˌæn.drə.prɑːˈdeʃ, -prəˈ-, ˌɑːn-, -ˈdeɪʃ
andiron ˈæn.daɪən (US) -daɪɚn **-s** -z
Andizhan ˈæn.dɪ.ʒæn (US) ˈɑːn.dɪ.ʒɑːn, ˈæn.dɪ.ʒæn
Andorra ænˈdɔː.rə, -ˈdɒr.ə (US) -ˈdɔːr.ə
Andorra la Vella ænˌdɔː.rə.ləˈveɪ.jə (US) -ˌdɔːr.ə.lɑːˈveɪl.jə
Andover ˈæn.dəʊ.vəʳ (US) -doʊ.vɚ
Andow ˈæn.daʊ
Andrade ˈæn.dreɪd, -drɑːd
Andrassy ænˈdræs.i
Andre, André ˈɑ̃ː*n*.dreɪ, ˈɑːn-, ˈæn- (US) ˈɑːn.dreɪ, ˈæn-, ˈɑ̃ː-
Andrea ˈæn.dri.ə; ænˈdreɪə (US) ˈæn.dri.ə, ˈɑːn-; ænˈdreɪə, ɑːn-
Andrea del Sarto ænˌdreɪə.delˈsɑː.təʊ (US) ɑːnˌdreɪə.delˈsɑːr.t̬oʊ, æn-
Andreas ˈæn.dri.əs, -dri.æs; ænˈdreɪəs (US) ɑːnˈdreɪəs, æn-
Andrei ˈɒn.dreɪ, ˈæn- (US) ˈɑːn-
Andrew ˈæn.druː
Andrewatha *Cornish family:* ænˈdruː.θə *Plymouth family:* ænˈdruː.ə.θə, ˌæn.druˈɒθ.ə (US) -ˈɑː.θə
Andrews, Andrewes ˈæn.druːz
Andrex® ˈæn.dreks
Andria ˈæn.dri.ə (US) ˈæn-, ˈɑːn-
andro- æn.drəʊ-; ænˈdrɒ- (US) æn.drə-, -droʊ-; ænˈdrɑː-
Note: Prefix. Either takes primary or secondary stress on the first syllable, e.g. **androgen** /ˈæn.drəʊ.dʒən (US) -drə-/ **androgenic** /ˌæn.drəʊˈdʒen.ɪk (US) -drəˈ-/, or primary stress on the first syllable, e.g. **androgynous** /ænˈdrɒdʒ.ᵊn.əs (US) -drɑː.dʒᵊn.əs/.
androcentric ˌæn.drəʊˈsen.trɪk (US) -drəˈ-
Androcles ˈæn.drəʊ.kliːz (US) -drə-
Androclus ænˈdrɒk.ləs (US) -ˈdrɑː.kləs
androeci|um ænˈdriː.si|.əm (US) -ʃi-, -si- **-ia** -ə
androgen ˈæn.drəʊ.dʒən, -dʒen, -dʒɪn (US) -drə-, -droʊ- **-s** -z
androgenic ˌæn.drəʊˈdʒen.ɪk (US) -drəˈ-, -droʊˈ-
androgenous ænˈdrɒdʒ.ᵊn.əs, ˈ-ɪ.nəs (US) -ˈdrɑː.dʒᵊn.əs
androgynous ænˈdrɒdʒ.ɪ.nəs, -ᵊn.əs (US) -ˈdrɑː.dʒᵊn-
androgyny ænˈdrɒdʒ.ɪ.ni, -ᵊn.i (US) -ˈdrɑː.dʒᵊn-
android ˈæn.drɔɪd **-s** -z
Andromache ænˈdrɒm.ə.ki (US) -ˈdrɑː.mə-
Andromeda ænˈdrɒm.ɪ.də, -ə.də (US) -ˈdrɑː.mə-
Andronicus *Byzantine emperors and other figures in ancient history:* ˌæn.drəˈnaɪ.kəs, ænˈdrɒn.ɪ.kəs (US) -ˈdrɑː.nə- *in Shakespeare's* **Titus Andronicus**: ænˈdrɒn.ɪ.kəs (US) -ˈdrɑː.nɪ-
Andropov ˈæn.drə.pɒf, ænˈdrɒp.ɒf, -əf (US) ɑːnˈdrɔː.pəf, -ˈdroʊ-, -pɔːf

Andros 'æn.drɒs (US) -'drɑːs
Andvari æn'dwɑː.ri (US) ɑːn-
Andy 'æn.di
-ane -eɪn
Note: Suffix. Does not normally affect word stress, e.g. **alkane** /'æl.keɪn/.
anecdotage 'æn.ɪk.dəʊ.tɪdʒ, -ək- (US) -doʊ.t̬ɪdʒ
anecdotal ˌæn.ɪk'dəʊ.təl, -ək- (US) -'doʊ.t̬əl
anecdote 'æn.ɪk.dəʊt, -ək- (US) -doʊt **-s** -s
anecdotic ˌæn.ɪk'dəʊ.tɪk, -ek-, -ək-, -'dɒt- (US) -ɪk'dɑː.t̬ɪk **-al** -əl **-ally** -əl.i, -li
anechoic ˌæn.ɪ'kəʊ.ɪk, -ek'əʊ-, -ə'kəʊ- (US) -ə'koʊ-, -ɪ'-, -ek'oʊ- *stress shift:* ˌanechoic 'chamber
anelectric ˌæn.ɪ'lek.trɪk, -ə'lek- **-s** -s
anelectrode ˌæn.ɪ'lek.trəʊd, -ə'lek- (US) -troʊd **-s** -z
anemia ə'niː.mi.ə
anemic ə'niː.mɪk
anemometer ˌæn.ɪ'mɒm.ɪ.təʳ, -ə.təʳ (US) -'mɑː.mə.t̬ɚ **-s** -z
anemometric ˌæn.ɪ.məʊ'met.rɪk (US) -moʊ'-
anemometry ˌæn.ɪ'mɒm.ɪ.tri, -ə.tri (US) -'mɑː.mə-
anemone ə'nem.ə.ni **-s** -z
anemoscope ə'nem.ə.skəʊp (US) -skoʊp **-s** -s
anent ə'nent
aneroid 'æn.ə.rɔɪd, -ɪ.rɔɪd **-s** -z
anesthesia ˌæn.əs'θiː.zi.ə, -ɪs'-, -iːs'-, -ʒi-, '-ʒə (US) '-ʒə
anesthesiolog|y ˌæn.əsˌθiː.zi'ɒl.ə.dʒ|i, -ɪsˌ-, -iːsˌ-, -ʒi'- (US) -zi'ɑː.lə- **-ist/s** -ɪst/s
anesthetic ˌæn.əs'θet.ɪk, -ɪs'-, -iːs'- (US) -θet̬- **-s** -s **-ally** -əl.i, -li *stress shift:* ˌanesthetic 'mask
anesthetist ə'niːs.θə.tɪst, æn'iːs-, -θɪ- (US) ə'nes.θə.t̬ɪst **-s** -s
anesthetiz|e, -is|e ə'niːs.θə.taɪz, æn'iːs-, -θɪ- (US) ə'nes.θə- **-es** -ɪz **-ing** -ɪŋ **-ed** -d
aneurin ə'njʊr.ɪn, -'njʊə.rɪn (US) 'æn.jɚ.ɪn, -jʊ.rɪn
Aneurin ə'naɪə.rɪn (US) -'naɪ-
aneurism 'æn.jʊə.rɪ.zəm (US) 'æn.jɚ.ɪ-, -jʊ.rɪ- **-s** -z
aneurismal ˌæn.jʊə'rɪz.məl (US) -jə'-, -jʊ'-
aneurysm 'æn.jʊə.rɪ.zəm (US) -jɚ.ɪ-, -jʊ.rɪ- **-s** -z
aneurysmal ˌæn.jʊə'rɪz.məl (US) -jə'-, -jʊ'-
anew ə'njuː (US) -'nuː, -'njuː
anfractuosity ˌæn.fræk.tju'ɒs.ə.ti, -ɪ.ti (US) -tʃu'ɑː.sə.t̬i
angel (A) 'eɪn.dʒəl **-s** -z **'angel ˌdust**
Angela 'æn.dʒəl.ə, -dʒɪ.lə
Angeleno ˌæn.dʒəl'iː.nəʊ (US) -dʒə'liː.noʊ
Angeles 'æn.dʒəl.iːz, -dʒɪ.liːz, -liz, -lis (US) -dʒəl.əs, -dʒə.liːz
angelfish 'eɪn.dʒəl.fɪʃ **-es** -ɪz
angel-food cake ˌeɪn.dʒəl'fuːdˌkeɪk (US) 'eɪn.dʒəlˌfuːd-
angelic æn'dʒel.ɪk **-al** -əl **-ally** -əl.i, -li
angelica (A) æn'dʒel.ɪ.kə
Angelico æn'dʒel.ɪ.kəʊ (US) -koʊ
Angelina ˌæn.dʒəl'iː.nə, -dʒel'- (US) -dʒə'liː-, -dʒel'iː-
Angelo 'æn.dʒəl.əʊ, -dʒɪ.ləʊ (US) -dʒə.loʊ
Angelou 'æn.dʒəl.uː (US) -dʒə.luː, -loʊ
angelus (A) 'æn.dʒəl.əs, -dʒɪ.ləs **-es** -ɪz
ang|er 'æŋ.g|əʳ (US) -g|ɚ **-ers** -əz (US) -ɚz **-ering** -ər.ɪŋ **-ered** -əd (US) -ɚd
Angers ɑ̃ːn'ʒeɪ
Angevin 'æn.dʒɪ.vɪn, -dʒə-
Angharad æŋ'hær.əd, æn-; 'æŋ.ər- (US) æŋ'her-, æn- (US) -'hær-
Angie 'æn.dʒi
Angier 'æn.dʒɪəʳ
angina æn'dʒaɪ.nə **-s** -z
angiogram 'æn.dʒi.əʊ.græm (US) -ə-, -oʊ- **-s** -z
angiographic ˌæn.dʒi.əʊ'græf.ɪk (US) -ə'-, -oʊ'-
angiography ˌæn.dʒi'ɒg.rə.fi (US) -'ɑː.grə-
angioplasty 'æn.dʒi.əʊ.plæs.ti (US) -ə-, -oʊ-
angiosperm 'æn.dʒi.əʊ.spɜːm (US) -ə.spɜːrm, -oʊ- **-s** -z
Angkor Thom ˌæŋ.kɔː'tɔːm (US) -kɔːr'tɑːm
angl|e (A) 'æŋ.gl̩ **-es** -z **-ing** -ɪŋ, '-glɪŋ **-ed** -d
Anglepoise® 'æŋ.gl̩.pɔɪz ˌ**Anglepoise 'lamp** (US) **'Anglepoise ˌlamp**
angler 'æŋ.gləʳ, -gl̩.əʳ (US) '-glɚ, -gl̩.ɚ **-s** -z
Anglesea 'æŋ.gl̩.si, -siː
Anglesey 'æŋ.gl̩.si, -siː
Angli|a 'æŋ.gli|.ə **-an/s** -ən/z
Anglican 'æŋ.glɪ.kən **-s** -z **-ism** -ɪ.zəm
anglice 'æŋ.glɪ.si, -glə-
anglicism 'æŋ.glɪ.sɪ.zəm, -glə- **-s** -z
anglicist 'æŋ.glɪ.sɪst, -glə- **-s** -s
anglicization, -isa- ˌæŋ.glɪ.saɪ'zeɪ.ʃən, -glə-, -ɪ'- (US) -ɪ'-
angliciz|e, -is|e 'æŋ.glɪ.saɪz, -glə- **-es** -ɪz **-ing** -ɪŋ **-ed** -d
angling 'æŋ.glɪŋ, -gl̩.ɪŋ
Anglo- æŋ.gləʊ- (US) æŋ.gloʊ-
Note: Prefix. Words containing **anglo-** normally carry either primary or secondary stress on the first syllable, e.g. **anglophobe** /'æŋ.gləʊ.fəʊb (US) -gloʊ.foʊb/, **anglophobia** /ˌæŋ.gləʊ'fəʊ.bi.ə (US) -gloʊ'foʊ-/. Where the prefix is used to mean "English and ...", it usually carries secondary stress, e.g. **Anglo-French** /ˌæŋ.gləʊ'frentʃ (US) -gloʊ'-/.
Anglo 'æŋ.gləʊ (US) -gloʊ **-s** -z
Anglo-American ˌæŋ.gləʊ.ə'mer.ɪ.kən (US) -gloʊ- **-s** -z
Anglo-French ˌæŋ.gləʊ'frentʃ (US) -gloʊ'-
Anglo-Irish ˌæŋ.gləʊ'aɪə.rɪʃ (US) -gloʊ'aɪ-
anglomania ˌæŋ.gləʊ'meɪ.ni.ə (US) -gloʊ'-
Anglo-Norman ˌæŋ.gləʊ'nɔː.mən (US) -gloʊ'nɔːr-
anglophile (A) 'æŋ.gləʊ.faɪl (US) -glə- **-s** -z
anglophilia ˌæŋ.gləʊ'fɪl.i.ə (US) -glə'-
anglophobe 'æŋ.gləʊ.fəʊb (US) -glə.foʊb **-s** -z
anglophobia ˌæŋ.gləʊ'fəʊ.bi.ə (US) -glə'foʊ-
anglophone 'æŋ.gləʊ.fəʊn (US) -glə.foʊn **-s** -z
Anglo-Saxon ˌæŋ.gləʊ'sæk.sən (US) -gloʊ'- **-s** -z
Anglo-Saxondom ˌæŋ.gləʊ'sæk.sən.dəm (US) -gloʊ'-
Anglo-Saxonism ˌæŋ.gləʊ'sæk.sən.ɪ.zəm (US) -gloʊ'- **-s** -z
Angmering 'æŋ.mə.rɪŋ
Angol|a æŋ'gəʊ.l|ə (US) -'goʊ-, æn- **-an/s** -ən/z
angora (A) *cat, rabbit, cloth:* æŋ'gɔː.rə (US) -'gɔːr.ə, æn- **-s** -z
Angora *old form of* **Ankara** *in Turkey:* 'æŋ.gə.rə, æŋ'gɔː.rə (US) æŋ'gɔːr.ə, æn-
angostura (A) ˌæŋ.gə'stjʊə.rə, -gɒs'tjʊə-, -'stjɔː- (US) -gə'stʊr.ə, -'stjʊr- ˌ**Angostura 'bitters®**
Angoulême ɑ̃ːŋ.gʊ'lem
angr|y 'æŋ.gr|i **-ier** -i.əʳ (US) -i.ɚ **-iest** -i.əst, -i.ɪst **-ily** -ɪ.li, -əl.i **-iness** -ɪ.nəs, -ɪ.nɪs ˌ**angry young 'man**
angst æŋkst (US) æŋkst, ɑːŋkst
angstrom 'æŋk.strəm **-s** -z
Anguill|a æŋ'gwɪl|.ə **-an/s** -ən/z
anguine 'æŋ.gwɪn
anguish 'æŋ.gwɪʃ **-es** -ɪz **-ing** -ɪŋ **-ed** -t
angular 'æŋ.gjʊ.ləʳ, -gjə- (US) -lɚ **-ly** -li **-ness** -nəs, -nɪs
angularit|y ˌæŋ.gjʊ'lær.ə.t|i, -gjə-, -ɪ.t|i (US) -'ler.ə.t̬|i, -'lær- **-ies** -iz
angulate 'æn.gjʊ.leɪt, -gjə-, -lɪt, -lət
angulated 'æŋ.gjʊ.leɪ.tɪd, -gjə- (US) -t̬ɪd
Angus 'æŋ.gəs
Angustura ˌæŋ.gə'stjʊə.rə, -'stjɔː-, -'stʊr.ə (US) -'stʊr-, -'stjʊr-

anharmonic ˌæn.hɑːˈmɒn.ɪk (US) -hɑːrˈmɑː.nɪk *stress shift:* ˌanharmonic ˈsystem
anhungered ənˈhʌŋ.gəd, æn- (US) -gɚd
anhydride ænˈhaɪ.draɪd **-s** -z
anhydrite ænˈhaɪ.draɪt
anhydrous ænˈhaɪ.drəs
anil ˈæn.ɪl
anile ˈeɪ.naɪl, ˈæn.aɪl
aniline ˈæn.ɪ.liːn, -lɪn, -laɪn (US) -lɪn, -liːn, -laɪn
anility ænˈɪl.ə.ti, əˈnɪl-, -ɪ.ti (US) -ə.t̬i
anima ˈæn.ɪ.mə
animadversion ˌæn.ɪ.mædˈvɜː.ʃᵊn, -mədˈ-, -ʒᵊn (US) -ˈvɜːr.ʒᵊn, -ʃᵊn **-s** -z
animad|vert ˌæn.ɪ.mæd|ˈvɜːt, -mədˈ- (US) -ˈvɜːrt **-verts** -ˈvɜːts (US) -ˈvɜːrts **-verting** -ˈvɜː.tɪŋ (US) -ˈvɜːr.t̬ɪŋ **-verted** -ˈvɜː.tɪd (US) -ˈvɜːr.t̬ɪd
animal ˈæn.ɪ.mᵊl, ˈ-ə- **-s** -z
animalcule ˌæn.ɪˈmæl.kjuːl **-s** -z
animalism ˈæn.ɪ.mᵊl.ɪ.zᵊm
animalistic ˌæn.ɪ.mᵊlˈɪs.tɪk (US) -məˈlɪs-, -məlˈ-
animate (*adj.*) ˈæn.ɪ.mət, -mɪt, -meɪt
ani|mate (*v.*) ˈæn.ɪ|.meɪt, ˈ-ə- **-mates** -meɪts **-mating** -meɪ.tɪŋ (US) -meɪ.t̬ɪŋ **-mated/ly** -meɪ.tɪd/li (US) -meɪ.t̬ɪd/li
animation ˌæn.ɪˈmeɪ.ʃᵊn, -əˈ- **-s** -z
animator ˈæn.ɪ.meɪ.təʳ, ˈ-ə- (US) -t̬ɚ **-s** -z
animatronic ˌæn.ɪ.məˈtrɒn.ɪk, ˌ-ə- (US) -ˈtrɑː.nɪk **-s** -s
anim|ism ˈæn.ɪ.m|ɪ.zᵊm, ˈ-ə- **-ist/s** -ɪst/s
animosit|y ˌæn.ɪˈmɒs.ə.t|i, -əˈ-, -ɪ.t|i (US) -ˈmɑː.sə.t̬|i **-ies** -iz
animus ˈæn.ɪ.məs
anion ˈæn.aɪən **-s** -z
anis ˈæn.iːs, -i; ænˈiːs (US) ˈæn.iːs, ˈɑː.niːs, -i; ænˈiːs, ɑːˈniːs
anise ˈæn.ɪs, ænˈiːs
aniseed ˈæn.ɪ.siːd, ˈ-ə-
anisette ˌæn.ɪˈset, -əˈ-, -ˈzet
anisometric ænˌaɪ.səʊˈmet.rɪk (US) -soʊˈ-
anisotropic ˌæn.aɪ.səʊˈtrɒp.ɪk, -ˈtrəʊ.pɪk (US) -soʊˈtrɑː.pɪk, -ˈtroʊ- **-ally** -ᵊl.i, -li
anisotropism ˌæn.aɪˈsɒt.rə.pɪ.zᵊm (US) -ˈsɑː.trə-
anisotropy ˌæn.aɪˈsɒt.rə.pi (US) -ˈsɑː.trə-
Anita əˈniː.tə (US) -t̬ə
Anjou ɑ̃ːnˈdʒuː, ɑːnˈ-
Ankara ˈæŋ.kᵊr.ə (US) ˈæŋ-, ˈɑːŋ-
ankerite ˈæŋ.kᵊr.aɪt (US) -kə.raɪt
ankh ɑːŋk, æŋk **-s** -s
ankle ˈæŋ.kl̩ **-s** -z ˈankle ˌsock
anklet ˈæŋ.klət, -klɪt **-s** -s
Ann æn
anna (A) ˈæn.ə **-s** -z
Annaba ænˈɑː.bə
Annabel ˈæn.ə.bel
Annabella ˌæn.əˈbel.ə
Annagh ænˈɑː, ˈæn.ɑː
Annakin ˈæn.ə.kɪn
annalist ˈæn.ᵊl.ɪst **-s** -s
annals ˈæn.ᵊlz
Annaly ˈæn.ə.li
Annam ænˈæm, ˈæn.æm
Annamese ˌæn.əˈmiːz
Annan ˈæn.ən
Annandale ˈæn.ən.deɪl
Annapolis əˈnæp.ᵊl.ɪs, ænˈæp-
Annapurna ˌæn.əˈpɜː.nə, -ˈpʊə- (US) -ˈpɜːr-, -ˈpʊr-
Ann Arbor ˌænˈɑː.bə (US) -ˈɑːr.bɚ
Annas ˈæn.æs, -əs
annatto əˈnæt.əʊ, ænˈæt- (US) əˈnɑː.toʊ, əˈnæt.oʊ
Anne æn
anneal əˈniːl **-s** -z **-ing** -ɪŋ **-ed** -d
Anneka ˈæn.ɪ.kə, -ə.kə
annelid ˈæn.ə.lɪd **-s** -z
Annesley ˈænz.li
Annett ˈæn.ɪt, -ət
Annette əˈnet, ænˈet (US) əˈnet
annex (*n.*) ˈæn.eks **-es** -ɪz
annex (*v.*) əˈneks, ænˈeks **-es** -ɪz **-ing** -ɪŋ **-ed** -t **-ment/s** -mənt/s
annexation ˌæn.ekˈseɪ.ʃᵊn, -ɪkˈ- **-s** -z
annex|e ˈæn.eks **-es** -ɪz
Annfield Plain ˌæn.fiːldˈpleɪn
Annie ˈæn.i
Annigoni ˌæn.ɪˈgəʊ.ni (US) -ˈgoʊ-
annihi|late əˈnaɪ.ɪ|.leɪt, ˈ-ə- (US) ˈ-ə- **-lates** -leɪts **-lating** -leɪ.tɪŋ (US) -leɪ.t̬ɪŋ **-lated** -leɪ.tɪd (US) -leɪ.t̬ɪd **-lator/s** -leɪ.təʳ/z (US) -leɪ.t̬ɚ/z
annihilation əˌnaɪ.ɪˈleɪ.ʃᵊn, -əˈ- (US) -əˈ- **-s** -z
Anning ˈæn.ɪŋ
Anniston ˈæn.ɪ.stən
anniversar|y ˌæn.ɪˈvɜː.sᵊr|.i (US) -ˈvɜːr- **-ies** -iz
anno Domini (A) ˌæn.əʊˈdɒm.ɪ.naɪ (US) -oʊˈdɑː.mə.niː, -ˈdoʊ-, -naɪ
anno|tate ˈæn.əʊ|.teɪt (US) ˈ-ə-, ˈ-oʊ- **-tates** -teɪts **-tating** -teɪ.tɪŋ (US) -teɪ.t̬ɪŋ **-tated** -teɪ.tɪd (US) -teɪ.t̬ɪd **-tator/s** -teɪ.təʳ/s (US) -teɪ.t̬ɚ/z **-tative** -teɪ.tɪv (US) -teɪ.t̬ɪv
annotation ˌæn.əʊˈteɪ.ʃᵊn (US) -əˈ-, -oʊˈ- **-s** -z
announc|e əˈnaʊnts **-es** -ɪz **-ing** -ɪŋ **-ed** -t **-ement/s** -mənt/s
announcer əˈnaʊnt.səʳ (US) -sɚ **-s** -z
annoy əˈnɔɪ **-s** -z **-ing/ly** -ɪŋ/li **-ed** -d
annoyanc|e əˈnɔɪ.ənts **-es** -ɪz
annual ˈæn.ju.əl **-s** -z **-ly** -i
annualiz|e, -is|e ˈæn.ju.ᵊl.aɪz (US) -ə.laɪz, -jul- **-es** -ɪz **-ing** -ɪŋ **-ed** -d
annuit|y əˈnjuː.ə.t|i, -ɪ.t|i (US) -ˈnuː.ə.t̬|i, -ˈnjuː- **-ies** -iz **-ant/s** -ᵊnt/s
annul əˈnʌl **-s** -z **-ling** -ɪŋ **-led** -d
annular ˈæn.jə.ləʳ, ˈ-jʊ- (US) -lɚ
annu|late ˈæn.jə|.leɪt, ˈ-jʊ- **-lated** -leɪ.tɪd (US) -leɪ.t̬ɪd
annulet ˈæn.jʊ.lət, ˈ-jə-, -lɪt **-s** -s
annulment əˈnʌl.mənt **-s** -s
annul|us æn.jə.l|əs, ˈ-jʊ- **-uses** -ə.sɪz **-i** -aɪ, -iː
annum ˈæn.əm
annunci|ate əˈnʌnt.si|.eɪt, -ʃi- **-ates** -eɪts **-ating** -eɪ.tɪŋ (US) -eɪ.t̬ɪŋ **-ated** -eɪ.tɪd (US) -eɪ.t̬ɪd
annunciation (A) əˌnʌnt.siˈeɪ.ʃᵊn **-s** -z
annus mirabilis (A) ˌæn.əs.mɪˈrɑː.bᵊl.ɪs, -məˈ- (US) ˌɑː.nəs-, ˌæn.əs-
anode ˈæn.əʊd (US) -oʊd **-s** -z
anodiz|e, -ise ˈæn.əʊ.daɪz (US) ˈ-oʊ-, ˈ-ə- **-es** -ɪz **-ing** -ɪŋ **-ed** -d
anodyne ˈæn.əʊ.daɪn (US) ˈ-oʊ-, ˈ-ə- **-s** -z
a|noint ə|ˈnɔɪnt **-noints** -ˈnɔɪnts **-nointing** -ˈnɔɪn.tɪŋ (US) -ˈnɔɪn.t̬ɪŋ **-nointed** -ˈnɔɪn.tɪd (US) -ˈnɔɪn.t̬ɪd **-nointment/s** -ˈnɔɪnt.mənt/s
anomalous əˈnɒm.ə.ləs (US) -ˈnɑː.mə- **-ly** -li
anomal|y əˈnɒm.ə.l|i (US) -ˈnɑː.mə- **-ies** -iz
anon (A) əˈnɒn (US) -ˈnɑːn
anonym ˈæn.ə.nɪm, -ɒn.ɪm (US) -ə.nɪm **-s** -z
anonymity ˌæn.əˈnɪm.ə.ti, -ɒnˈɪm-, -ɪ.ti (US) -əˈnɪm.ə.t̬i
anonymiz|e, -is|e əˈnɒn.ɪ.maɪz, ˈ-ə- (US) -ˈnɑː.nə- **-es** -ɪz **-ing** -ɪŋ **-ed** -d
anonymous əˈnɒn.ɪ.məs, ˈ-ə- (US) -ˈnɑː.nə- **-ly** -li
anopheles əˈnɒf.ɪ.liːz, ˈ-ə- (US) -ˈnɑː.fə-
anorak ˈæn.ᵊr.æk (US) -ə.ræk **-s** -s
anorectic ˌæn.ᵊrˈek.tɪk (US) -əˈrek- **-s** -s
anorexia ˌæn.ᵊrˈek.si.ə (US) -əˈrek- anoˌrexia nerˈvosa
anorexic ˌæn.ᵊrˈek.sɪk (US) -əˈrek- **-s** -s
anosmia ænˈɒz.mi.ə, -ˈnɒs- (US) ænˈɑːz-, -ˈɑːs-
another əˈnʌð.əʳ (US) -ɚ
A N Other ˌeɪ.enˈʌð.əʳ (US) -ɚ
Anouilh ˈæn.uː.iː, ˌæn.uːˈiː (US) ɑːˈnuː.jə, ænˈuː-, -iː; ˌɑː.nuːˈiː, ˌæn.uːˈ-
anoxia ænˈɒk.si.ə, eɪˈnɒk- (US) ænˈɑːk-
ansaphone® ˈɑːnt.sə.fəʊn (US) ˈæn.sə.foʊn **-s** -z
anschauung (A) ˈæn.ʃaʊ.ʊŋ (US) ˈɑːn.ʃaʊ.əŋ
anschluss (A) ˈæn.ʃlʊs (US) ˈɑːn-, ˈæn-
Ansell ˈænt.sᵊl
Anselm ˈænt.selm

anserine 'æn*t*.sə.raɪn, -riːn, -rɪn
Ansley 'ænz.li
Anson 'æn*t*.sən
Ansonia æn'səʊ.ni.ə (US) -'soʊ-, '-njə
Ansted 'æn*t*.sted, -stɪd
Anster 'æn*t*.stəʳ (US) -stɚ
Anstey 'æn*t*.sti
Anston 'æn*t*.stən
Anstruther 'æn*t*.strʌð.əʳ (US) -ɚ
answ|er 'ɑːn*t*.s|əʳ (US) 'æn*t*.s|ɚ **-ers** -əz (US) -ɚz **-ering** -ᵊr.ɪŋ **-ered** -əd (US) -ɚd **-erer/s** -ᵊr.əʳ/z (US) -ɚ.ɚ/z **'answering ma,chine**
answerability ,ɑːn*t*.sᵊr.ə'bɪl.ə.ti, -ɪ.ti (US) ,æn*t*.sɚ.ə'bɪl.ə.t̬i
answerab|le 'ɑːn*t*.sᵊr.ə.b|l̩ (US) 'æn*t*- **-ly** -li
answerphone 'ɑːn*t*.sə.fəʊn (US) 'æn*t*.sɚ.foʊn **-s** -z
ant- ænt-
Note: Prefix. Where **ant-** is attached to a free stem it often carries secondary stress, e.g. **antacid** /,æn'tæs.ɪd/. In other cases it may take primary, secondary or no stress at all, e.g. **antonym** /'æn.tə.nɪm (US) -tᵊn.ɪm/, **antonymic** /,æn.tə'nɪm.ɪk/, **antonymous** /æn'tɒn.ɪ.məs (US) -'tɑː.nə-/.
ant ænt **-s** -s **'ant ,lion**
-ant -ənt
Note: Suffix. Words containing **-ant** are stressed in a similar way to those containing **-ance**; see above.
Antabuse® 'æn.tə.bjuːs, -bjuːz
antacid ,æn'tæs.ɪd **-s** -z
Antaeus æn'tiː.əs, -'teɪ-
antagonism æn'tæg.ᵊn.ɪ.zᵊm **-s** -z
antagonist æn'tæg.ᵊn.ɪst **-s** -s
antagonistic æn,tæg.ᵊn'ɪs.tɪk, ,æn.tæg.ᵊn'- (US) -ə'nɪs- **-ally** -ᵊl.i, -li
antagoniz|e, -is|e æn'tæg.ᵊn.aɪz (US) -ə.naɪz **-es** -ɪz **-ing** -ɪŋ **-ed** -d
Antalya æn'tæl.jə (US) ,ɑːn.tᵊl'jɑː, ,æn-
Antananarivo ,æn.tə,næn.ə'riː.vəʊ (US) -voʊ
Antarctic æn'tɑːk.tɪk (US) -'tɑːrk-, -'tɑːr.t̬ɪk **Ant,arctic 'Circle** ; **Ant,arctic 'Ocean**
Antarctica æn'tɑːk.tɪ.kə (US) -'tɑːrk-, -'tɑːr.t̬ɪ-
Antares æn'teə.riːz (US) -'ter.iːz
ant-bear 'ænt.beəʳ (US) -ber **-s** -z
ante- æn.tɪ- (US) -t̬i-, -t̬ə-
Note: Prefix. Words containing **ante-** carry either primary or secondary stress on the first syllable, e.g. **antechamber** /'æn.tɪ,tʃeɪm.bəʳ (US) -t̬ɪ,tʃeɪm.bɚ/, **antenatal** /,æn.tɪ'neɪ.tᵊl (US) -t̬ᵊl/.
ante 'æn.ti (US) -t̬i **-s** -z **-ing** -ɪŋ **-d** -d
anteater 'ænt,iː.təʳ (US) -t̬ɚ **-s** -z
antebellum ,æn.tɪ'bel.əm (US) -t̬ə'-
antecedence ,æn.tɪ'siː.dᵊnts, 'æn.tɪ.siː- (US) ,æn.t̬ə'siː-
antecedent ,æn.tɪ'siː.dᵊnt, -t̬ə'- **-s** -s **-ly** -li
antechamber 'æn.tɪ,tʃeɪm.bəʳ (US) -t̬ɪ,tʃeɪm.bɚ **-s** -z
antechapel 'æn.tɪ,tʃæp.ᵊl (US) -t̬ɪ- **-s** -z
ante|date ,æn.tɪ|'deɪt (US) 'æn.t̬ɪ|.deɪt **-dates** -'deɪts (US) -deɪts **-dating** -'deɪ.tɪŋ (US) -deɪ.t̬ɪŋ **-dated** -'deɪ.tɪd (US) -deɪ.t̬ɪd
antediluvi|an ,æn.tɪ.dɪ'luː.vi|.ən, -də'-, -daɪ'-, -'ljuː- (US) -t̬ɪ.də'luː- **-ans** -ənz **-al** -ᵊl **-ally** -ᵊl.i
antelope 'æn.tɪ.ləʊp (US) -t̬ᵊl.oʊp **-s** -s
antemeridian ,æn.tɪ.mə'rɪd.i.ən (US) -t̬ɪ-
ante meridiem ,æn.tɪ.mə'rɪd.i.əm (US) -t̬ɪ-
antenatal ,æn.tɪ'neɪ.tᵊl (US) -t̬ɪ'neɪ.t̬ᵊl
antenn|a æn'ten|.ə **-ae** -iː **-as** -əz **-al** -ᵊl **-ary** -ᵊr.i
Antenor æn'tiː.nɔːʳ (US) -nɔːr
antenuptial ,æn.tɪ'nʌp.ʃᵊl, -tʃᵊl (US) -t̬ɪ'-
antepenult ,æn.tɪ.pɪ'nʌlt, -pen'ʌlt, -pə'nʌlt (US) ,æn.t̬ɪ'piː.nʌlt; -pɪ'nʌlt **-s** -s
antepenultimate ,æn.tɪ.pə'nʌl.tɪ.mət, -pɪ'nʌl-, -pen'ʌl-, -tə-, -mɪt (US) -t̬ɪ.pɪ'nʌl.t̬ə.mət **-s** -s
anteprandial ,æn.tɪ'præn.di.əl (US) -t̬ɪ'-
anterior æn'tɪə.ri.əʳ (US) -'tɪr.i.ɚ **-ly** -li
anteroom 'æn.tɪ.rʊm, -ruːm (US) -t̬ɪ.ruːm, -rʊm **-s** -z
Anthea 'æn*t*.θi.ə (US) æn'θiː-
ant-heap 'ænt.hiːp **-s** -s
antheli|on ænt'hiː.li|.ən, æn*t*'θiː- **-ons** -ənz **-a** -ə
anthelix ænt'hiː.lɪks, æn*t*'θiː- **-es** -ɪz
anthem 'æn*t*.θəm **-s** -z
anther 'æn*t*.θəʳ (US) -θɚ **-s** -z
anthill 'ænt.hɪl **-s** -z
anthological ,æn*t*.θə'lɒdʒ.ɪ.kᵊl (US) -'lɑː.dʒɪ-
anthologist æn'θɒl.ə.dʒɪst (US) -'θɑː.lə- **-s** -s
anthologiz|e, -is|e æn'θɒl.ə.dʒaɪz (US) -'θɑː.lə- **-es** -ɪz **-ing** -ɪŋ **-ed** -d
antholog|y æn'θɒl.ə.dʒ|i (US) -'θɑː.lə- **-ies** -iz
Anthon 'æn.tɒn (US) 'æn*t*.θən, 'æn.tɑːn
Anthony 'æn.tə.ni, 'æn*t*.θə.ni (US) 'æn.θə.ni, æn.tə.ni
anthracite 'æn*t*.θrə.saɪt
anthracitic ,æn*t*.θrə'sɪt.ɪk (US) -'sɪt̬-
anthrax 'æn*t*.θræks
anthropic æn'θrɒp.ɪk (US) -'θrɑː.pɪk **-al** -ᵊl
anthropo- ,æn*t*.θrəʊ.pəʊ-; ,æn*t*.θrəʊ'pɒ- (US) ,æn*t*.θrə.pə-, -poʊ-; ,æn*t*.θrə'pɑː-
Note: Prefix. Words containing **anthropo-** normally exhibit secondary stress on the first syllable, e.g. **anthropomorphic** /,æn*t*.θrə.pəʊ'mɔː.fɪk (US) -pə'mɔːr-/, but may also have primary stress on the third syllable, e.g., **anthropology** /,æn*t*.θrə'pɒl.ə.dʒi (US) -'pɑː.lə-/.
anthropocentric ,æn*t*.θrəʊ.pəʊ'sen.trɪk (US) -θrə.pə'-, -poʊ'-
anthropocentrism ,æn.θrəʊ.pəʊ'sen.trɪ.zᵊm (US) -θrə.pə'-, -poʊ'-
anthropoid 'æn*t*.θrəʊ.pɔɪd (US) -θrə-, -θroʊ- **-s** -z
anthropoidal ,æn*t*.θrəʊ'pɔɪd.ᵊl (US) -θrə'-, -θroʊ'-
anthropological ,æn*t*.θrə.pə'lɒdʒ.ɪ.kᵊl (US) -'lɑː.dʒɪ- **-ly** -i
anthropologist ,æn*t*.θrə'pɒl.ə.dʒɪst (US) -'pɑː.lə- **-s** -s
anthropology ,æn*t*.θrə'pɒl.ə.dʒi (US) -'pɑː.lə-
anthropometric ,æn*t*.θrəʊ.pəʊ'met.rɪk (US) -θrə.pə'-
anthropometry ,æn.θrə'pɒm.ɪ.tri, '-ə- (US) -'pɑː.mə-
anthropomorph|ic ,æn*t*.θrə.pəʊ'mɔː.f|ɪk (US) -pə'mɔːr- **-ous** -əs
anthropomorph|ism ,æn*t*.θrə.pəʊ'mɔː.f|ɪ.zᵊm (US) -pə'mɔːr- **-ist/s** -ɪst/s
anthropomorphiz|e, -is|e ,æn*t*.θrə.pəʊ'mɔː.faɪz (US) -pə'mɔːr- **-es** -ɪz **-ing** -ɪŋ **-ed** -d
anthropomorphosis ,æn*t*.θrə.pəʊ.mɔː'fəʊ.sɪs (US) -pə.mɔːr'foʊ-
anthropopha|gus ,æn*t*.θrəʊ'pɒf.ə|.gəs (US) -θrə'pɑː.fə- **-gi** -dʒaɪ, -gaɪ (US) -dʒaɪ
anthropopha|gy ,æn*t*.θrəʊ'pɒf.ə|.dʒi (US) -θrə'pɑː.fə- **-gous** -gəs
anthroposoph|y ,æn*t*.θrəʊ'pɒs.ə.f|i (US) -θrə'pɑː.sə- **-ist/s** -ɪst/s
anti- æn.tɪ-, -ti-; æn'tɪ- (US) -t̬ɪ-, -t̬i-, -taɪ-; æn'tɪ-
Note: Prefix. Numerous compounds may be formed by prefixing **anti-** to other words. Most often, these compounds carry primary or secondary stress on the first syllable, e.g. **antihero** /'æn.tɪ,hɪə.rəʊ (US) -t̬ɪ,hɪr.oʊ/, **anti-icer** /,æn.ti'aɪ.səʳ (US) -t̬i'aɪ.sɚ/, but there are also cases in which the second syllable takes the primary stress, e.g. **antinomy** /æn'tɪn.ə.mi/.
anti 'æn.ti (US) -t̬i, -taɪ **-s** -z
antiabortion ,æn.ti.ə'bɔː.ʃᵊn (US) -t̬i.ə'bɔːr-, -taɪ- **-ist/s** -ɪst/s

anti-aircraft ˌæn.ti'eə.krɑːft (US) -t̬i'er.kræft, -taɪ'-
antibacterial ˌæn.tɪ.bæk'tɪə.ri.əl (US) -t̬ɪ.bæk'tɪr.i-, -taɪ-
antiballistic ˌæn.tɪ.bə'lɪs.tɪk (US) -t̬ɪ-, -taɪ-
Antibes ɑːn'tiːb, æn-, ɒn'- (US) ɑːn'-
antibiosis ˌæn.tɪ.baɪ'əʊ.sɪs (US) -t̬ɪ.baɪ'oʊ-, -taɪ-
antibiotic ˌæn.tɪ.baɪ'ɒt.ɪk (US) -t̬ɪ.baɪ'ɑː.t̬ɪk, -taɪ- **-s** -s
antibod|y 'æn.tɪˌbɒd|.i (US) -t̬ɪˌbɑː.d|i, -taɪˌ- **-ies** -iz
antic 'æn.tɪk (US) -t̬ɪk **-s** -s
anticatholic ˌæn.tɪ'kæθ.ᵊl.ɪk (US) -t̬ɪ'-, -taɪ'- **-s** -s
anti-choice ˌæn.tɪ'tʃɔɪs (US) -t̬ɪ'-, -taɪ'-
antichrist (A) 'æn.tɪ.kraɪst (US) -t̬ɪ-, -taɪ- **-s** -s
antichristian *opposing Christianity:* ˌæn.tɪ'krɪs.tʃᵊn, -'krɪʃ- (US) -t̬ɪ'-, -taɪ'- **-s** -z *pertaining to Antichrist:* 'æn.tɪˌkrɪʃ.tʃᵊn (US) -t̬ɪˌ-, -taɪˌ- **-s** -z
anticipant æn'tɪs.ɪ.pənt, '-ə- **-s** -s
antici|pate æn'tɪs.ɪ|.peɪt, '-ə- (US) '-ə- **-pates** -peɪts **-pating** -peɪ.tɪŋ (US) -peɪ.t̬ɪŋ **-pated** -peɪ.tɪd (US) -peɪ.t̬ɪd **-pative/ly** -peɪ.tɪv/li (US) -peɪ.t̬ɪv/li
anticipation ænˌtɪs.ɪ'peɪ.ʃᵊn, -ə'-; ˌæn.tɪ.sɪ'-, -sə'- (US) ænˌtɪs.ə'- **-s** -z
anticipator|y ænˌtɪs.ɪ'peɪ.tᵊr|.i, -ə'-; ˌæn.tɪ.sɪ'-, -sə'- (US) æn'tɪs.ə.pə.tɔːr- **-ily** -ᵊl.i, -ɪ.li
anticiz|e, -is|e 'æn.tɪ.saɪz (US) -t̬ɪ-, -taɪ- **-es** -ɪz **-ing** -ɪŋ **-ed** -d
anticlerical ˌæn.tɪ'kler.ɪ.kᵊl (US) -t̬ɪ'-, -taɪ'- **-ism** -ɪ.zᵊm **-ist/s** -ɪst/s
anticlimactic ˌæn.tɪ.klaɪ'mæk.tɪk, -klɪ'- (US) -t̬ɪ.klaɪ'-, -taɪ- **-ally** -ᵊl.i, -li
anticlimatic ˌæn.tɪ.klaɪ'mæt.ɪk, -klɪ'- (US) -t̬ɪ.klaɪ'mæt̬-, -taɪ- **-al** -ᵊl **-ally** -ᵊl.i, -li
anticlimax ˌæn.tɪ'klaɪ.mæks, 'æn.tɪˌklaɪ- (US) ˌæn.t̬ɪ'klaɪ-, -taɪˌ- **-es** -ɪz
anticline 'æn.tɪ.klaɪn (US) -t̬ɪ- **-s** -z
anticlockwise ˌæn.tɪ'klɒk.waɪz (US) -t̬ɪ'klɑːk-, -taɪ'- *stress shift:* ˌanticlockwise 'action
anticoagulant ˌæn.tɪ.kəʊ'æg.jʊ.lənt, -jə- (US) -t̬ɪ.koʊ'æg.jə-, -taɪ- **-s** -s
anticonsumer|ism ˌæn.tɪ.kən'sjuː.mᵊr|.ɪ.zᵊm, -'suː- (US) -t̬ɪ.kən'suː- **-ist/s** -ɪst/s
anticonvulsant ˌæn.tɪ.kən'vʌl.sᵊnt (US) -t̬ɪ-, -taɪ- **-s** -s
anticonvulsive ˌæn.tɪ.kən'vʌl.sɪv (US) -t̬ɪ-, -taɪ- **-s** -z
anticyclone ˌæn.tɪ'saɪ.kləʊn, 'æn.tɪ.saɪ- (US) ˌæn.t̬ɪ'saɪ.kloʊn, -taɪ'- **-s** -z
anticyclonic ˌæn.tɪ.saɪ'klɒn.ɪk (US) -t̬ɪ.saɪ'klɑː.nɪk, -taɪ-
antidepressant ˌæn.tɪ.dɪ'pres.ᵊnt, -də'- (US) -t̬ɪ-, -taɪ- **-s** -s
antidotal ˌæn.tɪ'dəʊ.tᵊl, 'æn.tɪ.dəʊ- (US) 'æn.t̬ɪ.doʊ-
antidote 'æn.tɪ.dəʊt (US) -t̬ɪ.doʊt **-s** -s
Antietam æn'tiː.təm (US) -t̬əm
antifebrile ˌæn.tɪ'fiː.braɪl, -'feb.raɪl (US) -t̬ɪ'fiː.brɪl, -taɪ'-, -'feb.rɪl, -rəl
anti-federal ˌæn.tɪ'fed.ᵊr.ᵊl (US) -t̬ɪ'-, -taɪ'- **-ism** -ɪ.zᵊm **-ist/s** -ɪst/s
antifreeze 'æn.tɪ.friːz (US) -t̬ɪ-
antigen 'æn.tɪ.dʒən, -dʒen (US) -t̬ɪ- **-s** -z
Antigone æn'tɪg.ə.ni
Antigonus æn'tɪg.ə.nəs
Antigu|a æn'tiː.g|ə (US) -gw|ə, -g|ə, -'tɪg.w|ə, '-ə **-an/s** -ən/z
antihel|ix ˌæn.tɪ'hiː.l|ɪks (US) -t̬ɪ'-, -taɪ'- **-ixes** -ɪk.sɪz **-ices** -ɪ.siːz, -'hel.ɪs.iːz
antihero 'æn.tɪˌhɪə.rəʊ (US) -t̬ɪˌher.oʊ, -t̬i-, -taɪ-, -hiː.roʊ **-es** -z
antiheroic ˌæn.tɪ.hɪ'rəʊ.ɪk, -hə'-, -her'əʊ- (US) -t̬ɪ.hɪ'roʊ-, -t̬i-, -taɪ-
antiheroine 'æn.tɪˌher.əʊ.ɪn (US) -t̬ɪˌher.oʊ-, -taɪ- **-s** -z
antihistamine ˌæn.tɪ'hɪs.tə.mɪn, -miːn (US) -t̬ɪ'- **-s** -z
anti-icer ˌæn.ti'aɪ.səʳ (US) -t̬i'aɪ.sɚ **-s** -z
anti-inflammatory ˌæn.ti.ɪn'flæm.ə.tᵊr.i (US) -t̬i.ɪn'flæm.ə.tɔːr-, -taɪ-
Anti-Jacobin ˌæn.tɪ'dʒæk.ə.bɪn, -ɒb.ɪn (US) -t̬ɪ'dʒæk.ə.bɪn, -taɪ'-
antiknock ˌæn.tɪ'nɒk (US) 'æn.t̬ɪ'nɑːk, -t̬i-, -taɪ- **-ing** -ɪŋ
Antilles æn'tɪl.iːz
antilock ˌæn.tɪ'lɒk (US) -t̬ɪ'lɑːk, -t̬i-, -taɪ- *stress shift:* ˌantilock 'brakes
anti-locking ˌæn.tɪ'lɒk.ɪŋ (US) -t̬ɪ'lɑː.kɪŋ
antilog ˌæn.tɪ'lɒg (US) 'æn.t̬ɪ.lɑːg, -taɪ-, -lɔːg **-s** -z
antilogarithm ˌæn.tɪ'lɒg.ə.rɪ.ðᵊm, -θᵊm (US) -t̬ɪ'lɑː.gɚ.ɪ.ðᵊm, -taɪ'-, -'lɔː- **-s** -z
antilog|y æn'tɪl.ə.dʒ|i **-ies** -iz
antimacassar ˌæn.tɪ.mə'kæs.əʳ (US) -t̬ɪ.mə'kæs.ɚ **-s** -z
Antimachus æn'tɪm.ə.kəs
antimatter 'æn.tɪˌmæt.əʳ (US) -t̬ɪˌmæt̬.ɚ, -t̬i-, -taɪ-
anti-missile ˌæn.tɪ'mɪs.aɪl (US) -t̬ɪ'mɪs.ᵊl, -t̬i-, -taɪ'-
antimonarchical ˌæn.tɪ.mɒn'ɑː.kɪ.kᵊl, -mə'nɑː- (US) -t̬ɪ.mə'nɑːr-, -taɪ-
antimonarchist ˌæn.tɪ'mɒn.ə.kɪst (US) -t̬ɪ'mɑː.nɚ-, -taɪ'-, -nɑːr- **-s** -s
antimonial ˌæn.tɪ'məʊ.ni.əl (US) -t̬ɪ'moʊ- **-s** -z
antimonic ˌæn.tɪ'mɒn.ɪk (US) -t̬ɪ'mɑː.nɪk
antimony 'æn.tɪ.mə.ni, æn'tɪm.ə- (US) 'æn.t̬ə.moʊ-
antinode 'æn.tɪ.nəʊd (US) -t̬ɪ.noʊd
antinomian ˌæn.tɪ'nəʊ.mi.ən (US) -t̬ɪ'noʊ-, -taɪ'- **-s** -z
antinomic ˌæn.tɪ'nɒm.ɪk (US) -t̬ɪ'nɑː.mɪk **-al** -ᵊl **-ally** -ᵊl.i, -li
antinom|y æn'tɪn.ə.m|i **-ies** -iz
Antinous æn'tɪn.əʊ.əs (US) -oʊ-
antinovel 'æn.tɪˌnɒv.ᵊl (US) -t̬ɪˌnɑː.vᵊl, -t̬i-, -taɪˌ- **-s** -z
antinuclear ˌæn.tɪ'njuː.kli.ə (US) -t̬ɪ'nuː-, -t̬i-, -taɪ'-, -'njuː-
Antioch 'æn.ti.ɒk (US) -t̬i.ɑːk
Antiochus æn'taɪ.ə.kəs
Antioquia ˌæn.ti.əʊ'kiː.ə (US) -t̬i.ə'-; ɑːn'tjoʊ.kjɑː
antioxidant ˌæn.ti'ɒk.sɪ.dᵊnt (US) -t̬i'ɑːk-, -taɪ'- **-s** -s
Antipas 'æn.tɪ.pæs (US) -t̬ɪ-
antipasti ˌæn.tɪ'pæs.ti (US) ˌæn.t̬ɪ'pɑː.sti, ˌɑːn.t̬ɪ'-, -'pæs.ti
antipasto ˌæn.ti'pæs.təʊ (US) ˌæn.t̬i'pɑː.stoʊ, ˌɑːn-, -'pæs.toʊ **-s** -z
Antipater æn'tɪp.ə.təʳ (US) -t̬ɚ
antipathetic ˌæn.tɪ.pə'θet.ɪk, ænˌtɪp.ə'- (US) ˌæn.t̬ɪ.pə'θet̬.ɪk, ænˌtɪ.pə'- **-al** -ᵊl **-ally** -ᵊl.i, -li
antipath|y æn'tɪp.ə.θ|i **-ies** -iz
anti-personnel ˌæn.tɪˌpɜː.sᵊn'el (US) -t̬ɪˌpɜːr-, -t̬i-, -taɪˌ-
antiperspirant ˌæn.tɪ'pɜː.spᵊr.ənt, -spɪ.rənt (US) -t̬ɪ'pɜːr.spɚ.ənt, -t̬i-, -taɪ'- **-s** -s
Antipholus æn'tɪf.ə.ləs
antiphon 'æn.tɪ.fən, -fɒn (US) -t̬ə.fɑːn, -fən **-s** -z
antiphonal æn'tɪf.ə.nᵊl **-s** -z
antiphoner æn'tɪf.ᵊn.əʳ (US) -ɚ **-s** -z
antiphonic ˌæn.tɪ'fɒn.ɪk (US) -t̬ɪ'fɑː.nɪk **-al** -ᵊl **-ally** -ᵊl.i, -li
antiphon|y æn'tɪf.ə.n|i **-ies** -iz
antipodal æn'tɪp.ə.dᵊl
antipodean (A) ænˌtɪp.əʊ'diː.ən, ˌæn.tɪp- (US) -ə'-
antipodes æn'tɪp.ə.diːz
antipope 'æn.tɪ.pəʊp (US) -t̬ɪ.poʊp **-s** -s
antipyretic ˌæn.tɪ.paɪə'ret.ɪk, -pɪ'ret- (US) -t̬ɪ.paɪ'ret̬-, -t̬i-, -taɪ- **-s** -s
antipyrin ˌæn.tɪ'paɪə.rɪn, -riːn (US) -t̬ɪ'paɪ-, -taɪ'-
antiquarian ˌæn.tɪ'kweə.ri.ən (US) -t̬ə'kwer.i- **-s** -z **-ism** -ɪ.zᵊm
antiquar|y 'æn.tɪ.kwᵊr|.i (US) -t̬ə.kwer- **-ies** -iz
anti|quate 'æn.tɪ|.kweɪt (US) -t̬ə- **-quates** -kweɪts **-quating** -kweɪ.tɪŋ (US) -kweɪ.t̬ɪŋ **-quated** -kweɪ.tɪd (US) -kweɪ.t̬ɪd

antique æn'tiːk **-s** -s **-ly** -li **-ness** -nəs, -nɪs
antiquit|y æn'tɪk.wə.t|i, -wɪ- (US) -wə.t̬|i **-ies** -iz
anti-racial|ism ˌæn.tɪ'reɪ.ʃᵊl|.ɪ.zᵊm, -ʃi.ə.l|ɪ- (US) -t̬ɪ'reɪ.ʃᵊl|.ɪ-, -t̬i-, -taɪ'- **-ist/s** -ɪst/s
anti-rac|ism ˌæn.tɪ'reɪ.s|ɪ.zᵊm (US) -t̬ɪ'-, -taɪ'- **-ist/s** -ɪst/s
antirrhinum ˌæn.tɪ'raɪ.nəm, -tə'- (US) -t̬ə'- **-s** -z
antiscorbutic ˌæn.tɪ.skɔː'bjuː.tɪk (US) -t̬ɪ.skɔːr'bjuː.t̬ɪk, -taɪ- **-s** -s
anti-Semite ˌæn.tɪ'siː.maɪt, -'sem.aɪt (US) -t̬ɪ'sem.aɪt, -t̬i-, -taɪ'- **-s** -s
anti-Semitic ˌæn.tɪ.sɪ'mɪt.ɪk, -sə'- (US) -t̬ɪ.sə'mɪt̬-, -t̬i-, -taɪ- *stress shift:* ˌanti-Semitic 'views
anti-Semitism ˌæn.tɪ'sem.ɪ.tɪ.zᵊm, '-ə- (US) -t̬ɪ'sem.ə-, -t̬i-, -taɪ'-
antisepsis ˌæn.tɪ'sep.sɪs (US) -t̬ə'-
antiseptic ˌæn.tɪ'sep.tɪk (US) -t̬ə'- **-s** -s **-ally** -ᵊl.i, -li *stress shift:* ˌantiseptic 'lozenge
antiser|um ˌæn.tɪ'sɪə.r|əm (US) -t̬ɪ'sɪr|.əm, -taɪ'- **-ums** -əmz **-a** -ə
antisocial ˌæn.tɪ'səʊ.ʃᵊl (US) -t̬ɪ'soʊ-, -t̬i-, -taɪ'- **-ly** -i
antisocialist ˌæn.tɪ'səʊ.ʃᵊl.ɪst (US) -t̬ɪ'soʊ-, -t̬i-, -taɪ'- **-s** -s
antistatic ˌæn.tɪ'stæt.ɪk (US) -t̬ɪ'stæt̬-, -taɪ'- *stress shift:* ˌantistatic 'cloth
Antisthenes æn'tɪs.θə.niːz, -θɪ-
antistrophe æn'tɪs.trə.fi **-s** -z
antistrophic ˌæn.tɪ'strɒf.ɪk (US) -t̬ə'strɑː.fɪk
anti-tank ˌæn.tɪ'tæŋk (US) -t̬ɪ'-, -t̬i-, -taɪ'-
antithes|is æn'tɪθ.ə.s|ɪs, '-ɪ- **-es** -iːz
antithetic ˌæn.tɪ'θet.ɪk (US) -t̬ə'θet̬.ɪk **-al** -ᵊl **-ally** -ᵊl.i, -li
antitox|ic ˌæn.tɪ'tɒk.s|ɪk (US) -t̬ɪ'tɑːk-, -taɪ'- **-in/s** -sɪn/z
antiviral ˌæn.tɪ'vaɪə.rᵊl (US) -t̬ɪ'vaɪ-, -t̬i-, -taɪ'-
anti-vivisection ˌæn.tɪˌvɪv.ɪ'sek.ʃᵊn (US) -t̬ɪ'vɪv.ɪ.sek-, -taɪ'- **-ist/s** -ɪst/s
antler 'ænt.ləʳ (US) -lɚ **-s** -z **-ed** -d
Antofagasta ˌæn.tə.fə'gæs.tə
Antoine ɑːn'twæn, ɒn'- (US) 'æn.twɑːn, ɑːn-
Antoinette ˌæn.twɑː'net, ˌɑːn-, -twə'- (US) ˌæn.twə'-, ˌɑːn-
Anton 'æn.tɒn (US) -tɑːn
Antonia æn'təʊ.ni.ə (US) -'toʊ-; ˌæn.toʊ'niː-
Antonine 'æn.tə.naɪn (US) -t̬ə- **-s** -z
Antoninus ˌæn.təʊ'naɪ.nəs (US) -t̬ə'-
Antonio æn'təʊ.ni.əʊ (US) -'toʊ.ni.oʊ
Antonius æn'təʊ.ni.əs (US) -'toʊ-
Antony 'æn.tə.ni (US) -tᵊn.i
antonym 'æn.tə.nɪm (US) -tᵊn.ɪm **-s** -z
antonymic ˌæn.tə'nɪm.ɪk (US) -tᵊn'ɪm-
antonymous æn'tɒn.ɪ.məs, '-ə- (US) -'tɑː.nə-
antonymy æn'tɒn.ɪ.mi, '-ə- (US) -'tɑː.nə-
Antrim 'æn.trɪm
Antrobus 'æn.trə.bəs
Antron 'æn.trɒn (US) -trɑːn
antr|um 'æn.tr|əm **-ums** -əmz **-a** -ə
antsy 'ænt.si
Antwerp 'æn.twɜːp (US) -twɜːrp
ANU ˌeɪ.en'juː
Anubis ə'njuː.bɪs (US) -'nuː-, -'njuː-
anuresis ˌæn.jʊə'riː.sɪs, -jə- (US) -jʊ'-, -jə'-
anuria ˌæn'juː.ri.ə, -'jɔː- (US) -'jʊr.i-
anus 'eɪ.nəs **-es** -ɪz
anvil 'æn.vɪl (US) -vᵊl, -vɪl **-s** -z
Anwar 'æn.wɑːʳ (US) 'ɑːn.wɑːr, 'æn-
Anwick 'æn.ɪk (US) -wɪk
anxiet|y æŋ'zaɪ.ə.t|i, æŋg-, -ɪt|.i (US) -ə.t̬|i **-ies** -iz
anxious 'æŋk.ʃəs **-ly** -li **-ness** -nəs, -nɪs
any *normal form:* 'en.i *occasional weak form:* ə.ni *occasional weak form after t or d:* ᵊn.i

Note: The usual pronunciation is /'en.i/, but when the word follows immediately after a strongly stressed word it may be weakened to /ə.ni/ (e.g. 'Have you got any change?' /hæv.juˌgɒt.ə.ni'tʃeɪndʒ (US) -ˌgɑːt-/). In more rapid speech, and when preceded by an alveolar consonant, the first syllable may be reduced to syllabic /n̩/ (e.g. 'Got any more?' /ˌgɒt.n̩.i'mɔːʳ (US) ˌgɑːt̬.n̩.i'mɔːr/).

anybody 'en.iˌbɒd.i, -bə.di (US) -ˌbɑː.di
anyhow 'en.i.haʊ
anymore ˌen.i'mɔːʳ (US) -'mɔːr
anyone 'en.i.wʌn, -wən
anyplace 'en.i.pleɪs
anyroad 'en.i.rəʊd (US) -roʊd
anything 'en.i.θɪŋ
anytime 'en.i.taɪm
anyway 'en.i.weɪ **-s** -z
anywhere 'en.i.*h*weəʳ (US) -*h*wer
anywise 'en.i.waɪz
Anzac 'æn.zæk **-s** -s **'Anzac ˌDay**
Anzio 'æn.zi.əʊ (US) -oʊ
AOB ˌeɪ.əʊ'biː (US) -oʊ'-
A-OK, A-Okay ˌeɪ.əʊ'keɪ (US) -oʊ'-
A-one ˌeɪ'wʌn *stress shift:* ˌA-one con'dition
Aoni|a eɪ'əʊ.ni|.ə (US) -'oʊ- **-an/s** -ən/z
aorist 'eɪ.ə.rɪst, 'eə.rɪst (US) 'eɪ.ə- **-s** -s
aort|a eɪ'ɔː.t|ə (US) -'ɔːr.t̬|ə **-as** -əz **-ae** -iː **-al** -ᵊl **-ic** -ɪk
Aosta ɑː'ɒs.tə (US) -'ɔː.stə, -'oʊ-
Aouita aʊ'iː.tə (US) -t̬ə
apace ə'peɪs
Apache ə'pætʃ.i **-s** -z
apart ə'pɑːt (US) -'pɑːrt **-ness** -nəs, -nɪs
apartheid ə'pɑː.teɪt, -teɪd, -taɪt, -'pɑːt.heɪt, -heɪd, -haɪt (US) -'pɑːr.teɪt, -taɪt
apartment ə'pɑːt.mənt (US) -'pɑːrt- **-s** -s **a'partment ˌblock ; a'partment ˌhouse**
apathetic ˌæp.ə'θet.ɪk (US) -'θet̬- **-al** -ᵊl **-ally** -ᵊl.i, -li *stress shift:* ˌapathetic 'voters
apath|y 'æp.ə.θ|i **-ies** -iz
ap|e eɪp **-es** -s **-ing** -ɪŋ **-ed** -t
Apelles ə'pel.iːz
Apemantus æp.ɪ'mæn.təs (US) -t̬əs
Apennines 'æp.ə.naɪnz, -en.aɪnz
aperçu ˌæp.ɜː'sjuː, -ə'-, -'suː (US) -ɚ'suː, ˌɑː.pɚ'- **-s** -z
aperient ə'pɪə.ri.ənt (US) -'pɪr.i- **-s** -s
aperiodic ˌeɪ.pɪə.ri'ɒd.ɪk (US) -pɪr.i'ɑː.dɪk
aperiodicity ˌeɪ.pɪə.ri.ə'dɪs.ə.ti, -ɪ.ti (US) -pɪr.i.ə'dɪs.ə.t̬i
apéritif əˌper.ə'tiːf, æpˌer-, -ɪ'-, ə'per.ə.tɪf (US) ɑːˌper.ɪ'-, -ə'- **-s** -s
aperture 'æp.ə.tʃəʳ, -tjʊəʳ (US) -ɚ.tʃʊr, -tʃɚ **-s** -z
aper|y 'eɪ.pə.r|i **-ies** -iz
apeshit 'eɪp.ʃɪt
apex, APEX (A) 'eɪ.peks **-es** -ɪz
aphaeresis æf'ɪə.rə.sɪs, ə'fɪə-, -rɪ- (US) ə'fer.ə-
aphasia ə'feɪ.zi.ə, æf'eɪ-, eɪ'feɪ-, -ʒi.ə, -ʒə (US) ə'feɪ.ʒə, -ʒi.ə
aphasic ə'feɪ.zɪk, æf'eɪ-, eɪ'feɪ- (US) ə'feɪ-
apheli|on æf'iː.li.|ən **-a** -ə
apheresis æf'ɪə.rə.sɪs, ə'fɪə-, -rɪ- (US) ə'fer.ə-
aphes|is 'æf.ə.s|ɪs, '-ɪ- **-es** -iːz
aphid 'eɪ.fɪd (US) 'eɪ.fɪd, 'æf.ɪd, -əd **-s** -z
aphidian eɪ'fɪd.i.ən, æf'ɪd- **-s** -z
aph|is 'eɪ.f|ɪs, 'æf|.ɪs **-ides** -ɪ.diːz **-ises** -ɪ.sɪz
aphonia eɪ'fəʊ.ni.ə, æf'əʊ-, ə'fəʊ- (US) eɪ'foʊ-
aphonic eɪ'fɒn.ɪk, æf'ɒn-, ə'fɒn- (US) eɪ'fɑː.nɪk
aphony 'æf.ə.ni
aphorism 'æf.ᵊr.ɪ.zᵊm, -ɒr- (US) '-ɚ- **-s** -z
aphorist 'æf.ᵊr.ɪst, -ɒr- (US) '-ɚ- **-s** -s
aphoristic ˌæf.ᵊr'ɪs.tɪk, -ɒr'- (US) -ə'rɪs- **-ally** -ᵊl.i, -li
aphoriz|e, -is|e 'æf.ᵊr.aɪz, -ɒr- (US) -ə.raɪz **-es** -ɪz **-ing** -ɪŋ **-ed** -d **-er/s** -əʳ/z (US) -ɚ/z
Aphra 'æf.rə
aphrodisiac ˌæf.rəʊ'dɪz.i.æk (US) -rə'-, -roʊ'-, -'diː.zi- **-s** -s

aphrodisian ˌæf.rəʊˈdɪz.i.ən ⓤⓢ -rəˈdiː.zi-, -roʊˈ-, -ˈdɪz.i-, -ˈdɪʒ.ən **-s** -z
Aphrodite ˌæf.rəʊˈdaɪ.ti ⓤⓢ -rəˈdaɪ.t̬i, -roʊˈ-
aphtha ˈæf.θə
Apia ɑːˈpiː.ə
apian ˈeɪ.pi.ən
apiarian ˌeɪ.piˈeə.ri.ən ⓤⓢ -ˈer.i- **-s** -z
apiarist ˈeɪ.pi.ə.rɪst **-s** -s
apiar|y ˈeɪ.pi.ə.r|i ⓤⓢ -er|.i **-ies** -iz
apical ˈæp.ɪ.kəl, ˈeɪ.pɪ- **-ly** -i
apices (*alternative plur. of* **apex**) ˈeɪ.pɪ.siːz, ˈæp.ɪ-
apiculture ˈeɪ.pɪ.kʌl.tʃəʳ ⓤⓢ -tʃɚ
apiece əˈpiːs
apis ˈeɪ.pɪs
Apis ˈɑː.pɪs, ˈeɪ-
apish ˈeɪ.pɪʃ **-ly** -li **-ness** -nəs, -nɪs
aplenty əˈplen.ti ⓤⓢ -t̬i
aplomb əˈplɒm, æpˈlɒm ⓤⓢ əˈplɑːm, -ˈplʌm
apn(o)ea æpˈniː.ə, ˈæp.ni.ə
apn(o)eic æpˈniː.ɪk
apocalyps|e (A) əˈpɒk.ə.lɪps ⓤⓢ -ˈpɑː.kə- **-es** -ɪz
apocalypt|ic əˌpɒk.əˈlɪp.t|ɪk ⓤⓢ -ˌpɑː.kəˈ- **-ist/s** -ɪst/s **-ical** -ɪ.kəl *stress shift:* aˌpocalyptic ˈvision
apocope əˈpɒk.əʊ.pi ⓤⓢ -ˈpɑː.kə- **-s** -z
apocryph|a (A) əˈpɒk.rɪ.f|ə, -rə- ⓤⓢ -ˈpɑː.krə- **-al** -əl
apocryphal əˈpɒk.rɪ.fəl, -rə- ⓤⓢ -ˈpɑː.krə-
apodeictic ˌæp.əʊˈdaɪk.tɪk ⓤⓢ -əˈ-, -oʊˈ- **-al** -əl **-ally** -əl.i, -li
apodictic ˌæp.əʊˈdɪk.tɪk ⓤⓢ -əˈ-, -oʊˈ- **-al** -əl **-ally** -əl.i, -li
apodos|is əˈpɒd.ə.s|ɪs ⓤⓢ -ˈpɑː.də- **-es** -iːz
apogee ˈæp.əʊ.dʒiː ⓤⓢ -ə- **-s** -z
apolitical ˌeɪ.pəˈlɪt.ɪ.kəl, ˈ-ə- ⓤⓢ -ˈlɪt̬.ə-
Apollinaire əˌpɒl.ɪˈneəʳ ⓤⓢ -ˌpɑː.lɪˈner
Apollinaris əˌpɒl.ɪˈnɑː.rɪs, -ˈeə- ⓤⓢ -pɑː.lɪˈner.ɪs
Apollo əˈpɒl.əʊ ⓤⓢ -ˈpɑː.loʊ
Apollodorus əˌpɒl.əˈdɔː.rəs ⓤⓢ -ˌpɑː.ləˈdɔːr.əs
Apolloni|a ˌæp.əˈləʊ.ni.|ə, -ɒlˈəʊ- ⓤⓢ -əˈloʊ- **-an** -ən **-us** -əs
Apollos əˈpɒl.əs ⓤⓢ -ˈpɑː.ləs
Apollyon əˈpɒl.i.ən ⓤⓢ -ˈpɑː.li-
apologetic əˌpɒl.əˈdʒet.ɪk ⓤⓢ -ˌpɑː.ləˈdʒet̬.ɪk **-al** -əl **-ally** -əl.i, -li **-s** -s
apologia ˌæp.əˈləʊ.dʒə, -dʒi.ə ⓤⓢ -ˈloʊ- **-s** -z
apologist əˈpɒl.ə.dʒɪst ⓤⓢ -ˈpɑː.lə- **-s** -s
apologiz|e, -is|e əˈpɒl.ə.dʒaɪz ⓤⓢ -ˈpɑː.lə- **-es** -ɪz **-ing** -ɪŋ **-ed** -d **-er/s** -əʳ/z, -ɚ/z
apologue ˈæp.əʊ.lɒg ⓤⓢ -ə.lɑːg **-s** -z
apolog|y əˈpɒl.ə.dʒ|i ⓤⓢ -ˈpɑː.lə- **-ies** -iz
apophthegm ˈæp.ə.θem **-s** -z
apoplectic ˌæp.əˈplek.tɪk **-al** -əl **-ally** -əl.i, -li
apoplex|y ˈæp.ə.plek.s|i **-ies** -iz
aposiopes|is ˌæp.ə.saɪ.əʊˈpiː.s|ɪs, əˌpɒs.i.əʊˈ- ⓤⓢ ˌæp.oʊ.saɪ.oʊˈ-, -ə.saɪ.əˈ- **-es** -iːz
apostas|y əˈpɒs.tə.s|i ⓤⓢ -ˈpɑː.stə- **-ies** -iz
apostate əˈpɒs.teɪt, -tɪt, -tət ⓤⓢ -ˈpɑː.steɪt, -stɪt, -stət **-s** -s
apostatic ˌæp.əʊˈstæt.ɪk ⓤⓢ -əˈstæt̬- **-al** -əl
apostatiz|e, -is|e əˈpɒs.tə.taɪz ⓤⓢ -ˈpɑː.stə- **-es** -ɪz **-ing** -ɪŋ **-ed** -d
a posteriori ˌeɪ.pɒsˌter.iˈɔː.raɪ, ˌɑː-, -ˌtɪə.riˈ-, -riː ⓤⓢ ˌeɪ.pɑːˌstɪr-
apostil əˈpɒs.tɪl ⓤⓢ -ˈpɑː.stɪl **-s** -z
apostle əˈpɒs.l̩ ⓤⓢ -ˈpɑː.sl̩ **-s** -z **-ship** -ʃɪp
apostolate əˈpɒs.tə.lət, -lɪt, -leɪt ⓤⓢ -ˈpɑː.stə.lɪt, -leɪt **-s** -s
apostolic ˌæp.əˈstɒl.ɪk ⓤⓢ -ˈstɑː.lɪk **-al** -əl **-ally** -əl.i
apostolicism ˌæp.əˈstɒl.ɪ.sɪ.zəm ⓤⓢ -ˈstɑː.lɪ-
apostrophe əˈpɒs.trə.fi ⓤⓢ -ˈpɑː.strə- **-s** -z
apostrophiz|e, -is|e əˈpɒs.trə.faɪz ⓤⓢ -ˈpɑː.strə- **-es** -ɪz **-ing** -ɪŋ **-ed** -d
apothecar|y əˈpɒθ.ə.kər.|i, ˈ-ɪ- ⓤⓢ -ˈpɑː.θə- **-ies** -iz
apothegm ˈæp.ə.θem **-s** -z
apothegmatic ˌæp.ə.θegˈmæt.ɪk ⓤⓢ -ˈmæt̬- **-al** -əl
apotheos|is əˌpɒθ.iˈəʊ.s|ɪs, ˌæp.əʊ.θiˈ- ⓤⓢ əˌpɑː.θiˈoʊ-, ˌæp.əˈθiː.ə- **-es** -iːz
apotheosiz|e, -is|e əˈpɒθ.i.əʊ.saɪz, ˌæp.əˈθiː.əʊ.saɪz ⓤⓢ əˈpɑː.θi.oʊ-, ˌæp.əˈθiː.ə- **-es** -ɪz **-ing** -ɪŋ **-ed** -d
appal əˈpɔːl ⓤⓢ -ˈpɔːl, -ˈpɑːl **-s** -z **-ling/ly** -ɪŋ/li **-led** -d
Appalachi|a ˌæp.əˈleɪ.ʃ|ə, -tʃ|ə, -ʃi|.ə ⓤⓢ -ˈleɪ.tʃi-, -ˈlætʃ.i-, -ˈleɪ.tʃ|ə, -ˈlætʃ|.ə **-an/s** -ən/z
appall əˈpɔːl ⓤⓢ -ˈpɔːl, -ˈpɑːl **-s** -z **-ing/ly** -ɪŋ/li **-ed** -d
Appaloosa ˌæp.əˈluː.sə
appanag|e ˈæp.ə.nɪdʒ **-es** -ɪz
apparat ˌæp.əˈrɑːt ⓤⓢ ˌɑː.pəˈ-, ˈæp.ə.ræt **-s** -s
apparatchik ˌæp.əˈrætʃ.ɪk, -ˈræt.tʃɪk, -ˈrɑːt-, -ˈrɑː.tʃɪk ⓤⓢ ˌɑː.pəˈrɑː.tʃɪk, -ˈrɑːt.tʃɪk **-s** -s **-i** -i
apparatus ˌæp.ərˈeɪ.təs, -ˈæt.əs ⓤⓢ -əˈræt̬- **-es** -ɪz
apparel əˈpær.əl ⓤⓢ -ˈper-, -ˈpær- **-s** -z **-ling** -ɪŋ **-led** -d
apparent əˈpær.ənt, -ˈpeə.rənt ⓤⓢ -ˈper.ənt, -ˈpær- **-ly** -li **-ness** -nəs, -nɪs
apparition ˌæp.ərˈɪʃ.ən ⓤⓢ -əˈrɪʃ- **-s** -z
apparitor əˈpær.ɪ.təʳ ⓤⓢ -ˈper.ɪ.t̬ɚ, -ˈpær- **-s** -z
appassionata əˌpæs.i.əˈnɑː.tə, -ˌpæs.jəˈ- ⓤⓢ -ˌpɑː.si.əˈnɑː.t̬ə, -ˌpæs.i-
appeal əˈpiːl **-s** -z **-ing** -ɪŋ **-ed** -d **-er/s** -əʳ/z ⓤⓢ -ɚ/z **Apˈpeal ˌCourt**
appealing əˈpiː.lɪŋ **-ly** -li **-ness** -nəs, -nɪs
appear əˈpɪəʳ ⓤⓢ -ˈpɪr **-s** -z **-ing** -ɪŋ **-ed** -d **-er/s** -əʳ/z ⓤⓢ -ɚ/z
appearanc|e əˈpɪə.rənts ⓤⓢ -ˈpɪr.ənts **-es** -ɪz
appeas|e əˈpiːz **-es** -ɪz **-ing/ly** -ɪŋ/li **-ed** -d **-able** -ə.bl̩
appeasement əˈpiːz.mənt **-s** -s
appellant əˈpel.ənt **-s** -s
appellate əˈpel.ət, æpˈel-, -eɪt, -ɪt ⓤⓢ -ɪt
appellation ˌæp.əˈleɪ.ʃən, -ɪˈ-, -elˈeɪ- **-s** -z
appellation contrôlée *as if French:* æp.el.æsˌjɔ̃ːŋ.kɔ̃ːn.trəʊˈleɪ, æp.elˌæs.jɔ̃ːŋ-, -kɒnˈtrəʊ.leɪ ⓤⓢ æp.elˌɑː.sjoʊn.kɑːn.troʊˈleɪ
appellative əˈpel.ə.tɪv, æpˈel- ⓤⓢ -t̬ɪv **-ly** -li **-ness** -nəs, -nɪs
append əˈpend **-s** -z **-ing** -ɪŋ **-ed** -ɪd
appendag|e əˈpen.dɪdʒ **-es** -ɪz
appendant əˈpen.dənt **-s** -s
appendectom|y ˌæp.enˈdek.tə.m|i **-ies** -iz
appendicitis əˌpen.dɪˈsaɪ.tɪs, -dəˈ-
appendicular ˌæp.enˈdɪk.jʊ.ləʳ, -ənˈ-, -ɪnˈ-, -jə- ⓤⓢ -ju.lɚ
append|ix əˈpen.d|ɪks **-ixes** -ɪk.sɪz **-ices** -ɪ.siːz
appercep|tion ˌæp.əˈsep.|ʃən ⓤⓢ -ɚˈ- **-tive** -tɪv
Apperley ˈæp.ə.li ⓤⓢ -ɚ-
appertain ˌæp.əˈteɪn ⓤⓢ -ɚˈ- **-s** -z **-ing** -ɪŋ **-ed** -d
appertinent əˈpɜː.tɪ.nənt, æpˈɜː- ⓤⓢ əˈpɝː.tən.ənt
appeten|ce ˈæp.ɪ.tən|ts **-cy** *-t*.si **-t** -t
appetite ˈæp.ɪ.taɪt, ˈ-ə- ⓤⓢ ˈ-ə- **-s** -s
appetizer, -iser ˈæp.ɪ.taɪ.zəʳ, ˈ-ə- ⓤⓢ -ə.taɪ.zɚ **-s** -z
appetizing, -isi- ˈæp.ɪ.taɪ.zɪŋ, ˈ-ə- ⓤⓢ ˈ-ə- **-ly** -li
Appi|an ˈæp.i|.ən **-us** -əs
applaud əˈplɔːd ⓤⓢ -ˈplɑːd, -ˈplɔːd **-s** -z **-ing/ly** -ɪŋ/li **-ed** -ɪd **-er/s** -əʳ/z, -ɚ/z
applause əˈplɔːz ⓤⓢ -ˈplɑːz, -ˈplɔːz

apple 'æp.l̩ **-s** -z **'apple ˌblossom** ; **'apple ˌbutter; ˌapple 'sauce** Ⓤⓢ **'apple ˌsauce; 'apple ˌtree; the ˌapple of one's 'eye**
Appleby 'æp.l̩.bi
apple-cart 'æp.l̩.kɑːt Ⓤⓢ -kɑːrt
Appledore 'æp.l̩.dɔːʳ Ⓤⓢ -dɔːr
Appleford 'æp.l̩.fəd Ⓤⓢ -fɚd
Applegate 'æp.l̩.geɪt, -gɪt
applejack 'æp.l̩.dʒæk
apple-pie ˌæp.l̩'paɪ **-s** -z *stress shift, see compounds:* **ˌapple-pie 'bed** ; **in ˌapple-pie 'order**
Appleseed 'æp.l̩.siːd
Appleton 'æp.l̩.tən Ⓤⓢ -t̬ən
appliable ə'plaɪ.ə.bl̩ **-ness** -nəs, -nɪs
applianc|e ə'plaɪ.ənts **-es** -ɪz
applicability ˌæp.lɪ.kə'bɪl.ə.ti, əˌplɪk-, -ɪ.ti Ⓤⓢ -ə.t̬i
applicab|le ə'plɪk.ə.bl|, 'æp.lɪ- **-ly** -li **-leness** -l̩.nəs, -nɪs
applicant 'æp.lɪ.kənt, -lə- **-s** -s
applicate 'æp.lɪ.kət, -lə-, -kɪt, -keɪt
application ˌæp.lɪ'keɪ.ʃən, -lə'- **-s** -z
applicator 'æp.lɪ.keɪ.təʳ, -lə- Ⓤⓢ -t̬ɚ **-s** -z
appliqué æp'liː.keɪ, ə'pliː-; 'æp.lɪ.keɪ Ⓤⓢ 'æp.lə.keɪ, -lɪ- **-s** -z
appl|y ə'pl|aɪ **-ies** -aɪz **-ying** -aɪ.ɪŋ **-ied** -aɪd
appoggiatura əˌpɒdʒ.ə'tʊə.rə, -i.ə'-, -'tjʊə- Ⓤⓢ əˌpɑː.dʒə'tʊr.ə **-s** -z
ap|point ə|'pɔɪnt **-points** -'pɔɪnts **-pointing** -'pɔɪn.tɪŋ Ⓤⓢ -'pɔɪn.t̬ɪŋ **-pointed** -'pɔɪn.tɪd Ⓤⓢ -'pɔɪn.t̬ɪd
appointee əˌpɔɪn'tiː, ˌæp.ɔɪn'- **-s** -z
appointive ə'pɔɪn.tɪv Ⓤⓢ -t̬ɪv
appointment ə'pɔɪnt.mənt **-s** -s
Appomattox ˌæp.ə'mæt.əks Ⓤⓢ -'mæt̬-
ap|port ə|'pɔːt Ⓤⓢ -'pɔːrt **-ports** -'pɔːts Ⓤⓢ -'pɔːrts **-porting** -'pɔː.tɪŋ Ⓤⓢ -'pɔːr.t̬ɪŋ **-ported** -'pɔː.tɪd Ⓤⓢ -'pɔːr.t̬ɪd
apportion ə'pɔː.ʃən Ⓤⓢ -'pɔːr- **-s** -z **-ing** -ɪŋ **-ed** -d **-ment/s** -mənt/s
appos|e ə'pəʊz, æp'əʊz Ⓤⓢ ə'poʊz **-es** -ɪz **-ing** -ɪŋ **-ed** -d
apposite 'æp.ə.zɪt, -zaɪt Ⓤⓢ -zɪt **-ly** -li **-ness** -nəs, -nɪs
apposition ˌæp.ə'zɪʃ.ən **-s** -z
appositional ˌæp.ə'zɪʃ.ən.əl
appraisal ə'preɪ.zəl **-s** -z
apprais|e ə'preɪz **-es** -ɪz **-ing** -ɪŋ **-ed** -d **-er/s** -əʳ/z Ⓤⓢ -ɚ/s **-able** -ə.bl̩
appraisement ə'preɪz.mənt **-s** -s
appreciab|le ə'priː.ʃə.bl|, -ʃi.ə-, -si.ə- Ⓤⓢ '-ʃə-, '-ʃi.ə- **-ly** -li
appreci|ate ə'priː.ʃi|.eɪt, -si- Ⓤⓢ -ʃi- **-ates** -eɪts **-ating/ly** -eɪ.tɪŋ/li Ⓤⓢ -eɪ.t̬ɪŋ/li **-ated** -eɪ.tɪd Ⓤⓢ -eɪ.t̬ɪd **-ator/s** -eɪ.təʳ/z Ⓤⓢ -eɪ.t̬ɚ/z
appreciation əˌpriː.ʃi'eɪ.ʃən, -si'- Ⓤⓢ -ʃi'- **-s** -z
appreciative ə'priː.ʃi.ə.tɪv, -si-, -eɪ.tɪv, '-ʃə.tɪv Ⓤⓢ -'priː.ʃə.t̬ɪv, '-ʃi.ə-, -eɪ- **-ly** -li **-ness** -nəs, -nɪs
appreciatory ə'priː.ʃi.ə.təʳr.i, -ʃi.eɪ-, -si.ə- Ⓤⓢ '-ʃə.tɔːr-, '-ʃi.ə-
apprehend ˌæp.rɪ'hend, -rə'- **-s** -z **-ing** -ɪŋ **-ed** -ɪd
apprehensibility ˌæp.rɪˌhent.sɪ'bɪl.ə.ti, -rə-, -sə'-, -ɪ.ti Ⓤⓢ -ə.t̬i
apprehensible ˌæp.rɪ'hent.sɪ.bl̩, -rə'-, -sə-
apprehension ˌæp.rɪ'hen.tʃən, -rə'- Ⓤⓢ -'hent.ʃən **-s** -z
apprehensive ˌæp.rɪ'hent.sɪv, -rə'- **-ly** -li **-ness** -nəs, -nɪs
apprentic|e ə'pren.tɪs Ⓤⓢ -t̬ɪs **-es** -ɪz **-ing** -ɪŋ **-ed** -t
apprenticeship ə'pren.tɪ.ʃɪp, -tɪs- Ⓤⓢ -t̬əs.ʃɪp, -t̬ə- **-s** -s
appris|e, -iz|e ə'praɪz **-es** -ɪz **-ing** -ɪŋ **-ed** -d **-er/s** -əʳ/z Ⓤⓢ -ɚ/z
appro 'æp.rəʊ Ⓤⓢ -roʊ
approach ə'prəʊtʃ Ⓤⓢ -'proʊtʃ **-es** -ɪz **-ing** -ɪŋ **-ed** -t
approachability əˌprəʊ.tʃə'bɪl.ə.ti, -ɪ.ti Ⓤⓢ -ˌproʊ.tʃə'bɪl.ə.t̬i
approachable ə'prəʊ.tʃə.bl̩ Ⓤⓢ -'proʊ-
appro|bate 'æp.rəʊ|.beɪt Ⓤⓢ -rə- **-bates** -beɪts **-bating** -beɪ.tɪŋ Ⓤⓢ -beɪ.t̬ɪŋ **-bated** -beɪ.tɪd Ⓤⓢ -beɪ.t̬ɪd **-bative** -beɪ.tɪv Ⓤⓢ -beɪ.t̬ɪv
approbation ˌæp.rəʊ'beɪ.ʃən, Ⓤⓢ -rə'-, -roʊ'- **-s** -z
approbatory ˌæp.rəʊ'beɪ.təʳr.i Ⓤⓢ ə'proʊ.bə.tɔːr-
appropriate *(adj.)* ə'prəʊ.pri.ət, -ɪt Ⓤⓢ -'proʊ- **-ly** -li **-ness** -nəs, -nɪs
appropri|ate *(v.)* ə'prəʊ.pri|.eɪt Ⓤⓢ -'proʊ- **-ates** -eɪts **-ating** -eɪ.tɪŋ Ⓤⓢ -eɪ.t̬ɪŋ **-ated** -eɪ.tɪd Ⓤⓢ -eɪ.t̬ɪd **-ator/s** -eɪ.təʳ/z Ⓤⓢ -eɪ.t̬ɚ/z
appropriation əˌprəʊ.pri'eɪ.ʃən Ⓤⓢ -ˌproʊ- **-s** -z
approval ə'pruː.vəl **-s** -z
approv|e ə'pruːv **-es** -z **-ing/ly** -ɪŋ/li **-ed** -d **-er/s** -əʳ/z Ⓤⓢ -ɚ/z **-able** -ə.bl̩
approx *(abbrev. for* **approximate/ly***)* ə'prɒk.sɪ.mət/li, -sə-, -mɪt/li Ⓤⓢ -'prɑːk-
approximant ə'prɒk.sɪ.mənt, -sə- Ⓤⓢ -'prɑːk- **-s** -s
approximate *(adj.)* ə'prɒk.sɪ.mət, -sə-, -mɪt Ⓤⓢ -'prɑːk- **-ly** -li
approxi|mate *(v.)* ə'prɒk.sɪ|.meɪt, -sə- Ⓤⓢ -'prɑːk- **-mates** -meɪts **-mating** -meɪ.tɪŋ Ⓤⓢ -meɪ.t̬ɪŋ **-mated** -meɪ.tɪd Ⓤⓢ -meɪ.t̬ɪd
approximation əˌprɒk.sɪ'meɪ.ʃən, -sə'- Ⓤⓢ -ˌprɑːk- **-s** -z
approximative ə'prɒk.sɪ.mə.tɪv, -sə- Ⓤⓢ -'prɑːk.sə.mə.t̬ɪv
appui æp'wiː, ə'pwiː
appuls|e æp'ʌls, ə'pʌls, 'æp.ʌls **-es** -ɪz
appurtenan|ce ə'pɜː.tɪ.nən|ts, -tən.ən|ts Ⓤⓢ -'pɜːr.tən- **-ces** -t.sɪz **-t** -t
APR ˌeɪ.pi'ɑːʳ Ⓤⓢ -'ɑːr
Apr. *(abbrev. for* **April***)* 'eɪ.prəl, -prɪl
après 'æp.reɪ Ⓤⓢ ˌɑː'preɪ, ˌæp'reɪ
après-ski ˌæp.reɪ'skiː Ⓤⓢ ˌɑː.preɪ'-, ˌæp.reɪ'- *stress shift:* **ˌaprès-ski 'drinks**
apricot 'eɪ.prɪ.kɒt Ⓤⓢ -kɑːt, 'æp.rɪ- **-s** -s
April 'eɪ.prəl, -prɪl **-s** -z **ˌApril 'Fools' ˌDay**
a priori ˌeɪ.praɪ'ɔː.raɪ, ˌɑː.priː'ɔː.ri Ⓤⓢ ˌɑː.priː'ɔːr.aɪ, ˌeɪ-, -i
apriority ˌeɪ.praɪ'ɒr.ə.ti, -ɪ.ti Ⓤⓢ -'ɔːr.ə.t̬i
apron 'eɪ.prən **-s** -z **-ed** -d **'apron ˌstrings**
apropos ˌæp.rə'pəʊ Ⓤⓢ -'poʊ
aps|e æps **-es** -ɪz
apsidal 'æp.sɪ.dəl
Apsley 'æp.sli
apt æpt **-er** -əʳ Ⓤⓢ -ɚ **-est** -əst, -ɪst **-ly** -li **-ness** -nəs, -nɪs
apter|al 'æp.təʳr|.əl **-ous** -əs
apteryx 'æp.təʳr.ɪks **-es** -ɪz
aptitude 'æp.tɪ.tjuːd, -tə-, -tʃuːd Ⓤⓢ -tuːd, -tjuːd **-s** -z
aptitudinal ˌæp.tɪ'tjuː.dɪ.nəl, -tə'-, -'tʃuː- Ⓤⓢ -'tuː.dən.əl, -'tjuː- **-ly** -li
Apuli|a ə'pjuː.li|.ə **-an/s** -ən/z
apyretic ˌæp.aɪə'ret.ɪk, ˌeɪ.paɪə'-, -paɪ.ɪ'- Ⓤⓢ -paɪ'ret̬-
aquacultural ˌæk.wə'kʌl.tʃəʳr.əl Ⓤⓢ ˌɑː.kwə'-, ˌæk.wə'-
aquaculture 'æk.wəˌkʌl.tʃəʳ Ⓤⓢ 'ɑː.kwəˌkʌl.tʃɚ, 'æk.wəˌ-
aqua fortis ˌæk.wə'fɔː.tɪs Ⓤⓢ ˌɑː.kwə'fɔːr.t̬ɪs, ˌæk.wə'-
aquamarine ˌæk.wə.mə'riːn, 'æk.wə.mə.riːn Ⓤⓢ ˌɑː.kwə.mə'riːn, ˌæk.wə- **-s** -z
aquaplan|e 'æk.wə.pleɪn Ⓤⓢ 'ɑː.kwə-, 'æk.wə- **-es** -z **-ing** -ɪŋ **-ed** -d
aqua regia ˌæk.wə'riː.dʒi.ə Ⓤⓢ ˌɑː.kwə'-, ˌæk.wə'-
aquarell|e ˌæk.wə'rel Ⓤⓢ ˌɑː.kwə'-, ˌæk.wə'- **-es** -z **-ist/s** -ɪst/s
aquarist 'æk.wə.rɪst Ⓤⓢ ə'kwer.ɪst **-s** -s
aquari|um ə'kweə.ri.|əm Ⓤⓢ -'kwer.i- **-ums** -əmz **-a** -ə
Aquari|us ə'kweə.ri.|əs Ⓤⓢ -'kwer.i- **-an/s** -ən/z
Aquascutum® ˌæk.wə'skjuː.təm Ⓤⓢ ˌɑː.kwə'skuː.t̬əm, ˌæk.wə'-

aquatic ə'kwæt.ɪk, -'kwɒt- Ⓤⓢ -'kwæṭ-, -'kwɑː.ṭɪk **-s** -s **-ally** -əl.i, -li
aquatint 'æk.wə.tɪnt Ⓤⓢ 'ɑː.kwə-, 'æk.wə- **-s** -s
aquatube 'æk.wə.tjuːb, -tʃuːb Ⓤⓢ 'ɑː.kwə.tuːb, 'æk.wə-, -tjuːb **-s** -z
aquavit 'æk.wə.vɪt, -viːt Ⓤⓢ 'ɑː.kwə.viːt
aqua vitae ˌæk.wə'viː.taɪ, -'vaɪ.tiː Ⓤⓢ ˌɑː.kwə'vaɪ.ṭiː, ˌæk.wə'-
aqueduct 'æk.wɪ.dʌkt, -wə- **-s** -s
aqueous 'eɪ.kwi.əs, 'æk.wi- **-ly** -li
aquifer 'æk.wɪ.fəʳ, -wə.fəʳ Ⓤⓢ 'ɑː.kwə.fɚ, æk.wə- **-s** -z
Aquila 'æk.wɪ.lə, -wə-; ə'kwɪl.ə
aquilegia ˌæk.wɪ.liː.dʒi.ə, -wə-, -'liː.dʒə **-s** -z
aquiline 'æk.wɪ.laɪn, -wə- Ⓤⓢ -lən
Aquinas ə'kwaɪ.nəs, æk'waɪ-, -næs
Aquino ə'kiː.nəʊ Ⓤⓢ -noʊ
Aquitaine ˌæk.wɪ'teɪn, -wə'teɪn, '---
Aquitania ˌæk.wɪ'teɪ.ni.ə
aquiver ə'kwɪv.əʳ Ⓤⓢ -ɚ
ar- ə'r-; 'ær- Ⓤⓢ ə'r-; 'er-, 'ær-
Note: Prefix. Examples include **arrogate** /'ær.əʊ.geɪt Ⓤⓢ 'er.ə-/, in which it is stressed, and **array** /ə'reɪ/, where it is unstressed.
-ar -əʳ, -ɑːʳ Ⓤⓢ -ɚ, -ɑːr
Note: Suffix. Normally pronounced /-əʳ Ⓤⓢ -ɚ/, e.g. **molecular** /məʊ'lek.jə.ləʳ Ⓤⓢ moʊ'lek.juː.lɚ/, but in some cases /-ɑːʳ Ⓤⓢ -ɑːr/, e.g. **sonar** /'səʊ.nɑːʳ Ⓤⓢ 'soʊ.nɑːr/.
Arab 'ær.əb Ⓤⓢ 'er-, 'ær- **-s** -z
Arabella ˌær.ə'bel.ə Ⓤⓢ ˌer-, ˌær-
arabesque ˌær.ə'besk Ⓤⓢ ˌer-, ˌær- **-s** -s **-d** -t
Arabi|a ə'reɪ.bi|.ə **-an/s** -ən/z
Arabic *of Arabia:* 'ær.ə.bɪk Ⓤⓢ 'er-, 'ær- *name of ship:* 'ær.ə.bɪk; ə'ræb- Ⓤⓢ 'er.ə-, 'ær-; ə'ræb-
arabis 'ær.ə.bɪs Ⓤⓢ 'er-, 'ær-
Arabist 'ær.ə.bɪst Ⓤⓢ 'er-, 'ær- **-s** -s
arable 'ær.ə.bl̩ Ⓤⓢ 'er-, 'ær-
Araby 'ær.ə.bi Ⓤⓢ 'er-, 'ær-
Aracaju ˌær.ə.kæʒ'uː Ⓤⓢ ɑːˌrɑː.kə'ʒuː
Arachne ə'ræk.ni
arachnid ə'ræk.nɪd **-a** -ə **-s** -z
arachnoid ə'ræk.nɔɪd **-s** -z
arachnologist ˌær.æk'nɒl.ə.dʒɪst, -ək'- Ⓤⓢ ˌer.ək'nɑː.lə-, ˌær- **-s** -s
arachnopho|bia əˌræk.nəʊ'fəʊ.|bi.ə Ⓤⓢ -nə'foʊ-, -noʊ'- **-bic** -bɪk
Arafat 'ær.ə.fæt Ⓤⓢ 'er-, 'ær-
Arafura ˌær.ə'fʊə.rə Ⓤⓢ ˌɑːr.ə'fʊr.ə
Aragon 'ær.ə.gən Ⓤⓢ 'er.ə.gɑːn, 'ær-, -gən
aragonite ə'ræg.ən.aɪt, 'ær.ə.gən- Ⓤⓢ ə'ræg.ən-; 'er.ə.gən-, 'ær-
Aral 'ɑː.rəl, 'ær.əl, -æl Ⓤⓢ 'er.əl, 'ær-
Araldite® 'ær.əl.daɪt Ⓤⓢ 'er-, 'ær-
Aram *biblical name:* 'eə.ræm, -rəm Ⓤⓢ 'er.æm, 'ær-, 'eɪ.rəm, 'ɑːr.əm *surname:* 'eə.rəm Ⓤⓢ 'er.əm, 'ær-
Aramaean ˌær.ə'miː.ən Ⓤⓢ ˌer-, ˌær-
Arama|ic ˌær.ə'meɪ|.ɪk Ⓤⓢ ˌer-, ˌær- **-ism** -ɪ.zəm
Aramean ˌær.ə'miː.ən Ⓤⓢ ˌer-, ˌær- **-s** -z
aramid 'ær.ə.mɪd Ⓤⓢ 'er-, 'ær- **-s** -z
Aramite 'ær.ə.maɪt Ⓤⓢ 'er-, 'ær- **-s** -s
Aran 'ær.ən Ⓤⓢ 'er-, 'ær-
Arapaho ə'ræp.ə.həʊ Ⓤⓢ -hoʊ
Ararat 'ær.ə.ræt Ⓤⓢ 'er-, 'ær-
Araucani|a ˌær.ɔː'keɪ.ni|.ə Ⓤⓢ ˌer-, ˌær-, -ɑː'-; əˌraʊ.kɑː'niː- **-an/s** -ən/z
araucaria ˌær.ɔː'keə.ri.ə Ⓤⓢ ˌer.ɔː'ker.i-, ˌær-, -ɑː'- **-s** -z
Arawak 'ær.ə.wæk, -wɑːk Ⓤⓢ 'ɑːr.ə.wɑːk; 'ær.ə.wæk, 'er- **-s** -s
Arber 'ɑː.bəʳ Ⓤⓢ 'ɑːr.bɚ
Arberry 'ɑː.bər.i Ⓤⓢ 'ɑːr.ber-
Arbil 'ɑː.bɪl Ⓤⓢ 'ɑːr-
arbiter 'ɑː.bɪ.təʳ Ⓤⓢ 'ɑːr.bɪ.ṭɚ **-s** -z
arbitrage *arbitration:* 'ɑː.bɪ.trɪdʒ Ⓤⓢ 'ɑːr- *of stocks, etc.:* ˌɑː.bɪ'trɑːʒ, 'ɑː.bɪ.trɪdʒ Ⓤⓢ 'ɑːr.bɪ.trɑːʒ
arbitrageur ˌɑː.bɪ.trɑː'ʒɜːʳ Ⓤⓢ 'ɑːr.bɪ.trɑː.ʒɚ **-s** -z
arbitrament ɑː'bɪt.rə.mənt Ⓤⓢ ɑːr- **-s** -s
arbitrarily ˌɑː.bɪ'treə.rəl.i, 'ɑː.bɪ.trər.əl.i Ⓤⓢ ˌɑːr.bə'trer.əl-
arbitrar|y 'ɑː.bɪ.trər|.i Ⓤⓢ 'ɑːr.bə.trer- **-iness** -ɪ.nəs, -ɪ.nɪs
arbi|trate 'ɑː.bɪ|.treɪt Ⓤⓢ 'ɑːr.bə|.treɪt **-trates** -treɪts **-trating** -treɪ.tɪŋ Ⓤⓢ -treɪ.ṭɪŋ **-trated** -treɪ.tɪd Ⓤⓢ -treɪ.ṭɪd
arbitration ˌɑː.bɪ'treɪ.ʃən Ⓤⓢ ˌɑːr.bə'- **-s** -z
arbitrator 'ɑː.bɪ.treɪ.təʳ Ⓤⓢ 'ɑːr.bə- **-s** -z
Arblay 'ɑː.bleɪ Ⓤⓢ 'ɑːr-
arbor *tree:* 'ɑː.bɔːʳ, -bəʳ Ⓤⓢ 'ɑːr.bɚ *axle, shaft:* 'ɑː.bəʳ Ⓤⓢ 'ɑːr.bɚ **-s** -z
Arbor 'ɑː.bəʳ Ⓤⓢ 'ɑːr.bɚ **'Arbor ˌDay**
arboraceous ˌɑː.bər'eɪ.ʃəs, -bɔː'reɪ- Ⓤⓢ ˌɑːr.bə'reɪ-, -bɔː'-
arbore|al ɑː'bɔː.ri|.əl Ⓤⓢ ɑːr'bɔːr.i- **-ous** -əs
arborescen|ce ˌɑː.bər'es.ən|ts, -bɔː'res- Ⓤⓢ ˌɑːr.bə'res-, -bɔː'- **-t** -t
arbore|tum ˌɑː.bər'iː.|təm, -bɔː'riː- Ⓤⓢ ˌɑːr.bə'riː-, -bɔː'- **-tums** -təmz Ⓤⓢ -ṭəmz **-ta** -tə Ⓤⓢ -ṭə
arboriculture 'ɑː.bər.ɪˌkʌl.tʃəʳ, -bɔː-; ɑː'bɒr.ɪˌ- Ⓤⓢ 'ɑːr.bɚ.ɪˌkʌl.tʃɚ; ɑːr'bɔːr-
arborization, -isa- ˌɑː.bər.aɪ'zeɪ.ʃən, -bɔː.raɪ'-, -rɪ'- Ⓤⓢ ˌɑːr.bɚ.ɪ'-, -bɔːr-
arboriz|e, -is|e 'ɑː.bər.aɪz Ⓤⓢ 'ɑːr.bə.raɪz **-es** -ɪz **-ing** -ɪŋ **-ed** -d
arbor-vitae ˌɑː.bə'viː.taɪ, -bɔː-, -'vaɪ-, -tiː Ⓤⓢ ˌɑːr.bɚ'vaɪ.tiː, -'viː- **-s** -z
arbour 'ɑː.bəʳ Ⓤⓢ 'ɑːr.bɚ **-s** -z
Arbroath ɑː'brəʊθ Ⓤⓢ ɑːr'broʊθ
Arbus 'ɑː.bəs Ⓤⓢ 'ɑːr-
Arbuthnot(t) ɑː'bʌθ.nət, ə'bʌθ- Ⓤⓢ ɑːr-, -nɑːt
arbutus ɑː'bjuː.təs Ⓤⓢ ɑːr'bjuː.ṭəs **-es** -ɪz
arc (A) ɑːk Ⓤⓢ ɑːrk **-s** -s **-(k)ing** -ɪŋ **-(k)ed** -t **'arc ˌlamp; 'arc ˌlight**
arcade ɑː'keɪd Ⓤⓢ ɑːr- **-s** -z
Arcadi|a ɑː'keɪ.di|.ə Ⓤⓢ ɑːr- **-an/s** -ən/z
Arcady 'ɑː.kə.di Ⓤⓢ 'ɑːr-
arcane ɑː'keɪn Ⓤⓢ ɑːr-
arcan|um ɑː'keɪ.n|əm Ⓤⓢ ɑːr- **-a** -ə
arch- ɑːtʃ-, ɑːk- Ⓤⓢ ɑːrtʃ-, ɑːrk-
Note: Prefix. Words containing **arch-** normally carry secondary stress on the first syllable, e.g. **archbishop** /ˌɑːtʃ'bɪʃ.əp Ⓤⓢ ˌɑːrtʃ-/, with the obvious exception of **archangel**.
arch (*adj.*) ɑːtʃ Ⓤⓢ ɑːrtʃ **-est** -əst, -ɪst **-ly** -li **-ness** -nəs, -nɪs
arch (*n. v.*) ɑːtʃ Ⓤⓢ ɑːrtʃ **-es** -ɪz **-ing** -ɪŋ **-ed** -t
-arch -ɑːk, -ək Ⓤⓢ -ɑːrk, -ɚk
Note: Suffix. Normally /-ɑːk Ⓤⓢ -ɑːrk/, e.g. **oligarch** /'ɒl.ɪ.gɑːk Ⓤⓢ 'ɑː.lɪ.gɑːrk/, but /-ək, -ɚk/ is preferred in some words, e.g. **monarch** /'mɒn.ək Ⓤⓢ 'mɑː.nɚk -nɑːrk/.
archaean (A) ɑː'kiː.ən Ⓤⓢ ɑːr-
archaeo- ˌɑː.ki.əʊ-; ˌɑː.ki'ɒ- Ⓤⓢ ˌɑːr.ki.oʊ-, -ə-; ˌɑːr.ki'ɑː-
Note: Prefix. Words containing **archaeo-** normally carry secondary stress on the first syllable, and in the items which follow have primary stress on the second syllable, e.g. **archaeology** /ˌɑː.ki'ɒl.ə.dʒi Ⓤⓢ ˌɑːr.ki'ɑː.lə-/, with the exception of **archaeological**.
archaeologic|al ˌɑː.ki.ə'lɒdʒ.ɪ.k|əl Ⓤⓢ ˌɑːr.ki.ə'lɑː.dʒɪ- **-ally** -əl.i, -i
archaeologist ˌɑː.ki'ɒl.ə.dʒɪst Ⓤⓢ ˌɑːr.ki'ɑː.lə- **-s** -s
archaeology ˌɑː.ki'ɒl.ə.dʒi Ⓤⓢ ˌɑːr.ki'ɑː.lə-
archaeopteryx ˌɑː.ki'ɒp.tər.ɪks Ⓤⓢ ˌɑːr.ki'ɑːp- **-es** -ɪz
archaic ɑː'keɪ.ɪk Ⓤⓢ ɑːr- **-ally** -əl.i, -li
archaism ɑː'keɪ.ɪ.zəm, 'ɑː.keɪ- Ⓤⓢ 'ɑːr.ki-, -keɪ- **-s** -z
archangel ɑː'keɪn.dʒəl, 'ɑː.keɪn- Ⓤⓢ 'ɑːr.keɪn- **-s** -z
Archangel 'ɑːˌkeɪn.dʒəl, ˌɑː'keɪn- Ⓤⓢ 'ɑːr.keɪn-
archbishop ˌɑːtʃ'bɪʃ.əp Ⓤⓢ ˌɑːrtʃ- **-s** -s *stress shift:* ˌArchbishop of 'Canterbury

archbishopric ˌɑːtʃˈbɪʃ.ə.prɪk US ˌɑːrtʃ- **-s** -s
Archbold ˈɑːtʃ.bəʊld US ˈɑːrtʃ.boʊld
Archdale ˈɑːtʃ.deɪl US ˈɑːrtʃ-
archdeacon ˌɑːtʃˈdiː.kən US ˌɑːrtʃ- **-s** -z
archdeaconr|y ˌɑːtʃˈdiː.kᵊn.r|i US ˌɑːrtʃ- **-ies** -iz
archdioces|e ˌɑːtʃˈdaɪə.sɪs US ˌɑːrtʃ- **-es** -ɪz
archducal ˌɑːtʃˈdjuː.kᵊl US ˌɑːrtʃˈduː-, -ˈdjuː-
archduchess ˌɑːtʃˈdʌtʃ.ɪs, -əs US ˌɑːrtʃ- **-es** -ɪz
archduch|y ˌɑːtʃˈdʌtʃ.|i US ˌɑːrtʃ- **-ies** -iz
archduke ˌɑːtʃˈdjuːk US ˌɑːrtʃˈduːk, -ˈdjuːk **-s** -s *stress shift:* ˌArchduke ˈFerdinand
archdukedom ˌɑːtʃˈdjuːk.dəm US ˌɑːrtʃˈduːk-, -ˈdjuːk **-s** -z
Archelaus ˌɑː.kɪˈleɪ.əs, -kəˈ- US ˌɑːr-
archenem|y ˌɑːtʃˈen.ɪ.m|i, -ə.mi US ˌɑːrtʃ- **-ies** -iz
archeo- ˌɑː.ki.əʊ-; ˌɑː.kiˈɒ- US ˌɑːr.ki.oʊ-, -ə-; ˌɑːr.kiˈɑː-
Note: Prefix. See **archaeo-**.
archeologic|al ˌɑː.ki.əˈlɒdʒ.ɪ.k|ᵊl US ˌɑr.ki.əˈlɑː.dʒɪ- **-ally** -ᵊl.i, -li
archeologist ˌɑː.kiˈɒl.ə.dʒɪst US ˌɑːr.kiˈɑː.lə- **-s** -s
archeology ˌɑː.kiˈɒl.ə.dʒi US ˌɑːr.kiˈɑː.lə-
archeopteryx ˌɑː.kiˈɒp.tə.rɪks US ˌɑːr.kiˈɑːp- **-es** -ɪz
archer (A) ˈɑː.tʃəʳ US ˈɑːr.tʃɚ **-s** -z
archeress ˈɑː.tʃᵊr.ɪs, -es US ˈɑːr.tʃɚ.əs **-es** -ɪz
archery ˈɑː.tʃᵊr.i US ˈɑːr-
archetypal ˌɑː.kɪˈtaɪ.pᵊl, ˈɑː.kɪˌtaɪ- US ˌɑːr.kɪˈtaɪ-
archetype ˈɑː.kɪ.taɪp US ˈɑːr- **-s** -s
archetypic|al ˌɑː.kɪˈtɪp.ɪ.k|ᵊl US ˌɑːr.kəˈ- **-ally** -ᵊl.i, -li *stress shift:* ˌarchetypical ˈincident
archfiend ˌɑːtʃˈfiːnd US ˌɑːrtʃ- **-s** -z
arch-heretic ˌɑːtʃˈher.ə.tɪk, ˈ-ɪ- US ˌɑːrtʃˈher.ə- **-s** -s
archi- ɑː.tʃi- US ɑːr.tʃi-
Archibald ˈɑː.tʃɪ.bɔːld, -bᵊld US ˈɑːr.tʃə.bɔːld, -bɑːld
-archic -ɑː.kɪk US -ɑːr.kɪk
Archie ˈɑː.tʃi US ˈɑːr-
Archilochus ɑːˈkɪl.ə.kəs US ɑːr-
archimandrite ˌɑː.kɪˈmæn.draɪt US ˌɑːr.kəˈ- **-s** -s
archimedean ˌɑː.kɪˈmiː.di.ən, -miːˈdiː.ən US ˌɑːr.kə- *stress shift:* ˌarchimedean ˈscrew
Archimedes ˌɑː.kɪˈmiː.diːz US ˌɑːr.kəˈ-
archipelago ˌɑː.kɪˈpel.əg.əʊ US ˌɑːr.kəˈpel.ə.goʊ **-(e)s** -z
archiphoneme ˌɑː.kɪˈfəʊ.niːm US ˈɑːr.kɪˌfoʊ-, ˌɑːr.kɪˈfo- **-s** -z
architect ˈɑː.kɪ.tekt US ˈɑːr.kə- **-s** -s
architectonic ˌɑː.kɪ.tekˈtɒn.ɪk US ˌɑːr.kə.tekˈtɑː.nɪk **-s** -s
architectural ˌɑː.kɪˈtek.tʃᵊr.ᵊl US ˌɑːr.kəˈ- **-ly** -i
architecture ˈɑː.kɪ.tek.tʃəʳ US ˈɑːr.kə.tek.tʃɚ
architrave ˈɑː.kɪ.treɪv US ˈɑːr.kə- **-s** -z **-d** -d
archival ˌɑːˈkaɪ.vᵊl US ˌɑːr-
archive ˈɑː.kaɪv US ˈɑːr- **-s** -z
archivist ˈɑː.kɪ.vɪst US ˈɑːr.kaɪ-, -kə- **-s** -s
archon ˈɑː.kən, -kɒn US ˈɑːr.kɑːn **-s** -z
arch-prelate ˌɑːtʃˈprel.ət, -ɪt US ˌɑːrtʃ- **-s** -s
arch-priest ˌɑːtʃˈpriːst US ˌɑːrtʃ- **-s** -s *stress shift:* ˌarch-priest's ˈceremony
arch-traitor ˌɑːtʃˈtreɪ.təʳ US ˌɑːrtʃˈtreɪ.t̬ɚ **-s** -z *stress shift:* ˌarch-traitor ˈclique
archway (A) ˈɑːtʃ.weɪ US ˈɑːrtʃ- **-s** -z
archwise ˈɑːtʃ.waɪz US ˈɑːrtʃ-
Archytas ɑːˈkaɪ.təs, -tæs US ɑːrˈkaɪ.t̬əs
Arcite ˈɑː.saɪt US ˈɑːr-
Arcot ˈɑː.kɒt US ˈɑːr.kɑːt
arctic (A) ˈɑːk.tɪk US ˈɑːrk-; ˈɑːr.t̬ɪk ˌ**Arctic ˈCircle**; ˌ**Arctic ˈOcean**
Arcturus ɑːkˈtjʊə.rəs US ɑːrkˈtʊr.əs
arcuate ˈɑː.kju.ət, -eɪt, -ɪt US ˈɑːr-
arcuated ˈɑː.kju.eɪ.tɪd US ˈɑːr.kju.eɪ.t̬ɪd
Arcy ˈɑː.si US ˈɑːr-
-ard -əd, -ɑːd US -ɚd, -ɑːrd
Note: Suffix. In frequently occurring words, normally /-əd US -ɚd/, e.g. **wizard** /ˈwɪz.əd US -ɚd/, but may also be /-ɑːd US -ɑːrd/, e.g. **dullard** /ˈdʌl.əd, -ɑːd US -ɚd/. See individual items.
Ardagh ˈɑː.də, -dɑː US ˈɑːr-
Ardèche ɑːˈdeʃ US ɑːr-
Ardee ɑːˈdiː US ɑːr-
Arden ˈɑː.dᵊn US ˈɑːr-
ardency ˈɑː.dᵊnt.si US ˈɑːr-
Ardennes ɑːˈden, -denz US ɑːr-
ardent ˈɑː.dᵊnt US ˈɑːr- **-ly** -li
Arding ˈɑː.dɪŋ US ˈɑːr-
Ardingly ˈɑː.dɪŋ.laɪ, ˌ--ˈ- US ˈɑːr.dɪŋ-, ˌ--ˈ-
Ardleigh, Ardley ˈɑːd.li US ˈɑːrd-
Ardoch ˈɑː.dɒk, -dɒx US ˈɑːr.dɑːk
ardo(u)r ˈɑː.dəʳ US ˈɑːr.dɚ
Ardrishaig ɑːˈdrɪʃ.ɪg, -eɪg US ɑːr-
Ardrossan ɑːˈdrɒs.ᵊn US ɑːrˈdrɑː.sᵊn
Ards ɑːdz US ɑːrdz
Arduin ˈɑː.dwɪn US ˈɑːr-
arduous ˈɑː.dju.əs, -dʒu- US ˈɑːr.dʒu- **-ly** -li **-ness** -nəs, -nɪs
Ardwick ˈɑː.dwɪk US ˈɑːr-
are (*from* **be**) *strong form:* ɑːʳ US ɑːr *weak form:* əʳ US ɚ *occasional weak form before vowels:* r
Note: Weak form word. The strong form /ɑːʳ US ɑːr/ is used for emphasis (e.g. 'You **are** stupid.'), for contrast (e.g. 'You **are** rich, but you **aren't** handsome.') and in final position (e.g. 'Here you are.'). The weak form is usually /əʳ US ɚ/ (e.g. 'These are mine.' /ˌðiːz.əˈmaɪn US -ɚˈ-/; 'These are old.' /ˌðiːz.əʳˈəʊld US -ɚˈoʊld/), but when the weak form precedes a vowel, as in the last example, it often happens that the word is pronounced as a syllabic /r̩/ (e.g. /ˌðiːz. r̩ ˈəʊld US -ˈoʊld/).
are *surface measure:* ɑːʳ US ɑːr **-s** -z
area ˈeə.ri.ə US ˈer.i- **-s** -z ˈ**area** ˌ**code**
areca əˈriː.kə; ˈær.ɪ- US əˈriː.kə; ˈær.ɪ-, ˈer- **-s** -z
arena əˈriː.nə **-s** -z
Arendt ˈær.ənt, ˈɑː.rənt US ˈɑːr.ənt, ˈer-
aren't ɑːnt US ɑːrnt
areol|a əˈriː.ᵊl|.ə, ærˈiː- **-as** -əz **-ae** -iː
areometer ˌær.iˈɒm.ɪ.təʳ, ˌeə.riˈ-, ˈ-ə- US ˌer.iˈɑː.mə.t̬ɚ, ˌær- **-s** -z
areometry ˌær.iˈɒm.ɪ.tri, ˌeə.riˈ-, ˈ-ə- US ˌer.iˈɑː.mə-, ˌær-
Areopagite ˌær.iˈɒp.ə.gaɪt, -dʒaɪt US ˌer.iˈɑː.pə-, ˌær- **-s** -s
Areopagitic ˌær.i.ɒp.əˈdʒɪt.ɪk US ˌer.iˌɑː.pəˈ-, ˌær- **-a** -ə
Areopagus ˌær.iˈɒp.ə.gəs US ˌer.iˈɑː.pə-, ˌær-
Arequipa ˌær.ɪˈkiː.pə, -ekˈiː- US ˌɑː.rəˈkiː-, ˌer.əˈ-, ˌær-
Ares ˈeə.riːz US ˈer.iːz
arête ærˈet, əˈret
Aretha əˈriː.θə
Arethusa ˌær.ɪˈθjuː.zə, -eθˈjuː- US ˌɑːr.əˈθuː-
Arezzo ærˈet.səʊ, əˈret- US ɑːˈret.soʊ
Arfon ˈɑː.vᵊn, -vɒn US ˈɑːr-, -fᵊn
Argand ˈɑː.gænd, -gənd US ˌɑːrˈgɑːnd, -ˈgænd **-s** -z *stress shift, US only, see compound:* ˌ**Argand** ˈ**diagram**
argent (A) ˈɑː.dʒᵊnt US ˈɑːr-
Argentina ˌɑː.dʒᵊnˈtiː.nə, -dʒenˈ- US ˌɑːr-
argentine (A) ˈɑː.dʒᵊn.taɪn US ˈɑːr.dʒᵊn.taɪn, -tiːn, -tɪn
Argentinian ˌɑː.dʒᵊnˈtɪn.i.ən US ˌɑːr- **-s** -z
argillaceous ˌɑː.dʒɪˈleɪ.ʃəs US ˌɑːr.dʒəˈ-
Argive ˈɑː.gaɪv US ˈɑːr- **-s** -z
Argo ˈɑː.gəʊ US ˈɑːr.goʊ
argol ˈɑː.gɒl, -gᵊl US ˈɑːr.gɑːl, -gᵊl
Argolis ˈɑː.gᵊl.ɪs US ˈɑːr-

argon 'ɑː.gɒn, -gən ⓊⓈ 'ɑːr.gɑːn
Argonaut 'ɑː.gə.nɔːt ⓊⓈ 'ɑːr.gə.nɑːt, -nɔːt **-s** -s
Argonautic ˌɑː.gə'nɔː.tɪk ⓊⓈ ˌɑːr.gə'nɑː.t̬ɪk, -'nɔː-
Argos 'ɑː.gɒs ⓊⓈ 'ɑːr.gɑːs, -gəs
argos|y 'ɑː.gə.s|i ⓊⓈ 'ɑːr.gə.s|i **-ies** -iz
argot 'ɑː.gəʊ ⓊⓈ 'ɑːr.goʊ, -gət **-s** -z
arguab|le 'ɑːg.ju.ə.b|l̩ ⓊⓈ 'ɑːrg- **-ly** -li
argu|e 'ɑːg.juː ⓊⓈ 'ɑːrg- **-es** -z **-ing** -ɪŋ **-ed** -d **-er/s** -əʳ/z ⓊⓈ -ɚ/z
argument 'ɑːg.jə.mənt, -jʊ- ⓊⓈ 'ɑːrg.jə-, -jʊ- **-s** -s
argumental ˌɑːg.jə'men.tᵊl, -jʊ- ⓊⓈ ˌɑːrg.jə'men.t̬ᵊl, -jʊ-
argumentation ˌɑːg.jə.men'teɪ.ʃᵊn, -jʊ-, -mən- ⓊⓈ ˌɑːrg.jə-, -jʊ- **-s** -z
argumentative ˌɑːg.jə'men.tə.tɪv, -jʊ- ⓊⓈ ˌɑːrg.jə'men.t̬ə.t̬ɪv, -jʊ- **-ly** -li **-ness** -nəs, -nɪs
argus (A) 'ɑː.gəs ⓊⓈ 'ɑːr- **-es** -ɪz
argy-bargy ˌɑː.dʒi'bɑː.dʒi ⓊⓈ ˌɑːr.dʒi'bɑːr-
Argyle ɑː'gaɪl ⓊⓈ ɑːr-, '-- *stress shift:* ˌArgyle 'tartan
Argyllshire ɑː'gaɪl.ʃəʳ, -ˌʃɪəʳ ⓊⓈ ɑːr'gaɪl.ʃɚ, -ˌʃɪr
aria 'ɑː.ri.ə ⓊⓈ 'ɑːr.i- **-s** -z
Ariadne ˌær.i'æd.ni ⓊⓈ ˌær-, ˌer-
Arian 'eə.ri.ən ⓊⓈ 'er.i-, 'ær- **-s** -z **-ism** -ɪ.zᵊm
-arian -'eə.ri.ən ⓊⓈ -'er.i-, -'ær-
Note: Suffix. Always carries primary stress, e.g. **grammarian** /grə'meə.ri.ən ⓊⓈ -'mer.i-/.
arid 'ær.ɪd ⓊⓈ 'er-, 'ær- **-ly** -li **-ness** -nəs, -nɪs
aridity ær'ɪd.ə.ti, ə'rɪd-, -ɪ.ti ⓊⓈ er'ɪd.ə.t̬i, ær-
ariel (A) 'eə.ri.əl ⓊⓈ 'er.i- **-s** -z
Aries 'eə.riːz, -ri.iːz ⓊⓈ 'er.iːz
arietta ˌær.i'et.ə, ˌɑː.ri'- ⓊⓈ ˌɑːr.i'et̬-, ˌær.i'-, ˌer- **-s** -z
aright ə'raɪt
-arily -ᵊr.ə.li, -ɪ.li; -'er.ᵊl.i, -ɪ.li ⓊⓈ -er.ə.li, -ær-
Note: Suffix. The stress pattern of words containing **-arily** in British English is either unaffected by the affix or primary stress moves to the antepenultimate syllable, in which case it contains a full vowel, e.g. **momentarily** /'məʊ.mən.tᵊr.ᵊl.i, -ɪ.li; ˌməʊ.mən'ter-/. In American English, **-arily** normally has a full vowel, but the antepenultimate syllable may or may not take primary stress, e.g. **momentarily** /'moʊ.mən.ter.ᵊl.i, ˌmoʊ.mən'ter-/. See individual entries.
Arimathaea ˌær.ɪ.mə'θiː.ə ⓊⓈ ˌer.ə-, ˌær-
Arion ə'raɪən, ær'aɪən ⓊⓈ ə'raɪən
arioso ˌɑː.ri'əʊ.səʊ, ˌær.i'-, -zəʊ ⓊⓈ ˌɑːr.i'oʊ.soʊ
Ariosto ˌær.i'ɒs.təʊ ⓊⓈ ˌɑːr.i'ɑː.stoʊ, ˌer-, ˌær-, -'ɔː-, -'oʊ-
aris|e ə'raɪz **-es** -ɪz **-ing** -ɪŋ
arisen ə'rɪz.ᵊn
Aristaeus ˌær.ɪ'stiː.əs, -ə'- ⓊⓈ ˌer.ə'-, ˌær-
Aristarchus ˌær.ɪ'stɑː.kəs ⓊⓈ ˌer.ə'stɑːr-, ˌær-
Aristide ˌær.ɪ'stiːd ⓊⓈ ˌer-, ˌær-
Aristides ˌær.ɪ'staɪ.diːz ⓊⓈ ˌer.ə'-, ˌær-
aristo ə'rɪs.təʊ ⓊⓈ -toʊ **-s** -z
aristocrac|y ˌær.ɪ'stɒk.rə.s|i ⓊⓈ ˌer.ə'stɑː.krə-, ˌær- **-ies** -iz
aristocrat 'ær.ɪ.stə.kræt; ə'rɪs.tə- ⓊⓈ ə'rɪs-; 'er.ə.stə-, 'ær- **-s** -s
aristocratic ˌær.ɪ.stə'kræt.ɪk ⓊⓈ əˌrɪs.tə'kræt̬.ɪk; ˌer.ə.stə'-, ˌær- **-al** -ᵊl **-ally** -ᵊl.i, -li *stress shift, British:* ˌaristocratic 'airs *stress shift, US:* aˌristocratic 'airs, ˌaristocratic 'airs
aristocratism ˌær.ɪ'stɒk.rə.tɪ.zᵊm ⓊⓈ ˌer.ə'stɑː.krə-, ˌær-
Aristophanes ˌær.ɪ'stɒf.ə.niːz ⓊⓈ ˌer.ə'stɑː.fə-, ˌær-
aristophanic ˌær.ɪ.stə'fæn.ɪk, -tɒf'æn- ⓊⓈ ˌer.ə.stə'-, ˌær-
aristotelian (A) ˌær.ɪ.stɒt'iː.li.ən, -stə'tiː- ⓊⓈ ˌer.ə.stə'tiː-, ˌær- **-s** -z
Aristotle 'ær.ɪ.stɒt.l̩ ⓊⓈ 'er.ə.stɑː.t̬l̩, 'ær-
Aristoxenus ˌær.ɪ'stɒk.sɪ.nəs, -sə.nəs ⓊⓈ ˌer.ə'stɑːk.sə-, ˌær-
arithmetic (*n.*) ə'rɪθ.mə.tɪk, -mɪ- **-s** -s
arithmetic (*adj.*) ˌær.ɪθ'met.ɪk ⓊⓈ ˌer.ɪθ'met̬-, ˌær- **-al** -ᵊl **-ally** -ᵊl.i, -li *stress shift:* ˌarithmetic 'mean
arithmetician əˌrɪθ.mə'tɪʃ.ᵊn, -mɪ'-; ˌær.ɪθ- ⓊⓈ əˌrɪθ.mə'- **-s** -z
-arium -'eə.ri.əm ⓊⓈ -'er.i-
Note: Suffix. Always carries primary stress, e.g. **solarium** /səʊ'leə.ri.əm ⓊⓈ soʊ-, sə-/.
Arius 'eə.ri.əs; ə'raɪ- ⓊⓈ 'er.i-, 'ær-
Ariz. (*abbrev. for* **Arizona**) ˌær.ɪ'zəʊ.nə ⓊⓈ ˌer.ɪ'zoʊ-, ˌær-, -ə'-
Arizona ˌær.ɪ'zəʊ.nə ⓊⓈ ˌer.ɪ'zoʊ-, ˌær-, -ə'-
Arjuna ɑː'juː.nə ⓊⓈ ɑːr-, ɜːr-
ark (A) ɑːk ⓊⓈ ɑːrk **-s** -s
Ark. (*abbrev. for* **Arkansas**) 'ɑː.kən.sɔː; ɑː'kæn.zəs ⓊⓈ 'ɑːr.kən.sɑː, -sɔː; ɑːr'kæn.zəs
Arkansas *US state:* 'ɑː.kən.sɔː ⓊⓈ 'ɑːr.kən.sɑː, -sɔː *river:* ɑː'kæn.zəs ⓊⓈ ɑːr'kæn.zəs
Arkhangelsk ˌɑː.kæŋ'gelsk ⓊⓈ ɑːr'kɑːn.gelsk
Arklow 'ɑː.kləʊ ⓊⓈ 'ɑːr.kloʊ
Arkwright 'ɑː.kraɪt ⓊⓈ 'ɑːr-
Arlen 'ɑː.lən ⓊⓈ 'ɑːr-
Arlene 'ɑː.liːn ⓊⓈ ɑːr'liːn
Arlington 'ɑː.lɪŋ.tən ⓊⓈ 'ɑːr-
arm ɑːm ⓊⓈ ɑːrm **-s** -z **-ing** -ɪŋ **-ed** -d **cost an ˌarm and a 'leg ; ˌkeep someone at ˌarm's 'length ; ˌarmed to the 'teeth**
armada (A) ɑː'mɑː.də ⓊⓈ ɑːr'- **-s** -z
Armadale 'ɑː.mə.deɪl ⓊⓈ 'ɑːr-
armadillo ˌɑː.mə'dɪl.əʊ ⓊⓈ ˌɑːr.mə'dɪl.oʊ **-s** -z
Armado ɑː'mɑː.dəʊ ⓊⓈ ɑːr'mɑː.doʊ
Armageddon ˌɑː.mə'ged.ᵊn ⓊⓈ ˌɑːr-
Armagh ˌɑː'mɑː ⓊⓈ ˌɑːr-
Armagnac 'ɑː.mə.njæk ⓊⓈ 'ɑːr-, ˌ--'-
Armah 'ɑː.mə ⓊⓈ 'ɑːr-
Armalite® 'ɑː.mᵊl.aɪt ⓊⓈ 'ɑːr.mə.laɪt
armament 'ɑː.mə.mənt ⓊⓈ 'ɑːr- **-s** -s
Armani ˌɑː'mɑː.ni ⓊⓈ ˌɑːr-
Armatrading ˌɑː.mə'treɪ.dɪŋ, 'ɑː.mə.treɪ- ⓊⓈ 'ɑːr.mə.treɪ-, ˌɑːr.mə'treɪ-
armature 'ɑː.mə.tʃəʳ, -tʃʊəʳ, -tjʊəʳ, -tjəʳ ⓊⓈ 'ɑːr.mə.tʃɚ **-s** -z
armband 'ɑːm.bænd ⓊⓈ 'ɑːrm- **-s** -z
armchair ˌɑːm'tʃeəʳ, '-- ⓊⓈ 'ɑːrm.tʃer **-s** -z
Note: The latter British form is used when attributive.
armed ɑːmd ⓊⓈ ɑːrmd **ˌarmed 'robbery**
Armeni|a ɑː'miː.ni|.ə ⓊⓈ ɑːr- **-an/s** -ən/z
Armfield 'ɑːm.fiːld ⓊⓈ 'ɑːrm-
armful 'ɑːm.fʊl ⓊⓈ 'ɑːrm- **-s** -z
armhole 'ɑːm.həʊl ⓊⓈ 'ɑːrm.hoʊl **-s** -z
armiger (A) 'ɑː.mɪ.dʒəʳ ⓊⓈ 'ɑːr.mɪ.dʒɚ **-s** -z
Armin 'ɑː.mɪn ⓊⓈ 'ɑːr-
arm-in-arm ˌɑːm.ɪn'ɑːm ⓊⓈ ˌɑːrm.ɪn'ɑːrm
Arminian ɑː'mɪn.i.ən ⓊⓈ ɑːr- **-s** -z
Armistead 'ɑː.mɪ.sted, -stɪd ⓊⓈ 'ɑːr-
armistic|e 'ɑː.mɪ.stɪs ⓊⓈ 'ɑːr.mə- **-es** -ɪz **'Armistice ˌDay**
Armitage 'ɑː.mɪ.tɪdʒ, -mə- ⓊⓈ 'ɑːr.mə.t̬ɪdʒ
armless 'ɑːm.ləs, -lɪs ⓊⓈ 'ɑːrm-
armlet 'ɑːm.lət, -lɪt ⓊⓈ 'ɑːrm- **-s** -s
armload 'ɑːm.ləʊd ⓊⓈ 'ɑːrm.loʊd **-s** -z
armlock 'ɑːm.lɒk ⓊⓈ 'ɑːrm.lɑːk **-s** -s
arm|or 'ɑː.m|əʳ ⓊⓈ 'ɑːr.m|ɚ **-ors** -əz ⓊⓈ -ɚz **-oring** -ᵊr.ɪŋ **-ored** -əd ⓊⓈ -ɚd **ˌarmored 'vehicle**
armorer 'ɑː.mᵊr.əʳ ⓊⓈ 'ɑːr.mɚ.ɚ **-s** -z
armorial ɑː'mɔː.ri.əl ⓊⓈ ɑːr'mɔːr.i-
Armoric ɑː'mɒr.ɪk ⓊⓈ ɑːr'mɔːr-
Armoric|a ɑː'mɒr.ɪ.k|ə ⓊⓈ ɑːr'mɔːr- **-an/s** -ən/z
armor-pla|te ˌɑː.mə'pleɪ|t, '--- ⓊⓈ 'ɑːr.mɚ.pleɪ|t **-tes** -ts **-ting** -tɪŋ ⓊⓈ -t̬ɪŋ **-ted** -tɪd ⓊⓈ -t̬ɪd

armor|y 'ɑː.mᵊr|.i US 'ɑːr- **-ies** -iz

arm|our (A) 'ɑː.m|əʳ US 'ɑːr.m|ɚ **-ours** -əz US -ɚz **-ouring** -ᵊr.ɪŋ **-oured** -əd US -ɚd **ˌarmoured 'vehicle**

armourer 'ɑː.mᵊr.əʳ US 'ɑːr.mɚ.ɚ **-s** -z

armour-pla|te ˌɑː.mə'pleɪ|t, '--- US 'ɑːr.mɚ.pleɪ|t **-tes** -ts **-ting** -tɪŋ US -t̬ɪŋ **-ted** -tɪd US -t̬ɪd

Note: The latter British form is used attributively.

armour|y 'ɑː.mᵊr|.i US 'ɑːr- **-ies** -iz

armpit 'ɑːm.pɪt US 'ɑːrm- **-s** -s

armrest 'ɑːm.rest US 'ɑːrm- **-s** -s

arms ɑːmz US ɑːrmz **'arms conˌtrol** ; **'arms ˌrace** ; **ˌup in 'arms**

Armstead 'ɑːm.sted, -stɪd US 'ɑːrm-

Armstrong 'ɑːm.strɒŋ US 'ɑːrm.strɑːŋ, -strɔːŋ

Armthorpe 'ɑːm.θɔːp US 'ɑːrm.θɔːrp

arm|y 'ɑː.m|i US 'ɑːr- **-ies** -iz

army-corps *sing.:* 'ɑː.mi.kɔːʳ US 'ɑːr.mi.kɔːr *plur.:* -kɔːz US -kɔːrz

Arnald 'ɑː.nəld US 'ɑːr-

Arndale 'ɑːn.deɪl US 'ɑːrn-

Arne ɑːn US ɑːrn

Arnfield 'ɑːn.fiːld US 'ɑːrn-

Arnhem 'ɑː.nəm, 'ɑːn.həm US 'ɑːr.nəm, 'ɑːrn.hem

arnica 'ɑː.nɪ.kə US 'ɑːr-

Arno 'ɑː.nəʊ US 'ɑːr.noʊ

Arnold 'ɑː.nᵊld US 'ɑːr- **-son** -sᵊn

Arnot(t) 'ɑː.nət, -nɒt US 'ɑːr.nət, -nɑːt

Arolla ə'rɒl.ə US -'rɑː.lə

aroma ə'rəʊ.mə US -'roʊ- **-s** -z

aromatherap|y əˌrəʊ.mə'θer.ə.p|i US -ˌroʊ- **-ist/s** -ɪst/s

aromatic ˌær.əʊ'mæt.ɪk US ˌer.ə'mæt̬-, ˌær- **-s** -s *stress shift:* ˌaromatic 'oils

arose (*from* **arise**) ə'rəʊz US -'roʊz

around ə'raʊnd

arousal ə'raʊ.zᵊl **-s** -z

arous|e ə'raʊz **-es** -ɪz **-ing** -ɪŋ **-ed** -d

arpeggio ɑː'pedʒ.i.əʊ, -'pedʒ.əʊ US ɑːr'pedʒ.i.oʊ, -'peʒ-, -'pedʒ.oʊ **-s** -z

arquebus 'ɑː.kwɪ.bəs, -kwə.bəs, -bʌs US 'ɑːr- **-es** -ɪz

arr (*abbrev. for* **arranged by**) ə'reɪndʒdˌbaɪ (*abbrev. for* **arrives, arrival**) ə'raɪ|vz; -vᵊl

arrack 'ær.ək US 'er-, 'ær-; ə'ræk

arraign ə'reɪn **-s** -z **-ing** -ɪŋ **-ed** -d **-er/s** -əʳ/z US -ɚ/z **-ment/s** -mənt/s

Arran 'ær.ᵊn US 'er-, 'ær-

arrang|e ə'reɪndʒ **-es** -ɪz **-ing** -ɪŋ **-ed** -d **-er/s** -əʳ/z US -ɚ/z

arrangement ə'reɪndʒ.mənt **-s** -s

arrant 'ær.ᵊnt US 'er-, 'ær- **-ly** -li

arras 'ær.əs US 'er-, 'ær- **-es** -ɪz

Arras *French town:* 'ær.əs, -æs US 'er-, 'ær-

Arrau ə'raʊ; 'ær.aʊ US ə'raʊ

array ə'reɪ **-s** -z **-ing** -ɪŋ **-ed** -d

arrear ə'rɪəʳ US -'rɪr **-s** -z **-age** -ɪdʒ

arrest ə'rest **-s** -s **-ing** -ɪŋ **-ed** -ɪd **-ment/s** -mənt/s

arrestable ə'res.tə.bl̩

arrestation ˌær.es'teɪ.ʃᵊn US ˌer-, ˌær-; əˌres'- **-s** -z

arrhythm|ia ə'rɪð.m|i.ə **-ic** -ɪk **-ical** -ɪ.kᵊl **-ically** -ɪ.kᵊl.i, -ɪ.kli

Arrian 'ær.i.ən US 'er-, 'ær-

arrière-ban ˌær.i.eə'bæn US -er'bɑːn, -'bæn **-s** -z

arrière pensée ˌær.i.eə'pɑ̃ː*nt*.seɪ, -pɑː*nt*'seɪ US -er.pɑː*n*'seɪ

arris 'ær.ɪs US 'er-, 'ær- **-es** -ɪz

arrival ə'raɪ.vᵊl **-s** -z

arriv|e ə'raɪv **-es** -z **-ing** -ɪŋ **-ed** -d

arrivederci ˌær.i.və'deə.tʃi US əˌriː.və'der-

arriviste ˌær.iː'viːst US ˌer-, ˌær- **-s** -s

arroganc|e 'ær.ə.gən*t*s US 'er-, 'ær- **-y** -i

arrogant 'ær.ə.gənt US 'er-, 'ær- **-ly** -li

arro|gate 'ær.əʊ|.geɪt US 'er.ə-, 'ær- **-gates** -geɪts **-gating** -geɪ.tɪŋ US -geɪ.t̬ɪŋ **-gated** -geɪ.tɪd US -geɪ.t̬ɪd

arrogation ˌær.əʊ'geɪ.ʃᵊn US ˌer.ə'-, ˌær- **-s** -z

arrogative ə'rɒg.ə.tɪv US -'rɑː.gə.t̬ɪv

arrondissement ˌær.ɒn'diː.sᵊm.ɑ̃ː US erˌɑːn.diːs'mɑːn, ær-; əˌrɑːn- **-s** -s

arrow 'ær.əʊ US 'er.oʊ, 'ær- **-s** -z **'arrow ˌhead**

arrowroot 'ær.əʊ.ruːt US 'er.oʊ-, 'ær-

Arrowsmith 'ær.əʊ.smɪθ US 'er.oʊ-, 'ær-

arrowwood 'ær.əʊ.wʊd US 'er.oʊ-, 'ær-

ars ɑːz US ɑːrz

ars|e ɑːs US ɑːrs **-es** -ɪz

Note: In US dictionaries, **arse** is usually listed as a variant of **ass**, which is pronounced /æs/. **Arse** is a British term.

arsehole 'ɑːs.həʊl US 'ɑːrs.hoʊl **-s** -z

arsenal (A) 'ɑː.sᵊn.ᵊl US 'ɑːr- **-s** -z

arsenate 'ɑː.sᵊn.eɪt, -sɪ.neɪt, -nɪt, -nət US 'ɑːr- **-s** -s

arsenic (*n.*) 'ɑː.sᵊn.ɪk US 'ɑːr-

arsenic (*adj.*) ɑː'sen.ɪk US ɑːr- **-al** -ᵊl

arsenide 'ɑː.sᵊn.aɪd US 'ɑːr- **-s** -z

arsenite 'ɑː.sᵊn.aɪt, -sɪ.naɪt US 'ɑːr-

ars|is 'ɑː.s|ɪs US 'ɑːr- **-es** -iːz

arson 'ɑː.sᵊn US 'ɑːr-

arsonist 'ɑː.sᵊn.ɪst US 'ɑːr- **-s** -s

art (*n.*) ɑːt US ɑːrt **-s** -s **'art ˌgallery** ; **ˌarts and 'crafts** ; **'art ˌschool**

art (*v.*) (*from* **be**) *normal form:* ɑːt US ɑːrt *occasional weak form:* ət US ɚt

Artaxerxes ˌɑː.tə'zɜːk.siːz, -tək'sɜːk-, -təg'zɜːk-, 'ɑː.tə.zɜːk-, -tək.sɜːk-, -təg.zɜːk- US ˌɑːr.t̬ə'zɜːrk-

Art Deco ˌɑːt'dek.əʊ US ˌɑːrt.deɪ'koʊ, ˌɑːr-, -'deɪ.koʊ

artefact 'ɑː.tɪ.fækt, -tə.fækt US 'ɑːr.t̬ə- **-s** -s

Artemis 'ɑː.tɪ.mɪs, -tə.mɪs US 'ɑːr.t̬ə-

Artemus 'ɑː.tɪ.məs, -tə.məs US 'ɑːr.t̬ɪ-

arterial ɑː'tɪə.ri.əl US ɑːr'tɪr.i-

arteriolar ɑːˌtɪə.ri'əʊ.ləʳ US ɑːrˌtɪr.i'oʊ.lɚ

arteriol|e ɑː'tɪə.ri.əʊl US ɑːr'tɪr.i.oʊl **-es** -z

arteriosclerosis ɑːˌtɪə.ri.əʊ.sklə'rəʊ.sɪs, -sklɪə'- US ɑːrˌtɪr.i.oʊ.sklə'roʊ.səs

arteritis ˌɑː.tᵊr'aɪ.tɪs, -tɪ'raɪ-, -təs US ˌɑːr.t̬ə'raɪ.t̬əs

arter|y 'ɑː.tᵊr|.i US 'ɑːr.t̬ɚ- **-ies** -iz

artesian ɑː'tiː.zi.ən, -ʒi.ən, -ʒᵊn US ɑːr'tiː.ʒᵊn **arˌtesian 'well**

Artex® 'ɑː.teks US 'ɑːr-

artful 'ɑːt.fᵊl, -fʊl US 'ɑːrt- **-ly** -i **-ness** -nəs, -nɪs **ˌArtful 'Dodger**

arthritic ɑː'θrɪt.ɪk US ɑːr'θrɪt̬.ɪk **-s** -s

arthritis ɑː'θraɪ.tɪs, -təs US ɑːr'θraɪ.t̬əs

arthropod 'ɑː.θrə.pɒd US 'ɑːr.θrə.pɑːd **-s** -z

arthroscope 'ɑː.θrə.skəʊp US 'ɑːr.θrə.skoʊp **-s** -s

arthroscopic ˌɑː.θrə'skɒp.ɪk US ˌɑːr.θrə'skɑː.pɪk

arthroscopy ɑː'θrɒs.kə.pi US ɑːr'θrɑː.skə-

Arthur 'ɑː.θəʳ US 'ɑːr.θɚ

Arthurian ɑː'θjʊə.ri.ən, -'θʊə- US ɑːr'θʊr.i-, -'θɜːr-

artichoke 'ɑː.tɪ.tʃəʊk US 'ɑːr.t̬ə.tʃoʊk **-s** -s

articl|e 'ɑː.tɪ.kl̩ US 'ɑːr.t̬ɪ- **-es** -z **-ing** -ɪŋ, -klɪŋ **-ed** -d

articular ɑː'tɪk.jə.ləʳ, -jʊ- US ɑːr'tɪk.jə.lɚ

articulate (*adj.*) ɑː'tɪk.jə.lət, -jʊ-, -lɪt US ɑːr'tɪk.jə.lət **-ly** -li **-ness** -nəs, -nɪs

articu|late (*v.*) ɑː'tɪk.jə|.leɪt, -jʊ- US ɑːr'tɪk.jə- **-lates** -leɪts **-lating** -leɪ.tɪŋ US -leɪ.t̬ɪŋ **-lated** -leɪ.tɪd US -leɪ.t̬ɪd **-lator/s** -leɪ.təʳ/z US -leɪ.t̬ɚ/s **arˌticulated 'lorry**

articulation ɑːˌtɪk.jə'leɪ.ʃᵊn, -jʊ'- US ɑːrˌtɪk.jə'- **-s** -z

articulatory ɑː'tɪk.jə.lə.tᵊr.i, -jʊ-; ɑːˌtɪk.jə'leɪ-, -jʊ'- US ɑːr'tɪk.jə.lə.tɔːr-

artifact 'ɑː.tɪ.fækt ⓤⓢ 'ɑːr.t̬ə- **-s** -s
artific|e 'ɑː.tɪ.fɪs ⓤⓢ 'ɑːr.t̬ə- **-es** -ɪz
artificer ɑː'tɪf.ɪ.səʳ ⓤⓢ ɑːr'tɪf.ə.sɚ **-s** -z
artificial ˌɑː.tɪ'fɪʃ.ᵊl ⓤⓢ ˌɑːr.t̬ə'- **-ly** -i **-ness** -nəs, -nɪs *stress shift, see compounds:* **ˌartificial insemi'nation**; **ˌartificial in'telligence**; **ˌartificial respi'ration**
artificialit|y ˌɑː.tɪˌfɪʃ.i'æl.ə.t|i, -ɪ.t|i ⓤⓢ ˌɑːr.t̬əˌfɪʃ.i'æl.ə.t̬|i **-ies** -iz
artificializ|e, -is|e ˌɑː.tɪ'fɪʃ.ᵊl.aɪz ⓤⓢ ˌɑːr.t̬ə- **-es** -ɪz **-ing** -ɪŋ **-ed** -d
artiller|y ɑː'tɪl.ᵊr|.i ⓤⓢ ɑːr- **-ies** -iz **-ist/s** -ɪst/s
artillery|-man ɑː'tɪl.ᵊr.i|.mən, -mæn ⓤⓢ ɑːr'- **-men** -mən, -men
artisan ˌɑː.tɪ'zæn, -tə'zæn, '--- ⓤⓢ 'ɑːr.t̬ə.zᵊn, -sᵊn **-s** -z
artist 'ɑː.tɪst ⓤⓢ 'ɑːr.t̬əst, -t̬ɪst **-s** -s
artiste ɑː'tiːst ⓤⓢ ɑːr- **-s** -s
artistic ɑː'tɪs.tɪk ⓤⓢ ɑːr- **-al** -ᵊl **-ally** -ᵊl.i, -li
artistry 'ɑː.tɪ.stri ⓤⓢ 'ɑːr.t̬ə-, -t̬ɪ-
artless 'ɑːt.ləs, -lɪs ⓤⓢ 'ɑːrt- **-ly** -li **-ness** -nəs, -nɪs
Art Nouveau ˌɑːt.nuː'vəʊ, ˌɑː-, ˌ-'-- ⓤⓢ ˌɑːrt.nuː'voʊ, ˌɑːr-
Artois ɑː'twɑː, '-- ⓤⓢ ɑːr-
arts|man 'ɑːts|.mæn ⓤⓢ 'ɑːrts- **-men** -men
artsy 'ɑːt.si ⓤⓢ 'ɑːrt-
artwork 'ɑːt.wɜːk ⓤⓢ 'ɑːrt.wɜːrk
arty 'ɑː.ti ⓤⓢ 'ɑːr.t̬i
arty-farty ˌɑː.ti'fɑː.ti ⓤⓢ ˌɑːr.t̬i'fɑːr.t̬i *stress shift:* ˌarty-farty 'person
Arub|a ə'ruː.b|ə **-an/s** -ən/z
arum 'eə.rəm ⓤⓢ 'er- **-s** -z
Arun 'ær.ᵊn ⓤⓢ 'er-, 'ær-
Arundel 'ær.ᵊn.dᵊl; ə'rʌn- ⓤⓢ 'er.ᵊn-, 'ær-; ə'rʌn-
Arundell 'ær.ᵊn.del, -dᵊl ⓤⓢ 'er-, 'ær-
Arveragus ɑː'ver.ə.gəs ⓤⓢ ɑːr-
-ary -ᵊr.i ⓤⓢ -er.i, -ɚ.i
Note: Suffix. When added to a free stem, **-ary** does not normally affect the stress pattern, e.g. **imagine** /ɪ'mædʒ.ɪn/, **imaginary** /ɪ'mæʒd.ɪ.nᵊr.i ⓤⓢ -ə.ner-/. Otherwise words containing **-ary** normally carry stress one or two syllables before the suffix, e.g. **centenary** /sen'tiː.nᵊr.i, -'ten.ᵊr- ⓤⓢ 'sen.tᵊn.er-, sen'ten.ᵊr-/, **culinary** /'kʌl.ɪ.nᵊr.i ⓤⓢ -ə.ner-/. There are exceptions; see individual entries.
Aryan 'eə.ri.ən, 'ɑː- ⓤⓢ 'er.i-, 'ær-, 'ɑːr- **-s** -z **-ism** -ɪ.zᵊm
arytenoid ˌær.ɪ'tiː.nɔɪd, -rə'tiː-; ær'ɪt.ᵊn.ɔɪd ⓤⓢ ə'rɪt.ᵊn-; ˌer.ɪ'tiː.nɔɪd, ˌær- **-s** -z

as *(conj.) strong form:* æz *weak form:* əz
Note: Weak form word. The strong form /æz/ is used in contrastive or coordinative constructions (e.g. 'as and when it's ready'), and in sentence-final position (e.g. 'That's what I bought it as.'). Quite frequently the strong form is found when the word occurs in initial position in a sentence if the following word is not stressed (e.g. 'As I was saying, …'). The weak form is /əz/ (e.g. 'as good as gold' /əzˌgʊd.əz'gəʊld ⓤⓢ -'goʊld/).
as *(n.) coin:* æs **-es** -ɪz
AS (*abbrev. for* **airspeed** *or* **Anglo-Saxon** *or* **antisubmarine**) ˌeɪ'es
Asa *biblical name:* 'eɪ.sə, 'ɑː.sə *as modern first name:* 'eɪ.zə
asaf(o)etida ˌæs.ə'fet.ɪ.də, -'fiː.tɪ- ⓤⓢ -'fet̬.ə-
a.s.a.p., ASAP ˌeɪ.es.eɪ'piː, 'eɪ.sæp
Asaph 'æs.əf
ASAT 'eɪ.sæt
asbest|ic æs'bes.t|ɪk, əs-, æz-, əz- **-ous** -əs
asbestos æs'bes.tɒs, æz-, əs-, əz-, -təs ⓤⓢ -təs
asbestosis ˌæs.bes'təʊ.sɪs, ˌæz-, -bɪs- ⓤⓢ -'toʊ-
Ascalon 'æs.kə.lɒn, -lən ⓤⓢ -lɑːn
Ascanius æs'keɪ.ni.əs
ascend ə'send, æs'end **-s** -z **-ing** -ɪŋ **-ed** -ɪd
ascendan|ce ə'sen.dən|*t*s, æs'en- **-cy** -*t*.si **-t** -t
ascenden|ce ə'sen.dən|*t*s, æs'en- **-cy** -*t*.si **-t** -t
ascender ə'sen.dəʳ ⓤⓢ -dɚ **-s** -z
ascension (A) ə'sen.*t*ʃᵊn ⓤⓢ -'sen*t*.ʃᵊn **-s** -z **A'scension ˌDay**
ascensional ə'sen.*t*ʃᵊn.ᵊl ⓤⓢ -'sen*t*.ʃᵊn-
ascent ə'sent, æs'ent **-s** -s
ascertain ˌæs.ə'teɪn ⓤⓢ -ɚ'- **-s** -z **-ing** -ɪŋ **-ed** -d **-ment** -mənt **-able** -ə.bl̩
ascetic ə'set.ɪk, æs'et- ⓤⓢ ə'set̬.ɪk **-al** -ᵊl **-ally** -ᵊl.i, -li **-s** -s
asceticism ə'set.ɪ.sɪ.zᵊm, æs'et- ⓤⓢ ə'set̬.ə-
Asch æʃ
Ascham 'æs.kəm
ASCII 'æs.kiː, -ki
Asclepius ə'skliː.pi.əs, æs'kliː-
ascorbate ə'skɔː.beɪt, æs'kɔː- ⓤⓢ ə'skɔːr- **-s** -s
ascorbic ə'skɔː.bɪk, æs'kɔː- ⓤⓢ ə'skɔːr- **aˌscorbic 'acid**
Ascot *place in Berkshire:* 'æs.kət ⓤⓢ -kɑːt
ascot *item of clothing:* 'æs.kət ⓤⓢ -kɑːt, -kət **-s** -s

ascrib|e ə'skraɪb **-es** -z **-ing** -ɪŋ **-ed** -d **-able** -ə.bl̩
ascription ə'skrɪp.ʃᵊn, æs'krɪp-
ascriptive ə'skrɪp.tɪv
Asda® 'æz.də
asdic 'æz.dɪk **-s** -s
-ase -eɪz, -eɪs
Note: Suffix. Does not normally affect stress pattern, e.g. **amylase** /'æm.ɪ.leɪz/.
asepsis ˌeɪ'sep.sɪs, ə-, æs'ep-
aseptic ˌeɪ'sep.tɪk, ə-, æ'sep- **-s** -s
asexual ˌeɪ'sek.ʃʊəl, -ʃu.əl, -sjʊəl, -ʃᵊl ⓤⓢ -ʃu.əl **-ly** -i
asexuality ˌeɪ.sek.ʃu'æl.ɪ.ti, -sju'-, -ə.ti ⓤⓢ -ʃu'æl.ə.t̬i
Asgard 'æs.gɑːd, 'æz- ⓤⓢ -gɑːrd, 'ɑːs-, 'ɑːz-
Asgill 'æs.gɪl, 'æz-
ash (A) æʃ **-es** -ɪz **'ash ˌcan**; **ˌAsh 'Wednesday**
asham|ed ə'ʃeɪm|d **-edly** -ɪd.li **-edness** -ɪd.nəs, -nɪs
Ashanti ə'ʃæn.ti, æʃ'- ⓤⓢ ə'ʃæn-, -'ʃɑːn- **-s** -z
Ashbee 'æʃ.bi
Ashbery 'æʃ.bᵊr.i ⓤⓢ -ber-
Ashbourne 'æʃ.bɔːn ⓤⓢ -bɔːrn
Ashburne 'æʃ.bɜːn ⓤⓢ -bɜːrn
Ashburnham æʃ'bɜː.nəm ⓤⓢ -'bɜːr-
Ashburton æʃ'bɜː.tᵊn ⓤⓢ -'bɜːr-
Ashbury 'æʃ.bᵊr.i ⓤⓢ -ber-, -bɚ-
Ashby 'æʃ.bi
Ashby-de-la-Zouch ˌæʃ.bi.də.lɑː'zuːʃ, -de.lə'-
ashcan 'æʃ.kæn **-s** -z
Ashcombe 'æʃ.kəm
Ashcroft 'æʃ.krɒft ⓤⓢ -krɑːft
Ashdod 'æʃ.dɒd ⓤⓢ -dɑːd
Ashdown 'æʃ.daʊn
Ashe æʃ
ashen 'æʃ.ᵊn
Asher 'æʃ.əʳ ⓤⓢ -ɚ
asher|y 'æʃ.ᵊr|.i **-ies** -iz
Ashfield 'æʃ.fiːld
Ashford 'æʃ.fəd ⓤⓢ -fɚd
Ashington 'æʃ.ɪŋ.tən
Ashkenazy, Ashkenazi ˌæʃ.kə'nɑː.zi, -kɪ'nɑː- ⓤⓢ ɑːʃ-
Ashkhabad ˌɑːʃ.kə'bɑːd ⓤⓢ ˌɑːʃ.kɑː'bɑːd
Ashland 'æʃ.lənd
ashlar 'æʃ.ləʳ, -lɑːʳ ⓤⓢ -lɚ
Ashley, Ashlee, Ashleigh 'æʃ.li
Ashman 'æʃ.mən
Ashmole 'æʃ.məʊl ⓤⓢ -moʊl
Ashmolean æʃ'məʊ.li.ən, ˌæʃ.məʊ'liː.ən ⓤⓢ -'moʊ.li-
Ashmore 'æʃ.mɔːʳ ⓤⓢ -mɔːr
ashore ə'ʃɔːʳ ⓤⓢ -'ʃɔːr
Ashover 'æʃ.əʊ.vəʳ ⓤⓢ -oʊ.vɚ
ashpan 'æʃ.pæn **-s** -z

ashram ˈæʃ.rəm, -ræm **-s** -z
Ashtaroth ˈæʃ.tə.rɒθ (US) -rɑːθ, -rɔːθ
Ashton ˈæʃ.tᵊn
Ashton-in-Makerfield ˌæʃ.tᵊn.ɪnˈmeɪ.kə.fiːld (US) -kɚ-
Ashton-under-Lyne ˌæʃ.tᵊn.ʌn.dəˈlaɪn, -ˈʌn.dəˌlaɪn (US) -ʌn.dɚˈ-, -ˈʌn.dɚˌ-
Ashtoreth ˈæʃ.tə.reθ, -tɒr.eθ (US) -tə.reθ
ashtray ˈæʃˌtreɪ **-s** -z
Ashurbanipal ˌæʃ.ɜːˈbɑː.nɪ.pæl, -pᵊl (US) ˌɑː.ʃʊrˈbɑː.nɪ.pɑːl
Ashwell ˈæʃ.wel, -wᵊl
Ashworth ˈæʃ.wəθ, -wɜːθ (US) -wɚθ, -wɜːrθ
ash|y ˈæʃ|.i **-ier** -i.əʳ (US) -i.ɚ **-iest** -i.əst, -i.ɪst **-iness** -ɪ.nəs, -ɪ.nɪs
Asia ˈeɪ.ʃə, -ʒə (US) ˈeɪ.ʒə, -ʃə **ˌAsia ˈMinor**
Asian ˈeɪ.ʃᵊn, -ʒᵊn (US) ˈeɪ.ʒᵊn, -ʃᵊn **-s** -z **ˌAsian ˈflu**
Asiatic ˌeɪ.ʃiˈæt.ɪk, ˌeɪ.si-, ˌeɪ.ʒi-, ˌeɪ.zi- (US) ˌeɪ.ʒiˈæt̬.ɪk, -ʃiˈ- **-s** -s *stress shift:* ˌAsiatic ˈorigin
aside əˈsaɪd **-s** -z
Asimov ˈæz.ɪ.mɒf, ˈæs-, ˈ-ə-, -mɒv (US) ˈæz.ə.mɑːf, -mɑːv
asinine ˈæs.ɪ.naɪn, -ə.naɪn
asininit|y ˌæs.ɪˈnɪn.ə.t|i, -əˈnɪn-, -ɪ.t|i (US) -əˈnɪn.ə.t̬|i **-ies** -iz
ask (*v.*) ɑːsk (US) æsk **-s** -s **-ing** -ɪŋ **-ed** -t
askance əˈskænts, -ˈskɑːnts (US) əˈskænts
askant əˈskænt
Aske æsk
Askelon ˈæs.kɪ.lən, -kə.lən, -lɒn (US) -kə.lɑːn
Askern ˈæs.kɜːn, -kən (US) -kɜːrn, -kɚn
askew əˈskjuː
Askew ˈæs.kjuː
Askey ˈæs.ki
Askrigg ˈæs.krɪg
Askwith ˈæs.kwɪθ
Aslam ˈæz.ləm
aslant əˈslɑːnt (US) -ˈslænt
asleep əˈsliːp
ASLEF ˈæz.lef
Asmara æsˈmɑː.rə, æz- (US) -ˈmɑːr.ə
Asmodeus æsˈməʊ.di.əs (US) ˌæz.moʊˈdiː-, ˌæs-, -məˈ-
Note: For British English, the name must be pronounced /ˌæs.məʊˈdiː.əs/ in Milton's 'Paradise Lost', iv, 168.
asocial ˌeɪˈsəʊ.ʃᵊl (US) -ˈsoʊ-
Asoka əˈʃəʊ.kə, əˈsəʊ- (US) -ˈsoʊ-
asp æsp, ɑːsp (US) æsp **-s** -s
asparagus əˈspær.ə.gəs (US) -ˈsper-, -ˈspær-
aspartame əˈspɑː.teɪm; ˈæs.pə- (US) ˈæs.pɚ-; əˈspɑːr-
Aspasia æsˈpeɪ.zi.ə, əˈspeɪ-, -ʒə (US) -ʒə
ASPCA ˌeɪ.esˌpiː.siːˈeɪ
aspect ˈæs.pekt **-s** -s
aspectable æsˈpek.tə.bl̩
aspectual əˈspek.tʃu.əl, æsˈpek-, -tju- (US) -tʃu-
Aspel(l) ˈæs.pᵊl
aspen (**A**) ˈæs.pən **-s** -z
asper ˈæs.pəʳ (US) -pɚ
asperg|e əˈspɜːdʒ, æsˈpɜːdʒ (US) əˈspɜːrdʒ **-es** -ɪz **-ing** -ɪŋ **-ed** -d
asperges (**A**) *religious service:* æsˈpɜː.dʒiːz, əˈspɜː- (US) əˈspɜːr-
aspergill ˈæs.pə.dʒɪl (US) -pɚ- **-s** -z
asperit|y æsˈper.ə.t|i, əˈsper-, -ɪ.t|i (US) -ə.t̬|i **-ies** -iz
Aspern ˈæs.pɜːn (US) -pɜːrn
aspers|e əˈspɜːs, æsˈpɜːs (US) əˈspɜːrs **-es** -ɪz **-ing** -ɪŋ **-ed** -t
aspersion əˈspɜː.ʃᵊn, æsˈpɜː- (US) əˈspɜːr.ʒᵊn, -ʃᵊn **-s** -z
asphalt (*n.*) ˈæs.fælt, -fɔːlt, -fəlt (US) -fɑːlt, -fɔːlt **-s** -s **ˌasphalt ˈjungle**
asphal|t (*v.*) ˈæs.fæl|t, æsˈfæl|t (US) ˈæs.fɑːl|t, -fɔːl|t **-ts** -ts **-ting** -tɪŋ (US) -t̬ɪŋ **-ted** -tɪd (US) -t̬ɪd
asphaltic æsˈfæl.tɪk (US) -ˈfɑːl.t̬ɪk, -ˈfɔːl-
asphodel ˈæs.fəʊ.del (US) -fə- **-s** -z
asphyxia əsˈfɪks.i.ə, æs-
asphyxiant əsˈfɪk.si.ənt, æsˈ- **-s** -s
asphyxi|ate əsˈfɪk.si|.eɪt, æs- **-ates** -s **-ating** -eɪ.tɪŋ (US) -eɪ.t̬ɪŋ **-ated** -eɪ.tɪd (US) -eɪ.t̬ɪd **-ator/s** -eɪ.təʳ/z (US) -eɪ.t̬ɚ/z
asphyxiation əsˌfɪk.siˈeɪ.ʃᵊn, æs- **-s** -z
asphyx|y æsˈfɪk.s|i **-ies** -iz
aspic ˈæs.pɪk
aspidistra ˌæs.pɪˈdɪs.trə (US) -pəˈ- **-s** -z
Aspinall ˈæs.pɪ.nɔːl, -nᵊl
Aspinwall ˈæs.pɪn.wɔːl (US) -wɔːl, -wɑːl
aspirant ˈæs.pɪ.rᵊnt; əˈspaɪə- (US) ˈæs.pɚ.ᵊnt, -pɪ.rᵊnt **-s** -s
aspirate (*n. adj.*) ˈæs.pᵊr.ət, -pɪ.rət-, -rɪt **-s** -s
aspir|ate (*v.*) ˈæs.pᵊr.|eɪt, -pɪ.r|eɪt (US) -pə.r|eɪt, -pɪ- **-ates** -eɪts **-ating** -eɪ.tɪŋ (US) -eɪ.t̬ɪŋ **-ated** -eɪ.tɪd (US) -eɪ.t̬ɪd **-ator/s** -eɪ.təʳ/z (US) -eɪ.t̬ɚ/z
aspiration ˌæs.pᵊrˈeɪ.ʃᵊn, -pɪˈreɪ- (US) -pəˈreɪ-, -pɪˈ- **-s** -z
aspirational ˌæs.pᵊrˈeɪ.ʃᵊn.ᵊl, -pɪˈreɪ- (US) -pəˈreɪ-, -pɪˈ- **-ly** -i
aspir|e əˈspaɪəʳ (US) -spaɪɚ **-es** -z **-ing/ly** -ɪŋ/li **-ed** -d **-er/s** -əʳ/z (US) -ɚ/z
aspirin ˈæs.pᵊr.ɪn, ˈ-prɪn **-s** -z
aspirine ˈæs.pᵊr.iːn, -pɪ.riːn (US) -pə.riːn, -pɪ- **-s** -z
asplenium æsˈpliː.ni.əm, əˈspliː- **-s** -z
Asquith ˈæs.kwɪθ
ass æs **-es** -ɪz
assaf(o)etida ˌæs.əˈfet.ɪ.də, -ˈfiː.tɪ- (US) -ˈfet̬.ə-
assagai ˈæs.ə.gaɪ **-s** -z
assai æsˈaɪ
assail əˈseɪl **-s** -z **-ing** -ɪŋ **-ed** -d **-able** -ə.bl̩ **-ant/s** -ənt/s
Assam æsˈæm, ˈæs.æm
Assamese ˌæs.əˈmiːz, -æmˈiːz (US) -əˈmiːz, -ˈmiːs
assassin əˈsæs.ɪn (US) -ən **-s** -z
assassi|nate əˈsæs.ɪ|.neɪt, ˈ-ə- **-nates** -neɪts **-nating** -neɪ.tɪŋ (US) -neɪ.t̬ɪŋ **-nated** -neɪ.tɪd (US) -neɪ.t̬ɪd **-nator/s** -neɪ.təʳ/z (US) -neɪ.t̬ɚ/z
assassination əˌsæs.ɪˈneɪ.ʃᵊn, -əˈ- **-s** -z
assault əˈsɔːlt, -ˈsɒlt (US) -ˈsɔːlt, -ˈsɑːlt **-s** -s **-ing** -ɪŋ (US) əˈsɔːl.t̬ɪŋ **-ed** -ɪd (US) əˈsɔːl.t̬ɪd **-er/s** -əʳ/z (US) əˈsɔːl.t̬ɚ/z **aˌssault and ˈbattery; aˈssault ˌcourse**
assay (*n.*) əˈseɪ; ˈæs.eɪ (US) ˈæs.eɪ; əˈseɪ **-s** -z
assay (*v.*) əˈseɪ, æsˈeɪ **-s** -z **-ing** -ɪŋ **-ed** -d **-er/s** -əʳ/z (US) -ɚ/z
Assaye æsˈeɪ
assegai ˈæs.ə.gaɪ, ˈ-ɪ- (US) ˈ-ə- **-s** -z
assemblag|e əˈsem.blɪdʒ **-es** -ɪz
assembl|e əˈsem.bl̩ **-es** -z **-ing** -ɪŋ, ˈ-blɪŋ **-ed** -d **-er/s** -əʳ/z, ˈ-bləʳ/z (US) ˈ-bl̩.ɚ/z, -blɚ/z
assembl|y əˈsem.bl|i **-ies** -iz **asˈsembly ˌline**; **asˈsembly ˌroom**; **asˈsembly ˌlanguage**
assembly|man əˈsem.bli|.mæn, -mən **-men** -men, -mən
assen|t əˈsen|t, æsˈen|t **-ts** -ts **-ting/ly** -tɪŋ/li (US) -t̬ɪŋ/li **-ted** -tɪd (US) -t̬ɪd
Asser ˈæs.əʳ (US) -ɚ
as|sert ə|ˈsɜːt (US) -ˈsɜːrt **-serts** -ˈsɜːts (US) -ˈsɜːrts **-serting** -ˈsɜː.tɪŋ (US) -ˈsɜːr.t̬ɪŋ **-serted** -ˈsɜː.tɪd (US) -ˈsɜːr.t̬ɪd **-serter/s** -ˈsɜː.təʳ/z (US) -ˈsɜːr.t̬ɚ/s **-sertor/s** -ˈsɜː.təʳ/z (US) -ˈsɜːr.t̬ɚ/z **-sertable** -ˈsɜː.tə.bl̩ (US) -ˈsɜːr.t̬ə.bl̩
assertion əˈsɜː.ʃᵊn (US) -ˈsɜːr- **-s** -z
assertive əˈsɜː.tɪv (US) -sɜːr.t̬ɪv **-ly** -li **-ness** -nəs, -nɪs **asˈsertiveness ˌtraining**
assess əˈses **-es** -ɪz **-ing** -ɪŋ **-ed** -t **-or/s** -əʳ/z (US) -ɚ/z **-able** -ə.bl̩
assessment əˈses.mənt **-s** -s
asset ˈæs.et, -ɪt **-s** -s
asset-stripp|ing ˈæs.etˌstrɪp|.ɪŋ **-er/s** -əʳ/z (US) -ɚ/z
assev|er æsˈev|.əʳ, əˈsev- (US) -ɚ **-ers** -əz (US) -ɚs **-ering** -ᵊr.ɪŋ **-ered** -əd (US) -ɚd
assever|ate əˈsev.ᵊr|.eɪt, æsˈev- (US) -ə.r|eɪt **-ates** -eɪts **-ating** -eɪ.tɪŋ (US) -eɪ.t̬ɪŋ **-ated** -eɪ.tɪd (US) -eɪ.t̬ɪd
asseveration əˌsev.əˈreɪ.ʃᵊn, æsˌev- **-s** -z

asshole 'ɑːs.həʊl, 'æs- (US) 'æs.hoʊl **-s** -z
Note: Chiefly US; see note at **arse**.
assibi|late ə'sɪb.ɪ|.leɪt, æs'ɪb-, '-ə- **-lates** -leɪts **-lating** -leɪ.tɪŋ (US) -leɪ.t̬ɪŋ **-lated** -leɪ.tɪd (US) -leɪ.t̬ɪd
assibilation əˌsɪb.ɪ'leɪ.ʃᵊn, æsˌɪb-, -ə'- **-s** -z
assiduit|y ˌæs.ɪ'djuː.ə.t|i, -'dʒuː-, -ɪ.t|i (US) -'duː.ə.t̬|i, -'djuː- **-ies** -iz
assiduous ə'sɪd.ju.əs, -'sɪdʒ.u- (US) -'sɪdʒ.u- **-ly** -li **-ness** -nəs, -nɪs
assign ə'saɪn **-s** -z **-ing** -ɪŋ **-ed** -d **-er/s** -əʳ/z (US) -ɚ/z **-able** -ə.bl̩
assignat *as if French:* ˌæs.ɪn'jɑː, æs.ɪg'næt **-s** -z, -s
assignation ˌæs.ɪg'neɪ.ʃᵊn **-s** -z
assignee ˌæs.aɪ'niː, -ɪ'niː (US) əˌsaɪ'niː, ˌæs.ə'- **-s** -z
assignment ə'saɪn.mənt, -'saɪm- (US) -'saɪn- **-s** -s
assimilable ə'sɪm.ᵊl.ə.bl̩, -ɪ.lə-
assimil|ate ə'sɪm.ɪ.l|eɪt, -ᵊl|.eɪt (US) -ə.l|eɪt **-ates** -eɪts **-ating** -eɪ.tɪŋ (US) -eɪ.t̬ɪŋ **-ated** -eɪ.tɪd (US) -eɪ.t̬ɪd
assimilation əˌsɪm.ɪ'leɪ.ʃᵊn, -ᵊl'eɪ- (US) -ə'leɪ- **-s** -z
assimilative ə'sɪm.ɪ.lə.tɪv, -ᵊl.ə-, -ə.leɪ- (US) -ə.leɪ.t̬ɪv, -lə-
assimilatory ə'sɪm.ɪ.lə.tᵊr.i, -ᵊl.ə-; əˌsɪm.ɪ'leɪ-, -ə'- (US) ə'sɪm.ᵊl.ə.tɔːr-
Assiniboine ə'sɪn.ɪ.bɔɪn, -ə.bɔɪn **-s** -z
Assisi ə'siː.si, -zi, -'sɪs.i
assist ə'sɪst **-s** -s **-ing** -ɪŋ **-ed** -ɪd **-er/s** -əʳ/z (US) -ɚ/z
assistanc|e ə'sɪs.tᵊnts **-es** -ɪz
assistant ə'sɪs.tᵊnt **-s** -s
Assiut æs'juːt (US) ɑː'sjuːt
assiz|e ə'saɪz **-es** -ɪz **-er/s** -əʳ/z (US) -ɚ/z
assoc (*abbrev. for* **associated**) ə'səʊ.ʃi.eɪ.tɪd, -si- (US) -'soʊ.ʃi.eɪ.t̬ɪd, -si-
associable ə'səʊ.ʃi.ə.bl̩, -ʃə-, -si.ə- (US) -'soʊ-
associate (*n.*) ə'səʊ.ʃi.ət, -si.ət (US) -'soʊ.ʃi.ɪt, -si-, -ət **-s** -s
associ|ate (*v.*) ə'səʊ.ʃi|.eɪt, -si- (US) -'soʊ- **-ates** -eɪts **-ating** -eɪ.tɪŋ (US) -eɪ.t̬ɪŋ **-ated** -eɪ.tɪd (US) -eɪ.t̬ɪd
association əˌsəʊ.ʃi'eɪ.ʃᵊn, -si'- (US) -ˌsoʊ **-s** -z
associative ə'səʊ.ʃi.ə.tɪv, -si- (US) -'soʊ-
assonanc|e 'æs.ᵊn.ənts **-es** -ɪz
assonant 'æs.ᵊn.ənt **-s** -s
asson|ate 'æs.ᵊn|.eɪt (US) -ə.n|eɪt **-ates** -eɪts **-ating** -eɪ.tɪŋ (US) -eɪ.t̬ɪŋ **-ated** -eɪ.tɪd (US) -eɪ.t̬ɪd
as|sort ə|'sɔːt (US) -'sɔːrt **-sorts** -'sɔːts (US) -'sɔːrts **-sorting** -'sɔː.tɪŋ (US) -'sɔːr.t̬ɪŋ **-sorted** -'sɔː.tɪd (US) -'sɔːr.t̬ɪd
assortment ə'sɔːt.mənt (US) -'sɔːrt- **-s** -s
Assouan æs'wæn, ɑː'swæn, -'swɑːn (US) 'æs.wɑːn, 'ɑː.swɑːn *stress shift, British only, see compound:* ˌ**Assouan 'Dam**
asst (*abbrev. for* **assistant**) ə'sɪs.tᵊnt
assuag|e ə'sweɪdʒ **-es** -ɪz **-ing** -ɪŋ **-ed** -d **-ement** -mənt
assum|e ə'sjuːm, -suːm (US) -suːm **-es** -z **-ing/ly** -ɪŋ/li **-ed** -d **-edly** -ɪd.li, -əd- **-able** -ə.bl̩ **-ably** -ə.bli
assumpsit ə'sʌmp.sɪt
assumption (A) ə'sʌmp.ʃᵊn **-s** -z
assumptive ə'sʌmp.tɪv
assuranc|e ə'ʃʊə.rᵊnts, -'ʃɔː- (US) -'ʃʊr.ᵊnts, -'ʃɜːr- **-es** -ɪz
assur|e ə'ʃʊəʳ, -ʃɔːʳ (US) -'ʃʊr, -'ʃɜːr **-es** -z **-ing** -ɪŋ **-ed** -d **-edly** -ɪd.li, -əd- **-edness** -d.nəs, -nɪs **-er/s** -əʳ/z (US) -ɚ/z
Assyri|a ə'sɪr.i|.ə **-an/s** -ən/z
assyriologist (A) əˌsɪr.i'ɒl.ə.dʒɪst (US) -'ɑː.lə- **-s** -s
assyriology (A) əˌsɪr.i'ɒl.ə.dʒi (US) -'ɑː.lə-
Astaire ə'steəʳ (US) -'ster
Astarte æs'tɑː.ti (US) ə'stɑr.t̬i
astatine 'æs.tə.tiːn, -tɪn
Astbury 'æst.bᵊr.i (US) -ber-
aster 'æs.təʳ (US) -tɚ **-s** -z
asterisk 'æs.tᵊr.ɪsk **-s** -s
asterism 'æs.tᵊr.ɪ.zᵊm **-s** -z
Asterix 'æs.tᵊr.ɪks
astern ə'stɜːn (US) -'stɜːrn
asteroid 'æs.tᵊr.ɔɪd (US) -tə.rɔɪd **-s** -z
asthenia æs'θiː.ni.ə
asthenic æs'θen.ɪk **-al** -ᵊl
asthma 'æsθ.mə, 'æs.mə (US) 'æz.mə
asthmatic æsθ'mæt.ɪk, æs'mæt.ɪk (US) æz'mæt̬- **-al** -ᵊl **-ally** -ᵊl.i, -li **-s** -s
Asti 'æs.ti, -tiː (US) 'ɑː.sti
astigmatic ˌæs.tɪg'mæt.ɪk (US) -'mæt̬-
astigmatism ə'stɪg.mə.tɪ.zᵊm, æs'tɪg-
astir ə'stɜːʳ (US) -'stɜːr
Asti Spumante ˌæs.ti.spu'mæn.ti, -teɪ (US) ˌɑː.sti.spu'mɑːn-, ˌæs.ti-
Astle 'æs.l̩, 'æs.tl̩
Astley 'æst.li
Aston 'æs.tᵊn ˌ**Aston 'Martin ®**; ˌ**Aston 'Villa**
astonish ə'stɒn.ɪʃ (US) -'stɑː.nɪʃ **-es** -ɪz **-ed/ly** -t/li
astonishing ə'stɒn.ɪ.ʃɪŋ (US) -'stɑː.nɪ- **-ly** -li
astonishment ə'stɒn.ɪʃ.mənt (US) -'stɑː.nɪʃ-
Astor 'æs.təʳ, -tɔːʳ (US) -tɚ
Astoria ə'stɔː.ri.ə, æs'tɔː- (US) ə'stɔːr.i-, æs'tɔːr-
astound ə'staʊnd **-s** -z **-ing/ly** -ɪŋ **-ed** -ɪd
Astra® 'æs.trə
Astraea æs'triː.ə
astragal 'æs.trə.gᵊl **-s** -z
astrakhan (A) ˌæs.trə'kæn, -kɑːn
astral 'æs.trᵊl **-ly** -i
astray ə'streɪ
Astrid 'æs.trɪd
astride ə'straɪd
astring|e ə'strɪndʒ **-es** -ɪz **-ing** -ɪŋ **-ed** -d
astringency ə'strɪn.dʒənt.si
astringent ə'strɪn.dʒənt **-s** -s **-ly** -li
astro- æs.trəʊ-; ə'strɒ- (US) æs.troʊ-; ə'strɑː-
Note: Prefix. Either takes primary or secondary stress on the first syllable, e.g. **astrolabe** /'æs.trəʊ.leɪb (US) -trə-/, **astronomic** /ˌæs.trə'nɒm.ɪk (US) -'nɑː.mɪk/, or primary stress on the second syllable, e.g. **astronomy** /ə'strɒn.ə.mi (US) ə'strɑː.nə-/.
astrobiology ˌæs.trəʊ.baɪ'ɒl.ə.dʒi (US) -troʊ.baɪ'ɑː.lə-, -trə-
astrodome 'æs.trəʊ.dəʊm (US) -trə.doʊm **-s** -z
astrolabe 'æs.trəʊ.leɪb (US) -trə- **-s** -z
astrologer ə'strɒl.ə.dʒəʳ, æs'- (US) ə'strɑː.lə.dʒɚ **-s** -z
astrologic ˌæs.trə'lɒdʒ.ɪk (US) -'lɑː.dʒɪk **-al** -ᵊl **-ally** -ᵊl.i
astrologist ə'strɒl.ə.dʒɪst, æs'- (US) ə'strɑː.lə- **-s** -s
astrology ə'strɒl.ə.dʒi, æs'- (US) ə'strɑː.lə-
astromet|er ə'strɒm.ɪ.t|əʳ, æs'trɒm-, -ə.təʳ (US) ə'strɑː.mə.t̬|ɚ **-ers** -əz (US) -ɚz **-ry** -ri
astronaut 'æs.trə.nɔːt (US) -nɑːt, -nɔːt **-s** -s
astronautic|al ˌæs.trəʊ'nɔː.tɪ.k|ᵊl (US) -trə'nɑː.t̬ɪ-, -'nɔː- **-s** -s
astronomer ə'strɒn.ə.məʳ, æs'- (US) ə'strɑː.nə.mɚ **-s** -z
astronomic ˌæs.trə'nɒm.ɪk (US) -'nɑː.mɪk **-al** -ᵊl **-ally** -ᵊl.i, -li *stress shift* ˌastronomic 'increase
astronom|y ə'strɒn.ə.m|i, æs'- (US) ə'strɑː.nə- **-ies** -iz
Astrophil 'æs.trəʊ.fɪl (US) -trə-
astrophysical ˌæs.trəʊ'fɪz.ɪ.kᵊl (US) -troʊ'-, -trə'-
astrophysicist ˌæs.trəʊ'fɪz.ɪ.sɪst (US) -troʊ'-, -trə'- **-s** -s
astrophysics ˌæs.trəʊ'fɪz.ɪks (US) -troʊ'-
Astros 'æs.trəʊz (US) -troʊz
astroturf (A ®) 'æs.trəʊ.tɜːf (US) -troʊ.tɜːrf
Asturias æs'tʊə.ri.æs, ə'stʊə-, -stjʊə-, -əs (US) ə'stʊr.i-
astu|te ə'stjuː|t, æs'tjuː|t, -'tʃuː|t (US) ə'stuː|t, -'stjuː|t **-ter** -təʳ (US) -t̬ɚ **-test** -tɪst, -təst (US) -t̬ɪst, -t̬əst **-tely** -t.li **-teness** -t.nəs, -t.nɪs

Astyanax ə'staɪ.ə.næks, æs'taɪ-
astylar eɪ'staɪ.ləʳ, -lɑːʳ (US) -lɚ
Asunción əˌsʊnt.si'əʊn, -'ɒn (US) ɑːˌsuːnt.si'oʊn, ˌɑː.suːnt-
asunder ə'sʌn.dəʳ (US) -dɚ
Aswan æs'wæn, ɑː'swæn, -swɑːn (US) 'æs.wɑːn, 'ɑː.swɑːn *stress shift, British only, see compound:* ˌ**Aswan 'Dam**
asyllabic ˌeɪ.sɪ'læb.ɪk, -sə'- (US) -sɪ'- *stress shift:* ˌasyllabic 'vowel
asylum ə'saɪ.ləm **-s** -z
asymmetric ˌeɪ.sɪ'met.rɪk, ˌæs.ɪ'-, -sə'- **-al** -əl **-ally** -əl.i, -li *stress shift:* ˌasymmetric 'bars
asymmetry eɪ'sɪm.ə.tri, æs'ɪm-, '-ɪ-
asymptote 'æs.ɪmp.təʊt (US) -toʊt **-s** -s
asymptotic ˌæs.ɪmp'tɒt.ɪk (US) -'tɑː.t̬ɪk **-al** -əl **-ally** -əl.i, -li *stress shift:* ˌasymptotic 'curve
asyndet|on æs'ɪn.dɪ.t|ən, ə'sɪn- (US) ə'sɪn.də.t|ɑːn, ˌeɪ- **-a** -ə
at- ət-, æt-
Note: Prefix. Examples include **attestation** /ˌæt.es'teɪ.ʃən (US) æt̬-/, in which it is stressed, and **attest** /ə'test/, where it is unstressed.
at *(prep.) strong form:* æt *weak form:* ət
Note: Weak form word. The strong form is /æt/, and is used mainly in sentence-final position (e.g. 'What are you playing at?'). It may also be used in sentence-initial position. The weak form is /ət/ (e.g. 'She's at home.' /ʃiz.ət'həʊm (US) -'hoʊm/).
at *currency:* ɑːt, æt
Atalanta ˌæt.ə'læn.tə (US) ˌæt̬.ə'læn.t̬ə
Atall 'æt.ɔːl
AT&T ˌeɪ.tiː.ənd'tiː
Atari® ə'tɑː.ri (US) -'tɑːr.i
Atatürk 'æt.ə.tɜːk, ˌ--'- (US) 'æt̬.ə.tɝːk
atavism 'æt.ə.vɪ.zəm (US) 'æt̬-
atavistic ˌæt.ə'vɪs.tɪk (US) ˌæt̬.ə'- **-ally** -əl.i, -li *stress shift:* ˌatavistic 'feelings
ataxia ə'tæk.si.ə, æt'æk-, eɪ'-
atax|y ə'tæk.s|i, eɪ- **-ies** -iz **-ic** -ɪk
Atbara æt'bɑː.rə (US) -'bɑːr.ə
ATC ˌeɪ.tiː'siː
Atchison 'ætʃ.ɪ.sən, 'eɪ.tʃɪ- (US) 'ætʃ.ɪ-
Ate *(n.)* 'ɑː.ti, 'eɪ- (US) 'ɑː-
ate *(from* **eat***)* et, eɪt (US) eɪt
-ate -eɪt, -ət, -ɪt
Note: Suffix. When forming a verb, **-ate** is always pronounced with a full vowel, and the verb itself is usually stressed two syllables before the suffix, e.g. **demonstrate** /'dem.ən.streɪt/, unless it is a word containing two syllables, in which case the suffix normally carries primary stress in British English, e.g. **rotate** /rəʊ'teɪt (US) 'roʊ.teɪt, -'-/. In nouns, **-ate** is normally pronounced /-ət/ or /-ɪt/, e.g. **climate** /'klaɪ.mət, -mɪt/, but where the noun is a chemical term it generally has a full vowel, e.g. **nitrate** /'naɪ.treɪt, -trɪt (US) -treɪt/. There are numerous exceptions; see individual entries.
A-team 'eɪˌtiːm
atelic ə'tel.ɪk, æt'el.ɪk, -iː.lɪk (US) ˌeɪ'tiː.lɪk, ˌæt'iː-, -'el.ɪk
atelier ə'tel.i.eɪ, 'æt.el-, 'æt.ə.li-, -jeɪ (US) ə'təl.jeɪ, æt'el-; ˌæt.el'jeɪ **-s** -z
a tempo ˌɑː'tem.pəʊ (US) -poʊ
Atfield 'æt.fiːld
Athabasca ˌæθ.ə'bæs.kə
Athaliah ˌæθ.ə'laɪ.ə
Athanasian ˌæθ.ə'neɪ.zi.ən, '-ʒən, -si.ən, -ʒi- (US) -ʒən
Athanasius ˌæθ.ə'neɪ.zi.əs, '-ʒəs, -si.əs, -ʒi- (US) -ʒəs
Athawes 'æt.hɔːz, 'æθ.ɔːz (US) 'æt̬.hɑːz, -hɔːz, 'æθ.ɑːz, -ɔːz
atheism 'eɪ.θi.ɪ.zəm
atheist 'eɪ.θi.ɪst **-s** -s
atheistic ˌeɪ.θi'ɪs.tɪk **-al** -əl **-ally** -əl.i, -li *stress shift:* ˌatheistic 'culture
atheling (A) 'æθ.ə.lɪŋ **-s** -z
Athelney 'æθ.əl.ni
Athelstan 'æθ.əl.stən *as if Old English:* 'æð.əl.stɑːn
Athelston 'æθ.əl.stən
Athena ə'θiː.nə
Athenaeum ˌæθ.ɪ'niː.əm, -ə'- **-s** -z
Athene ə'θiː.ni, -niː
Athenian ə'θiː.ni.ən **-s** -z
Athenry ˌæθ.ən'raɪ, -ɪn'-
Athens 'æθ.ənz, -ɪnz
Atherley 'æθ.ə.li (US) '-ɚ-
atherosclerosis ˌæθ.ə.rəʊ.sklə'rəʊ.sɪs, -skler'əʊ-, sklɪr'- (US) -roʊ.sklə'roʊ.səs
atherosclerotic ˌæθ.ə.rəʊ.sklə'rɒt.ɪk, -skler'ɒt-, -sklɪr'- (US) -roʊ.sklə'rɑː.t̬ɪk
Atherston 'æθ.ə.stən (US) '-ɚ-
Atherstone 'æθ.ə.stəʊn, -stən (US) -ɚ.stoʊn, -stən
Atherton 'æθ.ə.tən (US) '-ɚ.t̬ən
athirst ə'θɜːst (US) -'θɝːst
Athlestaneford 'el.ʃən.fəd (US) -fɚd
athlete 'æθ.liːt **-s** -s ˌ**athlete's 'foot** (US) '**athlete's** ˌ**foot**
athletic æθ'let.ɪk, əθ- (US) -'let̬.ɪk **-al** -əl **-ally** -əl.i, -li **-s** -s
athleticism æθ'let.ɪ.sɪ.zəm, əθ-, '-ə- (US) -'let̬.ə-
Athlone æθ'ləʊn (US) -'loʊn *stress shift:* ˌAthlone 'Press
Athol 'æθ.əl, -ɒl (US) -ɑːl, -əl
Atholl, Athole 'æθ.əl
Athos 'æθ.ɒs, 'eɪ.θɒs (US) 'æθ.ɑːs, 'eɪ.θɑːs; 'æθ.oʊs
athwart ə'θwɔːt (US) -'θwɔːrt
Athy ə'θaɪ
-ation -'eɪ.ʃən
Note: Suffix. Always carries primary stress, e.g. **demonstration** /ˌdem.ən'streɪ.ʃən/.
atishoo ə'tɪʃ.uː
-ative -ə.tɪv, -eɪ- (US) -ə.t̬ɪv, -eɪ-
Note: Suffix. Words containing **-ative** are normally stressed one or two syllables before the suffix, e.g. **ablative** /'æb.lə.tɪv (US) -t̬ɪv/, **operative** /'ɒp.ər.ə.tɪv (US) 'ɑː.pɚ.ə.t̬ɪv/. See individual entries for exceptions.
Atkins 'æt.kɪnz
Atkinson 'æt.kɪn.sən
Atlanta ət'læn.tə, æt- (US) -t̬ə
atlantean ˌæt.læn'tiː.ən, -lən'-; ət'læn.ti-, æt- (US) ˌæt.læn'tiː-, -lən'-
Atlantes *statues:* ət'læn.tiːz, æt- *in Ariosto's 'Orlando Furioso':* ət'læn.tes, æt-
Atlantic ət'læn.tɪk, æt- (US) -t̬ɪk **At**ˌ**lantic 'City**
Atlantis ət'læn.tɪs, æt- (US) -t̬ɪs
atlas (A) 'æt.ləs **-es** -ɪz
ATM ˌeɪ.tiː'em **-s** -z
atman (A) 'ɑːt.mən
atmometer æt'mɒm.ɪ.təʳ, '-ə- (US) -'mɑː.mə.t̬ɚ **-s** -z
atmosphere 'æt.məs.fɪəʳ (US) -fɪr **-s** -z
atmospheric ˌæt.məs'fer.ɪk (US) -'fer-, -'fɪr- **-s** -s **-al** -əl **-ally** -əl.i, -li *stress shift:* ˌatmospheric 'pressure
atoll 'æt.ɒl; ə'tɒl (US) 'æt.ɑːl, 'eɪ.tɑːl, -tɔːl **-s** -z
atom 'æt.əm (US) 'æt̬- **-s** -z
atomic ə'tɒm.ɪk (US) -'tɑː.mɪk **-s** -s **-ally** -əl.i, -li **a**ˌ**tomic 'energy**
atom|ism 'æt.ə.m|ɪ.zəm (US) 'æt̬- **-ist/s** -ɪst/s
atomistic ˌæt.ə'mɪs.tɪk (US) ˌæt̬-
atomization, -isa- ˌæt.ə.maɪ'zeɪ.ʃən (US) ˌæt̬.ə.mɪ'-
atomiz|e, -is|e 'æt.ə.maɪz (US) 'æt̬- **-es** -ɪz **-ing** -ɪŋ **-ed** -d **-er/s** -əʳ/z (US) -ɚ/z
atonal eɪ'təʊ.nəl, ə-, æt'əʊ- (US) eɪ'toʊ-, æt'oʊ- **-ism** -ɪ.zəm **-ly** -i
atonality ˌeɪ.təʊ'næl.ə.ti, ə-, ˌæt.əʊ'-, -ɪ.ti (US) ˌeɪ.toʊ'næl.ə.t̬i, ˌæt.oʊ'-
aton|e ə'təʊn (US) -'toʊn **-es** -z **-ing/ly** -ɪŋ/li **-ed** -d **-er/s** -əʳ/z, -ɚ/z
atonement ə'təʊn.mənt, -'təʊm- (US) -'toʊn- **-s** -s
atonic eɪ'tɒn.ɪk, ə-, æt'ɒn- (US) eɪ'tɑː.nɪk, æt'ɑː- **-s** -s
atony 'æt.ən.i (US) 'æt̬-
atop ə'tɒp (US) -'tɑːp
-ator -ə.təʳ, -eɪ.təʳ (US) -ə.t̬ɚ, -eɪ.t̬ɚ

Note: Suffix. Words containing **-ator** behave similarly to verbs containing **-ate**, e.g. **demonstrator** /'dem.ən.streɪ.təʳ ⓤⓢ -t̬ɚ/.
-atory -ə.tᵊr.i, -eɪ- ⓤⓢ -ə.tɔːr.i
Note: Suffix. The pronunciation differs between British and American English. In British English, the penultimate syllable is always reduced, but the antepenultimate syllable may be stressed, and in either case may be pronounced with a full vowel, e.g. **articulatory** /ɑː'tɪk.jə.lə.tᵊr.i, -jʊ-; ɑːˌtɪk.jə'leɪ-, -jʊ'-/. In American English, the penultimate syllable is pronounced with a full vowel (but does not carry primary stress), e.g. **articulatory** /ɑːr'tɪk.jə.lə.tɔːr.i/.
ATP ˌeɪ.tiː'piː
atrabilious ˌæt.rə'bɪl.i.əs ⓤⓢ '-jəs
Atreus 'eɪ.tri.əs, -tri.uːs, -truːs
atri|um 'eɪ.tri.|əm, 'æt.ri- ⓤⓢ 'eɪ.tri- **-a** -ə **-ums** -əmz
atrocious ə'trəʊ.ʃəs ⓤⓢ -'troʊ- **-ly** -li **-ness** -nəs, -nɪs
atrocit|y ə'trɒs.ə.t|i, -ɪ.t|i, -'trɑː.sə.t̬|i **-ies** -iz
atrophic ə'trɒf.ɪk, æt'rɒf- ⓤⓢ ə'trɑː.fɪk
atroph|y 'æt.rə.f|i **-ies** -iz **-ying** -i.ɪŋ **-ied** -id
atropine 'æt.rə.pɪn, -piːn
Atropos 'æt.rə.pɒs, -pəs ⓤⓢ -pɑːs
attaboy 'æt.ə.bɔɪ ⓤⓢ 'æt̬-
attach ə'tætʃ **-es** -ɪz **-ing** -ɪŋ **-ed** -t **-able** -ə.bl̩
attaché ə'tæʃ.eɪ, æt'æʃ- ⓤⓢ ˌæt̬.ə'ʃeɪ, ə'tæʃ.eɪ **-s** -z **at'taché ˌcase** ⓤⓢ **atta'ché ˌcase, at'taché ˌcase,**
attachment ə'tætʃ.mənt **-s** -s
attack ə'tæk **-s** -s **-ing** -ɪŋ **-ed** -t **-er/s** -əʳ/z, -ɚ/z
attain ə'teɪn **-s** -z **-ing** -ɪŋ **-ed** -d **-able** -ə.bl̩
attainability əˌteɪ.nə'bɪl.ə.ti, -ɪ.ti ⓤⓢ -ə.t̬i
attainder ə'teɪn.dəʳ ⓤⓢ -dɚ **-s** -z
attainment ə'teɪn.mənt, -'teɪm- ⓤⓢ -'teɪn- **-s** -s
at|taint ə|'teɪnt **-taints** -'teɪnts **-tainting** -'teɪn.tɪŋ ⓤⓢ -'teɪn.t̬ɪŋ **-tainted** -'teɪn.tɪd ⓤⓢ -'teɪn.t̬ɪd
attar 'æt.əʳ ⓤⓢ 'æt̬.ɚ, -ɑːr
attempt ə'tempt **-s** -s **-ing** -ɪŋ **-ed** -ɪd **-er/s** -əʳ/z ⓤⓢ -ɚ/z **-able** -ə.bl̩
Attenborough 'æt.ᵊn.bᵊr.ə, -ᵊm-, -ˌbʌr.ə ⓤⓢ -ᵊnˌbɜːr.oʊ
attend ə'tend **-s** -z **-ing** -ɪŋ **-ed** -ɪd **-er/s** -əʳ/z ⓤⓢ -ɚ/z
attendanc|e ə'ten.dᵊnts **-es** -ɪz
attendant ə'ten.dᵊnt **-s** -s
attendee ə.ten'diː, ˌæt.en- **-s** -z
attention ə'ten.tʃᵊn **-s** -z
attentive ə'ten.tɪv ⓤⓢ -t̬ɪv **-ly** -li **-ness** -nəs, -nɪs
attenuate (*adj.*) ə'ten.ju.ɪt, -ət, -eɪt
attenu|ate (*v.*) ə'ten.ju|.eɪt **-ates** -eɪts **-ating** -eɪ.tɪŋ ⓤⓢ -eɪ.t̬ɪŋ **-ated** -eɪ.tɪd ⓤⓢ -eɪ.t̬ɪd
attenuation əˌten.ju'eɪ.ʃᵊn **-s** -z
attenuator ə'ten.ju.eɪ.təʳ ⓤⓢ -t̬ɚ **-s** -z
Atterbury 'æt.ə.bᵊr.i ⓤⓢ 'æt̬.ɚ.ber.i, -bɚ-
Attercliffe 'æt.ə.klɪf ⓤⓢ 'æt̬.ɚ-
attest ə'test **-s** -s **-ing** -ɪŋ **-ed** -ɪd **-or/s** -əʳ/z ⓤⓢ -ɚ/z **-able** -ə.bl̩
attestation ˌæt.es'teɪ.ʃᵊn ⓤⓢ ˌæt̬- **-s** -z
Attfield 'æt.fiːld
attic 'æt.ɪk ⓤⓢ 'æt̬- **-s** -s
Attica 'æt.ɪ.kə ⓤⓢ 'æt̬-
atticism 'æt.ɪ.sɪ.zᵊm ⓤⓢ 'æt̬- **-s** -z
atticiz|e, -is|e 'æt.ɪ.saɪz ⓤⓢ 'æt̬- **-es** -ɪz **-ing** -ɪŋ **-ed** -d
Attila ə'tɪl.ə; 'æt.ɪ.lə ⓤⓢ ə'tɪl.ə; 'æt̬.ɪ.lə
attir|e ə'taɪəʳ ⓤⓢ -'taɪɚ **-es** -z **-ing** -ɪŋ **-ed** -d **-ement** -mənt
Attis 'æt.ɪs ⓤⓢ 'æt̬-
attitude 'æt.ɪ.tjuːd, -tʃuːd ⓤⓢ 'æt̬.ə.tuːd, -tjuːd **-s** -z
attitudinal ˌæt.ɪ'tjuː.dɪ.nᵊl, -'tʃuː- ⓤⓢ ˌæt̬.ə'tuː.dᵊn.ᵊl, -'tjuː-
attitudinarian ˌæt.ɪ.tjuː.dɪ'neə.ri.ən, -tʃuː- ⓤⓢ ˌæt̬.əˌtuː.dɪ'ner.i-, -ˌtjuː- **-s** -z
attitudiniz|e, -is|e ˌæt.ɪ'tjuː.dɪ.naɪz, -'tʃuː- ⓤⓢ ˌæt̬.ə'tuː.dᵊn.aɪz, -'tjuː- **-es** -ɪz **-ing** -ɪŋ **-ed** -d **-er/s** -əʳ/z, -ɚ/z
Attleborough 'æt.ᵊl.bᵊr.ə, -ˌbʌr.ə ⓤⓢ -ˌbɜːr.oʊ
Attlee 'æt.li
Attock ə'tɒk ⓤⓢ -'tɑːk
attorn ə'tɜːn ⓤⓢ -'tɜːrn **-s** -z **-ing** -ɪŋ **-ed** -d
attorney ə'tɜː.ni ⓤⓢ -'tɜːr- **-s** -z **aˌttorney 'general**
attorney-at-law əˌtɜː.ni.ət'lɔː ⓤⓢ -ˌtɜːr.ni.ət'lɑː, -'lɔː **attorneys-at-law** əˌtɜː.niz.ət'lɔː ⓤⓢ -ˌtɜːr.niz.ət'lɑː, -'lɔː
attorneyship ə'tɜː.ni.ʃɪp ⓤⓢ -'tɜːr- **-s** -s
attract ə'trækt **-s** -s **-ing/ly** -ɪŋ/li **-ed** -ɪd **-or/s** -əʳ/z ⓤⓢ -ɚ/z **-able** -ə.bl̩
attractability əˌtræk.tə'bɪl.ə.ti, -ɪ.ti ⓤⓢ -ə.t̬i
attraction ə'træk.ʃᵊn **-s** -z
attractive ə'træk.tɪv **-ly** -li **-ness** -nəs, -nɪs
attributable ə'trɪb.jə.tə.bl̩, -jʊ- ⓤⓢ -jə.t̬ə-
attribute (*n.*) 'æt.rɪ.bjuːt **-s** -s
attri|bute (*v.*) ə'trɪ|.bjuːt **-butes** -bjuːts **-buting** -bjʊ.tɪŋ ⓤⓢ -bjə.t̬ɪŋ, -bjuː- **-buted** -bjʊ.tɪd ⓤⓢ -bjə.t̬ɪd, -bjuː-
attribution ˌæt.rɪ'bjuː.ʃᵊn **-s** -z
attributive ə'trɪb.jə.tɪv, -jʊ- ⓤⓢ -jə.t̬ɪv **-ly** -li
attrition ə'trɪʃ.ᵊn, æt'rɪʃ-
attun|e ə'tjuːn, æt'juːn ⓤⓢ ə'tuːn, -'tjuːn **-es** -z **-ing** -ɪŋ **-ed** -d
Attwell 'æt.wel, -wəl
At(t)wood 'æt.wʊd
ATV ˌeɪ.tiː'viː **-s** -z
Atwater 'æt.wɔː.təʳ ⓤⓢ -wɑː.t̬ɚ, -wɔː-
atypical ˌeɪ'tɪp.ɪ.kᵊl
aubade əʊ'bɑːd ⓤⓢ oʊ- **-s** -z
auberg|e əʊ'beəʒ, -'bɜːʒ ⓤⓢ oʊ'berʒ **-es** -ɪz
aubergine 'əʊ.bə.ʒiːn, -dʒiːn, ˌ--'- ⓤⓢ 'oʊ.bɚ- **-s** -z
Auberon 'ɔː.bə.rən, 'əʊ-, -rɒn, ˌ--'- ⓤⓢ 'ɑː.bə.rɑːn, 'ɔː-
aubretia ɔː'briː.ʃə, -ʃi.ə ⓤⓢ ɑː-, ɔː-
Aubrey 'ɔː.bri ⓤⓢ 'ɑː-, 'ɔː-
aubrietia ɔː'briː.ʃə, -ʃi.ə ⓤⓢ ɑː-, ɔː- **-s** -z
auburn (A) 'ɔː.bən, -bɜːn ⓤⓢ 'ɑː.bɚn, 'ɔː-
Auchindachie ˌɔː.kɪn'dæk.i, -xɪn'dæx- ⓤⓢ ˌɑː.kɪn'dæk-, ˌɔː-
Auchinleck ˌɔː.kɪn'lek, -xɪn'-, '--- ⓤⓢ ˌɑː.kɪn'lek, ˌɔː-, '---
Auchmuty ɔːk'mjuː.ti ⓤⓢ ɑːk-, ɔːk-
Auchtermuchty ˌɔːk.tə'mʌk.ti, ˌɒk.tə-, ˌɔːx.tə'mʌx.ti, ˌɒx.tə- ⓤⓢ ˌɑːk.tɚ'mʌk-, ˌɔːk-
Auckland 'ɔːk.lənd ⓤⓢ 'ɑːk-, 'ɔːk-
au contraire ˌəʊ.kɒn'treəʳ ⓤⓢ ˌoʊ.kɑːn'trer
au courant əʊ'kʊr.ɑ̃ːŋ ⓤⓢ ˌoʊ.kuː'rɑːn
auction 'ɔːk.ʃᵊn, 'ɒk- ⓤⓢ 'ɑːk.ʃᵊn, 'ɔːk- **-s** -z **-ing** -ɪŋ **-ed** -d
auctionary 'ɔːk.ʃᵊn.ᵊr.i, 'ɒk- ⓤⓢ 'ɑːk.ʃᵊn.er-, 'ɔːk-
auctioneer ˌɔːk.ʃᵊn'ɪəʳ, ˌɒk- ⓤⓢ ˌɑːk.ʃə'nɪr, ˌɔːk- **-s** -z **-ing** -ɪŋ **-ed** -d
audacious ɔː'deɪ.ʃəs ⓤⓢ ɑː-, ɔː- **-ly** -li **-ness** -nəs, -nɪs
audacit|y ɔː'dæs.ə.t|i, -ɪ.t|i ⓤⓢ ɑː'dæs.ə.t̬|i, ɔː- **-ies** -iz
Audelay 'ɔːd.leɪ ⓤⓢ 'ɑːd-, 'ɔːd-
Auden 'ɔː.dᵊn ⓤⓢ 'ɑː-, 'ɔː-
Audenshaw 'ɔː.dᵊn.ʃɔː ⓤⓢ 'ɑː.dᵊn.ʃɑː, 'ɔː-, -ʃɔː
Audi® 'aʊ.di ⓤⓢ 'aʊ-, 'ɑː-
audibility ˌɔː.dɪ'bɪl.ə.ti, -də'-, -ɪ.ti ⓤⓢ ˌɑː.də'bɪl.ə.t̬i, ˌɔː-
audib|le 'ɔː.də.b|l̩, '-dɪ- ⓤⓢ 'ɑː.də-, 'ɔː- **-ly** -li **-leness** -l̩.nəs, -nɪs

audienc|e 'ɔː.di.ən*t*s Ⓤⓢ 'ɑː-, 'ɔː- **-es** -ɪz
audio 'ɔː.di.əʊ Ⓤⓢ 'ɑː.di.oʊ, 'ɔː-
audiocassette ˌɔː.di.əʊ.kə'set Ⓤⓢ ˌɑː.di.oʊ-, ˌɔː- **-s** -s
audiologist ˌɔː.di'ɒl.ə.dʒɪst Ⓤⓢ ˌɑː.di'ɑː.lə-, ˌɔː- **-s** -s
audiology ˌɔː.di'ɒl.ə.dʒi Ⓤⓢ ˌɑː.di'ɑː.lə-, ˌɔː-
audiometer ˌɔː.di'ɒm.ɪ.təʳ, -ə.təʳ Ⓤⓢ ˌɑː.di'ɑː.mə.t̬ɚ, ˌɔː- **-s** -z
audiometry ˌɔː.di'ɒm.ɪ.tri, '-ə- Ⓤⓢ ˌɑː.di'ɑː.mə-, ˌɔː-
audiotape 'ɔː.di.əʊ.teɪp Ⓤⓢ 'ɑː.di.oʊ-, 'ɔː- **-s** -s
audio-typ|ing 'ɔː.di.əʊˌtaɪ.p|ɪŋ Ⓤⓢ 'ɑː.di.oʊ-, 'ɔː- **-ist/s** -ɪst/s
audio-visual ˌɔː.di.əʊ'vɪʒ.u.əl, -'vɪz.ju- Ⓤⓢ ˌɑː.di.oʊ'vɪʒ.ju-, ˌɔː-
audiphone 'ɔː.dɪ.fəʊn Ⓤⓢ 'ɑː.dɪ.foʊn, 'ɔː- **-s** -z
au|dit 'ɔː|.dɪt Ⓤⓢ 'ɑː-, 'ɔː- **-dits** -dɪts **-diting** -dɪ.tɪŋ Ⓤⓢ -də.t̬ɪŋ **-dited** -dɪ.tɪd Ⓤⓢ -də.t̬ɪd
audition ɔː'dɪʃ.ᵊn Ⓤⓢ ɑː-, ɔː- **-s** -z
auditor 'ɔː.dɪt.əʳ Ⓤⓢ 'ɑː.də.t̬ɚ, 'ɔː- **-s** -z
auditori|um ˌɔː.dɪ'tɔː.ri|.əm Ⓤⓢ ˌɑː.də'tɔːr.i-, ˌɔː- **-ums** -əmz **-a** -ə
auditorship 'ɔː.dɪt.ə.ʃɪp Ⓤⓢ 'ɑː.də.t̬ɚ-, 'ɔː- **-s** -s
auditor|y 'ɔː.dɪ.tᵊr|.i Ⓤⓢ 'ɑː.də.tɔːr-, 'ɔː- **-ies** -iz
Audley 'ɔːd.li Ⓤⓢ 'ɑːd-, 'ɔːd-
Audrey 'ɔː.dri Ⓤⓢ 'ɑː-, 'ɔː-
Audubon 'ɔː.də.bɒn, -bən Ⓤⓢ 'ɑː.də.bɑːn, 'ɔː-, -bən
au fait ˌəʊ'feɪ Ⓤⓢ ˌoʊ-
Aufidius ɔː'fɪd.i.əs Ⓤⓢ ɑː-, ɔː-
Aufklärung 'aʊf.kleə.rʊŋ Ⓤⓢ -kler.ʊŋ
Auf Wiedersehen ˌaʊf'viː.də.zeɪ.ən, -zeɪn Ⓤⓢ -'viː.dɚ-
Aug. (*abbrev. for* **August**) 'ɔː.gəst Ⓤⓢ 'ɑː-, 'ɔː-
Augean ɔː'dʒiː.ən Ⓤⓢ ɑː-, ɔː-
Augeas ɔː'dʒiː.æs Ⓤⓢ ɑː-, ɔː-
Augener 'aʊ.gᵊn.əʳ Ⓤⓢ -ɚ
auger 'ɔː.gəʳ Ⓤⓢ 'ɑː.gɚ, 'ɔː- **-s** -z
Aughrim 'ɔː.grɪm Ⓤⓢ 'ɑː-, 'ɔː-
aught ɔːt Ⓤⓢ ɑːt, ɔːt
Aughton *Humberside, S. Yorks & Nr. Ormskirk, Lancashire:* 'ɔː.tᵊn Ⓤⓢ 'ɑː-, 'ɔː- *Nr. Lancaster, Lancashire:* 'æf.tən
Augie 'ɔː.gi Ⓤⓢ 'ɑː-, 'ɔː-
augment (*n.*) 'ɔːg.mənt Ⓤⓢ 'ɑːg-, 'ɔːg- **-s** -s
aug|ment (*v.*) ɔːg|'ment Ⓤⓢ ɑːg-, ɔːg- **-ments** -'ments **-menting** -'men.tɪŋ Ⓤⓢ -'men.t̬ɪŋ **-mented** -'men.tɪd Ⓤⓢ -'men.t̬ɪd **-mentable** -'men.tə.bl̩ Ⓤⓢ -'men.t̬ə.bl̩
augmentation ˌɔːg.men'teɪ.ʃᵊn, -mən'- Ⓤⓢ ˌɑːg-, ˌɔːg- **-s** -z
augmentative ɔːg'men.tə.tɪv Ⓤⓢ ɑːg'men.t̬ə.t̬ɪv, ɔːg-
au gratin ˌəʊ'græt.æ̃ŋ Ⓤⓢ oʊ'grɑː.tᵊn, -'græt.ᵊn
Augsburg 'aʊgz.bɜːg, 'aʊks-, -bʊəg Ⓤⓢ 'ɑːgz.bɜːrg, 'ɔːgz-, -bʊrg
aug|ur 'ɔː.g|əʳ Ⓤⓢ 'ɑː.g|ɚ, 'ɔː- **-urs** -əz Ⓤⓢ -ɚz **-uring** -ᵊr.ɪŋ **-ured** -əd Ⓤⓢ -ɚd
augural 'ɔːg.jʊ.rᵊl, -jᵊr.ᵊl Ⓤⓢ 'ɑːg.jɚ.ᵊl, 'ɔːg-
augur|y 'ɔːg.jʊ.r|i, -jᵊr.|i Ⓤⓢ 'ɑːg.jɚ|.i, 'ɔːg- **-ies** -iz
August (*n.*) 'ɔː.gəst Ⓤⓢ 'ɑː-, 'ɔː- **-s** -s ˌ**August Bank 'Holiday**
august (*adj.*) ɔː'gʌst Ⓤⓢ ɑː-, ɔː-, '-- **-est** -ɪst **-ly** -li **-ness** -nəs, -nɪs
August|a ɔː'gʌs.t|ə, ə- Ⓤⓢ ə'-, ɑː-, ɔː- **-an** -ən
Augustine ɔː'gʌs.tɪn, ə- Ⓤⓢ ɑː-, ɔː-; 'ɑː.gə.stɪn, 'ɔː-
Augustinian ˌɔː.gə'stɪn.i.ən Ⓤⓢ ˌɑː-, ˌɔː-
Augustus ɔː'gʌs.təs, ə- Ⓤⓢ ə-, ɑː-, ɔː-
auk ɔːk Ⓤⓢ ɑːk, ɔːk **-s** -s
aul|a 'ɔː.l|ə, 'aʊ- Ⓤⓢ 'ɑː-, 'ɔː- **-ae** -iː, -aɪ, -eɪ
auld (A) ɔːld Ⓤⓢ ɑːld, ɔːld
auld lang syne ˌɔːld.læŋ'saɪn, -zaɪn Ⓤⓢ ˌɑːld-, ˌɔːld-
Aumerle ɔː'mɜːl Ⓤⓢ ɑː'mɜːrl, ɔː-
au naturel ˌəʊ.næt.jʊ'rel Ⓤⓢ ˌoʊ.nætʃ.ə'rel; -nɑː.tʊ'-
Aungier 'eɪn.dʒəʳ Ⓤⓢ -dʒɚ
aunt ɑːnt Ⓤⓢ ænt, ɑːnt **-s** -s
Note: Although **aunt** is generally /ænt/ in American English, regional and social subgroups have persistent /ɑːnt/.
auntie, aunty 'ɑːn.ti Ⓤⓢ 'æn.t̬i, 'ɑːn- **-s** -z
au pair ˌəʊ'peəʳ Ⓤⓢ oʊ'per
aura 'ɔː.rə Ⓤⓢ 'ɔːr.ə **-s** -z
aural 'ɔː.rᵊl, 'aʊ- Ⓤⓢ 'ɔːr.ᵊl **-ly** -i
aurate 'ɔː.reɪt, -rɪt Ⓤⓢ 'ɔːr.eɪt **-s** -s
aureate 'ɔː.ri.eɪt, -ət, -ɪt Ⓤⓢ 'ɔːr.i-
Aureli|a ɔː'riː.li.|ə **-an** -ən **-us** -əs
aureola ɔː'riː.ə.lə Ⓤⓢ ˌɔːr.i'oʊ- **-s** -z
aureole 'ɔː.ri.əʊl Ⓤⓢ 'ɔːr.i.oʊl **-s** -z
aureomycin ˌɔː.ri.əʊ'maɪ.sɪn Ⓤⓢ ˌɔːr.i-
au revoir ˌəʊ.rəv'wɑːʳ, -rɪv'- Ⓤⓢ ˌoʊ.rəv'wɑːr
auricle 'ɔː.rɪ.kl̩, 'ɒr.ɪ- Ⓤⓢ 'ɔːr.ɪ- **-s** -z
auricula ɔː'rɪk.jʊ.lə, ɒr'ɪk-, -jə- Ⓤⓢ ɔː'rɪk.jə- **-s** -z
auricular ɔː'rɪk.jʊ.ləʳ, ɒr'ɪk-, -jə- Ⓤⓢ ɔː'rɪk.jə.lɚ **-ly** -li
auricu|late ɔː'rɪk.jʊ|.lət, -jə-, -lɪt, -leɪt Ⓤⓢ -jə- **-lated** -leɪ.tɪd Ⓤⓢ -leɪ.t̬ɪd
Auriel 'ɔː.ri.əl Ⓤⓢ 'ɔːr.i-
auriferous ɔː'rɪf.ᵊr.əs
Auriga ɔː'raɪ.gə
Aurignacian ˌɔː.rɪg'neɪ.ʃᵊn, -ʃi.ən Ⓤⓢ ˌɔːr.ɪg-
aurist 'ɔː.rɪst Ⓤⓢ 'ɔːr.ɪst **-s** -s
aurochs 'ɔː.rɒks, 'aʊ- Ⓤⓢ 'ɔːr.ɑːks, 'aʊ.rɑːks **-es** -ɪz
auror|a (A) ɔː'rɔː.r|ə, ə- Ⓤⓢ -'rɔːr|.ə **-as** -əz **-al** -ᵊl
aurora australis ɔːˌrɔː.rə.ɒs'treɪ.lɪs, ə-, -'trɑː- Ⓤⓢ -ˌrɔːr.ə.ɔː'streɪ-
aurora borealis ɔːˌrɔː.rə.bɒr.i'eɪ.lɪs, ə-, -'ɑː.lɪs Ⓤⓢ -ˌrɔːr.ə.bɔːr.i'æl.ɪs, -'ɑː.lɪs
Auschwitz 'aʊʃ.wɪts *as if German:* -vɪts
auscul|tate 'ɔː.skᵊl|.teɪt, 'ɒs.kᵊl-, -kʌl- Ⓤⓢ 'ɑː.skᵊl-, 'ɔː- **-tates** -teɪts **-tating** -teɪ.tɪŋ Ⓤⓢ -teɪ.t̬ɪŋ **-tated** -teɪ.tɪd Ⓤⓢ -teɪ.t̬ɪd
auscultation ˌɔː.skᵊl'teɪ.ʃᵊn, ˌɒs.kᵊl'-, -kʌl'- Ⓤⓢ ˌɑː.skᵊl-, ˌɔː- **-s** -z
auscultator 'ɔː.skᵊl.teɪ.təʳ, 'ɒs.kᵊl-, -kʌl- Ⓤⓢ 'ɑː.skᵊl.teɪ.t̬ɚ, 'ɔː- **-s** -z
auspic|e 'ɔː.spɪs, 'ɒs.pɪs Ⓤⓢ 'ɑː.spɪs, 'ɔː- **-es** -ɪz
auspicious ɔː'spɪʃ.əs, ɒs'pɪʃ- Ⓤⓢ ɑː'spɪʃ-, ɔː- **-ly** -li **-ness** -nəs, -nɪs
Aussie 'ɒz.i Ⓤⓢ 'ɑː.zi, 'ɔː-, -si **-s** -z
Austell 'ɔː.stᵊl, 'ɒs.tᵊl *local Cornish pronunciation:* 'ɔː.sᵊl Ⓤⓢ 'ɑː.stᵊl, 'ɔː-
Austen 'ɒs.tɪn, 'ɔː.stɪn Ⓤⓢ 'ɑː.stɪn, 'ɔː-
Auster 'ɔː.stəʳ, ɒː.stəʳ Ⓤⓢ 'ɑː.stɚ, 'ɔː-
auster|e ɒs'tɪəʳ, ɔː'stɪəʳ Ⓤⓢ ɑː'stɪr, ɔː- **-er** -əʳ, -ɚ **-est** -ɪst, -əst **-ely** -li **-eness** -nəs, -nɪs
austerit|y ɒs'ter.ə.t|i, ɔː'ster-, -ɪ.t|i Ⓤⓢ 'ɑː.ster.ə.t̬|i, 'ɔː- **-ies** -iz
Austerlitz 'ɔː.stə.lɪts, 'aʊ- Ⓤⓢ 'ɑː.stɚ-, 'ɔː-
Austin 'ɒs.tɪn, 'ɔː.stɪn Ⓤⓢ 'ɑː.stɪn, 'ɔː- **-s** -z
austral 'ɒs.trᵊl, 'ɔː.strᵊl Ⓤⓢ 'ɑː.strᵊl, 'ɔː-
Australasi|a ˌɒs.trə'leɪ.ʒ|ə, ˌɔː.strə-, -zi|.ə, -ʃi|.ə, -ʃ|ə Ⓤⓢ ˌɑː.strə'-, ˌɔː- **-an/z** -ən/z
Australi|a ɒs'treɪ.li|.ə, ɔː'streɪ- Ⓤⓢ ɑː'streɪl.jə, ɔː'- **-an/s** -ən/z
australopithecus ˌɒs.trə.ləʊ'pɪθ.ɪ.kəs, ˌɔː.strə-, -ə.kəs Ⓤⓢ ˌɑː.strə.loʊ'-, ˌɔː-
Austri|a 'ɒs.tri|.ə, 'ɔː.stri- Ⓤⓢ 'ɑː.stri-, 'ɔː- **-an/s** -ən/z
Austro- ɒs.trəʊ-, ɔː.strəʊ- Ⓤⓢ ɑː.stroʊ-, ɔː-
Note: Prefix. Behaves as **Anglo-**.
Austro-German ˌɒs.trəʊ'dʒɜː.mən, ˌɔː.strəʊ'- Ⓤⓢ ˌɑː.stroʊ'dʒɜːr-, ˌɔː-
Austro-Hungarian ˌɒs.trəʊ.hʌŋ'geə.ri.ən, ˌɔː.strəʊ- Ⓤⓢ ˌɑː.stroʊ.hʌŋ'ger.i-, ˌɔː-

Austronesi|a ˌɒs.trəʊ'niː.ʒ|ə, ˌɔː.strəʊ'-, -zi|.ə, -si|.ə, -ʃ|ə (US) ˌɑː.stroʊ'-, ˌɔː- **-an/s** -ən/z
autarchic ɔː'tɑː.kɪk (US) ɑː'tɑːr-, ɔː- **-al** -əl
autarch|y 'ɔː.tɑː.k|i (US) 'ɑː.tɑːr-, 'ɔː- **-ies** -iz
autarkic ɔː'tɑː.kɪk (US) ɑː'tɑr-, ɔː- **-al** əl
authentic ɔː'θen.tɪk (US) ɑː'θen.t̬ɪk, ɔː- **-al** -əl **-ally** -əl.i, -li
authenti|cate ɔː'θen.tɪ|.keɪt (US) ɑː'θen.t̬ɪ-, ɔː- **-cates** -keɪts **-cating** -keɪ.tɪŋ (US) -keɪ.t̬ɪŋ **-cated** -keɪ.tɪd (US) -keɪ.t̬ɪd **-cator/s** -keɪ.təʳ/z (US) -keɪ.t̬ɚ/z
authentication ɔːˌθen.tɪ'keɪ.ʃən (US) ɑːˌθen.t̬ɪ'-, ɔː- **-s** -z
authenticit|y ˌɔː.θen'tɪs.ə.t|i, -θən'-, -ɪ.t|i (US) ˌɑː.θen'tɪs.ə.t̬|i, ˌɔː- **-ies** -iz
author 'ɔː.θəʳ (US) 'ɑː.θɚ, 'ɔː- **-s** -z
authoress 'ɔː.θər.es, -ɪs, -əs; ˌɔː.θər'es (US) 'ɑː.θɚ.ɪs, 'ɔː-, -əs **-es** -ɪz
authorial ɔː'θɔː.ri.əl (US) ɑː'θɔːr.i-, ɔː-
authoritarian ˌɔː.θɒr.ɪ'teə.ri.ən, ɔːˌθɒr-, -ə'- (US) əˌθɔːr.ə'ter.i-, ɑː-, ɔː- **-s** -z
authoritarianism ɔːˌθɒr.ɪ'teə.ri.ə.nɪ.zəm, -ə'- (US) əˌθɔːr.ə'ter.i-, ɑː-, ɔː-
authoritative ɔː'θɒr.ɪ.tə.tɪv, ə-, '-ə-, -teɪ- (US) ə'θɔːr.ə.teɪ.t̬ɪv, ɑː-, ɔː- **-ly** -li **-ness** -nəs, -nɪs
authorit|y ɔː'θɒr.ə.t|i, ə-, -ɪ.t|i (US) ə'θɔːr.ə.t̬|i, ɑː-, ɔː- **-ies** -iz
authorization, -isa- ˌɔː.θər.aɪ'zeɪ.ʃən, -ɪ'- (US) ˌɑː.θɚ.ɪ'-, ˌɔː- **-s** -z
authoriz|e, -is|e 'ɔː.θər.aɪz (US) 'ɑː-, 'ɔː- **-es** -ɪz **-ing** -ɪŋ **-ed** -d **-able** -ə.bl̩
authorship 'ɔː.θə.ʃɪp (US) 'ɑː.θɚ-, 'ɔː-
autism 'ɔː.tɪ.zəm (US) 'ɑː.tɪ-, 'ɔː-
autistic ɔː'tɪs.tɪk (US) ɑː-, ɔː-
auto- ɔː.təʊ-; ɔː'tɒ- (US) ɑː.t̬oʊ-, ɔː-; ɑː'tɑː-, ɔː-
Note: Prefix. Either takes primary or secondary stress on the first syllable. e.g. **autocrat** /'ɔː.tə.kræt (US) 'ɑː.t̬ə-, ɔː-/, **automatic** /ˌɔː.tə'mæt.ɪk (US) ˌɑː.t̬ə'mæt̬-, ɔː-/, or primary stress on the second syllable, e.g. **automaton** /ɔː'tɒm.ə.tən (US) ɑː'tɑː.mə-, ɔː-, -tɑːn/.
auto 'ɔː.təʊ (US) 'ɑː.t̬oʊ, 'ɔː- **-s** -z
autobahn 'ɔː.təʊ.bɑːn, 'aʊ- (US) 'ɑː.t̬oʊ-, 'ɔː-, -t̬ə- **-s** -z
autobiographer ˌɔː.tə.baɪ'ɒg.rə.fəʳ (US) ˌɑː.t̬ə.baɪ'ɑː.grə.fɚ, ˌɔː-, -t̬oʊ- **-s** -z
autobiographic ˌɔː.təˌbaɪ.əʊ'græf.ɪk (US) ˌɑː.t̬əˌbaɪ.ə'-, ˌɔː-, -t̬oʊˌ- **-al** -əl **-ally** -əl.i, -li *stress shift:* ˌautobiographic 'novel
autobiograph|y ˌɔː.tə.baɪ'ɒg.rə.f|i (US) ˌɑː.t̬ə.baɪ'ɑː.grə-, ˌɔː-, -t̬oʊ- **-ies** -iz
autocade 'ɔː.təʊ.keɪd (US) 'ɑː.t̬oʊ-, 'ɔː-
auto-car 'ɔː.təʊ.kɑːʳ (US) 'ɑː.t̬oʊ.kɑːr, 'ɔː- **-s** -z
autochthon ɔː'tɒk.θən, -θɒn (US) ɑː'tɑːk.θən, ɔː- **-s** -z
autochthonous ɔː'tɒk.θən.əs (US) ɑː'tɑːk-, ɔː-
autoclav|e 'ɔː.təʊ.kleɪv (US) 'ɑː.t̬oʊ-, 'ɔː- **-es** -z **-ing** -ɪŋ **-ed** -d
autocrac|y ɔː'tɒk.rə.s|i (US) ɑː'tɑː.krə-, ɔː- **-ies** -iz
autocrat 'ɔː.tə.kræt (US) 'ɑː.t̬ə-, 'ɔː- **-s** -s
autocratic ˌɔː.tə'kræt.ɪk (US) ˌɑː.t̬ə'kræt̬-, ˌɔː- **-al** -əl **-ally** -əl.i, -li *stress shift:* ˌautocratic 'government
autocross 'ɔː.təʊ.krɒs (US) 'ɑː.t̬oʊ.krɑːs, 'ɔː-
autocue (A®) 'ɔː.təʊ.kjuː (US) 'ɑː.t̬oʊ-, 'ɔː- **-s** -z
auto-da-fé ˌɔː.təʊ.dɑː'feɪ, ˌaʊ- (US) ˌɑː.t̬oʊ.də'-, ˌɔː- **-s** -z
autodestruct ˌɔː.təʊ.dɪ'strʌkt, -də'- (US) ˌɑː.t̬oʊ-, ˌɔː- **-s** -s **-ing** -ɪŋ **-ed** -ɪd
autodidact ˌɔː.təʊ'daɪ.dækt (US) ˌɑː.t̬oʊ-, ˌɔː- **-s** -s
autodidactic ˌɔː.təʊ.daɪ'dæk.tɪk, -dɪ'- (US) ˌɑː.t̬oʊ-, ˌɔː-
autoerotic ˌɔː.təʊ.ɪ'rɒt.ɪk, -ə'rɒt- (US) ˌɑː.t̬oʊ.ɪ'rɑː.t̬ɪk, ˌɔː- *stress shift:* ˌautoerotic 'fantasy
autoerot|ism ˌɔː.təʊ.ɪ'rɒt|.ɪ.zəm; -'er.ə.t|ɪ- (US) ˌɑː.t̬oʊ.ɪ'rɑː.t̬|ɪ-, ˌɔː- **-icism** -ɪ.sɪ.zəm (US) -ə.sɪ.zəm
autogam|ous ɔː'tɒg.ə.m|əs (US) ɑː'tɑː.gə-, ɔː- **-y** -i
autogenesis ˌɔː.təʊ'dʒen.ə.sɪs, '-ɪ- (US) ˌɑː.t̬oʊ'dʒen.ə-, ˌɔː-
autogenetic ˌɔː.təʊ.dʒən'et.ɪk (US) ˌɑː.t̬oʊ.dʒə'net̬-, ˌɔː-
autogenic ˌɔː.təʊ'dʒen.ɪk (US) ˌɑː.t̬oʊ'-, ˌɔː-
autogenous ɔː'tɒdʒ.ə.nəs (US) ɑː't̬ɑː.dʒə-, ɔː- **-ly** -li
autogiro ˌɔː.təʊ'dʒaɪə.rəʊ (US) ˌɑː.t̬oʊ'dʒaɪ.roʊ, ˌɔː- **-s** -z
autograph 'ɔː.tə.grɑːf, -græf (US) 'ɑː.t̬ə.græf, 'ɔː- **-s** -s
autographic ˌɔː.təʊ'græf.ɪk (US) ˌɑː.t̬ə'-, ˌɔː- **-al** -əl **-ally** -əl.i
autography ɔː'tɒg.rə.fi (US) ɑː'tɑː.grə-, ɔː-
autogyro ˌɔː.təʊ'dʒaɪə.rəʊ (US) ˌɑː.t̬oʊ'dʒaɪ.roʊ, ˌɔː- **-s** -z
Autoharp® 'ɔː.təʊ.hɑːp (US) 'ɑː.t̬oʊ.hɑːrp, 'ɔː-
auto-immun|e ˌɔː.təʊ.ɪ'mjuːn (US) ˌɑː.t̬oʊ-, ˌɔː- **-ity** -ə.ti, -ɪ.ti (US) -ə.t̬i
autolexic|al ˌɔː.təʊ'lek.sɪ.k|əl (US) ˌɑː.t̬oʊ'lek.sə-, ˌɔː- **-ally** -əl.i, -li
autolock 'ɔː.təʊ.lɒk (US) 'ɑː.t̬oʊ.lɑːk, 'ɔː-
Autolycus ɔː'tɒl.ɪ.kəs (US) ɑː'tɑː.lɪ-, ɔː-
automaker 'ɔː.təʊˌmeɪ.kəʳ (US) 'ɑː.t̬oʊˌmeɪ.kɚ, 'ɔː- **-s** -z
automat (A®) 'ɔː.tə.mæt (US) 'ɑː.t̬ə-, 'ɔː-
auto|mate 'ɔː.tə|.meɪt (US) 'ɑː.t̬ə-, 'ɔː- **-mates** -meɪts **-mating** -meɪ.tɪŋ (US) -meɪ.t̬ɪŋ **-mated** -meɪ.tɪd (US) -meɪ.t̬ɪd
automatic ˌɔː.tə'mæt.ɪk (US) ˌɑː.t̬ə'mæt̬-, ˌɔː- **-al** -əl **-ally** -əl.i, -li *stress shift, see compound:* ˌautomatic 'pilot
automation ˌɔː.tə'meɪ.ʃən (US) ˌɑː.t̬ə'-, ˌɔː-
automat|ism ɔː'tɒm.ə.t|ɪ.zəm (US) ɑː'tɑː.mə.t̬|ɪ-, ɔː- **-ist/s** -ɪst/s
automat|on ɔː'tɒm.ə.t|ən (US) ɑː'tɑː.mə-, ɔː-, -t|ɑːn **-ons** -ənz (US) -ənz, -ɑːnz **-a** -ə
automobile 'ɔː.tə.məʊ.biːl, ˌɔː.tə.məʊ'biːl (US) 'ɑː.t̬ə.moʊ.biːl, 'ɔː-, ˌɑː.t̬ə.moʊ'biːl, ˌɔː-, ˌɑː.t̬ə'moʊ-, 'ɔː- **-s** -z
automotive ˌɔː.tə'məʊ.tɪv (US) ˌɑː.t̬ə'moʊ.t̬ɪv, ˌɔː-
autonomic ˌɔː.tə'nɒm.ɪk (US) ˌɑː.t̬ə'nɑː.mɪk, ˌɔː- *stress shift:* ˌautonomic 'reflex
autonomous ɔː'tɒn.ə.məs (US) ɑː'tɑː.nə-, ɔː-
autonom|y ɔː'tɒn.ə.m|i (US) ɑː'tɑː.nə-, ɔː- **-ies** -iz
autonym 'ɔː.tə.nɪm (US) 'ɑː.t̬ə-, 'ɔː- **-s** -z
auto-pilot 'ɔː.təʊˌpaɪ.lət (US) 'ɑː.t̬oʊ-, 'ɔː- **-s** -s
autops|y 'ɔː.tɒp.s|i, -təp-, ɔː'tɒp.s|i (US) 'ɑː.tɑːp-, 'ɔː-, -t̬əp- **-ies** -iz
autoroute 'ɔː.təʊ.ruːt (US) 'ɑː.t̬oʊ-, 'ɔː-, -raʊt **-s** -s
autosegment 'ɔː.təʊ.seg.mənt (US) 'ɑː.t̬oʊ-, 'ɔː- **-s** -s
autosegmental ˌɔː.təʊ.seg'men.təl (US) ˌɑː.t̬oʊ.seg'men.t̬əl, ˌɔː- **-ly** -i
autosug|gestion ˌɔː.təʊ.sə|'dʒes.tʃən, -'dʒeʃ- (US) ˌɑː.t̬oʊ.səg'-, ˌɔː- **-gestive** -'dʒes.tɪv
autotroph 'ɔː.təʊ.trɒf (US) 'ɑː.t̬oʊ.trɑːf, 'ɔː-, -troʊf
autotyp|e 'ɔː.təʊ.taɪp (US) 'ɑː.t̬oʊ-, 'ɔː- **-es** -s **-ing** -ɪŋ **-ed** -t
autotypography ˌɔː.təʊ.taɪ'pɒg.rə.fi (US) ˌɑː.t̬oʊ.taɪ'pɑː.grə-, ˌɔː-
autoworker 'ɔː.təʊˌwɜː.kəʳ (US) 'ɑː.t̬oʊˌwɜːr.kɚ, 'ɔː- **-s** -z
autumn (A) 'ɔː.təm (US) 'ɑː.t̬əm, 'ɔː- **-s** -z

autumnal ɔːˈtʌm.nəl (US) ɑː-, ɔː- **-ly** -i
Auvergne əʊˈveən, -ˈvɜːn (US) oʊˈvern, -ˈvɜːrn
auxiliar|y ɔːgˈzɪl.i.ər|.i, ɔːkˈsɪl-, -jər|.i (US) ɑːgˈzɪl.jər-, ɔːg-, -ˈi.er|.i **-ies** -iz
auxin ˈɔːk.sɪn (US) ˈɑːk-, ˈɔːk-
Ava ˈɑː.və, ˈeɪ.və (US) ˈeɪ-
avail əˈveɪl **-s** -z **-ing/ly** -ɪŋ/li **-ed** -d
availability əˌveɪ.ləˈbɪl.ə.ti, -ɪ.ti (US) -ə.t̬i
availab|le əˈveɪ.lə.b|l̩ **-ly** -li **-leness** -l̩.nəs, -nɪs
avalanch|e ˈæv.əl.ɑːntʃ (US) -æntʃ **-es** -ɪz
Avalon ˈæv.əl.ɒn (US) -ə.lɑːn
avant-courier ˌævɑ̃ːŋˈkʊr.i.eɪ (US) ˌɑː.vɑːnt-, ˌæv.ɑːnt-; əˌvɑːnt- **-s** -z
avant-garde ˌæv.ɑ̃ːŋˈgɑːd (US) ˌɑː.vɑːntˈgɑːrd, ˌæv.ɑːnt-; əˌvɑːnt-
avarice ˈæv.ər.ɪs
avaricious ˌæv.ərˈɪʃ.əs (US) -əˈrɪʃ- **-ly** -li **-ness** -nəs, -nɪs
avast əˈvɑːst (US) əˈvæst
avatar ˌæv.əˈtɑːʳ, ˈ--- (US) ˈæv.ə.tɑːr **-s** -z
avaunt əˈvɔːnt (US) -ˈvɑːnt, -ˈvɔːnt
AVC ˌeɪ.viːˈsiː
ave *prayer:* ˈɑː.veɪ, -viː **-s** -z
Ave. (*abbrev. for* **avenue**) æv, ˈæv.ə.njuː, ˈ-ɪ- (US) ˈæv.ə.nuː, ˈ-ɪ-, -njuː
Avebury ˈeɪv.bər.i (US) -ber-, -bɚ-
Aveley ˈeɪv.li
Aveline ˈæv.ə.laɪn, -liːn
Aveling ˈeɪv.lɪŋ
Ave Maria ˌɑː.veɪ.məˈriː.ə, -viː- **-s** -z
Ave Maria Lane ˌɑː.vi.mə.riː.əˈleɪn *formerly:* ˌeɪ.vi.məˌraɪəˈleɪn
aveng|e əˈvendʒ **-es** -ɪz **-ing** -ɪŋ **-ed** -d **-er/s** -əʳ/z (US) -ɚ/z **-eful** -fʊl
avenue ˈæv.ə.njuː, ˈ-ɪ- (US) -nuː, -njuː **-s** -z
aver əˈvɜːʳ (US) -ˈvɜːr **-s** -z **-ring** -ɪŋ **-red** -d **-ment/s** -mənt/s
averag|e ˈæv.ər.ɪdʒ, ˈ-rɪdʒ **-es** -ɪz **-ing** -ɪŋ **-ed** -d **-ely** -li
averse əˈvɜːs (US) -ˈvɜːrs **-ly** -li **-ness** -nəs, -nɪs
aversion əˈvɜː.ʃən, -ʒən (US) -ˈvɜːr.ʒən, -ʃən **-s** -z
a|vert ə|ˈvɜːt (US) -ˈvɜːrt **-verts** -ˈvɜːts (US) -ˈvɜːrts **-verting** -ˈvɜː.tɪŋ (US) -ˈvɜːr.t̬ɪŋ **-verted** -ˈvɜː.tɪd (US) -ˈvɜːr.t̬ɪd **-vertible** -ˈvɜː.tə.bl̩, -tɪ- (US) -ˈvɜːr.t̬ə.bl̩
Avery ˈeɪ.vər.i, ˈeɪv.ri
Aves ˈeɪ.viːz
Avesta əˈves.tə
avgolemono ˌæv.gəʊˈlem.ə.nəʊ (US) ˌɑːv.goʊˈlem.ə.noʊ
Avia® ˈeɪ.vi.ə (US) əˈviː-
avian ˈeɪ.vi.ən **-s** -z
aviarist ˈeɪ.vi.ər.ɪst **-s** -s
aviar|y ˈeɪ.vi.ər|.i (US) -er- **-ies** -iz
aviation ˌeɪ.viˈeɪ.ʃən
aviator ˈeɪ.vi.eɪ.təʳ (US) -t̬ɚ **-s** -z
Avice ˈeɪ.vɪs
Avicenna ˌæv.ɪˈsen.ə
aviculture ˈeɪ.vɪˌkʌl.tʃəʳ, ˈæv.ɪ- (US) -tʃɚ
avid ˈæv.ɪd **-ly** -li
avidity əˈvɪd.ə.ti, ævˈɪd-, -ɪ.ti (US) -ə.t̬i
Aviemore ˈæv.ɪ.mɔːʳ, ˌ--ˈ- (US) ˌæv.ɪˈmɔːr
Avignon ˈæv.i.njɔ̃ːŋ (US) ˌæv.iːˈnjõʊn, -ˈnjɑːn
avionic ˌeɪ.viˈɒn.ɪk (US) -ˈɑː.nɪk **-s** -s *stress shift:* ˌavionic ˈsystem
Avis® ˈeɪ.vɪs
Avoca əˈvəʊ.kə (US) -ˈvoʊ-
avocado ˌæv.əˈkɑː.dəʊ (US) -doʊ, ɑː.vəˈ- **-s** -z
avocation ˌæv.əʊˈkeɪ.ʃən (US) -əˈ-, -oʊˈ- **-s** -z
avocet ˈæv.əʊ.set (US) ˈ-ə- **-s** -s
Avoch ɔːk, ɔːx
Avogadro ˌæv.əʊˈgæd.rəʊ, -ˈgɑː.drəʊ (US) -əˈgɑː.droʊ, ˌɑː.vəˈ-, -ˈgæd.roʊ
avoid əˈvɔɪd **-s** -z **-ing** -ɪŋ **-ed** -ɪd
avoidab|le əˈvɔɪ.də.bl̩ **-ly** -li
avoidanc|e əˈvɔɪ.dənts **-es** -ɪz
avoirdupois ˌæv.ə.dəˈpɔɪz, ˌæv.wɑː.djuˈpwɑː (US) ˌæv.ɚ.dəˈpɔɪz, ˈæv.ɚ.dəˌpɔɪz
Avon *in Avon:* ˈeɪ.vən (US) -vɑːn, -vən, ˈæv.ən *in Devon:* ˈæv.ən *in the Grampian region:* ɑːn *trademark:* ˈeɪ.vɒn (US) -vɑːn
Avondale ˈeɪ.vən.deɪl (US) ˈeɪ.vən-, ˈæv.ən-
Avonmouth ˈeɪ.vən.maʊθ, -vəm- (US) -vən-
Avory ˈeɪ.vər.i (US) ˈeɪv.ri
avow əˈvaʊ **-s** -z **-ing** -ɪŋ **-ed** -d **-edly** -ɪd.li, -əd-
avowal əˈvaʊ.əl **-s** -z
Avril ˈæv.rɪl, -rəl
avuncular əˈvʌŋ.kjə.ləʳ, -kjʊ- (US) -lɚ **-ly** -li
AWACS ˈeɪ.wæks
a|wait ə|ˈweɪt **-waits** -ˈweɪts **-waiting** -ˈweɪ.tɪŋ (US) -ˈweɪ.t̬ɪŋ **-waited** -ˈweɪ.tɪd (US) -ˈweɪ.t̬ɪd
awak|e əˈweɪk **-es** -s **-ing** -ɪŋ **-ed** -t **awoke** əˈwəʊk (US) -ˈwoʊk
awaken əˈweɪ.kən **-s** -z **-ing/s** -ɪŋ/z **-ed** -d **-ment/s** -mənt/s
awakening (*n.*) əˈweɪ.kən.ɪŋ **-s** -z
award əˈwɔːd (US) -ˈwɔːrd **-s** -z **-ing** -ɪŋ **-ed** -ɪd **-able** -ə.bl̩
aware əˈweəʳ (US) -ˈwer **-ness** -nəs, -nɪs
awash əˈwɒʃ (US) -ˈwɑːʃ, -ˈwɔːʃ
away əˈweɪ
aw|e (A) ɔː (US) ɑː, ɔː **-es** -z **-(e)ing** -ɪŋ **-ed** -d
awe-inspiring ˈɔː.ɪn.spaɪə.rɪŋ (US) ˈɑː-, ˈɔː- **-ly** -li
aweless ˈɔː.ləs, -lɪs (US) ˈɑː-, ˈɔː- **-ness** -nəs, -nɪs
awesome ˈɔː.səm (US) ˈɑː-, ˈɔː- **-ness** -nəs, -nɪs
awe-stricken ˈɔːˌstrɪk.ən (US) ˈɑː-, ˈɔː-
awe-struck ˈɔː.strʌk (US) ˈɑː-, ˈɔː-
awful *terrible:* ˈɔː.fəl, -fʊl (US) ˈɑː-, ˈɔː- **-ness** -nəs, -nɪs *inspiring awe:* ˈɔː.fʊl (US) ˈɑː-, ˈɔː- **-ness** -nəs, -nɪs
awfully ˈɔː.fəl.i, -fʊl- (US) ˈɑː-, ˈɔː-
awhile əˈhwaɪl
awkward ˈɔː.kwəd (US) ˈɑː.kwɚd, ˈɔː- **-est** -əst, -ɪst **-ly** -li **-ness** -nəs, -nɪs **-ish** -ɪʃ
awl ɔːl (US) ɔːl, ɑːl **-s** -z
awn ɔːn (US) ɑːn, ɔːn **-s** -z **-ed** -d
awning ˈɔː.nɪŋ (US) ˈɑː-, ˈɔː- **-s** -z
awoke (*from* **awake**) əˈwəʊk (US) -ˈwoʊk
awoken əˈwəʊ.kən (US) -ˈwoʊ-
AWOL, Awol ˈeɪ.wɒl (US) -wɑːl
Awooner əˈwuː.nəʳ (US) -nɚ
awry əˈraɪ
ax|e, ax æks **-es** -ɪz **-ing** -ɪŋ **-ed** -t **have an ˈaxe to ˌgrind**
axel (A) ˈæk.səl **-s** -z
axes (*plur. of* **axis**) ˈæk.siːz
axes (*plur. of* **axe**) ˈæk.sɪz
Axholm(e) ˈæks.həʊm, -əm (US) -hoʊm
axial ˈæk.si.əl **-ly** -i
axil ˈæk.sɪl, -səl **-s** -z
axill|a ækˈsɪl.|ə **-ae** -iː **-as** -əz **-ar** -əʳ (US) -ɚ **-ary** -ər.i
axiom ˈæk.si.əm **-s** -z
axiomatic ˌæk.si.əˈmæt.ɪk (US) -ˈmæt̬- **-al** -əl **-ally** -əl.i, -li
ax|is ˈæk.s|ɪs **-es** -iːz
axle ˈæk.sl̩ **-s** -z **-d** -d
axle-tree ˈæk.sl̩.triː **-s** -z
Axminster ˈæks.mɪn.stəʳ (US) -stɚ **-s** -z
axolotl ˈæk.sə.lɒt.l̩ (US) ˈæk.sə.lɑː.t̬l̩ **-s** -z
axon ˈæk.sɒn (US) -sɑːn **-s** -z
ay aɪ, eɪ **-es** -z
ayah ˈaɪ.ə, ˈɑː.jə **-s** -z
ayatollah ˌaɪ.əˈtɒl.ə (US) -ˈtoʊ.lə; -toʊˈlɑː **-s** -z
Ayckbourn ˈeɪk.bɔːn (US) -bɔːrn
Aycliffe ˈeɪ.klɪf
aye *ever:* eɪ *yes:* aɪ **-s** -z
aye-aye ˈaɪ.aɪ **-s** -z
Ayenbite of Inwyt ˌeɪ.ən.baɪt.əvˈɪn.wɪt
Ayer eəʳ (US) er

Ayers eəz (US) erz ˌ**Ayers 'Rock**
Ayesha aɪ'iː.ʃə
Aylesbury 'eɪlz.bᵊr.i (US) -ber-, -bɚ-
Aylesford 'eɪlz.fəd, 'eɪls- (US) -fɚd
Ayling 'eɪ.lɪŋ
Aylmer 'eɪl.məʳ (US) -mɚ
Aylsham 'eɪl.ʃəm
Aylward 'eɪl.wəd (US) -wɚd
Aylwin 'eɪl.wɪn
Aymer 'eɪ.məʳ (US) -mɚ
Ayot 'eɪ.ət
Ayr eəʳ (US) er **-shire** -ʃəʳ, -ˌʃɪəʳ (US) -ʃɚ, -ˌʃɪr
Ayre eəʳ (US) er **-s** -z
Ayrton 'eə.tᵊn (US) 'er-
Ayscough 'æs.kə, 'æsk.juː, 'eɪ.skəf, 'eɪz.kɒf (US) 'æs.kjuː
Ayscue 'eɪ.skjuː (US) 'æs.kjuː
Ayton, **Aytoun** 'eɪ.tᵊn
ayurved|a aɪ.ʊə'veɪ.d|ə, ɑː-, -'viː- (US) ˌɑː.jʊr'veɪ- **-ic** -ɪk
A-Z ˌeɪ.tə'zed (US) -t̬ə'ziː
azalea ə'zeɪ.li.ə (US) -'zeɪl.jə **-s** -z
Azani|a ə'zeɪ.ni|.ə **-an/s** -ən/z
Azariah ˌæz.ə'raɪ.ə
Azerbaijan ˌæz.ə.baɪ'dʒɑːn, -'ʒɑːn (US) ˌɑː.zɚ-, ˌæz.ɚ- **-i/s** -i/z
azimuth 'æz.ɪ.məθ, '-ə- **-s** -s
Aziz ə'ziːz, -'zɪz
azodye 'eɪ.zəʊ.daɪ, 'æz.əʊ- (US) -zoʊ- **-s** -z
azoic ə'zəʊ.ɪk, æz'əʊ-, eɪ'zəʊ- (US) ə'zoʊ-, eɪ-
Azores ə'zɔːz (US) 'eɪ.zɔːrz; ə'zɔːrz
Note: It is customary to pronounce /ə'zɔː.rɪz (US) -'zɔːr.ɪz/ (or /-'zɔː.rez (US) -'zɔːr.ez/) in reciting Tennyson's poem 'The Revenge'.
azote ə'zəʊt, æz'əʊt; 'æz.əʊt, 'eɪ.zəʊt (US) 'æz.oʊt, 'eɪ.zoʊt; ə'zoʊt
azotic ə'zɒt.ɪk, æz'ɒt-, eɪ'zɒt- (US) ə'zɑː.t̬ɪk
Azov 'ɑː.zɒv, 'eɪ-, 'æz.ɒv (US) 'ɑː.zɑːf, 'eɪ-, 'æz.ɑːf, -ɔːf
AZT ˌeɪ.zed'tiː (US) -ziː'-
Aztec 'æz.tek **-s** -s
azure 'æʒ.əʳ, 'eɪ.ʒəʳ, -ʒʊəʳ, 'æz.jʊəʳ; eɪ'zjʊəʳ, ə'zjʊəʳ (US) 'æʒ.ɚ, 'eɪ.ʒɚ
azygous ə'zaɪ.gəs, æz'aɪ-, ˌeɪ'zaɪ- (US) 'æz.ɪ-; ˌeɪ'zaɪ-

B

b (B) biː **-'s** -z

ba beɪ **-s** -z

BA ˌbiːˈeɪ

baa bɑː (US) bæ, bɑː **-s** -z **-ing** -ɪŋ **-ed** -d

Baader-Meinhof ˌbɑː.dəˈmaɪn.hɒf (US) -dɚˈmaɪn.hɑːf, -hoʊf

Baal ˈbeɪ.ᵊl *Jewish pronunciation:* bɑːl

BAAL bɑːl

baa-lamb ˈbɑː.læm (US) ˈbɑː-, ˈbæ- **-s** -z

Baalim ˈbeɪ.ᵊl.ɪm *Jewish pronunciation:* ˈbɑː.lɪm

baas *master:* bɑːs **-es** -ɪz

baas (*from* **baa**) bɑːz (US) bæz, bɑːz

baaskaap ˈbɑːs.kæp (US) -kɑːp

Ba'ath bɑːθ (US) bɑːθ, bæθ **-ist/s** -ɪst/s

Bab bɑːb

baba ˈbɑː.bɑː, -bə **-s** -z

Babar ˈbɑː.bɑːʳ (US) bəˈbɑːr; ˈbæb.ɑːr, ˈbɑː.bɑːr

Babbage ˈbæb.ɪdʒ

babbit (B) ˈbæb.ɪt **-s** -s

babbl|e ˈbæb.ḷ **-es** -z **-ing** -ɪŋ, ˈbæb.lɪŋ **-ed** -d **-er/s** -əʳ/z, ˈ-ləʳ/z (US) ˈ-ḷ.ɚ/z, ˈ-lɚ/z **-ement/s** -mənt/s

Babcock ˈbæb.kɒk (US) -kɑːk

babe beɪb **-s** -z

babel (B) ˈbeɪ.bᵊl (US) ˈbeɪ-, ˈbæb.ᵊl **-s** -z

Babington ˈbæb.ɪŋ.tən

Bab|ism ˈbɑː.b|ɪ.zᵊm **-ist/s** -ɪst/s **-ite** -aɪt

Babi Yar ˌbɑː.biˈjɑːʳ (US) -ˈjɑːr *stress shift:* ˌBabi Yar ˈmassacre

babka ˈbɑːb.kə **-s** -z

baboo (B) ˈbɑː.buː **-s** -z

baboon bəˈbuːn (US) bæbˈuːn, bəˈbuːn **-s** -z

babooner|y bəˈbuː.nᵊr|.i, bæbˈuː- **-ies** -iz

Babs bæbz

babu (B) ˈbɑː.buː **-s** -z

babushka bæbˈuːʃ.kə, bəˈbuːʃ-, -ˈbʊʃ- **-s** -z

bab|y (B) ˈbeɪ.b|i **-ies** -iz **ˈbaby ˌboom** ; **ˈbaby ˌboomer** ; **ˌbaby ˈgrand** ; **ˈbaby ˌtalk** ; **ˈbaby ˌcarriage** ; **throw the ˌbaby out with the ˈbath water**

Babycham® ˈbeɪ.bɪ.ʃæm

Babygro® ˈbeɪ.bɪ.grəʊ (US) -groʊ **-s** -z

babyhood ˈbeɪ.bɪ.hʊd

babyish ˈbeɪ.bi.ɪʃ **-ly** -li **-ness** -nəs, -nɪs

Babylon ˈbæb.ɪ.lɒn, -ə-, -lən (US) -lɑːn

Babyloni|a ˌbæb.ɪˈləʊ.ni|.ə, -əˈ- (US) -ˈloʊ- **-an/s** -ən/z

baby|sit ˈbeɪ.bɪ|.sɪt **-sitter/s** -ˌsɪt.əʳ/z (US) -ˌsɪt̬.ɚ/z **-sitting** -ˌsɪt.ɪŋ (US) -ˌsɪt̬.ɪŋ **-sat** -sæt

Bacall bəˈkɔːl (US) -ˈkɔːl, -ˈkɑːl

Bacardi® bəˈkɑː.di (US) -ˈkɑːr- **-s** -z

baccalaureate ˌbæk.əˈlɔː.ri.ət, -ɪt (US) -ˈlɔːr.i-, -ɪt **-s** -s

baccarat ˈbæk.ə.rɑː, ˌ--ˈ- (US) ˌbæk.əˈrɑː, ˌbɑː.kəˈ-, ˈ---

Bacchae ˈbæk.iː

bacchanal ˈbæk.ə.nᵊl; ˌbæk.əˈnæl (US) ˌbæk.əˈnæl **-s** -z

bacchanali|a ˌbæk.əˈneɪ.li|.ə (US) -jə **-an/s** -ən/z

bacchant ˈbæk.ənt **-s** -s

bacchante bəˈkæn.ti, bəˈkænt (US) -ˈkænt, -ˈkæn.ti, -ˈkɑːn- **-s** -z, -s

bacchic ˈbæk.ɪk

Bacchus ˈbæk.əs (US) ˈbæk.əs, ˈbɑː.kəs

Bacchylides bækˈɪl.ɪ.diːz, bəˈkɪl-

baccy ˈbæk.i

Bach *German composer:* bɑːk *as if German:* bɑːx (US) bɑːk *English surname:* beɪtʃ, bætʃ

bach *Welsh term of address:* bɑːk *as if Welsh:* bɑːx (US) bɑːk

Bacharach ˈbæk.ə.ræk

Bache beɪtʃ

bachelor (B) ˈbætʃ.ᵊl.əʳ, -ɪ.ləʳ (US) -ᵊl.ɚ **-s** -z **-hood** -hʊd **-ship** -ʃɪp **ˌBachelor of ˈArts** ; **ˌBachelor of ˈScience** ; **ˈbachelor ˌgirl**

baciliform bəˈsɪl.ɪ.fɔːm, bæsˈɪl- (US) bəˈsɪl.ə.fɔːrm

bacillary bəˈsɪl.ᵊr.i, bæsˈɪl- (US) bəˈsɪl-

bacill|us bəˈsɪl.|əs, bæsˈɪl- (US) bəˈsɪl- **-i** -aɪ, -iː

back (B) bæk **-s** -s **-ing** -ɪŋ **-ed** -t **ˈBack ˌBay** ; **ˌback ˈdoor** *stress shift:* ˌback door ˈdeal; **ˌback ˈgarden** ; **ˌback of beˈyond**; **ˌback ˈseat**; **ˌback seat ˈdriver**; **ˈback ˌtalk**; **ˌback ˈyard** *stress shift:* ˌback yard ˈspecial; **have one's ˌback to the ˈwall**; **ˌput someone's ˈback up**; **ˌturn one's ˈback on someone/something**

backache ˈbæk.eɪk **-s** -s

backbeat ˈbæk.biːt

backbench ˌbækˈbentʃ **-es** -ɪz *stress shift:* ˌbackbench ˈspeaker

backbencher ˌbækˈben.tʃəʳ (US) -tʃɚ **-s** -z *stress shift:* ˌbackbencher ˈvote

backbi|ting ˈbækˌbaɪ|.tɪŋ (US) -t̬ɪŋ **-ter/s** -təʳ/z (US) -t̬ɚ/z

backboard ˈbæk.bɔːd (US) -bɔːrd **-s** -z

backbone ˈbæk.bəʊn (US) -boʊn **-s** -z

backbreaker ˈbækˌbreɪ.kəʳ (US) -kɚ **-s** -z

backbreaking ˈbækˌbreɪ.kɪŋ **-ly** -li

backchat ˈbæk.tʃæt

back|cloth ˈbæk|.klɒθ (US) -klɑːθ **-cloths** -klɒθs, -klɒðz (US) -klɑːθs, -klɑːðz

backcomb ˈbæk.kəʊm, ˌ-ˈ- (US) ˈbæk.koʊm **-s** -z **-ing** -ɪŋ **-ed** -d

back|date ˌbæk|ˈdeɪt (US) ˈbæk|.deɪt **-dates** -ˈdeɪts (US) -deɪts **-dating** -ˈdeɪ.tɪŋ (US) -deɪ.t̬ɪŋ **-dated** -ˈdeɪ.tɪd (US) -deɪ.t̬ɪd *stress shift:* ˌbackdated ˈcheque

backdrop ˈbæk.drɒp (US) -drɑːp **-s** -s

backer ˈbæk.əʳ (US) -ɚ **-s** -z

backfield ˈbæk.fiːld

backfill ˈbæk.fɪl **-s** -z **-ing** -ɪŋ **-ed** -d

backfir|e ˌbækˈfaɪəʳ, ˈ-- (US) ˌbækˈfaɪɚ, ˈ-- **-es** -z **-ing** -ɪŋ **-ed** -d

back-formation ˈbæk.fɔːˌmeɪ.ʃᵊn (US) -fɔːrˌ- **-s** -z

backgammon ˈbæk.gæm.ən, ˌ-ˈ--

background ˈbæk.graʊnd **-s** -z **ˈbackground ˌnoise**, **ˌbackground ˈnoise** (US) **ˈbackground ˌnoise**

backhand ˈbæk.hænd **-s** -z

backhanded ˌbækˈhænd.ɪd **-ly** -li **-ness** -nəs, -nɪs *stress shift, see compound:* **ˌbackhanded ˈcompliment**

backhander ˌbækˈhænd.əʳ (US) -ɚ **-z** -z

backhoe ˈbæk.həʊ (US) -hoʊ **-s** -z

Backhouse ˈbæk.haʊs

backing ˈbæk.ɪŋ **-s** -z

backlash ˈbæk.læʃ

backless ˈbæk.ləs, -lɪs

back|light ˈbæk|.laɪt **-lights** -laɪts **-lighting** -ˌlaɪ.tɪŋ (US) -ˌlaɪ.t̬ɪŋ **-lighted** -ˌlaɪ.tɪd (US) -ˌlaɪ.t̬ɪd **backlit** ˈbæk.lɪt

backlist ˈbæk.lɪst **-s** -s **-ing** -ɪŋ **-ed** -ɪd

backlog ˈbæk.lɒg (US) -lɑːg, -lɔːg **-s** -z

backpack ˈbæk.pæk **-s** -s **-ing** -ɪŋ **-ed** -d **-er/s** -əʳ/z (US) -ɚ/z

back-pedal ˌbækˈped.ᵊl, ˈ-ˌ-- (US) ˈbæk.ped- **-s** -z **-(l)ing** -ɪŋ **-(l)ed** -d

backrest ˈbæk.rest **-s** -s

backroom ˌbækˈrʊm, -ˈruːm, ˈ-- (US) ˌbækˈruːm, -ˈrʊm, ˈ-- **ˈbackroom ˌboy**

backscratcher ˈbækˌskrætʃ.əʳ (US) -ɚ **-s** -z

backsheesh, **backshish** ˌbækˈʃiːʃ, ˈ--

backside ˌbækˈsaɪd, ˈ-- (US) ˈ-- **-s** -z

backslap ˈbæk.slæp **-s** -s **-ping** -ɪŋ **-ped** -t **-per/s** -əʳ/z (US) -ɚ/z

backslash ˈbæk.slæʃ **-es** -ɪz

backslid|e ˈbæk.slaɪd **-es** -z **-ing** -ɪŋ **-er/s** -əʳ/z (US) -ɚ/z **backslid** ˈbæk.slɪd

backspac|e ˈbæk.speɪs **-es** -ɪz **-ing** -ɪŋ **-ed** -t

backspin ˈbæk.spɪn

backstage ˌbækˈsteɪdʒ *stress shift:* ˌbackstage ˈpass

backstairs ˌbækˈsteəz (US) ˌbækˈsterz *stress shift:* ˌbackstairs ˈgossip

backstay ˈbæk.steɪ **-s** -z

backstitch ˈbæk.stɪtʃ **-es** -ɪz **-ing** -ɪŋ **-ed** -t

backstop ˈbæk.stɒp (US) -stɑːp **-s** -s **-ping** -ɪŋ **-ped** -t

backstrap 'bæk.stræp **-s** -s
backstreet 'bæk.striːt **-s** -s
backstroke 'bæk.strəuk (US) -strouk
back-to-back ˌbæk.tə'bæk *stress shift:* ˌback-to-back 'house
backtrack 'bæk.træk **-s** -s **-ing** -ɪŋ **-ed** -t
backup 'bæk.ʌp **-s** -s
backward 'bæk.wəd (US) -wɚd **-ly** -li **-ness** -nəs, -nɪs **-s** -z ˌ**bend over 'backwards**
backwash 'bæk.wɒʃ (US) -wɑːʃ, -wɔːʃ **-es** -ɪz
backwater 'bækˌwɔː.təʳ (US) -ˌwɑː.t̬ɚ, -ˌwɔː- **-s** -z
backwoods 'bæk.wudz
backwoods|man ˌbæk'wudz|.mən, '-ˌ-- **-men** -mən, -men
bacon (B) 'beɪ.kᵊn ˌ**bring home the 'bacon**
Baconian beɪ'kəu.ni.ən, bə'kəu- (US) -'kou- **-s** -z
bacteriological bækˌtɪə.ri.ə'lɒdʒ.ɪ.kᵊl (US) -ˌtɪr.i.ə'lɑː.dʒɪ-
bacteriolog|y bækˌtɪə.ri'ɒl.ə.dʒ|i (US) -ˌtɪr.i'ɑː.lə- **-ist/s** -ɪst/s
bacteriophag|e bæk'tɪə.ri.əu.feɪdʒ (US) -'tɪr.i.ə- **-es** -ɪz
Bactri|a 'bæk.tri|.ə **-an/s** -ən/z
Bacup 'beɪ.kəp
bad bæd ˌ**bad 'blood**; ˌ**bad 'language**; ˌ**bad 'news**; ˌ**bad 'temper**; **go from** ˌ**bad to 'worse**
Bad bæd, bɑːd (US) bɑːd
Badajoz ˌbæd.ə'hɒs *as if Spanish:* ˌbæd.ə'xɒθ (US) ˌbɑː.dɑː'houz, -ðɑː'houθ
badass 'bæd.æs **-ed** -t
Badcock 'bæd.kɒk (US) -kɑːk
Baddeley 'bæd.ᵊl.i
baddie 'bæd.i **-s** -z
baddish 'bæd.ɪʃ
badd|y 'bæd|.i **-ies** -iz
bade (*from* **bid**) bæd, beɪd
Badedas® 'bæd.ɪ.dæs; bə'deɪ.dəs
Badel bə'del
Badely 'bæd.ᵊl.i
Baden 'bɑː.dᵊn
Baden-Powell ˌbeɪ.dᵊn'pauəl, -'pəuəl, -'pəu.ɪl, -'pəu.el (US) -'pou.əl, -'pauəl
Baden-Württemberg ˌbɑː.dᵊn'vɜː.tᵊm.bɜːg (US) -'vɜːr.tᵊm.bɜːrg
Bader 'bɑː.dəʳ, 'beɪ- (US) -dɚ
badg|e bædʒ **-es** -ɪz **-ing** -ɪŋ **-ed** -d
badg|er (B) 'bædʒ|.əʳ (US) -ɚ **-ers** -əz (US) -ɚz **-ering** -ᵊr.ɪŋ **-ered** -əd (US) -ɚd
badger-baiting 'bædʒ.əˌbeɪ.tɪŋ (US) -ɚˌbeɪ.t̬ɪŋ
badger-dog 'bædʒ.ə.dɒg (US) -ɚ.dɑːg, -dɔːg **-s** -z
Bad Godesburg ˌbɑːd'gəu.dəz.bɜːg, -'gəudz-, -beəg (US) -'gou.dəz.bɜːrg
Badham 'bæd.əm
badinage 'bæd.ɪ.nɑːʒ, -nɑːdʒ, ˌ--'-
badlands 'bæd.lændz
badly 'bæd.li
badminton (B) 'bæd.mɪn.tən
bad-mouth 'bæd.mauθ **-s** -z **-ing** -ɪŋ **-ed** -d
badness 'bæd.nəs, -nɪs
Badoit® 'bæd.wɑː, -'- (US) bɑː'dwɑː
bad-tempered ˌbæd'tem.pəd (US) 'bædˌtem.pɚd **-ly** -li **-ness** -nəs, -nɪs *stress shift, British only:* ˌbad-tempered 'person
Baeda 'biː.də
Baedeker 'beɪ.dek.əʳ, 'baɪ-, -dɪ.kəʳ (US) 'beɪ.də.kɚ, 'baɪ- **-s** -z
Baez 'baɪ.ez, -'-
Baffin 'bæf.ɪn ˌ**Baffin 'Bay**; ˌ**Baffin 'Island**
baffl|e 'bæf.l̩ **-es** -z **-ing** -ɪŋ, '-lɪŋ **-ed** -d **-er/s** -əʳ/z, '-ləʳ/z (US) '-l̩.ɚ/z, '-lɚ/z **-ement** -mənt
BAFTA, Bafta 'bæf.tə
bag bæg **-s** -z **-ging** -ɪŋ **-ged** -d '**bag** ˌ**lady**; ˌ**bag of 'bones**
bagatelle ˌbæg.ə'tel **-s** -z
Bagdad *in Iraq:* ˌbæg'dæd, '-- (US) 'bæg.dæd *in Tasmania, Florida:* 'bæg.dæd
Bagehot 'bædʒ.ət, 'bæg-
bagel 'beɪ.gᵊl **-s** -z
bagful 'bæg.ful **-s** -z
baggag|e 'bæg.ɪdʒ **-es** -ɪz
Baggie® 'bæg.i **-s** -z
bagg|y 'bæg|.i **-ier** -i.əʳ (US) -i.ɚ **-iest** -i.ɪst, -i.əst **-ily** -ɪ.li, -ᵊl.i **-iness** -ɪ.nəs, -ɪ.nɪs
Baghdad bæg'dæd, '-- (US) 'bæg.dæd
Bagheera bæg'ɪə.rə, bə'gɪə- (US) bə'gɪr.ə
Bagley 'bæg.li
Bagnall 'bæg.nəl, -nɔːl
Bagnell 'bæg.nəl
bagnio 'bæn.jəu, 'bɑː.njəu (US) 'bɑː.njou, 'bæn.jou **-s** -z
Bagnold 'bæg.nəuld (US) -nould
Bagot 'bæg.ət
bagpip|e 'bæg.paɪp **-es** -s **-er/s** -əʳ/z (US) -ɚ/z
Bagshaw(e) 'bæg.ʃɔː (US) -ʃɑː, -ʃɔː
Bagshot 'bæg.ʃɒt (US) -ʃɑːt
bags|y 'bæg.z|i **-ies** -iz **-ing** -ɪŋ **-ied** -id
baguette, baguet bæg'et, bə'get **-s** -s
Bagworthy 'bædʒ.ᵊr.i
bah bɑː (US) bɑː, bæ
bahadur bə'hɑː.dəʳ (US) -dɚ **-s** -z
Baha'i bə'haɪ, bɑː-, -'hɑː.i, -'haɪ.i **-s** -z
Baha|ism bə'haɪ|.ɪ.zᵊm, bɑː-, -'hɑː- **-ist/s** -ɪst/s
Bahama bə'hɑː.mə **-s** -z
Bahamian bə'heɪ.mi.ən, -'hɑː- **-s** -z
Bahasa bə'hɑː.sə
Bahawalpur bɑː'hɑː.wəl.puəʳ, bə- (US) -pur
Bahia bə'hiː.ə
Bahrain, Bahrein bɑː'reɪn **-i** -i
baht bɑːt **-s** -s
baignoire 'beɪn.wɑːʳ (US) ben'wɑːr, beɪn- **-s** -z
Baikal 'baɪ.kæl, -kɑːl, -'-
bail beɪl **-s** -z **-ing** -ɪŋ **-ed** -d **-er/s** -əʳ/z (US) -ɚ/z
bailable 'beɪ.lə.bl̩
bail-bond 'beɪl.bɒnd, -'- (US) 'beɪl.bɑːnd **-s** -z
bail-bonds|man 'beɪlˌbɒndz|.mən (US) -ˌbɑːndz- **-men** -mən
Baildon 'beɪl.dən
bailee ˌbeɪ'liː **-s** -z
bailey (B) 'beɪ.li
bailie (B) 'beɪ.li **-s** -z
bailiff 'beɪ.lɪf **-s** -s
bailiwick 'beɪ.lɪ.wɪk **-s** -s
Baille 'beɪ.li
Baillie 'beɪ.li
Baillieu 'beɪ.ljuː (US) 'beɪl.juː
Bailly 'beɪ.li
bailment 'beɪl.mənt **-s** -s
Baily 'beɪ.li
Bain beɪn
Bainbridge 'beɪn.brɪdʒ, 'beɪm- (US) 'beɪn-
Baines beɪnz
bain-marie ˌbæn.mə'riː *as if French:* bǣm- (US) ˌbæn- **-s** -z
Baird beəd (US) berd
bairn beən (US) bern **-s** -z
Bairstow 'beə.stəu (US) 'ber.stou
bait beɪt **-s** -s **-ing** -ɪŋ (US) 'beɪ.t̬ɪŋ **-ed** -ɪd (US) 'beɪ.t̬ɪd
bai|za 'baɪ|.zə (US) -zɑː **-zas** -zəz
baiz|e beɪz **-es** -ɪz
Baja California ˌbɑː.hɑː.kæl.ɪ'fɔː.njə (US) -ə'fɔːr-
bak|e beɪk **-es** -s **-ing** -ɪŋ **-ed** -t ˌ**baked A'laska**; ˌ**baked 'beans**; '**baking** ˌ**powder**; '**baking** ˌ**soda**
bakehou|se 'beɪk.hau|s **-ses** -zɪz
Bakelite® 'beɪ.kᵊl.aɪt (US) 'beɪ.kə.laɪt, 'beɪk.laɪt
baker (B) 'beɪ.kəʳ (US) -kɚ **-s** -z
Bakerloo ˌbeɪ.kᵊl'uː (US) -kɚ'luː
Bakersfield 'beɪ.kəz.fiːld (US) -kɚz-
baker|y 'beɪ.kᵊr|.i **-ies** -iz
Bakewell 'beɪk.wel, -wəl
Bakke 'bɑː.ki
baklava 'bæk.lə.vɑː, 'bɑː.klə- *as if Greek:* ˌ--'- **-s** -z
baksheesh ˌbæk'ʃiːʃ, '--
Baku bæk'uː (US) bɑː'kuː
Bakunin bə'kuː.nɪn, bɑː- (US) bɑː'kuːn.jɪn, bə-
Bala 'bæl.ə
balaam (B) 'beɪ.læm, -ləm **-s** -z

balaclava (B) ˌbæl.əˈklɑː.və, ˌbɑː.ləˈ- **-s** -z
Balakirev bəˈlæk.ɪ.rev, -ˈlɑː.kɪ- Ⓤⓢ ˌbɑː.lɑːˈkɪr.*j*ef
balalaika ˌbæl.əˈlaɪ.kə **-s** -z
balanc|e ˈbæl.ən*t*s **-es** -ɪz **-ing** -ɪŋ **-ed** -t **ˈbalancing ˌact ; ˌbalance of ˈpayments ; ˈbalance ˌsheet**
Balanchine ˈbæl.ən.tʃiːn, ˌ--ˈ- Ⓤⓢ ˈbæl.ən*t*.ʃiːn
Balatka bəˈlæt.kə Ⓤⓢ -kɑː, -ˈlɑːt-
Balaton bælˈæt.ən *as if Hungarian:* bɒlˈɒt- Ⓤⓢ ˈbɑː.lɑː.tɑːn
Balboa bælˈbəʊ.ə Ⓤⓢ -ˈboʊ-
Balbriggan bælˈbrɪg.ən
Balbus ˈbæl.bəs
Balchin ˈbɔːl.tʃɪn, ˈbɒl- Ⓤⓢ ˈbɔːl-, ˈbɑːl-
balcon|y ˈbæl.kə.n|i **-ies** -iz
bald bɔːld Ⓤⓢ bɔːld, bɑːld **-er** -əʳ Ⓤⓢ -ɚ **-est** -ɪst, -əst **-ing** -ɪŋ **-ish** -ɪʃ **-ly** -li **-ness** -nəs, -nɪs **ˌbald ˈeagle**
baldachin, baldaquin ˈbɔːl.də.kɪn Ⓤⓢ ˈbɔːl-, ˈbɑːl- **-s** -z
Balder ˈbɔːl.dəʳ, ˈbɒl- Ⓤⓢ ˈbɔːl.dɚ, ˈbɑːl-
balderdash ˈbɔːl.də.dæʃ, ˈbɒl- Ⓤⓢ ˈbɔːl.dɚ-, ˈbɑːl-
baldfaced ˌbɔːldˈfeɪst Ⓤⓢ ˈbɔːld.feɪst, ˈbɑːld- *stress shift, British only:* ˌbaldfaced ˈliar
bald-headed ˌbɔːldˈhed.ɪd Ⓤⓢ ˌbɔːld-, ˌbɑːld- *stress shift:* ˌbald-headed ˈman
Baldock ˈbɔːl.dɒk Ⓤⓢ ˈbɔːl.dɑːk, ˈbɑːl-
baldric (B) ˈbɔːl.drɪk, ˈbɒl- Ⓤⓢ ˈbɔːl-, ˈbɑːl- **-s** -s
Baldry ˈbɔːl.dri Ⓤⓢ ˈbɔːl-, ˈbɑːl-
Baldwin ˈbɔːld.wɪn Ⓤⓢ ˈbɔːld-, ˈbɑːld-
bal|e (B) beɪl **-es** -z **-ing** -ɪŋ **-ed** -d
Bale, Bâle *in Switzerland:* bɑːl
Baleares ˌbæl.iˈɑː.rɪz Ⓤⓢ ˌbɑː.liˈ-, ˌbæl.iˈ-
Balearic ˌbæl.iˈær.ɪk Ⓤⓢ ˌbɑː.liˈ-, ˌbæl.iˈ-, -ˈer-
baleen bəˈliːn, bælˈiːn **-s** -z
baleful ˈbeɪl.fᵊl, -fʊl **-ly** -i **-ness** -nəs, -nɪs
baler ˈbeɪ.ləʳ Ⓤⓢ -lɚ **-s** -z
Balfour ˈbæl.fəʳ, -fɔːʳ Ⓤⓢ -fɚ, -fɔːr
Balguy ˈbɔːl.gi Ⓤⓢ ˈbɔːl-, ˈbɑːl-
Balham ˈbæl.əm
Bali ˈbɑː.li Ⓤⓢ ˈbɑː.li, ˈbæl.i
Balinese ˌbɑː.lɪˈniːz Ⓤⓢ ˌbɑː.ləˈ-, ˌbæl.əˈ-
Baliol ˈbeɪ.li.əl
balk bɔːlk, bɔːk Ⓤⓢ bɔːk, bɑːk **-s** -s **-ing** -ɪŋ **-ed** -t
Balkan ˈbɔːl.kən, bɒl- Ⓤⓢ ˈbɔːl-, ˈbɑːl- **-s** -z
Balkanization, -isa- ˌbɔːl.kə.naɪˈzeɪ.ʃᵊn, ˌbɒl-, -nɪˈ- Ⓤⓢ ˌbɔːl-, ˌbɑːl-
Balkaniz|e, -is|e ˈbɔːl.kə.naɪz, ˈbɒl- Ⓤⓢ ˈbɔːl-, ˈbɑːl- **-es** -ɪz **-ing** -ɪŋ **-ed** -d
Balkhash bælˈkæʃ Ⓤⓢ bɑːlˈkɑːʃ, bæl-, -ˈkæʃ
ball (B) bɔːl Ⓤⓢ bɔːl, bɑːl **-s** -z **ˌball and ˈchain ; ˌball ˈbearing; ˈball ˌboy; ˈball ˌgame; ˈball ˌgirl; ˈball ˌpark; ˌon the ˈball; ˌset the ball ˈrolling, ˌset the ˈball ˌrolling**
ballad ˈbæl.əd **-s** -z
ballade bælˈɑːd, bəˈlɑːd **-s** -z
balladeer ˌbæl.əˈdɪəʳ Ⓤⓢ -ˈdɪr **-s** -z
Ballantine, Ballantyne ˈbæl.ən.taɪn
Ballantrae ˌbæl.ənˈtreɪ
Ballarat ˌbæl.əˈræt, ˈ---
Ballard ˈbæl.əd, -ɑːd Ⓤⓢ -ɚd, -ɑːrd
ballast ˈbæl.əst **-s** -s
Ballater ˈbæl.ə.təʳ Ⓤⓢ -t̬ɚ
ballcarrier ˈbɔːlˌkær.i.əʳ Ⓤⓢ -ˌker.i.ɚ, ˈbɑːl-, -ˌkær- **-s** -z
ballcock ˈbɔːl.kɒk Ⓤⓢ ˈbɔːl.kɑːk, ˈbɑːl- **-s** -s
Balleine bælˈen
ballerina ˌbæl.ᵊrˈiː.nə Ⓤⓢ -əˈriː- **-s** -z
Ballesteros ˌbæl.ɪˈstɪə.rɒs, ˌbaɪ.ɪˈ-, -əˈ-, -ˈsteə- Ⓤⓢ ˌbaɪ.əˈster.oʊs, ˌbæl-
ballet ˈbæl.eɪ Ⓤⓢ bælˈeɪ, ˈ-- **-s** -z **ˈballet ˌdancer**
balletic bælˈet.ɪk, bəˈlet- Ⓤⓢ bəˈlet̬.ɪk
balletomane ˈbæl.ɪ.təʊ.meɪn, -et.əʊ- Ⓤⓢ bəˈlet̬.ə- **-s** -z
ballgown ˈbɔːl.gaʊn Ⓤⓢ ˈbɔːl-, ˈbɑːl- **-s** -z
Ballingry bəˈlɪŋ.gri
Balliol ˈbeɪ.li.əl
ballistic bəˈlɪs.tɪk **-s** -s
balloon bəˈluːn **-s** -z **-ist/s** -ɪst/s **go ˌdown/ˌover like a ˌlead baˈlloon**
ball|ot ˈbæl|.ət **-ots** -əts **-oting** -ə.tɪŋ Ⓤⓢ -ə.t̬ɪŋ **-oted** -ə.tɪd Ⓤⓢ -ə.t̬ɪd **ˈballot ˌbox ; ˈballot ˌpaper; ˈballot ˌrigging**
ball-park ˈbɔːl.pɑːk Ⓤⓢ -pɑːrk, ˈbɑːl- **ˌball-park ˈfigure**
ballplayer ˈbɔːlˌpleɪ.əʳ Ⓤⓢ -ɚ, ˈbɑːl- **-s** -z
ball|-point ˈbɔːl|.pɔɪnt Ⓤⓢ ˈbɔːl-, ˈbɑːl- **-points** -pɔɪnts **-pointed** -ˌpɔɪn.tɪd Ⓤⓢ -ˌpɔɪn.t̬ɪd **ˌball-point ˈpen**
ballroom ˈbɔːl.rʊm, -ruːm Ⓤⓢ ˈbɔːl-, ˈbɑːl- **-s** -z **ˌballroom ˈdancing** Ⓤⓢ **ˈballroom ˌdancing**
balls-up ˈbɔːlzˌʌp Ⓤⓢ ˈbɔːlz-, ˈbɑːlz-
balls|y ˈbɔːl.z|i Ⓤⓢ ˈbɔːl-, ˈbɑːl- **-ier** -i.əʳ Ⓤⓢ -i.ɚ **-iest** -i.əst, -i.ɪst
bally ˈbæl.i
Ballycastle ˌbæl.ɪˈkɑː.sl̩ Ⓤⓢ -ˈkæs.l̩
Ballyclare ˌbæl.ɪˈkleəʳ Ⓤⓢ -ˈkler
ballyhoo ˌbæl.ɪˈhuː Ⓤⓢ ˈ---
Ballymena ˌbæl.ɪˈmiː.nə
Ballymoney ˌbæl.ɪˈmʌn.i
balm bɑːm **-s** -z
Balmain ˈbæl.mæ̃n, -ˈ- Ⓤⓢ ˈbæl.meɪn, -ˈ-
Balm(e) bɑːm
Balmer ˈbɑː.məʳ Ⓤⓢ ˈbɑːl.mɚ, ˈbɑː-
Balmoral bælˈmɒr.ᵊl Ⓤⓢ -ˈmɔːr-
balm|y ˈbɑː.m|i **-ier** -i.əʳ Ⓤⓢ -i.ɚ **-iest** -i.ɪst, -i.əst **-ily** -ɪ.li, -ᵊl.i **-iness** -ɪ.nəs, -ɪ.nɪs
Balniel bælˈniː.ɪl
Balogh ˈbæl.ɒg Ⓤⓢ -ɑːg
baloney bəˈləʊ.ni Ⓤⓢ -ˈloʊ-
Baloo bəˈluː
balsa ˈbɔːl.sə, ˈbɒl- Ⓤⓢ ˈbɔːl-, ˈbɑːl- **ˈbalsa ˌwood**
balsam ˈbɔːl.səm, ˈbɒl- Ⓤⓢ ˈbɔːl-, ˈbɑːl- **-s** -z
balsamic bɔːlˈsæm.ɪk, bɒl- Ⓤⓢ bɔːl-, bɑːl- **balˌsamic ˈvinegar**
Balta ˈbæl.tə Ⓤⓢ ˈbæl-, ˈbɑːl-
Balthazar ˌbæl.θəˈzɑːʳ, ˈ---; bælˈθæz.əʳ Ⓤⓢ ˌbæl.θəˈzɑːr, ˈ---; bælˈθeɪ.zɚ
Note: In Shakespeare, normally /ˌbæl.θəˈzɑːʳ, ˈ--- Ⓤⓢ ˌbæl.θəˈzɑːr, ˈ---/.
balti (B) ˈbɔːl.ti, ˈbɒl- Ⓤⓢ ˈbɔːl-, ˈbɑːl-, ˈbʌl-
Baltic ˈbɔːl.tɪk, ˈbɒl- Ⓤⓢ ˈbɔːl-, ˈbɑːl- **ˌBaltic ˈSea ; ˌBaltic ˈStates**
Baltimore ˈbɔːl.tɪ.mɔːʳ, ˈbɒl- Ⓤⓢ ˈbɔːl.tə.mɔːr, ˈbɑːl-, -mɚ **-s** -z
Baluchistan bəˌluː.tʃɪˈstɑːn, bælˌuː-, -kɪˈ-, -ˈstæn Ⓤⓢ -tʃəˈstæn, -ˈstɑːn
baluster ˈbæl.ə.stəʳ Ⓤⓢ -stɚ **-s** -z **-ed** -d
balustrade ˌbæl.əˈstreɪd Ⓤⓢ ˈ--- **-s** -z
Balzac ˈbæl.zæk Ⓤⓢ ˈbɔːl-, ˈbɑːl-, ˈbæl-
Bamako ˌbæm.əˈkəʊ Ⓤⓢ ˌbæm.əˈkoʊ, ˌbɑː.mə-
Bambi ˈbæm.bi
bambin|o bæmˈbiː.n|əʊ Ⓤⓢ bæmˈbiː.n|oʊ, bɑːm- **-os** -əʊz Ⓤⓢ -oʊz **-i** -i
bamboo bæmˈbuː **-s** -z
bamboozl|e bæmˈbuː.zl̩ **-es** -z **-ing** -ɪŋ, -ˈbuːz.lɪŋ **-ed** -d
Bamborough ˈbæm.bᵊr.ə Ⓤⓢ -oʊ
Bamburgh ˈbæm.bᵊr.ə Ⓤⓢ -bɚ.ə, -bɝːg
Bamfield ˈbæm.fiːld
Bamford ˈbæm.fəd Ⓤⓢ -fɚd
ban *prohibit:* bæn **-s** -z **-ning** -ɪŋ **-ned** -d
ban *Romanian money:* bæn Ⓤⓢ bɑːn **bani** ˈbɑː.ni
banal bəˈnɑːl, bænˈɑːl, -ˈnæl
banalit|y bəˈnæl.ə.t|i, bænˈæl-, -ɪ.t|i Ⓤⓢ -ə.t̬|i **-ies** -iz
banana bəˈnɑː.nə Ⓤⓢ -ˈnæn.ə **-s** -z **baˌnana reˈpublic ; baˈnana ˌskin; baˌnana ˈsplit**
Banaras bəˈnɑː.rəs Ⓤⓢ -ˈnɑːr.əs
Banbridge ˈbæn.brɪdʒ, ˈbæm- Ⓤⓢ ˈbæn-

Banbury 'bæn.bᵊr.i, 'bæm- (US) 'bæn.ber-, -bɚ-

Banchory 'bæŋ.kᵊr.i

Bancroft 'bæŋ.krɒft (US) 'bæn.krɑːft, 'bæŋ-

band bænd **-s** -z **-ing** -ɪŋ **-ed** -ɪd **'band ˌshell**

Banda 'bæn.də (US) 'bɑːn-, 'bæn-

bandag|e 'bæn.dɪdʒ **-es** -ɪz **-ing** -ɪŋ **-ed** -d

Band-Aid®, band-aid 'bænd.eɪd **-s** -z

bandan(n)a bæn'dæn.ə **-s** -z

Bandaranaika ˌbæn.dᵊr.ə'naɪ.ɪ.kə, -'naɪ.kə (US) ˌbɑːn-

Bandar Seri Begawan ˌbæn.də.ser.i.bə'gɑː.wən, -be'-, -bɪ'-, -'gaʊ.ən (US) ˌbɑːn.dɚ-

B and B ˌbiː.ᵊnd'biː, -ᵊm'- (US) -ᵊnd'- **-s** -z

bandbox 'bænd.bɒks (US) -bɑːks **-es** -ɪz

bandeau 'bæn.dəʊ *as if French:* bɑ̃n'dəʊ (US) bæn'doʊ **bandeaux** 'bæn.dəʊ, -dəʊz *as if French:* bɑ̃n'dəʊ (US) bæn'doʊ, -doʊz

banderole 'bæn.dᵊr.əʊl (US) -də.roʊl **-s** -z

bandicoot 'bæn.dɪ.kuːt **-s** -s

bandit 'bæn.dɪt **-s** -s **-ry** -ri

bandleader 'bænd,liː.dəʳ (US) -dɚ **-s** -z

bandmaster 'bænd,mɑː.stəʳ (US) -,mæs.tɚ **-s** -z

bandog 'bæn.dɒg (US) -dɑːg, -dɔːg **-s** -z

bandoleer, bandolier ˌbæn.dᵊl'ɪəʳ (US) -də'lɪr **-s** -z

bandoline 'bæn.dəʊ.liːn (US) -də-, -doʊ-

bands|man 'bændz|.mən **-men** -mən, -men

bandstand 'bænd.stænd **-s** -z

Bandung 'bæn.dʊŋ, -'- (US) 'bɑːn-, 'bæn-

bandwagon 'bænd,wæg.ən **-s** -z

band|y 'bæn.d|i **-ier** -i.əʳ (US) -i.ɚ **-iest** -i.ɪst, -i.əst **-ies** -iz **-ying** -i.ɪŋ **-ied** -id

bandy-legged ˌbæn.di'legd, -'leg.ɪd, -'leg.əd *stress shift:* ˌbandy-legged 'child

bane beɪn **-s** -z

baneful 'beɪn.fᵊl, -fʊl **-ly** -i **-ness** -nəs, -nɪs

Banff bænf **-shire** -ʃəʳ, -ˌʃɪəʳ (US) -ʃɚ, -ˌʃɪr

Banfield 'bæn.fiːld

bang bæŋ **-s** -z **-ing** -ɪŋ **-ed** -d **go ˌoff with a 'bang**

Bangalore ˌbæŋ.gə'lɔːʳ (US) 'bæŋ.gə.lɔːr, ˌ--'-

banger 'bæŋ.əʳ (US) -ɚ **-s** -z

Banger 'beɪn.dʒəʳ (US) -dʒɚ

Bangkok bæŋ'kɒk (US) 'bæŋ.kɑːk, -'- *stress shift, British only:* ˌBangkok 'temple

Bangladesh ˌbæŋ.glə'deʃ, -'deɪʃ (US) ˌbæŋ.glə'deʃ, ˌbɑːŋ-

Bangladeshi ˌbæŋ.glə'deʃ.i, -'deɪ.ʃi (US) ˌbæŋ.glə'deʃ-, ˌbɑːŋ- **-s** -z

bangle 'bæŋ.gl̩ **-s** -z **-d** -d

bang-on ˌbæŋ'ɒn (US) 'bæŋ.ɑːn

Bangor *in Wales:* 'bæŋ.gəʳ (US) -gɚ *in US:* 'bæŋ.gɔːʳ, -gəʳ (US) -gɔːr, -gɚ

Bangui ˌbɑːŋ'giː (US) ˌbɑːŋ-

bang-up ˌbæŋ'ʌp (US) '--

Banham 'bæn.əm

bani (*plur. of* **ban**) 'bɑː.ni

banian 'bæn.i.ən, '-jæn **-s** -z

banish 'bæn.ɪʃ **-es** -ɪz **-ing** -ɪŋ **-ed** -t **-ment/s** -mənt/s

banister (B) 'bæn.ɪ.stəʳ (US) -ə.stɚ **-s** -z

Banja Luka ˌbæn.jə'luː.kə (US) ˌbɑː.njə'-

banjo 'bæn.dʒəʊ, -'- (US) 'bæn.dʒoʊ **-(e)s** -z

Banjul bæn'dʒuːl (US) 'bɑːn.dʒuːl

bank bæŋk **-s** -s **-ing** -ɪŋ **-ed** -t **'bank aˌccount ; 'bank ˌcard ; 'bank ˌclerk ; ˌbank 'holiday ; 'bank ˌmanager ; 'bank ˌrate ; 'bank ˌstatement ; ˌBank of 'England**

bankability ˌbæŋ.kə'bɪl.ə.ti, -ɪ.ti (US) -ə.t̬i

bankable 'bæŋ.kə.bl̩

banker 'bæŋ.kəʳ (US) -kɚ **-s** -z

Bankes bæŋks

Bankhead 'bæŋk.hed

bank-note 'bæŋk.nəʊt (US) -noʊt **-s** -s

bankroll 'bæŋk.rəʊl (US) -roʊl **-s** -z **-ing** -ɪŋ **-ed** -d

bankrupt 'bæŋ.krʌpt, -krəpt **-s** -s

bankruptc|y 'bæŋ.krəpt.s|i, -krʌpt- **-ies** -iz

Banks bæŋks

banksia 'bæŋk.si.ə **-s** -z

Ban-Lon® 'bæn.lɒn (US) -lɑːn

Bann bæn

Bannatyne 'bæn.ə.taɪn

banner (B) 'bæn.əʳ (US) -ɚ **-s** -z

Bannerman 'bæn.ə.mən (US) '-ɚ-

Banning 'bæn.ɪŋ

bannister (B) 'bæn.ɪ.stəʳ (US) -ə.stɚ **-s** -z

bannock 'bæn.ək **-s** -s

Bannockburn 'bæn.ək.bɜːn (US) -bɜːrn, -bɚn

Bannon 'bæn.ən

banns bænz

banque|t 'bæŋ.kwɪ|t (US) -kwə|t, -kwɪ|t **-ts** -ts **-ting** -tɪŋ (US) -t̬ɪŋ **-ted** -tɪd (US) -t̬ɪd **'banquet ˌroom ; 'banqueting ˌhall**

banquette bæŋ'ket **-s** -s

Banquo 'bæŋ.kwəʊ (US) -kwoʊ

banshee 'bæn.ʃiː, -'- **-s** -z

Banstead 'bænt.stɪd, -sted

bant bænt **-s** -s **-ing** -ɪŋ (US) 'bæn.t̬ɪŋ **-ed** -ɪd (US) 'bæn.t̬ɪd

bantam (B) 'bæn.təm (US) -t̬əm **-s** -z

bantamweight 'bæn.təm.weɪt (US) -t̬əm- **-s**

bant|er 'bæn.t|əʳ (US) -t̬|ɚ **-ers** -əz (US) -ɚz **-ering** -ᵊr.ɪŋ **-ered** -əd (US) -ɚd

Banting 'bæn.tɪŋ (US) -t̬ɪŋ

bantling 'bænt.lɪŋ **-s** -z

Bantry 'bæn.tri

Bantu ˌbæn'tuː, ˌbɑːn-, '-- (US) 'bæn.tuː

bantustan (B) ˌbæn.tu'stɑːn, ˌbɑːn-, -'stæn

banyan 'bæn.jæn, -ni.ən, '-jən (US) '-jən, '-jæn **-s** -z

Banyard 'bæn.jɑːd (US) -jɑːrd

banzai bæn'zaɪ, bɑːn-, '-- (US) bɑːn'zaɪ, '--

baobab 'beɪ.əʊ.bæb (US) '-oʊ-, 'bɑː- **-s** -z

bap bæp **-s** -s

baptism 'bæp.tɪ.zᵊm **-s** -z **ˌbaptism of 'fire**

baptismal bæp'tɪz.mᵊl **-ly** -i

baptist (B) 'bæp.tɪst **-s** -s **ˌJohn the 'Baptist**

baptister|y 'bæp.tɪ.stᵊr|.i **-ies** -iz

baptistr|y 'bæp.tɪ.str|i **-ies** -iz

baptiz|e, -is|e bæp'taɪz (US) '-- **-es** -ɪz **-ing** -ɪŋ **-ed** -d

bar (B) bɑːʳ (US) bɑːr **-s** -z **-ring** -ɪŋ **-red** -d **'bar ˌcode ; 'bar ˌgraph ; 'bar ˌmeal ; 'bar ˌstaff**

Barabbas bə'ræb.əs

barb bɑːb (US) bɑːrb **-s** -z **-ing** -ɪŋ **-ed** -d

Barbadian bɑː'beɪ.di.ən, -dʒən (US) bɑːr- **-s** -z

Barbados bɑː'beɪ.dɒs, -dəs (US) bɑːr'beɪ.doʊs

Barbara 'bɑː.bᵊr.ə, '-brə (US) 'bɑːr-

barbarian bɑː'beə.ri.ən (US) bɑːr'ber.i- **-s** -z

barbaric bɑː'bær.ɪk (US) bɑːr'ber-, -'bær- **-ally** -ᵊl.i, -li

barbarism 'bɑː.bᵊr.ɪ.zᵊm (US) 'bɑːr- **-s** -z

barbarit|y bɑː'bær.ə.t|i, -ɪ|.ti (US) bɑːr'ber.ə.t̬|i, -'bær- **-ies** -iz

barbariz|e, -ise 'bɑː.bᵊr.aɪz (US) 'bɑːr- **-es** -ɪz **-ing** -ɪŋ **-ed** -d

Barbarossa ˌbɑː.bᵊr'ɒs.ə (US) ˌbɑːr.bə'roʊ.sə, -'rɑː-

barbarous 'bɑː.bᵊr.əs (US) 'bɑːr- **-ly** -li **-ness** -nəs, -nɪs

Barbary 'bɑː.bᵊr.i (US) 'bɑːr- **ˌBarbary 'ape ; ˌBarbary 'Coast**

barbate 'bɑː.beɪt, -bɪt, -bət (US) 'bɑːr-

barbated 'bɑː.beɪ.tɪd, -bɪ-, -bə-; bɑː'beɪ- (US) bɑːr'beɪ.t̬ɪd

Barbauld 'bɑː.bᵊld (US) 'bɑːr-

barbecu|e 'bɑː.bɪ.kjuː, -bə- (US) 'bɑːr- **-es** -z **-ing** -ɪŋ **-ed** -d

barbed bɑːbd (US) bɑːrbd **ˌbarbed 'wire**

barbell 'bɑː.bel Ⓤⓢ 'bɑːr- **-s** -z
barber (B) 'bɑː.bəʳ Ⓤⓢ 'bɑːr.bɚ **-s** -z
barberr|y 'bɑː.bᵊr|.i Ⓤⓢ 'bɑːr.ber|.i **-ies** -iz
barbershop 'bɑː.bə.ʃɒp Ⓤⓢ 'bɑːr.bɚ.ʃɑːp **-s** -s ˌ**barbershop quar'tet**
barbette bɑː'bet Ⓤⓢ bɑːr- **-s** -s
barbican (B) 'bɑː.bɪ.kən Ⓤⓢ 'bɑːr.bə- **-s** -z
barbie (B) 'bɑː.bi Ⓤⓢ 'bɑːr- **'Barbie ˌdoll®**
Barbirolli ˌbɑː.bɪ'rɒl.i, -bə'- Ⓤⓢ ˌbɑːr.bə'rɑː.li
barbitone 'bɑː.bɪ.təʊn Ⓤⓢ 'bɑːr.bə.toʊn **-s** -z
barbiturate bɑː'bɪtʃ.ᵊr.ət, -'bɪt.jʊ.rət, -jᵊr.ət, -ɪt, -eɪt Ⓤⓢ bɑːr'bɪtʃ.ᵊr.ət, -eɪt **-s** -s
barbituric ˌbɑː.bɪ'tʃʊə.rɪk; ˌbɑː'bɪt.jʊ-, -jᵊr.ɪk Ⓤⓢ ˌbɑːr.bə'tʃʊr.ɪk, -'tʊr- **barbiˌturic 'acid**
Barbour® 'bɑː.bəʳ Ⓤⓢ 'bɑːr.bɚ **-s** -z
Barbuda bɑː'bjuː.də Ⓤⓢ bɑːr'buː-, -'bjuː-
barbule 'bɑː.bjuːl Ⓤⓢ 'bɑːr- **-s** -z
barbwire 'bɑːb.waɪəʳ Ⓤⓢ 'bɑːrb.waɪɚ
Barca 'bɑː.kə Ⓤⓢ 'bɑːr-
barcarol(l)e ˌbɑː.kə'rəʊl, -'rɒl, '--- Ⓤⓢ 'bɑːr.kə.roʊl **-s** -z
Barcelona ˌbɑː.sᵊl'əʊ.nə, -sɪ'ləʊ- Ⓤⓢ ˌbɑːr.sə'loʊ-
Barchester 'bɑː.tʃes.təʳ, -tʃɪ.stəʳ Ⓤⓢ 'bɑːr.tʃə.stɚ, -tʃes.tɚ
Barclay 'bɑː.kli, -kleɪ Ⓤⓢ 'bɑːr- **-'s** -z
Barclaycard® 'bɑː.kli.kɑːd, -kleɪ- Ⓤⓢ 'bɑːr.kli.kɑːrd
bar code 'bɑː.kəʊd Ⓤⓢ 'bɑːr.koʊd **-s** -z
Barcroft 'bɑː.krɒft Ⓤⓢ 'bɑːr.krɑːft
bard (B) bɑːd Ⓤⓢ bɑːrd **-s** -z **-ic** -ɪk
Bardell bɑː'del; 'bɑː.dᵊl, -del Ⓤⓢ bɑːr'del; 'bɑːr.dᵊl, -del
Note: In 'Pickwick' generally pronounced /bɑː'del Ⓤⓢ bɑːr-/.
bardolatry bɑː'dɒl.ə.tri Ⓤⓢ bɑːr'dɑː.lə-
Bardolph 'bɑː.dɒlf Ⓤⓢ 'bɑːr.dɑːlf
Bardot bɑː'dəʊ Ⓤⓢ bɑːr'doʊ
Bardsey 'bɑːd.si Ⓤⓢ 'bɑːrd-
Bardsley 'bɑːdz.li Ⓤⓢ 'bɑːrdz-
Bardswell 'bɑːdz.wəl, -wel Ⓤⓢ 'bɑːrdz-
Bardwell 'bɑːd.wəl, -wel Ⓤⓢ 'bɑːrd-
bar|e beəʳ Ⓤⓢ ber **-er** -əʳ Ⓤⓢ -ɚ **-est** -ɪst, -əst
bareback 'beə.bæk Ⓤⓢ 'ber- **-ed** -t
Barebones 'beə.bəʊnz Ⓤⓢ 'ber.boʊnz
barefaced beə'feɪst Ⓤⓢ 'ber.feɪst **-ly** -li, -ɪd.li **-ness** -nəs, -nɪs *stress shift, British only:* ˌbarefaced 'liar
barefoot beə'fʊt Ⓤⓢ 'ber.fʊt *stress shift, British only:* ˌbarefoot 'child
barefooted ˌbeə'fʊt.ɪd Ⓤⓢ 'ber.fʊt̬- *stress shift, British only:* ˌbarefooted 'child
barehanded ˌbeə'hæn.dɪd Ⓤⓢ 'berˌhæn- *stress shift, British only:* ˌbarehanded 'warrior
bare-headed ˌbeə'hed.ɪd Ⓤⓢ 'berˌhed- *stress shift, British only:* ˌbare-headed 'worshippers
Bareilly bə'reɪ.li
bare-legged ˌbeə'legd, -'leg.ɪd Ⓤⓢ 'berˌleg.ɪd, -legd *stress shift, British only:* ˌbare-legged 'child
bare|ly 'beə|.li Ⓤⓢ 'ber- **-ness** -nəs, -nɪs
Barenboim 'bær.ən.bɔɪm, 'bɑːr- Ⓤⓢ 'ber-, 'bær-
Barents 'bær.ənts Ⓤⓢ 'ber-, 'bær-
barf bɑːf Ⓤⓢ bɑːrf **-s** -s **-ing** -ɪŋ **-ed** -t
Barfield 'bɑː.fiːld Ⓤⓢ 'bɑːr-
bar|fly 'bɑː|.flaɪ Ⓤⓢ 'bɑːr- **-flies** -flaɪz
Barfoot 'bɑː.fʊt Ⓤⓢ 'bɑːr-
bargain 'bɑː.gɪn, -gən Ⓤⓢ 'bɑːr- **-s** -z **-ing** -ɪŋ **-ed** -d **-er/s** -əʳ/z Ⓤⓢ -ɚ/z ˌ**bargain 'basement** ; **'bargain ˌhunter**
barg|e bɑːdʒ Ⓤⓢ bɑːrdʒ **-es** -ɪz
bargee bɑː'dʒiː, '-- Ⓤⓢ bɑːr'dʒiː **-s** -z
barge|man 'bɑːdʒ|.mən, -mæn Ⓤⓢ 'bɑːrdʒ- **-men** -mən, -men
bargepole 'bɑːdʒ.pəʊl Ⓤⓢ 'bɑːrdʒ.poʊl **-s** -z
Barger 'bɑː.dʒəʳ Ⓤⓢ 'bɑːr.dʒɚ
Bargh bɑːdʒ, bɑːf Ⓤⓢ bɑːrdʒ, bɑːrf
Bargoed 'bɑː.gɔɪd Ⓤⓢ 'bɑːr-
Bargrave 'bɑː.greɪv Ⓤⓢ 'bɑːr-
Barham *surname:* 'bær.əm, 'bɑː.rəm Ⓤⓢ 'ber-, 'bær-, 'bɑːr.əm *in Kent:* 'bær.əm Ⓤⓢ 'ber-, 'bær-
Bari 'bɑː.ri Ⓤⓢ 'bɑːr.i
Baring 'beə.rɪŋ, 'bær.ɪŋ Ⓤⓢ 'ber.ɪŋ, 'bær- **-s** -z
Baring-Gould ˌbeə.rɪŋ'guːld Ⓤⓢ ˌber.ɪŋ'-
baritone 'bær.ɪ.təʊn Ⓤⓢ 'ber.ə.toʊn, 'bær- **-s** -z
barium 'beə.ri.əm Ⓤⓢ 'ber.i-, 'bær- ˌ**barium 'meal**
bark bɑːk Ⓤⓢ bɑːrk **-s** -s **-ing** -ɪŋ **-ed** -t **-er/s** -əʳ/z Ⓤⓢ -ɚ/z ˌ**bark up the wrong 'tree** ; **their ˌbark is ˌworse than their 'bite**
barkeep 'bɑː.kiːp Ⓤⓢ 'bɑːr- **-s** -s **-er/s** -əʳ/z Ⓤⓢ -ɚ/z
Barker 'bɑː.kəʳ Ⓤⓢ 'bɑːr.kɚ
Barking 'bɑː.kɪŋ Ⓤⓢ 'bɑːr-
Barkston 'bɑːk.stən Ⓤⓢ 'bɑːrk-
barley 'bɑː.li Ⓤⓢ 'bɑːr- **'barley ˌsugar** ; **'barley ˌwater** ; ˌ**barley 'wine**
barleycorn (B) 'bɑː.li.kɔːn Ⓤⓢ 'bɑːr.li.kɔːrn **-s** -z
Barlow(e) 'bɑː.ləʊ Ⓤⓢ 'bɑːr.loʊ
barm bɑːm Ⓤⓢ bɑːrm
barmaid 'bɑː.meɪd Ⓤⓢ 'bɑːr- **-s** -z
bar|man 'bɑː|.mən, -mæn Ⓤⓢ 'bɑːr- **-men** -mən, -men
Barmby 'bɑːm.bi Ⓤⓢ 'bɑːrm-
Barmecide 'bɑː.mɪ.saɪd Ⓤⓢ 'bɑːr.mə-
bar mi(t)zvah bɑː'mɪts.və Ⓤⓢ bɑːr-
Barmouth 'bɑː.məθ Ⓤⓢ 'bɑːr-
barm|y 'bɑː.m|i Ⓤⓢ 'bɑːr- **-ier** -i.əʳ Ⓤⓢ -i.ɚ **-iest** -i.ɪst, -i.əst **-iness** -ɪ.nəs, -ɪ.nɪs
barn bɑːn Ⓤⓢ bɑːrn **-s** -z **'barn ˌdance** ; ˌ**barn 'door**
Barnabas 'bɑː.nə.bəs, -bæs Ⓤⓢ 'bɑːr-
Barnaby 'bɑː.nə.bi Ⓤⓢ 'bɑːr-
barnacle 'bɑː.nə.kl̩ Ⓤⓢ 'bɑːr- **-s** -z
Barnard 'bɑː.nəd, -nɑːd Ⓤⓢ 'bɑːr.nɚd; bɑːr'nɑːrd
Barnardiston ˌbɑː.nə'dɪs.tən Ⓤⓢ ˌbɑːr.nɚ'-
Barnardo bə'nɑː.dəʊ, bɑː- Ⓤⓢ bɚ'nɑːr.doʊ
Barnby 'bɑːn.bi, 'bɑːm- Ⓤⓢ 'bɑːrn-
Barnes bɑːnz Ⓤⓢ bɑːrnz
Barnet(t) 'bɑː.nɪt Ⓤⓢ bɑːr'net, '--
barney (B) 'bɑː.ni Ⓤⓢ 'bɑːr- **-s** -z
Barnfield 'bɑːn.fiːld Ⓤⓢ 'bɑːrn-
Barnham 'bɑː.nəm Ⓤⓢ 'bɑːr-
Barnicott 'bɑː.nɪ.kət, -kɒt Ⓤⓢ 'bɑːr.nə.kɑːt, -nɪ-, -kət
Barnoldswick bɑː'nəʊldz.wɪk *locally also:* 'bɑː.lɪk Ⓤⓢ bɑːr'noʊldz.wɪk
Barnsley 'bɑːnz.li Ⓤⓢ 'bɑːrnz-
Barnstaple 'bɑːn.stə.pl̩ *locally also:* -bl̩ Ⓤⓢ 'bɑːrn.stə.pl̩
barnstorm 'bɑːn.stɔːm Ⓤⓢ 'bɑːrn.stɔːrm **-s** -z **-ing** -ɪŋ **-ed** -d **-er/s** -əʳ/z Ⓤⓢ -ɚ/z
Barnum 'bɑː.nəm Ⓤⓢ 'bɑːr-
barnyard 'bɑːn.jɑːd Ⓤⓢ 'bɑːrn.jɑːrd **-s** -z
Baroda bə'rəʊ.də Ⓤⓢ -'roʊ-
barograph 'bær.əʊ.grɑːf, -græf Ⓤⓢ 'ber.ə.græf, 'bær- **-s** -s
Barolo bə'rəʊ.ləʊ Ⓤⓢ -'roʊ.loʊ
Barolong ˌbɑː.rəʊ'ləʊŋ, ˌbær.əʊ-, -'lɒŋ Ⓤⓢ ˌbɑːr.ə'loʊŋ
barometer bə'rɒm.ɪ.təʳ, -ə.təʳ Ⓤⓢ -'rɑː.mə.t̬ɚ **-s** -z
barometric ˌbær.əʊ'met.rɪk Ⓤⓢ ˌber.ə'-, ˌbær- **-al** -ᵊl **-ally** -ᵊl.i, -li
barometry bə'rɒm.ɪ.tri, '-ə- Ⓤⓢ -'rɑː.mə-
baron (B) 'bær.ᵊn Ⓤⓢ 'ber-, 'bær- **-s** -z
baronag|e 'bær.ᵊn.ɪdʒ Ⓤⓢ 'ber-, 'bær- **-es** -ɪz
baroness (B) 'bær.ᵊn.es, -ɪs, -əs; ˌbær.ᵊn'es Ⓤⓢ 'ber.ᵊn.əs, 'bær- **-es** -ɪz
baronet 'bær.ᵊn.ɪt, -et, -ət; ˌbær.ᵊn'et Ⓤⓢ 'ber.ᵊn.ət, 'bær-, -ɪt **-s** -s

baronetag|e 'bær.ə.nɪ.tɪdʒ, ˌbær.ə'nɪt.ɪdʒ (US) 'ber.ə.nə.t̬ɪdʒ, 'bær- **-es** -ɪz

baronetc|y 'bær.ə.nɪt.s|i, -net- (US) 'ber-, 'bær- **-ies** -iz

baronial bə'rəʊ.ni.əl (US) -'roʊ-

baron|y 'bær.ᵊn|.i (US) 'ber-, 'bær- **-ies** -iz

baroque bə'rɒk, bær'ɒk (US) bə'roʊk, bær'oʊk, -'ɑːk

baroscope 'bær.əʊ.skəʊp (US) 'ber.ə.skoʊp, 'bær- **-s** -s

baroscopic ˌbær.əʊ'skɒp.ɪk (US) ˌber.ə'skɑː.pɪk, ˌbær-

Barossa bə'rɒs.ə (US) -'rɑː.sə **Baˌrossa 'Valley**

barouch|e bə'ruːʃ, bær'uːʃ (US) bə'ruːʃ **-es** -ɪz

barperson 'bɑːˌpɜː.sᵊn (US) 'bɑːrˌpɜːr- **-s** -z

barque bɑːk (US) bɑːrk **-s** -s

Barquisimeto ˌbɑː.kɪ.sɪ'meɪ.təʊ (US) bɑːrˌkə.sə'meɪ.toʊ

Barr bɑːʳ (US) bɑːr

Barra 'bær.ə (US) 'ber-, 'bær-

barrack 'bær.ək (US) 'ber-, 'bær- **-s** -s **-ing** -ɪŋ **-ed** -t

Barraclough 'bær.ə.klʌf (US) 'ber-, 'bær-

barracuda ˌbær.ə'kjuː.də, -'kuː- (US) ˌber.ə'kuː-, ˌbær- **-s**

barrag|e 'bær.ɑːdʒ (US) bə'rɑːdʒ **-es** -ɪz

barramund|a ˌbær.ə'mʌn.d|ə (US) ˌber-, ˌbær- **-as** -əz **-i** -i **-is** -ɪs

Barranquilla ˌbær.əŋ'kiː.ə (US) ˌbɑːr.ɑːn'kiː.jɑː, ˌber-, ˌbær-

barratry 'bær.ə.tri (US) 'ber-, 'bær-

Barrat(t) 'bær.ət (US) 'ber-, 'bær-

barre bɑːʳ (US) bɑːr **-s** -z

barrel 'bær.ᵊl (US) 'ber-, 'bær- **-s** -z

barrel-organ 'bær.ᵊlˌɔː.gən (US) 'ber.ᵊlˌɔːr-, 'bær- **-s** -z

barren 'bær.ᵊn (US) 'ber-, 'bær- **-est** -ɪst, -əst **-ly** -li **-ness** -nəs, -nɪs

Barrett 'bær.ət, -et, -ɪt (US) 'ber-, 'bær-

barrette bə'ret, bɑː- (US) bə'ret **-s** -s

Barrhead 'bɑː.hed (US) 'bɑːr-

barricad|e ˌbær.ɪ'keɪd, -ə'-, '--- (US) 'ber.ə.keɪd, 'bær-, ˌ--'- **-es** -z **-ing** -ɪŋ **-ed** -ɪd

Barrie 'bær.i (US) 'ber-, 'bær-

barrier (B) 'bær.i.əʳ (US) 'ber.i.ɚ, 'bær- **-s** -z **ˌGreat ˌBarrier 'Reef**

barring 'bɑː.rɪŋ (US) 'bɑːr.ɪŋ

Barrington 'bær.ɪŋ.tən (US) 'ber-

barrio 'bær.i.əʊ (US) 'bɑːr.i.oʊ, 'ber-, 'bær- **-s** -z

barrister 'bær.ɪ.stəʳ (US) 'ber.ɪ.stɚ, 'bær- **-s** -z

barrister-at-law ˌbær.ɪ.stəʳ.ət'lɔː (US) ˌber.ə.stɚ.ət'lɑː, ˌbær-, -'lɔː **barristers-at-law** ˌbær.ɪ.stəz.ət'lɔː (US) ˌber.ə.stɚz.ət'lɑː, ˌbær-, -'lɔː

barristerial ˌbær.ɪ'stɪə.ri.əl (US) ˌber.ə'stɪr.i-, ˌbær-

Barron 'bær.ən (US) 'ber-, 'bær-

barroom 'bɑː.rʊm, -ruːm (US) 'bɑːr.ruːm, -rʊm **-s** -z

barrow (B) 'bær.əʊ (US) 'ber.oʊ, 'bær- **-s** -z

Barrow-in-Furness ˌbær.əʊ.ɪn'fɜː.nɪs, -nes, -nəs (US) ˌber.oʊ.ɪn'fɜːr-, ˌbær-

Barry 'bær.i (US) 'ber-, 'bær-

Barrymore 'bær.ɪ.mɔːʳ (US) 'ber.ɪ.mɔːr, 'bær-

Barset 'bɑː.sɪt, -set, -sət (US) 'bɑːr- **-shire** -ʃəʳ, -ˌʃɪəʳ (US) -ʃɚ, -ˌʃɪr

barstool 'bɑː.stuːl (US) 'bɑːr- **-s** -z

Barstow 'bɑː.stəʊ (US) 'bɑːr.stoʊ

bart (B) bɑːt (US) bɑːrt **-s** -s

bartend 'bɑː.tend (US) 'bɑːr- **-s** -z **-ing** -ɪŋ **-ed** -ɪd

bartender 'bɑːˌten.dəʳ (US) 'bɑːrˌten.dɚ **-s** -z

bart|er (B) 'bɑː.t|əʳ (US) 'bɑːr.t̬|ɚ **-ers** -əz (US) -ɚz **-ering** -ᵊr.ɪŋ **-ered** -əd (US) -ɚd

Barth bɑːθ (US) bɑːrθ

Barthelme 'bɑː.tᵊl.meɪ (US) 'bɑːr.t̬ᵊl-

Barthes bɑːt (US) bɑːrt

Bartholomew bɑː'θɒl.ə.mjuː, bə'- (US) bɑːr'θɑː.lə-, bɚ-

Bartle 'bɑː.tl̩ (US) 'bɑːr.t̬l̩

Bartleby 'bɑː.tl̩.bi (US) 'bɑːr.t̬l̩-

Bartlett 'bɑːt.lət, -lɪt (US) 'bɑːrt-

Bartók 'bɑː.tɒk (US) 'bɑːr.tɑːk

Bartolommeo ˌbɑː.tɒl.ə'meɪ.əʊ (US) bɑːrˌtɑː.lə'meɪ.oʊ

Bartolozzi ˌbɑː.tə'lɒt.si (US) ˌbɑːr.t̬ə'lɑːt-

Barton 'bɑː.tᵊn (US) 'bɑːr-

Bartram 'bɑː.trəm (US) 'bɑːr-

Bart's bɑːts (US) bɑːrts

bartsia 'bɑːt.si.ə (US) 'bɑːrt-

Baruch *biblical name:* 'bɑː.rʊk, 'beə-, -rək (US) bə'ruːk; 'bɑːr.uːk, 'ber- *modern surname:* bə'ruːk

Barugh bɑːf (US) bɑːrf

Barum 'beə.rəm (US) 'ber.əm

Barwick *in the UK:* 'bær.ɪk (US) 'ber.ɪk, 'bær- *in the US:* 'bɑː.wɪk; 'bær.ɪk (US) 'bɑːr.wɪk

Baryshnikov bə'rɪʃ.nɪ.kɒf, bær'ɪʃ-, -kəf (US) bə'rɪʃ.nɪ.kɔːf, bɑː'-, -kɑːf

barysphere 'bær.ɪ.sfɪəʳ (US) 'ber.ɪ.sfɪr, 'bær- **-s** -z

barytone 'bar.ɪ.təʊn (US) 'ber.ə.toʊn, 'bær- **-s** -z

basal 'beɪ.sᵊl

basalt 'bæs.ɔːlt; -ᵊlt; bə'sɔːlt, -'sɒlt (US) bə'sɔːlt, -'sɑːlt; 'beɪ.sɔːlt, -sɑːlt

basaltic bə'sɔːl.tɪk, -'sɒl- (US) bə'sɔːl.t̬ɪk, -'sɑːl-

Basan 'beɪ.sæn

bascule 'bæs.kjuːl **-s** -z

bas|e beɪs **-es** -ɪz **-er** -əʳ (US) -ɚ **-est** -ɪst, -əst **-ely** -li **-eness** -nəs, -nɪs **-ing** -ɪŋ **-ed** -t ˌ**base 'metal**; '**base ˌrate**

baseball 'beɪs.bɔːl (US) -bɔːl, -bɑːl '**baseball ˌbat**; '**baseball ˌcap**

baseboard 'beɪs.bɔːd (US) -bɔːrd **-s** -z

baseborn 'beɪs.bɔːn (US) -bɔːrn

Baseden 'beɪz.dən

Basel 'bɑː.zᵊl

baseless 'beɪs.ləs, -lɪs **-ly** -li **-ness** -nəs, -nɪs

baseline 'beɪs.laɪn **-s** -z

base|man 'beɪs|.mən, -mæn **-men** -mən, -men

basement 'beɪs.mənt **-s** -s

bases (*plur. of* **base**) 'beɪ.sɪz (*plur. of* **basis**) 'beɪ.siːz

Basford *in Nottinghamshire:* 'beɪs.fəd (US) -fɚd *in Staffordshire:* 'bæs.fəd (US) -fɚd

bash bæʃ **-es** -ɪz **-ing** -ɪŋ **-ed** -t

Basham 'bæʃ.əm

Bashan 'beɪ.ʃæn

Bashford 'bæʃ.fəd (US) -fɚd

bashful 'bæʃ.fᵊl, -fʊl **-lest** -ɪst, -əst **-ly** -i **-ness** -nəs, -nɪs

basho 'bæʃ.əʊ (US) bɑː'ʃoʊ **-s** -z

basic (B) 'beɪ.sɪk **-ally** -ᵊl.i, -li

BASIC, **Basic** 'beɪ.sɪk

basicity bə'sɪs.ə.ti, -ɪ.ti (US) -ə.t̬i

Basie 'beɪ.si, -zi

basil (B) 'bæz.ᵊl, -ɪl (US) 'beɪ.zᵊl, -sᵊl; 'bæz.ᵊl

basilar 'bæz.ɪ.ləʳ, 'bæs-, -ᵊl.əʳ (US) -ɪ.lɚ, -ᵊl.ɚ ˌ**basilar 'membrane**

Basildon 'bæz.ᵊl.dən

basilect 'bæz.ɪ.lekt, '-ə- (US) 'bæz.ə-, 'beɪ.sə- **-s** -s **-al** -ᵊl

basilic|a bə'zɪl.ɪ.k|ə, -'sɪl- (US) -'sɪl- **-as** -əz **-an** -ən

basilisk 'bæz.ə.lɪsk, '-ɪ- (US) 'bæs-, 'bæz- **-s** -s

basin 'beɪ.sᵊn **-s** -z

basinet 'bæs.ɪ.net; '-ə-; -nɪt; ˌbæs.ɪ'net **-s** -s

Basinger 'beɪ.sɪŋ.gəʳ, 'bæs.ɪn.dʒəʳ (US) 'beɪ.sɪŋ.gɚ, 'bæs.ɪn.dʒɚ

Basingstoke 'beɪ.zɪŋ.stəʊk (US) -stoʊk

bas|is 'beɪ.s|ɪs **-es** -iːz

bask bɑːsk (US) bæsk **-s** -s **-ing** -ɪŋ **-ed** -t

Basker 'bɑː.skəʳ (US) 'bæs.kɚ

Baskervill(e) 'bæs.kə.vɪl (US) -kɚ-

basket 'bɑː.skɪt (US) 'bæs.kət **-s** -s **-ful/s** -fʊl/z '**basket ˌcase**; **put all one's ˌeggs in one 'basket**

basketball 'bɑː.skɪt.bɔːl (US) 'bæs.kət.bɔːl, -bɑːl

basketry 'bɑː.skɪ.tri (US) 'bæs.kə-

basketwork 'bɑː.skɪt.wɜːk (US) 'bæs.kət.wɜːrk

Baskin-Robbins® ˌbæs.kɪn'rɒb.ɪnz (US) -'rɑː.bɪnz

Basle bɑːl

basmati bəˈsmɑː.ti, bæsˈmɑː-, bəz-, bæz-

bas mi(t)zvah ˌbæsˈmɪts.və (US) ˌbɑːs- **-ing** -ɪŋ **-ed** -d

Basnett ˈbæz.nɪt, -nət, -net

Basotho bəˈsuː.tuː, -ˈsəʊ.təʊ (US) -ˈsoʊ.toʊ

basque (B) bæsk, bɑːsk (US) bæsk **-s** -s

Basra(h) ˈbæz.rə, ˈbʌz-, ˈbæs- (US) ˈbɑːz.rə, ˈbæs-, ˈbæz-, ˈbɑːs-

bas-relief ˌbɑː.rɪˈliːf, ˌbæs-, ˌbɑːs-, -rəˈliːf **-s** -s

bass (B) *fish, fibre, beer:* bæs

bass *in music:* beɪs **-es** -ɪz ˌ**bass clariˈnet** ; ˌ**bass ˈclef** ; ˌ**bass ˈdrum** ; ˌ**bass guiˈtar**

Bassanio bəˈsɑː.ni.əʊ, bæsˈɑː- (US) -oʊ

Bassenthwaite ˈbæs.ᵊn.θweɪt

basset ˈbæs.ɪt (US) -ət **-s** -s

ˈ**basset ˌhorn** ; ˈ**basset ˌhound**

Basseterre bæsˈteəʳ (US) -ˈter

Basset(t) ˈbæs.ɪt (US) -ət

Bassey ˈbæs.i

bassinet(te) ˌbæs.ɪˈnet, -əˈ- **-s** -s

Bassingbourne ˈbæs.ɪŋ.bɔːn (US) -bɔːrn

bassist ˈbeɪ.sɪst **-s** -s

bass|o ˈbæs|.əʊ (US) -oʊ, ˈbɑː.s|oʊ **-os** -z **-i** -iː

bassoon bəˈsuːn **-s** -z **-ist/s** -ɪst/s

basswood ˈbæs.wʊd

bast (B) bæst

Bastable ˈbæs.tə.bl̩

bastard ˈbɑː.stəd, ˈbæs.təd (US) ˈbæs.tɚd **-s** -z **-y** -i

bastardiz|e, -is|e ˈbɑː.stə.daɪz, ˈbæs.tə- (US) ˈbæs.tɚ- **-es** -ɪz **-ing** -ɪŋ **-ed** -d

bast|e beɪst **-es** -s **-ing** -ɪŋ **-ed** -ɪd

bastille (B) bæsˈtiːl **-s** -z

bastinado ˌbæs.tɪˈnɑː.dəʊ, -ˈneɪ- (US) -doʊ **-es** -z **-ing** -ɪŋ **-ed** -d

bastion ˈbæs.ti.ən (US) ˈ-tʃən, ˈ-ti.ən **-s** -z **-ed** -d

Basuto bəˈsuː.təʊ, -ˈzuː- (US) -toʊ **-s** -z

Basutoland bəˈsuː.təʊ.lænd, -ˈzuː- (US) -toʊ-

bat bæt **-s** -s **-ting** -ɪŋ (US) ˈbæt̬.ɪŋ **-ted** -ɪd (US) ˈbæt̬.ɪd

Baˈtaan bəˈtɑːn (US) -ˈtæn, -ˈtɑːn

Batavia bəˈteɪ.vi.ə

batboy ˈbæt.bɔɪ **-s** -z

batch bætʃ **-es** -ɪz

Batchelar, Batchelor ˈbætʃ.ᵊl.əʳ, -ɪ.ləʳ (US) -ᵊl.ɚ

bat|e (B) beɪt **-es** -s **-ing** -ɪŋ (US) ˈbeɪ.t̬ɪŋ **-ed** -ɪd (US) ˈbeɪ.t̬ɪd

Bateman ˈbeɪt.mən **-s** -s

Bates beɪts

Bateson ˈbeɪt.sᵊn

Batey ˈbeɪ.ti (US) -t̬i

ba|th (B) (*n.*) bɑː|θ (US) bæ|θ **-ths** -ðz ˌ**Bath ˈbun,** ˈ**Bath ˌbun** ; ˌ**bath ˈchair** ; ˈ**bath ˌcube** ; ˈ**bath ˌmat** ; ˈ**bath ˌsalts** ; ˈ**Bath ˌstone** ; ˌ**Bath ˈOliver**

bath (*v.*) bɑːθ (US) bæθ **-s** -s **-ing** -ɪŋ **-ed** -t

bath|e beɪð **-es** -z **-ing** -ɪŋ **-ed** -d ˈ**bathing ˌcostume** ; ˈ**bathing ˌbeauty** ; ˈ**bathing ˌsuit**

bather ˈbeɪ.ðəʳ (US) -ðɚ **-s** -z

bathetic bəˈθet.ɪk, bæθˈet- (US) bəˈθet̬-

Bathgate ˈbɑːθ.geɪt (US) ˈbæθ-

bathhou|se ˈbɑːθ.haʊ|s (US) ˈbæθ- **-ses** -zɪz

bathmat ˈbɑːθ.mæt (US) ˈbæθ- **-s** -s

Batho ˈbæθ.əʊ, ˈbeɪ.θəʊ (US) ˈbæθ.oʊ, ˈbeɪ.θoʊ

batholite ˈbæθ.əʊ.laɪt (US) ˈ-ə- **-s** -s

batholith ˈbæθ.əʊ.lɪθ (US) ˈ-ə- **-s** -s

bathors|e ˈbæt.hɔːs (US) -hɔːrs **-es** -ɪz

bathos ˈbeɪ.θɒs (US) -θɑːs

bathrobe ˈbɑːθ.rəʊb (US) ˈbæθ.roʊb **-s** -z

bathroom ˈbɑːθ.rʊm, -ruːm (US) ˈbæθ.ruːm, -rʊm **-s** -z

Bathsheba ˈbæθ.ʃɪ.bə; bæθˈʃiː-

bathtub ˈbɑːθ.tʌb (US) ˈbæθ- **-s**

Bathurst ˈbæθ.ɜːst, -əst, -hɜːst, ˈbɑː.θɜːst, -θəst, ˈbɑːθ.hɜːst (US) ˈbæθ.ɜːrst, -hɜːrst

bathyscaphe ˈbæθ.ɪ.skæf **-s** -s

bathysphere ˈbæθ.ɪ.sfɪəʳ (US) -sfɪr **-s** -z

batik bætˈiːk; ˈbæt.ɪk (US) bəˈtiːk; ˈbæt̬.ɪk

batiste bætˈiːst, bəˈtiːst

Batley ˈbæt.li

bat|man *military:* ˈbæt|.mən **-men** -mən

batman *oriental weight:* ˈbæt.mən **-s** -z

Batman® ˈbæt.mæn

baton ˈbæt.ᵊn; bætˈɒn (US) bəˈtɑːn **-s** -z

Baton Rouge ˌbæt.ᵊnˈruːʒ

bats bæts

bats|man ˈbæts|.mən **-men** -mən

battalion bəˈtæl.i.ən, ˈ-jən (US) ˈ-jən **-s** -z

Battambang ˈbæt.əm.bæŋ (US) ˈbæt̬-

battels ˈbæt.ᵊlz (US) ˈbæt̬-

batten (B) ˈbæt.ᵊn **-s** -z **-ing** -ɪŋ **-ed** -d

Battenberg ˈbæt.ᵊn.bɜːg, -ᵊm- (US) -ᵊn.bɜːrg ˈ**Battenberg ˌcake**

batt|er ˈbæt|.əʳ (US) ˈbæt̬|.ɚ **-ers** -əz (US) -ɚz **-ering** -ᵊr.ɪŋ **-ered** -əd (US) -ɚd ˈ**battering ˌram**

Battersby ˈbæt.əz.bi (US) ˈbæt̬.ɚz-

Battersea ˈbæt.ə.si (US) ˈbæt̬.ɚ-

batter|y ˈbæt.ᵊr|.i (US) ˈbæt̬- **-ies** -iz ˈ**battery ˌacid**

batting (*n.*) ˈbæt.ɪŋ (US) ˈbæt̬.ɪŋ ˈ**batting ˌaverage** ; ˈ**batting ˌorder**

Battishill ˈbæt.ɪ.ʃɪl, -ʃᵊl (US) ˈbæt̬-

battl|e (B) ˈbæt.l̩ (US) ˈbæt̬- **-es** -z **-ing** -ɪŋ, ˈbæt.lɪŋ **-ed** -d **-er/s** -əʳ/z, ˈ-ləʳ/z (US) ˈ-l̩.ɚ/z, ˈ-lɚ/z ˈ**battle ˌcry** ; ˌ**Battle of ˈBritain** ; ˌ**battle ˈroyal** ; ˈ**battle ˌstations**

battle-ax|e, battle-ax ˈbæt.l̩.æks (US) ˈbæt̬- **-es** -ɪz

battledore, battledoor ˈbæt.l̩.dɔːʳ (US) ˈbæt̬.l̩.dɔːr **-s** -z

battledress ˈbæt.l̩.dres

battlefield ˈbæt.l̩.fiːld (US) ˈbæt̬- **-s** -z

battleground ˈbæt.l̩.graʊnd **-s** -z

battlement ˈbæt.l̩.mənt (US) ˈbæt̬- **-s** -s **-ed** -ɪd (US) -mən.t̬ɪd

battleship ˈbæt.l̩.ʃɪp (US) ˈbæt̬- **-s** -s

battue bætˈuː, -ˈjuː **-s** -z

batt|y ˈbæt|.i (US) ˈbæt̬- **-ier** -i.əʳ (US) -i.ɚ **-iest** -i.ɪst, -i.əst

Battye ˈbæt.i (US) ˈbæt̬-

Batumi bɑːˈtuː.mi

batwing ˈbæt.wɪŋ ˌ**batwing ˈsleeve**

bauble ˈbɔː.bl̩ (US) ˈbɑː-, ˈbɔː- **-s** -z

Baucis ˈbɔː.sɪs (US) ˈbɑː-, ˈbɔː

Baudelaire ˈbəʊ.də.leəʳ, ˌ--ˈ- (US) ˌboʊ.dəˈler, ˌboʊdˈler

Baudouin ˈbəʊ.dwæ̃n (US) boʊˈdwɑːn

Bauer baʊəʳ (US) baʊɚ

Baugh bɔː (US) bɑː, bɔː

Baughan bɔːn (US) bɑːn, bɔːn

Bauhaus ˈbaʊ.haʊs

baulk bɔːk, bɔːlk (US) bɑːk, bɔːk **-s** -s **-ing** -ɪŋ **-ed** -t

Baum *US name:* bɔːm (US) bɑːm, bɔːm *German name:* baʊm

bauxite ˈbɔːk.saɪt (US) ˈbɑːk-, ˈbɔːk-

Bavari|a bəˈveə.ri|.ə (US) -ˈver.i- **-an/s** -ən/z

bawbee bɔːˈbiː, ˈ-- (US) ˈbɑː.biː, ˈbɔː-, -ˈ- **-s** -z

bawd bɔːd (US) bɑːd, bɔːd **-s** -z **-ry** -ri

Bawden ˈbɔː.dᵊn (US) ˈbɑː-, ˈbɔː-

bawd|y ˈbɔː.d|i (US) ˈbɑː-, ˈbɔː- **-ier** -i.əʳ (US) -i.ɚ **-iest** -i.ɪst, -i.əst **-ily** -ɪ.li, -ᵊl.i **-iness** -ɪ.nəs, -ɪ.nɪs ˈ**bawdy ˌhouse**

bawl bɔːl (US) bɑːl, bɔːl **-s** -z **-ing** -ɪŋ **-ed** -d **-er/s** -əʳ/z (US) -ɚ/z

Bax bæks

Baxandall ˈbæk.sᵊn.dɔːl (US) -dɔːl, -dɑːl

Baxter ˈbæk.stəʳ (US) -stɚ

bay (B) beɪ **-s** -z **-ing** -ɪŋ **-ed** -d ˈ**bay ˌleaf** ; ˌ**Bay of ˈPigs** ; ˈ**bay ˌtree** ; ˌ**bay ˈwindow**

bayard (B) *horse:* beɪəd (US) beɪɚd **-s** -z

Bayard *surname:* ˈbeɪ.ɑːd (US) -ɑːrd

Bayard *airship:* ˈbeɪ.ɑːd, -ˈ-; beɪəd (US) beɪɚd; ˈbeɪ.ɑːrd **-s** -z

bayberr|y ˈbeɪ.bᵊr|.i (US) -ˌber- **-ies** -iz

Bayeux baɪˈjɜː, beɪ- (US) ˈbeɪ.juː, ˈbaɪ- *stress shift, British only: see compound:* ˌ**Bayeux ˈTapestry**

Bayley ˈbeɪ.li

Bayliss ˈbeɪ.lɪs

Bayly ˈbeɪ.li

Baynes beɪnz

Baynham 'beɪ.nəm
Baynton 'beɪn.tən (US) -tᵊn
bayone|t 'beɪ.ə.nə|t, -nɪ|t, -ne|t; ˌbeɪ.ə'ne|t (US) ˌbeɪ.ə'ne|t, '--- **-ts** -ts **-t(t)ing** -tɪŋ (US) -t̬ɪŋ **-t(t)ed** -tɪd (US) -t̬ɪd
Bayonne *in France:* baɪ'ɒn (US) beɪ'oʊn, -'ɑːn, -'ɔːn *in New Jersey, U.S.A.:* beɪ'əʊn (US) -'oʊn, -'joʊn
bayou 'baɪ.uː, -əʊ (US) *-juː, -joʊ* **-s** -z
Bayreuth baɪ'rɔɪt, '--
bay-rum ˌbeɪ'rʌm
Bayston Hill ˌbeɪ.stᵊn'hɪl
Bayswater 'beɪzˌwɔː.təʳ (US) -ˌwɑː.t̬ɚ, -ˌwɔː-
bazaar bə'zɑːʳ (US) -'zɑːr **-s** -z
Bazalgette 'bæz.ᵊl.dʒɪt, -dʒet
bazooka bə'zuː.kə **-s** -z
BBC ˌbiː.biː'siː
BC biː'siː
BCG ˌbiː.siː'dʒiː
bdellium 'del.i.əm, bə'del-
be- bɪ-, bə-
Note: Prefix. Words containing **be-** are always stressed on the second syllable, e.g. **friend** /frend/, **befriend** /bɪ'frend/.
be *strong form:* biː *weak forms:* bi, bɪ **being** 'biː.ɪŋ **been** biːn, bɪn (US) bɪn
Note: Weak form word. The strong form /biː/ is used contrastively (e.g. "the **be** all and **end** all") and in sentence-final position (e.g. "What'll it be?"). The weak form is /bɪ/ before consonants (e.g. "We'll be going" /ˌwiːl.bɪ'gəʊ.ɪŋ (US) -'goʊ-/); before vowels it is /bi/ (e.g. "It'll be opening soon" /ˌɪt.l̩.bi'əʊ.pᵊn.ɪŋˌsuːn (US) -'oʊ-/). See note at **been** for further weak form information.
Bea biː
beach (B) biːtʃ (US) **-es** -ɪz **-ing** -ɪŋ **-ed** -t 'beach ˌball ; 'beach ˌbum
beachchair 'biːtʃ.tʃeəʳ (US) -tʃer **-s** -z
beachcomber (B) 'biːtʃˌkəʊ.məʳ (US) -ˌkoʊ.mɚ **-s** -z
beachhead 'biːtʃ.hed **-s** -z
beach-la-mar, **Beach-la-Mar** ˌbiːtʃ.lə'mɑːʳ (US) -'mɑːr
beachwear 'biːtʃ.weəʳ (US) -wer
beachy (B) 'biː.tʃi ˌ**Beachy 'Head**
beacon 'biː.kᵊn **-s** -z
Beaconsfield *place in Buckinghamshire:* 'bek.ᵊnz.fiːld *title of Benjamin Disraeli:* 'biː.kᵊnz.fiːld
bead biːd **-s** -z **-ing/s** -ɪŋ/z **-ed** -ɪd **-er/s** -əʳ/z (US) -ɚ/z
beadle (B) 'biː.dl̩ **-s** -z
Beadon 'biː.dᵊn
beadwork 'biːd.wɜːk (US) -wɜːrk
bead|y 'biː.d|i **-ier** -i.əʳ (US) -i.ɚ **-iest** -i.ɪst, -i.əst **-iness** -ɪ.nɪs, -ɪ.nəs
beagle 'biː.gl̩ **-s** -z
beak biːk **-s** -s **-ed** -t
beaker 'biː.kəʳ (US) -kɚ **-s** -z
Beal(e) biːl
beam biːm **-s** -z **-ing** -ɪŋ **-ed** -d **'beam ˌengine**
beam-ends ˌbiːm'endz, '--
Beaminster 'bem.ɪn*t*.stəʳ *locally also:* 'bem.ɪ.stəʳ (US) -stɚ
Note: /'biː.mɪn*t*-/ is sometimes heard from people unfamiliar with the place.
Beamish 'biː.mɪʃ
beam|y 'biː.m|i **-ily** -ɪ.li, -ᵊl.i **-iness** -ɪ.nɪs, -ɪ.nəs
bean biːn **-s** -z ˌ**full of 'beans** ; ˌ**spill the 'beans**
beanbag 'biːn.bæg, 'biːm- (US) 'biːn- **-s** -z
beanfeast 'biːn.fiːst **-s** -s **-er/s** -əʳ/z (US) -ɚ/z
beanie 'biː.ni **-s** -z
beano (B) 'biː.nəʊ (US) -noʊ **-s** -z
beanpole 'biːn.pəʊl, 'biːm- (US) 'biːn.poʊl **-s** -z
beanshoot 'biːn.ʃuːt **-s** -s
beansprout 'biːn.spraʊt **-s** -s
beanstalk 'biːn.stɔːk (US) -stɔːk, -stɑːk **-s** -s
bear beəʳ (US) ber **-s** -z **-ing/s** -ɪŋ/z **bore** bɔːʳ (US) bɔːr **borne** bɔːn (US) bɔːrn **'bear ˌgarden**
bearab|le 'beə.rə.b|l̩ (US) 'ber.ə- **-ly** -li **-leness** -l̩.nəs, -l̩.nɪs
bear-baiting 'beəˌbeɪ.tɪŋ (US) 'berˌbeɪ.t̬ɪŋ
beard (B) bɪəd (US) bɪrd **-s** -z **-ed** -ɪd
Bearder 'bɪə.dəʳ (US) 'bɪr.dɚ
beardless 'bɪəd.ləs, -lɪs (US) 'bɪrd-
Beardsley 'bɪədz.li (US) 'bɪrdz-
Beare bɪəʳ (US) bɪr
bearer 'beə.rəʳ (US) 'ber.ɚ **-s** -z
bearhug 'beə.hʌg (US) 'ber- **-s** -z
bearing (*n.*) 'beə.rɪŋ (US) 'ber.ɪŋ **-s** -z
bearing rein 'beə.rɪŋ.reɪn (US) 'ber.ɪŋ- **-s** -z
bearish 'beə.rɪʃ (US) 'ber.ɪʃ **-ly** -li **-ness** -nəs, -nɪs
béarnaise (B) ˌbeɪə'neɪz, -'nez (US) ˌber'neɪz, ˌbeɪ.ɑːr'-, ˌbeɪɚ'-
Bearsden beəz'den (US) berz-
bearskin 'beə.skɪn (US) 'ber- **-s** -z
Bearsted 'bɜː.sted, 'beə.sted (US) 'bɜːr-, 'ber-
Beasant 'beɪ.zᵊnt
Beasley 'biːz.li
beast biːst **-s** -s ˌ**beast of 'burden**
beastings 'biː.stɪŋz
beastl|y 'biːs*t*.l|i **-ier** -i.əʳ (US) -i.ɚ **-iest** -i.ɪst, -i.əst **-iness** -ɪ.nəs, -i.nɪs
beat biːt **-s** -s **-ing/s** -ɪŋ/z (US) 'biː.t̬ɪŋ/z **-en** -ᵊn (US) 'biː.t̬ᵊn **-er/s** -əʳ/z (US) 'biː.t̬ɚ/z ˌ**beat about the 'bush** ; **'Beat Geneˌration**
beatific ˌbiː.ə'tɪf.ɪk **-al** -ᵊl **-ally** -ᵊl.i, -li
beatification biˌæt.ɪ.fɪ'keɪ.ʃᵊn, ˌ-ə- (US) -ˌæt̬.ə- **-s** -z
beatif|y bi'æt.ɪ.f|aɪ, '-ə- (US) -'æt̬.ə- **-ies** -aɪz **-ying** -aɪ.ɪŋ **-ied** -aɪd
beatitude (B) bi'æt.ɪ.tjuːd, '-ə-, -tʃuːd (US) -'æt̬.ə.tuːd, -tjuːd **-s** -z
Beatles 'biː.tl̩z (US) -t̬l̩z
beatnik 'biːt.nɪk **-s** -s
Beaton 'biː.tᵊn (US) -t̬ᵊn
Beatrice 'bɪə.trɪs (US) 'biː.ə-
Beatrix 'bɪə.trɪks (US) 'biː.ə-
Beattie 'biː.ti (US) -t̬i, 'beɪ-
Beattock 'biː.tək (US) -t̬ək
Beatty 'biː.ti (US) 'beɪ.t̬i, 'biː-
beat-up ˌbiːt'ʌp
beau (B) bəʊ (US) boʊ **-s** -z ˌ**Beau 'Brummell**
Beauchamp 'biː.tʃəm
Beauclerc(k) 'bəʊ.kleəʳ (US) 'boʊ.kler, -klɜːrk
Beaufort *in South Carolina:* 'bjuː.fət, -fɔːt (US) 'bjuː.fɚt *other senses:* 'bəʊ.fət, -fɔːt (US) 'boʊ.fɚt
beau(x) geste(s) ˌbəʊ'ʒest (US) ˌboʊ-
Beauharnais ˌbəʊ.ɑː'neɪ (US) ˌboʊ.ɑːr'-
Beaujolais 'bəʊ.ʒᵊl.eɪ, -ʒɒl.eɪ (US) ˌboʊ.ʒə'leɪ
Beaujolais nouveau ˌbəʊ.ʒə.leɪ.nuː'vəʊ, -ʒɒl.eɪ- (US) ˌboʊ.ʒə.leɪ.nuː'voʊ
Beaulieu *in Hampshire:* 'bjuː.li *US family name:* 'bəʊ.juː (US) 'boʊ-, 'boʊl- *in France:* bəʊ'ljɜː (US) boʊ-
Beaumarchais 'bəʊ.mɑːˌʃeɪ, ˌ--'- (US) ˌboʊ.mɑːr'ʃeɪ
Beaumaris bəʊ'mær.ɪs, bjuː- (US) boʊ'mer-, -'mær-
beau(x) monde(s) bəʊ'mɒnd (US) ˌboʊ'mɑːnd
Beaumont 'bəʊ.mənt, -mɒnt (US) 'boʊ-, -mɑːnt
Beaune bəʊn (US) boʊn
Beauregard 'bəʊ.rɪ.gɑːd (US) 'boʊ.rə.gɑːrd
beaut bjuːt **-s** -s
beauteous 'bjuː.ti.əs (US) -t̬i- **-ly** -li **-ness** -nəs, -nɪs
beautician bjuː'tɪʃ.ᵊn **-s** -z
beautification ˌbjuː.tɪ.fɪ'keɪ.ʃᵊn, -tə- (US) -t̬ə-
beautiful 'bjuː.tɪ.fᵊl, -tə-, -fʊl (US) -t̬ə- **-ly** -i
beautif|y 'bjuː.tɪ.f|aɪ, -tə- (US) -t̬ə- **-ies** -aɪz **-ying** -aɪ.ɪŋ **-ied** -aɪd **-ier/s** -aɪ.əʳ/z (US) -aɪ.ɚ/z
beaut|y 'bjuː.t|i (US) -t̬|i **-ies** -iz **'beauty ˌcontest** ; **'beauty ˌmark** ; **'beauty ˌparlo(u)r** ; **'beauty ˌsleep** ; **'beauty ˌspot**
Beauvoir 'bəʊv.wɑː (US) boʊv'wɑːr
beaux-arts bəʊ'zɑːʳ (US) boʊ'zɑːr

Beaux' Stratagem ˌbəʊzˈstræt.ə.dʒəm US ˌboʊzˈstræt̬-
Beavan, Beaven ˈbev.ᵊn
beaver (B) ˈbiː.vəʳ US -vɚ **-s** -z
Beaverbrook ˈbiː.və.brʊk US -vɚ-
beaver|y ˈbiː.vᵊr|.i **-ies** -iz
Beavis ˈbiː.vɪs
Beazley ˈbiːz.li
Bebb beb
Bebington ˈbeb.ɪŋ.tən
bebop ˈbiː.bɒp US -bɑːp **-per/s** -əʳ/z US -ɚ/z
becalm bɪˈkɑːm, bə- **-s** -z **-ing** -ɪŋ **-ed** -d
became (*from* **become**) bɪˈkeɪm, bə-
because bɪˈkɒz, bə-, -ˈkəz *colloquially also:* kɒz, kəz US bɪˈkɑːz, bə-, -ˈkʌz, -ˈkəz, kəz
Note: The form /bɪˈkəz/ or /bə-/ is unusual in having a stressed schwa vowel. This is found only in a few phrases, most commonly in "because of the/a …" The pronunciation /kəz/ (also /kɒz/ in British English) is often spelt ''cos'.
Beccles ˈbek.l̩z
bechamel, béchamel ˌbeɪ.ʃəˈmel, ˌbeʃ.əˈ- *stress shift:* **ˌbechamel ˈsauce**
Becher ˈbiː.tʃəʳ US -tʃɚ
Bechstein ˈbek.staɪn **-s** -z
Bechuana ˌbetʃ.uˈɑː.nə **-s** -z **-land** -lænd
beck (B) bek **-s** -s **ˌbeck and ˈcall**
Becke bek
Beckenbauer ˈbek.ᵊn.baʊəʳ US -baʊɚ
Beckenham ˈbek.ᵊn.əm
Becker ˈbek.əʳ US -ɚ
Becket(t) ˈbek.ɪt
Beckford ˈbek.fəd US -fɚd
Beckinsale ˈbek.ɪn.seɪl
Beckles ˈbek.l̩z
Beckley ˈbek.li
beckon ˈbek.ᵊn **-s** -z **-ing** -ɪŋ **-ed** -d
Beckton ˈbek.tən
Beckwith ˈbek.wɪθ
Becky ˈbek.i
becloud bɪˈklaʊd, bə- **-s** -z **-ing** -ɪŋ **-ed** -ɪd
becom|e bɪˈkʌm, bə- **-es** -z **-ing** -ɪŋ **became** bɪˈkeɪm, bə-
becoming bɪˈkʌm.ɪŋ, bəˈ- **-ly** -li **-ness** -nəs, -nɪs
Becontree ˈbek.ən.triː
becquerel (B) ˌbek.əˈrel; ˈbek.ə.rel, -rᵊl **-s** -z
bed bed **-s** -z **-ding** -ɪŋ **-ded** -ɪd **ˈbed ˌrest**; **ˌbed and ˈbreakfast**; **ˌget out of ˌbed on the ˌwrong ˈside**
BEd biːˈed
bedad bɪˈdæd, bə-
Bedale ˈbiː.dᵊl, -deɪl
Bedales ˈbiː.deɪlz
bedaub bɪˈdɔːb, bə- US -ˈdɑːb, -ˈdɔːb **-s** -z **-ing** -ɪŋ **-ed** -d
bedazzl|e bɪˈdæz.l̩, bə- **-es** -z **-ing** -ɪŋ **-ed** -d
bedbug ˈbed.bʌg **-s** -z
bedchamber ˈbedˌtʃeɪm.bəʳ US -bɚ **-s** -z
bedclothes ˈbed.kləʊðz, -kləʊz US -kloʊðz, -kloʊz
Beddau ˈbeð.aɪ
bedder ˈbed.əʳ US -ɚ **-s** -z
Beddgelert beðˈgel.ət, bed-, beɪð-, -ɜːt US -ɚt
bedding (*n.*) ˈbed.ɪŋ
Beddoes ˈbed.əʊz US -oʊz
beddy-bye ˈbed.i.baɪ **-s** -z
Bede biːd
bedeck bɪˈdek, bə- **-s** -s **-ing** -ɪŋ **-ed** -t
Bedel ˈbiː.dᵊl; bɪˈdel, bə-
bedel(l) bedˈel, bɪˈdel, bə- **-s** -z
Bedevere ˈbed.ɪ.vɪəʳ, ˈ-ə- US -ə.vɪr
bedevil bɪˈdev.ᵊl, bə- **-s** -z **-(l)ing** -ɪŋ **-(l)ed** -d
bedevilment bɪˈdev.ᵊl.mənt, bə-
bedew bɪˈdjuː, bə- US -ˈduː, -ˈdjuː **-s** -z **-ing** -ɪŋ **-ed** -d
bedfellow ˈbedˌfel.əʊ US -oʊ **-s** -z
Bedford ˈbed.fəd US -fɚd **-shire** -ʃəʳ, -ˌʃɪəʳ US -ʃɚ, -ˌʃɪr
bedim bɪˈdɪm, bə- **-s** -z **-ming** -ɪŋ **-med** -d
Bedivere ˈbed.ɪ.vɪəʳ, ˈ-ə- US -ə.vɪr
bedizen bɪˈdaɪ.zᵊn, bə-, -ˈdɪz.ᵊn **-s** -z **-ing** -ɪŋ **-ed** -d
bedjacket ˈbedˌdʒæk.ɪt **-s** -s
bedlam (B) ˈbed.ləm
Bedlamite ˈbed.lə.maɪt **-s** -s
bedlinen ˈbedˌlɪn.ɪn, -ən US -ən
bedmaker ˈbedˌmeɪ.kəʳ US -kɚ **-s** -z
Bedouin ˈbed.u.ɪn **-s** -z
bedpan ˈbed.pæn **-s** -z
bedpost ˈbed.pəʊst US -poʊst **-s** -s
bedraggl|e bɪˈdræg.l̩, bə- **-es** -z **-ing** -ɪŋ **-ed** -d
bedridden ˈbedˌrɪd.ᵊn
bedrock ˈbed.rɒk US -rɑːk **-s** -s
bedroll ˈbed.rəʊl US -roʊl **-s** -z
bedroom ˈbed.rʊm, -ruːm US -ruːm, -rʊm **-s** -z
Beds. (*abbrev. for* **Bedfordshire**) bedz; ˈbed.fəd.ʃəʳ, -ˌʃɪəʳ US bedz; ˈbed.fɚd.ʃɚ, -ˌʃɪr
bedside ˈbed.saɪd **ˌbedside ˈmanner**; **ˌbedside ˈtable**
bedsit ˈbed.sɪt **-s** -s
bedsitter bedˈsɪt.əʳ, ˈ-ˌ-- US bedˈsɪt.ɚ, ˈ-ˌ-- **-s** -z
bedsore ˈbed.sɔːʳ US -sɔːr **-s** -z
bedspread ˈbed.spred **-s** -z
bedstead ˈbed.sted **-s** -z
bedstraw ˈbed.strɔː US -strɑː, -strɔː **-s** -z
bedtime ˈbed.taɪm
Bedwas ˈbed.wæs
Bedwell ˈbed.wel, -wəl
Bedworth ˈbed.wəθ US -wɚθ
bee (B) biː **-s** -z **ˈbee ˌsting**; **have a ˈbee in one's ˌbonnet**; **the ˌbee's ˈknees**
Beeb biːb
Beeby ˈbiː.bi
beech (B) biːtʃ **-es** -ɪz **-en** -ᵊn
Beecham ˈbiː.tʃəm **ˌBeecham's ˈPowders®**
Beecher ˈbiː.tʃəʳ US -tʃɚ
Beeching ˈbiː.tʃɪŋ
beechnut ˈbiːtʃ.nʌt **-s** -s
beechwood ˈbiːtʃ.wʊd
bee eater ˈbiːˌiː.təʳ US -t̬ɚ **-s** -z
beef (*n*) biːf **-s** -s **beeves** biːvz
beef (*v*) biːf **-s** -s **-ing** -ɪŋ **-ed** -t
beefalo ˈbiː.fᵊl.əʊ US -fə.loʊ **-(e)s** -z
beefburger ˈbiːfˌbɜː.gəʳ US -ˌbɜːr.gɚ **-s** -z
beefcake ˈbiːf.keɪk **-s** -s
beefeater (B) ˈbiːfˌiː.təʳ US -t̬ɚ **-s** -z
beefsteak ˈbiːf.steɪk, -ˈ- **-s** -s
beef|y ˈbiː.f|i **-ier** -i.əʳ US -i.ɚ **-iest** -i.ɪst, -i.əst **-ily** -ɪ.li, -ᵊl.i **-iness** -ɪ.nəs, -ɪ.nɪs
beehive ˈbiː.haɪv **-s** -z
bee-keep|ing ˈbiːˌkiː.p|ɪŋ **-er/s** -əʳ/z US -ɚ/z
beeline ˈbiː.laɪn **-s** -z
Beelzebub biːˈel.zɪ.bʌb, -zə-
been (*from* **be**) biːn, bɪn US bɪn
Note: Weak form word, British English. The pronunciation /bɪn/ may be used optionally as a weak form corresponding to /biːn/ (e.g. "Jane's been invited" /ˈdʒeɪnz.bɪn.ɪnˌvaɪ.tɪd/). In American English, /biːn/ does not usually occur.
beep biːp **-s** -s **-ing** -ɪŋ **-ed** -t
beeper ˈbiː.pəʳ US -pɚ **-s** -z
beer (B) bɪəʳ US bɪr **-s** -z **ˈbeer ˌgarden**; **ˈbeer ˌmat**
Beerbohm ˈbɪə.bəʊm US ˈbɪr.boʊm
Beersheba bɪəˈʃiː.bə, ˈbɪə.ʃɪ- US bɪrˈʃiː-, ber-
beer|y ˈbɪə.r|i US ˈbɪr|.i **-ier** -i.əʳ US -i.ɚ **-iest** -i.ɪst, -i.əst **-ily** -ɪ.li, -ᵊl.i **-iness** -ɪ.nəs, -ɪ.nɪs
Beesl(e)y ˈbiːz.li
beestings ˈbiː.stɪŋz
Beeston ˈbiː.stᵊn
beeswax ˈbiːz.wæks
beeswing ˈbiːz.wɪŋ
beet biːt **-s** -s
Beetham ˈbiː.θəm
Beethoven *composer:* ˈbeɪt.həʊ.vᵊn, ˈbeɪ.təʊ- US ˈbeɪ.toʊ- *London street:* ˈbiːt.həʊ.vᵊn, ˈbiː.təʊ- US ˈbiː.toʊ-
beetl|e ˈbiː.tl̩ US -t̬l̩ **-es** -z **-ing** -ɪŋ, ˈbiːt.lɪŋ **-ed** -d

Beeton 'biː.tᵊn
beetroot 'biːt.ruːt **-s** -s
beeves (*plur. of* **beef**) biːvz
befall bɪ'fɔːl, bə- Ⓤⓢ -'fɔːl, -'fɑːl **-s** -z **-ing** -ɪŋ **-en** -ən
befell (*from* **befall**) bɪ'fel, bə-
befit bɪ'fɪt, bə- **-s** -s **-ting/ly** -ɪŋ/li Ⓤⓢ -'fɪt̬.ɪŋ/li **-ted** -ɪd Ⓤⓢ -'fɪt̬.ɪd
before bɪ'fɔːʳ, bə- Ⓤⓢ -'fɔːr
beforehand bɪ'fɔː.hænd, bə- Ⓤⓢ -'fɔːr-
before-mentioned bɪ'fɔːˌmen.*t*ʃᵊnd, -ˌ-'-- Ⓤⓢ bə'fɔːrˌmen-
beforetime bɪ'fɔː.taɪm, bə- Ⓤⓢ -'fɔːr-
befoul bɪ'faʊl, bə- **-s** -z **-ing** -ɪŋ **-ed** -d
befriend bɪ'frend, bə- **-s** -z **-ing** -ɪŋ **-ed** -ɪd
befuddl|e bɪ'fʌd.l̩, bə- **-es** -z **-ing** -ɪŋ, -'fʌd.lɪŋ **-ed** -d
befuddlement bɪ'fʌd.l̩.mᵊnt, bə-
beg beg **-s** -z **-ging** -ɪŋ **-ged** -d
begad bɪ'gæd, bə-
began (*from* **begin**) bɪ'gæn, bə-
begat (*from* **beget**) bɪ'gæt, bə-
beget bɪ'get, bə- **-s** -s **-ting** -ɪŋ Ⓤⓢ -'get̬.ɪŋ **begat** bɪ'gæt, bə- **begot** bɪ'gɒt, bə- Ⓤⓢ -'gɑːt **begotten** bɪ'gɒt.ᵊn, bə- Ⓤⓢ -'gɑː.tᵊn
Begg beg
beggar 'beg.əʳ Ⓤⓢ -ɚ **-s** -z
beggarl|y 'beg.ᵊl|.i Ⓤⓢ -ɚ.l|i **-iness** -ɪ.nəs, -ɪ.nɪs
beggar-my-neighbour ˌbeg.ə.mɪ'neɪ.bəʳ, -maɪ'- Ⓤⓢ -ɚ.maɪ'neɪ.bɚ
beggarweed 'beg.ə.wiːd Ⓤⓢ '-ɚ- **-s** -z
beggary 'beg.ᵊr.i
Beggs begz
begin bɪ'gɪn, bə- **-s** -z **-ning/s** -ɪŋ/z
Begin 'beɪ.gɪn
beginner bɪ'gɪn.əʳ, bə- Ⓤⓢ -ɚ **-s** -z
Begley 'beg.li
begone bɪ'gɒn, bə- Ⓤⓢ -'gɑːn
begonia bɪ'gəʊ.ni.ə, bə- Ⓤⓢ -'goʊ.njə **-s** -z
begorra bɪ'gɒr.ə, bə- Ⓤⓢ -'gɔːr.ə
begot (*from* **beget**) bɪ'gɒt, bə- Ⓤⓢ -'gɑːt **-ten** -ᵊn Ⓤⓢ -'gɑː.t̬ᵊn
begrim|e bɪ'graɪm, bə- **-es** -z **-ing** -ɪŋ **-ed** -d
begrudg|e bɪ'grʌdʒ, bə- **-es** -ɪz **-ing** -ɪŋ **-ed** -d
beguil|e bɪ'gaɪl, bə- **-es** -z **-ing/ly** -ɪŋ/li **-ed** -d
beguine bɪ'giːn
begum (B) 'beɪ.gəm **-s** -z
begun (*from* **begin**) bɪ'gʌn, bə-
behalf bɪ'hɑːf, bə- Ⓤⓢ -'hæf
Behan 'biː.ən
behav|e bɪ'heɪv, bə- **-es** -z **-ing** -ɪŋ **-ed** -d
behavio(u)r bɪ'heɪ.vjəʳ, bə- Ⓤⓢ -vjɚ **-s** -z
behavio(u)r|ism bɪ'heɪ.vjᵊr|.ɪ.zᵊm, bə- **-ist/s** -ɪst/s
behead bɪ'hed, bə- **-s** -z **-ing** -ɪŋ **-ed** -ɪd
beheld (*from* **behold**) bɪ'held, bə-
behemoth (B) bɪ'hiː.mɒθ, bə-, -məθ Ⓤⓢ -mɑːθ, -məθ; 'biː.ə.məθ
behest bɪ'hest, bə- **-s** -s
behind bɪ'haɪnd, bə-
behindhand bɪ'haɪnd.hænd, bə-
behind-the-scenes bɪˌhaɪn*d*.ðə'siːnz Ⓤⓢ bə- *stress shift:* ˌbehind-the-scenes 'tour
Behn ben
behold bɪ'həʊld, bə- Ⓤⓢ -'hoʊld **-s** -z **-ing** -ɪŋ **beheld** bɪ'held, bə- **beholder/s** bɪ'həʊl.dəʳ/z, bə- Ⓤⓢ -'hoʊl.dɚ/z
beholden bɪ'həʊl.dᵊn, bə- Ⓤⓢ -'hoʊl-
behoof bɪ'huːf, bə-
behoov|e bɪ'huːv, bə- **-es** -z **-ing** -ɪŋ **-ed** -d
behov|e bɪ'həʊv, bə- Ⓤⓢ -'hoʊv **-es** -z **-ing** -ɪŋ **-ed** -d
Behrens 'beə.rənz Ⓤⓢ 'ber.ənz
Behrman 'beə.mən Ⓤⓢ 'ber-
Beiderbecke 'baɪ.də.bek Ⓤⓢ -dɚ-
beige beɪʒ
Beighton 'beɪ.tᵊn, 'baɪ-
beignet 'beɪ.njeɪ, -'- Ⓤⓢ ˌbeɪ'njeɪ **-s** -z
Beijing beɪ'*d*ʒɪŋ
being 'biː.ɪŋ **-s** -z
Beira 'baɪ.rə Ⓤⓢ 'beɪ-
Beirut beɪ'ruːt
Beit baɪt
Beith *surname:* biːθ *place in Scotland:* biːð
Bejam® 'biː.dʒæm
bejan 'biː.dʒᵊn **-s** -z
bejesus, bejezus bɪ'dʒiː.zəz, bə-, -zəs
bejewel bɪ'dʒuː.əl **-s** -z **-(l)ing** -ɪŋ **-(l)ed** -d
bel bel **-s** -z
belabo(u)r bɪ'leɪ.bəʳ, bə- Ⓤⓢ -bɚ **-s** -z **-ing** -ɪŋ **-ed** -d
Belarius bɪ'leə.ri.əs, bə-, -'lɑː- Ⓤⓢ -'ler.i-
Belasco bɪ'læs.kəʊ, bə- Ⓤⓢ -koʊ
belated bɪ'leɪ.tɪd, bə- Ⓤⓢ -t̬ɪd **-ly** -li **-ness** -nəs, -nɪs
belay bɪ'leɪ, bə- **-s** -z **-ing** -ɪŋ **-ed** -d
bel canto ˌbel'kæn.təʊ Ⓤⓢ -toʊ
belch (B) beltʃ **-es** -ɪz **-ing** -ɪŋ **-ed** -t **-er/s** -əʳ/z Ⓤⓢ -ɚ/z
Belcher 'bel.*t*ʃəʳ Ⓤⓢ -*t*ʃɚ
beldam(e) 'bel.dəm **-s** -z
beleagu|er bɪ'liː.g|əʳ, bə- Ⓤⓢ -g|ɚ **-ers** -əz Ⓤⓢ -ɚz **-ering** -ᵊr.ɪŋ **-ered** -əd Ⓤⓢ -ɚd **-erer/s** -əʳ/z Ⓤⓢ -ɚ/z
Belém bə'lem, bel'em
belemnite 'bel.əm.naɪt **-s** -s
Belfast bel'fɑːst, '-- Ⓤⓢ 'bel.fæst, ˌ-'-
belfr|y 'bel.fr|i **-ies** -iz
Belgian 'bel.dʒən **-s** -z
Belgic 'bel.dʒɪk
Belgium 'bel.dʒəm
Belgrade bel'greɪd Ⓤⓢ '-- *stress shift, British only:* ˌBelgrade 'streets
Belgrano bel'grɑː.nəʊ Ⓤⓢ -noʊ
Belgrave bel'greɪv Ⓤⓢ '-- *stress shift, British only:* ˌBelgrave 'Square
Belgravia bel'greɪ.vi.ə
Belial 'biː.li.əl
bel|ie bɪ'l|aɪ, bə- **-ies** -aɪz **-ying** -aɪ.ɪŋ **-ied** -aɪd
belief bɪ'liːf, bə- **-s** -s
believab|le bɪ'liː.və.b|l̩, bə- **-ly** -li
believ|e bɪ'liːv, bə- **-es** -z **-ing/ly** -ɪŋ/li **-ed** -d
believer bɪ'liː.vəʳ, bə- Ⓤⓢ -vɚ **-s** -z
belike bɪ'laɪk, bə-
Belinda bə'lɪn.də, bɪ-
Belisha bə'liː.ʃə, bɪ- **Beˌlisha 'beacon**
belittl|e bɪ'lɪt.l̩, bə- Ⓤⓢ -'lɪt̬- **-es** -z **-ing** -ɪŋ, -'lɪt.lɪŋ **-ed** -d
Belize bə'liːz, bel'iːz
bell (B) bel **-s** -z **-ing** -ɪŋ **-ed** -d **'bell ˌjar**; **'bell ˌpepper**; **'bell ˌtent**; **'bell ˌtower**
Bella 'bel.ə
belladonna ˌbel.ə'dɒn.ə Ⓤⓢ -'dɑː.nə
Bellamy 'bel.ə.mi
Bellatrix 'bel.ə.trɪks, bə'leɪ- Ⓤⓢ 'bel.ə-
bell-bottom 'belˌbɒt.əm Ⓤⓢ -ˌbɑː.t̬əm **-s** -z **-ed** -d
bellboy 'bel.bɔɪ **-s** -z
belle (B) bel **-s** -z **ˌSouthern 'belle**; **ˌbelle of the 'ball**
belle époque ˌbel.eɪ'pɒk Ⓤⓢ -'pɑːk
Belle Isle ˌbel'aɪl
Bellerophon bə'ler.ə.fən, bɪ- Ⓤⓢ -fən, -fɑːn
belles lettres ˌbel'let.rə
Bellevue bel'vjuː, '-- Ⓤⓢ 'bel.vjuː
Bellew 'bel.juː
bellhop 'bel.hɒp Ⓤⓢ -hɑːp **-s** -s
bellicose 'bel.ɪ.kəʊs, '-ə-, -kəʊz Ⓤⓢ -koʊs **-ly** -li
bellicosity ˌbel.ɪ'kɒs.ə.ti, -ɪ.ti Ⓤⓢ -ə'kɑː.sə.t̬i
belligeren|ce bə'lɪdʒ.ᵊr.ən*t*|s, bɪ'- **-cy** -si
belligerent bə'lɪdʒ.ᵊr.ənt, bɪ- **-s** -s **-ly** -li
Bellingham *in Northumberland:* 'bel.ɪn.*d*ʒəm *surname:* 'bel.ɪn.*d*ʒəm, -ɪŋ.əm, -hæm *in London:* 'bel.ɪŋ.əm *in the US:* 'bel.ɪŋ.hæm
Bellini bel'iː.ni, bə'liː-
bell|man 'bel|.mən, -mæn **-men** -mən, -men

Belloc 'bel.ɒk US -ɑːk
Bellot 'bel.əʊ US bel'oʊ
bellow (B) 'bel.əʊ US -oʊ **-s** -z **-ing** -ɪŋ **-ed** -d
bellringer 'bel,rɪŋ.əʳ US -ɚ **-s** -z
Bellshill belz'hɪl
bellwether 'bel,weð.əʳ US -ɚ **-s** -z
bell|y 'bel|.i **-ies** -iz **-ying** -i.ɪŋ **-ied** -id **'belly ,button** ; **'belly ,dance** ; **'belly ,flop** ; **'belly ,laugh**
bellyach|e 'bel.i.eɪk **-es** -s **-ing** -ɪŋ **-ed** -t
bellyful 'bel.ɪ.fʊl **-s** -z
belly-up ,bel.i'ʌp
Belmont 'bel.mɒnt, -mənt US -mɑːnt
Belmopan ,bel.məʊ'pæn US -moʊ'-
Belo Horizonte ,beɪ.ləʊ.hɒr.ɪ'zɒn.ti US -loʊ.hɔːr.ə'zɑːn-, ,bel.oʊ-
belong bɪ'lɒŋ, bə- US -'lɑːŋ, -'lɔːŋ **-s** -z **-ing** -ɪŋ **-ed** -d
Belorussi|a ,bel.əʊ'rʌʃ.ə, ,bjel-, -'ruː.si- US -oʊ'-, -ə'- **-an/s** -ən/z
beloved *used predicatively:* bɪ'lʌvd, bə- *used attributively or as a noun:* bɪ'lʌv.ɪd, bə-, -'lʌvd
below bɪ'ləʊ, bə- US -'loʊ
Bel Paese ,bel.pɑː'eɪ.zeɪ, -zi US -zi
Belper 'bel.pəʳ US -pɚ
Belsen 'bel.sᵊn
Belsham 'bel.ʃəm
Belshaw 'bel.ʃɔː US -ʃɑː, -ʃɔː
Belshazzar bel'ʃæz.əʳ US -ɚ
Belsize 'bel.saɪz
Belstead 'bel.stɪd, -sted
belt (B) belt **-s** -s **-ing/s** -ɪŋ/z US 'bel.t̬ɪŋ **-ed** -ɪd US 'bel.t̬ɪd **be,low the 'belt**
Beltingham 'bel.tɪn.dʒəm
Belton 'bel.tən
beltway 'belt.weɪ **-s** -z
Beluchistan bə'luː.tʃɪ.stɑːn, bɪ-, -stæn, bə,luː.tʃɪ'stɑːn, bə-, -kɪ'-, -'stæn
beluga bə'luː.gə, bɪ'-, bel'uː- **-s** -z
belvedere (B) 'bel.və.dɪəʳ, -vɪ-, ,--'- US 'bel.və.dɪr, ,--'- **-s** -z
Belvoir 'biː.vəʳ US -vɚ
bema 'biː.mə **-s** -z **-ta** -tə US -t̬ə
Bembridge 'bem.brɪdʒ
bemoan bɪ'məʊn, bə- US -'moʊn **-s** -z **-ing** -ɪŋ **-ed** -d
bemus|e bɪ'mjuːz, bə- **-es** -ɪz **-ing** -ɪŋ **-ed** -d
Ben ben
Benares bɪ'nɑː.rɪz, bə-, ben'ɑː- US bə'nɑːr.iːz
Benbecula ben'bek.jʊ.lə, bem-, -jə- US ben-
Benbow 'ben.bəʊ, 'bem- US 'ben.boʊ
bench ben*t*ʃ **-es** -ɪz
bencher 'ben.*t*ʃəʳ US -*t*ʃɚ **-s** -z
Benchley 'ben*t*ʃ.li
benchmark 'ben*t*ʃ.mɑːk US -mɑːrk **-s** -s **-ing** -ɪŋ
bend bend **-s** -z **-ing** -ɪŋ **-ed** -ɪd **bent** bent **bendable** 'ben.də.bl̩ **,round the 'bend**
Bendall 'ben.dᵊl, -dɔːl US -dᵊl, -dɔːl, -dɑːl
bender (B) 'ben.dəʳ US -dɚ **-s** -z
Bendix® 'ben.dɪks
bend|y 'ben.d|i **-ier** -i.əʳ US -i.ɚ **-iest** -i.ɪst, -i.əst **-iness** -ɪ.nəs, -ɪ.nɪs
beneath bɪ'niːθ, bə-
Benedicite ,ben.ɪ'daɪ.sɪ.ti, -'diː.tʃɪ-, -tʃə-, -teɪ US -ə'dɪs.ə.t̬i, ,beɪ.neɪ'diː.tʃiː.teɪ **-s** -z
Benedick 'ben.ɪ.dɪk, '-ə- **-s** -s
Benedict 'ben.ɪ.dɪkt, '-ə-
benedictine *liqueur:* ,ben.ɪ'dɪk.tiːn, -ə'- **-s** -z
Benedictine *monk:* ,ben.ɪ'dɪk.tɪn, -ə'-, -taɪn US -tɪn, -tiːn **-s** -z
Note: Members of the Order pronounce /-tɪn/.
benediction ,ben.ɪ'dɪk.ʃᵊn, -ə'- **-s** -z
Benedictus ,ben.ɪ'dɪk.təs, -ə'-, -tʊs **-es** -ɪz
benefaction ,ben.ɪ'fæk.ʃᵊn, -ə'- US ,ben.ə'fæk-, 'ben.ə.fæk- **-s** -z
benefactive 'ben.ɪ.fæk.tɪv, -ə-, ,ben.ɪ'fæk-, -ə'- US 'ben.ə.fæk-, ,ben.ə'fæk-
benefactor 'ben.ɪ.fæk.təʳ, '-ə- US -tɚ **-s** -z
benefactress 'ben.ɪ.fæk.trəs, '-ɪ-, -tres, ,ben.ɪ'fæk-, -ə'- US 'ben.ə.fæk- **-es** -ɪz
benefic bɪ'nef.ɪk
benefic|e 'ben.ɪ.fɪs, '-ə- **-es** -ɪz **-ed** -t
beneficen|ce bɪ'nef.ɪ.sᵊn|*t*s, bə- **-t/ly** -t/li
beneficial ,ben.ɪ'fɪʃ.ᵊl, -ə'- **-ly** -li **-ness** -nəs, -nɪs
beneficiar|y ,ben.ɪ'fɪʃ.ᵊr|.i, -ə'- **-ies** -iz
bene|fit 'ben.ɪ|.fɪt, '-ə- **-fits** -fɪts **-fit(t)ing** -fɪ.tɪŋ US -fɪ.t̬ɪŋ **-fit(t)ed** -fɪ.tɪd US -fɪ.t̬ɪd
Benelux 'ben.ɪ.lʌks
Benenden 'ben.ən.dən
Bene't 'ben.ɪt
Benet 'ben.ɪt
Benét *US surname:* ben'eɪ US bə'neɪ, ben'eɪ
Benetton® 'ben.ɪ.tᵊn, '-ə-, -tɒn US -ə.t̬ən, -tɑːn
benevolence bɪ'nev.ᵊl.ən*t*s, bə-
benevolent bɪ'nev.ᵊl.ənt, bɪ- **-ly** -li
Benfleet 'ben.fliːt
BEng ,biː'end*ʒ*
Bengal ,beŋ'gɔːl, ,ben- US -'gɔːl; 'beŋ.gᵊl, 'ben- *stress shift, British only:* ,Bengal 'tiger
Bengalese ,beŋ.gᵊl'iːz, ,ben-, -gɔː'- US -gə'liːz, -'liːs
Bengali beŋ'gɔː.li, ben- **-s** -z
Bengasi beŋ'gɑː.zi, ben-
Benge bend*ʒ*
Benghazi beŋ'gɑː.zi, ben-
Ben-Gurion ben'gʊə.ri.ən, beŋ-, -'gʊr.i- US -'gʊr.i-, ,ben.gʊr'jɑːn
Benham 'ben.əm
Ben-Hur ben'hɜːʳ US -'hɜːr
Benidorm 'ben.ɪ.dɔːm, '-ə- US -dɔːrm
benighted bɪ'naɪ.tɪd, bə- US -t̬ɪd
benign bɪ'naɪn, bə- **-est** -ɪst, -əst **-ly** -li
benignancy bɪ'nɪg.nən*t*.si, bə-
benignant bɪ'nɪg.nənt, bə- **-ly** -li
benignity bɪ'nɪg.nə.ti, bə-, -nɪ- US -nə.t̬i
Benin ben'iːn, bɪ'niːn, bə-
benison 'ben.ɪ.sᵊn, '-ə-, -zᵊn **-s** -z
Benis(s)on 'ben.ɪ.sᵊn, '-ə-
Benito ben'iː.təʊ, bə'niː- US bə'niː.t̬oʊ
Benjamin 'ben.dʒə.mɪn, -ən
Benjamite 'ben.dʒə.maɪt **-s** -s
Benn ben
Bennet(t) 'ben.ɪt
Bennette ben'et, bə'net
Ben Nevis ,ben'nev.ɪs
Bennington 'ben.ɪŋ.tən
Benny 'ben.i
Bensham 'ben*t*.ʃəm
Bensley 'benz.li
Benson 'ben*t*.sᵊn
Benstead 'ben*t*.stɪd, -sted
bent (B) (*from* **bend**) bent **-s** -s
Bentham 'ben.təm, 'ben*t*.θəm US 'ben*t*.θəm **-ism** -ɪ.zᵊm **-ite/s** -aɪt/s
benthic 'ben*t*.θɪk
Bentinck 'ben.tɪŋk
Bentine ben'tiːn, '--
Bentley 'bent.li **-s** -z
Benton 'ben.tən
bentwood 'bent.wʊd
benumb bɪ'nʌm, bə- **-s** -z **-ing** -ɪŋ **-ed** -d
Benvolio ben'vəʊ.li.əʊ US -'voʊ.li.oʊ
Benz benz, bents
Benzedrine® 'ben.zɪ.driːn, -zə-, -drɪn
benzene, benzine 'ben.ziːn, -'-
benzoate 'ben.zəʊ.eɪt US -zoʊ-
benzoic ben'zəʊ.ɪk US -'zoʊ-
benzoin 'ben.zəʊ.ɪn, -'-- US 'ben.zoʊ-, ben'zoʊ-
benzol 'ben.zɒl US -zɑːl
benzoline 'ben.zə*ʊ*.liːn US -zə-
benzyl 'ben.zɪl US -ziː.əl, -zᵊl
Beowulf 'beɪ.ə*ʊ*.wʊlf, 'biː- US 'beɪə.wʊlf
beque|ath bɪ'kwiː|ð, bə-, -'kwiː|θ **-ths** -ðz, -θs **-thing** -ðɪŋ **-thed** -ðd, -θt
bequest bɪ'kwest, bə- **-s** -s
be|rate bɪ|'reɪt, bə-, bɪ- **-rates** -'reɪts **-rating** -'reɪ.tɪŋ US -'reɪ.t̬ɪŋ **-rated** -'reɪ.tɪd US -'reɪ.t̬ɪd

Berber ˈbɜː.bəʳ (US) ˈbɝː.bɚ **-s** -z
berceuse beəˈsɜːz (US) berˈsʊz, -ˈsɜːz
Bere bɪəʳ (US) bɪr
Berea bəˈriː.ə, bɪ- (US) bə-
bereav|e bɪˈriːv, bə- (US) bɪ- **-es** -z **-ing** -ɪŋ **-ed** -d
bereavement bɪˈriːv.mənt, bə- **-s** -s
bereft bɪˈreft, bə-
Berengaria ˌber.ᵊŋˈgeə.ri.ə, -ɪŋˈ-, -eŋˈ- (US) -ˈger.i-
Berenice *in ancient Egypt, etc.:* ˌber.ɪˈnaɪ.si, -ki, -ˈniː.tʃeɪ *opera by Handel:* ˌber.ɪˈniː.tʃi *modern name:* ˌber.əˈniːs, -ɪˈ-
Berenson ˈber.ᵊn*t*.sən
Beresford ˈber.ɪs.fəd, -ɪz- (US) -fɚd
beret ˈber.eɪ, -i (US) bəˈreɪ **-s** -z
berg (B) bɜːg, beəg (US) bɝːg **-s** -z
bergamot ˈbɜː.gə.mɒt, -mət (US) ˈbɝː.gə.mɑːt **-s** -s
Bergen ˈbɜː.gən, ˈbeə- (US) ˈbɝː-
Berger *English surname:* ˈbɜː.dʒəʳ (US) ˈbɝː.dʒɚ *US surname:* ˈbɜː.gəʳ (US) ˈbɝː.gɚ
Bergerac ˈbɜː.ʒə.ræk (US) ˌbɝː.ʒəˈræk, -ˈrɑːk
Bergman ˈbɜːg.mən (US) ˈbɝːg-
Bergson ˈbɜːg.sən (US) ˈberg-, ˈbɝːg-
Bergsonian bɜːgˈsəʊ.ni.ən (US) bergˈsoʊ-, bɝːg-
beribboned bɪˈrɪb.ᵊnd, bə-
beriberi ˌber.ɪˈber.i
Bering ˈbeə.rɪŋ, ˈber- (US) ˈber.ɪŋ ˌ**Bering** ˈ**Strait**
Berisford ˈber.ɪs.fəd (US) -fɚd
berk bɜːk (US) bɝːk **-s** -z
Berkeleian bɑːkˈliː.ən (US) ˈbɝː.kli.ən
Berkeley *in England:* ˈbɑː.kli (US) ˈbɑːr-, ˈbɝː- *in US:* ˈbɜː.kli (US) ˈbɝː-
berkelium bɜːˈkiː.li.əm (US) ˈbɝː.kli.əm, bɝːˈkliː.əm
Berkhamsted, Berkhampstead ˈbɜː.kəm*p*.stɪd, -sted (US) ˈbɝː-
Note: The usual British pronunciation is /ˈbɜː-/, but the form /ˈbɑː-/ is used by some residents.
Berkley ˈbɜː.kli (US) ˈbɝː-
Berks. (*abbrev. for* **Berkshire**) bɑːks, ˈbɑːk.ʃəʳ, -ˌʃɪəʳ (US) bɝːrks; ˈbɝːk.ʃɚ, -ˌʃɪr
Berkshire ˈbɑːk.ʃəʳ, -ˌʃɪəʳ (US) ˈbɝːk.ʃɚ, -ˌʃɪr
Berlin *in Germany:* bɜːˈlɪn (US) bɝː- *stress shift, British only, see compound:* ˌ**Berlin** ˈ**Wall**
Berlin *surname:* ˈbɜː.lɪn, -ˈ- (US) ˈbɝː-, -ˈ- *town in US:* ˈbɜː.lɪn (US) ˈbɝː-
Berliner bɜːˈlɪn.əʳ (US) bɚˈlɪn.ɚ **-s** -z
Berlioz ˈbeə.li.əʊz, ˈbɜː- (US) ˈber.li.oʊz
Berlitz bɜːˈlɪts, ˈ-- (US) ˈbɝː.lɪts, ˌ-ˈ-
Bermondsey ˈbɜː.mən*d*.zi (US) ˈbɝː-
Bermuda bəˈmjuː.də (US) bɚ- **-s** -z Berˌ**muda** ˈ**shorts**; Berˌ**muda** ˈ**triangle**
Bern bɜːn, beən (US) bɝːn
Bernadette ˌbɜː.nəˈdet (US) ˌbɝː-
Bernard *first name:* ˈbɜː.nəd (US) ˈbɝː.nɚd *surname:* bɜːˈnɑːd, bəˈ-; ˈbɜː.nəd (US) bɚˈnɑːrd; ˈbɝː.nɚd
Berne bɜːn, beən (US) bɝːn
Berners ˈbɜː.nəz (US) ˈbɝː.nɚz
Bernese bɜːˈniːz (US) bɝː-, -ˈniːs *stress shift:* ˌBernese ˈOberland
Bernhardt ˈbɜːn.hɑːt (US) ˈbɝːn.hɑːrt
Bernice *biblical name:* bɜːˈnaɪ.si (US) bɚ- *modern name:* ˈbɜː.nɪs, bɜːˈniːs (US) ˈbɝː-; bɚˈniːs
Bernini bɜːˈniː.ni, bə- (US) bɚ-, ber-
Bernoulli bɜːˈnuː.ji, bəˈ-, -li (US) bɚˈnuː.li
Bernstein ˈbɜːn.staɪn, -stiːn (US) ˈbɝːn-
Berol® ˈbiː.rɒl, -rəʊl (US) -rɑːl, -roʊl
Berowne bəˈrəʊn (US) -ˈroʊn
Berra ˈber.ə
Berridge ˈber.ɪdʒ
berr|y (B) ˈber|.i **-ies** -iz
Berryman ˈber.ɪ.mæn, -mən
berserk bəˈzɜːk, -ˈsɜːk (US) bɚˈsɝːk, -ˈzɝːk **-s** -s
Bert bɜːt (US) bɝːt
berth (*n.*) bɜːθ (US) bɝːθ **-s** -s, bɜːðz (US) bɝːðz
berth (*v.*) bɜːθ (US) bɝːθ **-s** -s **-ing** -ɪŋ **-ed** -t
Bertha ˈbɜː.θə (US) ˈbɝː-
Bertie *first name:* ˈbɜː.ti (US) ˈbɝː.t̬i *surname:* ˈbɑː.ti, ˈbɜː- (US) ˈbɑːr.t̬i, ˈbɝː-
Bertolucci ˌbɜː.təʊˈluː.tʃi, -təˈ-, -ˈlʊtʃ.i (US) ˌbɝː.t̬əˈluː.tʃi, ˌber-
Bertram ˈbɜː.trəm (US) ˈbɝː-
Bertrand ˈbɜː.trənd (US) ˈbɝː-
Berwick ˈber.ɪk **-shire** -ʃəʳ, -ˌʃɪəʳ (US) -ʃɚ, -ˌʃɪr
Berwick-on-Tweed ˌber.ɪk.ɒnˈtwiːd (US) -ɑːnˈ-
beryl (B) ˈber.ᵊl, -ɪl (US) -ᵊl **-s** -z
beryllium bəˈrɪl.i.əm, berˈɪl- (US) bəˈrɪl-
Besançon bəˈzɑ̃ːn.sɔ̃ːŋ (US) -ˈzɑ̃ːn.sõʊn
Besant ˈbes.ᵊnt, ˈbez-; bɪˈzænt, bə-
beseech bɪˈsiːtʃ, bə- **-es** -ɪz **-ing/ly** -ɪŋ/li **-ed** -t **besought** bɪˈsɔːt, bə- (US) -ˈsɑːt, -ˈsɔːt
beseem bɪˈsiːm, bə- **-s** -z **-ing** -ɪŋ **-ed** -d
beset bɪˈset, bə- **-s** -s **-ting** -ɪŋ (US) -ˈset̬.ɪŋ
beshrew bɪˈʃruː, bə-
beside bɪˈsaɪd, bə- **-s** -z
besieg|e bɪˈsiːdʒ, bə- **-es** -ɪz **-ing** -ɪŋ **-ed** -d **-er/s** -əʳ/z (US) -ɚ/z
Besley ˈbez.li
besmear bɪˈsmɪəʳ, bə- (US) -ˈsmɪr **-s** -z **-ing** -ɪŋ **-ed** -d
besmirch bɪˈsmɜːtʃ, bə- (US) -ˈsmɝːtʃ **-es** -ɪz **-ing** -ɪŋ **-ed** -t
besom ˈbiː.zᵊm **-s** -z
besotted bɪˈsɒt.ɪd, bə- (US) -ˈsɑː.t̬ɪd **-ly** -li **-ness** -nəs, -nɪs
besought (*from* **beseech**) bɪˈsɔːt, bə- (US) -ˈsɑːt, -ˈsɔːt
bespangl|e bɪˈspæŋ.gl̩, bəˈspæŋ- **-es** -z **-ing** -ɪŋ, ˈ-glɪŋ **-ed** -d
bespatt|er bɪˈspæt|.əʳ, bə- (US) -ˈspæt̬|.ɚ **-ers** -əz (US) -ɚz **-ering** -ᵊr.ɪŋ **-ered** -əd (US) -ɚd
bespeak bɪˈspiːk, bə- **-s** -s **-ing** -ɪŋ **bespoke** bɪˈspəʊk, bə- (US) -ˈspoʊk **bespoken** bɪˈspəʊ.kᵊn, bə- (US) -ˈspoʊ-
bespectacled bɪˈspek.tə.kl̩d, -tɪ.kl̩d
besprinkl|e bɪˈsprɪŋ.kl̩, bə- **-es** -z **-ing** -ɪŋ, ˈ-klɪŋ **-ed** -d
Bess bes
Bessacarr ˈbes.ə.kəʳ (US) -kɚ
Bessarabia ˌbes.əˈreɪ.bi.ə
Bessborough ˈbez.bᵊr.ə (US) -oʊ
Bessemer ˈbes.ɪ.məʳ, ˈ-ə- (US) -mɚ
Besses o' th' Barn ˌbes.ɪz.əðˈbɑːn (US) -ˈbɑːrn
Bessie ˈbes.i
best (B) best **-s** -s **-ing** -ɪŋ **-ed** -ɪd ˌ**best** ˈ**man**; ˌ**make the** ˈ**best of** ˌ**something**; **the** ˌ**best of** ˈ**both** ˌ**worlds** (US) **the** ˌ**best of** ˌ**both** ˈ**worlds**
bestial ˈbes.ti.əl, ˈbiː.sti- (US) ˈbes.tʃᵊl, ˈbiːs-, -ti.əl **-ly** -i **-ism** -ɪ.zᵊm
bestialit|y ˌbes.tiˈæl.ə.t|i, ˌbiː.stiˈ-, -ɪ.t|i (US) ˌbes.tʃiˈæl.ə.t̬|i, ˌbiːs- **-ies** -iz
bestiar|y ˈbes.ti.ᵊr|.i, ˈbiː.sti- (US) -tʃi.er|.i **-ies** -iz
bestir bɪˈstɜːʳ, bə- (US) -ˈstɝː **-s** -z **-ring** -ɪŋ **-red** -d
bestow bɪˈstəʊ, bə- (US) -ˈstoʊ **-s** -z **-ing** -ɪŋ **-ed** -d
bestowal bɪˈstəʊ.əl, bə- (US) -ˈstoʊ- **-s** -z
bestrew bɪˈstruː, bə- **-s** -z **-ing** -ɪŋ **-ed** -d **bestrewn** bɪˈstruːn, bə-
bestrid|e bɪˈstraɪd, bə- **-es** -z **-ing** -ɪŋ **bestrode** bɪˈstrəʊd, bə- (US) -ˈstroʊd **bestridden** bɪˈstrɪ.dᵊn, bə-
bestseller ˌbestˈsel.əʳ (US) -ɚ **-s** -z *stress shift:* ˌbestseller ˈlistings
best-selling ˌbestˈsel.ɪŋ *stress shift:* ˌbest-selling ˈbook
Beswick ˈbez.ɪk
bet (B) bet **-s** -s **-ting** -ɪŋ (US) ˈbet̬.ɪŋ **-ted** -ɪd (US) ˈbet̬.ɪd ˌ**hedge one's** ˈ**bets**
beta ˈbiː.tə (US) ˈbeɪ.t̬ə **-s** -z
beta-blocker ˈbiː.təˌblɒk.əʳ (US) ˈbeɪ.t̬əˌblɑː.kɚ **-s** -z

betak|e bɪˈteɪk, bə- **-es** -s **-ing** -ɪŋ **betook** bɪˈtʊk, bə- **betaken** bɪˈteɪ.kᵊn, bə-

betel ˈbiː.tᵊl US -t̬ᵊl **-nut/s** -nʌt/s

Betelgeuse, Betelgeux ˈbiː.tᵊl.*d*ʒɜːz, ˈbet.ᵊl-, -*d*ʒuːz US ˈbiː.t̬ᵊl.dʒuːz, ˈbet̬.ᵊl-, -dʒuːs, -dʒɜːz

bête noire ˌbetˈnwɑːʳ US -ˈnwɑːr, ˌbeɪt- **bêtes noires** ˌbetˈnwɑːʳ, -ˈnwɑːz US -nwɑːr, beɪt-, -nwɑːrz

Beth beθ

Bethany ˈbeθ.ᵊn.i

Bethel ˈbeθ.ᵊl

Bethell ˈbeθ.ᵊl, bəˈθel

Bethesda beθˈez.də, bɪˈθez-, bə- US bəˈθez-, bɪ-

bethink bɪˈθɪŋk, bə- **-s** -s **-ing** -ɪŋ **bethought** bɪˈθɔːt, bə- US -ˈθɑːt, -ˈθɔːt

Bethlehem ˈbeθ.lɪ.hem, -lə- US -lə.hem, -həm

Bethnal ˈbeθ.nᵊl

bethought (*from* **bethink**) bɪˈθɔːt, bə- US -ˈθɑːt, -ˈθɔːt

Bethsaida beθˈseɪ.də, -ˈsaɪ-

Bethune *surname:* ˈbiː.tᵊn US bəˈθuːn *in names of streets, etc.:* beθˈjuːn, bɪˈθjuːn, bə- US bəˈθuːn, -ˈθjuːn

betide bɪˈtaɪd, bə-

betimes bɪˈtaɪmz, bə-

Betjeman ˈbetʃ.ə.mən

betoken bɪˈtəʊ.kᵊn, bə- US -ˈtoʊ- **-s** -z **-ing** -ɪŋ **-ed** -ᵊnd

betony ˈbet.ə.ni

betook (*from* **betake**) bɪˈtʊk, bəˈtʊk

betray bɪˈtreɪ, bə- **-s** -z **-ing** -ɪŋ **-ed** -d **-er/s** -əʳ/z US -ɚ/z

betrayal bɪˈtreɪ.əl, bə- **-s** -z

betro|th bɪˈtrəʊ|ð, bə-, -ˈtrəʊ|θ US -ˈtroʊ|ð, -ˈtrɑː|θ **-ths** -ðz, -θs **-thing** -ðɪŋ, -θɪŋ **-thed** -ðd, -θt

Note: In British English, the voiceless version is unlikely before **-ing**.

betrothal bɪˈtrəʊ.ðᵊl, bə- US -ˈtroʊ-, -θᵊl **-s** -z

Betsy ˈbet.si

Bette bet; ˈbet.i US bet; ˈbet̬.i

Betteley ˈbet.ᵊl.i US ˈbet̬-

bett|er ˈbet|.əʳ US ˈbet̬|.ɚ **-ers** -əz US -ɚz **-ering** -ᵊr.ɪŋ **-ered** -əd US -ɚd **for ˌbetter or (for) ˈworse**

betterment ˈbet.ə.mənt US ˈbet̬.ɚ-

betting ˈbet.ɪŋ US ˈbet̬- **-s** -z **ˈbetting ˌshop**

bettor ˈbet.əʳ US ˈbet̬.ɚ **-s** -z

Bettws ˈbet.əs US ˈbet̬-

Bettws-y-Coed ˌbet.ə.siˈkɔɪd, -ʊ.siˈ-, -kəʊ.ɪd, -əd US ˌbet̬.ə.siˈkɔɪd

Betty ˈbet.i US ˈbet̬-

between bɪˈtwiːn, bə-

betweentimes bɪˈtwiːn.taɪmz, bə-

betwixt bɪˈtwɪkst, bə-

Beulah ˈbjuː.lə

Bevan ˈbev.ᵊn

bevel ˈbev.ᵊl **-s** -z **-(l)ing** -ɪŋ **-(l)ed** -d

Beven ˈbev.ᵊn

beverag|e ˈbev.ᵊr.ɪdʒ, ˈ-rɪdʒ **-es** -ɪz

Beveridge ˈbev.ᵊr.ɪdʒ, ˈ-rɪdʒ

Beverley ˈbev.ᵊl.i US -ɚ.li

Beverly ˈbev.ᵊl.i US -ɚ.li **ˌBeverly ˈHills**

Beves ˈbiː.vɪs

Bevin ˈbev.ɪn

Bevis ˈbiː.vɪs, ˈbev.ɪs

bevv|y ˈbev|.i **-ies** -iz **-ied** -id

bev|y ˈbev|.i **-ies** -iz

bewail bɪˈweɪl, bə- **-s** -z **-ing** -ɪŋ **-ed** -d

beware bɪˈweəʳ, bə- US -ˈwer

Bewdley ˈbjuːd.li

bewhiskered bɪˈ*h*wɪs.kəd, bə- US -kɚd

Bewick(e) ˈbjuː.ɪk

bewigged bɪˈwɪgd, bə-

bewild|er bɪˈwɪl.d|əʳ, bə- US -d|ɚ **-ers** -əz US -ɚz **-ering/ly** -ᵊr.ɪŋ/li **-ered** -əd US -ɚd **-erment/s** -ə.mənt/s US -ɚ.mənt/s

bewitch bɪˈwɪtʃ, bə- **-es** -ɪz **-ing/ly** -ɪŋ/li **-ed** -t **-ment/s** -mənt/s

Bewley ˈbjuː.li

Bexhill beksˈhɪl *stress shift:* ˌBexhill ˈstation

Bexley ˈbek.sli

Bexleyheath ˌbek.slɪˈhiːθ

Bey beɪ **-s** -z

Beynon ˈbaɪ.nən, ˈbeɪ-

beyond biˈɒnd US -ˈ*j*ɑːnd

Beyrout(h) beɪˈruːt

bezant ˈbez.ᵊnt **-s** -s

bezel ˈbez.ᵊl **-s** -z

Béziers ˈbez.i.eɪ

bezique bɪˈziːk, bə-

BFPO ˌbiː.ef.piːˈəʊ US -ˈoʊ

Bhagavad-Gita ˌbæg.ə.vədˈgiː.tə, ˌbʌg-, -vædˈ- US ˌbɑː.gə.vɑːdˈ-

bhagwan (B) ˈbæg.wɑːn

bhang bæŋ

bhangra ˈbæŋ.grə, ˈbɑːŋ-

bhindi ˈbɪn.di

Bhopal bəʊˈpɑːl US boʊ-

Bhutan buːˈtɑːn, -ˈtæn

Bhutanese ˌbuː.təˈniːz

Bhutto ˈbuː.təʊ, ˈbʊt.əʊ US ˈbuː.t̬oʊ

bi- baɪ-

Note: Prefix. Words containing **bi-** normally take secondary stress, but sometimes primary stress, on the first syllable, e.g. **bimetallic** /ˌbaɪ.metˈæl.ɪk/, British English **bicarb** /ˈbaɪ.kɑːb/, or primary stress on the second syllable, e.g. **biathlete** /baɪˈæθ.liːt/.

Biafr|a biˈæf.r|ə, baɪˈ- **-an/s** -ən/z

Bialystok biˈæl.ɪ.stɒk; ˈ-ə-; ˌbiː.əˈlɪs.tɒk US biˈɑː.lə.stɑːk, -ˈæl.ə-

Bianca biˈæŋ.kə US -ˈæŋ-, -ˈɑːŋ-

biannual baɪˈæn.ju.əl **-s** -z **-ly** -li

Biarritz ˌbɪəˈrɪts, ˈ-- US ˌbiː.əˈrɪts, ˈ---

bias ˈbaɪəs **-(s)es** -ɪz **-(s)ing** -ɪŋ **-(s)ed** -t

biathlete baɪˈæθ.liːt **-s** -s

biathlon baɪˈæθ.lən, -lɒn US -lɑːn **-s** -z

biaxal baɪˈæk.sᵊl

biaxial baɪˈæk.si.əl

bib bɪb **-s** -z

Bibby ˈbɪb.i

bibelot ˈbɪb.ləʊ, -ᵊl.əʊ US -ə.loʊ, ˈbiː.bloʊ **-s** -z

Bible ˈbaɪ.bl̩ **-s** -z **ˈBible ˌBelt**

biblic|al ˈbɪb.lɪ.k|ᵊl **-ally** -ᵊl.i, -li

biblio- bɪb.li.əʊ-; ˌbɪb.liˈɒ- US bɪb.li.oʊ-, -ə-; ˌbɪb.liˈɑː-

Note: Prefix. Normally takes either primary or secondary stress on the first syllable, e.g. **bibliophile** /ˈbɪb.li.əʊ.faɪl US -ə-/, **bibliomania** /ˌbɪb.li.əʊˈmeɪ.ni.ə US -əˈ-/, or secondary stress on the first syllable, with primary stress occurring on the antepenultimate syllable of the resulting word, e.g. **bibliography** /ˌbɪb.liˈɒg.rə.fi US -ˈɑː.grə-/.

bibliograph|y ˌbɪb.liˈɒg.rə.f|i US -ˈɑː.grə- **-ies** -iz **-er/s** -əʳ/z US -ɚ/z

bibliolat|ry ˌbɪb.liˈɒl.ə.t|ri US -ˈɑː.lə- **-er/z** -əʳ/z US -ɚ/z

bibliomania ˌbɪb.li.əʊˈmeɪ.ni.ə US -əˈ-, -oʊˈ-

bibliomaniac ˌbɪb.li.əʊˈmeɪ.ni.æk US -əˈ-, -oʊˈ- **-s** -s

bibliophile ˈbɪb.li.əʊ.faɪl US -ə-, -oʊ- **-s** -z

bibulous ˈbɪb.jə.ləs, -jʊ- US -jə- **-ly** -li

Bic® bɪk

bicameral ˌbaɪˈkæm.ᵊr.ᵊl **-ism** -ɪ.zᵊm

bicarb ˈbaɪ.kɑːb US baɪˈkɑːrb

bicarbonate ˌbaɪˈkɑː.bᵊn.ət, -eɪt, -ɪt US -ˈkɑːr- **-s** -s **biˌcarbonate of ˈsoda**

bice baɪs

Bice ˈbiː.tʃi; baɪs

bicentenar|y ˌbaɪ.senˈtiː.nᵊr|.i, -sᵊnˈ-, -ˈten.ᵊr- US baɪˈsen.tᵊn.er|.i; ˌbaɪ.senˈten.ᵊr- **-ies** -iz

bicentennial ˌbaɪ.senˈten.i.əl, -sənˈ- **-s** -z

biceps ˈbaɪ.seps

Bicester ˈbɪs.təʳ US -tɚ

bichloride ˌbaɪˈklɔː.raɪd US -ˈklɔːr.aɪd

bichromate ˌbaɪˈkrəʊ.meɪt, -met, -mɪt US -ˈkroʊ-

bick|er ˈbɪk|.əʳ US -ɚ **-ers** -əz US -ɚz **-ering/s** -ᵊr.ɪŋ/z **-ered** -əd US -ɚd **-erer/s** -ᵊr.əʳ/z US -ɚ.ɚ/z

Bickerstaff ˈbɪk.ə.stɑːf US -ɚ.stæf

Bickersteth ˈbɪk.ə.steθ, -stɪθ US ˈ-ɚ-

Bickerton ˈbɪk.ə.tᵊn US ˈ-ɚ-

Bickford ˈbɪk.fəd US -fɚd

Bickleigh, Bickley ˈbɪk.li

Bicknell 'bɪk.nəl
bicoastal baɪ'kəʊ.stəl (US) -'koʊ-
bicuspid baɪ'kʌs.pɪd **-s** -z
bicyc|le 'baɪ.sɪ.kl̩, -sə- **-les** -l̩z **-ling** -lɪŋ **-led** -l̩d
bicyclist 'baɪ.sɪ.klɪst, -sə- **-s** -s
bid bɪd **-s** -z **-ding** -ɪŋ **-der/s** -əʳ/z (US) -ɚ/z **bade** bæd, beɪd **bidden** 'bɪd.ən
biddable 'bɪd.ə.bl̩
bidder (B) 'bɪd.əʳ (US) -ɚ **-s** -z
Biddle 'bɪd.l̩
Biddulph 'bɪd.ʌlf, -əlf
bidd|y (B) 'bɪd|.i **-ies** -iz
bid|e (B) baɪd **-es** -z **-ing** -ɪŋ **-ed** -ɪd
Bideford 'bɪd.ɪ.fəd (US) -fɚd
Biden 'baɪ.dən
bidet 'biː.deɪ (US) bɪ'deɪ, biː- **-s** -z
bidialectal ˌbaɪ.daɪə'lek.təl
bidialectalism ˌbaɪ.daɪə'lek.təl.ɪ.zəm
Bidwell 'bɪd.wel
Bielefeld 'biː.lə.felt, -feld
biennial baɪ'en.i.əl **-ly** -i
bier bɪəʳ (US) bɪr **-s** -z
Bierce bɪəs (US) bɪrs
biff bɪf **-s** -s **-ing** -ɪŋ **-ed** -t
Biffen 'bɪf.ɪn, -ən
bifocal baɪ'fəʊ.kəl (US) 'baɪˌfoʊ-, ˌ-'-- **-s** -z
bifur|cate 'baɪ.fə.keɪt, -fɜː- (US) -fɚ- **-cates** -keɪts **-cating** -keɪ.tɪŋ (US) -keɪ.t̬ɪŋ **-cated** -keɪ.tɪd (US) -keɪ.t̬ɪd
bifurcation ˌbaɪ.fə'keɪ.ʃən, -fɜː'- (US) -fɚ'- **-s** -z
big bɪg **-ger** -əʳ (US) -ɚ **-gest** -ɪst, -əst **-ness** -nəs, -nɪs ˌ**Big 'Apple** ; ˌ**Big 'Bang** ; ˌ**Big 'Ben** ; ˌ**big 'business** ; ˌ**Big 'Dipper** ; ˌ**big 'game** ; ˌ**big 'screen** ; ˌ**big 'wheel** ; ˌ**hit the 'big** ˌ**time**
bigamist 'bɪg.ə.mɪst **-s** -s
bigamous 'bɪg.ə.məs **-ly** -li
bigam|y 'bɪg.ə.m|i **-ies** -iz
Bigelow 'bɪg.əl.əʊ, -ɪ.ləʊ (US) -ə.loʊ
Bigfoot 'bɪg.fʊt
Bigge bɪg
biggie 'bɪg.i
Biggin 'bɪg.ɪn **-s**
biggish 'bɪg.ɪʃ
Biggles 'bɪg.l̩z
Biggleswade 'bɪg.l̩z.weɪd
Biggs bɪgz
biggl|y 'bɪgl|.i **-ies** -iz
Bigham 'bɪg.em
bighead 'bɪg.hed **-s** -z
bigheaded ˌbɪg'hed.ɪd, -əd (US) '-ˌ-- **-ly** -li **-ness** -nəs, -nɪs *stress shift:* ˌbigheaded 'bully
bighorn 'bɪg.hɔːn (US) -hɔːrn **-s** -z
bight baɪt **-s** -s **-ing** -ɪŋ (US) 'baɪ.t̬ɪŋ **-ed** -ɪd (US) 'baɪ.t̬ɪd
big-league 'bɪg.liːg
Biglow 'bɪg.ləʊ (US) -loʊ
Bignell 'bɪg.nəl
big|ot 'bɪg|.ət **-ots** -əts **-oted** -ə.tɪd (US) -ə.t̬ɪd
bigotr|y 'bɪg.ə.tr|i **-ies** -iz
bigraph 'baɪ.grɑːf, -græf (US) -græf **-s** -s
Big Sur ˌbɪg'sɜːʳ (US) -'sɜːr
big-ticket 'bɪgˌtɪk.ɪt
big-time 'bɪg.taɪm **-er/s** -əʳ/z (US) -ɚ/z
bigwig 'bɪg.wɪg **-s** -z
Bihar bɪ'hɑːʳ, biː- (US) -hɑːr
bijou 'biː.ʒuː, -'-
bik|e baɪk **-es** -s **-ing** -ɪŋ **-ed** -t
biker (B) 'baɪ.kəʳ (US) -kɚ **-s** -z
bikini (B) bɪ'kiː.ni, bə- **-s** -z
Biko 'biː.keʊ (US) -koʊ
bilabial (*n. adj.*) baɪ'leɪ.bi.əl **-s** -z **-ly** -i
bilateral baɪ'læt.ər.əl, '-rəl (US) -'læt̬.ɚ.əl **-y** -i **-ness** -nəs, -nɪs
Bilbao bɪl'baʊ, -'bɑː.əʊ (US) -'bɑː.oʊ, -'baʊ
bilberr|y 'bɪl.bər|.i (US) -ber- **-ies** -iz
Bilborough 'bɪl.bər.ə (US) -oʊ
Bilbrough 'bɪl.brə (US) -broʊ
Bildungsroman 'bɪl.dʊŋz.rəʊ.mɑːn (US) -roʊ- **-s** -z **-e** -ə
bile baɪl
bilg|e bɪldʒ **-es** -ɪz **-ing** -ɪŋ **-ed** -d **'bilge** ˌ**pump** ; **'bilge** ˌ**water**
bilgy 'bɪl.dʒi
bilharzia bɪl'hɑː.zi.ə, -'hɑːt.si- (US) -'hɑːr.zi-
biliary 'bɪl.i.ər.i
bilingual baɪ'lɪŋ.gwəl **-s** -z **-ly** -i **-ism** -ɪ.zəm *stress shift, see first compound:* ˌ**bilingual 'secretary,** **biˌlingual 'secretary**
bilious 'bɪl.i.əs (US) '-jəs, '-i.əs **-ly** -li **-ness** -nəs, -nɪs
bilirubin ˌbɪl.ɪ'ruː.bɪn
biliteral baɪ'lɪt.ər.əl, '-rəl (US) -'lɪt̬.ɚ.əl **-ly** -i
bilk bɪlk **-s** -s **-ing** -ɪŋ **-ed** -t
bill (B) bɪl **-s** -z **-ing** -ɪŋ **-ed** -d ˌ**bill of 'fare** ; ˌ**fit the 'bill**
billable 'bɪl.ə.bl̩
billabong 'bɪl.ə.bɒŋ (US) -bɑːŋ, -bɔːŋ **-s** -z
billboard 'bɪl.bɔːd (US) -bɔːrd **-s** -z
Billericay ˌbɪl.ə'rɪk.i
bille|t 'bɪl|.ɪt, -ət (US) -ət **-ts** -ts **-ting** -tɪŋ (US) -t̬ɪŋ **-ted** -tɪd (US) -t̬ɪd
billet-doux ˌbɪl.eɪ'duː **billets-doux** ˌbɪl.eɪ'duː, -duːz
billfold 'bɪl.fəʊld (US) -foʊld **-s** -z
billhook 'bɪl.hʊk **-s** -s
billiard 'bɪl.i.əd, '-jəd (US) '-jɚd **-s** -z **'billiard** ˌ**ball** ; **'billiard** ˌ**cue** ; **'billiard** ˌ**room** ; **'billiard** ˌ**table**
Billie 'bɪl.i
Billie-Jean ˌbɪl.i'dʒiːn
Billing 'bɪl.ɪŋ **-s** -z
Billinge 'bɪl.ɪndʒ
Billingham 'bɪl.ɪŋ.*h*əm
Billinghurst 'bɪl.ɪŋ.hɜːst (US) -hɜːrst
Billingsgate 'bɪl.ɪŋz.geɪt
Billington 'bɪl.ɪŋ.tən
billion 'bɪl.i.ən, -jən (US) -jən **-s** -z
billionaire ˌbɪl.i.ə'neəʳ, ˌ-jə'- (US) -jə'ner **-s** -z
billionth 'bɪl.i.ənθ, '-jənθ (US) '-jənθ **-s** -s
billow 'bɪl.əʊ (US) -oʊ **-s** -z **-ing** -ɪŋ **-ed** -d **-y** -i
billposter 'bɪlˌpəʊ.stəʳ (US) -ˌpoʊ.stɚ **-s** -z
billsticker 'bɪlˌstɪk.əʳ (US) -kɚ **-s** -z
bill|y (B) 'bɪl|.i **-ies** -iz **'billy** ˌ**can**; **'billy** ˌ**club**; **'billy** ˌ**goat**
billycock 'bɪl.i.kɒk (US) -kɑːk **-s** -s
billy-o 'bɪl.i.əʊ (US) -oʊ
Biloxi bɪ'lʌk.si, bə-, -'lɒk- (US) -'lɑːk-, -'lʌk-
Bilston(e) 'bɪl.stən
Bilton 'bɪl.tən
biltong 'bɪl.tɒŋ (US) -tɑːŋ, -tɔːŋ
bimbo 'bɪm.bəʊ (US) -boʊ **-(e)s** -z
bimestrial baɪ'mes.tri.əl
bimetallic ˌbaɪ.met'æl.ɪk, -mɪ'tæl-, -mə-
bimetall|ism baɪ'met.əl|.ɪ.zəm (US) -'met̬- **-ist/s** -ɪst/s
bimolecular ˌbaɪ.mə'lek.jə.ləʳ, -jʊ- (US) -lɚ
bimonthl|y baɪ'mʌn*t*θ.l|i **-ies** -iz
bin bɪn **-s** -z **-ning** -ɪŋ **-ned** -d
binar|y 'baɪ.nər|.i **-ies** -iz ˌ**binary 'number**
binaural baɪ'nɔː.rəl, bɪ- (US) -'nɔːr.əl
Binchy 'bɪn.*t*ʃi (US) 'bɪn*t*.ʃi
bind baɪnd **-s** -z **-ing** -ɪŋ **bound** baʊnd
binder 'baɪn.dəʳ (US) -dɚ **-s** -z
binder|y 'baɪn.dər|.i **-ies** -iz
bindweed 'baɪnd.wiːd
Binet 'biː.neɪ (US) bɪ'neɪ
Binet-Simon ˌbiː.neɪ'saɪ.mən (US) bɪˌneɪ.si'moʊn
Bing bɪŋ
bing|e bɪndʒ **-es** -ɪz **-(e)ing** -ɪŋ **-ed** -d
Bingen 'bɪŋ.ən
Bingham 'bɪŋ.əm
Bingley 'bɪŋ*g*.li
bingo 'bɪŋ.gəʊ (US) -goʊ
Bink(e)s bɪŋks
bin|man 'bɪn|.mæn, 'bɪm-, -mən (US) 'bɪn- **-men** -men, -mən
binnacle 'bɪn.ə.kl̩ **-s** -z
Binney, Binnie 'bɪn.i
Binns bɪnz
binocular (*adj.*) baɪ'nɒk.jə.ləʳ, bɪ-, bə-, -jʊ- (US) -'nɑː.kjə.lɚ, -kjʊ-

binoculars (*n.*) bɪˈnɒk.jə.ləz, baɪ-, bə-, -jʊ- (US) -ˈnɑː.kjə.lɚz, -kjʊ-
binomial baɪˈnəʊ.mi.əl (US) -ˈnoʊ- **-s** -z **-ly** -i
Binste(a)d ˈbɪn.stɪd, -sted
bint bɪnt **-s** -s
Binyon ˈbɪn.jən
bio- baɪ.əʊ-; baɪˈɒ- (US) baɪ.oʊ-, -ə-; baɪˈɑː-
Note: Prefix. Normally carries primary or secondary stress on the first syllable, e.g. **biograph** /ˈbaɪ.əʊ.grɑːf (US) -ə.græf/, **biographic** /ˌbaɪ.əʊˈgræf.ɪk (US) -əˈ-/, or primary stress on the second syllable, e.g. **biographer** /baɪˈɒg.rə.fəʳ (US) -ˈɑː.grə.fɚ/. There are exceptions; see individual entries.
biochemic|al ˌbaɪ.əʊˈkem.ɪ.k|əl (US) -oʊˈ- **-als** -əlz **-ally** -əl.i, -li
biochemist ˌbaɪ.əʊˈkem.ɪst (US) -oʊˈ- **-s** -s **-ry** -ri
biocoenosis ˌbaɪ.əʊ.sɪˈnəʊ.sɪs, -siːˈ- (US) -oʊ.sɪˈnoʊ-
biodegradability ˌbaɪ.əʊ.dɪ.greɪ.dəˈbɪl.ɪ.ti, -də.greɪ-, -ə.ti (US) -oʊ.dɪ.greɪ.dəˈbɪl.ə.t̬i, -də-
biodegradab|le ˌbaɪ.əʊ.dɪˈgreɪ.də.b|l̩, -dəˈ- (US) -oʊ- **-ly** -li
biodegradation ˌbaɪ.əʊ.deg.rəˈdeɪ.ʃən (US) ˌ-oʊ-
biodegrad|e ˌbaɪ.əʊ.dɪˈgreɪd, -dəˈ- (US) -oʊ- **-es** -z **-ing** -ɪŋ **-ed** -ɪd
biodiversity ˌbaɪ.əʊ.daɪˈvɜː.sə.ti, -dɪˈ-, -sɪ- (US) -oʊ.dɪˈvɝː.sə.t̬i, -daɪˈ-
bioengineer ˌbaɪ.əʊ.en.dʒɪˈnɪəʳ, -dʒəˈ- (US) -oʊ.en.dʒɪˈnɪr, -dʒəˈ- **-s** -z
bioengineering ˌbaɪ.əʊ.en.dʒɪˈnɪə.rɪŋ, -dʒəˈ- (US) -oʊ.en.dʒɪˈnɪr.ɪŋ, -dʒəˈ-
biofeedback ˌbaɪ.əʊˈfiːd.bæk (US) -oʊˈ-
biogenesis ˌbaɪ.əʊˈdʒen.ə.sɪs, ˈ-ɪ- (US) -oʊˈ-
biogenetic ˌbaɪ.əʊ.dʒəˈnet.ɪk, -dʒɪˈ- (US) -oʊ.dʒəˈnet̬- **-ally** -əl.i, -li
biogenic ˌbaɪ.əʊˈdʒen.ɪk (US) -oʊˈ-
biograph ˈbaɪ.əʊ.grɑːf, -græf (US) -ə.græf **-s** -s
biographer baɪˈɒg.rə.fəʳ (US) -ˈɑː.grə.fɚ **-s** -z
biographic ˌbaɪ.əʊˈgræf.ɪk (US) -əˈ- **-al** -əl **-ally** -əl.i, -li
biograph|y baɪˈɒg.rə.f|i (US) -ˈɑː.grə- **-ies** -iz
biolinguistics ˌbaɪ.əʊ.lɪŋˈgwɪs.tɪks (US) ˌ-oʊ-
biologic ˌbaɪ.əˈlɒdʒ.ɪk (US) -ˈlɑː.dʒɪk
biologic|al ˌbaɪ.əˈlɒdʒ.ɪ.k|əl (US) -ˈlɑː.dʒɪ- **-ally** -əl.i, -li **bioˌlogical ˈclock** ; **bioˌlogical ˈwarfare**
biologist baɪˈɒl.ə.dʒɪst (US) -ˈɑː.lə- **-s** -s
biology baɪˈɒl.ə.dʒi (US) -ˈɑː.lə-
biome ˈbaɪ.əʊm (US) -oʊm
biometric ˌbaɪ.əʊˈmet.rɪk (US) -oʊˈ- **-s** -s **-al** -əl
biometry baɪˈɒm.ɪ.tri, ˈ-ə- (US) -ˈɑː.mə-
bionic baɪˈɒn.ɪk (US) -ˈɑː.nɪk **-s** -s
biophysicist ˌbaɪ.əʊˈfɪz.ɪ.sɪst, -oʊˈ- **-s** -s
biophysic|s ˌbaɪ.əʊˈfɪz.ɪk|s (US) -oʊˈ- **-al** -əl
biopic ˈbaɪ.əʊ.pɪk (US) -oʊ- **-s** -s
biops|y ˈbaɪ.ɒp.s|i (US) -ɑːp- **-ies** -iz
biorhythm ˈbaɪ.əʊˌrɪð.əm (US) -oʊˌ- **-s** -z
bioscope ˈbaɪ.əʊ.skəʊp (US) -skoʊp **-s** -s
biosphere ˈbaɪ.əʊ.sfɪəʳ (US) -ə.sfɪr **-s** -z
biotech ˈbaɪ.əʊ.tek (US) -oʊ-
biotechnology ˌbaɪ.əʊ.tekˈnɒl.ə.dʒi (US) -oʊ.tekˈnɑː.lə-
biotope ˈbaɪ.əʊ.təʊp (US) -toʊp **-s** -s
biparous ˈbɪp.ər.əs
bipartisan ˌbaɪ.pɑː.tɪˈzæn; baɪˈpɑː.tɪ.zæn, -zən (US) baɪˈpɑːr.t̬ə.zən
bipartite baɪˈpɑː.taɪt (US) baɪˈpɑːr- *stress shift:* ˌbipartite ˈtreaty
biped ˈbaɪ.ped **-s** -z
bipedal baɪˈpiː.dəl, -ˈped.əl (US) -ˈped.əl **-ism** -ɪ.zəm
biplane ˈbaɪ.pleɪn **-s** -s
bipod ˈbaɪ.pɒd (US) -pɑːd **-s** -z
bipolar baɪˈpəʊ.ləʳ (US) -ˈpoʊ.lɚ
bipolarity ˌbaɪ.pəʊˈlær.ɪ.ti, -ə.ti (US) -poʊˈler.ə.t̬i, -ˈlær-
biquadratic ˌbaɪ.kwɒdˈræt.ɪk, -kwəˈdræt- (US) -kwɑːˈdræt̬.ɪk **-s** -s
birch (B) bɜːtʃ (US) bɝːtʃ **-es** -ɪz **-ing** -ɪŋ **-ed** -t
Birchall ˈbɜː.tʃɔːl, -tʃəl (US) ˈbɝː.tʃɔːl, -tʃɑːl, -tʃəl
Birchenough ˈbɜː.tʃɪ.nʌf (US) ˈbɝː-
Bircher ˈbɜː.tʃəʳ (US) ˈbɝː.tʃɚ
Birchwood ˈbɜːtʃ.wʊd (US) ˈbɝːtʃ-
Bircotes ˈbɜː.kəʊts (US) ˈbɝː.koʊts
bird (B) bɜːd (US) bɝːd **-s** -z **ˈbird ˌcage**; **ˈbird ˌdog**; **ˈbird ˌfancier**; **ˌbird of ˈparadise**; **ˌbird of ˈprey**; **ˌkill two ˌbirds with ˌone ˈstone**
bird-brained ˈbɜːdˌbreɪnd (US) ˈbɝːd-
birdhou|se ˈbɜːd.haʊ|s (US) ˈbɝːd- **-ses** -zɪz
birdie ˈbɜː.di (US) ˈbɝː- **-s** -z **-d** -d
birdlike ˈbɜːd.laɪk (US) ˈbɝːd-
birdlime ˈbɜːd.laɪm (US) ˈbɝːd-
birdseed ˈbɜːd.siːd (US) ˈbɝːd-
bird's-eye (*n. adj.*) ˈbɜːdz.aɪ (US) ˈbɝːdz- **-s** -z **ˌbird's-eye ˈview**
Birds Eye® ˈbɜːdz.aɪ (US) ˈbɝːdz-
bird's-nest ˈbɜːdz.nest (US) ˈbɝːdz- **-s** -s **-ing** -ɪŋ **-ed** -ɪd **ˌbird's nest ˈsoup**
birdwatch|ing ˈbɜːdˌwɒtʃ|.ɪŋ (US) ˈbɝːdˌwɑː.tʃ|ɪŋ, -ˌwɔː- **-er/s** -əʳ/z (US) -ɚ/z
bireme ˈbaɪ.riːm, -ˈ- (US) baɪˈriːm **-s** -z
biretta bɪˈret.ə (US) -ˈret̬- **-s** -z
Birgit ˈbɜː.gɪt, ˈbɪə- (US) ˈbɝː-, -giːt
biriani ˌbɪr.iˈɑː.ni **-s** -z
Birkbeck *surname:* ˈbɜː.bek, ˈbɜːk- (US) ˈbɝː-, ˈbɝːk- *college in London:* ˈbɜːk.bek (US) ˈbɝːk-
Birkenau ˈbɜː.kən.aʊ (US) ˈbɝː-
Birkenhead ˌbɜː.kənˈhed, ˈ--- (US) ˌbɝː.kənˈhed, ˈ---
Birkenstocks® ˈbɜː.kən.stɒks (US) ˈbɝː.kən.stɑːks
Birkett ˈbɜː.kɪt (US) ˈbɝː-
Birley ˈbɜː.li (US) ˈbɝː-
Birling ˈbɜː.lɪŋ (US) ˈbɝː-
Birmingham *place in UK:* ˈbɜː.mɪŋ.əm (US) ˈbɝː- *places in US:* ˈbɜː.mɪŋ.hæm (US) ˈbɝː-
Birnam ˈbɜː.nəm (US) ˈbɝː-
Birney ˈbɜː.ni (US) ˈbɝː-
Biro® ˈbaɪə.rəʊ (US) -roʊ **-s** -z
Biron ˈbaɪ.rən
Note: /bɪˈruːn/ in 'Love's Labour's Lost'.
birr bɜːʳ (US) bɝː **birrotch** ˈbɜː.rɒtʃ (US) ˈbɝː.ɑːtʃ
Birrell ˈbɪr.əl
birrotch (*plur. of* **birr**) ˈbɜː.rɒtʃ (US) ˈbɝː.ɑːtʃ
Birstall ˈbɜː.stɔːl (US) ˈbɝː.stɔːl, -stɑːl
Birt bɜːt (US) bɝːt
birth bɜːθ (US) bɝːθ **-s** -s **ˈbirth cerˌtificate** ; **ˈbirth conˌtrol** ; **ˈbirthing ˌcenter**
birthday ˈbɜːθ.deɪ, -di (US) ˈbɝːθ.deɪ **-s** -z **ˈbirthday ˌcake** ; **ˈbirthday ˌcard** ; **ˈbirthday ˌparty** ; **ˈbirthday ˌpresent** ; **in one's ˈbirthday ˌsuit**
birthmark ˈbɜːθ.mɑːk (US) ˈbɝːθ.mɑːrk **-s** -s
birthplac|e ˈbɜːθ.pleɪs (US) ˈbɝːθ- **-es** -ɪz
birthrate ˈbɜːθ.reɪt (US) ˈbɝːθ- **-s** -s
birthright ˈbɜːθ.raɪt (US) ˈbɝːθ- **-s** -s
Birtwistle ˈbɜː.twɪ.sl̩ (US) ˈbɝː-
biryani ˌbɪr.iˈɑː.ni **-s** -z
bis bɪs
Biscay ˈbɪs.keɪ, -ki **ˌBay of ˈBiscay**
biscuit ˈbɪs.kɪt **-s** -s **ˈbiscuit ˌbarrel**
bisect baɪˈsekt (US) ˈbaɪ.sekt, -ˈ- **-s** -s **-ing** -ɪŋ **-ed** -ɪd
bisection baɪˈsek.ʃən **-s** -z
bisector baɪˈsek.təʳ (US) -tɚ **-s** -z
bisexual baɪˈsek.ʃʊəl, -ʃu.əl, -sjʊəl, -sjʊ.əl (US) -ʃu.əl
bisexuality baɪˌsek.ʃuˈæl.ɪ.ti, -sjuˈæl-, -ə.ti (US) -ʃuˈæl.ə.t̬i
bishop (B) ˈbɪʃ.əp **-s** -s
bishopric ˈbɪʃ.ə.prɪk **-s** -s
Bishopsgate ˈbɪʃ.əps.geɪt, -gɪt

Bishop's Stortford ˌbɪʃ.əpsˈstɔːt.fəd, -ˈstɔː- US -ˈstɔːrt.fɚd, -ˈstɔːr-
Bishopstoke ˈbɪʃ.əp.stəʊk US -stoʊk
Bishopston ˈbɪʃ.əp.stən
Bishopton ˈbɪʃ.əp.tən
Bisley ˈbɪz.li **-s** -z
Bismarck ˈbɪz.mɑːk US -mɑːrk
bismuth ˈbɪz.məθ
bison ˈbaɪ.sᵊn **-s** -z
Bispham *surname:* ˈbɪs.fəm, ˈbɪs.pəm *place:* ˈbɪs.pəm
bisque biːsk, bɪsk US bɪsk **-s** -s
Bissau ˈbɪs.aʊ, -ˈ- US bɪˈsaʊ
Bissell ˈbɪs.ᵊl
Bissett ˈbɪs.ɪt, ˈbɪz-
bissextile bɪˈsek.staɪl US -stᵊl, -staɪl **-s** -z
bister ˈbɪs.təʳ US -tɚ
Bisto® ˈbɪs.təʊ US -toʊ
bistour|y ˈbɪs.tᵊr|.i **-ies** -iz
bistre ˈbɪs.təʳ US -tɚ
bistro, **bistrot** ˈbiː.strəʊ, ˈbɪs- US -stroʊ **-s** -z
bisulph|ate baɪˈsʌl.f|eɪt, -f|ɪt, -f|ət US -f|eɪt **-ite** -aɪt
bit bɪt **-s** -s **ˌbits and ˈpieces ; take the ˌbit between one's ˈteeth**
bitch bɪtʃ **-es** -ɪz
bitch|y ˈbɪtʃ|.i **-iness** -ɪ.nəs, -ɪ.nɪs
bit|e baɪt **-es** -s **-ing** -ɪŋ US ˈbaɪ.t̬ɪŋ **bit** bɪt **bitten** ˈbɪt.ᵊn **biter/s** ˈbaɪ.təʳ/z US -t̬ɚ/z **ˌbite ˈoff ˌmore than one can ˈchew ; ˌbite one's ˈtongue ; ˌbite someone's ˈhead off ; ˌbite the ˈbullet ; ˌbite the ˈdust ; ˌbite the ˌhand that ˈfeeds one**
Bithell ˈbɪθ.ᵊl, bɪˈθel
Bithynia bɪˈθɪn.i.ə, baɪ-
Bitola ˈbiː.təʊ.lə US -toʊ-, -t̬ᵊl.ə
Bitolj ˈbiː.təʊ.ljə US -toʊ-, -t̬ᵊl.jə
bitten (*from* **bite**) ˈbɪt.ᵊn **once ˌbitten twice ˈshy**
bitt|er ˈbɪt|.əʳ US ˈbɪt̬|.ɚ **-erer** -ᵊr.əʳ US -ɚ.ɚ **-erest** -ᵊr.ɪst, -əst **-erly** -ə.li US -ɚ.li **-erness** -ə.nəs, -nɪs US -ɚ.nəs, -nɪs **to the ˌbitter ˈend**
bittern ˈbɪt.ən, -ɜːn US ˈbɪt̬.ɚn **-s** -z
bitters ˈbɪt.əz US ˈbɪt̬.ɚz
bittersweet ˈbɪt.ə.swiːt, ˌ--ˈ- US ˈbɪt̬.ɚ.swiːt
bitt|y ˈbɪt|.i US ˈbɪt̬- **-ier** -i.əʳ US -i.ɚ **-iest** -i.ɪst, -i.əst **-iness** -ɪ.nəs, -ɪ.nɪs
bitumen ˈbɪtʃ.ə.mɪn, ˈ-ʊ-, -men, -mən US bɪˈtuː.mən, baɪ-, -ˈtjuː- **-s** -z
bituminous bɪˈtʃuː.mɪ.nəs, bə-, -ˈtjuː-, -mə- US -ˈtuː-, -ˈtjuː-
bivalen|ce ˌbaɪˈveɪ.lən|ts, bɪ- US ˌbaɪˈveɪ.lən|ts, ˈbaɪ.veɪ- **-cy** -*t*.si **-t** -t
bivalve ˈbaɪ.vælv **-s** -z
bivouac ˈbɪv.u.æk US -u.æk, ˈ-wæk **-s** -s **-king** -ɪŋ **-ked** -t
bi-weekl|y baɪˈwiː.kl|i **-ies** -iz *stress shift:* ˌbi-weekly ˈjournal
bizarre bɪˈzɑːʳ, bə- US -ˈzɑːr **-ly** -li **-ness** -nəs, -nɪs
Bizerte, Bizerta bɪˈzɜː.tə US -ˈzɜːr-
Bizet ˈbiː.zeɪ US -ˈ-
Björk bjɔːk, bjɜːk US bjɔːrk, bjɜːrk
Bjorn, **Björn** bjɔːn, bjɜːn; biˈɔːn, -ˈɜːn US bjɔːrn, bjɜːrn
BL ˌbiːˈel
blab blæb **-s** -z **-bing** -ɪŋ **-bed** -d **-ber/s** -əʳ/z US -ɚ/z
blabber|mouth ˈblæb.ə|.maʊθ US ˈ-ɚ- **-mouths** -maʊðz, -maʊθs
Blaby ˈbleɪ.bi
Blachford ˈblæʃ.fəd US -fɚd
black (B) blæk **-s** -s **-er** -əʳ US -ɚ **-est** -ɪst, -əst **-ish** -ɪʃ **-ly** -li **-ness** -nəs, -nɪs **-ing** -ɪŋ **-ed** -t **ˌblack ˈbelt ; ˌblack ˈbox ; ˌblack ˈeye ; ˌBlack ˈForest ; ˌBlack Forest ˈgateau ; ˌblack ˈhole ; ˌblack ˌhole of Calˈcutta ; ˌblack ˈice ; ˌblack ˈmagic ; ˌblack ˈmarket ; ˌblack ˈpepper ; ˌblack ˈpudding ; ˌBlack ˈRod ; ˌblack ˈtreacle ; ˌblack and ˈblue ; ˌblack and ˈtan ; ˌblack and ˈwhite ; ˌblack ˌsheep of the ˈfamily**
Blackadder ˈblækˌæd.əʳ, ˌ-ˈ-- US ˈblækˌæd.ɚ
blackamoor ˈblæk.ə.mɔːʳ US -mʊr **-s** -z
blackball (*v.*) ˈblæk.bɔːl US -bɔːl, -bɑːl **-s** -z **-ing** -ɪŋ **-ed** -d
blackbeetle ˌblækˈbiː.tl̩ US ˈblækˌbiː.t̬l̩ **-s** -z
blackberr|y ˈblæk.bᵊr|.i, -ˌber- US -ˌber- **-ies** -iz
blackberrying ˈblæk.bᵊr.i.ɪŋ, -ˌber- US -ˌber-
blackbird ˈblæk.bɜːd US -bɜːrd **-s** -z
blackboard ˈblæk.bɔːd US -bɔːrd **-s** -z
black box ˌblækˈbɒks US -ˈbɑːks **-es** -ɪz
Blackburn(e) ˈblæk.bɜːn US -bɜːrn
blackcap ˈblæk.kæp **-s** -s
blackcock ˈblæk.kɒk US -kɑːk **-s** -s
blackcurrant ˌblækˈkʌr.ᵊnt US ˈblækˌkɜːr- **-s** -s *stress shift, British only:* ˌblackcurrant ˈpie
Blackdown ˈblæk.daʊn
blacken ˈblæk.ᵊn **-s** -z **-ing** -ɪŋ **-ed** -d
Blackett ˈblæk.ɪt
black-eyed ˌblækˈaɪd *stress shift:* ˌblack-eyed ˈpeas
black|fly ˈblæk|.flaɪ **-flies** -flaɪz
Black|foot ˈblæk|.fʊt **-feet** -fiːt
Blackford ˈblæk.fəd US -fɚd
Blackfriars ˌblækˈfraɪəz US -ˈfraɪɚz *stress shift:* ˌBlackfriars ˈBobby
blackgame ˈblæk.geɪm **-s** -z
blackguard ˈblæg.ɑːd, ˈ-əd US -ɑːrd, -ɚd **-s** -z **-ly** -li
blackhead ˈblæk.hed **-s** -z
Blackheath ˌblækˈhiːθ *stress shift:* ˌBlackheath ˈHarriers
Blackie ˈblæk.i, ˈbleɪ.ki US ˈblæk.i
blacking (*n.*) ˈblæk.ɪŋ **-s** -z
blackjack ˈblæk.dʒæk **-s** -s
blacklead (*n.*) ˈblæk.led
blacklead (*v.*) ˌblækˈled, ˈ-- **-s** -z **-ing** -ɪŋ **-ed** -ɪd
blackleg ˈblæk.leg **-s** -z
Blackley *Manchester:* ˈbleɪ.kli *surname:* ˈblæk.li
blacklist ˈblæk.lɪst **-s** -s **-ing** -ɪŋ **-ed** -ɪd
blackmail ˈblæk.meɪl **-s** -z **-ing** -ɪŋ **-ed** -d **-er/s** -əʳ/z US -ɚ/z
Blackman ˈblæk.mən
Black Maria ˌblæk.məˈraɪə
Blackmoor, **Blackmore** ˈblæk.mɔːʳ US -mɔːr
blackout ˈblæk.aʊt **-s** -s
Blackpool ˈblæk.puːl
Blackpudlian ˌblækˈpʌd.li.ən **-s** -z
Blackrock ˈblæk.rɒk US -rɑːk
Blackshirt ˈblæk.ʃɜːt US -ʃɜːrt **-s** -s
blacksmith ˈblæk.smɪθ **-s** -s
Blackston ˈblæk.stᵊn
Blackstone ˈblæk.stəʊn, -stᵊn US -stoʊn, -stᵊn
blackthorn (B) ˈblæk.θɔːn US -θɔːrn **-s** -z
blacktop ˈblæk.tɒp US -tɑːp **-s** -s **-ping** -ɪŋ **-ped** -t
Blackwall ˈblæk.wɔːl US -wɔːl, -wɑːl
blackwater (B) ˈblækˌwɔː.təʳ US -ˌwɑː.t̬ɚ, -ˌwɔː-
Blackwell ˈblæk.wel, -wᵊl
Blackwood *surname:* ˈblæk.wʊd *place in Gwent:* ˌblækˈwʊd
bladder ˈblæd.əʳ US -ɚ **-s** -z
bladderwort ˈblæd.ə.wɜːt US -ɚ.wɜːrt, -wɔːrt **-s** -s
bladderwrack ˈblæd.ᵊr.æk
blade bleɪd **-s** -z
Bladon ˈbleɪ.dᵊn
blaeberr|y ˈbleɪ.bᵊr|.i US -ber- **-ies** -iz
Blaenau Ffestiniog ˌblaɪ.naɪ.fesˈtɪn.i.ɒg, ˌbleɪ.ni- US -ɑːg
Blaenau Gwent ˌblaɪ.naɪˈgwent, ˌbleɪ.ni-
Blaenavon blaɪˈnæv.ᵊn
blah-blah ˈblɑː.blɑː, ˌ-ˈ-
Blaikie ˈbleɪ.ki
Blaikley ˈbleɪ.kli
blain bleɪn **-s** -z
Blair bleəʳ US bler
Blair Atholl ˌbleəʳˈæθ.ᵊl US ˌbler-
Blairgowrie ˌbleəˈgaʊə.ri US ˌbler-
Blaise bleɪz
Blake bleɪk
Blakely ˈbleɪ.kli
Blakeney ˈbleɪk.ni

Blakey 'bleɪ.ki
Blakiston 'blæk.ɪ.stᵊn, 'bleɪ.kɪ-
blamab|le 'bleɪ.mə.bl̩ **-ly** -li **-leness** -l̩.nəs, -nɪs
blam|e bleɪm **-es** -z **-ing** -ɪŋ **-ed** -d
blameless 'bleɪm.ləs, -lɪs **-ly** -li **-ness** -nəs, -nɪs
blameworth|y 'bleɪm,wɜː.ðli (US) -,wɜːr- **-iness** -ɪ.nəs, -ɪ.nɪs
Blamires blə'maɪəz (US) -'maɪɚz
Blanc *Mont:* blɑ̃ːŋ (US) blɑ̃ːŋ, blɑːŋk
blanch blɑːntʃ (US) blæntʃ **-es** -ɪz **-ing** -ɪŋ **-ed** -t
Blanchard 'blæn.tʃəd, -tʃɑːd (US) 'blænt.ʃɚd, -ʃɑːrd
Blanche blɑːntʃ (US) blæntʃ
Blanchflower 'blɑːntʃ.flaʊəʳ (US) 'blæntʃ.flaʊɚ
blancmang|e blə'mɒndʒ, -'mɒ̃nʒ (US) -'mɑːndʒ, -'mɑːnʒ **-es** -ɪz
blanco 'blæŋ.kəʊ (US) -koʊ
bland (B) blænd **-er** -əʳ (US) -ɚ **-est** -ɪst, -əst **-ly** -li **-ness** -nəs, -nɪs
Blandford 'blænd.fəd (US) -fɚd
blandish 'blæn.dɪʃ **-es** -ɪz **-ing** -ɪŋ **-ed** -t
blandishment 'blæn.dɪʃ.mᵊnt **-s**
Blandy 'blæn.di
Blaney 'bleɪ.ni
blank (*n. adj. v.*) blæŋk **-s** -s **-er** -əʳ (US) -ɚ **-est** -ɪst, -əst **-ly** -li **-ness** -nəs, -nɪs **-ing** -ɪŋ **-ed** -t ,**blank 'cheque/check**; ,**blank 'verse**
blan|ket 'blæŋ|.kɪt **-kets** -kɪts **-keting** -kɪ.tɪŋ (US) -kɪ.t̬ɪŋ **-keted** -kɪ.tɪd (US) -kɪ.t̬ɪd
Blankley 'blæŋ.kli
blanquette ,blɒŋ'ket, ,blæŋ-, ,blɑ̃ːŋ- (US) ,blɑːŋ- **-s** -s
Blantyre blæn'taɪəʳ, '-- (US) blæn'taɪɚ
Note: In Malawi the preferred stress pattern is /'--/.
blar|e bleəʳ (US) bler **-es** -z **-ing** -ɪŋ **-ed** -d
blarney (B) 'blɑː.ni (US) 'blɑːr-
blasé 'blɑː.zeɪ, blɑː'zeɪ (US) -'-
blasphem|e ,blæs'fiːm, ,blɑːs- (US) 'blæs.fiːm **-es** -z **-ing/ly** -ɪŋ/li **-ed** -d **-er/s** -əʳ/z (US) -ɚ/z
blasphemous 'blæs.fə.məs, 'blɑːs-, -fɪ- (US) 'blæs- **-ly** -li
blasphem|y 'blæs.fə.m|i, 'blɑːs-, -fɪ- (US) 'blæs- **-ies** -iz
blast blɑːst (US) blæst **-s** -s **-ing** -ɪŋ **-ed** -ɪd **'blast ,furnace**
blastoderm 'blæs.təʊ.dɜːm (US) -tə.dɜːrm **-s** -z
blast-off 'blɑːst.ɒf (US) 'blæst.ɑːf **-s** -s
blatancy 'bleɪ.tᵊnt.si
blatant 'bleɪ.tᵊnt **-ly** -li
Blatchford 'blætʃ.fəd (US) -fɚd
blath|er 'blæð|.əʳ (US) -ɚ **-ers** -əz (US) -ɚz **-ering** -ᵊr.ɪŋ **-ered** -əd (US) -ɚd
Blawith *in Cumbria:* 'blɑːð *road in Harrow:* 'bleɪ.wɪθ
Blaydes bleɪdz
Blaydon 'bleɪ.dᵊn
blaz|e bleɪz **-es** -ɪz **-ing** -ɪŋ **-ed** -d
blazer 'bleɪ.zəʳ (US) -zɚ **-s** -z
Blazes 'bleɪ.zɪz
Blazey 'bleɪ.zi
blazon 'bleɪ.zᵊn *in original heraldic sense also:* 'blæz.ᵊn **-s** -z **-ing** -ɪŋ **-ed** -d
bleach bliːtʃ **-es** -ɪz **-ing** -ɪŋ **-ed** -t **'bleaching ,powder**
bleachers 'bliː.tʃəz (US) -tʃɚ/z
bleak bliːk **-er** -əʳ (US) -ɚ **-est** -ɪst, -əst **-ly** -li **-ness** -nəs, -nɪs
Bleakley 'bliː.kli
blear blɪəʳ (US) blɪr
blear|y 'blɪə.r|i (US) 'blɪr|.i **-ier** -i.əʳ (US) -i.ɚ **-iest** -i.ɪst (US) -i.əst **-ily** -ᵊl.i, -ɪ.li **-iness** -ɪ.nəs, -ɪ.nɪs
bleary-eyed ,blɪə.ri'aɪd (US) 'blɪr.i.aɪd- *stress shift, British only:* ,bleary-eyed 'child
Bleasedale 'bliːz.deɪl
bleat bliːt **-s** -s **-ing** -ɪŋ (US) 'bliː.t̬ɪŋ **-ed** -ɪd (US) 'bliː.t̬ɪd
bleb bleb **-s** -z
bled (*from* **bleed**) bled
Bledisloe 'bled.ɪ.sləʊ (US) -sloʊ
bleed bliːd **-s** -z **-ing** -ɪŋ **-er/s** -əʳ/z (US) -ɚ/z **bled** bled
bleep bliːp **-s** -s **-ing** -ɪŋ **-ed** -t
bleeper 'bliː.pəʳ (US) -pɚ **-s** -s
blemish 'blem.ɪʃ **-es** -ɪz **-ing** -ɪŋ **-ed** -t
blench (B) blentʃ **-es** -ɪz **-ing** -ɪŋ **-ed** -t
Blencowe 'bleŋ.kəʊ (US) -koʊ
blend blend **-s** -z **-ing** -ɪŋ **-ed** -ɪd
blende blend
blender 'blen.dəʳ (US) -dɚ **-s** -z
Blenheim 'blen.ɪm, -əm
Blenkinsop 'bleŋ.kɪn.sɒp (US) -sɑːp
Blennerhassett ,blen.ə'hæs.ɪt (US) 'blen.ɚ.hæs-
Blériot 'bler.i.əʊ (US) ,bler.i'oʊ, '--- **-s** -z
bless bles **-es** -ɪz **-ing** -ɪŋ **-ed** -t **blest** blest
blessed (*adj.*) 'bles.ɪd, -əd **-ly** -li **-ness** -nəs, -nɪs
blessing 'bles.ɪŋ **-s** -z **a ,blessing in dis'guise**
Blessington 'bles.ɪŋ.tən
blest (*from* **bless**) blest
Bletchley 'bletʃ.li
bleth|er 'bleð|.əʳ (US) -ɚ **-ers** -əz (US) -ɚz **-ering** -ᵊr.ɪŋ **-ered** -əd (US) -ɚd
blew (*from* **blow**) bluː
Blewett, Blewitt bluː.ɪt
Blickling 'blɪk.lɪŋ
Bligh blaɪ
blight blaɪt **-s** -s **-ing** -ɪŋ (US) 'blaɪ.t̬ɪŋ **-ed** -ɪd (US) 'blaɪ.t̬ɪd
blighter 'blaɪ.təʳ (US) -t̬ɚ **-s** -z
Blighty 'blaɪ.ti (US) -t̬i
blimey 'blaɪ.mi
blimp blɪmp **-s** -s **-ish** -ɪʃ
blind blaɪnd **-er** -əʳ (US) -ɚ **-est** -ɪst, -əst **-ly** -li **-ness** -nəs, -nɪs **-s** -z **-ing** -ɪŋ **-ed** -ɪd ,**blind 'date**; **'blind ,side**; **'blind ,spot**; **as ,blind as a 'bat**; **(a ,case of) the ,blind ,leading the 'blind**; ,**turn a ,blind 'eye (to)**
blinder 'blaɪn.dəʳ (US) -dɚ **-s** -z
blindfold 'blaɪnd.fəʊld (US) -foʊld **-s** -z **-ing** -ɪŋ **-ed** -ɪd
blindman's-buff ,blaɪnd.mænz'bʌf
blindworm 'blaɪnd.wɜːm (US) -wɜːrm **-s** -z
blini 'blɪn.i, 'bliː.ni **-s** -z
blink blɪŋk **-s** -s **-ing** -ɪŋ **-ed** -t
blinker 'blɪŋ.kəʳ (US) -kɚ **-s** -z **-ed** -d
blip blɪp **-s** -s **-ping** -ɪŋ **-ped** -t
bliss (B) blɪs
Blissett 'blɪs.ɪt
blissful 'blɪs.fᵊl, -fʊl **-ly** -i **-ness** -nəs, -nɪs
blist|er 'blɪs.t|əʳ (US) -t|ɚ **-ers** -əz (US) -ɚz **-ering** -ᵊr.ɪŋ **-ered** -əd (US) -ɚd
blith|e blaɪð **-er** -əʳ (US) -ɚ **-est** -ɪst, -əst **-ely** -li **-eness** -nəs, -nɪs
Blithedale 'blaɪð.deɪl
blithering 'blɪð.ᵊr.ɪŋ
blithesome 'blaɪð.səm **-ly** -li **-ness** -nəs, -nɪs
BLit(t) ,biː'lɪt
blitz blɪts **-es** -ɪz **-ing** -ɪŋ **-ed** -t
blitzkrieg 'blɪts.kriːg **-s** -z
Blixen 'blɪk.sᵊn
blizzard 'blɪz.əd (US) -ɚd **-s** -z
bloat bləʊt (US) bloʊt **-s** -s **-ing** -ɪŋ (US) 'bloʊ.t̬ɪŋ **-ed/ness** -ɪd/nəs, -nɪs (US) 'bloʊ.t̬ɪd/nəs, -nɪs
bloater 'bləʊ.təʳ (US) 'bloʊ.t̬ɚ **-s** -z
blob blɒb (US) blɑːb **-s** -z
blobb|y 'blɒb|.i (US) 'blɑː.b|i **-ier** -i.əʳ (US) -i.ɚ **-iest** -i.ɪst, -ɪ.əst
bloc blɒk (US) blɑːk **-s** -s
Bloch blɒk *as if German:* blox (US) blɑːk
block (B) blɒk (US) blɑːk **-s** -s **-ing** -ɪŋ **-ed** -t **-er/s** -əʳ/z (US) -ɚ/z ,**block 'capitals**; ,**block 'booking**
blockad|e blɒk'eɪd, blə'keɪd (US) blɑː'keɪd **-es** -z **-ing** -ɪŋ **-ed** -ɪd **-er/s** -əʳ/z (US) -ɚ/z
blockag|e 'blɒk.ɪdʒ (US) 'blɑː.kɪdʒ **-es** -ɪz
blockbust|er 'blɒk,bʌs.t|əʳ (US) 'blɑːk,bʌs.t|ɚ **-ers** -əz (US) -ɚz **-ering** -ᵊr.ɪŋ
blockhead 'blɒk.hed (US) 'blɑːk- **-s** -z
blockhou|se 'blɒk.hau|s (US) 'blɑːk- **-ses** -zɪz

Blodwen ˈblɒd.wɪn, -wen (US) ˈblɑːd-
Bloemfontein ˈbluːm.fən.teɪn, -fɒn- (US) -fɑːn-
Blofeld ˈbləʊ.felt, -feld (US) ˈbloʊ-
Blois *town in France:* blwɑː *surname:* blɔɪs
bloke bləʊk (US) bloʊk **-s** -s
Blom blɒm (US) blɑːm
Blomefield ˈbluːm.fiːld
Blomfield ˈblɒm.fiːld, ˈblʊm-, ˈblʌm-, ˈbluːm- (US) ˈblɑːm-, ˈblʊm-, ˈblʌm-, ˈbluːm-
blond(e) blɒnd (US) blɑːnd **-s** -z
Blondel(l) ˈblʌn.dᵊl, ˈblɒn-; blɒnˈdel (US) blɑːnˈdel; ˈblɑːn.dᵊl, ˈblʌn-
Blondin ˈblɒn.dɪn *as if French:* blɔ̃ːnˈdæ̃ŋ (US) blɑːnˈdæn
blood blʌd **-s** -z ˈ**blood ˌcell** ; ˈ**blood ˌdonor** ; ˈ**blood ˌgroup** ; ˈ**blood ˌmoney** ; ˈ**blood ˌpoisoning** ; ˈ**blood ˌpressure** ; ˌ**blood reˈlation** ; ˈ**blood ˌsport** ; ˈ**blood ˌtest** ; ˈ**blood transˌfusion** ; ˈ**blood ˌvessel** ; ˌ**blood is thicker than ˈwater** ; **get ˌblood out of a ˈstone** ; **in ˌcold ˈblood**
bloodba|th ˈblʌd.bɑː|θ (US) -bæ|θ **-ths** -ðz
bloodcurdling ˈblʌdˌkɜː.dl̩.ɪŋ, -ˌkɜːd.lɪŋ (US) -ˌkɜːr.dl̩.ɪŋ, -ˌkɜːrd.lɪŋ **-ly** -li
bloodhound ˈblʌd.haʊnd **-s** -z
bloodless ˈblʌd.ləs, -lɪs **-ly** -li **-ness** -nəs, -nɪs
bloodletting ˈblʌdˌlet.ɪŋ (US) -ˌlet̬.ɪŋ
bloodline ˈblʌd.laɪn
blood-red ˌblʌdˈred *stress shift:* ˌblood-red ˈlips
bloodshed ˈblʌd.ʃed
bloodshot ˈblʌd.ʃɒt (US) -ʃɑːt
bloodstain ˈblʌd.steɪn **-s** -z **-ed** -d
bloodstock ˈblʌd.stɒk (US) -stɑːk
bloodstone ˈblʌd.stəʊn (US) -stoʊn **-s** -z
bloodstream ˈblʌd.striːm **-s** -z
bloodsucker ˈblʌdˌsʌk.əʳ (US) -ɚ **-s** -z
bloodthirst|y ˈblʌdˌθɜː.st|i (US) -ˌθɜːr- **-ier** -i.əʳ (US) -i.ɚ **-iest** -i.ɪst, -i.əst **-ily** -ɪ.li, -ᵊl.i **-iness** -ɪ.nəs, -ɪ.nɪs
blood|y ˈblʌd|.i **-ier** -i.əʳ (US) -i.ɚ **-iest** -i.ɪst, -i.əst **-ily** -ɪ.li, -ᵊl.i **-iness** -ɪ.nəs, -ɪ.nɪs ˌ**Bloody ˈMary**
bloody-minded ˌblʌd.iˈmaɪn.dɪd *stress shift:* ˌbloody-minded ˈperson
bloom (B) bluːm **-s** -z **-ing** -ɪŋ **-ed** -d
bloomer (B) ˈbluː.məʳ (US) -mɚ **-s** -z
Bloomfield ˈbluːm.fiːld
Bloomingdale ˈbluː.mɪŋ.deɪl **-'s** -z
Bloomington ˈbluː.mɪŋ.tən
Bloomsbury ˈbluːmz.bᵊr.i (US) -ber-, -bɚ-
bloop bluːp **-s** -s **-ing** -ɪŋ **-ed** -t
blooper ˈbluː.pəʳ (US) -pɚ **-s** -z

Blore blɔːʳ (US) blɔːr
blossom (B) ˈblɒs.ᵊm (US) ˈblɑː.sᵊm **-s** -z **-ing** -ɪŋ **-ed** -d
blot blɒt (US) blɑːt **-s** -s **-ting** -ɪŋ (US) ˈblɑː.t̬ɪŋ **-ted** -ɪd (US) ˈblɑː.t̬ɪd
blotch blɒtʃ (US) blɑːtʃ **-es** -ɪz **-ing** -ɪŋ **-ed** -t
blotch|y ˈblɒtʃ|.i (US) ˈblɑː.tʃ|i **-ier** -i.əʳ (US) -i.ɚ **-iest** -i.ɪst, -i.əst **-ily** -ɪ.li, -ᵊl.i **-iness** -ɪ.nəs, -ɪ.nɪs
blotter ˈblɒt.əʳ (US) ˈblɑː.t̬ɚ **-s** -z
blotting ˈblɒt.ɪŋ (US) ˈblɑː.t̬.ɪŋ ˈ**blotting ˌpaper**
blotto ˈblɒt.əʊ (US) ˈblɑː.t̬oʊ
Blount blʌnt, blaʊnt
blous|e blaʊz (US) blaʊs **-es** -ɪz
blouson ˈbluː.zɒn (US) -sɑːn, ˈblaʊ-, -zɑːn **-s** -z
blow (B) bləʊ (US) bloʊ **-s** -z **-ing** -ɪŋ **blew** bluː **blown** bləʊn (US) bloʊn **blowed** bləʊd (US) bloʊd **blower/s** ˈbləʊ.əʳ/z (US) ˈbloʊ.ɚ/s
blow-by-blow ˌbləʊ.baɪˈbləʊ (US) ˌbloʊ.baɪˈbloʊ *stress shift:* ˌblow-by-blow acˈcount
blow|dry ˈbləʊ|.draɪ (US) ˈbloʊ- **-dries** -draɪz **-drying** -ˌdraɪ.ɪŋ **-dried** -draɪd **-drier/s** -ˌdraɪ.əʳ/z (US) -ˌdraɪ.ɚ/z
blowfl|y ˈbləʊ.fl|aɪ (US) ˈbloʊ- **-ies** -aɪz
blowgun ˈbləʊ.gʌn (US) ˈbloʊ- **-s** -z
blowhard ˈbləʊ.hɑːd (US) ˈbloʊ.hɑːrd **-s** -z
blowhole ˈbləʊ.həʊl (US) ˈbloʊ.hoʊl **-s** -z
blowlamp ˈbləʊ.læmp (US) ˈbloʊ- **-s** -s
blown (*from* **blow**) bləʊn (US) bloʊn
blowout ˈbləʊ.aʊt (US) ˈbloʊ- **-s** -s
blowpipe ˈbləʊ.paɪp (US) ˈbloʊ- **-s** -s
blows|y ˈblaʊ.z|i **-ier** -i.əʳ (US) -i.ɚ **-iest** -i.ɪst, -i.əst **-ily** -ɪ.li, -ᵊl.i **-iness** -ɪ.nəs, -ɪ.nɪs
blowtorch ˈbləʊ.tɔːtʃ (US) ˈbloʊ.tɔːrtʃ **-es** -ɪz
blow|y ˈbləʊ|.i (US) ˈbloʊ- **-ier** -i.əʳ (US) -i.ɚ **-iest** -i.ɪst, -i.əst **-ily** -ɪ.li, -ᵊl.i **-iness** -ɪ.nəs, -ɪ.nɪs
blowz|y ˈblaʊ.z|i **-ier** -i.əʳ (US) -i.ɚ **-iest** -i.ɪst, -i.əst **-ily** -ɪ.li, -ᵊl.i **-iness** -ɪ.nəs, -ɪ.nɪs
Blox(h)am ˈblɒk.səm (US) ˈblɑːk-
BLT ˌbiː.elˈtiː
blub blʌb **-s** -z **-bing** -ɪŋ **-bed** -d
blubb|er ˈblʌb|.əʳ (US) -ɚ **-ers** -əz (US) -ɚz **-ering** -ᵊr.ɪŋ **-ered** -əd (US) -ɚd **-erer/s** -ᵊr.əʳ/z
bludgeon ˈblʌdʒ.ᵊn **-s** -z **-ing** -ɪŋ **-ed** -d
blu|e bluː **-es** -z **-er** -əʳ (US) -ɚ **-est** -ɪst, -əst **-(e)ing** -ɪŋ **-ed** -d ˌ**blue ˈcheese** ; ˈ**blue ˌlaw**; ˌ**blue ˈmovie**; ˈ**blue ˌjay**; ˈ**blue ˌtit**; ˌ**out of the ˈblue**
Bluebeard ˈbluː.bɪəd (US) -bɪrd
bluebell ˈbluː.bel **-s** -z

blueberr|y ˈbluː.bᵊr|.i, -ˌber- (US) -ˌber- **-ies** -iz
bluebird ˈbluː.bɜːd (US) -bɜːrd **-s** -z
blue-blooded ˌbluːˈblʌd.ɪd (US) ˈ-ˌ-- *stress shift, British only:* ˌblue-blooded ˈmonarch
bluebottle ˈbluːˌbɒt.l̩ (US) -ˌbɑː.t̬l̩ **-s** -z
bluecoat ˈbluː.kəʊt (US) -koʊt **-s** -s
blue-collar ˌbluːˈkɒl.əʳ (US) ˈbluːˌkɑː.lɚ *stress shift, British only:* ˌblue-collar ˈworker
blue-eyed ˌbluːˈaɪd, ˈ-- *stress shift, British only: see compound:* ˌ**blue-eyed ˈboy**
bluegrass ˈbluː.grɑːs (US) -græs
bluejacket ˈbluːˌdʒæk.ɪt **-s** -s
bluejeans, blue jeans ˌbluːˈdʒiːnz (US) ˈ--
blueness ˈbluː.nəs, -nɪs
blue-pencil ˌbluːˈpent.sᵊl, -sɪl (US) ˈ-ˌ-- **-s** -z **-(l)ing** -ɪŋ **-(l)ed** -d
blueprint ˈbluː.prɪnt **-s** -s
bluestocking ˈbluːˌstɒk.ɪŋ (US) -ˌstɑː.kɪŋ **-s** -z
Bluett ˈbluː.ɪt
bluey ˈbluː.i
bluff blʌf **-s** -s **-er** -əʳ (US) -ɚ **-est** -ɪst, -əst **-ly** -li **-ness** -nəs, -nɪs **-ing** -ɪŋ **-ed** -t
bluish ˈbluː.ɪʃ
Blum bluːm
Blume bluːm
Blundell ˈblʌn.dᵊl; blʌnˈdel
Blunden ˈblʌn.dən
blund|er ˈblʌn.d|əʳ (US) -d|ɚ **-ers** -əz (US) -ɚz **-ering** -ᵊr.ɪŋ **-ered** -əd (US) -ɚd **-erer/s** -ᵊr.əʳ/z (US) -ɚ.ɚ/z
blunderbuss ˈblʌn.də.bʌs (US) -dɚ- **-es** -ɪz
Blunkett ˈblʌŋ.kɪt
Blunn blʌn
blunt (B) blʌnt **-er** -əʳ (US) ˈblʌn.t̬ɚ **-est** -ɪst, -əst (US) ˈblʌn.t̬ɪst, -t̬əst **-ly** -li **-ness** -nəs, -nɪs **-s** -s **-ing** -ɪŋ (US) ˈblʌn.t̬ɪŋ **-ed** -ɪd (US) ˈblʌn.t̬ɪd ˌ**blunt ˈinstrument**
blur (B) blɜːʳ (US) blɜːr **-s** -z **-ring** -ɪŋ **-red** -d
blurb blɜːb (US) blɜːrb **-s** -z
blurt blɜːt (US) blɜːrt **-s** -s **-ing** -ɪŋ (US) ˈblɜːr.t̬ɪŋ **-ed** -ɪd (US) ˈblɜːr.t̬ɪd
blush blʌʃ **-es** -ɪz **-ing/ly** -ɪŋ/li **-ed** -t
blusher ˈblʌʃ.əʳ (US) -ɚ **-s** -z
blust|er ˈblʌs.t|əʳ (US) -t|ɚ **-ers** -əz (US) -ɚz **-ering/ly** -ᵊr.ɪŋ/li **-ered** -əd (US) -ɚd **-erer/s** -ᵊr.əʳ/z (US) -ɚ.ɚ/z
bluster|y ˈblʌs.tᵊr|.i **-iness** -ɪ.nəs, -ɪ.nɪs
Blu-Tack® ˈbluː.tæk
Bly blaɪ
Blyth blaɪð, blaɪθ, blaɪ
Blythborough ˈblaɪ.bᵊr.ə (US) -oʊ

Blythe blaɪð
Blyton ˈblaɪ.tᵊn
B-movie ˈbiːˌmuː.vi **-s** -z
BMus ˌbiːˈmʌz
BMW® ˌbiː.emˈdʌb.l̩.ju
BMX ˌbiː.emˈeks *stress shift, see compound:* ˌ**BMX** ˈ**bike**
bn (*abbrev. for* **billion**) ˈbɪl.i.ən, ˈ-jən (US) ˈ-jən
Bo bəʊ (US) boʊ
BO ˌbiːˈəʊ (US) -ˈoʊ
boa bəʊə (US) boʊə **-s** -z
Boadicea ˌbəʊ.dɪˈsiː.ə, -dəˈ- (US) ˌboʊ.ə-
Boag bəʊg; ˈbəʊ.æg, -əg (US) boʊg
Boal bəʊl (US) boʊl
Boanas ˈbəʊ.nəs (US) ˈboʊ-
Boanerges ˌbəʊəˈnɜː.dʒiːz (US) ˌboʊəˈnɜːr-
boar bɔːʳ (US) bɔːr **-s** -z
board bɔːd (US) bɔːrd **-s** -z **-ing** -ɪŋ **-ed** -ɪd ˈ**board** ˌ**game** ; ˈ**boarding** ˌ**house** ; ˈ**boarding** ˌ**pass** ; ˈ**boarding** ˌ**school** ; ˌ**go by the** ˈ**board**
boarder ˈbɔː.dəʳ (US) ˈbɔːr.dɚ **-s** -z
boardroom ˈbɔːd.rʊm, -ruːm (US) ˈbɔːrd.ruːm, -rʊm **-s** -z
boardwalk ˈbɔːd.wɔːk (US) ˈbɔːrd.wɔːk, -wɑːk **-s** -s
boarish ˈbɔː.rɪʃ (US) ˈbɔːr.ɪʃ
Boas ˈbəʊ.æz, -əz, -æs, -əs (US) ˈboʊ-
Boase bəʊz (US) boʊz
boast bəʊst (US) boʊst **-s** -s **-ing/ly** -ɪŋ/li **-ed** -ɪd **-er/s** -əʳ/z (US) -ɚ/z
boastful ˈbəʊst.fᵊl, -fʊl (US) ˈboʊst- **-ly** -li **-ness** -nəs, -nɪs
boat bəʊt (US) boʊt **-s** -s **-er/s** -əʳ/z (US) ˈboʊ.t̬ɚ/z ˈ**boat** ˌ**race** ; ˈ**boat** ˌ**train** ; ˌ**burn one's** ˈ**boats**
Boateng ˈbwɑː.teŋ, ˈbəʊ- (US) ˈbwɑː-, ˈboʊ-
boathook ˈbəʊt.hʊk (US) ˈboʊt- **-s** -s
boathou|se ˈbəʊt.haʊ|s (US) ˈboʊt- **-ses** -zɪz
boating ˈbəʊ.tɪŋ (US) ˈboʊ.t̬ɪŋ
boatload ˈbəʊt.ləʊd (US) ˈboʊt.loʊd **-s** -z
boat|man ˈbəʊt|.mən (US) ˈboʊt- **-men** -mən, -men
boatswain ˈbəʊ.sᵊn, ˈbəʊt.sweɪn (US) ˈboʊ.sᵊn **-s** -z
boatyard ˈbəʊt.jɑːd (US) ˈboʊt.jɑːrd **-s** -z
Boaz ˈbəʊ.æz (US) ˈboʊ-
bob (B) bɒb (US) bɑːb **-s** -z **-bing** -ɪŋ **-bed** -d
Bobbie ˈbɒb.i (US) ˈbɑː.bi
bobbin ˈbɒb.ɪn (US) ˈbɑː.bɪn **-s** -z
bobbish ˈbɒb.ɪʃ (US) ˈbɑː.bɪʃ **-ly** -li **-ness** -nəs, -nɪs
bobble ˈbɒb.l̩ (US) ˈbɑː.bl̩ **-s** -z
bobb|y (B) ˈbɒb|.i (US) ˈbɑː.b|i **-ies** -iz ˈ**bobby** ˌ**pin**
bobbysox ˈbɒb.i.sɒks (US) ˈbɑː.bi.sɑːks **-er/s** -əʳ/z (US) -ɚ/z
bobcat ˈbɒb.kæt (US) ˈbɑːb- **-s** -s
Bobo Dioulasso ˌbəʊ.bəʊ.djuˈlæs.əʊ (US) ˌboʊ.boʊ.djuˈlæs.oʊ
bobolink ˈbɒb.ə.lɪŋk (US) ˈbɑː.bə- **-s** -s
bobsled ˈbɒb.sled (US) ˈbɑːb- **-s** -z **-ding** -ɪŋ **-ded** -ɪd
bobsleigh ˈbɒb.sleɪ (US) ˈbɑːb- **-s** -z
bobstay ˈbɒb.steɪ (US) ˈbɑːb- **-s** -z
bobtail ˈbɒb.teɪl (US) ˈbɑːb- **-s** -z
bobwig ˈbɒb.wɪg (US) ˈbɑːb- **-s** -z
Boca Raton ˌbəʊ.kə.rəˈtəʊn (US) ˌboʊ.kə.rəˈtoʊn
Boccaccio bɒkˈɑː.tʃi.əʊ, bəˈkɑː- (US) boʊˈkɑː-
Boccherini ˌbɒk.ᵊrˈiː.ni (US) ˌbɑː.kəˈriː-, ˌboʊ-
Boche(s) bɒʃ (US) bɑːʃ, bɔːʃ
Bochum ˈbəʊ.kᵊm (US) ˈboʊ-
bod bɒd (US) bɑːd **-s** -z
bodacious bəʊˈdeɪ.ʃəs (US) boʊ- **-ly** -li
Boddington ˈbɒd.ɪŋ.tən (US) ˈbɑː.dɪŋ-
Boddy ˈbɒd.i (US) ˈbɑː.di
bod|e (B) bəʊd (US) boʊd **-es** -z **-ing** -ɪŋ **-ed** -ɪd
bodega (B) bəˈdeɪ.gə, bɒdˈeɪ- (US) boʊˈdeɪ- **-s** -z
Boden ˈbəʊ.dᵊn (US) ˈboʊ-
Bodey ˈbəʊ.di (US) ˈboʊ-
bodg|e bɒdʒ (US) bɑːdʒ **-es** -ɪz **-ing** -ɪŋ **-ed** -d
bodger ˈbɒdʒ.əʳ (US) ˈbɑː.dʒɚ **-s** -z
Bodiam ˈbəʊ.di.əm (US) ˈboʊ-
bodic|e ˈbɒd.ɪs (US) ˈbɑː.dɪs **-es** -ɪz
Bodie ˈbəʊ.di (US) ˈboʊ-
-bodied -ˈbɒd.id (US) -ˈbɑː.did
Note: Suffix. Always carries primary stress unless used attributively, e.g. **full-bodied** /ˌfʊlˈbɒd.id (US) -ˈbɑː.did/, ˌ**full-bodied** ˈ**wine**.
bodily ˈbɒd.ɪ.li, -ᵊl.i (US) ˈbɑː.dᵊl.i ˌ**bodily** ˈ**function**
bodkin (B) ˈbɒd.kɪn (US) ˈbɑːd- **-s** -z
Bodleian ˈbɒd.li.ən, bɒdˈliː- (US) ˈbɑːd.li.ən, bɑːdˈliː-
Bodley ˈbɒd.li (US) ˈbɑːd-
Bodmin ˈbɒd.mɪn (US) ˈbɑːd-
Bodnant ˈbɒd.nænt (US) ˈbɑːd-
bod|y ˈbɒd|.i (US) ˈbɑː.d|i **-ies** -iz ˈ**body** ˌ**bag**; ˈ**body** ˌ**builder**; ˈ**body** ˌ**building**; ˈ**body** ˌ**language**; ˈ**body** ˌ**snatcher**; **keep** ˌ**body and** ˌ**soul to**ˈ**gether**; **over** ˌ**my** ˌ**dead** ˈ**body**
bodyguard ˈbɒd.i.gɑːd (US) ˈbɑː.di.gɑːrd **-s** -z
bodysurf ˈbɒd.i.sɜːf (US) ˈbɑː.di.sɜːrf **-s** -s **-ing** -ɪŋ **-ed** -t **-er/s** -əʳ/z (US) -ɚ/z
bodywarmer ˈbɒd.iˌwɔː.məʳ (US) ˈbɑː.diˌwɔːr.mɚ **-s** -z
bodywork ˈbɒd.i.wɜːk (US) ˈbɑː.di.wɜːrk
Boeing® ˈbəʊ.ɪŋ (US) ˈboʊ-
Boeoti|a biˈəʊ.ʃ|ə, -ʃi|.ə (US) -ˈoʊ.ʃ|ə **-an/s** -ən/z
Boer bəʊəʳ, bɔːʳ, bʊəʳ (US) bɔːr, boʊɚ, bʊr **-s** -z
Boethius bəʊˈiː.θi.əs (US) boʊ-
boeuf bourguignon ˌbɜːfˌbʊə.giːˈnjɔ̃ːŋ, -ˌbɔː-, -gɪˈ- (US) ˌbɜːfˌbʊr.giːˈnjõʊn
boffin (B) ˈbɒf.ɪn (US) ˈbɑː.fɪn **-s** -z
Bofors ˈbəʊ.fəz (US) ˈboʊ.fɔːrz, -fɔːrs
bog bɒg (US) bɑːg, bɔːg **-s** -z **-ging** -ɪŋ **-ged** -d
Bogan ˈbəʊ.gᵊn (US) ˈboʊ-
Bogarde ˈbəʊ.gɑːd (US) ˈboʊ.gɑːrd
Bogart ˈbəʊ.gɑːt (US) ˈboʊ.gɑːrt
Bogdan ˈbɒg.dæn (US) ˈbɑːg-, ˈbɔːg-
bogey ˈbəʊ.gi (US) ˈboʊ- **-s** -z
bogey|man ˈbəʊ.gi|.mæn (US) ˈboʊ- **-men** -men
boggl|e ˈbɒg.l̩ (US) ˈbɑː.gl̩ **-es** -z **-ing** -ɪŋ, ˈ-lɪŋ (US) ˈ-glɪŋ **-ed** -d **-er/s** -əʳ/z, ˈ-ləʳ/z (US) ˈbɑː.gl̩.ɚ/z, ˈbɑːg.lɚ/z
bogg|y ˈbɒg|.i (US) ˈbɑː.g|i **-ier** -i.əʳ (US) -i.ɚ **-iest** -i.ɪst, -i.əst **-iness** -ɪ.nəs, -ɪ.nɪs
bogie ˈbəʊ.gi (US) ˈboʊ- **-s** -z ˈ**bogie** ˌ**engine** ; ˈ**bogie** ˌ**wheel**
Bognor ˈbɒg.nəʳ (US) ˈbɑːg.nɚ, ˈbɔːg- ˌ**Bognor** ˈ**Regis**
bog-oak ˌbɒgˈəʊk (US) ˈbɑːg.oʊk, ˈbɔːg-
Bogota *in Columbia:* ˌbɒg.əʊˈtɑː, ˌbəʊ.gə- (US) ˌboʊ.gəˈtɑː, ˈ--- *in New Jersey:* bəˈgəʊ.tə (US) -ˈgoʊ.t̬ə
bogstandard ˌbɒgˈstæn.dəd (US) ˈbɑːgˌstæn.dɚd, ˈbɔːg-,
bogus ˈbəʊ.gəs (US) ˈboʊ-
bog|y ˈbəʊ.g|i (US) ˈboʊ- **-ies** -iz
bohea bəʊˈhiː (US) boʊ-
Bohème bəʊˈem, -ˈeɪm (US) boʊ-
Bohemia bəʊˈhiː.mi.ə (US) boʊ-
bohemian (B) bəʊˈhiː.mi.ən (US) boʊ- **-s** -z
Böhm bɜːm
Bohn bəʊn (US) boʊn
Bohr bɔːʳ (US) bɔːr
Bohun ˈbəʊ.ən, buːn (US) ˈboʊ-, buːn
Note: /buːn/ in Shaw's 'You never can tell'.
boil bɔɪl **-s** -z **-ing** -ɪŋ **-ed** -d ˈ**boiling** ˌ**point**
boiler ˈbɔɪ.ləʳ (US) -lɚ **-s** -z ˈ**boiler** ˌ**suit**
boilermaker ˈbɔɪ.ləˌmeɪ.kəʳ (US) -lɚˌmeɪ.kɚ **-s** -z
boilerplate ˈbɔɪ.lə.pleɪt (US) -lɚ- **-s** -s
boil-in-the-bag ˌbɔɪl.ɪn.ðəˈbæg *stress shift:* ˌboil-in-the-bag ˈmeal
boing bɔɪŋ
Boipatong ˌbɔɪ.pəˈtɒŋ, -pætˈɒŋ (US) ˈbɔɪ.pə.tɑːŋ, -tɔːŋ

Bois bɔɪs, bwɑː
Boise ˈbɔɪ.zi, ˈbɔɪ.si
boisterous ˈbɔɪ.stᵊr.əs **-ly** -li **-ness** -nəs, -nɪs
Boker ˈbəʊ.kəʳ ⓤⓢ ˈboʊ.kɚ
Bokhara bəʊˈkɑː.rə ⓤⓢ boʊˈkɑːr.ə
Bolan ˈbəʊ.lən ⓤⓢ ˈboʊ-
bolas ˈbəʊ.ləs, -læs ⓤⓢ ˈboʊ- **-es** -ɪz
bold bəʊld ⓤⓢ boʊld **-er** -əʳ ⓤⓢ -ɚ **-est** -ɪst, -əst **-ly** -li **-ness** -nəs, -nɪs
bold-face ˌbəʊldˈfeɪs ⓤⓢ ˈboʊld.feɪs, ˈboʊl- **-d** -t *stress shift, British only:* ˌbold-face ˈtype
Boldon ˈbəʊl.dᵊn ⓤⓢ ˈboʊl-
Boldre ˈbəʊl.dəʳ ⓤⓢ ˈboʊl.dɚ
bole bəʊl ⓤⓢ boʊl **-s** -z
bolero *dance:* bəˈleə.rəʊ, bɒlˈeə-, -ˈlɪə- ⓤⓢ bəˈler.oʊ, boʊ- **-s** -z *garment:* ˈbɒl.ə.rəʊ ⓤⓢ bəˈler.oʊ **-s** -z
bolet|us bəʊˈliː.t|əs ⓤⓢ boʊˈliː.t̬|əs **-uses** -ə.sɪz **-i** -aɪ
Boleyn bəˈlɪn; bʊ-; bəʊ-; -ˈliːn; ˈbʊl.ɪn ⓤⓢ ˈbʊ.lɪn, bʊˈlɪn
Bolingbroke ˈbɒl.ɪŋ.brʊk ⓤⓢ ˈbɑː.lɪŋ-, ˈboʊ-
Bolinger ˈbɒl.ɪn.dʒəʳ, ˈbəʊ.lɪn- ⓤⓢ ˈbɑː.lən.dʒɚ
Bolitho bəˈlaɪ.θəʊ, bɒlˈaɪ- ⓤⓢ bəˈlaɪ.θoʊ
Bolivar *S. American general:* ˈbɒl.ɪ.vɑːʳ; bɒlˈiː- ⓤⓢ ˈbɑː.lə.vɚ *places in US:* ˈbɒl.ɪ.vəʳ, ˈ-ə-, -vɑːʳ ⓤⓢ ˈbɑː.lə.vɚ
bolivar *money:* bɒlˈiː.vɑːʳ; ˈbɒl.ɪ.vəʳ ⓤⓢ boʊˈliː.vɑːr; ˈbɑː.lə.vɚ **-s** -z
bolivares (*alternative plur. of* **bolivar**) ˌbɒl.ɪˈvɑː.reɪz ⓤⓢ boʊˌliː.vɑːˈreɪs; ˌboʊ.lɪˈvɑːr.es
Bolivi|a bəˈlɪv.i|.ə, bɒlˈɪv- ⓤⓢ bəˈlɪv-, boʊ- **-an/s** -ən/z
bolivia|no bəʊˌlɪv.iˈɑː|.nəʊ, bɒlˌɪv-; ˌbəʊ.lɪ.viˈ-, ˌbɒl.ɪv- ⓤⓢ bəˌlɪv.iˈɑː.noʊ, boʊ- **-nos** -nɒs ⓤⓢ -noʊs
boll bəʊl, bɒl ⓤⓢ boʊl **-s** -z **-ed** -d ˌ**boll ˈweevil** ⓤⓢ ˈ**boll** ˌ**weevil**
Böll bɜːl ⓤⓢ bɜːl, boʊl
bollard ˈbɒl.ɑːd, -əd ⓤⓢ ˈbɑː.lɚd **-s** -z
Bolling ˈbəʊ.lɪŋ ⓤⓢ ˈboʊ-
Bollinger ˈbɒl.ɪn.dʒəʳ ⓤⓢ ˈbɑː.lən.dʒɚ
Bollington ˈbɒl.ɪŋ.tən ⓤⓢ ˈbɑː.lɪŋ-
bollix ˈbɒl.ɪks ⓤⓢ ˈbɑː.lɪks **-es** -ɪz **-ing** -ɪŋ **-ed** -t
bollocking ˈbɒl.ə.kɪŋ ⓤⓢ ˈbɑː.lə-
bollocks ˈbɒl.əks ⓤⓢ ˈbɑː.ləks
bolo ˈbəʊ.ləʊ ⓤⓢ ˈboʊ.loʊ **-s** -z
Bologna bəˈlɒn.jə, bɒlˈɒn-, -ˈləʊ.njə, -ni.ə ⓤⓢ bəˈloʊ.njə, -ˈlɑː-
bologna *sausage:* bəˈləʊ.ni ⓤⓢ -ˈloʊ-
bolognaise ˌbɒl.əˈneɪz, -ˈnjeɪz ⓤⓢ ˌboʊ.ləˈnjeɪz
Bolognese ˌbɒl.əˈneɪz *as if Italian:* -ˈnjeɪ.zeɪ ⓤⓢ ˌboʊ.ləˈniːz, -ˈnjiːz

bolometer bəʊˈlɒm.ɪ.təʳ, ˈ-ə- ⓤⓢ boʊˈlɑː.mə.t̬ɚ **-s** -z
boloney bəˈləʊ.ni ⓤⓢ -ˈloʊ-
Bolshevik ˈbɒl.ʃə.vɪk, -ʃɪ- ⓤⓢ ˈboʊl-, ˈbɑːl- **-s** -s
Bolshev|ist ˈbɒl.ʃə.v|ɪst, -ʃɪ- ⓤⓢ ˈboʊl-, ˈbɑːl- **-ism** -ɪ.zᵊm
bolshie ˈbɒl.ʃi ⓤⓢ ˈboʊl-, ˈbɑːl- **-s** -z
Bolshoi, Bolshoy bɒlˈʃɔɪ, ˈ-- ⓤⓢ ˈboʊl.ʃɔɪ, ˈbɑːl-; boʊlˈʃɔɪ
bolshy ˈbɒl.ʃi ⓤⓢ ˈboʊl-, ˈbɑːl- **-s** -z
Bolsover *surname, street in London:* ˈbɒl.səʊ.vəʳ ⓤⓢ ˈboʊl.soʊ.vɚ *in Derbyshire:* ˈbəʊl.zəʊ.vəʳ; ˈbəʊl.səʊ- ⓤⓢ ˈboʊl.zoʊ.vɚ
bolst|er ˈbəʊl.st|əʳ ⓤⓢ ˈboʊl.st|ɚ **-ers** -əz ⓤⓢ -ɚz **-ering** -ᵊr.ɪŋ **-ered** -əd ⓤⓢ -ɚd
bolt (B) bəʊlt ⓤⓢ boʊlt **-s** -s **-ing** -ɪŋ ⓤⓢ ˈboʊl.t̬ɪŋ **-ed** -ɪd ⓤⓢ ˈboʊl.t̬ɪd ˌ**bolt ˈupright**
bolter (B) ˈbəʊl.təʳ ⓤⓢ ˈboʊl.t̬ɚ **-s** -z
Bolton ˈbəʊl.tᵊn ⓤⓢ ˈboʊl-
Bolton-le-Sands ˌbəʊl.tən.ləˈsændz, -lɪˈ- ⓤⓢ ˌboʊl.tᵊn-
bolus ˈbəʊ.ləs ⓤⓢ ˈboʊ- **-es** -ɪz
Bolzano bɒlt*ˈ*zɑː.nəʊ ⓤⓢ boʊltˈsɑː.noʊ, boʊlˈzɑː-
bomb bɒm ⓤⓢ bɑːm **-s** -z **-ing** -ɪŋ **-ed** -d ˌ**bomb disˈposal** ˌ**unit,** ˈ**bomb di**ˌ**sposal** ˌ**unit**
bombard (*n.*) ˈbɒm.bɑːd ⓤⓢ ˈbɑːm.bɑːrd **-s** -z
bombard (*v.*) bɒmˈbɑːd ⓤⓢ bɑːmˈbɑːrd **-s** -z **-ing** -ɪŋ **-ed** -ɪd **-ment/s** -mənt/s
bombardier ˌbɒm.bəˈdɪəʳ ⓤⓢ ˌbɑːm.bəˈdɪr **-s** -z
bombardon ˈbɒm.bə.dᵊn; bɒmˈbɑː- ⓤⓢ ˈbɑːm.bɚ-; bɑːmˈbɑːr- **-s** -z
bombasine ˈbɒm.bə.ziːn, -siːn, ˌ--ˈ- ⓤⓢ ˌbɑːm.bəˈziːn
bombast ˈbɒm.bæst ⓤⓢ ˈbɑːm-
bombastic bɒmˈbæs.tɪk ⓤⓢ bɑːm- **-ally** -ᵊl.i, -li
Bombay ˌbɒmˈbeɪ ⓤⓢ ˌbɑːm- *stress shift, see compound:* ˌ**Bombay ˈduck**
bombe bɒm, bɒmb ⓤⓢ bɑːm **-s** -z
bomber ˈbɒm.əʳ ⓤⓢ ˈbɑː.mɚ **-s** -z
bombshell ˈbɒm.ʃel ⓤⓢ ˈbɑːm- **-s** -z
bombsite ˈbɒm.saɪt ⓤⓢ ˈbɑːm- **-s** -s
Bompas ˈbʌm.pəs
bon bɔ̃ː*ŋ* ⓤⓢ bɔ̃ːn
bona fid|e ˌbəʊ.nəˈfaɪ.d|i, -d|eɪ ⓤⓢ ˌboʊ.nəˈ- **-es** -iːz, -eɪz
bonanza bəˈnæn.zə **-s** -z
Bonapart|e ˈbəʊ.nə.pɑːt ⓤⓢ ˈboʊ.nə.pɑːrt **-ist/s** -ɪst/s
Bonar ˈbɒn.əʳ, ˈbəʊ.nəʳ ⓤⓢ ˈbɑː.nɚ, ˈboʊ-
bonbon ˈbɒn.bɒn, ˈbɒm- ⓤⓢ ˈbɑːn.bɑːn **-s** -z

Bonchurch ˈbɒn.tʃɜːtʃ ⓤⓢ ˈbɑːn.tʃɜːrtʃ
bond (B) bɒnd ⓤⓢ bɑːnd **-s** -z **-ing** -ɪŋ **-ed** -ɪd ˈ**bond** ˌ**holder**
bondage ˈbɒn.dɪdʒ ⓤⓢ ˈbɑːn-
Bondi *place in Australia:* ˈbɒn.daɪ ⓤⓢ ˈbɑːn- ˌ**Bondi ˈBeach**
Bondi *mathematician:* ˈbɒn.di ⓤⓢ ˈbɑːn-
bondmaid ˈbɒnd.meɪd ⓤⓢ ˈbɑːnd- **-s** -z
bond|man ˈbɒnd|.mən ⓤⓢ ˈbɑːnd- **-men** -mən, -men
bonds|man ˈbɒn*d*z|.mən ⓤⓢ ˈbɑːn*d*z- **-men** -mən, -men
bonds|woman ˈbɒn*d*z|ˌwʊm.ən ⓤⓢ ˈbɑːn*d*z- **-women** -ˌwɪm.ɪn
bond|woman ˈbɒnd|ˌwʊm.ən ⓤⓢ ˈbɑːnd- **-women** -ˌwɪm.ɪn
bon|e (B) bəʊn ⓤⓢ boʊn **-es** -z **-ing** -ɪŋ **-ed** -d **-er/s** -əʳ/z ⓤⓢ -ɚ/z **-less** -ləs, -lɪs ˈ**bone** ˌ**meal**; ˈ**bone** ˌ**marrow;** ˌ**chilled to the ˈbone; have a ˈbone to pick with** ˌ**someone;** ˌ**make no ˈbones about something**
bone-dry ˌbəʊnˈdraɪ ⓤⓢ ˌboʊ- *stress shift:* ˌbone-dry ˈdesert
bonehead ˈbəʊn.hed ⓤⓢ ˈboʊn- **-s** -z
bonesetter ˈbəʊnˌset.əʳ ⓤⓢ ˈboʊnˌset̬.ɚ **-s** -z
bone-shaker ˈbəʊnˌʃeɪ.kəʳ ⓤⓢ ˈboʊnˌʃeɪ.kɚ **-s** -z
Bo'ness bəʊˈnes ⓤⓢ boʊ-
bonfire ˈbɒn.faɪəʳ ⓤⓢ ˈbɑːn.faɪɚ **-s** -z ˈ**Bonfire** ˌ**Night**
bongo ˈbɒŋ.gəʊ ⓤⓢ ˈbɑːŋ.goʊ **-(e)s** -z ˈ**bongo** ˌ**drum**
Bonham ˈbɒn.əm ⓤⓢ ˈbɑː.nəm
Bonham-Carter ˌbɒn.əmˈkɑː.təʳ ⓤⓢ ˌbɑː.nəmˈkɑːr.t̬ɚ
bonhomie ˈbɒn.ɒm.i, -ə.mi, -miː, ˌ--ˈ- ⓤⓢ ˌbɑː.nəˈmiː, ˈ---
Boniface ˈbɒn.ɪ.feɪs, -fæs ⓤⓢ ˈbɑː.nɪ-
Bonifacio ˌbɒn.ɪˈfæʃ.i.əʊ, -ˈfæs- ⓤⓢ ˌboʊ.niˈfɑː.ʃoʊ, ˈ-ʃi.oʊ
Bonington ˈbɒn.ɪŋ.tən ⓤⓢ ˈbɑː.nɪŋ.t̬ən
bonk bɒŋk ⓤⓢ bɑːŋk, bɔːŋk **-s** -s **-ing** -ɪŋ **-ed** -t
bonkers ˈbɒŋ.kəz ⓤⓢ ˈbɑːŋ.kɚz, ˈbɔːŋ-
bon(s) mot(s) ˌbɔ̃ː*m*ˈməʊ ⓤⓢ ˌbɔ̃ːnˈmoʊ
Bonn bɒn ⓤⓢ bɑːn
Bonnard bɒnˈɑːʳ ⓤⓢ bɑːˈnɑːr, bɔː-
Bonner ˈbɒn.əʳ ⓤⓢ ˈbɑː.nɚ
bonn|et ˈbɒn|.ɪt ⓤⓢ ˈbɑː.n|ɪt **-ets** -ɪts **-eting** -ɪ.tɪŋ ⓤⓢ -ɪ.t̬ɪŋ **-eted** -ɪ.tɪd ⓤⓢ -ɪ.t̬ɪd
Bonnett ˈbɒn.ɪt ⓤⓢ ˈbɑː.nɪt
Bonnie ˈbɒn.i ⓤⓢ ˈbɑː.ni

bonn|y 'bɒn|.i (US) 'bɑː.n|i **-ier** -i.əʳ (US) -i.ɚ **-iest** -i.ɪst, -i.əst **-ily** -ɪ.li, -ᵊl.i **-iness** -ɪ.nəs, -ɪ.nɪs

bonsai 'bɒn.saɪ (US) ˌbɑːn'saɪ, ˌboʊn- **-s** -z

Bonsor 'bɒn*t*.səʳ, -zəʳ (US) 'bɑːn*t*.sɚ, -zɚ

bonus 'bəʊ.nəs (US) 'boʊ- **-es** -ɪz

bon(s) vivant(s) ˌbɔ̃ː*ŋ*.vi.'vɑ̃ː*ŋ* (US) ˌbɑːn.viː'vɑːnt, ˌbɔ̃ː-

bon(s) viveur(s) ˌbɔ̃ː*ŋ*.vi'vɜːʳ (US) ˌbɑːn.viː'vɜːr

bon voyage ˌbɔ̃ː*ŋ*.vɔɪ'ɑːʒ, -vwaɪ'- (US) ˌbɑːn.vwaɪ'-, -vɔɪ'-

bon|y 'bəʊ.n|i (US) 'boʊ- **-ier** -i.əʳ (US) -i.ɚ **-iest** -i.ɪst, -i.əst **-iness** -ɪ.nəs, -ɪ.nɪs

bonz|e bɒnz (US) bɑːnz **-es** -ɪz

bonzer 'bɒn.zəʳ (US) 'bɑːn.zɚ

boo buː **-s** -z **-ing** -ɪŋ **-ed** -d **-er/s** -əʳ/z (US) -ɚ/z **ˌcouldn't say ˌboo to a 'goose**

boob buːb **-s** -z **-ing** -ɪŋ **-ed** -d

boo-boo 'buː.buː **-s** -z

boob|y 'buː.b|i **-ies** -iz **-yish** -i.ɪʃ **'booby ˌprize ; 'booby ˌtrap**

boodle (B) 'buː.dl̩

boog|ie 'buː.g|i (US) 'bʊg-, 'buː- **-ies** -iz **-ieing** -i.ɪŋ **-ied** -id

boogie-woogie ˌbuː.gi'wuː.gi, 'buː.giˌwuː-, ˌbʊg.i'wʊg.i

boohoo ˌbuː'huː **-s** -z **-ing** -ɪŋ **-ed** -d

book bʊk **-s** -s **-ing** -ɪŋ **-ed** -t **-er/s** -əʳ/z (US) -ɚ/z **'book ˌclub ; 'book ˌtoken; ˌbring someone to 'book; in someone's 'good/bad ˌbooks, in someone's ˌgood/ˌbad 'books**

bookable 'bʊk.ə.bl̩

bookbind|er 'bʊkˌbaɪn.d|əʳ (US) -d|ɚ **-ers** -əz (US) -ɚz **-ing** -ɪŋ

bookcas|e 'bʊk.keɪs **-es** -ɪz

bookend 'bʊk.end **-s** -z

Booker 'bʊk.əʳ (US) -ɚ

Bookham 'bʊk.əm

bookie 'bʊk.i **-s** -z

booking 'bʊk.ɪŋ **-s** -z **'booking ˌoffice**

bookish 'bʊk.ɪʃ **-ly** -li **-ness** -nəs, -nɪs

bookkeep|er 'bʊkˌkiː.p|əʳ (US) -p|ɚ **-ers** -əz (US) -ɚz **-ing** -ɪŋ

bookland 'bʊk.lænd

book-learning 'bʊkˌlɜː.nɪŋ (US) -ˌlɜːr-

booklet 'bʊk.lət, -lɪt **-s** -s

bookmak|er 'bʊkˌmeɪ.k|əʳ (US) -k|ɚ **-ers** -əz (US) -ɚz **-ing** -ɪŋ

book|man 'bʊk|.mən, -mæn **-men** -mən, -men

bookmark 'bʊk.mɑːk (US) -mɑːrk **-s** -s **-er/s** -əʳ/z (US) -ɚ/z

bookmobile 'bʊk.m*əʊ*ˌbiːl (US) -mə-, -moʊ- **-s** -z

bookplate 'bʊk.pleɪt **-s** -s

booksell|er 'bʊkˌsel|.əʳ (US) -ɚ **-ers** -əz (US) -ɚz **-ing** -ɪŋ

bookshel|f 'bʊk.ʃel|f **-ves** -vz

bookshop 'bʊk.ʃɒp (US) -ʃɑːp **-s** -s

bookstall 'bʊk.stɔːl (US) -stɔːl, -stɑːl **-s** -z

bookstand 'bʊk.stænd **-s** -z

bookstore 'bʊk.stɔːʳ (US) -stɔːr **-s** -z

bookwork 'bʊk.wɜːk (US) -wɜːrk

bookworm 'bʊk.wɜːm (US) -wɜːrm **-s** -z

Boolean 'buː.li.ən **-s** -z

boom buːm **-s** -z **-ing** -ɪŋ **-ed** -d **'boom ˌbox**

boomerang 'buː.mᵊr.æŋ (US) -mə.ræŋ **-s** -z

boomlet 'buːm.lət, -lɪt **-s** -s

boon buːn **-s** -z

boondock 'buːn.dɒk (US) -dɑːk **-s** -s

boondoggl|e 'buːnˌdɒg.l̩ (US) -ˌdɑː.gl̩, -ˌdɔː- **-es** -z **-ing** -ɪŋ, ˌ-lɪŋ (US) -ˌdɑː.gl̩.ɪŋ, -ˌdɔː-, ˌ-glɪŋ **-ed** -d **-er/s** -əʳ/z, ˌ-ləʳ/z (US) -ˌdɑː.gl̩.ɚ/z, -ˌdɔː-, ˌ-glɚ/z

Boon(e) buːn

boonies 'buː.niz

boor bɔːʳ, bʊə (US) bʊr **-s** -z

Boord bɔːd (US) bɔːrd

boorish 'bɔː.rɪʃ, 'bʊə- (US) 'bʊr.ɪʃ **-ly** -li **-ness** -nəs, -nɪs

Boosey 'buː.zi

boost buːst **-s** -s **-ing** -ɪŋ **-ed** -ɪd

booster 'buː.stəʳ (US) -stɚ **-s** -z

boot (B) buːt **-s** -s **-ing** -ɪŋ (US) 'buː.t̬ɪŋ **-ed** -ɪd (US) 'buː.t̬ɪd **'boot ˌsale ; ˌput the 'boot in; too ˌbig for one's 'boots**

bootblack 'buːt.blæk **-s** -s

bootee ˌbuː'tiː; 'buː.ti (US) 'buː.t̬i **-s** -z

Boötes bəʊ'əʊ.tiːz (US) boʊ'oʊ-

booth (B) buːð, buːθ **-s** -z, -s

Boothby 'buːð.bi

Boothe buːð

Boothroyd 'buːθ.rɔɪd, 'buːð-

bootjack 'buːt.dʒæk **-s** -s

bootlac|e 'buːt.leɪs **-es** -ɪz

Bootle 'buː.tl̩ (US) 'buː.t̬l̩

bootleg 'buːt.leg **-s** -z **-ging** -ɪŋ **-ged** -d

bootlegger 'buːtˌleg.əʳ (US) -ɚ **-s** -z

bootless 'buːt.ləs, -lɪs **-ly** -li **-ness** -nəs, -nɪs

boots *(sing.) hotel servant:* buːts *(plur.)* buːts, 'buːt.sɪz

Boots® buːts

bootstrap 'buːt.stræp **-s** -s **-ping** -ɪŋ **-ped** -t

booty 'buː.ti (US) -t̬i

booz|e buːz **-es** -ɪz **-ing** -ɪŋ **-ed** -d **-er/s** -əʳ/z (US) -ɚ/z

booze-up 'buːz.ʌp **-s** -s

booz|y 'buː.z|i **-ier** -i.əʳ (US) -i.ɚ **-iest** -i.ɪst, -i.əst **-ily** -ɪ.li, -ᵊl.i

bop bɒp (US) bɑːp **-s** -s **-ping** -ɪŋ **-ped** -t **-py** -i

Bo-peep ˌbəʊ'piːp (US) ˌboʊ-

Bophuthatswana ˌbɒp.uː.tæt'swɑː.nə, ˌbəʊ.puː-, -tət'- (US) ˌboʊ.puː.tɑːt'swɑː-, -t̬ət'-

boracic bə'ræs.ɪk, bɒr'æs- (US) bə'ræs-, bɔː-

borage 'bɒr.ɪdʒ, 'bʌr- (US) 'bɔːr-

borate 'bɔː.reɪt, -rɪt, -rət (US) 'bɔːr.eɪt, -ɪt, -ət **-s** -s

borax 'bɔː.ræks (US) 'bɔːr.æks

borborygmus ˌbɔː.bə'rɪg.məs (US) ˌbɔːr-

Bord bɔːd (US) bɔːrd

Bordeaux bɔː'dəʊ (US) bɔːr'doʊ

bordello bɔː'del.əʊ (US) bɔːr'del.oʊ **-s** -z

bord|er 'bɔː.d|əʳ (US) 'bɔːr.d|ɚ **-ers** -əz (US) -ɚz **-ering** -ᵊr.ɪŋ **-ered** -əd (US) -ɚd **-erer/s** -ᵊr.əʳ/z (US) -ɚ.ɚ/z

borderland 'bɔː.dᵊl.ænd (US) 'bɔːr.dɚ.lænd **-s** -z

borderline 'bɔː.dᵊl.aɪn (US) 'bɔːr.dɚ.laɪn **-s** -z

Borders 'bɔː.dəz (US) 'bɔːr.dɚz

Bordon 'bɔː.dᵊn (US) 'bɔːr-

bordure 'bɔː.dj*ʊə*ʳ (US) 'bɔːr.djɚ, -dʒɚ **-s** -z

bor|e bɔːʳ (US) bɔːr **-es** -z **-ing** -ɪŋ **-ed** -d

bore *(from* **bear**) bɔːʳ (US) bɔːr

borealis ˌbɒr.i'ɑː.lɪs, ˌbɔː.ri'-, -'eɪ- (US) ˌbɔːr.i'æl.ɪs, -'eɪ.lɪs

Boreas 'bɒr.i.æs, 'bɔː.ri-, -əs (US) 'bɔːr.i-

boredom 'bɔː.dəm (US) 'bɔːr-

Boreham 'bɔː.rəm (US) 'bɔːr.əm

Borehamwood ˌbɔː.rəm'wʊd (US) ˌbɔːr.əm-

borehole 'bɔː.həʊl (US) 'bɔːr.hoʊl **-s** -z

borer 'bɔː.rəʳ (US) 'bɔːr.ɚ **-s** -z

Borg bɔːg (US) bɔːrg

Borges 'bɔː.ges, -xes (US) 'bɔːr.hes

Borgia 'bɔː.*dʒ*i.ə, -*dʒ*ə (US) 'bɔːr.*dʒ*ə

boric 'bɔː.rɪk, 'bɒr.ɪk (US) 'bɔːr.ɪk **ˌboric 'acid**

Boris 'bɒr.ɪs (US) 'bɔːr-

Borland 'bɔː.lənd (US) 'bɔːr-

borlotti (B) bɔː'lɒt.i (US) bɔːr'lɑː.t̬i

born bɔːn (US) bɔːrn

born-again ˌbɔːn.ə'gen, -'geɪn (US) ˌbɔːrn.ə'gen *stress shift, see compound:* **ˌborn-again 'Christian**

borne *(from* **bear**) bɔːn (US) bɔːrn

Borneo 'bɔː.ni.əʊ (US) 'bɔːr.ni.oʊ

Borodin 'bɒr.ə.dɪn (US) 'bɔːr-

boron 'bɔː.rɒn (US) 'bɔːr.ɑːn

borough 'bʌr.ə (US) 'bɜːr.oʊ, -ə **-s** -z

borrow (B) 'bɒr.əʊ (US) 'bɑːr.oʊ **-s** -z **-ing** -ɪŋ **-ed** -d **-er/s** -əʳ/z (US) -ɚ/z

Borrowash 'bɒr.əʊ.wɒʃ (US) 'bɑːr.oʊ.wɑːʃ, -wɔːʃ

Borrowdale 'bɒr.ə.deɪl (US) 'bɑːr-

Bors bɔːs (US) bɔːrs

borsch bɔːʃ (US) bɔːrʃ
borscht bɔːʃt (US) bɔːrʃt
borstal (B) 'bɔː.stᵊl (US) 'bɔːr- **-s** -z
borstch bɔːʃ, bɔːstʃ, bɔːʃtʃ (US) bɔːrʃt
Borthwick 'bɔːθ.wɪk (US) 'bɔːrθ-
Borwick 'bɒr.ɪk (US) 'bɔːr.wɪk
borzoi 'bɔː.zɔɪ, -'- (US) 'bɔːr- **-s** -z
Bosanquet 'bəʊ.zᵊn.ket, -kɪt (US) 'boʊ-
boscag|e 'bɒs.kɪdʒ (US) 'bɑːs- **-es** -ɪz
Boscastle 'bɒs.kɑː.sl̩, -kæs.l̩ (US) 'bɑː.skæs-
Boscawen bɒs'kəʊ.ən; -ɪn; -'kɔː-; 'bɒs.kwɪn (US) bɑː'skoʊ.ən; 'bɑː.skwɪn
Bosch bɒʃ (US) bɑːʃ
bosh bɒʃ (US) bɑːʃ
Bosham 'bɒz.əm, 'bɒs- (US) 'bɑː.zəm, -səm
Note: A new pronunciation /'bɒʃ.əm/ is also heard.
Bosher 'bəʊ.ʃəʳ (US) 'boʊ.ʃɚ
bosky 'bɒs.ki (US) 'bɑː.ski
bos'n, bo's'n 'bəʊ.sᵊn (US) 'boʊ- **-s** -z
Bosni|a 'bɒz.ni|.ə (US) 'bɑːz- **-an/s** -ən/z
Bosnia-Herzegovina ˌbɒz.ni.əˌhɜː.zə'gɒv.ɪ.nə; -gəʊ'viː- (US) ˌbɑːz.ni.əˌhert.sə.goʊ'viː.nə, -gə'-
bosom 'bʊz.ᵊm **-s** -z **-y** -i
Bosphorus 'bɒs.fᵊr.əs, -pᵊr- (US) 'bɑːs.fɚ-, 'bɑː.spɚ-
Bosporus 'bɒs.pᵊr.əs (US) 'bɑː.spɚ-
boss (B) bɒs (US) bɑːs **-es** -ɪz **-ing** -ɪŋ **-ed** -t
bossa nova ˌbɒs.ə'nəʊ.və (US) ˌbɑː.sə'noʊ-
boss-eyed ˌbɒs'aɪd (US) 'bɑːs.aɪd *stress shift:* ˌboss-eyed 'cat
Bossuet 'bɒs.u.eɪ (US) 'bɑː.sweɪ
boss|y 'bɒs|.i (US) 'bɑː.s|i **-ier** -i.əʳ (US) -i.ɚ **-iest** -i.ɪst, -i.əst **-ily** -ɪ.li, -ᵊl.i **-iness** -ɪ.nəs, -ɪ.nɪs
Bostik® 'bɒs.tɪk (US) 'bɑː.stɪk
Bostock 'bɒs.tɒk (US) 'bɑː.stɑːk
Boston 'bɒs.tᵊn (US) 'bɑː.stᵊn, 'bɔː-
Bostonian bɒs'təʊ.ni.ən (US) bɑː'stoʊ-, bɔː- **-s** -z
bosun 'bəʊ.sᵊn (US) 'boʊ- **-s** -z
Boswell 'bɒz.wəl, -wel (US) 'bɑːz-
Bosworth 'bɒz.wəθ, -wɜːθ (US) 'bɑːz.wɚθ, -wɜːrθ
botanic bə'tæn.ɪk, bɒt'æn- (US) bə'tæn- **-al** -ᵊl **-ally** -ᵊl.i, -li boˌtanic 'garden
botanist 'bɒt.ᵊn.ɪst (US) 'bɑː.tᵊn- **-s** -s
botaniz|e, -is|e 'bɒt.ᵊn.aɪz (US) 'bɑː.tᵊn- **-es** -ɪz **-ing** -ɪŋ **-ed** -d
botany 'bɒt.ᵊn.i (US) 'bɑː.tᵊn- ˌ**Botany 'Bay**
botch bɒtʃ (US) bɑːtʃ **-es** -ɪz **-ing** -ɪŋ **-ed** -t **-er/s** -əʳ/z (US) -ɚ/z
botch-up 'bɒtʃ.ʌp (US) 'bɑːtʃ- **-s** -s
both bəʊθ (US) boʊθ
Botha 'bəʊ.tə (US) 'boʊ.t̬ə
Botham 'bəʊ.θəm, 'bɒð.əm (US) 'boʊ.θəm, 'bɑː.ðəm
both|er 'bɒð|.əʳ (US) 'bɑː.ð|ɚ **-ers** -əz (US) -ɚz **-ering** -ᵊr.ɪŋ **-ered** -əd (US) -ɚd
botheration ˌbɒð.ᵊr'eɪ.ʃᵊn (US) ˌbɑː.ðə'reɪ-
bothersome 'bɒð.ə.sᵊm (US) 'bɑː.ðɚ-
Bothnia 'bɒθ.ni.ə (US) 'bɑːθ-
Bothwell 'bɒθ.wᵊl, 'bɒð-, -wel (US) 'bɑːθ-, 'bɑːð-
both|y 'bɒθ|.i, bɒð- (US) 'bɑː.θ|i, -ð|i **-ies** -iz
Botolph 'bɒt.ɒlf, -ᵊlf (US) 'bɑː.tɑːlf
botrytis bɒt'raɪ.tɪs (US) boʊ'traɪ.t̬əs
Botswana bɒt'swɑː.nə (US) bɑːt-
Botticelli ˌbɒt.ɪ'tʃel.i (US) ˌbɑː.t̬ə'- **-s** -z
bottl|e 'bɒt.l̩ (US) 'bɑː.t̬l̩ **-es** -z **-ing** -ɪŋ, '-lɪŋ (US) 'bɑː.t̬l̩.ɪŋ, 'bɑːt.lɪŋ **-ed** -d **-er/s** -əʳ/z, '-ləʳ/z (US) 'bɑː.t̬l̩.ɚ/z, 'bɑːt.lɚ/z **'bottle ˌbank**
bottle-green ˌbɒt.l̩'griːn (US) ˌbɑː.t̬l̩'- *stress shift:* ˌbottle-green 'jacket
bottleneck 'bɒt.l̩.nek (US) 'bɑː.t̬l̩- **-s** -s
bottle-nos|e 'bɒt.l̩.nəʊz (US) 'bɑː.t̬l̩.noʊz **-es** -ɪz **-ed** -d
bottle-wash|er 'bɒt.l̩ˌwɒʃ.əʳ (US) 'bɑː.t̬l̩ˌwɑː.ʃɚ **-ers** -əz (US) -ɚs **-ing** -ɪŋ
bottom (B) 'bɒt.əm (US) 'bɑː.t̬əm **-s** -z **-ing** -ɪŋ **-ed** -d
Bottome bə'təʊm (US) -'toʊm
bottomless 'bɒt.əm.ləs, -lɪs, -les (US) 'bɑː.t̬əm-
Bottomley 'bɒt.əm.li (US) 'bɑː.t̬əm-
bottomry 'bɒt.əm.ri (US) 'bɑː.t̬əm-
botulism 'bɒt.jʊ.lɪ.zᵊm, -jə-, 'bɒtʃ.ʊ-, '-ə- (US) 'bɑː.tʃə-
Bouaké 'bwɑː.keɪ
Boucicault 'buː.si.kəʊ *as if French:* ˌ--'- (US) 'buː.si.koʊ, -kɑːlt
bouclé 'buː.kleɪ (US) -'-
Boudicca 'buː.dɪ.kə, 'bəʊ- (US) buː'dɪk.ə
boudoir 'buːd.wɑːʳ (US) 'buːd.wɑːr, 'bʊd- **-s** -z
bouffant 'buː.fɑ̃ːŋ, -fɒnt (US) buː'fɑːnt, '--
bougainvillaea ˌbuː.gᵊn'vɪl.i.ə (US) -i.ə, '-jə **-s** -z
Bougainville 'buː.gᵊn.vɪl, -viːl
bougainvillea ˌbuː.gᵊn'vɪl.i.ə (US) -i.ə, '-jə **-s** -z
bough baʊ **-s** -z
Bough bɒf (US) bɑːf
Boughey 'bəʊ.i (US) 'boʊ-
bought (*from* **buy**) bɔːt (US) bɑːt, bɔːt
Boughton 'bɔː.tᵊn, 'baʊ- (US) 'bɑː.tᵊn, 'bɔː-, 'baʊ-
bougie 'buː.*d*ʒiː, -'- **-s** -z
bouillabaisse ˌbuː.jə'bes, ˌbwiː-, -jɑː'-, -'beɪs, '---
bouillon 'buː.jɔ̃ːŋ, 'bwiː-, -jɒn (US) 'bʊl.jɑːn, 'buː-, -jən
Boulanger ˌbuː.lɑ̃ːn'ʒeɪ, '---
Boulby 'bəʊl.bi (US) 'boʊl-
boulder 'bəʊl.dəʳ (US) 'boʊl.dɚ **-s** -z
Bouler 'buː.ləʳ (US) -lɚ
boules buːl
boulevard 'buː.lə.vɑːd, -lɪ-, 'buːl.vɑːʳ (US) 'bʊl.ə.vɑːrd **-s** -z
Boulez 'buː.lez, -leɪ (US) buː'lez
Boulogne bʊ'lɔɪn, bə- (US) -'loʊn, -'lɔɪn
Boult bəʊlt (US) boʊlt
Boulter 'bəʊl.təʳ (US) 'boʊl.t̬ɚ
Boulton 'bəʊl.tᵊn (US) 'boʊl-
bounc|e baʊn*t*s **-es** -ɪz **-ing** -ɪŋ **-ed** -t
bouncer (B) 'baʊn*t*.səʳ (US) -sɚ **-s** -z
bounc|y 'baʊn*t*.s|i **-ier** -i.əʳ (US) -i.ɚ **-iest** -i.ɪst, -i.əst
bound baʊnd **-s** -z **-ing** -ɪŋ **-ed** -ɪd
boundar|y 'baʊn.dᵊr|.i **-ies** -iz
bounden 'baʊn.dən ˌ**bounden 'duty**
bounder 'baʊn.dəʳ (US) -dɚ **-s** -z
Bounderby 'baʊn.də.bi (US) -dɚ-
boundless 'baʊnd.ləs, -lɪs **-ly** -li **-ness** -nəs, -nɪs
bounteous 'baʊn.ti.əs, -tʃəs (US) -t̬i.əs **-ly** -li **-ness** -nəs, -nɪs
bountiful 'baʊn.tɪ.fᵊl, -tə-, -fʊl (US) -t̬ə-, -t̬ɪ- **-ly** -i **-ness** -nəs, -nɪs
bount|y 'baʊn.t|i (US) -t̬|i **-ies** -iz **'bounty ˌhunter**
bouquet bʊ'keɪ; bəʊ-; 'buː.keɪ (US) boʊ'keɪ, buː- **-s** -z
bouquet(s) garni(s) bʊˌkeɪ.gɑː'niː, ˌbuː.keɪ- (US) ˌboʊ.keɪ.gɑːr'-
Bourbon *French royal house:* 'bʊə.bən, 'bɔː-, -bɒn (US) 'bʊr.bən, -bɔːn **-s** -z
bourbon *drink:* 'bɜː.bən, 'bʊə- (US) 'bɜːr- *biscuit:* 'bɔː.bən, 'bʊə-, -bɒn (US) 'bɜːr-
Bourchier 'baʊ.tʃəʳ (US) -tʃɚ
Bourdillon bə'dɪl.i.ən, bɔː-, -'dɪl.ən (US) bɔːr'dɪl.jən, bɚ-
bourdon 'bɔː.dᵊn, 'bʊə- (US) 'bʊr-, 'bɔːr- **-s** -z
bourgeois *middle class:* 'bɔːʒ.wɑː, 'bʊəʒ- (US) 'bʊrʒ- *printing type:* bɜː'dʒɔɪs (US) bɜːr-
bourgeoisie ˌbɔːʒ.wɑː'ziː, ˌbʊəʒ-, -wə'- (US) ˌbʊrʒ-
Bourke bɜːk (US) bɜːrk
bourn(e) bɔːn, bʊən (US) bɔːrn, bʊrn **-s** -z
Bourne bɔːn, bʊən *as surname also:* bɜːn (US) bɔːrn, bʊrn, bɜːrn
Bournemouth 'bɔːn.məθ (US) 'bɔːrn-
Bournville 'bɔːn.vɪl (US) 'bɔːrn-
bourrée 'bʊr.eɪ, 'bʊə.reɪ (US) bʊ'reɪ **-s** -z

bours|e (B) bʊəs, bɔːs (US) bʊrs, bɔːrs **-es** -ɪz
boustrophedon ˌbuː.strəˈfiː.dᵊn, ˌbaʊ-, -dɒn (US) -ɑːn
bout baʊt **-s** -s
boutique buːˈtiːk **-s** -s
Boutros-Ghali ˌbuː.trɒsˈɡɑː.li (US) -trousˈ-
Bouverie ˈbuː.vᵊr.i
bouzouki bʊˈzuː.ki, bə-, buː- **-s** -z
Bovary ˈbəʊ.vᵊr.i (US) ˈboʊ-
Bovey *place:* ˈbʌv.i *surname:* ˈbuː.vi, ˈbəʊ-, ˈbʌv.i (US) ˈbuː.vi, ˈboʊ-, ˈbʌv.i
Bovey Tracey ˌbʌv.iˈtreɪ.si
Bovill ˈbəʊ.vɪl (US) ˈboʊ-
bovine ˈbəʊ.vaɪn (US) ˈboʊ-, -viːn
Bovingdon ˈbʌv.ɪŋ.dən, ˈbɒv- (US) ˈbʌv-, ˈbɑː.vɪŋ-
Note: Locally /ˈbʌv-/.
Bovington ˈbɒv.ɪŋ.tən (US) ˈbɑː.vɪŋ-
Bovis ˈbəʊ.vɪs (US) ˈboʊ-
Bovril® ˈbɒv.rɪl, -rəl (US) ˈbɑːv-
bovver ˈbɒv.əʳ, ˈbɑː.vɚ ˈ**bovver** ˌ**boot** ; ˈ**bovver** ˌ**boy**
bow (*n.*) *bending, fore end of ship:* baʊ **-s** -z
bow (B) (*n.*) *for shooting, etc., knot:* bəʊ (US) boʊ **-s** -z ˌ**bow** ˈ**tie** ; ˌ**bow** ˈ**window**
bow (*v.*) *in playing the violin, etc.:* bəʊ (US) boʊ **-s** -z **-ing/s** -ɪŋ/z **-ed** -d
bow (*v.*) *bend body:* baʊ **-s** -z **-ing** -ɪŋ **-ed** -d
Bowater ˈbəʊˌwɔː.təʳ (US) ˈboʊˌwɑː.t̬ɚ, -ˌwɔː-
Bowden ˈbəʊ.dᵊn, ˈbaʊ- (US) ˈboʊ-, ˈbaʊ-
Bowdler ˈbaʊd.ləʳ (US) ˈboʊd.lɚ, ˈbaʊd-
bowdlerism ˈbaʊd.lᵊr.ɪ.zᵊm (US) ˈboʊd-, ˈbaʊd- **-s** -z
bowdlerization, -isa- ˌbaʊd.lᵊr.aɪˈzeɪ.ʃᵊn, -ɪˈ- (US) ˌboʊd.lɚ.ɪˈ-, ˌbaʊd-
bowdleriz|e, -is|e ˈbaʊd.lᵊr.aɪz (US) ˈboʊd.lə.raɪz, ˈbaʊd- **-es** -ɪz **-ing** -ɪŋ **-ed** -d
Bowdoin, Bowdon ˈbəʊ.dᵊn (US) ˈboʊ-
bowel baʊəl **-s** -z
Bowen ˈbəʊ.ɪn (US) ˈboʊ-
bower (B) baʊəʳ (US) baʊɚ **-s** -z
Bowering ˈbaʊə.rɪŋ (US) ˈbaʊɚ.ɪŋ
bowery (B) ˈbaʊə.ri (US) ˈbaʊɚ.i, ˈbaʊ.ri
Bowes bəʊz (US) boʊz
Bowie ˈbaʊ.i, ˈbəʊ- (US) ˈboʊ-, ˈbuː-
bowie-kni|fe ˈbəʊ.i.naɪ|f, ˈbuː- (US) ˈboʊ-, ˈbuː- **-ves** -vz
Bowker ˈbaʊ.kəʳ (US) -kɚ
bowl bəʊl (US) boʊl **-s** -z **-ing** -ɪŋ **-ed** -d ˈ**bowling** ˌ**alley** ; ˈ**bowling** ˌ**green**
Bowland ˈbəʊ.lənd (US) ˈboʊ-
bow-legged bəʊˈlegd, -ˈleg.ɪd, -əd (US) boʊ- *stress shift:* ˌbow-legged ˈchild
bowler (B) ˈbəʊ.ləʳ (US) ˈboʊ.lɚ **-s** -z
Bowles bəʊlz (US) boʊlz
bowline ˈbəʊ.lɪn (US) ˈboʊ- **-s** -z
Bowling ˈbəʊ.lɪŋ (US) ˈboʊ-
Bowlker ˈbəʊ.kəʳ (US) ˈboʊ.kɚ
bow|man (B) ˈbəʊ|.mən (US) ˈboʊ- **-men** -mən, -men
Bowmer ˈbəʊ.məʳ (US) ˈboʊ.mɚ
Bown baʊn
Bowness bəʊˈnes (US) boʊ-
Bowra ˈbaʊ.rə
Bowring ˈbaʊ.rɪŋ
bowshot ˈbəʊ.ʃɒt (US) ˈboʊ.ʃɑːt **-s** -s
bowsprit ˈbəʊ.sprɪt, ˈbaʊ- (US) ˈbaʊ-, ˈboʊ- **-s** -s
bowstring ˈbəʊ.strɪŋ (US) ˈboʊ- **-s** -z
Bowtell bəʊˈtel (US) boʊ-
bow-wow (*interj.*) *sound made by a dog:* ˌbaʊˈwaʊ **-s** -z (*n.*) *dog:* ˈbaʊ.waʊ **-s** -z
bowyer (B) ˈbəʊ.jəʳ (US) ˈboʊ.jɚ
box (B) bɒks (US) bɑːks **-es** -ɪz **-ing** -ɪŋ **-ed** -t ˌ**box** ˈ**bed** ; ˈ**box** ˌ**cloth** ; ˌ**box** ˈ**junction** ; ˈ**box** ˌ**number** ; ˈ**box** ˌ**office** ; ˈ**box** ˌ**seat** ; ˌ**boxed** ˈ**set** ; ˈ**box** ˌ**score**
boxcar ˈbɒks.kɑːʳ (US) ˈbɑːks.kɑːr **-s** -z
boxer (B) ˈbɒk.səʳ (US) ˈbɑːk.sɚ **-s** -z ˈ**boxer** ˌ**shorts**
boxing ˈbɒk.sɪŋ (US) ˈbɑːk- ˈ**Boxing** ˌ**Day** ; ˈ**boxing** ˌ**glove** ; ˈ**boxing** ˌ**match**
Boxmoor ˈbɒks.mɔːʳ *also locally:* -ˈ- (US) ˈbɑːks.mʊr, -mɔːr
boxroom ˈbɒks.rʊm, -ruːm (US) ˈbɑːks.ruːm, -rʊm **-s** -z
boxwood ˈbɒks.wʊd (US) ˈbɑːks-
box|y ˈbɒk.s|i (US) ˈbɑːk- **-iness** -ɪ.nəs, -ɪ.nɪs
boy bɔɪ **-s** -z ˌ**boy** ˈ**scout** (US) ˈ**boy** ˌ**scout**
boyar ˈbɔɪ.əʳ, -ɑːʳ; ˈbəʊ.jɑːʳ, -ˈ- (US) boʊˈjɑːr; ˈbɔɪ.ɚ **-s** -z
Boyce bɔɪs
boyco|tt (B) ˈbɔɪ.kɒ|t, -kə|t (US) -kɑː|t **-tts** -ts **-tting** -tɪŋ (US) -t̬ɪŋ **-tted** -tɪd (US) -t̬ɪd **-tter/s** -təʳ/z (US) -t̬ɚ/z
Boyd bɔɪd
Boyer ˈbwaɪ.eɪ; ˈbɔɪ.əʳ (US) bɔɪˈeɪ; ˈbɔɪ.ɚ
Boyet ˈbɔɪ.et, -ˈ- (US) bwɑːˈjeɪ
boyfriend ˈbɔɪ.frend **-s** -z
boyhood ˈbɔɪ.hʊd **-s** -z
boyish ˈbɔɪ.ɪʃ **-ly** -li **-ness** -nəs, -nɪs
Boyle bɔɪl
Boyne bɔɪn
boyo ˈbɔɪ.əʊ (US) -oʊ **-s** -z
boysenberr|y ˈbɔɪ.zᵊn.bᵊr|.i, -ˌber- (US) -ˌber- **-ies** -iz
Boyson ˈbɔɪ.sᵊn
Boyton ˈbɔɪ.tᵊn
Boz bɒz (US) bɑːz
Note: This pen-name of Charles Dickens was originally pronounced /bəʊz (US) boʊz/, but this pronunciation is not often heard now.
bozo ˈbəʊ.zəʊ (US) ˈboʊ.zoʊ **-s** -z
BP ˌbiːˈpiː
BPhil ˌbiːˈfɪl
BR ˌbiːˈɑːʳ (US) -ˈɑːr
bra brɑː **-s** -z
Brabant brəˈbænt; ˈbræb.ənt
Brabantio brəˈbæn.ti.əʊ, bræbˈæn-, -*t*ʃi- (US) brəˈbæn.t̬i.oʊ, -ˈbæn*t*.ʃi-
Brabazon ˈbræb.ə.zᵊn (US) -zɑːn
Brabham ˈbræb.əm
Brabourne *place:* ˈbreɪ.bɔːn (US) -bɔːrn *family name:* ˈbreɪ.bən, ˈbreɪ.bɔːn (US) -bɚn, -bɔːrn
brac|e (B) breɪs **-es** -ɪz **-ing** -ɪŋ **-ed** -t
Bracebridge ˈbreɪs.brɪdʒ
bracelet ˈbreɪs.lət, -lɪt **-s** -s
brach brætʃ (US) brætʃ, bræk **-es** -ɪz
brachial ˈbreɪ.ki.əl (US) ˈbreɪ-, ˈbræk.i-
brachy- ˈbræk.i-
brachycephalic ˌbræk.i.səˈfæl.ɪk, -sɪˈ-
brack bræk **-s** -s
bracken ˈbræk.ᵊn
Brackenbury ˈbræk.ᵊn.bᵊr.i (US) -ber-
Brackenridge ˈbræk.ᵊn.rɪdʒ
brack|et ˈbræk|.ɪt **-ets** -ɪts **-eting** -ɪ.tɪŋ (US) -ɪ.t̬ɪŋ **-eted** -ɪ.tɪd (US) -ɪ.t̬ɪd
brackish ˈbræk.ɪʃ **-ness** -nəs, -nɪs
Brackley ˈbræk.li
Bracknell ˈbræk.nəl
brad (B) bræd **-s** -z
bradawl ˈbræd.ɔːl (US) -ɑːl, -ɔːl **-s** -z
Bradbury ˈbræd.bᵊr.i, ˈbræb- (US) -ber-
Braddon ˈbræd.ᵊn
Braden ˈbreɪ.dᵊn
Bradfield ˈbræd.fiːld
Bradford ˈbræd.fəd (US) -fɚd
Bradgate ˈbræd.geɪt, -gɪt
Bradlaugh, Bradlaw ˈbræd.lɔː (US) -lɑː, -lɔː
Bradley ˈbræd.li
Bradman ˈbræd.mən
Bradshaw ˈbræd.ʃɔː (US) -ʃɑː, -ʃɔː
Bradstreet ˈbræd.striːt
Bradwardine ˈbræd.wə.diːn (US) -wɚ-
Brady ˈbreɪ.di
bradycardia ˌbræd.ɪˈkɑː.di.ə (US) -ˈkɑːr-
brae breɪ **-s** -z
Braemar breɪˈmɑːʳ (US) -ˈmɑːr *stress shift:* ˌBraemar ˈgames
brag bræg **-s** -z **-ging/ly** -ɪŋ/li **-ged** -d
Bragg bræg
braggadocio ˌbræg.əˈdəʊ.*t*ʃi.əʊ (US) -ˈdoʊ- **-s** -z
braggart ˈbræg.ət, -ɑːt (US) -ɚt **-s** -s

Braham ˈbreɪ.əm
Brahe ˈbrɑː.hə, -ə, -hi
brahma (B) *god:* ˈbrɑː.mə *breed of fowl or cattle:* ˈbreɪ.mə (US) ˈbrɑː-, ˈbreɪ-, ˈbræm.ə **-s** -z
Brahman ˈbrɑː.mən **-s** -z **-ism** -ɪ.zᵊm
Brahmaputra ˌbrɑː.məˈpuː.trə
Brahmin ˈbrɑː.mɪn **-s** -z **-ism** -ɪ.zᵊm
brahminical ˌbrɑːˈmɪn.ɪ.kᵊl
Brahms brɑːmz
braid (B) breɪd **-s** -z **-ing** -ɪŋ **-ed** -ɪd
brail breɪl **-s** -z
Braille breɪl
Brailsford ˈbreɪls.fəd (US) -fɚd
brain (B) breɪn **-s** -z ˈ**brain** ˌ**damage** ; ˈ**brain** ˌ**death** ; ˈ**brain** ˌ**drain**
brain|child ˈbreɪn|.tʃaɪld **-children** -ˌtʃɪl.drən
Braine breɪn
brainless ˈbreɪn.ləs, -lɪs **-ness** -nəs, -nɪs
brainsick ˈbreɪn.sɪk
brainstorm ˈbreɪn.stɔːm (US) -stɔːrm **-s** -z **-ing** -ɪŋ **-ed** -d
brainstorming ˈbreɪnˌstɔː.mɪŋ (US) -ˌstɔːr-
brainteaser ˈbreɪnˌtiː.zəʳ (US) -zɚ **-s** -z
Braintree ˈbreɪn.triː, -tri
brainwash ˈbreɪn.wɒʃ (US) -wɑːʃ, -wɔːʃ **-es** -ɪz **-ing** -ɪŋ **-ed** -t
brainwave ˈbreɪn.weɪv **-s** -z
brain|y ˈbreɪ.n|i **-ier** -i.əʳ (US) -i.ɚ **-iest** -i.ɪst, -i.əst
brais|e breɪz **-es** -ɪz **-ing** -ɪŋ **-ed** -d
Braithwaite ˈbreɪ.θweɪt
brak|e breɪk **-es** -s **-ing** -ɪŋ **-ed** -t ˈ**brake** ˌ**fluid** ; ˈ**brake** ˌ**light**
Brakenridge ˈbræk.ᵊn.rɪdʒ
Bram bræm
Bramah ˈbrɑː.mə, ˈbræm.ə
Bramall ˈbræm.ɔːl (US) -ɔːl, -ɑːl
Brambler ˈbræm.bləʳ (US) -blɚ
bramble ˈbræm.bl̩ **-s** -z ˈ**bramble** ˌ**bush**
brambly ˈbræm.bli
Bramhall ˈbræm.hɔːl (US) -hɔːl, -hɑːl
Bramley ˈbræm.li **-s** -z
Brampton ˈbræm*p*.tən
Bramwell ˈbræm.wel, -wəl
bran (B) bræn ˌ**bran** ˈ**mash** ; ˌ**bran** ˈ**pie**
Branagh ˈbræn.ə
branch (B) brɑːn*t*ʃ (US) bræn*t*ʃ **-es** -ɪz **-ing** -ɪŋ **-ed** -t
branchi|a ˈbræŋ.ki|.ə **-ae** -iː
branchial ˈbræŋ.ki.əl
branchiate ˈbræŋ.ki.eɪt, -ət
Brancusi bræŋˈkuː.zi (US) bræn-, brɑːŋ-
brand (B) brænd **-s** -z **-ing** -ɪŋ **-ed** -ɪd ˈ**brand** ˌ**name** ; ˌ**brand** ˈ**new** ; ˈ**branding** ˌ**iron**
Brandeis ˈbræn.daɪs
Brandenburg ˈbræn.dən.bɜːg (US) -bɜːrg ˌ**Brandenburg** ˈ**Gate**
Brandi ˈbræn.di
brandish ˈbræn.dɪʃ **-es** -ɪz **-ing** -ɪŋ **-ed** -t
Brando ˈbræn.dəʊ (US) -doʊ
Brandon ˈbræn.dən
Brandram ˈbræn.drəm
Brandt brænt
brand|y (B) ˈbræn.d|i **-ies** -iz **-ied** -id **-ying** -i.ɪŋ ˌ**brandy** ˈ**butter** (US) ˈ**brandy** ˌ**butter** ; ˈ**brandy** ˌ**snap**
brank bræŋk **-s** -s
Branksome ˈbræŋk.səm
Branson ˈbræn*t*.sᵊn
Branston ˈbræn*t*.stən
brant brænt **-s** -s
Brant brɑːnt (US) brænt
brant|-goose brænt|ˈguːs **-geese** -ˈgiːs
Braque brɑːk, bræk
Brasenose ˈbreɪz.nəʊz (US) -noʊz
brash bræʃ **-es** -ɪz **-ly** -li **-ness** -nəs, -nɪs
Brasher ˈbreɪ.ʃəʳ (US) -ʃɚ
brasier ˈbreɪ.zi.əʳ, ˈ-ʒəʳ (US) ˈ-ʒɚ **-s** -z
Brasilia brəˈzɪl.i.ə (US) -i.ə, ˈ-jə
Brasov ˈbræʃ.ɒv (US) ˈbrɑː.ʃɔv
brass brɑːs (US) bræs **-es** -ɪz ˌ**brass** ˈ**band** ; ˌ**brass** ˈ**knuckles** ; ˌ**brass** ˈ**monkey** ; ˌ**brassed** ˈ**off**
brassard ˈbræs.ɑːd, -ˈ- (US) ˈbræs.ɑːrd; brəˈsɑːrd **-s** -z
brasserie ˈbræs.ᵊr.i (US) ˌbræs.əˈriː **-s** -z
Brassey ˈbræs.i
brassica ˈbræs.ɪ.kə **-s** -z
brassière ˈbræs.i.əʳ, ˈbræz- (US) brəˈzɪr **-s** -z
Brasso® ˈbrɑː.səʊ (US) ˈbræs.oʊ
brass|y, brass|ie *golf club:* ˈbrɑː.s|i (US) ˈbræs|.i **-ies** -iz
brass|y *(adj.)* ˈbrɑː.s|i (US) ˈbræs|.i **-ier** -i.əʳ (US) -i.ɚ **-iest** -i.ɪst, -i.əst
Brasted ˈbreɪ.stɪd, ˈbræs.tɪd
brat bræt **-s** -s ˈ**brat** ˌ**pack**
Bratislava ˌbræt.ɪˈslɑː.və (US) ˌbrɑː.t̬ɪ-
Bratsk brætsk, brɑːtsk (US) brɑːtsk
Brattleboro ˈbræt.l̩.bᵊr.ə (US) -oʊ
Braughing ˈbræf.ɪŋ
Braun brɔːn, braʊn (US) brɑːn, brɔːn, braʊn
Note: The trademark is pronounced /brɔːn/ in British English, /brɑːn, brɔːn/ in American English.
Braunton ˈbrɔːn.tən (US) ˈbrɑːn-, ˈbrɔːn-
Brautigan ˈbraʊ.tɪ.gən, ˈbrɔː-, ˈbræt.ɪ- (US) ˈbrɑː.t̬ɪ-, ˈbrɔː-
bravado brəˈvɑː.dəʊ (US) -doʊ **-(e)s** -z
brav|e breɪv **-er** -əʳ (US) -ɚ **-est** -ɪst, -əst **-ely** -li **-es** -z **-ing** -ɪŋ **-ed** -d
braver|y ˈbreɪ.vᵊr|.i **-ies** -iz
Bravington ˈbræv.ɪŋ.tən
bravo brɑːˈvəʊ, ˈ-- (US) ˈbrɑː.voʊ, -ˈ- **-(e)s** -z
Note: Always /ˈ--/ in the ICAO alphabet.
bravura brəˈvjʊə.rə, -ˈvjɔː-, -ˈvʊə- (US) -ˈvjʊr.ə, -ˈvʊr-
brawl brɔːl (US) brɑːl, brɔːl **-s** -z **-ing** -ɪŋ **-ed** -d **-er/s** -əʳ/z (US) -ɚ/z
brawn brɔːn (US) brɑːn, brɔːn
Brawne brɔːn (US) brɑːn, brɔːn
brawn|y ˈbrɔː.n|i (US) ˈbrɑː-, ˈbrɔː- **-ier** -i.əʳ (US) -i.ɚ **-iest** -i.ɪst, -i.əst **-iness** -ɪ.nəs, -ɪ.nɪs
Braxton ˈbræk.stᵊn
bray (B) breɪ **-s** -z **-ing** -ɪŋ **-ed** -d
Braybrooke ˈbreɪ.brʊk
Brayley ˈbreɪ.li
braz|e breɪz **-es** -ɪz **-ing** -ɪŋ **-ed** -d
brazen ˈbreɪ.zᵊn **-ly** -li **-ness** -nəs, -nɪs
brazen-faced ˌbreɪ.zᵊnˈfeɪst *stress shift:* ˌbrazen-faced ˈchild
brazier ˈbreɪ.zi.əʳ, ˈ-ʒəʳ (US) ˈ-ʒɚ **-s** -z
Brazier ˈbreɪ.ʒəʳ (US) -ʒɚ
Brazil *country:* brəˈzɪl *English surname:* ˈbræz.ɪl, -ᵊl; brəˈzɪl **Bra**ˈ**zil** ˌ**nut**
Brazilian brəˈzɪl.i.ən (US) -jən **-s** -z
Brazzaville ˈbræz.ə.vɪl, ˈbrɑː.zə-
breach briːtʃ **-es** -ɪz **-ing** -ɪŋ **-ed** -t ˌ**breach of the** ˈ**peace**
bread bred **-s** -z **-ed** -ɪd ˈ**bread** ˌ**basket** ; ˌ**bread and** ˈ**butter**
Breadalbane *Earl:* brəˈdɔːl.bɪn, brɪ-, -bᵊn (US) -ˈdɔːl-, -ˈdɑːl- *place:* brəˈdæl.bɪn, -ˈdɔːl-, -bən (US) -ˈdæl-, -ˈdɔːl-, -ˈdɑːl-
breadboard ˈbred.bɔːd (US) -bɔːrd **-s** -z
breadbox ˈbred.bɒks (US) -bɑːks **-es** -ɪz
breadcrumb ˈbred.krʌm **-s** -z
breadfruit ˈbred.fruːt **-s** -s
breadline ˈbred.laɪn
breadth bretθ, bredθ **-s** -s
breadth|ways ˈbretθ|.weɪz, ˈbredθ- **-wise** -waɪz
breadwinner ˈbredˌwɪn.əʳ (US) -ɚ **-s** -z
break breɪk **-s** -s **-ing** -ɪŋ **broke** brəʊk (US) broʊk **broken** ˈbrəʊ.kᵊn (US) ˈbroʊ- ˌ**breaking and** ˈ**entering**
breakable ˈbreɪ.kə.bl̩ **-s** -z
breakag|e ˈbreɪ.kɪdʒ **-es** -ɪz
breakaway ˈbreɪ.kə.weɪ **-s** -z
breakdown ˈbreɪk.daʊn **-s** -z
breaker ˈbreɪ.kəʳ (US) -kɚ **-s** -z
break-even ˌbreɪkˈiː.vᵊn
breakfast ˈbrek.fəst **-s** -s **-ing** -ɪŋ **-ed** -ɪd
break-in ˈbreɪk.ɪn **-s** -z
breakneck ˈbreɪk.nek
breakout ˈbreɪk.aʊt **-s** -s
Breakspear ˈbreɪk.spɪəʳ (US) -spɪr
breakthrough ˈbreɪk.θruː **-s** -z
breakup ˈbreɪk.ʌp **-s** -s
breakwater ˈbreɪkˌwɔː.təʳ (US) -ˌwɑː.t̬ɚ, -ˌwɔː- **-s** -z
bream (B) briːm (US) briːm, brɪm **-s** -z

Breamore ˈbrem.əʳ (US) -ɚ
breast brest **-s** -s **-ing** -ɪŋ **-ed** -ɪd ˌ**make a** ˌ**clean** ˈ**breast of something**
breastbone ˈbres*t*.bəʊn (US) -boʊn **-s** -z
breast-feed ˈbres*t*.fiːd **-s** -z **-ing** -ɪŋ
breast-fed ˈbres*t*.fed
Breaston ˈbriː.stᵊn
breastplate ˈbres*t*.pleɪt **-s** -s
breaststroke ˈbres*t*.strəʊk (US) -stroʊk
breastwork ˈbrest.wɜːk (US) -wɜːrk **-s** -s
breath breθ **-s** -s ˈ**breath** ˌ**test** ; ˌ**take someone's** ˈ**breath away** ; ˌ**waste one's** ˈ**breath**
breathalyz|e, -ys|e ˈbreθ.ᵊl.aɪz (US) -ə.laɪz **-es** -ɪz **-ed** -d **-ing** -ɪŋ **-er/s** -əʳ/z (US) -ɚ/z
breath|e briːð **-es** -z **-ing** -ɪŋ **-ed** -d ˈ**breathing** ˌ**room** ; ˈ**breathing** ˌ**space** ; ˌ**breathe** ˌ**down someone's** ˈ**neck**
breathed *phonetic term:* breθt, briːðd
breather ˈbriː.ðəʳ (US) -ðɚ **-s** -z
breathiness ˈbreθ.ɪ.nəs, -nɪs
breathless ˈbreθ.ləs, -lɪs **-ly** -li **-ness** -nəs, -nɪs
breathtaking ˈbreθˌteɪ.kɪŋ **-ly** -li
breath|y ˈbreθ|.i **-ier** -i.əʳ (US) -i.ɚ **-iest** -i.ɪst, -i.əst **-iness** -ɪ.nəs, -ɪ.nɪs
Brebner ˈbreb.nəʳ (US) -nɚ
Brechin ˈbriː.kɪn, -xɪn (US) -kɪn
Brecht brekt *as if German:* brext **-ian** -i.ən
Breckenridge, -kin- ˈbrek.ᵊn.rɪdʒ, -ɪn-
Brecknock ˈbrek.nɒk, -nək (US) -nɑːk **-shire** -ʃəʳ, -ˌʃɪəʳ (US) -ʃɚ, -ˌʃɪr
Brecon ˈbrek.ᵊn ˌ**Brecon** ˈ**Beacons**
bred (*from* **breed**) bred
Bredbury ˈbred.bᵊr.i, ˈbreb- (US) ˈbred.ber-, -bɚ-
Bredon ˈbriː.dᵊn
bree briː
breech (*n.*) briːtʃ **-es** -ɪz **-ed** -t ˈ**breech** ˌ**birth,** ˌ**breech** ˈ**birth** (US) ˈ**breech** ˌ**birth**
breeches *trousers:* ˈbrɪtʃ.ɪz, ˈbriː.tʃɪz
breeching ˈbrɪtʃ.ɪŋ, ˈbriː.tʃɪŋ **-s** -z
breech-loader ˈbriːtʃˌləʊ.dəʳ (US) -ˌloʊ.dɚ **-s** -z
breed briːd **-s** -z **-ing** -ɪŋ **bred** bred ˈ**breeding** ˌ**ground**
breeder ˈbriː.dəʳ (US) -dɚ **-s** -z ˈ**breeder re**ˌ**actor**
breeks briːks
breez|e briːz **-es** -ɪz
breez|y ˈbriː.z|i **-ier** -i.əʳ (US) -i.ɚ **-iest** -i.ɪst, -i.əst **-ily** -ɪ.li, -ᵊl.i **-iness** -ɪ.nəs, -ɪ.nɪs
Bremen *in Germany:* ˈbreɪ.mən (US) ˈbrem.ən, ˈbreɪ.mən *in US:* ˈbri.ːmᵊn, ˈbrem.ən
Bremerhaven ˈbreɪ.məˌhɑː.vᵊn (US) ˈbrem.ɚ-, ˈbreɪ.mɚ-

Bren bren
Brenda ˈbren.də
Brendan ˈbren.dən
Brendel ˈbren.dᵊl
Brendon ˈbren.dən
Brennan ˈbren.ən
Brenner ˈbren.əʳ (US) -ɚ
Brent brent
Brentford ˈbrent.fəd (US) -fɚd
brent|-goose ˌbrent|ˈguːs **-geese** -giːs
Brenton ˈbren.tən
Brentwood ˈbrent.wʊd
bre'r, br'er (B) brɜːʳ, breəʳ (US) brɜːr, brer
Brereton ˈbrɪə.tᵊn (US) ˈbrɪr-
Brescia ˈbreʃ.ə, ˈbreɪ.ʃə (US) ˈbreʃ.ɑː, ˈbreɪ.ʃɑː
Breslau ˈbrez.laʊ, ˈbres-
Brest *in France:* brest
brethren ˈbreð.rən, -rɪn
Breton ˈbret.ᵊn *as if French:* bretˈɔ̃ːŋ (US) ˈbret.ᵊn **-s** -z
Bret(t) bret
Bretwalda bretˈwɔːl.də, -ˈwɒl-, ˈ--- (US) -ˈwɑːl-, -ˈwɔːl-
Breughel ˈbrɔɪ.gᵊl, ˈbrɜː-, ˈbruː- *as if Dutch:* -xəl (US) ˈbruː.gᵊl, ˈbrɔɪ-, ˈbrɔː-
breve briːv (US) briːv, brev **-s** -z
brev|et ˈbrev|.ɪt **-ets** -ɪts **-eting** -ɪ.tɪŋ (US) -ɪ.t̬ɪŋ **-eted** -ɪ.tɪd (US) -ɪ.t̬ɪd
breviar|y ˈbrev.i.ᵊr|.i, ˈbriː.vi- (US) -er|.i, -ɚ|.i **-ies** -iz
breviate ˈbriː.vi.ət, -ɪt **-s** -s
brevier brəˈvɪəʳ, brɪ- (US) -ˈvɪr
brevity ˈbrev.ə.ti, -ɪ.ti (US) -ə.t̬i
brew (B) bruː **-s** -z **-ing** -ɪŋ **-ed** -d
brewer (B) ˈbruː.əʳ (US) -ɚ **-s** -z ˌ**brewer's** ˈ**yeast**
brewer|y ˈbruː.ᵊr|.i (US) ˈbruː.ɚ|.i, ˈ-ri **-ies** -iz
Brewster ˈbruː.stəʳ (US) -stɚ
Brezhnev ˈbreʒ.nef, -njef (US) -nef, -nev
Brian braɪən
Note: /ˈbriː.ən/ for the novelist Brian Moore.
Bria(n)na briˈæn.ə
Brianne briˈæn
briar braɪəʳ (US) braɪɚ **-s** -z
Briareus ˌbraɪˈeə.ri.əs (US) -ˈer.i-
brib|e braɪb **-es** -z **-ing** -ɪŋ **-ed** -d **-er/s** -əʳ/z (US) -ɚ/z
briber|y ˈbraɪ.bᵊr|.i **-ies** -iz
bric-à-brac ˈbrɪk.əˌbræk
Brice braɪs
brick brɪk **-s** -s ˈ**brick** ˌ**dust** ; ˈ**brick** ˌ**field**
brickbat ˈbrɪk.bæt **-s** -s
brickie ˈbrɪk.i **-s** -z
brick-kiln ˈbrɪk.kɪln, -kɪl **-s** -z
Note: The pronunciation /-kɪl/ is used chiefly by those concerned with the working of kilns.

bricklay|er ˈbrɪkˌleɪ|.əʳ (US) -ɚ **-ers** -əz (US) -ɚz **-ing** -ɪŋ
brickmak|er ˈbrɪkˌmeɪ|.kəʳ (US) -kɚ **-ers** -əz (US) -ɚz **-ing** -ɪŋ
brickwork ˈbrɪk.wɜːk (US) -wɜːrk
bricolage ˌbrɪk.əʊˈlɑːʒ, ˈ--- (US) ˌbriː.koʊˈlɑːʒ, ˌbrɪk.oʊˈ-
bridal ˈbraɪ.dᵊl
bride braɪd **-s** -z
bridegroom ˈbraɪd.grʊm, -gruːm (US) -gruːm, -grʊm **-s** -z
Brideshead ˈbraɪdz.hed
bridesmaid ˈbraɪdz.meɪd **-s** -z
brides|man ˈbraɪdz|.mən **-men** -mən, -men
bride-to-be ˌbraɪd.təˈbiː (US) -tuːˈ- **brides-to-be** ˌbraɪdz.təˈbiː (US) -tuːˈ-
Bridewell ˈbraɪd.wel, -wəl
bridg|e (B) brɪdʒ **-es** -ɪz **-ing** -ɪŋ **-ed** -d ˌ**burn one's** ˈ**bridges**
bridgeable ˈbrɪdʒ.ə.bl̩
bridgehead ˈbrɪdʒ.hed **-s** -z
Bridgeman ˈbrɪdʒ.mən
Bridgend ˌbrɪdʒˈend, ˈ--
Bridgenorth ˈbrɪdʒ.nɔːθ, -ˈ- (US) ˈbrɪdʒ.nɔːrθ, -ˈ-
Bridgeport ˈbrɪdʒ.pɔːt (US) -pɔːrt
Bridger ˈbrɪdʒ.əʳ (US) -ɚ
Bridges ˈbrɪdʒ.ɪz
Bridget ˈbrɪdʒ.ɪt
Bridgetown ˈbrɪdʒ.taʊn
Bridgewater ˈbrɪdʒˌwɔː.təʳ (US) -ˌwɑː.t̬ɚ, -ˌwɔː-
bridgework ˈbrɪdʒ.wɜːk (US) -wɜːrk
Bridgnorth ˈbrɪdʒ.nɔːθ, ˌ-ˈ- (US) ˈbrɪdʒ.nɔːrθ, ˌ-ˈ-
Bridgwater ˈbrɪdʒˌwɔː.təʳ (US) -ˌwɑː.t̬ɚ, -ˌwɔː-
bridie (B) ˈbraɪ.di **-s** -z
bridl|e ˈbraɪ.dl̩ **-es** -z **-ing** -ɪŋ, ˈbraɪd.lɪŋ **-ed** -d ˈ**bridle** ˌ**path**
Bridlington ˈbrɪd.lɪŋ.tən
bridoon brɪˈduːn **-s** -z
Bridport ˈbrɪd.pɔːt (US) -pɔːrt
brie (B) briː
brief briːf **-s** -s **-er** -əʳ (US) -ɚ **-est** -ɪst, -əst **-ly** -li **-ness** -nəs, -nɪs **-ing** -ɪŋ **-ed** -t
briefcas|e ˈbriːf.keɪs **-es** -ɪz, -əz
brier braɪəʳ (US) braɪɚ **-s** -z
Brierfield ˈbraɪə.fiːld (US) ˈbraɪɚ-
Brierley ˈbraɪə.li, ˈbrɪə- (US) ˈbraɪɚ-, ˈbrɪr-
Briers braɪəz (US) braɪɚz
brig brɪg **-s** -z
brigade brɪˈgeɪd, brə- **-s** -z
brigadier ˌbrɪg.əˈdɪəʳ (US) -ˈdɪr **-s** -z *stress shift, see compound:* ˌ**brigadier** ˈ**general**
Brigadoon ˌbrɪg.əˈduːn
brigand ˈbrɪg.ᵊnd **-s** -z **-age** -ɪdʒ
brigantine ˈbrɪg.ᵊn.tiːn, -taɪn **-s** -z

Briges 'brɪdʒ.ɪz
Brigg brɪg **-s** -z
Brigham 'brɪg.əm
Brighouse 'brɪg.haʊs
bright (B) braɪt **-er** -əʳ (US) 'braɪ.t̬ɚ **-est** -ɪst, -əst (US) 'braɪ.t̬ɪst, -t̬əst **-ly** -li **-ness** -nəs, -nɪs
brighten 'braɪ.tᵊn **-s** -z **-ing** -ɪŋ **-ed** -d
Brightlingsea 'braɪt.lɪŋ.siː
Brighton 'braɪ.tᵊn
brights braɪts
Brigid 'brɪdʒ.ɪd
Brigit 'brɪdʒ.ɪt
Brignell 'brɪg.nəl
Brigstock(e) 'brɪg.stɒk (US) -stɑːk
brill (B) brɪl **-s** -z
brillian|ce 'brɪl.i.ən*t*|s (US) '-jən*t*|s **-cy** -si
brilliant 'brɪl.i.ənt (US) '-jənt **-s** -s **-ly** -li **-ness** -nəs, -nɪs
brilliantine 'brɪl.i.ən.tiːn (US) '-jən- **-d** -d
Brillo® 'brɪl.əʊ (US) -oʊ
Brillo pad® 'brɪl.əʊˌpæd (US) -oʊˌ-
brim brɪm **-s** -z **-ming** -ɪŋ **-med** -d
brimful brɪm'fʊl, '--
brimstone 'brɪm.stə*ʊ*n (US) -stoʊn
Brind brɪnd
Brindisi 'brɪn.dɪ.si, -də-, -zi
brindle (B) 'brɪn.dḷ **-s** -z **-d** -d
brine braɪn
bring brɪŋ **-s** -z **-ing** -ɪŋ **brought** brɔːt (US) brɑːt, brɔːt **bringer/s** 'brɪŋ.əʳ/z (US) -ɚ/z
brinjal 'brɪn.*d*ʒᵊl
brink (B) brɪŋk **-s** -s
brinkmanship 'brɪŋk.mən.ʃɪp
brinksmanship 'brɪŋ*k*s.mən.ʃɪp
Brinks-Mat® ˌbrɪŋks'mæt
Brinsley 'brɪnz.li
brin|y 'braɪ.n|i **-ier** -i.əʳ (US) -i.ɚ **-iest** -i.ɪst, -i.əst **-iness** -ɪ.nəs, -ɪ.nɪs
Bri-Nylon® ˌbraɪ'naɪ.lɒn (US) -lɑːn
brio 'briː.əʊ (US) -oʊ
brioch|e bri'ɒʃ, -'əʊʃ (US) -'oʊʃ, -'ɑːʃ **-es** -ɪz
Briony 'braɪə.ni
briquette brɪ'ket **-s** -s
Brisbane 'brɪz.bən (US) -bən, -beɪn
Note: /'brɪz.bən/ is the pronunciation in Australia.
Briscoe 'brɪs.kəʊ (US) -koʊ
brisk brɪsk **-er** -əʳ (US) -ɚ **-est** -ɪst, -əst **-ly** -li **-ness** -nəs, -nɪs
brisket 'brɪs.kɪt **-s** -s
bristl|e 'brɪs.ḷ **-es** -z **-ing** -ɪŋ, 'brɪs.lɪŋ **-ed** -d
brist|ly 'brɪs|.ḷ.i, 'brɪs.li **-liness** -ḷ.ɪ.nəs, 'brɪs.li-, -nɪs
Bristol 'brɪs.tᵊl
Bristow(e) 'brɪs.təʊ (US) -toʊ
Brit brɪt **-s** -s
Brit. (*abbrev. for* **Britain**) brɪt; 'brɪt.ᵊn
Brit. (*abbrev. for* **British**) brɪt; 'brɪt.ɪʃ (US) brɪt; 'brɪt̬.ɪʃ
Britain 'brɪt.ᵊn
Britannia brɪ'tæn.i.ə, '-jə (US) '-jə
Britannic brɪ'tæn.ɪk **-a** -ə
britches 'brɪtʃ.ɪz, -əz
Briticism 'brɪt.ɪ.sɪ.zᵊm (US) 'brɪt̬- **-s** -z
British 'brɪt.ɪʃ (US) 'brɪt̬- **-er/s** -əʳ/z (US) -ɚ/z ˌ**British** '**English**; ˌ**British** '**Isles**; ˌ**British** '**Summer** ˌ**Time**
Britishism 'brɪt.ɪ.ʃɪ.zᵊm (US) 'brɪt̬- **-s** -z
British Leyland® ˌbrɪt.ɪʃ'leɪ.lənd (US) ˌbrɪt̬-
Britling 'brɪt.lɪŋ
Britney 'brɪt.ni
Britomart 'brɪt.əʊ.mɑːt (US) -oʊ.mɑːrt
Briton 'brɪt.ᵊn **-s** -z
Britt brɪt
Brittain 'brɪt.ᵊn; brɪ'teɪn (US) 'brɪt.ᵊn; brɪ'teɪn
Brittan 'brɪt.ᵊn
Brittany 'brɪt.ᵊn.i
Britten 'brɪt.ᵊn
brittl|e 'brɪt.ḷ (US) 'brɪt̬- **-er** -əʳ (US) -ɚ **-est** -ɪst, -əst **-eness** -nəs, -nɪs
Brittney 'brɪt.ni
Britton 'brɪt.ᵊn
Britvic® 'brɪt.vɪk
Brixham 'brɪk.sᵊm
Brixton 'brɪk.stᵊn
Brize Norton ˌbraɪz'nɔː.tᵊn (US) -'nɔːr-
Brno 'bɜː.nəʊ *as if Czech:* 'bɚ- (US) 'bɜːr.noʊ
bro brəʊ (US) broʊ **-s** -z
broach brəʊtʃ (US) broʊtʃ **-es** -ɪz **-ing** -ɪŋ **-ed** -t
broad brɔːd (US) brɑːd, brɔːd **-er** -əʳ (US) -ɚ **-est** -ɪst, -əst **-ly** -li **-ness** -nəs, -nɪs ˌ**broad** '**bean**
Broad brɔːd (US) brɑːd, brɔːd **-s** -z
Broadbent 'brɔːd.bent (US) 'brɑːd-, 'brɔːd-
broadbrimmed ˌbrɔːd'brɪmd (US) ˌbrɑːd-, ˌbrɔːd- *stress shift:* ˌbroadbrimmed 'hat
broadcast 'brɔːd.kɑːst (US) 'brɑːd.kæst, 'brɔːd- **-s** -s **-ing** -ɪŋ **-er/s** -əʳ/z (US) -ɚ/z
broadcloth 'brɔːd.klɒθ (US) 'brɑːd.klɑːθ, 'brɔːd-
broaden 'brɔː.dᵊn (US) 'brɑː-, 'brɔː- **-s** -z **-ing** -ɪŋ **-ed** -d
broad-gauge 'brɔːd.geɪdʒ (US) 'brɑːd-, 'brɔːd-
Broadhurst 'brɔːd.hɜːst (US) 'brɑːd.hɜːrst, 'brɔːd-
Broadlands 'brɔːd.ləndz (US) 'brɑːd-, 'brɔːd-
broadloom 'brɔːd.luːm (US) 'brɑːd-, 'brɔːd-
broad-minded ˌbrɔːd'maɪn.dɪd (US) ˌbrɑːd-, ˌbrɔːd-, '-ˌ-- **-ness** -nəs, -nɪs *stress shift, British only:* ˌbroad-minded 'person
Broadmoor 'brɔːd.mɔːʳ (US) 'brɑːd.mʊr, 'brɔːd-, -mɔːr
broadsheet 'brɔːd.ʃiːt (US) 'brɑːd-, 'brɔːd- **-s** -s
broadside 'brɔːd.saɪd (US) 'brɑːd-, 'brɔːd- **-s** -z
Broadstairs 'brɔːd.steəz (US) 'brɑːd.sterz, 'brɔːd-
broadsword 'brɔːd.sɔːd (US) 'brɑːd.sɔːrd, 'brɔːd- **-s** -z
Broadwater 'brɔːdˌwɔː.təʳ (US) 'brɑːdˌwɑː.t̬ɚ, -ˌwɔː-
Broadway 'brɔːd.weɪ (US) 'brɑːd-, 'brɔːd-
Broadwood 'brɔːd.wʊd (US) 'brɑːd-, 'brɔːd- **-s** -z
Brobdingnag 'brɒb.dɪŋ.næg (US) 'brɑːb-
Brobdingnagian ˌbrɒb.dɪŋ'næg.i.ən (US) ˌbrɑːb- **-s** -z
brocade brə*ʊ*'keɪd (US) broʊ- **-s** -z **-d** -ɪd
brocard 'brəʊ.kəd, -kɑːd (US) 'broʊ.kɚd, 'brɑː-, -kɑːrd **-s** -z
broc(c)oli 'brɒk.ᵊl.i, -aɪ (US) 'brɑː.kᵊl-
Broch brɒk *as if German:* brox (US) broʊk
brochette brɒʃ'et (US) broʊ'ʃet **-s** -s
brochure 'brəʊ.ʃəʳ, -ʃʊəʳ, brɒʃ'ʊəʳ, brə'ʃʊəʳ (US) broʊ'ʃʊr **-s** -z
brock (B) brɒk (US) brɑːk **-s** -s
Brocken 'brɒk.ᵊn (US) 'brɑː.kᵊn
Brockenhurst 'brɒk.ᵊn.hɜːst (US) 'brɑː.kᵊn.hɜːrst
Brocket 'brɒk.ɪt (US) 'brɑː.kɪt
Brocklehurst 'brɒk.ḷ.hɜːst (US) 'brɑː.kḷ.hɜːrst
Brockley 'brɒk.li (US) 'brɑː.kli
Brockman 'brɒk.mən (US) 'brɑːk-
Brockwell 'brɒk.wəl, -wel (US) 'brɑː.kwəl, -kwel
Broderick 'brɒd.ᵊr.ɪk (US) 'brɑː.dᵊr-
broderie anglaise ˌbrəʊ.dᵊr.i'ɑ̃ː*ŋ*.gleɪz, ˌbrɒd.ᵊr-, -'glez, -ɑ̃ː*ŋ*'gleɪz, -'glez (US) ˌbroʊ.də.riː.ɑːŋ'gleɪz
Brodie 'brəʊ.di (US) 'broʊ-
Brodrick 'brɒd.rɪk (US) 'brɑː.drɪk
Brogan 'brəʊ.gᵊn (US) 'broʊ-
brogue brəʊg (US) broʊg **-s** -z
broil brɔɪl **-s** -z **-ing** -ɪŋ **-ed** -d
broiler 'brɔɪ.ləʳ (US) -lɚ **-s** -z
brok|e (*v.*) brəʊk (US) broʊk **-es** -s **-ing** -ɪŋ **-ed** -t
broke (*from* **break**) brəʊk (US) broʊk
Broke brʊk
broken 'brəʊ.kᵊn (US) 'broʊ- **-ly** -li
broken-down ˌbrəʊ.kᵊn'daʊn (US) ˌbroʊ- *stress shift:* ˌbroken-down 'car

broken-hearted ˌbrəʊ.kᵊnˈhɑː.tɪd US ˌbroʊ.kᵊnˈhɑːr.t̬ɪd *stress shift:* ˌbroken-hearted ˈsuitor
broker ˈbrəʊ.kəʳ US ˈbroʊ.kɚ **-s** -z **-ing** -ɪŋ **-ed** -d
brokerag|e ˈbrəʊ.kᵊr.ɪdʒ US ˈbroʊ- **-es** -ɪz
broll|y ˈbrɒl|.i US ˈbrɑː.l|i **-ies** -iz
bromate ˈbrəʊ.meɪt US ˈbroʊ- **-s** -s
brome brəʊm, bruːm US broʊm **-s** -z
Brome brəʊm, bruːm US broʊm, bruːm
bromeliad brəʊˈmiː.li.æd US broʊ-
Bromfield ˈbrɒm.fiːld US ˈbrɑːm-
Bromham ˈbrɒm.əm US ˈbrɑː.məm
bromic ˈbrəʊ.mɪk US ˈbroʊ-
bromide ˈbrəʊ.maɪd US ˈbroʊ- **-s** -z
bromine ˈbrəʊ.miːn, -mɪn US ˈbroʊ-
Bromley ˈbrɒm.li, ˈbrʌm- US ˈbrɑːm-
Brompton ˈbrɒmp.tən, ˈbrʌmp- US ˈbrɑːmp-
Bromsgrove ˈbrɒmz.grəʊv US ˈbrɑːmz.groʊv
Bromwich *in place names:* ˈbrɒm.ɪtʃ, ˈbrʌm-, -ɪdʒ US ˈbrɑːm.wɪtʃ *surname:* ˈbrʌm.ɪdʒ US -wɪtʃ
Bromyard ˈbrɒm.jɑːd, -jəd US ˈbrɑːm.jɑːrd, -jɚd
bronchi|a ˈbrɒŋ.ki|.ə, ˈbrɒn- US ˈbrɑːŋ-, ˈbrɑːn- **-ae** -iː
bronchial ˈbrɒŋ.ki.əl, ˈbrɒn- US ˈbrɑːŋ-, ˈbrɑːn-
bronchiole ˈbrɒŋ.ki.əʊl, ˈbrɒn- US ˈbrɑːŋ.ki.oʊl, ˈbrɑːn- **-s** -z
bronchitic brɒŋˈkɪt.ɪk, brɒn- US brɑːŋˈkɪt̬-, brɑːn-
bronchitis brɒŋˈkaɪ.tɪs, brɒn- US brɑːŋˈkaɪ.t̬ɪs, brɑːn-
broncho-pneumonia ˌbrɒŋ.kəʊ.njuːˈməʊ.ni.ə, ˌbrɒn-, -njʊˈ- US ˌbrɑːŋ.koʊ.nuːˈmoʊ.njə, ˌbrɑːn-, -njuːˈ-
bronch|us ˈbrɒŋ.k|əs, ˈbrɒn- US ˈbrɑːŋ-, ˈbrɑːn- **-i** -iː, -aɪ
bronco ˈbrɒŋ.kəʊ US ˈbrɑːŋ.koʊ **-s** -z
Bronson ˈbrɒnt.sən US ˈbrɑːnt-
Bronstein ˈbrɒn.stiːn US ˈbrɑːn-
Bronte, Brontë ˈbrɒn.teɪ, -ti US ˈbrɑːn.teɪ, -t̬i
brontosaur ˈbrɒn.tə.sɔːʳ US ˈbrɑːn.t̬ə.sɔːr **-s** -z
brontosaur|us ˌbrɒn.təˈsɔː.r|əs US ˌbrɑːn.t̬əˈsɔːr|.əs **-uses** -ə.sɪz **-i** -aɪ
Bronwen ˈbrɒn.wen, -wɪn US ˈbrɑːn-
Bronx brɒŋks US brɑːŋks **ˌBronx ˈcheer**
bronz|e brɒnz US brɑːnz **-es** -ɪz **-ing** -ɪŋ **-ed** -d **-y** -i **ˈBronze ˌAge**
bronzer ˈbrɒn.zəʳ US ˈbrɑːn.zɚ **-s** -z
brooch brəʊtʃ US broʊtʃ, bruːtʃ **-es** -ɪz
brood bruːd **-s** -z **-ing** -ɪŋ **-ed** -ɪd
brood|y ˈbruː.d|i **-ily** -ɪ.li, -ᵊl.i **-iness** -ɪ.nəs, -ɪ.nɪs
brook brʊk **-s** -s **-ing** -ɪŋ **-ed** -t
Brook(e) brʊk **-s** -s
Brooker ˈbrʊk.əʳ US -ɚ
Brookfield ˈbrʊk.fiːld
Brookland ˈbrʊk.lənd **-s** -z
brooklet ˈbrʊk.lət, -lɪt **-s** -s
Brookline ˈbrʊk.laɪn
Brooklyn ˈbrʊk.lɪn US -lɪn, -lən **ˌBrooklyn ˈBridge**
Brookner ˈbrʊk.nəʳ US -nɚ
Brooks brʊks
Brookside ˈbrʊk.saɪd
Brooksmith ˈbrʊk.smɪθ
Brookwood ˈbrʊk.wʊd
broom bruːm, brʊm **-s** -z
Broom(e) bruːm
Broomfield ˈbruːm.fiːld, ˈbrʊm-
broomstick ˈbruːm.stɪk, ˈbrʊm- **-s** -s
Brophy ˈbrəʊ.fi US ˈbroʊ-
Bros. ˈbrʌð.əz *sometimes humorously:* brɒs, brɒz US ˈbrʌð.ɚz
Broseley ˈbrəʊz.li US ˈbroʊz-
Brosnahan ˈbrɒz.nə.hən, ˈbrɒs- US ˈbrɑːz-, ˈbrɑːs-
broth brɒθ US brɑːθ **-s** -s
brothel ˈbrɒθ.ᵊl US ˈbrɑː.θᵊl **-s** -z
brother ˈbrʌð.əʳ US -ɚ **-s** -z
brotherhood ˈbrʌð.ə.hʊd US ˈ-ɚ- **-s** -z
broth|er-in-law ˈbrʌð|.əʳ.ɪn.lɔː US -ɚ.ɪn.lɑː, -lɔː **-ers-in-law** -əz.ɪn.lɔː US -ɚz.ɪn.lɑː, -lɔː
brotherl|y ˈbrʌð.ᵊl|.i US -ɚ.l|i **-iness** -ɪ.nəs, -ɪ.nɪs
Brotton ˈbrɒt.ᵊn US ˈbrɑː.tᵊn
Brough brʌf
brougham ˈbruː.əm, bruːm US broʊm, ˈbruː.əm, bruːm **-s** -z
Brougham brʊm, bruːm, ˈbruː.əm, ˈbrəʊ- US brʊm, bruːm, ˈbruː.əm, ˈbroʊ-
Brougham and Vaux ˌbrʊm.əndˈvɔːks US -ˈvɑːks, -ˈvɔːks
brought (*from* **bring**) brɔːt US brɑːt, brɔːt
Broughton *in Northamptonshire:* ˈbraʊ.tᵊn *all others in England:* ˈbrɔː.tᵊn US ˈbrɑː-, ˈbrɔː-
brouhaha ˈbruː.hɑː.hɑː **-s** -z
brow braʊ **-s** -z
brow|beat ˈbraʊ|.biːt **-beats** -biːts **-beating** -biː.tɪŋ US -biː.t̬ɪŋ **-beaten** -biː.tᵊn US -biː.t̬ᵊn
brown (B) braʊn **-s** -z **-er** -əʳ US -ɚ **-est** -ɪst, -əst **-ness** -nəs, -nɪs **-ing** -ɪŋ **-ed** -d **ˌbrown ˈale** ; **ˌbrown ˈBetty** ; **ˌbrown ˈbread** ; **ˌbrown ˈowl** ; **ˌbrown ˈsauce** ; **ˌbrown ˈsugar**
brown-bag ˌbraʊnˈbæg **-s** -z **-ging** -ɪŋ **-ged** -d
Browne braʊn
Brownhills ˈbraʊn.hɪlz
Brownian ˈbraʊ.ni.ən **ˌBrownian ˈmotion** US **ˈBrownian ˌmotion**; **ˌBrownian ˈmovement** US **ˈBrownian ˌmovement**
brownie (B) ˈbraʊ.ni **-s** -z **ˈBrownie ˌGuide** ; **ˈbrownie ˌpoint**
browning (B) ˈbraʊ.nɪŋ
brownish ˈbraʊ.nɪʃ
Brownjohn ˈbraʊn.dʒɒn US -dʒɑːn
Brownlee, Brownlie ˈbraʊn.li
Brownlow ˈbraʊn.ləʊ US -loʊ
brown-nos|e ˌbraʊnˈnəʊz US -ˈnoʊz **-es** -ɪz **-ing** -ɪŋ **-ed** -d
brownout ˈbraʊn.aʊt **-s** -s
Brownrigg ˈbraʊn.rɪg
brownshirt (B) ˈbraʊn.ʃɜːt US -ʃɜːrt **-s** -s
Brownsmith ˈbraʊn.smɪθ
Brownson ˈbraʊn.sᵊn
brownstone ˈbraʊn.stəʊn US -stoʊn **-s** -z
brows|e (B) braʊz **-es** -ɪz **-ing** -ɪŋ **-ed** -d
Broxbourne ˈbrɒks.bɔːn US ˈbrɑːks.bɔːrn
Broxburn ˈbrɒks.bɜːn US ˈbrɑːks.bɜːrn
Brubeck ˈbruː.bek
Bruce bruːs
brucellosis ˌbruː.sɪˈləʊ.sɪs, -səˈ- US -ˈloʊ-
Brucesmith ˈbruːs.smɪθ
Bruch brʊk *as if German:* brʊx
Bruckner ˈbrʊk.nəʳ US -nɚ
Brueg(h)el ˈbrɔɪ.gᵊl, ˈbrɜː-, ˈbruː- *as if Dutch:* -xəl US ˈbruː.gᵊl, ˈbrɔɪ-, ˈbrɔː-
Bruges bruːʒ
bruin (B) ˈbruː.ɪn, brʊɪn US ˈbruː.ɪn **-s** -z
bruis|e bruːz **-es** -ɪz **-ing** -ɪŋ **-ed** -d
bruiser ˈbruː.zəʳ US -zɚ **-s** -z
bruit bruːt **-s** -s **-ing** -ɪŋ US ˈbruː.t̬ɪŋ **-ed** -ɪd US ˈbruː.t̬ɪd
Brum brʌm
Brumaire bruˈmeəʳ US -ˈmer
brume bruːm
brummagem (B) ˈbrʌm.ə.dʒəm
Brummel ˈbrʌm.ᵊl
brunch brʌntʃ **-es** -ɪz
Brunei ˈbruː.naɪ, -ˈ- US -ˈ-
Brunel bruːˈnel
brunette, brunet bruːˈnet **-s** -s
Brünnhilde brʊnˈhɪl.də, ˈ-ˌ--
Brunning ˈbrʌn.ɪŋ
Bruno ˈbruː.nəʊ US -noʊ
Brunswick ˈbrʌnz.wɪk
brunt brʌnt
Brunton ˈbrʌn.tən
brush brʌʃ **-es** -ɪz **-ing** -ɪŋ **-ed** -t
brush-off ˈbrʌʃ.ɒf US -ɑːf **-s** -s **ˌgive someone the ˈbrush-off**

brushwood ˈbrʌʃ.wʊd
brushwork ˈbrʌʃ.wɜːk US -wɜːrk
brusque bruːsk, brʊsk, brʌsk US brʌsk **-ly** -li **-ness** -nəs, -nɪs
Brussels ˈbrʌs.ᵊlz ˌ**brussels ˈsprout(s)** US ˈ**brussels ˌsprout(s)**
brut, (B®) bruːt
brutal ˈbruː.tᵊl US -t̬ᵊl **-ly** -i
brutalit|y bruːˈtæl.ə.t|i, -ɪ.t|i US -ə.t̬|i **-ies** -iz
brutaliz|e, -is|e ˈbruː.tᵊl.aɪz US -t̬ᵊl- **-es** -ɪz **-ing** -ɪŋ **-ed** -d
brute bruːt **-s** -s
brutish ˈbruː.tɪʃ US -t̬ɪʃ **-ly** -li **-ness** -nəs, -nɪs
Brutnell ˈbruːt.nel, -nᵊl
Bruton ˈbruː.tᵊn US -tᵊn
Brutus ˈbruː.təs US -t̬əs
Bryan braɪən **-s** -z
Bryant braɪənt
Bryce braɪs
Brydon ˈbraɪ.dᵊn
Bryers braɪəz US braɪɚz
Brylcreem® ˈbrɪl.kriːm **-ed** -d
Brymbo ˈbrɪm.bəʊ, ˈbrʌm- US ˈbrɪm.boʊ
Bryn brɪn
Brynamman brɪˈnæm.ən
Bryncoch brɪnˈkəʊx US -ˈkoʊx
Brynhild ˈbrɪn.hɪld
Brynmawr *in Wales:* brɪnˈmaʊəʳ, brɪm- US -ˈmaʊɚ
Bryn Mawr *in US:* brɪnˈmɔːʳ US -ˈmɑːr
Brynmor ˈbrɪn.mɔːʳ, ˈbrɪm- US ˈbrɪn.mɔːr
bryony (B) ˈbraɪə.ni
Bryson ˈbraɪ.sᵊn
BS ˌbiːˈes
BSc ˌbiː.esˈsiː
BSE ˌbiː.esˈiː
BSkyB ˌbiː.skaɪˈbiː
BST ˌbiː.esˈtiː
BT ˌbiːˈtiː
bub bʌb **-s** -z
bubbl|e ˈbʌb.l̩ **-es** -z **-ing** -ɪŋ, ˈbʌb.lɪŋ **-ed** -d ˌ**bubble-and-ˈsqueak** ; ˈ**bubble ˌbath** ; ˈ**bubble ˌgum** ; ˈ**bubble ˌwrap**
Bubblejet® ˈbʌb.l̩.dʒet
bubbly ˈbʌb.l̩.i, -li
Buber ˈbuː.bəʳ US -bɚ
bubo ˈbjuː.bəʊ, ˈbuː- US -boʊ **-es** -z
bubonic bjuːˈbɒn.ɪk, buː- US -ˈbɑː.nɪk buˌ**bonic ˈplague**
Bucaramanga bʊˌkær.əˈmæŋ.gə US ˌbuː.kə.rɑːˈmɑːŋ.gɑː, -kɑːr.ɑːˈ-
buccal ˈbʌk.ᵊl
buccaneer ˌbʌk.əˈnɪəʳ US -ˈnɪr **-s** -z
Buccleuch bəˈkluː
Bucephalus bjuːˈsef.ᵊl.əs
Buchan ˈbʌk.ᵊn, ˈbʌx-
Buchanan bjuːˈkæn.ən, bə-
Bucharest ˌbuː.kəˈrest, ˌbjuː-, ˌbʊk.əˈ-, ˈ--- US ˈbuː.kə.rest, ˈbjuː-
Buchel ˈbjuː.ʃᵊl
Buchenwald ˈbuː.kᵊn.væld *as if German:* ˈbʊx.ən.vælt US ˈbuː.kᵊn.wɑːld, -wɔːld
Büchner ˈbuːk.nəʳ *as if German:* ˈbuːx- US ˈbʊk.nɚ, ˈbuːk-
buck (B) bʌk **-s** -s **-ing** -ɪŋ **-ed** -t ˌ**buck's ˈfizz** ; ˌ**buck ˈteeth** ; ˌ**pass the ˈbuck**
buckboard ˈbʌk.bɔːd US -bɔːrd **-s** -z
buck|et ˈbʌk|.ɪt **-ets** -ɪts **-eting** -ɪ.tɪŋ US -ɪ.t̬ɪŋ **-eted** -ɪ.tɪd US -ɪ.t̬ɪd ˌ**kick the ˈbucket**
bucketful ˈbʌk.ɪt.fʊl **-s** -z
Buckhaven ˈbʌkˌheɪ.vᵊn
buckhorn ˈbʌk.hɔːn US -hɔːrn
Buckhurst ˈbʌk.*h*ɜːst US -*h*ɜːrst
Buckie ˈbʌk.i
Buckingham ˈbʌk.ɪŋ.əm **-shire** -ʃəʳ, -ˌʃɪəʳ US -ʃɚ, -ˌʃɪr ˌ**Buckingham ˈPalace**
Buckland ˈbʌk.lənd
buckl|e (B) ˈbʌk.l̩ **-es** -z **-ing** -ɪŋ, ˈbʌk.lɪŋ **-ed** -d
buckler ˈbʌk.ləʳ US -lɚ **-s** -z
Buckley ˈbʌk.li
Buckmaster ˈbʌkˌmɑː.stəʳ US -ˌmæs.tɚ
Bucknall ˈbʌk.nəl
Bucknell ˈbʌk.nᵊl; bʌkˈnel
Bucknill ˈbʌk.nɪl, -nᵊl
buck-passing ˈbʌkˌpɑː.sɪŋ US -ˌpæs.ɪŋ
buckram ˈbʌk.rəm **-s** -z
Bucks. (*abbrev. for* **Buckinghamshire**) bʌks; ˈbʌk.ɪŋ.əm.ʃəʳ, -ˌʃɪəʳ US bʌks; ˈbʌk.ɪŋ.əm.ʃɚ, -ˌʃɪr
buckshee ˌbʌkˈʃiː, ˈ--
buckshot ˈbʌk.ʃɒt US -ʃɑːt
buckskin ˈbʌk.skɪn **-s** -z
Buckston ˈbʌk.stən
buckwheat ˈbʌk.*h*wiːt
bucolic bjuːˈkɒl.ɪk US -ˈkɑː.lɪk **-al** -ᵊl **-ally** -ᵊl.i, -li
Buczacki bʊˈtʃæt.ski, bjuː-
bud (B) bʌd **-s** -z **-ding** -ɪŋ **-ded** -ɪd ˌ**nip something in the ˈbud**
Budapest ˌbjuː.dəˈpest, ˌbuː- US ˈbuː.də.pest; ˌbuː.dəˈpeʃt
Budd bʌd
Buddha ˈbʊd.ə US ˈbuː.də, ˈbʊd.ə
Buddh|ism ˈbʊd|.ɪ.zᵊm US ˈbuː.d|ɪ-, ˈbʊd|.ɪ- **-ist/s** -ɪst/s
Buddhistic bʊˈdɪs.tɪk US buː-, bʊ-
budding ˈbʌd.ɪŋ
Buddle ˈbʌd.l̩, ˈbʊd-
buddleia ˈbʌd.li.ə US bədˈliː-; ˈbʌd.li- **-s** -z
budd|y ˈbʌd|.i **-ies** -iz
Bude bjuːd
budg|e (B) bʌdʒ **-es** -ɪz **-ing** -ɪŋ **-ed** -d
budgerigar ˈbʌdʒ.ᵊr.ɪ.gɑːʳ US -gɑːr **-s** -z
budg|et ˈbʌdʒ|.ɪt **-ets** -ɪts **-eting** -ɪ.tɪŋ US -ɪ.t̬ɪŋ **-eted** -ɪ.tɪd US -ɪ.t̬ɪd
budgetary ˈbʌdʒ.ɪ.tᵊr.i, ˈ-ə- US -ter.i
budgie ˈbʌdʒ.i **-s** -z
Budleigh ˈbʌd.li
Budweiser® ˈbʌd.waɪ.zəʳ US -zɚ
Buenos Aires ˌbweɪ.nɒsˈaɪə.rez, -nəs-, -riːz, -rɪs US ˌbweɪ.nəsˈer.iːz, -noʊsˈ-, ˌboʊ.nəsˈ-, -aɪ.riːz
buff bʌf
buffalo (B) ˈbʌf.ᵊl.əʊ US -ə.loʊ **-es** -z ˌ**Buffalo ˈBill**
buffer ˈbʌf.əʳ US -ɚ **-s** -z ˈ**buffer ˌzone**
buffet (*n.*) *blow:* ˈbʌf.ɪt **-s** -s
buffet (*n.*) *refreshment, sideboard:* ˈbʊf.eɪ, ˈbʌf-, -i US bəˈfeɪ, buː- **-s** -z
buff|et (*v.*) *hit against:* ˈbʌf|.ɪt **-ets** -ɪts **-eting** -ɪ.tɪŋ, -ə.tɪŋ US -ɪ.t̬ɪŋ, -ə.t̬ɪŋ **-eted** -ɪ.tɪd, -ə.tɪd US -ɪ.t̬ɪd, -ə.t̬ɪd
buffo ˈbʊf.əʊ US ˈbuː.foʊ **-s** -z
buffoon bəˈfuːn, bʌfˈuːn US bəˈfuːn **-s** -z
buffooner|y bəˈfuː.nᵊr|.i, bʌfˈuː- US bəˈfuː- **-ies** -iz
Buffs bʌfs
bug bʌg **-s** -z **-ging** -ɪŋ **-ged** -d
Bug *river:* buːg
bugaboo ˈbʌg.ə.buː **-s** -z
Buganda buːˈgæn.də
Bugatti bjʊˈgæt.i, bʊ- US -ˈgɑː.t̬i
bugbear ˈbʌg.beəʳ US -ber **-s** -z
bug-eyed ˌbʌgˈaɪd US ˈ-- *stress shift, British only:* ˌbug-eyed ˈmonster
bugg|er ˈbʌg|.əʳ US -ɚ **-ers** -əz US -ɚz **-ering** -ᵊr.ɪŋ **-ered** -əd US -ɚd
buggery ˈbʌg.ᵊr.i
Buggins ˈbʌg.ɪnz
Buggs bjuːgz, bʌgz
bugg|y ˈbʌg|.i **-ies** -iz
bugl|e (B) ˈbjuː.gl̩ **-es** -z **-ing** -ɪŋ, ˈbjuː.glɪŋ **-ed** -d
bugler ˈbjuː.gləʳ US -glɚ **-s** -z
bugloss ˈbjuː.glɒs US -glɑːs
Bugner ˈbʌg.nəʳ US -nɚ
Bugs Bunny ˌbʌgzˈbʌn.i
Buick® ˈbjuː.ɪk **-s** -s
build bɪld **-s** -z **-ing** -ɪŋ **built** bɪlt ˈ**building soˌciety**
builder ˈbɪl.dəʳ US -dɚ **-s** -z
build-up ˈbɪld.ʌp **-s** -s
built (*from* **build**) bɪlt
Builth bɪlθ
built-in ˌbɪltˈɪn US ˈbɪlt.ɪn *stress shift, British only:* ˌbuilt-in ˈmicrophone
Buist bjuːst, ˈbjuː.ɪst
Buitoni® bjuːˈtəʊ.ni, bwiː- US -ˈtoʊ-
Bujumbura ˌbuː.dʒəmˈbʊə.rə, -dʒʊmˈ- US -ˈbʊr.ə
Bukowski bjʊˈkɒf.ski, bjuː-, -ˈkaʊ- US bjuːˈkaʊ-

Bulawayo ˌbʊl.əˈweɪ.əʊ, ˌbuː.lə- (US) -oʊ

bulb bʌlb **-s** -z

bulbaceous bʌlˈbeɪ.ʃəs

bulbous ˈbʌl.bəs

bulbul ˈbʊl.bʊl **-s** -z

Bulford ˈbʊl.fəd (US) -fɚd

Bulgakov bʊlˈgɑː.kɒf (US) -kɔːf, -kɔːv

bulgar ˈbʌl.gəʳ, ˈbʊl- (US) -gɚ **ˈbulgar ˌwheat**

Bulgar ˈbʌl.gɑːʳ, ˈbʊl-, -gəʳ (US) -gɑːr, -gɚ **-s** -z

Bulgari|a bʌlˈgeə.ri|.ə (US) -ˈger.i- **-an/s** -ən/z

bulg|e bʌldʒ **-es** -ɪz **-ing** -ɪŋ **-ed** -d

bulgur ˈbʊl.gəʳ (US) -gɚ

bulg|y ˈbʌl.dʒ|i **-iness** -ɪ.nəs, -ɪ.nɪs

bulim|ia bʊˈlɪm|.i.ə, buː-, bjuː-, -ˈliː.m|i- (US) bjuːˈliː.m|i-, buː- **-ic/s** -ɪk **buˌlimia nerˈvosa**

Bulins ˈbjuː.lɪnz

bulk bʌlk **-s** -s **-ing** -ɪŋ **-ed** -t

bulkhead ˈbʌlk.hed **-s** -z

Bulkington ˈbʌl.kɪŋ.tən

bulk|y ˈbʌl.k|i **-ier** -i.əʳ (US) -i.ɚ **-iest** -i.ɪst, -i.əst **-ily** -ɪ.li, -əl.i **-iness** -ɪ.nəs, -ɪ.nɪs

bull (B) bʊl **-s** -z **-ing** -ɪŋ **-ed** -d **ˌbull ˈterrier ; ˈbull's ˌeye ; like a ˌbull in a ˈchina shop ; take the ˌbull by the ˈhorns**

bullac|e ˈbʊl.ɪs **-es** -ɪz

Bullard ˈbʊl.ɑːd, -əd (US) -ɑːrd, -ɚd

bull-baiting ˈbʊlˌbeɪ.tɪŋ (US) -t̬ɪŋ

bull-cal|f ˈbʊlˌkɑː|f, ˌ-ˈ- (US) ˈbʊl.kæ|f **-ves** -vz

bulldog ˈbʊl.dɒg (US) -dɑːg, -dɔːg **-s** -z

bulldoz|e ˈbʊl.dəʊz (US) -doʊz **-es** -ɪz **-ing** -ɪŋ **-ed** -d

bulldozer ˈbʊlˌdəʊ.zəʳ (US) -ˌdoʊ.zɚ **-s** -z

Bulleid ˈbʊl.iːd

Bullen ˈbʊl.ən, -ɪn

Buller ˈbʌl.əʳ (US) -ɚ

bullet ˈbʊl.ɪt, -ət **-s** -s

bulletin ˈbʊl.ə.tɪn, ˈ-ɪ- (US) -ə.t̬ɪn **-s** -z **ˈbulletin ˌboard**

bullet-proof ˈbʊl.ɪt.pruːf **ˌbullet-proof ˈvest**

bullfight ˈbʊl.faɪt **-s** -s

bullfight|er ˈbʊlˌfaɪ.t|əʳ (US) -t̬|ɚ **-ers** -əz (US) -ɚz **-ing** -ɪŋ

bullfinch ˈbʊl.fɪntʃ **-es** -ɪz

bullfrog ˈbʊl.frɒg (US) -frɑːg, -frɔːg **-s** -z

bullheaded ˌbʊlˈhed.ɪd (US) ˈ-ˌ-- **-ly** -li **-ness** -nəs, -nɪs *stress shift, British only:* ˌbullheaded ˈperson

bullhorn ˈbʊl.hɔːn (US) -hɔːrn **-s** -z

bullion ˈbʊl.i.ən, ˈ-jən (US) ˈ-jən

bullish ˈbʊl.ɪʃ **-ly** -li **-ness** -nəs, -nɪs

Bullman ˈbʊl.mən

bullock (B) ˈbʊl.ək **-s** -s

Bullokar ˈbʊl.ə.kɑːʳ, -kəʳ (US) -kɑːr

Bullough ˈbʊl.əʊ (US) -oʊ

bullpen ˈbʊl.pen **-s** -z

bullring ˈbʊl.rɪŋ **-s** -z

bullrush ˈbʊl.rʌʃ **-es** -ɪz

bull|shit ˈbʊl|.ʃɪt **-shits** -ʃɪts **-shitting** -ˌʃɪt.ɪŋ (US) -ˌʃɪt̬.ɪŋ **-shitted** -ˌʃɪt.ɪd (US) -ˌʃɪt̬.ɪd

bullshitter ˈbʊlˌʃɪt.əʳ (US) -ˌʃɪt̬.ɚ **-s** -z

bull|y ˈbʊl|.i **-ies** -iz **-ying** -i.ɪŋ **-ied** -id

Bulmer ˈbʊl.məʳ (US) -mɚ

bulrush ˈbʊl.rʌʃ **-es** -ɪz

Bulstrode ˈbʊl.strəʊd, ˈbʌl.strəʊd (US) -stroʊd

Bultitude ˈbʊl.tɪ.tjuːd, ˈ-tə- (US) -tuːd, -tjuːd

bulwark ˈbʊl.wək, ˈbʌl-, -wɜːk (US) -wɚk, -wɜːrk **-s** -s

Bulwer ˈbʊl.wəʳ (US) -wɚ

Bulwer-Lytton ˌbʊl.wəˈlɪt.ən (US) -wɚˈlɪt̬-

bum bʌm **-s** -z **-ming** -ɪŋ **-med** -d

bumbag ˈbʌm.bæg **-s** -z

bumbl|e ˈbʌm.bl̩ **-es** -z **-ing** -ɪŋ, ˈbʌm.blɪŋ **-ed** -d **-er/s** -əʳ/z, ˈ-bləʳ/z (US) ˈ-bl̩.ɚ/z, ˈ-blɚ/z

bumblebee ˈbʌm.bl̩.biː **-s** -z

bumboat ˈbʌm.bəʊt (US) -boʊt **-s** -s

bumf bʌm*p*f

Bumford ˈbʌm.fəd (US) -fɚd

bumkin ˈbʌm*p*.kɪn **-s** -z

bummaree ˌbʌm.əˈriː, ˈ--- (US) ˈbʌm.ə.riː **-s** -z

bummer ˈbʌm.əʳ (US) -ɚ **-s** -z

bump bʌmp **-s** -s **-ing** -ɪŋ **-ed** -t

bumper ˈbʌm.pəʳ (US) -pɚ **-s** -z **ˈbumper ˌcar ; ˈbumper ˌsticker ; ˌbumper to ˈbumper**

bumph bʌm*p*f

bumpkin ˈbʌmp.kɪn **-s** -z

bumptious ˈbʌmp.ʃəs **-ly** -li **-ness** -nəs, -nɪs

Bumpus ˈbʌm.pəs

bump|y ˈbʌm.p|i **-ier** -i.əʳ (US) -i.ɚ **-iest** -i.ɪst, -i.əst **-ily** -ɪ.li, -əl.i **-iness** -ɪ.nəs, -ɪ.nɪs

bun bʌn **-s** -z **have a ˈbun in the ˌoven**

Bunce bʌn*t*s

bunch (B) bʌn*t*ʃ **-es** -ɪz **-ing** -ɪŋ **-ed** -t

buncombe (B) ˈbʌŋ.kəm

Bundesbank ˈbʊn.dəz.bæŋk

Bundesrat ˈbʊn.dəz.rɑːt

Bundestag ˈbʊn.dəz.tɑːg *as if German:* -dəz.tɑːk (US) -dəz.tɑːg

bundl|e ˈbʌn.dl̩ **-les** -z **-ling** -ɪŋ, ˈbʌnd.lɪŋ **-led** -d

bung bʌŋ **-s** -z **-ing** -ɪŋ **-ed** -d

bungalow ˈbʌŋ.gəl.əʊ (US) -oʊ **-s** -z

Bungay ˈbʌŋ.gi

Bunge ˈbʌŋ.i

bungee ˈbʌn.dʒi **ˈbungee ˌjumping**

bungl|e ˈbʌŋ.gl̩ **-es** -z **-ing** -ɪŋ, ˈbʌŋ.glɪŋ **-ed** -d **-er/s** -əʳ/z, ˈ-gləʳ/z (US) ˈ-gl̩.ɚ/z, ˈ-glɚ/z

bunion ˈbʌn.jən **-s** -z

bunk bʌŋk **-s** -s **-ing** -ɪŋ **-ed** -t

bunk|er (B) ˈbʌŋ.k|əʳ (US) -k|ɚ **-ers** -əz (US) -ɚz **-ering** -ər.ɪŋ **-ered** -əd (US) -ɚd

bunkhou|se ˈbʌŋk.hau|s **-ses** -zɪz

bunkum ˈbʌŋ.kəm

Bunnett ˈbʌn.ɪt

bunn|y ˈbʌn|.i **-ies** -iz

Bunsen ˈbʌn*t*.sən (US) -sɪn **ˌBunsen ˈburner** (US) **ˈBunsen ˌburner**

bunt bʌnt **-s** -s

Bunter ˈbʌn.təʳ (US) -t̬ɚ

bunting (B) ˈbʌn.tɪŋ (US) -t̬ɪŋ **-s** -z

Bunty ˈbʌn.ti (US) -t̬i

Buñuel ˌbuː.njuˈel, ˈ---; ˌbuːnˈwel, ˌbʊn- (US) ˌbuːnˈwel, ˌbʊn-

Bunyan ˈbʌn.jən

buoy bɔɪ (US) bɔɪ, ˈbuː.i **-s** -z **-ing** -ɪŋ **-ed** -d

buoyancy ˈbɔɪ.ən*t*.si (US) ˈbɔɪ-, ˈbuː.jən*t*-

buoyant ˈbɔɪ.ənt (US) ˈbɔɪ-, ˈbuː.jənt **-ly** -li

BUPA ˈbuː.pə, ˈbjuː-

bur bɜːʳ (US) bɜːr **-s** -z

Burbage ˈbɜː.bɪdʒ (US) ˈbɜːr-

Burberr|y® ˈbɜː.bər|.i (US) ˈbɜːr.ber-, -bɚ- **-y's** -iz **-ies** -iz

burbl|e ˈbɜː.bl̩ (US) ˈbɜːr- **-es** -z **-ing** -ɪŋ, ˈ-blɪŋ **-ed** -d

Burbridge ˈbɜː.brɪdʒ (US) ˈbɜːr-

Burbury ˈbɜː.bər.i (US) ˈbɜːr.ber-, -bɚ-

Burch bɜːtʃ (US) bɜːrtʃ

Burchell, Burchall ˈbɜː.tʃəl (US) ˈbɜːr-

Burchill ˈbɜː.tʃəl, -tʃɪl (US) ˈbɜːr-

Burco ˈbɜː.kəʊ (US) ˈbɜːr.koʊ

burden (B) ˈbɜː.dən (US) ˈbɜːr- **-s** -z **-ing** -ɪŋ **-ed** -d

burdensome ˈbɜː.dən.səm (US) ˈbɜːr-

Burdett ˈbɜː.det, -ˈ- (US) bɜːrˈdet, ˈ--

Burdett-Coutts ˌbɜː.detˈkuːts, -ˌ-ˈ- (US) bɜːrˌdetˈ-

burdock ˈbɜː.dɒk (US) ˈbɜːr.dɑːk **-s** -s

Burdon ˈbɜː.dən (US) ˈbɜːr-

Bure bjʊəʳ (US) bjʊr

bureau ˈbjʊə.rəʊ, ˈbjɔː-, bjʊəˈrəʊ (US) ˈbjʊr.oʊ **-s** -z

bureaucrac|y bjʊəˈrɒk.rə.s|i, bjəˈ-, bjɔːˈ- (US) bjʊˈrɑː.krə- **-ies** -iz

bureaucrat ˈbjʊə.rəʊ.kræt, ˈbjɔː- (US) ˈbjʊr.ə- **-s** -s

bureaucratic ˌbjʊə.rəʊˈkræt.ɪk, ˌbjɔː- (US) ˌbjʊr.əˈkræt̬- **-ally** -əl.i, -li

bureaux (*alternative plur. of* **bureau**) ˈbjʊə.rəʊ, ˈbjɔː-, -rəʊz; ˌbjʊəˈrəʊ, -ˈrəʊz (US) ˈbjʊr.oʊ, -oʊz

burette, buret bjʊəˈret (US) bjʊrˈet **-s** -s

Burford ˈbɜː.fəd (US) ˈbɜːr.fɚd
burg bɜːg (US) bɜːrg **-s** -z
Burgar ˈbɜː.gəʳ (US) ˈbɜːr.gɚ
Burg|e bɜːdʒ (US) bɜːrdʒ **-es** -ɪz
burgee ˈbɜː.dʒiː, -ˈ- (US) ˈbɜːr.dʒi **-s** -z
burgeon ˈbɜː.dʒᵊn (US) ˈbɜːr- **-s** -z **-ing** -ɪŋ **-ed** -d
burger ˈbɜː.gəʳ (US) ˈbɜːr.gɚ **-s** -z
burgess (B) ˈbɜː.dʒəs, -dʒɪs, -dʒes (US) ˈbɜːr- **-es** -ɪz
burgh ˈbʌr.ə (US) bɜːrg, ˈbɜː.rə, ˈbɜːr.oʊ **-s** -z
Burgh bɜːg (US) bɜːrg *in Suffolk:* bɜːg; ˈbʌr.ə (US) bɜːrg; ˈbɜːr.oʊ *Baron, Heath in Surrey, place in Lincolnshire:* ˈbʌr.ə (US) ˈbɜːr.oʊ *Burgh-by-Sands:* brʌf
Burghclere ˈbɜː.kleəʳ (US) ˈbɜːr.kler
burgher ˈbɜː.gəʳ (US) ˈbɜːr.gɚ **-s** -z
Burghersh ˈbɜː.gəʃ (US) ˈbɜːr.gɚʃ
Burghley ˈbɜː.li (US) ˈbɜːr-
burglar ˈbɜː.gləʳ (US) ˈbɜːr.glɚ **-s** -z
burglariz|e ˈbɜː.glᵊr.aɪz (US) ˈbɜːr.glə.raɪz **-es** -ɪz **-ing** -ɪŋ **-ed** -d
burglar|y ˈbɜː.glᵊr|.i (US) ˈbɜːr- **-ies** -iz
burgl|e ˈbɜː.gl̩ (US) ˈbɜːr- **-es** -z **-ing** -ɪŋ, ˈ-glɪŋ **-ed** -d
burgomaster ˈbɜː.gəʊˌmɑː.stəʳ (US) ˈbɜːr.gəˌmæs.tɚ **-s** -z
Burgos ˈbʊə.gɒs (US) ˈbʊr.gɑːs
Burgoyne ˈbɜː.gɔɪn, -ˈ- (US) bɜːrˈgɔɪn, ˈ--
burgund|y (B) ˈbɜː.gᵊn.d|i (US) ˈbɜːr- **-ies** -iz
burial ˈber.i.əl **-s** -z ˈ**burial ˌground** ; ˈ**burial ˌplace**
burin ˈbjʊə.rɪn (US) ˈbʊr.ɪn, ˈbɜːr- **-s** -z
burk bɜːk (US) bɜːrk **-s** -s
burk|e (B) bɜːk (US) bɜːrk **-es** -s **-ing** -ɪŋ **-ed** -t
Burkina Faso bɜːˌkiː.nəˈfæs.əʊ (US) bʊrˌkiː.nəˈfɑː.soʊ
burlap ˈbɜː.læp (US) ˈbɜːr-
Burleigh ˈbɜː.li (US) ˈbɜːr-
burlesqu|e bɜːˈlesk (US) bɜːr- **-es** -s **-ing** -ɪŋ **-ed** -t
Burley ˈbɜː.li (US) ˈbɜːr-
Burling ˈbɜː.lɪŋ (US) ˈbɜːr-
Burlington ˈbɜː.lɪŋ.tən (US) ˈbɜːr-
burl|y (B) ˈbɜː.l|i (US) ˈbɜːr- **-ier** -i.əʳ (US) -i.ɚ **-iest** -i.ɪst, -i.əst **-iness** -ɪ.nəs, -ɪ.nɪs
Burma ˈbɜː.mə (US) ˈbɜːr-
Burman ˈbɜː.mən (US) ˈbɜːr- **-s** -z
Burmese bɜːˈmiːz (US) bɜːr-, -ˈmiːs
burn bɜːn (US) bɜːrn **-s** -z **-ing** -ɪŋ **-ed** -d **burnt** bɜːnt (US) bɜːrnt
Burnaby ˈbɜː.nə.bi (US) ˈbɜːr-
Burnand bɜːˈnænd, bə- (US) bɚ-
Burne bɜːn (US) bɜːrn
burner ˈbɜː.nəʳ (US) ˈbɜːr.nɚ **-s** -z ˌ**put something on a/the ˌback ˈburner**
burnet (B) ˈbɜː.nɪt (US) ˈbɜːr- **-s** -s
Burnett bɜːˈnet, bə-; ˈbɜː.nɪt (US) bɚˈnet; ˈbɜːr.nɪt
Burney ˈbɜː.ni (US) ˈbɜːr-
Burnham ˈbɜː.nəm (US) ˈbɜːr-
Burnham-on-Crouch ˌbɜː.nəm.ɒnˈkraʊtʃ (US) ˌbɜːr.nəm.ɑːnˈ-
Burnham-on-Sea ˌbɜː.nəm.ɒnˈsiː (US) ˌbɜːr.nəm.ɑːnˈ-
burnish ˈbɜː.nɪʃ (US) ˈbɜːr- **-es** -ɪz **-ing** -ɪŋ **-ed** -t **-er/s** -əʳ/z (US) -ɚ/z
Burnley ˈbɜːn.li (US) ˈbɜːrn-
burnous, burnous|e bɜːˈnuːs (US) bɚ- **-es** -ɪz
burnout ˈbɜːn.aʊt (US) ˈbɜːrn-
Burns bɜːnz (US) bɜːrnz
Burnside ˈbɜːn.saɪd (US) ˈbɜːrn-
burnt (*from* **burn**) bɜːnt (US) bɜːrnt ˌ**burnt ˈoffering**
Burntisland ˌbɜːntˈaɪ.lənd (US) ˌbɜːrnt-
Burntwood ˈbɜːnt.wʊd (US) ˈbɜːrnt-
burp bɜːp (US) bɜːrp **-s** -s **-ing** -ɪŋ **-ed** -t
burr (B) bɜːʳ (US) bɜːr **-s** -z
Burrell ˈbʌr.ᵊl, ˈbɜːr-
Burridge ˈbʌr.ɪdʒ (US) ˈbɜːr-
burrito bəˈriː.təʊ, bʊrˈiː- (US) bəˈriː.t̬oʊ **-s** -z
Burrough(e)s ˈbʌr.əʊz (US) ˈbɜːr.oʊz
burrow ˈbʌr.əʊ (US) ˈbɜːr.oʊ **-s** -z **-ing** -ɪŋ **-ed** -d
Burrows ˈbʌr.əʊz (US) ˈbɜːr.oʊz
Burry Port ˌbʌr.iˈpɔːt (US) ˌbɜːr.iˈpɔːrt
Bursa ˈbɜː.sə (US) bʊrˈsɑː, bɜːr-
bursar ˈbɜː.səʳ (US) ˈbɜːr.sɚ, -sɑːr **-s** -z
bursarship ˈbɜː.sə.ʃɪp (US) ˈbɜːr.sɚ-, -sɑːr- **-s** -s
bursar|y ˈbɜː.sᵊr|.i (US) ˈbɜːr- **-ies** -iz
Burscough Bridge ˌbɜː.skəʊˈbrɪdʒ (US) ˌbɜːr.skoʊˈ-
Bursledon ˈbɜː.zᵊl.dᵊn (US) ˈbɜːr-
Burslem ˈbɜːz.ləm (US) ˈbɜːrz-
burst bɜːst (US) bɜːrst **-s** -s **-ing** -ɪŋ
Burt bɜːt (US) bɜːrt
burthen ˈbɜː.ðᵊn (US) ˈbɜːr- **-s** -z
burton (B) ˈbɜː.tᵊn (US) ˈbɜːr-
Burundi bʊˈrʊn.di, bə- **-an/s** -ən/z
Burwash ˈbɜː.wɒʃ *locally also:* ˈbʌr.əʃ (US) ˈbɜːr.wɑːʃ, -wɔːʃ
bur|y (*v*) ˈber|.i **-ies** -iz **-ying** -i.ɪŋ **-ied** -id
Bury *place:* ˈber.i *surname:* ˈbjʊə.ri, ˈber.i (US) ˈbʊr.i, ˈber-
bus bʌs **-(s)es** -ɪz **-(s)ing** -ɪŋ **-(s)ed** -t ˈ**bus conˌductor** ; ˈ**bus ˌstop**
busbar ˈbʌs.bɑːʳ (US) -bɑːr **-s** -z
busboy ˈbʌs.bɔɪ **-s** -z
busb|y ˈbʌz.b|i **-ies** -iz
bush (B) bʊʃ **-es** -ɪz **-ing** -ɪŋ **-ed** -t ˈ**bush ˌbaby** ; ˌ**beat about the ˈbush**
bushel ˈbʊʃ.ᵊl **-s** -z
Bushell ˈbʊʃ.ᵊl (US) ˈbʊʃ.ᵊl, bʊˈʃel
Bushey ˈbʊʃ.i
Bushire bjuːˈʃaɪəʳ, buː-, -ˈʃɪəʳ (US) buːˈʃɪr
bush-league ˈbʊʃ.liːg **-s** -z
bush|man (B) ˈbʊʃ|.mən **-men** -mən, -men
Bushmills ˈbʊʃ.mɪlz
Bushnell ˈbʊʃ.nᵊl (US) -nᵊl, -nel
bushranger ˈbʊʃˌreɪn.dʒəʳ (US) -dʒɚ **-s** -z
bushwhack ˈbʊʃ.*h*wæk **-s** -s **-ing** -ɪŋ **-ed** -t
bushwhacker ˈbʊʃˌ*h*wæk.əʳ (US) -ɚ **-s** -z
bush|y (B) ˈbʊʃ|.i **-ily** -ɪ.li, -ᵊl.i **-iness** -ɪ.nəs, -ɪ.nɪs
business ˈbɪz.nɪs, -nəs **-es** -ɪz ˌ**mind one's ˌown ˈbusiness**
businesslike ˈbɪz.nɪs.laɪk, -nəs-
business|man ˈbɪz.nɪs|.mæn, -nəs-, -mən **-men** -men, -mən
business|person ˈbɪz.nɪs|ˌpɜː.sᵊn, -nəsˌ- **-people** -ˌpiː.pl̩
business|woman ˈbɪz.nɪs|ˌwʊm.ən, -nəsˌ- **-women** -ˌwɪm.ɪn
busk (B) bʌsk **-s** -s **-ing** -ɪŋ **-ed** -t **-er/s** -əʳ/z (US) -ɚ/z
buskin ˈbʌs.kɪn **-s** -z **-ed** -d
bus|man ˈbʌs|.mən, -mæn **-men** -mən, -men ˌ**busman's ˈholiday**
Busoni buːˈzəʊ.ni, bjuː-, -ˈsəʊ- (US) bʊˈzoʊ.ni, bjuː-
buss (B) bʌs **-es** -ɪz **-ing** -ɪŋ **-ed** -t
bust bʌst **-s** -s **-ing** -ɪŋ **-ed** -ɪd
bustard ˈbʌs.təd (US) -tɚd **-s** -z
buster (B) ˈbʌs.təʳ (US) -tɚ **-s** -z
bustier ˈbʌs.ti.əʳ, ˈbʊs-, ˈbuː.sti- (US) ˈbuː.sti.eɪ, ˈbʊs.tjeɪ **-s** -z
bustl|e ˈbʌs.l̩ **-es** -z **-ing** -ɪŋ, ˈbʌs.lɪŋ **-ed** -d
bust|y ˈbʌs.t|i **-ier** -i.əʳ (US) -i.ɚ **-iest** -i.ɪst, -i.əst **-iness** -ɪ.nəs, -ɪ.nɪs
bus|y ˈbɪz|.i **-ier** -i.əʳ (US) -i.ɚ **-iest** -i.ɪst, -i.əst **-ily** -ɪ.li, -ᵊl.i ˈ**busy ˌsignal**
busybod|y ˈbɪz.iˌbɒd|.i (US) -ˌbɑː.d|i **-ies** -iz
busyness ˈbɪz.i.nəs, -nɪs
but *strong form:* bʌt *weak form:* bət
Note: Weak form word. The strong form /bʌt/ is used contrastively (e.g. **ifs** and **buts**) and in sentence-final position (e.g. "It's anything but"). The weak form is /bət/ (e.g. "It's good but expensive" /ɪtsˌgʊd.bət.ɪkˈspen*t*.sɪv/).
butane ˈbjuː.teɪn (US) ˈbjuː.teɪn, -ˈ-
butch (B) bʊtʃ
butch|er (B) ˈbʊtʃ|.əʳ (US) -ɚ **-ers** -əz (US) -ɚz **-ering** -ᵊr.ɪŋ **-ered** -əd (US) -ɚd
butcher|y ˈbʊtʃ.ᵊr|.i **-ies** -iz
Bute bjuːt **-shire** -ʃəʳ, -ˌʃɪəʳ (US) -ʃɚ, -ˌʃɪr
Buthelezi ˌbuː.təˈleɪ.zi

butler (B) ˈbʌt.ləʳ ⓊⓈ -lɚ **-s** -z
butler|age ˈbʌt.lᵊr|.ɪdʒ **-y** -i **-ies** -iz
Butlin ˈbʌt.lɪn
butt (B) bʌt **-s** -s **-ing** -ɪŋ ⓊⓈ ˈbʌt̬.ɪŋ **-ed** -ɪd ⓊⓈ ˈbʌt̬.ɪd
butt-end ˈbʌt.end **-s** -z
butt|er ˈbʌt|.əʳ ⓊⓈ ˈbʌt̬|.ɚ **-ers** -əz ⓊⓈ -ɚz **-ering** -ᵊr.ɪŋ **-ered** -əd ⓊⓈ -ɚd **ˈbutter ˌbean ; ˈbutter ˌdish ; ˈbutter ˌknife ; ˌbutter wouldn't ˌmelt in his/her ˈmouth**
butterball ˈbʌt.ə.bɔːl ⓊⓈ ˈbʌt̬.ɚ.bɔːl, -bɑːl **-s** -z
buttercup ˈbʌt.ə.kʌp ⓊⓈ ˈbʌt̬.ɚ- **-s** -s
butterfat ˈbʌt.ə.fæt ⓊⓈ ˈbʌt̬.ɚ-
Butterfield ˈbʌt.ə.fiːld ⓊⓈ ˈbʌt̬.ɚ-
butterfinger|s ˈbʌt.əˌfɪŋ.gə|z ⓊⓈ ˈbʌt̬.ɚˌfɪŋ.gɚ|z **-ed** -d
butterfl|y ˈbʌt.ə.fl|aɪ ⓊⓈ ˈbʌt̬.ɚ- **-ies** -aɪz
Butterick ˈbʌt.ᵊr.ɪk ⓊⓈ ˈbʌt̬-
Butterleigh, Butterley ˈbʌt.ᵊl.i ⓊⓈ ˈbʌt̬.ɚ.li
Buttermere ˈbʌt.ə.mɪəʳ ⓊⓈ ˈbʌt̬.ɚ.mɪr
buttermilk ˈbʌt.ə.mɪlk ⓊⓈ ˈbʌt̬.ɚ-
butternut ˈbʌt.ə.nʌt ⓊⓈ ˈbʌt̬.ɚ- **-s** -s
butterscotch ˈbʌt.ə.skɒtʃ ⓊⓈ ˈbʌt̬.ɚ.skɑːtʃ
Butterwick ˈbʌt.ᵊr.ɪk, -ə.wɪk ⓊⓈ ˈbʌt̬.ɚ.ɪk, -wɪk
Butterworth ˈbʌt.ə.wəθ, -wɜːθ ⓊⓈ ˈbʌt̬.ɚ.wɚθ, -wɜːrθ
butter|y ˈbʌt.ᵊr|.i ⓊⓈ ˈbʌt̬- **-ies** -iz
buttock ˈbʌt.ək ⓊⓈ ˈbʌt̬- **-s** -s
button (B) ˈbʌt.ᵊn **-s** -z **-ing** -ɪŋ **-ed** -d
button-down ˌbʌt.ᵊnˈdaʊn *stress shift:* ˌbutton-down ˈcollar
buttonhol|e ˈbʌt.ᵊn.həʊl ⓊⓈ -hoʊl **-es** -z **-ing** -ɪŋ **-ed** -d
buttonhook ˈbʌt.ᵊn.hʊk **-s** -s
buttress (B) ˈbʌt.rəs, -rɪs **-es** -ɪz
butt|y ˈbʌt|.i ⓊⓈ ˈbʌt̬- **-ies** -iz
butut buːˈtuːt
butyric bjʊˈtɪr.ɪk ⓊⓈ bjuː-
buxom ˈbʌk.səm **-ness** -nəs, -nɪs
Buxtehude ˌbʊk.stəˈhuː.də
Buxton ˈbʌk.stən
buy baɪ **-s** -z **-ing** -ɪŋ **bought** bɔːt ⓊⓈ bɑːt, bɔːt
buyable ˈbaɪ.ə.bl̩
buyer ˈbaɪ.əʳ ⓊⓈ -ɚ **-s** -z
buyout ˈbaɪ.aʊt **-s** -s
Buzfuz ˈbʌz.fʌz
buzz bʌz **-es** -ɪz, -əz **-ing** -ɪŋ **-ed** -d
buzzard ˈbʌz.əd ⓊⓈ -ɚd **-s** -z
buzzer ˈbʌz.əʳ ⓊⓈ -ɚ **-s** -z
buzzword ˈbʌz.wɜːd ⓊⓈ -wɜːrd **-s** -z
bwana ˈbwɑː.nə
by *normal form:* baɪ *occasional weak forms:* bɪ, bə
Note: Weak form word. The strong form is /baɪ/. The weak forms /bɪ, bə/ are rarely used, but can be found occasionally, particularly in measurements (e.g. "two by three" /ˌtuː.bəˈθriː/).
by-and-by ˌbaɪ.ᵊnᵈˈbaɪ, -ᵊm- ⓊⓈ -ᵊnᵈ-
Byard baɪəd ⓊⓈ baɪɚd
Byars baɪəz ⓊⓈ baɪɚz
Byas(s) baɪəs
Byatt baɪət
Bydgoszcz ˈbɪd.gɒʃt *as if Polish:* -gɒtʃtʃ ⓊⓈ -gɔːʃtʃ
bye (B) baɪ **-s** -z
bye-bye *goodbye:* ˌbaɪˈbaɪ, bə-, bʌbˈaɪ; ˈbaɪ.baɪ, ˈbʌb.aɪ
bye-bye *sleep:* ˈbaɪ.baɪ **-s** -z
byelaw ˈbaɪ.lɔː ⓊⓈ -lɑː, -lɔː **-s** -z
by-election ˈbaɪ.ɪˌlek.ʃᵊn, -əˌ- **-s** -z
Byelorussi|a ˌbjel.əʊˈrʌʃ|.ə, ˌbel-, -ˈruː.si- ⓊⓈ -oʊˈ-, -əˈ- **-an/s** -ᵊn/z
Byers baɪəz ⓊⓈ baɪɚz
Byfleet ˈbaɪ.fliːt
Byford ˈbaɪ.fəd ⓊⓈ -fɚd
bygone ˈbaɪ.gɒn ⓊⓈ -gɑːn **-s** -z
Bygraves ˈbaɪ.greɪvz
bylaw ˈbaɪ.lɔː ⓊⓈ -lɑː, -lɔː **-s** -z
Byles baɪlz
byline ˈbaɪ.laɪn **-s** -z
Byng bɪŋ
Bynoe ˈbaɪ.nəʊ ⓊⓈ -noʊ
BYO ˌbiː.waɪˈəʊ ⓊⓈ -ˈoʊ
bypass ˈbaɪ.pɑːs ⓊⓈ -pæs **-es** -ɪz
bypa|th ˈbaɪ.pɑː|θ ⓊⓈ -pæ|θ **-ths** -ðz
byplay ˈbaɪ.pleɪ
by-product ˈbaɪˌprɒd.ʌkt, -əkt ⓊⓈ -ˌprɑː.dəkt **-s** -s
Byrd bɜːd ⓊⓈ bɜːrd
byre baɪəʳ ⓊⓈ baɪɚ **-s** -z
Byrne bɜːn ⓊⓈ bɜːrn
byroad ˈbaɪ.rəʊd ⓊⓈ -roʊd **-s** -z
Byrom ˈbaɪ.rəm
Byron ˈbaɪ.rən
Byronic baɪˈrɒn.ɪk ⓊⓈ -ˈrɑː.nɪk **-ally** -ᵊl.i, -li
Bysshe bɪʃ
bystander ˈbaɪˌstæn.dəʳ ⓊⓈ -dɚ **-s** -z
bystreet ˈbaɪ.striːt **-s** -s
byte baɪt **-s** -s
Bythesea ˈbaɪθ.siː
byway ˈbaɪ.weɪ **-s** -z
byword ˈbaɪ.wɜːd ⓊⓈ -wɜːrd **-s** -z
Byzantian baɪˈzæn.ti.ən, bɪ-, bə-, ˈ-*t*ʃᵊn ⓊⓈ bɪˈzæn.ti.ən, bə-, baɪ-, -ˈzæn*t*.ʃᵊn
Byzantine bɪˈzæn.taɪn, baɪ-, bə-, -tiːn; ˈbɪz.ᵊn- ⓊⓈ ˈbɪz.ᵊn.tiːn, -taɪn
Byzantium bɪˈzæn.ti.əm, baɪ-, bə-, ˈ-*t*ʃᵊm ⓊⓈ bɪˈzæn.ti.əm, bə-, baɪ-, -ˈzæn*t*.ʃᵊm

C

c (C) siː -'s -z
ca (*abbrev. for* **circa**) 'sɜː.kə (US) 'sɜːr-
CAA ˌsiː.eɪ'eɪ
cab kæb **-s** -z
CAB ˌsiː.eɪ'biː
cabal kə'bæl, kæb'æl (US) kə'bɑːl, -'bæl **-s** -z
cabala (C) kə'bɑː.lə, kæb'ɑː-
cabalism 'kæb.ə.lɪ.zᵊm
cabalistic ˌkæb.ə'lɪs.tɪk **-al** -ᵊl **-ally** -ᵊl.i, -li
caballero ˌkæb.ə'leə.rəʊ, -'ljeə- (US) -'ler.oʊ, -əl'jer- **-s** -z
cabana kə'bɑː.nə (US) -'bæn.ə, -'bɑː.nə, -njə **-s** -z
cabaret 'kæb.ə.reɪ, ˌ--'- (US) ˌkæb.ə'reɪ, '--- **-s** -z
cabbag|e 'kæb.ɪdʒ **-es** -ɪz **'cabbage ˌrose**
cabbala (C) kə'bɑː.lə, kæb'ɑː- **-s** -z
cabbal|ism 'kæb.ə.l|ɪ.zᵊm **-ist/s** -ɪst/s
cabbalistic ˌkæb.ə'lɪs.tɪk **-al** -ᵊl **-ally** -ᵊl.i, -li
cabb|ie, cabb|y 'kæb|.i **-ies** -iz
cabdriver 'kæbˌdraɪ.vəʳ (US) -vɚ **-s** -z
Cabell 'kæb.ᵊl
caber 'keɪ.bəʳ (US) -bɚ **-s** -z
cabernet sauvignon ˌkæb.ə.neɪ.səʊ.viː'njɔ̃ːŋ, -jɒn (US) -ɚ.neɪˌsoʊ.viː'njoʊn
cabin 'kæb.ɪn **-s** -z **'cabin ˌboy** ; **'cabin ˌcruiser** ; **'cabin ˌfever**
cabinet (C) 'kæb.ɪ.nət, -ə-, -nɪt **-s** -s **'Cabinet ˌMinister, ˌCabinet 'Minister**
cabinetmak|er 'kæb.ɪ.nətˌmeɪ.k|əʳ, -nɪt- (US) -k|ɚ **-ers** -əz (US) -ɚz **-ing** -ɪŋ
cabl|e (C) 'keɪ.bl̩ **-es** -z **-ing** -ɪŋ, '-blɪŋ **-ed** -d **'cable ˌcar** ; **ˌcable 'television, ˌcable tele'vision**
cablecast 'keɪ.bl̩.kɑːst (US) -kæst **-s** -s **-ing** -ɪŋ **-er/s** -əʳ/z (US) -ɚ/z
cablegram 'keɪ.bl̩.græm **-s** -z
cab|man 'kæb|.mən **-men** -mən, -men
caboodle kə'buː.dl̩
caboos|e kə'buːs **-es** -ɪz
Cabot 'kæb.ət
cabotage 'kæb.ə.tɑːʒ, -tɪdʒ
Cabrini kə'briː.ni
cabriole 'kæb.ri.əʊl (US) -oʊl **-s** -z
cabriolet 'kæb.ri.əʊ.leɪ, ˌkæb.ri.əʊ'leɪ (US) ˌkæb.ri.ə'leɪ **-s** -z
cabstand 'kæb.stænd **-s** -z
ca-ca 'kɑː.kɑː
cacao kə'kaʊ, kæk'aʊ; kə'kɑː.əʊ, kæk'ɑː-, -'eɪ- (US) -oʊ **-s** -z
cachalot 'kæʃ.ə.lɒt (US) -lɑːt, -loʊ **-s** -s, -z
cach|e kæʃ **-es** -ɪz
cachepot 'kæʃ.pəʊ, ˌkæʃ'pɒt (US) 'kæʃ.pɑːt, -poʊ **-s** -s, -z
cachet 'kæʃ.eɪ (US) -'- **-s** -z
cachinnat|e 'kæk.ɪ.neɪt, '-ə- **-es** -s **-ing** -ɪŋ **-ed** -ɪd
cachinnation ˌkæk.ɪ'neɪ.ʃᵊn
cachou kæʃ'uː, kə'ʃuː; 'kæʃ.uː **-s** -z
cachucha kə'tʃuː.tʃə **-s** -z
cacique kæs'iːk, kə'siːk **-s** -s
cack-handed ˌkæk'hæn.dɪd, '--- **-ly** -li **-ness** -nəs, -nɪs
cackl|e 'kæk.l̩ **-es** -z **-ing** -ɪŋ, '-lɪŋ **-ed** -d **-er/s** -əʳ/z, '-ləʳ/z (US) '-l̩.ɚ/z, '-lɚ/z
cacodyl 'kæk.əʊ.daɪl, -dɪl (US) 'kæk.oʊ.dɪl, '-ə-
cacoepy kæk'əʊ.ɪ.pi, -ep.i (US) -'oʊ.ə-
cacographic ˌkæk.əʊ'græf.ɪk (US) -oʊ'-, -ə'- **-al** -ᵊl
cacography kæk'ɒg.rə.fi, kə'kɒg- (US) kə'kɑː.grə-
cacology kæk'ɒl.ə.dʒi, kə'kɒl- (US) kə'kɑː.lə-
cacophonic ˌkæk.əʊ'fɒn.ɪk (US) -oʊ'fɑː.nɪk, -ə'- **-al** -ᵊl **-ally** -ᵊl.i, -li
cacophonous kə'kɒf.ə.nəs, kæk'ɒf- (US) kə'kɑː.fə-
cacophon|y kə'kɒf.ə.n|i, kæk'ɒf- (US) kə'kɑː.fə- **-ies** -iz
cactus 'kæk.təs **-es** -ɪz **cacti** 'kæk.taɪ
cacuminal kæk'juː.mɪ.nᵊl, kə'kjuː- (US) kə'kjuː.mə- **-s** -z
cad kæd **-s** -z
CAD kæd
cadaster kə'dæs.təʳ (US) -tɚ
cadastral kə'dæs.trəl
cadastre kə'dæs.təʳ (US) -tɚ
cadaver kə'dɑː.vəʳ, -'deɪ-, -'dæv.əʳ (US) -'dæv.ɚ **-s** -z
cadaveric kə'dæv.ə.rɪk (US) -ɚ.ɪk
cadaverous kə'dæv.ᵊr.əs **-ness** -nəs, -nɪs
Cadbury 'kæd.bᵊr.i (US) 'kæd.ber.i, -bɚ-
Cadby 'kæd.bi
CAD/CAM 'kæd.kæm
Caddell kə'del
caddie 'kæd.i **-s** -z
caddis 'kæd.ɪs **'caddis ˌfly**
caddish 'kæd.ɪʃ **-ly** -li **-ness** -nəs, -nɪs
cadd|y 'kæd|.i **-ies** -iz
cade (C) keɪd **-s** -z
Cadell 'kæd.ᵊl, kə'del
cadenc|e 'keɪ.dᵊnts **-es** -ɪz
cadency 'keɪ.dᵊnt.si
Cadenus kə'diː.nəs
cadenza kə'den.zə **-s** -z
Cader Idris ˌkæd.əʳ'ɪd.rɪs (US) -ɚ'-
cadet kə'det **-s** -s **ca'det ˌcorps**
cadetship kə'det.ʃɪp **-s** -s
cadg|e kædʒ **-es** -ɪz **-ing** -ɪŋ **-ed** -d **-er/s** -əʳ/z (US) -ɚ/z
cadi 'kɑː.di, 'keɪ- **-s** -z
Cadillac® 'kæd.ɪ.læk, -ᵊl.æk (US) -ə.læk, -ᵊl.æk **-s** -s
Cadiz *in Spain:* kə'dɪz *as if Spanish:* 'kæd.ɪθ (US) kə'dɪz; 'keɪ.dɪz *in Phillipines:* 'kɑː.diːs (US) kə'dɪz; 'keɪ.dɪz *in the US:* kæd'ɪz; 'keɪ.dɪz (US) kə'dɪz; 'keɪ.dɪz
Cadman 'kæd.mən
Cadmean 'kæd.mi.ən, kæd'miː- (US) kæd'miː-
cadmic 'kæd.mɪk
cadmium 'kæd.mi.əm, 'kæb- (US) 'kæd-
Cadmus 'kæd.məs
Cadogan kə'dʌg.ən
cadre 'kɑː.dəʳ, 'keɪ-, -drə (US) 'kæd.riː, 'kɑː.dri, -dreɪ **-s** -z
caduce|us kə'djuː.si|.əs, -'dʒuː- (US) -'duː-, -'djuː-, -ʃ|əs **-i** -aɪ
Cadwallader kæd'wɒl.ə.dəʳ (US) -'wɑː.lə.dɚ
CAE ˌsiː.eɪ'iː
caec|um 'siː.k|əm **-a** -ə
Caedmon 'kæd.mən
Caen kɑ̃ː (US) kɑːn
Caerleon kɑː'liː.ən, kə-, -'lɪən (US) kɑːr-
Caernarvon, Caernarfon kə'nɑː.vᵊn (US) kɑːr'nɑːr- **-shire** -ʃəʳ, -ˌʃɪəʳ (US) -ʃɚ, -ˌʃɪr
Caerphilly keə'fɪl.i, kɑː-, kə'fɪl- (US) kɑːr-
Caesar 'siː.zəʳ (US) -zɚ **-s** -z
Caesarea ˌsiː.zə'riː.ə
caesarean, caesarian *way of having a baby:* sɪ'zeə.ri.ən, sə- (US) sɪ'zer.i- **caeˌsarean 'section**
Caesarean *of Caesarea:* ˌsiː.zə'riː.ən *of Caesar:* siː'zeə.ri.ən, sɪ- (US) sɪ'zer.i-
caesium 'siː.zi.əm
caesura sɪ'zjʊə.rə, siː-, -'zjɔː-, -'ʒʊə- (US) sə'zʊr.ə, -'ʒʊr- **-s** -z
café, cafe 'kæf.eɪ (US) kæf'eɪ, kə'feɪ **-s** -z
cafeteria ˌkæf.ə'tɪə.ri.ə, -ɪ'- (US) -'tɪr.i- **-s** -z
cafetière, cafetiere ˌkæf.ə'tjeəʳ (US) -'tjer **-s** -z
caff kæf **-s** -s
caffein 'kæf.iːn, -eɪn (US) kæf'iːn
caffeinated 'kæf.ɪ.neɪ.tɪd, '-ə- (US) -ə.neɪ.t̬ɪd
caffeine 'kæf.iːn, -eɪn (US) kæf'iːn
caftan 'kæf.tæn (US) -tæn, -tən **-s** -z
cag|e (C) keɪdʒ **-es** -ɪz **-ing** -ɪŋ **-ed** -d
cageling 'keɪdʒ.lɪŋ **-s** -z
cager 'keɪ.dʒəʳ (US) -dʒɚ **-s** -z
cag|ey 'keɪ.dʒ|i **-ier** -i.əʳ (US) -i.ɚ **-iest** -i.ɪst, -i.əst **-ily** -ɪ.li, -ᵊl.i **-iness** -ɪ.nəs, -ɪ.nɪs

Cagliari ˌkæl.jiˈɑː.ri, ˈkæl.jə.ri
Ⓤⓢ ˈkɑːl.jɑːr.i, -jɚ-
Cagliostro kæl.jiˈɒs.trəʊ
Ⓤⓢ kɑːlˈjɔː.stroʊ
Cagney ˈkæg.ni
cagoule kəˈguːl, kægˈuːl **-s** -z
cag|y ˈkeɪ.dʒ|i **-ier** -i.əʳ Ⓤⓢ -i.ɚ **-iest** -i.ɪst, -i.əst **-ily** -ɪ.li, -ᵊl.i **-iness** -ɪ.nəs, -ɪ.nɪs
Cahal kəˈhæl, ˈkæ.hᵊl
Cahan kɑːn
Cahill ˈkɑː.hɪl, ˈkeɪ.hɪl
Cahoon kəˈhuːn, kæ-
cahoots kəˈhuːts
CAI ˌsiː.eɪˈaɪ
Caiaphas ˈkaɪ.ə.fæs, -fəs
Caicos ˈkeɪ.kɒs, -kəs Ⓤⓢ -kəs
Caillard ˈkaɪ.ɑːʳ Ⓤⓢ -ɑːr
caiman ˈkeɪ.mən, ˈkaɪ-, -mæn Ⓤⓢ ˈkeɪ- **-s** -z
Cain(e) keɪn
caique, caïque kaɪˈiːk, kɑː- Ⓤⓢ kɑːˈiːk **-s** -s
Caird keəd Ⓤⓢ kerd
Cairene ˈkaɪə.riːn Ⓤⓢ ˈkaɪ-, -ˈ-
cairn keən Ⓤⓢ kern **-s** -z
cairngorm (C) ˌkeənˈgɔːm, ˌkeəŋ-, ˈ-- Ⓤⓢ ˈkern.gɔːrm **-s** -z
Cairns keənz Ⓤⓢ kernz
Cairo *in Egypt:* ˈkaɪə.rəʊ Ⓤⓢ ˈkaɪ.roʊ *in the US:* ˈkeə.rəʊ Ⓤⓢ ˈker.oʊ
caisson ˈkeɪ.sɒn, -sᵊn *sometimes in engineering:* kəˈsuːn Ⓤⓢ ˈkeɪ.sᵊn, -sɑːn **-s** -z
Caister ˈkeɪ.stəʳ Ⓤⓢ -stɚ
Caister-on-Sea ˌkeɪ.stəʳ.ɒnˈsiː Ⓤⓢ -stɚ.ɑːnˈ-
Caistor ˈkeɪ.stəʳ Ⓤⓢ -stɚ
Caithness ˈkeɪθ.nes, -nəs; keɪθˈnes
caitiff ˈkeɪ.tɪf Ⓤⓢ -t̬ɪf **-s** -s
Caitlin, Caitlín ˈkeɪt.lɪn, ˈkæt.lɪn
Caius *Roman name, character in Shakespeare's Merry Wives:* ˈkaɪ.əs, ˈkeɪ.əs *as if Latin:* ˈgaɪ- *Cambridge college:* kiːz
cajol|e kəˈdʒəʊl Ⓤⓢ -ˈdʒoʊl **-es** -z **-ing** -ɪŋ **-ed** -d **-er/s** -əʳ/z Ⓤⓢ -ɚ/z
cajoler|y kəˈdʒəʊ.lᵊr|.i Ⓤⓢ -ˈdʒoʊ- **-ies** -iz
Cajun ˈkeɪ.dʒən **-s** -z
cak|e keɪk **-es** -s **-ing** -ɪŋ **-ed** -t **(sell/go) like ˌhot ˈcakes** Ⓤⓢ **(sell/go) like ˈhot ˌcakes ; ˌhave one's ˌcake and ˈeat it** Ⓤⓢ **ˌhave one's ˌcake and ˌeat it ˈtoo**
cakewalk ˈkeɪk.wɔːk Ⓤⓢ -wɑːk, -wɔːk **-s** -s
Cakovec tʃɑːˈkəʊ.vets Ⓤⓢ -ˈkoʊ-
CAL kæl, ˌsiː.eɪˈel
Calabar ˌkæl.əˈbɑːʳ, ˈ--- Ⓤⓢ ˈkæl.ə.bɑːr, ˌ--ˈ-
calabash ˈkæl.ə.bæʃ **-es** -ɪz, -əz
calaboos|e ˈkæl.ə.buːs, --ˈ- **-es** -ɪz
calabrese ˈkæl.ə.briːs, -briːz
Calabri|a kəˈlæb.ri|.ə, kælˈæb-, -ˈɑː.bri- Ⓤⓢ kəˈleɪ.bri-, -ˈlɑː- **-an/s** -ən/z
Calais ˈkæl.eɪ Ⓤⓢ kælˈeɪ
calamari ˌkæl.əˈmɑː.ri Ⓤⓢ -ˈmɑːr.i
calamine ˈkæl.ə.maɪn
calamitous kəˈlæm.ɪ.təs, -ə.təs Ⓤⓢ -ə.t̬əs **-ly** -li **-ness** -nəs, -nɪs
calamit|y kəˈlæm.ə.t|i, -ɪ.t|i Ⓤⓢ -ə.t̬|i **-ies** -iz **Caˌlamity ˈJane**
calamus ˈkæl.ə.məs
calash kəˈlæʃ **-es** -ɪz
calcareous kælˈkeə.ri.əs Ⓤⓢ -ˈker.i-, -ˈkær- **-ness** -nəs, -nɪs
calceolaria ˌkæl.si.əˈleə.ri.ə Ⓤⓢ -ˈler.i-, -ˈlær- **-s** -z
calces ˈkæl.siːz
Calchas ˈkæl.kæs
calciferol kælˈsɪf.ə.rɒl Ⓤⓢ -roʊl, -rɑːl
calciferous kælˈsɪf.ᵊr.əs
calcification ˌkæl.sɪ.fɪˈkeɪ.ʃᵊn, -sə-
calcifug|e ˈkæl.sɪ.fjuːdʒ **-es** -ɪz
calcifugous kælˈsɪf.jə.gəs
calcif|y ˈkæl.sɪ.f|aɪ, -sə- **-ies** -aɪz **-ying** -aɪ.ɪŋ **-ied** -aɪd
calcination ˌkæl.sɪˈneɪ.ʃᵊn, -səˈ-
calcin|e ˈkæl.saɪn, -sɪn **-es** -z **-ing** -ɪŋ **-ed** -d
calcite ˈkæl.saɪt **-s** -s
calcium ˈkæl.si.əm
Calcot(t) ˈkɔːl.kət, ˈkɒl-, ˈkæl- Ⓤⓢ ˈkɔːl.kɑːt, ˈkɑːl-, ˈkæl-
Note: In Calcot Row, Berkshire, the pronunciation is /ˈkæl.kət/.
calculab|le ˈkæl.kjə.lə.b|l̩, -kjʊ- Ⓤⓢ -kjə- **-ly** -li
calcu|late ˈkæl.kjə|.leɪt, -kjʊ- Ⓤⓢ -kjə- **-lates** -leɪts **-lating** -leɪ.tɪŋ Ⓤⓢ -leɪ.t̬ɪŋ **-lated** -leɪ.tɪd Ⓤⓢ -leɪ.t̬ɪd
calculation ˌkæl.kjəˈleɪ.ʃᵊn, -kjʊˈ- Ⓤⓢ -kjəˈ- **-s** -z
calculative ˈkæl.kjə.lə.tɪv, -kjʊ- Ⓤⓢ -kjə.lə.t̬ɪv
calculator ˈkæl.kjə.leɪ.təʳ, -kjʊ- Ⓤⓢ -kjə.leɪ.t̬ɚ **-s** -z
calcul|us ˈkæl.kjə.l|əs, -kjʊ- Ⓤⓢ -kjə- **-uses** -ə.sɪz **-i** -aɪ
Calcutt ˈkæl.kʌt
Calcutta kælˈkʌt.ə Ⓤⓢ -ˈkʌt̬-
Caldecote ˈkɔːl.dɪ.kət, ˈkɒl-, -də- Ⓤⓢ ˈkɑːl.də.koʊt, ˈkɔːl-, -kət
Caldecott ˈkɔːl.də.kət, ˈkɒl-, -dɪ-, -kɒt Ⓤⓢ ˈkɑːl.də.kɑːt, ˈkɔːl-, -kət
Calder ˈkɔːl.dəʳ, ˈkɒl- Ⓤⓢ ˈkɔːl.dɚ, ˈkɑːl-
caldera kælˈdeə.rə, ˈkɔːl.də.rə Ⓤⓢ kælˈder.ə
Calderon *English name:* ˈkɔːl.də.rən, ˈkɒl-, ˈkæl- Ⓤⓢ ˈkɔːl.də.rɑːn, ˈkɑːl- *Spanish name:* ˌkæl.dəˈrɒn Ⓤⓢ ˌkɑːl.ðəˈrɔːn
Caldicot(t) ˈkɔːl.dɪ.kɒt, ˈkɒl-, -də-, -kət Ⓤⓢ ˈkɑːl.də.kɑːt, ˈkɔːl-, -kət
caldron ˈkɔːl.drən, ˈkɒl- Ⓤⓢ ˈkɑːl-, ˈkɔːl- **-s** -z
Caldwell ˈkɔːld.wəl, ˈkɒld-, -wel Ⓤⓢ ˈkɔːld-, ˈkɑːld-
Caleb ˈkeɪ.leb, -lɪb, -ləb
Caledon ˈkæl.ɪ.dᵊn, ˈ-ə-
Caledoni|a ˌkæl.ɪˈdəʊ.ni|.ə, -əˈ- Ⓤⓢ -ˈdoʊ- **-an/s** -ən/z
calefaction ˌkæl.ɪˈfæk.ʃᵊn, -əˈ-
calefactor|y ˌkæl.ɪˈfæk.tᵊr|.i, -əˈ-, -tr|i **-ies** -iz
calendar ˈkæl.ən.dəʳ, -ɪn- Ⓤⓢ -dɚ **-s** -z
calend|er ˈkæl.ən.d|əʳ, -ɪn- Ⓤⓢ -d|ɚ **-ers** -əz Ⓤⓢ -ɚz **-ering** -ᵊr.ɪŋ **-ered** -əd Ⓤⓢ -ɚd
calends ˈkæl.ɪndz, -endz, -əndz Ⓤⓢ ˈkæl.ɪndz, ˈkeɪ.lɪndz, -lendz, -ləndz
calendula kəˈlen.djə.lə, kælˈen-, -djʊ- Ⓤⓢ -dʒə- **-s** -z
calenture ˈkæl.ən.tʃʊəʳ, -ɪn-, -tjʊəʳ, -tʃəʳ Ⓤⓢ -tʃɚ, -tʃʊr **-s** -z
cal|f kɑː|f Ⓤⓢ kæ|f **-ves** -vz **ˌcalf's-foot ˈjelly**
calfskin ˈkɑːf.skɪn Ⓤⓢ ˈkæf-
Calgary ˈkæl.gᵊr.i
Calhoun kælˈhuːn, -ˈhəʊn, kəˈhuːn Ⓤⓢ kælˈhuːn, -ˈhoʊn, kəˈhuːn
Cali ˈkɑː.li
Caliban ˈkæl.ɪ.bæn, ˈ-ə-, -bən
caliber ˈkæl.ɪ.bəʳ, ˈ-ə- Ⓤⓢ ˈkæl.ə.bɚ **-s** -z
Calibra® kəˈliː.brə
cali|brate ˈkæl.ɪ|.breɪt, ˈ-ə- **-brates** -breɪts **-brating** -breɪ.tɪŋ Ⓤⓢ -breɪ.t̬ɪŋ **-brated** -breɪ.tɪd Ⓤⓢ -breɪ.t̬ɪd
calibration ˌkæl.ɪˈbreɪ.ʃᵊn, -əˈ-
calibrator ˈkæl.ɪ.breɪ.təʳ, ˈ-ə- Ⓤⓢ -t̬ɚ **-s** -z
calibre ˈkæl.ɪ.bəʳ, ˈ-ə- Ⓤⓢ ˈkæl.ə.bɚ **-s** -z
calicle ˈkæl.ɪ.kl̩ **-s** -z
calico ˈkæl.ɪ.kəʊ, ˈ-ə- Ⓤⓢ -koʊ **-(e)s** -z
Calicut ˈkæl.ɪ.kət, ˈ-ə-, -kʌt
calif ˈkeɪ.lɪf, ˈkæl.ɪf **-s** -s
Calif. (*abbrev. for* **California**) ˌkæl.ɪˈfɔː.ni.ə, -əˈ-, ˈ-njə Ⓤⓢ -əˈfɔːr.njə, -ni.ə
Californi|a ˌkæl.ɪˈfɔː.ni|.ə, -əˈ-, ˈ-nj|ə Ⓤⓢ -əˈfɔːr.nj|ə, -ni|.ə **-an/s** -ən/z
californium ˌkæl.ɪˈfɔː.ni.əm, -əˈ- Ⓤⓢ -əˈfɔːr-
Caligula kəˈlɪg.jʊ.lə, -jə-
calipash ˈkæl.ɪ.pæʃ
calipee ˈkæl.ɪ.piː, ˌ--ˈ-
caliper ˈkæl.ɪ.pəʳ Ⓤⓢ -ə.pɚ **-s** -z
caliph ˈkeɪ.lɪf, ˈkæl.ɪf **-s** -s
caliphate ˈkæl.ɪ.feɪt, ˈkeɪ.lɪ-, -fɪt, -fət Ⓤⓢ ˈkeɪ.lɪ.fət, ˈkæl.ɪ.feɪt **-s** -s

calisthenic ˌkæl.ɪsˈθen.ɪk, -əsˈ- (US) -əsˈ- **-s** -s
Calisto kəˈlɪs.təʊ (US) -toʊ
cal|ix ˈkeɪ.l|ɪks, ˈkæl|.ɪks **-ices** -ɪs.iːz
calk kɔːk (US) kɔːk, kɑːk **-s** -s **-ing** -ɪŋ **-ed** -t
calkin ˈkæl.kɪn, ˈkɔː- (US) ˈkɔː-, ˈkɑː- **-s** -z
call kɔːl (US) kɔːl, kɑːl **-s** -z **-ing** -ɪŋ **-ed** -d ˈ**call** ˌ**girl**
Callaghan ˈkæl.ə.hən, -hæn, -gən (US) -hæn
Callahan ˈkæl.ə.hæn, -hən (US) -hæn
Callan ˈkæl.ən
Callander ˈkæl.ən.dəʳ (US) -dɚ
callanetics® ˌkæl.əˈnet.ɪks (US) -ˈneṭ-
Callao kəˈjaʊ (US) kəˈjɑː.oʊ
Callas ˈkæl.əs, -æs
callboy ˈkɔːl.bɔɪ (US) ˈkɔːl-, ˈkɑːl- **-s** -z
Callcott ˈkɔːl.kət, ˈkɒl- (US) ˈkɔːl.kɑːt, ˈkɑːl-
Callender ˈkæl.ɪn.dəʳ, -ən- (US) -dɚ
caller ˈkɔː.ləʳ (US) ˈkɔː.lɚ, ˈkɑː- **-s** -z
Caller ˈkæl.əʳ (US) -ɚ
Callie *surname:* ˈkɔː.li (US) ˈkɔː-, ˈkɑː-
Callie *girl's name:* ˈkæl.i
calligraphic ˌkæl.ɪˈgræf.ɪk, -əˈ- **-al** -ᵊl **-ally** -ᵊl.i, -li
calligraph|y kəˈlɪg.rə.f|i, kælˈɪg- **-ist/s** -ɪst/s **-er/s** -əʳ/z (US) -ɚ/z
calling ˈkɔː.lɪŋ (US) ˈkɔː-, ˈkɑː- **-s** -z ˈ**calling** ˌ**card**
Calliope kəˈlaɪə.pi, kælˈaɪə-
calliper ˈkæl.ɪ.pəʳ (US) -ə.pɚ **-s** -z
callipygian ˌkæl.ɪˈpɪdʒ.i.ən, -əˈ- (US) -əˈ-
callipygous ˌkæl.ɪˈpaɪ.gəs, -əˈ- (US) -əˈ-
Callirrhoe kælˈɪr.əʊ.iː, kəˈlɪr- (US) kəˈlɪr.oʊ-
Callisthenes kælˈɪs.θə.niːz, kəˈlɪs- (US) kəˈlɪs-
callisthenic ˌkæl.ɪsˈθen.ɪk **-s** -s
Callistratus kælˈɪs.trə.təs, kəˈlɪs- (US) kəˈlɪs-
callosit|y kælˈɒs.ə.t|i, kəˈlɒs-, -ɪt|.i (US) kəˈlɑː.sə.ṭ|i **-ies** -iz
callous ˈkæl.əs **-ly** -li **-ness** -nəs, -nɪs
callow (C) ˈkæl.əʊ (US) -oʊ **-er** -əʳ (US) -ɚ **-est** -ɪst, -əst
Calloway ˈkæl.ə.weɪ
call-up ˈkɔːl.ʌp (US) ˈkɔːl-, ˈkɑːl-
callus ˈkæl.əs **-es** -ɪz
calm kɑːm (US) kɑː*l*m **-s** -z **-er** -əʳ (US) -ɚ **-est** -ɪst, -əst **-ly** -li **-ness** -nəs, -nɪs **-ing** -ɪŋ **-ed** -d
calmative ˈkæl.mə.tɪv, ˈkɑː.mə- (US) ˈkɑː.mə.ṭɪv, ˈkæl- **-s** -z
calmodulin kælˈmɒd.jə.lɪn, -jʊ- (US) -ˈmɑː.dʒə-, -dʒʊ-
Calne kɑːn
calomel ˈkæl.əʊ.mel (US) -ə.mel, -məl
calor ˈkæl.əʳ (US) -ɚ ˈ**Calor** ˌ**gas®**
caloric kəˈlɒr.ɪk; ˈkæl.ᵊr- (US) kəˈlɔːr-
calorie ˈkæl.ᵊr.i **-s** -z
calorific ˌkæl.əˈrɪf.ɪk, -ɔːˈ- (US) -əˈ-
calorification kəˌlɒr.ɪ.fɪˈkeɪ.ʃᵊn; ˌkæl.ə.rɪ-, ˌkæl.ɔː-, ˌkæl.ɒr.ɪ- (US) kəˌlɔːr-, kælˌɔːr-
calorimeter ˌkæl.əˈrɪm.ɪ.təʳ, -ɔːˈ-, -ɒrˈɪm-, ˈ-ə- (US) -əˈrɪm.ə.ṭɚ **-s** -z
calorimetry ˌkæl.əˈrɪm.ɪ.tri, -ɔːˈ-, -ɒrˈɪm-, ˈ-ə- (US) -əˈrɪm.ə-
calotte kəˈlɒt (US) -lɑːt **-s** -s
caloyer ˈkæl.ɔɪ.əʳ (US) ˈkæl.ə.jɚ; kəˈlɔɪ- **-s** -z
Calpurnia ˌkælˈpɜː.ni.ə (US) -ˈpɜːr-
calque kælk **-s** -s
Calshot ˈkæl.ʃɒt (US) -ʃɑːt
Calthorpe *district in Birmingham:* ˈkæl.θɔːp (US) -θɔːrp *surname:* ˈkɔːl.θɔːp, ˈkɒl-, ˈkæl.θɔːp (US) ˈkɔːl.θɔːrp, ˈkɑːl-, ˈkæl-
Calton *in Edinburgh:* ˈkɔːl.tᵊn (US) ˈkɔːl-, ˈkɑːl- *in Glasgow:* ˈkɑːl.tᵊn
caltrop ˈkæl.trəp, -trɒp **-s** -s
calumet ˈkæl.jʊ.met (US) ˈkæl.jə.met, -mɪt; ˌkæl.jəˈmet **-s** -s
calumni|ate kəˈlʌm.ni|.eɪt **-ates** -eɪts **-ating** -eɪ.tɪŋ (US) -eɪ.ṭɪŋ **-ated** -eɪ.tɪd (US) -eɪ.ṭɪd **-ator/s** -eɪ.təʳ/z (US) -eɪ.ṭɚ/z
calumniation kəˌlʌm.niˈeɪ.ʃᵊn **-s** -z
calumn|y ˈkæl.əm.n|i **-ies** -iz
calvados (C) ˈkæl.və.dɒs (US) ˌkæl.vəˈdoʊs, ˌkɑːl-
calvar|y (C) ˈkæl.vᵊr|.i **-ies** -iz
calv|e kɑːv (US) kæv **-es** -z **-ing** -ɪŋ **-ed** -d
Calverley *surname:* ˈkæl.vᵊl.i (US) -vɚ.li *place in West Yorkshire:* ˈkɑː.və.li, ˈkɔːv.li (US) ˈkɑː.vɚ-, ˈkɔːv-
Calvert ˈkæl.vɜːt, -vət, ˈkɔːl.vət (US) ˈkæl.vɜːrt, -vɚt
Calverton ˈkæl.və.tᵊn, ˈkɔːl- (US) ˈkæl.vɚ.ṭən
calves'-foot ˈkɑːvz.fʊt (US) ˈkævz-
Calvin ˈkæl.vɪn
Calvin|ism ˈkæl.vɪ.n|ɪ.zᵊm, -və- **-ist/s** -ɪst/s
Calvinistic ˌkæl.vɪˈnɪs.tɪk, -vəˈ- **-al** -ᵊl **-ally** -ᵊl.i, -li
cal|x kæl|ks **-ces** -siːz **-xes** -k.sɪz
Calydon ˈkæl.ɪ.dᵊn, ˈ-ə-
calypso (C) kəˈlɪp.səʊ (US) -soʊ **-(e)s** -z
ca|lyx ˈkeɪ|.lɪks, ˈkæl|.ɪks **-lyces** -lɪ.siːz **-lyxes** -lɪk.sɪz
calzone kæltˈsoʊ.ni, kælˈzəʊ-, -neɪ (US) kælˈzoʊ.ni, -ˈzoʊn **-s** -z
cam (C) kæm **-s** -z
CAm (*abbrev. for* **Central America**) ˌsen.trᵊl.əˈmer.ɪ.kə
CAM kæm
Camalodunum ˌkæm.ə.ləʊˈdjuː.nəm (US) -loʊˈduː-, -ˈdjuː-
camaraderie ˌkæm.əˈrɑː.dᵊr.i, -ˈræd.ᵊr-, -iː (US) ˌkæm.əˈrɑː.dɚ.i, ˌkɑː.məˈ-, -ˈræd.ɚ-
Camargue kæmˈɑːg, kəˈmɑːg (US) kəˈmɑːrg
camarilla ˌkæm.əˈrɪl.ə **-s** -z
Camay® ˈkæm.eɪ (US) ˌkæmˈeɪ
camber (C) ˈkæm.bəʳ (US) -bɚ **-s** -z
Camberley ˈkæm.bᵊl.i (US) -bɚ.li
Camberwell ˈkæm.bə.wel, -wəl (US) -bɚ-
cambial ˈkæm.bi.əl
cambium ˈkæm.bi.əm
Cambodi|a ˌkæmˈbəʊ.di|.ə (US) -ˈboʊ- **-an/s** -ən
Camborne ˈkæm.bɔːn, -bən (US) -bɔːrn
Cambray ˈkɑ̃ː*m*.breɪ, ˈkɒm- (US) kɑːmˈbreɪ
Cambri|a ˈkæm.bri|.ə **-an/s** -ən/z
cambric ˈkæm.brɪk, ˈkeɪm-
Cambridge ˈkeɪm.brɪdʒ **-shire** -ʃəʳ, -ˌʃɪəʳ (US) -ʃɚ, -ˌʃɪr
Cambs. (*abbrev. for* **Cambridgeshire**) kæm*b*z; ˈkeɪm.brɪdʒ.ʃəʳ, -ˌʃɪəʳ (US) kæm*b*z; ˈkeɪm.brɪdʒ.ʃɚ, -ˌʃɪr
Cambyses kæmˈbaɪ.siːz
camcorder ˈkæmˌkɔː.dəʳ (US) -ˌkɔːr.dɚ **-s** -z
Camden ˈkæm.dən
came (*from* **come**) keɪm
camel ˈkæm.ᵊl **-s** -z
Camelford ˈkæm.ᵊl.fəd (US) -fɚd
camelhair ˈkæm.ᵊl.heəʳ (US) -her
camel(l)ia (C) kəˈmiː.li.ə, -ˈmel.i- (US) -ˈmiːl.jə, -ˈmiː.li.ə **-s** -z
Camelot ˈkæm.ə.lɒt, ˈ-ɪ- (US) -lɑːt
Camembert ˈkæm.əm.beəʳ (US) -ber
cameo ˈkæm.i.əʊ (US) -oʊ **-s** -z ˈ**cameo** ˌ**role**
camera ˈkæm.ᵊr.ə, ˈkæm.rə **-s** -z
cameral ˈkæm.ᵊr.ᵊl
camera|man ˈkæm.ᵊr.ə|.mæn, ˈkæm.rə-, -mən **-men** -men
camera obscura ˌkæm.ᵊr.ə.əbˈskjʊə.rə, ˌkæm.rə-, -ɒbˈ- (US) -əbˈskjʊr.ə
Camero kəˈmeə.rəʊ (US) -ˈmer.oʊ
Cameron ˈkæm.ᵊr.ən, ˈkæm.rən
Cameronian ˌkæm.ᵊrˈəʊ.ni.ən (US) -ˈroʊ- **-s** -z
Cameroon ˌkæm.əˈruːn, ˈ--- **-s** -z
camiknickers ˈkæm.iˌnɪk.əz, ˌkæm.iˈnɪk- (US) ˈkæm.iˌnɪk.ɚz
Camilla kəˈmɪl.ə
Camille kəˈmiːl, -ˈmɪl
camis|e kəˈmiːz **-es** -ɪz
camisole ˈkæm.ɪ.səʊl (US) -soʊl **-s** -z
Camlachie kæmˈlæk.i, -ˈlæx-
camomile ˈkæm.əʊ.maɪl (US) -ə.miːl
Camorra kəˈmɒr.ə (US) -ˈmɔːr-
camouflag|e ˈkæm.ə.flɑːʒ, ˈ-ʊ- (US) -flɑː*d*ʒ **-es** -ɪz **-ing** -ɪŋ **-ed** -d

Camoys kəˈmɔɪz
camp (C) kæmp **-s** -s **-ing** -ɪŋ **-ed** -t **ˌcamp ˈbed, ˈcamp ˌbed; ˌCamp ˈDavid; ˈcamp ˌfollower ; ˈcamp ˌstool**
Campagna kæmˈpɑː.njə (US) -njɑː
campaign kæmˈpeɪn **-s** -z **-ing** -ɪŋ **-ed** -d **-er/s** -əʳ/z (US) -ɚ/z
campanile ˌkæm.pəˈniː.leɪ (US) -leɪ, -li **-s** -z
campanolog|y ˌkæm.pəˈnɒl.ə.dʒ|i (US) -ˈnɑː.lə- **-ist/s** -ɪst/s
campanula kəmˈpæn.jʊ.lə, kæm-, -jə- **-s** -z
Campari® kæmˈpɑː.ri (US) -ˈpɑːr.i
Campbell ˈkæm.bᵊl **-s** -z
Campbellite ˈkæm.bᵊl.aɪt (US) -bə.laɪt **-s** -s
Campbeltown ˈkæm.bᵊl.taʊn
Campden ˈkæm*p*.dən
Campeche kæmˈpiː.tʃi
camper ˈkæm.pəʳ (US) -pɚ **-s** -z **ˈcamper ˌvan**
Camperdown ˈkæm.pə.daʊn (US) -pɚ-
campfire ˈkæmp.faɪəʳ (US) -faɪɚ **-s** -z
campground ˈkæmp.graʊnd **-s** -z
camphire ˈkæm*p*.faɪəʳ (US) -faɪɚ
camphor ˈkæm*p*.fəʳ (US) -fɚ **-s** -z
camphor|ate ˈkæm*p*.fə.r|eɪt **-ates** -eɪts **-ating** -eɪ.tɪŋ (US) -eɪ.t̬ɪŋ **-ated** -eɪ.tɪd (US) -eɪ.t̬ɪd **ˌcamphorated ˈoil**
camphoric kæmˈfɒr.ɪk (US) -ˈfɔːr-
camping ˈkæm.pɪŋ
campion (C) ˈkæm.pi.ən **-s** -z
Camps kæmps
campsite ˈkæmp.saɪt **-s** -s
campus ˈkæm.pəs **-es** -ɪz
CAMRA ˈkæm.rə
camshaft ˈkæm.ʃɑːft (US) -ʃæft **-s** -s
Camus kæmˈuː (US) kæmˈuː, kɑːˈmuː, kə-
camwood ˈkæm.wʊd
can (*n.*) kæn **-s** -z **ˈcan ˌopener ; (ˌopen a) ˌcan of ˈworms ; ˌcarry the ˈcan**
can (*v.*) *put in cans:* kæn **-s** -z **-ning** -ɪŋ **-ned** -d
can (*auxil. v.*) *strong form:* kæn *weak forms:* kən, kn̩, kŋ̍
Note: Weak form word. The strong form /kæn/ is used for emphasis (e.g. "You **can** do it", and for contrast (e.g. "I don't know if he can or he can't"). It is also used finally in a sentence (e.g. "I don't know if I can"). The form /kŋ̍/ occurs only before words beginning with /k/ or /g/.
Cana ˈkeɪ.nə
Canaan ˈkeɪ.nən, -ni.ən *Jewish pronunciation:* kəˈneɪ.ən
Canaanite ˈkeɪ.nə.naɪt, -ni.ə- *Jewish pronunciation:* kəˈneɪ.ə.naɪt **-s** -s
Canada ˈkæn.ə.də
Canadian kəˈneɪ.di.ən **-s** -z
canaille kəˈneɪəl, -naɪ (US) kəˈneɪl
canal kəˈnæl **-s** -z
Canaletto ˌkæn.ᵊlˈet.əʊ (US) -əˈlet̬.oʊ
canalization, -isa- ˌkæn.ᵊl.aɪˈzeɪ.ʃᵊn, -ɪˈ- (US) -ɪˈ-
canaliz|e, -is|e ˈkæn.ᵊl.aɪz (US) -ə.laɪz **-es** -ɪz **-ing** -ɪŋ **-ed** -d
Cananite ˈkæn.ə.naɪt, ˈkeɪ.nə- **-s** -s
canapé ˈkæn.ə.peɪ **-s** -z
canard ˈkæn.ɑːd, kəˈnɑːd, kænˈɑːd (US) kəˈnɑːrd **-s** -z
canar|y (C) kəˈneə.r|i (US) -ˈner|.i **-ies** -iz **Caˈnary ˌIslands**
canasta kəˈnæs.tə
canaster kəˈnæs.təʳ (US) -tɚ **-s** -z
Canaveral kəˈnæv.ᵊr.ᵊl
Canberra ˈkæn.bᵊr.ə, ˈkæm- (US) ˈkæn.ber-, -bɚ-
cancan ˈkæn.kæn, ˈkæŋ- **-s** -z
cancel ˈkæn*t*.sᵊl **-s** -z **-(l)ing** -ɪŋ **-(l)ed** -d
cancell|ate ˈkæn*t*.sᵊl|.eɪt, -sɪ.l|eɪt (US) -sə.l|eɪt **-ates** -eɪts **-ating** -eɪ.tɪŋ (US) -eɪ.t̬ɪŋ **-ated** -eɪ.tɪd (US) -eɪ.t̬ɪd
cancellation ˌkæn*t*.sᵊlˈeɪ.ʃᵊn, -sɪˈleɪ- (US) -səˈleɪ- **-s** -z
cancellous ˈkæn*t*.sᵊl.əs
cancer (C) ˈkæn*t*.səʳ (US) -sɚ **-s** -z
Cancerean, Cancerian kæn*t*ˈsɪə.ri.ən, -ˈseə- (US) -ˈser.i-, -ˈsɪr- **-s** -z
cancerous ˈkæn*t*.sᵊr.əs
cancroid ˈkæŋ.krɔɪd
Candace kænˈdeɪ.si, ˈkæn.dɪs, -dəs
candela kænˈdel.ə, -ˈdeɪ.lə, -ˈdiː- **-s** -z
candelabr|a ˌkæn.dᵊlˈɑː.br|ə, -dɪˈlɑː-, -ˈlæb.r|ə (US) -dəˈlɑː.br|ə, -ˈlæb.r|ə **-as** -əz **-um** -əm
Canderel® ˌkæn.dᵊrˈel, ˈ---
candescen|ce kænˈdes.ᵊn|*t*s **-t** -t
Candia ˈkæn.di.ə
Candice ˈkæn.dɪs, -diːs
candid ˈkæn.dɪd **-ly** -li **-ness** -nəs, -nɪs
Candida ˈkæn.dɪ.də
candida|cy ˈkæn.dɪ.də|.si **-cies** -siz
candidate ˈkæn.dɪ.dət, -deɪt, -dɪt **-s** -s
candidature ˈkæn.dɪ.də.tʃəʳ, ˈ-də-, -deɪ-, -dɪtʃ.əʳ (US) ˈkæn.də.də.tʃʊr, -tʃɚ **-s** -z
Candide kɑ̃ːnˈdiːd (US) kɑːn-, kæn-
candidias|is ˌkæn.dɪˈdaɪə.s|ɪs, -dəˈ- **-es** -iːz
candle ˈkæn.dl̩ **-s** -z **ˌburn the ˌcandle at ˌboth ˈends**
candlelight ˈkæn.dl̩.laɪt
candle-lit ˈkæn.dl̩.lɪt **ˌcandle-lit ˈdinner**
Candlemas ˈkæn.dl̩.məs, -mæs
candlepower ˈkæn.dl̩.paʊəʳ (US) -paʊɚ **-s** -z
candlestick ˈkæn.dl̩.stɪk **-s** -s
candlewick ˈkæn.dl̩.wɪk
cando(u)r ˈkæn.dəʳ (US) -dɚ
cand|y (C) ˈkæn.d|i **-ies** -iz **-ying** -i.ɪŋ **-ied** -id
candyfloss ˈkæn.di.flɒs (US) -flɑːs
candytuft ˈkæn.di.tʌft
cane (C) keɪn **-s** -z **ˈcane ˌsugar, ˌcane ˈsugar**
Canford ˈkæn.fəd (US) -fɚd
Canham ˈkæn.əm
canicular kəˈnɪk.jʊ.ləʳ, kænˈɪk-, -jə- (US) -jə.lɚ
canine ˈkeɪ.naɪn, ˈkæn.aɪn (US) ˈkeɪ.naɪn **-s** -z
Canis ˈkeɪ.nɪs, ˈkæn.ɪs
canister ˈkæn.ɪ.stəʳ (US) -ə.stɚ **-s** -z
cank|er ˈkæŋ.k|əʳ (US) -k|ɚ **-ers** -əz (US) -ɚz **-ering** -ᵊr.ɪŋ **-ered** -əd (US) -ɚd
cankerous ˈkæŋ.kᵊr.əs
canna ˈkæn.ə **-s** -z
cannabis ˈkæn.ə.bɪs
Cannan ˈkæn.ən
cannelloni ˌkæn.ᵊlˈəʊ.ni, -ɪˈləʊ- (US) -əˈloʊ-
canner|y ˈkæn.ᵊr|.i **-ies** -iz
Cannes kæn, kænz (US) kæn, kænz, kɑːn **ˌCannes ˈFilm ˌFestival**
cannibal ˈkæn.ɪ.bᵊl, ˈ-ə- **-s** -z
cannibalism ˈkæn.ɪ.bᵊl.ɪ.zᵊm, ˈ-ə-
cannibalistic ˌkæn.ɪ.bᵊlˈɪs.tɪk, ˌ-ə- (US) -bəˈlɪs-
cannibaliz|e, -is|e ˈkæn.ɪ.bᵊl.aɪz, ˈ-ə- (US) -bə.laɪz **-es** -ɪz **-ing** -ɪŋ **-ed** -d
cannikin ˈkæn.ɪ.kɪn (US) ˈ-ə- **-s** -z
Canning ˈkæn.ɪŋ
Cannizzaro ˌkæn.ɪˈzɑː.rəʊ, -əˈ- (US) -roʊ
Cannock ˈkæn.ək
cannon (C) ˈkæn.ən **-s** -z **ˈcannon ˌfodder**
cannonad|e ˌkæn.əˈneɪd **-es** -z **-ing** -ɪŋ **-ed** -ɪd
cannonball ˈkæn.ən.bɔːl (US) -bɔːl, -bɑːl **-s** -z **-ing** -ɪŋ **-ed** -d
cannoneer ˌkæn.əˈnɪəʳ (US) -ˈnɪr **-s** -z
cannonry ˈkæn.ən.ri
cannonshot ˈkæn.ən.ʃɒt (US) -ʃɑːt **-s** -s
cannot ˈkæn.ɒt, -ət (US) ˈkæn.ɑːt, kəˈnɑːt
Note: This word is usually contracted to /kɑːnt (US) kænt/. See **can't**.
cannul|a ˈkæn.jə.l|ə, -jʊ- (US) -jə- **-ae** -iː, -aɪ **-as** -əz
cann|y ˈkæn|.i **-ier** -i.əʳ (US) -i.ɚ **-iest** -i.ɪst, -i.əst **-ily** -ɪ.li, -ᵊl.i **-iness** -ɪ.nəs, -ɪ.nɪs
canoe kəˈnuː **-s** -z **-ing** -ɪŋ **-d** -d
canoeist kəˈnuː.ɪst **-s** -s
canon ˈkæn.ən **-s** -z **ˌcanon ˈlaw**
Canonbury ˈkæn.ən.bᵊr.i, -əm- (US) -ən.ber-, -bɚ-
canoness ˌkæn.əˈnes, ˈkæn.ə.nɪs, -nes (US) ˈkæn.ə.nəs **-es** -ɪz
canonic kəˈnɒn.ɪk, kænˈɒn- (US) kəˈnɑː.nɪk **-al/s** -ᵊl/z **-ally** -ᵊl.i, -li
canonization, -isa- ˌkæn.ə.naɪˈzeɪ.ʃᵊn, -nɪˈ- (US) -nɪˈ- **-s** -z

canoniz|e, -is|e 'kæn.ə.naɪz **-es** -ɪz **-ing** -ɪŋ **-ed** -d
canonr|y 'kæn.ən.r|i **-ies** -iz
canoodl|e kə'nuː.dḷ **-es** -z **-ing** -ɪŋ, -'nuːd.lɪŋ **-ed** -d
Canopus kə'nəʊ.pəs (US) -'noʊ-
canop|y 'kæn.ə.p|i **-ies** -iz
Canossa kə'nɒs.ə, kæn'ɒs- (US) kə'nɑː.sə
canst (*from* **can**) *strong form:* kænst *weak form:* kənst
cant (C) kænt **-s** -s **-ing** -ɪŋ **-ed** -ɪd **-er/s** -əʳ/z (US) -ɚ/z
can't kɑːnt (US) kænt
Cantab. 'kæn.tæb
cantabile kæn'tɑː.bɪ.leɪ, -bə-
Cantabria kæn'tæb.ri.ə (US) -'teɪ.bri-
Cantabrian kæn'tæb.ri.ən (US) -'teɪ.bri-
Cantabrigian ˌkæn.tə'brɪdʒ.i.ən **-s** -z
cantaloup(e) 'kæn.tə.luːp (US) -t̬ə.loʊp- **-s** -s
cantankerous ˌkæn'tæŋ.kᵊr.əs, kən- **-ly** -li **-ness** -nəs, -nɪs
cantata kæn'tɑː.tə, kən- (US) kən'tɑː.t̬ə **-s** -z
cantatrice 'kæn.tə.triːs *as if French:* ˌkɑ̃ːn.tæt'riːs *as if Italian:* ˌkɑːn.tə'triː.tʃeɪ (US) ˌkɑːn.tə'triːs **-s** -ɪz
canteen kæn'tiːn **-s** -z *stress shift:* ˌcanteen 'food
cant|er (C) 'kæn.t|əʳ (US) -t̬|ɚ **-ers** -əz (US) -ɚz **-ering** -ᵊr.ɪŋ **-ered** -əd (US) -ɚd
Canterbury 'kæn.tə.bᵊr.i, -ber- (US) -t̬ɚ.ber-, -bɚ- ˌ**Canterbury 'Tales**
cantharides kænt'θær.ɪ.diːz, kənt- (US) -'θer-, -'θær-
canticle 'kæn.tɪ.kḷ (US) -t̬ə- **-s** -z
Canticles *Song of Solomon:* 'kæn.tɪ.kḷz (US) -t̬ə-
cantilena ˌkæn.tɪ'leɪn.ə (US) -t̬ə'-
cantilever 'kæn.tɪ.liː.vəʳ, -tə- (US) -t̬ə.liː.vɚ, -lev.ɚ **-s** -z
Cantire kæn'taɪəʳ (US) -'taɪɚ
Cantling 'kænt.lɪŋ
canto 'kæn.təʊ (US) -toʊ **-s** -z
canton *Swiss state:* 'kæn.tɒn, ˌ-'- (US) 'kæn.tɑːn, -tᵊn; kæn'tɑːn **-s** -z *in heraldry:* 'kæn.tən
Canton *in China:* ˌkæn'tɒn (US) -'tɑːn *in Wales, surname, place in US:* 'kæn.tən (US) -tᵊn
canton (*v.*) *divide into portions or districts:* kæn'tɒn (US) -'tɑːn **-s** -z **-ing** -ɪŋ **-ed** -d
canton (*v.*) *provide accommodation:* kæn'tuːn, kən- (US) kæn'toʊn, -'tɑːn **-s** -z **-ing** -ɪŋ **-ed** -d **-ment/s** -mənt/s
Cantona 'kæn.tə.nɑː
cantonal 'kæn.tə.nᵊl, kæn'təʊ.nᵊl (US) 'kæn.tə.nᵊl, kæn'tɑː.nəl
Cantonese ˌkæn.tə'niːz, -tɒn'iːz (US) -tᵊn'iːz, -'iːs
cantor 'kæn.tɔːʳ (US) -tɚ, -tɔːr **-s** -z
cantoris kæn'tɔː.rɪs (US) -'tɔːr.ɪs
cantus 'kæn.təs (US) -t̬əs
Cantwell 'kænt.wel
Canty 'kæn.ti (US) -t̬i
Canuck kə'nʌk **-s** -s
Canute kə'njuːt (US) -'nuːt, -'njuːt
canvas 'kæn.vəs **-es** -ɪz
canvasback 'kæn.vəs.bæk **-s** -s
canvass 'kæn.vəs **-es** -ɪz **-ing** -ɪŋ **-ed** -t **-er/s** -əʳ/z (US) -ɚ/z
Canvey 'kæn.vi
canyon 'kæn.jən **-s** -z
Canyonlands 'kæn.jən.lændz
canzone kænt'səʊ.neɪ, kæn'zəʊ- (US) kæn'zoʊ.ni, kɑːnt'soʊ.neɪ **-s** -z
canzonet kænt'səʊ.net, kæn'zəʊ- (US) ˌkæn.zə'net **-s** -s
caoutchouc 'kaʊ.tʃʊk, -tʃuːk, -tʃuː, -'-
cap kæp **-s** -s **-ping** -ɪŋ **-ped** -t
CAP ˌsiː.eɪ'piː
capabilit|y ˌkeɪ.pə'bɪl.ə.t|i, -ɪ.t|i (US) -ə.t̬|i **-ies** -iz
capab|le 'keɪ.pə.b|ḷ **-ly** -li **-leness** -ḷ.nəs, -nɪs
capacious kə'peɪ.ʃəs **-ly** -li **-ness** -nəs, -nɪs
capacitance kə'pæs.ɪ.tᵊnts (US) '-ə-
capaci|tate kə'pæs.ɪ|.teɪt (US) '-ə- **-tates** -teɪts **-tating** -teɪ.tɪŋ (US) -teɪ.t̬ɪŋ **-tated** -teɪ.tɪd (US) -teɪ.t̬ɪd
capacitor kə'pæs.ɪ.təʳ, '-ə- (US) -ə.t̬ɚ **-s** -z
capacit|y kə'pæs.ə.t|i, -ɪ.t|i (US) -ə.t̬|i **-ies** -iz
cap-à-pie ˌkæp.ə'piː
caparison kə'pær.ɪ.sᵊn (US) -'per.ə-, -'pær- **-s** -z **-ing** -ɪŋ **-ed** -d
cape (C) keɪp **-s** -s **-d** -t ˌ**Cape Ca'naveral** ; ˌ**Cape 'Cod** ; ˌ**Cape 'Horn** ; ˌ**Cape of Good 'Hope** ; '**Cape** ˌ**Province** ; ˌ**caped cru'sader**
Capel *surname, places in Kent and Surrey:* 'keɪ.pᵊl *in Wales:* 'kæp.ᵊl
Capel Curig ˌkæp.ᵊl'kɪr.ɪg
Capell 'keɪ.pᵊl
capel(l)et 'kæp.ə.let, -lɪt **-s** -s
cap|er 'keɪ.p|əʳ (US) -p|ɚ **-ers** -əz (US) -ɚz **-ering** -ᵊr.ɪŋ **-ered** -əd (US) -ɚd **-erer/s** -ᵊr.əʳ/z (US) -ɚ.ɚ/z
caper *bird:* 'kæp.əʳ (US) -ɚ **-s** -z
capercailzie, capercaillie ˌkæp.ə'keɪ.li, -'keɪ.lji, -'keɪl.zi (US) -ɚ'keɪ.li, -'keɪl.ji, -zi **-s** -z
Capernaum kə'pɜː.ni.əm (US) -'pɜːr-
Cape Town, Capetown 'keɪp.taʊn
Cape Verde ˌkeɪp'vɜːd, -'veəd (US) -vɜːrd
Capgrave 'kæp.greɪv
capias 'keɪ.pi.æs, -pjæs, -pjəs (US) 'keɪ.pi.əs **-es** -ɪz
capillarity ˌkæp.ɪ'lær.ə.ti, -ə'-, -ɪ.ti (US) -'ler.ə.t̬i, -'lær-
capillary kə'pɪl.ᵊr.i (US) 'kæp.ə.ler-
capital 'kæp.ɪ.tᵊl (US) -ə.t̬ᵊl **-s** -z **-ly** -i ˌ**capital 'letter** ; ˌ**capital 'punishment**
capitalism 'kæp.ɪ.tᵊl.ɪ.zᵊm, kə'pɪt.ᵊl-, kæp'ɪt- (US) 'kæp.ə.t̬ᵊl-
capitalist 'kæp.ɪ.tᵊl.ɪst, kə'pɪt.ᵊl-, kæp'ɪt- (US) 'kæp.ə.t̬ᵊl- **-s** -s
capitalistic ˌkæp.ɪ.tᵊl'ɪs.tɪk (US) -ə.t̬ə'lɪs- **-ally** -ᵊl.i, -li
capitalization, -isa- ˌkæp.ɪ.tᵊl.aɪ'zeɪ.ʃᵊn, kæpˌɪt.ᵊl-, kəˌpɪt- (US) ˌkæp.ə.t̬ᵊl.ɪ'- **-s** -z
capitaliz|e, -is|e 'kæp.ɪ.tᵊl.aɪz, kæp'ɪt.ᵊl-, kə'pɪt- (US) 'kæp.ə.t̬ə.laɪz **-es** -ɪz **-ing** -ɪŋ **-ed** -d
capitation ˌkæp.ɪ'teɪ.ʃᵊn (US) -ə'- **-s** -z
capitol (C) 'kæp.ɪ.tᵊl (US) -ə.t̬ᵊl **-s** -z ˌ**Capitol 'Hill**
capitolian ˌkæp.ɪ'təʊ.li.ən (US) -ə'toʊ-
capitoline (C) kə'pɪt.əʊ.laɪn (US) 'kæp.ə.t̬ə.laɪn, -liːn
capitular kə'pɪt.jʊ.ləʳ, -jə-, -'pɪtʃ.ʊ-, '-ə- (US) -'pɪtʃ.ᵊl.ɚ **-s** -z
capitular|y kə'pɪt.jʊ.lə.r|i, -jə-, -'pɪtʃ.ʊ-, '-ə- (US) -'pɪtʃ.ə.ler|.i **-ies** -iz
capitu|late kə'pɪt.jʊ|.leɪt, -jə-, -'pɪtj.ʊ-, '-ə- (US) -'pɪtʃ.ə|.leɪt, '-ʊ- **-lates** -leɪts **-lating** -leɪ.tɪŋ (US) -leɪ.t̬ɪŋ **-lated** -leɪ.tɪd (US) -leɪ.t̬ɪd
capitulation kəˌpɪt.jʊ'leɪ.ʃᵊn, -jə'-, -ˌpɪtʃ.ʊ'-, -ə'- (US) -ˌpɪtʃ.ə'-, -jʊ'- **-s** -z
capitul|um kə'pɪt.jʊ.l|əm, -jə-, -'pɪtʃ.ʊ-, '-ə- (US) -'pɪtʃ.ə- **-a** -ə
capo *for guitar:* 'kæp.əʊ, 'keɪ.pəʊ (US) 'keɪ.poʊ **-s** -z *criminal chieftain:* 'kɑː.pəʊ, 'kæp.əʊ (US) 'kɑː.poʊ, 'kæp.oʊ
capon 'keɪ.pən, -pɒn (US) -pɑːn, -pᵊn **-s** -z
Capone kə'pəʊn, keɪ- (US) kə'poʊn
capot kə'pɒt (US) -'pɑːt **-s** -s **-ting** -ɪŋ (US) -'pɑː.t̬ɪŋ **-ted** -ɪd (US) -'pɑː.t̬ɪd
capote kə'pəʊt (US) -'poʊt **-s** -s
Capote kə'pəʊ.ti (US) -'poʊ.t̬i
Cappadoci|a ˌkæp.ə'dəʊ.si|.ə, -ʃi|.ə, -ʃ|ə (US) -'doʊ.ʃ|ə **-an/s** -ən/z
Capper 'kæp.əʳ (US) -ɚ
cappuccino ˌkæp.ʊ'tʃiː.nəʊ, -ə'- (US) ˌkæp.ə'tʃiː.noʊ, ˌkɑː.pə'- **-s** -z
Capra 'kæp.rə
Capri kæp'riː, kə'priː
capric 'kæp.rɪk
capriccio kə'prɪtʃ.i.əʊ, -'priː.tʃi- (US) -'priː.tʃoʊ **-s** -z
capriccioso kəˌprɪtʃ.i'əʊ.zəʊ, -ˌpriː.tʃi'-, -səʊ (US) ˌkɑː.priː'tʃoʊ.soʊ, -tʃi'oʊ-; kəˌpriː-
capric|e kə'priːs **-es** -ɪz

capricious kəˈprɪʃ.əs **-ly** -li **-ness** -nəs, -nɪs
Capricorn ˈkæp.rɪ.kɔːn (US) -rə.kɔːrn
Capricornus ˌkæp.rɪˈkɔː.nəs (US) -rəˈkɔːr-
capriol|e ˈkæp.ri.əʊl (US) -oʊl **-es** -z **-ing** -ɪŋ **-ed** -d
capsicum ˈkæp.sɪ.kəm
capsiz|e kæpˈsaɪz (US) ˈ--, -ˈ- **-es** -ɪz **-ing** -ɪŋ **-ed** -d
capstan ˈkæp.stən **-s** -z
capsular ˈkæp.sjʊ.ləʳ, -sjə- (US) -sə.lɚ, -sjʊ-
capsule ˈkæp.sjuːl (US) -səl, -sjʊl **-s** -z
captain ˈkæp.tɪn (US) -tən **-s** -z
captainc|y ˈkæp.tɪn.s|i, -tən- **-ies** -iz
caption ˈkæp.ʃən **-s** -z
captious ˈkæp.ʃəs **-ly** -li **-ness** -nəs, -nɪs
capti|vate ˈkæp.tɪ|.veɪt (US) -tə- **-vates** -veɪts **-vating** -veɪ.tɪŋ (US) -veɪ.t̬ɪŋ **-vated** -veɪ.tɪd (US) -veɪ.t̬ɪd
captivation ˌkæp.tɪˈveɪ.ʃən (US) -təˈ-
captive ˈkæp.tɪv **-s** -z
captivit|y kæpˈtɪv.ə.t|i, -ɪ.t|i (US) -ə.t̬|i **-ies** -iz
captor ˈkæp.təʳ, -tɔːʳ (US) -tɚ, -tɔːr **-s** -z
capt|ure ˈkæp.tʃ|əʳ (US) -tʃ|ɚ **-ures** -əz (US) -ɚz **-uring** -ər.ɪŋ **-ured** -əd (US) -ɚd
Capua ˈkæp.ju.ə
capuch|e kəˈpuːʃ, -ˈpuːtʃ **-es** -ɪz
capuchin (C) ˈkæp.jʊ.tʃɪn, -ʃɪn; kəˈpuː- (US) ˈkæp.jʊ.tʃɪn, -jə-, -ʃɪn; kəˈpjuː- **-s** -z
Capulet ˈkæp.jʊ.let, -jə-, -lət, -lɪt
capybara ˌkæp.ɪˈbɑː.rə (US) -ˈbɑːr.ə **-s** -z
car kɑːʳ (US) kɑːr **-s** -z ˈ**car a**ˌ**larm** ; ˈ**car** ˌ**ferry** ; ˈ**car** ˌ**park** ; ˈ**car** ˌ**pool** ; ˈ**car** ˌ**port** ; ˈ**car** ˌ**wash**
Cara ˈkɑː.rə (US) ˈker.ə, ˈkær-, ˈkɑːr-
carabineer ˌkær.ə.bɪˈnɪəʳ (US) ˌker.ə.bɪˈnɪr, ˌkær- **-s** -z
carabiner ˌkær.əˈbiː.nəʳ (US) ˌker.əˈbiː.nɚ, ˌkær- **-s** -z
carabinieri ˌkær.ə.bɪ.niˈeə.ri (US) ˌker.ə.bənˈjer.i, ˌkær-
caracal ˈkær.ə.kæl (US) ˈker-, ˈkær- **-s** -z
Caracas kəˈræk.əs, -ˈrɑː.kəs (US) -ˈrɑː-
caracole ˈkær.ə.kəʊl (US) ˈker.ə.koʊl, ˈkær- **-s** -z
Caractacus kəˈræk.tə.kəs
Caradoc kəˈræd.ək; ˈkær.ə.dɒk (US) ˈker.ə.dɑːk, ˈkær-; kəˈræd.ək
carafe kəˈræf, -ˈrɑːf **-s** -s
carambola ˌkær.əmˈbəʊ.lə (US) ˌker.əmˈboʊ-, ˌkær- **-s** -z
caramel ˈkær.ə.məl, -mel (US) ˈkɑːr.məl; ˈker.ə-, ˈkær- **-s** -z
carameliz|e, -is|e ˈkær.ə.məl.aɪz, -mel- (US) ˈkɑːr.mə.laɪz, ˈker.ə-, ˈkær- **-es** -ɪz **-ing** -ɪŋ **-ed** -d
Caran d'Ache® ˌkær.ənˈdæʃ (US) ˌkɑːr.ɑːnˈdɑːʃ
carapac|e ˈkær.ə.peɪs (US) ˈker-, ˈkær- **-es** -ɪz
carat ˈkær.ət (US) ˈker-, ˈkær- **-s** -s
Caratacus kəˈræt.ə.kəs (US) -ˈræt̬-
Caravaggio ˌkær.əˈvædʒ.i.əʊ, ˌkɑː.rəˈ-, -ˈvɑː.dʒi- (US) ˌker.əˈvɑː.dʒi.oʊ, ˌkær-
caravan ˈkær.ə.væn, ˌ--ˈ- (US) ˈker.ə.væn, ˈkær- **-s** -z **-ning** -ɪŋ
caravansar|y ˌkær.əˈvæn.sər|.i (US) ˌker-, ˌkær- **-ies** -iz
caravanserai ˌkær.əˈvæn.sər.aɪ, -eɪ, -i (US) ˌker-, ˌkær- **-s** -z
caravel ˈkær.ə.vel, ˌ--ˈ- (US) ˈker.ə.vel, ˈkær- **-s** -z
caraway ˈkær.ə.weɪ (US) ˈker-, ˈkær- **-s** -z ˈ**caraway** ˌ**seed**
Carbery ˈkɑː.bər.i (US) ˈkɑːr.ber-, -bɚ-
carbide ˈkɑː.baɪd (US) ˈkɑːr- **-s** -z
carbine ˈkɑː.baɪn (US) ˈkɑːr.biːn, -baɪn **-s** -z
carbineer ˌkɑː.bɪˈnɪəʳ, -bəˈ- (US) ˌkɑːr.bəˈnɪr **-s** -z
carbohydrate ˌkɑː.bəʊˈhaɪ.dreɪt, -drɪt (US) ˌkɑːr.boʊˈhaɪ.dreɪt, -bəˈ- **-s** -s
carbolic kɑːˈbɒl.ɪk (US) kɑːrˈbɑː.lɪk **car**ˌ**bolic** ˈ**acid**
carbon ˈkɑː.bən (US) ˈkɑːr- **-s** -z ˌ**carbon** ˈ**copy** (US) ˈ**carbon** ˌ**copy** ; ˌ**carbon di**ˈ**oxide**
carbonaceous ˌkɑː.bəʊˈneɪ.ʃəs (US) ˌkɑːr.bəˈ-
carbonade ˌkɑː.bəˈneɪd, ˈ--- (US) ˌkɑːr.bəˈneɪd **-s** -z
carbonara ˌkɑː.bəˈnɑː.rə (US) ˌkɑːr.bəˈnɑːr.ə
carbonate (*n.*) ˈkɑː.bən.eɪt, -ɪt, -ət (US) ˈkɑːr- **-s** -s
carbon|ate (*v.*) ˈkɑː.bən|.eɪt (US) ˈkɑːr- **-ates** -eɪts **-ating** -eɪ.tɪŋ (US) -eɪ.t̬ɪŋ **-ated** -eɪ.tɪd (US) -eɪ.t̬ɪd
carbon|-date ˌkɑː.bən|ˈdeɪt (US) ˌkɑːr- **-dates** -ˈdeɪts **-dating** -ˈdeɪ.tɪŋ (US) -ˈdeɪ.t̬ɪŋ **-dated** -ˈdeɪ.tɪd (US) -ˈdeɪ.t̬ɪd
carbonic kɑːˈbɒn.ɪk (US) kɑːrˈbɑː.nɪk
carboniferous ˌkɑː.bəˈnɪf.ər.əs (US) ˌkɑːr-
carbonization, -isa- ˌkɑː.bən.aɪˈzeɪ.ʃən, -ɪˈ- (US) ˌkɑːr.bən.ɪˈ-
carboniz|e, -is|e ˈkɑː.bən.aɪz (US) ˈkɑːr- **-es** -ɪz **-ing** -ɪŋ **-ed** -d
carbonnade ˌkɑː.bənˈeɪd, -ˈɑːd, ˈ--- (US) ˌkɑːr.bənˈeɪd **-s** -z
carbonyl ˈkɑː.bə.nɪl, -naɪl (US) ˈkɑːr-, -niːl **-s** -z
Carborundum® ˌkɑː.bərˈʌn.dəm (US) ˌkɑːr.bɚ-
carboxyl kɑːˈbɒk.sɪl, -saɪl (US) kɑːrˈbɑːk.səl
carboy ˈkɑː.bɔɪ (US) ˈkɑːr- **-s** -z
carbuncle ˈkɑː.bʌŋ.kl̩ (US) ˈkɑːr- **-s** -z
carburation ˌkɑː.bjəˈreɪ.ʃən, -bjʊˈ- (US) ˌkɑːr.bə-, -bjə-
carburetter, carburettor ˌkɑː.bjəˈret.əʳ, -bjʊˈ-, ˈkɑː.bjə.ret.ə (US) ˈkɑːr.bə.reɪ.t̬ɚ, -bjə- **-s** -z
carburization, -isa- ˌkɑː.bjə.raɪˈzeɪ.ʃən, -bjʊ-, -rɪˈ- (US) ˌkɑːr.bɚ.ɪˈ-, -bjɚ-
carburiz|e, -is|e ˈkɑː.bjə.raɪz, -bjʊ- (US) ˈkɑːr.bə-, -bjə- **-es** -ɪz **-ing** -ɪŋ **-ed** -d
carcanet ˈkɑː.kə.net, -nɪt (US) ˈkɑːr- **-s** -s
carcas|e ˈkɑː.kəs (US) ˈkɑːr- **-es** -ɪz
carcass ˈkɑː.kəs (US) ˈkɑːr- **-es** -ɪz
Carcassonne ˌkɑː.kəˈsɒn (US) ˌkɑːr.kəˈsoʊn, -ˈsɔːn
Carchemish ˈkɑː.kə.mɪʃ, -kɪ-; kɑːˈkiː- (US) ˈkɑːr.kə-; kɑːrˈkiː-
carcinogen kɑːˈsɪn.ə.dʒən, -dʒen; ˈkɑː.sɪ.nə-, -sən.ə- (US) kɑːrˈsɪn.ə-; ˈkɑːr.sən.ə- **-s** -z
carcinogenic ˌkɑː.sɪ.nəʊˈdʒen.ɪk, -sən.əʊˈ- (US) ˌkɑːr.sən.oʊˈ-; kɑːrˌsɪn-
carcinom|a ˌkɑː.sɪˈnəʊ.m|ə (US) ˌkɑːr.sənˈoʊ- **-as** -əz **-ata** -ə.tə (US) -ə.t̬ə
Carcroft ˈkɑː.krɒft (US) ˈkɑːr.krɑːft
card kɑːd (US) kɑːrd **-s** -z **-ing** -ɪŋ **-ed** -ɪd ˈ**card** ˌ**index** ; ˈ**card** ˌ**key** ; **put one's** ˌ**cards on the** ˈ**table**
cardamom, -mum ˈkɑː.də.məm (US) ˈkɑːr-, -mɑːm
cardboard ˈkɑːd.bɔːd (US) ˈkɑːrd.bɔːrd
card-carrying ˈkɑːdˌkær.i.ɪŋ (US) ˈkɑːrdˌker-, -ˌkær-
Cardenden ˌkɑː.dənˈdən (US) ˌkɑːr-
Cardew ˈkɑː.djuː (US) ˈkɑːr.duː
cardiac ˈkɑː.di.æk (US) ˈkɑːr- ˌ**cardiac a**ˈ**rrest**
cardiacal kɑːˈdaɪə.kəl (US) kɑːr-
Cardiff ˈkɑː.dɪf (US) ˈkɑːr-
cardigan ˈkɑː.dɪ.gən (US) ˈkɑːr- **-s** -z
Cardigan ˈkɑː.dɪ.gən (US) ˈkɑːr- **-shire** -ʃəʳ, -ˌʃɪəʳ (US) -ʃɚ, -ʃɪr
Cardin ˈkɑː.dæ̃n, -dæn (US) kɑːrˈdæn
cardinal ˈkɑː.dɪ.nəl, -dən.əl (US) ˈkɑːr- **-s** -z ˌ**cardinal** ˈ**number** ; ˌ**cardinal** ˈ**point** ; ˌ**cardinal** ˈ**rule** ; ˌ**cardinal** ˈ**vowel**
cardio- ˈkɑː.di.əʊ-, ˌkɑː.diˈɒ- (US) ˈkɑːr.di.oʊ-, ˌkɑːr.diˈɑː-
Note: Prefix. Normally takes either primary or secondary stress on the first syllable, e.g. **cardiogram** /ˈkɑː.di.əʊ.græm (US) ˈkɑːr.di.oʊ-/, **cardiological** /ˌkɑː.di.əʊˈlɒdʒ.ɪ.kəl (US) ˌkɑːr.di.əˈlɑː.dʒɪ-/, or primary stress on the third syllable, e.g.

cardiology /ˌkɑː.diˈɒl.ə.dʒi (US) ˌkɑːr.diˈɑː.lə-/.
cardiogram ˈkɑː.di.əʊ.græm (US) ˈkɑːr.di.oʊ- **-s** -z
cardiograph ˈkɑː.di.əʊ.grɑːf, -græf (US) ˈkɑːr.di.oʊ.græf **-s** -s
cardiography ˌkɑː.diˈɒg.rə.fi (US) ˌkɑːr.diˈɑː.grə-
cardioid ˈkɑː.di.ɔɪd (US) ˈkɑːr- **-s** -z
cardiological ˌkɑː.di.əʊˈlɒdʒ.ɪ.kəl (US) ˌkɑːr.di.əˈlɑː.dʒɪ-
cardiolog|y ˌkɑː.diˈɒl.ə.dʒ|i (US) ˌkɑːr.diˈɑː.lə- **-ist/s** -ɪst/s
cardiometer ˌkɑː.diˈɒm.ɪ.təʳ, -mə- (US) ˌkɑːr.diˈɑː.mə.t̬ɚ **-s** -z
cardiopulmonary ˌkɑː.di.əʊˈpʌl.mən.ər.i, -ˈpʊl- (US) ˌkɑːr.di.oʊˈpʊl.mə.ner-, -ˈpʌl-
cardiovascular ˌkɑː.di.əʊˈvæs.kjʊ.ləʳ, -kjə- (US) ˌkɑːr.di.oʊˈvæs.kjə.lɚ
cardoon kɑːˈduːn (US) kɑːr- **-s** -z
cardpunch ˈkɑːd.pʌntʃ (US) ˈkɑːrd- **-es** -ɪz
cardsharp ˈkɑːd.ʃɑːp (US) ˈkɑːrd.ʃɑːrp **-s** -z **-er/s** -əʳ/z (US) -ɚ/z
Cardwell ˈkɑːd.wəl, -wel (US) ˈkɑːrd-
Cardy ˈkɑː.di (US) ˈkɑːr-
car|e keəʳ (US) ker **-es** -z **-ing** -ɪŋ **-ed** -d **-er/s** -əʳ/z (US) -ɚ/z
careen kəˈriːn **-s** -z **-ing** -ɪŋ **-ed** -d
career kəˈrɪəʳ (US) -ˈrɪr **-s** -z **-ing** -ɪŋ **-ed** -d **caˈreers adˌvisor** ; **caˈreers ˌoffice**
careerist kəˈrɪə.rɪst (US) -ˈrɪr.ɪst **-s** -s
carefree ˈkeə.friː (US) ˈker-
careful ˈkeə.fəl, -fʊl (US) ˈker- **-lest** -ɪst **-ly** -i **-ness** -nəs, -nɪs
careless ˈkeə.ləs, -lɪs (US) ˈker- **-ly** -li **-ness** -nəs, -nɪs
caress kəˈres **-es** -ɪz **-ing/ly** -ɪŋ/li **-ed** -t
caret ˈkær.ət, -ɪt, -et (US) ˈker-, ˈkær- **-s** -s
caretaker ˈkeəˌteɪ.kəʳ (US) ˈkerˌteɪ.kɚ **-s** -z **ˌcaretaker ˈgovernment** (US) **ˈcaretaker ˌgovernment**
Carew kəˈruː; ˈkeə.ri (US) kəˈruː, ˈker.u, -i
careworn ˈkeə.wɔːn (US) ˈker.wɔːrn
Carey ˈkeə.ri (US) ˈker.i, ˈkær-
carfare ˈkɑː.feəʳ (US) ˈkɑːr.fer **-s** -z
Carfax ˈkɑː.fæks (US) ˈkɑːr-
Cargill ˈkɑː.gɪl, -ˈ- (US) ˈkɑːr.gɪl, -ˈ-
cargo ˈkɑː.gəʊ (US) ˈkɑːr.goʊ **-(e)s** -z
carhop ˈkɑː.hɒp (US) ˈkɑːr.hɑːp **-s** -s
Caria ˈkeə.ri.ə (US) ˈker.i-
Carib ˈkær.ɪb (US) ˈker-, ˈkær- **-s** -z
Caribbean ˌkær.ɪˈbiː.ən; kəˈrɪb.i.ən (US) ˌker.ɪˈbiː-, ˌkær-; kəˈrɪb.i-
Caribbees ˈkær.ɪ.biːz (US) ˈker-, ˈkær-
caribou (C) ˈkær.ɪ.buː (US) ˈker-, ˈkær- **-s** -z
caricatur|e ˈkær.ɪ.kə.tʃʊəʳ, -tʃɔːʳ, -tjʊəʳ, ˌkær.ɪ.kəˈtʃʊəʳ, -ˈtʃɔːʳ, -ˈtjʊəʳ (US) ˈker.ə.kə.tʃʊr, ˈkær-, -tʊr, -tʃɚ **-es** -z **-ing** -ɪŋ **-ed** -d
caricaturist ˈkær.ɪ.kə.tʃʊə.rɪst, -tʃɔː-, -tjʊə-, ˌkær.ɪ.kəˈtʃʊə.rɪst, -ˈtʃɔː-, -ˈtjʊə- (US) ˈker.ə.kə.tʃʊr.ɪst, ˈkær-, -tʊr-, -tʃɚ- **-s** -s
caries ˈkeə.riːz, -ri.iːz (US) ˈker.iːz, -i.iːz
carillon kærˈɪl.jən, kəˈrɪl-, -ɒn; ˈkær.ɪ.ljən, -əl.jən, -ɒn (US) ˈker.ə.lɑːn, ˈkær- **-s** -z
Carinthia kəˈrɪn*t*.θi.ə, kærˈɪn*t*- (US) kəˈrɪn*t*-
carious ˈkeə.ri.əs (US) ˈker.i-
Carisbrooke ˈkær.ɪs.brʊk, -ɪz- (US) ˈker-, ˈkær-
Carl kɑːl (US) kɑːrl
Carla ˈkɑː.lə (US) ˈkɑːr-
Carle kɑːl (US) kɑːrl **-s** -z
Carless ˈkɑː.ləs (US) ˈkɑːr-
Carleton ˈkɑːl.tən (US) ˈkɑːrl-
Carlile kɑːˈlaɪl (US) kɑːr-
Carlin ˈkɑː.lɪn (US) ˈkɑːr-
Carlingford ˈkɑː.lɪŋ.fəd (US) ˈkɑːr.lɪŋ.fɚd
Carlisle kɑːˈlaɪl *locally:* ˈ-- (US) kɑːrˈlaɪl, kɚˈ-; ˈkɑːr.laɪl
Carlist ˈkɑː.lɪst (US) ˈkɑːr- **-s** -s
Carlos ˈkɑː.lɒs (US) ˈkɑːr.ləs, -loʊs
Carlovingian ˌkɑː.ləʊˈvɪn.*d*ʒi.ən, -*d*ʒən (US) ˌkɑːr.lə-
Carlow ˈkɑː.ləʊ (US) ˈkɑːr.loʊ
Carlsbad ˈkɑːlz.bæd (US) ˈkɑːrlz-
Carlsberg® ˈkɑːlz.bɜːg (US) ˈkɑːrlz.bɜːrg **-s** -z
Carlson ˈkɑːl.sən (US) ˈkɑːrl-
Carlsruhe ˈkɑːlzˌruː.ə (US) ˈkɑːrlz-
Carlton ˈkɑːl.tən (US) ˈkɑːrl-
Carluccio kɑːˈluː.tʃi.əʊ (US) kɑːrˈluː.tʃi.oʊ
Carluke kɑːˈluːk (US) kɑːr-
Carly ˈkɑː.li (US) ˈkɑːr-
Carlyle kɑːˈlaɪl, ˈ-- (US) kɑːrˈlaɪl, ˈ--
car|man ˈkɑː|.mən (US) ˈkɑːr- **-men** -mən, -men
Carmarthen kəˈmɑː.ðən (US) kɑːrˈmɑːr- **-shire** -ʃəʳ, -ˌʃɪəʳ (US) -ʃɚ, -ʃɪr
Carmel ˈkɑː.mel, -məl, kɑːˈmel (US) ˈkɑːr.mel, -məl; kɑːrˈmel
Note: The form /kɑːˈmel (US) kɑːr-/ is preferred for the city in California.
Carmelite ˈkɑː.məl.aɪt, -mɪ.laɪt, -mel.aɪt (US) ˈkɑːr.mə.laɪt, -mɪ-, -mel.aɪt **-s** -s
Carmen ˈkɑː.men (US) ˈkɑːr-
Carmichael kɑːˈmaɪ.kəl, ˈ--- (US) ˈkɑːr.maɪ-
Carmina Burana ˌkɑː.mɪ.nə.bəˈrɑː.nə, kɑːˌmiː-, -bjʊˈ-, -bʊˈ- (US) kɑːrˌmiː.nə.bəˈ-
carminative ˈkɑː.mɪ.nə.tɪv, -mə- (US) ˈkɑːr.mə.nə.t̬ɪv **-s** -z
carmine ˈkɑː.maɪn, -mɪn (US) ˈkɑːr-
Carnaby ˈkɑː.nə.bi (US) ˈkɑːr- **ˈCarnaby ˌStreet**
Carnac ˈkɑː.næk (US) kɑːrˈnæk
carnage ˈkɑː.nɪdʒ (US) ˈkɑːr-
Carnaghan ˈkɑː.nə.gən, -hən (US) ˈkɑːr.nə.hæn
carnal ˈkɑː.nəl (US) ˈkɑːr- **-ly** -i
carnality kɑːˈnæl.ə.ti, -ɪ.ti (US) kɑːrˈnæl.ə.t̬i
Carnarvon kəˈnɑː.vən (US) kɑːrˈnɑːr-
Carnatic kɑːˈnæt.ɪk (US) kɑːrˈnæt̬-
carnation (C) kɑːˈneɪ.ʃən (US) kɑːr- **-s** -z
Carné kɑːˈneɪ (US) kɑːr-
Carnegie kɑːˈneg.i, -ˈneɪ.gi, -ˈniː-; ˈkɑː.nə.gi (US) ˈkɑːr.nə.gi; kɑːrˈneɪ-, -ˈneg.i, -ˈniː.gi **CarˌnegieˈHall**
carnelian kɑːˈniː.li.ən, kə- (US) kɑːr-, -ˈniːl.jən **-s** -z
carnet ˈkɑː.neɪ (US) kɑːrˈneɪ **-s** -z
Carnforth ˈkɑːn.fɔːθ, -fəθ (US) ˈkɑːrn.fɔːrθ, -fɚθ
carnival ˈkɑː.nɪ.vəl (US) ˈkɑːr.nə- **-s** -z
carnivore ˈkɑː.nɪ.vɔːʳ, -nə- (US) ˈkɑːr.nə.vɔːr **-s** -z
carnivorous kɑːˈnɪv.ər.əs (US) kɑːr-
Carnochan ˈkɑː.nə.kən, -nɒk.ən, -nɒx- (US) ˈkɑːr.nə.kən, -nɑː.kən
Carnoustie kɑːˈnuː.sti (US) kɑːr-
carob ˈkær.əb (US) ˈker-, ˈkær- **-s** -z
carol (C) ˈkær.əl (US) ˈker-, ˈkær- **-s** -z **-(l)ing** -ɪŋ **-(l)ed** -d **ˈcarol ˌsinger**
Carole ˈkær.əl (US) ˈker-, ˈkær-
Carolina ˌkær.əlˈaɪ.nə (US) ˌker.əˈlaɪ-, ˌkær-
Caroline ˈkær.əl.aɪn, -ɪn (US) ˈker.ə.laɪn, ˈkær-, -əl.ɪn
carolus (C) ˈkær.əl.əs (US) ˈker-, ˈkær- **-es** -ɪz
Carolyn ˈkær.əl.ɪn (US) ˈker-, ˈkær-
carotene ˈkær.ə.tiːn (US) ˈker-, ˈkær-
carotid kəˈrɒt.ɪd (US) -ˈrɑː.t̬ɪd **-s** -z
carotin ˈkær.ə.tɪn (US) ˈker-, ˈkær-
carousal kəˈraʊ.zəl **-s** -z
carous|e kəˈraʊz **-es** -ɪz **-ing** -ɪŋ **-ed** -d **-er/s** -əʳ/z (US) -ɚ/z
carousel ˌkær.əˈsel, -ʊˈ- (US) ˈker.ə.sel, ˈkær-, ˌ--ˈ- **-s** -z
carp kɑːp (US) kɑːrp **-s** -s **-ing** -ɪŋ **-ed** -t **-er/s** -əʳ/z (US) -ɚ/z
carpaccio kɑːˈpætʃ.i.əʊ, -ˈpætʃ.əʊ (US) kɑːrˈpɑːtʃ.oʊ
carpal ˈkɑː.pəl (US) ˈkɑːr- **-s** -z
Carpathian kɑːˈpeɪ.θi.ən (US) kɑːr- **-s** -z
carpe diem ˌkɑː.peɪˈdiː.em, -piˈ- (US) ˌkɑːr.pəˈ-, -peɪˈ-
carpel ˈkɑː.pel, -pəl (US) ˈkɑːr- **-s** -z
Carpentaria ˌkɑː.pənˈteə.ri.ə, -penˈ-, -pəmˈ- (US) ˌkɑːr.pənˈter.i-

carpent|er (C) ˈkɑː.pᵊn.t|əʳ, -pɪn- (US) ˈkɑːr.pᵊn.t̬|ɚ **-ers** -əz (US) -ɚz **-ering** -ᵊr.ɪŋ **-ered** -əd (US) -ɚd
carpentry ˈkɑː.pᵊn.tri, -pɪn- (US) ˈkɑːr.pᵊn-
carp|et ˈkɑː.p|ɪt (US) ˈkɑːr.p|ət **-ets** -ɪts (US) -əts **-eting** -ɪ.tɪŋ (US) -ə.t̬ɪŋ **-eted** -ɪ.tɪd (US) -ə.t̬ɪd ˈ**carpet** ˌ**broom** ; ˈ**carpet** ˌ**slipper** ; ˈ**carpet** ˌ**sweeper**
carpetbag ˈkɑː.pɪt.bæg (US) ˈkɑːr.pət- **-s** -z **-ging** -ɪŋ
carpetbagger ˈkɑː.pɪtˌbæg.əʳ (US) ˈkɑːr.pətˌbæg.ɚ **-s** -z
carpet-bomb ˈkɑː.pɪt.bɒm (US) ˈkɑːr.pət.bɑːm **-s** -z **-ing** -ɪŋ **-ed** -d
carp|us ˈkɑː.p|əs (US) ˈkɑːr- **-i** -aɪ, -iː
Carr kɑːʳ (US) kɑːr
carrag(h)een ˈkær.ə.giːn, --ˈ- (US) ˈker.ə.giːn, ˈkær-
Carrara kəˈrɑː.rə (US) kəˈrɑːr.ə
Carrauntoohill ˌkær.ənˈtuː.hᵊl (US) ˌker-, ˌkær-
carraway ˈkær.ə.weɪ (US) ˈker-, ˈkær- **-s** -z
Carrhae ˈkær.iː (US) ˈker-, ˈkær-
carriag|e ˈkær.ɪdʒ (US) ˈker-, ˈkær- **-es** -ɪz ˈ**carriage** ˌ**clock**
carriageway ˈkær.ɪdʒ.weɪ (US) ˈker-, ˈkær- **-s** -z
carrick (C) ˈkær.ɪk (US) ˈker-, ˈkær-
Carrickfergus ˌkær.ɪkˈfɜː.gəs (US) ˌker.ɪkˈfɜːr-, ˌkær-
Carrie ˈkær.i (US) ˈker-, ˈkær-
carrier ˈkær.i.əʳ (US) ˈker.i.ɚ, ˈkær- **-s** -z ˈ**carrier** ˌ**bag** ; ˈ**carrier** ˌ**pigeon**
Carrington ˈkær.ɪŋ.tən (US) ˈker-, ˈkær-
carrion ˈkær.i.ən (US) ˈker-, ˈkær- ˌ**carrion** ˈ**crow** (US) ˈ**carrion** ˌ**crow**
Carrodus ˈkær.ə.dəs (US) ˈker-, ˈkær-
Carroll ˈkær.ᵊl (US) ˈker-, ˈkær-
Carron ˈkær.ᵊn (US) ˈker-, ˈkær-
carrot ˈkær.ət (US) ˈker-, ˈkær- **-s** -s
carroty ˈkær.ə.ti (US) ˈker.ə.t̬i, ˈkær-
carrousel ˌkær.əˈsel, -ʊˈ- (US) ˌker.əˈsel, ˌkær-, ˈ--- **-s** -z
Carruthers kəˈrʌð.əz (US) -ɚz
carr|y ˈkær|.i (US) ˈker-, ˈkær **-ies** -iz **-ying** -i.ɪŋ **-ied** -id **-ier/s** -i.əʳ/z (US) -i.ɚ/z
carryall ˈkær.i.ɔːl (US) ˈker.i.ɔːl, ˈkær-, -ɑːl **-s** -z
carrycot ˈkær.i.kɒt (US) ˈker.i.kɑːt, ˈkær- **-s** -s
carryings-on ˌkær.i.ɪŋzˈɒn (US) ˌker.i.ɪŋzˈɑːn, ˌkær-
carry-on ˈkær.i.ɒn (US) ˈker.i.ɑːn, ˈkær- **-s** -z
carryout ˈkær.i.aʊt (US) ˈker-, ˈkær- **-s** -z
Carse kɑːs (US) kɑːrs
Carshalton kɑːˈʃɔːl.tᵊn, kəˈ- *old-fashioned local pronunciation:* keɪsˈhɔː.tᵊn (US) kɑːrˈʃɔːl-, kɚ-, -ˈʃɑːl-
carsick ˈkɑː.sɪk (US) ˈkɑːr- **-ness** -nəs, -nɪs
Carson ˈkɑː.sᵊn (US) ˈkɑːr-
Carstairs ˈkɑː.steəz, ˌ-ˈ- (US) ˈkɑːr.sterz
cart (C) kɑːt (US) kɑːrt **-s** -s **-ing** -ɪŋ (US) ˈkɑːr.t̬ɪŋ **-ed** -ɪd (US) ˈkɑːr.t̬ɪd **-er/s** -əʳ/z (US) ˈkɑːr.t̬ɚ/z **put the** ˌ**cart before the** ˈ**horse**
Carta ˈkɑː.tə (US) ˈkɑːr.t̬ə
cartage ˈkɑː.tɪdʒ (US) ˈkɑːr.t̬ɪdʒ
Cartagena ˌkɑː.təˈgeɪ.nə (US) ˌkɑːr.t̬əˈdʒiː.nə, -ˈheɪ-, -ˈgeɪ-
carte (C) kɑːt (US) kɑːrt
carte blanche ˌkɑːtˈblɑ̃ːntʃ (US) ˌkɑːrtˈblɑːnʃ, -ˈblæntʃ
cartel kɑːˈtel (US) kɑːr- **-s** -z
Carter ˈkɑː.təʳ (US) ˈkɑːr.t̬ɚ
Carteret *surname:* ˈkɑː.tə.ret, -rɪt (US) ˈkɑːr.t̬ɚ.ɪt *US place name:* ˌkɑː.təˈret (US) ˌkɑːr.t̬əˈ-
Cartesian kɑːˈtiː.zi.ən, -ʒᵊn (US) kɑːrˈtiː.ʒᵊn **-ism** -ɪ.zᵊm
Carteton ˈkɑː.tə.tᵊn (US) ˈkɑːr.t̬ə.tən
Carthage ˈkɑː.θɪdʒ (US) ˈkɑːr-
Carthaginian ˌkɑː.θəˈdʒɪn.i.ən (US) ˌkɑːr- **-s** -z
cart-hors|e ˈkɑːt.hɔːs (US) ˈkɑːrt.hɔːrs **-es** -ɪz
Carthusian kɑːˈθjuː.zi.ən, -ˈθuː- (US) kɑːrˈθuː.ʒᵊn, -ˈθjuː- **-s** -z
Cartier ˈkɑː.ti.eɪ (US) ˌkɑːr.tiˈeɪ; kɑːrˈtjeɪ
Cartier-Bresson ˌkɑː.ti.eɪˈbres.ɔ̃ːn (US) ˌkɑːr.tjeɪ.breɪˈsõʊn, -bresˈõʊn
cartilag|e ˈkɑː.tɪ.lɪdʒ, -tᵊl.ɪdʒ (US) ˈkɑːr.t̬ᵊl.ɪdʒ **-es** -ɪz
cartilaginous ˌkɑː.tɪˈlædʒ.ɪ.nəs, -tᵊlˈædʒ-, -ᵊn.əs (US) ˌkɑːr.t̬əˈlædʒ.ᵊn.əs
carting ˈkɑː.tɪŋ (US) ˈkɑːr.t̬ɪŋ
Cartland ˈkɑːt.lənd (US) ˈkɑːrt-
cartload ˈkɑːt.ləʊd (US) ˈkɑːrt.loʊd **-s** -z
Cartmel(e) ˈkɑːt.mel, -mᵊl (US) ˈkɑːrt-
cartographic ˌkɑː.təʊˈgræf.ɪk, ˌkɑːr.t̬əˈ- **-ally** -ᵊl.i, -li
cartograph|y kɑːˈtɒg.rə.f|i (US) kɑːrˈtɑː.grə- **-er/s** -əʳ/z (US) -ɚ/z
cartomancy ˈkɑː.təʊ.mænt.si (US) ˈkɑːr.t̬ə-
carton ˈkɑː.tᵊn (US) ˈkɑːr- **-s** -z
cartoon kɑːˈtuːn (US) kɑːr- **-s** -z **-ist/s** -ɪst/s
cartouch|e, cartouch kɑːˈtuːʃ (US) kɑːr- **-es** -ɪz
cartridg|e ˈkɑː.trɪdʒ (US) ˈkɑːr- **-es** -ɪz ˈ**cartridge** ˌ**paper**
cartwheel ˈkɑːt.hwiːl (US) ˈkɑːrt- **-s** -z **-ing** -ɪŋ **-ed** -d
cartwright (C) ˈkɑːt.raɪt (US) ˈkɑːrt- **-s** -s
caruncle ˈkær.əŋ.kl̩; kəˈrʌŋ- (US) kəˈrʌŋ-, kerˈʌŋ-, kær- **-s** -z
Carus ˈkeə.rəs (US) ˈker.əs, ˈkɑːr-
Caruso kəˈruː.zəʊ, -səʊ (US) -soʊ, -zoʊ
Caruthers kəˈrʌð.əz (US) -ɚz
carv|e kɑːv (US) kɑːrv **-es** -z **-ing** -ɪŋ **-ed** -d ˈ**carving** ˌ**knife**
carver (C) ˈkɑː.vəʳ (US) ˈkɑːr.vɚ **-s** -z
carver|y ˈkɑː.vᵊr|.i (US) ˈkɑːr- **-ies** -iz
Carville ˈkɑː.vɪl (US) ˈkɑːr-
Carwardine ˈkɑː.wə.diːn (US) ˈkɑːr.wɚ-
carwash ˈkɑː.wɒʃ (US) ˈkɑːr.wɑːʃ, -wɔːʃ **-es** -ɪz
Cary *surname:* ˈkeə.ri (US) ˈker.i *first name:* ˈkær.i (US) ˈker.i, ˈkær-
caryatid ˌkær.iˈæt.ɪd, ˈkær.i.ə.tɪd (US) ˌker.iˈæt̬.ɪd, ˌkær-; kəˈraɪ.ə.t̬ɪd **-s** -z **-es** -iːz
Caryll ˈkær.ɪl, -ᵊl (US) ˈker-, ˈkær-
Carysfort ˈkær.ɪs.fɔːt, -əs- (US) ˈker.ɪs.fɔːrt, ˈkær-
Casablanca ˌkæs.əˈblæŋ.kə (US) ˌkæs.əˈblæŋ.kə, ˌkɑː.səˈblɑːŋ.kə
Casals kəˈsæls (US) -ˈsɑːlz, -ˈsælz
Casamassima ˌkæs.əˈmæs.ɪ.mə
Casanova ˌkæs.əˈnəʊ.və, ˌkæz- (US) ˌkæs.əˈnoʊ-, ˌkæz-
Casaubon kəˈsɔː.bᵊn; ˈkæz.ə.bɒn, -ɔː- (US) kəˈsɑː.bᵊn, -ˈsɔː-; ˈkæz.ə.bɑːn
casbah (C) ˈkæz.bɑː (US) ˈkæz.bɑː, ˈkɑːz- **-s** -z
cascad|e kæsˈkeɪd **-es** -z **-ing** -ɪŋ **-ed** -ɪd
cascara kæsˈkɑː.rə, kəˈskɑː- (US) kæsˈker.ə, -ˈkær- **-s** -z
cascarilla ˌkæs.kəˈrɪl.ə
cas|e (C) keɪs **-es** -ɪz **-ing** -ɪŋ **-ed** -t ˈ**case** ˌ**ending** ; ˌ**case** ˈ**history** ; ˈ**case** ˌ**knife** ; ˈ**case** ˌ**law** ; ˈ**case** ˌ**shot** ; ˈ**case** ˌ**study**
casebook ˈkeɪs.bʊk **-s** -s
casein ˈkeɪ.siːn, -siː.ɪn (US) -siː.ɪn, -siːn
caseload ˈkeɪs.ləʊd (US) -loʊd **-s** -z
casemate ˈkeɪs.meɪt **-s** -s
casement ˈkeɪs.mənt **-s** -s
Casement ˈkeɪs.mənt
casern kəˈzɜːn (US) -ˈzɜːrn **-s** -z
casework ˈkeɪs.wɜːk (US) -wɜːrk **-er/s** -əʳ/z (US) -ɚ/z
Casey ˈkeɪ.si
cash (C) kæʃ **-es** -ɪz **-ing** -ɪŋ **-ed** -t **-less** -ləs, -lɪs ˈ**cash** ˌ**crop** ; ˈ**cash** ˌ**desk** ; ˈ**cash dis**ˌ**penser** ; ˈ**cash** ˌ**flow** ; ˈ**cash ma**ˌ**chine** ; ˈ**cash** ˌ**register**
cash-and-carry ˌkæʃ.ᵊndˈkær.i, -ᵊŋˈ- (US) -ᵊndˈker-, -ˈkær-
cashbook ˈkæʃ.bʊk **-s** -s
cashbox ˈkæʃ.bɒks (US) -bɑːks **-es** -ɪz
cashew ˈkæʃ.uː; -ˈ-, kəˈʃuː (US) ˈkæʃ.uː; kəˈʃuː **-s** -z ˈ**cashew** ˌ**nut**, **ca**ˈ**shew** ˌ**nut** (US) **ca**ˈ**shew** ˌ**nut**

cashier (*n.*) kæʃˈɪəʳ, kəˈʃɪəʳ ⓤⓢ kæʃˈɪr **-s** -z
cashier (*v.*) kəˈʃɪəʳ, kæʃˈɪəʳ ⓤⓢ kəˈʃɪr, kæʃˈɪr **-s** -z **-ing** -ɪŋ **-ed** -d
cash-in-hand ˌkæʃ.ɪnˈhænd *stress shift:* ˌcash-in-hand ˈpayment
cashless ˈkæʃ.ləs, -lɪs
Cashmere *place:* ˈkæʃ.mɪəʳ, ˌ-ˈ- ⓤⓢ ˈkæʃ.mɪr **-s** -z
cashmere *fabric:* ˈkæʃ.mɪəʳ, ˌ-ˈ- ⓤⓢ ˈkæʒ.mɪr, ˈkæʃ-
Cashmore ˈkæʃ.mɔːʳ ⓤⓢ -mɔːr
cashpoint ˈkæʃ.pɔɪnt **-s** -s
Casimir ˈkæs.ɪ.mɪəʳ ⓤⓢ -ə.mɪr
casing ˈkeɪ.sɪŋ **-s** -z
casino kəˈsiː.nəʊ ⓤⓢ -noʊ **-s** -z
Casio® ˈkæs.i.əʊ ⓤⓢ -oʊ
cask kɑːsk ⓤⓢ kæsk **-s** -s **-ing** -ɪŋ **-ed** -t
casket ˈkɑː.skɪt ⓤⓢ ˈkæs.kɪt **-s** -s
Caslon ˈkæz.lᵊn, -lɒn ⓤⓢ -lᵊn, -lɑːn
Caspar ˈkæs.pəʳ, -pɑːʳ ⓤⓢ -pɚ
Caspian ˈkæs.pi.ən
casque kæsk, kɑːsk ⓤⓢ kæsk **-s** -s
Cass kæs
Cassandra kəˈsæn.drə, -ˈsɑːn-
cassareep ˈkæs.ə.riːp
cassata kəˈsɑː.tə, kæsˈɑː- ⓤⓢ kəˈsɑː.t̬ə
cassation kæsˈeɪ.ʃᵊn, kəˈseɪ- ⓤⓢ kəˈseɪ- **-s** -z
Cassatt kəˈsæt
cassava kəˈsɑː.və
Cassavetes ˌkæs.əˈviː.tiːz ⓤⓢ -t̬iːz
Cassel(l) ˈkæs.ᵊl
casserole ˈkæs.ᵊr.əʊl ⓤⓢ -ə.roʊl **-s** -z
cassette kəˈset, kæsˈet ⓤⓢ kəˈset **-s** -s caˈssette reˌcorder
cassia ˈkæs.i.ə
Cassidy ˈkæs.ə.di, -ɪ.di ⓤⓢ -ə.di
Cassie ˈkæs.i
Cassil(l)is ˈkæs.ᵊlz, ˈkɑː.sᵊlz
Cassio ˈkæs.i.əʊ ⓤⓢ -oʊ
Cassiopeia ˌkæs.i.əʊˈpiː.ə *as name of constellation also:* ˌkæs.iˈəʊ.pi- ⓤⓢ ˌkæs.i.əˈpiː-
cassis kæsˈiːs, ˈ-- ⓤⓢ kæsˈiːs
Cassius ˈkæs.i.əs ⓤⓢ ˈkæʃ.əs, ˈkæs.i-
Cassivelaunus ˌkæs.ɪ.vɪˈlɔː.nəs, ˌ-ə-, -vəˈ- ⓤⓢ -ɪ.vəˈlɑː-, -ˈlɔː-
cassock ˈkæs.ək **-s** -s **-ed** -t
cassoulet ˌkæs.ʊˈleɪ, ˈ--- ⓤⓢ ˌkæs.ʊˈleɪ **-s** -z
cassowar|y ˈkæs.ə.weə.r|i, -wə- ⓤⓢ -wer|.i **-ies** -iz
Cass Timberlane ˌkæsˈtɪm.bə.leɪn ⓤⓢ -bɚ-
cast kɑːst ⓤⓢ kæst **-s** -s **-ing** -ɪŋ ˌcast-ˈiron
Castali|a kæsˈteɪ.li|.ə ⓤⓢ -li|.ə, -ˈteɪl.j|ə **-an/s** -ən/z
castanet ˌkæs.təˈnet **-s** -s

castaway ˈkɑː.stə.weɪ ⓤⓢ ˈkæs.tə- **-s** -z
caste kɑːst ⓤⓢ kæst **-s** -s
Castel Gandolfo ˌkæs.tel.gænˈdɒl.fəʊ ⓤⓢ -ˈdɑːl.foʊ, -ˈdɔːl-
castellated ˈkæs.tə.leɪ.tɪd, -tɪ-, -tel.eɪ- ⓤⓢ -tə.leɪ.t̬ɪd
Castelnau ˈkɑː.sᵊl.nɔː, -nəʊ ⓤⓢ ˈkæs.ᵊl.nɔː, -noʊ
caster ˈkɑː.stəʳ ⓤⓢ ˈkæs.tɚ **-s** -z ˈcaster ˌsugar
Casterbridge ˈkɑː.stə.brɪdʒ ⓤⓢ ˈkæs.tɚ-
casti|gate ˈkæs.tɪ|.geɪt, -tə|.geɪt ⓤⓢ -tə- **-gates** -geɪts **-gating** -geɪ.tɪŋ ⓤⓢ -geɪ.t̬ɪŋ **-gated** -geɪ.tɪd ⓤⓢ -geɪ.t̬ɪd **-gator/s** -geɪ.təʳ/z ⓤⓢ -geɪ.t̬ɚ/z
castigation ˌkæs.tɪˈgeɪ.ʃᵊn, -təˈ- ⓤⓢ -əˈ- **-s** -z
Castile kæsˈtiːl
Castilian kæsˈtɪl.i.ən, kəˈstɪl- ⓤⓢ -i.ən, -jən **-s** -z
casting ˈkɑː.stɪŋ ⓤⓢ ˈkæs.tɪŋ **-s** -z ˈ**casting** ˌ**couch** ; ˈ**casting** ˌ**net** ; ˌ**casting** ˈ**vote**
castl|e (C) ˈkɑː.sl̩ ⓤⓢ ˈkæs.l̩ **-es** -z **-ing** -ɪŋ **-ed** -d
Castlebar ˌkɑː.sl̩ˈbɑːʳ ⓤⓢ ˌkæs.l̩ˈbɑːr
Castleford ˈkɑː.sl̩.fəd ⓤⓢ ˈkæs.l̩.fɚd
Castlemaine ˈkɑː.sl̩.meɪn ⓤⓢ ˈkæs.l̩-
Castlenau ˈkɑː.sl̩.nɔː ⓤⓢ ˈkæs.l̩.nɑː, -nɔː
Castlerea(gh) ˈkɑː.sl̩.reɪ, ˌ--ˈ- ⓤⓢ ˈkæs.l̩-
Castleton ˈkɑː.sl̩.tən ⓤⓢ ˈkæs.l̩.t̬ən
Castlewellan ˌkɑː.sl̩ˈwel.ən ⓤⓢ ˌkæs.l̩ˈ-
cast-off ˈkɑːst.ɒf, ˌ-ˈ- ⓤⓢ ˈkæst.ɑːf **-s** -s
castor (C) ˈkɑː.stəʳ ⓤⓢ ˈkæs.tɚ **-s** -z ˌ**castor** ˈ**oil** ; ˈ**castor** ˌ**sugar**
cas|trate kæs|ˈtreɪt ⓤⓢ ˈ-- **-trates** -ˈtreɪts ⓤⓢ -treɪts **-trating** -ˈtreɪ.tɪŋ ⓤⓢ -treɪ.t̬ɪŋ **-trated** -ˈtreɪ.tɪd ⓤⓢ -treɪ.t̬ɪd
castration kæs|ˈtreɪ.ʃᵊn **-s** -z
castrat|o kæsˈtrɑː.t|əʊ ⓤⓢ -t|oʊ **-i** -iː
Castries kæsˈtriːz, -ˈtriːs
Castro ˈkæs.trəʊ ⓤⓢ -troʊ
Castrol® ˈkæs.trɒl ⓤⓢ -trɑːl, -troʊl
casual ˈkæʒ.ju.əl, -zju- ⓤⓢ ˈ-uː- **-ly** -i ˌ**casual** ˈ**sex**
casualt|y ˈkæʒ.ju.əl.t|i, ˈkæz- ⓤⓢ ˈkæʒ.uː- **-ies** -iz
casuarina ˌkæz.jʊəˈriː.nə, ˌkæʒ-, ˈkæʒ.jʊə.riː- ⓤⓢ ˌkæʒ.uː.əˈriː- **-s** -z
casuist ˈkæz.ju.ɪst, ˈkæʒ- ⓤⓢ ˈkæʒ.u- **-s** -s
casuistic ˌkæz.juˈɪs.tɪk, ˌkæʒ- ⓤⓢ ˌkæʒ.uˈ- **-al** -ᵊl

casuistry ˈkæz.ju.ɪ.stri, ˈkæʒ- ⓤⓢ ˈkæʒ.u-
casus belli ˌkɑː.sʊsˈbel.iː, ˌkeɪ.səsˈbel.aɪ ⓤⓢ ˌkeɪ.səsˈbel.i, ˌkɑː-
Caswell ˈkæz.wəl, -wel ⓤⓢ ˈkæz-, ˈkæs-
cat kæt **-s** -s ˈ**cat** ˌ**burglar** ; ˌ**cat's** ˈ**whiskers** ; **let the** ˌ**cat out of the** ˈ**bag** ; **play** ˌ**cat and** ˈ**mouse with** ; **set the** ˌ**cat among the** ˈ**pigeons**
CAT kæt ˈ**CAT** ˌ**scan**
cata- ˈkæt.ə- ⓤⓢ ˈkæt̬.ə-, kəˈtæ-
Note: Prefix. This usually takes primary or secondary stress on the first syllable, e.g. **catalogue** /ˈkæt.ə.lɒg ⓤⓢ ˈkæt̬.ə.lɑːg/, or on the second syllable, e.g. **catastrophe** /kəˈtæs.trə.fi/.
catabolic ˌkæt.əˈbɒl.ɪk ⓤⓢ ˌkæt̬.əˈbɑː.lɪk **-ally** -ᵊl.i, -li
catabolism kəˈtæb.ᵊl.ɪ.zᵊm
catachresis ˌkæt.əˈkriː.sɪs ⓤⓢ ˌkæt̬.əˈ-
cataclysm ˈkæt.ə.klɪ.zᵊm ⓤⓢ ˈkæt̬- **-s** -z
cataclysmal ˌkæt.əˈklɪz.məl ⓤⓢ ˌkæt̬.əˈ- **-ly** -li
cataclysmic ˌkæt.əˈklɪz.mɪk ⓤⓢ ˌkæt̬.əˈ- **-ally** -ᵊl.i, -li
catacomb ˈkæt.ə.kuːm, -kəʊm ⓤⓢ ˈkæt̬.ə.koʊm **-s** -z
catafalque ˈkæt.ə.fælk ⓤⓢ ˈkæt̬.ə.fælk, -fɔːlk, -fɑːlk **-s** -s
Catalan ˌkæt.əˈlæn, ˈ---, -lən ⓤⓢ ˈkæt̬.ə.læn, -ᵊl.ən **-s** -z
catalectic ˌkæt.əˈlek.tɪk ⓤⓢ ˌkæt̬.əˈlet̬.ɪk
catalep|sy ˈkæt.ə.lep.s|i ⓤⓢ ˈkæt̬.ə- **-ies** -iz
cataleptic ˌkæt.əˈlep.tɪk ⓤⓢ ˌkæt̬.əˈ-
catalexis ˈkæt.ə.lek.sɪs ⓤⓢ ˈkæt̬.ə-
catalog ˈkæt.ᵊl.ɒg ⓤⓢ ˈkæt̬.ə.lɑːg, -lɔːg **-s** -z **-ing** -ɪŋ **-ed** -d **-er/s** -əʳ/z ⓤⓢ -ɚ/z **-ist/s** -ɪst/s
catalogu|e ˈkæt.ᵊl.ɒg ⓤⓢ ˈkæt̬.ə.lɑːg, -lɔːg **-es** -z **-ing** -ɪŋ **-ed** -d **-er/s** -əʳ/z ⓤⓢ -ɚ/z **-ist/s** -ɪst/s
Cataloni|a ˌkæt.əˈləʊ.ni|.ə, -nj|ə ⓤⓢ -ˈloʊ-, -nj|ə **-an/s** -ən/z
catalpa kəˈtæl.pə **-s** -z
catalysis kəˈtæl.ə.sɪs, ˈ-ɪ-
catalyst ˈkæt.ᵊl.ɪst ⓤⓢ ˈkæt̬- **-s** -s
catalytic ˌkæt.əˈlɪt.ɪk ⓤⓢ ˌkæt̬ˈə- *stress shift, see compound:* ˌ**catalytic** **conˈverter**
catamaran ˌkæt.ə.məˈræn, ˈkæt.ə.mə.ræn ⓤⓢ ˌkæt̬.ə.məˈræn **-s** -z
Catania kəˈteɪ.ni.ə, -ˈtɑː-, -njə ⓤⓢ -njə, -ni.ə
cataphora kəˈtæf.ᵊr.ə
cataphoric ˌkæt.əˈfɒr.ɪk ⓤⓢ ˌkæt̬.əˈfɔːr-

cataplasm 'kæt.ə.plæz.ᵊm US 'kæt̬- **-s** -z

cata|pult 'kæt.ə|.pʌlt US 'kæt̬- **-pults** -pʌlts **-pulting** -pʌl.tɪŋ US -pʌl.t̬ɪŋ **-pulted** -pʌl.tɪd US -pʌl.t̬ɪd

cataract 'kæt.ᵊr.ækt US 'kæt̬.ər.ækt **-s** -s

catarrh kə'tɑːʳ, kæt'ɑːʳ US kə'tɑːr **-s** -z **-al** -ᵊl

catastas|is kə'tæs.tə.s|ɪs **-es** -iːz

catastrophe kə'tæs.trə.fi **-s** -z

catastrophic ˌkæt.ə'strɒf.ɪk US ˌkæt̬.ə'strɑː.fɪk **-ally** -ᵊl.i, -li

catatonia ˌkæt.ə'təʊ.ni.ə US ˌkæt̬.ə'toʊ-

catatonic ˌkæt.ə'tɒn.ɪk US ˌkæt̬.ə'tɑː.nɪk

catawba (C) kə'tɔː.bə US -'tɔː-, -'tɑː-

catbird 'kæt.bɜːd US -bɜːrd **-s** -z

catboat 'kæt.bəʊt US -boʊt **-s** -s

catcall 'kæt.kɔːl US -kɔːl, -kɑːl **-s** -z **-ing** -ɪŋ **-ed** -d

catch kætʃ **-es** -ɪz **-ing** -ɪŋ **caught** kɔːt US kɑːt, kɔːt

catch-22 (C) ˌkætʃˌtwen.ti'tuː US -t̬i'-

catchall 'kætʃ.ɔːl US -ɔːl, -ɑːl **-s** -z

catcher 'kætʃ.əʳ US -ɚ **-s** -z

catching 'kætʃ.ɪŋ

catchment 'kætʃ.mənt **-s** -s **'catchment ˌarea**

catchpenn|y 'kætʃ.pen|.i **-ies** -iz

catchphras|e 'kætʃ.freɪz **-es** -ɪz

catchpole (C) 'kætʃ.pəʊl US -poʊl **-s** -z

catchpoll 'kætʃ.pəʊl US -poʊl **-s** -z

catchword 'kætʃ.wɜːd US -wɜːrd **-s** -z

catch|y 'kætʃ|.i **-iness** -ɪ.nəs, -ɪ.nɪs

catechism 'kæt.ə.kɪ.zᵊm, '-ɪ- US 'kæt̬.ə- **-s** -z

catechist 'kæt.ə.kɪst, '-ɪ- US 'kæt̬.ə- **-s** -s

catechiz|e, -is|e 'kæt.ə.kaɪz, '-ɪ- US 'kæt̬.ə- **-es** -ɪz **-ing** -ɪŋ **-ed** -d **-er/s** -əʳ/z US -ɚ/z

catechu 'kæt.ə.tʃuː, '-ɪ- US 'kæt̬.ə.tʃuː, -kjuː

catechumen ˌkæt.ɪ'kjuː.men, -ə'-, -mɪn US ˌkæt̬.ə'kjuː.mən **-s** -z

categoric|al ˌkæt.ə'gɒr.ɪ.k|ᵊl, -ɪ'- US ˌkæt̬.ə'gɔːr- **-ally** -ᵊl.i, -li

categorization, -isa- ˌkæt.ə.gᵊr.aɪ'zeɪ.ʃᵊn, ˌ-ɪ-, -ɪ'- US ˌkæt̬.ə.gɚ.ɪ'- **-s** -z

categoriz|e, -is|e 'kæt.ə.gᵊr.aɪz, '-ɪ- US 'kæt̬.ə.gə.raɪz **-es** -ɪz **-ing** -ɪŋ **-ed** -d

categor|y 'kæt.ə.gᵊr|.i, '-ɪ- US 'kæt̬.ə.gɔːr- **-ies** -iz

catenar|y kə'tiː.nᵊr|.i **-ies** -iz

caten|ate 'kæt.ɪ.n|eɪt, '-ə- US 'kæt.ᵊn|.eɪt **-ates** -eɪts **-ating** -eɪ.tɪŋ US -eɪ.t̬ɪŋ **-ated** -eɪ.tɪd US -eɪ.t̬ɪd

catenation ˌkæt.ɪ'neɪ.ʃᵊn, -ə'- US ˌkæt.ən'eɪ- **-s** -z

catenative kə'tiː.nə.tɪv

cateniz|e, -is|e 'kæt.ɪ.naɪz, '-ə- US 'kæt.ᵊn.aɪz **-es** -ɪz **-ing** -ɪŋ **-ed** -d

cat|er (C) 'keɪ.t|əʳ US -t̬|ɚ **-ers** -əz US -ɚz **-ering** -ᵊr.ɪŋ **-ered** -əd US -ɚd **-erer/s** -ᵊr.əʳ/z US -ɚ.ɚ/z

Caterham 'keɪ.tᵊr.əm US -t̬ɚ-

Caterina ˌkæt.ᵊr'iː.nə US ˌkæt̬-

caterpillar 'kæt.ə.pɪl.əʳ US 'kæt̬.ɚ.pɪl.ɚ, '-ə- **-s** -z

caterwaul 'kæt.ə.wɔːl US 'kæt̬.ɚ-, -wɑːl **-s** -z **-ing** -ɪŋ **-ed** -d

Catesby 'keɪts.bi

catfish 'kæt.fɪʃ **-es** -ɪz

Catford 'kæt.fəd US -fɚd

catgut 'kæt.gʌt

Cathar 'kæθ.əʳ, -ɑːʳ US -ɑːr **-ism** -ɪ.zᵊm **-ist/s** -ɪst/s

Catharine 'kæθ.ᵊr.ɪn, 'kæθ.rɪn

cathars|is kə'θɑː.s|ɪs, kæθ'ɑː- US kə'θɑːr- **-es** -iːz

cathartic kə'θɑː.tɪk, kæθ'ɑː- US kə'θɑːr.t̬ɪk **-s** -s

Cathay kæθ'eɪ, kə'θeɪ

Cathcart 'kæθ.kət, -kɑːt; kæθ'kɑːt, kəθ- US 'kæθ.kɑːrt, -kɚt; kæθ'kɑːrt, kəθ-

cathead 'kæt.hed **-s** -z

cathedra kə'θiː.drə, -'θed.rə US kə'θiː.drə, 'kæθ.ə- **-s** -z

cathedra (*in phrase* **ex cathedra**) kə'θiː.drə, kæθ'ed.rɑː, kə'θed-

cathedral kə'θiː.drᵊl **-s** -z

Cather 'kæð.əʳ US -ɚ

Catherine 'kæθ.ᵊr.ɪn, 'kæθ.rɪn **'catherine ˌwheel**

catheter 'kæθ.ɪ.təʳ, '-ə- US -ə.t̬ɚ **-s** -z

catheterization, -isa- ˌkæθ.ɪ.tᵊr.aɪ'zeɪ.ʃᵊn, ˌ-ə-, -ɪ'- US -ə.t̬ɚ.ɪ'-

catheteriz|e, -is|e 'kæθ.ɪ.tᵊr.aɪz, '-ə- US '-ə.t̬ɚ- **-es** -ɪz **-ing** -ɪŋ **-ed** -d

cathetometer ˌkæθ.ɪ'tɒm.ɪ.təʳ, -ə'-, '-ə- US -ə'tɑː.mə.t̬ɚ **-s** -z

cathex|is kə'θek.s|ɪs, kæθ'ek- **-es** -iːz

Cathleen 'kæθ.liːn, -'- US -'-, '--

cathode 'kæθ.əʊd US -oʊd **-s** -z ˌ**cathode 'ray** ; ˌ**cathode-'ray ˌtube**

catholic (C) 'kæθ.ᵊl.ɪk **-s** -s

catholicism (C) kə'θɒl.ɪ.sɪ.zᵊm, '-ə- US -'θɑː.lə-

catholicity (C) ˌkæθ.əʊ'lɪs.ə.ti, -ɪ.ti US ˌkæθ.ə'lɪs.ə.t̬i

catholiciz|e, -is|e kə'θɒl.ɪ.saɪz, '-ə- US -'θɑː.lə- **-es** -ɪz **-ing** -ɪŋ **-ed** -d

Cathy 'kæθ.i

Catiline 'kæt.ɪ.laɪn, -ᵊl.aɪn US -ɪ.laɪn, '-ə-

cation 'kæt.aɪən **-s** -z

catkin 'kæt.kɪn **-s** -z

catlike 'kæt.laɪk

catmint 'kæt.mɪnt

catnap 'kæt.næp **-s** -s **-ping** -ɪŋ **-ped** -t

catnip 'kæt.nɪp

Cato 'keɪ.təʊ US -t̬oʊ

cat-o'-nine-tails ˌkæt.ə'naɪn.teɪlz US ˌkæt̬-

Cator 'keɪ.təʳ US -t̬ɚ

Catriona kə'trɪː.ə.nə, kæ'triː-, -'triː.nə, ˌkæt.ri'əʊ.nə US -'oʊ-

cat's-cradle ˌkæts'kreɪ.dl̩ US ˌ-'--, '-ˌ--

cat's-eye 'kæts.aɪ **-s** -z

Catshill kæts'hɪl *stress shift:* ˌCatshill 'stores

Catskill 'kæt.skɪl

catsuit 'kæt.suːt, -sjuːt US -suːt **-s** -s

catsup 'kæt.səp, 'kætʃ.əp, 'ketʃ.əp **-s** -s

Cattegat 'kæt.ɪ.gæt US 'kæt̬-

Cattell kæt'el, kə'tel

Catterick 'kæt.ᵊr.ɪk US 'kæt̬-

Cattermole 'kæt.ə.məʊl US 'kæt̬.ɚ.moʊl

catter|y 'kæt.ᵊr|.i US 'kæt̬- **-ies** -iz

cattish 'kæt.ɪʃ US 'kæt̬-

cattle 'kæt.l̩ US 'kæt̬- **'cattle ˌgrid** ; **'cattle ˌmarket** ; **'cattle ˌpen** ; **'cattle ˌtruck**

cattle-show 'kæt.l̩.ʃəʊ US 'kæt̬.l̩.ʃoʊ **-s** -z

catt|y 'kæt|.i US 'kæt̬- **-ier** -i.əʳ US -i.ɚ **-iest** -i.ɪst, -i.əst **-ily** -ɪ.li, -ᵊl.i **-iness** -ɪ.nəs, -ɪ.nɪs

Catullus kə'tʌl.əs

catwalk 'kæt.wɔːk US -wɑːk, -wɔːk **-s** -s

Caucasi|a kɔː'keɪ.ʒ|ə, -ʒi|.ə, -zi- US kɑː'keɪ.ʒ|ə, kɔː-, -ʃ|ə **-an/s** -ən/z

Caucasus 'kɔː.kə.səs, -zəs US 'kɑː-, 'kɔː-

caucus 'kɔː.kəs US 'kɑː-, 'kɔː- **-es** -ɪz

caudal 'kɔː.dᵊl US 'kɑː-, 'kɔː-

caudate 'kɔː.deɪt US 'kɑː-, 'kɔː-

caudillo kaʊ'diː.əʊ, kɔː'dɪl-, -jəʊ US kaʊ'diː.joʊ, -'dɪl- **-s** -z

Caudine 'kɔː.daɪn US 'kɑː-, 'kɔː-

caudle (C) 'kɔː.dl̩ US 'kɑː-, 'kɔː-

caught (*from* **catch**) kɔːt US kɑːt, kɔːt

caul kɔːl US kɑːl, kɔːl **-s** -z

cauldron 'kɔːl.drᵊn, 'kɒl- US 'kɑːl-, 'kɔːl- **-s** -z

Caulfield 'kɔː.fiːld, 'kɔːl- US 'kɑː-, 'kɔː-, 'kɑːl-, 'kɔːl-

cauliflower 'kɒl.ɪˌflaʊəʳ US 'kɑː.lɪˌflaʊɚ, 'kɔː- **-s** -z ˌ**cauliflower 'ear**

caulk kɔːk US kɑːk, kɔːk **-s** -s **-ing** -ɪŋ **-ed** -t

caulker 'kɔː.kəʳ US 'kɑː.kɚ, 'kɔː- **-s** -z

causa 'kaʊ.sɑː, -zɑː

causal 'kɔː.zᵊl US 'kɑː-, 'kɔː- **-ly** -i

causality kɔː'zæl.ə.ti, -ɪ.ti US kɑː'zæl.ə.t̬i, kɔː-

causa mortis ˌkaʊ.sɑːˈmɔː.tɪs, -zɑːˈ- ⓊⓈ -mɔːr.t̬ɪs
causation kɔːˈzeɪ.ʃᵊn ⓊⓈ kɑː-, kɔː-
causative ˈkɔː.zə.tɪv ⓊⓈ ˈkɑː.zə.t̬ɪv, ˈkɔː- **-ly** -li
caus|e kɔːz ⓊⓈ kɑːz, kɔːz **-es** -ɪz **-ing** -ɪŋ **-ed** -d
cause(s) célèbre(s) ˌkɔːz.selˈeb.rə, ˌkəʊz-, -səˈleb-, -ˈleɪ.brə ⓊⓈ ˌkɑːz.səˈleb.rə, ˌkɔːz-, ˌkoʊz-
causeless ˈkɔːz.ləs, -lɪs ⓊⓈ ˈkɑːz-, ˈkɔːz- **-ly** -li
causerie ˈkəʊ.zᵊr.i, -iː ⓊⓈ ˌkoʊ.zəˈriː **-s** -z
causeway ˈkɔːz.weɪ ⓊⓈ ˈkɑːz-, ˈkɔːz- **-s** -z
caustic ˈkɔː.stɪk, ˈkɒs.tɪk ⓊⓈ ˈkɑː.stɪk, ˈkɔː- **-al** -ᵊl **-ally** -ᵊl.i, -li ˌ**caustic** ˈ**soda**
causticity kɔːˈstɪs.ə.ti, kɒsˈtɪs-, -ɪ.ti ⓊⓈ kɑːˈstɪs.ə.t̬i, kɔː-
cauterization, -isa- ˌkɔː.tᵊr.aɪˈzeɪ.ʃᵊn, -ɪˈ- ⓊⓈ ˌkɑː.t̬ɚ.ɪˈ-, ˌkɔː- **-s** -z
cauteriz|e, -is|e ˈkɔː.tᵊr.aɪz ⓊⓈ ˈkɑː.t̬ə.raɪz, ˈkɔː- **-es** -ɪz **-ing** -ɪŋ **-ed** -d
cauter|y ˈkɔː.tᵊr|.i ⓊⓈ ˈkɑː.t̬ɚ-, ˈkɔː- **-ies** -iz
Cauthen ˈkɔː.θᵊn ⓊⓈ ˈkɑː-, ˈkɔː-
caution ˈkɔː.ʃᵊn ⓊⓈ ˈkɑː-, ˈkɔː- **-s** -z **-ing** -ɪŋ **-ed** -d **-er/s** -əʳ/z ⓊⓈ -ɚ/z ˈ**caution** ˌ**money**; **throw** ˌ**caution to the** ˈ**wind**
cautionary ˈkɔː.ʃᵊn.ᵊr.i, -ʃᵊn.ri ⓊⓈ ˈkɑː.ʃᵊn.er-, ˈkɔː- ˌ**cautionary** ˈ**tale**
cautious ˈkɔː.ʃəs ⓊⓈ ˈkɑː-, ˈkɔː- **-ly** -li **-ness** -nəs, -nɪs
cavalcade ˌkæv.ᵊlˈkeɪd, ˈ--- **-s** -z
cavalier ˌkæv.ᵊlˈɪəʳ ⓊⓈ -əˈlɪr **-s** -z
Cavalleria Rusticana kə.væl.əˌriː.ə.rʊs.tɪˈkɑː.nə, ˌkæv.ᵊl-, -ˌrɪə-
cavalr|y ˈkæv.ᵊl.r|i **-ies** -iz
cavalry|man ˈkæv.ᵊl.ri|.mən, -mæn **-men** -mən, -men
Cavan ˈkæv.ᵊn
Cavanagh ˈkæv.ə.nə
Cavanaugh ˈkæv.ə.nɔː ⓊⓈ -nɑː, -nɔː
cavatina ˌkæv.əˈtiː.nə **-s** -z
cav|e (C) (*n. v.*) keɪv **-es** -z **-ing** -ɪŋ **-ed** -d **-er/s** -əʳ/z ⓊⓈ -ɚ/z ˈ**cave** ˌ**dweller**
cave *beware:* ˈkeɪ.vi
caveat ˈkæv.i.æt, ˈkeɪ.vi- ⓊⓈ ˈkæv.i-, ˈkeɪ.vi-, ˈkɑː- **-s** -s
caveat emptor ˌkæv.i.ætˈemp.tɔːʳ, ˌkeɪ.vi-, -təʳ ⓊⓈ -tɔːr, ˌkɑː-, -ɑːtˈ-, -tɚ
Cavell ˈkæv.ᵊl, kəˈvel
Note: The family of Nurse Edith Cavell pronounces /ˈkæv.ᵊl/.

cave|man ˈkeɪv|.mæn **-men** -men
Cavendish ˈkæv.ᵊn.dɪʃ
cavern ˈkæv.ᵊn, -ɜːn ⓊⓈ -ɚn **-s** -z
cavernous ˈkæv.ᵊn.əs ⓊⓈ -ɚn- **-ly** -li
Caversham ˈkæv.ə.ʃəm ⓊⓈ ˈ-ɚ-
caviar(e) ˈkæv.i.ɑːʳ, ˌ--ˈ- ⓊⓈ ˈkæv.i.ɑːr
cavil ˈkæv.ᵊl, -ɪl **-s** -z **-(l)ing** -ɪŋ **-(l)ed** -d **-(l)er/s** -əʳ/z ⓊⓈ -ɚ/z
cavit|y ˈkæv.ə.t|i, -ɪ.t|i ⓊⓈ -ə.t̬|i **-ies** -iz
ca|vort kə|ˈvɔːt ⓊⓈ -ˈvɔːrt **-vorts** -ˈvɔːts ⓊⓈ -ˈvɔːrts **-vorting** -ˈvɔː.tɪŋ ⓊⓈ -ˈvɔːr.t̬ɪŋ **-vorted** -ˈvɔː.tɪd ⓊⓈ -ˈvɔːr.t̬ɪd
cav|y ˈkeɪ.v|i **-ies** -iz
caw kɔː ⓊⓈ kɑː, kɔː **-s** -z **-ing** -ɪŋ **-ed** -d
Cawdor ˈkɔː.dəʳ, -dɔːʳ ⓊⓈ ˈkɑː.dɚ, ˈkɔː-, -dɔːr
Cawdrey ˈkɔː.dri ⓊⓈ ˈkɑː-, ˈkɔː-
Cawley ˈkɔː.li ⓊⓈ ˈkɑː-, ˈkɔː-
Cawse kɔːz ⓊⓈ kɑːz, kɔːz
Caxton ˈkæk.stᵊn
cay kiː, keɪ **-s** -z
cayenne (C) keɪˈen ⓊⓈ kaɪ-, keɪ- *stress shift:* ˌ**cayenne** ˈ**pepper**
Cayley ˈkeɪ.li
cayman (C) ˈkeɪ.mən **-s** -z ˈ**Cayman** ˌ**Islands**
Cazenove ˈkæz.ᵊn.əʊv ⓊⓈ -oʊv
CB ˌsiːˈbiː
CBC ˌsiː.biːˈsiː
CBE ˌsiː.biːˈiː
CBI ˌsiː.biːˈaɪ
CBS ˌsiː.biːˈes *stress shift:* ˌCBS ˈrecords
cc ˌsiːˈsiː
CD ˌsiːˈdiː **-s** -z ˌ**C**ˈ**D** ˌ**player**
CDI ˌsiː.diːˈaɪ
Cdr. (*abbrev. for* **commander**) kəˈmɑːn.dəʳ ⓊⓈ -ˈmæn.dɚ
CD-ROM ˌsiː.diːˈrɒm ⓊⓈ -ˈrɑːm **-s** -z
CDT ˌsiː.diːˈtiː
ceas|e siːs **-es** -ɪz **-ing** -ɪŋ **-ed** -t
cease-fire ˈsiːs.faɪəʳ ⓊⓈ -faɪɚ
ceaseless ˈsiː.sləs, -slɪs **-ly** -li **-ness** -nəs, -nɪs
Ceausescu ˌtʃaʊˈʃes.kuː
Cebu siˈbuː
Cecil ˈses.ᵊl, -ɪl, ˈsɪs.ᵊl, -ɪl ⓊⓈ ˈsiː.sᵊl, ˈses.ᵊl
Note: The family name of the Marquess of Exeter and that of the Marquess of Salisbury is /ˈsɪs.ᵊl, -ɪl/.
Cecile sesˈiːl, ˈ--, ˈses.ɪl, -ᵊl ⓊⓈ sɪˈsiːl
Cecilia sɪˈsiː.li.ə, sə-, -ˈsɪl.i- ⓊⓈ -ˈsiːl.jə, -ˈsɪl-
Cecily ˈses.ɪ.li, ˈsɪs-, -ᵊl.i ⓊⓈ ˈses-
cec|um ˈsiː.k|əm **-a** -ə
cedar ˈsiː.dəʳ ⓊⓈ -dɚ **-s** -z
ced|e siːd **-es** -z **-ing** -ɪŋ **-ed** -ɪd
cedi ˈsiː.di **-s** -z
cedilla səˈdɪl.ə, sɪ- **-s** -z

Cedric ˈsed.rɪk, ˈsiː.drɪk
Ceefax® ˈsiː.fæks
Cefn-Mawr ˌkev.ᵊnˈmaʊəʳ ⓊⓈ -ˈmaʊɚ
CEGB ˌsiː.iː.dʒiːˈbiː
ceilidh ˈkeɪ.li **-s** -z
ceiling ˈsiː.lɪŋ **-s** -z
celadon ˈsel.ə.dɒn, -dən ⓊⓈ -dɑːn
celandine ˈsel.ən.daɪn, -diːn **-s** -z
Celanese® ˌsel.əˈniːz ⓊⓈ -ˈniːz, -ˈniːs
celeb səˈleb, sɪ- **-s** -z
Celebes selˈiː.biz, səˈliː-, sɪ- ⓊⓈ ˈsel.ə.biːz, səˈliː.biz
celebrant ˈsel.ə.brᵊnt, ˈ-ɪ- **-s** -s
cele|brate ˈsel.ə|.breɪt, ˈ-ɪ- **-brates** -breɪts **-brating** -breɪ.tɪŋ ⓊⓈ -breɪ.t̬ɪŋ **-brated** -breɪ.tɪd ⓊⓈ -breɪ.t̬ɪd **-brator/s** -breɪ.təʳ/z ⓊⓈ -breɪ.t̬ɚ/z
celebration ˌsel.əˈbreɪ.ʃᵊn, -ɪˈ- **-s** -z
celebratory ˌsel.əˈbreɪ.tᵊr.i, -ɪˈ-, -tri; ˈsel.ɪ.brə-, ˈ-ə- ⓊⓈ ˈsel.ə.brə.tɔːr.i; səˈleb.rə-
celebrit|y səˈleb.rə.t|i, sɪ-, -rɪ- ⓊⓈ səˈleb.rə.t̬|i **-ies** -iz
celeriac səˈler.i.æk, sɪ-; ˈsel.ᵊr-
celerity səˈler.ə.ti, sɪ-, -ɪ.ti ⓊⓈ -ə.t̬i
celery ˈsel.ᵊr.i
celeste (C) səˈlest, sɪ- **-s** -s
celestial (C) səˈles.ti.əl, sɪ- ⓊⓈ ˈ-tʃᵊl **-ly** -i
celestine ˈsel.ə.staɪn, ˈ-ɪ-, -stɪn
Celestine ˈsel.ə.staɪn, ˈ-ɪ-; sɪˈles.taɪn, sə-, -tɪn, -tiːn **-s** -z
Celia ˈsiː.li.ə
celiac ˈsiː.li.æk
celibacy ˈsel.ə.bə.si, ˈ-ɪ-
celibatarian ˌsel.ə.bəˈteə.ri.ən, ˌ-ɪ- ⓊⓈ -ˈter.i- **-s** -z
celibate ˈsel.ə.bət, ˈ-ɪ-, -bɪt **-s** -s
Céline selˈiːn, seɪˈliːn
cell sel **-s** -z
cellar ˈsel.əʳ ⓊⓈ -ɚ **-s** -z
cellarage ˈsel.ᵊr.ɪdʒ
cellarer ˈsel.ᵊr.əʳ ⓊⓈ -ɚ **-s** -z
cellaret ˌsel.ᵊrˈet, ˈsel.ᵊr.et ⓊⓈ ˌsel.ɚˈet **-s** -s
cellarist ˈsel.ᵊr.ɪst **-s** -s
cellar|man ˈsel.ə|.mən, -mæn ⓊⓈ -ɚ- **-men** -mən, -men
Cellini tʃelˈiː.ni, tʃɪˈliː-, tʃə-
cellist ˈtʃel.ɪst **-s** -s
cellmate ˈsel.meɪt **-s** -s
Cellnet® ˈsel.net
cello ˈtʃel.əʊ ⓊⓈ -oʊ **-s** -z
Cellophane® ˈsel.ə.feɪn
cellphone ˈsel.fəʊn ⓊⓈ -foʊn **-s** -z
cellular ˈsel.jə.ləʳ, -jʊ- ⓊⓈ -lɚ ˌ**cellular** ˈ**phone**; ˌ**cellular** ˈ**radio**
cellule ˈsel.juːl **-s** -z
cellulite ˈsel.jə.laɪt, -jʊ-
celluloid (C) ˈsel.jə.lɔɪd, -jʊ-
cellulose ˈsel.jə.ləʊs, -jʊ- ⓊⓈ -loʊs

Celsius 'sel.si.əs (US) 'sel.si.əs, -ʃəs
celt *axe:* selt **-s** -s
Celt *people, tribe:* kelt, selt **-s** -s *member of football or baseball team:* selt **-s** -s
Celtic *of the people or tribe:* 'kel.tɪk, 'sel.tɪk
Note: In names of football and baseball teams /'sel.tɪk/; for **Sea** /'kel.tɪk/.
cembal|o 'tʃem.bə.l|əʊ, 'sem- (US) -loʊ **-os** -əʊz (US) -oʊz **-i** -iː
cement sɪ'ment, sə- **-s** -s **-ing** -ɪŋ **-ed** -ɪd **ce'ment-ˌmixer**
cementation ˌsiː.men'teɪ.ʃən **-s** -z
cementium sɪ'men.ʃi.əm, sə-, '-ti- (US) -ti-
cemeter|y 'sem.ə.tr|i, '-ɪ- (US) -ə.ter|.i **-ies** -iz
Cenci 'tʃen.tʃi
CENELEC 'sen.ɪ.lek, '-ə-
cenematics ˌsen.ɪ'mæt.ɪks, -ə'- (US) -'mæt-
cenetics sə'net.ɪks, sɪ- (US) -'net-
CEng (*abbrev. for* **Chartered Engineer**) ˌsiː'endʒ, ˌtʃɑː.təd,en.dʒɪ'nɪər, -dʒə'- (US) ˌsiː'endʒ, ˌtʃɑːr.tɚd,en.dʒɪ'nɪr, -dʒə'-
Cenis sə'niː, sen'iː
cenobite 'siː.nə.baɪt, 'sen.ə- (US) 'sen.ə- **-s** -s
cenotaph 'sen.əʊ.tæf, -tɑːf (US) -ə.tæf **-s** -s
cens|e sents **-es** -ɪz **-ing** -ɪŋ **-ed** -t
censer 'sent.sər (US) -sɚ **-s** -z
cens|or 'sent.s|ər (US) -s|ɚ **-ors** -əz (US) -ɚz **-oring** -ər.ɪŋ **-ored** -əd (US) -ɚd
censorial sent'sɔː.ri.əl (US) -'sɔːr.i- **-ly** -i
censorian sent'sɔː.ri.ən (US) -'sɔːr.i-
censorious sent'sɔː.ri.əs (US) -'sɔːr.i- **-ly** -li **-ness** -nəs, -nɪs
censorship 'sent.sə.ʃɪp (US) -sɚ- **-s** -s
censurable 'sent.sjər.ə.bl̩, -ʃər- (US) -ʃɚ-
cens|ure 'sent.sj|ər, -ʃ|ər (US) 'sent.ʃ|ɚ **-ures** -əz (US) -ɚz **-uring** -ər.ɪŋ **-ured** -əd (US) -ɚd
census 'sent.səs **-es** -ɪz **'census ˌpaper**
cent sent **-s** -s
centage 'sen.tɪdʒ
cental 'sen.təl **-s** -z
centaur 'sen.tɔːr (US) -tɔːr **-s** -z
Centaur|us sen'tɔː.r|əs (US) -'tɔːr|.əs **-i** -aɪ, -iː
centaur|y 'sen.tɔː.r|i (US) -tɔːr|.i **-ies** -iz
centavo sen'tɑː.vəʊ (US) -voʊ **-s** -z
centenarian ˌsen.tɪ'neə.ri.ən, -tə'- (US) -tən'er.i- **-s** -z
centenar|y sen'tiː.nər|.i, sən-, -'ten.ər- (US) 'sen.tən.er-; sen'ten.ər- **-ies** -iz
centennial sen'ten.i.əl, sən- **-s** -z **-ly** -i
cent|er 'sen.t|ər (US) -t|ɚ **-ers** -əz (US) -ɚz **-ering** -ər.ɪŋ **-ered** -əd (US) -ɚd **ˌcenter of 'gravity ; ˌcenter 'stage**
centerboard 'sen.tə.bɔːd (US) -tɚ.bɔːrd **-s** -z
center-field ˌsen.tə'fiːld (US) -tɚ'- **-s** -z **-er/s** -ər/z (US) -ɚ/z
centerfold 'sen.tə.fəʊld (US) -tɚ.foʊld **-s** -z
center-forward ˌsen.tə'fɔː.wəd (US) -tɚ'fɔːr.wɚd **-s** -z
center-|half ˌsen.tə|'hɑːf (US) -tɚ|'hæf **-halves** -'hɑːvz (US) -'hævz
centerpiec|e 'sen.tə.piːs (US) -tɚ- **-es** -ɪz
centesimal sen'tes.ɪ.məl, '-ə- **-ly** -i
centesim|o sen'tes.ɪ.m|əʊ, '-ə- (US) -m|oʊ **-i** -aɪ, -iː **-os** -əʊz (US) -oʊz
centigrade 'sen.tɪ.greɪd (US) -tə-
centigram, **centigramme** 'sen.tɪ.græm (US) -tə- **-s** -z
centigram(me) 'sen.tɪ.græm (US) -tə- **-s** -z
centilitre, **centiliter** 'sen.tɪˌliː.tər (US) -təˌliː.tɚ **-s** -z
centime 'sɑ̃ːn.tiːm, 'sɔ̃ːn-, 'sɑːn-; -'- (US) 'sɑːn-, 'sen- **-s** -z
centimetre, **centimeter** 'sen.tɪˌmiː.tər (US) -təˌmiː.tɚ **-s** -z
centimo 'sen.tɪ.məʊ (US) -moʊ **-s** -z
centipede 'sen.tɪ.piːd (US) -tə- **-s** -z
centipois|e 'sen.tɪ.pɔɪz (US) -tə- **-es** -ɪz
centner 'sent.nər (US) -nɚ **-s** -z
cento 'sen.təʊ (US) -toʊ **-s** -z
CENTO 'sen.təʊ (US) -toʊ
central (C) 'sen.trəl **-ly** -i **ˌCentral ˌAfrican Re'public ; ˌCentral A'merica ; ˌCentral 'Daylight ˌTime ; ˌcentral 'heating ; ˌcentral reser'vation ; ˌCentral 'Standard ˌTime**
centralism 'sen.trəl.ɪ.zəm
centralist 'sen.trəl.ɪst **-s** -s
centrality sen'træl.ə.ti, -ɪ.ti (US) -ə.ti
centralization, -isa- ˌsen.trəl.aɪ'zeɪ.ʃən, -lɪ'- (US) -lɪ'-
centraliz|e, -is|e 'sen.trəl.aɪz **-es** -ɪz **-ing** -ɪŋ **-ed** -d
cent|re 'sen.t|ər (US) -t|ɚ **-res** -əz (US) -ɚz **-ring** -ər.ɪŋ **-red** -əd (US) -ɚd **ˌcentre of 'gravity ; ˌcentre 'stage**
centreboard 'sen.tə.bɔːd (US) -tɚ.bɔːrd **-s** -z
centre-field ˌsen.tə'fiːld (US) -tɚ- **-s** -z **-er/s** -ər/z (US) -ɚ/z
centrefold 'sen.tə.fəʊld (US) -tɚ.foʊld **-s** -z
centre-forward ˌsen.tə'fɔː.wəd (US) -tɚ'fɔːr.wɚd **-s** -z
centre-|half ˌsen.tə|'hɑːf (US) -tɚ|'hæf **-halves** -'hɑːvz (US) -'hævz
centrepiec|e 'sen.tə.piːs (US) -tɚ- **-es** -ɪz
centric 'sen.trɪk **-al** -əl **-ally** -əl.i, -li
centrifugal ˌsen.trɪ'fjuː.gəl, -trə'-, sen'trɪf.jʊ-, -jə- (US) sen'trɪf.jə.gəl, '-ə-, -juː-
centrifug|e 'sen.trɪ.fjuːdʒ, -trə- (US) -trə- **-es** -ɪz **-ing** -ɪŋ **-ed** -d
centriole 'sen.tri.əʊl (US) -oʊl **-s** -z
centripetal sen'trɪp.ɪ.təl, '-ə-, ˌsen.trɪ'piː- (US) sen'trɪ.pə.təl
centr|ism 'sen.tr|ɪ.zəm **-ist/s** -ɪst/s
centro- 'sen.trəʊ- (US) 'sen.trə-
centr|um 'sen.tr|əm **-a** -ə
centumvirate sen'tʌm.vɪ.rət, -və-, -rɪt (US) sen'tʌm.vɚ.ət, ken-, -vɪ.rət **-s** -s
Centumviri ˌsen.tʌm'vɪ.riː (US) 'sen.təm.vɪ-, 'ken.tʊm-, -raɪ
centuple 'sen.tjʊ.pl̩; sen'tjuː- (US) 'sen.tə-; sen'tuː-, -'tjuː-
centurion sen'tjʊə.ri.ən, -'tʃʊə-, -'tjɔː-, -'tʃɔː- (US) -'tʊr.i-, -'tjʊr- **-s** -z
centur|y 'sen.tʃər|.i **-ies** -iz
CEO ˌsiː.iː'əʊ (US) -'oʊ
cep sep **-s** -s
cèpe sep **-s** -s
cephalic sef'æl.ɪk, sɪf-, sə'fæl-, kef'æl-, kɪf- (US) sə'fæl.ɪk
Cephalonia ˌsef.ə'ləʊ.ni.ə (US) -'loʊ-
cephalopod 'sef.əl.əʊ.pɒd (US) -ə.pɑːd **-s** -z
cephalopoda ˌsef.ə'lɒp.ə.də (US) -'lɑː.pə-
cephalous 'sef.əl.əs
Cephas 'siː.fæs
Cepheid 'siː.fi.ɪd, 'sef.i- **-s** -z
Cepheus 'siː.fi.əs, -fjəs
ceramic sə'ræm.ɪk, sɪ-, kɪ-, kə- (US) sə'ræm- **-s** -s
Note: In the UK, experts tend to use the forms with /kɪ-, kə-/.
ceramicist sə'ræm.ɪ.sɪst, sɪ-, '-ə- (US) sə'ræm.ə- **-s** -s
ceramist 'ser.ə.mɪst, sə'ræm.ɪst **-s** -s
cerastes sə'ræs.tiːz, sɪ- (US) sə-
cerate 'sɪə.reɪt, -rɪt, -rət (US) 'sɪr.eɪt, -ɪt **-s** -s
Cerberus 'sɜː.bər.əs (US) 'sɜːr-
cercari|a sɜː'keə.ri|.ə (US) sɚ'ker.i- **-ae** -iː
cer|e sɪər (US) sɪr **-es** -z **-ing** -ɪŋ **-ed** -d
cereal 'sɪə.ri.əl (US) 'sɪr.i- **-s** -z
cerebell|um ˌser.ɪ'bel|.əm, -ə'- (US) -ə'- **-ums** -əmz **-a** -ə
Cerebos® 'ser.ə.bɒs, '-ɪ- (US) -bɑːs
cerebral 'ser.ə.brəl, '-ɪ-; sə'riː-, sɪ- (US) 'ser.ə-; sə'riː- **-s** -z **ˌcerebral 'palsy**
cere|brate 'ser.ə|.breɪt, '-ɪ- (US) '-ə- **-brates** -breɪts **-brating** -breɪ.tɪŋ (US) -breɪ.tɪŋ **-brated** -breɪ.tɪd (US) -breɪ.tɪd
cerebration ˌser.ɪ'breɪ.ʃən, -ə'- (US) -ə'- **-s** -z
cerebr|um sə'riː.br|əm, sɪ-; ser.ɪ-, '-ə- (US) 'ser.ə-; sə'riː- **-a** -ə **-ums** -əmz
Ceredigion ˌker.ə'dɪg.i.ɒn, -ɪ'- (US) -ɑːn

cerement 'sɪə.mənt, 'ser.ə.mənt (US) 'sɪr.mənt **-s** -s
ceremonial ˌser.ɪ'məʊ.ni.əl, -ə'- (US) -ə'moʊ- **-s** -z **-ly** -i **-ism** -ɪ.zᵊm
ceremonious ˌser.ɪ'məʊ.ni.əs, -ə'- (US) -ə'moʊ- **-ly** -li **-ness** -nəs, -nɪs
ceremon|y 'ser.ɪ.mə.n|i, '-ə- (US) '-ə.moʊ.n|i **-ies** -iz
Ceres 'sɪə.riːz (US) 'sɪr.iːz
cerif 'ser.ɪf **-s** -s
cerise sə'riːz, sɪ-, -'riːs (US) sə-
cerium 'sɪə.ri.əm (US) 'sɪr.i-
ceroplastic ˌsɪə.rəʊ'plæs.tɪk, -'plɑː.stɪk (US) 'sɪr.oʊ.plæs-, 'ser-
cert sɜːt (US) sɜːrt **-s** -s
certain 'sɜː.tᵊn, -tɪn (US) 'sɜːr- **-ly** -li
certaint|y 'sɜː.tᵊn.t|i, -tɪn- (US) 'sɜːr- **-ies** -iz
certes 'sɜː.tiːz, -tɪz, sɜːts (US) 'sɜːr.tiːz
certifiab|le ˌsɜː.tɪ'faɪ.ə.b|l̩, -tə'-, 'sɜː.tɪ.faɪ-, -tə- (US) 'sɜːr.t̬ə.faɪ- **-ly** -li
certificate (*n.*) sə'tɪf.ɪ.kət, sɜː-, '-ə-, -kɪt (US) sɚ- **-s** -s
certifi|cate (*v.*) sə'tɪf.ɪ|.keɪt, sɜː-, '-ə- (US) sɚ- **-cates** -keɪts **-cating** -keɪ.tɪŋ (US) -keɪ.t̬ɪŋ **-cated** -keɪ.tɪd, -kə.tɪd, -kɪ- (US) -keɪ.t̬ɪd
certification *act of certifying:* ˌsɜː.tɪ.fɪ'keɪ.ʃᵊn, -fə'- (US) ˌsɜːr.t̬ə- **-s** -z *providing with a certificate:* ˌsɜː.tɪ.fɪ'keɪ.ʃᵊn, səˌtɪ- (US) ˌsɜːr.t̬ə- **-s** -z
certificatory sə'tɪf.ɪ.kə.tᵊr.i, sɜː-, -keɪ-, -tri (US) sɚ'tɪf.ɪ.kə.tɔːr.i
certif|y 'sɜː.tɪ.f|aɪ, -tə- (US) -t̬ə- **-ies** -aɪz **-ying** -aɪ.ɪŋ **-ied** -aɪd **-ier/s** -aɪ.əʳ/z (US) -aɪ.ɚ/z ˌ**certified 'mail**
certiorari ˌsɜː.ʃi.ɔː'reə.raɪ, -ti.ə'-, -'rɑː.ri (US) ˌsɜːr.ʃi.ə'rer.i, -'rɑːr- **-s** -z
certitude 'sɜː.tɪ.tjuːd (US) 'sɜːr.t̬ə.tuːd, -tjuːd **-s**
cerulean sə'ruː.li.ən, sɪ- (US) sə'ruː-
cerumen sə'ruː.men, sɪ-, -mən (US) sə'ruː-
Cervantes sɜː'væn.tiːz, -tɪz (US) sɚ-
cervical sə'vaɪ.kᵊl, sɜː-; 'sɜː.vɪ- (US) 'sɜːr.vɪ- **cerˌvical 'smear, ˌcervical 'smear** (US) **ˌcervical 'smear**
cervine 'sɜː.vaɪn (US) 'sɜːr-
cer|vix 'sɜː|.vɪks (US) 'sɜːr- **-vices** -vɪs.iːz **-vixes** -vɪk.sɪz
Cerynean sə'rɪn.i.ən (US) ˌser.ə'niː.ən
César 'seɪ.zɑːʳ, -zəʳ (US) seɪ'zɑːr
cesarean, cesarian sɪ'zeə.ri.ən, sə- (US) sə'zer.i- **-s** -z **ceˌsarean 'section**
Cesarewitch *Russian prince:* sɪ'zɑː.rə.vɪtʃ, sə- (US) -'zɑːr.ə- *race:* sɪ'zær.ə.wɪtʃ, -'zɑː.rə-, -rɪ- (US) -'zɑːr.ə-
Cesario siː'zɑː.ri.əʊ, -'zær.i- (US) -'zɑːr.i.oʊ

cesium 'siː.zi.əm
cess ses **-es** -ɪz
cessation ses'eɪ.ʃᵊn, sɪ'seɪ-, sə- **-s** -z
cession 'seʃ.ᵊn **-s** -z
cessionar|y 'seʃ.ᵊn.ᵊr|.i, -ᵊn.r|i (US) -er- **-ies** -iz
Cessna® 'ses.nə
cesspit 'ses.pɪt **-s** -s
cesspool 'ses.puːl **-s** -z
c'est la vie ˌseɪ.lɑː'viː, -læ'-, -lə'-
cestui que trust ˌset.ɪ.kɪ'trʌst (US) ˌset̬-, ˌses.twɪ- **-s** -s
cestui que vie ˌset.ɪ.kɪ'viː (US) ˌset̬-, ˌses.twɪ- **-s** -z
cestuis que trust ˌset.ɪz.kɪ'trʌst (US) ˌset̬-, ˌses.twɪz-
cestuis que vie ˌset.ɪz.kɪ'viː (US) ˌset̬-, ˌses.twɪz-
cestus 'ses.təs **-es** -ɪz
cesura sɪ'zjʊə.rə, siː-, -'zjɔː-, -'ʒʊə- (US) sə'zʊr.ə, -'ʒʊr- **-s** -z
Cetacea sɪ'teɪ.ʃə, sə-, -ʃi.ə, -si.ə (US) -ʃə
cetacean sɪ'teɪ.ʃᵊn, sə-, -ʃi.ən, -si.ən (US) -ʃᵊn **-s** -z
cetaceous sɪ'teɪ.ʃəs, sə-, -ʃi.əs, -si.əs (US) -ʃəs
cetane 'siː.teɪn
Cetewayo ketʃ'waɪ.əʊ, ˌket.i'waɪ-, -wɑː.jəʊ (US) -'waɪ.oʊ
Ceuta 'sjuː.tə (US) 'seɪ.uː.t̬ə
Cévennes sev'en, sə'ven, sɪ-, -venz (US) seɪ'ven
ceviche sə'viː.tʃeɪ, -tʃiː
Ceylon sɪ'lɒn, sə- (US) sɪ'lɑːn, seɪ-
Ceylonese ˌsel.ə'niːz, ˌsiː.lə- (US) ˌsiː.lə'niːz, ˌseɪ-, -'niːs
Cézanne seɪ'zæn, sɪ-, sez'æn (US) seɪ'zɑːn
cf. (*abbrev. for* **compare**) kəm'peəʳ, kən'fɜːʳ; ˌsiː'ef (US) kəm'per, kən'fɜːr; ˌsiː'ef
CFC ˌsiː.ef'siː **-s** -z
cg (*abbrev. for* **centigramme, centigram**) 'sen.tɪ.græm (US) -t̬ə-
Chablis 'ʃæb.liː, -bli, -'- (US) ʃæb'li, ʃɑː'bli
Chabrier 'ʃæb.ri.eɪ, 'ʃɑː.bri-, --'- (US) ˌʃɑː.bri'eɪ
cha-cha 'tʃɑː.tʃɑː **-s** -z **-ing** -ɪŋ **-ed** -d
cha-cha-cha ˌtʃɑː.tʃɑː'tʃɑː **-s** -z
chaconne ʃæk'ɒn, ʃə'kɒn (US) ʃɑː'kɑːn, ʃæk'ɑːn, -'ɔːn **-s** -z
chacun à son goût ˌʃæk.ɜːn.ɑː.sɔ̃ːŋ'guː, -æ.sɒŋ'- (US) ʃɑːˌkuːn.ɑː.sɑːn'-, ʃækˌuːn-, -sɔːn'-
Chad tʃæd **-ian/s** -i.ən/z
Chadband 'tʃæd.bænd
Chadderton 'tʃæd.ə.tᵊn (US) -ɚ.t̬ən
Chadwick 'tʃæd.wɪk
chaf|e tʃeɪf **-es** -s **-ing** -ɪŋ **-ed** -t

chafer 'tʃeɪ.fəʳ (US) -fɚ **-s** -z
chaff tʃæf, tʃɑːf (US) tʃæf **-s** -s **-ing/ly** -ɪŋ/li **-ed** -t
chaff|er 'tʃæf|.əʳ (US) -ɚ **-ers** -əz (US) -ɚz **-ering** -ᵊr.ɪŋ **-ered** -əd (US) -ɚd
Chaffey 'tʃeɪ.fi
chaffinch 'tʃæf.ɪntʃ **-es** -ɪz
chaff|y 'tʃæf|.i, 'tʃɑː.f|i (US) 'tʃæf|.i **-iness** -ɪ.nəs, -ɪ.nɪs
chafing-dish 'tʃeɪ.fɪŋ.dɪʃ **-es** -ɪz
Chagall ʃæg'æl, ʃə'gæl, -gɑːl (US) ʃə'gɑːl
chagrin (*n.*) 'ʃæg.rɪn, -rᵊn (US) ʃə'grɪn
chagrin (*v.*) 'ʃæg.rɪn, ʃə'griːn (US) ʃə'grɪn **-s** -z **-ing** -ɪŋ **-ed** -d
Chaim haɪm, xaɪm
chain tʃeɪn **-s** -z **-ing** -ɪŋ **-ed** -d **'chain ˌgang ; ˌchain 'letter ; 'chain ˌmail ; ˌchain re'action ; 'chain ˌstore**
chainless 'tʃeɪn.ləs, -lɪs
chain-link 'tʃeɪn.lɪŋk **ˌchain-link 'fence**
chainsaw 'tʃeɪn.sɔː (US) -sɑː, -sɔː **-s** -z **-ing** -ɪŋ **-ed** -d
chain-smok|e 'tʃeɪn.sməʊk (US) -smoʊk **-es** -s **-ing** -ɪŋ **-ed** -t **-er/s** -əʳ/z (US) -ɚ/z
chainstitch 'tʃeɪn.stɪtʃ
chainwork 'tʃeɪn.wɜːk (US) -wɜːrk
chair tʃeəʳ (US) tʃer **-s** -z **-ing** -ɪŋ **-ed** -d
chairlift 'tʃeə.lɪft (US) 'tʃer- **-s** -s
chair|man 'tʃeə|.mən (US) 'tʃer- **-men** -mən
chairmanship 'tʃeə.mən.ʃɪp (US) 'tʃer- **-s** -s
chairperson 'tʃeəˌpɜː.sᵊn (US) 'tʃerˌpɜːr- **-s** -z
chair|woman 'tʃeə|ˌwʊm.ən (US) 'tʃer- **-women** -ˌwɪm.ɪn
chais|e ʃeɪz (US) ʃeɪz, tʃeɪs **-es** -ɪz
chaise(s) longue(s) ˌʃeɪz'lɒŋ, ˌʃez-, -'lɒŋg, -'lɔ̃ːŋg (US) ˌʃeɪz'lɔːŋ, ˌtʃeɪs-, -'lɑːŋ
Chalcedon 'kæl.sɪ.dᵊn, -dɒn (US) -sə.dɑːn
chalcedony kæl'sed.ᵊn.i (US) kæl'sed.ᵊn.i, 'kæl.sə.doʊ.ni
chalcedonyx ˌkæl.sɪ'dɒn.ɪks (US) -'dɑː.nɪks; kæl'sed.ᵊn.ɪks **-es** -ɪz
Chalcis 'kæl.sɪs
chalcography kæl'kɒg.rə.fi (US) -'kɑː.grə-
Chalde|a kæl'diː|.ə, kɔːl- (US) kæl- **-an/s** -ən/z
Chaldee kæl'diː, kɔːl- (US) kæl- **-s** -z
chaldron 'tʃɔːl.drᵊn (US) 'tʃɔːl-, 'tʃɑːl- **-s** -z
chalet 'ʃæl.eɪ, 'ʃæl.i (US) ʃæl'eɪ **-s** -z
Chalfont *in Buckinghamshire:* 'tʃæl.fənt, -fɒnt *old-fashioned:* 'tʃɑː- (US) -fɑːnt
chalic|e 'tʃæl.ɪs **-es** -ɪz **-ed** -t

chalk (C) tʃɔːk ⓊⓈ tʃɔːk, tʃɑːk **-s** -s **-ing** -ɪŋ **-ed** -t **ˈchalk ˌpit** ; **as ˌdifferent as ˌchalk and ˈcheese**
chalkboard ˈtʃɔːk.bɔːd ⓊⓈ -bɔːrd, ˈtʃɑːk- **-s** -z
Chalker ˈtʃɔː.kəʳ ⓊⓈ ˈtʃɔː.kɚ, ˈtʃɑː-
chalkface ˈtʃɔːk.feɪs ⓊⓈ ˈtʃɔːk-, ˈtʃɑːk-
Chalkley ˈtʃɔːk.li ⓊⓈ ˈtʃɔːk-, ˈtʃɑːk-
chalkstone ˈtʃɔːk.stəʊn ⓊⓈ ˈtʃɔːk.stoʊn, ˈtʃɑːk- **-s** -z
chalk|y ˈtʃɔː.k|i ⓊⓈ ˈtʃɔː-, ˈtʃɑː- **-ier** -i.əʳ ⓊⓈ -i.ɚ **-iest** -i.ɪst, -i.əst **-ily** -ɪ.li, -əl.i **-iness** -ɪ.nəs, -ɪ.nɪs
challeng|e ˈtʃæl.ɪndʒ, -əndʒ **-es** -ɪz **-ing** -ɪŋ **-ed** -d **-er/s** -əʳ/z ⓊⓈ -ɚ/z
Challenor ˈtʃæl.ə.nəʳ, ˈ-ɪ- ⓊⓈ -ə.nɚ
challis (C) ˈʃæl.ɪs, ˈʃæl.i
Challoner ˈtʃæl.ə.nəʳ ⓊⓈ -nɚ
Chalmers ˈtʃɑː.məz, ˈtʃæl- ⓊⓈ -mɚz
Chaloner ˈtʃæl.ə.nəʳ ⓊⓈ -nɚ
chalybeate kəˈlɪb.i.ət, -ɪt, -eɪt
chamber ˈtʃeɪm.bəʳ ⓊⓈ -bɚ **-s** -z **-ed** -d **ˈchamber ˌmusic** ; **ˈchamber ˌpot**
chamberlain ˈtʃeɪm.bəl.ɪn, -ən ⓊⓈ -bɚ- **-s** -z
Chamberlain ˈtʃeɪm.bəl.ɪn, -ən, -eɪn ⓊⓈ -bɚ-
chamberlainship ˈtʃeɪm.bəl.ɪn.ʃɪp, -ən- ⓊⓈ -bɚ- **-s** -s
chambermaid ˈtʃeɪm.bə.meɪd ⓊⓈ -bɚ- **-s** -z
Chambers ˈtʃeɪm.bəz ⓊⓈ -bɚz
Chambourcy® ʃæmˈbʊə.si, -ˈbɔː- ⓊⓈ ˌʃɑːm.bʊrˈsiː
chambray ˈʃæm.breɪ
chambré ˈʃɑːm.breɪ ⓊⓈ ʃɑːmˈbreɪ
chameleon kəˈmiː.li.ən ⓊⓈ -li.ən, -ˈmiːl.jən **-s** -s
chamfer ˈʃæmp.fəʳ, ˈtʃæmp- ⓊⓈ -fɚ **-s** -z
chamois (*sing.*) *goat-antelope:* ˈʃæm.wɑː ⓊⓈ ˈʃæm.i, ʃæmˈwɑː (*plur.*) ˈʃæm.wɑːz ⓊⓈ ˈʃæm.iz, ʃæmˈwɑːz
chamois *leather:* ˈʃæm.i **ˈchamois ˌleather, ˌchamois ˈleather**
chamomile ˈkæm.ə.maɪl ⓊⓈ -miːl, -maɪl
Chamonix ˈʃæm.ə.niː, -ɒn.iː ⓊⓈ ˌʃæm.əˈniː
champ tʃæmp **-s** -s **-ing** -ɪŋ **-ed** -t
champagne (C) ʃæmˈpeɪn **-s** -z *stress shift:* ˌchampagne ˈsocialist
champaign ˈtʃæm.peɪn **-s** -z
champers ˈʃæm.pəz ⓊⓈ -pɚz
champerty ˈtʃæm.pɜː.ti, -pə- ⓊⓈ -pɝː.t̬i
champignon ˈʃæm.piː.njɔ̃ː, ˈʃɑ̃ːm-, ˌ--ˈ-; ʃæmˈpɪn.jən, ˈ--- ⓊⓈ ʃæmˈpɪn.jən, tʃæm- **-s** -z
champion (C) ˈtʃæm.pi.ən ⓊⓈ -pi.ən, -pjən **-s** -z **-ing** -ɪŋ **-ed** -d
championship ˈtʃæm.pi.ən.ʃɪp ⓊⓈ ˈtʃæm.pi.ən.ʃɪp, -pjən- **-s** -s
Champlain *French explorer:* ʃæmˈpleɪn; ʃɔ̃ːŋˈplɑ̃ːŋ ⓊⓈ ʃæmˈpleɪn; ʃɑ̃ːˈplɑ̃ːŋ *lake in US:* ʃæmˈpleɪn
Champneys ˈtʃæmp.niz
Champs Elysées ˌʃɑ̃ːnz.elˈiː.zeɪ, ˌʃɔ̃ːnz-, ⓊⓈ ˌʃɑːnz.eɪ.liːˈzeɪ
chanc|e tʃɑːnts ⓊⓈ tʃænts **-es** -ɪz **-ing** -ɪŋ **-ed** -t **-er/s** -əʳ/z ⓊⓈ -ɚ/z
chancel ˈtʃɑːnt.səl ⓊⓈ ˈtʃænt- **-s** -z
chanceller|y ˈtʃɑːnt.səl.ər|.i ⓊⓈ ˈtʃænt- **-ies** -iz
chancellor (C) ˈtʃɑːnt.səl.əʳ, -sɪ.ləʳ ⓊⓈ ˈtʃænt- **-s** -z **-ship/s** -ʃɪp/s **ˌchancellor of the exˈchequer**
Chancellorsville ˈtʃɑːnt.səl.əz.vɪl ⓊⓈ ˈtʃænt.səl.ɚz-
chancer|y (C) ˈtʃɑːnt.sər|.i ⓊⓈ ˈtʃænt- **-ies** -iz
chancre ˈʃæŋ.kəʳ ⓊⓈ -kɚ
chancroid ˈʃæŋ.krɔɪd **-s** -z
chanc|y ˈtʃɑːnt.s|i ⓊⓈ ˈtʃænt- **-ier** -i.əʳ ⓊⓈ -i.ɚ **-iest** -i.ɪst, -i.əst
chandelier ˌʃæn.dəˈlɪəʳ, -dɪˈ- ⓊⓈ -ˈlɪr **-s** -z
Chandigarh ˌtʃæn.dɪˈgɜːʳ, ˌtʃʌn-, -ˈgɑːʳ, ˈ--- ⓊⓈ -ˈgɜːr, -ˈgɑːr
chandler (C) ˈtʃɑːnd.ləʳ ⓊⓈ ˈtʃænd.lɚ **-s** -z
Chandos ˈʃæn.dɒs, ˈtʃæn.dɒs ⓊⓈ -dɑːs
Note: Lord Chandos pronounces /ˈʃæn-/. **Chandos Street** in London is generally pronounced with /ˈtʃæn-/.
Chanel ʃəˈnel, ʃænˈel
Chaney ˈtʃeɪ.ni
Chang tʃæŋ
chang|e tʃeɪndʒ **-es** -ɪz **-ing** -ɪŋ **-ed** -d **-er/s** -əʳ/z ⓊⓈ -ɚ/z
changeability ˌtʃeɪn.dʒəˈbɪl.ə.ti, -ɪ.ti ⓊⓈ -ə.t̬i
changeab|le ˈtʃeɪn.dʒə.b|l̩ **-ly** -li **-leness** -l̩.nəs, -l̩.nɪs
changeful ˈtʃeɪndʒ.fəl, -fʊl **-ly** -i **-ness** -nəs, -nɪs
changeless ˈtʃeɪndʒ.ləs, -lɪs
changeling ˈtʃeɪndʒ.lɪŋ **-s** -z
changeover ˈtʃeɪndʒˌəʊ.vəʳ ⓊⓈ -ˌoʊ.vɚ **-s** -z
Chang Jiang ˌtʃæŋ.dʒiˈæŋ ⓊⓈ ˌtʃɑːŋ.dʒiˈɑːŋ, ˌtʃæŋ-, -ˈæŋ
channel ˈtʃæn.əl **-s** -z **-(l)ing** -ɪŋ **-(l)ed** -d **ˈChannel ˌIslands** ; **ˌChannel ˈTunnel**
channelization, -isa- ˌtʃæn.əl.aɪˈzeɪ.ʃən, -ɪˈ- ⓊⓈ -ɪˈ-
channeliz|e, -is|e ˈtʃæn.əl.aɪz ⓊⓈ -ə.laɪz **-es** -ɪz **-ing** -ɪŋ **-ed** -d
Channell ˈtʃæn.əl
Channing ˈtʃæn.ɪŋ
Channon ˈtʃæn.ən, ˈʃæn.ən
chanson ˈʃɑ̃ːn.sɔ̃ːŋ, -sɒn, -ˈ- ⓊⓈ ʃɑ̃ːnˈsoʊn, -ˈsɑːn, -ˈsɔːn **-s** -z
chant (C) tʃɑːnt ⓊⓈ tʃænt **-s** -s **-ing** -ɪŋ ⓊⓈ ˈtʃæn.t̬ɪŋ **-ed** -ɪd ⓊⓈ ˈtʃæn.t̬ɪd **-er/s** -əʳ/z ⓊⓈ ˈtʃæn.t̬ɚ/z
Chantal ʃɑ̃ːnˈtɑːl, ʃæn-, -tæl ⓊⓈ ʃɑːnˈtɑːl
Chantelle ʃɑ̃ːnˈtel, ʃæn- ⓊⓈ ʃɑːnˈtel, ʃæn-
Chanter ˈtʃɑːn.təʳ ⓊⓈ ˈtʃæn.t̬ɚ
chanterelle ˌʃɑ̃ːn.təˈrel, ˌʃæn-, ˌtʃæn- ⓊⓈ ˌʃæn.t̬əˈ-, ˌʃɑːn- **-s** -z
chanteus|e ʃɑ̃ːnˈtɜːz, ʃɑːn- ⓊⓈ ʃɑ̃ːnˈtuːz, ʃæn-, -ˈtuːs **-es** -ɪz
chanticleer (C) ˈtʃɑːn.tɪ.klɪəʳ, ˈtʃænt-, ˈʃɑːn-, -tə-, ˌ--ˈ- ⓊⓈ ˈtʃæn.t̬ə.klɪr, ˈʃæn- **-s** -z
Chantilly *in France:* ʃænˈtɪl.i, ʃɑ̃ːn- ⓊⓈ ʃænˈtɪl.i; ˌʃɑːn.tiˈji
Note: In the song "Chantilly Lace", it is pronounced /ʃænˈtɪl.i/.
Chantilly *in US:* ʃænˈtɪli
Chantrey ˈtʃɑːn.tri ⓊⓈ ˈtʃæn-
chantr|y ˈtʃɑːn.tr|i ⓊⓈ ˈtʃæn- **-ies** -iz
chant|y ˈtʃɑːn.t|i ⓊⓈ ˈtʃæn.t̬|i **-ies** -iz
Chanukah ˈhɑː.nuː.kɑː, ˈxɑː- ⓊⓈ ˈhɑː.nə.kə, ˈxɑː-, -nʊ.kɑː
chaos ˈkeɪ.ɒs ⓊⓈ -ɑːs
chaotic keɪˈɒt.ɪk ⓊⓈ -ˈɑː.t̬ɪk **-ally** -əl.i, -li
chap tʃæp **-s** -s **-ping** -ɪŋ **-ped** -t
chapat(t)i tʃəˈpɑː.ti, -ˈpæt.i **-(e)s** -z
chapbook ˈtʃæp.bʊk **-s** -s
chape tʃeɪp **-s** -s
chapeau ˈʃæp.əʊ, -ˈ- ⓊⓈ ʃæpˈoʊ **-s** -z
chapeaux (*alternative plur. of* **chapeau**) ˈʃæp.əʊ, -əʊz ⓊⓈ ʃæpˈoʊ, -ˈoʊz
chapel ˈtʃæp.əl **-s** -z
Chapel-en-le-Frith ˌtʃæp.əl.ən.ləˈfrɪθ, -en.ləˈ-
chapelr|y ˈtʃæp.əl.r|i **-ies** -iz
Chapeltown ˈtʃæp.əl.taʊn
chaperon|e, chaperon ˈʃæp.ər.əʊn ⓊⓈ -ə.roʊn **-s** -z **-ing** -ɪŋ **-ed** -d **-age** -ɪdʒ
chapfallen ˈtʃæpˌfɔː.lən ⓊⓈ -ˌfɔː-, -ˌfɑː-
chaplain ˈtʃæp.lɪn **-s** -z
chaplainc|y ˈtʃæp.lɪnt.s|i, -lənt- **-ies** -iz
chaplet ˈtʃæp.lət, -lɪt, -let **-s** -s
Chaplin ˈtʃæp.lɪn
Chapman ˈtʃæp.mən
Chapone ʃəˈpəʊn ⓊⓈ -poʊn
Chappaquiddick ˌtʃæp.əˈkwɪd.ɪk
Chappell ˈtʃæp.əl
chappie ˈtʃæp.i **-s** -z
Chapple ˈtʃæp.l̩
chapstick ˈtʃæp.stɪk **-s** -s
chapter ˈtʃæp.təʳ ⓊⓈ -tɚ **-s** -z **ˈchapter ˌhouse** ; **ˌchapter and ˈverse**
Chapultepec tʃəˈpuːl.təˌpek, -ˈpʊl-
char tʃɑːʳ ⓊⓈ tʃɑːr **-s** -z **-ring** -ɪŋ **-red** -d
charabanc ˈʃær.ə.bæŋ, -bɑ̃ːŋ ⓊⓈ -bæŋ **-s** -s

character 'kær.ək.təʳ, -ɪk- Ⓤⓢ 'ker.ək.tɚ, 'kær- **-s** -z
characteristic ˌkær.ək.tə'rɪs.tɪk, -ɪk- Ⓤⓢ ˌker.ək-, ˌkær- **-s** -s **-al** -əl **-ally** -əl.i, -li
characterization, -isa- ˌkær.ək.tᵊr.aɪ'zeɪ.ʃᵊn, -ɪk-, -ɪ'- Ⓤⓢ ˌker.ək.tɚ.ɪ'-, ˌkær- **-s** -z
characteriz|e, -is|e 'kær.ək.tᵊr.aɪz, -ɪk- Ⓤⓢ 'ker.ək.tə.raɪz, 'kær- **-es** -ɪz **-ing** -ɪŋ **-ed** -d
characterless 'kær.ək.tə.ləs, -ɪk-, -lɪs Ⓤⓢ 'ker.ək.tɚ-, 'kær- **-ness** -nəs, -nɪs
charade ʃə'rɑːd Ⓤⓢ -'reɪd **-s** -z
charbroil 'tʃɑː.brɔɪl Ⓤⓢ 'tʃɑːr- **-s** -z **-ing** -ɪŋ **-ed** -d
charcoal 'tʃɑː.kəʊl Ⓤⓢ 'tʃɑːr.koʊl
chard (C) tʃɑːd Ⓤⓢ tʃɑːrd
chardonnay (C) 'ʃɑː.dᵊn.eɪ Ⓤⓢ 'ʃɑːr-, ˌ--'- **-s** -z
char|e tʃeəʳ Ⓤⓢ tʃer **-es** -z **-ing** -ɪŋ **-ed** -d
charg|e tʃɑːdʒ Ⓤⓢ tʃɑːrdʒ **-es** -ɪz **-ing** -ɪŋ **-ed** -d **'charge ˌcard**
chargeab|le 'tʃɑː.dʒə.b|l̩ Ⓤⓢ 'tʃɑːr- **-ly** -li **-leness** -l̩.nəs, -nɪs
chargé(s) d'affaires ˌʃɑː.ʒeɪ.dæf'eəʳ, -də'feəʳ Ⓤⓢ ˌʃɑːr.ʒeɪ.də'fer, -dæf'er
charger 'tʃɑː.dʒəʳ Ⓤⓢ 'tʃɑːr.dʒɚ **-s** -z
chargé(s) d'affaires *sing:* ˌʃɑː.ʒeɪ.dæf'eəʳ, -də'feəʳ Ⓤⓢ ˌʃɑːr.ʒeɪ.də'fer, -dæf'er *plur:* -z
Charing Cross ˌtʃær.ɪŋ'krɒs, ˌtʃeər- Ⓤⓢ ˌtʃer.ɪŋ'krɑːs, ˌtʃær-
chariot 'tʃær.i.ət Ⓤⓢ 'tʃer-, 'tʃær- **-s** -s
charioteer ˌtʃær.i.ə'tɪəʳ Ⓤⓢ ˌtʃer.i.ə'tɪr, ˌtʃær- **-s** -z
charisma kə'rɪz.mə
charismatic ˌkær.ɪz'mæt.ɪk Ⓤⓢ ˌker.ɪz'mæţ-, ˌkær-
charitab|le 'tʃær.ɪ.tə.b|l̩, '-ə- Ⓤⓢ 'tʃer-, 'tʃær- **-ly** -li **-leness** -l̩.nəs, -nɪs
charit|y (C) 'tʃær.ɪ.t|i, -ə.t|i Ⓤⓢ 'tʃer.ə.ţ|i, 'tʃær- **-ies** -iz
charivari ˌʃɑː.rɪ'vɑː.ri Ⓤⓢ ʃəˌrɪv.ə'riː; ˌʃɑː.rɪ'vɑː.ri, ˌʃɪv.ə'riː **-s** -z
charivaria ˌʃɑː.rɪv'ɑː.ri.ə Ⓤⓢ ˌʃɑːr.ɪ'vɑːr.i-
charlad|y 'tʃɑːˌleɪ.d|i Ⓤⓢ 'tʃɑːr- **-ies** -iz
charlatan 'ʃɑː.lə.tᵊn, -tæn Ⓤⓢ 'ʃɑːr.lə.tᵊn **-s** -z
charlatanism 'ʃɑː.lə.tᵊn.ɪ.zᵊm Ⓤⓢ 'ʃɑːr.lə.tᵊn-, -ţə.nɪ- **-s** -z
charlatanry 'ʃɑː.lə.tᵊn.ri Ⓤⓢ 'ʃɑːr.lə.tᵊn-, -ţən-
Charlbury 'tʃɑːl.bᵊr.i Ⓤⓢ 'tʃɑːrl.ber.i, -bɚ-
Charlecote 'tʃɑːl.kəʊt Ⓤⓢ 'tʃɑːrl.koʊt
Charlemagne 'ʃɑː.lə.meɪn, -maɪn, ˌ--'- Ⓤⓢ 'ʃɑːr.lə.meɪn
Charlemont 'tʃɑː.lɪ.mənt, 'tʃɑːl.mənt Ⓤⓢ 'tʃɑːr.lɪ.mənt, 'tʃɑːrl.mənt
Charlene 'tʃɑː.liːn, 'ʃɑː-, ʃɑː'liːn Ⓤⓢ ʃɑːr'liːn, '--
Charleroi 'ʃɑː.lə.rɔɪ *as if French:* ˌʃɑː.lə'rwɑː Ⓤⓢ 'ʃɑːr-
Charles tʃɑːlz Ⓤⓢ tʃɑːrlz
Charleston 'tʃɑːl.stən Ⓤⓢ 'tʃɑːrl-
Charlestown 'tʃɑːlz.taʊn Ⓤⓢ 'tʃɑːrlz-
Charlesworth 'tʃɑːlz.wəθ, -wɜːθ Ⓤⓢ 'tʃɑːrlz.wɚθ, -wɜːrθ
Charleville 'ʃɑː.lə.vɪl Ⓤⓢ 'ʃɑːr-
Charley 'tʃɑː.li Ⓤⓢ 'tʃɑːr- **'charley ˌhorse**
charlie (C) 'tʃɑː.li Ⓤⓢ 'tʃɑːr- **-s** -z
charlock 'tʃɑː.lɒk Ⓤⓢ 'tʃɑːr.lɑːk
charlotte (C) 'ʃɑː.lət Ⓤⓢ 'ʃɑːr- **-s** -s
Charlottenburg ʃɑː'lɒt.ᵊn.bɜːg Ⓤⓢ ʃɑːr'lɑː.tᵊn.bɜːrg
Charlottesville 'ʃɑː.ləts.vɪl Ⓤⓢ 'ʃɑːr-
Charlton 'tʃɑːl.tᵊn Ⓤⓢ 'tʃɑːrl-
charm tʃɑːm Ⓤⓢ tʃɑːrm **-s** -z **-ed** -d **-ing** -ɪŋ **-er/s** -əʳ/z Ⓤⓢ -ɚ/z
Charmaine ʃɑː'meɪn Ⓤⓢ ʃɑːr-
Charmian 'tʃɑː.mi.ən, 'ʃɑː-, 'kɑː- Ⓤⓢ 'tʃɑːr-, 'ʃɑːr-, 'kɑːr-
Charmin® 'tʃɑː.mɪn Ⓤⓢ 'ʃɑːr-
charming 'tʃɑː.mɪŋ Ⓤⓢ 'tʃɑːr- **-ly** -li
charnel 'tʃɑː.nᵊl Ⓤⓢ 'tʃɑːr- **'charnel ˌhouse**
Charnock 'tʃɑː.nɒk, -nək Ⓤⓢ 'tʃɑːr.nɑːk
Charnwood 'tʃɑːn.wʊd, -wəd Ⓤⓢ 'tʃɑːrn-
Charolais *sing:* 'ʃær.ə.leɪ Ⓤⓢ ˌʃɑːr.ə'leɪ *plur:* 'ʃær.ə.leɪ, -leɪz Ⓤⓢ ˌʃɑːr.ə'leɪ, -'leɪz
Charon 'keə.rᵊn, -rɒn Ⓤⓢ 'ker.ᵊn
Charpentier ʃɑː'pɑ̃ːn.ti'eɪ Ⓤⓢ ˌʃɑːr.pɑ̃ːn.ti'eɪ, -'tjeɪ
Charrington 'tʃær.ɪŋ.tən Ⓤⓢ 'tʃer-, 'tʃær-
chart tʃɑːt Ⓤⓢ tʃɑːrt **-s** -s **-ing** -ɪŋ Ⓤⓢ 'tʃɑːr.ţɪŋ **-ed** -ɪd Ⓤⓢ 'tʃɑːr.ţɪd
chart|er (C) 'tʃɑː.t|əʳ Ⓤⓢ 'tʃɑːr.ţ|ɚ **-ers** -əz Ⓤⓢ -ɚz **-ering** -ᵊr.ɪŋ **-ered** -əd Ⓤⓢ -ɚd **-erer/s** -ᵊr.əʳ/z Ⓤⓢ -ɚ.ɚ/z **'charter ˌflight**; **ˌchartered a'ccountant**
Charterhouse 'tʃɑː.tə.haʊs Ⓤⓢ 'tʃɑːr.ţɚ-
Charteris 'tʃɑː.təz, -tᵊr.ɪs Ⓤⓢ 'tʃɑːr.ţɚ.ɪs
charterpart|y 'tʃɑː.təˌpɑː.t|i Ⓤⓢ 'tʃɑːr.ţɚˌpɑːr.ţ|i **-ies** -iz
chart|ism (C) 'tʃɑː.t|ɪ.zᵊm Ⓤⓢ 'tʃɑːr.ţ|ɪ- **-ist/s** -ɪst/s
Chartres 'ʃɑː.trə; ʃɑːt Ⓤⓢ 'ʃɑːr.trə; ʃɑːrt
Chartreuse® ʃɑː'trɜːz Ⓤⓢ ʃɑːr'truːz
Chartwell 'tʃɑːt.wel, -wəl Ⓤⓢ 'tʃɑːrt-
char|woman 'tʃɑː|ˌwʊm.ən Ⓤⓢ 'tʃɑːr- **-women** -ˌwɪm.ɪn
char|y 'tʃeə.r|i Ⓤⓢ 'tʃer|.i **-ier** -i.əʳ Ⓤⓢ -i.ɚ **-iest** -i.ɪst, -i.əst **-ily** -ɪ.li, -ᵊl.i **-iness** -ɪ.nəs, -ɪ.nɪs
Charybdis kə'rɪb.dɪs
Chas tʃæz, tʃɑːlz Ⓤⓢ tʃæz, tʃɑːrlz
chas|e (C) tʃeɪs **-es** -ɪz **-ing** -ɪŋ **-ed** -t **-er/s** -əʳ/z Ⓤⓢ -ɚ/z
chasm 'kæz.ᵊm **-s** -z
chassé 'ʃæs.eɪ Ⓤⓢ -'- **-s** -z
chasseur ʃæs'ɜːʳ Ⓤⓢ -'ɜːr **-s** -z
chassis *sing:* 'ʃæs.i, -iː Ⓤⓢ 'tʃæs-, 'ʃæs- *plur:* 'ʃæs.iz, -iːz Ⓤⓢ 'tʃæs-, 'ʃæs-
chaste tʃeɪst **-ly** -li **-ness** -nəs, -nɪs
chasten 'tʃeɪ.sᵊn **-s** -z **-ing** -ɪŋ **-ed** -d
chastis|e tʃæs'taɪz Ⓤⓢ '-- **-es** -ɪz **-ing** -ɪŋ **-ed** -d
chastisement tʃæs'taɪz.mənt, 'tʃæs.tɪz- Ⓤⓢ 'tʃæs.taɪz-, -'-- **-s** -s
chastiser tʃæs'taɪ.zəʳ Ⓤⓢ -zɚ **-s** -z
chastity (C) 'tʃæs.tə.ti, -tɪ- Ⓤⓢ -tə.ţi **'chastity ˌbelt**
chasuble 'tʃæz.jʊ.bl̩, -jə- Ⓤⓢ -jə-, '-ə- **-s** -z
chat tʃæt **-s** -s **-ting** -ɪŋ Ⓤⓢ 'tʃæţ.ɪŋ **-ted** -ɪd Ⓤⓢ 'tʃæţ.ɪd **'chat ˌshow**
Chataway 'tʃæt.ə.weɪ Ⓤⓢ 'tʃæţ-
château 'ʃæt.əʊ, -'- Ⓤⓢ ʃæt'oʊ **-s** -z
chateaubriand (C) ˌʃæt.əʊ.bri'ɑ̃ː*nd*, ˌʃæt.əʊ'briː-, ʃæt'əʊ- Ⓤⓢ ˌʃæt.oʊ.bri'ɑ̃ː*nd*, ˌʃɑː.toʊ- **-s** -z
Châteauneuf-du-Pape ˌʃæt.əʊ.nɜːf.dju'pæp Ⓤⓢ -oʊˌnɜːf.du-, -dju-, -'pɑːp
châteaux (*alternative plur. of* **chateau**) 'ʃæt.əʊ, -əʊz, -'- Ⓤⓢ ʃæt'oʊ, -'oʊz
chatelain 'ʃæt.ᵊl.eɪn, -æ̃ŋ Ⓤⓢ 'ʃæţ.ə.leɪn **-s** -z
chatelaine 'ʃæt.ᵊl.eɪn Ⓤⓢ 'ʃæţ.ə.leɪn **-s** -z
Chater 'tʃeɪ.təʳ Ⓤⓢ -tɚ
Chatham 'tʃæt.əm Ⓤⓢ 'tʃæţ-
chatline 'tʃæt.laɪn **-s** -z
Chatsworth 'tʃæts.wəθ, -wɜːθ Ⓤⓢ -wɚθ, -wɜːrθ
Chattanooga ˌtʃæt.ᵊn'uː.gə Ⓤⓢ ˌtʃæţ.ə'nuː-, ˌtʃæt.ᵊn'uː-
chattel 'tʃæt.ᵊl Ⓤⓢ 'tʃæţ- **-s** -z
chatt|er 'tʃæt|.əʳ Ⓤⓢ 'tʃæţ|.ɚ **-ers** -əz Ⓤⓢ -ɚz **-ering** -ᵊr.ɪŋ **-ered** -əd Ⓤⓢ -ɚd **-erer/s** -ᵊr.əʳ/z Ⓤⓢ -ɚ.ɚ/z **'chattering ˌclasses**
chatterbox 'tʃæt.ə.bɒks Ⓤⓢ 'tʃæţ.ɚ.bɑːks **-es** -ɪz
Chatteris 'tʃæt.ᵊr.ɪs
Chatterley 'tʃæt.ᵊl.i Ⓤⓢ 'tʃæţ.ɚ.li
Chatterton 'tʃæt.ə.tᵊn Ⓤⓢ 'tʃæţ.ɚ-
Chatto 'tʃæt.əʊ Ⓤⓢ -oʊ, 'tʃæţ-
chatt|y 'tʃæt|.i Ⓤⓢ 'tʃæţ|.i **-ier** -i.əʳ Ⓤⓢ -i.ɚ **-iest** -i.ɪst, -i.əst **-ily** -ɪ.li, -ᵊl.i **-iness** -ɪ.nəs, -ɪ.nɪs
Chatwin 'tʃæt.wɪn

Chaucer ˈtʃɔː.səʳ Ⓤⓢ ˈtʃɑː.sɚ, ˈtʃɔː-

Chaucerian tʃɔːˈsɪə.ri.ən Ⓤⓢ tʃɑːˈsɪr.i-, tʃɔː-, -ˈser-

chaudfroid ˈʃəʊ.fwɑː, -frwɑː Ⓤⓢ ˈʃoʊ-

Chaudhuri ˈtʃaʊ.dᵊr.i

chauffer ˈtʃɔː.fəʳ Ⓤⓢ ˈtʃɑː.fɚ, ˈtʃɔː- **-s** -z

chauffeur ˈʃəʊ.fəʳ, ʃəʊˈfɜːʳ Ⓤⓢ ʃoʊˈfɜːr **-s** -z

Chauncey ˈtʃɔːnt.si Ⓤⓢ ˈtʃɑːnt-, ˈtʃɔːnt-

chauvin|ism ˈʃəʊ.vɪ.n|ɪ.zᵊm, -və- Ⓤⓢ ˈʃoʊ- **-ist/s** -ɪst/s

chauvinistic ˌʃəʊ.vɪˈnɪs.tɪk, -vəˈ- Ⓤⓢ ˌʃoʊ- **-ally** -ᵊl.i, -li

Chavez ˈtʃæv.es Ⓤⓢ ˈʃɑː.vez, ˈtʃɑː-, -ves

Chaworth ˈtʃɑː.wəθ, -wɜːθ Ⓤⓢ -wɚθ, -wɜːrθ

Chayefsky tʃaɪˈef.ski

Che tʃeɪ

Cheadle ˈtʃiː.dl̩

Cheam tʃiːm

cheap tʃiːp **-er** -əʳ Ⓤⓢ -ɚ **-est** -ɪst, -əst **-ly** -li **-ness** -nəs, -nɪs ˌ**cheap** ˈ**shot**

cheapen ˈtʃiː.pᵊn **-s** -z **-ing** -ɪŋ **-ed** -d

cheapie ˈtʃiː.pi **-s** -z

cheap-jack ˈtʃiːp.dʒæk **-s** -s

cheapo ˈtʃiː.pəʊ Ⓤⓢ -poʊ **-s** -z

Cheapside ˈtʃiːp.saɪd, tʃiːpˈsaɪd

cheapskate ˈtʃiːp.skeɪt **-s** -s

cheat tʃiːt **-s** -s **-ing** -ɪŋ Ⓤⓢ ˈtʃiː.t̬ɪŋ **-ed** -ɪd Ⓤⓢ ˈtʃiː.t̬ɪd

Cheatham ˈtʃiː.təm Ⓤⓢ -t̬əm

Chechen ˌtʃetʃˈen **-s** -z *stress shift:* ˌChechen ˈfighters

Chechenia ˈtʃetʃ.ni.ɑː, -ni.ə; tʃetʃ.ɪˈnjɑː Ⓤⓢ -ni.ə

Chechnya ˈtʃetʃ.ni.ɑː, -ni.ə; tʃetʃ.ɪˈnjɑː Ⓤⓢ -ni.ə

check tʃek **-s** -s **-ing** -ɪŋ **-ed** -t ˈ**checking ac**ˌ**count**

checkbook ˈtʃek.bʊk **-s** -s

check|er (C) ˈtʃek|.əʳ Ⓤⓢ -ɚ **-ers** -əz Ⓤⓢ -ɚz **-ering** -ᵊr.ɪŋ **-ered** -əd Ⓤⓢ -ɚd

checkerboard ˈtʃek.ə.bɔːd Ⓤⓢ -ɚ.bɔːrd **-s** -z

checkers ˈtʃek.əz Ⓤⓢ -ɚz

check-in ˈtʃek.ɪn **-s** -z ˈ**check-in** ˌ**desk**

Checkland ˈtʃek.lənd

checklist ˈtʃek.lɪst **-s** -s

checkma|te ˈtʃek.meɪ|t, ˌ-ˈ- **-tes** -ts **-ting** -tɪŋ Ⓤⓢ -t̬ɪŋ **-ted** -tɪd Ⓤⓢ -t̬ɪd

checkout ˈtʃek.aʊt **-s** -s

checkpoint ˈtʃek.pɔɪnt **-s** -s ˌ**Checkpoint** ˈ**Charlie**

checkrein ˈtʃek.reɪn **-s** -z

checkroom ˈtʃek.rʊm, -ruːm Ⓤⓢ -ruːm **-s** -z

checkup ˈtʃek.ʌp **-s** -s

cheddar (C) ˈtʃed.əʳ Ⓤⓢ -ɚ **-s** -z **-ing** -ɪŋ **-ed** -d

cheek tʃiːk **-s** -s **-ing** -ɪŋ **-ed** -t ˌ**turn the other** ˈ**cheek**

cheekbone ˈtʃiːk.bəʊn Ⓤⓢ -boʊn **-s** -z

Cheeke tʃiːk

cheek|y ˈtʃiː.k|i **-ier** -i.əʳ Ⓤⓢ -i.ɚ **-iest** -i.ɪst, -i.əst **-ily** -ɪ.li, -ᵊl.i **-iness** -ɪ.nəs, -ɪ.nɪs

cheep tʃiːp **-s** -s **-ing** -ɪŋ **-ed** -t

cheer tʃɪəʳ Ⓤⓢ tʃɪr **-s** -z **-ing** -ɪŋ **-ed** -d

cheerful ˈtʃɪə.fᵊl, -fʊl Ⓤⓢ ˈtʃɪr- **-ly** -i **-ness** -nəs, -nɪs

cheerio ˌtʃɪə.riˈəʊ Ⓤⓢ ˌtʃɪr.iˈoʊ **-s** -z

Cheerios® ˈtʃɪə.ri.əʊz, ˈtʃɪr.i.oʊz

cheerleader ˈtʃɪəˌliː.dəʳ Ⓤⓢ ˈtʃɪrˌliː.dɚ **-s** -z

cheerless ˈtʃɪə.ləs, -lɪs Ⓤⓢ ˈtʃɪr- **-ly** -li **-ness** -nəs, -nɪs

cheer|y ˈtʃɪə.r|i Ⓤⓢ ˈtʃɪr|.i **-ier** -i.əʳ Ⓤⓢ -i.ɚ **-iest** -i.ɪst, -i.əst **-ily** -ɪ.li, -ᵊl.i **-iness** -ɪ.nəs, -ɪ.nɪs

chees|e tʃiːz **-es** -ɪz **-ed** -d ˌ**cheesed** ˈ**off**

cheeseboard ˈtʃiːz.bɔːd Ⓤⓢ -bɔːrd **-s** -z

cheeseburger ˈtʃiːzˌbɜː.gəʳ Ⓤⓢ -ˌbɜːr.gɚ **-s** -z

cheesecake ˈtʃiːz.keɪk **-s** -s

cheesecloth ˈtʃiːz.klɒθ Ⓤⓢ -klɑːθ

Cheeseman ˈtʃiːz.mən

cheesemonger ˈtʃiːzˌmʌŋ.gəʳ Ⓤⓢ -gɚ, -ˌmɑːŋ- **-s** -z

cheeseparing ˈtʃiːzˌpeə.rɪŋ Ⓤⓢ -ˌper.ɪŋ

Cheesewright ˈtʃiːz.raɪt, ˈtʃez-

chees|y ˈtʃiː.z|i **-iness** -ɪ.nəs, -ɪ.nɪs

cheetah ˈtʃiː.tə Ⓤⓢ -t̬ə **-s** -z

Cheetham ˈtʃiː.təm Ⓤⓢ -t̬əm

Cheever ˈtʃiː.vəʳ Ⓤⓢ -vɚ

chef ʃef **-s** -s

chef d'équipe ˌʃef.dekˈiːp

chef(s) d'oeuvre, chef(s)-d'oeuvre ˌʃeɪˈdɜːv.rə, -əʳ Ⓤⓢ ˌʃeɪˈdɜːv.rə, -ˈdɜːrv

Cheke tʃiːk

Chekhov ˈtʃek.ɒf, -ɒv Ⓤⓢ -ɑːf, -ɔːf, -ɑːv

chela ˈtʃeɪ.lə, ˈtʃiː.lə **-s** -z

chela|te kiːˈleɪ|t, kə-, tʃiː-, kɪ-; ˈkiː.leɪ|t, ˈtʃiː- Ⓤⓢ ˈkiː.leɪ|t **-tes** -ts **-ting** -tɪŋ Ⓤⓢ -t̬ɪŋ **-ted** -tɪd Ⓤⓢ -t̬ɪd

chelation kiːˈleɪ.ʃᵊn, kə-, tʃiː-, kɪ-

Chelmer ˈtʃel.məʳ Ⓤⓢ -mɚ

Chelmsford ˈtʃelmz.fəd, ˈtʃelmps- *old-fashioned local pronunciations:* ˈtʃemz-, ˈtʃɒmz- Ⓤⓢ -fɚd

Chelsea ˈtʃel.si ˌ**Chelsea** ˈ**bun**, ˈ**Chelsea** ˌ**bun** ; ˌ**Chelsea** ˈ**pensioner**

Chelsey ˈtʃel.si

Cheltenham ˈtʃel.tᵊn.əm

Chelyabinsk tʃelˈjɑː.bɪnsk

chemic ˈkem.ɪk

chemical ˈkem.ɪ.kᵊl **-ly** -i **-s** -z ˌ**chemical engi**ˈ**neering** ; ˌ**chemical** ˈ**warfare**

chemis|e ʃəˈmiːz **-es** -ɪz

chemist ˈkem.ɪst **-s** -s

chemistry ˈkem.ɪ.stri, -ə-

Chemnitz ˈkem.nɪts

chemo- ˈkiː.məʊ-, ˈkem.əʊ- Ⓤⓢ ˈkiː.moʊ-, ˈkem.oʊ-

chemotherapy ˌkiː.məʊˈθer.ə.pi, ˌkem.əʊ- Ⓤⓢ ˌkiː.moʊˈ-, ˌkem.oʊˈ-

Chenevix ˈtʃen.ə.vɪks, ˈʃen.ə.vɪks

Cheney ˈtʃiː.ni, ˈtʃeɪ- Ⓤⓢ ˈtʃeɪ-

Chengdu ˌtʃʌŋˈduː

Chenies *in Buckinghamshire:* ˈtʃeɪ.niz *street in London:* ˈtʃiː.niz

chenille ʃəˈniːl

cheongsam ˌtʃɒŋˈsæm, tʃi‚ɒŋ- Ⓤⓢ ˌtʃɔːŋ-, ˌtʃɑːŋ- **-s** -z

Cheops ˈkiː.ɒps Ⓤⓢ -ɑːps

Chepstow ˈtʃep.stəʊ Ⓤⓢ -stoʊ

cheque tʃek **-s** -s ˈ**cheque** ˌ**card**

chequebook ˈtʃek.bʊk **-s** -s

chequecard ˈtʃek.kɑːd Ⓤⓢ -kɑːrd **-s** -z

chequ|er ˈtʃek|.əʳ Ⓤⓢ -ɚ **-ers** -əz Ⓤⓢ -ɚz **-ering** -ᵊr.ɪŋ **-ered** -əd Ⓤⓢ -ɚd

Chequers ˈtʃek.əz Ⓤⓢ -ɚz

Cher ʃeəʳ Ⓤⓢ ʃer

Cherbourg ˈʃeə.bʊəg, ʃɜː-, -bɔːg, -bɜːg Ⓤⓢ ˈʃer.bʊrg, -bʊr, -ˈ-

cherish ˈtʃer.ɪʃ **-es** -ɪz **-ing** -ɪŋ **-ed** -t

Cheriton ˈtʃer.ɪ.tᵊn

Chernobyl tʃɜːˈnəʊ.bᵊl, tʃə-, -ˈnɒb.ᵊl, -ɪl Ⓤⓢ tʃɚˈnoʊ.bᵊl

Cherokee ˈtʃer.ə.kiː, ˌ--ˈ- **-s** -z

cheroot ʃəˈruːt **-s** -s

cherr|y (C) ˈtʃer|.i **-ies** -iz ˌ**cherry** ˈ**brandy** ; ˌ**cherry** ˈ**pie** ; ˌ**cherry to**ˈ**mato**

cherrystone ˈtʃer.i.stəʊn Ⓤⓢ -stoʊn **-s** -z

chersonese ˈkɜː.sə.niːs, -niːz, ˌ--ˈ- Ⓤⓢ ˌkɜːr.sə.niːz, -niːs

Chertsey ˈtʃɜːt.si Ⓤⓢ ˈtʃɜːrt-

cherub ˈtʃer.əb **-s** -z

cherubic tʃəˈruː.bɪk, tʃerˈuː- Ⓤⓢ tʃəˈruː- **-ally** -ᵊl.i, -li

cherubim ˈtʃer.ə.bɪm, ˈ-ʊ-

Cherubini ˌker.ʊˈbiː.niː, -əˈ-, -ni

chervil ˈtʃɜː.vɪl, -vᵊl Ⓤⓢ ˈtʃɜːr-

Cherwell ˈtʃɑː.wəl, -wel Ⓤⓢ ˈtʃɑːr-

Cheryl ˈtʃer.ᵊl, ˈʃer-, -ɪl

Chesapeake ˈtʃes.ə.piːk

Chesebro, Chesebrough ˈtʃiːz.brə

Chesham ˈtʃeʃ.ᵊm *old-fashioned local pronunciation:* ˈtʃes-

Cheshire ˈtʃeʃ.əʳ, -ɪəʳ Ⓤⓢ -ɚ, -ɪr ˌ**Cheshire** ˈ**cat** ; ˌ**Cheshire** ˈ**cheese**

Cheshunt ˈtʃes.ᵊnt, ˈtʃeʃ-

Chesil ˈtʃez.ᵊl ˌ**Chesil** ˈ**Bank** ; ˌ**Chesil** ˈ**Beach**

Chesney ˈtʃes.ni, ˈtʃez.ni

Chesnutt ˈtʃes.nʌt

chess tʃes

chessboard ˈtʃes.bɔːd Ⓤⓢ -bɔːrd **-s** -z

chess|man 'tʃes|.mæn, -mən **-men** -men, -mən
chest tʃest **-s** -s **-ed** -ɪd ˌ**chest of 'drawers**
Chester 'tʃes.təʳ ⓤⓢ -tɚ
chesterfield (C) 'tʃes.tə.fiːld ⓤⓢ -tɚ- **-s** -z
Chester-le-Street ˌtʃes.tə.lɪ'striːt ⓤⓢ -tɚ-
Chesterton 'tʃes.tə.tᵊn ⓤⓢ -tɚ.t̬ən
chestnut 'tʃes.nʌt, 'tʃest- **-s** -s
Chestre 'tʃes.təʳ ⓤⓢ -tɚ
chest|y 'tʃes.t|i **-ier** -i.əʳ ⓤⓢ -i.ɚ **-iest** -i.ɪst, -i.əst **-ily** -ɪ.li, -ᵊl.i **-iness** -ɪ.nəs, -ɪ.nɪs
Chetham 'tʃet.əm
chetrum 'tʃet.rʊm, -rəm
Chettle 'tʃet.l̩ ⓤⓢ 'tʃet̬-
Chetwode 'tʃet.wʊd
Chetwynd 'tʃet.wɪnd
cheval-glass ʃə'væl.glɑːs ⓤⓢ -glæs **-es** -ɪz
chevalier ˌʃev.ə'lɪəʳ ⓤⓢ -'lɪr **-s** -z
Chevalier *surname:* ʃə'væl.i.eɪ, ʃɪ- ⓤⓢ -i.eɪ, -jeɪ
Chevening 'tʃiːv.nɪŋ
Cheves tʃiːvz
Chevette® ʃə'vet, ʃev'et **-s** -s
Cheviot *hills, sheep:* 'tʃiː.vi.ət, 'tʃev.i-, 'tʃɪv.i- ⓤⓢ 'ʃev.i- *cloth:* 'tʃev.i.ət ⓤⓢ 'ʃev-
Chevis 'tʃev.ɪs
Chevrolet® 'ʃev.rə.leɪ, ˌ--'- ⓤⓢ ˌʃev.rə'leɪ **-s** -z
chevron 'ʃev.rᵊn, -rɒn ⓤⓢ -rᵊn **-s** -z
chev|y (C) 'tʃev|.i **-ies** -iz **-ying** -i.ɪŋ **-ied** -id
Chevy 'ʃev.i
chew tʃuː **-s** -z **-ing** -ɪŋ **-ed** -d **'chewing ˌgum**
chew|y 'tʃuː|.i **-ier** -i.əʳ ⓤⓢ -i.ɚ **-iest** -i.ɪst, -i.əst **-iness** -ɪ.nəs, -ɪ.nɪs
Cheyenne ˌʃaɪ'æn, -'en ⓤⓢ -'en, -'æn
Cheyne 'tʃeɪ.ni, tʃeɪn
Cheyney 'tʃeɪ.ni
chez ʃeɪ
Chiang Kai-Shek ˌtʃæŋ.kaɪ'ʃek ⓤⓢ ˌtʃæŋ-, dʒæŋ-
Chiang Mai tʃiˌæŋ'maɪ ⓤⓢ ˌdʒɑːŋ'maɪ, tʃiˌɑːŋ-
chianti (C) ki'æn.ti ⓤⓢ -'ɑːn.t̬i, -'æn-
Chiantishire ki'æn.ti.ʃəʳ, -ˌʃɪəʳ ⓤⓢ -'ɑːn.t̬i.ʃɚ, -'æn-, -ˌʃɪr
Chiapas tʃi'æp.əs ⓤⓢ -'ɑː.pəs
chiaroscuro kiˌɑː.rə'skʊə.rəʊ, -rɒs'kʊə-, -'kjʊə- ⓤⓢ -ˌɑːr.ə'skjʊr.oʊ
chias|ma kaɪ'æz|.mə **-mata** -mə.tə ⓤⓢ -mə.t̬ə **-mas** -məz
chiasmus kaɪ'æz.məs
chic ʃiːk, ʃɪk
Chicago ʃɪ'kɑː.gəʊ, ʃə- ⓤⓢ -goʊ, -'kɔː-
chican|e ʃɪ'keɪn, ʃə- **-es** -z **-ing** -ɪŋ **-ed** -d **-er/s** -əʳ/z ⓤⓢ -ɚ/z
chicaner|y ʃɪ'keɪ.nᵊr|.i, ʃə- **-ies** -iz
chicano tʃɪ'kɑː.nəʊ ⓤⓢ -noʊ **-s** -z
Chichele 'tʃɪtʃ.ᵊl.i, -ɪ.li
Chichén Itzá tʃiˌtʃen.ɪt'sɑː ⓤⓢ -iːt'-
Chichester 'tʃɪtʃ.ɪ.stəʳ, '-ə- ⓤⓢ -stɚ
chi-chi 'ʃiː.ʃiː
chick (C) tʃɪk **-s** -s
chickabidd|y 'tʃɪk.əˌbɪd|.i **-ies** -iz
chickadee 'tʃɪk.əˌdiː, ˌ--'- **-s** -z
Chickasaw 'tʃɪk.ə.sɔː ⓤⓢ -sɔː, -sɑː **-s** -z
chicken 'tʃɪk.ɪn, -ᵊn **-s** -z **-ing** -ɪŋ **-ed** -d **'chicken ˌfeed** ; ˌ**chicken 'Kiev** ; **'chicken ˌpox** ; ˌ**don't count your ˌchickens before they 'hatch**
chickenhearted ˌtʃɪk.ɪn'hɑː.tɪd, -ᵊn'-, -təd, 'tʃɪk.ɪnˌhɑː-, -ᵊnˌ- ⓤⓢ ˌtʃɪk.ɪn'hɑːr.t̬ɪd, -ᵊn'-, -t̬əd
chickenshit 'tʃɪk.ɪn.ʃɪt, -ᵊn- **-s** -s
Chicklets® 'tʃɪk.ləts, -lɪts
chickpea 'tʃɪk.piː **-s** -z
chickweed 'tʃɪk.wiːd
Chiclayo tʃi'klɑː.jəʊ ⓤⓢ -joʊ
chicory 'tʃɪk.ᵊr.i
Chiddingly ˌtʃɪd.ɪŋ'laɪ, '---
chid|e tʃaɪd **-es** -z **-ing** -ɪŋ **-ed** -ɪd **chid** tʃɪd **chidden** 'tʃɪd.ᵊn
chief tʃiːf **-s** -s **-ly** -li ˌ**chief in'spector** ; ˌ**chief of 'staff**
chieftain 'tʃiːf.tᵊn, -tɪn **-s** -z
chieftanc|y 'tʃiːf.tᵊn*t*.s|i, -tɪn*t*- **-ies** -iz
chiff-chaff 'tʃɪf.tʃæf **-s** -s
chiffon 'ʃɪf.ɒn, ʃɪ'fɒn ⓤⓢ ʃɪ'fɑːn **-s** -z
chiffon(n)ier ˌʃɪf.ə'nɪəʳ, -ni.eɪ *as if French:* ʃiː.fɔ̃ː'nje ⓤⓢ -'nɪr **-s** -z
chifforobe 'ʃɪf.ə.rəʊb ⓤⓢ 'ʃɪf.roʊb **-s** -z
chignon 'ʃiː.njɒn, -njɒŋ, -njɔ̃ː *old-fashioned:* ʃɪ'nɒn ⓤⓢ 'ʃiː.njɑːn **-s** -z
Chigwell 'tʃɪg.wel, -wəl
chihuahua (C) tʃɪ'wɑː.wə, tʃə-, ʃɪ-, ʃə-, -wɑː **-s** -z
chilblain 'tʃɪl.bleɪn **-s** -z
child (C) tʃaɪld **children** 'tʃɪl.drᵊn **'child aˌbuse** ; ˌ**child 'benefit** ; **'child's ˌplay** ; ˌ**child 'prodigy** ; ˌ**child sup'port**
childbearing 'tʃaɪldˌbeə.rɪŋ ⓤⓢ -ˌber.ɪŋ
childbed 'tʃaɪld.bed
childbirth 'tʃaɪld.bɜːθ ⓤⓢ -bɜːrθ
childcare 'tʃaɪld.keəʳ ⓤⓢ -ker
Childe tʃaɪld
Childermas 'tʃɪl.də.mæs, -məs ⓤⓢ -dɚ.mæs
Childers 'tʃɪl.dəz ⓤⓢ -dɚz
childhood 'tʃaɪld.hʊd ˌ**childhood 'sweetheart**
childish 'tʃaɪl.dɪʃ **-ly** -li **-ness** -nəs, -nɪs
childless 'tʃaɪld.ləs, -lɪs **-ness** -nəs, -nɪs
childlike 'tʃaɪld.laɪk
childmind|er 'tʃaɪldˌmaɪn.d|əʳ ⓤⓢ -d|ɚ **-ers** -əz ⓤⓢ -ɚz **-ing** -ɪŋ
childproof 'tʃaɪld.pruːf
children (*from* **child**) 'tʃɪl.drᵊn **'children's ˌhome**
Childs tʃaɪldz
Chile 'tʃɪl.i, 'tʃiː.leɪ
Chilean 'tʃɪl.i.ən, tʃɪ'liː.ən ⓤⓢ tʃɪ'liː-, 'tʃɪl.i- **-s** -z
chili 'tʃɪl.i **-s** -z
chiliad 'kɪl.i.æd, 'kaɪ.li-, -əd **-s** -z
chili|asm 'kɪl.i|.æz.ᵊm **-ast/s** -æst/s
chilidog 'tʃɪl.i.dɒg ⓤⓢ -dɑːg, -dɔːg **-s** -z
chill tʃɪl **-s** -z **-ing/ly** -ɪŋ/li **-ed** -d **-ness** -nəs, -nɪs **-er** -əʳ ⓤⓢ -ɚ
chiller 'tʃɪl.əʳ ⓤⓢ -ɚ **-s** -z
chilli 'tʃɪl.i **-es** -z **'chilli ˌpepper** ; **'chilli ˌpowder**
chilli con carne ˌtʃɪl.i.kɒn'kɑː.ni, -kɒŋ'-, -kən'-, -kəŋ'-, -neɪ ⓤⓢ -kɑːn'kɑːr.ni, -kən'-
Chillingham 'tʃɪl.ɪŋ.əm
Chillingly 'tʃɪl.ɪŋ.li
Chillingworth 'tʃɪl.ɪŋ.wəθ, -wɜːθ ⓤⓢ -wɚθ, -wɜːrθ
Chillon ʃɪ'lɒn, ʃə-; 'ʃɪl.ən, -ɒn ⓤⓢ ʃə'lɑːn, ʃɪ-; 'ʃɪl.ən; ʃi'joʊn
Note: In Byron's 'Castle of Chillon' it is usual to pronounce /'ʃɪl.ən/ or /'ʃɪl.ɒn ⓤⓢ -ɑːn/.
chill|y 'tʃɪl|.i **-ier** -i.əʳ ⓤⓢ -i.ɚ **-iest** -i.ɪst, -i.əst **-iness** -ɪ.nəs, -ɪ.nɪs
Chiltern 'tʃɪl.tᵊn ⓤⓢ -tɚn ˌ**Chiltern 'Hills** ; ˌ**Chiltern 'Hundreds**
Chilton 'tʃɪl.tᵊn
chimaera kaɪ'mɪə.rə, kɪ-, kə-, ʃɪ-, ʃə-, -'meə-; 'kɪm.ᵊr.ə ⓤⓢ kaɪ'mɪr.ə, kɪ- **-s** -z
Chimborazo ˌtʃɪm.bə'rɑː.zəʊ, ˌʃɪm-, -bɒr'ɑː- ⓤⓢ -bə'rɑː.zoʊ
chim|e tʃaɪm **-es** -z **-ing** -ɪŋ **-ed** -d **-er/s** -əʳ/z ⓤⓢ -ɚ/z
chimera kaɪ'mɪə.rə, kɪ-, kə-, ʃɪ-, ʃə-, -'meə-; 'kɪm.ᵊr.ə ⓤⓢ kaɪ'mɪr.ə, kɪ- **-s** -z
chimere tʃɪ'mɪəʳ, ʃɪ-, kɪ-, kaɪ- ⓤⓢ -'mɪr **-s** -z
chimeric kaɪ'mer.ɪk, kɪ-, kə- **-al** -ᵊl **-ally** -ᵊl.i, -li
Chimkent tʃɪm'kent
chimney 'tʃɪm.ni **-s** -z **'chimney ˌbreast** ; **'chimney ˌpot** ; **'chimney ˌstack** ; **'chimney ˌsweep** ; **'chimney ˌsweeper**
chimneypiec|e 'tʃɪm.ni.piːs **-es** -ɪz
chimp tʃɪmp **-s** -s
chimpanzee ˌtʃɪm.pᵊn'ziː, -pæn'- ⓤⓢ tʃɪm'pæn.ziː, ˌtʃɪm.pᵊn'zi **-s** -z
chin tʃɪn **-s** -z ˌ**chin-'deep**

china (C) ˈtʃaɪ.nə ˈ**china** ˌ**clay**, ˌ**china** ˈ**clay**; **like a** ˌ**bull in a** ˈ**china shop**
China|man ˈtʃaɪ.nə|.mən **-men** -mən
Chinatown ˈtʃaɪ.nə.taʊn
chinchilla tʃɪnˈtʃɪl.ə **-s** -z
Chindit ˈtʃɪn.dɪt **-s** -s
chin|e tʃaɪn **-es** -z **-ing** -ɪŋ **-ed** -d
Chinese tʃaɪˈniːz (US) -ˈniːz, -ˈniːs *stress shift, see compounds:* ˌ**Chinese** ˈ**gooseberry**; ˌ**Chinese** ˈ**lantern**; ˌ**Chinese** ˈ**restaurant**
Chingford ˈtʃɪŋ.fəd (US) -fɚd
chink (C) tʃɪŋk **-s** -s
Chinkie, Chinky ˈtʃɪŋ.ki
chinless ˈtʃɪn.ləs, -lɪs ˌ**chinless** ˈ**wonder**
Chinnock ˈtʃɪn.ək
Chinnor ˈtʃɪn.əʳ (US) -ɚ
chino ˈtʃiː.nəʊ (US) -noʊ **-s** -z
Chinook tʃɪˈnʊk, -ˈnuːk (US) ʃəˈnʊk, tʃə-
chinstrap ˈtʃɪn.stræp **-s** -s
chintz tʃɪnts **-es** -ɪz **-y** -i
chinwag ˈtʃɪn.wæg **-s** -s **-ging** -ɪŋ
Chios ˈkaɪ.ɒs, ˈkiː- (US) -ɑːs
chip tʃɪp **-s** -s **-ping** -ɪŋ **-ped** -t ˈ**chip** ˌ**shop**; **have a** ˈ**chip on one's** ˌ**shoulder**
chipboard ˈtʃɪp.bɔːd (US) -bɔːrd
chipmunk ˈtʃɪp.mʌŋk **-s** -s
chipolata ˌtʃɪp.əlˈɑː.tə (US) -əˈlɑː.ţə **-s** -z
Chipp tʃɪp
Chippendale ˈtʃɪp.ən.deɪl **-s** -z
Chippenham ˈtʃɪp.ən.əm
chipper ˈtʃɪp.əʳ (US) -ɚ
Chippewa ˈtʃɪp.ɪ.wɑː, -wə **-s** -z
chippie ˈtʃɪp.i **-s** -z
Chipping ˈtʃɪp.ɪŋ
Chipping Sodbury ˌtʃɪp.ɪŋˈsɒd.bər.i (US) -ˈsɑːd.ber-, -bɚ-
chipp|y ˈtʃɪp|.i **-ier** -i.əʳ (US) -i.ɚ **-iest** -i.ɪst, -i.əst **-iness** -ɪ.nəs, -ɪ.nɪs
Chips tʃɪps
Chirk tʃɜːk (US) tʃɜːrk
chirograph ˈkaɪə.rəʊ.grɑːf, -græf (US) ˈkaɪ.rə.græf **-s** -s
chirographer kaɪəˈrɒg.rə.fəʳ (US) kaɪˈrɑː.grə.fɚ **-s** -z
chirographic ˌkaɪə.rəʊˈgræf.ɪk (US) ˌkaɪ.roʊˈ-
chirographist kaɪəˈrɒg.rə.fɪst (US) kaɪˈrɑː.grə- **-s** -s
chirography kaɪəˈrɒg.rə.fi (US) kaɪˈrɑː.grə-
Chirol ˈtʃɪr.əl
chiromancer ˈkaɪə.rəʊ.mænt.səʳ (US) ˈkaɪ.roʊ.mænt.sɚ **-s** -z
chiromancy ˈkaɪə.rəʊ.mænt.si (US) ˈkaɪ.roʊ-
Chiron ˈkaɪə.rən (US) ˈkaɪ-
chiropodist kɪˈrɒp.ə.dɪst, ʃɪ-, tʃɪ- (US) kɪˈrɑː.pə-, kaɪ-, ʃɪ- **-s** -s
chiropody kɪˈrɒp.ə.di, ʃɪ-, tʃɪ- (US) kɪˈrɑː.pə-, kaɪ-, ʃɪ-
chiropractic ˌkaɪə.rəʊˈpræk.tɪk (US) ˌkaɪ.roʊˈ-, ˈkaɪ.roʊ.præk-
chiropractor ˈkaɪə.rəʊ.præk.təʳ (US) ˈkaɪ.roʊ.præk.tɚ **-s** -z
chirp tʃɜːp (US) tʃɜːrp **-s** -s **-ing** -ɪŋ **-ed** -t
chirp|y ˈtʃɜː.p|i (US) ˈtʃɜːr- **-ier** -i.əʳ (US) -i.ɚ **-iest** -i.ɪst, -i.əst **-ily** -ɪ.li, -əl.i **-iness** -ɪ.nəs, -ɪ.nɪs
chirr tʃɜːʳ (US) tʃɜːr **-s** -z **-ing** -ɪŋ **-ed** -d
chirrup ˈtʃɪr.əp (US) ˈtʃɪr-, ˈtʃɜːr- **-s** -s **-ing** -ɪŋ **-ed** -t
chisel ˈtʃɪz.əl **-s** -z **-(l)ing** -ɪŋ **-(l)ed** -d **-(l)er/s** -əʳ/z (US) -ɚ/z
Chisholm ˈtʃɪz.əm
Chislehurst ˈtʃɪz.l̩.hɜːst (US) -hɜːrst
Chiswick ˈtʃɪz.ɪk
chit tʃɪt **-s** -s
chit-chat, chitchat ˈtʃɪt.tʃæt
chitin ˈkaɪ.tɪn, -tən (US) -tən
Chittagong ˈtʃɪt.ə.gɒŋ (US) ˈtʃɪţ.ə.gɑːŋ, -gɔːŋ
Chittenden ˈtʃɪt.ən.dən
chitterling ˈtʃɪt.əl.ɪŋ (US) ˈtʃɪţ.ɚ.lɪŋ **-s** -z
Chitty ˈtʃɪt.i (US) ˈtʃɪţ-
chivalric ˈʃɪv.əl.rɪk (US) ʃɪˈvæl-; ˈʃɪv.əl-
chivalrous ˈʃɪv.əl.rəs **-ly** -li **-ness** -nəs, -nɪs
chivalry ˈʃɪv.əl.ri
chive tʃaɪv **-s** -z
Chivers ˈtʃɪv.əz (US) -ɚz
chivv|y ˈtʃɪv|.i **-ies** -iz **-ying** -i.ɪŋ **-ied** -id
chiv|y ˈtʃɪv|.i **-ies** -iz **-ying** -i.ɪŋ **-ied** -id
chlamid|ia, chlamyd|ia kləˈmɪd|.i.ə **-iae** -i.i **-ial** -i.əl
chlamy|s ˈklæm.ɪ|s, ˈkleɪ.mɪ|s **-des** -diːz
Chloe, Chloë ˈkləʊ.i (US) ˈkloʊ-
chloral ˈklɔː.rəl (US) ˈklɔːr.əl
chloramine ˈklɔː.rə.miːn; klɔːˈræm.iːn (US) ˈklɔːr.ə.miːn, ˌ--ˈ-; klɔːˈræm.iːn, -ɪn
chlorate ˈklɔː.reɪt, -rɪt (US) ˈklɔːr.eɪt, -ɪt **-s** -s
chloric ˈklɔː.rɪk, ˈklɒr.ɪk (US) ˈklɔːr.ɪk
chloride ˈklɔː.raɪd (US) ˈklɔːr.aɪd **-s** -z
chlori|nate ˈklɔː.rɪ|.neɪt, ˈklɒr.ɪ- (US) ˈklɔːr.ɪ- **-nates** -neɪts **-nating** -neɪ.tɪŋ (US) -neɪ.ţɪŋ **-nated** -neɪ.tɪd (US) -neɪ.ţɪd
chlorine ˈklɔː.riːn (US) ˈklɔːr.iːn, -ɪn
Chloris ˈklɔː.rɪs, ˈklɒr.ɪs (US) ˈklɔːr.ɪs
chlorite ˈklɔː.raɪt (US) ˈklɔːr.aɪt **-s** -s
chloro- ˈklɔː.rəʊ-, ˈklɒr.əʊ- (US) ˈklɔːr.ə-, ˈ-oʊ-
chlorodyne ˈklɔː.rə.daɪn, ˈklɒr.ə- (US) ˈklɔːr.ə-
chlorofluorocarbon ˌklɔː.rəʊˌflɔː.rəʊˈkɑː.bən, ˌklɒr.əʊ-, -ˌflʊə- (US) ˌklɔːr.oʊˌflɔːr.oʊˈkɑːr-, -ˌflʊr- **-s** -z
chloroform ˈklɔː.rə.fɔːm, ˈklɒr.ə- (US) ˈklɔːr.ə.fɔːrm **-s** -z **-ing** -ɪŋ **-ed** -d
Chloromycetin® ˌklɔː.rəʊ.maɪˈsiː.tɪn, ˌklɒr.əʊ- (US) ˌklɔːr.oʊ.maɪˈsiː.tən
chlorophyl(l) ˈklɔː.rə.fɪl, ˈklɒr.ə- (US) ˈklɔːr.ə-
chlorophyllose ˌklɔː.rəˈfɪl.əʊs, ˌklɒr.əˈ- (US) ˌklɔːr.əˈfɪl.oʊs
chloroplast ˈklɒr.ə.plɑːst, -plæst (US) ˈklɔːr.ə.plæst
chlorous ˈklɔː.rəs (US) ˈklɔːr.əs
Choate tʃəʊt (US) tʃoʊt
choc tʃɒk (US) tʃɑːk **-s** -s
choc-ic|e ˈtʃɒk.aɪs (US) ˈtʃɑːk- **-es** -ɪz
chock tʃɒk (US) tʃɑːk **-s** -s ˌ**chock-**ˈ**full**
chock-a-block ˌtʃɒk.əˈblɒk, ˈ--- (US) ˈtʃɑːk.ə.blɑːk
chocoholic, chocaholic ˌtʃɒk.əˈhɒl.ɪk (US) ˌtʃɑː.kəˈhɑː.lɪk **-s** -s
chocolate ˈtʃɒk.əl.ət, -ɪt, ˈ-lət, -lɪt (US) ˈtʃɑːk.lət, ˈtʃɔːk-, ˈtʃɑː.kəl.ət, ˈtʃɔː-, -ɪt **-s** -s ˌ**chocolate** ˈ**cake**, ˈ**chocolate** ˌ**cake**; ˌ**chocolate chip** ˈ**cookie**; ˈ**drinking** ˌ**chocolate**
Choctaw ˈtʃɒk.tɔː (US) ˈtʃɑːk.tɔː, -tɑː
choic|e tʃɔɪs **-es** -ɪz **-er** -əʳ (US) -ɚ **-est** -ɪst, -əst **-ely** -li **-eness** -nəs, -nɪs
choir kwaɪəʳ (US) kwaɪɚ **-s** -z ˈ**choir** ˌ**screen**
choirboy ˈkwaɪə.bɔɪ (US) ˈkwaɪɚ- **-s** -z
choirmaster ˈkwaɪəˌmɑː.stəʳ (US) ˈkwaɪɚˌmæs.tɚ **-s** -z
chok|e tʃəʊk (US) tʃoʊk **-es** -s **-ing** -ɪŋ **-ed** -t
choker ˈtʃəʊ.kəʳ (US) ˈtʃoʊ.kɚ **-s** -z
chok|y ˈtʃəʊ.k|i (US) ˈtʃoʊ- **-ier** -i.əʳ (US) -i.ɚ **-iest** -i.ɪst, -i.əst **-iness** -ɪ.nəs, -ɪ.nɪs
Cholderton ˈtʃəʊl.də.tən (US) ˈtʃoʊl.dɚ.ţən
choler ˈkɒl.əʳ (US) ˈkɑː.lɚ
cholera ˈkɒl.ər.ə (US) ˈkɑː.lɚ-
choleraic ˌkɒl.əˈreɪ.ɪk (US) ˌkɑː.ləˈ-
choleric ˈkɒl.ər.ɪk; kɒlˈer- (US) ˈkɑː.lɚ-; kəˈler-
cholesterol kəˈles.tər.ɒl, kɒlˈes-, -əl (US) kəˈles.tə.rɑːl, -rɔːl, -roʊl
choliamb ˈkəʊ.li.æm*b* (US) ˈkoʊ- **-s** -z
choliambic ˌkəʊ.liˈæm.bɪk (US) ˌkoʊ-
choline ˈkəʊ.liːn (US) ˈkoʊ-, -lɪn
Cholmeley ˈtʃʌm.li
Cholmondeley ˈtʃʌm.li
Cholsey ˈtʃəʊl.zi, ˈtʃɒl.si (US) ˈtʃoʊl-
Chomley ˈtʃʌm.li
chomp tʃɒmp (US) tʃɑːmp **-s** -s **-ing** -ɪŋ **-ed** -t
Chomsky ˈtʃɒm*p*.ski (US) ˈtʃɑːm*p*- **-an** -ən
chon tʃəʊn (US) tʃoʊn
Chongquing ˌtʃʊŋˈtʃɪŋ
choo-choo ˈtʃuː.tʃuː **-s** -z

choos|e tʃuːz **-es** -ɪz **-ing** -ɪŋ **chose** tʃəuz ⓤⓢ tʃouz **chosen** 'tʃəu.zᵊn ⓤⓢ 'tʃou- **chooser/s** 'tʃuː.zəʳ/z ⓤⓢ -zɚ/z

choos|y, choos|ey 'tʃuː.z|i **-ier** -i.əʳ ⓤⓢ -i.ɚ **-iest** -i.ɪst, -i.əst **-iness** -ɪ.nəs, -ɪ.nɪs

chop tʃɒp ⓤⓢ tʃɑːp **-s** -s **-ping** -ɪŋ **-ped** -t **'chopping ˌboard** ; **ˌchop 'suey**

chop-chop ˌtʃɒp'tʃɒp ⓤⓢ ˌtʃɑːp'tʃɑːp

chophou|se 'tʃɒp.hau|s ⓤⓢ 'tʃɑːp- **-ses** -zɪz

Chopin 'ʃɒp.æ̃ŋ, 'ʃəu.pæ̃ŋ, -pæŋ ⓤⓢ 'ʃou.pæn; ʃou'pæ̃n

chopper 'tʃɒp.əʳ ⓤⓢ 'tʃɑː.pɚ **-s** -z

chopp|y 'tʃɒp|.i ⓤⓢ 'tʃɑː.p|i **-ier** -i.əʳ ⓤⓢ -i.ɚ **-iest** -i.ɪst, -i.əst **-ily** -ɪ.li, -ᵊl.i **-iness** -ɪ.nəs, -ɪ.nɪs

chopstick 'tʃɒp.stɪk ⓤⓢ 'tʃɑːp- **-s** -s

chop-suey ˌtʃɒp'suː.i ⓤⓢ ˌtʃɑːp-

choral 'kɔː.rᵊl ⓤⓢ 'kɔːr.ᵊl **-ly** -i

chorale kɒr'ɑːl, kə'rɑːl, kɔː- ⓤⓢ kə'ræl, -'rɑːl **-s** -z

chord kɔːd ⓤⓢ kɔːrd **-s** -z

chordate 'kɔː.deɪt, -dɪt, -dət ⓤⓢ 'kɔːr-

chore tʃɔːʳ ⓤⓢ tʃɔːr **-s** -z

chorea kɒr'ɪə, kɔː'rɪə, kə- ⓤⓢ kə'riː.ə, kɔːr'iː-

choreograph 'kɒr.i.ə.grɑːf, 'kɔː.ri-, -græf ⓤⓢ 'kɔːr.i.ə.græf **-s** -s **-ing** -ɪŋ **-ed** -t

choreographer ˌkɒr.i'ɒg.rə.fəʳ, ˌkɔː.ri- ⓤⓢ ˌkɔːr.i'ɑː.grə.fɚ **-s** -z

choreographic ˌkɒr.i.əʊ'græf.ɪk, ˌkɔː.ri- ⓤⓢ ˌkɔːr.i.ə'-

choreography ˌkɒr.i'ɒg.rə.fi, ˌkɔː.ri- ⓤⓢ ˌkɔːr.i'ɑː.grə-

choriamb 'kɒr.i.æmb, 'kɔː.ri- ⓤⓢ 'kɔːr.i- **-s** -z

choriambic ˌkɒr.i'æm.bɪk, ˌkɔː.ri- ⓤⓢ ˌkɔːr.i'-

choric 'kɒr.ɪk ⓤⓢ 'kɔːr-

chorion 'kɔː.ri.ən, -ɒn ⓤⓢ 'kɔːr.i.ɑːn **-s** -z

chorionic ˌkɔː.ri'ɒn.ɪk ⓤⓢ ˌkɔːr.i'ɑː.nɪk

chorister 'kɒr.ɪ.stəʳ ⓤⓢ 'kɔːr.ɪ.stɚ **-s** -z

chorizo tʃə'riː.zəu, tʃɒr'iː- ⓤⓢ tʃə'riː.zou, tʃou-, -sou **-s** -z

Chorley 'tʃɔː.li ⓤⓢ 'tʃɔːr-

Chorleywood ˌtʃɔː.li'wud ⓤⓢ ˌtʃɔːr-

choroid 'kɔː.rɔɪd ⓤⓢ 'kɔːr.ɔɪd

chortl|e 'tʃɔː.tḷ ⓤⓢ 'tʃɔːr.ţḷ **-es** -z **-ing** -ɪŋ, 'tʃɔːt.lɪŋ ⓤⓢ 'tʃɔːr.ţḷ.ɪŋ, 'tʃɔːrt.lɪŋ **-ed** -d

chorus 'kɔː.rəs ⓤⓢ 'kɔːr.əs **-es** -ɪz **-ing** -ɪŋ **-ed** -t

chose *legal term:* ʃəuz ⓤⓢ ʃouz

chose (*from* **choose**) tʃəuz ⓤⓢ tʃouz

Chosen *Japanese name for Korea:* ˌtʃəu'sen ⓤⓢ ˌtʃou-

chosen (*from* **choose**) 'tʃəu.zᵊn ⓤⓢ 'tʃou-

Chou En-lai ˌtʃəu.en'laɪ, ˌdʒəu- ⓤⓢ ˌdʒou-

chough tʃʌf **-s** -s

choux ʃuː **ˌchoux 'pastry**

chow tʃau **-s** -z

chow-chow ˌtʃau'tʃau, '-- **-s** -z

chowder 'tʃau.dəʳ ⓤⓢ -dɚ **-s** -z

Chowles tʃəulz ⓤⓢ tʃoulz

chow mein ˌtʃau'meɪn

chrestomath|y kres'tɒm.ə.θ|i ⓤⓢ -'tɑː.mə- **-ies** -iz

Chrétien de Troyes kreɪˌtjæ̃n.də'trwɑː

Chris krɪs **-'s** -ɪz

chrism 'krɪz.ᵊm

chrisom 'krɪz.ᵊm **-s** -z

Chrissie 'krɪs.i

Christ kraɪst **-s** -s

Christa 'krɪs.tə

Christabel 'krɪs.tə.bel, -bᵊl

Christadelphian ˌkrɪs.tə'del.fi.ən **-s** -z

Christchurch 'kraɪst.tʃɜːtʃ ⓤⓢ -tʃɜːrtʃ

Christdom 'kraɪst.dəm

christen 'krɪs.ᵊn **-s** -z **-ing** -ɪŋ **-ed** -d

Christendom 'krɪs.ᵊn.dəm

christening 'krɪs.ᵊn.ɪŋ **-s** -z

Christensen 'krɪs.tᵊn.sᵊn

Christi (*in* **Corpus Christi**) 'krɪs.ti

Christian 'krɪs.tʃən, 'krɪʃ-; 'krɪs.ti.ən ⓤⓢ 'krɪs.tʃən, -ti.ən **-s** -z **'Christian ˌname** ; **ˌChristian 'Science** ; **ˌChristian 'Scientist**

Christiana ˌkrɪs.ti'ɑː.nə ⓤⓢ -ti'æn.ə, -tʃi'-, -'ɑː.nə

Christiania ˌkrɪs.ti'ɑː.ni.ə ⓤⓢ -ti'æn.i-, -tʃi'-, -'ɑː.ni-

Christianism 'krɪs.tʃᵊn.ɪ.zᵊm, 'krɪʃ-; 'krɪs.ti.ə.nɪ- ⓤⓢ 'krɪs.tʃᵊn.ɪ-, -ti.ə.nɪ-

Christianity ˌkrɪs.ti'æn.ə.ti, -'tʃæn-, -ɪ.ti ⓤⓢ -tʃi'æn.ə.ţi, -ti'-

christianiz|e, -is|e (C) 'krɪs.tʃə.naɪz, 'krɪʃ-; 'krɪs.ti.ə- ⓤⓢ 'krɪs.tʃə- **-es** -ɪz **-ing** -ɪŋ **-ed** -d

christianly (C) 'krɪs.tʃən.li, 'krɪʃ-; 'krɪs.ti.ən- ⓤⓢ 'krɪs.tʃən-

Christie 'krɪs.ti **-'s** -z

Christina krɪ'stiː.nə

Christine 'krɪs.tiːn, krɪ'stiːn

Christlike 'kraɪst.laɪk **-ness** -nəs, -nɪs

Christmas 'krɪst.məs ⓤⓢ 'krɪs- **-es** -ɪz **'Christmas ˌbox** ; **'Christmas ˌcake** ; **'Christmas ˌcard** ; **ˌChristmas 'Day** ; **ˌChristmas 'Eve** ; **'Christmas ˌpresent** ; **ˌChristmas 'pudding** ; **'Christmas ˌtree**

Christmassy 'krɪst.mə.si ⓤⓢ 'krɪs-

Christmastide 'krɪst.məs.taɪd ⓤⓢ 'krɪs-

Christminster 'kraɪstˌmɪnt.stəʳ, 'krɪst- ⓤⓢ -stɚ

Christobel 'krɪs.tə.bel

Christophe krɪ'stɒf; 'krɪs.tɒf ⓤⓢ kriː'stɑːf, krɪ-, -'stɔːf

christophene 'krɪs.tə.fiːn **-s** -z

Christopher 'krɪs.tə.fəʳ ⓤⓢ -fɚ

Christopherson krɪ'stɒf.ə.sᵊn ⓤⓢ -'stɑː.fɚ-

Christy 'krɪs.ti

chroma 'krəu.mə ⓤⓢ 'krou-

chromate 'krəu.meɪt, -mɪt ⓤⓢ 'krou- **-s** -s

chromatic krəʊ'mæt.ɪk ⓤⓢ krou'mæţ-, krə- **-ally** -ᵊl.i, -li

chromaticity ˌkrəu.mə'tɪs.ə.ti, -ɪ.ti ⓤⓢ ˌkrou.mə'tɪs.ə.ţi

chromatin 'krəu.mə.tɪn ⓤⓢ 'krou-

chromatogram 'krəu.mə.tə.græm, krəu'mæt.ə- ⓤⓢ krou'mæţ- **-s** -z

chromatographic ˌkrəu.mə.tə'græf.ɪk, krəuˌmæt.ə'- ⓤⓢ krouˌmæţ-

chromatography ˌkrəu.mə'tɒg.rə.fi ⓤⓢ ˌkrou.mə'tɑː.grə-

chrome krəum ⓤⓢ kroum

chrom|ic 'krəu.m|ɪk ⓤⓢ 'krou- **-ous** -əs

chromite 'krəu.maɪt ⓤⓢ 'krou- **-s** -s

chromium 'krəu.mi.əm ⓤⓢ 'krou-

chromolithograph ˌkrəu.məʊ'lɪθ.əʊ.grɑːf, -græf ⓤⓢ ˌkrou.mou'lɪθ.ə.græf **-s** -s

chromolithography ˌkrəu.məu.lɪ'θɒg.rə.fi ⓤⓢ ˌkrou.mou.lɪ'θɑː.grə-

chromosomal ˌkrəu.mə'səu.mᵊl ⓤⓢ ˌkrou.mə'sou-

chromosome 'krəu.mə.səum ⓤⓢ 'krou.mə.soum **-s** -z

chromosphere 'krəu.mə.sfɪəʳ ⓤⓢ 'krou.mə.sfɪr **-s** -z

chromotype 'krəu.məʊ.taɪp ⓤⓢ 'krou.mou-

chronic 'krɒn.ɪk ⓤⓢ 'krɑː.nɪk **-al** -ᵊl **-ally** -ᵊl.i, -li

chronicl|e 'krɒn.ɪ.kḷ ⓤⓢ 'krɑː.nɪ- **-es** -z **-ing** -ɪŋ, -klɪŋ **-ed** -d **-er/s** -kləʳ/z ⓤⓢ -klɚ/z

Chronicles 'krɒn.ɪ.kḷz ⓤⓢ 'krɑː.nɪ-

chrono- 'krɒn.əʊ-, 'krəu.nəʊ-, krə'nɒ- ⓤⓢ 'krɑː.nou-, 'krou.nou-, '-nə-, krə'nɑː-

Note: Prefix. This may take primary or secondary stress on the first syllable (e.g. **chronograph** /'krɒn.əʊ.grɑːf ⓤⓢ 'krɑː.nə.græf/) or primary stress on the second syllable (e.g. **chronometer** /krə'nɒm.ɪ.təʳ ⓤⓢ krə'nɑː.mə.ţɚ/.

chronogram 'krɒn.ə.græm, 'krəu.nə- ⓤⓢ 'krɑː.nə-, 'krou- **-s** -z

chronograph 'krɒn.ə.grɑːf, 'krəu.nə-, -græf ⓤⓢ 'krɑː.nə.græf, 'krou- **-s** -s

chronologic ˌkrɒn.ə'lɒdʒ.ɪk ⓤⓢ ˌkrɑː.nə'lɑː.dʒɪk **-al** -ᵊl **-ally** -ᵊl.i, -li

chronolog|y krɒn'ɒl.ə.dʒ|i, krə'nɒl- ⓤⓢ krə'nɑː.lə-, krɑː- **-ies** -iz **-ist/s** -ɪst/s
chronometer krɒn'ɒm.ɪ.təʳ, krə'nɒm-, -ə.təʳ ⓤⓢ krə'nɑː.mə.t̬ɚ, krɑː- **-s** -z
chronometric ˌkrɒn.ə'met.rɪk ⓤⓢ ˌkrɑː.nə'- **-al** -ᵊl **-ally** -ᵊl.i
chronometry krɒn'ɒm.ɪ.tri, krə'nɒm-, -ə.tri ⓤⓢ krə'nɑː.mə-, krɑː-
chrysalid 'krɪs.ᵊl.ɪd **-s** -z
chrysalides krɪ'sæl.ɪ.diːz, krə-, '-ə-
chrysalis 'krɪs.ᵊl.ɪs **-es** -ɪz
chrysanth krɪ'sænʈθ, krə-, -'zænʈθ **-s** -s
chrysanthemum krɪ'sænʈθ.ə.məm, krə-, -'zænʈθ-, '-ɪ- **-s** -z
chryselephantine ˌkrɪs.el.ɪ'fæn.taɪn, -ə'- ⓤⓢ -taɪn, -tiːn, -tɪn
Chrysler® 'kraɪz.ləʳ ⓤⓢ 'kraɪs.lɚ **-s** -z
chrysolite 'krɪs.əʊ.laɪt ⓤⓢ '-ə- **-s** -s
chrysopras|e 'krɪs.əʊ.preɪz ⓤⓢ '-ə- **-es** -ɪz
Chrysostom 'krɪs.ə.stəm ⓤⓢ 'krɪs.ə.stəm, krɪ'sɑː-
Chryston 'kraɪ.stən
chthonian 'θəʊ.ni.ən, 'kθəʊ- ⓤⓢ 'θoʊ-
chthonic 'θɒn.ɪk, 'kθɒn- ⓤⓢ 'θɑː.nɪk
chub tʃʌb **-s** -z
Chubb tʃʌb
chubb|y 'tʃʌb|.i **-ier** -i.əʳ ⓤⓢ -i.ɚ **-iest** -i.ɪst, -i.əst **-ily** -ɪ.li, -ᵊl.i **-iness** -ɪ.nəs, -ɪ.nɪs
Chuchulain(n) kuː'kʌl.ɪn
chuck (C) tʃʌk **-s** -s **-ing** -ɪŋ **-ed** -t 'chuck ˌwagon
chuckl|e 'tʃʌk.l̩ **-es** -z **-ing** -ɪŋ, '-lɪŋ **-ed** -d
Chudleigh 'tʃʌd.li
chuff tʃʌf **-s** -s **-ing** -ɪŋ **-ed** -t
Chuffey 'tʃʌf.i
chug tʃʌg **-s** -z **-ging** -ɪŋ **-ged** -d
chugalug 'tʃʌg.ə.lʌg **-s** -z **-ging** -ɪŋ **-ged** -d
chukka 'tʃʌk.ə **-s** -z
chukker 'tʃʌk.əʳ ⓤⓢ -ɚ **-s** -z
chum tʃʌm **-s** -z **-ming** -ɪŋ **-med** -d
Chumbi 'tʃʊm.bi
chumm|y 'tʃʌm|.i **-ier** -i.əʳ ⓤⓢ -i.ɚ **-iest** -i.ɪst, -i.əst **-ily** -ɪ.li, -ᵊl.i **-iness** -ɪ.nəs, -ɪ.nɪs
chump tʃʌmp **-s** -s
chund|er 'tʃʌn.d|əʳ ⓤⓢ -d|ɚ **-ers** -əz ⓤⓢ -ɚz **-ering** -ᵊr.ɪŋ **-ered** -əd ⓤⓢ -ɚd
Chungking ˌtʃʊŋ'kɪŋ, ˌtʃʌŋ- ⓤⓢ ˌtʃʊŋ'kɪŋ, ˌtʃʌŋ-, ˌdʒʊŋ-, ˌdʒʌŋ-, -'gɪŋ *stress shift:* ˌChungking 'Mansions
chunk tʃʌŋk **-s** -s
chunk|y 'tʃʌŋ.k|i **-ier** -i.əʳ ⓤⓢ -i.ɚ **-iest** -i.ɪst, -i.əst **-ily** -ɪ.li, -ᵊl.i **-iness** -ɪ.nəs, -ɪ.nɪs
Chunnel 'tʃʌn.ᵊl
chunt|er 'tʃʌn.t|əʳ ⓤⓢ -t̬|ɚ **-ers** -əz ⓤⓢ -ɚz **-ering** -ᵊr.ɪŋ **-ered** -əd ⓤⓢ -ɚd
church (C) tʃɜːtʃ ⓤⓢ tʃɜːrtʃ **-es** -ɪz ˌChurch of 'England
Churchdown 'tʃɜːtʃ.daʊn ⓤⓢ 'tʃɜːrtʃ-
Note: There was until recently a local pronunciation /'tʃəʊ.zᵊn/, which is preserved as the name of a hill near by, which is now written **Chosen**.
churchgo|er 'tʃɜːtʃˌgəʊ|.əʳ ⓤⓢ 'tʃɜːrtʃˌgoʊ|.ɚ **-ers** -əz ⓤⓢ -ɚz **-ing** -ɪŋ
Churchill 'tʃɜː.tʃɪl ⓤⓢ 'tʃɜːr-
Churchillian tʃɜː'tʃɪl.i.ən ⓤⓢ tʃɜːr-
church|man (C) 'tʃɜːtʃ|.mən ⓤⓢ 'tʃɜːrtʃ- **-men** -mən
churchwarden ˌtʃɜːtʃ'wɔː.dᵊn ⓤⓢ ˌtʃɜːrtʃ'wɔːr- **-s** -z *stress shift:* ˌchurchwarden 'pipe
church|y 'tʃɜː.tʃ|i ⓤⓢ 'tʃɜːr- **-ier** -i.əʳ ⓤⓢ -i.ɚ **-iest** -i.ɪst, -i.əst **-ily** -ɪ.li, -ᵊl.i **-iness** -ɪ.nəs, -ɪ.nɪs
churchyard *outside church:* 'tʃɜːtʃ.jɑːd ⓤⓢ 'tʃɜːrtʃ.jɑːrd **-s** -z
Churchyard *surname:* 'tʃɜː.tʃəd ⓤⓢ 'tʃɜːr.tʃɚd
churl tʃɜːl ⓤⓢ tʃɜːrl **-s** -z
churlish 'tʃɜː.lɪʃ ⓤⓢ 'tʃɜːr- **-ly** -li **-ness** -nəs, -nɪs
churn tʃɜːn ⓤⓢ tʃɜːrn **-s** -z **-ing** -ɪŋ **-ed** -d
chute ʃuːt **-s** -s
Chute tʃuːt
Chuter 'tʃuː.təʳ ⓤⓢ -t̬ɚ
chutney 'tʃʌt.ni **-s** -z
chutzpa(h) 'hʊt.spɑː, 'xʊt-, -spə
Chuzzlewit 'tʃʌz.l̩.wɪt
chyle kaɪl
chyme kaɪm
CIA ˌsiː.aɪ'eɪ
ciabatta tʃə'bæt.ə, -'bɑː.tə
Cian 'kiː.ən
ciao tʃaʊ
Ciara 'kɪə.rə ⓤⓢ 'kɪr.ə
Ciaran 'kɪə.rᵊn ⓤⓢ 'kɪr.ᵊn
Ciba-Geigy® ˌsiː.bə'gaɪ.gi
Cibber 'sɪb.əʳ ⓤⓢ -ɚ
cibori|um sɪ'bɔː.ri|.əm, sə- ⓤⓢ -'bɔːr.i- **-ums** -əmz **-a** -ə
cicada sɪ'kɑː.də, -'keɪ- ⓤⓢ -'keɪ-, -'kɑː- **-s** -z
cicala sɪ'kɑː.lə **-s** -z
cicatric|e 'sɪk.ə.trɪs **-es** -ɪz
cicatrix 'sɪk.ə.trɪks; sə'keɪ-, sɪ- **cicatrices** ˌsɪk.ə'traɪ.siːz; sə'keɪ.trɪ-, sɪ-
cicatriz|e, -is|e 'sɪk.ə.traɪz **-es** -ɪz **-ing** -ɪŋ **-ed** -d
cicel|y (C) 'sɪs.ᵊl|.i, -ɪ.l|i **-ies** -iz
Cicero 'sɪs.ᵊr.əʊ ⓤⓢ -ə.roʊ
cicerone ˌtʃɪtʃ.ə'rəʊ.ni, ˌsɪs.ə'-, ˌtʃiː.tʃə'- ⓤⓢ ˌsɪs.ə'roʊ- **-s** -z
Ciceronian ˌsɪs.ᵊr'əʊ.ni.ən ⓤⓢ -ə'roʊ- **-s** -z
cicisbe|o ˌtʃɪtʃ.ɪz'beɪ|.əʊ ⓤⓢ sɪ'sɪs.biː|.oʊ **-i** -iː
Cid sɪd
CID ˌsiː.aɪ'diː
-cidal -'saɪ.dᵊl
-cide -saɪd
cider 'saɪ.dəʳ ⓤⓢ -dɚ **-s** -z 'cider-ˌcup
cig sɪg **-s** -z
cigar sɪ'gɑːʳ, sə- ⓤⓢ -gɑːr **-s** -z ci'gar-ˌshaped
cigarette ˌsɪg.ᵊr'et, '--- ⓤⓢ ˌsɪg.ə'ret **-s** -s ciga'rette ˌholder ⓤⓢ 'cigarette ˌholder ; ciga'rette ˌlighter ⓤⓢ 'cigarette ˌlighter
cigarillo ˌsɪg.ə'rɪl.əʊ ⓤⓢ -oʊ **-s** -z
cigg|y 'sɪg|.i **-ies** -iz
cilia 'sɪl.i.ə
ciliary 'sɪl.i.ᵊr.i ⓤⓢ -er-
cilic|e 'sɪl.ɪs **-es** -ɪz
Cilicia saɪ'lɪʃ.i.ə, sɪ-, -'lɪs- ⓤⓢ sə'lɪʃ.ə
cilium 'sɪl.i.əm
Cilla 'sɪl.ə
Ciller 'sɪl.əʳ ⓤⓢ -ɚ
Cimabue ˌtʃɪm.ə'buː.eɪ, ˌtʃiː.mə'-, -i
Cimmeri|an sɪ'mɪə.ri|.ən ⓤⓢ -'mɪr.i- **-i** -aɪ
C-in-C ˌsiː.ɪn'siː **-s** -z
cinch sɪntʃ **-es** -ɪz
cinchona sɪŋ'kəʊ.nə ⓤⓢ -'koʊ-, sɪn- **-s** -z
cinchonic sɪŋ'kɒn.ɪk ⓤⓢ -'kɑː.nɪk, sɪn-
Cincinnati ˌsɪnʈ.sɪ'næt.i, -sə'- ⓤⓢ -'næt̬-
Cincinnatus ˌsɪnʈ.sɪ'nɑː.təs, -'neɪ- ⓤⓢ -'næt̬.əs-, -'nɑː.t̬əs, -'neɪ-
cincture 'sɪŋk.tʃəʳ ⓤⓢ -tʃɚ **-s** -z
cinder 'sɪn.dəʳ ⓤⓢ -dɚ **-s** -z 'cinder ˌblock ; 'cinder ˌpath ; 'cinder ˌtrack
Cinderella ˌsɪn.dᵊr'el.ə
Cinderford 'sɪn.də.fəd ⓤⓢ -dɚ.fɚd
Cindy 'sɪn.di
cine- 'sɪn.i-
cinecamera 'sɪn.iˌkæm.ᵊr.ə, -ˌkæm.rə, ˌsɪn.i'kæm- **-s** -z
cinefilm 'sɪn.i.fɪlm **-s** -z
cinema 'sɪn.ə.mə, '-ɪ-, -mɑː ⓤⓢ -mə **-s** -z
cinemago|er 'sɪn.ə.məˌgəʊ|.əʳ, '-ɪ- ⓤⓢ -goʊ|.ɚ **-ers** -əz ⓤⓢ -ɚz **-ing** -ɪŋ
CinemaScope® 'sɪn.ə.mə.skəʊp, '-ɪ- ⓤⓢ -skoʊp **-s** -s
cinematic ˌsɪn.ɪ'mæt.ɪk, -ə'- ⓤⓢ -ə'mæt̬- **-ally** -ᵊl.i, -li
cinematograph ˌsɪn.ɪ'mæt.ə.grɑːf, -ə'-, -græf ⓤⓢ -ə'mæt̬.ə.græf **-s** -s
cinematographic ˌsɪn.ɪ.mæt.ə'græf.ɪk, ˌ-ə-; sɪ.nɪˌmæt- ⓤⓢ ˌsɪn.əˌmæt̬- **-al** -ᵊl **-ally** -ᵊl.i, -li
cinematograph|y ˌsɪn.ɪ.mə'tɒg.rə.f|i, ˌ-ə- ⓤⓢ -ə.mə'tɑː.grə- **-er/s** -əʳ/z ⓤⓢ -ɚ/z

cinema verité ˌsɪn.ɪ.mɑː'ver.ɪ.teɪ, ˌ-ə-, -ə.mə'- US ˌsɪn.ɪ.mɑː.ver.ə'teɪ, -mə'ver.ə.teɪ
cine-projector 'sɪn.i.prəˌdʒek.təʳ US -tɚ **-s** -z
Cinerama® ˌsɪn.ə'rɑː.mə, -ɪ'- US -ə'rɑː-, -'ræm.ə
cineraria ˌsɪn.ə'reə.ri.ə US -'rer.i- **-s** -z
cinerari|um ˌsɪn.ə'reə.ri|.əm US -'rer.i- **-a** -ə
cinerary 'sɪn.ə.rᵊr.i US -rer-
cineration ˌsɪn.ə'reɪ.ʃᵊn
cinnabar 'sɪn.ə.bɑːʳ US -bɑːr
cinnamon 'sɪn.ə.mən
cinque (C) sɪŋk **'Cinque ˌPorts**
Cinquecento® ˌtʃɪŋ.kweɪ'tʃen.təʊ, -kwɪ'- US -toʊ
cinquefoil 'sɪŋk.fɔɪl
Cinzano® tʃɪn'zɑː.nəʊ, sɪn-, tʃɪnt'sɑː-, sɪnt'sɑː- US -noʊ
ciph|er 'saɪ.f|əʳ US -f|ɚ **-ers** -əz US -ɚz **-ering** -ᵊr.ɪŋ **-ered** -əd US -ɚd **'cipher ˌkey**
Cipriani ˌsɪp.ri'ɑː.ni
circa 'sɜː.kə US 'sɜːr-
circadian sɜː'keɪ.di.ən, sə- US sɚ-; ˌsɜːr.kə'diː.ən
Circassi|a sɜː'kæs.i|.ə, sə-, -'kæʃ|.ə, -i|.ə US sɚ- **-an/s** -ən/z
Circe 'sɜː.si US 'sɜːr-
circl|e 'sɜː.kḷ US 'sɜːr- **-es** -z **-ing** -ɪŋ, '-klɪŋ US '-kḷ.ɪŋ, '-klɪŋ **-ed** -d
circlet 'sɜː.klət, -klɪt US 'sɜːr- **-s** -s
circuit 'sɜː.kɪt US 'sɜːr- **-s** -s **-ry** -ri **'circuit ˌbreaker** ; **'circuit ˌtraining**
circuitous sə'kjuː.ɪ.təs, sɜː-, '-ə- US sɚ'kjuː.ə.t̬əs **-ly** -li **-ness** -nəs, -nɪs
circular 'sɜː.kjə.ləʳ, -kjʊ- US 'sɜːr.kjə.lɚ **-s** -z **'circular ˌsaw, ˌcircular 'saw**
circularity ˌsɜː.kjə'lær.ə.ti, -kjʊ'-, -ɪ.ti US -kjə'ler.ə.t̬i, -'lær-
circulariz|e, -is|e 'sɜː.kjə.lᵊr.aɪz, -kjʊ- US 'sɜːr.kjə.lə.raɪz **-es** -ɪz **-ing** -ɪŋ **-ed** -d
circu|late 'sɜː.kjə|.leɪt, -kjʊ- US 'sɜːr.kjə- **-lates** -leɪts **-lating** -leɪ.tɪŋ US -leɪ.t̬ɪŋ **-lated** -leɪ.tɪd US -leɪ.t̬ɪd **-lator/s** -leɪ.təʳ/z US -leɪ.t̬ɚ/z
circulation ˌsɜː.kjə'leɪ.ʃᵊn, -kjʊ'- US ˌsɜːr- **-s** -z
circulatory ˌsɜː.kjə'leɪ.tᵊr.i, -kjʊ'-, -tri; 'sɜː.kjə.lə-, -kjʊ- US 'sɜːr.kjə.lə.tɔːr.i
circum- 'sɜː.kəm-, sə'kʌm- US 'sɜːr.kəm-, sɚ'kʌm-
Note: Prefix. This may have primary or secondary stress on the first syllable, e.g. **circumstance** /'sɜː.kəm.stɑːnts US 'sɜːr.kəm.stæns/ or on the second syllable, e.g. **circumference** /sə'kʌmp.fᵊr.ᵊnts US sɚ-/.
circumambient ˌsɜː.kəm'æm.bi.ənt US ˌsɜːr-
circumambu|late ˌsɜː.kəm'æm.bjə|.leɪt, -bjʊ- US ˌsɜːr.kəm'æm.bjə- **-lates** -leɪts **-lating** -leɪ.tɪŋ US -leɪ.t̬ɪŋ **-lated** -leɪ.tɪd US -leɪ.t̬ɪd
circumcis|e 'sɜː.kəm.saɪz US 'sɜːr- **-es** -ɪz **-ing** -ɪŋ **-ed** -d
circumcision ˌsɜː.kəm'sɪʒ.ᵊn US ˌsɜːr- **-s** -z
circumferenc|e sə'kʌmp.fᵊr.ᵊnts US sɚ- **-es** -ɪz
circumferential səˌkʌmp.fᵊ'ren.tʃᵊl US sɚˌkʌmp.fɚ'rent.ʃᵊl
circumflex 'sɜː.kəm.fleks US 'sɜːr- **-es** -ɪz
circumlocution ˌsɜː.kəm.lə'kjuː.ʃᵊn US ˌsɜːr- **-s** -z
circumlocutory ˌsɜː.kəm.lə'kjuː.tᵊr.i, -tri; -'lɒk.jʊ- US ˌsɜːr.kəm'lɑː.kjuː.tɔːr.i
circumnavi|gate ˌsɜː.kəm'næv.ɪ|.geɪt US ˌsɜːr- **-gates** -geɪts **-gating** -geɪ.tɪŋ US -geɪ.t̬ɪŋ **-gated** -geɪ.tɪd US -geɪ.t̬ɪd **-gator/s** -geɪ.təʳ/z US -geɪ.t̬ɚ/z
circumnavigation ˌsɜː.kəmˌnæv.ɪ'geɪ.ʃᵊn US ˌsɜːr- **-s** -z
circumpolar ˌsɜː.kəm'pəʊ.ləʳ US ˌsɜːr.kəm'poʊ.lɚ
circumscrib|e 'sɜː.kəm.skraɪb, ˌ--'- US 'sɜːr-, ˌ--'- **-es** -z **-ing** -ɪŋ **-ed** -d
circumscription ˌsɜː.kəm'skrɪp.ʃᵊn US ˌsɜːr- **-s** -z
circumspect 'sɜː.kəm.spekt US 'sɜːr- **-ly** -li **-ness** -nəs, -nɪs
circumspection ˌsɜː.kəm'spek.ʃᵊn US ˌsɜːr-
circumstanc|e 'sɜː.kəm.stænts, -stənts, -stɑːnts US 'sɜːr.kəm.stænts, -stənts **-es** -ɪz **-ed** -t
circumstantial ˌsɜː.kəm'stæn.tʃᵊl US ˌsɜːr.kəm'stænt.ʃᵊl- **-ly** -i **ˌcircumstantial 'evidence**
circumstantiality ˌsɜː.kəmˌstæn.tʃi'æl.ə.ti, -ɪ.ti US ˌsɜːr.kəmˌstænt.ʃi'æl.ə.t̬i
circumstanti|ate ˌsɜː.kəm'stæn.tʃi|.eɪt US ˌsɜːr.kəm'stænt.ʃi-- **-ates** -eɪts **-ating** -eɪ.tɪŋ US -eɪ.t̬ɪŋ **-ated** -eɪ.tɪd US -eɪ.t̬ɪd
circumvallation ˌsɜː.kəm.və'leɪ.ʃᵊn, -væl'eɪ- US ˌsɜːr- **-s** -z
circum|vent ˌsɜː.kəm|'vent, '--|- US ˌsɜːr- **-vents** -'vents **-venting** -'ven.tɪŋ US -'ven.t̬ɪŋ **-vented** -'ven.tɪd US -'ven.t̬ɪd
circumvention ˌsɜː.kəm'ven.tʃᵊn US ˌsɜːr.kəm'vent.ʃᵊn **-s** -z
circus (C) 'sɜː.kəs US 'sɜːr- **-es** -ɪz
Cirencester 'saɪə.rᵊn.ses.təʳ, 'sɪs.ɪ.təʳ, -stəʳ US 'saɪ.rᵊn.ses.tɚ
Note: The pronunciation most usually heard in the town is /'saɪə.rᵊn.ses.təʳ/ (or /-tər/ with the dialectal retroflex /r/).
cirque sɜːk, sɪək US sɜːrk **-s** -s
cirrhosis sɪ'rəʊ.sɪs, sə- US sə'roʊ-
cirrocumulus ˌsɪr.əʊ'kjuː.mjə.ləs, -mjʊ- US -oʊ'kjuː.mjə-
cirrostratus ˌsɪr.əʊ'strɑː.təs, -'streɪ- US -oʊ'streɪ.t̬əs, -'stræt̬.əs
cirrus 'sɪr.əs
CIS ˌsiː.aɪ'es
Cisalpine sɪ'sæl.paɪn
Ciskei sɪ'skaɪ, 'sɪs.kaɪ US 'sɪs.kaɪ
Cissie 'sɪs.i
cissoid 'sɪs.ɔɪd **-s** -z
cissy (C) 'sɪs.i
cist sɪst **-s** -s
Cistercian sɪ'stɜː.ʃᵊn, sə- US -'stɜːr- **-s** -z
cistern 'sɪs.tən US -tɚn **-s** -z
cistus 'sɪs.təs **-es** -ɪz
citadel 'sɪt.ə.dᵊl, -del US 'sɪt̬- **-s** -z
citation saɪ'teɪ.ʃᵊn **-s** -z
citatory 'saɪ.tə.tᵊr.i, 'sɪ-, -tri; saɪ'teɪ- US 'saɪ.t̬ə.tɔːr.i
cit|e saɪt **-es** -s **-ing** -ɪŋ US 'saɪ.t̬ɪŋ **-ed** -ɪd US 'saɪ.t̬ɪd
cithar|a 'sɪθ.ᵊr|.ə **-ae** -iː
cither 'sɪθ.əʳ US -ɚ, 'sɪð- **-s** -z
Citibank® 'sɪt.i.bæŋk US 'sɪt̬-
citizen 'sɪt.ɪ.zᵊn, '-ə- US 'sɪt̬- **-s** -z **ˌcitizen's ar'rest**
citizenry 'sɪt.ɪ.zᵊn.ri, '-ə- US 'sɪt̬-
citizenship 'sɪt.ɪ.zᵊn.ʃɪp, '-ə- US 'sɪt̬-
citole 'sɪt.əʊl, sɪ'təʊl US 'sɪt.oʊl, sɪ'toʊl **-s** -z
citrate 'sɪt.reɪt, 'saɪ.treɪt, -trɪt **-s** -s
citric 'sɪt.rɪk **ˌcitric 'acid**
citrine sɪ'triːn, sə-
Citroën® 'sɪt.rəʊən, 'sɪt.rᵊn US ˌsɪt.roʊ'en, ˌsiː.troʊ'- **-s** -z
citron 'sɪt.rᵊn **-s** -z
citronella ˌsɪt.rᵊn'el.ə US -rə'nel-
citrous 'sɪt.rəs
citrus 'sɪt.rəs **-es** -ɪz **'citrus ˌfruit**
cittern 'sɪt.ɜːn, -ən US 'sɪt̬.ɚn **-s** -z
cit|y (C) 'sɪt|.i US 'sɪt̬|.i **-ies** -iz **ˌcity 'father** ; **ˌcity 'gent** ; **ˌcity 'hall** ; **ˌcity 'slicker** US **'city ˌslicker**
city-dweller 'sɪt.iˌdwel.əʳ US 'sɪt̬.iˌdwel.ɚ **-s** -z
Ciudad Bolívar θjʊˌdɑːd.bɒl'iː.vɑːʳ, θiː.ʊˌdɑːd- US sjuːˌdɑːd.boʊ'liː.vɑːr, ˌsiː.uː-
Ciudad Guayana θjʊˌdɑːd.gwaɪ'jɑː.nə, θiː.ʊˌdɑːd-

(US) sjuːˌdɑːd.ɡə'-, ˌsiː.uː-, -ɡwə'-, -ɡwɑː'-
Ciudad Juárez θjʊˌdɑːd'hwɑː.rez, θiː.ʊ-, -'wɑː- (US) sjuːˌdɑːd'hwɑːr.es, ˌsiː.uː-, -'wɑːr.eʒ
civet 'sɪv.ɪt **-s** -s
civic 'sɪv.ɪk **-s** -s **ˌcivic 'centre** (US) **'civic ˌcenter**
civil 'sɪv.ᵊl, -ɪl **-ly** -i **ˌcivil de'fence** ; **ˌcivil diso'bedience** ; **ˌcivil engi'neer** ; **ˌcivil engi'neering** ; **ˌcivil 'liberty** ; **ˌcivil 'rights ˌmovement** ; **ˌcivil 'servant** ; **ˌcivil 'service** ; **ˌcivil 'war**
civilian sɪ'vɪl.i.ən, sə- (US) '-jən **-s** -z
civilit|y sɪ'vɪl.ə.t|i, sə-, -ɪ.t|i (US) -ə.ţ|i **-ies** -iz
civilizable, -isa- 'sɪv.ɪ.laɪ.zə.bl̩, '-ə-
civilization, -isa- ˌsɪv.ᵊl.aɪ'zeɪ.ʃᵊn, -ɪ.laɪ'-, -lɪ'- (US) -ᵊl.ɪ'- **-s** -z
civiliz|e, -is|e 'sɪv.ᵊl.aɪz, -ɪ.laɪz (US) -ə.laɪz, '-ɪ- **-es** -ɪz **-ing** -ɪŋ **-ed** -d
civitas 'sɪv.ɪ.tæs, 'kɪv-
civv|y 'sɪv|.i **-ies** -iz **'civvy ˌstreet**
CJD ˌsiː.dʒeɪ'diː
cl (*abbrev. for* **centilitre/s**) *singular:* 'sen.tɪˌliː.təʳ (US) -ţəˌliː.ţɚ *plural:* -z
clack klæk **-s** -s **-ing** -ɪŋ **-ed** -t
Clackmannan klæk'mæn.ən **-shire** -ʃəʳ, -ˌʃɪəʳ (US) -ʃɚ, -ˌʃɪr
Clacton 'klæk.tən
clad klæd
cladding 'klæd.ɪŋ
cladistics klə'dɪs.tɪks, klæd'ɪs-
Claggart 'klæɡ.ət (US) -ɚt
Claiborne 'kleɪ.bɔːn (US) -bɔːrn
claim kleɪm **-s** -z **-ing** -ɪŋ **-ed** -d
claimant 'kleɪ.mənt **-s** -s
claimer 'kleɪ.məʳ (US) -mɚ **-s** -z
clairaudien|ce ˌkleə'rɔː.di.ən|*t*s (US) ˌkler'ɑː-, -'ɔː- **-t** -t
Claire kleəʳ (US) kler
Clairol® 'kleə.rɒl (US) 'kler.ɑːl
clairvoyan|ce ˌkleə'vɔɪ.ən*t*|s (US) ˌkler- **-cy** -si
clairvoyant ˌkleə'vɔɪ.ənt (US) ˌkler- **-s** -s
clam klæm **-s** -z **-ming** -ɪŋ **-med** -d
clamant 'kleɪ.mənt, 'klæm.ənt **-ly** -li
clambake 'klæm.beɪk **-s** -s
clamb|er 'klæm.b|əʳ (US) -b|ɚ **-ers** -əz (US) -ɚz **-ering** -ᵊr.ɪŋ **-ered** -əd (US) -ɚd
clamm|y 'klæm|.i **-ier** -i.əʳ (US) -i.ɚ **-iest** -i.ɪst, -i.əst **-ily** -ɪ.li, -ᵊl.i **-iness** -ɪ.nəs, -ɪ.nɪs
clam|or 'klæm|.əʳ (US) -ɚ **-ors** -əz (US) -ɚz **-oring** -ᵊr.ɪŋ **-ored** -əd (US) -ɚd **-orer/s** -ᵊr.əʳ/z (US) -ɚ.ɚ/z
clamorous 'klæm.ᵊr.əs **-ly** -li **-ness** -nəs, -nɪs
clam|our 'klæm|.əʳ (US) -ɚ **-ours** -əz (US) -ɚz **-ouring** -ᵊr.ɪŋ **-oured** -əd (US) -ɚd **-ourer/s** -ᵊr.əʳ/z (US) -ɚ.ɚ/z
clamp klæmp **-s** -s **-ing** -ɪŋ **-ed** -t
clampdown 'klæmp.daʊn **-s** -z
clan klæn **-s** -z
clandestine klæn'des.tɪn, -taɪn, 'klæn.dɪs- (US) klæn'des.tɪn **-ly** -li
clang klæŋ **-s** -z **-ing** -ɪŋ **-ed** -d
clanger 'klæŋ.əʳ (US) -ɚ **-s** -z
clangor 'klæŋ.ɡəʳ, -əʳ (US) -ɚ, -ɡɚ
clangorous 'klæŋ.ɡᵊr.əs, -ᵊr- (US) '-ɚ-, -ɡɚ- **-ly** -li
clangour 'klæŋ.ɡəʳ, -əʳ (US) -ɚ, -ɡɚ
clank klæŋk **-s** -s **-ing** -ɪŋ **-ed** -t
Clanmaurice klæn'mɒr.ɪs, klæm- (US) -'mɔːr-, -'mɑːr-
Clanmorris klæn'mɒr.ɪs, klæm- (US) klæn'mɔːr-
clannish 'klæn.ɪʃ **-ly** -li **-ness** -nəs, -nɪs
Clanricarde klæn'rɪk.əd (US) -ɚd
clanship 'klæn.ʃɪp
clans|man 'klænz|.mən **-men** -mən
clap klæp **-s** -s **-ping** -ɪŋ **-ped** -t **ˌclapped 'out** *stress shift:* ˌclapped-out 'car
clapboard 'klæp.bɔːd (US) -bɔːrd; 'klæb.ɚd **-s** -z
Clapham 'klæp.ᵊm **ˌClapham 'omnibus**
clapometer klæp'ɒm.ɪ.təʳ (US) -'ɑː.mə.ţɚ **-s** -z
clapper 'klæp.əʳ (US) -ɚ **-s** -z
clapperboard 'klæp.ə.bɔːd (US) -ɚ.bɔːrd **-s** -z
Clapton 'klæp.tən
claptrap 'klæp.træp
claque klæk **-s** -s
Clara 'klɑː.rə, 'kleə- (US) 'kler.ə, 'klær-
clarabella (C) ˌklær.ə'bel.ə (US) ˌkler-, ˌklær- **-s** -z
Clare kleəʳ (US) kler
Clarel 'kleə.rᵊl (US) 'kler.ᵊl, 'klær.ᵊl; klə'rel
Claremont 'kleə.mɒnt, -mənt (US) 'kler.mɑːnt
Clarence 'klær.ᵊn*t*s (US) 'kler-, 'klær-
Clarenc(i)eux 'klær.ᵊn.suː, -sjuː (US) 'kler-, 'klær-
clarendon (C) 'klær.ᵊn.dən (US) 'kler-, 'klær-
claret 'klær.ət, -ɪt (US) 'kler-, 'klær- **-s** -s
Clarges 'klɑː.dʒɪz, -dʒəz (US) 'klɑːr-
Clarice 'klær.ɪs (US) 'kler-, 'klær-; kler'iːs, klær-
Claridge 'klær.ɪdʒ (US) 'kler-, 'klær- **-'s** -ɪz
clarification ˌklær.ɪ.fɪ'keɪ.ʃᵊn, ˌ-ə- (US) ˌkler-, ˌklær-
clari|fy 'klær.ɪ|.faɪ, '-ə- (US) 'kler-, 'klær- **-fies** -faɪz **-fying** -faɪ.ɪŋ **-fied** -faɪd **-fier/s** -faɪ.əʳ/z (US) -faɪ.ɚ/z
Clarina klə'raɪ.nə
clarinet ˌklær.ɪ'net, -ə'- (US) ˌkler-, ˌklær- **-s** -s
clarinettist ˌklær.ɪ'net.ɪst, -ə'- (US) ˌkler.ə'neţ-, ˌklær- **-s** -s
clarion 'klær.i.ən (US) 'kler-, 'klær- **-s** -z **'clarion ˌcall**
Clarissa klə'rɪs.ə, klær'ɪs- (US) klə'rɪs-
clarity 'klær.ə.ti, -ɪ.ti (US) 'kler.ə.ţi, 'klær-
Clark(e) klɑːk (US) klɑːrk
clarkia 'klɑː.ki.ə (US) 'klɑːr- **-s** -z
Clarkson 'klɑːk.sᵊn (US) 'klɑːrk-
Clarrie 'klær.i (US) 'kler-, 'klær-
Clary 'kleə.ri (US) 'kler.i, 'klær-
clash klæʃ **-es** -ɪz **-ing** -ɪŋ **-ed** -t
clasp klɑːsp (US) klæsp **-s** -s **-ing** -ɪŋ **-ed** -t **'clasp ˌknife**
class klɑːs (US) klæs **-es** -ɪz **-ing** -ɪŋ **-ed** -t **'class ˌsystem** ; **'class ˌwar, ˌclass 'war**
class-conscious 'klɑːsˌkɒn.*t*ʃəs, ˌ-'-- (US) 'klæsˌkɑːn*t*.ʃəs **-ness** -nəs, -nɪs
classic 'klæs.ɪk **-s** -s
classic|al 'klæs.ɪ.k|ᵊl, '-ə- **-ally** -ᵊl.i, -li **-alness** -ᵊl.nəs, -nɪs **ˌclassical 'music**
classicism 'klæs.ɪ.sɪ.zᵊm, '-ə- **-s** -z
classicist 'klæs.ɪ.sɪst, '-ə- **-s** -s
classifiable 'klæs.ɪ.faɪ.ə.bl̩, ˌklæs.ɪ'faɪ- (US) 'klæs.ə.faɪ-
classification ˌklæs.ɪ.fɪ'keɪ.ʃᵊn, ˌ-ə- (US) ˌ-ə- **-s** -z
classificatory ˌklæs.ɪ.fɪ'keɪ.tᵊr.i, ˌ-ə-, -tri; 'klæs.ɪ.fɪ.kə-, '-ə- (US) 'klæs.ə.fɪ.kə.tɔːr.i; klə'sɪf.ə-
classi|fy 'klæs.ɪ|.faɪ, '-ə- **-fies** -faɪz **-fying** -faɪ.ɪŋ **-fied** -faɪd **-fier/s** -faɪ.əʳ/z (US) -faɪ.ɚ/z **ˌclassified 'ad** (US) **'classified ˌad** ; **ˌclassified infor'mation**
class|ism 'klɑː.s|ɪ.zᵊm (US) 'klæs|.ɪ- **-ist/s** -ɪst/s
classless 'klɑːs.ləs, -lɪs (US) 'klæs- **-ness** -nəs, -nɪs
class|man 'klɑːs|.mæn, -mən (US) 'klæs- **-men** -men, -mən
classmate 'klɑːs.meɪt (US) 'klæs- **-s** -s
classroom 'klɑːs.rʊm, -ruːm (US) 'klæs.ruːm, -rʊm **-s** -z
classwork 'klɑːs.wɜːk (US) 'klæs.wɜːrk
class|y 'klɑː.s|i (US) 'klæs|.i **-ier** -i.əʳ (US) -i.ɚ **-iest** -i.ɪst, -i.əst **-ily** -ɪ.li, -ᵊl.i **-iness** -ɪ.nəs, -ɪ.nɪs
clatt|er 'klæt|.əʳ (US) 'klæţ|.ɚ **-ers** -əz (US) -ɚz **-ering** -ᵊr.ɪŋ **-ered** -əd (US) -ɚd
Claud(e) klɔːd (US) klɑːd, klɔːd
Claudette klɔː'det (US) klɑː-, klɔː-
Claudi|a 'klɔː.di|.ə, 'klaʊ- (US) 'klɑː-, 'klɔː-, 'klaʊ- **-an** -ən
Claudine klɔː'diːn (US) klɑː-, klɔː-
Claudio 'klaʊ.di.əʊ, 'klɔː- (US) 'klɑː.di.oʊ, 'klɔː-, 'klaʊ-
Claudius 'klɔː.di.əs (US) 'klɑː-, 'klɔː-
claus|e klɔːz (US) klɑːz, klɔːz **-es** -ɪz **-al** -ᵊl

Clausewitz ˈklaʊ.sə.vɪts, -zə-
claustral ˈklɔː.strᵊl (US) ˈklɑː-, ˈklɔː-
claustrophob|ia ˌklɔː.strəˈfəʊ.b|i.ə, ˌklɒs.trə- (US) ˌklɑː.strəˈfoʊ-, ˌklɔː- **-ic** -ɪk
clave (*archaic past of* cleave) kleɪv
clavecin ˈklæv.sɪn, -ə.sɪn, ˈ-ɪ- **-s** -z
Claverhouse ˈkleɪ.və.haʊs (US) -vɚ-
Clavering ˈkleɪ.vᵊr.ɪŋ, ˈklæv.ᵊr-
clavichord ˈklæv.ɪ.kɔːd (US) -kɔːrd **-s** -z
clavicle ˈklæv.ɪ.kl̩ **-s** -z
clavicular kləˈvɪk.jʊ.ləʳ, klævˈɪk-, -jə- (US) -jə.lɚ
clavier *keyboard:* ˈklæv.i.əʳ; klævˈɪəʳ, kləˈvɪəʳ (US) ˈklæv.i.ɚ; kləˈvɪr **-s** -z *instrument:* kləˈvɪəʳ, klævˈɪəʳ (US) ˈklæv.i.ɚ; kləˈvɪr **-s** -z
claw klɔː (US) klɑː, klɔː **-s** -z **-ing** -ɪŋ **-ed** -d
clawback ˈklɔː.bæk (US) ˈklɑː-, ˈklɔː- **-s** -s
Claxton ˈklæk.stᵊn
clay (C) kleɪ **-s** -z ˌ**clay ˈpigeon**
Clayden, **Claydon** ˈkleɪ.dᵊn
clayey ˈkleɪ.i
Clayhanger ˈkleɪ.hæŋ.əʳ (US) -ɚ
claymore ˈkleɪ.mɔːʳ (US) -mɔːr **-s** -z
Clayton ˈkleɪ.tᵊn
Clayton-le-Moors ˌkleɪ.tᵊn.liˈmɔːʳ (US) -ˈmɔːr
clean kliːn **-s** -z **-ing** -ɪŋ **-ed** -d **-est** -ɪst, -əst **-ly** -li **-ness** -nəs, -nɪs
clean-cut ˌkliːnˈkʌt, ˌkliːŋ- (US) ˌkliːn- *stress shift:* ˌclean-cut ˈimage
cleaner ˈkliː.nəʳ (US) -nɚ **-s** -z
cleanliness ˈklen.lɪ.nəs, -nɪs
cleanl|y ˈklen.l|i **-ier** -i.əʳ (US) -i.ɚ **-iest** -i.ɪst, -i.əst
cleans|e klenz **-es** -ɪz **-ing** -ɪŋ **-ed** -d **-er/s** -əʳ/z (US) -ɚ/z **-able** -ə.bl̩
cleanshaven ˌkliːnˈʃeɪ.vᵊn *stress shift:* ˌcleanshaven ˈchin
clean-up ˈkliːn.ʌp **-s** -s
clear klɪəʳ (US) klɪr **-er** -əʳ (US) -ɚ **-est** -ɪst, -əst **-ly** -li **-ness** -nəs, -nɪs **-s** -z **-ing** -ɪŋ **-ed** -d ˌ**clear-ˈheaded** (US) ˈ**clear-ˌheaded** *stress shift, British only:* ˌclear-headed ˈthinking ˌ**clear-ˈsighted** (US) ˈ**clear-ˌsighted** *stress shift, British only:* ˌclear-sighted ˈplanning
clearage ˈklɪə.rɪdʒ (US) ˈklɪr.ɪdʒ
clearanc|e ˈklɪə.rᵊnts (US) ˈklɪr.ᵊnts **-es** -ɪz ˈ**clearance ˌsale**
clear-cut ˌklɪəˈkʌt (US) ˌklɪr- *stress shift:* ˌclear-cut ˈdifference
clearing-hou|se ˈklɪə.rɪŋ.haʊ|s (US) ˈklɪr.ɪŋ- **-ses** -zɪz
clearout ˈklɪə.raʊt (US) ˈklɪr- **-s** -s
clearway ˈklɪə.weɪ (US) ˈklɪr- **-s** -z
Cleary ˈklɪə.ri (US) ˈklɪr.i
cleat kliːt **-s** -s
Cleator Moor ˌkliː.təˈmɔːʳ (US) -tɚˈmɔːr
cleavag|e ˈkliː.vɪdʒ **-es** -ɪz
cleav|e kliːv **-es** -z **-ing** -ɪŋ **-ed** -d **clove** kləʊv (US) kloʊv **cleft** kleft **cloven** ˈkləʊ.vᵊn (US) ˈkloʊ- **clave** kleɪv
cleaver (C) ˈkliː.vəʳ (US) -vɚ **-s** -z
Cleckheaton klekˈhiː.tᵊn (US) -t̬ᵊn
Clee kliː
cleek kliːk **-s** -s **-ing** -ɪŋ **-ed** -t
Cleese kliːz
Cleethorpes ˈkliː.θɔːps (US) -θɔːrps
clef klef **-s** -s
cleft kleft **-s** -s ˌ**cleft ˈpalate**
cleg kleg **-s** -z
Clegg kleg
Cleland ˈklel.ənd, ˈkliː.lənd
Clem klem
clematis ˈklem.ə.tɪs, klɪˈmeɪ.tɪs, klə-, klemˈeɪ- (US) ˈklem.ə.t̬əs; kləˈmæt̬.əs, -ˈmɑː.t̬əs
Clemence ˈklem.ən*t*s
Clemenceau ˈklem.ən.səʊ, -ɑ̃ːn- (US) -soʊ
clemency ˈklem.ən*t*.si
Clemens ˈklem.ənz
clement (C) ˈklem.ənt **-ly** -li
Clementi klɪˈmen.ti, klə-, klemˈen- (US) -t̬i
Clementina ˌklem.ənˈtiː.nə
clementine (C) ˈklem.ən.tiːn, -taɪn (US) -taɪn, -tiːn **-s** -z
Clemo ˈklem.əʊ (US) -oʊ
clench klen*t*ʃ **-es** -ɪz **-ing** -ɪŋ **-ed** -t
Cleo ˈkliː.əʊ (US) -oʊ
Cleobury *places in Shropshire:* ˈklɪb.ᵊr.i, ˈkleb-, ˈklɪə.bᵊr- (US) -er-, ˈ-ɚ-
Cleobury *surname:* ˈkləʊ.bᵊr.i, ˈkliː- (US) ˈkloʊ.ber-, ˈkliː-, -bɚ-
Cleopatra ˌkli.əˈpæt.rə, -ˈpɑː.trə (US) ˌkli.oʊˈpæt.rə, -əˈ-, -ˈpeɪ.trə, -ˈpɑː-
clepsydr|a ˈklep.sɪ.dr|ə, klepˈsɪd.r|ə (US) ˈklep.sɪ.dr|ə **-ae** -iː
clerestor|y ˈklɪə.stɔː.r|i, -stə- (US) ˈklɪr.stɔːr|.i **-ies** -iz
clergy ˈklɜː.dʒi (US) ˈklɜːr-
clergy|man ˈklɜː.dʒɪ|.mən (US) ˈklɜːr- **-men** -mən
clergy|woman ˈklɜː.dʒɪ|ˌwʊm.ən (US) ˈklɜːr- **-women** -ˌwɪm.ɪn
cleric ˈkler.ɪk **-s** -s
clerical ˈkler.ɪ.kᵊl **-s** -z **-ly** -i
clerihew (C) ˈkler.ɪ.hjuː, ˈ-ə- (US) ˈ-ə- **-s** -z
clerisy ˈkler.ɪ.si, ˈ-ə- (US) ˈ-ə-
clerk (C) klɑːk (US) klɜːrk **-s** -s
Clerke klɑːk (US) klɜːrk, klɑːrk
Clerkenwell ˈklɑː.kᵊn.wel, -wəl (US) ˈklɜːr-, klɑːr-
clerkship ˈklɑːk.ʃɪp (US) ˈklɜːrk- **-s** -s
Clermont *towns in Ireland, village in Norfolk:* ˈkleə.mɒnt, -mənt (US) ˈkler.mɑːnt *in US:* ˈkleə.mɒnt, ˈklɜː- (US) ˈkler.mɑːnt, ˈklɜːr-
Clermont-Ferrand ˌkleə.mɔ̃ː*n*.ferˈɑ̃ː*ŋ* (US) ˌkler.mɑːn.ferˈɑ̃ː*n*
Clery ˈklɪə.ri (US) ˈklɪr.i
Clevedon ˈkliːv.dən
Cleveland ˈkliːv.lənd
Cleveleys ˈkliːv.liz
clev|er ˈklev|.əʳ (US) -ɚ **-erer** -ᵊr.əʳ (US) -ɚ.ɚ **-erest** -ᵊr.ɪst, -əst **-erly** -ᵊl.i (US) -ɚ.li **-erness** -ə.nəs, -nɪs (US) -ɚ.nəs, -nɪs **-erish** -ᵊr.ɪʃ ˈ**clever** ˌ**clogs**; **too** ˌ**clever by ˈhalf**
clever-dick ˈklev.ə.dɪk (US) ˈ-ɚ- **-s** -s
Cleverdon ˈklev.ə.dᵊn (US) ˈ-ɚ-
Cleves kliːvz
clew kluː **-s** -z **-ing** -ɪŋ **-ed** -d
Clews kluːz
Cley klaɪ, kleɪ
cliché ˈkliː.ʃeɪ, -ˈ- (US) -ˈ- **-s** -z **-d** -d
click klɪk **-s** -s **-ing** -ɪŋ **-ed** -t
client klaɪənt **-s** -s
clientage ˈklaɪən.tɪdʒ
clientele ˌkliː.ɑ̃ː*n*ˈtel, -ɑːnˈ-, -ənˈ- (US) ˌklaɪ.ənˈtel, ˌkliː-, -ɑːnˈ- **-s** -z
cliff klɪf **-s** -s
Cliff(e) klɪf
cliff-hanger ˈklɪfˌhæŋ.əʳ (US) -ɚ **-s** -z
Clifford ˈklɪf.əd (US) -ɚd
clift (C) klɪft **-s** -s
Clifton ˈklɪf.tᵊn
climacteric klaɪˈmæk.tᵊr.ɪk; ˌklaɪ.mækˈter- (US) klaɪˈmæk.tɚ.ɪk; ˌklaɪ.mækˈter-, -ˈtɪr- **-s** -s
climacterical ˌklaɪ.mækˈter.ɪ.kᵊl
climactic klaɪˈmæk.tɪk **-al** -ᵊl **-ally** -ᵊl.i, -li
climate ˈklaɪ.mət, -mɪt **-s** -s
climatic klaɪˈmæt.ɪk (US) -ˈmæt̬- **-al** -ᵊl **-ally** -ᵊl.i, -li
climatolog|y ˌklaɪ.məˈtɒl.ə.dʒ|i (US) -ˈtɑː.lə- **-ist/s** -ɪst/s
climax ˈklaɪ.mæks **-es** -ɪz **-ing** -ɪŋ **-ed** -t
climb klaɪm **-s** -z **-ing** -ɪŋ **-ed** -d **-able** -ə.bl̩ ˈ**climbing** ˌ**frame**
climb-down ˈklaɪm.daʊn **-s** -z
climber ˈklaɪ.məʳ (US) -mɚ **-s** -z
clime klaɪm **-s** -z
clinch (C) klɪn*t*ʃ **-es** -ɪz **-ing** -ɪŋ **-ed** -t **-er/s** -əʳ/z (US) -ɚ/z
cline (C) klaɪn **-s** -z
cling klɪŋ **-s** -z **-ing** -ɪŋ **clung** klʌŋ
clingfilm (C®) ˈklɪŋ.fɪlm
clingstone ˈklɪŋ.stəʊn (US) -stoʊn **-s** -z
cling|y ˈklɪŋ|.i **-ier** -i.əʳ (US) -i.ɚ **-iest** -i.ɪst, -i.əst **-iness** -ɪ.nəs, -ɪ.nɪs
clinic ˈklɪn.ɪk **-s** -s **-al** -ᵊl **-ally** -ᵊl.i, -li
clinician klɪˈnɪʃ.ᵊn (US) klɪ-, klə- **-s** -z
clink klɪŋk **-s** -s **-ing** -ɪŋ **-ed** -t
clinker (C) ˈklɪŋ.kəʳ (US) -kɚ **-s** -z
clinometer klaɪˈnɒm.ɪ.təʳ, klɪ-, ˈ-ə- (US) -ˈnɑː.mə.t̬ɚ **-s** -s

clinometric ˌklaɪ.nəʊˈmet.rɪk, ˌklɪn.əʊˈ- ⓤⓢ -noʊˈ-
clinometry klaɪˈnɒm.ɪ.tri, klɪ-, ˈ-ə- ⓤⓢ klaɪˈnɑː.mə-
Clint klɪnt
Clinton ˈklɪn.tən ⓤⓢ ˈklɪn.tən, -tᵊn
Clio ˈkliː.əʊ, ˈklaɪ- ⓤⓢ -oʊ
Note: The pronunciation /ˈkliː.əʊ ⓤⓢ -oʊ/ is suitable for the motor car.
clip klɪp **-s** -s **-ping** -ɪŋ **-ped** -t **ˈclip ˌjoint**
clipboard ˈklɪp.bɔːd ⓤⓢ -bɔːrd **-s** -z
clip-clop ˈklɪp.klɒp ⓤⓢ -klɑːp **-s** -s **-ping** -ɪŋ **-ped** -t
clipper ˈklɪp.əʳ ⓤⓢ -ɚ **-s** -z
clippie ˈklɪp.i **-s** -z
clipping ˈklɪp.ɪŋ **-s** -z
clique kliːk ⓤⓢ kliːk, klɪk **-s** -s **-y** -i
cliquish ˈkliː.kɪʃ ⓤⓢ ˈkliː.kɪʃ, ˈklɪk.ɪʃ **-ly** -li **-ness** -nəs, -nis
cliqu|y ˈkliː.k|i ⓤⓢ ˈkliː.k|i, ˈklɪk|.i **-ier** -i.əʳ ⓤⓢ -i.ɚ **-iest** -i.ɪst, -i.əst **-iness** -ɪ.nəs, -ɪ.nɪs
Clissold ˈklɪs.ᵊld, -əʊld ⓤⓢ -oʊld
Clitheroe ˈklɪð.ə.rəʊ ⓤⓢ -roʊ
clitic ˈklɪt.ɪk ⓤⓢ ˈklɪt̬- **-s** -s
clitoral ˈklɪt.ᵊr.ᵊl ⓤⓢ ˈklɪt̬.ɚ-, ˈklaɪ.t̬ɚ-
clitoridectom|y ˌklɪt.ᵊr.ɪˈdek.tə.m|i ⓤⓢ ˌklɪt- **-ies** -iz
clitor|is ˈklɪt.ᵊr|.ɪs ⓤⓢ ˈklɪt̬.ɚ|.əs, ˈklaɪ.t̬ɚ-; klɪˈtɔːr- **-ic** -ɪk
Clive klaɪv
Cliveden ˈklɪv.dᵊn, ˈkliːv-
cloa|ca kləʊˈeɪ|.kə ⓤⓢ kloʊ- **-cae** -kiː, -siː ⓤⓢ -siː, -kiː **-cal** -kᵊl
cloak (C) kləʊk ⓤⓢ kloʊk **-s** -s **-ing** -ɪŋ **-ed** -t
cloak-and-dagger ˌkləʊk.ᵊnˈdæg.əʳ ⓤⓢ ˌkloʊk.ᵊnˈdæg.ɚ
cloakroom ˈkləʊk.rʊm, -ruːm ⓤⓢ ˈkloʊk.ruːm, -rʊm **-s** -z
clobb|er ˈklɒb|.əʳ ⓤⓢ ˈklɑː.b|ɚ **-ers** -əz ⓤⓢ -ɚz **-ering** -ᵊr.ɪŋ **-ered** -əd ⓤⓢ -ɚd
cloch|e klɒʃ, kləʊʃ ⓤⓢ kloʊʃ **-es** -ɪz
clock klɒk ⓤⓢ klɑːk **-s** -s **-ing** -ɪŋ **-ed** -t **ˈclock ˌface ; put the ˈclock ˌback**
clockwise ˈklɒk.waɪz ⓤⓢ ˈklɑːk-
clockwork ˈklɒk.wɜːk ⓤⓢ ˈklɑːk.wɜːrk
clod klɒd ⓤⓢ klɑːd **-s** -z **-dy** -i
clodhopp|ing ˈklɒdˌhɒp|.ɪŋ ⓤⓢ ˈklɑːdˌhɑː.p|ɪŋ **-er/s** -əʳ/z ⓤⓢ -ɚ/z
Cloete kləʊˈiː.ti; ˈkluː.ti ⓤⓢ ˈkluː.t̬i; kloʊˈiː.t̬i
clog klɒg ⓤⓢ klɑːg, klɔːg **-s** -z **-ging** -ɪŋ **-ged** -d
clogg|y ˈklɒg|.i ⓤⓢ ˈklɑː.g|i **-ier** -i.əʳ ⓤⓢ -i.ɚ **-iest** -i.ɪst, -i.əst **-ily** -ɪ.li, -ᵊl.i **-iness** -ɪ.nəs, -ɪ.nɪs
Clogher ˈklɒ.həʳ, ˈklɒx.əʳ, ˈklɔː-, klɔːʳ ⓤⓢ ˈklɑː.hɚ, -xɚ
cloisonné klwɑːˈzɒn.eɪ, klwʌzˈɒn-; ˌklɔɪ.zəˈneɪ ⓤⓢ ˌklɔɪ.zəˈneɪ
cloist|er ˈklɔɪ.st|əʳ ⓤⓢ -st|ɚ **-ers** -əz ⓤⓢ -ɚz **-ering** -ᵊr.ɪŋ **-ered** -əd ⓤⓢ -ɚd
cloistral ˈklɔɪ.strᵊl
clonal ˈkləʊ.nᵊl ⓤⓢ ˈkloʊ- **-ly** -i
clon|e kləʊn ⓤⓢ kloʊn **-es** -z **-ing** -ɪŋ **-ed** -d
Clonmel ˈklɒn.mel, -ˈ- ⓤⓢ ˈklɑːn.mel, -ˈ-
clos|e (*v.*) kləʊz ⓤⓢ kloʊz **-es** -ɪz **-ing** -ɪŋ **-ed** -d **-er/s** -əʳ/z ⓤⓢ -ɚ/z **ˌclosed ˈbook ; ˌclosed ˈcircuit** *stress shift:* ˌclosed circuit ˈtelevision ; **ˌclosed ˈshop**
clos|e (*n.*) *end:* kləʊz ⓤⓢ kloʊz **-es** -ɪz
clos|e (*adj.*) *near:* kləʊs ⓤⓢ kloʊs **-er** -əʳ ⓤⓢ -ɚ **-est** -ɪst, -əst **-ely** -li **-eness** -nəs, -nɪs **ˌclose ˈquarters ; ˌclose ˈseason**
close-cut ˌkləʊsˈkʌt ⓤⓢ ˌkloʊs-
closefisted ˌkləʊsˈfɪs.tɪd ⓤⓢ ˌkloʊs- *stress shift:* ˌclosefisted ˈmiser
close-grained ˌkləʊsˈgreɪnd ⓤⓢ ˌkloʊs- *stress shift:* ˌclose-grained ˈwood
close-hauled ˌkləʊsˈhɔːld ⓤⓢ ˌkloʊsˈhɔːld, -ˈhɑːld *stress shift:* ˌclose-hauled ˈsailing
close-knit ˌkləʊsˈnɪt ⓤⓢ ˌkloʊs- *stress shift:* ˌclose-knit ˈfamily
closely ˈkləʊ.sli ⓤⓢ ˈkloʊ-
closely-guarded ˌkləʊ.sliˈgɑː.dɪd ⓤⓢ ˌkloʊ.sliˈgɑːr- *stress shift:* closely-guarded secret
clos|et ˈklɒz|.ɪt ⓤⓢ ˈklɑː.z|ɪt **-ets** -ɪts **-eting** -ɪ.tɪŋ ⓤⓢ -ɪ.t̬ɪŋ, ˈ-ə- **-eted** -ɪ.tɪd ⓤⓢ -ɪ.t̬ɪd, ˈ-ə- **come ˌout of the ˈcloset**
close-up ˈkləʊs.ʌp ⓤⓢ ˈkloʊs- **-s** -s
closure ˈkləʊ.ʒəʳ ⓤⓢ ˈkloʊ.ʒɚ **-s** -z
clot klɒt ⓤⓢ klɑːt **-s** -s **-ting** -ɪŋ ⓤⓢ ˈklɑː.t̬ɪŋ **-ted** -ɪd ⓤⓢ ˈklɑː.t̬ɪd **ˌclotted ˈcream**
cloth klɒθ ⓤⓢ klɑːθ **-s** klɒθs, klɒðz ⓤⓢ klɑθs, klɑːðz **ˈcloth ˌyard ; cut one's ˌcoat according to one's ˈcloth**
cloth|e kləʊð ⓤⓢ kloʊð **-es** -z **-ing** -ɪŋ **-ed** -d **clad** klæd
cloth-eared ˌklɒθˈɪəd ⓤⓢ ˌklɑːθˈɪrd *stress shift:* ˌcloth-eared ˈlistener
clothes kləʊðz ⓤⓢ kloʊðz **ˈclothes ˌbrush ; ˈclothes ˌhanger**
clotheshors|e ˈkləʊðz.hɔːs ⓤⓢ ˈkloʊðz.hɔːrs **-es** -ɪz
clothesline ˈkləʊðz.laɪn ⓤⓢ ˈkloʊðz- **-s** -z
clothespeg ˈkləʊðz.peg ⓤⓢ ˈkloʊðz- **-s** -z
clothespin ˈkləʊðz.pɪn ⓤⓢ ˈkloʊðz- **-s** -z
clothier ˈkləʊ.ði.əʳ ⓤⓢ ˈkloʊ.ði.ɚ **-s** -z
Clothilde ˈklɒt.ɪld, -ˈ- ⓤⓢ kloʊˈtɪl.də
clothing ˈkləʊ.ðɪŋ ⓤⓢ ˈkloʊ-
Clotho ˈkləʊ.θəʊ ⓤⓢ ˈkloʊ.θoʊ
cloud klaʊd **-s** -z **-ing** -ɪŋ **-ed** -ɪd **ˈcloud-ˌcapped**
cloudberr|y ˈklaʊd.bᵊr|.i, ˈklaʊb-, -ber- ⓤⓢ ˈklaʊd.ber- **-ies** -iz
cloudburst ˈklaʊd.bɜːst ⓤⓢ -bɜːrst **-s** -s
cloud-cuckoo-land ˌklaʊdˈkʊk.uː.lænd ⓤⓢ -ˈkuː.kuː-, -ˈkʊk.ʊ-
Cloudesley ˈklaʊdz.li
cloudless ˈklaʊd.ləs, -lɪs **-ly** -li **-ness** -nəs, -nɪs
cloud|y ˈklaʊ.d|i **-ier** -i.əʳ ⓤⓢ -i.ɚ **-iest** -i.ɪst, -i.əst **-ily** -ɪ.li, -ᵊl.i **-iness** -ɪ.nəs, -ɪ.nɪs
clough klʌf **-s** -s
Clough *surname:* klʌf, kluː *in Ireland:* klɒx ⓤⓢ klʌf
Clouseau kluːˈsəʊ, ˈ-- ⓤⓢ kluːˈzoʊ, ˈ--
clout klaʊt **-s** -s **-ing** -ɪŋ ⓤⓢ ˈklaʊ.t̬ɪŋ **-ed** -ɪd ⓤⓢ ˈklaʊ.t̬ɪd
clove (*n.*) kləʊv ⓤⓢ kloʊv **-s** -z
clov|e (*from* **cleave**) kləʊv ⓤⓢ kloʊv **-en** -ᵊn
Clovelly kləˈvel.i
cloven ˈkləʊ.vᵊn ⓤⓢ ˈkloʊ- **ˌcloven-ˈfooted** *stress shift:* ˌcloven-footed ˈbeast
clover (C) ˈkləʊ.vəʳ ⓤⓢ ˈkloʊ.vɚ **-s** -z
Clovis ˈkləʊ.vɪs ⓤⓢ ˈkloʊ-
Clow kləʊ ⓤⓢ kloʊ, klaʊ
Clowes *in Norfolk:* kluːz *surname:* klaʊz, kluːz
clown klaʊn **-s** -z **-ing** -ɪŋ **-ed** -d
Clowne klaʊn
clownish ˈklaʊ.nɪʃ **-ly** -li **-ness** -nəs, -nɪs
cloy klɔɪ **-s** -z **-ing/ly** -ɪŋ/li **-ed** -d
cloze kləʊz ⓤⓢ kloʊz
club klʌb **-s** -z **-bing** -ɪŋ **-bed** -d **ˌclub ˈsandwich ; ˌclub ˈsoda ; ˌclub ˈmoss** ⓤⓢ **ˈclub ˌmoss**
clubbable ˈklʌb.ə.bl̩
club|foot ˌklʌb|ˈfʊt, ˈ-- ⓤⓢ ˈ-- **-feet** -ˈfiːt ⓤⓢ -fiːt
clubfooted ˌklʌbˈfʊt.ɪd, ˈ--- ⓤⓢ ˈklʌbˌfʊt̬.ɪd
clubhou|se ˈklʌb.haʊ|s **-ses** -zɪz
clubland ˈklʌb.lænd, -lənd
club|man ˈklʌb|.mən, -mæn **-men** -mən, -men
Club Med ˌklʌbˈmed
Club Méditerranée ® ˌklʌbˌmed.ɪˌter.əˈneɪ
club-room ˈklʌb.rʊm, -ruːm ⓤⓢ -ruːm, -rʊm **-s** -z
cluck klʌk **-s** -s **-ing** -ɪŋ **-ed** -t
clu|e kluː **-es** -z **-(e)ing** -ɪŋ **-ed** -d **ˌclued ˈup**
clueless ˈkluː.ləs, -lɪs **-ness** -nəs, -nɪs
Cluj kluːʒ

clumber (C) ˈklʌm.bəʳ (US) -bɚ **-s** -z
clump klʌmp **-s** -s **-ing** -ɪŋ **-ed** -t
clumpy ˈklʌm.pi
clums|y ˈklʌm.z|i **-ier** -i.əʳ (US) -i.ɚ **-iest** -i.ɪst, -i.əst **-ily** -ɪ.li, -ᵊl.i **-iness** -ɪ.nəs, -ɪ.nɪs
Clun klʌn
clunch klʌntʃ
clung (*from* **cling**) klʌŋ
clunk klʌŋk **-s** -s **-ing** -ɪŋ **-ed** -t
clust|er ˈklʌs.t|əʳ (US) -tɚ **-ers** -əz (US) -ɚz **-ering** -ᵊr.ɪŋ **-ered** -əd (US) -ɚd
clutch klʌtʃ **-es** -ɪz **-ing** -ɪŋ **-ed** -t ˈ**clutch** ˌ**bag**
clutt|er ˈklʌt|.əʳ (US) ˈklʌţ|.ɚ **-ers** -əz (US) -ɚz **-ering** -ᵊr.ɪŋ **-ered** -əd (US) -ɚd
Clutterbuck ˈklʌt.ə.bʌk (US) ˈklʌţ.ɚ-
Clutton ˈklʌt.ᵊn (US) ˈklʌţ-
Clwyd ˈkluː.ɪd
Clwydian kluˈɪd.i.ən
Clydach ˈklɪd.ək, ˈklʌd-, -əx (US) -ək
Clyde klaɪd
Clydebank ˈklaɪd.bæŋk, -ˈ-
Clydesdale ˈklaɪdz.deɪl **-s** -z
Clydeside ˈklaɪd.saɪd
Clym klɪm
clyster ˈklɪs.təʳ (US) -tɚ **-s** -z
Clytemnestra ˌklaɪ.təmˈnes.trə, ˌklɪt.əmˈ-, -ɪmˈ-, -emˈ-, -ˈniː.strə (US) ˌklaɪ.ţəmˈnes.trə
Clytie *in Greek mythology:* ˈklɪt.i.iː, ˈklaɪ.tiː (US) ˈklaɪ.ţi.iː, ˈklɪţ.i.iː *modern first name, chignon:* ˈklaɪ.ti, -tiː (US) ˈklaɪ.ţi, klɪˈʃiː.ə
cm (*abbrev. for* **centimetre/s**) *singular:* ˈsen.tɪˌmiː.təʳ (US) -ţəˌmiː.ţɚ *plural:* -z
CND ˌsiː.enˈdiː
Cnidus ˈnaɪ.dəs, ˈknaɪ-
CNN ˌsiː.enˈen
Cnut kəˈnjuːt, knuːt
co- kəʊ- (US) koʊ-
Co. (*abbrev. for* **company**) kəʊ, ˈkʌm.pᵊn.i (US) koʊ, ˈkʌm.pᵊn.i
CO ˌsiːˈəʊ (US) -ˈoʊ
c/o (*abbrev. for* **care of**) ˈkeəʳ.ɒv (US) ˈker.ɑːv, -əv
c/o (*abbrev. for* **carried over**) ˌkær.idˈəʊ.vəʳ (US) ˌker.idˈoʊ.vɚ, ˌkær-
coach kəʊtʃ (US) koʊtʃ **-es** -ɪz **-ing** -ɪŋ **-ed** -t ˈ**coach** ˌ**horse** ; ˈ**coach** ˌ**house** ; ˈ**coach** ˌ**party** ; ˈ**coach** ˌ**station**
coach|man ˈkəʊtʃ|.mən (US) ˈkoʊtʃ- **-men** -mən
coac|tion kəʊˈæk|.ʃᵊn (US) koʊ- **-tive** -tɪv
coadjacent ˌkəʊ.əˈdʒeɪ.sᵊnt (US) ˌkoʊ-
coadjutant kəʊˈædʒ.ʊ.tᵊnt, ˈ-ə- (US) koʊˈædʒ.ə.ţᵊnt **-s** -s
coadjutor kəʊˈædʒ.ʊ.təʳ, ˈ-ə- (US) koʊˈædʒ.ə.ţɚ **-s** -z
co-administrator ˌkəʊ.ədˈmɪn.ɪ.streɪ.təʳ (US) ˌkoʊ.ædˈmɪn.ɪ.streɪ.ţɚ, -ədˈ- **-s** -z
coagulant kəʊˈæg.jʊ.lənt, -jə- (US) koʊˈæg.jə- **-s** -s
coagu|late kəʊˈæg.jə|.leɪt, -jʊ- (US) koʊˈæg.jə- **-lates** -leɪts **-lating** -leɪ.tɪŋ (US) -leɪ.ţɪŋ **-lated** -leɪ.tɪd (US) -leɪ.ţɪd
coagulation kəʊˌæg.jəˈleɪ.ʃᵊn, -jʊˈ- (US) koʊˌæg.jəˈ-
coal kəʊl (US) koʊl **-s** -z **-ing** -ɪŋ **-ed** -d ˈ**coal** ˌ**bed** ; ˌ**coal** ˈ**black** ; ˈ**coal** ˌ**bunker** ; ˈ**coal** ˌ**scuttle** ; ˈ**coal** ˌ**tar** ; ˌ**haul someone over the** ˈ**coals**
coalesc|e kəʊəˈles (US) koʊə- **-es** -ɪz **-ing** -ɪŋ **-ed** -t
coalescen|ce kəʊəˈles.ᵊn|ts (US) koʊə- **-t** -t
coalfac|e ˈkəʊl.feɪs (US) ˈkoʊl- **-es** -ɪz
coalfield ˈkəʊl.fiːld (US) ˈkoʊl- **-s** -z
coalhole ˈkəʊl.həʊl (US) ˈkoʊl.hoʊl **-s** -z
coalhou|se ˈkəʊl.haʊ|s (US) ˈkoʊl- **-ses** -zɪz
Coalite® ˈkəʊ.laɪt (US) ˈkoʊ-
coalition kəʊəˈlɪʃ.ᵊn (US) koʊə- **-s** -z
coal|man ˈkəʊl|.mæn, -mən (US) ˈkoʊl- **-men** -men, -mən
coalmine ˈkəʊl.maɪn (US) ˈkoʊl- **-s** -z
coalminer ˈkəʊlˌmaɪ.nəʳ (US) ˈkoʊlˌmaɪ.nɚ **-s** -z
coalpit ˈkəʊl.pɪt (US) ˈkoʊl- **-s** -s
Coalville ˈkəʊl.vɪl (US) ˈkoʊl-
coanchor ˈkəʊˌæŋ.kəʳ (US) ˈkoʊˌæŋ.kɚ **-s** -z
coars|e kɔːs (US) kɔːrs **-er** -əʳ (US) -ɚ **-est** -ɪst, -əst **-ely** -li **-eness** -nəs, -nɪs ˈ**coarse** ˌ**fishing**, ˌ**coarse** ˈ**fishing**
coarse-grained ˌkɔːsˈgreɪnd (US) ˈkɔːrs.greɪnd *stress shift:* ˌcoarse-grained ˈpicture
coarsen ˈkɔː.sᵊn (US) ˈkɔːr- **-s** -z **-ing** -ɪŋ **-ed** -d
coarticulation ˌkəʊ.ɑː.tɪ.kjəˈleɪ.ʃᵊn, -jʊˈ- (US) ˌkoʊ.ɑːr.tɪ.kjəˈ-
coast kəʊst (US) koʊst **-s** -s **-ing** -ɪŋ **-ed** -ɪd
coastal ˈkəʊs.tᵊl (US) ˈkoʊ-
coaster ˈkəʊ.stəʳ (US) ˈkoʊ.stɚ **-s** -z
coastguard ˈkəʊs*t*.gɑːd (US) ˈkoʊs*t*.gɑːrd **-s** -z
coastline ˈkəʊst.laɪn (US) ˈkoʊst- **-s** -z
coastwise ˈkəʊst.waɪz (US) ˈkoʊst-
coat kəʊt (US) koʊt **-s** -s **-ing** -ɪŋ **-ed** -ɪd ˈ**coat** ˌ**check** ; ˈ**coat** ˌ**hanger** ; ˌ**coat of** ˈ**arms** ; ˈ**coat** ˌ**room** ; ˈ**coat** ˌ**tail(s)** ; ˌ**cut one's** ˌ**coat according to one's** ˈ**cloth**
Coatbridge ˈkəʊt.brɪdʒ (US) ˈkoʊt-
Coat(e)s kəʊts (US) koʊts
coati kəʊˈɑː.ti (US) koʊˈɑː.ţi **-s** -z
coating ˈkəʊ.tɪŋ (US) ˈkoʊ.ţɪŋ **-s** -z
coauthor kəʊˈɔː.θəʳ, ˈ--- (US) koʊˈɑː.θɚ, -ˈɔː- **-s** -z **-ing** -ɪŋ **-ed** -d
coax kəʊks (US) koʊks **-es** -ɪz **-ing/ly** -ɪŋ/li **-ed** -t **-er/s** -əʳ/z (US) -ɚ/z
co-axial ˌkəʊˈæk.si.əl (US) ˌkoʊ- **-ly** -i
cob kɒb (US) kɑːb **-s** -z
Cobain kəʊˈbeɪn (US) ˈkoʊ-, ˌkoʊˈbeɪn
cobalt ˈkəʊ.bɔːlt, -bɒlt (US) ˈkoʊ.bɔːlt, -bɑːlt
Cobb(e) kɒb (US) kɑːb
cobber ˈkɒb.əʳ (US) ˈkɑː.bɚ **-s** -z
Cobbett ˈkɒb.ɪt (US) ˈkɑː.bɪt
cobbl|e ˈkɒb.l̩ (US) ˈkɑː.bl̩ **-es** -z **-ing** -ɪŋ, ˈ-blɪŋ (US) ˈkɑː.bl̩.ɪŋ, ˈ-blɪŋ **-ed** -d
Cobbleigh ˈkɒb.li (US) ˈkɑː.bli
cobbler ˈkɒb.ləʳ, ˈkɒb.l̩.əʳ (US) ˈkɑː.blɚ **-s** -z
cobblestone ˈkɒb.l̩.stəʊn (US) ˈkɑː.bl̩.stoʊn **-s** -z
Cobbold ˈkɒb.əʊld, -ᵊld (US) ˈkɑː.boʊld
Cobden ˈkɒb.dᵊn (US) ˈkɑːb-
Cobh kəʊv (US) koʊv
Cobham ˈkɒb.ᵊm (US) ˈkɑː.bᵊm
Coblenz kəʊˈblen*t*s, ˈkəʊ.blen*t*s (US) ˈkoʊ-
cobnut ˈkɒb.nʌt (US) ˈkɑːb- **-s** -s
COBOL, Cobol ˈkəʊ.bɒl (US) ˈkoʊ.bɔːl, -bɑːl
cobra ˈkəʊ.brə, ˈkɒb.rə (US) ˈkoʊ.brə **-s** -z
Coburg ˈkəʊ.bɜːg (US) ˈkoʊ.bɜːrg **-s** -z
cobweb ˈkɒb.web (US) ˈkɑːb- **-s** -z
coca ˈkəʊ.kə (US) ˈkoʊ.kə **-s** -z
Coca-Cola® ˌkəʊ.kəˈkəʊ.lə (US) ˌkoʊ.kəˈkoʊ-
cocaine kəʊˈkeɪn (US) koʊ-, ˈ--
coccal ˈkɒk.ᵊl (US) ˈkɑː.kᵊl
coccid ˈkɒk.sɪd (US) ˈkɑːk-
cocciferous kɒkˈsɪf.ᵊr.əs (US) kɑːk-
coccoid ˈkɒk.ɔɪd (US) ˈkɑː.kɔɪd
coccus ˈkɒk.əs (US) ˈkɑː.kəs **cocci** ˈkɒk.aɪ, ˈkɒk.saɪ (US) ˈkɑːk.saɪ
coccyx ˈkɒk.sɪks (US) ˈkɑːk- **-es** -ɪz **coccyges** -saɪ.dʒiːz
Cochabamba ˌkəʊ.tʃəˈbæm.bə (US) ˌkoʊ.tʃəˈbɑːm-
Cochin ˈkəʊ.tʃɪn, ˈkɒtʃ.ɪn (US) ˈkoʊ.tʃɪn
Cochin-China ˌkɒtʃ.ɪnˈtʃaɪ.nə (US) ˌkoʊ.tʃɪnˈ-, ˌkɑː-
cochineal ˌkɒtʃ.ɪˈniːl, -əˈ-, ˈ--- (US) ˈkɑː.tʃə.niːl, ˌ--ˈ-
Cochise kəʊˈtʃiːs (US) koʊ-, -ˈtʃiːz
cochle|a ˈkɒk.li|.ə (US) ˈkɑːk-, ˈkoʊk- **-as** -əz **-ae** -iː **-ar** -əʳ (US) -ɚ
Cochran(e) ˈkɒk.rən, ˈkɒx- (US) ˈkɑːk-
cock kɒk (US) kɑːk **-s** -s **-ing** -ɪŋ **-ed** -t
cockade kɒkˈeɪd (US) kɑːˈkeɪd **-s** -z
cock-a-doodle-doo ˌkɒk.ə.duː.dl̩ˈduː (US) ˌkɑːk-

cock-a-hoop ˌkɒk.əˈhuːp Ⓤⓢ ˌkɑːk-
Cockaigne kɒkˈeɪn, kəˈkeɪn Ⓤⓢ kɑːˈkeɪn
cock-a-leekie ˌkɒk.əˈliː.ki Ⓤⓢ ˌkɑːk-
cockalorum ˌkɒk.əˈlɔː.rᵊm Ⓤⓢ ˌkɑː.kəˈlɔːr.ᵊm **-s** -z
cockamamie ˌkɒk.əˈmeɪ.mi Ⓤⓢ ˈkɑː.kə.meɪ-
cock-and-bull ˌkɒk.ᵊndˈbʊl, -ᵊmˈ- Ⓤⓢ ˌkɑːk.ᵊnd- *stress shift, British only, see compound:* ˌ**cock-and-bull ˈstory** Ⓤⓢ ˌ**cock-and-ˈbull ˌstory**
cockateel, cockatiel ˌkɒk.əˈtiːl Ⓤⓢ ˌkɑː.kəˈ- **-s** -z
cockatoo ˌkɒk.əˈtuː Ⓤⓢ ˈkɑː.kə.tuː **-s** -z
cockatric|e ˈkɒk.ə.traɪs, -trɪs, -trəs Ⓤⓢ ˈkɑː.kə- **-es** -ɪz
Cockaygne kɒkˈeɪn, kəˈkeɪn Ⓤⓢ kɑːˈkeɪn
Cockburn ˈkəʊ.bɜːn, -bən Ⓤⓢ ˈkoʊ.bɝːn
cockchafer ˈkɒkˌtʃeɪ.fəʳ Ⓤⓢ ˈkɑːkˌtʃeɪ.fɚ **-s** -z
Cockcroft ˈkəʊk.krɒft, ˈkɒk.*k*rɒft Ⓤⓢ ˈkɑːk.*k*rɑːft, ˈkoʊ.krɑːft
cockcrow ˈkɒk.krəʊ Ⓤⓢ ˈkɑːk.kroʊ
Cocke *place:* kɒk Ⓤⓢ kɑːk *surname:* kəʊk, kɒk Ⓤⓢ koʊk, kɑːk
Cockell ˈkɒk.ᵊl Ⓤⓢ ˈkɑː.kᵊl
cocker (C) ˈkɒk.əʳ Ⓤⓢ ˈkɑː.kɚ **-s** -z ˌ**cocker ˈspaniel**
cockerel ˈkɒk.ᵊr.ᵊl Ⓤⓢ ˈkɑː.kɚ- **-s** -z
Cockerell ˈkɒk.ᵊr.ᵊl Ⓤⓢ ˈkɑː.kɚ-
Cockermouth ˈkɒk.ə.məθ, -maʊθ *locally:* -məθ Ⓤⓢ ˈkɑː.kɚ
cockeye ˈkɒk.aɪ Ⓤⓢ ˈkɑːk.aɪ **-d** kɒkˈaɪd Ⓤⓢ ˈkɑːk.aɪd *stress shift, British only:* ˌcockeyed ˈoptimist
cock|fight ˈkɒk|.faɪt Ⓤⓢ ˈkɑːk- **-fights** -faɪts **-fighting** -ˌfaɪ.tɪŋ Ⓤⓢ -ˌfaɪ.t̬ɪŋ
Cockfosters ˌkɒkˈfɒs.təz, ˈ-ˌ-- Ⓤⓢ ˈkɑːkˌfɑː.stɚz, ˌ-ˈ--
cockhors|e ˌkɒkˈhɔːs Ⓤⓢ ˈkɑːk.hɔːrs **-es** -ɪz
cockl|e (C) ˈkɒk.l̩ Ⓤⓢ ˈkɑː.kl̩ **-es** -z **-ing** -ɪŋ, ˈ-lɪŋ Ⓤⓢ ˈkɑː.kl̩.ɪŋ, ˈ-klɪŋ **-ed** -d
cockleshell ˈkɒk.l̩.ʃel Ⓤⓢ ˈkɑː.kl̩- **-s** -z
cockney (C) ˈkɒk.ni Ⓤⓢ ˈkɑːk- **-s** -z
cockneyism ˈkɒk.ni.ɪ.zᵊm Ⓤⓢ ˈkɑːk- **-s** -z
cockpit ˈkɒk.pɪt Ⓤⓢ ˈkɑːk- **-s** -s
cockroach ˈkɒk.rəʊtʃ Ⓤⓢ ˈkɑːk.roʊtʃ **-es** -ɪz
Cockroft ˈkɒk.rɒft, ˈkəʊ.krɒft Ⓤⓢ ˈkɑː.krɑːft, ˈkoʊ-
cockscomb ˈkɒk.skəʊm Ⓤⓢ ˈkɑːk.skoʊm **-s** -z
Cocksedge ˈkɒk.sɪdʒ, ˈkɒs.ɪdʒ, -edʒ, ˈkəʊ.sɪdʒ Ⓤⓢ ˈkɑːk.sɪdʒ, ˈkɑː-, ˈkoʊ-, -sedʒ
Cockshott ˈkɒk.ʃɒt Ⓤⓢ ˈkɑːk.ʃɑːt
cocksh|y ˈkɒk.ʃ|aɪ Ⓤⓢ ˈkɑːk- **-ies** -aɪz
cockspur (C) ˈkɒk.spɜːʳ, -spəʳ Ⓤⓢ ˈkɑːk.spɝːr **-s** -z
cocksure ˌkɒkˈʃʊəʳ, -ˈʃɔːʳ Ⓤⓢ ˌkɑːkˈʃʊr, -ˈʃɝːr
cocktail ˈkɒk.teɪl Ⓤⓢ ˈkɑːk- **-s** -z **ˈcocktail ˌdress** ; **ˈcocktail ˌlounge** ; **ˈcocktail ˌparty** ; **ˈcocktail ˌstick**
cock-up ˈkɒk.ʌp Ⓤⓢ ˈkɑːk- **-s** -s
Cockwood ˈkɒk.wʊd Ⓤⓢ ˈkɑːk-
Note: There exists also a local pronunciation /ˈkɒk.ʊd Ⓤⓢ ˈkɑː.kʊd/.
cock|y ˈkɒk|.i Ⓤⓢ ˈkɑː.k|i **-ier** -i.əʳ Ⓤⓢ -i.ɚ **-iest** -i.ɪst, -i.əst **-ily** -ɪ.li, -ᵊl.i **-iness** -ɪ.nəs, -ɪ.nɪs
cocky-leeky ˌkɒk.iˈliː.ki Ⓤⓢ ˌkɑː.ki-
coco ˈkəʊ.kəʊ Ⓤⓢ ˈkoʊ.koʊ **-s** -z
cocoa ˈkəʊ.kəʊ Ⓤⓢ ˈkoʊ.koʊ **-s** -z **ˈcocoa ˌbutter**
cocoanut ˈkəʊ.kə.nʌt Ⓤⓢ ˈkoʊ- **-s** -s
co-conspirator ˌkəʊ.kənˈspɪr.ə.təʳ, ˈ-ɪ- Ⓤⓢ ˌkoʊ.kənˈspɪr.ə.t̬ɚ **-s** -z
coconut ˈkəʊ.kə.nʌt Ⓤⓢ ˈkoʊ- **-s** -s ˌ**coconut ˈice** ; **ˈcoconut ˌshy**
cocoon kəˈkuːn **-s** -z **-ing** -ɪŋ **-ed** -d
Cocos ˈkəʊ.kəs, -kɒs Ⓤⓢ ˈkoʊ.koʊs, -kəs
cocotte kəˈkɒt, kəʊ-, kɒkˈɒt Ⓤⓢ koʊˈkɑːt **-s** -s
Cocteau ˈkɒk.təʊ Ⓤⓢ kɑːkˈtoʊ
Cocytus kə*ʊ*ˈsaɪ.təs Ⓤⓢ koʊˈsaɪ.t̬əs
cod (C) kɒd Ⓤⓢ kɑːd **-s** -z **-ding** -ɪŋ **-ded** -ɪd ˌ**cod-liver ˈoil**
COD ˌsiː.əʊˈdiː Ⓤⓢ -oʊˈ-
coda ˈkəʊ.də Ⓤⓢ ˈkoʊ- **-s** -z
Coddington ˈkɒd.ɪŋ.tən Ⓤⓢ ˈkɑː.dɪŋ-
coddl|e ˈkɒd.l̩ Ⓤⓢ ˈkɑː.dl̩ **-es** -z **-ing** -ɪŋ, ˈ-lɪŋ Ⓤⓢ ˈkɑː.dl̩.ɪŋ, ˈkɑːd.lɪŋ **-ed** -d
cod|e kəʊd Ⓤⓢ koʊd **-es** -z **-ing** -ɪŋ **-ed** -ɪd **-er/s** -əʳ/z Ⓤⓢ -ɚ/s
co-defendant ˌkəʊ.dɪˈfen.dənt, -dəˈ- Ⓤⓢ ˌkoʊ- **-s**
codeine ˈkəʊ.diːn Ⓤⓢ ˈkoʊ-
co-determination ˌkəʊ.dɪ.tɜː.mɪˈneɪ.ʃᵊn, -də- Ⓤⓢ ˌkoʊ.dɪ.tɝːr-, -də-
cod|ex ˈkəʊ.d|eks Ⓤⓢ ˈkoʊ- **-exes** -ek.sɪz, -səz **-ices** -ɪ.siːz, ˈkɒd.ɪ.siːz Ⓤⓢ ˈkoʊ.də.siːz, ˈkɑː-
codger ˈkɒdʒ.əʳ Ⓤⓢ ˈkɑː.dʒɚ **-s** -z
codicil ˈkəʊ.dɪ.sɪl, ˈkɒd.ɪ-, ˈ-ə- Ⓤⓢ ˈkɑː.də.sᵊl, -sɪl **-s** -z
codicillary ˌkəʊ.dɪˈsɪl.ᵊr.i, ˌkɒd.ɪˈ- Ⓤⓢ ˌkɑː.dəˈ-
Codicote ˈkəʊ.dɪ.kəʊt, ˈkɒd.ɪ.kət Ⓤⓢ ˈkoʊ.dɪ.koʊt, ˈkɑː.dɪ.kət
codification ˌkəʊ.dɪ.fɪˈkeɪ.ʃᵊn, -də- Ⓤⓢ ˌkɑː-, ˌkoʊ- **-s** -z
codi|fy ˈkəʊ.dɪ|.faɪ, -də- Ⓤⓢ ˈkɑː-, ˈkoʊ- **-fies** -faɪz **-fying** -faɪ.ɪŋ **-fied** -faɪd
codling ˈkɒd.lɪŋ Ⓤⓢ ˈkɑːd- **-s** -z
codpiec|e ˈkɒd.piːs Ⓤⓢ ˈkɑːd- **-es** -ɪz
Codrington ˈkɒd.rɪŋ.tən Ⓤⓢ ˈkɑːd-
Codsall ˈkɒd.sᵊl Ⓤⓢ ˈkɑːd-
codswallop ˈkɒdzˌwɒl.əp Ⓤⓢ ˈkɑːdzˌwɑː.ləp, -ˌwɔː-
Cody ˈkəʊ.di Ⓤⓢ ˈkoʊ-
Coe kəʊ Ⓤⓢ koʊ
coed ˌkəʊˈed Ⓤⓢ ˈkoʊ.ed **-s** -z *stress shift, British only:* ˌcoed ˈschool
Coed kɔɪd
coeducation ˌkəʊ.edʒ.ʊˈkeɪ.ʃᵊn, -ed.jʊˈ- Ⓤⓢ ˌkoʊ.edʒ.ʊˈ-, -əˈ-
coeducational ˌkəʊ.edʒ.ʊˈkeɪ.ʃᵊn.ᵊl, -ed.jʊˈ-, -ˈkeɪʃ.nᵊl Ⓤⓢ ˌkoʊ.edʒ.əˈ- **-ly** -li
coefficient ˌkəʊ.ɪˈfɪʃ.ᵊnt, -əˈfɪʃ- Ⓤⓢ ˌkoʊ- **-s** -s
coelacanth ˈsiː.lə.kæn*t*θ **-s** -s
coeliac ˈsiː.li.æk
coenobite ˈsiː.nə*ʊ*.baɪt Ⓤⓢ ˈsen.ə- **-s** -s
coequal ˌkəʊˈiː.kwᵊl Ⓤⓢ ˌkoʊ- **-ly** -i
coequality ˌkəʊ.ɪˈkwɒl.ə.ti, -ɪ.ti Ⓤⓢ ˌkoʊ.iːˈkwɑː.lə.t̬i
coerc|e kəʊˈɜːs Ⓤⓢ koʊˈɝːrs **-es** -ɪz **-ing** -ɪŋ **-ed** -t
coercib|le kəʊˈɜː.sɪ.b|l̩, -sə- Ⓤⓢ koʊˈɝːr- **-ly** -li
coercion kəʊˈɜː.ʃᵊn Ⓤⓢ koʊˈɝːr.ʒᵊn, -ʃᵊn
coercionist kəʊˈɜː.ʃᵊn.ɪst Ⓤⓢ koʊˈɝːr.ʒᵊn-, -ʃᵊn- **-s** -s
coercive kəʊˈɜː.sɪv Ⓤⓢ koʊˈɝːr- **-ly** -li
co-eternal ˌkəʊ.ɪˈtɜː.nᵊl Ⓤⓢ ˌkoʊ.ɪˈtɝːr-
Coetzee kuːtˈsɪə, -siː
Coeur de Lion ˌkɜː.dəˈliː.ɔ̃ːŋ, -dᵊlˈiː-, -ɒn Ⓤⓢ ˌkɝːr.dəˈliː.ən, -ˈlaɪən
coeval kəʊˈiː.vᵊl Ⓤⓢ koʊ- **-s** -z
co-executor ˌkəʊ.ɪɡˈzek.jʊ.təʳ, -eɡˈ-, -jə-; -ɪkˈsek-, -ekˈ- Ⓤⓢ ˌkoʊ.ɪɡˈzek.juː.t̬ɚ, -eɡˈ- **-s** -z
co-exist ˌkəʊ.ɪɡˈzɪst, -eɡˈ-, -əɡˈ-; -ɪkˈsɪst, -ekˈ-, -əkˈ- Ⓤⓢ ˌkoʊ.ɪɡˈzɪst, -eɡˈ- **-s** -s **-ing** -ɪŋ **-ed** -ɪd
co-existen|ce ˌkəʊ.ɪɡˈzɪs.tᵊn|*t*s, -eɡˈ-, -əɡˈ-; -ɪkˈsɪs-, -ekˈ-, -əkˈ- Ⓤⓢ ˌkoʊ.ɪɡˈ-, -eɡˈ- **-t** -t
co-extend ˌkəʊ.ɪkˈstend, -ekˈ-, -əkˈ- Ⓤⓢ ˌkoʊ.ɪkˈ-, -ekˈ- **-s** -z **-ing** -ɪŋ **-ed** -ɪd
co-extension ˌkəʊ.ɪkˈsten.*t*ʃᵊn, -ekˈ-, -əkˈ- Ⓤⓢ ˌkoʊ.ɪkˈ-, -ekˈ- **-s** -z
co-extensive ˌkəʊ.ɪkˈsten*t*.sɪv, -ekˈ-, -əkˈ- Ⓤⓢ ˌkoʊ.ɪkˈ-, -ekˈ-
Coey ˈkəʊ.i Ⓤⓢ ˈkoʊ-
C of E (*abbrev. for* **Church of England**) ˌsiː.əvˈiː
coffee ˈkɒf.i Ⓤⓢ ˈkɑː.fi, ˈkɔː- **-s** -z **ˈcoffee ˌbar** ; **ˈcoffee ˌbean** ; **ˈcoffee ˌbreak** ; **ˈcoffee ˌcup** ; **ˈcoffee ˌmill** ; **ˈcoffee ˌtable**

coffeehou|se ˈkɒf.i.haʊ|s (US) ˈkɑː.fi-, ˈkɔː- **-ses** -zɪz

coffee klatch, coffee klatsch ˈkɒf.iˌklætʃ (US) ˈkɑː.fi-, ˈkɔː-

coffeemaker ˈkɒf.iˌmeɪ.kəʳ (US) ˈkɑː.fiˌmeɪ.kɚ, ˈkɔː- **-s** -z

coffeepot ˈkɒf.i.pɒt (US) ˈkɑː.fi.pɑːt, ˈkɔː- **-s** -s

coffer ˈkɒf.əʳ (US) ˈkɑː.fɚ, ˈkɔː- **-s** -z

Coffey ˈkɒf.i (US) ˈkɑː.fi, ˈkɔː-

coffin (C) ˈkɒf.ɪn (US) ˈkɔː.fɪn, ˈkɑː- **-s** -z **-ing** -ɪŋ **-ed** -d

cog kɒg (US) kɑːg, kɔːg **-s** -z **-ging** -ɪŋ **-ged** -d

cogen|ce ˈkəʊ.dʒᵊnt|s (US) ˈkoʊ- **-cy** -si

Cogenhoe ˈkʊk.nəʊ (US) -noʊ

cogent ˈkəʊ.dʒᵊnt (US) ˈkoʊ- **-ly** -li

Coggeshall *in Essex:* ˈkɒg.ɪ.ʃᵊl; ˈkɒk.sᵊl (US) ˈkɑː.gɪ.ʃᵊl, ˈkɔː-; ˈkɑːk.sᵊl *surname:* ˈkɒg.zɔːl (US) ˈkɑːg.zɔːl, ˈkɔːg-, -zɑːl

Coggin ˈkɒg.ɪn (US) ˈkɑː.gɪn, ˈkɔː-

Coghill ˈkɒg.ɪl, -hɪl (US) ˈkɑː.gɪl, ˈkɔː-, ˈkɑːg.hɪl, ˈkɔːg-

cogi|tate ˈkɒdʒ.ɪ|.teɪt, ˈ-ə- (US) ˈkɑː.dʒə- **-tates** -teɪts **-tating** -teɪ.tɪŋ (US) -teɪ.t̬ɪŋ **-tated** -teɪ.tɪd (US) -teɪ.t̬ɪd **-tator/s** -teɪ.təʳ/z (US) -teɪ.t̬ɚ/z

cogitation ˌkɒdʒ.ɪˈteɪ.ʃᵊn, -əˈ- (US) ˌkɑː.dʒəˈ- **-s** -z

cogitative ˈkɒdʒ.ɪ.tə.tɪv, ˈ-ə-, -teɪ- (US) ˈkɑː.dʒə.teɪ.t̬ɪv

cogito ergo sum ˌkɒg.ɪ.təʊˌɜː.gəʊˈsʊm (US) ˌkɑː.giː.toʊˌer.goʊˈsʌm, ˌkoʊ.gə-, -dʒiː-, -ˌɜːr-, -ˈsʊm

cognac ˈkɒn.jæk (US) ˈkoʊ.njæk **-s** -s

cognate ˈkɒg.neɪt, -ˈ- (US) ˈkɑːg.neɪt, ˈkɔːg- **-s** -s

cognation kɒgˈneɪ.ʃᵊn (US) kɑːg-, kɔːg-

cognition kɒgˈnɪʃ.ᵊn (US) kɑːg-, kɔːg- **-s** -z

cognitive ˈkɒg.nə.tɪv, -nɪ- (US) ˈkɑːg.nə.t̬ɪv, ˈkɔːg-

cognizable, -isa- ˈkɒg.nɪ.zə.bl̩, ˈkɒn.ɪ-; kɒgˈnaɪ- (US) ˈkɑːg.nɪ-, ˈkɔːg-, ˈkɑː-, kɑːgˈnaɪ-, kɔːg-

cognizanc|e, -isa- ˈkɒg.nɪ.zᵊnts, ˈkɒn.ɪ-; kɒgˈnaɪ- (US) ˈkɑːg.nə-, ˈkɔːg-, ˈkɑː- **-es** -ɪz

cognizant, -isa- ˈkɒg.nɪ.zᵊnt, ˈkɒn.ɪ-; kɒgˈnaɪ- (US) ˈkɑːg.nə-, ˈkɔːg-, ˈkɑː-

cognomen kɒgˈnəʊ.men, -mən (US) kɑːgˈnoʊ-, kɔːg- **-s** -z

cognominal kɒgˈnəʊ.mɪ.nᵊl, -ˈnɒm.ɪ- (US) kɑːgˈnɑː.mə-, kɔːg-

cognoscent|e ˌkɒn.jəʊˈʃen.t|i, ˌkɒg.nəʊˈ-, -ˈsen- (US) ˌkɑːg.nəˈʃen.t̬|i, ˌkɔːg-, ˌkɑː.njəˈ- **-i** -iː, -i

cognovit kɒgˈnəʊ.vɪt (US) kɑːgˈnoʊ-, kɔːg- **-s** -s

cogwheel ˈkɒg.wiːl, -hwiːl (US) ˈkɑːg-, ˈkɔːg- **-s** -z

cohab|it kəʊˈhæb|.ɪt (US) koʊ- **-its** -ɪts **-iting** -ɪ.tɪŋ (US) -ɪ.t̬ɪŋ **-ited** -ɪ.tɪd (US) -ɪ.t̬ɪd

cohabitant kəʊˈhæb.ɪ.tᵊnt (US) koʊˈhæb.ɪ.t̬ᵊnt **-s** -s

cohabitation kəʊˌhæb.ɪˈteɪ.ʃᵊn, ˌkəʊ.hæb- (US) koʊˌhæb-

cohabitee ˌkəʊ.hæb.ɪˈtiː, kəʊˌhæb.ɪˈtiː (US) ˌkoʊ- **-s** -z

co-heir ˌkəʊˈeəʳ, ˈ-- (US) ˈkoʊ.er, -ˈ- **-s** -z

co-heiress ˌkəʊˈeə.res, -rɪs, -rəs, ˌ--ˈ- (US) ˈkoʊ.er.əs, ˌ-ˈ-- **-es** -ɪz

Cohen ˈkəʊ.ɪn, -ən (US) ˈkoʊ.ən

coher|e kəʊˈhɪəʳ (US) koʊˈhɪr **-es** -z **-ing** -ɪŋ **-ed** -d

coheren|ce kəʊˈhɪə.rᵊn*t*|s (US) koʊˈhɪr.ᵊn*t*|s **-cy** -si

coherent kəʊˈhɪə.rᵊnt (US) koʊˈhɪr.ᵊnt **-ly** -li

cohesion kəʊˈhiː.ʒᵊn (US) koʊ-

cohesive kəʊˈhiː.sɪv, -zɪv (US) koʊ- **-ly** -li **-ness** -nəs, -nɪs

Cohn kəʊn (US) koʊn

Cohn-Bendit ˌkəʊnˈben.dɪt, ˌkəʊm- (US) ˌkoʊn-

cohort ˈkəʊ.hɔːt (US) ˈkoʊ.hɔːrt **-s** -s

COHSE ˈkəʊ.zi (US) ˈkoʊ-

coif (*n.*) kɔɪf **-s** -s

coif (*v.*) kwɑːf **-s** -s **-fing** -ɪŋ **-fed** -t

coiffé ˈkwɑː.feɪ, ˈkwɒf.eɪ, ˈkwæf-, -ˈ- (US) kwɑːˈfeɪ **-s** -z **-ing** -ɪŋ **-d** -d

coiffeur kwɑːˈfɜːʳ, kwɒfˈɜːʳ, kwæf- (US) kwɑːˈfɜːr **-s** -z

coiffeus|e kwɑːˈfɜːz, kwɒfˈɜːz, kwæf- (US) kwɑːˈfɜːz **-es** -ɪz

coiffure kwɒːˈfjʊəʳ, kwɒfˈjʊəʳ, kwæf- (US) kwɑːˈfjʊr **-s** -z

coign kɔɪn **-s** -z

coil kɔɪl **-s** -z **-ing** -ɪŋ **-ed** -d

Coimbra ˈkwɪm.brə, ˈkwiːm-

coin kɔɪn **-s** -z **-ing** -ɪŋ **-ed** -d **-er/s** -əʳ/z (US) -ɚ/z

coinag|e ˈkɔɪ.nɪdʒ **-es** -ɪz

coin-box ˈkɔɪn.bɒks, ˈkɔɪm- (US) ˈkɔɪn.bɑːks **-es** -ɪz

coincid|e ˌkəʊ.ɪnˈsaɪd, -ənˈ- (US) ˌkoʊ- **-es** -z **-ing** -ɪŋ **-ed** -ɪd

coincidenc|e kəʊˈɪn*t*.sɪ.dᵊn*t*s (US) koʊ- **-es** -ɪz

coincidental kəʊˌɪn*t*.sɪˈden.tᵊl, ˌkəʊ.ɪn- (US) koʊˌɪn*t*.sɪˈden.t̬ᵊl **-ly** -i

co-inheritor ˌkəʊ.ɪnˈher.ɪ.təʳ, ˈ-ə- (US) ˌkoʊ.ɪnˈher.ə.t̬ɚ **-s** -z

coinsurance ˌkəʊ.ɪnˈʃʊə.rᵊn*t*s, -ˈʃɔː- (US) ˌkoʊ.ɪnˈʃʊr.ᵊn*t*s, -ˈʃɜːr-

coinsur|e ˌkəʊ.ɪnˈʃʊəʳ, -ˈʃɔːʳ (US) ˌkoʊ.ɪnˈʃʊr, -ˈʃɜːr **-es** -z **-ing** -ɪŋ **-ed** -d **-er/s** -əʳ/z (US) -ɚ/z

Cointreau® ˈkwɒn.trəʊ, ˈkwɑːn-, ˈkwæn- (US) ˈkwɑːn.troʊ

coir kɔɪəʳ (US) kɔɪr

coition kəʊˈɪʃ.ᵊn (US) koʊ-

coit|us ˈkəʊ.ɪ.t|əs, ˈkɔɪ.t|əs (US) ˈkoʊ.ə.t̬|əs **-al** -ᵊl **-ally** -ᵊl.i

coitus interruptus ˌkəʊ.ɪ.təs.ɪn.təˈrʌp.təs, ˌkɔɪ- (US) ˌkoʊ.ə.t̬əs.ɪn.t̬əˈ-

coke kəʊk (US) koʊk

Coke *surname:* kəʊk, kʊk (US) koʊk

Note: Members of the Essex family pronounce /kʊk/. So also the family name of the Earl of Leicester.

Coke® kəʊk (US) koʊk

Coker ˈkəʊ.kəʳ (US) ˈkoʊ.kɚ

col kɒl (US) kɑːl **-s** -z

Col. (*abbrev. for* **Colonel**) ˈkɜː.nᵊl (US) ˈkɜːr-

cola ˈkəʊ.lə (US) ˈkoʊ- **-s**

colander ˈkʌl.ən.dəʳ, ˈkɒl- (US) ˈkʌl.ən.dɚ, ˈkɑː.lən- **-s** -z

Colbert kɒlˈbeəʳ (US) kɔːlˈber, koʊl-

Colby ˈkəʊl.bi, ˈkɒl- (US) ˈkoʊl-

colcannon kəlˈkæn.ən, ˈkɒl.kæn- (US) kəlˈkæn.ən, ˈkɑːl.kæn-

Colchester ˈkəʊl.tʃɪ.stəʳ, -tʃə- (US) ˈkoʊl.tʃes.tɚ

colchicum ˈkɒl.tʃɪ.kəm, -kɪ- (US) ˈkɑːl-

Colchis ˈkɒl.kɪs (US) ˈkɑːl-

Colclough ˈkɒl.klʌf, ˈkəʊl-, ˈkəʊ.kli, (US) ˈkɑːl.klʌf, ˈkoʊl-, ˈkoʊ.kli

cold kəʊld (US) koʊld **-s** -z **-er** -əʳ (US) -ɚ **-est** -ɪst, -əst **-ly** -li **-ness** -nəs, -nɪs **ˌcold ˈcomfort ; ˈcold ˌcream ; ˌcold ˈfeet ; ˈcold ˌframe ; ˈcold ˌsore ; ˌcold ˈstorage ; ˌcold ˈturkey ; ˌcold ˈwar ; ˌcold ˈwater ; blow ˌhot and ˈcold**

cold-blooded ˌkəʊldˈblʌd.ɪd (US) ˌkoʊld- **-ly** -li **-ness** -nəs, -nɪs *stress shift:* ˌcold-blooded ˈkiller

cold-call (*v.*) ˈkəʊld.kɔːl (US) ˈkoʊld-, -kɑːl **-s** -z **-ing** -ɪŋ **-ed** -d

cold-hearted ˌkəʊldˈhɑː.tɪd (US) ˌkoʊldˈhɑːr.t̬ɪd **-ness** -nəs, -nɪs

coldish ˈkəʊl.dɪʃ (US) ˈkoʊl-

Colditz ˈkəʊl.dɪts (US) ˈkoʊl-, ˈkɑːl-

cold-should|er ˌkəʊldˈʃəʊl.d|əʳ (US) ˌkoʊldˈʃoʊl.d|ɚ **-ers** -əz (US) -ɚz **-ering** -ᵊr.ɪŋ **-ered** -əd (US) -ɚd

Coldstream ˈkəʊl*d*.striːm (US) ˈkoʊl*d*-

cole (C) kəʊl (US) koʊl **-s** -z

Colebrook(e) ˈkəʊl.brʊk (US) ˈkoʊl-

Coleby ˈkəʊl.bi (US) ˈkoʊl-

Coleclough ˈkəʊl.klaʊ, -klʌf (US) ˈkoʊl-

Coleford ˈkəʊl.fəd (US) ˈkoʊl.fɚd

Coleman ˈkəʊl.mən (US) ˈkoʊl-

Colenso kəˈlen.zəʊ (US) -zoʊ

coleopter|a ˌkɒl.iˈɒp.tᵊr|.ə (US) ˌkɑː.liˈɑːp- **-al** -ᵊl

Coleraine kəʊlˈreɪn (US) koʊl-

Coleridge ˈkəʊ.lᵊr.ɪdʒ US ˈkoʊ-
Coles kəʊlz US koʊlz
Coleshill ˈkəʊlz.hɪl US ˈkoʊlz-
coleslaw ˈkəʊl.slɔː US ˈkoʊl.slɑː, -slɔː
Colet ˈkɒl.ɪt US ˈkɑː.lɪt
cole-tit ˈkəʊl.tɪt US ˈkoʊl- **-s** -s
Colette kɒlˈet, kəˈlet US koʊˈlet, kɑː-
coley (C) ˈkəʊ.li US ˈkoʊ- **-s** -z
Colgan ˈkɒl.gən US ˈkɑːl-
Colgate® ˈkəʊl.geɪt, ˈkɒl-, -gət, -gɪt US ˈkoʊl.geɪt
colic ˈkɒl.ɪk US ˈkɑː.lɪk **-ky** -i
Colin ˈkɒl.ɪn US ˈkɑː.lɪn
Colindale ˈkɒl.ɪn.deɪl, -ən- US ˈkɑː.lɪn-, -lən-
Coling ˈkəʊ.lɪŋ US ˈkoʊ-
coliseum (C) ˌkɒl.ɪˈsiː.əm, -əˈ- US ˌkɑː.ləˈ-
colitis kɒlˈaɪ.tɪs, kə*ʊ*ˈlaɪ- US koʊˈlaɪ.t̬əs, kə-
collabor|ate kəˈlæb.ᵊr|.eɪt, kɒlˈæb- US kəˈlæb.ə.r|eɪt **-ates** -eɪts **-ating** -eɪ.tɪŋ US -eɪ.t̬ɪŋ **-ated** -eɪ.tɪd US -eɪ.t̬ɪd
collaboration kəˌlæb.əˈreɪ.ʃᵊn, kɒlˌæb- US kəˌlæb- **-s** -z
collaborator kəˈlæb.ᵊr.eɪ.təʳ, kɒlˈæb- US kəˈlæb.ə.reɪ.t̬ɚ **-s** -z
collag|e kɒlˈɑːʒ, kəˈlɑːʒ; ˈkɒl.ɑːʒ US kəˈlɑːʒ, kɑː-, koʊ- **-es** -ɪz
collagen ˈkɒl.ə.dʒən, -dʒɪn US ˈkɑː.lə-
collagenic ˌkɒl.əˈdʒen.ɪk US ˌkɑː.ləˈ-
collagenous kəˈlædʒ.ɪ.nəs, ˈ-ə-
collaps|e kəˈlæps **-es** -ɪz **-ing** -ɪŋ **-ed** -t
collapsible kəˈlæp.sɪ.bl̩, -sə-
coll|ar ˈkɒl|.əʳ US ˈkɑː.l|ɚ **-ars** -əz US -ɚz **-aring** -ər.ɪŋ **-ared** -əd US -ɚd ˌ**hot under the** ˈ**collar**
collarbone ˈkɒl.ə.bəʊn US ˈkɑː.lɚ.boʊn **-s** -z
Collard ˈkɒl.əd US ˈkɑː.lɚd
coll|ate kəˈl|eɪt, kɒlˈ|eɪt US kəˈl|eɪt, koʊ-, kɑː- **-ates** -eɪts **-ating** -eɪ.tɪŋ US -eɪ.t̬ɪŋ **-ated** -eɪ.tɪd US -eɪ.t̬ɪd **-ator/s** -eɪ.təʳ/z US -eɪ.t̬ɚ/z
collateral kəˈlæt.ᵊr.ᵊl, kɒlˈæt- US kəˈlæt̬- **-s** -z **-ly** -i
collation kəˈleɪ.ʃᵊn, kɒlˈeɪ- US kɑːˈleɪ-, kə-, koʊ- **-s** -z
colleague ˈkɒl.iːg US ˈkɑː.liːg **-s** -z
collect (*n.*) ˈkɒl.ˈekt, -ɪkt US ˈkɑːl.ekt, -ɪkt **-s** -s
collect (*v.*) kəˈlekt **-s** -s **-ing** -ɪŋ **-ed** -ɪd
collectable kəˈlek.tə.bl̩ **-s** -z
collectanea ˌkɒl.ekˈteɪ.ni.ə, -ˈtɑː- US ˌkɑː.lekˈ-
collected kəˈlek.tɪd, -təd **-ly** -li **-ness** -nəs, -nɪs
collectible kəˈlek.tə.bl̩, -tɪ- **-s** -z
collection kəˈlek.ʃᵊn **-s** -z
collective kəˈlek.tɪv coˌ**llective** ˈ**bargaining**
collectiv|ism kəˈlek.tɪ.v|ɪ.zᵊm US -tə- **-ist/s** -ɪst/s
collectivity ˌkɒl.ekˈtɪv.ɪ.ti, kəˌlek-, -ə.ti US ˌkɑː.lekˈtɪv.ə.t̬i, kəˌlekˈ-
collectivization, -isa- kəˌlek.tɪ.vaɪˈzeɪ.ʃᵊn, -tə-, -vɪˈ- US -tɪ.vɪˈzeɪ-
collectiviz|e, -is|e kəˈlek.tɪ.vaɪz, -tə- **-es** -ɪz **-ing** -ɪŋ **-ed** -d
collector kəˈlek.təʳ US -tɚ **-s** -z coˈ**llector's** ˌ**item**, coˌ**llector's** ˈ**item**
colleen (C) ˈkɒl.iːn *in Ireland:* -ˈ- US kɑːˈliːn, ˈ-- **-s** -z
colleg|e (C) ˈkɒl.ɪdʒ US ˈkɑː.lɪdʒ **-es** -ɪz ˈ**College** ˌ**Board** ; ˌ**college** ˈ**try**
collegian kəˈliː.dʒi.ən, kɒlˈiː-, ˈ-dʒᵊn US kəˈliː.dʒən, ˈ-dʒi.ən **-s** -z
collegiate kəˈliː.dʒi.ət, kɒlˈiː-, -dʒət US kəˈliː.dʒɪt, -dʒi.ɪt
Colles ˈkɒl.ɪs, -əs US ˈkɑː.lɪs
collet (C) ˈkɒl.ɪt, -ət US ˈkɑː.lɪt **-s** -s
Collett ˈkɒl.ɪt, -et, -ət US ˈkɑː.lɪt
Colley ˈkɒl.i US ˈkɑː.li
collid|e kəˈlaɪd **-es** -z **-ing** -ɪŋ **-ed** -ɪd
collie (C) ˈkɒl.i US ˈkɑː.li **-s** -z
collier (C) ˈkɒl.i.əʳ, ˈ-jəʳ US ˈkɑːl.jɚ **-s** -z
collier|y ˈkɒl.jə.r|i, -i.ᵊr|.i US ˈkɑːl.jɚ|.i **-ies** -iz
colli|gate ˈkɒl.ɪ|.geɪt, ˈ-ə- US ˈkɑː.lə- **-gates** -geɪts **-gating** -geɪ.tɪŋ US -geɪ.t̬ɪŋ **-gated** -geɪ.tɪd US -geɪ.t̬ɪd
colligation ˌkɒl.ɪˈgeɪ.ʃᵊn, -əˈ- US ˌkɑː.ləˈ-
colli|mate ˈkɒl.ɪ|.meɪt, ˈ-ə- US ˈkɑː.lə- **-mates** -meɪts **-mating** -meɪ.tɪŋ US -meɪ.t̬ɪŋ **-mated** -meɪ.tɪd US -meɪ.t̬ɪd
collimation ˌkɒl.ɪˈmeɪ.ʃᵊn, -əˈ- US ˌkɑː.ləˈ-
collimator ˈkɒl.ɪ.meɪ.təʳ, ˈ-ə- US ˈkɑː.lə.meɪ.t̬ɚ **-s** -z
collinear kɒlˈɪn.i.əʳ, kə*ʊ*ˈlɪn- US kəˈlɪn.i.ɚ, kɑː-
Collingham ˈkɒl.ɪŋ.əm US ˈkɑː.lɪŋ-
Collings ˈkɒl.ɪŋz US ˈkɑː.lɪŋz
Collingwood ˈkɒl.ɪŋ.wʊd US ˈkɑː.lɪŋ-
Collins ˈkɒl.ɪnz US ˈkɑː.lɪnz
Collinson ˈkɒl.ɪn.sᵊn, -ən- US ˈkɑː.lɪn-
Collis ˈkɒl.ɪs US ˈkɑː.lɪs
collision kəˈlɪʒ.ᵊn **-s** -z coˈ**llision** ˌ**course**
collo|cate ˈkɒl.əʊ|.keɪt US ˈkɑː.lə- **-cates** -keɪts **-cating** -keɪ.tɪŋ US -keɪ.t̬ɪŋ **-cated** -keɪ.tɪd US -keɪ.t̬ɪd
collocation ˌkɒl.ə*ʊ*ˈkeɪ.ʃᵊn US ˌkɑː.ləˈ- **-s** -z
collodi|on kəˈləʊ.di|.ən US -ˈloʊ- **-um** -əm
colloid ˈkɒl.ɔɪd US ˈkɑː.lɔɪd **-s** -z
colloidal kəˈlɔɪ.dᵊl, kɒlˈɔɪ- US kəˈlɔɪ-
collop ˈkɒl.əp US ˈkɑː.ləp **-s** -s
colloquial kəˈləʊ.kwi.əl US -ˈloʊ- **-ly** -i **-ism/s** -ɪ.zᵊm/z
colloquium kəˈləʊ.kwi.əm US -ˈloʊ-
colloqu|y ˈkɒl.ə.kw|i US ˈkɑː.lə- **-ies** -iz
collotype ˈkɒl.ə*ʊ*.taɪp US ˈkɑː.lə- **-s** -s
Colls kɒlz US kɑːlz
collud|e kəˈluːd, -ˈljuːd US -ˈluːd **-es** -z **-ing** -ɪŋ **-ed** -ɪd **-er/s** -əʳ/z US -ɚ/z
collusion kəˈluː.ʒᵊn, -ˈljuː- US -ˈluː- **-s** -z
collusive kəˈluː.sɪv, -ˈljuː- US -ˈluː- **-ly** -li
Collyns ˈkɒl.ɪnz US ˈkɑː.lɪnz
collywobbles ˈkɒl.iˌwɒb.l̩z US ˈkɑː.liˌwɑː-
Colman ˈkəʊl.mən, ˈkɒl- US ˈkoʊl-, ˈkɑːl-
Colnaghi kɒlˈnɑː.gi US kɑːl-
Colnbrook ˈkəʊln.brʊk, ˈkəʊn- US ˈkoʊln-, ˈkoʊn-
Colne kəʊn, kəʊln US koʊn, koʊln
Colney ˈkəʊ.ni US ˈkoʊ-
Colo. (*abbrev. for* **Colorado**) ˌkɒl.ᵊrˈɑː.dəʊ US ˌkɑː.ləˈræd.oʊ, -ˈrɑː.doʊ
cologne (C) kəˈləʊn US -ˈloʊn **-s** -z
Colombi|a kəˈlɒm.bi|.ə, -ˈlʌm- US -ˈlʌm- **-an/s** -ən/z
Colombo kəˈlʌm.bəʊ, -ˈlɒm- US -ˈlʌm.boʊ
colon *punctuation, part of intestine:* ˈkəʊ.lɒn, -lən US ˈkoʊ.lən **-s** -z **cola** ˈkəʊ.lə US ˈkoʊ-
colon, colón *currency:* kɒlˈɒn, kəˈlɒn US kəˈloʊn **-s** -z **-es** -es, -əs
colonel (C) ˈkɜː.nᵊl US ˈkɝː- **-s** -z ˌ**Colonel** ˈ**Blimp**
colonelc|y ˈkɜː.nᵊl.s|i US ˈkɝː- **-ies** -iz
colonelship ˈkɜː.nᵊl.ʃɪp US ˈkɝː- **-s** -s
colonial kəˈləʊ.ni.əl US -ˈloʊ- **-s** -z
colonial|ism kəˈləʊ.ni.ə.l|ɪ.zᵊm US -ˈloʊ- **-ist/s** -ɪst/s
colonist ˈkɒl.ə.nɪst US ˈkɑː.lə- **-s** -s
colonization, -isa- ˌkɒl.ə.naɪˈzeɪ.ʃᵊn, -nɪˈ- US ˌkɑː.lə.nɪˈ-
coloniz|e, -is|e ˈkɒl.ə.naɪz US ˈkɑː.lə- **-es** -ɪz **-ing** -ɪŋ **-ed** -d **-er/s** -əʳ/z US -ɚ/z
colonnade ˌkɒl.əˈneɪd US ˌkɑː.ləˈ- **-s** -z
Colonus kəˈləʊ.nəs US -ˈloʊ-
colon|y ˈkɒl.ə.n|i US ˈkɑː.lə- **-ies** -iz
colophon ˈkɒl.ə.fən, -fɒn US ˈkɑː.lə.fən, -fɑːn **-s** -z
col|or ˈkʌl|.əʳ US -ɚ **-ors** -əz US -ɚz **-oring** -ᵊr.ɪŋ **-ored** -əd US -ɚd **-orer/s** -ᵊr.əʳ/z US -ɚ.ɚ/z **-orist/s** -ᵊr.ɪst/s
colorab|le ˈkʌl.ᵊr.ə.bl̩| **-ly** -li
Colorado ˌkɒl.ᵊrˈɑː.dəʊ US ˌkɑː.ləˈræd.oʊ, -ˈrɑː.doʊ *stress*

shift, see compounds: ˌ**Colorado 'beetle** ; ˌ**Colorado 'Springs**
colorant 'kʌl.ᵊr.ənt **-s** -s
coloration ˌkʌl.ə'reɪ.ʃᵊn
coloratura ˌkɒl.ᵊr.ə'tjʊə.rə, -'tʊə- (US) ˌkʌl.ɚ.ə'tʊr.ə, ˌkɑː.lɚ-, -'tjʊr-
color|-blind 'kʌl.ə|.blaɪnd (US) '-ɚ- **-blindness** -ˌblaɪn*d*.nəs, -nɪs
colorcast 'kʌl.ə.kɑːst (US) -ɚ.kæst **-s** -s **-ing** -ɪŋ **-ed** -ɪd
color-coded 'kʌl.əˌkəʊ.dɪd (US) -ɚ.koʊ-
colorfast 'kʌl.ə.fɑːst (US) -ɚ.fæst **-ness** -nəs, -nɪs
colorful 'kʌl.ə.fᵊl, -fʊl (US) '-ɚ- **-ly** -i
colorific ˌkɒl.ə'rɪf.ɪk, ˌkʌl- (US) ˌkʌl-
coloring 'kʌl.ᵊr.ɪŋ **-s** -z
Colorization® ˌkɒl.ə.raɪ'zeɪ.ʃᵊn, ˌkʌl-, -rɪ'- (US) ˌkʌl.ɚ.ɪ'-
colorless 'kʌl.ə.ləs, -lɪs (US) '-ɚ- **-ly** -li **-ness** -nəs, -nɪs
colossal kə'lɒs.ᵊl (US) -'lɑː.sᵊl **-ly** -i
colosseum (C) ˌkɒl.ə'siː.əm (US) ˌkɑː.lə'-
Colossian kə'lɒs.i.ən, -'lɒʃ.i.ən, -'lɒʃ.ᵊn (US) -'lɑː.ʃᵊn **-s** -z
coloss|us kə'lɒs|.əs (US) -'lɑː.s|əs **-i** -aɪ **-uses** -ə.sɪz
colostom|y kə'lɒs.tə.m|i, kɒl'ɒs- (US) kə'lɑː.stə- **-ies** -iz
colostrum kə'lɒs.trəm, kɒl'ɒs- (US) kə'lɑː.strəm
col|our 'kʌl|.əʳ (US) -ɚ **-ours** -əz (US) -ɚz **-ouring** -ᵊr.ɪŋ **-oured** -əd (US) -ɚd **-ourer/s** -ᵊr.əʳ/z (US) -ɚ.ɚ/z **-ourist/s** -ᵊr.ɪst/s
colourab|le 'kʌl.ᵊr.ə.b|l̩ **-ly** -li
colourant 'kʌl.ᵊr.ənt **-s** -s
colouration ˌkʌl.ə'reɪ.ʃᵊn
colour|-blind 'kʌl.ə|.blaɪnd (US) '-ɚ- **-blindness** -ˌblaɪn*d*.nəs, -nɪs
colourcast 'kʌl.ə.kɑːst (US) -ɚ.kæst **-s** -s
colour-coded 'kʌl.əˌkəʊ.dɪd (US) -ɚˌkoʊ-
colourfast 'kʌl.ə.fɑːst (US) -ɚ.fæst **-ness** -nəs, -nɪs
colourful 'kʌl.ə.fᵊl, -fʊl (US) '-ɚ- **-ly** -i
colouring 'kʌl.ᵊr.ɪŋ **-s** -z
colourless 'kʌl.ə.ləs, -lɪs (US) '-ɚ- **-ly** -li **-ness** -nəs, -nɪs
colourway 'kʌl.ə.weɪ (US) -ɚ- **-s** -z
colpo- 'kɒl.pə*ʊ*-; kɒl'pɒ- (US) 'kɑːl.pə-, 'kɑːl.poʊ-; kɑːl'pɑː-
Note: Prefix. This may carry primary or secondary stress on the first syllable, e.g. **colposcope** /'kɒl.pə.skəʊp (US) 'kɑːl.pə.skoʊp/, or on the second syllable, e.g. **colposcopy** /kɒl'pɒs.kə.pi (US) kɑːl'pɑː- /.
colporteur 'kɒl.pɔː.təʳ, ˌkɒl.pɔː'tɜːʳ (US) 'kɑːl.pɔːr.t̬ɚ, ˌkɑːl.pɔːr'tɜːr **-s** -z
colposcope 'kɒl.pə.skəʊp (US) 'kɑːl.pə.skoʊp **-s** -s
colposcopic ˌkɒl.pə'skɒp.ɪk (US) ˌkɑːl.pə'skɑː.pɪk
colposcopy kɒl'pɒs.kə.pi (US) kɑːl'pɑː.skə-
Colquhoun kə'huːn
Cols. (*abbrev. for* **Colonels**) 'kɜː.nᵊlz (US) 'kɜːr-
Colson 'kəʊl.sᵊn (US) 'koʊl-
Colston 'kəʊl.stᵊn (US) 'koʊl-
colt kəʊlt (US) koʊlt **-s** -s
coltish 'kəʊl.tɪʃ (US) 'koʊl.t̬ɪʃ **-ly** -li **-ness** -nəs, -nɪs
Coltrane kɒl'treɪn, kəʊl- (US) 'koʊl.treɪn
coltsfoot 'kəʊlts.fʊt (US) 'koʊlts- **-s** -s
colubrine 'kɒl.jʊ.braɪn, -brɪn (US) 'kɑː.lə-, 'kɑːl.jə-
Columba kə'lʌm.bə
columbari|um ˌkɒl.əm'beə.ri|.əm (US) ˌkɑː.ləm'ber.i- **-ums** -əmz **-a** -ə
Columbi|a kə'lʌm.bi|.ə **-an/s** -ən/z
Columbiad kə'lʌm.bi.æd
columbine (C) 'kɒl.əm.baɪn (US) 'kɑː.ləm- **-s** -z
Columbo kə'lʌm.bəʊ (US) -boʊ
Columbus kə'lʌm.bəs
column 'kɒl.əm (US) 'kɑː.ləm **-s** -z **-ed** -d
column|al kə'lʌm.n|ᵊl **-ar** -əʳ (US) -ɚ
columnist 'kɒl.əm.nɪst, -ə.mɪst (US) 'kɑː.ləm.nɪst, -lə.mɪst **-s** -s
colure kə'ljʊəʳ, -'lʊəʳ; 'kəʊ.ljʊəʳ, -lʊəʳ (US) koʊ'lʊr, kə-; 'koʊ.lʊr **-s** -z
Colwyn 'kɒl.wɪn (US) 'kɑːl- ˌ**Colwyn 'Bay**
Colyton 'kɒl.ɪ.tᵊn (US) 'kɑː.lɪ.t̬ᵊn
colza 'kɒl.zə (US) 'kɑːl-
com- kɒm-, kəm- (US) kɑːm-, kəm-
Note: Prefix. This may carry primary or secondary stress, e.g. **combat** /'kɒm.bæt (US) 'kɑːm.bæt/ or be unstressed, e.g. **complete** /kəm'pliːt/.
coma *deep sleep:* 'kəʊ.mə (US) 'koʊ- **-s** -z
com|a *tuft:* 'kəʊ.m|ə (US) 'koʊ- **-as** -əz **-ae** -iː
Coma Berenices ˌkəʊ.məˌber.i'naɪ.siːz (US) ˌkoʊ.məˌber.ə'-
Comanche kə'mæn.*t*ʃi, kəʊ- (US) kə- **-s** -z
Comaneci ˌkɒm.ə'netʃ.i, -'netʃ (US) ˌkoʊ.mə.'niː.tʃi, -'netʃ.i
comatose 'kəʊ.mə.təʊs, -təʊz (US) 'koʊ.mə.toʊs, 'kɑː-
comb kəʊm (US) koʊm **-s** -z **-ing/s** -ɪŋ/z **-ed** -d
combat (*n.*) 'kɒm.bæt, 'kʌm-, -bət (US) 'kɑːm.bæt **-s** -s
comba|t (*v.*) 'kɒm.bæ|t, 'kʌm-, -bə|t; kəm'bæ|t (US) kəm'bæ|t, kɑːm-; 'kɑːm.bæ|t **-ts** -ts **-(t)ting** -tɪŋ (US) -t̬ɪŋ **-(t)ted** -tɪd (US) -t̬ɪd
combatant 'kɒm.bə.tᵊnt, 'kʌm-; kəm'bæt.ᵊnt (US) kəm'bæt.ᵊnt; 'kɑːm.bə.tᵊnt **-s** -s
combative 'kɒm.bə.tɪv, 'kʌm-; kəm'bæt.ɪv (US) kəm'bæt̬.ɪv; 'kɑːm.bə.t̬ɪv **-ly** -li **-ness** -nəs, -nɪs
combe (C) kuːm, kəʊm (US) kuːm, koʊm **-s** -z
comber *combing machine:* 'kəʊ.məʳ (US) 'koʊ.mɚ **-s** -z
comber (C) *fish:* 'kɒm.bəʳ (US) 'kɑːm.bɚ **-s** -z
combination ˌkɒm.bɪ'neɪ.ʃᵊn, -bə'- (US) ˌkɑːm.bə'-, -bɪ'- **-s** -z ˌ**combi'nation ˌlock** ; ˌ**combi'nation ˌroom**
combinative 'kɒm.bɪ.nə.tɪv, -bə-, -neɪ- (US) 'kɑːm.bə.neɪ.t̬ɪv, -nə-, -bɪ-, kəm'baɪ.nə.t̬ɪv
combinatorial ˌkɒm.bɪ.nə'tɔː.ri.əl, -bᵊn.ə'- (US) ˌkɑːm.bə.nə'tɔːr.i-, -bɪn.ə'-; kəmˌbaɪ-
combinatory 'kɒm.bɪ.nə.tᵊr.i, -tri; ˌkɒm.bɪ'neɪ- (US) 'kɑːm.bə.nə.tɔːr.i, -bɪ-; kəm'baɪ-
combine (*n.*) 'kɒm.baɪn; kəm'baɪn (US) 'kɑːm.baɪn **-s** -z
combin|e (*v.*) *join:* kəm'baɪn **-es** -z **-ing** -ɪŋ **-ed** -d *harvest:* 'kɒm.baɪn (US) 'kɑːm- **-es** -z **-ing** -ɪŋ **-ed** -d ˌ**combine 'harvester**
combo 'kɒm.bəʊ (US) 'kɑːm.boʊ **-s** -z
Combs kəʊmz, kuːmz (US) koʊmz
combust kəm'bʌst **-s** -s **-ing** -ɪŋ **-ed** -ɪd **-er/s** -əʳ/z (US) -ɚ/z
combustibility kəmˌbʌs.tə'bɪl.ə.ti, -tɪ'-, -ɪ.ti (US) -ə.t̬i
combustible kəm'bʌs.tə.bl̩, -tɪ- **-ness** -nəs, -nɪs
combustion kəm'bʌs.tʃᵊn **-s** -z com'bustion ˌengine
com|e kʌm **-es** -z **-ing** -ɪŋ **came** keɪm
come-at-able ˌkʌm'æt.ə.bl̩ (US) -'æt̬-
comeback 'kʌm.bæk **-s** -s
Comecon 'kɒm.ɪ.kɒn (US) 'kɑː.mɪ.kɑːn
comedian kə'miː.di.ən **-s** -z
comedic kə'miː.dɪk **-ally** -ᵊl.i, -li
comedienne kəˌmiː.di'en, ˌkɒm.iː- (US) kəˌmiː- **-s** -z
comedown 'kʌm.daʊn, ˌ-'- (US) '-- **-s** -z
comed|y 'kɒm.ə.d|i, '-ɪ- (US) 'kɑː.mə- **-ies** -iz
come-hither ˌkʌm'hɪð.əʳ (US) ˌkʌm'hɪð.ɚ *stress shift:* ˌcome-hither 'look
comel|y 'kʌm.l|i **-ier** -i.əʳ (US) -i.ɚ **-iest** -i.ɪst, -i.əst **-iness** -ɪ.nəs, -ɪ.nɪs
Comenius kə'meɪ.ni.əs, kɒm'eɪ-, -'iː- (US) kə'miː-
come-on 'kʌm.ɒn (US) -ɑːn **-s** -z
-comer -ˌkʌm.əʳ (US) -ɚ
comer 'kʌm.əʳ (US) -ɚ **-s** -z

comestible kə'mes.tɪ.bl̩, -tə- **-s** -z
comet 'kɒm.ɪt US 'kɑː.mɪt **-s** -s **-ary** -ᵊr.i US -er.i
come-uppanc|e kʌm'ʌp.ənts **-es** -ɪz
comfit 'kʌm.fɪt, 'kɒm- US 'kʌm-, 'kɑːm- **-s** -s
com|fort 'kʌmp|.fət US -fɚt **-forts** -fəts US -fɚts **-forting/ly** -fə.tɪŋ/li US -fɚ.t̬ɪŋ/li **-forted** -fə.tɪd US -fɚ.t̬ɪd **-forter/s** -fə.təʳ/z US -fɚ.t̬ɚ/z **'comfort ˌstation**
comfortab|le 'kʌmpf.tə.b|l̩, 'kʌmp.fə.tə- US 'kʌmp.fɚ.t̬ə-, 'kʌmpf.tə- **-ly** -li
comforter 'kʌmp.fə.təʳ US -fɚ.t̬ɚ **-s** -z
comfortless 'kʌmp.fət.ləs, -lɪs US -fɚt-
comfrey 'kʌmp.fri
comf|y 'kʌmp.f|i **-ier** -i.əʳ US -i.ɚ **-iest** -i.ɪst, -i.əst **-ily** -ɪ.li, -ᵊl.i **-iness** -ɪ.nəs, -ɪ.nɪs
comic 'kɒm.ɪk US 'kɑː.mɪk **-s** -s **'comic ˌbook** ; **'comic ˌstrip**, **ˌcomic 'strip**
comic|al 'kɒm.ɪ.k|ᵊl US 'kɑː.mɪ- **-ally** -ᵊl.i, -li **-alness** -ᵊl.nəs, -nɪs
Cominform 'kɒm.ɪn.fɔːm, -ən-, ˌ--'- US 'kɑː.mən.fɔːrm
Comintern 'kɒm.ɪn.tɜːn, -ən-, ˌ--'- US 'kɑː.mən.tɜːrn
comity 'kɒm.ɪ.ti, -ə.ti US 'kɑː.mə.t̬i, 'koʊ-
comma 'kɒm.ə US 'kɑː.mə **-s** -z
command kə'mɑːnd US -'mænd **-s** -z **-ing** -ɪŋ **-ed** -ɪd
commandant 'kɒm.ən.dænt, -dɑːnt, ˌ--'- US 'kɑː.mən.dænt, -dɑːnt **-s** -s
commandantship ˌkɒm.ən'dænt.ʃɪp, -'dɑːnt-, 'kɒm.ən.dænt.ʃɪp, -dɑːnt- US 'kɑː.mən.dænt-, -dɑːnt- **-s** -s
commandeer ˌkɒm.ən'dɪəʳ US ˌkɑː.mən'dɪr **-s** -z **-ing** -ɪŋ **-ed** -d
commander kə'mɑːn.dəʳ US -'mæn.dɚ **-s** -z
commander-in-chief kəˌmɑːn.də.rɪn'tʃiːf US -ˌmæn.dɚ- **commanders-in-chief** kəˌmɑːn.dəz.ɪn'tʃiːf US -ˌmænd.ɚz-
commandership kə'mɑːn.də.ʃɪp US -'mæn.dɚ- **-s** -s
commanding kə'mɑːn.dɪŋ US -'mæn- **-ly** -li
commandment kə'mɑːnd.mənt, -'mɑːm- US -'mænd- **-s** -s
commando kə'mɑːn.dəʊ US -'mæn.doʊ **-(e)s** -z
Comme des Garçons ˌkɒm.deɪ.gɑː'sɔ̃ːŋ, ˌkɒm.deɪ'gɑː.sɔ̃ŋ US ˌkɑːm.deɪ.gɑːr'soʊ̃n
commedia dell'arte kɒmˌeɪ.di.ə.del'ɑː.teɪ, kəˌmeɪ-, -ˌmed.i- US kəˌmeɪ.di.ə.del'ɑːr.t̬i
comme il faut ˌkɒm.iːl'fəʊ US ˌkʌm.iːl'foʊ, ˌkɑːm-
commemo|rate kə'mem.ə|.reɪt **-rates** -reɪts **-rating** -reɪ.tɪŋ US -reɪ.t̬ɪŋ **-rated** -reɪ.tɪd US -reɪ.t̬ɪd **-rator/s** -reɪ.təʳ/z US -reɪ.t̬ɚ/z
commemoration kəˌmem.ə'reɪ.ʃᵊn **-s** -z
commemorative kə'mem.ᵊr.ə.tɪv, -eɪ- US -ə.t̬ɪv, -eɪ- **-ly** -li
commenc|e kə'ments **-es** -ɪz **-ing** -ɪŋ **-ed** -t
commencement kə'ments.mənt **-s** -s
commend kə'mend **-s** -z **-ing** -ɪŋ **-ed** -ɪd
commendab|le kə'men.də.b|l̩ **-ly** -li **-leness** -l̩.nəs, -nɪs
commendation ˌkɒm.en'deɪ.ʃᵊn, -ən'- US ˌkɑː.mən'- **-s** -z
commendatory kə'men.də.tᵊr.i, -tri; ˌkɒm.en'deɪ-, -ən'- US kə'men.də.tɔːr.i
commensal kə'ment.sᵊl
commensalism kə'ment.sᵊl.ɪ.zᵊm
commensurability kəˌment.ʃᵊr.ə'bɪl.ə.ti, -ʃʊ.rə-, -sjᵊr.ə-, -ɪ.ti US -sɚ.ə'bɪl.ə.t̬i, -ʃɚ-
commensurab|le kə'ment.ʃᵊr.ə.b|l̩, -ʃʊ.rə-, -sjᵊr.ə- US -sɚ.ə-, -ʃɚ- **-ly** -li **-leness** -l̩.nəs, -nɪs
commensurate kə'ment.ʃᵊr.ət, -ʃʊ.rət, -sjᵊr.ət, -ɪt US -sɚ.ət, -ʃɚ- **-ly** -li **-ness** -nəs, -nɪs
comment *(n.)* 'kɒm.ent US 'kɑː.ment **-s** -s
commen|t *(v.)* 'kɒm.en|t, -ən|t; kɒm'ent, kə'men|t; US 'kɑː.men|t **-ts** -ts **-ting** -tɪŋ US -t̬ɪŋ **-ted** -tɪd US -t̬ɪd
commentar|y 'kɒm.ən.tᵊr|.i, -tr|i US 'kɑː.mən.ter|.i **-ies** -iz
commen|tate 'kɒm.ən|.teɪt, -en- US 'kɑː.mən- **-tates** -teɪts **-tating** -teɪ.tɪŋ US -teɪ.t̬ɪŋ **-tated** -teɪ.tɪd US -teɪ.t̬ɪd
commentator 'kɒm.ən.teɪ.təʳ, -en- US 'kɑː.mən.teɪ.t̬ɚ **-s** -z
commerce 'kɒm.ɜːs US 'kɑː.mɜːrs
commercial kə'mɜː.ʃᵊl US -'mɜːr- **-s** -z **-ly** -i
commercialese kəˌmɜː.ʃᵊl'iːz US -ˌmɜːr.ʃə'liːz
commercial|ism kə'mɜː.ʃᵊl|.ɪ.zᵊm US -'mɜːr- **-ist/s** -ɪst/s
commerciality kəˌmɜː.ʃi'æl.ə.ti, -ɪ.ti US -ˌmɜːr.ʃi'æl.ə.t̬i
commercializ|e, -is|e kə'mɜː.ʃᵊl.aɪz US -'mɜːr.ʃə.laɪz **-es** -ɪz **-ing** -ɪŋ **-ed** -d
commie 'kɒm.i US 'kɑː.mi **-s** -z
commi|nate 'kɒm.ɪ|.neɪt US 'kɑː.mə- **-nates** -neɪts **-nating** -neɪ.tɪŋ US -neɪ.t̬ɪŋ **-nated** -neɪ.tɪd US -neɪ.t̬ɪd
commination ˌkɒm.ɪ'neɪ.ʃᵊn US ˌkɑː.mə'- **-s** -z
comminatory 'kɒm.ɪ.nə.tᵊr.i, -neɪ-, -tri US 'kɑː.mɪ.nə.tɔːr.i; kə'mɪn.ə-
comming|le kɒm'ɪŋ.gl̩, kə'mɪŋ- US kə'mɪŋ-, kɑː- **-es** -z **-ing** -ɪŋ, '-glɪŋ **-ed** -d
commi|nute 'kɒm.ɪ.njuːt US 'kɑː.mə.nuːt, -njuːt **-nutes** -njuːts US -nuːts, -njuːts **-nuting** -njuː.tɪŋ US -nuː.t̬ɪŋ, -njuː- **-nuted** -njuː.tɪd US -nuː.t̬ɪd, -njuː-
comminution ˌkɒm.ɪ'njuː.ʃᵊn US ˌkɑː.mə'nuː-, -'njuː-
commis 'kɒm.i, -ɪs US ˌkɑː'mi *stress shift, American only, see compound:* **'commis ˌchef**, **ˌcommis 'chef**
commiser|ate kə'mɪz.ᵊr|.eɪt, kɒm'ɪz- US kə'mɪz- **-ates** -eɪts **-ating** -eɪ.tɪŋ US -eɪ.t̬ɪŋ **-ated** -eɪ.tɪd US -eɪ.t̬ɪd
commiseration kəˌmɪz.ᵊr'eɪ.ʃᵊn, kɒmˌɪz- US kəˌmɪz- **-s**
commissar ˌkɒm.ɪ'sɑːʳ, -ə'-, '--- US 'kɑː.mə.sɑːr **-s** -z
commissarial ˌkɒm.ɪ'seə.ri.əl, -ə'-, -'sɑː-, -'sær.i- US ˌkɑː.mə'ser-
commissariat ˌkɒm.ɪ'seə.ri.ət, -ə'-, -'sɑː-, -'sær.i-, -æt US ˌkɑː.mə'ser-
commissar|y 'kɒm.ɪ.sᵊr|.i, kə'mɪs.ᵊr- US 'kɑː.mə.ser- **-ies** -iz
commission kə'mɪʃ.ᵊn **-s** -z **-ing** -ɪŋ **-ed** -d **-er/s** -əʳ/z, '-nəʳ/z US '-ᵊn.ɚ/z, '-nɚ/z **com'mission ˌagent** ; **comˌmissioned 'officer**
commissionaire kəˌmɪʃ.ᵊn'eəʳ US -'er **-s** -z
commissive kə'mɪs.ɪv, 'kɒm.ɪ.sɪv US kə'mɪs-
commissure 'kɒm.ɪ.sjʊəʳ, '-ə-, -ʃʊəʳ US 'kɑː.mə.ʃʊr **-s** -z
com|mit kə|'mɪt **-mits** -s **-mitting** -'mɪt.ɪŋ US -'mɪt̬.ɪŋ **-mitted** -'mɪt.ɪd US -'mɪt̬.ɪd **-mitter/s** -'mɪt.əʳ/z US -'mɪt̬.ɚ/z
commitment kə'mɪt.mənt **-s** -s
committal kə'mɪt.ᵊl US -'mɪt̬- **-s** -z
committee *council:* kə'mɪt.i US -'mɪt̬- **-s** -z **com'mittee ˌmeeting**
committee *one committed:* ˌkɒm.ɪ'tiː US ˌkɑː.mɪ'tiː **-s** -z
committor ˌkɒm.ɪ'tɔːʳ, kə'mɪt.əʳ US ˌkɑː.mɪ't̬ɔːr; kə'mɪt̬.ɚ **-s** -z
commixture kə'mɪks.tʃəʳ US -tʃɚ **-s** -z
commode kə'məʊd US -'moʊd **-s** -z
commodious kə'məʊ.di.əs US -'moʊ- **-ly** -li **-ness** -nəs, -nɪs
commodit|y kə'mɒd.ə.t|i, -ɪ.t|i US -'mɑː.də.t̬|i **-ies** -iz
commodore 'kɒm.ə.dɔːʳ US 'kɑː.mə.dɔːr **-s** -z
Commodus 'kɒm.ə.dəs US 'kɑː.mə-

common ˈkɒm.ən (US) ˈkɑː.mən **-s** -z **-er** -əʳ (US) -ɚ **-est** -ɪst, -əst **-ly** -li **-ness** -nəs, -nɪs ˌ**common de'nominator** ; ˌ**Common 'Market** ; **'common ˌroom** ; ˌ**common 'sense** ; **'common ˌtouch**
commonage ˈkɒm.ə.nɪdʒ (US) ˈkɑː.mə-
commonality ˌkɒm.əˈnæl.ə.ti, -ɪ.ti (US) ˌkɑː.məˈnæl.ə.t̬i
commonalt|y ˈkɒm.ə.nᵊl.t|i (US) ˈkɑː.mə- **-ies** -iz
Commondale ˈkɒm.ən.deɪl (US) ˈkɑː.mən-
commoner ˈkɒm.ə.nəʳ (US) ˈkɑː.mə.nɚ **-s** -z
common-law ˌkɒm.ənˈlɔː (US) ˈkɑː.mən.lɑː, -lɔː *stress shift, British only:* ˌcommon-law 'wife
common-or-garden ˌkɒm.ən.ɔːˈgɑː.dᵊn, -əˈgɑː- (US) ˌkɑː.mən.ɔːrˈgɑːr-
commonplac|e ˈkɒm.ən.pleɪs, -əm- (US) ˈkɑː.mən- **-es** -ɪz
commons (C) ˈkɒm.ənz (US) ˈkɑː.mənz
commonsense ˌkɒm.ənˈsen*t*s (US) ˌkɑː.mənˈ-
commonsensical ˌkɒm.ənˈsen*t*.sɪ.kᵊl (US) ˌkɑː.mənˈ-
commonwealth (C) ˈkɒm.ən.welθ (US) ˈkɑː.mən- **-s** -s
commotion kəˈməʊ.ʃᵊn (US) -ˈmoʊ- **-s** -z
communal ˈkɒm.jʊ.nᵊl, -jə-; kəˈmjuː- (US) kəˈmjuː-; ˈkɑː.mjə- **-ly** -i
communard (C) ˈkɒm.jʊ.nɑːd, ˌkɒm.jʊˈnɑː (US) ˈkɑː.mjʊ.nɑːrd, -nɑːr **-s** -z
commune (*n.*) ˈkɒm.juːn (US) ˈkɑː.mjuːn **-s** -z
commun|e (*v.*) kəˈmjuːn **-es** -z **-ing** -ɪŋ **-ed** -d
communicab|le kəˈmjuː.nɪ.kə.b|l̩ **-ly** -li **-leness** -l̩.nəs, -nɪs
communicant kəˈmjuː.nɪ.kənt **-s** -s
communi|cate kəˈmjuː.nɪ|.keɪt, -nə- **-cates** -keɪts **-cating** -keɪ.tɪŋ (US) -keɪ.t̬ɪŋ **-cated** -keɪ.tɪd (US) -keɪ.t̬ɪd **-cator/s** -keɪ.təʳ/z (US) -keɪ.t̬ɚ/z
communication kəˌmjuː.nɪˈkeɪ.ʃᵊn, -nəˈ- **-s** -z
communicative kəˈmjuː.nɪ.kə.tɪv, -nə-, -keɪ- (US) -nə.keɪ.t̬ɪv, -kə- **-ly** -li **-ness** -nəs, -nɪs
communion kəˈmjuː.ni.ən (US) -njən **-s** -z
communiqué kəˈmjuː.nɪ.keɪ, kɒmˈjuː-, -nə- (US) kəˌmjuː.nɪˈkeɪ, kəˈmjuː.nɪ.keɪ **-s** -z
commun|ism ˈkɒm.jə.n|ɪ.zᵊm, -jʊ- (US) ˈkɑː.mjə- **-ist/s** -ɪst/s
communit|y kəˈmjuː.nə.t|i, -nɪ- (US) -nə.t̬|i **-ies** -iz **com'munity ˌcentre** ; **com'munity ˌchest** (US) **community 'chest** ; **com'munity ˌcollege**
commutability kəˌmjuː.təˈbɪl.ə.ti, -ɪ.ti (US) -t̬əˈbɪl.ə.t̬i
commutable kəˈmjuː.tə.bl̩ (US) -t̬ə-
commu|tate ˈkɒm.jʊ|.teɪt (US) ˈkɑː.mjə- **-tates** -teɪts **-tating** -teɪ.tɪŋ (US) -teɪ.t̬ɪŋ **-tated** -teɪ.tɪd (US) -teɪ.t̬ɪd **-tator/s** -teɪ.təʳ/z (US) -teɪ.t̬ɚ/z
commutation ˌkɒm.jʊˈteɪ.ʃᵊn (US) ˌkɑː.mjəˈ- **-s** -z
commutative kəˈmjuː.tə.tɪv, ˈkɒm.jʊ.teɪ- (US) ˈkɑː.mjə.teɪ.t̬ɪv, kəˈmjuː.t̬ə- **-ly** -li
com|mute kə|ˈmjuːt **-mutes** -ˈmjuːts **-muting** -ˈmjuː.tɪŋ (US) -ˈmjuː.t̬ɪŋ **-muted** -ˈmjuː.tɪd (US) -ˈmjuː.t̬ɪd
commuter kəˈmjuː.təʳ (US) -t̬ɚ **-s** -z
Como ˈkəʊ.məʊ (US) ˈkoʊ.moʊ
Comorin ˈkɒm.ə.rɪn (US) ˈkɑː.mɚ.ɪn
Comoros ˈkɒm.ə.rəʊz (US) ˈkɑː.mə.roʊz
comose ˈkəʊ.məʊs, -əʊz, -ˈ- (US) ˈkoʊ.moʊs
compact (*n.*) ˈkɒm.pækt (US) ˈkɑːm- **-s** -s
compact (*adj. v.*) kəmˈpækt (US) kəm-, kɑːm- **-er** -əʳ (US) -ɚ **-est** -ɪst, -əst **-ly** -li **-ness** -nəs, -nɪs **-s** -s **-ing** -ɪŋ **-ed** -ɪd *stress shift, see compound:* ˌ**compact 'disc/**ˌ**compact 'disk**
companion kəmˈpæn.jən **-s** -z **-ship** -ʃɪp
companionab|le kəmˈpæn.jə.nə.b|l̩ **-ly** -li **-leness** -l̩.nəs, -nɪs
companionate kəmˈpæn.jə.nət, -nɪt
companionway kəmˈpæn.jən.weɪ **-s** -z
compan|y ˈkʌm.pə.n|i **-ies** -iz
comparability ˌkɒm.pᵊr.əˈbɪl.ə.ti; kəmˌpær-, -ɪ.ti (US) ˌkɑːm.pɚ.əˈbɪl.ə.t̬i
comparab|le ˈkɒm.pᵊr.ə.b|l̩ (US) ˈkɑːm-; kəmˈper.ə-, -ˈpær- **-ly** -li **-leness** -l̩.nəs, -nɪs
comparative kəmˈpær.ə.tɪv (US) -ˈper.ə.t̬ɪv, -ˈpær- **-s** -z **-ly** -li
compar|e kəmˈpeəʳ (US) -per **-es** -z **-ing** -ɪŋ **-ed** -d
comparison kəmˈpær.ɪ.sᵊn (US) -ˈper-, -ˈpær- **-s** -z
compartment kəmˈpɑːt.mənt (US) -ˈpɑːrt- **-s** -s
compartmentalization, -isa- ˌkɒm.pɑːt.men.tᵊl.aɪˈzeɪ.ʃᵊn, kɒm.pɑːtˌmen-, -ɪˈ- (US) kəm.pɑːrtˌmen.t̬ᵊl.ɪˈ-, ˌkɑːm-
compartmentaliz|e, -is|e ˌkɒm.pɑːtˈmen.tᵊl.aɪz (US) kəm.pɑːrtˈmen.t̬ə.laɪz, ˌkɑːm- **-es** -ɪz **-ing** -ɪŋ **-ed** -d
compass ˈkʌm.pəs (US) ˈkʌm-, ˈkɑːm- **-es** -ɪz **-ing** -ɪŋ **-ed** -t
compassion kəmˈpæʃ.ᵊn
compassionate kəmˈpæʃ.ᵊn.ət, -ɪt **-ly** -li **-ness** -nəs, -nɪs
compatibility kəmˌpæt.əˈbɪl.ə.ti, -ɪˈ-, -ɪ.ti (US) -ˌpæt̬.əˈbɪl.ə.t̬i
compatib|le kəmˈpæt.ɪ.b|l̩, ˈ-ə- (US) -ˈpæt̬- **-ly** -li **-leness** -l̩.nəs, -nɪs
compatriot kəmˈpæt.ri.ət, kɒm- (US) kəmˈpeɪ.tri-, kɑːm- **-s** -s
compeer ˈkɒm.pɪəʳ, -ˈ- (US) ˈkɑːm.pɪr; -ˈ-, kəm- **-s** -z
compel kəmˈpel **-s** -z **-ling/ly** -ɪŋ/li **-led** -d **-lable** -ə.bl̩
compendious kəmˈpen.di.əs **-ly** -li **-ness** -nəs, -nɪs
compendi|um kəmˈpen.di|.əm **-ums** -əmz **-a** -ə
compen|sate ˈkɒm.pən|.seɪt, -pen- (US) ˈkɑːm- **-sates** -seɪts **-sating** -seɪ.tɪŋ (US) -seɪ.t̬ɪŋ **-sated** -seɪ.tɪd (US) -seɪ.t̬ɪd
compensation ˌkɒm.pənˈseɪ.ʃᵊn, -pen- (US) ˌkɑːm- **-s** -z
compensative kəmˈpen*t*.sə.tɪv, ˌkɒm.pənˈseɪ- (US) kəmˈpen*t*.sə.t̬ɪv, ˈkɑːm.pən.seɪ-
compensatory ˌkɒm.pənˈseɪ.tᵊr.i, -tri; kəmˈpen*t*.sə-; ˈkɒm.pen.seɪ-, -pən- (US) kəmˈpen*t*.sə.tɔːr.i
comper|e, compèr|e ˈkɒm.peəʳ (US) ˈkɑːm.per **-es** -z **-ing** -ɪŋ **-ed** -d
com|pete kəmˈpiːt **-petes** -ˈpiːts **-peting** -ˈpiː.tɪŋ (US) -ˈpiː.t̬ɪŋ **-peted** -ˈpiː.tɪd (US) -ˈpiː.t̬ɪd
competen|ce ˈkɒm.pɪ.tᵊn*t*|s, -pə- (US) ˈkɑːm- **-cies** -siz **-cy** -si
competent ˈkɒm.pɪ.tᵊnt, -pə- (US) ˈkɑːm.pɪ.t̬ᵊnt, -pə- **-ly** -li
competition ˌkɒm.pəˈtɪʃ.ᵊn, -pɪˈ- (US) ˌkɑːm- **-s** -z
competitive kəmˈpet.ɪ.tɪv, ˈ-ə- (US) -ˈpet̬.ə.t̬ɪv
competitor kəmˈpet.ɪ.təʳ, ˈ-ə- (US) -ˈpet̬.ə.t̬ɚ **-s** -z
compilation ˌkɒm.pɪˈleɪ.ʃᵊn, -pəˈ-, -paɪˈ- (US) ˌkɑːm.pəˈ- **-s** -z
compil|e kəmˈpaɪl **-es** -z **-ing** -ɪŋ **-ed** -d **-er/s** -əʳ/z (US) -ɚ/z
complacen|ce kəmˈpleɪ.sᵊn*t*|s **-cy** -si
complacent kəmˈpleɪ.sᵊnt **-ly** -li
complain kəmˈpleɪn **-s** -z **-ing** -ɪŋ **-ed** -d **-er/s** -əʳ/z (US) -ɚ/z
complainant kəmˈpleɪ.nənt **-s** -s
complaint kəmˈpleɪnt **-s** -s
complaisance kəmˈpleɪ.zᵊn*t*s (US) -sᵊn*t*s
complaisant kəmˈpleɪ.zᵊnt (US) -sᵊnt **-ly** -li
compleat kəmˈpliːt
complement (*n.*) ˈkɒm.plɪ.mənt, -plə- (US) ˈkɑːm- **-s** -s
comple|ment (*v.*) ˈkɒm.plɪ|.ment, ˌkɒm.plɪˈment (US) ˈkɑːm.plɪ-

-ments -ments, -'ments ⓤⓢ -ments -menting -men.tɪŋ, -'men.tɪŋ ⓤⓢ -men.t̬ɪŋ -mented -men.tɪd, -'men.tɪd ⓤⓢ -men.t̬ɪd

complemental ˌkɒm.plɪ'men.tᵊl ⓤⓢ ˌkɑːm.plɪ'men.t̬ᵊl

complementary ˌkɒm.plɪ'men.tᵊr.i, -plə'-, '-tri ⓤⓢ ˌkɑːm.plə'men.t̬ɚ.i, '-tri

complementation ˌkɒm.plɪ.men'teɪ.ʃᵊn, -plə-, -mən'- ⓤⓢ ˌkɑːm-

complementiser, -izer 'kɒm.plɪ.men.taɪ.zəʳ, -plə-, -mən- ⓤⓢ 'kɑːm.plə.mən.taɪ.zɚ, -men- **-s** -z

com|plete kəm|'pliːt **-pletest** -'pliː.tɪst, -təst ⓤⓢ -'pliː.t̬ɪst, -t̬əst **-pletely** -'pliːt.li **-pleteness** -'pliːt.nəs, -nɪs **-pletes** -'pliːts **-pleting** -'pliː.tɪŋ ⓤⓢ -'pliː.t̬ɪŋ **-pleted** -'pliː.tɪd ⓤⓢ -'pliː.t̬ɪd

completion kəm'pliː.ʃᵊn

complex (*adj.*) 'kɒm.pleks, kəm'pleks ⓤⓢ kɑːm'pleks, kəm-; 'kɑːm.pleks

complex (*n.*) 'kɒm.pleks ⓤⓢ 'kɑːm- **-es** -ɪz

complexion kəm'plek.ʃᵊn **-s** -z **-ed** -d

complexit|y kəm'plek.sə.t|i, -sɪ- ⓤⓢ -sə.t̬|i **-ies** -iz

complianc|e kəm'plaɪ.ənts **-es** -ɪz

compliant kəm'plaɪ.ənt **-ly** -li

compli|cate 'kɒm.plɪ|.keɪt ⓤⓢ 'kɑːm.plə- **-cates** -keɪts **-cating** -keɪ.tɪŋ ⓤⓢ -keɪ.t̬ɪŋ **-cated** -keɪ.tɪd ⓤⓢ -keɪ.t̬ɪd

complication ˌkɒm.plɪ'keɪ.ʃᵊn ⓤⓢ ˌkɑːm.plə'- **-s** -z

complicity kəm'plɪs.ə.ti, -ɪ.ti ⓤⓢ -ə.t̬i

compliment (*n.*) 'kɒm.plɪ.mənt, -plə- ⓤⓢ 'kɑːm.plə- **-s** -s

compli|ment (*v.*) 'kɒm.plɪ|.ment, -plə-, ˌkɒm.plɪ|'ment ⓤⓢ 'kɑːm.plə- **-ments** -ments, -'ments ⓤⓢ -ments **-menting** -men.tɪŋ, -'men.tɪŋ ⓤⓢ -men.t̬ɪŋ **-mented** -men.tɪd, -'men.tɪd ⓤⓢ -men.t̬ɪd

complimentarily ˌkɒm.plɪ'men.tᵊr.ᵊl.i, -plə- ⓤⓢ ˌkɑːm.plə.men'ter-; -'men.t̬ɚ-

complimentar|y ˌkɒm.plɪ'men.tᵊr|.i, -plə'-, '-tr|i ⓤⓢ ˌkɑːm.plə'men.t̬ɚ|.i, '-tr|i **-ies** -iz

complin 'kɒm.plɪn ⓤⓢ 'kɑːm- **-s** -z

compline 'kɒm.plɪn, -plaɪn ⓤⓢ 'kɑːm- **-s** -z

compl|y kəm'pl|aɪ **-ies** -aɪz **-ying** -aɪ.ɪŋ **-ied** -aɪd **-ier/s** -aɪ.əʳ/z ⓤⓢ -aɪ.ɚ/z

compo 'kɒm.pəʊ ⓤⓢ 'kɑːm.poʊ

component kəm'pəʊ.nənt ⓤⓢ -'poʊ- **-s** -s

componential ˌkɒm.pəʊ'nen.tʃᵊl ⓤⓢ ˌkɑːm.pə'- **ˌcompoˌnential a'nalysis**

com|port kəm|'pɔːt ⓤⓢ -'pɔːrt **-ports** -'pɔːts ⓤⓢ -'pɔːrts **-porting** -'pɔː.tɪŋ ⓤⓢ -'pɔːr.t̬ɪŋ **-ported** -'pɔː.tɪd ⓤⓢ -'pɔːr.t̬ɪd

comportment kəm'pɔːt.mənt ⓤⓢ -'pɔːrt-

compos|e kəm'pəʊz ⓤⓢ -'poʊz **-es** -ɪz **-ing** -ɪŋ **-ed** -d

compos|ed kəm'pəʊz|d ⓤⓢ -'poʊz|d **-edly** -ɪd.li, -əd.li **-edness** -ɪd.nəs, -d.nəs, -nɪs

composer kəm'pəʊ.zəʳ ⓤⓢ -'poʊ.zɚ **-s** -z

composite 'kɒm.pə.zɪt, -sɪt, -zaɪt, -saɪt ⓤⓢ kəm'pɑː.zɪt **-ly** -li **-ness** -nəs, -nɪs

composition ˌkɒm.pə'zɪʃ.ᵊn ⓤⓢ ˌkɑːm- **-s** -z

compositor kəm'pɒz.ɪ.təʳ ⓤⓢ -'pɑː.zɪ.t̬ɚ **-s** -z

compos mentis ˌkɒm.pəs'men.tɪs, -pɒs- ⓤⓢ ˌkɑːm.pəs'men.t̬əs

compost 'kɒm.pɒst ⓤⓢ 'kɑːm.poʊst **-s** -s **'compost ˌheap**

composure kəm'pəʊ.ʒəʳ ⓤⓢ -'poʊ.ʒɚ

compote 'kɒm.pəʊt, -pɒt ⓤⓢ 'kɑːm.poʊt **-s** -s

compound (*n. adj.*) 'kɒm.paʊnd ⓤⓢ 'kɑːm- **-s** -z **ˌcompound 'fracture**

compound (*v.*) kəm'paʊnd, kɒm-; 'kɒm.paʊnd ⓤⓢ kɑːm'paʊnd, kəm-; 'kɑːm.paʊnd **-s** -z **-ing** -ɪŋ **-ed** -ɪd **-able** -ə.bl̩

comprehend ˌkɒm.prɪ'hend, -prə'- ⓤⓢ ˌkɑːm- **-s** -z **-ing** -ɪŋ **-ed** -ɪd

comprehensibility ˌkɒm.prɪ.hent.sə'bɪl.ə.ti, -prə-, -sɪ'-, -ɪ.ti ⓤⓢ ˌkɑːm.prə.hent.sə'bɪl.ə.t̬i, -prɪ-

comprehensib|le ˌkɒm.prɪ'hent.sə.b|l̩, -prə'-, -sɪ- ⓤⓢ ˌkɑːm- **-ly** -li **-leness** -l̩.nəs, -nɪs

comprehension ˌkɒm.prɪ'hen.tʃᵊn, -prə'- ⓤⓢ ˌkɑːm.prɪ'hent.ʃᵊn-, -prə'-

comprehensive ˌkɒm.prɪ'hent.sɪv, -prə'- ⓤⓢ ˌkɑːm.prə-, -prɪ- **-ly** -li **-ness** -nəs, -nɪs **compre'hensive ˌschool**

compress (*n.*) 'kɒm.pres ⓤⓢ 'kɑːm- **-es** -ɪz

compress (*v.*) kəm'pres **-es** -ɪz **-ing** -ɪŋ **-ed** -t **-or/s** -əʳ/z ⓤⓢ -ɚ/z

compressibility kəmˌpres.ə'bɪl.ə.ti, -ɪ'-, -ɪ.ti ⓤⓢ -ə.t̬i

compressible kəm'pres.ə.bl̩, '-ɪ- **-ness** -nəs, -nɪs

compression kəm'preʃ.ᵊn **-s** -z **-al** -ᵊl

compressive kəm'pres.ɪv

compris|e kəm'praɪz **-es** -ɪz **-ing** -ɪŋ **-ed** -d **-able** -ə.bl̩

compromis|e 'kɒm.prə.maɪz ⓤⓢ 'kɑːm- **-es** -ɪz **-ing/ly** -ɪŋ/li **-ed** -d **-er/s** -əʳ/z ⓤⓢ -ɚ/z

Comptometer® ˌkɒmp'tɒm.ɪ.təʳ, '-ə- ⓤⓢ ˌkɑːmp'tɑː.mə.t̬ɚ **-s** -z

Compton 'kɒmp.tən, 'kʌmp- ⓤⓢ 'kɑːmp-

Note: For British English, as surname more often /'kʌmp-/, as place name more often /'kɒmp-/. The London street is generally /'kɒmp-/.

Compton-Burnett ˌkɒmp.tən.bɜː'net, -'bɜː.nɪt ⓤⓢ ˌkɑːmp.tən.bɝː'net

comptroller kən'trəʊ.ləʳ, kəmp-, kɒmp- ⓤⓢ kən'troʊ.lɚ, kəmp-, kɑːmp-; 'kɑːmp.troʊ- **-s** -z

compulsion kəm'pʌl.ʃᵊn **-s**

compulsive kəm'pʌl.sɪv **-ly** -li

compulsor|y kəm'pʌl.sᵊr|.i **-ily** -ᵊl.i, -ɪ.li

compunction kəm'pʌŋk.ʃᵊn

compunctious kəm'pʌŋk.ʃəs

compurgation ˌkɒm.pɜː'geɪ.ʃᵊn ⓤⓢ ˌkɑːm.pɚ'-

computability kəmˌpjuː.tə'bɪl.ə.ti, ˌkɒm.pjʊ-, -ɪ.ti ⓤⓢ kəmˌpjuː.t̬ə'bɪl.ə.t̬i

computable kəm'pjuː.tə.bl̩; 'kɒm.pjʊ- ⓤⓢ kəm'pjuː.t̬ə-

computation ˌkɒm.pjə'teɪ.ʃᵊn, -pjʊ'- ⓤⓢ ˌkɑːm.pjə'- **-s** -z

computational ˌkɒm.pjə'teɪ.ʃᵊn.ᵊl, -pjʊ'-, -'teɪʃ.nᵊl ⓤⓢ ˌkɑːm- **-ly** -i **compuˌtational lin'guistics**

computator 'kɒm.pjə.teɪ.təʳ, -pjʊ- ⓤⓢ 'kɑːm.pjə.teɪ.t̬ɚ **-s** -z

com|pute kəm|'pjuːt **-putes** -'pjuːts **-puting** -'pjuː.tɪŋ ⓤⓢ -'pjuː.t̬ɪŋ **-puted** -'pjuː.tɪd ⓤⓢ -'pjuː.t̬ɪd

computer kəm'pjuː.təʳ ⓤⓢ -t̬ɚ **-s** -z **com'puter ˌgame ; comˌputer 'programmer ; comˌputer aided de'sign**

computerate kəm'pjuː.tᵊr.ət ⓤⓢ -t̬ɚ-

computerization, -isa- kəmˌpjuː.tᵊr.aɪ'zeɪ.ʃᵊn, -ɪ'- ⓤⓢ -t̬ɚ.ɪ'-

computeriz|e, -is|e kəm'pjuː.tᵊr.aɪz ⓤⓢ -t̬ə.raɪz **-es** -ɪz **-ing** -ɪŋ **-ed** -d

computist kəm'pjuː.tɪst ⓤⓢ -t̬ɪst **-s** -s

comrade 'kɒm.reɪd, 'kʌm-, -rɪd ⓤⓢ 'kɑːm.ræd, -rəd **-s** -z **-ship** -ʃɪp

Comsat® 'kɒm.sæt ⓤⓢ 'kɑːm- **-s** -s

Comte kɔ̃ːnt, kɔːnt, kɒnt ⓤⓢ kɔ̃ːnt, koʊnt

Comus 'kəʊ.məs ⓤⓢ 'koʊ-

Comyn 'kʌm.ɪn

con- kɒn-, kən- ⓤⓢ kɑːn-, kən-

Note: Prefix. This may carry primary or secondary stress, e.g. **concept**

/'kɒn.sept US 'kɑːn-/, or may be unstressed, e.g. **consume** /kən'sjuːm US kən'suːm/.

con kɒn US kɑːn **-s** -z **-ning** -ɪŋ **-ned** -d **'con ˌman** ; **'con ˌtrick**

Conakry ˌkɒn.ə'kriː, 'kɒn.ə.kri US 'kɑː.nə.kri

Conall 'kɒn.ᵊl US 'kɑː.nᵊl

Conan *personal name:* 'kəʊ.nən, 'kɒn.ən US 'koʊ.nən, 'kɑː- *place in Scotland:* 'kɒn.ən, 'kəʊ.nən US 'kɑː-, 'koʊ-

Note: The members of the family of Sir Arthur Conan Doyle pronounce /'kəʊ.nən/.

Conant 'kɒn.ənt US 'koʊ.nənt

conation kəʊ'neɪ.ʃᵊn US koʊ-

conative 'kəʊ.nə.tɪv US 'koʊ.nə.t̬ɪv

Concannon kɒn'kæn.ən, kɒŋ- US kɑːn-

concaten|ate kən'kæt.ᵊn|.eɪt, kəŋ-, kɒn-, kɒŋ-, '-ɪ- US kən'kæt̬-, kɑːn- **-ates** -eɪts **-ating** -eɪ.tɪŋ US -eɪ.t̬ɪŋ **-ated** -eɪ.tɪd US -eɪ.t̬ɪd

concatenation kənˌkæt.ə'neɪ.ʃᵊn, kəŋ-, kɒn-, kɒŋ-, -ɪ'-; 'kɒn.kæt-, 'kɒŋ- US kənˌkæt̬.ə'-; ˌkɑːn.kæt̬- **-s** -z

concave kɒŋ'keɪv, kəŋ-, kɒn-, kən-; 'kɒŋ.keɪv US kɑːn'keɪv, 'kɑːn- *stress shift:* ˌconcave 'lens

concavit|y kɒn'kæv.ə.t|i, kən-, kɒŋ-, kəŋ-, -ɪ.t|i US kɑːn'kæv.ə.t̬|i **-ies** -iz

conceal kən'siːl **-s** -z **-ing** -ɪŋ **-ed** -d **-able** -ə.bl̩ **-er/s** -əʳ/z US -ɚ/z

concealment kən'siːl.mənt **-s** -s

conced|e kən'siːd **-es** -z **-ing** -ɪŋ **-ed** -ɪd

conceit kən'siːt **-s** -s

conceited kən'siː.tɪd US -t̬ɪd **-ly** -li **-ness** -nəs, -nɪs

conceivab|le kən'siː.və.b|l̩ **-ly** -li **-leness** -l̩.nəs, -nɪs

conceiv|e kən'siːv **-es** -z **-ing** -ɪŋ **-ed** -d

concele|brate kɒn'sel.ə|.breɪt, kən-, '-ɪ- US kən-, kɑːn- **-brates** -breɪts **-brating** -breɪ.tɪŋ US -breɪ.t̬ɪŋ **-brated** -breɪ.tɪd US -breɪ.t̬ɪd

concelebration ˌkɒn.sel.ə'breɪ.ʃᵊn, -ɪ'-; kənˌsel- US kənˌsel-; ˌkɑːn.sel- **-s** -z

concent kən'sent, ˌkɒn- US kən-

concent|er kɒn'sen.t|əʳ US kən'sen.t̬|ɚ, kɑːn- **-ers** -əz US -ɚz **-ering** -ᵊr.ɪŋ **-ered** -əd US -ɚd

concen|trate 'kɒnt.sᵊn|.treɪt, -sɪn-, -sen- US 'kɑːnt.sᵊn- **-trates** -treɪts **-trating** -treɪ.tɪŋ US -treɪ.t̬ɪŋ **-trated** -treɪ.tɪd US -treɪ.t̬ɪd

concentration ˌkɒnt.sᵊn'treɪ.ʃᵊn, -sɪn'-, -sen'- US ˌkɑːnt.sᵊn'- **-s** -z **concen'tration ˌcamp**

concentrative 'kɒnt.sᵊn.treɪ.tɪv, -sɪn-, -sen- US 'kɑːnt.sən.treɪ.t̬ɪv; kən'sen.trə-

concent|re kɒn'sen.t|əʳ US kən'sen.t̬|ɚ, kɑːn- **-res** -əz US -ɚz **-ring** -rɪŋ **-ering** -ᵊr.ɪŋ **-red** -əd US -ɚd

concentric kən'sen.trɪk, kɒn- US kən- **-ally** -ᵊl.i, -li

Concepción kənˌsep.si'əʊn, ˌkɒn.sep- US kən-, kɑːn-, -'oʊn

concept 'kɒn.sept US 'kɑːn- **-s** -s

conception kən'sep.ʃᵊn **-s** -z

conceptual kən'sep.tʃu.əl, -ʃu-, -tju- US -tʃu- **-ly** -i

conceptualization, -isa- kənˌsep.tʃu.ə.laɪ'zeɪ.ʃᵊn, -ʃu-, -tju-, -ɪ'- US -tʃu.ᵊl.ɪ'-

conceptualiz|e, -is|e kən'sep.tʃu.ə.laɪz, -ʃu-, -tju-, -tʃʊ.laɪz, -tʃə- US -tʃu.ə- **-es** -ɪz **-ing** -ɪŋ **-ed** -d

conceptually kən'sep.tʃu.ə.li, -ʃu-, -tju- US -tʃu-

conceptus kən'sep.təs **-es** -ɪz

concern kən'sɜːn US -'sɜːrn **-s** -z **-ing** -ɪŋ **-ed** -d **-ment/s** -mənt/s

concern|ed kən'sɜːn|d US -'sɜːrn|d **-edly** -ɪd.li **-edness** -ɪd.nəs, -d.nəs, -nɪs

concert (*n.*) *musical entertainment:* 'kɒn.sət US 'kɑːn.sɚt **-s** -s

concert (C) (*n.*) *union:* 'kɒn.sɜːt, -sət US 'kɑːn.sɚt **-s** -s

con|cert (*v.*) kən|'sɜːt US -'sɜːrt **-certs** -'sɜːts US -'sɜːrts **-certing** -'sɜː.tɪŋ US -'sɜːr.t̬ɪŋ **-certed** -'sɜː.tɪd US -'sɜːr.t̬ɪd

concerti (*plur. of* **concerto**) kən'tʃeə.ti, -'tʃɜː- US -'tʃer.t̬i

concertina ˌkɒn*t*.sə'tiː.nə US ˌkɑːn*t*.sɚ'- **-s** -z **-ing** -ɪŋ **-ed** -d

concertino ˌkɒn.*t*ʃə'tiː.nəʊ US ˌkɑːn.tʃɚ'tiː.noʊ **-s** -z

concerto kən'tʃeə.təʊ, -'tʃɜː- US -'tʃer.t̬oʊ **-s** -z **concerti** kən'tʃeə.ti, -'tʃɜː- US -'tʃer.t̬i

concerto grosso kənˌtʃeə.təʊ'grɒs.əʊ, kɒn-, -ˌtʃɜː- US kənˌtʃer.t̬oʊ'groʊ.soʊ, kɑːn- US **concerti grossi** kənˌtʃeə.ti'grɒs.i US -ˌtʃer.t̬i'groʊ.si

concession kən'seʃ.ᵊn **-s** -z

concessionaire kənˌseʃ.ᵊn'eəʳ US -'er **-s** -z

concessional kən'seʃ.ᵊn.ᵊl, '-nᵊl US -ən.ᵊl **-ly** -i

concessionary kən'seʃ.ᵊn.ᵊr.i, -ᵊn.ri US -ʃᵊn.er.i

concessive kən'ses.ɪv **-ly** -li

conch kɒn*t*ʃ, kɒŋk US kɑːŋk, kɑːntʃ **conches** 'kɒn.*t*ʃɪz US 'kɑːn.tʃɪz **conchs** kɒŋks US kɑːŋks

concha 'kɒŋ.kə US 'kɑːŋ-, 'kɔːŋ- **-s** -z

Conchobar 'kɒŋ.kəʊ.əʳ, 'kɒn.u.əʳ US 'kɑː.nu.ɚ, 'kɑːŋ.koʊ.ɚ, 'kɔːŋ-

conchoid 'kɒŋ.kɔɪd US 'kɑːn- **-s** -z

conchologist kɒŋ'kɒl.ə.dʒɪst US kɑːŋ'kɑː.lə-, kɔːŋ- **-s** -s

conchology kɒŋ'kɒl.ə.dʒi US kɑːŋ'kɑː.lə-, kɔːŋ-

concierge ˌkɒn.si'eəʒ, ˌkɔːn-, ˌkɔ̃ːn-, '--- US koʊn'sjerʒ, kɑːn-, -si'erʒ **-s** -ɪz

concili|ate kən'sɪl.i|.eɪt **-ates** -eɪts **-ating** -eɪ.tɪŋ US -eɪ.t̬ɪŋ **-ated** -eɪ.tɪd US -eɪ.t̬ɪd

conciliation kənˌsɪl.i'eɪ.ʃᵊn

conciliative kən'sɪl.i.ə.tɪv, -eɪ- US -eɪ.t̬ɪv

conciliator kən'sɪl.i.eɪ.təʳ US -t̬ɚ **-s** -z

conciliatory kən'sɪl.i.ə.tᵊr.i, -eɪ-, -tri; kənˌsɪl.i'eɪ- US kən'sɪl.i.ə.tɔːr.i

concis|e kən'saɪs **-er** -əʳ US -ɚ **-est** -ɪst, -əst **-ely** -li **-eness** -nəs, -nɪs

concision kən'sɪʒ.ᵊn **-s** -z

conclave 'kɒŋ.kleɪv, 'kɒn- US 'kɑːn- **-s** -z

conclud|e kən'kluːd, kəŋ- US kən- **-es** -z **-ing** -ɪŋ **-ed** -ɪd

conclusion kən'kluː.ʒᵊn, kəŋ- US kən- **-s** -z

conclusive kən'kluː.sɪv, kəŋ- US kən- **-ly** -li **-ness** -nəs, -nɪs

concoct kən'kɒkt, kəŋ- US kən'kɑːkt **-s** -s **-ing** -ɪŋ **-ed** -ɪd **-er/s** -əʳ/z US -ɚ/z

concoction kən'kɒk.ʃᵊn, kəŋ- US kən'kɑːk- **-s** -z

concomitan|ce kən'kɒm.ɪ.tᵊn*t*|s, kəŋ-, '-ə- US kən'kɑː.mə.t̬ᵊn*t*|s **-cy** -si

concomitant kən'kɒm.ɪ.tᵊnt, kəŋ-, '-ə- US kən'kɑː.mə.t̬ᵊnt **-ly** -li

concord (*n.*) 'kɒŋ.kɔːd, 'kɒn- US 'kɑːn.kɔːrd, 'kɑːŋ-, 'kɔːŋ- **-s** -z

concord (*v.*) kən'kɔːd, kəŋ- US kən'kɔːrd **-s** -z **-ing** -ɪŋ **-ed** -ɪd

Concord *place in the US, type of grape:* 'kɒŋ.kəd US 'kɑːŋ.kɚd

concordanc|e kən'kɔː.dᵊn*t*s, kəŋ- US kən'kɔːr- **-es** -ɪz

concordant kən'kɔː.dᵊnt, kəŋ- US kən'kɔːr- **-ly** -li

concordat kɒn'kɔː.dæt, kɒŋ-, kən-, kəŋ- US kən'kɔːr- **-s** -s

Concorde 'kɒŋ.kɔːd, 'kɒn- US 'kɑːn.kɔːrd, 'kɑːŋ- **-s** -z

concours|e 'kɒŋ.kɔːs, 'kɒn-, -kʊəs US 'kɑːn.kɔːrs **-es** -ɪz

concrete (*n. adj.*) 'kɒŋ.kriːt, 'kɒn- US 'kɑːn- ˌ**concrete 'jungle**

con|crete (*v.*) *cover with concrete:* 'kɒŋ|.kriːt, 'kɒn- US 'kɑːn- **-cretes** -kriːts **-creting** -kriː.tɪŋ US -t̬ɪŋ **-creted** -kriː.tɪd US -kriː.t̬ɪd

con|crete (*v.*) *solidify:* kən|'kriːt, kəŋ- US kən- **-cretes** -'kriːts **-creting** -'kriː.tɪŋ US -'kriː.t̬ɪŋ **-creted** -'kriː.tɪd US -'kriː.t̬ɪd

concrete|ly kɒŋ'kriːt|.li, kɒn- Ⓤⓢ kɑːn- **-ness** -nəs, -nɪs
concretion kən'kriː.ʃᵊn, kəŋ-, kɒn- Ⓤⓢ kən-, kɑːn- **-s** -z
concretiz|e, -is|e 'kɒŋ.kriː.taɪz, 'kɒn-, -krɪ- Ⓤⓢ 'kɑːn.kriː-, kɑːn'kriː.taɪz, kɑːŋ- **-es** -ɪz **-ing** -ɪŋ **-ed** -d
concubinage kɒn'kjuː.bɪ.nɪdʒ, kɒŋ-, kən-, kəŋ- Ⓤⓢ kən'kjuː.bə-, kɑːn-
concubine 'kɒŋ.kjʊ.baɪn, 'kɒn-, -kjə- Ⓤⓢ 'kɑːŋ-, 'kɑːn- **-s** -z
concupiscen|ce kən'kjuː.pɪ.sᵊn|ts, kəŋ-, ˌkɒn-, ˌkɒŋ- Ⓤⓢ kɑːn-, kən'kjuː.pə- **-t** -t
concur kən'kɜːʳ, kəŋ- Ⓤⓢ -'kɜːr **-s** -z **-ring** -ɪŋ **-red** -d
concurren|ce kən'kʌr.ᵊnt|s, kəŋ- Ⓤⓢ kən- **-cy** -si
concurrent kən'kʌr.ᵊnt, kəŋ- Ⓤⓢ kən- **-ly** -li
concuss kən'kʌs, kəŋ- Ⓤⓢ kən- **-es** -ɪz **-ing** -ɪŋ **-ed** -t
concussion kən'kʌʃ.ᵊn, kəŋ- Ⓤⓢ kən- **-s** -z
condemn kən'dem **-s** -z **-ing** -ɪŋ **-ed** -d **-able** -*n*ə.bl̩
condemnation ˌkɒn.dem'neɪ.ʃᵊn, -dəm'- Ⓤⓢ ˌkɑːn- **-s** -z
condemnatory kən'dem.nə.tᵊr.i, -tri; ˌkɒn.dem'neɪ-, -dəm'- Ⓤⓢ kən'dem.nə.tɔːr.i
condensation ˌkɒn.den'seɪ.ʃᵊn, -dən'- Ⓤⓢ ˌkɑːn- **-s** -z
condens|e kən'den*t*s **-es** -ɪz **-ing** -ɪŋ **-ed** -t **-able** -ə.bl̩ **conˌdensed 'milk**
condenser kən'den.səʳ Ⓤⓢ -sɚ **-s** -z
condescend ˌkɒn.dɪ'send, -də'- Ⓤⓢ ˌkɑːn- **-s** -z **-ing** -ɪŋ **-ed** -ɪd
condescending ˌkɒn.dɪ'sen.dɪŋ, -də'- Ⓤⓢ ˌkɑːn- **-ly** -li
condescension ˌkɒn.dɪ'sen.ʃᵊn, -də'- Ⓤⓢ ˌkɑːn-
condign kən'daɪn, kɒn- Ⓤⓢ kən'daɪn, 'kɑːn.daɪn **-ly** -li **-ness** -nəs, -nɪs
condiment 'kɒn.dɪ.mənt Ⓤⓢ 'kɑːn.də- **-s** -s
condition kən'dɪʃ.ᵊn **-s** -z **-ing** -ɪŋ **-ed** -d
conditional kən'dɪʃ.ᵊn.ᵊl, '-nᵊl **-ly** -i
conditioner kən'dɪʃ.ᵊn.əʳ, '-nəʳ Ⓤⓢ '-ᵊn.ɚ, '-nɚ **-s** -z
condo 'kɒn.dəʊ Ⓤⓢ 'kɑːn.doʊ **-s** -z
condol|e kən'dəʊl Ⓤⓢ -'doʊl **-es** -z **-ing** -ɪŋ **-ed** -d **-ement/s** -mənt/s
condolenc|e kən'dəʊ.lənts Ⓤⓢ -'doʊ- **-es** -ɪz
condolent kən'dəʊ.lənt Ⓤⓢ -'doʊ-
condom 'kɒn.dɒm, -dəm Ⓤⓢ 'kɑːn.dəm, 'kʌn- **-s** -z
condominium ˌkɒn.də'mɪn.i.əm Ⓤⓢ ˌkɑːn.də'- **-s** -z
condonation ˌkɒn.dəʊ'neɪ.ʃᵊn Ⓤⓢ ˌkɑːn.doʊ'- **-s** -z
condon|e kən'dəʊn Ⓤⓢ -'doʊn **-es** -z **-ing** -ɪŋ **-ed** -d
condor (C) 'kɒn.dɔːʳ, -dəʳ Ⓤⓢ 'kɑːn.dɚ, -dɔːr **-s** -z
conduc|e kən'djuːs Ⓤⓢ -'duːs, -'djuːs **-es** -ɪz **-ing** -ɪŋ **-ed** -t **-ement/s** -mənt/s
conducive kən'djuː.sɪv Ⓤⓢ -'duː-, -'djuː- **-ly** -li **-ness** -nəs, -nɪs
conduct (*n.*) 'kɒn.dʌkt, -dəkt Ⓤⓢ 'kɑːn- **-s** -s
conduct (*v.*) kən'dʌkt **-s** -s **-ing** -ɪŋ **-ed** -ɪd
conductance kən'dʌk.tᵊnts
conductibility kənˌdʌk.tə'bɪl.ə.ti, -tɪ'-, -ɪ.ti Ⓤⓢ -ə.t̬i
conductible kən'dʌk.tə.bl̩, -tɪ-
conduction kən'dʌk.ʃᵊn
conductive kən'dʌk.tɪv
conductivity ˌkɒn.dʌk'tɪv.ə.ti, -dək'-, -ɪ.ti Ⓤⓢ ˌkɑːn.dʌk'tɪv.ə.t̬i
conductor kən'dʌk.təʳ Ⓤⓢ -tɚ **-s** -z
conductress kən'dʌk.trəs, -trɪs **-es** -ɪz
conduit 'kɒn.dju.ɪt, 'kʌn-, -du-, -dʒu-, -dɪt Ⓤⓢ 'kɑːn.du.ɪt, -dɪt **-s** -s
Conduit *street:* 'kɒn.dɪt, 'kʌn- Ⓤⓢ 'kɑːn-
Condy 'kɒn.di Ⓤⓢ 'kɑːn-
condyle 'kɒn.dɪl, -daɪl Ⓤⓢ 'kɑːn- **-s** -z
cone kəʊn Ⓤⓢ koʊn **-s** -z
Conestoga ˌkɒn.ə'stəʊ.gə Ⓤⓢ ˌkɑː.nə'stoʊ- **Cones'toga ˌwagon**
coney (C) 'kəʊ.ni Ⓤⓢ 'koʊ- **-s** -z **ˌConey 'Island** *stress shift:* ˌConey Island 'resident
confab 'kɒn.fæb; kɒn'fæb, kən- Ⓤⓢ 'kɑːn.fæb **-s** -z
confabu|late kən'fæb.jʊ|.leɪt, kɒn- Ⓤⓢ kən'fæb.jə- **-lates** -leɪts **-lating** -leɪ.tɪŋ Ⓤⓢ -leɪ.t̬ɪŋ **-lated** -leɪ.tɪd Ⓤⓢ -leɪ.t̬ɪd
confabulation kənˌfæb.jʊ'leɪ.ʃᵊn, kɒn- Ⓤⓢ kənˌfæb.jə'- **-s** -z
confect (*n.*) 'kɒn.fekt Ⓤⓢ 'kɑːn- **-s** -s
confect (*v.*) kən'fekt **-s** -s **-ing** -ɪŋ **-ed** -ɪd
confection kən'fek.ʃᵊn **-s** -z **-ing** -ɪŋ **-ed** -d **-er/s** -əʳ/z Ⓤⓢ -ɚ/z
confectionery kən'fek.ʃᵊn.ᵊr.i, -ʃᵊn.ri Ⓤⓢ -er-
confederac|y (C) kən'fed.ᵊr.ə.s|i **-ies** -iz
confederate (C) (*n. adj.*) kən'fed.ᵊr.ət, -ɪt **-s** -s
confede|rate (*v.*) kən'fed.ə|.reɪt **-rates** -reɪts **-rating** -reɪ.tɪŋ Ⓤⓢ -reɪ.t̬ɪŋ **-rated** -reɪ.tɪd Ⓤⓢ -reɪ.t̬ɪd
confederation kənˌfed.ə'reɪ.ʃᵊn **-s** -z
confer kən'fɜːʳ Ⓤⓢ -'fɜːr **-s** -z **-ring** -ɪŋ **-red** -d **-rable** -ə.bl̩ **-ment** -mənt
conferenc|e 'kɒn.fᵊr.ᵊnts Ⓤⓢ 'kɑːn.fɚ- **-es** -ɪz
conferral kən'fɜː.rᵊl Ⓤⓢ -'fɜːr.ᵊl **-s** -z
confess kən'fes **-es** -ɪz **-ing** -ɪŋ **-ed** -t **-edly** -ɪd.li
Confessio Amantis kɒnˌfes.i.əʊ.ə'mæn.tɪs, kən- Ⓤⓢ kɑːnˌfes.i.oʊ.ə'mɑːn-
confession kən'feʃ.ᵊn **-s** -z
confessional kən'feʃ.ᵊn.ᵊl, '-nᵊl **-s** -z
confessor kən'fes.əʳ, kɒn- Ⓤⓢ kən'fes.ɚ **-s** -z
Note: In British English, may also be pronounced /kɒn'fes.ɔːʳ/ in the sense of "Father Confessor".
confetti kən'fet.i, kɒn- Ⓤⓢ kən'fet̬-
confidant(e) 'kɒn.fɪ.dænt, -fə-, -dᵊnt; ˌkɒn.fɪ'dænt, -'dɑːnt Ⓤⓢ 'kɑːn.fə.dænt, -dɑːnt, ˌ--'- **-s** -s
confid|e kən'faɪd **-es** -z **-ing/ly** -ɪŋ/li **-ed** -ɪd **-er/s** -əʳ/z Ⓤⓢ -ɚ/z
confidenc|e 'kɒn.fɪ.dᵊnts, -fə- Ⓤⓢ 'kɑːn.fə- **-es** -ɪz
confident 'kɒn.fɪ.dᵊnt, -fə- Ⓤⓢ 'kɑːn.fə- **-ly** -li
confidential ˌkɒn.fɪ'den.*t*ʃᵊl Ⓤⓢ ˌkɑːn.fə'den*t*.ʃᵊl **-ly** -i
confidentiality ˌkɒn.fɪ.den.*t*ʃi'æl.ə.ti, -fə-, -ɪ.ti Ⓤⓢ ˌkɑːn.fə.den*t*.ʃi'æl.ə.t̬i
configuration kənˌfɪg.ə'reɪ.ʃᵊn, ˌkɒn.fɪg-, -jə'- Ⓤⓢ kənˌfɪg.jə'- **-s** -z
config|ure kən'fɪg|.əʳ, -jləʳ Ⓤⓢ -jlɚ **-ures** -əz Ⓤⓢ -ɚz **-uring** -ᵊr.ɪŋ **-ured** -əd Ⓤⓢ -ɚd
confine (*n.*) 'kɒn.faɪn Ⓤⓢ 'kɑːn- **-s** -z
confin|e (*v.*) kən'faɪn **-es** -z **-ing** -ɪŋ **-ed** -d
confinement kən'faɪn.mənt **-s** -s
confirm kən'fɜːm Ⓤⓢ -'fɜːrm **-s** -z **-ing** -ɪŋ **-ed** -d **-er/s** -əʳ/z Ⓤⓢ -ɚ/z
confirmation ˌkɒn.fə'meɪ.ʃᵊn Ⓤⓢ ˌkɑːn.fɚ'- **-s** -z
confirma|tive kən'fɜː.mə|.tɪv Ⓤⓢ -'fɜːr.mə|.t̬ɪv **-tory** -tᵊr.i, -tri Ⓤⓢ -tɔːr.i
confi|scate 'kɒn.fɪ|.skeɪt, -fə- Ⓤⓢ 'kɑːn.fə-, -fɪ- **-scates** -skeɪts **-scating** -skeɪ.tɪŋ Ⓤⓢ -skeɪ.t̬ɪŋ **-scated** -skeɪ.tɪd Ⓤⓢ -skeɪ.t̬ɪd **-scator/s** -skeɪ.təʳ/z Ⓤⓢ -skeɪ.t̬ɚ/z
confiscation ˌkɒn.fɪ'skeɪ.ʃᵊn, -fə'- Ⓤⓢ ˌkɑːn.fə'-, -fɪ- **-s** -z
confiscatory kən'fɪs.kə.tᵊr.i, kɒn-, -tri; ˌkɒn.fɪ'skeɪ-, -fə'-, 'kɒn.fɪ.skeɪ-, -fə- Ⓤⓢ kən'fɪs.kə.tɔːr.i
confit kɒn'fiː Ⓤⓢ koʊn-, kɔ̃ːn- **-s** -z
confiteor (C) kɒn'fɪt.i.ɔːʳ, kən-, '-eɪ- Ⓤⓢ kən'fɪt̬.i.ɔːr, -'fiː.t̬i- **-s** -z
confiture 'kɒn.fɪ.tjʊəʳ, -tjɔːʳ Ⓤⓢ 'kɑːn.fə.tʃʊr **-s** -z
conflagration ˌkɒn.flə'greɪ.ʃᵊn Ⓤⓢ ˌkɑːn- **-s** -z

con|flate kənˈfleɪt, kɒn- ⓤⓢ kən- **-flates** -ˈfleɪts **-flating** -ˈfleɪ.tɪŋ ⓤⓢ -ˈfleɪ.t̬ɪŋ **-flated** -ˈfleɪ.tɪd ⓤⓢ -ˈfleɪ.t̬ɪd
conflation kənˈfleɪ.ʃən, kɒn- ⓤⓢ kən-
conflict (*n.*) ˈkɒn.flɪkt ⓤⓢ ˈkɑːn- **-s** -s
conflict (*v.*) kənˈflɪkt **-s** -s **-ing** -ɪŋ **-ed** -ɪd
confluenc|e ˈkɒn.flu.ənts ⓤⓢ ˈkɑːn- **-es** -ɪz
confluent ˈkɒn.flu.ənt ⓤⓢ ˈkɑːn- **-s** -s **-ly** -li
conform kənˈfɔːm ⓤⓢ -ˈfɔːrm **-s** -z **-ing** -ɪŋ **-ed** -d **-er/s** -əʳ/z ⓤⓢ -ɚ/z
conformability kənˌfɔː.məˈbɪl.ə.ti, -ɪ.ti ⓤⓢ -ˌfɔːr.məˈbɪl.ə.t̬i
conformab|le kənˈfɔː.mə.bl̩ ⓤⓢ -ˈfɔːr- **-ly** -li
conformation ˌkɒn.fɔːˈmeɪ.ʃən, -fəˈ- ⓤⓢ ˌkɑːn.fɚˈ-, -fɔːrˈ- **-s** -z
conformist kənˈfɔː.mɪst ⓤⓢ -ˈfɔːr- **-s** -s
conformit|y kənˈfɔː.mə.t|i, -ɪ.t|i ⓤⓢ -ˈfɔːr.mə.t̬|i **-ies** -iz
confound kənˈfaʊnd, ˌkɒn- ⓤⓢ kən-, ˌkɑːn- **-s** -z **-ing** -ɪŋ **-ed/ly** -ɪd/li
confraternit|y ˌkɒn.frəˈtɜː.nə.t|i, -nɪ- ⓤⓢ ˌkɑːn.frəˈtɜːr.nə.t̬|i **-ies** -iz
confrère ˈkɒn.freəʳ ⓤⓢ kɑːnˈfrer **-s** -z
con|front kənˈfrʌnt **-fronts** -ˈfrʌnts **-fronting** -ˈfrʌn.tɪŋ ⓤⓢ -ˈfrʌn.t̬ɪŋ **-fronted** -ˈfrʌn.tɪd ⓤⓢ -ˈfrʌn.t̬ɪd
confrontation ˌkɒn.frʌnˈteɪ.ʃən, -frənˈ- ⓤⓢ ˌkɑːn.frənˈ- **-s** -z
confrontational ˌkɒn.frʌnˈteɪ.ʃən.əl, -frənˈ-, -ˈteɪʃ.nəl ⓤⓢ ˌkɑːn.frənˈ- **-ly** -i
Confucian kənˈfjuː.ʃən **-s** -z
Confucian|ism kənˈfjuː.ʃən|ɪ.zəm **-ist/s** -ɪst/s
confus|e kənˈfjuːz **-es** -ɪz **-ing/ly** -ɪŋ/li **-ed** -d **-edly** -ɪd.li, -d.li **-edness** -ɪd.nəs, -d.nəs, -nɪs
confusing kənˈfjuː.zɪŋ **-ly** -li
confusion kənˈfjuː.ʒən **-s** -z
confutable kənˈfjuː.tə.bl̩ ⓤⓢ -t̬ə-
confutation ˌkɒn.fjʊˈteɪ.ʃən ⓤⓢ ˌkɑːn.fjuːˈ- **-s** -z
con|fute kənˈfjuːt **-futes** -ˈfjuːts **-futing** -ˈfjuː.tɪŋ ⓤⓢ -ˈfjuː.t̬ɪŋ **-futed** -ˈfjuː.tɪd ⓤⓢ -ˈfjuː.t̬ɪd
conga ˈkɒŋ.gə ⓤⓢ ˈkɑːŋ-, ˈkɔːŋ- **-s** -z
congé ˈkɔ̃ːn.ʒeɪ, ˈkɔːn-, ˈkɒn- ⓤⓢ koʊnˈʒeɪ, kɑːn-, ˈ-- **-s** -z
congeal kənˈdʒiːl **-s** -z **-ing** -ɪŋ **-ed** -d **-able** -ə.bl̩
congee ˈkɒn.dʒiː ⓤⓢ ˈkɑːn- **-s** -z
congelation ˌkɒn.dʒɪˈleɪ.ʃən, -dʒəˈ- ⓤⓢ ˌkɑːn.dʒəˈ-
congener kənˈdʒiː.nəʳ; ˈkɒn.dʒɪ-, -dʒə- ⓤⓢ ˈkɑːn.dʒən.ɚ; kənˈdʒiː.nɚ **-s** -z

congenial kənˈdʒiː.ni.əl ⓤⓢ ˈ-njəl, ˈ-ni.əl **-ly** -i
congeniality kənˌdʒiː.niˈæl.ə.ti, -ɪ.ti ⓤⓢ -ə.t̬i
congenital kənˈdʒen.ɪ.təl ⓤⓢ -ə.t̬əl **-ly** -i
conger ˈkɒŋ.gəʳ ⓤⓢ ˈkɑːŋ.gɚ, ˈkɔːŋ- **-s** -z ˌ**conger ˈeel**, ˈ**conger ˌeel**
congeries ˈkɒn.dʒər.iːz, -ɪz; kənˈdʒɪə.riːz, -rɪz ⓤⓢ ˈkɑːn.dʒə.riːz
congest kənˈdʒest **-s** -s **-ing** -ɪŋ **-ed** -ɪd **-ive** -ɪv
congestion kənˈdʒes.tʃən, -ˈdʒeʃ- **-s** -z
Congleton ˈkɒŋ.gl̩.tən ⓤⓢ ˈkɑːŋ-, ˈkɔːŋ-
conglo|bate ˈkɒŋ.gləʊ|.beɪt, ˈkɒn- ⓤⓢ kənˈgloʊ|.beɪt; ˈkɑːŋ.gloʊ-, ˈkɔːŋ- **-bates** -beɪts **-bating** -beɪ.tɪŋ ⓤⓢ -beɪ.t̬ɪŋ **-bated** -beɪ.tɪd ⓤⓢ -beɪ.t̬ɪd
conglobation ˌkɒn.gləʊˈbeɪ.ʃən, ˌkɒŋ- ⓤⓢ ˌkɑːn.gloʊˈ-, kɑːŋ-, ˌkɔːŋ-
conglomerate (*n. adj.*) kənˈglɒm.ər.ət, kəŋ-, kɒn-, -eɪt, -ɪt ⓤⓢ kənˈglɑː.mɚ- **-s** -s
conglomer|ate (*v.*) kənˈglɒm.ər|.eɪt, kəŋ-, kɒn- ⓤⓢ kənˈglɑː.mə.r|eɪt **-ates** -eɪts **-ating** -eɪ.tɪŋ ⓤⓢ -eɪ.t̬ɪŋ **-ated** -eɪ.tɪd ⓤⓢ -eɪ.t̬ɪd
conglomeration kənˌglɒm.əˈreɪ.ʃən, kəŋ-, kɒn-, ˌkɒn.glɒm-, ˌkɒŋ.glɒm- ⓤⓢ kənˌglɑː.məˈ- **-s** -z
Congo ˈkɒŋ.gəʊ ⓤⓢ ˈkɑːŋ.goʊ, ˈkɔːŋ-
Congolese ˌkɒŋ.gəʊˈliːz ⓤⓢ ˌkɑːŋ.gəˈ-, ˌkɔːŋ-, -ˈliːs
congratu|late kənˈgrætʃ.ʊ|.leɪt, kəŋ-, -ˈgræt.jʊ-, -jə- ⓤⓢ -ˈgrætʃ.ə-, -ˈgrædʒ-, ˈ-ʊ- **-lates** -leɪts **-lating** -leɪ.tɪŋ ⓤⓢ -leɪ.t̬ɪŋ **-lated** -leɪ.tɪd ⓤⓢ -leɪ.t̬ɪd **-lator/s** -leɪ.təʳ/z ⓤⓢ -leɪ.t̬ɚ/z
congratulation kənˌgrætʃ.ʊˈleɪ.ʃən, kəŋ-, -ˌgræt.jʊˈ-, -jəˈ- ⓤⓢ -ˌgrætʃ.əˈ-, -ˌgrædʒ-, -ʊˈ- **-s** -z
congratulatory kənˌgrætʃ.ʊˈleɪ.tər.i, kəŋ-, -ˌgræt.jʊˈ-, -jəˈ-, -tri; kənˈgrætʃ.əl.ə- ⓤⓢ kənˈgrætʃ.əl.ə.tɔːr.i, -ˈgrædʒ-
congre|gate ˈkɒŋ.grɪ|.geɪt, -grə- ⓤⓢ ˈkɑːŋ-, ˈkɔːŋ- **-gates** -geɪts **-gating** -geɪ.tɪŋ ⓤⓢ -geɪ.t̬ɪŋ **-gated** -geɪ.tɪd ⓤⓢ -geɪ.t̬ɪd
congregation ˌkɒŋ.grɪˈgeɪ.ʃən, -grəˈ- ⓤⓢ ˌkɑːŋ-, ˌkɔːŋ- **-s** -z
congregational (**C**) ˌkɒŋ.grɪˈgeɪ.ʃən.əl, -grəˈ-, -ˈgeɪʃ.nəl ⓤⓢ ˌkɑːŋ-, ˌkɔːŋ- **-ism** -ɪ.zəm **-ist/s** -ɪst/s
Congresbury ˈkɒŋz.bri, ˈkuːmz.bər.i ⓤⓢ ˈkɑːŋz.ber-, ˈkɔːŋz-, ˈkuːmz-, -bɚ-
congress (**C**) ˈkɒŋ.gres ⓤⓢ ˈkɑːŋ-, ˈkɔːŋ-, -grəs **-es** -ɪz

congressional (**C**) kənˈgreʃ.ən.əl, kəŋ-, kɒŋ-, ˈ-nəl ⓤⓢ kəŋ-
congress|man ˈkɒŋ.gres|.mən ⓤⓢ ˈkɑːŋ-, ˈkɔːŋ-, -grəs- **-men** -mən, -men
congress|woman ˈkɒŋ.gres|ˌwʊm.ən ⓤⓢ ˈkɑːŋ-, ˈkɔːŋ-, -grəs- **-women** -ˌwɪm.ɪn
Congreve ˈkɒŋ.griːv ⓤⓢ ˈkɑːn-, ˈkɑːŋ-
congruenc|e ˈkɒŋ.gru.ənts ⓤⓢ ˈkɑːŋ-, ˈkɔːŋ-, kənˈgruː- **-es** -ɪz **-y** -i **-ies** -iz
congruent ˈkɒŋ.gru.ənt ⓤⓢ ˈkɑːŋ-; kənˈgruː- **-ly** -li
congruit|y kɒŋˈgruː.ə.t|i, kən-, kəŋ-, -ɪ.t|i ⓤⓢ kɑːnˈgruː.ə.t̬|i, kən- **-ies** -iz
congruous ˈkɒŋ.gru.əs ⓤⓢ ˈkɑːŋ-, ˈkɔːŋ- **-ly** -li **-ness** -nəs, -nɪs
conic ˈkɒn.ɪk ⓤⓢ ˈkɑː.nɪk **-s** -s
conical ˈkɒn.ɪ.kəl ⓤⓢ ˈkɑː.nɪ- **-ly** -i **-ness** -nəs, -nɪs
conifer ˈkɒn.ɪ.fəʳ, ˈkəʊ.nɪ-, -nə- ⓤⓢ ˈkɑː.nə.fɚ, ˈkoʊ- **-s** -z
coniferous kəʊˈnɪf.ər.əs, kɒnˈɪf- ⓤⓢ koʊˈnɪf-, kə-
coniform ˈkəʊ.nɪ.fɔːm ⓤⓢ ˈkoʊ.nɪ.fɔːrm
Coningham ˈkʌn.ɪŋ.əm ⓤⓢ -hæm
Coningsby ˈkɒn.ɪŋz.bi, ˈkʌn- ⓤⓢ ˈkʌn-
Conisbrough ˈkɒn.ɪs.brə, ˈkʌn- ⓤⓢ ˈkɑː.nɪs.bɚ.oʊ
Coniston ˈkɒn.ɪ.stən ⓤⓢ ˈkɑː.nɪ-
conjecturable kənˈdʒek.tʃər.ə.bl̩
conjectural kənˈdʒek.tʃər.əl **-ly** -i
conject|ure kənˈdʒek.tʃ|əʳ ⓤⓢ -tʃ|ɚ **-ures** -əz ⓤⓢ -ɚz **-uring** -ər.ɪŋ **-ured** -əd ⓤⓢ -ɚd
conjoin kənˈdʒɔɪn, kɒn- ⓤⓢ kən- **-s** -z **-ing** -ɪŋ **-ed** -d
conjoint kənˈdʒɔɪnt, kɒn- ⓤⓢ kən- **-ly** -li
conjugal ˈkɒn.dʒʊ.gəl, -dʒə- ⓤⓢ ˈkɑːn.dʒə- **-ly** -i ˌ**conjugal ˈrights**
conjugality ˌkɒn.dʒʊˈgæl.ə.ti, -ɪ.ti ⓤⓢ ˌkɑːn.dʒəˈgæl.ə.t̬i
conjugate (*n. adj*) ˈkɒn.dʒʊ.gət, -dʒə-, -gɪt, -geɪt ⓤⓢ ˈkɑːn.dʒə- **-s** -s
conju|gate (*v.*) ˈkɒn.dʒʊ|.geɪt, -dʒə- ⓤⓢ ˈkɑːn.dʒə- **-gates** -geɪts **-gating** -geɪ.tɪŋ ⓤⓢ -geɪ.t̬ɪŋ **-gated** -geɪ.tɪd ⓤⓢ -geɪ.t̬ɪd
conjugation ˌkɒn.dʒʊˈgeɪ.ʃən, -dʒəˈ- ⓤⓢ ˌkɑːn.dʒəˈ- **-s** -z
conjunct (*n.*) ˈkɒn.dʒʌŋ*k*t ⓤⓢ ˈkɑːn- **-s** -s
conjunct (*adj.*) kənˈdʒʌŋ*k*t, kɒn- ⓤⓢ kən-; ˈkɑːn.dʒʌŋ*k*t **-ly** -li
conjunction kənˈdʒʌŋk.ʃən **-s** -z
conjunctiva ˌkɒn.dʒʌŋ*k*ˈtaɪ.və ⓤⓢ ˌkɑːn.dʒəŋˈ-
conjunctive kənˈdʒʌŋ*k*.tɪv **-ly** -li
conjunctivitis kənˌdʒʌŋ*k*.tɪˈvaɪ.tɪs, -təˈ- ⓤⓢ -təˈvaɪ.t̬ɪs

conjuncture kən'dʒʌŋ*k*.tʃəʳ (US) -tʃɚ **-s** -z
conjuration ˌkɒn.dʒʊə'reɪ.ʃᵊn (US) ˌkɑːn.dʒʊ'reɪ- **-s** -z
conjur|e *charge solemnly:* kən'dʒʊəʳ (US) -'dʒʊr **-es** -z **-ing** -ɪŋ **-ed** -d
conj|ure *summon by magic:* 'kʌn.dʒ|əʳ (US) -dʒ|ɚ **-ures** -əz (US) -ɚz **-uring** -ᵊr.ɪŋ **-ured** -əd (US) -ɚd **-urer/s** -ᵊr.əʳ/z (US) -ɚ.ɚ/z **-uror/s** -ᵊr.əʳ/z (US) -ɚ.ɚ/z **'conjuring ˌtrick**
conk kɒŋk (US) kɑːŋk, kɔːŋk **-s** -s **-ing** -ɪŋ **-ed** -t
conker 'kɒŋ.kəʳ (US) 'kɑːŋ.kɚ, 'kɔːŋ- **-s** -z
Conleth 'kɒn.ləθ (US) 'kɑːn-
Conley 'kɒn.li (US) 'kɑːn-
Conlon 'kɒn.lən (US) 'kɑːn-
con|man 'kɒn|.mæn (US) 'kɑːn- **-men** -men
Conn. (*abbrev. for* **Connaught**) 'kɒn.ɔːt (US) 'kɑː.nɑːt, -nɔːt
Conn. (*abbrev. for* **Connecticut**) kə'net.ɪ.kət (US) -'net̬-, -kɪt
Connah's Quay ˌkɒn.əz'kiː (US) ˌkɑː.nəz'kiː, -'keɪ, -'kweɪ
Connally 'kɒn.ᵊl.i (US) 'kɑː.nᵊl-
connate 'kɒn.eɪt, -'- (US) 'kɑː.neɪt, -'-
Connaught 'kɒn.ɔːt (US) 'kɑː.nɑːt, -nɔːt
connect kə'nekt **-s** -s **-ing** -ɪŋ **-ed/ly** -ɪd/li **-able** -ə.bl̩ **-or/s** -əʳ/z (US) -ɚ/z
connectible kə'nek.tə.bᵊl, -tɪ-
Connecticut kə'net.ɪ.kət (US) -'net̬-, -kɪt
connection kə'nek.ʃᵊn **-s** -z
connective kə'nek.tɪv **-s** -z **-ly** -li
Connelly 'kɒn.ᵊl.i (US) 'kɑː.nᵊl-
Connemara ˌkɒn.ɪ'mɑː.rə, -ə'- (US) ˌkɑː.nə'-
Conner 'kɒn.əʳ (US) 'kɑː.nɚ
Connery 'kɒn.ᵊr.i (US) 'kɑː.nɚ-
connexion kə'nek.ʃᵊn **-s** -z
Connie 'kɒn.i (US) 'kɑː.ni
conning tower 'kɒn.ɪŋˌtaʊəʳ (US) 'kɑː.nɪŋˌtaʊɚ **-s** -z
connivance kə'naɪ.vᵊn*t*s
conniv|e kə'naɪv **-es** -z **-ing** -ɪŋ **-ed** -d **-er/s** -əʳ/z (US) -ɚ/z
connoisseur ˌkɒn.ə'sɜːʳ, -ɪ'- (US) ˌkɑː.nə'sɜːr **-s** -z
Connolly 'kɒn.ᵊl.i (US) 'kɑː.nᵊl-
Connor 'kɒn.əʳ (US) 'kɑː.nɚ **-s**
conno|tate 'kɒn.əʊ|.teɪt (US) 'kɑː.nə- **-tates** -teɪts **-tating** -teɪ.tɪŋ (US) -teɪ.t̬ɪŋ **-tated** -teɪ.tɪd (US) -teɪ.t̬ɪd
connotation ˌkɒn.əʊ'teɪ.ʃᵊn (US) ˌkɑː.nə'- **-s** -z
connotative 'kɒn.əʊ.teɪ.tɪv; kə'nəʊ.tə- (US) kə'noʊ.t̬ə.t̬ɪv, 'kɑː.nə.teɪ-
connot|e kə'nəʊt, kɒn'əʊt (US) kə'noʊt **-es** -s **-ing** -ɪŋ (US) kə'noʊ.t̬ɪŋ **-ed** -ɪd (US) kə'noʊ.t̬ɪd
connubial kə'njuː.bi.əl, kɒn'juː- (US) kə'nuː-, -'njuː- **-ly** -i
connubiality kəˌnjuː.bi'æl.ə.ti, kɒnˌjuː-, -ɪ.ti (US) kəˌnuː.bi'æl.ə.t̬i, -ˌnjuː-
conoid 'kəʊ.nɔɪd (US) 'koʊ- **-s** -z
conoidal kəʊ'nɔɪ.dᵊl (US) koʊ-
Conolly 'kɒn.ᵊl.i (US) 'kɑː.nᵊl-
conqu|er 'kɒŋ.k|əʳ (US) 'kɑːŋ.k|ɚ, 'kɔːŋ- **-ers** -əz (US) -ɚz **-ering** -ᵊr.ɪŋ **-ered** -əd (US) -ɚd **-erable** -ᵊr.ə.bl̩
conqueror 'kɒŋ.kᵊr.əʳ (US) 'kɑːŋ.kɚ.ɚ, 'kɔːŋ- **-s** -z
conquest (**C**) 'kɒŋ.kwest (US) 'kɑːn-, 'kɑːŋ- **-s** -s
conquistador kɒn'kɪs.tə.dɔːʳ, kɒŋ-, -'kwɪs-; ˌkɒn.kɪ.stə'dɔːʳ, kɒŋ-, -kwɪ- (US) kɑːŋ'kiː.stə.dɔːr, kɔːŋ-, kɑːn-, -'kwɪs.tə- **-s** -z
Conrad 'kɒn.ræd (US) 'kɑːn-
Conran 'kɒn.rən, -ræn (US) 'kɑːn-
Conroy 'kɒn.rɔɪ (US) 'kɑːn-
consanguine kɒn'sæŋ.gwɪn (US) kɑːn-
consanguineous ˌkɒn.sæŋ'gwɪn.i.əs (US) ˌkɑːn.sæŋ'-
consanguinity ˌkɒn.sæŋ'gwɪn.ə.ti, -ɪ.ti (US) ˌkɑːn.sæŋ'gwɪn.ə.t̬i
conscienc|e 'kɒn.*t*ʃᵊn*t*s (US) 'kɑːn- **-es** -ɪz **'conscience-ˌstricken**
conscientious ˌkɒn.*t*ʃi'en.*t*ʃəs (US) ˌkɑːn.*t*ʃi'en*t*.ʃəs **-ly** -li **-ness** -nəs, -nɪs **consciˌentious ob'jector**
conscionab|le 'kɒn.*t*ʃᵊn.ə.b|l̩ (US) 'kɑːn- **-ly** -li **-leness** -l̩.nəs, -nɪs
conscious 'kɒn.*t*ʃəs (US) 'kɑːn*t*.ʃəs **-ly** -li **-ness** -nəs, -nɪs **'consciousness ˌraising**
conscrib|e kən'skraɪb **-es** -z **-ing** -ɪŋ **-ed** -d
conscript (*n.*) 'kɒn.skrɪpt (US) 'kɑːn- **-s** -s
conscript (*v.*) kən'skrɪpt **-s** -s **-ing** -ɪŋ **-ed** -ɪd
conscription kən'skrɪp.ʃᵊn **-s** -z
conse|crate 'kɒn*t*.sɪ|.kreɪt, -sə- (US) 'kɑːn*t*.sə- **-crates** -kreɪts **-crating** -kreɪ.tɪŋ (US) -kreɪ.t̬ɪŋ **-crated** -kreɪ.tɪd (US) -kreɪ.t̬ɪd **-crator/s** -kreɪ.təʳ/z (US) -kreɪ.t̬ɚ/z
consecration ˌkɒn*t*.sɪ'kreɪ.ʃᵊn, -sə'- (US) ˌkɑːn*t*.sə'- **-s** -z
consecutive kən'sek.jʊ.tɪv, -jə- (US) -jə.t̬ɪv **-ly** -li **-ness** -nəs, -nɪs
consensual kən'sen*t*.sju.ᵊl, kɒn-, -'sen.*t*ʃu- (US) kən'sen*t*.ʃu-, '-ʃᵊl **-ly** -li
consensus kən'sen*t*.səs, kɒn- (US) kən-
con|sent kən|'sent **-sents** -'sents **-senting** -'sen.tɪŋ (US) -'sen.t̬ɪŋ **-sented** -'sen.tɪd (US) -'sen.t̬ɪd
consequenc|e 'kɒn*t*.sɪ.kwən*t*s, -sə- (US) 'kɑːn*t*- **-es** -ɪz
consequent 'kɒn*t*.sɪ.kwənt, -sə- (US) 'kɑːn*t*- **-ly** -li
consequential ˌkɒn*t*.sɪ'kwen.*t*ʃᵊl, -sə'- (US) ˌkɑːn*t*- **-ly** -i
conservable kən'sɜː.və.bl̩ (US) -'sɜːr-
conservanc|y kən'sɜː.vᵊn*t*.s|i (US) -'sɜːr- **-ies** -iz
conservation ˌkɒn*t*.sə'veɪ.ʃᵊn (US) ˌkɑːn*t*.sɚ'-
conservationist ˌkɒn*t*.sə'veɪ.ʃᵊn.ɪst (US) ˌkɑːn*t*.sɚ'- **-s** -s
conservatism kən'sɜː.və.tɪ.zᵊm (US) -'sɜːr-
conservative (**C**) kən'sɜː.və.tɪv (US) -'sɜːr.və.t̬ɪv **-s** -z **-ly** -li **-ness** -nəs, -nɪs
conservatoire kən'sɜː.və.twɑːʳ, kɒn- (US) kən'sɜːr.və.twɑːr, -ˌsɜːr.və'twɑːr **-s** -z
conservator *preserver:* 'kɒn*t*.sə.veɪ.təʳ (US) 'kɑːn*t*.sɚ.veɪ.t̬ɚ **-s** -z
conservator *official guardian:* kən'sɜː.və.təʳ (US) -'sɜːr.və.t̬ɚ **-s** -z
conservator|y kən'sɜː.və.tr|i (US) -'sɜːr.və.tɔːr|.i **-ies** -iz
conserve (*n.*) kən'sɜːv; 'kɒn.sɜːv (US) 'kɑːn.sɜːrv **-s** -z
conserv|e (*v.*) kən'sɜːv (US) -'sɜːrv **-es** -z **-ing** -ɪŋ **-ed** -d
Consett 'kɒn.sɪt, -set, -sət (US) 'kɑːn-
consid|er kən'sɪd|.əʳ (US) -ɚ **-ers** -əz (US) -ɚz **-ering** -ᵊr.ɪŋ **-ered** -əd (US) -ɚd
considerab|le kən'sɪd.ᵊr.ə.b|l̩ **-ly** -li **-leness** -l̩.nəs, -nɪs
considerate kən'sɪd.ᵊr.ət, -ɪt **-ly** -li **-ness** -nəs, -nɪs
consideration kənˌsɪd.ᵊr'eɪ.ʃᵊn **-s** -z
consign kən'saɪn **-s** -z **-ing** -ɪŋ **-ed** -d **-er/s** -əʳ/z (US) -ɚ/z **-able** -ə.bl̩
consignation ˌkɒn.saɪ'neɪ.ʃᵊn (US) ˌkɑːn.sɪg'-, -sɪ'-
consignee ˌkɒn.saɪ'niː, -sɪ'- (US) ˌkɑːn- **-s** -z
consignment kən'saɪn.mənt, -'saɪm- (US) -'saɪn- **-s** -s
consist kən'sɪst **-s** -s **-ing** -ɪŋ **-ed** -ɪd
consisten|ce kən'sɪs.tᵊn*t*|s **-cy** -si **-cies** -siz
consistent kən'sɪs.tᵊnt **-ly** -li
consistorial ˌkɒn.sɪ'stɔː.ri.əl (US) ˌkɑːn.sɪ'stɔːr.i-
consistor|y kən'sɪs.tᵊr|.i, -tr|i (US) -tɚ|.i **-ies** -iz
consolable kən'səʊ.lə.bl̩ (US) -'soʊ-
consolation ˌkɒn.sə'leɪ.ʃᵊn (US) ˌkɑːn- **-s** -z ˌ**conso'lation ˌprize**
consolatory kən'sɒl.ə.tᵊr.i, -'səʊ.lə-, -tri (US) -'sɑː.lə.tɔːr.i, -'soʊ-
console (*n.*) 'kɒn.səʊl (US) 'kɑːn.soʊl **-s** -z

consol|e (*v.*) kən'səʊl US -'soʊl **-es** -z **-ing** -ɪŋ **-ed** -d **-er/s** -əʳ/z US -ɚ/z

consoli|date kən'sɒl.ɪ|.deɪt, '-ə- US -'sɑː.lə- **-dates** -deɪts **-dating** -deɪ.tɪŋ US -deɪ.t̬ɪŋ **-dated** -deɪ.tɪd US -deɪ.t̬ɪd **-dator/s** -deɪ.təʳ/z US -deɪ.t̬ɚ/z **-dative** -deɪ.tɪv US -deɪ.t̬ɪv

consolidation kənˌsɒl.ɪ'deɪ.ʃᵊn, -ə'- US -ˌsɑː.lə'- **-s** -z

consols kən'sɒlz; 'kɒnt.sᵊlz US 'kɑːn.sɑːlz; kən'sɑːlz

consommé kən'sɒm.eɪ, kɒn-; 'kɒnt.sə.meɪ US ˌkɑːnt.sə'meɪ, '---

consonanc|e 'kɒnt.sᵊn.ənts US 'kɑːnt- **-es** -ɪz

consonant 'kɒnt.sᵊn.ənt US 'kɑːnt- **-s** -s **-ly** -li

consonantal ˌkɒnt.sᵊn'æn.tᵊl US ˌkɑːnt.sə'næn.t̬ᵊl **-ly** -i

consort (*n.*) 'kɒn.sɔːt US 'kɑːn.sɔːrt **-s** -s

con|sort (*v.*) kən|'sɔːt, kɒn- US kən|'sɔːrt **-sorts** -'sɔːts US -'sɔːrts **-sorting** -'sɔː.tɪŋ US -'sɔːr.t̬ɪŋ **-sorted** -'sɔː.tɪd US -'sɔːr.t̬ɪd

consorti|um kən'sɔː.ti|.əm, -ʃi-, '-ʃ|əm US -'sɔːr.t̬i|.əm, -ʃi-, '-ʃ|əm **-ums** -əmz **-a** -ə

conspectus kən'spek.təs **-es** -ɪz

conspicuous kən'spɪk.ju.əs **-ly** -li **-ness** -nəs, -nɪs

conspirac|y kən'spɪr.ə.s|i **-ies** -iz **con'spiracy ˌtheory**

conspirator kən'spɪr.ə.təʳ, -ɪ.təʳ US -ə.t̬ɚ **-s** -z

conspiratorial kənˌspɪr.ə'tɔː.ri.əl, kɒn- US kənˌspɪr.ə'tɔːr.i-

conspir|e kən'spaɪəʳ US -'spaɪɚ **-es** -z **-ing** -ɪŋ **-ed** -d **-er/s** -əʳ/z US -ɚ/z

constable (**C**) 'kʌnt.stə.bḷ, 'kɒnt- US 'kɑːnt-, 'kʌnt- **-s** -z

constabular|y kən'stæb.jʊ.lᵊr|.i, -jə- US -jə.ler|.i **-ies** -iz

Constance 'kɒnt.stənts US 'kɑːnt-

constancy 'kɒnt.stənt.si US 'kɑːnt-

constant 'kɒnt.stənt US 'kɑːnt- **-s** -s **-ly** -li **-ness** -nəs, -nɪs

Constanta kən'stæn.tə US -t̬ə

Constantine *Kings and Emperors:* 'kɒnt.stᵊn.taɪn, -tiːn US 'kɑːnt.stᵊn.tiːn, -taɪn *city:* 'kɒnt.stᵊn.taɪn, -tiːn US 'kɑːnt-

Constantinople ˌkɒn.stæn.tɪ'nəʊ.pḷ US ˌkɑːn.stæn.tᵊn'oʊ-

constative kən'stæt.ɪv US -'stæt̬-

constellation ˌkɒnt.stə'leɪ.ʃᵊn, -stɪ'- US ˌkɑːnt- **-s** -z

conster|nate 'kɒnt.stə|.neɪt US 'kɑːnt.stɚ- **-nates** -neɪts **-nating** -neɪ.tɪŋ US -neɪ.t̬ɪŋ **-nated** -neɪ.tɪd US -neɪ.t̬ɪd

consternation ˌkɒnt.stə'neɪ.ʃᵊn US ˌkɑːnt.stɚ'-

consti|pate 'kɒnt.stɪ|.peɪt, -stə- US 'kɑːnt.stə- **-pates** -peɪts **-pating** -peɪ.tɪŋ US -peɪ.t̬ɪŋ **-pated** -peɪ.tɪd US -peɪ.t̬ɪd

constipation ˌkɒnt.stɪ'peɪ.ʃᵊn, -stə'- US ˌkɑːnt.stə'-

constituen|cy kən'stɪt.ju.ənt|.si, kɒn-, -'stɪtʃ.u- US kən'stɪtʃ.u- **-cies** -siz

constituent kən'stɪt.ju.ənt, kɒn-, -'stɪtʃ.u- US kən'stɪtʃ.u- **-s** -s

consti|tute 'kɒnt.stɪ|.tjuːt, -stə-, -tʃuːt US 'kɑːnt.stə|.tuːt, -tjuːt **-tutes** -tjuːts, -tʃuːts US -tuːts, -tjuːts **-tuting** -tjuː.tɪŋ, -tʃuː.tɪŋ US -tuː.t̬ɪŋ, -tjuː- **-tuted** -tjuː.tɪd, -tʃuː.tɪd US -tuː.t̬ɪd, -tjuː-

constitution ˌkɒnt.stɪ'tjuː.ʃᵊn, -stə'-, -'tʃuː- US ˌkɑːnt.stə'tuː-, -'tjuː- **-s** -z

constitutional ˌkɒnt.stɪ'tjuː.ʃᵊn.ᵊl, -stə'-, -'tʃuː-, -'tjuːʃ.nᵊl, -'tʃuːʃ- US ˌkɑːnt.stə'tuː-, -'tjuː-, -'tuːʃ.nᵊl, -'tjuːʃ- **-ly** -i

constitutional|ism ˌkɒnt.stɪ'tjuː.ʃᵊn.ᵊl|.ɪ.zᵊm, -stə'-, -'tʃuː- US ˌkɑːnt.stə'tuː-, -'tjuː- **-ist/s** -ɪst/s

constitutionaliz|e, -is|e ˌkɒnt.stɪ'tjuː.ʃᵊn.ᵊl.aɪz, -stə'-, -'tʃuː- US ˌkɑːnt.stə'tuː.ʃᵊn.ə.laɪz, -'tjuː- **-es** -ɪz **-ing** -ɪŋ **-ed** -d

constitutive kən'stɪt.jʊ.tɪv, kɒn-, -'stɪtʃ.ə-; 'kɒnt.stɪ.tjuː-, -stə-, -tʃuː- US 'kɑːnt.stə.tuː.t̬ɪv, -tjuː-; kən'stɪtʃ.ə-

constrain kən'streɪn **-s** -z **-ing** -ɪŋ **-ed** -d **-edly** -ɪd.li, -d.li **-able** -ə.bḷ

constraint kən'streɪnt **-s** -s

constrict kən'strɪkt **-s** -s **-ing** -ɪŋ **-ed** -ɪd **-or/s** -əʳ/z US -ɚ/z **-ive** -ɪv

constriction kən'strɪk.ʃᵊn **-s** -z

construct (*n.*) 'kɒn.strʌkt US 'kɑːn- **-s** -s

construct (*v.*) kən'strʌkt **-s** -s **-ing** -ɪŋ **-ed** -ɪd

construction kən'strʌk.ʃᵊn **-s** -z

constructional kən'strʌk.ʃᵊn.ᵊl **-ly** -i

constructionist kən'strʌk.ʃᵊn.ɪst **-s** -s

constructive kən'strʌk.tɪv **-ly** -li **-ness** -nəs, -nɪs

constructor kən'strʌk.təʳ US -tɚ **-s** -z

constru|e kən'struː, kɒn- US kən- **-es** -z **-ing** -ɪŋ **-ed** -d

consubstantial ˌkɒn.səb'stæn.tʃᵊl, -'stɑːn- US ˌkɑːn.səb'stænt.ʃᵊl **-ly** -i

consubstanti|ate ˌkɒn.səb'stæn.tʃi|.eɪt, -'stɑːn-, -'stænt.si-, -'stɑːnt.si- US ˌkɑːn.səb'stænt.ʃi- **-ates** -eɪts **-ating** -eɪ.tɪŋ US -eɪ.t̬ɪŋ **-ated** -eɪ.tɪd US -eɪ.t̬ɪd

consubstantiation ˌkɒn.səbˌstæn.tʃi'eɪ.ʃᵊn, -ˌstɑːn-, -ˌstænt.si'-, -ˌstɑːnt.si'- US ˌkɑːn.səbˌstænt.ʃi'-

consuetude 'kɒnt.swɪ.tjuːd, -tʃuːd US 'kɑːnt.swɪ.tuːd, -tjuːd

consuetudinary ˌkɒnt.swɪ'tjuː.dɪ.nᵊr.i US ˌkɑːnt.swɪ'tuː.dɪ.ner-, -'tjuː-

consul 'kɒnt.sᵊl US 'kɑːnt- **-s** -z **-ship/s** -ʃɪp/s

consular 'kɒnt.sjʊ.ləʳ, -sjə- US 'kɑːnt-

consulate 'kɒnt.sjʊ.lət, -sjə-, -lɪt US 'kɑːnt- **-s** -s

con|sult kən|'sʌlt **-sults** -'sʌlts **-sulting** -'sʌl.tɪŋ US -'sʌl.t̬ɪŋ **-sulted** -'sʌl.tɪd US -'sʌl.t̬ɪd

consultanc|y kən'sʌl.tᵊnt.s|i **-ies** -iz

consultant kən'sʌl.tᵊnt **-s** -s

consultation ˌkɒn.sᵊl'teɪ.ʃᵊn, -sʌl'- US ˌkɑːn- **-s** -z

consultative kən'sʌl.tə.tɪv US -t̬ə.t̬ɪv; 'kɑːnt.səl.teɪ-

consultatory kən'sʌl.tə.tᵊr.i, -tri; ˌkɒnt.sᵊl'teɪ- US kən'sʌl.t̬ə.tɔːr.i

consumable kən'sjuː.mə.bḷ, -'suː- US -'suː- **-s** -z

consum|e kən'sjuːm, -'suːm US -'suːm **-es** -z **-ing** -ɪŋ **-ed** -d

consumer kən'sjuː.məʳ, -'suː- US -'suː.mɚ **-s** -z **con'sumer ˌgoods**; **con'sumer soˌciety**

consumer|ism kən'sjuː.mə.r|ɪ.zᵊm, -'suː- US -'suː.mɚ.ɪ- **-ist** -ɪst

consummate (*adj.*) kən'sʌm.ət, -ɪt; 'kɒnt.sə.mət, -sjʊ-, -mɪt US 'kɑːnt.sə.mɪt; kən'sʌm.ɪt **-ly** -li

consum|mate (*v.*) 'kɒnt.sə|.meɪt, -sjʊ- US 'kɑːnt.sə- **-mates** -meɪts **-mating** -meɪ.tɪŋ US -meɪ.t̬ɪŋ **-mated** -meɪ.tɪd US -meɪ.t̬ɪd **-mator/s** -meɪ.təʳ/z US -meɪ.t̬ɚ/z

consummation ˌkɒnt.sə'meɪ.ʃᵊn, -sjʊ'- US ˌkɑːnt.sə'- **-s** -z

consummative 'kɒnt.sə.meɪ.tɪv, -sʌm.eɪ-, -sjʊ.meɪ-; kən'sʌm.ə- US 'kɑːnt.sə.meɪ.t̬ɪv; kən'sʌm.ə-

consumption kən'sʌmp.ʃᵊn

consumptive kən'sʌmp.tɪv **-s** -z **-ly** -li **-ness** -nəs, -nɪs

contact (*n. adj.*) 'kɒn.tækt US 'kɑːn- **-s** -s **'contact ˌlens**

contact (*v.*) 'kɒn.tækt; -'-, kən- US 'kɑːn.tækt **-s** -s **-ing** -ɪŋ **-ed** -ɪd

contagion kən'teɪ.dʒᵊn **-s** -z

contagious kən'teɪ.dʒəs **-ly** -li **-ness** -nəs, -nɪs

contain kən'teɪn **-s** -z **-ing** -ɪŋ **-ed** -d **-able** -ə.bḷ

container kən'teɪ.nəʳ US -nɚ **-s** -z **con'tainer ˌship**

containerization, -isa- kənˌteɪ.nᵊr.aɪˈzeɪ.ʃᵊn, -ɪˈ- ⓤⓢ -ɪˈ-
containeriz|e, is|e kənˈteɪ.nᵊr.aɪz ⓤⓢ -nə.raɪz **-es** -ɪz **-ing** -ɪŋ **-ed** -d
containment kənˈteɪn.mənt, -ˈteɪm- ⓤⓢ -ˈteɪn-
contaminant kənˈtæm.ɪ.nənt, ˈ-ə- **-s** -s
contami|nate kənˈtæm.ɪ|.neɪt, ˈ-ə- **-nates** -neɪts **-nating** -neɪ.tɪŋ ⓤⓢ -neɪ.t̬ɪŋ **-nated** -neɪ.tɪd ⓤⓢ -neɪ.t̬ɪd **-nater/s** -neɪ.təʳ/z ⓤⓢ -neɪ.t̬ɚ/z
contamination kənˌtæm.ɪˈneɪ.ʃᵊn, -əˈ- **-s** -z
contaminative kənˈtæm.ɪ.nə.tɪv, ˈ-ə-, -neɪ- ⓤⓢ -t̬ɪv
contango kənˈtæŋ.gəʊ, kɒn- ⓤⓢ kənˈtæŋ.goʊ **-s** -z
contd (*abbrev. for* **continued**) kənˈtɪn.juːd, -jud
contemn kənˈtem **-s** -z **-ing** -ɪŋ **-ed** -d **-er/s** -əʳ/z, -nəʳ/z ⓤⓢ -ɚ/z, -nɚ/z
contem|plate ˈkɒn.təm|.pleɪt, -tem- ⓤⓢ ˈkɑːn.t̬əm-, -tem- **-plates** -pleɪts **-plating** -pleɪ.tɪŋ ⓤⓢ -pleɪ.t̬ɪŋ **-plated** -pleɪ.tɪd ⓤⓢ -pleɪ.t̬ɪd **-plator/s** -pleɪ.təʳ/z ⓤⓢ -pleɪ.t̬ɚ/z
contemplation ˌkɒn.təmˈpleɪ.ʃᵊn, -temˈ- ⓤⓢ ˌkɑːn.t̬əmˈ-, -temˈ- **-s** -z
contemplative *pensive:* ˈkɒn.tem.pleɪ.tɪv, -təm-, -plə-; kənˈtem.plə- ⓤⓢ kənˈtem.plə.t̬ɪv; ˈkɑːn.t̬əm.pleɪ- **-ly** -li **-ness** -nəs, -nɪs
contemplative *of religious orders:* kənˈtem.plə.tɪv ⓤⓢ -t̬ɪv
contemporaneity kənˌtem.pᵊr.əˈniː.ə.ti, kɒn-, -ˈneɪ-, -ɪ.ti; ˌkɒn.tem- ⓤⓢ kənˌtem.pɚ.əˈniː.ə.t̬i, -ˈneɪ-
contemporaneous kənˌtem.pᵊrˈeɪ.ni.əs, kɒn-; ˌkɒn.tem- ⓤⓢ kən- **-ly** -li **-ness** -nəs, -nɪs
contemporar|y kənˈtem.pᵊr.ᵊr|.i ⓤⓢ -pə.rer- **-ies** -iz **-ily** -ᵊl.i, -ɪ.li
contempt kənˈtemp*t*
contemptibility kənˌtemp*.*təˈbɪl.ə.ti, -tɪˈ-, -ɪ.ti ⓤⓢ -təˈbɪl.ə.t̬i
contemptib|le kənˈtemp*.*tə.b|l̩, -tɪ- **-ly** -li **-leness** -l̩.nəs, -nɪs
contemptuous kənˈtemp*.*tʃu.əs, -tju- ⓤⓢ -tʃu- **-ly** -li **-ness** -nəs, -nɪs
contend kənˈtend **-s** -z **-ing** -ɪŋ **-ed** -ɪd **-er/s** -əʳ/z ⓤⓢ -ɚ/z
content (*n.*) *what is contained:* ˈkɒn.tent ⓤⓢ ˈkɑːn- **-s** *contentment:* kənˈtent
con|tent (*adj. v.*) kən|ˈtent **-tents** -ˈtents **-tenting** -ˈten.tɪŋ ⓤⓢ -ˈten.t̬ɪŋ **-tented/ly** -ˈten.tɪd/li ⓤⓢ -ˈten.t̬ɪd/li **-tentedness** -ˈten.tɪd.nəs, -nɪs ⓤⓢ -ˈten.t̬ɪd-
contention kənˈten.*t*ʃᵊn **-s** -z
contentious kənˈten.*t*ʃəs **-ly** -li **-ness** -nəs, -nɪs
contentment kənˈtent.mənt
contents (*n.*) *what is contained:* ˈkɒn.tents, kənˈtents ⓤⓢ ˈkɑːn.tents
contermin|al kɒnˈtɜː.mɪ.n|ᵊl, kən-, -mə- ⓤⓢ kənˈtɜːr- **-ous** -əs
contest (*n.*) ˈkɒn.test ⓤⓢ ˈkɑːn- **-s** -s
contest (*v.*) kənˈtest **-s** -s **-ing** -ɪŋ **-ed** -ɪd **-able** -ə.bl̩
contestant kənˈtes.tᵊnt **-s** -s
contestation ˌkɒn.tesˈteɪ.ʃᵊn ⓤⓢ ˌkɑːn- **-s** -z
context ˈkɒn.tekst ⓤⓢ ˈkɑːn- **-s** -s
contextual kənˈtek.stju.əl, kɒn-, -ˈteks.tʃu- ⓤⓢ kənˈteks.tʃu-, kɑːn-, -tʃᵊl **-ly** -i
contextualization, -isa- kənˌtek.stju.ə.laɪˈzeɪ.ʃᵊn, -ˌteks.tʃu-, -lɪˈ- ⓤⓢ kənˌteks.tʃu.ə.lɪˈ-, kɑːn-, -tʃᵊl.ɪˈ-
contextualiz|e, is|e kənˈtek.stju.ə.laɪz, -ˈteks.tʃu- ⓤⓢ kənˈteks.tʃu-, -tʃə.laɪz **-es** -ɪz **-ing** -ɪŋ **-ed** -d
Conti ˈkɒn.ti ⓤⓢ ˈkɑːn.t̬i
contiguity ˌkɒn.tɪˈgjuː.ə.ti, -təˈ-, -ɪ.ti ⓤⓢ ˌkɑːn.t̬əˈgjuː.ə.t̬i
contiguous kənˈtɪg.ju.əs **-ly** -li **-ness** -nəs, -nɪs
continen|ce ˈkɒn.tɪ.nən*t*|s ⓤⓢ ˈkɑːn.tᵊn.ən*t*|s **-cy** -si
continent (C) ˈkɒn.tɪ.nənt ⓤⓢ ˈkɑːn.tᵊn.ənt **-s** -s **-ly** -li
continental ˌkɒn.tɪˈnen.tᵊl, -təˈ- ⓤⓢ ˌkɑːn.t̬ᵊnˈen.t̬ᵊl **ˌcontinental ˈbreakfast** ; **ˌcontinental ˈquilt**
contingen|ce kənˈtɪn.dʒᵊn*t*|s **-cy** -si **-cies** -siz
contingent kənˈtɪn.dʒᵊnt **-s** -s **-ly** -li
continual kənˈtɪn.ju.əl **-ly** -i
continuan|ce kənˈtɪn.ju.ən*t*|s **-t/s** -t/s
continuation kənˌtɪn.juˈeɪ.ʃᵊn **-s** -z
continuative kənˈtɪn.ju.ə.tɪv, -eɪ.tɪv ⓤⓢ kənˈtɪn.ju.eɪ.t̬ɪv, -ə-
continuator kənˈtɪn.ju.eɪ.təʳ ⓤⓢ -t̬ɚ **-s** -z
contin|ue kənˈtɪn|.juː, -ju **-ues** -juːz, -juz **-uing** -ju.ɪŋ **-ued** -juːd, -jud **-uer/s** -ju.əʳ/z ⓤⓢ -ju.ɚ/z
continuity ˌkɒn.tɪˈnjuː.ə.ti, -təˈ-, -ɪ.ti ⓤⓢ ˌkɑːn.tᵊnˈuː.ə.t̬i, -ˈjuː-
continuo kənˈtɪn.ju.əʊ, kɒn-, -u.əʊ ⓤⓢ kənˈtɪn.ju.oʊ
continuous kənˈtɪn.ju.əs **-ly** -li **-ness** -nəs, -nɪs **conˌtinuous asˈsessment**
continu|um kənˈtɪn.ju|.əm **-ums** -əmz **-a** -ə
contoid ˈkɒn.tɔɪd ⓤⓢ ˈkɑːn- **-s** -z
con|tort kən|ˈtɔːt ⓤⓢ -ˈtɔːrt **-torts** -ˈtɔːts ⓤⓢ -ˈtɔːrts **-torting** -ˈtɔː.tɪŋ ⓤⓢ -ˈtɔːr.t̬ɪŋ **-torted** -ˈtɔː.tɪd ⓤⓢ -ˈtɔːr.t̬ɪd
contortion kənˈtɔː.ʃᵊn ⓤⓢ -ˈtɔːr- **-s** -z
contortionist kənˈtɔː.ʃᵊn.ɪst, kɒn- ⓤⓢ kənˈtɔːr- **-s** -s
contour ˈkɒn.tʊəʳ, -tɔːʳ ⓤⓢ ˈkɑːn.tʊr **-s** -z **-ing** -ɪŋ **-ed** -d
contra- ˈkɒn.trə- ⓤⓢ ˈkɑːn.trə-
Note: Prefix. In the sense of "against", this always carries primary or secondary stress on the first syllable.
contra (C) ˈkɒn.trə, -trɑː ⓤⓢ ˈkɑːn.trə **-s** -z
contraband ˈkɒn.trə.bænd ⓤⓢ ˈkɑːn- **-ist/s** -ɪst/s
contrabass ˌkɒn.trəˈbeɪs, ˈ--- ⓤⓢ ˈkɑːn.trə.beɪs **-es** -ɪz
contra bonos mores ˌkɒn.trɑːˌbəʊ.nəʊsˈmɔː.reɪs, -ˌbɒn.əʊs- ⓤⓢ ˌkɑːn.trɑːˌboʊ.noʊsˈmɔːr.iːz
contraception ˌkɒn.trəˈsep.ʃᵊn ⓤⓢ ˌkɑːn-
contraceptive ˌkɒn.trəˈsep.tɪv ⓤⓢ ˌkɑːn- **-s** -z
contract (*n.*) ˈkɒn.trækt ⓤⓢ ˈkɑːn- **-s** -s
contract (*v.*) kənˈtrækt **-s** -s **-ing** -ɪŋ **-ed** -ɪd **-ive** -ɪv
contractibility kənˌtræk.təˈbɪl.ə.ti, -tɪˈ-, -ɪ.ti ⓤⓢ kənˌtræk.təˈbɪl.ə.t̬i; ˌkɑːn.træk-
contractib|le kənˈtræk.tə.b|l̩, -tɪ- **-ly** -li **-leness** -l̩.nəs, -nɪs
contractile kənˈtræk.taɪl ⓤⓢ -tᵊl, -taɪl
contraction kənˈtræk.ʃᵊn **-s** -z
contractionary kənˈtræk.ʃᵊn.ᵊr.i, -ʃᵊn.ri ⓤⓢ -ʃᵊn.er.i
contractor *builder:* kənˈtræk.təʳ; ˈkɒn.træk- ⓤⓢ ˈkɑːn.træk.tɚ **-s** -z *other senses:* kənˈtræk.təʳ ⓤⓢ -tɚ **-s** -z
contractual kənˈtræk.tʃu.ᵊl, -tju- ⓤⓢ kənˈtræk.tʃu-, kɑːn-, -*t*ʃᵊl **-ly** -i
contracture kənˈtræk.tʃəʳ, -tjʊəʳ, -ʃəʳ ⓤⓢ -tʃɚ **-s** -z
contradict ˌkɒn.trəˈdɪkt ⓤⓢ ˌkɑːn- **-s** -s **-ing** -ɪŋ **-ed** -ɪd
contradiction ˌkɒn.trəˈdɪk.ʃᵊn ⓤⓢ ˌkɑːn- **-s** -z
contradictor|y ˌkɒn.trəˈdɪk.tᵊr|.i, -tr|i ⓤⓢ ˌkɑːn- **-ily** -ᵊl.i, -ɪ.li **-iness** -ɪ.nəs, -ɪ.nɪs
contradistinc|tion ˌkɒn.trə.dɪˈstɪŋ*k*|.ʃᵊn, -dəˈ- ⓤⓢ ˌkɑːn.trə.dɪˈ-, -dəˈ- **-tive** -tɪv
contradistinguish ˌkɒn.trə.dɪˈstɪŋ.gwɪʃ, -dəˈ- ⓤⓢ ˌkɑːn.trə.dɪˈ-, -dəˈ- **-es** -ɪz **-ing** -ɪŋ **-ed** -t
contrafactive ˌkɒn.trəˈfæk.tɪv ⓤⓢ ˌkɑːn-
contraflow ˈkɒn.trə.fləʊ ⓤⓢ ˈkɑːn.trə.floʊ **-s** -z

contraindi|cate ˌkɒn.trəˈɪn.dɪ|.keɪt US ˌkɑːn.trə- **-cates** -keɪts **-cating** -keɪ.tɪŋ US -keɪ.t̬ɪŋ **-cated** -keɪ.tɪd US -keɪ.t̬ɪd

contraindication ˌkɒn.trə.ɪn.dɪˈkeɪ.ʃᵊn US ˌkɑːn.trə- **-s** -z

contraindicative ˌkɒn.trə.ɪnˈdɪk.ə.tɪv US ˌkɑːn.trə.ɪnˈdɪk.ə.t̬ɪv

contralti (*plur. of* **contralto**) kənˈtræl.ti, -ˈtrɑːl- US -ˈtræl.t̬i

contralto kənˈtræl.təʊ, -ˈtrɑːl- US -ˈtræl.t̬oʊ **-s** -z

contra pacem ˌkɒn.trɑːˈpɑː.kem, -ˈpɑː.tʃem US ˌkɑːn.trɑːˈpɑː.kem, -ˈpeɪ.sem

contraposition ˌkɒn.trə.pəˈzɪʃ.ᵊn US ˌkɑːn-

contraption kənˈtræp.ʃᵊn **-s** -z

contrapuntal ˌkɒn.trəˈpʌn.tᵊl US ˌkɑːn.trəˈpʌn.t̬ᵊl **-ly** -i

contrapuntist ˌkɒn.trəˈpʌn.tɪst US ˌkɑːn.trəˈpʌn.t̬ɪst **-s** -s

contrariety ˌkɒn.trəˈraɪ.ə.ti, -ɪ.ti US ˌkɑːn.trəˈraɪ.ə.t̬i

contrariwise kənˈtreə.ri.waɪz; ˈkɒn.trə- US kənˈtrer.i-, ˈkɑːn.trɚ-

contrar|y *opposed:* ˈkɒn.trᵊr|.i US ˈkɑːn.trɚ|.i **-ies** -iz **-ily** -ᵊl.i, -ɪ.li

contrar|y *perverse, obstinate:* kənˈtreə.r|i US -ˈtrer|.i **-ies** -iz **-ily** -ɪ.li, -ᵊl.i **-iness** -ɪ.nəs, -ɪ.nɪs

contrast (*n.*) ˈkɒn.trɑːst US ˈkɑːn.træst **-s** -s

contrast (*v.*) kənˈtrɑːst US -ˈtræst **-s** -s **-ing/ly** -ɪŋ/li **-ed** -ɪd

contrastive kənˈtrɑː.stɪv US -ˈtræs.tɪv

contraven|e ˌkɒn.trəˈviːn US ˌkɑːn- **-es** -z **-ing** -ɪŋ **-ed** -d

contravention ˌkɒn.trəˈven.*t*ʃᵊn US ˌkɑːn- **-s** -z

contretemps (*sing.*) ˈkɒn.trə.tɑ̃ː*ŋ*, ˈkɔːn-, ˈkɔ̃ː*n*- US ˈkɑːn.trə.tɑ̃ː (*plur.*) ˈkɒn.trə.tɑ̃ː, -z US ˈkɑːn.trə.tɑ̃ː, -z

contrib|ute kənˈtrɪb|.juːt, ˈkɒn.trɪ.b|juːt, -jət US kənˈtrɪb|.juːt, -jət **-utes** -juːts US -juːts, -jəts **-uting** -jʊ.tɪŋ US -juː.t̬ɪŋ, -jə- **-uted** -jʊ.tɪd US -juː.t̬ɪd, -jə-

contribution ˌkɒn.trɪˈbjuː.ʃᵊn US ˌkɑːn- **-s** -z

contributive kənˈtrɪb.jʊ.tɪv, -jə- US -jə.t̬ɪv

contributor kənˈtrɪb.jʊ.təʳ, -jə-; ˈkɒn.trɪ.bjuː- US kənˈtrɪb.jə.t̬ɚ **-s**

contributory kənˈtrɪb.jʊ.tᵊr.i, -jə-, -tri; ˌkɒn.trɪˈbjuː- US kənˈtrɪb.jə.tɔːr.i

contrite kənˈtraɪt, kɒn- US kən-, kɑːn- **-ly** -li **-ness** -nəs, -nɪs

contrition kənˈtrɪʃ.ᵊn

contrivanc|e kənˈtraɪ.vᵊn*t*s **-es** -ɪz

contriv|e kənˈtraɪv **-es** -z **-ing** -ɪŋ **-ed** -d **-er/s** -əʳ/z US -ɚ/z

control (*n.*) kənˈtrəʊl *in machinery also:* ˈkɒn.trəʊl US kənˈtroʊl **-s** -z

control (*v.*) kənˈtrəʊl US -ˈtroʊl **-s** -z **-ling** -ɪŋ **-led** -d **-lable** -ə.bl̩

controller kənˈtrəʊ.ləʳ US -ˈtroʊ.lɚ **-s** -z

controversial ˌkɒn.trəˈvɜː.ʃᵊl, ˈ-si.əl US ˌkɑːn.trəˈvɜːr.ʃᵊl **-ly** -i

controversialist ˌkɒn.trəˈvɜː.ʃᵊl.ɪst, ˈ-si.ᵊl- US ˌkɑːn.trəˈvɜːr.ʃᵊl- **-s** -s

controvers|y ˈkɒn.trə.vɜː.s|i, -və.s|i; kənˈtrɒv.ə.s|i US ˈkɑːn.trə.vɜːr- **-ies** -iz

controver|t ˌkɒn.trəˈvɜː|t, ˈ--- US ˈkɑːn.trə.vɜːr|t, ˌ--ˈ- **-ts** -ts **-ting** -tɪŋ US -t̬ɪŋ **-ted** -tɪd US -t̬ɪd

controvertib|le ˌkɒn.trəˈvɜː.tə.b|l̩, -tɪ- US ˌkɑːn.trəˈvɜːr.t̬ə- **-ly** -li

contumacious ˌkɒn.tjʊˈmeɪ.ʃəs US ˌkɑːn.tʊˈ-, -tjuːˈ-, -t̬əˈ-, -tjəˈ- **-ly** -li **-ness** -nəs, -nəs

contumacy ˈkɒn.tjʊ.mə.si US ˈkɑːn.tuː-, -tjʊ-; kənˈtuː-

contumelious ˌkɒn.tjʊˈmiː.li.əs US ˌkɑːn.tʊˈ-, -tjuːˈ-, -təˈ-, -tjəˈ- **-ly** -li **-ness** -nəs, -nɪs

contumel|y ˈkɒn.tjuː.mᵊl|.i, -tjʊ-, -mɪ.l|i; kənˈtjʊm.ɪ.l|i, -ᵊl|.i, -ˈtjuː.mɪ.l|i, -mᵊl|.i US ˈkɑːn.tuː.mᵊl|.i, -tjuː-, ˈ-t̬əm.l|i; kənˈtuː.mə.l|i, -ˈtjuː-, -ˈtʊm.ə- **-ies** -iz

contus|e kənˈtjuːz US -ˈtuːz, -ˈtjuːz **-es** -ɪz **-ing** -ɪŋ **-ed** -d

contusion kənˈtjuː.ʒᵊn US -ˈtuː-, -ˈtjuː- **-s** -z

conundrum kəˈnʌn.drəm **-s** -z

conurbation ˌkɒn.ɜːˈbeɪ.ʃᵊn, -əˈ- US ˌkɑː.nɜːrˈ-, -nɚˈ- **-s** -z

convalesc|e ˌkɒn.vəˈles US ˌkɑːn- **-es** -ɪz **-ing** -ɪŋ **-ed** -t

convalescence ˌkɒn.vəˈles.ᵊn*t*s US ˌkɑːn-

convalescent ˌkɒn.vəˈles.ᵊnt US ˌkɑːn- **-s** -s

convection kənˈvek.ʃᵊn

convector kənˈvek.təʳ US -tɚ **-s** -z

convenanc|e ˈkɔ̃ː*n*.və.nɑ̃ː*n*s, ˈkɒn-, -nɑːn*t*s US ˈkɑːn.və.nən*t*s, -næn*t*s **-es** -ɪz

conven|e kənˈviːn **-es** -z **-ing** -ɪŋ **-ed** -d **-er/s** -əʳ/z US -ɚ/z **-or/s** -əʳ/z US -ɚ/z

convenienc|e kənˈviː.ni.ən*t*s US -ˈviːn.jən*t*s **-es** -ɪz **conˈvenience ˌfood** ; **conˈvenience ˌstore**

convenient kənˈviː.ni.ənt US -ˈviːn.jənt **-ly** -li

convent ˈkɒn.vənt, -vent US ˈkɑːn- **-s** -s

conventicle kənˈven.tɪ.kᵊl US -t̬ə- **-s** -z

convention kənˈven.*t*ʃᵊn US -ˈven*t*.ʃᵊn **-s** -z

conventional kənˈven.*t*ʃᵊn.ᵊl US -ˈven*t*.ʃᵊn- **-ly** -i

conventional|ism kənˈven.*t*ʃᵊn.ᵊl|.ɪ.zᵊm US -ˈven*t*.ʃᵊn- **-ist/s** -ɪst/s

conventionalit|y kənˌven.*t*ʃəˈnæl.ə.t|i, -ɪ.t|i US -ˌven*t*.ʃəˈnæl.ə.t̬|i **-ies** -iz

conventionaliz|e, -is|e kənˈven.*t*ʃᵊn.ᵊl.aɪz US -ˈven*t*.ʃᵊn.ə.laɪz **-es** -ɪz **-ing** -ɪŋ **-ed** -d

conventual kənˈven.tju.əl, -tʃu-, -tʃᵊl US -tʃu.əl **-s** -z

converg|e kənˈvɜːdʒ, kɒn- US kənˈvɜːrdʒ **-es** -ɪz **-ing** -ɪŋ **-ed** -d

convergen|ce kənˈvɜː.dʒᵊn*t*|s, kɒn- US kənˈvɜːr- **-ces** -sɪz **-cy** -si

convergent kənˈvɜː.dʒᵊnt, kɒn- US kənˈvɜːr- **-ly** -li

conversable kənˈvɜː.sə.bl̩ US -ˈvɜːr-

conversan|ce kənˈvɜː.sᵊn*t*|s; ˈkɒn.və- US kənˈvɜːr-; ˈkɑːn.vɚ- **-cy** -si

conversant kənˈvɜː.sᵊnt; ˈkɒn.və- US kənˈvɜːr-; ˈkɑːn.vɚ- **-ly** -li

conversation ˌkɒn.vəˈseɪ.ʃᵊn US ˌkɑːn.vɚˈ- **-s** -z **converˈsation ˌpiece**

conversational ˌkɒn.vəˈseɪ.ʃᵊn.ᵊl, -ˈseɪʃ.nᵊl US ˌkɑːn.vɚˈ- **-ly** -i

conversationalist ˌkɒn.vəˈseɪ.ʃᵊn.ᵊl.ɪst, -ˈseɪʃ.nᵊl- US ˌkɑːn.vɚˈ- **-s** -s

conversazione ˌkɒn.və.sæt.siˈəʊ.neɪ, -ni US ˌkɑːn.vɚ.sɑːt.siˈoʊ.ni, ˌkoʊn- **-s** -z

convers|e (*n. adj.*) ˈkɒn.vɜːs; kənˈvɜːs US ˈkɑːn.vɜːrs; kənˈvɜːrs **-es** -ɪz **-ely** -li

convers|e (*v.*) kənˈvɜːs US -ˈvɜːrs **-es** -ɪz **-ing** -ɪŋ **-ed** -t

conversion kənˈvɜː.ʃᵊn, -ʒᵊn US -ˈvɜːr.ʒᵊn, -ʃᵊn **-s** -z **conˈversion ˌcourse**

convert (*n.*) ˈkɒn.vɜːt US ˈkɑːn.vɜːrt **-s** -s

con|vert (*v.*) kən|ˈvɜːt US -ˈvɜːrt **-verts** -ˈvɜːts US -ˈvɜːrts **-verting** -ˈvɜː.tɪŋ US -ˈvɜːr.t̬ɪŋ **-verted** -ˈvɜː.tɪd US -ˈvɜːr.t̬ɪd **-verter/s** -ˈvɜː.təʳ/z US -ˈvɜːr.t̬ɚ/z **-vertor/s** -ˈvɜː.təʳ/z US -ˈvɜːr.t̬ɚ/z

convertibility kənˌvɜː.təˈbɪl.ə.ti, -tɪˈ-, -ɪ.ti US -ˌvɜːr.t̬əˈbɪl.ə.t̬i

convertib|le kənˈvɜː.tə.b|l̩, -tɪ- US -ˈvɜːr.t̬ə- **-ly** -li

convex kɒnˈveks, ˈ-- US ˈkɑːn.veks; kənˈveks **-ly** -li

convexit|y kɒn'vek.sə.t|i, kən-, -ɪt|.i (US) kən'vek.sə.ţ|i **-ies** -iz
convey kən'veɪ **-s** -z **-ing** -ɪŋ **-ed** -d **-er/s** -əʳ/z (US) -ɚ/z **-or/s** -əʳ/z (US) -ɚ/z **-able** -ə.bl̩ **con'veyor ˌbelt**
conveyanc|e kən'veɪ.ənts **-es** -ɪz
conveyanc|er kən'veɪ.ənt.s|əʳ (US) -s|ɚ **-ers** -əz (US) -ɚz **-ing** -ɪŋ
convict (*n.*) 'kɒn.vɪkt (US) 'kɑːn- **-s** -s
convict (*v.*) kən'vɪkt **-s** -s **-ing** -ɪŋ **-ed** -ɪd
conviction kən'vɪk.ʃən **-s** -z
convinc|e kən'vɪnts **-es** -ɪz **-ing** -ɪŋ **-ed** -t
convincible kən'vɪnt.sə.bl̩
convincing kən'vɪnt.sɪŋ **-ly** -li
convivial kən'vɪv.i.əl **-ly** -i
conviviality kənˌvɪv.i'æl.ə.ti, -ɪ.ti (US) -ə.ţi
convocation ˌkɒn.vəʊ'keɪ.ʃən (US) ˌkɑːn.və'- **-s** -z
convok|e kən'vəʊk (US) -'voʊk **-es** -s **-ing** -ɪŋ **-ed** -t
convolu|te 'kɒn.və.luː|t, -ljuː|t, ˌ--'- (US) 'kɑːn.və.luː|t **-ted/ly** -tɪd/li (US) -ţɪd/li
convolution ˌkɒn.və'luː.ʃən, -'ljuː- (US) ˌkɑːn.və'luː- **-s** -z
convolv|e kən'vɒlv (US) -'vɑːlv, -'vɔːlv **-es** -z **-ing** -ɪŋ **-ed** -d
convolvul|us kən'vɒl.vjʊ.l|əs, -vjə- (US) -'vɑːl.vjuː-, -vjə- **-i** -aɪ **-uses** -ə.sɪz
convoy 'kɒn.vɔɪ (US) 'kɑːn- **-s** -z **-ing** -ɪŋ **-ed** -d
convulsant kən'vʌl.sənt **-s** -s
convuls|e kən'vʌls **-es** -ɪz **-ing** -ɪŋ **-ed** -t
convulsion kən'vʌl.ʃən **-s** -z
convulsive kən'vʌl.sɪv **-ly** -li **-ness** -nəs, -nɪs
Conway 'kɒn.weɪ (US) 'kɑːn-
Conwy 'kɒn.wi (US) 'kɑːn-
con|y 'kəʊ.n|i (US) 'koʊ- **-ies** -iz
Conybeare 'kɒn.ɪ.bɪəʳ, 'kʌn- (US) 'kɑː.nɪ.bɪr, 'kʌn.ɪ-
coo kuː **-es** -z **-ing** -ɪŋ **-ed** -d
Coober Pedy ˌkuː.bə'piː.di (US) -bɚ'-
Cooch kuːtʃ
cooee 'kuː.i, -iː, ˌ-'- **-s** -z **-ing** -ɪŋ **-d** -d
cook kʊk **-s** -s **-ing** -ɪŋ **-ed** -t
cookbook 'kʊk.bʊk **-s** -s
cook-chill ˌkʊk'tʃɪl **-s** -z **-ing** -ɪŋ **-ed** -d
Cook(e) kʊk
cooker 'kʊk.əʳ (US) -ɚ **-s** -z
cookery 'kʊk.ər.i **'cookery ˌbook**
Cookham 'kʊk.əm (US) -əm, -hæm
cookhou|se 'kʊk.haʊ|s **-ses** -zɪz
cookie 'kʊk.i **-s** -z
cookout 'kʊk.aʊt **-s** -s
Cookson 'kʊk.sən
Cookstown 'kʊks.taʊn
cookware 'kʊk.weəʳ (US) -wer
cook|y 'kʊk|.i **-ies** -iz

cool kuːl **-er** -əʳ (US) -ɚ **-est** -ɪst, -əst **-ly** -li, -i **-ness** -nəs, -nɪs **-s** -z **-ing** -ɪŋ **-ed** -d
coolant 'kuː.lənt **-s** -s
coolbox 'kuːl.bɒks (US) -bɑːks **-es** -ɪz
cooler 'kuː.ləʳ (US) -lɚ **-s** -z
coolheaded ˌkuːl'hed.ɪd **-ness** -nəs, -nɪs *stress shift:* ˌcoolheaded 'thinking
coolibah 'kuː.lɪ.bɑː, -lə- **-s** -z
Coolidge 'kuː.lɪdʒ
coolie 'kuː.li **-s** -z
Cooling 'kuː.lɪŋ
cooling-off period ˌkuː.lɪŋ'ɒfˌpɪə.ri.əd (US) -'ɑːfˌpɪr.i- **-s** -z
coom kuːm **-s** -z
coomb kuːm **-s** -z
Coomb(e) kuːm
Coomber 'kuːm.bəʳ (US) -bɚ
Coombes kuːmz
coon kuːn **-s** -z
coop kuːp **-s** -s **-ing** -ɪŋ **-ed** -t
co-op 'kəʊ.ɒp, -'- (US) 'koʊ.ɑːp **-s** -s
coop|er (C) 'kuː.p|əʳ (US) -p|ɚ **-ers** -əz (US) -ɚz **-ering** -ər.ɪŋ **-ered** -əd (US) -ɚd
cooperag|e 'kuː.pər.ɪdʒ **-es** -ɪz
cooper|ate kəʊ'ɒp.ər|.eɪt (US) koʊ'ɑː.pə.r|eɪt **-ates** -eɪts **-ating** -eɪ.tɪŋ (US) -eɪ.ţɪŋ **-ated** -eɪ.tɪd (US) -eɪ.ţɪd **-ator/s** -eɪ.təʳ/z (US) -eɪ.ţɚ/z
cooperation kəʊˌɒp.ə'reɪ.ʃən, ˌkəʊ.ɒp- (US) koʊˌɑː.pə'- **-s** -z
cooperative kəʊ'ɒp.ər.ə.tɪv (US) koʊ'ɑː.pɚ.ə.ţɪv **-s** -z **-ly** -li
Cooperstown 'kuː.pəz.taʊn (US) -pɚz-
coopery 'kuː.pər.i
Coopman 'kuːp.mən
co-opt kəʊ'ɒpt (US) koʊ'ɑːpt, '-- **-s** -s **-ing** -ɪŋ **-ed** -ɪd
co-optation ˌkəʊ.ɒp'teɪ.ʃən (US) ˌkoʊ.ɑːp'- **-s**
co-option kəʊ'ɒp.ʃən (US) koʊ'ɑːp- **-s** -z
coordinate (*n. adj.*) kəʊ'ɔː.dɪ.nət, -dən.ət (US) koʊ'ɔːr.dən-, -eɪt **-s** -s **-ly** -li **-ness** -nəs, -nɪs
coordin|ate (*v.*) kəʊ'ɔː.dɪ.n|eɪt, -dən|.eɪt (US) koʊ'ɔːr.dən- **-ates** -eɪts **-ating** -eɪ.tɪŋ (US) -eɪ.ţɪŋ **-ated** -eɪ.tɪd (US) -eɪ.ţɪd **-ator/s** -eɪ.təʳ/z (US) -eɪ.ţɚ/z
coordination kəʊˌɔː.dɪ'neɪ.ʃən, -dən'eɪ- (US) koʊˌɔːr.dən'eɪ-
coordinative kəʊ'ɔː.dɪ.nə.tɪv, -dən.ə-, -eɪ- (US) koʊ'ɔːr.dən.ə.ţɪv
Coors® kɔːz, kʊəz (US) kʊrz
coot kuːt **-s** -s
Coote kuːt
co-ownership ˌkəʊ'əʊ.nə.ʃɪp (US) ˌkoʊ'oʊ.nɚ-
cop kɒp (US) kɑːp **-s** -s **-ping** -ɪŋ **-ped** -t

Copacabana ˌkəʊ.pə.kə'bæn.ə (US) ˌkoʊ-, -'bɑː.nə
copaiba kəʊ'paɪ.bə, kɒp'aɪ- (US) koʊ'paɪ-
copal 'kəʊ.pəl; kəʊ'pæl (US) 'koʊ.pəl, -pæl
coparcener ˌkəʊ'pɑː.sən.əʳ, -sɪ.nəʳ (US) ˌkoʊ'pɑːr.sən.ɚ **-s** -z
copartner ˌkəʊ'pɑːt.nəʳ (US) 'koʊˌpɑːrt.nɚ, ˌ-'-- **-s** -z **-ship/s** -ʃɪp/s
cop|e (C) kəʊp (US) koʊp **-es** -s **-ing** -ɪŋ **-ed** -t
copeck 'kəʊ.pek, 'kɒp.ek (US) 'koʊ.pek **-s** -s
Copeland 'kəʊp.lənd (US) 'koʊp-
Copenhagen ˌkəʊ.pən'heɪ.gən, -'hɑː-, 'kəʊ.pənˌheɪ-, -ˌhɑː- (US) 'koʊ.pənˌheɪ.gən, -ˌhɑː-, ˌkoʊpən'heɪ-, -'hɑː-
coper 'kəʊ.pəʳ (US) 'koʊ.pɚ **-s** -z
Copernican kəʊ'pɜː.nɪ.kən (US) koʊ'pɜːr-, kə-
Copernicus kəʊ'pɜː.nɪ.kəs (US) koʊ'pɜːr-, kə-
copestone 'kəʊp.stəʊn (US) 'koʊp.stoʊn **-s** -z
Cophetua kəʊ'fet.ju.ə (US) koʊ-
copier 'kɒp.i.əʳ (US) 'kɑː.pi.ɚ **-s** -z
co-pilot 'kəʊˌpaɪ.lət, ˌ-'-- (US) 'koʊˌpaɪ- **-s** -s
coping 'kəʊ.pɪŋ (US) 'koʊ- **-s** -z
copingstone 'kəʊ.pɪŋ.stəʊn (US) 'koʊ.pɪŋ.stoʊn **-s** -z
copious 'kəʊ.pi.əs (US) 'koʊ- **-ly** -li **-ness** -nəs, -nɪs
Copland 'kɒp.lənd, 'kəʊp- (US) 'kɑːp-, 'koʊp-
Note: The name of the composer Aaron Copland is pronounced /'kəʊp.lənd (US) 'koʊp-/.
Copleston 'kɒp.l̩.stən (US) 'kɑː.pl̩-
Copley 'kɒp.li (US) 'kɑː.pli
cop-out 'kɒp.aʊt (US) 'kɑːp- **-s** -s
Copp kɒp (US) kɑːp
copp|er 'kɒp|.əʳ (US) 'kɑː.p|ɚ **-ers** -əz (US) -ɚz **-ering** -ər.ɪŋ **-ered** -əd (US) -ɚd ˌcopper 'beech ; ˌcopper 'sulphate
copperas 'kɒp.ər.əs (US) 'kɑː.pɚ-
copper-bottomed ˌkɒp.ə'bɒt.əmd (US) ˌkɑː.pɚ'bɑː.ţəmd *stress shift:* ˌcopper-bottomed 'prospect
Copperfield 'kɒp.ə.fiːld (US) 'kɑː.pɚ-
copperhead 'kɒp.ə.hed (US) 'kɑː.pɚ- **-s** -z
copperplate 'kɒp.ə.pleɪt, ˌ--'- (US) 'kɑː.pɚ-
coppersmith (C) 'kɒp.ə.smɪθ (US) 'kɑː.pɚ- **-s** -s
coppery 'kɒp.ər.i (US) 'kɑː.pɚ-
coppic|e 'kɒp.ɪs (US) 'kɑː.pɪs **-es** -ɪz **-ing** -ɪŋ **-ed** -t

Copping 'kɒp.ɪŋ ⓊⓈ 'kɑː.pɪŋ
Coppola 'kɒp.ᵊl.ə, 'kɑː.pᵊl.ə ⓊⓈ 'kɑː.pᵊl.ə, 'koʊ.pᵊl.ə
Coppull 'kɒp.ᵊl ⓊⓈ 'kɑː.pᵊl
copra 'kɒp.rə ⓊⓈ 'kɑː.prə
copro- 'kɒp.rəʊ- ⓊⓈ 'kɑː.proʊ-, -prə-
coproduc|e ˌkəʊ.prə'djuːs, -'dʒuːs ⓊⓈ ˌkoʊ.prə'duːs, -'djuːs **-es** -ɪz **-ing** -ɪŋ **-ed** -t **-er/s** -əʳ/z ⓊⓈ -ɚ/z
coproduction ˌkəʊ.prə'dʌk.ʃᵊn ⓊⓈ ˌkoʊ- **-s** -z
cops|e kɒps ⓊⓈ kɑːps **-es** -ɪz
Copt kɒpt ⓊⓈ kɑːpt **-s** -s
Copthall 'kɒp.tɔːl, 'kɒpt.hɔːl ⓊⓈ 'kɑːp.tɔːl, -tɑːl, 'kɑːpt.hɔːl, -hɑːl
Coptic 'kɒp.tɪk ⓊⓈ 'kɑːp-
copul|a 'kɒp.jə.l|ə, -jʊ- ⓊⓈ 'kɑː.pjə- **-ae** -iː **-as** -əz
copu|late 'kɒp.jə|.leɪt, -jʊ- ⓊⓈ 'kɑː.pjə- **-lates** -leɪts **-lating** -leɪ.tɪŋ ⓊⓈ -leɪ.t̬ɪŋ **-lated** -leɪ.tɪd ⓊⓈ -leɪ.t̬ɪd
copulation ˌkɒp.jə'leɪ.ʃᵊn, -jʊ'- ⓊⓈ ˌkɑː.pjə'- **-s** -z
copula|tive 'kɒp.jə.lə|.tɪv, -jʊ-, -leɪ- ⓊⓈ 'kɑː.pjə.lə|.t̬ɪv **-tory** -tᵊr.i, -tri ⓊⓈ -tɔːr.i
cop|y 'kɒp|.i ⓊⓈ 'kɑː.p|i **-ies** -iz **-ying** -i.ɪŋ **-ied** -id **-ier/s**
copybook 'kɒp.i.bʊk ⓊⓈ 'kɑː.pi- **-s** -s ˌ**blot one's** '**copybook**
copycat 'kɒp.i.kæt ⓊⓈ 'kɑː.pi- **-s** -s
Copydex® 'kɒp.i.deks ⓊⓈ 'kɑː.pi-
copy-ed|it 'kɒp.iˌed|.ɪt ⓊⓈ 'kɑː.pi- **-its** -ɪts **-iting** -ɪ.tɪŋ ⓊⓈ -ɪ.t̬ɪŋ **-ited** -ɪ.tɪd ⓊⓈ -ɪ.t̬ɪd **-itor/s** -ɪ.təʳ/z ⓊⓈ -ɪ.t̬ɚ/z
copyhold 'kɒp.i.həʊld ⓊⓈ 'kɑː.pi.hoʊld **-s** -z **-er/s** -əʳ/z ⓊⓈ -ɚ/z
copyist 'kɒp.i.ɪst ⓊⓈ 'kɑː.pi- **-s** -s
copy|right 'kɒp.i|.raɪt ⓊⓈ 'kɑː.pi- **-rights** -raɪts **-righting** -ˌraɪ.tɪŋ ⓊⓈ -ˌraɪ.t̬ɪŋ **-righted** -ˌraɪ.tɪd ⓊⓈ -ˌraɪ.t̬ɪd
copywrit|er 'kɒp.iˌraɪ.t|əʳ ⓊⓈ 'kɑː.piˌraɪ.t̬|ɚ **-ers** -əz ⓊⓈ -ɚz **-ing** -ɪŋ
coq au vin ˌkɒk.əʊ'væn, -'væ̃ŋ ⓊⓈ ˌkoʊk.oʊ'-, ˌkɑːk-
Coquelles kɒk'el, kəʊ'kel ⓊⓈ koʊ'kel
coqu|et kɒk|'et, kəʊ'k|let ⓊⓈ koʊ'k|let **-ets** -ets **-etting** -et.ɪŋ ⓊⓈ -et̬.ɪŋ **-etted** -et.ɪd ⓊⓈ -et̬.ɪd
Coquet 'kəʊ.kɪt ⓊⓈ 'koʊ-
coquetr|y 'kɒk.ɪ.tr|i, 'kəʊ.kɪ-, -kə- ⓊⓈ 'koʊ.kə.tr|i, koʊ'ket.r|i **-ies** -iz
coquette kɒk'et, kəʊ'ket ⓊⓈ koʊ'ket **-s** -s
coquettish kɒk'et.ɪʃ, kəʊ'ket- ⓊⓈ koʊ'ket̬- **-ly** -li **-ness** -nəs, -nɪs
cor kɔːʳ ⓊⓈ kɔːr **-s** -z
Cora 'kɔː.rə ⓊⓈ 'kɔːr.ə
coracle 'kɒr.ə.kl̩ ⓊⓈ 'kɔːr- **-s** -z
coral 'kɒr.əl ⓊⓈ 'kɔːr- **-s** -z ˌ**coral** '**reef**
corallaceous ˌkɒr.ə'leɪ.ʃəs ⓊⓈ ˌkɔːr-
corall|ine 'kɒr.ᵊl|.aɪn ⓊⓈ 'kɔːr.ə.l|aɪn **-ite** -aɪt
Coram 'kɔː.rəm ⓊⓈ 'kɔːr.əm
coram nobis ˌkɔː.rəm'nəʊ.bɪs, -ræm- ⓊⓈ ˌkɔːr.æm'noʊ.bɪs
cor(s) anglais ˌkɔː'rɒŋ.gleɪ, -'rɑːŋ- ⓊⓈ ˌkɔːr.ɑːŋ'gleɪ
corban 'kɔː.bæn, -bᵊn ⓊⓈ 'kɔːr-
corbel 'kɔː.bᵊl ⓊⓈ 'kɔːr- **-s** -z
Corbett 'kɔː.bɪt, -bet, -bət ⓊⓈ 'kɔːr-
Corbishley 'kɔː.bɪʃ.li ⓊⓈ 'kɔːr-
Corbridge 'kɔː.brɪdʒ ⓊⓈ 'kɔːr-
Corbusier kɔː'bjuː.zi.eɪ, -'buː- ⓊⓈ ˌkɔːr.buː'zjeɪ
Corby 'kɔː.bi ⓊⓈ 'kɔːr-
Corbyn 'kɔː.bɪn ⓊⓈ 'kɔːr-
Corcoran 'kɔː.kᵊr.ᵊn ⓊⓈ 'kɔːr-
Corcyra ˌkɔː'saɪə.rə ⓊⓈ ˌkɔːr'saɪ-
cord kɔːd ⓊⓈ kɔːrd **-s** -z **-ing** -ɪŋ **-ed** -ɪd **-age** -ɪdʒ
Cordelia kɔː'diː.li.ə ⓊⓈ kɔːr'diːl.jə
cordelier (C) ˌkɔː.dɪ'lɪəʳ ⓊⓈ ˌkɔːr.dɪ'lɪr **-s** -z
cordial 'kɔː.di.əl ⓊⓈ 'kɔːr.dʒəl, -djəl **-s** -z **-ly** -i
cordialit|y ˌkɔː.di'æl.ə.t|i, -ɪ.t|i ⓊⓈ ˌkɔːr.dʒi'æl.ə.t̬|i, -'djæl.ə- **-ies** -iz
cordillera (C) ˌkɔː.dɪ'ljeə.rə, -dᵊl'jeə-, -'eə- ⓊⓈ ˌkɔːr.dᵊl'jer.ə; kɔːr'dɪl.ɚ-
cordite 'kɔː.daɪt ⓊⓈ 'kɔːr-
cordless 'kɔːd.ləs, -lɪs ⓊⓈ 'kɔːrd-
Cordoba, **Córdoba** 'kɔː.də.bə ⓊⓈ 'kɔːr-
cordon 'kɔː.dᵊn ⓊⓈ 'kɔːr- **-s** -z **-ing** -ɪŋ **-ed** -d
cordon bleu ˌkɔː.dɔ̃ːm'blɜː, -dɒn'- ⓊⓈ ˌkɔːr.dɔ̃ː'bluː
cordon(s) sanitaire(s) ˌkɔː.dɔ̃ːn.sæn.ɪ'teəʳ, -dɒn-, -ə'- ⓊⓈ kɔːrˌdɔ̃ː.sɑː.ni'ter
Cordov|a 'kɔː.də.v|ə ⓊⓈ 'kɔːr- **-an/s** -ən/z
corduroy 'kɔː.djə.rɔɪ, -djʊ-, -dʒə-, -dʒʊ-, ˌ--'- ⓊⓈ 'kɔːr.də- **-s** -z
cordwainer 'kɔːdˌweɪ.nəʳ ⓊⓈ 'kɔːrdˌweɪ.nɚ **-s** -z
cor|e kɔːʳ ⓊⓈ kɔːr **-es** -z **-ing** -ɪŋ **-ed** -d **-er/s** -əʳ/z ⓊⓈ -ɚ/z
CORE kɔːʳ ⓊⓈ kɔːr
co-referential ˌkəʊ.ref.ə'ren.tʃᵊl ⓊⓈ ˌkoʊ.ref.ə'rent.ʃᵊl
co-regent ˌkəʊ'riː.dʒᵊnt ⓊⓈ ˌkoʊ- **-s** -s
coreligionist ˌkəʊ.rɪ'lɪdʒ.ᵊn.ɪst, -rə'- ⓊⓈ ˌkoʊ.rə'-, -rɪ'- **-s** -s
Corelli kə'rel.i, kɒr'el- ⓊⓈ koʊ'rel-, kə'-
co-representational ˌkəʊ.rep.rɪ.zen'teɪ.ʃᵊn.ᵊl, -rə-, -'teɪʃ.nᵊl ⓊⓈ koʊ-
co-respondent ˌkəʊ.rɪ'spɒn.dənt, -rə'- ⓊⓈ ˌkoʊ.rɪ'spɑːn-, -rə'- **-s** -s
Corey 'kɔː.ri ⓊⓈ 'kɔːr.i
corf kɔːf ⓊⓈ kɔːrf **-s** -s
Corfe kɔːf ⓊⓈ kɔːrf
Corfu kɔː'fuː, -'fjuː ⓊⓈ 'kɔːr.fuː, -fjuː, -'-
corgi (C) 'kɔː.gi ⓊⓈ 'kɔːr- **-s** -z
coriander ˌkɒr.i'æn.dəʳ, 'kɒr.i.æn- ⓊⓈ 'kɔːr.i.æn.dɚ, ˌkɔːr.i'æn-
Corin 'kɒr.ɪn, -ᵊn ⓊⓈ 'kɔːr-
Corinne kə'rɪn
Corinth 'kɒr.ɪntθ ⓊⓈ 'kɔːr-
Corinthian kə'rɪnt.θi.ən **-s** -z
Coriolanus ˌkɒr.i.əʊ'leɪ.nəs, -'lɑː- ⓊⓈ ˌkɔːr.i.ə'-
Corioles kə'raɪə.liːz, kɒr'aɪə- ⓊⓈ kə'raɪə-
Coriolis kə'raɪə.lɪs, kɒr'aɪə- ⓊⓈ kə'raɪə-
cork (C) kɔːk ⓊⓈ kɔːrk **-s** -s **-ing** -ɪŋ **-ed** -t
corkage 'kɔː.kɪdʒ ⓊⓈ 'kɔːr-
corker (C) 'kɔː.kəʳ ⓊⓈ 'kɔːr.kɚ **-s** -z
Corkery 'kɔː.kᵊr.i ⓊⓈ 'kɔːr-
corkscrew 'kɔːk.skruː ⓊⓈ 'kɔːrk- **-s** -z **-ing** -ɪŋ **-ed** -d
corky 'kɔː.ki ⓊⓈ 'kɔːr-
corm kɔːm ⓊⓈ kɔːrm **-s** -z
Cormac 'kɜː.mæk, 'kɔː- ⓊⓈ 'kɔːr-
Cormack 'kɔː.mæk ⓊⓈ 'kɔːr-
cormorant 'kɔː.mᵊr.ənt ⓊⓈ 'kɔːr- **-s** -s
corn kɔːn ⓊⓈ kɔːrn **-s** -z **-ing** -ɪŋ **-ed** -d '**Corn** ˌ**Belt**; '**corn** ˌ**dolly**; ˌ**corned** '**beef**; '**corn** ˌ**exchange**
cornball 'kɔːn.bɔːl, 'kɔːm- ⓊⓈ 'kɔːrn-, -bɑːl **-s** -z
cornbread 'kɔːn.bred, 'kɔːm- ⓊⓈ 'kɔːrn-
Cornbury 'kɔːn.bᵊr.i, 'kɔːm- ⓊⓈ 'kɔːrn.ber-, -bɚ-
corncrake 'kɔːn.kreɪk, 'kɔːŋ- ⓊⓈ 'kɔːrn- **-s** -s
corndog 'kɔːn.dɒg ⓊⓈ 'kɔːrn.dɑːg, -dɔːg **-s** -z
corne|a 'kɔː.ni|.ə; kɔː'niː- ⓊⓈ 'kɔːr.ni- **-as** -əz **-al** -ᵊl
Corneille kɔː'neɪ, -'neɪl ⓊⓈ kɔːr'neɪ
Cornelia kɔː'niː.li.ə ⓊⓈ kɔːr'niːl.jə
cornelian kɔː'niː.li.ən ⓊⓈ kɔːr'niːl.jən **-s** -z
Cornelius kɔː'niː.li.əs ⓊⓈ kɔːr'niːl.jəs
Cornell kɔː'nel ⓊⓈ kɔːr-
corn|er 'kɔː.n|əʳ ⓊⓈ 'kɔːr.n|ɚ **-ers** -əz ⓊⓈ -ɚz **-ering** -ᵊr.ɪŋ **-ered** -əd ⓊⓈ -ɚd ˌ**corner** '**shop**
-cornered -'kɔː.nəd ⓊⓈ -'kɔr.nɚd
cornerstone 'kɔː.nə.stəʊn ⓊⓈ 'kɔːr.nɚ.stoʊn **-s** -z

cornet ˈkɔː.nɪt US kɔːrˈnet **-s** -s
Cornetto® kɔːˈnet.əʊ US kɔːrˈnet̬.oʊ
cornfield ˈkɔːn.fiːld US ˈkɔːrn- **-s** -z
cornflakes ˈkɔːn.fleɪks US ˈkɔːrn-
cornflour ˈkɔːn.flaʊəʳ US ˈkɔːrn.flaʊɚ
cornflower ˈkɔːn.flaʊəʳ US ˈkɔːrn.flaʊɚ **-s** -z
Cornhill ˌkɔːnˈhɪl US ˈkɔːrn.hɪl, ˌ-ˈ-
cornic|e ˈkɔː.nɪs US ˈkɔːr- **-es** -ɪz
cornich|e (C) kɔːˈniːʃ; ˈ--, -nɪʃ US kɔːrˈniːʃ **-es** -ɪz
Cornish ˈkɔː.nɪʃ US ˈkɔːr- **-man** -mən **-men** -mən, -men **-woman** -ˌwʊm.ən **-women** -ˌwɪm.ɪn ˌ**Cornish** ˈ**pasty**
cornmeal ˈkɔːn.miːl, ˈkɔːm- US ˈkɔːrn-
cornstarch ˈkɔːn.stɑːtʃ US ˈkɔːrn.stɑːrtʃ
cornsyrup ˈkɔːnˌsɪr.əp US ˈkɔːrnˌsɪr-, -ˌsɜːr-
cornucopi|a ˌkɔː.njʊˈkəʊ.pi|.ə US ˌkɔːr.nəˈkoʊ-, -njəˈ- **-as** -əz **-an** -ən
Cornwall ˈkɔːn.wɔːl, -wəl US ˈkɔːrn.wɔːl, -wɑːl
Cornwallis kɔːnˈwɒl.ɪs US kɔːrnˈwɑː.lɪs
Cornwell ˈkɔːn.wel, -wəl US ˈkɔːrn-
corn|y ˈkɔː.n|i US ˈkɔːr- **-ier** -i.əʳ US -i.ɚ **-iest** -i.ɪst, -i.əst
corolla (C) kəˈrɒl.ə, -ˈrəʊ.lə US -ˈroʊ-, -ˈrɑː- **-s** -z
Note: The suitable pronunciation for the car in Amercian English is /kəˈroʊ-/.
corollar|y kəˈrɒl.ᵊr|.i US ˈkɔːr.ə.ler- **-ies** -iz
Coromandel ˌkɒr.əʊˈmæn.dᵊl US ˌkɔːr.oʊˈ-
coron|a kəˈrəʊ.n|ə US -ˈroʊ- **-ae** -iː **-as** -əz
Corona *female name:* ˈkɒr.ə.nə US ˈkɔːr-
coronach (C) ˈkɒr.ə.nək, -nəx, -næk US ˈkɔːr.ə.nək **-s** -s
coronal *(n.)* ˈkɒr.ə.nᵊl US ˈkɔːr- **-s** -z
coronal *(adj.) pertaining to the sun's corona:* kəˈrəʊ.nᵊl US -ˈroʊ- *medical, botanical and phonetic senses:* ˈkɒr.ə.nᵊl; kəˈrəʊ- US ˈkɔːr.ə-; kəˈroʊ-
coronar|y ˈkɒr.ə.nᵊr|.i US ˈkɔːr.ə.ner- **-ies** -iz
coronation ˌkɒr.əˈneɪ.ʃᵊn US ˌkɔːr- **-s** -z
Coronel ˈkɒr.ə.nel US ˈkɔːr-
coroner ˈkɒr.ə.nəʳ US ˈkɔːr.ᵊn.ɚ **-s** -z
coronet ˈkɒr.ə.nɪt, -net, -nət; ˌkɒr.əˈnet US ˌkɔːr.əˈnet **-s** -s
corpora *(plur. of* **corpus***)* ˈkɔː.pᵊr.ə, -pə.rɑː US ˈkɔːr.pɚ.ə
corporal ˈkɔː.pᵊr.ᵊl, ˈ-prᵊl US ˈkɔːr- **-s** -z **-ly** -i ˌ**corporal** ˈ**punishment**
corporality ˌkɔː.pəˈræl.ə.ti, -ɪ.ti US ˌkɔːr.pəˈræl.ə.t̬i
corporate ˈkɔː.pᵊr.ət, -ɪt, ˈ-prət, ˈ-prɪt US ˈkɔːr- **-ly** -li **-ness** -nəs, -nɪs
corporation ˌkɔː.pᵊrˈeɪ.ʃᵊn US ˌkɔːr.pəˈreɪ- **-s** -z
corporative ˈkɔː.pᵊr.ə.tɪv US ˈkɔːr.pɚ.ə.t̬ɪv
corporator ˈkɔː.pᵊr.eɪ.təʳ US ˈkɔːr.pə.reɪ.t̬ɚ **-s** -z
corporeal kɔːˈpɔː.ri.əl US kɔːrˈpɔːr- **-ly** -i
corps *(sing.)* kɔːʳ US kɔːr *(plur.)* kɔːz US kɔːrz
corps de ballet ˌkɔː.dəˈbæl.eɪ, -li US ˌkɔːr.də.bælˈeɪ
corps|e kɔːps US kɔːrps **-es** -ɪz **-ing** -ɪŋ **-ed** -t
corpulen|ce ˈkɔː.pjʊ.lənt|s, -pjə- US ˈkɔːr.pjə- **-cy** -si
corpulent ˈkɔː.pjʊ.lənt, -pjə- US ˈkɔːr.pjə-
corp|us ˈkɔː.p|əs US ˈkɔːr- **-ora** -ə.rə US -ɚ.ə **-uses** -ə.sɪz
Corpus Christi ˌkɔː.pəsˈkrɪs.ti US ˌkɔːr-
corpuscle ˈkɔː.pʌs.l̩, -pə.sl̩; kɔːˈpʌs- US ˈkɔːr.pʌs.l̩, -pə.sl̩ **-s** -z
corpuscular kɔːˈpʌs.kjə.ləʳ, -kjʊ- US kɔːrˈpʌs.kjə.lɚ
corpuscule kɔːˈpʌs.kjuːl, -kjʊl US kɔːrˈpʌs.kjuːl **-s** -z
corpus delicti ˌkɔː.pʌs.dɪˈlɪk.taɪ, -pəs- US ˌkɔːr-
corpus juris ˌkɔː.pʌsˈdʒʊə.rɪs, -pəs- US ˌkɔːr.pʌsˈdʒʊr.ɪs
corral kəˈrɑːl, kɒrˈɑːl US kəˈræl **-s** -z **-ling** -ɪŋ **-led** -d
correct kəˈrekt **-est** -ɪst, -əst **-ly** -li **-ness** -nəs, -nɪs **-s** -s **-ing** -ɪŋ **-ed** -ɪd **-or/s** -əʳ/z US -ɚ/z
correction kəˈrek.ʃᵊn **-s** -z
correctional kəˈrek.ʃᵊn.ᵊl
correctitude kəˈrek.tɪ.tjuːd, -tʃuːd US -tə.tuːd, -tjuːd
corrective kəˈrek.tɪv **-s** -z
Correggio kəˈredʒ.i.əʊ US ˈ-oʊ
correlate *(n.)* ˈkɒr.ᵊl.ət, -ɪ.lət, -leɪt US ˈkɔːr.ə.leɪt **-s** -s
corre|late *(v.)* ˈkɒr.əl.leɪt, ˈ-ɪ- US ˈkɔːr.ə- **-lates** -leɪts **-lating** -leɪ.tɪŋ US -leɪ.t̬ɪŋ **-lated** -leɪ.tɪd US -leɪ.t̬ɪd **-latable** -leɪ.tə.bl̩ US -leɪ.t̬ə.bl̩
correlation ˌkɒr.əˈleɪ.ʃᵊn, -ɪˈ- US ˌkɔːr.əˈ- **-s** -z
correlative kɒrˈel.ə.tɪv, kəˈrel- US kəˈrel.ə.t̬ɪv **-ly** -li **-ness** -nəs, -nɪs
correspond ˌkɒr.ɪˈspɒnd, -əˈ- US ˌkɔːr.əˈ- **-s** -z **-ing** -ɪŋ **-ed** -ɪd
correspondenc|e ˌkɒr.ɪˈspɒn.dənts, -əˈ- US ˌkɔːr.əˈspɑːn- **-es** -ɪz corre'spondence ˌcourse
correspondent ˌkɒr.ɪˈspɒn.dᵊnt, -əˈ- US ˌkɔːr.əˈspɑːn- **-s** -s
corresponding ˌkɒr.ɪˈspɒn.dɪŋ, -əˈ- US ˌkɔːr.əˈspɑːn- **-ly** -li
corridor ˈkɒr.ɪ.dɔːʳ, ˈ-ə-, -dəʳ US ˈkɔːr.ə.dɚ, ˈ-ɪ-, -dɔːr **-s** -z
corrie (C) ˈkɒr.i US ˈkɔːr-
Corrientes ˌkɒr.iˈen.tes US ˌkɔːr-
Corrigan ˈkɒr.ɪ.gᵊn, ˈ-ə- US ˈkɔːr.ə-, ˈ-ɪ-
corrigend|um ˌkɒr.ɪˈdʒen.d|əm, -əˈ-, -ˈgen- US ˌkɔːr- **-a** -ə
corrigible ˈkɒr.ɪ.dʒə.bl̩, -dʒɪ- US ˈkɔːr-
Corringham ˈkɒr.ɪŋ.əm US ˈkɔːr-, -hæm
corroborant kəˈrɒb.ᵊr.ᵊnt US -ˈrɑː.bɚ- **-s** -s
corrobor|ate kəˈrɒb.ᵊr|.eɪt US -ˈrɑː.bə.r|eɪt **-ates** -eɪts **-ating** -eɪ.tɪŋ US -eɪ.t̬ɪŋ **-ated** -eɪ.tɪd US -eɪ.t̬ɪd **-ator/s** -eɪ.təʳ/z US -eɪ.t̬ɚ/z
corroboration kəˌrɒb.əˈreɪ.ʃᵊn US -ˌrɑː.bəˈ- **-s** -z
corroborative kəˈrɒb.ᵊr.ə.tɪv, -eɪ- US -ˈrɑː.bɚ.ə.t̬ɪv
corroboratory kəˈrɒb.ᵊr.ə.tᵊr.i, -tri; kəˌrɒb.əˈreɪ- US -ˈrɑː.bɚ.ə.tɔːr.i
corroboree kəˈrɒb.ᵊr.i, kəˌrɒb.əˈriː US -ˌrɑː.bəˈriː **-s** -z
corrod|e kəˈrəʊd US -ˈroʊd **-es** -z **-ing** -ɪŋ **-ed** -ɪd
corrodible kəˈrəʊ.də.bl̩, -dɪ- US -ˈroʊ.də-
corrosion kəˈrəʊ.ʒᵊn US -ˈroʊ- **-s** -z
corrosive kəˈrəʊ.sɪv, -zɪv US -ˈroʊ- **-s** -z **-ly** -li **-ness** -nəs, -nɪs
corru|gate ˈkɒr.ə|.geɪt, ˈ-ʊ- US ˈkɔːr.ə- **-gates** -geɪts **-gating** -geɪ.tɪŋ US -geɪ.t̬ɪŋ **-gated** -geɪ.tɪd US -geɪ.t̬ɪd ˌ**corrugated** ˈ**iron**
corrugation ˌkɒr.əˈgeɪ.ʃᵊn, -ʊˈ- US ˌkɔːr.əˈ- **-s** -z
corrupt kəˈrʌpt **-est** -ɪst, -əst **-ly** -li **-ness** -nəs, -nɪs **-s** -s **-ing** -ɪŋ **-ed** -ɪd **-er/s** -əʳ/z US -ɚ/z
corruptibility kəˌrʌp.təˈbɪl.ə.ti, -tɪˈ-, -ɪ.ti US -təˈbɪl.ə.t̬i
corruptib|le kəˈrʌp.tə.bl|̩, -tɪ- US -tə- **-ly** -li **-leness** -l̩.nəs, -nɪs
corruption kəˈrʌp.ʃᵊn **-s** -z
corruptive kəˈrʌp.tɪv
Corry ˈkɒr.i US ˈkɔːr-
Corsa® ˈkɔː.sə US ˈkɔːr-
corsag|e kɔːˈsɑːʒ, ˈ-- US kɔːrˈsɑːʒ, -sɑːdʒ **-es** -ɪz
corsair ˈkɔː.seəʳ, -ˈ- US ˈkɔːr.ser, -ˈ- **-s** -z
cors|e kɔːs US kɔːrs **-es** -ɪz
corselet ˈkɔː.slət, -slɪt US ˈkɔːr- **-s** -s
corset ˈkɔː.sət, -sɪt US ˈkɔːr- **-s** -s
corsetry ˈkɔː.sə.tri, -sɪ- US ˈkɔːr-
Corsham ˈkɔː.ʃəm US ˈkɔːr-

Corsic|a ˈkɔː.sɪ.kl̩ə (US) ˈkɔːr- **-an/s** -ən/z
corslet ˈkɔː.slət, -slɪt (US) ˈkɔːr- **-s** -s
cortèg|e kɔːˈteɪʒ, -ˈteʒ, ˈ-- (US) kɔːrˈteʒ **-es** -ɪz
Cortes, Cortés ˈkɔː.tes, -tez, -ˈ- (US) kɔːrˈtez
cort|ex ˈkɔː.t|eks (US) ˈkɔːr- **-exes** -ek.sɪz **-ices** -ɪ.siːz
Corti ˈkɔː.ti (US) ˈkɔːr.ti
cortical ˈkɔː.tɪ.kᵊl (US) ˈkɔːr.t̬ɪ-
corticosteroid ˌkɔː.tɪ.kəʊˈstɪə.rɔɪd, -ˈster.ɔɪd (US) ˌkɔːr.t̬ɪ.koʊˈster.ɔɪd, -ˈstɪr- **-s** -z
Cortina® kɔːˈtiː.nə (US) kɔːr- **-s** -z
cortisone ˈkɔː.tɪ.zəʊn, -tə-, -səʊn (US) ˈkɔːr.t̬ə.zoʊn, -soʊn
Cortney ˈkɔːt.ni (US) ˈkɔːrt-
corundum kəˈrʌn.dəm
Corunna kɒrˈʌn.ə, kəˈrʌn- (US) kəˈrʌn-
corus|cate ˈkɒr.ə.s|keɪt, -ʌs|.keɪt (US) ˈkɔːr.ə.s|keɪt **-cates** -keɪts **-cating** -keɪ.tɪŋ (US) -keɪ.t̬ɪŋ **-cated** -keɪ.tɪd (US) -keɪ.t̬ɪd
coruscation ˌkɒr.əˈskeɪ.ʃᵊn, -ʌsˈkeɪ- (US) ˌkɔːr.əˈskeɪ- **-s** -z
corvée ˈkɔː.veɪ (US) kɔːrˈveɪ **-s** -z
corvette kɔːˈvet (US) kɔːr- **-s** -s
Corwen ˈkɔː.wen, -wɪn (US) ˈkɔːr-
Cory ˈkɔː.ri (US) ˈkɔːr.i
Corybant ˈkɒr.ɪ.bænt (US) ˈkɔːr- **-s** -s **Corybantes** ˌkɒr.ɪˈbæn.tiːz (US) ˌkɔːr-
Corydon ˈkɒr.ɪ.dᵊn, ˈ-ə-, -dɒn (US) ˈkɔːr.ə.dᵊn, -dɑːn
corymb ˈkɒr.ɪmb, -ɪm (US) ˈkɔːr-
coryphae|us ˌkɒr.ɪˈfiː|.əs (US) ˌkɔːr.əˈ- **-i** -aɪ
coryphée ˌkɒr.ɪˈfeɪ (US) ˌkɔːr-
Coryton *in Devon:* ˈkɒr.ɪ.tᵊn, ˈ-ə- (US) ˈkɔːr- *in Essex:* ˈkɔː.rɪ.tən, ˈ-rə- (US) ˈkɔːr-
cos *because:* kəz, kəs, kɒz, kɒs (US) kəz, kəs, kɑːz, kɑːs
Note: Weak form word.
cos (C) *lettuce:* kɒs, kɒz (US) kɑːs, koʊs
Cosa Nostra ˌkəʊ.zəˈnɒs.trə (US) ˌkoʊ.səˈnoʊ.strə, -zəˈ-
Cosby ˈkɒz.bi (US) ˈkɑːz-
cosec ˈkəʊ.sek (US) ˈkoʊ-
cosecant ˌkəʊˈsiː.kᵊnt (US) ˌkoʊ- **-s** -s
co-set ˈkəʊ.set (US) ˈkoʊ- **-s** -s
Cosgrave ˈkɒz.greɪv (US) ˈkɑːz-
cosh kɒʃ (US) kɑːʃ **-es** -ɪz **-ing** -ɪŋ **-ed** -t
Cosham ˈkɒs.əm (US) ˈkɑː.səm
cosh|er *feast, pamper:* ˈkɒʃ|.əʳ (US) ˈkɑː.ʃ|ɚ **-ers** -əz (US) -ɚz **-ering** -ᵊr.ɪŋ **-ered** -əd (US) -ɚd
cosher *according to Jewish law:* ˈkəʊ.ʃəʳ, ˈkɒʃ.əʳ (US) ˈkoʊ.ʃɚ
Cosi Fan Tutte ˌkəʊ.si.fænˈtʊt.eɪ, -zi-, kəʊˌsiː-, -i (US) koʊˌsiː.fɑːnˈtuː.teɪ
cosignator|y ˌkəʊˈsɪg.nə.tᵊr|.i, -tr|i (US) ˌkoʊˈsɪg.nə.tɔːr|.i **-ies** -iz

Cosima ˈkəʊ.sɪ.mə (US) ˈkoʊ.zi-, -mɑː
cosine ˈkəʊ.saɪn (US) ˈkoʊ- **-s** -z
CoSIRA kəʊˈsaɪə.rə (US) koʊˈsaɪə-
cosmetic kɒzˈmet.ɪk (US) kɑːzˈmet̬- **-s** -s **-al** -ᵊl **-ally** -ᵊl.i, -li
cosmic ˈkɒz.mɪk (US) ˈkɑːz- **-al** -ᵊl **-ally** -ᵊl.i, -li
cosm|ism ˈkɒz.m|ɪ.zᵊm (US) ˈkɑːz- **-ist/s** -ɪst/s
cosmo- ˈkɒz.məʊ-, kɒzˈmɒ- (US) ˈkɑːz.moʊ-, -mə-, kɑːzˈmɑː-
Note: Prefix. This may be stressed on the initial syllable (as in **cosmonaut** /ˈkɒz.mə.nɔːt (US) ˈkɑːz.mə.nɑːt/) or on the second syllable (e.g. **cosmology** /kɒzˈmɒl.ə.dʒi (US) kɑːzˈmɑː.lə.dʒi/).
Cosmo ˈkɒz.məʊ (US) ˈkɑːz.moʊ
cosmogonic ˌkɒz.məʊˈgɒn.ɪk (US) ˌkɑːz.məˈgɑː.nɪk **-al** -ᵊl **-ally** -ᵊl.i, -li
cosmogon|y kɒzˈmɒg.ᵊn|.i (US) kɑːzˈmɑː.gᵊn- **-ist/s** -ɪst/s
cosmographic ˌkɒz.məʊˈgræf.ɪk (US) ˌkɑːz.məˈ- **-al** -ᵊl **-ally** -ᵊl.i, -li
cosmograph|y kɒzˈmɒg.rə.f|i (US) kɑːzˈmɑː.grə- **-er/s** -əʳ/z (US) -ɚ/z
cosmological ˌkɒz.məˈlɒdʒ.ɪ.kᵊl (US) ˌkɑːz.məˈlɑː.dʒɪ-
cosmolog|y kɒzˈmɒl.ə.dʒ|i (US) kɑːzˈmɑː.lə- **-ist/s** -ɪst/s
cosmonaut ˈkɒz.mə.nɔːt (US) ˈkɑːz.mə.nɑːt, -nɔːt **-s** -s
cosmopolitan (C®) ˌkɒz.məˈpɒl.ɪ.tᵊn, ˈ-ə- (US) ˌkɑːz.məˈpɑː.lɪ- **-s** -z
cosmopolitanism ˌkɒz.məˈpɒl.ɪ.tᵊn.ɪ.zᵊm, ˈ-ə-, -tɪ.nɪ- (US) ˌkɑːz.məˈpɑː.lɪ.tᵊn.ɪ-
cosmos (C®) ˈkɒz.mɒs (US) ˈkɑːz.moʊs, -məs, -mɑːs
Cossack ˈkɒs.æk (US) ˈkɑː.sæk **-s** -s
coss|et ˈkɒs|.ɪt (US) ˈkɑː.s|ɪt **-ets** -ɪts **-eting** -ɪ.tɪŋ (US) -ɪ.t̬ɪŋ **-eted** -ɪ.tɪd (US) -ɪ.t̬ɪd
cost kɒst (US) kɑːst **-s** -s **-ing** -ɪŋ ˌ**cost-efˈfective** ; ˌ**cost of ˈliving**
Costa ˈkɒs.tə (US) ˈkɑː.stə
Costa Blanca ˌkɒs.təˈblæŋ.kə (US) ˌkɑː.stəˈblɑːŋ-, ˌkoʊ-
Costa Brava ˌkɒs.təˈbrɑː.və (US) ˌkɑː.stə-, ˌkoʊ-
Costa del Sol ˌkɒs.tə.delˈsɒl (US) ˌkɑː.stə.delˈsoʊl, ˌkoʊ-
Costain kɒsˈteɪn, ˈ-- (US) ˈkɑː.steɪn, -ˈ-
costal ˈkɒs.tᵊl (US) ˈkɑː.stᵊl
co-star (*n.*) ˈkəʊ.stɑːʳ (US) ˈkoʊ.stɑːr **-s** -z
co-star (*v.*) kəʊˈstɑːʳ (US) ˈkoʊ.stɑːr **-s** -z **-ring** -ɪŋ **-red** -d
costard ˈkʌs.təd, ˈkɒs- (US) ˈkɑː.stɚd **-s** -z
Costard ˈkɒs.təd, -tɑːd (US) ˈkɑː.stɚd, -stɑːrd

Costa Ric|a ˌkɒs.təˈriː.k|ə (US) ˌkoʊ.stəˈ-, ˌkɑː- **-an/s** -ən/z
cost-effective ˌkɒst.ɪˈfek.tɪv, -əˈ-, ˈkɒst.ɪ.fek-, ˈ-ə- (US) ˈkɑːst.ɪˌfek-, -əˌ-, ˌkɑːst.ɪˈfekt-, -əˈ- **-ly** -li **-ness** -nəs, -nɪs
Costello kɒsˈtel.əʊ, kəˈstel-, ˈkɒs.tᵊl.əʊ (US) kɑːˈstel.oʊ, kə-; ˈkɑː.stə.loʊ
coster ˈkɒs.təʳ (US) ˈkɑː.stɚ **-s** -z
costermonger ˈkɒs.təˌmʌŋ.gəʳ (US) ˈkɑː.stɚˌmʌŋ.gɚ, -ˌmɑːŋ- **-s** -z
costive ˈkɒs.tɪv (US) ˈkɑː.stɪv **-ly** -li **-ness** -nəs, -nɪs
costl|y ˈkɒst.l|i (US) ˈkɑːst- **-ier** -i.əʳ (US) -i.ɚ **-iest** -i.ɪst, -i.əst **-iness** -ɪ.nəs, -ɪ.nɪs
costmary ˈkɒst.meə.ri (US) ˈkɑːst.mer.i
Costner ˈkɒs*t*.nəʳ (US) ˈkɑːs*t*.nɚ
cost-plus ˌkɒs*t*ˈplʌs (US) ˌkɑːs*t*-
costum|e ˈkɒs.tjuːm (US) ˈkɑː.stuːm, -stjuːm **-es** -z **-ing** -ɪŋ **-ed** -d ˌ**costume ˈjewellery**
costumier kɒsˈtjuː.mi.əʳ, -eɪ (US) kɑːˈstuː.mi.eɪ, -ˈstjuː-, -ɚ **-s** -z
Cosway ˈkɒz.weɪ (US) ˈkɑːz- **-s** -z
cos|y ˈkəʊ.z|i (US) ˈkoʊ- **-ies** -iz **-ier** -i.əʳ (US) -i.ɚ **-iest** -i.ɪst, -i.əst **-ily** -ɪ.li, -ᵊl.i **-iness** -ɪ.nəs, -ɪ.nɪs
cot kɒt (US) kɑːt **-s** -s ˈ**cot** ˌ**death**
cotangent ˌkəʊˈtæn.dʒənt, ˈ-ˌ-- (US) ˌkoʊˈtæn-, ˈ-ˌ-- **-s** -s
cot|e kəʊt (US) koʊt **-es** -s **-ing** -ɪŋ (US) ˈkoʊ.t̬ɪŋ **-ed** -ɪd (US) ˈkoʊ.t̬ɪd
Côte d'Azur ˌkəʊt.dæˈzʊəʳ, -dəˈ- (US) ˌkoʊt.dəˈzʊr, -dɑːˈ-
Côte d'Ivoire ˌkəʊt.diːˈvwɑːʳ (US) ˌkoʊt.diːˈvwɑːr
Côte d'Or ˌkəʊtˈdɔːʳ (US) ˌkoʊtˈdɔːr
cotenancy ˌkəʊˈten.ən*t*.si (US) ˌkoʊ-
coterie ˈkəʊ.tᵊr.i (US) ˈkoʊ.t̬ɚ- **-s** -z
coterminous ˌkəʊˈtɜː.mɪ.nəs (US) ˌkoʊˈtɜːr- **-ly** -li
Cotgrave ˈkɒt.greɪv (US) ˈkɑːt-
cotill(i)on kəˈtɪl.i.ən, kəʊ-, kɒtˈɪl- (US) koʊˈtɪl.jən, kə- **-s** -z
Coton ˈkəʊ.tᵊn (US) ˈkoʊ-
cotoneaster kəˌtəʊ.niˈæs.təʳ (US) -ˌtoʊ.niˈæs.tɚ **-s** -z
Cotonou ˌkəʊ.təˈnuː, ˌkɒt.ɒnˈuː (US) ˌkoʊ.toʊˈnuː, -tᵊnˈuː
Cotopaxi ˌkɒt.əʊˈpæk.si, ˌkəʊ.təʊˈ- (US) ˌkoʊ.t̬əˈ-
Cotswold ˈkɒt.swəʊld, -swəld (US) ˈkɑːt.swoʊld **-s** -z
Cotsworth ˈkɒt.swəθ, -wɜːθ (US) ˈkɑːt.swɜːrθ, -swɚθ
cottag|e ˈkɒt.ɪdʒ (US) ˈkɑː.t̬ɪdʒ **-es** -ɪz **-ing** -ɪŋ **-ey** -i ˌ**cottage ˈcheese** ; ˌ**cottage ˈindustry** ; ˌ**cottage ˈpie**
cottager ˈkɒt.ɪ.dʒəʳ (US) ˈkɑː.t̬ɪ.dʒɚ **-s** -z

Cottam 'kɒt.əm Ⓤⓢ 'kɑː.t̬əm
Cottbus 'kɒt.bəs, -bʊs Ⓤⓢ 'kɑːt.bəs, -bʊs
Cottenham 'kɒt.ən.əm Ⓤⓢ 'kɑː.tən-, -hæm
cotter (C) 'kɒt.əʳ Ⓤⓢ 'kɑː.t̬ɚ **-s** -z
Cotterell 'kɒt.ər.əl Ⓤⓢ 'kɑː.t̬ɚ-
Cotterill 'kɒt.ər.əl, -ɪl Ⓤⓢ 'kɑː.t̬ɚ-
Cottesloe 'kɒt.sləʊ, -əz.ləʊ Ⓤⓢ 'kɑːt.sloʊ, -əz.loʊ
Cottian 'kɒt.i.ən Ⓤⓢ 'kɑː.t̬i-
Cottingham 'kɒt.ɪŋ.əm Ⓤⓢ 'kɑː.t̬ɪŋ-, -hæm
cotton (C) 'kɒt.ən Ⓤⓢ 'kɑː.tən **-s** -z **-ing** -ɪŋ **-ed** -d **'Cotton ˌBelt** ; **ˌcotton 'candy** ; **ˌcotton 'wool**
cotton grass 'kɒt.ən.grɑːs Ⓤⓢ 'kɑː.tən.græs
cottonseed 'kɒt.ən.siːd Ⓤⓢ 'kɑː.tən-
cottontail 'kɒt.ən.teɪl Ⓤⓢ 'kɑː.tən- **-s** -z
cottony 'kɒt.ən.i Ⓤⓢ 'kɑː.tən-
Cottrell 'kɒt.rəl; kə'trel Ⓤⓢ 'kɑː.trəl; kə'trel
cotyledon ˌkɒt.ɪ'liː.dən, -əl'iː- Ⓤⓢ ˌkɑː.t̬ə'liː- **-s** -z
cotyledonous ˌkɒt.ɪ'liː.dən.əs, -əl'iː- Ⓤⓢ ˌkɑː.t̬ə'liː-
couch *all verb senses, item of furniture:* kaʊtʃ **-es** -ɪz **-ing** -ɪŋ **-ed** -t **'couch poˌtato**, **ˌcouch po'tato**
couch *grass:* kuːtʃ, kaʊtʃ
Couch kuːtʃ
couchant 'kaʊ.tʃənt, 'kuː-
couchée 'kuː.ʃeɪ, -'- Ⓤⓢ kuː'ʃeɪ **-s** -z
couchette kuː'ʃet **-s** -s
Coué 'kuː.eɪ **-ism** -ɪ.zəm
cougar 'kuː.gəʳ Ⓤⓢ -gɚ **-s** -z
cough kɒf Ⓤⓢ kɑːf, kɔːf **-s** -s **-ing** -ɪŋ **-ed** -t **-er/s** -əʳ/z Ⓤⓢ -ɚ/z **'cough ˌdrop** ; **'cough ˌmixture** ; **'cough ˌsyrup**
Coughlan 'kɒg.lən, 'kɒf-, 'kɒk-, 'kɒx-, 'kəʊ- Ⓤⓢ 'kɑː.glən, 'koʊ.lən
Coughlin 'kɒg.lɪn, 'kɒf-, 'kɒk-, 'kɒx- Ⓤⓢ 'kɑː.glɪn, 'kɑːf-
could (*from* **can**) *strong form:* kʊd *weak form:* kəd
Note: Weak form word. The strong form is used for emphasis, e.g. "You **could** be right", for contrast, e.g. "whether she could or not", and in sentence-final position, e.g. " as well as he could.".
couldn't 'kʊd.ənt
couldst kʊdst
coulee 'kuː.li **-s** -z
coulisse kuː'liːs, kʊ- **-s** -ɪz
couloir 'kuːl.wɑːʳ, -wɔːʳ Ⓤⓢ kuːl'wɑːr **-s** -z
coulomb (C) 'kuː.lɒm Ⓤⓢ -lɑːm, -loʊm **-s** -z
Coulsdon 'kəʊlz.dən, 'kuːlz- Ⓤⓢ 'koʊlz-, 'kuːlz-
Note: /'kəʊlz- Ⓤⓢ 'koʊlz-/ is the traditional local pronunciation. People unfamiliar with the place generally pronounce /'kuːlz-/, as also do new residents in the district.
Coulson 'kəʊl.sən, 'kuːl- Ⓤⓢ 'koʊl-, 'kuːl-
coulter 'kəʊl.təʳ, 'kuː- Ⓤⓢ 'koʊl.t̬ɚ **-s** -z
Coulton 'kəʊl.tən Ⓤⓢ 'koʊl-
council 'kaʊnt.səl, -sɪl **-s** -z **'council ˌhouse** ; **'council ˌtax**
councillor 'kaʊnt.səl.əʳ, -sɪ.ləʳ Ⓤⓢ -səl.ɚ **-s** -z
council|man 'kaʊnt.səl|.mən, -sɪl-, -mæn **-men** -mən, -men **-woman** -ˌwʊm.ən **-women** -ˌwɪm.ɪn
counsel 'kaʊnt.səl **-s** -z **-(l)ing** -ɪŋ **-(l)ed** -d
counsel(l)or 'kaʊnt.səl.əʳ Ⓤⓢ -ɚ **-s** -z
count (C) kaʊnt **-s** -s **-ing** -ɪŋ Ⓤⓢ 'kaʊn.t̬ɪŋ **-ed** -ɪd Ⓤⓢ 'kaʊn.t̬ɪd
countab|le 'kaʊn.tə.b|l̩ Ⓤⓢ -t̬ə- **-ly** -li
countdown 'kaʊnt.daʊn
countenanc|e 'kaʊn.tən.ənts, -tɪ.nənts Ⓤⓢ -tən.ənts **-es** -ɪz **-ing** -ɪŋ **-ed** -t
counter- 'kaʊn.təʳ- Ⓤⓢ 'kaʊn.t̬ɚ-
count|er 'kaʊn.t|əʳ Ⓤⓢ 'kaʊn.t̬|ɚ **-ers** -əz Ⓤⓢ -ɚz **-ering** -ər.ɪŋ **-ered** -əd Ⓤⓢ -ɚd
ˌCounter-Refor'mation
counteract ˌkaʊn.tər'ækt, '--- Ⓤⓢ ˌkaʊn.t̬ɚ'ækt **-s** -s **-ing** -ɪŋ **-ed** -ɪd
counteraction *counteracting:* ˌkaʊn.tər'æk.ʃən Ⓤⓢ -t̬ɚ'- **-s** -z
counter-action *action by way of reply:* 'kaʊn.tərˌæk.ʃən Ⓤⓢ -t̬ɚˌ- **-s** -z
counteractive ˌkaʊn.tər'æk.tɪv Ⓤⓢ -t̬ɚ'- **-ly** -li
counterargument 'kaʊn.tərˌɑːg.jə.mənt, -jʊ- Ⓤⓢ -t̬ɚˌɑːrg.jə- **-s** -s
counterattack 'kaʊn.tər.əˌtæk, ˌkaʊn.tər.ə'tæk Ⓤⓢ 'kaʊn.t̬ɚ.əˌtæk, ˌkaʊn.t̬ɚ.ə'tæk **-s** -s
counterattraction ˌkaʊn.tər.ə'træk.ʃən, 'kaʊn.tər.ə.træk- Ⓤⓢ ˌkaʊn.t̬ɚ.ə'træk-, 'kaʊn.t̬ɚ.əˌtræk- **-s** -z
counterbalanc|e (*n.*) 'kaʊn.təˌbæl.ənts Ⓤⓢ -t̬ɚ- **-es** -ɪz
counterbalanc|e (*v.*) ˌkaʊn.tə'bæl.ənts Ⓤⓢ -t̬ɚ'- **-es** -ɪz **-ing** -ɪŋ **-ed** -t
counterblast 'kaʊn.tə.blɑːst Ⓤⓢ -t̬ɚ.blæst **-s** -s
counterblow 'kaʊn.tə.bləʊ Ⓤⓢ -t̬ɚ.bloʊ **-s** -z
countercharg|e 'kaʊn.tə.tʃɑːdʒ Ⓤⓢ -t̬ɚ.tʃɑːrdʒ **-es** -ɪz **-ing** -ɪŋ **-ed** -d
counterclaim 'kaʊn.tə.kleɪm Ⓤⓢ -t̬ɚ- **-s** -z **-ing** -ɪŋ **-ed** -d
counterclockwise ˌkaʊn.tə'klɒk.waɪz Ⓤⓢ -t̬ɚ'klɑː.kwaɪz
counterespionage ˌkaʊn.tər'es.pi.ə.nɑːʒ, -nɑːdʒ Ⓤⓢ -t̬ɚ'-
counter|feit 'kaʊn.tə|.fɪt, -fiːt Ⓤⓢ -t̬ɚ|.fɪt **-feits** -fɪts, -fiːts Ⓤⓢ -fɪts **-feiting** -fɪ.tɪŋ, -fiː- Ⓤⓢ -fɪ.t̬ɪŋ **-feited** -fɪ.tɪd, -fiː- Ⓤⓢ -fɪ.t̬ɪd **-feiter/s** -fɪ.təʳ/z, -fiː- Ⓤⓢ -fɪ.t̬ɚ/z
counterfoil 'kaʊn.tə.fɔɪl Ⓤⓢ -t̬ɚ- **-s** -z
counterinsurgen|cy ˌkaʊn.tər.ɪn'sɜː.dʒən|t.si Ⓤⓢ -t̬ɚ.ɪn'sɝːr- **-t** -t
counterintelligence ˌkaʊn.tər.ɪn'tel.ɪ.dʒənts, 'kaʊn.tər.ɪn.tel- Ⓤⓢ ˌkaʊn.t̬ɚ.ɪn'tel-, 'kaʊn.t̬ɚ.ɪnˌtel-
counterintuitive ˌkaʊn.tər.ɪn'tjuː.ə.tɪv, -ɪ.tɪv Ⓤⓢ -t̬ɚ.ɪn'tuː.ə.t̬ɪv, -'tjuː- **-ly** -li
countermand ˌkaʊn.tə'mɑːnd, '--- Ⓤⓢ ˌkaʊn.t̬ɚ'mænd, '--- **-s** -z **-ing** -ɪŋ **-ed** -ɪd
countermeasure 'kaʊn.təˌmeʒ.əʳ Ⓤⓢ -t̬ɚˌmeʒ.ɚ **-s** -z
countermove 'kaʊn.tə.muːv Ⓤⓢ -t̬ɚ- **-s** -z
counteroffensive ˌkaʊn.tər.ə'fent.sɪv, 'kaʊn.tər.əˌfent- Ⓤⓢ 'kaʊn.t̬ɚ.əˌfent- **-s** -z
counterpane 'kaʊn.tə.peɪn, -pɪn Ⓤⓢ -t̬ɚ- **-s** -z
counterpart 'kaʊn.tə.pɑːt Ⓤⓢ -tɚ.pɑːrt **-s** -s
counterplot 'kaʊn.tə.plɒt Ⓤⓢ -tɚ.plɑːt **-s** -s
counterpoint 'kaʊn.tə.pɔɪnt Ⓤⓢ -tɚ-
counterpois|e 'kaʊn.tə.pɔɪz Ⓤⓢ -tɚ- **-es** -ɪz **-ing** -ɪŋ **-ed** -d
counterproductive ˌkaʊn.tə.prə'dʌk.tɪv Ⓤⓢ -tɚ- **-ly** -li **-ness** -nəs, -nɪs
counterrevolution ˌkaʊn.tə.rev.ə'luː.ʃən, -'ljuː-, 'kaʊn.tə.rev.əˌluː-, -ˌljuː- Ⓤⓢ ˌkaʊn.t̬ɚ.rev.ə'luː-, 'kaʊn.t̬ɚ.rev.əˌluː- **-s** -z
counterrevolutionar|y ˌkaʊn.tə.rev.ə'luː.ʃən.ər|.i, -'ljuː-, 'kaʊn.tə.rev.əˌluː-, -ˌljuː- Ⓤⓢ ˌkaʊn.t̬ɚ.rev.ə'luː.ʃən.er-, 'kaʊn.t̬ɚ.rev.əˌluː- **-ies** -iz
counterscarp 'kaʊn.tə.skɑːp Ⓤⓢ -t̬ɚ.skɑːrp **-s** -s
countersign (*n.*) 'kaʊn.tə.saɪn Ⓤⓢ -t̬ɚ- **-s** -z **-ed** -d
countersign (*v.*) 'kaʊn.tə.saɪn, ˌ--'- Ⓤⓢ -tɚ- **-s** -z **-ing** -ɪŋ **-ed** -d
counter|sink 'kaʊn.tə|.sɪŋk Ⓤⓢ -tɚ- **-sinks** -sɪŋks **-sinking** -sɪŋ.kɪŋ **-sunk** -sʌŋk

countertenor ˌkaʊn.təˈten.əʳ, ˈkaʊn.təˌten- Ⓤⓢ ˈkaʊn.t̬ɚˌten.ɚ **-s** -z
counterterror|ism ˌkaʊn.təˈter.ə.r|ɪ.zᵊm Ⓤⓢ -t̬ɚˈter.ɚ|.ɪ- **-ist/s** -ɪst/s
countervail ˌkaʊn.təˈveɪl, ˈ--- Ⓤⓢ ˈkaʊn.tɚ.veɪl, ˌ--ˈ- **-s** -z **-ing** -ɪŋ **-ed** -d
counterweight ˈkaʊn.tə.weɪt Ⓤⓢ -tɚ- **-s** -s
countess (C) ˈkaʊn.tɪs, -tes, -təs; ˌkaʊnˈtes Ⓤⓢ ˈkaʊn.t̬ɪs, -təs **-es** -ɪz
Countesthorpe ˈkaʊn.tɪs.θɔːp Ⓤⓢ -θɔːrp
countinghou|se ˈkaʊn.tɪŋ.haʊ|s **-ses** -zɪz
countless ˈkaʊnt.ləs, -lɪs
countrified ˈkʌn.trɪ.faɪd
countr|y ˈkʌn.tr|i **-ies** -iz ˌ**country and** ˈ**western** ; ˌ**country** ˈ**bumpkin** ; ˌ**country** ˈ**dancing** Ⓤⓢ ˈ**country** ˌ**dancing** ; ˌ**country** ˈ**house** ; ˌ**country** ˈ**seat**
country-danc|e ˌkʌn.triˈdɑːnts Ⓤⓢ -ˈdænts **-es** -ɪz **-ing** -ɪŋ
country|man ˈkʌn.trɪ|.mən **-men** -mən
countryside ˈkʌn.trɪ.saɪd
country|woman ˈkʌn.trɪ|ˌwʊm.ən **-women** -ˌwɪm.ɪn
count|y ˈkaʊn.t|i Ⓤⓢ -t̬|i **-ies** -iz ˌ**county** ˈ**court** ; ˌ**county** ˈ**fair** ; ˌ**county** ˈ**hall** ; ˌ**county** ˈ**town**
coup kuː **-s** -z
coup(s) de foudre ˌkuː.dəˈfuː.drə
coup(s) de grâce ˌkuː.dəˈgrɑːs
coup(s) de main ˌkuː.dəˈmæ̃ŋ, -ˈmæn
coup(s) d'état ˌkuː.deɪˈtɑː, -detˈɑː
coup(s) de théâtre ˌkuː.də.teɪˈɑː.trə
coupé, coupe ˈkuː.peɪ, -ˈ- Ⓤⓢ kuːˈpeɪ, koʊp **-s** -z
Couper ˈkuː.pəʳ Ⓤⓢ -pɚ
Couperin ˈkuː.pə.ræ̃ŋ, -ræn
Coupland ˈkuːp.lənd, ˈkəʊp- Ⓤⓢ ˈkuːp-, ˈkoʊp-
coupl|e ˈkʌp.l̩ **-es** -z **-ing** -ɪŋ, ˈ-lɪŋ **-ed** -d
coupler ˈkʌp.ləʳ Ⓤⓢ -lɚ **-s** -z
couplet ˈkʌp.lət, -lɪt **-s** -s
coupling ˈkʌp.lɪŋ **-s** -z
coupon ˈkuː.pɒn Ⓤⓢ ˈkuː.pɑːn, ˈkjuː- **-s** -z
courage (C) ˈkʌr.ɪdʒ
courageous kəˈreɪ.dʒəs **-ly** -li **-ness** -nəs, -nɪs
courante kʊˈrɑ̃ːnt, -ˈrɑːnt, -ˈrænt Ⓤⓢ -ˈrɑːnt **-s** -s
courgette kɔːˈʒet, kʊə- Ⓤⓢ kʊr- **-s** -s
courier (C) ˈkʊr.i.əʳ, ˈkʌr- Ⓤⓢ ˈkʊr.i.ɚ, ˈkɜːr- **-s** -z
Courland ˈkʊə.lənd, -lænd Ⓤⓢ ˈkʊr-
cours|e (C) kɔːs Ⓤⓢ kɔːrs **-es** -ɪz **-ing** -ɪŋ **-ed** -t
courser ˈkɔː.səʳ Ⓤⓢ ˈkɔːr.sɚ **-s** -s
coursework ˈkɔːs.wɜːk Ⓤⓢ ˈkɔːrs.wɜːrk
court (C) kɔːt Ⓤⓢ kɔːrt **-s** -s **-ing** -ɪŋ Ⓤⓢ ˈkɔːr.t̬ɪŋ **-ed** -ɪd Ⓤⓢ ˈkɔːr.t̬ɪd ˈ**court** ˌ**card** ; ˌ**court of ap**ˈ**peal** ; ˈ**court** ˌ**order**, ˌ**court** ˈ**order** ; ˈ**court** ˌ**shoe**
Courtauld ˈkɔː.təʊld, ˈkɔː.təʊ Ⓤⓢ ˈkɔːr.toʊld, -toʊ
court-bouillon ˌkɔːtˈbuː.jɒn, ˈkʊət-, ˈkʊə-, ˌ--ˈ- Ⓤⓢ ˌkɔːr.buːˈjɑːn
Courtelle® kɔːˈtel, kʊə- Ⓤⓢ kɔːr-
Courtenay ˈkɔːt.ni Ⓤⓢ ˈkɔːrt-
courteous ˈkɜː.ti.əs Ⓤⓢ ˈkɜːr.t̬i- **-ly** -li **-ness** -nəs, -nɪs
courtesan ˌkɔː.tɪˈzæn, ˌkʊə-, -təˈ-, ˈ--- Ⓤⓢ ˈkɔːr.t̬ə.zᵊn, -zæn **-s** -z
courtes|y ˈkɜː.tə.s|i, -tɪ- Ⓤⓢ ˈkɜːr.t̬ə- **-ies** -iz
Courthope ˈkɔː.təp, ˈkɔːt.həʊp Ⓤⓢ ˈkɔːr.təp, ˈkɔːrt.hoʊp
courthou|se ˈkɔːt.haʊ|s Ⓤⓢ ˈkɔːrt- **-ses** -zɪz
courtier ˈkɔː.ti.əʳ Ⓤⓢ ˈkɔːr.t̬i.ɚ **-s** -z
courtl|y ˈkɔːt.l|i Ⓤⓢ ˈkɔːrt- **-ier** -i.əʳ Ⓤⓢ -i.ɚ **-iest** -i.ɪst, -i.əst **-iness** -ɪ.nəs, -ɪ.nɪs
court-martial ˌkɔːtˈmɑː.ʃᵊl Ⓤⓢ ˈkɔːrtˌmɑːr- **-s** -z **-(l)ing** -ɪŋ **-(l)ed** -d **courts-martial** ˌkɔːts- Ⓤⓢ ˈkɔːrts-
Courtneidge ˈkɔːt.nɪdʒ Ⓤⓢ ˈkɔːrt-
Courtney ˈkɔːt.ni Ⓤⓢ ˈkɔːrt-
courtroom ˈkɔːt.rʊm, -ruːm Ⓤⓢ ˈkɔːrt.ruːm, -rʊm **-s** -z
courtship ˈkɔːt.ʃɪp Ⓤⓢ ˈkɔːrt- **-s** -s
courtyard ˈkɔːt.jɑːd Ⓤⓢ ˈkɔːrt.jɑːrd **-s** -z
Courvoisier® kʊəˈvwæz.i.eɪ, kɔːˈ-, -ˈvwɑː.zi- Ⓤⓢ ˌkɔːr.vwɑː.ziˈeɪ
couscous ˈkuːs.kuːs
cousin ˈkʌz.ᵊn **-s** -z
Cousins ˈkʌz.ᵊnz
Cousteau kuːˈstəʊ, ˈ-- Ⓤⓢ kuːˈstoʊ
couth kuːθ **-ly** -li **-ness** -nəs, -nɪs
Coutts kuːts
couture kuːˈtjʊəʳ, -ˈtʊəʳ Ⓤⓢ kuːˈtʊr
couturier kuːˈtjʊə.ri.eɪ, -ˈtʊə-, -əʳ Ⓤⓢ -ˈtʊr.i.eɪ, -ɚ **-s** -z
Couzens ˈkʌz.ᵊnz
covalenc|y ˌkəʊˈveɪ.lənt.s|i, ˈkəʊ.veɪ- Ⓤⓢ ˌkoʊˈveɪ.lənt- **-ies** -iz
covalent ˌkəʊˈveɪ.lənt, ˈ--- Ⓤⓢ ˌkoʊˈveɪ-
covariance ˌkəʊˈveə.ri.ənts, ˈkəʊ.veə- Ⓤⓢ ˌkoʊˈver.i-, -ˈvær-
cove (C) kəʊv Ⓤⓢ koʊv **-s** -z
coven ˈkʌv.ᵊn **-s** -z
coven|ant ˈkʌv.ᵊn|.ənt Ⓤⓢ -ænt **-ants** -ənts Ⓤⓢ -ænts **-anting** -ən.tɪŋ Ⓤⓢ -ən.t̬ɪŋ, -æn- **-anted** -ən.tɪd Ⓤⓢ -ən.t̬ɪd, -æn- **-anter/s** -ən.təʳ/z Ⓤⓢ -ən.t̬ɚ/z, -æn-
covenantee ˌkʌv.ᵊn.ənˈtiː Ⓤⓢ -ænˈtiː, -ənˈ- **-s** -z
covenantor ˈkʌv.ᵊn.ən.təʳ Ⓤⓢ ˈkʌv.ən.æn.t̬ɚ; ˌkʌv.ən.ænˈtɔːr **-s** -z
Covent ˈkɒv.ᵊnt, ˈkʌv- Ⓤⓢ ˈkʌv-, ˈkɑː.vᵊnt ˌ**Covent** ˈ**Garden**
Coventry ˈkɒv.ᵊn.tri, ˈkʌv- Ⓤⓢ ˈkʌv-, ˈkɑː.vᵊn-
cov|er ˈkʌv|.əʳ Ⓤⓢ -ɚ **-ers** -əz Ⓤⓢ -ɚz **-ering/s** -ᵊr.ɪŋ/z **-ered** -əd Ⓤⓢ -ɚd ˈ**cover** ˌ**charge** ; ˈ**cover** ˌ**girl** ; ˌ**covered** ˈ**wagon**
Coverack ˈkɒv.ᵊr.æk, ˈkʌv-, -ək Ⓤⓢ ˈkʌv.ə.ræk, ˈkɑː.və-
coverage ˈkʌv.ᵊr.ɪdʒ
coverall ˈkʌv.ᵊr.ɔːl Ⓤⓢ -ɔːl, -ɑːl **-s** -z
Coverdale ˈkʌv.ə.deɪl Ⓤⓢ ˈ-ɚ-
coverlet ˈkʌv.ə.lət, -lɪt Ⓤⓢ ˈ-ɚ- **-s** -s
Coverley ˈkʌv.ə.li Ⓤⓢ ˈ-ɚ-
cover-point ˌkʌv.əˈpɔɪnt Ⓤⓢ -ɚˈ- **-s** -s
covert (*n.*) *shelter, cloth:* ˈkʌv.ət, -ə Ⓤⓢ ˈkʌv.ɚt, ˈkoʊ.vɚt **-s** -z
covert (*adj.*) ˈkʌv.ət; ˈkəʊ.vɜːt, -ˈ- Ⓤⓢ ˈkoʊ.vɜːrt, ˈkʌv.ɚt; koʊˈvɜːrt **-ly** -li
coverture ˈkʌv.ə.tʃəʳ, -tʃʊəʳ, -tjʊəʳ Ⓤⓢ -ɚ.tʃɚ
cover-up ˈkʌv.əʳ.ʌp Ⓤⓢ ˈ-ɚ- **-s** -s
cov|et ˈkʌv|.ɪt, -ət **-ets** -ɪts, -əts **-eting/ly** -ɪ.tɪŋ/li, -ə.tɪŋ/li Ⓤⓢ -ə.t̬ɪŋ/li **-eted** -ɪ.tɪd, -ə.tɪd Ⓤⓢ -ə.t̬ɪd **-etable** -ɪ.tə.bl̩, -ə.tə.bl̩ Ⓤⓢ -ə.t̬ə.bl̩
covetous ˈkʌv.ɪ.təs, -ə.təs Ⓤⓢ -ə.t̬əs **-ly** -li **-ness** -nəs, -nɪs
covey ˈkʌv.i **-s** -z
Covington ˈkʌv.ɪŋ.tən
cow kaʊ **-s** -z **-ing** -ɪŋ **-ed** -d ˈ**cow** ˌ**parsley**, ˌ**cow** ˈ**parsley** ; **till the** ˈ**cows come** ˌ**home**
Cowan kaʊən
coward (C) kaʊəd Ⓤⓢ kaʊɚd **-s** -z
cowardice ˈkaʊə.dɪs Ⓤⓢ ˈkaʊɚ-
cowardl|y ˈkaʊəd.l|i Ⓤⓢ ˈkaʊɚd- **-iness** -ɪ.nəs, -ɪ.nɪs
cowbane ˈkaʊ.beɪn
cowbell ˈkaʊ.bel **-s** -z
cowboy ˈkaʊ.bɔɪ **-s** -z ˈ**cowboy** ˌ**boots** ; ˈ**cowboy** ˌ**hat**
cowcatcher ˈkaʊˌkætʃ.əʳ Ⓤⓢ -ɚ **-s** -z
Cowden ˈkaʊ.den, -dᵊn; kaʊˈden
Cowdenbeath ˌkaʊ.dᵊnˈbiːθ
Cowdray ˈkaʊ.dreɪ, -dri
Cowdrey ˈkaʊ.dri
Cowell kaʊəl, kaʊl, kəʊəl Ⓤⓢ kaʊəl, kaʊl, koʊəl
Cowen kaʊən, kaʊɪn, kəʊən, kəʊɪn Ⓤⓢ kaʊən, kaʊɪn, koʊən, koʊɪn

cower kaʊəʳ ⓤⓢ kaʊɚ **-s** -z **-ing** -ɪŋ **-ed** -d
Cowes kaʊz
cowgirl ˈkaʊ.ɡɜːl ⓤⓢ -ɡɜːrl **-s** -z
cowhand ˈkaʊ.hænd **-s** -z
cowherd ˈkaʊ.hɜːd ⓤⓢ -hɜːrd **-s** -z
cowhide ˈkaʊ.haɪd
Cowie ˈkaʊ.i
cowl kaʊl **-s** -z **-ing** -ɪŋ **-ed** -d
Cowley ˈkaʊ.li
cowlick ˈkaʊ.lɪk **-s** -s
cowlike ˈkaʊ.laɪk
Cowling ˈkaʊ.lɪŋ
cow|-man ˈkaʊ|.mən **-men** -mən
co-worker ˌkəʊˈwɜː.kəʳ ⓤⓢ ˈkoʊˌwɜːr.kɚ, ˌ-ˈ-- **-s** -z
cowpat ˈkaʊ.pæt **-s** -s
Cowper ˈkaʊ.pəʳ, ˈkuː- ⓤⓢ ˈkaʊ.pɚ, ˈkuː-
Note: The poet called himself /ˈkuː.pəʳ ⓤⓢ -pɚ/. /ˈkuː.pəʳ ⓤⓢ -pɚ/ is also the pronunciation in **Cowper Powys** /ˌkuː.pəˈpəʊ.ɪs ⓤⓢ -pɚˈpoʊ-/ and **Cowper-Black** /ˌkuː.pəˈblæk ⓤⓢ -pɚˈ-/.
cowpoke ˈkaʊ.pəʊk ⓤⓢ -poʊk **-s** -s
cowpox ˈkaʊ.pɒks ⓤⓢ -pɑːks
cowpuncher ˈkaʊˌpʌn.*t*ʃəʳ ⓤⓢ -ˌpʌn*t*.ʃɚ **-s** -z
cowr|ie, cowr|y ˈkaʊ.r|i **-ies** -iz
co-writer ˈkəʊˌraɪ.təʳ ⓤⓢ ˈkoʊˌraɪ.t̬ɚ, ˌ-ˈ-- **-s** -z
cowshed ˈkaʊ.ʃed **-s** -z
cowslip ˈkaʊ.slɪp **-s** -s
cox (C) kɒks ⓤⓢ kɑːks **-es** -ɪz
Coxall ˈkɒk.sᵊl, -sɑːl ⓤⓢ ˈkɑːk-
coxcomb ˈkɒk.skəʊm ⓤⓢ ˈkɑːk.skoʊm **-s** -z
coxswain ˈkɒk.sᵊn, -sweɪn ⓤⓢ ˈkɑːk- **-s** -z
coy kɔɪ **-er** -əʳ ⓤⓢ -ɚ **-est** -ɪst, -əst **-ly** -li **-ness** -nəs, -nɪs
coyish ˈkɔɪ.ɪʃ **-ly** -li **-ness** -nəs, -nɪs
Coyle kɔɪl
coyote kɔɪˈəʊ.ti, kaɪ-; ˈkɔɪ.əʊt, ˈkaɪ- ⓤⓢ kaɪˈoʊ.t̬i; ˈkaɪ.oʊt **-s** -z
coypu ˈkɔɪ.puː, -pjuː, -ˈ- **-s** -z
coz kʌz
cozen ˈkʌz.ᵊn **-s** -z **-ing** -ɪŋ **-ed** -d **-er/s** -əʳ/z ⓤⓢ -ɚ/z
Cozens, Cozzens ˈkʌz.ᵊnz
CPU ˌsiː.piːˈjuː
crab kræb **-s** -z **-bing** -ɪŋ **-bed** -d ˈcrab ˌapple
Crabbe kræb
crabbed ˈkræb.ɪd, -əd, kræbd **-ly** -li **-ness** -nəs, -nɪs
crabb|y ˈkræb|.i **-ier** -i.əʳ ⓤⓢ -i.ɚ **-iest** -i.ɪst, -i.əst **-ily** -ɪ.li, -ᵊl.i **-iness** -ɪ.nəs, -ɪ.nɪs
crabtree (C) ˈkræb.triː **-s** -z
crabwise ˈkræb.waɪz
crack kræk **-s** -s **-ing** -ɪŋ **-ed** -t ˌ**crack of** ˈ**dawn**
crackdown ˈkræk.daʊn **-s** -z
Crackenthorpe ˈkræk.ᵊn.θɔːp ⓤⓢ -θɔːrp
cracker ˈkræk.əʳ ⓤⓢ -ɚ **-s** -z
cracker-barrel ˈkræk.əˌbær.ᵊl ⓤⓢ -ɚˌber.ᵊl, -ˌbær-
crackerjack (*adj.*) ˈkræk.ə.dʒæk ⓤⓢ ˈ-ɚ-
Cracker Jack® ˈkræk.ə.dʒæk ⓤⓢ ˈ-ɚ-
crackhead ˈkræk.hed **-s** -z
crackhou|se ˈkræk.haʊ|s **-ses** -zɪz
crackl|e ˈkræk.l̩ **-es** -z **-ing** -ɪŋ, ˈ-lɪŋ **-ed** -d
crackling ˈkræk.lɪŋ
crackly ˈkræk.l̩.i, ˈkræk.li
cracknel ˈkræk.nᵊl **-s** -z
Cracknell ˈkræk.nᵊl
crackpot ˈkræk.pɒt ⓤⓢ -pɑːt **-s** -s
cracks|man ˈkræks|.mən **-men** -mən
Cracow ˈkræk.ɒf, -ɒv, -aʊ, -əʊ ⓤⓢ ˈkrɑː.kaʊ, ˈkræk.aʊ; ˈkrɑː.kʊf
-cracy -krə.si
Craddock ˈkræd.ək
cradl|e ˈkreɪ.dl̩ **-es** -z **-ing** -ɪŋ, ˈkreɪd.lɪŋ **-ed** -d
cradlesnatch ˈkreɪ.dl̩.snætʃ **-ing** -ɪŋ **-er/s** -əʳ/z ⓤⓢ -ɚ/z
Cradley ˈkreɪd.li, ˈkræd-
craft krɑːft ⓤⓢ kræft **-s** -s
-craft -krɑːft ⓤⓢ -kræft
crafts|man ˈkrɑːfts|.mən ⓤⓢ ˈkræfts- **-men** -mən **-manship** -mən.ʃɪp
crafts|woman ˈkrɑːfts|ˌwʊm.ən ⓤⓢ ˈkræfts- **-women** -ˌwɪm.ɪn
craft|y ˈkrɑːf.t|i ⓤⓢ ˈkræf- **-ier** -i.əʳ ⓤⓢ -i.ɚ **-iest** -i.ɪst, -i.əst **-ily** -ɪ.li, -ᵊl.i **-iness** -ɪ.nəs, -ɪ.nɪs
crag kræɡ **-s** -z
Cragg kræɡ
cragg|y ˈkræɡ|.i **-ier** -i.əʳ ⓤⓢ -i.ɚ **-iest** -i.ɪst, -i.əst **-ily** -ɪ.li, -ᵊl.i **-iness** -ɪ.nəs, -ɪ.nɪs
crags|man ˈkræɡz|.mən **-men** -mən, -men
Craig kreɪɡ
Craigavon ˌkreɪˈɡæv.ᵊn
Craigie ˈkreɪ.ɡi
Craik kreɪk
Craiova krəˈjəʊ.və, krɑː- ⓤⓢ krɑːˈjoʊ-
crak|e kreɪk **-es** -s **-ing** -ɪŋ **-ed** -t
cram (C) kræm **-s** -z **-ming** -ɪŋ **-med** -d
crambo ˈkræm.bəʊ ⓤⓢ -boʊ
Cramer ˈkrɑː.məʳ, ˈkreɪ- ⓤⓢ ˈkreɪ.mɚ
cram-full ˌkræmˈfʊl
Cramlington ˈkræm.lɪŋ.tən
crammer ˈkræm.əʳ ⓤⓢ -ɚ **-s** -z
cramp (C) kræmp **-s** -s **-ing** -ɪŋ **-ed** -t
cramp-iron ˈkræmp.aɪən ⓤⓢ -aɪɚn **-s** -z
crampon ˈkræm.pɒn, -pən ⓤⓢ -pɑːn **-s** -z
Crampton ˈkræm*p*.tən
cran kræn **-s** -z
cranage ˈkreɪ.nɪdʒ
Cranage ˈkræn.ɪdʒ
cranberr|y ˈkræn.bᵊr|.i, ˈkræm- ⓤⓢ -ˌber- **-ies** -iz
Cranborne ˈkræn.bɔːn, ˈkræm- ⓤⓢ ˈkræn.bɔːrn
Cranbourn(e) ˈkræn.bɔːn, ˈkræm- ⓤⓢ ˈkræn.bɔːrn
Cranbrook ˈkræn.brʊk, ˈkræm- ⓤⓢ ˈkræn-
cran|e (C) kreɪn **-es** -z **-ing** -ɪŋ **-ed** -d ˈ**crane** ˌ**fly**
cranesbill ˈkreɪnz.bɪl **-s** -z
Cranfield ˈkræn.fiːld
Cranford ˈkræn.fəd ⓤⓢ -fɚd
cranial ˈkreɪ.ni.əl
cranio- ˈkreɪ.ni.əʊ- ⓤⓢ ˈkreɪ.ni.oʊ-, -ə-
craniolog|y ˌkreɪ.niˈɒl.ə.dʒ|i ⓤⓢ -ˈɑː.lə- **-ist/s** -ɪst/s
crani|um ˈkreɪ.ni|.əm **-ums** -əmz **-a** -ə
crank kræŋk **-s** -s
crankshaft ˈkræŋk.ʃɑːft ⓤⓢ -ʃæft **-s** -s
Crankshaw ˈkræŋk.ʃɔː ⓤⓢ -ʃɑː, -ʃɔː
crank|y ˈkræŋ.k|i **-ier** -i.əʳ ⓤⓢ -i.ɚ **-iest** -i.ɪst, -i.əst **-ily** -ɪ.li, -ᵊl.i **-iness** -ɪ.nəs, -ɪ.nɪs
Cranleigh, Cranley ˈkræn.li
Cranmer ˈkræn.məʳ, ˈkræm- ⓤⓢ ˈkræn.mɚ
crann|y ˈkræn|.i **-ies** -iz **-ied** -id
Cranston ˈkræn.stən
Cranwell ˈkræn.wəl, -wel
Cranworth ˈkræn.wəθ, -wɜːθ ⓤⓢ -wɚθ, -wɜːrθ
crap kræp **-s** -s **-ping** -ɪŋ **-ped** -t
crape kreɪp **-s** -s
crapper ˈkræp.əʳ ⓤⓢ -ɚ **-s** -z
crapp|y ˈkræp|.i **-ier** -i.əʳ ⓤⓢ -i.ɚ **-iest** -i.ɪst, -i.əst
craps kræps
crapshooter ˈkræpˌʃuː.təʳ ⓤⓢ -t̬ɚ **-s** -z
crapulen|ce ˈkræp.jə.lən|*t*s, -jʊ- **-t/ly** -t/li
crapulous ˈkræp.jə.ləs, -jʊ- **-ly** -li
crash kræʃ **-es** -ɪz **-ing** -ɪŋ **-ed** -t ˈcrash ˌbarrier ; ˈcrash ˌhelmet, ˌcrash ˈhelmet
Crashaw ˈkræʃ.ɔː ⓤⓢ -ɑː, -ɔː
crash-div|e ˈkræʃ.daɪv, ˌ-ˈ- **-es** -z **-ing** -ɪŋ **-ed** -d **crash-dove** ˈkræʃ.dəʊv ⓤⓢ -doʊv
crash-land ˌkræʃˈlænd ⓤⓢ ˈkræʃ.lænd, ˌ-ˈ- **-s** -z **-ing/s** -ɪŋ/z **-ed** -ɪd *stress shift, British only:* ˌcrash-land ˈheavily
cra|sis ˈkreɪ|.sɪs **-ses** -siːz
crass kræs **-er** -əʳ ⓤⓢ -ɚ **-est** -ɪst, -əst **-ly** -li **-ness** -nəs, -nɪs
-crat -kræt
cratch krætʃ **-es** -ɪz
Cratchit ˈkrætʃ.ɪt

crate kreɪt **-s** -s
crater ˈkreɪ.təʳ US -t̬ɚ **-s** -z
Crathie ˈkræθ.i
-cratic -ˈkræt.ɪk US -ˈkræt̬.ɪk
cra|vat krə|ˈvæt **-vats** -væts **-vatted** -væt.ɪd US -væt̬.ɪd
crav|e kreɪv **-es** -z **-ing** -ɪŋ **-ed** -d **-er/s** -əʳ/z US -ɚ/z
craven (C) ˈkreɪ.vᵊn **-s** -z **-ly** -li
craving ˈkreɪ.vɪŋ **-s** -z
craw krɔː US krɑː, krɔː **-s** -z
crawfish ˈkrɔː.fɪʃ US ˈkrɑː-, ˈkrɔː- **-es** -ɪz
Crawford ˈkrɔː.fəd US ˈkrɑː.fɚd, ˈkrɔː-
crawl krɔːl US krɑːl, krɔːl **-s** -z **-ing** -ɪŋ **-ed** -d **-er/s** -əʳ/z US -ɚ/z
Crawley ˈkrɔː.li US ˈkrɑː-, ˈkrɔː-
crawl|y ˈkrɔː.l|i US ˈkrɑː-, ˈkrɔː- **-ier** -i.əʳ US -i.ɚ **-iest** -i.ɪst, -i.əst **-iness** -ɪ.nəs, -ɪ.nɪs
Craxi ˈkræk.si
Cray kreɪ
crayfish ˈkreɪ.fɪʃ **-es** -ɪz
Crayford ˈkreɪ.fəd US -fɚd
Crayola® kreɪˈəʊ.lə US -ˈoʊ-
crayon ˈkreɪ.ɒn, -ən US -ɑːn, -ən **-s** -z **-ing** -ɪŋ **-ed** -d
craz|e kreɪz **-es** -ɪz **-ed** -d
craz|y ˈkreɪ.z|i **-ier** -i.əʳ US -i.ɚ **-iest** -i.ɪst, -i.əst **-ily** -ɪ.li, -ᵊl.i **-iness** -ɪ.nəs, -ɪ.nɪs **ˈCrazy ˌHorse** ; **ˌcrazy ˈpaving**
CRE ˌsiː.ɑːrˈiː US -ɑːrˈ-
Creagh kreɪ
creak kriːk **-s** -s **-ing** -ɪŋ **-ed** -t
creak|y ˈkriː.k|i **-ier** -i.əʳ US -i.ɚ **-iest** -i.ɪst, -i.əst **-ily** -ɪ.li, -ᵊl.i **-iness** -ɪ.nəs, -ɪ.nɪs
cream kriːm **-s** -z **-ing** -ɪŋ **-ed** -d **-er/s** -əʳ/z US -ɚ/z **ˌcream ˈcheese** ; **ˌcream ˈcracker** ; **ˌcream ˈsoda** ; **ˌcream ˈtea**
creamer|y ˈkriː.mᵊr|.i **-ies** -iz
cream|y ˈkriː.m|i **-ier** -i.əʳ US -i.ɚ **-iest** -i.ɪst, -i.əst **-ily** -ɪ.li, -ᵊl.i **-iness** -ɪ.nəs, -ɪ.nɪs
creas|e kriːs **-es** -ɪz **-ing** -ɪŋ **-ed** -t
Creas(e)y ˈkriː.si
creasy ˈkriː.si
cre|ate kri|ˈeɪt **-ates** -eɪts **-ating** -eɪ.tɪŋ US -eɪ.t̬ɪŋ **-ated** -eɪ.tɪd US -eɪ.t̬ɪd
creation (C) kriˈeɪ.ʃᵊn **-s** -z
creation|ism kriˈeɪ.ʃᵊn|.ɪ.zᵊm **-ist/s** -ɪst/s
creative kriˈeɪ.tɪv US -t̬ɪv **-ly** -li **-ness** -nəs, -nɪs
creativity ˌkriː.eɪˈtɪv.ə.ti, -ɪ.ti US -ə.t̬i
creator (C) kriˈeɪ.təʳ US -t̬ɚ **-s** -z
creature ˈkriː.tʃəʳ US -tʃɚ **-s** -z **ˌcreature ˈcomfort** US **ˈcreature ˌcomfort**
crèch|e kreʃ, kreɪʃ **-es** -ɪz
Crécy ˈkres.i US kreɪˈsiː
cred kred
Creda® ˈkriː.də
credence ˈkriː.dᵊnts
credential krɪˈden.*t*ʃᵊl, krə- US -ˈden*t*.ʃᵊl **-s** -z
credibility ˌkred.əˈbɪl.ə.ti, -ɪˈ-, -ɪ.ti US -əˈbɪl.ə.t̬i
credib|le ˈkred.ə.b|l̩, ˈ-ɪ- **-ly** -li **-leness** -l̩.nəs, -nɪs
cred|it ˈkred|.ɪt **-its** -ɪts **-iting** -ɪ.tɪŋ US -ɪ.t̬ɪŋ **-ited** -ɪ.tɪd US -ɪ.t̬ɪd **ˈcredit ˌcard**
creditab|le ˈkred.ɪ.tə.b|l̩ US -t̬ə- **-ly** -li **-leness** -l̩.nəs, -nɪs
Crediton ˈkred.ɪ.tᵊn
creditor ˈkred.ɪ.təʳ US -t̬ɚ **-s** -z
creditworth|y ˈkred.ɪtˌwɜː.ð|i US -ˌwɜːr- **-iness** -ɪ.nəs, -ɪ.nɪs
credo ˈkreɪ.dəʊ, ˈkriː- US ˈkriː.doʊ, ˈkreɪ- **-s** -z
credulity krəˈdjuː.lə.ti, krɪ-, kredˈjuː-, -lɪ- US krəˈduː.lə-, -ˈdjuː-
credulous ˈkred.jʊ.ləs, -jə- US ˈkredʒ.ə-, ˈkred.jə- **-ly** -li **-ness** -nəs, -nɪs
Cree kriː
creed (C) kriːd **-s** -z
creek (C) kriːk **-s** -s
creel kriːl **-s** -z
creep kriːp **-s** -s **-ing** -ɪŋ **crept** krept
creeper ˈkriː.pəʳ US -pɚ **-s** -z
creep|y ˈkriː.p|i **-ier** -i.əʳ US -i.ɚ **-iest** -i.ɪst, -i.əst **-ily** -ɪ.li, -ᵊl.i **-iness** -ɪ.nəs, -ɪ.nɪs
creepy-crawl|y ˌkriː.piˈkrɔː.l|i, ˈkriː.piˌkrɔː- US ˌkriː.piˈkrɑː-, -ˈkrɔː-, ˈkriː.piˌkrɑː-, -ˌkrɔː- **-ies** -iz
Crees kriːs, kriːz
Creevey ˈkriː.vi
Creighton ˈkraɪ.tᵊn, ˈkreɪ- US ˈkreɪ-, ˈkraɪ-
crema|te krɪˈmeɪ|t, krə- US ˈkriː.meɪ|t; krɪˈmeɪ|t **-tes** -ts **-ting** -tɪŋ US -t̬ɪŋ **-ted** -tɪd US -t̬ɪd **-tor/s** -təʳ/z US -t̬ɚ/z
cremation krɪˈmeɪ.ʃᵊn, krə- US krɪ-, kriː- **-s** -z
crematori|um ˌkrem.əˈtɔː.ri|.əm US ˌkriː.məˈtɔːr.i-, ˌkrem.əˈ- **-ums** -əmz **-a** -ə
cremator|y ˈkrem.ə.tᵊr|.i, -tr|i US ˈkriː.mə.tɔːr|.i, ˈkrem.ə- **-ies** -iz
creme krem, kriːm
crème brulée ˌkrem.bruːˈleɪ, ˌkreɪm-, ˌ-ˈ--
crème caramel ˌkrem.kær.əˈmel, ˌkreɪm-, -ˈkær.ə.mel US -ker.əˈmel, -kær-, -ˈker.ə.mel, -ˈkær-
crème de la crème ˌkrem.də.lɑːˈkrem, ˌkreɪm-, -ˈkreɪm
crème de menthe ˌkrem.dəˈmɑ̃ː*n*θ, ˌkreɪm-, -ˈmɑːntθ, -ˈmɒn*t*θ, -ˈmɒnt US -ˈmɑːnt, -ˈmen*t*θ
crème fraîche ˌkremˈfreɪʃ, ˌkreɪm- US -ˈfreɪʃ, -ˈfreʃ
Cremona krɪˈməʊ.nə, krə- US -ˈmoʊ-
Cremora® krɪˈmɔː.rə, krə-
crenate ˈkriː.neɪt
crenel(l)|ate ˈkren.ᵊl|.eɪt, -ɪ.l|eɪt US -ə.l|eɪt **-ates** -eɪts **-ating** -eɪ.tɪŋ US -eɪ.t̬ɪŋ **-ated** -eɪ.tɪd US -eɪ.t̬ɪd
crenel(l)ation ˌkren.ᵊlˈeɪ.ʃᵊn, -ɪˈleɪ- US -əˈleɪ- **-s** -z
creole (C) ˈkriː.əʊl, ˈkreɪ-, -ˈ- US ˈkriː.oʊl, -ˈ- **-s** -z
Creolian kriːˈəʊ.li.ən, kreɪ- US -ˈoʊ-
Creon ˈkriː.ən, -ɒn US -ɑːn
creo|sote ˈkriː.ə|.səʊt US -soʊt **-sotes** -səʊts US -soʊts **-soting** -səʊ.tɪŋ US -soʊ.t̬ɪŋ **-soted** -səʊ.tɪd US -soʊ.t̬ɪd
crêpe, crepe kreɪp **-s** -s **ˌcrepe ˈpaper** US **ˈcrepe ˌpaper**
crêpe de chine ˌkreɪp.dəˈʃiːn, ˌkrep-
crêpe(s) suzette ˌkreɪp.suːˈzet, ˌkrep-
crepi|tate ˈkrep.ɪ|.teɪt **-tates** -teɪts **-tating** -teɪ.tɪŋ US -teɪ.t̬ɪŋ **-tated** -teɪ.tɪd US -teɪ.t̬ɪd
crepitation ˌkrep.ɪˈteɪ.ʃᵊn **-s** -z
crépon ˈkrep.ɔ̃ː*ŋ*, ˈkreɪ.pɔ̃ː*ŋ*, -pɒn US ˈkreɪ.pɑːn
crept (*from* **creep**) krept
crepuscular krɪˈpʌs.kjə.ləʳ, krə-, krepˈʌs-, -kjʊ- US -kjə.lɚ
crepuscule ˈkrep.ə.skjuːl US krɪˈpʌs.kjuːl
crescendo krɪˈʃen.dəʊ, krə- US -doʊ **-s** -z
crescent *moon, shape:* ˈkres.ᵊnt, ˈkrez- US ˈkres- **-s** -s
crescent *growing, when applied to objects other than the moon:* ˈkres.ᵊnt
Crespigny *surname:* ˈkrep.ɪ.ni, ˈkrep.ni, ˈkres.pɪ.ni *in London streets:* kresˈpɪn.i
cress kres **-es** -ɪz
Cressida ˈkres.ɪ.də
Cresswell ˈkrez.wəl, -wel, ˈkres- US ˈkres.wel, ˈkrez-, -wəl
Cressy ˈkres.i
crest krest **-s** -s **-ing** -ɪŋ **-ed** -ɪd
Cresta ˈkres.tə **ˌCresta ˈRun**
crestfallen ˈkrestˌfɔː.lᵊn US -ˌfɔː-, -ˌfɑː- **-ness** -nəs, -nɪs
Creswell ˈkres.wəl, -wel, ˈkrez-
Creswick ˈkrez.ɪk US ˈkres.wɪk; ˈkrez.ɪk
cretaceous (C) krɪˈteɪ.ʃəs, krə-, kretˈeɪ-, -ʃi.əs
Cretan ˈkriː.tᵊn **-s** -z
Crete kriːt
Cretic ˈkriː.tɪk US -t̬ɪk **-s** -s

cretin 'kret.ɪn (US) 'kriː.tᵊn **-s** -z
cretinism 'kret.ɪ.nɪ.zᵊm, -ᵊn.ɪ- (US) 'kriː.tᵊn-
cretinous 'kret.ɪ.nəs, -ᵊn.əs (US) 'kriː.tᵊn- **-ly** -li
cretonne kret'ɒn, krɪ'tɒn, krə-; 'kret.ɒn (US) 'kriː.tɑːn, krɪ'tɑːn **-s** -z
Creusa kri'uː.zə (US) -sə
Creuse krɜːz (US) krɜːrz
Creutzfeldt-Jacob ˌkrɔɪts.felt'jæk.ɒb (US) -'jɑː.koʊb, -kɑːb ˌ**Creutzfeldt-'Jacob di**ˌ**sease**
crevass|e krɪ'væs, krə- (US) krə- **-es** -ɪz **-ed** -t
Crèvecoeur krev'kɜːʳ (US) -'kʊr
crevic|e 'krev.ɪs **-es** -ɪz
crew kruː **-s** -z **'crew** ˌ**cut** ; ˌ**crew 'neck**, **'crew** ˌ**neck**
Crewe kruː
crewel 'kruː.əl, -ɪl **-s** -z
Crewkerne 'kruː.kɜːn, 'krʊk.ən, kruː'kɜːn (US) 'kruː.kɜːn
Crianlarich ˌkriː.ən'lær.ɪk, -ɪx (US) -'ler.ɪk, -'lær-
crib krɪb **-s** -z **-bing** -ɪŋ **-bed** -d **-ber/s** -əʳ/z (US) -ɚ/z **'crib** ˌ**death**
cribbage 'krɪb.ɪdʒ
Cribbins 'krɪb.ɪnz
Criccieth 'krɪk.i.eθ, -əθ
Crich kraɪtʃ
Crichel 'krɪtʃ.ᵊl
Crichton 'kraɪ.tᵊn
crick (C) krɪk **-s** -s **-ing** -ɪŋ **-ed** -t
crick|et 'krɪk|.ɪt **-ets** -ɪts **-eter/s** -ɪ.təʳ/z (US) -ɪ.t̬ɚ/z **-eting** -ɪ.tɪŋ (US) -ɪ.t̬ɪŋ
Crickhowell krɪk'haʊəl, -'haʊl
cricoid 'kraɪ.kɔɪd
cri(s) de coeur ˌkriː.də'kɜːʳ (US) -'kɜːr
cried (*from* **cry**) kraɪd
Crieff kriːf
crier 'kraɪ.əʳ (US) -ɚ **-s** -z
cries (*from* **cry**) kraɪz
crikey 'kraɪ.ki
crime kraɪm **-s** -z ˌ**crime of 'passion**
Crime|a kraɪ'miː|.ə **-an** -ən
crimen falsi ˌkrɪm.en'fæl.si
crime(s) passionel(s) ˌkriːm.pæs.i.ə'nel, -pæʃ.ə'-
criminal 'krɪm.ɪ.nᵊl, '-ə- **-s** -z **-ly** -li ˌ**criminal 'damage** ; ˌ**criminal 'law**, (US) **'criminal** ˌ**law**
criminality ˌkrɪm.ɪ'næl.ə.ti, -ə'-, -ɪ.ti (US) -ə'næl.ə.t̬i
criminalization, -isa- ˌkrɪm.ɪ.nᵊl.aɪ'zeɪ.ʃᵊn, -ɪ'- (US) -ɪ'-
criminaliz|e, -is|e 'krɪm.ɪ.nᵊl.aɪz (US) -nə.laɪz **-es** -ɪz **-ing** -ɪŋ **-ed** -d
crimi|nate 'krɪm.ɪ|.neɪt, '-ə- **-nates** -neɪts **-nating** -neɪ.tɪŋ (US) -neɪ.t̬ɪŋ **-nated** -neɪ.tɪd (US) -neɪ.t̬ɪd
crimination ˌkrɪm.ɪ'neɪ.ʃᵊn, -ə'- **-s** -z
criminolog|y ˌkrɪm.ɪ'nɒl.ə.dʒ|i, -ə'- (US) -'nɑː.lə- **-ist/s** -ɪst/s
crimp krɪmp **-s** -s **-ing** -ɪŋ **-ed** -t
Crimplene® 'krɪm.pliːn
crimson 'krɪm.zᵊn **-s** -z **-ing** -ɪŋ **-ed** -d
cring|e krɪndʒ **-es** -ɪz **-ing** -ɪŋ **-ed** -d **-er/s** -əʳ/z (US) -ɚ/z
crinkl|e 'krɪŋ.kl̩ **-es** -z **-ing** -ɪŋ, '-klɪŋ **-ed** -d
crinkly 'krɪŋ.kli
crinoid 'kraɪ.nɔɪd, 'krɪn.ɔɪd **-s** -z
crinoline 'krɪn.ᵊl.ɪn **-s** -z
cripes kraɪps
Crippen 'krɪp.ɪn, -ᵊn
crippl|e 'krɪp.l̩ **-es** -z **-ing** -ɪŋ, '-lɪŋ **-ed** -d
Cripplegate 'krɪp.l̩.geɪt
Crisco® 'krɪs.kəʊ (US) -koʊ
Criseyde krɪ'seɪ.də
cris|is 'kraɪ.s|ɪs **-es** -iːz **'crisis** ˌ**management**
crisp (C) krɪsp **-er** -əʳ (US) -ɚ **-est** -ɪst, -əst **-ly** -li **-ness** -nəs, -nɪs
crispbread 'krɪsp.bred **-s** -z
Crispian 'krɪs.pi.ən
Crispin 'krɪs.pɪn
crisp|y 'krɪs.p|i **-ier** -i.əʳ (US) -i.ɚ **-iest** -i.ɪst, -i.əst **-ily** -ɪ.li, -ᵊl.i **-iness** -ɪ.nəs, -ɪ.nɪs
crisscross 'krɪs.krɒs (US) -krɑːs **-es** -ɪz **-ing** -ɪŋ **-ed** -t
Cristina krɪ'stiː.nə
Critchley 'krɪtʃ.li
criteri|on (C) kraɪ'tɪə.ri|.ən (US) -'tɪr.i- **-ons** -ənz **-a** -ə
critic 'krɪt.ɪk (US) 'krɪt̬- **-s** -s
critic|al 'krɪt.ɪ.k|ᵊl (US) 'krɪt̬- **-ally** -ᵊl.i, -li **-alness** -ᵊl.nəs, -nɪs
criticism 'krɪt.ɪ.sɪ.zᵊm, '-ə- (US) 'krɪt̬- **-s** -z
criticizable, -isa- 'krɪt.ɪ.saɪ.zə.bl̩, '-ə-, ˌkrɪt.ɪ'saɪ-, -ə'- (US) 'krɪt̬.ɪ.saɪ-
criticiz|e, -is|e 'krɪt.ɪ.saɪz, '-ə- (US) 'krɪt̬- **-es** -ɪz **-ing** -ɪŋ **-ed** -d
critique krɪ'tiːk, krə- **-s** -s
Crittenden 'krɪt.ᵊn.dən
critter 'krɪt.əʳ (US) 'krɪt̬.ɚ **-s** -z
croak krəʊk (US) kroʊk **-s** -s **-ing/s** -ɪŋ/z **-ed** -t **-er/s** -əʳ/z (US) -ɚ/z
croak|y 'krəʊ.k|i (US) 'kroʊ- **-ier** -i.əʳ (US) -i.ɚ **-iest** -i.ɪst, -i.əst **-ily** -ɪ.li, -ᵊl.i **-iness** -ɪ.nəs, -ɪ.nɪs
Croat 'krəʊ.æt, -ət (US) 'kroʊ- **-s** -s
Croatia krəʊ'eɪ.ʃə (US) kroʊ-
Croatian krəʊ'eɪ.ʃᵊn (US) kroʊ- **-s** -z
crochet 'krəʊ.ʃeɪ, -ʃi (US) kroʊ'ʃeɪ **-s** -z **-ing** -ɪŋ **-ed** -d **'crochet** ˌ**hook** (US) **cro'chet** ˌ**hook**
crock krɒk (US) krɑːk **-s** -s
Crocker 'krɒk.əʳ (US) 'krɑː.kɚ
crockery 'krɒk.ᵊr.i (US) 'krɑː.kɚ-
crocket 'krɒk.ɪt (US) 'krɑː.kɪt **-s** -s
Crockett 'krɒk.ɪt (US) 'krɑː.kɪt
Crockford 'krɒk.fəd (US) 'krɑːk.fɚd
Crockpot® 'krɒk.pɒt (US) 'krɑːk.pɑːt
crocodile 'krɒk.ə.daɪl (US) 'krɑː.kə- **-s** -z ˌ**crocodile 'tears** (US) **'crocodile** ˌ**tears**
crocodilian ˌkrɒk.ə'dɪl.i.ən (US) ˌkrɑː.kə'dɪl.jən **-s** -z
crocus 'krəʊ.kəs (US) 'kroʊ- **-es** -ɪz
Croesus 'kriː.səs
croft (C) krɒft (US) krɑːft **-s** -s
crofter 'krɒf.təʳ (US) 'krɑːf.tɚ **-s** -z
Crofton 'krɒf.tᵊn (US) 'krɑːf-
Crohn krəʊn (US) kroʊn **'Crohn's di**ˌ**sease**
croissant 'kwæs.ɑ̃ːŋ, 'krwæs-, -ɒnt (US) kwɑː'sɑ̃ː, krə-, krwɑː-, -'sɑːnt **-s** -z
Croker 'krəʊ.kəʳ (US) 'kroʊ.kɚ
Cro-Magnon ˌkrəʊ'mæn.jɔ̃ːŋ, -jən, -'mæg.nən, -nɒn (US) kroʊ'mæg.nən, -nɑːn, -'mæn.jən, -jɑːn
Cromarty 'krɒm.ə.ti (US) 'krɑː.mɚ.t̬i
Crombie 'krɒm.bi, 'krʌm- (US) 'krɑːm-, 'krʌm-
Crome krəʊm (US) kroʊm
Cromer 'krəʊ.məʳ (US) 'kroʊ.mɚ
cromlech 'krɒm.lek (US) 'krɑːm- **-s** -s
Crommelin 'krʌm.lɪn, 'krɒm- (US) 'krɑːm-, 'krʌm-
Crompton 'krʌmp.tən, 'krɒmp- (US) 'krɑːmp-
Cromwell 'krɒm.wəl, 'krʌm-, -wel (US) 'krɑːm-
Cromwellian krɒm'wel.i.ən, krʌm- (US) krɑːm-
crone krəʊn (US) kroʊn **-s** -z
Cronin 'krəʊ.nɪn (US) 'kroʊ-
Cronkite 'krɒŋ.kaɪt (US) 'krɑːn.kaɪt, 'krɑːŋ-
Cronos 'krəʊ.nɒs (US) 'kroʊ.nɑːs
cron|y 'krəʊ.n|i (US) 'kroʊ- **-ies** -iz
cronyism 'krəʊ.ni.ɪ.zᵊm (US) 'kroʊ-
crook (C) krʊk **-s** -s **-ing** -ɪŋ **-ed** -t **by** ˌ**hook or by 'crook**
Crookback 'krʊk.bæk
crookbacked 'krʊk.bækt
Crooke krʊk **-s** -s
crooked *not straight:* 'krʊk.ɪd **-er** -əʳ (US) -ɚ **-est** -ɪst, -əst **-ly** -li **-ness** -nəs, -nɪs
crooked *having a crook:* krʊkt
Croome kruːm
croon kruːn **-s** -z **-ing** -ɪŋ **-ed** -d **-er/s** -əʳ/z (US) -ɚ/z
crop krɒp (US) krɑːp **-s** -s **-ping** -ɪŋ **-ped** -t
cropper 'krɒp.əʳ (US) 'krɑː.pɚ **-s** -z
croquet 'krəʊ.keɪ, -ki (US) kroʊ'keɪ **-s** -z **-ing** -ɪŋ **-ed** -d
croquette krɒk'et, krəʊ'ket (US) kroʊ'ket **-s** -s
crore krɔːʳ (US) krɔːr **-s** -z
Crosby 'krɒz.bi, 'krɒs- (US) 'krɑːz-

Crosfield 'krɒs.fiːld ⓊⓈ 'krɑːs-
Croshaw 'krəʊ.ʃɔː ⓊⓈ 'kroʊ.ʃɑː, -ʃɔː
crosier (C) 'krəʊ.zi.əʳ, -ʒəʳ ⓊⓈ 'kroʊ.ʒɚ **-s** -z
cross- krɒs- ⓊⓈ krɑːs-
cross (C) krɒs ⓊⓈ krɑːs **-es** -ɪz **-er** -əʳ ⓊⓈ -ɚ **-est** -ɪst, -əst **-ly** -li **-ness** -nəs, -nɪs **-ing** -ɪŋ **-ed** -t **'cross ˌaction ; 'cross ˌbench**
crossbar 'krɒs.bɑːʳ ⓊⓈ 'krɑːs.bɑːr **-s** -z
crossbeam 'krɒs.biːm ⓊⓈ 'krɑːs- **-s** -z
crossbencher 'krɒsˌben.*t*ʃəʳ, ˌ-'-- ⓊⓈ 'krɑːsˌben*t*.ʃɚ **-s** -z
crossbill 'krɒs.bɪl ⓊⓈ 'krɑːs- **-s** -z
crossbones 'krɒs.bəʊnz ⓊⓈ 'krɑːs.boʊnz
crossbow 'krɒs.bəʊ ⓊⓈ 'krɑːs.boʊ **-s** -z
crossbred 'krɒs.bred ⓊⓈ 'krɑːs-
crossbreed 'krɒs.briːd ⓊⓈ 'krɑːs- **-s** -z
cross-Channel ˌkrɒs'tʃæn.əl ⓊⓈ ˌkrɑːs- *stress shift:* ˌcross-Channel 'ferry
crosscheck (*n*) 'krɒs.tʃek ⓊⓈ 'krɑːs-
crosscheck (*v*) ˌkrɒs'tʃek, '-- ⓊⓈ 'krɑːs.tʃek **-s** -s **-ing** -ɪŋ **-ed** -t
cross-claim 'krɒs.kleɪm ⓊⓈ 'krɑːs- **-s** -z
cross-country ˌkrɒs'kʌn.tri ⓊⓈ ˌkrɑːs- *stress shift:* ˌcross-country 'runner
crosscourt 'krɒs.kɔːt ⓊⓈ 'krɑːs.kɔːrt
cross-cultural ˌkrɒs'kʌl.tʃə.rəl ⓊⓈ ˌkrɑːs'kʌl.tʃɚ.əl **-ly** -li
crosscut 'krɒs.kʌt, ˌ-'- ⓊⓈ 'krɑːs.kʌt **-s** -s
cross-dress|ing ˌkrɒs'dres|.ɪŋ ⓊⓈ ˌkrɑːs- **-er/s** -əʳ/z ⓊⓈ -ɚ/z
Crosse krɒs ⓊⓈ krɑːs
cross-examination ˌkrɒs.ɪgˌzæm.ɪ'neɪ.ʃən, -egˌ-, -ɪkˌsæm-, -ekˌ-, -ə'- ⓊⓈ ˌkrɑːs.ɪgˌzæm-, -egˌ- **-s** -z
cross-examin|e ˌkrɒs.ɪg'zæm.ɪn, -eg'-, -ɪk'sæm-, -ek'- ⓊⓈ ˌkrɑːs.ɪg'zæm-, -eg'- **-es** -z **-ing** -ɪŋ **-ed** -d **-er/s** -əʳ/z ⓊⓈ -ɚ/z
cross-eyed ˌkrɒs'aɪd, '-- ⓊⓈ 'krɑːsˌaɪd *stress shift, British only:* ˌcross-eyed 'stare
cross-fertilization, -isa- ˌkrɒsˌfɜː.tɪ.laɪ'zeɪ.ʃən, -tə-, -lɪ'-, -lə'- ⓊⓈ ˌkrɑːsˌfɜːr.t̬əl.ɪ'-
cross-fertiliz|e, -is|e ˌkrɒs'fɜː.tɪ.laɪz, -tə- ⓊⓈ ˌkrɑːs'fɜːr.t̬ə- **-es** -ɪz **-ing** -ɪŋ **-ed** -d
cross-fire 'krɒs.faɪəʳ ⓊⓈ 'krɑːs.faɪɚ
cross-grained ˌkrɒs'greɪnd ⓊⓈ ˌkrɑːs-, '-ˌ- *stress shift:* ˌcross-grained 'cutting
crosshatch 'krɒs.hætʃ ⓊⓈ 'krɑːs- **-es** -ɪz **-ing** -ɪŋ **-ed** -t
crossing 'krɒs.ɪŋ ⓊⓈ 'krɑː.sɪŋ **-s** -z
cross-legged ˌkrɒs'legd, '--; ˌkrɒs'leg.ɪd, -əd ⓊⓈ ˌkrɑːs'leg.əd, -'legd
Crossley 'krɒs.li ⓊⓈ 'krɑː.sli
Crossman 'krɒs.mən ⓊⓈ 'krɑːs-
crossover 'krɒsˌəʊ.vəʳ ⓊⓈ 'krɑːsˌoʊ.vɚ **-s** -z
crosspatch 'krɒs.pætʃ ⓊⓈ 'krɑːs- **-es** -ɪz
cross-purpos|e ˌkrɒs'pɜː.pəs ⓊⓈ ˌkrɑːs'pɜːr-, '-ˌ-- **-es** -ɪz
cross-question ˌkrɒs'kwes.tʃən, -'kweʃ- ⓊⓈ ˌkrɑːs-, '-ˌ-- **-s** -z **-ing** -ɪŋ **-ed** -d
cross-refer ˌkrɒs.rɪ'fɜːʳ, -rə'- ⓊⓈ ˌkrɑːs.rə'fɜːr **-s** -z **-ring** -ɪŋ **-red** -d
cross-referenc|e ˌkrɒs'ref.ər.ən*t*s, '-rən*t*s ⓊⓈ ˌkrɑːs-, 'krɑːsˌref.ɚ.ən*t*s, ˌ-rən*t*s **-es** -ɪz
crossroad 'krɒs.rəʊd ⓊⓈ 'krɑːs.roʊd **-s** -z
cross-section 'krɒs.sek.ʃən, ˌ-'-- ⓊⓈ 'krɑːs.sek- **-s** -z
cross-stitch 'krɒs.stɪtʃ ⓊⓈ 'krɑːs-
crosswalk 'krɒs.wɔːk ⓊⓈ 'krɑːs.wɑːk, -wɔːk **-s** -s
crossway 'krɒs.weɪ ⓊⓈ 'krɑːs- **-s** -z
crosswind 'krɒs.wɪnd ⓊⓈ 'krɑːs- **-s** -z
crosswise 'krɒs.waɪz ⓊⓈ 'krɑːs-
crossword 'krɒs.wɜːd ⓊⓈ 'krɑːs.wɜːrd **-s** -z **'crossword ˌpuzzle**
Crosthwaite 'krɒs.θweɪt ⓊⓈ 'krɑːs-
crotch (C) krɒtʃ ⓊⓈ krɑːtʃ **-es** -ɪz
crotch|et (C) 'krɒtʃ|.ɪt, -ət ⓊⓈ 'krɑː.tʃ|ət **-ets** -ɪts, -əts ⓊⓈ -əts
crotchet|y 'krɒtʃ.ɪ.t|i, -ə.t|i ⓊⓈ 'krɑː.tʃə.t̬|i **-iness** -ɪ.nəs, -ɪ.nɪs
Crothers 'krʌð.əz ⓊⓈ -ɚz
croton (C) 'krəʊ.tən ⓊⓈ 'kroʊ-
crouch (C) (*v.*) kraʊtʃ **-es** -ɪz **-ing** -ɪŋ **-ed** -t
Crouch *village in Kent:* kruːtʃ
Crouchback 'kraʊtʃ.bæk
croup kruːp **-s** -s
croupier 'kruː.pi.əʳ, -eɪ ⓊⓈ -eɪ, -ɚ **-s** -z
croustade kruː'stɑːd **-s** -z
crouton 'kruː.tɒn, -tɔ̃ːŋ ⓊⓈ 'kruː.tɑːn, -'- **-s** -z
crow (C) krəʊ ⓊⓈ kroʊ **-s** -z **-ing** -ɪŋ **-ed** -d **crew** kruː **'crow's ˌnest, ˌcrow's 'nest ; as the ˌcrow 'flies**
crowbar 'krəʊ.bɑːʳ ⓊⓈ 'kroʊ.bɑːr **-s** -z
Crowborough 'krəʊ.bər.ə ⓊⓈ 'kroʊ.bɚ.oʊ
crowd kraʊd **-s** -z **-ing** -ɪŋ **-ed** -ɪd
Crowe krəʊ ⓊⓈ kroʊ
crow|foot 'krəʊ|.fʊt ⓊⓈ 'kroʊ- **-foots** -fʊts **-feet** -fiːt
Crowhurst 'krəʊ.hɜːst ⓊⓈ 'kroʊ.hɜːrst
Crowland 'krəʊ.lənd ⓊⓈ 'kroʊ-
Crowley 'krəʊ.li, 'kraʊ- ⓊⓈ 'kroʊ-, 'kraʊ-
crown kraʊn **-s** -z **-ing** -ɪŋ **-ed** -d **ˌCrown 'Court ; ˌcrown 'glass ; ˌcrown 'jewels ; ˌcrown 'land ; ˌcrown 'prince**
Crowndale 'kraʊn.deɪl
crow's|-foot 'krəʊz|.fʊt ⓊⓈ 'kroʊz- **-feet** -fiːt
Crowther 'kraʊ.ðəʳ ⓊⓈ -ðɚ
Crowthorne 'krəʊ.θɔːn ⓊⓈ 'kroʊ.θɔːrn
Croxteth 'krɒk.stəθ ⓊⓈ 'krɑːk-
Croyden, Croydon 'krɔɪ.dən
crozier (C) 'krəʊ.zi.əʳ, -ʒəʳ ⓊⓈ 'kroʊ.ʒɚ **-s** -z
CRT ˌsiː.ɑː'tiː ⓊⓈ -ɑːr'-
cru kruː
crucial 'kruː.ʃəl **-ly** -i
crucible 'kruː.sɪ.bl̩, -sə- **-s** -z
crucifer 'kruː.sɪ.fəʳ, -sə- ⓊⓈ -fɚ **-s** -z
cruciferous kruː'sɪ.fər.əs
crucifix 'kruː.sɪ.fɪks, -sə- **-es** -ɪz
crucifixion (C) ˌkruː.sə'fɪk.ʃən, -sɪ'- **-s** -z
cruciform 'kruː.sɪ.fɔːm, -sə- ⓊⓈ -fɔːrm
cruci|fy 'kruː.sɪ|.faɪ, -sə- **-fies** -faɪz **-fying** -faɪ.ɪŋ **-fied** -faɪd **-fier/s** -faɪ.əʳ/z ⓊⓈ -faɪ.ɚ/z
crud krʌd **-s** -z **-ding** -ɪŋ **-ded** -ɪd
crudd|y 'krʌd|.i **-ier** -i.əʳ ⓊⓈ -i.ɚ **-iest** -i.ɪst, -i.əst
crud|e kruːd **-er** -əʳ ⓊⓈ -ɚ **-est** -ɪst, -əst **-ely** -li **-eness** -nəs, -nɪs
Cruden 'kruː.dən
crudité(s) 'kruː.dɪ.teɪ, -də- ⓊⓈ ˌkruː.dɪ'teɪ
crudit|y 'kruː.də.t|i, -dɪ.t|i ⓊⓈ -də.t̬|i **-ies** -iz
cruel 'kruː.əl, krʊəl ⓊⓈ 'kruː.əl **-ler** -əʳ ⓊⓈ -ɚ **-lest** -ɪst, -əst **-ly** -li **-ness** -nəs, -nɪs
cruelt|y 'kruː.əl.t|i, 'krʊəl- ⓊⓈ 'kruː.əl.t̬|i **-ies** -iz
cruet 'kruː.ɪt **-s** -s
Cruft krʌft **-s** -s
Crui(c)kshank 'krʊk.ʃæŋk
cruis|e (C) kruːz **-es** -ɪz **-ing** -ɪŋ **-ed** -d **-er/s** -əʳ/z ⓊⓈ -ɚ/z **'cruise conˌtrol ; ˌcruise 'missile** ⓊⓈ **'cruise ˌmissile**
cruller 'krʌl.əʳ ⓊⓈ -ɚ **-s** -z
crumb krʌm **-s** -z **-ing** -ɪŋ **-ed** -d
crumbl|e 'krʌm.bl̩ **-es** -z **-ing** -ɪŋ, '-blɪŋ **-ed** -d
crumbl|y 'krʌm.bl|i, -bl̩|.i **-ier** -i.əʳ ⓊⓈ -i.ɚ **-iest** -i.ɪst, -i.əst **-iness**
crumby 'krʌm.i
crumhorn 'krʌm.hɔːn ⓊⓈ -hɔːrn **-s** -z
Crumlin 'krʌm.lɪn
Crummock 'krʌm.ək
crummy 'krʌm.i
crump (C) krʌmp **-s** -s **-ing** -ɪŋ **-ed** -t

crumpet 'krʌm.pɪt **-s** -s
crumpl|e 'krʌm.pl̩ **-es** -z **-ing** -ɪŋ, '-plɪŋ **-ed** -d
crunch krʌntʃ **-es** -ɪz **-ing** -ɪŋ **-ed** -t
Crunchie® 'krʌn.tʃi
crunch|y 'krʌn.tʃ|i **-ier** -i.əʳ (US) -i.ɚ **-iest** -i.ɪst, -i.əst **-iness** -ɪ.nəs, -ɪ.nɪs
Crundale 'krʌn.dəl (US) -deɪl
crupper 'krʌp.əʳ (US) -ɚ **-s** -z
crusade (C) kruː'seɪd **-s** -z
crusader kruː'seɪ.dəʳ (US) -dɚ **-s** -z
crus|e kruːz **-es** -ɪz
crush krʌʃ **-es** -ɪz **-ing** -ɪŋ **-ed** -t **-er/s** -əʳ/z (US) -ɚ/z **-able** -ə.bl̩
Crusoe 'kruː.səʊ (US) -soʊ
crust krʌst **-s** -s
crustace|an krʌs'teɪ.ʃ|ən, -ʃi|.ən **-a** -ə **-ans** -ənz
crustaceous krʌs'teɪ.ʃəs, -ʃi.əs
crustate 'krʌs.teɪt
crustated krʌs'teɪ.tɪd (US) -t̬ɪd
crustation krʌs'teɪ.ʃən **-s** -z
crusted 'krʌs.tɪd
crust|y 'krʌs.t|i **-ier** -i.əʳ (US) -i.ɚ **-iest** -i.ɪst, -i.əst **-ily** -ɪ.li, -əl.i **-iness** -ɪ.nəs, -ɪ.nɪs
crutch krʌtʃ **-es** -ɪz **-ed** -t
Crutched Friars ˌkrʌtʃt'fraɪəz, ˌkrʌtʃ.ɪd'- (US) -'fraɪɚz
Cruttwell 'krʌt.wəl, -wel
crux krʌks **-es** -ɪz
Cruyff kraɪf, krɔɪf (US) krɔɪf
Cruz kruːz
cruzado kruː'zɑː.dəʊ (US) -doʊ, -'zeɪ- **-(e)s** -z
cruzeiro kruː'zeə.rəʊ (US) -'zer.oʊ **-s** -z
cr|y kr|aɪ **-ies** -aɪz **-ying** -aɪ.ɪŋ **-ied** -aɪd
cry-bab|y 'kraɪˌbeɪ.b|i **-ies** -iz
cryo- ˌkraɪ.əʊ- (US) ˌkraɪ.oʊ-, -ə-
cryogenic ˌkraɪ.əʊ'dʒen.ɪk (US) -ə'- **-s** -s
cryonic kraɪ'ɒn.ɪk (US) -'ɑː.nɪk **-s** -s
crypt- krɪpt-
crypt krɪpt **-s** -s
cryptic 'krɪp.tɪk **-al** -əl **-ally** -əl.i, -li
crypto 'krɪp.təʊ (US) -toʊ **-s** -z
cryptogam 'krɪp.təʊ.gæm (US) -tə- **-s** -z
cryptogram 'krɪp.təʊ.græm (US) -tə- **-s** -z **-ic** -ɪk
cryptograph 'krɪp.təʊ.grɑːf, -græf (US) -tə.græf **-s** -s
cryptographer krɪp'tɒg.rə.fəʳ (US) -'tɑː.grə.fɚ **-s** -z
cryptography krɪp'tɒg.rə.fi (US) -'tɑː.grə-
cryptolog|y krɪp'tɒl.ə.dʒ|i (US) -'tɑː.lə- **-ist/s** -ɪst/s
crystal (C) 'krɪs.təl **-s** -z ˌ**crystal 'ball** ; '**crystal** ˌ**gazing**
crystalizable, -isa- 'krɪs.təl.aɪ.zə.bl̩ (US) -tə.laɪ-
crystalline 'krɪs.təl.aɪn (US) -tə.laɪn
crystallization, -isa- ˌkrɪs.təl.aɪ'zeɪ.ʃən, -ɪ'- (US) -ɪ'- **-s** -z
crystalliz|e, -is|e 'krɪs.təl.aɪz (US) -tə.laɪz **-es** -ɪz **-ing** -ɪŋ **-ed** -d
crystallographer ˌkrɪs.təl'ɒg.rə.fəʳ (US) -tə'lɑː.grə.fɚ **-s** -z
crystallography krɪs.təl'ɒg.rə.fi (US) -tə'lɑː.grə-
crystalloid 'krɪs.təl.ɔɪd (US) -tə.lɔɪd **-s** -z
CSE ˌsiː.es'iː
C-section 'siːˌsek.ʃən **-s** -z
ct (*abbrev. for* **carat**) 'kær.ət (US) 'ker-, 'kær-
cub kʌb **-s** -z **-bing** -ɪŋ **-bed** -d
Cub|a 'kjuː.b|ə **-an/s** -ən/z ˌ**Cuban 'heel**
cubage 'kjuː.bɪdʒ
cubb|y 'kʌb|.i **-ies** -iz
cubbyhole 'kʌb.i.həʊl (US) -hoʊl **-s** -z
cub|e kjuːb **-es** -z **-ing** -ɪŋ **-ed** -d
cubic 'kjuː.bɪk **-al** -əl **-ally** -əl.i, -li
cubicle 'kjuː.bɪ.kl̩ **-s** -z
cub|ism 'kjuː.b|ɪ.zəm **-ist/s** -ɪst/s
cubistic kjuː'bɪs.tɪk
cu|bit 'kjuː|.bɪt **-bits** -bɪts **-bital** -bɪ.təl, -bɪ.t̬əl
Cubitt 'kjuː.bɪt
cuboid 'kjuː.bɔɪd **-s** -z
cuchul(l)inn, cuchulain (C) kuː'kʊl.ɪn, -'xʊl- (US) -'kʊl-
Cuckfield 'kʊk.fiːld
Cuckmere 'kʊk.mɪəʳ (US) -mɪr
cuckold 'kʌk.əʊld, -əld (US) -oʊld, -əld **-s** -z **-ing** -ɪŋ **-ed** -ɪd **-er/s** -əʳ/z (US) -ɚ/z **-ry** -ri
cuckoo 'kʊk.uː (US) 'kuː.kuː, 'kʊk.uː **-s** -z **-ing** -ɪŋ **-ed** -d '**cuckoo** ˌ**clock** ; '**cuckoo** ˌ**spit**
cuckooflower 'kʊk.uː.flaʊəʳ (US) 'kuː.kuː.flaʊɚ, 'kʊk.uːˌ- **-s** -z
cuckoopint 'kʊk.uː.paɪnt (US) 'kuː.kuː-, 'kʊk.uː **-s** -s
cucumber 'kjuː.kʌm.bəʳ (US) -bɚ **-s** -z
cud kʌd **-s** -z
cuddl|e 'kʌd.l̩ **-es** -z **-ing** -ɪŋ, '-lɪŋ **-ed** -d **-y** -i
cudd|y 'kʌd|.i **-ies** -iz
cudgel 'kʌdʒ.əl **-s** -z **-(l)ing** -ɪŋ **-(l)ed** -d
Cudworth 'kʌd.wəθ, -wɜːθ (US) -wɚθ, -wɜːrθ
cue kjuː **-s** -z
Cuenca 'kweŋ.kɑː, -kə
Cuernavaca ˌkweə.nə'væk.ə (US) ˌkwer.nə'vɑː.kə, -nɑː'vɑː.kɑː
cuff kʌf **-s** -s **-ing** -ɪŋ **-ed** -t
Cuffley 'kʌf.li
cufflink 'kʌf.lɪŋk **-s** -s
cui bono ˌkuː.i'bəʊn.əʊ, ˌkwiː-, -'bɒn.əʊ (US) ˌkwiː'boʊ.noʊ
cuirass kwɪ'ræs, kjʊə- (US) kwɪ'ræs **-es** -ɪz
cuirassier ˌkwɪ.rə'si.əʳ, ˌkjʊə.rə'- (US) ˌkwiː.rə'sɪr, 'kwɪr.ə.sɪr **-s** -z
cuisenaire ˌkwiː.zən'eəʳ (US) -er
Cuisinart® 'kwiː.zən.ɑːt (US) -ɑːrt
cuisine kwɪz'iːn, kwə'ziːn
cuisine minceur kwɪˌziːn.mæ̃n'sɜːʳ, kwə- (US) -'sɜːr
cuiss|e kwɪs **-es** -ɪz
Culcheth 'kʌl.tʃəθ, -tʃɪθ
cul-de-sac 'kʌl.də.sæk, 'kʊl-, ˌ--'- **-s** -s
Culham 'kʌl.əm
culinary 'kʌl.ɪ.nər.i, '-ə-, 'kjuː.lɪ- (US) 'kʌl.ə.ner-
Culkin 'kʌl.kɪn
cull kʌl **-s** -z **-ing** -ɪŋ **-ed** -d
Cullen 'kʌl.ən, -ɪn
cullender 'kʌl.ən.dəʳ, -ɪn- (US) -dɚ **-s** -z
Culley 'kʌl.i
Cullinan 'kʌl.ɪ.nən, '-ə-, -næn
Culloden kə'lɒd.ən, kʌl'ɒd-; kə'laʊ.dən (US) kə'loʊ.dən, -'lɑː-
Cullompton kə'lʌmp.tən, 'kʌl.əmp-
Cullum 'kʌl.əm
culm (C) kʌlm **-s** -z
Culme kʌlm
culmi|nate 'kʌl.mɪ|.neɪt **-nates** -neɪts **-nating** -neɪ.tɪŋ (US) -neɪ.t̬ɪŋ **-nated** -neɪ.tɪd (US) -neɪ.t̬ɪd
culmination ˌkʌl.mɪ'neɪ.ʃən, -mə'- **-s** -z
culottes kjuː'lɒts, kuː- (US) 'kuː.lɑːts, 'kjuː-, -'-
culpability ˌkʌl.pə'bɪl.ə.ti, -ɪ.ti (US) -ə.t̬i
culpab|le 'kʌl.pə.b|l̩ **-ly** -li **-leness** -l̩.nəs, -nɪs
culprit 'kʌl.prɪt **-s** -s
Culross *Scottish surname & place:* 'kuː.rɒs, -rəs (US) -rɑːs
Culross *English surname and London street:* 'kʌl.rɒs, -'- (US) 'kʌl.rɑːs, -'-
cult kʌlt **-s** -s
Culter 'kuː.təʳ (US) -t̬ɚ
cultivable 'kʌl.tɪ.və.bl̩, -tə- (US) -t̬ə-
culti|vate 'kʌl.tɪ|.veɪt, -tə- (US) -t̬ə- **-vates** -veɪts **-vating** -veɪ.tɪŋ (US) -veɪ.t̬ɪŋ **-vated** -veɪ.tɪd (US) -veɪ.t̬ɪd **-vatable** -veɪ.tə.bl̩ (US) -veɪ.t̬ə-
cultivation ˌkʌl.tɪ'veɪ.ʃən, -tə'- (US) -t̬ə'-
cultivator 'kʌl.tɪ.veɪ.təʳ, -tə- (US) -t̬ə.veɪ.t̬ɚ **-s** -z
Cults kʌlts
cultural 'kʌl.tʃər.əl **-ly** -i
culturality ˌkʌl.tʃər'æl.ɪ.ti, -ə.ti (US) -tʃə'ræl.ə.t̬i
culture 'kʌl.tʃəʳ (US) -tʃɚ **-s** -z **-d** -d '**culture** ˌ**shock**
culver (C) 'kʌl.vəʳ (US) -vɚ **-s** -z
culverin 'kʌl.vər.ɪn **-s** -z
culvert 'kʌl.vət (US) -vɚt **-s** -s **-age** -ɪdʒ (US) 'kʌl.vɚ.t̬ɪdʒ

Culzean kə'leɪn
cum kʌm, kʊm
Cumaean kjuː'miː.ən
cumbent 'kʌm.bᵊnt
cumb|er 'kʌm.b|əʳ (US) -b|ɚ **-ers** -əz (US) -ɚz **-ering** -ᵊr.ɪŋ **-ered** -əd (US) -ɚd **-erer/s** -ᵊr.əʳ/z (US) -ɚ.ɚ/z
Cumberland 'kʌm.bᵊl.ənd (US) -bɚ.lənd
Cumbernauld ˌkʌm.bə'nɔːld, '--- (US) ˌkʌm.bɚ'nɑːld, -'nɔːld
cumbersome 'kʌm.bə.səm (US) -bɚ- **-ly** -li **-ness** -nəs, -nɪs
Cumbri|a 'kʌm.bri|.ə **-an/s** -ən/z
cumbrous 'kʌmb.rəs **-ly** -li **-ness** -nəs, -nɪs
cumin 'kʌm.ɪn, 'kuː.mɪn, 'kjuː-
cum laude ˌkʌm'laʊ.deɪ, ˌkʊm-, -'lɔː.di (US) ˌkʊm'laʊ.deɪ, -'lɑː-, -'lɔː-, -di, -də
cummerbund 'kʌm.ə.bʌnd (US) '-ɚ- **-s** -z
cummin 'kʌm.ɪn
Cumming 'kʌm.ɪŋ **-s** -z
cummings (C) 'kʌm.ɪŋz
Cumnock 'kʌm.nək
Cumnor 'kʌm.nəʳ (US) -nɚ
cumulate (*adj.*) 'kjuː.mjə.lət, -mjʊ-, -lɪt, -leɪt (US) -mjə-
cumu|late (*v.*) 'kjuː.mjə|.leɪt, -mjʊ- (US) -mjə- **-lates** -leɪts **-lating** -leɪ.tɪŋ (US) -leɪ.t̬ɪŋ **-lated** -leɪ.tɪd (US) -leɪ.t̬ɪd
cumulation ˌkjuː.mjə'leɪ.ʃᵊn, -mjʊ'- (US) -mjə'- **-s** -z
cumulative 'kjuː.mjə.lə.tɪv, -mjʊ-, -leɪ- (US) -mjə.lə.t̬ɪv **-ly** -li **-ness** -nəs, -nɪs
cumulonimbus ˌkjuː.mjə.ləʊ'nɪm.bəs, -mjʊ- (US) -mjə.loʊ'- **-es** -ɪz
cumul|us 'kjuː.mjə.l|əs, -mjʊ- (US) -mjə- **-i** -aɪ, -iː (US) -aɪ
Cunard ˌkjuː'nɑːd (US) ˌkuː'nɑːrd, ˌkjuː- **-er/s** -əʳ/z (US) -ɚ/z
cunctation kʌŋk'teɪ.ʃᵊn **-s** -z
cunctator kʌŋk'teɪ.təʳ (US) -t̬ɚ **-s** -z
cuneiform 'kjuː.nɪ.fɔːm, -ni.ɪ-, -ə.fɔːm (US) 'kjuː.nə.fɔːrm, -ni.ə-
Cunliffe 'kʌn.lɪf
cunnilingus ˌkʌn.ɪ'lɪŋ.gəs (US) -ə'-
cunning 'kʌn.ɪŋ **-est** -ɪst **-ly** -li **-ness** -nəs, -nɪs
Cunningham 'kʌn.ɪŋ.əm (US) -hæm
cunt kʌnt **-s** -s
cup kʌp **-s** -s **-ping** -ɪŋ **-ped** -t **'Cup ˌFinal**, **ˌCup 'Final**
Cupar 'kuː.pəʳ (US) -pɚ
cupbearer 'kʌpˌbeə.rəʳ (US) -ˌber.ɚ **-s** -z
cupboard 'kʌb.əd (US) -ɚd **-s** -z **'cupboard ˌlove**
cupcake 'kʌp.keɪk **-s** -s
cupful 'kʌp.fʊl **-s** -z
cupid (C) 'kjuː.pɪd **-s** -z
cupidity kju'pɪd.ə.ti, -ɪ.ti (US) -ə.t̬i
cupola 'kjuː.pᵊl.ə **-s** -z
cuppa 'kʌp.ə **-s** -z
cupreous 'kjuː.pri.əs
cupric 'kjuː.prɪk
Cuprinol® 'kjuː.prɪ.nɒl, -prə- (US) -nɑːl
cuprous kjuː.prəs
cur kɜːʳ (US) kɜːr **-s** -z
curability ˌkjʊə.rə'bɪl.ə.ti, ˌkjɔː-, -ɪ.ti (US) ˌkjʊr.ə'bɪl.ə.t̬i
curable 'kjʊə.rə.bl̩, 'kjɔː- (US) 'kjʊr-
curaç|ao (C) 'kjʊə.rə.s|aʊ, 'kjɔː-, -s|əʊ, ˌ--'- (US) 'kjʊr.ə.s|oʊ, 'kʊr-, -s|aʊ, ˌ--'- **-oa** -əʊə (US) -oʊə
curac|y 'kjʊə.rə.s|i, 'kjɔː- (US) 'kjʊr.ə- **-ies** -iz
Curan 'kʌr.ən
curare kjʊə'rɑː.ri (US) kjʊ'rɑːr.i
curate 'kjʊə.rət, 'kjɔː-, -rɪt (US) 'kjʊr.ət, -eɪt **-s** -s ˌ**curate's 'egg**
curative 'kjʊə.rə.tɪv, 'kjɔː- (US) 'kjʊr.ə.t̬ɪv **-ly** -li
curator kjʊə'reɪ.təʳ, kjɔː- (US) 'kjʊr.eɪ.t̬ɚ, 'kjɜːr- **-s** -z **-ship/s** -ʃɪp/s
curb kɜːb (US) kɜːrb **-s** -z **-ing** -ɪŋ **-ed** -d
curbstone 'kɜːb.stəʊn (US) 'kɜːrb.stoʊn **-s** -z
curd kɜːd (US) kɜːrd **-s** -z
curdl|e 'kɜː.dl̩ (US) 'kɜːr- **-es** -z **-ing** -ɪŋ, 'kɜːd.lɪŋ (US) 'kɜːr.dl̩.ɪŋ, 'kɜːrd.lɪŋ **-ed** -d
curd|y 'kɜː.d|i (US) 'kɜːr- **-ier** -i.əʳ (US) -i.ɚ **-iest** -i.ɪst, -i.əst **-iness** -ɪ.nəs, -ɪ.nɪs
cur|e kjʊəʳ, kjɔːʳ (US) kjʊr **-es** -z **-ing** -ɪŋ **-ed** -d **-er/s** -əʳ/z (US) -ɚ/z
cure-all 'kjʊəʳ.ɔːl, 'kjɔːʳ- (US) 'kjʊr.ɑːl, 'kjɜːr-, -ɔːl **-s** -z
cu|ret kjʊə|'ret (US) kjʊ|'ret **-rets** -'rets **-retting** -'ret.ɪŋ (US) -'ret̬.ɪŋ **-retted** -'ret.ɪd (US) -'ret̬.ɪd
curettage ˌkjʊə.rɪ'tɑːʒ, kjʊə'ret.ɪdʒ (US) kjʊ'ret̬.ɪdʒ, ˌkjʊr.ə'tɑːʒ
cu|rette kjʊə|'ret (US) kjʊ- **-rettes** -'rets **-retting** -'ret.ɪŋ (US) -'ret̬.ɪŋ **-retted** -'ret.ɪd (US) -'ret̬.ɪd
curettment kjʊə'ret.mənt (US) kjʊ-
curfew 'kɜː.fjuː (US) 'kɜːr- **-s** -z
cur|ia 'kjʊə.r|i.ə, 'kjɔː-, 'kʊə- (US) 'kjʊr|.i- **-iae** -i.iː, -i.aɪ
curie (C) 'kjʊə.ri, -iː (US) 'kjʊr.i, -iː **-s** -z
curio 'kjʊə.ri.əʊ, 'kjɔː- (US) 'kjʊr.i.oʊ **-s** -z
curiosit|y ˌkjʊə.ri'ɒs.ə.t|i, ˌkjɔː-, -ɪ.t|i (US) ˌkjʊr.i'ɑː.sə.t̬|i **-ies** -iz
curious 'kjʊə.ri.əs, 'kjɔː- (US) 'kjʊr.i- **-ly** -li **-ness** -nəs, -nɪs
curium 'kjʊə.ri.əm, 'kjɔː- (US) 'kjʊr.i-
curl kɜːl (US) kɜːrl **-s** -z **-ing** -ɪŋ **-ed** -d **'curling ˌtongs**
curler 'kɜː.ləʳ (US) 'kɜːr.lɚ **-s** -z
curlew 'kɜː.ljuː (US) 'kɜːr.luː, 'kɜːrl.juː **-s** -z
curlicue 'kɜː.lɪ.kjuː (US) 'kɜːr- **-s** -z
curling 'kɜː.lɪŋ (US) 'kɜːr-
curl|y 'kɜː.l|i (US) 'kɜːr- **-ier** -i.əʳ (US) -i.ɚ **-iest** -i.ɪst, -i.əst **-iness** -ɪ.nəs, -ɪ.nɪs
curmudgeon kɜː'mʌdʒ.ᵊn, kə- (US) kɚ- **-s** -z **-ly** -li
curragh, **currach** (C) 'kʌr.ə (US) 'kɜːr- **-s** -z
Curran 'kʌr.ᵊn (US) 'kɜːr-
currant 'kʌr.ᵊnt (US) 'kɜːr- **-s** -s
currenc|y 'kʌr.ᵊnt.s|i (US) 'kɜːr- **-ies** -iz
current 'kʌr.ᵊnt (US) 'kɜːr- **-s** -s **-ly** -li **-ness** -nəs, -nɪs ˌ**current ac'count** ; ˌ**current af'fairs**
Currer 'kʌr.əʳ (US) 'kɜːr.ɚ
curricle 'kʌr.ɪ.kl̩ (US) 'kɜːr- **-s** -z
curricul|um kə'rɪk.jə.l|əm, -jʊ- (US) -jə- **-a** -ə **-ums** -əmz **-ar** -əʳ (US) -ɚ
curriculum vitae kəˌrɪk.jə.ləm'viː.taɪ, -jʊ-, -teɪ (US) -jə.ləm'viː.taɪ, -tiː, -'vaɪ.t̬i **-s** -s **curricula vitae** kəˌrɪk.jə.lə'viː.taɪ, -jʊ-, -teɪ (US) -jə.lə'viː.taɪ, -tiː, -'vaɪ.t̬i
Currie 'kʌr.i (US) 'kɜːr.i
Currier 'kʌr.i.əʳ (US) 'kɜːr.i.ɚ
currish 'kɜː.rɪʃ (US) 'kɜːr.ɪʃ **-ly** -li **-ness** -nəs, -nɪs
curr|y (C) 'kʌr|.i (US) 'kɜːr- **-ies** -iz **-ying** -i.ɪŋ **-ied** -id **-ier/s** -i.əʳ/z (US) -i.ɚ/z **'curry ˌpowder**
curs|e kɜːs (US) kɜːrs **-es** -ɪz **-ing** -ɪŋ **-ed** -t
cursed (*adj.*) 'kɜː.sɪd (US) 'kɜːr- **-ly** -li **-ness** -nəs, -nɪs
cursive 'kɜː.sɪv (US) 'kɜːr- **-ly** -li **-ness** -nəs, -nɪs
cursor 'kɜː.səʳ (US) 'kɜːr.sɚ **-s** -z
Cursor Mundi ˌkɜː.sɔː'mʊn.diː, -'mʌn.daɪ (US) ˌkɜːr.sɔːr'mʊn.di, -sɚ'-
cursor|y 'kɜː.sᵊr|.i (US) 'kɜːr- **-ily** -ᵊl.i, -ɪ.li **-iness** -ɪ.nəs, -ɪ.nɪs
curst kɜːst (US) kɜːrst
cursus 'kɜː.səs (US) 'kɜːr-
curt kɜːt (US) kɜːrt **-er** -əʳ (US) 'kɜːr.t̬ɚ **-est** -ɪst, -əst (US) 'kɜːr.t̬ɪst, -t̬əst **-ly** -li **-ness** -nəs, -nɪs
curtail kɜː'teɪl (US) kɚ- **-s** -z **-ing** -ɪŋ **-ed** -d **-ment/s** -mənt/s
curtain 'kɜː.tᵊn, -tɪn (US) 'kɜːr.tᵊn **-s** -z **-ed** -d **'curtain ˌcall** ; **'curtain ˌraiser**
curtes|y 'kɜː.tə.s|i, -tɪ.s|i (US) 'kɜːr.t̬ə- **-ies** -ɪz
Curtice 'kɜː.tɪs (US) 'kɜːr.t̬ɪs
curtilage 'kɜː.tᵊl.ɪdʒ, -tɪ.lɪdʒ (US) 'kɜːr.t̬ᵊl-
Curtis(s) 'kɜː.tɪs (US) 'kɜːr.t̬ɪs
curtsey 'kɜːt.si (US) 'kɜːrt- **-s** -z **-ing** -ɪŋ **-ed** -d
curts|y 'kɜːt.s|i (US) 'kɜːrt- **-ies** -iz **-ying** -i.ɪŋ **-ied** -id

curvaceous kɜːˈveɪ.ʃəs (US) kɜːr- **-ly** -li **-ness** -nəs, -nɪs
curvation kɜːˈveɪ.ʃən (US) kɜːr- **-s** -z
curvature ˈkɜː.və.tʃər, -tjʊər (US) ˈkɜːr.və.tʃɚ **-s** -z
curv|e kɜːv (US) kɜːrv **-es** -z **-ing** -ɪŋ **-ed** -d ˈ**curve** ˌ**ball**
cur|vet kɜːˈvet (US) kɜːr- **-vets** -ˈvets **-vet(t)ing** -ˈvet.ɪŋ (US) -ˈveţ.ɪŋ **-vet(t)ed** -ˈvet.ɪd (US) -ˈveţ.ɪd
curviline|al ˌkɜː.vɪˈlɪn.i|.əl, -vəˈ- (US) ˌkɜːr.vəˈ- **-ar** -ər (US) -ɚ
Curwen ˈkɜː.wɪn, -wən (US) ˈkɜːr-
Curzon ˈkɜː.zən (US) ˈkɜːr-
Cusack ˈkjuː.sæk, -zæk, -zək (US) ˈkuː-, ˈkjuː-
Cush kʊʃ, kʌʃ **-ite/s** -aɪt/s
Cushing ˈkʊʃ.ɪŋ
cushion ˈkʊʃ.ən **-s** -z **-ing** -ɪŋ **-ed** -d
cush|y ˈkʊʃ|.i **-ily** -ɪ.li, -əl.i **-iness** -ɪ.nəs, -ɪ.nɪs
cusp kʌsp **-s** -s
cuspid ˈkʌs.pɪd
cuspidor ˈkʌs.pɪ.dɔːr (US) -ə.dɔːr **-s** -z
cuss kʌs **-es** -ɪz **-ing** -ɪŋ **-ed** -t
cussed *(adj.)* ˈkʌs.ɪd, -əd **-ly** -li **-ness** -nəs, -nɪs
custard ˈkʌs.təd (US) -tɚd **-s** -z ˈ**custard** ˌ**apple** ; ˌ**custard** ˈ**pie**
Custer ˈkʌs.tər (US) -tɚ
custodial kʌsˈtəʊ.di.əl (US) -ˈtoʊ-
custodian kʌsˈtəʊ.di.ən (US) -ˈtoʊ- **-s** -z
custody ˈkʌs.tə.di
custom ˈkʌs.təm **-s** -z
customarily ˈkʌs.tə.mər.əl.i, -ɪ.li; ˌkʌs.təˈmer- (US) ˌkʌs.təˈmer-
customar|y ˈkʌs.tə.mər|.i (US) -mer- **-iness** -ɪ.nəs, -ɪ.nɪs
customer ˈkʌs.tə.mər (US) -mɚ **-s** -z
customhou|se ˈkʌs.təm.hau|s **-ses** -zɪz
customiz|e, -is|e ˈkʌs.tə.maɪz **-es** -ɪz **-ing** -ɪŋ **-ed** -d **-er/s** -ər/z (US) -ɚ/z
custom-made ˌkʌs.təmˈmeɪd (US) ˈ--,- *stress shift, British only:* ˌcustom-made ˈsuit
custos *(sing.)* ˈkʌs.tɒs, -təʊs (US) -tɑːs; ˈkʊs.toʊs *(plur.)* **custodes** kʌsˈtəʊ.diːz (US) -ˈtoʊ-
cut kʌt **-s** -s **-ting** -ɪŋ (US) ˈkʌţ.ɪŋ **-ter/s** -ər/z (US) ˈkʌţ.ɚ/z
cut-and-|dried ˌkʌt.ənˈ|draɪd **-dry** -ˈdraɪ
cut-and-paste ˌkʌt.əndˈpeɪst, -əmˈ- (US) -əndˈ-
cutaneous kjuːˈteɪ.ni.əs **-ly** -li
cutaway ˈkʌt.ə.weɪ (US) ˈkʌţ-
cutback ˈkʌt.bæk **-s** -s
Cutch kʌtʃ
cut|e kjuːt **-er** -ər (US) ˈkjuː.ţɚ **-est** -ɪst, -əst (US) ˈkjuː.ţɪst, -ţəst **-ely** -li **-eness** -nəs, -nɪs
cutey ˈkjuː.ti (US) -ţi **-s** -z
Cutforth ˈkʌt.fɔːθ (US) -fɔːrθ
Cuthbert ˈkʌθ.bət (US) -bɚt
Cuthbertson ˈkʌθ.bət.sən (US) -bɚt-
cuticle ˈkjuː.tɪ.kl̩ (US) -ţə- **-s** -z
cuticular kjuːˈtɪk.jə.lər, -jʊ- (US) -lɚ
Cuticura® ˌkjuː.tɪˈkjʊə.rə, -ˈkjɔː- (US) -ţəˈkjʊr.ə
cutie ˈkjuː.ti (US) -ţi **-s** -z
cutie-pie ˈkjuː.ti.paɪ (US) -ţi-
cutis ˈkjuː.tɪs (US) -ţɪs
cutlass ˈkʌt.ləs **-es** -ɪz
cutler (C) ˈkʌt.lər (US) -lɚ **-s** -z
cutlery ˈkʌt.lər.i
cutlet ˈkʌt.lət, -lɪt **-s** -s
cutoff ˈkʌt.ɒf (US) ˈkʌţ.ɑːf, -ɔːf **-s** -s
cutout ˈkʌt.aʊt (US) ˈkʌţ- **-s** -s
cut-price ˌkʌtˈpraɪs *stress shift:* ˌcut-price ˈgoods
Cuttell kəˈtel
cutter ˈkʌt.ər (US) ˈkʌţ.ɚ **-s** -z
cutthroat ˈkʌt.θrəʊt (US) -θroʊt **-s** -s
cutting ˈkʌt.ɪŋ (US) ˈkʌţ- **-s** -z ˌ**cutting** ˈ**edge**
cuttle (C) ˈkʌt.l̩ (US) ˈkʌţ- **-s** -z **-bone** -bəʊn (US) -boʊn
cuttlefish ˈkʌt.l̩.fɪʃ (US) ˈkʌţ- **-es** -ɪz
cutt|y ˈkʌt|.i (US) ˈkʌţ- **-ies** -iz ˌ**Cutty** ˈ**Sark**
cutwater ˈkʌtˌwɔː.tər (US) -ˌwɑː.ţɚ, -ˌwɔː- **-s** -z
cutworm ˈkʌt.wɜːm (US) -wɜːrm **-s** -z
cuvette kjuːˈvet (US) kjuː-, kuː- **-s** -s
Cuvier ˈkjuː.vi.eɪ, ˈkuː- (US) ˈkjuː.vi.eɪ; ˌkuːˈvjeɪ
Cuxhaven ˈkʊksˌhɑː.vən
Cuyahoga ˌkaɪ.əˈhəʊ.gə (US) -ˈhoʊ-, -ˈhɑː-, -ˈhɔː-
Cuyp kaɪp, kɔɪp (US) kɔɪp **-s** -s
Cuzco ˈkʊs.kəʊ, ˈkuː.skəʊ (US) ˈkuː.skoʊ
CV ˌsiːˈviː **-s** -z
cwm kʊm, kuːm **-s** -z
Cwm Avon kʊmˈæv.ən, kuːm-
Cwmbach kʊmˈbɑːx, kuːm- (US) -ˈbɑːk
Cwmbran kʊmˈbrɑːn, kuːm-
cwt *(abbrev. for* **hundredweight***)* ˈhʌn.drəd.weɪt, -drɪd- **-s** -s
cyan ˈsaɪ.æn, -ən
cyanate ˈsaɪə.neɪt
cyanic saɪˈæn.ɪk
cyanide ˈsaɪə.naɪd **-s** -z
cyanogen saɪˈæn.ə.dʒən, -dʒɪn, -dʒen
cyanosis ˌsaɪəˈnəʊ.sɪs (US) -ˈnoʊ-
cybernetic ˌsaɪ.bəˈnet.ɪk (US) -bɚˈneţ- **-s** -s
cycad ˈsaɪ.kæd, -kəd **-s** -z
Cyclades ˈsaɪ.klə.diːz, ˈsɪk.lə-
cyclamate ˈsaɪ.klə.meɪt, ˈsɪk.lə- (US) ˈsaɪ.klə- **-s** -s
cyclamen ˈsɪk.lə.mən, ˈsaɪ.klə-, -men (US) ˈsaɪ.klə- **-s** -z
cycl|e ˈsaɪ.kl̩ **-es** -z **-ing** -ɪŋ, ˈ-klɪŋ **-ed** -d
cyclic ˈsaɪ.klɪk, ˈsɪk.lɪk **-al** -əl **-ally** -əl.i, -li
cyclist ˈsaɪ.klɪst **-s** -s
cyclo- ˈsaɪ.kləʊ-, saɪˈklɒ-, ˈsɪk.ləʊ- (US) ˈsaɪ.kloʊ-, saɪˈklɑː-
Note: Prefix. This may be stressed on the initial syllable, e.g. **cyclostyle** /ˈsaɪ.kləʊ.staɪl (US) ˈsaɪ.kloʊ-/ or on the second syllable, e.g. **cyclometer** /saɪˈklɒm.ɪ.tə (US) saɪˈklɑː.mə.tɚ/.
cyclograph ˈsaɪ.kləʊ.grɑːf, -græf (US) -klə.græf **-s** -s
cycloid ˈsaɪ.klɔɪd **-s** -z
cycloidal saɪˈklɔɪ.dəl
cyclometer saɪˈklɒm.ɪ.tər, ˈ-ə- (US) -ˈklɑː.mə.ţɚ **-s** -z
cyclone ˈsaɪ.kləʊn (US) -kloʊn **-s** -z
cyclonic saɪˈklɒn.ɪk (US) -ˈklɑː.nɪk
cyclopaed|ia ˌsaɪ.kləʊˈpiː.d|i.ə (US) -kloʊˈ-, -kləˈ- **-ias** -i.əz **-ic** -ɪk
cyclopean ˌsaɪ.kləʊˈpiː.ən; saɪˈkləʊ.pi- (US) ˌsaɪ.kloʊˈpiː-, -kləˈ-; saɪˈkloʊ.pi-
cycloped|ia ˌsaɪ.kləʊˈpiː.d|i.ə (US) -kloʊˈ-, -kləˈ- **-ias** -i.əz **-ic** -ɪk
cyclops *(sing.)* ˈsaɪ.klɒps (US) -klɑːps *(plur.)* **cyclopes** saɪˈkləʊ.piːz (US) -ˈkloʊ-
cyclorama ˌsaɪ.kləˈrɑː.mə (US) -kloʊˈræm.ə, -kləˈ-, -ˈrɑː.mə **-s** -z
cyclostyl|e ˈsaɪ.kləʊ.staɪl (US) -klə- **-es** -z **-ing** -ɪŋ **-ed** -d
cyclothymia ˌsaɪ.kləʊˈθaɪ.mi.ə, ˌsɪk.ləʊˈ- (US) ˌsaɪ.kloʊˈ-, -kləˈ-
cyclotron ˈsaɪ.kləʊ.trɒn (US) -klə.trɑːn **-s** -z
cyder ˈsaɪ.dər (US) -dɚ **-s** -z
cygnet ˈsɪg.nət, -nɪt **-s** -s
Cygnus ˈsɪg.nəs
cylinder ˈsɪl.ɪn.dər, -ən- (US) -dɚ **-s** -z
cylindric səˈlɪn.drɪk, sɪ- **-al** -əl **-ally** -əl.i, -li
cylindriform səˈlɪn.drɪ.fɔːm, sɪ- (US) -drɪ.fɔːrm, -drə-
cylindroid ˈsɪl.ɪn.drɔɪd, səˈlɪn-, sɪ- **-s** -z
cyli|x ˈsaɪ.lɪ|ks, ˈsɪl.ɪ|ks **-ces** -siːz
cy|ma ˈsaɪ|.mə **-mae** -miː
cymbal ˈsɪm.bəl **-s** -z
cymbal|o ˈsɪm.bə.l|əʊ (US) -l|oʊ **-o(e)s** -əʊz (US) -oʊz
Cymbeline ˈsɪm.bə.liːn, -bɪ-
cyme saɪm **-s** -z
Cymric ˈkɪm.rɪk, ˈkʌm- (US) ˈkɪm-
Cymru ˈkɪm.ri, ˈkʌm- (US) ˈkʌm-
Cymry ˈkɪm.ri, ˈkʌm- (US) ˈkɪm-
Cynewulf ˈkɪn.ɪ.wʊlf, ˈ-ə-
cynic ˈsɪn.ɪk **-s** -s
cynical ˈsɪn.ɪ.kəl **-ly** -i
cynicism ˈsɪn.ɪ.sɪ.zəm, ˈ-ə- **-s** -z
cynocephalic ˌsaɪ.nəʊ.sefˈæl.ɪk, -kefˈ- (US) -noʊ-

cynocephalous ˌsaɪ.nəʊˈsef.ə.ləs, -ˈkef- ⓊⓈ -noʊˈ-
Cynon ˈkɪn.ən, ˈkʌn-
cynosure ˈsaɪ.nə.sjʊəʳ, ˈsɪn.ə-, -ˌʃʊəʳ ⓊⓈ -ʃʊr **-s** -z
Cynthi|a ˈsɪnt.θi|.ə **-us** -əs
cyph|er ˈsaɪ.f|əʳ ⓊⓈ -f|ɚ **-ers** -əz ⓊⓈ -ɚz **-ering** -ᵊr.ɪŋ **-ered** -əd ⓊⓈ -ɚd
cy près ˌsiːˈpreɪ, ˌsaɪ-
cypress ˈsaɪ.prəs, -prɪs **-es** -ɪz
Cyprian ˈsɪp.ri.ən **-s** -z
Cypriot ˈsɪp.ri.ət **-s** -s
Cypriote ˈsɪp.ri.əʊt ⓊⓈ -oʊt **-s** -s
Cyprus ˈsaɪ.prəs
Cyrano ˈsɪr.ə.nəʊ; sɪˈrɑː-, sə- ⓊⓈ ˈsɪr.ə.noʊ **ˌCyrano de ˈBergerac**
Cyrenaica ˌsɪr.əˈneɪ.ɪ.kə, ˌsaɪə.rəˈ-, -ɪˈ-, -ˈnaɪ- ⓊⓈ ˌsaɪ.rəˈ-
Cyrene saɪəˈriː.ni ⓊⓈ saɪ-
Cyrenian saɪəˈriː.ni.ən ⓊⓈ saɪ-
Cyrenius saɪəˈriː.ni.əs ⓊⓈ saɪ-
Cyril ˈsɪr.ᵊl, -ɪl
Cyrillic səˈrɪl.ɪk, sɪ- ⓊⓈ sə-
Cyrus ˈsaɪə.rəs ⓊⓈ ˈsaɪ-
cyst sɪst **-s** -s
cystic ˈsɪs.tɪk **ˌcystic fibˈrosis**
cystitis sɪˈstaɪ.tɪs ⓊⓈ -t̬ɪs
cystoid ˈsɪs.tɔɪd
Cythera sɪˈθɪə.rə, sə- ⓊⓈ -ˈθɪr.ə
cyto- ˈsaɪ.təʊ-, saɪˈtɒ- ⓊⓈ ˈsaɪ.t̬oʊ-, -t̬ə-, saɪˈtɑː-
Note: Prefix. This may carry primary or secondary stress on the initial syllable, e.g. **cytoplasm** /ˈsaɪ.tə.plæz.ᵊm ⓊⓈ ˈsaɪ.t̬ə- / or on the second syllable, e.g. **cytology** /saɪˈtɒl.ə.dʒi ⓊⓈ saɪˈtɑːl- /.
cytogenetics ˌsaɪ.təʊ.dʒəˈnet.ɪks, -dʒenˈet-, -dʒɪˈnet- ⓊⓈ ˌsaɪ.t̬oʊ.dʒəˈnet̬-
cytology saɪˈtɒl.ə.dʒi ⓊⓈ -ˈtɑː.lə-
cytoplasm ˈsaɪ.təʊ.plæz.ᵊm ⓊⓈ -t̬ə- **-s** -z
cytoplasmic ˌsaɪ.təʊˈplæz.mɪk ⓊⓈ -t̬əˈ-
czar (**C**) zɑːʳ, tsɑːʳ ⓊⓈ zɑːr, tsɑːr **-s** -z
czardas ˈtʃɑː.dæʃ, ˈzɑː.dæs, -dəs ⓊⓈ ˈtʃɑːr.dɑːʃ, -dæʃ **-es** -ɪz
czarevitch (**C**) ˈzɑː.rə.vɪtʃ, -rɪ- ⓊⓈ ˈzɑːr.ə-, ˈtsɑːr- **-es** -ɪz
czarevna (**C**) zɑːˈrev.nə, tsɑː- **-s** -z
czarina zɑːˈriː.nə, tsɑː- **-s** -z
czarist ˈzɑː.rɪst, ˈtsɑː- ⓊⓈ ˈzɑːr.ɪst, ˈtsɑːr- **-s** -s
Czech tʃek **-s** -s
Czechoslovak ˌtʃek.əʊˈsləʊ.væk ⓊⓈ -oʊˈsloʊ.vɑːk, -væk **-s** -s
Czechoslovaki|a ˌtʃek.əʊ.sləʊˈvæk.i|.ə, -ˈvɑː.ki- ⓊⓈ -oʊ.sloʊˈvɑː.ki-, -ˈvæk.i- **-an** -ən
Czerny ˈtʃɜː.ni, ˈzɜː-, ˈtʃeə- ⓊⓈ ˈtʃer-

D

d (D) diː **-'s** -z
d' (*from* **do**) də, d
Note: See also **d'you.**
'd (*from* **had, would**) d
DA ˌdiːˈeɪ **-s** -z
dab dæb **-s** -z **-bing** -ɪŋ **-bed** -d **-ber/s** -əʳ/z (US) -ɚ/z ˌ**dab** ˈ**hand**
dabbl|e ˈdæb.l̩ **-es** -z **-ing** -ɪŋ, ˈdæb.lɪŋ **-ed** -d **-er/s** -əʳ/z, ˈdæb.ləʳ/z (US) -ɚ/z
dabchick ˈdæb.tʃɪk **-s** -s
da capo dɑːˈkɑː.pəʊ, də- (US) -poʊ
Dacca ˈdæk.ə (US) ˈdæk.ə, ˈdɑː.kə
dace deɪs
dacha ˈdætʃ.ə (US) ˈdɑː.tʃə **-s** -z
Dachau *as if German:* ˈdæx.aʊ, ˈdæk- (US) ˈdɑː.kaʊ
dachshund ˈdæk.sᵊnd, ˈdæʃ.ᵊnd, -hʊnd, -hʊnt (US) ˈdɑːks.hʊnd, ˈdɑːk.sənd **-s** -z
Daci|a ˈdeɪ.si|.ə, -ʃi-, ˈ-ʃ|ə (US) ˈ-ʃ|ə **-an/s** -ən/z
dacoit dəˈkɔɪt **-s** -s
Dacre ˈdeɪ.kəʳ (US) -kɚ **-s** -z
Dacron® ˈdæk.rɒn, ˈdeɪ.krɒn (US) ˈdeɪ.krɑːn, ˈdæk.rɑːn
dactyl ˈdæk.tɪl, -tᵊl **-s** -z
dactylic dækˈtɪl.ɪk
dactylogram dækˈtɪl.əʊ.græm; ˈdæk.tɪ.ləʊ-, -tᵊl.əʊ- (US) dækˈtɪl.ə- **-s** -z
dactylography ˌdæk.tɪˈlɒg.rə.fi (US) -təˈlɑː.grə-
dad (D) dæd **-s** -z
Dada ˈdɑː.dɑː, -də **-ism** -ɪ.zᵊm **-ist/s** -ɪst/s
dadaistic (D) ˌdɑː.dɑːˈɪs.tɪk
Daddies® ˈdæd.iz
dadd|y ˈdæd|.i **-ies** -iz
daddy longlegs ˌdæd.iˈlɒŋ.legz (US) -ˈlɑːŋ-, -ˈlɔːŋ-
dado ˈdeɪ.dəʊ (US) -doʊ **-s** -z
Daedalus ˈdiː.dᵊl.əs (US) ˈded.ᵊl-
daemon ˈdiː.mən, ˈdaɪ-, ˈdeɪ- **-s** -z
daemonic diːˈmɒn.ɪk, dɪ-, də- (US) -ˈmɑː.nɪk
D'Aeth deɪθ, deθ, diːθ
DAF® dæf
daffodil ˈdæf.ə.dɪl **-s** -z
daff|y ˈdæf|.i **-ier** -i.əʳ (US) -i.ɚ **-iest** -i.ɪst, -i.əst **-iness** -ɪ.nəs, -ɪ.nɪs
Daffyd ap Gwilym ˌdæv.ɪð.ɑːpˈgwɪl.ɪm, -ɪd- (US) ˌdɑː.vɪð-
daft dɑːft (US) dæft **-er** -əʳ (US) -ɚ **-est** -ɪst, -əst **-ly** -li **-ness** -nəs, -nɪs
Dafydd ˈdæv.ɪð, ˈdæf-
dag dæg **-s** -z **-ging** -ɪŋ **-ged** -d
da Gama dəˈgɑː.mə (US) -ˈgɑː-, -ˈgæm.ə
Dagenham ˈdæg.ᵊn.əm
Dagestan ˌdɑː.gɪˈstɑːn, -gəˈ-
dagga ˈdæx.ə, ˈdʌx-, ˈdɑː.xə (US) ˈdæg.ə, ˈdɑː.gə
dagger ˈdæg.əʳ (US) -ɚ **-s** -z **at** ˌ**daggers** ˈ**drawn** ; **look** ˈ**daggers at someone**
Daggett ˈdæg.ɪt
dagg|y ˈdæg|.i **-ier** -i.əʳ (US) -i.ɚ **-iest** -i.ɪst, -i.əst
Dagmar ˈdæg.mɑːʳ (US) -mɑːr
dago ˈdeɪ.gəʊ (US) -goʊ **-(e)s** -z
Dagobert ˈdæg.əʊ.bɜːt (US) -ə.bɜːrt
Dagon ˈdeɪ.gɒn, -gən (US) -gɑːn
Dagonet ˈdæg.ə.nət, -nɪt
daguerreotype dəˈger.əʊ.taɪp (US) ˈ-ə- **-s** -s
Dagwood ˈdæg.wʊd
dahl (D) dɑːl
dahlia (D) ˈdeɪ.li.ə, ˈ-ljə (US) ˈdæl.jə, ˈdɑːl-, ˈdeɪl- **-s** -z
Dahomey dəˈhəʊ.mi (US) -ˈhoʊ-
Dahrendorf ˈdɑː.rᵊn.dɔːf, ˈdær.ᵊn- (US) -dɔːrf
Dai daɪ
Daiches ˈdeɪ.*t*ʃɪz, -*t*ʃəz, -*t*ʃɪs, -*t*ʃəs
Daihatsu® ˌdaɪˈhæt.suː (US) -ˈhɑːt-
daikon ˈdaɪ.kɒn, -kən (US) -kən, -kɑːn **-s** -z
Dail, Dáil dɔɪl
Dáil Eireann ˌdɔɪlˈeə.rən (US) -ˈer.ən, -ˈeɪ.rən
dail|y ˈdeɪ.l|i **-ies** -iz
Daimler® ˈdeɪm.ləʳ (US) -lɚ **-s** -z
Daintree ˈdeɪn.triː, -tri
daint|y ˈdeɪn.t|i (US) -t̬|i **-ies** -iz **-ier** -i.əʳ (US) -i.ɚ **-iest** -i.ɪst, -i.əst **-ily** -ɪ.li, -ᵊl.i **-iness** -ɪ.nəs, -ɪ.nɪs
daiquiri (D) ˈdaɪ.kɪ.ri, ˈdæk.ɪ-, -ᵊr.i; daɪˈkɪə.ri, də- (US) ˈdæk.ɚ.i, ˈdaɪ.kɚ-
dair|y ˈdeə.r|i (US) ˈder|.i **-ies** -iz **-ying** -i.ɪŋ ˈ**dairy** ˌ**farm** ; ˈ**dairy** ˌ**products**
Dairylea® ˌdeə.riˈliː, ˈ--- (US) ˌder.iˈliː, ˈ---
dairymaid ˈdeə.riˌmeɪd (US) ˈder.i- **-s** -z
dairy|man ˈdeə.ri|.mən, -mæn (US) ˈder.i- **-men** -mən, -men
dais ˈdeɪ.ɪs, deɪs (US) ˈdeɪ.ɪs, ˈdaɪ- **-es** -ɪz
dais|y (D) ˈdeɪ.z|i **-ies** -iz ˈ**daisy** ˌ**chain** ; ˈ**daisy** ˌ**wheel**
Dakar ˈdæk.ɑːʳ, -əʳ (US) dəˈkɑːr; ˈdæk.ɑːr
Dakota dəˈkəʊ.tə (US) -ˈkoʊ.t̬ə **-s** -z
dal *food:* dɑːl
dal *in Italian phrases:* dæl, dɑːl (US) dɑːl
Dalai Lama ˌdæl.aɪˈlɑː.mə, ˌdɑː.laɪˈ- (US) ˌdɑː.laɪˈ- **-s** -z
dalasi dəˈlɑː.si **-s** -z
Dalbeattie dælˈbiː.ti, dəl- (US) -t̬i
Dalby ˈdɔːl.bi, ˈdɒl-, ˈdæl- (US) ˈdɑːl-, ˈdɔːl-, ˈdæl-
Daldy ˈdæl.di (US) ˈdɑːl.di
dale (D) deɪl **-s** -z
Dalek ˈdɑː.lek, -lɪk **-s** -s
dales|man ˈdeɪlz|.mən, -mæn **-men** -mən, -men **-woman** -ˌwʊm.ən **-women** -ˌwɪm.ɪn
Daley ˈdeɪ.li
Dalgety dælˈget.i, dəl- (US) -ˈget̬- *stress shift, see compound:* ˌ**Dalgety** ˈ**Bay**
Dalgleish, Dalglish dælˈgliːʃ, dəl-
Dalhousie dælˈhaʊ.zi, -ˈhuː-
Dali ˈdɑː.li
Dalkeith dælˈkiːθ
Dalkey ˈdɔː.ki, ˈdɔːl-
Dallas ˈdæl.əs
dallianc|e ˈdæl.i.ən*t*s **-es** -ɪz
Dalloway ˈdæl.ə.weɪ
dall|y ˈdæl|.i **-ies** -iz **-ying** -i.ɪŋ **-ied** -id **-ier/s** -i.əʳ/z (US) -i.ɚ/z
Dalmatia dælˈmeɪ.ʃə, -ʃi.ə
dalmatian (D) dælˈmeɪ.ʃᵊn, -ʃi.ən **-s** -z
Dalmeny dælˈmen.i, dəl-
Dalny ˈdæl.ni
Dalry dælˈraɪ, dəl-
Dalrymple dælˈrɪm.pl̩, dəl-; ˈdæl.rɪm- (US) ˈdæl.rɪm-
Note: The family name of the Earl of Stair is /dælˈrɪm-, dəl-/.
dal segno dælˈsen.jəʊ, dɑːl- (US) dɑːlˈseɪ.njoʊ, -ˈsen.joʊ
Dalston ˈdɔːl.stᵊn, ˈdɒl- (US) ˈdɔːl-, ˈdɑːl-
Dalton ˈdɔːl.tᵊn, ˈdɒl- (US) ˈdɔːl-, ˈdɑːl-
Dalton-in-Furness ˌdɔːl.tᵊn.ɪnˈfɜː.nɪs, ˌdɒl- (US) ˌdɔːl.tᵊn.ɪnˈfɜːr-, ˌdɑːl-
Daltonism ˈdɔːl.tᵊn.ɪ.zᵊm, ˈdɒl- (US) ˈdɔːl-, ˈdɑːl-
Daltr(e)y ˈdɔːl.tri, ˈdɒl- (US) ˈdɔːl-, ˈdɑːl-
Dalwhinnie dælˈ*h*wɪn.i, dəl-
Daly ˈdeɪ.li
Dalyell diːˈel
Dalzell diːˈel; ˈdæl.zel
Dalziel diːˈel; ˈdæl.ziːl, -zi.əl
Note: The form /diːˈel/ is chiefly used in Scotland.
dam dæm **-s** -z **-ming** -ɪŋ **-med** -d
damag|e ˈdæm.ɪdʒ **-es** -ɪz **-ing/ly** -ɪŋ/li **-ed** -d
damaging ˈdæm.ɪ.dʒɪŋ **-ly** -li
Damaraland dəˈmɑː.rə.lænd; ˈdæm.ə.rə- (US) dəˈmɑːr.ə-
Damart® ˈdæm.ɑːt, ˈdeɪ.mɑːt (US) ˈdæm.ɑːrt, ˈdeɪ.mɑːrt
damascene ˈdæm.ə.siːn **-s** -z
Damascus dəˈmæs.kəs, -ˈmɑː.skəs (US) -ˈmæs.kəs
damask ˈdæm.əsk **-s** -s
dame (D) deɪm **-s** -z
Damian, Damien ˈdeɪ.mi.ən
Damman ˈdæm.æn (US) dæmˈæn
dammit ˈdæm.ɪt

damn dæm **-s** -z **-ing** -ɪŋ **-ed** -d
damnab|le ˈdæm.nə.b|l̩ **-ly** -li **-leness** -l̩.nəs, -l̩.nɪs
damnation dæmˈneɪ.ʃᵊn **-s** -z
damnatory ˈdæm.nə.tᵊr.i, -tri (US) -tɔːr.i
damnedest ˈdæm.dɪst, -dəst
damni|fy ˈdæm.nɪ|.faɪ **-fies** -faɪz **-fying** -faɪ.ɪŋ **-fied** -faɪd
damnum sine injuria ˌdæm.nəmˌsiː.neɪ.ɪnˈdʒʊə.ri.ə (US) -ˈdʒʊr.i.ə
Damoclean ˌdæm.əˈkliː.ən
Damocles ˈdæm.ə.kliːz
Damon ˈdeɪ.mən
damosel, damozel ˌdæm.əʊˈzel (US) -əˈ-, -oʊˈ- **-s** -z
damp dæmp **-er** -əʳ (US) -ɚ **-est** -ɪst, -əst **-ly** -li **-ness** -nəs, -nɪs **-ish** -ɪʃ **-s** -s **-ing** -ɪŋ **-ed** -t ˈ**damp** ˌ**course** ; ˌ**damp** ˈ**squib**
dampen ˈdæm.pən **-s** -z **-ing** -ɪŋ, ˈdæmp.nɪŋ **-ed** -d
damper ˈdæm.pəʳ (US) -pɚ **-s** -z
Dampier ˈdæm.pi.əʳ, -pɪəʳ (US) -pi.ɚ
damp-proof ˈdæmp.pruːf **-s** -s **-ing** -ɪŋ **-ed** -d
damsel ˈdæm.zᵊl **-s** -z
damson ˈdæm.zᵊn **-s** -z
dan (**D**) dæn **-s** -z
Dana *first name in UK:* ˈdɑː.nə *in US:* ˈdeɪ.nə *in Canada:* ˈdæn.ə
Danaan ˈdæn.i.ən **-s** -z
Danaë ˈdæn.eɪ.iː, ˈ-i-
Danaides, Danäides dəˈneɪ.ɪ.diːz, dænˈeɪ-, ˈ-ə-
Dan-Air® ˌdænˈeəʳ (US) -ˈer
Danakil ˌdæn.əˈkiːl, -ˈkɪl (US) ˈdæn.ə.kɪl; dəˈnɑː.kiːl
Da Nang ˌdɑːˈnæŋ (US) dəˈnæŋ, dɑːˈnɑːŋ
Danbury ˈdæn.bᵊr.i, ˈdæm- (US) ˈdæn.ber-, -bɚ-
Danby ˈdæn.bi, ˈdæm- (US) ˈdæn-
danc|e dɑːnts (US) dænts **-es** -ɪz **-ing** -ɪŋ **-ed** -t **-er/s** -əʳ/z (US) -ɚ/z
Dance dɑːnts, dænts (US) dænts
Dancer ˈdɑːnt.səʳ (US) ˈdænt.sɚ
dandelion ˈdæn.dɪ.laɪən (US) -də-, -dɪ- **-s** -z
dandi|fy ˈdæn.dɪ|.faɪ (US) -də- **-fies** -faɪz **-fying** -faɪ.ɪŋ **-fied** -faɪd
dandl|e ˈdæn.dl̩ **-es** -z **-ing** -ɪŋ, ˈdænd.lɪŋ **-ed** -d
Dando ˈdæn.dəʊ (US) -doʊ
dandruff ˈdæn.drʌf (US) -drəf
dand|y ˈdæn.d|i **-ies** -iz **-yish** -i.ɪʃ **-yism** -i.ɪ.zᵊm
Dane deɪn **-s** -z
Danebury ˈdeɪn.bᵊr.i, ˈdeɪm- (US) ˈdeɪn.ber-, -bɚ-
danegeld ˈdeɪn.geld, ˈdeɪŋ- (US) ˈdeɪn-
Danelaw ˈdeɪn.lɔː (US) -lɑː, -lɔː
danger ˈdeɪn.dʒəʳ (US) -dʒɚ **-s** -z
Dangerfield ˈdeɪn.dʒə.fiːld (US) -dʒɚ-
dangerous ˈdeɪn.dʒᵊr.əs **-ly** -li **-ness** -nəs, -nɪs
dangerously ˈdeɪn.dʒᵊr.ə.sli
dangl|e (**D**) ˈdæŋ.gl̩ **-es** -z **-ing** -ɪŋ, ˈdæŋ.glɪŋ **-ed** -d **-er/s** -əʳ/z, ˈ-gləʳ/z (US) ˈ-gl̩.ɚ/z, ˈ-glɚ/z
dangly ˈdæŋ.gl̩.i, ˈ-gli
Daniel ˈdæn.jəl **-s** -z
Danielle ˌdæn.iˈel, dænˈjel
Danish ˈdeɪ.nɪʃ ˌ**Danish** ˈ**blue** ; ˌ**Danish** ˈ**pastry**
dank dæŋk **-er** -əʳ (US) -ɚ **-est** -ɪst, -əst **-ly** -li **-ness** -nəs, -nɪs
Danks dæŋks
Dankworth ˈdæŋk.wəθ, -wɜːθ (US) -wɚθ, -wɜːrθ
Dann dæn
d'Annunzio dænˈʊnt.si.əʊ (US) dɑːˈnʊnt.si.oʊ
Danny ˈdæn.i
danse(s) macabre(s) ˌdɑ̃ns.məˈkɑː.brə, -mækˈɑː- (US) ˌdɑːnts.məˈkɑː.brə
danseuse(s) ˌdɑ̃nˈsɜːz (US) ˌdɑːntˈsuːz, -ˈsʊz
Dansville ˈdænz.vɪl
Dante ˈdæn.ti, ˈdɑːn-, -teɪ (US) ˈdɑːn.teɪ
Dantesque dænˈtesk (US) dɑːn-
Danton ˈdæn.tɒn, -tən; *as if French:* dɑ̃nˈtɔ̃ŋ (US) dɑːnˈtɑːn, -toʊn; ˈ--, -tən
Danube ˈdæn.juːb
Danubian dænˈjuː.bi.ən, dəˈnjuː-
Danuta dəˈnuː.tə, dænˈuː- (US) dəˈnuː.t̬ə
Danvers ˈdæn.vəz (US) -vɚz
Danville ˈdæn.vɪl
Danzig ˈdænt.sɪg, -sɪk
daphne (**D**) ˈdæf.ni
Daphnis ˈdæf.nɪs
dapp|er (**D**) ˈdæp|.əʳ (US) -ɚ **-erest** -ᵊr.ɪst, -ᵊr.əst
dappl|e ˈdæp.l̩ **-es** -z **-ing** -ɪŋ, ˈ-lɪŋ **-ed** -d
dapple-grey ˌdæp.l̩ˈgreɪ
DAR ˌdiː.eɪˈɑːʳ (US) -ˈɑːr
Darbishire ˈdɑː.bi.ʃəʳ, -ˌʃɪəʳ (US) ˈdɑːr.bi.ʃɚ, -ˌʃɪr
Darby ˈdɑː.bi (US) ˈdɑːr- ˌ**Darby and** ˈ**Joan**
d'Arc dɑːk (US) dɑːrk
D'Arcy, Darcy ˈdɑː.si (US) ˈdɑːr-
Dardanelles ˌdɑː.dᵊnˈelz (US) ˌdɑːr-
Dardanus ˈdɑː.dᵊn.əs (US) ˈdɑːr-
dar|e (**D**) deəʳ (US) der **-es** -z **-ing** -ɪŋ **-ed** -d **durst** dɜːst (US) dɜːrst
daredevil ˈdeəˌdev.ᵊl (US) ˈder- **-s** -z
daren't deənt (US) dernt
Darent ˈdær.ᵊnt (US) ˈder-, ˈdær-
Darenth ˈdær.ənθ (US) ˈder-, ˈdær-
Dares ˈdeə.riːz (US) ˈder.iːz
daresay, dare say ˌdeəˈseɪ (US) ˌder-
Daresbury ˈdɑːz.bᵊr.i (US) ˈdɑːrz.ber-, -bɚ-
Dar es Salaam ˌdɑː.res.səˈlɑːm, -rɪs-, -rez-, -rɪz- (US) ˌdɑːr.es-
Darfield ˈdɑː.fiːld (US) ˈdɑːr-
Darien ˈdeə.ri.ən, ˈdær.i.ən (US) ˈder.i-, ˈdær-; ˌder.iˈen, ˌdær-
Darin ˈdær.ɪn (US) ˈder-, ˈdær-
daring ˈdeə.rɪŋ (US) ˈder.ɪŋ **-ly** -li
Dario ˈdær.i.əʊ (US) dɑːˈriː.oʊ
dariole ˈdær.i.əʊl (US) ˈder.i.oʊl, ˈdær- **-s** -z
Darius dəˈraɪ.əs, ˈdeə.ri-, ˈdær.i-, ˈdɑː.ri- (US) dəˈraɪ-; ˈder.i-, ˈdær-
Darjeeling dɑːˈdʒiː.lɪŋ (US) dɑːr-
dark dɑːk (US) dɑːrk **-er** -əʳ (US) -ɚ **-est** -ɪst, -əst **-ly** -li **-ness** -nəs, -nɪs ˈ**Dark** ˌ**Ages**; ˌ**dark** ˈ**glasses**; ˌ**dark** ˈ**horse**
darken ˈdɑː.kᵊn (US) ˈdɑːr- **-s** -z **-ing** -ɪŋ, ˈdɑːk.nɪŋ (US) ˈdɑːr.kᵊn.ɪŋ, ˈdɑːrk.nɪŋ **-ed** -d
dark|ie ˈdɑː.k|i (US) ˈdɑːr- **-ies** -iz
darkish ˈdɑː.kɪʃ (US) ˈdɑːr-
darkling ˈdɑː.klɪŋ (US) ˈdɑːr-
darkroom ˈdɑːk.rʊm, -ruːm (US) ˈdɑːrk.ruːm, -rʊm **-s** -z
darksome ˈdɑːk.səm (US) ˈdɑːrk-
dark|y ˈdɑː.k|i (US) ˈdɑːr- **-ies** -iz
Darlaston ˈdɑː.lə.stən (US) ˈdɑːr-
Darleen, Darlene ˈdɑː.liːn (US) dɑːrˈliːn
Darley ˈdɑː.li (US) ˈdɑːr-
darling (**D**) ˈdɑː.lɪŋ (US) ˈdɑːr- **-s** -z
Darlington ˈdɑː.lɪŋ.tən (US) ˈdɑːr-
Darlow ˈdɑː.ləʊ (US) ˈdɑːr.loʊ
Darmstadt ˈdɑːm.stæt *as if German:* -ʃtæt (US) ˈdɑːrm-
darn dɑːn (US) dɑːrn **-s** -z **-ing** -ɪŋ **-ed** -d **-er/s** -əʳ/z (US) -ɚ/z ˈ**darning** ˌ**needle**
darnation dɑːˈneɪ.ʃᵊn (US) dɑːr-
darnel ˈdɑː.nᵊl (US) ˈdɑːr-
Darnell dɑːˈnel (US) dɑːr-, ˈ--
Darney ˈdɑː.ni (US) ˈdɑːr-
Darnley ˈdɑːn.li (US) ˈdɑːrn-
Darracq ˈdær.ək, dærˈæk (US) ˈder-, ˈdær-
Darragh ˈdær.ə, -əx (US) ˈder.ə, ˈdær-
Darreil ˈdær.ᵊl (US) ˈder-, ˈdær-
Darren, Darron ˈdær.ᵊn (US) ˈder-, ˈdær-
Darrow ˈdær.əʊ (US) ˈder.oʊ, ˈdær-
Darryl ˈdær.ᵊl, -ɪl (US) ˈder-, ˈdær-
dart (**D**) dɑːt (US) dɑːrt **-s** -s **-ing** -ɪŋ (US) ˈdɑːr.t̬ɪŋ **-ed** -ɪd (US) ˈdɑːr.t̬ɪd
D'Artagnan dɑːˈtæn.jən, -jɑ̃ŋ (US) dɑːrˈtæn.jən; ˌdɑːr.tᵊnˈjɑːn
dartboard ˈdɑːt.bɔːd (US) ˈdɑːrt.bɔːrd **-s** -z
darter ˈdɑː.təʳ (US) ˈdɑːr.t̬ɚ **-s** -z
Dartford ˈdɑːt.fəd (US) ˈdɑːrt.fɚd
Darth Vader ˌdɑːθˈveɪ.dəʳ (US) ˌdɑːrθˈveɪ.dɚ

Dartie 'dɑː.ti (US) 'dɑːr.t̬i
Dartle 'dɑː.tl̩ (US) 'dɑːr.t̬l̩
Dartmoor 'dɑːt.mɔːʳ, -mʊəʳ (US) 'dɑːrt.mʊr, -mɔːr
Dartmouth 'dɑːt.məθ (US) 'dɑːrt-
Darton 'dɑː.tᵊn (US) 'dɑːr-
darts dɑːts (US) dɑːrts
Darwen 'dɑː.wɪn (US) 'dɑːr-
Darwin 'dɑː.wɪn (US) 'dɑːr- **-ism** -ɪ.zᵊm
Darwinian dɑː'wɪn.i.ən (US) dɑːr-
Daryl(l) 'dær.ᵊl, -ɪl (US) 'der-, 'dær-
Dasent 'deɪ.sᵊnt
dash (D) dæʃ **-es** -ɪz **-ing** -ɪŋ **-ed** -t **-er/s** -əʳ/z (US) -ɚ/z
dashboard 'dæʃ.bɔːd (US) -bɔːrd **-s** -z
dashing 'dæʃ.ɪŋ **-ly** -li
Dashwood 'dæʃ.wʊd
dastard 'dæs.təd, 'dɑː.stəd (US) 'dæs.tɚd **-s** -z **-ly** -li **-liness** -lɪ.nəs, -nɪs
DAT dæt; ˌdiː.eɪ'tiː
data 'deɪ.tə, 'dɑː- (US) 'deɪ.t̬ə, 'dæt̬.ə, 'dɑː.t̬ə
databank 'deɪ.tə.bæŋk, 'dɑː- (US) 'deɪ.t̬ə-, 'dæt̬.ə-, 'dɑː.t̬ə- **-s** -s
databas|e 'deɪ.tə.beɪs, 'dɑː- (US) 'deɪ.t̬ə-, 'dæt̬.ə-, 'dɑː.t̬ə- **-es** -ɪz
databus 'deɪ.tə.bʌs, 'dɑː- (US) 'deɪ.t̬ə-, 'dæt̬.ə-, 'dɑː.t̬ə- **-es** -ɪz
datafile 'deɪ.tə.faɪl, 'dɑː- (US) 'deɪ.t̬ə-, 'dæt̬.ə-, 'dɑː.t̬ə- **-s** -z
dataflow 'deɪ.tə.fləʊ, 'dɑː- (US) 'deɪ.t̬ə.floʊ, 'dæt̬.ə-, 'dɑː.t̬ə-
dataglove 'deɪ.tə.glʌv, 'dɑː- (US) 'deɪ.t̬ə-, 'dæt̬.ə- (US) 'dɑː.t̬ə- **-s** -z
Datapost® 'deɪ.tə.pəʊst, 'dɑː- (US) -t̬ə.poʊst
Datchery 'dætʃ.ᵊr.i
Datchet 'dætʃ.ɪt
dat|e deɪt **-es** -s **-ing** -ɪŋ (US) 'deɪ.t̬ɪŋ **-ed** -ɪd (US) 'deɪ.t̬ɪd **'dating ˌagency**
dated 'deɪ.tɪd (US) -t̬ɪd
Datel® 'deɪ.tel
Dateline® 'deɪt.laɪn **-s** -z
date-stamp 'deɪt.stæmp **-s** -s **-ing** -ɪŋ **-ed** -t
datival də'taɪ.vᵊl, deɪ-
dative 'deɪ.tɪv (US) -t̬ɪv **-s** -z
Datsun® 'dæt.sᵊn (US) 'dɑːt-, 'dæt-
dat|um 'deɪ.t|əm, 'dɑː- (US) 'deɪ.t̬|əm, 'dæt̬|.əm, 'dɑː.t̬|əm **-a** -ə
daub dɔːb (US) dɑːb, dɔːb **-s** -z **-ing** -ɪŋ **-ed** -d **-er/s** -əʳ/z (US) -ɚ/z
daube dəʊb (US) doʊb **-s** -z
Daubeney 'dɔː.bᵊn.i (US) 'dɑː-, 'dɔː-
Daudet 'dəʊ.deɪ (US) doʊ'deɪ
Daugavpils 'daʊ.gæf.pɪls (US) 'doʊ.gʌv-, 'daʊ-, -gʌf-, -gɑːf-, -pɪlz, -piːlz
daughter 'dɔː.təʳ (US) 'dɑː.t̬ɚ, 'dɔː- **-s** -z
daughter-in-law 'dɔː.təʳ.ɪn.lɔː (US) 'dɑː.t̬ɚ.ɪn.lɑː, 'dɔː-, -lɔː **daughters-in-law** 'dɔː.təz.ɪn.lɔː (US) 'dɑː.t̬ɚz.ɪn.lɑː, 'dɔː-, -lɔː
daughterl|y 'dɔː.tə.l|i (US) 'dɑː.t̬ɚ-, 'dɔː- **-iness** -ɪ.nəs, -ɪ.nɪs
Daun dɔːn (US) dɑːn, dɔːn
daunt (D) dɔːnt (US) dɑːnt, dɔːnt **-s** -s **-ing** -ɪŋ (US) 'dɑːn.t̬ɪŋ, 'dɔːn- **-ed** -ɪd (US) 'dɑːn.t̬ɪd, 'dɔːn-
dauntless 'dɔːnt.ləs, -lɪs (US) 'dɑːnt-, 'dɔːnt **-ly** -li **-ness** -nəs, -nɪs
dauphin (D) 'dɔː.fɪn, 'dəʊ-, -fæ̃ (US) 'dɑː.fɪn, 'dɔː-; doʊ'fæn **-s** -z
Dauphiné 'dɔː.fɪ.neɪ, 'dəʊ-, --'- (US) ˌdoʊ.fiː'neɪ
dauphine (D) 'dɔː.fiːn, 'dəʊ-, -fɪn (US) dɑː'fiːn, dɔː-, doʊ- **-s** -z
Davao dæv'ɑː.əʊ, də'vɑː- (US) dɑː'vaʊ
Dave deɪv
Davenant, D'Avenant 'dæv.ᵊn.ənt, -ɪ.nənt
davenport (D) 'dæv.ᵊn.pɔːt, -ᵊm- (US) -ᵊn.pɔːrt **-s** -s
Daventry 'dæv.ᵊn.tri *old-fashioned local pronunciation:* 'deɪn.tri
Davey 'deɪ.vi
David 'deɪ.vɪd **-s** -z
Davidge 'dæv.ɪdʒ
Davidson 'deɪ.vɪd.sᵊn
Davie 'deɪ.vi
Davies 'deɪ.vɪs (US) -viːz
Davina də'viː.nə
da Vinci də'vɪn.*t*ʃi
Davis 'deɪ.vɪs
Davison 'deɪ.vɪ.sᵊn
davit 'dæv.ɪt, 'deɪ.vɪt **-s** -s
Davos dæv'əʊs, dɑː'vəʊs, -'vɒs; 'dɑː.vɒs, -vəʊs (US) dɑː'voʊs
dav|y (D) 'deɪ.v|i **-ies** -iz **'davy ˌlamp** ; **ˌDavy ˌJones's 'locker**
daw (D) dɔː (US) dɑː, dɔː **-s** -z
dawdl|e 'dɔː.dl̩ (US) 'dɑː-, 'dɔː- **-es** -z **-ing** -ɪŋ, 'dɔːd.lɪŋ (US) 'dɑːd-, 'dɔːd- **-ed** -d **-er/s** -əʳ/z, 'dɔːd.ləʳ/z (US) 'dɑː.dl̩.ɚ/z, 'dɔː- (US) 'dɑːd.lɚ/z, 'dɔːd-
Dawe dɔː (US) dɑː, dɔː **-s** -z
Dawkes dɔːks (US) dɑːks, dɔːks
Dawkins 'dɔː.kɪnz (US) 'dɑː-, 'dɔː-
Dawley 'dɔː.li (US) 'dɑː-, 'dɔː-
Dawlish 'dɔː.lɪʃ (US) 'dɑː-, 'dɔː-
dawn (D) dɔːn (US) dɑːn, dɔːn **-s** -z **-ing** -ɪŋ **-ed** -d
Dawson 'dɔː.sᵊn (US) 'dɑː-, 'dɔː-
day (D) deɪ **-s** -z **'day ˌboy** ; **'day ˌcamp** ; **'day ˌgirl** ; **'day ˌjob** ; **'day ˌlily** ; **'day ˌnursery** ; **ˌday 'out** ; **'day ˌroom** ; **'day ˌschool** ; **at the ˌend of the 'day** ; **ˌcall it a 'day**
daybreak 'deɪ.breɪk **-s** -s
daycare 'deɪ.keəʳ (US) -ker
day|dream 'deɪ|.driːm **-dreams** -driːmz **-dreaming** -ˌdriː.mɪŋ **-dreamed** -drempt, -driːmd **-dreamt** -drempt **-dreamer/s** -ˌdriː.məʳ/z (US) -ˌdriː.mɚ/z
Day-Glo®, dayglo 'deɪ.gləʊ (US) -gloʊ
Daylesford 'deɪlz.fəd, 'deɪls- (US) -fɚd
Day-Lewis ˌdeɪ'luː.ɪs
daylight 'deɪ.laɪt **-s** -s **ˌdaylight 'robbery** ; **ˌdaylight 'saving** ; **'daylight ˌtime** ; **ˌbeat the living 'daylights out of sb**
dayspring 'deɪ.sprɪŋ
daystar 'deɪ.stɑːʳ (US) -stɑːr **-s** -z
daytime 'deɪ.taɪm
day-to-day ˌdeɪ.tə'deɪ (US) -t̬ə'-
Dayton 'deɪ.tᵊn
Daytona deɪ'təʊ.nə (US) -'toʊ- **Dayˌtona 'Beach**
daywork 'deɪ.wɜːk (US) -wɜːrk
Daz® dæz
daz|e deɪz **-es** -ɪz **-ing** -ɪŋ **-ed** -d **-edly** -əd.li, -ɪd.li
dazzl|e 'dæz.l̩ **-es** -z **-ing/ly** -ɪŋ/li, 'dæz.lɪŋ/li **-ed** -d **-er/s** -əʳ/z, '-ləʳ/z (US) '-l̩.ɚ/z, '-lɚ/z
DBMS ˌdiː.biː.em'es
DC ˌdiː'siː
D-Day 'diː.deɪ
DDT ˌdiː.diː'tiː
de- diː-, dɪ-, də-
Note: Prefix. In verbs containing **de-** where the stem is free, usually a noun, it is normally pronounced /ˌdiː-/, e.g. **debag** /ˌdiː'bæg/, **declutch** /ˌdiː'klʌtʃ/. Attached to bound stems the pronunciation is normally /dɪ-/ or /də-/, e.g . **debilitate** /dɪ'bɪl.ɪ.teɪt/, **demand** /dɪ'mɑːnd (US) -mænd/. There are exceptions; see individual entries.
de *in French names:* də, dɪ, di
deacon (D) 'diː.kən **-s** -z
deaconess ˌdiː.kə'nes; '---, -nɪs (US) 'diː.kᵊn.əs **-es** -ɪz
deacon|hood 'diː.kən|.hʊd **-ship/s** -ʃɪp/s
deaconr|y 'diː.kən.r|i **-ies** -iz
deacti|vate ˌdi'æk.tɪ|.veɪt, -tə- **-vates** -veɪts **-vating** -veɪ.tɪŋ (US) -veɪ.t̬ɪŋ **-vated** -veɪ.tɪd (US) -veɪ.t̬ɪd
deactivation diˌæk.tɪ'veɪ.ʃᵊn, ˌdiː.æk-, -tə'- (US) diˌæk-
dead ded **-ness** -nəs, -nɪs **ˌdead 'end** ; **ˌdead 'heat**; **ˌdead 'letter**; **ˌdead or a'live**; **ˌdead 'reckoning**; **ˌdead 'ringer**; **ˌDead 'Sea**; **ˌdead 'set**; **as ˌdead as a 'door-nail**
dead-and-alive ˌded.ᵊn*d*.ə'laɪv
deadbeat (*n.*) 'ded.biːt, 'deb- (US) 'ded- **-s** -s
dead beat (*adj.*) ˌded'biːt, ˌdeb- (US) ˌded- *stress shift:* ˌdead beat 'worker

deadbolt ˈded.bəʊlt, ˈdeb- Ⓤⓢ ˈded.boʊlt **-s** -s
deaden ˈded.ᵊn **-s** -z **-ing** -ɪŋ **-ed** -d
dead-end ˌdedˈend *stress shift:* ˌdead-end ˈstreet
deadeye (D) ˈded.aɪ **-s** -z
deadhead ˈded.hed, -ˈ- **-s** -z
deadline ˈded.laɪn **-s** -z
deadlock ˈded.lɒk Ⓤⓢ -lɑːk **-s** -s **-ed** -t
deadl|y ˈded.l|i **-ier** -i.əʳ Ⓤⓢ -i.ɚ **-iest** -i.ɪst, -i.əst **-iness** -ɪ.nəs, -ɪ.nɪs ˌ**deadly** ˈ**nightshade**
deadnettle ˈded.net.l̩, ˌ-ˈ-- Ⓤⓢ ˌdedˈnet̬-, ˈ-ˌ-- **-s** -z
deadpan ˈded.pæn, ˈdeb-, ˌ-ˈ- Ⓤⓢ ˈded.pæn
deadweight ˌdedˈweɪt, ˈ-- **-s** -s
deadwood ˈded.wʊd, ˌ-ˈ-
deaf def **-er** -əʳ Ⓤⓢ -ɚ **-est** -ɪst, -əst **-ly** -li **-ness** -nəs, -nɪs ˌ**fall on** ˌ**deaf** ˈ**ears**
deaf-aid ˈdef.eɪd **-s** -z
deaf-and-dumb ˌdef.ᵊndˈdʌm
deafen ˈdef.ᵊn **-s** -z **-ing/ly** -ɪŋ/li, ˈ-nɪŋ/li **-ed** -d
deaf-mute ˌdefˈmjuːt, ˈ-- **-s** -s
Deakin ˈdiː.kɪn
deal (D) diːl **-s** -z **-ing** -ɪŋ **dealt** delt
dealer ˈdiː.ləʳ Ⓤⓢ -lɚ **-s** -z
dealership ˈdiː.lə.ʃɪp Ⓤⓢ -lɚ- **-s** -s
dealing ˈdiː.lɪŋ **-s** -z
dealt (*from* **deal**) delt
Dealtry *surname:* ˈdɔːl.tri, ˈdɪəl- Ⓤⓢ ˈdɑːl-, ˈdɔːl-, ˈdiːl- *road in London:* ˈdel.tri
deami|nate diˈæm.ɪ.neɪt, ˌdiː-, ˈ-ə- Ⓤⓢ ˈ-ə- **-nates** -neɪts **-nating** -neɪ.tɪŋ Ⓤⓢ -neɪ.t̬ɪŋ **-nated** -neɪ.tɪd Ⓤⓢ -neɪ.t̬ɪd
deamination diˌæm.ɪˈneɪ.ʃᵊn, ˌdiː-, -əˈ- Ⓤⓢ -əˈ-
dean diːn **-s** -z **-ship/s** -ʃɪp/s
Dean(e) diːn
deaner|y ˈdiː.nᵊr|.i **-ies** -iz
Deanna diˈæn.ə; ˈdiː.nə Ⓤⓢ diˈæn.ə
Deans diːnz
dear (D) dɪəʳ Ⓤⓢ dɪr **-s** -z **-er** -əʳ Ⓤⓢ -ɚ **-est** -ɪst, -əst **-ly** -li **-ness** -nəs, -nɪs
dear|ie ˈdɪə.r|i Ⓤⓢ ˈdɪr|.i **-ies** -iz
Dearne dɜːn Ⓤⓢ dɜːrn
dearth (D) dɜːθ Ⓤⓢ dɜːrθ **-s** -s
dear|y ˈdɪə.r|i Ⓤⓢ ˈdɪr|.i **-ies** -iz
death deθ **-s** -s ˈ**death** ˌ**duty**; ˈ**death** ˌ**mask**; ˈ**death** ˌ**penalty**; ˈ**death** ˌ**rate**; ˈ**death** ˌ**rattle**; ˌ**death** ˈ**row**; ˈ**death** ˌ**toll**; ˈ**death** ˌ**trap**; ˈ**death** ˌ**warrant**; ˌ**Death** ˈ**Valley**; ˈ**death** ˌ**wish**; **like** ˌ**death warmed** ˈ**up**; **like** ˌ**grim** ˈ**death**
Death *surname:* deɪθ, deθ, diːθ; diːˈæθ, deɪ-, -ˈɑːθ
deathbed ˈdeθ.bed **-s** -z
deathblow ˈdeθ.bləʊ Ⓤⓢ -bloʊ **-s** -z
deathless ˈdeθ.ləs, -lɪs
deathlike ˈdeθ.laɪk
deathl|y ˈdeθ.l|i **-ier** -i.əʳ Ⓤⓢ -i.ɚ **-iest** -i.ɪst, -i.əst **-iness** -ɪ.nəs, -ɪ.nɪs
death's-head ˈdeθs.hed **-s** -z
deathwatch ˈdeθ.wɒtʃ Ⓤⓢ -wɑːtʃ, -wɔːtʃ ˌ**deathwatch** ˈ**beetle**
Deauville ˈdəʊ.vɪl, -viːl Ⓤⓢ ˈdoʊ-
Deayton ˈdiː.tᵊn
deb deb **-s** -z
débâcle deɪˈbɑː.kl̩, də-, debˈɑː-, dɪˈbɑː-; ˈdeɪ.bɑː- Ⓤⓢ dɪˈbɑː-, də-, deɪ-, -ˈbæk.l̩ **-s** -z
debag ˌdiːˈbæg **-s** -z **-ging** -ɪŋ **-ged** -d
debar ˌdiːˈbɑːʳ, dɪ- Ⓤⓢ -ˈbɑːr **-s** -z **-ring** -ɪŋ **-red** -d
debark ˌdiːˈbɑːk, dɪ- Ⓤⓢ -ˈbɑːrk **-s** -s **-ing** -ɪŋ **-ed** -t
debarkation ˌdiː.bɑːˈkeɪ.ʃᵊn Ⓤⓢ -bɑːrˈ- **-s** -z
debas|e dɪˈbeɪs **-es** -ɪz **-ing/ly** -ɪŋ/li **-ed** -t **-ement** -mənt
debatab|le dɪˈbeɪ.tə.b|l̩, də- Ⓤⓢ dɪˈbeɪ.t̬ə- **-ly** -li
de|bate dɪ|ˈbeɪt, də- Ⓤⓢ dɪ- **-bates** -ˈbeɪts **-bating** -ˈbeɪ.tɪŋ Ⓤⓢ -ˈbeɪ.t̬ɪŋ **-bated** -ˈbeɪ.tɪd Ⓤⓢ -ˈbeɪ.t̬ɪd **-bater/s** -ˈbeɪ.təʳ/z Ⓤⓢ -ˈbeɪ.t̬ɚ/z
debauch dɪˈbɔːtʃ Ⓤⓢ -ˈbɑːtʃ, -ˈbɔːtʃ **-es** -ɪz **-ing** -ɪŋ **-ed** -t **-er/s** -əʳ/z Ⓤⓢ -ɚ/z
debauchee ˌdeb.ɔːˈtʃiː, -ˈʃiː, ˌdɪb-; dɪˌbɔː-, də- Ⓤⓢ ˌdeb.ɑːˈʃiː, -ɔːˈ-; dɪˌbɑːˈtʃiː, -ˌbɔːˈ- **-s** -z
debaucher|y dɪˈbɔː.tʃᵊr|.i, dəˈ- Ⓤⓢ dɪˈbɑː-, -ˈbɔː- **-ies** -iz
de Beauvoir dəˈbəʊ.vwɑːʳ Ⓤⓢ -ˌboʊˈvwɑːr
Deben ˈdiː.bᵊn
de bene esse ˌdeɪˌben.iˈes.i, dəˌbiː.niːˈes.iː
Debenham ˈdeb.ᵊn.əm Ⓤⓢ -hæm **-'s** -z
debenture dɪˈben.tʃəʳ, də- Ⓤⓢ dɪˈbent.ʃɚ **-s** -z
debili|tate dɪˈbɪl.ɪ|.teɪt, də-, ˈ-ə- Ⓤⓢ dɪ- **-tates** -teɪts **-tating** -teɪ.tɪŋ Ⓤⓢ -teɪ.t̬ɪŋ **-tated** -teɪ.tɪd Ⓤⓢ -teɪ.t̬ɪd
debilitation dɪˌbɪl.ɪˈteɪ.ʃᵊn, də-, -əˈ- Ⓤⓢ dɪ-
debility dɪˈbɪl.ə.ti, də-, -ɪ.ti Ⓤⓢ dɪˈbɪl.ə.t̬i
deb|it ˈdeb|.ɪt **-its** -ɪts **-iting** -ɪ.tɪŋ Ⓤⓢ -ɪ.t̬ɪŋ **-ited** -ɪ.tɪd Ⓤⓢ -ɪ.t̬ɪd
Debnam ˈdeb.nəm
debonair ˌdeb.əˈneəʳ Ⓤⓢ -ˈner **-ly** -li **-ness** -nəs, -nɪs
de Bono dəˈbəʊ.nəʊ Ⓤⓢ -ˈboʊ.noʊ
Deborah ˈdeb.ᵊr.ə, ˈ-rə
debouch dɪˈbaʊtʃ, ˌdiː-, -buːʃ **-es** -ɪz **-ing** -ɪŋ **-ed** -t **-ment** -mənt
Debra ˈdeb.rə
Debrecen ˈdeb.rət.sᵊn Ⓤⓢ ˌdeb.rətˈsen, ˈ---
Debrett dəˈbret, dɪ- **-'s** -s
debridement, débridement dɪˈbriːd.mənt, ˌdiː-, deɪ-; *as if French:* -ˌbriːdˈmɑ̃ŋ Ⓤⓢ dɪˈbriːd.mənt, deɪ-, -ˈbriːd.mɑ̃ŋ
debrief ˌdiːˈbriːf **-s** -s **-ing** -ɪŋ **-ed** -t
debris ˈdeɪ.briː, ˈdeb.riː Ⓤⓢ dəˈbriː; ˈdeɪ.briː
debt det **-s** -s
debtor ˈdet.əʳ Ⓤⓢ ˈdet̬.ɚ **-s** -z
debug ˌdiːˈbʌg **-s** -z **-ging** -ɪŋ **-ged** -d
debunk ˌdiːˈbʌŋk **-s** -s **-ing** -ɪŋ **-ed** -t
De Burgh dəˈbɜːg Ⓤⓢ -ˈbɜːrg
Debussy dəˈbuː.siː, -ˈbjuː- Ⓤⓢ ˈdeɪ.bjuː.si, ˌdeɪ.bjuːˈsiː, dəˈbjuː.si
Note: US street names are always /də-/.
début ˈdeɪ.bjuː, -buː; ˈdeb.juː Ⓤⓢ deɪˈbjuː, ˈ-- **-s** -z
débutant ˈdeb.jʊ.tɑ̃ːŋ, ˈdeɪ.buː- Ⓤⓢ ˈdeb.juː.tɑːnt, ˌ--ˈ- **-s** -z
débutante ˈdeb.juː.tɑ̃ːŋt, ˈdeɪ.bjuː- Ⓤⓢ ˈdeb.juː.tɑːnt, ˌ--ˈ- **-s** -s
Dec. (*abbrev. for* **December**) dɪˈsem.bəʳ, də- Ⓤⓢ dɪˈsem.bɚ
deca- dek.ə-
Note: Prefix. Normally carries primary or secondary stress on the first syllable, e.g. **decagon** /ˈdek.ə.gən Ⓤⓢ -gɑːn/, **decahedron** /ˌdek.əˈhiː.drən/.
decachord ˈdek.ə.kɔːd Ⓤⓢ -kɔːrd **-s** -z
decade *ten years:* ˈdek.eɪd; dekˈeɪd, dɪˈkeɪd **-s** -z *division of the rosary:* ˈdek.əd
decaden|ce ˈdek.ə.dᵊnt|s Ⓤⓢ ˈdek.ə-; dɪˈkeɪ- **-cy** -si
decadent ˈdek.ə.dᵊnt Ⓤⓢ ˈdek.ə-; dɪˈkeɪ- **-ly** -li
decaf, decaff ˈdiː.kæf
decaffei|nate dɪˈkæf.ɪ|.neɪt, ˌdiː-, ˈ-ə- **-nates** -neɪts **-nating** -neɪ.tɪŋ Ⓤⓢ -neɪ.t̬ɪŋ **-nated** -neɪ.tɪd Ⓤⓢ -neɪ.t̬ɪd
decagon ˈdek.ə.gən Ⓤⓢ -gɑːn **-s** -z
decagram, decagramme ˈdek.ə.græm **-s** -z
decahedr|on ˌdek.əˈhiː.dr|ən, -ˈhed.r|ən Ⓤⓢ -ˈhiː.dr|ən **-ons** -ənz **-a** -ə **-al** -ᵊl
decal ˈdiː.kæl; dɪˈkæl **-s** -z
decalcification ˌdiːˌkæl.sɪ.fɪˈkeɪ.ʃᵊn, -sə-
decalci|fy ˌdiːˈkæl.sɪ|.faɪ, -sə- **-fies** -faɪz **-fying** -faɪ.ɪŋ **-fied** -faɪd
decalitre, decaliter ˈdek.əˌliː.təʳ Ⓤⓢ -t̬ɚ **-s** -z
Decalogue ˈdek.ə.lɒg Ⓤⓢ -lɑːg, -lɔːg **-s** -z

Decameron dɪ'kæm.ᵊr.ᵊn, dek'æm-, də'kæm-
decametre, decameter 'dek.əˌmiː.təʳ (US) -t̬ɚ -s -z
decamp ˌdiː'kæmp, dɪ- -s -s -ing -ɪŋ -ed -t
decanal dɪ'keɪ.nᵊl, dek'eɪ-, də'keɪ-; 'dek.ᵊn.ᵊl
decani dɪ'keɪ.naɪ, dek'eɪ-
de|cant dɪ|'kænt, ˌdiː- -cants -'kænts -canting -'kæn.tɪŋ (US) -'kæn.t̬ɪŋ -canted -'kæn.tɪd (US) -'kæn.t̬ɪd
decantation ˌdiː.kæn'teɪ.ʃᵊn -s -z
decanter dɪ'kæn.təʳ, də- (US) dɪ'kæn.t̬ɚ -s -z
decapi|tate dɪ'kæp.ɪ|.teɪt, ˌdiː-, 'ə- -tates -teɪts -tating -teɪ.tɪŋ (US) -teɪ.t̬ɪŋ -tated -teɪ.tɪd (US) -teɪ.t̬ɪd
decapitation dɪˌkæp.ɪ'teɪ.ʃᵊn, ˌdiː-, -ə'- -s -z
decapod 'dek.ə.pɒd (US) -pɑːd -s -z
Decapolis dek'æp.ə.lɪs, dɪ'kæp-
decarbo|nate ˌdiː'kɑː.bə|.neɪt (US) -'kɑːr- -nates -neɪts -nating -neɪ.tɪŋ (US) -neɪ.t̬ɪŋ -nated -neɪ.tɪd (US) -neɪ.t̬ɪd
decarbonization, -isa- diːˌkɑː.bᵊn.aɪ'zeɪ.ʃᵊn, ˌdɪ.kɑː-, -ɪ'- (US) ˌdiː.kɑːr.bə.nɪ'-
decarboniz|e, -is|e ˌdiː'kɑː.bə.naɪz (US) -'kɑːr- -es -ɪz -ing -ɪŋ -ed -d
decarburiz|e, -is|e ˌdiː'kɑː.bjʊ.raɪz, -bjᵊr.aɪz (US) -'kɑːr.bə.raɪz, -bjə-, -bjʊ- -es -ɪz -ing -ɪŋ -ed -d
decasyllabic ˌdek.ə.sɪ'læb.ɪk, -sə'-
decasyllable 'dek.əˌsɪl.ə.bl̩, ˌdek.ə'sɪl.ə- -s -z
decathlete dɪ'kæθ.liːt, dek'æθ-, də'kæθ- -s -s
decathlon dɪ'kæθ.lɒn, dek'æθ-, də'kæθ-, -lən (US) dɪ'kæθ.lɑːn, -lən, də- -s -z
decay dɪ'keɪ, də- -s -z -ing -ɪŋ -ed -d
Decca 'dek.ə
Deccan 'dek.ən, -æn
deceas|e dɪ'siːs, də- (US) dɪ- -es -ɪz -ing -ɪŋ -ed -t
decedent dɪ'siː.dᵊnt, də- (US) dɪ- -s -s
deceit dɪ'siːt, də- (US) dɪ- -s -s
deceitful dɪ'siːt.fᵊl, də-, -fʊl (US) dɪ- -ly -i -ness -nəs, -nɪs
deceivable dɪ'siː.və.bl̩, də- (US) dɪ-
deceiv|e dɪ'siːv, də- (US) dɪ- -es -z -ing -ɪŋ -ed -d -er/s -əʳ/z (US) -ɚ/z
deceler|ate dɪ'sel.ᵊr|.eɪt, ˌdiː- (US) -ə.r|eɪt -ates -eɪts -ating -eɪ.tɪŋ (US) -eɪ.t̬ɪŋ -ated -eɪ.tɪd (US) -eɪ.t̬ɪd
deceleration dɪˌsel.ə'reɪ.ʃᵊn, ˌdiː.sel- -s -z
December dɪ'sem.bəʳ, də- (US) dɪ'sem.bɚ -s -z
decemvir dɪ'sem.vəʳ, də-, -vɜːʳ (US) diː'sem.vɪr -s -z
decemvirate dɪ'sem.vɪ.rət, də-, -vᵊr.ət, -ɪt, -eɪt (US) diː'sem.vɚ.ɪt, -və.reɪt -s -s
decenc|y 'diː.sᵊnt.s|i -ies -iz
decennial dɪ'sen.i.əl, des'en-, də'sen-, diː- (US) dɪ'sen-, diː-
decent 'diː.sᵊnt -ly -li
decentralization, -isa- diːˌsen.trᵊl.aɪ'zeɪ.ʃᵊn, ˌdɪ.sen-, -ɪ'- (US) -ɪ'-
decentraliz|e, -is|e diː'sen.trə.laɪz, ˌdɪ- -es -ɪz -ing -ɪŋ -ed -d
deception dɪ'sep.ʃᵊn, də- (US) dɪ- -s -z
deceptive dɪ'sep.tɪv, də- (US) dɪ- -ly -li -ness -nəs, -nɪs
deci- des.i-
Note: Prefix. Normally carries primary or secondary stress on the first syllable, e.g. **decimal** /'des.ɪ.mᵊl/, **decimalization** /ˌdes.ɪ.mᵊl.aɪ'zeɪ.ʃᵊn (US) -ɪ'-/. There are exceptions; see individual entries.
decibel 'des.ɪ.bel, -bəl, -bᵊl -s -z
decid|e dɪ'saɪd, də- (US) dɪ- -es -z -ing -ɪŋ -ed/ly -ɪd/li -er/s -əʳ/z (US) -ɚ/z
deciduous dɪ'sɪd.ju.əs, də- (US) dɪ'sɪdʒ.u- -ly -li -ness -nəs, -nɪs
decigram, decigramme 'des.ɪ.græm -s -z
decilitre, deciliter 'des.ɪˌliː.təʳ (US) -t̬ɚ -s -z
decillion dɪ'sɪl.i.ən, '-jən (US) '-jən -s -z
decimal 'des.ɪ.mᵊl, '-ə- -s -z -ly -i ˌdecimal 'point (US) 'decimal ˌpoint
decimalization, -isa- ˌdes.ɪ.mᵊl.aɪ'zeɪ.ʃᵊn, ˌ-ə-, -ɪ'- (US) -ɪ'-
decimaliz|e, -is|e 'des.ɪ.mᵊl.aɪz, -ə- (US) -mə.laɪz -es -ɪz -ing -ɪŋ -ed -d
deci|mate 'des.ɪ|.meɪt, '-ə- -mates -meɪts -mating -meɪ.tɪŋ (US) -meɪ.t̬ɪŋ -mated -meɪ.tɪd (US) -meɪ.t̬ɪd -mator/s -meɪ.təʳ/z (US) -meɪ.t̬ɚ/z
decimation ˌdes.ɪ'meɪ.ʃᵊn, -ə'-
decimetre, decimeter 'des.ɪˌmiː.təʳ (US) -t̬ɚ -s -z
deciph|er dɪ'saɪ.f|əʳ, ˌdiː- (US) -f|ɚ -ers -əz (US) -ɚz -ering -ᵊr.ɪŋ -ered -əd (US) -ɚd
decipherable dɪ'saɪ.fᵊr.ə.bl̩, ˌdiː-
decision dɪ'sɪʒ.ᵊn, də- (US) dɪ- -s -z
decision-mak|er dɪ'sɪʒ.ᵊnˌmeɪ.k|əʳ, də-, -ᵊm- (US) dɪ'sɪʒ.ᵊnˌmeɪ.k|ɚ -ers -əz (US) -ɚz -ing -ɪŋ
decisive dɪ'saɪ.sɪv, də-, -zɪv (US) dɪ'saɪ.sɪv -ly -li -ness -nəs, -nɪs
Decius 'diː.ʃi.əs, '-ʃəs, '-si.əs; 'dek.i.əs, 'des- (US) 'diː.ʃi.əs, '-ʃəs, '-si.əs; 'des.i.əs
deck dek -s -s -ing -ɪŋ -ed -t -er/s -əʳ/z (US) -ɚ/z ˌclear the 'decks; ˌhit the 'deck
deckchair 'dek.tʃeəʳ (US) -tʃer -s -z
Decker 'dek.əʳ (US) -ɚ
deckhand 'dek.hænd -s -z
deckhou|se 'dek.hau|s -ses -zɪz
deckle 'dek.l̩ -s -z ˌdeckle 'edged
declaim dɪ'kleɪm, də- (US) dɪ- -s -z -ing -ɪŋ -ed -d -er/s -əʳ/z (US) -ɚ/z -ant/s -ənt/s
declamation ˌdek.lə'meɪ.ʃᵊn -s -z
declamatory dɪ'klæm.ə.tᵊr.i, də-, -tri (US) dɪ'klæm.ə.tɔːr.i
Declan 'dek.lən
declarable dɪ'kleə.rə.bl̩, də- (US) dɪ'kler.ə-, -'klær-
declaration ˌdek.lə'reɪ.ʃᵊn -s -z
declarative dɪ'klær.ə.tɪv, də-, -kleə.rə- (US) dɪ'kler.ə.t̬ɪv, -'klær- -ly -li
declaratory dɪ'klær.ə.tᵊr.i, də-, -'kleə.rə-, -tri (US) dɪ'kler.ə.tɔːr.i, -'klær-
declar|e dɪ'kleəʳ, də- (US) dɪ'kler -es -z -ing -ɪŋ -ed -d -er/s -əʳ/z (US) -ɚ/z
declaredly dɪ'kleə.rɪd.li, də-, -rəd- (US) dɪ'kler-
declass ˌdiː'klɑːs (US) -'klæs -es -ɪz -ing -ɪŋ -ed -t
declassification ˌdiːˌklæs.ɪ.fɪ'keɪ.ʃᵊn, ˌ-ə-
declassi|fy ˌdiː'klæs.ɪ|.faɪ, '-ə- -fies -faɪz -fying -faɪ.ɪŋ -fied -faɪd
declension dɪ'klen.tʃᵊn, də- (US) dɪ'klent.ʃᵊn -s -z
declination ˌdek.lɪ'neɪ.ʃᵊn, -lə'- -s -z
declin|e dɪ'klaɪn, də- (US) dɪ- -es -z -ing -ɪŋ -ed -d -able -ə.bl̩
declivit|y dɪ'klɪv.ə.t|i, də-, -ɪ.t|i (US) dɪ'klɪv.ə.t̬|i -ies -iz
declutch ˌdiː'klʌtʃ -es -ɪz -ing -ɪŋ -ed -t
decoct dɪ'kɒkt, ˌdiː- (US) -'kɑːkt -s -s -ing -ɪŋ -ed -ɪd
decod|e ˌdiː'kəʊd (US) -'koʊd -es -z -ing -ɪŋ -ed -ɪd
decok|e ˌdiː'kəʊk (US) -'koʊk -es -s -ing -ɪŋ -ed -t
décolletage ˌdeɪ.kɒl'tɑːʒ; -kɒl.ɪ'-, -ə'- (US) -kɑː.lə'-, -kɑːl'-
décolleté(e) ˌdeɪ.kɒl'teɪ; -kɒl.ɪ'-, -ə'- (US) -kɑː.lə'-, -kɑːl'-
decolonization ˌdiːˌkɒl.ɪ.naɪ'zeɪ.ʃᵊn, -nɪ'- (US) -ˌkɑː.lə.nɪ'-
decoloniz|e, -is|e ˌdiː'kɒl.ə.naɪz (US) -'kɑː.lə- -es -ɪz -ing -ɪŋ -ed -d
decolo(u)rization, -isa- ˌdiː.kʌl.ə.raɪ'zeɪ.ʃᵊn, dɪˌkʌl-, -ᵊr.ɪ'- (US) dɪˌkʌl.ɚ.ɪ'-
decolo(u)riz|e, -is|e ˌdiː'kʌl.ᵊr.aɪz (US) -ə.raɪz -es -ɪz -ing -ɪŋ -ed -d
decommission ˌdiː.kə'mɪʃ.ᵊn -s -z -ing -ɪŋ -ed -d

decompos|e ˌdiː.kəmˈpəʊz (US) -ˈpoʊz **-es** -ɪz **-ing** -ɪŋ **-ed** -d **-able** -ə.bl̩
decomposition ˌdiː.kɒm.pəˈzɪʃ.ᵊn, dɪˌkɒm- (US) ˌdiː.kɑːm- **-s** -z
decompound ˌdiː.kəmˈpaʊnd **-s** -z **-ing** -ɪŋ **-ed** -ɪd
decompress ˌdiː.kəmˈpres **-es** -ɪz **-ing** -ɪŋ **-ed** -t **-er/s** -əʳ/z (US) -ɚ/z
decompression ˌdiː.kəmˈpreʃ.ᵊn
decongestant ˌdiː.kənˈdʒest.ᵊnt **-s** -s
deconsecrat|e ˌdiːˈkɒn*t*.sɪ.kreɪt, -sə- (US) -ˈkɑːn*t*- **-es** -s **-ing** -ɪŋ **-ed** -ɪd
deconsecration ˌdiː.kɒn*t*.sɪˈkreɪ.ʃᵊn, dɪˌkɒn*t*-, -səˈ- (US) ˌdiː.kɑːn*t*- **-s** -z
deconstruct ˌdiː.kənˈstrʌkt **-s** -s **-ing** -ɪŋ **-ed** -ɪd **-ive** -ɪv
deconstruction ˌdiː.kənˈstrʌk.ʃᵊn **-ism** -ɪ.zᵊm **-ist/s** -ɪst/s
decontami|nate ˌdiː.kənˈtæm.ɪ|.neɪt, ˈ-ə- **-nates** -neɪts **-nating** -neɪ.tɪŋ (US) -neɪ.t̬ɪŋ **-nated** -neɪ.tɪd (US) -neɪ.t̬ɪd
decontamination ˌdiː.kənˌtæm.ɪˈneɪ.ʃᵊn, -əˈ-
decontrol ˌdiː.kənˈtrəʊl (US) -ˈtroʊl **-s** -z **-ling** -ɪŋ **-led** -d
decor, décor ˈdeɪ.kɔːʳ, ˈdek.ɔːʳ, ˈdɪk- (US) deɪˈkɔːr, ˈ-- **-s** -z
decor|ate ˈdek.ᵊr|.eɪt (US) -ə.r|eɪt **-ates** -eɪts **-ating** -eɪ.tɪŋ (US) -eɪ.t̬ɪŋ **-ated** -eɪ.tɪd (US) -eɪ.t̬ɪd
decoration ˌdek.ᵊˈreɪ.ʃᵊn (US) -əˈreɪ- **-s** -z
decorative ˈdek.ᵊr.ə.tɪv (US) -t̬ɪv **-ly** -li **-ness** -nəs, -nɪs
decorator ˈdek.ᵊr.eɪ.təʳ (US) -ə.reɪ.t̬ɚ **-s** -z
decorous ˈdek.ᵊ.rəs; dɪˈkɔː- (US) ˈdek.ɚ.əs **-ly** -li **-ness** -nəs, -nɪs
decorum dɪˈkɔː.rəm, də- (US) dɪˈkɔːr-
De Courcy dəˈkʊə.si, -ˈkɔː-, -ˈkɜː- (US) -ˈkʊr-, -ˈkɔːr-, -ˈkɜːr-
decoy (*n.*) ˈdiː.kɔɪ; dɪˈkɔɪ, də- (US) ˈdiː.kɔɪ; dɪˈkɔɪ **-s** -z
decoy (*v.*) dɪˈkɔɪ, də- (US) dɪ- **-s** -z **-ing** -ɪŋ **-ed** -d
decreas|e (*n.*) ˈdiː.kriːs; dɪˈ-, diː-, də- (US) ˈdiː.kriːs **-es** -ɪz
decreas|e (*v.*) dɪˈkriːs, diː-, də-; ˈdiː.kriːs (US) dɪˈkriːs; ˈdiː.kriːs **-es** -ɪz **-ing/ly** -ɪŋ/li **-ed** -t
decree dɪˈkriː, də- (US) dɪ- **-s** -z **-ing** -ɪŋ **-d** -d
decree nisi dɪˌkriːˈnaɪ.saɪ, -si
decrement ˈdek.rɪ.mənt, -rə- **-s** -s
decrepit dɪˈkrep.ɪt, də- (US) dɪ- **-est** -ɪst, -əst
decrepitation dɪˌkrep.ɪˈteɪ.ʃᵊn, də-, -əˈ- (US) dɪ- **-s** -z
decrepitude dɪˈkrep.ɪ.tjuːd, də-, ˈ-ə-, -tʃuːd (US) dɪˈkrep.ɪ.tuːd, ˈ-ə-, -tjuːd
decrescendo ˌdiː.krɪˈʃen.dəʊ, ˌdeɪ-, -krəˈ- (US) -doʊ **-s** -z
De Crespigny dəˈkrep.ɪ.ni, -ˈkres.pɪ-
decrial dɪˈkraɪ.əl **-s** -z
decriminalization, -isa- diːˌkrɪm.ɪ.nᵊl.aɪˈzeɪ.ʃᵊn, ˌdɪ.krɪ.mɪ-, -mᵊn.ᵊl-, -ɪˈ- (US) ˌdiː.krɪ.mɪ.nᵊl.ɪˈ-
decriminaliz|e, -is|e ˌdiːˈkrɪm.ɪ.nᵊl.aɪz, dɪ-, -ᵊn.ᵊl- (US) -ɪ.nᵊl- **-es** -ɪz **-ing** -ɪŋ **-ed** -d
decr|y dɪˈkr|aɪ, də- (US) dɪ- **-ies** -aɪz **-ying** -aɪ.ɪŋ **-ied** -aɪd **-ier/s** -aɪ.əʳ/z (US) -aɪ.ɚ/z
decumben|ce dɪˈkʌm.bən*t*|s, ˌdiː- **-cy** -si
decumbent dɪˈkʌm.bənt, ˌdiː- **-ly** -li
decuple ˈdek.jʊ.pl̩ (US) -jʊ-, -jə- **-es** -z **-ing** -ɪŋ, ˈdek.jʊ.plɪŋ, -juː- **-ed** -d
Dedalus ˈdiː.dᵊl.əs (US) ˈded.ᵊl.əs, ˈdiː.dᵊl-
Deddington ˈded.ɪŋ.tᵊn
Dedham ˈded.əm
dedi|cate ˈded.ɪ|.keɪt **-cates** -keɪts **-cating** -keɪ.tɪŋ (US) -keɪ.t̬ɪŋ **-cated/ly** -keɪ.tɪd/li (US) -keɪ.t̬ɪd/li **-cator/s** -keɪ.təʳ/z (US) -keɪ.t̬ɚ/z
dedicatee ˌded.ɪ.kəˈtiː **-s** -z
dedication ˌded.ɪˈkeɪ.ʃᵊn **-s** -z
dedicatory ˈded.ɪ.kə.tᵊr.i, -keɪ-, -tri; ˌded.ɪˈkeɪ- (US) ˈded.ɪ.kə.tɔːr-
de Dion dəˈdiː.ən, -ɒn *as if French:* -ɔ̃ŋ (US) dəˈdiː.ɑːn *as if French:* -ɔ̃ŋ **-s** -z
Dedlock ˈded.lɒk (US) -lɑːk
Dedman ˈded.mən, ˈdeb-, -mæn (US) ˈded-
deduc|e dɪˈdjuːs, də- (US) dɪˈduːs, -ˈdjuːs **-es** -ɪz **-ing** -ɪŋ **-ed** -t
deducibility dɪˌdjuː.səˈbɪl.ə.ti, də-, -sɪˈ-, -ɪ.ti (US) dɪˌduː.səˈbɪl.ə.t̬i, -ˌdjuː-
deducible dɪˈdjuː.sə.bl̩, də-, -sɪ- (US) dɪˈduː-, -ˈdjuː-
deduct dɪˈdʌkt, də- (US) dɪ- **-s** -s **-ing** -ɪŋ **-ed** -ɪd **-ible** -ə.bl̩
deduction dɪˈdʌk.ʃᵊn, də- (US) dɪ- **-s** -z
deductive dɪˈdʌk.tɪv, də- (US) dɪ- **-ly** -li
Dee diː
deed diːd **-s** -z ˈ**deed** ˌ**poll**
Deedes diːdz
deejay ˈdiː.dʒeɪ **-s** -z
Deek(e)s diːks
Deeley ˈdiː.li
deem diːm **-s** -z **-ing** -ɪŋ **-ed** -d
Deems diːmz
deemster ˈdiːm.stəʳ (US) -stɚ **-s** -z
deep diːp **-s** -s **-er** -əʳ (US) -ɚ **-est** -ɪst, -əst **-ly** -li **-ness** -nəs, -nɪs ˌ**deep** ˈ**freeze** (US) ˈ**deep** ˌ**freeze**; ˌ**Deep** ˈ**South**; **go off the** ˈ**deep** ˌ**end**; ˌ**throw (someone) in at the** ˈ**deep** ˌ**end**
deepen ˈdiː.pᵊn **-s** -z **-ing** -ɪŋ **-ed** -d
deep-fr|y ˌdiːpˈfr|aɪ, ˈ-- **-ies** -aɪz **-ying** -aɪ.ɪŋ **-ied** -aɪd *stress shift:* ˌdeep-fried ˈchicken
deep-laid ˌdiːpˈleɪd *stress shift:* ˌdeep-laid ˈplans
deep-rooted ˌdiːpˈruː.tɪd (US) -t̬ɪd *stress shift:* ˌdeep-rooted ˈfears
deep-sea ˌdiːpˈsiː *stress shift:* ˌdeep-sea ˈdiving
deep-seated ˌdiːpˈsiː.tɪd (US) -t̬ɪd *stress shift:* ˌdeep-seated ˈsorrow
deep-six ˌdiːpˈsɪks **-es** -ɪz **-ing** -ɪŋ **-ed** -t
deer dɪəʳ (US) dɪr ˈ**deer** ˌ**forest**; ˈ**deer** ˌ**park**; ˈ**Deer** ˌ**Park**
Deerfield ˈdɪə.fiːld (US) ˈdɪr-
deerhound ˈdɪə.haʊnd (US) ˈdɪr- **-s** -z
deerskin ˈdɪə.skɪn (US) ˈdɪr-
Deerslayer ˈdɪəˌsleɪ.əʳ (US) ˈdɪrˌsleɪ.ɚ
deerstalk|ing ˈdɪəˌstɔː.k|ɪŋ (US) ˈdɪr-, -ˌstɑː-, -ˌstɔː- **-er/s** -əʳ/z (US) -ɚ/z
Deery ˈdɪə.ri (US) ˈdɪr.i
de-escal|ate ˌdiːˈes.kᵊl|.eɪt (US) -kə.l|eɪt **-ates** -eɪts **-ating** -eɪ.tɪŋ (US) -eɪ.t̬ɪŋ **-ated** -eɪ.tɪd (US) -eɪ.t̬ɪd
de-escalation ˌdiː.es.kəˈleɪ.ʃᵊn, diːˌes- (US) diːˌes-
Deeside ˈdiː.saɪd
defac|e dɪˈfeɪs **-es** -ɪz **-ing** -ɪŋ **-ed** -t **-er/s** -əʳ/z (US) -ɚ/z **-ement/s** -mənt/s
de facto ˌdeɪˈfæk.təʊ, ˌdiː- (US) -toʊ
defae|cate ˈdef.ə|.keɪt, ˈdiː.fə-, -fɪ- (US) ˈdef.ə-, ˈ-ɪ- **-cates** -keɪts **-cating** -keɪ.tɪŋ (US) -keɪ.t̬ɪŋ **-cated** -keɪ.tɪd (US) -keɪ.t̬ɪd
defaecation ˌdef.əˈkeɪ.ʃᵊn, ˌdiː.fəˈ-, -fɪˈ- (US) ˌdef.əˈ-, -ɪˈ-
defal|cate ˈdiː.fæl|.keɪt, diːˈfæl-; ˈdiː.fɔːl- (US) diːˈfæl-, -ˈfɔːl- **-cates** -keɪts **-cating** -keɪ.tɪŋ (US) -keɪ.t̬ɪŋ **-cated** -keɪ.tɪd (US) -keɪ.t̬ɪd
defalcation ˌdiː.fælˈkeɪ.ʃᵊn, -fɔːlˈ- **-s** -z
defamation ˌdef.əˈmeɪ.ʃᵊn, ˌdiː.fəˈ- (US) ˌdef.əˈ- **-s** -z
defamatory dɪˈfæm.ə.tᵊr.i, də-, -tri (US) dɪˈfæm.ə.tɔːr.i
defam|e dɪˈfeɪm, də- (US) dɪ- **-es** -z **-ing** -ɪŋ **-ed** -d **-er/s** -əʳ/z (US) -ɚ/z
Defarge dəˈfɑːʒ (US) -ˈfɑːrʒ
default (*n*) dɪˈfɔːlt, də-, -ˈfɒlt; ˈdiː.fɔːlt, -fɒlt (US) dɪˈfɑːlt, -ˈfɔːlt
defaul|t (*v*) dɪˈfɔːl|t, də-, -ˈfɒl|t (US) dɪˈfɑːl|t, -ˈfɔːl|t **-ts** -ts **-ting** -tɪŋ (US) -t̬ɪŋ **-ted** -tɪd (US) -t̬ɪd **-ter/s** -təʳ/z (US) -t̬ɚ/z
defeasance dɪˈfiː.zᵊn*t*s, də- (US) dɪ-
defeasib|le dɪˈfiː.zə.b|l̩, də-, -zɪ- (US) dɪ- **-ly** -li **-leness** -l̩.nəs, -nɪs
de|feat dɪ|ˈfiːt, də- (US) dɪ- **-s** -ˈfiːts **-ing** -ˈfiː.tɪŋ (US) -ˈfiː.t̬ɪŋ **-ed** -ˈfiː.tɪd (US) -ˈfiː.t̬ɪd
defeat|ism dɪˈfiː.t|ɪ.zᵊm, də- (US) dɪˈfiː.t̬|ɪ- **-ist/s** -ɪst/s

defe|cate ˈdef.ə|.keɪt, ˈdiː.fə-, -fɪ- ⓤⓢ ˈdef.ə-, ˈ-ɪ- **-cates** -keɪts **-cating** -keɪ.tɪŋ ⓤⓢ -keɪ.t̬ɪŋ **-cated** -keɪ.tɪd ⓤⓢ -keɪ.t̬ɪd
defecation ˌdef.əˈkeɪ.ʃᵊn, ˌdiː.fəˈ-, -fɪˈ- ⓤⓢ ˌdef.əˈ-, -ɪˈ- **-s** -z
defect (*n.*) ˈdiː.fekt; dɪˈfekt, də- ⓤⓢ ˈdiː.fekt; dɪˈfekt **-s** -s
defect (*v.*) dɪˈfekt, də- ⓤⓢ dɪ- **-s** -s **-ing** -ɪŋ **-ed** -ɪd
defection dɪˈfek.ʃᵊn, də- ⓤⓢ dɪ- **-s** -z
defective dɪˈfek.tɪv, də- ⓤⓢ dɪ- **-ly** -li **-ness** -nəs, -nɪs
defector dɪˈfek.təʳ, də- ⓤⓢ dɪˈfek.tɚ **-s** -z
defenc|e dɪˈfen*t*s, də- ⓤⓢ dɪ- **-es** -ɪz
defenceless dɪˈfen*t*.sləs, də-, -slɪs ⓤⓢ dɪ- **-ly** -li **-ness** -nəs, -nɪs
defend dɪˈfend, də- ⓤⓢ dɪ- **-s** -z **-ing** -ɪŋ **-ed** -ɪd **-able** -ə.bl̩
defendant dɪˈfen.dənt, də- ⓤⓢ dɪ- **-s** -s
defender dɪˈfen.dəʳ, də- ⓤⓢ dɪˈfen.dɚ **-s** -z
defens|e dɪˈfen*t*s, də- ⓤⓢ dɪ-; ˈdiː.fen*t*s *esp. in sports:* ˈdiː.fen*t*s **-es** -ɪz
defenseless dɪˈfen*t*.sləs, də-, -slɪs ⓤⓢ dɪ- **-ly** -li **-ness** -nəs, -nɪs
defense|man dɪˈfen*t*s|.mən, də- ⓤⓢ dɪ-, -mæn **-men** -mən
defensibility dɪˌfen*t*.səˈbɪl.ə.ti, də-, -sɪˈ-, -ɪ.ti ⓤⓢ dɪˌfen*t*.səˈbɪl.ə.t̬i
defensib|le dɪˈfen*t*.sə.b|l̩, də-, -sɪ- ⓤⓢ dɪ- **-ly** -li
defensive dɪˈfen*t*.sɪv, də- ⓤⓢ dɪ- **-ly** -li **-ness** -nəs, -nɪs
defer dɪˈfɜːʳ, də- ⓤⓢ dɪˈfɜːr **-s** -z **-ring** -ɪŋ **-red** -d **-rer/s** -əʳ/z ⓤⓢ -ɚ/z
deferen|ce ˈdef.ᵊr.ᵊn|*t*s **-t** -t
deferential ˌdef.ᵊˈren.*t*ʃᵊl ⓤⓢ -ˈren*t*.ʃᵊl **-ly** -i
deferment dɪˈfɜː.mənt, də- ⓤⓢ dɪˈfɜːr- **-s** -s
deferral dɪˈfɜː.rᵊl, də- ⓤⓢ dɪˈfɜːr.ᵊl **-s** -z
defiance dɪˈfaɪ.ən*t*s, də- ⓤⓢ dɪ-
defiant dɪˈfaɪ.ənt, də- ⓤⓢ dɪ- **-ly** -li **-ness** -nəs, -nɪs
defibrill|ate ˌdiːˈfɪb.rɪ.l|eɪt, -ˈfaɪ.brɪ-, -brᵊl|.eɪt ⓤⓢ -rɪ.l|eɪt, -rə- **-ates** -eɪts **-ating** -eɪ.tɪŋ ⓤⓢ -eɪ.t̬ɪŋ **-ated** -eɪ.tɪd ⓤⓢ -eɪ.t̬ɪd
defibrillation diːˌfɪb.rɪˈleɪ.ʃᵊn, -ˌfaɪ.brɪˈ-, -brəˈ-; ˌdiː.fɪ.brɪˈ-
defibrillator ˌdiːˈfɪb.rɪ.leɪ.təʳ, -ˈfaɪ.brɪ-, -brə- ⓤⓢ -t̬ɚ **-s** -z
deficienc|y dɪˈfɪʃ.ᵊn*t*.s|i, də- ⓤⓢ dɪ- **-ies** -iz
deficient dɪˈfɪʃ.ᵊnt, də- ⓤⓢ dɪ- **-ly** -li
deficit ˈdef.ɪ.sɪt, ˈ-ə-; dəˈfɪs-, dɪ- ⓤⓢ ˈdef.ɪ.sɪt, ˈ-ə- **-s** -s
defilad|e ˌdef.ɪˈleɪd, -əˈ-, ˈ--- **-es** -z **-ing** -ɪŋ **-ed** -ɪd
defile (*n.*) dɪˈfaɪl, ˌdiː-; ˈdiː.faɪl **-s** -z
defil|e (*v.*) dɪˈfaɪl, də- ⓤⓢ dɪ- **-es** -z **-ing** -ɪŋ **-ed** -d **-er/s** -əʳ/z ⓤⓢ -ɚ/z **-ement** -mənt
definable dɪˈfaɪ.nə.bl̩, də- ⓤⓢ dɪ-
defin|e dɪˈfaɪn, də- ⓤⓢ dɪ- **-es** -z **-ing** -ɪŋ **-ed** -d **-er/s** -əʳ/z ⓤⓢ -ɚ/z
definite ˈdef.ɪ.nət, -ᵊn.ət, -ɪt **-ly** -li **-ness** -nəs, -nɪs
definition ˌdef.ɪˈnɪʃ.ᵊn, -əˈ- **-s** -z
definitive dɪˈfɪn.ə.tɪv, də-, ˈ-ɪ- ⓤⓢ dɪˈfɪn.ə.t̬ɪv **-ly** -li **-ness** -nəs, -nɪs
defla|grate ˈdiː.flə|.greɪt, ˈdef.lə- ⓤⓢ ˈdef.lə- **-grates** -greɪts **-grating** -greɪ.tɪŋ ⓤⓢ -greɪ.t̬ɪŋ **-grated** -greɪ.tɪd ⓤⓢ -greɪ.t̬ɪd **-grator/s** -greɪ.təʳ/z ⓤⓢ -greɪ.t̬ɚ/z
deflagration ˌdiː.fləˈgreɪ.ʃᵊn, ˌdef.ləˈ- ⓤⓢ ˌdef.ləˈ- **-s** -z
de|flate dɪ|ˈfleɪt, ˌdiː- **-flates** -ˈfleɪts **-flating** -ˈfleɪ.tɪŋ ⓤⓢ -ˈfleɪ.t̬ɪŋ **-flated** -ˈfleɪ.tɪd ⓤⓢ -ˈfleɪ.t̬ɪd
deflation dɪˈfleɪ.ʃᵊn, ˌdiː- **-ary** -ᵊr.i ⓤⓢ -er.i
deflect dɪˈflekt, də- ⓤⓢ dɪ- **-s** -s **-ing** -ɪŋ **-ed** -ɪd **-or/s** -əʳ/z ⓤⓢ -ɚ/z
deflection, deflexion dɪˈflek.ʃᵊn, də- ⓤⓢ dɪ- **-s** -z
defloration ˌdiː.flɔːˈreɪ.ʃᵊn, ˌdef.lɔːˈ- ⓤⓢ ˌdef.ləˈ-, ˌdiː.fləˈ-, -flɔːˈ- **-s** -z
deflower dɪˈflaʊəʳ, ˌdiː- ⓤⓢ -ˈflaʊɚ **-s** -z **-ing** -ɪŋ **-ed** -d
Defoe dɪˈfəʊ, də- ⓤⓢ -ˈfoʊ
defog ˌdiːˈfɒg ⓤⓢ -ˈfɑːg, -ˈfɔːg **-s** -z **-ging** -ɪŋ **-ged** -d **-ger/s** -əʳ/z ⓤⓢ -ɚ/z
defoliant ˌdiːˈfəʊ.li.ənt, dɪ- ⓤⓢ -ˈfoʊ- **-s** -s
defoli|ate ˌdiːˈfəʊ.li|.eɪt, dɪ- ⓤⓢ -ˈfoʊ- **-ates** -eɪts **-ating** -eɪ.tɪŋ ⓤⓢ -eɪ.t̬ɪŋ **-ated** -eɪ.tɪd ⓤⓢ -eɪ.t̬ɪd
defoliation ˌdiː.fəʊ.liˈeɪ.ʃᵊn; diːˌfəʊ-, dɪ- ⓤⓢ diːˌfoʊ-, dɪ-
deforest ˌdiːˈfɒr.ɪst, dɪ-, -əst ⓤⓢ -ˈfɔːr- **-s** -s **-ing** -ɪŋ **-ed** -ɪd
deforestation diːˌfɒr.ɪˈsteɪ.ʃᵊn, dɪ-; ˌdiː.fɔːr-, -əˈ- ⓤⓢ diːˌfɔːr-, dɪ-
deform dɪˈfɔːm, də-, ˌdiː- ⓤⓢ dɪˈfɔːrm, ˌdiː- **-s** -z **-ing** -ɪŋ **-ed** -d **-er/s** -əʳ/z ⓤⓢ -ɚ/z
deformation ˌdiː.fɔːˈmeɪ.ʃᵊn, ˌdef.əˈ- ⓤⓢ ˌdiː.fɔːrˈ-, ˌdef.ɚˈ- **-s** -z
deformit|y dɪˈfɔː.mə.t|i, də-, -mɪ- ⓤⓢ dɪˈfɔːr.mə.t̬|i **-ies** -iz
defraud dɪˈfrɔːd, ˌdiː-, də- ⓤⓢ dɪˈfrɑːd, ˌdiː-, -ˈfrɔːd **-s** -z **-ing** -ɪŋ **-ed** -ɪd **-er/s** -əʳ/z ⓤⓢ -ɚ/z
defray dɪˈfreɪ, də- ⓤⓢ dɪ- **-s** -z **-ing** -ɪŋ **-ed** -d **-er/s** -əʳ/z ⓤⓢ -ɚ/z **-ment** -mənt
defrayal dɪˈfreɪ.əl, də- ⓤⓢ dɪ- **-s** -z
De Freitas dəˈfreɪ.təs ⓤⓢ -t̬əs
defrock ˌdiːˈfrɒk ⓤⓢ -ˈfrɑːk **-s** -s **-ing** -ɪŋ **-ed** -t
defrost ˌdiːˈfrɒst, dɪ- ⓤⓢ -ˈfrɑːst **-s** -s **-ing** -ɪŋ **-ed** -ɪd **-er/s** -əʳ/z ⓤⓢ -ɚ/z
deft deft **-er** -əʳ ⓤⓢ -ɚ **-est** -ɪst, -əst **-ly** -li **-ness** -nəs, -nɪs
defunct dɪˈfʌŋ*k*t, də-; ˈdiː.fʌŋ*k*t ⓤⓢ dɪˈfʌŋ*k*t, ˌdiː- **-s** -s
defus|e ˌdiːˈfjuːz, dɪ-, də- ⓤⓢ ˌdiː-, dɪ- **-es** -ɪz **-ing** -ɪŋ **-ed** -d
def|y dɪˈf|aɪ, də- ⓤⓢ dɪ- **-ies** -aɪz **-ying** -aɪ.ɪŋ **-ied** -aɪd **-ier/s** -aɪ.əʳ/z ⓤⓢ -aɪ.ɚ/z
Deganwy dɪˈgæn.wi, də-
Degas dəˈgɑː, ˈdeɪ.gɑː
De Gaulle dəˈgəʊl, dɪ-, -ˈgɔːl ⓤⓢ -ˈgoʊl, -ˈgɔːl, -ˈgɑːl
degauss ˌdiːˈgaʊs, -ˈgɔːs ⓤⓢ -ˈgaʊs **-es** -ɪz **-ing** -ɪŋ **-ed** -t
degeneracy dɪˈdʒen.ᵊr.ə.si, də- ⓤⓢ dɪ-
degenerate (*adj.*) dɪˈdʒen.ᵊr.ət, də-, -ɪt ⓤⓢ dɪ- **-ly** -li **-ness** -nəs, -nɪs
degener|ate (*v.*) dɪˈdʒen.ᵊr|.eɪt, də- ⓤⓢ dɪˈdʒen.ə.r|eɪt **-ates** -eɪts **-ating** -eɪ.tɪŋ ⓤⓢ -eɪ.t̬ɪŋ **-ated** -eɪ.tɪd ⓤⓢ -eɪ.t̬ɪd
degeneration dɪˌdʒen.əˈreɪ.ʃᵊn, də- ⓤⓢ dɪ-
degenerative dɪˈdʒen.ᵊr.ə.tɪv, də-, -ə.reɪ- ⓤⓢ dɪˈdʒen.ɚ.ə.t̬ɪv, -ə.reɪ-
deglutin|ate ˌdiːˈgluː.tɪ.n|eɪt, dɪ- ⓤⓢ -tᵊn|.eɪt **-ates** -eɪts **-ating** -eɪ.tɪŋ ⓤⓢ -eɪ.t̬ɪŋ **-ated** -eɪ.tɪd ⓤⓢ -eɪ.t̬ɪd
deglutition ˌdiː.gluːˈtɪʃ.ᵊn
degradation ˌdeg.rəˈdeɪ.ʃᵊn **-s** -z
degrad|e dɪˈgreɪd, də- ⓤⓢ dɪ- **-es** -z **-ed** -ɪd **-able** -ə.bl̩
degrading dɪˈgreɪ.dɪŋ, də- ⓤⓢ dɪ- **-ly** -li
degree dɪˈgriː, də- ⓤⓢ dɪ- **-s** -z
dehisc|e dɪˈhɪs, ˌdiː- ⓤⓢ ˌdiː-, dɪ- **-es** -ɪz **-ing** -ɪŋ **-ed** -t
dehiscen|ce dɪˈhɪs.ᵊn|*t*s, ˌdiː- ⓤⓢ ˌdiː-, dɪ- **-t** -t
Dehra Dun ˌdeə.rəˈduːn, ˌdeɪᵊ- ⓤⓢ ˌder.əˈ-
dehumaniz|e, -is|e ˌdiːˈhjuː.mə.naɪz **-es** -ɪz **-ing** -ɪŋ **-ed** -d
dehumidifier ˌdiː.hjuːˈmɪd.ɪ.faɪ.əʳ ⓤⓢ -ə.faɪ.ɚ **-s** -z
dehy|drate ˌdiː.haɪ|ˈdreɪt, ˈ--- **-drates** -ˈdreɪts **-drating** -ˈdre.tɪŋ ⓤⓢ -ˈdreɪ.t̬ɪŋ **-drated** -ˈdreɪ.tɪd ⓤⓢ -ˈdreɪ.t̬ɪd
dehydration ˌdiː.haɪˈdreɪ.ʃᵊn
dehypnotiz|e, -is|e ˌdiːˈhɪp.nə.taɪz **-es** -ɪz **-ing** -ɪŋ **-ed** -d
de-ic|e ˌdiːˈaɪs **-es** -ɪz **-ing** -ɪŋ **-ed** -t **-er/s** -əʳ/z ⓤⓢ -ɚ/z
deicide ˈdeɪ.ɪ.saɪd, ˈdiː-, ˈ-ə- ⓤⓢ ˈdiː.ə- **-s** -z
dei|ctic ˈdaɪ|k.tɪk, ˈdeɪ- **-xis** -k.sɪs
deification ˌdeɪ.ɪ.fɪˈkeɪ.ʃᵊn, ˌdiː-, ˌ-ə- ⓤⓢ ˌdiː.ə- **-s** -z

dei|fy 'deɪ.ɪ|.faɪ, 'diː-, '-ə- (US) 'diː- **-fies** -faɪz **-fying** -faɪ.ɪŋ **-fied** -faɪd
Deighton *surname:* 'deɪ.tᵊn, 'daɪ- *place in North Yorkshire:* 'diː.tᵊn
deign deɪn **-s** -z **-ing** -ɪŋ **-ed** -d
deindustrialization, -isa- ˌdiː.ɪnˌdʌs.tri.ᵊl.aɪ'zeɪ.ʃᵊn, -ɪ'- (US) -ɪ'-
Deirdre 'dɪə.dri, -dreɪ (US) 'dɪr.drə, -dri
de|ism 'deɪ|.ɪ.zᵊm, 'diː- (US) 'diː- **-ist/s** -ɪst/s
deistic deɪ'ɪs.tɪk, diː- (US) diː- **-al** -ᵊl
deit|y (D) 'deɪ.ɪ.t|i, 'diː-, '-ə- (US) 'diː.ə.t̬|i **-ies** -iz
déjà vu ˌdeʒ.ɑː'vuː, -'vjuː (US) ˌdeɪ.ʒɑː'vuː, -vjuː
deject dɪ'dʒekt, də- (US) dɪ- **-s** -s **-ing** -ɪŋ **-ed/ly** -ɪd/li **-edness** -ɪd.nəs, -nɪs
dejection dɪ'dʒek.ʃᵊn, də- (US) dɪ-
déjeuner 'deɪ.ʒə.neɪ, -ʒɜː- (US) -ʒə- **-s** -z
de jure ˌdeɪ'dʒʊə.reɪ, di-, ˌdiː-, -ri (US) diː'dʒʊr.i, deɪ-
Dekker 'dek.əʳ (US) -ɚ
dekko 'dek.əʊ (US) -oʊ **-s** -z
de Klerk də'klɜːk, də'kleək (US) -'klerk, -'klɜːrk
de Kooning də'kəʊ.nɪŋ, -'kuː- (US) -'kuː-
Del. (*abbrev. for* **Delaware**) 'del.ə.weəʳ (US) -wer
de la Bère də.lə'bɪəʳ (US) də.lə'bɪr
Delacroix 'del.ə.krwɑː, ˌ--'-
Delafield 'del.ə.fiːld
Delagoa ˌdel.ə'gəʊə (US) -'goʊə
Delamain 'del.ə.meɪn
de la Mare də.lɑː'meəʳ, ˌdel.ə'- (US) də.lə'mer, ˌdel.ə'-
Delamere 'del.ə.mɪəʳ (US) -mɪr
De Lancey də'lɑːnt.si (US) -'lænt-
Delane də'leɪn, dɪ-
Delany də'leɪ.ni, dɪ-
De la Pole ˌdel.ə'pəʊl, də.lɑː'- (US) də.lə'poʊl
de la Roche ˌdel.ə'rɒʃ, -'rəʊʃ; də.lə'- (US) də.lɑː'roʊʃ, -lə-, -'rɑːʃ
De la Rue ˌdel.ə'ruː; də.lɑː'-; 'del.ə.ruː
de la Torre ˌdel.ə'tɔːʳ, də.lɑː'- (US) -'tɔːr
Delaunay də'lɔː.neɪ (US) -lɔː'neɪ
Delaware 'del.ə.weəʳ (US) -wer
De la Warr ˌdel.ə'weəʳ, də.lɑː'- (US) -'wer
delay dɪ'leɪ, də- (US) dɪ- **-s** -z **-ing** -ɪŋ **-ed** -d **-er/s** -əʳ/z (US) -ɚ/z
Delbert 'del.bət (US) -bɚt
del credere ˌdel'kred.ᵊr.eɪ, -'kreɪ.dᵊr-, -i (US) -'kreɪ.dɚ-
dele 'diː.liː, -li
delectab|le dɪ'lek.tə.b|l̩, də- (US) dɪ- **-ly** -li **-leness** -l̩.nəs, -nɪs
delectation ˌdiː.lek'teɪ.ʃᵊn
delegac|y 'del.ɪ.gə.s|i, '-ə- **-ies** -iz
delegate (*n.*) 'del.ɪ.gət, '-ə-, -geɪt, -gɪt (US) -gət, -gɪt, -geɪt **-s** -s
dele|gate (*v.*) 'del.ɪ|.geɪt, '-ə- **-gates** -geɪts **-gating** -geɪ.tɪŋ (US) -geɪ.t̬ɪŋ **-gated** -geɪ.tɪd (US) -geɪ.t̬ɪd
delegation ˌdel.ɪ'geɪ.ʃᵊn, -ə'- **-s** -z
delend|um dɪ'len.d|əm, diː- **-a** -ə
de|lete dɪ|'liːt, də- (US) dɪ- **-letes** -'liːts **-leting** -'liː.tɪŋ (US) -'liː.t̬ɪŋ **-leted** -'liː.tɪd (US) -'liː.t̬ɪd
deleterious ˌdel.ɪ'tɪə.ri.əs, ˌdɪl-, ˌdiː.lɪ'-, -lə'tɪə- (US) ˌdel.ə'tɪr.i- **-ly** -li **-ness** -nəs, -nɪs
deletion dɪ'liː.ʃᵊn, də- (US) dɪ- **-s** -z
delf delf
Delft delft **-ware** -weəʳ (US) -wer
Delham 'del.əm
Delhi 'del.i
deli 'del.i **-s** -z
Deli|a 'diː.li|.ə (US) 'diːl.j|ə, -li|.ə **-an/s** -ən/z
deliberate (*adj.*) dɪ'lɪb.ᵊr.ət, də-, -ɪt (US) dɪ- **-ly** -li **-ness** -nəs, -nɪs
deliber|ate (*v.*) dɪ'lɪb.ᵊr|.eɪt, də- (US) dɪ'lɪb.ə.r|eɪt **-ates** -eɪts **-ating** -eɪ.tɪŋ (US) -eɪ.t̬ɪŋ **-ated** -eɪ.tɪd (US) -eɪ.t̬ɪd **-ator/s** -eɪ.təʳ/z (US) -eɪ.t̬ɚ/z
deliberation dɪˌlɪb.ə'reɪ.ʃᵊn, də- (US) dɪ- **-s** -z
deliberative dɪ'lɪb.ᵊr.ə.tɪv, də- (US) dɪ'lɪb.ɚ.ə.t̬ɪv, -rə.t̬ɪv **-ly** -li
Delibes də'liːb, dɪ-
delicac|y 'del.ɪ.kə.s|i, '-ə- **-ies** -iz
delicate 'del.ɪ.kət, '-ə-, -kɪt **-ly** -li **-ness** -nəs, -nɪs
delicatessen ˌdel.ɪ.kə'tes.ᵊn, ˌ-ə- **-s** -z
delicious dɪ'lɪʃ.əs, də- (US) dɪ- **-ly** -li **-ness** -nəs, -nɪs
delict dɪ'lɪkt; 'diː.lɪkt (US) dɪ'lɪkt **-s** -s
de|light dɪ|'laɪt, də- (US) dɪ- **-lights** -'laɪts **-lighting** -'laɪ.tɪŋ (US) -'laɪ.t̬ɪŋ **-lighted/ly** -'laɪ.tɪd/li (US) -'laɪ.t̬ɪd/li
delightful dɪ'laɪt.fᵊl, də-, -fʊl (US) dɪ- **-ly** -i **-ness** -nəs, -nɪs
delightsome dɪ'laɪt.səm, də- (US) dɪ-
Delilah dɪ'laɪ.lə, də- (US) dɪ-
delim|it dɪ'lɪm|.ɪt, ˌdiː-, də- (US) dɪ- **-its** -ɪts **-iting** -ɪ.tɪŋ (US) -ɪ.t̬ɪŋ **-ited** -ɪ.tɪd (US) -ɪ.t̬ɪd
delimitation dɪˌlɪm.ɪ'teɪ.ʃᵊn, ˌdiː-, də- (US) dɪ- **-s** -z
deline|ate dɪ'lɪn.i|.eɪt, də- (US) dɪ- **-ates** -eɪts **-ating** -eɪ.tɪŋ (US) -eɪ.t̬ɪŋ **-ated** -eɪ.tɪd (US) -eɪ.t̬ɪd **-ator/s** -eɪ.təʳ/z (US) -eɪ.t̬ɚ/z
delineation dɪˌlɪn.i'eɪ.ʃᵊn, də- (US) dɪ- **-s** -z
delinquenc|y dɪ'lɪŋ.kwənt.s|i, də- (US) dɪ- **-ies** -iz
delinquent dɪ'lɪŋ.kwənt, də- (US) dɪ- **-s** -s
deliquesc|e ˌdel.ɪ'kwes, -ə'- **-es** -ɪz **-ing** -ɪŋ **-ed** -t
deliquescen|ce ˌdel.ɪ'kwes.ᵊn|ts **-t** -t
delirious dɪ'lɪr.i.əs, də-, -'lɪə.ri- (US) dɪ'lɪr.i- **-ly** -li **-ness** -nəs, -nɪs
delirium dɪ'lɪr.i.əm, də-, -'lɪə.ri- (US) dɪ'lɪr.i-
delirium tremens dɪˌlɪr.i.əm'triː.menz, -'trem.enz, -ənz
De l'Isle *English name:* də'laɪl
Delisle *French name:* də'liːl
Delius 'diː.li.əs
deliv|er dɪ'lɪv|.əʳ, də- (US) dɪ'lɪv|.ɚ **-ers** -əz (US) -ɚz **-ering** -ᵊr.ɪŋ **-ered** -əd (US) -ɚd **-erer/s** -ᵊr.əʳ/z (US) -ɚ.ɚ/z
deliverable dɪ'lɪv.ᵊr.ə.bl̩, də- (US) dɪ- **-s** -z
deliveranc|e dɪ'lɪv.ᵊr.ᵊnts, də- (US) dɪ- **-es** -ɪz
deliver|y dɪ'lɪv.ᵊr|.i, də- (US) dɪ- **-ies** -iz
delivery|man dɪ'lɪv.ᵊr.ɪ|.mən, də-, -mæn (US) dɪ- **-men** -mən, -men
dell (D) del **-s** -z
Della 'del.ə
Dellar 'del.əʳ (US) -ɚ
della Robbia ˌdel.ə'rɒb.i.ə (US) ˌdel.ə'roʊ.biə, -ɑː'-, -'rɑː-, -bjə
Delma 'del.mə
Delmar del'mɑːʳ, '-- (US) 'del.mɑːr, -'-
Delmarva del'mɑː.və (US) -'mɑːr- Del'marva Peˌninsula
Del Monte® del'mɒn.teɪ, -ti (US) -'mɑːn.t̬i
Delores də'lɔː.rɪz, dɪ- (US) dɪ'lɔːr.ɪs, də-
Deloria də'lɔː.ri.ə (US) -'lɔːr.i-
Delors də'lɔːʳ (US) -'lɔːr
Delos 'diː.lɒs (US) -lɑːs, 'del.oʊs
delouse ˌdiː'laʊs (US) -'laʊs, -'laʊz **-es** -ɪz **-ing** -ɪŋ **-ed** -t (US) -t, -d
Delph delf
Delphi *in Greece:* 'del.faɪ, -fi *city in US:* 'del.faɪ
Delph|ian 'del.f|i.ən **-ic** -ɪk ˌDelphic 'oracle
Delphine del'fiːn
delphinium del'fɪn.i.əm **-s** -z
Delroy 'del.rɔɪ
delta 'del.tə (US) -t̬ə **-s** -z
deltoid 'del.tɔɪd
delud|e dɪ'luːd, də-, -'ljuːd (US) dɪ'luːd **-es** -z **-ing** -ɪŋ **-ed** -ɪd **-er/s** -əʳ/z (US) -ɚ/z
delug|e 'del.juːdʒ **-es** -ɪz **-ing** -ɪŋ **-ed** -d
delusion dɪ'luː.ʒᵊn, də-, -'ljuː- (US) dɪ'luː- **-s** -z

delusive dɪˈluː.sɪv, də-, -ˈljuː- US dɪˈluː- **-ly** -li **-ness** -nəs, -nɪs
delusory dɪˈluː.sᵊr.i, də-, -ˈljuː-, -zᵊr- US dɪˈluː-
de luxe, **deluxe** dəˈlʌks, dɪ-, -ˈluːks, -ˈlʊks US dɪˈlʌks, də-, -ˈlʊks
delv|e delv **-es** -z **-ing** -ɪŋ **-ed** -d **-er/s** -əʳ/z US -ɚ/z
Delyn ˈdel.ɪn
Dem (*abbrev. for* **Democrat**) ˈdem.ə.kræt (*abbrev. for* **Democratic**) ˌdem.əˈkræt.ɪk
demagnetization, -isa- diːˌmæg.nə.taɪˈzeɪ.ʃᵊn, ˌdiː.mæg-, -nɪ-, -ɪˈ- US diːˌmæg.nə.t̬ɪˈ- **-s** -z
demagnetiz|e, -is|e ˌdiːˈmæg.nə.taɪz, -nɪ- **-es** -ɪz **-ing** -ɪŋ **-ed** -d
demagog ˈdem.ə.gɒg US -gɑːg, -gɔːg **-s** -z
demagogic ˌdem.əˈgɒg.ɪk, -ˈgɒdʒ- US -ˈgɑː.dʒɪk, -gɪk; -goʊ.dʒɪk **-al** -ᵊl **-ally** -ᵊl.i, -li
demagogue ˈdem.ə.gɒg US -gɑːg, -gɔːg **-s** -z
demagoguery ˈdem.ə.gɒg.ᵊr.i US -gɑː.gɚ-
demagogy ˈdem.ə.gɒg.i, -gɒdʒ- US -gɑː.dʒi, -gi; -goʊ.dʒi
demand dɪˈmɑːnd, də- US dɪˈmænd **-s** -z **-ing/ly** -ɪŋ/li **-ed** -ɪd
demanding dɪˈmɑːn.dɪŋ, də- US dɪˈmæn- **-ly** -li
demar|cate ˈdiː.mɑː|.keɪt US diːˈmɑːr|.keɪt, ˈdiː.mɑːr- **-cates** -keɪts **-cating** -keɪ.tɪŋ US -keɪ.t̬ɪŋ **-cated** -keɪ.tɪd US -keɪ.t̬ɪd
demarcation ˌdiː.mɑːˈkeɪ.ʃᵊn US -mɑːrˈ-
demarcative ˌdiːˈmɑː.kə.tɪv US -ˈmɑːr.kə.t̬ɪv
démarch|e ˈdeɪ.mɑːʃ, -ˈ- US deɪˈmɑːrʃ, dɪ- **-es** -ɪz
demark dɪˈmɑːk, ˌdiː- US -ˈmɑːrk **-s** -s **-ing** -ɪŋ **-ed** -t
demarkation ˌdiː.mɑːˈkeɪ.ʃᵊn US -mɑːrˈ-
Demas ˈdiː.mæs
dematerializ|e, -is|e ˌdiː.məˈtɪə.ri.ə.laɪz US -ˈtɪr.i- **-es** -ɪz **-ing** -ɪŋ **-ed** -d
demean dɪˈmiːn, də- US dɪ- **-s** -z **-ing** -ɪŋ **-ed** -d
demeano(u)r dɪˈmiː.nəʳ, də- US dɪˈmiː.nɚ **-s** -z
Demelza dɪˈmel.zə, də-, demˈel-
de|ment dɪ|ˈment, də- US dɪ- **-ments** -ˈments **-menting** -ˈmen.tɪŋ US -ˈmen.t̬ɪŋ **-mented/ly** -ˈmen.tɪd/li US -ˈmen.t̬ɪd/li
dementia dɪˈmen.*t*ʃə, də-, -*t*ʃi.ə US dɪˈmen*t*.ʃə
dementia praecox dɪˌmen.*t*ʃəˈpriː.kɒks, -ˈpraɪ- US -men*t*.ʃəˈpriː.kɑːks
demerara *sugar:* ˌdem.ᵊˈreə.rə, -ˈrɑː- US -ˈrɑːr.ə
Demerara *district in Guyana:* ˌdem.əˈrɑː.rə US -ˈrɑːr.ə
demerger ˌdiːˈmɜː.dʒəʳ US -ˈmɜːr.dʒɚ **-s** -z
demerit ˌdiːˈmer.ɪt, ˈdiː.mer- US dɪˈmer-, diː- **-s** -s
Demerol® ˈdem.ə.rɒl US -rɑːl
demesne dɪˈmeɪn, də-, -ˈmiːn US dɪ- **-s** -z
Demeter dɪˈmiː.təʳ, də- US -t̬ɚ
Demetrius dɪˈmiː.tri.əs, də-
demi- dem.i-
Note: Prefix. Normally carries primary or secondary stress on the first syllable, e.g. **demigod** /ˈdem.i.gɒd US -gɑːd/, **demisemiquaver** /ˌdem.iˈsem.iˌkweɪ.vəʳ US -vɚ/.
demigod ˈdem.i.gɒd US -gɑːd **-s** -z
demigoddess ˈdem.iˌgɒd.es US -ˌgɑː.des **-es** -ɪz
demijohn ˈdem.i.dʒɒn US -dʒɑːn **-s** -z
demilitarization, -isa- diːˌmɪl.ɪ.tᵊr.aɪˈzeɪ.ʃᵊn, ˌdiː.mɪ.lɪ-, -lə-, -ɪˈ- US diːˌmɪl.ɪ.t̬ɚ.ɪˈ-
demilitariz|e, -is|e ˌdiːˈmɪl.ɪ.tᵊr.aɪz, ˈ-ə- US -t̬ə.raɪz **-es** -ɪz **-ing** -ɪŋ **-ed** -d
de Mille dəˈmɪl, dɪ-
demimondaine ˌdem.i.mɒnˈdeɪn US -mɑːnˈ- **-s** -z
demimonde ˌdem.iˈmɔ̃ːnd, -ˈmɔːnd, -ˈmɒnd, ˈ--- US ˈdem.i.mɑːnd
de minimis ˌdeɪˈmɪn.ɪ.miːs, ˈ-ə-
demis|e dɪˈmaɪz, də- US dɪ- **-es** -ɪz **-ing** -ɪŋ **-ed** -d
demisemiquaver ˈdem.i.sem.iˌkweɪ.vəʳ, ˌdem.iˈsem.i- US ˌdem.iˈsem.iˌkweɪ.vɚ **-s** -z
demission dɪˈmɪʃ.ᵊn **-s** -z
demist ˌdiːˈmɪst **-s** -s **-ing** -ɪŋ **-ed** -ɪd **-er/s** -əʳ/z US -ɚ/z
demitass|e ˈdem.i.tæs, -tɑːs **-es** -ɪz
demiurg|e ˈdem.i.ɜːdʒ, ˈdiː.mi- US -ɜːrdʒ **-es** -ɪz
demo ˈdem.əʊ US -oʊ **-s** -z
demob ˌdiːˈmɒb US -ˈmɑːb **-s** -z **-bing** -ɪŋ **-bed** -d
demobilization, -isa- diːˌməʊ.bᵊl.aɪˈzeɪ.ʃᵊn, dɪ-, -bɪ.laɪˈ-, -lɪˈ- US -ˌmoʊ.bᵊl.ɪˈ-, -bɪ.lɪˈ- **-s** -z
demobiliz|e, -is|e ˌdiːˈməʊ.bᵊl.aɪz, dɪ-, -bɪ.laɪz US -ˈmoʊ.bə.laɪz, -bɪ- **-es** -ɪz **-ing** -ɪŋ **-ed** -d
democrac|y dɪˈmɒk.rə.s|i, də- US dɪˈmɑː- **-ies** -iz
democrat (D) ˈdem.ə.kræt **-s** -s
democratic (D) ˌdem.əˈkræt.ɪk US -ˈkræt̬- **-al** -ᵊl **-ally** -ᵊl.i, -li
democratization, -isa- dɪˌmɒk.rə.taɪˈzeɪ.ʃᵊn, də-, -tɪˈ- US dɪˌmɑː.krə.t̬ɪˈ-
democratiz|e, -is|e dɪˈmɒk.rə.taɪz, də- US dɪˈmɑː.krə- **-es** -ɪz **-ing** -ɪŋ **-ed** -d
Democritus dɪˈmɒk.rɪ.təs, də-, -rə- US dɪˈmɑːk.krə.t̬əs
démodé ˌdeɪˈməʊ.deɪ US -moʊˈdeɪ
demodu|late ˌdiːˈmɒd.jə|.leɪt, dɪ-, -jʊ-; -ˈmɒdʒ.ə-, ˈ-ʊ- US -ˈmɑː.dʒə-, -dʒʊ- **-lates** -leɪts **-lating** -leɪ.tɪŋ US -leɪ.t̬ɪŋ **-lated** -leɪ.tɪd US -leɪ.t̬ɪd
demodulation ˌdiːˌmɒd.jəˈleɪ.ʃᵊn, dɪ-, -jʊˈ-; -mɒdʒ.əˈ-, -ʊˈ- US -ˌmɑː.dʒəˈ-, -dʒʊ-
demodulator ˌdiːˈmɒd.jə.leɪ.təʳ, dɪ-, -jʊ-; -ˈmɒdʒ.ə-, ˈ-ʊ- US -ˈmɑː.dʒə.leɪ.t̬ɚ, -dʒʊ- **-s** -z
demographer dɪˈmɒg.rə.fəʳ, də-, ˌdiː- US dɪˈmɑː.grə.fɚ, ˌdiː- **-s** -z
demographic ˌdem.əʊˈgræf.ɪk, ˌdiː.məʊˈ- US ˌdem.əˈ-, ˌdiː.məˈ- **-s** -s
demography dɪˈmɒg.rə.fi, də-, ˌdiː- US dɪˈmɑː.grə-, ˌdiː-
demoiselle ˌdem.wɑːˈzel, -wəˈ- **-s** -z
De Moivre dəˈmɔɪ.vəʳ, dɪ- US -vɚ
demolish dɪˈmɒl.ɪʃ, də- US dɪˈmɑː.lɪʃ **-es** -ɪz **-ing** -ɪŋ **-ed** -t **-er/s** -əʳ/z US -ɚ/z
demolition ˌdem.əˈlɪʃ.ᵊn, ˌdiː.məˈ- **-s** -z
demon ˈdiː.mən **-s** -z
demonetization, -isa- ˌdiːˌmʌn.ɪ.taɪˈzeɪ.ʃᵊn, -ˌmɒn-, -ə-, -tɪˈ- US -ˌmɑː.nə.tɪˈ-
demonetiz|e, -is|e ˌdiːˈmʌn.ɪ.taɪz, -ˈmɒn-, ˈ-ə- US -ˈmɑː.nə- **-es** -ɪz **-ing** -ɪŋ **-ed** -d
demoniac dɪˈməʊ.ni.æk, də-, diː- US dɪˈmoʊ-, diː- **-s** -s
demoniac|al ˌdiː.məʊˈnaɪə.k|ᵊl US -məˈ- **-ally** -ᵊl.i, -li
demonic dɪˈmɒn.ɪk, də-, diː- US dɪˈmɑː.nɪk, diː- **-al** -ᵊl **-ally** -ᵊl.i, -li
demon|ism ˈdiː.mə.n|ɪ.zᵊm **-ist/s** -ɪst/s
demoniz|e ˈdiː.mᵊn.aɪz **-es** -ɪz **-ing** -ɪŋ **-ed** -d
demonology ˌdiː.məˈnɒl.ə.dʒi US -ˈnɑː.lə-
demonstrability dɪˌmɒn*t*.strəˈbɪl.ə.ti, də-, -ɪ.ti; ˌdem.ən- US dɪˌmɑːn*t*.strəˈbɪl.ə.t̬i; ˌdem.ən-
demonstrab|le dɪˈmɒn*t*.strə.b|l̩, də-; ˈdem.ən- US dɪˈmɑːn*t*-, də-; ˈdem.ən- **-ly** -li
demon|strate ˈdem.ən|.streɪt **-strates** -streɪts **-strating** -streɪ.tɪŋ US -streɪ.t̬ɪŋ **-strated** -streɪ.tɪd US -streɪ.t̬ɪd
demonstration ˌdem.ənˈstreɪ.ʃᵊn **-s** -z

demonstrative dɪˈmɒnt.strə.tɪv, də- (US) dɪˈmɑːnt.strə.t̬ɪv **-s** -z **-ly** -li **-ness** -nəs, -nɪs
demonstrator ˈdem.ən.streɪ.təʳ (US) -t̬ɚ **-s** -z
de Montfort dəˈmɒnt.fət, -fɔːt (US) -ˈmɑːnt.fɚt, -fɔːrt
demoralization, -isa- dɪˌmɒr.əl.aɪˈzeɪ.ʃən, ˌdiː.mɒr-, -ɪˈ- (US) dɪˌmɔːr.əl.ɪˈ-
demoraliz|e, -is|e dɪˈmɒr.ə.laɪz, ˌdiː- (US) -ˈmɔːr- **-es** -ɪz **-ing** -ɪŋ **-ed** -d
De Morgan dəˈmɔː.gən (US) -ˈmɔːr-
Demos ˈdiː.mɒs (US) -mɑːs
Demosthenes dɪˈmɒs.θə.niːz, də-, -θɪ- (US) -ˈmɑːs-
de|mote dɪ|ˈməʊt, ˌdiː- (US) -ˈmoʊt **-motes** -ˈməʊts (US) -ˈmoʊts **-moting** -ˈməʊ.tɪŋ (US) -ˈmoʊ.t̬ɪŋ **-moted** -ˈməʊ.tɪd (US) -ˈmoʊ.t̬ɪd
demotic dɪˈmɒt.ɪk, də-, diː- (US) dɪˈmɑː.t̬ɪk, diː-
demotion dɪˈməʊ.ʃən, ˌdiː- (US) -ˈmoʊ-
demoti|vate ˌdiːˈməʊ.tɪ|.veɪt, -tə- (US) -ˈmoʊ.t̬ə- **-vates** -veɪts **-vating** -veɪ.tɪŋ (US) -veɪ.t̬ɪŋ **-vated** -veɪ.tɪd (US) -veɪ.t̬ɪd
Dempsey ˈdemp.si
Dempster ˈdemp.stəʳ (US) -stɚ
demulcent dɪˈmʌl.sənt, də-, ˌdiː- (US) dɪ-, ˌdiː- **-s** -s
demur dɪˈmɜːʳ, də- (US) dɪˈmɜːr **-s** -z **-ring** -ɪŋ **-red** -d
demur|e dɪˈmjʊəʳ, də-, -mjɔːʳ (US) dɪˈmjʊr **-er** -əʳ (US) -ɚ **-est** -ɪst, -əst **-ely** -li **-eness** -nəs, -nɪs
demurrage dɪˈmʌr.ɪdʒ, də- (US) dɪˈmɜːr-
demurrer *person who demurs:* dɪˈmɜː.rəʳ, də- (US) -ˈmɜːr.ɚ **-s** -z
demurrer *objection on grounds of irrelevance:* dɪˈmʌr.əʳ, də- (US) dɪˈmɜːr.ɚ **-s** -z
dem|y dɪˈm|aɪ, də- (US) dɪ- **-ies** -aɪz
demystification ˌdiː.mɪ.stɪ.fɪˈkeɪ.ʃən, -stə-; diːˌmɪs.tɪ-, -tə- (US) diːˌmɪs-
demysti|fy ˌdiːˈmɪs.tɪ|.faɪ, -tə- **-fies** -faɪz **-fying** -faɪ.ɪŋ **-fied** -faɪd
demythologiz|e, -is|e ˌdiː.mɪˈθɒl.ə.dʒaɪz, -maɪˈ-, -məˈ- (US) -mɪˈθɑː.lə- **-es** -ɪz **-ing** -ɪŋ **-ed** -d
den den **-s** -z
Denali dəˈnɑː.li
denari|us dɪˈneə.ri|.əs, də-, denˈeə-, -ˈɑː- (US) dɪˈner.i-, -ˈnær- **-i** -aɪ, -iː
denary ˈdiː.nər.i, ˈden.ər-
denationalization, -isa- diːˌnæʃ.ən.əl.aɪˈzeɪ.ʃən, ˌdiː.næʃ-, -nəl.aɪ-, -ɪˈ- (US) diːˌnæʃ.ən.əl.ɪˈ-, -nəl.ɪ-
denationaliz|e, -is|e ˌdiːˈnæʃ.ən.əl.aɪz, ˈ-nəl- **-es** -ɪz **-ing** -ɪŋ **-ed** -d
denaturalization, -isa- diːˌnætʃ.ər.əl.aɪˈzeɪ.ʃən, ˌdiː.nætʃ-, -ɪˈ- (US) diːˌnætʃ.ɚ.əl.ɪˈ-
denaturaliz|e, -is|e ˌdiːˈnætʃ.ər.əl.aɪz **-es** -ɪz **-ing** -ɪŋ **-ed** -d
denatur|e ˌdiːˈneɪ.tʃəʳ (US) -tʃɚ **-es** -z **-ing** -ɪŋ **-ed** -d
Denbigh ˈden.bi, ˈdem- (US) ˈden- **-shire** -ʃəʳ, -ˌʃɪəʳ (US) -ʃɚ, -ˌʃɪr
Denby ˈden.bi, ˈdem- (US) ˈden-
Dench den*t*ʃ
dendrite ˈden.draɪt **-s** -s
dendritic denˈdrɪt.ɪk (US) -ˈdrɪt̬- **-al** -əl
dendroid ˈden.drɔɪd
dendrology denˈdrɒl.ə.dʒi (US) -ˈdrɑː.lə-
dendron ˈden.drən (US) -drən, -drɑːn **-s** -z
dene (D) diːn **-s** -z
Deneb ˈden.eb
Denebola dɪˈneb.ə.lə, denˈeb-, dəˈneb-
dengue ˈdeŋ.gi, -geɪ
Deng Xiaoping ˌdeŋ.ʃaʊˈpɪŋ (US) ˌdʌŋ-, ˌdeŋ-
Denham ˈden.əm
Denholm *place in West Yorkshire:* ˈden.hɒlm (US) -hoʊlm
Denholm(e) *name:* ˈden.əm
Denia ˈdiː.ni.ə **-s** -z
deniable dɪˈnaɪ.ə.bl̩, də- (US) dɪ-
denial dɪˈnaɪ.əl, də- (US) dɪ- **-s** -z
denier *coin:* ˈden.i.əʳ, -eɪ; dəˈnɪəʳ (US) dəˈnɪr **-s** -z
denier *thickness of yarn:* ˈden.i.əʳ, -eɪ (US) ˈden.jɚ
denier *person who denies:* dɪˈnaɪ.əʳ, də- (US) dɪˈnaɪ.ɚ **-s** -z
deni|grate ˈden.ɪ|.greɪt, ˈ-ə- **-grates** -greɪts **-grating** -greɪ.tɪŋ (US) -greɪ.t̬ɪŋ **-grated** -greɪ.tɪd (US) -greɪ.t̬ɪd
denigration ˌden.ɪˈgreɪ.ʃən, -əˈ-
denim ˈden.ɪm, -əm **-s** -z
De Niro dəˈnɪə.rəʊ (US) -ˈnɪr.oʊ
Denis ˈden.ɪs
Denise dəˈniːz, denˈiːz, dɪˈniːz, -ˈniːs (US) dəˈniːs, denˈiːs, dɪˈniːs, -ˈniːz
Denison ˈden.ɪ.sən
denizen ˈden.ɪ.zən, ˈ-ə- **-s** -z
Denman ˈden.mən, ˈdem- (US) ˈden-
Denmark ˈden.mɑːk, ˈdem- (US) ˈden.mɑːrk
Denning ˈden.ɪŋ
Dennis ˈden.ɪs
Dennison ˈden.ɪ.sən
Denny ˈden.i **-s** -z
denomi|nate dɪˈnɒm.ɪ|.neɪt, dəˈ-, ˈ-ə- (US) dɪˈnɑː.mə- **-nates** -neɪts **-nating** -neɪ.tɪŋ (US) -neɪ.t̬ɪŋ **-nated** -neɪ.tɪd (US) -neɪ.t̬ɪd
denomination dɪˌnɒm.ɪˈneɪ.ʃən, də-, -əˈ- (US) dɪˌnɑː.məˈ- **-s** -z
denominational dɪˌnɒm.ɪˈneɪ.ʃən.əl, də-, -əˈ- (US) dɪˌnɑː.məˈ-
denominationalism dɪˌnɒm.ɪˈneɪ.ʃən.əl.ɪ.zəm, də-, -əˈ- (US) dɪˌnɑː.məˈ-
denominative dɪˈnɒm.ɪ.nə.tɪv, də-, ˈ-ə- (US) dɪˈnɑː.mə.nə.t̬ɪv
denominator dɪˈnɒm.ɪ.neɪ.təʳ, də-, ˈ-ə- (US) dɪˈnɑː.mə.neɪ.t̬ɚ **-s** -z
denotation ˌdiː.nəʊˈteɪ.ʃən (US) -noʊˈ-, -nəˈ- **-s** -z
denotative dɪˈnəʊ.tə.tɪv, də-; ˈdiː.nəʊ.teɪ- (US) ˈdiː.noʊ.teɪ.t̬ɪv; dɪˈnoʊ.t̬ə-
de|note dɪ|ˈnəʊt, də- (US) dɪ|ˈnoʊt **-notes** -ˈnəʊts (US) -ˈnoʊts **-noting** -ˈnəʊ.tɪŋ (US) -ˈnoʊ.t̬ɪŋ **-noted** -ˈnəʊ.tɪd (US) -ˈnoʊ.t̬ɪd
dénouement deɪˈnuː.mɑ̃ŋ, dɪ-, də- (US) ˌdeɪ.nuːˈmɑ̃ŋ
dénouements deɪˈnuː.mɑ̃ŋ, dɪ-, də-, -mɑ̃ŋz (US) ˌdeɪ.nuːˈmɑ̃ŋ, -ˈmɑ̃ŋz
denounc|e dɪˈnaʊn*t*s, də- (US) dɪ- **-es** -ɪz **-ing** -ɪŋ **-ed** -t **-er/s** -əʳ/z (US) -ɚ/z **-ement/s** -mənt/s
de novo deɪˈnəʊ.vəʊ, diː-, də- (US) -ˈnoʊ.voʊ
dens|e den*t*s **-er** -əʳ (US) -ɚ **-est** -ɪst, -əst **-ely** -li **-eness** -nəs, -nɪs
densit|y ˈden*t*.sɪ.t|i, -sə- (US) -sə.t̬|i **-ies** -iz
dent (D) dent **-s** -s **-ing** -ɪŋ **-ed** -ɪd
dental ˈden.təl **-s** -z **ˈdental ˌfloss** ; **ˈdental ˌsurgeon**
dentaliz|e, -is|e ˈden.təl.aɪz (US) -t̬ə.laɪz **-es** -ɪz **-ing** -ɪŋ **-ed** -d
dentate ˈden.teɪt
dentated denˈteɪ.tɪd, ˈden.teɪ- (US) -t̬ɪd
denticle ˈden.tɪ.kl̩ (US) -t̬ɪ- **-s** -z
dentifric|e ˈden.tɪ.friːs, -tə-, -frɪs (US) -t̬ə.frɪs **-es** -ɪz
dentil ˈden.tɪl, -təl (US) -təl **-s** -z
dentilingual ˌden.tiˈlɪŋ.gwəl (US) -t̬iˈ- **-s** -z
dentine ˈden.tiːn
dentist ˈden.tɪst (US) -t̬ɪst **-s** -s
dentistry ˈden.tɪ.stri, -tə- (US) -t̬ɪ-
dentition denˈtɪʃ.ən
Denton ˈden.tən (US) -tən
denture ˈden.*t*ʃəʳ (US) ˈden*t*.ʃɚ **-s** -z
denudation ˌdiː.njuːˈdeɪ.ʃən, ˌden.juːˈ- (US) ˌdiː.nuːˈ-, -njuːˈ-; ˌden.juːˈ- **-s** -z
denud|e dɪˈnjuːd, də-, ˌdiː- (US) dɪˈnuːd, ˌdiː-, -ˈnjuːd **-es** -z **-ing** -ɪŋ **-ed** -ɪd
denunci|ate dɪˈnʌn*t*.si|.eɪt, də-, -ʃi- (US) dɪˈnʌn*t*.si- **-ates** -eɪts **-ating** -eɪ.tɪŋ (US) -eɪ.t̬ɪŋ **-ated** -eɪ.tɪd (US) -eɪ.t̬ɪd **-ator/s** -eɪ.təʳ/z (US) -eɪ.t̬ɚ/z

denunciation dɪˌnʌnt.si'eɪ.ʃ°n, də-, -ʃi'- (US) dɪˌnʌnt.si'- **-s** -z
denunciatory dɪ'nʌnt.si.ə.t°r.i, də-, -ʃi-, -tri (US) dɪ'nʌnt.si.ə.tɔːr.i
Denver 'den.vəʳ (US) -vɚ
den|y dɪ'n|aɪ, də- (US) dɪ- **-ies** -aɪz **-ying** -aɪ.ɪŋ **-ied** -aɪd **-ier/s** -aɪ.əʳ/z (US) -aɪ.ɚ/z
Denys 'den.ɪs
Denzil 'den.zɪl, -z°l (US) -z°l
deodand 'diː.əʊ.dænd (US) '-ə- **-s** -z
deodar 'diː.əʊ.dɑːʳ (US) -ə.dɑːr **-s** -z
deodorant di'əʊ.d°r.°nt (US) -'oʊ- **-s** -s
deodorization, -isa- diˌəʊ.d°r.aɪ'zeɪ.ʃ°n, -ɪ'- (US) -oʊ.dɚ.ɪ'- **-s** -z
deodoriz|e, -is|e di'əʊ.d°r.aɪz (US) -'oʊ.də.raɪz **-es** -ɪz **-ing** -ɪŋ **-ed** -d **-er/s** -əʳ/z (US) -ɚ/z
deontic di'ɒn.tɪk, diː-, deɪ- (US) -'ɑːn.t̬ɪk
deoxidization, -isa- diˌɒk.sɪ.daɪ'zeɪ.ʃ°n, ˌdiː-, -sə-, -dɪ'- (US) -ˌɑːk.sə.dɪ'- **-s** -z
deoxidiz|e, -is|e di'ɒk.sɪ.daɪz, ˌdiː-, -sə- (US) -'ɑːk.sə- **-es** -ɪz **-ing** -ɪŋ **-ed** -d **-er/s** -əʳ/z (US) -ɚ/z
Depardieu ˌdep.ɑː'djɜː, də.pɑː'-; 'dep.ɑː.djɜː (US) ˌdep.ɑːr'djɜː, '---
de|part dɪ|'pɑːt, də- (US) dɪ|'pɑːrt **-parts** -'pɑːts (US) -'pɑːrts **-parting** -'pɑː.tɪŋ (US) -'pɑːr.t̬ɪŋ **-parted** -'pɑː.tɪd (US) -'pɑːr.t̬ɪd
department dɪ'pɑːt.mənt, də- (US) dɪ'pɑːrt- **-s** -s **de'partment ˌstore**
departmental ˌdiː.pɑːt'men.t°l (US) -pɑːrt'men.t̬°l **-ism** -ɪ.z°m
departure dɪ'pɑː.tʃəʳ, də- (US) dɪ'pɑːr.tʃɚ **-s** -z **de'parture ˌlounge**
depast|ure ˌdiː'pɑːs.tʃ|əʳ (US) -'pæs.tʃ|ɚ **-ures** -əz (US) -ɚz **-uring** -°r.ɪŋ **-ured** -əd (US) -ɚd
depend dɪ'pend, də- (US) dɪ- **-s** -z **-ing** -ɪŋ **-ed** -ɪd
dependability dɪˌpen.də'bɪl.ə.ti, də-, -ɪ.ti (US) dɪˌpen.də'bɪl.ə.t̬i
dependab|le dɪ'pen.də.b|l̩, də-, dɪ- **-ly** -li **-leness** -l̩.nəs, -nɪs
dependant dɪ'pen.dənt, də- (US) dɪ- **-s** -s
dependenc|e dɪ'pen.dənts, də- (US) dɪ- **-y** -i **-ies** -iz
dependent dɪ'pen.dənt, də- (US) dɪ- **-s** -s **-ly** -li
De Pere dɪ'pɪəʳ, də- (US) -'pɪr
depersonaliz|e, is|e ˌdiː'pɜː.s°n.°l.aɪz (US) -'pɜːr- **-es** -ɪz **-ing** -ɪŋ **-ed** -d
Depew dɪ'pjuː, də-
depict dɪ'pɪkt, də- (US) dɪ- **-s** -s **-ing** -ɪŋ **-ed** -ɪd
depiction dɪ'pɪk.ʃ°n, də- (US) dɪ- **-s** -z
depi|late 'dep.ɪ|.leɪt, '-ə- **-lates** -leɪts **-lating** -leɪ.tɪŋ (US) -leɪ.t̬ɪŋ **-lated** -leɪ.tɪd (US) -leɪ.t̬ɪd
depilation ˌdep.ɪ'leɪ.ʃ°n, -ə'-
depilator|y dɪ'pɪl.ə.t°r|.i, də-, -tr|i (US) dɪ'pɪl.ə.tɔːr|.i **-ies** -iz
de|plete dɪ|'pliːt, də- (US) dɪ- **-pletes** -'pliːts **-pleting** -'pliː.tɪŋ (US) -'pliː.t̬ɪŋ **-pleted** -'pliː.tɪd (US) -'pliː.t̬ɪd
depletion dɪ'pliː.ʃ°n, də- (US) dɪ- **-s** -z
deplet|ive dɪ'pliː.t|ɪv, də- (US) dɪ'pliː.t̬|ɪv **-ory** -°r.i
deplorab|le dɪ'plɔː.rə.b|l̩, də- (US) dɪ'plɔːr.ə- **-ly** -li **-leness** -l̩.nəs, -nɪs
deplor|e dɪ'plɔːʳ, də- (US) dɪ'plɔːr **-es** -z **-ing** -ɪŋ **-ed** -d
deploy dɪ'plɔɪ, də- (US) dɪ- **-s** -z **-ing** -ɪŋ **-ed** -d
deployment dɪ'plɔɪ.mənt, də-, dɪ- **-s** -s
depolarization, -isa- diːˌpəʊ.l°r.aɪ'zeɪ.ʃ°n, ˌdiː.pəʊ-, -ɪ'- (US) diːˌpoʊ.lɚ.ɪ'-
depolariz|e, -is|e ˌdiː'pəʊ.l°r.aɪz (US) -'poʊ.lə.raɪz **-es** -ɪz **-ing** -ɪŋ **-ed** -d
depoliticization ˌdiː.pəˌlɪt.ɪ.saɪ'zeɪ.ʃ°n, ˌ-ə-, -sɪ'- (US) ˌ-lɪt̬.ɪ.sɪ'-, ˌ-ə-
depoliticiz|e, -is|e ˌdiː.pə'lɪt.ɪ.saɪz, '-ə- (US) -'lɪt̬- **-es** -ɪz **-ing** -ɪŋ **-ed** -d
de Pompadour də'pɒm.pə.dɔːʳ, -dʊəʳ (US) -'pɑːm.pə.dɔːr
deponent dɪ'pəʊ.nənt, də- (US) dɪ'poʊ- **-s** -s
Depo-Provera® ˌdep.əʊ.prəʊ'vɪə.rə (US) -oʊ.proʊ'ver.ə
depopu|late ˌdiː'pɒp.jə|.leɪt, -jʊ- (US) -'pɑː.pjə- **-lates** -leɪts **-lating** -leɪ.tɪŋ (US) -leɪ.t̬ɪŋ **-lated** -leɪ.tɪd (US) -leɪ.t̬ɪd **-lator/s** -leɪ.təʳ/z (US) -leɪ.t̬ɚ/z
depopulation diːˌpɒp.jə'leɪ.ʃ°n, ˌdiː.pɒp-, -jʊ'- (US) diːˌpɑː.pjə'-
de|port dɪ|'pɔːt, də- (US) dɪ|'pɔːrt **-ports** -'pɔːts (US) -'pɔːrts **-porting** -'pɔː.tɪŋ (US) -'pɔːr.t̬ɪŋ **-ported** -'pɔː.tɪd (US) -'pɔːr.t̬ɪd
deportation ˌdiː.pɔː'teɪ.ʃ°n (US) -pɔːr'- **-s** -z
deportee ˌdiː.pɔː'tiː (US) -pɔːr'- **-s** -z
deportment dɪ'pɔːt.mənt, də- (US) dɪ'pɔːrt-
deposal dɪ'pəʊ.z°l, də- (US) dɪ'poʊ- **-s** -z
depos|e dɪ'pəʊz, də- (US) dɪ'poʊz **-es** -ɪz **-ing** -ɪŋ **-ed** -d
depos|it dɪ'pɒz|.ɪt, də- (US) dɪ'pɑː.z|ɪt **-its** -ɪts **-iting** -ɪ.tɪŋ (US) -ɪ.t̬ɪŋ **-ited** -ɪ.tɪd (US) -ɪ.t̬ɪd **de'posit acˌcount**
depositar|y dɪ'pɒz.ɪ.t°r|.i, də-, '-ə- (US) dɪ'pɑː.zə.ter- **-ies** -iz
deposition ˌdep.ə'zɪʃ.°n, ˌdiː.pə'- **-s** -z
depositor dɪ'pɒz.ɪ.təʳ, də-, '-ə- (US) dɪ'pɑː.zə.t̬ɚ **-s** -z
depositor|y dɪ'pɒz.ɪ.t°r|.i, də-, '-ə-, -tr|i (US) dɪ'pɑː.zə.tɔːr|.i **-ies** -iz
depot 'dep.əʊ (US) 'diː.poʊ, 'dep.oʊ **-s** -z
Depp dep
depravation ˌdep.rə'veɪ.ʃ°n
deprav|e dɪ'preɪv, də- (US) dɪ- **-es** -z **-ing** -ɪŋ **-ed** -d **-edly** -d.li, -ɪd.li **-edness** -d.nəs, -ɪd.nəs, -nɪs
depravity dɪ'præv.ə.ti, də-, -ɪ.ti (US) dɪ'præv.ə.t̬i
depre|cate 'dep.rə|.keɪt, -rɪ- **-cates** -keɪts **-cating/ly** -keɪ.tɪŋ/li (US) -keɪ.t̬ɪŋ/li **-cated** -keɪ.tɪd (US) -keɪ.t̬ɪd **-cator/s** -keɪ.təʳ/z (US) -keɪ.t̬ɚ/z
deprecation ˌdep.rə'keɪ.ʃ°n, -prɪ'- **-s** -z
deprecatory 'dep.rə.kə.t°r.i, -rɪ-, -tri; ˌdep.rə'keɪ- (US) 'dep.rə.kə.tɔːr.i
depreciable dɪ'priː.ʃi.ə.bl̩, də-, -si- (US) dɪ'priː.ʃi.ə.bl̩, '-ʃə.bl̩
depreci|ate dɪ'priː.ʃi|.eɪt, də-, -si- (US) dɪ'priː.ʃi- **-ates** -eɪts **-ating/ly** -eɪ.tɪŋ/li (US) -eɪ.t̬ɪŋ/li **-ated** -eɪ.tɪd (US) -eɪ.t̬ɪd **-ator/s** -eɪ.təʳ/z (US) -eɪ.t̬ɚ/z
depreciation dɪˌpriː.ʃi'eɪ.ʃ°n, də-, -si'- (US) dɪˌpriː.ʃi'-
depreciatory dɪ'priː.ʃi.ə.t°r.i, də-, -si-, '-ʃə.t°r-, -tri (US) dɪ'priː.ʃi.ə.tɔːr.i, '-ʃə.tɔːr-
depre|date 'dep.rə|.deɪt, -rɪ- **-dates** -deɪts **-dating** -deɪ.tɪŋ (US) -deɪ.t̬ɪŋ **-dated** -deɪ.tɪd (US) -deɪ.t̬ɪd **-dator/s** -deɪ.təʳ/z (US) -deɪ.t̬ɚ/z
depredation ˌdep.rə'deɪ.ʃ°n, -rɪ'- **-s** -z
depredatory dɪ'pred.ə.t°r.i, də-, -tri; ˌdep.rə'deɪ- (US) 'dep.rə.də.tɔːr.i, -deɪ.t̬ɚ-; dɪ'pred.ə.tɔːr-
depress dɪ'pres, də- (US) dɪ- **-es** -ɪz **-ing** -ɪŋ **-ed** -t **-or/s** -əʳ/z (US) -ɚ/z **-ant/s** -°nt/s
depressing dɪ'pres.ɪŋ, də- (US) dɪ- **-ly** -li
depression dɪ'preʃ.°n, də- (US) dɪ- **-s** -z
depressive dɪ'pres.ɪv, də- (US) dɪ- **-s** -z
depressor dɪ'pres.əʳ, də- (US) dɪ'pres.ɚ **-s** -z
depressurization, -isation diːˌpreʃ.°r.aɪ'zeɪ.ʃ°n, ˌdiː.preʃ-, -ɪ'- (US) diːˌpreʃ.ɚ.ɪ'-
depressuriz|e, -is|e ˌdiː'preʃ.°r.aɪz (US) -ə.raɪz **-es** -ɪz **-ing** -ɪŋ **-ed** -d
deprivation ˌdep.rɪ'veɪ.ʃ°n, -rə'-; ˌdiː.praɪ'- **-s** -z
depriv|e dɪ'praɪv, də- (US) dɪ- **-es** -z **-ing** -ɪŋ **-ed** -d
de profundis ˌdeɪ.prɒf'ʊn.diːs, -prə'fʊn- (US) -proʊ'fʊn.dɪs
deprogram ˌdiː'prəʊ.græm (US) -'proʊ- **-s** -z **-(m)ing** -ɪŋ **-(m)ed** -d

deprogramm|e ˌdiːˈprəʊ.græm (US) -ˈproʊ- **-s** -z **-ing** -ɪŋ **-er** -d
dept (*abbrev. for* **department**) dɪˈpɑːt.mənt, də- (US) dɪˈpɑːrt-
Deptford ˈdet.fəd, ˈdep.fəd (US) -fɚd
depth depθ **-s** -s ˈ**depth** ˌ**charge**
deputation ˌdep.jəˈteɪ.ʃən, -jʊˈ- (US) -jəˈ- **-s** -z
de|pute dɪ|ˈpjuːt, də- (US) dɪ- **-putes** -ˈpjuːts **-puting** -ˈpjuː.tɪŋ (US) -ˈpjuː.t̬ɪŋ **-puted** -ˈpjuː.tɪd (US) -ˈpjuː.t̬ɪd
deputiz|e, -is|e ˈdep.jə.taɪz, -jʊ- **-es** -ɪz **-ing** -ɪŋ **-ed** -d
deput|y ˈdep.jə.t|i, -jʊ- (US) -t̬|i **-ies** -iz
De Quincey dəˈkwɪnt.si, dɪ-
deraci|nate dɪˈræs.ɪ|.neɪt, ˌdiː-, ˈ-ə- **-nates** -neɪts **-nating** -neɪ.tɪŋ (US) -neɪ.t̬ɪŋ **-nated** -neɪ.tɪd, -neɪ.t̬ɪd
deracination diːˌræs.ɪˈneɪ.ʃən, ˌdiː.ræs-, -əˈ- (US) diːˌræs-
derail dɪˈreɪl, ˌdiː- **-s** -z **-ing** -ɪŋ **-ed** -d
derailleur dɪˈreɪ.ljəʳ, də-, -ləʳ (US) dɪˈreɪ.lɚ
derailment dɪˈreɪl.mənt, ˌdiː- **-s** -s
derang|e dɪˈreɪndʒ, də- (US) dɪ- **-es** -ɪz **-ing** -ɪŋ **-ed** -d **-ement/s** -mənt/s
de|rate ˌdiː|ˈreɪt **-rates** -ˈreɪts **-rating** -ˈreɪ.tɪŋ (US) -ˈreɪ.t̬ɪŋ **-rated** -ˈreɪ.tɪd (US) -ˈreɪ.t̬ɪd
deration ˌdiːˈræʃ.ən **-s** -z **-ing** -ɪŋ **-ed** -d
derb|y ˈdɑː.b|i (US) ˈdɜːr- **-ies** -iz
Der|by ˈdɑː|.bi (US) ˈdɑːr-, ˈdɜːr- **-byshire** -bɪ.ʃəʳ, -ˌʃɪəʳ (US) -ʃɚ, -ˌʃɪr
Note: American pronunciation uses ˈdɑːr- for British references.
Derbys. (*abbrev. for* **Derbyshire**) ˈdɑː.bɪ.ʃəʳ, -ˌʃɪəʳ (US) ˈdɑːr.bɪ.ʃɚ, ˈdɜːr-, -ˌʃɪr
Note: American pronunciation uses ˈdɑːr- for British references.
deregu|late ˌdiːˈreg.jə|.leɪt, -jʊ- (US) -jə- **-lates** -leɪts **-lating** -leɪ.tɪŋ (US) -leɪ.t̬ɪŋ **-lated** -leɪ.tɪd (US) -leɪ.t̬ɪd
deregulation ˌdiː.reg.jəˈleɪ.ʃən, -jʊˈ- (US) -jəˈ-
Dereham ˈdɪə.rəm (US) ˈdɪr.əm
Derek ˈder.ɪk
derelict ˈder.ə.lɪkt, ˈ-ɪ- **-s** -s
dereliction ˌder.əˈlɪk.ʃən, -ɪˈ-
derequisition diːˌrek.wɪˈzɪʃ.ən, ˌdiː.rek-, -wəˈ- (US) diːˌrek- **-s** -z **-ing** -ɪŋ **-ed** -d
De Reszke dəˈres.ki
Derg(h) dɜːg (US) dɜːrg
Derham ˈder.əm
derid|e dɪˈraɪd, də- (US) dɪ- **-es** -z **-ing/ly** -ɪŋ/li **-ed** -ɪd **-er/s** -əʳ/z (US) -ɚ/z
de rigueur də.rɪˈgɜːʳ, ˌdeɪ-, ˌdiː-, -riːˈ- (US) -ˈgɜːr
Dering ˈdɪə.rɪŋ (US) ˈdɪr.ɪŋ
derision dɪˈrɪʒ.ən, də- (US) dɪ-
derisive dɪˈraɪ.sɪv, dəˈraɪ-, -zɪv, -ˈrɪz.ɪv (US) dɪˈraɪ.sɪv, -zɪv **-ly** -li **-ness** -nəs, -nɪs
derisory dɪˈraɪ.sər.i, də-, -zər- (US) dɪˈraɪ-
derivation ˌder.ɪˈveɪ.ʃən, -əˈ- **-s** -z **-al** -əl
derivative dɪˈrɪv.ə.tɪv, də- (US) dɪˈrɪv.ə.t̬ɪv **-s** -z **-ly** -li
deriv|e dɪˈraɪv, də- (US) dɪ- **-es** -z **-ing** -ɪŋ **-ed** -d **-able** -ə.bl̩
d'Erlanger ˌdeə.lɑ̃ŋˈʒeɪ (US) ˌder.lɑːnˈ-
derm dɜːm (US) dɜːrm **-al** -əl
-derm -dɜːm (US) -dɜːrm
Note: Suffix. Does not normally carry stress, e.g. **pachyderm** /ˈpæk.ɪ.dɜːm (US) -ə.dɜːrm/.
dermabrasion ˌdɜː.məˈbreɪ.ʒən (US) ˌdɜːr-
-dermal -dɜː.məl (US) -dɜːr-
Note: Suffix. May or may not carry stress, e.g. **epidermal** /ˌep.ɪˈdɜː.məl (US) -ˈdɜːr-/; see individual entries.
dermatitis ˌdɜː.məˈtaɪ.tɪs (US) ˌdɜːr.məˈtaɪ.t̬əs
dermatolog|y ˌdɜː.məˈtɒl.ə.dʒ|i (US) ˌdɜːr.məˈtɑː.lə- **-ist/s** -ɪst/s
dermatos|is ˌdɜː.məˈtəʊ.s|ɪs (US) ˌdɜːr.məˈtoʊ- **-es** -iːz
dermis ˈdɜː.mɪs (US) ˈdɜːr-
Dermot(t) ˈdɜː.mət (US) ˈdɜːr-
dernier cri ˌdɜː.ni.eɪˈkriː, ˌdeə- (US) ˌder.njeɪˈ-, ˌdɜːr-
dero|gate ˈder.əʊ|.geɪt, ˈdiː.rəʊ- (US) ˈder.ə- **-gates** -geɪts **-gating** -geɪ.tɪŋ (US) -geɪ.t̬ɪŋ **-gated** -geɪ.tɪd (US) -geɪ.t̬ɪd
derogation ˌder.əʊˈgeɪ.ʃən, ˌdiː.rəʊˈ- (US) ˌder.əˈ-
derogator|y dɪˈrɒg.ə.tər|.i, də-, -tr|i (US) dɪˈrɑː.gə.tɔːr|.i **-ily** -əl.i, -ɪ.li **-iness** -ɪ.nəs, -ɪ.nɪs
Deronda dəˈrɒn.də, dɪ- (US) dəˈrɑːn-
derrick (D) ˈder.ɪk **-s** -s
Derrida dəˈriː.də, derˈiː-; ˈder.ɪ- (US) ˈder.iː.dɑː
derrière ˈder.i.eəʳ, ˌ--ˈ- (US) ˌder.iˈer, ˈ--- **-s** -z
derring-do ˌder.ɪŋˈduː, ˌdeə.rɪŋˈ- (US) ˌder.ɪŋˈ-
derringer (D) ˈder.ɪn.dʒəʳ, -ən- (US) -dʒɚ **-s** -z
Derry ˈder.i
derv dɜːv (US) dɜːrv
dervish (D) ˈdɜː.vɪʃ (US) ˈdɜːr- **-es** -ɪz
Dervla ˈdɜːv.lə (US) ˈdɜːrv-
Derwent ˈdɜː.wənt, ˈdɑː-, -went, -wɪnt (US) ˈdɜːr-, ˈdɑːr- ˈ**Derwent** ˌ**Water**
Note: /ˈdɑː- (US) ˈdɑːr-/ is the normal pronunciation for the Baron.
Des dez (US) des
DES ˌdiː.iːˈes
Desai desˈaɪ; ˈdeɪ.saɪ
desali|nate ˌdiːˈsæl.ɪ|.neɪt, ˈ-ə- **-nates** -neɪts **-nating** -neɪ.tɪŋ (US) -neɪ.t̬ɪŋ **-nated** -neɪ.tɪd (US) -neɪ.t̬ɪd
desalination diːˌsæl.ɪˈneɪ.ʃən, ˌdiː.sæl-, -əˈ- (US) diːˌsæl- **-s** -z
desalinization, -isa- diːˌsæl.ɪ.naɪˈzeɪ.ʃən, ˌdiː.sæl-, ˌ-ə-, -nɪˈ- (US) diːˌsæl.ə.nɪˈ-
desaliniz|e, -is|e ˌdiːˈsæl.ɪ.naɪz, ˈ-ə- **-es** -ɪz **-ing** -ɪŋ **-ed** -d
Desart ˈdez.ət (US) -ɚt
Desborough ˈdez.brə (US) -bɚ.oʊ, ˈ-brə
descal|e ˌdiːˈskeɪl **-es** -z **-ing** -ɪŋ **-ed** -d
descant (*n.*) ˈdes.kænt **-s** -s
descan|t (*v.*) dɪˈskæn|t, desˈkæn|t (US) ˈdes.kæn|t, -ˈ- **-ts** -ts **-ting** -tɪŋ (US) -t̬ɪŋ **-ted** -tɪd (US) -t̬ɪd
Descartes ˈdeɪ.kɑːt, deɪˈkɑːt (US) deɪˈkɑːrt
descend dɪˈsend, də- (US) dɪ- **-s** -z **-ing** -ɪŋ **-ed** -ɪd
descendant, descendent dɪˈsen.dənt, də- (US) dɪ- **-s** -s
descender dɪˈsen.dəʳ, də- (US) dɪˈsen.dɚ **-s** -z
descent dɪˈsent, də- (US) dɪ- **-s** -s
describ|e dɪˈskraɪb, də- (US) dɪ- **-es** -z **-ing** -ɪŋ **-ed** -d **-er/s** -əʳ/z (US) -ɚ/z **-able** -ə.bl̩
description dɪˈskrɪp.ʃən, də- (US) dɪ- **-s** -z
descriptive dɪˈskrɪp.tɪv, də- (US) dɪ- **-ly** -li **-ness** -nəs, -nɪs
descriptiv|ism dɪˈskrɪp.tɪ.v|ɪ.zəm, də- (US) dɪ- **-ist** -ɪst
descr|y dɪˈskr|aɪ, də- (US) dɪ- **-ies** -aɪz **-ying** -aɪ.ɪŋ **-ied** -aɪd
Desdemona ˌdez.dɪˈməʊ.nə, -dəˈ- (US) -dəˈmoʊ-
dese|crate ˈdes.ɪ|.kreɪt, ˈ-ə- **-crates** -kreɪts **-crating** -kreɪ.tɪŋ (US) -kreɪ.t̬ɪŋ **-crated** -kreɪ.tɪd (US) -kreɪ.t̬ɪd **-crator/s** -kreɪ.təʳ/z (US) -kreɪ.t̬ɚ/z
desecration ˌdes.ɪˈkreɪ.ʃən, -əˈ- **-s** -z
deseed ˌdiːˈsiːd **-s** -z **-ing** -ɪŋ **-ed** -d
desegre|gate ˌdiːˈseg.rɪ|.geɪt, -rə- **-gates** -geɪts **-gating** -geɪ.tɪŋ (US) -geɪ.t̬ɪŋ **-gated** -geɪ.tɪd (US) -geɪ.t̬ɪd
desegregation diːˌseg.rɪˈgeɪ.ʃən, ˌdiː.seg-, -rəˈ- (US) diːˌseg-
deselect ˌdiː.səˈlekt, -sɪˈ- **-s** -s **-ing** -ɪŋ **-ed** -ɪd
deselection ˌdiː.səˈlek.ʃən, -sɪˈ-
de Selincourt dəˈsel.ɪŋ.kɔːt, -ɪn- (US) -kɔːrt
desensitization diːˌsent.sɪ.taɪˈzeɪ.ʃən, ˌdiː.sent-, -sə-, -tɪˈ- (US) diːˌsent.sɪ.tɪˈ-, ˌ-sə-

desensitiz|e, -is|e ˌdiːˈsent.sɪ.taɪz, -sə- **-es** -ɪz **-ing** -ɪŋ **-ed** -d

desert (*n. adj.*) *dry place:* ˈdez.ət Ⓤⓢ -ɚt **-s** -s ˌ**desert ˈisland** ; ˈ**desert** ˌ**rat**

desert (*n.*) *what is deserved:* dɪˈzɜːt, də- Ⓤⓢ dɪˈzɜːrt **-s** -s **get one's** ˌ**just deˈserts**

de|sert (*v.*) dɪ|ˈzɜːt, də- Ⓤⓢ dɪ|ˈzɜːrt **-serts** -ˈzɜːts Ⓤⓢ -ˈzɜːrts **-serting** -ˈzɜː.tɪŋ Ⓤⓢ -ˈzɜːr.t̬ɪŋ **-serted** -ˈzɜː.tɪd Ⓤⓢ -ˈzɜːr.t̬ɪd **-serter/s** -ˈzɜː.təʳ/z Ⓤⓢ -ˈzɜːr.t̬ɚ/z

desertification dɪˌzɜː.tɪ.fɪˈkeɪ.ʃᵊn, də-, -tə- Ⓤⓢ dɪˌzɜːr.t̬ə-

desertion dɪˈzɜː.ʃᵊn, də- Ⓤⓢ dɪˈzɜːr- **-s** -z

deserv|e dɪˈzɜːv, də- Ⓤⓢ dɪˈzɜːrv **-es** -z **-ing/ly** -ɪŋ/li **-ed** -d **-edly** -ɪd.li

desex ˌdiːˈseks **-es** -ɪz **-ing** -ɪŋ **-ed** -t

desexualiz|e, -is|e diːˈsek.ʃʊə.laɪz, -ʃu.ᵊl.aɪz, -sjʊə.laɪz, -sjʊ.ᵊl.aɪz Ⓤⓢ -ʃu.ə.laɪz **-es** -ɪz **-ing** -ɪŋ **-ed** -d

deshabille ˌdez.æbˈiːl, ˌdeɪ.zæbˈ-, ˌdes.æbˈ-, -əˈbiːl, ˈ--- Ⓤⓢ ˌdes.æbˈ-, ˌdez-; ˈdɪs.ə.biːl

déshabillé ˌdeɪ.zæbˈiː.eɪ, ˌdez.æb-, ˌdes-, -əˈbiː-, -ˈbiːl

desiccant ˈdes.ɪ.kᵊnt, ˈ-ə- **-s** -s

desic|cate ˈdes.ɪ|.keɪt, ˈ-ə- **-cates** -keɪts **-cating** -keɪ.tɪŋ Ⓤⓢ -keɪ.t̬ɪŋ **-cated** -keɪ.tɪd Ⓤⓢ -keɪ.t̬ɪd

desiccation ˌdes.ɪˈkeɪ.ʃᵊn, -əˈ-

desiccative ˈdes.ɪ.kə.tɪv; desˈɪk.ə-, dɪˈsɪk- Ⓤⓢ ˈdes.ɪ.keɪ.t̬ɪv; dəˈsɪk.ə-

desiccator ˈdes.ɪ.keɪ.təʳ, ˈ-ə- Ⓤⓢ -t̬ɚ **-s** -z

desider|ate dɪˈzɪd.ᵊr|.eɪt, də-, -ˈsɪd- Ⓤⓢ dɪˈsɪd.ə.r|eɪt, -ˈzɪd- **-ates** -eɪts **-ating** -eɪ.tɪŋ Ⓤⓢ -eɪ.t̬ɪŋ **-ated** -eɪ.tɪd Ⓤⓢ -eɪ.t̬ɪd

desideration dɪˌzɪd.ᵊˈreɪ.ʃᵊn, də-, -ˌsɪd- Ⓤⓢ dɪˌsɪd-, -ˌzɪd- **-s** -z

desiderative dɪˈzɪd.ᵊr.ə.tɪv, də-, -ˈsɪd- Ⓤⓢ dɪˈsɪd.ɚ.ə.t̬ɪv, -ˈzɪd-

desiderat|um dɪˌzɪd.ᵊˈrɑː.t|əm, də-, -ˌsɪd-, -ˈreɪ- Ⓤⓢ dɪˌsɪd.əˈrɑː.t̬|əm, -ˌzɪd-, -ˈreɪ- **-a** -ə

design dɪˈzaɪn, də- Ⓤⓢ dɪ- **-s** -z **-ing** -ɪŋ **-ed** -d **-edly** -ɪd.li **-able** -ə.bl̩

designate (*adj.*) ˈdez.ɪg.neɪt, -nɪt, -nət

desig|nate (*v.*) ˈdez.ɪg|.neɪt **-nates** -neɪts **-nating** -neɪ.tɪŋ Ⓤⓢ -neɪ.t̬ɪŋ **-nated** -neɪ.tɪd Ⓤⓢ -neɪ.t̬ɪd **-nator/s** -neɪ.təʳ/z Ⓤⓢ -neɪ.t̬ɚ/z

designation ˌdez.ɪgˈneɪ.ʃᵊn **-s** -z

designer dɪˈzaɪ.nəʳ, də- Ⓤⓢ dɪˈzaɪ.nɚ **-s** -z

desinenc|e ˈdes.ɪ.nən*t*s, ˈdez-, -ᵊn.ən*t*s **-es** -ɪz

desirability dɪˌzaɪə.rəˈbɪl.ə.ti, də-, -ɪ.ti Ⓤⓢ dɪˌzaɪ.rəˈbɪl.ə.t̬i

desirab|le dɪˈzaɪə.rə.b|l̩, də- Ⓤⓢ dɪˈzaɪ- **-ly** -li **-leness** -l̩.nəs, -nɪs

desir|e dɪˈzaɪəʳ, də Ⓤⓢ dɪˈzaɪɚ **-es** -z **-ing** -ɪŋ **-ed** -d **-er/s** -əʳ/z Ⓤⓢ -ɚ/z

Désirée deɪˈzɪə.reɪ, dezˈɪə- Ⓤⓢ ˌdez.əˈreɪ

desirous dɪˈzaɪə.rəs, də- Ⓤⓢ dɪˈzaɪ.rəs **-ly** -li

desist dɪˈsɪst, də-, dɪˈzɪst **-s** -s **-ing** -ɪŋ **-ed** -ɪd

desistance dɪˈsɪs.tᵊn*t*s, dəˈ-, dɪˈzɪs-

desk desk **-s** -s ˈ**desk** ˌ**job**

de-skill ˌdiːˈskɪl **-s** -z **-ing** -ɪŋ **-ed** -d

desktop ˈdesk.tɒp Ⓤⓢ -tɑːp ˌ**desktop ˈpublishing**

Des Moines dəˈmɔɪn, dɪ-, -ˈmɔɪnz Ⓤⓢ -ˈmɔɪn

Desmond ˈdez.mənd

desolate (*adj.*) ˈdes.ᵊl.ət, ˈdez-, -ɪt **-ly** -li **-ness** -nəs, -nɪs

desol|ate (*v.*) ˈdes.ᵊl|.eɪt, ˈdez.ə.l|eɪt **-ates** -eɪts **-ating** -eɪ.tɪŋ Ⓤⓢ -eɪ.t̬ɪŋ **-ated** -eɪ.tɪd Ⓤⓢ -eɪ.t̬ɪd **-ator/s** -eɪ.təʳ/z Ⓤⓢ -eɪ.t̬ɚ/z

desolation ˌdes.ᵊlˈeɪ.ʃᵊn, ˌdez- **-s** -z

de Soto dəˈsəʊ.təʊ Ⓤⓢ -ˈsoʊ.toʊ

despair dɪˈspeəʳ, də- Ⓤⓢ dɪˈsper **-s** -z **-ing/ly** -ɪŋ/li **-ed** -d

Despard ˈdes.pəd, -pɑːd Ⓤⓢ -pɚd, -pɑːrd

despatch dɪˈspætʃ, də- Ⓤⓢ dɪ- **-es** -ɪz **-ing** -ɪŋ **-ed** -t **-er/s** -əʳ/z Ⓤⓢ -ɚ/z **desˈpatch** ˌ**box** ; **desˈpatch** ˌ**rider**

desperado ˌdes.pəˈrɑː.dəʊ, -ˈreɪ- Ⓤⓢ -doʊ **-(e)s** -z

desperate ˈdes.pᵊr.ət, -ɪt **-ly** -li **-ness** -nəs, -nɪs

desperation ˌdes.pᵊˈreɪ.ʃᵊn

despicability dɪˌspɪk.əˈbɪl.ə.ti, də-, -ɪ.ti; ˌdes.pɪ.kəˈ- Ⓤⓢ dɪˌspɪk.əˈbɪl.ə.t̬i; ˌdes.pɪ.kəˈ-

despicab|le dɪˈspɪk.ə.b|l̩, də-; ˈdes.pɪ.kə- Ⓤⓢ dɪˈspɪk.ə-; ˈdes.pɪ.kə- **-ly** -li **-leness** -l̩.nəs, -nɪs

despis|e dɪˈspaɪz, də- Ⓤⓢ dɪ- **-es** -ɪz **-ing** -ɪŋ **-ed** -d **-er/s** -əʳ/z Ⓤⓢ -ɚ/z

despite dɪˈspaɪt, də- Ⓤⓢ dɪ-

despiteful dɪˈspaɪt.fᵊl, də-, -fʊl Ⓤⓢ dɪ- **-ly** -li

despoil dɪˈspɔɪl, də- Ⓤⓢ dɪ- **-s** -z **-ing** -ɪŋ **-ed** -d **-er/s** -əʳ/z Ⓤⓢ -ɚ/z

despoliation dɪˌspəʊ.liˈeɪ.ʃᵊn, də-, -ˌspɒl.iˈ- Ⓤⓢ dɪˌspoʊ.liˈ-

despond (D) dɪˈspɒnd, də- Ⓤⓢ dɪˈspɑːnd **-s** -z **-ing/ly** -ɪŋ/li **-ed** -ɪd

desponden|ce dɪˈspɒn.dən*t*|s, də- Ⓤⓢ dɪˈspɑːn- **-cy** -si

despondent dɪˈspɒn.dənt, də- Ⓤⓢ dɪˈspɑːn- **-ly** -li

despot ˈdes.pɒt, -pət Ⓤⓢ -pət **-s** -s

despotic dɪˈspɒt.ɪk, desˈpɒt-, dəˈspɒt- Ⓤⓢ desˈpɑː.t̬ɪk **-al** -ᵊl **-ally** -ᵊl.i, -li **-alness** -ᵊl.nəs, -nɪs

despotism ˈdes.pə.tɪ.zᵊm Ⓤⓢ -tɪ- **-s** -z

desqua|mate ˈdes.kwə|.meɪt **-mates** -meɪts **-mating** -meɪ.tɪŋ Ⓤⓢ -meɪ.t̬ɪŋ **-mated** -meɪ.tɪd Ⓤⓢ -meɪ.t̬ɪd

des res ˌdezˈrez

dessert dɪˈzɜːt, də- Ⓤⓢ dɪˈzɜːrt **-s** -s **desˈsert** ˌ**wine, des**ˌ**sert ˈwine**

dessertspoon dɪˈzɜːt.spuːn, də- Ⓤⓢ dɪˈzɜːrt- **-s** -z

dessert|spoonful dɪˈzɜːt|ˌspuːn.fʊl, də- Ⓤⓢ dɪˈzɜːrt- **-spoonsful** -ˌspuːnz.fʊl **-spoonfuls** -ˌspuːn.fʊlz

destabilization ˌdiːˌsteɪ.bᵊl.aɪˈzeɪ.ʃᵊn, dɪ-, -bɪ.laɪˈ- Ⓤⓢ -bᵊl.ɪˈ-, -bɪ.lɪˈ-

destabiliz|e, -is|e ˌdiːˈsteɪ.bᵊl.aɪz, dɪ-, -bɪ.laɪz **-es** -ɪz **-ing** -ɪŋ **-ed** -d

destination ˌdes.tɪˈneɪ.ʃᵊn, -təˈ- **-s** -z

destin|e ˈdes.tɪn, -tᵊn **-es** -z **-ing** -ɪŋ **-ed** -d

destin|y ˈdes.tɪ.n|i, -tᵊn|.i **-ies** -iz

destitute ˈdes.tɪ.tjuːt, -tə- Ⓤⓢ -tuːt, -tjuːt **-ly** -li **-ness** -nəs, -nɪs

destitution ˌdes.tɪˈtjuː.ʃᵊn, -təˈ- Ⓤⓢ -ˈtuː-, -ˈtjuː-

destroy dɪˈstrɔɪ, də- Ⓤⓢ dɪ- **-s** -z **-ing** -ɪŋ **-ed** -d

destroyer dɪˈstrɔɪ.əʳ, də- Ⓤⓢ dɪˈstrɔɪ.ɚ **-s** -z

destruct dɪˈstrʌkt, də- Ⓤⓢ dɪ- **-s** -s **-ing** -ɪŋ **-ed** -ɪd

destructibility dɪˌstrʌk.təˈbɪl.ə.ti, də-, -tɪˈ-, -ɪ.ti Ⓤⓢ dɪˌstrʌk.təˈbɪl.ə.t̬i, -tɪˈ-

destructible dɪˈstrʌk.tə.bl̩, də-, -tɪ- Ⓤⓢ dɪ-

destruction dɪˈstrʌk.ʃᵊn, də- Ⓤⓢ dɪ- **-s** -z

destructive dɪˈstrʌk.tɪv, də- Ⓤⓢ dɪ- **-ly** -li **-ness** -nəs, -nɪs

destructor dɪˈstrʌk.təʳ, də- Ⓤⓢ dɪˈstrʌk.tɚ **-s** -z

desuetude dɪˈsjuː.ɪ.tjuːd, -tʃuːd; ˈdes.wɪ-, ˈdiː.swɪ- Ⓤⓢ ˈdes.wɪ.tuːd, -tjuːd; dɪˈsuː.ə-

desultor|y ˈdes.ᵊl.tᵊr|.i, ˈdez-, -tr|i Ⓤⓢ -tɔːr|.i **-ily** -ᵊl.i, -ɪ.li **-iness** -ɪ.nəs, -ɪ.nɪs

Des Vœux deɪˈvɜː

detach dɪˈtætʃ, də- Ⓤⓢ dɪ- **-es** -ɪz **-ing** -ɪŋ **-ed** -t **-edly** -t.li, -ɪd.li **-able** -ə.bl̩

detachment dɪˈtætʃ.mənt, də- Ⓤⓢ dɪ- **-s** -s

detail ˈdiː.teɪl; dɪˈteɪl, də- Ⓤⓢ dɪˈteɪl; ˈdiː.teɪl **-s** -z **-ing** -ɪŋ **-ed** -d

detain dɪˈteɪn, də- Ⓤⓢ dɪ- **-s** -z **-ing** -ɪŋ **-ed** -d **-er/s** -əʳ/z Ⓤⓢ -ɚ/z

detainee ˌdiː.teɪˈniː; dɪˌteɪˈ-, də- (US) ˌdiː.teɪˈ- **-s** -z
detect dɪˈtekt, də- (US) dɪ- **-s** -s **-ing** -ɪŋ **-ed** -ɪd
detectab|le dɪˈtek.tə.bl̩|, də- (US) dɪ- **-ly** -li
detection dɪˈtek.ʃᵊn, də- (US) dɪ- **-s** -z
detective dɪˈtek.tɪv, də- (US) dɪ- **-s** -z
detector dɪˈtek.təʳ, də- (US) dɪˈtek.tɚ **-s** -z
detent dɪˈtent, də- (US) dɪ- **-s** -s
détente ˈdeɪ.tɑ̃nt (US) deɪˈtɑːnt, ˈ--
detention dɪˈten.*t*ʃᵊn, də- (US) dɪ- **-s** -z **deˈtention ˌcentre**
deter dɪˈtɜːʳ, də- (US) dɪˈtɜːr **-s** -z **-ring** -ɪŋ **-red** -d
Deterding ˈdet.ə.dɪŋ (US) ˈdet̬.ɚ-
detergent dɪˈtɜː.dʒᵊnt, də- (US) dɪˈtɜːr- **-s** -s
deterior|ate dɪˈtɪə.ri.ᵊr|.eɪt, də- (US) dɪˈtɪr.i.ə.r|eɪt **-ates** -eɪts **-ating** -eɪ.tɪŋ (US) -eɪ.t̬ɪŋ **-ated** -eɪ.tɪd (US) -eɪ.t̬ɪd
deterioration dɪˌtɪə.ri.əˈreɪ.ʃᵊn, də- (US) dɪˌtɪr.i-
determinable dɪˈtɜː.mɪ.nə.bl̩, də-, -mᵊn.ə- (US) dɪˈtɜːr-
determinant dɪˈtɜː.mɪ.nənt, də- (US) dɪˈtɜːr- **-s** -s
determinate dɪˈtɜː.mɪ.nət, də-, -nɪt (US) dɪˈtɜːr- **-ly** -li **-ness** -nəs, -nɪs
determination dɪˌtɜː.mɪˈneɪ.ʃᵊn, də-, -məˈ- (US) dɪˌtɜːr- **-s** -z
determinative dɪˈtɜː.mɪ.nə.tɪv, də-, -mᵊn.ə- (US) dɪˈtɜːr.mɪ.neɪ.t̬ɪv, -nə-
determin|e dɪˈtɜː.mɪn, də-, -mən (US) dɪˈtɜːr- **-es** -z **-ing** -ɪŋ **-ed/ly** -d/li
determined dɪˈtɜː.mɪnd, də- (US) dɪˈtɜːr- **-ly** -li
determiner dɪˈtɜː.mɪ.nəʳ, də-, -mə- (US) dɪˈtɜːr.mɪ.nɚ **-s** -z
determin|ism dɪˈtɜː.mɪ.n|ɪ.zᵊm, də-, -mə- (US) dɪˈtɜːr- **-ist/s** -ɪst/s
deterrence dɪˈter.ᵊn*t*s, də- (US) dɪ-
deterrent dɪˈter.ᵊnt, də- (US) dɪ- **-s** -s
detest dɪˈtest, də- (US) dɪ- **-s** -s **-ing** -ɪŋ **-ed** -ɪd
detestab|le dɪˈtes.tə.bl̩|, də- (US) dɪ- **-ly** -li **-leness** -l̩.nəs, -nɪs
detestation ˌdiː.tesˈteɪ.ʃᵊn, dɪˌtes- (US) ˌdiː.tes-
dethron|e diːˈθrəʊn, ˌdiː-, də- (US) dɪˈθroʊn, ˌdiː- **-es** -z **-ing** -ɪŋ **-ed** -d **-ement** -mənt
detinue ˈdet.ɪ.njuː (US) -ᵊn.juː, -uː
Detlev ˈdet.lef (US) -ləf, -lef
Detmold ˈdet.məʊld (US) -moʊld
de Tocqueville dəˈtəʊk.vɪl, -ˈtɒk-, -viːl (US) -ˈtoʊk.vɪl, -ˈtɑːk-
deton|ate ˈdet.ᵊn|.eɪt **-ates** -eɪts **-ating** -eɪ.tɪŋ (US) -eɪ.t̬ɪŋ **-ated** -eɪ.tɪd (US) -eɪ.t̬ɪd
detonation ˌdet.ᵊnˈeɪ.ʃᵊn **-s** -z
detonator ˈdet.ᵊn.eɪ.təʳ (US) -t̬ɚ **-s** -z
detour ˈdiː.tʊəʳ, ˈdeɪ-, -tɔːʳ (US) ˈdiː.tʊr; -ˈ-, dɪ- **-s** -z
detox ˌdiːˈtɒks, dɪ-; ˈdiː.tɒks (US) diːˈtɑːks, ˈ-- **-es** -ɪz **-ing** -ɪŋ **-ed** -t
detoxi|cate ˌdiːˈtɒk.sɪ|.keɪt, dɪ-, -sə- (US) -ˈtɑːk- **-cates** -keɪts **-cating** -keɪ.tɪŋ (US) -keɪ.t̬ɪŋ **-cated** -keɪ.tɪd (US) -keɪ.t̬ɪd
detoxification diːˌtɒk.sɪ.fɪˈkeɪ.ʃᵊn, dɪ-, -sə-; ˌdiː.tɒk- (US) diːˌtɑːk-
detoxi|fy ˌdiːˈtɒk.sɪ|.faɪ, dɪ-, -sə- (US) ˌdiːˈtɑːk- **-fies** -faɪz **-fying** -faɪ.ɪŋ **-fied** -faɪd
detract dɪˈtrækt, də- (US) dɪ- **-s** -s **-ing/ly** -ɪŋ/li **-ed** -ɪd
detraction dɪˈtræk.ʃᵊn, də- (US) dɪ- **-s** -z
detract|ive dɪˈtræk.t|ɪv, də- (US) dɪ- **-ory** -ᵊr.i
detractor dɪˈtræk.təʳ, də- (US) dɪˈtræk.tɚ **-s** -z
detrain ˌdiːˈtreɪn **-s** -z **-ing** -ɪŋ **-ed** -d
detriment ˈdet.rɪ.mənt, -rə- **-s** -s
detrimental ˌdet.rɪˈmen.tᵊl, -rəˈ- (US) -t̬ᵊl
detrition dɪˈtrɪʃ.ᵊn, də- (US) dɪ-
detritus dɪˈtraɪ.təs, də- (US) dɪˈtraɪ.t̬əs
Detroit dəˈtrɔɪt, dɪ-
de trop dəˈtrəʊ (US) -troʊ
detrun|cate ˌdiːˈtrʌŋ|.keɪt, ˈ--- (US) ˌdiːˈtrʌŋ- **-cates** -keɪts **-cating** -keɪ.tɪŋ (US) -keɪ.t̬ɪŋ **-cated** -keɪ.tɪd (US) -keɪ.t̬ɪd
detruncation ˌdiː.trʌŋˈkeɪ.ʃᵊn **-s** -z
Dettol® ˈdet.ɒl, -ᵊl (US) -tɑːl, -t̬ᵊl
detumescen|ce ˌdiː.tjuːˈmes.ᵊn|*t*s, -tjʊˈ- (US) -tuːˈ-, -tjuːˈ- **-t** -t
Deucalion djuːˈkeɪ.li.ən (US) duː-, djuː-
deuc|e djuːs, dʒuːs (US) duːs, djuːs **-es** -ɪz
deuc|ed djuːs|t, dʒuːs|t; ˈdjuː.s|ɪd, ˈdʒuː- (US) ˈduː.s|ɪd, ˈdjuː-; duːs|t, djuːs|t **-edly** -ɪd.li
deus ex machina ˌdeɪ.əs.eksˈmɑːk.ɪ.nə, -ˈmæk-, ˌdiː-, -ʊs-
deuterium djuːˈtɪə.ri.əm (US) duːˈtɪr.i-, djuː-
deuteronomic ˌdjuː.tᵊr.əˈnɒm.ɪk (US) ˌduː.t̬ɚ.əˈnɑː.mɪk, ˌdjuː-
Deuteronomy ˌdjuː.təˈrɒn.ə.mi (US) ˌduː.t̬əˈrɑː.nə-, ˌdjuː-
Deutsche Mark ˌdɔɪ.tʃəˈmɑːk (US) -ˈmɑːrk **-s** -s
deutschmark (D) ˈdɔɪtʃ.mɑːk (US) -mɑːrk **-s** -s
deutzia ˈdjuːt.si.ə, ˈdɔɪt- (US) ˈduːt-, ˈdjuːt- **-s** -z
deux chevaux ˌdɜː.ʃəˈvəʊ, -ʃɪˈ- (US) -ˈvoʊ
deva ˈdeɪ.və, ˈdiː.və **-s** -z
de Valera də.vəˈleə.rə, -ˈlɪə-; ˌdev.əˈ- (US) -ler.ə, -ˈlɪr-
de Valois dəˈvæl.wɑː
devaluation ˌdiː.væl.juˈeɪ.ʃᵊn; dɪˌvæl- (US) ˌdiː.væl- **-s** -z
devalu|e ˌdiːˈvæl.juː, dɪ- **-es** -z **-ing** -ɪŋ **-ed** -d
Devanagari ˌdeɪ.vəˈnɑː.gᵊr.i, ˌdev.əˈ-
Devant dəˈvænt, dɪ-
deva|state ˈdev.ə|.steɪt **-states** -steɪts **-stating/ly** -steɪ.tɪŋ/li (US) -steɪ.t̬ɪŋ/li **-stated** -steɪ.tɪd (US) -steɪ.t̬ɪd
devastation ˌdev.əˈsteɪ.ʃᵊn **-s** -z
develop dɪˈvel.əp, də- (US) dɪ- **-s** -s **-ing** -ɪŋ **-ed** -t **deˌveloping ˈcountry**
developer dɪˈvel.ə.pəʳ, də- (US) -pɚ **-s** -z
development dɪˈvel.əp.mənt, də- **-s** -s
developmental dɪˌvel.əpˈmen.tᵊl, də- (US) -t̬ᵊl **-ly** -li
Devenish ˈdev.ᵊn.ɪʃ
Deventer ˈdev.ᵊn.təʳ (US) -tɚ
De Vere dəˈvɪəʳ, dɪ- (US) -ˈvɪr
Devereux ˈdev.ə.ruː, -ruːks, -rɜː, -rəʊ, -reks, ˈ-ᵊr.ə (US) -ə.ruː, -rɜː, -rə, -uːks
Deveron ˈdev.ə.rᵊn (US) -ɚ.ᵊn
Devers ˈdiː.vəz, ˈdev.əz (US) ˈdiː.vɚz, ˈdev.ɚz
Devi ˈdeɪ.vi
devian|ce ˈdiː.vi.ən*t*|s **-cy** -si
deviant ˈdiː.vi.ənt **-s** -s
devi|ate ˈdiː.vi|.eɪt **-ates** -eɪts **-ating** -eɪ.tɪŋ (US) -eɪ.t̬ɪŋ **-ated** -eɪ.tɪd (US) -eɪ.t̬ɪd **-ator/s** -eɪ.təʳ/z (US) -eɪ.t̬ɚ/z
deviation ˌdiː.viˈeɪ.ʃᵊn **-s** -z
deviation|ism ˌdiː.viˈeɪ.ʃᵊn|.ɪ.zᵊm **-ist/s** -ɪst/s
devic|e dɪˈvaɪs, də- (US) dɪ- **-es** -ɪz **ˌleave someone to their ˌown deˈvices**
devil ˈdev.ᵊl **-s** -z **-(l)ing** -ɪŋ **-(l)ed** -d **ˌdevil's ˈadvocate** ; **ˌdevil's ˈfood ˌcake**, **ˈdevil's food ˌcake** (US) **ˈdevil's food ˌcake; between the ˌdevil and the ˌdeep blue ˈsea** ; **give the ˌdevil his ˈdue**; **ˌtalk of the ˈdevil**
devilfish ˈdev.ᵊl.fɪʃ **-es** -ɪz
devilish ˈdev.ᵊl.ɪʃ **-ly** -li **-ness** -nəs, -nɪs
devil-may-care ˌdev.ᵊl.meɪˈkeəʳ (US) -ˈker *stress shift:* ˌdevil-may-care ˈattitude
devilment ˈdev.ᵊl.mənt **-s** -s
devilr|y ˈdev.ᵊl.r|i **-ies** -iz
Devine dəˈvaɪn, dɪ-
devious ˈdiː.vi.əs **-ly** -li **-ness** -nəs, -nɪs
devis|e dɪˈvaɪz, də- (US) dɪ- **-es** -ɪz **-ing** -ɪŋ **-ed** -d **-er/s** -əʳ/z (US) -ɚ/z **-able** -ə.bl̩
devisee dɪˌvaɪˈziː, də-; ˌdev.ɪˈ- (US) dɪˌvaɪˈ-; ˌdev.əˈ- **-s** -z
devisor dɪˈvaɪ.zəʳ, də-; dəˌvaɪˈzɔːʳ, dɪ-; ˌdev.aɪˈ- (US) dɪˈvaɪ.zɚ; ˌdev.əˈzɔːr **-s** -z

devitalization, **-isa-** diː,vaɪ.tᵊl.aɪ'zeɪ.ʃᵊn, ,diː.vaɪ-, -ɪ'- (US) diː,vaɪ.t̬ᵊl.ɪ'-
devitaliz|e, **-is|e** ,diː'vaɪ.tᵊl.aɪz (US) -t̬ᵊl- **-es** -ɪz **-ing** -ɪŋ **-ed** -d
Devizes dɪ'vaɪ.zɪz, də-, -zəz
Devlin 'dev.lɪn, -lən
devocalization, **-isa-** diː,vəʊ.kᵊl.aɪ'zeɪ.ʃᵊn, ,diː.vəʊ-, -ɪ'- (US) diː,voʊ- **-s** -z
devocaliz|e, **-is|e** ,diː'vəʊ.kᵊl.aɪz (US) -'voʊ- **-es** -ɪz **-ing** -ɪŋ **-ed** -d
devoic|e ,diː'vɔɪs **-es** -ɪz **-ing** -ɪŋ **-ed** -t
devoid dɪ'vɔɪd, də- (US) dɪ-
devolution ,diː.və'luː.ʃᵊn, ,dev.ə'-, -'ljuː- (US) ,dev.ə'luː-, ,diː.və'- **-s** -z
devolv|e dɪ'vɒlv, də- (US) dɪ'vɑːlv **-es** -z **-ing** -ɪŋ **-ed** -d
Devon 'dev.ᵊn **-shire** -ʃəʳ, -,ʃɪəʳ (US) -ʃɚ, -,ʃɪr
Devonian dev'əʊ.ni.ən, dɪ'vəʊ-, də- (US) dɪ'voʊ- **-s** -z
Devonport 'dev.ᵊn.pɔːt, -ᵊm- (US) -ᵊn.pɔːrt
de|vote dɪ|'vəʊt, də- (US) dɪ|'voʊt **-votes** -vəʊts (US) -voʊts **-voting** -vəʊ.tɪŋ (US) -voʊ.t̬ɪŋ **-voted** -vəʊ.tɪd (US) -voʊ.t̬ɪd
devoted dɪ'vəʊ.tɪd, də- (US) dɪ'voʊ.t̬ɪd **-ly** -li **-ness** -nəs, -nɪs
devotee ,dev.əʊ'tiː (US) -ə'tiː, -'teɪ, -oʊ- **-s** -z
devotion dɪ'vəʊ.ʃᵊn, də- (US) dɪ'voʊ- **-s** -z
devotional dɪ'vəʊ.ʃᵊn.ᵊl, də- (US) dɪ'voʊ- **-ly** -i
devour dɪ'vaʊəʳ, də- (US) dɪ'vaʊɚ **-s** -z **-ing** -ɪŋ **-ed** -d **-er/s** -əʳ/z (US) -ɚ/z
de|vout dɪ|'vaʊt, də- (US) dɪ- **-vouter** -'vaʊ.təʳ (US) -'vaʊ.t̬ɚ **-voutest** -'vaʊ.tɪst, -təst (US) -'vaʊ.t̬ɪst, -t̬əst **-voutly** -'vaʊt.li **-voutness** -'vaʊt.nəs, -nɪs
dew djuː, dʒuː (US) duː, djuː **-s** -z **'dew ,pond** ; **'dew ,point**
Dewali dɪ'wɑː.li (US) də-, dɪ-
Dewar 'djuː.əʳ, 'dʒuː-; djʊəʳ, dʒʊəʳ (US) 'duː.ɚ, 'djuː-
dewberr|y 'djuː.bᵊr|.i, 'dʒuː-, -ber- (US) 'duː.ber-, 'djuː- **-ies** -iz
dewclaw 'djuː.klɔː, 'dʒuː- (US) 'duː.klɑː, 'djuː-, -klɔː **-s** -z
dewdrop 'djuː.drɒp, 'dʒuː- (US) 'duː.drɑːp, 'djuː- **-s** -s
D'Ewes djuːz, dʒuːz (US) duːz, djuːz
De Wet də'vet, -'wet
Dewey 'djuː.i, 'dʒuː- (US) 'duː-, 'djuː-
Dewhurst 'djuː.hɜːst, 'dʒuː- (US) 'duː.hɜːrst, 'djuː-
Dewi 'de.wi
Note: This is a Welsh place name. The anglicized pronunciation /'djuː.i/ should be considered incorrect.
dewlap 'djuː.læp, 'dʒuː- (US) 'duː-, 'djuː- **-s** -s
Dewsbury 'djuːz.bᵊr.i, 'dʒuːz- (US) 'duːz.ber-, 'djuːz-, -bɚ-
dew|y 'djuː|.i, 'dʒuː- (US) 'duː-, 'djuː- **-iness** -ɪ.nəs, -ɪ.nɪs
Dexedrine® 'dek.sɪ.driːn, -sə-
dexter (D) 'dek.stəʳ (US) -stɚ
dexterity dek'ster.ə.ti, -ɪ.ti (US) -ə.t̬i
dexterous 'dek.stᵊr.əs **-ly** -li **-ness** -nəs, -nɪs
dextrose 'dek.strəʊs, -strəʊz (US) -stroʊs
dextrous 'dek.strəs **-ly** -li **-ness** -nəs, -nɪs
De Zoete də'zuːt
de Zoete Wedd də,zuːt'wed
dg (*abbrev. for* **decigram**) 'des.ɪ.græm
Dhaka 'dæk.ə (US) 'dæk.ə, 'dɑː.kɑː
dhal dɑːl
dharma 'dɑː.mə (US) 'dɑːr-
dhobi 'dəʊ.bi (US) 'doʊ- **-es** -z
dhoti 'dəʊ.ti (US) 'doʊ.t̬i **-es** -z
dhow daʊ **-s** -z
DHSS ,diː.eɪtʃ.es'es
dhurrie 'dʌr.i (US) 'dɜːr- **-s** -z
di- daɪ-, dɪ-
Note: Prefix. Where the meaning is **two**, it may carry either primary or secondary stress and is pronounced /daɪ-/, e.g. **digraph** /'daɪ.grɑːf (US) -græf/, **diglossia** /,daɪ'glɒs.i.ə (US) -'glɑː.si-/. In other instances, it may be pronounced /daɪ-/, /dɪ-/ or occasionally /də-/, and is not normally stressed in verbs and adjectives, e.g. **digest** /daɪ'dʒest/, **diverse** /daɪ'vɜːs (US) dɪ'vɜːrs/. In nouns, however, it may carry stress, e.g. **digest** /'daɪ.dʒest/. There are exceptions; see individual entries.
Di daɪ
dia- daɪə-; daɪ'æ-
Note: Prefix. Normally carries primary or secondary stress on the first syllable, e.g. **diadem** /'daɪə.dem/, **diabolic** /,daɪə'bɒl.ɪk (US) -'bɑː.lɪk/, or primary stress on the second syllable, e.g. **diagonal** /daɪ'æg.ᵊn.ᵊl/.
diabetes ,daɪə'biː.tiːz, -tɪz, -tɪs (US) -t̬əs, -t̬iːz
diabetic ,daɪə'bet.ɪk (US) -'bet̬- **-s** -s
diabolic ,daɪə'bɒl.ɪk (US) -'bɑː.lɪk **-al** -ᵊl **-ally** -ᵊl.i, -li
diabolism daɪ'æb.ᵊl.ɪ.zᵊm
diaboliz|e, **-is|e** daɪ'æb.ᵊl.aɪz (US) -ə.laɪz **-es** -ɪz **-ing** -ɪŋ **-ed** -d
diabolo di'æb.ᵊl.əʊ, daɪ-, -ɑː.bᵊl- (US) daɪ'æb.ə.loʊ
diachronic ,daɪ.ə'krɒn.ɪk (US) -'krɑː.nɪk **-ally** -ᵊl.i, -li
diacid daɪ'æs.ɪd **-s** -z
diaconal daɪ'æk.ə.nᵊl, di-
diaconate daɪ'æk.ə.neɪt, di-, -nɪt, -nət **-s** -s
diacritic ,daɪə'krɪt.ɪk (US) -'krɪt̬- **-s** -s **-al** -ᵊl
diadem 'daɪə.dem, -dəm **-s** -z
diaeres|is daɪ'er.ə.s|ɪs, -'ɪr-, -'ɪə.rə-, -rɪ- (US) -'er.ə-, -'ɪr **-es** -iːz
Diaghilev di'æg.ɪ.lef, '-ə- (US) -'ɑː.gə.lef, -gɪ-
diagnos|e 'daɪəg.nəʊz, ,--'- (US) ,daɪəg'noʊs, -'noʊz, '--- **-es** -ɪz **-ing** -ɪŋ **-ed** -d
diagnos|is ,daɪəg'nəʊ.s|ɪs (US) -'noʊ- **-es** -iːz
diagnostic ,daɪəg'nɒs.tɪk (US) -'nɑː.stɪk **-s** -s
diagnostician ,daɪəg.nɒs'tɪʃ.ᵊn (US) -nɑː'stɪʃ- **-s** -z
diagonal daɪ'æg.ᵊn.ᵊl **-s** -z **-ly** -i
diagram 'daɪə.græm **-s** -z
diagrammatic ,daɪə.grə'mæt.ɪk (US) -'mæt̬- **-al** -ᵊl **-ally** -ᵊl.i, -li
dial daɪəl (US) daɪəl **-s** -z **-(l)ing** -lɪŋ **-(l)ed** -d **'dialling ,code** ; **'dialling ,tone** ; **'dial ,tone**
dialect 'daɪə.lekt **-s** -s
dialectal ,daɪə'lek.tᵊl
dialectic ,daɪə'lek.tɪk **-s** -s **-al** -ᵊl **-ally** -ᵊl.i, -li
dialectician ,daɪə.lek'tɪʃ.ᵊn **-s** -z
dialectolog|y ,daɪə.lek'tɒl.ə.dʒ|i (US) -'tɑː.lə- **-ist/s** -ɪst/s
diallage *figure of speech:* daɪ'æl.ə.gi, -dʒi
diallage *mineral:* 'daɪə.lɪdʒ
dialog|ism daɪ'æl.ə.dʒ|ɪ.zᵊm **-ist/s** -ɪst/s
dialogue, **dialog** 'daɪə.lɒg (US) -lɑːg **-s** -z
dialys|is daɪ'æl.ə.s|ɪs, '-ɪ- **-es** -iːz
diamagnetic ,daɪə.mæg'net.ɪk, -məg'- (US) -mæg'net̬- **-s** -s **-ally** -ᵊl.i, -li
diamagnetism ,daɪə'mæg.nə.tɪ.zᵊm, -nɪ-
diamanté ,diː.ə'mɑ̃ːŋ.teɪ, ,daɪə'-, -'mæn-, -ti (US) ,diː.ə.mɑːn'teɪ, -'mɑːn.teɪ
diameter daɪ'æm.ɪ.təʳ, '-ə- (US) -ə.t̬ɚ **-s** -z
diametral daɪ'æm.ɪ.trəl, '-ə- **-ly** -i
diametric ,daɪə'met.rɪk **-al** -ᵊl **-ally** -ᵊl.i, -li
diamond (D) 'daɪə.mənd (US) 'daɪə-, 'daɪ- **-s** -z
diamondback 'daɪə.mənd.bæk (US) 'daɪə-, 'daɪ- **-s** -s
Diana daɪ'æn.ə
Diane daɪ'æn, di-
dianthus daɪ'ænt.θəs **-es** -ɪz
diapason ,daɪə'peɪ.zᵊn, -sᵊn **-s** -z
diap|er 'daɪə.p|əʳ (US) -p|ɚ **-ers** -əz (US) -ɚz **-ering** -ᵊr.ɪŋ **-ered** -əd (US) -ɚd

diaphanous daɪˈæf.ᵊn.əs
diaphone ˈdaɪə.fəʊn US -foʊn **-s** -z
diaphragm ˈdaɪə.fræm, -frəm US -fræm **-s** -z
diaphragmatic ˌdaɪə.fræɡˈmæt.ɪk, -frəɡˈ- US -ˈmæt̬-
diapositive ˌdaɪəˈpɒz.ɪ.tɪv, ˈ-ə- US -ˈpɑː.zə.t̬ɪv **-s** -z
diarch|y ˈdaɪ.ɑː.k|i US -ɑːr- **-ies** -iz
diarist ˈdaɪə.rɪst **-s** -s
diarrh(o)ea ˌdaɪəˈrɪə US -ˈriː.ə
diar|y ˈdaɪə.r|i **-ies** -iz
diaspora (**D**) daɪˈæs.pᵊr.ə
diastase ˈdaɪə.steɪs, -steɪz
diastas|is daɪˈæs.tə.s|ɪs, ˌdaɪəˈsteɪ.s|ɪs **-es** -iːz
diastole daɪˈæs.tᵊl.i **-s** -z
diastolic ˌdaɪəˈstɒl.ɪk US -ˈstɑː.lɪk
diasystem ˈdaɪəˌsɪs.təm
diatherm|ic ˌdaɪəˈθɜː.m|ɪk US -ˈθɜːr- **-ous** -əs
diatom ˈdaɪə.təm, -tɒm US -tɑːm **-s** -z
diatomaceous ˌdaɪə.təˈmeɪ.ʃəs
diatomic ˌdaɪəˈtɒm.ɪk US -ˈtɑː.mɪk
diatomite daɪˈæt.ə.maɪt US -ˈæt̬-
diatonic ˌdaɪəˈtɒn.ɪk US -ˈtɑː.nɪk **-ally** -ᵊl.i, -li
diatribe ˈdaɪə.traɪb **-s** -z
diatype ˈdaɪə.taɪp
Diaz ˈdiː.əs, -æs, -æθ US -ɑːs, -ɑːz, -əs, -æz
diazepam daɪˈæz.ə.pæm, -ˈeɪ.zə-, -zɪ- US -ˈæz.ə-
dib dɪb **-s** -z **-bing** -ɪŋ **-bed** -d **-ber/s** -əʳ/z US -ɚ/z
dibasic daɪˈbeɪ.sɪk
dibasicity ˌdaɪ.beɪˈsɪs.ə.ti, -ɪ.ti US -ə.t̬i
Dibb dɪb
dibbl|e ˈdɪb.l̩ **-es** -z **-ing** -ɪŋ, ˈdɪb.lɪŋ **-ed** -d **-er/s** -əʳ/z, ˈ-ləʳ/z US ˈ-l̩.ɚ/z, ˈ-lɚ/z
Dibdin ˈdɪb.dɪn
dibs dɪbz
dicast ˈdɪk.æst US ˈdɪk.æst, ˈdaɪ.kæst **-s** -s
dice (*plur. of* **die**) daɪs
dic|e (*v.*) daɪs **-es** -ɪz **-ing** -ɪŋ **-ed** -t
dicey (**D**) ˈdaɪ.si
dichloride ˌdaɪˈklɔː.raɪd US -ˈklɔːr.aɪd **-s** -z
dichotom|y daɪˈkɒt.ə.m|i, dɪ- US -ˈkɑː.t̬ə- **-ies** -iz
dichromate ˌdaɪˈkrəʊ.meɪt US -ˈkroʊ- **-s** -s
dick (**D**) dɪk
dickens (**D**) ˈdɪk.ɪnz
Dickensian dɪˈken.zi.ən, də-, -si-
dick|er (**D**) ˈdɪk|.əʳ US -ɚ **-ers** -əz US -ɚz **-ering** -ᵊr.ɪŋ **-ered** -əd US -ɚd
Dickerson ˈdɪk.ə.sᵊn US ˈ-ɚ-
dickey (**D**) ˈdɪk.i **-s** -z ˈ**dickey** ˌ**bow**
dickhead ˈdɪk.hed **-s** -z
Dickie ˈdɪk.i
Dickins ˈdɪk.ɪnz
Dickinson ˈdɪk.ɪn.sᵊn
Dickson ˈdɪk.sᵊn
dick|y (**D**) ˈdɪk|.i **-ies** -iz
dickybird ˈdɪk.i.bɜːd US -bɜːrd **-s** -z
dicotyledon ˌdaɪ.kɒt.ɪˈliː.dᵊn, -ᵊlˈiː- US -kɑː.t̬ᵊlˈ- **-s** -z
Dictaphone® ˈdɪk.tə.fəʊn US -foʊn **-s** -z
dictate (*n.*) ˈdɪk.teɪt **-s** -s
dic|tate (*v.*) dɪk|ˈteɪt US ˈdɪk|.teɪt, -|ˈ- **-tates** -ˈteɪts US -teɪts, -ˈteɪts **-tating** -ˈteɪ.tɪŋ US -teɪ.t̬ɪŋ, -ˈteɪ- **-tated** -ˈteɪ.tɪd US -teɪ.t̬ɪd, -ˈteɪ-
dictation dɪkˈteɪ.ʃᵊn **-s** -z
dictator dɪkˈteɪ.təʳ US ˈdɪk.teɪ.t̬ɚ, -ˈ-- **-s** -z
dictatorial ˌdɪk.təˈtɔː.ri.əl US -ˈtɔːr.i- **-ly** -i
dictatorship dɪkˈteɪ.tə.ʃɪp US -t̬ɚ- **-s** -s
diction ˈdɪk.ʃᵊn
dictionar|y ˈdɪk.ʃᵊn.ᵊr|.i, -ʃᵊn.r|i US -er|.i **-ies** -iz
dict|um ˈdɪk.t|əm **-a** -ə **-ums** -əmz
did (*from* **do**) dɪd
Didache ˈdɪd.ə.ki
didact ˈdaɪ.dækt **-s** -s
didactic dɪˈdæk.tɪk, daɪ-, də- US daɪ-, dɪ- **-al** -ᵊl **-ally** -ᵊl.i, -li
didacticism dɪˈdæk.tɪ.sɪ.zᵊm, daɪ-, də- US daɪ-, dɪ- -tə-
Didcot ˈdɪd.kət, -kɒt US -kɑːt
diddl|e ˈdɪd.l̩ **-es** -z **-ing** -ɪŋ, ˈ-lɪŋ **-ed** -d **-er/s** -əʳ/z, ˈ-ləʳ/z US ˈ-l̩.ɚ/z, ˈ-lɚ/z
diddly ˈdɪd.l̩.i, ˈ-li
diddlysquat ˌdɪd.l̩.iˈskwɒt, -liˈ- US -ˈskwɑːt
diddums ˈdɪd.əmz
Diderot ˈdiː.də.rəʊ US ˌdiː.dəˈroʊ
didgeridoo ˌdɪdʒ.ᵊr.iˈduː **-s** -z
Didier ˈdɪd.i.eɪ, ˈdiː.di-
didn't ˈdɪd.ᵊnt
Dido ˈdaɪ.dəʊ US -doʊ
didst dɪdst
Didymus ˈdɪd.ɪ.məs, ˈ-ə-
die (*n.*) *stamp:* daɪ **-s** -z
die (*n.*) *cube:* daɪ **dice** daɪs
die (*v.*) daɪ **-s** -z **dying** ˈdaɪ.ɪŋ **died** daɪd
die-casting ˈdaɪˌkɑː.stɪŋ US -ˌkæs.tɪŋ
Diego diˈeɪ.ɡəʊ US -ɡoʊ
diehard ˈdaɪ.hɑːd US -hɑːrd **-s** -z
dielectric ˌdaɪ.ɪˈlek.trɪk, -əˈ- **-s** -s
Dieppe diːˈep, di-
dieres|is daɪˈer.ə.s|ɪs, -ˈɪr-, -ˈɪə.rə-, -rɪ- US -ˈer.ə- **-es** -iːz
dieretic ˌdaɪəˈret.ɪk US -ˈret̬-
diesel ˈdiː.zᵊl US -sᵊl, -zᵊl **-s** -z ˈ**diesel** ˌ**engine**
diesink ˈdaɪ.sɪŋk **-er/s** -əʳ/z US -ɚ/z **-ing** -ɪŋ
dies irae ˌdiː.eɪzˈɪə.raɪ, -ezˈ-, -esˈ-, -reɪ US -eɪzˈɪr.eɪ, -esˈ-
dies|is ˈdaɪ.ə.s|ɪs, ˈ-ɪ- **-es** -iːz
dies non ˌdaɪ.iːzˈnɒn, ˌdiː.eɪz- US ˈdiː.eɪs.nɑːn, -es-; ˌdiː.eɪzˈnɑːn, ˌdaɪ.iːzˈ- **-s** -z
diet daɪət **-s** -s **-ing** -ɪŋ US ˈdaɪə.t̬ɪŋ **-ed** -ɪd US ˈdaɪə.t̬ɪd **-er/s**
dietar|y ˈdaɪə.tᵊr|.i, ˈdaɪ.ɪ-, -tr|i US ˈdaɪə.ter- **-ies** -iz ˌ**dietary** ˈ**fibre**
dietetic ˌdaɪəˈtet.ɪk, ˌdaɪ.ɪˈ- US -ˈtet̬- **-s** -s **-al** -ᵊl **-ally** -ᵊl.i, -li
dietician, dietitian ˌdaɪəˈtɪʃ.ᵊn, ˌdaɪ.ɪˈ- US ˌdaɪəˈ- **-s** -z
Dietrich ˈdiː.trɪk, -trɪx, -trɪʃ
Dieu et mon droit ˌdjɜː.eɪ.mɔ̃ːnˈdrwɑː
diff|er ˈdɪf|.əʳ US -ɚ **-ers** -əz US -ɚz **-ering** -ᵊr.ɪŋ **-ered** -əd US -ɚd
differenc|e ˈdɪf.ᵊr.ᵊnts, ˈ-rᵊnts **-es** -ɪz
different ˈdɪf.ᵊr.ᵊnt, ˈ-rᵊnt **-ly** -li
differenti|a ˌdɪf.ᵊˈren.*t*ʃi|.ə, ˈ-*t*ʃ|ə US -ˈren*t*.ʃi|.ə, ˈ-ʃə **-ae** -iː
differentiable ˌdɪf.ᵊˈren.*t*ʃi.ə.bl̩, ˈ-*t*ʃə- US -ˈren*t*.ʃi.ə-, ˈ-ʃə-
differential ˌdɪf.ᵊˈren.*t*ʃᵊl US -ˈren*t*.ʃᵊl **-s** -z **-ly** -i
differenti|ate ˌdɪf.ᵊˈren.*t*ʃi|.eɪt US -ˈren*t*.ʃi- **-ates** -eɪts **-ating** -eɪ.tɪŋ US -eɪ.t̬ɪŋ **-ated** -eɪ.tɪd US -eɪ.t̬ɪd
differentiation ˌdɪf.ᵊr.en.*t*ʃiˈeɪ.ʃᵊn, -en*t*.siˈ- US -ə.ren*t*.ʃiˈ-, -siˈ- **-s** -z
difficult ˈdɪf.ɪ.kᵊlt, ˈ-ə-
difficult|y ˈdɪf.ɪ.kᵊl.t|i, ˈ-ə- US -t̬|i **-ies** -iz
diffidence ˈdɪf.ɪ.dᵊnts
diffident ˈdɪf.ɪ.dᵊnt **-ly** -li
diffract dɪˈfrækt **-s** -s **-ing** -ɪŋ **-ed** -ɪd
diffraction dɪˈfræk.ʃᵊn
diffuse (*adj.*) dɪˈfjuːs **-ly** -li **-ness** -nəs, -nɪs
diffus|e (*v.*) dɪˈfjuːz **-es** -ɪz **-ing** -ɪŋ **-ed** -d **-edly** -ɪd.li, -d.li **-edness** -ɪd.nəs, -d.nəs, -nɪs **-er/s** -əʳ/z US -ɚ/z
diffusibility dɪˌfjuː.zəˈbɪl.ə.ti, -zɪˈ-, -ɪ.ti US -zəˈbɪl.ə.t̬i
diffusible dɪˈfjuː.zə.bl̩, -zɪ-
diffusion dɪˈfjuː.ʒᵊn
diffusive dɪˈfjuː.sɪv **-ly** -li **-ness** -nəs, -nɪs
dig (*n. v.*) dɪɡ **-s** -z **-ging** -ɪŋ **-ged** -d **dug** dʌɡ
dig. (*in phrase* **infra dig.**) dɪɡ
digamma daɪˈɡæm.ə, ˈ--- **-s** -z
Digby ˈdɪɡ.bi
digest (*n.*) ˈdaɪ.dʒest **-s** -s
digest (*v.*) daɪˈdʒest, dɪ-, də- **-s** -s **-ing** -ɪŋ **-ed** -ɪd

digestibility daɪˌdʒes.tə'bɪl.ə.ti, dɪ-, də-, -tɪ'-, -ɪ.ti US -ə.t̬i

digestible daɪ'dʒes.tə.bl̩, dɪ-, də-, -tɪ-

digestif ˌdiː.ʒes'tɪf **-s** -s

digestion daɪ'dʒes.tʃᵊn, dɪ-, də-, -'dʒeʃ- **-s** -z

digestive daɪ'dʒes.tɪv, dɪ-, də- **-s** -z **-ly** -li **-ness** -nəs, -nɪs **diˌgestive 'biscuit, di'gestive ˌbiscuit**

digger 'dɪg.əʳ US -ɚ **-s** -z

Digges dɪgz

diggings 'dɪg.ɪŋz

Diggle 'dɪg.l̩ **-s** -z

Diggory 'dɪg.ᵊr.i

dight daɪt

Dighton 'daɪ.tᵊn

digit 'dɪdʒ.ɪt **-s** -s

digital 'dɪdʒ.ɪ.tᵊl, '-ə- US -t̬ᵊl **-s** -z **-ly**

digitalin ˌdɪdʒ.ɪ'teɪ.lɪn, -ə'-, -'tɑː- US -'tæl.ɪn, -'teɪ.lɪn

digitalis ˌdɪdʒ.ɪ'teɪ.lɪs, -ə'-, -'tɑː- US -'tæl.ɪs, -'teɪ.lɪs

digitalization, -isa- ˌdɪdʒ.ɪ.tᵊl.aɪ'zeɪ.ʃᵊn, ˌ-ə-, -ɪ'- US -t̬ᵊl.ɪ'-

digitaliz|e, -is|e 'dɪdʒ.ɪ.tᵊl.aɪz, '-ə- US -t̬ə.laɪz **-es** -ɪz **-ing** -ɪŋ **-ed** -d

digitization, -isa- ˌdɪdʒ.ɪ.taɪ'zeɪ.ʃᵊn, ˌ-ə-, -tɪ'- US -t̬ɪ'-

digitiz|e, -is|e 'dɪdʒ.ɪ.taɪz, '-ə- **-es** -ɪz **-ing** -ɪŋ **-ed** -d

digloss|ia daɪ'glɒs|.i.ə US -'glɑː.s|i- **-ic** -ɪk

digni|fy 'dɪg.nɪ|.faɪ, -nə- **-fies** -faɪz **-fying** -faɪ.ɪŋ **-fied** -faɪd

dignitar|y 'dɪg.nɪ.tᵊr|.i, -nə- US -nə.ter- **-ies** -iz

dignit|y 'dɪg.nə.t|i, -nɪ- US -t̬|i **-ies** -iz

digraph 'daɪ.grɑːf US -græf **-s** -s

digress daɪ'gres, dɪ- **-es** -ɪz **-ing** -ɪŋ **-ed** -t

digression daɪ'greʃ.ᵊn, dɪ- **-s** -z

digressive daɪ'gres.ɪv, dɪ- **-ly** -li **-ness** -nəs, -nɪs

digs dɪgz

Dijon 'diː.ʒ̃ɔ̃ŋ US diː'ʒoʊn, -'ʒɔːn

dik|e daɪk **-es** -s **-ing** -ɪŋ **-ed** -t

diktat 'dɪk.tæt, -tɑːt US dɪk'tɑːt, '-- **-s** -s

dilapi|date dɪ'læp.ɪ|.deɪt, də-, '-ə- **-dates** -deɪts **-dating** -deɪ.tɪŋ US -deɪ.t̬ɪŋ **-dated** -deɪ.tɪd US -deɪ.t̬ɪd

dilapidation dɪˌlæp.ɪ'deɪ.ʃᵊn, də-, -ə'- **-s** -z

dilatability daɪˌleɪ.tə'bɪl.ə.ti, dɪ-, də-, -ɪ.ti US -t̬ə'bɪl.ə.t̬i

dilatation ˌdɪl.ə'teɪ.ʃᵊn, ˌdaɪ-, -leɪ'- US ˌdɪl.ə'teɪ.ʃᵊn; ˌdaɪ.lə.teɪ- **-s** -z

dila|te daɪ'leɪ|t, dɪ-, də- US 'daɪ.leɪ|t; -'-, də- **-tes** -ts **-ting** -tɪŋ US -t̬ɪŋ **-ted** -tɪd US -t̬ɪd **-ter/s** -təʳ/z US -t̬ɚ/z **-table** -tə.bl̩ US -t̬ə.bl̩

dilation daɪ'leɪ.ʃᵊn, dɪ-, də- **-s** -z

dilator daɪ'leɪ.təʳ, dɪ-, də- US -t̬ɚ **-s** -z

dilator|y 'dɪl.ə.tᵊr|.i, -tr|i US -tɔːr|.i **-ily** -ᵊl.i, -ɪ.li **-iness** -i.nəs, -i.nɪs

dildo 'dɪl.dəʊ US -doʊ **-(e)s** -z

dilemma dɪ'lem.ə, daɪ-, də- **-s** -z

dilettante ˌdɪl.ɪ'tæn.ti, -ə'-, -teɪ US ˌdɪl.ə'tɑːnt, -'tænt, '---, ˌdɪl.ə'tæn.ti, -'tɑːn- **-s** -z

dilettanti (*alternative plur. of* **dilettante**) ˌdɪl.ɪ'tæn.ti, -ə'-, -teɪ US ˌdɪl.ə'tɑːn.taɪ, -'tæn-, -ti

dilettantism ˌdɪl.ɪ'tæn.tɪ.zᵊm, -ə'- US -'tɑːn-, -'tæn-

diligenc|e 'dɪl.ɪ.dʒᵊnts, '-ə- **-es**

diligent 'dɪl.ɪ.dʒᵊnt, '-ə- **-ly** -li

Dilke dɪlk **-s** -s

dill (D) dɪl **-s** -z

Diller 'dɪl.əʳ US -ɚ

Dilley 'dɪl.i

Dillinger 'dɪl.ɪn.dʒəʳ US -dʒɚ

Dillon 'dɪl.ən

Dillwyn 'dɪl.ɪn, 'dɪl.wɪn

dill|y 'dɪl|.i **-ies** -iz

dillydall|y 'dɪl.iˌdæl|.i, ˌ--'-- **-ies** -iz **-ying** -i.ɪŋ **-ied** -id

diluent 'dɪl.ju.ənt **-s** -s

dilu|te daɪ'luː|t, dɪ-, -'ljuː|t US -'luː|t **-tes** -ts **-ting** -tɪŋ US -t̬ɪŋ **-ted** -tɪd US -t̬ɪd **-teness** -t.nəs, -t.nɪs

dilution daɪ'luː.ʃᵊn, dɪ-, -'ljuː- US -'luː- **-s** -z

diluvi|al daɪ'luː.vi|.əl, dɪ-, -'ljuː- US dɪ'luː-, daɪ- **-an** -ən

diluvi|um daɪ'luː.vi|.əm, dɪ-, -'ljuː- US dɪ'luː-, daɪ- **-a** -ə

Dilwyn, Dilwen 'dɪl.wɪn

Dilys 'dɪl.ɪs

dim dɪm **-mer/s** -əʳ/z US -ɚ/z **-mest** -ɪst, -əst **-ly** -li **-ness** -nəs, -nɪs **-s** -z **-ming** -ɪŋ **-med** -d

Di Maggio dɪ'mædʒ.i.əʊ US -oʊ, '-oʊ

Dimbleby 'dɪm.bl̩.bi

dime daɪm **-s** -z

dimension ˌdaɪ'men.*t*ʃᵊn, dɪ-, də- US dɪ'men*t*.ʃᵊn, də-, ˌdaɪ- **-s** -z

dimensional ˌdaɪ'men.*t*ʃᵊ.nᵊl, dɪ-, də- US dɪ'men*t*.ʃᵊn-, də-, ˌdaɪ-

dimeter 'dɪm.ɪ.təʳ, '-ə- US -ə.t̬ɚ **-s** -z

diminish dɪ'mɪn.ɪʃ, də- **-es** -ɪz **-ing** -ɪŋ **-ed** -t **-able** -ə.bl̩

diminuendo dɪˌmɪn.ju'en.dəʊ, də- US -doʊ **-s** -z

diminution ˌdɪm.ɪ'njuː.ʃᵊn US -ə'nuː-, -'njuː- **-s** -z

diminutive dɪ'mɪn.jə.tɪv, də-, -jʊ- US -jə.t̬ɪv **-ly** -li **-ness** -nəs, -nɪs

dimity 'dɪm.ɪ.ti, -ə.ti US -ə.t̬i, -ɪ.t̬i

dimmer 'dɪm.əʳ US -ɚ **-s** -z

Dimmesdale 'dɪmz.deɪl

dimmish 'dɪm.ɪʃ

dimorphism daɪ'mɔː.fɪ.zᵊm US -'mɔːr-

dimorphous daɪ'mɔː.fəs US -'mɔːr-

dimout 'dɪm.aʊt **-s** -s

dimpl|e 'dɪm.pl̩ **-es** -z **-ing** -ɪŋ, 'dɪm.plɪŋ **-ed** -d

Dimplex® 'dɪm.pleks

dimply 'dɪm.pli

dim sum ˌdɪm'sʊm, -'sʌm

dimwit 'dɪm.wɪt **-s** -s

dim-witted ˌdɪm'wɪt.ɪd US 'dɪmˌwɪt̬-, ˌ-'-- **-ly** -li **-ness** -nəs, -nɪs *stress shift, British only:* ˌdimwitted 'idiot

din dɪn **-s** -z **-ning** -ɪŋ **-ned** -d

Dina 'diː.nə, 'daɪ.nə

Dinah 'daɪ.nə

dinar 'diː.nɑːʳ, -'- US diː'nɑːr, '-- **-s** -z

Dinaric dɪ'nær.ɪk, də-, daɪ- US -'ner-, -'nær-

Dinas Powis ˌdiː.næs'paʊ.ɪs

din|e (D) daɪn **-es** -z **-ing** -ɪŋ **-ed** -d **'dining ˌcar ; 'dining ˌroom ; 'dining ˌtable**

Dinefwr dɪ'nev.ʊəʳ US -ʊr

diner 'daɪ.nəʳ US -nɚ **-s** -z

Dinesen 'dɪn.ɪ.sᵊn, '-ə- US 'diː.nə-, 'dɪn.ə-, '-ɪ-, -sɪn

dinette daɪ'net, dɪ- US daɪ- **-s** -s

ding dɪŋ **-s** -z **-ing** -ɪŋ **-ed** -d

ding-a-ling 'dɪŋ.ə.lɪŋ **-s** -z

dingbat 'dɪŋ.bæt **-s** -s

ding-dong 'dɪŋ.dɒŋ US -dɑːŋ, -dɔːŋ

dingh|y 'dɪŋ.g|i, -i US 'dɪŋ|.i, -g|i **-ies** -iz

dingle (D) 'dɪŋ.gl̩ **-s** -z

Dingley 'dɪŋ.li

dingo 'dɪŋ.gəʊ US -goʊ **-es** -z

Dingwall 'dɪŋ.wɔːl, -wəl US -wɑːl, -wɔːl, -wəl

ding|y 'dɪn.dʒ|i **-ier** -i.əʳ US -i.ɚ **-iest** -i.ɪst, -i.əst **-ily** -ɪ.li, -ᵊl.i **-iness** -ɪ.nəs, -ɪ.nɪs

dink dɪŋk **-s** -s

Dinkins 'dɪŋ.kɪnz US 'dɪŋ-, 'dɪn-

dinkum 'dɪŋ.kəm

dink|y 'dɪŋ.k|i **-ier** -i.əʳ US -i.ɚ **-iest** -i.ɪst, -i.əst **-iness** -ɪ.nəs, -ɪ.nɪs

Dinmont 'dɪn.mɒnt, 'dɪm-, -mənt US 'dɪn.mɑːnt, -mənt

Dinneford 'dɪn.ɪ.fəd US -fɚd

dinner 'dɪn.əʳ US -ɚ **-s** -z **'dinner ˌhour ; 'dinner ˌjacket ; 'dinner ˌlady ; 'dinner ˌparty ; 'dinner ˌplate ; 'dinner ˌservice ; 'dinner ˌset ; 'dinner ˌtable ; 'dinner ˌtime**

Dinnington 'dɪn.ɪŋ.tᵊn

Dinocrates daɪ'nɒk.rə.tiːz, dɪ- US -'nɑː.krə-

Dinorah dɪ'nɔː.rə US -'nɔːr.ə

dinosaur 'daɪ.nə.sɔːʳ US -sɔːr **-s** -z

dinosaur|us ˌdaɪ.nə'sɔː.r|əs US -'sɔːr|.əs **-i** -aɪ

dinotheri|um ˌdaɪ.nəʊˈθɪə.rɪ|.əm Ⓤⓢ -oʊˈ-,-əˈ-, -ˈθɪr.i- **-a** -ə
dint dɪnt
Dinwiddie dɪnˈwɪd.i, ˈ---
diocesan daɪˈɒs.ɪ.sᵊn, ˈ-ə-, -zᵊn Ⓤⓢ -ˈɑː.sə-
dioces|e ˈdaɪə.sɪs, -siːs, -siːz **-es** -ɪz
Diocles ˈdaɪə.kliːz
Diocletian ˌdaɪəˈkliː.ʃᵊn, -ʃi.ən
diode ˈdaɪ.əʊd Ⓤⓢ -oʊd **-s** -z
Diodorus ˌdaɪəˈdɔː.rəs Ⓤⓢ -ˈdɔːr.əs
Diogenes daɪˈɒdʒ.ɪ.niːz, ˈ-ə- Ⓤⓢ -ˈɑː.dʒə-
Diomede ˈdaɪə.miːd
Diomedes ˌdaɪəˈmiː.diːz; daɪˈɒm.ɪ- Ⓤⓢ ˌdaɪəˈmiː-
Dion *Greek:* ˈdaɪ.ən Ⓤⓢ -ɑːn *French:* ˈdiː.ən,ˈ-ɔ̃ŋ, -ɒŋ, -ɒn Ⓤⓢ diˈoʊn
Dionne diːˈɒn, di-; ˈdiː.ɒn Ⓤⓢ -ˈɑːn
Dionysi|a ˌdaɪəˈnɪs.i|.ə, -ˈnɪz- Ⓤⓢ -ˈnɪʃ.i|.ə, -ˈnɪs-, -ˈnɪz-, -ˈnɪʃ|.ə **-an** -ən
Dionysiac ˌdaɪəˈnɪs.i.æk, -ˈnɪz-
Dionysius ˌdaɪəˈnɪs.i.əs, -ˈnɪz- Ⓤⓢ -ˈnɪʃ.əs, ˈ-i.əs, -ˈnɪs.i-, -ˈnaɪ.si-
Dionysus ˌdaɪəˈnaɪ.səs Ⓤⓢ -ˈnaɪ.səs, -ˈniː-
dioptre, **diopter** daɪˈɒp.təʳ Ⓤⓢ -ˈɑːp.tɚ **-s** -z
dioptric daɪˈɒp.trɪk Ⓤⓢ -ˈɑːp-
Dior ˈdiː.ɔːʳ, diˈɔːʳ Ⓤⓢ diˈɔːr
diorama ˌdaɪəˈrɑː.mə Ⓤⓢ -ˈræm.ə, -ˈrɑː.mə **-s** -z
dioramic ˌdaɪəˈræm.ɪk
Dioscuri ˌdaɪəˈskjʊə.ri; ˌdaɪ.ɒsˈkjʊə-; daɪˈɒs.kjʊ.ri, -raɪ Ⓤⓢ ˌdaɪ.ɑːˈskjʊr.aɪ
Diosy diˈəʊ.si Ⓤⓢ -ˈoʊ-
dioxide daɪˈɒk.saɪd Ⓤⓢ -ˈɑːk- **-s** -z
dioxin daɪˈɒk.sɪn Ⓤⓢ -ˈɑːk- **-s** -z
dip dɪp **-s** -s **-ping** -ɪŋ **-ped** -t **-per/s** -əʳ/z Ⓤⓢ -ɚ/z
diphenyl daɪˈfiː.naɪl, -ˈfen.aɪl, -ᵊl, -ɪl, -ˈfen.ɪl Ⓤⓢ -ˈfen.ᵊl, -ˈfiː.nᵊl
diphtheria dɪfˈθɪə.ri.ə, dɪp- Ⓤⓢ -ˈθɪr.i-
diphthong ˈdɪf.θɒŋ, ˈdɪp- Ⓤⓢ -θɑːŋ, -θɔːŋ **-s** -z
diphthongal ˈdɪf.θɒŋ.ᵊl, ˈdɪp-, -gᵊl, -ˈ-- Ⓤⓢ dɪfˈθɑːŋ.ᵊl, dɪp-, -ˈθɔːŋ-, -gᵊl **-ly** -i
diphthongization, **-isa-** ˌdɪf.θɒŋ.aɪˈzeɪ.ʃᵊn, ˌdɪp-, -gaɪˈ-, -gɪˈ- Ⓤⓢ -θɑːŋ.ɪˈ-, -θɔːŋ-, -gɪˈ- **-s** -z
diphthongiz|e, **-is|e** ˈdɪf.θɒŋ.aɪz, ˈdɪp-, -gaɪz Ⓤⓢ -θɑːŋ.aɪz, -θɔːŋ-, -gaɪz **-es** -ɪz **-ing** -ɪŋ **-ed** -d
Diplock ˈdɪp.lɒk Ⓤⓢ -lɑːk
diplodoc|us dɪˈplɒd.ə.k|əs, ˌdɪp.ləʊˈdəʊ- Ⓤⓢ dɪˈplɑː.də-, -ˈploʊ- **-uses** -ə.sɪz **-i** -aɪ
diploid ˈdɪp.lɔɪd **-s** -z
diploma dɪˈpləʊ.mə Ⓤⓢ -ˈploʊ-, də- **-s** -z
diplomacy dɪˈpləʊ.mə.si Ⓤⓢ -ˈploʊ-, də-
diplomat ˈdɪp.lə.mæt **-s** -s
diplomatic ˌdɪp.ləˈmæt.ɪk Ⓤⓢ -ˈmæt̬- **-s** -s **-al** -ᵊl **-ally** -ᵊl.i, -li
diplomatist dɪˈpləʊ.mə.tɪst Ⓤⓢ -ˈploʊ.mə.tɪst, də- **-s** -s
diplomatiz|e, **-is|e** dɪˈpləʊ.mə.taɪz Ⓤⓢ -ˈploʊ-, də- **-es** -ɪz **-ing** -ɪŋ **-ed** -d
diplosis dɪˈpləʊ.sɪs Ⓤⓢ -ˈploʊ-
dipole ˈdaɪ.pəʊl Ⓤⓢ -poʊl **-s** -z
dipper ˈdɪp.əʳ Ⓤⓢ -ɚ **-s** -z
dipp|y ˈdɪp|.i **-ier** -i.əʳ Ⓤⓢ -i.ɚ **-iest** -i.ɪst, -i.əst
dipsomania ˌdɪp.səʊˈmeɪ.ni.ə Ⓤⓢ -səˈ-, -soʊˈ-
dipsomaniac ˌdɪp.səʊˈmeɪ.ni.æk Ⓤⓢ -səˈ-, -soʊˈ- **-s** -s
dipstick ˈdɪp.stɪk **-s** -s
dipswitch ˈdɪp.swɪtʃ **-es** -ɪz
dipteran ˈdɪp.tə.rən Ⓤⓢ -tɚ.ən **-s** -z
dipter|on ˈdɪp.tə.r|ən Ⓤⓢ -r|ɑːn **-ons** -ənz Ⓤⓢ -ɑːnz **-a** -ə **-ous** -əs
diptych ˈdɪp.tɪk **-s** -s
dir|e daɪəʳ Ⓤⓢ daɪɚ **-er** -əʳ Ⓤⓢ -ɚ **-est** -ɪst, -əst **-ely** -li **-eness** -nəs, -nɪs
direct dɪˈrekt, daɪ-, də- Ⓤⓢ dɪˈrekt, daɪ- **-s** -s **-ing** -ɪŋ **-ed** -ɪd **-est** -ɪst, -əst **-ness** -nəs, -nɪs *stress shift: see compound:* ˌ**direct** ˈ**mail** ; ˌ**direct** ˈ**object**
direction dɪˈrek.ʃᵊn, daɪ-, də- Ⓤⓢ dɪˈrek-, daɪ- **-s** -z **-less** -ləs, -lɪs
directional dɪˈrek.ʃᵊn.ᵊl, daɪ-, də- Ⓤⓢ dɪˈrek-, daɪ-
directive dɪˈrek.tɪv, daɪ-, də- Ⓤⓢ dɪˈrek-, daɪ- **-s** -z
directly dɪˈrekt.li, daɪ-, də- Ⓤⓢ dɪ-, daɪ-
director dɪˈrek.təʳ, daɪ-, də- Ⓤⓢ dɪˈrek.tɚ, daɪ- **-s** -z
directorate dɪˈrek.tᵊr.ət, daɪ-, də-, -ɪt Ⓤⓢ dɪˈrek-, daɪ- **-s** -s
directorial dɪˌrekˈtɔː.ri.əl, daɪ-, də- Ⓤⓢ dɪˌrekˈtɔːr.i-, daɪ-
directorship dɪˈrek.tə.ʃɪp, daɪ-, də- Ⓤⓢ dɪˈrek.tɚ-, daɪ- **-s** -s
director|y dɪˈrek.tᵊr|.i, daɪ-, də- Ⓤⓢ dɪˈrek-, daɪ- **-ies** -iz
direful ˈdaɪə.fᵊl, -fʊl Ⓤⓢ ˈdaɪɚ- **-ly** -i **-ness** -nəs, -nɪs
dirg|e dɜːdʒ Ⓤⓢ dɝːdʒ **-es** -ɪz
dirham ˈdɪ.ræm, ˈdɪər.æm, -əm Ⓤⓢ dɪrˈhæm; dəˈræm **-s** -z
dirigible ˈdɪr.ɪ.dʒə.bl̩, -dʒɪ-; dɪˈrɪdʒ-, də- Ⓤⓢ ˈdɪr.ə.dʒə-; dɪˈrɪdʒ.ə-, də- **-s** -z
dirigisme ˌdɪr.ɪˈʒiː.zᵊm; ˈdɪr.ɪ.ʒɪ- Ⓤⓢ ˌdɪr.ɪˈʒiː-
dirigiste ˌdɪr.ɪˈʒiːst; ˈdɪr.ɪ.ʒɪst Ⓤⓢ ˈdɪr.ɪ.ʒɪst; ˌdɪr.ɪˈʒiːst **-s** -s
dirk (D) dɜːk Ⓤⓢ dɝːk **-s** -s
dirndl ˈdɜːn.dl̩ Ⓤⓢ ˈdɝːn- **-s** -z
dirt dɜːt Ⓤⓢ dɝːt ˌ**dirt** ˈ**cheap** ; ˌ**dirt** ˈ**poor** ; ˈ**dirt** ˌ**track**
dirt|y ˈdɜː.t|i Ⓤⓢ ˈdɝː.t̬|i **-ies** -iz **-ying** -i.ɪŋ **-ied** -id **-ier** -i.əʳ Ⓤⓢ -i.ɚ **-iest** -i.ɪst, -i.əst **-ily** -ɪ.li, -ᵊl.i **-iness** -ɪ.nəs, -ɪ.nɪs ˌ**dirty** ˈ**trick** ; **do someone's** ˈ**dirty** ˌ**work**
dis- dɪs-, dɪz-
Note: Prefix. In words containing **dis-**, the prefix will normally either not be stressed, e.g. **disable** /dɪˈseɪ.bl̩/, or will take secondary stress if the stem is stressed on its second syllable, e.g. **ability** /əˈbɪl.ə.ti Ⓤⓢ -t̬i/, **disability** /ˌdɪs.əˈbɪl.ə.ti Ⓤⓢ -t̬i/. There is sometimes a difference in stress between nouns and verbs, e.g. **discharge**, noun /ˈdɪs.tʃɑːdʒ Ⓤⓢ -tʃɑːrdʒ/, verb /dɪsˈtʃɑːdʒ Ⓤⓢ -ˈtʃɑːrdʒ/. There are exceptions; see individual entries.
Dis dɪs
disabilit|y ˌdɪs.əˈbɪl.ə.t|i, -ɪ.t|i Ⓤⓢ -ə.t̬|i **-ies** -iz
disabl|e dɪˈseɪ.bl̩ **-es** -z **-ing** -ɪŋ, -ˈeɪ.blɪŋ **-ed** -d **-ement** -mənt
disabus|e ˌdɪs.əˈbjuːz **-es** -ɪz **-ing** -ɪŋ **-ed** -d
disaccharide daɪˈsæk.ᵊr.aɪd, -ɪd Ⓤⓢ -ə.raɪd **-s** -z
disaccustom ˌdɪs.əˈkʌs.təm **-s** -z **-ing** -ɪŋ **-ed** -d
disadvantag|e ˌdɪs.ədˈvɑːn.tɪdʒ Ⓤⓢ -ˈvæn.t̬ɪdʒ **-es** -ɪz **-ed** -d
disadvantageous ˌdɪs,æd.vənˈteɪ.dʒəs, -əd-, -vɑːnˈ-, -vænˈ-; dɪˌsæd- Ⓤⓢ ˌdɪs,æd.vænˈ-, -vənˈ- **-ly** -li **-ness** -nəs, -nɪs
disaffect ˌdɪs.əˈfekt **-s** -s **-ing** -ɪŋ **-ed/ly** -ɪd/li **-edness** -ɪd.nəs, -nɪs
disaffection ˌdɪs.əˈfek.ʃᵊn
disafforest ˌdɪs.əˈfɒr.ɪst, -əst Ⓤⓢ -ˈfɔːr- **-s** -s **-ing** -ɪŋ **-ed** -ɪd
disafforestation ˌdɪs.əˌfɒr.ɪˈsteɪ.ʃᵊn, -əˈ- Ⓤⓢ -ˌfɔːr-
disagree ˌdɪs.əˈgriː **-s** -z **-ing** -ɪŋ **-d** -d
disagreeab|le ˌdɪs.əˈgriː.ə.b|l̩ **-ly** -li **-leness** -l̩.nəs, -nɪs
disagreement ˌdɪs.əˈgriː.mᵊnt **-s** -s
disallow ˌdɪs.əˈlaʊ **-s** -z **-ing** -ɪŋ **-ed** -d
disallowable ˌdɪs.əˈlaʊ.ə.bl̩ *stress shift:* ˌdisallowable ˈgoals
disallowance ˌdɪs.əˈlaʊ.ən*t*s
disambigu|ate ˌdɪs.æmˈbɪg.ju|.eɪt **-ates** -eɪts **-ating** -eɪ.tɪŋ Ⓤⓢ -eɪ.t̬ɪŋ **-ated** -eɪ.tɪd Ⓤⓢ -eɪ.t̬ɪd
disambiguation ˌdɪs.æmˌbɪg.juˈeɪ.ʃᵊn
disappear ˌdɪs.əˈpɪəʳ Ⓤⓢ -ˈpɪr **-s** -z **-ing** -ɪŋ **-ed** -d
disappearanc|e ˌdɪs.əˈpɪə.rᵊn*t*s Ⓤⓢ -ˈpɪr.ᵊn*t*s **-es** -ɪz

disap|point ˌdɪs.əˈpɔɪnt **-points** -ˈpɔɪnts **-pointing/ly** -ˈpɔɪn.tɪŋ/li US -ˈpɔɪn.t̬ɪŋ/li **-pointed** -ˈpɔɪn.tɪd US -ˈpɔɪn.t̬ɪd

disappointment ˌdɪs.əˈpɔɪnt.mənt **-s** -s

disapprobation ˌdɪs.æp.rəʊˈbeɪ.ʃən, -rʊˈ-; dɪˌsæp- US ˌdɪsˌæp.rəˈ-, -roʊˈ-

disapproval ˌdɪs.əˈpruː.vəl

disapprov|e ˌdɪs.əˈpruːv **-es** -z **-ing/ly** -ɪŋ/li **-ed** -d

disarm dɪˈsɑːm, -ˈzɑːm US -ˈsɑːrm **-s** -z **-ing/ly** -ɪŋ/li **-ed** -d **-er/s** -əʳ/z US -ɚ/z

disarmament dɪˈsɑː.mə.mənt, -ˈzɑː- US -ˈsɑːr-

disarrang|e ˌdɪs.əˈreɪndʒ **-es** -ɪz **-ing** -ɪŋ **-ed** -d

disarrangement ˌdɪs.əˈreɪndʒ.mənt **-s** -s

disarray ˌdɪs.əˈreɪ **-s** -z **-ing** -ɪŋ **-ed** -d

disarticu|late ˌdɪs.ɑːˈtɪk.jəl.leɪt, -jʊ- US -ɑːrˈ- **-lates** -leɪts **-lating** -leɪ.tɪŋ US -leɪ.t̬ɪŋ **-lated** -leɪ.tɪd US -leɪ.t̬ɪd

disarticulation ˌdɪs.ɑːˌtɪk.jəˈleɪ.ʃən, -jʊˈ- US -ɑːr-

disassoci|ate ˌdɪs.əˈsəʊ.si|.eɪt, -ʃi- US -ˈsoʊ.ʃi-, -si- **-ates** -eɪts **-ating** -eɪ.tɪŋ US -eɪ.t̬ɪŋ **-ated** -eɪ.tɪd US -eɪ.t̬ɪd

disassociation ˌdɪs.ə.səʊ.siˈeɪ.ʃən, -ʃiˈ- US -soʊ.ʃiˈ-, -siˈ-

disaster dɪˈzɑː.stəʳ, də- US dɪˈzæs.tɚ **-s** -z

disastrous dɪˈzɑː.strəs, də- US dɪˈzæs.trəs **-ly** -li **-ness** -nəs, -nɪs

disavow ˌdɪs.əˈvaʊ **-s** -z **-ing** -ɪŋ **-ed** -d **-al** -əl

disband dɪsˈbænd **-s** -z **-ing** -ɪŋ **-ed** -ɪd **-ment** -mənt

disbar dɪsˈbɑːʳ US -ˈbɑːr **-s** -z **-ring** -ɪŋ **-red** -d

disbark dɪsˈbɑːk US -ˈbɑːrk **-s** -s **-ing** -ɪŋ **-ed** -t

disbelief ˌdɪs.bɪˈliːf, -bəˈ-

disbeliev|e ˌdɪs.bɪˈliːv, -bəˈ- **-es** -z **-ing** -ɪŋ **-ed** -d **-er/s** -əʳ/z US -ɚ/z

disburden dɪsˈbɜː.dən US -ˈbɜːr- **-s** -z **-ing** -ɪŋ **-ed** -d

disburdenment dɪsˈbɜː.dən.mənt US -ˈbɜːr-

disburs|e dɪsˈbɜːs US -ˈbɜːrs **-es** -ɪz **-ing** -ɪŋ **-ed** -t

disbursement dɪsˈbɜːs.mənt US -ˈbɜːrs- **-s** -s

disc dɪsk **-s** -s ˈ**disc** ˌ**jockey**

discard (*n.*) ˈdɪs.kɑːd US -kɑːrd **-s** -z

discard (*v.*) dɪˈskɑːd US -ˈskɑːrd **-s** -z **-ing** -ɪŋ **-ed** -ɪd

discern dɪˈsɜːn, də- US dɪˈsɜːrn, -ˈzɜːrn **-s** -z **-ing** -ɪŋ **-ed** -d **-er/s** -əʳ/z US -ɚ/z

discernib|le dɪˈsɜː.nə.bl|, də-, -nɪ- US dɪˈsɜːr-, -ˈzɜːr- **-ly** -li **-leness** -l̩.nəs, -nɪs

discerning dɪˈsɜː.nɪŋ, də- US dɪˈsɜːr-, -ˈzɜːr- **-ly** -li

discernment dɪˈsɜːn.mənt, də- US dɪˈsɜːrn-, -ˈzɜːrn-

discharg|e (*n.*) ˈdɪs.tʃɑːdʒ, -ˈ- US ˈdɪs.tʃɑːrdʒ, -ˈ- **-es** -ɪz

discharg|e (*v.*) dɪsˈtʃɑːdʒ US -ˈtʃɑːrdʒ **-es** -ɪz **-ing** -ɪŋ **-ed** -d **-er/s** -əʳ/z US -ɚ/z

disciple dɪˈsaɪ.pl̩, də- US dɪ- **-s** -z **-ship** -ʃɪp

disciplinarian ˌdɪs.ə.plɪˈneə.ri.ən, ˌ-ɪ-, -pləˈ- US -ˈner.i- **-s** -z

disciplinary ˌdɪs.əˈplɪ.nər.i, -ɪˈ-, ˈdɪs.ə.plɪ-, ˈ-ɪ- US ˈdɪs.ə.plɪ.ner- ˌ**disciplinary** ˈ**action**, **disci**ˌ**plinary** ˈ**action** US ˈ**disciplinary** ˌ**action**

disciplin|e ˈdɪs.ə.plɪn, ˈ-ɪ- **-es** -z **-ing** -ɪŋ **-ed** -d

disclaim dɪsˈkleɪm **-s** -z **-ing** -ɪŋ **-ed** -d

disclaimer dɪsˈkleɪm.əʳ US -mɚ **-s** -z

disclos|e dɪsˈkləʊz US -ˈkloʊz **-es** -ɪz **-ing** -ɪŋ **-ed** -d

disclosure dɪsˈkləʊ.ʒəʳ US -ˈkloʊ.ʒɚ **-s** -z

disco ˈdɪs.kəʊ US -koʊ **-s** -z **-ing** -ɪŋ

discobol|us dɪˈskɒb.əl|.əs US -ˈskɑː.bəl- **-i** -aɪ

discol|o(u)r dɪˈskʌl|.əʳ US -ˈskʌl|.ɚ **-o(u)rs** -əz US -ɚz **-o(u)ring** -ər.ɪŋ **-o(u)red** -əd US -ɚd

discolo(u)ration dɪˌskʌl.əˈreɪ.ʃən; ˌdɪs.kʌl- US dɪˌskʌl- **-s** -z

discombobu|late ˌdɪs.kəmˈbɒb.jəl.leɪt, -jʊ- US -ˈbɑː.bjə-, -bjʊ- **-lates** -leɪts **-lating** -leɪ.tɪŋ US -leɪ.t̬ɪŋ **-lated** -leɪ.tɪd US -leɪ.t̬ɪd

discom|fit dɪˈskʌmp|.fɪt **-fits** -fɪts **-fiting** -fɪ.tɪŋ US -fɪ.t̬ɪŋ **-fited** -fɪ.tɪd US -fɪ.t̬ɪd

discomfiture dɪˈskʌmp.fɪ.tʃəʳ, -fə- US -tʃɚ

discom|fort dɪˈskʌmp|.fət US -fɚt **-forts** -fəts US -fɚts **-forting** -fə.tɪŋ US -fɚ.t̬ɪŋ **-forted** -fə.tɪd US -fɚ.t̬ɪd

discommod|e ˌdɪs.kəˈməʊd US -ˈmoʊd **-es** -z **-ing** -ɪŋ **-ed** -ɪd

discompos|e ˌdɪs.kəmˈpəʊz US -ˈpoʊz **-es** -ɪz **-ing** -ɪŋ **-ed** -d

discomposure ˌdɪs.kəmˈpəʊ.ʒəʳ US -ˈpoʊ.ʒɚ

discon|cert ˌdɪs.kən|ˈsɜːt US -ˈsɜːrt **-certs** -ˈsɜːts US -ˈsɜːrts **-certing/ly** -ˈsɜː.tɪŋ/li US -ˈsɜːr.t̬ɪŋ/li **-certed** -ˈsɜː.tɪd US -ˈsɜːr.t̬ɪd

disconnect ˌdɪs.kəˈnekt **-s** -s **-ing** -ɪŋ **-ed** -ɪd

disconnection ˌdɪs.kəˈnek.ʃən

disconsolate dɪˈskɒnt.səl.ət, -ɪt US -ˈskɑːnt- **-ly** -li **-ness** -nəs, -nɪs

discon|tent ˌdɪs.kən|ˈtent **-tented** -ˈten.tɪd US -ˈten.t̬ɪd **-tentedly** -ˈten.tɪd.li US -ˈten.t̬ɪd.li **-tentedness** -ˈten.tɪd.nəs, -nɪs US -ˈten.t̬ɪd.nəs, -nɪs **-tentment** -ˈtent.mənt

discontinuance ˌdɪs.kənˈtɪn.ju.ənts

discontinuation ˌdɪs.kənˌtɪn.juˈeɪ.ʃən

discontinu|e ˌdɪs.kənˈtɪn.juː **-es** -z **-ing** -ɪŋ **-ed** -d

discontinuit|y ˌdɪsˌkɒn.tɪˈnjuː.ə.t|i, -kɒn-, -ɪ.t|i; dɪˌskɒn- US ˌdɪs.kɑːn.tənˈuː.ə.t̬|i, -ˈjuː- **-ies** -iz

discontinuous ˌdɪs.kənˈtɪn.ju.əs **-ly** -li

discord (*n.*) ˈdɪs.kɔːd US -kɔːrd **-s** -z

discord (*v.*) dɪˈskɔːd US -ˈskɔːrd **-s** -z **-ing** -ɪŋ **-ed** -ɪd

discordan|ce dɪˈskɔː.dənt|s US -ˈskɔːr- **-cy** -si

discordant dɪˈskɔː.dənt US -ˈskɔːr- **-ly** -li

discotheque, **discothèque** ˈdɪs.kə.tek **-s** -s

discount (*n.*) ˈdɪs.kaʊnt **-s** -s

dis|count (*v.*) dɪˈs|kaʊnt **-counts** -kaʊnts **-counting** -kaʊn.tɪŋ US -kaʊn.t̬ɪŋ **-counted** -kaʊn.tɪd US -kaʊn.t̬ɪd **-counter/s** -kaʊn.təʳ/z US -kaʊn.t̬ɚ/z

discountenanc|e dɪˈskaʊn.tɪ.nənts, -tə- US -tən.ənts **-es** -ɪz **-ing** -ɪŋ **-ed** -t

discourag|e dɪˈskʌr.ɪdʒ US -ˈskɜːr- **-es** -ɪz **-ing/ly** -ɪŋ/li **-ed** -d

discouragement dɪˈskʌr.ɪdʒ.mənt US -ˈskɜːr- **-s** -s

discours|e (*n.*) ˈdɪs.kɔːs US -kɔːrs **-es** -ɪz

discours|e (*v.*) dɪˈskɔːs US -ˈskɔːrs **-es** -ɪz **-ing** -ɪŋ **-ed** -t **-er/s** -əʳ/z US -ɚ/z

discourteous dɪˈskɜː.ti.əs US -ˈskɜːr.t̬i- **-ly** -li **-ness** -nəs, -nɪs

discourtesy dɪˈskɜː.tə.si, -tɪ- US -ˈskɜːr.t̬ə-

discov|er dɪˈskʌv|.əʳ US -ɚ **-ers** -əz US -ɚz **-ering** -ər.ɪŋ **-ered** -əd US -ɚd **-erer/s** -ər.əʳ/z US -ɚ.ɚ/z

discoverable dɪˈskʌv.ər.ə.bl̩

discovert dɪˈskʌv.ət US -ɚt

discover|y dɪˈskʌv.ər|.i **-ies** -iz

discred|it dɪˈskred|.ɪt **-its** -ɪts **-iting** -ɪ.tɪŋ US -ɪ.t̬ɪŋ **-ited** -ɪ.tɪd US -ɪ.t̬ɪd

discreditab|le dɪˈskred.ɪ.tə.bl|̩ US -t̬ə- **-ly** -li **-leness** -l̩.nəs, -nɪs

dis|creet dɪˈs|kriːt **-creetest** -ˈkriː.tɪst, -təst US -ˈkriː.t̬ɪst, -t̬əst **-creetly** -ˈkriːt.li **-creetness** -ˈkriːt.nəs, -nɪs

discrepan|cy dɪ'skrep.ᵊn|*t*.si **-cies** -*t*.siz **-t** -t
discrete dɪ'skriːt **-ly** -li **-ness** -nəs, -nɪs
discretion dɪ'skreʃ.ᵊn **-s** -z
discretional dɪ'skreʃ.ᵊn.ᵊl **-ly** -i
discretionar|y dɪ'skreʃ.ᵊn.ᵊr|.i, -r|i US -er|.i **-ily** -ᵊl.i, -ɪ.li
discriminate (*adj.*) dɪ'skrɪm.ɪ.nət, '-ə-, -nɪt **-ly** -li
discrimi|nate (*v.*) dɪ'skrɪm.ɪ|.neɪt, '-ə- **-nates** -neɪts **-nating/ly** -neɪ.tɪŋ/li US -neɪ.t̬ɪŋ/li **-nated** -neɪ.tɪd US -neɪ.t̬ɪd
discrimination dɪˌskrɪm.ɪ'neɪ.ʃᵊn, -ə'- **-s** -z
discriminative dɪ'skrɪm.ɪ.nə.tɪv, '-ə-, -neɪ- US -neɪ.t̬ɪv, -nə- **-ly** -li
discriminatory dɪ'skrɪm.ɪ.nə.tᵊr.i, '-ə-, -tri; dɪˌskrɪm.ɪ'neɪ-, -ə'- US dɪ'skrɪm.ɪ.nə.tɔːr.i
discursion dɪ'skɜː.ʃᵊn, -ʒᵊn US -'skɜːr.ʒᵊn, -ʃᵊn **-s** -z
discursive dɪ'skɜː.sɪv US -skɜːr- **-ly** -li **-ness** -nəs, -nɪs
discursory dɪ'skɜː.sᵊr.i US -'skɜːr-
disc|us 'dɪs.k|əs **-i** -aɪ **-uses** -ə.sɪz
discuss dɪ'skʌs **-es** -ɪz **-ing** -ɪŋ **-ed** -t **-able** -ə.bl̩
discussant dɪ'skʌs.ᵊnt **-s** -s
discussion dɪ'skʌʃ.ᵊn **-s** -z
disdain dɪs'deɪn, dɪz- **-s** -z **-ing** -ɪŋ **-ed** -d
disdainful dɪs'deɪn.fᵊl, dɪz-, -fʊl **-ly** -i **-ness** -nəs, -nɪs
diseas|e dɪ'ziːz, də- US dɪ- **-es** -ɪz **-ed** -d
disembark ˌdɪs.ɪm'bɑːk, -em'- US -'bɑːrk, '--- **-s** -s **-ing** -ɪŋ **-ed** -t
disembarkation ˌdɪs.ɪm.bɑː'keɪ.ʃᵊn, -em- US -bɑːr'- **-s** -z
disembarkment ˌdɪs.ɪm'bɑːk.mənt, -em'- US -'bɑːrk- **-s** -s
disembarrass ˌdɪs.ɪm'bær.əs, -em'- US -'ber-, -'bær- **-es** -ɪz **-ing** -ɪŋ **-ed** -t
disembarrassment ˌdɪs.ɪm'bær.əs.mənt, -em'- US -'ber-, -'bær- **-s** -s
disembod|y ˌdɪs.ɪm'bɒd|.i, -em'- US -'bɑː.d|i **-ies** -iz **-ying** -i.ɪŋ **-ied** -id
disembowel ˌdɪs.ɪm'baʊəl, -em'- **-s** -z **-(l)ing** -ɪŋ **-(l)ed** -d
disen|chant ˌdɪs.ɪn|'tʃɑːnt, -en'-, -ᵊn'- US -'tʃænt **-chants** -'tʃɑːnts US -'tʃænts **-chanting** -'tʃɑːn.tɪŋ US -'tʃæn.t̬ɪŋ **-chanted** -'tʃɑːn.tɪd US -'tʃæn.t̬ɪd
disenchantment ˌdɪs.ɪn'tʃɑːnt.mənt, -en'-, -ᵊn'- US -'tʃænt- **-s** -s
disencumb|er ˌdɪs.ɪn'kʌm.b|əʳ, -ɪŋ'-, -en'-, -eŋ'- US -b|ɚ **-ers** -əz US -ɚz **-ering** -ᵊr.ɪŋ **-ered** -əd US -ɚd
disendow ˌdɪs.ɪn'daʊ, -en'- **-s** -z **-ing** -ɪŋ **-ed** -d
disendowment ˌdɪs.ɪn'daʊ.mənt, -en'-
disenfranchis|e ˌdɪs.ɪn'fræn.*t*ʃaɪz, -en'- **-es** -ɪz **-ing** -ɪŋ **-ed** -d
disenfranchisement ˌdɪs.ɪn'fræn.*t*ʃɪz.mənt, -en'-, -*t*ʃaɪz- US -*t*ʃaɪz-, -*t*ʃɪz-
disengag|e ˌdɪs.ɪn'geɪdʒ, -ɪŋ'-, -en'-, -eŋ'- US -ɪn'-, - en'- **-es** -ɪz **-ing** -ɪŋ **-ed** -d
disengagement ˌdɪs.ɪn'geɪdʒ.mənt, -ɪŋ'-, -en'-, -eŋ'- US -ɪn'-, -en'-
disentail ˌdɪs.ɪn'teɪl, -en'-, -ᵊn'- **-s** -z **-ing** -ɪŋ **-ed** -d
disentangl|e ˌdɪs.ɪn'tæŋ.gl̩, -en'- **-es** -z **-ing** -ɪŋ, -'tæŋ.glɪŋ **-ed** -d
disentanglement ˌdɪs.ɪn'tæŋ.gl̩.mənt, -en'-
disequilibrium ˌdɪs.ek.wɪ'lɪb.ri.əm, -iː.kwɪ'-, -kwə'- US ˌdɪs.iː.kwɪ'-; dɪˌsek.wɪ'-
disestablish ˌdɪs.ɪ'stæb.lɪʃ, -es'tæb-, -ə'stæb- US -ɪ'stæb-, -es'tæb-, 'dɪs.ɪ.stæb-, -es.tæb- **-es** -ɪz **-ing** -ɪŋ **-ed** -t
disestablishment ˌdɪs.ɪ'stæb.lɪʃ.mənt, -es'tæb-, -ə'stæb- US -ɪ'stæb-, -es'tæb-
disestablishmentarian ˌdɪs.ɪˌstæb.lɪʃ.mən'teə.ri.ən, -esˌtæb-, -əˌstæb- US -ɪˌstæb.lɪʃ.mən'ter.i-, -esˌtæb-
disfavo(u)r dɪs'feɪ.vəʳ US -vɚ
disfiguration dɪsˌfɪg.ə'reɪ.ʃᵊn, ˌdɪs.fɪg-, -jʊ'- US dɪsˌfɪg.jə'- **-s** -z
disfig|ure dɪs'fɪg|.əʳ US -j|ɚ **-ures** -əz US -ɚz **-uring** -ᵊr.ɪŋ **-ured** -əd US -ɚd **-urement/s** -ə.mənt/s US -ɚ.mənt/s
disforest dɪs'fɒr.ɪst, -əst US -'fɔːr- **-s** -s **-ing** -ɪŋ **-ed** -ɪd
disfranchis|e dɪs'fræn.*t*ʃaɪz **-es** -ɪz **-ing** -ɪŋ **-ed** -d
disfranchisement dɪs'fræn.*t*ʃɪz.mənt, -*t*ʃəz-, -*t*ʃaɪz- US -tʃaɪz-, -tʃɪz-
disgorg|e dɪs'gɔːdʒ US -'gɔːrdʒ **-es** -ɪz **-ing** -ɪŋ **-ed** -d
disgrac|e dɪs'greɪs, dɪz- US dɪs- **-es** -ɪz **-ing** -ɪŋ **-ed** -t
disgraceful dɪs'greɪs.fᵊl, dɪz-, -fʊl US dɪs- **-ly** -i **-ness** -nəs, -nɪs
disgruntled dɪs'grʌn.tl̩d US -t̬l̩d
disgruntlement dɪs'grʌn.tl̩.mənt US -t̬l̩-
disguis|e dɪs'gaɪz, dɪz- US dɪs- **-es** -ɪz **-ing** -ɪŋ **-ed** -d **-er/s** -əʳ/z US -ɚ/z
disgust dɪs'gʌst, dɪz- US dɪs- **-s** -s **-ing** -ɪŋ **-ed/ly** -ɪd/li
disgusting dɪs'gʌs.tɪŋ, dɪz- US dɪs- **-ly** -li
dish dɪʃ **-es** -ɪz **-ing** -ɪŋ **-ed** -t
dishabille ˌdɪs.æb'iːl, -ə'biːl US -ə'-
disharmony dɪs'hɑː.mᵊn.i US -'hɑːr-
dish|cloth 'dɪʃ|.klɒθ US -klɑːθ **-cloths** -klɒθs, -klɒðz US -klɑːθs, -klɑːðz
dishearten dɪs'hɑː.tᵊn US -'hɑːr- **-s** -z **-ing/ly** -ɪŋ/li **-ed** -d
dishevel dɪ'ʃev.ᵊl **-s** -z **-(l)ing** -ɪŋ **-(l)ed** -d
dishful 'dɪʃ.fʊl **-s** -z
dishonest dɪ'sɒn.ɪst, -'zɒn-, -əst US -'sɑː.nɪst, -nəst **-ly** -li
dishonest|y dɪ'sɒn.ɪ.st|i, -'zɒn-, '-ə- US -'sɑː.nə- **-ies** -iz
dishono(u)r dɪ'sɒn.əʳ, -'zɒn- US -'sɑː.nɚ **-s** -z **-ing** -ɪŋ **-ed** -d **-er/s** -əʳ/z US -ɚ/z
dishono(u)rab|le dɪ'sɒn.ᵊr.ə.bl|, -'zɒn- US -'sɑː.nɚ- **-ly** -li **-leness** -l̩.nəs, -nɪs
dishrag 'dɪʃ.ræg **-s** -z
dishtowel 'dɪʃ.taʊəl **-s** -z
dishwash|er 'dɪʃˌwɒʃ|.əʳ US -ˌwɑː.ʃ|ɚ, -ˌwɔː- **-ers** -əz US -ɚz **-ing** -ɪŋ
dishwater 'dɪʃˌwɔː.təʳ US -ˌwɑː.t̬ɚ, -ˌwɔː-
dish|y 'dɪʃ|.i **-ier** -i.əʳ US -i.ɚ **-iest** -i.ɪst, -i.əst
disillusion ˌdɪs.ɪ'luː.ʒᵊn, -ə'-, -'ljuː- US -'luː- **-s** -z **-ing** -ɪŋ **-ed** -d **-ment/s** -mənt/s
disincentive ˌdɪs.ɪn'sen.tɪv US -t̬ɪv **-s** -z
disinclination ˌdɪs.ɪn.klɪ'neɪ.ʃᵊn, -ɪŋ-, -klə'- US -ɪn-
disinclin|e ˌdɪs.ɪn'klaɪn, -ɪŋ'- US -ɪn- **-es** -z **-ing** -ɪŋ **-ed** -d
disinfect ˌdɪs.ɪn'fekt **-s** -s **-ing** -ɪŋ **-ed** -ɪd
disinfectant ˌdɪs.ɪn'fek.tənt **-s** -s
disinfection ˌdɪs.ɪn'fek.ʃᵊn **-s** -z
disinfestation ˌdɪs.ɪn.fes'teɪ.ʃᵊn
disinflation ˌdɪs.ɪn'fleɪ.ʃᵊn
disinformation ˌdɪs.ɪn.fə'meɪ.ʃᵊn, -fɔː'- US -fɚ'-
disingenuous ˌdɪs.ɪn'dʒen.ju.əs **-ly** -li **-ness** -nəs, -nɪs
disinher|it ˌdɪs.ɪn'her|.ɪt **-its** -ɪts **-iting** -ɪ.tɪŋ US -ɪ.t̬ɪŋ **-ited** -ɪ.tɪd US -ɪ.t̬ɪd
disinheritance ˌdɪs.ɪn'her.ɪ.tᵊn*t*s US -t̬ᵊn*t*s
disintegrable dɪ'sɪn.tɪ.grə.bl̩, -tə- US -t̬ə-
disinte|grate dɪ'sɪn.tɪ|.greɪt, -tə- US -t̬ə- **-grates** -greɪts **-grating** -greɪ.tɪŋ US -greɪ.t̬ɪŋ **-grated** -greɪ.tɪd US -greɪ.t̬ɪd **-grator/s** -greɪ.təʳ/z US -greɪ.t̬ɚ/z
disintegration dɪˌsɪn.tɪ'greɪ.ʃᵊn, -tə'-; ˌdɪs.ɪn- US ˌdɪs.ɪn.t̬ə'- **-s** -z
disinter ˌdɪs.ɪn'tɜːʳ US -'tɜːr **-s** -z **-ring** -ɪŋ **-red** -d
disinterest dɪ'sɪn.trəst, -trest, -trɪst; '-tᵊr.əst, -est, -ɪst US -'sɪn.trɪst, -trəst, -trest; '-t̬ɚ.ɪst, -əst, -est

disinterested dɪ'sɪn.trə.stɪd, -tres.tɪd, -trɪ.stɪd; '-tᵊr.ə.stɪd, -es.tɪd, -ɪ.stɪd US -'sɪn.trɪ.stɪd, -trə-, -tres.tɪd; '-t̬ɚ.ɪ.stɪd, -ə-, -es.tɪd **-ly** -li **-ness** -nəs, -nɪs
disinterment ˌdɪs.ɪn'tɜː.mənt US -'tɜːr- **-s** -s
disinvest ˌdɪs.ɪn'vest **-s** -s **-ing** -ɪŋ **-ed** -ɪd **-ment** -mənt
disjoin dɪs'dʒɔɪn, dɪz- US dɪs- **-s** -z **-ing** -ɪŋ **-ed** -d
disjoint dɪs'dʒɔɪnt, dɪz- US dɪs- **-s** -s **-ing** -ɪŋ **-ed** -ɪd
disjointed dɪs'dʒɔɪn.tɪd, dɪz- US dɪs'dʒɔɪn.t̬ɪd **-ly** -li **-ness** -nəs, -nɪs
disjunct dɪs'dʒʌŋ*k*t, '--
disjunction dɪs'dʒʌŋ*k*.ʃᵊn **-s** -z
disjunctive dɪs'dʒʌŋ*k*.tɪv **-ly** -li
disk dɪsk **-s** -s **'disk ˌdrive**
diskette dɪ'sket **-s** -s
dislik|e dɪ'slaɪk, dɪz'laɪk US dɪ'slaɪk **-es** -s **-ing** -ɪŋ **-ed** -t **-able** -ə.bl̩
Note: The stress /'--/ is, however, used in the expression **likes and dislikes.**
dislo|cate 'dɪs.ləʊ|.keɪt US dɪ'sloʊ-; 'dɪs.loʊ- **-cates** -keɪts **-cating** -keɪ.tɪŋ US -keɪ.t̬ɪŋ **-cated** -keɪ.tɪd US -keɪ.t̬ɪd
dislocation ˌdɪs.ləʊ'keɪ.ʃᵊn US -loʊ'- **-s** -z
dislodg|e dɪ'slɒdʒ US -'slɑːdʒ **-es** -ɪz **-ing** -ɪŋ **-ed** -d **-(e)ment** -mənt
disloyal dɪ'slɔɪəl; ˌdɪs'lɔɪəl **-ly** -i
disloyalt|y dɪ'slɔɪəl.t|i; ˌdɪs'lɔɪəl- US -t̬|i **-ies** -iz
dismal 'dɪz.məl **-ly** -i **-ness** -nəs, -nɪs
dismantl|e dɪ'smæn.tl̩, dɪz'mæn- US dɪ'smæn.t̬l̩ **-es** -z **-ing** -ɪŋ, dɪ'smænt.lɪŋ, dɪz'mænt- US dɪ'smæn.t̬l̩.ɪŋ, -'smænt.lɪŋ **-ed** -d
dismast ˌdɪs'mɑːst US -'mæst **-s** -s **-ing** -ɪŋ **-ed** -ɪd
dismay dɪ'smeɪ, dɪz'meɪ **-s** -z **-ing** -ɪŋ **-ed** -d
dismemb|er dɪ'smem.b|əʳ US -b|ɚ **-ers** -əz US -ɚz **-ering** -ᵊr.ɪŋ **-ered** -əd US -ɚd **-erment** -ə.mənt US -ɚ.mənt
dismiss dɪ'smɪs **-es** -ɪz **-ing** -ɪŋ **-ed** -t
dismissal dɪ'smɪs.ᵊl **-s** -z
dismissive dɪ'smɪs.ɪv **-ly** -li **-ness** -nəs, -nɪs
dis|mount dɪ's|maʊnt **-s** -maʊnts **-mounting** -maʊn.tɪŋ US -maʊn.t̬ɪŋ **-mounted** -maʊn.tɪd US -maʊn.t̬ɪd
Disney 'dɪz.ni **'Disney ˌWorld®**
Disneyland® 'dɪz.ni.lænd
disobedience ˌdɪs.əʊ'biː.di.ən*t*s US -ə'-, -oʊ'-
disobedient ˌdɪs.əʊ'biː.di.ənt US -ə'-, -oʊ'- **-ly** -li
disobey ˌdɪs.əʊ'beɪ US -ə'-, -oʊ'- **-s** -z **-ing** -ɪŋ **-ed** -d
disoblig|e ˌdɪs.ə'blaɪdʒ **-es** -ɪz **-ing/ly** -ɪŋ/li **-ingness** -ɪŋ.nəs, -nɪs **-ed** -d
disord|er dɪ'sɔː.d|əʳ, -'zɔː- US -'sɔːr.d|ɚ, -'zɔːr- **-ers** -əz US -ɚz **-ering** -ᵊr.ɪŋ **-ered** -əd US -ɚd
disorderl|y dɪ'sɔː.dᵊl|.i, -'zɔː- US -'sɔːr.dɚ.l|i, -'zɔːr- **-iness** -ɪ.nəs, -ɪ.nɪs
disorganization, -isa- dɪˌsɔː.gə.naɪ'zeɪ.ʃᵊn, -ˌzɔː-, -nɪ'-; ˌdɪs.ɔː-, ˌdɪz- US dɪˌsɔːr.gə.nɪ'-, -ˌzɔːr-
disorganiz|e, -is|e dɪ'sɔː.gə.naɪz, -'zɔː-; ˌdɪs'ɔː-, ˌdɪz'ɔː- US dɪ'sɔːr-, -'zɔːr- **-es** -ɪz **-ing** -ɪŋ **-ed** -d
disorien|t dɪ'sɔː.ri.ən|t, -en|t US -'sɔːr.i.en|t **-ts** -ts **-ting** -tɪŋ US -t̬ɪŋ **-ted** -tɪd US -t̬ɪd
disorien|tate dɪ'sɔː.ri.ən|.teɪt, -en-; ˌdɪs'ɔːr- US dɪ'sɔːr.i- **-tates** -teɪts **-tating** -teɪ.tɪŋ US -teɪ.t̬ɪŋ **-tated** -teɪ.tɪd US -teɪ.t̬ɪd
disorientation dɪˌsɔː.ri.ən'teɪ.ʃᵊn, -en'-; ˌdɪsˌɔː- US dɪˌsɔːr.i-
disown dɪ'səʊn; ˌdɪs'əʊn US dɪ'soʊn **-s** -z **-ing** -ɪŋ **-ed** -d
disparag|e dɪ'spær.ɪdʒ US -'sper-, -'spær- **-es** -ɪz **-ing/ly** -ɪŋ/li **-ed** -d **-er/s** -əʳ/z US -ɚ/z **-ement** -mənt
disparate 'dɪs.pᵊr.ət, -ɪt, -eɪt US -ət, -ɪt; dɪ'sper-, -'spær- **-s** -s
disparit|y dɪ'spær.ə.t|i, -ɪ.t|i US -'per.ə.t̬|i, -'pær- **-ies** -iz
dispassionate dɪ'spæʃ.ᵊn.ət, -ɪt **-ly** -li **-ness** -nəs, -nɪs
dispatch (*n*) dɪ'spætʃ, də-; 'dɪs.pætʃ US dɪ'spætʃ; 'dɪs.pætʃ **-es** -ɪz **dis'patch ˌbox** ; **dis'patch ˌrider**
dispatch (*v*) dɪ'spætʃ, də- US dɪ- **-es** -ɪz **-ing** -ɪŋ **-ed** -t **-er/s** -əʳ/z US -ɚ/z
dispel dɪ'spel **-s** -z **-(l)ing** -ɪŋ **-(l)ed** -d
dispensable dɪ'spen*t*.sə.bl̩
dispensar|y dɪ'spen*t*.sᵊr|.i **-ies** -iz
dispensation ˌdɪs.pen'seɪ.ʃᵊn, -pən'- **-s** -z
dispensator|y dɪ'spen.sə.tᵊr|.i, -tr|i US -tɔːr|.i **-ies** -iz
dispens|e dɪ'spen*t*s **-es** -ɪz **-ing** -ɪŋ **-ed** -t **-er/s** -əʳ/z US -ɚ/z
dispersal dɪ'spɜː.sᵊl US -'spɜːr- **-s** -z
dispers|e dɪ'spɜːs US -spɜːrs **-es** -ɪz **-ing** -ɪŋ **-ed** -t **-er/s** -əʳ/z US -ɚ/z **-ant/s** -ᵊnt/s
dispersion (D) dɪ'spɜː.ʃᵊn US -'spɜːr.ʒᵊn, -ʃᵊn **-s** -z
dispersive dɪ'spɜː.sɪv US -'spɜːr.zɪv, -sɪv
dispir|it dɪ'spɪr|.ɪt **-its** -ɪts **-iting** -ɪ.tɪŋ US -ɪ.t̬ɪŋ **-ited/ly** -ɪ.tɪd/li US -ɪ.t̬ɪd/li **-itedness** -ɪ.tɪd.nəs, -nɪs US -ɪ.t̬ɪd.nəs, -nɪs
displac|e dɪ'spleɪs **-es** -ɪz **-ing** -ɪŋ **-ed** -t
displacement dɪ'spleɪs.mənt
display dɪ'spleɪ **-s** -z **-ing** -ɪŋ **-ed** -d **-er/s** -əʳ/z US -ɚ/z
displeas|e dɪ'spliːz **-es** -ɪz **-ing/ly** -ɪŋ/li **-ed** -d
displeasure dɪ'spleʒ.əʳ US -ɚ
di|sport dɪ|'spɔːt US -|'spɔːrt **-sports** -'spɔːts US -'spɔːrts **-sporting** -'spɔː.tɪŋ US -'spɔːr.t̬ɪŋ **-sported** -'spɔː.tɪd US -'spɔːr.t̬ɪd
disposable dɪ'spəʊ.zə.bl̩, də- US dɪ'spoʊ-
disposal dɪ'spəʊ.zᵊl, də- US dɪ'spoʊ- **-s** -z
Disposall® dɪ'spəʊ.zɔːl, də- US dɪ'spoʊ.zɑːl, -zɔːl
dispos|e dɪ'spəʊz, də- US -'spoʊz **-es** -ɪz **-ing** -ɪŋ **-ed** -d **-er/s** -əʳ/z US -ɚ/z
disposition ˌdɪs.pə'zɪʃ.ᵊn **-s** -z
dispossess ˌdɪs.pə'zes **-es** -ɪz **-ing** -ɪŋ **-ed** -t
dispossession ˌdɪs.pə'zeʃ.ᵊn
Disprin® 'dɪs.prɪn **-s** -z
disproof dɪ'spruːf
disproportion ˌdɪs.prə'pɔː.ʃᵊn US -'pɔːr- **-ed** -d
disproportional ˌdɪs.prə'pɔː.ʃᵊn.ᵊl, -'pɔːʃ.nᵊl US -'pɔːr.ʃᵊn.ᵊl, -'pɔːrʃ.nᵊl **-ly** -i
disproportionate ˌdɪs.prə'pɔː.ʃᵊn.ət, -ɪt US -'pɔːr- **-ly** -li **-ness** -nəs, -nɪs
disproval dɪ'spruː.vᵊl; ˌdɪs'pruː-
disprov|e dɪ'spruːv; ˌdɪs'pruːv **-es** -z **-ing** -ɪŋ **-ed** -d
disputable dɪ'spjuː.tə.bl̩, də-; 'dɪs.pjʊ- US dɪ'spjuː.t̬ə-; 'dɪs.pjʊ-, -pjə-
disputableness dɪ'spjuː.tə.bl̩.nəs, də-, -nɪs US dɪ'spjuː.t̬ə-
disputant dɪ'spjuː.tᵊnt; 'dɪs.pjʊ- US 'dɪs.pjʊ.tᵊnt, -pjə-; dɪ'spjuː- **-s** -s
disputation ˌdɪs.pjʊ'teɪ.ʃᵊn US -pjuː'- **-s** -z
disputatious ˌdɪs.pjʊ'teɪ.ʃəs US -pjuː'- **-ly** -li **-ness** -nəs, -nɪs
disputative dɪ'spjuː.tə.tɪv US -t̬ə.t̬ɪv
dispute (*n.*) dɪ'spjuːt; 'dɪs.pjuːt US dɪ'spjuːt **-s** -s
di|spute (*v.*) dɪ|'spjuːt **-sputes** -'spjuːts **-sputing** -'spjuː.tɪŋ US -'spjuː.t̬ɪŋ **-sputed** -'spjuː.tɪd US -'spjuː.t̬ɪd **-sputer/s** -'spjuː.təʳ/z US -'spjuː.t̬ɚ/z
disqualification dɪˌskwɒl.ɪ.fɪ'keɪ.ʃᵊn, -ˌ-ə-; ˌdɪsˌkwɒl- US dɪˌskwɑː.lə- **-s** -z
disquali|fy dɪ'skwɒl.ɪ|.faɪ '-ə-; ˌdɪs'kwɒl- US dɪ'skwɑː.lə- **-fies** -faɪz **-fying** -faɪ.ɪŋ **-fied** -faɪd

di|squiet (*n. v.*) dɪ|ˈskwaɪət **-squiets** -ˈskwaɪəts **-squieting** -ˈskwaɪə.tɪŋ Ⓤⓢ -ˈskwaɪə.t̬ɪŋ **-squieted** -ˈskwaɪə.tɪd Ⓤⓢ -ˈskwaɪə.t̬ɪd
disquietude dɪˈskwaɪə.tjuːd, -ˈskwaɪ.ɪ- Ⓤⓢ -ˈskwaɪə.tuːd, -tjuːd
disquisition ˌdɪs.kwɪˈzɪʃ.ᵊn, -kwəˈ- **-s** -z
disquisitional ˌdɪs.kwɪˈzɪʃ.ᵊn.ᵊl, -kwəˈ-, ˈ-nᵊl
disquisitive dɪˈskwɪz.ə.tɪv, -ɪ.tɪv Ⓤⓢ -ə.t̬ɪv
Disraeli dɪzˈreɪ.li, dɪs-
d'Israeli dɪzˈreɪ.li, dɪs-
disregard ˌdɪs.rɪˈgɑːd, -rəˈ- Ⓤⓢ -rɪˈgɑːrd **-s** -z **-ing** -ɪŋ **-ed** -ɪd
disregardful ˌdɪs.rɪˈgɑːd.fᵊl, -rəˈ-, -fʊl Ⓤⓢ -rɪˈgɑːrd- **-ly** -i
disrepair ˌdɪs.rɪˈpeəʳ, -rəˈ- Ⓤⓢ -rɪˈper
disreputability dɪsˌrep.jə.təˈbɪl.ə.ti, -jʊ-, -ɪ.ti Ⓤⓢ -jə.t̬əˈ-
disreputab|le dɪsˈrep.jə.tə.b|l̩, -jʊ- Ⓤⓢ -jə.t̬ə- **-ly** -li **-leness** -l̩.nəs, -nɪs
disrepute ˌdɪs.rɪˈpjuːt, -rəˈ- Ⓤⓢ -rɪˈ-
disrespect ˌdɪs.rɪˈspekt, -rəˈ- Ⓤⓢ -rɪˈ-
disrespectful ˌdɪs.rɪˈspekt.fᵊl, -rəˈ-, -fʊl Ⓤⓢ -rɪˈ- **-ly** -i **-ness** -nəs, -nɪs
disrob|e dɪsˈrəʊb Ⓤⓢ -ˈroʊb **-es** -z **-ing** -ɪŋ **-ed** -d
disrupt dɪsˈrʌpt **-s** -s **-ing** -ɪŋ **-ed** -ɪd
disruption dɪsˈrʌp.ʃᵊn **-s** -z
disruptive dɪsˈrʌp.tɪv **-ly** -li **-ness** -nəs, -nɪs
Diss dɪs
dissatisfaction dɪsˌsæt.ɪsˈfæk.ʃᵊn, ˌdɪs.sæt-, -əsˈ- Ⓤⓢ ˌdɪs.sæt̬.əsˈ-
dissatisfactor|y dɪsˌsæt.ɪsˈfæk.tᵊr|.i, ˌdɪs.sæt-, -əsˈ- Ⓤⓢ ˌdɪs.sæt̬.əsˈ- **-ily** -ᵊl.i, -ɪ.li **-iness** -i.nəs, -i.nɪs
dissatis|fy dɪsˈsæt.ɪs|.faɪ, ˌdɪs-, -əs- Ⓤⓢ -ˈsæt̬.əs- **-fies** -faɪz **-fying** -faɪ.ɪŋ **-fied** -faɪd
dissect dɪˈsekt, də-, daɪ- Ⓤⓢ dɪˈsekt, daɪ-; ˈdaɪ.sekt **-s** -s **-ing** -ɪŋ **-ed** -ɪd **-or/s** -əʳ/z Ⓤⓢ -ɚ/z **-ible** -ə.bl̩, -ɪ.bl̩
dissection dɪˈsek.ʃᵊn, də-, daɪ- Ⓤⓢ dɪˈsek-, daɪ-; ˈdaɪ.sek- **-s** -z
dissemblanc|e dɪˈsem.blənts **-es** -ɪz
dissembl|e dɪˈsem.bl̩ **-es** -z **-ing** -ɪŋ, ˈ-blɪŋ **-ed** -d **-er/s** -əʳ/z, ˈ-bləʳ/z Ⓤⓢ -ə/z
dissemi|nate dɪˈsem.ɪ|.neɪt, ˈ-ə- **-nates** -neɪts **-nating** -neɪ.tɪŋ Ⓤⓢ -neɪ.t̬ɪŋ **-nated** -neɪ.tɪd Ⓤⓢ -neɪ.t̬ɪd **-nator/s** -neɪ.təʳ/z Ⓤⓢ -neɪ.t̬ɚ/z
dissemination dɪˌsem.ɪˈneɪ.ʃᵊn, -əˈ-
dissension dɪˈsen.tʃᵊn **-s** -z
dis|sent dɪ|ˈsent **-sents** -ˈsents **-senting** -ˈsen.tɪŋ Ⓤⓢ -ˈsen.t̬ɪŋ **-sented** -ˈsen.tɪd Ⓤⓢ -ˈsen.t̬ɪd **-senter/s** -ˈsen.təʳ/z Ⓤⓢ -ˈsen.t̬ɚ/z
dissentient dɪˈsen.tʃi.ənt, -tʃᵊnt Ⓤⓢ -ˈsent.ʃᵊnt **-s** -s
dissertation ˌdɪs.əˈteɪ.ʃᵊn, -ɜːˈ- Ⓤⓢ -ɚˈ- **-s** -z
dissservic|e ˌdɪsˈsɜː.vɪs, dɪ- Ⓤⓢ -ˈsɜːr- **-es** -ɪz
dissev|er dɪsˈsev|.əʳ Ⓤⓢ -ɚ **-ers** -əz Ⓤⓢ -ɚz **-ering** -ᵊr.ɪŋ **-ered** -əd Ⓤⓢ -ɚd **-erment** -ə.mənt Ⓤⓢ -ɚ.mənt **-erance** -ᵊr.ᵊnts
dissidence ˈdɪs.ɪ.dᵊnts, ˈ-ə-
dissident ˈdɪs.ɪ.dᵊnt, ˈ-ə- **-s** -s
dissimilar ˌdɪsˈsɪm.ɪ.ləʳ, dɪ-, ˈ-ə- Ⓤⓢ -lɚ **-ly** -li
dissimilarit|y ˌdɪsˌsɪm.ɪˈlær.ə.t|i, dɪ-, -əˈ-, -ɪ.t|i Ⓤⓢ -ˈler.ə.t̬|i, -ˈlær- **-ies** -iz
dissimi|late dɪˈsɪm.ɪ|.leɪt, ˌdɪs-, ˈ-ə- **-lates** -leɪts **-lating** -leɪ.tɪŋ Ⓤⓢ -leɪ.t̬ɪŋ **-lated** -leɪ.tɪd Ⓤⓢ -leɪ.t̬ɪd
dissimilation ˌdɪsˌsɪm.ɪˈleɪ.ʃᵊn, dɪ-, -əˈ- **-s** -z
dissimilitude ˌdɪs.sɪˈmɪl.ɪ.tjuːd, -ɪˈ-, ˈ-ə- Ⓤⓢ -tuːd, -tjuːd
dissimu|late dɪˈsɪm.jə|.leɪt, ˌdɪs-, -jʊ- **-lates** -leɪts **-lating** -leɪ.tɪŋ Ⓤⓢ -leɪ.t̬ɪŋ **-lated** -leɪ.tɪd Ⓤⓢ -leɪ.t̬ɪd **-lator/s** -leɪ.təʳ/z Ⓤⓢ -leɪ.t̬ɚ/z
dissimulation ˌdɪsˌsɪm.jəˈleɪ.ʃᵊn, dɪ-, -jʊˈ- **-s** -z
dissi|pate ˈdɪs.ɪ|.peɪt, ˈ-ə- **-pates** -peɪts **-pating** -peɪ.tɪŋ Ⓤⓢ -peɪ.t̬ɪŋ **-pated** -peɪ.tɪd Ⓤⓢ -peɪ.t̬ɪd **-pative** -peɪ.tɪv Ⓤⓢ -peɪ.t̬ɪv
dissipation ˌdɪs.ɪˈpeɪ.ʃᵊn, -əˈ- **-s** -z
dissociable *separable*: dɪˈsəʊ.ʃi.ə.bl̩, ˌdɪs- Ⓤⓢ -ˈsoʊ-, -ʃə.bl̩ *unsociable*: ˌdɪsˈsəʊ.ʃə.bl̩, dɪ- Ⓤⓢ -ˈsoʊ-
dissoci|ate dɪˈsəʊ.ʃi|.eɪt, -si- Ⓤⓢ -ˈsoʊ- **-ates** -eɪts **-ating** -eɪ.tɪŋ Ⓤⓢ -eɪ.t̬ɪŋ **-ated** -eɪ.tɪd Ⓤⓢ -eɪ.t̬ɪd
dissociation dɪˌsəʊ.ʃiˈeɪ.ʃᵊn, ˌdɪs-, -siˈ- Ⓤⓢ -ˌsoʊ-
dissolubility dɪˌsɒl.jəˈbɪl.ə.ti, -jʊˈ-, -ɪ.ti Ⓤⓢ -ˌsɑːl.jəˈbɪl.ə.t̬i, -jʊˈ-
dissolub|le dɪˈsɒl.jə.b|l̩, -jʊ- Ⓤⓢ -ˈsɑːl- **-ly** -li **-leness** -l̩.nəs, -nɪs
dissolute ˈdɪs.ə.luːt, -ljuːt Ⓤⓢ -luːt **-s** -s **-ly** -li **-ness** -nəs, -nɪs
dissolution ˌdɪs.əˈluː.ʃᵊn, -ˈljuː- Ⓤⓢ -ˈluː- **-s** -z
dissolvability dɪˌzɒl.vəˈbɪl.ə.ti, dəˌzɒl-, -ˌsɒl-, -ɪ.ti Ⓤⓢ dɪˌzɑːl.vəˈbɪl.ə.t̬i, -ˌzɔːl-
dissolv|e dɪˈzɒlv, -ˈsɒlv Ⓤⓢ -ˈzɑːlv, -ˈzɔːlv **-es** -z **-ing** -ɪŋ **-ed** -d **-able** -ə.bl̩
dissolvent dɪˈzɒl.vənt, -ˈsɒl- Ⓤⓢ -ˈzɑːl-, -ˈzɔːl- **-s** -s
dissonanc|e ˈdɪs.ᵊn.ənts **-es** -ɪz
dissonant ˈdɪs.ᵊn.ənt **-ly** -li
dissuad|e dɪˈsweɪd **-es** -z **-ing** -ɪŋ **-ed** -ɪd
dissuasion dɪˈsweɪ.ʒᵊn
dissuasive dɪˈsweɪ.sɪv, -zɪv Ⓤⓢ -sɪv **-ly** -li **-ness** -nəs, -nɪs
dissymmetry dɪˈsɪm.ɪ.tri, ˌdɪs-, ˈ-ə-
dissymmetric ˌdɪs.ɪˈmet.rɪk, -sɪmˈ-
distaff ˈdɪs.tɑːf Ⓤⓢ -tæf **-s** -s
distanc|e ˈdɪs.tᵊnts **-es** -ɪz **-ing** -ɪŋ **-ed** -t
distant ˈdɪs.tᵊnt **-ly** -li
distaste dɪˈsteɪst **-s** -s
distasteful dɪˈsteɪst.fᵊl, -fʊl **-ly** -i **-ness** -nəs, -nɪs
distemp|er dɪˈstem.p|əʳ Ⓤⓢ -p|ɚ **-ers** -əz Ⓤⓢ -ɚz **-ering** -ᵊr.ɪŋ **-ered** -əd Ⓤⓢ -ɚd
distend dɪˈstend **-s** -z **-ing** -ɪŋ **-ed** -ɪd
distensible dɪˈstent.sə.bl̩, -sɪ-
distension dɪˈsten.tʃᵊn Ⓤⓢ -ˈstent.ʃᵊn
distich ˈdɪs.tɪk **-s** -s **-ous** -əs
distil(l) dɪˈstɪl, də- Ⓤⓢ dɪ- **-s** -z **-ing** -ɪŋ **-ed** -d
distillate ˈdɪs.tɪ.lət, -tᵊl.ət, -eɪt, -ɪt Ⓤⓢ -tə.leɪt, -tᵊl.ɪt; dɪˈstɪl.ɪt **-s** -s
distillation ˌdɪs.tɪˈleɪ.ʃᵊn, -təˈ- **-s** -z
distillatory dɪˈstɪl.ə.tᵊr.i, də-, -tri Ⓤⓢ dɪˈstɪl.ə.tɔːr.i
distiller dɪˈstɪl.əʳ, də- Ⓤⓢ dɪˈstɪl.ɚ **-s** -z
distiller|y dɪˈstɪl.ᵊr|.i, də- Ⓤⓢ dɪ- **-ies** -iz
distinct dɪˈstɪŋkt, də- Ⓤⓢ dɪ- **-est** -ɪst, -əst **-ly** -li **-ness** -nəs, -nɪs
distinction dɪˈstɪŋk.ʃᵊn, də- Ⓤⓢ dɪ- **-s** -z
distinctive dɪˈstɪŋk.tɪv, də- Ⓤⓢ dɪ- **-ly** -li **-ness** -nəs, -nɪs
distinguish dɪˈstɪŋ.gwɪʃ, də- Ⓤⓢ dɪ- **-es** -ɪz **-ing** -ɪŋ **-ed** -t
distinguishab|le dɪˈstɪŋ.gwɪ.ʃə.b|l̩, də- Ⓤⓢ dɪ- **-ly** -li
di|stort dɪ|ˈstɔːt Ⓤⓢ -ˈstɔːrt **-storts** -ˈstɔːts Ⓤⓢ -ˈstɔːrts **-storting** -ˈstɔː.tɪŋ Ⓤⓢ -ˈstɔːr.t̬ɪŋ **-storted** -ˈstɔː.tɪd Ⓤⓢ -ˈstɔːr.t̬ɪd
distortion dɪˈstɔː.ʃᵊn Ⓤⓢ -ˈstɔːr- **-s** -z
distract dɪˈstrækt, dəˈstrækt Ⓤⓢ dɪ- **-s** -s **-ing** -ɪŋ **-ed/ly** -ɪd/li **-edness** -ɪd.nəs, -nɪs
distraction dɪˈstræk.ʃᵊn, də- **-s** -z
distrain dɪˈstreɪn, də- Ⓤⓢ dɪ- **-s** -z **-ing** -ɪŋ **-ed** -d **-er/s** -əʳ/z Ⓤⓢ -ɚ/z **-able** -ə.bl̩
distrainee ˌdɪs.treɪˈniː **-s** -z
distrainor ˌdɪs.treɪˈnɔːʳ Ⓤⓢ -ˈnɔːr, dɪˈstreɪ.nɚ **-s** -z
distraint dɪˈstreɪnt **-s** -s
distrait dɪˈstreɪ; ˈdɪs.treɪ Ⓤⓢ dɪˈstreɪ
distraught dɪˈstrɔːt Ⓤⓢ -ˈstrɑːt, -ˈstrɔːt
distress dɪˈstres **-es** -ɪz **-ing/ly** -ɪŋ/li **-ed** -t
distressful dɪˈstres.fᵊl, -fʊl **-ly** -i
distributable dɪˈstrɪb.jə.tə.bl̩, -jʊ- Ⓤⓢ -t̬ə-

distribu|te dɪˈstrɪb.juː|t; ˈdɪs.trɪ.bjuː|t, -trə- US dɪˈstrɪb.juː|t, -jʊ|t, -jə|t **-tes** -ts **-ting** -tɪŋ US -t̬ɪŋ **-ted** -tɪd US -t̬ɪd
distribution ˌdɪs.trɪˈbjuː.ʃᵊn, -trəˈ- **-s** -z
distributive dɪˈstrɪb.jə.tɪv, -jʊ- US -jə.t̬ɪv **-ly** -li
distributor dɪˈstrɪb.jə.təʳ, -jʊ- US -t̬ɚ **-s** -z
district ˈdɪs.trɪkt **-s** -s ˌ**district atˈtorney** ; ˌ**District of Coˈlumbia**
distrust dɪˈstrʌst; ˌdɪsˈtrʌst **-s** -s **-ing** -ɪŋ **-ed** -ɪd
distrustful dɪˈstrʌst.fᵊl, -fʊl; ˌdɪsˈtrʌst- **-ly** -i **-ness** -nəs, -nɪs
disturb dɪˈstɜːb US -ˈstɜːrb **-s** -z **-ing/ly** -ɪŋ/li **-ed** -d **-er/s** -əʳ/z US -ɚ/z
disturbanc|e dɪˈstɜː.bᵊnts US -ˈstɜːr- **-es** -ɪz
distyle ˈdɪs.taɪl; ˈdaɪ.staɪl **-s** -z
disulphate daɪˈsʌl.feɪt, -fɪt **-s** -s
disulphide daɪˈsʌl.faɪd **-s** -z
disunion dɪˈsjuː.njən, -ni.ən US ˈ-njən **-s** -z
disu|nite ˌdɪs.juː|ˈnaɪt **-nites** -ˈnaɪts **-niting** -ˈnaɪ.tɪŋ US -ˈnaɪ.t̬ɪŋ **-nited** -ˈnaɪ.tɪd US -ˈnaɪ.t̬ɪd
disunity dɪˈsjuː.nɪ.ti, -nə- US -t̬i
disuse (*n.*) dɪˈsjuːs
disus|e (*v.*) dɪˈsjuːz **-es** -ɪz **-ing** -ɪŋ **-ed** -d
disyllabic ˌdaɪ.sɪˈlæb.ɪk, ˌdɪs.ɪˈ-, -əˈ-
disyllable daɪˈsɪl.ə.bl̩, dɪ- **-s** -z
ditch dɪtʃ **-es** -ɪz **-ing** -ɪŋ **-ed** -t **-er/s** -əʳ/z US -ɚ/z
Ditchling ˈdɪtʃ.lɪŋ
ditchwater ˈdɪtʃˌwɔː.təʳ US -ˌwɑː.t̬ɚ, -ˌwɔː- **as ˌdull as ˈditch-water**
dith|er ˈdɪð|.əʳ US -ɚ **-ers** -əz US -ɚz **-ering** -ᵊr.ɪŋ **-ered** -əd US -ɚd **-erer/s** -ᵊr.əʳ/z US -ɚ.ɚ/z **-ery** -ᵊr.i
dithyramb ˈdɪθ.ɪ.ræm*b*, ˈ-ə- **-s** -z
Note: The /b/ is rarely pronounced.
dithyramb|us ˌdɪθ.ɪˈræm.b|əs, -əˈ- **-i** -aɪ **-ic/s** -ɪk/s
ditransitive ˌdaɪˈtræn.sɪ.tɪv, -ˈtrɑːn-, -sə- US -ˈtræn.sə.t̬ɪv **-s** -z **-ly** -li
dits|y ˈdɪt.s|i **-ier** -i.əʳ US -i.ɚ **-iest** -i.ɪst, -i.əst
ditto ˈdɪt.əʊ US ˈdɪt̬.oʊ **-s** -z
Ditton ˈdɪt.ᵊn
ditt|y ˈdɪt|.i US ˈdɪt̬- **-ies** -iz
diures|is ˌdaɪ.jʊəˈriː.s|ɪs, -jəˈ- US -jəˈ-, -əˈ-, -jʊrˈ- **-es** -iːz
diuretic ˌdaɪ.jʊəˈret.ɪk, -jəˈ- US -jəˈret̬-, -əˈ- **-s** -s
diurnal ˌdaɪˈɜː.nᵊl US -ˈɜːr- **-s** -z **-ly** -i
diva ˈdiː.və **-s** -z
diva|gate ˈdaɪ.və|.geɪt; -veɪ-; ˈdɪv.ə- US ˈdaɪ.və-, ˈdɪv.ə- **-gates** -geɪts **-gating** -geɪ.tɪŋ US -geɪ.t̬ɪŋ **-gated** -geɪ.tɪd US -geɪ.t̬ɪd
divagation ˌdaɪ.vəˈgeɪ.ʃᵊn, -veɪˈ- US ˌdaɪ.vəˈ-, ˌdɪv.əˈ- **-s** -z
divalent ˌdaɪˈveɪ.lənt, ˈdaɪ.veɪ-
Divali dɪˈvɑː.li
divan dɪˈvæn, də-, daɪ-; ˈdaɪ.væn US dɪˈvæn, daɪ-; ˈdaɪ.væn **-s** -z
div|e daɪv **-es** -z **-ing** -ɪŋ **-ed** -d **dove** dəʊv US doʊv **ˈdiving ˌbell** ; **ˈdiving ˌboard** ; **ˈdiving ˌsuit**
dive-bomb ˈdaɪv.bɒm US -bɑːm **-s** -z **-ing** -ɪŋ **-ed** -d **-er/s** -əʳ/z US -ɚ/z
diver (D) ˈdaɪ.vəʳ US -vɚ **-s** -z
diverg|e daɪˈvɜːdʒ, dɪ- US dɪˈvɜːrdʒ, daɪ- **-es** -ɪz **-ing** -ɪŋ **-ed** -d
divergenc|e daɪˈvɜː.dʒᵊnts, dɪ- US dɪˈvɜːr-, daɪ- **-es** -ɪz **-y** -i **-ies** -iz
divergent daɪˈvɜː.dʒənt, dɪ- US dɪˈvɜːr-, daɪ- **-ly** -li
divers ˈdaɪ.vəz, -vɜːz, -vɜːs; daɪˈvɜːs US ˈdaɪ.vɚz
diverse daɪˈvɜːs, ˈ-- US dɪˈvɜːrs, daɪ-; ˈdaɪ.vɜːrs **-ly** -li
diversification daɪˌvɜː.sɪ.fɪˈkeɪ.ʃᵊn, dɪ-, də-, -sə- US dɪˌvɜːr-, daɪ- **-s** -z
diversi|fy daɪˈvɜː.sɪ|.faɪ, dɪ- US dɪˈvɜːr-, daɪ- **-fies** -faɪz **-fying** -faɪ.ɪŋ **-fied** -faɪd
diversion daɪˈvɜː.ʃᵊn, dɪ-, -ʒən US dɪˈvɜːr-, daɪ- **-s** -z
diversionary daɪˈvɜː.ʃᵊn.ᵊr.i, dɪ-, -ʒᵊn- US dɪˈvɜːr.ʒᵊn.er.i, daɪ-, -ʃᵊn-
diversionist daɪˈvɜː.ʃᵊn.ɪst, dɪ-, -ʒᵊn- US dɪˈvɜːr-, daɪ- **-s** -s
diversit|y daɪˈvɜː.sə.t|i, dɪ-, -ɪ.t|i US dɪˈvɜːr.sə.t̬|i, daɪ- **-ies** -iz
di|vert daɪ|ˈvɜːt, dɪ- US dɪ|ˈvɜːrt, daɪ- **-verts** -ˈvɜːts US -ˈvɜːrts **-verting/ly** -ˈvɜː.tɪŋ/li US -ˈvɜːr.t̬ɪŋ/li **-verted** -ˈvɜː.tɪd US -ˈvɜːr.t̬ɪd
diverticulitis ˌdaɪ.vəˌtɪk.jʊˈlaɪ.tɪs, -vɜːˌ-, -jəˈ- US -vɚˌtɪk.jəˈlaɪ.t̬əs, -jʊˈ-
diverticulosis ˌdaɪ.vəˌtɪk.jʊˈləʊ.sɪs, -vɜːˌ-, -jəˈ- US -vɚˌtɪk.jəˈloʊ-, -jʊˈ-
diverticulum ˌdaɪ.vəˈtɪk.jʊ.ləm, -vɜːˈ-, -jə- US -vɚˈtɪk.jə-, -jʊ-
divertimento dɪˌvɜː.tɪˈmen.təʊ, -ˌveə-, -təˈ- US -ˌvɜːr.t̬əˈmen.toʊ
divertissement ˌdiː.veəˈtiːs.mɑ̃ŋ, -vəˈ-, -vɜːˈ-, dɪˈvɜː.tɪs.mənt US ˌdɪv.erˈtiːs.mɑ̃
Dives *in Bible:* ˈdaɪ.viːz *surname:* daɪvz
divest daɪˈvest, dɪ- US dɪ-, daɪ- **-s** -s **-ing** -ɪŋ **-ed** -ɪd
divestiture daɪˈves.tɪ.tʃəʳ, dɪ- US dɪˈves.tɪ.tʃɚ, daɪ-
divestment daɪˈvest.mənt, dɪ- US dɪ-, daɪ- **-s** -s
divid|e dɪˈvaɪd, də- **-es** -z **-ing** -ɪŋ **-ed/ly** -ɪd/li **-able** -ə.bl̩
dividend ˈdɪv.ɪ.dend, ˈ-ə-, -dənd **-s** -z
divider dɪˈvaɪ.dəʳ, də- US -dɚ **-s** -z
divination ˌdɪv.ɪˈneɪ.ʃᵊn, -əˈ- **-s** -z
divin|e (*n. adj.*) dɪˈvaɪn, də- **-es** -z **-er** -əʳ US -ɚ **-est** -ɪst, -əst **-ely** -li **-eness** -nəs, -nɪs **diˌvine ˈright**
divin|e (*v.*) dɪˈvaɪn, də- **-es** -z **-ing** -ɪŋ **-ed** -d **-er/s** -əʳ/z US -ɚ/z **diˈvining ˌrod**
divinit|y dɪˈvɪn.ə.t|i, də-, -ɪ.t|i US -ə.t̬|i **-ies** -iz
divisibility dɪˌvɪz.ɪˈbɪl.ə.ti, də-, -əˈ-, -ɪ.ti US -əˈbɪl.ə.t̬i
divisib|le dɪˈvɪz.ə.bl|̩, də-, ˈ-ɪ- **-ly** -li
division dɪˈvɪʒ.ᵊn, də- **-s** -z
divisional dɪˈvɪʒ.ᵊn.ᵊl, də-, ˈ-nᵊl
divisive dɪˈvaɪ.sɪv, də- **-ly** -li **-ness** -nəs, -nɪs
divisor dɪˈvaɪ.zəʳ, də- US -zɚ **-s** -z
divorc|e dɪˈvɔːs, də- US -ˈvɔːrs **-es** -ɪz **-ing** -ɪŋ **-ed** -t **-er/s** -əʳ/z US -ɚ/z
divorcé(e), divorcee dɪˌvɔːˈsiː, də-, -ˈseɪ; ˌdɪv.ɔːˈ- US dɪˌvɔːrˈseɪ, də-, -ˈsiː; -ˈvɔːr.seɪ, -siː **-s** -z
divot ˈdɪv.ət **-s** -s
divulg|e daɪˈvʌldʒ, dɪ- US dɪ-, daɪ- **-es** -ɪz **-ing** -ɪŋ **-ed** -d
divulsion daɪˈvʌl.ʃᵊn, dɪ- US dɪ-, daɪ- **-s** -z
divv|y ˈdɪv|.i **-ies** -iz **-ying** -i.ɪŋ **-ied** -id
divvy-up ˌdɪv.iˈʌp
Diwali dɪˈwɑː.li
Dix dɪks
Dixey, Dixie ˈdɪk.si
dixieland (D) ˈdɪk.si.lænd
Dixon ˈdɪk.sᵊn
Dixwell ˈdɪk.swəl, -swel
DIY ˌdiː.aɪˈwaɪ
dizz|y ˈdɪz|.i **-ier** -i.əʳ US -i.ɚ **-iest** -i.ɪst, -i.əst **-ily** -ɪ.li, -ᵊl.i **-iness** -ɪ.nəs, -ɪ.nɪs **-ies** -iz **-ying/ly** -i.ɪŋ **-ied** -id
DJ ˌdiːˈdʒeɪ US ˈ-- **-s** -z *stress shift, British only:* ˌDJ ˈculture
Djakarta dʒəˈkɑː.tə US -ˈkɑːr.t̬ə
djellaba(h) dʒəˈlɑː.bə **-s** -z
Djibouti dʒɪˈbuː.ti, dʒə- US -t̬i
djinn dʒɪn **-s** -z
djinni dʒɪˈni, ˈdʒɪn.i
dl (*abbrev. for* **decilitre/s, deciliter/s**) *singular:* ˈdes.ɪˌliː.təʳ US -t̬ɚ *plural:* -z
DLit(t) ˌdiːˈlɪt
dm (*abbrev. for* **decimetre/s, decimeter/s**) *singular:* ˈdes.ɪˌmiː.təʳ US -t̬ɚ *plural:* -z
D-mark ˈdɔɪtʃ.mɑːk US -mɑːrk **-s** -s
DNA ˌdiː.enˈeɪ
Dnepropetrovsk ˌ*d*njep.rɒp.jetˈrɒfsk US ˌnep.roʊ.pəˈtrɔːfsk, ˌdjnep-, -pjəˈ-
Dnieper ˈ*d*niː.pəʳ US -pɚ

D-notic|e ˈdiːˌnəʊ.tɪs ⓤⓢ -ˌnoʊ.t̬ɪs **-es** -ɪz

do (*v.*) *strong form:* duː *weak forms:* də, du **dost** *strong form:* dʌst *weak form:* dəst **doth** *strong form:* dʌθ *weak form:* dəθ **doeth** ˈduː.ɪθ **does** *strong form:* dʌz *weak form:* dəz **doing** ˈduː.ɪŋ **did** dɪd **done** dʌn **doer/s** ˈduː.əʳ/z ⓤⓢ -ɚ/z

Note: Weak form word. The strong form /duː/ is normally used in final position (e.g. "Yes, I do"), when it is used as a full verb rather than as an auxiliary (e.g. "Do it yourself"), for emphasis (e.g. "Why **do** you like him?") or for contrast (e.g. "I do and I don't"). There are two weak forms: /də/ before consonants (e.g. "How do they do it" /ˌhaʊ.də.ðeɪˈduː.ɪt/) and /du/ before vowels (e.g. "Why do all the books disappear?" /ˌwaɪ.duˌɔːl.ðəˈbʊks.dɪs.ə.pɪəʳ ⓤⓢ -pɪɚ/).

do (*n.*) *entertainment:* duː **-s** -z

do (*n.*) *musical note:* dəʊ ⓤⓢ doʊ **-s** -z

do. (*abbrev. for* **ditto**) ˈdɪt.əʊ ⓤⓢ ˈdɪt̬.oʊ

DOA ˌdiː.əʊˈeɪ ⓤⓢ -oʊˈ-

doable ˈduː.ə.bl̩

Doane dəʊn ⓤⓢ doʊn

Dobb dɒb ⓤⓢ dɑːb **-s** -z

dobbin (D) ˈdɒb.ɪn ⓤⓢ ˈdɑː.bɪn **-s** -z

Dobell dəʊˈbel, ˈdəʊ.bəl ⓤⓢ ˈdoʊ.bəl, -bel

doberman (D) ˈdəʊ.bə.mən ⓤⓢ ˈdoʊ.bɚ- **-s** -z

Doberman pinscher ˌdəʊ.bə.mənˈpɪn.*t*ʃəʳ ⓤⓢ ˌdoʊ.bɚ.mənˈpɪn*t*.ʃɚ

Dobie ˈdəʊ.bi ⓤⓢ ˈdoʊ-

dobra ˈdəʊ.brə ⓤⓢ ˈdoʊ- **-s** -z

Dobrée ˈdəʊ.breɪ ⓤⓢ ˈdoʊ-

Dobson ˈdɒb.sən ⓤⓢ ˈdɑːb-

doc dɒk ⓤⓢ dɑːk **-s** -s

docent ˈdəʊ.sənt, dəʊˈsent ⓤⓢ ˈdoʊ.sənt, -sent; doʊˈsent **-s** -s

Docet|ism dəʊˈsiː.t|ɪ.zəm; ˈdəʊ.sɪ- ⓤⓢ doʊˈsiː.t|ɪ-; ˈdoʊ.sə.t̬|ɪ- **-ist/s** -ɪst/s

Docherty ˈdɒk.ə.ti, ˈdɒx- ⓤⓢ ˈdɑː.kɚ.t̬i

docile ˈdəʊ.saɪl, ˈdɒs.aɪl ⓤⓢ ˈdɑː.səl, -saɪl **-ly** -li

docility dəʊˈsɪl.ə.ti, -ɪ.ti ⓤⓢ dɑːˈsɪl.ə.t̬i, doʊ-

dock dɒk ⓤⓢ dɑːk **-s** -s **-ing** -ɪŋ **-ed** -t

dockage ˈdɒk.ɪdʒ ⓤⓢ ˈdɑː.kɪdʒ

docker (D) ˈdɒk.əʳ ⓤⓢ ˈdɑː.kɚ **-s** -z

Dockerill ˈdɒk.ər.əl ⓤⓢ ˈdɑː.kɚ-

dock|et ˈdɒk|.ɪt ⓤⓢ ˈdɑː.k|ɪt **-ets** -ɪts **-eting** -ɪ.tɪŋ ⓤⓢ -ɪ.t̬ɪŋ **-eted** -ɪ.tɪd ⓤⓢ -ɪ.t̬ɪd

dockland (D) ˈdɒk.lænd, -lənd ⓤⓢ ˈdɑːk- **-s**

dockside ˈdɒk.saɪd ⓤⓢ ˈdɑːk-

dockworker ˈdɒkˌwɜː.kəʳ ⓤⓢ ˈdɑːkˌwɜːr.kɚ **-s** -z

dockyard ˈdɒk.jɑːd ⓤⓢ ˈdɑːk.jɑːrd **-s** -z

Doc Martens® ˌdɒkˈmɑː.tɪnz ⓤⓢ ˌdɑːkˈmɑːr.tənz

doct|or ˈdɒk.t|əʳ ⓤⓢ ˈdɑːk.t|ɚ **-ors** -əz ⓤⓢ -ɚz **-oring** -ər.ɪŋ **-ored** -əd ⓤⓢ -ɚd

doctoral ˈdɒk.tər.əl ⓤⓢ ˈdɑːk-

doctorate ˈdɒk.tər.ət, -ɪt ⓤⓢ ˈdɑːk- **-s** -s

Doctorow ˈdɒk.tər.əʊ ⓤⓢ ˈdɑːk.tə.roʊ

doctrinaire ˌdɒk.trɪˈneəʳ, -trəˈ- ⓤⓢ ˌdɑːk.trəˈner **-s** -z

doctrinal dɒkˈtraɪ.nəl; ˈdɒk.trɪ- ⓤⓢ ˈdɑːk.trɪ- **-ly** -i

doctrinarian ˌdɒk.trɪˈneə.ri.ən, -trəˈ- ⓤⓢ ˌdɑːk.trɪˈner.i- **-s** -z

doctrine ˈdɒk.trɪn ⓤⓢ ˈdɑːk- **-s** -z

docudrama ˈdɒk.jʊˌdrɑː.mə ⓤⓢ ˈdɑː.kjʊˌdrɑː.mə, -ˌdræm.ə **-s** -z

document (*n.*) ˈdɒk.jə.mənt, -jʊ- ⓤⓢ ˈdɑː.kjə-, -jʊ- **-s** -s

docu|ment (*v.*) ˈdɒk.jə|.ment, -jʊ- ⓤⓢ ˈdɑː.kjə-, -jʊ- **-ments** -ments **-menting** -men.tɪŋ ⓤⓢ -men.t̬ɪŋ **-mented** -men.tɪd ⓤⓢ -men.t̬ɪd

documental ˌdɒk.jəˈmen.təl, -jʊˈ- ⓤⓢ ˌdɑː.kjəˈmenˈt̬əl, -jʊ-

documentar|y (*n. adj.*) ˌdɒk.jəˈmen.tər|.i, -jʊˈ-, ˈ-tr|i ⓤⓢ ˌdɑː.kjəˈmen.t̬ɚ|.i, -kjʊˈ- **-ies** -iz

documentation ˌdɒk.jə.menˈteɪ.ʃən, -jʊ-, -mənˈ- ⓤⓢ ˌdɑː.kjə-, -jʊ-

Docwra ˈdɒk.rə ⓤⓢ ˈdɑːk-

Dod(d) dɒd ⓤⓢ dɑːd **-s** -z

dodd|er ˈdɒd|.əʳ ⓤⓢ ˈdɑː.d|ɚ **-ers** -əz ⓤⓢ -ɚz **-ering** -ər.ɪŋ **-ered** -əd ⓤⓢ -ɚd **-erer/s** -ər.əʳ/z ⓤⓢ -ɚ.ɚ/z

doddery ˈdɒd.ər.i ⓤⓢ ˈdɑː.dɚ-

Doddington ˈdɒd.ɪŋ.tən ⓤⓢ ˈdɑː.dɪŋ-

doddle ˈdɒd.l̩ ⓤⓢ ˈdɑː.dl̩ **-s** -z

Doddridge ˈdɒd.rɪdʒ ⓤⓢ ˈdɑː.drɪdʒ

dodecagon ˌdəʊˈdek.ə.gən ⓤⓢ ˌdoʊ- **-s** -z

dodecahedr|on ˌdəʊ.dek.əˈhiː.dr|ən, -dɪk-, -ˈhed.r|ən ⓤⓢ ˌdoʊ.dek.əˈhiː.dr|ən **-ons** -ənz **-a** -ə **-al** -əl

Dodecanese ˌdəʊ.dɪ.kəˈniːz, -dek.əˈ- ⓤⓢ ˌdoʊ.dek-, -ˈniːs

dodg|e (D) dɒdʒ ⓤⓢ dɑːdʒ **-es** -ɪz **-ing** -ɪŋ **-ed** -d **-er/z** -əʳ/z ⓤⓢ -ɚ/z ˌ**Dodge** ˈ**City**

dodgem ˈdɒdʒ.əm ⓤⓢ ˈdɑː.dʒəm **-s** -z

Dodgson ˈdɒdʒ.sən ⓤⓢ ˈdɑːdʒ-

dodg|y ˈdɒdʒ|.i ⓤⓢ ˈdɑː.dʒ|i **-ier** -i.əʳ ⓤⓢ -i.ɚ **-iest** -i.ɪst, -i.əst **-ily** -ɪ.li, -əl.i **-iness** -ɪ.nəs, -ɪ.nɪs

Dodington ˈdɒd.ɪŋ.tən ⓤⓢ ˈdɑː.dɪŋ-

dodo (D) ˈdəʊ.dəʊ ⓤⓢ ˈdoʊ.doʊ **-(e)s** -z

Dodoma ˈdəʊ.də.mə, -mɑː ⓤⓢ ˈdoʊ.də.mɑː, -doʊ-, doʊˈ-

Dodona dəʊˈdəʊ.nə ⓤⓢ dəˈdoʊ-

Dodsley ˈdɒdz.li ⓤⓢ ˈdɑːdz-

Dodson ˈdɒd.sən ⓤⓢ ˈdɑːd-

Dodsworth ˈdɒdz.wəθ, -wɜːθ ⓤⓢ ˈdɑːdz.wɚθ, -wɜːrθ

Dodwell ˈdɒd.wəl, -wel ⓤⓢ ˈdɑːd-

doe (D) dəʊ ⓤⓢ doʊ **-s** -z

doer ˈduː.əʳ ⓤⓢ -ɚ **-s** -z

-doer -ˌduː.əʳ ⓤⓢ -ɚ

Note: Suffix. Normally carries secondary stress, e.g. **wrongdoer** /ˈrɒŋˌduː.əʳ ⓤⓢ ˈrɑːŋˌduː.ɚ/.

does (*from* **do**) *strong form:* dʌz *weak form:* dəz

Note: Weak form word. The strong form is used when **does** is used as a full verb (e.g. "That's what he does for a living"), for emphasis (e.g. "That **does** look nice") and for contrast (e.g. "It **does** cost a lot, but it **doesn't** need repairing"). The strong form also occurs in final position (e.g. "I don't like it as much as she does"). When **does** occurs in other positions as an auxiliary, the weak form is normally used (e.g. "Why does it stop?" /ˌwaɪ.dəz.ɪtˈstɒp ⓤⓢ -stɑːp/).

doeskin ˈdəʊ.skɪn ⓤⓢ ˈdoʊ- **-s** -z

doesn't ˈdʌz.ənt

doeth (*from* **do**) ˈduː.ɪθ

Note: Archaic.

doff (D) dɒf ⓤⓢ dɑːf, dɔːf **-s** -s **-ing** -ɪŋ **-ed** -t **-er/s** -əʳ/z ⓤⓢ -ɚ/z

dog dɒg ⓤⓢ dɑːg, dɔːg **-s** -z **-ging** -ɪŋ **-ged** -d ˈ**dog** ˌ**biscuit**; ˈ**dog** ˌ**collar**; ˈ**dog** ˌ**days**; ˈ**dog** ˌ**paddle**; ˈ**dog** ˌ**rose**; ˌ**dog's** ˈ**breakfast**; ˈ**Dog** ˌ**Star**; **dressed up like a** ˌ**dog's** ˈ**dinner**; **it's a** ˈ**dog's** ˌ**life**; **let** ˌ**sleeping dogs** ˈ**lie**; ˌ**go to the** ˈ**dogs**

dogbane ˈdɒg.beɪn ⓤⓢ ˈdɑːg-, ˈdɔːg-

Dogberry ˈdɒg.ber.i, -bər- ⓤⓢ ˈdɑːg.ber-, ˈdɔːg-

dogcart ˈdɒg.kɑːt ⓤⓢ ˈdɑːg.kɑːrt, ˈdɔːg- **-s** -s

dogcatcher ˈdɒgˌkætʃ.əʳ ⓤⓢ ˈdɑːgˌkætʃ.ɚ, ˈdɔːg- **-s** -z

dog|e dəʊdʒ, dəʊʒ ⓤⓢ doʊdʒ **-es** -ɪz

dog-ear ˈdɒg.ɪəʳ ⓤⓢ ˈdɑːg.ɪr, ˈdɔːg- **-s** -z **-ing** -ɪŋ **-ed** -d

dog-eat-dog ˌdɒg.iːtˈdɒg ⓤⓢ ˌdɑːg.iːtˈdɑːg; ˌdɔːg.iːtˈdɔːg

dog-end ˈdɒg.end ⓤⓢ ˈdɑːg-, ˈdɔːg- **-s** -z

dogfight ˈdɒg.faɪt ⓤⓢ ˈdɑːg-, ˈdɔːg- **-s** -s

dogfish ˈdɒg.fɪʃ ⓤⓢ ˈdɑːg-, ˈdɔːg- **-es** -ɪz

Doggart ˈdɒg.ət ⓤⓢ ˈdɑː.gɚt, ˈdɔː-

dogged ˈdɒg.ɪd ⓤⓢ ˈdɑː.gɪd, ˈdɔː- **-ly** -li **-ness** -nəs, -nɪs
dogger (D) ˈdɒg.əʳ ⓤⓢ ˈdɑː.gɚ, ˈdɔː- **-s** -z ˌ**Dogger ˈBank** ⓤⓢ ˈ**Dogger ˌBank**
doggerel ˈdɒg.ᵊr.ᵊl, -ɪl ⓤⓢ ˈdɑː.gɚ.ᵊl, ˈdɔː-, ˈ-grᵊl
Doggert ˈdɒg.ət ⓤⓢ ˈdɑː.gɚt, ˈdɔː-
Doggett ˈdɒg.ɪt ⓤⓢ ˈdɑː.gɪt, ˈdɔː-
doggo ˈdɒg.əʊ ⓤⓢ ˈdɑː.goʊ, ˈdɔː-
doggone ˈdɒg.ɒn ⓤⓢ ˈdɑː.gɑːn; ˈdɔː.gɔːn **-d** -d
dogg|y, dogg|ie ˈdɒg|.i ⓤⓢ ˈdɑː.g|i, ˈdɔː- **-ies** -iz ˈ**doggie ˌbag**
doghou|se ˈdɒg.haʊ|s ⓤⓢ ˈdɑːg-, ˈdɔːg- **-ses** -zɪz
dogie ˈdəʊ.gi ⓤⓢ ˈdoʊ- **-s** -z
dogleg ˈdɒg.leg ⓤⓢ ˈdɑːg-, ˈdɔːg- **-s** -z **-ging** -ɪŋ **-ged** -ɪd, -legd
dogma ˈdɒg.mə ⓤⓢ ˈdɑːg-, ˈdɔːg- **-s** -z
dogmatic dɒgˈmæt.ɪk ⓤⓢ dɑːgˈmæţ-, dɔːg- **-s** -s **-al** -ᵊl **-ally** -ᵊl.i, -li
dogmat|ism ˈdɒg.mə.t|ɪ.zᵊm ⓤⓢ ˈdɑːg.mə.t|ɪ-, ˈdɔːg- **-ist/s** -ɪst/s
dogmatiz|e, -is|e ˈdɒg.mə.taɪz ⓤⓢ ˈdɑːg-, ˈdɔːg- **-es** -ɪz **-ing** -ɪŋ **-ed** -d **-er/s** -əʳ/z ⓤⓢ -ɚ/z
do-good|er ˌduːˈgʊd|.əʳ ⓤⓢ ˈduːˌgʊd|.ɚ **-ers** -əz ⓤⓢ -ɚz **-ing** -ɪŋ
dogsbod|y ˈdɒgz.bɒd|.i ⓤⓢ ˈdɑːgz.bɑː.d|i, ˈdɔːgz- **-ies** -iz
dogsled ˈdɒg.sled ⓤⓢ ˈdɑːg-, ˈdɔːg- **-s** -z
dog-tired ˌdɒgˈtaɪəd ⓤⓢ ˌdɑːgˈtaɪɚd, ˌdɔːg- *stress shift:* ˌdog-tired ˈworker
dog|tooth ˈdɒg|.tuːθ ⓤⓢ ˈdɑːg-, ˈdɔːg- **-teeth** -tiːθ
dogwatch ˈdɒg.wɒtʃ ⓤⓢ ˈdɑːg.wɑːtʃ, ˈdɔːg- **-es** -ɪz
dogwood ˈdɒg.wʊd ⓤⓢ ˈdɑːg-, ˈdɔːg-
doh dəʊ ⓤⓢ doʊ **-s** -z
Doha ˈdəʊ.hɑː, -ə ⓤⓢ ˈdoʊ-
Doherty ˈdəʊ.ə.ti; ˈdɒ.hə-; ˈdɒx.ə-; dəʊˈhɜː- ⓤⓢ ˈdɔːr.ə.ţi, ˈdoʊ.ɚ-
Dohnanyi dɒkˈnɑːn.jiː, dɒx-, -ji ⓤⓢ ˈdoʊ.ɑː.nji; dɑːkˈnɑːn.ji, dɑːx-
Doig dɔɪg, ˈdəʊ.ɪg ⓤⓢ dɔɪg, ˈdoʊ.ɪg
doil|y ˈdɔɪ.l|i **-ies** -iz
doing (*from* **do**) ˈduː.ɪŋ **-s** -z
Doister ˈdɔɪ.stəʳ ⓤⓢ -stɚ
doit dɔɪt **-s** -s
do-it-yourself ˌduː.ɪt.jɔːˈself, -ɪ.tʃəˈ-, -jəˈ- ⓤⓢ ˌduː.ɪt.jɚˈself, -ɪ.tʃɚˈ-
Dolan ˈdəʊ.lən ⓤⓢ ˈdoʊl-
Dolby ˈdɒl.bi ⓤⓢ ˈdɑːl-, ˈdoʊl-
dolce ˈdɒl.tʃi, ˈdəʊl-, -tʃeɪ ⓤⓢ ˈdoʊl.tʃeɪ
dolce vita ˌdɒl.tʃiˈviː.tə, ˌdəʊ-, -tʃeɪˈ- ⓤⓢ ˌdoʊl.tʃeɪˈviː.tə
Dolcis® ˈdɒl.sɪs, -tʃɪs ⓤⓢ ˈdɑːl-
doldrum ˈdɒl.drəm ⓤⓢ ˈdoʊl-, ˈdɑːl- **-s** -z
dol|e (D) dəʊl ⓤⓢ doʊl **-es** -z **-ing** -ɪŋ **-ed** -d
doleful ˈdəʊl.fᵊl, -fʊl ⓤⓢ ˈdoʊl- **-ly** -i **-ness** -nəs, -nɪs
dolerite ˈdɒl.ə.raɪt ⓤⓢ ˈdɑː.lə-
Dolgellau, Dolgelley dɒlˈgeθ.laɪ, -li ⓤⓢ dɑːl-
dolichocephalic ˌdɒl.ɪ.kəʊ.sefˈæl.ɪk, -sɪˈfæl-, -səˈ-, -kefˈæl-, -kɪˈfæl- ⓤⓢ ˌdɑː.lɪ.koʊ-
Dolittle ˈduː.lɪ.tl̩ ⓤⓢ -ţl̩
doll dɒl ⓤⓢ dɑːl **-s** -z ˈ**doll's ˌhouse**
dollar (D) ˈdɒl.əʳ ⓤⓢ ˈdɑː.lɚ **-s** -z ˌ**bet one's ˌbottom ˈdollar**
Dollond ˈdɒl.ənd ⓤⓢ ˈdɑː.lənd
dollop ˈdɒl.əp ⓤⓢ ˈdɑː.ləp **-s** -s
doll|y (D) ˈdɒl|.i ⓤⓢ ˈdɑː.l|i **-ies** -iz ˈ**dolly ˌmixture**
dolman ˈdɒl.mən ⓤⓢ ˈdoʊl- **-s** -z
dolmen ˈdɒl.men ⓤⓢ ˈdoʊl- **-s** -z
dolomite (D) ˈdɒl.ə.maɪt ⓤⓢ ˈdoʊ.lə-, ˈdɑː- **-s** -s
dolor ˈdɒl.əʳ, ˈdəʊ.ləʳ ⓤⓢ ˈdoʊ.lɚ, ˈdɑː-
Dolores dəˈlɔː.res, dɒlˈɔː-, -rɪs, -rəs, -rez, -rɪz, -rəz ⓤⓢ dəˈlɔːr.əs, -ɪs
dolorous ˈdɒl.ᵊr.əs ⓤⓢ ˈdoʊ.lɚ-, ˈdɑː- **-ly** -li **-ness** -nəs, -nɪs
dolour ˈdɒl.əʳ, ˈdəʊ.ləʳ ⓤⓢ ˈdoʊ.lɚ, ˈdɑː-
dolphin ˈdɒl.fɪn ⓤⓢ ˈdɑːl- **-s** -z
dolt dəʊlt ⓤⓢ doʊlt **-s** -s
doltish ˈdəʊl.tɪʃ ⓤⓢ ˈdoʊl- **-ly** -li **-ness** -nəs, -nɪs
-dom -dəm
Note: Suffix. Normally unstressed, e.g. **kingdom** /ˈkɪŋ.dəm/.
domain dəʊˈmeɪn ⓤⓢ doʊ-, də- **-s** -z
Dombey ˈdɒm.bi ⓤⓢ ˈdɑːm-
dome dəʊm ⓤⓢ doʊm **-s** -z **-d** -d
Domesday ˈduːmz.deɪ ˈ**Domesday ˌbook**
domestic dəˈmes.tɪk **-s** -s **-ally** -ᵊl.i, -li doˌ**mestic ˈanimal** ; doˌ**mestic ˈviolence**
domesti|cate dəˈmes.tɪ|.keɪt **-cates** -keɪts **-cating** -keɪ.tɪŋ ⓤⓢ -keɪ.ţɪŋ **-cated** -keɪ.tɪd ⓤⓢ -keɪ.ţɪd
domestication dəˌmes.tɪˈkeɪ.ʃᵊn
domesticity ˌdəʊ.mesˈtɪs.ə.ti, ˌdɒm.es-, -ɪ.ti ⓤⓢ ˌdoʊ.mesˈ-, dəˌmesˈ-
Domestos® dəˈmes.tɒs, dəʊ- ⓤⓢ dəˈmes.toʊs
domett dəʊˈmet ⓤⓢ də-, doʊ-; ˈdɑː.mət
Domett ˈdɒm.ɪt ⓤⓢ ˈdɑː.mɪt
domicil|e ˈdɒm.ɪ.saɪl, ˈdəʊ.mɪ-, -sɪl ⓤⓢ ˈdɑː.mə-, ˈdoʊ.mə- **-es** -z **-ing** -ɪŋ **-ed** -d
domiciliary ˌdɒm.ɪˈsɪl.i.ᵊr.i, -əˈ- ⓤⓢ ˌdɑː.məˈsɪl.i.er-, ˌdoʊ-
dominance ˈdɒm.ɪ.nənts, ˈ-ə- ⓤⓢ ˈdɑː.mə-
dominant ˈdɒm.ɪ.nənt, ˈ-ə- ⓤⓢ ˈdɑː.mə- **-s** -s **-ly** -li
domi|nate ˈdɒm.ɪ|.neɪt, ˈ-ə- ⓤⓢ ˈdɑː.mə- **-nates** -neɪts **-nating** -neɪ.tɪŋ ⓤⓢ -neɪ.ţɪŋ **-nated** -neɪ.tɪd ⓤⓢ -neɪ.ţɪd **-nator/s** -neɪ.təʳ/z ⓤⓢ -neɪ.ţɚ/z
domination ˌdɒm.ɪˈneɪ.ʃᵊn, -əˈ- ⓤⓢ ˌdɑː.məˈ- **-s** -z
dominatr|ix ˌdɒm.ɪˈneɪ.tr|ɪks, -əˈ- ⓤⓢ ˌdɑː.məˈ- **-ixes** -ɪk.sɪz **-ices** -ɪ.siːz
domineer ˌdɒm.ɪˈnɪəʳ, -əˈ- ⓤⓢ ˌdɑː.məˈnɪr **-s** -z **-ing/ly** -ɪŋ/li **-ed** -d
Domingo dəˈmɪŋ.gəʊ, dɒmˈɪŋ- ⓤⓢ dəˈmɪŋ.goʊ
Dominic ˈdɒm.ɪ.nɪk, ˈ-ə- ⓤⓢ ˈdɑː.mə-
Dominica ˌdɒm.ɪˈniː.kə; -əˈ-; dəˈmɪn.ɪ- ⓤⓢ ˌdɑː.mɪˈniː-, dəˈmɪn.ɪ-
dominical dəˈmɪn.ɪ.kᵊl, dɒmˈɪn-, dəʊˈmɪn- ⓤⓢ doʊˈmɪn-, də-
Dominican *republic, religious order:* dəˈmɪn.ɪ.kən, dɒmˈɪn- ⓤⓢ doʊˈmɪn-, də- **-s** -z *of Dominica:* ˌdɒm.ɪˈniː.kən ⓤⓢ ˌdɑː.mɪˈniː- **-s** -z
dominie ˈdɒm.ɪ.ni, ˈ-ə- ⓤⓢ ˈdɑː.mɪ- **-s** -z
dominion (D) dəˈmɪn.jən, -i.ən ⓤⓢ ˈ-jən **-s** -z
Dominique ˌdɒm.ɪˈniːk, -əˈ-, ˈ--- ⓤⓢ ˌdɑː.məˈ-, ˈ---
domino (D) ˈdɒm.ɪ.nəʊ, ˈ-ə- ⓤⓢ ˈdɑː.mə.noʊ **-(e)s** -z ˈ**domino efˌfect**
Domitian dəʊˈmɪʃ.i.ən, dɒmˈɪʃ-, -ˈɪʃ.ən ⓤⓢ dəˈmɪʃ.ən, -i.ən
don (D) dɒn ⓤⓢ dɑːn **-s** -z **-ning** -ɪŋ **-ned** -d
doña, dona ˈdɒn.jə ⓤⓢ ˈdoʊ.njə, -nə
dona(h) ˈdəʊ.nə ⓤⓢ ˈdoʊ- **-s** -z
Donal ˈdəʊ.nᵊl ⓤⓢ ˈdoʊ-
Donalbain ˈdɒn.ᵊl.beɪn ⓤⓢ ˈdɑː.nᵊl-
Donald ˈdɒn.ᵊld ⓤⓢ ˈdɑː.nᵊld
Donaldson ˈdɒn.ᵊld.sᵊn ⓤⓢ ˈdɑː.nᵊld-
Donat ˈdəʊ.næt ⓤⓢ ˈdoʊ-
do|nate dəʊ|ˈneɪt ⓤⓢ ˈdoʊ|.neɪt, -|ˈ- **-nates** -ˈneɪts ⓤⓢ -neɪts, -ˈneɪts **-nating** -ˈneɪ.tɪŋ ⓤⓢ -neɪ.ţɪŋ, -ˈneɪ- **-nated** -ˈneɪ.tɪd ⓤⓢ -neɪ.ţɪd, -ˈneɪ-
Donatello ˌdɒn.əˈtel.əʊ ⓤⓢ ˌdɑː.nəˈtel.oʊ
donatio dəʊˈnɑː.ti.əʊ ⓤⓢ doʊˈnɑː.ti.oʊ, -ˈneɪ-, -ʃi-
donation dəʊˈneɪ.ʃᵊn ⓤⓢ doʊˈneɪ- **-s** -z
Donatist ˈdəʊ.nə.tɪst, ˈdɒn.ə- ⓤⓢ ˈdoʊ.nə-, ˈdɑː- **-s** -s
donative ˈdəʊ.nə.tɪv, ˈdɒn.ə- ⓤⓢ ˈdoʊ.nə.ţɪv, ˈdɑː- **-s** -z
donator dəʊˈneɪ.təʳ ⓤⓢ ˈdoʊ.neɪ.ţɚ, ˌdoʊˈneɪ- **-s** -z
donatory ˈdəʊ.nə.tᵊr.i, ˈdɒn.ə-; -tri, dəʊˈneɪ- ⓤⓢ ˈdoʊ.nə.tɔːr.i

Donatus dəʊ'neɪ.təs, -'nɑː-
Ⓤⓢ doʊ'neɪ.t̬əs, -'nɑː-
Don Carlos ˌdɒn'kɑː.lɒs, ˌdɒŋ-
Ⓤⓢ ˌdɑːn'kɑːr.loʊs
Doncaster 'dɒŋ.kə.stəʳ, -ˌkɑː-, -ˌkæs.təʳ Ⓤⓢ 'dɑːŋˌkæs.tɚ, -kə.stɚ, 'dɑːn-
done (*from* **do**) dʌn
Done dəʊn Ⓤⓢ doʊn
donee dəʊ'niː Ⓤⓢ doʊ- **-s** -z
Donegal ˌdɒn.ɪ'gɔːl, ˌdʌn-, '---
Ⓤⓢ ˌdɑː.nɪ'gɔːl, -'gɑːl, '---
Note: /ˌdʌn.ɪ'gɔːl/ appears to be the most usual pronunciation in Ireland.
Donelson 'dɒn.əl.sən Ⓤⓢ 'dɑː.nəl-
doner 'dɒn.əʳ Ⓤⓢ 'doʊ.nɚ ˌ**doner ke'bab**
Donetsk dɒn'*j*etsk Ⓤⓢ də'njetsk, doʊ-
Donetz dɒn'*j*ets Ⓤⓢ də'nets, dɑː'njets
dong (*v.*) dɒŋ Ⓤⓢ dɑːŋ, dɔːŋ **-s** -z **-ing** -ɪŋ **-ed** -d
dông *Vietnam currency:* dɒŋ Ⓤⓢ dɑːŋ, dɔːŋ
donga 'dɒŋ.gə Ⓤⓢ 'dɑːŋ.gə, 'dɔːŋ- **-s** -z
Dönges 'dɜːn.jes
Don Giovanni ˌdɒn.dʒəʊ'vɑː.ni, -dʒi.əʊ'-, -'væn.i
Ⓤⓢ ˌdɑːn.dʒi.ə'vɑː.ni, -dʒoʊ'-
Dongola 'dɒŋ.gə.lə Ⓤⓢ 'dɑːŋ-
Donington 'dɒn.ɪŋ.tən, 'dʌn-
Ⓤⓢ 'dɑː.nɪŋ-
Donizetti ˌdɒn.ɪ'zet.i, -ɪd'ze-, -ɪt'set-
Ⓤⓢ ˌdɑː.nə'zet̬.i, -nət'set̬-
donjon 'dɒn.*d*ʒən, 'dʌn- Ⓤⓢ 'dɑːn- **-s** -z
Don Juan ˌdɒn'dʒuː.ən, -'*h*wɑːn
Ⓤⓢ ˌdɑːn-
donkey 'dɒŋ.ki Ⓤⓢ 'dɑːŋ-, 'dɔːŋ-, 'dʌŋ- **-s** -z **'donkey ˌengine**; **'donkey ˌjacket**; **'donkey's ˌyears**
donkeywork 'dɒŋ.ki.wɜːk
Ⓤⓢ 'dɑːŋ.ki.wɜːrk, 'dɔːŋ-, 'dʌŋ-
Donleavy, Donlevy dɒn'liː.vi, -'lev.i
Ⓤⓢ 'dɑːn.liː.vi, 'dʌn-, -lev.i, -'--
donna (D) 'dɒn.ə Ⓤⓢ 'dɑː.nə
Donnan 'dɒn.ən Ⓤⓢ 'dɑː.nən
Donne dʌn, dɒn Ⓤⓢ dʌn, dɑːn
Donnell 'dɒn.əl Ⓤⓢ 'dɑː.nəl
Donnelly 'dɒn.əl.i Ⓤⓢ 'dɑː.nəl-
Donnington 'dɒn.ɪŋ.tən Ⓤⓢ 'dɑː.nɪŋ-
donnish 'dɒn.ɪʃ Ⓤⓢ 'dɑː.nɪʃ **-ly** -li **-ness** -nəs, -nɪs
Donny 'dɒn.i Ⓤⓢ 'dɑː.ni
Donnybrook 'dɒn.i.brʊk Ⓤⓢ 'dɑː.ni-
Donoghue 'dʌn.ə.hjuː, 'dɒn-, -huː
Ⓤⓢ 'dɑː.nə.hjuː, 'dʌn.ə-, -huː
Donohoe 'dʌn.ə.həʊ, 'dɒn-, -huː
Ⓤⓢ 'dɑː.nə.hoʊ, 'dʌn.ə-, -huː
Donohue 'dʌn.ə.hjuː, 'dɒn-, -huː
Ⓤⓢ 'dɑː.nə.hjuː, 'dʌn.ə-, -huː
donor 'dəʊ.nəʳ, -nɔːʳ Ⓤⓢ 'doʊ.nɚ **-s** -z
Donovan 'dɒn.ə.vən Ⓤⓢ 'dɑː.nə-, 'dʌn.ə-
Don Pasquale ˌdɒn.pæs'kwɑː.leɪ, 'dɒm-, -li Ⓤⓢ ˌdɑːn.pə'-
Don Quixote ˌdɒn'kwɪk.sət, ˌdɒŋ-, -səʊt, -sɒt; *as if Spanish:* ˌdɒn.ki'həʊ.teɪ, ˌdɒŋ-, -ti
Ⓤⓢ ˌdɑːn.kiː'hoʊ.teɪ, -t̬i; -'kwɪk.sət
donship 'dɒn.ʃɪp Ⓤⓢ 'dɑːn- **-s** -s
don't dəʊnt Ⓤⓢ doʊnt
Note: Weak forms /dən, dn̩/ may sometimes be heard in the expression "I don't know", and a weak form /dəm/ in the expression "I don't mind".
do|nut 'dəʊ|.nʌt Ⓤⓢ 'doʊ- **-nuts** -nʌts **-nutting** -nʌt.ɪŋ Ⓤⓢ -nʌt̬.ɪŋ
Doo duː
Doobie 'duː.bi
doodad 'duː.dæd **-s** -z
doodah 'duː.dɑː **-s** -z
doodl|e 'duː.dl̩ **-es** -z **-ing** -ɪŋ, 'duːd.lɪŋ **-ed** -d **-er/s** -əʳ/z, 'duːd.ləʳ/z
Ⓤⓢ 'duː.dl̩.ɚ/z, 'duːd.lɚ/z
doodlebug 'duː.dl̩.bʌg **-s** -z
doohickey 'duːˌhɪk.i **-s** -z
Doolittle 'duː.lɪ.tl̩ Ⓤⓢ -t̬l̩
doom duːm **-s** -z **-ing** -ɪŋ **-ed** -d
doomsayer 'duːmˌseɪ.əʳ Ⓤⓢ -ɚ **-s** -z
doomsday (D) 'duːmz.deɪ
Doon(e) duːn
door dɔːʳ Ⓤⓢ dɔːr **-s** -z ˌ**shut the ˌdoor in someone's 'face**; ˌ**show someone the 'door**
doorbell 'dɔː.bel Ⓤⓢ 'dɔːr- **-s** -z
doorframe 'dɔː.freɪm Ⓤⓢ 'dɔːr- **-s** -z
doorjamb 'dɔː.dʒæm Ⓤⓢ 'dɔːr- **-s** -z
doorkeeper 'dɔːˌkiː.pəʳ
Ⓤⓢ 'dɔːrˌkiː.pɚ **-s** -z
doorknob 'dɔː.nɒb Ⓤⓢ 'dɔːr.nɑːb **-s** -z
doorknocker 'dɔːˌnɒk.əʳ
Ⓤⓢ 'dɔːrˌnɑː.kɚ **-s** -z
door|man 'dɔː|.mən, -mæn Ⓤⓢ 'dɔːr- **-men** -mən, -men
doormat 'dɔː.mæt Ⓤⓢ 'dɔːr- **-s** -s
doornail 'dɔː.neɪl Ⓤⓢ 'dɔːr- **-s** -z **as ˌdead as a 'doornail**
doorplate 'dɔː.pleɪt Ⓤⓢ 'dɔːr- **-s** -s
doorpost 'dɔː.pəʊst Ⓤⓢ 'dɔːr.poʊst **-s** -s
doorstep 'dɔː.step Ⓤⓢ 'dɔːr- **-s** -s **-ping** -ɪŋ **-ped** -t **-per/s** -əʳ/z Ⓤⓢ -ɚ/z
doorstop 'dɔː.stɒp Ⓤⓢ 'dɔːr.stɑːp **-s** -s
door-to-door ˌdɔː.tə'dɔːʳ
Ⓤⓢ ˌdɔːr.t̬ə'dɔːr
doorway 'dɔː.weɪ Ⓤⓢ 'dɔːr- **-s** -z
doo-wop 'duː.wɒp Ⓤⓢ -wɑːp
dopa 'dəʊ.pə Ⓤⓢ 'doʊ-, -pɑː
dopamine 'dəʊ.pə.miːn, -mɪn
Ⓤⓢ 'doʊ-
dop|e dəʊp Ⓤⓢ doʊp **-es** -s **-ing** -ɪŋ **-ed** -t **-er/s** -əʳ/z Ⓤⓢ -ɚ/z
dop|ey 'dəʊ.p|i Ⓤⓢ 'doʊ- **-ier** -i.əʳ Ⓤⓢ -i.ɚ **-iest** -i.ɪst, -i.əst **-ily** -ɪ.li, -əl.i **-iness** -ɪ.nəs, -ɪ.nɪs
doppelganger 'dɒp.əlˌgæŋ.əʳ
Ⓤⓢ 'dɑː.pəlˌgæŋ.ɚ **-s** -z
doppelgänger 'dɒp.əlˌgeŋ.əʳ
Ⓤⓢ 'dɑː.pəlˌgeŋ.ɚ **-s** -z
Doppler 'dɒp.ləʳ Ⓤⓢ 'dɑː.plɚ **'Doppler efˌfect**
dop|y 'dəʊ.p|i Ⓤⓢ 'doʊ- **-ier** -i.əʳ Ⓤⓢ -i.ɚ **-iest** -i.ɪst, -i.əst **-ily** -ɪ.li, -əl.i **-iness** -ɪ.nəs, -ɪ.nɪs
Dora 'dɔː.rə Ⓤⓢ 'dɔːr.ə
dorado (D) də'rɑː.dəʊ, dɒr'ɑː-
Ⓤⓢ doʊ'rɑː.doʊ, də'- **-s** -z
Doran 'dɔː.rən Ⓤⓢ 'dɔːr.ən
Dorando də'ræn.dəʊ, dɒr'æn-
Ⓤⓢ dɔːr'æn.doʊ
Dorcas 'dɔː.kəs, -kæs Ⓤⓢ 'dɔːr-
Dorchester 'dɔː.tʃɪ.stəʳ
Ⓤⓢ 'dɔːr.tʃes.tɚ
Dordogne dɔː'dɔɪn Ⓤⓢ dɔːr'doʊn
Dordon 'dɔː.dən Ⓤⓢ 'dɔːr-
Dordrecht 'dɔː.drext, -drekt
Ⓤⓢ 'dɔːr.drekt, -drext
Dore dɔːʳ Ⓤⓢ dɔːr
Doreen 'dɔː.riːn; -'-, də-, dɒr'iːn
Ⓤⓢ dɔː'riːn
Dorian 'dɔː.ri.ən Ⓤⓢ 'dɔːr.i- **-s** -z
Doric 'dɒr.ɪk Ⓤⓢ 'dɔːr-
Doricism 'dɒr.ɪ.sɪ.zəm, '-ə- Ⓤⓢ 'dɔːr- **-s** -z
Dorigen 'dɒr.ɪ.gən Ⓤⓢ 'dɔːr-
Doris *modern first name:* 'dɒr.ɪs
Ⓤⓢ 'dɔːr-, 'dɑːr- *district and female name in Greek history:* 'dɔː.rɪs, 'dɒr.ɪs Ⓤⓢ 'dɔːr.ɪs, 'dɑːr-
dork dɔːk Ⓤⓢ dɔːrk **-s** -s
Dorking 'dɔː.kɪŋ Ⓤⓢ 'dɔːr-
dorm dɔːm Ⓤⓢ dɔːrm **-s** -z
dormancy 'dɔː.mən*t*.si Ⓤⓢ 'dɔːr-
dormant 'dɔː.mənt Ⓤⓢ 'dɔːr-
dormer (D) 'dɔː.məʳ Ⓤⓢ 'dɔːr.mɚ **-s** -z ˌ**dormer 'window**
dormie 'dɔː.mi Ⓤⓢ 'dɔːr-
dormitor|y 'dɔː.mɪ.tər|.i, -mə-, -tr|i
Ⓤⓢ 'dɔːr.mə.tɔːr|.i **-ies** -iz
Dormobile® 'dɔː.mə.biːl Ⓤⓢ 'dɔːr- **-s** -z
dor|mouse 'dɔː|.maʊs Ⓤⓢ 'dɔːr- **-mice** -maɪs
dormy 'dɔː.mi Ⓤⓢ 'dɔːr-
Dornoch 'dɔː.nɒk, -nək, -nɒx, -nəx
Ⓤⓢ 'dɔːr.nɑːk, -nək
Dornton 'dɔːn.tən Ⓤⓢ 'dɔːrn-
Dorothea ˌdɒr.ə'θi.ə Ⓤⓢ ˌdɔːr-, ˌdɑːr-
Dorothy 'dɒr.ə.θi Ⓤⓢ 'dɔːr-, 'dɑːr-
Dorr dɔːʳ Ⓤⓢ dɔːr
Dorriforth 'dɒr.ɪ.fɔːθ Ⓤⓢ 'dɔːr.ɪ.fɔːrθ, 'dɑːr-
Dorrit 'dɒr.ɪt Ⓤⓢ 'dɔːr-
Dors dɔːz Ⓤⓢ dɔːrz
dorsal 'dɔː.səl Ⓤⓢ 'dɔːr- **-ly** -i
Dorset 'dɔː.sɪt, -sət Ⓤⓢ 'dɔːr- **-shire** -ʃəʳ, -ˌʃɪəʳ Ⓤⓢ -ʃɚ, -ˌʃɪr
Dorsey 'dɔː.si Ⓤⓢ 'dɔːr-

dorsum ˈdɔː.səm US ˈdɔːr-

Dortmund ˈdɔːt.mənd, -mʊnd US ˈdɔːrt-

dor|y (D) ˈdɔː.r|i US ˈdɔːr|.i **-ies** -iz

DOS dɒs US dɑːs

dosag|e ˈdəʊ.sɪdʒ US ˈdoʊ- **-es** -ɪz

dos|e dəʊs US doʊs **-es** -ɪz **-ing** -ɪŋ **-ed** -t **like a ˌdose of ˈsalts**

dosh dɒʃ US dɑːʃ

do-si-do ˌdəʊ.siˈdəʊ, -saɪˈ- US ˌdoʊ.siˈdoʊ **-s** -z

Dos Passos ˌdɒsˈpæs.ɒs US ˌdoʊsˈpæs.oʊs, dəs-, ˌdɑːs-

doss dɒs US dɑːs **-es** -ɪz **-ing** -ɪŋ **-ed** -t **-er/s** -əʳ/z US -ɚ/z

dossal ˈdɒs.ᵊl US ˈdɑː.sᵊl **-s** -z

dosshou|se ˈdɒs.haʊ|s US ˈdɑːs- **-ses** -zɪz

dossier ˈdɒs.i.eɪ, -əʳ US ˈdɑː.si.eɪ, -ɚ **-s** -z

dost (*from* **do**) *strong form:* dʌst *weak form:* dəst

Dostoievski, Dostoevsky ˌdɒs.tɔɪˈef.ski US ˌdɔː.stəˈjef-, ˌdɑː-, ˈdʌs.təˈ-, -tɔɪˈ-

dot (D) dɒt US dɑːt **-s** -s **-ting** -ɪŋ US ˈdɑː.t̬ɪŋ **-ted** -ɪd US ˈdɑː.t̬ɪd **ˌdotted ˈline**

dotage ˈdəʊ.tɪdʒ US ˈdoʊ.t̬ɪdʒ

dotard ˈdəʊ.təd, -ɑːd US ˈdoʊ.t̬ɚd **-s** -z

dot|e dəʊt US doʊt **-es** -s **-ing/ly** -ɪŋ/li US ˈdoʊ.t̬ɪŋ/li **-ed** -ɪd US ˈdoʊ.t̬ɪd **-er/s** -əʳ/z US ˈdoʊ.t̬ɚ/z

doth (*from* **do**) *strong form:* dʌθ *weak form:* dəθ

Dotheboys Hall ˌduː.ðə.bɔɪzˈhɔːl US -ˈhɔːl, -ˈhɑːl

dot-matrix ˌdɒtˈmeɪ.trɪks, ˈ-ˌ-- US ˌdɑːtˈmeɪ- **ˌdot-matrix ˈprinter, dot-ˌmatrix ˈprinter** US **ˌdot ˈmatrix printer**

dotterel ˈdɒt.rᵊl US ˈdɑː.trᵊl **-s** -z

dottle ˈdɒt.l̩ US ˈdɑː.t̬l̩ **-s** -z

dott|y ˈdɒt|.i US ˈdɑː.t̬|i **-ier** -i.əʳ US -i.ɚ **-iest** -i.ɪst, -i.əst **-ily** -ɪ.li, -ᵊl.i **-iness** -ɪ.nəs, -ɪ.nɪs

Douai *French town:* ˈduː.eɪ US -ˈ- *school near Reading:* ˈdaʊ.eɪ, ˈduː-, -i US duːˈeɪ *version of Bible:* ˈdaʊ.eɪ, ˈduː-, -i US duːˈeɪ, ˈ--

Douala duˈɑː.lə

doubl|e ˈdʌb.l̩ **-y** -i, ˈ-li **-eness** -nəs, -nɪs **-es** -z **-ing** -ɪŋ, ˈ-lɪŋ **-ed** -d **ˌdouble ˈagent ; ˌdouble ˈbass; ˌdouble ˈchin; ˌdouble ˈdutch; ˌdouble ˈentry; ˌdouble ˈfirst; ˌDouble ˈGloucester; ˌdouble inˈdemnity; ˌdouble ˈjeopardy; ˌdouble ˈtake** US **ˈdouble ˌtake**

double-barrel(l)ed ˌdʌb.l̩ˈbær.l̩d US -ˈber-, -ˈbær- *stress shift:* ˌdouble-barrel(l)ed ˈname

double-breasted ˌdʌb.l̩ˈbres.tɪd *stress shift:* ˌdouble-breasted ˈjacket

double-check ˌdʌb.l̩ˈtʃek US ˈdʌb.l̩ˌtʃek, ˌ--ˈ- **-s** -s **-ing** -ɪŋ **-ed** -t

double-cross ˌdʌb.l̩ˈkrɒs US -ˈkrɑːs **-es** -ɪz **-ing** -ɪŋ **-ed** -t

Doubleday ˈdʌb.l̩.deɪ

double-deal|er ˌdʌb.l̩ˈdiː.l|əʳ US -l|ɚ **-ers** -əʳ/z US -ɚ/z **-ing** -ɪŋ

double-decker ˌdʌb.l̩ˈdek.əʳ US ˈdʌb.l̩ˌdek.ɚ, ˌdʌb.l̩ˈdek- **-s** -z *stress shift, British only:* ˌdouble-decker ˈbus

double-dip ˌdʌb.l̩ˈdɪp **-s** -s **-ping** -ɪŋ **-ped** -t

double-edged ˌdʌb.l̩ˈedʒd *stress shift:* ˌdouble-edged ˈsword

double entendre ˌduː.bl̩ɑ̃ːnˈtɑ̃ːn.drə, -ɑːnˈtɑːn- US ˌdʌb.l̩.ɑːnˈtɑːn.drə, ˌduː.blɑːnˈtrɑːn

double-glaz|e ˌdʌb.l̩ˈɡleɪz **-es** -ɪz **-ing** -ɪŋ **-ed** -d *stress shift:* ˌdouble-glazed ˈwindows

double-glazing ˌdʌb.l̩ˈɡleɪ.zɪŋ

double-header ˌdʌb.l̩ˈhed.əʳ US -ɚ **-s** -z

double-jointed ˌdʌb.l̩ˈdʒɔɪn.tɪd US -t̬ɪd *stress shift:* ˌdouble-jointed ˈgymnast

double-park ˌdʌb.l̩ˈpɑːk US -ˈpɑːrk **-s** -s **-ing** -ɪŋ **-ed** -t

double-quick ˌdʌb.l̩ˈkwɪk *stress shift:* ˌdouble-quick ˈtime

doublespeak ˈdʌb.l̩.spiːk

double-stop ˌdʌb.l̩ˈstɒp US -ˈstɑːp **-s** -s **-ping** -ɪŋ **-ped** -t

doublet ˈdʌb.lɪt, -lət **-s** -s

doubletalk ˈdʌb.l̩.tɔːk US -tɔːk, -tɑːk

doublethink ˈdʌb.l̩.θɪŋk

double-tongued ˌdʌb.l̩ˈtʌŋd

doubloon dʌbˈluːn **-s** -z

doubt daʊt **-s** -s **-ing/ly** -ɪŋ/li US ˈdaʊ.t̬ɪŋ/li **-ed** -ɪd US ˈdaʊ.t̬ɪd **-er/s** -əʳ/z US ˈdaʊ.t̬ɚ/z **ˌdoubting ˈThomas**

doubtful ˈdaʊt.fᵊl, -fʊl **-lest** -ɪst, -əst **-ly** -i **-ness** -nəs, -nɪs

doubtless ˈdaʊt.ləs, -lɪs **-ly** -li

douch|e duːʃ **-es** -ɪz **-ing** -ɪŋ **-ed** -t

Doug dʌɡ

Dougal(l) ˈduː.ɡᵊl

Dougan ˈduː.ɡən

dough dəʊ US doʊ

Dougherty ˈdɒx.ə.ti, ˈdəʊ-, ˈdaʊ- US ˈdɔːr.ə.t̬i, ˈdɔːr.t̬i, ˈdoʊ.ɚ-, ˈdaʊ-, ˈdɑː.kɚ-

doughfaced ˈdəʊ.feɪst US ˈdoʊ-

dough|nut ˈdəʊ|.nʌt US ˈdoʊ- **-nuts** -nʌts **-nutting** -nʌt.ɪŋ US -nʌt̬.ɪŋ

dought|y (D) ˈdaʊ.t|i US -t̬|i **-ier** -i.əʳ US -i.ɚ **-iest** -i.ɪst, -i.əst **-ily** -ɪ.li, -ᵊl.i **-iness** -ɪ.nəs, -ɪ.nɪs

dough|y ˈdəʊ|.i US ˈdoʊ- **-ily** -ɪ.li, -ᵊl.i **-iness** -ɪ.nəs, -ɪ.nɪs

Douglas-Home ˌdʌɡ.ləsˈhjuːm

Douglas(s) ˈdʌɡ.ləs

douloureux ˌduː.ləˈrɜː, -luːˈ-, -lʊˈ-

Doulton ˈdəʊl.tᵊn US ˈdoʊl-

Dounreay ˈduːn.reɪ, -ˈ-

dour dʊəʳ, daʊəʳ US dʊr, daʊɚ **-ly** -li **-ness** -nəs, -nɪs

Douro ˈdʊə.rəʊ US ˈdɔːr.oʊ

dous|e daʊs **-es** -ɪz **-ing** -ɪŋ **-ed** -t

dove (D) dʌv **-s** -z

dove (*from* **dive**) dəʊv US doʊv

dovecot(e) ˈdʌv.kɒt US -kɑːt **-s** -s

Dovedale ˈdʌv.deɪl

Dover ˈdəʊ.vəʳ US ˈdoʊ.vɚ **ˌDover ˈsole**

dovetail ˈdʌv.teɪl **-s** -z **-ing** -ɪŋ **-ed** -d

Dovey ˈdʌv.i

Dow daʊ **ˌDow ˈJones ; ˌDow Jones ˈindex**

dowager ˈdaʊə.dʒəʳ, ˈdaʊɪ- US -dʒɚ **-s** -z

Dowden ˈdaʊ.dᵊn

Dowds daʊdz

dow|dy ˈdaʊ.d|i **-ies** -iz **-ier** -i.əʳ US -i.ɚ **-iest** -i.ɪst, -i.əst **-ily** -ɪ.li, -ᵊl.i **-iness** -ɪ.nəs, -ɪ.nɪs

dowel daʊəl **-s** -z **-(l)ing** -ɪŋ **-(l)ed** -d

Dowell daʊəl; ˈdaʊ.ɪl, -el

dower daʊəʳ US daʊɚ **-s** -z **-less** -ləs, -lɪs

Dowgate ˈdaʊ.ɡɪt, -ɡeɪt

Dowie ˈdaʊ.i

Dowland ˈdaʊ.lənd

dowlas (D) ˈdaʊ.ləs

Dowler ˈdaʊ.ləʳ US -lɚ

Dowling ˈdaʊ.lɪŋ

down (D) daʊn **-s** -z **-ing** -ɪŋ **-ed** -d **ˌdown ˈpayment ; ˈDown's ˌsyndrome ; ˌdown ˈunder**

Down *county:* daʊn **-shire** -ʃəʳ, -ˌʃɪəʳ US -ʃɚ, -ˌʃɪr

down-and-out ˌdaʊn.ənˈdaʊt **-s** -s *stress shift:* ˌdown-and-out ˈperson

down-at-heel ˌdaʊn.ətˈhiːl *stress shift:* ˌdown-at-heel ˈperson

downbeat ˈdaʊn.biːt, ˈdaʊm- US ˈdaʊn- **-s** -s

downcast ˈdaʊn.kɑːst, ˈdaʊŋ-, ˌ-ˈ- US ˈdaʊn.kæst

downdraught ˈdaʊn.drɑːft US -dræft **-s** -s

downdrift ˈdaʊn.drɪft

Downe daʊn **-s** -z

downer ˈdaʊ.nəʳ US -nɚ **-s** -z

Downey ˈdaʊ.ni

downfall ˈdaʊn.fɔːl US -fɔːl, -fɑːl **-s** -z

downgrad|e ˌdaʊnˈɡreɪd, ˌdaʊŋ- US ˈdaʊn.ɡreɪd **-es** -z **-ing** -ɪŋ **-ed** -ɪd *stress shift, British only:* ˌdowngraded ˈworker

Downham 'daʊ.nəm
downhearted ˌdaʊn'hɑː.tɪd Ⓤⓢ -'hɑːr.t̬ɪd **-ly** -li **-ness** -nəs, -nɪs *stress shift:* ˌdownhearted 'person
downhill ˌdaʊn'hɪl *stress shift:* ˌdownhill 'slide
down-home ˌdaʊn'həʊm Ⓤⓢ -'hoʊm
Downie 'daʊ.ni
Downing 'daʊ.nɪŋ **'Downing ˌStreet**
downland (D) 'daʊn.lænd, -lənd
download ˌdaʊn'ləʊd, '-- Ⓤⓢ 'daʊn.loʊd **-s** -z **-ing** -ɪŋ **-ed** -ɪd
downmarket ˌdaʊn'mɑː.kɪt, ˌdaʊm- Ⓤⓢ 'daʊnˌmɑːr- *stress shift, British only:* ˌdownmarket 'area
Downpatrick ˌdaʊn'pæt.rɪk, ˌdaʊm- Ⓤⓢ ˌdaʊn-
downpipe 'daʊn.paɪp, 'daʊm- Ⓤⓢ 'daʊn- **-s** -s
downplay ˌdaʊn'pleɪ, ˌdaʊm- Ⓤⓢ 'daʊn.pleɪ **-s** -z **-ing** -ɪŋ **-ed** -d *stress shift, British only:* ˌdownplayed 'incident
downpour 'daʊn.pɔːʳ, 'daʊm- Ⓤⓢ 'daʊn.pɔːr **-s** -z
downright 'daʊn.raɪt **-ness** -nəs, -nɪs
downriver ˌdaʊn'rɪv.əʳ, -ɚ *stress shift:* ˌdownriver 'settlement
downrush 'daʊn.rʌʃ **-es** -ɪz
Downs daʊnz
downside (D) 'daʊn.saɪd
downsiz|e ˌdaʊn'saɪz Ⓤⓢ '-- **-es** -ɪz **-ing** -ɪŋ **-ed** -d *stress shift, British only:* ˌdownsized 'payments
downspout 'daʊn.spaʊt **-s** -s
downstage ˌdaʊn'steɪdʒ Ⓤⓢ '-- *stress shift, British only:* ˌdownstage 'action
downstairs ˌdaʊn'steəz Ⓤⓢ -'sterz *stress shift:* ˌdownstairs 'bathroom
downstream ˌdaʊn'striːm *stress shift:* ˌdownstream 'settlement
downswing 'daʊn.swɪŋ **-s** -z
downtime 'daʊn.taɪm
down-to-earth ˌdaʊn.tu'ɜːθ Ⓤⓢ -'ɜːrθ *stress shift:* ˌdown-to-earth 'person
Downton 'daʊn.tən Ⓤⓢ -tᵊn
downtown ˌdaʊn'taʊn Ⓤⓢ ˌdaʊn'taʊn, '-- *stress shift, British only:* ˌdowntown 'area
downtrodden 'daʊnˌtrɒd.ᵊn, ˌ-'-- Ⓤⓢ 'daʊnˌtrɑː.dᵊn
downturn 'daʊn.tɜːn Ⓤⓢ -tɜːrn **-s** -z
downward 'daʊn.wəd Ⓤⓢ -wɚd **-s** -z
downwind ˌdaʊn'wɪnd Ⓤⓢ ˌdaʊn'wɪnd, '--
down|y 'daʊ.n|i **-ier** -i.əʳ Ⓤⓢ -i.ɚ **-iest** -i.ɪst, -i.əst
dowr|y 'daʊ.r|i **-ies** -iz
dows|e daʊz, daʊs **-es** -ɪz **-ing** -ɪŋ **-ed** -d **-er/s** -əʳ/z Ⓤⓢ -ɚ/z **'dowsing ˌrod**
Dowse daʊs
Dowson 'daʊ.sᵊn
Dowton 'daʊ.tᵊn
doxolog|y dɒk'sɒl.ə.dʒ|i Ⓤⓢ dɑːk'sɑː.lə- **-ies** -iz
dox|y 'dɒk.s|i Ⓤⓢ 'dɑːk- **-ies** -iz
doyen 'dɔɪ.en, -ən; 'dwaɪ.æ̃ŋ; dɔɪ'en Ⓤⓢ 'dɔɪ.ən, -ən, dwɑː'jen **-s** -z
doyenne dɔɪ'en; dwaɪ'æŋ Ⓤⓢ dɔɪ'en, -'jen, dwɑː'jen **-s** -z
Doyle dɔɪl
doyley 'dɔɪ.li **-s** -z
D'Oyl(e)y 'dɔɪ.li
d'Oyly Carte ˌdɔɪ.li'kɑːt Ⓤⓢ -'kɑːrt
doz|e dəʊz Ⓤⓢ doʊz **-es** -ɪz **-ing** -ɪŋ **-ed** -d **-er/s** -əʳ/z Ⓤⓢ -ɚ/z
dozen 'dʌz.ᵊn **-s** -z **-th** -θ
doz|y 'dəʊ.z|i Ⓤⓢ 'doʊ- **-ier** -i.əʳ Ⓤⓢ -i.ɚ **-iest** -i.ɪst, -i.əst **-ily** -ɪ.li, -ᵊl.i **-iness** -ɪ.nəs, -ɪ.nɪs
DPhil ˌdiː'fɪl
dr (*abbrev. for* **dram**) dræm
Dr. (*abbrev. for* **Doctor**) 'dɒk.təʳ Ⓤⓢ 'dɑːk.tɚ
drab dræb **-s** -z **-ber** -əʳ Ⓤⓢ -ɚ **-best** -ɪst, -əst **-ness** -nəs, -nɪs
drabbl|e (D) 'dræb.l̩ **-es** -z **-ing** -ɪŋ, '-lɪŋ **-ed** -d
dracaena drə'siː.nə **-s** -z
drachm dræm **-s** -z
drachm|a 'dræk.m|ə **-as** -əz **-ae** -iː, -eɪ
Draco *Greek legislator:* 'dreɪ.kəʊ Ⓤⓢ -koʊ *English surname:* 'drɑː.kəʊ Ⓤⓢ -koʊ
draconian (D) drə'kəʊ.ni.ən, dræk'əʊ- Ⓤⓢ drə'koʊ-, dreɪ-
Dracula 'dræk.jə.lə, -jʊ-
draff dræf, drɑːf Ⓤⓢ dræf
draft drɑːft Ⓤⓢ dræft **-s** -s **-ing** -ɪŋ **-ed** -ɪd **-er/s** -əʳ/z Ⓤⓢ -ɚ/z **'draft ˌdodger**
draftee ˌdrɑːf'tiː Ⓤⓢ ˌdræf- **-s** -z
drafts|man 'drɑːfts|.mən Ⓤⓢ 'dræfts- **-men** -mən, -men **-manship** -mən.ʃɪp
drafts|woman 'drɑːfts|ˌwʊm.ən Ⓤⓢ 'dræfts- **-women** -ˌwɪm.ɪn
draft|y 'drɑːf.t|i Ⓤⓢ 'dræf- **-ier** -i.əʳ Ⓤⓢ -i.ɚ **-iest** -i.ɪst, -i.əst **-iness** -ɪ.nəs, -ɪ.nɪs
drag dræg **-s** -z **-ging** -ɪŋ **-ged** -d **'drag ˌrace** ; **'drag ˌqueen**
Drage dreɪdʒ
dragee, dragée dræʒ'eɪ Ⓤⓢ dræʒ'eɪ, drɑː'ʒeɪ **-s** -z
draggl|e 'dræg.l̩ **-es** -z **-ing** -ɪŋ, '-lɪŋ **-ed** -d
dragg|y 'dræg|.i **-ier** -i.əʳ Ⓤⓢ -i.ɚ **-iest** -i.ɪst, -i.əst
dragnet 'dræg.net **-s** -s
drago|man 'dræg.əʊ|.mən, -mæn Ⓤⓢ -ə-, -oʊ- **-mans** -mənz, -mænz **-men** -mən, -men
dragon 'dræg.ᵊn **-s** -z **'dragon's ˌblood, ˌdragon's 'blood**
dragonet 'dræg.ə.nɪt, -net **-s** -s
dragonfl|y 'dræg.ᵊn.fl|aɪ **-ies** -aɪz
dragonnade ˌdræg.ə'neɪd **-s** -z
dragoon drə'guːn **-s** -z
dragster 'dræg.stəʳ Ⓤⓢ -stɚ **-s** -z
drain dreɪn **-s** -z **-ing** -ɪŋ **-ed** -d **-er/s** -əʳ/z Ⓤⓢ -ɚ/z **'draining ˌboard**
drainage 'dreɪ.nɪdʒ
drainpipe 'dreɪn.paɪp, 'dreɪm- Ⓤⓢ 'dreɪn- **-s** -s
drake (D) dreɪk **-s** -s
Drakensberg 'dræk.ənz.bɜːg Ⓤⓢ 'drɑː.kənz.bɜːrg
Dralon® 'dreɪ.lɒn Ⓤⓢ -lɑːn
dram dræm **-s** -z **-ming** -ɪŋ **-med** -d
drama 'drɑː.mə Ⓤⓢ 'drɑːm.ə, 'dræm.ə **-s** -z
Dramamine® 'dræm.ə.miːn
dramatic drə'mæt.ɪk Ⓤⓢ -'mæt̬- **-al** -ᵊl **-ally** -ᵊl.i, -li **-s** -s
dramatis personae ˌdrɑː.mə.tɪs.pɜː'səʊ.naɪ, ˌdræm.ə-, -pə'- Ⓤⓢ ˌdrɑː.mə.t̬ɪs.pɚ'soʊ-, ˌdræm.ə-, -ni
dramatist 'dræm.ə.tɪst, 'drɑː.mə- Ⓤⓢ 'drɑː.mə.t̬ɪst, 'dræm.ə- **-s** -s
dramatization, -isa- ˌdræm.ə.taɪ'zeɪ.ʃᵊn, ˌdrɑː.mə-, -tɪ'- Ⓤⓢ ˌdrɑː.mə.t̬ɪ'-, ˌdræm.ə- **-s** -z
dramatiz|e, -is|e 'dræm.ə.taɪz, 'drɑː.mə- Ⓤⓢ 'drɑː.mə-, 'dræm.ə- **-es** -ɪz **-ing** -ɪŋ **-ed** -d **-able** -ə.bl̩
dramaturg|e 'dræm.ə.tɜːdʒ, 'drɑː.mə- Ⓤⓢ 'drɑː.mə-, 'dræm.ə.tɜːrdʒ **-es** -ɪz
dramaturgic ˌdræm.ə'tɜː.dʒɪk, ˌdrɑː.mə- Ⓤⓢ 'drɑː.mə.tɜːr-; ˌdræm.ə'tɜːr- **-al** -ᵊl **-ally** -ᵊl.i, -li
dramaturgy 'dræm.ə.tɜː.dʒi, 'drɑː.mə- Ⓤⓢ 'drɑː.mə.tɜːr-, 'dræm.ə-
Drambuie® dræm'bjuː.i, -'buː-
Drane dreɪn
drank (*from* **drink**) dræŋk
drap|e dreɪp **-es** -s **-ing** -ɪŋ **-ed** -t
draper (D) 'dreɪ.pəʳ Ⓤⓢ -pɚ **-s** -z
draper|y 'dreɪ.pᵊr|.i **-ies** -iz
Drapier 'dreɪ.pi.əʳ Ⓤⓢ -ɚ
drastic 'dræs.tɪk, 'drɑː.stɪk Ⓤⓢ 'dræs.tɪk **-ally** -ᵊl.i, -li
drat dræt
draught drɑːft Ⓤⓢ dræft **-s** -s
draughtboard 'drɑːf*t*.bɔːd Ⓤⓢ 'dræf*t*.bɔːrd **-s** -z
draught-proof 'drɑːf*t*.pruːf Ⓤⓢ 'dræf*t*- **-s** -s **-ing** -ɪŋ **-d** -t
draughts|man 'drɑːf*t*s|.mən Ⓤⓢ 'dræf*t*s- **-men** -mən
draughts|woman 'drɑːfts|ˌwʊm.ən Ⓤⓢ 'dræfts- **-women** -ˌwɪm.ɪn

draught|y ˈdrɑːf.t|i (US) ˈdræf- **-ier** -i.əʳ (US) -i.ɚ **-iest** -i.ɪst, -i.əst **-ily** -ɪ.li, -ᵊl.i **-iness** -ɪ.nəs, -ɪ.nɪs

Drava ˈdrɑː.və

Dravidian drəˈvɪd.i.ən **-s** -z

draw drɔː (US) drɑː, drɔː **-s** -z **-ing** -ɪŋ **drew** druː **drawn** drɔːn (US) drɑːn, drɔːn **drawable** ˈdrɔː.ə.bl̩ (US) ˈdrɑː-, ˈdrɔː- **ˈdrawing ˌboard** ; **ˈdrawing ˌpin** ; **ˈdrawing ˌroom** ; **ˈdrawing ˌtable** ; **go ˌback to the ˈdrawing ˌboard**

drawback ˈdrɔː.bæk (US) ˈdrɑː-, ˈdrɔː- **-s** -s

drawbridg|e ˈdrɔː.brɪdʒ (US) ˈdrɑː-, ˈdrɔː- **-es** -ɪz

drawee ˌdrɔːˈiː (US) ˌdrɑː-, ˌdrɔː- **-s** -z

drawer *sliding box:* drɔːʳ (US) drɔːr **-s** -z

drawer *person who draws:* ˈdrɔː.əʳ (US) ˈdrɑː.ɚ, ˈdrɔː- **-s** -z

drawers *garment*: drɔːz (US) drɔːrz

drawl drɔːl (US) drɑːl, drɔːl **-s** -z **-ing** -ɪŋ **-ed** -d **-er/s** -əʳ/z (US) -ɚ/z

drawn (*from* **draw**) drɔːn (US) drɑːn, drɔːn

drawstring ˈdrɔː.strɪŋ (US) ˈdrɑː-, ˈdrɔː- **-s** -z

Drax dræks

dray dreɪ **-s** -z

dray|man ˈdreɪ|.mən, -mæn **-men** -mən, -men

Drayton ˈdreɪ.tᵊn

dread dred **-s** -z **-ing** -ɪŋ **-ed** -ɪd

dreadful ˈdred.fᵊl, -fʊl **-ly** -i **-ness** -nəs, -nɪs

dreadlocks ˈdred.lɒks (US) -lɑːks

dreadnought, dreadnaught (D) ˈdred.nɔːt (US) -nɑːt, -nɔːt **-s** -s

dream driːm **-s** -z **-ing/ly** -ɪŋ/li **-ed** dremp*t*, driːmd (US) driːmd, dremp*t* **-t** dremp*t* **-er/s** ˈdriː.məʳ/z (US) -mɚ/z **-like** -laɪk **ˈdream ˌworld**

dreamboat ˈdriːm.bəʊt (US) -boʊt **-s** -s

dreamland ˈdriːm.lænd

dreamless ˈdriːm.ləs, -lɪs **-ly** -li

dreamtime ˈdriːm.taɪm

dream|y ˈdriː.m|i **-ier** -i.əʳ (US) -i.ɚ **-iest** -i.ɪst, -i.əst **-ily** -ɪ.li, -ᵊl.i **-iness** -ɪ.nəs, -ɪ.nɪs

drear drɪəʳ (US) drɪr

drear|y ˈdrɪə.r|i (US) ˈdrɪr|.i **-ier** -i.əʳ (US) -i.ɚ **-iest** -i.ɪst, -i.əst **-ily** -ɪ.li, -ᵊl.i **-iness** -ɪ.nəs, -ɪ.nɪs

dredg|e dredʒ **-es** -ɪz **-ing** -ɪŋ **-ed** -d

dredger ˈdredʒ.əʳ (US) -ɚ **-s** -z

Dre-fach Felindre drevˌɑːx.velˈɪn.drə

dregg|y ˈdreg|.i **-ily** -ɪ.li, -ᵊl.i **-iness** -ɪ.nəs, -ɪ.nɪs

dregs dregz

Dreiser ˈdraɪ.zəʳ, -səʳ (US) -zɚ, -sɚ

drench drentʃ **-es** -ɪz **-ing** -ɪŋ **-ed** -t **-er/s** -əʳ/z (US) -ɚ/z

Dresden ˈdrez.dᵊn

dress dres **-es** -ɪz **-ing** -ɪŋ **-ed** -t **ˌdress ˈcircle** (US) **ˈdress ˌcircle** ; **ˌdress ˈcoat** (US) **ˈdress ˌcoat**; **ˈdress ˌcode**; **ˌdress reˈhearsal** (US) **ˈdress reˌhearsal**; **ˈdress ˌsense**; **ˌdress ˈsuit** (US) **ˈdress ˌsuit**

dressage ˈdres.ɑːʒ; -ɑːdʒ; -ɪdʒ; drəˈsɑːʒ (US) drəˈsɑːʒ, dresˈɑːʒ

dresser ˈdres.əʳ (US) -ɚ **-s** -z

dressing ˈdres.ɪŋ **-s** -z **ˈdressing ˌgown** ; **ˈdressing ˌroom** ; **ˈdressing ˌtable**

dressing-down ˌdres.ɪŋˈdaʊn **-s** -z

dressmak|er ˈdresˌmeɪ.k|əʳ (US) -k|ɚ **-ers** -əz (US) -ɚz **-ing** -ɪŋ

dress|y ˈdres|.i **-ier** -i.əʳ (US) -i.ɚ **-iest** -i.ɪst, -i.əst **-ily** -ɪ.li, -ᵊl.i **-iness** -ɪ.nəs, -ɪ.nɪs

drew (*from* **draw**) druː

Drew druː **-s** -z

Dreyfus ˈdreɪ.fəs, ˈdraɪ-, -fʊs

dribbl|e ˈdrɪb.l̩ **-es** -z **-ing** -ɪŋ **-ed** -d, ˈ-lɪŋ **-er/s** -əʳ/z, ˈ-ləʳ/z (US) ˈ-l̩.ɚ/z, ˈ-lɚ/z

driblet ˈdrɪb.lət, -lɪt **-s** -s

dribs and drabs ˌdrɪbz.ənˈdræbz

dried (*from* **dry**) draɪd

drier ˈdraɪ.əʳ (US) -ɚ **-s** -z

dries (*from* **dry**) draɪz

driest ˈdraɪ.ɪst, -əst

Driffield ˈdrɪf.iːld

drift drɪft **-s** -s **-ing** -ɪŋ **-ed** -ɪd

drifter ˈdrɪf.təʳ (US) -tɚ **-s** -z

driftless ˈdrɪft.ləs, -lɪs

driftwood ˈdrɪft.wʊd

drifty ˈdrɪf.ti

drill drɪl **-s** -z **-ing** -ɪŋ **-ed** -d **ˈdrill ˌsergeant**

drily ˈdraɪ.li

drink drɪŋk **-s** -s **-ing** -ɪŋ **drank** dræŋk **drunk** drʌŋk **drinker/s** ˈdrɪŋ.kəʳ/z (US) -kɚ/z **ˈdrinking ˌfountain** ; **ˈdrinking ˌhorn** ; **ˈdrinking ˌwater**

drinkable ˈdrɪŋ.kə.bl̩

drink-driv|ing ˌdrɪŋkˈdraɪ.v|ɪŋ **-er/s** -əʳ/z (US) -ɚ/z

Drinkwater ˈdrɪŋkˌwɔː.təʳ (US) -ˌwɑː.t̬ɚ, -ˌwɔː-

drip drɪp **-s** -s **-ping** -ɪŋ **-ped** -t

drip|-dry ˈdrɪp|.draɪ, ˌ-ˈ- **-dries** -draɪz **-drying** -ˌdraɪ.ɪŋ **-dried** -draɪd

drip|-feed ˈdrɪp|.fiːd **-feeds** -fiːdz **-feeding** -ˌfiː.dɪŋ **-fed** -fed

dripping ˈdrɪp.ɪŋ **-s** -z

dripp|y ˈdrɪp|.i **-ier** -i.əʳ (US) -i.ɚ **-iest** -i.ɪst, -i.əst

dripstone ˈdrɪp.stəʊn (US) -stoʊn **-s** -z

Driscoll ˈdrɪs.kᵊl

driv|e draɪv **-es** -z **-ing** -ɪŋ **drove** drəʊv (US) droʊv **driven** ˈdrɪv.ᵊn **ˈdriving ˌiron** ; **ˈdriving ˌlicence/license** ; **ˈdriving ˌseat** ; **ˈdriving ˌtest**

driveaway ˈdraɪv.əˌweɪ

drive-by ˈdraɪv.baɪ

drive-in ˈdraɪv.ɪn **-s** -z

drivel ˈdrɪv.ᵊl **-s** -z **-(l)ing** -ɪŋ **-(l)ed** -d **-(l)er/s** -əʳ/z (US) -ɚ/z

driven (*from* **drive**) ˈdrɪv.ᵊn

driver (D) ˈdraɪ.vəʳ (US) -vɚ **-s** -z **ˈdriver's ˌlicense** ; **in the ˈdriver's ˌseat**

driveway ˈdraɪv.weɪ **-s** -z

Driza-bone® ˈdraɪ.zə.bəʊn (US) -boʊn

drizzl|e ˈdrɪz.l̩ **-es** -z **-ing** -ɪŋ, ˈ-lɪŋ **-ed** -d

drizzly ˈdrɪz.l̩.i, ˈ-li

Drogheda *place:* ˈdrɔɪ.ɪ.də, ˈdrɔː-, ˈ-ə-, ˈdrɒ.hə- (US) ˈdrɔː.ɪ-, ˈdrɑː-, ˈ-ə- *Earl:* ˈdrɔɪ.ɪ.də

droid drɔɪd **-s** -z

droit drɔɪt, drwɑː **-s** -s

droit de seigneur ˌdrwɑː.də.seɪˈnjɜːʳ, -senˈjɜːʳ, -siːˈnjɜːʳ (US) -seɪˈnjʊr, -senˈjʊr, -ˈjɜːr

Droitwich ˈdrɔɪ.twɪtʃ

droll drəʊl (US) droʊl **-ness** -nəs, -nɪs **-er** -əʳ (US) -ɚ **-est** -ɪst, -əst **-y** -li, ˈdrəʊ.li (US) ˈdroʊ.li

droller|y ˈdrəʊ.lᵊr|.i (US) ˈdroʊ- **-ies** -iz

-drome -drəʊm (US) -droʊm

Note: Suffix. Normally unstressed, e.g. **aerodrome** /ˈeə.rə.drəʊm (US) ˈer.ə.droʊm/.

dromedar|y ˈdrɒm.ə.dᵊr|.i, ˈdrʌm-, ˈ-ɪ- (US) ˈdrɑː.mə.der-, ˈdrʌm.ə- **-ies** -iz

Dromio ˈdrəʊ.mi.əʊ (US) ˈdroʊ.mi.oʊ

Dromore ˈdrəʊ.mɔːʳ; drəˈmɔːʳ (US) ˈdroʊ.mɔːr; drəˈmɔːr

dron|e drəʊn (US) droʊn **-es** -z **-ing** -ɪŋ **-ed** -d

Dronfield ˈdrɒn.fiːld (US) ˈdrɑːn-

drongo ˈdrɒŋ.gəʊ (US) ˈdrɑːŋ.goʊ **-(e)s** -z

Drood druːd

drool druːl **-s** -z **-ing** -ɪŋ **-ed** -d

droop druːp **-s** -s **-ing/ly** -ɪŋ/li **-ed** -t

droop|y ˈdruː.p|i **-ier** -i.əʳ (US) -i.ɚ **-iest** -i.ɪst, -i.əst **-ily** -ɪ.li, -ᵊl.i **-iness** -ɪ.nəs, -ɪ.nɪs

drop drɒp (US) drɑːp **-s** -s **-ping** -ɪŋ **-ped** -t **ˈdrop ˌscone** ; **ˈdrop ˌshot** ; **a ˌdrop in the ˈocean** ; **at the ˌdrop of a ˈhat**

drop-in ˈdrɒp.ɪn (US) ˈdrɑːp-

dropkick ˈdrɒp.kɪk (US) ˈdrɑːp- **-s** -s

droplet ˈdrɒp.lət, -lɪt (US) ˈdrɑːp- **-s** -s

dropout ˈdrɒp.aʊt (US) ˈdrɑːp- **-s** -s

dropper ˈdrɒp.əʳ (US) ˈdrɑː.pɚ **-s** -z

dropping ˈdrɒp.ɪŋ (US) ˈdrɑː.pɪŋ **-s** -z

dropsic|al ˈdrɒp.sɪ.k|ᵊl (US) ˈdrɑːp- **-ally** -ᵊl.i, -li **-alness** -ᵊl.nəs, -nɪs

dropsy ˈdrɒp.si (US) ˈdrɑːp-

droshk|y ˈdrɒʃ.k|i (US) ˈdrɑːʃ- **-ies** -iz

drosophila drəˈsɒf.ɪ.lə, drɒsˈɒf-, -ᵊl.ə (US) droʊˈsɑː.fᵊl.ə, drə- **-s** -z

dross drɒs ⓊⓈ drɑːs **-y** -i
drought draʊt **-s** -s **-y** -i
drove drəʊv ⓊⓈ droʊv **-s** -z
drover 'drəʊ.vəʳ ⓊⓈ 'droʊ.vɚ **-s** -z
Drower draʊəʳ ⓊⓈ draʊɚ
drown draʊn **-s** -z **-ing** -ɪŋ **-ed** -d
drows|e draʊz **-es** -ɪz **-ing** -ɪŋ **-ed** -d
drows|y 'draʊ.z|i **-ier** -i.əʳ ⓊⓈ -i.ɚ **-iest** -i.ɪst, -i.əst **-ily** -ɪ.li, -əl.i **-iness** -ɪ.nəs, -ɪ.nɪs
Droylsden 'drɔɪlz.dən
Drs. (*abbrev. for* **Doctors**) 'dɒk.təz ⓊⓈ 'dɑːk.tɚz
drub drʌb **-s** -z **-bing** -ɪŋ **-bed** -d
Druce druːs
Drucker 'drʊk.əʳ ⓊⓈ 'drʌk.ɚ, 'drʊk-
drudg|e drʌdʒ **-es** -ɪz **-ing/ly** -ɪŋ/li **-ed** -d
drudgery 'drʌdʒ.ər.i
drug drʌg **-s** -z **-ging** -ɪŋ **-ged** -d
drugget 'drʌg.ɪt **-s** -s
druggie 'drʌg.i **-s** -z
druggist 'drʌg.ɪst **-s** -s
drugg|y 'drʌg|.i **-ies** -iz
drugstore 'drʌg.stɔːʳ ⓊⓈ -stɔːr **-s** -z
druid 'druː.ɪd **-s** -z **-ess/es** -ɪs/ɪz, -es/ɪz **-ism** -ɪ.zəm
druidic dru'ɪd.ɪk **-al** -əl
drum drʌm **-s** -z **-ming** -ɪŋ **-med** -d **ˌdrum 'major** ⓊⓈ **'drum ˌmajor** ; **ˌdrum major'ette**
drumbeat 'drʌm.biːt **-s** -s
drumfire 'drʌm.faɪəʳ ⓊⓈ -faɪɚ
drumhead 'drʌm.hed **-s** -z
drummer 'drʌm.əʳ ⓊⓈ -ɚ **-s** -z
Drummond 'drʌm.ənd
drumroll 'drʌm.rəʊl ⓊⓈ -roʊl **-s** -z
drumstick 'drʌm.stɪk **-s** -s
drunk (*n. adj.*) (*also from* **drink**) drʌŋk **-s** -s
drunkard 'drʌŋ.kəd ⓊⓈ -kɚd **-s** -z
drunk-driv|ing ˌdrʌŋk'draɪ.v|ɪŋ **-er/s** -əʳ/z ⓊⓈ -ɚ/z
drunken 'drʌŋ.kən **-ly** -li **-ness** -nəs, -nɪs
drupe druːp **-s** -s
Drury 'drʊə.ri ⓊⓈ 'drʊr.i
drus|e *geological term:* druːz **-es** -ɪz
Druse *surname:* druːz, druːs
Drus|e, Druz|e *member of sect in Syria and Lebanon:* druːz **-es** -ɪz
Drusilla druː'sɪl.ə, drʊ-
druthers 'drʌð.əz ⓊⓈ -ɚz
dr|y dr|aɪ **-ier** -aɪ.əʳ ⓊⓈ -aɪ.ɚ **-iest** -aɪ.ɪst, -əst **-yly** -aɪ.li **-yness** -aɪ.nəs, -nɪs **-ies** -aɪz **-ying** -aɪ.ɪŋ **-ied** -aɪd **ˌdry 'goods** ⓊⓈ **'dry ˌgoods** ; **ˌdry 'ice**; **ˌdry 'land**; **ˌdry 'rot**
dryad 'draɪ.æd, -əd **-s** -z
Dryburgh 'draɪ.bər.ə ⓊⓈ -bɜːrg, -bɚ.ə
dry-clean ˌdraɪ'kliːn ⓊⓈ '-- **-s** -z **-ing** -ɪŋ **-ed** -d **-er/s** -əʳ/z ⓊⓈ -ɚ/z
Dryden 'draɪ.dən
dry-dock ˌdraɪ'dɒk, '-- ⓊⓈ 'draɪ.dɑːk **-s** -s **-ing** -ɪŋ **-ed** -t
dryer 'draɪ.əʳ ⓊⓈ -ɚ **-s** -z
Dryfesdale 'draɪfs.deɪl
Dryhurst 'draɪ.hɜːst ⓊⓈ -hɜːrst
drying (*from* **dry**) 'draɪ.ɪŋ
dryly 'draɪ.li
dryness 'draɪ.nəs, -nɪs
dry-nurs|e 'draɪ.nɜːs ⓊⓈ -nɜːrs **-es** -ɪz **-ing** -ɪŋ **-ed** -t
drypoint 'draɪ.pɔɪnt
Drysdale 'draɪz.deɪl
dryshod 'draɪ.ʃɒd ⓊⓈ ʃɑːd
drywall 'draɪ.wɔːl ⓊⓈ -wɔːl, -wɑːl **-s** -z **-ing** -ɪŋ **-ed** -d
DTI ˌdiː.tiː'aɪ
DTP ˌdiː.tiː'piː
DTs ˌdiː'tiːz
dual 'djuː.əl, 'dʒuː-; djʊəl, dʒʊəl ⓊⓈ 'duː.əl, 'djuː- **ˌdual 'carriageway**
dual|ism 'djuː.ə.l|ɪ.zəm, 'dʒuː-; 'djʊə.l|ɪ-, 'dʒʊə- ⓊⓈ 'duː.əl|.ɪ-, 'djuː- **-ist/s** -ɪst/s
dualistic ˌdjuː.ə'lɪs.tɪk, ˌdʒuː-; ˌdjʊə'lɪs-, ˌdʒʊə- ⓊⓈ ˌduː.əl'ɪs-, ˌdjuː-
dualit|y dju'æl.ə.t|i, dʒu-, -ɪ.t|i ⓊⓈ du'æl.ə.ţ|i, dju- **-ies** -iz
dual-purpose ˌdjuː.əl'pɜː.pəs, ˌdʒuː-; ˌdjʊəl-, ˌdʒʊəl- ⓊⓈ ˌduː.əl'pɜːr-, ˌdjuː- *stress shift:* ˌdual-purpose 'implement
Duane dweɪn; du'eɪn
dub dʌb **-s** -z **-bing** -ɪŋ **-bed** -d
Dubai duː'baɪ, dʊ-, djʊ- ⓊⓈ duː-, də-
Du Barry djuː'bær.i, duː- ⓊⓈ duː'ber-, djuː-, -'bær-
dubbin 'dʌb.ɪn
Dubcek 'dʊb.tʃek ⓊⓈ 'duːb-
dubiety djuː'baɪ.ə.ti, djʊ-, dʒuː-, dʒʊ-, -ɪ.ti ⓊⓈ duː'baɪ.ə.ţi, djuː-
dubious 'djuː.bi.əs, 'dʒuː- ⓊⓈ 'duː-, 'djuː- **-ly** -li **-ness** -nəs, -nɪs
dubi|tate 'djuː.bɪ.teɪt, 'dʒuː- ⓊⓈ 'duː.bə-, 'djuː- **-tates** -teɪts **-tating** -teɪ.tɪŋ ⓊⓈ -teɪ.ţɪŋ **-tated** -teɪ.tɪd ⓊⓈ -teɪ.ţɪd
dubitation ˌdjuː.bɪ'teɪ.ʃən, ˌdʒuː- ⓊⓈ ˌduː.bə'-, ˌdjuː- **-s** -z
dubitative 'djuː.bɪ.tə.tɪv, 'dʒuː-, -teɪ- ⓊⓈ 'duː.bə-, 'djuː- **-ly** -li
Dublin 'dʌb.lɪn
Dubliner 'dʌb.lɪ.nəʳ ⓊⓈ -nɚ **-s** -z
DuBois, Du Bois duː'bwɑː, djuː-
Dubonnet® djuː'bɒn.eɪ, duː-, '--- ⓊⓈ ˌduː.bə'neɪ, ˌdjuː-
Dubrovnik djʊ'brɒv.nɪk, dʊ- ⓊⓈ duː'brɑːv-
ducal 'djuː.kəl, 'dʒuː- ⓊⓈ 'duː-, 'djuː- **-ly** -i
Du Cane djuː'keɪn, duː- ⓊⓈ du-, djuː-
ducat 'dʌk.ət **-s** -s
duce (**D**) 'duː.tʃeɪ, -tʃi ⓊⓈ 'duː.tʃeɪ
duces tecum ˌduː.kes'teɪ.kʊm ⓊⓈ -siːz'-
Duchesne djuː'ʃeɪn, duː-
duchess (**D**) 'dʌtʃ.ɪs, -es; dʌtʃ'es ⓊⓈ 'dʌtʃ.ɪs **-es** -ɪz
duchesse duː'ʃes; 'dʌtʃ.ɪs, -es ⓊⓈ 'dʌtʃ.ɪs
duch|y 'dʌtʃ|.i **-ies** -iz
Ducie 'djuː.si, 'dʒuː- ⓊⓈ 'duː-, 'djuː-
duck dʌk **-s** -s **-ing** -ɪŋ **-ed** -t **'duck ˌpond** ; **ˌducks and 'drakes** ; **ˌtake to something like a ˌduck to 'water**
duckbill 'dʌk.bɪl **-s** -z **-ed** -d **ˌduckbilled 'platypus**
duckboard 'dʌk.bɔːd ⓊⓈ -bɔːrd **-s** -z
duck-egg 'dʌk.eg **-s** -z
duckling 'dʌk.lɪŋ **-s** -z
duckweed 'dʌk.wiːd
Duckworth 'dʌk.wəθ, -wɜːθ ⓊⓈ -wɚθ, -wɜːrθ
duck|y 'dʌk|.i **-ies** -iz
duct dʌkt **-s** -s
ductile 'dʌk.taɪl ⓊⓈ -tɪl, -taɪl
ductility dʌk'tɪl.ə.ti, -ɪ.ti ⓊⓈ -ə.ţi
ductless 'dʌkt.ləs, -lɪs **ˌductless 'gland**
dud dʌd **-s** -z
Duddeston 'dʌd.ɪ.stən
Duddington 'dʌd.ɪŋ.tən
Duddon 'dʌd.ən
dude duːd, djuːd **-s** -z **'dude ˌranch**
Dudeney 'duːd.ni, 'djuːd-
dudgeon 'dʌdʒ.ən **-s** -z
Dudley 'dʌd.li
due djuː, dʒuː ⓊⓈ duː, djuː **-s** -z
duel 'djuː.əl, 'dʒuː- ⓊⓈ 'duː.əl, 'djuː- **-s** -z **-(l)ing** -ɪŋ **-(l)ed** -d **-(l)er/s** -əʳ/z ⓊⓈ -ɚ/z
duel(l)ist 'djuː.əl.ɪst, 'dʒuː- ⓊⓈ 'duː-, 'djuː- **-s** -s
duenna dju'en.ə, du- ⓊⓈ du-, dju- **-s** -z
Duer 'djuː.əʳ, 'dʒuː- ⓊⓈ 'duː.ɚ, 'djuː-
Duessa dju'es.ə, dʒu- ⓊⓈ du-, dju-
duet dju'et, dʒu- ⓊⓈ du-, dju- **-s** -s
duettino ˌdjuː.et'iː.nəʊ, ˌdʒuː- ⓊⓈ ˌduː.et'iː.noʊ, ˌdjuː- **-s** -z
duettist dju'et.ɪst, dʒu- ⓊⓈ du'eţ-, dju- **-s** -s
duetto dju'et.əʊ, dʒu- ⓊⓈ du'eţ.oʊ, dju- **-s** -z
duff (**D**) dʌf
duffel 'dʌf.əl **'duffel ˌbag** ; **'duffel ˌcoat**
duffer 'dʌf.əʳ ⓊⓈ -ɚ **-s** -z
Dufferin 'dʌf.ər.ɪn
Duffield 'dʌf.iːld
Duffin 'dʌf.ɪn
Duffy 'dʌf.i
Dufy 'duː.fi ⓊⓈ duː'fiː
dug (*n.*) (*also from* **dig**) dʌg **-s** -z
Dugald 'duː.gəld

Dugan ˈduː.gᵊn
Dugdale ˈdʌg.deɪl
Duggan ˈdʌg.ᵊn
Dugmore ˈdʌg.mɔːʳ (US) -mɔːr
dugong ˈdjuː.gɒŋ, ˈduː- (US) ˈduː.gɑːŋ, -gɔːŋ **-s** -z
dugout ˈdʌg.aʊt **-s** -s
Duguid ˈdjuː.gɪd, ˈduː.gɪd (US) ˈduː-, ˈdjuː-
DUI ˌdiː.juːˈaɪ
duiker ˈdaɪ.kəʳ (US) -kɚ **-s** -z
Duisburg ˈdjuːz.bɜːg, ˈdjuːs- (US) ˈduːs.bɜːrg, ˈduːz-
Dukakis dʊˈkɑː.kɪs, djʊ-, dʒʊ-, də- (US) dʊˈkɑː.kəs, də-
Dukas ˈdjuː.kɑː, ˈduː-, -ˈ- (US) duːˈkɑː, djuː-
duke (D) djuːk, dʒuːk (US) duːk, djuːk **-s** -s
dukedom ˈdjuːk.dəm, ˈdʒuːk- (US) ˈduːk-, ˈdjuːk- **-s** -z
duker|y ˈdjuː.kᵊr|.i, ˈdʒuː- (US) ˈduː-, ˈdjuː- **-ies** -iz
Dukinfield ˈdʌk.ɪn.fiːld
Dulce ˈdʌl.si
dulcet ˈdʌl.sɪt, -sət
Dulcie ˈdʌl.si
dulci|fy ˈdʌl.sɪ|.faɪ, -sə- **-fies** -faɪz **-fying** -faɪ.ɪŋ **-fied** -faɪd
dulcimer ˈdʌl.sɪ.məʳ, -sə- (US) -mɚ **-s** -z
Dulcinea ˌdʌl.sɪˈniː.ə, -ˈneɪ-; dʌlˈsɪn.i- (US) ˌdʌl.səˈniː-; dʌlˈsɪn.i-
dulia djʊˈlaɪə, dʊ- (US) duːˈlaɪə, djuː-; ˈduː.li.ə
dull dʌl **-er** -əʳ (US) -ɚ **-est** -ɪst, -əst **-y** -li, -i **-ness** -nəs, -nɪs **-s** -z **-ing** -ɪŋ **-ed** -d **as ˌdull as ˈditch-water**
dullard ˈdʌl.əd, -ɑːd (US) -ɚd **-s** -z
Dulles ˈdʌl.ɪs, -əs
dullish ˈdʌl.ɪʃ
dullsville ˈdʌlz.vɪl
dulness ˈdʌl.nəs, -nɪs
Duluth dəˈluːθ, djʊ-, dʊ-, də- (US) də-
Dulux® ˈdjuː.lʌks
Dulwich ˈdʌl.ɪdʒ, -ɪtʃ
duly ˈdjuː.li, ˈdʒuː- (US) ˈduː-, ˈdjuː-
Duma ˈduː.mə, ˈdjuː- (US) ˈduː-
Dumain djʊˈmeɪn, dʒʊ- (US) duː-, djuː-
Dumas ˈdjuː.mɑː, ˈduː-; dʊˈmɑː (US) duːˈmɑː, djuː-
Du Maurier djuːˈmɔː.ri.eɪ, duː-, -ˈmɒr.i- (US) duːˈmɔːr.i-, djuː-
dumb dʌm **-ly** -li **-ness** -nəs, -nɪs **-s** -z **-ing** -ɪŋ **-ed** -d **ˈdumb ˌshow ; ˌdumb ˈwaiter** (US) **ˈdumb ˌwaiter**
Dumbarton dʌmˈbɑː.tᵊn, dəm- (US) -ˈbɑːr-
Note: In **Dumbarton Oaks** (Washington DC), however, the pronunciation is /ˌdʌm.bɑːr.tᵊnˈəʊks (US) -bɑːr.tᵊnˈoʊks/.
dumbbell ˈdʌm.bel **-s** -z
dumbfound ˌdʌmˈfaʊnd, ˈ-- (US) ˈdʌm.faʊnd, ˌ-ˈ- **-s** -z **-ing** -ɪŋ **-ed** -ɪd
dumbo (D) ˈdʌm.bəʊ (US) -boʊ
dumbstricken ˈdʌmˌstrɪk.ᵊn
dumbstruck ˈdʌm.strʌk
dum-dum ˈdʌm.dʌm **-s** -z
dumfound ˌdʌmˈfaʊnd, ˈ-- (US) ˈdʌm.faʊnd, ˌ-ˈ- **-s** -z **-ing** -ɪŋ **-ed** -ɪd
Dumfries dʌmˈfriːs, dəm- **-shire** -ʃəʳ, -ˌʃɪəʳ, dʌmˈfriːʃ.ʃəʳ (US) dʌmˈfriːs.ʃɚ, -ˌʃɪr
dumm|y ˈdʌm|.i **-ies** -iz
dump dʌmp **-s** -s **-ing** -ɪŋ **-ed** -t **ˈdump ˌtruck**
dumper ˈdʌm.pəʳ (US) -pɚ **-s** -z
Dumphreys ˈdʌm*p*.frɪz, -friz
dumpish ˈdʌm.pɪʃ **-ly** -li **-ness** -nəs, -nɪs
dumpling ˈdʌm.plɪŋ **-s** -z
dumps dʌmps
Dumpster® ˈdʌmp.stəʳ (US) -stɚ
dump|y ˈdʌm.p|i **-ier** -i.əʳ (US) -i.ɚ **-iest** -i.ɪst, -i.əst **-iness** -ɪ.nəs, -ɪ.nɪs
dun dʌn **-s** -z **-ning** -ɪŋ **-ned** -d
Dunalley dʌnˈæl.i
Dunaway ˈdʌn.ə.weɪ
Dunbar dʌnˈbɑːʳ, dʌm-, ˈ-- (US) ˈdʌn.bɑːr, -ˈ-
Note: In Scotland always -ˈ-.
Dunbarton dʌnˈbɑː.tᵊn, dʌm- (US) dʌnˈbɑːr- **-shire** -ʃəʳ, -ˌʃɪəʳ (US) -ʃɚ, -ˌʃɪr
Dunblane dʌnˈbleɪn, dʌm- (US) dʌn-
Duncan ˈdʌŋ.kən, ˈdʌn-
Duncannon dʌnˈkæn.ən, dʌŋ- (US) dʌn-
Duncansby ˈdʌŋ.kənz.bi, ˈdʌn-
dunc|e dʌn*t*s **-es** -ɪz
Dunciad ˈdʌn*t*.si.æd
Duncombe ˈdʌn.kəm, ˈdʌŋ-
Dundalk dʌnˈdɔːk, -ˈdɔːlk (US) -ˈdɔːk, -ˈdɑːk
Dundas dʌnˈdæs, ˈdʌn.dæs, ˈdʌn.dəs (US) dʌnˈdæs, ˈdʌn.dəs
Dundee dʌnˈdiː, ˌdʌn- *stress shift:* ˌDundee ˈstation
dunderhead ˈdʌn.də.hed (US) -dɚ- **-s** -z
Dundonald dʌnˈdɒn.ᵊld (US) -ˈdɑː.nᵊld
dundrear|y (D) dʌnˈdrɪə.r|i (US) -ˈdrɪr|.i **-ies** -iz
Dundrum dʌnˈdrʌm, ˈdʌn.drəm
dune djuːn, dʒuːn (US) duːn, djuːn **-s** -z
Dunedin dʌnˈiː.dɪn, -dᵊn
Dunell djʊˈnel, ˌdjuː-, dʒʊ-, ˌdʒuː- (US) duː-, djuː-
Dunfermline dʌnˈfɜːm.lɪn, -lən (US) -ˈfɜːrm-
dung dʌŋ
Dungannon dʌnˈgæn.ən, dʌŋ-
dungaree ˌdʌŋ.gəˈriː, ˈ--- **-s** -z
Dungarvan dʌnˈgɑː.vən, dʌŋ- (US) dʌnˈgɑːr-
Dungeness ˌdʌn.*d*ʒəˈnes, -*d*ʒɪˈ-
dungeon ˈdʌn.dʒᵊn **-s** -z
dunghill ˈdʌŋ.hɪl **-s** -z
Dunglison ˈdʌŋ.glɪ.sᵊn
dungy ˈdʌŋ.i
Dunham ˈdʌn.ᵊm
Dunhill ˈdʌn.hɪl
Dunholme ˈdʌn.əm
dunk (D) dʌŋk **-s** -s **-ing** -ɪŋ **-ed** -t
Dunkeld dʌnˈkeld, dʌŋ- (US) dʌn-
Dunker ˈdʌŋ.kəʳ (US) -kɚ **-s** -z
Dunkirk dʌnˈkɜːk, ˌdʌn-, dʌŋ-, ˌdʌŋ- (US) ˈdʌn.kɜːrk, dʌnˈkɜːrk, ˌdʌn-
Dunkley ˈdʌŋ.kli
Dun Laoghaire dʌnˈlɪə.ri, duːn-, ˈleə-, -rə (US) -ˈler.ə, -i
Dunlap ˈdʌn.ləp, -læp (US) -læp, -ləp
dunlin ˈdʌn.lɪn, -lən **-s** -z
Dunlop *surname:* ˈdʌn.lɒp, -ˈ- (US) ˈdʌn.lɑːp, -ˈ-
Dunlop® ˈdʌn.lɒp (US) -lɑːp **-s** -s
Dunmail dʌnˈmeɪl, dʌm- (US) dʌn-
Dunmore dʌnˈmɔːʳ, dʌm- (US) dʌnˈmɔːr
Dunmow ˈdʌn.məʊ, ˈdʌm- (US) ˈdʌn.moʊ
dunnage ˈdʌn.ɪdʒ
Dunn(e) dʌn
Dunnet(t) ˈdʌn.ɪt
Dunning ˈdʌn.ɪŋ
dunno dəˈnəʊ (US) -ˈnoʊ
dunnock ˈdʌn.ək **-s** -s
Dunnottar dʌnˈɒt.əʳ, dəˈnɒt- (US) dʌnˈɑː.t̬ɚ, dəˈnɑː-
dunn|y ˈdʌn|.i **-ies** -ɪz
Dunoon dʌnˈuːn, dəˈnuːn
Dunraven dʌnˈreɪ.vᵊn
Dunrobin dʌnˈrɒb.ɪn (US) -ˈrɑː.bɪn
Dunsany dʌnˈseɪ.ni, -ˈsæn.i
Dunse dʌn*t*s
Dunsinane dʌnˈsɪn.ən
Note: This name has to be pronounced /ˌdʌn*t*.sɪˈneɪn/ in Shakespeare's 'Macbeth'.
Duns Scotus ˌdʌnzˈskɒt.əs, -ˈskəʊ.təs (US) -ˈskoʊ.t̬əs
Dunstable ˈdʌn*t*.stə.bl̩
Dunstaffnage dʌnˈstæf.nɪdʒ, -ˈstɑːf- (US) -ˈstæf-
Dunstan ˈdʌn*t*.stᵊn
Dunster ˈdʌn*t*.stəʳ (US) -stɚ
Dunston ˈdʌn*t*.stᵊn
Dunton ˈdʌn.tən (US) -tᵊn
Dunwich ˈdʌn.ɪtʃ
Dunwoody dʌnˈwʊd.i
duo- djuː.əʊ-, dʒuː.əʊ-; djuˈɒ-, dʒuˈɒ- (US) duː.oʊ-, djuː-, -ə-; duˈɑː-, djuˈɑː-
Note: Prefix. Either carries primary or secondary stress on the first syllable, e.g. **duologue** /ˈdjuː.ə.lɒg (US)

'duː.ə.lɑːg/, **duodecimal** /ˌdjuː.əʊ'des.ɪ.məl (US) ˌduː.oʊ'-/, or primary stress on the second syllable, e.g. **duopoly** /dju'ɒp.əl.i (US) du'ɑː.pəl-/.

duo 'djuː.əʊ, 'dʒuː- (US) 'duː.oʊ, 'djuː- **-s** -z

duodecennial ˌdjuː.əʊ.dɪ'sen.i.əl, ˌdʒuː-, -də'- (US) ˌduː.oʊ.də'-, ˌdjuː-

duodecimal ˌdjuː.əʊ'des.ɪ.məl, ˌdʒuː-, '-ə- (US) ˌduː.oʊ'-, ˌdjuː- **-s** -z

duodecimo ˌdjuː.əʊ'des.ɪ.məʊ, ˌdʒuː- (US) ˌduː.oʊ'des.ə.moʊ, ˌdjuː- **-s** -z

duodenal ˌdjuː.əʊ'diː.nəl, ˌdʒuː- (US) ˌduː.ə'-, ˌdjuː-; duː'ɑː.dən.əl, djuː-

duodenary ˌdjuː.əʊ'diː.nər.i, ˌdʒuː- (US) ˌduː.ə'-, ˌdjuː-, -'dən.ɚ.i

duoden|um ˌdjuː.əʊ'diː.n|əm, ˌdʒuː- (US) ˌduː.ə'-, ˌdjuː-; duː'ɑː.dən|.əm, djuː- **-ums** -əmz **-a** -ə

duologue 'djuː.ə.lɒg, 'dʒuː- (US) 'duː.ə.lɑːg, 'djuː- **-s** -z

duopol|y dju'ɒp.əl|.i, dʒu- (US) du'ɑː.pəl-, dju- **-ies** -iz

dup|e djuːp, dʒuːp (US) duːp, djuːp **-es** -s **-ing** -ɪŋ **-ed** -t

dupery 'djuː.pər.i, 'dʒuː- (US) 'duː-, 'djuː-

duple 'djuː.pl̩, 'dʒuː- (US) 'duː-, 'djuː-

Dupleix *governor in India:* djuː'pleɪks (US) duː'pleɪks, djuː- *historian:* djuː'pleɪ (US) duː'pleɪ, djuː-

duplex 'djuː.pleks, 'dʒuː- (US) 'duː-, 'djuː- **-es** -ɪz

duplicate (*n. adj.*) 'djuː.plɪ.kət, 'dʒuː-, -plə-, -kɪt (US) 'duː-, 'djuː- **-s** -s

dupli|cate (*v.*) 'djuː.plɪ|.keɪt, 'dʒuː-, -plə- (US) 'duː-, 'djuː- **-cates** -keɪts **-cating** -keɪ.tɪŋ (US) -keɪ.t̬ɪŋ **-cated** -keɪ.tɪd (US) -keɪ.t̬ɪd **-cator/s** -keɪ.tər/z (US) -keɪ.t̬ɚ/z

duplication ˌdjuː.plɪ'keɪ.ʃən, ˌdʒuː-, -plə'- (US) ˌduː-, ˌdjuː- **-s** -z

duplicature 'djuː.plɪ.keɪ.tʃər, 'dʒuː-, -kə- (US) 'duː.plə.kə.tʃʊr, 'djuː-, -keɪ-, -tʃɚ **-s** -z

duplicitous djʊ'plɪs.ɪ.təs, dʒʊ-, '-ə- (US) duː'plɪs.ə.t̬əs, djuː- **-ly** -li **-ness** -nəs, -nɪs

duplicity djʊ'plɪs.ə.ti, dʒʊ-, -ɪ.ti (US) duː'plɪs.ə.t̬i, djuː-

dupl|y djʊ'pl|aɪ, dʒʊ- (US) duː-, djuː- **-ies** -aɪz

Dupont djʊ'pɒnt; 'djuː.pɒnt (US) duː'pɑːnt, djuː-, '--

Dupré(e) dʊ'preɪ, djʊ-, -'priː (US) duː-, djuː-

du Pré dʊ'preɪ, djʊ- (US) duː-, djuː-

Dupuytren dʊ'pwiː.trən, djʊ-; 'djuː.pɪ.træ̃ŋ, ˌ--'- (US) 'duː.pwiː.træn, 'djuː-

Duquesne *French naval commander:* djʊ'keɪn, dʊ- (US) duː-, djuː- *place in US:* djuː'keɪn, duː- (US) duː-, dju-

durability ˌdjʊə.rə'bɪl.ə.ti, ˌdjɔː-, ˌdʒʊə-, ˌdʒɔː-, -ɪ.ti (US) ˌdʊr.ə'bɪl.ə.t̬i, ˌdjʊr-, ˌdɜːr-

durab|le 'djʊə.rə.b|l̩, 'djɔː-, 'dʒʊə-, 'dʒɔː- (US) 'dʊr.ə-, 'djʊr-, 'dɜːr- **-ly** -li **-leness** -l̩.nəs, -nɪs

Duracell® 'djʊə.rə.sel, 'dʒʊə-, 'djɔː-, 'dʒɔː- (US) 'dʊr.ə-, 'djʊr-, 'dɜːr-

Duraglit® 'djʊə.rə.glɪt, 'dʒʊə- (US) 'dʊr.ə-, 'djʊr-

dural 'djʊə.rəl, 'djɔː-, 'dʒʊə-, 'dʒɔː- (US) 'dʊr.əl, 'djʊr-

Duralumin® djʊə'ræl.jʊ.mɪn, djɔː-, dʒʊə-, dʒɔː-, -jə- (US) duː'ræl.jə-, djuː-

duramen djʊə'reɪ.men, dʒʊə- (US) dʊ-, djʊ-, -mən

Duran djʊə'ræn, dʊə-, dʒʊə- (US) dʊ'ræn, də- **Duˌran Du'ran**

durance 'djʊə.rənts, 'dʒʊə- (US) 'dʊr.ənts, 'djʊr-

Durand djʊə'rænd, dʒʊə- (US) dʊ'rænd, də-

Durango də'ræŋ.gəʊ, dʊ- (US) -goʊ

Durant djʊ'rɑːnt, dʒʊ-, -'rænt (US) 'duː.rænt; də'rænt

Durante djʊ'ræn.ti, dʒʊ-, -teɪ (US) də'ræn.t̬i, dʊ-

duration djʊə'reɪ.ʃən, djɔː-, dʒʊə-, dʒɔː- (US) dʊ-, djʊ-, də- **-s** -z

durative 'djʊə.rə.tɪv, 'djɔː-, 'dʒʊə-, 'dʒɔː- (US) 'dʊr.ə.t̬ɪv, 'djʊr-

Durban 'dɜː.bən (US) 'dɜːr-

durbar 'dɜː.bɑːr, ˌ-'- (US) 'dɜːr.bɑːr **-s** -z

d'Urberville 'dɜː.bə.vɪl (US) 'dɜːr.bɚ- **-s** -z

Durbin 'dɜː.bɪn (US) 'dɜːr-

Durden 'dɜː.dən (US) 'dɜːr-

durdle 'dɜː.dl̩ (US) 'dɜːr- **-s** -z

Durell djʊə'rel, dʒʊə- (US) duː-, djuː-

Dürer 'djʊə.rər (US) 'djuː.rɚ **-s** -z

duress djʊ'res, dʒʊ- (US) dʊ-, djʊ-

durex (D®) 'djʊə.reks, 'djɔː-, 'dʒʊə-, 'dʒɔː- (US) 'dʊr.eks, 'djʊr- **-es** -ɪz

Durham 'dʌr.əm (US) 'dɜːr-

durian, durion 'djʊə.ri.ən, 'dʊr.i-, -æn (US) 'dʊr.i- **-s** -z

during 'djʊə.rɪŋ, 'djɔː-, 'dʒʊə-, 'dʒɔː- (US) 'dʊr.ɪŋ, 'djʊr-, 'dɜːr-

Durnford 'dɜːn.fəd (US) 'dɜːrn.fɚd

Durocher də'rəʊ.ʃər, -tʃər (US) -'roʊ.ʃɚ, -tʃɚ

Durran dʌr'æn, də'ræn (US) də'ræn

Durrant 'dʌr.ənt (US) 'dɜːr-; də'rænt

Durrell 'dʌr.əl (US) 'dɜːr-

Dürrenmat 'djʊə.rən.mæt, 'dʊə- (US) 'dʊr.ən.mɑːt

durrie 'dʌr.i (US) 'dɜːr- **-s** -z

Durrington 'dʌr.ɪŋ.tən (US) 'dɜːr-

Dursley 'dɜːz.li (US) 'dɜːrz-

durst (*from* **dare**) dɜːst (US) dɜːrst **-n't** 'dɜː.sənt (US) 'dɜːr-

durum 'djʊə.rəm, 'dʒʊə-, 'djɔː-, 'dʒɔː- (US) 'dʊr.əm, 'dɜːr-

Durward 'dɜː.wəd (US) 'dɜːr.wɚd

Duse 'duː.zi

Dushanbe duː'ʃæn.bə, -'ʃæm-, -'ʃɑːn-, -'ʃɑːm-, -bi (US) duː'ʃɑːn.bi

dusk dʌsk **-s** -s **-ing** -ɪŋ **-ed** -t

dusk|y 'dʌs.k|i **-ier** -i.ər (US) -i.ɚ **-iest** -i.ɪst, -i.əst **-ily** -ɪ.li, -əl.i **-iness** -ɪ.nəs, -ɪ.nɪs

Düsseldorf 'dʊs.əl.dɔːf (US) 'duː.səl.dɔːrf, 'dʊs.əl-

dust dʌst **-s** -s **-ing** -ɪŋ **-ed** -ɪd **'Dust ˌBowl** ; **'dust ˌcover** ; **'dust ˌjacket** ; **ˌbite the 'dust**

dustbin 'dʌst.bɪn **-s** -z

dustcart 'dʌst.kɑːt (US) -kɑːrt **-s** -s

dustcoat 'dʌst.kəʊt (US) -koʊt **-s** -s

duster 'dʌs.tər (US) -tɚ **-s** -z

Dustin 'dʌs.tɪn

dust|man 'dʌst|.mən **-men** -mən

dustpan 'dʌst.pæn **-s** -z

dustproof 'dʌst.pruːf

dustsheet 'dʌst.ʃiːt **-s** -s

dust-up 'dʌst.ʌp **-s** -s

dust|y (**D**) 'dʌs.t|i **-ier** -i.ər (US) -i.ɚ **-iest** -i.ɪst, -i.əst **-ily** -ɪ.li, -əl.i **-iness** -ɪ.nəs, -ɪ.nɪs

Dutch dʌtʃ **-man** -mən **-men** -mən **ˌDutch 'cap** ; **ˌDutch 'courage** ; **ˌDutch 'elm diˌsease** ; **ˌDutch 'oven** ; **ˌDutch 'treat**

Dutch|woman 'dʌtʃ|ˌwʊm.ən **-women** -ˌwɪm.ɪn

duteous 'djuː.ti.əs, 'dʒuː- (US) 'duː.t̬i-, 'djuː- **-ly** -li **-ness** -nəs, -nɪs

Duthie 'dʌθ.i

dutiable 'djuː.ti.ə.bl̩, 'dʒuː- (US) 'duː.t̬i-, 'djuː-

dutiful 'djuː.tɪ.fəl, 'dʒuː-, -fʊl (US) 'duː.t̬ɪ-, 'djuː- **-ly** -i **-ness** -nəs, -nɪs

Dutton 'dʌt.ən

dut|y 'djuː.t|i, 'dʒuː- (US) 'duː.t̬|i, 'djuː- **-ies** -iz

duty-free ˌdjuː.ti'friː, ˌdʒuː- (US) ˌduː.t̬i-, ˌdjuː- **ˌduty-'free shop**

duumvir dju'ʌm.vər, du-, -'ʊm-; 'djuː.əm.vər, 'duː- (US) du'ʌm.vɚ, dju- **-s** -z **-i** -aɪ, -iː

duumvirate dju'ʌm.vɪ.rət, du-, -vər.ət, -ɪt, -eɪt (US) du'ʌm.vɪ.rət, dju-, -vɚ.ət, -ɪt **-s** -s

Duvalier djʊ'væl.i.eɪ, dʊ- (US) duː'vɑːl.jeɪ, djuː-

Duveen djʊ'viːn (US) duː-, djuː-, də-

duvet 'djuː.veɪ, 'duː- (US) duː'veɪ, djuː- **-s** -z

dux dʌks **-es** -ɪz

Duxbury 'dʌks.bᵊr.i (US) -ber-, -bɚ-
Duxford 'dʌks.fəd (US) -fɚd
DV ˌdiː'viː
Dvoràk *Czech composer:* 'dvɔː.ʒɑːk, 'vɔː-, -ʒæk (US) 'dvɔːr.ʒɑːk
Dvorak *US family name:* 'dvɔː.ræk (US) 'dvɔːr.æk
dwale dweɪl
dwar|f (*n.*) dwɔː|f (US) dwɔːr|f **-s** -s **-ves** -vz
dwarf (*v.*) dwɔːf (US) dwɔːrf **-s** -s **-ing** -ɪŋ **-ed** -t
dwarfish 'dwɔː.fɪʃ (US) 'dwɔːr- **-ly** -li **-ness** -nəs, -nɪs
Dwayne dweɪn
dweeb dwiːb **-s** -z
dwell dwel **-s** -z **-ing** -ɪŋ **-ed** -t, -d **dwelt** dwelt **dweller/s** 'dwel.əʳ/z (US) -ɚ/z
dwelling 'dwel.ɪŋ **-s** -z
dwelt (*from* **dwell**) dwelt
DWI ˌdiːˌdʌb.l̩.juː'aɪ (US) -juː'-, -jə'-
Dwight dwaɪt
dwindl|e 'dwɪn.dl̩ **-es** -z **-ing** -ɪŋ **-ed** -d
Dworkin 'dwɔː.kɪn (US) 'dwɔːr-
Dwyer dwaɪəʳ (US) dwaɪɚ
dyad 'daɪ.æd, -əd **-s** -z
Dyak 'daɪ.æk, -ək **-s** -s
dyarch|y 'daɪ.ɑː.k|i (US) -ɑːr- **-ies** -iz
Dyce daɪs
dy|e (D) daɪ **-es** -z **-eing** -ɪŋ **-ed** -d **-er/s** -əʳ/z (US) -ɚ/z
dyed-in-the-wool ˌdaɪd.ɪn.ðə'wʊl
Dyer daɪəʳ (US) daɪɚ
dyestuff 'daɪ.stʌf **-s** -s
dyewood 'daɪ.wʊd
dyeworks 'daɪ.wɜːks (US) -wɜːrks
Dyfed 'dʌv.ɪd, -ed, -əd
Dyffryn 'dʌf.rɪn, -rᵊn
dying (*from* **die**) 'daɪ.ɪŋ
dyk|e (D) daɪk **-es** -s **-ing** -ɪŋ **-ed** -t
Dylan 'dɪl.ən, 'dʌl- (US) 'dɪl-
Dymchurch 'dɪm.tʃɜːtʃ (US) -tʃɜːrtʃ
Dymock, Dymoke 'dɪm.ək
Dymond 'daɪ.mənd
Dymphna 'dɪmp.nə
dynameter daɪ'næm.ɪ.təʳ, dɪ-, '-ə- (US) -ə.t̬ɚ **-s** -z
dynamic daɪ'næm.ɪk, dɪ- **-al** -ᵊl **-ally** -ᵊl.i, -li **-s** -s
dynamism 'daɪ.nə.mɪ.zᵊm
dyna|mite 'daɪ.nə|.maɪt **-mites** -maɪts **-miting** -maɪ.tɪŋ (US) -maɪ.t̬ɪŋ **-mited** -maɪ.tɪd (US) -maɪ.t̬ɪd **-miter/s** -maɪ.təʳ/z (US) -maɪ.t̬ɚ/z
dynamo 'daɪ.nə.məʊ (US) -moʊ **-s** -z
dynamometer ˌdaɪ.nə'mɒm.ɪ.təʳ, '-ə- (US) -'mɑː.mə.t̬ɚ **-s** -z
dynamometric ˌdaɪ.nə.məʊ'met.rɪk (US) -moʊ'- **-al** -ᵊl
dynast 'dɪn.əst, 'daɪ.nəst, -næst (US) 'daɪ.næst, -nəst **-s** -s
dynastic dɪ'næs.tɪk, daɪ-, də- (US) daɪ-
dynast|y 'dɪn.ə.st|i, 'daɪ.nə- (US) 'daɪ.nə- **-ies** -iz
dynatron 'daɪ.nə.trɒn (US) -trɑːn **-s** -z
dyne daɪn **-s** -s
Dynevor 'dɪn.ɪ.vəʳ, '-ə- (US) -vɚ
d'you *strong forms:* dʒuː, djuː *weak forms:* dʒə, djə, dʒu, dju
Note: Abbreviated form of "do you": the spelling represents a pronunciation that is usually unstressed, and the pronunciation therefore parallels that of unstressed **you**, which has weak forms /jə/ before a consonant and /ju/ before vowels. When used contrastively, the strong form /djuː/ or /dʒuː/ may be used (e.g. "I don't like it. **D'you** like it?").
Dysart 'daɪ.sət, -zət, -sɑːt, -zɑːt (US) -sɑːrt, -zɑːrt, -sɚt
dysarthria dɪ'sɑː.θri.ə (US) -'sɑːr-
dysenteric ˌdɪs.ᵊn'ter.ɪk, -en'- (US) -en'-
dysentery 'dɪs.ᵊn.tᵊr.i, -tri (US) -ter.i
dysfunction dɪs'fʌŋk.ʃᵊn **-s** -z **-ing** -ɪŋ **-ed** -d **-al** -ᵊl
dysfunctional dɪs'fʌŋ*k*.ʃᵊn.ᵊl
dysgraphia dɪs'græf.i.ə
dysgraphic dɪs'græf.ɪk
dyslalia dɪ'sleɪ.li.ə, -'slæl.i-
dyslexia dɪ'slek.si.ə
dyslexic dɪ'slek.sɪk
dysmenorrh(o)ea ˌdɪs.men.ə'rɪə (US) -'riː.ə
Dyson 'daɪ.sᵊn
dyspepsia dɪ'spep.si.ə
dyspeptic dɪ'spep.tɪk **-s** -s
dysphagia dɪs'feɪ.dʒi.ə (US) -dʒə, -dʒi.ə
dysphasia dɪs'feɪ.zi.ə, -ʒi-, '-ʒə (US) '-ʒə, '-ʒi.ə
dysphasic dɪs'feɪ.zɪk **-s** -s
dysphonia dɪs'fəʊ.ni.ə (US) -'foʊ-
dysphonic dɪs'fɒn.ɪk (US) -'fɑː.nɪk
dyspn(o)ea dɪs*p*'niː.ə
dysprosium dɪ'sprəʊ.zi.əm, -si- (US) -'sproʊ-
dystrophic dɪ'strɒf.ɪk (US) -'strɑː.fɪk, -'stroʊ-
dystrophy 'dɪs.trə.fi
dysuria dɪ'sjʊə.ri.ə (US) -'sjʊr.i-
dziggetai '*d*zɪg.ɪ.taɪ, '-ə-, ˌ--'- (US) 'dʒɪg.ɪ.taɪ **-s** -z

E

e (E) iː **-'s** -z **'E ˌnumber**
E (*abbrev. for* **east**) iːst
E111 ˌiːˌwʌn.ɪ'lev.ən, -ə'-
each iːtʃ **ˌeach 'other**
EACSO iː'æk.səʊ, -'ɑːk- US -soʊ
Eadie, Eady 'iː.di
eager 'iː.gəʳ US -gɚ **-ly** -li **-ness** -nəs, -nɪs **ˌeager 'beaver**
eagle (E) 'iː.gl̩ **-s** -z **'eagle ˌowl** ; **ˌEagle 'Scout** US **'Eagle ˌScout**
eagle-eyed ˌiː.gl̩'aɪd, 'iː.gl̩.aɪd
Eaglefield 'iː.gl̩.fiːld
Eaglehawk 'iː.gl̩.hɔːk US -hɑːk, -hɔːk
Eaglescliffe 'iː.gl̩z.klɪf
eaglet 'iː.glɪt, -lət **-s** -s
eagre 'eɪ.gəʳ, 'iː- US 'iː.gɚ, 'eɪ- **-s** -z
Eakin 'eɪ.kɪn, 'iː- **-s** -z
Ealing 'iː.lɪŋ
Eames iːmz, eɪmz
Eamon(n) 'eɪ.mən
-ean -iː.ən, -i.ən
Note: Suffix. **-ean** may take primary stress or alternatively words containing it may be stressed on the syllable before the prefix. An example where both possibilities occur is **Caribbean**, which is either /ˌkær.ɪ'biː.ən US ˌker-/, or /kə'rɪb.i.ən/.
ear ɪəʳ US ɪr **-s** -z **'ear ˌtrumpet** ; **ˌturn a ˌdeaf 'ear to** ; **ˌkeep one's ˌear to the 'ground** ; **ˌprick up one's 'ears** ; **ˌgive someone a ˌthick 'ear**
earache 'ɪə.reɪk US 'ɪr-
Eardley 'ɜːd.li US 'ɜːrd-
eardrop 'ɪə.drɒp US 'ɪr.drɑːp **-s** -s
eardrum 'ɪə.drʌm US 'ɪr- **-s** -z
eared ɪəd US ɪrd
earful 'ɪə.fʊl US 'ɪr-
Earhart 'eə.hɑːt US 'er.hɑːrt
earl (E) ɜːl US ɜːrl **-s** -z **-dom/s** -dəm/z **ˌEarl's 'Court** ; **ˌEarl 'Grey** ; **ˌearl 'marshal**
Earl(e) ɜːl US ɜːrl
earl|y 'ɜː.l|i US 'ɜːr- **-ier** -i.əʳ US -i.ɚ **-iest** -i.ɪst, -i.əst **-iness** -ɪ.nəs, -ɪ.nɪs **'early ˌbird** ; **ˌearly 'warning ˌsystem**
earmark 'ɪə.mɑːk US 'ɪr.mɑːrk **-s** -s **-ing** -ɪŋ **-ed** -t
earmuffs 'ɪə.mʌfs US 'ɪr-
earn (E) ɜːn US ɜːrn **-s** -z **-ing** -ɪŋ **-ed** -d, ɜːnt US ɜːrnt
earnest 'ɜː.nɪst, -nəst US 'ɜːr- **-s** -s **-ly** -li **-ness** -nəs, -nɪs
earnings 'ɜː.nɪŋz US 'ɜːr-
Earnshaw 'ɜːn.ʃɔː US 'ɜːrn.ʃɑː, -ʃɔː
Earp ɜːp US ɜːrp
earphone 'ɪə.fəʊn US 'ɪr.foʊn **-s** -z
earpiec|e 'ɪə.piːs US 'ɪr- **-es** -ɪz
earplug 'ɪə.plʌg US 'ɪr- **-s** -z
earring 'ɪə.rɪŋ US 'ɪr.ɪŋ, -rɪŋ **-s** -z
earshot 'ɪə.ʃɒt US 'ɪr.ʃɑːt
earsplitting 'ɪəˌsplɪt.ɪŋ US 'ɪrˌsplɪt̬.ɪŋ **-ly** -li
earth (E) (*n.*) ɜːθ US ɜːrθ **-s** -s, ɜːðz US ɜːrðz **'earth ˌmother**
earth (*v.*) ɜːθ US ɜːrθ **-s** -s **-ing** -ɪŋ **-ed** -t
earthborn 'ɜːθ.bɔːn US 'ɜːrθ.bɔːrn
earthbound 'ɜːθ.baʊnd US 'ɜːrθ-
earthen 'ɜː.θᵊn, -ðᵊn US 'ɜːr-
earthenware 'ɜː.θᵊn.weəʳ, -ðᵊn- US 'ɜːr.θᵊn.wer, -ðᵊn-
earthiness 'ɜː.θɪ.nəs, -nɪs US 'ɜːr-
earthling 'ɜːθ.lɪŋ US 'ɜːrθ- **-s** -z
earthl|y 'ɜːθ.l|i US 'ɜːrθ- **-ier** -i.əʳ US -i.ɚ **-iest** -i.ɪst, -i.əst **-iness** -ɪ.nəs, -ɪ.nɪs
earthmover 'ɜːθˌmuː.vəʳ US 'ɜːrθˌmuː.vɚ **-s** -z
earthquake 'ɜːθ.kweɪk US 'ɜːrθ- **-s** -s
Earthsea 'ɜːθ.siː US 'ɜːrθ-
earthshaking 'ɜːθˌʃeɪ.kɪŋ US 'ɜːrθ-
earth-shattering 'ɜːθˌʃæt.ᵊr.ɪŋ US 'ɜːrθˌʃæt̬- **-ly** -li
earthward 'ɜːθ.wəd US 'ɜːrθ.wɚd **-s** -z
earthwork 'ɜːθ.wɜːk US 'ɜːrθ.wɜːrk **-s** -s
earthworm 'ɜːθ.wɜːm US 'ɜːrθ.wɜːrm **-s** -z
earth|y 'ɜː.θ|i US 'ɜːr- **-ily** -ɪ.li, -ᵊl.i **-iness** -ɪ.nəs, -ɪ.nɪs
earwax 'ɪə.wæks US 'ɪr-
earwig 'ɪə.wɪg US 'ɪr- **-s** -z **-ging** -ɪŋ **-ged** -d
Easdale 'iːz.deɪl
eas|e iːz **-es** -ɪz **-ing** -ɪŋ **-ed** -d
Easebourne 'iːz.bɔːn US -bɔːrn
easeful 'iːz.fᵊl, -fʊl **-ly** -li **-ness** -nəs, -nɪs
easel 'iː.zᵊl **-s** -z
easement 'iːz.mənt **-s** -s
Easey 'iː.zi
easiness (*from* **easy**) 'iː.zɪ.nəs, -nɪs
Easington 'iː.zɪŋ.tən
east (E) iːst **ˌEast 'Anglia** ; **ˌEast 'End** *stress shift:* ˌEast End 'pub ; **ˌEast 'Coast** *stress shift:* ˌEast Coast 'accent
East Bergholt ˌiːst'bɜːg.həʊlt US -'bɜːrg.hoʊlt
eastbound 'iːst.baʊnd
Eastbourne 'iːs*t*.bɔːn US -bɔːrn
Eastcheap 'iːs*t*.tʃiːp
Eastender ˌiːst'en.dəʳ US -dɚ **-s** -z
Easter 'iː.stəʳ US -stɚ **-s** -z **ˌEaster 'bonnet** US **'Easter ˌbonnet** ; **ˌEaster 'Bunny** US **'Easter ˌBunny** ; **ˌEaster 'Day** ; **'Easter ˌegg** ; **'Easter ˌIsland** ; **ˌEaster 'Sunday**
easterl|y 'iː.stᵊl|.i US -stɚ.l|i **-ies** -iz
eastern (E) 'iː.stᵊn US -stɚn **-most** -məʊst, -məst US -moʊst, -məst **ˌEastern 'Shore** ; **ˌEastern 'Standard ˌTime**
easterner (E) 'iːs.tᵊn.əʳ US -tɚ.nɚ **-s** -z
Eastertide 'iː.stə.taɪd US -stɚ-
Eastfield 'iːst.fiːld
Eastham 'iːst.*h*əm
Easthampton ˌiːst'hæm*p*.tən
easting 'iː.stɪŋ **-s** -z
East Kilbride ˌiːst.kɪl'braɪd
Eastlake 'iːst.leɪk
Eastleigh 'iːst.liː, ˌiːst'liː
Eastman 'iːs*t*.mən
east-northeast ˌiːst.nɔːθ'iːst US -nɔːrθ'- *in nautical usage also:* -nɔː'riːst US -nɔːr'iːst
Easton 'iː.stən
Easton-in-Gordano ˌiː.stᵊn.ɪn.gɔː'dɑː.nəʊ, -ɪŋ- US -gɔːr'dɑː.noʊ
Eastport 'iːs*t*.pɔːt US -pɔːrt
east-southeast ˌiːst.saʊθ'iːst *in nautical usage also:* -saʊ'-
eastward 'iːst.wəd US -wɚd **-ly** -li **-s** -z
East-West ˌiːst'west *stress shift, see compound:* **ˌEast-West re'lations**
Eastwood 'iːst.wʊd
eas|y (E) 'iː.z|i **-ier** -i.əʳ US -i.ɚ **-iest** -i.ɪst, -i.əst **-ily** -ɪ.li, -ᵊl.i **-iness** -ɪ.nəs, -ɪ.nɪs **'easy ˌchair** ; **as ˌeasy as 'pie** ; **ˌtake it 'easy** ; **on 'easy ˌstreet**
easygoing ˌiː.zi'gəʊ.ɪŋ US -'goʊ- *stress shift:* ˌeasygoing 'person
eat iːt **-s** -s **-ing** -ɪŋ US 'iː.t̬ɪŋ **ate** et, eɪt US eɪt **eaten** 'iː.tᵊn US -t̬ən **eater/s** 'iː.təʳ/z US -t̬ɚ/z **'eating diˌsorder** ; **ˌeat one's 'heart out** ; **ˌeat one's 'words** ; **ˌeat someone out of ˌhouse and 'home**
eatable 'iː.tə.bl̩ US -t̬ə- **-s** -z
eater|y 'iː.tᵊr|.i US -t̬ɚ- **-ies** -iz
Eaton 'iː.tᵊn
Eaton Socon ˌiː.tᵊn'səʊ.kᵊn US -'soʊ-
eau de cologne ˌəʊ.də.kə'ləʊn, -dɪ- US ˌoʊ.də.kə'loʊn *stress shift:* ˌeau de cologne 'spray
eau de nil ˌəʊ.də'niːl US ˌoʊ- *stress shift:* ˌeau de nil 'paint
eau de parfum ˌəʊ.də.pɑː'fʌm US ˌoʊ.də.pɑːr'-
eau de toilette ˌəʊ.də.twɑː'let, -twə'- US ˌoʊ-
eau-de-vie ˌəʊ.də'viː US ˌoʊ-
eave (E) iːv **-s** -z

eavesdrop 'iːvz.drɒp (US) -drɑːp **-s** -s **-ping** -ɪŋ **-ped** -t **-per/s** -əʳ/z (US) -ɚ/z
ebb eb **-s** -z **-ing** -ɪŋ **-ed** -d ˌ**ebb 'tide**
Ebbsfleet 'ebz.fliːt
Ebbw 'eb.uː, -ə
Ebel eb'el, 'iː.bəl
Ebenezer ˌeb.ə'niː.zəʳ, -ɪ'- (US) -zɚ *stress shift:* ˌEbenezer 'Scrooge
Eberhart 'eɪ.bə.hɑːt (US) 'eb.ɚ.hɑːrt, 'eɪ.bɚ-
Ebionite 'iː.bjə.naɪt, -bɪə- **-s** -s
Eblis 'eb.lɪs
ebon 'eb.ən
ebonite 'eb.ə.naɪt
ebonizle, -isle 'eb.ə.naɪz **-es** -ɪz **-ing** -ɪŋ **-ed** -d
ebony (E) 'eb.ən.i
Eboracum iː'bɒr.ə.kəm, ɪ- (US) ɪ'bɔːr-
Ebrington 'eb.rɪŋ.tən
Ebro 'iː.brəʊ, 'eb.rəʊ (US) 'eɪ.broʊ, 'iː-, 'eb.roʊ
ebullien|ce ɪ'bʌl.i.ən*t*s, -'bʊl- (US) -'bʊl.jən*t*s, -'bʌl- **-cy** -*t*si
ebullient ɪ'bʌl.i.ənt, -'bʊl- (US) -'bʊl.jənt, -'bʌl- **-ly** -li
ebullition ˌeb.ə'lɪʃ.ən, -ʊ'- (US) -ə'-, -juː'- **-s** -z
Ebury 'iː.bər.i (US) -ˌber-, -bɚ-
EC ˌiː'siː
écarté eɪ'kɑː.teɪ (US) ˌeɪ.kɑːr'teɪ
Ecbatana ek'bæt.ən.ə, ˌek.bə'tɑː.nə (US) ek'bæt.ən.ə
ecce homo ˌek.eɪ'həʊ.məʊ, ˌetʃ-, -'hɒm.əʊ (US) -'hoʊ.moʊ
eccentric ɪk'sen.trɪk, ek- **-s** -s **-al** -əl **-ally** -əl.i, -li
eccentricit|y ˌek.sen'trɪs.ə.t|i, -sən'-, -ɪ.t|i (US) -ə.t̬|i **-ies** -iz
Ecclefechan ˌek.l̩'fek.ən, -'fex-
Eccles 'ek.l̩z **'Eccles ˌcake**
Ecclesfield 'ek.l̩z.fiːld
ecclesi|a ɪ'kliː.zi|.ə (US) ɪ'kliː-, ek'liː-, -'leɪ- **-ast/s** -æst/s
Ecclesiastes ɪˌkliː.zi'æs.tiːz (US) ɪˌkliː-, ekˌliː-
ecclesiastic ɪˌkliː.zi'æs.tɪk (US) ɪˌkliː-, ekˌliː- **-s** -s **-al** -əl **-ally** -əl.i, -li
ecclesiasticism ɪˌkliː.zi'æs.tɪ.sɪ.zəm (US) ɪˌkliː-, ekˌliː-
Ecclesiasticus ɪˌkliː.zi'æs.tɪ.kəs (US) ɪˌkliː-, ekˌliː-
Eccleston 'ek.l̩.stən
eccrine 'ek.rɪn, -riːn, -rən, -raɪn
ECG ˌiː.siː'dʒiː
echelon 'eʃ.ə.lɒn, 'eɪ.ʃə- (US) 'eʃ.ə.lɑːn **-s** -z **-ned** -d
echidn|a ek'ɪd.n|ə, ɪ'kɪd- (US) iː'kɪd- **-ae** -iː **-as** -əz
echin|us ek'aɪ.n|əs; ɪ'kaɪ-; ə-; 'ek.ɪn|.əs (US) ɪ'kaɪ.n|əs **-i** -aɪ
echo 'ek.əʊ (US) -oʊ **-es** -z **-ing** -ɪŋ **-ed** -d
echocardio|gram ˌek.əʊ'kɑː.di.əʊ|.græm (US) -oʊ'kɑːr.di.ə-, -oʊ- **-s** -z **-graph/s** -grɑːf/s, -græf/s (US) -græf/s
echoic ek'əʊ.ɪk, ɪ'kəʊ-, ə- (US) ek'oʊ-
echolalia ˌek.əʊ'leɪ.li.ə (US) -oʊ'-
echolo|cate ˌek.əʊ.ləʊ|'keɪt (US) -oʊ.loʊ'- **-cates** -'keɪts **-cating** -'keɪ.tɪŋ (US) -'keɪ.t̬ɪŋ **-cated** -'keɪ.tɪd (US) -'keɪ.t̬ɪd
echolocation ˌek.əʊ.ləʊ'keɪ.ʃən (US) -oʊ.loʊ'-
echt ext, ekt
Eckersl(e)y 'ek.əz.li (US) -ɚz-
Eckert 'ek.ət (US) -ɚt
Eckertford 'ek.ət.fəd (US) -ɚt.fɚd
Eckington 'ek.ɪŋ.tən
éclair eɪ'kleəʳ, ɪ-; 'eɪ.kleəʳ (US) eɪ'kler, ɪ- **-s** -z
eclampsia ɪ'klæm*p*.si.ə, ek'læm*p*-, ə'klæm*p*-
éclat eɪ'klɑː, '-- **-s** -z
eclectic ek'lek.tɪk, ɪ'klek-, iː- (US) ek'lek- **-s** -s **-al** -əl **-ally** -əl.i, -li
eclecticism ek'lek.tɪ.sɪ.zəm, ɪ'klek-, iː-, -tə- (US) ek'lek.tə-
eclips|e ɪ'klɪps, ə-, iː- **-es** -ɪz **-ing** -ɪŋ **-ed** -t
ecliptic ɪ'klɪp.tɪk, ə-, iː- **-s** -s
eclogue 'ek.lɒg (US) -lɑːg, -lɔːg **-s** -z
eco- iː.kəʊ-, ek.əʊ-; ɪ.kɒ- (US) ek.oʊ-, -ə-, iː.koʊ-, -kə-; ɪ.kɑː-
Note: Prefix. Either takes primary or secondary stress on the first syllable, e.g. **ecosphere** /'iː.kəʊ.sfɪəʳ (US) 'ek.oʊ.sfɪr/, **economic** /ˌiː.kə'nɒm.ɪk (US) ˌiː.kə'nɑː.mɪk/, or primary or secondary stress on the second syllable, e.g. **ecology** /iː'kɒl.ə.dʒi (US) -'kɑː.lə-/, **econometric** /ɪˌkɒn.ə'met.rɪk (US) -kɑː.nə'-/.
eco-friendly 'iː.kəʊˌfrend.li (US) 'ek.oʊˌ-, 'iː.koʊˌ-
E coli ˌiː'kəʊ.laɪ (US) -'koʊ-
ecologic|al ˌiː.kə'lɒdʒ.ɪ.k|əl, ˌek.ə'- (US) -'lɑː.dʒɪ- **-ally** -əl.i, -li ˌ**ecoˌlogically 'sound**
ecolog|y iː'kɒl.ə.dʒ|i, ɪ-, ek'ɒl- (US) iː'kɑː.lə-, ɪ'kɑː-, ek'ɑː- **-ist/s** -ɪst/s
econometric ɪˌkɒn.ə'met.rɪk, iː- (US) -ˌkɑː.nə'- **-s** -s
econometrician ɪˌkɒn.ə.met'rɪʃ.ən, iː-, -mə'trɪʃ- (US) -ˌkɑː.nə.mə'- **-s** -z
econometrics ɪˌkɒn.ə'met.rɪks, iː- (US) -ˌkɑː.nə'-
economic ˌiː.kə'nɒm.ɪk, ˌek.ə'- (US) -'nɑː.mɪk **-s** -s **-al** -əl **-ally** -əl.i, -li ˌ**economic 'growth**
economist ɪ'kɒn.ə.mɪst, iː- (US) -'kɑː.nə- **-s** -s
economiz|e, -is|e ɪ'kɒn.ə.maɪz, ə'kɒn- (US) ɪ'kɑː.nə-, iː- **-es** -ɪz **-ing** -ɪŋ **-ed** -d **-er/s** -əʳ/z (US) -ɚ/z
econom|y ɪ'kɒn.ə.m|i, ə'kɒn- (US) ɪ'kɑː.nə-, iː- **-ies** -iz **e'conomy ˌclass**
ecosphere 'iː.kəʊ.sfɪəʳ, 'ek.əʊ- (US) 'ek.oʊ.sfɪr, 'iː.koʊ-
ecosystem 'iː.kəʊˌsɪs.təm, 'ek.əʊ-, -tɪm (US) 'ek.oʊˌsɪs.təm, 'iː.koʊ- **-s** -z
ecru 'eɪ.kruː, 'ek.ruː
ecstas|y 'ek.stə.s|i **-ies** -iz
ecstatic ɪk'stæt.ɪk, ek-, ək- (US) ek'stæt̬-, ɪk- **-al** -əl **-ally** -əl.i, -li
ECT ˌiː.siː'tiː
ecto- ek.təʊ- (US) ek.toʊ-, -tə-
Note: Prefix. Normally takes primary or secondary stress on the first syllable, e.g. **ectomorph** /'ek.təʊ.mɔːf (US) 'ek.toʊ.mɔːrf/, **ectomorphic** /ˌek.təʊ'mɔː.fɪk (US) ˌek.toʊ'mɔːr-/.
ectoderm 'ek.təʊ.dɜːm (US) -toʊ.dɜːrm, -tə-
ectoderm|al ˌek.təʊ'dɜː.m|əl (US) -toʊ'dɜːr-, -tə'- **-ic** -ɪk
ectomorph 'ek.təʊ.mɔːf (US) -toʊ.mɔːrf, -tə- **-s** -s
ectomorph|ic ˌek.təʊ'mɔː.f|ɪk (US) -toʊ'mɔːr-, -tə'- **-ism** -ɪ.zəm **-y** -i
-ectomy -'ek.tə.mi
Note: Suffix. Always carries primary stress, e.g. **appendix** /ə'pen.dɪks/, **appendectomy** /ˌæp.en'dek.tə.mi/.
ectopic ek'tɒp.ɪk, ˌek-, ɪk- (US) ek'tɑː.pɪk **ecˌtopic 'pregnancy**
ectoplasm 'ek.təʊ.plæz.əm (US) -toʊ-, -tə-
ecu, ECU (*abbrev. for* **European Currency Unit**) 'ek.juː, 'eɪ.kjuː, 'iː-; ˌiː.siː'juː (US) 'eɪ.kuː; ˌiː.siː'juː **-s** -z
Ecuador 'ek.wə.dɔːʳ (US) -dɔːr
ecumenic ˌiː.kjʊ'men.ɪk, ˌek.jʊ'-, -jə'- (US) ˌek.jʊ'-, -jə'- **-al** -əl
ecumenicism ˌiː.kjʊ'men.ɪ.sɪ.zəm, ˌek.jʊ'-, -jə'- (US) ˌek.jʊ'-, -jə'-
ecumen|ism iː'kjuː.mə.n|ɪ.zəm; ɪ-; 'ek.jʊ-, -jə- (US) 'ek.juː-, -jə-; ek'juː-, ɪ'kjuː- **-ist/s** -ɪst/s
eczema 'ek.sɪ.mə, -səm.ə (US) 'ek.sə.mə; 'eg.zə-; ɪg'ziː.mə
eczematous ek'sem.ə.təs, ɪk-; ɪg'zem- (US) ɪg'zem.ə.t̬əs, eg-; ɪk'sem-
Ed ed
-ed -t, -d, -ɪd
Note: Suffix. Unstressed. When preceded by /t/ or /d/, the pronunciation is /-ɪd/, e.g. **batted** /'bæt.ɪd (US) 'bæt̬.ɪd/. When preceded by a voiceless consonant other than /t/, the pronunciation is /t/, e.g. **picked** /pɪkt/.

When preceded by a voiced sound, including vowels and consonants, the pronunciation is /d/, e.g. **rigged** /rɪgd/. There are, however, exceptions, particularly in adjectival forms, including **dogged** /'dɒg.ɪd ⓊⓈ 'dɑː.gɪd/, and **learned** /'lɜː.nɪd ⓊⓈ 'lɜːr-/; see individual entries.

edacious ɪ'deɪ.ʃəs, iː-, ed'eɪ- ⓊⓈ ɪ'deɪ-, iː-

Edam 'iː.dæm ⓊⓈ 'iː.dəm, -dæm

edaphic ɪ'dæf.ɪk, iː-

Edda 'ed.ə **-s** -z

Eddie 'ed.i

Eddington 'ed.ɪŋ.tən

edd|y (E) 'ed|.i **-ies** -iz **-ying** -i.ɪŋ **-ied** -id

Eddystone 'ed.ɪ.stᵊn, -stəʊn ⓊⓈ -stoʊn, -stən

Ede iːd

edelweiss 'eɪ.dᵊl.vaɪs

edem|a ɪ'diː.m|ə, iː- **-as** -əz **-ata** -ə.tə ⓊⓈ -ə.t̬ə

edematous ɪ'diː.mə.təs, iː- ⓊⓈ -t̬əs

Eden 'iː.dᵊn ˌ**Garden of 'Eden**

Edenbridge 'iː.dᵊn.brɪdʒ

Edenfield 'iː.dᵊn.fiːld

edentate iː'den.teɪt, ɪ- **-s** -s

Edessa ɪ'des.ə, iː-

Edgar 'ed.gəʳ ⓊⓈ -gɚ

Edgbaston 'edʒ.bə.stᵊn, -bæs.tᵊn

edg|e (E) edʒ **-es** -ɪz **-ing** -ɪŋ **-ed** -d

Edgecomb(e) 'edʒ.kəm

Edgecote 'edʒ.kəʊt, -kət ⓊⓈ -koʊt

Edgecumbe 'edʒ.kəm, -kuːm

Edgehill *name of a hill:* ˌedʒ'hɪl *surname:* 'edʒ.hɪl

edgeless 'edʒ.ləs, -lɪs

Edgerton 'edʒ.ə.tᵊn ⓊⓈ -ɚ.t̬ən

edge|ways 'edʒ|.weɪz **-wise** -waɪz

Edgeworth 'edʒ.wəθ, -wɜːθ ⓊⓈ -wɚθ, -wɜːrθ

edging 'edʒ|.ɪŋ **-s** -z

Edgington 'edʒ.ɪŋ.tən

Edgley 'edʒ.li

Edgware 'edʒ.weəʳ ⓊⓈ -wer

edg|y 'edʒ|.i **-ier** -i.əʳ ⓊⓈ -i.ɚ **-iest** -i.ɪst, -i.əst **-ily** ɪ.li, ᵊl.i

edibility ˌed.ɪ'bɪl.ə.ti, -ə'-, -ɪ.ti ⓊⓈ -ə.t̬i

edible 'ed.ɪ.bl̩, '-ə- **-s** -z **-ness** -nəs, -nɪs

edict 'iː.dɪkt **-s** -s

Edie 'iː.di

edification ˌed.ɪ.fɪ'keɪ.ʃᵊn, ˌ-ə-

edific|e 'ed.ɪ.fɪs, '-ə- **-es** -ɪz

edi|fy 'ed.ɪ|.faɪ, '-ə- **-fies** -faɪz **-fying** -faɪ.ɪŋ **-fied** -faɪd

Edina ɪ'daɪ.nə, iː-, ed'aɪ-, -'iː-

Edinburgh 'ed.ɪn.bᵊr.ə, -ɪm-, -ᵊn-, -bʌr- ⓊⓈ -bʌr.ə, -oʊ

Edington 'ed.ɪŋ.tən

Edison 'ed.ɪ.sᵊn, '-ə-

ed|it 'ed|.ɪt **-its** -ɪts **-iting** -ɪ.tɪŋ ⓊⓈ -ɪ.t̬ɪŋ **-ited** -ɪ.tɪd ⓊⓈ -ɪ.t̬ɪd

Edith 'iː.dɪθ

edition ɪ'dɪʃ.ᵊn, ə- ⓊⓈ ɪ- **-s** -z

editor 'ed.ɪ.təʳ ⓊⓈ -tɚ **-s** -z

editorial ˌed.ɪ'tɔː.ri.əl, -ə'- ⓊⓈ -ə'tɔːr.i- **-s** -z **-ly** -i

editorializ|e, -is|e ˌed.ɪ'tɔː.ri.ᵊl.aɪz, -ə'- ⓊⓈ -ə'tɔːr.i.ə.laɪz **-es** -ɪz **-ing** -ɪŋ **-ed** -d

editor-in-chief ˌed.ɪ.təʳ.ɪn'tʃiːf ⓊⓈ -t̬ɚ-

editorship 'ed.ɪ.tə.ʃɪp ⓊⓈ -t̬ɚ- **-s** -s

Edmond 'ed.mənd **-s** -z

Edmonton 'ed.mən.tən

Edmund 'ed.mənd **-s** -z

Edna 'ed.nə

Edom 'iː.dəm **-ite/s** -aɪt/s

Edridge 'ed.rɪdʒ

Edsall 'ed.sᵊl

educability ˌedʒ.ʊ.kə'bɪl.ə.ti, ˌed.jʊ-, -ɪt.i ⓊⓈ ˌedʒ.ʊ.kə'bɪl.ə.t̬i, ˌ-ə-

educable 'edʒ.ʊ.kə.bl̩, 'ed.jʊ- ⓊⓈ 'edʒ.ʊ-, '-ə-

edu|cate 'edʒ.ʊ|.keɪt, 'ed.jʊ- ⓊⓈ 'edʒ.ʊ|.keɪt, '-ə- **-cates** -keɪts **-cating** -keɪ.tɪŋ ⓊⓈ -keɪ.t̬ɪŋ **-cated** -keɪ.tɪd ⓊⓈ -keɪ.t̬ɪd **-cator/s** -keɪ.təʳ/z ⓊⓈ -keɪ.t̬ɚ/z

education ˌedʒ.ʊ'keɪ.ʃᵊn, ˌed.jʊ'- ⓊⓈ ˌedʒ.ʊ'keɪ.ʃᵊn, -ə'-

educational ˌedʒ.ʊ'keɪ.ʃᵊn.ᵊl, ˌed.jʊ'- ⓊⓈ ˌedʒ.ʊ'keɪ.ʃᵊn.ᵊl, -ə'- **-ly** -i

educationalist ˌedʒ.ʊ'keɪ.ʃᵊn.ᵊl.ɪst, ˌed.jʊ'- ⓊⓈ ˌedʒ.ʊ'keɪ.ʃᵊn.ᵊl.ɪst, -ə'- **-s** -s

educationist ˌedʒ.ʊ'keɪ.ʃᵊn.ɪst, ˌed.jʊ'- ⓊⓈ ˌedʒ.ʊ'keɪ.ʃᵊn.ɪst, -ə'- **-s** -s

educative 'edʒ.ʊ.kə.tɪv, 'ed.jʊ-, -keɪ- ⓊⓈ 'edʒ.ʊ.keɪ.t̬ɪv, '-ə-

educ|e ɪ'djuːs, iː-, -'dʒuːs ⓊⓈ -'duːs, -'djuːs **-es** -ɪz **-ing** -ɪŋ **-ed** -t

eduction ɪ'dʌk.ʃᵊn, iː- **-s** -z

Edward 'ed.wəd ⓊⓈ -wɚd **-(e)s** -z

Edwardian ed'wɔː.di.ən ⓊⓈ -'wɔːr-, -'wɑːr- **-s** -z

Edwin 'ed.wɪn

Edwina ed'wiː.nə

Edwinstowe 'ed.wɪn.stəʊ ⓊⓈ -stoʊ

-ee -iː, -i

Note: Suffix. May be stressed or unstressed, e.g. **employee** /ˌem.plɔɪ'iː, ɪm'plɔɪ.iː/, **committee** /kə'mɪt.i ⓊⓈ -'mɪt̬-/.

-ée, -ee -eɪ

Note: Suffix. May be stressed or unstressed in British English, e.g. **soirée** /'swɑː.reɪ, -'-/, but normally stressed in American English, e.g. /swɑː'reɪ/.

EEC ˌiː.iː'siː

EEG ˌiː.iː'dʒiː

eel iːl **-s** -z

eelgrass 'iːl.grɑːs ⓊⓈ -græs

eelworm 'iːl.wɜːm ⓊⓈ -wɜːrm **-s** -z

e'en iːn

eeny, meeny, miney, mo ˌiː.niˌmiː.niˌmaɪ.ni'məʊ ⓊⓈ -'moʊ

e'er eəʳ ⓊⓈ er

-eer -'ɪəʳ ⓊⓈ -'ɪr

Note: Suffix. Normally carries stress, e.g., **musket** /'mʌskɪt/, **musketeer** /ˌmʌs.kɪ'tɪəʳ ⓊⓈ -kə'tɪr/.

eer|ie 'ɪə.r|i ⓊⓈ 'ɪr|.i **-y** -i **-ily** -ɪ.li, -ᵊl.i **-iness** -ɪ.nəs, -ɪ.nɪs

Eeyore 'iː.ɔːʳ ⓊⓈ -ɔːr

eff ef **-ing** -ɪŋ ˌ**eff 'off** ; ˌ**effing and 'blinding**

effac|e ɪ'feɪs, ef'eɪs ⓊⓈ ɪ'feɪs, ə- **-es** -ɪz **-ing** -ɪŋ **-ed** -t **-ement** -mənt **-eable** -ə.bl̩

effect ɪ'fekt ⓊⓈ ɪ'fekt, ə-, iː- **-s** -s **-ing** -ɪŋ **-ed** -ɪd

effective ɪ'fek.tɪv ⓊⓈ ɪ'fek-, ə-, iː- **-s** -z **-ly** -li **-ness** -nəs, -nɪs

effectual ɪ'fek.tʃu.əl, -tju-, -tʃʊl, -tjʊl ⓊⓈ ɪ'fek.tʃuː.əl, ə-, iː- **-ly** -i

effectuality ɪˌfek.tʃu'æl.ə.ti, -tju'-, -ɪ.ti ⓊⓈ ɪˌfek.tʃuː'æl.ə.t̬i, ə-, iː-

effectu|ate ɪ'fek.tʃu|.eɪt, -tju- ⓊⓈ ɪ'fek.tʃuː-, ə-, iː- **-ates** -eɪts **-ating** -eɪ.tɪŋ ⓊⓈ -eɪ.t̬ɪŋ **-ated** -eɪ.tɪd ⓊⓈ -eɪ.t̬ɪd

effeminacy ɪ'fem.ɪ.nə.si, ef'em-, ə'fem-, '-ə-

effeminate (*adj.*) ɪ'fem.ɪ.nət, ef'em-, ə'fem-, '-ə-, -nɪt **-ly** -li **-ness** -nəs, -nɪs

effemi|nate (*v.*) ɪ'fem.ɪ|.neɪt, ef'em-, '-ə- **-nates** -neɪts **-nating** -neɪ.tɪŋ ⓊⓈ -neɪ.t̬ɪŋ **-nated** -neɪ.tɪd ⓊⓈ -neɪ.t̬ɪd

effendi ef'en.di, ɪ'fen-

efferent 'ef.ᵊr.ᵊnt, 'iː.fᵊr- ⓊⓈ 'ef.ᵊr-

effervesc|e ˌef.ə'ves ⓊⓈ -ɚ'- **-es** -ɪz **-ing** -ɪŋ **-ed** -t

effervescen|t ˌef.ə'ves.ən|t ⓊⓈ -ɚ'- **-ce** -ts *stress shift:* ˌeffervescent 'powder

effete ɪ'fiːt, ef'iːt

efficacious ˌef.ɪ'keɪ.ʃəs, -ə'- **-ly** -li **-ness** -nəs, -nɪs

efficacity ˌef.ɪ'kæs.ə.ti, -ə'-, -ɪ.ti ⓊⓈ -ə.t̬i

efficacy 'ef.ɪ.kə.si, '-ə-

efficiency ɪ'fɪʃ.ᵊnt.si, ə- ⓊⓈ ɪ'fɪʃ-, ə-, iː-

efficient ɪ'fɪʃ.ᵊnt, ə- ⓊⓈ ɪ'fɪʃ-, ə-, iː- **-ly** -li

Effie 'ef.i

effig|y 'ef.ɪ.dʒ|i, '-ə- **-ies** -iz

Effingham *in the UK:* 'ef.ɪŋ.əm ⓊⓈ 'ef.ɪŋ.əm, -hæm *in the US:* 'ef.ɪŋ.hæm

effloresc|e ˌef.lɔːˈres, -lɒrˈes, -ləˈres (US) -ləˈres, -lɔːr'- **-es** -ɪz **-ing** -ɪŋ **-ed** -t
efflorescen|t ˌef.lɔːˈres.ᵊn|t (US) -lə'-, -lɔːr'- **-ce** -*t*s
effluence ˈef.lu.ən*t*s
effluent ˈef.lu.ənt **-s** -s
effluvi|um ɪˈfluː.vi|.əm, efˈluː- **-a** -ə **-al** -əl
efflux ˈef.lʌks **-es** -ɪz
effluxion efˈluk.ʃᵊn, ɪˈflʌk- **-s** -z
effort ˈef.ət (US) -ɚt **-s** -s
effortless ˈef.ət.ləs, -lɪs (US) -ɚt- **-ly** -li **-ness** -nəs, -nɪs
effronter|y ɪˈfrʌn.tᵊr|.i, efˈrʌn- (US) efˈrʌn-, ɪˈfrʌn- **-ies** -iz
effulg|e ɪˈfʌldʒ, efˈʌldʒ **-es** -ɪz **-ing** -ɪŋ **-ed** -d
effulgen|ce ɪˈfʌl.dʒᵊn|*t*s, efˈʌl- **-t/ly** -t/li
effuse (*adj.*) ɪˈfjuːs, efˈjuːs
effus|e (*v.*) ɪˈfjuːz, efˈjuːz **-es** -ɪz **-ing** -ɪŋ **-ed** -d
effusion ɪˈfjuː.ʒᵊn, efˈjuː- **-s** -z
effusive ɪˈfjuː.sɪv, efˈjuː- **-ly** -li **-ness** -nəs, -nɪs
Efik ˈef.ɪk
EFL ˌiː.efˈel
eft eft **-s** -s
EFTA ˈef.tə
e.g. ˌiːˈdʒiː; fᵊr.ɪgˈzɑːm.pl̩ (US) ˌiːˈdʒiː; fɚ.ɪgˈzæm.pl̩
egad iːˈgæd, ɪ-
egalitarian ɪˌgæl.ɪˈteə.ri.ən, iː-, -əˈ-; ˌiː.gæl- (US) -ˈter.i- **-ism** -ɪ.zᵊm
Egan ˈiː.gᵊn
Egbert ˈeg.bət, -bɜːt (US) -bɚt, -bɜːrt
Egdon ˈeg.dən
Egeria ɪˈdʒɪə.ri.ə, iː- (US) -ˈdʒɪr.i-
Egerton ˈedʒ.ə.tᵊn (US) ˈ-ɚ-
Egeus *in Greek mythology:* ˈiː.dʒuːs; ɪˈdʒiː.əs, iː- (US) iːˈdʒiː.əs *Shakespearean character:* iːˈdʒiː.əs, ɪ-
egg eg **-s** -z **-ing** -ɪŋ **-ed** -d **-y** ˈ**egg** ˌ**timer** ; **have** ˈ**egg on one's** ˌ**face** ; **put** ˌ**all one's** ˌ**eggs in one** ˈ**basket**
eggcup ˈeg.kʌp **-s** -s
egghead ˈeg.hed **-s** -z
Eggleston ˈeg.l̩z.tᵊn (US) -l̩.stᵊn
Eggleton ˈeg.l̩.tᵊn
eggnog ˌegˈnɒg, ˈ-- (US) ˈeg.nɑːg **-s** -z
eggplant ˈeg.plɑːnt (US) -plænt **-s** -s
egg-shaped ˈeg.ʃeɪpt
eggshell ˈeg.ʃel **-s** -z
Egham ˈeg.əm
Eglamore, Eglamour ˈeg.lə.mɔːʳ (US) -mɔːr
eglantine (E) ˈeg.lən.taɪn, -tiːn
Eglingham ˈeg.lɪn.dʒəm
Eglinton ˈeg.lɪn.tən
Eglon ˈeg.lɒn (US) -lɑːn
Egmont ˈeg.mɒnt, -mənt (US) -mɑːnt
ego ˈiː.gəʊ, ˈeg.əʊ (US) ˈiː.goʊ, ˈeg.oʊ **-s** -z ˈ**ego** ˌ**trip**
egocentric ˌiː.gəʊˈsen.trɪk, ˌeg.əʊˈ- (US) ˌiː.goʊˈ-, ˌeg.oʊˈ- **-ally** -ᵊl.i, -li
egocentricity ˌiː.gəʊ.senˈtrɪs.ɪ.ti, ˌeg.əʊ-, -ə.ti (US) ˌiː.goʊ.senˈtrɪs.ə.t̬i, ˌeg.oʊ-
egocentrism ˌiː.gəʊˈsen.trɪ.zᵊm, ˌeg.əʊˈ- (US) ˌiː.goʊˈ-, ˌeg.oʊˈ-
ego|ism ˈiː.gəʊ|.ɪ.zᵊm, ˈeg.əʊ- (US) ˈiː.goʊ-, ˈeg.oʊ- **-ist/s** -ɪst/s
egoistic ˌiː.gəʊˈɪs.tɪk, ˌeg.əʊˈ- (US) ˌiː.goʊˈ-, ˌeg.oʊˈ- **-al** -ᵊl **-ally** -ᵊl.i, -li
egomania ˌiː.gəʊˈmeɪ.ni.ə, ˌeg.əʊˈ- (US) ˌiː.goʊˈ-, ˌeg.oʊˈ-
egomaniac ˌiː.gəʊˈmeɪ.ni.æk, ˌeg.əʊˈ- (US) ˌiː.goʊˈ-, ˌeg.oʊˈ- **-s** -s
Egon ˈeg.ən, ˈiː.gən, -gɒn (US) ˈeɪ.gɑːn, -gən
Note: The restaurant critic Egon Ronay is popularly pronounced as /ˈiː.gɒn/ in the UK.
egot|ism ˈiː.gəʊ.t|ɪ.zᵊm, ˈeg.əʊ- (US) ˈiː.goʊ-, ˈeg.oʊ- **-ist/s** -ɪst/s •
egotistic ˌiː.gəʊˈtɪs.tɪk, ˌeg.əʊˈ- (US) ˌiː.goʊˈ-, ˌeg.oʊˈ- **-al** -ᵊl **-ally** -ᵊl.i, -li
egregious ɪˈgriː.dʒəs, əˈgriː-, -dʒi.əs (US) iː-, ɪ- **-ly** -li **-ness** -nəs, -nɪs
Egremont ˈeg.rə.mənt, -rɪ-, -mɒnt (US) -mɑːnt
egress ˈiː.gres **-es** -ɪz
egression ɪˈgreʃ.ᵊn, iː- **-s** -z
egressive ɪˈgres.ɪv, iː-
egret ˈiː.grət, -grɪt, -gret (US) ˈiː.gret, ˈeg.ret, -rɪt **-s** -s
Egton ˈeg.tən
Egypt ˈiː.dʒɪpt
Egyptian ɪˈdʒɪp.ʃᵊn, ə-, iː- **-s** -z
Egyptolog|y ˌiː.dʒɪpˈtɒl.ə.dʒ|i (US) -ˈtɑː.lə- **-ist/s** -ɪst/s
eh eɪ
Ehrlich *European family name:* ˈeə.lɪk, -lɪx (US) ˈer- *US family name:* ˈɜː.lɪk (US) ˈɜːr-, ˈer-
eider ˈaɪ.dəʳ (US) -dɚ **-s** -z ˈ**eider** ˌ**duck**
eiderdown ˈaɪ.də.daʊn (US) -dɚ- **-s** -z
Eifel ˈaɪ.fᵊl
Eiffel Tower ˌaɪ.fᵊlˈtaʊəʳ (US) -ˈtaʊɚ **-s** -z
Eiger ˈaɪ.gəʳ (US) -gɚ
eight eɪt **-s** -s
eighteen eɪˈtiːn **-s** -z **-th/s** -θ/s *stress shift:* ˌeighteen ˈmonths
eightfold ˈeɪt.fəʊld (US) -foʊld
eighth eɪtθ **-s** -s
eightieth ˈeɪ.ti.əθ, -ti.ɪθ (US) -t̬i.əθ **-s** -s
eightsome ˈeɪt.sᵊm
eight|y ˈeɪ.t|i (US) -t̬|i **-ies** -iz
eightyfold ˈeɪ.ti.fəʊld (US) -t̬i.foʊld
eighty-six ˌeɪ.tiˈsɪks (US) -t̬iˈ- **-es** -ɪz **-ing** -ɪŋ **-ed** -t
Eilat eɪˈlɑːt, -ˈlæt (US) -ˈlɑːt
Eilean ˈel.ən, ˈiː.lən
Eileen ˈaɪ.liːn (US) aɪˈliːn
Eiloart ˈaɪ.ləʊ.ɑːt (US) -loʊ.ɑːrt
Eindhoven ˈaɪnd.həʊ.vᵊn (US) -hoʊ-
Einstein ˈaɪn.staɪn
einsteinium ˌaɪnˈstaɪ.ni.əm
Eire ˈeə.rə (US) ˈer.ə, -iː; ˈaɪ.rə, -riː
eirenicon aɪəˈriː.nɪ.kɒn, -ˈren.ɪ- (US) aɪˈriː.nɪ.kɑːn **-s** -z
Eisenhower ˈaɪ.zᵊn.haʊəʳ (US) -haʊɚ
eisteddfod (E) aɪˈsteð.vɒd, ɪ-, -ˈsted.fəd (US) -ˈsteð.vɑːd, eɪ- **-s** -z
either ˈaɪ.ðəʳ, ˈiː- (US) ˈiː.ðɚ, ˈaɪ-
ejacu|late (*v.*) ɪˈdʒæk.jə|.leɪt, iː-, -jʊ- **-lates** -leɪts **-lating** -leɪ.tɪŋ (US) -leɪ.t̬ɪŋ **-lated** -leɪ.tɪd (US) -leɪ.t̬ɪd
ejaculate (*n.*) ɪˈdʒæk.jə.lət, iː-, -jʊ-, -lɪt, -leɪt (US) -lət, -lɪt
ejaculation ɪˌdʒæk.jəˈleɪ.ʃᵊn, iː-, -jʊˈ- **-s** -z
ejaculative ɪˈdʒæk.jə.lə.tɪv, -jʊ-, -leɪ.tɪv (US) -jə.lə.t̬ɪv
ejaculatory ɪˈdʒæk.jə.lə.tᵊr.i, iː-, -jʊ-, -leɪ-, -tri; ɪˌdʒæk.jəˈleɪ-, iː-, -jʊˈ- (US) ɪˈdʒæk.jə.lə.tɔːr.i, iː-, -jʊ-
eject ɪˈdʒekt, iː- **-s** -s **-ing** -ɪŋ **-ed** -ɪd
ejection ɪˈdʒek.ʃᵊn, iː- **-s** -z
ejective ɪˈdʒek.tɪv, iː- **-s** -z
ejectment ɪˈdʒekt.mənt, iː- **-s** -s
ejector ɪˈdʒek.təʳ, iː- (US) -tɚ **-s** -z
ejusdem generis eɪˌʊs.demˈgen.ᵊr.ɪs (US) edʒˌuːs.demˈgen.ɚ.əs; iː.dʒəs.demˈdʒen-
Ekaterinburg ɪˌkæt.ᵊrˈiːn.bɜːg (US) -bɜːrg
ek|e iːk **-es** -s **-ing** -ɪŋ **-ed** -t
EKG ˌiː.keɪˈdʒiː
Ekron ˈek.rɒn (US) -rɑːn
Ektachrome® ˈek.tə.krəʊm (US) -kroʊm
el el
elaborate (*adj.*) ɪˈlæb.ᵊr.ət, -ɪt **-ly** -li **-ness** -nəs, -nɪs
elabor|ate (*v.*) ɪˈlæb.ᵊ.r|eɪt **-ates** -eɪts **-ating** -eɪ.tɪŋ (US) -eɪ.t̬ɪŋ **-ated** -eɪ.tɪd (US) -eɪ.t̬ɪd **-ator/s** -eɪ.təʳ/z (US) -eɪ.t̬ɚ/z
elaboration ɪˌlæb.əˈreɪ.ʃᵊn **-s** -z
elaborative ɪˈlæb.ᵊr.ə.tɪv, -eɪ- (US) -ə.t̬ɪv
Elaine ɪˈleɪn, ə-, elˈeɪn
El Al® ˌelˈæl
El Alamein ˌelˈæl.ə.meɪn; elˌæl.əˈmeɪn (US) ˌelˈæl.ə.mein, -ˈɑː.lə-; elˌæl.əˈmeɪn, -ˌɑː.ləˈ-
Elam ˈiː.ləm **-ite/s** -aɪt/s
élan eɪˈlɑ̃ːŋ, ɪ-, -ˈlɑːn (US) -ˈlɑːn, -ˈlɑ̃ːŋ, -ˈlæn *stress shift, see compound:* ˌ**élan vi**ˈ**tal**
eland (E) ˈiː.lənd **-s** -z
elaps|e ɪˈlæps **-es** -ɪz **-ing** -ɪŋ **-ed** -t

elastic ɪ'læs.tɪk, -'lɑː.stɪk (US) -'læs.tɪk **-s** -s **-ally** -ᵊl.i, -li **eˌlastic 'band**

elasti|cate ɪ'læs.tɪ.keɪt, -'lɑː.stɪ-, -stə- (US) -'læs.tɪ- **-cates** -keɪts **-cating** -keɪ.tɪŋ (US) -keɪ.t̬ɪŋ **-cated** -keɪ.tɪd (US) -keɪ.t̬ɪŋ

elasticity ˌɪl.æs'tɪs.ə.ti, ˌel-, ˌiː.læs-, -lə'stɪs-, -lɑː'-, -ɪ.ti; ɪˌlæs'tɪs-, -ˌlɑː'stɪs- (US) ɪˌlæs'tɪs.ə.t̬i, ˌiː.læs'-

elastin ɪ'læs.tɪn, ə-, -'lɑː.stɪn (US) ɪ'læs.tɪn

Elastoplast® ɪ'læs.təʊ.plɑːst, el-, iː'læs-, -plæst; -'lɑː.stəʊ.plɑːst (US) ɪ'læs.toʊ.plæst, iː-, -tə-

e|late ɪ|'leɪt, iː- **-lates** -leɪts **-lating** -leɪ.tɪŋ (US) -leɪ.t̬ɪŋ **-lated/ly** -leɪ.tɪd/li (US) -leɪ.t̬ɪd/li

elation ɪ'leɪ.ʃᵊn, iː-

Elba 'el.bə

Elbe 'el.bə, elb

elbow 'el.bəʊ (US) -boʊ **-s** -z **-ing** -ɪŋ **-ed** -d **'elbow ˌgrease**; **'elbow ˌroom**

El Cid ˌel'sɪd

elder (E) 'el.dəʳ (US) -dɚ **-s** -z **ˌelder 'statesman**

elderberr|y 'el.dəˌber|.i, -bᵊr- (US) -dɚˌber- **-ies** -iz

elderflower 'el.dəˌflaʊəʳ (US) -dɚ.ˌflaʊɚ **-s** -z

elderl|y 'el.dᵊl|.i (US) -dɚ.l|i **-iness** -ɪ.nəs, -ɪ.nɪs

eldest 'el.dɪst, -dəst

Eldon 'el.dᵊn

El Dorado, Eldorado ˌel.də'rɑː.dəʊ, -dɒr'ɑː- (US) -də'rɑː.doʊ, -'reɪ-

Eldred 'el.drɪd, -dred, -drəd

Eldridge 'el.drɪdʒ

Eleanor 'el.ɪ.nəʳ, '-ə- (US) -nɚ, -nɔːr

Eleanora ˌel.i.ə'nɔː.rə (US) -'nɔːr.ə-

Eleazar ˌel.i'eɪ.zəʳ (US) -zɚ

elecampane ˌel.ɪ.kæm'peɪn, ˌ-ə- **-s** -z

elect ɪ'lekt **-s** -s **-ing** -ɪŋ **-ed** -ɪd **-able** -ə.bl̩

election ɪ'lek.ʃᵊn **-s** -z

electioneer ɪˌlek.ʃə'nɪəʳ (US) -'nɪr **-s** -z **-ing** -ɪŋ **-ed** -d **-er/s** -əʳ/z (US) -ɚ/z

elective ɪ'lek.tɪv **-ly** -li

elector ɪ'lek.təʳ (US) -tɚ **-s** -z

electoral ɪ'lek.tᵊr.ᵊl, '-trᵊl

electorate ɪ'lek.tᵊr.ət, -ɪt, '-trət, '-trɪt **-s** -s

Electra ɪ'lek.trə **E'lectra ˌcomplex**

electric ɪ'lek.trɪk **-al** -ᵊl **-ally** -ᵊl.i, -li **-s** -s **eˌlectric 'blanket**; **eˌlectric 'chair**; **eˌlectric gui'tar**; **eˌlectric 'shock**; **eˌlectric 'shock ˌtherapy**

electrician ˌel.ɪk'trɪʃ.ᵊn, ˌiː.lek'-; ɪˌlek'- (US) ɪˌlek'-, ˌiː.lek'- **-s** -z

electricity ˌel.ɪk'trɪs.ə.ti, ˌiː.lek-, -ɪ.ti; ɪˌlek'- (US) ɪˌlek'-; ˌiː.lek'-

electrification ɪˌlek.trɪ.fɪ'keɪ.ʃᵊn, -trə- **-s** -z

electri|fy ɪ'lek.trɪ|.faɪ, -trə- **-fies** -faɪz **-fying** -faɪ.ɪŋ **-fied** -faɪd **-fiable** -faɪ.ə.bl̩

electro- ɪ.lek.trəʊ-; ˌel.ɪk'trɒ-, ˌiː.lek'-; ɪˌlek'- (US) ɪ.lek.troʊ-; ɪˌlek'trɑː-; ˌiː.lek'-

Note: Prefix. Either takes primary or secondary stress on the second syllable, e.g. **electrocute** /ɪ'lek.trə.kjuːt/, **electrocution** /ɪˌlek.trə'kjuː.ʃᵊn/, or primary stress on the third syllable, with secondary stress on either the first or second syllable, e.g. **electrolysis** /ˌel.ɪk'trɒl.ɪ.sɪs, ɪˌlek'- (US) ɪˌlek'trɑː.lə-, ˌiː.lek'-/.

electrobiology ɪˌlek.trəʊ.baɪ'ɒl.ə.dʒi (US) -troʊ.baɪ'ɑː.lə-

electrocardiogram ɪˌlek.trəʊ'kɑː.di.əʊ.græm (US) -troʊ'kɑːr.di.ə- **-s** -z

electrocardiograph ɪˌlek.trəʊ'kɑː.di.əʊ.grɑːf, -græf (US) -troʊ'kɑːr.di.ə.græf **-s** -s

electrochemistry ɪˌlek.trəʊ'kem.ɪ.stri, -ə.stri (US) -troʊ'kem.ə-

electroconvulsive ɪˌlek.trəʊ.kən'vʌl.sɪv (US) -troʊ- **eˌlectroconˌvulsive 'therapy**

electro|cute ɪ'lek.trə|.kjuːt **-cutes** -kjuːts **-cuting** -kjuː.tɪŋ (US) -kjuː.t̬ɪŋ **-cuted** -kjuː.tɪd (US) -kjuː.t̬ɪd

electrocution ɪˌlek.trə'kjuː.ʃᵊn **-s** -z

electrode ɪ'lek.trəʊd (US) -troʊd **-s** -z

electrodynamic ɪˌlek.trəʊ.daɪ'næm.ɪk, -dɪ'- (US) -troʊ.daɪ'- **-s** -s

electroencephalo|gram ɪˌlek.trəʊ.en'sef.ᵊl.əʊ|.græm, -ɪn'-, -'kef-, -eŋ'kef-, -ɪŋ'kef- (US) -troʊ.en'sef.ə.loʊ-, -lə- **-s** -z **-graph/s** -grɑːf/s, -græf/s (US) -græf/s

electrokinetic ɪˌlek.trəʊ.kɪ'net.ɪk, -kaɪ'- (US) -troʊ.kɪ'net̬-, -trə- **-s** -s

electrolier ɪˌlek.trəʊ'lɪəʳ (US) -trə'lɪr **-s** -z

Electrolux® ɪ'lek.trəʊ.lʌks (US) -trə-

electrolys|is ˌel.ɪk'trɒl.ə.s|ɪs, ˌiː.lek-, -ɪ.s|ɪs; ɪˌlek'-, ə- (US) ɪˌlek'trɑː.lə-; ˌiː.lek- **-es** -iːz

electrolyte ɪ'lek.trə.laɪt **-s** -s

electrolytic ɪˌlek.trə'lɪt.ɪk (US) -'lɪt̬-

electrolyz|e, -ys|e ɪ'lek.trᵊl.aɪz (US) -trə.laɪz **-es** -ɪz **-ing** -ɪŋ **-ed** -d

electromagnet ɪˌlek.trəʊ'mæg.nɪt, -nət (US) -troʊ'-, -trə'- **-s** -s **-ism** -ɪ.zᵊm

electromagnetic ɪˌlek.trəʊ.mæg'net.ɪk, -məg'- (US) -troʊ.mæg'net̬-, -trə-

electrometer ˌel.ɪk'trɒm.ɪ.təʳ, ˌiː.lek-, -mə.təʳ; ɪˌlek'- (US) ɪ.lek'trɑː.mə.t̬ɚ; ˌiː.lek'- **-s** -z

electromotive ɪˌlek.trəʊ'məʊ.tɪv (US) -troʊ'moʊ.t̬ɪv, -trə'-

electromotor ɪˌlek.trəʊ'məʊ.təʳ (US) -troʊ'moʊ.t̬ɚ, -trə'- **-s** -z

electron ɪ'lek.trɒn (US) -trɑːn **-s** -z

electronic ˌel.ek'trɒn.ɪk, -ɪk'-, ˌiː.lek'-; ɪˌlek'- (US) ɪˌlek'trɑː.nɪk; ˌiː.lek'- **-s** -s **-ally** -ᵊl.i, -li *stress shift, see compound:* **ˌelectronic 'mail**

electropalatogram ɪˌlek.trəʊ'pæl.ə.təʊ.græm (US) -troʊ'pæl.ə.t̬ə- **-s** -z

electropalatography ɪˌlek.trəʊˌpæl.ə'tɒg.rə.fi (US) -troʊˌpæl.ə'tɑː.grə-

electrophone ɪ'lek.trə.fəʊn (US) -foʊn **-s** -z

electrophorus ˌel.ɪk'trɒf.ᵊr.əs, ˌiː.lek'- (US) ɪˌlek'trɑː.fɚ-; ˌiː.lek'- **-es** -ɪz

electropla|te ɪ'lek.trəʊ.pleɪ|t, ɪˌlek.trəʊ'pleɪ|t (US) ɪ'lek.troʊ.pleɪ|t, iː-, -trə- **-tes** -ts **-ting** -tɪŋ (US) -t̬ɪŋ **-ted** -tɪd (US) -t̬ɪd **-ter/s** -təʳ/z (US) -t̬ɚ/z

electropolar ɪˌlek.trəʊ'pəʊ.ləʳ (US) -troʊ'poʊ.lɚ

electropositive ɪˌlek.trəʊ'pɒz.ə.tɪv, -ɪ.tɪv (US) -troʊ'pɑː.zə.t̬ɪv

electroscope ɪ'lek.trəʊ.skəʊp (US) -troʊ.skoʊp, -trə- **-s** -s

electrostatic ɪˌlek.trəʊ'stæt.ɪk (US) -troʊ'stæt̬- **-s** -s

electrotherapeutic ɪˌlek.trəʊˌθer.ə'pjuː.tɪk (US) -troʊˌθer.ə'pjuː.t̬ɪk **-s** -s

electrotherapy ɪˌlek.trəʊ'θer.ə.pi (US) -troʊ'-

electrothermal ɪˌlek.trəʊ'θɜː.mᵊl (US) -troʊ'θɜːr-

electrotype ɪ'lek.trəʊ.taɪp (US) -troʊ- **-s** -s

electrovalency ɪˌlek.trəʊ'veɪ.lənt.si (US) -troʊ'-

electrum ɪ'lek.trəm

electuar|y ɪ'lek.tjʊə.r|i (US) -tʃuː.er|.i **-ies** -iz

eleemosynary ˌel.i.iː'mɒs.ɪ.nᵊr.i, ˌel.iː'-, ˌel.ɪ'-, -'mɒz-, -'məʊ.zɪ-, -zᵊn.ᵊr- (US) ˌel.ɪ'mɑː.sə.ner.i, -iː.ə'-

elegance 'el.ɪ.gᵊnts (US) '-ə-

elegant 'el.ɪ.gᵊnt (US) '-ə- **-ly** -li

elegiac ˌel.ɪ'dʒaɪ.ək, -ə'-, -æk (US) ˌel.ɪ'dʒaɪ.ək, -ə'-, -æk; ɪ'liː.dʒiː.æk **-s** -s **-al** -ᵊl

elegist 'el.ɪ.dʒɪst, '-ə- **-s** -s

elegit ɪ'liː.dʒɪt, el'iː-

elegiz|e, -is|e 'el.ɪ.dʒaɪz, '-ə- **-es** -ɪz **-ing** -ɪŋ **-ed** -d

eleg|y 'el.ɪ.dʒ|i, '-ə- **-ies** -iz

element 'el.ɪ.mənt, '-ə- (US) '-ə- **-s** -s

elemental ˌel.ɪ'men.tᵊl, -ə'- (US) -ə'men.t̬ᵊl **-s** -z **-ly** -i

elementar|y ˌel.ɪˈmen.tᵊr|.i, -əˈ-, ˈ-tr|i (US) -əˈmen.t̬ɚ|.i, ˈ-tr|i **-ily** -ɪ.li, -ᵊl.i **-iness** -ɪ.nəs, -ɪ.nɪs **eleˈmentary ˌschool**
elemi ˈel.ɪ.mi
elenchus ɪˈleŋ.kəs, ə-
Eleonora ˌel.i.əˈnɔː.rə (US) -ˈnɔːr.ə
Eleonore ˈel.i.ə.nɔːʳ (US) -nɔːr
elephant ˈel.ɪ.fənt, ˈ-ə- **-s** -s
elephantiasis ˌel.ɪ.fənˈtaɪə.sɪs, ˌ-ə-, -fænˈ-
elephantine ˌel.ɪˈfæn.taɪn, -əˈ- (US) -taɪn, tiːn, ˈel.ə.fən-
Eleusinian ˌel.juːˈsɪn.i.ən, -uːˈ-
Eleusis elˈjuː.sɪs, ɪˈljuː-, ə-, -ˈluː- (US) ɪˈluː.sɪs
Eleuthera ɪˈluː.θᵊr.ə, elˈuː-, -ˈjuː- (US) ɪˈluː-
ele|vate ˈel.ɪ|.veɪt, ˈ-ə- **-vates** -veɪts **-vating** -veɪ.tɪŋ (US) -veɪ.t̬ɪŋ **-vated** -veɪ.tɪd (US) -veɪ.t̬ɪd
elevation ˌel.ɪˈveɪ.ʃᵊn, -əˈ- **-s** -z
elevator ˈel.ɪ.veɪ.təʳ, ˈ-ə- (US) -t̬ɚ **-s** -z
elevatory ˌel.ɪˈveɪ.tᵊr.i, -əˈ-, ˈ-tri (US) -t̬ɚ.i
eleven ɪˈlev.ᵊn, ə- **-s** -z **-th/s** -θ/s
eleven-plus ɪˌlev.ᵊnˈplʌs, ə-, -əmˈ- (US) -ənˈ- **-es** -ɪz
elevenses ɪˈlev.ᵊn.zɪz, ə-
el|f el|f **-ves** -vz
elfin ˈel.fɪn **-s** -z
elfish ˈel.fɪʃ **-ly** -li
Elfrida elˈfriː.də
Elgar *composer:* ˈel.gɑːʳ (US) -gɑːr *surname:* ˈel.gɑːʳ, -gəʳ (US) -gɑːr, -gɚ
Elgin ˈel.gɪn (US) -gɪn, -dʒɪn ˌ**Elgin ˈMarbles**
El Greco ˌelˈgrek.əʊ (US) -oʊ
Elham ˈiː.ləm
Eli ˈiː.laɪ
Elia ˈiː.li.ə
Elias ɪˈlaɪəs, elˈaɪ-, əˈlaɪ-, -ˈlaɪ.æs
Elibank ˈel.ɪ.bæŋk
elic|it ɪˈlɪs|.ɪt, ə-, iː- **-its** -ɪts **-iting** -ɪ.tɪŋ (US) -ɪ.t̬ɪŋ **-ited** -ɪ.tɪd (US) -ɪ.t̬ɪd
elicitation ɪˌlɪs.ɪˈteɪ.ʃᵊn, ə-, iː-, -əˈ-
elid|e ɪˈlaɪd, iː- **-es** -z **-ing** -ɪŋ **-ed** -ɪd **-able** -ə.bl̩
Elie ˈiː.li
eligibility ˌel.ɪ.dʒəˈbɪl.ə.ti, ˌ-ə-, -dʒɪˈ-, -ɪ.ti (US) -dʒəˈbɪl.ə.t̬i
eligib|le ˈel.ɪ.dʒə.b|l̩, ˈ-ə-, -dʒɪ- (US) -dʒə- **-ly** -li **-leness** -l̩.nəs, -nɪs
Elihu ɪˈlaɪ.hjuː, elˈaɪ- (US) ˈel.ɪ-; iːˈlaɪ-, ɪ-
Elijah ɪˈlaɪ.dʒə
Eliman ˈel.ɪ.mən
elimi|nate ɪˈlɪm.ɪ|.neɪt, ə-, ˈ-ə- **-nates** -neɪts **-nating** -neɪ.tɪŋ (US) -neɪ.t̬ɪŋ **-nated** -neɪ.tɪd (US) -neɪ.t̬ɪd **-nator/s** -neɪ.təʳ/z (US) -neɪ.t̬ɚ/z
elimination ɪˌlɪm.ɪˈneɪ.ʃᵊn, ə-, -əˈ- **-s** -z
Elinor ˈel.ɪ.nəʳ, ˈ-ə- (US) -nɚ, nɔːr
Eliot ˈel.i.ət
Eliotson ˈel.i.ət.sᵊn
Eliott ˈel.i.ət
Eliphaz ˈel.ɪ.fæz
Elis ˈiː.lɪs
Elisabeth ɪˈlɪz.ə.bəθ, ə-
Elise ɪˈliːz (US) ɪˈliːz, -ˈliːs
Elisha *prophet:* ɪˈlaɪ.ʃə *place in Northumberland:* elˈɪʃ.ə
elision ɪˈlɪʒ.ᵊn **-s** -z
elite, élite ɪˈliːt, eɪ-
elitism, élitism ɪˈliː.tɪ.zᵊm, eɪˈliː-
elitist, élitist ɪˈliː.tɪst, eɪˈliː- **-s** -s
elixir ɪˈlɪk.səʳ, elˈɪk-, əˈlɪk-, iː-, -sɪəʳ (US) -sɚ **-s** -z
Eliza ɪˈlaɪ.zə
Elizabeth ɪˈlɪz.ə.bəθ, ə-
Elizabethan ɪˌlɪz.əˈbiː.θᵊn, ə- **-s** -z *stress shift:* Eˌlizabethan ˈpoet
Elizabethian ɪˌlɪz.əˈbiː.θi.ən, ə- **-s** -z *stress shift:* Eˌlizabethian ˈpoet
elk elk **-s** -s
Elkhart ˈelk.hɑːt (US) -hɑːrt
Elkin ˈel.kɪn
Elkington ˈel.kɪŋ.tən
Elkins ˈel.kɪnz
ell el **-s** -z
Ella ˈel.ə
Elland ˈel.ənd
Ellangowan ˌel.ənˈgaʊən, -əŋˈ-
Ellen ˈel.ən, -ɪn
Ellenborough ˈel.ən.bᵊr.ə, -ɪn- (US) -oʊ
Ellery ˈel.ᵊr.i
Ellesmere ˈelz.mɪəʳ (US) -mɪr
Ellice ˈel.ɪs
Ellicott ˈel.ɪ.kət, -kɒt (US) -kət, -kɑːt
Elliman ˈel.ɪ.mən
Ellingham *in Northumberland:* ˈel.ɪn.dʒəm *surname:* ˈel.ɪŋ.əm
Ellington ˈel.ɪŋ.tən
Elliot ˈel.i.ət
Elliotson ˈel.i.ət.sᵊn
Elliott ˈel.i.ət
ellipse ɪˈlɪps **-s** -ɪz
ellips|is ɪˈlɪp.s|ɪs **-es** -iːz
ellipsoid ɪˈlɪp.sɔɪd **-s** -z
ellipsoidal ˌel.ɪpˈsɔɪ.dᵊl; ɪˌlɪpˈ-, elˌɪp- (US) ɪˌlɪpˈ-; ˌel.ɪpˈ-
elliptic ɪˈlɪp.tɪk **-al** -ᵊl **-ally** -ᵊl.i, -li
ellipticity ˌel.ɪpˈtɪs.ə.ti, ˌɪl-, -ɪ.ti (US) ɪˌlɪpˈtɪs.ə.t̬i; ˌel.ɪpˈ-
Ellis ˈel.ɪs
Ellison ˈel.ɪ.sᵊn
Elliston ˈel.ɪ.stᵊn
Ellon ˈel.ən
Ellsworth ˈelz.wəθ, -wɜːθ (US) -wɚθ, -wɜːrθ
Ellwood ˈel.wʊd
elm (E) elm **-s** -z
Elmer ˈel.məʳ (US) -mɚ
Elmer Gantry ˌel.məˈgæn.tri (US) -mɚˈ-
Elmes elmz
Elmhurst ˈelm.hɜːst (US) -hɜːrst
Elmina elˈmiː.nə
Elmo ˈel.məʊ (US) -moʊ
Elmore ˈel.mɔːʳ (US) -mɔːr
Elmsley ˈelmz.li
Elmwood ˈelm.wʊd
elocution ˌel.əˈkjuː.ʃᵊn
elocutionary ˌel.əˈkjuː.ʃᵊn.ᵊr.i, -ri (US) -er.i
elocutionist ˌel.əˈkjuː.ʃᵊn.ɪst **-s** -s
Elohim elˈəʊ.hɪm, ɪˈləʊ-, ə-, -hiːm; ˌel.əʊˈhiːm (US) elˈoʊ.hɪm, ɪˈloʊ-, ə-, -hiːm, ˌel.oʊˈhɪm, -ˈoʊ-
Eloi ɪˈləʊ.aɪ; ˈiː.ləʊ.aɪ, -lɔɪ (US) ˈiː.lɔɪ, ˈeɪ-
Eloisa ˌel.əʊˈiː.zə, -sə (US) -oʊˈ-
Éloise, Eloise ˌel.əʊˈiːz (US) -oʊˈ-
elon|gate ˈiː.lɒŋ|.geɪt (US) ɪˈlɑːŋ-, -ˈlɔːŋ- **-gates** -geɪts **-gating** -geɪ.tɪŋ (US) -geɪ.t̬ɪŋ **-gated** -geɪ.tɪd (US) -geɪ.t̬ɪd
elongation ˌiː.lɒŋˈgeɪ.ʃᵊn (US) ˌiː.lɑːŋˈ-, -lɔːŋˈ-; ɪˌlɑːŋˈ-, -ˌlɔːŋˈ- **-s** -z
elop|e ɪˈləʊp (US) -ˈloʊp **-es** -s **-ing** -ɪŋ **-ed** -t **-ement/s** -mənt/s
eloquence ˈel.ə.kwən*t*s
eloquent ˈel.ə.kwənt **-ly** -li
El Paso ˌelˈpæs.əʊ (US) -oʊ
Elphick ˈel.fɪk
Elphin ˈel.fɪn
Elphinstone ˈel.fɪn.stən
Elsa *English name:* ˈel.sə *German name:* ˈel.zə
El Salvador ˌelˈsæl.və.dɔːʳ (US) -dɔːr
Elsan® ˈel.sæn
else els **-ˈs** -ɪz
elsewhere ˌelsˈ*h*weəʳ, ˈ-- (US) ˈels.*h*wer
Elsie ˈel.si
Elsinore ˈel.sɪ.nɔːʳ, ˌ--ˈ- (US) ˈel.sə.nɔːr, ˌ--ˈ-
Note: The stressing /ˌ--ˈ-/ has to be used in Shakespeare's 'Hamlet'.
Elsmere ˈelz.mɪəʳ (US) -mɪr
Elson ˈel.sᵊn
Elspeth ˈel.spəθ, -speθ
Elstree ˈel.striː, ˈelz.triː, -tri
Elswick ˈel.sɪk, ˈel.zɪk, ˈelz.wɪk
Note: **Elswick** in Tyne and Wear is locally /ˈel.sɪk/ or /ˈel.zɪk/.
Elsworthy ˈelz.wɜː.ði (US) -wɜːr-
ELT ˌiː.elˈtiː
Eltham ˈel.təm
Elton ˈel.tᵊn
eluci|date ɪˈluː.sɪ|.deɪt, əˈluː-, -ˈljuː-, -sə- (US) ɪˈluː.sɪ-, -sə- **-dates** -deɪts **-dating** -deɪ.tɪŋ (US) -deɪ.t̬ɪŋ **-dated** -deɪ.tɪd (US) -deɪ.t̬ɪd **-dator/s** -deɪ.təʳ/z (US) -deɪ.t̬ɚ/z
elucidation ɪˌluː.sɪˈdeɪ.ʃᵊn, əˌluː-, -ˌljuː-, -səˈ- (US) ɪˌluː.sɪˈdeɪ-, -səˈ- **-s** -z

elucidative ɪ'luː.sɪ.deɪ.tɪv, ə'luː-, -'ljuː-, -sə-, -də- (US) ɪ'luː.sɪ.deɪ.t̬ɪv, -sə-
elucidatory ɪ'luː.sɪ.deɪ.tᵊr.i, ə'luː-, -'ljuː-, -sə-, -tri; ɪˌluː.sɪ'deɪ-, ə-, -ˌljuː-, -sə'- (US) ɪ'luː.sɪ.deɪ.tɔːr.i, -sə-; ɪˌluː.sɪ'deɪ.t̬ɚ-, -sə'-
elud|e ɪ'luːd, ə'luːd, -'ljuːd (US) ɪ'luːd **-es** -z **-ing** -ɪŋ **-ed** -ɪd
elusion ɪ'luː.ʒᵊn, ə'luː, -'ljuː- (US) ɪ'luː- **-s** -z
elusive ɪ'luː.sɪv, ə'luː-, -'ljuː- (US) ɪ'luː- **-ly** -li **-ness** -nəs, -nɪs
elusory ɪ'luː.sᵊr.i, ə'luː-, -'ljuː- (US) ɪ'luː-
elvan 'el.vən
Elvedon 'elv.dən, 'el.dən
elver 'el.vəʳ (US) -vɚ **-s** -z
elves (*plur. of* **elf**) elvz
Elvey 'el.vi
Elvin 'el.vɪn
Elvira el'vɪə.rə, -'vaɪə- (US) -'vaɪ.rə, -'vɪr.ə
Elvis 'el.vɪs
Elwell 'el.wel, -wəl
Elwes 'el.wɪz, -wɪs, -wez
Ely *cities:* 'iː.li *first name in US:* 'iː.laɪ
Elyot 'el.i.ət
Elyse el'iːz (US) ɪ'liːs
Elysée eɪ'liː.zeɪ, ɪ-, ə- (US) ˌeɪ.liː'zeɪ
Elysi|an ɪ'lɪz.i|.ən, iː- (US) ɪ'lɪʒ|.ən **-um** -əm **Eˌlysian 'fields**
elzevir (E) 'el.zɪ.vɪəʳ, -sɪ-, -zə-, -sə- (US) -vɪr
em- em-, ɪm-
Note: Prefix. Either takes primary or secondary stress and is pronounced /em-/, e.g. **emblem** /'em.bləm/, **emblematic** /ˌem.blə'mæt.ɪk (US) -'mæt̬-/, or is unstressed and may be pronounced either /ɪm-/ or /em-/, e.g. **embed** /ɪm'bed, em- (US) em-, ɪm-/.
em em **-s** -z
'em (*weak form of* **them**) əm, m
emaci|ate ɪ'meɪ.ʃi|.eɪt, iː-, -si- **-ates** -eɪts **-ating** -eɪ.tɪŋ (US) -eɪ.t̬ɪŋ **-ated** -eɪ.tɪd (US) -eɪ.t̬ɪd
emaciation ɪˌmeɪ.ʃi'eɪ.ʃᵊn, iː-, -si'-
e-mail, E-mail 'iː.meɪl **-s** -z **-ing** -ɪŋ **-ed** -d
emalangeni (*plur. of* **lilangeni**) 'em.ə.lɑːŋˌgen.i (US) ˌem.ə.lən'gen-
ema|nate 'em.ə|.neɪt **-nates** -neɪts **-nating** -neɪ.tɪŋ (US) -neɪ.t̬ɪŋ **-nated** -neɪ.tɪd (US) -neɪ.t̬ɪd **-native** -neɪ.tɪv (US) -neɪ.t̬ɪv
emanation ˌem.ə'neɪ.ʃᵊn **-s** -z
emanci|pate ɪ'mænt.sɪ|.peɪt, -sə- **-pates** -peɪts **-pating** -peɪ.tɪŋ (US) -peɪ.t̬ɪŋ **-pated** -peɪ.tɪd (US) -peɪ.t̬ɪd **-pator/s** -peɪ.təʳ/z (US) -peɪ.t̬ɚ/z
emancipation ɪˌmænt.sɪ'peɪ.ʃᵊn, -sə'- **-s** -z
Emanuel ɪ'mæn.ju.əl, -el
emasculate (*adj.*) ɪ'mæs.kjʊ.lɪt, iː-, -kjə-, -lət
emascu|late (*v.*) ɪ'mæs.kjʊ|.leɪt, iː-, -kjə- **-lates** -leɪts **-lating** -leɪ.tɪŋ (US) -leɪ.t̬ɪŋ **-lated** -leɪ.tɪd (US) -leɪ.t̬ɪd **-lator/s** -leɪ.təʳ/z (US) -leɪ.t̬ɚ/z
emasculation ɪˌmæs.kjʊ'leɪ.ʃᵊn, iː-, -kjə'- **-s** -z
embalm ɪm'bɑːm, em- (US) em-, ɪm- **-s** -z **-ing** -ɪŋ **-ed** -d **-er/s** -əʳ/z (US) -ɚ/z **-ment/s** -mənt/s
embank ɪm'bæŋk, em- (US) em-, ɪm- **-s** -s **-ing** -ɪŋ **-ed** -t
embankment (E) ɪm'bæŋk.mənt, em- (US) em-, ɪm- **-s** -s
embarcation ˌem.bɑː'keɪ.ʃᵊn (US) -bɑːr'- **-s** -z
embargo ɪm'bɑː.gəʊ, em- (US) em'bɑːr.goʊ, ɪm- **-es** -z **-ing** -ɪŋ **-ed** -d
embark ɪm'bɑːk, em- (US) em'bɑːrk, ɪm- **-s** -s **-ing** -ɪŋ **-ed** -t
embarkation ˌem.bɑː'keɪ.ʃᵊn (US) -bɑːr'- **-s** -z
embarras de richesses ˌɑːm.bærˌɑː.də.riː'ʃes, ɑ̃ːm- (US) ˌɑːm.bɑː.rɑː-
embarrass ɪm'bær.əs, em- (US) em'ber-, ɪm-, -'bær- **-es** -ɪz **-ing/ly** -ɪŋ/li **-ed** -t
embarrassment ɪm'bær.əs.mənt, em- (US) em'ber-, ɪm-, -'bær- **-s** -s
embass|y 'em.bə.s|i **-ies** -iz
embattl|e ɪm'bæt.l̩, em- (US) em'bæt̬-, ɪm- **-es** -z **-ing** -ɪŋ, -'bæt.lɪŋ **-ed** -d
embay ɪm'beɪ, em- (US) em-, ɪm- **-s** -z **-ing** -ɪŋ **-ed** -d
embed ɪm'bed, em- (US) em-, ɪm- **-s** -z **-ding** -ɪŋ **-ded** -ɪd **-ment** -mənt
embellish ɪm'bel.ɪʃ, em- (US) em-, ɪm- **-es** -ɪz **-ing** -ɪŋ **-ed** -t **-er/s** -əʳ/z (US) -ɚ/z
embellishment ɪm'bel.ɪʃ.mənt, em- (US) em-, ɪm- **-s** -s
ember (E) 'em.bəʳ (US) -bɚ **-s** -z **'Ember ˌday**
embezzl|e ɪm'bez.l̩, em- (US) em-, ɪm- **-es** -z **-ing** -ɪŋ, -'-lɪŋ **-ed** -d **-er/s** -əʳ/z, '-ləʳ/z (US) -ɚ/z, '-lɚ/z
embezzlement ɪm'bez.l̩.mənt, em- (US) em-, ɪm-
embitt|er ɪm'bɪt|.əʳ, em- (US) em'bɪt̬|.ɚ, ɪm- **-ers** -əz (US) -ɚz **-ering** -ᵊr.ɪŋ **-ered** -əd (US) -ɚd **-erment** -ə.mənt (US) -ɚ.mənt
emblazon ɪm'bleɪ.zᵊn, em- (US) em-, ɪm- **-s** -z **-ing** -ɪŋ **-ed** -d **-ment/s** -mənt/s **-ry** -ri
emblem 'em.bləm, -blem, -blɪm (US) -bləm **-s** -z
emblematic ˌem.blə'mæt.ɪk, -blɪ'- (US) -blə'mæt̬- **-al** -ᵊl **-ally** -ᵊl.i, -li
emblematiz|e, -is|e em'blem.ə.taɪz, '-ɪ-; 'em.blem.ə- (US) em'blem.ə- **-es** -ɪz **-ing** -ɪŋ **-ed** -d
emblements 'em.blə.mənts, -bl̩- (US) -blə-
embodiment ɪm'bɒd.ɪ.mənt, em- (US) em'bɑː.di-, ɪm- **-s** -s
embod|y ɪm'bɒd|.i, em- (US) em'bɑː.d|i, ɪm- **-ies** -iz **-ying** -i.ɪŋ **-ied** -id
embolden ɪm'bəʊl.dᵊn, em- (US) em'boʊl-, ɪm- **-s** -z **-ing** -ɪŋ **-ed** -d
embolism 'em.bə.lɪ.zᵊm **-s** -z
embonpoint ˌɑ̃ːm.bɔ̃ːm'pwɑ̃ːŋ (US) ˌɑ̃ːm.bõʊn'pwæ̃n, -'pwɑ̃ːn
embosom ɪm'bʊz.ᵊm, em- (US) em-, ɪm- **-s** -z **-ing** -ɪŋ **-ed** -d
emboss ɪm'bɒs, em- (US) em'bɑːs, ɪm- **-es** -ɪz **-ing** -ɪŋ **-ed** -t **-er/s** -əʳ/z (US) -ɚ/z **-ment/s** -mənt/s
embouchure ˌɑ̃ːm.buː'ʃʊəʳ, '--- (US) ˌɑːm.buː'ʃʊr, '--- **-s** -z
embowel ɪm'baʊəl, em- (US) em'baʊᵊl, ɪm- **-s** -z **-(l)ing** -ɪŋ **-(l)ed** -d
embower ɪm'baʊəʳ, em- (US) em'baʊɚ, ɪm- **-s** -z **-ing** -ɪŋ **-ed** -d
embrac|e ɪm'breɪs, em- (US) em-, ɪm- **-es** -ɪz **-ing** -ɪŋ **-ed** -t
embracery ɪm'breɪ.sᵊr.i, em- (US) em-, ɪm-
embranchment ɪm'brɑːntʃ.mənt, em- (US) em'bræntʃ-, ɪm- **-s** -s
embrasure ɪm'breɪ.ʒəʳ, em-, -ʒʊəʳ (US) em'breɪ.ʒɚ, ɪm- **-s** -z
embro|cate 'em.brəʊ|.keɪt (US) -broʊ-, -brə- **-cates** -keɪts **-cating** -keɪ.tɪŋ (US) -keɪ.t̬ɪŋ **-cated** -keɪ.tɪd (US) -keɪ.t̬ɪd
embrocation ˌem.brəʊ'keɪ.ʃᵊn (US) -broʊ'-, -brə'- **-s** -z
embroglio ɪm'brəʊ.li.əʊ, em- (US) em'broʊ.ljoʊ, ɪm- **-s** -z
embroid|er ɪm'brɔɪ.d|əʳ, em- (US) em'brɔɪ.d|ɚ, ɪm- **-ers** -əz (US) -ɚz **-ering** -ᵊr.ɪŋ **-ered** -əd (US) -ɚd **-erer/s** -ᵊr.əʳ/z (US) -ɚ.ɚ/z
embroider|y ɪm'brɔɪ.dᵊr|.i, em- (US) em-, ɪm- **-ies** -iz
embroil ɪm'brɔɪl, em- (US) em-, ɪm- **-s** -z **-ing** -ɪŋ **-ed** -d **-ment/s** -mənt/s
embryo 'em.bri.əʊ (US) -oʊ **-s** -z
embryolog|y ˌem.bri'ɒl.ə.dʒ|i (US) -'ɑː.lə- **-ist/s** -ɪst/s
embryonic ˌem.bri'ɒn.ɪk (US) -'ɑː.nɪk
Embury, Emburey 'em.bᵊr.i, -bjʊ.ri, -bjə.ri (US) -bɚ.i
emcee ˌem'siː **-s** -z **-ing** -ɪŋ **-d** -d

-eme -iːm
Note: Suffix. Unstressed, e.g. **lexeme** /'lek.siːm/.

Emeline 'em.ɪ.liːn, '-ə- (US) -ə.laɪn, -liːn

emend ɪ'mend, iː- **-s** -z **-ing** -ɪŋ **-ed** -ɪd **-able** -ə.bl̩

emen|date 'iː.men|.deɪt, 'em.en- (US) 'iː.men-, -mən-; ɪ'men- **-dates** -deɪts **-dating** -deɪ.tɪŋ (US) -deɪ.t̬ɪŋ **-dated** -deɪ.tɪd (US) -deɪ.t̬ɪd **-dator/s** -deɪ.təʳ/z (US) -deɪ.t̬ɚ/z

emendation ˌiː.men'deɪ.ʃᵊn, ˌem.en'-, -ən'- **-s** -z

emendatory ɪ'men.də.tᵊr.i, iː-, -tri (US) -tɔːr.i

emerald 'em.ᵊr.ᵊld, '-rᵊld **-s** -z **'Emerald ˌIsle**

emerg|e ɪ'mɜːdʒ, iː- (US) -'mɜːrdʒ **-es** -ɪz **-ing** -ɪŋ **-ed** -d

emergen|ce ɪ'mɜː.dʒᵊn|*t*s, iː- (US) -'mɜːr- **-t** -t

emergenc|y ɪ'mɜː.dʒᵊn*t*.s|i, iː- (US) -'mɜːr- **-ies** -iz **e'mergency ˌroom**

emeritus ɪ'mer.ɪ.təs, iː-, -ə.təs (US) -ə.t̬əs

emersion ɪ'mɜː.ʃᵊn, iː-, -ʒᵊn (US) -'mɜːr.ʒᵊn, -ʃᵊn **-s** -z

Emerson 'em.ə.sᵊn (US) '-ɚ-

emery (E) 'em.ᵊr.i **'emery ˌboard** ; **'emery ˌpaper**

emetic ɪ'met.ɪk, iː- (US) -'met̬- **-s** -s **-al** -ᵊl **-ally** -ᵊl.i, -li

émeute eɪ'mɜːt **-s** -s

EMF ˌiː.em'ef

EMI® ˌiː.em'aɪ

emigrant 'em.ɪ.grənt (US) '-ɪ-, '-ə- **-s** -s

emi|grate 'em.ɪ|.greɪt (US) '-ɪ-, '-ə- **-grates** -greɪts **-grating** -greɪ.tɪŋ (US) -greɪ.t̬ɪŋ **-grated** -greɪ.tɪd (US) -greɪ.t̬ɪd **-grator/s** -greɪ.təʳ/z (US) -greɪ.t̬ɚ/z

emigration ˌem.ɪ'greɪ.ʃᵊn (US) -ɪ'-, -ə'- **-s** -z

emigratory 'em.ɪ.grə.tᵊr.i, -greɪ-, -tri; ˌem.ɪ'greɪ- (US) 'em.ɪ.grə.tɔːr.i, '-ə-

émigré 'em.ɪ.greɪ **-s** -z

Emil em'iːl, eɪ'miːl (US) 'iː.məl, 'eɪ-

Emile, Émile em'iːl, eɪ'miːl (US) 'iː.məl; eɪ'miːl

Emilia ɪ'mɪl.i.ə, -'jə, em'iː.li.ə (US) ɪ'mɪl.jə, em'iː.ljə

Emily 'em.ɪ.li, '-ə-

eminen|ce 'em.ɪ.nən*t*|s, '-ə- **-ces** -sɪz **-cy** -si

éminence grise ˌem.ɪ.nən*t*s'griːz *as if French:* ˌeɪ.mɪˌnɑ̃ː*nt*s'griːz (US) ˌeɪ.miː.nɑːn*t*s'-

eminent 'em.ɪ.nənt, '-ə- **-ly** -li

emir (E) em'ɪəʳ, ɪ'mɪr, ə-, eɪ-; 'em.ɪəʳ (US) em'ɪr, ə'mɪr; ˌeɪ'mɪr **-s** -z

emirate 'em.ɪ.rət, -ᵊr.ət, -ɪt, -eɪt; em'ɪə.rət, ɪ'mɪə-, ə-, eɪ-, -rɪt, -reɪt (US) em'ɪr.eɪt, ə'mɪr-, -ət **-s** -s

emissar|y 'em.ɪ.sᵊr|.i (US) -ser- **-ies** -iz

emission ɪ'mɪʃ.ᵊn, iː- **-s** -z

emissive ɪ'mɪs.ɪv, iː-

e|mit ɪ|'mɪt, iː- **-mits** -'mɪts **-mitting** -'mɪt.ɪŋ (US) -'mɪt̬- **-mitted** -'mɪt.ɪd (US) -'mɪt̬- **-mitter/s** -'mɪt.əʳ/z (US) -'mɪt̬.ɚ/z

Emley 'em.li

Emlyn 'em.lɪn

Emma 'em.ə

Emmanuel ɪ'mæn.ju.əl, em'æn-, -el, -jʊl

Emmaus em'eɪ.əs, ɪ'meɪ-

Emmeline 'em.ɪ.liːn, '-ə- (US) -ə.laɪn, -liːn

Emmental, Emmenthal 'em.ən.tɑːl

Emmerdale 'em.ə.deɪl (US) '-ɚ-

emmet (E) 'em.ɪt **-s** -s

Emmie 'em.i

Emmy 'em.i **-s** -z **'Emmy Aˌward**

emollient ɪ'mɒl.i.ənt, iː- (US) -'mɑːl.jənt **-s** -s

emolument ɪ'mɒl.jʊ.mənt, -jə- (US) -'mɑːl- **-s** -s

Emory 'em.ᵊr.i

e|mote ɪ|'məʊt, iː- (US) -'moʊt **-motes** -'məʊts (US) -'moʊts **-moting** -'məʊ.tɪŋ (US) -'moʊ.t̬ɪŋ **-moted** -'məʊ.tɪd (US) -'moʊ.t̬ɪd

emotion ɪ'məʊ.ʃᵊn (US) -'moʊ- **-s** -z **-less** -ləs, -lɪs

emotional ɪ'məʊ.ʃᵊn.ᵊl (US) -'moʊ- **-ly** -i

emotionalism ɪ'məʊ.ʃᵊn.ᵊl.ɪ.zᵊm (US) -'moʊ-

emotionaliz|e, -is|e ɪ'məʊ.ʃᵊn.ᵊl.aɪz (US) -'moʊ.ʃᵊn.ə.laɪz **-es** -ɪz **-ing** -ɪŋ **-ed** -d

emotive ɪ'məʊ.tɪv (US) -'moʊ.t̬ɪv **-ly** -li

empanel ɪm'pæn.ᵊl, em- (US) em-, ɪm- **-s** -z **-(l)ing** -ɪŋ **-(l)ed** -d **-ment/s** -mənt/s

empathetic ˌem.pə'θet.ɪk (US) -'θet̬-

empathic em'pæθ.ɪk, ɪm-

empathiz|e, -is|e 'em.pə.θaɪz **-es** -ɪz **-ing** -ɪŋ **-ed** -d

empathy 'em.pə.θi

Empedocles em'ped.ə.kliːz, ɪm-

emperor (E) 'em.pᵊr.əʳ (US) -ɚ.ɚ **-s** -z

emphas|is 'em*p*.fə.s|ɪs **-es** -iːz

emphasiz|e, -is|e 'em*p*.fə.saɪz **-es** -ɪz **-ing** -ɪŋ **-ed** -d

emphatic ɪm'fæt.ɪk, em- (US) em'fæt̬-, ɪm- **-al** -ᵊl **-ally** -ᵊl.i, -li

emphysema ˌem*p*.fɪ'siː.mə (US) -fə'siː-, -'ziː- **-s** -z

empire (E) 'em.paɪəʳ (US) -paɪɚ **-s** -z **ˌEmpire 'State ˌBuilding**

empiric ɪm'pɪr.ɪk, em- (US) em-, ɪm- **-s** -s **-al** -ᵊl **-ally** -ᵊl.i, -li

empiric|ism ɪm'pɪr.ɪ.s|ɪ.zᵊm, em-, '-ə- (US) em-, ɪm- **-ist/s** -ɪst/s

emplacement ɪm'pleɪs.mənt, em- (US) em-, ɪm- **-s** -s

employ ɪm'plɔɪ, em- (US) em-, ɪm- **-s** -z **-ing** -ɪŋ **-ed** -d **-able** -ə.bl̩

employé ɑ̃ː*m*'plɔɪ.eɪ, ɔ̃ː*m*- **-s** -z

employee ɪm'plɔɪ.iː, em-, əm-; ˌem.plɔɪ'iː (US) em'plɔɪ.iː, ɪm-, ˌem.plɔɪ'iː **-s** -z

employer ɪm'plɔɪ.əʳ, em- (US) em'plɔɪ.ɚ, ɪm- **-s** -z

employment ɪm'plɔɪ.mənt, em- (US) em-, ɪm- **-s** -s **em'ployment ˌagency**

empori|um em'pɔː.ri|.əm, ɪm- (US) -'pɔːr.i- **-ums** -əmz **-a** -ə

empower ɪm'paʊəʳ, em- (US) em'paʊɚ, ɪm- **-s** -z **-ing** -ɪŋ **-ed** -d

empowerment ɪm'paʊə.mənt, em- (US) em'paʊɚ-, ɪm-

empress (E) 'em.prəs, -prɪs, -pres **-es** -ɪz

Empson 'emp.sᵊn

emption 'em*p*.ʃᵊn

empt|y 'em*p*.t|i **-ier** -i.əʳ (US) -i.ɚ **-iest** -i.ɪst, -i.əst **-ily** -ɪ.li, -ᵊl.i **-iness** -ɪ.nəs, -ɪ.nɪs **-ies** -iz **-ying** -i.ɪŋ **-ied** -id

empty-handed ˌem*p*.ti'hæn.dɪd *stress shift:* ˌempty-handed 'beggar

empty-headed ˌem*p*.ti'hed.ɪd **-ness** -nəs, -nɪs *stress shift:* ˌempty-headed 'nonsense

empyema ˌem.paɪ'iː.mə (US) -paɪ'-, -pi'-

empyre|al ˌem.paɪə'riː|.əl, -pɪ'- (US) em'pɪr.i-, -'paɪ.ri-; ˌem.paɪ'riː-, -pə'- **-an** -ən

EMS ˌiː.em'es

Emsworth 'emz.wəθ, -wɜːθ (US) -wɚθ, -wɜːrθ

emu 'iː.mjuː (US) -mjuː, -muː **-s** -z

EMU ˌiː.em'juː, 'iː.mjuː

emu|late 'em.jə|.leɪt, -jʊ- **-lates** -leɪts **-lating** -leɪ.tɪŋ (US) -leɪ.t̬ɪŋ **-lated** -leɪ.tɪd (US) -leɪ.t̬ɪd **-lator/s** -leɪ.təʳ/z (US) -leɪ.t̬ɚ/z

emulation ˌem.jə'leɪ.ʃᵊn, -jʊ'-

emulative 'em.jə.lə.tɪv, -jʊ-, -leɪ- (US) -leɪ.t̬ɪv

emulous 'em.jə.ləs, -jʊ- **-ly** -li

emulsifier ɪ'mʌl.sɪ.faɪ.əʳ, -sə- (US) -ɚ **-s** -z

emulsi|fy ɪ'mʌl.sɪ|.faɪ, -sə- **-fies** -faɪz **-fying** -faɪ.ɪŋ **-fied** -faɪd

emulsion ɪ'mʌl.ʃᵊn **-s** -z

emunctor|y ɪ'mʌŋ*k*.tᵊr|.i **-ies** -iz

en *in French phrases:* ɑ̃ːŋ, ɒn, ɑːn

en- ɪn-, en-, ən-
Note: Prefix. Either takes primary or secondary stress and is pronounced

/en-/, e.g. **energy** /ˈen.ə.dʒi (US) ˈ-ɚ-/, **energetic** /ˌen.əˈdʒet.ɪk (US) -ɚˈdʒeţ.ɪk/, or is unstressed and may be pronounced either /ɪn-/ or /en-/, e.g. **endear** /ɪnˈdɪəʳ, en- (US) -ˈdɪr/. NB When followed by a /k/ or /g/, assimilation may take place, e.g. **encage** may also be /ɪŋˈkeɪdʒ, eŋ-/.

enabl|e ɪˈneɪ.bl̩, enˈeɪ- **-es** -z **-ing** -ɪŋ, ˈ-blɪŋ **-ed** -d

enabler ɪˈneɪ.bləʳ, enˈeɪ-, -bl̩.əʳ (US) ˈ-blɚ, ˈ-bl̩.ɚ **-s** -z

enact ɪˈnækt, enˈækt **-s** -s **-ing** -ɪŋ **-ed** -ɪd **-or/s** -əʳ/z (US) -ɚ/z **-ment/s** -mənt/s **-ive** -ɪv

enaction ɪˈnæk.ʃən, enˈæk- **-s** -z

enamel ɪˈnæm.əl **-s** -z **-(l)ing** -ɪŋ **-(l)ed** -d **-(l)er/s** -əʳ/z (US) -ɚ/z **-(l)ist/s** -ɪst/s

enamelware ɪˈnæm.əl.weəʳ (US) -wer

enamo(u)r ɪˈnæm.əʳ, enˈæm- (US) -ɚ **-s** -z **-ing** -ɪŋ **-ed** -d

en banc ɑ̃ːmˈbɑ̃ːŋk (US) ɑ̃ːnˈbɑ̃ːŋ

en bloc ˌɑ̃ːmˈblɒk (US) ɑ̃ːnˈblɑːk, en-

Encaenia enˈsiː.ni.ə

encag|e ɪnˈkeɪdʒ, ɪŋ-, en-, eŋ- (US) en-, ɪn- **-es** -ɪz **-ing** -ɪŋ **-ed** -d

encamp ɪnˈkæmp, ɪŋ-, en-, eŋ- (US) en-, ɪn- **-s** -s **-ing** -ɪŋ **-ed** -t, -kæmt **-ment/s** -mənt/s

encapsu|late ɪnˈkæp.sjə|.leɪt, ɪŋ-, en-, eŋ-, -sjʊ- (US) en-, ɪn- **-lates** -leɪts **-lating** -leɪ.tɪŋ (US) -leɪ.ţɪŋ **-lated** -leɪ.tɪd (US) -leɪ.ţɪd

encapsulation ɪnˌkæp.sjəˈleɪ.ʃən, ɪŋ-, en-, eŋ-, -sjʊˈ- (US) en-, ɪn-

encas|e ɪnˈkeɪs, ɪŋ-, en-, eŋ- (US) en-, ɪn- **-es** -ɪz **-ing** -ɪŋ **-ed** -t **-ement/s** -mənt/s

encaustic ɪnˈkɔː.stɪk, ɪŋ-, en-, eŋ-, enˈkɒs.tɪk (US) enˈkɑː.stɪk, -ˈkɔː-, ɪn- **-s** -s **-ally** -əl.i, -li

-ence -ənts

Note: Suffix. Normally, **-ence** does not affect the stress pattern of the word it is attached to, e.g. **depend** /dɪˈpend/, **dependence** /dɪˈpen.dənts/. In other cases, the stress may be on the penultimate or antepenultimate syllable, e.g. **excellence** /ˈek.səl.ənts/. See individual entries.

enceinte ˌɑ̃ːnˈsæ̃nt (US) ˌɑ̃ːn-; enˈseɪnt **-s** -s

Enceladus enˈsel.ə.dəs

encephalic ˌen.kəˈfæl.ɪk, ˌeŋ-, ˌɪn-, ˌɪŋ-, -kɪˈ-; ˌen.səˈ-, ˌɪn-, -sefˈæl-, -sɪˈfæl- (US) ˌen.səˈfæl.ɪk, -sɪˈ-

encephalitis ˌen.kef.əˈlaɪ.tɪs, ˌeŋ-, ˌɪn-, ˌɪŋ-, -kɪ.fəˈ-; ˌen.sə-, ˌɪn-, -sef.əˈ-; enˌkef-, eŋ-, ɪn-, ɪŋ-; enˌsef-, ɪn- (US) enˌsef.əˈlaɪ.ţɪs

encephalogram enˈkef.ə.lə.græm, eŋ-, ɪn-, ɪŋ-; enˈsef-, ɪn- (US) enˈsef.ə.loʊ- **-s** -z

encephalograph enˈkef.ə.lə.grɑːf, eŋ-, ɪn-, ɪŋ; enˈsef-, ɪn-, -græf (US) enˈsef.ə.loʊ.græf **-s** -s

encephalomyelitis enˌkef.ə.ləʊ.maɪəˈlaɪ.tɪs, eŋ-, ɪn-, ɪŋ-; enˌsef-, ɪnˌsef-; ˌen.kef-, ˌeŋ-, ˌɪn-, ˌɪŋ-; ˌen.sef-, ˌɪn.sef- (US) enˌsef.ə.loʊ.maɪəˈlaɪ.ţɪs

encephalopathic enˌkef.ə.ləʊˈpæθ.ɪk, eŋ-, ɪn-, ɪŋ-, enˌsef-, ɪnˌsef- (US) enˌsef.ə.loʊˈ-

encephalopathy enˌkef.əˈlɒp.ə.θi, eŋ-, ɪn-, ɪŋ-; enˌsef-, ɪnˌsef-; ˌen.kef-, ˌeŋ-, ˌɪn-, ˌɪŋ-; ˌen.sef-, ˌɪn.sef- (US) enˌsef.əˈlɑː.pə-

enchain ɪnˈtʃeɪn, en- (US) en-, ɪn- **-s** -z **-ing** -ɪŋ **-ed** -d **-ment** -mənt

enchan|t ɪnˈtʃɑːn|t, en- (US) enˈtʃæn|t, ɪn- **-ts** -ts **-ting/ly** -tɪŋ/li (US) -ţɪŋ/li **-ted** -tɪd (US) -ţɪd **-ter/s** -təʳ/z (US) -ţɚ/z **-tress/es** -trɪs/ɪz **-tment/s** -t.mənt/s

enchilada ˌen.tʃɪˈlɑː.də **-s** -z

enchiridion ˌen.kaɪˈrɪd.i.ən, ˌeŋ-, -kɪˈ-, -ɒn (US) ˌen.kaɪˈrɪd.i.ən, -kɪˈ- **-s** -z

enciph|er ɪnˈsaɪ.f|əʳ, en- (US) enˈsaɪ.f|ɚ, ɪn- **-ers** -əz (US) -ɚz **-ering** -ər.ɪŋ **-ered** -əd (US) -ɚd

encircl|e ɪnˈsɜː.kl̩, en- (US) enˈsɜːr-, ɪn- **-es** -z **-ing** -ɪŋ, ˈ-klɪŋ **-ed** -d **-ement/s** -mənt/s

Encke ˈeŋ.kə

enclasp ɪnˈklɑːsp, ɪŋ-, en-, eŋ- (US) enˈklæsp, ɪn- **-s** -s **-ing** -ɪŋ **-ed** -t

enclave ˈen.kleɪv, ˈeŋ- (US) ˈen-, ˈɑːn- **-s** -z

enclitic ɪnˈklɪt.ɪk, ɪŋ-, en-, eŋ- (US) enˈklɪţ-, ɪn- **-s** -s **-ally** -əl.i, -li

enclos|e ɪnˈkləʊz, ɪŋ-, en-, eŋ- (US) enˈkloʊz, ɪn- **-es** -ɪz **-ing** -ɪŋ **-ed** -d

enclosure ɪnˈkləʊ.ʒəʳ, ɪŋ-, en-, eŋ- (US) enˈkloʊ.ʒɚ, ɪn- **-s** -z

encod|e ɪnˈkəʊd, en-, eŋ-, ɪŋ- (US) enˈkoʊd, ɪn- **-es** -z **-ing** -ɪŋ **-ed** -ɪd **-er/s** -əʳ/z (US) -ɚ/z

encomi|ast ɪnˈkəʊ.mi|.æst, ɪŋ-, en-, eŋ- (US) enˈkoʊ-, ɪn- **-asts** -æsts **-um/s** -əm/z **-a** -ə

encompass ɪnˈkʌm.pəs, ɪŋ-, en-, eŋ- (US) en-, ɪn- **-es** -ɪz **-ing** -ɪŋ **-ed** -t

encore ˈɒŋ.kɔːʳ, ˈɑ̃ːŋ-, -ˈ- (US) ˈɑːn.kɔːr, -ˈ- **-es** -z **-ing** -ɪŋ **-ed** -d

encoun|ter ɪnˈkaʊn|.təʳ, ɪŋ-, en-, eŋ- (US) enˈkaʊn|.ţɚ, ɪn- **-ters** -təz (US) -ţɚz **-tering** -tər.ɪŋ (US) -ţɚ.ɪŋ **-tered** -təd (US) -ţɚd

encourag|e ɪnˈkʌr.ɪdʒ, ɪŋ-, en-, eŋ- (US) en.kɜːr-, ɪn- **-es** -ɪz **-ing/ly** -ɪŋ/li **-ed** -d

encouragement ɪnˈkʌr.ɪdʒ.mənt, ɪŋ-, en-, eŋ- (US) en.kɜːr-, ɪn- **-s** -s

encroach ɪnˈkrəʊtʃ, ɪŋ-, en-, eŋ- (US) enˈkroʊtʃ, ɪn- **-es** -ɪz **-ing** -ɪŋ **-ed** -t **-ment/s** -mənt/s

en croûte ˌɑ̃ːŋˈkruːt (US) ˌɑːnˈkruːt

encrust ɪnˈkrʌst, ɪŋ-, en-, eŋ- (US) en-, ɪn- **-s** -s **-ing** -ɪŋ **-ed** -ɪd

encrustation ˌen.krʌsˈteɪ.ʃən, ˌeŋ- (US) ˌen- **-s** -z

encrypt ɪnˈkrɪpt, ɪŋ-, en-, eŋ- (US) en-, ɪn- **-s** -s **-ing** -ɪŋ **-ed** -ɪd

encryption ɪnˈkrɪp.ʃən, ɪŋ-, en-, eŋ- (US) en-, ɪn-

encumb|er ɪnˈkʌm.b|əʳ, ɪŋ-, en-, eŋ- (US) enˈkʌm.b|ɚ, ɪn- **-ers** -əz (US) -ɚz **-ering** -ər.ɪŋ **-ered** -əd (US) -ɚd

encumbranc|e ɪnˈkʌm.brənts, ɪŋ-, en-, eŋ- (US) en-, ɪn- **-es** -ɪz

-ency -ənt.si

Note: Suffix. Words containing **-ency** are stressed in a similar way to those containing **-ence**; see above.

encyclic ɪnˈsɪk.lɪk, en-, -ˈsaɪ.klɪk (US) en-, ɪn- **-s** -s **-al/s** -əl/z

encyclop(a)edia ɪnˌsaɪ.kləˈpiː.di.ə, enˌsaɪ-, ˌɪn.saɪ-, ˌen- (US) enˌsaɪ-, ɪn-, ˌen.saɪ-, ˌɪn- **-s** -z

encyclop(a)edic ɪnˌsaɪ.kləˈpiː.dɪk, enˌsaɪ-, ˌɪn.saɪ-, ˌen- (US) enˌsaɪ-, ɪn-, ˌen.saɪ-, ˌɪn- **-ally** -əl.i, -li

encyclop(a)ed|ism ɪnˌsaɪ.kləˈpiː.d|ɪ.zəm, enˌsaɪ-, ˌɪn.saɪ-, ˌen- (US) enˌsaɪ-, ɪn-, ˌen.saɪ-, ˌɪn- **-ist/s** -ɪst/s

end end **-s** -z **-ing** -ɪŋ **-ed** -ɪd **ˌend ˈproduct ; ˈend ˌuser ; be at a ˌloose ˈend ; be at ˌloose ˈends ; ˌmake ends ˈmeet** (US) **ˌmake ˈends ˌmeet ; go off the ˈdeep ˌend ; ˌthrown in at the ˈdeep ˌend ; at the ˌend of the ˈday**

endang|er ɪnˈdeɪn.dʒ|əʳ, en- (US) enˈdeɪn.dʒ|ɚ, ɪn- **-ers** -əz (US) -ɚz **-ering** -ər.ɪŋ **-ered** -əd (US) -ɚd **-erment** -ə.mənt (US) -ɚ.mənt

endear ɪnˈdɪəʳ, en- (US) enˈdɪr, ɪn- **-s** -z **-ing/ly** -ɪŋ/li **-ed** -d **-ment** -mənt

endeav|o(u)r ɪnˈdev|.əʳ, en- (US) enˈdev|.ɚ, ɪn- **-o(u)rs** -əz (US) -ɚz **-o(u)ring** -ər.ɪŋ **-o(u)red** -əd (US) -ɚd

Endell ˈen.dəl

endemic enˈdem.ɪk **-s** -s **-al** -əl **-ally** -əl.i, -li

Enderby ˈen.də.bi (US) -dɚ-

endermic enˈdɜː.mɪk (US) -ˈdɜːr- **-al** -əl **-ally** -əl.i, -li

endgame ˈend.geɪm, ˈeŋ- (US) ˈend- **-s** -z

Endicott 'en.dɪ.kət, -də-, -kɒt US -kɑːt, -kət

ending 'en.dɪŋ **-s** -z

endive 'en.dɪv, -daɪv US 'en.daɪv, 'ɑːn.diːv **-s** -z

endless 'end.ləs, -lɪs **-ly** -li **-ness** -nəs, -nɪs

endlong 'end.lɒŋ US -lɑːŋ, -lɔːŋ

endmost 'en*d*.məʊst US -moʊst

endnote 'end.nəʊt US -noʊt **-s** -s

endo- en.d*əʊ*-; en'dɒ-, ɪn- US en.doʊ-, -də-; en'dɑː-, ɪn-

Note: Prefix. Either carries primary or secondary stress on the first syllable, e.g. **endomorph** /'en.d*əʊ*.mɔːf US -doʊ.mɔːrf/, **endomorphic** /ˌen.d*əʊ*'mɔː.fɪk US -doʊ'mɔːr-/, or primary stress on the second syllable, e.g. **endogenous** /ɪn'dɒdʒ.ɪ.nəs US /en'dɑː.dʒə-/.

endocentric ˌen.dəʊ'sen.trɪk US -doʊ'-

endocrine 'en.d*əʊ*.kraɪn, -krɪn, -kriːn US -də.krɪn, -kriːn, -kraɪn **'endocrine ˌgland**

endocrinolog|y ˌen.d*əʊ*.kraɪ'nɒl.ə.dʒ|i, -krɪ'- US -doʊ.krɪ'nɑː.lə- **-ist/s** -ɪst/s

endoderm 'en.dəʊ.dɜːm US -doʊ.dɜːrm

endoderm|al ˌen.dəʊ'dɜː.m|ᵊl US -doʊ'dɜːr- **-ic** -ɪk

endogamy ɪn'dɒg.ə.mi, en- US en'dɑː.gə-, ɪn-

endogenous ɪn'dɒdʒ.ə.nəs, en-, '-ɪ- US en'dɑː.dʒə-, ɪn-

endometrial ˌen.dəʊ'miː.tri.əl US -doʊ'-

endometriosis ˌen.dəʊˌmiː.tri'əʊ.sɪs US -doʊˌmiː.tri'oʊ-

endometri|um ˌen.dəʊ'miː.tri|.əm US -doʊ'- **-a** -ə

endomorph 'en.d*əʊ*.mɔːf US -doʊ.mɔːrf **-s** -s **-y** -i

endomorph|ic ˌen.d*əʊ*'mɔː.f|ɪk US -doʊ'mɔːr- **-ism** -ɪ.zᵊm

endophoric ˌen.dəʊ'fɒr.ɪk US -doʊ'fɔːr-

endoplasm 'en.dəʊ.plæz.ᵊm US -doʊ-

endoplasmic ˌen.dəʊ'plæz.mɪk US -doʊ'-

Endor 'en.dɔːʳ US -dɔːr

endorphin en'dɔː.fɪn US -'dɔːr-, ɪn- **-s** -z

endors|e ɪn'dɔːs, en- US en'dɔːrs, ɪn- **-es** -ɪz **-ing** -ɪŋ **-ed** -t **-er/s** -əʳ/z US -ɚ/z **-ement/s** -mənt/s **-able** -ə.bl̩

endorsee ˌen.dɔː'siː US -dɔːr'- **-s** -z

endoscope 'en.d*əʊ*.skəʊp US -doʊ.skoʊp, -də- **-s** -s

endoscop|y en'dɒs.kə.p|i US -'dɑː.skə- **-ies** -iz

endoskeleton ˌen.dəʊ'skel.ɪ.tᵊn, '-ə- US -doʊ'- **-s** -z

endosperm 'en.dəʊ.spɜːm US -doʊ.spɜːrm **-s** -z

endow ɪn'daʊ, en- US en-, ɪn- **-s** -z **-ing** -ɪŋ **-ed** -d **-ment/s** -mənt/s

endpaper 'endˌpeɪ.pəʳ US -pɚ **-s** -z

endpoint 'end.pɔɪnt **-s** -s

end-stopped 'end.stɒpt US -stɑːpt

endu|e ɪn'djuː, en- US en'duː, ɪn-, -'djuː **-es** -z **-ing** -ɪŋ **-ed** -d

endurab|le ɪn'djʊə.rə.b|l̩, en-, -'djɔː- US en'dʊr.ə-, ɪn-, -'djʊr- **-ly** -li

endurance ɪn'djʊə.rᵊn*t*s, en-, -'djɔː- US en'dʊr.ᵊn*t*s, ɪn-, -'djʊr-

endur|e ɪn'djʊəʳ, en-, -'djɔːʳ US en'dʊr, ɪn, -'djʊr **-es** -z **-ing/ly** -ɪŋ/li **-ed** -d

end|ways 'end|.weɪz **-wise** -waɪz

Endymion en'dɪm.i.ən, ɪn-

-ene -iːn

Note: Suffix. **-ene** is not stressed, e.g. **ethylene** /'eθ.ɪ.liːn/.

ENE ˌiːst.nɔːθ'iːst US -nɔːrθ- *in nautical usage also:* -nɔː'riːst US -nɔːr'iːst

Eneas iː'niː.əs, ɪ-, -æs

Eneid 'iː.ni.ɪd, ɪ'niː-

enema 'en.ɪ.mə, '-ə- US '-ə- **-s** -z

enem|y 'en.ə.m|i, '-ɪ- **-ies** -iz

energetic ˌen.ə'dʒet.ɪk US -ɚ'dʒet̬- **-s** -s **-ally** -ᵊl.i, -li

energiz|e, -is|e 'en.ə.dʒaɪz US '-ɚ- **-es** -ɪz **-ing** -ɪŋ **-ed** -d **-er/s** -əʳ/z US -ɚ/z

energumen ˌen.ə'gjuː.men US -ɚ'- **-s** -z

energ|y 'en.ə.dʒ|i US '-ɚ- **-ies** -iz

ener|vate 'en.ə|.veɪt, -ɜː- US '-ɚ- **-vates** -veɪts **-vating** -veɪ.tɪŋ US -veɪ.t̬ɪŋ **-vated** -veɪ.tɪd US -veɪ.t̬ɪd

enervation ˌen.ə'veɪ.ʃᵊn, -ɜː'- US -ɚ'-

en famille ˌɑ̃ː*n*.fæm'iː US ˌɑ̃ːn.fɑː'miː.jə

enfant(s) terrible(s) ˌɑ̃ː*n*.fɑ̃ː*n*.ter'iː.blə, ˌɒn.fɒn-, -tə'riː- US ˌɑːn.fɑːn.ter'iː-, ˌɑ̃*n*.fɑ̃*n*-

enfeebl|e ɪn'fiː.bl̩, en- US en-, ɪn- **-es** -z **-ing** -ɪŋ, '-blɪŋ **-ed** -d **-ement** -mənt

enfeoff ɪn'fiːf, en-, -'fef US en-, ɪn- **-s** -s **-ing** -ɪŋ **-ed** -t **-ment/s** -mənt/s

Enfield 'en.fiːld

enfilad|e ˌen.fɪ'leɪd, '--- US 'en.fə.leɪd **-es** -z **-ing** -ɪŋ **-ed** -ɪd

enfold ɪn'fəʊld, en- US en'foʊld, ɪn- **-s** -z **-ing** -ɪŋ **-ed** -ɪd **-ment** -mənt

enforc|e ɪn'fɔːs, en- US en'fɔːrs, ɪn- **-es** -ɪz **-ing** -ɪŋ **-ed** -t **-edly** -ɪd.li **-eable** -ə.bl̩

enforcement ɪn'fɔːs.mənt, en- US en'fɔːrs-, ɪn-

enfranchis|e ɪn'fræn.*t*ʃaɪz, en- US en-, ɪn- **-es** -ɪz **-ing** -ɪŋ **-ed** -d

enfranchisement ɪn'fræn.*t*ʃɪz.mənt, en-, -*t*ʃəz- US en'fræn.*t*ʃaɪz-, ɪn-, -*t*ʃəz- **-s** -s

Engadine 'eŋ.gə.diːn, ˌ--'-

engag|e ɪn'geɪdʒ, ɪŋ-, en-, eŋ- US en-, ɪn- **-es** -ɪz **-ing/ly** -ɪŋ/li **-ed** -d

engagement ɪn'geɪdʒ.mənt, ɪŋ-, en-, eŋ- US en-, ɪn- **-s** -s **en'gagement ˌring**

en garde ɑ̃ː*ŋ*'gɑːd US ˌɑːn'gɑːrd, ˌɑ̃ːn-

Engels 'eŋ.gᵊlz

engend|er ɪn'dʒen.d|əʳ, en- US en'dʒen.d|ɚ, ɪn- **-ers** -əz US -ɚz **-ering** -ᵊr.ɪŋ **-ered** -əd US -ɚd

engine 'en.dʒɪn **-s** -z **'engine ˌdriver**

engineer ˌen.dʒɪ'nɪəʳ, -dʒə'- US -'nɪr **-s** -z **-ing** -ɪŋ **-ed** -d

engird ɪn'gɜːd, ɪŋ-, en-, eŋ- US en'gɜːrd, ɪn- **-s** -z **-ing** -ɪŋ **-ed** -ɪd

England 'ɪŋ.glənd **-er/s** -əʳ/z US -ɚ/z

Englefield 'eŋ.gl̩.fiːld

Englewood 'eŋ.gl̩.wʊd

English 'ɪŋ.glɪʃ **ˌEnglish 'Channel**; **ˌEnglish 'horn** US **'English ˌhorn**

English|man 'ɪŋ.glɪʃ|.mən **-men** -mən, -men

English|woman 'ɪŋ.glɪʃ|ˌwʊm.ən **-women** -ˌwɪm.ɪn

engorged ɪn'gɔːdʒd, ɪŋ-, en-, eŋ- US en'gɔːrdʒd, ɪn-

engraft ɪn'grɑːft, ɪŋ-, en-, eŋ- US en'græft, ɪn- **-s** -s **-ing** -ɪŋ **-ed** -ɪd **-ment** -mənt

engrailed ɪn'greɪld, ɪŋ-, en-, eŋ- US en-, ɪn-

engrain ɪn'greɪn, ɪŋ-, en-, eŋ- US en-, ɪn- **-s** -z **-ing** -ɪŋ **-ed** -d

engrav|e ɪn'greɪv, ɪŋ-, en-, eŋ- US en-, ɪn- **-es** -z **-ing/s** -ɪŋ/z **-ed** -d **-er/s** -əʳ/z US -ɚ/z **-ery** -ᵊr.i

en gros ˌɑ̃ː*ŋ*'grəʊ, ˌɑːn'groʊ

engross ɪn'grəʊs, ɪŋ-, en-, eŋ- US en'groʊs, ɪn- **-es** -ɪz **-ing** -ɪŋ **-ed** -t **-ment** -mənt

engulf ɪn'gʌlf, ɪŋ-, en-, eŋ- US en-, ɪn- **-s** -s **-ing** -ɪŋ **-ed** -t **-ment** -mənt

enhanc|e ɪn'hɑːn*t*s, en- US -'hæn*t*s **-es** -ɪz **-ing** -ɪŋ **-ed** -t **-ement/s** -mənt/s **-er/s** -əʳ/z US -ɚ/z

enharmonic ˌen.hɑː'mɒn.ɪk US -hɑːr'mɑː.nɪk **-al** -ᵊl **-ally** -ᵊl.i, -li

Enid 'iː.nɪd

enigma ɪ'nɪg.mə, en'ɪg-, ə'nɪg- US ɪ'nɪg.mə, ə-, en'ɪg- **-s** -z

enigmatic ˌen.ɪg'mæt.ɪk US -'mæt̬- **-al** -ᵊl **-ally** -ᵊl.i, -li *stress shift:* ˌenigmatic 'smile

enigmatist ɪ'nɪg.mə.tɪst, en'ɪg-, ə'nɪg- US ɪ'nɪg-, ə-, en'ɪg- **-s** -s

enigmatiz|e, -is|e ɪ'nɪg.mə.taɪz, en'ɪg-, ə'nɪg- Ⓤⓢ ɪ'nɪg-, ə-, en'ɪg- **-es** -ɪz **-ing** -ɪŋ **-ed** -d
enjamb(e)ment ɪn'dʒæm*b*.mənt, en- Ⓤⓢ en-, ɪn- **-s** -s
enjoin ɪn'dʒɔɪn, en- Ⓤⓢ en-, ɪn- **-s** -z **-ing** -ɪŋ **-ed** -d
enjoy ɪn'dʒɔɪ, en- Ⓤⓢ en-, ɪn- **-s** -z **-ing** -ɪŋ **-ed** -d
enjoyab|le ɪn'dʒɔɪ.ə.bl̩, en- Ⓤⓢ en-, ɪn- **-ly** -li **-leness** -l̩.nəs, -nɪs
enjoyment ɪn'dʒɔɪ.mənt, en- Ⓤⓢ en-, ɪn- **-s** -s
enkindl|e ɪn'kɪn.dl̩, en-, ɪŋ-, eŋ- Ⓤⓢ en-, ɪn- **-es** -z **-ing** -ɪŋ, '-lɪŋ **-ed** -d
enlac|e ɪn'leɪs, en- Ⓤⓢ en-, ɪn- **-es** -ɪz **-ing** -ɪŋ **-ed** -t **-ement/s** -mənt/s
Enlai ˌen'laɪ
enlarg|e ɪn'lɑːdʒ, en- Ⓤⓢ en'lɑːrdʒ, ɪn- **-es** -ɪz **-ing** -ɪŋ **-ed** -d **-er/s** -əʳ/z Ⓤⓢ -ɚ/z **-ement/s** -mənt/s
enlighten ɪn'laɪ.tᵊn, en- Ⓤⓢ en-, ɪn- **-s** -z **-ing** -ɪŋ **-ed** -d
enlightenment (E) ɪn'laɪ.tᵊn.mənt, en- Ⓤⓢ en-, ɪn-
enlist ɪn'lɪst, en- Ⓤⓢ en-, ɪn- **-s** -s **-ing** -ɪŋ **-ed** -ɪd **-ment/s** -mənt/s
enliven ɪn'laɪ.vᵊn, en- Ⓤⓢ en-, ɪn- **-s** -z **-ing** -ɪŋ **-ed** -d
en masse ɑ̃ː*m*'mæs, ɒn- Ⓤⓢ ɑːn-, ɑ̃ːn-
enmesh ɪn'meʃ, en- Ⓤⓢ en-, ɪn- **-es** -ɪz **-ing** -ɪŋ **-ed** -t
enmit|y 'en.mə.t|i, -mɪ- **-ies** -iz
Ennis 'en.ɪs
Enniscorthy ˌen.ɪ'skɔː.θi Ⓤⓢ -'skɔːr-
Enniskillen ˌen.ɪ'skɪl.ən, -ə'-, -ɪn
Ennius 'en.i.əs
ennobl|e ɪ'nəʊ.bl̩, en'əʊ- Ⓤⓢ en'oʊ-, ɪ'noʊ- **-es** -z **-ing** -ɪŋ, '-blɪŋ **-ed** -d **-ement** -mənt
ennui 'ɑ̃ːn.wiː, 'ɒn-, -'- Ⓤⓢ ˌɑːn'wiː, '--
Eno® 'iː.nəʊ Ⓤⓢ -noʊ **-'s** -z
Enoch 'iː.nɒk Ⓤⓢ -nɑːk, -nək
enormit|y ɪ'nɔː.mə.t|i, ə-, -mɪ- Ⓤⓢ -'nɔːr.mə.t̬|i **-ies** -iz
enormous ɪ'nɔː.məs, ə- Ⓤⓢ -'nɔːr- **-ly** -li **-ness** -nəs, -nɪs
Enos 'iː.nɒs Ⓤⓢ -nɑːs, -nəs
enough ɪ'nʌf, ə-
enounc|e ɪ'naʊn*t*s **-es** -ɪz **-ing** -ɪŋ **-ed** -t
enow ɪ'naʊ
en passant ˌɑ̃ː*m*'pæs.ɑ̃ː*ŋ*, ˌ--'- Ⓤⓢ ˌɑ̃ːn.pɑː'sɑ̃ːn, -pə'-
enquir|e ɪn'kwaɪəʳ, ɪŋ-, en-, eŋ- Ⓤⓢ en'kwaɪɚ, ɪn- **-es** -z **-ing/ly** -ɪŋ/li **-ed** -d **-er/s** -əʳ/z Ⓤⓢ -ɚ/z
enquir|y ɪn'kwaɪə.r|i, ɪŋ-, en-, eŋ- Ⓤⓢ en'kwaɪ-, ɪn-; 'ɪn.kwɚ.i **-ies** -iz
enrag|e ɪn'reɪdʒ, en- Ⓤⓢ en-, ɪn- **-es** -ɪz **-ing** -ɪŋ **-ed** -d
enrapt ɪn'ræpt, en- Ⓤⓢ en-, ɪn-
enrapt|ure ɪn'ræp.tʃ|əʳ, en- Ⓤⓢ en'ræp.tʃ|ɚ, ɪn- **-ures** -əz Ⓤⓢ -ɚz **-uring** -ᵊr.ɪŋ **-ured** -əd Ⓤⓢ -ɚd
enregist|er ɪn'redʒ.ɪ.st|əʳ, en-, '-ə- Ⓤⓢ en'redʒ.ɪ.st|ɚ, ɪn-, '-ə- **-ers** -əz Ⓤⓢ -ɚz **-ering** -ᵊr.ɪŋ **-ered** -əd Ⓤⓢ -ɚd
enrich ɪn'rɪtʃ, en- Ⓤⓢ en-, ɪn- **-es** -ɪz **-ing** -ɪŋ **-ed** -t **-ment** -mənt
Enright 'en.raɪt
enrob|e ɪn'rəʊb, en- Ⓤⓢ en'roʊb, ɪn- **-es** -z **-ing** -ɪŋ **-ed** -d
enrol ɪn'rəʊl, en- Ⓤⓢ en'roʊl, ɪn- **-s** -z **-ling** -ɪŋ **-led** -d
enroll ɪn'rəʊl, en- Ⓤⓢ en'roʊl, ɪn- **-s** -z **-ing** -ɪŋ **-ed** -d
enrol(l)ment ɪn'rəʊl.mənt, en- Ⓤⓢ en'roʊl-, ɪn- **-s** -s
en route ˌɑ̃ː*n*'ruːt, ˌɒn- Ⓤⓢ ˌɑːn-
en|s en|z **-tia** -ʃi.ə, -ʃə, -ti.ə
ENSA 'en*t*.sə
ensample en'sɑːm.pl̩, ɪn- Ⓤⓢ -'sæm- **-s** -z
ensanguined ɪn'sæŋ.gwɪnd, en- Ⓤⓢ en-, ɪn-
ensconc|e ɪn'skɒn*t*s, en- Ⓤⓢ en'skɑːn*t*s, ɪn- **-es** -ɪz **-ing** -ɪŋ **-ed** -t
ensemble ɑ̃ː*n*'sɑ̃ː*m*.bᵊl, ɒn'sɒm- Ⓤⓢ ˌɑːn'sɑːm- **-s** -z
enshrin|e ɪn'ʃraɪn, en- Ⓤⓢ en-, ɪn- **-es** -z **-ing** -ɪŋ **-ed** -d **-ement** -mənt
enshroud ɪn'ʃraʊd, en- Ⓤⓢ en-, ɪn- **-s** -z **-ing** -ɪŋ **-ed** -ɪd
ensign *flag:* 'en.saɪn *in the navy:* 'en*t*.sᵊn **-s** -z
ensign *officer:* 'en.saɪn Ⓤⓢ 'en.sɪn **-s** -z
ensign (*v.*) en'saɪn, ɪn- **-s** -z **-ing** -ɪŋ **-ed** -d
ensilag|e 'en*t*.sɪ.lɪdʒ, -sə; ɪn'saɪ-, en- Ⓤⓢ 'en*t*.sə- **-es** -ɪz
ensil|e en'saɪl, 'en*t*.saɪl **-es** -z **-ing** -ɪŋ **-ed** -d
enslav|e ɪn'sleɪv, en- Ⓤⓢ en-, ɪn- **-es** -z **-ing** -ɪŋ **-ed** -d **-er/s** -əʳ/z Ⓤⓢ -ɚ/z **-ement** -mənt
ensnar|e ɪn'sneəʳ, en- Ⓤⓢ en'sner, ɪn- **-es** -z **-ing** -ɪŋ **-ed** -d **-er/s** -əʳ/z Ⓤⓢ -ɚ/z
ensoul ɪn'səʊl, en- Ⓤⓢ en'soʊl, ɪn- **-s** -z **-ing** -ɪŋ **-ed** -d
ensu|e ɪn'sjuː, en-, -'suː Ⓤⓢ en'suː, ɪn-, -'sjuː **-es** -z **-ing** -ɪŋ **-ed** -d
en suite ˌɑ̃ː*n*'swiːt, ˌɒn- Ⓤⓢ ˌɑːn- *stress shift:* ˌen suite 'bathroom
ensur|e ɪn'ʃɔːʳ, en-, -'ʃʊəʳ, -'sjʊəʳ Ⓤⓢ en'ʃʊr, ɪn- **-es** -z **-ing** -ɪŋ **-ed** -d
-ent -ᵊnt
Note: Suffix. Words containing **-ent** are stressed in a similar way to those containing **-ence**; see above.
entablature en'tæb.lə.tʃəʳ, ɪn-, -lɪ-, -tʃʊəʳ, -tjʊəʳ Ⓤⓢ -lə.tʃɚ **-s** -z
entail ɪn'teɪl, en- Ⓤⓢ en-, ɪn- **-s** -z **-ing** -ɪŋ **-ed** -d **-er/s** -əʳ/z Ⓤⓢ -ɚ/z **-ment** -mənt
entangl|e ɪn'tæŋ.gl̩, en- Ⓤⓢ en-, ɪn- **-es** -z **-ing** -ɪŋ, '-glɪŋ **-ed** -d **-ement/s** -mənt/s
Entebbe en'teb.i, ɪn- Ⓤⓢ -ə
entendre ɑ̃ː*n*'tɑ̃ː*n*.drə Ⓤⓢ ɑːn'tɑːn.drə
entente ɑ̃ː*n*'tɑ̃ː*n*t Ⓤⓢ ɑːn'tɑːnt **-s** -s
entente cordiale ˌɑ̃ː*n*.tɑ̃ː*n*t.kɔː.di'ɑːl Ⓤⓢ ˌɑːn.tɑːnt.kɔːr-
ent|er 'en.t|əʳ Ⓤⓢ -t̬|ɚ **-ers** -əz Ⓤⓢ -ɚz **-ering** -ᵊr.ɪŋ **-ered** -əd Ⓤⓢ -ɚd
enteric en'ter.ɪk
enteritis ˌen.tə'raɪ.tɪs Ⓤⓢ -t̬ɪs
enterokinas|e ˌen.tᵊr.əʊ'kaɪ.neɪz Ⓤⓢ -t̬ə.roʊ'kaɪ.neɪs, -'kɪn.eɪs, -eɪz **-es** -ɪz
enterology ˌen.tə'rɒl.ə.dʒi Ⓤⓢ -t̬ə'rɑː.lə-
enterotomy ˌen.tə'rɒt.ə.mi Ⓤⓢ -t̬ə'rɑː.t̬ə-
enterovirus ˌen.tᵊr.əʊ'vaɪə.rəs Ⓤⓢ -t̬ə.roʊ'vaɪ.rəs **-es** -ɪz
enterpris|e 'en.tə.praɪz Ⓤⓢ -t̬ɚ- **-es** -ɪz **-ing/ly** -ɪŋ/li
entertain ˌen.tə'teɪn Ⓤⓢ -t̬ɚ'- **-s** -z **-ing/ly** -ɪŋ/li **-ed** -d **-er/s** -əʳ/z Ⓤⓢ -ɚ/z
entertainment ˌen.tə'teɪn.mənt Ⓤⓢ -t̬ɚ'- **-s** -s
enthral ɪn'θrɔːl, en- Ⓤⓢ en'θrɔːl, ɪn-, -'θrɑːl **-s** -z **-ling** -ɪŋ **-led** -d **-ment** -mənt
enthrall ɪn'θrɔːl, en- Ⓤⓢ en'θrɔːl, ɪn-, -'θrɑːl **-s** -z **-ing** -ɪŋ **-ed** -d **-ment** -mənt
enthron|e ɪn'θrəʊn, en- Ⓤⓢ en'θroʊn, ɪn- **-es** -z **-ing** -ɪŋ **-ed** -d **-ement/s** -mənt/s
enthus|e ɪn'θjuːz, en- Ⓤⓢ en'θuːz, ɪn-, -'θjuːz **-es** -ɪz **-ing** -ɪŋ **-ed** -d
enthusi|asm ɪn'θjuː.zi|.æz.ᵊm, en-, -'θuː- Ⓤⓢ en'θuː-, ɪn-, -'θjuː- **-ast/s** -æst/s
enthusiastic ɪnˌθjuː.zi'æs.tɪk, en-, -ˌθuː- Ⓤⓢ enˌθuː-, ɪn-, -ˌθjuː- **-ally** -ᵊl.i, -li
entia (*plur. of* **ens**) 'en.ʃi.ə, -ʃə, -ti.ə
entic|e ɪn'taɪs, en- Ⓤⓢ en-, ɪn- **-es** -ɪz **-ing/ly** -ɪŋ/li **-ed** -t **-ement/s** -mənt/s
entire ɪn'taɪəʳ, en- Ⓤⓢ en'taɪɚ, ɪn- **-ly** -li **-ness** -nəs, -nɪs
entiret|y ɪn'taɪə.rə.t|i, en- Ⓤⓢ en'taɪ.rə.t̬|i, -'taɪr.t̬|i, ɪn- **-ies** -iz
entitl|e ɪn'taɪ.tl̩, en- Ⓤⓢ en'taɪ.t̬l̩, ɪn- **-es** -z **-ing** -ɪŋ, -'taɪt.lɪŋ **-ed** -d
entitlement ɪn'taɪ.tl̩.mənt, en- Ⓤⓢ en'taɪ.t̬l̩-, ɪn- **-s** -s
entit|y 'en.tɪ.t|i, -tə- Ⓤⓢ -t̬ə.t̬|i **-ies** -iz
entomb ɪn'tuːm, en- Ⓤⓢ en-, ɪn- **-s** -z **-ing** -ɪŋ **-ed** -d **-ment/s** -mənt/s
entomological ˌen.tə.mə'lɒdʒ.ɪ.kl̩ Ⓤⓢ -t̬ə.mə'lɑː.dʒɪ- **-ly** -i

entomologiz|e, -is|e ˌen.tə'mɒl.ə.dʒaɪz (US) -t̬ə'mɑː.lə- **-es** -ɪz **-ing** -ɪŋ **-ed** -d
entomolog|y ˌen.tə'mɒl.ə.dʒ|i (US) -t̬ə'mɑː.lə- **-ist/s** -ɪst/s
entourag|e 'ɒn.tʊ.rɑːʒ, 'ɑ̃ːn-, -tʊə-, ˌ--'- (US) ˌɑːn.tʊ'rɑːʒ **-es** -ɪz
entr'acte 'ɒn.trækt, 'ɑ̃ːn-, ˌ-'- (US) 'ɑːnˌtrækt, ɑ̃ːn-, ˌ-'- **-s** -s
entrails 'en.treɪlz
entrain ɪn'treɪn, en- (US) en-, ɪn- **-s** -z **-ing** -ɪŋ **-ed** -d
entrammel ɪn'træm.əl, en- (US) en-, ɪn- **-s** -z **-(l)ing** -ɪŋ **-(l)ed** -d
entranc|e (*n.*) *entry, place of entry, etc.:* 'en.trənts **-es** -ɪz
entranc|e (*v.*) *put in state of trance, delight:* ɪn'trɑːnts, en- (US) en'trænts, ɪn- **-es** -ɪz **-ing** -ɪŋ **-ed** -t **-ement/s** -mənt/s
entrant 'en.trənt **-s** -s
entrap ɪn'træp, en- (US) en-, ɪn- **-s** -s **-ping** -ɪŋ **-ped** -t **-ment** -mənt
en|treat ɪn|'triːt, en- (US) en-, ɪn- **-treats** -'triːts **-treating/ly** -'triː.tɪŋ/li (US) -'triː.t̬ɪŋ/li **-treated** -'triː.tɪd (US) -'triː.t̬ɪd **-treatment** -'triːt.mənt
entreat|y ɪn'triː.t|i, en- (US) en'triː.t̬|i, ɪn- **-ies** -iz
entrechat 'ɑ̃ːn.trə.ʃɑː, 'ɒn- (US) ˌɑːn.trə'ʃɑː, '--- **-s** -z
entrecôte 'ɑ̃ːn.trə.kəʊt, 'ɒn- (US) 'ɑːn.trə.koʊt, 'ɑ̃ːn-, ˌ--'- **-s** -s
entrée 'ɑ̃ːn.treɪ, 'ɒn- (US) 'ɑːn-, ˌ-'- **-s** -z
entremets (*sing.*) 'ɑ̃ːn.trə.meɪ, 'ɒnt- (US) 'ɑːn.trə-, ˌ--'- (*plur.*) -z
entrench ɪn'trentʃ, en- (US) en-, ɪn- **-es** -ɪz **-ing** -ɪŋ **-ed** -t **-ment/s** -mənt/s
entre nous ˌɑ̃ːn.trə'nuː, ˌɒn- (US) ˌɑːn-
entrepôt 'ɑ̃ːn.trə.pəʊ, 'ɒn- (US) 'ɑːn.trə.poʊ; ˌ--'- **-s** -z
entrepreneur ˌɒn.trə.prə'nɜːr, ˌɑ̃ːn-, -pren'ɜːr (US) ˌɑːn.trə.prə'nɜːr, -'nʊr, -'njʊr **-s** -z
entrepreneurial ˌɒn.trə.prə'nɜː.ri.əl, ˌɑ̃ːn- (US) ˌɑːn.trə.prə'nɜːr.i-, -'nʊr-, -'njʊr-
entresol 'ɑ̃ːn.trə.sɒl, 'ɒn- (US) 'ɑːn.trə.sɑːl, ˌ--'- **-s** -z
entropy 'en.trə.pi
entrust ɪn'trʌst, en- (US) en-, ɪn- **-s** -s **-ing** -ɪŋ **-ed** -ɪd
entr|y 'en.tr|i **-ies** -iz
entry|ism 'en.tri|.ɪ.zəm **-ist/s** -ɪst/s
entryphone 'en.tri.fəʊn (US) -foʊn **-s** -z
entryway 'en.tri.weɪ **-s** -z
entwin|e ɪn'twaɪn, en- (US) en-, ɪn- **-es** -z **-ing** -ɪŋ **-ed** -d
entwist ɪn'twɪst, en- (US) en-, ɪn- **-s** -s **-ing** -ɪŋ **-ed** -ɪd
enumerable ɪ'njuː.mər.ə.bl̩ (US) -'nuː-, -'njuː-
enumer|ate ɪ'njuː.mər|.eɪt (US) -'nuː.mə.r|eɪt, -'njuː- **-ates** -eɪts **-ating** -eɪ.tɪŋ (US) -eɪ.t̬ɪŋ **-ated** -eɪ.tɪd (US) -eɪ.t̬ɪd **-ator/s** -eɪ.tər/z (US) -eɪ.t̬ɚ/z
enumeration ɪˌnjuː.mər'eɪ.ʃən (US) -ˌnuː.mə'reɪ-, -ˌnjuː- **-s** -z
enumerative ɪ'njuː.mər.ə.tɪv, -eɪ.tɪv (US) -'nuː.mɚ.ə.t̬ɪv, -'njuː-
enunciable ɪ'nʌnt.si.ə.bl̩, -ʃi.ə-
enunci|ate ɪ'nʌnt.si|.eɪt, -ʃi- **-ates** -eɪts **-ating** -eɪ.tɪŋ (US) -eɪ.t̬ɪŋ **-ated** -eɪ.tɪd (US) -eɪ.t̬ɪd **-ator/s** -eɪ.tər/z (US) -eɪ.t̬ɚ/z
enunciation ɪˌnʌnt.si'eɪ.ʃən **-s** -z
enunciative ɪ'nʌnt.si.ə.tɪv, -ʃi.ə-, -eɪ.tɪv (US) -ə.t̬ɪv
enur|e ɪ'njʊər (US) -'njʊr **-es** -z **-ing** -ɪŋ **-ed** -d
enuresis ˌen.jʊə'riː.sɪs (US) -juː'-
envelop ɪn'vel.əp, en- (US) en-, ɪn- **-s** -s **-ing** -ɪŋ **-ed** -t **-ment/s** -mənt/s
envelope 'en.və.ləʊp, 'ɒn- (US) 'en.və.loʊp, 'ɑːn- **-s** -s
envenom ɪn'ven.əm, en- (US) en-, ɪn- **-s** -z **-ing** -ɪŋ **-ed** -d
enviab|le 'en.vi.ə.b|l̩ **-ly** -li **-leness** -l̩.nəs, -nɪs
envious 'en.vi.əs **-ly** -li **-ness** -nəs, -nɪs
environ (*v.*) ɪn'vaɪə.rən, en- (US) en'vaɪ-, ɪn-, -ɚn **-s** -z **-ing** -ɪŋ **-ed** -d
environment ɪn'vaɪə.rən.mənt, en- (US) en'vaɪ-, ɪn-, -ɚn- **-s** -s
environmental ɪnˌvaɪə.rən'men.təl, en-, -rəm'- (US) enˌvaɪ.rən'men.t̬əl, ɪn-, -ɚn'- **-ly** -i
environmental|ism ɪnˌvaɪə.rən'men.təl|.ɪ.zəm, en-, -rəm'- (US) enˌvaɪ.rən'men.t̬əl-, ɪn-, -ɚn'- **-ist/s** -ɪst/s
environmentally-friendly ɪnˌvaɪə.rənˌmen.təl.i'frend.li, en-, -rəmˌ- (US) enˌvaɪ.rən.men.t̬əl-, ɪn-, ˌ-ɚn-
environs (*n.*) ɪn'vaɪə.rənz, en-; 'en.vɪ-, -vər.ənz (US) en'vaɪ.rənz, ɪn-, -ɚnz
envisag|e ɪn'vɪz.ɪdʒ, en- (US) en-, ɪn- **-es** -ɪz **-ing** -ɪŋ **-ed** -d
envision ɪn'vɪʒ.ən, en- (US) en-, ɪn- **-s** -z **-ing** -ɪŋ **-ed** -d
envoy 'en.vɔɪ (US) 'ɑːn-, 'en- **-s** -z
env|y 'en.v|i **-ies** -iz **-ying** -i.ɪŋ **-ied** -id
enwrap ɪn'ræp, en- (US) en-, ɪn- **-s** -s **-ping** -ɪŋ **-ped** -t
enwreath|e ɪn'riːð, en- (US) en-, ɪn- **-es** -z **-ing** -ɪŋ **-ed** -d
enzyme 'en.zaɪm **-s** -z
enzymolog|y ˌen.zaɪ'mɒl.ə.dʒ|i (US) -zɪ'-, -'mɑː.lə- **-ist/s** -ɪst/s
Eocene 'iː.əʊ.siːn (US) -oʊ-, -ə-
eolian (E) i'əʊ.li.ən (US) -'oʊ-
eolith 'iː.əʊ.lɪθ (US) -oʊ-, -ə- **-s** -s
eolithic ˌiː.əʊ'lɪθ.ɪk (US) -oʊ'-, -ə'-
-eous -i.əs, -əs
Note: Suffix. Words containing **-eous** are normally stressed on the syllable preceding the suffix, e.g. **advantage** /əd'vɑːn.tɪdʒ (US) -'væn.t̬ɪdʒ/, **advantageous** /ˌæd.vən'teɪ.dʒəs (US) -væn'-/.
EP ˌiː'piː
EPA ˌiː.piː'eɪ
epact 'iː.pækt, 'ep.ækt **-s** -s
Epaminondas epˌæm.ɪ'nɒn.dæs, ɪˌpæm-, -ə'- (US) ɪˌpæm.ə'nɑːn-
eparch 'ep.ɑːk (US) -ɑːrk **-s** -s **-y** -i **-ies** -iz
epaulette, epaulet ˌep.ə'let, -ɔː'-, '--- (US) ˌep.ə'let, '--- **-s** -s
Epcot® 'ep.kɒt (US) -kɑːt **'Epcot ˌCenter**
epee, épée 'ep.eɪ, 'eɪ.peɪ, -'- (US) eɪ'peɪ; 'ep.eɪ **-s** -z **-ist/s** -ɪst/s
epenthes|is ep'ent.θə.s|ɪs, ɪ'pent-, -θɪ- (US) ɪ'pent.θə- **-es** -iːz
epenthetic ˌep.en'θet.ɪk, -ən'- (US) -en'θet̬-
epergne ɪ'pɜːn, ep'ɜːn, -'eən (US) iː'pɜːrn, eɪ- **-s** -z
epexegesis epˌek.sɪ'dʒiː.sɪs, ɪˌpek-, -sə'- (US) -sə'-
epexegetic epˌek.sɪ'dʒet.ɪk, ɪˌpek-, -sə'- (US) -sə'dʒet̬- **-al** -əl **-ally** -əl.i, -li
ephah 'iː.fə **-s** -z
ephedrine 'ef.ə.drɪn, '-ɪ-, -driːn, ɪ'fed.rɪn, -riːn (US) ɪ'fed.rin; 'ef.ə.driːn, -drɪn
ephemer|a ɪ'fem.ər|.ə, ef'em-, ə'fem-, -'fiː.mər- (US) ɪ'fem.ɚ-, ef'em-, '-r|ə **-as** -əz **-al** -əl
ephemeralit|y ɪˌfem.ə'ræl.ə.t|i, efˌem-, əˌfem-, -ˌfiː.mə'-, -ɪ.t|i (US) ɪˌfem.ə'ræl.ə.t̬|i, efˌem- **-ies** -iz
ephemeris ɪ'fem.ər.ɪs, ef'em-, ə'fem-, -'fiː.mər- (US) ɪ'fem-, ef'em-
ephemerides ˌef.ɪ'mer.ɪ.diːz (US) -ə'mer.ə-
ephemeron ɪ'fem.ər.ɒn, ef'em-, ə'fem-, -'fiː.mər-, -ən (US) ɪ'fem.ə.rɑːn, ef'em-, -rən **-s** -z
ephemerous ɪ'fem.ər.əs, ef'em-, ə'fem-, -'fiː.mər- (US) ɪ'fem.ɚ-, ef'em-
Ephesian ɪ'fiː.ʒən, ef'iː-, -ʒi.ən, -zi- **-s** -z
Ephesus 'ef.ə.səs, '-ɪ-
ephod 'iː.fɒd, 'ef.ɒd (US) -ɑːd **-s** -z
Ephraim 'iː.freɪ.ɪm, -fri-, -əm, -frəm (US) 'iː.fri.əm, -frəm
Ephron 'ef.rɒn, 'iː.frɒn (US) -frɑːn
epi- ep.i-, ep.ə-; ep'ɪ-
Note: Prefix. Normally takes either

primary or secondary stress on the first syllable, e.g. **epicycle** /'ep.ɪ.saɪ.kl̩/, **epicyclic** /ˌep.ɪ'sɪk.lɪk/, but may also be stressed on the second syllable, e.g. **epigraphy** /e'pɪg.rə.fi/.

epiblast 'ep.ɪ.blæst **-s** -s
epic 'ep.ɪk **-s** -s
epicanth|ic ˌep.ɪ'kæn*t*.θ|ɪk **-us/es** -əs/ɪz **-i** -aɪ
epicene 'ep.ɪ.siːn **-s** -z
epicenter 'ep.ɪ.sen.təʳ ⓤⓢ -t̬ɚ **-s** -z
epicentral ˌep.ɪ'sen.trəl
epicentre 'ep.ɪ.sen.təʳ ⓤⓢ -t̬ɚ **-s** -z
epicentr|um ˌep.ɪ'sen.tr|əm **-ums** -əmz **-a** -ə
Epicharmus ˌep.ɪ'kɑː.məs ⓤⓢ -'kɑːr-
epic|ism 'ep.ɪ.s|ɪ.zᵊm **-ist/s** -ɪst/s
Epicoene 'ep.ɪ.siː.ni ⓤⓢ 'ep.ɪ.siːn
epicotyl 'ep.ɪ.kɒt.ɪl ⓤⓢ -kɑː.t̬ᵊl **-s** -z
Epictetus ˌep.ɪk'tiː.təs ⓤⓢ -t̬əs
epicure 'ep.ɪ.kjʊəʳ, -kjɔːʳ ⓤⓢ -kjʊr **-s** -z
Epicurean ˌep.ɪ.kjʊə'riː.ən, -kjɔː'- ⓤⓢ -kjʊr'iː- **-s** -z
epicurism 'ep.ɪ.kjʊə.rɪ.zᵊm, -kjɔː- ⓤⓢ -kjʊr.ɪ-
Epicurus ˌep.ɪ'kjʊə.rəs, -'kjɔː- ⓤⓢ -ə'kjʊr.əs
epicycle 'ep.ɪ.saɪ.kl̩ ⓤⓢ '-ə- **-s** -z
epicyclic ˌep.ɪ'saɪ.klɪk, -'sɪk.lɪk ⓤⓢ -ə'-
epicycloid ˌep.ɪ'saɪ.klɔɪd ⓤⓢ -ə'- **-s** -z
Epidaurus ˌep.ɪ'dɔː.rəs ⓤⓢ -ə'dɔːr.əs
epideictic ˌep.ɪ'daɪk.tɪk ⓤⓢ -ə'-
epidemic ˌep.ɪ'dem.ɪk ⓤⓢ -ə'- **-s** -s **-al** -ᵊl **-ally** -ᵊl.i, -li
epidemiological ˌep.ɪˌdiː.mi.ə'lɒdʒ.ɪ.kᵊl ⓤⓢ -əˌdiː.mi.ə'lɑː.dʒɪ-, -ˌdem.i- **-ly** -i
epidemiolog|y ˌep.ɪˌdiː.mi'ɒl.ə.dʒ|i ⓤⓢ -əˌdiː.mi'ɑː.lə-, -ˌdem.i'- **-ist/s** -ɪst/s
epiderm|al ˌep.ɪ'dɜː.m|ᵊl ⓤⓢ -ə'dɜːr- **-ic** -ɪk **-oid** -ɔɪd
epidermis ˌep.ɪ'dɜː.mɪs ⓤⓢ -ə'dɜːr-
epidiascope ˌep.ɪ'daɪə.skəʊp ⓤⓢ -ə'daɪə.skoʊp **-s** -s
epididymis ˌep.ɪ'dɪd.ə.mɪs, '-ɪ- ⓤⓢ -ə'- **epididymides** ˌep.ɪ.dɪ'dɪm.ɪ.diːz ⓤⓢ -ə-
epidural ˌep.ɪ'djʊə.rᵊl, -'djɔː- ⓤⓢ -ə'dʊr.ᵊl, -'djʊr- **-s** -z
epige|al ˌep.ɪ'dʒiː|.əl ⓤⓢ -ə'- **-an** -ən
epigene 'ep.ɪ.dʒiːn ⓤⓢ '-ə-
epigenesis ˌep.ɪ'dʒen.ə.sɪs, '-ɪ- ⓤⓢ -ə'-
epiglott|al ˌep.ɪ'glɒt|.ᵊl, 'ep.ɪ.glɒt- ⓤⓢ ˌep.ə'glɑː.t̬|ᵊl **-ic** -ɪk
epiglottis ˌep.ɪ'glɒt.ɪs, 'ep.ɪ.glɒt- ⓤⓢ -ə'glɑː.t̬ɪs **-es** -ɪz
epigone 'ep.ɪ.gəʊn ⓤⓢ -ə.goʊn **-s** -z
Epigoni ep'ɪ.gə.naɪ, ɪ'pɪg-, -niː
epigram 'ep.ɪ.græm ⓤⓢ '-ə- **-s** -z
epigrammatic ˌep.ɪ.grə'mæt.ɪk ⓤⓢ -ə.grə'mæt̬- **-al** -ᵊl **-ally** -ᵊl.i, -li
epigrammatist ˌep.ɪ'græm.ə.tɪst ⓤⓢ -ə'græm.ə.t̬ɪst **-s** -s
epigrammatiz|e, -is|e ˌep.ɪ'græm.ə.taɪz ⓤⓢ -ə'- **-es** -ɪz **-ing** -ɪŋ **-ed** -d
epigraph 'ep.ɪ.grɑːf, -græf ⓤⓢ -ə.græf **-s** -s
epigrapher ep'ɪg.rə.fəʳ, ɪ'pɪg- ⓤⓢ -fɚ **-s** -z
epigraphic ˌep.ɪ'græf.ɪk ⓤⓢ -ə'-
epigraph|y ep'ɪg.rə.f|i, ɪ'pɪg- **-ist/s** -ɪst/s
epilepsy 'ep.ɪ.lep.si, '-ə-
epileptic ˌep.ɪ'lep.tɪk, -ə'- **-s** -s **-al** -ᵊl
epilog 'ep.ɪ.lɒg ⓤⓢ -ə.lɑːg, -lɔːg **-s** -z
epilogic ˌep.ɪ'lɒdʒ.ɪk, -ə'- ⓤⓢ -ə'lɑː.dʒɪk
epilogiz|e, -is|e ep'ɪl.ə.dʒaɪz, ɪ'pɪl- **-es** -ɪz **-ing** -ɪŋ **-ed** -d
epilogue 'ep.ɪ.lɒg ⓤⓢ -ə.lɑːg, -lɔːg **-s** -z
Epimenides ˌep.ɪ'men.ɪ.diːz, -ə.diːz ⓤⓢ -ə'-
Epinal 'ep.ɪ.nᵊl ⓤⓢ ˌeɪ.piː'nɑːl
epiphan|y (E) ɪ'pɪf.ᵊn|.i, ep'ɪf-, ə'pɪf- ⓤⓢ ɪ'pɪf.ə.n|i **-ies** -iz
epiphyte 'ep.ɪ.faɪt ⓤⓢ '-ə- **-s** -s
Epirus ep'aɪə.rəs, ɪ'paɪə- ⓤⓢ ɪ'paɪ-
episcopac|y ɪ'pɪs.kə.pə.s|i, ep'ɪs- **-ies** -iz
episcopal ɪ'pɪs.kə.pᵊl, ep'ɪs- **-ly** -i
episcopalian (E) ɪˌpɪs.kə'peɪ.li.ən, epˌɪs- ⓤⓢ -'peɪ.li.ən, -'peɪl.jən **-s** -z **-ism** -ɪ.zᵊm
episcopate ɪ'pɪs.kə.pət, ep'ɪs-, -pɪt, -peɪt **-s** -s
episcope 'ep.ɪ.skəʊp ⓤⓢ -ə.skoʊp **-s** -s
episcopiz|e, -is|e ɪ'pɪs.kə.paɪz, ep'ɪs- **-es** -ɪz **-ing** -ɪŋ **-ed** -d
episiotom|y ɪˌpɪz.i'ɒt.ə.m|i, epˌɪz-, -ˌiː.zi'-; ˌep.ɪ.zi'- ⓤⓢ ɪˌpiː.ziː'ɑː.t̬ə-; ˌep.ɪ.saɪ'- **-ies** -iz
episode 'ep.ɪ.səʊd ⓤⓢ -ə.soʊd **-s** -z
episodic ˌep.ɪ'sɒd.ɪk ⓤⓢ -ə'sɑː.dɪk **-al** -ᵊl **-ally** -ᵊl.i, -li
epistemic ˌep.ɪ'stiː.mɪk, -'stem.ɪk
epistemological ɪˌpɪs.tɪ.mə'lɒdʒ.ɪ.kᵊl, epˌɪs-, -tə-, -tiː- ⓤⓢ -'lɑː.dʒɪ- **-ly** -li
epistemology ɪˌpɪs.tə'mɒl.ə.dʒi, epˌɪs-, -tɪ'- ⓤⓢ -tə'mɑː.lə-
epistle (E) ɪ'pɪs.l̩, ep'ɪs- ⓤⓢ ɪ'pɪs- **-s** -z
epistler ɪ'pɪs*t*.ləʳ, ep'ɪs- ⓤⓢ ɪ'pɪs*t*.lɚ **-s** -z
epistolary ɪ'pɪs.tᵊl.ᵊr.i, ep'ɪs- ⓤⓢ ɪ'pɪs.tᵊl.er-
epistoler ɪ'pɪs.tᵊl.əʳ, ep'ɪs- ⓤⓢ ɪ'pɪs.tᵊl.ɚ **-s** -z
epistoliz|e, -is|e ɪ'pɪs.tᵊl.aɪz, ep'ɪs- ⓤⓢ ɪ'pɪs.tə.laɪz **-es** -ɪz **-ing** -ɪŋ **-ed** -d
epistyle 'ep.ɪ.staɪl **-s** -z
epitaph 'ep.ɪ.tɑːf, -tæf ⓤⓢ -ə.tæf **-s** -s
Epithalamion ˌep.ɪ.θə'leɪ.mi.ən
epithalami|um ˌep.ɪ.θə'leɪ.mi|.əm **-a** -ə **-ums** -əmz
epitheli|um ˌep.ɪ'θiː.li|.əm **-ums** -əmz **-a** -ə
epithet 'ep.ɪ.θet ⓤⓢ -θet, -θət **-s** -s
epithetic ˌep.ɪ'θet.ɪk ⓤⓢ -ə'θet̬-
epitome ɪ'pɪt.ə.mi, ep'ɪt-, ə'pɪt- ⓤⓢ ɪ'pɪt̬- **-s** -z
epitomic ˌep.ɪ'tɒm.ɪk ⓤⓢ -'tɑː.mɪk **-al** -ᵊl
epitomist ɪ'pɪt.ə.mɪst, ep'ɪt- ⓤⓢ ɪ'pɪt̬- **-s** -s
epitomiz|e, -is|e ɪ'pɪt.ə.maɪz, ep'ɪt- ⓤⓢ ɪ'pɪt̬- **-es** -ɪz **-ing** -ɪŋ **-ed** -d
epoch 'iː.pɒk, 'ep.ək ⓤⓢ 'ep.ək, -ɑːk, ˌiː'pɑːk **-s** -s
epochal 'iː.pɒk.ᵊl, 'ep.ɒk-, -ə.kᵊl; iː'pɒk.ᵊl ⓤⓢ 'ep.ə.kᵊl; -ɑː.kᵊl
epoch-making 'iː.pɒkˌmeɪ.kɪŋ ⓤⓢ 'ep.əkˌ-, -ɑːkˌ-
epode 'ep.əʊd ⓤⓢ -oʊd **-s** -z
eponym 'ep.ə.nɪm **-s** -z
eponymous ɪ'pɒn.ɪ.məs, ep'ɒn-, '-ə- ⓤⓢ ɪ'pɑː.nə-
eponymy ɪ'pɒn.ɪ.mi, ep'ɒn-, '-ə- ⓤⓢ ɪ'pɑː.nə-
epos 'ep.ɒs, 'iː.pɒs ⓤⓢ 'ep.ɑːs **-es** -ɪz
Epos, EPOS 'iː.pɒs ⓤⓢ -pɑːs
epoxy ɪ'pɒk.si, ep'ɒk- ⓤⓢ ɪ'pɑːk- **eˌpoxy 'resin**
Epping 'ep.ɪŋ
Epps eps
EPROM 'iː.prɒm ⓤⓢ -prɑːm **-s** -z
epsilon ep'saɪ.lən, -lɒn; 'ep.sɪ.lən, -sə-, -lɒn ⓤⓢ 'ep.sə.lɑːn, -lən **-s** -z
Epsom 'ep.səm **'Epsom ˌsalts, ˌEpsom 'salts**
Epstein 'ep.staɪn
Epstein-Barr ˌep.staɪn'bɑːʳ, -staɪm'- ⓤⓢ -staɪn.'bɑːr
Epworth 'ep.wəθ, -wɜːθ ⓤⓢ -wɚθ, -wɜːrθ
epylli|on ep'ɪl.i|.ɒn, ɪ'pɪl-, -ən ⓤⓢ -ɑːn, -ən **-a** -ə
equability ˌek.wə'bɪl.ə.ti, ˌiː.kwə'-, -ɪ.ti ⓤⓢ -ə.t̬i
equab|le 'ek.wə.b|l̩, 'iː.kwə- **-ly** -li **-leness** -l̩.nəs, -nɪs
equal 'iː.kwəl **-ly** -i **-ness** -nəs, -nɪs **-s** -z **-(l)ing** -ɪŋ **-(l)ed** -d **ˌEqual Oppor'tunities Comˌmission ; ˌEqual 'Rights Aˌmendment ; ˌequal 'rights ; 'equals ˌsign**
equalit|y ɪ'kwɒl.ə.t|i, iː-, -ɪ.t|i ⓤⓢ -'kwɑː.lə.t̬|i, -'kwɔː- **-ies** -iz
equalization, -isa- ˌiː.kwᵊl.aɪ'zeɪ.ʃᵊn, -ɪ'- ⓤⓢ -ɪ'- **-s** -z
equaliz|e, -is|e 'iː.kwᵊl.aɪz ⓤⓢ -kwə.laɪz **-es** -ɪz **-ing** -ɪŋ **-ed** -d

equalizer, -iser 'iː.kwə.laɪ.zəʳ (US) -zɚ **-s** -z

equanimity ˌek.wə'nɪm.ə.ti, ˌiː.kwə'-, -ɪ.ti (US) -ə.t̬i

equanimous ɪ'kwæn.ɪ.məs, iː-, ek'wæn-, -'wɒn-, -ə.məs (US) ɪ'kwæn-, iː-, ek'wæn- **-ly** -li **-ness** -nəs, -nɪs

e|quate ɪ'kweɪt, iː- **-quates** -kweɪts **-quating** -kweɪ.tɪŋ (US) -kweɪ.t̬ɪŋ **-quated** -kweɪ.tɪd (US) -kweɪ.t̬ɪd **-quatable** -kweɪ.tə.bl̩ (US) -kweɪ.t̬ə.bl̩

equation ɪ'kweɪ.ʒᵊn (US) ɪ'-, iː'- **-s** -z

equational ɪ'kweɪ.ʒᵊn.ᵊl, iː-

equative ɪ'kweɪ.tɪv (US) -t̬ɪv

equator ɪ'kweɪ.təʳ (US) -t̬ɚ **-s** -z

equatorial ˌek.wə'tɔː.ri.əl, ˌiː.kwə'- (US) -'tɔːr.i- **-ly** -i

equerr|y 'ek.wə.r|i; ɪ'kwer|.i (US) 'ek.wɚ|.i; ɪ'kwer- **-ies** -iz

Note: The pronunciation at court is /ɪ'kwer.i/.

equestrian ɪ'kwes.tri.ən, ek'wes- (US) ɪ'kwes- **-s** -z **-ism** -ɪ.zᵊm

equestrienne ɪˌkwes.tri'en, ekˌwes- (US) ɪˌkwes- **-s** -z

equi- iː.kwɪ-, ek.wɪ-, -wi-, -wə-; ɪ'kwɪ-

Note: Prefix. Either takes primary or secondary stress on the first syllable, e.g. **equinox** /'iː.kwɪ.nɒks (US) -nɑːks/, **equinoctial** /ˌiː.kwɪn'ɒk.ʃᵊl (US) -'nɑːk-/, or primary or secondary stress on the second syllable, e.g. **equivocate** /ɪ'kwɪv.ə.keɪt/, **equivocation** /ɪˌkwɪv.ə'keɪ.ʃᵊn/.

equiangular ˌiː.kwi'æŋ.gjʊ.ləʳ, -gjə- (US) -lɚ

equidistant ˌiː.kwɪ'dɪs.tᵊnt, ˌek.wɪ'-, -wə'- **-ly** -li

equilateral ˌiː.kwɪ'læt.ᵊr.ᵊl, -kwə'- (US) -'læt̬-, ˌek.wə'-

equilib|rate ˌiː.kwɪ'laɪ.b|reɪt, ˌek.wɪ'-, -wə'-, -'lɪb|.reɪt; iː'kwɪl.ɪ.b|reɪt, ɪ- (US) ɪ'kwɪl-, iː- **-rates** -reɪts **-rating** -reɪ.tɪŋ (US) -reɪ.t̬ɪŋ **-rated** -reɪ.tɪd (US) -reɪ.t̬ɪd

equilibration ˌiː.kwɪ.laɪ'breɪ.ʃᵊn, ˌek.wɪ-, -wə-, -lɪ'breɪ-; iːˌkwɪl.ɪ'-, ɪ- (US) ɪˌkwɪl.ɪ'-, iːˌ-

equilibrist iː'kwɪl.ɪ.brɪst, ɪ-; ˌiː.kwɪ'lɪb.rɪst, ˌek.wɪ'-, -wə'- (US) ɪ'kwɪl.ə.brɪst, iː-, ˌiː.kwə'lɪb.rɪst **-s** -s

equilibrium ˌiː.kwɪ'lɪb.ri.əm, ˌek.wɪ'-, -wə'-

equimultiple ˌiː.kwɪ'mʌl.tɪ.pl̩, ˌek.wɪ'-, -wə'-, -tə- (US) -t̬ə- **-s** -z

equine 'ek.waɪn, 'iː.kwaɪn (US) 'iː.kwaɪn, 'ek.waɪn

equinoctial ˌiː.kwɪ'nɒk.ʃᵊl, ˌek.wɪ'-, -wə'- (US) -'nɑːk- **-s** -z

equinox 'iː.kwɪ.nɒks, 'ek.wɪ-, -wə- (US) -nɑːks **-es** -ɪz

equip ɪ'kwɪp **-s** -s **-ping** -ɪŋ **-ped** -t

equipag|e 'ek.wɪ.pɪdʒ, -wə- **-es** -ɪz

equipment ɪ'kwɪp.mənt

equipois|e 'ek.wɪ.pɔɪz, 'iː.kwɪ-, -kwə- **-es** -ɪz **-ing** -ɪŋ **-ed** -d

equipollent ˌiː.kwɪ'pɒl.ənt, ˌek.wɪ'-, -wə'- (US) -'pɑː.lənt

equitab|le 'ek.wɪ.tə.b|l̩, -wə- (US) -t̬ə- **-ly** -li **-leness** -l̩.nəs, -nɪs

equitation ˌek.wɪ'teɪ.ʃᵊn, -wə'-

equit|y (E) 'ek.wɪ.t|i, -wə- (US) -t̬|i **-ies** -iz

equivalen|ce ɪ'kwɪv.ᵊl.ən*t*|s **-cy** -si

equivalent ɪ'kwɪv.ᵊl.ənt **-s** -s **-ly** -li

equivocal ɪ'kwɪv.ə.kᵊl, '-ɪ- **-ly** -i **-ness** -nəs, -nɪs

equivo|cate ɪ'kwɪv.ə|.keɪt **-cates** -keɪts **-cating** -keɪ.tɪŋ (US) -keɪ.t̬ɪŋ **-cated** -keɪ.tɪd (US) -keɪ.t̬ɪd **-cator/s** -keɪ.tɚ/z (US) -keɪ.t̬ɚ/z

equivocation ɪˌkwɪv.ə'keɪ.ʃᵊn **-s** -z

equivoque, equivoke 'ek.wɪ.vəʊk, -wə- (US) -voʊk **-s** -s

Equuleus ek'wʊl.i.əs

er ɜːʳ (US) ɜːr

-er -əʳ (US) -ɚ

Note: Suffix. Normally unstressed, e.g. **paint** /peɪnt/, **painter** /'peɪn.təʳ (US) -t̬ɚ/, **soon** /suːn/, **sooner** /'suː.nəʳ (US) -nɚ/.

ER ˌiː'ɑːʳ (US) -'ɑːr

era 'ɪə.rə (US) 'ɪr.ə, 'er- **-s** -z

ERA ˌiː.ɑːʳ'eɪ (US) -ɑːr'-

eradi|ate ɪ'reɪ.di|.eɪt, iː- **-ates** -eɪts **-ating** -eɪ.tɪŋ (US) -eɪ.t̬ɪŋ **-ated** -eɪ.tɪd (US) -eɪ.t̬ɪd

eradiation ɪˌreɪ.di'eɪ.ʃᵊn, iː-

eradicable ɪ'ræd.ɪ.kə.bl̩

eradi|cate ɪ'ræd.ɪ|.keɪt **-cates** -keɪts **-cating** -keɪ.tɪŋ (US) -keɪ.t̬ɪŋ **-cated** -keɪ.tɪd (US) -keɪ.t̬ɪd

eradication ɪˌræd.ɪ'keɪ.ʃᵊn

eradicative ɪ'ræd.ɪ.kə.tɪv, -keɪ- (US) -kə.t̬ɪv

Érard 'er.ɑːd (US) eɪ'rɑːrd, 'er.ɑːr*d* **-s** -z

eras|e ɪ'reɪz (US) -'reɪs **-es** -ɪz **-ing** -ɪŋ **-ed** -d **-er/s** -əʳ/z (US) -ɚ/z **-able** -ə.bl̩

erasion ɪ'reɪ.ʒᵊn **-s** -z

Erasmian ɪ'ræz.mi.ən, er'æz- **-s** -z **-ism** -ɪ.zᵊm

Erasmus ɪ'ræz.məs, er'æz-

Erastian ɪ'ræs.ti.ən, er'æs- **-s** -z **-ism** -ɪ.zᵊm

Erastus ɪ'ræs.təs, er'æs-

erasure ɪ'reɪ.ʒəʳ (US) -ʃɚ **-s** -z

erbium 'ɜː.bi.əm (US) 'ɜːr-

Erdington 'ɜː.dɪŋ.tən (US) 'ɜːr-

ere eəʳ (US) er

Erebus 'er.ɪ.bəs, '-ə-

Erec 'ɪə.rek (US) 'iː.rek, 'er.ek

Erechtheum ˌer.ek'θiː.əm, -ɪk'-, -ək'-

Erechtheus ɪ'rek.θjuːs, er'ek-, -θi.əs

erect ɪ'rekt **-ly** -li **-ness** -nəs, -nɪs **-s** -s **-ing** -ɪŋ **-ed** -ɪd

erectile ɪ'rek.taɪl (US) -təl, -taɪl

erection ɪ'rek.ʃᵊn **-s** -z

erector ɪ'rek.təʳ (US) -tɚ **-s** -z

eremite 'er.ɪ.maɪt, '-ə- **-s** -s

eremitic ˌer.ɪ'mɪt.ɪk, -ə'- (US) -ə'mɪt̬- **-al** -ᵊl

erepsin ɪ'rep.sɪn

Eretri|a ɪ'ret.ri|.ə, er'et- **-an/s** -ən/z

erewhile eə'*h*waɪl (US) er'-

Erewhon 'er.ɪ.*h*wɒn (US) -*h*wɑːn, -*h*wʌn

Erfurt 'eə.fɜːt *as if German:* -fʊət (US) 'er.fʊrt, -fɜːrt

erg ɜːg (US) ɜːrg **-s** -z

ergative 'ɜː.gə.tɪv (US) 'ɜːr.gə.t̬ɪv

ergativity ˌɜː.gə'tɪv.ə.ti, -ɪ.ti (US) ˌɜːr.gə'tɪv.ə.t̬i

ergo 'ɜː.gəʊ, 'eə- (US) 'er.goʊ, 'ɜːr-

ergon 'ɜː.gɒn (US) 'ɜːr.gɑːn **-s** -z

ergonic ɜː'gɒn.ɪk (US) ɜːr'gɑː.nɪk **-s** -s **-ally** -ᵊl.i, -li

ergonomic ˌɜː.gə'nɒm.ɪk (US) ˌɜːr.gə'nɑː.mɪk **-s** -s

ergonomical ˌɜː.gə'nɒm.ɪ.kᵊl (US) ˌɜːr.gə'nɑː.mɪ- **-ly** -i

ergonomist ɜː'gɒn.ə.mɪst (US) ɜːr'gɑː.nə- **-s** -s

ergosterol ɜː'gɒs.tə.rɒl, -tɪᵊ- (US) ɜːr'gɑː.stə.rɑːl, -rɔːl, -roʊl

ergot 'ɜː.gət, -gɒt (US) 'ɜːr.gət, -gɑːt **-ism** -ɪ.zᵊm

Eric 'er.ɪk

Erica, erica 'er.ɪ.kə

ericaceous ˌer.ɪ'keɪ.ʃəs

Ericht 'er.ɪxt

Eric(k)son 'er.ɪk.sᵊn

Erie 'ɪə.ri (US) 'ɪr.i

Erik 'er.ɪk

Erika 'er.ɪ.kə

Erin 'ɪə.rɪn, 'er.ɪn, 'eə.rɪn (US) 'er.ɪn, 'ɪr-

Eris 'er.ɪs (US) 'ɪr-, 'er-

eristic er'ɪs.tɪk (US) ɪ'rɪs-, er'ɪs- **-s** -s

Erith 'ɪə.rɪθ (US) 'ɪr.ɪθ

Eritre|a ˌer.ɪ'treɪ|.ə, -ə'treɪ-, -'triː- (US) -'triː- **-an/s** -ən/z

Erle ɜːl (US) ɜːrl

erl-king 'ɜːl.kɪŋ, ˌ-'- (US) 'ɜːrl.kɪŋ, 'erl- **-s** -z

ERM ˌiː.ɑːʳ'em (US) -ɑːr'-

ermine 'ɜː.mɪn (US) 'ɜːr- **-s** -z **-d** -d

erne (E) ɜːn (US) ɜːrn **-s** -z

Ernest 'ɜː.nɪst, -nəst (US) 'ɜːr-

Ernie 'ɜː.ni (US) 'ɜːr-

Ernle 'ɜːn.li (US) 'ɜːrn-

Ernst ɜːn*t*st *as if German:* eən*t*st (US) ɜːrn*t*st *as if German:* ernst

erod|e ɪ'rəʊd (US) -'roʊd **-es** -z **-ing** -ɪŋ **-ed** -ɪd

erogenous ɪ'rɒdʒ.ɪ.nəs, er'ɒdʒ-, ə'rɒdʒ-, '-ə- US ɪ'rɑː.dʒɪ-, -dʒə-
Eroica er'əʊ.ɪ.kə, ɪ'rəʊ-, ə'rəʊ- US ɪ'roʊ-, er'oʊ-
Eros 'ɪə.rɒs, 'er.ɒs US 'er.ɑːs, 'ɪr-
erosion ɪ'rəʊ.ʒᵊn US -'roʊ- **-s** -z
erosive ɪ'rəʊ.sɪv, -zɪv US -'roʊ-
erotic ɪ'rɒt.ɪk US -'rɑː.t̬ɪk **-s** -s **-a** -ə **-ally** -ᵊl.i, -li
eroticism ɪ'rɒt.ɪ.sɪ.zᵊm, '-ə- US -'rɑː.t̬ə-
eroticization, -isa- ɪˌrɒt.ɪ.saɪ'zeɪ.ʃᵊn, ˌ-ə-, -sɪ'- US -ˌrɑː.t̬ə.sɪ'-
eroticiz|e, -is|e ɪ'rɒt.ɪ.saɪz, '-ə- US -'rɑː.t̬ə- **-es** -ɪz **-ing** -ɪŋ **-ed** -d
erotogenic ɪˌrɒt.ə'dʒen.ɪk, -ˌrəʊ.tə'- US ɪˌrɑː.t̬ə'dʒen-, -ˌroʊ- **-ally** -ᵊl.i, -li
erotomani|a ɪˌrɒt.əʊ'meɪ.ni|.ə, -ˌrəʊ.təʊ'- US ɪˌrɑː.t̬ə'meɪ.ni|.ə, -ˌroʊ- **-ac/s** -æk/s
err ɜːʳ US ɜːr, er **-s** -z **-ing** -ɪŋ **-ed** -d
errand 'er.ənd **-s** -z
errant 'er.ənt **-ly** -li **-ry** -ri
errata (*plur. of* **erratum**) er'ɑː.tə, ɪ'rɑː-, -'reɪ- US -t̬ə
erratic ɪ'ræt.ɪk, er'æt- US ɪ'ræt̬- **-ally** -ᵊl.i, -li
errat|um er'ɑː.t|əm, ɪ'rɑː-, -'reɪ- US -t̬|əm **-a** -ə
Errol(l) 'er.əl
erroneous ɪ'rəʊ.ni.əs, er'əʊ- US ə'roʊ-, er'oʊ-, ɪ'roʊ- **-ly** -li **-ness** -nəs, -nɪs
error 'er.əʳ US -ɚ **-s** -z
ersatz 'ɜː.sæts *as if German:* 'eə.zɑːts US 'er.zɑːts, -'-
Erse ɜːs US ɜːrs
Erskine 'ɜː.skɪn US 'ɜːr-
erst ɜːst US ɜːrst
erstwhile 'ɜːst.*h*waɪl US 'ɜːrst-
erubescen|ce ˌer.ʊ'bes.ᵊn|*t*s, -uː'- **-cy** -*t*si **-t** -t
eruct ɪ'rʌkt, iː- **-s** -s **-ing** -ɪŋ **-ed** -ɪd
eruc|tate ɪ'rʌk|.teɪt, iː- **-tates** -teɪts **-tating** -teɪ.tɪŋ US -teɪ.t̬ɪŋ **-tated** -teɪ.tɪd US -teɪ.t̬ɪd
eructation ˌiː.rʌk'teɪ.ʃᵊn, ˌer.ʌk-, -ək'-; ɪˌrʌk'- US ˌiː.rʌk'-, ɪˌrʌk'- **-s** -z
erudite 'er.ʊ.daɪt, -jʊ- US -jə-, -ə-, -juː-, -uː- **-ly** -li **-ness** -nəs, -nɪs
erudition ˌer.ʊ'dɪʃ.ᵊn, -jʊ'- US -juː'-, -uː'-, -jə'-, -ə'-
erupt ɪ'rʌpt **-s** -s **-ing** -ɪŋ **-ed** -ɪd
eruption ɪ'rʌp.ʃᵊn **-s** -z
eruptive ɪ'rʌp.tɪv **-ly** -li **-ness** -nəs, -nɪs
Ervine 'ɜː.vɪn US 'ɜːr-
Erving 'ɜː.vɪŋ US 'ɜːr-
erysipelas ˌer.ɪ'sɪp.ᵊl.əs, -ə'-, -ɪ.ləs, -lɪs
erythema ˌer.ɪ'θiː.mə, -ə'-
erythrocyte ɪ'rɪθ.rəʊ.saɪt US er'ɪθ.roʊ- **-s** -s
erythrocytic ɪˌrɪθ.rəʊ'sɪt.ɪk US erˌɪθ.roʊ'sɪt̬-
erythromycin ɪˌrɪθ.rəʊ'maɪ.sɪn, əˌrɪθ- US ɪ.rɪθ.roʊ'-, -rə'-
Erzerum 'eə.zə.ruːm US 'er-
Esau 'iː.sɔː US -sɑː, -sɔː
Esbjerg 'es.bjɜːg US -bjerg
escalad|e ˌes.kə'leɪd, '--- **-es** -z **-ing** -ɪŋ **-ed** -ɪd
esca|late 'es.kə|.leɪt **-lates** -leɪts **-lating** -leɪ.tɪŋ US -leɪ.t̬ɪŋ **-lated** -leɪ.tɪd US -leɪ.t̬ɪd
escalation ˌes.kə'leɪ.ʃᵊn
escalator 'es.kə.leɪ.təʳ US -t̬ɚ **-s** -z
escal(l)op ɪ'skɒl.əp, es'kɒl-, -'kæl-, -ɒp; 'es.kə.lɒp US es'kɑː.ləp, ɪ'skɑː-, -'skæl- **-ed** -t
escalope 'es.kə.lɒp, 'ɪs-, -ləp; es'kæl.əp, -ɒp US ˌes.kə'loʊp **-s** -s
escapade ˌes.kə'peɪd, '--- **-s** -z
escap|e ɪ'skeɪp, es'keɪp, ə'skeɪp **-es** -s **-ing** -ɪŋ **-ed** -t **-ement/s** -mənt/s
escapee ɪˌskeɪ'piː, ˌes.keɪ'- **-s** -z
escap|ism ɪ'skeɪ.p|ɪ.zᵊm, es'keɪ- **-ist/s** -ɪst/s
escapolog|y ˌes.kə'pɒl.ə.dʒ|i, -keɪ'- US -keɪ'pɑː.lə- **-ist/s** -ɪst/s
escargot ɪ'skɑː.gəʊ, es'kɑː- *as if French:* ˌes.kɑː'gəʊ US ˌes.kɑːr'goʊ **-s** -z
escarole 'es.kə.rəʊl US -kə.roʊl
escarp ɪ'skɑːp, es'kɑːp US es'kɑːrp **-s** -s **-ing** -ɪŋ **-ed** -t
escarpment ɪ'skɑːp.mənt, es'kɑːp- US es'kɑːrp- **-s** -s
-esce -'es
Note: Suffix. Always carries primary stress, e.g. **convalesce** /ˌkɒn.və'les US ˌkɑːn-/.
-escen|ce -'es.ᵊn|*t*s **-t** -t
Note: Suffix. Always carries primary stress, e.g. **convalescence** /ˌkɒn.və'les.ᵊn*t*s US ˌkɑːn-/.
eschar 'es.kɑːʳ US -kɑːr, -kɚ **-s** -z
eschatological ˌes.kə.tə'lɒdʒ.ɪ.kᵊl, -kæt.ə'- US -kə.t̬ə'lɑː.dʒɪ-; esˌkæt̬.ᵊl'ɑː-
eschatolog|y ˌes.kə'tɒl.ə.dʒ|i US -'tɑː.lə- **-ist/s** -ɪst/s
es|cheat ɪs|'tʃiːt, es- **-cheats** -'tʃiːts **-cheating** -'tʃiː.tɪŋ US -'tʃiː.t̬ɪŋ **-cheated** -'tʃiː.tɪd US -'tʃiː.t̬ɪd
Escher 'eʃ.əʳ US -ɚ
eschew ɪs'tʃuː, es- US es-, ɪs- **-s** -z **-ing** -ɪŋ **-ed** -d
eschscholtzia ɪ'skɒl.ʃə, es'kɒl-, -tʃə; ɪʃ'ɒlt.si.ə, eʃ-, ə'ʃɒlt-, -'skɒlt- US eʃ'oʊlt.si.ə **-s** -z
Escoffier ɪ'skɒf.i.eɪ, es'kɒf- US ˌes.kɑː'fjeɪ
Escom 'es.kɒm, -kɑːm US -kɑːm
Escombe 'es.kəm
Escondido ˌes.kən'diː.dəʊ US -doʊ
Escorial ˌes.kɒr.i'ɑːl, -'æl; es'kɔː.ri.æl, -ɑːl US es'kɔːr.i.əl; esˌkɔːr.i'æl
escort (E®) (*n.*) 'es.kɔːt US -kɔːrt **-s** -s
escor|t (*v.*) ɪ'skɔː|t, es'kɔː|t; 'es.kɔː|t US es'kɔːr|t, ɪ'skɔːr|t; 'es.kɔːr|t **-ts** -ts **-ting** -tɪŋ US -t̬ɪŋ **-ted** -tɪd US -t̬ɪd
Escott 'es.kɒt US -kɑːt
Escow 'es.kəʊ US -koʊ
escritoire ˌes.kriː'twɑːʳ, '--- US ˌes.kriː'twɑːr **-s** -z
escrow 'es.krəʊ, -'- US 'es.kroʊ, -'-
escudo es'kuː.dəʊ, ɪ'skuː-, -'skjuː-; ɪʃ'kuː-, eʃ- US es'kuː.doʊ, ɪ'skuː- **-s** -z
esculent 'es.kjə.lənt, -kjʊ- **-s** -s
Escurial es'kjʊə.ri.əl US -'kjʊr.i-
escutcheon ɪ'skʌtʃ.ᵊn, es'kʌtʃ- **-s** -z
Esda 'es.də, 'ez- **'Esda ˌtest**
Esdaile 'ez.deɪl
Esdras 'ez.dræs, -drəs
-ese -'iːz US -'iːz, -'iːs
Note: Suffix. Always carries primary stress, e.g. **Japan** /dʒə'pæn/, **Japanese** /ˌdʒæp.ə'niːz/.
ESE ˌiːst.saʊθ'iːst *in nautical usage also:* -saʊ'-
Esfahan 'eʃ.fə.hɑːn, 'es- US ˌes.fə'hɑːn
Esher 'iː.ʃəʳ US -ʃɚ
Esias ɪ'zaɪ.əs, ez'aɪ-, -æs
Esk esk
Eskimo 'es.kɪ.məʊ US -kə.moʊ **-s** -z
ESL ˌiː.es'el
Esmé 'ez.mi, -meɪ
Esmeralda ˌez.mə'ræl.də, -mɪ'-
Esmond(e) 'ez.mənd
ESN ˌiː.es'en
ESOL 'iː.sɒl US -sɑːl
ESOP 'iː.sɒp US -sɑːp
esophageal ɪˌsɒf.ə'dʒiː.əl, iː-, ə-; ˌiː.sɒf- US ɪˌsɑː.fə'-; ˌiː.sɑː-
esopha|gus iː'sɒf.ə|.gəs, ɪ-, ə- US ɪ'sɑː.fə-, iː- **-gi** -gaɪ, -dʒaɪ **-guses** -gə.sɪz
esoteric ˌes.əʊ'ter.ɪk, ˌiː.səʊ'- US ˌes.ə'- **-al** -ᵊl **-ally** -ᵊl.i, -li
ESP ˌiː.es'piː
Espace® es'pæs
espadrille ˌes.pə'drɪl, '--- US 'es.pə.drɪl **-s** -z
espalier ɪ'spæl.i.eɪ, es'pæl-, -i.əʳ US -'spæl.jɚ, -jeɪ **-s** -z **-ing** -ɪŋ **-ed** -d
esparto es'pɑː.təʊ, ɪ'spɑː- US es'pɑːr.t̬oʊ **-s** -z
especial ɪ'speʃ.ᵊl, es'peʃ-, ə'speʃ- **-ly** -i
Esperant|o ˌes.pᵊr'æn.t|əʊ US -pə'ræn.t|oʊ, -'rɑːn- **-ist/s** -ɪst/s

espial ɪ'spaɪ.əl, es'paɪ-
espionage 'es.pi.ə.nɑːʒ, -nɑːdʒ, -nɪdʒ; ˌes.pi.ə'nɑːʒ, -'nɑːdʒ
esplanade ˌes.plə'neɪd, -'nɑːd, '--- ⓤⓢ 'es.plə.nɑːd, -neɪd **-s** -z
Esplanade *in Western Australia:* 'es.plə.nɑːd
ESPN ˌiː.esˌpiː'en
Espoo 'es.pəʊ ⓤⓢ -poʊ
espous|e ɪ'spaʊz, es'paʊz **-es** -ɪz **-ing** -ɪŋ **-ed** -d **-er/s** -əʳ/z ⓤⓢ -ɚ/z **-al/s** -ᵊl/z
espressivo ˌes.pres'iː.vəʊ ⓤⓢ -voʊ
espresso es'pres.əʊ, ɪ'spres- ⓤⓢ -oʊ **-s** -z
esprit es'priː, ɪ'spriː, ə'spriː; 'es.priː ⓤⓢ es'priː, ɪ'spriː
esprit de corps esˌpriː.də'kɔːʳ, ɪˌspriː-, əˌspriː-; ˌes.priː- ⓤⓢ esˌpriː.də'kɔːr, ɪˌspriː-
esp|y ɪ'splaɪ, es'plaɪ **-ies** -aɪz **-ying** -aɪ.ɪŋ **-ied** -aɪd
Espy 'es.pi
Esq. (*abbrev. for* **Esquire**) ɪ'skwaɪəʳ, es'kwaɪəʳ ⓤⓢ 'es.kwaɪɚ; ɪ'skwaɪɚ, es'kwaɪɚ
-esque -'esk
Note: Suffix. Always carries primary stress, e.g. **picturesque** /ˌpɪk.tʃᵊr'esk/.
Esquiline 'es.kwɪ.laɪn, -kwᵊl.aɪn ⓤⓢ -kwə.laɪn
Esquimalt es'kwaɪ.mɔːlt, ɪ'skwaɪ-, -mɒlt ⓤⓢ -mɑːlt, -mɔːlt
esquire ɪ'skwaɪəʳ, es'kwaɪəʳ ⓤⓢ 'es.kwaɪɚ; ɪ'skwaɪɚ, es'kwaɪɚ **-s** -z
ess es **-es** -ɪz
essay (*n.*) *piece of writing:* 'es.eɪ **-s** -z **-ist/s** -ɪst/s
essay (*n. v.*) *attempt:* es'eɪ, '-- **-s** -z **-ing** -ɪŋ **-ed** -d **-er/s** -əʳ/z ⓤⓢ -ɚ/z
esse 'es.i
Essen 'es.ᵊn
essenc|e 'es.ᵊnts **-es** -ɪz
Essene 'es.iːn, -'- **-s** -z
essential ɪ'sen.*t*ʃᵊl ⓤⓢ ɪ'sen*t*.ʃᵊl, es'en*t*- **-s** -z **-ly** -i **-ness** -nəs, -nɪs esˌsential 'oil
essentiality ɪˌsen.*t*ʃi'æl.ə.ti, esˌen-, -ɪ.ti ⓤⓢ -ə.t̬i
Essex 'es.ɪks
essive 'es.ɪv **-s** -z
Esso® 'es.əʊ ⓤⓢ -oʊ
-est -ɪst, -əst
Note: Suffix. Does not affect the stress pattern of the word, e.g. **happy** /'hæp.i/, **happiest** /'hæp.i.ɪst/.
EST ˌiː.es'tiː
establish ɪ'stæb.lɪʃ, es'tæb- **-es** -ɪz **-ing** -ɪŋ **-ed** -t **-er/s** -əʳ/z ⓤⓢ -ɚ/z **-ment/s** -mənt/s

estate ɪ'steɪt, es'teɪt **-s** -s es'tate ˌagent ; es'tate ˌcar
Estcourt 'est.kɔːt ⓤⓢ -kɔːrt
Este 'es.ti ⓤⓢ -teɪ
Estée 'es.teɪ, -tiː ⓤⓢ -teɪ
esteem ɪ'stiːm, es'tiːm **-s** -z **-ing** -ɪŋ **-ed** -d
Estelle ɪ'stel, es'tel
ester 'es.təʳ ⓤⓢ -tɚ **-s** -z
Esterhazy 'es.tə.hɑː.zi ⓤⓢ -tɚ.hɑː.zi
Esther 'es.təʳ, -θəʳ ⓤⓢ -tɚ
esthete 'iːs.θiːt ⓤⓢ 'es- **-s** -s
esthetic iːs'θet.ɪk, ɪs- ⓤⓢ es'θet̬- **-al** -ᵊl **-ally** -ᵊl.i, -li **-s** -s
esthetic|ism iːs'θet.ɪ.s|ɪ.zᵊm, ɪs- ⓤⓢ es'θet̬- **-ist/s** -ɪst/s
estimab|le 'es.tɪ.mə.b|l̩, -tə- **-ly** -li **-leness** -l̩.nəs, -nɪs
estimate (*n.*) 'es.tɪ.mət, -tə-, -mɪt, -meɪt ⓤⓢ -mɪt, -mət **-s** -s
esti|mate (*v.*) 'es.tɪ|.meɪt, -tə-, -mət ⓤⓢ -meɪt **-mates** -meɪts, -məts ⓤⓢ -meɪts **-mating** -meɪ.tɪŋ, -mə- ⓤⓢ -meɪ.t̬ɪŋ **-mated** -meɪ.tɪd, -mə- ⓤⓢ -meɪ.t̬ɪd **-mator/s** -meɪ.təʳ/z, -mə- ⓤⓢ -meɪ.t̬ɚ/z
estimation ˌes.tɪ'meɪ.ʃᵊn, -tə'- **-s**
estival iː'staɪ.vᵊl, es'taɪ- ⓤⓢ 'es.tə-, es'taɪ-
Eston 'es.tən
Estoni|a es'təʊ.ni|.ə, ɪ'stəʊ- ⓤⓢ es'toʊ- **-an/s** -ən/z
estop ɪ'stɒp, es'tɒp ⓤⓢ es'tɑːp **-s** -s **-ping** -ɪŋ **-ped** -t **-page** -ɪdʒ **-pel/s** -ᵊl/z
Estoril ˌes.tᵊr'ɪl ⓤⓢ ˌiː.stə'rɪl
estovers ɪ'stəʊ.vəz, es'təʊ- ⓤⓢ es'toʊ.vɚz
estrade es'trɑːd, ɪ'strɑːd ⓤⓢ es'trɑːd **-s** -z
Estragon 'es.trə.gɒn ⓤⓢ -gɑːn
estrang|e ɪ'streɪndʒ, es'treɪndʒ **-es** -ɪz **-ing** -ɪŋ **-ed** -d
estrangement ɪ'streɪndʒ.mənt, es'treɪndʒ- **-s** -s
estrea|t ɪ'striːt, es'triːt ⓤⓢ es'triː|t **-ts** -ts **-ting** -tɪŋ ⓤⓢ -t̬ɪŋ **-ted** -tɪd ⓤⓢ -t̬ɪd
Estremadura ˌes.trə.mə'dʊə.rə, -'dɔː- ⓤⓢ -'dʊr.ə
estrogen 'iː.strə.dʒᵊn, 'es.trə- ⓤⓢ 'es.trə.dʒᵊn, -dʒen
estr(o)us 'iː.strəs, 'es.trəs ⓤⓢ 'es.trəs **-es** -ɪz
estuarine 'es.tju.ə.raɪn, -riːn, -rɪn ⓤⓢ 'es.tʃuː.ə.raɪn, -ɚ.ɪn
estuar|y 'es.tjʊə.r|i, -tju.ə-, -tʃʊə-, -tʃu.ə-, -tjʊr|.i, -tʃʊr|.i ⓤⓢ 'es.tʃuː.er|.i **-ies** -iz
esurien|ce ɪ'sjʊə.ri.ən|ts ⓤⓢ iː'sʊr.i-, -'sjʊr- **-cy** -*t*.si **-t** -t
eta *Greek alphabet:* 'iː.tə ⓤⓢ 'eɪ.t̬ə, 'iː-
ETA *estimated time of arrival:* ˌiː.tiː'eɪ

ETA *Basque separatist group:* 'et.ə ⓤⓢ 'et̬-
étagère, etagere ˌeɪ.tə'ʒeəʳ, ˌet.ə-, -tæʒ'eəʳ, -tɑː'ʒeəʳ ⓤⓢ -tɑː'ʒer **-s** -z
Etah 'iː.tə ⓤⓢ -t̬ə
Etain 'et.eɪn
et al et'æl ⓤⓢ et'ɑːl, -'æl, -'ɔːl
Etam® 'iː.tæm
etc. ɪt'set.ᵊr.ə, et-, ət- ⓤⓢ -'set̬.ɚ-
etcetera ɪt'set.ᵊr.ə, et-, ət- ⓤⓢ -'set̬.ɚ- **-s** -z
etch etʃ **-es** -ɪz **-ing/s** -ɪŋ/z **-ed** -t **-er/s** -əʳ/z ⓤⓢ -ɚ/z
eternal ɪ'tɜː.nᵊl ⓤⓢ -'tɜːr- **-ly** -i
eternaliz|e, -is|e ɪ'tɜː.nᵊl.aɪz ⓤⓢ -'tɜːr.nə.laɪz **-es** -ɪz **-ing** -ɪŋ **-ed** -d
eternit|y ɪ'tɜː.nə.t|i, -nɪ.t|i ⓤⓢ -'tɜːr.nə.t̬|i **-ies** -iz
eterniz|e, -is|e ɪ'tɜː.naɪz ⓤⓢ -'tɜːr- **-es** -ɪz **-ing** -ɪŋ **-ed** -d
Etesian ɪ'tiː.ʒi.ən, -zi-, -ʒᵊn
Ethan 'iː.θᵊn
ethane 'iː.θeɪn, 'eθ.eɪn ⓤⓢ 'eθ.eɪn
ethanoic ˌeθ.ə'nəʊ.ɪk, 'iː.θə'- ⓤⓢ ˌeθ.ə'noʊ-
ethanol 'eθ.ə.nɒl, 'iː.θə- ⓤⓢ 'eθ.ə.nɑːl, -noʊl
Ethel 'eθ.ᵊl
Ethelbald 'eθ.ᵊl.bɔːld ⓤⓢ -bɔːld, -bɑːld
Ethelbert 'eθ.ᵊl.bɜːt, -bət ⓤⓢ -bɜːrt, -bɚt
Ethelberta ˌeθ.ᵊl'bɜː.tə, 'eθ.ᵊlˌbɜː- ⓤⓢ ˌeθ.ᵊl'bɜːr.t̬ə
Ethelburga ˌeθ.ᵊl'bɜː.gə, 'eθ.ᵊlˌbɜː- ⓤⓢ ˌeθ.ᵊl'bɜːr-
Ethelred 'eθ.ᵊl.red
Ethelwulf 'eθ.ᵊl.wʊlf
ethene 'eθ.iːn
ether 'iː.θəʳ ⓤⓢ -θɚ **-s** -z
ethereal ɪ'θɪə.ri.əl, iː-, ə- ⓤⓢ -'θɪr.i- **-ly** -i
etherealiz|e, -is|e ɪ'θɪə.ri.ᵊl.aɪz, iː-, ə- ⓤⓢ -'θɪr.i.ə.laɪz **-es** -ɪz **-ing** -ɪŋ **-ed** -d
Etherege 'eθ.ᵊr.ɪdʒ
etheric iː'θer.ɪk, ɪ- **-s** -s **-ally** -ᵊl.i, -li
Etherington 'eð.ᵊr.ɪŋ.tən
etheriz|e, -is|e 'iː.θᵊr.aɪz ⓤⓢ -θə.raɪz **-es** -ɪz **-ing** -ɪŋ **-ed** -d
ethic 'eθ.ɪk **-s** -s **-al** -ᵊl **-ally** -ᵊl.i, -li
Ethiop 'iː.θi.ɒp ⓤⓢ -ɑːp **-s** -s
Ethiopi|a ˌiː.θi'əʊ.pi|.ə ⓤⓢ -'oʊ- **-an/s** -ən/z
Ethiopic ˌiː.θi'ɒp.ɪk, -'əʊ.pɪk ⓤⓢ -'ɑː-, -'oʊ-
ethnic 'eθ.nɪk **-al** -ᵊl **-ally** -ᵊl.i, -li
ethnicity eθ'nɪs.ə.ti, -ɪ.ti ⓤⓢ -ə.t̬i
ethno- eθ.nəʊ-; eθ'nɒ- ⓤⓢ eθ.noʊ-; eθ'nɑː-
Note: Prefix. Either takes primary or secondary stress on the first syllable, e.g. **ethnographic** /ˌeθ.nəʊ'græf.ɪk ⓤⓢ -noʊ'-/, or primary stress on the

second syllable, e.g. **ethnographer** /eθ'nɒg.rə.fəʳ ⓤⓢ -'nɑː.grə.fɚ/.
ethnocentr|ic ˌeθ.nəʊ'sen.tr|ɪk ⓤⓢ -noʊ'-, -nə'- **-ism** -ɪ.zᵊm **-ically** -ɪ.kᵊl.i, -ɪ.kli
ethnocentricity ˌeθ.nəʊ.sen'trɪs.ə.ti, -ɪ.ti ⓤⓢ -noʊ.sen'trɪs.ə.t̬i
ethnographer eθ'nɒg.rə.fəʳ ⓤⓢ -'nɑː.grə.fɚ **-s** -z
ethnographic ˌeθ.nəʊ'græf.ɪk ⓤⓢ -noʊ'-, -nə'- **-al** -ᵊl
ethnography eθ'nɒg.rə.fi ⓤⓢ -'nɑː.grə-
ethnologic ˌeθ.nəʊ'lɒdʒ.ɪk ⓤⓢ -noʊ'lɑː.dʒɪk, -nə'- **-al** -ᵊl **-ally** -ᵊl.i, -li
ethnolog|y eθ'nɒl.ə.dʒ|i ⓤⓢ -'nɑː.lə- **-ist/s** -ɪst/s
ethologic ˌiː.θə'lɒdʒ.ɪk ⓤⓢ -'lɑː.dʒɪk **-al** -ᵊl
etholog|y iː'θɒl.ə.dʒ|i, ɪ- ⓤⓢ iː'θɑː.lə-, ɪ'- **-ist/s** -ɪst/s
ethos 'iː.θɒs ⓤⓢ -θɑːs, 'eθ.ɑːs, -oʊs
ethyl *commercial and general pronunciation:* 'eθ.ɪl, -ᵊl ⓤⓢ -ᵊl *chemists' pronunciation:* 'iː.θaɪl
ethylene 'eθ.ɪ.liːn, -ᵊl.iːn ⓤⓢ -ə.liːn
etio|late 'iː.ti.əʊ|.leɪt ⓤⓢ -ə- **-lates** -leɪts **-lating** -leɪ.tɪŋ ⓤⓢ -leɪ.t̬ɪŋ **-lated** -leɪ.tɪd ⓤⓢ -leɪ.t̬ɪd
etiolog|y ˌiː.ti'ɒl.ə.dʒ|i ⓤⓢ -'ɑː.lə- **-ist/s** -ɪst/s
etiquette 'et.ɪ.ket, -kət; ⓤⓢ 'et̬.ɪ.kɪt, -ket
Etna 'et.nə
Eton 'iː.tᵊn
Etonian iː'təʊ.ni.ən, ɪ- ⓤⓢ -'toʊ- **-s** -z
Etruri|a ɪ'trʊə.ri|.ə ⓤⓢ -'trʊr.i- **-an/s** -ən/z
Etruscan ɪ'trʌs.kᵊn **-s** -z
-ette -et
Note: Suffix. Normally takes primary stress, e.g. **majorette** /ˌmeɪ.dʒᵊr'et/; there are exceptions, however, e.g. **etiquette** /'et.ɪ.ket ⓤⓢ 'et̬.ɪ.kɪt/. See individual entries.
Ettrick 'et.rɪk
Etty 'et.i ⓤⓢ 'et̬-
étude 'eɪ.tjuːd, -'- ⓤⓢ 'eɪ.tuːd, -tjuːd **-s** -z
etui et'wiː ⓤⓢ eɪ'twiː **-s** -z
etymologic ˌet.ɪ.mə'lɒdʒ.ɪk, ˌ-ə- ⓤⓢ ˌet̬.ɪ.mə'lɑː.dʒɪk **-al** -ᵊl **-ally** -ᵊl.i, -li
etymologist ˌet.ɪ'mɒl.ə.dʒɪst, -ə'- ⓤⓢ ˌet̬.ɪ'mɑː.lə- **-s** -s
etymologiz|e, -is|e ˌet.ɪ'mɒl.ə.dʒaɪz, -ə'- ⓤⓢ ˌet̬.ɪ'mɑː.lə- **-es** -ɪz **-ing** -ɪŋ **-ed** -d
etymolog|y ˌet.ɪ'mɒl.ə.dʒ|i, -ə'- ⓤⓢ ˌet̬.ɪ'mɑː.lə- **-ies** -iz
etymon 'et.ɪ.mɒn, '-ə- ⓤⓢ 'et̬.ə.mɑːn **-s** -z
EU ˌiː'juː
Eubank 'juː.bæŋk
Euboea juː'biː.ə
eucalyptus ˌjuː.kᵊl'ɪp.təs **-es** -ɪz
Eucharist 'juː.kᵊr.ɪst **-s** -s
eucharistic ˌjuː.kᵊr'ɪs.tɪk **-al** -ᵊl **-ally** -ᵊl.i, -li
euchre 'juː.kəʳ ⓤⓢ -kɚ **-s** -z **-ing** -ɪŋ **-d** -d
Euclid 'juː.klɪd **-s** -z
Euclidean juː'klɪd.i.ən
eud(a)emon|ism juː'diː.mə.n|ɪ.zᵊm **-ist/s** -ɪst/s
eudiometer ˌjuː.di'ɒm.ɪ.təʳ, '-ə- ⓤⓢ -'ɑː.mə.t̬ɚ **-s** -z
Eudocia juː'dəʊ.ʃi.ə, -ʃə, -si.ə ⓤⓢ -'doʊ-
Eudora juː'dɔː.rə ⓤⓢ -'dɔːr.ə
Eudoxia juː'dɒk.si.ə ⓤⓢ -'dɑːk-
Eudoxus juː'dɒk.səs ⓤⓢ -'dɑːk-
Eugen *English name:* 'juː.dʒen, -dʒɪn, -dʒən *German name:* 'ɔɪ.gən
Eugene juː'dʒiːn, -'dʒeɪn; 'juː.dʒiːn ⓤⓢ juː'dʒiːn, '--
Eugene Onegin ˌjuː.dʒiːn.ɒn'jeɪ.gɪn ⓤⓢ -ɑːn'-, -oʊn'-
Eugénia juː'dʒiː.ni.ə, -'ʒiː-, -'dʒeɪ-, -'ʒeɪ-
eugenic juː'dʒen.ɪk **-s** -s
eugenicist juː'dʒen.ɪ.sɪst, '-ə- **-s** -s
Eugénie juː'ʒeɪ.ni, -'ʒiː-, -'dʒiː-
Eugenius juː'dʒiː.ni.əs, -'ʒiː-, -'dʒeɪ- ⓤⓢ -'ʒeɪ-
Eulalia juː'leɪ.li.ə
Eulenspiegel 'ɔɪ.lᵊn,ʃpiː.gᵊl
Euler *English name:* 'juː.ləʳ ⓤⓢ -lɚ *German name:* 'ɔɪ.ləʳ ⓤⓢ -lɚ
eulogist 'juː.lə.dʒɪst **-s** -s
eulogistic ˌjuː.lə'dʒɪs.tɪk **-al** -ᵊl **-ally** -ᵊl.i, -li
eulogi|um juː'ləʊ.dʒi|.əm ⓤⓢ -'loʊ- **-ums** -z **-a** -ə
eulogiz|e, -is|e 'juː.lə.dʒaɪz **-es** -ɪz **-ing** -ɪŋ **-ed** -d
eulog|y 'juː.lə.dʒ|i **-ies** -iz
Eumenides juː'men.ɪ.diːz, '-ə-
Eunice *modern Christian name:* 'juː.nɪs *biblical name:* juː'naɪ.si
eunuch 'juː.nək **-s** -s **-ism** -ɪ.zᵊm
euonymus juː'ɒn.ɪ.məs, '-ə- ⓤⓢ -'ɑː.nə- **-es** -ɪz
eupepsia juː'pep.si.ə
eupeptic juː'pep.tɪk
Euphemia juː'fiː.mi.ə
euphemism 'juː.fə.mɪ.zᵊm, -fɪ- **-s** -z
euphemistic ˌjuː.fə'mɪs.tɪk, -fɪ'- **-al** -ᵊl **-ally** -ᵊl.i, -li
euphemiz|e, -is|e 'juː.fə.maɪz, -fɪ- **-es** -ɪz **-ing** -ɪŋ **-ed** -d
euphonic juː'fɒn.ɪk ⓤⓢ -'fɑː.nɪk **-al** -ᵊl **-ally** -ᵊl.i, -li
euphonious juː'fəʊ.ni.əs ⓤⓢ -'foʊ- **-ly** -li
euphonium juː'fəʊ.ni.əm ⓤⓢ -'foʊ- **-s** -z
euphoniz|e, -is|e 'juː.fə.naɪz **-es** -ɪz **-ing** -ɪŋ **-ed** -d
euphony 'juː.fᵊn.i
euphorbia juː'fɔː.bi.ə ⓤⓢ -'fɔːr-
euphoria juː'fɔː.ri.ə ⓤⓢ -'fɔːr.i-
euphoric juː'fɒr.ɪk ⓤⓢ -'fɔːr.ɪk **-ally** -ᵊl.i, -li
euphrasy 'juː.frə.si
Euphrates juː'freɪ.tiːz ⓤⓢ -t̬iːz
Euphronius juː'frəʊ.ni.əs ⓤⓢ -'froʊ-
Euphrosyne juː'frɒz.ɪ.niː, '-ə- ⓤⓢ -'frɑː.zə-
Euphues 'juː.fju.iːz
euphu|ism 'juː.fju.|ɪ.zᵊm **-isms** -ɪ.zᵊmz **-ist/s** -ɪst/s
euphuistic ˌjuː.fju'ɪs.tɪk
eupnoea 'juːp.niː.ə ⓤⓢ -'--
Eurasi|a jʊə'reɪ.ʒ|ə, jɔː'-, '-ʒi|.ə, '-ʃ|ə ⓤⓢ jʊ'reɪ.ʒ|ə **-a** -ᵊn
Euratom jʊə'ræt.əm, jɔː-' ⓤⓢ jʊ'ræt̬-
eureka (E) jʊə'riː.kə, jɔː'- ⓤⓢ jʊ-
eurhythm|ic jʊə'rɪð.m|ɪk, jɔː'-, -'rɪθ- ⓤⓢ jʊ'rɪð- **-ics** -ɪks **-y** -i
Euripides jʊə'rɪp.ɪ.diːz, jɔː'-, '-ə- ⓤⓢ jʊ-
Euripus jʊə'raɪ.pəs, jɔː'- ⓤⓢ jʊ-
Euro- 'jʊə.rəʊ-, jɔː-; jʊə'rɒ- ⓤⓢ 'jʊr.oʊ-, -ə-; jʊ'roʊ-
Note: Prefix. Usually takes primary stress on the first syllable, e.g. **Eurocrat** /'jʊə.rəʊ.kræt ⓤⓢ 'jʊr.ə-/.
Eurobond 'jʊə.rəʊ.bɒnd, 'jɔː- ⓤⓢ 'jʊr.oʊ.bɑːnd **-s** -z
eurocentric ˌjʊə.rəʊ'sen.trɪk, ˌjɔː- ⓤⓢ ˌjʊr.oʊ'-
Eurocheque® 'jʊə.rəʊ.tʃek, 'jɔː- ⓤⓢ 'jʊr.oʊ- **-s** -s
Eurocommun|ism ˌjʊə.rəʊ'kɒm.jə.n|ɪ.zᵊm, ˌjɔː-, -jʊ-, 'jʊə.rəʊˌkɒm-, 'jɔː- ⓤⓢ ˌjʊr.oʊ'kɑːm.jə-, -ə'- **-ist/s** -ɪst/s
Eurocrat 'jʊə.rəʊ.kræt, 'jɔː- ⓤⓢ 'jʊr.ə- **-s** -s
Eurodisney® 'jʊə.rəʊˌdɪz.ni, 'jɔː- ⓤⓢ 'jʊr.oʊ-
Eurodollar® 'jʊə.rəʊˌdɒl.əʳ, 'jɔː- ⓤⓢ 'jʊr.oʊˌdɑː.lɚ **-s** -z
Europa jʊə'rəʊ.pə, jɔː'- ⓤⓢ jʊ'roʊ-
Europe 'jʊə.rəp, 'jɔː- ⓤⓢ 'jʊr.əp
European ˌjʊə.rə'piː.ən, ˌjɔː- ⓤⓢ ˌjʊr.ə'- **-s** -z *stress shift:* ˌEuropean Com'munity ; ˌ**European Eco'nomic Com'munity** ; ˌ**European 'Monetary System**
europeaniz|e, -is|e ˌjʊə.rə'piː.ə.naɪz, ˌjɔː- ⓤⓢ ˌjʊr.ə'- **-es** -ɪz **-ing** -ɪŋ **-ed** -d

europium jʊə'rəʊ.pi.əm, jɔː'- Ⓤⓢ jʊ'roʊ-
Eurosceptic 'jʊə.rəʊˌskep.tɪk, 'jɔː- Ⓤⓢ 'jʊr.oʊ-, '-ə- **-s** -s
Eurotunnel® 'jʊə.rəʊˌtʌn.əl, 'jɔː- Ⓤⓢ 'jʊr.oʊ-, '-ə-
Eurovision® 'jʊə.rəʊ.vɪ.ʒən, 'jɔː- Ⓤⓢ 'jʊr.ə-, -oʊ- **ˌEurovision 'Song ˌContest**
Eurus 'jʊə.rəs, 'jɔː- Ⓤⓢ 'jʊr.əs
Eurydice jʊə'rɪd.ɪ.si, jɔː'-, '-ə- Ⓤⓢ jʊ-
eurythm|ic jʊə'rɪð.m|ɪk, jɔː'-, -'rɪθ- Ⓤⓢ jʊ'rɪð- **-ics** -ɪks **-y** -i
Eusden 'juːz.dən
Eusebius juː'siː.bi.əs
Eustace 'juː.stəs, -stɪs
eustachian juː'steɪ.ʃən, -ʃi.ən, -ki.ən **euˌstachian 'tube** Ⓤⓢ **eu'stachian ˌtube**
Eustachius juː'steɪ.ki.əs
Eustacia juː'steɪ.si.ə, -ʃə
Euston 'juː.stən
Euterpe juː'tɜː.pi Ⓤⓢ -'tɜːr-
euthanasia ˌjuː.θə'neɪ.zi.ə, '-ʒə Ⓤⓢ '-ʒə, '-zi.ə
Eutropius juː'trəʊ.pi.əs Ⓤⓢ -'troʊ-
Euxine 'juːk.saɪn
Euxton 'ek.stən
Eva 'iː.və Ⓤⓢ 'iː.və, 'eɪ-
evacu|ate ɪ'væk.ju|.eɪt **-ates** -eɪts **-ating** -eɪ.tɪŋ Ⓤⓢ -eɪ.t̬ɪŋ **-ated** -eɪ.tɪd Ⓤⓢ -eɪ.t̬ɪd **-ator/s** -eɪ.tər/z Ⓤⓢ -eɪ.t̬ɚ/z
evacuation ɪˌvæk.ju'eɪ.ʃən **-s** -z
evacuee ɪˌvæk.ju'iː **-s** -z
evad|e ɪ'veɪd **-es** -z **-ing** -ɪŋ **-ed** -ɪd **-er/s** -ər/z Ⓤⓢ -ɚ/z
Evadne ɪ'væd.ni
evalu|ate ɪ'væl.ju|.eɪt **-ates** -eɪts **-ating** -eɪ.tɪŋ Ⓤⓢ -eɪ.t̬ɪŋ **-ated** -eɪ.tɪd Ⓤⓢ -eɪ.t̬ɪd
evaluation ɪˌvæl.ju'eɪ.ʃən **-s** -z
evaluative ɪ'væl.ju.ə.tɪv Ⓤⓢ -eɪ.t̬ɪv **-ly** -li
Evan 'ev.ən
Evander ɪ'væn.dər Ⓤⓢ -dɚ
evanesc|e ˌiː.və'nes, ˌev.ə'- Ⓤⓢ ˌev.ə'- **-es** -ɪz **-ing** -ɪŋ **-ed** -t
evanescen|ce ˌiː.və'nes.ən|ts, ˌev.ə'- Ⓤⓢ ˌev.ə'- **-t/ly** -t/li
evangel ɪ'væn.dʒəl, -dʒel **-s** -z
evangelic ˌiː.væn'dʒel.ɪk, ˌev.æn'-, -ən'- **-s** -s
evangelic|al ˌiː.væn'dʒel.ɪ.k|əl, ˌev.æn'-, -ən'- **-als** -əlz **-ally** -li **-alism** -əl.ɪ.zəm
Evangeline ɪ'væn.dʒɪ.liːn, -dʒəl.iːn, -aɪn Ⓤⓢ -dʒə.lɪn, -dʒɪ-, -liːn, -laɪn
evangel|ism ɪ'væn.dʒə.l|ɪ.zəm, -dʒɪ- **-ist/s** -ɪst/s
evangelistic ɪˌvæn.dʒə'lɪs.tɪk, -dʒɪ'-
evangelization, -isa- ɪˌvæn.dʒəl.aɪ'zeɪ.ʃən, -dʒɪ.laɪ'-, -lɪ'- Ⓤⓢ -dʒəl.ɪ'-
evangeliz|e, -is|e ɪ'væn.dʒəl.aɪz, -dʒɪ- Ⓤⓢ -dʒə.laɪz, -dʒɪ- **-es** -ɪz **-ing** -ɪŋ **-ed** -d
Evans 'ev.ənz
Evanson 'ev.ən.sən
Evanston 'ev.ən.stən
Evansville 'ev.ənz.vɪl
evaporable ɪ'væp.ər.ə.bl̩
evapor|ate ɪ'væp.ər|.eɪt Ⓤⓢ -ə.r|eɪt **-ates** -eɪts **-ating** -eɪ.tɪŋ Ⓤⓢ -eɪ.t̬ɪŋ **-ated** -eɪ.tɪd Ⓤⓢ -eɪ.t̬ɪd **-ator/s** -eɪ.tər/z Ⓤⓢ -eɪ.t̬ɚ/z **eˌvaporated 'milk**
evaporation ɪˌvæp.ə'reɪ.ʃən **-s** -z
evasion ɪ'veɪ.ʒən **-s** -z
evasive ɪ'veɪ.sɪv **-ly** -li **-ness** -nəs, -nɪs
eve (E) iːv **-s** -z
Evele(i)gh 'iːv.li
Evelina ˌev.ɪ'liː.nə, -ə'-
Eveline 'iːv.lɪn, 'ev.lɪn, 'ev.ɪ.liːn
Evelyn 'iːv.lɪn, 'ev.lɪn, 'ev.ə- Ⓤⓢ 'ev.ə-, 'ev.lɪn, 'iːv-
Note: The pronunciation /'iːv.lɪn/ is used in the US only for British people of that name.
even 'iː.vən **-ly** -li **-ness** -nəs, -nɪs **-s** -z **-ing** -ɪŋ **-ed** -d
Evenden 'ev.ən.dən
evenhanded ˌiː.vən'hæn.dɪd **-ly** -li **-ness** -nəs, -nɪs *stress shift:* ˌevenhanded ad'ministrator
evening *(n.)* 'iːv.nɪŋ **-s** -z **'evening ˌdress**, **ˌevening 'dress** ; **'evening ˌgown** ; **ˌevening 'primrose** ; **ˌevening 'primrose ˌoil**
Evens 'ev.ənz
evensong 'iː.vən.sɒŋ Ⓤⓢ -sɑːŋ, -sɔːŋ **-s** -z
even-steven ˌiː.vən'stiː.vən **-s** -z
e|vent ɪ|'vent **-vents** -'vents **-venting** -'ven.tɪŋ Ⓤⓢ -'ven.t̬ɪŋ **-vented** -'ven.tɪd Ⓤⓢ -'ven.t̬ɪd **-venter/s** -'ven.tər/z Ⓤⓢ -'ven.t̬ɚ/z
eventful ɪ'vent.fəl, -fʊl **-ly** -i
eventide 'iː.vən.taɪd **-s** -z
eventive ɪ'ven.tɪv Ⓤⓢ -t̬ɪv
eventual ɪ'ven.tʃu.əl, -tju-, -tʃʊl, -tjʊl Ⓤⓢ -tʃu.əl **-ly** -i
eventualit|y ɪˌven.tʃu'æl.ə.t|i, -tju'-, -ɪ.t|i Ⓤⓢ -tʃu'æl.ə.t̬|i **-ies** -iz
eventu|ate ɪ'ven.tʃu|.eɪt, -tju- Ⓤⓢ -tʃu- **-ates** -eɪts **-ating** -eɪ.tɪŋ Ⓤⓢ -eɪ.t̬ɪŋ **-ated** -eɪ.tɪd Ⓤⓢ -eɪ.t̬ɪd
ever 'ev.ər Ⓤⓢ -ɚ
Everard 'ev.ər.ɑːd Ⓤⓢ -ə.rɑːrd
Everest 'ev.ər.est Ⓤⓢ -ə.rest, -ɚ.ɪst, '-rɪst
Everett 'ev.ər.et Ⓤⓢ -ə.ret, 'ev.rɪt
Everglades 'ev.ə.gleɪdz Ⓤⓢ '-ɚ-
evergreen 'ev.ə.griːn Ⓤⓢ '-ɚ- **-s** -z
Everitt 'ev.ər.ɪt
everlasting ˌev.ə'lɑː.stɪŋ Ⓤⓢ -ɚ'læs.tɪŋ **-ly** -li **-ness** -nəs, -nɪs
Everl(e)y 'ev.ə.li Ⓤⓢ '-ɚ-
evermore ˌev.ə'mɔːr Ⓤⓢ -ɚ'mɔːr
EverReady® 'ev.əˌred.i Ⓤⓢ -ɚˌ-
Evers 'ev.əz Ⓤⓢ -ɚz
Evershed 'ev.ə.ʃed Ⓤⓢ '-ɚ-
eversion ɪ'vɜː.ʃən, iː- Ⓤⓢ -'vɜːr.ʒən, -ʃən
Eversley 'ev.əz.li Ⓤⓢ -ɚz-
e|vert ɪ|'vɜːt, iː- Ⓤⓢ -'vɜːrt **-verts** -'vɜːts Ⓤⓢ -'vɜːrts **-verting** -'vɜː.tɪŋ Ⓤⓢ -'vɜːr.t̬ɪŋ **-verted** -'vɜː.tɪd Ⓤⓢ -'vɜːr.t̬ɪd
Evert 'ev.ət Ⓤⓢ -ɚt
Everton 'ev.ə.tən Ⓤⓢ '-ɚ-
every 'ev.ri **ˌevery ˌwhich 'way** Ⓤⓢ **ˌevery 'which ˌway**, **'every ˌwhich ˌway**
Note: The meaning is slightly different in American English depending on the stress pattern. **ˌEvery 'which ˌway** means "akimbo". **'Every ˌwhich ˌway** means "in all possible ways".
everybody 'ev.riˌbɒd.i Ⓤⓢ -ˌbɑː.di
everyday 'ev.ri.deɪ, ˌ--'-
Everyman 'ev.ri.mæn
everyone 'ev.ri.wʌn
everyplace 'ev.ri.pleɪs
everything 'ev.ri.θɪŋ
everywhere 'ev.ri.*h*weər Ⓤⓢ -*h*wer
Evesham 'iːv.ʃəm *locally also:* 'iː.vɪ-
Evett 'ev.ɪt
evict ɪ'vɪkt **-s** -s **-ing** -ɪŋ **-ed** -ɪd
eviction ɪ'vɪk.ʃən **-s** -z
evidenc|e 'ev.ɪ.dənts, '-ə- **-es** -ɪz **-ing** -ɪŋ **-ed** -t
evident 'ev.ɪ.dənt, '-ə- **-ly** -li
evidential ˌev.ɪ'den.*t*ʃəl, -ə'- Ⓤⓢ -ʃəl **-ly** -i
evidentiary ˌev.ɪ'den.*t*ʃər.i, -ə'- Ⓤⓢ -'den*t*.ʃɚ.i
evil 'iː.vəl, -vɪl Ⓤⓢ -vəl **-s** -z **-ly** -i **ˌevil 'eye** Ⓤⓢ **'evil ˌeye**
evildoer 'iː.vəlˌduː.ər, -vɪlˌ-, ˌiː.vəl'duː-, -vɪl'- Ⓤⓢ 'iː.vəlˌduː.ɚ, ˌiː.vəl'duː- **-s** -z
evil-minded ˌiː.vəl'maɪn.dɪd, -vɪl'-, 'iː.vəlˌmaɪn-, -vɪlˌ- Ⓤⓢ ˌiː.vəl'maɪn-, 'iː.vəlˌmaɪn- **-ness** -nəs, -nɪs
evinc|e ɪ'vɪn*t*s **-es** -ɪz **-ing** -ɪŋ **-ed** -t **-ive** -ɪv
evincib|le ɪ'vɪn*t*.sə.b|l̩, -sɪ- **-ly** -li
evi|rate 'iː.vɪ|.reɪt, 'ev.ɪ- **-rates** -reɪts **-rating** -reɪ.tɪŋ Ⓤⓢ -reɪ.t̬ɪŋ **-rated** -reɪ.tɪd Ⓤⓢ -reɪ.t̬ɪd
evisce|rate ɪ'vɪs.ə|.reɪt, iː- **-rates** -reɪts **-rating** -reɪ.tɪŋ Ⓤⓢ -reɪ.t̬ɪŋ **-rated** -reɪ.tɪd Ⓤⓢ -reɪ.t̬ɪd
evisceration ɪˌvɪs.ə'reɪ.ʃən, iːˌvɪs-
Evita ev'iː.tə, ɪ'viː- Ⓤⓢ -tə, -t̬ə

evo|cate 'ev.əʊ|.keɪt, 'iː.vəʊ- ⓊⓈ 'ev.ə-, 'iː.voʊ- **-cates** -keɪts **-cating** -keɪ.tɪŋ ⓊⓈ -keɪ.t̬ɪŋ **-cated** -keɪ.tɪd ⓊⓈ -keɪ.t̬ɪd
evocation ˌev.əʊ'keɪ.ʃᵊn, ˌiː.vəʊ'- ⓊⓈ ˌev.ə'-, ˌiː.voʊ'- **-s** -z
evocative ɪ'vɒk.ə.tɪv ⓊⓈ -'vɑː.kə.t̬ɪv **-ly** -li
evok|e ɪ'vəʊk ⓊⓈ -'voʊk **-es** -s **-ing** -ɪŋ **-ed** -t
evolute ˌiː.və'luːt, ˌev.ə'-, -'ljuːt ⓊⓈ ˌev.ə'luːt, ˌiː.və'- **-s** -s
evolution ˌiː.və'luː.ʃᵊn, ˌev.ə'-, -'ljuː- ⓊⓈ ˌev.ə'luː.ʃᵊn, ˌiː.və'- **-s** -z
evolutional ˌiː.və'luː.ʃᵊn.ᵊl, ˌev.ə'-, -'ljuː- ⓊⓈ ˌev.ə'luː-, ˌiː.və'-
evolutionary ˌiː.və'luː.ʃᵊn.ᵊr.i, ˌev.ə'-, -'ljuː-, -ri ⓊⓈ ˌev.ə'luː.ʃᵊn.er-, ˌiː.və'-
evolution|ism ˌiː.və'luː.ʃᵊn|.ɪ.zᵊm, ˌev.ə'-, -'ljuː- ⓊⓈ ˌev.ə'luː-, ˌiː.və'- **-ist/s** -ɪst/s
evolutive ɪ'vɒl.jə.tɪv, iː-, -jʊ- ⓊⓈ ˌev.ə'luː.t̬ɪv, ˌiː.və'-; iː'vɑːl.jə-
evolv|e ɪ'vɒlv ⓊⓈ -'vɑːlv **-es** -z **-ing** -ɪŋ **-ed** -d **-able** -ə.bl̩
Évora 'ev.ə.rə ⓊⓈ ev'ʊr.ə
Evo-stik® 'iː.vəʊ.stɪk ⓊⓈ -voʊ-
evulsion ɪ'vʌl.ʃᵊn, iː- **-s** -z
Ewan 'juː.ən
Ewart 'juː.ət, jʊət ⓊⓈ 'juː.ɚt
Ewbank 'juː.bæŋk
ewe juː **-s** -z
Ewell 'juː.əl, jʊəl ⓊⓈ 'juː.əl
Ewen 'juː.ən, -ɪn; jʊən ⓊⓈ 'juː.ən
ewer 'juː.əʳ, jʊəʳ ⓊⓈ 'juː.ɚ **-s** -z
Ewing 'juː.ɪŋ
ex- eks-, ɪks-, egz-, ɪgz-
Note: Prefix. Takes either primary or secondary stress, e.g. **excellent** /'ek.sᵊl.ᵊnt/, **excitation** /ˌek.sɪ'teɪ.ʃᵊn ⓊⓈ -saɪ'-/ or may be unstressed, e.g. **excel** /ɪk'sel/.
ex eks
exacer|bate ɪg'zæs.ə|.beɪt, eg-; ɪk'sæs-, ek- ⓊⓈ ɪg'zæs.ɚ-, eg'- **-bates** -beɪts **-bating** -beɪ.tɪŋ ⓊⓈ -beɪ.t̬ɪŋ **-bated** -beɪ.tɪd ⓊⓈ -beɪ.t̬ɪd
exacerbation ɪgˌzæs.ə'beɪ.ʃᵊn, egˌ-; ɪkˌsæs-, ekˌ- ⓊⓈ ɪgˌzæs.ɚ'-, eg'- **-s** -z
exact ɪg'zækt, eg'-; ɪk'sækt, ek'- ⓊⓈ ɪg'zækt, eg'- **-ly** -li, -'zæk.li, -'sæk- ⓊⓈ -'zæk- **-ness** -nəs, -nɪs **-s** -s **-ing/ly** -ɪŋ/li **-ed** -ɪd **-er/s** -əʳ/z ⓊⓈ -ɚ/z **-or/s** -əʳ/z ⓊⓈ -ɚ/z
exaction ɪg'zæk.ʃᵊn, eg'-; ɪk'sæk-, ek'- ⓊⓈ ɪg'zæk-, eg'- **-s** -z
exactitude ɪg'zæk.tɪ.tjuːd, eg'-, -tə-; ɪk'sæk-, ek'- ⓊⓈ ɪg'zæk.tə.tuːd, eg'-, -tjuːd
exactly ɪg'zækt.li, eg'-; ɪk'sækt-, ek'- ⓊⓈ ɪg'zækt-, eg'-
exagger|ate ɪg'zædʒ.ᵊr|.eɪt, eg'-; ɪk'sædʒ-, ek'- ⓊⓈ ɪg'zædʒ.ə.r|eɪt, eg'- **-ates** -eɪts **-ating** -eɪ.tɪŋ ⓊⓈ -eɪ.t̬ɪŋ **-ated/ly** -eɪ.tɪd/li ⓊⓈ -eɪ.t̬ɪd/li **-ator/s** -eɪ.təʳ/z ⓊⓈ -eɪ.t̬ɚ/z
exaggeration ɪgˌzædʒ.ᵊr'eɪ.ʃᵊn, egˌ-; ɪkˌsædʒ-, ekˌ- ⓊⓈ ɪgˌzædʒ-, egˌ- **-s** -z
exaggerative ɪg'zædʒ.ᵊr.ə.tɪv, eg'-; ɪk'sædʒ-, ek'- ⓊⓈ ɪg'zædʒ.ɚ.ə.t̬ɪv, eg'-
exal|t ɪg'zɔːl|t, eg'-, -'zɒl|t; ɪk'sɔːl|t, ek'-, -'sɒl|t ⓊⓈ ɪg'zɔːl|t, eg-, -'zɑːl|t **-ts** -ts **-ting** -tɪŋ ⓊⓈ -t̬ɪŋ **-ted/ly** -tɪd/li ⓊⓈ -t̬ɪd/li **-tedness** -tɪd.nəs ⓊⓈ -t̬ɪd.nəs, -nɪs
exaltation ˌeg.zɔːl'teɪ.ʃᵊn, ˌek.sɔːl'-, -sɒl'- ⓊⓈ ˌeg.zɔːl'-, -zɑːl'-; ˌek.sɔːl'-, -sɑːl'- **-s** -z
exam ɪg'zæm, eg'-; ɪk'sæm, ek'- ⓊⓈ ɪg'zæm, eg'- **-s** -z
examen eg'zeɪ.men, ɪg'- **-s** -z
examination ɪgˌzæm.ɪ'neɪ.ʃᵊn, egˌ-; ɪkˌsæm-, ekˌ-, -ə'- ⓊⓈ ɪgˌzæm-, egˌ- **-s** -z **exˌami'nation ˌpaper**
examin|e ɪg'zæm.ɪn, eg'-; ɪk'sæm-, ek'- ⓊⓈ ɪg'zæm-, eg'- **-es** -z **-ing** -ɪŋ **-ed** -d **-er/s** -əʳ/z ⓊⓈ -ɚ/z
examinee ɪgˌzæm.ɪ'niː, egˌ-; ɪkˌsæm-, ekˌ-, -ə'- ⓊⓈ ɪgˌzæm-, egˌ- **-s** -z
exampl|e ɪg'zɑːm.pl̩, eg'-; ɪk'sɑːm-, ek'- ⓊⓈ ɪg'zæm-, eg'- **-es** -z **-ing** -ɪŋ, '-plɪŋ **-ed** -d
exarch 'ek.sɑːk ⓊⓈ -sɑːrk **-s** -s **-ate/s** -eɪt/s
exasper|ate ɪg'zæs.pᵊr|.eɪt, eg'-; ɪk'sæs-, ek'-, -'zɑː.spᵊr- ⓊⓈ ɪg'zæs.pə.r|eɪt, eg'- **-ates** -eɪts **-ating/ly** -eɪ.tɪŋ/li ⓊⓈ -eɪ.t̬ɪŋ/li **-ated/ly** -eɪ.tɪd/li ⓊⓈ -eɪ.t̬ɪd/li
exasperation ɪgˌzæs.pə'reɪ.ʃᵊn, egˌ-; ɪkˌsæs-, ekˌ-, -ˌzɑː.spə'- ⓊⓈ ɪg'zæs.pə'-, eg-
Excalibur ek'skæl.ɪ.bəʳ, ɪk'-, '-ə- ⓊⓈ -bɚ
ex cathedra ˌeks.kə'θiː.drə, -'θed.rə, -rɑː ⓊⓈ -kə'θiː.drə, -'kæθ.ɪ-
exca|vate 'ek.skə|.veɪt **-vates** -veɪts **-vating** -veɪ.tɪŋ ⓊⓈ -veɪ.t̬ɪŋ **-vated** -veɪ.tɪd ⓊⓈ -veɪ.t̬ɪd **-vator/s** -veɪ.təʳ/z ⓊⓈ -veɪ.t̬ɚ/z
excavation ˌeks.kə'veɪ.ʃᵊn **-s** -z
exceed ɪk'siːd, ek- **-s** -z **-ing/ly** -ɪŋ/li **-ed** -ɪd
exceeding ɪk'siː.dɪŋ, ek- **-ly** -li
excel ɪk'sel, ek- **-s** -z **-ling** -ɪŋ **-led** -d
excellenc|e 'ek.sᵊl.ᵊn*t*s **-es** -ɪz
excellenc|y (E) 'ek.sᵊl.ᵊn*t*.s|i **-ies** -iz
excellent 'ek.sᵊl.ᵊnt **-ly** -li
excelsior ek'sel.si.ɔːʳ, ɪk-, -əʳ ⓊⓈ -ɔːr, -ɚ
except ɪk'sept, ek- **-s** -s **-ing** -ɪŋ **-ed** -ɪd
exception ɪk'sep.ʃᵊn, ek- **-s** -z
exceptionab|le ɪk'sep.ʃᵊn.ə.bl|̩, ek- **-ly** -li **-leness** -l̩.nəs, -nɪs
exceptional ɪk'sep.ʃᵊn.ᵊl, ek- **-ly** -i
excerpt (*n.*) 'ek.sɜːpt, 'eg.zɜːpt ⓊⓈ 'ek.sɜːrpt, 'eg.zɜːrpt **-s** -s
excerpt (*v.*) ek'sɜːpt, ɪk'- ⓊⓈ ek'sɜːrpt, eg'zɜːrpt **-s** -s **-ing** -ɪŋ **-ed** -ɪd
excerption ek'sɜːp.ʃᵊn, ɪk- ⓊⓈ ek'sɜːrp-, eg'zɜːrp- **-s** -z
excess ɪk'ses, ek'- **-es** -ɪz **-ing** -ɪŋ **-ed** -t *stress shift:* ˌexcess 'baggage
excessive ɪk'ses.ɪv, ek'- **-ly** -li **-ness** -nəs, -nɪs
exchang|e ɪks'tʃeɪndʒ, eks'- **-es** -ɪz **-ing** -ɪŋ **-ed** -d **-er/s** -əʳ/z ⓊⓈ -ɚ/z **-eable** -ə.bl̩ **ex'change ˌrate** ; **Ex'change ˌRate ˌMechanism**
exchangeability ɪksˌtʃeɪn.dʒə'bɪl.ə.ti, eksˌ-, -ɪ.ti ⓊⓈ -ə.t̬i
exchangee ˌeks.tʃeɪn'dʒiː; ɪksˌtʃeɪn'- **-s** -z
exchequer (E) ɪks'tʃek.əʳ, eks'- ⓊⓈ -ɚ **-s** -z ˌ**Chancellor of the Ex'chequer**
excisable ek'saɪ.zə.bl̩, ɪk'- ⓊⓈ ek'saɪ-, 'ek.saɪ-
excise (*n.*) *tax:* 'ek.saɪz; ek'saɪz, ɪk'- ⓊⓈ 'ek.saɪz, -saɪs **-man** -mæn **-men** -men
excis|e (*v.*) *cut out:* ek'saɪz, ɪk- **-es** -ɪz **-ing** -ɪŋ **-ed** -d
excision ek'sɪʒ.ᵊn, ɪk'- **-s** -z
excitability ɪkˌsaɪ.tə'bɪl.ə.ti, ekˌ-, -ɪ.ti ⓊⓈ -ə.t̬i
excitab|le ɪk'saɪ.tə.bl|̩, ek'- ⓊⓈ -t̬ə- **-ly** -li **-leness** -l̩.nəs, -nɪs
excitant 'ek.sɪ.tᵊnt; ɪk'saɪ-, ek'- ⓊⓈ ɪk'saɪ.tᵊnt **-s** -s
excitation ˌek.sɪ'teɪ.ʃᵊn, -sə'-, -saɪ'- ⓊⓈ ˌek.saɪ'- **-s** -z
excita|tive ek'saɪ.tə|.tɪv, ɪk'- ⓊⓈ -t̬ə|.t̬ɪv **-tory** -tᵊr.i, -tri ⓊⓈ -tɔːr.i
ex|cite ɪk|'saɪt, ek|'- **-es** -'saɪts **-ing/ly** -'saɪ.tɪŋ/li ⓊⓈ -'saɪ.t̬ɪŋ/li **-ed** -'saɪ.tɪd ⓊⓈ -'saɪ.t̬ɪd **-er/s** -'saɪ.təʳ/z ⓊⓈ -'saɪ.t̬ɚ/z
excitement ɪk'saɪt.mənt, ek'- **-s** -s
exclaim ɪks'kleɪm, eks'- **-s** -z **-ing** -ɪŋ **-ed** -d
exclamation ˌeks.klə'meɪ.ʃᵊn **-s** -z **excla'mation ˌmark** ; **excla'mation ˌpoint**
exclamatory eks'klæm.ə.tᵊr.i, ɪks'-, -tri ⓊⓈ -tɔːr.i
exclave 'eks.kleɪv **-s** -z
exclud|e ɪks'kluːd, eks'- **-es** -z **-ing** -ɪŋ **-ed** -ɪd
exclusion ɪks'kluː.ʒᵊn, eks'- **-s** -z
exclusionary ɪks'kluː.ʒᵊn.ᵊr.i, eks'- ⓊⓈ -er-
exclusionist ɪks'kluː.ʒᵊn.ɪst, eks'- **-s** -s
exclusive ɪks'kluː.sɪv, eks'- **-ly** -li **-ness** -nəs, -nɪs

exclusiv|ism ɪks'kluː.sɪ.v|ɪ.zᵊm, eks'-, -sə- **-ist/s** -ɪst/s
exclusivistic ɪksˌkluː.sɪ'vɪs.tɪk, eks'-, -sə'-
exclusivity ˌeks.kluː'sɪv.ə.ti, -ɪ.ti ⓊⓈ -ə.t̬i
excogi|tate ek'skɒdʒ.ɪ|.teɪt, ɪk'- ⓊⓈ -'skɑː.dʒɪ- **-tates** -teɪts **-tating** -teɪ.tɪŋ ⓊⓈ -teɪ.t̬ɪŋ **-tated** -teɪ.tɪd ⓊⓈ -teɪ.t̬ɪd
excogitation ˌek.skɒdʒ.ɪ'teɪ.ʃᵊn; ɪkˌskɒdʒ.ɪ'-, ekˌ- ⓊⓈ ɪkˌskɑː.dʒɪ'-, ekˌ- **-s** -z
excommuni|cate ˌek.skə'mjuː.nɪ|.keɪt, -nə- **-cates** -keɪts **-cating** -keɪ.tɪŋ ⓊⓈ -keɪ.t̬ɪŋ **-cated** -keɪ.tɪd ⓊⓈ -keɪ.t̬ɪd
excommunication ˌek.skəˌmjuː.nɪ'keɪ.ʃᵊn, -nə'- **-s** -z
excori|ate ek'skɔː.ri|.eɪt, ɪk'-, -'skɒr.i- ⓊⓈ -'skɔːr.i- **-ates** -eɪts **-ating** -eɪ.tɪŋ ⓊⓈ -eɪ.t̬ɪŋ **-ated** -eɪ.tɪd ⓊⓈ -eɪ.t̬ɪd
excoriation ekˌskɔː.ri'eɪ.ʃᵊn, ɪkˌ-, -ˌskɒr.i'- ⓊⓈ -ˌskɔːr.i'- **-s** -z
excrement 'ek.skrə.mənt, -skrɪ- **-s** -s
excremental ˌek.skrə'men.tᵊl, -skrɪ'- ⓊⓈ -t̬ᵊl
excrescen|ce ɪk'skres.ᵊn|*t*s, ek'- **-ces** -*t*.sɪz **-t** -t
excreta ɪk'skriː.tə, ek'- ⓊⓈ -t̬ə
ex|crete ɪk's|kriːt, ek'- **-cretes** -kriːts **-creting** -kriː.tɪŋ ⓊⓈ -kriː.t̬ɪŋ **-creted** -kriː.tɪd ⓊⓈ -kriː.t̬ɪd **-cretive** -kriː.tɪv ⓊⓈ -kriː.t̬ɪv **-cretory** -kriː.tᵊr.i ⓊⓈ -kriː.t̬ɚ.i
excretion ɪk'skriː.ʃᵊn, ek'- **-s** -z
excret|um ɪk'skriː.t|əm, ek'- ⓊⓈ -t̬|əm **-a** -ə
excruci|ate ɪk'skruː.ʃi|.eɪt, ek'-, -si- ⓊⓈ -ʃi- **-ates** -eɪts **-ating/ly** -eɪ.tɪŋ/li ⓊⓈ -eɪ.t̬ɪŋ/li **-ated** -eɪ.tɪd ⓊⓈ -eɪ.t̬ɪd
excruciation ɪkˌskruː.ʃi'eɪ.ʃᵊn, ekˌ-, -si'- ⓊⓈ -ʃi'-
excul|pate 'ek.skʌl|.peɪt; ɪk'skʌl-, ek'- **-pates** -peɪts **-pating** -peɪ.tɪŋ ⓊⓈ -peɪ.t̬ɪŋ **-pated** -peɪ.tɪd ⓊⓈ -peɪ.t̬ɪd
exculpation ˌek.skʌl'peɪ.ʃᵊn
exculpatory ek'skʌl.pə.tᵊr.i, -tri ⓊⓈ -tɔːr.i
excurs|e ɪk'skɜːs, ek'- ⓊⓈ -'skɜːrs **-es** -ɪz **-ing** -ɪŋ **-ed** -t
excursion ɪk'skɜː.ʃᵊn, ek'-, -ʒᵊn ⓊⓈ -'skɜːr.ʒᵊn **-s** -z
excursionist ɪk'skɜː.ʃᵊn.ɪst, ek'-, -ʒᵊn- ⓊⓈ -'skɜːr.ʒᵊn- **-s** -s
excursioniz|e, -is|e ɪk'skɜː.ʃᵊn.aɪz, ek'-, -ʒᵊn- ⓊⓈ -'skɜːr.ʒᵊn- **-es** -ɪz **-ing** -ɪŋ **-ed** -d
excursive ɪk'skɜː.sɪv, ek'- ⓊⓈ -'skɜːr- **-ly** -li **-ness** -nəs, -nɪs
excursus ek'skɜː.səs, ɪk'- ⓊⓈ -'skɜːr- **-es** -ɪz
excusab|le ɪk'skjuː.zə.b|l̩, ek'- **-ly** -li **-leness** -l̩.nəs, -nɪs
excusatory ɪk'skjuː.zə.tᵊr.i, ek'-, -tri ⓊⓈ -tɔːr.i
excus|e (*n.*) ɪk'skjuːs, ek'- **-es** -ɪz
excus|e (*v.*) ɪk'skjuːz, ek'- **-es** -ɪz **-ing** -ɪŋ **-ed** -d
ex delicto ˌeks.del'ɪk.təʊ ⓊⓈ -diː'lɪk.toʊ, -dɪ'-
ex-directory ˌeks.də'rek.tᵊr.i, -dɪ'-, -daɪ'-, '-tri
Exe eks
exeat 'ek.si.æt, -seɪ- **-s** -s
execrab|le 'ek.sɪ.krə.b|l̩, -sə- **-ly** -li **-leness** -l̩.nəs, -nɪs
exe|crate 'ek.sɪ|.kreɪt, -sə- **-crates** -kreɪts **-crating** -kreɪ.tɪŋ ⓊⓈ -kreɪ.t̬ɪŋ **-crated** -kreɪ.tɪd ⓊⓈ -kreɪ.t̬ɪd
execration ˌek.sɪ'kreɪ.ʃᵊn, -sə'- **-s** -z
execra|tive 'ek.sɪ.kreɪ|.tɪv, -sə- ⓊⓈ -t̬ɪv **-tively** -tɪv.li ⓊⓈ -t̬ɪv.li **-tory** -tᵊr.i, -tri ⓊⓈ -tɔːr.i
executant ɪg'zek.jə.tənt, eg-, -jʊ-; ɪk'sek-, ek- ⓊⓈ ɪg'zek.jə-, eg- **-s** -s
exe|cute 'ek.sɪ|.kjuːt, -sə- **-cutes** -kjuːts **-cuting** -kjuː.tɪŋ ⓊⓈ -kjuː.t̬ɪŋ **-cuted** -kjuː.tɪd ⓊⓈ -kjuː.t̬ɪd **-cuter/s** -kjuː.təʳ/z ⓊⓈ -kjuː.t̬ɚ/z **-cutable** -kjuː.tə.bl̩ ⓊⓈ -kjuː.t̬ə.bl̩
execution ˌek.sɪ'kjuː.ʃᵊn, -sə'- **-s** -z
executioner ˌek.sɪ'kjuː.ʃᵊn.əʳ, -sə'- ⓊⓈ -ɚ **-s** -z
executive ɪg'zek.jə.tɪv, eg-, -jʊ-; ɪk'sek-, ek- ⓊⓈ ɪg'zek.jə.t̬ɪv, eg- **-s** -z **-ly** -li exˌecutive 'privilege
executor ɪg'zek.jə.təʳ, eg-, -jʊ-; ɪk'sek-, ek- ⓊⓈ ɪg'zek.jə.t̬ɚ, eg- **-s** -z **-ship/s** -ʃɪp/s
executory ɪg'zek.jə.tᵊr.i, eg-, -jʊ-, -tri, ɪk'sek-, ek- ⓊⓈ ɪg'zek.jə.tɔːr.i, eg-
executr|ix ɪg'zek.jə.tr|ɪks, eg-, -jʊ-; ɪk'sek-, ek- ⓊⓈ ɪg'zek.jə-, eg- **-ixes** -ɪk.sɪz **executrices** ɪgˌzek.jə'traɪ.siːz, eg-, -jʊ-; ɪkˌsek-, ek- ⓊⓈ ɪgˌzek.jə'-, eg-
exeges|is ˌek.sɪ'dʒiː.s|ɪs, -sə'- **-es** -iːz
exegetic ˌek.sɪ'dʒet.ɪk, -sə'-, 'dʒiː.tɪk ⓊⓈ -'dʒet̬- **-al** -ᵊl **-ally** -ᵊl.i, -li **-s** -s
exemplar ɪg'zem.plɑːʳ, eg-; ɪk'sem-, ek-, -plɑːʳ ⓊⓈ ɪg'zem.plɚ, eg-, -plɑːr **-s** -z
exemplarity ˌeg.zem'plær.ə.ti, -ɪ.ti ⓊⓈ -'pler-, -'plær-, -ə.t̬i
exemplar|y ɪg'zem.plᵊr|.i, eg-; ɪk'sem-, ek- ⓊⓈ ɪg'zem-, eg- **-ily** -ᵊl.i, -ɪ.li **-iness** -ɪ.nəs, -ɪ.nɪs
exemplification ɪgˌzem.plɪ.fɪ'keɪ.ʃᵊn, eg-, -plə-; ɪkˌsem-, ek- ⓊⓈ ɪgˌzem.plə-, eg- **-s** -z
exempli|fy ɪg'zem.plɪ|.faɪ, eg-, -plə-; ɪk'sem-, ek- ⓊⓈ ɪg'zem-, eg- **-fies** -faɪz **-fying** -faɪ.ɪŋ **-fied** -faɪd
exemplum ɪg'zem.pləm, eg'-; ɪk'sem-, ek'-
exempt ɪg'zempt, eg'-; ɪk'sempt, ek'- ⓊⓈ ɪg'zempt, eg'- **-s** -s **-ing** -ɪŋ **-ed** -ɪd
exemption ɪg'zemp.ʃᵊn, eg'-; ɪk'semp-, ek'- ⓊⓈ ɪg'zemp-, eg' **-s** -z
exequatur ˌek.sɪ'kweɪ.təʳ, -sə'- ⓊⓈ -t̬ɚ **-s** -z
exequies 'ek.sɪ.kwɪz, -sə- ⓊⓈ -kwiːz
exercis|e 'ek.sə.saɪz ⓊⓈ -sɚ- **-es** -ɪz **-ing** -ɪŋ **-ed** -d **-er/s** -əʳ/z ⓊⓈ -ɚ/z 'exercise ˌbook
exercitation egˌzɜː.sɪ'teɪ.ʃᵊn, ɪgˌ- ⓊⓈ -ˌzɜːr-
exergue ek'sɜːg, '-- ⓊⓈ 'ek.sɜːrg, 'eg.zɜːrg **-s** -z
exer|t ɪg'zɜː|t, eg-; ɪk'sɜː|t, ek- ⓊⓈ ɪg'zɜːr|t, eg- **-ts** -ts **-ting** -tɪŋ ⓊⓈ -t̬ɪŋ **-ted** -tɪd ⓊⓈ -t̬ɪd **-tive** -tɪv ⓊⓈ -t̬ɪv
exertion ɪg'zɜː.ʃᵊn, eg-; ɪk'sɜː-, ek- ⓊⓈ ɪg'zɜːr-, eg- **-s** -z
Exeter 'ek.sɪ.təʳ, -sə- ⓊⓈ -t̬ɚ
exeunt 'ek.si.ʌnt, -seɪ-, -ʊnt, -si.ənt ⓊⓈ -si.ʌnt, -ənt
exfoli|ate eks'fəʊ.li|.eɪt ⓊⓈ -'foʊ- **-ates** -eɪts **-ating** -eɪ.tɪŋ ⓊⓈ -eɪ.t̬ɪŋ **-ated** -eɪ.tɪd ⓊⓈ -eɪ.t̬ɪd **-ator** -eɪ.təʳ ⓊⓈ -eɪ.t̬ɚ/z
exfoliation eksˌfəʊ.li'eɪ.ʃᵊn, ˌeks.fəʊ- ⓊⓈ eksˌfoʊ- **-s** -z
ex gratia eks'greɪ.ʃə, -ʃi.ə
exhalant, exhalent eks'heɪ.lənt, ɪks-; eg'zeɪ- ⓊⓈ eks'heɪ-
exhalation ˌeks.*h*ə'leɪ.ʃᵊn **-s** -z
exhal|e eks'heɪl, ɪks-; eg'zeɪl ⓊⓈ eks'heɪl, '-- **-es** -z **-ing** -ɪŋ **-ed** -d
exhaust ɪg'zɔːst, eg'-; ɪk'sɔːst, ek'- ⓊⓈ ɪg'zɑːst, eg'-, -'zɔːst **-s** -s **-ing** -ɪŋ **-ed** -ɪd **-er/s** -əʳ/z ⓊⓈ -ɚ/z **-ible** -ə.bl̩, -ɪ.bl̩ **-less** -ləs, -lɪs ex'haust ˌpipe
exhaustion ɪg'zɔːs.tʃᵊn, eg-; ɪk'sɔː-, ek- ⓊⓈ ɪg'zɑː-, eg-, -'zɔː-
exhaustive ɪg'zɔː.stɪv, eg-; ɪk'sɔː-, ek- ⓊⓈ ɪg'zɑː-, eg-, -'zɔː- **-ly** -li **-ness** -nəs, -nɪs
exhibit (*n.*) ɪg'zɪb.ɪt, eg-; ɪk'sɪb-, ek-; 'eg.zɪb-, 'ek.sɪb- ⓊⓈ ɪg'zɪb-, eg- **-s** -s
exhib|it (*v.*) ɪg'zɪb|.ɪt, eg-; ɪk'sɪb-, ek- ⓊⓈ ɪg'zɪb-, eg- **-its** -ɪts **-iting** -ɪ.tɪŋ ⓊⓈ -ɪ.t̬ɪŋ **-ited** -ɪ.tɪd ⓊⓈ -ɪ.t̬ɪd **-itor/s** -ɪ.təʳ/z ⓊⓈ -ɪ.t̬ɚ/z **-itive** -ɪ.tɪv ⓊⓈ -ɪ.t̬ɪv **-itory** -ɪ.tᵊr.i, -ɪ.tri ⓊⓈ -ɪ.tɔːr.i

exhibition ˌek.sɪˈbɪʃ.ᵊn, -səˈ- **-s** -z
exhibitioner ˌek.sɪˈbɪʃ.ᵊn.əʳ, -səˈ- Ⓤⓢ -ɚ **-s** -z
exhibitionism ˌek.sɪˈbɪʃ.ᵊn.ɪ.zᵊm, -səˈ-
exhibitionist ˌek.sɪˈbɪʃ.ᵊn.ɪst, -səˈ- **-s** -s
exhibitionistic ˌek.sɪ.bɪ.ʃᵊnˈɪs.tɪk, -sə- **-ally** -ᵊl.i, -li
exhilarant ɪgˈzɪl.ᵊr.ᵊnt, eg-; ɪkˈsɪl-, ek- Ⓤⓢ ɪgˈzɪl-, eg- **-s** -s
exhilar|ate ɪgˈzɪl.ᵊr|.eɪt, eg-; ɪkˈsɪl-, ek- Ⓤⓢ ɪgˈzɪl-, eg- **-ates** -eɪts **-ating** -eɪ.tɪŋ Ⓤⓢ -eɪ.t̬ɪŋ **-ated** -eɪ.tɪd Ⓤⓢ -eɪ.t̬ɪd
exhilaration ɪgˌzɪl.ᵊrˈeɪ.ʃᵊn, eg-; ɪkˌsɪl-, ek- Ⓤⓢ ɪgˌzɪl-, eg-
exhilarative ɪgˈzɪl.ᵊr.ə.tɪv, eg-, -eɪ-; ɪkˈsɪl-, ek- Ⓤⓢ ɪgˈzɪl.ə.reɪ.t̬ɪv, eg-
exhor|t ɪgˈzɔː|t, eg-; ɪkˈsɔː|t, ek- Ⓤⓢ ɪgˈzɔːr|t, eg- **-ts** -ts **-ting** -tɪŋ Ⓤⓢ -t̬ɪŋ **-ted** -tɪd Ⓤⓢ -t̬ɪd
exhortation ˌeg.zɔːˈteɪ.ʃᵊn, ˌek.sɔːˈ- Ⓤⓢ ˌeg.zɔːrˈ-, -zɚˈ-; ˌek.sɔːrˈ-, -sɚˈ- **-s** -z
exhorta|tive ɪgˈzɔː.tə|.tɪv, eg-; ɪkˈsɔː-, ek- Ⓤⓢ ɪgˈzɔːr.t̬ə|.t̬ɪv, eg- **-tory** -tᵊr.i, -tri Ⓤⓢ -tɔːr.i
exhumation ˌeks.*h*juːˈmeɪ.ʃᵊn Ⓤⓢ ˌeks.*h*juːˈ-, ˌeg.zjuːˈ- **-s** -z
exhum|e eksˈ*h*juːm, ɪksˈ-; ɪgˈzjuːm, egˈ- Ⓤⓢ egˈzuːm, ɪgˈ-, -ˈzjuːm **-es** -z **-ing** -ɪŋ **-ed** -d **-er/s** -əʳ/z Ⓤⓢ -ɚ/z
exigen|ce ˈek.sɪ.dʒən*t*|s, -sə-; ˈeg.zɪ-, -zə- **-ces** -sɪz
exigenc|y ˈek.sɪ.dʒən*t*.s|i, -sə-; ˈeg.zɪ-, -zə-; ɪgˈzɪdʒ.ən*t*-, eg-; ɪkˈsɪdʒ-, ek- **-ies** -iz
exigent ˈek.sɪ.dʒənt, -sə-; ˈeg.zɪ-, -zə- **-ly** -li
exiguity ˌek.sɪˈgjuː.ə.ti, -ɪ.ti Ⓤⓢ ˌek.sɪˈgjuː.ə.t̬i, ˌeg.zɪˈ-
exiguous egˈzɪg.ju.əs, ɪg-; ekˈsɪg-, ɪk- Ⓤⓢ egˈzɪg-, ɪg- **-ness** -nəs, -nɪs
exil|e ˈek.saɪl, ˈeg.zaɪl **-es** -z **-ing** -ɪŋ **-ed** -d
exility egˈzɪl.ə.ti, ekˈsɪl-, -ɪ.ti Ⓤⓢ -ə.t̬i
exist ɪgˈzɪst, eg-; ɪkˈsɪst, ek- Ⓤⓢ ɪgˈzɪst, eg- **-s** -s **-ing** -ɪŋ **-ed** -ɪd
existen|ce ɪgˈzɪs.tᵊn|*t*s, eg-; ɪkˈsɪs-, ek- Ⓤⓢ ɪgˈzɪs-, eg- **-ces** -*t*.sɪz
existent ɪgˈzɪs.tᵊnt, eg-; ɪkˈsɪs-, ek- Ⓤⓢ ɪgˈzɪs-, eg-
existential ˌeg.zɪˈsten.*t*ʃᵊl, -zəˈ-; ˌek.sɪˈ-, -səˈ-
existential|ism ˌeg.zɪˈsten.*t*ʃᵊl|.ɪ.zᵊm, -zəˈ-; ˌek.sɪˈ-, -səˈ- **-ist/s** -ɪst/s
exit ˈek.sɪt, ˈeg.zɪt **-s** -s **ˈexit ˌpoll**
ex libris ˌeksˈlɪb.riːs, -rɪs, -ˈlaɪ.brɪs Ⓤⓢ -ˈliː.brɪs
Exmoor ˈek.smɔːʳ, -smʊəʳ Ⓤⓢ -smʊr
Exmouth *in Devon:* ˈek.smaʊθ, -sməθ *in Australia:* ˈek.smaʊθ
exo- ek.səʊ-; ɪkˈsɒ-, ek- Ⓤⓢ ek.soʊ-; ɪkˈsɑː-, ek-
Note: Prefix. Either carries primary or secondary stress on the first syllable, e.g. **exocrine** /ˈek.səʊ.kraɪn Ⓤⓢ -sə.krən/, **exocentric** /ˌek.səʊˈsen.trɪk Ⓤⓢ -soʊˈ-/, or primary stress on the second syllable, e.g. **exogamy** /ekˈsɒg.ə.mi Ⓤⓢ -ˈsɑː.gə-/.
exocentric ˌek.səʊˈsen.trɪk Ⓤⓢ -soʊˈ- **-ally** -ᵊ.li, -li
Exocet® ˈek.səʊ.set Ⓤⓢ -soʊ- **-s** -s
exocrine ˈek.səʊ.kraɪn, -krɪn Ⓤⓢ ˈek.sə.krən, -soʊ-, -kraɪn, -kriːn
exode ˈek.səʊd Ⓤⓢ -soʊd **-s** -z
exodus (**E**) ˈek.sə.dəs **-es** -ɪz
ex officio ˌeks.əˈfɪʃ.i.əʊ, -ɒfˈɪʃ-, -ˈɪs- Ⓤⓢ -əˈfɪʃ.i.oʊ, -ˈfɪs-
exogam|y ekˈsɒg.ə.m|i Ⓤⓢ -ˈsɑː.gə- **-ous** -əs
exogenous ɪkˈsɒdʒ.ə.nəs, ek-, -ɪ.nəs Ⓤⓢ -ˈsɑː.dʒə-
exon ˈek.sɒn Ⓤⓢ -sɑːn **-s** -z
exoner|ate ɪgˈzɒn.ᵊr|.eɪt, eg-; ɪkˈsɒn-, ek- Ⓤⓢ ɪgˈzɑː.nə.r|eɪt, eg- **-ates** -eɪts **-ating** -eɪ.tɪŋ Ⓤⓢ -eɪ.t̬ɪŋ **-ated** -eɪ.tɪd Ⓤⓢ -eɪ.t̬ɪd
exoneration ɪgˌzɒn.əˈreɪ.ʃᵊn, eg-; ɪkˌsɒn-, ek- Ⓤⓢ ɪgˌzɑː.nəˈ-, eg-
exonerative ɪgˈzɒn.ᵊr.ə.tɪv, eg-, -eɪ-; ɪkˈsɒn-, ek-, -eɪ.tɪv Ⓤⓢ ɪgˈzɑː.nə.reɪ.t̬ɪv, eg-
exophora ekˈsɒf.ᵊr.ə Ⓤⓢ -ˈsɑː.fɚ-
exophoric ˌek.səʊˈfɒr.ɪk Ⓤⓢ -səˈfɔːr-
exorbitan|ce ɪgˈzɔː.bɪ.tᵊn*t*|s, eg-, -bə-; ɪkˈsɔː-, ek- Ⓤⓢ ɪgˈzɔːr.bə.t̬ᵊn*t*|s, eg- **-cy** -si
exorbitant ɪgˈzɔː.bɪ.tᵊnt, eg-, -bə-; ɪkˈsɔː-, ek- Ⓤⓢ ɪgˈzɔːr.bə.t̬ᵊnt, eg- **-ly** -li
exorc|ism ˈek.sɔː.s|ɪ.zᵊm, -sə-; ˈeg.zɔː-, -zə- Ⓤⓢ ˈek.sɔːr-, -sɚ- **-ist/s** -ɪst/s
exorciz|e, -is|e ˈek.sɔː.saɪz, -sə-; ˈeg.zɔː-, -zə- Ⓤⓢ ˈek.sɔːr-, -sɚ- **-es** -ɪz **-ing** -ɪŋ **-ed** -d
exordi|um ekˈsɔː.di|.əm; egˈzɔː- Ⓤⓢ egˈzɔːr.di-, ɪg-; ekˈsɔːr-, ɪk- **-ums** -əmz **-a** -ə
exoskelet|on ˌek.səʊˈskel.ɪ.t|ᵊn, ˈ-ə-, ˈek.səʊˌskel- Ⓤⓢ ˌek.soʊˈskel.ə- **-ons** -ənz **-al** -ᵊl
exoteric ˌek.səʊˈter.ɪk Ⓤⓢ -səˈ-, -soʊˈ- **-s** -s **-al** -ᵊl **-ally** -ᵊl.i, -li
exotic ɪgˈzɒt.ɪk, eg-; ɪkˈsɒt-, ek- Ⓤⓢ ɪgˈzɑː.t̬ɪk, eg- **-s** -s **-a** -ə **-ally** -ᵊl.i, -li
exoticism ɪgˈzɒt.ɪ.sɪ.zᵊm, eg-, ˈ-ə-; ɪkˈsɒt-, ek-, ək- Ⓤⓢ ɪgˈzɑː.t̬ə-, eg-
expand ɪkˈspænd, ek- **-s** -z **-ing** -ɪŋ **-ed** -ɪd **-er/s** -əʳ/z Ⓤⓢ -ɚ/z **-able** -ə.bl̩
expans|e ɪkˈspæn*t*s, ek- **-es** -ɪz
expansibility ɪkˌspæn*t*.səˈbɪl.ə.ti, ek-, -sɪˈ-, -ɪ.ti Ⓤⓢ -ə.t̬i
expansib|le ɪkˈspæn*t*.sə.b|l̩, ek-, -sɪ- **-ly** -li **-leness** -l̩.nəs, -nɪs
expansile ɪkˈspæn*t*.saɪl, ek- Ⓤⓢ -sɪl
expansion ɪkˈspæn.*t*ʃᵊn, ek- **-s** -z
expansion|ism ɪkˈspæn.*t*ʃᵊn|.ɪ.zᵊm, ek-, ək- **-ist/s** -ɪst/s
expansive ɪkˈspæn*t*.sɪv, ek- **-ly** -li **-ness** -nəs, -nɪs
ex parte ˌeksˈpɑː.teɪ, -ti Ⓤⓢ -ˈpɑːr.ti
expat ˌekˈspat **-s** -s *stress shift:* ˌexpat comˈmunity
expati|ate ekˈspeɪ.ʃi|.eɪt, ɪk- **-ates** -eɪts **-ating** -eɪ.tɪŋ Ⓤⓢ -eɪ.t̬ɪŋ **-ated** -eɪ.tɪd Ⓤⓢ -eɪ.t̬ɪd
expatiation ekˌspeɪ.ʃiˈeɪ.ʃᵊn, ɪk- **-s** -z
expatia|tive ekˈspeɪ.ʃi.ə|.tɪv, ɪk-, -tɪv Ⓤⓢ -eɪ|.t̬ɪv **-tory** -tᵊr.i, -tri Ⓤⓢ -tɔːr.i
expatriate (*n. adj.*) ɪkˈspæt.ri.ət, ekˈ-, -ˈspeɪ.tri-, -ɪt, -eɪt Ⓤⓢ ekˈspeɪ-, ɪkˈ- **-s** -s
expatri|ate (*v.*) ɪkˈspæt.ri|.eɪt, ekˈ-, -ˈspeɪ.tri- Ⓤⓢ ekˈspeɪ-, ɪkˈ- **-ates** -eɪts **-ating** -eɪ.tɪŋ Ⓤⓢ -eɪ.t̬ɪŋ **-ated** -eɪ.tɪd Ⓤⓢ -eɪ.t̬ɪd
expatriation ekˌspæt.riˈeɪ.ʃᵊn, ɪk-, -ˌspeɪ.triˈ-, ˌek.speɪ-, ˌek.spæt.riˈ- Ⓤⓢ ekˌspeɪ.triˈeɪ-, ɪk-
expect ɪkˈspekt, ek- **-s** -s **-ing** -ɪŋ **-ed** -ɪd
expectan|cy ɪkˈspek.tᵊn*t*|si, ek- **-ce** -s **-cies** -siz
expectant ɪkˈspek.tᵊnt, ek- **-ly** -li
expectation ˌek.spekˈteɪ.ʃᵊn **-s** -z
expectorant ɪkˈspek.tᵊr.ᵊnt, ek- **-s** -s
expector|ate ɪkˈspek.tᵊr|.eɪt, ek- **-ates** -eɪts **-ating** -eɪ.tɪŋ Ⓤⓢ -eɪ.t̬ɪŋ **-ated** -eɪ.tɪd Ⓤⓢ -eɪ.t̬ɪd
expectoration ɪkˌspek.tᵊrˈeɪ.ʃᵊn, ek-
expedien|cy ɪkˈspiː.di.ən*t*|si, ek- **-ce** -s
expedient ɪkˈspiː.di.ənt, ek- **-s** -s **-ly** -li
expe|dite ˈek.spɪ|.daɪt, -spə- **-dites** -daɪts **-diting** -daɪ.tɪŋ Ⓤⓢ -daɪ.t̬ɪŋ **-dited** -daɪ.tɪd Ⓤⓢ -daɪ.t̬ɪd
expediter ˈek.spɪ.daɪ.təʳ, -spə- Ⓤⓢ -t̬ɚ **-s** -z
expedition ˌek.spɪˈdɪʃ.ᵊn, -spəˈ- **-s** -z
expeditionary ˌek.spɪˈdɪʃ.ᵊn.ᵊr.i, -spɪˈ-, -ri Ⓤⓢ -er-
expeditious ˌek.spɪˈdɪʃ.əs, -spəˈ- **-ly** -li **-ness** -nəs, -nɪs
expeditor ˈek.spɪ.daɪ.təʳ, -spə- Ⓤⓢ -t̬ɚ **-s** -z
expel ɪkˈspel, ek- **-s** -z **-ling** -ɪŋ **-led** -d **-lable** -ə.bl̩
expend ɪkˈspend, ek- **-s** -z **-ing** -ɪŋ **-ed** -ɪd
expendable ɪkˈspen.də.bl̩, ek- **-s** -z
expenditure ɪkˈspen.dɪ.tʃəʳ, ek-, -də-

Ⓤⓢ -tʃɚ -s -z
expens|e ɪk'spen*t*s, ek- **-es** -ɪz
ex'pense ac,count
expensive ɪk'spen*t*.sɪv, ek- **-ly** -li **-ness** -nəs, -nɪs
experienc|e ɪk'spɪə.ri.ən*t*s, ek- Ⓤⓢ -'spɪr.i- **-es** -ɪz **-ing** -ɪŋ **-ed** -t
experiential ɪk,spɪə.ri'en.*t*ʃᵊl, ek- Ⓤⓢ -,spɪr.i'- **-ly** -li
experiment (*n.*) ɪk'sper.ɪ.mənt, ek-, '-ə- **-s** -s
experiment (*v.*) ɪk'sper.ɪ.ment, ek-, '-ə- **-s** -s **-ing** -ɪŋ **-ed** -ɪd
experimental ɪk,sper.ɪ'men.tᵊl, ek-, -ə'-; ,ek.sper- Ⓤⓢ ek,sper-, ɪk- **-ly** -i
experimental|ism ɪk,sper.ɪ'ment.ᵊl|.ɪ.zᵊm, ek-, -ə'-; ,ek.sper-, -ə'men- Ⓤⓢ ek,sper-, ɪk- **-ist/s** -ɪst/s
experimentaliz|e, -is|e ɪk,sper.ɪ'men.tᵊl.aɪz, ek-, -ə'-; ,ek.sper- Ⓤⓢ ek,sper.ɪ'men.t̬ᵊ.laɪz, ɪk- **-es** -ɪz **-ing** -ɪŋ **-ed** -d
experimentation ɪk,sper.ɪ.men'teɪ.ʃᵊn, ek-, ,-ə- **-s** -z
expert 'ek.spɜːt Ⓤⓢ -spɜːrt **-s** -s **-ly** -li **-ness** -nəs, -nɪs
expertise ,ek.spɜː'tiːz, -spə'tiːz Ⓤⓢ -spɜːr'-, -spɚ'-
expiable 'ek.spi.ə.bl̩
expi|ate 'ek.spi|.eɪt **-ates** -eɪts **-ating** -eɪ.tɪŋ Ⓤⓢ -eɪ.t̬ɪŋ **-ated** -eɪ.tɪd Ⓤⓢ -eɪ.t̬ɪd **-ator/s** -eɪ.tər/z Ⓤⓢ -eɪ.t̬ɚ/z
expiation ,ek.spi'eɪ.ʃᵊn **-s** -z
expiatory 'ek.spi.ə.tᵊr.i, -eɪ-, -tri; ,ek.spi'eɪ- Ⓤⓢ 'ek.spi.ə.tɔːr.i
expiration ,ek.spɪ'reɪ.ʃᵊn, -spə'-, -spaɪə'- Ⓤⓢ -spə'- **-s** -z
expiratory ɪk'spɪr.ə.tᵊr.i, ek-, -'spaɪə.rə-, -tri Ⓤⓢ -'spaɪ.rə.tɔːr.i
expir|e ɪk'spaɪəʳ, ek'- Ⓤⓢ -'spaɪɚ **-es** -z **-ing** -ɪŋ **-ed** -d
expiry ɪk'spaɪə.ri, ek- Ⓤⓢ -'spaɪ-; 'ek.spɚ.i ex'piry ,date
explain ɪk'spleɪn, ek'- **-s** -z **-ing** -ɪŋ **-ed** -d **-er/s** -əʳ/z Ⓤⓢ -ɚ/z **-able** -ə.bl̩
explanation ,ek.splə'neɪ.ʃᵊn **-s** -z
explanator|y ɪk'splæn.ə.tᵊr|.i, ek'-, '-ɪ-, -tr|i Ⓤⓢ -ə.tɔːr|.i **-ily** -ᵊl.i, -ɪ.li **-iness** -ɪ.nəs, -ɪ.nɪs
expletive ɪk'spliː.tɪv, ek'- Ⓤⓢ 'ek.splə.t̬ɪv **-s** -z
expletory ɪk'spliː.tᵊr.i, ek'-, '-tri Ⓤⓢ -t̬ɚ.i
explicab|le ɪk'splɪk.ə.bl|̩, ek-; 'ek.splɪ.kə- **-ly** -li
expli|cate 'ek.splɪ|.keɪt **-cates** -keɪts **-cating** -keɪ.tɪŋ Ⓤⓢ -keɪ.t̬ɪŋ **-cated** -keɪ.tɪd Ⓤⓢ -keɪ.t̬ɪd
explication ,ek.splɪ'keɪ.ʃᵊn **-s** -z
explicative ek'splɪk.ə.tɪv, ɪk-; 'ek.splɪ.keɪ.tɪv Ⓤⓢ -t̬ɪv
explicatory ek'splɪk.ə.tᵊr.i, ɪk-, -tri; 'ek.splɪ.keɪ-, ,ek.splɪ'keɪ- Ⓤⓢ 'ek.splɪ.kə.tɔːr.i; ɪk'splɪk.ə-, ek-
explicit ɪk'splɪs.ɪt, ek- **-ly** -li **-ness** -nəs, -nɪs
explod|e ɪk'spləʊd, ek- Ⓤⓢ -'sploʊd **-es** -z **-ing** -ɪŋ **-ed** -ɪd **-er/s** -əʳ/z Ⓤⓢ -ɚ/z
exploit (*n.*) 'ek.splɔɪt **-s** -s
exploi|t (*v.*) ɪk'splɔɪ|t, ek- **-ts** -ts **-ting** -tɪŋ Ⓤⓢ -t̬ɪŋ **-ted** -tɪd Ⓤⓢ -t̬ɪd **-ter/s** -təʳ/z Ⓤⓢ -t̬ɚ/z
exploitation ,ek.splɔɪ'teɪ.ʃᵊn
exploitative ɪk'splɔɪ.tə.tɪv, ek- Ⓤⓢ -t̬ə.t̬ɪv **-ly** -li
exploitive ɪk'splɔɪ.tɪv, ek- Ⓤⓢ -t̬ɪv **-ly** -li
exploration ,ek.splə'reɪ.ʃᵊn, -splɔː'- Ⓤⓢ -splɔːr **-s** -z
explorative ɪk'splɒr.ə.tɪv, ek-, -'splɔː.rə- Ⓤⓢ -'splɔːr.ə.t̬ɪv
exploratory ɪk'splɒr.ə.tᵊr.i, ek-, -'splɔː.rə-, -tri Ⓤⓢ -'splɔːr.ə.tɔːr.i
explor|e ɪk'splɔːʳ, ek- Ⓤⓢ -'splɔːr **-es** -z **-ing** -ɪŋ **-ed** -d **-er/s** -əʳ/z Ⓤⓢ -ɚ/z
explosion ɪk'spləʊ.ʒᵊn, ek- Ⓤⓢ -'sploʊ- **-s** -z
explosive ɪk'spləʊ.sɪv, ek-, -zɪv Ⓤⓢ -'sploʊ.sɪv **-s** -z **-ly** -li **-ness** -nəs, -nɪs
expo 'ek.spəʊ Ⓤⓢ -spoʊ **-s** -z
exponent ɪk'spəʊ.nənt, ek- Ⓤⓢ -'spoʊ- **-s** -s
exponential ,ek.spə*ʊ*'nen.*t*ʃᵊl Ⓤⓢ -spoʊ'nen*t*.ʃᵊl **-ly** -li
export (*n.*) 'ek.spɔːt Ⓤⓢ -spɔːrt **-s** -s
expor|t (*v.*) ɪk'spɔː|t, ek-; 'ek.spɔː|t Ⓤⓢ ɪk'spɔːr|t, ek-; 'ek.spɔːr|t **-ts** -ts **-ting** -tɪŋ Ⓤⓢ -t̬ɪŋ **-ted** -tɪd Ⓤⓢ -t̬ɪd **-ter/s** -təʳ/z Ⓤⓢ -t̬ɚ/z
exportable ɪk'spɔː.tə.bᵊl, ek- Ⓤⓢ -'spɔːr.t̬ə-
exportation ,ek.spɔː'teɪ.ʃᵊn Ⓤⓢ -spɔːr'-
expos|e ɪk'spəʊz, ek- Ⓤⓢ -'spoʊz **-es** -ɪz **-ing** -ɪŋ **-ed** -d **-edness** -d.nəs, -nɪs **-er/s** -əʳ/z Ⓤⓢ -ɚ/z
exposé ek'spəʊ.zeɪ, ɪk- Ⓤⓢ ,ek.spoʊ'zeɪ, '--- **-s** -z
exposition ,ek.spə*ʊ*'zɪʃ.ᵊn Ⓤⓢ -pə'- **-s** -z
expositive ɪk'spɒz.ɪ.tɪv, ek-, -ə.tɪv Ⓤⓢ -'spɑː.zə.t̬ɪv
exposi|tor ɪk'spɒz.ɪ|.təʳ, ek-, -ə|.təʳ Ⓤⓢ -'spɑː.zə|.t̬ɚ **-tors** -təz Ⓤⓢ -t̬ɚz **-tory** -tᵊr.i, -tri Ⓤⓢ -tɔːr.i
ex post facto ,eks.pəʊs*t*'fæk.təʊ Ⓤⓢ -poʊst'fæk.toʊ
expostu|late ɪk'spɒs.tʃə|.leɪt, ek-, -tʃʊ-, -tjə-, -tjʊ- Ⓤⓢ -'spɑːs.tʃə- **-lates** -leɪts **-lating** -leɪ.tɪŋ Ⓤⓢ -leɪ.t̬ɪŋ **-lated** -leɪ.tɪd Ⓤⓢ -leɪ.t̬ɪd **-lator/s** -leɪ.təʳ/z Ⓤⓢ -leɪ.t̬ɚ/z
expostulation ɪk,spɒs.tʃə'leɪ.ʃᵊn, ek-, -tʃʊ'-, -tjə'-, -tjʊ'- Ⓤⓢ -,pɑːs.tʃə'- **-s** -z
expostulative ɪk'spɒs.tʃə.lə.tɪv, ek-, -tʃʊ-, -tjə-, -tjʊ-, -leɪ- Ⓤⓢ -'pɑːs.tʃə.leɪ.t̬ɪv
expostulatory ɪk'spɒs.tʃə.lə.tᵊr.i, ek-, -tʃʊ-, -tjə-, -tjʊ-, -leɪ-, -tri Ⓤⓢ -'spɑːs.tʃə.lə.tɔːr.i
exposure ɪk'spəʊ.ʒəʳ, ek- Ⓤⓢ -'spoʊ.ʒɚ **-s** -z
expound ɪk'spaʊnd, ek- **-s** -z **-ing** -ɪŋ **-ed** -ɪd **-er/s** -əʳ/z Ⓤⓢ -ɚ/z
express ɪk'spres, ek- **-es** -ɪz **-ly** -li **-ness** -nəs, -nɪs **-ing** -ɪŋ **-ed** -t ,express de'livery, ex,press de'livery Ⓤⓢ ,express de'livery
expressible ɪk'spres.ə.bl̩, ek-, -sɪ-
expression ɪk'spreʃ.ᵊn, ek- **-s** -z
expressional ɪk'spreʃ.ᵊn.ᵊl, ek-
expression|ism ɪk'spreʃ.ᵊn|.ɪ.zᵊm, ek- **-ist/s** -ɪst/s
expressionistic ɪk,spreʃ.ə'nɪs.tɪk, ek- **-ally** -ᵊl.i, -li
expressionless ɪk'spreʃ.ᵊn.ləs, ek-, -lɪs **-ly** -li **-ness** -nəs, -nɪs
expressive ɪk'spres.ɪv, ek- **-ly** -li **-ness** -nəs, -nɪs
expresso ɪk'spres.əʊ, ek- Ⓤⓢ -oʊ **-s** -z
expressway ɪk'spres.weɪ, ek- **-s** -z
expropri|ate ɪk'sprəʊ.pri|.eɪt, ek- Ⓤⓢ -'sproʊ- **-ates** -eɪts **-ating** -eɪ.tɪŋ Ⓤⓢ -eɪ.t̬ɪŋ **-ated** -eɪ.tɪd Ⓤⓢ -eɪ.t̬ɪd **-ator/s** -eɪ.təʳ/z Ⓤⓢ -eɪ.t̬ɚ/z
expropriation ɪk,sprəʊ.pri'eɪ.ʃᵊn, ek-; ,ek.sprəʊ- Ⓤⓢ ɪk,sproʊ-, ek- **-s** -z
expulsion ɪk'spʌl.ʃᵊn, ek- **-s** -z
expulsive ɪk'spʌl.sɪv, ek-
expung|e ɪk'spʌn*d*ʒ, ek- **-es** -ɪz **-ing** -ɪŋ **-ed** -d
expur|gate 'ek.spə|.geɪt, -spɜː- Ⓤⓢ -spɚ- **-gates** -geɪts **-gating** -geɪ.tɪŋ Ⓤⓢ -geɪ.t̬ɪŋ **-gated** -geɪ.tɪd Ⓤⓢ -geɪ.t̬ɪd **-gator/s** -geɪ.təʳ/z Ⓤⓢ -geɪ.t̬ɚ/z
expurgation ,ek.spə'geɪ.ʃᵊn, -spɜː'- Ⓤⓢ -spɚ'- **-s** -z
expurgatory ek'spɜː.gə.tᵊr.i, ɪk'-, -tri Ⓤⓢ -'spɜːr.gə.tɔːr.i
exquisite ɪk'skwɪz.ɪt, ek-; 'ek.skwɪ.zɪt, -zət **-s** -s **-ly** -li **-ness** -nəs, -nɪs

exscind ek'sɪnd, ɪk- **-s** -z **-ing** -ɪŋ **-ed** -ɪd
exsect ek'sekt, ɪk- **-s** -s **-ing** -ɪŋ **-ed** -ɪd
exsection ek'sek.ʃᵊn, ɪk- **-s** -z
ex-service ˌeks'sɜː.vɪs, ⓤⓢ ˌeks'sɜːr-
exsic|cate 'ek.sɪ|.keɪt, 'eks- **-cates** -keɪts **-cating** -keɪ.tɪŋ ⓤⓢ -keɪ.t̬ɪŋ **-cated** -keɪ.tɪd ⓤⓢ -keɪ.t̬ɪd **-cator/s** -keɪ.təʳ/z ⓤⓢ -keɪ.t̬ɚ/z
extant ek'stænt, ɪk-, 'ek.stᵊnt ⓤⓢ 'ek.stᵊnt; ˌek'stænt
extemporaneous ɪkˌstem.pə'reɪ.ni.əs, ek-; ˌek.stem- ⓤⓢ ɪkˌstem.pə'-, ek- **-ly** -li **-ness** -nəs, -nɪs
extemporary ɪk'stem.pᵊr.ə.ri, ek- ⓤⓢ -er.i
extempore ɪk'stem.pᵊr.i, ek-
extemporization, -isa- ɪkˌstem.pᵊr.aɪ'zeɪ.ʃᵊn, ek-, -ɪ'- ⓤⓢ -ɪ'- **-s** -z
extemporiz|e, -is|e ɪk'stem.pᵊr.aɪz, ek- ⓤⓢ -pə.raɪz **-es** -ɪz **-ing** -ɪŋ **-ed** -d **-er/s** -əʳ/z ⓤⓢ -ɚ/z
extend ɪk'stend, ek- **-s** -z **-ing** -ɪŋ **-ed** -ɪd **-able** -ə.bl̩ **exˌtended 'family**
extensibility ɪkˌstent*t*.sə'bɪl.ə.ti, ek-, -sɪ'-, -ɪ.ti ⓤⓢ -ə.t̬i
extensible ɪk'stent*t*.sə.bl̩, ek-, -sɪ-
extensile ɪk'stent*t*.saɪl, ek- ⓤⓢ -sɪl
extension ɪk'sten.*t*ʃᵊn, ek- **-s** -z **ex'tension ˌlead**
extensive ɪk'stent*t*.sɪv, ek- **-ly** -li **-ness** -nəs, -nɪs
extensor ɪk'stent*t*.səʳ, ek- ⓤⓢ -sɚ **-s** -z
extent ɪk'stent, ek- **-s** -s
extenu|ate ɪk'sten.ju|.eɪt, ek- **-ates** -eɪts **-ating/ly** -eɪ.tɪŋ/li ⓤⓢ -eɪ.t̬ɪŋ/li **-ated** -eɪ.tɪd ⓤⓢ -eɪ.t̬ɪd **exˌtenuating 'circumstances**
extenuation ɪkˌsten.ju'eɪ.ʃᵊn, ek- **-s** -z
extenuative ɪk'sten.ju.ə.tɪv, ek-, -eɪ- ⓤⓢ -eɪ.t̬ɪv
extenuatory ɪk'sten.ju.ə.tᵊr.i, ek-, -eɪ-, -tri ⓤⓢ -ə.tɔːr.i
exterior ɪk'stɪə.ri.əʳ, ek- ⓤⓢ -'stɪr.i.ɚ **-s** -z **-ly** -li
exteriority ɪkˌstɪə.ri'ɒr.ə.ti, ek-, -ɪ.ti; ˌek.stɪə- ⓤⓢ ɪkˌstɪr.i'ɔːr.ə.t̬i, ek-
exterioriz|e, -is|e ɪk'stɪə.ri.ᵊr.aɪz, ek- ⓤⓢ -'stɪr.i.ə.raɪz **-es** -ɪz **-ing** -ɪŋ **-ed** -d
exterminable ɪk'stɜː.mɪ.nə.bl̩, ek-, -mə- ⓤⓢ -'stɜːr-
extermi|nate ɪk'stɜː.mɪ|.neɪt, ek-, -mə- ⓤⓢ -'stɜːr- **-nates** -neɪts **-nating** -neɪ.tɪŋ ⓤⓢ -neɪ.t̬ɪŋ **-nated** -neɪ.tɪd ⓤⓢ -neɪ.t̬ɪd **-nator/s** -neɪ.təʳ/z ⓤⓢ -neɪ.t̬ɚ/z
extermination ɪkˌstɜː.mɪ'neɪ.ʃᵊn, ek-, -mə'- ⓤⓢ -ˌstɜːr- **-s** -z
exterminative ɪk'stɜː.mɪ.nə.tɪv, ek-, -mə-, -neɪ- ⓤⓢ -'stɜːr.mə.neɪ.t̬ɪv, -nə-
exterminatory ɪk'stɜː.mɪ.nə.tᵊr.i, ek-, -mə-, -neɪ-, -tri ⓤⓢ -'stɜːr.mə.nə.tɔːr.i
extern 'ek.stɜːn; ɪk'stɜːn, ek- ⓤⓢ 'ek.stɜːrn **-s** -z
external ɪk'stɜː.nᵊl, ek-; 'ek.stɜː- ⓤⓢ ɪk'stɜːr-, ek-; 'ek.stɜːr- **-s** -z **-ly** -i
external|ism ɪk'stɜː.nᵊl|.ɪ.zᵊm, ek- ⓤⓢ -'stɜːr- **-ist/s** -ɪst/s
externality ˌek.stɜː'næl.ə.ti, -ɪ.ti ⓤⓢ -stɜːr'næl.ə.t̬i
externalization, -isa- ɪkˌstɜː.nᵊl.aɪ'zeɪ.ʃᵊn, ek-, -ɪ'- ⓤⓢ -ˌstɜːr.nᵊl.ɪ'-
externaliz|e, -is|e ɪk'stɜː.nᵊl.aɪz, ek- ⓤⓢ -'stɜːr.nə.laɪz **-es** -ɪz **-ing** -ɪŋ **-ed** -d
exterritorial ˌek.ster.ɪ'tɔː.ri.əl ⓤⓢ -'tɔːr.i-
extinct ɪk'stɪŋkt, ek-
extinction ɪk'stɪŋk.ʃᵊn, ek- **-s** -z
extinctive ɪk'stɪŋk.tɪv, ek-
extinguish ɪk'stɪŋ.gwɪʃ, ek- **-es** -ɪz **-ing** -ɪŋ **-ed** -t **-er/s** -əʳ/z ⓤⓢ -ɚ/z **-ment** -mənt **-able** -ə.bl̩
extir|pate 'ek.stɜː|.peɪt, -stə- ⓤⓢ -stɚ-; ɪk'stɜːr-, ek- **-pates** -peɪts **-pating** -peɪ.tɪŋ ⓤⓢ -peɪ.t̬ɪŋ **-pated** -peɪ.tɪd ⓤⓢ -peɪ.t̬ɪd **-pator/s** -peɪ.təʳ/z ⓤⓢ -peɪ.t̬ɚ/z
extirpation ˌek.stɜː'peɪ.ʃᵊn, -stə'- ⓤⓢ -stɚ'- **-s** -z
extol ɪk'stəʊl, ek-, -'stɒl ⓤⓢ -'stoʊl, -'stɑːl **-s** -z **-ling** -ɪŋ **-led** -d
extoll ɪk'stəʊl, ek-, -stɒl ⓤⓢ -'stoʊl, -'stɑːl **-s** -z **-ing** -ɪŋ **-ed** -d
Exton 'ek.stən
extor|t ɪk'stɔː|t, ek- ⓤⓢ -'stɔːr|t **-ts** -ts **-ting** -tɪŋ ⓤⓢ -t̬ɪŋ **-ted** -tɪd ⓤⓢ -t̬ɪd **-ter/s** -təʳ/z ⓤⓢ -t̬ɚ/z
extortion ɪk'stɔː.ʃᵊn, ek- ⓤⓢ -'stɔːr- **-s** -z
extortionate ɪk'stɔː.ʃᵊn.ət, ek-, -ɪt ⓤⓢ -'stɔːr- **-ly** -li
extortioner ɪk'stɔː.ʃᵊn.əʳ, ek- ⓤⓢ -'stɔːr.ʃᵊn.ɚ **-s** -z
extortionist ɪk'stɔː.ʃᵊn.ɪst, ek- ⓤⓢ -'stɔːr- **-s** -s
extra- 'ek.strə-; ɪk'stræ-, ek-

Note: Prefix. Normally takes either primary or secondary stress on the first syllable, e.g. **extradite** /'ek.strə.daɪt/, **extramural** /ˌeks.trə'mjʊə.rᵊl ⓤⓢ -'mjʊr.ᵊl/, but may also take primary stress on the second syllable, e.g. **extrapolate** /ɪk'stræp.ə.leɪt/. In some cases, the second syllable seems to disappear altogether, e.g. **extraordinary** /ek'strɔː.dᵊn.ᵊr.i ⓤⓢ -'strɔːr.dᵊn.er-/.

extra 'ek.strə **-s** -z **ˌextra 'time**
extract (*n.*) 'ek.strækt **-s** -s
extract (*v.*) ɪk'strækt, ek- **-s** -s **-ing** -ɪŋ **-ed** -ɪd **-able** -ə.bl̩ **ex'tractor ˌfan**
extraction ɪk'stræk.ʃᵊn, ek- **-s** -z
extractive ɪk'stræk.tɪv, ek- **-ly** -li
extractor ɪk'stræk.təʳ, ek- ⓤⓢ -tɚ **-s** -z **ex'tractor ˌfan**
extracurricular ˌek.strə.kə'rɪk.jə.ləʳ, -jʊ- ⓤⓢ -kə'rɪk.jə.lɚ **ˌextracurˌricular ac'tivities**
extra|dite 'ek.strə|.daɪt **-dites** -daɪts **-diting** -daɪ.tɪŋ ⓤⓢ -daɪ.t̬ɪŋ **-dited** -daɪ.tɪd ⓤⓢ -daɪ.t̬ɪd **-ditable** -daɪ.tə.bl̩ ⓤⓢ -daɪ.t̬ə.bl̩
extradition ˌek.strə'dɪʃ.ᵊn **-s** -z
extrados ek'streɪ.dɒs ⓤⓢ -dɑːs, -doʊs **-es** -ɪz
extragalactic ˌek.strə.gə'læk.tɪk
extrajudicial ˌek.strə.dʒuː'dɪʃ.ᵊl **-ly** -i
extramarital ˌek.strə'mær.ɪ.tᵊl ⓤⓢ -'mer.ə.t̬ᵊl, -'mær- **ˌextramarital 'sex**
extramural ˌek.strə'mjʊə.rᵊl, -'mjɔː- ⓤⓢ -'mjʊr.ᵊl
extraneous ɪk'streɪ.ni.əs, ek- **-ly** -li
extraordinaire ɪkˌstrɔː.dɪ'neəʳ, ek-, -dᵊn'eəʳ ⓤⓢ -ˌstrɔːr.də'ner
extraordinar|y ɪk'strɔː.dᵊn.ᵊr|.i, ek-, -dɪ.nᵊr-; ˌek.strə'ɔː- ⓤⓢ ɪk'strɔːr.dᵊn.er-, ek-; ˌek.strə'ɔːr- **-ily** -ᵊl.i, -ɪ.li **-iness** -ɪ.nəs, -ɪ.nɪs
extrapo|late ɪk'stræp.ə|.leɪt, ek- **-es** -leɪts **-lating** -leɪ.tɪŋ ⓤⓢ -leɪ.t̬ɪŋ **-lated** -leɪ.tɪd ⓤⓢ -leɪ.t̬ɪd
extrapolation ɪkˌstræp.ə'leɪ.ʃᵊn, ek- **-s** -z
extrasensory ˌek.strə'sent*t*.sᵊr.i **ˌextraˌsensory per'ception**
extraterrestrial ˌeks.trə.tə'res.tri.əl, -ter'es-, -tɪ'res- ⓤⓢ -tə'- **-s** -z
extraterritorial ˌeks.trəˌter.ɪ'tɔː.ri.əl, -ə'- ⓤⓢ -'tɔːr.i-
extravagan|ce ɪk'stræv.ə.gən*t*|s, ek-, '-ɪ- **-ces** -sɪz
extravagant ɪk'stræv.ə.gənt, '-ɪ- **-ly** -li
extravaganza ɪkˌstræv.ə'gæn.zə, ek-; ˌek.stræv- ⓤⓢ ɪkˌstræv-, ek- **-s** -z
extrava|sate ek'stræv.ə|.seɪt, ɪk- **-sates** -seɪts **-sating** -seɪ.tɪŋ ⓤⓢ -seɪ.t̬ɪŋ **-sated** -seɪ.tɪd ⓤⓢ -seɪ.t̬ɪd
extravasation ekˌstræv.ə'seɪ.ʃᵊn, ɪk-; -'zeɪ-, ˌek.stræv- ⓤⓢ ɪkˌstræv-, ek- **-s** -z
extra|vert 'ek.strə|.vɜːt ⓤⓢ -vɜːrt **-verts** -vɜːts ⓤⓢ -vɜːrts **-verted** -vɜː.tɪd ⓤⓢ -vɜːr.t̬ɪd
Extremadura ˌek.strə.mə'djʊə.rə ⓤⓢ -'dʊr.ə, -'djʊr.ə

extrem|e ɪk'striːm, ek- **-es** -z **-est** -ɪst, -əst **-ly** -li **-eness** -nəs, -nɪs
extrem|ism ɪk'striː.m|ɪ.zᵊm, ek- **-ist/s** -ɪst/s
extremit|y ɪk'strem.ə.t|i, ek-, -ɪ.t|i ⓤⓢ -ə.t̬|i **-ies** -iz
extricable ɪk'strɪk.ə.bl̩, ek-; 'ek.strɪ.kə-
extri|cate 'ek.strɪ|.keɪt **-cates** -keɪts **-cating** -keɪ.tɪŋ ⓤⓢ -keɪ.t̬ɪŋ **-cated** -keɪ.tɪd ⓤⓢ -keɪ.t̬ɪd
extrication ˌek.strɪ'keɪ.ʃᵊn
extrinsic ek'strɪnt.sɪk, ɪk-, -'strɪn.zɪk **-al** -ᵊl **-ally** -ᵊl.i, -li
extroversion ˌek.strə'vɜː.ʃᵊn, -ʒᵊn ⓤⓢ 'ek.strə.vɚ.ʒən, -stroʊ-
extro|vert 'ek.strə|.vɜːt ⓤⓢ -strə|.vɜːrt, -stroʊ- **-verts** -vɜːts ⓤⓢ -vɜːrts **-verted** -vɜː.tɪd ⓤⓢ -vɜːr.t̬ɪd
extrud|e ɪk'struːd, ek- **-es** -z **-ing** -ɪŋ **-ed** -ɪd
extrusion ɪk'struː.ʒᵊn, ek- **-s** -z
extrus|ive ɪk'struː.s|ɪv, ek- **-ory** -ᵊr.i ⓤⓢ -ɔːr.i
exuberan|ce ɪg'zjuː.bᵊr.ᵊnt|s, eg-, -'zuː-; ɪk'sjuː-, ek-, -'suː- ⓤⓢ ɪg'zuː-, eg- **-cy** -si
exuberant ɪg'zjuː.bᵊr.ᵊnt, eg-, -'zuː-; ɪk'sjuː-, ek-, -'suː- ⓤⓢ ɪg'zuː-, eg- **-ly** -li
exuber|ate ɪg'zjuː.bᵊr|.eɪt, eg-, -'zuː-; ɪk'sjuː-, ek-, -'suː- ⓤⓢ ɪg'zuː.bə.r|eɪt, eg- **-ates** -eɪts **-ating** -eɪ.tɪŋ ⓤⓢ -eɪ.t̬ɪŋ **-ated** -eɪ.tɪd ⓤⓢ -eɪ.t̬ɪd
exudation ˌek.sjuː'deɪ.ʃᵊn, ˌeg.zjuː'- ⓤⓢ ˌek.sjuː'-, -suː'-, -sə'-, ˌeg.zjuː'-, -zuː'- **-s** -z
exud|e ɪg'zjuːd, eg-, -'zuːd; ɪk'sjuːd, ek-, -'suːd ⓤⓢ ɪg'zuːd, ɪk'suːd, ek- **-es** -z **-ing** -ɪŋ **-ed** -ɪd
exul|t ɪg'zʌl|t, eg-; ɪk'sʌl|t, ek- ⓤⓢ ɪg'zʌl|t, eg- **-ts** -ts **-ting/ly** -tɪŋ/li ⓤⓢ -t̬ɪŋ/li **-ted** -tɪd ⓤⓢ -t̬ɪd
exultan|ce ɪg'zʌl.tᵊnt|s, eg-; ɪk'sʌl-, ek- ⓤⓢ ɪg'zʌl-, eg- **-cy** -si
exultant ɪg'zʌl.tᵊnt, eg-; ɪk'sʌl-, ek- ⓤⓢ ɪg'zʌl-, eg- **-ly** -li
exultation ˌeg.zʌl'teɪ.ʃᵊn, -zᵊl'-; ˌek.sʌl'-, -sᵊl'- ⓤⓢ ˌek.sʌl'-, -sᵊl'-; ˌeg.zʌl'-, -zᵊl'- **-s** -z
exurb 'ek.sɜːb; 'eg.zɜːb ⓤⓢ 'ek.sɜːrb; 'eg.zɜːrb
exur|ban ek'sɜː|.bᵊn; eg'zɜː- ⓤⓢ ek'sɜːr-; eg'zɜːr- **-banite** -bᵊn.aɪt **-bia** -bi.ə
exuviae ɪg'zjuː.vi.iː, eg-, -'zuː-; ɪk'sjuː-, ek-, -'suː-, -aɪ ⓤⓢ ɪg'zuː.vi.iː, ek'suː-, eg'zuː-, -aɪ
exuvial ɪg'zjuː.vi.əl, eg-, -'zuː-; ɪk'sjuː-, ek-, -'suː- ⓤⓢ ɪg'zuː-, ek'suː-, eg'zuː-
exuvi|ate ɪg'zjuː.vi|.eɪt, eg-, -'zuː-; ɪk'sjuː-, ek-, -'suː- ⓤⓢ ɪg'zuː-, ek'suː-, eg'zuː- **-ates** -eɪts **-ating** -eɪ.tɪŋ ⓤⓢ -eɪ.t̬ɪŋ **-ated** -eɪ.tɪd ⓤⓢ -eɪ.t̬ɪd
exuviation ɪgˌzjuː.vi'eɪ.ʃᵊn, eg-, -ˌzuː-; ɪkˌsjuː-, ek-, -ˌsuː- ⓤⓢ ɪg'zuː-, ek'suː-, eg'zuː-
ex voto ˌeks'vəʊ.təʊ ⓤⓢ -'voʊ.t̬oʊ
Exxon® 'ek.sɒn ⓤⓢ -sɑːn
Eyam 'iː.əm, iːm
eyas aɪəs **-es** -ɪz
Eyck aɪk
eye (*n. v.*) aɪ **-s** -z **-ing** -ɪŋ **-d** -d **have ˌeyes in the ˌback of one's 'head ; in a ˌpig's 'eye ; ˌone in the 'eye ; ˌup to one's 'eyes ; ˌgive one's ˌeye 'teeth ; see ˌeye to 'eye**
Eye *place:* aɪ
eyeball 'aɪ.bɔːl ⓤⓢ -bɔːl, -bɑːl **-s** -z **-ing** -ɪŋ **-ed** -d
eyebath 'aɪ.bɑːθ ⓤⓢ -bæθ **-s** -s
eyebright 'aɪ.braɪt
eyebrow 'aɪ.braʊ **-s** -z **'eyebrow ˌpencil**
eye-catching 'aɪˌkætʃ.ɪŋ **-ly** -li
eyeful 'aɪ.fʊl **-s** -z
eyeglass 'aɪ.glɑːs ⓤⓢ -glæs **-es** -ɪz
eyelash 'aɪ.læʃ **-es** -ɪz
eyelet 'aɪ.lət, -lɪt **-s** -s
eyelid 'aɪ.lɪd **-s** -z
eyeliner 'aɪˌlaɪ.nəʳ ⓤⓢ -nɚ **-s** -z
Eyemouth 'aɪ.maʊθ
eye-open|er 'aɪˌəʊ.pᵊn|.əʳ, -ˌəʊp.n|əʳ ⓤⓢ -ˌoʊ.pᵊn|.ɚ **-ers** -əz, -ɚz **-ing** -ɪŋ
eyepatch 'aɪ.pætʃ **-es** -ɪz
eyepiec|e 'aɪ.piːs **-es** -ɪz
eyeshade 'aɪ.ʃeɪd **-s** -z
eyeshot 'aɪ.ʃɒt ⓤⓢ -ʃɑːt
eyesight 'aɪ.saɪt
eyesore 'aɪ.sɔːʳ ⓤⓢ -sɔːr **-s** -z
eyestrain 'aɪ.streɪn
Eyetie 'aɪ.taɪ **-s** -z
eye|tooth 'aɪ|.tuːθ **-teeth** -tiːθ
eyewash 'aɪ.wɒʃ ⓤⓢ -wɑːʃ, -wɔːʃ
eyewitness ˌaɪ'wɪt.nɪs, -nəs, '--- **-es** -ɪz
Eynon 'aɪ.nən ⓤⓢ -nɑːn
Eynsford 'eɪnz.fəd, 'eɪnts- ⓤⓢ -fɚd
Eynsham *in Oxfordshire:* 'eɪn.ʃᵊm *locally:* 'en.ʃᵊm
eyot eɪt, eɪət, aɪt **-s** -s
Note: The local pronunciation in the Thames valley is /eɪt/.
Eyre, eyre eəʳ ⓤⓢ er
eyr|ie, eyr|y 'aɪə.r|i, 'ɪə-, 'eə- ⓤⓢ 'er.i, 'ɪr- **-ies** -iz
Eysenck 'aɪ.zeŋk
Eyton *in Shropshire:* 'aɪ.tᵊn *in Hereford and Worcester:* 'eɪ.tᵊn *surname:* 'aɪ.tᵊn, 'iː-
Ezekiel ɪ'ziː.ki.əl, ez'iː-
Ezra 'ez.rə

F

f (F) ef **-'s** -s
fa fɑː
FA ˌef'eɪ *stress shift:* ˌFA 'cup ; **ˌsweet ˌF'A**
fab fæb
Faber *English name:* 'feɪ.bəʳ (US) -bɚ *German name:* 'fɑː.bəʳ (US) -bɚ
Fabergé 'fæb.ə.ʒeɪ, -dʒeɪ (US) ˌfæb.ɚ'ʒeɪ
Fabian 'feɪ.bi.ən **-s** -z **-ism** -ɪ.zᵊm **'Fabian Soˌciety**
Fabius 'feɪ.bi.əs
fable 'feɪ.bl̩ **-s** -z **-d** -d
fabliau 'fæb.li.əʊ (US) -oʊ **-x** -z
Fablon® 'fæb.lɒn (US) -lɑːn
fabric 'fæb.rɪk **-s** -s **'fabric ˌsoftener**
fabri|cate 'fæb.rɪ|.keɪt **-cates** -keɪts **-cating** -keɪ.tɪŋ (US) -keɪ.t̬ɪŋ **-cated** -keɪ.tɪd (US) -keɪ.t̬ɪd **-cator/s** -keɪ.təʳ/z (US) -keɪ.t̬ɚ/z
fabrication ˌfæb.rɪ'keɪ.ʃᵊn, -rə'- **-s** -z
Fabricius fə'brɪʃ.i.əs, -ʃəs
fabulist 'fæb.jə.lɪst, -jʊ- (US) -jə- **-s** -s
fabulous 'fæb.jə.ləs, -jʊ- (US) -jə- **-ly** -li **-ness** -nəs, -nɪs
Fabyan 'feɪ.bi.ən
facade, façade fə'sɑːd, fæs'ɑːd (US) fə'sɑːd **-s** -z
fac|e (*n. v.*) feɪs **-es** -ɪz **-ing** -ɪŋ **-ed** -t **'face ˌpack** ; **ˌface 'value** ; **ˌcut off one's ˌnose to ˌspite one's 'face** ; **put a ˌbrave 'face on** ; **ˌfly in the 'face of** ; **ˌlaugh on the other ˌside of one's 'face**
face|cloth 'feɪs|.klɒθ (US) -klɑːθ **-cloths** -klɒθs, -klɒðz (US) -klɑːθs, -klɑːðz
faceless 'feɪs.ləs, -lɪs **-ness** -nəs, -nɪs
face-lift 'feɪs.lɪft **-s** -s
facemask 'feɪs.mɑːsk (US) -mæsk **-s** -s
face-off 'feɪs.ɒf (US) -ɑːf **-s** -s
faceplate 'feɪs.pleɪt **-s** -s
facer 'feɪ.səʳ (US) -sɚ **-s** -z
face-sav|er 'feɪsˌseɪ|.vəʳ (US) -vɚ **-ers** -z **-ing** -ɪŋ
fac|et 'fæs|.ɪt, -ət, -et (US) -ɪt **-ets** -ɪts **-et(t)ed** -ɪ.tɪd (US) -ɪ.t̬ɪd
facetiae fə'siː.ʃi.iː, -ʃiː (US) -ʃi.iː
facetious fə'siː.ʃəs **-ly** -li **-ness** -nəs, -nɪs
face-to-face ˌfeɪs.tə'feɪs (US) -t̬ə- *stress shift:* ˌface-to-face 'talk
facia 'feɪ.ʃə (US) -ʃi.ə, -ʃə **-s** -z
facial 'feɪ.ʃᵊl **-ly** -i **-s** -z
facies 'feɪ.ʃi.iːz, -ʃiːz
facile 'fæs.aɪl (US) -ɪl, -əl **-ly** -li **-ness** -nəs, -nɪs
facili|tate fə'sɪl.ɪ|.teɪt, '-ə- **-tates** -teɪts **-tating** -teɪ.tɪŋ (US) -teɪ.t̬ɪŋ **-tated** -teɪ.tɪd (US) -teɪ.t̬ɪd **-tator/s** -teɪ.təʳ/z (US) -teɪ.t̬ɚ/z
facilitation fəˌsɪl.ɪ'teɪ.ʃᵊn, -ə'-
facilit|y fə'sɪl.ə.t|i, -ɪ.t|i (US) -ə.t̬|i **-ies** -iz
facing 'feɪ.sɪŋ **-s** -z
facsimile fæk'sɪm.ᵊl.i, -ɪ.li **-s** -z
fact fækt **-s** -s **ˌfact of 'life**
fact-find|ing 'fæktˌfaɪn.d|ɪŋ **-er/s** -əʳ/z (US) -ɚ/z
faction 'fæk.ʃᵊn **-s** -z
factional 'fæk.ʃᵊn.ᵊl
factional|ism 'fæk.ʃᵊn.ᵊl|.ɪ.zᵊm **-ist/s** -ɪst/s
factionalization, -isa- ˌfæk.ʃᵊn.ᵊl.aɪ'zeɪ.ʃᵊn, -ɪ'- (US) -ɪ'-
factionaliz|e, -is|e 'fæk.ʃᵊn.ᵊl.aɪz (US) -ə.laɪz **-es** -ɪz **-ing** -ɪŋ **-ed** -d
factious 'fæk.ʃəs **-ly** -li **-ness** -nəs, -nɪs
factitious fæk'tɪʃ.əs **-ly** -li **-ness** -nəs, -nɪs
factitive 'fæk.tɪ.tɪv, -tə.tɪv (US) -tə.t̬ɪv
factive 'fæk.tɪv
factivity fæk'tɪv.ə.ti, -ɪ.ti (US) -ə.t̬i
fact|or 'fæk.t|əʳ (US) -t|ɚ **-ors** -əz (US) -ɚz **-oring** -ᵊr.ɪŋ **-ored** -ᵊrd **-orage** -ᵊr.ɪdʒ **ˌFactor '5**
factorial fæk'tɔː.ri.əl (US) -'tɔːr.i-
factorization, -isa- ˌfæk.tᵊr.aɪ'zeɪ.ʃᵊn, -ɪ'- (US) -ɪ'-
factoriz|e, -is|e 'fæk.tᵊr.aɪz (US) -tə.raɪz **-es** -ɪz **-ing** -ɪŋ **-ed** -d
factor|y 'fæk.tᵊr|.i, '-tr|i **-ies** -iz **'factory ˌfarming**, **ˌfactory 'farming** ; **ˌfactory 'floor**
factotum fæk'təʊ.təm (US) -'toʊ.t̬əm **-s** -z
factsheet 'fækt.ʃiːt **-s** -s
factual 'fæk.tʃʊəl, -tjʊəl (US) -tʃuː.əl **-ly** -li **-ness** -nəs, -nɪs
factum 'fæk.təm
factum probandum ˌfæk.təm.prəʊ'bæn.dəm (US) -proʊ'bɑːn-
facul|a 'fæk.jə.l|ə, -jʊ- (US) -jə-, -juː- **-ae** -iː
facultative 'fæk.ᵊl.tə.tɪv, -teɪ- (US) -teɪ.t̬ɪv **-ly** -li
facult|y 'fæk.ᵊl.t|i (US) -t̬|i **-ies** -iz
fad fæd **-s** -z
faddish 'fæd.ɪʃ **-ly** -li **-ness** -nəs, -nɪs
fadd|ism 'fæd|.ɪ.zᵊm **-ist/s** -ɪst/s
fadd|y 'fæd|.i **-ier** -i.əʳ (US) -i.ɚ **-iest** -i.ɪst, -i.əst **-ily** -ɪ.li, -ᵊl.i **-iness** -ɪ.nəs, -ɪ.nɪs
fad|e feɪd **-es** -z **-ing** -ɪŋ **-ed** -ɪd
fadeout 'feɪd.aʊt **-s** -s
fado 'fɑː.du (US) 'fɑː.ðuː, -ðoʊ, -doʊ **-s** -z
faecal 'fiː.kᵊl
faeces 'fiː.siːz
Faed feɪd
faerie, faery (F) 'feə.ri, 'feɪ.ᵊr.i (US) 'fer.i
Faeroe 'feə.rəʊ (US) 'fer.oʊ **-s** -z
Faeroese ˌfeə.rəʊ'iːz (US) ˌfer.oʊ'-
faff fæf **-s** -s **-ing** -ɪŋ **-ed** -t
Fafner 'fɑːf.nəʳ, 'fæf- (US) -nɚ
Fafnir 'fæf.nɪəʳ, 'fæv- (US) -nɪr
fag fæg **-s** -z **-ging** -ɪŋ **-ged** -d **'fag ˌend**, **ˌfag 'end** ; **'fag ˌhag**
Fagan 'feɪ.gən
Fagg(e) fæg
faggot 'fæg.ət **-s** -s
Fagin 'feɪ.gɪn
fagot 'fæg.ət **-s** -s
fah fɑː
Fahd fɑːd
Fahey, Fahie 'feɪ.i; feɪ
Fahrenheit 'fær.ᵊn.haɪt, 'fɑː.rᵊn- (US) 'fer.ᵊn-, 'fær-
Fahy 'fɑː.i, -hi; feɪ (US) 'feɪ.i; feɪ
faience, faïence faɪ'ɑ̃ːns, feɪ-, -ɑːnts (US) faɪ'ɑːnts, feɪ'-, 'faɪ.ənts
fail feɪl **-s** -z **-ing/s** -ɪŋ/z **-ed** -d
faille feɪəl (US) faɪl, feɪl
failsafe 'feɪl.seɪf, -'- (US) '--
Failsworth 'feɪlz.wəθ, -wɜːθ (US) -wɚθ, -wɜːrθ
failure 'feɪ.ljəʳ (US) 'feɪl.jɚ **-s** -z
fain feɪn
Fainall 'feɪ.nɔːl (US) -nɔːl, -nɑːl
faint feɪnt **-er** -əʳ (US) 'feɪn.t̬ɚ **-est** -ɪst, -əst (US) 'feɪn.t̬ɪst, 'feɪn.t̬əst **-ly** -li **-ness** -nəs, -nɪs **-s** -s **-ing** -ɪŋ (US) 'feɪn.t̬ɪŋ **-ed** -ɪd (US) 'feɪn.t̬ɪd
fainthearted ˌfeɪnt'hɑː.tɪd (US) -'hɑːr.t̬ɪd **-ly** -li **-ness** -nəs, -nɪs *stress shift:* ˌfainthearted 'hero
Fainwell 'feɪn.wel, -wəl
fair (F) feəʳ (US) fer **-s** -z **-er** -əʳ (US) -ɚ **-est** -ɪst, -əst **-ness** -nəs, -nɪs **ˌfair 'do's** ; **ˌfair 'dinkum** ; **ˌfair 'game** ; **'Fair ˌIsle** ; **ˌfair 'play** ; **ˌfair's 'fair** ; **ˌfair and 'square**
Fairbairn 'feə.beən (US) 'fer.bern **-s** -z
Fairbank 'feə.bæŋk (US) 'fer- **-s** -s
Fairbeard 'feə.bɪəd (US) 'fer.bɪrd
Fairbrother 'feəˌbrʌð.əʳ (US) 'ferˌbrʌð.ɚ
Fairburn 'feə.bɜːn (US) 'fer.bɜːrn
Fairbury 'feə.bᵊr.i (US) 'ferˌber-, -bɚ-
Fairchild 'feə.tʃaɪld (US) 'fer-
Fairclough 'feə.klʌf, -kləʊ (US) 'fer.klʌf
fairfaced ˌfeə'feɪst (US) ˌfer- *stress shift:* ˌfairfaced 'child
Fairfax 'feə.fæks (US) 'fer-
Fairfield 'feə.fiːld (US) 'fer-
Fairford 'feə.fəd (US) 'fer.fɚd
Fairgrieve 'feə.griːv (US) 'fer-

fairground ˈfeə.graʊnd ⓤⓢ ˈfer- **-s** -z
fair-haired ˌfeəˈheəd ⓤⓢ ˌferˈherd
stress shift: ˌfair-haired ˈchild
Fairhaven ˈfeəˌheɪ.vᵊn ⓤⓢ ˈfer-
Fairholme ˈfeə.həʊm ⓤⓢ ˈfer.hoʊm, -hoʊlm
Fairholt ˈfeə.həʊlt ⓤⓢ ˈfer.hoʊlt
fairish ˈfeə.rɪʃ ⓤⓢ ˈfer.ɪʃ
Fairleigh ˈfeə.li, -liː ⓤⓢ ˈfer-
Fairlight ˈfeə.laɪt ⓤⓢ ˈfer-
fairly ˈfeə.li ⓤⓢ ˈfer-
Fairman ˈfeə.mən ⓤⓢ ˈfer-
fair-minded ˌfeəˈmaɪn.dɪd ⓤⓢ ˌfer- **-ly** -li **-ness** -nəs, -nɪs *stress shift:* ˌfair-minded ˈjudge
Fairmont ˈfeə.mɒnt, -mənt ⓤⓢ ˈfer.mɑːnt
Fairmount ˈfeə.maʊnt ⓤⓢ ˈfer-
Fairport ˈfeə.pɔːt ⓤⓢ ˈfer.pɔːrt
Fairscribe ˈfeə.skraɪb ⓤⓢ ˈfer-
Fairview ˈfeə.vjuː ⓤⓢ ˈfer-
fairway ˈfeə.weɪ ⓤⓢ ˈfer- **-s** -z
Fairweather ˈfeəˌweð.əʳ ⓤⓢ ˈferˌweð.ɚ
fair-weather ˈfeəˌweð.əʳ ⓤⓢ ˈferˌweð.ɚ
fair|y ˈfeə.r|i ⓤⓢ ˈfer|.i **-ies** -iz ˌ**fairy ˈgodmother** ; ˈ**fairy ˌlight** ; ˌ**fairy ˈring** ⓤⓢ ˈ**fairy ˌring** ; ˈ**fairy ˌstory** ; ˈ**fairy ˌtale**
fairyland ˈfeə.ri.lænd ⓤⓢ ˈfer.i-
fairylike ˈfeə.ri.laɪk ⓤⓢ ˈfer.i-
Faisal ˈfaɪ.sᵊl
Faisalabad ˈfaɪ.sᵊl.ə.bæd, -zᵊl- ⓤⓢ ˌfaɪ.sɑː.ləˈbɑːd, -sæl.əˈbæd
fait accompli ˌfeɪt.əˈkɒm.pliː, ˌfet-, -ˈkʌm- *as if French:* -kɔ̃ːmˈpliː ⓤⓢ ˌfeɪt.ə.kɑːmˈpliː, ˌfet- **faits accomplis** ˌfeɪz-, ˌfeɪts-, ˌfeɪt-, ˌfez-, -pliːz ⓤⓢ ˌfeɪt.ə.kɑːmˈpliː, ˌfet-, -ˈpliːz
faith (F) feɪθ **-s** -s ˈ**faith ˌhealer**
faithful (F) ˈfeɪθ.fᵊl, -fʊl **-ly** -i **-ness** -nəs, -nɪs
Faithfull ˈfeɪθ.fᵊl, -fʊl
faithless ˈfeɪθ.ləs, -lɪs **-ly** -li **-ness** -nəs, -nɪs
Faithorne ˈfeɪ.θɔːn ⓤⓢ -θɔːrn
fajita fæˈhiː.tə ⓤⓢ fæ-, fə-, -t̬ə
fak|e feɪk **-es** -s **-ing** -ɪŋ **-ed** -t **-er/s** -əʳ/z ⓤⓢ -ɚ/z
Fakenham ˈfeɪ.kᵊn.əm
fakir ˈfeɪ.kɪəʳ, ˈfɑː-, ˈfæk.ɪəʳ, fəˈkɪəʳ, fækˈɪəʳ ⓤⓢ fɑːˈkɪr, fækˈɪr; ˈfeɪ.kɚ **-s** -z **-ism** -ɪ.zᵊm
Fal fæl
falafel fəˈlɑː.fᵊl, -ˈlæf.ᵊl ⓤⓢ -ˈlɑː.fᵊl
Falange fəˈlændʒ; ˈfæl.ændʒ ⓤⓢ fəˈlændʒ, -ˈlɑːndʒ
Falangist fəˈlæn.dʒɪst **-s** -s
Falasha fəˈlæʃ.ə ⓤⓢ -ˈlɑː.ʃə, fɑːˈ- **-s** -z
fal|cate ˈfæl|.keɪt **-cated** -keɪ.tɪd ⓤⓢ -keɪ.t̬ɪd
falchion ˈfɔːl.tʃᵊn ⓤⓢ ˈfɔːl-, ˈfɑːl- **-s** -z
falcon (F) ˈfɔːl.kᵊn, ˈfɔː-, ˈfɒl-, ˈfæl- ⓤⓢ ˈfæl-, ˈfɔːl-, ˈfɑːl-, ˈfɔː- **-s** -z **-er/s** -əʳ/z ⓤⓢ -ɚ/z
Note: /ˈfɔː-/ is the usual British pronunciation among people who practise the sport of falconry, with /ˈfɔː-/ and /ˈfɔːl-/ most usual among them in the US.
Falconbridge ˈfɔːl.kᵊn.brɪdʒ, ˈfɔː-, ˈfɒl-, ˈfæl-, -kᵊm- ⓤⓢ ˈfɔː.kᵊn-, ˈfɔːl-, ˈfæl-, ˈfɑːl-
Falconer ˈfɔːl.kᵊn.əʳ, ˈfɔː-, ˈfɒl-, ˈfæl- ⓤⓢ ˈfɔː.kᵊn.ɚ, ˈfɔːl-, ˈfæl-, ˈfɑːl-
falconry ˈfɔːl.kᵊn.ri, ˈfɔː-, ˈfɒl-, ˈfæl- ⓤⓢ ˈfæl-, ˈfɔːl-, ˈfɑːl-, ˈfɔː-
Note: See note at **falcon**.
Falder ˈfɔːl.dəʳ, ˈfɒl- ⓤⓢ ˈfɑːl.dɚ, ˈfɔːl-
falderal ˈfæl.də.ræl, -dɪ-, ˌ--ˈ- ⓤⓢ ˈfɑːl.də.rɑːl, ˈfæl.də.ræl **-s** -z
Faldo ˈfæl.dəʊ ⓤⓢ -doʊ
faldstool ˈfɔːl*d*.stuːl **-s** -z
Falerii fəˈlɪə.ri.aɪ, fælˈɪə-, -iː ⓤⓢ fəˈlɪr.i-
Falernian fəˈlɜː.ni.ən ⓤⓢ -ˈlɜːr-
Falk fɔːk, fɔːlk ⓤⓢ fɔːk, fɔːlk, fɑːlk
Falkenbridge ˈfɔː.kᵊn.brɪdʒ, ˈfɔːl-, ˈfɒl-, ˈfæl-, -kᵊm- ⓤⓢ ˈfɔː.kᵊn-, ˈfɔːl-, ˈfæl-, ˈfɑːl-
Falkender ˈfɔːl.kən.dəʳ ⓤⓢ -dɚ
Falkirk ˈfɔːl.kɜːk, ˈfɒl-, -kək ⓤⓢ ˈfɔːl.kɜːrk, -kɚk
Falkland *Viscount:* ˈfɔː.klənd, ˈfɒl- ⓤⓢ ˈfɔː- *place in Scotland:* ˈfɔːl.klənd, ˈfɒl- ⓤⓢ ˈfɔːl-
Falkland Islands ˈfɔː.kləndˌaɪ.ləndz, ˈfɔːl-, ˈfɒl- ⓤⓢ ˈfɔː-, ˈfɔːl-
Falkner ˈfɔːk.nəʳ, ˈfɔːlk-, ˈfɒlk-, ˈfælk- ⓤⓢ ˈfɔːk.nɚ, ˈfɔːlk-, ˈfɑːlk-, ˈfælk-
fall fɔːl ⓤⓢ fɔːl, fɑːl **-s** -z **-ing** -ɪŋ **fell** fel **fallen** ˈfɔː.lən ⓤⓢ ˈfɔː-, ˈfɑː- ˈ**fall ˌguy** ; ˌ**falling ˈstar**
Falla ˈfaɪ.jə; ˈfɑː.ljə, ˈfæl.jə, -ə ⓤⓢ ˈfaɪ.jə; ˈfɑːl.jɑː
fallacious fəˈleɪ.ʃəs **-ly** -li **-ness** -nəs, -nɪs
fallac|y ˈfæl.ə.s|i **-ies** -iz
fallal fælˈæl, -ˈlæl ⓤⓢ fælˈæl, fɑːˈlɑːl **-s** -z
fallback ˈfɔːl.bæk ⓤⓢ ˈfɔːl-, ˈfɑːl- **-s** -s
Faller ˈfæl.əʳ ⓤⓢ -ɚ
fallibility ˌfæl.əˈbɪl.ə.ti, -ɪˈ-, -ɪ.ti ⓤⓢ -ə.t̬i
fallib|le ˈfæl.ə.b|l̩, ˈ-ɪ- **-ly** -li **-leness** -l̩.nəs, -nɪs
falling-out ˌfɔː.lɪŋˈaʊt ⓤⓢ ˌfɔː-, ˌfɑː- **fallings-out** ˌfɔː.lɪŋzˈaʊt ⓤⓢ ˌfɔː-, ˌfɑː- **falling-outs** ˌfɔː.lɪŋˈaʊts ⓤⓢ ˌfɔː-, ˌfɑː-
fall-off ˈfɔːl.ɒf ⓤⓢ -ɑːf, ˈfɑːl- **-s** -s
Fallon ˈfæl.ən
fallopian (F) fəˈləʊ.pi.ən, fælˈəʊ- ⓤⓢ fəˈloʊ- **faˌllopian ˈtube**
fallout ˈfɔːl.aʊt ⓤⓢ ˈfɔːl-, ˈfɑːl-
fallow (F) ˈfæl.əʊ ⓤⓢ -oʊ **-s** -z **-ness** -nəs, -nɪs **-ing** -ɪŋ **-ed** -d ˈ**fallow ˌdeer**, ˌ**fallow ˈdeer**
Fallowfield ˈfæl.əʊ.fiːld ⓤⓢ -oʊ-
Fallows ˈfæl.əʊz ⓤⓢ -oʊz
Falls fɔːlz ⓤⓢ fɔːlz, fɑːlz ˌ**Falls ˈRoad**
Falmer ˈfæl.məʳ, ˈfɔːl- ⓤⓢ ˈfɑːl.mɚ, ˈfɔːl-
Falmouth ˈfæl.məθ
fals|e fɔːls, fɒls ⓤⓢ fɔːls, fɑːls **-er** -əʳ ⓤⓢ -ɚ **-est** -ɪst, -əst **-eness** -nəs, -nɪs ˌ**false aˈlarm** ; ˌ**false preˈtences** ; ˌ**false ˈstart** ; ˌ**false ˈteeth**
falsehood ˈfɔːls.*h*ʊd, ˈfɒls- ⓤⓢ ˈfɔːls.hʊd, ˈfɑːls- **-s** -z
falsely ˈfɔːl.sli, ˈfɒl- ⓤⓢ ˈfɔːl-, ˈfɑːl-
falsetto fɒlˈset.əʊ, fɔːl- ⓤⓢ fɔːlˈset̬.oʊ, fɑːl- **-s** -z
Falshaw ˈfɔːl.ʃɔː, ˈfɒl- ⓤⓢ ˈfɔːl.ʃɑː, ˈfɑːl-, -ʃɔː
falsification ˌfɔːl.sɪ.fɪˈkeɪ.ʃᵊn, ˌfɒl-, -sə- ⓤⓢ ˌfɔːl-, ˌfɑːl- **-s** -z
falsi|fy ˈfɔːl.sɪ|.faɪ, ˈfɒl-, -sə- ⓤⓢ ˈfɔːl-, ˈfɑːl- **-fies** -faɪz **-fying** -faɪ.ɪŋ **-fied** -faɪd **-fier/s** -faɪ.əʳ/z ⓤⓢ -faɪ.ɚ/z
falsit|y ˈfɔːl.sə.t|i, ˈfɒl-, -ɪ.t|i ⓤⓢ ˈfɔːl.sə.t̬|i, ˈfɑːl- **-ies** -iz
Falstaff ˈfɔːl.stɑːf, ˈfɒl- ⓤⓢ ˈfɔːl.stæf, ˈfɑːl-
Falstaffian fɔːlˈstɑː.fi.ən, fɒl- ⓤⓢ fɔːlˈstæf.i-, fɑːl-
falt|er ˈfɔːl.t|əʳ, ˈfɒl- ⓤⓢ ˈfɔːl.t̬|ɚ, ˈfɑːl- **-ers** -əz ⓤⓢ -ɚz **-ering/ly** -ᵊr.ɪŋ/li **-ered** -əd ⓤⓢ -ɚd **-erer/s** -ᵊr.əʳ/z ⓤⓢ -ɚ.ɚ/z
Famagusta ˌfæm.əˈgʊs.tə, ˌfɑː.məˈ- ⓤⓢ ˌfɑː.məˈguː.stə
fame feɪm **-d** -d
familial fəˈmɪl.i.əl
familiar fəˈmɪl.i.əʳ ⓤⓢ ˈ-jɚ, -i.ɚ **-s** -z **-ly** -li
familiarit|y fəˌmɪl.iˈær.ə.t|i, -ɪ.t|i ⓤⓢ -ˈer.ə.t̬|i, -ˈær- **-ies** -iz
familiariz|e, -is|e fəˈmɪl.i.ᵊr.aɪz ⓤⓢ ˈ-jə.raɪz, ˈ-i.ə- **-es** -ɪz **-ing** -ɪŋ **-ed** -d
famil|y ˈfæm.ᵊl|.i, -ɪ.l|i **-ies** -iz ˌ**family alˈlowance** ; ˌ**family ˈcredit** ; ˈ**family ˌman** ; ˌ**family ˈplanning** ; ˈ**family ˌroom** ; ˈ**family ˌstyle** ; ˌ**family ˈtree**
famine ˈfæm.ɪn **-s** -z
famish ˈfæm.ɪʃ **-es** -ɪz **-ing** -ɪŋ **-ed** -t
famosus libellus fæmˌəʊ.səs.lɪˈbel.əs ⓤⓢ -ˌoʊ-
famous ˈfeɪ.məs **-ly** -li **-ness** -nəs, -nɪs
fan fæn **-s** -z **-ning** -ɪŋ **-ned** -d
Fan *Welsh mountains:* væn
fan-assisted ˌfæn.əˈsɪs.tɪd *stress shift:* ˌfan-assisted ˈoven

fanatic fəˈnæt.ɪk ⓤⓢ -ˈnæt̬- **-s** -s **-al** -ᵊl **-ally** -ᵊl.i, -li
fanaticism fəˈnæt.ɪ.sɪ.zᵊm, ˈ-ə- ⓤⓢ -ˈnæt̬-
fanaticiz|e, -is|e fəˈnæt.ɪ.saɪz ⓤⓢ -ˈnæt̬- **-es** -ɪz **-ing** -ɪŋ **-ed** -d
fanbelt ˈfæn.belt **-s** -s
fanciful ˈfænt.sɪ.fᵊl, -fʊl **-ly** -i **-ness** -nəs, -nɪs
Fancourt ˈfæn.kɔːt, ˈfæŋ- ⓤⓢ -kɔːrt
fanc|y ˈfænt.s|i **-ies** -iz **-ying** -i.ɪŋ **-ied** -id **-ier/s** -i.əʳ/z ⓤⓢ -i.ɚ/z ˌ**fancy** ˈ**dress**
fancy-free ˌfænt.siˈfriː ˌ**footloose and** ˌ**fancy-**ˈ**free** ⓤⓢ ˈ**footloose and** ˌ**fancy** ˌ**free**
fancywork ˈfænt.si.wɜːk ⓤⓢ -wɜːrk
fandango fænˈdæŋ.gəʊ ⓤⓢ -goʊ **-s** -z
fane (F) feɪn **-s** -z
Faneuil ˈfæn.ᵊl, -jəl, -juəl ⓤⓢ -jə.wəl
fanfare ˈfæn.feəʳ ⓤⓢ -fer **-s** -z
fanfaronade ˌfæn.fær.əˈnɑːd, -fᵊr-, -ˈneɪd ⓤⓢ -fər.əˈneɪd, -ˈnɑːd **-s** -z
fang (F) fæŋ **-s** -z **-ed** -d
fanjet ˈfæn.dʒet **-s** -s
fanlight ˈfæn.laɪt **-s** -s
fanner ˈfæn.əʳ ⓤⓢ -ɚ **-s** -z
Fanning ˈfæn.ɪŋ
fann|y (F) ˈfæn|.i **-ies** -iz ˈ**fanny** ˌ**pack**
Fanshawe ˈfæn.ʃɔː ⓤⓢ -ʃɑː, -ʃɔː
Fanta® ˈfæn.tə ⓤⓢ -t̬ə
fantabulous fænˈtæb.jə.ləs, -jʊ-
fantail ˈfæn.teɪl **-s** -z
fantasia fænˈteɪ.zi.ə, -ˈtɑː-, ˈ-ʒə; ˌfæn.təˈziː.ə, -ˈsiː- ⓤⓢ fænˈteɪ.ʒə, -ʒi.ə; ˌfæn.t̬əˈziː.ə **-s** -z
fantasiz|e, -is|e ˈfæn.tə.saɪz ⓤⓢ -t̬ə- **-es** -ɪz **-ing** -ɪŋ **-ed** -d
fantasm ˈfæn.tæz.ᵊm **-s** -z
fantastic fænˈtæs.tɪk, fən- ⓤⓢ fæn- **-al** -ᵊl **-ally** -ᵊl.i, -li **-alness** -ᵊl.nəs, -nɪs
fantas|y ˈfæn.tə.s|i, -z|i ⓤⓢ -t̬ə- **-ies** -iz
Fanti, Fante ˈfæn.ti ⓤⓢ ˈfæn.ti, ˈfɑːn- **-s** -z
fanzine ˈfæn.ziːn **-s** -z
far fɑːʳ ⓤⓢ fɑːr ˌ**Far** ˈ**East**
farad ˈfær.əd, -æd ⓤⓢ ˈfer-, ˈfær- **-s** -z
faraday (F) ˈfær.ə.deɪ ⓤⓢ ˈfer-, ˈfær- **-s** -z
faradic fəˈræd.ɪk
faraway ˌfɑː.rəˈweɪ ⓤⓢ ˌfɑːr.əˈ- *stress shift:* ˌfaraway ˈlook
farc|e fɑːs ⓤⓢ fɑːrs **-es** -ɪz
farceur ˌfɑːˈsɜːʳ ⓤⓢ ˌfɑːrˈsɜːr **-s** -z
farci(e) ˌfɑːˈsiː ⓤⓢ ˌfɑːr-
farcical ˈfɑː.sɪ.kᵊl, -sə- ⓤⓢ ˈfɑːr- **-ly** -i
farcy ˈfɑː.si ⓤⓢ ˈfɑːr-
far|e (*n. v.*) feəʳ ⓤⓢ fer **-es** -z **-ing** -ɪŋ **-ed** -d
Far East ˌfɑːrˈiːst ⓤⓢ ˌfɑːr-
Farebrother ˈfeəˌbrʌð.əʳ ⓤⓢ ˈferˌbrʌð.ɚ

Fareham ˈfeə.rəm ⓤⓢ ˈfer.əm
farewell ˌfeəˈwel ⓤⓢ ˌfer- **-s** -z *stress shift:* ˌfarewell ˈkiss
Farewell ˈfeə.wel, -wᵊl ⓤⓢ ˈfer-
farfalle fɑːˈfæl.eɪ ⓤⓢ fɑːr-
far-fetched ˌfɑːˈfetʃt ⓤⓢ ˌfɑːr- *stress shift:* ˌfar-fetched ˈtale
far-flung ˌfɑːˈflʌŋ ⓤⓢ ˌfɑːr- *stress shift:* ˌfar-flung ˈplaces
Fargo ˈfɑː.gəʊ ⓤⓢ ˈfɑːr.goʊ
Faribault ˈfær.ɪ.bəʊ ⓤⓢ ˈfer.ɪ.boʊ, ˈfær-
farina fəˈriː.nə, -ˈraɪ- ⓤⓢ -ˈriː-
Farina fəˈriː.nə
farinaceous ˌfær.ɪˈneɪ.ʃəs, -əˈ- ⓤⓢ ˌfer-, ˌfær-
Faringdon ˈfær.ɪŋ.dən ⓤⓢ ˈfer-, ˈfær-
Faringford ˈfær.ɪŋ.fəd ⓤⓢ ˈfer.ɪŋ.fɚd, ˈfær-
Farington ˈfær.ɪŋ.tən ⓤⓢ ˈfer-, ˈfær-
farinose ˈfær.ɪ.nəʊs, -nəʊz ⓤⓢ ˈfer.ə.noʊs, ˈfær-
Farjeon ˈfɑː.dʒᵊn ⓤⓢ ˈfɑːr-
Farleigh, Farley ˈfɑː.li ⓤⓢ ˈfɑːr-
farm fɑːm ⓤⓢ fɑːrm **-s** -z **-ing** -ɪŋ **-ed** -d
Farman ˈfɑː.mən ⓤⓢ ˈfɑːr-
Farmaner ˈfɑː.mə.nəʳ ⓤⓢ ˈfɑːr.mə.nɚ
farmer (F) ˈfɑː.məʳ ⓤⓢ ˈfɑːr.mɚ **-s** -z
farmhou|se ˈfɑːm.haʊ|s ⓤⓢ ˈfɑːrm- **-ses** -zɪz
Farmington ˈfɑː.mɪŋ.tən ⓤⓢ ˈfɑːr-
farmland ˈfɑːm.lænd, -lənd ⓤⓢ ˈfɑːrm.lænd
farmstead ˈfɑːm.sted ⓤⓢ ˈfɑːrm- **-s** -z
farmyard ˈfɑːm.jɑːd ⓤⓢ ˈfɑːrm.jɑːrd **-s** -z
Farnaby ˈfɑː.nə.bi ⓤⓢ ˈfɑːr-
Farnborough ˈfɑːn.bᵊr.ə, ˈfɑːm- ⓤⓢ ˈfɑːrn-, -oʊ
Farn(e) fɑːn ⓤⓢ fɑːrn
Farnham ˈfɑː.nəm ⓤⓢ ˈfɑːr-
Farnhamworth ˈfɑː.nəm.wəθ, -wɜːθ ⓤⓢ ˈfɑːr.nəm.wɚθ, -wɜːrθ
faro *gambling game:* ˈfeə.rəʊ ⓤⓢ ˈfer.oʊ, ˈfær-
Faro *in Portugal:* ˈfɑː.rəʊ, ˈfeə- ⓤⓢ ˈfɑːr.oʊ, ˈfer-
Faroe ˈfeə.rəʊ ⓤⓢ ˈfer.oʊ
Faroese ˌfeə.rəʊˈiːz ⓤⓢ ˌfer.oʊˈ-
far-off ˌfɑːrˈɒf ⓤⓢ ˌfɑːrˈɑːf *stress shift:* ˌfar-off ˈtown
farouche fəˈruːʃ, fɑː-
Farouk fəˈruːk, færˈuːk ⓤⓢ fəˈruːk
far-out ˌfɑːrˈaʊt ⓤⓢ ˌfɑːr- *stress shift:* ˌfar-out ˈmusic
Farquhar ˈfɑː.kwəʳ, -kəʳ ⓤⓢ ˈfɑːr.kwɚ, -kwɑːr, -kɚ
Farquharson ˈfɑː.kwə.sᵊn, -kə- ⓤⓢ ˈfɑːr.kwɚ-, -kɚ-
Farr fɑːʳ ⓤⓢ fɑːr
farraginous fəˈreɪ.dʒɪ.nəs, -ˈrædʒ.ɪ-, -ᵊn.əs ⓤⓢ fəˈrædʒ.ɪ.nəs, ˈ-ə-

farrago fəˈrɑː.gəʊ, -ˈreɪ- ⓤⓢ fəˈrɑː.goʊ, -ˈreɪ- **-es** -z
Farragut ˈfær.ə.gət ⓤⓢ ˈfer-, ˈfær-
Farrah ˈfær.ə ⓤⓢ ˈfer-, ˈfær-
Farrant ˈfær.ᵊnt ⓤⓢ ˈfer-, ˈfær-
far-reaching ˌfɑːˈriː.tʃɪŋ ⓤⓢ ˌfɑːr- *stress shift:* ˌfar-reaching ˈconsequences
Farrell ˈfær.ᵊl ⓤⓢ ˈfer-, ˈfær-
Farren ˈfær.ᵊn ⓤⓢ ˈfer-, ˈfær-
Farrener ˈfær.ə.nəʳ ⓤⓢ ˈfer.ə.nɚ, ˈfær-
farrier ˈfær.i.əʳ ⓤⓢ ˈfer.i.ɚ, ˈfær- **-s** -z **-y** -i **-ies** -iz
Farringdon ˈfær.ɪŋ.dən ⓤⓢ ˈfer-, ˈfær-
Farringford ˈfær.ɪŋ.fəd ⓤⓢ ˈfer.ɪŋ.fɚd, ˈfær-
Farrington ˈfær.ɪŋ.tən ⓤⓢ ˈfer-, ˈfær-
farrow (F) ˈfær.əʊ ⓤⓢ ˈfer.oʊ, ˈfær- **-s** -z **-ing** -ɪŋ **-ed** -d
farseeing ˌfɑːˈsiː.ɪŋ ⓤⓢ ˌfɑːr- *stress shift:* ˌfarseeing ˈleader
Farsi ˈfɑː.siː, ˌ-ˈ- ⓤⓢ ˈfɑːr- **-s** -z
farsighted fɑːˈsaɪ.tɪd ⓤⓢ fɑːrˈsaɪ.t̬ɪd **-ly** -li **-ness** -nəs, -nɪs
Farsley ˈfɑːz.li ⓤⓢ ˈfɑːrz-
fart fɑːt ⓤⓢ fɑːrt **-s** -s **-ing** -ɪŋ ⓤⓢ ˈfɑːr.t̬ɪŋ **-ed** -ɪd ⓤⓢ ˈfɑːr.t̬ɪd
farth|er ˈfɑː.ð|əʳ ⓤⓢ ˈfɑːr.ð|ɚ **-est** -ɪst, -əst
farthing ˈfɑː.ðɪŋ ⓤⓢ ˈfɑːr- **-s** -z
farthingale ˈfɑː.ðɪŋ.geɪl ⓤⓢ ˈfɑːr- **-s** -z
fartlek ˈfɑːt.lek ⓤⓢ ˈfɑːrt- **-s** -s
Faruk fəˈruːk, færˈuːk ⓤⓢ fəˈruːk
Farwell ˈfɑː.wel, -wəl ⓤⓢ ˈfɑːr-
fasces ˈfæs.iːz
fasci|a *medical term:* ˈfæʃ.i|.ə, -ʃ|ə ⓤⓢ -ʃi|.ə **-as** -əs **-ae** -iː *other senses:* ˈfeɪ.ʃ|ə, -ʃi|.ə ⓤⓢ ˈfæʃ.i|.ə, ˈfæʃ|.ə *also when referring to classical architecture:* ˈfeɪ.si|.ə ⓤⓢ -ʃi- **-as** -əz **-ae** -iː
fasciated ˈfæʃ.i.eɪ.tɪd ⓤⓢ -t̬ɪd
fascicle ˈfæs.ɪ.kl̩, ˈ-ə- **-s** -z
fascicule ˈfæs.ɪ.kjuːl, ˈ-ə- **-s** -z
fascin|ate ˈfæs.ɪ.n|eɪt, -ᵊn|.eɪt ⓤⓢ -ᵊn|.eɪt **-ates** -eɪts **-ated** -eɪ.tɪd ⓤⓢ -eɪ.t̬ɪd **-ator/s** -eɪ.təʳ/z ⓤⓢ -eɪ.t̬ɚ/z
fascinating ˈfæs.ɪ.neɪ.tɪŋ, -ᵊn.eɪ- ⓤⓢ -ᵊn.eɪ.t̬ɪŋ **-ly** -li
fascination ˌfæs.ɪˈneɪ.ʃᵊn, -ᵊnˈeɪ- ⓤⓢ -ᵊnˈeɪ- **-s** -z
fascine fæsˈiːn, fəˈsiːn **-s** -z
fascism (F) ˈfæʃ.ɪ.zᵊm
fascist (F) ˈfæʃ.ɪst **-s** -s
Fascisti fæʃˈɪs.tiː, fəˈʃɪs-
fascistic (F) fæʃˈɪs.tɪk, fəˈʃɪs- **-ally** -ᵊl.i, -li
fash fæʃ **-es** -ɪz **-ing** -ɪŋ **-ed** -t
fashion ˈfæʃ.ᵊn **-s** -z **-ing** -ɪŋ **-ed** -d **-er/s** -əʳ/z ⓤⓢ -ɚ/z ˈ**fashion** ˌ**plate**

fashionab|le 'fæʃ.ᵊn.ə.bl̩, 'fæʃ.nə- **-ly** -li **-leness** -l̩.nəs, -nɪs
Faslane fæz'leɪn, fə'sleɪn
Fassbinder 'fæs.bɪn.dəʳ Ⓤⓢ 'fɑːs.bɪn.dɚ
fast (F) fɑːst Ⓤⓢ fæst **-s** -s **-est** -ɪst, -əst **-ness** -nəs, -nɪs **-ing** -ɪŋ **-ed** -ɪd **-er/s** -əʳ/z Ⓤⓢ -ɚ/z ˌ**fast and 'loose** ; '**fast ˌday** ; ˌ**fast 'food** ; '**fast ˌlane** ; ˌ**fast re'actor** ; '**fast ˌtrack** ; ˌ**life in the 'fast ˌlane** ; ˌ**pull a 'fast ˌone**
fastball 'fɑːst.bɔːl Ⓤⓢ 'fæst-, -bɑːl **-s** -z
fasten 'fɑː.sᵊn Ⓤⓢ 'fæs.ᵊn **-s** -z **-ing** -ɪŋ, 'fɑːs.nɪŋ Ⓤⓢ 'fæs- **-ed** -d
fastener 'fɑː.sᵊn.əʳ Ⓤⓢ 'fæs.ᵊn.ɚ **-s** -z
fastening 'fɑː.sᵊn.ɪŋ; 'fɑːs.nɪŋ Ⓤⓢ 'fæs.ᵊn.ɪŋ, 'fæs.nɪŋ **-s** -z
fast-forward ˌfɑːst'fɔː.wəd Ⓤⓢ ˌfæst'fɔːr.wɚd **-s** -z **-ing** -ɪŋ **-ed** -ɪd
fasti (F) 'fæs.tiː, -taɪ
fastidious fæs'tɪd.i.əs, fə'stɪd- **-ly** -li **-ness** -nəs, -nɪs
fastness 'fɑːst.nəs, -nɪs Ⓤⓢ 'fæst- **-es** -ɪz
Fastnet 'fɑːst.net, -nɪt Ⓤⓢ 'fæst-
fast-talk ˌfɑːst'tɔːk Ⓤⓢ ˌfæst-, -'tɑːk **-s** -s **-ing** -ɪŋ **-ed** -t **-er/s** -əʳ/z Ⓤⓢ -ɚ/z
fat fæt **-ter** -əʳ Ⓤⓢ 'fæṭ.ɚ **-test** -ɪst, -əst Ⓤⓢ 'fæṭ.ɪst, -əst **-ness** -nəs, -nɪs '**fat ˌcat** ; ˌ**fat 'city**
fatal 'feɪ.tᵊl Ⓤⓢ -ṭᵊl **-ly** -i
fatal|ism 'feɪ.tᵊl|.ɪ.zᵊm Ⓤⓢ -ṭᵊl- **-ist/s** -ɪst/s
fatalistic ˌfeɪ.tᵊl'ɪs.tɪk Ⓤⓢ -ṭᵊl'- **-ally** -ᵊl.i, -li
fatalit|y fə'tæl.ə.t|i, feɪ-, -ɪ.t|i Ⓤⓢ -ə.ṭ|i **-ies** -iz
fat|e (F) feɪt **-es** -s **-ed** -ɪd Ⓤⓢ 'feɪ.ṭɪd
fateful 'feɪt.fᵊl, -fʊl **-ly** -i
fathead 'fæt.hed **-s** -z
fath|er (F) 'fɑː.ð|əʳ Ⓤⓢ -ð|ɚ **-ers** -əz Ⓤⓢ -ɚz **-ering** -ᵊr.ɪŋ **-ered** -əd Ⓤⓢ -ɚd ˌ**Father 'Christmas** ; '**father ˌfigure**
fatherhood 'fɑː.ðə.hʊd Ⓤⓢ -ðɚ-
father-in-law 'fɑː.ðəʳ.ɪn.lɔː Ⓤⓢ -ðɚ.ɪn.lɑː, -lɔː **fathers-in-law** 'fɑː.ðəz- Ⓤⓢ -ðɚz-
fatherland 'fɑː.ðə.lænd Ⓤⓢ -ðɚ- **-s** -z
fatherless 'fɑː.ðə.ləs, -lɪs Ⓤⓢ -ðɚ-
fatherl|y 'fɑː.ðᵊl|.i Ⓤⓢ -ðɚ.l|i **-iness** -ɪ.nəs, -ɪ.nɪs
fathom 'fæð.əm **-s** -z **-ing** -ɪŋ **-ed** -d **-able** -ə.bl̩ **-less** -ləs, -lɪs
fatigu|e fə'tiːg **-es** -z **-ing/ly** -ɪŋ/li **-ed** -d ˌ**chronic fa'tigue ˌsyndrome**
Fatima 'fæt.ɪ.mə Ⓤⓢ 'fæṭ-, 'fɑː.ṭɪ-; fə'tiː-
fatling 'fæt.lɪŋ **-s** -z
fatsia 'fæt.si.ə **-s** -z
fatso 'fæt.səʊ Ⓤⓢ -soʊ **-es** -z
fatted 'fæt.ɪd Ⓤⓢ 'fæṭ- ˌ**fatted 'calf**
fatten 'fæt.ᵊn **-s** -z **-ing** -ɪŋ **-ed** -d **-er/s** -əʳ/z Ⓤⓢ -ɚ/z
fattish 'fæt.ɪʃ Ⓤⓢ 'fæṭ-
fatt|y 'fæt|.i Ⓤⓢ 'fæṭ- **-ies** -iz **-ier** -i.əʳ Ⓤⓢ -i.ɚ **-iest** -i.ɪst, -i.əst **-iness** -ɪ.nəs, -ɪ.nɪs ˌ**fatty 'acid**
fatuity fə'tjuː.ə.ti, fæt'juː-, -ɪ.ti Ⓤⓢ fə'tuː.ə.ṭi, -'tjuː-
fatuous 'fæt.ju.əs Ⓤⓢ 'fætʃ.u- **-ly** -li **-ness** -nəs, -nɪs
fatwa 'fæt.wɑː, -wə Ⓤⓢ 'fæt.wɑː, 'fʌt- **-s** -z
fatwood 'fæt.wʊd
faubourg 'fəʊ.bʊəg, -bɜːg Ⓤⓢ 'foʊ.bʊr, -bʊrg **-s** -z
faucal 'fɔː.kᵊl Ⓤⓢ 'fɑː-, 'fɔː-
fauces 'fɔː.siːz Ⓤⓢ 'fɑː-, 'fɔː-
faucet 'fɔː.sɪt, -sət Ⓤⓢ 'fɑː-, 'fɔː- **-s** -s
Faucett, Faucit 'fɔː.sɪt, -ət Ⓤⓢ 'fɑː-, 'fɔː-
Faulconbridge 'fɔː.kᵊn.brɪdʒ, 'fɔːl-, -kᵊm- Ⓤⓢ 'fɑː.kᵊn-, 'fɑːl-, 'fɔː-, 'fɔːl-
Fauldhouse 'fɔːld.haʊs Ⓤⓢ 'fɑːld-, 'fɔːld-
Faulds fəʊldz, fɔːldz Ⓤⓢ foʊldz, fɑːldz, fɔːldz
Faulhorn 'faʊl.hɔːn Ⓤⓢ -hɔːrn
Faulk fɔːk Ⓤⓢ fɑːk, fɔːk, fɑːlk
Faulkes fɔːks, fɔːlks Ⓤⓢ fɑːks, fɑːlks, fɔːks, fɔːlks
Faulkland 'fɔː.klənd, 'fɔːl- Ⓤⓢ 'fɑː-, 'fɑːl-, 'fɔː-, 'fɔːl-
Faulkner 'fɔːk.nəʳ Ⓤⓢ 'fɑːk.nɚ, 'fɔːk-, 'fɑːlk-
Faulks fəʊks Ⓤⓢ foʊks
faul|t fɔːl|t, fɒl|t Ⓤⓢ fɔːl|t, fɑːl|t **-ts** -ts **-ting** -tɪŋ Ⓤⓢ -ṭɪŋ **-ted** -tɪd Ⓤⓢ -ṭɪd
faultfind|er 'fɔːltˌfaɪn.d|əʳ, 'fɒlt- Ⓤⓢ 'fɔːltˌfaɪn.d|ɚ, 'fɑːlt- **-ers** -əz Ⓤⓢ -ɚz **-ing** -ɪŋ
faultless 'fɔːlt.ləs, 'fɒlt-, -lɪs Ⓤⓢ 'fɔːlt-, 'fɑːlt- **-ly** -li **-ness** -nəs, -nɪs
fault|y 'fɔːl.t|i, 'fɒl- Ⓤⓢ 'fɔːl.ṭ|i, 'fɑːl- **-ier** -i.əʳ Ⓤⓢ -i.ɚ **-iest** -i.ɪst, -i.əst **-ily** -ɪ.li, -ᵊl.i **-iness** -ɪ.nəs, -ɪ.nɪs
faun fɔːn Ⓤⓢ fɑːn, fɔːn **-s** -z
fauna 'fɔː.nə Ⓤⓢ 'fɑː-, 'fɔː-
Faunch fɔːntʃ Ⓤⓢ fɑːntʃ, fɔːntʃ
Fauntleroy 'fɔːnt.lə.rɔɪ, 'fɒnt- Ⓤⓢ 'fɑːnt-, 'fɔːnt-
Fauré 'fɔː.reɪ, 'fɒr.eɪ Ⓤⓢ foʊ'reɪ, fɔː-
Faust faʊst
Faustian 'faʊ.sti.ən
Faustina fɔː'stiː.nə, faʊ- Ⓤⓢ faʊ-, fɔː-
Faustus 'fɔː.stəs, 'faʊ- Ⓤⓢ 'faʊ-, 'fɔː-
fauteuil 'fəʊ.tɜː.i, fəʊ'tɜː.i, -'tɜːl Ⓤⓢ 'foʊ.tɪl; foʊ'tɜː.jə **-s** -z
fauve fəʊv Ⓤⓢ foʊv
fauv|ism (F) 'fəʊ.v|ɪ.zᵊm Ⓤⓢ 'foʊ- **-ist/s** -ɪst/s
Faux fəʊ, fɔːks Ⓤⓢ foʊ
faux ami ˌfəʊz.æm'i Ⓤⓢ ˌfoʊz- **-s** -z
faux-naïf ˌfəʊ.naɪ'iːf Ⓤⓢ ˌfoʊ.nɑː'- **-s** -s
faux pas *singular:* ˌfəʊ'pɑː Ⓤⓢ ˌfoʊ-
faux pas *plural:* ˌfəʊ'pɑː, -'pɑːz Ⓤⓢ ˌfoʊ-
fave feɪv **-s** -z
Favel 'feɪ.vᵊl
Faversham 'fæv.ə.ʃəm Ⓤⓢ '-ɚ-
Favoni|an fə'vəʊ.ni|.ən, feɪ- Ⓤⓢ -'voʊ- **-us** -əs
Favorit® 'fæv.ᵊr.ɪt
fav|o(u)r 'feɪ.v|əʳ Ⓤⓢ -v|ɚ **-o(u)rs** -əz Ⓤⓢ -ɚz **-o(u)ring** -ᵊr.ɪŋ **-o(u)red** -əd Ⓤⓢ -ɚd **-o(u)rer/s** -ᵊr.əʳ/z Ⓤⓢ -ɚ.ɚ/z
favo(u)rab|le 'feɪ.vᵊr.ə.bl̩ **-ly** -li **-leness** -l̩.nəs, -nɪs
favo(u)rit|e 'feɪ.vᵊr.ɪt, -ət **-es** -s **-ism** -ɪ.zᵊm ˌ**favo(u)rite 'son**
favo(u)rless 'feɪ.və.ləs, -lɪs Ⓤⓢ -vɚ-
Fawcett 'fɔː.sɪt, -sət, 'fɒs.ɪt, -ət Ⓤⓢ 'fɑː.sɪt, 'fɔː-, -sət
Fawkes fɔːks Ⓤⓢ fɑːks, fɔːks
Fawkner 'fɔːk.nəʳ Ⓤⓢ 'fɑːk.nɚ, 'fɔːk-
Fawley 'fɔː.li Ⓤⓢ 'fɑː-, 'fɔː-
Fawlty 'fɔːl.ti Ⓤⓢ 'fɑːl-, 'fɔːl-
fawn fɔːn Ⓤⓢ fɑːn, fɔːn **-s** -z **-ing/ly** -ɪŋ/li **-ed** -d **-er/s** -əʳ/z Ⓤⓢ -ɚ/z
Fawssett 'fɔː.sɪt, -sət Ⓤⓢ 'fɑː.sɪt, 'fɔː-, -sət
fax fæks **-es** -ɪz **-ing** -ɪŋ **-ed** -t '**fax maˌchine**
fay (F) feɪ **-s** -z
Faye feɪ
Fayette feɪ'et *stress shift, see compound:* ˌ**Fayette 'City**
Fayetteville 'feɪ.et.vɪl, -ɪt-, -ət- Ⓤⓢ *locally also:* 'feɪt.vəl
Faygate 'feɪ.geɪt
Faza(c)kerley fə'zæk.ᵊl.i Ⓤⓢ -ɚ.li
faz|e feɪz **-es** -ɪz **-ing** -ɪŋ **-ed** -d
FBI ˌef.biː'aɪ
FC ˌef'siː
FCO ˌef.siː'əʊ Ⓤⓢ -'oʊ
FDA ˌef.diː'eɪ
fe *name of note in Tonic Sol-fa:* fiː
fe *syllable used in Tonic Sol-fa for counting a short note off the beat:* fi
FE (*abbrev. for* **Further Education**) ˌef'iː
fealty 'fiːl.ti
fear fɪəʳ Ⓤⓢ fɪr **-s** -z **-ing** -ɪŋ **-ed** -d
fearful 'fɪə.fᵊl, -fʊl Ⓤⓢ 'fɪr- **-ly** -i **-ness** -nəs, -nɪs
Fearghal 'fɜː.gᵊl Ⓤⓢ 'fɜːr-
Feargus 'fɜː.gəs Ⓤⓢ 'fɜːr-
Fearing 'fɪə.rɪŋ Ⓤⓢ 'fɪr.ɪŋ
fearless 'fɪə.ləs, -lɪs Ⓤⓢ 'fɪr- **-ly** -li **-ness** -nəs, -nɪs
Fearn(e) fɜːn Ⓤⓢ fɜːrn
Fearnside 'fɜːn.saɪd Ⓤⓢ 'fɜːrn-

Fearon 'fɪə.rᵊn (US) 'fɪr.ᵊn
fearsome 'fɪə.səm (US) 'fɪr- **-ly** -li **-ness** -nəs, -nɪs
feasibility ˌfiː.zə'bɪl.ə.ti, -zɪ'-, -ɪ.ti (US) -ə.t̬i
feasib|le 'fiː.zə.bl̩, -zɪ- **-ly** -li **-leness** -l̩.nəs, -nɪs
feast (F) fiːst **-s** -s **-ing** -ɪŋ **-ed** -ɪd **-er/s** -əʳ/z (US) -ɚ/z
feat fiːt **-s** -s
feath|er 'feð|.əʳ (US) -ɚ **-ers** -əz (US) -ɚz **-ering** -ᵊr.ɪŋ **-ered** -əd (US) -ɚd **ˌfeather 'bed**
featherbed 'feð.ə.bed, ˌ--'- (US) -ɚ- **-s** -z **-ding** -ɪŋ **-ded** -ɪd
featherbrain 'feð.ə.breɪn (US) '-ɚ- **-s** -z **-ed** -d
featheredg|e 'feð.əʳ.edʒ, ˌ--'- (US) -ɚ- **-es** -ɪz
featherhead 'feð.ə.hed (US) '-ɚ- **-s** -z **-ed** -ɪd
featherstitch 'feð.ə.stɪtʃ (US) '-ɚ- **-es** -ɪz **-ing** -ɪŋ **-ed** -t
Featherston 'feð.ə.stən (US) '-ɚ-
Featherstone 'feð.ə.stən, -stəʊn (US) -ɚ.stən, -stoʊn
Featherstonehaugh 'feð.ə.stᵊn.hɔː; 'fæn.ʃɔː; 'fes.tᵊn.hɔː, 'fɪə.stᵊn-; 'fiː.sᵊn.heɪ (US) 'feð.ɚ.stᵊn.θɑː, -hɔː; 'fæn.ʃɑː, -ʃɔː; 'fes.tᵊn.hɑː, 'fɪr.stᵊn-, -hɔː; 'fiː.sᵊn.heɪ
featherweight 'feð.ə.weɪt (US) '-ɚ- **-s** -s
feather|y 'feð.ᵊr|.i **-iness** -ɪ.nəs, -ɪ.nɪs
Featley 'fiːt.li
featly 'fiːt.li
feat|ure 'fiː.tʃ|əʳ (US) -tʃ|ɚ **-ures** -əz (US) -ɚz **-uring** -ᵊr.ɪŋ **-ured** -əd (US) -ɚd **-ureless** -ə.ləs, -lɪs (US) -ɚ.ləs, -lɪs
Feaver 'fiː.vəʳ (US) -vɚ
Feb. (*abbrev. for* **February**) feb, 'feb.ru.ᵊr.i, '-jʊ.ᵊr.i, '-jʊ.ri, '-jᵊr.i (US) 'feb.ruː.er.i, '-juː-, '-jə.wer-
febrifug|e 'feb.rɪ.fjuːdʒ, -rə- **-es** -ɪz
febrile 'fiː.braɪl (US) -brɪl, 'feb.rɪl
February 'feb.ru.ᵊr.i, '-ju.ᵊr.i, '-jʊ.ri, '-jᵊr.i (US) 'feb.ruː.er.i, '-juː-, '-jə.wer- **-s**
fecal 'fiː.kᵊl
feces 'fiː.siːz
fecit 'fiː.sɪt, 'feɪ.kɪt
Feckenham 'fek.ᵊn.əm
feckless 'fek.ləs, -lɪs **-ly** -li **-ness** -nəs, -nɪs
feculen|t 'fek.jə.lən|t, -jʊ- (US) -jə-, -juː- **-ce** -*t*s
fecund 'fek.ənd, 'fiː.kənd, -kʌnd
fecun|date 'fek.ᵊn|.deɪt, 'fiː.kᵊn-, -kʌn- **-dates** -deɪts **-dating** -deɪ.tɪŋ (US) -deɪ.t̬ɪŋ **-dated** -deɪ.tɪd (US) -deɪ.t̬ɪd
fecundation ˌfek.ᵊn'deɪ.ʃᵊn, ˌfiː.kᵊn'-, -kʌn'-
fecundity fɪ'kʌn.də.ti, fiː'kʌn-, fek'ʌn-, -dɪ.ti (US) -də.t̬i
fed (*from* **feed**) fed **ˌfed 'up**
Fed fed
federal (F) 'fed.ᵊr.ᵊl, '-rəl **-ly** -i **ˌFederal Re'serve**
federal|ism 'fed.ᵊr.ᵊl|.ɪ.zᵊm, '-rᵊl- **-ist/s** -ɪst/s
federalization, -isa- ˌfed.ᵊr.ᵊl.aɪ'zeɪ.ʃᵊn, ˌ-rᵊl-, -ɪ'- (US) -ɪ'-
federaliz|e, -is|e 'fed.ᵊr.ᵊl.aɪz, '-rᵊl- (US) '-ɚ.ə.laɪz, '-rə- **-es** -ɪz **-ing** -ɪŋ **-ed** -d
federate (*n. adj.*) 'fed.ᵊr.ət, -ɪt, -eɪt **-s** -s
feder|ate (*v.*) 'fed.ᵊr|.eɪt **-ates** -eɪts **-ating** -eɪ.tɪŋ (US) -eɪ.t̬ɪŋ **-ated** -eɪ.tɪd (US) -eɪ.t̬ɪd
federation ˌfed.ᵊr'eɪ.ʃᵊn (US) -ə'reɪ- **-s** -z
federative 'fed.ᵊr.ə.tɪv, -eɪ- (US) -ɚ.ə.t̬ɪv, -ə.reɪ- **-ly** -li
fedora (F) fɪ'dɔː.rə, fə-, fed'ɔː- (US) fə'dɔːr.ə **-s** -z
fed up ˌfed'ʌp
fee fiː **-s** -z **-ing** -ɪŋ **-d** -d **ˌfee 'simple** ; **ˌfee 'tail**
feeb|le 'fiː.bl̩ **-ler** -ləʳ (US) -lɚ **-lest** -l̩.ɪst, -əst, -lɪst, -ləst **-ly** -li **-leness** -l̩.nəs, -nɪs
feebleminded ˌfiː.bl̩'maɪn.dɪd (US) ˌfiː.bl̩'maɪn.dɪd, 'fiː.bl̩ˌmaɪn.dɪd **-ness** -nəs, -nɪs *stress shift, British only:* ˌfeebleminded 'simpleton
feed fiːd **-s** -z **-ing** -ɪŋ **fed** fed **feeder/s** 'fiː.dəʳ/z (US) -dɚ/z **'feeding ˌbottle** ; **'feed ˌpipe** ; **'feed ˌtank**
feedback 'fiːd.bæk
feedbag 'fiːd.bæg **-s** -z
feel fiːl **-s** -z **-ing** -ɪŋ **felt** felt
feeler 'fiː.ləʳ (US) -lɚ **-s** -z
feelgood 'fiːl.gʊd **'feelgood ˌfactor**
feeling 'fiː.lɪŋ **-s** -z **-ly** -li
Feeney 'fiː.ni
feet (*plur. of* **foot**) fiːt **ˌdrag one's 'feet** ; **ˌfall on one's 'feet** ; **ˌfind one's 'feet** ; **have/keep ˌboth feet on the 'ground** ; **be ˌrushed off one's 'feet** ; **ˌsweep someone off their 'feet**
Fegan 'fiː.gən
Feiffer 'faɪ.fəʳ (US) -fɚ
feign feɪn **-s** -z **-ing** -ɪŋ **-ed** -d **-edly** -ɪd.li **-edness** -ɪd.nəs, -nɪs
Feilden 'fiːl.dən
Feilding 'fiːl.dɪŋ
Feinstein 'faɪn.staɪn
feint feɪnt **-s** -s **-ing** -ɪŋ (US) 'feɪn.t̬ɪŋ **-ed** -ɪd (US) 'feɪn.t̬ɪd
Feisal 'faɪ.sᵊl, 'feɪ-
Feist fiːst
feist|y 'faɪ.st|i **-ier** -i.əʳ (US) -i.ɚ **-iest** -i.ɪst, -i.əst **-ily** -ɪ.li, -ᵊl.i
felafel fə'lɑː.fᵊl, -'læf.ᵊl (US) -'lɑː.fᵊl
feldspar 'feld.spɑːʳ, 'fel- (US) 'feld.spɑːr
Felicia fə'lɪs.i.ə, fel'ɪs-, fɪ'lɪs-, -'lɪʃ- (US) fə'lɪʃ.ə, -i.ə, -'liː.ʃə, -'lɪs.i.ə
felicitat|e fɪ'lɪs.ɪ|.teɪt, fə-, fel'ɪs-, '-ə- (US) fə'lɪs- **-es** -teɪts **-ing** -teɪ.tɪŋ (US) -teɪ.t̬ɪŋ **-ed** -teɪ.tɪd (US) -teɪ.t̬ɪd
felicitation fɪˌlɪs.ɪ'teɪ.ʃᵊn, fə-, felˌɪs-, -ə'- (US) fəˌlɪs- **-s** -z
felicitous fɪ'lɪs.ɪ.təs, fə-, fel'ɪs-, '-ə- (US) fə'lɪs.ɪ.t̬əs, '-ə- **-ly** -li **-ness** -nəs, -nɪs
felicity (F) fɪ'lɪs.ə.ti, fə-, fel'ɪs-, -ɪ.ti (US) fə'lɪs.ə.t̬i
feline 'fiː.laɪn **-s** -z
felinity fɪ'lɪn.ə.ti, fiː-, fə-, -ɪ.ti (US) -ə.t̬i, -ɪ.t̬i
Felix 'fiː.lɪks
Felixstowe 'fiː.lɪk.stəʊ (US) -stoʊ
Felkin 'fel.kɪn
fell (F) fel **-s** -z **-ing** -ɪŋ **-ed** -d
fella 'fel.ə **-s** -z
fellah 'fel.ə (US) 'fel.ə; fə'lɑː **-in** -hiːn, ˌfel.ə'hiːn (US) -hiːn **-een** -hiːn, ˌfel.ə'hiːn (US) -hiːn
fella|te fel'eɪ|t, fə'leɪ|t, fɪ- (US) 'fel.eɪ|t, -'- **-tes** -ts **-ting** -tɪŋ (US) -t̬ɪŋ **-ted** -tɪd (US) -t̬ɪd **-tor/s** -təʳ/z (US) -t̬ɚ/z **-trix/es** -trɪks/ɪz **-trice/s** -trɪs/ɪz
fellatio fə'leɪ.ʃi.əʊ, fel'eɪ-, fɪ'leɪ- (US) fə'leɪ.ʃi.oʊ, -ʃoʊ; -'lɑː.ti.oʊ
fellation fə'leɪ.ʃᵊn, fel'eɪ-, fɪ'leɪ- (US) fə-
feller 'fel.əʳ (US) -ɚ **-z** -z
Felling 'fel.ɪŋ
Fellini fel'iː.ni, fə'liː-, fɪ- (US) fə-
felloe 'fel.əʊ (US) -oʊ **-s** -z
fellow 'fel.əʊ (US) -oʊ **-s** -z **ˌfellow 'citizen** ; **ˌfellow 'feeling** ; **ˌfellow 'traveller**
Fellow(e)s 'fel.əʊz (US) -oʊz
fellowship 'fel.əʊ.ʃɪp (US) -oʊ- **-s** -s
Felltham 'fel.θəm
felo-de-se ˌfiː.ləʊ.diː'siː, ˌfel.əʊ-, -dɪ'-, -'seɪ (US) ˌfiː.loʊ.dɪ'siː, ˌfel.oʊ- **felos-de-se** ˌfiː.ləʊz-, ˌfel.əʊz- (US) ˌfiː.loʊz-, ˌfel.oʊz- **felones-de-se** ˌfiː.ləʊ.niːz-, ˌfel.əʊ.niːz- (US) ˌfel.oʊ.niː.dɪ'siː, ˌfiː.loʊ-
felon 'fel.ən **-s** -z
felonious fə'ləʊ.ni.əs, fel'əʊ-, fɪ'ləʊ- (US) fə'loʊ- **-ly** -li **-ness** -nəs, -nɪs
felon|y 'fel.ə.n|i **-ies** -iz
Felpham 'fel.pəm
felspar 'fel.spɑːʳ (US) -spɑːr
Felste(a)d 'fel.stɪd, -sted
felt felt **-s** -s
Feltham *place:* 'fel.təm *personal name:* 'fel.θəm
felting 'fel.tɪŋ **-s** -z

Felton 'fel.tᵊn
felt-tip ˌfelt'tɪp **-s** -s *stress shift, see compound:* ˌ**felt-tip 'pen**
felucca fel'ʌk.ə, fə'lʌk-, fɪ- US fə'lʌk-, -'luː.kə **-s** -z
female 'fiː.meɪl **-s** -z **-ness** -nəs, -nɪs
feme fiːm, fem US fem **-s** -z
Femidom® 'fem.ɪ.dɒm US -dɑːm
feminine 'fem.ɪ.nɪn, '-ə- **-ly** -li **-ness** -nəs, -nɪs
femininit|y ˌfem.ɪ'nɪn.ə.t|i, -ə'-, -ɪ.t|i US -ə.t̬|i **-ies** -iz
femin|ism 'fem.ɪ.n|ɪ.zᵊm, '-ə- **-ist/s** -ɪst/s
feminiz|e, -is|e 'fem.ɪ.naɪz, '-ə- **-es** -ɪz **-ing** -ɪŋ **-ed** -d
femme(s) fatale(s) ˌfæm.fə'tɑːl US ˌfem.fə'tæl
femora (*alternative plur. of* **femur**) 'fem.ᵊr.ə, 'fiː.mᵊr- US 'fem.ᵊr-
femoral 'fem.ᵊr.ᵊl, 'fiː.mᵊr- US 'fem.ᵊr-
femur 'fiː.məʳ US -mɚ **-s** -z **femora** 'fem.ᵊr.ə, 'fiː.mᵊr- US 'fem.ᵊr-
fen (F) fen **-s** -z
fenc|e fen*t*s **-es** -ɪz **-ing** -ɪŋ **-ed** -t **-er/s** -əʳ/z US -ɚ/z **-eless** -ləs, -lɪs ˌ**sit on the 'fence**
fencesitt|er 'fen*t*sˌsɪt|.əʳ US -ˌsɪt̬- **-ers** -əʳ/z US -ɚ/z **-ing** -ɪŋ
Fenchurch 'fen.tʃɜːtʃ US -tʃɜːrtʃ
fend fend **-s** -z **-ing** -ɪŋ **-ed** -ɪd
fender 'fen.dəʳ US -dɚ **-s** -z
fender-bender 'fen.dəˌben.dəʳ US -dɚˌben.dɚ **-s** -z
Fenella fɪ'nel.ə, fə-
fenestr|a fɪ'nes.tr|ə, fə- **-ae** -iː **-al** -ᵊl
fenes|trate fɪ'nes|.treɪt, fə'nes-; 'fen.ɪ.s|treɪt, '-ə- US 'fen.ɪ.s|treɪt; fə'nes|.treɪt **-trates** -treɪts **-trating** -treɪ.tɪŋ US -treɪ.t̬ɪŋ **-trated** -treɪ.tɪd US -treɪ.t̬ɪd
fenestration ˌfen.ɪ'streɪ.ʃᵊn, -ə'- **-s** -z
feng shui ˌfeŋ'ʃuːi US ˌfʌŋ'ʃweɪ
Fenham 'fen.əm
Fenian 'fiː.ni.ən **-s** -z **-ism** -ɪ.zᵊm
Fenimore 'fen.ɪ.mɔːʳ US -mɔːr
fenland (F) 'fen.lənd, -lænd
Fenn fen
fennec 'fen.ek, -ɪk **-s** -s
fennel 'fen.ᵊl
Fennell 'fen.ᵊl
Fennessy 'fen.ɪ.si, '-ə-
Fennimore 'fen.ɪ.mɔːʳ US -mɔːr
fenny (F) 'fen.i
Fenrir 'fen.rɪəʳ US -rɪr
Fenton 'fen.tən US -tᵊn
fenugreek 'fen.jʊ.griːk, -ʊ- US -juː-, -jə-
Fenwick *English surname:* 'fen.ɪk, -wɪk *American surname:* 'fen.wɪk *places in UK:* 'fen.ɪk
Feodor 'fiː.əʊ.dɔːʳ US -ə.dɔːr
Feodora ˌfiː.əʊ'dɔː.rə US -ə'dɔːr.ə
feoff fiːf, fef **-s** -s **-ing** -ɪŋ **-ed** -t **-er/s** -əʳ/z US -ɚ/z **-ment/s** -mənt/s
feoffee fiː'fiː, fef'iː **-s** -z
feoffor fiː'fɔːʳ, fef'ɔːʳ US fiː'fɔːr, fef'ɔːr **-s** -z
ferae naturae ˌfer.aɪˌnɑː'tjʊə.raɪ, -'tjɔː- US ˌfiː.riː.nə'tuː.riː, -'tʊr.iː
feral 'fer.ᵊl, 'fɪə.rᵊl US 'fer.ᵊl, 'fɪr-
Ferdinand 'fɜː.dɪ.nænd, -də-, -dᵊn.ænd, -ənd US 'fɜːr.dᵊn.ænd
feretor|y 'fer.ɪ.tᵊr|.i, -tr|i US -tɔːr|.i **-ies** -iz
Fergal 'fɜː.gᵊl US 'fɜːr-
Fergie 'fɜː.gi US 'fɜːr-
Fergus 'fɜː.gəs US 'fɜːr-
Fergus(s)on 'fɜː.gə.sᵊn US 'fɜːr-
feri|a 'fer.i.ə, 'fɪə.ri- US 'fɪr-, 'fer- **-al** -əl
Feringhee fə'rɪŋ.gi **-s** -z
Fermanagh fə'mæn.ə, fɜː- US fɚ-, fɜːr-
ferment (*n.*) 'fɜː.ment US 'fɜːr- **-s** -s
fer|ment (*v.*) fə|'ment, fɜː- US fɚ- **-ments** -'ments **-menting** -'men.tɪŋ US -'men.t̬ɪŋ **-mented** -'men.tɪd US -'men.t̬ɪd **-mentable** -'men.tə.bl̩ US -'men.t̬ə.bl̩
fermentation ˌfɜː.men'teɪ.ʃᵊn, -mən'- US ˌfɜːr- **-s** -z
fermentative fə'men.tə.tɪv US -t̬ə.t̬ɪv **-ly** -li **-ness** -nəs, -nɪs
Fermi 'feə.mi US 'fer-
fermium 'fɜː.mi.əm US 'fɜːr-
Fermor 'fɜː.mɔːʳ US 'fɜːr.mɔːr
Fermoy *near Cork:* fə'mɔɪ, fɜː- US fɚ-, fɜːr- *street in London:* 'fɜː.mɔɪ US 'fɜːr-
fern (F) fɜːn US fɜːrn **-s** -z
Fernandez fɜː'næn.dez, fə- US fɚ-
Fernando fə'næn.dəʊ US fɚ'næn.doʊ
Ferndale 'fɜːn.deɪl US 'fɜːrn-
Ferndown 'fɜːn.daʊn US 'fɜːrn-
ferner|y 'fɜː.nᵊr|.i US 'fɜːr- **-ies** -iz
Fernhough 'fɜːn.həʊ US 'fɜːrn.hoʊ
Fernihough, Fernyhough 'fɜː.ni.hʌf, -həʊ US 'fɜːr.ni.hʌf, -hoʊ
ferny 'fɜː.ni US 'fɜːr-
ferocious fə'rəʊ.ʃəs, fɪ- US fə'roʊ- **-ly** -li **-ness** -nəs, -nɪs
ferocity fə'rɒs.ə.ti, fɪ-, -ɪ.ti US fə'rɑː.sə.t̬i
-ferous -fᵊr.əs
Note: Suffix. Words containing **-ferous** are normally stressed on the preceding syllable, e.g. **conifer** /'kɒn.ɪ.fəʳ US 'kɑː.nə.fɚ/, **coniferous** /kəʊ'nɪf.ᵊr.əs US koʊ'nɪf-/.
Ferrand 'fer.ᵊnd
Ferranti fə'ræn.ti, fɪ-, fer'æn- US fə'rɑːn.t̬i
Ferrar 'fer.əʳ; fə'rɑːʳ US 'fer.ɚ; fə'rɑːr
Ferrara fə'rɑː.rə, fɪ'-, fer'ɑː- US -'rɑːr.ə
Ferrari® fə'rɑː.ri, fɪ'-, fer'ɑː- US fə'rɑːr.i
Ferraro fə'rɑː.rəʊ, fɪ'-, fer'ɑː- US fə'rɑːr.oʊ
Ferraud fə'rəʊ, fer'əʊ US fə'roʊ
ferrel (F) 'fer.ᵊl **-s** -z
ferreous 'fer.i.əs
Ferrer 'fer.əʳ; fə'reəʳ US 'fer.ɚ; fə'rer **-s** -z
ferre|t (F) 'fer.ɪ|t, -ə|t **-ts** -ts **-ting** -tɪŋ US -t̬ɪŋ **-ted** -tɪd US -t̬ɪd
ferri- 'fer.i-
ferric 'fer.ɪk
Ferrier 'fer.i.əʳ US -ɚ
ferris (F) 'fer.ɪs '**ferris** ˌ**wheel**
Ferrisburg 'fer.ɪs.bɜːg US -bɜːrg
ferrite 'fer.aɪt
ferritic fer'ɪt.ɪk, fə'rɪt- US fə'rɪt̬-, fer'ɪt̬-
ferro- fer.əʊ- US fer.oʊ-
Note: Prefix. Normally carries either primary or secondary stress on the first syllable, e.g. **ferrotype** /'fer.əʊ.taɪp US -oʊ-/, **ferromagnetic** /ˌfer.əʊ.mæg'net.ɪk US -oʊ.mæg'net̬-/.
ferroconcrete ˌfer.əʊ'kɒŋ.kriːt US -oʊ'kɑːn.kriːt
ferromagnetic ˌfer.əʊ.mæg'net.ɪk US -oʊ.mæg'net̬-
ferromagnetism ˌfer.əʊ'mæg.nə.tɪ.zᵊm US -oʊ'-
ferrotype 'fer.əʊ.taɪp US -oʊ- **-s** -s
ferrous 'fer.əs
ferruginous fer'uː.dʒɪ.nəs, fə'ruː-, fɪ-, -dʒᵊn- US fə'ruː.dʒɪ.nəs, fer'uː-
ferrule 'fer.uːl, -ᵊl, -juːl US -ᵊl, -uːl **-s** -z
Note: /'fer.ᵊl/ is the pronunciation used by those connected with the umbrella trade.
ferr|y (F) 'fer|.i **-ies** -iz **-ying** -i.ɪŋ **-ied** -id
ferryboat 'fer.i.bəʊt US -boʊt **-s** -s
Ferryhill 'fer.i.hɪl
ferry|man 'fer.i|.mən, -mæn **-men** -mən, -men
fertile 'fɜː.taɪl US 'fɜːr.t̬ᵊl **-ly** -li
fertility fə'tɪl.ə.ti, fɜː-, -ɪ.ti US fɚ'tɪl.ə.t̬i
fertilization, -isa- ˌfɜː.tɪ.laɪ'zeɪ.ʃᵊn, -tᵊl.aɪ'-, -ɪ'- US ˌfɜːr.t̬ᵊl.ɪ'-
fertiliz|e, -is|e 'fɜː.tɪ.laɪz, -tᵊl.aɪz US 'fɜːr.t̬ə.laɪz **-es** -ɪz **-ing** -ɪŋ **-ed** -d
fertilizer, -ise- 'fɜː.tɪ.laɪ.zəʳ, -tᵊl.aɪ- US 'fɜːr.t̬ᵊl- **-s** -z
ferule 'fer.uːl, -ᵊl, -juːl US -ᵊl, -uːl **-s** -z
fervency 'fɜː.vᵊnt.si US 'fɜːr-
fervent 'fɜː.vᵊnt US 'fɜːr- **-ly** -li **-ness** -nəs, -nɪs

fervid 'fɜː.vɪd Ⓤ 'fɜːr- **-ly** -li **-ness** -nəs, -nɪs
fervo(u)r 'fɜː.vəʳ Ⓤ 'fɜːr.vɚ
fescue 'fes.kjuː **-s** -z
fess|e fes **-es** -ɪz
Fessenden 'fes.ᵊn.dən
festal 'fes.tᵊl **-ly** -i
Feste 'fes.ti Ⓤ -teɪ
fest|er 'fes.t|əʳ Ⓤ -t|ɚ **-ers** -əz Ⓤ -ɚz **-ering** -ᵊr.ɪŋ **-ered** -əd Ⓤ -ɚd
Festiniog fes'tɪn.i.ɒg Ⓤ -ɑːg, -ɔːg
festival 'fes.tɪ.vᵊl, -tə- **-s** -z
festive 'fes.tɪv **-ly** -li **-ness** -nəs, -nɪs
festivit|y fes'tɪv.ə.t|i, -ɪ.t|i Ⓤ -ə.ţ|i **-ies** -iz
festoon fes'tuːn Ⓤ fes'tuːn, fə'stuːn **-s** -z **-ing** -ɪŋ **-ed** -d
festschrift 'fest.ʃrɪft, 'feʃ- **-en** -ən **-s** -s
Festus 'fes.təs
feta 'fet.ə Ⓤ 'feţ- ˌ**feta 'cheese**
fetal 'fiː.tᵊl Ⓤ -ţᵊl **'fetal poˌsition**
fetch fetʃ **-es** -ɪz **-ing** -ɪŋ **-ed** -t **-er/s** -əʳ/z Ⓤ -ɚ/z
fetching 'fetʃ.ɪŋ **-ly** -li
fet|e, fêt|e feɪt Ⓤ feɪt, fet **-es** -s **-ing** -ɪŋ Ⓤ 'feɪ.ţɪŋ, 'feţ.ɪŋ **-ed** -ɪd Ⓤ 'feɪ.ţɪd, 'feţ.ɪd ˌ**garden 'fete** Ⓤ **'garden ˌfete**
fête(s) champêtre(s) ˌfet.ʃɑ̃ːm'pet.rə Ⓤ -ʃɑːm'-
fetich 'fet.ɪʃ Ⓤ 'feţ- **-es** -ɪz
fetich|ism 'fet.ɪ.ʃ|ɪ.zᵊm Ⓤ 'feţ- **-ist/s** -ɪst/s
fetichistic ˌfet.ɪ'ʃɪs.tɪk Ⓤ ˌfeţ- **-ally** -ᵊl.i, -li
fetid 'fet.ɪd, 'fiː.tɪd Ⓤ 'feţ.ɪd, 'fiː.ţɪd **-ly** -li **-ness** -nəs, -nɪs
fetish 'fet.ɪʃ Ⓤ 'feţ- **-es** -ɪz
fetish|ism 'fet.ɪ.ʃ|ɪ.zᵊm Ⓤ 'feţ- **-ist/s** -ɪst/s
fetishistic ˌfet.ɪ'ʃɪs.tɪk Ⓤ ˌfeţ- **-ally** -ᵊl.i, -li
fetlock 'fet.lɒk Ⓤ -lɑːk **-s** -s **-ed** -t
fetolog|y fiː'tɒl.ə.dʒ|i Ⓤ -'tɑː.lə- **-ist/s** -ɪst/s
fetta 'fet.ə Ⓤ 'feţ- ˌ**fetta 'cheese**
fett|er (F) 'fet|.əʳ Ⓤ 'feţ|.ɚ **-ers** -əz Ⓤ -ɚz **-ering** -ᵊr.ɪŋ **-ered** -əd Ⓤ -ɚd
Fettes *place:* 'fet.ɪs Ⓤ 'feţ- *surname:* 'fet.ɪs, -ɪz Ⓤ 'feţ-
Fettesian fet'iː.zi.ən, -ʒᵊn **-s** -z
fettl|e 'fet.ḷ Ⓤ 'feţ- **-es** -z **-ing** -ɪŋ, '-lɪŋ Ⓤ 'feţ.ḷ.ɪŋ, 'fet.lɪŋ **-ed** -d
fettuccine ˌfet.ʊ'tʃiː.ni Ⓤ ˌfeţ.ə'-
fetus 'fiː.təs Ⓤ -ţəs **-es** -ɪz
feu fjuː **-s** -z **-ing** -ɪŋ **-ed** -d
feud fjuːd **-s** -z
feudal 'fjuː.dᵊl **-ly** -i
feudal|ism 'fjuː.dᵊl|ɪ.zᵊm **-ist/s** -ɪst/s
feudality fjuː'dæl.ə.ti, -ɪ.ti Ⓤ -ə.ţi
feudalization, -isa- ˌfjuː.dᵊl.aɪ'zeɪ.ʃᵊn, -ɪ'- Ⓤ -ɪ'-
feudaliz|e, -is|e 'fjuː.dᵊl.aɪz Ⓤ -də.laɪz **-es** -ɪz **-ing** -ɪŋ **-ed** -d
feudatory 'fjuː.də.tᵊr.i, -tri Ⓤ -tɔːr.i
feuilleton 'fɜː.ɪ.tɔ̃ːŋ, 'fɜːl.tɔ̃ːŋ Ⓤ 'fɜː.jə.tɑːn, 'fɜːr-, -tɔ̃ːn **-s** -z
fever 'fiː.vəʳ Ⓤ -vɚ **-s** -z **-ed** -d **'fever ˌblister**; **'fever ˌpitch**
feverfew 'fiː.və.fjuː Ⓤ -vɚ-
feverish 'fiː.vᵊr.ɪʃ **-ly** -li **-ness** -nəs, -nɪs
Feversham 'fev.ə.ʃᵊm Ⓤ '-ɚ-
few (F) fjuː **-er** -əʳ Ⓤ -ɚ **-est** -ɪst, -əst **-ness** -nəs, -nɪs
fey feɪ **-ness** -nəs, -nɪs
Feydeau 'feɪ.dəʊ Ⓤ feɪ'doʊ
Feynman 'faɪn.mən
fez (F) fez **-(z)es** -ɪz
Fezzan fez'ɑːn, -'æn Ⓤ -'æn
Ffestiniog fes'tɪn.i.ɒg Ⓤ -ɑːg, -ɔːg
Ffitch fɪtʃ
Ffoulkes fəʊks, fəʊlks, faʊks, fuːks Ⓤ foʊks, foʊlks, faʊks, fuːks
Ffrangcon 'fræŋ.kᵊn
-fiable -faɪ.ə.bḷ
Note: Suffix. Normally unstressed, e.g. **rectifiable** /'rek.tɪ.faɪ.ə.bḷ Ⓤ -tə-/, although some words containing **-fiable** may also be stressed on the antepenultimate syllable, especially in British English (e.g. **justifiable** /ˌdʒʌs.tɪ'faɪ.ə.bḷ/); see also entry for **-fy**.
fiacre fi'ɑː.krə Ⓤ -kɚ **-s** -z
fiancé(e) fi'ɑ̃ːn.seɪ, -'ɒnt- Ⓤ ˌfiː.ɑːn'seɪ, -'-- **-s** -z
Fianna Fail, Fianna Fáil ˌfiː.ə.nə'fɔɪl, ˌfiː.nə'-, -'fɔːl Ⓤ -'fɔɪl, -'fiːl
fiasco fi'æs.kəʊ Ⓤ -koʊ **-(e)s** -z
fiat *decree:* 'faɪ.æt Ⓤ 'fiː.ət, -æt, -ɑːt **-s** -s
Fiat® fɪət, 'fiː.æt Ⓤ 'fiː.ɑːt **-s** -s
fiat justicia ˌfiː.æt.jʊs'tɪs.i.ə Ⓤ ˌfiː.ɑːt'jʊs.tɪ.ʃə
fib fɪb **-s** -z **-bing** -ɪŋ **-bed** -d **-ber/s** -əʳ/z Ⓤ -ɚ/z
fiber 'faɪ.bəʳ Ⓤ -bɚ **-s** -z
fiberglass 'faɪ.bə.glɑːs Ⓤ -bɚ.glæs
fiberlike 'faɪ.bə.laɪk Ⓤ -bɚ-
Fibonacci ˌfɪb.ə'nɑː.tʃi, ˌfiː.bə'-
fibre 'faɪ.bəʳ Ⓤ -bɚ **-s** -z **-d** -d **-less** -ləs, -lɪs
fibreglass 'faɪ.bə.glɑːs Ⓤ -bɚ.glæs
fibreoptic ˌfaɪ.bəʳ'ɒp.tɪk Ⓤ -bɚ'ɑːp- **-s** -s
fibre optics ˌfaɪ.bəʳ'ɒp.tɪks Ⓤ -bɚ'ɑːp-
fibriform 'faɪ.brɪ.fɔːm, 'fɪb.rɪ- Ⓤ -fɔːrm
fibril 'faɪ.brɪl, -brəl Ⓤ 'faɪ.brɪl, 'fɪb.rɪl **-s** -s **-lar** -əʳ Ⓤ -ɚ **-lose** -əʊs Ⓤ -oʊs
fibril|late 'faɪ.brɪ|.leɪt, 'fɪb.rɪ-, -rə- Ⓤ 'fɪb.rɪ-, 'faɪ.brɪ- **-lates** -leɪts **-lating** -leɪ.tɪŋ Ⓤ -leɪ.ţɪŋ **-lated** -leɪ.tɪd Ⓤ -leɪ.ţɪd
fibrillation ˌfaɪ.brɪ'leɪ.ʃᵊn, ˌfɪb.rɪ'-, -rə'- Ⓤ ˌfɪb.rɪ'-, ˌfaɪ.brɪ'- **-s** -z
fibrilliform faɪ'brɪl.ɪ.fɔːm, fɪ- Ⓤ fɪ'-, faɪ'-, -fɔːrm
fibrin 'fɪb.rɪn, 'faɪ.brɪn Ⓤ 'faɪ- **-ous** -əs
fibrinogen fɪ'brɪn.əʊ.dʒᵊn, faɪ-, -dʒen Ⓤ faɪ'brɪn.ə-
fibro- faɪ.brəʊ-; faɪ'brəʊ- Ⓤ faɪ.broʊ-, -brə-; faɪ'broʊ-
Note: Prefix. Normally carries primary or secondary stress on the first syllable, e.g. **fibrositis** /ˌfaɪ.brəʊ'saɪ.tɪs Ⓤ -broʊ'saɪ.ţɪs/, or primary stress on the second syllable, e.g. **fibrosis** /faɪ'brəʊ.sɪs Ⓤ -'broʊ-/.
fibroid 'faɪ.brɔɪd **-s** -z
fibroma faɪ'brəʊ.mə Ⓤ -'broʊ- **-s** -z **-ta** -tə Ⓤ -ţə
fibrosis faɪ'brəʊ.sɪs Ⓤ -'broʊ-
fibrositis ˌfaɪ.brəʊ'saɪ.tɪs Ⓤ -broʊ'saɪ.ţɪs
fibrous 'faɪ.brəs **-ly** -li **-ness** -nəs, -nɪs
fibul|a 'fɪb.jə.l|ə, -jʊ- Ⓤ -jə- **-as** -əz **-ae** -iː
FICA 'fiː.kə Ⓤ 'faɪ-, 'fiː-
fich|e fiːʃ **-es** -ɪz
fichu 'fiː.ʃuː, 'fɪʃ.uː Ⓤ 'fɪʃ.uː; fiː'ʃuː **-s** -z
fickl|e 'fɪk.ḷ **-er** -əʳ, '-ləʳ Ⓤ '-lɚ, -ḷ.ɚ **-est** -ɪst, -əst **-eness** -nəs, -nɪs
fiction 'fɪk.ʃᵊn **-s** z
fictional 'fɪk.ʃᵊn.ᵊl **-ly** -i
fictionalization ˌfɪk.ʃᵊn.ᵊl.aɪ'zeɪ.ʃᵊn, -ɪ'- Ⓤ -ɪ'-
fictionaliz|e, -is|e 'fɪk.ʃᵊn.ᵊl.aɪz Ⓤ -ə.laɪz **-es** -ɪz **-ing** -ɪŋ **-ed** -d
fictionist 'fɪk.ʃᵊn.ɪst **-s** -s
fictitious fɪk'tɪʃ.əs **-ly** -li **-ness** -nəs, -nɪs
fictive 'fɪk.tɪv
fid fɪd **-s** -z
fiddl|e 'fɪd.ḷ **-es** -z **-ing** -ɪŋ, '-lɪŋ **-ed** -d **-er/s** -əʳ/z, '-ləʳ/z, '-ḷ.ɚ/z Ⓤ '-lɚ/z **as ˌfit as a 'fiddle**
fiddlededee ˌfɪd.ḷ.dɪ'diː Ⓤ -diː'diː
fiddle-faddl|e 'fɪd.ḷˌfæd.ḷ **-es** -z **-ing** -ɪŋ, ˌ-lɪŋ **-ed** -d
fiddlesticks 'fɪd.ḷ.stɪks
fiddl|y 'fɪd.ḷ|.i, 'fɪd.l|i **-ier** -i.əʳ Ⓤ -i.ɚ **-iest** -i.ɪst, -i.əst **-iness** -ɪ.nəs, -ɪ.nɪs
Fidel fɪ'del, fiː-, 'fɪd.el
Fidelia fɪ'diː.li.ə, fə-, -'deɪ- Ⓤ -'diː.li.ə, -'diːl.jə
Fidelio fɪ'deɪ.li.əʊ Ⓤ -oʊ
fidelity fɪ'del.ə.ti, fə-, -ɪ.ti Ⓤ -ə.ţi
fidg|et 'fɪdʒ|.ɪt **-ets** -ɪts **-eting** -ɪ.tɪŋ Ⓤ -ɪ.ţɪŋ **-eted** -ɪ.tɪd Ⓤ -ɪ.ţɪd
fidget|y 'fɪdʒ.ɪ.t|i, '-ə- **-ier** -i.əʳ Ⓤ -i.ɚ **-iest** -i.ɪst, -i.əst **-iness** -ɪ.nəs, -ɪ.nɪs

Fido ˈfaɪ.dəʊ US -doʊ
fiducial fɪˈdjuː.ʃi.əl, fə-, faɪ-, -si- US -ˈduː.ʃᵊl, -ˈdjuː- **-ly** -i
fiduciar|y fɪˈdjuː.ʃi.ə.r|i, fə-, faɪ-, -si-, -ʃᵊr|.i US fɪˈduː.ʃi.er-, -ʃᵊr-, -ˈdjuː- **-ies** -iz
fie faɪ
Fiedler ˈfiːd.ləʳ US -lɚ
fief fiːf **-s** -s
fiefdom ˈfiːf.dəm **-s** -z
field (F) fiːld **-s** -z **-ing** -ɪŋ **-ed** -ɪd **-er/s** -əʳ/z US -ɚ/z **ˈfield ˌglass** ; **ˈfield ˌgoal** ; **ˈfield ˌgun** ; **ˌfield ˈhospital** US **ˈfield ˌhospital** ; **ˌfield ˈmarshal** US **ˈfield ˌmarshal** ; **ˈfield ˌmouse** ; **ˈfield ˌofficer** ; **ˌfield of ˈvision** ; **ˈfield ˌtrip** ; **have a ˈfield ˌday**
Fielden ˈfiːl.dᵊn
Fieldener ˈfiːl.dᵊn.əʳ US -ɚ
fielder (F) ˈfiːl.dəʳ US -dɚ **-s** -z
fieldfare ˈfiːld.feəʳ US -fer **-s** -z
Fielding ˈfiːl.dɪŋ
Fields fiːldz
fields|man ˈfiːldz|.mən **-men** -mən, -men
field-test ˈfiːld.test **-s** -s **-ing** -ɪŋ **-ed** -ɪd
fieldwork ˈfiːld.wɜːk US -wɜːrk **-s** -s **-er/s** -əʳ/z US -ɚ/z
fiend (F) fiːnd **-s** -z
fiendish ˈfiːn.dɪʃ **-ly** -li **-ness** -nəs, -nɪs
Fiennes faɪnz
fierc|e fɪəs US fɪrs **-er** -əʳ US -ɚ **-est** -ɪst, -əst **-ely** -li **-eness** -nəs, -nɪs
fier|y ˈfaɪə.r|i US ˈfaɪ-, ˈfaɪɚ|.i **-ily** -ɪ.li, -ᵊl.i **-iness** -ɪ.nəs, -ɪ.nɪs
fiesta (F®) fiˈes.tə **-s** -z
FIFA ˈfiː.fə
fif|e (F) faɪf **-es** -s **-ing** -ɪŋ **-ed** -t **-er/s** -əʳ/z US -ɚ/z
Fife faɪf **-shire** -ʃəʳ, -ˌʃɪəʳ US -ʃɚ, -ʃɪr
Fifi ˈfiː.fiː
Fifield ˈfaɪ.fiːld
fifteen fɪfˈtiːn **-s** -z **-th/s** -θ/s *stress shift:* ˌfifteen ˈyears
fifth fɪfθ **-s** -s **-ly** -li **ˌFifth Aˈmendment** ; **ˌFifth ˈAvenue**
fifth-column ˌfɪfθˈkɒl.əm US -ˈkɑː.ləm **-ist/s** -ɪst/s, -nɪst/s **-ism** -ɪ.zᵊm, -nɪ.zᵊm
fiftieth ˈfɪf.ti.əθ **-s** -s
fift|y ˈfɪf.t|i **-ies** -iz
fifty-fifty ˌfɪf.tiˈfɪf.ti
fiftyfold ˈfɪf.ti.fəʊld US -foʊld
fig fɪg **-s** -z **ˈfig ˌleaf** ; **ˈfig ˌtree**
Figaro ˈfɪg.ə.rəʊ US -roʊ
Figes ˈfɪg.ɪs
Figg fɪg
Figgis ˈfɪg.ɪs
fight faɪt **-s** -s **-ing** -ɪŋ US ˈfaɪ.t̬ɪŋ **fought** fɔːt US fɑːt, fɔːt **ˈfighting ˌcock**
fighter ˈfaɪ.təʳ US -t̬ɚ **-s** -z

figment ˈfɪg.mənt **-s** -s
Figueroa ˌfɪg.əˈrəʊ.ə US -ˈroʊ-
figurability ˌfɪg.jᵊr.əˈbɪl.ə.ti, -ᵊr-, -jʊ.rəˈ-, -ɪ.ti US -jɚ.əˈbɪl.ə.t̬i, -jʊ.rəˈ-
figurable ˈfɪg.jᵊr.ə.bl̩, -ᵊr-, -jʊ.rə- US -jɚ.ə-, -jʊ.rə-
figurative ˈfɪg.jᵊr.ə.tɪv, -ᵊr-, -jʊ.rə- US -jɚ.ə.t̬ɪv, -jʊ.rə- **-ly** -li **-ness** -nəs, -nɪs
figur|e ˈfɪg.əʳ US -jɚ, -jʊr **-es** -z **-ing** -ɪŋ **-ed** -d **ˌfigure ˈeight** ; **ˌfigure of ˈeight** ; **ˌfigure of ˈspeech** ; **ˈfigure ˌskating**
figurehead ˈfɪg.ə.hed US -jɚ- **-s** -z
figurine ˈfɪg.jə.riːn, ˈ-ə-, -jʊ-, ˌ--ˈ- US ˌfɪg.juːˈriːn, -jəˈ- **-s** -z
Fiji ˈfiː.dʒiː, -ˈ- US ˈ--
Fijian fɪˈdʒiː.ən, fiː- US ˈfiː.dʒiː-, -ˈ-- **-s** -z
filament ˈfɪl.ə.mənt **-s** -s
filamentous ˌfɪl.əˈmen.təs
filari|a fɪˈleə.ri|.ə US -ˈler.i- **-ae** -iː **-al** -əl
filarias|is ˌfɪl.əˈraɪə.s|ɪs; fɪˌleə.riˈeɪ-, fə- US ˌfɪl.əˈraɪ.ə.s|ɪs **-es** -iːz
filature ˈfɪl.ə.tʃəʳ, -tjəʳ US -tʃɚ **-s** -z
filbert ˈfɪl.bət US -bɚt **-s** -s
filch fɪltʃ **-es** -ɪz **-ing** -ɪŋ **-ed** -t
Fildes faɪldz
fil|e faɪl **-es** -z **-ing/s** -ɪŋ/z **-ed** -d **ˈfiling ˌclerk**
filemot ˈfɪl.ɪ.mɒt US -mɑːt
filet ˈfɪl.eɪ, ˈfiː.leɪ US fɪˈleɪ, ˈfɪl.eɪ **-s** -z
filet(s) mignon(s) ˌfɪl.eɪˈmiː.njɔ̃ːŋ, ˌfiː.leɪ-, -ˈmɪn.jɒn US ˌfɪl.eɪ.miːˈnjɑːn, -ˈnjoʊn; fɪˌleɪ-
Filey ˈfaɪ.li
filial ˈfɪl.i.əl **-ly** -i **-ness** -nəs, -nɪs
filiation ˌfɪl.iˈeɪ.ʃᵊn
filibeg ˈfɪl.ɪ.beg, ˈ-ə- **-s** -z
filibust|er ˈfɪl.ɪ.bʌs.t|əʳ, ˈ-ə- US -t|ɚ **-ers** -əz US -ɚz **-ering** -ᵊr.ɪŋ **-ered** -əd US -ɚd
filigree ˈfɪl.ɪ.griː, ˈ-ə- **-s** -z **-ing** -ɪŋ **-d** -d
filing ˈfaɪ.lɪŋ **-s** -z **ˈfiling ˌcabinet**
Filioque ˌfiː.liˈəʊ.kwi, ˌfaɪ-, ˌfɪl.iˈ- US -ˈoʊ-
Filipino ˌfɪl.ɪˈpiː.nəʊ, -əˈ- US -noʊ **-s** -z
Filkin ˈfɪl.kɪn **-s** -z
fill fɪl **-s** -z **-ing/s** -ɪŋ/z **-ed** -d **ˈfilling ˌstation** ; **ˌfill the ˈbill**
filler *thing or person that fills:* ˈfɪl.əʳ US -ɚ **-s** -z
filler, fillér *Hungarian currency:* ˈfiː.leəʳ US ˈfɪl.er, ˈfiː.ler **-s** -z
fill|et ˈfɪl|.ɪt **-ets** -ɪts **-eting** -ɪ.tɪŋ US -ɪ.t̬ɪŋ **-eted** -ɪ.tɪd US -ɪ.t̬ɪd
fillibeg ˈfɪl.ɪ.beg, ˈ-ə- **-s** -z
fillip ˈfɪl.ɪp **-s** -s **-ing** -ɪŋ **-ed** -t
Fillmore ˈfɪl.mɔːʳ US -mɔːr

fill|y ˈfɪl|.i **-ies** -iz
film fɪlm **-s** -z **-ing** -ɪŋ **-ed** -d **ˈfilm ˌstar**
filmgoer ˈfɪlmˌgəʊ.əʳ US -ˌgoʊ.ɚ **-s** -z
filmgoing ˈfɪlmˌgəʊ.ɪŋ US -ˌgoʊ-
filmic ˈfɪl.mɪk
filmmaker ˈfɪlmˌmeɪ.kəʳ US -kɚ **-s** -z
film(s) noir(s) ˌfɪlmˈnwɑː, -ˈnwɑːr
film|set ˈfɪlm|.set **-sets** -sets **-setting** -ˌset.ɪŋ US -ˌset̬.ɪŋ
filmstrip ˈfɪlm.strɪp **-s** -s
film|y ˈfɪl.m|i **-ier** -i.əʳ US -i.ɚ **-iest** -i.ɪst, -i.əst **-ily** -ɪ.li, -ᵊl.i **-iness** -ɪ.nəs, -ɪ.nɪs
filo ˈfaɪ.ləʊ, ˈfiː-, ˈfɪl.əʊ US ˈfiː.loʊ, ˈfaɪ- **ˌfilo ˈpastry** US **ˈfilo ˌpastry**
Filofax® ˈfaɪ.ləʊ.fæks US -loʊ-
Filon ˈfaɪ.lən, -lɒn US ˌfiːˈlɑːn
fils *son:* fiːs
fils *monetary unit:* fɪls
filt|er (*n. v.*) ˈfɪl.t|əʳ US -t̬|ɚ **-ers** -əz US -ɚz **-ering** -ᵊr.ɪŋ **-ered** -əd US -ɚd **ˈfilter ˌcoffee** ; **ˈfilter ˌpaper** ; **ˈfilter ˌtip**
filth fɪlθ
filth|y ˈfɪl.θ|i **-ier** -i.əʳ US -i.ɚ **-iest** -i.ɪst, -i.əst **-ily** -ɪ.li, -ᵊl.i **-iness** -ɪ.nəs, -ɪ.nəs
filtrate (*n.*) ˈfɪl.treɪt **-s** -s
fil|trate (*v.*) fɪl|ˈtreɪt US ˈ-- **-trates** -ˈtreɪts US -treɪts **-trating** -ˈtreɪ.tɪŋ US -treɪ.t̬ɪŋ **-trated** -ˈtreɪ.tɪd US -treɪ.t̬ɪd
filtration fɪlˈtreɪ.ʃᵊn **-s** -z
FIMBRA ˈfɪm.brə
fin fɪn **-s** -z
Fina® ˈfiː.nə, ˈfaɪ-
finable ˈfaɪ.nə.bl̩
finagl|e fɪˈneɪ.gl̩ **-es** -z **-ing** -ɪŋ, ˈ-glɪŋ **-ed** -d **-er/s** -əʳ/z, ˈ-gləʳ/z US ˈ-ɚ/z, ˈ-glɚ/z
final ˈfaɪ.nᵊl **-s** -z **-ly** -i
finale fɪˈnɑː.li, fə-, -leɪ US -ˈnæl.i, -ˈnɑː.leɪ, -li **-s** -z
finalist ˈfaɪ.nᵊl.ɪst **-s** -s
finality faɪˈnæl.ə.ti, -ɪ.ti US faɪˈnæl.ə.t̬i, fə-
finaliz|e, -is|e ˈfaɪ.nᵊl.aɪz US -nə.laɪz **-es** -ɪz **-ing** -ɪŋ **-ed** -d
financ|e ˈfaɪ.nænts; faɪˈnænts, fɪ-, fə- **-es** -ɪz **-ing** -ɪŋ **-ed** -t
financial faɪˈnæn.tʃᵊl, fɪ-, fə- US -ˈnænt.ʃᵊl **-ly** -i **Fiˌnancial ˈTimes**
financier faɪˈnænt.si.əʳ, fɪ-, fə- US fɪˈnænt.si.ɚ, fə-; ˌfɪn.ənˈsɪr, ˌfaɪ.nænˈ-, -nənˈ- **-s** -z
Finbar ˈfɪn.bɑːʳ, ˈfɪm- US ˈfɪn.bɑːr
finch (F) fɪntʃ **-es** -ɪz
Finchale ˈfɪŋ.kᵊl
Fincham ˈfɪn.tʃəm
Finchampsted ˈfɪn.tʃəm.sted, -tʃəmp-, -stɪd
Finchley ˈfɪntʃ.li

find faɪnd **-s** -z **-ing/s** -ɪŋ/z **found** faʊnd **finder/s** ˈfaɪn.dəʳ/z (US) -dɚ/z

fin de siècle ˌfæ̃n.dəˈsjek.l̩, ˌfæn-, -siˈek-, -lə (US) ˌfæ̃n.də.siˈek.lə, -ˈsjek-, -l̩

Findlater ˈfɪnd.lə.təʳ, -leɪ.təʳ (US) -t̬ɚ

Findlay ˈfɪnd.leɪ, -li

Findley ˈfɪnd.li

Findus ˈfɪn.dəs

fin|e faɪn **-es** -z **-er** -əʳ (US) -ɚ **-est** -ɪst, -əst **-eness** -nəs, -nɪs **-ing** -ɪŋ **-ed** -d **ˌfine ˈart**; **ˈfine ˌprint**, **ˌfine ˈprint**

finely ˈfaɪn.li

finery ˈfaɪ.nᵊr.i

fines herbes ˌfiːnˈeəb, -ˈɜːb (US) ˌfiːnˈzerb

finespun ˌfaɪnˈspʌn (US) ˈ-- *stress shift, British only:* ˌfinespun ˈyarn

finess|e (*n. v.*) fɪˈnes, fə- **-es** -ɪz **-ing** -ɪŋ **-ed** -t

fine-tooth ˌfaɪnˈtuːθ **-ed** -t **ˌfine-toothed ˈcomb**

fine-tun|e ˌfaɪnˈtjuːn, -ˈtʃuːn (US) -ˈtuːn, -ˈtjuːn **-es** -z **-ing** -ɪŋ **-ed** -d *stress shift:* ˌfine-tuned ˈinstrument

Fingal ˈfɪŋ.gᵊl **ˌFingal's ˈCave**

Fingall ˈfɪŋ.gɔːl (US) -gɔːl, -gɑːl

fing|er ˈfɪŋ.g|əʳ (US) -g|ɚ **-ers** -əz (US) -ɚz **-ering/s** -ᵊr.ɪŋ/z **-ered** -əd (US) -ɚd **ˈfinger ˌbowl**; **ˈFinger ˌLakes**; **ˌburn one's ˈfingers**; **ˌall ˌfingers and ˈthumbs**; **have a ˌfinger in every ˈpie**; **keep one's ˈfingers ˌcrossed**; **ˌtwist someone round one's ˌlittle ˈfinger**; **ˌwork one's ˌfingers to the ˈbone**

fingerboard ˈfɪŋ.gə.bɔːd (US) -gɚ.bɔːrd **-s** -z

fingermark ˈfɪŋ.gə.mɑːk (US) -gɚ.mɑːrk **-s** -s

fingernail ˈfɪŋ.gə.neɪl (US) -gɚ- **-s** -z

fingerplate ˈfɪŋ.gə.pleɪt (US) -gɚ- **-s** -s

fingerpost ˈfɪŋ.gə.pəʊst (US) -gɚ.poʊst **-s** -s

fingerprint ˈfɪŋ.gə.prɪnt (US) -gɚ- **-s** -s

fingerstall ˈfɪŋ.gə.stɔːl (US) -gɚ.stɔːl, -stɑːl **-s** -z

fingertip ˈfɪŋ.gə.tɪp (US) -gɚ- **-s** -s

Fingest ˈfɪn.dʒɪst

finial ˈfɪn.i.əl, ˈfaɪ.ni- (US) ˈfɪn.i- **-s** -z

finical ˈfɪn.ɪ.kᵊl **-ly** -i **-ness** -nəs, -nəs

finicking ˈfɪn.ɪ.kɪŋ

finick|y ˈfɪn.ɪ.k|i **-ier** -i.əʳ (US) -i.ɚ **-iest** -i.ɪst, -i.əst **-ily** -ɪ.li, -ᵊl.i **-iness** -ɪ.nəs, -ɪ.nɪs

finis ˈfɪn.ɪs, ˈfiː.nɪs (US) ˈfɪn.ɪs; fiːˈniː; ˈfaɪ.nɪs

finish ˈfɪn.ɪʃ **-es** -ɪz **-ing** -ɪŋ **-ed** -t **-er/s** -əʳ/z (US) -ɚ/z **ˈfinishing ˌschool**

Finisterre ˌfɪn.ɪˈsteəʳ, -əˈ-, ˈ--- (US) ˌfɪn.ɪˈster

finite ˈfaɪ.naɪt **-ly** -li **-ness** -nəs, -nɪs

finito fɪˈniː.təʊ, fə- (US) -toʊ

finitude ˈfaɪ.nɪ.tjuːd, ˈfɪn.ɪ-, -tʃuːd (US) ˈfɪn.ɪ.tuːd, -tjuːd

fink fɪŋk **-s** -s **-ing** -ɪŋ **-ed** -t

Finlaison ˈfɪn.lɪ.sᵊn

Finland ˈfɪn.lənd **-er/s** -əʳ/z (US) -ɚ/z

Finlandization, -isa- ˌfɪn.lən.daɪˈzeɪ.ʃᵊn, -dɪˈ- (US) -dɪˈ-

Finlandiz|e, -is|e ˈfɪn.lən.daɪz **-es** -ɪz **-ing** -ɪŋ **-ed** -d

Finlay ˈfɪn.leɪ, -li

Finlayson ˈfɪn.lɪ.sᵊn

Finley ˈfɪn.li

Finn fɪn **-s** -z

Finnan ˈfɪn.ən

Finnegan ˈfɪn.ɪ.gən, ˈ-ə-

Finney ˈfɪn.i

Finnic ˈfɪn.ɪk

Finnie ˈfɪn.i

Finnish ˈfɪn.ɪʃ

Finnon ˈfɪn.ən

Finno-Ugrian ˌfɪn.əʊˈjuː.gri.ən (US) -oʊˈuː-, -ˈjuː-

Finno-Ugric ˌfɪn.əʊˈjuː.grɪk (US) -oʊˈuː-, -ˈjuː-

fino ˈfiː.nəʊ (US) -noʊ **-s** -z

Finsberg ˈfɪnz.bɜːg (US) -bɜːrg

Finsbury ˈfɪnz.bᵊr.i (US) -ˌber-, -bɚ- **ˌFinsbury ˈPark**

Finzi ˈfɪn.zi

Fiona fiˈəʊ.nə (US) -ˈoʊ-

fiord fjɔːd; fiˈɔːd; ˈfiː.ɔːd (US) fjɔːrd; fiˈɔːrd **-s** -z

fiorin ˈfaɪə.rɪn (US) ˈfaɪɚ.ɪn

Fiorino® ˌfiː.ɔːˈriː.nəʊ (US) -noʊ

fioritur|a ˌfjɔː.riˈtjʊə.r|ə, ˌfiː.ə.ri- (US) ˌfjɔː.riːˈtuː.r|ɑː **-e** -eɪ

fir fɜːʳ (US) fɜːr **-s** -z **ˈfir ˌtree**

Firbank ˈfɜː.bæŋk (US) ˈfɜːr-

fir|e faɪəʳ (US) faɪɚ **-es** -z **-ing** -ɪŋ **-ed** -d **-er/s** -əʳ/z (US) -ɚ/z **ˈfire aˌlarm**; **ˈfire briˌgade**; **ˈfire conˌtrol**; **ˈfire deˌpartment**; **ˈfire ˌdrill**; **ˈfire ˌengine**; **ˈfire esˌcape**; **ˈfire exˌtinguisher**; **ˈfire ˌfighter**; **ˈfire ˌhydrant**; **ˈfire ˌiron**; **ˈfire ˌscreen**; **ˌout of the ˌfrying pan ˌinto the ˈfire**

firearm ˈfaɪəʳ.ɑːm (US) ˈfaɪɚ.ɑːrm **-s** -z

fireball ˈfaɪə.bɔːl (US) ˈfaɪɚ.bɔːl, -bɑːl **-s** -z

firebomb ˈfaɪə.bɒm (US) ˈfaɪɚ.bɑːm **-s** -z **-ing** -ɪŋ **-ed** -d

firebox ˈfaɪə.bɒks (US) ˈfaɪɚ.bɑːks **-es** -ɪz

firebrand ˈfaɪə.brænd (US) ˈfaɪɚ- **-s** -z

firebreak ˈfaɪə.breɪk (US) ˈfaɪɚ- **-s** -s

firebrick ˈfaɪə.brɪk (US) ˈfaɪɚ- **-s** -s

firebug ˈfaɪə.bʌg (US) ˈfaɪɚ- **-s** -z

fireclay ˈfaɪə.kleɪ (US) ˈfaɪɚ-

firecracker ˈfaɪəˌkræk.əʳ (US) ˈfaɪɚˌkræk.ɚ **-s** -z

firecrest ˈfaɪə.krest (US) ˈfaɪɚ- **-s** -s

firedamp ˈfaɪə.dæmp (US) ˈfaɪɚ-

firedog ˈfaɪə.dɒg (US) ˈfaɪɚ.dɑːg, -dɔːg **-s** -z

fire-eat|er ˈfaɪəʳˌiː.t|əʳ (US) ˈfaɪɚˌiː.t̬|ɚ **-ers** -əz (US) -ɚz **-ing** -ɪŋ

firefl|y ˈfaɪə.fl|aɪ (US) ˈfaɪɚ- **-ies** -aɪz

fireguard ˈfaɪə.gɑːd (US) ˈfaɪɚ.gɑːrd **-s** -z

firehou|se ˈfaɪə.haʊ|s (US) ˈfaɪɚ- **-ses** -zɪz

fire|light ˈfaɪə|.laɪt (US) ˈfaɪɚ- **-lighter/s** -ˌlaɪ.təʳ/z (US) -ˌlaɪ.t̬ɚ/z

firelock ˈfaɪə.lɒk (US) ˈfaɪɚ.lɑːk **-s** -s

fire|man ˈfaɪə|.mən (US) ˈfaɪɚ- **-men** -mən, -men

fireplac|e ˈfaɪə.pleɪs (US) ˈfaɪɚ- **-es** -ɪz

fireplug ˈfaɪə.plʌg (US) ˈfaɪɚ- **-s** -z

firepower ˈfaɪəˌpaʊəʳ (US) ˈfaɪɚˌpaʊɚ

fireproof ˈfaɪə.pruːf (US) ˈfaɪɚ-

fireship ˈfaɪə.ʃɪp (US) ˈfaɪɚ- **-s** -s

fireside ˈfaɪə.saɪd (US) ˈfaɪɚ- **-s** -z

firestone ˈfaɪə.stəʊn (US) ˈfaɪɚ.stoʊn

firestorm ˈfaɪə.stɔːm (US) ˈfaɪɚ.stɔːrm **-s** -z

firetrap ˈfaɪə.træp (US) ˈfaɪɚ- **-s** -s

firewarden ˈfaɪəˌwɔː.dᵊn (US) ˈfaɪɚˌwɔːr- **-s** -z

firewater ˈfaɪəˌwɔː.təʳ (US) ˈfaɪɚˌwɑː.t̬ɚ, -ˌwɔː-

firewood ˈfaɪə.wʊd (US) ˈfaɪɚ-

firework ˈfaɪə.wɜːk (US) ˈfaɪɚ.wɜːrk **-s** -s

firing ˈfaɪə.rɪŋ (US) ˈfaɪɚ.ɪŋ **ˈfiring ˌline**; **ˈfiring ˌparty**; **ˈfiring ˌsquad**

firkin ˈfɜː.kɪn (US) ˈfɜːr- **-s** -z

firm fɜːm (US) fɜːrm **-s** -z **-er** -əʳ (US) -ɚ **-est** -ɪst, -əst **-ly** -li **-ness** -nəs, -nɪs

firmament ˈfɜː.mə.mənt (US) ˈfɜːr- **-s** -s

firmware ˈfɜːm.weəʳ (US) ˈfɜːrm.wer

Firsby ˈfɜːz.bi (US) ˈfɜːrz-

first ˈfɜːst (US) ˈfɜːrst **-s** -s **-ly** -li **ˌfirst ˈaid**; **ˌfirst ˈbase**; **ˌfirst ˈclass**; **ˌfirst ˈfloor**; **ˌfirst ˈlady**; **ˌFirst ˌWorld ˈWar**

first base ˌfɜːs*t*ˈbeɪs (US) ˌfɜːs*t*-

firstborn ˈfɜːs*t*.bɔːn (US) ˈfɜːrs*t*.bɔːrn

first-degree ˌfɜːs*t*.dɪˈgriː, -dəˈ- (US) ˌfɜːrs*t*.dɪˈ- *stress shift, see compound:* **ˌfirst-degree ˈmurder**

firstfruits ˈfɜːs*t*.fruːts (US) ˈfɜːrs*t*-

firsthand ˌfɜːstˈhænd (US) ˌfɜːrst- *stress shift:* ˌfirsthand acˈcount

firstling ˈfɜːs*t*.lɪŋ (US) ˈfɜːrs*t*- **-s** -z

firstly ˈfɜːs*t*.li (US) ˈfɜːrs*t*-

first-past-the-post ˌfɜːs*t*ˌpɑːs*t*.ðəˈpəʊst (US) ˌfɜːrs*t*ˌpæs*t*.ðəˈpoʊst *stress shift:* ˌfirst-past-the-post ˈsystem

first-rate ˌfɜːs*t*ˈreɪt (US) ˌfɜːrst- *stress shift:* ˌfirst-rate ˈgame

first-time ˌfɜːs*t*ˈtaɪm (US) ˌfɜːrs*t*- *stress shift, see compound:* **ˌfirst-time ˈbuyer**

firth (F) fɜːθ (US) fɜːrθ **-s** -s
fisc fɪsk
fiscal 'fɪs.kᵊl **-s** -z
Fischer 'fɪʃ.əʳ (US) -ɚ
fish (F) fɪʃ **-es** -ɪz **-ing** -ɪŋ **-ed** -t ˌ**fish and 'chips** ; ˌ**fish 'finger** ; '**fishing** ˌ**rod** ; '**fishing** ˌ**tackle** ; '**fish** ˌ**knife** ; '**fish** ˌ**slice** ; '**fish** ˌ**stick** ; **have other** '**fish to** ˌ**fry** ; **like a** ˌ**fish out of 'water** ; **a 'pretty** ˌ**kettle of** ˌ**fish**
fishbone 'fɪʃ.bəʊn (US) -boʊn **-s** -z
fishbowl 'fɪʃ.bəʊl (US) -boʊl **-s** -z
fishcake 'fɪʃ.keɪk **-s** -s
fisher (F) 'fɪʃ.əʳ (US) -ɚ **-s** -z
fisher|man 'fɪʃ.ə|.mən (US) '-ɚ- **-men** -mən, -men
fisher|y 'fɪʃ.ᵊr|.i **-ies** -iz
fisheye 'fɪʃ.aɪ ˌ**fisheye 'lens**
Fishguard 'fɪʃ.gɑːd (US) -gɑːrd
fishhook 'fɪʃ.*h*ʊk (US) -hʊk **-s** -s
Fishkill 'fɪʃ.kɪl
fishmonger 'fɪʃˌmʌŋ.gəʳ (US) -ˌmʌŋ.gɚ, -ˌmɑːŋ- **-s** -z
fish 'n' chips ˌfɪʃ.ᵊn'tʃɪps
fishnet 'fɪʃ.net **-s** -s ˌ**fishnet 'stockings**
fishplate 'fɪʃ.pleɪt **-s** -s
fishpond 'fɪʃ.pɒnd (US) -pɑːnd **-s** -z
fishtail 'fɪʃ.teɪl **-s** -z **-ing** -ɪŋ **-ed** -d
fishtank 'fɪʃ.tæŋk **-s** -s
Fishwick 'fɪʃ.wɪk
fish|wife 'fɪʃ|.waɪf **-wives** -waɪvz
fish|y 'fɪʃ|.i **-ier** -i.əʳ (US) -i.ɚ **-iest** -i.ɪst, -i.əst **-ily** -ɪ.li, -ᵊl.i **-iness** -ɪ.nəs, -ɪ.nɪs
Fisk(e) fɪsk
Fison 'faɪ.sᵊn
fissile 'fɪs.aɪl (US) -ɪl
fission 'fɪʃ.ᵊn (US) 'fɪʃ-, 'fɪʒ- **-s** -z **-al** -ᵊl
fissionable 'fɪʃ.ᵊn.ə.bl̩ (US) 'fɪʃ-, 'fɪʒ-
fissiparous fɪ'sɪp.ᵊr.əs, fə-
fiss|ure 'fɪʃ|.əʳ, -ʊəʳ (US) -ɚ **-ures** -əz (US) -ɚz **-uring** -ᵊr.ɪŋ **-ured** -əd (US) -ɚd
fist fɪst **-s** -s **-ing** -ɪŋ **-ed** -ɪd **-ic** -ɪk
fistfight 'fɪst.faɪt **-s** -s
fistful 'fɪst.fʊl **-s** -z
fisticuffs 'fɪs.tɪ.kʌfs
fistul|a 'fɪs.tjə.l|ə, -tjʊ-, -tʃə-, -tʃʊ- (US) -tjə-, -tʃuː- **-as** -əz **-ae** -iː **-ous** -əs
fit fɪt **-s** -s **-ting/ly** -ɪŋ/li (US) 'fɪt̬.ɪŋ/li **-ted** -ɪd (US) 'fɪt̬.ɪd **-ter/s** -əʳ/z (US) 'fɪt̬.ɚ/z **-test** -ɪst (US) 'fɪt̬.ɪst, -əst **-ly** -li ˌ**fitted 'kitchen** ; '**fitting** ˌ**room** ; **as** ˌ**fit as a 'fiddle**
fitch (F) fɪtʃ **-es** -ɪz
Fitchburg 'fɪtʃ.bɜːg (US) -bɜːrg
fitchew 'fɪtʃ.uː **-s** -z
fitful 'fɪt.fᵊl, -fʊl **-ly** -i **-ness** -nəs, -nɪs
fitment 'fɪt.mənt **-s** -s
fitness 'fɪt.nəs, -nɪs
fitt fɪt **-s** -s
Fitzalan fɪts'æl.ən
Fitzcharles fɪts'tʃɑːlz (US) -'tʃɑːrlz
Fitzclarence fɪts'klær.ən*t*s (US) -'kler-, -'klær-
Fitzgeorge fɪts'dʒɔːdʒ (US) -'dʒɔːrdʒ
Fitzgerald, **FitzGerald** fɪts'dʒer.əld (US) fɪts'dʒer.əld, '---
Fitzgibbon fɪts'gɪb.ən
Fitzhardinge fɪts'hɑː.dɪŋ (US) -'hɑːr-
Fitzharris fɪts'hær.ɪs (US) -'her-, -'hær-
Fitzherbert fɪts'hɜː.bət (US) -'hɜːr.bɚt
Fitzhugh fɪts'hjuː
Fitzjames fɪts'dʒeɪmz
Note: In **James Fitzjames** often /'fɪts.dʒeɪmz/.
Fitzjohn fɪts'dʒɒn (US) -'dʒɑːn
Fitzmaurice fɪts'mɒr.ɪs (US) -'mɑːr-, -'mɔːr-
Fitzpatrick fɪts'pæt.rɪk
Fitzroy *surname:* fɪts'rɔɪ, '-- *square and street in London:* 'fɪts.rɔɪ
Fitzsimmons fɪt*s*'sɪm.ənz
Fitzstephen fɪt*s*'stiː.vᵊn
Fitzwalter fɪts'wɔːl.təʳ, -'wɒl- (US) -'wɔːl.t̬ɚ, -'wɑːl-
Fitzwilliam fɪts'wɪl.jəm, '-i.əm (US) '-jəm
five faɪv **-s** -z **-fold** -fəʊld (US) -foʊld
five-and-dime ˌfaɪv.ᵊnd'daɪm **-s** -z
fivepen|ce 'faɪf.pən*t*|s, 'faɪv- **-ces** -sɪz
fivepenny 'faɪv.pᵊn.i
fiver 'faɪ.vəʳ (US) -vɚ **-s** -z
fix fɪks **-es** -ɪz **-ing** -ɪŋ **-ed** -t **-edness** -ɪd.nəs, -nɪs **-er/s** -əʳ/z (US) -ɚ/z
fixable 'fɪk.sə.bl̩
fixa|te fɪk'seɪ|t (US) '-- **-tes** -ts **-ting** -tɪŋ (US) -t̬ɪŋ **-ted** -tɪd (US) -t̬ɪd
fixation fɪk'seɪ.ʃᵊn **-s** -z
fixative 'fɪk.sə.tɪv (US) -t̬ɪv **-s** -z
fixedly 'fɪk.sɪd.li, -səd-
fixit|y 'fɪk.sə.t|i, -ɪ.t|i (US) -ə.t̬|i **-ies** -iz
fixture 'fɪks.tʃəʳ (US) -tʃɚ **-s** -z
fizz fɪz **-es** -ɪz **-ing** -ɪŋ **-ed** -d **-er/s** -əʳ/z (US) -ɚ/z
fizzl|e 'fɪz.l̩ **-es** -z **-ing** -ɪŋ, '-lɪŋ **-ed** -d
fizz|y 'fɪz|.i **-ier** -i.əʳ (US) -i.ɚ **-iest** -i.ɪst, -i.əst **-iness** -ɪ.nəs, -ɪ.nɪs
fjord fjɔːd; fi'ɔːd; 'fiː.ɔːd (US) fjɔːrd **-s** -z
Fla. (*abbrev. for* **Florida**) 'flɒr.ɪ.də (US) 'flɔːr-, 'flɑːr-
flab flæb
flabbergast 'flæb.ə.gɑːst (US) -ɚ.gæst **-s** -s **-ing** -ɪŋ **-ed** -ɪd
flabb|y 'flæb|.i **-ier** -i.əʳ (US) -i.ɚ **-iest** -i.ɪst, -i.əst **-ily** -ɪ.li, -ᵊl.i **-iness** -ɪ.nəs, -ɪ.nɪs
flaccid 'flæk.sɪd, 'flæs.ɪd **-ly** -li **-ness** -nəs, -nɪs
flaccidity flæk'sɪd.ə.ti, flæs'ɪd-, -ɪ.ti (US) -ə.t̬i
flack (F) flæk **-s** -s
Flackwell 'flæk.wel, -wəl
flag flæg **-s** -z **-ging** -ɪŋ **-ged** -d '**flag** ˌ**day** ; '**flag** ˌ**officer**
flagellant 'flædʒ.ᵊl.ənt, -ɪ.lənt; flə'dʒel.ənt, flædʒ'el- (US) 'flædʒ.ᵊl.ənt, -ɪ.lənt; flə'dʒel.ənt **-s** -s
flagellate (*n, adj*) 'flædʒ.ᵊl.ət, -ɪ.lət, -ɪt, -eɪt (US) 'flædʒ.ᵊl.eɪt, -ɪt; flə'dʒel.ɪt **-s** -s
flagell|ate (*v*) 'flædʒ.ᵊl|.eɪt, '-ɪ- (US) -ə.l|eɪt **-ates** -eɪts **-ating** -eɪ.tɪŋ (US) -eɪ.t̬ɪŋ **-ated** -eɪ.tɪd (US) -eɪ.t̬ɪd **-ator/s** -eɪ.təʳ/z (US) -eɪ.t̬ɚ/z
flagellation ˌflædʒ.ə'leɪ.ʃᵊn, -ɪ'- **-s** -z
flagell|um flə'dʒel|.əm, flædʒ'el- (US) flə'dʒel- **-ums** -əmz **-a** -ə
flageolet ˌflæd.ʒəʊ'let, -'leɪ, '--- (US) ˌflædʒ.ə'let, -'leɪ **-s** -s
Flagg flæg
flag|man 'flæg|.mən, -mæn **-men** -mən, -men
flagon 'flæg.ən **-s** -z
flagpole 'flæg.pəʊl (US) -poʊl **-s** -z
flagrancy 'fleɪ.grən*t*.si
flagrant 'fleɪ.grənt **-ly** -li
flagrante delicto fləˌgræn.teɪ.dɪ'lɪk.təʊ, flægˌræn-, -ti-, -də'-, -deɪ'- (US) fləˌgræn.ti.diː'lɪk.toʊ
flagship 'flæg.ʃɪp **-s** -s
flagstaff 'flæg.stɑːf (US) -stæf **-s** -s
flagstone 'flæg.stəʊn (US) -stoʊn **-s** -z
flag-waving 'flægˌweɪ.vɪŋ
Flaherty 'fleə.ti, 'flɑː.*h*ə.ti, 'flæ.hə.ti (US) 'flæ.ɚ.t̬i, 'flɑː-; 'fler.ə-
flail fleɪl **-s** -z **-ing** -ɪŋ **-ed** -d
flair fleəʳ (US) fler **-s** -z
flak flæk
flak|e fleɪk **-es** -s **-ing** -ɪŋ **-ed** -t ˌ**flake 'white**
flak|y 'fleɪ.k|i **-ily** -ɪ.li, -ᵊl.i **-iness** -ɪ.nəs, -ɪ.nɪs ˌ**flaky 'pastry**
flam flæm **-s** -z
Flambard 'flæm.bɑːd, -bəd (US) -bɑːrd, -bɚd
flambé, **flambe** 'flɑ̃ː*m*.beɪ (US) flɑːm'beɪ **-ed** -d
flambeau (F) 'flæm.bəʊ (US) -boʊ **-s** -z
flambée, **flambee** 'flɑ̃ː*m*.beɪ (US) flɑːm'beɪ **-d** -d
Flamborough 'flæm.bᵊr.ə (US) -oʊ
flamboyance flæm'bɔɪ.ən*t*s
flamboyant flæm'bɔɪ.ənt **-ly** -li
flam|e fleɪm **-es** -z **-ing** -ɪŋ **-ed** -d
flamen 'fleɪ.men **-s** -z
flamenco flə'meŋ.kəʊ (US) -koʊ **-s** -z
flameproof 'fleɪm.pruːf **-s** -s **-ing** -ɪŋ **-ed** -t
flamethrower 'fleɪmˌθrəʊ.əʳ (US) -ˌθroʊ.ɚ **-s** -z
flamingo flə'mɪŋ.gəʊ, flæm'ɪŋ- (US) flə'mɪŋ.goʊ **-(e)s** -z
Flaminius flə'mɪn.i.əs, flæm'ɪn- (US) flə'mɪn-

flammability ˌflæm.əˈbɪl.ə.ti, -ɪ.ti ⓊⓈ -ə.t̬i
flammable ˈflæm.ə.bl̩
Flamstead ˈflæm.stiːd, -stɪd
flan flæn **-s** -z
Flanagan ˈflæn.ə.gᵊn
Flanders ˈflɑːn.dəz ⓊⓈ ˈflæn.dɚz
flang|e flændʒ **-es** -ɪz **-ing** -ɪŋ **-ed** -d
flank flæŋk **-s** -s **-ing** -ɪŋ **-ed** -t **-er/s** -əʳ/z ⓊⓈ -ɚ/z
Flann flæn
flannel ˈflæn.ᵊl **-s** -z **-(l)ing** -ɪŋ **-(l)ed** -d
flannelette, flannelet ˌflæn.ᵊlˈet ⓊⓈ ˌflæn.ᵊlˈet, -əˈlet
flannelly ˈflæn.ᵊl.i
flap flæp **-s** -s **-ping** -ɪŋ **-ped** -t
flapdoodle ˈflæpˌduː.dl̩
flapjack ˈflæp.dʒæk **-s** -s
flapper ˈflæp.əʳ ⓊⓈ -ɚ **-s** -z
flar|e fleəʳ ⓊⓈ fler **-es** -z **-ing/ly** -ɪŋ/li **-ed** -d
flarepa|th ˈfleə.pɑː|θ ⓊⓈ ˈfler.pæ|θ **-ths** -ðz
flare-up ˈfleəʳ.ʌp ⓊⓈ ˈfler- **-s** -s
flash (F) flæʃ **-es** -ɪz **-ing** -ɪŋ **-ed** -t **ˈflash ˌcard** ; **ˈflash ˌpoint** ; **ˌflash in the ˈpan** ; **ˌquick as a ˈflash**
flashback ˈflæʃ.bæk **-s** -s
flashbulb ˈflæʃ.bʌlb **-s** -z
flasher ˈflæʃ.əʳ ⓊⓈ -ɚ **-s** -z
flashgun ˈflæʃ.gʌn **-s** -z
flashlight ˈflæʃ.laɪt **-s** -s
Flashman ˈflæʃ.mən
flash|y ˈflæʃ|.i **-ier** -i.əʳ ⓊⓈ -i.ɚ **-iest** -i.ɪst, -i.əst **-ily** -ɪ.li, -ᵊl.i **-iness** -ɪ.nəs, -ɪ.nɪs
flask flɑːsk ⓊⓈ flæsk **-s** -s
flat flæt **-s** -s **-ter** -əʳ ⓊⓈ ˈflæt̬.ɚ **-test** -ɪst, -əst ⓊⓈ ˈflæt̬.ɪst, -əst **-ly** -li **-ness** -nəs, -nɪs
Flatbush ˈflæt.bʊʃ
flat-chested ˌflætˈtʃes.tɪd **-ness** -nəs, -nɪs *stress shift:* ˌflat-chested ˈwaif
flatfish ˈflæt.fɪʃ **-es** -ɪz
flatfoot ˈflæt.fʊt
flat-footed ˌflætˈfʊt.ɪd ⓊⓈ -ˈfʊt̬-, ˈ--- **-ly** -li **-ness** -nəs, -nɪs *stress shift, British only:* ˌflat-footed ˈperson
Flathead ˈflæt.hed **-s** -z
flatiron ˈflætˌaɪən ⓊⓈ ˈflætˌaɪɚn **-s** -z
Flatland ˈflæt.lænd
flatlet ˈflæt.lət, -lɪt **-s** -s
flatmate ˈflæt.meɪt **-s** -s
flat-out ˌflætˈaʊt ⓊⓈ ˌflæt- *stress shift:* ˌflat-out ˈdash
flatten ˈflæt.ᵊn **-s** -z **-ing** -ɪŋ **-ed** -d
flatt|er ˈflæt|.əʳ ⓊⓈ ˈflæt̬|.ɚ **-ers** -əz, -ɚz **-ering/ly** -ᵊr.ɪŋ/li **-ered** -əd, -ɚd **-erer/s** -ᵊr.əʳ/z ⓊⓈ -ɚ.ɚ/z
flatter|y ˈflæt.ᵊr|.i ⓊⓈ ˈflæt̬- **-ies** -iz
flatties ˈflæt.iz ⓊⓈ ˈflæt̬-
flattish ˈflæt.ɪʃ ⓊⓈ ˈflæt̬-
flattop ˈflæt.tɒp ⓊⓈ -tɑːp **-s** -s
flatulen|ce ˈflæt.jə.lənt|s, -jʊ-, ˈflætʃ.ə- ⓊⓈ ˈflætʃ.ə- **-cy** -si
flatulent ˈflæt.jə.lənt, -jʊ-, ˈflætʃ.ə-, ˈ-ʊ- ⓊⓈ ˈflætʃ.ə- **-ly** -li
flatus ˈfleɪ.təs ⓊⓈ -t̬əs **-es** -ɪz
flatware ˈflæt.weəʳ ⓊⓈ -wer
flat|ways ˈflæt|.weɪz **-wise** -waɪz
flatworm ˈflæt.wɜːm ⓊⓈ -wɜːrm **-s** -z
Flaubert ˈfləʊ.beəʳ ⓊⓈ ˈfloʊ.ber, -ˈ-
flaun|t flɔːn|t ⓊⓈ flɑːn|t, flɔːn|t **-ts** -ts **-ting/ly** -tɪŋ/li ⓊⓈ -t̬ɪŋ/li **-ted** -tɪd ⓊⓈ -t̬ɪd
flautist ˈflɔː.tɪst ⓊⓈ ˈflɑː.t̬ɪst, ˈflɔː-, ˈflaʊ- **-s** -s
Flavel ˈflæv.ᵊl, ˈfleɪ.vᵊl
Flavell fləˈvel, ˈfleɪ.vᵊl
Flavi|a ˈfleɪ.vi|.ə **-an** -ən
flavin ˈfleɪ.vɪn, ˈflæv.ɪn ⓊⓈ ˈfleɪ.vɪn **-s** -z
flavin(e) ˈfleɪ.viːn, ˈflæv.iːn, -ɪn ⓊⓈ ˈfleɪ.viːn
Flavius ˈfleɪ.vi.əs
flav|or ˈfleɪ.v|əʳ ⓊⓈ -v|ɚ **-ors** -əz ⓊⓈ -ɚz **-oring/s** -ᵊr.ɪŋ/z **-ored** -əd ⓊⓈ -ɚd **ˌflavor of the ˈmonth**
flavorful ˈfleɪ.və.fᵊl, -fʊl ⓊⓈ -vɚ-
flavoring ˈfleɪ.vᵊr.ɪŋ
flavorless ˈfleɪ.və.ləs, -lɪs ⓊⓈ -vɚ- **-ness** -nəs, -nɪs
flavorous ˈfleɪ.vᵊr.əs
flavorsome ˈfleɪ.və.səm ⓊⓈ -vɚ-
flav|our (*n. v.*) ˈfleɪ.v|əʳ ⓊⓈ -v|ɚ **-ours** -əz ⓊⓈ -ɚz **-ouring/s** -ᵊr.ɪŋ/z **-oured** -əd ⓊⓈ -ɚd **ˌflavour of the ˈmonth**
flavourful ˈfleɪ.və.fᵊl, -fʊl ⓊⓈ -vɚ-
flavouring ˈfleɪ.vᵊr.ɪŋ **-s** -z
flavourless ˈfleɪ.və.ləs, -lɪs ⓊⓈ -vɚ- **-ness** -nəs, -nɪs
flavoursome ˈfleɪ.və.səm ⓊⓈ -vɚ-
flaw flɔː ⓊⓈ flɑː, flɔː **-s** -z **-ing** -ɪŋ **-ed** -d
flawless ˈflɔː.ləs, -lɪs ⓊⓈ ˈflɑː-, ˈflɔː- **-ly** -li **-ness** -nəs, -nɪs
flax flæks **-en** -ᵊn
Flaxman ˈflæks.mən
flay fleɪ **-s** -z **-ing** -ɪŋ **-ed** -d **-er/s** -əʳ/z ⓊⓈ -ɚ/z
flea fliː **-s** -z **ˈflea ˌmarket**
fleabag ˈfliː.bæg **-s** -z
fleabane ˈfliː.beɪn
flea|bite ˈfliː|.baɪt **-bites** -baɪts **-bitten** -bɪt.ᵊn ⓊⓈ -bɪt̬-
fleadh flɑː
fleam fliːm **-s** -z
fleapit ˈfliː.pɪt **-s** -s
flèch|e, flech|e fleɪʃ, fleʃ **-es** -ɪz
fleck flek **-s** -s **-ing** -ɪŋ **-ed** -t
Flecker ˈflek.əʳ ⓊⓈ -ɚ
Flecknoe ˈflek.nəʊ ⓊⓈ -noʊ
flection ˈflek.ʃᵊn **-s** -z
flectional ˈflek.ʃᵊn.ᵊl
fled (*from* **flee**) fled
fledg|e fledʒ **-es** -ɪz **-ing** -ɪŋ **-ed** -d
fledg(e)ling ˈfledʒ.lɪŋ **-s** -z
flee fliː **-s** -z **-ing** -ɪŋ **fled** fled
fleec|e fliːs **-es** -ɪz **-ing** -ɪŋ **-ed** -t
fleec|y ˈfliː.s|i **-ier** -i.əʳ ⓊⓈ -i.ɚ **-iest** -i.ɪst, -i.əst **-iness** -ɪ.nəs, -ɪ.nɪs
fleer flɪəʳ ⓊⓈ flɪr **-s** -z **-ing** -ɪŋ **-ed** -d
fleet (F) fliːt **-s** -s **-er** -əʳ ⓊⓈ ˈfliː.t̬ɚ **-est** -ɪst, -əst ⓊⓈ ˈfliː.t̬ɪst, -t̬əst **-ly** -li **-ness** -nəs, -nɪs **-ing** -ɪŋ ⓊⓈ ˈfliː.t̬ɪŋ **-ed** -ɪd ⓊⓈ ˈfliː.t̬ɪd **ˈFleet ˌStreet**
fleeting ˈfliː.tɪŋ ⓊⓈ -t̬ɪŋ **-ly** -li
Fleetwood ˈfliːt.wʊd
Fleming ˈflem.ɪŋ **-s** -z
Flemings ˈflem.ɪŋz
Flemington ˈflem.ɪŋ.tən
Flemish ˈflem.ɪʃ
Flemming ˈflem.ɪŋ
flens|e flenz, flen*t*s ⓊⓈ flen*t*s **-es** -ɪz **-ing** -ɪŋ **-ed** -d
flesh fleʃ **-es** -ɪz **-ing/s** -ɪŋ/z **-ed** -t **ˌflesh and ˈblood** ; **ˈflesh ˌwound** ; **ˌmake someone's ˈflesh ˌcreep**
fleshless ˈfleʃ.ləs, -lɪs
freshl|y ˈfleʃ.l|i **-iness** -ɪ.nəs, -ɪ.nɪs
fleshpot ˈfleʃ.pɒt ⓊⓈ -pɑːt **-s** -s
flesh|y ˈfleʃ|.i **-iness** -ɪ.nəs, -ɪ.nɪs
fletcher (F) ˈfletʃ.əʳ ⓊⓈ -ɚ **-s** -z
Flete fliːt
fletton (F) ˈflet.ᵊn ⓊⓈ ˈflet̬-
fleur-de-lis ˌflɜː.dəˈliː, -liːs ⓊⓈ ˌflɜːr-, flʊr-
fleuron ˈflʊə.rɒn, ˈflɜː-, -rən ⓊⓈ ˈflɜːr.ɑːn, ˈflʊr- **-s** -z
flew (*from* **fly**) fluː
flex fleks **-es** -ɪz **-ing** -ɪŋ **-ed** -t
flexibility ˌflek.sɪˈbɪl.ə.ti, -səˈ-, -ɪ.ti ⓊⓈ -ə.t̬i
flexib|le ˈflek.sɪ.b|l̩, -sə- **-ly** -li **-leness** -l̩.nəs, -nɪs
flexion ˈflek.ʃᵊn **-s** -z
flexitime ˈflek.si.taɪm
flexor ˈflek.səʳ ⓊⓈ -sɚ, -sɔːr **-s** -z
flextime ˈfleks.taɪm
flexure ˈflek.ʃəʳ ⓊⓈ -ʃɚ **-s** -z
flibbertigibbet ˌflɪb.ə.tiˈdʒɪb.ɪt, -ət ⓊⓈ ˈflɪb.ɚ.t̬iˌdʒɪb- **-s** -s
flick flɪk **-s** -s **-ing** -ɪŋ **-ed** -t
flick|er ˈflɪk|.əʳ ⓊⓈ -ɚ **-ers** -əz ⓊⓈ -ɚz **-ering** -ᵊr.ɪŋ **-ered** -əd ⓊⓈ -ɚd
flick-kni|fe ˈflɪk.naɪ|f **-ves** -vz
flier ˈflaɪ.əʳ ⓊⓈ -ɚ **-s** -z
flight (F) flaɪt **-s** -s **-less** -ləs, -lɪs **ˈflight atˌtendant** ; **ˈflight ˌdeck** ; **ˈflight ˌpath**
flight|y ˈflaɪ.t|i ⓊⓈ -t̬|i **-ier** -i.əʳ ⓊⓈ -i.ɚ **-iest** -i.ɪst, -i.əst **-ily** -ɪ.li, -ᵊl.i **-iness** -ɪ.nəs, -ɪ.nɪs

flimflam 'flɪm.flæm **-s** -z **-ming** -ɪŋ **-med** -d

flims|y 'flɪm.z|i **-ier** -i.əʳ (US) -i.ɚ **-iest** -i.ɪst, -i.əst **-ily** -ɪ.li, -əl.i **-iness** -ɪ.nəs, -ɪ.nɪs

flinch flɪntʃ **-es** -ɪz **-ing/ly** -ɪŋ/li **-ed** -t **-er/s** -əʳ/z (US) -ɚ/z

flinders (F) 'flɪn.dəz (US) -dɚz

fling flɪŋ **-s** -z **-ing** -ɪŋ **flung** flʌŋ

flint flɪnt **-s** -s **'flint ˌglass**

Flint flɪnt **-shire** -ʃəʳ, -ˌʃɪəʳ (US) -ʃɚ, -ˌʃɪr

flintlock 'flɪnt.lɒk (US) -lɑːk **-s** -s

Flintshire 'flɪnt.ʃəʳ, -ˌʃɪəʳ (US) -ʃɚ, -ˌʃɪr

flintstone (F) 'flɪnt.stəʊn (US) -stoʊn **-s** -z

flint|y 'flɪn.t|i (US) -ţ|i **-ier** -i.əʳ (US) -i.ɚ **-iest** -i.ɪst, -i.əst **-ily** -ɪ.li, -əl.i **-iness** -ɪ.nəs, -ɪ.nɪs

flip flɪp **-s** -s **-ping** -ɪŋ **-ped** -t **'flip ˌside**

flip-flap 'flɪp.flæp **-s** -s **-ping** -ɪŋ **-ped** -t

flip-flop 'flɪp.flɒp (US) -flɑːp **-s** -s **-ping** -ɪŋ **-ped** -t

flippancy 'flɪp.ənt.si

flippant 'flɪp.ənt **-ly** -li **-ness** -nəs, -nɪs

flipper 'flɪp.əʳ (US) -ɚ **-s** -z

flirt flɜːt (US) flɜːrt **-s** -s **-ing/ly** -ɪŋ/li (US) 'flɜːr.ţɪŋ/li **-ed** -ɪd (US) 'flɜːr.ţɪd

flirtation flɜː'teɪ.ʃən (US) flɜːr- **-s** -z

flirtatious flɜː'teɪ.ʃəs (US) flɜːr- **-ly** -li **-ness** -nəs, -nɪs

flirty 'flɜː.ti (US) 'flɜːr.ţi

flit flɪt **-s** -s **-ting** -ɪŋ (US) 'flɪţ.ɪŋ **-ted** -ɪd (US) 'flɪţ.ɪd

flitch (F) flɪtʃ **-es** -ɪz

flitt|er 'flɪt|.əʳ (US) 'flɪţ|.ɚ **-ers** -əz (US) -ɚz **-ering** -ər.ɪŋ **-ered** -əd (US) -ɚd

Flitwick 'flɪt.ɪk (US) 'flɪţ-

flivver 'flɪv.əʳ (US) -ɚ **-s** -z

Flixton 'flɪk.stən

float fləʊt (US) floʊt **-s** -s **-ing** -ɪŋ (US) 'floʊ.ţɪŋ **-ed** -ɪd (US) 'floʊ.ţɪd **-er/s** -əʳ/z (US) 'floʊ.ţɚ/z **-age** -ɪdʒ (US) 'floʊ.ţɪdʒ **ˌfloating 'bridge** ; **ˌfloating 'dock**

floatation fləʊ'teɪ.ʃən (US) floʊ-

floatplane 'fləʊt.pleɪn (US) 'floʊt- **-s** -z

floccu|late 'flɒk.jə|.leɪt, -jʊ- (US) 'flɑː.kjuː-, -kjə- **-lates** -leɪts **-lating** -leɪ.tɪŋ (US) -leɪ.ţɪŋ **-lated** -leɪ.tɪd (US) -leɪ.ţɪd

flocculent 'flɒk.jə.lənt, -jʊ- (US) 'flɑː.kjuː-, -kjə-

flock flɒk (US) flɑːk **-s** -s **-ing** -ɪŋ **-ed** -t

Flockton 'flɒk.tən (US) 'flɑːk-

Flodden 'flɒd.ən (US) 'flɑː.dən

floe fləʊ (US) floʊ **-s** -z

Floella fləʊ'el.ə (US) floʊ-

flog flɒg (US) flɑːg, flɔːg **-s** -z **-ging/s** -ɪŋ/z **-ged** -d

Flo-Jo 'fləʊ.dʒəʊ (US) 'floʊ.dʒoʊ

flood (F) flʌd **-s** -z **-ing** -ɪŋ **-ed** -ɪd **ˌflood 'tide**

floodgate 'flʌd.geɪt **-s** -s

flood|light 'flʌd|.laɪt **-lights** -laɪts **-lighting** -laɪ.tɪŋ (US) -laɪ.ţɪŋ **-lit** -lɪt

floodwater 'flʌdˌwɔː.təʳ (US) -ˌwɑː.ţɚ, -ˌwɔː- **-s** -z

Flook flʊk, fluːk

floor flɔːʳ (US) flɔːr **-s** -z **-ing** -ɪŋ **-ed** -d **-er/s** -əʳ/z (US) -ɚ/z **'floor ˌcloth** ; **'floor ˌplan** ; **'floor ˌshow**

floorboard 'flɔː.bɔːd (US) 'flɔːr.bɔːrd **-s** -z

floorwalker 'flɔːˌwɔː.kəʳ (US) 'flɔːrˌwɔː.kɚ, -ˌwɑː- **-s** -z

floosie 'fluː.zi **-s** -z

flooz|y, flooz|ie 'fluː.z|i **-ys** -iz **-ies** -iz

flop flɒp (US) flɑːp **-s** -s **-ping** -ɪŋ **-ped** -t

flophou|se 'flɒp.haʊ|s (US) 'flɑːp- **-ses** -zɪz

flopp|y 'flɒp|.i (US) 'flɑː.p|i **-ier** -i.əʳ (US) -i.ɚ **-iest** -i.ɪst, -i.əst **-ily** -ɪ.li, -əl.i **-iness** -ɪ.nəs, -ɪ.nɪs **ˌfloppy 'disk**

Flopsy 'flɒp.si (US) 'flɑːp-

floptical 'flɒp.tɪ.kəl (US) 'flɑːp- **ˌfloptical 'disk**

flor|a (F) 'flɔː.r|ə (US) 'flɔːr|.ə, 'floʊ.r|ə **-as** -əz **-ae** -iː

floral 'flɔː.rəl, 'flɒr.əl (US) 'flɔːr-, 'floʊ.rəl

Florence 'flɒr.ənts (US) 'flɔːr-

florentine (F) 'flɒr.ən.taɪn, -tiːn (US) 'flɔːr- **-s** -z

Flores 'flɔː.rɪz (US) 'flɔːr.es, -ɪz

florescen|ce flɔː'res.ən|ts, flɒr'es-, flə'res- (US) flɔː'res-, flə-, floʊ- **-t** -t

floret 'flɒr.ɪt, 'flɔː.rɪt, -ret (US) 'flɔːr.ɪt-, 'floʊ.rɪt **-s** -s

Florian 'flɔː.ri.ən (US) 'flɔːr.i-

flori|ate 'flɔː.ri|.eɪt (US) 'flɔːr.i-, 'floʊ.ri- **-ates** -eɪts **-ating** -eɪ.tɪŋ (US) -eɪ.ţɪŋ **-ated** -eɪ.tɪd (US) -eɪ.ţɪd

floribunda ˌflɒr.ɪ'bʌn.də, ˌflɔː.rɪ'- (US) ˌflɔːr.ɪ'-, ˌfloʊ.rɪ'-

floricultur|al ˌflɔː.rɪ'kʌl.tʃər|.əl, ˌflɒr.ɪ'-, -tʃʊ.r|əl (US) ˌflɔːr.ɪ'kʌl.tʃɚ|.əl, ˌfloʊ.rɪ'- **-ist/s** -ɪst/s

floriculture 'flɔː.rɪ.kʌl.tʃəʳ, 'flɒr.ɪ- (US) 'flɔːr.ɪ.kʌl.tʃɚ, 'floʊ.rɪ-

florid 'flɒr.ɪd (US) 'flɔːr- **-est** -ɪst, -əst **-ly** -li **-ness** -nəs, -nɪs

Florida 'flɒr.ɪ.də (US) 'flɔːr-, 'flɑːr- **ˌFlorida 'Keys**

Floridian flɒr'ɪd.i.ən, flə'rɪd- (US) flɔː'rɪd-, flɑː'- **-s** -z

floridity flɒr'ɪd.ə.ti, flə'rɪd-, flɔː-, -ɪ.ti (US) flɔː'rɪd.ə.ţi

floriferous flɔː'rɪf.ər.əs, flɒr'ɪf-, flə'rɪf- (US) flɔː'rɪf-, floʊ'-

florin 'flɒr.ɪn (US) 'flɔːr- **-s** -z

Florinda flɔː'rɪn.də, flɒr'ɪn-, flə'rɪn- (US) flɔː'rɪn-, floʊ-

Florio 'flɔː.ri.əʊ (US) 'flɔːr.i.oʊ

florist 'flɒr.ɪst, 'flɔː.rɪst (US) 'flɔːr.ɪst, 'floʊ.rɪst **-s** -s

floristry 'flɒr.ɪ.stri, 'flɔː.rɪ- (US) 'flɔːr.ɪ-, 'floʊ.rɪ-

Florrie 'flɒr.i (US) 'flɔːr-

floruit 'flɔː.ru.ɪt, 'flɒr.u- (US) 'flɔːr.ju-, 'floʊr-

floss (F) flɒs (US) flɑːs **-y** -i **-es** -ɪz **-ing** -ɪŋ **-ed** -t

Flossie 'flɒs.i (US) 'flɑː.si

flotage 'fləʊ.tɪdʒ (US) 'floʊ.ţɪdʒ

flotation fləʊ'teɪ.ʃən (US) floʊ- **-s** -z

flotilla fləʊ'tɪl.ə (US) floʊ- **-s** -z

flotsam 'flɒt.səm (US) 'flɑːt- **ˌflotsam and 'jetsam**

Flotta 'flɒt.ə (US) 'flɑː.ţə

flounc|e flaʊnts **-es** -ɪz **-ing** -ɪŋ **-ed** -t

flouncy 'flaʊnt.si

flound|er 'flaʊn.d|əʳ (US) -d|ɚ **-ers** -əz (US) -ɚz **-ering** -ər.ɪŋ **-ered** -əd (US) -ɚd

flour flaʊəʳ (US) flaʊɚ **-s** -z **-ing** -ɪŋ **-ed** -d

flourish 'flʌr.ɪʃ (US) 'flɜːr.ɪʃ **-es** -ɪz **-ing/ly** -ɪŋ/li **-ed** -t

floury 'flaʊə.ri (US) 'flaʊə.ri

flout flaʊt **-s** -s **-ing** -ɪŋ (US) 'flaʊ.ţɪŋ **-ed** -ɪd (US) 'flaʊ.ţɪd

flow fləʊ (US) floʊ **-s** -z **-ing/ly** -ɪŋ/li **-ingness** -ɪŋ.nəs, -nɪs **-ed** -d **'flow ˌchart** ; **'flow ˌdiagram**

flower (F) flaʊəʳ (US) flaʊɚ **-s** -z **-ing** -ɪŋ **-ed** -d **-er/s** -əʳ/z (US) -ɚ/z **'flower ˌchild** ; **'flower ˌgarden** ; **'flower ˌgirl** ; **'flower ˌpower**

flowerbed 'flaʊə.bed (US) 'flaʊɚ- **-s** -z

floweret 'flaʊə.rɪt, -ret (US) 'flaʊɚ.ɪt, -et **-s** -s

flowerless 'flaʊə.ləs, -lɪs (US) 'flaʊɚ-

flowerpot 'flaʊə.pɒt (US) 'flaʊɚ.pɑːt **-s** -s

flowery 'flaʊə.ri

flown (*from* **fly**) fləʊn (US) floʊn

Floyd flɔɪd

Floyder 'flɔɪ.dəʳ (US) -dɚ

fl oz (*abbrev. for* **fluid ounce**) *singular:* ˌfluː.ɪd'aʊnts *plural:* -'aʊnt.sɪz

flu, 'flu fluː

flub flʌb **-s** -z **-bing** -ɪŋ **-bed** -d

fluctuant 'flʌk.tʃu.ənt, -tju- (US) -tʃu-, -tʃə.wənt

fluctu|ate 'flʌk.tʃu|.eɪt, -tju- (US) -tʃu-, -tʃə.w|eɪt **-ates** -eɪts **-ating** -eɪ.tɪŋ (US) -eɪ.ţɪŋ **-ated** -eɪ.tɪd (US) -eɪ.ţɪd

fluctuation ˌflʌk.tʃu'eɪ.ʃən, -tju'- (US) -tʃu-, -tʃə'weɪ- **-s** -z

Flud(d) flʌd

Fludyer 'flʌd.jəʳ, -i.əʳ (US) 'flʌd.jɚ

flue fluː **-s** -z **'flue ˌpipe**

Fluellen flu'el.ɪn, -ən

fluency 'fluː.ənt.si

fluent 'fluː.ənt **-ly** -li **-ness** -nəs, -nɪs
fluff flʌf **-s** -s **-ing** -ɪŋ **-ed** -t
fluff|y 'flʌf|.i **-ier** -i.əʳ ⓤⓢ -i.ɚ **-iest** -i.ɪst, -i.əst **-iness** -ɪ.nəs, -ɪ.nɪs
flugelhorn, **flügelhorn** 'fluː.gᵊl.hɔːn ⓤⓢ -hɔːrn **-s** -z
fluid 'fluː.ɪd **-s** -z ˌ**fluid** '**ounce**
fluidity flu'ɪd.ə.ti, -ɪ.ti ⓤⓢ -ə.t̬i
fluidization, **-isa-** ˌfluː.ɪ.daɪ'zeɪ.ʃᵊn, -dɪ'- ⓤⓢ -dɪ'-
fluidiz|e, **-is|e** 'fluː.ɪ.daɪz **-es** -ɪz **-ing** -ɪŋ **-ed** -d **-er/s** -əʳ/z ⓤⓢ -ɚ/z
fluk|e fluːk **-es** -s **-ing** -ɪŋ **-ed** -t **-er/s** -əʳ/z ⓤⓢ -ɚ/z **-ish** -ɪʃ
fluk|y, **fluk|ey** 'fluː.k|i **-ier** -i.əʳ ⓤⓢ -i.ɚ **-iest** -i.ɪst, -i.əst **-iness** -ɪ.nəs, -ɪ.nɪs
flume fluːm **-s** -z
flummery 'flʌm.ᵊr.i
flummox 'flʌm.əks **-es** -ɪz **-ing** -ɪŋ **-ed** -t
flung (*from* **fling**) flʌŋ
flunk flʌŋk **-s** -s **-ing** -ɪŋ **-ed** -t
flunkey 'flʌŋ.ki **-s** -z **-ism** -ɪ.zᵊm
flunk|y 'flʌŋ.k|i **-ys** -iz **-ies** -iz **-yism** -i.ɪ.zᵊm
fluor 'fluː.ɔːʳ, -əʳ ⓤⓢ -ɔːr, -ɚ
fluorescence flɔː'res.ᵊnts, flʊə-, flə-; ⓤⓢ flɔː-, flʊ-, fluː-, floʊ-
fluorescent flɔː'res.ᵊnt, flʊə-, flə- ⓤⓢ flɔː-, flʊ-, fluː-, floʊ-
fluoric flu'ɒr.ɪk ⓤⓢ -'ɔːr-
fluori|date 'flɔː.rɪ|.deɪt, 'flʊə-, -rə- ⓤⓢ 'flɔːr.ə-, 'flʊr- **-dates** -deɪts **-dating** -deɪ.tɪŋ ⓤⓢ -deɪ.t̬ɪŋ **-dated** -deɪ.tɪd ⓤⓢ -deɪ.t̬ɪd
fluoridation ˌflɔː.rɪ'deɪ.ʃᵊn, ˌflʊə-, -raɪ'-, -rə'- ⓤⓢ ˌflɔːr.ə'-, ˌflʊr.ə'-
fluoride 'flɔː.raɪd, 'flʊə- ⓤⓢ 'flɔːr.aɪd, 'flʊr- **-s** -z
fluoridization, **-isa-** ˌflɔː.rɪ.daɪ'zeɪ.ʃᵊn, ˌflʊə-, -raɪ-, -dɪ'- ⓤⓢ ˌflɔːr.ə.dɪ'-, ˌflʊr-
fluoridiz|e, **-is|e-** 'flɔː.rɪ.daɪz, 'flʊə- ⓤⓢ 'flɔːr.ə-, 'flʊr- **-es** -ɪz **-ing** -ɪŋ **-ed** -d
fluori|nate 'flɔː.rɪ|.neɪt, 'flʊə-, 'flɒr.ɪ-, '-ə- ⓤⓢ 'flɔːr.ə-, 'flʊr- **-nates** -neɪts **-nating** -neɪ.tɪŋ ⓤⓢ -neɪ.t̬ɪŋ **-nated** -neɪ.tɪd ⓤⓢ -neɪ.t̬ɪd
fluorination ˌflɔː.rɪ'neɪ.ʃᵊn, ˌflʊə-, ˌflɒr.ɪ'-, -ə'- ⓤⓢ ˌflɔːr.ə'-, ˌflʊr-
fluorine 'flɔː.riːn, 'flʊə- ⓤⓢ 'flɔːr.iːn, 'flʊr-, -ɪn
fluorisis flɔː'raɪ.sɪs, flʊə-, flə- ⓤⓢ flɔː-, flʊ-
fluorite 'flɔː.raɪt, 'flʊə- ⓤⓢ 'flɔːr.aɪt, 'flʊr-
fluoro- flɔː.rəʊ-, flʊə-; flɔː'rɒ-, flʊə-, flə-, 'rəʊ- ⓤⓢ flɔːr.ə-, flʊr-, '-oʊ-; flɔː'rɑː-, flʊ-, -'roʊ-
Note: Prefix. Either takes primary or secondary stress on the first syllable, e.g. **fluoroscope** /'flɔː.rəʊ.skəʊp ⓤⓢ 'flɔːr.ə.skoʊp/, **fluoroscopic** /ˌflɔː.rəʊ'skɒp.ɪk ⓤⓢ ˌflɔːr.ə'skɑː.pɪk/, or primary stress on the second syllable, e.g. **fluoroscopy** /flɔː'rɒs.kə.pi ⓤⓢ -'rɑː.skə-/.
fluorocarbon ˌflɔː.rəʊ'kɑː.bᵊn, ˌflʊə- ⓤⓢ ˌflɔːr.ə'kɑːr-, ˌflʊr-, -oʊ'- **-s** -z
stress shift: ˌfluorocarbon 'dating techˌnique
fluoroscop|e 'flɔː.rəʊ.skəʊp, 'flʊə- ⓤⓢ 'flɔːr.ə-, 'flʊr-, -oʊ- **-es** -s **-ing** -ɪŋ **-ed** -t
fluoroscopic ˌflɔː.rəʊ'skɒp.ɪk, ˌflʊə- ⓤⓢ ˌflɔːr.ə'-, ˌflʊr-, -oʊ'- **-ally** -ᵊl.i, -li
fluoroscop|y flɔː'rɒs.kə.p|i, flʊə-, flə- ⓤⓢ flɔː'rɑː.skə-, flʊ- **-ies** -iz **-ist/s** -ɪst/s
fluorosis flɔː'rəʊ.sɪs, flʊə-, flə- ⓤⓢ flɔː'roʊ-, flʊ-
fluorspar 'flɔː.spɑːʳ, 'flʊə- ⓤⓢ 'flɔːr.spɑːr, 'fluː.ɔːr-
flurr|y 'flʌr|.i ⓤⓢ 'flɜːr- **-ies** -iz **-ying** -i.ɪŋ **-ied** -id
flush flʌʃ **-es** -ɪz **-ing** -ɪŋ **-ed** -t
flushing (**F**) 'flʌʃ.ɪŋ **-s** -z
flust|er 'flʌs.t|əʳ ⓤⓢ -t|ɚ **-ers** -əz ⓤⓢ -ɚz **-ering** -ᵊr.ɪŋ **-ered** -əd ⓤⓢ -ɚd
flut|e (**F**) fluːt **-es** -s **-ing** -ɪŋ ⓤⓢ 'fluː.t̬ɪŋ **-ed** -ɪd ⓤⓢ 'fluː.t̬ɪd **-y** -i ⓤⓢ 'fluː.t̬i **-ier** -i.əʳ ⓤⓢ 'fluː.t̬i.ɚ **-iest** -i.ɪst, -i.əst ⓤⓢ 'fluː.t̬i.ɪst, -əst **-iness** -ɪ.nəs, -ɪ.nɪs ⓤⓢ 'fluː.t̬ɪ.nəs, -nɪs
flutist 'fluː.tɪst ⓤⓢ -t̬ɪst **-s** -s
flutt|er (**F**) 'flʌt|.əʳ ⓤⓢ 'flʌt̬|.ɚ **-ers** -əz ⓤⓢ -ɚz **-ering** -ᵊr.ɪŋ **-ered** -əd ⓤⓢ -ɚd **-erer/s** -ᵊr.əʳ/z ⓤⓢ -ɚ.ɚ/z
fluvial 'fluː.vi.əl
flux flʌks **-es** -ɪz
fluxion 'flʌk.ʃᵊn **-s** -z
fluxional 'flʌk.ʃᵊn.ᵊl
fl|y (**F**) fl|aɪ **-ies** -aɪz **-ying** -aɪ.ɪŋ **flew** fluː **flown** fləʊn ⓤⓢ floʊn **flier/s** 'flaɪ.əʳ/z ⓤⓢ -ɚ/z '**fly** ˌ**ball** ; ˌ**flying** '**buttress** ; '**flying** ˌ**fish** ; '**flying** ˌ**officer** ; ˌ**flying** '**saucer** ; '**flying** ˌ**squad** ; ˌ**flying** '**start** ; '**fly** ˌ**sheet** ; **he/she** ˌ**wouldn't** ˌ**harm a** '**fly**
flyable 'flaɪ.ə.bl̩
flyaway 'flaɪ.ə.weɪ
fly-by-night 'flaɪ.baɪ.naɪt **-s** -s **-er/s** -əʳ/z ⓤⓢ ɚ/z
fly-by-wire 'flaɪ.baɪ.waɪəʳ, ˌ--'- ⓤⓢ -waɪɚ
flycatcher 'flaɪˌkætʃ.əʳ ⓤⓢ -ɚ **-s** -z
fly-drive 'flaɪ.draɪv, ˌ-'- **-s** -z
flyer 'flaɪ.əʳ ⓤⓢ -ɚ **-s** -z
fly-fishing 'flaɪˌfɪʃ.ɪŋ
flyingsaucer ˌflaɪ.ɪŋ'sɔː.səʳ ⓤⓢ -'sɑː.sɚ, -'sɔː- **-s** -z
flying squad 'flaɪ.ɪŋ.skwɒd ⓤⓢ -skwɑːd **-s** -z
flylea|f 'flaɪ.liː|f **-ves** -vz
Flymo® 'flaɪ.məʊ ⓤⓢ -moʊ
Flyn(n) flɪn
Flynt flɪnt
flyover 'flaɪˌəʊ.vəʳ ⓤⓢ -ˌoʊ.vɚ **-s** -z
flypaper 'flaɪˌpeɪ.pəʳ ⓤⓢ -pɚ **-s** -z
flypast 'flaɪ.pɑːst ⓤⓢ -pæst **-s** -s
flyposter 'flaɪˌpəʊ.stəʳ ⓤⓢ -ˌpoʊ.stɚ **-s** -z
flyswatter 'flaɪˌswɒt.əʳ ⓤⓢ -ˌswɑː.t̬ɚ **-s** -z
Flyte flaɪt
flyway 'flaɪ.weɪ **-s** -z
flyweight 'flaɪ.weɪt **-s** -s
flywheel 'flaɪ.*h*wiːl **-s** -z
FM ˌef'em
Fo fəʊ ⓤⓢ foʊ
foal fəʊl ⓤⓢ foʊl **-s** -z **-ing** -ɪŋ **-ed** -d
foam fəʊm ⓤⓢ foʊm **-s** -z **-ing** -ɪŋ **-ed** -d **-y** -i **-iness** -ɪ.nəs, -ɪ.nɪs
Foard fɔːd ⓤⓢ fɔːrd
fob fɒb ⓤⓢ fɑːb **-s** -z **-bing** -ɪŋ **-bed** -d
focal 'fəʊ.kᵊl ⓤⓢ 'foʊ- '**focal** ˌ**point**, ˌ**focal** '**point**
Foch fɒʃ ⓤⓢ fɑːʃ, fɔːʃ
Fochabers 'fɒk.ə.bəz, 'fɒx- ⓤⓢ 'fɑːk.ə.bɚz
Focke fɒk ⓤⓢ fɑːk
fo'c'sle 'fəʊk.sᵊl ⓤⓢ 'foʊk- **-s** -z
fo|cus (*n.*) 'fəʊ|.kəs ⓤⓢ 'foʊ- **-cuses** -kə.sɪz **-ci** -saɪ, -kiː
focus (*v.*) 'fəʊ.kəs ⓤⓢ 'foʊ- **-(s)es** -ɪz **-(s)ing** -ɪŋ **-(s)ed** -t
fodder 'fɒd.əʳ ⓤⓢ 'fɑː.dɚ
foe fəʊ ⓤⓢ foʊ **-s** -z
FoE (*abbrev. for* **Friends of the Earth**) ˌef.əʊ'iː ⓤⓢ -oʊ'-
foehn fɜːn ⓤⓢ feɪn, fɜːn
foe|man 'fəʊ|.mən, -mæn ⓤⓢ 'foʊ- **-men** -mən, -men
foetal 'fiː.tᵊl ⓤⓢ -t̬ᵊl '**foetal po**ˌ**sition**
foetid 'fiː.tɪd, 'fet.ɪd ⓤⓢ 'fet̬.ɪd, 'fiː.t̬ɪd **-ly** -li **-ness** -nəs, -nɪs
foetus 'fiː.təs ⓤⓢ -t̬əs **-es** -ɪz
fog fɒg ⓤⓢ fɑːg, fɔːg **-s** -z **-ging** -ɪŋ **-ged** -d '**fog** ˌ**lamp**
fogbound 'fɒg.baʊnd ⓤⓢ 'fɑːg-, 'fɔːg-
Fogerty 'fəʊ.gə.ti, 'fɒg.ə.ti ⓤⓢ 'foʊ.gɚ.t̬i
fogey 'fəʊ.gi ⓤⓢ 'foʊ- **-s** -z **-ish** -ɪʃ **-ism** -ɪ.zᵊm
Fogg fɒg ⓤⓢ fɑːg, fɔːg
fogg|y 'fɒg|.i ⓤⓢ 'fɑː.gli, 'fɔː- **-ier** -i.əʳ ⓤⓢ -i.ɚ **-iest** -i.ɪst, -i.əst **-ily** -ɪ.li, -ᵊl.i **-iness** -ɪ.nəs, -ɪ.nɪs ˌ**Foggy** '**Bottom**
foghorn 'fɒg.hɔːn ⓤⓢ 'fɑːg.hɔːrn, 'fɔːg- **-s** -z
fog|y 'fəʊ.g|i ⓤⓢ 'foʊ- **-ies** -iz **-yish** -i.ɪʃ **-yism** -i.ɪ.zᵊm
fohn, **föhn** fɜːn ⓤⓢ feɪn, fɜːn
foible 'fɔɪ.bl̩ **-s** -z
foie gras ˌfwɑː'grɑː

foil fɔɪl **-s** -z **-ing** -ɪŋ **-ed** -d
foist fɔɪst **-s** -s **-ing** -ɪŋ **-ed** -ɪd
Fokker® ˈfɒk.əʳ US ˈfɑː.kɚ
fold fəʊld US foʊld **-s** -z **-ing** -ɪŋ **-ed** -ɪd
foldaway ˈfəʊld.ə.weɪ US ˈfoʊld-
folder ˈfəʊl.dəʳ US ˈfoʊl.dɚ **-s** -z
folderol ˈfɒl.dɪ.rɒl, -də- US ˈfɑːl.də.rɑːl **-s** -z
foldout ˈfəʊld.aʊt US ˈfoʊld- **-s** -s
Foley ˈfəʊ.li US ˈfoʊ-
Folgate ˈfɒl.gɪt, -geɪt US ˈfɑːl.geɪt
Folger ˈfəʊl.dʒəʳ, ˈfɒl- US ˈfoʊl.dʒɚ
foliage ˈfəʊ.li.ɪdʒ US ˈfoʊ- **-d** -d
foliar ˈfəʊ.li.ə US ˈfoʊ.li.ɚ
foliate *(adj.)* ˈfəʊ.li.ət, -ɪt, -eɪt US ˈfoʊ-
foli|ate *(v.)* ˈfəʊ.li|.eɪt US ˈfoʊ- **-ates** -eɪts **-ating** -eɪ.tɪŋ US -eɪ.t̬ɪŋ **-ated** -eɪ.tɪd US -eɪ.t̬ɪd
foliation ˌfəʊ.liˈeɪ.ʃᵊn US ˌfoʊ- **-s** -z
folic ˈfɒl.ɪk, ˈfəʊ.lɪk US ˈfoʊ- ˌ**folic** ˈ**acid**
Folies Bergère ˌfɒl.i.bɜːˈʒeəʳ, -bəˈ-, -beəˈ- US ˌfoʊ.li.berˈʒer
folio ˈfəʊ.li.əʊ US ˈfoʊ.li.oʊ **-s** -z
Foliot ˈfɒl.i.ət US ˈfɑː.li-
folk fəʊk US foʊk **-s** -s ˈ**folk** ˌ**dance** ; ˈ**folk** ˌ**song**
Folkes fəʊlks, fuːks US foʊlks
Folkestone ˈfəʊk.stən US ˈfoʊk-
folklore ˈfəʊk.lɔːʳ US ˈfoʊk.lɔːr
folklorist ˈfəʊkˌlɔː.rɪst US ˈfoʊkˌlɔːr.ɪst **-s** -s
folksinger ˈfəʊkˌsɪŋ.əʳ US ˈfoʊkˌsɪŋ.ɚ **-s** -z
folks|y ˈfəʊk.s|i US ˈfoʊk- **-ier** -i.əʳ US -i.ɚ **-iest** -i.ɪst, -i.əst **-ily** -ɪ.li, -ᵊl.i **-iness** -ɪ.nəs, -ɪ.nɪs
folktale ˈfəʊk.teɪl US ˈfoʊk- **-s** -z
Follen ˈfɒl.ɪn, -ən US ˈfɑː.lɪn, -lən
Follett ˈfɒl.ɪt, -ət US ˈfɑː.lɪt, -lət
Follick ˈfɒl.ɪk US ˈfɑː.lɪk
follicle ˈfɒl.ɪ.kl̩ US ˈfɑː.lɪ- **-s** -z
follow ˈfɒl.əʊ US ˈfɑː.loʊ **-s** -z **-ing/s** -ɪŋ/z **-ed** -d **-er/s** -əʳ/z US -ɚ/z
follow-my-leader ˌfɒl.əʊ.məˈliː.dəʳ, -mɪˈ-, -maɪˈ- US ˌfɑː.loʊ.maɪˈliː.dɚ
follow-on ˈfɒl.əʊ.ɒn US ˈfɑː.loʊ.ɑːn **-s** -z
follow-the-leader ˌfɒl.əʊ.ðəˈliː.dəʳ US ˌfɑː.loʊ.ðəˈliː.dɚ
follow-through ˌfɒl.əʊˈθruː US ˈ---, ˈfɑː.loʊ.θruː **-s** -z
follow-up ˈfɒl.əʊ.ʌp US ˈfɑː.loʊ- **-s** -s
foll|y (F) ˈfɒl|.i US ˈfɑː.l|i **-ies** -iz
Fomalhaut ˈfəʊ.mə.ləʊt, ˈfɒm-, -ᵊl.hɔːt US ˈfoʊ.mᵊl.hɑːt, -hɔːt, -mə.loʊ
fo|ment fəʊ|ˈment US foʊ- **-ments** -ˈments **-menting** -ˈmen.tɪŋ US -ˈmen.t̬ɪŋ **-mented** -ˈmen.tɪd US -ˈmen.t̬ɪd **-menter/s** -ˈmen.təʳ/z US -ˈmen.t̬ɚ/z
fomentation ˌfəʊ.menˈteɪ.ʃᵊn, -mənˈ- US ˌfoʊ- **-s** -z
fond fɒnd US fɑːnd **-er** -əʳ US -ɚ **-est** -ɪst, -əst **-ly** -li **-ness** -nəs, -nɪs
Fonda ˈfɒn.də US ˈfɑːn-
fondant ˈfɒn.dənt US ˈfɑːn- **-s** -s
fondl|e ˈfɒn.dl̩ US ˈfɑːn- **-es** -z **-ing** -ɪŋ, ˈfɒnd.lɪŋ US ˈfɑːnd- **-ed** -d
fondly ˈfɒnd.li US ˈfɑːnd-
fondu(e) ˈfɒn.djuː, -duː, -ˈ- US fɑːnˈduː, -ˈdjuː, ˈ-- **-s** -z
font fɒnt US fɑːnt **-s** -s **-al** -ᵊl US ˈfɑːn.t̬ᵊl
Fontainebleau ˈfɒn.tɪn.bləʊ, -tɪm-, -təm- US ˈfɑːn.tᵊn.bloʊ
Fontane ˈfɒn.teɪn *as if German:* fɒnˈtɑː.nə US ˈfɑːn-
fontanelle, fontanel ˌfɒn.təˈnel US ˌfɑːn.tᵊnˈel **-s** -z
Fontenoy ˈfɒn.tə.nɔɪ, -tɪ.nɔɪ US ˈfɑːn.tᵊn.ɔɪ
Fonteyn fɒnˈteɪn, ˈ-- US fɑːnˈteɪn, ˈ--
Fonthill ˈfɒnt.hɪl US ˈfɑːnt-
Foochow ˌfuːˈtʃaʊ
food fuːd **-s** -z **-less** -ləs, -lɪs ˈ**food** ˌ**poisoning** ; ˈ**food** ˌ**processor**
foodie ˈfuː.di **-s** -z
foodstuff ˈfuːd.stʌf **-s** -s
fool fuːl **-s** -z **-ing** -ɪŋ **-ed** -d ˌ**fool's** ˈ**gold**, ˈ**fool's** ˌ**gold** ; ˌ**make a** ˈ**fool of one**ˌ**self**
fooler|y ˈfuː.lᵊr|.i **-ies** -iz
foolhard|y ˈfuːlˌhɑː.d|i US -ˌhɑːr- **-iest** -i.ɪst, -i.əst **-ily** -ɪ.li, -ᵊl.i **-iness** -ɪ.nəs, -ɪ.nɪs
foolish ˈfuː.lɪʃ **-ly** -li **-ness** -nəs, -nɪs
foolproof ˈfuːl.pruːf
foolscap, fool's cap *hat:* ˈfuːlz.kæp **-s** -s
foolscap *paper size:* ˈfuːl.skæp, ˈfuːlz.kæp
foot (F) *(n.)* fʊt **feet** fiːt ˈ**foot** ˌ**fault** ; ˈ**foot** ˌ**passenger** ; ˈ**foot** ˌ**soldier** ; ˌ**one** ˌ**foot in the** ˈ**grave** ; **put one's** ˌ**best foot** ˈ**forward** ; ˌ**put one's** ˈ**foot down** ; ˌ**put one's** ˈ**foot in it**
foot *(v.)* fʊt **-s** -s **-ing** -ɪŋ US ˈfʊt̬.ɪŋ **-ed** -ɪd US ˈfʊt̬.ɪd
footage ˈfʊt.ɪdʒ US ˈfʊt̬-
foot-and-mouth ˌfʊt.ᵊndˈmaʊθ, -ᵊmˈ- US -ᵊndˈ- ˌ**foot-and-**ˈ**mouth di**ˌ**sease**
football ˈfʊt.bɔːl US -bɔːl, -bɑːl **-s** -z **-ing** -ɪŋ **-er/s** -əʳ/z US -ɚ/z ˈ**football** ˌ**match** ; ˈ**football** ˌ**pools**
footba|th ˈfʊt.bɑː|θ US -bæ|θ **-ths** -ðz
footboard ˈfʊt.bɔːd US -bɔːrd **-s** -z
footbridg|e ˈfʊt.brɪdʒ **-es** -ɪz
Foote fʊt
footer ˈfʊt.əʳ US ˈfʊt̬.ɚ
footfall ˈfʊt.fɔːl US -fɔːl, -fɑːl **-s** -z
foothill ˈfʊt.hɪl **-s** -z
foothold ˈfʊt.həʊld US -hoʊld **-s** -z
footie ˈfʊt.i US ˈfʊt̬-
footing ˈfʊt.ɪŋ US ˈfʊt̬- **-s** -z
footl|e ˈfuː.tl̩ US -t̬l̩ **-es** -z **-ing** -ɪŋ, ˈfuːt.lɪŋ **-ed** -d
footlight ˈfʊt.laɪt **-s** -s
footlocker ˈfʊtˌlɒk.əʳ US -ˌlɑː.kɚ **-s** -z
footloose ˈfʊt.luːs ˌ**footloose and** ˌ**fancy-**ˈ**free**
foot|man ˈfʊt|.mən **-men** -mən
footmark ˈfʊt.mɑːk US -mɑːrk **-s** -s
footnote ˈfʊt.nəʊt US -noʊt **-s** -s
footpad ˈfʊt.pæd **-s** -z
footpa|th ˈfʊt.pɑː|θ US -pæ|θ **-ths** -ðz
footplate ˈfʊt.pleɪt **-s** -s
foot-pound ˈfʊt.paʊnd **-s** -z
footprint ˈfʊt.prɪnt **-s** -s
footrac|e ˈfʊt.reɪs **-es** -ɪz
footrest ˈfʊt.rest **-s** -s
footrule ˈfʊt.ruːl **-s** -z
footsie (F) ˈfʊt.si
footsore ˈfʊt.sɔːʳ US -sɔːr
footstep ˈfʊt.step **-s** -s
footstool ˈfʊt.stuːl **-s** -z
footsure ˈfʊt.ʃʊəʳ, -ʃɔːʳ US -ʃʊr, -ʃɜːr **-ness** -nəs, -nɪs
footwear ˈfʊt.weəʳ US -wer
footwork ˈfʊt.wɜːk US -wɜːrk
footy ˈfʊt.i US ˈfʊt̬-
foozl|e (F) ˈfuː.zl̩ **-es** -z **-ing** -ɪŋ, ˈfuːz.lɪŋ **-ed** -d **-er/s** -əʳ/z, ˈfuːz.ləʳ/z US ˈfuː.zl̩.ɚ/z, ˈfuːz.lɚ/z
fop fɒp US fɑːp **-s** -s
fopper|y ˈfɒp.ᵊr|.i US ˈfɑː.pɚ- **-ies** -iz
foppish ˈfɒp.ɪʃ US ˈfɑː.pɪʃ **-ly** -li **-ness** -nəs, -nɪs
for *(prep. conj.) strong form:* fɔːʳ US fɔːr *weak form:* fəʳ US fɚ *alternative weak form before vowels:* fr̩
Note: Weak form word. The strong form /fɔːʳ US fɔːr/ is used contrastively (e.g. "**for** and **against**") and in sentence-final position (e.g. "That's what it's for"). The weak form is /fə US fɚ/ before consonants (e.g. "Thanks for coming" /ˌθæŋks.fəˈkʌm.ɪŋ US -fɚˈ-/); before vowels it is /fər US fɚ/ (e.g. "One for all" /ˌwʌn.fərˈɔːl US -fɚˈɑːl/) or, in rapid speech, /fr̩/ (e.g. "Time for another" /ˌtaɪm.fr̩.əˈnʌð.əʳ US -ɚ/).
forag|e ˈfɒr.ɪdʒ US ˈfɔːr- **-es** -ɪz **-ing** -ɪŋ **-ed** -d **-er/s** -əʳ/z US -ɚ/z
foramen fəˈreɪ.men, fɒrˈeɪ-, -mən US fəˈreɪ.mən, fɔː-, foʊ- **foramina** fəˈræm.ɪ.nə, fɒrˈeɪ- US fəˈræm.ə-, fɔː-, foʊ-
forasmuch fᵊr.əzˈmʌtʃ, ˌfɔː.rəz-, ˌfɒr.əz- US ˌfɔːr.æzˈ-, ˌfɚ-, -əzˈ-
foray ˈfɒr.eɪ US ˈfɔːr- **-s** -z **-ing** -ɪŋ **-ed** -d
forbad *(from* **forbid***)* fəˈbæd, fɔː- US fɚ-, fɔːr-

forbade (*from* **forbid**) fə'bæd, fɔː-, -beɪd ⓤⓢ fɚ'bæd, fɔːr-

forbear (*n.*) 'fɔː.beəʳ ⓤⓢ 'fɔːr.ber -**s** -z

for|bear (*v.*) fɔː|'beəʳ, fə- ⓤⓢ fɔːr|'ber -**bears** -'beəz ⓤⓢ -'berz -**bearing/ly** -'beə.rɪŋ/li ⓤⓢ -'ber.ɪŋ/li -**bore** -'bɔːʳ ⓤⓢ -'bɔːr -**borne** -'bɔːn ⓤⓢ -'bɔːrn

forbearance fɔː'beə.rənts, fə- ⓤⓢ fɔːr'ber.ənts

Forbes fɔːbz, 'fɔː.bɪs ⓤⓢ fɔːrbz

for|bid fə|'bɪd, fɔː- ⓤⓢ fɚ-, fɔːr- -**bids** -'bɪdz -**bidding/ly** -'bɪd.ɪŋ/li -**bad** -'bæd -**bade** -'bæd, -'beɪd ⓤⓢ -'bæd -**bidden** -'bɪd.ᵊn

forbore (*from* **forbear**) fɔː'bɔːʳ ⓤⓢ fɔːr'bɔːr

forc|e (F) fɔːs ⓤⓢ fɔːrs -**es** -ɪz -**ing** -ɪŋ -**ed** -t -**edly** -ɪd.li -**edness** -ɪd.nəs, -nɪs **'force ˌpump ; ˌforced 'march**

forcefeed ˌfɔːs'fiːd, '-- ⓤⓢ 'fɔːrs.fiːd, ˌ-'- -**s** -z -**ing** -ɪŋ **forcefed** ˌfɔːs'fed, '-- ⓤⓢ 'fɔːrs.fed, ˌ-'-

forceful 'fɔːs.fᵊl, -fʊl ⓤⓢ 'fɔːrs- -**ly** -i -**ness** -nəs, -nɪs

force majeure ˌfɔːs.mæʒ'ɜːʳ, -mædʒ'ʊəʳ ⓤⓢ ˌfɔːrs.mɑː'ʒɜːr

forcemeat 'fɔːs.miːt ⓤⓢ 'fɔːrs-

forceps 'fɔː.seps, -sɪps, -səps ⓤⓢ 'fɔːr-

forcer 'fɔː.səʳ ⓤⓢ 'fɔːr.sɚ -**s** -z

forcib|le 'fɔː.sə.b|l̩, -sɪ- ⓤⓢ 'fɔːr- -**ly** -li -**leness** -l̩.nəs, -nɪs

ford (F) fɔːd ⓤⓢ fɔːrd -**s** -z -**ing** -ɪŋ -**ed** -ɪd -**able** -ə.bl̩

Fordcombe 'fɔːd.kəm ⓤⓢ 'fɔːrd-

Forde fɔːd ⓤⓢ fɔːrd

Forder 'fɔː.dəʳ ⓤⓢ 'fɔːr.dɚ

Fordham 'fɔː.dəm ⓤⓢ 'fɔːr-

Fordingbridge 'fɔː.dɪŋ.brɪdʒ ⓤⓢ 'fɔːr-

Fordoun 'fɔː.dᵊn ⓤⓢ 'fɔːr-

Fordyce 'fɔː.daɪs ⓤⓢ 'fɔːr-

fore fɔːʳ ⓤⓢ fɔːr

forearm (*n.*) 'fɔːʳ.ɑːm ⓤⓢ 'fɔːr.ɑːrm -**s** -z

forearm (*v.*) fɔːʳ'ɑːm ⓤⓢ fɔːr'ɑːrm -**s** -z -**ing** -ɪŋ -**ed** -d

forebear 'fɔː.beəʳ ⓤⓢ 'fɔːr.ber -**s** -s

forebod|e fɔː'bəʊd, fə- ⓤⓢ fɔːr'boʊd, fɚ- -**es** -z -**ing/ly** -ɪŋ/li -**ed** -ɪd -**er/s** -əʳ/z ⓤⓢ -ɚ/z

foreboding fɔː'bəʊ.dɪŋ, fə- ⓤⓢ fɔːr'boʊ-, fɚ- -**s** -z

forecast (*n.*) 'fɔː.kɑːst ⓤⓢ 'fɔːr.kæst -**s** -s

forecast (*v.*) 'fɔː.kɑːst ⓤⓢ 'fɔːr.kæst -**s** -s -**ing** -ɪŋ -**ed** -ɪd -**er/s** -əʳ/z ⓤⓢ -ɚ/z

forecastle 'fəʊk.sᵊl ⓤⓢ 'foʊk- -**s** -z

foreclos|e fɔː'kləʊz ⓤⓢ fɔːr'kloʊz -**es** -ɪz -**ing** -ɪŋ -**ed** -d

foreclosure fɔː'kləʊ.ʒəʳ ⓤⓢ fɔːr'kloʊ.ʒɚ -**s** -z

forecourt 'fɔː.kɔːt ⓤⓢ 'fɔːr.kɔːrt -**s** -s

forefather 'fɔːˌfɑː.ðəʳ ⓤⓢ 'fɔːrˌfɑː.ðɚ -**s** -z

forefinger 'fɔːˌfɪŋ.gəʳ ⓤⓢ 'fɔːrˌfɪŋ.gɚ -**s** -z

fore|foot 'fɔː|.fʊt ⓤⓢ 'fɔːr- -**feet** -fiːt

forefront 'fɔː.frʌnt ⓤⓢ 'fɔːr-

fore|go fɔː|'gəʊ ⓤⓢ fɔːr|'goʊ -**goes** -'gəʊz ⓤⓢ -'goʊz -**going** -'gəʊ.ɪŋ ⓤⓢ -'goʊ.ɪŋ -**went** -'went -**gone** -'gɒn ⓤⓢ -'gɑːn -**goer/s** -'gəʊ.əʳ/z ⓤⓢ -'goʊ.ɚ/z

foregone (*from* **forego**) fɔː'gɒn ⓤⓢ fɔːr'gɑːn

foregone (*adj.*) 'fɔː.gɒn ⓤⓢ 'fɔːr.gɑːn **ˌforegone con'clusion**

foreground 'fɔː.graʊnd ⓤⓢ 'fɔːr- -**s** -z

foregrounding 'fɔːˌgraʊn.dɪŋ ⓤⓢ 'fɔːr-

forehand 'fɔː.hænd ⓤⓢ 'fɔːr- -**s** -z

forehanded fɔː'hæn.dɪd ⓤⓢ 'fɔːrˌ-, ˌ-'-- -**ly** -li -**ness** -nəs, -nɪs *stress shift, British only:* ˌforehanded 'volley

forehead 'fɒr.ɪd, -ed; 'fɔː.hed ⓤⓢ 'fɔːr.ed, -hed -**s** -z

foreign 'fɒr.ɪn, -ən ⓤⓢ 'fɔːr- **ˌforeign af'fairs ; ˌforeign corre'spondent ; ˌforeign ex'change ; ˌforeign 'legion ; 'Foreign ˌOffice ; ˌforeign 'policy ; ˌforeign 'secretary ; ˌForeign 'Service**

foreigner 'fɒr.ɪ.nəʳ, '-ə- ⓤⓢ 'fɔːr- -**s** -z

forejudg|e fɔː'dʒʌdʒ ⓤⓢ fɔːr- -**es** -ɪz -**ing** -ɪŋ -**ed** -d

fore|know fɔː|'nəʊ ⓤⓢ fɔːr|'noʊ -**knows** -'nəʊz ⓤⓢ -'noʊz -**knowing** -'nəʊ.ɪŋ ⓤⓢ -'noʊ.ɪŋ -**knew** -'njuː ⓤⓢ -'nuː, -'njuː -**known** -'nəʊn ⓤⓢ -'noʊn

foreknowledge fɔː'nɒl.ɪdʒ ⓤⓢ fɔːr'nɑː.lɪdʒ

foreland (F) 'fɔː.lənd ⓤⓢ 'fɔːr- -**s** -z

foreleg 'fɔː.leg ⓤⓢ 'fɔːr- -**s** -z

forelock 'fɔː.lɒk ⓤⓢ 'fɔːr.lɑːk -**s** -s

fore|man (F) 'fɔː|.mən ⓤⓢ 'fɔːr- -**men** -mən

foremast 'fɔː.mɑːst ⓤⓢ 'fɔːr.mæst *nautical pronunciation:* -məst -**s** -s

foremost 'fɔː.məʊst, -məst ⓤⓢ 'fɔːr.moʊst

forename 'fɔː.neɪm ⓤⓢ 'fɔːr- -**s** -z

forenoon 'fɔː.nuːn ⓤⓢ 'fɔːr-, ˌ-'- -**s** -z

forensic fə'rent.sɪk, fɒr'ent-, -'en.zɪk ⓤⓢ fə'rent.sɪk, -'ren.zɪk -**s** -s

foreordain ˌfɔːʳ.ɔː'deɪn ⓤⓢ ˌfɔːr.ɔːr'- -**s** -z -**ing** -ɪŋ -**ed** -d

forepart 'fɔː.pɑːt ⓤⓢ 'fɔːr.pɑːrt -**s** -s

foreplay 'fɔː.pleɪ ⓤⓢ 'fɔːr-

fore|run fɔː|'rʌn ⓤⓢ fɔːr- -**runs** -'rʌnz -**running** -'rʌn.ɪŋ -**ran** -'ræn

forerunner 'fɔːˌrʌn.əʳ, ˌ-'-- ⓤⓢ 'fɔːrˌrʌn.ɚ, ˌ-'-- -**s** -z

foresail 'fɔː.seɪl ⓤⓢ 'fɔːr- *nautical pronunciation:* -sᵊl -**s** -z

fore|see fɔː|'siː, fə- ⓤⓢ fɔːr-, fɚ- -**sees** -'siːz -**seeing** -'siː.ɪŋ -**saw** -'sɔː ⓤⓢ -'sɑː, -'sɔː -**seen** -'siːn -**seeable** -'siː.ə.bl̩

foreseeability fɔːˌsiː.ə'bɪl.ə.ti, ˌfɔː.siː-; fəˌsiː- ⓤⓢ fɔːrˌsiː.ə'bɪl.ə.t̬i, fɚ-

foreshadow fɔː'ʃæd.əʊ ⓤⓢ fɔːr'ʃæd.oʊ -**s** -z -**ing** -ɪŋ -**ed** -d -**er/s** -əʳ/z ⓤⓢ -ɚ/z

foreshore 'fɔː.ʃɔːʳ ⓤⓢ 'fɔːr.ʃɔːr -**s** -z

foreshorten fɔː'ʃɔː.tᵊn ⓤⓢ fɔːr'ʃɔːr- -**s** -z -**ing** -ɪŋ -**ed** -d

foreshow fɔː'ʃəʊ ⓤⓢ fɔːr'ʃoʊ -**s** -z -**ing** -ɪŋ -**ed** -d -**n** -n

foresight 'fɔː.saɪt ⓤⓢ 'fɔːr- -**s** -s

foreskin 'fɔː.skɪn ⓤⓢ 'fɔːr- -**s** -z

forest (F) 'fɒr.ɪst ⓤⓢ 'fɔːr- -**s** -s **ˌForest 'Hills ; ˌforest 'ranger** ⓤⓢ **'forest ˌranger ; not see the ˌforest for the 'trees**

forestall fɔː'stɔːl ⓤⓢ fɔːr'stɔːl, -'stɑːl -**s** -z -**ing** -ɪŋ -**ed** -d -**er/s** -əʳ/z ⓤⓢ -ɚ/z

forester (F) 'fɒr.ɪ.stəʳ, '-ə- ⓤⓢ 'fɔːr- -**s** -z

forestry 'fɒr.ɪ.stri, '-ə- ⓤⓢ 'fɔːr-

foretaste (*n.*) 'fɔː.teɪst ⓤⓢ 'fɔːr- -**s** -s

foretast|e (*v.*) fɔː'teɪst ⓤⓢ fɔːr- -**es** -s -**ing** -ɪŋ -**ed** -ɪd

fore|tell fɔː|'tel ⓤⓢ fɔːr- -**tells** -'telz -**telling** -'tel.ɪŋ -**told** -'təʊld ⓤⓢ -'toʊld -**teller/s** -'tel.əʳ/z ⓤⓢ -'tel.ɚ/z

forethought 'fɔː.θɔːt ⓤⓢ 'fɔːr.θɑːt, -θɔːt

foretop, fore-top 'fɔː.tɒp ⓤⓢ 'fɔːr.tɑːp *nautical pronunciation:* -təp -**s** -s

fore-topmast fɔː'tɒp.mɑːst ⓤⓢ fɔːr'tɑːp.mæst *nautical pronunciation:* -məst -**s** -s

fore-topsail fɔː'tɒp.seɪl ⓤⓢ fɔːr'tɑːp- *nautical pronunciation:* -sᵊl -**s** -z

forever fə're.vəʳ ⓤⓢ fɔːr'ev.ɚ, fɚ-

forewarn fɔː'wɔːn ⓤⓢ fɔːr'wɔːrn -**s** -z -**ing** -ɪŋ -**ed** -d

forewent (*from* **forego**) fɔː'went ⓤⓢ fɔːr-

fore|woman 'fɔː|ˌwʊm.ən ⓤⓢ 'fɔːr- -**women** -ˌwɪm.ɪn

foreword 'fɔː.wɜːd ⓤⓢ 'fɔːr.wɜːrd -**s** -z

Forfar 'fɔː.fəʳ, -fɑːʳ ⓤⓢ 'fɔːr.fɚ, -fɑːr

forfei|t 'fɔː.fɪ|t ⓤⓢ 'fɔːr-, -fə|t -**ts** -ts -**ting** -tɪŋ ⓤⓢ -t̬ɪŋ -**ted** -tɪd ⓤⓢ -t̬ɪd -**ter/s** -təʳ/z ⓤⓢ -t̬ɚ/z -**table** -tə.bl̩ ⓤⓢ -t̬ə.bl̩

forfeiture 'fɔː.fɪ.tʃəʳ ⓤⓢ 'fɔːr.fə- -**s** -z

forfend fɔː'fend ⓤⓢ fɔːr- -**s** -z -**ing** -ɪŋ -**ed** -ɪd

forgath|er fɔː'gæð|.əʳ US fɔːr'gæð|.ɚ **-ers** -əz US -ɚz **-ering** -ᵊr.ɪŋ **-ered** -əd US -ɚd
forgave (*from* **forgive**) fə'geɪv US fɚ-, fɔːr-
forg|e fɔːdʒ US fɔːrdʒ **-es** -ɪz **-ing** -ɪŋ **-ed** -d **-er/s** -əʳ/z US -ɚ/z
forger|y 'fɔː.dʒᵊr|.i US 'fɔːr- **-ies** -iz
for|get fə|'get US fɚ-, fɔːr- **-gets** -'gets **-getting** -'get.ɪŋ US -'geţ.ɪŋ **-got** -'gɒt US -'gɑːt **-gotten** -'gɒt.ᵊn US -'gɑː.tᵊn
forgetful fə'get.fᵊl, -fʊl US fɚ-, fɔːr- **-ly** -i **-ness** -nəs, -nɪs
forget-me-not fə'get.mi.nɒt US fɚ'get.mi.nɑːt, fɔːr- **-s** -s
forgettab|le fə'get.ə.b|l̩ US fɚ'geţ-, fɔːr- **-ly** -li
for|give fə|'gɪv US fɚ-, fɔːr- **-gives** -'gɪvz **-giving** -'gɪv.ɪŋ **-gave** -'geɪv **-given** -'gɪv.ᵊn **-givable** -'gɪv.ə.bl̩ **-giveness** -'gɪv.nəs, -nɪs
for|go fɔː|'gəʊ US fɔːr|'goʊ **-goes** -'gəʊz US -'goʊz **-going** -'gəʊ.ɪŋ US -'goʊ.ɪŋ **-went** -'went **-gone** -'gɒn US -'gɑːn
forgot (*from* **forget**) fə'gɒt US fɚ'gɑːt, fɔːr-
forgotten (*from* **forget**) fə'gɒt.ᵊn US fɚ'gɑː.tᵊn, fɔːr-
Forington 'fɒr.ɪŋ.tən US 'fɔːr-
forint 'fɒr.ɪnt US 'fɔːr- **-s** -s
fork fɔːk US fɔːrk **-s** -s **-ing** -ɪŋ **-ed** -t
forklift 'fɔːk.lɪft, ˌ-'- US 'fɔːrk.lɪft **-s** -s **-ing** -ɪŋ **-ed** -ɪd ˌ**forklift 'truck**
forlorn fə'lɔːn, fɔː- US fɔːr'lɔːrn, fɚ- **-ly** -li **-ness** -nəs, -nɪs
form fɔːm US fɔːrm **-s** -z **-ing** -ɪŋ **-ed** -d
formal 'fɔː.mᵊl US 'fɔːr- **-ly** -i
formaldehyde fɔː'mæl.dɪ.haɪd, -də- US fɔːr-, fɚ-
formalin 'fɔː.mᵊl.ɪn US 'fɔːr.mə.lɪn
formal|ism 'fɔː.mᵊl|.ɪ.zᵊm US 'fɔːr- **-ist/s** -ɪst/s
formalit|y fɔː'mæl.ə.t|i, -ɪ.t|i US -ə.ţ|i **-ies** -iz
formalization, -isa- ˌfɔː.mᵊl.aɪ'zeɪ.ʃᵊn, -ɪ'- US ˌfɔːr.mᵊl.ɪ'- **-s** -z
formaliz|e, -is|e 'fɔː.mᵊl.aɪz US 'fɔːr.mə.laɪz **-es** -ɪz **-ing** -ɪŋ **-ed** -d
Forman 'fɔː.mən US 'fɔːr-
formant 'fɔː.mənt US 'fɔːr- **-s** -s
for|mat 'fɔː|.mæt US 'fɔːr- **-mats** -mæts **-matting** -mæt.ɪŋ US -mæţ.ɪŋ **-matted** -mæt.ɪd US -mæţ.ɪd **-matter/s** -mæt.əʳ/z US -mæţ.ɚ/z
formation fɔː'meɪ.ʃᵊn US fɔːr- **-s** -z
formative 'fɔː.mə.tɪv US 'fɔːr.mə.ţɪv **-ly** -li **-ness** -nəs, -nɪs
Formby 'fɔːm.bi US 'fɔːrm-
forme fɔːm US fɔːrm **-s** -z
former 'fɔː.məʳ US 'fɔːr.mɚ **-ly** -li
formic 'fɔː.mɪk US 'fɔːr- ˌ**formic 'acid**
Formica® fɔː'maɪ.kə, fə'maɪ- US fɔːr-, fɚ-
formidab|le 'fɔː.mɪ.də.b|l̩; fɔː'mɪd.ə-, fə- US 'fɔːr.mə.də.b|l̩; fɔːr'mɪd.ə-, fɚ- **-ly** -li **-leness** -l̩.nəs, -nɪs
Formidable *name of ship:* fɔː'mɪd.ə.bl̩; 'fɔː.mɪ.də- US 'fɔːr.mə.də-; fɔːr'mɪd.ə-
formless 'fɔːm.ləs US 'fɔːrm-, -lɪs **-ness** -nəs, -nɪs
Formos|a fɔː'məʊ.s|ə, -z|ə US fɔːr'moʊ- **-an/s** -ən/z
formul|a 'fɔː.mjə.l|ə, -mjʊ- US 'fɔːr.mjʊ-, -mjə- **-ae** -iː **-as** -əz
formulaic ˌfɔː.mjə'leɪ.ɪk, -mjʊ'- US ˌfɔːr.mjʊ'-, -mjə'-
formular|y 'fɔː.mjə.lə.r|i, -mjʊ- US 'fɔːr.mjʊ.ler|.i, -mjə- **-ies** -iz
formu|late 'fɔː.mjə|.leɪt, -mjʊ- US 'fɔːr.mjʊ-, -mjə- **-lates** -leɪts **-lating** -leɪ.tɪŋ US -leɪ.ţɪŋ **-lated** -leɪ.tɪd US -leɪ.ţɪd
formulation ˌfɔː.mjə'leɪ.ʃᵊn, -mjʊ'- US ˌfɔːr.mjʊ'-, -mjə'- **-s** -z
Fornax 'fɔː.næks US 'fɔːr-
Forney 'fɔː.ni US 'fɔːr-
forni|cate 'fɔː.nɪ|.keɪt, -nə- US 'fɔːr- **-cates** -keɪts **-cating** -keɪ.tɪŋ US -keɪ.ţɪŋ **-cated** -keɪ.tɪd US -keɪ.ţɪd **-cator/s** -keɪ.təʳ/z US -keɪ.ţɚ/z
fornication ˌfɔː.nɪ'keɪ.ʃᵊn, -nə'- US ˌfɔːr-
Forres 'fɒr.ɪs US 'fɔːr-
Forrest 'fɒr.ɪst US 'fɔːr-
Forrester 'fɒr.ɪ.stəʳ US 'fɔːr.ɪ.stɚ
for|sake fə|'seɪk, fɔː- US fɔːr-, fɚ- **-sakes** -'seɪks **-saking** -'seɪ.kɪŋ **-sook** -'sʊk **-saken** -'seɪ.kᵊn
Forshaw 'fɔː.ʃɔː US 'fɔːr.ʃɑː, -ʃɔː
forsooth fə'suːθ, fɔː- US fɔːr-, fɚ-
Forster 'fɔː.stəʳ US 'fɔːr.stɚ
for|swear fɔː|'sweəʳ US fɔːr|'swer **-swears** -'sweəz US -'swerz **-swearing** -'sweə.rɪŋ US -'swer.ɪŋ **-swore** -'swɔːʳ US -'swɔːr **-sworn** -'swɔːn US -'swɔːrn
Forsyte 'fɔː.saɪt US 'fɔːr-
Forsyth 'fɔː.saɪθ, -'- US 'fɔːr-, -'-
forsythia fɔː'saɪ.θi.ə, fə-, -'sɪθ.i- US fɔːr'sɪθ-, -'saɪ.θi- **-s** -z
fort fɔːt US fɔːrt **-s** -s ˌ**Fort 'Knox** ; ˌ**Fort 'Lauderdale** ; ˌ**Fort 'Worth** ; ˌ**hold the 'fort**
Fortaleza ˌfɔː.tə'leɪ.zə US ˌfɔːr.ţə'-
forte *strong point:* 'fɔː.teɪ, -ti US fɔːrt, 'fɔːr.teɪ **-s** -z US fɔːrts; 'fɔːr.teɪz
forte *in music:* 'fɔː.teɪ, -ti US 'fɔːr- **-s** -z
Fortescue 'fɔː.tɪ.skjuː, -tə- US 'fɔːr.ţə-
Forteviot fɔː'tiː.vi.ət US fɔːr-
forth (F) fɔːθ US fɔːrθ
forthcoming ˌfɔːθ'kʌm.ɪŋ US ˌfɔːrθ'-, '-ˌ-- *stress shift, British only:* ˌforthcoming 'book
forthright 'fɔːθ.raɪt, ˌ-'- US 'fɔːrθ-, ˌ-'- **-ness** -nəs, -nɪs
forthwith ˌfɔːθ'wɪθ, -'wɪð US ˌfɔːrθ'-
Forties *area in the North Sea:* 'fɔː.tiz, -tɪz US 'fɔːr.ţiz
fortieth 'fɔː.ti.əθ, -ɪθ US 'fɔːr.ţi- **-s** -s
fortification ˌfɔː.tɪ.fɪ'keɪ.ʃᵊn, -tə- US ˌfɔːr.ţə- **-s** -z
forti|fy 'fɔː.tɪ|.faɪ, -tə- US 'fɔːr.ţə- **-fies** -faɪz **-fying** -faɪ.ɪŋ **-fied** -faɪd **-fier/s** -faɪ.əʳ/z US -faɪ.ɚ/z **-fiable** -faɪ.ə.bl̩
Fortinbras 'fɔː.tɪn.bræs, -tɪm- US 'fɔːr.tᵊn-, -ţɪn-
fort|is 'fɔː.t|ɪs US 'fɔːr.ţ|ɪs **-es** -iːz, -eɪz
fortissimo fɔː'tɪs.ɪ.məʊ, -ə- US fɔːr'tɪs.ə.moʊ **-s** -z
fortition fɔː'tɪʃ.ᵊn US fɔːr-
fortitude 'fɔː.tɪ.tjuːd, -tʃuːd US 'fɔːr.ţə.tuːd, -tjuːd
fortnight 'fɔːt.naɪt US 'fɔːrt- **-s** -s
fortnightl|y (F) 'fɔːt.naɪt.l|i US 'fɔːrt- **-ies** -iz
Fortnum 'fɔːt.nəm US 'fɔːrt-
Fortran, FORTRAN 'fɔː.træn US 'fɔːr-
fortress 'fɔː.trəs, -trɪs US 'fɔːr- **-es** -ɪz
fortuitous fɔː'tjuː.ɪ.təs, -'tʃuː-, '-ə- US fɔːr'tuː.ə.ţəs, -'tjuː- **-ly** -li **-ness** -nəs, -nɪs
fortuit|y fɔː'tjuː.ɪ.t|i, -'tʃuː-, '-ə- US fɔːr'tuː.ə.ţ|i, -'tjuː- **-ies** -iz
Fortuna fɔː'tjuː.nə US fɔːr'tuː-, -'tjuː-
fortunate 'fɔː.tʃᵊn.ət, -ɪt US 'fɔːr- **-ly** -li **-ness** -nəs, -nɪs
Fortunatus ˌfɔː.tjuː'neɪ.təs, -'nɑː- US ˌfɔːr.tuː'nɑː.ţəs, -'neɪ-
fortune (F) 'fɔː.tʃuːn, -tjuːn, -tʃən US 'fɔːr.tʃən **-s** -z **-less** -ləs, -lɪs **'fortune ˌcookie**
fortune-teller 'fɔː.tʃuːnˌtel.əʳ, -tjuːnˌ-, -tʃənˌ- US 'fɔːr.tʃənˌtel.ɚ **-s** -z
fort|y 'fɔː.t|i US 'fɔːr.ţ|i **-ies** -iz ˌ**forty 'winks**
forty-five ˌfɔː.ti'faɪv US ˌfɔːr.ţɪ'- **-s** -z
fortyfold 'fɔː.ti.fəʊld US 'fɔːr.ţi-
forty-niner ˌfɔː.ti'naɪ.nəʳ US ˌfɔːr.ţi'naɪ.nɚ **-s** -z
forum 'fɔː.rəm US 'fɔːr.əm **-s** -z
forward 'fɔː.wəd US 'fɔːr.wɚd *nautical pronunciation:* 'fɒr.əd US 'fɔːr- **-ly** -li **-ness** -nəs, -nɪs **-er** -əʳ US -ɚ **-est** -ɪst, -əst **-s** -z **-ing** -ɪŋ **-ed** -ɪd ˌ**backwards and 'forwards**

forwards ˈfɔː.wədz (US) ˈfɔːr.wɚdz

forwent (*from* **forgo**) fɔːˈwent (US) fɔːr-

Fosbery ˈfɒz.bᵊr.i (US) ˈfɑːzˌber-, -bɚ-

Fosbroke ˈfɒz.brʊk (US) ˈfɑːz-

Fosbury ˈfɒz.bᵊr.i (US) ˈfɑːzˌber-, -bɚ-

Fosco ˈfɒs.kəʊ (US) ˈfɑː.skoʊ

Foss fɒs (US) fɑːs

foss|e fɒs (US) fɑːs **-es** -ɪz

fossick ˈfɒs.ɪk (US) ˈfɑː.sɪk **-s** -s **-ing** -ɪŋ **-ed** -t

fossil ˈfɒs.ᵊl, -ɪl (US) ˈfɑː.sᵊl **-s** -z

fossilization, -isa- ˌfɒs.ᵊl.aɪˈzeɪ.ʃᵊn, -ɪ.laɪˈ-, -lɪˈ- (US) ˌfɑː.sᵊl.ɪˈ-

fossiliz|e, -is|e ˈfɒs.ᵊl.aɪz, -ɪ.laɪz (US) ˈfɑː.sə.laɪz **-es** -ɪz **-ing** -ɪŋ **-ed** -d

fost|er (F) ˈfɒs.t|əʳ (US) ˈfɑː.st|ɚ **-ers** -əz (US) -ɚz **-ering** -ᵊr.ɪŋ **-ered** -əd (US) -ɚd **-erer/s** -ᵊr.əʳ/z (US) -ɚ.ɚ/z **-erage** -ᵊr.ɪdʒ **ˈfoster ˌbrother** ; **ˈfoster ˌchild** ; **ˈfoster ˌchildren** ; **ˈfoster ˌfather** ; **ˈfoster ˌhome** ; **ˈfoster ˌmother** ; **ˈfoster ˌparent** ; **ˈfoster ˌsister**

Fothergill ˈfʌð.ə.gɪl (US) ˈfɑː.ðɚ-

Fotheringay ˈfɒð.ᵊr.ɪŋ.heɪ, -geɪ (US) ˈfɑː.ðɚ-

Fotheringham ˈfɒð.ᵊr.ɪŋ.əm (US) ˈfɑː.ðɚ-

Foucault ˈfuː.kəʊ, -ˈ- (US) ˌfuːˈkoʊ

fouetté ˈfuː.ə.teɪ (US) fwetˈeɪ **-s** -z

fought (*from* **fight**) fɔːt (US) fɑːt, fɔːt

foul faʊl **-er** -əʳ (US) -ɚ **-est** -ɪst, -əst **-ly** -li, ˈfaʊ.li **-ness** -nəs, -nɪs **-s** -z **-ing** -ɪŋ **-ed** -d ˌ**foul ˈplay**

foulard ˈfuː.lɑːʳ, -lɑːd, -ˈ- (US) fuːˈlɑːrd

Foulden ˈfəʊl.dən (US) ˈfoʊl-

Foulds fəʊldz (US) foʊldz

Foulerton ˈfʊl.ə.tᵊn (US) ˈ-ɚ-

Foulger ˈfuːl.dʒəʳ, -gəʳ (US) ˈfuːl.dʒɚ, ˈfoʊl-, -gɚ

Foulis faʊlz

Foulkes fəʊks, faʊks (US) foʊks, faʊks

foulmouthed ˌfaʊlˈmaʊðd, -ˈmaʊθt (US) ˌ-ˈ-, ˈ-ˌ- *stress shift, British only:* ˌfoulmouthed ˈlanguage

foulness ˈfaʊl.nəs, -nɪs

Foulness ˌfaʊlˈnes *stress shift:* ˌFoulness ˈbeach

Foulsham ˈfəʊl.ʃᵊm (US) ˈfoʊl-

foul-up ˈfaʊl.ʌp **-s** -s

found faʊnd **-s** -z **-ing** -ɪŋ **-ed** -ɪd

found (*from* **find**) faʊnd

foundation faʊnˈdeɪ.ʃᵊn **-s** -z **founˈdation ˌcourse** ; **founˈdation ˌstone**

foundationer faʊnˈdeɪ.ʃᵊn.əʳ (US) -ɚ **-s** -z

found|er ˈfaʊn.d|əʳ (US) -d|ɚ **-ers** -əz (US) -ɚz **-ering** -ᵊr.ɪŋ **-ered** -əd (US) -ɚd ˌ**founder ˈmember**

foundling (F) ˈfaʊnd.lɪŋ **-s** -z

foundr|y ˈfaʊn.dr|i **-ies** -iz

fount *fountain, source:* faʊnt **-s** -s

fount *in printing:* faʊnt, fɒnt (US) faʊnt, fɑːnt **-s** -s

Note: Those connected with the printing trade generally pronounce /fɒnt (US) fɑːnt/.

fountain (F) ˈfaʊn.tɪn, -tən (US) -tᵊn **-s** -z **ˈfountain ˌpen**

fountainhead ˈfaʊn.tɪn.hed, -tən-, ˌ--ˈ- (US) ˈfaʊn.tᵊn.hed **-s** -z

four fɔːʳ (US) fɔːr **-s** -z **-th/s** -θ/s **-thly** -θ.li ˌ**Four ˈCorners**

four-cornered ˌfɔːˈkɔː.nəd (US) ˌfɔːrˈkɔːr.nɚd *stress shift:* ˌfour-cornered ˈhat

four-dimensional ˌfɔː.dɪˈmen.*t*ʃᵊn.ᵊl, -daɪˈ- (US) ˌfɔːr.dəˈmen*t*.ʃᵊn- *stress shift:* ˌfour-dimensional ˈmodel

fourfold ˈfɔː.fəʊld (US) ˈfɔːr.foʊld

four-footed ˌfɔːˈfʊt.ɪd (US) ˌfɔːrˈfʊt̬- *stress shift:* ˌfour-footed ˈbeast

Fourier ˈfʊə.ri.əʳ, ˈfʊr.i-, -eɪ (US) ˈfʊr.i.eɪ

four-in-hand ˌfɔːr.ɪnˈhænd (US) ˈfɔːr.ɪnˌhænd **-s** -z

four-legged ˌfɔːˈlegd, -ˈleg.ɪd (US) ˌfɔːr-, ˈfɔːrˌ- *stress shift:* ˌfour-legged ˈfriend

four-letter ˌfɔːˈlet.əʳ (US) ˌfɔːrˈlet̬.ɚ *stress shift, see compound:* ˌ**four-letter ˈword**

fourpence ˈfɔː.pᵊn*t*s (US) ˈfɔːr-

fourpenny ˈfɔː.pᵊn.i (US) ˈfɔːr-

four-ply ˈfɔː.plaɪ, ˌ-ˈ- (US) ˈfɔːr.plaɪ, ˌ-ˈ-

four-poster ˌfɔːˈpəʊ.stəʳ (US) ˌfɔːrˈpoʊ.stɚ **-s** -z *stress shift, see compound:* ˌ**four-poster ˈbed**

fourscore ˌfɔːˈskɔːʳ (US) ˌfɔːrˈskɔːr *stress shift:* ˌfourscore ˈyears

foursome ˈfɔː.səm (US) ˈfɔːr- **-s** -z

foursquare ˌfɔːˈskweəʳ, ˈ-- (US) ˌfɔːrˈskwer, ˈ--

fourteen ˌfɔːˈtiːn (US) ˌfɔːr- **-s** -z **-th/s** -θ/s *stress shift:* ˌfourteen ˈyears

fourteener fɔːˈtiː.nəʳ (US) fɔːrˈtiː.nɚ **-s** -z

fourth fɔːθ (US) fɔːrθ **-s** -s **-ly** -li ˌ**Fourth of Juˈly**

four-wheel drive ˌfɔː.*h*wiːlˈdraɪv (US) ˌfɔːr- *stress shift, British only:* ˌfour-wheel drive ˈcar

four-wheeler ˌfɔːˈ*h*wiː.ləʳ (US) ˌfɔːrˈ*h*wiː.lɚ **-s** -z

fov|ea ˈfɒv|.i.ə, ˈfəʊ.v|i- (US) ˈfoʊ- **-eae** -i.iː

Fowey fɔɪ, ˈfəʊ.i (US) fɔɪ, ˈfoʊ.i

Fowke faʊk, fəʊk (US) faʊk, foʊk

Fowkes fəʊks, faʊks (US) foʊks, faʊks

fowl faʊl **-s** -z **-ing** -ɪŋ **-ed** -d **-er/s** -əʳ/z (US) -ɚ/z **ˈfowling ˌpiece**

Fowler ˈfaʊ.ləʳ (US) -lɚ

Fowles faʊlz

fox (F) fɒks (US) fɑːks **-es** -ɪz **-ing** -ɪŋ **-ed** -t ˌ**fox ˈterrier**

Foxboro' ˈfɒks.bᵊr.ə (US) ˈfɑːks.bɚ.oʊ

Foxcroft ˈfɒks.krɒft (US) ˈfɑːks.krɑːft

Foxe fɒks (US) fɑːks

Foxfield ˈfɒks.fiːld (US) ˈfɑːks-

foxglove ˈfɒks.glʌv (US) ˈfɑːks- **-s** -z

foxhole ˈfɒks.həʊl (US) ˈfɑːks.hoʊl **-s** -z

foxhound ˈfɒks.haʊnd (US) ˈfɑːks- **-s** -z

fox|hunt ˈfɒks|.hʌnt (US) ˈfɑːks- **-hunts** -hʌnts **-hunting** -ˌhʌn.tɪŋ (US) -ˌhʌn.t̬ɪŋ

foxtrot ˈfɒks.trɒt (US) ˈfɑːks.trɑːt **-s** -s

Foxwell ˈfɒks.wəl, -wel (US) ˈfɑːks-

fox|y ˈfɒk.s|i (US) ˈfɑːk- **-ier** -i.əʳ (US) -i.ɚ **-iest** -i.ɪst, -i.əst **-ily** -ɪ.li, -ə.li **-iness** -ɪ.nəs, -ɪ.nɪs

Foy fɔɪ

foyer ˈfɔɪ.eɪ, -əʳ; ˈfwaɪ.eɪ (US) ˈfɔɪ.ɚ, -eɪ; fɔɪˈeɪ, fwɑːˈ- **-s** -z

Foyers ˈfɔɪ.əz (US) -ɚz

Foyle fɔɪl

Fr. (*abbrev. for* **Father**) ˈfɑː.ðəʳ (US) -ðɚ

frabjous ˈfræb.dʒəs

fracas *singular:* ˈfræk.ɑː (US) ˈfreɪ.kəs, ˈfræk.əs *plural:* ˈfræk.ɑːz (US) ˈfreɪ.kəs, ˈfræk.əs **-es** -ɪz

fractal ˈfræk.tᵊl **-s** -z

fraction ˈfræk.ʃᵊn **-s** -z

fractional ˈfræk.ʃᵊn.ᵊl **-ly** -i

fraction|ate ˈfræk.ʃᵊn|.eɪt **-ates** -eɪts **-ating** -eɪ.tɪŋ (US) -eɪ.t̬ɪŋ **-ated** -eɪ.tɪd (US) -eɪ.t̬ɪd

fractious ˈfræk.ʃəs **-ly** -li **-ness** -nəs, -nɪs

fract|ure ˈfræk.*t*ʃ|əʳ (US) -*t*ʃ|ɚ **-ures** -əz (US) -ɚz **-uring** -ᵊr.ɪŋ **-ured** -əd (US) -ɚd

fragile ˈfrædʒ.aɪl (US) ˈfrædʒ.ᵊl **-ly** -li

fragility frəˈdʒɪl.ə.ti, frædʒˈɪl-, -ɪ.ti (US) frəˈdʒɪl.ə.t̬i

fragment (*n.*) ˈfræg.mənt **-s** -s

fragmen|t (*v.*) frægˈmen|t (US) ˈfræg.men|t, -ˈ- **-ts** -ts **-ting** -tɪŋ (US) -t̬ɪŋ **-ted** -tɪd (US) -t̬ɪd

fragmental frægˈmen.tᵊl (US) -t̬ᵊl

fragmentar|y ˈfræg.mən.tᵊr|.i, -tr|i; frægˈmen- (US) ˈfræg.mən.ter|.i **-ily** -ᵊl.i, -ɪ.li **-iness** -ɪ.nəs, -ɪ.nɪs

fragmentation ˌfræg.mənˈteɪ.ʃᵊn, -menˈ-

Fragonard ˈfræg.ɒn.ɑːʳ, -ən- (US) ˌfræg.əˈnɑːr, ˌfrɑː.goʊˈ-

fragranc|e ˈfreɪ.grən*t*s **-es** -ɪz **-ed** -t

fragrant ˈfreɪ.grənt **-ly** -li **-ness** -nəs, -nɪs

frail freɪl **-er** -əʳ (US) -ɚ **-est** -ɪst, -əst **-ly** -li **-ness** -nəs, -nɪs

frailt|y ˈfreɪl.t|i (US) -t̬|i **-ies** -iz

frambesia, framboesia fræmˈbiː.zi.ə, -ʒə, ʒi.ə (US) -ʒə, -ʒi.ə

fram|e (F) freɪm **-es** -z **-ing** -ɪŋ **-ed** -d **-er/s** -əʳ/z (US) -ɚ/z

frame-up 'freɪm.ʌp **-s** -s
framework 'freɪm.wɜːk Ⓤⓢ -wɜːrk **-s** -s
Framingham *in UK:* 'freɪ.mɪŋ.əm *in US:* 'fræm.ɪŋ.hæm
Framley 'fræm.li
Framlingham 'fræm.lɪŋ.əm
Frampton 'fræm*p*.tən
Fran fræn
franc fræŋk **-s** -s
France frɑːn*t*s Ⓤⓢ frænts
Frances 'frɑːn*t*.sɪs Ⓤⓢ 'frænt-
Francesca fræn'tʃes.kə Ⓤⓢ fræn-, frɑːn-
Franche-Comté ˌfrɑ̃ːnʃ.kɔ̃ːn'teɪ Ⓤⓢ -koʊ̃n'-
franchis|e 'fræn.*t*ʃaɪz **-es** -ɪz **-ing** -ɪŋ **-ed** -d
franchisee ˌfræn.*t*ʃaɪ'ziː **-s** -z
Francie 'frɑːn*t*.si Ⓤⓢ 'frænt-
Francis 'frɑːn*t*.sɪs Ⓤⓢ 'frænt-
Franciscan fræn'sɪs.kən **-s** -z
Francisco fræn'sɪs.kəʊ Ⓤⓢ -koʊ *in San Francisco:* frən'sɪs.kəʊ, fræn- Ⓤⓢ -koʊ
francium 'frænt.si.əm
Franck frɑ̃ːŋk, frɑːŋk, fræŋk Ⓤⓢ frɑ̃ːŋk
Franco-, franco- fræŋ.kəʊ- Ⓤⓢ fræŋ.koʊ-, -kə-
Note: Prefix. Normally either takes primary or secondary stress on the first syllable, e.g. **francophile** /'fræŋ.kəʊ.faɪl Ⓤⓢ -koʊ-/, **Franco-German** /ˌfræŋ.kəʊ'dʒɜː.mən Ⓤⓢ -koʊ'dʒɜːr-/.
Franco 'fræŋ.kəʊ Ⓤⓢ -koʊ
Franco-German ˌfræŋ.kəʊ'dʒɜː.mən Ⓤⓢ -koʊ'dʒɜːr-
François 'frɑ̃ːn.swɑː, -'- Ⓤⓢ frɑ̃ːnt'swɑː, frænt'-, 'ˌ-
francolin 'fræŋ.kəʊ.lɪn Ⓤⓢ -koʊ- **-s** -z
Franconi|a fræŋ'kəʊ.ni|.ə Ⓤⓢ fræŋ'koʊ-, fræn- **-an** -ən
francophile 'fræŋ.kəʊ.faɪl Ⓤⓢ -koʊ-, -kə- **-s** -z
francophobe 'fræŋ.kəʊ.fəʊb Ⓤⓢ -koʊ.foʊb, -kə- **-s** -z
francophone (F) 'fræŋ.kəʊ.fəʊn Ⓤⓢ -koʊ.foʊn, -kə- **-s** -z
francophonic (F) ˌfræŋ.kəʊ'fɒn.ɪk Ⓤⓢ -koʊ'fɑː.nɪk, -kə'-
frangibility ˌfræn.dʒɪ'bɪl.ə.ti, -dʒə'-, -ɪ.ti Ⓤⓢ -ə.ṭi
frangible 'fræn.dʒɪ.bl̩, -dʒə- **-ness** -nəs, -nɪs
frangipani ˌfræn.dʒɪ'pɑː.ni, -'pæn.i **-s** -z
franglais 'frɑ̃ː*ŋ*.gleɪ, 'frɒŋ- Ⓤⓢ frɑ̃ːn'gleɪ
frank (F) fræŋk **-er** -əʳ Ⓤⓢ -ɚ **-est** -ɪst, -əst **-ly** -li **-ness** -nəs, -nɪs **-s** -s **-ing** -ɪŋ **-ed** -t

Frankau 'fræŋ.kəʊ, -kaʊ Ⓤⓢ -kaʊ
Frankenstein 'fræŋ.kᵊn.staɪn, -kɪn-
Frankfort *places in US:* 'fræŋk.fət Ⓤⓢ -fɚt
Frankfurt *in Germany:* 'fræŋk.fɜːt, -fət Ⓤⓢ -fɜːrt, -fɚt
frankfurter (F) 'fræŋk.fɜː.təʳ Ⓤⓢ -fɜːr.ṭɚ **-s** -z
Frankie 'fræŋ.ki
frankincense 'fræŋ.kɪn.sen*t*s, -kᵊn-
Frankish 'fræŋ.kɪʃ
Frankland 'fræŋk.lənd
franklin (F) 'fræŋk.lɪn **-s** -z
Franklyn 'fræŋk.lɪn
frantic 'fræn.tɪk Ⓤⓢ -ṭɪk **-ally** -ᵊl.i, -li **-ness** -nəs, -nɪs
Franz *German name:* frænts, frɑːnts *US name:* frænz
frap fræp **-s** -s **-ping** -ɪŋ **-ped** -t
frappé 'fræp.eɪ Ⓤⓢ -'-
Frascati fræs'kɑː.ti
Fraser 'freɪ.zəʳ Ⓤⓢ -zɚ
Fraserburgh 'freɪ.zə.bᵊr.ə, -bʌr- Ⓤⓢ -zɚ.bɚ-
frat fræt **-s** -s
fraternal frə'tɜː.nᵊl Ⓤⓢ -'tɜːr- **-ly** -i
fraternit|y frə'tɜː.nə.t|i, -ɪ.t|i Ⓤⓢ -'tɜːr.nə.ṭ|i **-ies** -iz
fraternization, -isa- ˌfræt.ᵊn.aɪ'zeɪ.ʃᵊn, -ɪ'- Ⓤⓢ -ɚ.nɪ'-
fraterniz|e, -is|e 'fræt.ə.naɪz Ⓤⓢ '-ɚ- **-es** -ɪz **-ing** -ɪŋ **-ed** -d **-er/s** -əʳ/z Ⓤⓢ -ɚ/z
fratricidal ˌfræt.rɪ'saɪ.dᵊl, ˌfreɪ.trɪ'-, -trə'- Ⓤⓢ ˌfræt.rə'saɪ-
fratricide 'fræt.rɪ.saɪd, 'freɪ.trɪ-, -trə- Ⓤⓢ 'fræt.rə- **-s** -z
Fratton 'fræt.ᵊn
Frau fraʊ
fraud frɔːd Ⓤⓢ frɑːd, frɔːd **-s** -z
fraudster 'frɔːd.stəʳ Ⓤⓢ 'frɑːd.stɚ, 'frɔːd- **-s** -z
fraudulence 'frɔː.djə.lənts, -djʊ-, -dʒə-, -dʒʊ- Ⓤⓢ 'frɑː.dʒə-, 'frɔː-, -djuː-, -djə-
fraudulent 'frɔː.djə.lənt, -djʊ-, -dʒə-, -dʒʊ- Ⓤⓢ 'frɑː.dʒə-, 'frɔː-, -djuː-, -djə- **-ly** -li
fraught frɔːt Ⓤⓢ frɑːt, frɔːt
fraülein 'frɔɪ.laɪn, 'fraʊ- **-s** -z
fray freɪ **-s** -z **-ing** -ɪŋ **-ed** -d
Fray Bentos® ˌfreɪ'ben.tɒs Ⓤⓢ -toʊs
Frayn freɪn
Frazer 'freɪ.zəʳ Ⓤⓢ -zɚ
Frazier 'freɪ.zi.əʳ Ⓤⓢ -ʒɚ, -ʒi.ɚ
frazil 'freɪ.zɪl, 'fræz.ɪl, -ᵊl Ⓤⓢ 'freɪ.zɪl; 'fræz.ᵊl; frə'zɪl, -'ziːl
frazzl|e 'fræz.l̩ **-es** -z **-ing** -ɪŋ, '-lɪŋ **-ed** -d
freak friːk **-s** -s **-ing** -ɪŋ **-ed** -t
Freake friːk
freakish 'friː.kɪʃ **-ly** -li **-ness** -nəs, -nɪs

freak|y 'friː.k|i **-ier** -i.əʳ Ⓤⓢ -i.ɚ **-iest** -i.ɪst, -i.əst **-ily** -ɪ.li, -ᵊl.i **-iness** -ɪ.nəs, -ɪ.nɪs
Frean friːn
Frears frɪəz, freəz Ⓤⓢ frɪrz, frerz
freckl|e 'frek.l̩ **-es** -z **-ing** -ɪŋ, '-lɪŋ **-ed** -d
Freckleton 'frek.l̩.tən
freckly 'frek.l̩.i, 'frek.li
Fred fred
Freddie, Freddy 'fred.i
Frederica ˌfred.ᵊr'iː.kə Ⓤⓢ -ə'riː-
Frederic(k) 'fred.ᵊr.ɪk
Fredericksburg 'fred.ᵊr.ɪks.bɜːg Ⓤⓢ -bɜːrg
free (F) friː **-r** -əʳ Ⓤⓢ -ɚ **-st** -ɪst, əst **-ly** -li **-s** -z **-ing** -ɪŋ **-d** -d **-r/s** -əʳ/z Ⓤⓢ -ɚ/z ˌ**free 'enterprise** ; '**free ˌhouse** ; ˌ**free 'kick** ; ˌ**free 'market** ; ˌ**free 'ride** ; ˌ**free 'trade** ; ˌ**free 'will** ; **gives someone a** ˌ**free 'hand**
freebas|e 'friː.beɪs **-es** -ɪz **-ing** -ɪŋ **-ed** -t
freebie, freebee 'friː.bi **-s** -z
freeboard 'friː.bɔːd Ⓤⓢ -bɔːrd
freebooter 'friːˌbuː.təʳ Ⓤⓢ -ṭɚ **-s** -z
freeborn ˌfriː'bɔːn Ⓤⓢ -'bɔːrn *stress shift:* ˌfreeborn 'citizen
Freeborn 'friː.bɔːn Ⓤⓢ -bɔːrn
Freeburn 'friː.bɜːn Ⓤⓢ -bɜːrn
freed|man 'friːd|.mæn, -mən **-men** -men, -mən
freedom 'friː.dəm **-s** -z '**freedom** ˌ**fighter**
free-fall (*v.*) 'friː.fɔːl, ˌ-'- Ⓤⓢ 'friː.fɔːl, -fɑːl **-ing** -ɪŋ **-er/s** -əʳ/z Ⓤⓢ -ɚ/z
Freefone® 'friː.fəʊn Ⓤⓢ -foʊn
free-for-all 'friː.fəʳˌɔːl, ˌ--'- Ⓤⓢ 'friː.fɚ.ɔːl, -ɑːl
freehand 'friː.hænd
freehearted ˌfriː'hɑː.tɪd Ⓤⓢ -'hɑːr.ṭɪd, 'ˌ-- **-ly** -li **-ness** -nəs, -nɪs *stress shift, British only:* ˌfreehearted 'friend
freehold 'friː.həʊld Ⓤⓢ -hoʊld **-s** -z **-er/s** -əʳ/z Ⓤⓢ -ɚ/z
freelanc|e 'friː.lɑːn*t*s, ˌ-'- Ⓤⓢ 'friː.læn*t*s **-es** -ɪz **-er/s** -əʳ/z Ⓤⓢ -ɚ/z
Freeling 'friː.lɪŋ
freeload 'friː.ləʊd Ⓤⓢ -loʊd **-s** -z **-ing** -ɪŋ **-ed** -ɪd **-er/s** -əʳ/z Ⓤⓢ -ɚ/z
free|man 'friː|.mən, -mæn **-men** -mən, -men
Freeman *surname:* 'friː.mən
free-market (*adj.*) 'friːˌmɑː.kɪt Ⓤⓢ -ˌmɑːr-
free market (*n.*) ˌfriː'mɑː.kɪt Ⓤⓢ -'mɑːr-
freemason 'friːˌmeɪ.sᵊn **-s** -z
freemasonry 'friːˌmeɪ.sᵊn.ri, ˌfriː'meɪ-
freephone 'friː.fəʊn Ⓤⓢ -foʊn

Freeport 'friː.pɔːt (US) -pɔːrt
Freepost® 'friː.pəʊst (US) -poʊst
free-range ˌfriː'reɪndʒ *stress shift, see compounds:* **ˌfree-range 'eggs** ; **ˌfree-range 'chickens**
freesheet 'friː.ʃiːt **-s** -s
freesia 'friː.zi.ə, -ʒə, -ʒi.ə (US) -ʒi.ə, -ʒə **-s** -z
free-spoken ˌfriː'spəʊ.kᵊn (US) ˌfriː'spoʊ-, 'ˌ-ˌ-- *stress shift, British only:* ˌfree-spoken 'person
free-standing ˌfriː'stæn.dɪŋ (US) ˌfriː'stæn.dɪŋ, '-ˌ-- *stress shift, British only:* ˌfree-standing 'column
freestone (F) 'friː.stəʊn (US) -stoʊn
freestyle 'friː.staɪl
Freeth friːθ
freethinker ˌfriː'θɪŋ.kəʳ (US) -kɚ, '-ˌ-- **-s** -z
Freetown 'friː.taʊn
freeway 'friː.weɪ **-s** -z
freewheel ˌfriː'*h*wiːl (US) 'friː.*h*wiːl **-s** -z **-ing** -ɪŋ **-ed** -d *stress shift, British only:* ˌfreewheel 'mechanism
freewill ˌfriː'wɪl, '--
freez|e friːz **-es** -ɪz **-ing** -ɪŋ **froze** frəʊz (US) froʊz **frozen** 'frəʊ.zᵊn (US) 'froʊ- **freezer/s** 'friː.zəʳ/z (US) -zɚ/z **'freeze ˌframe**, **ˌfreeze 'frame**
freeze|-dry 'friːz|.draɪ **-dries** -draɪz **-drying** -ˌdraɪ.ɪŋ **-dried** -draɪd
Freiburg 'fraɪ.bɜːg (US) -bɜːrg
freight freɪt **-s** -s **-ing** -ɪŋ (US) 'freɪ.t̬ɪŋ **-ed** -ɪd (US) 'freɪ.t̬ɪd **-age** -ɪdʒ (US) 'freɪ.t̬ɪdʒ **'freight ˌcar**
freighter 'freɪ.təʳ (US) -t̬ɚ **-s** -z
freightliner 'freɪtˌlaɪ.nəʳ (US) -nɚ **-s** -z
Fremantle 'friː.mæn.tl̩ (US) -t̬l̩
fremitus 'frem.ɪ.təs (US) -t̬əs
Fremont 'friː.mɒnt, frɪ'mɒnt (US) 'friː.mɑːnt
French, french frentʃ **ˌFrench 'bean** ; **ˌFrench 'bread** ; **ˌFrench 'dressing** ; **ˌfrench 'fry** (US) **'french ˌfry** ; **ˌFrench 'loaf** ; **ˌFrench Revo'lution** ; **ˌFrench 'stick** ; **ˌFrench 'windows**
frenchi|fy 'fren.*t*ʃɪ|.faɪ (US) 'frent.ʃɪ- **-fies** -faɪz **-fying** -faɪ.ɪŋ **-fied** -faɪd
French|man 'fren*t*ʃ|.mən **-men** -mən
french-polish ˌfren*t*ʃ'pɒl.ɪʃ (US) -'pɑː.lɪʃ **-es** -ɪz **-ing** -ɪŋ **-ed** -t **-er/s** -əʳ/z (US) -ɚ/z
French|woman 'fren*t*ʃ|ˌwʊm.ən **-women** -ˌwɪm.ɪn
frenetic frə'net.ɪk, frɪ-, fren'et- (US) frə'net̬- **-ally** -ᵊl.i, -li
frenz|y 'fren.z|i **-ies** -iz **-ied/ly** -ɪd/li
frequen|ce 'friː.kwən*t*|s **-cy** -si **-cies** -siz
frequent *(adj.)* 'friː.kwənt **-ly** -li **-ness** -nəs, -nɪs
frequen|t *(v.)* frɪ'kwen|t, friː-, frə- (US) friː-; 'friː.kwen|t, -kwən|t **-ts** -ts **-ting** -tɪŋ (US) -t̬ɪŋ **-ted** -tɪd (US) -t̬ɪd **-ter/s** -təʳ/z (US) -t̬ɚ/z
frequentative frɪ'kwen.tə.tɪv, friː-, frə- (US) friː'kwen.t̬ə.t̬ɪv **-s** -z
Frere frɪəʳ (US) frer
fresco 'fres.kəʊ (US) -koʊ **-(e)s** -z
fresh freʃ **-er** -əʳ (US) -ɚ **-est** -ɪst, -əst **-ly** -li **-ness** -nəs, -nɪs
freshen 'freʃ.ᵊn **-s** -z **-ing** -ɪŋ **-ed** -d
fresher 'freʃ.əʳ (US) -ɚ **-s** -z
freshet 'freʃ.ɪt, -ət **-s** -s
fresh|man 'freʃ|.mən **-men** -mən
freshwater (F) 'freʃˌwɔː.təʳ, ˌ-'-- (US) 'freʃˌwɑː.t̬ɚ, -ˌwɔː-
Fresno 'frez.nəʊ (US) -noʊ
fret fret **-s** -s **-ting** -ɪŋ (US) 'fret̬.ɪŋ **-ted** -ɪd (US) 'fret̬.ɪd
fretful 'fret.fᵊl, -fʊl **-ly** -i **-ness** -nəs, -nɪs
fretsaw 'fret.sɔː (US) -sɑː, -sɔː **-s** -z
Fretwell 'fret.wel, -wəl
fretwork 'fret.wɜːk (US) -wɜːrk
Freud frɔɪd **-ian** -i.ən **ˌFreudian 'slip**
Frew fruː
Frey freɪ
Freya freɪə
Freyberg 'fraɪ.bɜːg (US) -bɜːrg
Freyer frɪəʳ; 'fraɪ.əʳ (US) 'fraɪ.ɚ, -ɚ; frɪr
Freyja freɪə
Fri. *(abbrev. for* **Friday***)* 'fraɪ.deɪ, -di
friability ˌfraɪ.ə'bɪl.ə.ti, -ɪ.ti (US) -ə.t̬i
friable 'fraɪ.ə.bl̩ **-ness** -nəs, -nɪs
friar fraɪəʳ (US) fraɪɚ **-s** -z
friar|y 'fraɪə.r|i **-ies** -iz
fribbl|e 'frɪb.l̩ **-es** -z **-ing** -ɪŋ, '-lɪŋ **-ed** -d
fricandeau 'frɪk.ən.dəʊ, -*ɑ̃ːn*- (US) ˌfrɪk.ən'doʊ, '--- **-s** -z
fricandeaux *(alternative plur. of* **fricandeau***)* 'frɪk.ən.dəʊ, -*ɑ̃ːn*-, -dəʊz (US) ˌfrɪk.ən'doʊ, -'doʊz, '---
fricassee ˌfrɪk.ə'siː, -'seɪ, '--- (US) ˌfrɪk.ə'siː, '--- **-s** -z **-ing** -ɪŋ **-d** -d
fricative 'frɪk.ə.tɪv (US) -t̬ɪv **-s** -z
friction 'frɪk.ʃᵊn **-s** -z **-less** -ləs, -les, -lɪs
frictional 'frɪk.ʃᵊn.ᵊl
Friday 'fraɪ.deɪ, -di **-s** -z
fridg|e frɪdʒ **-es** -ɪz **ˌfridge-'freezer**
fried *(from* **fry***)* fraɪd
Friedan friː'dæn, frɪ-
Friedland 'friːd.lənd, -lænd
Friedman 'friːd.mən
Friel friːl
friend (F) frend **-s** -z
friendless 'frend.ləs, -lɪs **-ness** -nəs, -nɪs
friendl|y (F) 'frend.l|i **-ies** -iz **-ier** -i.əʳ (US) -i.ɚ **-iest** -i.ɪst, -i.əst **-iness** -ɪ.nəs, -ɪ.nɪs
Friendl|y 'frend.l|i **-ies** -iz
friendship 'fren*d*.ʃɪp **-s** -s
Friern 'fraɪ.ən, 'friː- (US) -ɚn
fries *(from* **fry***)* fraɪz
Fries friːs, friːz
Friesian 'friː.zi.ən, -ʒi-, '-ʒᵊn (US) 'friː.ʒᵊn
Friesland 'friːz.lənd, -lænd **-er/s** -əʳ/z (US) -ɚ/z
friez|e (F) friːz **-es** -ɪz
frig frɪg **-s** -z **-ging** -ɪŋ **-ged** -d
frigate 'frɪg.ət, -ɪt **-s** -s
fright fraɪt **-s** -s **-ing** -ɪŋ (US) 'fraɪ.t̬ɪŋ **-ed** -ɪd (US) 'fraɪ.t̬ɪd
frighten 'fraɪ.tᵊn **-s** -z **-ing/ly** -ɪŋ/li **-ed** -d **-er/s** -əʳ/z (US) -ɚ/z
frightful 'fraɪt.fᵊl, -fʊl **-ly** -i **-ness** -nəs, -nɪs
frigid 'frɪdʒ.ɪd **-ly** -li **-ness** -nəs, -nɪs
Frigidaire® ˌfrɪdʒ.ɪ'deəʳ, -ə'- (US) -'der, '--ˌ-
frigidity frɪ'dʒɪd.ə.ti, -ɪ.ti (US) -ə.t̬i
Friis friːs
frijole frɪ'həʊ.li, -eɪ (US) friː'hoʊ.liː, -'hoʊ, -'hoʊl **-s** -z
frill frɪl **-s** -z **-ing** -ɪŋ **-ed** -d
frill|y 'frɪl|.i **-ier** -i.əʳ (US) -i.ɚ **-iest** -i.ɪst, -i.əst **-iness** -ɪ.nəs, -ɪ.nɪs
Frimley 'frɪm.li
fring|e frɪn*d*ʒ **-es** -ɪz **-ing** -ɪŋ **-ed** -d **-eless** -ləs, -lɪs **'fringe ˌbenefit**, **ˌfringe 'benefit** ; **ˌfringe 'theatre/'theater**
Frinton 'frɪn.tən
fripper|y 'frɪp.ᵊr|.i **-ies** -iz
Frisbee® 'frɪz.bi **-s** -z
frisé(e) 'friːz.eɪ (US) friː'zeɪ, frɪ- **-s** -z
frisette frɪ'zet, friː- **-s** -s
Frisian 'frɪz.i.ən, 'friː.zi-, -ʒi-, -ʒᵊn (US) 'frɪʒ.ᵊn, 'friː.ʒᵊn **-s** -z
frisk frɪsk **-s** -s **-ing** -ɪŋ **-ed** -t **-er/s** -əʳ/z (US) -ɚ/z
frisket 'frɪs.kɪt **-s** -s
frisk|y 'frɪs.k|i **-ier** -i.əʳ (US) -i.ɚ **-iest** -i.ɪst, -i.əst **-ily** -ɪ.li, -ᵊl.i **-iness** -ɪ.nəs, -ɪ.nɪs
frisson 'friː.s*ɔ̃ːŋ*, -'- (US) friː'sõʊn **-s** -z
Friston 'frɪs.tᵊn
Friswell 'frɪz.wəl, -wel
frit frɪt **-s** -s **-ting** -ɪŋ (US) 'frɪt̬.ɪŋ **-ted** -ɪd (US) 'frɪt̬.ɪd
frith (F) frɪθ **-s** -s
Frithsden 'friːz.dən, 'frɪz-, 'frɪθs.dən
fritillar|y frɪ'tɪl.ᵊr|.i, frə- (US) 'frɪt̬.ᵊl.er|.i **-ies** -iz
Fritos® 'friː.təʊz (US) -t̬oʊz, -toʊz
fritt|er 'frɪt|.əʳ (US) 'frɪt̬|.ɚ **-ers** -əz (US) -ɚz **-ering** -ᵊr.ɪŋ **-ered** -əd (US) -ɚd
fritz (F) frɪts
Friuli fri'uː.li
frivol 'frɪv.ᵊl **-s** -z **-(l)ing** -ɪŋ **-(l)ed** -d
frivolit|y frɪ'vɒl.ə.t|i, frə-, -ɪ.t|i (US) -'vɑː.lə.t̬|i **-ies** -iz

frivolous 'frɪv.ᵊl.əs **-ly** -li **-ness** -nəs, -nɪs
Frizelle frɪ'zel
friz(z) frɪz **-es** -ɪz **-ing** -ɪŋ **-ed** -d
frizzl|e 'frɪz.l̩ **-es** -z **-ing** -ɪŋ, '-lɪŋ **-ed** -d
frizzl|y 'frɪz.l̩|.i, 'frɪz.l|i **-iness** -ɪ.nəs, -ɪ.nɪs
frizz|y 'frɪz|.i **-ier** -i.əʳ (US) -i.ɚ **-iest** -i.ɪst, -i.əst **-iness** -ɪ.nəs, -ɪ.nɪs
fro frəʊ (US) froʊ
Frobisher 'frəʊ.bɪ.ʃəʳ (US) 'froʊ.bɪ.ʃɚ
frock frɒk (US) frɑːk **-s** -s ˌ**frock 'coat**
Frodo 'frəʊ.dəʊ (US) 'froʊ.doʊ
Frodsham 'frɒd.ʃᵊm (US) 'frɑːd-
Froebel 'frəʊ.bᵊl, 'frɜː- (US) 'frɜː-, 'froʊ-
frog frɒg (US) frɑːg, frɔːg **-s** -z **have a 'frog in one's ˌthroat**
Froggatt 'frɒg.ɪt, -ət (US) 'frɑː.gɪt, -gət
frogg|y 'frɒg|.i (US) 'frɑː.g|i **-ies** -iz
frog|man 'frɒg|.mən (US) 'frɑːg-, 'frɔːg- **-men** -mən
frogmarch 'frɒg.mɑːtʃ (US) 'frɑːg.mɑːrtʃ, 'frɔːg- **-es** -ɪz **-ing** -ɪŋ **-ed** -t
Frogmore 'frɒg.mɔːʳ (US) 'frɑːg.mɔːr, 'frɔːg-
frogspawn 'frɒg.spɔːn (US) 'frɑːg.spɑːn, 'frɔːg-, -spɔːn
Froissart 'frɔɪ.sɑːt, 'frwæs.ɑː (US) -sɑːrt; *as if French:* ˌfrwɑː'sɑːr
frolic 'frɒl.ɪk (US) 'frɑː.lɪk **-s** -s **-king** -ɪŋ **-ked** -t
frolicsome 'frɒl.ɪk.səm (US) 'frɑː.lɪk- **-ness** -nəs, -nɪs
from *strong form:* frɒm (US) frɑːm *weak forms:* frəm, frm̩
Note: Weak form word. The strong from /frɒm (US) frɑːm/ is used contrastively (e.g. "Travelling **to** and **from** London") and in sentence-final position (e.g. "Where is it from?"). The weak form is /frəm/ (e.g. "back from abroad" /ˌbæk.frəm.ə'brɔːd (US) -'brɑːd/). In rapid speech this may be further weakened to /frm̩/ (e.g. "one from each" /ˌwʌn.frm̩'iːtʃ/).
fromage frais ˌfrɒm.ɑːʒ'freɪ (US) frəˌmɑːʒ'-; ˌfrɑː.mɑːʒ'-
Frome *in Somerset:* fruːm *lake in Australia:* frəʊm (US) froʊm
Note: /frəʊm (US) froʊm/ is suitable in the Edith Wharton novel "Ethan Frome".
Fromm frɒm (US) frɑːm
frond frɒnd (US) frɑːnd **-s** -z
front frʌnt **-s** -s **-ing** -ɪŋ (US) 'frʌn.t̬ɪŋ **-ed** -ɪd (US) 'frʌn.t̬ɪd ˌ**front 'line**; **'front ˌmatter**; **'front ˌmoney**
frontag|e 'frʌn.tɪdʒ (US) -t̬ɪdʒ **-es** -ɪz
frontal 'frʌn.tᵊl (US) -t̬ᵊl **-s** -z
frontbench ˌfrʌnt'bentʃ **-er/s** -əʳ/z (US) -ɚ/z *stress shift:* ˌfrontbench 'spokesman
Frontera® frʌn'teə.rə, frɒn- (US) frʌn'ter.ə, frɑːn-
frontier frʌn'tɪəʳ; '--, 'frɒn- (US) frʌn'tɪr, frɑːn- **-s** -z
frontispiec|e 'frʌn.tɪs.piːs, -təs- (US) -t̬ɪs- **-es** -ɪz
frontless 'frʌnt.ləs, -lɪs, -les
frontlet 'frʌnt.lɪt, -lət **-s** -s
front-load ˌfrʌnt'ləʊd (US) -'loʊd, '-- **-s** -z **-ing** -ɪŋ **-ed** -ɪd **-er/s** -əʳ/z (US) -ɚ/z *stress shift, British only:* ˌfront-loading 'drier
front-page ˌfrʌnt'peɪdʒ *stress shift, see compound:* ˌ**front-page 'news**
front-runner 'frʌntˌrʌn.əʳ, ˌ-'-- (US) 'frʌntˌrʌn.ɚ **-s** -z
frost (F) frɒst (US) frɑːst **-s** -s **-ing/s** -ɪŋ/z **-ed** -ɪd
frost|bite 'frɒst|.baɪt (US) 'frɑːst- **-bitten** -ˌbɪt.ᵊn (US) -ˌbɪt̬-
Frosties® 'frɒs.tiz (US) 'frɑː.stiz
frostwork 'frɒst.wɜːk (US) 'frɑːst.wɜːrk
frost|y 'frɒs.t|i (US) 'frɑː.st|i **-ier** -i.əʳ (US) -i.ɚ **-iest** -i.ɪst, -i.əst **-ily** -ɪ.li, -ᵊl.i **-iness** -ɪ.nəs, -ɪ.nɪs
froth (*n.*) frɒθ (US) frɑːθ **-s** -s
fro|th (*v.*) frɒ|θ (US) frɑː|θ, frɑː|ð **-ths** -θs (US) -θs, -ðz **-thing** -θɪŋ (US) -θɪŋ, -ðɪŋ **-thed** -θt (US) -θt, -ðd
Frothingham 'frɒð.ɪŋ.əm (US) 'frɑː.ðɪŋ-
froth|y 'frɒθ|.i (US) 'frɑː.θ|i, -ð|i **-ier** -i.əʳ (US) -i.ɚ **-iest** -i.ɪst, -i.əst **-ily** -ɪ.li, -ᵊl.i **-iness** -ɪ.nəs, -ɪ.nɪs
frottage 'frɒt.ɑːʒ, -ɪdʒ; frɒt'ɑːʒ (US) frə'tɑːʒ, frɑː-
Froud fraʊd, fruːd
Froude fruːd
froufrou 'fruː.fruː
froward 'frəʊ.əd (US) 'froʊ.ɚd **-ly** -li **-ness** -nəs, -nɪs
frown fraʊn **-s** -z **-ing/ly** -ɪŋ/li **-ed** -d
frowst fraʊst **-s** -s **-ing** -ɪŋ **-ed** -ɪd
frowst|y 'fraʊ.st|i **-iness** -ɪ.nəs, -ɪ.nɪs
frows|y, frowz|y 'fraʊ.z|i **-ier** -i.əʳ (US) -i.ɚ **-iest** -i.ɪst, -i.əst **-iness** -ɪ.nəs, -ɪ.nɪs
froz|e (*from* **freeze**) frəʊz (US) froʊz **-en** -ᵊn
fructiferous frʌk'tɪf.ᵊr.əs (US) frʌk-, frʊk-
fructification ˌfrʌk.tɪ.fɪ'keɪ.ʃᵊn (US) ˌfrʌk.tə-, ˌfrʊk-
fructi|fy 'frʌk.tɪ|.faɪ (US) 'frʌk.tə-, 'frʊk- **-fies** -faɪz **-fying** -faɪ.ɪŋ **-fied** -faɪd
fructose 'frʌk.təʊs, 'frʊk-, -təʊz (US) -toʊs
frugal 'fruː.gᵊl **-ly** -i
frugality fruː'gæl.ə.ti, -ɪ.ti (US) -ə.t̬i
fruit fruːt **-s** -s **-ing** -ɪŋ (US) 'fruː.t̬ɪŋ **-ed** -ɪd (US) 'fruː.t̬ɪd **'fruit maˌchine**
fruitarian fruː'teə.ri.ən (US) -'ter.i- **-s** -z
fruitcake 'fruːt.keɪk **-s** -s
fruiterer 'fruː.tᵊr.əʳ (US) -t̬ɚ.ɚ **-s** -z
fruitful 'fruːt.fᵊl, -fʊl **-ly** -i **-ness** -nəs, -nɪs
fruition fru'ɪʃ.ᵊn
fruitless 'fruːt.ləs, -lɪs **-ly** -li **-ness** -nəs, -nɪs
fruit|y 'fruː.t|i (US) -t̬|i **-ier** -i.əʳ (US) -i.ɚ **-iest** -i.ɪst, -i.əst **-iness** -ɪ.nəs, -ɪ.nɪs
frumenty 'fruː.mən.ti (US) -t̬i
frump frʌmp **-s** -s **-ish** -ɪʃ
frump|y 'frʌm.p|i **-ier** -i.əʳ (US) -i.ɚ **-iest** -i.ɪst, -i.əst **-ily** -ɪ.li, -ᵊl.i **-iness** -ɪ.nəs, -ɪ.nɪs
frustra|te frʌs'treɪ|t, '-- (US) 'frʌs.treɪ|t **-tes** -ts **-ting** -tɪŋ (US) -t̬ɪŋ **-ted** -tɪd (US) -t̬ɪd
frustration frʌs'treɪ.ʃᵊn **-s** -z
frust|um 'frʌs.t|əm **-a** -ə **-ums** -əmz
fr|y (F) fr|aɪ **-ies** -aɪz **-ying** -aɪ.ɪŋ **-ied** -aɪd **-yer** -aɪ.əʳ (US) -aɪ.ɚ **'frying ˌpan**; ˌ**out of the ˌfrying pan ˌinto the 'fire**
Frye fraɪ
ft (*abbrev. for* **foot** *or* **feet**) *singular:* fʊt *plural:* fiːt
FT ˌef'tiː
FTSE, FT-SE 'fʊt.si **'FT-SE ˌIndex**
FT-SE 100 ˌfʊt.si.wʌn'hʌn.drəd, -drɪd
Fuad fuː'ɑːd, -'æd (US) 'fuː.ɑːd
fuchsia 'fjuː.ʃə **-s** -z
fuchsine 'fuːk.siːn, -sɪn (US) 'fuːk.sɪn, 'fjuːk-, 'fʊk-, -siːn
fuck fʌk **-s** -s **-ing** -ɪŋ **-ed** -t **-er/s** -əʳ/z (US) -ɚ/z
fu|cus 'fjuː|.kəs **-ci** -saɪ **-cuses** -kə.sɪz
fuddl|e 'fʌd.l̩ **-es** -z **-ing** -ɪŋ, '-lɪŋ **-ed** -d
fuddy-duddl|y 'fʌd.iˌdʌd|.i **-ies** -iz
fudg|e fʌdʒ **-es** -ɪz **-ing** -ɪŋ **-ed** -d
Fudge fʌdʒ, fjuːdʒ
fuehrer 'fjʊə.rə, 'fjɔː- (US) 'fjʊr.ɚ
fuel 'fjuː.əl, fjʊəl (US) 'fjuː.əl, fjuːl **-s** -z **-(l)ing** -ɪŋ **-(l)ed** -d **add ˌfuel to the 'fire**
Fuentes 'fwen.tes, -teɪz
fug fʌg **-s** -z
fugacious fjuː'geɪ.ʃəs **-ly** -li **-ness** -nəs, -nɪs
fugacity fjuː'gæs.ə.ti, -ɪ.ti (US) -ə.t̬i
fugal 'fjuː.gᵊl
Fugard 'fuː.gɑːd, 'fjuː- (US) -gɑːrd
fuggles 'fʌg.l̩z
fugg|y 'fʌg|.i **-ier** -i.əʳ (US) -i.ɚ **-iest** -i.ɪst, -i.əst **-iness** -ɪ.nəs, -ɪ.nɪs
fugitive 'fjuː.dʒə.tɪv, -dʒɪ- (US) -t̬ɪv **-s** -z **-ly** -li **-ness** -nəs, -nɪs
fugle|man 'fjuː.gl̩|.mæn, -mən **-men** -men, -mən
fugue fjuːg **-s** -z

führer (F) ˈfjʊə.rəʳ, ˈfjɔː- (US) ˈfjʊr.ɚ -s -z

Fujairah fuːˈdʒaɪə.rə (US) -ˈdʒaɪ-

Fuji ˈfuː.dʒi

Fujian fuːˈdʒɑːn

Fuji-san ˈfuː.dʒi.sæn (US) -sɑːn

Fujitsu fʊˈdʒɪt.suː, fuː- (US) fuː-ˈ, fʊ-

Fujiyama ˌfuː.dʒiˈjɑː.mə

Fukuoka ˌfʊk.uːˈəʊ.kə, ˌfuː.kuːˈ- (US) ˌfuː.kuːˈoʊ-, ˌfʊk.uːˈ-

-ful -fᵊl, -fʊl

Note: Two suffixes are covered by this entry, both of which are not stressed. The first forms an adjective, e.g. **beauty** /ˈbjuː.ti (US) -t̬i/, **beautiful** /ˈbjuː.tɪ.fᵊl (US) -t̬ɪ-/; in this the pronunciation /-fᵊl/ is preferred. The second forms a measuring noun, e.g. **bucket** /ˈbʌk.ɪt/, **bucketful** /ˈbʌk.ɪt.fʊl/, and is normally /-fʊl/.

Fulani fuːˈlɑː.ni, ˈ--- -s -z

Fulbright ˈfʊl.braɪt -s -s

Fulcher ˈfʊl.tʃəʳ (US) -tʃɚ

fulcr|um ˈfʊl.kr|əm, ˈfʌl- -a -ə -ums -əmz

fulfil fʊlˈfɪl -s -z -ling -ɪŋ -led -d -ment -mənt

fulfill fʊlˈfɪl -s -z -ing -ɪŋ -ed -d -ment -mənt

Fulford ˈfʊl.fəd (US) -fɚd

fulgent ˈfʌl.dʒənt -ly -li

Fulham ˈfʊl.əm

fuliginous fjuːˈlɪdʒ.ɪ.nəs -ly -li

Fulke fʊlk

full fʊl -er -əʳ (US) -ɚ -est -ɪst, -əst -ness -nəs, -nɪs ˌ**full ˈboard** ; ˌ**full ˈface** ; ˌ**full ˈmoon** ; ˌ**full ˈstop**

fullback ˈfʊl.bæk, ˌ-ˈ- (US) ˈ-- -s -s

full-blooded ˌfʊlˈblʌd.ɪd *stress shift:* ˌfull-blooded ˈmale

full-blown ˌfʊlˈbləʊn (US) -ˈbloʊn *stress shift:* ˌfull-blown ˈargument

full-bodied ˌfʊlˈbɒd.ɪd (US) -ˈbɑː.did *stress shift:* ˌfull-bodied ˈwine

fuller (F) ˈfʊl.əʳ (US) -ɚ -s -z

Fullerton ˈfʊl.ə.tᵊn (US) -ɚ-

full-face ˌfʊlˈfeɪs *stress shift:* ˌfull-face ˈphotograph

full-fledged ˌfʊlˈfledʒd *stress shift:* ˌfull-fledged ˈbird

full-grown ˌfʊlˈgrəʊn (US) -ˈgroʊn *stress shift:* ˌfull-grown ˈman

full-length ˌfʊlˈleŋ*k*θ *stress shift:* ˌfull-length ˈcoat

full-scale ˌfʊlˈskeɪl *stress shift:* ˌfull-scale ˈwar

full-time ˌfʊlˈtaɪm *stress shift:* ˌfull-time ˈmother

fully ˈfʊl.i

-fully -fᵊl.i, -fʊl.i

Note: Suffix. Words containing **-fully** are stressed in a similar way to adjectives containing **-ful**; see above.

fully-fledged ˌfʊl.iˈfledʒd *stress shift:* ˌfully-fledged ˈbird

fulmar ˈfʊl.məʳ, -mɑːʳ (US) -mɚ, -mɑːr -s -z

Fulmer ˈfʊl.məʳ (US) -mɚ

fulmi|nate ˈfʊl.mɪ|.neɪt, ˈfʌl-, -mə- -nates -neɪts -nating -neɪ.tɪŋ (US) -neɪ.t̬ɪŋ -nated -neɪ.tɪd (US) -neɪ.t̬ɪd

fulmination ˌfʊl.mɪˈneɪ.ʃᵊn, ˌfʌl-, -məˈ- -s -z

fulness ˈfʊl.nəs, -nɪs

fulsome ˈfʊl.səm -ly -li -ness -nəs, -nɪs

Fulton ˈfʊl.tᵊn

Fulvia ˈfʊl.vi.ə, ˈfʌl-

fulvous ˈfʌl.vəs, ˈfʊl-

Fulwood ˈfʊl.wʊd

Fu Manchu ˌfuː.mænˈtʃuː

fumbl|e ˈfʌm.bl̩ -es -z -ing -ɪŋ, ˈ-blɪŋ -ed -d -er/s -əʳ/z, ˈ-bləʳ/z (US) ˈ-bl̩.ɚ/z, ˈ-blɚ/z

fum|e fjuːm -es -z -ing -ɪŋ -ed -d

fumi|gate ˈfjuː.mɪ|.geɪt, -mə- -gates -geɪts -gating -geɪ.tɪŋ (US) -geɪ.t̬ɪŋ -gated -geɪ.tɪd (US) -geɪ.t̬ɪd -gator/s -geɪ.təʳ/z (US) -geɪ.t̬ɚ/z

fumigation ˌfjuː.mɪˈgeɪ.ʃᵊn, -məˈ- -s -z

fun fʌn

Funafuti ˌfuː.nəˈfuː.ti

funambulist fjuːˈnæm.bjə.lɪst, fjʊ-, -bjʊ- (US) fjuːˈnæm.bjə-, -bjuː- -s -s

Funchal fʊnˈʃɑːl, -ˈtʃɑːl

function ˈfʌŋ*k*.ʃᵊn -s -z -ing -ɪŋ -ed -d

functional ˈfʌŋ*k*.ʃᵊn.ᵊl -ly -i

functional|ism ˈfʌŋ*k*.ʃᵊn.ᵊl|.ɪ.zᵊm -ist/s -ɪst/s

functionality ˌfʌŋ*k*.ʃᵊnˈæl.ɪ.ti, -ə.ti (US) -ə.t̬i

functionar|y ˈfʌŋ*k*.ʃᵊn.ᵊr.|i, -r|i (US) -er|.i -ies -iz

functor ˈfʌŋ*k*.təʳ, -tɔːʳ (US) -tɚ, -tɔːr -s -z

fund fʌnd -s -z -ing -ɪŋ -ed -ɪd

fundament ˈfʌn.də.mənt -s -s

fundamental ˌfʌn.dəˈmen.tᵊl (US) -t̬ᵊl -s -z -ly -i

fundamental|ism (F) ˌfʌn.dəˈmen.tᵊl|.ɪ.zᵊm (US) -t̬ᵊl- -ist/s -ɪst/s

fundamentality ˌfʌn.də.menˈtæl.ə.ti, -ɪ.ti (US) -ə.t̬i

fundless ˈfʌnd.ləs, -lɪs, -les

fundrais|er ˈfʌndˌreɪ.z|əʳ (US) -z|ɚ -er/s -əz (US) -ɚz -ing -ɪŋ

Fundy ˈfʌn.di

funeral ˈfjuː.nᵊr.əl -s -z ˈ**funeral** ˌ**home** ; ˈ**funeral** ˌ**parlo(u)r**

funerary ˈfjuː.nᵊr.ə.ri (US) -er.i

funereal fjuːˈnɪə.ri.əl (US) -ˈnɪr.i- -ly -i

funfair ˈfʌn.feəʳ (US) -fer -s -z

fungal ˈfʌŋ.gᵊl

fungible ˈfʌn.dʒɪ.bl̩, -dʒə- -s -z

fungicidal ˌfʌŋ.gɪˈsaɪ.dᵊl, ˌfʌn.dʒɪˈ- (US) ˌfʌn.dʒɪˈ-, ˌfʌŋ.gəˈ- -li -i

fungicide ˈfʌŋ.gɪ.saɪd, ˈfʌn.dʒɪ- (US) ˈfʌn.dʒɪ-, ˈfʌŋ.gə- -s -z

fungo ˈfʌŋ.gəʊ (US) -goʊ -es -z

fun|gus ˈfʌŋ.|gəs -gi -gaɪ, -giː, ˈfʌn.dʒiː, -dʒaɪ -guses -gə.sɪz -goid -gɔɪd -gous -gəs

funicle ˈfjuː.nɪ.kl̩ -s -z

funicular fjuːˈnɪk.jə.ləʳ, fə-, -jʊ- (US) -juː.lɚ -s -z

funicul|us fjuːˈnɪk.jə.l|əs, fə-, -jʊ- (US) -juː- -i -aɪ

funk (F) fʌŋk -s -s -ing -ɪŋ -ed -t

funk|y ˈfʌŋ.k|i -ier -i.əʳ (US) -i.ɚ -iest -i.ɪst, -i.əst -ily -ɪ.li, -ᵊl.i -iness -ɪ.nəs, -ɪ.nɪs

funnel ˈfʌn.ᵊl -s -z -(l)ing -ɪŋ -(l)ed -d

funnies ˈfʌn.iz

funn|y ˈfʌn|.i -ier -i.əʳ (US) -i.ɚ -iest -i.ɪst, -i.əst -ily -ɪ.li, -ᵊl.i -iness -ɪ.nəs, -ɪ.nɪs ˈ**funny** ˌ**bone** ; ˈ**funny** ˌ**business**

fur fɜːʳ (US) fɜːr -s -z -ring -ɪŋ -red -d

fur (*abbrev. for* **furlong**) ˈfɜː.lɒŋ (US) ˈfɜːr.lɑːŋ, -lɔːŋ

Furbear ˈfɜː.beəʳ (US) ˈfɜːr.ber

furbelow ˈfɜː.bɪ.ləʊ, -bə- (US) ˈfɜːr.bɪ.loʊ, -bə- -s -z

furbish ˈfɜː.bɪʃ (US) ˈfɜːr- -es -ɪz -ing -ɪŋ -ed -t

furcate (*adj.*) ˈfɜː.keɪt, -kɪt, -kət (US) ˈfɜːr-

fur|cate (*v.*) ˈfɜː|.keɪt, -|ˈ- (US) ˈfɜːr|.keɪt -cates -keɪts, -ˈkeɪts (US) -keɪts -cating -keɪ.tɪŋ, -ˈkeɪ- (US) -keɪ.t̬ɪŋ -cated -keɪ.tɪd, -ˈkeɪ- (US) -keɪ.t̬ɪd

furcation fɜːˈkeɪ.ʃᵊn (US) fɜːr- -s -z

furibund ˈfjʊə.rɪ.bʌnd, ˈfjɔː-, -bənd (US) ˈfjʊr.ɪ-

furioso ˌfjʊə.riˈəʊ.zəʊ, ˌfjɔː-, -səʊ (US) ˌfjʊr.iˈoʊ.soʊ, ˌfjɜːr-, -zoʊ

furious ˈfjʊə.ri.əs, ˈfjɔː- (US) ˈfjʊr.i-, ˈfjɜːr- -ly -li

furl fɜːl (US) fɜːrl -s -z -ing -ɪŋ -ed -d

furlong ˈfɜː.lɒŋ (US) ˈfɜːr.lɑːŋ, -lɔːŋ -s -z

furlough ˈfɜː.ləʊ (US) ˈfɜːr.loʊ -s -z

furnac|e ˈfɜː.nɪs, -nəs (US) ˈfɜːr- -es -ɪz

Furneaux ˈfɜː.nəʊ (US) fɜːrˈnoʊ

Furness ˈfɜː.nɪs, fɜːˈnes (US) ˈfɜːr.nɪs, fɜːrˈnes

Furneux ˈfɜː.nɪks, -nəʊ (US) ˈfɜːr.nɪks, -nuː, -noʊ

Note: /ˈfɜː.nɪks/ is the more usual local pronunciation.

furnish ˈfɜː.nɪʃ (US) ˈfɜːr- -es -ɪz -ing/s -ɪŋ/z -ed -t -er/s -əʳ/z (US) -ɚ/z

furniture ˈfɜː.nɪ.tʃəʳ (US) ˈfɜːr.nɪ.tʃɚ

Furnival(l) ˈfɜː.nɪ.vᵊl (US) ˈfɜːr-

furor ˈfjʊr.ɔː (US) ˈfjʊr.ɔːr, -ɚ

furore fjʊə'rɔː.ri, -reɪ; 'fjʊə.rɔːʳ, 'fjɔː- (US) 'fjʊr.ɔːr, -ɚ **-s** -z
furph|y (F) 'fɜː.f|i (US) 'fɜːr- **-ies** -iz
furrier 'fʌr.i.əʳ (US) 'fɜːr.i.ɚ **-s** -z
furrier|y 'fʌr.i.ᵊr|.i (US) 'fɜːr- **-ies** -iz
furrow 'fʌr.əʊ (US) 'fɜːr.oʊ **-s** -z **-ing** -ɪŋ **-ed** -d
furr|y 'fɜː.r|i (US) 'fɜːr|.i **-ier** -i.əʳ (US) -i.ɚ **-iest** -i.ɪst, -i.əst **-iness** -ɪ.nəs, -ɪ.nɪs
furth|er 'fɜː.ð|əʳ (US) 'fɜːr.ð|ɚ **-ers** -əz (US) -ɚz **-ering** -ᵊr.ɪŋ **-ered** -əd (US) -ɚd **-erer/s** -ᵊr.əʳ/z (US) -ɚ.ɚ/z ˌ**further edu'cation**
furtherance 'fɜː.ðᵊr.ᵊnts (US) 'fɜːr-
furthermore ˌfɜː.ðə'mɔːʳ, '--- (US) 'fɜːr.ðɚ.mɔːr
furthermost 'fɜː.ðə.məʊst (US) 'fɜːr.ðɚ.moʊst
furthest 'fɜː.ðɪst, -ðəst (US) 'fɜːr-
furtive 'fɜː.tɪv (US) 'fɜːr.t̬ɪv **-ly** -li **-ness** -nəs, -nɪs
furuncle 'fjʊə.rʌŋ.kᵊl, 'fjɔː- (US) 'fjʊr.ʌŋ- **-s** -z
fur|y (F) 'fjʊə.r|i, 'fjɔː- (US) 'fjʊr|.i **-ies** -iz
furze fɜːz (US) fɜːrz
fus|e fjuːz **-es** -ɪz **-ing** -ɪŋ **-ed** -d **'fuse ˌbox**
fusee fjuː'ziː (US) fjuː'ziː, '-- **-s** -z
fusel 'fjuː.zᵊl (US) 'fjuː.zᵊl, -sᵊl **'fusel ˌoil, ˌfusel 'oil**
fuselag|e 'fjuː.zᵊl.ɑːʒ, -zɪ.lɑːʒ (US) -sə.lɑːʒ, -zə-, -lɑːdʒ **-es** -ɪz
fusibility ˌfjuː.zɪ'bɪl.ə.ti, -zə'-, -ɪ.ti (US) -ə.t̬i
fusible 'fjuː.zɪ.bḷ, -zə-
fusil 'fjuː.zɪl (US) -zɪl, -sɪl **-s** -z
fusile 'fjuː.saɪl, -zaɪl (US) -zᵊl, -zaɪl, -sɪl
fusilier ˌfjuː.zᵊl'ɪəʳ, -zɪ'lɪəʳ (US) -zɪ'lɪr **-s** -z
fusillade ˌfjuː.zə'leɪd, -zɪ'- (US) ˌfjuː.sə'lɑːd, -zə'-, -'leɪd, '--- **-s** -z
fusilli fʊ'siː.li, fjʊ'zɪl.i (US) 'fjuː.siː.li, -zə-
fusion 'fjuː.ʒᵊn **-s** -z
fuss fʌs **-es** -ɪz **-ing** -ɪŋ **-ed** -t **-er/s** -əʳ/z (US) -ɚ/z
fussbudget 'fʌsˌbʌdʒ.ɪt **-s** -s
fusspot 'fʌs.pɒt (US) -pɑːt **-s** -s
fuss|y 'fʌs|.i **-ier** -i.əʳ (US) -i.ɚ **-iest** -i.ɪst, -i.əst **-ily** -ɪ.li, -ᵊl.i **-iness** -ɪ.nəs, -ɪ.nɪs
fustian 'fʌs.ti.ən (US) -tʃᵊn
fustic 'fʌs.tɪk
fusti|gate 'fʌs.tɪ|.geɪt, -tə- **-gates** -geɪts **-gating** -geɪ.tɪŋ (US) -geɪ.t̬ɪŋ **-gated** -geɪ.tɪd (US) -geɪ.t̬ɪd
fustigation ˌfʌs.tɪ'geɪ.ʃᵊn, -tə'- **-s** -z
fust|y 'fʌs.t|i **-ier** -i.əʳ (US) -i.ɚ **-iest** -i.ɪst, -i.əst **-ily** -ɪ.li, -ᵊl.i **-iness** -ɪ.nəs, -ɪ.nɪs
futhark 'fuː.θɑːk (US) -θɑːrk
futile 'fjuː.taɪl (US) -t̬əl, -taɪl **-ly** -li **-ness** -nəs, -nɪs
futilit|y fjuː'tɪl.ə.t|i, -ɪ.t|i (US) -ə.t̬|i **-ies** -iz
futon 'fuː.tɒn, 'fjuː-, 'fʊt.ɒn, -ᵊn; ˌfuː'tɒn (US) 'fuː.tɑːn **-s** -z
futtock 'fʌt.ək (US) 'fʌt̬- **-s** -s
future 'fjuː.tʃəʳ (US) -tʃɚ **-s** -z
futur|ism 'fjuː.tʃᵊr|.ɪ.zᵊm **-ist/s** -ɪst/s
futuristic ˌfjuː.tʃə'rɪs.tɪk **-ally** -ᵊl.i, -li
futurit|y fjuː'tjʊə.rə.t|i, -'tjɔː-, -'tʃʊə-, -'tʃɔː-, -ɪ.t|i (US) fjuː'tʊr.ə.t̬|i, -'tjʊr-, -'tʃʊr-, -'tʃɜːr- **-ies** -iz
futurolog|ist ˌfjuː.tʃə'rɒl.ə.dʒ|ɪst (US) -'rɑː.lə- **-ists** -ɪsts **-y** -i
fuz|e fjuːz **-es** -ɪz **-ing** -ɪŋ **-ed** -d
fuzee fjuː'ziː (US) fjuː'ziː, '-- **-s** -z
Fuzhou 'fuː.dʒəʊ (US) -dʒoʊ
fuzz fʌz **-es** -ɪz **-ing** -ɪŋ **-ed** -d
fuzz|y 'fʌz|.i **-ier** -i.əʳ (US) -i.ɚ **-iest** -i.ɪst, -i.əst **-ily** -ɪ.li, -ᵊl.i **-iness** -ɪ.nəs, -ɪ.nɪs
fuzzy-wuzz|y 'fʌz.iˌwʌz|.i, ˌ--'-- **-ies** -iz
f-word 'efˌwɜːd (US) -ˌwɜːrd
Fyf(f)e faɪf
Fyfield 'faɪ.fiːld
Fylingdales 'faɪ.lɪŋ.deɪlz
Fyne faɪn

G

g (G) dʒiː **-'s** -z
g (*abbrev. for* **gram/s**) *singular:* græm *plural:* -z
Ga. (*abbrev. for* **Georgia**) ˈdʒɔː.dʒə US ˈdʒɔːr-
gab gæb **-s** -z **-bing** -ɪŋ **-bed** -d
gabardine ˌgæb.əˈdiːn, ˈ--- US ˈgæb.ɚ.diːn, ˌ--ˈ- **-s** -z
Gabbatha ˈgæb.ə.θə
gabbl|e ˈgæb.l̩ **-es** -z **-ing** -ɪŋ, ˈ-lɪŋ **-ed** -d **-er/s** -əʳ/z, ˈ-ləʳ/z US ˈ-l̩.ɚ/z, ˈ-lɚ/z
gabbro ˈgæb.rəʊ US -roʊ **-s** -z
gabb|y ˈgæb|.i **-ier** -i.əʳ US -i.ɚ **-iest** -i.ɪst, -i.əst
gaberdine ˌgæb.əˈdiːn, ˈ--- US ˈgæb.ɚ.diːn, ˌ--ˈ- **-s** -z
gaberlunzie ˌgæb.əˈlʌn.zi, -ˈluː.nji, ˈgæb.ə.lʌn.zi, -luː.nji US ˌgæb.ɚˈlʌn.zi **-s** -z
gabfest ˈgæbˌfest **-s** -s
Gabii ˈgæb.i.iː, -bi.aɪ US ˈgæb.i.aɪ, ˈgeɪ.bi-
gabion ˈgeɪ.bi.ən **-s** -z
gable (G) ˈgeɪ.bl̩ **-s** -z **-d** -d
gablet ˈgeɪ.blɪt, -blət US -blət **-s** -s
Gabon gæbˈɒn, gəˈbɒn; ˈgæb.ɒn *as if French:* gæbˈɔ̃ːŋ US gæbˈoʊn, gəˈboʊn
Gabonese ˌgæb.ɒnˈiːz, -əˈniːz US -əˈniːz
Gaboon gəˈbuːn
Gabor gəˈbɔːʳ; ˈgɑː.bɔːʳ US gəˈbɔːr; ˈgɑː.bɔːr
Gaborone ˌgæb.əˈrəʊ.ni US ˌgɑː.bəˈroʊ.neɪ, -ni
Gabriel ˈgeɪ.bri.əl
Gabriella ˌgæb.riˈel.ə, ˌgeɪ.briˈ-
Gabrielle ˌgæb.riˈel, ˌgeɪ.briˈ-
gab|y ˈgeɪ.b|i **-ies** -iz
Gaby ˈgæb.i, ˈgɑː.bi
gad (G) gæd **-s** -z **-ding** -ɪŋ **-ded** -ɪd
gadabout ˈgæd.ə.baʊt **-s** -s
Gadara ˈgæd.ᵊr.ə
Gadarene ˌgæd.əˈriːn, ˈ--- US ˈ--- **-s** -z
Gaddafi gəˈdæf.i, -ˈdɑː.fi US -ˈdɑː-
Gaddesden ˈgædz.dᵊn
Gaddis ˈgæd.ɪs
Gade *English river:* geɪd *Danish composer:* ˈgɑː.də
Gades ˈgeɪ.diːz
gadfl|y ˈgæd.fl|aɪ **-ies** -aɪz
gadget ˈgædʒ.ɪt, -ət **-s** -s
gadgetry ˈgædʒ.ɪ.tri, ˈ-ə-
Gadhel ˈgæd.el US -əl **-s** -z
Gadhelic gædˈel.ɪk, gəˈdel-
gadolinium ˌgæd.əʊˈlɪn.i.əm, -ᵊlˈɪn- US -oʊˈlɪn-, gædˈlɪn-
gadroon gəˈdruːn **-s** -z
Gadsby ˈgædz.bi
Gadsden ˈgædz.dᵊn
Gadshill ˈgædz.hɪl
gadwall ˈgæd.wɔːl US -wɔːl **-s** -z
gadzooks ˌgædˈzuːks, gæd- US -ˈzuːks, -ˈzʊks
Gael geɪl **-s** -z
Gaelic ˈgeɪ.lɪk, ˈgæl.ɪk
Gaeltacht ˈgeɪl.tæxt, -təxt
Gaetulia *in Ireland:* giːˈtjuː.li.ə, gaɪ-, dʒi-, -ˈtuː- US dʒiˈtuː-, giː- *in Libya:* dʒɪˈtjuː.li.ə US -ˈtuː-, -ˈtjuː-
gaff gæf **-s** -s **-ing** -ɪŋ **-ed** -t
gaffe gæf **-s** -s
gaffer ˈgæf.əʳ US -ɚ **-s** -z
gag gæg **-s** -z **-ging** -ɪŋ **-ged** -d
gaga ˈgɑː.gɑː, ˈgæg.ɑː US ˈgɑː.gɑː **-s** -z
Gagarin gəˈgɑː.rɪn, gægˈɑː- US gəˈgɑːr.ɪn
gag|e (G) geɪdʒ **-es** -ɪz **-ing** -ɪŋ **-ed** -d
gaggle ˈgæg.l̩ **-s** -z
Gaia ˈgaɪ.ə, ˈgeɪ-
gaiet|y (G) ˈgeɪ.ə.t|i, -ɪ.t|i US -ə.t̬|i **-ies** -iz
Gail ˈgeɪl
gaily (*from* **gay**) ˈgeɪ.li
gain geɪn **-s** -z **-ing/s** -ɪŋ/z **-ed** -d **-er/s** -əʳ/z US -ɚ/z
Gaines geɪnz
Gainesville ˈgeɪnz.vɪl US -vɪl, -vəl
gainful ˈgeɪn.fᵊl, -fʊl **-ly** -i **-ness** -nəs, -nɪs
gain|say ˌgeɪn|ˈseɪ **-says** -ˈseɪz, -ˈsez **-saying** -ˈseɪ.ɪŋ **-sayed** -ˈseɪd **-said** -ˈsed, -ˈseɪd **-sayer/s** -ˈseɪ.əʳ/z US -ˈseɪ.ɚ/z
Gainsborough ˈgeɪnz.bᵊr.ə US -oʊ, -ə **-s** -z
Gairdner ˈgeəd.nəʳ, ˈgɑːd- US ˈgerd.nɚ, ˈgɑːrd-
Gairloch ˈgeə.lɒx, -lɒk US ˈger.lɑːk
Gaisford ˈgeɪs.fəd US -fɚd
gait geɪt **-s** -s
gaiter ˈgeɪ.təʳ US -t̬ɚ **-s** -z
Gaitskell ˈgeɪt.skᵊl, -skɪl
Gaius ˈgaɪ.əs US ˈgeɪ-, ˈgaɪ-
gal *girl:* gæl **-s** -z
gal (*abbrev. for* **gallon**) ˈgæl.ən
gala *special occasion:* ˈgɑː.lə, ˈgeɪ- US ˈgeɪ-, ˈgæl.ə, ˈgɑː.lə **-s** -z
Gala *river:* ˈgɑː.lə US ˈgɑː.lə, ˈgæl.ə
galactic gəˈlæk.tɪk **-ally** -ᵊl.i, -li
galacto- gəˈlæk.təʊ- US ˈ-tə-, ˈ-toʊ-
galactose gəˈlæk.təʊs, -təʊz US -toʊs
galah gəˈlɑː **-s** -z
Galahad ˈgæl.ə.hæd
galantine ˈgæl.ən.tiːn, ˌ--ˈ- **-s** -z
Galapagos gəˈlæp.ə.gəs, -gɒs US gəˈlɑː.pə.goʊs, -gəz
Galashiels ˌgæl.əˈʃiːlz *stress shift:* ˌGalashiels ˈstreets
Galata ˈgæl.ə.tə US -t̬ə
Galatea ˌgæl.əˈti.ə
Galatia gəˈleɪ.ʃə, -ʃi.ə, ˌgæl.əˈti.ə
Galatian gəˈleɪ.ʃᵊn, -ʃi.ən, ˌgæl.əˈti.ən **-s** -z
galax|y ˈgæl.ək.s|i **-ies** -iz
Galba ˈgæl.bə
galbanum ˈgæl.bə.nəm
Galbraith gælˈbreɪθ US ˈ--
gale (G) geɪl **-s** -z
Galen ˈgeɪ.lən, -lɪn
galena (G) gəˈliː.nə
Galenic gəˈlen.ɪk, geɪ-, -ˈliː.nɪk **-al** -əl
Galerius gəˈlɪə.ri.əs US -ˈlɪr.i-
Galesburg ˈgeɪlz.bɜːg US -bɜːrg
Galic|ia gəˈlɪs|.i.ə, gælˈɪs-, -ˈɪʃ|.ə, -ˈɪʃ|.i.ə US gəˈlɪʃ|.ə **-ian/s** -i.ən/z US -ən/z, -i.ən/z
Galilean ˌgæl.ɪˈliː.ən, -əˈ- US -əˈ- **-s** -z
Galilee ˈgæl.ɪ.liː, ˈ-ə- US ˈ-ə-
Galileo ˌgæl.ɪˈleɪ.əʊ, -əˈ-, -ˈliː.əʊ US -əˈliː-, -ˈleɪ-
galingale ˈgæl.ɪŋ.geɪl
Galion ˈgæl.i.ən US ˈgæl.jən
galipot ˈgæl.ɪ.pɒt US -pɑːt
gall gɔːl US gɔːl, gɑːl **-s** -z **-ing** -ɪŋ **-ed** -d **ˈgall ˌbladder**
Gallacher ˈgæl.ə.həʳ, -xəʳ US -hɚ
Gallagher ˈgæl.ə.həʳ, -xəʳ US -gɚ, -hɚ
Gallaher ˈgæl.ə.həʳ, -xəʳ US -hɚ
gallant (*n.*) ˈgæl.ənt **-s** -s
gallant (*adj.*) *brave:* ˈgæl.ənt **-ly** -li **-ness** -nəs, -nɪs
gallant (*adj.*) *attentive to women:* ˈgæl.ənt; gəˈlænt US ˈgæl.ənt; gəˈlænt, -ˈlɑːnt **-ly** -li **-ness** -nəs, -nɪs
Gallant gəˈlɔ̃ːŋ
gallantr|y ˈgæl.ən.tr|i **-ies** -iz
Gallatin ˈgæl.ə.tɪn
Gallaudet gæl.əˈdet *stress shift:* ˌGallaudet ˈCollege
Galle *port in Sri Lanka:* gɑːl US gɑːl, gæl
Galle *German astronomer:* ˈgæl.ə
galleon ˈgæl.i.ən US -i.ən, ˈ-jən **-s** -z
galler|y ˈgæl.ᵊr|.i **-ies** -iz **-ied** -id
galley ˈgæl.i **-s** -z **ˈgalley ˌproof** ; **ˈgalley ˌslave**
gallfl|y ˈgɔːl.fl|aɪ US ˈgɔːl-, ˈgɑːl- **-ies** -aɪz
Gallia ˈgæl.i.ə
galliambic ˌgæl.iˈæm.bɪk **-s** -s
galliard ˈgæl.i.ɑːd, -əd US ˈ-jɚd **-s** -z
gallic (G) ˈgæl.ɪk
Gallican ˈgæl.ɪ.kən **-s** -z
gallice ˈgæl.ɪ.siː, -si
gallicism ˈgæl.ɪ.sɪ.zᵊm, ˈ-ə- US ˈ-ə- **-s** -z
gallicizle, -is|e ˈgæl.ɪ.saɪz, ˈ-ə- US ˈ-ə- **-es** -ɪz **-ing** -ɪŋ **-ed** -d
gallimaufr|y ˌgæl.ɪˈmɔː.fr|i, -əˈ- US -əˈmɑː-, -ˈmɔː- **-ies** -iz

gallinaceous ˌgæl.ɪˈneɪ.ʃəs, -əˈ- (US) -əˈ-
Gallio ˈgæl.i.əʊ (US) -oʊ
galliot ˈgæl.i.ət **-s** -s
Gallipoli gəˈlɪp.ᵊl.i, gæˈlɪp-
Gallipolis *in US:* ˌgæl.ɪ.pəˈliːs (US) ˌ-ə-, -ˈlɪs
gallipot ˈgæl.ɪ.pɒt (US) -ə.pɑːt **-s** -s
gallium ˈgæl.i.əm
gallivant ˈgæl.ɪ.vænt, ˈ-ə-, ˌ--ˈ- (US) ˈgæl.ə.vænt, ˌ--ˈ- **-s** -s **-ing** -ɪŋ **-ed** -ɪd
gallnut ˈgɔːl.nʌt (US) ˈgɔːl-, ˈgɑːl- **-s** -s
gallon ˈgæl.ən **-s** -z
galloon gəˈluːn
gallop ˈgæl.əp **-s** -s **-ing** -ɪŋ **-ed** -t **-er/s** -əʳ/z (US) -ɚ/s
gallopade ˌgæl.əˈpeɪd, -ˈpɑːd (US) -ˈpeɪd **-s** -z
Gallovidian ˌgæl.əʊˈvɪd.i.ən (US) -əˈ- **-s** -z
galloway (G) ˈgæl.ə.weɪ **-s** -z
gallows ˈgæl.əʊz (US) -oʊz
gallstone ˈgɔːl.stəʊn (US) -stoʊn, ˈgɑːl- **-s** -z
Gallup ˈgæl.əp **ˈGallup ˌpoll**
Gallus ˈgæl.əs
galoot gəˈluːt **-s** -s
galop ˈgæl.əp; gælˈɒp (US) ˈgæl.əp **-s** -s
galore gəˈlɔːʳ (US) -ˈlɔːr
galosh gəˈlɒʃ (US) -ˈlɑːʃ **-es** -ɪz
Galpin ˈgæl.pɪn
Galsham ˈgɔːl.səm, ˈgɒl- (US) ˈgɔːl-, ˈgɑːl-
Galston ˈgɔːl.stᵊn, ˈgɒl- (US) ˈgɔːl-, ˈgɑːl-
Galsworthy ˈgɔːlz.wɜː.ði, ˈgɒlz-, ˈgælz- (US) ˈgɔːlz.wɜːr-, ˈgɑːlz-, ˈgælz-
Note: John Galsworthy, the author, is commonly called /ˈgɔːlz.wɜː.ði (US) -wɜːr-/.
Galt gɔːlt, gɒlt (US) gɑːlt, gɔːlt
Galton ˈgɔːl.tᵊn, ˈgɒl- (US) ˈgɔːl-, ˈgɑːl-
Galvani gælˈvɑː.ni
galvanic gælˈvæn.ɪk
galvanism ˈgæl.və.nɪ.zᵊm
galvaniz|e, -is|e ˈgæl.və.naɪz **-es** -ɪz **-ing** -ɪŋ **-ed** -d **-er/s** -əʳ/z (US) -ɚ/z
galvanometer ˌgæl.vəˈnɒm.ɪ.təʳ, -ə.təʳ (US) -ˈnɑː.mə.t̬ɚ **-s** -z
Galveston, Galvestone ˈgæl.vɪ.stᵊn, -və-
Galway ˈgɔːl.weɪ (US) ˈgɔːl-, ˈgɑːl-
gam gæm **-s** -z
Gama ˈgɑː.mə
Gamage ˈgæm.ɪdʒ **-ˈs** -ɪz
Gamaliel gəˈmeɪ.li.əl *in Jewish usage also:* -ˈmɑː-; ˌgæm.əˈliː.əl
Gamay ˈgæm.eɪ, -ˈ- (US) gæmˈeɪ
gamba ˈgæm.bə (US) ˈgɑːm-, ˈgæm- **-s** -z
gambado *jump:* gæmˈbeɪ.dəʊ, -ˈbɑː- (US) -ˈbeɪ.doʊ **-(e)s** -z
gambadoes *leggings:* gæmˈbeɪ.dəʊz (US) -doʊz
Gambetta gæmˈbet.ə (US) -ˈbet̬-
Gambia ˈgæm.bi.ə **-n/s** -n/z
gambier *substance used in dyeing:* ˈgæm.bɪəʳ (US) ˈgæm.bɪr
Gambier *surname:* ˈgæm.bi.əʳ, -bɪəʳ, -bi.eɪ (US) ˈgæm.bɪr
gambit ˈgæm.bɪt **-s** -s
gambl|e (G) ˈgæm.bl̩ **-es** -z **-ing** -ɪŋ, ˈ-blɪŋ **-ed** -d **-er/s** -əʳ/z, ˈ-bləʳ/z (US) ˈ-bl̩.ɚ/z, ˈ-blɚ/z
gamboge gæmˈbəʊʒ, -ˈbəʊdʒ, -ˈbuːʒ (US) -ˈboʊdʒ
gambol ˈgæm.bᵊl **-s** -z **-(l)ing** -ɪŋ **-(l)ed** -d
gambrel ˈgæm.brəl **-s** -z
gam|e geɪm **-es** -z **-er** -əʳ (US) -ɚ **-est** -ɪst, -əst **-ely** -li **-eness** -nəs, -nɪs **-ing** -ɪŋ **-ed** -d **ˈgame ˌshow**
gamebag ˈgeɪm.bæg **-s** -z
gamecock ˈgeɪm.kɒk (US) -ˈkɑːk **-s** -s
gamekeeper ˈgeɪmˌkiː.pəʳ (US) -pɚ **-s** -z
gamelan ˈgæm.ə.læn, ˈ-ɪ- **-s** -z
gamesmanship ˈgeɪmz.mən.ʃɪp
games|-master ˈgeɪmzˌmɑː.stəʳ (US) -ˌmæs.tɚ **-masters** -ˌmɑː.stəz (US) -ˌmæs.tɚz **-mistress/es** -ˌmɪs.trəs/ɪz, -trɪs/ɪz
gamester ˈgeɪm.stəʳ (US) -stɚ **-s** -z
gamete ˈgæm.iːt, gəˈmiːt **-s** -s
gametic gəˈmet.ɪk, gæmˈet- (US) gəˈmet̬-
gamin ˈgæm.ɪn, gæˈmæ̃ŋ **-s** -z
gamine ˈgæm.iːn, -ˈ- **-s** -z
gamma ˈgæm.ə **-s** -z **ˈgamma ˌray**
Gammell ˈgæm.ᵊl
gammer ˈgæm.əʳ (US) -ɚ **-s** -z
gammon ˈgæm.ən **-s** -z **-ing** -ɪŋ **-ed** -d
gamm|y ˈgæm|.i **-ier** -i.əʳ (US) -i.ɚ **-iest** -i.ɪst, -i.əst
-gamous -gə.məs
Note: Suffix. Usually unstressed, e.g. **monogamous** /məˈnɒg.ə.məs (US) -ˈnɑː.gə-/.
gamp (G) gæmp **-s** -s
gamut ˈgæm.ət, -ʌt **-s** -s
gam|y ˈgeɪ.m|i **-ier** -i.əʳ (US) -i.ɚ **-iest** -i.ɪst, -i.əst **-iness** -ɪ.nəs, -ɪ.nɪs
-gamy -gə.mi
Note: Suffix. Normally unstressed, e.g. **monogamy** /məˈnɒg.ə.mi (US) -ˈnɑː.gə-/.
Gandalf ˈgæn.dælf (US) -dælf, -dɑːlf
gander (G) ˈgæn.dəʳ (US) -dɚ **-s** -z
Gandh|i ˈgæn.d|i, ˈgɑːn- (US) ˈgɑːn-, ˈgæn- **-ian** -i.ən
Ganes(h)a gænˈiː.sə, -ˈeɪ.sə (US) -ʃə
gang gæŋ **-s** -z **-ing** -ɪŋ **-ed** -d
gang-bang ˈgæŋˌbæŋ **-s** -z **-ing** -ɪŋ **-ed** -d
Ganges ˈgæn.dʒiːz
gangland ˈgæŋ.lænd, -lənd
gangling ˈgæŋ.glɪŋ
gangli|on ˈgæŋ.gli|.ən, -ɒn (US) -ən **-a** -ə **-ons** -ənz, -ɒnz (US) -ənz
gangl|y ˈgæŋ.gl|i **-ier** -i.əʳ (US) -i.ɚ **-iest** -i.ɪst, -i.əst
gangplank ˈgæŋ.plæŋk **-s** -s
gangren|e ˈgæŋ.griːn (US) ˈ--, ˌ-ˈ- **-es** -z **-ing** -ɪŋ **-ed** -d
gangrenous ˈgæŋ.grɪ.nəs (US) -grə-
gangster ˈgæŋ*k*.stəʳ (US) -stɚ **-s** -z **-ism** -ɪ.zᵊm
gangway ˈgæŋ.weɪ **-s** -z
ganister ˈgæn.ɪ.stəʳ (US) -stɚ
ganja ˈgæn.dʒə, ˈgɑːn- (US) ˈgɑːn-
gannet ˈgæn.ɪt, -ət **-s** -s
Gannett ˈgæn.ɪt, -ət
gannister ˈgæn.ɪ.stəʳ (US) -stɚ
Gannon ˈgæn.ən
gantr|y (G) ˈgæn.tr|i **-ies** -iz
Ganymede ˈgæn.ɪ.miːd (US) ˈ-ə-
gaol dʒeɪl **-s** -z **-ing** -ɪŋ **-ed** -d
gaolbird ˈdʒeɪl.bɜːd (US) -bɜːrd **-s** -z
gaoler ˈdʒeɪ.ləʳ (US) -lɚ **-s** -z
gap gæp **-s** -s
gap|e geɪp **-es** -s **-ing** -ɪŋ **-ed** -t
garag|e ˈgær.ɑːʒ, -ɪdʒ, -ɑːdʒ *occasionally:* gəˈrɑːdʒ, -rɑːʒ (US) gəˈrɑːʒ, -ˈrɑːdʒ **-es** -ɪz **-ing** -ɪŋ **-ed** -d **ˈgarage ˌsale** (US) **gaˈrage ˌsale**
garam masala ˌgɑː.rəm.məˈsɑː.lə, -mɑːˈsɑː-
Garamond ˈgær.ə.mɒnd (US) ˈger-, ˈgær-, -mɑːnd
garb gɑːb (US) gɑːrb **-s** -z **-ed** -d
garbage ˈgɑː.bɪdʒ (US) ˈgɑːr- **ˈgarbage ˌcan**; **ˈgarbage disˌposal**; **ˈgarbage ˌman**
garbanzo gɑːˈbæn.zəʊ (US) gɑːrˈbɑːn.zoʊ **-s** -z
garbl|e ˈgɑː.bl̩ (US) ˈgɑːr- **-es** -z **-ing** -ɪŋ, ˈ-blɪŋ **-ed** -d
Garbo ˈgɑː.bəʊ (US) ˈgɑːr.boʊ
Garcia *English surname:* ˈgɑː.si.ə, ˈgɑː.ʃi.ə (US) gɑːrˈsiː.ə, ˈgɑːr.si-
García, Garcia *Spanish surname:* gɑːˈsiː.ə (US) gɑːr-
García Lorca gɑːˌsiː.əˈlɔː.kə (US) gɑːrˌsiː.əˈlɔːr.kə
García Márquez gɑːˌsiː.əˈmɑː.kez, -kes (US) gɑːrˌsiː.ə.mɑːrˈkez, -ˈkes, -ˈkeθ
garçon, garcon ˈgɑː.sɒn, -sɒn; gɑːˈsɔ̃ŋ (US) gɑːrˈsoʊn, -ˈsɔ̃ː **-s** -z
garda *Irish police:* ˈgɑː.də (US) ˈgɑːr- **gardai** gɑːˈdiː (US) gɑːr-
Garda *Italian lake:* ˈgɑː.də (US) ˈgɑːr-
garden (G) ˈgɑː.dᵊn (US) ˈgɑːr- **-s** -z **-ing** -ɪŋ **-ed** -d **ˈgarden ˌcentre**; **ˌgarden ˈcity**; **ˈgarden ˌparty**
gardener ˈgɑː.dᵊn.əʳ; ˈgɑːd.nəʳ (US) ˈgɑːr.dᵊn.ɚ; ˈgɑːrd.nɚ **-s** -z

gardenia gɑːˈdiː.ni.ə (US) gɑːr-, ˈ-njə **-s** -z
Gardiner ˈgɑː.dᵊn.əʳ; ˈgɑːd.nəʳ (US) ˈgɑːr.dᵊn.ɚ; ˈgɑːrd.nɚ
Gardner ˈgɑːd.nəʳ (US) ˈgɑːrd.nɚ
Gare du Nord ˌgɑː.djuːˈnɔːʳ (US) ˌgɑːr.duːˈnɔːr, -djuːˈ-
garefowl ˈgeə.faʊl (US) ˈger- **-s** -z
Gareth ˈgær.əθ, -eθ, -ɪθ (US) ˈger-, ˈgær-
Garfield ˈgɑː.fiːld (US) ˈgɑːr-
garfish ˈgɑː.fɪʃ (US) ˈgɑːr-
Garforth ˈgɑː.fəθ, -fɔːθ (US) ˈgɑːr.fɚθ, -fɔːrθ
Garfunkel ˌgɑːˈfʌŋ.kᵊl, ˈ--- (US) ˈgɑːr.fʌŋ-
garganey ˈgɑː.gᵊn.i (US) ˈgɑːr- **-s** -z
Gargantua gɑːˈgæn.tju.ə, -tʃu- (US) gɑːrˈgæn.tʃu-, -tju-
gargantuan gɑːˈgæn.tju.ən, -tʃu- (US) gɑːrˈgæn.tʃu-, -tʃu-
Gargery ˈgɑː.dʒᵊr.i (US) ˈgɑːr-
gargl|e ˈgɑː.gl̩ (US) ˈgɑːr- **-es** -z **-ing/s** -ɪŋ/z, ˈ-glɪŋ **-ed** -d
gargoyle ˈgɑː.gɔɪl (US) ˈgɑːr- **-s** -z
garibaldi (G) ˌgær.ɪˈbɔːl.di, -əˈ-, -ˈbæl-, -ˈbɒl- (US) ˌger-, ˌgær-, -ˈbɑːl- **-s** -z
Garioch ˈgær.i.ɒk, -ɒx (US) ˈger.i.ɑːk, ˈgær-
garish ˈgeə.rɪʃ, ˈgɑː- (US) ˈger.ɪʃ, ˈgær- **-ly** -li **-ness** -nəs, -nɪs
garland (G) ˈgɑː.lənd (US) ˈgɑːr- **-s** -z
garlic ˈgɑː.lɪk (US) ˈgɑːr- **-ky** -i
Garlick ˈgɑː.lɪk (US) ˈgɑːr-
Garman ˈgɑː.mən (US) ˈgɑːr-
gar|ment ˈgɑː|.mənt (US) ˈgɑːr- **-ments** -mənts **-mented** -mən.tɪd (US) -mən.t̬ɪd
garner (G) ˈgɑː.nəʳ (US) ˈgɑːr.nɚ **-s** -z **-ing** -ɪŋ **-ed** -d
garnet ˈgɑː.nɪt, -nət (US) ˈgɑːr- **-s** -s
Garnet(t) ˈgɑː.nɪt, -nət (US) ˈgɑːr-
Garnham ˈgɑː.nəm (US) ˈgɑːr-
garnish ˈgɑː.nɪʃ (US) ˈgɑːr- **-es** -ɪz **-ing** -ɪŋ **-ed** -t
garnishee ˌgɑː.nɪˈʃiː (US) ˌgɑːr- **-s** -z **-ing** -ɪŋ **-d** -d
garnishment ˈgɑː.nɪʃ.mənt (US) ˈgɑːr- **-s** -s
garniture ˈgɑː.nɪ.tʃəʳ (US) ˈgɑːr.nɪ.tʃɚ
Garonne gærˈɒn (US) -ˈɔːn, -ˈɑːn
Garrard ˈgær.əd, -ɑːd (US) ˈger.ɚd, ˈgær-; gəˈrɑːrd
Garratt ˈgær.ət (US) ˈger-, ˈgær-
Garraway ˈgær.ə.weɪ (US) ˈger-, ˈgær-
garret ˈgær.ət, -ɪt (US) ˈger-, ˈgær- **-s** -s
Garret(t) ˈgær.ət, -ɪt (US) ˈger-, ˈgær-
Garrick ˈgær.ɪk (US) ˈger-, ˈgær-
Garrioch *district in Scotland:* ˈgɪə.ri (US) ˈger.i *surname:* ˈgær.i.ək, -əx (US) ˈger-, ˈgær-
garrison (G) ˈgær.ɪ.sᵊn, ˈ-ə- (US) ˈger.ə-, ˈgær- **-s** -z **-ing** -ɪŋ **-ed** -d
Garrod ˈgær.əd (US) ˈger-, ˈgær-
Garrold ˈgær.ᵊld (US) ˈger-, ˈgær-
garrot ˈgær.ət (US) ˈger-, ˈgær- **-s** -s
garro|t(t)e gəˈrɒ|t (US) -ˈrɑː|t, -ˈroʊ|t; ˈger.ə|t **-t(t)es** -ts **-t(t)ing** -tɪŋ (US) -t̬ɪŋ **-t(t)ed** -tɪd (US) -t̬ɪd **-t(t)er/s** -təʳ/z (US) -t̬ɚ/z
garrulity gærˈuː.lə.ti, gəˈruː-, -ˈrjuː-, -lɪ- (US) gerˈuː.lə.t̬i, gær-
garrulous ˈgær.ᵊl.əs, -ʊl-, -jʊl- (US) ˈger.ᵊl-, -jᵊl- **-ly** -li **-ness** -nəs, -nɪs
Garston ˈgɑː.stᵊn (US) ˈgɑːr-
gart|er ˈgɑː.t|əʳ (US) ˈgɑːr.t̬|ɚ **-ers** -əz (US) -ɚz **-ering** -ᵊr.ɪŋ **-ered** -əd (US) -ɚd
garth (G) gɑːθ (US) gɑːrθ **-s** -s
Gartward ˈgɑːt.wəd, -wɔːd (US) ˈgɑːrt.wɚd
Garuda gærˈuː.də (US) ger-, gær-
Garvagh ˈgɑː.və (US) ˈgɑːr-
Garwood ˈgɑː.wʊd (US) ˈgɑːr-
Gary ˈgær.i (US) ˈger-, ˈgær-
Garza ˈgɑː.zə (US) ˈgɑːr-
gas (*n.*) gæs **-(s)es** -ɪz ˈ**gas** ˌ**chamber** ; ˈ**gas** ˌ**mask** ; ˈ**gas** ˌ**station**
gas (*v.*) gæs **-ses** -ɪz **-sing** -ɪŋ **-sed** -t
gasbag ˈgæs.bæg **-s** -z
Gascoigne ˈgæs.kɔɪn (US) gæsˈkɔɪn, ˈ--
Gascon ˈgæs.kən **-s** -z
gasconad|e ˌgæs.kəˈneɪd **-es** -z **-ing** -ɪŋ **-ed** -ɪd
Gascony ˈgæs.kə.ni
Gascoyne ˈgæs.kɔɪn (US) gæsˈkɔɪn, ˈ--
gaselier ˌgæs.əˈlɪəʳ (US) -ˈlɪr **-s** -z
gaseous ˈgæs.i.əs, ˈgeɪ.si-, ˈ-ʃəs; ˈgæʃ.əs (US) ˈgæs.i.əs, ˈgæʃ-; ˈgæʃ.əs **-ness** -nəs, -nɪs
gas-guzzler ˈgæsˌgʌz.ləʳ, -ˌgʌz.l̩.əʳ (US) ˌ-l̩.ɚ, ˌ-lɚ **-s** -z
gash gæʃ **-es** -ɪz **-ing** -ɪŋ **-ed** -t
gasholder ˈgæsˌhəʊl.dəʳ (US) -ˌhoʊl.dɚ **-s** -z
gasi|fy ˈgæs.ɪ|.faɪ, ˈ-ə- (US) ˈ-ə- **-fies** -faɪz **-fying** -faɪ.ɪŋ **-fied** -faɪd
Gaskell ˈgæs.kᵊl, -kel
gasket ˈgæs.kɪt **-s** -s
gaskin (G) ˈgæs.kɪn **-s** -z
gaslight ˈgæs.laɪt **-s** -s
gas|man ˈgæs|.mæn **-men** -men
gasohol ˈgæs.ə.hɒl (US) -hɔːl, -hɑːl
gasoline, gasolene ˈgæs.ᵊl.iːn, ˌ--ˈ-
gasometer gæsˈɒm.ɪ.təʳ, gəˈsɒm-, -ə.təʳ (US) gæsˈɑː.mə.t̬ɚ **-s** -z
gasp gɑːsp (US) gæsp **-s** -s **-ing** -ɪŋ **-ed** -t
Gaspé gæsˈpeɪ
gasper ˈgɑː.spəʳ (US) ˈgæs.pɚ **-s** -z
gass|y ˈgæs|.i **-ier** -i.əʳ (US) -i.ɚ **-iest** -i.ɪst, -i.əst **-iness** -ɪ.nəs, -ɪ.nɪs
gasteropod ˈgæs.tᵊr.əʊ.pɒd (US) -ə.pɑːd **-s** -z
Gaston ˈgæs.tɒn, gæsˈtɔ̃ːŋ (US) -tən, gæsˈtɑːn, -ɔ̃ːn
gastric ˈgæs.trɪk
gastrin ˈgæs.trɪn
gastritis gæsˈtraɪ.tɪs (US) -t̬əs
gastro- gæs.trəʊ-; gæsˈtrɒ- (US) gæs.troʊ-, -trə-; gæsˈtrɑː-
Note: Prefix. Normally takes either primary or secondary stress on the first syllable, e.g. **gastronome** /ˈgæs.trə.nəʊm (US) -noʊm/, **gastronomic** /ˌgæs.trəˈnɒm.ɪk (US) -ˈnɑː.mɪk/, or primary stress on the second syllable, e.g. **gastronomy** /gæsˈtrɒn.ə.mi (US) -ˈtrɑː.nə-/.
gastroenteritis ˌgæs.trəʊˌen.təˈraɪ.tɪs (US) -troʊˌen.t̬əˈraɪ.t̬əs
gastroenterolog|ist ˌgæs.trəʊˌen.təˈrɒl.ə.dʒ|ɪst (US) -troʊˌen.t̬əˈrɑː.lə.dʒ|ɪst **-ists** -ɪsts **-y** -i
gastrointestinal ˌgæs.trəʊˌɪn.tesˈtaɪ.nᵊl, -ɪnˈtes.tɪ.nᵊl, -tᵊn.ᵊl (US) -troʊ.ɪnˈtes.tᵊn.ᵊl
gastronome ˈgæs.trə.nəʊm (US) -noʊm **-s** -z
gastronomic ˌgæs.trəˈnɒm.ɪk (US) -ˈnɑː.mɪk **-al** -ᵊl
gastronom|y gæsˈtrɒn.ə.m|i (US) -ˈtrɑː.nə- **-ist/s** -ɪst/s
gastropod ˈgæs.trəʊ.pɒd (US) -trə.pɑːd **-s** -z
gasworks ˈgæs.wɜːks (US) -wɜːrks
gat|e geɪt **-es** -s **-ing** -ɪŋ (US) ˈgeɪ.t̬ɪŋ **-ed** -ɪd (US) ˈgeɪ.t̬əd
gâteau, gateau ˈgæt.əʊ (US) gætˈoʊ **-s** -z
gâteaux, gateaux ˈgæt.əʊ (US) gætˈoʊ, -z
gatecrash ˈgeɪt.kræʃ **-es** -ɪz **-ing** -ɪŋ **-ed** -t **-er/s** -əʳ/z (US) -ɚ/z
gatehou|se ˈgeɪt.haʊ|s **-ses** -zɪz
gatekeeper ˈgeɪtˌkiː.pəʳ (US) -pɚ **-s** -z
gateleg ˈgeɪt.leg **-s** -z
gate-legged ˈgeɪtˌlegd
gateless ˈgeɪt.ləs, -lɪs
gatepost ˈgeɪt.pəʊst (US) -poʊst **-s** -s
Gates geɪts
Gateshead ˈgeɪts.hed, ˌgeɪtsˈhed
gateway (G) ˈgeɪt.weɪ **-s** -z
Gath gæθ
gath|er ˈgæð|.əʳ (US) -ɚ **-ers** -əz (US) -ɚz **-ering/s** -ᵊr.ɪŋ/z **-ered** -əd (US) -ɚd **-erer/s** -ᵊr.əʳ/z (US) -ɚ.ɚ/z
Gatley ˈgæt.li
Gatling ˈgæt.lɪŋ
gator ˈgeɪ.tə (US) -t̬ɚ **-s** -z
Gatorade® ˌgeɪ.tᵊrˈeɪd (US) ˈgeɪ.t̬əˌreɪd
Gatsby ˈgæts.bi
Gatt, GATT gæt

Gatting 'gæt.ɪŋ (US) 'gæt̬-
Gatty 'gæt.i (US) 'gæt̬-
Gatwick 'gæt.wɪk ˌ**Gatwick 'Airport**
gauche gəʊʃ (US) goʊʃ **-ly** -li **-ness** -nəs, -nɪs
gaucherie 'gəʊ.ʃᵊr.i; ˌgəʊ.ʃᵊr'iː (US) ˌgoʊ.ʃə'riː **-s** -z
gaucho 'gaʊ.tʃəʊ (US) -tʃoʊ **-s** -z
gaud gɔːd (US) gɑːd, gɔːd **-s** -z
Gauden 'gɔː.dᵊn (US) 'gɑː-, 'gɔː-
Gaudí 'gaʊ.di, -'-
gaud|y 'gɔː.d|i (US) 'gɑː-, 'gɔː- **-ier** -i.əʳ (US) -i.ɚ **-iest** -i.ɪst, -i.əst **-ily** -ɪ.li, -ᵊl.i **-iness** -ɪ.nəs, -ɪ.nɪs
gaug|e geɪdʒ **-es** -ɪz **-ing** -ɪŋ **-ed** -d **-eable** -ə.bl̩
gauger 'geɪ.dʒəʳ (US) -dʒɚ **-s** -z
Gauguin 'gəʊ.gæ̃n, -gæn (US) goʊ'gæ̃, -'gæn
Gaul gɔːl **-s** -z **-ish** -ɪʃ
gauleiter 'gaʊ.laɪ.təʳ (US) -t̬ɚ **-s** -z
Gaull|ism 'gəʊ.l|ɪ.zᵊm (US) 'gɑː-, 'goʊ- **-ist/s** -ɪst/s
Gauloise(s)® 'gəʊl.wɑːz, ˌ-'- (US) goʊl'wɑːz, gɑːl-
Gault gɔːlt, gɒlt (US) gɔːlt, gɑːlt
Gaultier 'gɔːl.ti.eɪ (US) 'gɔːl-, 'gɑːl-
Gaumont® 'gəʊ.mɒnt, -mənt (US) 'goʊ.mɑːnt
gaun|t (G) gɔːn|t (US) gɑːn|t, gɔːn|t **-ter** -təʳ (US) -t̬ɚ **-test** -tɪst, -təst (US) -t̬ɪst, -t̬əst **-tly** -t.li **-tness** -t.nəs, -nɪs
gauntle|t (G) 'gɔːnt.lə|t, -lɪ|t (US) 'gɑːnt-, 'gɔːnt- **-ts** -ts **-ted** -tɪd (US) -t̬ɪd
Gauntlett 'gɔːnt.lət, -lɪt (US) 'gɑːnt-, 'gɔːnt
gauss (G) gaʊs **-es** -ɪz
gauz|e gɔːz (US) gɑːz, gɔːz **-es** -ɪz **-y** -i **-iness** -ɪ.nəs, -ɪ.nɪs
gave (*from* **give**) geɪv
gavel 'gæv.ᵊl **-s** -z
gavelkind 'gæv.ᵊl.kaɪnd, -kɪnd
gavel-to-gavel ˌgæv.ᵊl.tə'gæv.ᵊl
Gaveston 'gæv.ɪ.stᵊn, '-ə-
Gavey 'geɪ.vi
Gavin 'gæv.ɪn
gavotte gə'vɒt, gæ- (US) -'vɑːt **-s** -s
Gawain 'gɑː.weɪn, 'gæw.eɪn, -ɪn; gə'weɪn
gawd gɔːd (US) gɔːd, gɑːd
Gawith 'geɪ.wɪθ, 'gaʊ.ɪθ
gawk gɔːk (US) gɑːk, gɔːk **-s** -s
gawk|y 'gɔː.k|i (US) 'gɑː-, 'gɔː- **-ier** -i.əʳ (US) -i.ɚ **-iest** -i.ɪst, -i.əst **-iness** -ɪ.nəs, -ɪ.nɪs
gawp gɔːp (US) gɑːp, gɔːp **-s** -s **-ing** -ɪŋ **-ed** -t
Gawthrop 'gɔː.θrɒp, -θrəp (US) 'gɑː.θrɑːp, 'gɔː-, -θrəp
gay (G) geɪ **-er** -əʳ (US) -ɚ **-est** -ɪst, -əst **gaily** 'geɪ.li **gayness** 'geɪ.nəs, -nɪs
Gaye geɪ
Gayle geɪl
Gaylord 'geɪ.lɔːd (US) -lɔːrd
Gay-Lussac ˌgeɪ'luː.sæk (US) -lə'sæk
Gaynham 'geɪ.nəm
Gaynor 'geɪ.nəʳ (US) -nɚ
Gaza *in Israel:* 'gɑː.zə *in biblical use also:* 'geɪ.zə (US) 'gɑː.zə, 'gæz.ə, 'geɪ.zə ˌ**Gaza 'Strip**
Gaza *Greek scholar:* 'gɑː.zə
gaz|e geɪz **-es** -ɪz **-ing** -ɪŋ **-ed** -d **-er/s** -əʳ/z (US) -ɚ/z
gazebo gə'ziː.bəʊ (US) -'ziː.boʊ, -'zeɪ- **-s** -z
gazelle gə'zel **-s** -z
ga|zette gə|'zet **-zettes** -'zets **-zetting** -'zet.ɪŋ (US) -'zet̬.ɪŋ **-zetted** -'zet.ɪd (US) -'zet̬.əd
gazetteer ˌgæz.ə'tɪəʳ, -ɪ'- (US) -'tɪr **-s** -z
Gaziantep ˌgɑː.zi.ɑːn'tep
gazogene 'gæz.əʊ.dʒiːn (US) '-ə-
gazpacho gæs'pætʃ.əʊ (US) gə'spɑː.tʃoʊ, gəz'pɑː-
gazump gə'zʌmp **-s** -s **-ing** -ɪŋ **-ed** -t, -'zʌmt
gazunder gə'zʌn.dəʳ (US) -dɚ **-s** -s **-ing** -ɪŋ **-ed** -d
Gazza 'gæz.ə
GB ˌdʒiː'biː
GBH ˌdʒiː.biː'eɪtʃ
GCE ˌdʒiː.siː'iː **-s** -z
GCHQ ˌdʒiː.siː.eɪtʃ'kjuː
GCSE ˌdʒiː.siː.es'iː **-s** -z
Gdansk gə'dænt̮sk, -'daɪnt̮sk (US) -'dɑːnt̮sk, -'dænt̮sk
g'day gə'deɪ
GDP ˌdʒiː.diː'piː
GDR ˌdʒiː.diː'ɑːʳ (US) -'ɑːr
GE® ˌdʒiː'iː
gear gɪəʳ (US) gɪr **-s** -z **-ing** -ɪŋ **-ed** -d **'gear ˌlever**
gearbox 'gɪə.bɒks (US) 'gɪr.bɑːks **-es** -ɪz
Geare gɪəʳ (US) gɪr
gearshift 'gɪə.ʃɪft (US) 'gɪr- **-s** -s
Geary 'gɪə.ri (US) 'gɪr.i
Geat giːt **-s** -s
gecko 'gek.əʊ (US) -oʊ **-(e)s** -z
Ged ged, dʒed
GED ˌdʒiː.iː'diː
Geddes 'ged.ɪs (US) -iːz
geddit 'ged.ɪt (US) -ət
gee (G) dʒiː **-s** -z **-ing** -ɪŋ **-d** -d ˌ**gee 'whiz**
geegaw 'giː.gɔː (US) -gɑː, -gɔː **-s** -z
geegee 'dʒiː.dʒiː **-s** -z
geek giːk **-s** -s
geek|y 'giː.k|i **-ier** -i.əʳ (US) -i.ɚ **-iest** -i.ɪst, -i.əst
Geelong dʒɪ'lɒŋ, dʒə- (US) -'lɑːŋ, -'lɔːŋ
Geering 'gɪə.rɪŋ (US) 'gɪr.ɪŋ
geese (*plur. of* **goose**) giːs
Geeson 'dʒiː.sᵊn, 'giː-
gee-up ˌdʒiː'ʌp, 'dʒiː.ʌp
geezer 'giː.zəʳ (US) -zɚ **-s** -z
gefilte gə'fɪl.tə, gɪ- **ge'filte ˌfish, geˌfilte 'fish**
Gehazi gɪ'heɪ.zaɪ, ge-, gə-, -'hɑː-, -zi
Gehenna gɪ'hen.ə, gə-
Gehrig 'ger.ɪg
Geierstein 'gaɪə.staɪn (US) 'gaɪɚ-
Geiger 'gaɪ.gəʳ (US) -gɚ **'Geiger ˌcounter**
Geikie 'giː.ki
geisha 'geɪ.ʃə (US) 'geɪ-, 'giː- **-s** -z
gel *girl:* gel **-s** -z
gel *jelly:* dʒel **-s** -s **-ling** -ɪŋ **-led** -d
gelatin 'dʒel.ə.tɪn
gelatine 'dʒel.ə.tiːn, -tɪn, ˌ--'-
gelatiniz|e, -is|e dʒə'læt.ɪ.naɪz, dʒel'æt-, dʒɪ'læt-, -ᵊn.aɪz (US) dʒə'læt.ᵊn.aɪz **-es** -ɪz **-ing** -ɪŋ **-ed** -d
gelatinous dʒə'læt.ɪ.nəs, dʒel'æt-, dʒɪ'læt-, -ᵊn.əs (US) dʒə'læt.ᵊn.əs **-ly** -li
geld geld **-s** -z **-ing** -ɪŋ **-ed** -ɪd
Gelderland 'gel.də.lænd (US) -dɚ-
gelding 'gel.dɪŋ **-s** -z
Geldof 'gel.dɒf (US) -dɑːf
gelid 'dʒel.ɪd **-ly** -li **-ness** -nəs, -nɪs
gelignite 'dʒel.ɪg.naɪt, -əg-
Gell gel, dʒel
Gellan 'gel.ən
Gellatl(e)y 'gel.ət.li, gel'æt-, gə'læt- (US) gel'æt-, gə'læt-
Geller 'gel.əʳ (US) -ɚ
Gelligaer ˌgeθ.li'geəʳ, -'gaɪ.əʳ (US) -'ger, -'gaɪɚ
gem (G) dʒem **-s** -z
Gemara gə'mɑː.rə, gem'ɑː-, gɪ'mɑː-
gemi|nate (*v.*) 'dʒem.ɪ|.neɪt, '-ə- **-nates** -neɪts **-nating** -neɪ.tɪŋ (US) -neɪ.t̬ɪŋ **-nated** -neɪ.tɪd (US) -neɪ.t̬əd
geminate (*adj.*) 'dʒem.ɪ.nət
gemination ˌdʒem.ɪ'neɪ.ʃᵊn, -ə'-
Gemini *constellation:* 'dʒem.ɪ.naɪ, '-ə-, -niː *aircraft:* 'dʒem.ɪ.ni, '-ə-
Geminian ˌdʒem.ɪ'naɪ.ən, -ə'-, -'niː- **-s** -z
gem|ma (G) 'dʒem|.ə **-mae** -iː
gemmiferous dʒə'mɪf.ᵊr.əs, dʒem'ɪf-
gemmology dʒem'ɒl.ə.dʒi (US) -'ɑː.lə-
gemmule 'dʒem.juːl **-s** -z
gemology dʒem'ɒl.ə.dʒi (US) -'ɑː.lə-
gemsbok 'gemz.bɒk, -bʌk (US) -bɑːk **-s** -s
gemshorn 'gemz.hɔːn (US) -hɔːrn **-s** -z
gemstone 'dʒem.stəʊn (US) -stoʊn **-s** -z
gen dʒen **-s** -z **-ning** -ɪŋ **-ed** -d
gendarme 'ʒɑ̃ː*n*.dɑːm, 'ʒɔ̃ː*n*-, 'ʒɑːn- (US) 'ʒɑːn.dɑːrm **-s** -z
gender 'dʒen.dəʳ (US) -dɚ **-s** -z **-ing** -ɪŋ **-ed** -d

gender-bender 'dʒen.dəˌben.dəʳ ⓊⓈ -dɚˌben.dɚ **-s** -z

gene (G) dʒiːn **-s** -z

genealogical ˌdʒiː.ni.ə'lɒdʒ.ɪ.kᵊl ⓊⓈ ˌdʒiː.ni.ə'lɑː.dʒɪ-, ˌdʒen.i- **-ly** -i

genealogist ˌdʒiː.ni'æl.ə.dʒɪst ⓊⓈ ˌdʒiː.ni'-, ˌdʒen.i'- **-s** -s

genealog|y ˌdʒiː.ni'æl.ə.dʒ|i ⓊⓈ ˌdʒiː.ni'-, ˌdʒen.i'- **-ies** -iz

genera (*plur. of* **genus**) 'dʒen.ᵊr.ə

general 'dʒen.ᵊr.ᵊl **-s** -z **-ly** -i ˌ**general as'sembly** ; ˌ**general e'lection** ; ˌ**general prac'titioner** ; ˌ**general 'store** ; ˌ**General 'Motors®**

generalissimo ˌdʒen.ᵊr.ə'lɪs.ɪ.məʊ, '-ə- ⓊⓈ -ə.moʊ **-s** -z

generalist 'dʒen.ᵊr.ᵊl.ɪst, 'dʒen.rᵊl- **-s** -s

generalit|y ˌdʒen.ᵊ'ræl.ə.t|i, -ɪ.t|i ⓊⓈ -ə.ţ|i **-ies** -iz

generalization, -isa- ˌdʒen.ᵊr.ᵊl.aɪ'zeɪ.ʃᵊn, -ɪ'- ⓊⓈ -ɪ'- **-s** -z

generaliz|e, -is|e 'dʒen.ᵊr.ᵊl.aɪz ⓊⓈ -ə.laɪz **-es** -ɪz **-ing** -ɪŋ **-ed** -d **-able** -ə.bl̩

generalship 'dʒen.ᵊr.ᵊl.ʃɪp **-s** -s

gener|ate 'dʒen.ᵊr|.eɪt ⓊⓈ -ə.r|eɪt **-ates** -eɪts **-ating** -eɪ.tɪŋ ⓊⓈ -eɪ.ţɪŋ **-ated** -eɪ.tɪd ⓊⓈ -eɪ.ţɪd

generation ˌdʒen.ə'reɪ.ʃᵊn **-s** -z **gene'ration ˌgap**

generative 'dʒen.ᵊr.ə.tɪv ⓊⓈ -ə.ţɪv, '-ə.reɪ.ţɪv

generator 'dʒen.ᵊ.reɪ.təʳ ⓊⓈ -ţɚ **-s** -z

generatri|x 'dʒen.ᵊ.reɪ.trɪ|ks ⓊⓈ ˌdʒen.ə'reɪ- **-ces** -siːz

generic dʒə'ner.ɪk, dʒɪ-, dʒen'er- **-ally** -ᵊl.i, -li

generosity ˌdʒen.ᵊ'rɒs.ə.ti, -ɪ.ti ⓊⓈ -'rɑː.sə.ţi

generous 'dʒen.ᵊr.əs **-ly** -li **-ness** -nəs, -nɪs

gene|sis (G) 'dʒen.ə|.sɪs, '-ɪ- **-ses** -siːz

Genesius dʒə'niː.si.əs, dʒen'iː-, dʒɪ'niː- ⓊⓈ -si-, -ʃi-, -zi-

Genesta dʒə'nes.tə, dʒen'es-, dʒɪ'nes-

genet *animal:* 'dʒen.ɪt ⓊⓈ 'dʒen.ɪt, dʒə'net **-s** -s

Genet *French writer:* ʒə'neɪ

genetic dʒə'net.ɪk, dʒɪ- ⓊⓈ -'neţ.ɪk **-s** -s **-ally** -ᵊl.i, -li **geˌnetic engi'neering** ; **geˌnetic 'fingerprint**

geneticist dʒə'net.ɪ.sɪst, dʒɪ-, '-ə- ⓊⓈ -'neţ.ə- **-s** -s

Geneva dʒə'niː.və, dʒɪ- **Geˌneva Con'vention**

Geneviève *French name:* ˌʒen.ə'vjev ⓊⓈ ˌʒən.ə'vjev, 'dʒen.ə.viːv

Genevieve *English name:* 'dʒen.ə.viːv, '-ɪ-, ˌ--'-

Genghis Khan ˌgeŋ.gɪs'kɑːn, ˌdʒeŋ-, -gɪz'-

genial *amiable:* 'dʒiː.ni.əl **-ly** -i **-ness** -nəs, -nɪs

genial *of the chin:* dʒɪ'niː.əl, dʒə-, -'naɪ-

geniality ˌdʒiː.ni'æl.ə.ti, -ɪ.ti ⓊⓈ -ə.ţi

-genic -'dʒen.ɪk, -'dʒiː.nɪk

Note: Suffix. Words ending **-genic** normally carry primary stress on the penultimate syllable, e.g. **photogenic** /ˌfəʊ.təʊ'dʒen.ɪk ⓊⓈ ˌfoʊ.ţoʊ'-/.

genie (G) 'dʒiː.ni **-s** -z

genii (*from* **genius**) 'dʒiː.ni.aɪ

genista dʒə'nɪs.tə, dʒɪ-, dʒen'ɪs- **-s** -s

genital 'dʒen.ɪ.tᵊl, '-ə- ⓊⓈ -əţ.ᵊl **-s** -z **-ly** -li

genitalia ˌdʒen.ɪ'teɪ.li.ə, -ə'- ⓊⓈ -'teɪ.li.ə, -'teɪl.jə

genitival ˌdʒen.ɪ'taɪ.vᵊl, -ə'-

genitive 'dʒen.ɪ.tɪv, '-ə- ⓊⓈ -ə.ţɪv **-s** -z

genito-urinary ˌdʒen.ɪ.təʊ'jʊə.rɪ.nᵊr.i, ˌ-ə-, -'jɔː-, -rᵊn.ᵊr- ⓊⓈ -ə.ţoʊ'jʊr.ə.ner.i

geni|us 'dʒiː.ni|.əs **-i** -aɪ **-uses** -ə.sɪz

genius loci ˌdʒiː.ni.əs'ləʊ.saɪ ⓊⓈ -'loʊ- **genii loci** ˌdʒiː.ni.aɪ'-

Gennadi dʒə'nɑː.di, ge-

Gennesare|t gə'nez.ᵊr.ɪ|t, gɪ-, gen'ez-, -e|t, -ə|t ⓊⓈ gə'nes-, dʒə- **-th** -θ

Genoa 'dʒen.əʊ.ə, dʒə'nəʊ-, dʒɪ-, dʒen'əʊ- ⓊⓈ 'dʒen.ə.wə, dʒə'noʊ.ə

genocide 'dʒen.ə.saɪd

Genoese ˌdʒen.əʊ'iːz ⓊⓈ -oʊ'iːz *stress shift:* ˌGenoese 'sailor

genome 'dʒiː.nəʊm ⓊⓈ -noʊm **-s** -z

genotype 'dʒen.əʊ.taɪp ⓊⓈ '-oʊ-

-genous -dʒə.nəs, -dʒɪ.nəs

Note: Suffix. Words containing **-genous** are normally stressed on the antepenultimate syllable, e.g. **androgenous** /æn'drɒdʒ.ᵊn.əs ⓊⓈ -'drɑː.dʒᵊn-/. Exceptions exist: see individual entries.

genre 'ʒɑ̃ː*n*.rə ⓊⓈ 'ʒɑː*n*.rə

gen|s dʒen|z **-tes** -tiːz

Genseric 'gen.sᵊr.ɪk, 'dʒen-

Gensing 'gen.zɪŋ, 'gen*t*.sɪŋ

gent *gentleman:* dʒent **-s** -s

Gent *surname:* gent

Gent *place in Belgium:* gent, xent

genteel dʒen'tiːl, dʒən- **-ly** -li **-ness** -nəs, -nɪs

gentes (*plur. of* **gens**) 'dʒen.tiːz

gentian 'dʒen.*t*ʃᵊn, -*t*ʃi.ən **-s** -z

gentile (G) 'dʒen.taɪl **-s** -z

gentility ˌdʒen'tɪl.ə.ti ⓊⓈ -ţi

gent|le (G) 'dʒen.t|l̩ **-ler** -l̩.əʳ, 'dʒent.ləʳ ⓊⓈ 'dʒen.ţl̩.ɚ, 'dʒent.lɚ **-lest** -l̩.əst, -ɪst, 'dʒent.lɪst, -ləst **-ly** -li **-leness** -l̩.nəs, -nɪs ˈ**gentle ˌsex**

gentlefolk 'dʒen.tl̩.fəʊk ⓊⓈ 'dʒen.ţl̩-foʊk **-s** -s

gentle|man 'dʒen.tl̩|.mən ⓊⓈ 'dʒen.ţl̩- **-men** -mən, -men ˌ**gentleman's 'gentleman**

gentle|man-at-arms ˌdʒen.tl̩|.mən.ət'ɑːmz ⓊⓈ -ţl̩|.mən.ət'ɑːrmz **-men-at-arms** -mən.ət'ɑːmz, -men- ⓊⓈ -'ɑːrmz

gentlemanlike 'dʒen.tl̩.mən.laɪk ⓊⓈ 'dʒen.ţl̩.-

gentlemanl|y 'dʒen.tl̩.mən.l|i ⓊⓈ 'dʒen.ţl̩- **-iness** -ɪ.nəs, -ɪ.nɪs

gentle|woman 'dʒen.tl̩|ˌwʊm.ən ⓊⓈ 'dʒen.ţl̩- **-women** -ˌwɪm.ɪn

gentrification ˌdʒen.trɪ.fɪ'keɪ.ʃᵊn, -trə- **-s** -z

gentrifier 'dʒen.trɪ.faɪ.əʳ, -trə- ⓊⓈ -ɚ **-s** -z

gentrif|y 'dʒen.trɪ.f|aɪ, -trə- **-ies** -aɪz **-ying** -aɪ.ɪŋ **-ied** -aɪd

gentry (G) 'dʒen.tri

genuflect 'dʒen.jʊ.flekt, -jə- **-s** -s **-ing** -ɪŋ **-ed** -ɪd

genuflection, genuflexion ˌdʒen.jʊ'flek.ʃᵊn, -jə- **-s** -z

genuine 'dʒen.ju.ɪn **-ly** -li **-ness** -nəs, -nɪs

genus 'dʒiː.nəs, 'dʒen.əs **genera** 'dʒen.ᵊr.ə

-geny -dʒə.ni, -dʒɪ.ni

Note: Suffix. Words containing **-geny** are stressed in a similar way to those containing **-genous**; see above.

geo- dʒiː.əʊ-; dʒi'ɒ-, 'dʒɒ- ⓊⓈ dʒiː.oʊ-, -ə-; dʒi'ɑː-

Note: Prefix. Normally takes either primary or secondary stress on the first syllable, e.g. **geomancy** /'dʒiː.əʊ.mæn*t*.si ⓊⓈ '-ə-/, **geocentric** /ˌdʒiː.əʊ'sen.trɪk ⓊⓈ -oʊ'-/, or primary stress on the second syllable, e.g. **geography** /dʒi'ɒg.rə.fi ⓊⓈ -'ɑː.grə-/.

geocentric ˌdʒiː.əʊ'sen.trɪk ⓊⓈ -oʊ'- **-al** -ᵊl **-ally** -ᵊl.i, -li

geochemical ˌdʒiː.əʊ'kem.ɪ.kᵊl ⓊⓈ -oʊ'-

geochemist ˌdʒiː.əʊ'kem.ɪst, 'dʒiː.əʊˌkem- ⓊⓈ ˌdʒiː.oʊ'kem- **-s** -s

geochemistry ˌdʒiː.əʊ'kem.ɪ.stri ⓊⓈ -oʊ'-

geode 'dʒiː.əʊd ⓊⓈ -oʊd **-s** -z

geodesic ˌdʒiː.əʊ'des.ɪk, -'diː.sɪk ⓊⓈ -ə'- **-al** -ᵊl

geodesy dʒi'ɒd.ɪ.si, '-ə- ⓊⓈ -'ɑː.də-

geodic dʒi'ɒd.ɪk ⓊⓈ -'ɑː.dɪk

Geoff dʒef

Geoffr(e)y 'dʒef.ri

Geoghegan 'geɪ.gᵊn, 'gəʊ.gᵊn, gɪ'heɪ.gᵊn ⓊⓈ 'goʊ.gᵊn

geographer dʒi'ɒg.rə.fəʳ ⓊⓈ -'ɑː.grə.fɚ **-s** -z

geographic ˌdʒiː.əʊ'græf.ɪk ⓊⓈ -ə'- **-al** -ᵊl **-ally** -ᵊl.i, -li

geograph|y dʒiˈɒɡ.rə.f|i; ˈdʒɒɡ-
(US) dʒiˈɑː.ɡrə- **-ies** -iz
geologic ˌdʒi.əʊˈlɒdʒ.ɪk
(US) -əˈlɑː.dʒɪk **-al** -ᵊl **-ally** -ᵊl.i, -li
geologist dʒiˈɒl.ə.dʒɪst (US) -ˈɑː.lə- **-s** -s
geologiz|e, -is|e dʒiˈɒl.ə.dʒaɪz
(US) -ˈɑː.lə- **-es** -ɪz **-ing** -ɪŋ **-ed** -d
geology dʒiˈɒl.ə.dʒi (US) -ˈɑː.lə-
geomagnetic ˌdʒiː.əʊ.mæɡˈnet.ɪk,
-məɡˈ- (US) -oʊ.mæɡˈneṭ.ɪk
geomagnetism
ˌdʒiː.əʊˈmæɡ.nɪ.tɪ.zᵊm, -nə-
(US) -oʊˈmæɡ.nə-
geomancy ˈdʒiː.əʊ.mænt.si (US) ˈ-ə-
geometer dʒiˈɒm.ɪ.təʳ, ˈ-ə-
(US) -ˈɑː.mə.ṭɚ **-s** -z
geometric ˌdʒiː.əʊˈmet.rɪk (US) -əˈ- **-al**
-ᵊl **-ally** -ᵊl.i, -li
geometrician ˌdʒiː.əʊ.məˈtrɪʃ.ᵊn,
dʒiˌɒm.əˈ-, -ɪˈ- (US) ˌdʒiː.ə.məˈ-;
dʒiˌɑː- **-s** -z
geometr|y dʒiˈɒm.ɪ.tr|i, ˈ-ə-; ˈdʒɒm-
(US) dʒiˈɑː.mə- **-ies** -iz
geomorphologic
ˌdʒiː.əʊˌmɔː.fəˈlɒdʒ.ɪk
(US) -oʊˌmɔːr.fəˈlɑː.dʒɪk **-al** -ᵊl **-ally**
-ᵊl.i, -li
geomorphology|y
ˌdʒiː.əʊ.mɔːˈfɒl.ə.dʒ|i
(US) -oʊ.mɔːrˈfɑː.lə- **-ist/s** -ɪst/s
geophysical ˌdʒiː.əʊˈfɪz.ɪ.kᵊl (US) -oʊˈ-
geophysicist ˌdʒi.əʊˈfɪz.ɪ.sɪst
(US) -oʊˈ- **-s** -s
geophysics ˌdʒiː.əʊˈfɪz.ɪks (US) -oʊˈ-
geopolitical ˌdʒiː.əʊ.pəˈlɪt.ɪ.kᵊl
(US) -oʊ.pəˈlɪṭ- **-ly** -i
geopolitics ˌdʒiː.əʊˈpɒl.ə.tɪks, ˈ-ɪ-
(US) -oʊˈpɑː.lə-
Geordie ˈdʒɔː.di (US) ˈdʒɔːr- **-s** -z
George dʒɔːdʒ (US) dʒɔːrdʒ
Georgetown ˈdʒɔːdʒ.taʊn (US) ˈdʒɔːrdʒ-
georgette dʒɔːˈdʒet (US) dʒɔːr-
Georgi|a ˈdʒɔː.dʒ|ə, -dʒi|.ə (US) ˈdʒɔːr-
-an/s -ən/z
Georgiana ˌdʒɔː.dʒiˈɑː.nə
(US) ˌdʒɔːrˈdʒæn.ə, -dʒiˈæn-
georgic (G) ˈdʒɔː.dʒɪk (US) ˈdʒɔːr- **-s** -s
Georgina dʒɔːˈdʒiː.nə (US) dʒɔːrˈ-
geoscience ˌdʒiː.əʊˈsaɪ.ənts (US) -oʊˈ-
geostationary ˌdʒiː.əʊˈsteɪ.ʃᵊn.ᵊr.i, -ri
(US) -oʊˈsteɪ.ʃᵊn.er-
geothermal ˌdʒiː.əʊˈθɜː.mᵊl
(US) -oʊˈθɜːr-
geotropic ˌdʒiː.əʊˈtrɒp.ɪk
(US) -əˈtrɑː.pɪk
geotropism dʒiˈɒt.rə.pɪ.zᵊm
(US) -ˈɑː.trə- **-s** -z
Geraint ˈɡer.aɪnt, -ˈ- (US) dʒəˈreɪnt
Gerald ˈdʒer.ᵊld
Geraldine ˈdʒer.ᵊl.diːn, -daɪn
Note: /ˈdʒer.ᵊl.daɪn/ in Coleridge's
'Christabel'.
Geraldton ˈdʒer.ᵊld.tᵊn
geranium dʒəˈreɪ.ni.əm, dʒɪ- **-s** -z
Gerard ˈdʒer.ɑːd, ˈdʒer.əd, dʒerˈɑːd,
dʒəˈrɑːd (US) dʒəˈrɑːrd
gerbil ˈdʒɜː.bᵊl, -bɪl (US) ˈdʒɜːr.bᵊl **-s** -z
gerfalcon ˈdʒɜːˌfɔːl.kᵊn, -ˌfɔː.kᵊn
(US) ˈdʒɜːrˌfɑːl-, -ˌfæl-, -ˌfɔː- **-s** -z
Note: In British English, those who
practise the sport of falconry
pronounce /-ˌfɔː-/.
Gergesene ˈɡɜː.ɡɪ.siːn, -ɡə-, -ɡes.iːn,
ˌ-ˈ-- (US) ˈɡɜːr.ɡə- **-s** -z
Gerhardt ˈɡeə.hɑːt (US) ˈɡer.hɑːrd,
-hɑːrt
geriatric ˌdʒer.iˈæt.rɪk **-s** -s
geriatrician ˌdʒer.i.əˈtrɪʃ.ᵊn **-s** -z
geriatry ˈdʒer.i.ə.tri, -æt.ri
Geritol® ˈdʒer.ɪ.tɒl (US) -tɑːl
Gerizim ɡerˈaɪ.zɪm, ɡəˈraɪ-, -ˈriː-;
ˈɡer.ɪ.zɪm
germ dʒɜːm (US) dʒɜːrm **-s** -z ˌ**germ**
ˈ**warfare**
Germain ˈdʒɜː.mən, -meɪn (US) ˈdʒɜːr-
Germaine dʒəˈmeɪn, dʒɜː- (US) dʒɚ-
German ˈdʒɜː.mən (US) ˈdʒɜːr- **-s** -z
ˌ**German** ˈ**measles**
germander dʒəˈmæn.dəʳ, dʒɜː-
(US) dʒɚˈmæn.dɚ
germane (G) dʒəˈmeɪn, dʒɜː-;
ˈdʒɜː.meɪn (US) dʒɚˈmeɪn **-ly** -li **-ness**
-nəs, -nɪs
Germanic dʒəˈmæn.ɪk, dʒɜː- (US) dʒɚ-
German|ism ˈdʒɜː.mə.n|ɪ.zᵊm
(US) ˈdʒɜːr- **-isms** -ɪ.zᵊmz **-ist/s** -ɪst/s
germanium dʒəˈmeɪ.ni.əm, dʒɜː-
(US) dʒɚ-
germanization, -isa-
ˌdʒɜː.mə.naɪˈzeɪ.ʃᵊn, -ɪˈ-
(US) ˌdʒɜːr.mə.nɪˈ-
germaniz|e, -is|e ˈdʒɜː.mə.naɪz
(US) ˈdʒɜːr- **-es** -ɪz **-ing** -ɪŋ **-ed** -d
German|y ˈdʒɜː.mə.n|i (US) ˈdʒɜːr-
-ies -iz
germicidal ˌdʒɜː.mɪˈsaɪ.dᵊl, -məˈ-,
ˈdʒɜː.mɪ.saɪ-, -mə- (US) ˌdʒɜːr.məˈsaɪ-
germicide ˈdʒɜː.mɪ.saɪd, -mə-
(US) ˈdʒɜːr.mə- **-s** -z
germinal ˈdʒɜː.mɪ.nᵊl, -mə-
(US) ˈdʒɜːr.mə-
germi|nate ˈdʒɜː.mɪ|.neɪt, -mə-
(US) ˈdʒɜːr.mə- **-nates** -neɪts **-nating**
-neɪ.tɪŋ (US) -neɪ.ṭɪŋ **-nated** -neɪ.tɪd
(US) -neɪ.ṭɪd
germination ˌdʒɜː.mɪˈneɪ.ʃᵊn, -məˈ-
(US) ˌdʒɜːr.məˈ- **-s** -z
Germiston ˈdʒɜː.mɪ.stᵊn
(US) ˈdʒɜːr.mɪ-, -mə-
Germolene® ˈdʒɜː.mə.liːn (US) ˈdʒɜːr-
Geronimo dʒəˈrɒn.ɪ.məʊ, dʒɪ-,
dʒerˈɒn-, ˈ-ə- (US) -ˈrɑː.nə.moʊ
Gerontius ɡəˈrɒn.ti.əs, ɡɪ-, dʒə-, dʒɪ-,
ɡerˈɒn-, -ʃi.əs, -ʃəs (US) dʒəˈrɑːn-
gerontocrac|y ˌdʒer.ɒnˈtɒk.rə.s|i,
-ənˈ- (US) -ᵊnˈtɑː.krə- **-cies** -iz
gerontocratic dʒəˌrɒn.təˈkræt.ɪk,
ˌdʒer.ɒn-, -ən.təˈ-
(US) dʒəˌrɑːn.ṭəˈkræṭ.ɪk
gerontolog|y ˌdʒer.ɒnˈtɒl.ə.dʒ|i, ˌɡer-,
-ənˈ- (US) ˌdʒer.ᵊnˈtɑː.lə- **-ist/s** -ɪst/s
Gerrard ˈdʒer.əd, -ɑːd; dʒerˈɑːd,
dʒəˈrɑːd (US) ˈdʒer.ɚd ˌ**Gerrard's**
ˈ**Cross**
Gerry ˈdʒer.i
gerrymand|er ˈdʒer.i.mæn.d|əʳ,
ˌdʒer.iˈmæn- (US) -d|ɚ **-ers** -əz
(US) -ɚz **-ering** -ᵊr.ɪŋ **-ered** -əd (US) -ɚd
Gershwin ˈɡɜː.ʃwɪn (US) ˈɡɜːrʃ-, -wən
Gertie ˈɡɜː.ti (US) ˈɡɜːr.ṭi
Gertrude ˈɡɜː.truːd (US) ˈɡɜːr-
Gerty ˈɡɜː.ti (US) ˈɡɜːr.ṭi
gerund ˈdʒer.ᵊnd, -ʌnd **-s** -z
gerundival ˌdʒer.ᵊnˈdaɪ.vᵊl
gerundive dʒəˈrʌn.dɪv, dʒɪ-, dʒerˈʌn-
-s -z
Gerva(i)se ˈdʒɜː.veɪz, -vɪz; dʒɜːˈveɪz,
-ˈveɪs (US) ˈdʒɜːr-
Geryon ˈɡer.i.ən (US) ˈdʒɪr-, ˈɡer-
gesso ˈdʒes.əʊ (US) -oʊ **-es** -z
gest dʒest **-s** -s
gestalt ɡəˈʃtælt, -ʃtɑːlt; ˈɡeʃ.tælt
(US) ɡəˈʃtɑːlt
Gestapo ɡesˈtɑː.pəʊ, ɡeʃ-
(US) ɡəˈstɑː.poʊ, ɡəʃˈtɑː-
Gesta Romanorum
ˌdʒes.tə.rəʊ.məˈnɔː.rəm, -mɑː-,
ˌɡes- (US) -roʊ.mə.nɔːr.əm, -mɑ-
ges|tate dʒes|ˈteɪt, ˈ-- (US) ˈdʒes|.teɪt
-tates -ˈteɪts (US) -teɪts **-tating**
-ˈteɪ.tɪŋ (US) -teɪ.ṭɪŋ **-tated** -ˈteɪ.tɪd
(US) -teɪ.ṭɪd
gestation dʒesˈteɪ.ʃᵊn **-s** -z
gestatorial ˌdʒes.təˈtɔː.ri.əl
gestatory dʒesˈteɪ.tᵊr.i; ˈdʒes.tə-
(US) ˈdʒes.tə.tɔːr-
Gestetner® ɡesˈtet.nəʳ, ɡɪˈstet-, ɡə-
(US) -nɚ
gesticu|late dʒesˈtɪk.jə|.leɪt, -jʊ-
(US) -jə- **-lates** -leɪts **-lating** -leɪ.tɪŋ
(US) -leɪ.ṭɪŋ **-lated** -leɪ.tɪd (US) -leɪ.ṭɪd
-lator/s -leɪ.təʳ/z (US) -leɪ.ṭɚ/z
gesticulation dʒesˌtɪk.jəˈleɪ.ʃᵊn, -jʊˈ-
(US) -jəˈ- **-s** -z
gesticulatory dʒesˈtɪk.jʊ.leɪ.tᵊr.i, -lə-,
-je- (US) -jə.lə.tɔːr-
gesture ˈdʒes.tʃəʳ (US) -tʃɚ **-s** -z
-ing -ɪŋ **-ed** -d
Gesundheit ɡəˈzʊnd.haɪt
get ɡet **-s** -s **-ting** -ɪŋ (US) ˈɡeṭ.ɪŋ
got ɡɒt (US) ɡɑːt **gotten** ˈɡɒt.ᵊn
(US) ˈɡɑː.tᵊn ˌ**give as** ˌ**good as one**
ˈ**gets**
Getae ˈɡeɪ.taɪ, ˈdʒiː.tiː
getatable ɡetˈæt.ə.bl̩ (US) ɡeṭˈæṭ-
getaway ˈɡet.ə.weɪ (US) ˈɡeṭ- **-s** -z

Gethin ˈgeθ.ɪn
Gethsemane geθˈsem.ə.ni
get-rich-quick ˌget.rɪtʃˈkwɪk
get-together ˈget.tə.geð.ə ⓤⓢ -geð.ɚ **-s** -z
Getty ˈget.i ⓤⓢ ˈget̬.i
Gettysburg ˈget.iz.bɜːg ⓤⓢ ˈget̬.iz.bɜːrg ˌ**Gettysburg Adˈdress**
getup ˈget.ʌp ⓤⓢ ˈget̬- **-s** -s
get-up-and-go ˌget.ʌp.ənˈgəʊ, -əŋˈ- ⓤⓢ ˌget̬.ʌp.ənˈgoʊ
geum ˈdʒiː.əm **-s** -z
gewgaw ˈgjuː.gɔː ⓤⓢ ˈguː.gɑː, ˈgjuː-, -gɔː **-s** -z
Gewürztraminer gəˈvʊət.strəˌmiː.nə, -ˈvɜːt- ⓤⓢ -ˈvɜːrt.strəˌmiː.nɚ
geyser *hot spring:* ˈgaɪ.zəʳ, ˈgiː- ⓤⓢ ˈgaɪ.zɚ, -sɚ **-s** -z
Note: In New Zealand the pronunciation is /ˈgaɪ.zəʳ/. *apparatus for heating water:* ˈgiː.zəʳ ⓤⓢ -zɚ **-s** -z
Ghana ˈgɑː.nə
Ghanaian gɑːˈneɪ.ən ⓤⓢ -ˈniː-, -ˈneɪ- **-s** -z
ghastl|y ˈgɑːst.l|i ⓤⓢ ˈgæst.l|i **-ier** -i.əʳ ⓤⓢ -i.ɚ **-iest** -i.ɪst, -i.əst **-iness** -ɪ.nəs, -ɪ.nɪs
Ghat gɑːt, gɔːt **-s** -s
ghee giː
Ghent gent
gherkin ˈgɜː.kɪn ⓤⓢ ˈgɜːr- **-s** -z
ghetto ˈget.əʊ ⓤⓢ ˈget̬.oʊ **-(e)s** -z **ˈghetto ˌblaster**
Ghia ˈgiː.ə
Ghibelline ˈgɪb.ɪ.laɪn, ˈ-ə-, -liːn **-s** -z
ghillie ˈgɪl.i **-s** -z
ghost gəʊst ⓤⓢ goʊst **-s** -s **-ing** -ɪŋ **-ed** -ɪd **-like** -laɪk **ˈghost ˌtown** ; ˌ**give up the ˈghost**
ghostl|y ˈgəʊst.l|i ⓤⓢ ˈgoʊst- **-iness** -ɪ.nəs, -ɪ.nɪs
ghost|write ˈgəʊst|.raɪt ⓤⓢ ˈgoʊst- **-writes** -raɪts **-writing** -ˌraɪ.tɪŋ ⓤⓢ -ˌraɪ.t̬ɪŋ **-wrote** -rəʊt ⓤⓢ -roʊt
ghostwriter ˈgəʊstˌraɪ.təʳ ⓤⓢ ˈgoʊstˌraɪ.t̬ɚ **-s** -z
ghoul guːl **-s** -z **-ish/ly** -ɪʃ/li
ghyll gɪl **-s** -z
GI ˌdʒiːˈaɪ *stress shift:* ˌ**GI** ˈbride
giant dʒaɪənt **-s** -s **-like** -laɪk ˌ**Giant's ˈCauseway**
giantess ˈdʒaɪən.tes, -tɪs, -təs; ˌdʒaɪənˈtes ⓤⓢ ˈdʒaɪən.t̬əs **-es** -ɪz
Giaour ˈdʒaʊəʳ ⓤⓢ -ɚ
Gibb gɪb
gibb|er ˈdʒɪb|.əʳ ⓤⓢ -ɚ **-ers** -əz ⓤⓢ -ɚz **-ering** -ər.ɪŋ **-ered** -əd ⓤⓢ -ɚd
gibberish ˈdʒɪb.ə.rɪʃ
gibbet ˈdʒɪb.ɪt, -ət **-s** -s **-ing** -ɪŋ ⓤⓢ ˈdʒɪb.ɪ.t̬ɪŋ **-ed** -ɪd ⓤⓢ ˈdʒɪb.ɪ.t̬ɪd
Gibbie ˈdʒɪb.i
Gibbins ˈgɪb.ɪnz
gibbon (G) ˈgɪb.ən **-s** -z
gibbosity gɪˈbɒs.ə.ti, dʒɪ-, -ɪ.ti ⓤⓢ gɪˈbɑː.sə.t̬i
gibbous ˈgɪb.əs, ˈdʒɪb- ⓤⓢ ˈgɪb- **-ly** -li **-ness** -nəs, -nɪs
Gibbs gɪbz
gib|e dʒaɪb **-es** -z **-ing/ly** -ɪŋ/li **-ed** -d **-er/s** -əʳ/z ⓤⓢ -ɚ/z
Gibeon ˈgɪb.i.ən
giblet ˈdʒɪb.lət, -lɪt **-s** -s
Gibraltar dʒɪˈbrɔːl.təʳ, dʒə-, -ˈbrɒl- ⓤⓢ -ˈbrɑːl.tɚ, -ˈbrɔːl-
Gibraltarian ˌdʒɪb.rɔːlˈteə.ri.ən, -rɒlˈ-; dʒɪˌbrɔːlˈ-, dʒə-, -ˌbrɒlˈ- ⓤⓢ ˌdʒɪb.rɑːlˌter.i-, -rɔːlˈ- **-s** -z
Gibson ˈgɪb.sən
Gidding ˈgɪd.ɪŋ **-s** -z
Giddis ˈgɪd.ɪs
gidd|y (G) ˈgɪd|.i **-ier** -i.əʳ ⓤⓢ -i.ɚ **-iest** -i.ɪst, -i.əst **-ily** -ɪ.li, -əl.i **-iness** -ɪ.nəs, -ɪ.nɪs
Gide ʒiːd
Gidea ˈgɪd.i.ə
Gideon ˈgɪd.i.ən
Gielgud ˈgiːl.gʊd
Giffard ˈdʒɪf.əd, ˈgɪf- ⓤⓢ -ɚd
Giffen ˈgɪf.ɪn, ˈdʒɪf.ɪn, -ən
Giffnock ˈgɪf.nək
Gifford *place near Haddington:* ˈgɪf.əd ⓤⓢ -ɚd *surname:* ˈgɪf.əd, ˈdʒɪf.əd ⓤⓢ -ɚd
gift gɪft **-s** -s **-ed** -ɪd **ˈgift cerˌtificate** ; **ˈgift ˌtoken** ; ˌ**gift of the ˈgab** ; ˌ**look a ˌgift horse in the ˈmouth**
gift-wrap ˈgɪft.ræp **-s** -s **-ping** -ɪŋ **-ped** -t
gig gɪg **-s** -z
giga- ˈgɪg.ə-, ˈgaɪ.gə-, ˈdʒɪg.ə-
gigabyte ˈgɪg.ə.baɪt, ˈgaɪ.gə-, ˈdʒɪg.ə- **-s** -s
gigahertz ˈgɪg.ə.hɜːts, ˈgaɪ.gə-, ˈdʒɪg.ə- ⓤⓢ -hɜːrts
gigantesque ˌdʒaɪ.gænˈtesk, -gən-
gigantic dʒaɪˈgæn.tɪk, ˌdʒaɪ- ⓤⓢ -t̬ɪk **-ally** -əl.i, -li
gigantism dʒaɪˈgæn.tɪ.zəm, ˈdʒaɪ.gæn- ⓤⓢ -t̬ɪ-
giggl|e (*n. v.*) ˈgɪg.l̩ **-es** -z **-ing** -ɪŋ, ˈ-lɪŋ **-ed** -d **-er/s** -əʳ/z, ˈ-ləʳ/z ⓤⓢ ˈ-l̩.ɚ/z, ˈ-lɚ/z
giggleswick (G) ˈgɪg.l̩z.wɪk
giggly ˈgɪg.l̩.i, ˈgɪg.li
Gight gɪkt, gɪxt
Gigi ˈʒiː.ʒiː
Gigli ˈdʒiː.li, -lji ⓤⓢ ˈdʒiː.li, ˈdʒiːl.ji
Giglio ˈdʒiː.li.əʊ, ˈ-ljəʊ ⓤⓢ ˈ-li.oʊ
GIGO ˈgaɪ.gəʊ, ˈdʒaɪ- ⓤⓢ ˈgɪg.oʊ, ˈgaɪ.goʊ, ˈgiː-
gigolo ˈdʒɪg.ə.ləʊ, ˈʒɪg- ⓤⓢ -loʊ **-s** -z
gigot ˈdʒɪg.ət, ˈzɪg-, -əʊ, ˈdʒiː.gəʊ ⓤⓢ ziːˈgoʊ **-s** -s
gigue ʒiːg, ʒɪg **-s** -z
Gihon ˈgaɪ.hɒn *in Jewish usage sometimes:* ˈgiː.həʊn
gila (G) ˈhiː.lə, ˈgiː- ⓤⓢ ˈhɪː- **-s** -z
Gilbert ˈgɪl.bət ⓤⓢ -bɚt
Gilbertian gɪlˈbɜː.ti.ən, -ʃən ⓤⓢ -ˈbɜːr.t̬i.ən
Gilbey ˈgɪl.bi
Gilboa gɪlˈbəʊ.ə ⓤⓢ -ˈboʊ-
Gilchrist ˈgɪl.krɪst
gild gɪld **-s** -z **-ing** -ɪŋ **-ed** -ɪd **gilt** gɪlt
Gildas ˈgɪl.dæs
gilder (G) ˈgɪl.dəʳ ⓤⓢ -dɚ **-s** -z
Gildersleeve ˈgɪl.də.sliːv ⓤⓢ -dɚ-
Gildersome ˈgɪl.də.səm ⓤⓢ -dɚ-
Gilding ˈgɪl.dɪŋ
Gildredge ˈgɪl.drɪdʒ, -dredʒ
Gilead ˈgɪl.i.æd ⓤⓢ -əd
Giles dʒaɪlz
Gilfil ˈgɪl.fɪl
Gilfillan gɪlˈfɪl.ən
Gilford ˈgɪl.fəd ⓤⓢ -fɚd
Gilgal ˈgɪl.gæl, -gɔːl
Gilgamesh ˈgɪl.gə.meʃ
Gilham ˈgɪl.əm
Gilkes dʒɪlks
gill *respiratory organ, ravine:* gɪl **-s** -z *measure:* dʒɪl **-s** -z
Gill gɪl, dʒɪl
Gillam ˈgɪl.əm
Gillard ˈgɪl.ɑːd, -əd; gɪˈlɑːd ⓤⓢ ˈgɪl.ɚd
Gillen ˈgɪl.ən
Gilleney ˈgɪl.ən.i
Gillespie gɪˈles.pi, gə-
Gillett ˈgɪl.ɪt, ˈgɪl.et, gɪˈlet, dʒɪˈlet, dʒəˈlet
Gillette® dʒɪˈlet ⓤⓢ dʒəˈlet, dʒɪ- **-s** -s
Gilley ˈgɪl.i
Gilliam ˈgɪl.i.əm
Gillian ˈdʒɪl.i.ən, ˈgɪl-
Gilliat ˈgɪl.i.ət, -æt
Gillick ˈgɪl.ɪk
gillie (G) ˈgɪl.i **-s** -z
Gillies ˈgɪl.ɪs
Gilliland ˈgɪl.ɪ.lænd
Gilling ˈgɪl.ɪŋ **-s** -z
Gillingham *in Kent:* ˈdʒɪl.ɪŋ.əm *in Dorset & Norfolk:* ˈgɪl- *surname:* ˈgɪl-, ˈdʒɪl-
Gillison ˈgɪl.ɪ.sən
Gillmore ˈgɪl.mɔːʳ ⓤⓢ -mɔːr
Gillon ˈgɪl.ən
Gillott ˈdʒɪl.ət, ˈgɪl.ət
Gillow ˈgɪl.əʊ ⓤⓢ -oʊ
Gillray ˈgɪl.reɪ
Gills gɪlz
Gillson ˈdʒɪl.sən
gilly ˈgɪl.i **-s** -z

gillyflower 'dʒɪl.ɪˌflaʊəʳ ⓤⓈ -ˌflaʊɚ **-s** -z
Gilman 'gɪl.mən
Gilmer 'gɪl.məʳ ⓤⓈ -mɚ
Gilmore 'gɪl.mɔːʳ, -məʳ ⓤⓈ -mɔːr
Gilmour 'gɪl.mɔːʳ, -məʳ ⓤⓈ -mɔːr
Gilpatrick gɪl'pæt.rɪk
Gilpin 'gɪl.pɪn
Gilroy 'gɪl.rɔɪ
Gilson 'dʒɪl.sᵊn, 'gɪl.sᵊn
gilt gɪlt **-s**
gilt-edged ˌgɪlt'edʒd *stress shift:* ˌgilt-edged 'stocks
gimbal 'gɪm.bəl, 'dʒɪm- **-s** -z
gimbl|e 'gɪm.bl̩ **-es** -z **-ing** -ɪŋ, '-blɪŋ **-ed** -d
Gimblett 'gɪm.*b*lɪt, -ət
gimcrack 'dʒɪm.kræk **-s** -s
gimlet 'gɪm.lət, -lɪt **-s** -s
gimme 'gɪm.i
gimmick 'gɪm.ɪk **-s** -s **-ry** -ri **-y** -i
gimp gɪmp
Gimson 'gɪm*p*.sᵊn, 'dʒɪm*p*.sᵊn
gin dʒɪn **-s** -z **'gin ˌmill** ; ˌ**gin 'rummy** ; ˌ**gin 'sling**
Gina 'dʒiː.nə
Gingell 'gɪn.dʒᵊl
ginger 'dʒɪn.dʒəʳ ⓤⓈ -dʒɚ **-s** -z ˌ**ginger 'ale** ; ˌ**ginger 'beer**
gingerbread (G) 'dʒɪn.dʒə.bred ⓤⓈ -dʒɚ- **-s** -z **'gingerbread ˌman**
gingerly 'dʒɪn.dʒᵊl.i ⓤⓈ -dʒɚ.li
ginger|y 'dʒɪn.dʒᵊr|.i **-iness** -ɪ.nəs, -ɪ.nɪs
gingham 'gɪŋ.əm **-s** -z
gingival dʒɪn'dʒaɪ.vᵊl, 'dʒɪn.dʒɪ.vᵊl
gingivitis ˌdʒɪn.dʒɪ'vaɪ.tɪs, -dʒə'- ⓤⓈ -dʒə'vaɪ.t̬əs
gingko 'gɪŋ.kəʊ ⓤⓈ -koʊ **-s** -z
Gingold 'gɪŋ.gəʊld ⓤⓈ -goʊld
Ginkel(l) 'gɪŋ.kᵊl
ginkgo 'gɪŋ.kəʊ, 'gɪŋk.gəʊ ⓤⓈ 'gɪŋ.koʊ, 'gɪŋk.goʊ **-es** -z
Ginn gɪn
ginnel 'gɪn.ᵊl, 'dʒɪn- **-s** -z
Ginny 'dʒɪn.i
ginormous dʒaɪ'nɔː.məs ⓤⓈ -'nɔːr-
Ginsberg 'gɪnz.bɜːg ⓤⓈ -bɜːrg
ginseng 'dʒɪn.seŋ
Gioconda ˌdʒɪə'kɒn.də ⓤⓈ -'kɑːn-
Giotto 'dʒɒt.əʊ, dʒi'ɒt- ⓤⓈ 'dʒɑː.t̬oʊ
Giovanni ˌdʒiː.əʊ'vɑː.ni, dʒəʊ'-, -'væn.i ⓤⓈ dʒoʊ'vɑː-, dʒə-
gip gɪp **-s** -s **-ping** -ɪŋ **-ped** -t
Gipp gɪp
Gippsland 'gɪps.lænd
gippy 'dʒɪp.i
gips|y 'dʒɪp.s|i **-ies** -iz
giraffe dʒɪ'rɑːf, dʒə-, -'ræf ⓤⓈ dʒə'ræf **-s** -s
Giralda dʒɪ'ræl.də, hɪ-
girandole 'dʒɪr.ən.dəʊl ⓤⓈ -doʊl **-s** -z
gird gɜːd ⓤⓈ gɜːrd **-s** -z **-ing** -ɪŋ **-ed** -ɪd **girt** gɜːt ⓤⓈ gɜːrt

girder 'gɜː.dəʳ ⓤⓈ 'gɜːr.dɚ **-s** -z
girdl|e 'gɜː.dl̩ ⓤⓈ 'gɜːr- **-es** -z **-ing** -ɪŋ, 'gɜːd.lɪŋ ⓤⓈ 'gɜːr.dl̩.ɪŋ, 'gɜːrd.lɪŋ **-ed** -d
Girdlestone 'gɜː.dl̩.stᵊn ⓤⓈ 'gɜːr-
girl gɜːl ⓤⓈ gɜːrl **-s** -z **-hood** -hʊd
girlfriend 'gɜːl.frend ⓤⓈ 'gɜːrl- **-s** -z
girlie 'gɜː.li ⓤⓈ 'gɜːr-
girlish 'gɜː.lɪʃ ⓤⓈ 'gɜːr- **-ly** -li **-ness** -nəs, -nɪs
girly 'gɜː.li ⓤⓈ 'gɜːr-
giro (G) 'dʒaɪə.rəʊ ⓤⓈ 'dʒaɪ.roʊ **-s** -z
Girobank® 'dʒaɪə.rəʊ.bæŋk ⓤⓈ 'dʒaɪ.roʊ-
Gironde dʒɪ'rɒnd, ʒɪ-; -'rɔ̃ː*n*d ⓤⓈ dʒə'rɑːnd
Girondist dʒɪ'rɒn.dɪst, ʒɪ- ⓤⓈ dʒə'rɑːn- **-s** -s
girt (*n.*) gɜːt ⓤⓈ gɜːrt **-s** -s
girt (*from* **gird**) gɜːt ⓤⓈ gɜːrt
girth gɜːθ ⓤⓈ gɜːrθ **-s** -s
Girtin 'gɜː.tɪn ⓤⓈ 'gɜːr.tɪn, -tᵊn
Girton 'gɜː.tᵊn ⓤⓈ 'gɜːr-
Girtonian gɜː'təʊ.ni.ən ⓤⓈ gɚ'toʊ- **-s** -z
Girvan 'gɜː.vən ⓤⓈ 'gɜːr.vᵊn
Gisbourne 'gɪz.bɔːn, -bən ⓤⓈ -bɔːrn
Giscard d'Estaing *d*ʒɪs.kɑː.des.'tæŋ, -'tæ̃*ŋ* ⓤⓈ ʒisˌkɑːr.des'tæ̃*ŋ*
Giselle ʒɪ'zel, dʒɪ-
Gish gɪʃ
gismo 'gɪz.məʊ ⓤⓈ -moʊ **-s** -z
Gissing 'gɪs.ɪŋ
gist dʒɪst **-s** -s
git gɪt **-s** -s
Gita 'giː.tə ⓤⓈ -t̬ə
Gitane® ʒɪ'tɑːn ⓤⓈ -'tɑːn, -'tæn **-s** -z
gîte, gite ʒiːt **-s** -s
gittern 'gɪt.ɜːn ⓤⓈ -ɚn **-s** -z
Gitty 'gɪt.i ⓤⓈ 'gɪt̬.i
Giuseppe dʒu'sep.i
giv|e gɪv **-es** -z **-ing** -ɪŋ **gave** geɪv **giv|en** 'gɪv|.ᵊn **-er/s** -əʳ/z ⓤⓈ -ɚ/z **'given ˌname** ; ˌ**give as ˌgood as one 'gets**
give-and-take ˌgɪv.ᵊn*d*'teɪk
giveaway 'gɪv.ə.weɪ **-s** -z
giveback 'gɪv.bæk **-s** -s
Givenchy® ʒiː'vɑ̃ː*n*.ʃi, gɪ- ⓤⓈ ʒiː'.vɑ̃ːn-, -'ʃi
Giza, Gîza 'giː.zə
Gizeh 'giː.zeɪ, -zə
gizmo 'gɪz.məʊ ⓤⓈ -moʊ **-s** -z
gizzard 'gɪz.əd ⓤⓈ -ɚd **-s** -z
glabrous 'gleɪ.brəs
glacé, glace 'glæs.eɪ ⓤⓈ glæs'eɪ **-ed** -d
glacial 'gleɪ.si.əl, -ʃᵊl; 'glæs.i.əl ⓤⓈ 'gleɪ.ʃəl **-ly** -i
glaciation ˌgleɪ.si'eɪ.ʃᵊn, ˌglæs- ⓤⓈ ˌgleɪ.ʃi'-
glacier 'glæs.i.əʳ, 'gleɪ.si- ⓤⓈ 'gleɪ.ʃɚ **-s** -z

glacis 'glæs.ɪs, -i ⓤⓈ 'gleɪ.sɪs, 'glæs.ɪs, glæs'iː (*plur.*) 'glæs.ɪz ⓤⓈ 'gleɪ.siːz, 'glæs.iːz, -'-
glacises (*alternative plur. of* **glacis**) 'glæs·ɪ·sɪz ⓤⓈ 'gleɪ·sɪ·ziːz, 'glæs·ɪ-
glad glæd **-der** -əʳ ⓤⓈ -ɚ **-dest** -ɪst, -əst **-ness** -nəs, -nɪs **'glad ˌrags**
gladden 'glæd.ᵊn **-s** -z **-ing** -ɪŋ **-ed** -d
glade gleɪd **-s** -z
glad-hand 'glædˌhænd, ˌ-'- **-s** -z **-ing** -ɪŋ **-ed** -ɪd **-er/s** -ə/z
gladiator 'glæd.i.eɪ.təʳ ⓤⓈ -t̬ɚ **-s** -z
gladiatorial ˌglæd.i.ə'tɔː.ri.əl ⓤⓈ -tɔːr.i.əl
gladiole 'glæd.i.əʊl ⓤⓈ -oʊl **-s** -z
gladiol|us ˌglæd.i'əʊ.l|əs ⓤⓈ -'oʊ- **-i** -aɪ **-uses** -əs.ɪz
gladly 'glæd.li
gladsome 'glæd.səm **-ly** -li **-ness** -nəs, -nɪs
Gladstone 'glæd.stᵊn ⓤⓈ -stoʊn, -stᵊn
Gladstonian glæd'stəʊ.ni.ən ⓤⓈ -'stoʊ-
Gladwin 'glæd.wɪn
Gladys 'glæd.ɪs
glagolitic (G) ˌglæg.əʊ'lɪt.ɪk ⓤⓈ -ə'lɪt̬-
glair gleəʳ ⓤⓈ gler
Glaisdale 'gleɪz.deɪl *locally:* -dᵊl
Glaisher 'gleɪ.ʃəʳ ⓤⓈ -ʃɚ
glam glæm
Glam. (*abbrev.for* **Glamorgan**) glə'mɔː.gən ⓤⓈ -'mɔːr
Glamis glɑːmz
Note: In Shakespeare /'glæm.ɪs/.
Glamorgan glə'mɔː.gən ⓤⓈ -'mɔːr- **-shire** -ʃə, -ˌʃɪəʳ ⓤⓈ -ʃɚ, -ˌʃɪr
glamoriz|e, -is|e 'glæm.ᵊr.aɪz ⓤⓈ -ə.raɪz **-es** -ɪz **-ing** -ɪŋ **-ed** -d
glamorous 'glæm.ᵊr.əs **-ly** -li **-ness** -nəs, -nɪs
glamour 'glæm.əʳ ⓤⓈ -ɚ
glamourous 'glæm.ᵊr.əs **-ly** -li **-ness** -nəs, -nɪs
glanc|e glɑːn*t*s ⓤⓈ glæn*t*s **-es** -ɪz **-ing/ly** -ɪŋ/li **-ed** -t
gland glænd **-s** -z
glander|s 'glæn.də|z, 'glɑːn- ⓤⓈ 'glæn.dɚ|z **-ed** -d
glandes (*plur. of* **glans**) 'glæn.diːz
glandular 'glæn.djʊ.ləʳ, -dʒə.ləʳ ⓤⓈ -dʒə.lɚ ˌ**glandular 'fever**
glandule 'glæn.djuːl ⓤⓈ -dʒuːl **-s** -z
glans glænz **glandes** 'glæn.diːz
Glanvill(e) 'glæn.vɪl
Glapthorne 'glæp.θɔːn ⓤⓈ -θɔːrn
glar|e gleəʳ ⓤⓈ gler **-es** -z **-ing/ly** -ɪŋ/li **-ingness** -ɪŋ.nəs, -nɪs **-ed** -d
Glarus *place in US:* 'glær.əs ⓤⓈ 'gler-, 'glær- *other senses:* 'glɑː.rəs
Glasgow 'glɑːz.gəʊ, 'glɑːs-, 'glɑːs.kəʊ, 'glæz.gəʊ, 'glæs-, 'glæs.kəʊ ⓤⓈ 'glæs.koʊ, 'glæz.goʊ

glasier (G) ˈgleɪ.zi.əʳ, -ʒəʳ Ⓤⓢ -ʒɚ **-s** -z
glasnost ˈglæs.nɒst, ˈglæz- Ⓤⓢ ˈglæs.nɑːst, -noʊst
glass (G) glɑːs Ⓤⓢ glæs **-es** -ɪz ˌ**glass** ˈ**ceiling** ; ˈ**glass** ˌ**cutter**
glassblow|er ˈglɑːsˌbləʊ|.əʳ Ⓤⓢ ˈglæsˌbloʊ|.ɚ **-ers** -əz Ⓤⓢ -ɚz **-ing** -ɪŋ
Glasscock ˈglɑːs.kɒk, -kəʊ Ⓤⓢ ˈglæs.kɑːk, -koʊ
glassful ˈglɑːs.fʊl, -fᵊl Ⓤⓢ ˈglæs- **-s** -z
glasshou|se ˈglɑːs.haʊ|s Ⓤⓢ ˈglæs- **-ses** -zɪz
glasspaper, **glass-paper** ˈglɑːsˌpeɪ.pəʳ Ⓤⓢ ˈglæsˌpeɪ.pɚ
glassware ˈglɑːs.weəʳ Ⓤⓢ ˈglæs.wer
glasswork ˈglɑːs.wɜːk Ⓤⓢ ˈglæs.wɜːrk **-s** -s
glasswort ˈglɑːs.wɜːt Ⓤⓢ ˈglæs.wɜːrt
glass|y ˈglɑː.s|i Ⓤⓢ ˈglæs|.i **-ier** -i.əʳ Ⓤⓢ -i.ɚ **-iest** -i.ɪst, -i.əst **-ily** -ɪ.li, -ᵊl.i **-iness** -ɪ.nəs, -ɪ.nɪs
Glastonbury ˈglæs.tᵊn.bᵊr.i, ˈglɑː.stᵊn- Ⓤⓢ ˈglæs.tᵊnˌber.i, -bᵊr.i
Glaswegian glæzˈwiː.dʒᵊn, glɑːz-, glæs-, glɑːs-, -dʒi.ən Ⓤⓢ glæs-, glæz- **-s** -z
glaucoma glɔːˈkəʊ.mə, glaʊ- Ⓤⓢ glɑːˈkoʊ-, glɔː- **-tous** -təs
glaucous ˈglɔː.kəs Ⓤⓢ ˈglɑː-, ˈglɔː-
Glaxo® ˈglæk.səʊ Ⓤⓢ -soʊ
glaz|e gleɪz **-es** -ɪz **-ing** -ɪŋ **-ed** -d **-er/s** -əʳ/z Ⓤⓢ -ɚ/z
Glazebrook ˈgleɪz.brʊk
glazier ˈgleɪ.zi.əʳ, ˈ-ʒəʳ Ⓤⓢ ˈ-ʒɚ **-s** -z
Glazunov ˈglæz.u.nɒf Ⓤⓢ ˈglæz.ə.nɑːf, ˈglɑː.zə-, -noʊf
gleam gliːm **-s** -z **-ing** -ɪŋ **-ed** -d **-y** -i
glean gliːn **-s** -z **-ing/s** -ɪŋ/z **-ed** -d **-er/s** -əʳ/z Ⓤⓢ **-er/z** -ɚ/z
Gleason ˈgliː.sᵊn
glebe gliːb **-s** -z
glee gliː ˈ**glee** ˌ**club**
gleeful ˈgliː.fᵊl, -fʊl **-ly** -i **-ness** -nəs, -nɪs
glee|man ˈgliː|.mən, -mæn **-men** -mən, -men
Glegg gleg
Gleichen ˈglaɪ.kən
Glemsford ˈglems.fəd, ˈglemz- Ⓤⓢ -fɚd
glen (G) glen **-s** -z
Glenallan glenˈæl.ən
Glenalmond glenˈɑː.mənd
Glenavon glenˈæv.ᵊn
Glenavy glenˈeɪ.vi
Glencairn glenˈkeən, gleŋ- Ⓤⓢ glenˈkern
Glencoe glenˈkəʊ, gleŋ- Ⓤⓢ glenˈkoʊ
Glenda ˈglen.də
Glendale glenˈdeɪl, ˈglen.deɪl Ⓤⓢ ˈglen-
Glendenning glenˈden.ɪŋ
Glendin(n)ing glenˈdɪn.ɪŋ
Glendower glenˈdaʊ.əʳ Ⓤⓢ -ɚ
Gleneagles glenˈiː.glz
Glenelg glenˈelg
Glenfiddich glenˈfɪd.ɪk, -ɪx
Glenfinnan glenˈfɪn.ən
glengarr|y (G) glenˈgær|.i, gleŋ- Ⓤⓢ glenˈger-, -ˈgær-, ˈ--- **-ies** -iz
Glenlivet glenˈlɪv.ɪt, -ət
Glenmorangie ˌglen.məˈræn.dʒi, ˌglem- Ⓤⓢ ˌglen-
Glenmore glenˈmɔːʳ, glem- Ⓤⓢ ˈglen.mɔːr, -ˈ-
Glenn glen
Glenrothes glenˈrɒθ.ɪs Ⓤⓢ -ˈrɑː.θəs
Glen Trool ˌglenˈtruːl
Glenwood ˈglen.wʊd
Glenys ˈglen.ɪs
glib glɪb **-ber** -əʳ Ⓤⓢ -ɚ **-best** -ɪst, -əst **-ly** -li **-ness** -nəs, -nɪs
glid|e glaɪd **-es** -z **-ing/ly** -ɪŋ/li **-ed** -ɪd
glider ˈglaɪ.dəʳ Ⓤⓢ -dɚ **-s** -z
glimmer ˈglɪm.əʳ Ⓤⓢ -ɚ **-s** -z **-ing/s** -ɪŋ/z **-ingly** -ɪŋ.li **-ed** -d
glimps|e glɪmps **-es** -ɪz **-ing** -ɪŋ **-ed** -t
glinch glɪntʃ **-es** -ɪz
Glinka ˈglɪŋ.kə
glint glɪnt **-s** -s **-ing** -ɪŋ **-ed** -ɪd
gliom|a glaɪˈəʊ.m|ə Ⓤⓢ -ˈoʊ-, gli- **-as** -əz **-ata** -ə.tə Ⓤⓢ -ə.t̬ə
glissad|e (*n. v.*) glɪˈsɑːd, -ˈseɪd **-es** -z **-ing** -ɪŋ **-ed** -ɪd
glissand|o glɪˈsæn.d|əʊ Ⓤⓢ -ˈsɑːn.d|oʊ **-i** -iː **-os** -əʊz Ⓤⓢ -oʊz
Glisson ˈglɪs.ᵊn
glisten ˈglɪs.ᵊn **-s** -z **-ing** -ɪŋ **-ed** -d
glist|er ˈglɪs.t|əʳ Ⓤⓢ -t|ɚ **-ers** -əz Ⓤⓢ -ɚz **-ering** -ᵊr.ɪŋ **-ered** -əd Ⓤⓢ -ɚd
glitch glɪtʃ **-es** -ɪz
glitt|er ˈglɪt|.əʳ Ⓤⓢ ˈglɪt̬|.ɚ **-ers** -əz Ⓤⓢ -ɚz **-ering/ly** -ᵊr.ɪŋ/li **-ered** -əd Ⓤⓢ -ɚd **-ery** -ᵊr.i
glitterati ˌglɪt.əˈrɑː.tiː, -ti Ⓤⓢ ˌglɪt̬.əˈrɑː.t̬i
glitz glɪts
glitz|y ˈglɪt.s|i **-ier** -i.əʳ Ⓤⓢ -i.ɚ **-iest** -i.ɪst, -i.əst **-iness** -ɪ.nəs, -ɪ.nɪs
Gloag gləʊg Ⓤⓢ gloʊg
gloaming ˈgləʊ.mɪŋ Ⓤⓢ ˈgloʊ-
gloat gləʊt Ⓤⓢ gloʊt **-s** -s **-ing/ly** -ɪŋ Ⓤⓢ ˈgloʊ.t̬ɪŋ **-ed** -ɪd Ⓤⓢ ˈgloʊ.t̬əd
glob glɒb Ⓤⓢ glɑːb **-s** -z
global ˈgləʊ.bᵊl Ⓤⓢ ˈgloʊ- **-ly** -i **-ism** -ɪ.zᵊm ˌ**global** ˈ**village** ; ˌ**global** ˈ**warming**
globalization, **-isa-** ˌgləʊ.bᵊl.aɪˈzeɪ.ʃᵊn, -ɪˈ- Ⓤⓢ ˌgloʊ.bᵊl.ɪˈ-
globaliz|e, **-is|e** ˈgləʊ.bᵊl.aɪz Ⓤⓢ ˈgloʊ.bə.laɪz **-es** -ɪz **-ing** -ɪŋ **-ed** -d
globe gləʊb Ⓤⓢ gloʊb **-s** -z
globe-trott|er ˈgləʊbˌtrɒt|.əʳ Ⓤⓢ ˈgloʊbˌtrɑː.t̬|ɚ **-ers** -əz Ⓤⓢ -ɚz **-ing** -ɪŋ
globose ˈgləʊ.bəʊs, gləʊˈbəʊs Ⓤⓢ ˈgloʊ.boʊs, -ˈ-
globosity gləʊˈbɒs.ə.ti, -ɪ.ti Ⓤⓢ gloʊˈbɑː.sə.t̬i
globous ˈgləʊ.bəs Ⓤⓢ ˈgloʊ-
globular ˈglɒb.jʊ.ləʳ, -jə- Ⓤⓢ ˈglɑː.bjə.lɚ **-ly** -li
globule ˈglɒb.juːl Ⓤⓢ ˈglɑː.bjuːl **-s** -z
globulin ˈglɒb.jʊ.lɪn, -jə- Ⓤⓢ ˈglɑː.bjə- **-s** -z
glockenspiel ˈglɒk.ᵊn.ʃpiːl, -spiːl Ⓤⓢ ˈglɑː.kᵊn.spiːl, -ʃpiːl **-s** -z
glom glɒm Ⓤⓢ glɑːm **-s** -z **-ming** -ɪŋ **-med** -d
gloom gluːm **-s** -z **-ing** -ɪŋ **-ed** -d
gloom|y ˈgluː.m|i **-ier** -i.əʳ Ⓤⓢ -i.ɚ **-iest** -i.ɪst, -i.əst **-ily** -ɪ.li, -ᵊl.i **-iness** -ɪ.nəs, -ɪ.nɪs
glop glɒp Ⓤⓢ glɑːp **-py** -i
Gloria ˈglɔː.ri.ə Ⓤⓢ ˈglɔːr.i- **-s** -z
Gloriana ˌglɔː.riˈɑː.nə Ⓤⓢ ˌglɔːr.iˈæn.ə, -ˈeɪ.nə
glorification ˌglɔː.rɪ.fɪˈkeɪ.ʃᵊn, -rə- Ⓤⓢ ˌglɔːr.ə.fəˈ-
glori|fy ˈglɔː.rɪ|.faɪ, -rə- Ⓤⓢ ˈglɔːr.ə- **-fies** -faɪz **-fying** -faɪ.ɪŋ **-fied** -faɪd **-fier/s** -faɪ.əʳ/z Ⓤⓢ -faɪ.ɚ/z
glorious ˈglɔː.ri.əs Ⓤⓢ ˈglɔːr.i- **-ly** -li **-ness** -nəs, -nɪs
glor|y ˈglɔː.r|i Ⓤⓢ ˈglɔːr|.i **-ies** -iz **-ying** -i.ɪŋ **-ied** -id ˈ**glory** ˌ**hole**
Glos. (*abbrev. for* **Gloucestershire**) ˈglɒs.tə.ʃəʳ, -ˌʃɪəʳ Ⓤⓢ ˈglɑː.stɚ.ʃɚ, -ˌʃɪr
gloss glɒs Ⓤⓢ glɑːs **-es** -ɪz **-ing** -ɪŋ **-ed** -t **-er/s** -əʳ/z Ⓤⓢ -ɚ/z
glossal ˈglɒs.ᵊl Ⓤⓢ ˈglɑː.sᵊl
glossarial glɒsˈeə.ri.əl Ⓤⓢ glɑːˈser.i-
glossar|y ˈglɒs.ᵊr|.i Ⓤⓢ ˈglɑː.sᵊr- **-ies** -iz
glossectomy glɒsˈek.tə.mi Ⓤⓢ glɑːˈsek-
glossematics ˌglɒs.ɪˈmæt.ɪks, -əˈ- Ⓤⓢ ˌglɑː.səˈmæt̬.ɪks
glosseme ˈglɒs.iːm Ⓤⓢ ˈglɑː.siːm **-s** -z
glossitis glɒsˈaɪ.tɪs Ⓤⓢ glɑːˈsaɪ-
glossolalia ˌglɒs.əʊˈleɪ.li.ə Ⓤⓢ ˌglɑː.səˈ-
Glossop ˈglɒs.əp Ⓤⓢ ˈglɑː.səp
glossopharyngeal ˌglɒs.əʊˌfær.ɪnˈdʒiː.əl, -fəˈrɪn.dʒi.əl Ⓤⓢ ˌglɑː.soʊˌfer.ᵊnˈdʒiː.əl, -ˌfær-
gloss|y ˈglɒs|.i Ⓤⓢ ˈglɑː.s|i **-ies** -iz **-ier** -i.əʳ Ⓤⓢ -i.ɚ **-iest** -i.ɪst, -i.əst **-ily** -ɪ.li, -ᵊl.i **-iness** -ɪ.nəs, -ɪ.nɪs
Gloster ˈglɒs.təʳ Ⓤⓢ ˈglɑː.stɚ
glottal ˈglɒt.ᵊl Ⓤⓢ ˈglɑː.t̬əl ˌ**glottal** ˈ**stop**
glottalic glɒtˈæl.ɪk, gləˈtæl- Ⓤⓢ glɑːˈtæl-

glott|is ˈglɒt|.ɪs (US) ˈglɑː.t̬|əs **-ises** -ɪ.sɪz, -ə.sɪz **-ides** -ɪ.diːz
glottochronology ˌglɒt.əʊ.krəˈnɒl.ə.dʒi (US) ˌglɑː.t̬oʊ.krəˈnɑː.lə-
glottology glɒtˈɒl.ə.dʒi (US) glɑːˈtɑː.lə-
Gloucester *in the UK:* ˈglɒs.təʳ (US) ˈglɑː.stɚ **-shire** -ʃəʳ, -ˌʃɪəʳ (US) -ʃɚ, -ˌʃɪr *in the US:* ˈglaʊ.stəʳ (US) -stɚ
glove glʌv **-s** -z **-d** -d ˈ**glove comˌpartment** ; ˈ**glove ˌpuppet**
glover (G) ˈglʌv.əʳ (US) -ɚ **-s** -z
glow gləʊ (US) gloʊ **-s** -z **-ing/ly** -ɪŋ/li **-ed** -d
glower glaʊəʳ (US) glaʊɚ **-s** -z **-ing** -ɪŋ **-ed** -d
glowworm ˈgləʊ.wɜːm (US) ˈgloʊ.wɜːrm **-s** -z
gloxinia glɒkˈsɪn.i.ə (US) glɑːkˈ- **-s** -z
gloz|e gləʊz (US) gloʊz **-es** -ɪz **-ing** -ɪŋ **-ed** -d
Gluck glʊk, gluːk, glʌk
glucose ˈgluː.kəʊs, -kəʊz (US) -koʊs, -koʊz
glu|e gluː **-es** -z **-eing** -ɪŋ **-ed** -d **-er/s** -əʳ/z (US) -ɚ/z
gluesniff|ing ˈgluːˌsnɪf|.ɪŋ **-er/s** -əʳ/z (US) -ɚz
gluey ˈgluː.i **-ness** -nəs, -nɪs
glühwein ˈgluː.vaɪn
glum glʌm **-mer** -əʳ (US) -ɚ **-mest** -ɪst, -əst **-ly** -li **-ness** -nəs, -nɪs
Glusburn ˈglʌz.bɜːn (US) -bɜːrn
glut glʌt **-s** -s **-ting** -ɪŋ (US) ˈglʌt̬.ɪŋ **-ted** -ɪd (US) ˈglʌt̬.əd
glutamate ˈgluː.tə.meɪt (US) -t̬ə- **-s** -s
gluteal ˈgluː.ti.əl (US) -t̬i-
gluten ˈgluː.tᵊn, -tɪn
glute|us ˈgluː.ti|.əs (US) -t̬i- **-i** -aɪ
gluteus maximus ˌgluː.ti.əsˈmæk.sɪm.əs (US) -t̬i-
glutinous ˈgluː.tɪ.nəs, -tᵊn.əs (US) -tᵊn- **-ly** -li **-ness** -nəs, -nɪs
glutton ˈglʌt.ᵊn **-s** -z
gluttoniz|e, -is|e ˈglʌt.ᵊn.aɪz **-es** -ɪz **-ing** -ɪŋ **-ed** -d
gluttonous ˈglʌt.ᵊn.əs **-ly** -li
gluttony ˈglʌt.ᵊn.i
glyceride ˈglɪs.ᵊ.raɪd **-s** -z
glycerin ˈglɪs.ᵊr.ɪn, -iːn; ˌglɪs.əˈriːn
glycerine ˈglɪs.ᵊr.iːn, -ɪn; ˌglɪs.əˈriːn
glycerol ˈglɪs.ᵊ.rɒl (US) -rɑːl, -roʊl
glycogen ˈglaɪ.kəʊ.dʒən, ˈglɪk.əʊ-, -dʒen (US) ˈglaɪ.koʊ-, -kə-
glycol ˈglaɪ.kɒl, ˈglɪk.ɒl (US) ˈglaɪ.kɑːl, -koʊl
Glyde glaɪd
Glyn glɪn
Glynde glaɪnd
Glyndebourne ˈglaɪnd.bɔːn, ˈglaɪm- (US) ˈglaɪnd.bɔːrn
Glyndwr glɪnˈdaʊəʳ, glen- (US) -ˈdaʊɚ
Glynis ˈglɪn.ɪs
Glynne glɪn
Glyn-Neath ˌglɪnˈniːθ
glyph glɪf **-s** -s
glyptic ˈglɪp.tɪk
gm (*abbrev. for* **gram/s**) *singular:* græm *plural:* -z
G|-man ˈdʒiː|.mæn **-men** -ˌmen
GMT ˌdʒiː.emˈtiː
gnarl nɑːl (US) nɑːrl **-s** -z **-ed** -d
gnash næʃ **-es** -ɪz **-ing** -ɪŋ **-ed** -t
gnat næt **-s** -s
gnathic ˈnæθ.ɪk
gnaw nɔː (US) nɑː, nɔː **-s** -z **-ing** -ɪŋ **-ed** -d
gneiss naɪs, gəˈnaɪs
gnocchi ˈnjɒk.i (US) ˈnjɑː.ki
gnome *goblin:* nəʊm (US) noʊm **-s** -z
gnome *maxim:* ˈnəʊ.miː (US) ˈnoʊ- **-s** -z
gnomic ˈnəʊ.mɪk (US) ˈnoʊ-
gnomish ˈnəʊ.mɪʃ (US) ˈnoʊ-
gnomon ˈnəʊ.mɒn, -mən (US) ˈnoʊ.mɑːn, -mən **-s** -z
gnomonic nəʊˈmɒn.ɪk (US) noʊˈmɑː.nɪk **-al** -ᵊl **-ally** -ᵊl.i, -li
Gnosall ˈnəʊ.səl (US) ˈnoʊ-
gnostic (G) ˈnɒs.tɪk (US) ˈnɑː.stɪk **-s** -s
gnosticism (G) ˈnɒs.tɪ.sɪ.zᵊm (US) ˈnɑː.stə-
gnu nuː, njuː; gəˈnuː, -njuː **-s** -z
go gəʊ (US) goʊ **-es** -z **-ing** -ɪŋ **went** went **gone** gɒn (US) gɑːn, gɔːn **goer/s** ˈgəʊ.əʳ/z (US) ˈgoʊ.ɚ/z
Goa gəʊə (US) goʊə
goad gəʊd (US) goʊd **-s** -z **-ing** -ɪŋ **-ed** -ɪd
go-ahead (*adj.*) ˈgəʊ.ə.hed, ˌ--ˈ- (US) ˈgoʊ-
go-ahead (*n.*) ˈgəʊ.ə.hed (US) ˈgoʊ-
goal gəʊl (US) goʊl **-s** -z
goalie ˈgəʊ.li (US) ˈgoʊ.li **-s** -z
goalkeeper ˈgəʊlˌkiː.pəʳ (US) ˈgoʊlˌkiː.pɚ **-s** -z
goalmouth ˈgəʊl.maʊθ (US) ˈgoʊl- **-s**
goalpost ˈgəʊl.pəʊst (US) ˈgoʊl.poʊst **-s** -s
Goan gəʊ.ən (US) goʊ.ən
Goanese ˌgəʊ.əˈniːz (US) ˌgoʊ.ə-
goanna gəʊˈæn.ə (US) goʊ- **-s** -z
goat gəʊt (US) goʊt **-s** -s ˌ**get someone's** ˈ**goat**
goatee gəʊˈtiː (US) goʊ- **-s** -z *stress shift, British only, see compounds:* ˌ**goatee** ˈ**beard** (US) **goaˈtee** ˌ**beard**
goatherd ˈgəʊt.hɜːd (US) ˈgoʊt.hɜːrd **-s** -z
Goathland ˈgəʊθ.lənd (US) ˈgoʊθ-
goatish ˈgəʊ.tɪʃ (US) ˈgoʊ-
goatskin ˈgəʊt.skɪn (US) ˈgoʊt- **-s** -z
goatsucker ˈgəʊtˌsʌk.əʳ (US) ˈgoʊtˌsʌk.ɚ **-s** -z
gob gɒb (US) gɑːb **-s** -z **-bing** -ɪŋ **-bed** -d
gobbet ˈgɒb.ɪt (US) ˈgɑː.bɪt **-s** -s
Gobbi ˈgɒb.i (US) ˈgɑː.bi
gobbl|e ˈgɒb.l̩ (US) ˈgɑː.bl̩ **-es** -z **-ing** -ɪŋ, ˈgɒb.lɪŋ (US) ˈgɑː.bl̩.ɪŋ, ˈ-blɪŋ **-ed** -d **-er/s** -əʳ/z, ˈgɒb.ləʳ/z (US) ˈgɑː.bl̩.ɚ/z, ˈ-blɚ/z
gobbledygook, gobbledegook ˈgɒb.l̩.di.guːk, -gʊk (US) ˈgɑː.bl̩-
Gobbo ˈgɒb.əʊ (US) ˈgɑː.boʊ
Gobelin ˈgəʊ.bᵊl.ɪn, ˈgɒb.ᵊl- (US) ˈgoʊ.bᵊl-
go-between ˈgəʊ.bɪˌtwiːn, -bə- (US) ˈgoʊ.bə- **-s** -z
Gobi ˈgəʊ.bi (US) ˈgoʊ-
goblet ˈgɒb.lət, -lɪt (US) ˈgɑː.blət **-s** -s
goblin ˈgɒb.lɪn (US) ˈgɑː.blɪn **-s** -z
gobsmack ˈgɒb.smæk (US) ˈgɑːb- **-s** -s **-ing** -ɪŋ **-ed** -t
gobstopper ˈgɒbˌstɒp.əʳ (US) ˈgɑːbˌstɑː.pɚ **-s** -z
gob|y ˈgəʊ.b|i (US) ˈgoʊ- **-ies** -iz
go-by ˈgəʊˌbaɪ (US) ˈgoʊ-
go-cart ˈgəʊ.kɑːt (US) ˈgoʊ.kɑːrt **-s** -s
god (G) gɒd (US) gɑːd **-s** -z
Godalming ˈgɒd.ᵊl.mɪŋ (US) ˈgɑː.dᵊl-
Godard ˈgɒd.ɑː (US) goʊˈdɑːr
god-awful ˌgɒdˈɔː.fᵊl (US) ˌgɑːdˈɑː-, -ˈɔː- *stress shift:* ˌgod-awful ˈnoise
god|child ˈgɒd|.tʃaɪld (US) ˈgɑːd- **-children** -ˌtʃɪl.drᵊn
goddam(n) ˈgɒd.æm, ˈgɒd.dæm (US) ˌgɑːdˈdæm, ˈgɑːd-
goddamned ˈgɒd.æmd, ˈgɒd.dæmd (US) ˈgɑːd.æmd
Goddard ˈgɒd.ɑːd, -əd (US) ˈgɑː.dɚd, -dɑːrd
goddaughter ˈgɒdˌdɔː.təʳ (US) ˈgɑːdˌdɑː.t̬ɚ, -ˌdɔː- **-s** -z
Godden ˈgɒd.ᵊn (US) ˈgɑː.dᵊn
goddess ˈgɒd.es, -ɪs, -əs (US) ˈgɑː.dɪs, -dəs **-es** -ɪz
Goderich ˈgəʊ.drɪtʃ (US) ˈgoʊ-
godetia gəʊˈdiː.ʃə, -ʃi.ə (US) gə- **-s** -z
godfather (G) ˈgɒd.fɑː.ðəʳ (US) ˈgɑːdˌfɑː.ðɚ **-s** -z
god-fearing (G) ˈgɒdˌfɪə.rɪŋ (US) ˈgɑːd.fɪr.ɪŋ
godforsaken ˈgɒd.fəˌseɪ.kᵊn (US) ˈgɑːd.fɚ-
Godfrey ˈgɒd.fri (US) ˈgɑːd-
god-given ˈgɒdˌgɪv.ᵊn (US) ˈgɑːd-
godhead (G) ˈgɒd.hed (US) ˈgɑːd- **-s** -z
Godiva gəˈdaɪ.və
Godkin ˈgɒd.kɪn (US) ˈgɑːd-
godless ˈgɒd.ləs, -lɪs (US) ˈgɑːd- **-ly** -li **-ness** -nəs, -nɪs
godlike ˈgɒd.laɪk (US) ˈgɑːd-
godl|y ˈgɒd.l|i (US) ˈgɑːd- **-ier** -i.əʳ (US) -i.ɚ **-iest** -i.ɪst, -i.əst **-iness** -ɪ.nəs, -ɪ.nɪs
Godman ˈgɒd.mən (US) ˈgɑːd-

Godmanchester 'gɒd.mən,tʃes.təʳ (US) 'gɑːd.mən,tʃes.tɚ
godmother 'gɒd,mʌð.əʳ (US) 'gɑːd,mʌð.ɚ **-s** -z
Godolphin gə'dɒl.fɪn (US) -'dɑːl-
Godot 'gɒd.əʊ (US) gə'doʊ, gɑː-
godown 'gəʊ.daʊn (US) 'goʊ- **-s** -z
godparent 'gɒd,peə.rᵊnt (US) 'gɑːd,per.ᵊnt, -,pær- **-s** -s
godsend 'gɒd.send (US) 'gɑːd- **-s** -z
God-slot 'gɒd,slɒt (US) 'gɑːd,slɑːt **-s** -s
godson 'gɒd.sʌn (US) 'gɑːd- **-s** -z
Godspeed ,gɒd'spiːd (US) ,gɑːd-
Godunov 'gɒd.ə.nɒf, 'gʊd-, -u- (US) 'gʊd.ə.nɑːf
Godward 'gɒd.wəd (US) 'gɑːd.wɚd
Godwin 'gɒd.wɪn (US) 'gɑːd-
godwit 'gɒd.wɪt (US) 'gɑːd- **-s** -s
Godzilla gɒd'zɪl.ə (US) gɑːd-
Goebbels 'gɜː.bᵊlz, -bᵊls
Goering 'gɜː.rɪŋ (US) 'gɜːr-
Goethe 'gɜː.tə
gofer 'gəʊ.fəʳ (US) 'goʊ.fɚ **-s** -z
Goff(e) gɒf (US) gɑːf
goff|er 'gəʊ.f|əʳ, 'gɒf|.əʳ (US) 'gɑː.f|ɚ **-ers** -əz (US) -ɚz **-ering** -ᵊr.ɪŋ **-ered** -əd (US) -ɚd
Gog gɒg (US) gɑːg, gɔːg
Gogarty 'gəʊ.gə.ti (US) 'goʊ.gɚ.t̬i
go-getter 'gəʊ,get.əʳ, ,-'-- (US) 'goʊ,get̬.ɚ **-s** -z
goggl|e 'gɒg.l̩ (US) 'gɑː.gl̩ **-es** -z **-ing** -ɪŋ, '-lɪŋ (US) '-gl̩.ɪŋ, '-glɪŋ **-ed** -d
goggle-box 'gɒg.l̩.bɒks (US) 'gɑː.gl̩.bɑːks **-es** -ɪz
goggle-eyed ,gɒg.l̩'aɪd (US) 'gɑː.gl̩,aɪd *stress shift, British only:* ,goggle-eyed 'crowd
Gogmagog 'gɒg.mə.gɒg (US) 'gɑːg.mə.gɑːg, 'gɔːg-, -gɔːg
go-go 'gəʊ.gəʊ (US) 'goʊ.goʊ **'go-go ,dancer**
Gogo 'gəʊ.gəʊ (US) 'goʊ.goʊ
Gogol 'gəʊ.gɒl (US) 'goʊ.gɑːl, -gᵊl
Goiânia gɔɪ'ɑː.ni.ə
Goidelic gɔɪ'del.ɪk
goings 'gəʊ.ɪŋz (US) 'goʊ- **,comings and 'goings ; ,goings-'on**
goiter 'gɔɪ.təʳ (US) -t̬ɚ **-s** -z **-ed** -d
goitre 'gɔɪ.təʳ (US) -t̬ɚ **-s** -z **-d** -d
goitrous 'gɔɪ.trəs
go-kart 'gəʊ.kɑːt (US) 'goʊ.kɑːrt **-s** -s
Golan 'gəʊ.læn, -lɑːn; gəʊ'lɑːn (US) 'goʊ.lɑːn **,Golan 'Heights**
Golborne 'gəʊl.bɔːn (US) 'goʊl.bɔːrn
Golby 'gəʊl.bi (US) 'goʊl-
Golconda gɒl'kɒn.də (US) gɑːl'kɑːn.də
gold (G) gəʊld (US) goʊld **'Gold ,Coast ; 'gold ,dust ; ,gold 'leaf ; ,gold 'medal ; 'gold ,mine ; 'gold ,rush ; as ,good as 'gold**
Golda 'gəʊl.də (US) 'goʊl-
Goldberg 'gəʊl*d*.bɜːg (US) 'goʊl*d*.bɜːrg
goldbrick 'gəʊl*d*.brɪk (US) 'goʊl*d*- **-s** -s **-ing** -ɪŋ **-ed** -d **-er/s** -əʳ/z (US) -ɚ/z
goldcrest 'gəʊl*d*.krest (US) 'goʊl*d*- **-s** -s
gold-digger 'gəʊl*d*,dɪg.əʳ (US) 'goʊl*d*,dɪg.ɚ **-s** -z
golden (G) 'gəʊl.dᵊn (US) 'goʊl- **,golden 'age** (US) **'golden ,age ; ,golden 'handshake ; ,golden 'rule ; ,golden 'syrup**
goldeneye 'gəʊl.dᵊn.aɪ (US) 'goʊl- **-s** -z
goldfield 'gəʊl*d*.fiːld (US) 'goʊl*d*- **-s** -z
goldfinch 'gəʊl*d*.fɪn*t*ʃ (US) 'goʊl*d*- **-es** -ɪz
goldfish 'gəʊl*d*.fɪʃ (US) 'goʊl*d*- **-es** -ɪz **'goldfish ,bowl**
Goldilocks 'gəʊl.dɪ.lɒks (US) 'goʊl.di.lɑːks
Golding 'gəʊl.dɪŋ (US) 'goʊl-
Goldsborough 'gəʊldz.bᵊr.ə (US) 'goʊldz.bɚ.oʊ
Goldschmidt 'gəʊld.ʃmɪt (US) 'goʊld-
goldsmith (G) 'gəʊld.smɪθ (US) 'goʊld- **-s** -s
Goldstein 'gəʊld.staɪn, -stiːn (US) 'goʊld-
Goldwyn 'gəʊl.dwɪn (US) 'goʊl-
golem 'gəʊ.lem (US) 'goʊ- **-s** -z
golf *(n. v.)* gɒlf *old-fashioned, sometimes used by players:* gɒf (US) gɑːlf **-s** -s **-ing** -ɪŋ **-ed** -t **'golf ,club ; 'golf ,course ; 'golf ,links**
golfer 'gɒl.fəʳ, 'gɒf.əʳ (US) 'gɑːl.fɚ **-s** -z
Golgotha 'gɒl.gə.θə (US) 'gɑːl-
Goliath gəʊ'laɪ.əθ (US) gə-
Golightly gəʊ'laɪt.li (US) goʊ-
Gollancz gə'lænts, -'læŋ*k*s, gɒl'ænts, -'æŋ*k*s, 'gɒl.ənts, -æŋ*k*s (US) gə'lænts, 'gɑː.lənts, -lænts
golliwog 'gɒl.ɪ.wɒg (US) 'gɑː.li.wɔːg, -wɑːg **-s** -z
golly 'gɒl.i (US) 'gɑː.li
gollywog 'gɒl.ɪ.wɒg (US) 'gɑː.lɪ.wɔːg, -wɑːg **-s** -z
golosh gə'lɒʃ (US) gə'lɑːʃ **-es** -ɪz
Gomar 'gəʊ.məʳ (US) 'goʊ.mɚ
Gomer 'gəʊ.məʳ (US) 'goʊ.mɚ
Gomersal 'gɒm.ə.sᵊl (US) 'gɑː.mɚ.sᵊl
Gomes 'gəʊ.mez (US) 'goʊ-
Gomez, **Gómez** 'gəʊ.mez (US) 'goʊ-
Gomme gɒm (US) gɑːm
Gomorrah gə'mɒr.ə (US) -'mɔːr.ə, -'mɑːr-
Gompers 'gɒm.pəz (US) 'gɑːm.pɚz
Gomshall 'gʌm.ʃᵊl, 'gɒm- (US) 'gɑːm-
gonad 'gəʊ.næd (US) 'goʊ- **-s** -z
Goncourt ,gɒn'kʊəʳ, ,gɒŋ-, ,gɔ̃ːŋ- (US) ,goʊn'kur
gondola 'gɒn.dᵊl.ə (US) 'gɑːn- **-s** -z
gondolier ,gɒn.də'lɪəʳ, -dᵊl'ɪəʳ (US) ,gɑːn.də'lɪr **-s** -z
Gondwana gɒnd'wɑː.nə (US) gɑːnd- **-land** -lænd
gone *(from* **go**) gɒn (US) gɑːn
goner 'gɒn.əʳ (US) 'gɑː.nɚ **-s** -z
Goneril 'gɒn.ᵊr.ɪl, -ᵊl (US) 'gɑː.nᵊr.əl
gonfalon 'gɒn.fᵊl.ən (US) 'gɑːn- **-s** -z
gong gɒŋ (US) gɑːŋ, gɔːŋ **-s** -z
goniometer ,gəʊ.ni'ɒm.ɪ.təʳ, '-ə- (US) ,goʊ.ni'ɑː.mə.t̬ɚ **-s** -z
goniometric ,gəʊ.ni.ə'met.rɪk (US) ,goʊ-
gonk gɒŋk (US) gɑːŋk, gɔːŋk **-s** -s
gonna gᵊn.ə, 'gɒn.ə (US) 'gɑː.nə, 'gɔː-
gonorrh(o)e|a ,gɒn.ə'riː|.ə (US) ,gɑː.nə'- **-al** -əl
Gonville 'gɒn.vɪl (US) 'gɑːn-
Gonzales gɒn'zɑː.lɪs, gən-, -lez (US) gən'zɑː.ləs, gɑːn-, -'sɑː-, -leɪs
Gonzalez gɒn'zɑː.lɪs, gən-, -lez (US) gən'zɑːl.əs, gɑːn-, -'sɑː-, -leɪs
gonzo 'gɒn.zəʊ (US) 'gɑːn.zoʊ
goo guː
goober 'guː.bəʳ (US) -bɚ **-s** -z
Gooch guːtʃ
good (G) *(n. adj. interj.)* gʊd **-s** -z **-ness** -nəs, -nɪs **,good 'day ; ,Good 'Friday ; ,good 'grief! ; ,Good 'Heavens! ; 'goods ,train ; as ,good as 'gold**
Goodale 'gʊd.eɪl
Goodall 'gʊd.ɔːl (US) -ɔːl, -ɑːl
Goodbody 'gʊd.bɒd.i (US) -bɑː.di
goodbye *(n.)* gʊd'baɪ **-s** -z
goodbye *(interj.)* gʊd'baɪ
Goodchild 'gʊd.tʃaɪld
Goode gʊd
Goodell gʊ'del
Goodenough 'gʊd.ɪ.nʌf, '-ə-, -ᵊn.ʌf
Goodfellow 'gʊd,fel.əʊ (US) -oʊ
good-for-nothing 'gʊd.fə,nʌθ.ɪŋ, ,gʊd.fə'nʌθ- (US) 'gʊd.fɚ,nʌθ-, ,gʊd.fɚ'nʌθ- **-s** -z
Goodge guːdʒ, gʊdʒ
Goodhart 'gʊd.hɑːt (US) -hɑːrt
good-hearted ,gʊd'hɑː.tɪd (US) -'hɑːr.t̬əd **-ness** -nəs, -nɪs *stress shift:* ,good-hearted 'person
good-humo(u)red ,gʊd'hjuː.məd (US) -'hjuː.mɚd, -'juː- **-ly** -li **-ness** -nəs, -nɪs *stress shift:* ,good-humo(u)red 'friend
goodie 'gʊd.i **-s** -z
goodish 'gʊd.ɪʃ
Goodliffe 'gʊd.lɪf
good-looking ,gʊd'lʊk.ɪŋ *stress shift:* ,good-looking 'guy
goodl|y 'gʊd.l|i **-ier** -i.əʳ (US) -i.ɚ **-iest** -i.ɪst, -i.əst **-iness** -ɪ.nəs, -ɪ.nɪs
good|man 'gʊd|.mæn **-men** -men
Goodman 'gʊd.mən
good morning gʊd'mɔː.nɪŋ (US) -'mɔːr-

good-natured ˌgʊdˈneɪ.tʃəd Ⓤⓢ -tʃɚd **-ly** -li **-ness** -nəs, -nɪs *stress shift:* ˌgood-natured ˈsmile
goodness ˈgʊd.nəs, -nɪs
good night ˌgʊdˈnaɪt
Goodrich ˈgʊd.rɪtʃ
Goodson ˈgʊd.sᵊn
goods-train ˈgʊdz.treɪn **-s** -z
good-tempered ˌgʊdˈtem.pəd Ⓤⓢ -pɚd **-ly** -li **-ness** -nəs, -nɪs *stress shift:* ˌgood-tempered ˈhorse
goodwill gʊdˈwɪl **-s** -z
Goodwin ˈgʊd.wɪn
Goodwood ˈgʊd.wʊd
good|y (G) ˈgʊd|.i **-ies** -iz **ˌgoody-ˈtwo-shoes**
Goodyear® ˈgʊd.jɪəʳ, -jəʳ, -jɜːʳ Ⓤⓢ -jɪr, -jɚ, ˈgʊdʒ.ɪr
Goodyer ˈgʊd.jəʳ
goody-good|y ˈgʊd.iˌgʊd|.i **-ies** -iz
goo|ey ˈguː|.i **-ier** -i.əʳ Ⓤⓢ -i.ɚ **-iest** -i.ɪst, -i.əst **-iness** -ɪ.nəs, -ɪ.nɪs
goof guːf **-s** -s **-ing** -ɪŋ **-ed** -t
goofball ˈguːf.bɔːl Ⓤⓢ -bɔːl, -bɑːl **-s** -z
goof|y (G) ˈguː.f|i **-ier** -i.əʳ Ⓤⓢ -i.ɚ **-iest** -i.ɪst, -i.əst **-ily** -ɪ.li, -ᵊl.i **-iness** -ɪ.nəs, -ɪ.nɪs
Googe guːdʒ, gʊdʒ
Googie ˈguː.gi
googl|y ˈguː.gl|i **-ies** -iz
googol ˈguː.gɒl, -gᵊl Ⓤⓢ -gɑːl, -gəl **-s** -z
googolplex ˈguː.gɒl.pleks, -gᵊl- Ⓤⓢ -gɑːl-, -gᵊl-
Goole guːl
gool|ie, gool|y ˈguː.l|i **-ies** -iz
goon guːn **-s** -z
Goonhilly ˌguːnˈhɪl.i, ˌgʊn- *stress shift:* ˌGoonhilly ˈDown
goop guːp
goop|y ˈguː.p|i **-ier** -i.əʳ Ⓤⓢ -i.ɚ **-iest** -i.ɪst, -i.əst **-ily** -ɪ.li, -ᵊl.i **-iness** -ɪ.nəs, -ɪ.nɪs
goosander guːˈsæn.dəʳ Ⓤⓢ -dɚ **-s** -z
goose *bird:* guːs **geese** giːs **ˈgoose ˌbumps ; ˈgoose ˌgrass ; ˈgoose ˌpimples ; ˌcook someone's ˈgoose ; (kill) the ˌgoose that ˌlays the ˌgolden ˈeggs ; ˌcouldn't say ˌboo to a ˈgoose**
goos|e (*v.*) guːs **-es** -ɪz **-ing** -ɪŋ **-ed** -t
goos|e *tailor's iron:* guːs **-es** -ɪz
gooseberr|y ˈgʊz.bᵊr|.i, ˈguːz-, ˈ-br|i Ⓤⓢ ˈguːsˌber|.i, ˈguːz-, -bɚ- **-ies** -iz **ˌgooseberry ˈfool**
gooseflesh ˈguːs.fleʃ
goose-step ˈguːsˌstep **-s** -s **-ping** -ɪŋ **-ped** -t
goosey ˈguː.si **-s** -z
GOP ˌdʒiː.əʊˈpiː Ⓤⓢ -oʊˈ-
gopher ˈgəʊ.fəʳ Ⓤⓢ ˈgoʊ.fɚ **-s** -z
Gorazde gɔːˈræʒ.deɪ, gəˈ-
Gorbachev ˈgɔː.bə.tʃɒf, ˌ--ˈ- Ⓤⓢ ˈgɔːr.bə.tʃɑːf, ˌ--ˈ-
Gorbals ˈgɔː.bᵊlz Ⓤⓢ ˈgɔːr-
gorblimey ˌgɔːˈblaɪ.mi Ⓤⓢ ˌgɔːr-
Gorboduc ˈgɔː.bə.dʌk Ⓤⓢ ˈgɔːr-
Gordale ˈgɔː.deɪl Ⓤⓢ ˈgɔːr-
Gordian knot ˌgɔː.di.ənˈnɒt Ⓤⓢ ˌgɔːr.di.ənˈnɑːt
Gordimer ˈgɔː.dɪ.məʳ Ⓤⓢ ˈgɔːr-
Gordon ˈgɔː.dᵊn Ⓤⓢ ˈgɔːr-
Gordonstoun ˈgɔː.dᵊn.stən Ⓤⓢ ˈgɔːr-
gor|e (G) gɔːʳ Ⓤⓢ gɔːr **-es** -z **-ing** -ɪŋ **-ed** -d
Gorebridge ˈgɔː.brɪdʒ Ⓤⓢ ˈgɔːr-
Gorell ˈgɒr.ᵊl Ⓤⓢ ˌgɔːˈrel, ˈgɑː.rᵊl
Gore-Tex® ˈgɔː.teks Ⓤⓢ ˈgɔːr-
gorg|e gɔːdʒ Ⓤⓢ gɔːrdʒ **-es** -ɪz **-ing** -ɪŋ **-ed** -d
gorgeous ˈgɔː.dʒəs Ⓤⓢ ˈgɔːr- **-ly** -li **-ness** -nəs, -nɪs
Gorges ˈgɔː.dʒɪz Ⓤⓢ ˈgɔːr-
gorget ˈgɔː.dʒɪt, -dʒət Ⓤⓢ ˈgɔːr.dʒət **-s** -s
Gorgie ˈgɔː.gi Ⓤⓢ ˈgɔːr-
gorgon (G) ˈgɔː.gən Ⓤⓢ ˈgɔːr- **-s** -z
Gorgonzola ˌgɔː.gᵊnˈzəʊ.lə Ⓤⓢ ˌgɔːr.gᵊnˈzoʊ-
Gorham ˈgɔː.rəm Ⓤⓢ ˈgɔːr.əm
gorilla gəˈrɪl.ə **-s** -z
Goring ˈgɔː.rɪŋ Ⓤⓢ ˈgɔːr.ɪŋ **Göring** ˈgɜː.rɪŋ Ⓤⓢ ˈgɜːr.ɪŋ, ˈgɔːr-
Gorki, Gorky ˈgɔː.ki Ⓤⓢ ˈgɔːr-
Gorleston ˈgɔːl.stᵊn Ⓤⓢ ˈgɔːrl-
gormandiz|e, -is|e ˈgɔː.mən.daɪz Ⓤⓢ ˈgɔːr- **-es** -ɪz **-ing** -ɪŋ **-ed** -d **-er/s** -əʳ/z Ⓤⓢ -ɚ/z
gormless ˈgɔːm.ləs, -lɪs Ⓤⓢ ˈgɔːrm- **-ly** -li **-ness** -nəs, -nɪs
Gormley ˈgɔːm.li Ⓤⓢ ˈgɔːrm-
Goronwy gəˈrɒn.wi Ⓤⓢ -ˈrɑːn-
gorp gɔːp Ⓤⓢ gɔːrp
Gorringe ˈgɒr.ɪndʒ, -əndʒ Ⓤⓢ ˈgɑː.rɪndʒ, ˈgɔː-
gorse gɔːs Ⓤⓢ gɔːrs
Gorseinon gɔːˈsaɪ.nən Ⓤⓢ gɔːr-
Gorst gɔːst Ⓤⓢ gɔːrst
Gorton ˈgɔː.tᵊn Ⓤⓢ ˈgɔːr-
gor|y ˈgɔː.r|i Ⓤⓢ ˈgɔːr|.i **-ier** -i.əʳ Ⓤⓢ -i.ɚ **-iest** -i.ɪst, -i.əst **-ily** -ᵊl.i, -ɪ.li **-iness** -ɪ.nəs, -ɪ.nɪs
Goschen ˈgəʊ.ʃᵊn, ˈgɒʃ.ᵊn Ⓤⓢ ˈgoʊ-
gosh gɒʃ Ⓤⓢ gɑːʃ
goshawk ˈgɒs.hɔːk Ⓤⓢ ˈgɑːs.hɑːk, -hɔːk **-s** -s
Goshen ˈgəʊ.ʃᵊn, ˈgɒʃ.ᵊn Ⓤⓢ ˈgoʊ-
gosling (G) ˈgɒz.lɪŋ Ⓤⓢ ˈgɑːz- **-s** -z
go-slow ˌgəʊˈsləʊ, ˈ-- Ⓤⓢ ˈgoʊ.sloʊ **-s** -z
gospel (G) ˈgɒs.pᵊl, -pel Ⓤⓢ ˈgɑːs- **-s** -z **ˈgospel ˌmusic**
gospel(l)er ˈgɒs.pᵊl.əʳ Ⓤⓢ ˈgɑː.spᵊl.ɚ **-s** -z
Gosport ˈgɒs.pɔːt Ⓤⓢ ˈgɑːs.pɔːrt
gossamer ˈgɒs.ə.məʳ Ⓤⓢ ˈgɑː.sə.mɚ
Goss(e) gɒs Ⓤⓢ gɑːs
gossip (*n. v.*) ˈgɒs.ɪp Ⓤⓢ ˈgɑː.səp **-s** -s **-ing** -ɪŋ **-ed** -t **-y** -i
got (*from* **get**) gɒt Ⓤⓢ gɑːt
Göteborg ˈjɜː.tə.bɔː Ⓤⓢ -bɔːr
Goth gɒθ Ⓤⓢ gɑːθ **-s** -s
Gotha *in Germany:* ˈgəʊ.θə, ˈgəʊ.tə Ⓤⓢ ˈgoʊ.t̬ə *old-fashioned English spelling of* **Göta** *in Sweden:* ˈgəʊ.tə Ⓤⓢ ˈgoʊ.t̬ə
Gotham *in Nottinghamshire:* ˈgəʊ.təm Ⓤⓢ ˈgoʊ.t̬əm *New York:* ˈgɒθ.əm Ⓤⓢ ˈgɑː.θəm
Gothenburg ˈgɒθ.ᵊn.bɜːg, ˈgɒt-, -ᵊm- Ⓤⓢ ˈgɑː.θᵊn.bɜːrg, -tᵊn-
Gothic ˈgɒθ.ɪk Ⓤⓢ ˈgɑː.θɪk
Gothicism ˈgɒθ.ɪ.sɪ.zᵊm, ˈ-ə- Ⓤⓢ ˈgɑː.θə-
gothiciz|e, -is|e ˈgɒθ.ɪ.saɪz, ˈ-ə- Ⓤⓢ ˈgɑː.θə- **-es** -ɪz **-ing** -ɪŋ **-ed** -d
Gothland ˈgɒθ.lənd Ⓤⓢ ˈgɑːt-
Gotland ˈgɒt.lənd Ⓤⓢ ˈgɑːt-
gotta ˈgɒt.ə Ⓤⓢ ˈgɑː.t̬ə
gotten (*from* **get**) ˈgɒt.ᵊn Ⓤⓢ ˈgɑː.tᵊn
götterdämmerung (G) ˌgɜː.təˈdem.ə.rʊŋ, -ˈdeɪ.mə- Ⓤⓢ ˌgɜː.t̬ɚˈdem-
Gotthard ˈgɒt.ɑːd Ⓤⓢ ˈgɑː.tɑːrd
Gotti ˈgɒt.i Ⓤⓢ ˈgɑː.t̬i
Göttingen ˈgɜː.tɪŋ.ən Ⓤⓢ ˈgɜːr-
gouache guˈɑːʃ, -ˈæʃ, gwɑːʃ, gwæʃ
Gouda ˈgaʊ.də Ⓤⓢ ˈguː-
Goudie ˈgaʊ.di
goug|e gaʊdʒ, guːdʒ Ⓤⓢ gaʊdʒ **-es** -ɪz **-ing** -ɪŋ **-ed** -d
Gough gɒf Ⓤⓢ gɑːf
goujon ˈguː.dʒɒn, -ʒɒn, -ʒɔ̃ːŋ Ⓤⓢ guːˈʒoʊn **-s** -z
goulash ˈguː.læʃ Ⓤⓢ -lɑːʃ, -læʃ **-es** -ɪz
Goulburn *place-name:* ˈgəʊl.bɜːn Ⓤⓢ ˈgoʊl.bɜːrn *surname:* ˈguːl.bɜːn, ˈgəʊl.bən Ⓤⓢ ˈguːl.bɜːrn, ˈgoʊl.bɚn
Gould guːld
Goulden ˈguːl.dən
Goulding ˈguːl.dɪŋ
Gouler ˈguː.ləʳ Ⓤⓢ -lɚ
Gounod ˈguː.nəʊ Ⓤⓢ -noʊ
gourd gʊəd, gɔːd Ⓤⓢ gɔːrd, gʊrd **-s** -z
gourde gʊəd, gɔːd Ⓤⓢ gɔːrd, gʊrd **-s** -z
Gourl|ay ˈgʊə.l|eɪ, -l|i Ⓤⓢ ˈgʊr.l|i **-ey** -i
gourmand ˈgʊə.mənd, ˈgɔː-, -mãŋ Ⓤⓢ ˈgʊr.mɑːnd, -mənd; gʊrˈmɑːnd **-s** -z
gourmet ˈgʊə.meɪ, ˈgɔː- Ⓤⓢ ˈgʊr.meɪ, -ˈ- **-s** -z
Gourock ˈgʊə.rək Ⓤⓢ ˈgʊr.ək
gout gaʊt **-y** -i Ⓤⓢ ˈgaʊ.t̬i **-ily** -ɪ.li, -ᵊl.i Ⓤⓢ ˈgaʊ.t̬ɪ.li, -t̬ᵊl.i **-iness** -ɪ.nəs, -ɪ.nɪs Ⓤⓢ ˈgaʊ.t̬ɪ.nəs, -t̬ɪ-
Govan ˈgʌv.ᵊn
Gover ˈgəʊ.vəʳ Ⓤⓢ ˈgoʊ.vɚ

govern 'gʌv.ən (US) -ɚn **-s** -z **-ing** -ɪŋ **-ed** -d **-able** -ə.bl̩
governance 'gʌv.ən.ənts (US) -ɚ.nənts
governess 'gʌv.ən.əs, -ɪs, -es (US) -ɚ.nəs **-es** -ɪz
government 'gʌv.ən.mənt, -əm.mənt, -və.mənt (US) -ɚn- **-s** -s
governmental ˌgʌv.ən'men.təl, -əm'men-, -ə'men- (US) -ɚn'men.t̬əl
governor 'gʌv.ən.əʳ (US) -ɚ.nɚ **-s** -z
governor-general ˌgʌv.ən.ə'dʒen.ər.əl (US) -ɚ.nɚ'- **-s** -z
governorship 'gʌv.ən.ə.ʃɪp (US) -ɚ.nɚ- **-s** -s
Govey 'gəʊ.vi (US) 'goʊ-
Govier 'gəʊ.vi.əʳ (US) 'goʊ.vi.ɚ
Gow gaʊ
Gowan gaʊən
Gowdy 'gaʊ.di
Gowen gaʊən, gaʊɪn
Gower gaʊəʳ, gɔːʳ (US) gaʊɚ
Note: /gaʊəʳ/ is used in **Gower Street** and for the place in Wales. /gɔːʳ/ is the family name of the Duke of Sutherland; this pronunciation is also used in **Leveson-Gower**.
Gowing 'gaʊ.ɪŋ
gowk gaʊk **-s** -s
Gowlett 'gaʊ.lət, -lɪt
gown gaʊn **-s** -z **-ed** -d
gowns|man 'gaʊnz|.mən **-men** -mən, -men
Gowrie 'gaʊ.ri
Gowther 'gaʊ.ðəʳ (US) -ðɚ
Gowy 'gaʊ.i
goy gɔɪ **-s** -z **-im** -ɪm **-ish** -ɪʃ
Goya 'gɔɪ.ə
Gozo 'gəʊ.zəʊ (US) 'goʊ.zoʊ
GP ˌdʒiː'piː **-s** -z
GPA ˌdʒiː.piː'eɪ
GPO ˌdʒiː.piː'əʊ (US) -'oʊ
GPS ˌdʒiː.piː'es
grab græb **-s** -z **-bing** -ɪŋ **-bed** -d **-ber/s** -əʳ/z (US) -ɚ/z **'grab ˌbag** ; **ˌup for 'grabs**
grabbl|e 'græb.l̩ **-es** -z **-ing** -ɪŋ, '-lɪŋ **-ed** -d
grabb|y 'græb|.i **-ier** -i.əʳ (US) -i.ɚ **-iest** -i.ɪst, -i.əst
Grabham 'græb.əm
Gracch|us 'græk|.əs **-i** -iː, -aɪ
grac|e (G) greɪs **-es** -ɪz **-ing** -ɪŋ **-ed** -t **'grace ˌnote** ; **ˌfall from 'grace**
Gracechurch 'greɪs.tʃɜːtʃ (US) -tʃɜːrtʃ
graceful 'greɪs.fəl, -fʊl **-ly** -i **-ness** -nəs, -nɪs
Graceland 'greɪs.lænd, -lənd
graceless 'greɪ.sləs, -slɪs **-ly** -li **-ness** -nəs, -nɪs
Gracie 'greɪ.si
gracious 'greɪ.ʃəs **-ly** -li **-ness** -nəs, -nɪs
grackle 'græk.l̩ **-s** -z
grad græd **-s** -z **'grad ˌschool**
gradable 'greɪ.də.bl̩
gra|date grə|'deɪt (US) 'greɪ|.deɪt **-dates** -'deɪts (US) -deɪts **-dating** -'deɪ.tɪŋ (US) -deɪ.t̬ɪŋ **-dated** -'deɪ.tɪd (US) -deɪ.t̬əd
gradation grə'deɪ.ʃən (US) greɪ- **-s** -z
gradational grə'deɪ.ʃən.əl (US) greɪ-
grad|e greɪd **-es** -z **-ing** -ɪŋ **-ed** -ɪd **ˌgrade point 'average** (US) **'grade point ˌaverage** ; **'grade ˌschool** ; **ˌmake the 'grade**
gradeable 'greɪ.də.bl̩
gradely 'greɪd.li
Gradgrind 'græd.graɪnd
gradient 'greɪ.di.ənt **-s** -s
gradin 'greɪ.dɪn **-s** -z
graditative 'greɪ.dɪ.tə.tɪv, -də- (US) -də-
gradual 'grædʒ.u.əl, 'græd.ju.əl (US) 'grædʒ.u.əl **-s** -z **-ly** -i
graduate (*n.*) 'grædʒ.u.ət, 'græd.ju-, -ɪt (US) 'grædʒ.u.ət, -ɪt **-s** -s
gradu|ate (*v.*) 'græd.ju|.eɪt, 'grædʒ.u- (US) 'grædʒ.u- **-ates** -eɪts **-ating** -eɪ.tɪŋ (US) -eɪ.t̬ɪŋ **-ated** -eɪ.tɪd (US) -eɪ.t̬ɪd
graduation ˌgrædʒ.u'eɪ.ʃən, ˌgræd.ju'- (US) ˌgrædʒ.u'- **-s** -z
graduator 'grædʒ.u.eɪ.təʳ, 'græd.ju- (US) 'grædʒ.u.eɪ.t̬ɚ **-s** -z
gradus 'græd.əs, 'greɪ.dəs **-es** -ɪz
Grady 'greɪ.di
Graecism 'griː.sɪ.zəm
Graeco- 'griː.kəʊ-, 'grek.əʊ- (US) 'grek.oʊ-, 'griː.koʊ-
Graeme greɪəm, greɪm
Graf(f)ham 'græf.əm
graffiti grə'fiː.ti, græf'iː- (US) grə'fiː.t̬i
graft grɑːft (US) græft **-s** -s **-ing** -ɪŋ **-ed** -ɪd **-er/s** -əʳ/z (US) -ɚ/z
Grafton 'grɑːf.tən (US) 'græf-
graham cracker 'greɪəmˌkræk.əʳ (US) -ɚ, 'græm- **-s** -z
Graham(e) 'greɪəm
graham flour 'greɪəmˌflaʊəʳ (US) -ˌflaʊɚ
Grahamston 'greɪəm.stən
Grahamstown 'greɪəmz.taʊn
grail (G) greɪl **-s** -z
grain greɪn **-s** -z **-ing** -ɪŋ **-ed** -d **-er/s** -əʳ/z (US) -ɚ/z **ˌgo aˌgainst the 'grain**
Grainger 'greɪn.dʒəʳ (US) -dʒɚ
grain|y 'greɪ.n|i **-ier** -i.əʳ (US) -i.ɚ **-iest** -i.ɪst, -i.əst
gram græm **-s** -z
gramercy grə'mɜː.si (US) -'mɜːr-
graminaceous ˌgræm.ɪ'neɪ.ʃəs, ˌgreɪ.mɪ'-, -mə'- (US) ˌgræm.ə'-
gramineous grə'mɪn.i.əs, græm'ɪn-
graminivorous ˌgræm.ɪ'nɪv.ər.əs, ˌgreɪ-
grammalogue 'græm.ə.lɒg (US) -lɑːg, -lɔːg **-s** -z
grammar 'græm.əʳ (US) -ɚ **-s** -z **'grammar ˌschool**
grammarian grə'meə.ri.ən (US) -'mer.i- **-s** -z
grammatical grə'mæt.ɪ.kəl (US) -mæt̬.ɪ- **-ly** -i
grammaticality grəˌmæt.ɪ'kæl.ə.ti, -ɪ.ti (US) -ˌmæt̬.ə'kæl.ə.t̬i
grammaticiz|e, -is|e grə'mæt.ɪ.saɪz, '-ə- (US) -'mæt̬.ə- **-es** -ɪz **-ing** -ɪŋ **-ed** -d
gramme græm **-s** -z
Gramm|y 'græm|.i **-ys** -iz **-ies** -iz
gramophone 'græm.ə.fəʊn (US) -foʊn **-s** -z
Grampian 'græm.pi.ən **-s** -z
gramps græmps
grampus 'græm.pəs **-es** -ɪz
gran græn **-s** -z
Granada grə'nɑː.də
granar|y 'græn.ər|.i **-ies** -iz **'granary ˌbread**
Granbury 'græn.bər.i, 'græm- (US) 'grænˌber-, -bɚ-
Granby 'græn.bi, 'græm- (US) 'græn-
Gran Canaria ˌgræn.kə'neə.ri.ə, ˌgræŋ- (US) ˌgrɑːn.kə'nɑː-, -'ner-
Gran Chaco ˌgræn'tʃɑː.kəʊ, -'tʃæk.əʊ (US) ˌgrɑːn'tʃɑː.koʊ
grand grænd **-er** -əʳ (US) -ɚ **-est** -ɪst, -əst **-ly** -li **-ness** -nəs, -nɪs, 'græn.nəs, -nɪs **ˌGrand Ca'nary** ; **ˌGrand 'Canyon** ; **ˌgrand 'duchess** ; **ˌgrand 'duke** ; **ˌGrand 'Forks** ; **ˌgrand 'jury** ; **ˌGrand 'National** ; **ˌgrand pi'ano**
grandad (G) 'græn.dæd **-s** -z
grandadd|y 'græn.dæd|.i **-ies** -iz
grandam 'græn.dæm, -dəm **-s** -z
grandaunt 'grændˌɑːnt (US) -ˌænt, -ˌɑːnt **-s** -s
grand|child 'grænd|.tʃaɪld **-children** -ˌtʃɪl.drən
granddad (G) 'grænd.dæd **-s** -z
granddadd|y 'grænd.dæd|.i **-ies** -iz
granddaughter 'grændˌdɔː.təʳ (US) -ˌdɑː.t̬ɚ, -ˌdɔː- **-s** -z
grande dame ˌgrɑːnd'dɑːm, ˌgrɑ̃ːn-, -'dæm **-s** -z
grandee græn'diː **-s** -z
grandeur 'græn.djəʳ, -dʒəʳ, -djʊəʳ (US) -dʒɚ, -dʒʊr
grandfather 'grændˌfɑː.ðəʳ (US) -ðɚ **-s** -z **'grandfather ˌclause** ; **ˌgrandfather 'clock** (US) **'grandfather ˌclock**
Grand Guignol ˌgrɑ̃ːŋ.giː'njɒl (US) ˌgrɑ̃ː.giː'njoʊl, ˌgrɑːn-, -'njɑːl

grandiloquen|ce græn'dɪl.ə.kwənl*t*s **-t/ly** -t/li
grandiose 'græn.di.əʊs, -əʊz ⓤⓢ -oʊs, -oʊz, ˌ--'- **-ly** -li
grandiosity ˌgræn.di'ɒs.ə.ti, -ɪ.ti ⓤⓢ -'ɑː.sə.t̬i
Grandison 'græn.dɪ.sᵊn
Grandissimes 'grænd.ɪ.siːmz
grandma 'græn*d*.mɑː, 'græm- **-s** -z **ˌGrandma 'Moses**
grand mal ˌgrɑ̃ː*nd*'mæl ⓤⓢ ˌgrɑːn*d*'mɑːl, ˌgræn*d*-, -'mæl
grandmamma 'græn*d*.məˌmɑː, 'græm- **-s** -z
Grand Marnier® ˌgrɑ̃ː*nd*'mɑː.ni.eɪ ⓤⓢ ˌgrɑːn.mɑːr'njeɪ **-s** -z
grandmaster 'græn*d*ˌmɑː.stəʳ, 'græm- ⓤⓢ 'græn*d*ˌmæs.tɚ **-s** -z
grandmother 'græn*d*ˌmʌð.əʳ, 'græm- ⓤⓢ 'græn*d*ˌmʌð.ɚ **-s** -z
grandnephew 'græn*d*ˌnev.juː, -ˌnef-, ˌ-'-- ⓤⓢ 'græn*d*ˌnef.juː **-s** -z
grandniec|e 'græn*d*.niːs, ˌ-'- **-es** -ɪz
grandpa 'græn*d*.pɑː, 'græm- **-s** -z
grandpapa 'græn*d*.pəˌpɑː, 'græm- **-s** -z
grandparent 'græn*d*ˌpeə.rᵊnt, 'græm- ⓤⓢ 'græn*d*ˌper.ᵊnt, -ˌpær- **-s** -s
grand prix ˌgrɑ̃ː*n*'priː, ˌgrɒn-, ˌgrɒm- ⓤⓢ ˌgrɑːn- **grands prix** ˌgrɑ̃ː'priː, ˌgrɒn-, ˌgrɒm- ⓤⓢ ˌgrɑːn-
grandsire 'græn*d*.saɪəʳ ⓤⓢ -saɪɚ **-s** -z
grandson 'græn*d*.sʌn **-s** -z
grands prix ˌgrɑ̃ː'priː, ˌgrɒn-, ˌgrɒm- ⓤⓢ ˌgrɑːn
grandstand 'græn*d*.stænd **-s** -z **-ing** -ɪŋ **-ed** -ɪd
granduncle 'grændˌʌŋ.kl̩ **-s** -z
grang|e (G) 'greɪndʒ **-es** -ɪz
Grangemouth 'greɪndʒ.məθ, -maʊθ
Granger 'greɪn.dʒəʳ ⓤⓢ -dʒɚ
grangeriz|e, -is|e 'greɪn.dʒᵊr.aɪz ⓤⓢ -dʒə.raɪz **-es** -ɪz **-ing** -ɪŋ **-ed** -d
Grangetown 'greɪndʒ.taʊn
Grangeville 'greɪndʒ.vɪl
granite (G) 'græn.ɪt, -ət **-s** -s
granitic græn'ɪt.ɪk, grə'nɪt- ⓤⓢ grə'nɪt̬-
grann|y 'grænl.i **-ies** -iz **'granny ˌflat**; **'granny ˌknot**; **ˌGranny 'Smith**
granola grə'nəʊ.lə, græn'əʊ- ⓤⓢ grə'noʊ-
granolithic ˌgræn.əʊ'lɪθ.ɪk ⓤⓢ -ə'-
grant (G) grɑːnt ⓤⓢ grænt **-s** -s **-ing** -ɪŋ ⓤⓢ 'græn.t̬ɪŋ **-ed** -ɪd ⓤⓢ 'græn.t̬ɪd
Granta 'græn.tə, 'grɑːn- ⓤⓢ 'græn-
Grantchester 'grɑːn.tʃɪ.stəʳ, 'græn-, -tʃə, -tʃes.təʳ ⓤⓢ 'grænˌtʃes-
grantee ˌgrɑːn'tiː ⓤⓢ ˌgræn- **-s** -z
Granth grʌnt
Grantham 'græn*t*.θəm
Granton 'grɑːn.tən, 'græn- ⓤⓢ 'græn-
grantor ˌgrɑːn'tɔːʳ; 'grɑːn.təʳ ⓤⓢ 'græn.t̬ɚ; ˌgræn'tɔːr **-s** -z
Grantown 'græn.taʊn
granular 'græn.jə.ləʳ, -jʊ- ⓤⓢ -jə.lɚ **-ly** -li
granularity ˌgræn.jə'lær.ə.ti, -jʊ'-, -ɪ.ti ⓤⓢ -jə'ler.ə.t̬i, -'lær-
granu|late 'græn.jəl.leɪt, -jʊ- ⓤⓢ -jə- **-es** -leɪts **-ing** -leɪtɪŋ ⓤⓢ -leɪt̬.ɪŋ **-ed** -leɪtɪd ⓤⓢ -leɪ.t̬ɪd
granulation ˌgræn.jə'leɪ.ʃᵊn, -jʊ'- ⓤⓢ -jə'- **-s** -z
granule 'græn.juːl **-s** -z
granulite 'græn.jə.laɪt, -jʊ- ⓤⓢ -jə-
granulitic ˌgræn.jə'lɪt.ɪk, -jʊ'- ⓤⓢ -jə'lɪt̬-
Granville 'græn.vɪl
Granville-Barker ˌgræn.vɪl'bɑː.kəʳ ⓤⓢ -'bɑːr.kɚ
grape (G) greɪp **-s** -s
grapefruit 'greɪp.fruːt **-s** -s
grapeshot 'greɪp.ʃɒt ⓤⓢ -ʃɑːt
grapevine 'greɪp.vaɪn **-s** -z
graph grɑːf, græf ⓤⓢ græf **-s** -s **'graph ˌpaper**
grapheme 'græf.iːm **-s** -z
graphemic græf'iː.mɪk, grə'fiː- **-ally** -ᵊl.i, -li
-grapher -grə.fəʳ ⓤⓢ -grə.fɚ
Note: Suffix. Words containing **-grapher** are normally stressed on the antepenultimate syllable, e.g. **photographer** /fə'tɒg.rə.fəʳ ⓤⓢ -'tɑː.grə.fɚ/.
graphic (G) 'græf.ɪk **-s** -s **-al** -ᵊl **-ally** -ᵊl.i, -li **ˌgraphic de'sign**
-graphic -'græf.ɪk
Note: Suffix. Normally carries primary stress, e.g. **photographic** /ˌfəʊ.tə'græf.ɪk ⓤⓢ ˌfoʊ.t̬ə'-/.
graphite 'græf.aɪt
graphitic græf'ɪt.ɪk, grə'fɪt- ⓤⓢ grə'fɪt̬-
graphological ˌgræf.ə'lɒdʒ.ɪ.kᵊl ⓤⓢ -'lɑː.dʒɪ **-ly** -i
grapholog|y græf'ɒl.ə.dʒl i, grə'fɒl- ⓤⓢ grə'fɑː.lə- **-ist/s** -ɪst/s
graphometer græf'ɒm.ɪ.təʳ, grə'fɒm-, '-ə- ⓤⓢ grə'fɑː.mə.t̬ɚ **-s** -z
-graphy -grə.fi
Note: Suffix. Words containing **-graphy** are normally stressed on the antepenultimate syllable, e.g. **photography** /fə'tɒg.rə.fi ⓤⓢ -'tɑː.grə-/.
grapnel 'græp.nᵊl **-s** -z
grappa 'græp.ə ⓤⓢ 'grɑː.pə **-s** -z
Grappelli græp'el.i, grəp'-
grappl|e 'græp.l̩ **-es** -z **-ing** -ɪŋ, '-lɪŋ **-ed** -d **-er/s** -əʳ/z, '-ləʳ/z ⓤⓢ '-l̩.ɚ/z, '-lɚ/z **'grappling ˌiron**
grapy 'greɪ.pi
Grasmere 'grɑːs.mɪəʳ ⓤⓢ 'græs.mɪr
grasp grɑːsp ⓤⓢ græsp **-s** -s **-ing** -ɪŋ **-ed** -t **-er/s** -əʳ/z ⓤⓢ -ɚ/z **-able** -ə.bl̩
grass (G) grɑːs ⓤⓢ græs **-es** -ɪz **-ing** -ɪŋ **-ed** -t **ˌgrass 'widow**; **let the ˌgrass ˌgrow under one's 'feet**
grasshopper 'grɑːsˌhɒp.əʳ ⓤⓢ 'græsˌhɑː.pɚ **-s** -z
grassland 'grɑːs.lænd, -lənd ⓤⓢ 'græs-
grass-roots (*adj.*) ˌgrɑːs'ruːts ⓤⓢ ˌgræs- *stress shift:* ˌgrass-roots 'feeling
grass roots (*n.*) ˌgrɑːs'ruːts ⓤⓢ ˌgræs-
grass|y 'grɑː.sl i ⓤⓢ 'græsl.i **-ier** -i.əʳ ⓤⓢ -i.ɚ **-iest** -i.ɪst, -i.əst
grat|e (*n. v.*) greɪt **-es** -s **-ing/ly** -ɪŋ/li ⓤⓢ 'greɪ.t̬ɪŋ/li **-ed** -ɪd ⓤⓢ 'greɪ.t̬ɪd **-er/s** -əʳ/z ⓤⓢ 'greɪ.t̬ɚ/z
grateful 'greɪt.fᵊl, -fʊl **-ly** -i **-ness** -nəs, -nɪs
Gratian 'greɪ.ʃᵊn, -ʃi.ən
graticule 'græt.ɪ.kjuːl, '-ə- ⓤⓢ '-ə- **-s** -z
gratification ˌgræt.ɪ.fɪ'keɪ.ʃᵊn, ˌ-ə- ⓤⓢ ˌgræt̬.ə- **-s** -z
grati|fy 'græt.ɪl.faɪ, '-ə- ⓤⓢ 'græt̬.ə- **-fies** -faɪz **-fying/ly** -faɪ.ɪŋ/li **-fied** -faɪd
gratin 'græ.tæ̃ŋ, -tæn ⓤⓢ 'grɑː.tᵊn
grating (*n.*) 'greɪ.tɪŋ ⓤⓢ -t̬ɪŋ **-s** -z
Gratiot 'græʃ.i.ət, 'græʃ.ət, 'greɪ.ʃi.ət, -ʃət ⓤⓢ 'græʃ.ət
gratis 'grɑː.tɪs, 'greɪ-, 'græt.ɪs, -əs ⓤⓢ 'græt̬.əs, 'grɑː.t̬əs, 'greɪ-
gratitude 'græt.ɪ.tjuːd, -tʃuːd, '-ə- ⓤⓢ 'græt̬.ə.tuːd, -tjuːd
Grattan 'græt.ᵊn
gratuitous grə'tjuː.ɪ.təs, -'tʃuː- ⓤⓢ -'tuː.ə.t̬əs, -'tjuː- **-ly** -li **-ness** -nəs, -nɪs
gratuit|y grə'tjuː.ə.tl i, -'tʃuː-, -ɪ.tl i ⓤⓢ -'tuː.ə.t̬l i, -'tjuː- **-ies** -iz
graupel 'graʊ.pᵊl
gravadlax 'græv.əd.læks ⓤⓢ 'grɑː.vəd.lɑːks
gravamen grə'veɪ.men, -'vɑː-, -mən ⓤⓢ -mən **-s** -z **gravamina** grə'veɪ.mɪn.ə, -'vɑː- ⓤⓢ -'væm.ɪn-
grave *accent above a letter:* grɑːv ⓤⓢ grɑːv, greɪv
grav|e *other senses:* greɪv **-es** -z **-er** -əʳ ⓤⓢ -ɚ **-est** -ɪst, -əst **-ely** -li **-eness** -nəs, -nɪs **-ing** -ɪŋ **-ed** -d **-er/s** -əʳ/z ⓤⓢ -ɚ/z **ˌturn in one's 'grave**
graveclothes 'greɪv.kləʊðz ⓤⓢ -kloʊðz
gravedigger 'greɪvˌdɪg.əʳ ⓤⓢ -ɚ **-s** -z
gravel 'græv.ᵊl **-s** -z **-(l)ing** -ɪŋ **-(l)ed** -d **-ly** -i
graven 'greɪ.vᵊn **ˌgraven 'image**
Graves *surname:* greɪvz *wine:* grɑːv

Gravesend ˌgreɪvz'end
graveside 'greɪv.saɪd
gravestone 'greɪv.stəʊn (US) -stoʊn -s -z
graveyard 'greɪv.jɑːd (US) -jɑːrd **-s** -z **'graveyard ˌshift, ˌgraveyard 'shift**
gravid 'græv.ɪd **-ly** -li **-ness** -nəs, -nɪs
gravid|a 'græv.ɪ.d|ə **-as** -əz **-ae** -iː
gravidity græv'ɪd.ɪ.ti, grə'vɪd- (US) grə'vɪd.ə.t̬i
gravitas 'græv.ɪ.tæs, '-ə-, -tɑːs
gravi|tate 'græv.ɪ|.teɪt, '-ə- **-tates** -teɪts **-tating** -teɪ.tɪŋ (US) -teɪ.t̬ɪŋ **-tated** -teɪ.tɪd (US) -teɪ.t̬ɪd
gravitation ˌgræv.ɪ'teɪ.ʃᵊn, -ə'- **-al** -ᵊl **-ally** -ᵊl.i
gravitative 'græv.ɪ.teɪ.tɪv, '-ə-, -tə.tɪv (US) -teɪ.t̬ɪv
gravity 'græv.ə.ti, -ɪ.ti (US) -ə.t̬i
gravlax 'græv.læks (US) 'grɑːv.lɑːks
gravure grə'vjʊəʳ, -'vjɔːʳ (US) -'vjʊr
grav|y 'greɪ.v|i **-ies** -iz **'gravy ˌtrain**
gray (G) greɪ **-s** -z **-er** -əʳ (US) -ɚ **-est** -ɪst, -əst **-ness** -nəs, -nɪs **-ing** -ɪŋ
grayish 'greɪ.ɪʃ
grayling 'greɪ.lɪŋ **-s** -z
Grayson 'greɪ.sᵊn
graystone (G) 'greɪ.stəʊn (US) -stoʊn
Graz grɑːts
graz|e greɪz **-es** -ɪz **-ing** -ɪŋ **-ed** -d
grazier 'greɪ.zi.əʳ, -ʒəʳ (US) -ʒɚ **-s** -z
GRE ˌdʒiː.ɑːr'iː **-s** -z
Greasby 'griːz.bi
greas|e griːs **-es** -ɪz **-ing** -ɪŋ **-ed** -t
greasepaint 'griːs.peɪnt
greaseproof 'griːs.pruːf **ˌgreaseproof 'paper**
greaser 'griː.səʳ (US) -sɚ, -zɚ **-s** -z
Greasley 'griːz.li
greas|y 'griː.s|i **-ier** -i.əʳ (US) -i.ɚ **-iest** -i.ɪst, -i.əst **-ily** -ɪ.li, -ᵊl.i **-iness** -ɪ.nəs, -ɪ.nɪs
great greɪt **-er** -əʳ (US) 'greɪ.t̬ɚ **-est** -ɪst, -əst (US) 'greɪ.t̬ɪst, -t̬əst **-ness** -nəs, -nɪs **ˌGreat ˌBarrier 'Reef** ; **ˌGreat 'Britain** ; **ˌGreat 'Falls** ; **ˌGreat 'Lakes** ; **ˌGreat 'Plains**
great-aunt ˌgreɪt'ɑːnt (US) ˌgreɪt'ænt, -'ɑːnt **-s** -s *stress shift:* ˌgreat-aunt 'Maud
greatcoat 'greɪt.kəʊt (US) -koʊt **-s** -s
great-grand|child ˌgreɪt'grænd|.tʃaɪld **-children** -ˌtʃɪl.drᵊn
great-granddaughter ˌgreɪt'grænd̸ˌdɔː.təʳ (US) -ˌdɑː.t̬ɚ, -ˌdɔː- **-s** -z
great-grandfather ˌgreɪt'grænd̸ˌfɑː.ðəʳ (US) -ðɚ **-s** -z
great-grandmother ˌgreɪt'grænd̸ˌmʌð.əʳ, -'græm- (US) -'grænd̸ˌmʌð.ɚ **-s** -z
great-grandparent ˌgreɪt'grænd̸ˌpeə.rᵊnt (US) -ˌper.ᵊnt, -ˌpær- **-s** -s
great-grandson ˌgreɪt'grænd̸.sʌn **-s** -z
Greatham *in Durham:* 'griː.təm (US) 'griː.t̬əm *in Northamptonshire, Hampshire, and West Sussex:* 'gret.əm (US) 'greɪ.t̬əm
Greathead 'greɪt.hed
Greatheart 'greɪt.hɑːt (US) -hɑːrt
greathearted ˌgreɪt'hɑː.tɪd (US) -'hɑːr.t̬ɪd *stress shift:* ˌgreathearted 'warrior
greatly 'greɪt.li
Greatorex 'greɪ.tə.reks (US) -t̬ə-
Greats greɪts
great-uncle ˌgreɪt'ʌŋ.kl̩, '-ˌ-- **-s** -z *stress shift:* ˌgreat-uncle 'John
Great Yarmouth ˌgreɪt'jɑː.məθ (US) -'jɑːr-
greave griːv **-s** -z
Greaves griːvz, greɪvz
grebe griːb **-s** -z
Grecian 'griː.ʃᵊn **-s** -z
Grecism 'griː.sɪ.zᵊm
Greco- 'griː.kəʊ-, 'grek.əʊ- (US) 'grek.oʊ-, 'griː.koʊ-
Greece griːs
greed griːd
greed|y 'griː.d|i **-ier** -i.əʳ (US) -i.ɚ **-iest** -i.ɪst, -i.əst **-ily** -ɪ.li, -ᵊl.i **-iness** -ɪ.nəs, -ɪ.nɪs **'greedy ˌguts**
Greek griːk **-s** -s **ˌGreek ˌOrthodox 'Church**
Greel(e)y 'griː.li
green (G) griːn **-s** -z **-er** -əʳ (US) -ɚ **-est** -ɪst, -əst **-ly** -li **-ness** -nəs, -nɪs **-ing** -ɪŋ **-ed** -d **ˌgreen 'bean** (US) **'green ˌbean** ; **ˌGreen Be'ret** ; **'green ˌcard** ; **ˌgreen cross 'code** ; **'Green ˌParty**
Greenall 'griː.nɔːl
Greenaway 'griː.nə.weɪ
greenback 'griːn.bæk, 'griːm- (US) 'griːn- **-s** -s
greenbelt (G) 'griːn.belt, 'griːm- (US) 'griːn- **-s** -s
Green(e) griːn
greenery 'griː.nᵊr.i
green-eyed ˌgriːn'aɪd (US) 'griːn.aɪd *stress shift, British only:* ˌgreen-eyed 'monster
greenfield (G) 'griːn.fiːld
greenfinch 'griːn.fɪntʃ **-es** -ɪz
green|fly 'griːn|.flaɪ **-flies** -flaɪz
Greenford 'griːn.fəd (US) -fɚd
greengag|e 'griːn.geɪdʒ, 'griːŋ- (US) 'griːn- **-es** -ɪz
greengrocer 'griːnˌgrəʊ.səʳ, 'griːŋ- (US) 'griːnˌgroʊ.sɚ **-s** -z
Greenhalgh 'griːn.hælʃ, -hældʒ, -hɔː
Greenham 'griː.nəm **ˌGreenham 'Common**
Greenhaulgh 'griːn.hɔː
Greenhill 'griːn.hɪl
Greenhithe 'griːn.haɪð
greenhorn 'griːn.hɔːn (US) -hɔːrn **-s** -z
greenhou|se 'griːn.haʊ|s **-ses** -zɪz **'greenhouse efˌfect** ; **ˌgreenhouse 'gas**
greenish (G) 'griː.nɪʃ
Greenland 'griːn.lənd, -lænd **-er/s** -əʳ/z
Greenleaf 'griːn.liːf
greenmarket 'griːnˌmɑː.kɪt, 'griːm- (US) 'griːnˌmɑːr.kɪt **-s** -s
Greenock 'griː.nək, 'grɪn.ək, 'gren-
Greenore 'griː.nɔːʳ (US) -nɔːr
Greenough 'griː.nəʊ (US) -noʊ
Greenpeace 'griːn.piːs, 'griːm- (US) 'griːn-
Greenpoint 'griːn.pɔɪnt, 'griːm- (US) 'griːn-
Greenport 'griːn.pɔːt, 'griːm- (US) 'griːn.pɔːrt
greenroom 'griːn.rʊm, -ruːm (US) -ruːm, -rʊm **-s** -z
greensand 'griːn.sænd
greenshank 'griːn.ʃæŋk **-s** -s
Greenslade 'griːn.sleɪd
Greensleeves 'griːn.sliːvz
greenstick 'griːn.stɪk **-s** -z **ˌgreenstick 'fracture**
greenstone 'griːn.stəʊn (US) -stoʊn
greensward 'griːn.swɔːd (US) -swɔːrd
Greenville 'griːn.vɪl
Greenway 'griːn.weɪ
Greenwell 'griːn.wᵊl, -wel
Greenwich 'gren.ɪdʒ, 'grɪn-, -ɪtʃ (US) 'gren.ɪdʒ, 'grɪn-, -nɪtʃ, -wɪtʃ **ˌGreenwich 'Mean Time, ˌGreenwich ˌMean 'Time**
greenwood (G) 'griːn.wʊd **-s** -z
Greer grɪəʳ (US) grɪr
greet (G) griːt **-s** -s **-ing/s** -ɪŋ/z (US) 'griː.t̬ɪŋ/z **-ed** -ɪd (US) 'griː.t̬ɪd **'greetings ˌcard** (US) **'greeting ˌcard**
Greetland 'griːt.lənd
gregarious grɪ'geə.ri.əs, grə- (US) -'ger.i- **-ly** -li **-ness** -nəs, -nɪs
Greg(g) greg
Gregor 'greg.əʳ (US) -ɚ
Gregorian grɪ'gɔː.ri.ən, grə-, greg'ɔː- **-s** -z **Greˌgorian 'chant**
Gregory 'greg.ᵊr.i
Greig greg
greige greɪʒ
greisen 'graɪ.zᵊn
gremlin 'grem.lɪn **-s** -z
grenache gren'æʃ
Grenada grə'neɪ.də, grɪ-, gren'eɪ-
grenade grə'neɪd, grɪ-, gren'eɪd **-s** -z
grenadier (G) ˌgren.ə'dɪəʳ (US) -'dɪr **-s** -z
grenadine 'gren.ə.diːn, ˌgren.ə'diːn
Grenadines ˌgren.ə'diːnz
Grendel 'gren.dᵊl

Grenfell 'gren.fel, -fᵊl
Grenoble grə'nəʊ.bl̩, grɪ'nəʊ- ⓤⓢ grə'noʊ-
Grenville 'gren.vɪl, -vᵊl
Gresham 'greʃ.əm
Gresley 'grez.li
Greswell 'grez.wᵊl, -wel
Greta 'griː.tə, 'gret.ə, 'greɪ.tə ⓤⓢ 'gret̬.ə, 'griː.t̬ə, 'greɪ.t̬ə
Gretchen 'gretʃ.ᵊn
Gretel 'gret.ᵊl
Gretna 'gret.nə ˌ**Gretna 'Green**
Greuz|e grɜːz ⓤⓢ grɜːz **-es** -ɪz
Greville 'grev.ɪl, -ᵊl
grew (G) (*from* **grow**) gruː
grey (G) greɪ **-s** -z **-er** -əʳ ⓤⓢ -ɚ **-est** -ɪst, -əst **-ness** -nəs, -nɪs **-ing** -ɪŋ
greybeard 'greɪ.bɪəd ⓤⓢ -bɪrd **-s** -z
greycoat (G) 'greɪ.kəʊt ⓤⓢ -koʊt **-s** -s
grey-haired ˌgreɪ'heəd ⓤⓢ -'herd *stress-shift:* ˌgrey-haired 'person
greyhound 'greɪ.haʊnd **-s** -z ˌ**Greyhound 'bus®**
greyish 'greɪ.ɪʃ
greylag 'greɪ.læg **-s** -z
Greylock 'greɪ.lɒk ⓤⓢ -lɑːk
Greyson 'greɪ.sᵊn
Greystoke 'greɪ.stəʊk ⓤⓢ -stoʊk
Gribbin 'grɪb.ɪn
gribble (G) 'grɪb.l̩ **-s** -z
Grice graɪs
grid grɪd **-s** -z
griddl|e 'grɪd.l̩ **-es** -z **-ing** -ɪŋ **-ed** -d
gridiron 'grɪd.aɪən ⓤⓢ -aɪɚn **-s** -z
Gridley 'grɪd.li
gridlock 'grɪd.lɒk ⓤⓢ -lɑːk **-s** -s **-ed** -t
grief griːf **-s** -z **'grief-ˌstricken**
Grieg griːg
Grierson 'grɪə.sᵊn ⓤⓢ 'grɪr-
grievanc|e 'griː.vᵊnts **-es** -ɪz
griev|e (G) griːv **-es** -z **-ing** -ɪŋ **-ed** -d **-er/s** -əʳ/z ⓤⓢ -ɚ/z
grievous 'griː.vəs **-ly** -li **-ness** -nəs, -nɪs ˌ**grievous ˌbodily 'harm**
griffin (G) 'grɪf.ɪn **-s** -z
Griffith 'grɪf.ɪθ **-s** -s
griffon 'grɪf.ᵊn **-s** -z
grift grɪft **-s** -s **-ing** -ɪŋ **-ed** -ɪd
grifter 'grɪf.təʳ ⓤⓢ -tɚ **-s** -z
grig grɪg **-s** -z
Grigg grɪg **-s** -z
Grigson 'grɪg.sᵊn
grill grɪl **-s** -z **-ing** -ɪŋ **-ed** -d **-er/s** -əʳ/z ⓤⓢ -ɚ/z
grillag|e 'grɪl.ɪdʒ **-es** -ɪz
grille grɪl **-s** -z
grillroom 'grɪl.rʊm, -ruːm ⓤⓢ -ruːm, -rʊm **-s** -z
grilse grɪls
grim grɪm **-mer** -əʳ ⓤⓢ -ɚ **-mest** -ɪst, -əst **-ly** -li **-ness** -nəs, -nɪs ˌ**Grim 'Reaper**

grimac|e grɪ'meɪs, grə-; 'grɪm.əs, -ɪs ⓤⓢ 'grɪm.əs; grɪ'meɪs **-es** -ɪz **-ing** -ɪŋ **-ed** -t
Grimald 'grɪm.ᵊld
Grimaldi grɪ'mɔːl.di, grə-, -'mɒl-, -'mæl- ⓤⓢ -'mɑːl-, -'mɔːl-
grimalkin grɪ'mæl.kɪn, -'mɔːl- **-s** -z
grim|e graɪm **-es** -z **-ing** -ɪŋ **-ed** -d
Grimes graɪmz
Grimethorpe 'graɪm.θɔːp ⓤⓢ -θɔːrp
Grimké 'grɪm.ki
Grimm grɪm
Grimond 'grɪm.ənd
Grimsby 'grɪmz.bi
Grimshaw 'grɪm.ʃɔː ⓤⓢ -ʃɑː, -ʃɔː
Grimwood 'grɪm.wʊd
grim|y 'graɪ.m|i **-ier** -i.əʳ ⓤⓢ -i.ɚ **-iest** -i.ɪst, -i.əst **-ily** -ɪ.li, -ᵊl.i **-iness** -ɪ.nəs, -ɪ.nɪs
grin grɪn **-s** -z **-ning** -ɪŋ **-ned** -d
Grinch grɪntʃ
grind graɪnd **-s** -z **-ing** -ɪŋ **ground** graʊnd **grinder/s** 'graɪn.dəʳ/z ⓤⓢ -dɚ/z
Grindal 'grɪnd.ᵊl
Grindelwald 'grɪn.dᵊl.vɑːld, -væld ⓤⓢ -vɑːld, -væld, -wɔːld
Grindon 'grɪn.dən
grindstone 'graɪn*d*.stəʊn ⓤⓢ -stoʊn **-s** -z ˌ**keep one's ˌnose to the 'grindstone**
gringo 'grɪŋ.gəʊ ⓤⓢ -goʊ **-s** -z
Grinnell grɪ'nel
Grinstead 'grɪn.stɪd, -sted ⓤⓢ -sted
grip grɪp **-s** -s **-ping** -ɪŋ **-ped** -t
grip|e graɪp **-es** -s **-ing** -ɪŋ **-ed** -t **'gripe ˌwater**
gripes graɪps
grippe griːp, grɪp ⓤⓢ grɪp
grisaille grɪ'zeɪl, grə-, griː-, -'zaɪ, -'zaɪl ⓤⓢ -'zaɪ, -'zeɪl
Griselda grɪ'zel.də, grə-
grisette grɪ'zet **-s** -s
Grisewood 'graɪz.wʊd
griskin 'grɪs.kɪn
grisl|y 'grɪz.l|i **-ier** -i.əʳ ⓤⓢ -i.ɚ **-iest** -i.ɪst, -i.əst **-iness** -ɪ.nəs, -ɪ.nɪs
Grisons griː'zɔ̃ːŋ, -'zɔːŋ ⓤⓢ griː'zɔ̃ːŋ, -'zɔːŋ
Grissel 'grɪs.ᵊl
grist grɪst
gristle 'grɪs.l̩
gristly 'grɪs.l̩.i, 'grɪs.li
Griswold 'grɪz.wəʊld, -wᵊld ⓤⓢ -wɔːld, -wᵊld
grit grɪt **-s** -s **-ting** -ɪŋ ⓤⓢ 'grɪt̬.ɪŋ **-ted** -ɪd ⓤⓢ 'grɪt̬.ɪd
Gritton 'grɪt.ᵊn
gritt|y 'grɪt|.i ⓤⓢ 'grɪt̬|.i **-ier** -i.əʳ ⓤⓢ -i.ɚ **-iest** -i.ɪst, -i.əst **-ily** -ɪ.li, -ᵊl.i **-iness** -ɪ.nəs, -ɪ.nɪs
Grizedale 'graɪz.deɪl

Grizel grɪ'zel
grizzl|e 'grɪz.l̩ **-es** -z **-ing** -ɪŋ, '-lɪŋ **-ed** -d
grizzl|y 'grɪz.l|i **-ies** -iz **-ier** -i.əʳ ⓤⓢ -i.ɚ **-iest** -i.ɪst, -i.əst **'grizzly ˌbear**
Gro grəʊ, gruː, grɔː ⓤⓢ groʊ, grɔː
groan grəʊn ⓤⓢ groʊn **-s** -z **-ing/s** -ɪŋ/z **-ed** -d
groat grəʊt ⓤⓢ groʊt **-s** -s
grocer 'grəʊ.səʳ ⓤⓢ 'groʊ.sɚ **-s** -z
grocer|y 'grəʊ.sᵊr|.i ⓤⓢ 'groʊ- **-ies** -iz
grockle 'grɒk.l̩ ⓤⓢ 'grɑː.kl̩ **-s** -z
Grocott 'grɒk.ət, 'grəʊ.kɒt ⓤⓢ 'grɑː.kət, 'groʊ-
Grocyn 'grəʊ.sɪn ⓤⓢ 'groʊ-
grog grɒg ⓤⓢ grɑːg, grɔːg
grogg|y 'grɒg|.i ⓤⓢ 'grɑː.g|i, 'grɔː- **-ier** -i.əʳ ⓤⓢ -i.ɚ **-iest** -i.ɪst, -i.əst **-ily** -ɪ.li, -ᵊl.i **-iness** -ɪ.nəs, -ɪ.nɪs
grogram 'grɒg.rəm ⓤⓢ 'grɑː.grəm
groin grɔɪn **-s** -z
grommet 'grɒm.ɪt, 'grʌm- ⓤⓢ 'grɑː.mɪt **-s** -s
gromwell 'grɒm.wᵊl, -wel ⓤⓢ 'grɑːm-
Gromyko grə'miː.kəʊ ⓤⓢ -koʊ
Grongar 'grɒŋ.gəʳ ⓤⓢ 'grɑːŋ.gɚ, 'grɔːŋ-
Groningen 'grəʊ.nɪŋ.ən, 'grɒn.ɪŋ- ⓤⓢ 'groʊ-
groom (G) gruːm, grʊm **-s** -z **-ing** -ɪŋ **-ed** -d
grooms|man 'gruːmz|.mən, 'grʊmz- **-men** -mən, -men
groov|e gruːv **-es** -z **-ing** -ɪŋ **-ed** -d
groov|y 'gruː.v|i **-ier** -i.əʳ ⓤⓢ -i.ɚ **-iest** -i.ɪst, -i.əst **-iness** -ɪ.nəs, -ɪ.nɪs
grop|e grəʊp ⓤⓢ groʊp **-es** -s **-ing/ly** -ɪŋ/li **-ed** -t **-er/s** -əʳ/z ⓤⓢ -ɚ/z
Gropius 'grəʊ.pi.əs ⓤⓢ 'groʊ-
Grosart 'grəʊ.zɑːt ⓤⓢ 'groʊ.zɑːrt
grosbeak 'grəʊs.biːk, 'grɒs-, 'grɒz- ⓤⓢ 'groʊs- **-s** -s
groschen 'grɒʃ.ᵊn, 'grəʊʃ.ᵊn ⓤⓢ 'groʊ.ʃᵊn
Grose grəʊs, grəʊz ⓤⓢ groʊs, groʊz
grosgrain 'grəʊ.greɪn ⓤⓢ 'groʊ-
Grosmont *in North Yorkshire:* 'grəʊ.mənt, -mɒnt *locally also:* 'grəʊs.mənt ⓤⓢ 'groʊ.mɑːnt, 'groʊs- *in Gwent:* 'grɒs.mənt ⓤⓢ 'grɑːs-
gros point ˌgrəʊ'pɔɪnt ⓤⓢ 'groʊ.pɔɪnt
gross grəʊs ⓤⓢ groʊs **-er** -əʳ ⓤⓢ -ɚ **-est** -ɪst, -əst **-ly** -li **-ness** -nəs, -nɪs **-es** -ɪz **-ing** -ɪŋ **-ed** -t ˌ**gross doˌmestic 'product** ; ˌ**gross ˌnational 'product**
Gross *surname:* grɒs, grəʊs ⓤⓢ grɑːs, groʊs
Grosseteste 'grəʊs.test ⓤⓢ 'groʊs-
Grossmith 'grəʊ.smɪθ ⓤⓢ 'groʊ-
grosso modo ˌgrɒs.əʊ'mɒd.əʊ, -'məʊ.dəʊ ⓤⓢ ˌgroʊ.soʊ'moʊ.doʊ
Grosvenor 'grəʊv.nəʳ ⓤⓢ 'groʊv.nɚ

grosz grɔːʃ (US) grɑːʃ, grɔːʃ **groszy** ˈgrɔː.ʃi (US) ˈgrɑː-, ˈgrɔː-
Grote grəʊt (US) groʊt
grotesque grəʊˈtesk (US) groʊ- **-ly** -li **-ness** -nəs, -nɪs
Grotius ˈgrəʊ.ti.əs (US) ˈgroʊ.ʃəs, -ʃi.əs
grotto ˈgrɒt.əʊ (US) ˈgrɑː.t̬oʊ **-(e)s** -z
grott|y ˈgrɒt|.i (US) ˈgrɑː.t̬|i **-ier** -i.əʳ (US) -i.ɚ **-iest** -i.ɪst, -i.əst **-ily** -ɪ.li, -əl.i **-iness** -ɪ.nəs, -ɪ.nɪs
grouch graʊtʃ **-es** -ɪz **-ing** -ɪŋ **-ed** -t
Groucho ˈgraʊ.tʃəʊ (US) -tʃoʊ
grouch|y ˈgraʊ.tʃ|i **-ier** -i.əʳ (US) -i.ɚ **-iest** -i.ɪst, -i.əst **-ily** -ɪ.li, -əl.i **-iness** -ɪ.nəs, -ɪ.nɪs
ground graʊnd **-s** -z **-ing** -ɪŋ **-ed** -ɪd **-er/s** -əʳ/z (US) -ɚ/z ˈ**ground** ˌ**plan**; ˈ**ground** ˌ**rule**; ˈ**ground** ˌ**stroke**; ˈ**ground** ˌ**swell**; ˌ**suit someone** ˌ**down to the** ˈ**ground**
groundbreaking ˈgraʊndˌbreɪ.kɪŋ
groundcover ˈgraʊn*d*ˌkʌv.əʳ, ˈgraʊŋ- (US) ˈgraʊn*d*ˌkʌv.ɚ
groundhog ˈgraʊnd.hɒg (US) -hɑːg, -hɔːg **-s** -z ˈ**Groundhog** ˌ**Day**
groundless ˈgraʊnd.ləs, -lɪs **-ly** -li **-ness** -nəs, -nɪs
groundling ˈgraʊnd.lɪŋ **-s** -z
groundnut ˈgraʊnd.nʌt **-s** -s
groundsel ˈgraʊn*d*.səl
groundsheet ˈgraʊnd.ʃiːt **-s** -s
grounds|man ˈgraʊndz|.mən **-men** -mən, -men
groundspeed ˈgraʊnd.spiːd **-s** -z
groundwork ˈgraʊnd.wɜːk (US) -wɜːrk
group gruːp **-s** -s **-ing/s** -ɪŋ/z **-ed** -t
grouper ˈgruː.pəʳ (US) -pɚ **-s** -z
groupie ˈgruː.pi **-s** -z
grous|e (G) graʊs **-es** -ɪz **-ing** -ɪŋ **-ed** -t **-er/s** -əʳ/z (US) -ɚ/z
grout graʊt **-s** -s **-ing** -ɪŋ (US) ˈgraʊ.t̬ɪŋ **-ed** -ɪd (US) ˈgraʊ.t̬ɪd **-er/s** -əʳ/z (US) ˈgraʊ.t̬ɚ/z
grove (G) grəʊv (US) groʊv **-s** -z
grovel ˈgrɒv.əl (US) ˈgrɑː.vəl, ˈgrʌv.əl **-s** -z **-(l)ing** -ɪŋ **-(l)ed** -d **-(l)er/s** -əʳ/z (US) -ɚ/z
Grover ˈgrəʊ.vəʳ (US) ˈgroʊ.vɚ
grow grəʊ (US) groʊ **-s** -z **-ing** -ɪŋ **grew** gruː **grown** grəʊn (US) groʊn ˈ**grow** ˌ**bag**; ˈ**growing** ˌ**pains**
grow-bag ˈgrəʊ.bæg (US) ˈgroʊ- **-s** -z
grower ˈgrəʊ.əʳ (US) ˈgroʊ- **-s** -z
growl graʊl **-s** -z **-ing** -ɪŋ **-ed** -d **-er/s** -əʳ/z (US) -ɚ/z
grown (*from* **grow**) grəʊn (US) groʊn
grown-up (*n.*) ˈgrəʊn.ʌp (US) ˈgroʊn- **-s** -s
grown-up (*adj.*) ˌgrəʊnˈʌp (US) ˌgroʊnˈ- *stress shift:* ˌgrown-up ˈlanguage
growth grəʊθ (US) groʊθ **-s** -s
groyne grɔɪn **-s** -z
Grozny ˈgrɒz.ni (US) ˈgrɑːz-
grub grʌb **-s** -z **-bing** -ɪŋ **-bed** -d **-ber/s** -əʳ/z (US) -ɚ/z
grubb|y ˈgrʌb|.i **-ier** -i.əʳ (US) -i.ɚ **-iest** -i.ɪst, -i.əst **-iness** -ɪ.nəs, -ɪ.nɪs
grubstak|e ˈgrʌb.steɪk **-es** -s **-ing** -ɪŋ **-ed** -t
grudg|e grʌdʒ **-es** -ɪz **-ing/ly** -ɪŋ/li **-ed** -d
gruel grʊəl, ˈgruː.əl (US) ˈgruː.əl
gruel(l)ing ˈgrʊə.lɪŋ, ˈgruː.əl.ɪŋ (US) ˈgruː.lɪŋ, -əl.ɪŋ
Gruenther ˈgrʌn.θəʳ (US) -θɚ
gruesome ˈgruː.səm **-ly** -li **-ness** -nəs, -nɪs
gruff grʌf **-er** -əʳ (US) -ɚ **-est** -ɪst, -əst **-ly** -li **-ness** -nəs, -nɪs
grumbl|e ˈgrʌm.bl̩ **-es** -z **-ing** -ɪŋ, ˈ-blɪŋ **-ed** -d **-er/s** -əʳ/z, ˈ-bləʳ/z (US) ˈ-bl̩.ɚ/z, ˈ-blɚ/z
grummet ˈgrʌm.ɪt, -ət **-s** -s
grump grʌmp **-s** -s
grump|y ˈgrʌm.p|i **-ier** -i.əʳ (US) -i.ɚ **-iest** -i.ɪst, -i.əst **-ily** -ɪ.li, -əl.i **-iness** -ɪ.nəs, -ɪ.nɪs
Grundig® ˈgrʌn.dɪg, ˈgrʊn-
Grundtvig ˈgrʊnt.vɪg
Grundy ˈgrʌn.di
grunge grʌndʒ
grung|y ˈgrʌn.dʒ|i **-ier** -i.əʳ (US) -i.ɚ **-iest** -i.ɪst, -i.əst
grunt grʌnt **-s** -s **-ing** -ɪŋ (US) ˈgrʌn.t̬ɪŋ **-ed** -ɪd (US) ˈgrʌn.t̬ɪd **-er/s** -əʳ/z (US) ˈgrʌn.t̬ɚz
Gruyère ˈgruː.jeəʳ, -jəʳ; gruˈjeəʳ (US) gruˈjer
Gryll grɪl
gryphon ˈgrɪf.ən **-s** -z
G-seven ˌdʒiːˈsev.ən
g-spot ˈdʒiː.spɒt (US) -spɑːt
Gstaad kʃtɑːd; gəˈʃtɑːd (US) gəˈʃtɑːt, -ˈʃtɑːd
G-string ˈdʒiː.strɪŋ **-s** -z
GTI ˌdʒiː.tiːˈaɪ **-s** -z
guacamole ˌgwɑː.kəˈməʊ.li, ˌgwæk-, -leɪ (US) ˌgwɑːk.əˈmoʊ.li
Guadalajara ˌgwɑː.dəl.əˈhɑː.rə, ˌgwæd.əl- (US) ˌgwɑː.dəl.əˈhɑːr.ə
Guadalquivir ˌgwɑː.dəl.kwɪˈvɪəʳ, ˌgwæd.əl-, -kɪˈ- (US) ˌgwɑː.dəlˈkwɪ.vɚ, -kɪˈvɪr
Guadeloupe ˌgwɑː.dəˈluːp, -dəlˈuːp, ˈ---
Guam gwɑːm
Guangzhou ˌgwæŋˈʒəʊ (US) ˈgwɑːŋ.dʒoʊ
guano ˈgwɑː.nəʊ (US) -noʊ **-s** -z
Guarani, **Guaraní** ˌgwɑː.rəˈniː, ˈgwɑː.rən.i **-s** -z
guarantee ˌgær.ənˈtiː (US) ˌger-, ˌgær-, ˈ--- **-s** -z **-ing** -ɪŋ **-d** -d
guarantor ˌgær.ənˈtɔːʳ (US) ˈger.ən.tɔːr, ˈgær-, ˌ--ˈ- **-s** -z
guarant|y ˈgær.ən.t|i (US) ˈger.ən.t̬|i, ˈgær- **-ies** -iz
guard (G) gɑːd (US) gɑːrd **-s** -z **-ing** -ɪŋ **-ed/ly** -ɪd/li **-edness** -ɪd.nəs, -nɪs ˈ**guard's** ˌ**van**
guardian (G) ˈgɑː.di.ən (US) ˈgɑːr- **-s** -z **-ship** -ʃɪp
guardrail ˈgɑːd.reɪl (US) ˈgɑːrd- **-s** -z
guardroom ˈgɑːd.rʊm, -ruːm (US) ˈgɑːrd.ruːm, -rʊm **-s** -z
guards|man ˈgɑːdz|.mən, -mæn (US) ˈgɑːrdz- **-men** -mən, -men
Guarneri gwɑːˈneə.ri (US) gwɑːrˈner.i
Guatemal|a ˌgwɑː.təˈmɑː.l|ə, ˌgwæt.əˈ-, -ɪmˈɑː- (US) ˌgwɑː.t̬əˈ- **-an/s** -ən/z
guava ˈgwɑː.və **-s** -z
Guayaquil ˌgwaɪ.əˈkiːl, -ˈkɪl
Guayra ˈgwaɪ.rə
gubbins (G) ˈgʌb.ɪnz
gubernatorial ˌguː.bən.əˈtɔː.ri.əl, ˌgjuː- (US) ˌguː.bɚ.nəˈtɔːr.i-
Gucci® ˈguː.tʃi
gudgeon ˈgʌdʒ.ən **-s** -z
Gudrun ˈgʊd.ruːn, gʊˈdruːn
Gue gjuː
guelder-ros|e ˈgel.də.rəʊz, ˌ--ˈ- (US) ˈgel.dɚ.roʊz, ˌ--ˈ- **-es** -ɪz
Guelph, **Guelf** gwelf **-s** -s
Guenevere ˈgwɪn.ɪ.vɪəʳ, ˈgwen-, ˈ-ə- (US) -vɪr
guerdon ˈgɜː.dən (US) ˈgɜːr- **-s** -z
guerilla gəˈrɪl.ə, gjə-, gɜː- (US) gə- **-s** -z
Guernica ˈgɜː.nɪk.ə, ˈgwɜː-; gɜːˈniː.kə (US) ˈgwer.nɪk-
guernsey (G) ˈgɜːn.zi (US) ˈgɜːrn- **-s** -z
guerrilla gəˈrɪl.ə, gjə-, gɜː- (US) gə- **-s** -z
guess ges **-es** -ɪz **-ing** -ɪŋ **-ed** -t **-er/s** -əʳ/z (US) -ɚ/z **-able** -ə.bl̩ ˈ**guessing** ˌ**game**
guesstimate (*n.*) ˈges.tɪ.mət, -tə-, -mɪt, -meɪt **-s** -s
guessti|mate (*v.*) ˈges.tɪ|.meɪt, -tə- (US) -tə- **-mates** -meɪts **-mating** -meɪ.tɪŋ (US) -meɪ.t̬ɪŋ **-mated** -meɪ.tɪd (US) -meɪ.t̬ɪd
guesswork ˈges.wɜːk (US) -wɜːrk
guest (G) gest **-s** -s **-ing** -ɪŋ **-ed** -ɪd ˈ**guest** ˌ**night**; ˈ**guest** ˌ**room**
guesthou|se ˈgest.haʊ|s **-ses** -zɪz
Guevara gəˈvɑː.rə, gɪ-, gevˈɑː-
guff gʌf
guffaw gʌfˈɔː, gəˈfɔː (US) gʌfˈɑː, -ˈɔː, gəˈfɑː, -ˈfɔː **-s** -z **-ing** -ɪŋ **-ed** -d
Guggenheim ˈgʊg.ən.haɪm, ˈguː.gən-
Guggisberg ˈgʌg.ɪs.bɜːg (US) -bɜːrg
Guiana gaɪˈæn.ə, giˈɑː.nə (US) giˈæn.ə, gaɪ-, -ˈɑː.nə **-s** -z
Guianese ˌgaɪ.əˈniːz (US) ˌgiː.əˈniːz, ˌgaɪ-, -ˈniːs *stress shift:* ˌGuianese ˈpeople

guidance ˈgaɪ.dᵊnts
guid|e gaɪd **-es** -z **-ing** -ɪŋ **-ed** -ɪd **ˈguide ˌdog**
guidebook ˈgaɪd.bʊk **-s** -s
guideline ˈgaɪd.laɪn **-s** -z
guidepost ˈgaɪd.pəʊst US -poʊst **-s** -s
Guido ˈgwiː.dəʊ, ˈgiː- US -doʊ
guidon ˈgaɪ.dᵊn **-s** -z
guild gɪld **-s** -z
Guildenstern ˈgɪl.dᵊn.stɜːn US -stɜːrn
guilder ˈgɪl.dəʳ US -dɚ **-s** -z
Guildford ˈgɪl.fəd US -fɚd
guildhall (G) ˈgɪldˌhɔːl, ˌ-ˈ- US -hɔːl, -hɑːl **-s** -z
Guilding ˈgɪl.dɪŋ
guile gaɪl
guileful ˈgaɪl.fᵊl, -fʊl **-ly** -i **-ness** -nəs, -nɪs
guileless ˈgaɪl.ləs, -lɪs **-ly** -li **-ness** -nəs, -nɪs
Guilford ˈgɪl.fəd US -fɚd
guillemot ˈgɪl.ɪ.mɒt, ˈ-ə- US -ə.mɑːt **-s** -s
Guillim ˈgwɪl.ɪm
guillotin|e ˈgɪl.ə.tiːn, ˌ--ˈ- **-es** -z **-ing** -ɪŋ **-ed** -d
Note: Some people use /ˈgɪl.ə.tiːn/ for the noun and /ˌgɪl.əˈtiːn/ for the verb.
guilt gɪlt
guiltless ˈgɪlt.ləs, -lɪs **-ly** -li **-ness** -nəs, -nɪs
guilt|y ˈgɪl.t|i US -t̬|i **-ier** -i.əʳ US -i.ɚ **-iest** -i.ɪst, -i.əst **-ily** -ɪ.li, -ᵊl.i **-iness** -ɪ.nəs, -ɪ.nɪs
guimpe gɪmp, gæmp **-s** -s
guinea (G) ˈgɪn.i **-s** -z **ˈguinea ˌfowl** ; **ˈguinea ˌpig**
Guinea-Bissau ˌgɪn.i.bɪˈsaʊ
Guiness ˈgɪn.ɪs
Guinevere ˈgwɪn.ɪ.vɪəʳ, ˈgɪn-, ˈ-ə- US ˈgwɪn.ɪ.vɪr, ˈ-ə-
Guinness ˈgɪn.ɪs, -əs; gɪˈnes
Note: The beer (®) is called /ˈgɪn.ɪs/.
guipure gɪˈpjʊəʳ US -ˈpjʊr, -ˈpʊr
Guisborough ˈgɪz.bᵊr.ə US -bɚ.oʊ, -bɚ.ə
guis|e gaɪz **-es** -ɪz
Guise giːz, gwiːz
Guiseley ˈgaɪz.li
guitar gɪˈtɑːʳ US -ˈtɑːr **-s** -z
guitarist gɪˈtɑː.rɪst, gə- US -ˈtɑːr.ɪst **-s** -s
Gujarat ˌgʊdʒ.əˈrɑːt, ˌguː.dʒəˈ-
Gujarati ˌgʊdʒ.əˈrɑː.ti, ˌguː.dʒəˈ- US -t̬i
Gujranwala guːdʒˈrɑːn.wʌl.ə US -rənˈwɑː.lə
gulag (G) ˈguː.læg, -lɑːg US -lɑːg **-s** -z
Gulbenkian gʊlˈbeŋ.ki.ən
gulch gʌltʃ **-es** -ɪz
gulden ˈgʊl.dən, ˈguːl- **-s** -z
gules gjuːlz, dʒuːlz
gulf gʌlf **-s** -s **-y** -i **ˌGulf ˈStates** ; **ˈGulf ˌStream** ; **ˈGulf ˌWar** ; **ˌGulf ˈWar**
gull (G) gʌl **-s** -z **-ing** -ɪŋ **-ed** -d
gullet ˈgʌl.ɪt, -ət **-s** -s
gullibility ˌgʌl.ɪˈbɪl.ə.ti, -əˈ-, -ɪ.ti US -əˈbɪl.ə.t̬i
gullible ˈgʌl.ɪ.bl̩, ˈ-ə- US ˈ-ə-
Gulliver ˈgʌl.ɪ.vəʳ, ˈ-ə- US -ə.vɚ
gull|y (G) ˈgʌl|.i **-ies** -iz
gulp gʌlp **-s** -s **-ing** -ɪŋ **-ed** -t
gum gʌm **-s** -z **-ming** -ɪŋ **-med** -d **-mer/s** -əʳ/z US -ɚ/z
gumball ˈgʌm.bɔːl US -bɔːl, -bɑːl **-s** -z
Gumbley ˈgʌm.bli
gumbo (G) ˈgʌm.bəʊ US -boʊ **-s** -z
gumboil ˈgʌm.bɔɪl **-s** -z
gumboot ˈgʌm.buːt **-s** -s
gumdrop ˈgʌm.drɒp US -drɑːp **-s** -s
Gummidge ˈgʌm.ɪdʒ
gumm|y ˈgʌm|.i **-ier** -i.əʳ US -i.ɚ **-iest** -i.ɪst, -i.əst **-iness** -ɪ.nəs, -ɪ.nɪs
gumption ˈgʌm*p*.ʃᵊn
gumshield ˈgʌm.ʃiːld **-s** -z
gumshoe ˈgʌm.ʃuː **-s** -z **-ing** -ɪŋ **-d** -d
gumtree ˈgʌm.triː **-s** -z
gun gʌn **-s** -z **-ning** -ɪŋ **-ned** -d **-ner/s** -əʳ/z US -ɚ/z **ˈgun ˌcarriage** ; **ˈgun ˌdog** ; **ˈgun ˌroom** ; **ˌjump the ˈgun**
gunboat ˈgʌn.bəʊt, ˈgʌm- US ˈgʌn.boʊt **-s** -s
Gunby Hadath ˌgʌn.biˈhæd.əθ, ˌgʌm- US ˌgʌn-
guncatcher ˈgʌnˌkætʃ.əʳ, ˈgʌŋ- US ˈgʌnˌkætʃ.ɚ
guncotton ˈgʌn.kɒt.ᵊn, ˈgʌŋ- US ˈgʌn.kɑː.tᵊn
gunfight ˈgʌn.faɪt **-s** -s **-er/s** -əʳ/z US ɚ/z
gunfire ˈgʌn.faɪəʳ US -faɪɚ
Gunga Din ˌgʌŋ.gəˈdɪn
gung|e gʌndʒ **-y** -i
gung ho ˌgʌŋˈhəʊ US -ˈhoʊ
gunk gʌŋk **-y** -i
gun|man ˈgʌn|.mən, ˈgʌm-, -mæn US ˈgʌn- **-men** -mən, -men
gunmetal ˈgʌnˌmet.ᵊl, ˈgʌm- US ˈgʌnˌmet̬.ᵊl
Gunn gʌn
Gunnar ˈgʊn.ɑːʳ US -ɑːr
gunnel (G) ˈgʌn.ᵊl **-s** -z
Gunnell ˈgʌn.əl
Gunner ˈgʌn.əʳ US -ɚ
Gunnersbury ˈgʌn.əz.bᵊr.i US -ɚzˌber-, -bᵊr-
gunnery ˈgʌn.ᵊr.i
Gunning ˈgʌn.ɪŋ
Gunnison ˈgʌn.ɪ.sᵊn
gunny ˈgʌn.i
gunpoint ˈgʌn.pɔɪnt, ˈgʌm- US ˈgʌn-
gunpowder ˈgʌnˌpaʊ.dəʳ, ˈgʌm- US ˈgʌnˌpaʊ.dɚ **ˌGunpowder ˈPlot** US **ˈGunpowder ˌPlot**
gunrunn|er ˈgʌnˌrʌn|.əʳ US -ɚ **-ers** -əz US -ɚz **-ing** -ɪŋ
gunshot ˈgʌn.ʃɒt US -ʃɑːt **-s** -s
gunslinger ˈgʌn.slɪŋ.əʳ **-s** -z
gunsmith ˈgʌn.smɪθ **-s** -s
Gunter ˈgʌn.təʳ US -tɚ
Guntram ˈgʌn.trəm
gunwale ˈgʌn.ᵊl **-s** -z
gupp|y (G) ˈgʌp|.i **-ies** -iz
Gupta ˈgʊp.tə, ˈgʌp.tə
gurgl|e ˈgɜː.gl̩ US ˈgɜːr- **-es** -z **-ing** -ɪŋ, ˈ-glɪŋ **-ed** -d
Gurkha ˈgɜː.kə US ˈgɜːr- **-s** -z
Gurkhali ˌgɜːˈkɑː.li, ˌgʊə- US ˌgɜːr-
Gurley ˈgɜː.li US ˈgɜːr-
Gurnall ˈgɜː.nᵊl US ˈgɜːr-
gurnard (G) ˈgɜː.nəd US ˈgɜːr.nɚd **-s** -z
gurnet ˈgɜː.nɪt, -nət US ˈgɜːr- **-s** -s
Gurney ˈgɜː.ni US ˈgɜːr-
Gurton ˈgɜː.tᵊn US ˈgɜːr-
guru ˈgʊr.uː, ˈguː.ruː, ˈgʊə- US ˈguː.ruː **-s** -z
Gus gʌs
gush gʌʃ **-es** -ɪz **-ing/ly** -ɪŋ/li **-ed** -t **-er/s** -əʳ/z US -ɚ/z
Gushington ˈgʌʃ.ɪŋ.tən
gusset ˈgʌs.ɪt **-s** -s **-ing** -ɪŋ **-ed** -ɪd
Gussie, Gussy ˈgʌs.i
gust gʌst **-s** -s
Gustafson ˈgʊs.tæf.sᵊn US ˈgʌs.təf-, -tɑːf-
gustation gʌsˈteɪ.ʃᵊn
gustatory ˈgʌs.tə.tᵊr.i; gʌsˈteɪ- US ˈgʌs.tə.tɔːr-
Gustav, Gustave ˈgʊs.tɑːv, ˈgʌs- US ˈgʌs-
Gustavus gʊsˈtɑː.vəs, gʌs-, gəˈstɑː- US gʌsˈteɪ.vəs, -ˈtɑː-
gusto ˈgʌs.təʊ US -toʊ
gust|y ˈgʌs.t|i **-ier** -i.əʳ US -i.ɚ **-iest** -i.ɪst, -i.əst **-ily** -ɪ.li, -ᵊl.i **-iness** -ɪ.nəs, -ɪ.nɪs
gut gʌt **-s** -s **-ting** -ɪŋ US ˈgʌt̬.ɪŋ **-ted** -ɪd US ˈgʌt̬.ɪd
Gutenberg ˈguː.tᵊn.bɜːg US -bɜːrg
Guthrie ˈgʌθ.ri
Gutierrez guːˈtjer.ez
gutless ˈgʌt.ləs, -lɪs **-ly** -li **-ness** -nəs, -nɪs
guts|y ˈgʌt.s|i **-ier** -i.əʳ US -i.ɚ **-iest** -i.ɪst, -i.əst **-ily** -ɪ.li, -ᵊl.i **-iness** -ɪ.nəs, -ɪ.nɪs
gutt|a ˈgʌt|.ə US ˈgʌt̬|.ə **-ae** -iː
gutta-percha ˌgʌt.əˈpɜː.tʃə US ˌgʌt̬.əˈpɜːr-
gutt|er ˈgʌt|.əʳ US ˈgʌt̬|.ɚ **-ers** -əz US -ɚz **-ering** -ᵊr.ɪŋ **-ered** -əd US -ɚd **ˌgutter ˈpress** US **ˈgutter ˌpress**
guttersnipe ˈgʌt.ə.snaɪp US ˈgʌt̬.ɚ- **-s** -s
guttural ˈgʌt.ᵊr.ᵊl US ˈgʌt̬- **-s** -z **-ly** -i
guv gʌv
guvnor ˈgʌv.nəʳ US -nɚ

guy (G) gaɪ **-s** -z
Guyana gaɪˈæn.ə, giˈɑː.nə (US) giˈæn.ə, gaɪ-, -ˈɑː.nə
Guyanese ˌgaɪ.əˈniːz (US) ˌgiː.əˈniːz, ˌgaɪ-, -ˈniːs *stress shift:* ˌGuyanese ˈpeople
Guy Fawkes ˌgaɪˈfɔːks, ˈ-- (US) -ˈfɔːks, -ˈfɑːks *stress shift, see compound:* **ˈGuy Fawkes ˌnight**
Guysborough ˈgaɪz.bᵊr.ə (US) -bɚ.oʊ
guzzl|e ˈgʌz.l̩ **-es** -z **-ing** -ɪŋ, ˈ-lɪŋ **-ed** -d **-er/s** -əʳ/z, ˈ-ləʳ/z (US) ˈ-l̩.ɚ/z, ˈ-lɚ/z
Gwalia ˈgwɑː.li.ə
Gwalior ˈgwɑː.li.ɔːʳ (US) -ɔːr
Gwatkin ˈgwɒt.kɪn (US) ˈgwɑːt-
Gwaun-Cae-Gurwen ˌgwaɪn.kəˈgɜː.wən, ˌgwaɪŋ- (US) -ˈgɜːr-
Gwen gwen
Gwenda ˈgwen.də
Gwendol|en ˈgwen.də.l|ɪn, -dᵊl.|ɪn **-ine** -ɪn, -iːn **-yn** -ɪn
Gwent gwent
Gwersyllt ˌgweəˈsɪlt (US) ˌgwer-
Gwinnett gwɪˈnet
Gwladys ˈglæd.ɪs
Gwrych gʊˈriːk, -ˈriːx
Gwydion ˈgwɪd.i.ən
Gwydyr ˈgwɪd.ɪəʳ, -əʳ; ˈgwaɪ.dəʳ (US) ˈgwɪd.ɪr
Gwynedd ˈgwɪn.əð, -ɪð, -eð
Gwyneth ˈgwɪn.əθ, -ɪθ, -eθ
gwyniad ˈgwɪn.i.æd **-s** -z
Gwyn(ne) gwɪn
gyb|e dʒaɪb **-es** -z **-ing** -ɪŋ **-ed** -d
Gye dʒaɪ, gaɪ
Gyges ˈgaɪ.dʒiːz
Gyle gaɪl
Gyles gaɪlz
gym dʒɪm **-s** -z
gymkhana dʒɪmˈkɑː.nə **-s** -z
gymnas|ium dʒɪmˈneɪ.z|i.əm **-iums** -z **-ia** -i.ə
gymnast ˈdʒɪm.næst (US) -næst, -nəst **-s** -s
gymnastic dʒɪmˈnæs.tɪk **-s** -s **-al** -ᵊl **-ally** -ᵊl.i, -li
gymnosophist dʒɪmˈnɒs.ə.fɪst (US) -ˈnɑː.sə- **-s** -s
gymnosperm ˈdʒɪm.nəʊ.spɜːm, ˈgɪm- (US) -nə.spɜːrm **-s** -z
gymnospermous ˌdʒɪm.nəʊˈspɜː.məs, ˌgɪm- (US) -nəˈspɜːr-
Gympie ˈgɪm.pi
gymslip ˈdʒɪm.slɪp **-s** -s
gyn(a)ecological ˌgaɪ.nə.kəˈlɒdʒ.ɪ.kᵊl, -nɪ- (US) -ˈlɑː.dʒɪ- **-li** -i
gyn(a)ecolog|y ˌgaɪ.nəˈkɒl.ə.dʒ|i, -ɪˈ- (US) -ˈkɑː.lə- **-ist/s** -ɪst/s
gyneci|um ˌdʒaɪˈniː.si|əm, ˌgaɪ- **-a** -ə
Gyngell ˈgɪn.dʒᵊl
gynoeci|um ˌdʒaɪˈniː.si|.əm, ˌgaɪ- **-a** -ə
Györ djɜːʳ (US) djɜːr, djɔːr
gyp dʒɪp **-s** -s
Gyp *nickname:* dʒɪp *French novelist:* ʒiːp
gypsophila dʒɪpˈsɒf.ɪ.lə, -ᵊl.ə (US) -ˈsɑː.fɪ- **-s** -z
gypsum ˈdʒɪp.səm
gyps|y ˈdʒɪp.s|i **-ies** -iz
gyrate (*adj.*) ˈdʒaɪə.rət, -reɪt, -rɪt (US) ˈdʒaɪ.reɪt
gy|rate (*v.*) dʒaɪə|ˈreɪt (US) ˈdʒaɪ|.reɪt **-rates** -ˈreɪts (US) -reɪts **-rating** -ˈreɪ.tɪŋ (US) -reɪ.t̬ɪŋ **-rated** -ˈreɪ.tɪd (US) -reɪ.t̬ɪd
gyration dʒaɪəˈreɪ.ʃᵊn (US) dʒaɪ- **-s** -z
gyratory ˈdʒaɪə.rə.tᵊr.i; dʒaɪəˈreɪ- (US) ˈdʒaɪ.rə.tɔːr-
gyr|e dʒaɪəʳ (US) dʒaɪɚ **-es** -z **-ing** -ɪŋ **-ed** -d
gyrfalcon ˈdʒɜːˌfɔːl.kᵊn, ˈdʒɪə-, -ˌfɔː- (US) ˈdʒɜːr.fæl-, -fɔːl- **-s** -z
gyro- dʒaɪə.rəʊ- (US) dʒaɪ.roʊ-, -rə-
Note: Prefix. Normally takes either primary or secondary stress on the first syllable, e.g. **gyroscope** /ˈdʒaɪə.rə.skəʊp (US) ˈdʒaɪ.rə.skoʊp/, **gyroscopic** /ˌdʒaɪə.rəˈskɒp.ɪk (US) ˌdʒaɪ.rəˈskɑː.pɪk/.
gyro dʒaɪə.rəʊ (US) ˈdʒaɪ.roʊ, ˈgɪr.oʊ **-s** -z
gyrocompass ˈdʒaɪə.rəʊˌkʌm.pəs (US) ˈdʒaɪ.roʊ- **-es** -ɪz
gyromagnetic ˌdʒaɪə.rəʊ.mægˈnet.ɪk, -məgˈ- (US) ˌdʒaɪ.roʊ.mægˈnet̬.ɪk
gyron ˈdʒaɪə.rən, -rɒn (US) ˈdʒaɪ.rən, -rɑːn **-s** -z
gyroscope ˈdʒaɪə.rə.skəʊp (US) ˈdʒaɪ.rə.skoʊp **-s** -s
gyroscopic ˌdʒaɪə.rəˈskɒp.ɪk (US) ˌdʒaɪ.rəˈskɑː.pɪk **-ally** -ᵊl.i, -li
gyrostat ˈdʒaɪə.rəʊ.stæt (US) ˈdʒaɪ.rə-, -roʊ- **-s** -s
gyrostatic ˌdʒaɪə.rəʊˈstæt.ɪk (US) ˌdʒaɪ.rəˈstæt̬- **-s** -s
gyv|e dʒaɪv **-es** -z **-ing** -ɪŋ **-ed** -d

H

h (H) eɪtʃ **-'s** -ɪz
H_2O ˌeɪtʃ.tuː'əʊ (US) -'oʊ
ha *exclamation:* hɑː
ha (*abbrev. for* **hectare**) 'hek.teəʳ, -tɑːʳ, -təʳ (US) -ter
Haagen Dazs® ˌhɑː.gən'dɑːz (US) 'hɑː.gənˌdæs
Haakon 'hɔː.kɒn, 'hɑː-, -kᵊn (US) 'hɔː.kun, 'hɑː-, -kɑːn, -kən
Haarlem 'hɑː.ləm, -lem (US) 'hɑːr-
Habacuc, Habakkuk 'hæb.ə.kək, -kʌk; hə'bæk.ək
Habberton 'hæb.ə.tən (US) -ɚ.t̬ən
habeas corpus ˌheɪ.bi.əs'kɔː.pəs, -æs'- (US) -'kɔːr-
haberdasher 'hæb.ə.dæʃ.əʳ (US) -ɚ.dæʃ.ɚ **-s** -z
haberdashery 'hæb.ə.dæʃ.ᵊr.i, ˌhæb.ə'dæʃ- (US) 'hæb.ɚ.dæʃ.ɚ-
Habgood 'hæb.gʊd
habiliment hə'bɪl.ɪ.mənt, hæb'ɪl-, '-ə- (US) hə'bɪl.ə- **-s** -s
habili|tate hə'bɪl.ɪ|teɪt, hæb'ɪl-, '-ə- (US) hə'bɪl.ə- **-tates** -teɪts **-tating** -teɪ.tɪŋ (US) -teɪ.t̬ɪŋ **-tated** -teɪ.tɪd (US) -teɪ.t̬ɪd
habilitation həˌbɪl.ɪ'teɪ.ʃᵊn, hæbˌɪl-, -ə'- (US) həˌbɪl.ə'-
Habington 'hæb.ɪŋ.tən
habit 'hæb.ɪt **-s** -s
habitab|le 'hæb.ɪ.tə.b|l̩ (US) -t̬ə- **-ly** -li **-leness** -l̩.nəs, -nɪs
habitant *inhabitant:* 'hæb.ɪ.tᵊnt (US) -t̬ᵊnt **-s** -s
habitant *in Canada and Louisiana:* 'hæb.ɪ.tɔ̃ːŋ, 'æb-, -tɒŋ (US) 'hæb.ɪ.tɑːnt, -tənt; ˌæb.ɪ'tɑːn **-s** -z
habitat (H®) 'hæb.ɪ.tæt, '-ə- **-s** -s
habitation ˌhæb.ɪ'teɪ.ʃᵊn, -ə'- **-s** -z
habit-forming 'hæb.ɪtˌfɔː.mɪŋ (US) -ˌfɔːr-
habit|ual hə'bɪtʃ|.u.əl, hæb'ɪtʃ-, -'bɪt.j|u- (US) hə'bɪtʃ|.u.əl **-ually** -ʊ.li, -ə.li
habitu|ate hə'bɪtʃ.u|.eɪt, hæb'ɪtʃ-, -'bɪt.ju- (US) hə'bɪtʃ.u- **-ates** -eɪts **-ating** -eɪ.tɪŋ (US) -eɪ.t̬ɪŋ **-ated** -eɪ.tɪd (US) -eɪ.t̬ɪd
habitude 'hæb.ɪ.tjuːd, -tʃuːd (US) -tuːd, -tjuːd **-s** -z
habitué hə'bɪt.ju.eɪ, hæb'ɪt-, -'bɪtʃ.u.eɪ (US) həˌbɪtʃ.u'eɪ, hə'bɪtʃ.u.eɪ **-s** -z
Note: Also occasionally /ə'bɪt.ju.eɪ/ in British English, when not initial.
Habsburg 'hæps.bɜːg (US) -bɜːrg
hacek 'hɑː.tʃek, 'hætʃ.ek
hachure hæʃ'jʊəʳ, -'ʊəʳ (US) hæʃ'ʊr, -'jʊr, 'hæʃ.ʊr **-s** -z
hacienda ˌhæs.i'en.də (US) ˌhɑː.si'- **-s** -z
hack (H) hæk **-s** -s **-ing** -ɪŋ **-ed** -t
hackamore 'hæk.ə.mɔːʳ (US) -mɔːr **-s** -z
hackberr|y 'hækˌber|.i, -bᵊr|.i (US) -ˌber- **-ies** -iz
hacker (H) 'hæk.əʳ (US) -ɚ **-s** -z
Hackett 'hæk.ɪt
hackl|e 'hæk.l̩ **-es** -z **-ing** -ɪŋ, 'hæk.lɪŋ **-ed** -d
hackney (H) 'hæk.ni **-s** -z **-ed** -d
hacksaw 'hæk.sɔː (US) -sɑː, -sɔː **-s** -z
hackwork 'hæk.wɜːk (US) -wɜːrk
had (*from* **have**) *strong form:* hæd *weak forms:* həd, əd, d
Note: The strong form is used when **had** is used as a full verb rather than an auxiliary, e.g. 'We had some tea.' The auxiliary verb is a weak form word: the strong form /hæd/ is used contrastively, e.g. 'I don't know if she had or she hadn't', in final position, e.g. 'I'd read as much as he had' and quite frequently in initial position, e.g. 'Had anyone seen it before?'. It is also used for emphasis, e.g. 'It had to break down when it was raining'. Elsewhere, the weak form is usually /həd/ or /əd/. The form /d/ is usually used only after vowels.
Hadar 'heɪ.dɑːʳ (US) -dɑːr
hadarim (*plur. of* **heder**) ˌhæd.ɑː'riːm (US) ˌhɑː- *as if Hebrew:* ˌxæd- (US) ˌxɑː-
Hadden 'hæd.ᵊn
Haddington 'hæd.ɪŋ.tən
haddock (H) 'hæd.ək **-s** -s
Haddon 'hæd.ᵊn
had|e heɪd **-es** -z **-ing** -ɪŋ **-ed** -ɪd
Haden 'heɪ.dᵊn
Hades 'heɪ.diːz
Hadfield 'hæd.fiːld
hadj hædʒ, hɑːdʒ (US) hædʒ **-es** -ɪz
hadji 'hædʒ.i, 'hɑː.dʒi, -dʒiː (US) 'hædʒ.iː **-s** -z
Hadleigh, Hadley 'hæd.li
Hadlow 'hæd.ləʊ (US) -loʊ
hadn't 'hæd.ᵊnt
Hadrian 'heɪ.dri.ən ˌ**Hadrian's 'Wall**
hadst *strong form:* hædst *weak form:* hədst
Note: Weak form word, rarely used. See the note for **had**.
haecceity hek'siː.ə.ti, hiːk-, haɪk-, -ɪ.ti (US) hek'siː.ə.t̬i, hiːk-
haem hiːm
haematite 'hiː.mə.taɪt, 'hem.ə- (US) 'hiː.mə-
haematologic ˌhiː.mə.tə'lɒdʒ.ɪk (US) -t̬ə'lɑːdʒ- **-al** -ᵊl
haematolog|y ˌhiː.mə'tɒl.ə.dʒ|i (US) -'tɑː.lə- **-ist/s** -ɪst/s
haematoma ˌhiː.mə'təʊ.mə, ˌhem.ə'- (US) ˌhiː.mə'toʊ- **-s** -əz **-ta** -tə
haemoglobin ˌhiː.məʊ'gləʊ.bɪn, ˌhem.əʊ'- (US) 'hiː.mə.gloʊ-, -mə-
haemophili|a ˌhiː.mə'fɪl.i|.ə, ˌhem.ə'- (US) ˌhiː.moʊ'-, -mə'-, -'fiːl.j|ə **-ac/s** -æk/s
haemorrhag|e 'hem.ᵊr.ɪdʒ (US) -ɚ.ɪdʒ, '-rɪdʒ **-es** -ɪz **-ing** -ɪŋ **-ed** -d
haemorrhoid 'hem.ᵊr.ɔɪd (US) -ə.rɔɪd, '-rɔɪd **-s** -z
haemosta|sis ˌhiː.mə'steɪ|.sɪs, ˌhem.ə'- (US) ˌhiː.mə'- **-ses** -siːz
hafnium 'hæf.ni.əm
haft hɑːft (US) hæft **-s** -s
hag hæg **-s** -s
Hag® hɑːg
Hagan 'heɪ.gᵊn (US) 'heɪ-, 'hɑː-
Hagar *biblical name:* 'heɪ.gɑːʳ, -gəʳ (US) -gɑːr *modern personal name:* 'heɪ.gəʳ (US) -gɑːr, -gɚ
Hagarene 'hæg.ᵊr.iːn, 'heɪ.gᵊr-, ˌ--'- (US) 'hæg.ə.riːn, 'heɪ.gə- **-s** -z
Hagerstown 'heɪ.gəz.taʊn (US) -gɚz-
Haggada(h) hæg'ʌd.ə, -'ɒd- (US) hə'gɑː.dɑː, -də; ˌhɑː.gɑː'dɑː
Haggai 'hæg.eɪ.aɪ, -i.aɪ, 'hæg.aɪ; hæg'eɪ.aɪ (US) 'hæg.i.aɪ, 'hæg.aɪ
Haggar 'hæg.ɑːʳ, -əʳ (US) -ɑːr, -ɚ
haggard (H) 'hæg.əd (US) -ɚd **-ly** -li **-ness** -nəs, -nɪs
Hagger 'hæg.əʳ (US) -ɚ
Haggerston 'hæg.ə.stᵊn (US) '-ɚ-
haggis 'hæg.ɪs **-es** -ɪz
haggl|e 'hæg.l̩ **-es** -z **-ing** -ɪŋ, 'hæg.lɪŋ **-ed** -d **-er/s** -əʳ/z (US) -ɚ/z, 'hæg.ləʳ/z (US) -lɚ/z
hagiograph|y ˌhæg.i'ɒg.rə.f|i, ˌheɪ.dʒi'- (US) -'ɑː.grə- **-er/s** -əʳ/z (US) -ɚ/z
hagiolatry ˌhæg.i'ɒl.ə.tri, ˌheɪ.dʒi'- (US) -'ɑː.lə-
hagiolog|y ˌhæg.i'ɒl.ə.dʒ|i, ˌheɪ.dʒi'- (US) -'ɑː.lə- **-ist/s** -ɪst/s
hagioscope 'hæg.i.ə.skəʊp, 'heɪ.dʒi- (US) -skoʊp **-s** -s
Hagley 'hæg.li
Hagman 'hæg.mən
hagridden 'hægˌrɪd.ᵊn
Hague heɪg
ha-ha (*interj.*) hɑː'hɑː, '--
ha-ha *sunken fence:* 'hɑː.hɑː **-s** -z
Hahn hɑːn
hahnium 'hɑː.ni.əm
Haifa 'haɪ.fə
Haig heɪg
Haigh heɪg, heɪ
Haight-Ashbury ˌheɪt'æʃ.bᵊr.i (US) -ˌber-
haiku 'haɪ.kuː
hail heɪl **-s** -z **-ing** -ɪŋ **-ed** -d ˌ**Hail 'Mary**
Hailes heɪlz

Haile Selassie ˌhaɪ.li.səˈlæs.i, -sɪˈ- Ⓤ -ˈlæs.i, -ˈlɑː.si
Hailey ˈheɪ.li
Haileybury ˈheɪ.lɪ.bᵊr.i Ⓤ -ˌber-
hail-fellow-well-met ˌheɪlˌfel.əʊˌwelˈmet Ⓤ ˌ-oʊˌ-
Hailsham ˈheɪl.ʃəm
hailstone ˈheɪl.stəʊn Ⓤ -stoʊn **-s** -z
hailstorm ˈheɪl.stɔːm Ⓤ -stɔːrm **-s** -z
Hainan ˌhaɪˈnæn
Hainault ˈheɪ.nɔːt, -nɔːlt, -nɒlt Ⓤ -nɑːlt, -nɔːlt
Haines heɪnz
Haiphong ˌhaɪˈfɒŋ Ⓤ -ˈfɑːŋ
hair heəʳ Ⓤ her **-s** -z **ˈhair ˌgel** ; **ˈhair's ˌbreadth** ; **ˈhair ˌpiece** ; **ˌhair ˈshirt** ; **ˈhair ˌslide** ; **ˌhair ˈtrigger** ; **let one's ˈhair ˌdown** ; **ˌmake someone's ˈhair stand on ˌend**
hairball ˈheə.bɔːl Ⓤ ˈher-, -bɑːl **-s** -z
hairbreadth ˈheə.bretθ, -bredθ Ⓤ ˈher- **-s** -s
hairbrush ˈheə.brʌʃ Ⓤ ˈher- **-es** -ɪz
haircloth ˈheə.klɒθ Ⓤ ˈher.klɑːθ
haircut ˈheə.kʌt Ⓤ ˈher- **-s** -s
haircutt|er ˈheəˌkʌt|.əʳ Ⓤ ˈherˌkʌţ|.ɚ **-ers** -əz Ⓤ -ɚz **-ing** -ɪŋ
hairdo ˈheə.duː Ⓤ ˈher- **-s** -z
hairdress|er ˈheəˌdres|.əʳ Ⓤ ˈherˌdres|.ɚ **-ers** -ez Ⓤ -ɚz **-ing** -ɪŋ
hairdryer, hairdrier ˈheəˌdraɪ.əʳ Ⓤ ˈherˌdraɪ.ɚ **-s** -z
-haired -ˈheəd Ⓤ -herd
Note: Suffix. Compounds ending **-haired** normally carry primary stress on the suffix in British English, but there is a stress shift when such words are used attributively, e.g. ˌgoldenhaired ˈchild. In American English, compounds ending **-haired** are normally stressed on the first element, e.g. **goldenhaired** /Ⓤ ˈgoʊl.dᵊn.herd/.
hairgrass ˈheə.grɑːs Ⓤ ˈher.græs
hairgrip ˈheə.grɪp Ⓤ ˈher- **-s** -s
hairless ˈheə.ləs, -lɪs Ⓤ ˈher- **-ness** -nəs, -nɪs
hairline ˈheə.laɪn Ⓤ ˈher- **-s** -z
hairnet ˈheə.net Ⓤ ˈher- **-s** -s
hairpiec|e ˈheə.piːs Ⓤ ˈher- **-es** -ɪz
hairpin ˈheə.pɪn Ⓤ ˈher- **-s** -z **ˌhairpin ˈbend** ; **ˌhairpin ˈturn**
hair-raising ˈheəˌreɪ.zɪŋ Ⓤ ˈher-
hairsplitting ˈheəˌsplɪt.ɪŋ Ⓤ ˈherˌsplɪţ-
hairspray ˈheə.spreɪ Ⓤ ˈher- **-s** -z
hairspring ˈheə.sprɪŋ Ⓤ ˈher- **-s** -z
hairstyle ˈheə.staɪl Ⓤ ˈher- **-s** -z
hairstylist ˈheəˌstaɪ.lɪst Ⓤ ˈher- **-s** -s
hair|y ˈheə.r|i Ⓤ ˈher|.i **-ier** -i.əʳ Ⓤ -i.ɚ **-iest** -i.ɪst, -i.əst **-iness** -ɪ.nəs, -ɪ.nɪs
Haiti ˈheɪ.ti, ˈhaɪ-; haɪˈiː.ti, hɑː- Ⓤ ˈheɪ.ţi, -ti
Haitian ˈheɪ.ʃᵊn, -ʃi.ən, -ti-; haɪˈiː.ʃᵊn, hɑː-, -ʃi.ən Ⓤ ˈheɪ.ʃᵊn, -ti.ən **-s** -z
hajj hædʒ, hɑːdʒ Ⓤ hædʒ
hajji ˈhædʒ.i, ˈhɑː.dʒi, -dʒiː Ⓤ ˈhædʒ.iː **-s** -z
haka ˈhɑː.kə **-s** -z
hake heɪk **-s** -s
hakim *doctor:* hɑːˈkiːm, hə-, hækˈiːm Ⓤ hɑːˈkiːm **-s** -z *ruler:* ˈhɑː.kiːm, -ˈ- Ⓤ ˈhɑː.kiːm, -kɪm
Hakluyt ˈhæk.luːt
Hakodate ˌhæk.əʊˈdɑː.ti Ⓤ ˌhɑː.koʊˈdɑː.teɪ
Hal hæl
Halakah hælˈʌk.ə Ⓤ ˌhɑː.lɑːˈkɑː, -ˈxɑː; həˈlɑː.kə, -xə
halal hælˈæl; həˈlɑːl
halala, halalah həˈlæl.ə, hælˈæl.ə Ⓤ həˈlɑː.lə **-s** -z
halation həˈleɪ.ʃᵊn, hælˈeɪ- Ⓤ həˈleɪ- **-s** -z
halberd ˈhæl.bəd, ˈhɔːl-, -bɜːd Ⓤ ˈhæl.bɚd, ˈhɑːl- **-s** -z
halberdier ˌhæl.bəˈdɪəʳ Ⓤ -bɚˈdɪr **-s** -z
halcyon ˈhæl.si.ən **-s** -z
Halcyone hælˈsaɪə.ni
Haldane ˈhɔːl.deɪn, ˈhɒl- Ⓤ ˈhɔːl-, ˈhɑːl-
Haldon ˈhɔːl.dᵊn
hal|e (H) (*adj. v.*) heɪl **-er** -əʳ Ⓤ -ɚ **-est** -ɪst, -əst **-es** -z **-ing** -ɪŋ **-ed** -d
haler ˈhɑː.ləʳ Ⓤ -lɚ, -ler **-s** -z **-u** -uː
Hales heɪlz
Halesowen ˌheɪlzˈəʊ.ɪn, -ən Ⓤ -ˈoʊ-
Halesworth ˈheɪlz.wəθ, -wɜːθ Ⓤ -wɜːrθ, -wɚθ
Halex® ˈheɪ.leks
Haley ˈheɪ.li
hal|f hɑː|f Ⓤ hæ|f **-ves** -vz
Note: Compound words beginning with **half-** usually have secondary stress on this syllable and primary stress later in the compound word (e.g. **half-baked** has the stress pattern ˌ-ˈ-); however, the word is liable to undergo stress shift when a strongly stressed syllable follows (e.g. **half-baked plan** often has the pattern ˌ--ˈ-). Since there are many such words, notes about this stress shift for individual words are not given.
ˌhalf a ˈdozen ; **ˌhalf an ˈhour** ; **ˌhalf ˈcock** ; **ˌhalf ˈmeasures** ; **ˌhalf ˈnelson** ; **ˌhalf ˈpay** ; **ˌhalf ˈterm**
half-a-crown ˌhɑːf.əˈkraʊn Ⓤ ˌhæf-
halfback ˈhɑːf.bæk Ⓤ ˈhæf- **-s** -s
half-baked ˌhɑːfˈbeɪkt Ⓤ ˌhæf-
half-blood ˈhɑːf.blʌd Ⓤ ˈhæf-
half-board ˌhɑːfˈbɔːd Ⓤ ˌhæfˈbɔːrd
half-bred ˈhɑːf.bred Ⓤ ˈhæf-
half-breed ˈhɑːf.briːd Ⓤ ˈhæf- **-s** -z
half-brother ˈhɑːfˌbrʌð.əʳ Ⓤ ˈhæfˌbrʌð.ɚ **-s** -z
half-caste ˈhɑːf.kɑːst Ⓤ ˈhæf.kæst **-s** -s
half-crown ˌhɑːfˈkraʊn Ⓤ ˌhæf- **-s** -z
half-dozen ˌhɑːfˈdʌz.ᵊn Ⓤ ˌhæf- **-s** -z
half-hardy ˌhɑːfˈhɑː.di Ⓤ ˌhæfˈhɑːr-
half-hearted ˌhɑːfˈhɑː.tɪd Ⓤ ˌhæfˈhɑːr.ţɪd
half-hearted|ly ˌhɑːfˈhɑː.tɪd|.li Ⓤ ˌhæfˈhɑːr.ţɪd- **-ness** -nəs, -nɪs
half-holiday ˌhɑːfˈhɒl.ə.deɪ, ˈ-ɪ-, -di Ⓤ ˌhæfˈhɑː.lə.deɪ **-s** -z
half-hour ˌhɑːfˈaʊəʳ Ⓤ ˌhæfˈaʊr, -ˈaʊɚ **-s** -z
half-hourly ˌhɑːfˈaʊə.li Ⓤ ˌhæfˈaʊr-, -ˈaʊɚ-
half-length ˌhɑːfˈleŋθ, -ˈleŋkθ Ⓤ ˌhæf- **-s** -s
half-li|fe ˈhɑːf.laɪ|f Ⓤ ˈhæf- **-ves** -vz
half-mast ˌhɑːfˈmɑːst Ⓤ ˌhæfˈmæst
half-moon ˌhɑːfˈmuːn Ⓤ ˌhæf- **-s** -z
Halford ˈhæl.fəd, ˈhɔːl-, ˈhɒl- Ⓤ ˈhæl.fɚd, ˈhɔːl-, ˈhɑːl-
halfpence ˈheɪ.pᵊnts
halfpenn|y ˈheɪp.n|i, ˈheɪ.pᵊn|.i **-ies** -iz
Halfpenny ˈhɑːf.pen.i, -pə.ni Ⓤ ˈhæf-
halfpennyworth ˈheɪp.ni.wəθ, ˈheɪ.pᵊn.i-, -wɜːθ; ˌhɑːfˈpen.əθ Ⓤ ˈheɪ.pᵊn.i.wɜːrθ **-s** -s
half-pint ˌhɑːfˈpaɪnt Ⓤ ˌhæf- **-s** -s
half-price ˌhɑːfˈpraɪs Ⓤ ˌhæf-
half-sister ˈhɑːfˌsɪs.təʳ Ⓤ ˈhæfˌsɪs.tɚ **-s** -z
half-size ˌhɑːfˈsaɪz Ⓤ ˈhæf.saɪz
half-time ˌhɑːfˈtaɪm Ⓤ ˈhæf.taɪm
halftone ˌhɑːfˈtəʊn Ⓤ ˈhæf.toʊn **-s** -z
half-tru|th ˌhɑːfˈtruː|θ Ⓤ ˈhæf.truː|θ **-ths** -ðz
half-volley ˌhɑːfˈvɒl.i Ⓤ ˈhæfˌvɑː.li **-s** -z
halfway ˌhɑːfˈweɪ Ⓤ ˌhæf- **ˌhalfway ˈhouse** Ⓤ **ˈhalfway ˌhouse**
half-wit ˈhɑːf.wɪt Ⓤ ˈhæf- **-s** -s
half-witted ˌhɑːfˈwɪt.ɪd Ⓤ ˌhæfˈwɪţ-
half-year ˌhɑːfˈjɪəʳ Ⓤ ˌhæfˈjɪr **-s** -z **-ly** -li
Haliburton ˌhæl.ɪˈbɜː.tᵊn Ⓤ ˈhæl.ɪ.bɜːr-
halibut ˈhæl.ɪ.bət, -bʌt **-s** -s
Halicarnassus ˌhæl.ɪ.kɑːˈnæs.əs Ⓤ -kɑːrˈ-
halidom ˈhæl.ɪ.dəm
Halidon ˈhæl.ɪ.dᵊn
Halifax ˈhæl.ɪ.fæks
halitosis ˌhæl.ɪˈtəʊ.sɪs Ⓤ -ˈtoʊ-
Halkett ˈhɔːl.kɪt, ˈhæl.kɪt, ˈhæk.ɪt
hall (H) hɔːl Ⓤ hɔːl, hɑːl **-s** -z **ˌHall of ˈFame** ; **ˌhall of ˈresidence** ; **ˈresidence ˌhall**
hallal hælˈæl, həˈlɑːl

Hallam 'hæl.əm
Hallé 'hæl.eɪ, -i (US) 'hæl.eɪ
Halle 'hæl.ə (US) 'hɑː.lə
hallelujah (H) ˌhæl.ɪ'luː.jə, -ə'- **-s** -z
Haller 'hæl.əʳ (US) -ɚ
Hallett 'hæl.ɪt
Halley 'hæl.i, 'hɔː.li (US) 'hæl.i, 'heɪ.li
Note: Halley's Comet is usually referred to as /'hæl.iz/, with the popular variant /'heɪ.liz/ in the US. **ˌHalley's 'Comet**
halliard 'hæl.jəd, -i.əd (US) -jɚd **-s** -z
Halliday 'hæl.ɪ.deɪ, '-ə-
Halliwell 'hæl.ɪ.wel
hallmark 'hɔːl.mɑːk (US) -mɑːrk, 'hɑːl- **-s** -s **-ing** -ɪŋ **-ed** -t
hallo(a) hə'ləʊ, hæl'əʊ, hel'-, 'hʌl.əʊ (US) hə'loʊ
halloo hə'luː, hæl'uː (US) hə'luː **-s** -z **-ing** -ɪŋ **-ed** -d
hallow 'hæl.əʊ (US) -oʊ **-s** -z **-ing** -ɪŋ **-ed** -d
Halloween, Hallowe'en ˌhæl.əʊ'iːn (US) ˌhæl.oʊ'-, ˌhɑː.loʊ'-, -lə'wiːn
Hallowmas 'hæl.əʊ.mæs, -məs (US) -oʊ- **-es** -ɪz
Hallows 'hæl.əʊz (US) -oʊz
hallstand 'hɔːl.stænd (US) 'hɔːl-, 'hɑːl- **-s** -z
halluci|nate hə'luː.sɪ.neɪt, -'ljuː-, -sə- (US) -'luː- **-nates** -neɪts **-nating** -neɪ.tɪŋ (US) -neɪ.t̬ɪŋ **-nated** -neɪ.tɪd (US) -neɪ.t̬ɪd
hallucination həˌluː.sɪ'neɪ.ʃᵊn, -ˌljuː-, -sə'- (US) -ˌluː- **-s** -z
hallucinatory hə'luː.sɪ.nə.tᵊr.i, -'ljuː-, -sᵊn.ə-, -tri; həˌluː.sɪ'neɪ-, -ˌljuː-, -sᵊn'eɪ- (US) hə'luː.sɪ.nə.tɔːr.i
hallucinogen ˌhæl.uː'sɪn.ə.dʒᵊn, -dʒen; hə'luː.sɪ.nə-, -'ljuː-, -sᵊn.ə- (US) hə'luː.sɪ.nə.dʒen; ˌhæl.juː'sɪn.ə-, -jə'- **-s** -z
hallucinogenic həˌluː.sɪ.nəʊ'dʒen.ɪk, -ˌljuː-, -sᵊn.ə'- (US) -ˌluː.sɪ.noʊ'-
hallway 'hɔːl.weɪ (US) 'hɔːl-, 'hɑːl- **-s** -z
halma 'hæl.mə
halo 'heɪ.ləʊ (US) -loʊ **-(e)s** -z **-ing** -ɪŋ **-ed** -d
halogen 'hæl.ə.dʒen, 'heɪ.lə-, -dʒən (US) 'hæl.oʊ-, '-ə- **-s** -z
halogenous hə'lɒdʒ.ɪ.nəs, -ᵊn.əs (US) -'lɑː.dʒə.nəs
Halper 'hæl.pəʳ (US) -pɚ
Halpern 'hæl.pən (US) -pɚn
Hals hæls, hælz (US) hɑːls, hɑːlz
Halsbury 'hɔːlz.bᵊr.i, 'hɒlz- (US) 'hɔːlzˌber-, 'hɑːlz-
Halsey 'hɔːl.si, 'hæl-, -zi (US) 'hɔːl.zi, 'hɑːl-
Halstead 'hɔːl.sted, 'hɒl-, 'hæl-, -stɪd (US) 'hɔːl-, 'hɑːl-, 'hæl-
halt hɒlt, hɔːlt (US) hɔːlt, hɑːlt **-s** -s **-ing/ly** -ɪŋ/li (US) 'hɔːl.t̬ɪŋ/li, 'hɑːl- **-ed** -ɪd (US) 'hɔːl.t̬ɪd, 'hɑːl-
halter 'hɔːl.təʳ, 'hɒl- (US) 'hɔːl.t̬ɚ, 'hɑːl- **-s** -z
halterneck 'hɒl.tə.nek, 'hɔːl- (US) 'hɔːl.t̬ɚ-, 'hɑːl- **-s** -s
halva(h) 'hæl.və, -vɑː (US) hɑːl'vɑː; '--, -və
halv|e hɑːv (US) hæv **-es** -z **-ing** -ɪŋ **-ed** -d
Halvergate 'hæl.və.geɪt (US) -vɚ-
halves (*plur. of* **half**) hɑːvz (US) hævz
halyard 'hæl.jəd (US) -jɚd **-s** -z
ham (H) hæm **-s** -z **-ming** -ɪŋ **-med** -d
hamadryad ˌhæm.ə'draɪ.əd, -'draɪ.æd **-s** -z
Hamah 'hæm.ə (US) 'hɑː.mɑː
Haman *biblical name:* 'heɪ.mæn, -mən (US) -mən *modern surname:* 'heɪ.mən
Hamar 'heɪ.mɑːʳ (US) -mɑːr
hamartia ˌhɑː.mɑː'tiː.ə (US) -mɑːr'-
Hamas 'hæm.æs, -'-
Hamble 'hæm.bl̩
Hambleden 'hæm.bl̩.dən
Hambledon 'hæm.bl̩.dən
Hambleton 'hæm.bl̩.tən
Hamblin 'hæmb.lɪn
Hambro 'hæm.brəʊ, -brə (US) 'hæm.brə, -broʊ
Hamburg 'hæm.bɜːg (US) -bɜːrg, 'hɑːm.bʊrg
hamburger 'hæmˌbɜː.gəʳ (US) -ˌbɜːr.gɚ **-s** -z
Hamelin 'hæm.lɪn, -ᵊl.ɪn, -ɪ.lɪn
Hamer 'heɪ.məʳ (US) -mɚ
Hamerton 'hæm.ə.tᵊn (US) '-ɚ-
ham-fisted ˌhæm'fɪs.tɪd (US) '--- **-ly** -li **-ness** -nəs, -nɪs *stress shift, British only:* ˌham-fisted 'effort
ham-handed ˌhæm'hæn.dɪd (US) 'hæmˌhæn- **-ly** -li **-ness** -nəs, -nɪs *stress shift, British only:* ˌham-handed 'gesture
Hamhung ˌhɑːm'hʊŋ
Hamilcar hæm'ɪl.kɑːʳ, hə'mɪl-; 'hæm.ɪl-, -ᵊl- (US) -kɑːr
Hamill 'hæm.ᵊl
Hamilton 'hæm.ᵊl.tən, -ɪl-
Hamiltonian ˌhæm.ᵊl'təʊ.ni.ən, -ɪl'- (US) -'toʊ-
Hamish 'heɪ.mɪʃ
Hamite 'hæm.aɪt **-s** -s
Hamitic hæm'ɪt.ɪk, hə'mɪt- (US) hæm'ɪt̬-, hə'mɪt̬-
hamlet (H) 'hæm.lət, -lɪt **-s** -s
Hamley 'hæm.li
Hamlin, Hamlyn 'hæm.lɪn
hammam 'hæm.æm, -əm, 'hʌm.ʌm; hə'mɑːm (US) 'hæm.əm **-s** -z
Hammarskjöld 'hæm.ə.ʃəʊld (US) -ɚ.ʃoʊld, 'hɑː.mɚ-
hamm|er (H) 'hæm|.əʳ (US) -ɚ **-ers** -əz (US) -ɚz **-ering** -ᵊr.ɪŋ **-ered** -əd (US) -ɚd **ˌgo at it ˌhammer and 'tongs**
Hammerfest 'hæm.ə.fest (US) '-ɚ-
hammerhead 'hæm.ə.hed (US) '-ɚ- **-s** -z
hammerlock 'hæm.ə.lɒk (US) -ɚ.lɑːk **-s** -s
Hammersmith 'hæm.ə.smɪθ (US) '-ɚ-
Hammerstein 'hæm.ə.staɪn, -stiːn (US) '-ɚ-
Hammett 'hæm.ɪt
hammock 'hæm.ək **-s** -s
Ham(m)ond 'hæm.ənd
Hammurabi ˌhæm.ʊ'rɑː.bi (US) ˌhɑː.mʊ'-, ˌhæm.ə'-
hamm|y 'hæm|.i **-ier** -i.əʳ (US) -i.ɚ **-iest** -i.ɪst, -i.əst **-ily** -ɪ.li, -ᵊl.i **-iness** -ɪ.nəs, -ɪ.nɪs
Hampden 'hæm*p*.dən
hamp|er 'hæm.p|əʳ (US) -p|ɚ **-ers** -əz (US) -ɚz **-ering** -ᵊr.ɪŋ **-ered** -əd (US) -ɚd
Hampshire 'hæmp.ʃəʳ, -ˌʃɪəʳ (US) -ʃɚ, -ˌʃɪr
Hampstead 'hæm*p*.sted, -stɪd **ˌHampstead 'Heath**
Hampton 'hæm*p*.tən **ˌHampton 'Court**
Hamshaw 'hæm.ʃɔː (US) -ʃɑː, -ʃɔː
hamster 'hæm*p*.stəʳ (US) -stɚ **-s** -z
hamstring 'hæm.strɪŋ **-s** -z **-ing** -ɪŋ **-strung** -strʌŋ
hamza 'hæm.zə **-s** -z
Han hæn (US) hɑːn
Hanan 'hæn.ən
Hananiah ˌhæn.ə'na.ə
Hanbury 'hæn.bᵊr.i, 'hæm- (US) 'hænˌber-
Hancock 'hæn.kɒk, 'hæŋ- (US) 'hæn.kɑːk
Hancox 'hæn.kɒks, 'hæŋ- (US) 'hæn.kɑːks
hand (H) hænd **-s** -z **-ing** -ɪŋ **-ed** -ɪd **-er/s** -əʳ/z (US) -ɚ/z **-edness** -ɪd.nəs, -nɪs **'hand ˌcream ; 'hand greˌnade ; ˌknow somewhere like the ˌback of one's 'hand ; ˌbite the ˌhand that 'feeds ˌone ; ˌforce someone's 'hand ; ˌhand in 'glove (with) ; ˌwait on someone ˌhand and 'foot**
handbag 'hæn*d*.bæg, 'hæm- (US) 'hæn*d*- **-s** -z **-ging** -ɪŋ **-ged** -d
handball 'hæn*d*.bɔːl, 'hæm- (US) 'hæn*d*.bɔːl, -bɑːl **-s** -z
handbarrow 'hæn*d*ˌbær.əʊ, 'hæm- (US) 'hæn*d*ˌber.oʊ, -ˌbær- **-s** -z
handbasin 'hæn*d*ˌbeɪ.sᵊn, 'hæm-, -sɪn (US) 'hæn*d*- **-s** -z
handbell 'hæn*d*.bel, 'hæm- (US) 'hæn*d*- **-s** -z
handbill 'hæn*d*.bɪl, 'hæm- (US) 'hæn*d*- **-s** -z

handbook 'hænd.bʊk, 'hæm- Ⓤⓢ 'hænd- **-s** -s
handbrake 'hænd.breɪk, 'hæm- Ⓤⓢ 'hænd- **-s** -s
handcart 'hænd.kɑːt, 'hæŋ- Ⓤⓢ 'hænd.kɑːrt **-s** -s
Handcock 'hænd.kɒk Ⓤⓢ -kɑːk
handcuff 'hænd.kʌf **-s** -s **-ing** -ɪŋ **-ed** -t
Handel 'hæn.dəl
Handelian hæn'diː.li.ən Ⓤⓢ -'del.i-, -'diː.li-
handful 'hænd.fʊl **-s** -z
handgrip 'hænd.grɪp, 'hæŋ- Ⓤⓢ 'hænd- **-s** -s
handgun 'hænd.gʌn, 'hæŋ- Ⓤⓢ 'hænd- **-s** -z
hand-held ˌhænd'held Ⓤⓢ ˌ-'-, '-- *stress shift, British only:* ˌhand-held 'camera
handhold 'hænd.həʊld Ⓤⓢ -hoʊld **-s** -z
hand-holding 'hændˌhəʊl.ding Ⓤⓢ -ˌhoʊl-
handicap 'hæn.dɪ.kæp Ⓤⓢ '-dɪ-,'-di- **-s** -s **-ping** -ɪŋ **-ped** -t **-per/s** -ər/z Ⓤⓢ -ɚ/z
handicraft 'hæn.dɪ.krɑːft Ⓤⓢ -dɪ.kræft,'-di- **-s** -s
handiwork 'hæn.dɪ.wɜːk Ⓤⓢ -dɪ.wɜːrk,'-di-
handkerchie|f 'hæŋ.kə.tʃiː|f, -tʃɪ|f Ⓤⓢ -kɚ.tʃɪ|f, -tʃiː|f **-fs** -fs **-ves** -vz
handknit ˌhænd'nɪt **-s** -'nɪts **-ting** -'nɪt.ɪŋ Ⓤⓢ -'nɪt̬.ɪŋ **-ted** -'nɪt.ɪd Ⓤⓢ -'nɪt̬.ɪd *stress shift:* ˌhandknit 'sweater
handl|e 'hæn.dl̩ **-es** -z **-ing** -ɪŋ, -'hænd.lɪŋ **-ed** -d **-er/s** -ər/z Ⓤⓢ -ɚ/z, 'hænd.lər/z Ⓤⓢ -lɚ/z
handlebar 'hæn.dl̩.bɑːr Ⓤⓢ -bɑːr **-s** -z
Handley 'hænd.li
handmade ˌhænd'meɪd, ˌhæm- Ⓤⓢ ˌhænd- *stress shift:* ˌhandmade 'sweets
handmaid 'hænd.meɪd, 'hæm- Ⓤⓢ 'hænd- **-s** -z
handmaiden 'hændˌmeɪ.dən, 'hæm- Ⓤⓢ 'hænd- **-s** -z
hand-me-down 'hænd.mi.daʊn, 'hæm- Ⓤⓢ 'hænd- **-s** -z
handout 'hænd.aʊt **-s** -s
hand-pick ˌhænd'pɪk, ˌhæm- Ⓤⓢ ˌhænd- **-s** -s **-ing** -ɪŋ **-ed** -t
handrail 'hænd.reɪl **-s** -z
Hands hændz
handsaw 'hænd.sɔː Ⓤⓢ -sɑː, -sɔː **-s** -z
handsel 'hænd.səl **-s** -z **-ling** -ɪŋ **-led** -d
handset 'hænd.set **-s** -s
handsful (*plur. of* **handful**) 'hændz.fʊl
handshak|e 'hænd.ʃeɪk **-es** -s **-ing** -ɪŋ
hands-off ˌhændz'ɒf Ⓤⓢ -'ɑːf, -'ɔːf *stress shift:* ˌhands-off 'manner
handsom|e 'hænd.səm **-er** -ər Ⓤⓢ -ɚ **-est** -ɪst, -əst **-ely** -li **-eness** -nəs, -nɪs
hands-on ˌhændz'ɒn Ⓤⓢ -'ɑːn *stress shift:* ˌhands-on 'practice
handspring 'hænd.sprɪŋ **-s** -z
handstand 'hænd.stænd **-s** -z
hand-to-hand ˌhænd.tə'hænd *stress shift:* ˌhand-to-hand 'fighting
hand-to-mouth ˌhænd.tə'maʊθ *stress shift:* ˌhand-to-mouth 'living
handwork 'hænd.wɜːk Ⓤⓢ -wɜːrk
handwriting 'hændˌraɪ.tɪŋ Ⓤⓢ -t̬ɪŋ **-s** -z
handwritten ˌhænd'rɪt.ən *stress shift:* ˌhandwritten 'note
hand|y (H) 'hæn.d|i **-ier** -i.ər Ⓤⓢ -i.ɚ **-iest** -i.ɪst, -i.əst **-ily** -ɪ.li, -əl.i **-iness** -ɪ.nəs, -ɪ.nɪs
handy|man 'hæn.di|.mæn, -mən **-men** -men
hang hæŋ **-s** -z **-ing/s** -ɪŋ/z **-ed** -d **hung** hʌŋ
hangar 'hæŋ.gər, -ər Ⓤⓢ -ɚ **-s** -z
hangdog 'hæŋ.dɒg Ⓤⓢ -dɑːg, -dɔːg **-s** -z
hanger (H) 'hæŋ.ər Ⓤⓢ -ɚ **-s** -z
hanger-on ˌhæŋ.ər'ɒn Ⓤⓢ -ɚ'ɑːn **hangers-on** ˌhæŋ.əz'ɒn Ⓤⓢ -ɚz'-
hang-glid|er 'hæŋˌglaɪ.d|ər Ⓤⓢ -ɚ **-ers** -əz Ⓤⓢ -ɚz **-ing** -ɪŋ
hang|man 'hæŋ|.mən, -mæn **-men** -mən
hangnail 'hæŋ.neɪl **-s** -z
hangout 'hæŋ.aʊt **-s** -s
hangover 'hæŋ.əʊ.vər Ⓤⓢ -oʊ.vɚ **-s** -z
hang-up 'hæŋ.ʌp **-s** -s
hank (H) hæŋk **-s** -s
hank|er 'hæŋ.k|ər Ⓤⓢ -k|ɚ **-ers** -əz Ⓤⓢ -ɚz **-ering** -ər.ɪŋ **-ered** -əd Ⓤⓢ -ɚd
hankie 'hæŋ.ki **-s** -z
Hankow ˌhæn'kaʊ, ˌhæŋ- Ⓤⓢ ˌhæn-, ˌhɑːn-, -'koʊ
Hanks hæŋks
hank|y 'hæŋ.k|i **-ies** -iz
hanky-panky ˌhæŋ.ki'pæŋ.ki Ⓤⓢ ˌhæŋ.ki'pæŋ-, 'hæŋ.kiˌpæŋ-
Hanley 'hæn.li
Hanna(h) 'hæn.ə
Hannay 'hæn.eɪ
Hannen 'hæn.ən
Hannibal 'hæn.ɪ.bəl, '-ə-
Hannington 'hæn.ɪŋ.tən
Hanoi hæn'ɔɪ, hə'nɔɪ Ⓤⓢ hæn'ɔɪ, hɑː'nɔɪ, hə- *stress shift:* ˌHanoi 'Rocks
Hanover 'hæn.əʊ.vər Ⓤⓢ -oʊ.vɚ
Hanoverian ˌhæn.əʊ'vɪə.ri.ən, -'veə- Ⓤⓢ -ə'vɪr.i-, -'ver **-s** -z
Hansa 'hænt.sə, 'hæn.zə
Hansard 'hænt.sɑːd, -səd Ⓤⓢ -sɚd
Hansberry 'hænz.bər.i Ⓤⓢ -ˌber-
Hans|e hænts **-es** -ɪz
Hanseatic ˌhænt.si'æt.ɪk, ˌhæn.zi'- Ⓤⓢ -'æt̬-
hansel (H) 'hænt.səl **-s** -z **-(l)ing** -ɪŋ **-(l)ed** -d
Hänsel 'hænt.səl, 'hent-
Hansell 'hænt.səl
Hansen 'hænt.sen
hansom (H) 'hænt.səm **-s** -z **'hansom ˌcab**
Hanson 'hænt.sən
Hants. (*abbrev. for* **Hampshire**) hænts
Hanuk(k)ah 'hɑː.nə.kə, 'hɒn.ə-, 'hæn-, '-ʊ-, '-uː-, -kɑː Ⓤⓢ 'hɑː.nə.kə, 'xɑː-, -nuː-, -kɑː
Hanuman ˌhʌn.ʊ'mɑːn Ⓤⓢ ˌhɑː.nʊ'mɑːn, '---
Hanway 'hæn.weɪ
Hanwell 'hæn.wəl, -wel
hào haʊ
hap hæp **-s** -s **-ping** -ɪŋ **-ped** -t
haphazard ˌhæp'hæz.əd Ⓤⓢ -ɚd **-ly** -li **-ness** -nəs, -nɪs
hapless 'hæp.ləs, -lɪs **-ly** -li **-ness** -nəs, -nɪs
haploid 'hæp.lɔɪd **-s** -z
haplology hæp'lɒl.ə.dʒi Ⓤⓢ -'lɑː.lə-
haply 'hæp.li
hap'orth 'heɪ.pəθ Ⓤⓢ -pɚθ **-s** -s
happ|en 'hæp|.ən **-ens** -ənz **-ening/s** -ən.ɪŋ/z, 'hæp.nɪŋ/z **-ened** -ənd
happenstance 'hæp.ən.stænts, -əm-, -stɑːnts Ⓤⓢ -ən.stænts
Happisburgh 'heɪz.bər.ə
happ|y 'hæp|.i **-ier** -i.ər Ⓤⓢ -i.ɚ **-iest** -i.ɪst, -i.əst **-ily** -ɪ.li, -əl.i **-iness** -ɪ.nəs, -ɪ.nɪs **'happy ˌhour** ; **ˌhappy 'medium**
happy-go-lucky ˌhæp.i.gəʊ'lʌk.i Ⓤⓢ -goʊ'- *stress shift:* ˌhappy-go-lucky 'fellow
Hapsburg 'hæps.bɜːg Ⓤⓢ -bɜːrg
hara-kiri ˌhær.ə'kɪr.i, -'kɪə.ri Ⓤⓢ ˌhɑːr.ə'kɪr.i, ˌhær-
harangu|e hə'ræŋ **-es** -z **-ing** -ɪŋ **-ed** -d **-er/s** -ər/z Ⓤⓢ -ɚ/z
Harare hə'rɑː.ri, -reɪ Ⓤⓢ hɑː'rɑːr.i, hə-, -eɪ
harass 'hær.əs; hə'ræs Ⓤⓢ hə'ræs; 'her.əs, 'hær- **-es** -ɪz **-ing** -ɪŋ **-ed** -t **-er/s** -ər/z Ⓤⓢ -ɚ/z **-ment** -mənt
Harben 'hɑː.bən Ⓤⓢ 'hɑːr-
Harberton 'hɑː.bə.tən Ⓤⓢ 'hɑːr.bɚ.t̬ən
Harbin hɑː'biːn, -'bɪn Ⓤⓢ 'hɑːr.bɪn
harbinger 'hɑː.bɪn.dʒər Ⓤⓢ 'hɑːr.bɪn.dʒɚ **-s** -z
harb|or 'hɑː.b|ər Ⓤⓢ 'hɑːr.b|ɚ **-ors** -əz Ⓤⓢ -ɚz **-oring** -ər.ɪŋ **-ored** -əd Ⓤⓢ -ɚd **-orage** -ər.ɪdʒ **-orless** -ə.ləs, -lɪs Ⓤⓢ -ɚ.ləs, -lɪs **'harbor ˌmaster**
Harborough 'hɑː.bər.ə Ⓤⓢ 'hɑːr.bə.roʊ
harb|our 'hɑː.b|ər Ⓤⓢ 'hɑːr.b|ɚ **-ours** -əz Ⓤⓢ -ɚz **-ouring** -ər.ɪŋ

-oured -əd ⓊⓈ -ɚd -ourage -ər.ɪdʒ -ourless -ə.ləs, -lɪs ⓊⓈ -ɚ.ləs, -lɪs ˈharbour ˌmaster
Harcourt ˈhɑː.kət, -kɔːt ⓊⓈ ˈhɑːr.kɔːrt, -kɚt
hard (H) hɑːd ⓊⓈ hɑːrd **-er** -əʳ ⓊⓈ -ɚ **-est** -ɪst, -əst **-ness** -nəs, -nɪs **ˌhard ˈcopy, ˈhard ˌcopy ; ˌhard ˈcurrency ; ˌhard ˈdisk ; ˌno ˌhard ˈfeelings ; ˌhard ˈlabour ˌhard ˈluck ; ˌhard ˈluck ˌstory ; ˌhard of ˈhearing ; ˌhard ˈsell ; ˌhard ˈshoulder**
hardback ˈhɑːd.bæk ⓊⓈ ˈhɑːrd- **-s** -s
hardbake ˈhɑːd.beɪk ⓊⓈ ˈhɑːrd-
hard-baked ˌhɑːdˈbeɪkt ⓊⓈ ˌhɑːrd- *stress shift:* ˌhard-baked ˈcharacter
hard-bitten ˌhɑːdˈbɪt.ən ⓊⓈ ˌhɑːrd- *stress shift:* ˌhard-bitten ˈcynic
hardboard ˈhɑːd.bɔːd ⓊⓈ ˈhɑːrd.bɔːrd
hard-boiled ˌhɑːdˈbɔɪld ⓊⓈ ˌhɑːrd- *stress shift:* ˌhard-boiled ˈegg
Hardcastle ˈhɑːdˌkɑː.sl̩ ⓊⓈ ˈhɑːrdˌkæs-
hard-core *(adj.)* ˌhɑːdˈkɔːʳ, ˈ-- ⓊⓈ ˌhɑːrdˈkɔːr *stress shift:* ˌhard-core ˈporn
hard core *(n.) nucleus:* ˌhɑːdˈkɔː ⓊⓈ ˌhɑːrdˈkɔːr
hardcore *(n.) rubble:* ˈhɑːd.kɔːʳ ⓊⓈ ˈhɑːrd.kɔːr
hardcover ˈhɑːdˌkʌv.əʳ ⓊⓈ ˈhɑːrdˌkʌv.ɚ **-s** -z
hard-earned ˌhɑːdˈɜːnd ⓊⓈ ˌhɑːrdˈɜːrnd *stress shift:* ˌhard-earned ˈcash
harden (H) ˈhɑː.dən ⓊⓈ ˈhɑːr- **-s** -z **-ing** -ɪŋ, ˈhɑːd.nɪŋ ⓊⓈ ˈhɑːrd- **-ed** -d
hard-fought ˌhɑːdˈfɔːt ⓊⓈ ˌhɑːrdˈfɑːt, -ˈfɔːt *stress shift:* ˌhard-fought ˈbattle
hardheaded ˌhɑːdˈhed.ɪd ⓊⓈ ˌhɑːrd- **-ness** -nəs, -nɪs *stress shift:* ˌhardheaded ˈbargaining
hardhearted ˌhɑːdˈhɑː.tɪd ⓊⓈ ˌhɑːrdˈhɑːr.t̬ɪd **-ly** -li **-ness** -nəs, -nɪs *stress shift:* ˌhardhearted ˈvillain
hard-hit ˌhɑːdˈhɪt ⓊⓈ ˌhɑːrd- **-ting** -ɪŋ *stress shift:* ˌhard-hit ˈregion
Hardicanute ˈhɑː.dɪ.kəˌnjuːt, -də-; ˌhɑː.dɪ.kəˈnjuːt ⓊⓈ ˌhɑːr.dɪ.kəˈnuːt, -ˈnjuːt
Hardie ˈhɑː.di ⓊⓈ ˈhɑːr-
hardihood ˈhɑː.di.hʊd ⓊⓈ ˈhɑːr-
Harding ˈhɑː.dɪŋ ⓊⓈ ˈhɑːr-
Hardinge ˈhɑː.dɪŋ, -dɪndʒ ⓊⓈ ˈhɑːr-
hardline ˌhɑːdˈlaɪn ⓊⓈ ˌhɑːrd- *stress shift:* ˌhardline ˈleader
hardliner ˌhɑːdˈlaɪ.nəʳ, ˈ-ˌ-- ⓊⓈ ˌhɑːrdˈlaɪ.nɚ, ˈ-ˌ-- **-s** -z
hardly ˈhɑːd.li ⓊⓈ ˈhɑːrd-
hard-nosed ˌhɑːdˈnəʊzd ⓊⓈ ˌhɑːrdˈnoʊzd *stress shift:* ˌhard-nosed ˈpolicy
hard-on ˈhɑːd.ɒn ⓊⓈ ˈhɑːrd.ɑːn
hard-pressed ˌhɑːdˈprest ⓊⓈ ˌhɑːrd- *stress shift:* ˌhard-pressed ˈleader
hardship ˈhɑːd.ʃɪp ⓊⓈ ˈhɑːrd- **-s** -s
hard-up ˌhɑːdˈʌp ⓊⓈ ˌhɑːrd- *stress shift:* ˌhard-up ˈpensioner
hardware ˈhɑːd.weəʳ ⓊⓈ ˈhɑːrd.wer
hard-wearing ˌhɑːdˈweə.rɪŋ ⓊⓈ ˌhɑːrdˈwer.ɪŋ *stress shift:* ˌhard-wearing ˈcarpet
Hardwick(e) ˈhɑːd.wɪk ⓊⓈ ˈhɑːrd-
hardwood ˈhɑːd.wʊd ⓊⓈ ˈhɑːrd- **-s** -z
hard-working ˌhɑːdˈwɜː.kɪŋ ⓊⓈ ˌhɑːrdˈwɜːr- *stress shift:* ˌhard-working ˈsecretary
hard|y (H) ˈhɑː.d|i ⓊⓈ ˈhɑːr- **-ier** -i.əʳ ⓊⓈ -i.ɚ **-iest** -i.ɪst, -i.əst **-ily** -ɪ.li, -əl.i **-iness** -ɪ.nəs, -ɪ.nɪs
hare (H) heəʳ ⓊⓈ her **-s** -z
harebell ˈheə.bel ⓊⓈ ˈher- **-s** -z
harebrained ˈheə.breɪnd ⓊⓈ ˈher-
Harefield ˈheə.fiːld ⓊⓈ ˈher-
Hare Krishna ˌhær.iˈkrɪʃ.nə, ˌhɑː.riˈ- ⓊⓈ ˌhɑː.riˈ- **-s** -z
harelip ˌheəˈlɪp ⓊⓈ ˌher- **-s** -s **-ped** -t
harem ˈhɑː.riːm, ˈheə-, -rəm; həˈriːm, hɑː- ⓊⓈ ˈher.əm, ˈhær- **-s** -z
Harewood ˈhɑː.wʊd, ˈheə.wʊd ⓊⓈ ˈhɑːr-, ˈher-

Note: The Earl of Harewood pronounces /ˈhɑː.wʊd ⓊⓈ ˈhɑːr-/, and his house is called /ˌhɑː.wʊdˈhaʊs ⓊⓈ ˌhɑːr-/. The village in West Yorkshire is now generally pronounced /ˈheə.wʊd ⓊⓈ ˈher-/, though /ˈhɑː.wʊd ⓊⓈ ˈhɑːr-/ may sometimes be heard from old people there. Other people with the surname **Harewood** pronounce /ˈheə.wʊd ⓊⓈ ˈher-/.

Harford ˈhɑː.fəd ⓊⓈ ˈhɑːr.fɚd
Hargraves ˈhɑː.greɪvz ⓊⓈ ˈhɑːr-
Hargreaves ˈhɑː.griːvz, -greɪvz ⓊⓈ ˈhɑːr-
haricot ˈhær.ɪ.kəʊ ⓊⓈ ˈher.ɪ.koʊ, ˈhær- **-s** -z **ˌharicot ˈbean, ˈharicot ˌbean**
Haringey ˈhær.ɪŋ.geɪ ⓊⓈ ˈher-, ˈhær-
Harington ˈhær.ɪŋ.tən ⓊⓈ ˈher-, ˈhær-
Hariot ˈhær.i.ət ⓊⓈ ˈher-, ˈhær-, -ɑːt
hark hɑːk ⓊⓈ hɑːrk **-s** -s **-ing** -ɪŋ **-ed** -t
Harker ˈhɑː.kəʳ ⓊⓈ ˈhɑːr.kɚ
Harkin ˈhɑː.kɪn ⓊⓈ ˈhɑːr-
Harkinson ˈhɑː.kɪn*t*.sən ⓊⓈ ˈhɑːr-
Harkness ˈhɑːk.nəs, -nɪs ⓊⓈ ˈhɑːrk-
Harlech ˈhɑː.lek, -lex, -lək, -ləx ⓊⓈ ˈhɑːr.lek
Harleian hɑːˈliː.ən; ˈhɑː.li- ⓊⓈ ˈhɑːr.li-; hɑːrˈliː-
Harlem ˈhɑː.ləm, -lem ⓊⓈ ˈhɑːr- **ˌHarlem ˈGlobetrotters**
harlequin ˈhɑː.lɪ.kwɪn, -lə-, -kɪn ⓊⓈ ˈhɑːr.lɪ- **-s** -z
harlequinade ˌhɑː.lɪ.kwɪˈneɪd, -lə-, -kɪˈ- ⓊⓈ ˌhɑːr.lɪ- **-s** -z
Harlesden ˈhɑːlz.dən ⓊⓈ ˈhɑːrlz-
Harley ˈhɑː.li ⓊⓈ ˈhɑːr- **ˈHarley ˌStreet**
Harley Davidson® ˌhɑː.liˈdeɪ.vɪd.sən ⓊⓈ ˌhɑːr-
Harlock ˈhɑː.lɒk ⓊⓈ ˈhɑːr.lɑːk
harlot ˈhɑː.lət ⓊⓈ ˈhɑːr- **-s** -s **-ry** -ri
Harlow(e) ˈhɑː.ləʊ ⓊⓈ ˈhɑːr.loʊ
harm hɑːm ⓊⓈ hɑːrm **-s** -z **-ing** -ɪŋ **-ed** -d **ˌout of ˌharm's ˈway**
Harman ˈhɑː.mən ⓊⓈ ˈhɑːr-
Harmer ˈhɑː.məʳ ⓊⓈ ˈhɑːr.mɚ
harmful ˈhɑːm.fəl, -fʊl ⓊⓈ ˈhɑːrm- **-ly** -i **-ness** -nəs, -nɪs
harmless ˈhɑːm.ləs, -lɪs ⓊⓈ ˈhɑːrm- **-ly** -li **-ness** -nəs, -nɪs
Harmon ˈhɑː.mən ⓊⓈ ˈhɑːr-
Harmondsworth ˈhɑː.mən*d*z.wəθ, -wɜːθ ⓊⓈ ˈhɑːr.mən*d*z.wɜːrθ
Harmonia hɑːˈməʊ.ni.ə ⓊⓈ hɑːrˈmoʊ-
harmonic hɑːˈmɒn.ɪk ⓊⓈ hɑːrˈmɑː.nɪk **-s** -s **-al** -əl **-ally** -əl.i, -li
harmonica hɑːˈmɒn.ɪ.kə ⓊⓈ hɑːrˈmɑː.nɪ- **-s** -z
harmonious hɑːˈməʊ.ni.əs ⓊⓈ hɑːrˈmoʊ- **-ly** -li **-ness** -nəs, -nɪs
harmonist ˈhɑː.mə.nɪst ⓊⓈ ˈhɑːr- **-s** -s
harmonium hɑːˈməʊ.ni.əm ⓊⓈ hɑːrˈmoʊ- **-s** -z
harmonization, -isa- ˌhɑː.mə.naɪˈzeɪ.ʃən, -nɪˈ- ⓊⓈ ˌhɑːr.mə.nɪˈ- **-s** -z
harmoniz|e, -is|e ˈhɑː.mə.naɪz ⓊⓈ ˈhɑːr- **-es** -ɪz **-ing** -ɪŋ **-ed** -d **-er/s** -əʳ/z ⓊⓈ -ɚ/z
harmon|y ˈhɑː.mə.n|i ⓊⓈ ˈhɑːr- **-ies** -iz
Harmsworth ˈhɑːmz.wəθ, -wɜːθ ⓊⓈ ˈhɑːrmz.wɜːrθ
Harnack ˈhɑː.næk ⓊⓈ ˈhɑːr-
harness (H) ˈhɑː.nɪs, -nəs ⓊⓈ ˈhɑːr- **-es** -ɪz **-ing** -ɪŋ **-ed** -t **-er/s** -əʳ/z ⓊⓈ -ɚ/z
Harold ˈhær.əld ⓊⓈ ˈher-, ˈhær-
harp hɑːp ⓊⓈ hɑːrp **-s** -s **-ing** -ɪŋ **-ed** -t
Harpenden ˈhɑː.pən.dən ⓊⓈ ˈhɑːr-
Harper ˈhɑː.pəʳ ⓊⓈ ˈhɑːr.pɚ
Harpham ˈhɑː.pəm ⓊⓈ ˈhɑːr-
Harpic® ˈhɑː.pɪk ⓊⓈ ˈhɑːr-
harpist ˈhɑː.pɪst ⓊⓈ ˈhɑːr- **-s** -s
harpoon ˌhɑːˈpuːn ⓊⓈ ˌhɑːr- **-s** -z **-ing** -ɪŋ **-ed** -d **-er/s** -əʳ/z ⓊⓈ -ɚ/z
harpsichord ˈhɑːp.sɪ.kɔːd ⓊⓈ ˈhɑːrp.sɪ.kɔːrd **-s** -z
harp|y (H) ˈhɑː.p|i ⓊⓈ ˈhɑːr- **-ies** -iz
harquebus ˈhɑː.kwɪ.bəs, -kwə- ⓊⓈ ˈhɑːr.kwə- **-es** -ɪz
Harraden ˈhær.ə.dən, -den ⓊⓈ ˈher-, ˈhær-
Harrap ˈhær.əp ⓊⓈ ˈher-, ˈhær-
Harrell ˈhær.əl ⓊⓈ ˈher-, ˈhær-
harridan ˈhær.ɪ.dən, ˈ-ə- ⓊⓈ ˈher-, ˈhær- **-s** -z

Harrie ˈhær.i ⓊⓈ ˈher-, ˈhær-
harrier ˈhær.i.əʳ ⓊⓈ ˈher.i.ɚ, ˈhær- **-s** -z
Harries ˈhær.ɪs, -iz ⓊⓈ ˈher-, ˈhær-
Harriet ˈhær.i.ət ⓊⓈ ˈher-, ˈhær-
Harriman ˈhær.ɪ.mən ⓊⓈ ˈher-, ˈhær-
Harrington ˈhær.ɪŋ.tən ⓊⓈ ˈher-, ˈhær-
Harriot ˈhær.i.ət ⓊⓈ ˈher-, ˈhær-
Harris ˈhær.ɪs ⓊⓈ ˈher-, ˈhær- ˌ**Harris ˈTweed**
Harrisburg ˈhær.ɪs.bɜːg ⓊⓈ ˈher.ɪs.bɜːrg, ˈhær-
Harris(s)on ˈhær.ɪ.sᵊn ⓊⓈ ˈher-, ˈhær-
Harrod ˈhær.əd ⓊⓈ ˈher-, ˈhær- **-s** -z
Harrogate ˈhær.ə.gət, -geɪt, -gɪt ⓊⓈ ˈher-, ˈhær-
Harrop ˈhær.əp ⓊⓈ ˈher-, ˈhær-
Harrovian hærˈəʊ.vi.ən, həˈrəʊ- ⓊⓈ həˈroʊ- **-s** -z
harrow (H) ˈhær.əʊ ⓊⓈ ˈher.oʊ, ˈhær- **-s** -z **-ing/ly** -ɪŋ/li **-ed** -d
Harrowby ˈhær.əʊ.bi ⓊⓈ ˈher.oʊ-, ˈhær-
harr|y (H) ˈhær|.i ⓊⓈ ˈher-, ˈhær- **-ies** -iz **-ying** -i.ɪŋ **-ied** -id
harsh hɑːʃ ⓊⓈ hɑːrʃ **-er** -əʳ ⓊⓈ -ɚ **-est** -ɪst, -əst **-ly** -li **-ness** -nəs, -nɪs
hart (H) hɑːt ⓊⓈ hɑːrt **-s** -s
Harte hɑːt ⓊⓈ hɑːrt
hartebeest ˈhɑː.tɪ.biːst, -tə- ⓊⓈ ˈhɑːr.t̬ə-, -tə- **-s** -s
Hartford ˈhɑːt.fəd ⓊⓈ ˈhɑːrt.fɚd
Harthan ˈhɑː.ðᵊn, ˈhɑː.θᵊn ⓊⓈ ˈhɑːr-
Hartington ˈhɑː.tɪŋ.tən ⓊⓈ ˈhɑːr.t̬ɪŋ-
Hartland ˈhɑːt.lənd ⓊⓈ ˈhɑːrt-
Hartlepool ˈhɑːt.lɪ.puːl, -lə- ⓊⓈ ˈhɑːrt-
Hartley ˈhɑːt.li ⓊⓈ ˈhɑːrt-
Hartman ˈhɑːt.mən ⓊⓈ ˈhɑːrt-
Hartnell ˈhɑːt.nᵊl ⓊⓈ ˈhɑːrt-
Hartshill ˈhɑːts.hɪl ⓊⓈ ˈhɑːrts-
hartshorn (H) ˈhɑːts.hɔːn ⓊⓈ ˈhɑːrts.hɔːrn
hart's-tongue ˈhɑːts.tʌŋ ⓊⓈ ˈhɑːrts- **-s** -z
Hartz hɑːts ⓊⓈ hɑːrts
harum-scarum ˌheə.rəmˈskeə.rəm ⓊⓈ ˌher.əmˈsker.əm, ˌhær-, -ˈskær-
Harun-al-Rashid hærˌuːn.æl.ræʃˈiːd, hɑːˌruːn-; ˌhær.uːn.ælˈræʃ.iːd, ˌhɑː.ruːn-, -ɪd ⓊⓈ hɑːˌruːn.ɑːl.rɑːˈʃiːd
haruspex həˈrʌs.peks, hærˈʌs-; ˈhær.ə.speks **haruspices** həˈrʌs.pɪ.siːz, hærˈʌs-
Harvard ˈhɑː.vəd ⓊⓈ ˈhɑːr.vɚd
Harverson ˈhɑː.və.sᵊn ⓊⓈ ˈhɑːr.vɚ-
harvest ˈhɑː.vɪst, -əst ⓊⓈ ˈhɑːr- **-s** -s **-ing** -ɪŋ **-ed** -ɪd **-er/s** -əʳ/z ⓊⓈ -ɚ/z ˌ**harvest ˈfestival** ; ˈ**harvest ˌmite** ; ˌ**harvest ˈmoon** ; ˈ**harvest ˌmouse**
Harvey ˈhɑː.vi ⓊⓈ ˈhɑːr-
Harwich ˈhær.ɪtʃ, -ɪdʒ ⓊⓈ ˈhær-, ˈher-
Harwood ˈhɑː.wʊd ⓊⓈ ˈhɑːr-
Harworth ˈhɑː.wəθ ⓊⓈ ˈhɑːr.wɚθ
Haryana ˌhær.iˈɑː.nə ⓊⓈ ˌhɑːrˈjɑː-
Harz hɑːts ⓊⓈ hɑːrts
has (*from* **have**) *strong form:* hæz *weak forms:* həz, əz, z, s
Note: The strong form is used when **has** is used as a full verb rather than as an auxiliary, e.g. 'He has some money'. The auxiliary verb is a weak form word: the strong form /hæz/ is used contrastively, e.g. 'I don't know if she has or she hasn't', in final position, e.g. 'I've read as much as he has' and quite frequently in initial position, e.g. 'Has anyone seen my glasses?'. It is also used for emphasis, e.g. 'She **has** to have one'. Elsewhere, the weak form is usually /həz/ or /əz/. The shortest weak forms are /s/ and /z/: the form /s/ is used only after voiceless consonants other than /s, ʃ, tʃ/, while the form /z/ is used only after a vowel or a voiced consonant other than /z, ʒ, dʒ/. After /s, z, ʃ, ʒ, tʃ, dʒ/, the weak form is usually /əz/.
has-been ˈhæz.biːn, -bɪn ⓊⓈ -bɪn **-s** -z
Hasdrubal ˈhæz.drʊ.bᵊl, -druː-, -bæl
Haselden ˈhæz.ᵊl.dən, ˈheɪz-
hash hæʃ **-es** -ɪz **-ing** -ɪŋ **-ed** -t ˌ**hash ˈbrown**
hashish ˈhæʃ.ɪʃ, -iːʃ; hæsˈiːʃ
Hasid hæsˈiːd, hɑːˈsiːd **-im** -ɪm
Hasidic hæsˈɪd.ɪk, hɑːˈsɪd- ⓊⓈ hæsˈɪd-, həˈsɪd-, hɑː-
Hasidism hæsˈɪd.ɪ.zᵊm, ˈhæs- ⓊⓈ ˈhæs.ɪ.dɪ-, ˈhɑː.sɪ-; hæsˈɪd.ɪ-, həˈsɪd-, hɑː-
Haslam ˈhæz.ləm
Haslemere ˈheɪ.zl̩.mɪəʳ ⓊⓈ -mɪr
haslet ˈhæz.lət, ˈheɪz-, -lɪt ⓊⓈ ˈhæs-, ˈheɪz-
Haslett ˈhæz.lət, ˈheɪz.lət, -lɪt
Haslingden ˈhæz.lɪŋ.dən
Hasluck ˈhæz.lʌk, -lək
hasn't ˈhæz.ᵊnt
hasp hɑːsp, hæsp ⓊⓈ hæsp **-s** -s **-ing** -ɪŋ **-ed** -t
Hassall ˈhæs.ᵊl
Hassan *district in India:* ˈhʌs.ᵊn, ˈhæs- *Arabic name:* həˈsɑːn, hæsˈɑːn; ˈhæs.ᵊn, ˈhʌs- ⓊⓈ ˈhɑː.sɑːn; həˈsɑːn
Hasselhoff ˈhæs.ᵊl.hɒf ⓊⓈ -hɑːf
hassl|e ˈhæs.l̩ **-es** -z **-ing** -ɪŋ, ˈhæs.lɪŋ **-ed** -d
hassock (H) ˈhæs.ək **-s** -s
hast (H) (*from* **have**) *strong form:* hæst *weak forms:* həst, əst, st
Note: This weak form word is little used. See the note for **have** for guidance on when to use the strong form.
hast|e heɪst **-es** -s **-ing** -ɪŋ **-ed** -ɪd
hasten ˈheɪ.sᵊn **-s** -z **-ing** -ɪŋ, ˈheɪs.nɪŋ **-ed** -d
Hastie ˈheɪ.sti
Hastings ˈheɪ.stɪŋz
hast|y ˈheɪ.st|i **-ier** -i.əʳ ⓊⓈ -i.ɚ **-iest** -i.ɪst, -i.əst **-ily** -ɪ.li, -ᵊl.i **-iness** -ɪ.nəs, -ɪ.nɪs
hat hæt **-s** -s ˈ**hat ˌrack** ; ˈ**hat ˌstand** ; ˈ**hat ˌtrick** ; **at the ˌdrop of a ˈhat** ; ˌ**keep something ˌunder one's ˈhat** ; **I'll ˌeat my ˈhat**
hatband ˈhæt.bænd **-s** -z
hatbox ˈhæt.bɒks ⓊⓈ -bɑːks **-es** -ɪz
hatch (H) (*n. v.*) hætʃ **-es** -ɪz **-ing** -ɪŋ **-ed** -t
hatchback ˈhætʃ.bæk **-s** -s
hatcher|y ˈhætʃ.ᵊr|.i **-ies** -iz
hatchet ˈhætʃ.ɪt **-s** -s ˈ**hatchet ˌjob** ; ˌ**bury the ˈhatchet**
hatchling ˈhætʃ.lɪŋ **-s** -z
hatchment ˈhætʃ.mənt **-s** -s
hatchway (H) ˈhætʃ.weɪ **-s** -z
hat|e heɪt **-es** -s **-ing** -ɪŋ ⓊⓈ ˈheɪ.t̬ɪŋ **-ed** -ɪd ⓊⓈ ˈheɪ.t̬ɪd **-er/s** -əʳ/z ⓊⓈ ˈheɪ.t̬ɚ/z
hateful ˈheɪt.fᵊl, -fʊl **-ly** -i **-ness** -nəs, -nɪs
Hatfield ˈhæt.fiːld
hath (*from* **have**) *strong form:* hæθ *weak forms:* həθ, əθ
Note: This weak form word is little used. See the note for **has** for guidance on when to use the strong form.
hatha ˈhæθ.ə, ˈhʌθ-
Hathaway ˈhæθ.ə.weɪ
Hatherell ˈhæð.ᵊr.ᵊl
Hatherleigh ˈhæð.ə.li ⓊⓈ ˈ-ɚ-
Hatherley ˈhæð.ə.li ⓊⓈ ˈ-ɚ-
Hathersage ˈhæð.ə.seɪdʒ, -sɪdʒ, -sedʒ ⓊⓈ ˈ-ɚ-
Hatherton ˈhæð.ə.tᵊn ⓊⓈ -ɚ.t̬ᵊn
Hathorn(e) ˈhɔː.θɔːn ⓊⓈ ˈhɑː.θɔːrn, ˈhɔː-
Hathway ˈhæθ.weɪ
hatless ˈhæt.ləs, -lɪs, -les
hatpin ˈhæt.pɪn **-s** -z
hatred ˈheɪ.trɪd, -trəd
hatter ˈhæt.əʳ ⓊⓈ ˈhæt̬.ɚ **-s** -z **as ˌmad as a ˈhatter**
Hatteras ˈhæt.ᵊr.əs ⓊⓈ ˈhæt̬.ɚ-
Hattersley ˈhæt.əz.li ⓊⓈ ˈhæt̬.ɚz-
Hattie ˈhæt.i ⓊⓈ ˈhæt̬-
Hatton ˈhæt.ᵊn
hauberk ˈhɔː.bɜːk ⓊⓈ ˈhɑː.bɜːrk, ˈhɔː- **-s** -s
haugh hɔː ⓊⓈ hɑː, hɔː **-s** -z
Haughey ˈhɔː.hi, ˈhɒ- ⓊⓈ ˈhɑː-, ˈhɔː-
Haughton ˈhɔː.tᵊn ⓊⓈ ˈhɑː-, ˈhɔː-
haught|y ˈhɔː.t|i ⓊⓈ ˈhɑː.t̬|i, ˈhɔː- **-ier** -i.əʳ ⓊⓈ -i.ɚ **-iest** -i.ɪst, -i.əst **-ily** -ɪ.li, -ᵊl.i **-iness** -ɪ.nəs, -ɪ.nɪs
haul hɔːl ⓊⓈ hɑːl, hɔːl **-s** -z **-ing** -ɪŋ **-ed** -d **-er/s** -əʳ/z ⓊⓈ -ɚ/z
haulage ˈhɔː.lɪdʒ ⓊⓈ ˈhɑː-, ˈhɔː-

haulier ˈhɔː.li.əʳ (US) ˈhɑːl.jɚ, ˈhɔː- -s -z
haulm hɔːm (US) hɔːm, hɑːm -s -z
haunch hɔːntʃ (US) hɑːntʃ, hɔːntʃ -es -ɪz
haunt hɔːnt (US) hɑːnt, hɔːnt -s -s -ing/ly -ɪŋ/li (US) ˈhɑːn.t̬ɪŋ/li, ˈhɔːn- -ed -ɪd (US) ˈhɑːn.t̬ɪd, ˈhɔːn-
Hausa ˈhaʊ.sə, -zə -s -z
hausfrau ˈhaʊs.fraʊ -s -z -en -ᵊn
Haussmann ˈhaʊs.mæn (US) -mæn, -mən
hautbois (*sing.*) ˈəʊ.bɔɪ, ˈhəʊ-, ˈhɔːt- (US) ˈhoʊ-, ˈoʊ- (*plur.*) ˈəʊ.bɔɪz, ˈhəʊ-, ˈhɔːt- (US) ˈhoʊ-, ˈoʊ-
hautboy ˈəʊ.bɔɪ, ˈhəʊ-, ˈhɔːt- (US) ˈhoʊ-, ˈoʊ- -s -z
haute couture ˌəʊt.kuˈtjʊəʳ, -kuːˈ-, -ˈtʊəʳ (US) ˌoʊt.kuːˈtʊr
haute cuisine ˌəʊt.kwɪˈziːn, -kwəˈ- (US) ˌoʊt-
hauteur əʊˈtɜːʳ, ˈ-- (US) hoʊˈtɜːr, oʊˈ-
Havana həˈvæn.ə, hævˈæn-, -ˈvɑː.nə (US) -ˈvæn.ə -s -z
Havant ˈhæv.ᵊnt
Havard ˈhæv.ɑːd, -əd (US) -ɑːrd, -ɚd
Havarti həˈvɑː.ti (US) -ˈvɑːr-
have *one who has:* hæv -s -z
Note: This word usually occurs only in conjuction with **have-not**, in expressions such as 'There's a conflict between the haves and have-nots'.
have (*v.*) *strong form:* hæv *weak forms:* həv, əv, v **hast** *strong form:* hæst *weak forms:* həst, əst, st **has** *strong form:* hæz *weak forms:* həz, əz, z, s **having** ˈhæv.ɪŋ **had** *strong form:* hæd *weak forms:* həd, əd, d
Note: When **have** occurs as a full verb, e.g. 'to have and to hold', the strong form is used. As an auxiliary verb, it is a weak form word: the strong form is used contrastively, e.g. 'I don't know if you have or haven't', for emphasis, e.g. 'You **have** to see it', and also in final position, e.g. 'I've got as much as you have'. It is also quite often used in initial position, e.g. 'Have you seen my book?'. Elsewhere the weak form is commonly used; the form /v/ is only found after vowels. For **hast**, **has**, **had** and **hadst**, see notes provided for those word entries.
Havel ˈhɑː.vᵊl (US) -fᵊl
Havell ˈhæv.ᵊl
Havelo(c)k ˈhæv.lɒk, -lək (US) -lɑːk, -lək
haven ˈheɪ.vᵊn -s -z
have-not ˈhæv.nɒt, ˌ-ˈ- (US) ˈhæv.nɑːt, ˌ-ˈ- -s -s
haven't ˈhæv.ᵊnt
hav|er ˈheɪ.v|əʳ (US) -v|ɚ -ers -əz (US) -ɚz -ering -ᵊr.ɪŋ -ered -əd (US) -ɚd
Haverford ˈhæv.ə.fəd (US) -ɚ.fɚd
Haverfordwest ˌhæv.ə.fədˈwest, ˌhɑː.fədˈwest (US) ˌhæv.ɚ.fɚdˈ-, ˌhɑː.fɚdˈ-
Havergal ˈhæv.ə.gᵊl (US) ˈ-ɚ-
Haverhill ˈheɪ.vᵊr.ɪl, -ᵊl; ˈheɪ.və.hɪl (US) -vɚ-
Havering ˈheɪ.vᵊr.ɪŋ
Havers ˈheɪ.vəz (US) -vɚz
haversack ˈhæv.ə.sæk (US) ˈ-ɚ- -s -s
haversian canal (H) həˌvɜː.ʃᵊn.kəˈnæl, hævˌɜː-, -ʒᵊn- (US) həˌvɜːr.ʒᵊn
Haverstock ˈhæv.ə.stɒk (US) -ɚ.stɑːk
Havilah ˈhæv.ɪ.lə (US) -lə, -lɑː
Haviland ˈhæv.ɪ.lænd, ˈ-ə-, -lənd
Havisham ˈhæv.ɪ.ʃᵊm
havoc ˈhæv.ək
Havre *place in France:* ˈhɑː.vrə, -vəʳ (US) -vrə, -vɚ *place in Maryland:* ˈhɑː.vəʳ (US) -vɚ, ˈhæv.ɚ *place in Montana:* ˈhæv.əʳ (US) -ɚ
Havre de Grace ˌhɑː.və.dəˈgrɑːs, ˌhæv.ə-, -ˈgræs, -ˈgreɪs (US) ˌhɑː.vɚ-, ˌhæv.ɚ-
haw hɔː (US) hɑː, hɔː -s -z -ing -ɪŋ -ed -d
Hawaii həˈwaɪ.iː, hɑː-, -i (US) həˈwɑː-, -ˈwaɪ-
Hawaiian həˈwaɪ.ən, hɑː-, ˈ-i.ən (US) həˈwɑː.jən -s -z
Haward ˈheɪ.wəd, ˈhɔː.əd, hɑːd, hɔːd (US) ˈheɪ.wɚd, ˈhɔː.ɚd, hɑːrd, hɔːrd
Hawarden *in Clwyd:* ˈhɑː.dᵊn, ˈhɔː- (US) ˈhɑːr-, ˈhɔːr *Viscount:* ˈheɪˌwɔː.dᵊn (US) -ˌwɔːr- *town in US:* ˈheɪˌwɑː.dᵊn (US) -ˌwɑːr-
Haweis ˈhɔː.ɪs (US) ˈhɔː.ɪs, hɔɪs
Hawes hɔːz (US) hɑːz, hɔːz
hawfinch ˈhɔː.fɪntʃ (US) ˈhɑː-, ˈhɔː- -es -ɪz
haw-haw ˈhɔːˌhɔː, ˌ-ˈ- (US) ˈhɑː.hɑː, ˈhɔː.hɔː, ˌ-ˈ- -s -z
Hawick ˈhɔː.ɪk, hɔɪk (US) ˈhɑː.ɪk, ˈhɔː-, hɔɪk
hawk hɔːk (US) hɑːk, hɔːk -s -s -ing -ɪŋ -ed -t -er/s -əʳ/z (US) -ɚ/z
Hawke hɔːk (US) hɑːk, hɔːk -s -s
Hawker-Siddeley® ˌhɔː.kəˈsɪd.ᵊl.i, ˈ-li (US) ˌhɑː.kɚˈ-, ˌhɔː-
Hawkeye ˈhɔːk.aɪ (US) ˈhɑːk-, ˈhɔːk-
hawk-eyed ˈhɔːk.aɪd (US) ˈhɑːk-, ˈhɔːk-
Hawking ˈhɔː.kɪŋ (US) ˈhɑː-, ˈhɔː-
Hawkins ˈhɔː.kɪnz (US) ˈhɑː-, ˈhɔː-
hawkish ˈhɔː.kɪʃ (US) ˈhɑː-, ˈhɔː- -ly -li -ness -nes, -nɪs
hawkmoth ˈhɔːk.mɒθ (US) ˈhɑːk.mɑːθ, ˈhɔːk- -s -s
Hawks hɔːks (US) hɑːks, hɔːks
hawksbill ˈhɔːks.bɪl (US) ˈhɑːks-, ˈhɔːks- -s -z
Hawkshaw ˈhɔːk.ʃɔː (US) ˈhɑːk.ʃɑː, ˈhɔːk-, -ʃɔː
Hawksley ˈhɔːk.sli (US) ˈhɑːks-, ˈhɔːks-
Hawksmoor ˈhɔːks.mɔːʳ (US) ˈhɑːks.mɔːr, ˈhɔːks-, -mʊr
hawkweed ˈhɔːk.wiːd (US) ˈhɑːk-, ˈhɔːk-
Hawkwood ˈhɔːk.wʊd (US) ˈhɑːk-, ˈhɔːk-
Hawley ˈhɔː.li (US) ˈhɑː-, ˈhɔː-
Hawn hɔːn (US) hɑːn, hɔːn
Haworth *place in Yorkshire:* ˈhaʊ.əθ, ˈhɔː.əθ (US) ˈhɔː.wɚθ *surname:* ˈhaʊ.əθ (US) ˈheɪ.wɚθ, ˈhaʊ.ɚθ, ˈhoʊ-; hɑːrθ *place in New Jersey:* ˈhɔː.wəθ (US) -wɚθ
haws|e hɔːz (US) hɑːz, hɔːz -es -ɪz
hawser ˈhɔː.zəʳ (US) ˈhɑː.zɚ, ˈhɔː- -s -z
hawthorn ˈhɔː.θɔːn (US) ˈhɑː.θɔːrn, ˈhɔː- -s -z
Hawthornden ˈhɔː.θɔːn.dən (US) ˈhɑː.θɔːrn-, ˈhɔː-
Hawthorne ˈhɔː.θɔːn (US) ˈhɑː.θɔːrn, ˈhɔː-
Haxby ˈhæks.bi
hay (H) heɪ ˈ**hay** ˌ**fever**
haybox ˈheɪ.bɒks (US) -bɑːks -es -ɪz
haycart ˈheɪ.kɑːt (US) -kɑːrt -s -s
haycock (H) ˈheɪ.kɒk (US) -kɑːk -s -s
Hayden ˈheɪ.dᵊn
Haydn *English surname:* ˈheɪ.dᵊn *Austrian composer:* ˈhaɪ.dᵊn
Haydock ˈheɪ.dɒk (US) -dɑːk
Haydon ˈheɪ.dᵊn
Hayes heɪz
Hayesford ˈheɪz.fəd (US) -fɚd
Hayhurst ˈhaɪ.əst, ˈheɪ.hɜːst (US) ˈhaɪ.ɚst, ˈheɪ.hɜːrst
Hayle heɪl
Hayles heɪlz
Hayley ˈheɪ.li
Hayling Island ˌheɪ.lɪŋˈaɪ.lənd, ˈheɪ.lɪŋˌaɪ-
hayloft ˈheɪ.lɒft (US) -lɑːft -s -s
haymak|er ˈheɪˌmeɪ.k|əʳ (US) -k|ɚ -ers -əz (US) -ɚz -ing -ɪŋ
Haymarket ˈheɪˌmɑː.kɪt (US) -ˌmɑːr-
Haynes heɪnz
hayrick ˈheɪ.rɪk -s -s
Hays heɪz
hayseed ˈheɪ.siːd -s -z
haystack ˈheɪ.stæk -s -s
Hayter, Haytor ˈheɪ.təʳ (US) -t̬ɚ
hayward (H) ˈheɪ.wəd (US) -wɚd -s -z
haywire ˈheɪ.waɪəʳ (US) -waɪr
Haywood ˈheɪ.wʊd
hazard (H) ˈhæz.əd (US) -ɚd -s -z -ing -ɪŋ -ed -ɪd
hazardous ˈhæz.ə.dəs (US) ˈ-ɚ- -ly -li -ness -nəs, -nɪs
haz|e heɪz -es -ɪz -ing -ɪŋ -ed -d
hazel ˈheɪ.zᵊl -s -z

Hazelhurst ˈheɪ.zəl.hɜːst (US) -hɜːrst
hazelnut ˈheɪ.zəl.nʌt -s -s
Hazen ˈheɪ.zən
Hazledean ˈheɪ.zl̩.diːn
Hazlemere ˈheɪ.zl̩.mɪəʳ (US) -mɪr
Hazlett ˈheɪz.lɪt, ˈhæz-, -lət
Hazlitt ˈheɪz.lɪt, ˈhæz-
Note: William Hazlitt, the essayist, called himself /ˈheɪz.lɪt/, and the present members of his family pronounce the name thus. He is, however, commonly referred to as /ˈhæz.lɪt/. In the **Hazlitt Gallery** in London the pronunciation is /ˈhæz.lɪt/.
Hazor ˈheɪ.zɔːʳ (US) -zɔːr
haz|y ˈheɪ.z|i **-ier** -i.əʳ (US) -i.ɚ **-iest** -i.ɪst, -i.əst **-ily** -ɪ.li, -əl.i **-iness** -ɪ.nəs, -ɪ.nɪs
Hazzard ˈhæz.əd (US) -ɚd
H-Block ˈeɪtʃ.blɒk (US) -blɑːk
H-bomb ˈeɪtʃ.bɒm (US) -bɑːm **-s** -z
HDTV ˌeɪtʃ.diː.tiːˈviː
he *strong form:* hiː *weak forms:* hi, i
Note: Weak form word. The strong form /hiː/ is usually used contrastively, e.g. 'I'm not interested in what **he** says, it's **her** I'm listening to' or for emphasis, e.g. '**He**'s the one'. The weak form is /hi/ in careful speech, e.g. 'Does he live here?' /ˌdʌz.hiˌlɪvˈhɪə (US) -ˈhɪr/; in rapid speech it may be pronounced /i/ when following a consonant, e.g. 'What does he want?' /ˌwɒt.dəz.iˈwɒnt (US) ˌwɑːt.dəz.iˈwɑːnt/.
head (H) hed **-s** -z **-ing** -ɪŋ **-ed** -ɪd **ˌhead of ˈstate** ; **ˌhead ˈstart** ; **ˌhead ˈteacher** ; **ˌbite someone's ˈhead off** ; **have ˌeyes in the ˌback of one's ˈhead** ; **ˌbang one's ˌhead against a ˌbrick ˈwall** ; **ˌbury one's ˌhead in the ˈsand** ; **ˌhave one's ˈhead screwed on** ; **ˌhead over ˈheels** ; **keep one's ˌhead above ˈwater** ; **make ˌhead or ˈtail of** ; **ˌhold one's ˌhead ˈhigh**
head|ache ˈhed|.eɪk **-aches** -eɪks **-achy** -ˌeɪ.ki
headband ˈhed.bænd **-s** -z
headbang ˈhed.bæŋ **-s** -z **-ing** -ɪŋ **-ed** -d **-er/s** -əʳ/z (US) -ɚ/z
headboard ˈhed.bɔːd (US) -bɔːrd **-s** -z
headcheese ˈhed.tʃiːz
headdress ˈhed.dres **-es** -ɪz
header ˈhed.əʳ (US) -ɚ **-s** -z
headfirst ˌhedˈfɜːst (US) -ˈfɜːrst *stress shift:* ˌheadfirst ˈleap
headgear ˈhed.gɪəʳ (US) -gɪr **-s** -z
head-hunt|er ˈhedˌhʌn.t|əʳ (US) -t̬|ɚ **-ers** -əz (US) -ɚz **-ing** -ɪŋ
heading (H) ˈhed.ɪŋ **-s** -z
Headingl(e)y ˈhed.ɪŋ.li
Headlam ˈhed.ləm
headlamp ˈhed.læmp **-s** -s
headland ˈhed.lənd, -lænd **-s** -z
headless ˈhed.ləs, -lɪs **-ness** -nəs, -nɪs
headlight ˈhed.laɪt **-s** -s
headlin|e ˈhed.laɪn **-es** -z **-ing** -ɪŋ **-ed** -d
headlock ˈhed.lɒk (US) -lɑːk
headlong ˈhed.lɒŋ (US) -lɑːŋ, -lɔːŋ
headman *of group of workers:* ˌhedˈmæn, ˈ-- **headmen** ˌhedˈmen, ˈ-- **head|man** *of tribe:* ˈhed|.mæn, -mən **-men** -men, -mən
headmaster ˌhedˈmɑː.stəʳ, ˈ-ˌ-- (US) ˈhedˌmæs.tɚ **-s** -z
headmistress ˌhedˈmɪs.trəs, -trɪs, ˈ-ˌ-- (US) ˈhedˌ-- **-es** -ɪz
headnote ˈhed.nəʊt (US) -noʊt **-s** -s
head-on ˌhedˈɒn (US) -ˈɑːn *stress shift:* ˌhead-on ˈimpact
headphones ˈhed.fəʊnz (US) -foʊnz
headpiec|e ˈhed.piːs **-es** -ɪz
headquarters ˌhedˈkwɔː.təz, ˈ--- (US) ˈhedˌkwɔːr.t̬ɚz
headrest ˈhed.rest **-s** -s
headroom ˈhed.rʊm, -ruːm (US) -ruːm, -rʊm
headscar|f ˈhed.skɑː|f (US) -skɑːr|f **-ves** -vz
headset ˈhed.set **-s** -s
headship ˈhed.ʃɪp **-s** -s
heads|man ˈhedz|.mən **-men** -mən
headstand ˈhed.stænd **-s** -z
headstone (H) ˈhed.stəʊn (US) -stoʊn **-s** -z
headstrong ˈhed.strɒŋ (US) -strɑːŋ
headwater ˈhedˌwɔː.təʳ (US) -ˌwɑː.t̬ɚ, -ˌwɔː- **-s** -z
headway ˈhed.weɪ
headwind ˈhed.wɪnd **-s** -z
headword ˈhed.wɜːd (US) -wɜːrd **-s** -z
headwork ˈhed.wɜːk (US) -wɜːrk
head|y ˈhed|.i **-ier** -i.əʳ (US) -i.ɚ **-iest** -i.ɪst, -i.əst **-ily** -ɪ.li, -əl.i **-iness** -ɪ.nəs, -ɪ.nɪs
Heagerty ˈheg.ə.ti (US) -ɚ.t̬i
heal (H) hiːl **-s** -z **-ing** -ɪŋ **-ed** -d **-er/s** -əʳ/z (US) -ɚ/z
Healey ˈhiː.li
health helθ **ˌhealth and ˈsafety** ; **ˈhealth ˌfarm** ; **ˈhealth ˌfood** ; **ˈhealth ˌservice** ; **ˈhealth ˌvisitor**
healthcare ˈhelθ.keəʳ (US) -ker
healthful ˈhelθ.fəl, -fʊl **-ly** -i **-ness** -nəs, -nɪs
health-giving ˈhelθˌgɪv.ɪŋ
health|y ˈhel.θ|i **-ier** -i.əʳ (US) -i.ɚ **-iest** -i.ɪst, -i.əst **-ily** -ɪ.li, -əl.i **-iness** -ɪ.nəs, -ɪ.nɪs
Healy ˈhiː.li
Heaney ˈhiː.ni
Heanor ˈhiː.nəʳ (US) -nɚ
heap hiːp **-s** -s **-ing** -ɪŋ **-ed** -t
hear hɪəʳ (US) hɪr **-s** -z **-ing/s** -ɪŋ/z **heard** hɜːd (US) hɜːrd **hearer/s** ˈhɪə.rəʳ/z (US) ˈhɪr.ɚ/z **ˈhearing ˌaid** ; **ˌhard of ˈhearing**
heard (H) (*from* **hear**) hɜːd (US) hɜːrd
hearing-impaired ˈhɪə.rɪŋ.ɪmˌpeəd (US) ˈhɪr.ɪŋ.ɪmˌperd
hearken ˈhɑː.kən (US) ˈhɑːr- **-s** -z **-ing** -ɪŋ, ˈhɑːk.nɪŋ (US) ˈhɑːr.kən.ɪŋ, ˈhɑːrk.nɪŋ **-ed** -d
Hearn(e) hɜːn (US) hɜːrn
hearsay ˈhɪə.seɪ (US) ˈhɪr-
hears|e hɜːs (US) hɜːrs **-es** -ɪz
Hearsey ˈhɜː.si (US) ˈhɜːr-
Hearst hɜːst (US) hɜːrst
heart hɑːt (US) hɑːrt **-s** -s **ˈheart atˌtack** ; **ˈheart ˌfailure** ; **ˌeat one's ˈheart out** ; **have one's ˌheart in the ˌright ˈplace** ; **in one's ˌheart of ˈhearts** ; **ˌset one's ˈheart on something** ; **ˌwear one's ˌheart on one's ˈsleeve**
heartache ˈhɑːt.eɪk (US) ˈhɑːrt-
heartbeat ˈhɑːt.biːt (US) ˈhɑːrt- **-s** -s
heartbreak ˈhɑːt.breɪk (US) ˈhɑːrt-
heartbreaking ˈhɑːtˌbreɪ.kɪŋ (US) ˈhɑːrt- **-ly** -li
heartbroken ˈhɑːtˌbrəʊ.kən (US) ˈhɑːrtˌbroʊ-
heartburn ˈhɑːt.bɜːn (US) ˈhɑːrt.bɜːrn **-ing** -ɪŋ
-hearted -ˈhɑː.tɪd (US) -ˈhɑːr.t̬ɪd
Note: Suffix. Compounds containing **-hearted** are normally stressed on the suffix as shown, but a stress shift occurs when the word is used attributively, e.g. ˌbrokenhearted ˈlover.
hearten ˈhɑː.tən (US) ˈhɑːr- **-s** -z **-ing/ly** -ɪŋ/li, ˈhɑːt.nɪŋ/li (US) ˈhɑːrt- **-ed** -d
heartfelt ˈhɑːt.felt (US) ˈhɑːrt-
hear|th hɑː|θ (US) hɑːr|θ **-ths** -θs, -ðz **ˈhearth ˌrug**
hearthstone ˈhɑːθ.stəʊn (US) ˈhɑːrθ.stoʊn **-s** -z
heartland ˈhɑːt.lænd (US) ˈhɑːrt- **-s** -z
heartless ˈhɑːt.ləs, -lɪs (US) ˈhɑːrt- **-ly** -li **-ness** -nəs, -nɪs
heart-rending ˈhɑːtˌren.dɪŋ (US) ˈhɑːrt- **-ly** -li
heart-searching ˈhɑːtˌsɜː.tʃɪŋ (US) ˈhɑːrtˌsɜː- **-s** -z
heart's-ease ˈhɑːts.iːz (US) ˈhɑːrts-
heart-shaped ˈhɑːt.ʃeɪpt (US) ˈhɑːrt-
heartsick ˈhɑːt.sɪk (US) ˈhɑːrt- **-ness** -nəs, -nɪs
heartsore ˈhɑːt.sɔːʳ (US) ˈhɑːrt.sɔːr
heartstrings ˈhɑːt.strɪŋz (US) ˈhɑːrt-
heart-throb ˈhɑːt.θrɒb (US) ˈhɑːrt.θrɑːb **-s** -z
heart-to-heart ˌhɑːt.təˈhɑːt (US) ˌhɑːrt.tuːˈhɑːrt, -təˈ- **-s** -s *stress shift:* ˌheart-to-heart ˈtalk
heart-warming ˈhɑːtˌwɔː.mɪŋ (US) ˈhɑːrtˌwɔːr- **-ly** -li

heartwood 'hɑːt.wʊd (US) 'hɑːrt-
heart|y 'hɑː.t|i (US) 'hɑːr.t̬|i **-ier** -i.əʳ (US) -i.ɚ **-iest** -i.ɪst, -i.əst **-ily** -ɪ.li, -əl.i **-iness** -ɪ.nəs, -ɪ.nɪs
heat hiːt **-s** -s **-ing** -ɪŋ (US) 'hiː.t̬ɪŋ **-ed/ly** -ɪd (US) 'hiː.t̬ɪd **'heat ˌrash** ; **'heat ˌspot** ; **'heat ˌwave**
heater 'hiː.təʳ (US) -t̬ɚ **-s** -z
heath (H) hiːθ **-s** -s **ˌHeath 'Robinson**
Heathcliff(e) 'hiːθ.klɪf
Heathcoat 'hiːθ.kəʊt (US) -koʊt
Heathcote 'heθ.kət, 'hiːθ.kət (US) 'hiːθ.koʊt, -kət
heathen 'hiː.ðən **-s** -z **-ish** -ɪʃ **-dom** -dəm
heathenism 'hiː.ðən.ɪ.zəm
heatheniz|e, -is|e 'hiː.ðən.aɪz **-es** -ɪz **-ing** -ɪŋ **-ed** -d
heath|er (H) *shrub, girl's name:* 'heð|.əʳ (US) -ɚ **-ers** -əz (US) -ɚz **-ery** -ər.i
Heather *place in Leicestershire:* 'hiː.ðəʳ (US) -ðɚ
Heathfield 'hiːθ.fiːld
Heathrow ˌhiːθ'rəʊ, '-- (US) -roʊ **ˌHeathrow 'Airport**
Heath-Stubbs ˌhiːθ'stʌbz
heath|y 'hiː.θ|i **-ier** -i.əʳ (US) -i.ɚ **-iest** -i.ɪst, -i.əst
Heaton 'hiː.tən
heat-seeking 'hiːtˌsiː.kɪŋ
heatstroke 'hiːt.strəʊk (US) -stroʊk
heav|e hiːv **-es** -z **-ing** -ɪŋ **-ed** -d **hove** həʊv (US) hoʊv **heaver/s** 'hiː.vəʳ/z (US) -vɚ/z
heave-ho ˌhiːv'həʊ (US) -hoʊ
heaven (H) 'hev.ən **-s** -z **move ˌheaven and 'earth**
heavenl|y 'hev.ən.l|i **-iness** -ɪ.nəs, -ɪ.nɪs
heaven-sent ˌhev.ən'sent (US) '--- *stress shift, British only:* ˌheaven-sent 'chance
heavenward 'hev.ən.wəd (US) -wɚd **-s** -z
Heaviside 'hev.ɪ.saɪd
heav|y 'hev|.i **-ier** -i.əʳ (US) -i.ɚ **-iest** -i.ɪst, -i.əst **-ily** -ɪ.li, -əl.i **-iness** -ɪ.nəs, -ɪ.nɪs **ˌheavy 'breather** ; **ˌheavy 'cream** ; **ˌheavy 'metal**
heavy-duty ˌhev.i'djuː.ti (US) -'duː.t̬i, -'djuː- *stress shift:* ˌheavy-duty 'battery
heavy-handed ˌhev.i'hæn.dɪd **-ly** -li **-ness** -nəs, -nɪs *stress shift:* ˌheavy-handed 'criticism
heavy-hearted ˌhev.i'hɑː.tɪd (US) -'hɑːr.t̬ɪd **-ly** -li **-ness** -nəs, -nɪs *stress shift:* ˌheavy-hearted 'lover
heavyweight 'hev.i.weɪt **-s** -s
Heazell 'hiː.zəl
Hebburn 'heb.ɜːn, -ən (US) -ɜːrn, -ɚn
Hebden 'heb.dən
hebdomadal heb'dɒm.ə.dəl (US) -'dɑː.mə- **-ly** -li
Hebe 'hiː.bi
Heber 'hiː.bəʳ (US) -bɚ
Heberden 'heb.ə.dən (US) '-ɚ-
Hebraic hiː'breɪ.ɪk, hɪ'breɪ-, heb'reɪ- (US) hiː'breɪ-, hɪ- **-al** -əl **-ally** -əl.i, -li
Hebra|ism 'hiː.breɪ|.ɪ.zəm, -bri- **-isms** -ɪ.zəmz **-ist/s** -ɪst/s
Hebraistic ˌhiː.breɪ'ɪst.ɪk, -bri'-
hebraiz|e, -is|e 'hiː.breɪ.aɪz, -bri- **-es** -ɪz **-ing** -ɪŋ **-ed** -d
Hebrew 'hiː.bruː **-s** -z
Hebrides 'heb.rɪ.diːz, -rə-
Hebron *biblical place-name:* 'heb.rɒn, 'hiː.brɒn, -brən (US) 'hiː.brən, 'heb- *modern surname:* 'heb.rən, -rɒn (US) -rən, -rɑːn
Hecate 'hek.ə.ti *in Shakespeare sometimes:* 'hek.ət
hecatomb 'hek.ə.tuːm, -təʊm, -təm (US) -toʊm, -tʊm **-s** -z
Hecht hekt
heck hek
heckl|e 'hek.l̩ **-es** -z **-ing** -ɪŋ, 'hek.lɪŋ **-ed** -d **-er/s** -əʳ/z (US) -ɚ/z, 'hek.ləʳ/z (US) -lɚ/z
Heckmondwike 'hek.mənd.waɪk
Hecla 'hek.lə
hectare 'hek.teəʳ, -tɑːʳ, -təʳ (US) -ter **-s** -z
hectic 'hek.tɪk **-ally** -əl.i, -li
hectogram, hectogramme 'hek.təʊ.græm (US) -toʊ-, -tə- **-s** -z
hectogramme, -gram 'hek.təʊ.græm (US) -toʊ-, -tə- **-s** -z
hectograph 'hek.təʊ.grɑːf, -græf (US) -toʊ.græf, -tə- **-s** -s **-ing** -ɪŋ **-ed** -t
hectographic ˌhek.təʊ'græf.ɪk (US) -toʊ'-, -tə'-
hectolitre, hectoliter 'hek.təʊˌliː.təʳ (US) -toʊˌliː.t̬ɚ, -təˌ- **-s** -z
hectometre, hectometer 'hek.təʊˌmiː.təʳ (US) -toʊˌmiː.t̬ɚ, -təˌ- **-s** -z
hector (H) 'hek.təʳ (US) -tɚ **-s** -z **-ing** -ɪŋ **-ed** -d
Hecuba 'hek.jə.bə, -jʊ-
heder 'heɪ.dəʳ (US) 'heɪ.dɚ *as if Hebrew:* 'xeɪ- **-s** -z **hadarim** ˌhæd.ɑː'riːm (US) ˌhɑː- *as if Hebrew:* ˌxæd- (US) ˌxɑː-
Hedgcock 'hedʒ.kɒk (US) -kɑːk
hedg|e hedʒ **-es** -ɪz **-ing** -ɪŋ **-ed** -d **-er/s** -əʳ/z (US) -ɚ/z **'hedge ˌsparrow** ; **ˌhedge one's 'bets**
hedgehog 'hedʒ.hɒg (US) -hɑːg, -hɔːg **-s** -z
hedgehop 'hedʒ.hɒp (US) -hɑːp **-s** -s **-ping** -ɪŋ **-ped** -t
Hedgeley 'hedʒ.li
Hedger 'hedʒ.əʳ (US) -ɚ
Hedgerley 'hedʒ.ə.li (US) '-ɚ-
hedgerow 'hedʒ.rəʊ (US) -roʊ **-s** -z
Hedges 'hedʒ.ɪz
Hedley 'hed.li
hedon|ism 'hiː.dən|.ɪ.zəm, 'hed.ən- (US) 'hiː.dən- **-ist/s** -ɪst/s
hedonistic ˌhiː.dən'ɪs.tɪk, ˌhed.ən'- (US) ˌhiː.dən'- **-ally** -əl.i, -li
heebie-jeebies ˌhiː.bi'dʒiː.biz
heed hiːd **-s** -z **-ing** -ɪŋ **-ed** -ɪd
heedful 'hiːd.fəl, -fʊl **-ly** -i **-ness** -nəs, -nɪs
heedless 'hiːd.ləs, -lɪs **-ly** -li **-ness** -nəs, -nɪs
heehaw 'hiː.hɔː, ˌ-'- (US) 'hiː.hɑː, -hɔː, ˌ-'- **-s** -z **-ing** -ɪŋ **-ed** -d
heel hiːl **-s** -z **-ing** -ɪŋ **-ed** -d **ˌcool one's 'heels** ; **ˌdig one's 'heels in** ; **ˌdrag one's 'heels** ; **ˌhard on the 'heels of** ; **ˌkick one's 'heels**
Heeley 'hiː.li
Heenan 'hiː.nən
Heep hiːp
Heffer 'hef.əʳ (US) -ɚ
Hefner 'hef.nəʳ (US) -nɚ
heft|y 'hef.t|i **-ier** -i.əʳ (US) -i.ɚ **-iest** -i.ɪst, -i.əst **-ily** -ɪ.li, -əl.i **-iness** -ɪ.nəs, -ɪ.nɪs
Hegarty 'heg.ə.ti (US) -ɚ.t̬i
Hegel 'heɪ.gəl
Hegelian hɪ'geɪ.li.ən, heg'eɪ-; heɪ'giː-, heg'iː- **-ism** -ɪ.zəm
hegemonic ˌheg.ɪ'mɒn.ɪk, ˌhiː.gɪ'-, ˌhedʒ.ɪ'-, -ə'- (US) ˌhedʒ.ɪ'mɑː.nɪk
hegemony hɪ'gem.ə.ni, hiː'gem-, -'dʒem-; 'heg.ɪ.mə-, 'hedʒ- (US) hɪ'dʒem.ə-; 'hedʒ.ə.moʊ-
hegira (H) 'hedʒ.ɪ.rə, -ər.ə, hɪ'dʒaɪə.rə, hedʒ'aɪə- (US) 'hedʒ.ɪ.rə, -ɚ.ə, hɪ'dʒaɪ-, hedʒ'aɪ- **-s** -z
Hegley 'heg.li
Heidegger 'haɪ.deg.əʳ, -dɪ.gəʳ (US) -dɪ.gɚ
Heidelberg 'haɪ.dəl.bɜːg (US) -bɜːrg
Heidi 'haɪ.di
heifer 'hef.əʳ (US) -ɚ **-s** -z
heigh heɪ
heigh-ho ˌheɪ'həʊ (US) -'hoʊ
Heighington 'heɪ.ɪŋ.tən, 'hiː-
height haɪt **-s** -s
heighten 'haɪ.tən **-s** -z **-ing** -ɪŋ, 'haɪt.nɪŋ **-ed** -d
Heighton 'heɪ.tən
Heighway 'haɪ.weɪ, 'heɪ-
Heimlich manoeuvre, Heimlich maneuver 'haɪm.lɪk.məˌnuː.vəʳ, -lɪx- (US) -vɚ
Heineken® 'haɪ.nɪ.kən, -nə-
Heinekey 'haɪ.nɪ.ki
Heinemann 'haɪ.nə.mən, -mæn

Heinlein 'haɪn.laɪn
heinous 'heɪ.nəs, 'hiː- (US) 'heɪ- **-ly** -li **-ness** -nəs, -nɪs
Heinz haɪnts, haɪnz
Note: The trademark is always pronounced /haɪnz/.
heir eəʳ (US) er **-s** -z **-dom** -dəm **-less** -ləs, -lɪs, -les ˌ**heir ap'parent** ; ˌ**heir pre'sumptive**
heiress 'eə.res, -rɪs, -res; eə'res (US) 'er.ɪs **-es** -ɪz
heirloom 'eə.luːm (US) 'er- **-s** -z
heirship 'eə.ʃɪp (US) 'er-
heist haɪst **-s** -s **-ing** -ɪŋ **-ed** -ɪd
heister 'haɪ.stəʳ (US) -stɚ **-s** -z
hejira (H) 'hedʒ.ɪ.rə, -ᵊr.ə; hɪ'dʒaɪᵊ.rə, hə- **-s** -z
Hekla 'hek.lə
Hel hel
held (*from* **hold**) held
Helen 'hel.ən, -ɪn
Helena 'hel.ɪ.nə, '-ə-; hel'iː.nə, hɪ'liː-, hə-
Note: /'hel.ɪ.nə, 'hel.ə.nə/ are the more usual pronunciations, except in the name of the island **St. Helena**; the city in Montana is normally /'hel-/.
Helene hel'eɪn, hɪ'leɪn, hə-, -'liːn
Helensburgh 'hel.ənzˌbᵊr.ə, -ɪnzˌ-, -ˌbʌr- (US) -bɜːrg
Helenus 'hel.ɪ.nəs, '-ə-
Helga 'hel.gə
heliacal hɪ'laɪə.kᵊl, hiː-, hel'aɪə- **-ly** -i
Heliades hel'aɪə.diːz, hɪ'laɪə-
helianth|us ˌhiː.li'ænt.θ|əs, ˌhel.i'- **-i** -aɪ **-uses** -ə.sɪz
helical 'hel.ɪ.kᵊl, 'hiː.lɪ- **-ly** -i
helices (*plur. of* **helix**) 'hiː.lɪ.siːz, 'hel.ɪ-, -lə-
Helicon 'hel.ɪ.kᵊn, '-ə-, -ɪ.kɒn (US) -kɑːn, -kᵊn
helicopter 'hel.ɪ.kɒp.təʳ, '-əˌ- (US) -kɑːp.tɚ **-s** -z
Heligoland 'hel.ɪ.gəʊ.lænd, '-ə- (US) -goʊ-
heliocentric ˌhiː.li.əʊ'sen.trɪk (US) -oʊ'-, -ə'- **-al** -ᵊl **-ally** -ᵊl.i, -li *stress shift:* ˌheliocentric 'force
Heliogabalus ˌhiː.li.əʊ'gæb.ᵊl.əs (US) -oʊ'-, -ə'-
heliogram 'hiː.li.əʊ.græm (US) -oʊ-, -ə- **-s** -z
heliograph 'hiː.li.əʊ.grɑːf, -græf (US) -oʊ.græf, -ə- **-s** -s
heliograph|er ˌhiː.li'ɒg.rə.f|əʳ (US) -'ɑː.grə.f|ɚ **-ers** -əz (US) -ɚz **-y** -i
heliographic ˌhiː.li.əʊ'græf.ɪk (US) -oʊ-', -ə'- **-al** -ᵊl
heliometer ˌhiː.li'ɒm.ɪ.təʳ, '-ə- (US) -'ɑː.mə.t̬ɚ **-s** -z
heliometric ˌhiː.li.əʊ'met.rɪk (US) -oʊ'- **-ally** -ᵊl.i, -li
Heliopolis ˌhiː.li'ɒp.ᵊl.ɪs (US) -'ɑː.pᵊl-
Helios 'hiː.li.ɒs (US) -ɑːs
helioscope 'hiː.li.əʊ.skəʊp (US) -oʊ.skoʊp, -ə- **-s** -s
heliostat 'hiː.li.əʊ.stæt (US) -oʊ-, -ə- **-s** -s
heliotrope 'hiː.li.ə.trəʊp, 'hel.i- (US) 'hiː.li.ə.troʊp **-s** -s
heliotropic ˌhiː.li.ə'trɒp.ɪk (US) -'trɑː.pɪk **-ally** -ᵊl.i, -li
heliotropism ˌhiː.li'ɒt.rə.pɪ.zᵊm; 'hiː.li.əˌtrəʊ-, ˌhiː.li.ə'trəʊ- (US) ˌhiː.li'ɑː.trə-
helipad 'hel.ɪ.pæd **-s** -z
heliport 'hel.ɪ.pɔːt (US) -pɔːrt **-s** -s
helium 'hiː.li.əm
helix 'hiː.lɪks **-es** -ɪz **helices** 'hiː.lɪ.siːz, 'hel.ɪ-, -lə-
hell (H) hel **-s** -z ˌ**Hell's 'Angel** ; **come** ˌ**hell or** ˌ**high 'water**
he'll (= **he will**) hiːl
hellacious hel'eɪ.ʃəs
Hellas 'hel.æs (US) -æs, -əs
hellbent ˌhel'bent (US) '-ˌ-
hellebore 'hel.ɪ.bɔːʳ, '-ə- (US) -bɔːr
helleborine 'hel.ɪ.bə.raɪn, '-ə-, -riːn; ˌhel.ɪ'bɔː.riːn, -ə'- (US) ˌhel.ə'bɔːr.ɪn, -iːn
Hellene 'hel.iːn **-s** -z
Hellenic hel'iː.nɪk, hɪ'liː-, hə-, -'len- (US) hə'len-
Hellen|ism 'hel.ɪ.n|ɪ.zᵊm, '-ə- **-isms** -ɪ.zᵊmz **-ist/s** -ɪst/s
Hellenistic ˌhel.ɪ'nɪs.tɪk, -ə'- **-al** -ᵊl **-ally** -ᵊl.i, -li
helleniz|e, -is|e 'hel.ɪ.naɪz, '-ə- **-es** -ɪz **-ing** -ɪŋ **-ed** -d
Heller 'hel.əʳ (US) -ɚ
Hellespont 'hel.ɪ.spɒnt, '-ə- (US) -spɑːnt
hellfire ˌhel'faɪəʳ, '-- (US) 'hel.faɪr
hellhole 'hel.həʊl (US) -hoʊl **-s** -z
hellhound 'hel.haʊnd **-s** -z
Hellingly ˌhel.ɪŋ'laɪ
hellish 'hel.ɪʃ **-ly** -li **-ness** -nəs, -nɪs
Hellman 'hel.mən
hello hel'əʊ, hə'ləʊ (US) hel'oʊ, hə'loʊ, 'hel.oʊ **-(e)s** -z **-ing** -ɪŋ **-ed** -d
helluva 'hel.ə.və
hellward 'hel.wəd (US) -wɚd
helm helm **-s** -z
helme|t 'hel.mə|t, -mɪ|t **-ts** -ts **-ted** -tɪd (US) -t̬ɪd
Helmholtz 'helm.həʊlts (US) -hoʊlts
helminth 'hel.mɪntθ **-s** -s
helminthiasis ˌhel.mɪnt'θaɪə.sɪs
Helmsley 'helmz.li *locally:* 'hemz-
helms|man 'helmz|.mən **-men** -mən, -men
Helmut 'hel.mʊt
Héloïse ˌel.əʊ'iːz (US) -oʊ'-; 'el.ə.wiːz
hel|ot 'hel|.ət **-ots** -əts **-otage** -ə.tɪdʒ (US) -ə.t̬ɪdʒ **-otism** -ə.tɪ.zᵊm (US) -ə.t̬ɪ.zᵊm **-otry** -ət.ri
help help **-s** -s **-ing** -ɪŋ **-ed** -t **-er/s** -əʳ/z (US) -ɚ/z
helpful 'help.fᵊl, -fʊl **-ly** -i **-ness** -nəs, -nɪs
helpless 'help.ləs, -lɪs **-ly** -li **-ness** -nəs, -nɪs
helpline 'help.laɪn **-s** -z
helpmate 'help.meɪt **-s** -s
helpmeet 'help.miːt **-s** -s
Helsingborg 'hel.sɪŋ.bɔːg (US) -bɔːrg
Helsinki hel'sɪŋ.ki, '--- (US) 'hel.sɪŋ.ki, -'--
Helston(e) 'hel.stən
helter-skelter ˌhel.tə'skel.təʳ (US) -t̬ɚ'skel.t̬ɚ **-s** -z
helve helv **-s** -z
Helvellyn hel'vel.ɪn
Helveti|a hel'viː.ʃ|ə, -ʃi|.ə **-an/s** -ən/z
Helvetic hel'vet.ɪk (US) -'vet̬-
Helvétius hel'viː.ʃəs, -ʃi.əs (US) -'viː-, -'veɪ-
Hely 'hiː.li
hem (*n. v.*) hem **-s** -z **-ming** -ɪŋ **-med** -d
hemal 'hiː.mᵊl
he|-man 'hiː|.mæn **-men** -men
Hemans 'hem.ənz
hematite 'hiː.mə.taɪt, 'hem.ə- (US) 'hiː.mə-
hematologic ˌhiː.mə.tə'lɒdʒ.ɪk (US) -'lɑː.dʒɪk **-al** -ᵊl
hematolog|y ˌhiː.mə'tɒl.ə.dʒ|i (US) -'tɑː.lə- **-ist/s** -ɪst/s
hematoma ˌhiː.mə'təʊ.mə, ˌhem.ə'- (US) ˌhiː.mə'toʊ- **-s** -z **-ta** -tə
heme hiːm
Hemel Hempstead ˌhem.ᵊl'hemp.stɪd, -stəd, -sted
hemicycle 'hem.iˌsaɪ.kl̩ **-s** -z
hemidemisemiquaver ˌhem.iˌdem.i'sem.iˌkweɪ.vəʳ (US) -vɚ **-s** -z
Heming 'hem.ɪŋ
Hemingway 'hem.ɪŋ.weɪ
hemipleg|ia ˌhem.i'pliː.dʒ|i.ə, -dʒ|ə **-ic** -ɪk
hemisphere 'hem.ɪ.sfɪəʳ, '-ə- (US) -sfɪr **-s** -z
hemispheric ˌhem.ɪ'sfer.ɪk, -ə'- (US) -'sfɪr-, -'sfer- **-al** -ᵊl **-ally** -ᵊl.i, -li
hemistich 'hem.i.stɪk **-s** -s
hemline 'hem.laɪn **-s** -z
hemlock 'hem.lɒk (US) -lɑːk **-s** -s
Hemming 'hem.ɪŋ
Hemmings 'hem.ɪŋz
hemoglobin ˌhiː.məʊ'gləʊ.bɪn, ˌhem.əʊ'- (US) 'hiː.moʊ.gloʊ-, '-ə-
hemophili|a ˌhiː.mə'fɪl.i|.ə, ˌhem.ə'- (US) ˌhiː.moʊ'-, -mə'- **-ac/s** -æk/s

hemorrhag|e 'hem.ᵊr.ɪdʒ (US) -ɚ.ɪdʒ, '-rɪdʒ **-es** -ɪz **-ing** -ɪŋ **-ed** -d

hemorrhoid 'hem.ᵊr.ɔɪd (US) -ə.rɔɪd, '-rɔɪd **-s** -z

hemosta|sis ˌhiː.mə'steɪ|.sɪs, ˌhem.ə'- (US) ˌhiː.mə'- **-ses** -siːz

hemp hemp **-en** -ən

Hemp(e)l 'hem.pᵊl

hemstitch 'hem.stɪtʃ **-es** -ɪz **-ing** -ɪŋ **-ed** -t

Hemy 'hem.i

hen hen **-s** -z ˈ**hen** ˌ**party**

henbane 'hen.beɪn, 'hem- (US) 'hen-

hence hen*t*s

henceforth ˌhen*t*s'fɔːθ (US) 'hen*t*s.fɔːrθ

henceforward ˌhen*t*s'fɔː.wəd (US) -'fɔːr.wɚd

Henchard 'hen.tʃɑːd, -tʃəd (US) -tʃɚd, -tʃɑːrd

hench|man 'hen*t*ʃ|.mən **-men** -mən

hencoop 'hen.kuːp **-s** -s

hendecagon hen'dek.ə.gən (US) -gɑːn **-s** -z

hendecagonal ˌhen.dɪ'kæg.ᵊn.ᵊl, -dek'æg-

hendecasyllabic henˌdek.ə.sɪ'læb.ɪk, -sə'- **-s** -s

hendecasyllable ˌhen.dek.ə'sɪl.ə.bᵊl **-s** -z

Henderson 'hen.də.sᵊn (US) -dɚ-

hendiadys hen'daɪə.dɪs

Hendon 'hen.dən

Hendricks 'hen.drɪks

Hendrickson 'hen.drɪk.sᵊn

Hendrix 'hen.drɪks

Hendry 'hen.dri

Heneage 'hen.ɪdʒ

heng|e hendʒ **-es** -ɪz

Hengist 'heŋ.gɪst

Henley 'hen.li

Henlow 'hen.ləʊ (US) -loʊ

henna 'hen.ə **-s** -z **-ing** -ɪŋ **-ed** -d

henner|y 'hen.ᵊr|.i **-ies** -iz

Henness(e)y 'hen.ə.si, '-ɪ-

Henniker 'hen.ɪ.kəʳ (US) -kɚ

Henning 'hen.ɪŋ

henpeck 'hen.pek, 'hem- (US) 'hen- **-s** -s **-ing** -ɪŋ **-ed** -t

Henri *French name:* 'ɑ̃ːn.riː, -'- (US) ɑ̃ːn'riː *US surname:* 'hen.ri

Henrietta ˌhen.ri'et.ə (US) -'eţ-

Henriques hen'riː.kɪz

henr|y (**H**) 'hen.r|i **-ys** -iz **-ies** -iz

Henryson 'hen.rɪ.sᵊn

Hensen 'hen*t*.sᵊn

Hensley 'henz.li

Henslow(e) 'henz.ləʊ (US) -loʊ

Henson 'hen*t*.sᵊn

Henty 'hen.ti (US) -ţi

Hentzau 'hent.zaʊ

hepatic hɪ'pæt.ɪk, hep'æt- (US) hɪ'pæţ-

hepatica hɪ'pæt.ɪ.kə, hep'æt- (US) hɪ'pæţ- **-s** -z

hepatite 'hep.ə.taɪt

hepati|tis ˌhep.ə'taɪ|.tɪs, -təs (US) -ţɪs **-tides** -tɪ.diːz

Hepburn 'heb.ɜːn, -bən; 'hep.bɜːn (US) 'hep.bɝːn, -bɚn

Note: The names of Katharine and Audrey Hepburn are usually pronounced /'hep.bɜːn (US) -bɝːn/.

Hephaestus hɪ'fiː.stəs, hef'iː-, hə'fiː- (US) hɪ'fes.təs

Hephzibah 'hef.sɪ.bɑː, 'hep-, -sə-

Hepplewhite 'hep.l̩.*h*waɪt

hepta- 'hep.tə-; hep'tæ-

Note: Prefix. Normally takes either primary or secondary stress on the first syllable, e.g. **heptagon** /'hep.tə.gᵊn (US) -gɑːn/, **heptahedron** /ˌhep.tə'hiː.drᵊn/, or primary stress on the second syllable, e.g. **heptathlete** /hep'tæθ.liːt/.

heptagon 'hep.tə.gᵊn, -gɒn (US) -gɑːn **-s** -z

heptagonal hep'tæg.ᵊn.ᵊl

heptahedr|on ˌhep.tə'hiː.dr|ən, -'hed.r|ən, -r|ɒn; 'hep.təˌhiː.dr|ən, -ˌhed.r|ən, -r|ɒn (US) ˌhep.tə'hiː.dr|ən **-ons** -ənz **-a** -ə **-al** -ᵊl

heptameter hep'tæm.ɪ.təʳ, '-ə- (US) -ə.ţɚ **-s** -z

heptarch 'hep.tɑːk (US) -tɑːrk **-s** -s **-y** -i **-ies** -iz

Heptateuch 'hep.tə.tjuːk (US) -tuːk, -tjuːk

heptathlete hep'tæθ.liːt **-s** -s

heptathlon hep'tæθ.lɒn, -lən (US) -lɑːn **-s** -z

Hepworth 'hep.wəθ, -wɜːθ (US) -wɝːθ, -wɚθ

her *strong form:* hɜːʳ (US) hɝː *weak forms:* həʳ, əʳ (US) hɚ, ɚ **-s** -z

Note: Weak form word. The strong form /hɜːʳ (US) hɝː/ is used for emphasis, e.g. 'it was **her** fault' or contrast, e.g. 'his or her bank'. There is a weak form /həʳ (US) hɚ/ which is used at the beginning of sentences, e.g. 'Her train was late' /hə'treɪn.wəzˌleɪt (US) hɚ-/ and elsewhere in slow, careful speech, e.g. 'I admired her skill', /aɪ.ədˌmaɪəd.hə'skɪl (US) -ˌmaɪrd.hɚ'-/. In rapid speech the weak form is likely to be /əʳ (US) ɚ/, e.g. 'Let her through', /ˌlet.ə'θruː (US) ˌleţ.ɚ'-/.

Hera 'hɪə.rə (US) 'hɪr.ə, 'hiː.rə

Heraclean ˌher.ə'kliː.ən

Heracles 'her.ə.kliːz, 'hɪə.rə- (US) 'her.ə-

Heraclitus ˌher.ə'klaɪ.təs (US) -ţəs

Heraklion her'æk.li.ən

herald 'her.əld **-s** -z **-ing** -ɪŋ **-ed** -ɪd

heraldic hɪ'ræl.dɪk, hə'ræl-, her'æl- (US) hə'ræl-, her'æl- **-ally** -ᵊl.i, -li

heraldr|y 'her.ᵊl.dr|i **-ies** -iz

Herat her'æt, hɪ'ræt, hə'ræt, -'rɑːt (US) her'ɑːt

herb (**H**) hɜːb (US) ɝːb, hɝːb **-s** -z **-age** -ɪdʒ **-y** -i

Note: The US pronunciation for the name **Herb** is always /hɝːb/.

herbaceous hɜː'beɪ.ʃəs, hə- (US) hɚ'-, ɚ'- **her**ˌ**baceous** '**border**

herbal 'hɜː.bᵊl (US) 'hɝː-, 'ɝː-

herbal|ism 'hɜː.bᵊl|.ɪ.zᵊm (US) 'hɝː-, 'ɝː- **-ist/s** -ɪst/s

herbarium hɜː'beə.ri.əm (US) hɝː'ber.i-, ɝː- **-s** -z

Herbert 'hɜː.bət (US) 'hɝː.bɚt

herbicidal ˌhɜː.bɪ'saɪ.dᵊl (US) ˌhɝː-, ˌɝː-

herbicide 'hɜː.bɪ.saɪd (US) 'hɝː-, 'ɝː- **-s** -z

Herbie 'hɜː.bi (US) 'hɝː-

herbivore 'hɜː.bɪ.vɔːʳ (US) 'hɝː.bə.vɔːr, 'ɝː- **-s** -z

herbivorous hɜː'bɪv.ᵊr.əs, hə- (US) hɝː-, hɚ-, ɝː-, ɚ-

herboriz|e, -is|e 'hɜː.bᵊr.aɪz (US) 'hɝː-, 'ɝː- **-es** -ɪz **-ing** -ɪŋ **-ed** -d

Herbst hɜːbst (US) hɝːpst

Herculaneum ˌhɜː.kjə'leɪ.ni.əm, -kjʊ'- (US) ˌhɝː.kjə'-

Hercule 'eə.kjuːl, 'ɜː-, ˌ-'- (US) er'kjuːl, ɝː- ˌ**Hercule 'Poirot**, ˌ**Hercule Poi'rot**

herculean (**H**) ˌhɜː.kjə'liː.ən, -kjʊ'-; hɜː'kjuː.li- (US) ˌhɝː.kjuː'liː-; hɚ'kjuː.li-

Hercules 'hɜː.kjə.liːz, -kjʊ- (US) 'hɝː.kjə-

herd (**H**) hɜːd (US) hɝːd **-s** -z **-ing** -ɪŋ **-ed** -ɪd ˌ**herd 'instinct**

herds|man 'hɜːdz|.mən (US) 'hɝːdz- **-men** -mən

here hɪəʳ (US) hɪr ˌ**here**, ˌ**there**, **and 'everywhere** ; ˌ**neither** ˌ**here nor 'there**

hereabouts ˌhɪəʳ.ə'baʊts, '--- (US) ˌhɪr.ə'baʊts, '---

hereafter ˌhɪəʳ'ɑːf.təʳ (US) ˌhɪr'æf.tɚ

hereby ˌhɪə'baɪ, '-- (US) ˌhɪr'baɪ, '--

hereditable hɪ'red.ɪ.tə.bl̩, hə-, her'ed-, '-ə- (US) hə'red.ɪ.ţə-

hereditament ˌher.ɪ'dɪt.ə.mənt, -ə'-, '-ɪ- (US) -ə'dɪţ.ə- **-s** -s

hereditar|y hɪ'red.ɪ.tᵊr|.i, hə-, her'ed-, '-ə- (US) hə'red.ɪ.ter- **-ily** -ᵊl.i, -ɪ.li **-iness** -ɪ.nəs, -ɪ.nɪs

heredity hɪ'red.ə.ti, hə-, her'ed-, -ɪ.ti (US) hə'red.ɪ-

Hereford *place in UK:* 'her.ɪ.fəd, -ə.fəd US -ə.fɚd **-shire** -ʃəʳ, -ˌʃɪəʳ US -ʃɚ, -ˌʃɪr *in US:* 'hɜː.fəd US 'hɜːr.fɚd

herein ˌhɪəʳ'ɪn US ˌhɪr-

hereinabove ˌhɪəʳ.ɪn.ə'bʌv US ˌhɪr-

hereinafter ˌhɪəʳ.ɪn'ɑːf.təʳ US ˌhɪr.ɪn'æf.tɚ

hereinbefore ˌhɪəʳ.ɪn.bɪ'fɔːʳ, -bə'fɔːʳ US ˌhɪr.ɪn.bɪ'fɔːr, -bə'-

hereinbelow ˌhɪəʳ.ɪn.bɪ'ləʊ, -bə'- US ˌhɪr.ɪn.bɪ'loʊ, -bə'-

hereof ˌhɪəʳ'ɒv US ˌhɪr'ɑːv

hereon ˌhɪəʳ'ɒn US ˌhɪr'ɑːn

Herero hə'reə.rəʊ, her'eə-, -'ɪə-; 'hɪə.rə.rəʊ, 'her.ə- US hə'rer.oʊ; 'her.ə.roʊ **-s** -z

heresiarch hə'riː.zi.ɑːk, hɪ-, her'iː-; -si-, 'her.ə.si- US hə'riː.zi.ɑːrk; 'her.ə.si- **-s** -s

heres|y 'her.ə.s|i, '-ɪ- **-ies** -iz

heretic 'her.ə.tɪk, -ɪ.tɪk US '-ə- **-s** -s

heretic|al hə'ret.ɪ.k|əl, hɪ'-, her'et- US hə'reţ- **-ally** -əl.i, -li

hereto ˌhɪə'tuː US ˌhɪr-

heretofore ˌhɪə.tuː'fɔːʳ US ˌhɪr.tuː'fɔːr, '---

hereunder ˌhɪəʳ'ʌn.dəʳ US ˌhɪr'ʌn.dɚ, '---

hereunto ˌhɪəʳ.ʌn'tuː, -'ʌn.tuː US ˌhɪr-, '---

hereupon ˌhɪəʳ.ə'pɒn US ˌhɪr.ə'pɑːn, '---

Hereward 'her.ɪ.wəd, -ə- US -wɚd

herewith ˌhɪə'wɪð, -'wɪθ US ˌhɪr'wɪð, '--

Herford 'hɜː.fəd, 'hɑː- US 'hɜːr.fɚd

Hergé eə'ʒeɪ US er-

heriot (H) 'her.i.ət, -ɒt US -ət **-s** -s

Heriot-Watt ˌher.i.ət'wɒt US -'wɑːt

heritable 'her.ɪ.tə.bl̩, '-ə- US -ɪ.ţə-

heritag|e 'her.ɪ.tɪdʒ, '-ə- US -ɪ.ţɪdʒ **-es** -ɪz

heritor 'her.ɪ.təʳ, '-ə- US -ɪ.ţɚ **-s** -z

Herkomer 'hɜː.kə.məʳ US 'hɜːr.kə.mɚ **-s** -z

Herman 'hɜː.mən US 'hɜːr-

hermaphrodite hɜː'mæf.rə.daɪt, hə- US hɚ'mæf.roʊ-, -rə- **-s** -s

hermaphroditic hɜːˌmæf.rə'dɪt.ɪk, hə- US hɚˌmæf.roʊ'dɪţ-, -rə'- **-ally** -əl.i, -li

hermeneutic ˌhɜː.mɪ'njuː.tɪk, -mə'- US ˌhɜːr.mə'nuː.ţɪk, -'njuː- **-s** -s **-al** -əl **-ally** -əl.i, -li

Hermes 'hɜː.miːz US 'hɜːr-

Hermès® eə'mes US er-

Hermesetas® ˌhɜː.mɪ'siː.təz, -mə'-, -təs US ˌhɜːr.mə'siː.ţəz, -təs

hermetic hɜː'met.ɪk, hə- US hɚ'meţ- **-al** -əl **-ally** -əl.i, -li

Hermia 'hɜː.mi.ə US 'hɜːr-

Hermione hɜː'maɪə.ni, hə- US hɚ-

Hermiston 'hɜː.mɪ.stən US 'hɜːr-

hermit 'hɜː.mɪt US 'hɜːr- **-s** -s ˈ**hermit** ˌ**crab**

hermitag|e (H) 'hɜː.mɪ.tɪdʒ, -mə- *as if French:* ˌeə.mɪ'tɑːʒ US 'hɜːr.mɪ.ţɪdʒ **-es** -ɪz

hermitic hɜː'mɪt.ɪk, hə- US hɚ'mɪţ-

Hermocrates hɜː'mɒk.rə.tiːz, hə- US hɚ'mɑː.krə-

Hermogenes hɜː'mɒdʒ.ɪ.niːz, hə-, -ən.iːz US hɚ'mɑː.dʒə.niːz

Hermon 'hɜː.mən US 'hɜːr-

hern hɜːn US hɜːrn **-s** -z

Hernandez hɜː'næn.dez US hɚ-; er'nɑːn.des

Herne hɜːn US hɜːrn

herni|a 'hɜː.ni|.ə US 'hɜːr- **-as** -əz **-ae** -iː **-al** -əl

herni|ate 'hɜː.ni|.eɪt US 'hɜːr- **-ates** -eɪts **-ating** -eɪ.tɪŋ US -ţɪŋ **-ated** -eɪ.tɪd US -ţɪd

herniation ˌhɜː.ni'eɪ.ʃən US ˌhɜːr- **-s** -z

hero (H) 'hɪə.rəʊ US 'hɪr.oʊ, 'hiː.roʊ **-es** -z ˈ**hero** ˌ**worship**

Herod 'her.əd ˌ**Herod** ˈ**Antipas**

Herodian her'əʊ.di.ən, hə'rəʊ-, hɪ- US hə'roʊ- **-s** -z

Herodias her'əʊ.di.æs, hə'rəʊ-, hɪ-, -əs US hə'roʊ-

Herodotus her'ɒd.ə.təs, hə'rɒd-, hɪ- US hə'rɑː.də.ţəs

heroic hɪ'rəʊ.ɪk, hə-, her'əʊ- US hɪ'roʊ-, hiː- **-s** -s **-al** -əl **-ally** -əl.i, -li **he**ˌ**roic** ˈ**verse**

heroin 'her.əʊ.ɪn US -oʊ-

heroine 'her.əʊ.ɪn US -oʊ- **-s** -z

heroism 'her.əʊ.ɪ.zəm US -oʊ-

heron (H) 'her.ən **-s** -z **-ry** -ri **-ries** -riz

herpes 'hɜː.piːz US 'hɜːr-

herpetologic ˌhɜː.pɪ.tə'lɒdʒ.ɪk, -pə- US ˌhɜːr.pə.ţə'lɑː.dʒɪk **-al** -əl **-ally** -əl.i, -li

herpetolog|y ˌhɜː.pɪ'tɒl.ə.dʒ|i, -pə'- US -pə'tɑː.lə- **-ist/s** -ɪst/s

Herr heəʳ US her

Herrick 'her.ɪk

Herries 'her.ɪs, -ɪz

herring (H) 'her.ɪŋ **-s** -z

herringbone 'her.ɪŋ.bəʊn US -boʊn **-s** -z

Herriot 'her.i.ət

Herron 'her.ən

hers hɜːz US hɜːrz

Herschel(l) 'hɜː.ʃəl US 'hɜːr-

herself hə'self US hɚ- *when not initial:* ə- US ɚ-

Hershey 'hɜː.ʃi US 'hɜːr-

Herstmonceux ˌhɜːst.mən'zuː, -mɒn-, -'sjuː, -'suː US ˌhɜːrst.mən'-, -mɑːn'-

Hertford *in England:* 'hɑːt.fəd, 'hɑː- US 'hɑːrt.fɚd, 'hɑːr- **-shire** -ʃəʳ, -ˌʃɪəʳ US -ʃɚ, -ʃɪr

Hertford *in US:* 'hɜːt.fəd US 'hɜːrt.fɚd

Herts. (*abbrev. for* **Hertfordshire**) hɑːts; 'hɑːt.fəd.ʃəʳ, 'hɑː-, -ˌʃɪəʳ US hɑːrts; 'hɑːrt.fɚd.ʃɚ, 'hɑːr-, -ˌʃɪr

Hertslet 'hɜːt.slɪt US 'hɜːrt-

hertz hɜːts US hɜːrts

Hertz hɜːts, heəts US hɜːrts, herts **-ian** -i.ən

Note: The trademark is pronounced /hɜːts US hɜːrts/.

Hertzog 'hɜːt.sɒg US 'hɜːrt.sɑːg, -sɔːg

Hervey 'hɑː.vi, 'hɜː.vi US 'hɜːr-

Herzegovina ˌhɜːt.sə.gəʊ'viː.nə, ˌheət-, -sɪ.gəʊ'-; -sɪ'gɒv.ɪ.nə US ˌhɜːrt.sə.goʊ'viː.nə

Herzog 'hɜːt.sɒg US 'hɜːrt.sɑːg, -sɔːg

he's (he is *or* he has) *strong form:* hiːz *occasional weak forms:* hiz, iz

Note: See note for **he**.

Hesba 'hez.bə

Heseltine 'hes.əl.taɪn, 'hez-

Heshbon 'heʃ.bɒn US -bɑːn

Hesiod 'hiː.si.əd, 'hes.i-, -ɒd US -əd

hesitan|ce 'hez.ɪ.tənt|s, '-ə- **-cy** -si

hesitant 'hez.ɪ.tənt, '-ə- **-ly** -li

hesi|tate 'hez.ɪ|.teɪt, '-ə- **-tates** -teɪts **-tating/ly** -teɪ.tɪŋ/li US -teɪ.ţɪŋ/li **-tated** -teɪ.tɪd US -teɪ.ţɪd

hesitation ˌhez.ɪ'teɪ.ʃən, -ə'- **-s** -z

Hesketh 'hes.kəθ, -kɪθ

Hesperian hes'pɪə.ri.ən US -'pɪr.i-

Hesperides hes'per.ɪ.diːz, hɪ'sper-, hə-, '-ə- US hes'per.ɪ-

Hesperus 'hes.pər.əs

Hess hes

Hessayon 'hes.i.ən

Hesse 'hes.ə, hes

hessian (H) 'hes.i.ən US 'heʃ.ən **-s** -z

Hester 'hes.təʳ US -tɚ

Heston 'hes.tən

Heswall 'hez.wəl US 'hes.wɔːl

Hesychius hes'ɪk.i.əs

hetero 'het.ər.əʊ US 'heţ.ə.roʊ **-s** -z

heteroclite 'het.ər.əʊ.klaɪt US 'het.ɚ.ə- **-s** -s

heterodox 'het.ər.əʊ.dɒks US 'heţ.ɚ.ə.dɑːks **-y** -i

heterodyne 'het.ər.əʊ.daɪn US 'heţ.ɚ.ə-

heterogeneity ˌhet.ər.əʊ.dʒə'niː.ə.ti, -dʒɪ'-, -ɪ.ti US ˌheţ.ə.roʊ.dʒə'niː.ə.ţi, '-ɚ.ə-

heterogeneous ˌhet.ər.əʊ'dʒiː.ni.əs US ˌheţ.ə.roʊ'-, -ɚ.ə'- **-ly** -li **-ness** -nəs, -nɪs

heterogenesis ˌhet.ər.əʊ'dʒen.ə.sɪs, '-ɪ- US ˌheţ.ə.roʊ'dʒen.ə.sɪs, -ɚ.ə'-

heteronym ˈhet.ᵊr.əʊ.nɪm
(US) ˈhet̬.ə.roʊ-, -ɚ.ə- **-s** -z
heteronym|ous ˌhet.əˈrɒn.ɪ.m|əs, ˈ-ə-
(US) ˌhet̬.əˈrɑː.nɪ- **-y** -i
heterosex|ism ˌhet.ᵊr.əʊˈsek.s|ɪ.zᵊm
(US) ˌhet̬.ə.roʊˈ-, -ɚ.əˈ- **-ist/s** -ɪst/s
heterosexual ˌhet.ᵊr.əʊˈsek.ʃu.ᵊl, ˈ-sju-, -ʃᵊl (US) ˌhet̬.ə.roʊˈsek.ʃu.ᵊl, -ɚ.əˈ- **-s** -z **-ly** -i
heterosexuality ˌhet.ᵊr.əʊˌsek.ʃuˈæl.ə.ti, -sjuˈ-
(US) ˌhet̬.ə.roʊˌsek.ʃuˈæl.ə.t̬i, -ɚ.əˌ-
heterozygous ˌhet.ᵊr.əʊˈzaɪ.gəs
(US) ˌhet̬.ə.roʊˈ-, -ɚ.əˈ-
Hetherington ˈheð.ᵊr.ɪŋ.tən
Hetton-le-Hole ˌhet.ᵊn.ləˈhəʊl, -lɪˈ-
(US) ˌhet̬.ᵊn.ləˈhoʊl
Hetty ˈhet.i (US) ˈhet̬-
het up ˌhetˈʌp (US) ˌhet̬- *stress shift:* ˌhet up ˈteenager
Heugh *place:* hjuːf *surname:* hjuː
heuristic hjʊəˈrɪs.tɪk (US) hjuːˈ- **-s** -s **-ally** -ᵊl.i, -li
Hever ˈhiː.vəʳ (US) -vɚ
hew hjuː **-s** -z **-ing** -ɪŋ **-ed** -d **-n** -n **-er/s** -əʳ/z (US) -ɚ/z
Heward ˈhjuː.əd (US) -ɚd
Hewart ˈhjuː.ət (US) -ɚt
Hewetson ˈhjuː.ɪt.sᵊn
Hewett, Hewitt ˈhjuː.ɪt
Hewke hjuːk
Hewlett ˈhjuː.lɪt, -lət
Hewlettson ˈhjuː.lɪt.sᵊn, -lət-
hewn (*from* **hew**) hjuːn
hex heks **-es** -ɪz **-ing** -ɪŋ **-ed** -t
hexa- ˈhek.sə-; hekˈsæ-
Note: Prefix. Normally either takes primary or secondary stress on the first syllable, e.g. **hexagon** /ˈhek.sə.gᵊn (US) -gɑːn/, **hexahedron** /ˌhek.səˈhiː.drᵊn/, or primary stress on the second syllable, e.g. **hexagonal** /hekˈsæg.ᵊn.ᵊl/.
hexachord ˈhek.sə.kɔːd (US) -kɔːrd **-s** -z
hexagon ˈhek.sə.gən (US) -gɑːn **-s** -z
hexagonal hekˈsæg.ᵊn.ᵊl **-ly** -i
hexagram ˈhek.sə.græm **-s** -z
hexahedr|on ˌhek.səˈhiː.dr|ən, -ˈhed.r|ən (US) -ˈhiː.dr|ən **-ons** -ənz **-a** -ə **-al** -əl
Hexam ˈhek.səm
hexameter hekˈsæm.ɪ.təʳ, hɪkˈ-, ˈ-ə-
(US) -ə.t̬ɚ **-s** -z
Hexateuch ˈhek.sə.tjuːk (US) -tuːk, -tjuːk
Hexham ˈhek.səm
Hextable ˈhek.stə.bl̩
hey heɪ
Heycock ˈheɪ.kɒk (US) -kɑːk
heyday ˈheɪ.deɪ
Heyer heɪəʳ (US) heɪɚ
Heyerdahl ˈheɪə.dɑːl (US) ˈheɪɚ-, ˈhaɪɚ-
hey presto ˌheɪˈpres.təʊ (US) -toʊ
Heysham ˈhiː.ʃᵊm
Heyward ˈheɪ.wəd (US) -wɚd
Heywood ˈheɪ.wʊd
Hezbollah ˌhɪz.bɒlˈɑː, ˈhez-
(US) ˌhez.bəˈlɑː
Hezekiah ˌhez.ɪˈkaɪə, -əˈ-
Hezlewood ˈhez.l̩.wʊd
HGV ˌeɪtʃ.dʒiːˈviː
hi haɪ
hiatus haɪˈeɪ.təs, hi- (US) haɪˈeɪ.t̬əs **-es** -ɪz
Hiawatha ˌhaɪ.əˈwɒθ.ə (US) -ˈwɑː.θə
hibachi hɪˈbɑː.tʃi, hiː- **-s** -z
Hibbert ˈhɪb.ət, -ɜːt (US) -ɚt, -ɜːrt
hibernal haɪˈbɜː.nᵊl (US) -ˈbɜːr-
hiber|nate ˈhaɪ.bə|.neɪt (US) -bɚ- **-nates** -neɪts **-nating** -neɪ.tɪŋ (US) -neɪ.t̬ɪŋ **-nated** -neɪ.tɪd (US) -neɪ.t̬ɪd
hibernation ˌhaɪ.bəˈneɪ.ʃᵊn (US) -bɚˈ- **-s** -z
Hibernia haɪˈbɜː.ni.ə, hɪ- (US) -ˈbɜːr-
Hibernian (*n. adj.*) haɪˈbɜː.ni.ən (US) -ˈbɜːr- **-s** -z *in name of football club:* hɪˈbɜː.ni.ən (US) -ˈbɜːr- **-s** -z
Hibernicism haɪˈbɜː.nɪ.sɪ.zᵊm, -nə- (US) -ˈbɜːr- **-s** -z
hibiscus haɪˈbɪs.kəs, hɪ-, hə- (US) haɪ-, hɪ-
hiccough ˈhɪk.ʌp, -əp **-s** -s **-ing** -ɪŋ **-ed** -t
hiccup ˈhɪk.ʌp, -əp **-s** -s **-(p)ing** -ɪŋ **-(p)ed** -t
hick hɪk **-s** -s
hickey ˈhɪk.i **-s** -z
Hickman ˈhɪk.mən
Hickok ˈhɪk.ɒk (US) -ɑːk
hickory (H) ˈhɪk.ᵊr.i (US) -ɚ.i, ˈ-ri
Hicks hɪks
Hickson ˈhɪk.sᵊn
hid (*from* **hide**) hɪd
hidalgo (H) hɪˈdæl.gəʊ (US) -goʊ **-s** -z
hid|e haɪd **-es** -z **-ing/s** -ɪŋ/z **hid** hɪd **hidden** ˈhɪd.ᵊn ˌ**hide-and-ˈseek**; ˈ**hiding** ˌ**place**
hideaway ˈhaɪd.ə.weɪ **-s** -z
hidebound ˈhaɪd.baʊnd
hideous ˈhɪd.i.əs **-ly** -li **-ness** -nəs, -nɪs
hideout ˈhaɪd.aʊt **-s** -s
hid(e)y-hole ˈhaɪ.di.həʊl (US) -hoʊl **-s** -z
hie haɪ **-s** -z **-ing** -ɪŋ **-d** -d
Hierapolis ˌhaɪəˈræp.ᵊl.ɪs (US) ˌhaɪˈræp.ə.lɪs
hierarch ˈhaɪə.rɑːk (US) ˈhaɪ.rɑːrk **-s** -s
hierarchal ˌhaɪəˈrɑː.kᵊl (US) ˌhaɪˈrɑːr-
hierarchic ˌhaɪəˈrɑː.kɪk (US) ˌhaɪˈrɑːr- **-al** -ᵊl **-ally** -ᵊl.i, -li
hierarch|y ˈhaɪə.rɑː.k|i (US) ˈhaɪ.rɑːr- **-ies** -iz
hieratic ˌhaɪəˈræt.ɪk (US) ˌhaɪˈræt̬-
hieroglyph ˈhaɪə.rəʊ.glɪf (US) ˈhaɪ.roʊ- **-s** -s
hieroglyphic ˌhaɪə.rəʊˈglɪf.ɪk (US) ˌhaɪ.roʊˈ- **-s** -s **-al** -ᵊl **-ally** -ᵊl.i, -li
Hieronimo hɪəˈrɒn.ɪ.məʊ (US) hɪˈrɑː.nɪ.moʊ
Hieronymus hɪəˈrɒn.ɪ.məs, haɪəˈ- (US) haɪˈrɑː.nɪ-
hierophant ˈhɪə.rəʊ.fænt, ˈhaɪə- (US) ˈhaɪ.roʊ- **-s** -s
hifalutin ˌhaɪ.fəˈluː.tɪn, -tᵊn *stress shift:* ˌhifalutin ˈattitude
hi-fi ˈhaɪ.faɪ, ˌ-ˈ- **-s** -z
Higginbotham ˈhɪg.ɪnˌbɒt.əm, -ᵊnˌ-, -ᵊmˌ-, -ˌbɒθ.əm (US) -ˌbɑː.t̬əm, -θəm
Higginbottom ˈhɪg.ɪnˌbɒt.əm, -ᵊnˌ-, -ᵊmˌ- (US) -ˌbɑː.t̬əm
Higgins ˈhɪg.ɪnz
Higginson ˈhɪg.ɪn.sᵊn
higgl|e ˈhɪg.l̩ **-es** -z **-ing** -ɪŋ, ˈhɪg.lɪŋ **-ed** -d **-er/s** -əʳ/z (US) -ɚ/z, ˈhɪg.ləʳ/z (US) -lɚ/z
higgledy-piggledy ˌhɪg.l̩.diˈpɪg.l̩.di
Higgs hɪgz
high haɪ **-er** -əʳ (US) -ɚ **-est** -ɪst, -əst **-ly** -li **-ness** -nəs, -nɪs ˌ**High ˈCourt** *stress shift, British only:* ˌHigh Court ˌjudge; ˈ**high** ˌ**chair**; ˌ**high ˈchurch**; ˌ**high ˈchurchman**; ˈ**high** ˌ**day**; ˌ**high ˈfrequency**; ˌ**high ˈheels**; ˌ**high ˈhorse**; ˈ**high** ˌ**jump**; ˌ**high ˈroller**; ˈ**high** ˌ**school**; ˈ**high** ˌ**street**; ˌ**high ˈtide**; ˌ**high ˈwater**; ˌ**high ˈwater mark**; ˌ**high and ˈdry**; ˌ**high and ˈlow**; ˌ**higher eduˈcation**
Higham ˈhaɪ.əm **-s** -z
high-and-mighty ˌhaɪ.ənˈmaɪ.ti, -əmˈ- (US) -ənˈmaɪ.t̬i *stress shift:* ˌhigh-and-mighty ˈmanners
highball ˈhaɪ.bɔːl (US) -bɔːl, -bɑːl **-s** -z **-ing** -ɪŋ **-ed** -d
highborn ˌhaɪˈbɔːn (US) ˈhaɪ.bɔːrn *stress shift, British only:* ˌhighborn ˈlady
highboy ˈhaɪ.bɔɪ **-s** -z
Highbridge ˈhaɪ.brɪdʒ
highbrow ˈhaɪ.braʊ **-s** -z
highchair ˈhaɪ.tʃeəʳ, ˌ-ˈ- (US) -tʃer **-s** -z
High Church ˌhaɪˈtʃɜːtʃ (US) -ˈtʃɜːrtʃ **-man** -mən **-men** -mən, -men *stress shift:* ˌHigh Church ˈmannerism
high-class ˌhaɪˈklɑːs (US) -ˈklæs *stress shift:* ˌhigh-class ˈbutcher
Highclere ˈhaɪ.klɪəʳ (US) -klɪr
highfalut|in ˌhaɪ.fəˈluː.t|ɪn, -t|ᵊn **-ing** -ɪŋ *stress shift:* ˌhighfalutin ˈattitude
highflier, highflyer ˌhaɪˈflaɪ.əʳ (US) -ɚ **-s** -z
highflown ˌhaɪˈfləʊn (US) -ˈfloʊn *stress shift:* ˌhigh-flown ˈrhetoric

Highgate ˈhaɪ.geɪt, -gɪt, -gət
Highgrove ˈhaɪ.grəʊv ⓤⓢ -groʊv
high-handed ˌhaɪˈhæn.dɪd **-ly** -li **-ness** -nəs, -nɪs *stress shift:* ˌhigh-handed ˈruler
high-heeled ˌhaɪˈhiːld *stress shift:* ˌhigh-heeled ˈshoes
highjack ˈhaɪ.dʒæk **-s** -s **-ing** -ɪŋ **-ed** -t **-er/s** -əʳ/z ⓤⓢ -ɚ/z
highland (H) ˈhaɪ.lənd **-s** -z **-er/s** -əʳ/z ⓤⓢ -ɚ/z ˌ**Highland** ˈ**fling**
high-level ˌhaɪˈlev.əl *stress shift:* ˌhigh-level ˈlanguage
high|light ˈhaɪ|.laɪt **-lights** -laɪts **-lighting** -ˌlaɪ.tɪŋ ⓤⓢ -ˌlaɪ.t̬ɪŋ **-lighted** -ˌlaɪ.tɪd ⓤⓢ -ˌlaɪ.t̬ɪd
highlighter ˈhaɪˌlaɪ.təʳ ⓤⓢ -t̬ɚ **-s** -z
highly ˈhaɪ.li
high-minded ˌhaɪˈmaɪn.dɪd **-ness** -nəs, -nɪs *stress shift:* ˌhigh-minded ˈthinker
Highness ˈhaɪ.nəs, -nɪs **-es** -ɪz
high-octane ˌhaɪˈɒk.teɪn ⓤⓢ -ˈɑːk- *stress shift:* ˌhigh-octane ˈfuel
high-pitched ˌhaɪˈpɪtʃt *stress shift:* ˌhigh-pitched ˈvoice
high-powered ˌhaɪˈpaʊəd ⓤⓢ -ˈpaʊ.ɚd *stress shift:* ˌhigh-powered ˈengine
high-pressure ˌhaɪˈpreʃ.əʳ ⓤⓢ -ɚ *stress shift:* ˌhigh-pressure ˈsalesman
high-priced ˌhaɪˈpraɪst *stress shift:* ˌhigh-priced ˈgoods
high-priest ˌhaɪˈpriːst **-s** -s **-hood/s** -hʊd/z
high-priestess ˌhaɪ.priːˈstes, ˌ-ˈ-- ⓤⓢ ˌhaɪˈpriː- **-es** -ɪz
high-profile ˌhaɪˈprəʊ.faɪl ⓤⓢ -ˈproʊ- *stress shift:* ˌhigh-profile ˈmission
high-ranking ˌhaɪˈræŋ.kɪŋ, ˈ--- *stress shift:* ˌhigh-ranking ˈofficer
high-ris|e ˌhaɪˈraɪz, ˈ-- ⓤⓢ ˈ-- **-s** -ɪz *stress shift:* ˌhigh-rise ˈflats
high-risk ˌhaɪˈrɪsk *stress shift:* ˌhigh-risk ˈstrategy
highroad ˈhaɪ.rəʊd ⓤⓢ -roʊd **-s** -z
high-speed ˌhaɪˈspiːd *stress shift:* ˌhigh-speed ˈchase
high-spirited ˌhaɪˈspɪr.ɪ.tɪd ⓤⓢ -t̬ɪd **-ly** -li **-ness** -nəs, -nɪs
highspot ˈhaɪ.spɒt ⓤⓢ -spɑːt **-s** -s
hightail ˈhaɪ.teɪl **-s** -z **-ing** -ɪŋ **-ed** -d
high-tech ˌhaɪˈtek *stress shift:* ˌhigh-tech ˈoffice
Highton ˈhaɪ.tən
high-up ˌhaɪˈʌp **-s** -s *stress shift:* ˌhigh-up ˈsource
highway ˈhaɪ.weɪ **-s** -z ˌ**Highway** ˈ**Code**, ˈ**Highway** ˌ**Code** ; ˌ**highway** ˈ**robbery**
highway|man ˈhaɪ.weɪ|.mən **-men** -mən
Highworth ˈhaɪ.wəθ, -wɜːθ ⓤⓢ -wɚθ
High Wycombe ˌhaɪˈwɪk.əm
hijack ˈhaɪ.dʒæk **-s** -s **-ing** -ɪŋ **-ed** -t **-er/s** -əʳ/z ⓤⓢ -ɚ/z
hik|e haɪk **-es** -s **-ing** -ɪŋ **-ed** -t **-er/s** -əʳ/z ⓤⓢ -ɚ/z
Hilaire hɪˈleəʳ; ˈhɪl.eəʳ ⓤⓢ hɪˈler; ˈhɪl.er
hilarious hɪˈleə.ri.əs, hə- ⓤⓢ hɪˈler.i-, -ˈlær- **-ly** -li **-ness** -nəs, -nɪs
hilarity hɪˈlær.ə.ti, hə-, -ɪ.ti ⓤⓢ hɪˈler.ə.t̬i, -ˈlær-
Hilary ˈhɪl.ər.i
Hilda ˈhɪl.də
Hildebrand ˈhɪl.də.brænd, -dɪ-
Hildegard(e) ˈhɪl.də.gɑːd, -dɪ- ⓤⓢ -gɑːrd
hill (H) hɪl **-s** -z ˌ**over the** ˈ**hill** ; **as** ˌ**old as the** ˈ**hills**
Hillary ˈhɪl.ər.i
hillbill|y ˈhɪlˌbɪl|.i **-ies** -iz
Hillborn ˈhɪl.bɔːn ⓤⓢ -bɔːrn
Hillel ˈhɪl.el, -əl; hɪˈlel
Hillhead hɪlˈhed, ˈ--
Note: The pronunciation in Scotland is /-ˈ-/.
Hilliard ˈhɪl.i.əd, -ɑːd ⓤⓢ ˈ-jɚd
Hillingdon ˈhɪl.ɪŋ.dən
hill|man ˈhɪl|.mæn, -mən **-men** -men
Hillman ˈhɪl.mən **-s** -z
hillock ˈhɪl.ək **-s** -s
Hillsboro ˈhɪlz.bər.ə ⓤⓢ -oʊ
Hillsborough ˈhɪlz.bər.ə ⓤⓢ -oʊ
hillside (H) ˈhɪl.saɪd, ˌ-ˈ- **-s** -z
hilltop ˈhɪl.tɒp ⓤⓢ -tɑːp **-s** -s
hill|y ˈhɪl|.i **-ier** -i.əʳ ⓤⓢ -i.ɚ **-iest** -i.ɪst, -i.əst **-iness** -ɪ.nəs, -ɪ.nɪs
Hillyard ˈhɪl.jəd, -jɑːd ⓤⓢ -jɚd
Hillyer ˈhɪl.i.əʳ ⓤⓢ ˈ-jɚ
hilt hɪlt **-s** -s **-ed** -ɪd ⓤⓢ ˈhɪl.t̬ɪd
Hilton ˈhɪl.tən
hil|um ˈhaɪ.l|əm **-ums** -əmz **-a** -ə **-i** -aɪ **-us** -əs
Hilversum ˈhɪl.və.sʊm, -səm ⓤⓢ -vɚ-
him *strong form:* hɪm *weak form:* ɪm
Note: Weak form word. The strong form is mainly used for contrastive purposes, e.g. 'The gift is for **him**, not **her**'.
Himachal Pradesh hɪˌmɑː.tʃəl.prɑːˈdeʃ ⓤⓢ -prəˈ-
Himalaya ˌhɪm.əˈleɪə, hɪˈmɑː.li.ə, -lə.jə **-as** -əz **-an** -ən
Himes haɪmz
Himmler ˈhɪm.ləʳ ⓤⓢ -lɚ
himself hɪmˈself *when not initial:* ɪm-
Himyaritic ˌhɪm.jəˈrɪt.ɪk ⓤⓢ -ˈrɪt̬-
Hinayana ˌhiː.nəˈjɑː.nə, ˌhɪn.əˈ- ⓤⓢ ˌhiː.nəˈ-
Hinchcliffe ˈhɪn*t*ʃ.klɪf
Hinchingbrooke ˈhɪn.*t*ʃɪŋ.brʊk
Hinchliffe ˈhɪn*t*ʃ.lɪf
Hinckley ˈhɪŋ.kli
hind (H) haɪnd **-s** -z
Hinde haɪnd
Hindemith ˈhɪnd.ə.mɪt, -mɪθ
Hindenburg ˈhɪn.dən.bɜːg, -dəm- ⓤⓢ -bɜːrg
hinder *(adj.)* ˈhaɪn.dəʳ ⓤⓢ -dɚ **-most** -məʊst ⓤⓢ -moʊst
hind|er *(v.)* ˈhɪn.d|əʳ ⓤⓢ -d|ɚ **-ers** -əz ⓤⓢ -ɚz **-ering** -ər.ɪŋ **-ered** -əd ⓤⓢ -ɚd **-erer/s** -ər.əʳ/z ⓤⓢ -ɚ.ɚ/z
Hinderwell ˈhɪn.də.wel, -wəl ⓤⓢ -dɚ-
Hindhead ˈhaɪnd.hed
Hindi ˈhɪn.diː, -di
Hindle ˈhɪn.dl̩
Hindley *surname:* ˈhɪnd.li, ˈhaɪnd- *town in Greater Manchester:* ˈhɪnd.li
Hindlip ˈhɪnd.lɪp
hindmost ˈhaɪn*d*.məʊst ⓤⓢ -moʊst
hindquarters ˌhaɪn*d*ˈkwɔː.təz, ˌhaɪŋ-, ˈ--- ⓤⓢ ˈhaɪndˌkwɔːr.t̬ɚz
hindranc|e ˈhɪn.drən*t*s **-es** -ɪz
hindsight ˈhaɪnd.saɪt
Hindu ˌhɪnˈduː ⓤⓢ ˈhɪn.duː **-s** -z *stress shift, British only:* ˌHindu ˈdeity
Hinduism ˈhɪn.duː.ɪ.zəm, ˌhɪnˈduː- ⓤⓢ ˈhɪn.duː-
Hindu Kush ˌhɪn.duːˈkuːʃ, -ˈkʊʃ
Hindustan ˌhɪn.dʊˈstɑːn, -ˈstæn **-i** -i
Hines haɪnz
hing|e ˈhɪndʒ **-es** -ɪz **-ing** -ɪŋ **-ed** -d
Hingston ˈhɪŋ*k*.stən
Hinkson ˈhɪŋk.sən
hinn|y ˈhɪn|.i **-ies** -iz **-ying** -i.ɪŋ **-ied** -id
hint hɪnt **-s** -s **-ing** -ɪŋ ⓤⓢ ˈhɪn.t̬ɪŋ **-ed** -ɪd ⓤⓢ ˈhɪn.t̬ɪd
hinterland ˈhɪn.tə.lænd, -lənd ⓤⓢ -t̬ɚ-
Hinton ˈhɪn.tən
hip hɪp **-s** -s **-ped** -t **-per** -əʳ ⓤⓢ -ɚ **-pest** -ɪst, -əst ˈ**hip** ˌ**bath** ; ˈ**hip** ˌ**joint**
hipbone ˈhɪp.bəʊn ⓤⓢ -boʊn **-s** -z
hip-hop ˈhɪp.hɒp ⓤⓢ -hɑːp
Hipomenes haɪˈpɒm.ɪ.niːz ⓤⓢ -ˈpɑː.mɪ-
Hipparchus hɪˈpɑː.kəs ⓤⓢ -ˈpɑːr-
Hippias ˈhɪp.i.æs ⓤⓢ -æs, -əs
hippie ˈhɪp.i **-s** -z
hippo ˈhɪp.əʊ ⓤⓢ -oʊ **-s** -z
hippocamp|us ˌhɪp.əʊˈkæm.p|əs ⓤⓢ -oʊˈ- **-i** -aɪ
Hippocrates hɪˈpɒk.rə.tiːz ⓤⓢ -ˈpɑː.krə-
Hippocratic ˌhɪp.əʊˈkræt.ɪk ⓤⓢ -əˈkræt̬- ˌ**Hippocratic** ˈ**oath**
Hippocrene ˌhɪp.əʊˈkriː.niː, -ni *also in poetry:* ˈhɪp.əʊ.kriːn ⓤⓢ ˈhɪp.oʊ.kriːn, ˌhɪp.oʊˈkriː.ni
hippodrome (H) ˈhɪp.ə.drəʊm ⓤⓢ -droʊm **-s** -z
Hippolyta hɪˈpɒl.ɪ.tə, ˈ-ə- ⓤⓢ -ˈpɑː.lɪ.tə
Hippolyte hɪˈpɒl.ɪ.tiː, ˈ-ə- ⓤⓢ -ˈpɑː.lɪ.tiː

Hippolytus hɪˈpɒl.ɪ.təs, ˈ-ə- (US) -ˈpɑː.lɪ.təs

hippopotam|us ˌhɪp.əˈpɒt.ə.m|əs (US) -ˈpɑː.t̬ə- **-uses** -ə.sɪz **-i** -aɪ

hipp|y ˈhɪp|.i **-ies** -iz

hipster ˈhɪp.stəʳ (US) -stɚ **-s** -z

Hiram *biblical name:* ˈhaɪə.rəm, -ræm (US) ˈhaɪ.rəm *modern names:* ˈhaɪə.rəm (US) ˈhaɪ-

hircine ˈhɜː.saɪn (US) ˈhɜːr-, -sɪn

Hird hɜːd (US) hɜːrd

hir|e haɪəʳ (US) haɪr **-es** -z **-ing** -ɪŋ **-ed** -d **-er/s** -əʳ/z (US) -ɚ/z **-eling/s** -lɪŋ/z ˌ**hire ˈpurchase**; ˌ**hired ˈhand**

hireling ˈhaɪə.lɪŋ (US) ˈhaɪr- **-s** -z

Hirohito ˌhɪr.əʊˈhiː.təʊ (US) -oʊˈhiː.toʊ

Hiroshima hɪˈrɒʃ.ɪ.mə, hə-, ˈ-ə-; ˌhɪr.ɒʃˈiː-, -əˈʃiː- (US) ˌhɪr.əˈʃiː-, hɪˈroʊ.ʃɪ-

Hirst hɜːst (US) hɜːrst

hirsute ˈhɜː.sjuːt, -suːt, -ˈ- (US) ˈhɜːr.suːt, ˈhɪr-; hɚˈsuːt **-ness** -nəs, -nɪs

hirsutism ˈhɜː.sjuː.tɪ.zᵊm, -suː-; hɜːˈsjuː-, -ˈsuː- (US) ˈhɜːr.suː.t̬ɪ-, ˈhɪr-; hɚˈsuː-

his *strong form:* hɪz *weak form:* ɪz

Note: Weak form word. The strong form /hɪz/ is always used when the word occurs contrastively, e.g. 'It's **his**, not **hers**' and when it is in final position, e.g. 'He said it was **his**'. When the word is unstressed the weak pronuciation is usually /ɪz/, e.g. 'on his back', /ɒn.ɪzˈbæk (US) ɑːn-/, though /hɪz/ occurs when it is the first word in a sentence, e.g. 'His shoes were wet', /hɪzˈʃuːz.wəˌwet (US) -wɚ-/, and when the style of speech is slow and careful.

Hislop ˈhɪz.lɒp, -ləp (US) -lɑːp

his'n'hers ˌhɪz.ᵊnˈhɜːz (US) -ˈhɜːrz

Hispanic hɪˈspæn.ɪk **-s** -s

Hispanic|ism hɪˈspæn.ɪ.s|ɪ.zᵊm, ˈ-ə- **-ist/s** -ɪst/s

Hispaniola ˌhɪs.pæn.iˈəʊ.lə, -pænˈjəʊ-; hɪˌspæn- (US) ˌhɪs.pənˈjoʊ-

hiss (H) hɪs **-es** -ɪz **-ing** -ɪŋ **-ed** -t **-er/s** -əʳ/z (US) -ɚ/z

hist sːt, hɪst

Note: This spelling is used to represent the hissing sound made to attract someone's attention; it has a connotation of secrecy.

histamine ˈhɪs.tə.miːn, -mɪn **-s** -z

histogram ˈhɪs.tə.græm (US) -toʊ-, -tə- **-s** -z

histological ˌhɪs.təˈlɒdʒ.ɪ.kᵊl (US) -toʊˈlɑː.dʒɪ-, -təˈ- **-ly** -li

histolog|y hɪˈstɒl.ə.dʒ|i (US) ˈtɑː.lə- **-ist/s** -ɪst/s

Histon ˈhɪs.tᵊn

historian hɪˈstɔː.ri.ən (US) -ˈstɔːr.i- **-s** -z

historic hɪˈstɒr.ɪk (US) hɪˈstɔːr.ɪk **-al** -ᵊl **-ally** -ᵊl.i, -li

Note: In British English, the pronounciation /ɪsˈtɒr.ɪk/ is sometimes used, though only after 'an' /ən/.

historicism hɪˈstɒr.ɪ.sɪ.zᵊm, ˈ-ə- (US) -ˈstɔːr.ə-

historicity ˌhɪs.tɒrˈɪs.ə.ti, -təˈrɪs-, -ɪ.ti (US) -təˈrɪs.ə.t̬i

historiograph|y hɪˌstɒr.iˈɒg.rə.f|i (US) -ˌstɔːr.iˈɑː.grə- **-er/s** -əʳ/z (US) -ɚ/z

histor|y ˈhɪs.tᵊr|.i **-ies** -iz

histrionic ˌhɪs.triˈɒn.ɪk (US) -ˈɑː.nɪk **-s** -s **-al** -ᵊl **-ally** -ᵊl.i, -li

histrionism ˈhɪs.tri.ə.nɪ.zᵊm

hit hɪt **-s** -s **-ting** -ɪŋ (US) ˈhɪt̬.ɪŋ **-ter/s** -əʳ/z (US) ˈhɪt̬.ɚ/z ˈ**hit** ˌ**list**; ˈ**hit paˌrade**

Hitachi® hɪˈtɑː.tʃi, -ˈtætʃ.i (US) -ˈtɑː.tʃi

hit-and-miss ˌhɪt.ᵊnˈmɪs, -ᵊmˈ- (US) -ᵊnˈ-

hit-and-run ˌhɪt.ᵊnˈrʌn, -ᵊmˈ- (US) -ᵊnˈ- *stress shift, see compound:* ˌ**hit-and-run ˈdriver**

hitch hɪtʃ **-es** -ɪz **-ing** -ɪŋ **-ed** -t

Hitchcock ˈhɪtʃ.kɒk (US) -kɑːk

Hitchens ˈhɪtʃ.ɪnz

hitchhik|e ˈhɪtʃ.haɪk **-es** -s **-ing** -ɪŋ **-ed** -t **-er/s** -əʳ/z (US) -ɚ/z

Hitchin ˈhɪtʃ.ɪn **-s** -z

hi-tech ˌhaɪˈtek *stress shift:* ˌhi-tech ˈproduct

hither (H) ˈhɪð.əʳ (US) -ɚ

hithermost ˈhɪð.ə.məʊst (US) -ɚ.moʊst

hitherto ˌhɪð.əˈtuː (US) -ɚˈ- *stress shift:* ˌhitherto ˈnamed

hitherwards ˈhɪð.ə.wədz (US) -ɚ.wɚdz

Hitler ˈhɪt.ləʳ (US) -lɚ

Hitlerian hɪtˈlɪə.ri.ən (US) -ˈlɪr.i-

Hitlerism ˈhɪt.ləʳ.ɪ.zᵊm (US) -lɚ-

Hitlerite ˈhɪt.ləʳ.aɪt (US) -lɚ.aɪt **-s** -s

hit|man ˈhɪt|.mæn **-men** -men

Hittite ˈhɪt.aɪt (US) ˈhɪt̬- **-s** -s

HIV ˌeɪtʃ.aɪˈviː *stress shift, see compound:* ˌ**HIV ˈpositive**

hiv|e (*n. v.*) haɪv **-es** -z **-ing** -ɪŋ **-ed** -d

Hivite ˈhaɪ.vaɪt **-s** -s

Hizbollah ˌhɪz.bɒlˈɑː (US) ˌhez.bəˈlɑː

HMO ˌeɪtʃ.emˈəʊ (US) -ˈoʊ

HMS ˌeɪtʃ.emˈes

HNC ˌeɪtʃ.enˈsiː

HND ˌeɪtʃ.enˈdiː

ho həʊ (US) hoʊ

Hoadl(e)y ˈhəʊd.li (US) ˈhoʊd-

hoag|ie, hoag|y ˈhəʊ.g|i (US) ˈhoʊ- **-ies** -iz

hoar (H) hɔːʳ (US) hɔːr

hoard hɔːd (US) hɔːrd **-s** -z **-ing** -ɪŋ **-ed** -ɪd **-er/s** -əʳ/z (US) -ɚ/z

hoarding ˈhɔː.dɪŋ (US) ˈhɔːr- **-s** -z

Hoare hɔːʳ (US) hɔːr

hoarfrost ˈhɔː.frɒst, ˌ-ˈ- (US) ˈhɔːr.frɑːst **-s** -s

hoars|e hɔːs (US) hɔːrs **-er** -əʳ (US) -ɚ **-est** -ɪst, -əst **-ely** -li **-eness** -nəs, -nɪs

hoar|y ˈhɔː.r|i (US) ˈhɔːr|.i **-ier** -i.əʳ (US) -i.ɚ **-iest** -i.ɪst, -i.əst **-ily** -ᵊl.i, -ɪ.li **-iness** -ɪ.nəs, -ɪ.nɪs

hoax həʊks (US) hoʊks **-es** -ɪz **-ing** -ɪŋ **-ed** -t **-er/s** -əʳ/z (US) -ɚ/z

hob hɒb (US) hɑːb **-s** -z

Hoban ˈhəʊ.bən (US) ˈhoʊ-

Hobart ˈhəʊ.bɑːt, -bət; ˈhʌb.ət (US) ˈhoʊ.bɑːrt, -bɚt; ˈhʌb.ɚt

Hobbema ˈhɒb.ɪ.mə (US) ˈhɑː.bə.mɑː, -mə **-s** -z

Hobbes hɒbz (US) hɑːbz

hobbit (H) ˈhɒb.ɪt (US) ˈhɑː.bɪt **-s** -s

hobbl|e ˈhɒb.l̩ (US) ˈhɑː.b|l̩ **-es** -z **-ing** -ɪŋ, ˈhɒb.lɪŋ (US) ˈhɑː.blɪŋ **-ed** -d **-er/s** -əʳ/z (US) -ɚ/z, ˈhɒb.ləʳ/z (US) ˈhɑː.blɚ/z

hobbledehoy ˌhɒb.l̩.diˈhɔɪ, ˈhɒb.l̩.di.hɔɪ (US) ˈhɑː.bl̩.di.hɔɪ **-s** -z

Hobbs hɒbz (US) hɑːbz

hobb|y ˈhɒb|.i (US) ˈhɑː.b|i **-ies** -iz

hobbyhors|e ˈhɒb.i.hɔːs (US) ˈhɑː.bi.hɔːrs **-es** -ɪz

Hobday ˈhɒb.deɪ (US) ˈhɑːb-

hobgoblin ˌhɒbˈgɒb.lɪn, ˈ-ˌ-- (US) ˈhɑːbˌgɑːb- **-s** -z

Hobhouse ˈhɒb.haʊs (US) ˈhɑːb-

hobnail ˈhɒb.neɪl (US) ˈhɑːb- **-s** -z **-ed** -d ˌ**hobnail ˈboots**

hobnob ˈhɒb.nɒb, ˌ-ˈ- (US) ˈhɑːb.nɑːb **-s** -z **-bing** -ɪŋ **-bed** -d

hobo ˈhəʊ.bəʊ (US) ˈhoʊ.boʊ **-(e)s** -z

Hoboken ˈhəʊ.bəʊ.kᵊn (US) ˈhoʊ.boʊ-

Hobsbaum ˈhɒbz.baʊm (US) ˈhɑːbz-

Hobsbawm ˈhɒbz.bɔːm (US) ˈhɑːbz.bɑːm, -bɔːm

Hobson ˈhɒb.sᵊn (US) ˈhɑːb- ˌ**Hobson's ˈchoice**

Hobson-Jobson ˌhɒb.sᵊnˈdʒɒb.sᵊn (US) ˌhɑːb.sᵊnˈdʒɑːb-

Hoby ˈhəʊ.bi (US) ˈhoʊ-

Hoccleve ˈhɒk.liːv (US) ˈhɑːk-

Ho Chi Minh ˌhəʊ.tʃiːˈmɪn (US) ˌhoʊ-

Ho Chi Minh City ˌhəʊ.tʃiː.mɪnˈsɪt.i (US) ˌhoʊ.tʃiː.mɪnˈsɪt̬-

hock hɒk (US) hɑːk **-s** -s

hockey ˈhɒk.i (US) ˈhɑː.ki ˈ**hockey** ˌ**stick**

Hockin ˈhɒk.ɪn (US) ˈhɑː.kɪn

Hocking ˈhɒk.ɪŋ (US) ˈhɑː.kɪŋ

Hockley ˈhɒk.li (US) ˈhɑːk-

Hockney ˈhɒk.ni (US) ˈhɑːk-

hockshop ˈhɒk.ʃɒp (US) ˈhɑːk.ʃɑːp **-s** -s

hocus 'həʊ.kəs ⓊⓈ 'hoʊ- **-es** -ɪz **-(s)ing** -ɪŋ **-(s)ed** -t
hocus-pocus ˌhəʊ.kəs'pəʊ.kəs ⓊⓈ ˌhoʊ.kəs'poʊ-
hod hɒd ⓊⓈ hɑːd **-s** -z
Hodder 'hɒd.əʳ ⓊⓈ 'hɑː.dɚ
Hoddesdon 'hɒdz.dən ⓊⓈ 'hɑːdz-
Hoddinott 'hɒd.ɪ.nɒt, -ᵊn.ɒt ⓊⓈ 'hɑː.dᵊn.ɑːt
Hoddle 'hɒd.l̩ ⓊⓈ 'hɑː.dl̩
Hodge hɒdʒ ⓊⓈ hɑːdʒ
hodgepodge 'hɒdʒ.pɒdʒ ⓊⓈ 'hɑːdʒ.pɑːdʒ
Hodges 'hɒdʒ.ɪz ⓊⓈ 'hɑː.dʒɪz
Hodgetts 'hɒdʒ.ɪts ⓊⓈ 'hɑː.dʒɪts
Hodgins 'hɒdʒ.ɪnz ⓊⓈ 'hɑː.dʒɪnz
Hodgkin 'hɒdʒ.kɪn ⓊⓈ 'hɑːdʒ- **'Hodgkin's diˌsease**
Hodgkins 'hɒdʒ.kɪnz ⓊⓈ 'hɑːdʒ-
Hodgkinson 'hɒdʒ.kɪn.sᵊn ⓊⓈ 'hɑːdʒ-
Hodgkiss 'hɒdʒ.kɪs ⓊⓈ 'hɑːdʒ-
Hodgson 'hɒdʒ.sᵊn *in the North of England also:* 'hɒdʒ.ᵊn ⓊⓈ 'hɑːdʒ.sᵊn
hodometer hɒd'ɒm.ɪ.təʳ, -ə.təʳ ⓊⓈ hɑː'dɑː.mə.t̬ɚ **-s** -z
Hodson 'hɒd.sᵊn ⓊⓈ 'hɑːd-
hoe (H) həʊ ⓊⓈ hoʊ **-s** -z **-ing** -ɪŋ **-d** -d
hoedown 'həʊ.daʊn ⓊⓈ 'hoʊ- **-s** -z
Hoey hɔɪ, 'həʊ.i ⓊⓈ 'hoʊ.i
Hoffa 'hɒf.ə ⓊⓈ 'hɑː.fə
Hoffman(n) 'hɒf.mən ⓊⓈ 'hɑːf-
Hofmannsthal 'hɒf.mᵊn.stɑːl ⓊⓈ 'hɑːf.mɑːn-, 'hɔːf-
Hofmeister 'hɒfˌmaɪ.stəʳ ⓊⓈ 'hɑːfˌmaɪ.stɚ
hog hɒg ⓊⓈ hɑːg, hɔːg **-s** -z **-ging** -ɪŋ **-ged** -d
Hogan 'həʊ.gᵊn ⓊⓈ 'hoʊ-
Hogarth 'həʊ.gɑːθ, 'hɒg.ət ⓊⓈ 'hoʊ.gɑːrθ
Hogarthian həʊ'gɑː.θi.ən ⓊⓈ hoʊ'gɑːr-
Hogben 'hɒg.bᵊn, -ben ⓊⓈ 'hɑːg-, 'hɔːg
Hogg hɒg ⓊⓈ hɑːg, hɔːg
Hoggart 'hɒg.ət ⓊⓈ 'hɑː.gɚt, 'hɔː-
hogget (H) 'hɒg.ɪt ⓊⓈ 'hɑː.gɪt, 'hɔː- **-s** -s
hoggish 'hɒg.ɪʃ ⓊⓈ 'hɑː.gɪʃ, 'hɔː- **-ly** -li **-ness** -nəs, -nɪs
hogmanay (H) 'hɒg.mə.neɪ, ˌ--'- ⓊⓈ 'hɑːg.mə.neɪ, 'hɔːg-
hogshead 'hɒgz.hed ⓊⓈ 'hɑːgz-, 'hɔːgz- **-s** -z
hogwash 'hɒg.wɒʃ ⓊⓈ 'hɑːg.wɑːʃ, 'hɔːg-, -wɔːʃ
hogweed 'hɒg.wiːd ⓊⓈ 'hɑːg-, 'hɔːg- **-s** -z
Hohenlinden ˌhəʊ.ən'lɪn.dən ⓊⓈ ˌhoʊ.ən'-, 'hoʊ.ənˌlɪn-
Hohenzollern ˌhəʊ.ən'zɒl.ən ⓊⓈ 'hoʊ.ənˌzɑː.lɚn **-s** -z
hoi(c)k hɔɪk **-s** -s **-ing** -ɪŋ **-ed** -t
hoi polloi ˌhɔɪ.pə'lɔɪ, -pɒl'ɔɪ; -'pɒl.ɔɪ ⓊⓈ ˌhɔɪ.pə'lɔɪ
hoisin 'hɔɪ.sɪn, -'- **ˌhoisin 'sauce**
hoist hɔɪst **-s** -s **-ing** -ɪŋ **-ed** -ɪd
hoity-toity ˌhɔɪ.ti'tɔɪ.ti ⓊⓈ ˌhɔɪ.t̬i'tɔɪ.t̬i
hokey 'həʊ.ki ⓊⓈ 'hoʊ- **ˌhokey 'cokey**
hokey-pokey ˌhəʊ.ki'pəʊ.ki ⓊⓈ ˌhoʊ.ki'poʊ-
Hokkaido hɒk'aɪ.dəʊ ⓊⓈ hɑː'kaɪ.doʊ
hokum 'həʊ.kəm ⓊⓈ 'hoʊ-
Holbeach 'hɒl.biːtʃ, 'həʊl- ⓊⓈ 'hɑːl-, 'hoʊl-
Holbech 'həʊl.biːtʃ, 'hɒl- ⓊⓈ 'hoʊl-
Holbeck 'hɒl.bek, 'həʊl- ⓊⓈ 'hoʊl-
Holbein 'hɒl.baɪn ⓊⓈ 'hoʊl- **-s** -z
Holborn 'həʊ.bən, 'həʊl-, 'hɒl- ⓊⓈ 'hoʊl.bɚn, 'hoʊ-
Holbrook(e) 'həʊl.brʊk, 'hɒl- ⓊⓈ 'hoʊl-
Holburn 'hɒl.bɜːn, 'həʊl- ⓊⓈ 'hoʊl.bɜːrn
Holcroft 'həʊl.krɒft ⓊⓈ 'hoʊl.krɑːft
hold həʊld ⓊⓈ hoʊld **-s** -z **-ing/s** -ɪŋ/z **held** held **ˌno ˌholds 'barred** ; **'holding ˌcompany** ; **ˌhold one's 'own**
holdall 'həʊld.ɔːl ⓊⓈ 'hoʊld-, -ɑːl **-s** -z
Holden 'həʊl.dᵊn ⓊⓈ 'hoʊl-
holder (H) 'həʊl.dəʳ ⓊⓈ 'hoʊl.dɚ **-s** -z
Holderness 'həʊl.də.nəs, -nɪs, -nes ⓊⓈ 'hoʊl.dɚ-
holdover 'həʊldˌəʊ.vəʳ ⓊⓈ 'hoʊldˌoʊ.vɚ **-s** -z
Holdsworth 'həʊldz.wəθ, -wɜːθ ⓊⓈ 'hoʊldz.wɚθ, -wɜːrθ
holdup 'həʊld.ʌp ⓊⓈ 'hoʊld- **-s** -s
hol|e (H) həʊl ⓊⓈ hoʊl **-es** -z **-ing** -ɪŋ **-ed** -d **ˌhole in 'one** ⓊⓈ **'hole in ˌone** ; **ˌneed something like a ˌhole in the 'head** ⓊⓈ **ˌneed something like a 'hole in the ˌhead**
hole-and-corner ˌhəʊl.ənd'kɔː.nəʳ, -əŋ'- ⓊⓈ ˌhoʊl.ənd'kɔːr.nɚ
hole-in-the-wall ˌhəʊl.ɪn.ðə'wɔːl ⓊⓈ ˌhoʊl.ɪn.ðə'wɔːl, -wɑːl
Holford 'həʊl.fəd, 'hɒl- ⓊⓈ 'hoʊl.fɚd
holiday (H) 'hɒl.ə.deɪ, '-ɪ-, -di ⓊⓈ 'hɑː.lə.deɪ **-s** -z **'holiday ˌcamp**
holidaymaker 'hɒl.ə.diˌmeɪ.kəʳ, '-ɪ-, -deɪˌ- ⓊⓈ 'hɑː.lə.deɪˌmeɪ.kɚ **-s** -z
holier-than-thou ˌhəʊ.li.ə.ðᵊn'ðaʊ ⓊⓈ ˌhoʊ.li.ɚ- *stress shift:* ˌholier-than-thou 'attitude
Holies 'həʊ.lɪz ⓊⓈ 'hoʊ-
Holifield 'hɒl.ɪ.fiːld ⓊⓈ 'hoʊ.lɪ-, 'hɑː-
Holinshed 'hɒl.ɪn.ʃed ⓊⓈ 'hɑː.lɪn-
holism 'həʊ.lɪ.zᵊm, 'hɒl.ɪ- ⓊⓈ 'hoʊ.lɪ-
holistic həʊ'lɪs.tɪk, hɒl'ɪs- ⓊⓈ hoʊ'lɪs- **-ally** -ᵊl.i, -li
Holland, holland 'hɒl.ənd ⓊⓈ 'hɑː.lənd **-s** -z
hollandaise ˌhɒl.ən'deɪz ⓊⓈ ˌhɑː.lən'- *stress shift, see compound:* **ˌhollandaise 'sauce** ⓊⓈ **'hollandaise ˌsauce**
Hollander 'hɒl.ən.dəʳ ⓊⓈ 'hɑː.lən.dɚ **-s** -z
holl|er 'hɒl|.əʳ ⓊⓈ 'hɑː.l|ɚ **-ers** -əz ⓊⓈ -ɚz **-ering** -ᵊr.ɪŋ **-ered** -əd ⓊⓈ -ɚd
Holles 'hɒl.ɪs ⓊⓈ 'hɑː.lɪs
Holliday 'hɒl.ɪ.deɪ, '-ə-, -di ⓊⓈ 'hɑː.lə-
Hollings 'hɒl.ɪŋz ⓊⓈ 'hɑː.lɪŋz
Hollingsworth 'hɒl.ɪŋz.wəθ, -wɜːθ ⓊⓈ 'hɑː.lɪŋz.wɚθ, -wɜːrθ
Hollingworth 'hɒl.ɪŋ.wəθ, -wɜːθ ⓊⓈ 'hɑː.lɪŋ.wɚθ, -wɜːrθ
Hollins 'hɒl.ɪnz ⓊⓈ 'hɑː.lɪnz
Hollis 'hɒl.ɪs ⓊⓈ 'hɑː.lɪs
hollo 'hɒl.əʊ ⓊⓈ 'hɑː.loʊ; hə'loʊ **-es** -z **-ing** -ɪŋ **-ed** -d
hollo(a) 'hɒl.əʊ ⓊⓈ 'hɑː.loʊ; hə'loʊ **-s** -z **-ing** -ɪŋ **-ed** -d
Hollom 'hɒl.əm ⓊⓈ 'hɑː.ləm
hollow 'hɒl.əʊ ⓊⓈ 'hɑː.loʊ **-s** -z **-er** -əʳ ⓊⓈ -ɚ **-est** -ɪst, -əst **-ly** -li **-ness** -nəs, -nɪs **-ing** -ɪŋ **-ed** -d
Holloway 'hɒl.ə.weɪ ⓊⓈ 'hɑː.lə-
holl|y (H) 'hɒl|.i ⓊⓈ 'hɑː.l|i **-ies** -iz
hollyhock 'hɒl.i.hɒk ⓊⓈ 'hɑː.li.hɑːk **-s** -s
Hollywood 'hɒl.i.wʊd ⓊⓈ 'hɑː.li-
holm (H) həʊm ⓊⓈ hoʊ*l*m **-s** -z **'holm ˌoak**
Holman 'həʊl.mən, 'hɒl- ⓊⓈ 'hoʊl-
Holmby 'həʊm.bi ⓊⓈ 'hoʊ*l*m-
Holmer 'həʊl.məʳ, 'həʊ- ⓊⓈ 'hoʊ*l*.mɚ
Holmes həʊmz ⓊⓈ hoʊ*l*mz
Holmesdale 'həʊmz.deɪl ⓊⓈ 'hoʊ*l*mz-
Holmfirth 'həʊm.fəθ, -fɜːθ ⓊⓈ 'hoʊ*l*m.fɚθ, -fɜːrθ
holmium 'həʊl.mi.əm, 'hɒl- ⓊⓈ 'hoʊl-
holo- hɒl.əʊ-; hɒl'ɒ- ⓊⓈ hɑː.loʊ-, hoʊ-, -lə-; hoʊ'lɑː-
Note: Prefix. Normally either takes primary or secondary stress on the first syllable, e.g. **holograph** /'hɒl.ə.grɑːf ⓊⓈ 'hɑː.lə.græf/, **holographic** /ˌhɒl.ə'græf.ɪk ⓊⓈ ˌhɑː.lə'-/, or primary stress on the second syllable, e.g. **holography** /hɒl'ɒg.rə.fi ⓊⓈ hoʊ'lɑː.grə-/.
holocaust (H) 'hɒl.ə.kɔːst, -kɒst ⓊⓈ 'hɑː.lə.kɑːst, 'hoʊ-, -kɔːst **-s** -s
Holofernes ˌhɒl.əʊ'fɜː.niːz, hə'lɒf.ə- ⓊⓈ ˌhɑː.lə'fɜːr-
hologram 'hɒl.ə.græm ⓊⓈ 'hɑː.lə-, 'hoʊ- **-s** -z
holograph 'hɒl.ə.grɑːf, -græf ⓊⓈ 'hɑː.lə.græf, 'hoʊ- **-s** -s
holographic ˌhɒl.ə'græf.ɪk ⓊⓈ ˌhɑː.lə-, ˌhoʊ- **-ally** -ᵊl.i, -li

holography hɒlˈɒg.rə.fi Ⓤⓢ hoʊˈlɑː.grə-
Holon ˈhɒl.ən Ⓤⓢ ˈhɑː.lən; ˈhoʊ.lɑːn
holophras|e ˈhɒl.ə.freɪz Ⓤⓢ ˈhɑː.lə-, ˈhoʊ- **-es** -ɪz
holophrastic ˌhɒl.əˈfræs.tɪk Ⓤⓢ ˌhɑː.ləˈ-, ˌhoʊ-
holpen (*archaic past of* **help**) ˈhəʊl.pᵊn, ˈhɒl- Ⓤⓢ ˈhoʊl-
Holroyd ˈhɒl.rɔɪd, ˈhəʊl- Ⓤⓢ ˈhɑːl-
Holst həʊlst Ⓤⓢ hoʊlst
holstein (H) ˈhɒl.staɪn, ˈhəʊl- Ⓤⓢ ˈhoʊl.staɪn, -stiːn
holster ˈhəʊl.stəʳ Ⓤⓢ ˈhoʊl.stɚ **-s** -z **-ed** -d
holt (H) həʊlt Ⓤⓢ hoʊlt **-s** -s
Holtby ˈhəʊlt.bi Ⓤⓢ ˈhoʊlt-
Holtham ˈhəʊl.θəm, ˈhɒl-, ˈhəʊ- Ⓤⓢ ˈhoʊl-
holus-bolus ˌhəʊ.ləsˈbəʊ.ləs Ⓤⓢ ˌhoʊ.ləsˈboʊ-
hol|y (H) ˈhəʊ.l|i Ⓤⓢ ˈhoʊ- **-ier** -i.əʳ Ⓤⓢ -i.ɚ **-iest** -i.ɪst, -i.əst **-iness** -ɪ.nəs, -ɪ.nɪs ˌ**Holy ˈBible** ; ˌ**Holy Comˈmunion** ; ˌ**Holy ˈGhost** ; ˌ**Holy ˈGrail** ; ˈ**Holy ˌLand** ; ˌ**Holy ˌRoman ˈEmpire** ; ˌ**Holy ˈSpirit** ; ˈ**Holy ˌWeek**
Holycross ˈhəʊ.li.krɒs Ⓤⓢ ˈhoʊl.i.krɑːs
Holyhead ˌhɒl.iˈhed, ˈ--- Ⓤⓢ ˈhɑː.li-
Holyoake *place in Massachusetts:* ˈhəʊl.jəʊk Ⓤⓢ ˈhoʊl.joʊk *all other senses:* ˈhəʊ.li.əʊk Ⓤⓢ ˈhoʊ.li.oʊk
Holyrood ˈhɒl.i.ruːd Ⓤⓢ ˈhɑː.li-
holyston|e ˈhəʊl.i.stəʊn Ⓤⓢ ˈhoʊl.i.stoʊn **-es** -z **-ing** -ɪŋ **-ed** -d
Holywell ˈhɒl.i.wəl, -wel Ⓤⓢ ˈhɑː.li-
homage ˈhɒm.ɪdʒ Ⓤⓢ ˈhɑː.mɪdʒ, ˈɑː-
hombre ˈɒm.breɪ, -bri Ⓤⓢ ˈɑːm- **-s** -z
homburg (H) ˈhɒm.bɜːg Ⓤⓢ ˈhɑːm.bɜːrg **-s** -z
home həʊm Ⓤⓢ hoʊm **-s** -z ˌ**home ˈbrew** ; ˌ**Home ˈCounties** ; ˌ**home ecoˈnomics** ; ˌ**home ˈfree** ; ˌ**home ˈfront** Ⓤⓢ ˈ**home ˌfront** ; ˌ**home ˈhelp** ; ˈ**Home ˌOffice** ; ˈ**home ˌpage** ; ˌ**home ˈrule** ; ˌ**Home ˈSecretary** ; ˌ**home ˈtruth** ; ˌ**close to ˈhome** ; ˌ**home from ˈhome**
Home həʊm, hjuːm Ⓤⓢ hoʊm, hjuːm
Note: /hjuːm/ in **Milne-Home, Douglas-Home,** and Baron Home of the Hirsel
homeboy ˈhəʊm.bɔɪ Ⓤⓢ ˈhoʊm- **-s** -z
homebred ˌhəʊmˈbred Ⓤⓢ ˌhoʊm- *stress shift:* ˌhomebred ˈlivestock
homecoming ˈhəʊmˌkʌm.ɪŋ Ⓤⓢ ˈhoʊm- **-s** -z
homegrown ˌhəʊmˈgrəʊn Ⓤⓢ ˌhoʊmˈgroʊn *stress shift:* ˌhomegrown ˈfood
homeland (H) ˈhəʊm.lænd, -lənd Ⓤⓢ ˈhoʊm- **-s** -z
homeless ˈhəʊm.ləs, -lɪs Ⓤⓢ ˈhoʊm- **-ness** -nəs, -nɪs
homelike ˈhəʊm.laɪk Ⓤⓢ ˈhoʊm-
homel|y ˈhəʊm.l|i Ⓤⓢ ˈhoʊm- **-ier** -i.əʳ Ⓤⓢ -i.ɚ **-iest** -i.ɪst, -i.əst **-iness** -ɪ.nəs, -ɪ.nɪs
homemade ˌhəʊmˈmeɪd Ⓤⓢ ˌhoʊm- *stress shift:* ˌhomemade ˈjam
homemaker ˈhəʊmˌmeɪ.kəʳ Ⓤⓢ ˈhoʊmˌmeɪ.kɚ **-s** -z
homeo- ˈhəʊ.mi.əʊ-, ˈhɒm.i.əʊ-; ˌhəʊ.miˈɒ-, ˌhɒm.iˈɒ- Ⓤⓢ ˈhoʊ.mi.oʊ-, -ə-; ˌhoʊ.miˈɑː-
Note: Prefix. Normally ether takes primary or secondary stress on the first syllable, e.g. **homeopath** /ˈhəʊ.mi.əʊ.pæθ Ⓤⓢ ˈhoʊ.mi.oʊ-/, **homeopathic** /ˌhəʊ.mi.əʊˈpæθ.ɪk Ⓤⓢ ˌhoʊ.mi.oʊˈ-/, or primary stress on the third syllable with secondary stress on the first, e.g. **homeopathy** /ˌhəʊ.miˈɒp.ə.θi Ⓤⓢ ˌhoʊ.miˈɑː.pə-/.
homeopath ˈhəʊ.mi.əʊ.pæθ, ˈhɒm.i- Ⓤⓢ ˈhoʊ.mi.oʊ- **-s** -s
homeopathic ˌhəʊ.mi.əʊˈpæθ.ɪk, ˌhɒm.i- Ⓤⓢ ˌhoʊ.mi.oʊˈ- **-al** -ᵊl **-ally** -ᵊl.i, -li
homeopathy ˌhəʊ.miˈɒp.ə.θi, ˌhɒm.iˈ- Ⓤⓢ ˌhoʊ.miˈɑː.pə-
homeostasis ˌhəʊ.mi.əʊˈsteɪ.sɪs, ˈhɒm.i-, ˌ--ˈɒs.tə- Ⓤⓢ ˌhoʊ.mi.oʊˈ-, -ˈstæs.ɪs
homeostatic ˌhəʊ.mi.əʊˈstæt.ɪk, ˌhɒm.i- Ⓤⓢ ˌhoʊ.mi.oʊˈstæt̬- **-ally** -ᵊl.i, -li
homeowner ˈhəʊmˌəʊ.nəʳ Ⓤⓢ ˈhoʊmˌoʊ.nɚ **-s** -z
Homer ˈhəʊ.məʳ Ⓤⓢ ˈhoʊ.mɚ
Homeric *relating to Homer:* həʊˈmer.ɪk Ⓤⓢ hoʊ- *name of ship:* ˈhəʊ.mᵊr.ɪk Ⓤⓢ ˈhoʊ-
Homerton ˈhɒm.ə.tᵊn Ⓤⓢ ˈhɑː.mɚ-
homesick ˈhəʊm.sɪk Ⓤⓢ ˈhoʊm- **-ness** -nəs, -nɪs
homespun ˈhəʊm.spʌn Ⓤⓢ ˈhoʊm- **-s** -z
homestead ˈhəʊm.sted, -stɪd Ⓤⓢ ˈhoʊm- **-s** -z
homesteader ˈhəʊmˌsted.əʳ Ⓤⓢ ˈhoʊmˌsted.ɚ **-s** -z
homeward ˈhəʊm.wəd Ⓤⓢ ˈhoʊm.wɚd **-s** -z
homework ˈhəʊm.wɜːk Ⓤⓢ ˈhoʊm.wɜːrk
homey ˈhəʊ.mi Ⓤⓢ ˈhoʊ-
homicidal ˌhɒm.ɪˈsaɪ.dᵊl, -əˈ- Ⓤⓢ ˌhɑː.məˈ-, ˌhoʊ- *stress shift:* ˌhomicidal ˈmaniac
homicide ˈhɒm.ɪ.saɪd, ˈ-ə- Ⓤⓢ ˈhɑː.mə-, ˈhoʊ- **-s** -z
homil|y ˈhɒm.ɪ.l|i, ˈ-ə- Ⓤⓢ ˈhɑː.mə- **-ies** -iz
homing ˈhəʊ.mɪŋ Ⓤⓢ ˈhoʊ- ˈ**homing deˌvice** ; ˈ**homing ˌpigeon**
hominid ˈhɒm.ɪ.nɪd, ˈ-ə- Ⓤⓢ ˈhɑː.mɪ-, -mə- **-s** -z
hominoid ˈhɒm.ɪ.nɔɪd, -ə- Ⓤⓢ ˈhɑː.mɪ-, -mə- **-s** -z
hominy ˈhɒm.ɪ.ni, ˈ-ə- Ⓤⓢ ˈhɑː.mɪ-, -mə-
homo ˈhəʊ.məʊ, ˈhɒm.əʊ Ⓤⓢ ˈhoʊ.moʊ **-s** -z
homo- həʊ.məʊ-, hɒm.əʊ-; həˈmɒ-, hɒmˈɒ- Ⓤⓢ hoʊ.moʊ-, hɑː-, -mə-; həˈmɑː-, hoʊ-
Note: Prefix. Normally either takes primary or secondary stress on the first syllable, e.g. **homonym** /ˈhɒm.ə.nɪm Ⓤⓢ ˈhɑː.mə-/, **homophobia** /ˌhɒm.əˈfəʊ.bi.ə Ⓤⓢ ˌhoʊ.məˈfoʊ-/, or primary stress on the second syllable, e.g. **homonymy** /həˈmɒn.ɪ.mi Ⓤⓢ hoʊˈmɑː.nə-/.
homoeopath ˈhəʊ.mi.əʊ.pæθ, ˈhɒm.i- Ⓤⓢ ˈhoʊ.mi.oʊ- **-s** -s
homoeopathic ˌhəʊ.mi.əʊˈpæθ.ɪk, ˌhɒm.i- Ⓤⓢ ˌhoʊ.mi.oʊˈ- **-al** -ᵊl **-ally** -ᵊl.i, -li
homoeopathy ˌhəʊ.miˈɒp.ə.θi, ˌhɒm.iˈ- Ⓤⓢ ˌhoʊ.miˈɑː.pə-
homoeostasis ˌhəʊ.mi.əʊˈsteɪ.sɪs, ˌ--ˈɒs.tə- Ⓤⓢ ˌhoʊ.mi.oʊˈ-, -ˈstæs.ɪs
homoeostatic ˌhəʊ.mi.əʊˈstæt.ɪk Ⓤⓢ ˌhoʊ.mi.oʊˈstæt̬- **-ally** -ᵊl.i, -li
homoerotic ˌhəʊ.məʊ.ɪˈrɒt.ɪk, ˌhɒm.əʊ-, -əˈ- Ⓤⓢ ˌhoʊ.moʊ.ɪˈrɑː.t̬ɪk, -əˈ-
homoeroticism ˌhəʊ.məʊ.ɪˈrɒt.ɪ.sɪ.z.ᵊm, ˌhɒm.əʊ-, -əˈ-, ˈ-ə- Ⓤⓢ ˌhoʊ.moʊ.ɪˈrɑː.t̬ə-, -əˈ-
homogeneity ˌhəʊ.məʊ.dʒəˈniː.ə.ti, ˌhɒm.əʊ-, -dʒenˈiː-, -dʒɪˈniː-, -ɪ.ti Ⓤⓢ ˌhoʊ.moʊ.dʒəˈniː.ə.t̬i, ˌhɑː-, -mə-, -ˈneɪ-
homogeneous ˌhɒm.əˈdʒiː.ni.əs, ˌhəʊ.mə- Ⓤⓢ ˌhoʊ.moʊˈdʒiː-, ˌhɑː-, -məˈ- **-ly** -li **-ness** -nəs, -nɪs
homogeniz|e, is|e həˈmɒdʒ.ə.naɪz, hɒmˈɒdʒ-, ˈ-ɪ- Ⓤⓢ həˈmɑː.dʒə- **-es** -ɪz **-ing** -ɪŋ **-ed** -d
homograph ˈhɒm.ə.grɑːf, ˈhəʊ.mə-, -græf Ⓤⓢ ˈhɑː.mə.græf, ˈhoʊ- **-s** -s
homographic ˌhɒm.əˈgræf.ɪk, ˌhəʊ.məˈ- Ⓤⓢ ˌhɑː.məˈ-, ˌhoʊ-
homoiotherm həˈmɔɪ.ə.θɜːm, hɒmˈɔɪ- Ⓤⓢ hoʊˈmɔɪ.oʊ.θɜːrm **-s** -z
homoiothermic həˌmɔɪ.əˈθɜː.mɪk, hɒmˌɔɪ- Ⓤⓢ hoʊˌmɔɪ.oʊˈθɜːr-
homolog ˈhɒm.ə.lɒg Ⓤⓢ ˈhɑː.mə.lɑːg, ˈhoʊ-, -lɔːg **-s** -z
homologous həˈmɒl.ə.gəs, hɒmˈɒl- Ⓤⓢ hoʊˈmɑː.lə-, hə-
homologue ˈhɒm.ə.lɒg Ⓤⓢ ˈhɑː.mə.lɑːg, ˈhoʊ-, -lɔːg **-s** -z

homolog|y hə'mɒl.ə.dʒ|i, hɒm'ɒl- (US) hoʊ'mɑː.lə-, hə- **-ies** -iz
homonym 'hɒm.ə.nɪm (US) 'hɑː.mə- **-s** -z
homonymous hə'mɒn.ɪ.məs, hɒm'ɒn-, -ə.məs (US) hoʊ'mɑː.nə-, hə- **-ly** -li
homonymy hə'mɒn.ɪ.mi, hɒm'ɒn-, -ə.mi (US) hoʊ'mɑː.nə-, hə-
homophobe 'hɒm.ə.fəʊb (US) 'hoʊ.mə.foʊb **-s** -z
homophobia ˌhɒm.ə'fəʊ.bi.ə (US) ˌhoʊ.mə'foʊ-
homophobic ˌhɒm.ə'fəʊ.bɪk (US) ˌhoʊ.mə'foʊ-
homophone 'hɒm.ə.fəʊn, 'həʊ.mə- (US) 'hɑː.mə.foʊn, 'hoʊ- **-s** -z
homophonic ˌhɒm.ə'fɒn.ɪk, ˌhəʊ.mə'- (US) ˌhɑː.mə'fɑː.nɪk, ˌhoʊ- **-ally** -əl.i, -li
homophon|ous hə'mɒf.ən|.əs, hɒm'ɒf- (US) hoʊ'mɑː.fən-, hə- **-y** -i
homorganic ˌhɒm.ɔː'gæn.ɪk (US) ˌhoʊ.mɔːr'-, ˌhɑː-
homo sapiens ˌhəʊ.məʊ'sæp.i.enz, -ənz (US) ˌhoʊ.moʊ'-
homosexual ˌhəʊ.məʊ'sek.ʃu.əl, ˌhɒm.əʊ'-, '-sju-, -ʃəl (US) ˌhoʊ.moʊ'sek.ʃu.əl, -mə'- **-s** **-ist/s** -ɪst/s
homosexuality ˌhəʊ.məʊˌsek.ʃu'æl.ə.ti, ˌhɒm.əʊ-, -sju'-, -ɪ.ti (US) ˌhoʊ.moʊ.sek.ʃu'æl.ə.t̬i, -mə-
homozygous ˌhɒm.ə'zaɪ.gəs (US) ˌhoʊ.mə'-, ˌhɑː-
Homs hɒmz (US) hɔːmz
homuncul|us hɒm'ʌŋ.kjə.l|əs, hə'mʌŋ-, -kjʊ- (US) hoʊ'mʌŋ.kjə-, hə- **-i** -aɪ
hon. (H) (*abbrev. for* **honourable**) 'ɒn.ər.ə.bl̩ (US) 'ɑː.nɚ- (*abbrev. for* **honorary**) 'ɒn.ər.ə.ri, '-ər.i (US) 'ɑː.nɚ.er.i
honcho 'hɒn.tʃəʊ (US) 'hɑːn.tʃoʊ **-s** -z **-ing** -ɪŋ **-ed** -d
Honda® 'hɒn.də (US) 'hɑːn.də
Hondur|as hɒn'djʊə.r|əs, -'dʊə-, -'djɔː-, -r|æs (US) hɑːn'dʊr|.əs, -'djʊr- **-an/s** -ən/z
hon|e (H) həʊn (US) hoʊn **-es** -z **-ing** -ɪŋ **-ed** -d
Honecker 'hɒn.ɪ.kər, -ek.ər (US) 'hɑː.nɪ.kɚ
Honegger 'hɒn.ɪ.gər, -eg.ər (US) 'hɑː.nɪ.gɚ, 'hoʊ-
honest 'ɒn.ɪst, -əst (US) 'ɑː.nɪst **-ly** -li
honest-to-goodness ˌɒn.ɪst.tə'gʊd.nəs, -əst-, -tuː-, -nɪs (US) ˌɑː.nɪst.tə'-
honesty 'ɒn.ɪ.sti, '-ə- (US) 'ɑː.nɪ-
hon|ey 'hʌn|.i **-eyed** -id **-ied** -id
honeybee 'hʌn.i.biː **-s** -z
Honeybourne 'hʌn.i.bɔːn (US) -bɔːrn
honeybun 'hʌn.i.bʌn **-s** -z
honeybunch 'hʌn.i.bʌntʃ **-es** -ɪz
Honeychurch 'hʌn.i.tʃɜːtʃ (US) -tʃɜːrtʃ
honeycomb (H) 'hʌn.i.kəʊm (US) -koʊm **-s** -z **-ed** -d
honeydew 'hʌn.i.djuː (US) -duː, -djuː ˌ**honeydew 'melon**
honeymoon 'hʌn.i.muːn **-s** -z **-ing** -ɪŋ **-ed** -d **-er/s** -ər/z (US) -ɚ/z
honeysucker 'hʌn.iˌsʌk.ər (US) -ɚ **-s** -z
honeysuckle 'hʌn.iˌsʌk.l̩ **-s** -z
hong hɒŋ (US) hɑːŋ **-s** -z
Hong Kong ˌhɒŋ'kɒŋ (US) 'hɑːŋˌkɑːŋ, 'hɔːŋ-, -ˌkɔːŋ, ˌ-'-
Honiara ˌhəʊ.ni'ɑː.rə (US) ˌhoʊ.ni'ɑːr.ə
Honi soit qui mal y pense ˌɒn.iˌswɑː.kiːˌmæl.i'pɑ̃ːnts (US) ˌɔː.ni-
Honiton 'hɒn.ɪ.tən *locally:* 'hʌn- (US) 'hɑː.nə.t̬ən
honk hɒŋk (US) hɑːŋk, hɔːŋk **-s** -s **-ing** -ɪŋ **-ed** -t
honk|ie, honk|y 'hɒŋ.k|i (US) 'hɑːŋ-, 'hɔːŋ- **-ies** -iz
honky-tonk 'hɒŋ.ki.tɒŋk, ˌ--'- (US) 'hɑːŋ.ki.tɑːŋk, 'hɔːŋ-, -tɔːŋk
Honolulu ˌhɒn.əl'uː.luː (US) ˌhɑː.nə'luː-
hon|or (H) 'ɒn|.ər (US) 'ɑː.n|ɚ **-ors** -əz (US) -ɚz **-oring** -ər.ɪŋ **-ored** -əd (US) -ɚd
honorab|le 'ɒn.ər.ə.b|l̩ (US) 'ɑː.nɚ- **-ly** -li **-leness** -l̩.nəs, -nɪs
honorarium ˌɒn.ə'reə.ri.əm, -'rɑː- (US) ˌɑː.nə'rer.i- **-s** -z
honorary 'ɒn.ər.ə.ri, '-ər.i (US) 'ɑː.nə.rer.i
honorific ˌɒn.ər'ɪf.ɪk (US) ˌɑː.nə'rɪf- **-s** -s
Honorius hə'nɔː.ri.əs, hɒn'ɔː- (US) hoʊ'nɔːr.i-, hə-
hon|our 'ɒn|.ər (US) 'ɑː.n|ɚ **-ours** -əz (US) -ɚz **-ouring** -ər.ɪŋ **-oured** -əd (US) -ɚd **'honours ˌlist**
honourab|le (H) 'ɒn.ər.ə.b|l̩ (US) 'ɑː.nɚ- **-ly** -li **-leness** -l̩.nəs, -nɪs
Honshu 'hɒn.ʃuː (US) 'hɑːn-
Honyman 'hʌn.i.mən
Hoo huː
hooch huːtʃ
hood (H) hʊd **-s** -z **-ing** -ɪŋ **-ed** -ɪd **-less** -ləs, -lɪs
-hood -hʊd
Note: Suffix. Normally unstressed, e.g. **womanhood** /'wʊm.ən.hʊd/.
hoodlum 'huːd.ləm, 'hʊd- **-s** -z
hoodwink 'hʊd.wɪŋk **-s** -s **-ing** -ɪŋ **-ed** -t
hooey 'huː.i
hoo|f huː|f (US) hʊ|f, huː|f **-fs** -fs **-ves** -vz **-fing** -fɪŋ **-fed** -ft **-fer/s** -fər/z (US) -fɚ/z
Hoog(h)ly 'huː.gli
hook (H) hʊk **-s** -s **-ing** -ɪŋ **-ed** -t ˌ**hook and 'eye** ; ˌ**Hook of 'Holland** ; **by ˌhook or by 'crook** ; ˌ**hook, ˌline, and 'sinker**
hookah 'hʊk.ə, -ɑː (US) 'hʊk.ə, 'huː.kə, -kɑː **-s** -z
Hooke hʊk
hooker (H) 'hʊk.ər (US) -ɚ **-s** -z
hookey 'hʊk.i
hookup 'hʊk.ʌp **-s** -s
hookworm 'hʊk.wɜːm (US) -wɜːrm **-s** -z
hooky 'hʊk.i
Hooley 'huː.li
hooligan (H) 'huː.lɪ.gən, -lə- (US) -lɪ- **-s** -z **-ism** -ɪ.zəm
hoop huːp (US) huːp, hʊp **-s** -s **-ing** -ɪŋ **-ed** -t
hooper (H) 'huː.pər (US) -pɚ **-s** -z
hoopla 'huːp.lɑː, 'hʊp-
hoopoe 'huː.puː **-s** -z
hooray hʊ'reɪ, hə-, ˌhuː-
hooray Henr|y ˌhuː.reɪ'hen.r|i **-ies** -iz
hoot huːt **-s** -s **-ing** -ɪŋ (US) 'huː.t̬ɪŋ **-ed** -ɪd (US) 'huː.t̬ɪd
hootch huːtʃ
hootenan|ny 'huː.tən.æn|.i **-nies** -iz
hooter 'huː.tər (US) -t̬ɚ **-s** -z
hoov|er (H®) 'huː.v|ər (US) -v|ɚ **-ers** -əz (US) -ɚz **-ering** -ər.ɪŋ **-ered** -əd (US) -ɚd
hooves (*from* **hoof**) huːvz (US) hʊvz, huːvz
hop hɒp (US) hɑːp **-s** -s **-ping** -ɪŋ **-ped** -t ˌ**hopping 'mad**
Hopcraft 'hɒp.krɑːft (US) 'hɑːp.kræft
hop|e (H) həʊp (US) hoʊp **-es** -s **-ing** -ɪŋ **-ed** -t **'hope ˌchest**
hopeful (H) 'həʊp.fəl, -fʊl (US) 'hoʊp- **-ly** -i **-ness** -nəs, -nɪs
hopeless 'həʊp.ləs, -lɪs (US) 'hoʊp- **-ly** -li **-ness** -nəs, -nɪs
Hopi 'həʊ.pi (US) 'hoʊ-
Hopkins 'hɒp.kɪnz (US) 'hɑːp-
Hopkinson 'hɒp.kɪn.sən (US) 'hɑːp-
hoplite 'hɒp.laɪt (US) 'hɑː.plaɪt **-s** -s
hopper (H) 'hɒp.ər (US) 'hɑː.pɚ **-s** -z
hop-pick|er 'hɒpˌpɪk|.ər (US) 'hɑːpˌpɪk|.ɚ **-ers** -əz (US) -ɚz **-ing** -ɪŋ
Hoppner 'hɒp.nər (US) 'hɑːp.nɚ **-s** -z
hopscotch 'hɒp.skɒtʃ (US) 'hɑːp.skɑːtʃ
Hopton 'hɒp.tən (US) 'hɑːp-
Hor hɔːr (US) hɔːr
Horace 'hɒr.ɪs, -əs (US) 'hɔːr.ɪs
Horae 'hɔː.riː (US) 'hoʊ.riː, 'hɔːr.iː
Horatian hə'reɪ.ʃən, hɒr'eɪ-, -ʃi.ən (US) hɔː'reɪ-, hə-
Horatio hə'reɪ.ʃi.əʊ, hɒr'eɪ- (US) hɔː'reɪ-, hə-
Horati|us hə'reɪ.ʃ|əs, hɒr'eɪ-, -ʃi|.əs (US) hɔː'reɪ-, hə-
Horbury 'hɔː.bər.i (US) 'hɔːrˌber-
horde hɔːd (US) hɔːrd **-s** -z
Horeb 'hɔː.reb (US) 'hɔːr.eb

horehound 'hɔː.haʊnd (US) 'hɔːr- **-s** -z
horizon hə'raɪ.zᵊn **-s** -z
horizontal ˌhɒr.ɪ'zɒn.tᵊl, -ə'- (US) ˌhɔːr.ɪ'zɑːn- **-ly** -i
Horley 'hɔː.li (US) 'hɔːr-
Horlick 'hɔː.lɪk (US) 'hɔːr-
Horlicks® 'hɔː.lɪks (US) 'hɔːr-
hormonal hɔː'məʊ.nᵊl (US) hɔːr'moʊ-
hormone 'hɔː.məʊn (US) 'hɔːr.moʊn **-s** -z **ˌhormone re'placement ˌtherapy**
Hormuz ˌhɔː'muːz, 'hɔː.məz (US) 'hɔːr.mʌz, -muːz
horn (H) hɔːn (US) hɔːrn **-s** -z **ˌHorn of 'Africa ; ˌhorn of 'plenty ; take the ˌbull by the 'horns**
hornbeam 'hɔːn.biːm, 'hɔːm- (US) 'hɔːrn- **-s** -z
hornbill 'hɔːn.bɪl, 'hɔːm- (US) 'hɔːrn- **-s** -z
hornblende 'hɔːn.blend, 'hɔːm- (US) 'hɔːrn-
Hornblower 'hɔːnˌbləʊ.əʳ, 'hɔːm- (US) 'hɔːrnˌbloʊ.ɚ
hornbook 'hɔːn.bʊk, 'hɔːm- (US) 'hɔːrn- **-s** -s
Horncastle 'hɔːnˌkɑː.sᵊl, 'hɔːŋ- (US) 'hɔːrnˌkæs.ᵊl
Hornchurch 'hɔːn.tʃɜːtʃ (US) 'hɔːrn.tʃɜːrtʃ
Horne hɔːn (US) hɔːrn
horned *of cattle, birds, etc.:* hɔːnd (US) hɔːrnd *poetic:* 'hɔː.nɪd (US) 'hɔːr-
Hornell hɔː'nel (US) hɔːr-
Horner 'hɔː.nəʳ (US) 'hɔːr.nɚ
hornet 'hɔː.nɪt, -nət (US) 'hɔːr- **-s** -s **'hornet's ˌnest, ˌhornet's 'nest**
Horniman 'hɔː.nɪ.mən (US) 'hɔːr-
hornpipe 'hɔːn.paɪp, 'hɔːm- (US) 'hɔːrn- **-s** -s
horn-rimmed ˌhɔːn'rɪmd (US) 'hɔːrn.rɪmd *stress shift, British only:* ˌhorn-rimmed 'spectacles
Hornsea 'hɔːn.siː (US) 'hɔːrn-
Hornsey 'hɔːn.zi (US) 'hɔːrn-
hornswoggl|e 'hɔːnˌswɒg.l̩ (US) 'hɔːrnˌswɑː.gl̩ **-es** -z **-ing** -ɪŋ **-ed** -d
Hornung 'hɔː.nəŋ (US) 'hɔːr-
hornwork 'hɔːn.wɜːk (US) 'hɔːrn.wɜːrk **-s** -s
horn|y 'hɔː.n|i (US) 'hɔːr- **-ier** -i.əʳ (US) -i.ɚ **-iest** -i.ɪst, -i.əst **-iness** -ɪ.nəs, -ɪ.nɪs
horography hɒr'ɒg.rə.fi, hɔː'rɒg-, hə- (US) hɔː'rɑːg-
horolog|e 'hɒr.ə.lɒdʒ, 'hɔː.rə-, -ləʊdʒ (US) 'hɔːr.ə.loʊdʒ **-es** -ɪz
horologic ˌhɒr.ə'lɒdʒ.ɪk, ˌhɔː.rə'- (US) ˌhɔːr.ə'lɑː.dʒɪk **-al** -ᵊl
horological ˌhɒr.ə'lɒdʒ.ɪ.kᵊl, ˌhɔː.rə'- (US) ˌhɔːr.ə'lɑː.dʒɪ-
horolog|y hɒr'ɒl.ə.dʒ|i, hɔː'rɒl-, hə- (US) hɔːr'ɑː.lə- **-er/s** -əʳ/z (US) -ɚ/z **-ist/s** -ɪst/s
horoscope 'hɒr.ə.skəʊp (US) 'hɔːr.ə.skoʊp **-s** -s
horoscopic ˌhɒr.ə'skɒp.ɪk (US) ˌhɔːr.ə'skɑː.pɪk
Horovitz 'hɒr.ə.vɪts (US) 'hɔːr-
Horowitz 'hɒr.ə.vɪts, -wɪts (US) 'hɔːr.ə.wɪts
horrendous hɒr'en.dəs, hə'ren- (US) hɔː'ren-, hə- **-ly** -li **-ness** -nəs, -nɪs
horrib|le 'hɒr.ə.b|l̩, '-ɪ- (US) 'hɔːr- **-ly** -li **-leness** -l̩.nəs, -nɪs
horrid 'hɒr.ɪd (US) 'hɔːr- **-er** -əʳ (US) -ɚ **-est** -ɪst, -əst **-ly** -li **-ness** -nəs, -nɪs
horrific hɒr'ɪf.ɪk, hə'rɪf- (US) hɔː'rɪf-, hə- **-ally** -ᵊl.i, -li
horri|fy 'hɒr.ɪ|.faɪ, '-ə- (US) 'hɔːr- **-fies** -faɪz **-fying/ly** -faɪ.ɪŋ/li **-fied** -faɪd
horripilation hɒrˌɪp.ɪ'leɪ.ʃᵊn, -ə'-; ˌhɒr.ɪ.pɪ'-, ˌ-ə- (US) ˌhɔːr.ɪ.pə'leɪ-
Horrocks 'hɒr.əks (US) 'hɔːr-
horror 'hɒr.əʳ (US) 'hɔːr.ɚ **-s** -z
horror|-stricken 'hɒr.əlˌstrɪk.ᵊn (US) 'hɔːr.ɚˌ- **-struck** -strʌk
Horsa 'hɔː.sə (US) 'hɔːr-
hors de combat ˌ*h*ɔː.də'kɔ̃ː*m*.bɑː, -'kɔːm-, -'kɒm-, -bæt (US) ˌɔːr.də.kɔ̃ː*m*'bɑː
hors d'oeuvre ˌɔː'dɜːv, -'dɜːv.rə (US) ˌɔːr'dɜːrv, -'dɜːrv.rə **-s** -z
hors|e hɔːs (US) hɔːrs **-es** -ɪz **-ing** -ɪŋ **-ed** -t **ˌhorse 'chestnut ; 'horse ˌopera ; 'horse ˌsense ; 'horse ˌshow ; 'horse ˌtrials ; ˌflog a ˌdead 'horse ; ˌhold your 'horses ; (ˌstraight) from the ˌhorse's 'mouth**
horse-and-buggy ˌhɔːs.ᵊn*d*'bʌg.i, -ᵊm'- (US) ˌhɔːrs-
horseback 'hɔːs.bæk (US) 'hɔːrs- **'horseback ˌriding**
horsebox 'hɔːs.bɒks (US) 'hɔːrs.bɑːks **-es** -ɪz
horseflesh 'hɔːs.fleʃ (US) 'hɔːrs-
horsefl|y 'hɔːs.fl|aɪ (US) 'hɔːrs- **-ies** -aɪz
Horseguard 'hɔːs.gɑːd (US) 'hɔːrs.gɑːrd **-s** -z
horsehair 'hɔːs.heəʳ (US) 'hɔːrs.her **-s** -z
horselaugh 'hɔːs.lɑːf (US) 'hɔːrs.læf **-s** -s
horse|man (H) 'hɔːs|.mən (US) 'hɔːrs- **-men** -mən, -men **-manship** -mən.ʃɪp
horseplay 'hɔːs.pleɪ (US) 'hɔːrs-
horsepower 'hɔːsˌpaʊəʳ (US) 'hɔːrsˌpaʊr
horseradish 'hɔːsˌræd.ɪʃ (US) 'hɔːrs- **-es** -ɪz
horseshoe 'hɔːs.ʃuː, 'hɔːʃ- (US) 'hɔːrs-, 'hɔːrʃ- **-s** -z
horsetail 'hɔːs.teɪl (US) 'hɔːrs- **-s** -z
horsetrad|e 'hɔːs.treɪd (US) 'hɔːrs- **-es** -z **-ing** -ɪŋ **-ed** -ɪd **-er/s** -əʳ/z (US) -ɚ/z
horse-trading 'hɔːsˌtreɪ.dɪŋ (US) 'hɔːrs-
horsewhip 'hɔːs.*h*wɪp (US) 'hɔːrs- **-s** -s **-ping** -ɪŋ **-ped** -t
horse|woman 'hɔːs|ˌwʊm.ən (US) 'hɔːrs- **-women** -ˌwɪm.ɪn
hors|ey 'hɔː.s|i (US) 'hɔːr- **-ier** -i.əʳ (US) -i.ɚ **-iest** -i.ɪst, -i.əst **-ily** -ɪ.li, -ᵊl.i **-iness** -ɪ.nəs, -ɪ.nɪs
Horsfall 'hɔːs.fɔːl (US) 'hɔːrs.fɔːl, -fɑːl
Horsforth 'hɔːs.fəθ (US) 'hɔːrs.fɚθ
Horsham 'hɔː.ʃᵊm (US) 'hɔːr-
Horsley 'hɔːz.li, 'hɔːs- (US) 'hɔːrz-, 'hɔːrs-
Horsmonden *in Kent:* ˌhɔːz.mən'den *old-fashioned local pronunciation:* ˌhɔː.sᵊn- (US) ˌhɔːrz.mᵊn'-
hors|y 'hɔː.s|i (US) 'hɔːr- **-ier** -i.əʳ (US) -i.ɚ **-iest** -i.ɪst, -i.əst **-ily** -ɪ.li, -ᵊl.i **-iness** -ɪ.nəs, -ɪ.nɪs
horta|tive 'hɔː.tə|.tɪv (US) 'hɔːr.t̬ə|.t̬ɪv **-tory** -tᵊr.i (US) -tɔːr.i
Hortensi|a hɔː'tent.si|.ə, -'ten.*t*ʃi|.ə, -*t*ʃ|ə (US) hɔːr'ten.*t*ʃi- **-us** -əs
horticultur|al ˌhɔː.tɪ'kʌl.tʃᵊr|.ᵊl, -tə'-, -tʃʊ.r|ᵊl (US) ˌhɔːr.t̬ə'kʌl.tʃɚ|.ᵊl **-ist/s** -ɪst/s
horticulture 'hɔː.tɪ.kʌl.tʃəʳ, -tə- (US) 'hɔːr.t̬ə.kʌl.tʃɚ
Horton 'hɔː.tᵊn (US) 'hɔːr-
Horus 'hɔː.rəs (US) 'hɔːr.əs
Horwich 'hɒr.ɪtʃ (US) 'hɔːr.ɪtʃ
Hosack 'hɒs.ək (US) 'hɑː.sək
hosanna həʊ'zæn.ə (US) hoʊ- **-s** -z
hos|e həʊz (US) hoʊz **-es** -ɪz **-ing** -ɪŋ **-ed** -d
Hosea həʊ'zɪə (US) hoʊ'zeɪ.ə, -'ziː-
hosepipe 'həʊz.paɪp (US) 'hoʊz- **-s** -s
hosier (H) 'həʊ.zi.əʳ, -ʒəʳ (US) 'hoʊ.ʒɚ **-s** -z
hosiery 'həʊ.zi.ə.ri, -ʒᵊr.i (US) 'hoʊ.ʒɚ.i
Hoskins 'hɒs.kɪnz (US) 'hɑː.skɪnz
Hosmer 'hɒz.məʳ (US) 'hɑːz.mɚ
hospic|e 'hɒs.pɪs (US) 'hɑː.spɪs **-es** -ɪz
hospitab|le hɒs'pɪt.ə.b|l̩, hə'spɪt-; 'hɒs.pɪ.tə- (US) 'hɑː.spɪ.t̬ə-; hɑː'spɪt̬.ə- **-ly** -li **-leness** -l̩.nəs, -nɪs
hospital 'hɒs.pɪ.tᵊl (US) 'hɑː.spɪ.t̬ᵊl **-s** -z
Hospitaler 'hɒs.pɪ.tᵊl.əʳ (US) 'hɑː.spɪ.t̬ᵊl.ɚ **-s** -z
hospitalit|y ˌhɒs.pɪ'tæl.ə.t|i, -pə'-, -ɪ.t|i (US) ˌhɑː.spɪ'tæl.ə.t̬|i **-ies** -iz
hospitalization, -isa- ˌhɒs.pɪ.tᵊl.aɪ'zeɪ.ʃᵊn, -pə-, -ɪ'- (US) ˌhɑː.spɪ.t̬ᵊl.ɪ'-
hospitaliz|e, -is|e 'hɒs.pɪ.tᵊl.aɪz, -pə- (US) 'hɑː.spɪ.t̬ᵊl- **-es** -ɪz **-ing** -ɪŋ **-ed** -d
Hospitaller 'hɒs.pɪ.tᵊl.əʳ (US) 'hɑː.spɪ.t̬ᵊl.ɚ **-s** -z
host (H) həʊst (US) hoʊst **-s** -s

hosta ˈhɒs.tə, ˈhəʊ.stə (US) ˈhɑː-, ˈhoʊ- **-s** -z

hostag|e ˈhɒs.tɪdʒ (US) ˈhɑː.stɪdʒ **-es** -ɪz

hostel ˈhɒs.tᵊl (US) ˈhɑː.stᵊl **-s** -z

hostell|er ˈhɒs.tᵊl|.əʳ (US) ˈhɑː.stᵊl|.ɚ **-ers** -əz (US) -ɚz **-ing** -ɪŋ

hostelr|y ˈhɒs.tᵊl.r|i (US) ˈhɑː.stᵊl- **-ies** -iz

hostess ˈhəʊ.stɪs, -stes, -stəs; ˌhəʊˈstes (US) ˈhoʊ.stɪs, -stəs **-es** -ɪz

hostile ˈhɒs.taɪl (US) ˈhɑː.stᵊl, -staɪl **-ly** -li

hostilit|y hɒsˈtɪl.ə.t|i, -ɪ.t|i (US) hɑːˈstɪl.ə.t̬|i **-ies** -iz

hostler ˈɒs.ləʳ, ˈhɒs- (US) ˈhɑː.slɚ, ˈɑː- **-s** -z

hot hɒt (US) hɑːt **-ter** -əʳ (US) ˈhɑː.t̬ɚ **-test** -ɪst, -əst (US) ˈhɑː.t̬ɪst, -t̬əst **-ly** -li **-ness** -nəs, -nɪs **-s** -s **-ting** -ɪŋ (US) ˈhɑː.t̬ɪŋ **-ted** -ɪd (US) ˈhɑː.t̬ɪd **ˌhot ˈair** ; **ˌhot cross ˈbun** ; **ˈhot ˌdog** , **ˌhot ˈdog** ; **ˈhot ˌpants** ; **ˌhot poˈtato** ; **ˈhot ˌseat**, **ˌhot ˈseat** ; **ˌhot ˈstuff** ; **ˌhot ˈticket** ; **ˌhot ˈwater** ; **ˌblow ˌhot and ˈcold** ; **ˌsell like ˌhot ˈcakes** (US) **ˌsell like ˈhot ˌcakes**

hotbed ˈhɒt.bed (US) ˈhɑːt- **-s** -z

hot-blooded ˌhɒtˈblʌd.ɪd (US) ˌhɑːt- *stress shift:* ˌhot-blooded ˈyouth

Hotchkiss ˈhɒtʃ.kɪs (US) ˈhɑːtʃ-

hotchpot ˈhɒtʃ.pɒt (US) ˈhɑːtʃ.pɑːt **-s** -s

hotchpotch ˈhɒtʃ.pɒtʃ (US) ˈhɑːtʃ.pɑːtʃ **-es** -ɪz

hotdog ˈhɒt.dɒg (US) ˈhɑːt.dɑːg, -dɔːg **-s** -z **-ging** -ɪŋ **-ged** -d

hotel həʊˈtel, əʊ- (US) hoʊ- **-s** -z

Note: Some British speakers use the form /əʊˈtel/ always; others use it occasionally when the word is not initial, with 'an' as preceding indefinite article.

hotelier həʊˈtel.i.eɪ, əʊ-, -əʳ (US) ˌhoʊ.tᵊlˈjeɪ, ˌoʊ-; hoʊˈtel.jɚ **-s** -z

hotfoo|t ˌhɒtˈfʊt, ˈ-- (US) ˈhɑːt.fʊt **-ts** -ts **-ting** -tɪŋ (US) -t̬ɪŋ **-ted** -tɪd (US) -t̬ɪd

Hotham ˈhʌð.əm

hothead ˈhɒt.hed (US) ˈhɑːt- **-s** -z

hotheaded ˌhɒtˈhed.ɪd, ˈ-ˌ-- (US) ˈhɑːtˌhed.ɪd, ˌ-ˈ-- **-ly** -li **-ness** -nəs, -nɪs

hothou|se ˈhɒt.haʊ|s (US) ˈhɑːt- **-ses** -zɪz

hotline ˈhɒt.laɪn (US) ˈhɑːt- **-s** -z

Hotol ˈhɒt.ɒl, ˈhoʊ.tɒl (US) ˈhɑː.tɑːl, ˈhoʊ-

hotplate ˈhɒt.pleɪt (US) ˈhɑːt- **-s** -s

Hotpoint® ˈhɒt.pɔɪnt (US) ˈhɑːt-

hotpot ˈhɒt.pɒt (US) ˈhɑːt.pɑːt **-s** -s

hotrod ˈhɒt.rɒd (US) ˈhɑːt.rɑːd **-s** -z **-ding** -ɪŋ **-ded** -ɪd **-der/s** -əʳ/z (US) -ɚ/z

hotshot ˈhɒt.ʃɒt (US) ˈhɑːt.ʃɑːt **-s** -s

hotspur (**H**) ˈhɒt.spɜːʳ, -spəʳ (US) ˈhɑːt.spɜːr, -spɚ **-s** -z

hot-tempered ˌhɒtˈtem.pəd (US) ˌhɑːtˈtem.pɚd *stress shift:* ˌhot-tempered ˈfighter

Hottentot ˈhɒt.ᵊn.tɒt (US) ˈhɑː.tᵊn.tɑːt **-s** -s

hot-water bottle ˌhɒtˈwɔː.təˌbɒt.l̩ (US) ˌhɑːtˈwɑː.t̬ɚˌbɑː.t̬l̩, -ˈwɔː- **-s** -z

Houdini huːˈdiː.ni

hough hɒk (US) hɑːk **-s** -s **-ing** -ɪŋ **-ed** -t

Hough hʌf, hɒf, haʊ (US) hʌf, hɔːf, hɑːf

Houghall ˈhɒf.ᵊl (US) ˈhɑː.fᵊl

Hougham ˈhʌf.əm

Houghton ˈhɔː.tᵊn, ˈhaʊ-, ˈhəʊ- (US) ˈhoʊ-, ˈhɔː-, ˈhɑː-, ˈhaʊ-

Note: /ˈhɔː.tᵊn, ˈhaʊ.tᵊn/ are more usual in British English when the word is a surname. The city in Michigan is /ˈhəʊ- (US) ˈhoʊ-/.

Houghton-le-Spring ˌhəʊ.tᵊn.ləˈsprɪŋ, ˌhaʊ-, -liˈ- (US) ˌhoʊ-, ˌhaʊ-

Houltby ˈhəʊlt.bi (US) ˈhoʊlt-

houm(o)us ˈhuː.mʊs, ˈhʊm.ʊs, -əs (US) ˈhʌm.əs, ˈhʊm-

hound haʊnd **-s** -z **-ing** -ɪŋ **-ed** -ɪd

Houndsditch ˈhaʊndz.dɪtʃ

houndstooth ˈhaʊndz.tuːθ, ˌ-ˈ- (US) ˈ--

Hounslow ˈhaʊnz.ləʊ (US) -loʊ

hour aʊəʳ (US) aʊr, aʊɚ **-s** -z **-ly** -li

hourglass ˈaʊə.glɑːs (US) ˈaʊr.glæs, ˈaʊɚ- **-es** -ɪz

houri ˈhʊə.ri (US) ˈhʊr.i, ˈhuːr- **-s** -z

Housden ˈhaʊz.dən

hou|se (**H**) (*n.*) haʊ|s **-ses** -zɪz **ˌhouse arˈrest** ; **ˈhouse ˌhusband** ; **ˈhouse ˌmartin** ; **ˈhouse ˌmusic** ; **ˌHouse of ˈCommons** ; **ˌHouse of ˈLords** ; **ˌHouse of RepreˈsentatIves** ; **ˌHouses of ˈParliament** ; **ˈhouse ˌparty** ; **ˈhouse ˌsparrow** ; **ˌeat one out of ˌhouse and ˈhome** ; **ˌbring the ˈhouse ˌdown** ; **get ˌon like a ˈhouse on ˌfire** ; **ˌset one's ˈhouse in ˌorder**

hous|e (*v.*) haʊz **-es** -ɪz **-ing** -ɪŋ **-ed** -d

houseboat ˈhaʊs.bəʊt (US) -boʊt **-s** -s

housebound ˈhaʊs.baʊnd

housebreak|er ˈhaʊsˌbreɪ.k|əʳ (US) -k|ɚ **-ers** -əz (US) -ɚz **-ing** -ɪŋ

house-broken ˈhaʊsˌbrəʊ.kᵊn (US) -ˌbroʊ-

housebuy|er ˈhaʊsˌbaɪ|.əʳ (US) -ɚ **-ers** -z **-ing** -ɪŋ

housecoat ˈhaʊs.kəʊt (US) -koʊt **-s** -s

housefather ˈhaʊsˌfɑː.ðəʳ (US) -ðɚ **-s** -z

housefl|y ˈhaʊs.fl|aɪ **-ies** -aɪz

houseful ˈhaʊs.fʊl **-s** -z

household (**H**) ˈhaʊs.*h*əʊld (US) -*h*oʊld **-s** -z **-er/s** -əʳ/z (US) -ɚ/z

housekeeper ˈhaʊsˌkiː.pəʳ (US) -pɚ **-s** -z (US) -z

housekeeping ˈhaʊsˌkiː.pɪŋ

Housel ˈhaʊ.zᵊl

houseleek ˈhaʊs.liːk **-s** -s

housemaid ˈhaʊs.meɪd **-s** -z

house|man ˈhaʊs|.mən, -mæn **-men** -mən, -men

housemaster ˈhaʊsˌmɑː.stəʳ (US) -ˌmæs.tɚ **-s** -z

housemother ˈhaʊsˌmʌð.əʳ (US) -ɚ **-s** -z

houseplant ˈhaʊs.plɑːnt (US) -plænt **-s** -s

houseproud ˈhaʊs.praʊd

houseroom ˈhaʊs.rʊm, -ruːm (US) -ruːm, -rʊm

house|sit ˈhaʊs|.sɪt **-sits** -sɪts **-sitting** -ˌsɪt.ɪŋ (US) -ˌsɪt̬.ɪŋ **-sat** -sæt **-sitter/s** -ˌsɪt.əʳ/z (US) -ˌsɪt̬.ɚ/z

Housestead's Fort ˌhaʊs.stedzˈfɔːt (US) -ˈfɔːrt

house-to-house ˌhaʊs.təˈhaʊs *stress shift:* ˌhouse-to-house ˈsearch

housetop ˈhaʊs.tɒp (US) -tɑːp **-s** -s

housewarming ˈhaʊsˌwɔː.mɪŋ (US) -ˌwɔːr- **-s** -z

housewife *woman:* ˈhaʊs.waɪf; *old-fashioned:* ˈhʌz.ɪf **housewives** ˈhaʊs.waɪvz; *old-fashioned:* -ɪvz **housewifes** *old-fashioned:* ˈhʌz.ɪfs

housewi|fe *needle-case:* ˈhʌz.ɪ|f **-fes** -fs **-ves** -vz

housewifel|y ˈhaʊsˌwaɪf.l|i **-iness** -ɪ.nəs, -ɪ.nɪs

housewifery ˈhaʊsˌwɪf.ᵊr.i; *old-fashioned:* ˈhʌz.ɪ.fri (US) ˈhaʊsˌwaɪ.fɚ.i, ˌ-fri

housework ˈhaʊs.wɜːk (US) -wɜːrk

housey-housey, housie-housie ˌhaʊ.siˈhaʊ.si, -ziˈhaʊ.zi

housing ˈhaʊ.zɪŋ **ˈhousing asˌsociation** ; **ˈhousing deˌvelopment** ; **ˈhousing eˌstate** ; **ˈhousing ˌlist**

Housman ˈhaʊs.mən

Houston *English surname:* ˈhuː.stᵊn, ˈhaʊ- *Scottish surname:* ˈhuː.stᵊn *in US:* ˈhjuː.stᵊn

Houyhnhnm ˈhuː.ɪ.nᵊm (US) ˈhwɪn.ᵊm, huˈɪn- **-s** -z

hove (**H**) (*from* **heave**) həʊv (US) hoʊv

hovel ˈhɒv.ᵊl, ˈhʌv- (US) ˈhʌv-, ˈhɑː.vᵊl **-s** -z

Hovell ˈhəʊ.vᵊl, ˈhɒv.ᵊl, həʊˈvel (US) ˈhoʊ.vᵊl, ˈhɑː-, hoʊˈvel

Hovenden ˈhɒv.ᵊn.dən (US) ˈhoʊ.vᵊn-

hov|er ˈhɒv|.əʳ (US) ˈhʌv|.ɚ, ˈhɑː.v|ɚ **-ers** -əz (US) -ɚz **-ering** -ᵊr.ɪŋ **-ered** -əd (US) -ɚd

hovercraft ˈhɒv.ə.krɑːft (US) ˈhʌv.ɚ.kræft, ˈhɑː.vɚ- **-s** -s

hoverfl|y ˈhɒv.ə.fl|aɪ (US) ˈhʌv.ɚ-, ˈhɑː.vɚ- **-ies** -aɪz

hoverport 'hɒv.ə.pɔːt
(US) 'hʌv.ɚ.pɔːrt, 'hɑː.vɚ- **-s** -s
Hovis® 'həʊ.vɪs (US) 'hoʊ-
how (H) haʊ
Howard haʊəd (US) haʊɚd
Howarth haʊəθ (US) haʊɚθ
howdah 'haʊ.də **-s** -z
Howden 'haʊ.dᵊn
how-do-you-do ˌhaʊ.djʊ'duː, -djə'-, -dʒʊ'-, -dʒə'-, '---
(US) 'haʊ.də.juː.duː, '-djə.duː
howdy 'haʊ.di
howdy-do ˌhaʊ.di'duː **-s** -z
Howe haʊ
Howell haʊəl **-s** -z
Howerd haʊəd (US) haʊɚd
Howers haʊəz (US) haʊɚz
Howes haʊz
however haʊ'ev.əʳ (US) -ɚ
Howick 'haʊ.ɪk
Howie 'haʊ.i
Howitt 'haʊ.ɪt
howitzer 'haʊ.ɪt.səʳ (US) -sɚ **-s** -z
howl haʊl **-s** -z **-ing** -ɪŋ **-ed** -d
howler 'haʊ.ləʳ (US) -lɚ **-s** -z
Howlett 'haʊ.lɪt
Howley 'haʊ.li
Howorth haʊəθ (US) haʊɚθ
Howse haʊz
howsoever ˌhaʊ.səʊ'ev.əʳ
(US) -soʊ'ev.ɚ
Howson 'haʊ.sᵊn
Howth həʊθ (US) hoʊθ
how-to 'haʊ.tuː **-s** -z
Hoxha 'hɒdʒ.ə (US) 'hɔː.ʒdɑː
Hoxton 'hɒk.stᵊn (US) 'hɑːk-
hoy (H) hɔɪ **-s** -z
hoyden (H) 'hɔɪ.dᵊn **-s** -z
Hoylake 'hɔɪ.leɪk
Hoyland Nether ˌhɔɪ.lənd'neð.əʳ
(US) -ɚ
HP ˌeɪtʃ'piː
HQ ˌeɪtʃ'kjuː
HRH ˌeɪtʃ.ɑːʳ'eɪtʃ (US) -ɑːr'-
HRT ˌeitʃ.ɑː'tiː (US) -ɑːr'-
Huang Ho ˌhwæŋ'həʊ (US) ˌhwɑːŋ'hoʊ, ˌhwæŋ-
hub hʌb **-s** -z
Hubbard 'hʌb.əd (US) -ɚd
Hubble 'hʌb.l̩
hubble-bubble 'hʌb.l̩ˌbʌb.l̩ **-s** -z
hubbub 'hʌb.ʌb, -əb (US) -ʌb **-s** -z
hubb|y 'hʌb|.i **-ies** -iz
hubcap 'hʌb.kæp **-s** -s
Hubert 'hjuː.bət (US) -bɚt
hubris 'hjuː.brɪs, 'huː- (US) 'hjuː-
hubristic hjuː'brɪs.tɪk, huː- (US) hjuː-
huckaback 'hʌk.ə.bæk **-s** -s
Huckle 'hʌk.l̩
huckleberr|y (H) 'hʌk.l̩.bᵊr|.i, -ˌber|.i
(US) -'ber- **-ies** -iz
Hucknall, Hucknell 'hʌk.nᵊl
huckster 'hʌk.stəʳ (US) -stɚ **-s** -z
Huddersfield 'hʌd.əz.fiːld (US) -ɚz-
huddl|e 'hʌd.l̩ **-es** -z **-ing** -ɪŋ, 'hʌd.lɪŋ **-ed** -d
Hud(d)leston(e) 'hʌd.l̩.stᵊn
Hudibras 'hjuː.dɪ.bræs, -də-
Hudnott 'hʌd.nɒt, -nət (US) -nɑːt
Hudson 'hʌd.sᵊn
hue hjuː **-s** -z ˌ**hue and 'cry**
Hueffer 'hef.əʳ (US) -ɚ
Huelva 'wel.və (US) -və, -vɑː
huevos rancheros
ˌweɪ.vɒs.ræn'tʃeə.rɒs
(US) -voʊs.ræn'tʃer.oʊs
huff (H) hʌf **-s** -s **-ing** -ɪŋ **-ed** -t
huffish 'hʌf.ɪʃ **-ly** -li **-ness** -nəs, -nɪs
Huffman 'hʌf.mən
huff|y 'hʌf|.i **-ier** -i.əʳ (US) -i.ɚ **-iest** -i.ɪst, -i.əst **-ily** -ɪ.li, -ᵊl.i **-iness** -ɪ.nəs, -ɪ.nɪs
hug hʌg **-s** -z **-ging** -ɪŋ **-ged** -d
Hugall 'hjuː.gᵊl
hug|e hjuːdʒ **-er** -əʳ (US) -ɚ **-est** -ɪst, -əst **-ely** -li **-eness** -nəs, -nɪs
hugger-mugger 'hʌg.əˌmʌg.əʳ, ˌhʌg.ə'mʌg- (US) 'hʌg.ɚˌmʌg.ɚ
Huggin 'hʌg.ɪn **-s** -z
Hugh hjuː
Hughenden 'hjuː.ᵊn.dᵊn
Hughes hjuːz
Hugo 'hjuː.gəʊ (US) -goʊ
Hugon 'hjuː.gᵊn, -gɒn (US) -gɑːn
Huguenot 'hjuː.gə.nəʊ, 'huː-, -nɒt
(US) 'hjuː.gə.nɑːt **-s** -z
Huish 'hjuː.ɪʃ
hula 'huː.lə **-s** -z
Hula-Hoop® 'huː.lə.huːp **-s** -s
Hulbert 'hʌl.bət (US) -bɚt
hulk hʌlk **-s** -s **-ing** -ɪŋ
hull (H) hʌl **-s** -z **-ing** -ɪŋ **-ed** -d
hullabaloo ˌhʌl.ə.bə'luː **-s** -z
Hullah 'hʌl.ə
Hullbridge 'hʌl.brɪdʒ
hullo hə'ləʊ, hʌl'əʊ (US) hə'loʊ, hʌl'oʊ **-s** -z
Hulme hjuːm, huːm
Hulse hʌls
Hulsean hʌl'siː.ən
hum (*n. v.*) hʌm **-s** -z **-ming** -ɪŋ **-med** -d
'**humming** ˌ**top**
human (H) 'hjuː.mən **-s** -z **-ly** -li
ˌ**human 'being** ; ˌ**human 'nature** ; ˌ**human 'race** ; ˌ**human 'rights**
human|e hjuː'meɪn **-er** -əʳ (US) -ɚ **-est** -ɪst, -əst **-ely** -li **-eness** -nəs, -nɪs
human|ism 'hjuː.mə.n|ɪ.zᵊm **-ist/s** -ɪst/s
humanistic ˌhjuː.mə'nɪs.tɪk
humanitarian hjuːˌmæn.ɪ'teə.ri.ən, -ə'-; ˌhjuː.mæn-
(US) hjuːˌmæn.ə'ter.i- **-s** -z **-ism** -ɪ.zᵊm
humanit|y hjuː'mæn.ə.t|i, -ɪ.t|i
(US) -ə.t̬|i **-ies** -iz
humanization, -isa-
ˌhjuː.mə.naɪ'zeɪ.ʃᵊn, -nɪ'- (US) -nɪ'-
humaniz|e, -is|e 'hjuː.mə.naɪz **-es** -ɪz **-ing** -ɪŋ **-ed** -d
humankind ˌhjuː.mən'kaɪnd, -məŋ'-
(US) -mən'-
humanoid 'hjuː.mə.nɔɪd **-s** -z
Humber 'hʌm.bəʳ (US) -bɚ **-s** -z **-side** -saɪd
Humberston 'hʌm.bə.stᵊn (US) -bɚ-
Humbert 'hʌm.bət (US) -bɚt
humb|le 'hʌm.b|l̩ **-ler** -ləʳ (US) -lɚ **-lest** -lɪst, -ləst **-ly** -li **-leness** -l̩.nəs, -nɪs **-les** -l̩z **-ling** -l̩.ɪŋ (US) -lɪŋ **-led** -l̩d **eat** ˌ**humble 'pie**
Humblethwaite 'hʌm.bl̩.θweɪt
Humboldt 'hʌm.bəʊlt, 'hʊm-
(US) -boʊlt
Humbrol® 'hʌm.brɒl (US) -brɑːl
humbug 'hʌm.bʌg **-s** -z **-ging** -ɪŋ **-ged** -d
humdinger ˌhʌm'dɪŋ.əʳ (US) -ɚ **-s** -z
humdrum 'hʌm.drʌm
Hume hjuːm
humectant hjuː'mek.tᵊnt **-s** -s
humer|us 'hjuː.mᵊr|.əs **-i** -aɪ **-al** -ᵊl
Humian 'hjuː.mi.ən
humid 'hjuː.mɪd **-ness** -nəs, -nɪs
humidification hjuːˌmɪd.ɪ.fɪ'keɪ.ʃᵊn, ˌ-ə-
humidifier hjuː'mɪd.ɪ.faɪ.əʳ, '-ə- **-s** -z
humidif|y hjuː'mɪd.ɪ.f|aɪ, '-ə- **-ies** -aɪz **-ying** -aɪ.ɪŋ **-ied** -aɪd **-ier/s** -aɪ.əʳ/z
(US) -aɪ.ɚ/z
humidity hjuː'mɪd.ə.ti, -ɪ.ti (US) -ə.t̬i
humili|ate hjuː'mɪl.i|.eɪt **-ates** -eɪts **-ating/ly** -eɪ.tɪŋ/li (US) -eɪ.t̬ɪŋ/li **-ated** -eɪ.tɪd (US) -eɪ.t̬ɪd
humiliation hjuːˌmɪl.i'eɪ.ʃᵊn, ˌhjuː.mɪ.li'- (US) hjuːˌmɪl.i'- **-s** -z
humility hjuː'mɪl.ə.ti, -ɪt.i (US) -ə.t̬i
hummingbird 'hʌm.ɪŋ.bɜːd (US) -bɜːrd **-s** -z
hummock 'hʌm.ək **-s** -s **-y** -i
hummus 'hʊm.ʊs, 'hʌm-, -əs, 'huː.məs
(US) 'hʌm.əs, 'hʊm-
humongous hjuː'mʌŋ.gəs
hum|or 'hjuː.m|əʳ (US) -m|ɚ **-ors** -əz
(US) -ɚz **-oring** -ᵊr.ɪŋ **-ored** -əd (US) -ɚd **-orless/ly** -ə.ləs/li, -ɚ.lɪs/li
humoral 'hjuː.mᵊr.ᵊl
humoresque ˌhjuː.mᵊr'esk
(US) -mə'resk **-s** -s
humorist 'hjuː.mᵊr.ɪst **-s** -s
humoristic ˌhjuː.mᵊr'ɪs.tɪk
humorous 'hjuː.mᵊr.əs **-ly** -li **-ness** -nəs, -nɪs
hum|our 'hjuː.m|əʳ (US) -m|ɚ **-ours** -əz
(US) -ɚz **-ouring** -ᵊr.ɪŋ **-oured** -əd
(US) -ɚd **-ourless/ly** -ə.ləs/li, -ɚ.lɪs/li
humoursome 'hjuː.mə.sᵊm (US) -mɚ- **-ly** -li **-ness** -nəs, -nɪs

hump hʌmp **-s** -s **-ing** -ɪŋ **-ed** -t
humpback ˈhʌmp.bæk **-s** -s **-ed** -t
ˌ**humpbacked ˈbridge**
Humperdinck ˈhʌm.pə.dɪŋk (US) -pɚ-
humph (*interj.*) m̥m, hə̃h, hʌmf
Note: Interjection indicating annoyance or disapproval, with rapid fall in pitch. The transcriptions reflect a wide range of possible pronunciations. The small circle uncer the /m/ symbol indicates a voiceless consonant.
Humphr(e)y ˈhʌm*p*.fri **-s** -z
Humphries ˈhʌm*p*.friz
Humpty Dumpty ˌhʌm*p*.ti ˈdʌm*p*.ti
hump|y ˈhʌm.p|i **-ier** -i.əʳ (US) -i.ɚ **-iest** -i.ɪst, -i.əst **-iness** -ɪ.nəs, -ɪ.nɪs
humus ˈhjuː.məs
Hun hʌn **-s** -z
hunch hʌntʃ **-es** -ɪz **-ing** -ɪŋ **-ed** -t
hunchback ˈhʌn*t*ʃ.bæk **-s** -s **-ed** -t
hundred ˈhʌn.drəd, -drɪd **-s** -z
hundredfold ˈhʌn.drəd.fəʊld, -drɪd- (US) -foʊld
hundredth ˈhʌn.drədθ, -drɪdθ, -drətθ, -drɪtθ **-s** -s
hundredweight ˈhʌn.drəd.weɪt, -drɪd- **-s** -s
hung (*from* **hang**) hʌŋ ˌ**hung ˈjury** ; ˌ**hung ˈparliament**
Hungarian hʌŋˈgeə.ri.ən (US) -ˈger.i- **-s** -z
Hungary ˈhʌŋ.gᵊr.i
hung|er ˈhʌŋ.g|əʳ (US) -g|ɚ **-ers** -əz (US) -ɚz **-ering** -ᵊr.ɪŋ **-ered** -əd (US) -ɚd **ˈhunger ˌstrike** ; **ˈhunger ˌstriker**
Hungerford ˈhʌŋ.gə.fəd (US) -gɚ.fɚd
hungerstrik|e ˈhʌŋ.gə.straɪk (US) -gɚ- **-es** -s **-ing** -ɪŋ **hungerstruck** ˈhʌŋ.gə.strʌk (US) -gɚ-
hungover ˌhʌŋˈəʊ.vəʳ (US) -ˈoʊ.vɚ
hungr|y ˈhʌŋ.gr|i **-ier** -i.əʳ (US) -i.ɚ **-iest** -i.ɪst, -i.əst **-ily** -ᵊl.i, -ɪ.li **-iness** -ɪ.nəs, -ɪ.nɪs
hunk hʌŋk **-s** -s
hunk|y ˈhʌŋ.k|i **-ier** -i.əʳ (US) -i.ɚ **-iest** -i.ɪst, -i.əst
hunky-dory ˌhʌŋ.kiˈdɔː.ri (US) -ˈdɔːr.i
hunnish (**H**) ˈhʌn.ɪʃ
Hunslet ˈhʌnz.lət, -lɪt, ˈhʌn.slɪt, -slət
Hunstanton hʌnˈstæn.tən *locally:* ˈhʌn.stən
Hunsworth ˈhʌnz.wəθ (US) -wɚθ
hunt (**H**) hʌnt **-s** -s **-er/s** -əʳ/z (US) -ɚ/z **-ing** -ɪŋ (US) ˈhʌn.t̬ɪŋ **-ed** -ɪd (US) ˈhʌn.t̬ɪd **ˈhunting ˌground** ; **ˈhunting ˌhorn** ; **ˈhunting ˌknife**
hunter-gatherer ˌhʌn.təˈgæð.ᵊr.əʳ (US) -t̬ɚˈgæð.ɚ.ɚ **-s** -z
Hunterian hʌnˈtɪə.ri.ən (US) -ˈtɪr.i-
Huntingdon ˈhʌn.tɪŋ.dən **-shire** -ʃəʳ, -ˌʃɪəʳ (US) -ʃɚ, -ˌʃɪr
Huntingdonian ˌhʌn.tɪŋˈdəʊ.ni.ən (US) -ˈdoʊ- **-s** -z
Huntingford ˈhʌn.tɪŋ.fəd (US) -fɚd
Huntington ˈhʌn.tɪŋ.tən ˌ**Huntington's choˈrea**
Huntl(e)y ˈhʌnt.li
Hunton ˈhʌn.tən (US) -tᵊn
huntress ˈhʌn.trəs, -trɪs **-es** -ɪz
Hunts. (*abbrev. for* **Huntingdonshire**) hʌnts; ˈhʌn.tɪŋ.dən.ʃəʳ, -ˌʃɪəʳ (US) hʌnts; ˈhʌn.tɪŋ.dən.ʃɚ, -ˌʃɪr
hunts|man ˈhʌnts|.mən **-men** -mən, -men **-manship** -mən.ʃɪp
Huntsville ˈhʌnts.vɪl
Hunyadi ˈhʊn.jɑː.di, ˈhʌn-, -ˈ-- (US) ˈhʊn.jɑː.di
Hurd hɜːd (US) hɜːrd
hurdl|e ˈhɜː.dl̩ **-es** -z **-ing** -ɪŋ, ˈhɜːd.lɪŋ (US) ˈhɜːrd- **-ed** -d **-er/s** -əʳ/z (US) -ɚ/z
hurdy-gurd|y ˈhɜː.diˌgɜː.d|i, ˌhɜː.diˈgɜː- (US) ˌhɜːr.diˈgɜːr.d|i, ˈhɜːr.diˌgɜːr- **-ies** -iz
Hurford ˈhɜː.fəd (US) ˈhɜːr.fɚd
hurl hɜːl (US) hɜːrl **-s** -z **-ing** -ɪŋ **-ed** -d **-er/s** -əʳ/z (US) -ɚ/z
hurley (**H**) ˈhɜː.li (US) ˈhɜːr- **-s** -z
hurling ˈhɜː.lɪŋ (US) ˈhɜːr-
Hurlingham ˈhɜː.lɪŋ.əm (US) ˈhɜːr-
Hurlstone ˈhɜːl.stᵊn (US) ˈhɜːrl-
hurly-burly ˈhɜː.liˌbɜː.li, ˌhɜː.liˈbɜː- (US) ˈhɜːr.liˌbɜːr-, ˌhɜːr.liˈbɜːr-
Huron ˈhjʊə.rᵊn, -rɒn (US) ˈhjʊr.ɑːn, -ən
hurrah həˈrɑː, hʊ- (US) -ˈrɑː, -ˈrɔː **-s** -z **-ing** -ɪŋ **-ed** -d
hurray həˈreɪ, hʊ- **-s** -z
Hurrell ˈhʌr.ᵊl, ˈhʊə.rᵊl (US) ˈhɜːr.ᵊl
hurricane ˈhʌr.ɪ.kən, ˈ-ə-, -keɪn (US) ˈhɜːr.ɪ.keɪn, -kən **-s** -z **ˈhurricane ˌlamp**
hurried ˈhʌr.id (US) ˈhɜːr- **-ly** -li
hurr|y (**H**) ˈhʌr|.i (US) ˈhɜːr- **-ies** -i.z **-ying** -i.ɪŋ
hurry-scurry ˌhʌr.iˈskʌr.i (US) ˌhɜːr.iˈskɜːr-
hurst (**H**) hɜːst (US) hɜːrst **-s** -s
Hurstmonceux ˌhɜːs*t*.mənˈzuː, -mɒnˈ-, -ˈsjuː, -ˈsuː (US) ˈhɜːrs*t*.mən.suː, ˌ--ˈ-
Hurston ˈhɜː.stᵊn (US) ˈhɜːr-
Hurstpierpoint ˌhɜːs*t*.pɪəˈpɔɪnt (US) ˌhɜːrs*t*.pɪrˈ-
hurt (**H**) hɜːt (US) hɜːrt **-s** -s **-ing** -ɪŋ (US) ˈhɜːr.t̬ɪŋ
hurtful ˈhɜːt.fᵊl, -fʊl (US) ˈhɜːrt- **-ly** -i **-ness** -nəs, -nɪs
hurtl|e ˈhɜː.tl̩ (US) -t̬l̩ **-es** -z **-ing** -ɪŋ, ˈhɜːt.lɪŋ (US) ˈhɜːrt- **-ed** -d
husband ˈhʌz.bənd **-s** -z **-ing** -ɪŋ **-ed** -ɪd **-ly** -li
husband|man ˈhʌz.bən*d*|.mən **-men** -mən, -men
husbandry ˈhʌz.bən.dri
hush hʌʃ **-es** -ɪz **-ing** -ɪŋ **-ed** -t **ˈhush ˌmoney**
hushaby ˈhʌʃ.ə.baɪ
hush-hush ˌhʌʃˈhʌʃ *stress shift:* ˌhush-hush ˈservice
Hush Puppies® ˈhʌʃˌpʌp.iz
husk (**H**) hʌsk **-s** -s
Huskisson ˈhʌs.kɪ.sᵊn, -kə-
husk|y ˈhʌs.k|i **-ier** -i.əʳ (US) -i.ɚ **-iest** -i.ɪst, -i.əst **-ily** -ɪ.li, -ᵊl.i **-iness** -ɪ.nəs, -ɪ.nɪs
Hussain hʊˈseɪn (US) huː-
hussar hʊˈzɑːʳ, hə- (US) -ˈzɑːr **-s** -z
Hussein hʊˈseɪn (US) huː-
Hussey ˈhʌs.i
Hussite ˈhʌs.aɪt, ˈhʊs- (US) ˈhʌs- **-s** -s
huss|y (**H**) ˈhʌs|.i, ˈhʌz- **-ies** -iz
hustings ˈhʌs.tɪŋz
hustl|e ˈhʌs.l̩ **-es** -z **-ing** -ɪŋ, ˈhʌs.lɪŋ **-ed** -d **-er/s** -əʳ/z (US) -ɚ/z, ˈhʌs.ləʳ/z (US) -lɚ/z
Huston ˈhjuː.stᵊn
hut hʌt **-s** -s
hutch hʌtʃ **-es** -ɪz
Hutcheson ˈhʌtʃ.ɪ.sᵊn, ˈ-ə-
Hutchings ˈhʌtʃ.ɪŋz
Hutchinson ˈhʌtʃ.ɪn.sən
Hutchinsonian ˌhʌtʃ.ɪnˈsəʊ.ni.ən (US) -ˈsoʊ- **-s** -z
Hutchison ˈhʌtʃ.ɪ.sᵊn
Huth huːθ
Huthwaite ˈhuːθ.weɪt
hutment ˈhʌt.mənt **-s** -s
Hutton ˈhʌt.ᵊn
Hutu ˈhuː.tuː **-s** -z
hutzpah ˈhʊt.spɑː, ˈxʊt-, -spə
Huw hjuː
Huxley ˈhʌk.sli
Huxtable ˈhʌk.stə.bl̩
Huygens ˈhaɪ.gᵊnz
Huyton ˈhaɪ.tᵊn
huzza(h) hʊˈzɑː, hʌzˈɑː-, həˈzɑː (US) həˈzɑː, -ˈzɔː **-s** -z
Hwang-ho ˌhwæŋˈhəʊ (US) ˌhwɑːŋˈhoʊ
hwyl ˈhuː.ɪl, -əl
hyacinth (**H**) ˈhaɪə.sɪn*t*θ **-s** -s
hyacinthine ˌhaɪəˈsɪn*t*.θaɪn (US) -θaɪn, -θɪn
Hyades ˈhaɪ.ə.diːz
hyaena haɪˈiː.nə **-s** -z
hyalin ˈhaɪ.ə.lɪn
hyaline ˈhaɪə.lɪn, -liːn, -laɪn
hyalite ˈhaɪə.laɪt
hyaloid ˈhaɪə.lɔɪd
Hyam haɪəm
Hyamson ˈhaɪəm.sən
Hyannis haɪˈæn.ɪs
hybrid ˈhaɪ.brɪd **-s** -z **-ism** -ɪ.zᵊm
hybridity haɪˈbrɪd.ə.ti, -ɪ.ti (US) -ə.t̬i
hybridization, -isa- ˌhaɪ.brɪ.daɪˈzeɪ.ʃᵊn, ˌ-brə-, -dɪˈ- (US) -dɪˈ-

hybridiz|e, -is|e ˈhaɪ.brɪ.daɪz, -brə- **-es** -ɪz **-ing** -ɪŋ **-ed** -d **-er/s** -əʳ/z (US) -ɚ/z

Hyde haɪd ˌ**Hyde ˈPark** ; ˌ**Hyde ˌPark ˈCorner**

Hyderabad ˈhaɪ.dᵊr.ə.bæd, -bɑːd, ˌhaɪ.dᵊr.əˈbæd, -ˈbɑːd (US) ˈhaɪ.dɚ.ə.bæd, -bɑːd, ˈ-drə.bæd, -bɑːd

hydra (H) ˈhaɪ.drə **-s** -z

hydrangea haɪˈdreɪn.dʒə, -dʒi.ə (US) -ˈdreɪn-, -ˈdræn- **-s** -z

hydrant ˈhaɪ.drᵊnt **-s** -s

hydrate (*n.*) ˈhaɪ.dreɪt, -drɪt **-s** -s

hydra|te (*v.*) haɪˈdreɪ|t, ˈ-- (US) ˈ-- **-tes** -ts **-ting** -tɪŋ (US) -t̬ɪŋ **-ted** -tɪd (US) -t̬ɪd

hydration haɪˈdreɪ.ʃᵊn

hydraulic haɪˈdrɔː.lɪk, -ˈdrɒl.ɪk (US) -ˈdrɑː-, -ˈdrɔː- **-s** -s

hydrazine ˈhaɪ.drə.ziːn, -zɪn

hydro- haɪ.drəʊ-; haɪˈdrɒ- (US) haɪ.droʊ-, -drə-; haɪˈdrɑː-

Note: Prefix. Normally either takes primary or secondary stress on the first syllable, e.g. **hydrofoil** /ˈhaɪ.drəʊ.fɔɪl (US) -droʊ-/, **hydrochloric** /ˌhaɪ.drəʊˈklɒr.ɪk (US) -droʊˈklɔːr-/, or primary stress on the second syllable, e.g. **hydrogenate** /haɪˈdrɒdʒ.ɪ.neɪt (US) -ˈdrɑː.dʒə-/.

hydro ˈhaɪ.drəʊ (US) -droʊ **-s** -z

hydrocarbon ˌhaɪ.drəʊˈkɑː.bᵊn (US) -droʊˈkɑːr-, -drəˈ- **-s** -z

hydrocephalus ˌhaɪ.drəʊˈsef.ᵊl.əs, -ˈkef- (US) -droʊˈsef-

hydrochloric ˌhaɪ.drəʊˈklɒr.ɪk, -ˈklɔː.rɪk (US) -droʊˈklɔːr.ɪk, -drəˈ- *stress shift, see compound:* ˌ**hydrochloric ˈacid**

hydrodynamic ˌhaɪ.drəʊ.daɪˈnæm.ɪk, -dɪˈ- (US) -droʊ.daɪˈ-, -drə- **-al** -ᵊl **-ally** -ᵊl.i, -li **-s** -s

hydroelectric ˌhaɪ.drəʊ.ɪˈlek.trɪk, -əˈ- (US) -droʊ- **-s** -s *stress shift:* ˌhydroelectric ˈpower

hydroelectricity ˌhaɪ.drəʊ.ɪ.lekˈtrɪs.ɪ.ti, -ə- (US) -droʊ.ɪ.lekˈtrɪs.ɪ.t̬i, -ə.t̬i

hydrofoil ˈhaɪ.drəʊ.fɔɪl (US) -droʊ-, -drə- **-s** -z

hydrogen ˈhaɪ.drə.dʒən, -drɪ-, -dʒɪn (US) -drə.dʒən ˈ**hydrogen ˌbomb** ; ˌ**hydrogen ˈchloride** ; ˌ**hydrogen ˈfluoride** ; ˌ**hydrogen peˈroxide**

hydroge|nate haɪˈdrɒdʒ.ɪ|.neɪt, ˈ-ə-; ˈhaɪ.drə.dʒɪ-, -dʒə- (US) haɪˈdrɑː.dʒə-; ˈhaɪ.drə- **-nates** -neɪts **-nating** -neɪ.tɪŋ (US) -neɪ.t̬ɪŋ **-nated** -neɪ.tɪd (US) -neɪ.t̬ɪd

hydrogenation ˌhaɪ.drə.dʒəˈneɪ.ʃᵊn, -dʒɪˈ- (US) haɪˌdrɑː.dʒəˈ-

hydrogenous haɪˈdrɒdʒ.ɪ.nəs, ˈ-ə- (US) -ˈdrɑː.dʒɪ-, -dʒə-

hydrographic ˌhaɪ.drəʊˈgræf.ɪk (US) -droʊˈgræf- **-al** -ᵊl **-ally** -ᵊl.i, -li

hydrograph|y haɪˈdrɒg.rə.f|i (US) -ˈdrɑː.grə- **-er/s** -əʳ/z (US) -ɚ/z

hydrology haɪˈdrɒl.ə.dʒi (US) -ˈdrɑː.lə-

hydrolysis haɪˈdrɒl.ə.sɪs, ˈ-ɪ- (US) -ˈdrɑː.lɪ-

hydrolytic ˌhaɪ.drəˈlɪt.ɪk (US) -ˈlɪt̬- **-ally** -ᵊl.i, -li

hydrolyz|e, -ys|e ˈhaɪ.drə.laɪz **-es** -ɪz **-ing** -ɪŋ **-ed** -d

hydromechanics ˌhaɪ.drəʊ.mɪˈkæn.ɪks, -məˈ- (US) -droʊ.məˈ-

hydrometer haɪˈdrɒm.ɪ.təʳ, ˈ-ə- (US) -ˈdrɑː.mə.t̬ɚ **-s** -z

hydrometric ˌhaɪ.drəʊˈmet.rɪk (US) -droʊˈ-, -drəˈ- **-al** -ᵊl **-ally** -ᵊl.i, -li

hydrometry haɪˈdrɒm.ə.tri, ˈ-ɪ- (US) -ˈdrɑː.mə-

hydropathic ˌhaɪ.drəʊˈpæθ.ɪk (US) -droʊˈ-, -drəˈ- **-s** -s **-al** -ᵊl **-ally** -ᵊl.i, -li

hydropath|y haɪˈdrɒp.ə.θ|i (US) -ˈdrɑː.pə- **-ist/s** -ɪst/s

hydrophilic ˌhaɪ.drəʊˈfɪl.ɪk (US) -droʊˈ-, -drəˈ-

hydrophobia ˌhaɪ.drəʊˈfəʊ.bi.ə (US) -droʊˈfoʊ-, -drəˈ-

hydrophobic ˌhaɪ.drəʊˈfəʊ.bɪk (US) -droʊˈfoʊ-, -drəˈ-

hydrophyte ˈhaɪ.drəʊ.faɪt (US) -droʊ-, -drə- **-s** -s

hydroplane ˈhaɪ.drəʊ.pleɪn (US) -droʊ-, -drə- **-s** -z

hydroponic ˌhaɪ.drəʊˈpɒn.ɪk (US) -droʊˈpɑː.nɪk, -drəˈ- **-s** -s **-ally** -ᵊl.i, -li

hydroscope ˈhaɪ.drəʊ.skəʊp (US) -droʊ.skoʊp, -drə- **-s** -s

hydrostat ˈhaɪ.drəʊ.stæt (US) -droʊ-, -drə- **-s** -s

hydrostatic ˌhaɪ.drəʊˈstæt.ɪk (US) -droʊˈstæt̬-, -drəˈ- **-al** -ᵊl **-ally** -ᵊl.i, -li **-s** -s

hydrotherapy ˌhaɪ.drəʊˈθer.ə.pi (US) -droʊˈ-, -drəˈ-

hydrotropism haɪˈdrɒt.rə.pɪ.zᵊm (US) -ˈdrɑː.trə-

hydrous ˈhaɪ.drəs

hydroxide haɪˈdrɒk.saɪd (US) -ˈdrɑːk- **-s** -z

hydroxyl haɪˈdrɒk.sɪl (US) -ˈdrɑːk-

hyena haɪˈiː.nə **-s** -z

Hygeia haɪˈdʒiː.ə

hygiene ˈhaɪ.dʒiːn

hygienic haɪˈdʒiː.nɪk (US) ˌhaɪ.dʒiˈen.ɪk; haɪˈdʒen-, -ˈdʒiː.nɪk **-ally** -ᵊl.i, -li

hygienist ˈhaɪ.dʒiː.nɪst (US) ˈhaɪ.dʒiː.nɪst; -ˈ--, -ˈdʒen.ɪst **-s** -s

hygrometric ˌhaɪ.grəʊˈmet.rɪk (US) -groʊˈ-, -grəˈ- **-al** -ᵊl **-ally** -ᵊl.i, -li

hygromet|ry haɪˈgrɒm.ə.t|ri (US) -ˈgrɑː.mə- **-er/s** -əʳ/z (US) -ɚ/z

hygroscope ˈhaɪ.grəʊ.skəʊp (US) -groʊ.skoʊp, -grə- **-s** -s

hygroscopic ˌhaɪ.grəʊˈskɒp.ɪk (US) -groʊˈskɑː.pɪk, -grəˈ- **-ally** -ᵊl.i, -li

Hyksos ˈhɪk.sɒs (US) -sɑːs

Hylas ˈhaɪ.læs, -ləs

Hylton ˈhɪl.tən

Hyman ˈhaɪ.mən

hymen (H) ˈhaɪ.men, -mən (US) -mən **-s** -z

hymene|al ˌhaɪ.menˈiː|.əl, -məˈniː-, -mɪˈ- (US) -məˈ- **-an** -ən

Hymettus haɪˈmet.əs (US) -ˈmet̬-

hymn hɪm **-s** -z **-ing** -ɪŋ **-ed** -d ˈ**hymn ˌbook**

hymnal ˈhɪm.nᵊl **-s** -z

hymnar|y ˈhɪm.nᵊr|.i **-ies** -iz

hymnic ˈhɪm.nɪk

hymnody ˈhɪm.nə.di

hymnolog|y hɪmˈnɒl.ə.dʒi (US) -nɑː.lə- **-ist/s** -ɪst/s

Hyndley ˈhaɪnd.li

Hyndman ˈhaɪnd.mən

Hynes haɪnz

hyoid ˈhaɪ.ɔɪd

hyoscine ˈhaɪ.əʊ.siːn (US) -ə.siːn, -sɪn

hypallage haɪˈpæl.ə.gi, -dʒi (US) haɪ-, hə-; ˌhaɪ.pəˈlædʒ.i, ˌhɪp.əˈ-

Hypatia haɪˈpeɪ.ʃə, -ʃi.ə

hyp|e haɪp **-es** -s **-ing** -ɪŋ **-ed** -t ˌ**hyped ˈup**

hyper- haɪ.pəʳ-; haɪˈpɜː- (US) haɪ.pɚ-; haɪˈpɜːr-

Note: Prefix. Normally either takes primary or secondary stress on the first syllable, e.g. **hypermarket** /ˈhaɪ.pəˌmɑː.kɪt (US) -pɚˌmɑːr-/, **hyperactive** /ˌhaɪ.pəʳˈæk.tɪv (US) -pɚˈ-/, or primary stress on the second syllable, e.g. **hyperbole** /haɪˈpɜː.bᵊl.i (US) -ˈpɜːr-/. Note also that, although /r/ is normally assigned to a following strong syllable in US transcriptions, in **hyper-** it is perceived to be morphemically linked to that morpheme and is retained in the prefix as /ɚ/.

hyper ˈhaɪ.pəʳ (US) -pɚ

hyperactive ˌhaɪ.pəʳˈæk.tɪv (US) -pɚˈ- *stress shift* ˌhyperactive ˈchild

hyperactivity ˌhaɪ.pᵊr.ækˈtɪv.ə.ti, -ɪ.ti (US) -pɚ.ækˈtɪv.ə.t̬i

hyperacute ˌhaɪ.pər.əˈkjuːt (US) -pɚ- **-ness** -nəs, -nɪs

hyperbol|a haɪˈpɜː.bᵊl|.ə (US) -ˈpɜːr- **-ae** -iː **-as** -əz

hyperbole haɪˈpɜː.bᵊl.i US -ˈpɜːr- **-s** -z
hyperbolic ˌhaɪ.pəˈbɒl.ɪk
US -pɚˈbɑː.lɪk **-al** -ᵊl **-ally** -ᵊl.i, -li
hyperbol|ism haɪˈpɜː.bᵊl|.ɪ.zᵊm
US -ˈpɜːr- **-ist/s** -ɪst/s
hyperboliz|e, -is|e haɪˈpɜː.bᵊl.aɪz
US -ˈpɜːr- **-es** -ɪz **-ing** -ɪŋ **-ed** -d
hyperboloid haɪˈpɜː.bᵊl.ɔɪd US -ˈpɜːr- **-s** -z
hyperborean ˌhaɪ.pəˈbɔː.ri.ən; -bɔːˈriː.ən, -bɒrˈiː.ən
US -pɚ.bɔːˈriː-, -bəˈ- **-s** -z
hypercorrect ˌhaɪ.pə.kəˈrekt
US -pɚ.kəˈrekt **-ly** -li **-ness** -nəs, -nɪs
hypercorrection ˌhaɪ.pə.kəˈrek.ʃᵊn
US -pɚ.kəˈrek- **-s** -z
hypercritic|al ˌhaɪ.pəˈkrɪt.ɪ.k|ᵊl
US -pɚˈkrɪt̬- **-ally** -ᵊl.i US -li
hypercriticism ˌhaɪ.pəˈkrɪt.ɪ.sɪ.zᵊm
US -pɚˈkrɪt̬.ɪ-
hypercriticiz|e, -is|e ˌhaɪ.pəˈkrɪt.ɪ.saɪz
US -pɚˈkrɪt̬- **-es** -ɪz **-ing** -ɪŋ **-ed** -d
hyperglycaem|ia ˌhaɪ.pə.glaɪˈsiː.m|i.ə
US -pɚ- **-ic** -ɪk
hypericum haɪˈper.ɪ.kəm **-s** -z
Hyperides haɪˈper.ɪ.diːz; ˌhaɪ.pəˈraɪ-
US haɪˈper.ɪ-, hɪ-
hyperinflation ˌhaɪ.pᵊr.ɪnˈfleɪ.ʃᵊn
US -pɚ-
Hyperion haɪˈpɪə.ri.ən, -ˈper.i-
US -ˈpɪr-
hypermarket ˈhaɪ.pəˌmɑː.kɪt
US -pɚˌmɑːr- **-s** -s
hypernym ˈhaɪ.pə.nɪm US -pɚ- **-s** -z
hypersensitive ˌhaɪ.pəˈsent.sə.tɪv, -sɪ- US -pɚˈsent.sə.t̬ɪv
hypersensitivity
ˌhaɪ.pəˌsent.səˈtɪv.ə.ti, -sɪˈ-, -ɪ.ti
US -pɚˌsent.səˈtɪv.ə.t̬i
hyperspace ˈhaɪ.pə.speɪs US -pɚ-
hypertension ˌhaɪ.pəˈten.tʃᵊn, ˈhaɪ.pəˌten-, US ˌhaɪ.pɚˈtent.ʃᵊn
hypertext ˈhaɪ.pə.tekst US -pɚ-
hyperthyroid ˌhaɪ.pəˈθaɪ.rɔɪd
US -pɚˈ- **-ism** -ɪ.zᵊm
hypertroph|y haɪˈpɜː.trə.f|i US -ˈpɜːr- **-ied** -id
hyperventi|late ˌhaɪ.pəˈven.tɪ|.leɪt, -tə- US -pɚˈven.t̬ə- **-lates** -leɪts **-lating** -leɪ.tɪŋ US -leɪ.t̬ɪŋ **-lated** -leɪ.tɪd US -leɪ.t̬ɪd
hyperventilation ˌhaɪ.pəˌven.tɪˈleɪ.ʃᵊn, -təˈ- US -pɚˌven.t̬əˈ-
hyph|a ˈhaɪ.f|ə **-ae** -iː
hyphal ˈhaɪ.fᵊl
hyphen ˈhaɪ.fᵊn **-s** -z **-ing** -ɪŋ **-ed** -d
hyphen|ate ˈhaɪ.fᵊn|.eɪt, -fɪ.n|eɪt
US -fə- **-ates** -eɪts **-ating** -eɪ.tɪŋ
US -eɪ.t̬ɪŋ **-ated** -eɪ.tɪd US -eɪ.t̬ɪd
hyphenation ˌhaɪ.fᵊnˈeɪ.ʃᵊn
hypno- ˈhɪp.nəʊ-; hɪpˈnɒ-, -ˈnəʊ-
US ˈhɪp.noʊ-, -nə-; hɪpˈnɑː-, -ˈnoʊ-

Note: Prefix. Normally either takes primary or secondary stress on the first syllable, e.g. **hypnotism** /ˈhɪp.nə.tɪ.zᵊm/, **hypnotherapy** /ˌhɪp.nəʊˈθer.ə.pi US -noʊˈ-/, or primary stress on the second syllable, e.g. **hypnotic** /hɪpˈnɒt.ɪk US -ˈnɑː.t̬ɪk/.

hypnosis hɪpˈnəʊ.sɪs US -ˈnoʊ-
hypnotherapist ˌhɪp.nəʊˈθer.ə.pɪst
US -noʊˈ- **-s** -s
hypnotherapy ˌhɪp.nəʊˈθer.ə.pi
US -noʊˈ-
hypnotic hɪpˈnɒt.ɪk US -ˈnɑː.t̬ɪk
hypnot|ism ˈhɪp.nə.t|ɪ.zᵊm **-ist/s** -ɪst/s
hypnotization, -isa-
ˌhɪp.nə.taɪˈzeɪ.ʃᵊn, -tɪˈ- US -tɪˈ-
hypnotiz|e, -is|e ˈhɪp.nə.taɪz **-es** -ɪz **-ing** -ɪŋ **-ed** -d **-er/s** -əʳ/z US -ɚ/z
hypo- ˈhaɪ.pəʊ-; haɪˈpɒ- US ˈhaɪ.poʊ-, -pə-; haɪˈpɑː-, hɪ-

Note: Prefix. Normally either takes primary or secondary stress on the first syllable, e.g. **hypocaust** /ˈhaɪ.pəʊ.kɔːst US -poʊ-/, **hypothetic** /ˌhaɪ.pəʊˈθet.ɪk US -poʊˈθet̬-/, or primary stress on the second syllable, e.g. **hypotenuse** /haɪˈpɒt.ᵊn.juːz US -ˈpɑː.tᵊn.uːs/.

hypo ˈhaɪ.pəʊ US -poʊ **-s** -z
hypoallergenic ˌhaɪ.pəʊˌæl.əˈdʒen.ɪk, -ɜːˈ- US -poʊˌæl.ɚˈ-
hypocaust ˈhaɪ.pəʊ.kɔːst, -kɒst
US -poʊ.kɔːst, -pə-, -kɑːst **-s** -s
hypochondri|a ˌhaɪ.pəʊˈkɒn.dri|.ə
US -poʊˈkɑːn-, -pəˈ- **-ac/s** -æk/s
hypochondriacal
ˌhaɪ.pəʊ.kɒnˈdraɪ.ə.kᵊl, -kənˈ-
US -poʊ.kɑːnˈ-, -pə-
hypochondriasis
ˌhaɪ.pəʊ.kɒnˈdraɪ.ə.sɪs, -kənˈ-
US -poʊ.kɑːnˈ-, -pə-
hypocotyl ˌhaɪ.pəˈkɒt.ɪl
US -poʊˈkɑː.t̬ᵊl
hypocris|y hɪˈpɒk.rə.s|i, -rɪ-
US -ˈpɑː.krə- **-ies** -iz
hypocrite ˈhɪp.ə.krɪt **-s** -s
hypocritic|al ˌhɪp.əʊˈkrɪt.ɪ.k|ᵊl
US -əˈkrɪt̬- **-ally** -ᵊl.i, -li
hypocycloid ˌhaɪ.pəʊˈsaɪ.klɔɪd
US -poʊˈ-, -pəˈ- **-s** -z
hypodermic ˌhaɪ.pəʊˈdɜː.mɪk
US -poʊˈdɜːr-, -pəˈ- *stress shift, see compounds:* ˌ**hypodermic ˈneedle** ; ˌ**hypodermic syˈringe**
hypodermis ˌhaɪ.pəʊˈdɜː.mɪs
US -poʊˈdɜːr-, -pəˈ-
hypogeal ˌhaɪ.pəʊˈdʒiː.əl US -poʊˈ-
hypoglyc(a)em|ia ˌhaɪ.pəʊ.glaɪˈsiː.m|i.ə
US -poʊ- **-ic** -ɪk
hypophosphate ˌhaɪ.pəʊˈfɒs.feɪt, -fɪt
US -poʊˈfɑːs-, -pəˈ- **-s** -s
hyposta|sis haɪˈpɒs.tə|.sɪs
US -ˈpɑː.stə-, hɪ- **-ses** -siːz
hypostatiz|e, -is|e haɪˈpɒs.tə.taɪz
US -ˈpɑː.stə-, hɪ- **-es** -ɪz **-ing** -ɪŋ **-ed** -d
hypostyle ˈhaɪ.pəʊ.staɪl US -poʊ-
hyposulphite ˌhaɪ.pəʊˈsʌl.faɪt
US -poʊˈ-, -pəˈ- **-s** -s
hypotactic ˌhaɪ.pəʊˈtæk.tɪk
US -poʊˈ-, -pəˈ-
hypotax|is ˌhaɪ.pəʊˈtæk.s|ɪs, ˈhaɪ.pəʊ.tæk- US ˌhaɪ.poʊˈtæk-, -pəˈ- **-es** -iːz
hypotension ˌhaɪ.pəʊˈten.tʃᵊn
US ˈhaɪ.poʊˌten-, -pəˌ-
hypotenus|e haɪˈpɒt.ᵊn.juːz, -ɪ.njuːz, -juːs US -ˈpɑː.tᵊn.uːs, -tɪ.nuːs, -njuːs **-es** -ɪz
hypothalamus ˌhaɪ.pəʊˈθæl.ə.məs
US -poʊˈ-, -pəˈ-
hypothe|cate haɪˈpɒθ.ə|.keɪt, ˈ-ɪ-
US -ˈpɑː.θə-, hɪ- **-cates** -keɪts **-cating** -keɪ.tɪŋ US -keɪ.t̬ɪŋ **-cated** -keɪ.tɪd US -keɪ.t̬ɪd
hypothecation haɪˌpɒθ.əˈkeɪ.ʃᵊn, -ɪˈ-
US -pɑː.θəˈ-, hɪ- **-s** -z
hypothermal ˌhaɪ.pəʊˈθɜː.mᵊl
US -poʊˈθɜːr-, -pəˈ-
hypothermia ˌhaɪ.pəʊˈθɜː.mi.ə
US -poʊˈθɜːr-, -pəˈ-
hypothes|is haɪˈpɒθ.ə.s|ɪs, ˈ-ɪ-
US -ˈpɑː.θə-, hɪ- **-es** -iːz
hypothesiz|e, -is|e haɪˈpɒθ.ə.saɪz
US -ˈpɑː.θə-, hɪ- **-es** -ɪz **-ing** -ɪŋ **-ed** -d
hypothetic ˌhaɪ.pəʊˈθet.ɪk
US -poʊˈθet̬-, -pəˈ- **-al** -ᵊl **-ally** -ᵊl.i, -li
hypothyroid ˌhaɪ.pəʊˈθaɪ.rɔɪd
US -poʊˈ- **-ism** -ɪ.zᵊm
hypoxia haɪˈpɒk.si.ə US -ˈpɑːk-, hɪ-
hypoxic haɪˈpɒk.sɪk US -ˈpɑːk-, hɪ-
hypsome|try hɪpˈsɒm.ə|.tri
US -ˈsɑː.mə- **-ter/s** -təʳ/z US -t̬ɚ/z
hyrax ˈhaɪ.ræks **-es** -ɪz
Hyslop ˈhɪz.ləp, -lɒp US -lɑːp, -ləp
hyson (H) ˈhaɪ.sᵊn
hyssop ˈhɪs.əp
hysterectom|y ˌhɪs.tᵊrˈek.tə.m|i
US -təˈrek- **-ies** -iz
hysteria hɪˈstɪə.ri.ə US -ˈster.i-, -ˈstɪr-
hysteric hɪˈster.ɪk **-s** -s **-al** -ᵊl **-ally** -ᵊl.i, -li
hysteron proteron
ˌhɪs.tə.rɒnˈprɒt.ə.rɒn, -rɒmˈ-, -ˈprəʊ.tə- US -rɑːnˈprɑː.t̬ə.rɑːn
hythe (H) haɪð **-s** -z
Hyundai® ˈhaɪ.ʌn.daɪ, -ən-, ˈhjʊn-
US ˈhjʌn.deɪ, ˈhʌn-
Hywel haʊəl
Hz (*abbrev. for* **Hertz**) hɜːts, heəts
US hɜːrts, herts

I

i (I) aɪ **-'s** -z
Ia. (*abbrev. for* **Iowa**) ˈaɪ.əʊə; ˈaɪə.wə (US) ˈaɪə.wə; ˈaɪ.oʊ-
Iachimo iˈæk.ɪ.məʊ, aɪ- (US) -moʊ
Iago iˈɑː.ɡəʊ (US) -ɡoʊ
Iain ˈiː.ən
-ial -i.əl, -əl
Note: Suffix. Normally stressed on the syllable before the prefix, e.g. **facial** /ˈfeɪ.ʃᵊl/.
iamb ˈaɪ.æm*b* **-s** -z
iamb|ic aɪˈæm.b|ɪk **-us/es** -əs/ɪz
Ian ˈiː.ən
-ian -i.ən
Note: Suffix. Words ending **-ian** are stressed in a similar way to those ending **-ial**; see above.
I'Anson aɪˈæn*t*.sən
Ianthe aɪˈæn*t*.θi
IATA aɪˈɑː.tə, iː- (US) ˌaɪ.eɪ.tiːˈeɪ, aɪˈɑː.t̬ə
iatrogenic aɪ.æt.rəʊˈdʒen.ɪk, ˌaɪ.æt- (US) aɪ.æt.roʊˈ-, iː-, -rəˈ- **-ally** -ᵊl.i, -li
Ibadan ɪˈbæd.ᵊn (US) iːˈbɑː.dɑːn, -dᵊn
Ibbertson ˈɪb.ət.sᵊn (US) -ɚt-
Ibbetson ˈɪb.ɪt.sᵊn, -ət-
I-beam ˈaɪ.biːm **-s** -z
Iberi|a aɪˈbɪə.ri|.ə (US) -ˈbɪr.i- **-an/s** -ən/z
iberis aɪˈbɪə.rɪs (US) -ˈbɪr.ɪs
Iberus aɪˈbɪə.rəs (US) -ˈbɪr.əs
ibex ˈaɪ.beks **-es** -ɪz
ibid ɪˈbɪd, ˈɪb.ɪd
ibidem ˈɪb.ɪ.dem, ˈ-ə-; ɪˈbaɪ.dem (US) ˈɪb.ɪ.dem, ˈ-ə-; ɪˈbiː.dem, -ˈbaɪ-
-ibility -ɪˈbɪl.ɪ.ti, -əˈ-, -ə.ti (US) -ə.t̬i
Note: Suffix. Words containing **-ibility** always exhibit primary stress as shown above, e.g. **eligibility** /ˌel.ɪ.dʒəˈbɪl.ə.ti (US) -t̬i/.
ibis ˈaɪ.bɪs **-es** -ɪz
Ibiza ɪˈbiː.θə, iː- (US) ɪˈbiː.zə, -sə; -ˈviː.θə, -θɑː
-ible -ə.bl̩, -ɪ-
Note: Suffix. Words containing **-ible** are normally stressed either on the antepenultimate syllable, e.g. **susceptible** /səˈsep.tə.bl̩/, or two syllables preceding the suffix, e.g. **eligible** /ˈel.ɪ.dʒə.bl̩/.
IBM® ˌaɪ.biːˈem
Ibo ˈiː.bəʊ (US) -boʊ **-s** -z
Ibrahim ˈɪb.rə.hiːm, -hɪm, ˌ--ˈ-
Ibrox ˈaɪ.brɒks (US) -brɑːks
Ibsen ˈɪb.sᵊn
Ibstock ˈɪb.stɒk (US) -stɑːk
ibuprofen ˌaɪ.bjuːˈprəʊ.fen, -fᵊn; aɪˈbjuː.prəʊ- (US) ˌaɪ.bjuːˈproʊ.fᵊn

IC ˌaɪˈsiː **-s** -z
-ic -ɪk
Note: Suffix. Words containing **-ic** are normally stressed on the penultimate syllable, e.g. **music** /ˈmjuː.zɪk/.
-ic|al -ɪ.k|ᵊl **-ally** -ᵊl.i, -li
Note: Suffix. Words containing **-ical** are normally stressed on the antepenultimate syllable, e.g. **musical** /ˈmjuː.zɪ.kᵊl/.
Icari|a ɪˈkeə.ri|.ə, aɪ- (US) -ˈker.i- **-an** -ən
Icarus ˈɪk.ᵊr.əs, ˈaɪ.kᵊr- (US) ˈɪk.ɚ-
ICBM ˌaɪ.siː.biːˈem
ic|e aɪs **-es** -ɪz **-ing** -ɪŋ **-ed** -t ˈ**ice ˌage** ; ˈ**ice ˌaxe** ; ˈ**ice ˌbucket** ; ˈ**ice ˌcap** ; ˈ**ice ˌfield** ; ˈ**ice ˌfloe** ; ˈ**ice ˌhockey**, ˌ**ice ˈhockey** ; ˈ**ice ˌlolly**, ˌ**ice ˈlolly** ; ˈ**ice ˌpack** ; ˈ**ice ˌrink** ; ˌ**break the ˈice** ; ˌ**skate on ˌthin ˈice**
iceberg ˈaɪs.bɜːɡ (US) -bɜːrɡ **-s** -z ˌ**iceberg ˈlettuce**
icebound ˈaɪs.baʊnd
icebox ˈaɪs.bɒks (US) -bɑːks **-es** -ɪz
icebreaker ˈaɪsˌbreɪ.kəʳ (US) -kɚ **-s** -z
ice cream ˌaɪsˈkriːm, ˈ-- **-s** -z ˌ**ice ˈcream ˌparlo(u)r** ; ˌ**ice cream ˈsoda**
icefall ˈaɪs.fɔːl (US) -fɔːl, -fɑːl **-s** -z
icehou|se ˈaɪs.haʊ|s **-ses** -zɪz
Iceland ˈaɪs.lənd
Icelander ˈaɪs.lən.dəʳ, -læn- (US) -dɚ **-s** -z
Icelandic aɪsˈlæn.dɪk
icemaker ˈaɪsˌmeɪ.kəʳ (US) -kɚ **-s** -z
ice|man ˈaɪs|.mæn, -mən **-men** -men, -mən
Iceni aɪˈsiː.naɪ, -ni
icepick ˈaɪs.pɪk **-s** -s
ice|skate ˈaɪs|.skeɪt **-skates** -skeɪts **-skating** -ˌskeɪ.tɪŋ (US) -ˌskeɪ.t̬ɪŋ **-skated** -ˌskeɪ.tɪd (US) -ˌskeɪ.t̬ɪd **-skater/s** -ˌskeɪ.təʳ/z (US) -ˌskeɪ.t̬ɚ/z
Ichabod ˈɪk.ə.bɒd, ˈɪx- (US) ɪk-, -bɑːd
ich dien ˌɪxˈdiːn
I Ching ˌiːˈtʃɪŋ, ˌaɪ-, -ˈdʒɪŋ (US) ˌiː-
ich-laut ˈɪx.laut, ˈɪk-
ichneumon ɪkˈnjuː.mən (US) -ˈnuː-, -ˈnjuː- **-s** -z
ichnographic ˌɪk.nəʊˈɡræf.ɪk (US) -noʊˈ- **-al** -ᵊl **-ally** -ᵊl.i, -li
ichnography ɪkˈnɒɡ.rə.fi (US) -ˈnɑː.ɡrə-
ichnological ˌɪk.nəʊˈlɒdʒ.ɪ.kᵊl (US) -noʊˈlɑː.dʒɪ-
ichnology ɪkˈnɒl.ə.dʒi (US) -ˈnɑː.lə-
ichor ˈaɪ.kɔːʳ (US) -kɔːr, -kɚ
ichthyologic|al ˌɪk.θi.əˈlɒdʒ.ɪ.k|ᵊl (US) -ˈlɑː.dʒɪ- **-ally** -ᵊl.i, -li
ichthyolog|y ˌɪk.θiˈɒl.ə.dʒ|i (US) -ˈɑː.lə- **-ist/s** -ɪst/s
ichthyosaur ˈɪk.θi.ə.sɔːʳ (US) -sɔːr **-s** -z
ichthyosaur|us ˌɪk.θi.əʊˈsɔː.r|əs (US) -oʊˈsɔːr|.əs, -əˈ- **-i** -aɪ **-uses** -ə.sɪz

ICI® ˌaɪ.siːˈaɪ
-ician -ˈɪʃ.ᵊn
Note: Suffix. Normally carries primary stress as shown above, e.g. **musician** /mjuːˈzɪʃ.ᵊn/, **technician** /tekˈnɪʃ.ᵊn/.
icicle ˈaɪ.sɪ.kl̩, -sə- **-s** -z
icing ˈaɪ.sɪŋ ˈ**icing ˌsugar**
Icke aɪk, ɪk
Icknield ˈɪk.niːld
ick|y ˈɪk|.i **-ier** -i.əʳ (US) -i.ɚ **-iest** -i.ɪst, -i.əst
icon ˈaɪ.kɒn, -kən (US) -kɑːn, -kən **-s** -z
iconic aɪˈkɒn.ɪk (US) -ˈkɑː.nɪk
Iconium aɪˈkəʊ.ni.əm, ɪ- (US) aɪˈkoʊ-
iconoclasm aɪˈkɒn.əʊˌklæz.ᵊm (US) -ˈkɑː.nə-
iconoclast aɪˈkɒn.əʊ.klæst, -klɑːst (US) -ˈkɑː.nə.klæst **-s** -s
iconoclastic aɪˌkɒn.əʊˈklæs.tɪk, ˌaɪ.kɒn- (US) aɪˌkɑː.nəˈ- **-ally** -ᵊl.i, -li
iconographic ˌaɪ.kə.nəʊˈɡræf.ɪk (US) -noʊ-
iconograph|y ˌaɪ.kəˈnɒɡ.rə.f|i, -kɒnˈɒɡ- (US) -kəˈnɑː.ɡrə- **-er/s** -əʳ/z (US) -ɚ/z
iconoscope aɪˈkɒn.ə.skəʊp (US) -ˈkɑː.nə.skoʊp **-s** -s
icosahedr|on ˌaɪ.kɒs.əˈhiː.dr|ən, -kə.səˈ-; aɪˌkɒs- (US) ˌaɪ.koʊ.səˈ-; aɪˌkɑː- **-ons** -ənz **-a** -ə **-al** -əl
ictus ˈɪk.təs **-es** -ɪz
ICU ˌaɪ.siːˈjuː
ic|y ˈaɪ.s|i **-ier** -i.əʳ (US) -i.ɚ **-iest** -i.ɪst, -i.əst **-ily** -ɪ.li, -ᵊl.i **-iness** -ɪ.nəs, -ɪ.nɪs
id ɪd
'Id iːd
ID ˌaɪˈdiː ˌ**IˈD ˌcard**
I'd (= **I would, I should** *or* **I had**) aɪd
Ida ˈaɪ.də
Ida. (*abbrev. for* **Idaho**) ˈaɪ.də.həʊ (US) -hoʊ
Idaho ˈaɪ.də.həʊ (US) -hoʊ
Iddesleigh ˈɪdz.li
Ide iːd
-ide -aɪd
Note: Suffix. Words containing **-ide** are normally stressed on the penultimate or antepenultimate syllable, e.g. **hydroxide** /haɪˈdrɒk.saɪd (US) -ˈdrɑːk-/.
idea aɪˈdɪə (US) -ˈdiː.ə **-s** -z
Note: In British English, the pronunciation /ˈaɪ.dɪə/ is also sometimes heard, especially when a stress immediately follows, e.g. "I thought of the ˌidea ˈfirst".
ideal (*n.*) aɪˈdɪəl, -ˈdiː.əl (US) -ˈdiː- **-s** -z
ideal (*adj.*) aɪˈdɪəl, -ˈdiː.əl, ˈ-- (US) -ˈdiː- *stress shift:* ˌideal ˈhome
ideal|ism aɪˈdɪə.l|ɪ.zᵊm; ˈaɪ.dɪə- (US) aɪˈdiː.ə.l|ɪ- **-ist/s** -ɪst/s

idealistic aɪˌdɪəˈlɪs.tɪk; ˌaɪ.dɪə- Ⓤⓢ ˌaɪ.di.əˈ- **-ally** -ᵊl.i, -li
ideality ˌaɪ.diˈæl.ə.ti, -ɪ.ti Ⓤⓢ -ə.t̬i
idealization, -isa- aɪˌdɪə.laɪˈzeɪ.ʃᵊn, -lɪˈ-; ˌaɪ.dɪə- Ⓤⓢ aɪˌdiː.ə.ləˈ- **-s** -z
idealiz|e, -is|e aɪˈdɪə.laɪz Ⓤⓢ -ˈdiː.ə- **-es** -ɪz **-ing** -ɪŋ **-ed** -d **-er/s** -əʳ/z Ⓤⓢ -ɚ/z
ideally aɪˈdɪə.li, -ˈdɪəl.li Ⓤⓢ -ˈdiː.li, -ə.li
ide|ate ˈaɪ.di|.eɪt **-ates** -eɪts **-ating** -eɪ.tɪŋ Ⓤⓢ -t̬ɪŋ **-ated** -eɪ.tɪd Ⓤⓢ -t̬ɪd
ideational ˌaɪ.diˈeɪ.ʃᵊn.ᵊl, -ˈeɪʃ.nᵊl
idée fixe ˌiː.deɪˈfiːks **idées fixes** ˌiː.deɪˈfiːks, -deɪzˈ-
idée reçue ˌiː.deɪ.rəˈsuː **idées reçues** ˌiː.deɪ.rəˈsuː, -deɪz-
idem ˈɪd.em, ˈiː.dem, ˈaɪ- Ⓤⓢ ˈaɪ-, ˈiː-, ˈɪd.em
idempotent ˌɪd.əmˈpəʊ.tᵊnt, ˌiː.dəm-, ˌaɪ-, -demˈ- Ⓤⓢ ˌaɪ.demˈpoʊ-, ˌiː-, ˌɪd.emˈ-
identic|al aɪˈden.tɪ.k|ᵊl, ɪ- Ⓤⓢ -t̬ə- **-ally** -ᵊl.i, -li **-alness** -ᵊl.nəs, -ᵊl.nɪs
identifiable aɪˈden.tɪ.faɪ.ə.bl̩, -təˈ-, aɪˌden.tɪˈfaɪ-, -tə- Ⓤⓢ aɪˌden.t̬əˈ-
identification aɪˌden.tɪ.fɪˈkeɪ.ʃᵊn, -tə- Ⓤⓢ -t̬ə- **-s** -z
identi|fy aɪˈden.tɪ|.faɪ, -tə- Ⓤⓢ -t̬ə- **-fies** -faɪz **-fying** -faɪ.ɪŋ **-fied** -faɪd **-fier/s** -faɪ.əʳ/z Ⓤⓢ -faɪ.ɚ/z
identikit (I) aɪˈden.tɪ.kɪt Ⓤⓢ -t̬ə- **-s** -s
identit|y aɪˈden.tə.t|i, -ɪ.t|i Ⓤⓢ -t̬ə.t̬|i **-ies** -iz **iˈdentity ˌcard** ; **iˈdentity ˌcrisis** ; **iˈdentity paˌrade** ; **iˈdentity ˌlineup**
ideogram ˈɪd.i.əʊ.græm, ˈaɪ.di- Ⓤⓢ -oʊ-, -ə- **-s** -z
ideograph ˈɪd.i.əʊ.grɑːf, ˈaɪ.di-, -græf Ⓤⓢ -oʊ.græf, -ə- **-s** -s
ideographic ˌɪd.i.əʊˈgræf.ɪk, ˌaɪ.di- Ⓤⓢ -oʊˈ-, -əˈ- **-al** -ᵊl **-ally** -ᵊl.i, -li
ideography ˌɪd.iˈɒg.rə.fi, ˌaɪ.diˈ- Ⓤⓢ -ˈɑː.grə-
ideologic|al ˌaɪ.di.əˈlɒdʒ.ɪ.k|ᵊl, ˌɪd.i- Ⓤⓢ -ˈlɑː.dʒɪ- **-ally** -ᵊl.i, -li
ideologue ˈaɪ.di.əʊ.lɒg, ˈɪd.i- Ⓤⓢ -ə.lɑːg **-s** -z
ideolog|y ˌaɪ.diˈɒl.ə.dʒ|i, ˌɪd.iˈ- Ⓤⓢ -ˈɑː.lə- **-ies** -iz **-ist/s** -ɪst/s
ides (I) aɪdz ˌ**Ides of ˈMarch**
Idi Amin ˌiː.di.ɑːˈmiːn
idio- ɪd.i.əʊ-; ˌɪd.iˈɒ- Ⓤⓢ ɪd.i.oʊ-, -ə-; ˌɪd.iˈɑː-

Note: Prefix. Normally takes either primary or secondary stress on the first syllable, e.g. **idiolect** /ˈɪd.i.əʊ.lekt Ⓤⓢ -oʊ-/, **idiomatic** /ˌɪd.i.əʊˈmæt.ɪk Ⓤⓢ -əˈmæt̬-/, or secondary stress on the first syllable and primary stress on the third, e.g. **idiotic** /ˌɪd.iˈɒt.ɪk Ⓤⓢ -ˈɑː.t̬ɪk/.

idioc|y ˈɪd.i.ə.s|i **-ies** -iz
idiolect ˈɪd.i.əʊ.lekt Ⓤⓢ -oʊ-, -ə- **-s** -s **-al** -ᵊl
idiom ˈɪd.i.əm **-s** -z
idiomatic ˌɪd.i.əʊˈmæt.ɪk Ⓤⓢ -əˈmæt̬- **-al** -ᵊl **-ally** -ᵊl.i, -li
idiophone ˈɪd.i.əʊ.fəʊn Ⓤⓢ -oʊ.foʊn, -ə- **-s** -z
idiosyncras|y ˌɪd.i.əʊˈsɪŋ.krə.s|i Ⓤⓢ -oʊˈsɪn-, -əˈ-, -ˈsɪŋ- **-ies** -iz
idiosyncratic ˌɪd.i.əʊ.sɪŋˈkræt.ɪk Ⓤⓢ -oʊ.sɪnˈkræt̬-, -ə-, -sɪŋˈ- **-ally** -ᵊl.i, -li
idiot ˈɪd.i.ət **-s** -s ˈ**idiot ˌbox**
idiotic ˌɪd.iˈɒt.ɪk Ⓤⓢ -ˈɑː.t̬ɪk **-al** -ᵊl **-ally** -ᵊl.i, -li
idiotism ˈɪd.i.ə.tɪ.zᵊm Ⓤⓢ -t̬ɪ- **-s** -z
idiot-proof ˈɪd.i.ət.pruːf
idiot(s) savant(s) ˌiː.di.əʊ.sævˈɑ̃ːŋ, ˌɪd.i.ətˈsæv.ᵊnt Ⓤⓢ ˌiː.diː.oʊ.sævˈɑːnt, -ˈænt
Idist ˈiː.dɪst **-s** -s
id|le (I) ˈaɪ.d|l̩ **-ly** -li **-lest** -lɪst, -ləst **-leness** -l̩.nəs, -nɪs **-les** -l̩z **-ling** -lɪŋ **-led** -l̩d **-ler/s** -ləʳ/z Ⓤⓢ -lɚ/z
Ido ˈiː.dəʊ Ⓤⓢ -doʊ
idol ˈaɪ.dᵊl **-s** -z
idolater aɪˈdɒl.ə.təʳ Ⓤⓢ -ˈdɑː.lə.t̬ɚ **-s** -z
idolatrous aɪˈdɒl.ə.trəs Ⓤⓢ -ˈdɑː.lə- **-ly** -li **-ness** -nəs, -nɪs
idolatr|y aɪˈdɒl.ə.tr|i Ⓤⓢ -ˈdɑː.lə- **-ies** -iz
idolization, -isa- ˌaɪ.dᵊl.aɪˈzeɪ.ʃᵊn, -ɪˈ- Ⓤⓢ -ɪˈ-
idoliz|e, -is|e ˈaɪ.dᵊl.aɪz **-es** -ɪz **-ing** -ɪŋ **-ed** -d **-er/s** -əʳ/z Ⓤⓢ -ɚ/z
Idomeneus aɪˈdɒm.ɪ.njuːs, ɪˈ-, ˈ-ə-; ɪˌdɒm.ɪˈniː.əs, aɪˌ-, -əˈ- Ⓤⓢ -ˈdɑː.mə.nuːs, -njuːs
Idris ˈɪd.rɪs, ˈaɪ.drɪs
Idumea ˌaɪ.djʊˈmiː.ə, ˌɪd.jʊˈ- Ⓤⓢ ˌɪd.juːˈmiː.ə, ˌiː.djuːˈ-, ˌiː.dʒuːˈ-
idyll ˈɪd.ᵊl, ˈaɪ.dᵊl, -dɪl Ⓤⓢ ˈaɪ.dᵊl **-s** -z
idyllic ɪˈdɪl.ɪk, aɪ- Ⓤⓢ aɪ- **-ally** -ᵊl.i, -li
idyllist ˈɪd.ᵊl.ɪst, ˈaɪ.dᵊl-, -dɪl- Ⓤⓢ ˈaɪ.dᵊl- **-s** -s
i.e. ˌaɪˈiː
if ɪf
Ife *surname:* aɪf *town in Nigeria:* ˈiː.feɪ
Iffley ˈɪf.li
iffy ˈɪf.i
Ifor ˈaɪ.vəʳ, -fəʳ, ˈiː.vɔːʳ Ⓤⓢ ˈaɪ.vɚ, ˈiː-
-ify -ɪ.faɪ, -ə-

Note: Suffix. Words containing **-ify** normally carry stress on the antepenultimate syllable, e.g. **person** /ˈpɜː.sᵊn Ⓤⓢ ˈpɜːr-/, **personify** /pəˈsɒn.ɪ.faɪ Ⓤⓢ pɚˈsɑː.nɪ-/. Exceptions exist; see individual entries.

Igbo ˈiː.bəʊ Ⓤⓢ -boʊ **-s** -z
Ightham ˈaɪ.təm Ⓤⓢ -t̬əm

igloo ˈɪg.luː **-s** -z
Ignatius ɪgˈneɪ.ʃəs
igneous ˈɪg.ni.əs
ignis fatu|us ˌɪg.nɪsˈfæt.ju|.əs Ⓤⓢ -ˈfætʃ.uː- **-i** -iː
ig|nite ɪg|ˈnaɪt **-nites** -ˈnaɪts **-niting** -ˈnaɪ.tɪŋ Ⓤⓢ -ˈnaɪ.t̬ɪŋ **-nited** -ˈnaɪ.tɪd Ⓤⓢ -ˈnaɪ.t̬ɪd **-nitable** -ˈnaɪ.tə.bl̩ Ⓤⓢ -ˈnaɪ.t̬ə.bl̩
ignition ɪgˈnɪʃ.ᵊn **-s** -z
ignobility ˌɪg.nəʊˈbɪl.ə.ti, -ɪ.ti Ⓤⓢ -noʊˈbɪl.ə.t̬i, -nəˈ-
ignob|le ɪgˈnəʊ.bl̩ Ⓤⓢ -ˈnoʊ- **-ly** -li **-leness** -l̩.nəs, -nɪs
ignominious ˌɪg.nəʊˈmɪn.i.əs Ⓤⓢ -nəˈ- **-ly** -li **-ness** -nəs, -nɪs
ignominy ˈɪg.nə.mɪ.ni, -mə.ni Ⓤⓢ -nə.mɪ-
ignoramus ˌɪg.nəˈreɪ.məs **-es** -ɪz
ignorance ˈɪg.nᵊr.ᵊnts
ignorant ˈɪg.nᵊr.ᵊnt **-ly** -li
ignor|e ɪgˈnɔːʳ Ⓤⓢ -ˈnɔːr **-es** -z **-ing** -ɪŋ **-ed** -d **-able** -ə.bl̩
Igoe ˈaɪ.gəʊ Ⓤⓢ -goʊ
Igor ˈiː.gɔːʳ Ⓤⓢ -gɔːr
Igorot ˌiː.gəˈrəʊt, ˌɪg.əˈ- Ⓤⓢ ˌiː.goʊˈroʊt, ˌɪg.oʊˈ- **-s** -z
Igraine ɪˈgreɪn, iː-
Iguaçú ˌiː.gwɑːˈsuː
iguana ɪˈgwɑː.nə, ˌɪg.juˈɑː- Ⓤⓢ ɪˈgwɑː-, iː- **-s** -z
iguanodon ɪˈgwɑː.nə.dɒn, ˌɪg.juˈɑː-, -ˈæn.ə-, -dən Ⓤⓢ ɪˈgwɑː.nə.dɑːn, iː- **-s** -z
Iguazú ˌiː.gwɑːˈsuː
ikat ˈiː.kɑːt
IKBS ˌaɪ.keɪ.biːˈes
Ike aɪk
Ikea® aɪˈkiː.ə *as if Swedish:* ɪˈkeɪ.ə
ikon ˈaɪ.kɒn, -kən Ⓤⓢ -kɑːn, -kən **-s** -z
Ilchester ˈɪl.tʃɪs.təʳ Ⓤⓢ -tɚ
ILEA ˈɪl.i.ə, ˌaɪ.el.iːˈeɪ
ilea (*plur. of* **ileum**) ˈɪl.i.ə
ileostom|y ˌɪl.iˈɒs.tə.m|i Ⓤⓢ -ˈɑː.stə- **-ies** -iz
ile|um ˈɪl.i|.əm **-a** -ə **-al** -əl
ilex ˈaɪ.leks **-es** -ɪz
Ilford ˈɪl.fəd Ⓤⓢ -fɚd
Ilfracombe ˈɪl.frə.kuːm
ilia (*plur. of* **ilium**) ˈɪl.i.ə
iliac ˈɪl.i.æk
Iliad ˈɪl.i.æd, -əd Ⓤⓢ -əd, -æd
Iliffe ˈaɪ.lɪf
ili|um ˈɪl.i|.əm **-a** -ə
Ilium ˈɪl.i.əm, ˈaɪ.li-
ilk ɪlk
Ilkeston(e) ˈɪl.kɪ.stᵊn, -kə-
Ilkley ˈɪl.kli
ill ɪl **-s** -z ˌ**ill at ˈease** ; ˌ**ill ˈwill**
I'll (**= I will** *or* **I shall**) aɪl
Ill. (*abbrev. for* **Illinois**) ˌɪl.ɪˈnɔɪ, -əˈ-

ill-advised ˌɪl.ədˈvaɪzd *stress shift:* ˌill-advised ˈplan
ill-advisedly ˌɪl.ədˈvaɪ.zɪd.li
ill-assorted ˌɪl.əˈsɔː.tɪd (US) -ˈsɔːr.t̬ɪd *stress shift:* ˌill-assorted ˈcandidates
illative ɪˈleɪ.tɪv, ˈɪl.ə.tɪv (US) -t̬ɪv **-ly** -li
ill-bred ˌɪlˈbred *stress shift:* ˌill-bred ˈlout
ill-breeding ˌɪlˈbriː.dɪŋ
ill-conceived ˌɪl.kənˈsiːvd *stress shift:* ˌill-conceived ˈplan
ill-conditioned ˌɪl.kənˈdɪʃ.ənd *stress shift:* ˌill-conditioned ˈcrew
ill-considered ˌɪl.kənˈsɪd.əd (US) -ɚd *stress shift:* ˌill-considered ˈaction
ill-disposed ˌɪl.dɪˈspəʊzd (US) -ˈspoʊzd *stress shift:* ˌill-disposed ˈpatient
illegal ɪˈliː.gəl (US) ɪˈliː-, ˌɪl- **-ly** -i **ilˌlegal ˈalien ; ilˌlegal ˈimmigrant**
illegalit|y ˌɪl.iːˈgæl.ə.t|i, -ɪˈ-, -ɪ.t|i (US) -ə.t̬|i **-ies** -iz
illegibility ɪˌledʒ.əˈbɪl.ə.ti, ˌɪl.ledʒ-, -ɪˈ-, -ɪ.ti (US) -ə.t̬i
illegib|le ɪˈledʒ.ə.b|l̩, ˌɪlˈledʒ-, ˈ-ɪ- **-ly** -li **-leness** -l̩.nəs, -nɪs
illegitimacy ˌɪl.ɪˈdʒɪt.ə.mə.si, -əˈ-, ˈ-ɪ- (US) -ˈdʒɪt̬.ə-
illegitimate ˌɪl.ɪˈdʒɪt.ə.mət, -əˈ-, ˈ-ɪ-, -mɪt (US) -ˈdʒɪt̬.ə- **-ly** -li
ill-equipped ˌɪl.ɪˈkwɪpt *stress shift:* ˌill-equipped ˈproject
ill-fated ˌɪlˈfeɪ.tɪd (US) -t̬ɪd *stress shift:* ˌill-fated ˈlovers
ill-favoured ˌɪlˈfeɪ.vəd (US) -vɚd **-ly** -li **-ness** -nəs, -nɪs *stress shift:* ˌill-favoured ˈcouple
ill-feeling ˌɪlˈfiː.lɪŋ
ill-founded ˌɪlˈfaʊn.dɪd *stress shift:* ˌill-founded ˈrumo(u)r
ill-gotten ˌɪlˈgɒt.ən (US) -ˈgɑː.tən *stress shift, see compound:* **ˌill-gotten ˈgains**
illiberal ɪˈlɪb.ər.əl, ˌɪl- **-ly** -i **-ness** -nəs, -nɪs
illiberalism ɪˈlɪb.ər.əl.ɪ.zəm, ˌɪl-
illiberality ɪˌlɪb.əˈræl.ə.ti, ˌɪl-, -ɪ.ti (US) -ə.t̬i
illicit ɪˈlɪs.ɪt, ˌɪl- **-ly** -li **-ness** -nəs, -nɪs
illimitab|le ɪˈlɪm.ɪ.tə.b|l̩, ˌɪl- (US) -t̬ə- **-ly** -li **-leness** -l̩.nəs, -nɪs
Illingworth ˈɪl.ɪŋ.wəθ, -wɜːθ (US) -wɚθ, -wɜːrθ
Illinois ˌɪl.ɪˈnɔɪ, -əˈ-
illiteracy ɪˈlɪt.ər.ə.si, ˌɪl- (US) -ˈlɪt̬-
illiterate ɪˈlɪt.ər.ət, ˌɪl-, -ɪt (US) -ˈlɪt̬- **-s** -s **-ly** -li **-ness** -nəs, -nɪs
ill-judged ˌɪlˈdʒʌdʒd *stress shift:* ˌill-judged ˈmove
ill-mannered ˌɪlˈmæn.əd (US) -ɚd *stress shift:* ˌill-mannered ˈman
ill-natured ˌɪlˈneɪ.tʃəd (US) -tʃɚd **-ly** -li *stress shift:* ˌill-natured ˈdog
illness ˈɪl.nəs, -nɪs **-es** -ɪz
illocution ˌɪl.əˈkjuː.ʃən **-s** -z **-ary** -ər.i (US) -er-
Illogan ɪˈlʌg.ən
illogic|al ɪˈlɒdʒ.ɪ.k|əl, ˌɪl- (US) -ˈlɑː.dʒɪ- **-ally** -əl.i, -li **-alness** -əl.nəs, -nɪs
illogicalit|y ɪˌlɒdʒ.ɪˈkæl.ə.t|i, ˌɪl-, -ɪ.t|i (US) -ˌlɑː.dʒɪˈkæl.ə.t̬|i **-ies** -iz
ill-omened ˌɪlˈəʊ.mend, -mənd, -mɪnd (US) -ˈoʊ- *stress shift:* ˌill-omened ˈvoyage
ill-starred ˌɪlˈstɑːd (US) -ˈstɑːrd *stress shift:* ˌill-starred ˈlove
ill-tempered ˌɪlˈtem.pəd (US) -pɚd *stress shift:* ˌill-tempered ˈcustomer
ill-timed ˌɪlˈtaɪmd *stress shift:* ˌill-timed ˈentrance
ill|-treat ˌɪl|ˈtriːt, ɪl- **-treats** -ˈtriːts **-treating** -ˈtriː.tɪŋ (US) -ˈtriː.t̬ɪŋ **-treated** -ˈtriː.tɪd (US) -ˈtriː.t̬ɪd **-treatment** -ˈtriːt.mənt
illum|e ɪˈljuːm, -ˈluːm (US) -ˈluːm **-es** -z **-ing** -ɪŋ **-ed** -d
illuminant ɪˈluː.mɪ.nənt, -ˈljuː-, -mə- (US) -ˈluː.mə- **-s** -s
illumi|nate ɪˈluː.mɪ|.neɪt, -ˈljuː-, -mə- (US) -ˈluː.mə- **-nates** -neɪts **-nating** -neɪ.tɪŋ (US) -neɪ.t̬ɪŋ **-nated** -neɪ.tɪd (US) -neɪ.t̬ɪd **-nator/s** -neɪ.təʳ/z (US) -neɪ.t̬ɚ/z
illuminati (I) ɪˌluː.mɪˈnɑː.tiː, -məˈ- (US) -ˈnɑː.t̬i
illumination ɪˌluː.mɪˈneɪ.ʃən, -ˌljuː-, -məˈ- (US) -ˌluː- **-s** -z
illuminative ɪˈluː.mɪ.nə.təv, -ˈljuː-, -mə-, -neɪ- (US) -ˈluː.mɪ.neɪ.t̬ɪv, -mə-
illumin|e ɪˈljuː.mɪn, -ˈluː- (US) -ˈluː- **-es** -z **-ing** -ɪŋ **-ed** -d
ill-usage ˌɪlˈjuː.zɪdʒ, -sɪdʒ (US) -sɪdʒ, -zɪdʒ **-s** -ɪz
ill-used ˌɪlˈjuːzd *stress shift:* ˌill-used ˈservant
illusion ɪˈluː.ʒən, -ˈljuː- (US) -ˈluː- **-s** -z
illusion|ism ɪˈluː.ʒən|.ɪ.zəm, -ˈljuː- (US) -ˈluː- **-ist/s** -ɪst/s
illusive ɪˈluː.sɪv, -ˈljuː- (US) -ˈluː- **-ly** -li **-ness** -nəs, -nɪs
illusor|y ɪˈluː.sər|.i, -ˈljuː-, -zər- (US) -ˈluː- **-ily** -əl.i, -ɪ.li **-iness** -ɪ.nəs, -ɪ.nɪs
illu|strate ˈɪl.ə|.streɪt **-strates** -streɪts **-strating** -streɪ.tɪŋ (US) -streɪ.t̬ɪŋ **-strated** -streɪ.tɪd (US) -streɪ.t̬ɪd **-strator/s** -streɪ.təʳ/z (US) -streɪ.t̬ɚ/z
illustration ˌɪl.əˈstreɪ.ʃən **-s** -z
illustrative ˈɪl.ə.strə.tɪv, -streɪ-; ɪˈlʌs.trə.tɪv (US) ɪˈlʌs.trə.t̬ɪv; ˈɪl.ə.streɪ- **-ly** -li
illustrious ɪˈlʌs.tri.əs **-ly** -li **-ness** -nəs, -nɪs
illuvi|um ɪˈluː.vi|.əm **-ums** -əmz **-a** -ə **-al** -əl
Illyri|a ɪˈlɪr.i|.ə **-an/s** -ən/z
Illyricum ɪˈlɪr.ɪ.kəm
Ilminster ˈɪl.mɪn.stəʳ (US) -stɚ
Ilorin ɪˈlɒr.ɪn (US) -ˈlɔːr-
Ilyushin ɪˈljuː.ʃɪn, -ʃən (US) ɪlˈjuː-, ɪˈluː-
im- ɪm-
Note: Prefix. The form of **in-** where the stem begins with /p/, /b/, or /m/. When a negative prefix, **im-** does not affect the stress pattern of the stem, e.g. **balance** /ˈbæl.ənts/, **imbalance** /ɪmˈbæl.ənts/. In other cases, the prefix is normally stressed in nouns but not in verbs, e.g. **imprint**, noun /ˈɪm.prɪnt/, verb /ɪmˈprɪnt/.
I'm (= I am) aɪm
imag|e ˈɪm.ɪdʒ **-es** -ɪz **-ing** -ɪŋ **-ed** -d
imager|y ˈɪm.ɪ.dʒər|.i, ˈ-ə- **-ies** -iz
imaginab|le ɪˈmædʒ.ɪ.nə.b|l̩, -ən.ə- **-ly** -li **-leness** -l̩.nəs, -nɪs
imaginar|y ɪˈmædʒ.ɪ.nər|.i, -ən.ər-, -ˈ-nər|.i (US) -ə.ner- **-ily** -əl.i, -ɪ.li **-iness** -ɪ.nəs, -ɪ.nɪs
imagination ɪˌmædʒ.ɪˈneɪ.ʃən, -əˈ- **-s** -z
imaginative ɪˈmædʒ.ɪ.nə.tɪv, ˈ-ə- (US) -nə.t̬ɪv, -neɪ- **-ly** -li **-ness** -nəs, -nɪs
imagin|e ɪˈmædʒ.ɪn, -ən **-es** -z **-ing/s** -ɪŋ/z **-ed** -d
imagines (*plur. of* **imago**) ɪˈmeɪ.dʒɪ.niːz, ɪˈmɑː-, -neɪz (US) -niːz
imagism ˈɪm.ɪ.dʒɪ.zəm
ima|go ɪˈmeɪ|.gəʊ, ɪˈmɑː- (US) -goʊ **-goes** -gəʊz (US) -goʊz **-gines** -dʒɪ.niːz, -neɪz (US) -niːz
imam ɪˈmɑːm, ˈiː.mɑːm (US) ɪˈmɑːm **-s** -z
imbalanc|e ˌɪmˈbæl.ənts **-es** -ɪz
imbecile ˈɪm.bə.siːl, -bɪ-, -saɪl (US) -sɪl, -səl **-s** -z
imbecilic ˌɪm.bəˈsɪl.ɪk, -bɪˈ-
imbecilit|y ˌɪm.bəˈsɪl.ə.t|i, -bɪˈ-, -ɪ.t|i (US) -ə.t̬|i **-ies** -iz
Imbert ˈɪm.bət (US) -bɚt
imbib|e ɪmˈbaɪb **-es** -z **-ing** -ɪŋ **-ed** -d **-er/s** -əʳ/z (US) -ɚ/z
imbroglio ɪmˈbrəʊ.li.əʊ (US) -ˈbroʊ.li.oʊ **-s** -z
imbru|e ɪmˈbruː **-es** -z **-ing** -ɪŋ **-ed** -d
imbu|e ɪmˈbjuː **-es** -z **-ing** -ɪŋ **-ed** -d
Imelda ɪˈmel.də
Imeson ˈaɪ.mɪ.sən
IMF ˌaɪ.emˈef
imitability ˌɪm.ɪ.təˈbɪl.ə.ti, ˌ-ə-, -ɪ.ti (US) -ə.t̬i
imitable ˈɪm.ɪ.tə.bl̩, ˈ-ə- (US) -ə.t̬ə-
imi|tate ˈɪm.ɪ|.teɪt, ˈ-ə- **-tates** -teɪts **-tating** -teɪ.tɪŋ (US) -teɪ.t̬ɪŋ **-tated** -teɪ.tɪd (US) -teɪ.t̬ɪd **-tator/s** -teɪ.təʳ/z (US) -teɪ.t̬ɚ/z
imitation ˌɪm.ɪˈteɪ.ʃən, -əˈ- **-s** -z **-al** -əl

imitative 'ɪm.ɪ.tə.tɪv, '-ə-, -teɪ- (US) -teɪ.t̬ɪv **-ly** -li **-ness** -nəs, -nɪs
Imlay 'ɪm.leɪ
immaculate ɪ'mæk.jə.lət, -jʊ-, -lɪt **-ly** -li **-ness** -nəs, -nɪs **Im,maculate Con'ception**
immanen|ce 'ɪm.ə.nən*t*s **-t** -t
Immanuel ɪ'mæn.ju.əl (US) -el, -ᵊl
immaterial ,ɪm.ə'tɪə.ri.əl (US) -'tɪr.i- **-ly** -i **-ness** -nəs, -nɪs
immaterial|ism ,ɪm.ə'tɪə.ri.əl|.ɪ.zᵊm (US) -'tɪr.i- **-ist/s** -ɪst/s
immateriality ,ɪm.ə,tɪə.ri'æl.ə.ti, -ɪ.ti (US) -,tɪr.i'æl.ə.t̬i
immaterializ|e, -is|e ,ɪm.ə'tɪə.ri.ᵊl.aɪz (US) -'tɪr.i- **-es** -ɪz **-ing** -ɪŋ **-ed** -d
immature ,ɪm.ə'tjʊəʳ, -'tʃʊəʳ, -'tjɔːʳ, -'tʃɔːʳ (US) -'tʊr, -'tjʊr, -'tʃʊr **-ly** -li **-ness** -nəs, -nɪs
immaturit|y ,ɪm.ə'tjʊə.rə.t|i, -'tʃʊə-, -'tjɔː-, -'tʃɔː-, -rɪ- (US) -'tʊr.ə.t̬|i, -'tjʊr-, -'tʃʊr- **-ies** -iz
immeasurab|le ɪ'meʒ.ᵊr.ə.b|l̩, ,ɪm- **-ly** -li **-leness** -l̩.nəs, -nɪs
immediacy ɪ'miː.di.ə.si
immediate ɪ'miː.di.ət, -ɪt, -dʒət (US) -di.ɪt **-ly** -li
immemorial ,ɪm.ɪ'mɔː.ri.əl, -ə'- (US) -'mɔːr.i- **-ly** -li
immense ɪ'men*t*s **-ly** -li **-ness** -nəs, -nɪs
immensit|y ɪ'men*t*.sə.t|i, -sɪ- (US) -sə.t̬|i **-ies** -iz
immers|e ɪ'mɜːs (US) -'mɜːrs **-es** -ɪz **-ing** -ɪŋ **-ed** -t
immersion ɪ'mɜː.ʃᵊn, -ʒᵊn (US) -'mɜːr- **-s** -z **im'mersion ,heater**
immigrant 'ɪm.ɪ.grənt, '-ə- **-s** -s
immi|grate 'ɪm.ɪ|.greɪt, '-ə- **-grates** -greɪts **-grating** -greɪ.tɪŋ (US) -greɪ.t̬ɪŋ **-grated** -greɪ.tɪd (US) -greɪ.t̬ɪd
immigration ,ɪm.ɪ'greɪ.ʃᵊn, -ə'- **-s** -z
imminence 'ɪm.ɪ.nən*t*s, '-ə-
imminent 'ɪm.ɪ.nənt, '-ə- **-ly** -li
Immingham 'ɪm.ɪŋ.əm (US) -hæm, -həm, -əm
immiscibility ɪ,mɪs.ɪ'bɪl.ə.ti, ,ɪm-, -ə'-, -ɪ.ti (US) -ə.t̬i
immiscib|le ɪ'mɪs.ə.b|l̩, ,ɪm-, '-ɪ- **-ly** -li
immobile ɪ'məʊ.baɪl, ɪm- (US) -'moʊ.bᵊl, -bɪl, -baɪl
immobility ,ɪm.əʊ'bɪl.ə.ti, -ɪ.ti (US) -moʊ'bɪl.ə.t̬i
immobilization, -isa- ɪ,məʊ.bᵊl.aɪ'zeɪ.ʃᵊn, ,ɪm-, -bɪ.laɪ'-, -lɪ'- (US) -,moʊ.bə.lɪ'-
immobiliz|e, -is|e ɪ'məʊ.bᵊl.aɪz, ,ɪm-, -bɪ.laɪz (US) -'moʊ- **-es** -ɪz **-ing** -ɪŋ **-ed** -d
immobilizer ɪ'məʊ.bᵊl.aɪ.zəʳ (US) -zɚ **-s** -z
immoderate ɪ'mɒd.ᵊr.ət, ,ɪm-, -ɪt (US) -'mɑː.dɚ- **-ly** -li **-ness** -nəs, -nɪs
immoderation ɪ,mɒd.ə'reɪ.ʃᵊn, ,ɪm- (US) -,mɑː.də'-
immodest ɪ'mɒd.ɪst, ,ɪm- (US) -'mɑː.dɪst **-ly** -li
immodesty ɪ'mɒd.ə.sti, ,ɪm-, '-ɪ- (US) -'mɑː.də-
immo|late 'ɪm.əʊ|.leɪt (US) '-ə- **-lates** -leɪts **-lating** -leɪ.tɪŋ (US) -leɪ.t̬ɪŋ **-lated** -leɪ.tɪd (US) -leɪ.t̬ɪd **-lator/s** -leɪ.təʳ/z (US) -leɪ.t̬ɚ/z
immolation ,ɪm.əʊ'leɪ.ʃᵊn (US) -ə'- **-s** -z
immoral ɪ'mɒr.ᵊl, ,ɪm- (US) -'mɔːr- **-ly** -i
immoralit|y ,ɪm.ə'ræl.ə.t|i, -ɒr'æl-, -ɪ.t|i (US) -mɔː'ræl.ə.t̬|i, -mə'- **-ies** -iz
immortal ɪ'mɔː.tᵊl, ,ɪm- (US) -'mɔːr.t̬ᵊl **-s** -z **-ly** -i
immortality ,ɪm.ɔː'tæl.ə.ti, -ɪ.ti (US) -ɔːr'tæl.ə.t̬i
immortaliz|e, -is|e ɪ'mɔː.tᵊl.aɪz, ,ɪm- (US) -'mɔːr.t̬ᵊl- **-es** -ɪz **-ing** -ɪŋ **-ed** -d
immortelle ,ɪm.ɔː'tel (US) -ɔːr'- **-s** -z
immovability ɪ,muː.və'bɪl.ə.ti, ,ɪm-, -ɪ.ti (US) -ə.t̬i
immovab|le ɪ'muː.və.b|l̩, ,ɪm- **-ly** -li **-leness** -l̩.nəs, -nɪs
immune ɪ'mjuːn **im'mune ,system**
immunit|y ɪ'mjuː.nə.t|i, -nɪ- (US) -nə.t̬|i **-ies** -iz
immunization, -isa- ,ɪm.jə.naɪ'zeɪ.ʃᵊn, -jʊ-, -nɪ'- (US) -nɪ'- **-s** -z
immuniz|e, -is|e 'ɪm.jə.naɪz, -jʊ- **-es** -ɪz **-ing** -ɪŋ **-ed** -d
immuno- ,ɪm.jə.nəʊ-, -jʊ-; ɪ,mjuː.nəʊ- (US) -noʊ-
immunodeficiency ,ɪm.jə.nəʊ.dɪ'fɪʃ.ᵊn*t*.si, -jʊ-; ɪ,mjuː- (US) -noʊ-
immunologic|al ,ɪm.jə.nəʊ'lɒdʒ.ɪ.k|ᵊl, -jʊ-; ɪ,mjuː.nəʊ'- (US) ,ɪm.jə.noʊ'lɑː.dʒɪ-, -jʊ- **-ally** -ᵊl.i, -li
immunolog|y ,ɪm.jə'nɒl.ə.dʒ|i, -jʊ'- (US) -'nɑː.lə- **-ist/s** -ɪst/s
immunosuppress|ant ,ɪm.jə.nəʊ.sə'pres|.ᵊnt, -jʊ-; ɪ,mjuː- (US) -noʊ- **-ive** -ɪv
immunosuppression ,ɪm.jə.nəʊ.sə'preʃ.ᵊn, -jʊ-; ɪ,mjuː- (US) -noʊ-
immur|e ɪ'mjʊəʳ, -'mjɔːʳ (US) -'mjʊr **-es** -z **-ing** -ɪŋ **-ed** -d **-ement** -mənt
immutability ɪ,mjuː.tə'bɪl.ə.ti, -ɪ.ti; ,ɪm.jə-, -jʊ- (US) ɪ,mjuː.t̬ə'bɪl.ə.t̬i
immutab|le ɪ'mjuː.tə.b|l̩ (US) -t̬ə- **-ly** -li **-leness** -l̩.nəs, -nɪs
Imogen 'ɪm.ə.dʒᵊn, -dʒen, -dʒɪn (US) -dʒen, -dʒᵊn
Imogene 'ɪm.ə.dʒiːn
imp ɪmp **-s** -s **-ing** -ɪŋ **-ed** -t
impact (*n.*) 'ɪm.pækt **-s** -s
impact (*v.*) ɪm'pækt, '-- **-s** -s **-ing** -ɪŋ **-ed** -ɪd
impair ɪm'peəʳ (US) -'per **-s** -z **-ing** -ɪŋ **-ed** -d
impairment ɪm'peə.mənt (US) -'per- **-s** -s
impala ɪm'pɑː.lə (US) -'pɑː.lə, -'pæl.ə **-s** -z
impal|e ɪm'peɪl **-es** -z **-ing** -ɪŋ **-ed** -d **-ement** -mənt
impalpab|le ɪm'pæl.pə.b|l̩, ,ɪm- **-ly** -li
impanel ɪm'pæn.ᵊl **-s** -z **-(l)ing** -ɪŋ **-(l)ed** -d
imparisyllabic ɪm,pær.ɪ.sɪ'læb.ɪk, ,ɪm.pær-, ,-ə- (US) ɪm,per-, -,pær-
im|part ɪm|'pɑːt (US) -'pɑːrt **-parts** -'pɑːts (US) -'pɑːrts **-parting** -'pɑː.tɪŋ (US) -'pɑːr.t̬ɪŋ **-parted** -'pɑː.tɪd (US) -'pɑːr.t̬ɪd
impartation ,ɪm.pɑː'teɪ.ʃᵊn (US) -pɑːr'-
impartial ɪm'pɑː.ʃᵊl, ,ɪm- (US) -'pɑːr- **-ly** -i **-ness** -nəs, -nɪs
impartiality ɪm,pɑː.ʃi'æl.ə.ti, ,ɪm.pɑː-, ,ɪm,pɑː-, -ɪ.ti (US) ɪm,pɑːr-, ,ɪm-
impassability ɪm,pɑː.sə'bɪl.ə.ti, ,ɪm.pɑː-, ,ɪm,pɑː-, -ɪ.ti (US) ɪm,pæs.ə'bɪl.ə.t̬i, ,ɪm-
impassable ɪm'pɑː.sə.bl̩, ,ɪm- (US) -'pæs.ə- **-ness** -nəs, -nɪs
impasse 'æ̃m.pɑːs, 'æm-, 'ɪm-, -pæs, -'- (US) 'ɪm.pæs, -'- **-es** -ɪz
impassibility ɪm,pæs.ə'bɪl.ə.ti, ,ɪm.pæs-, -sɪ'-, -ɪ.ti (US) ɪm,pæs-
impassible ɪm'pæs.ə.bl̩, '-ɪ-
impassioned ɪm'pæʃ.ᵊnd
impassive ɪm'pæs.ɪv **-ly** -li **-ness** -nəs, -nɪs
impassivity ,ɪm.pæs'ɪv.ə.ti, -ɪ.ti (US) -ə.t̬i
impasto ɪm'pæs.təʊ (US) -toʊ, -'pɑː.stoʊ **-ed** -d
impatience ɪm'peɪ.ʃᵊn*t*s
impatiens ɪm'peɪ.ʃi.enz, -'pæt.i-
impatient ɪm'peɪ.ʃᵊnt **-ly** -li
impeach ɪm'piːtʃ **-es** -ɪz **-ing** -ɪŋ **-ed** -t **-er/s** -əʳ/z (US) -ɚ/z **-ment/s** -mənt/s **-able** -ə.bl̩
impeccability ɪm,pek.ə'bɪl.ə.ti, ,ɪm.pek-, -ɪ.ti (US) ɪm,pek.ə'bɪl.ə.t̬i
impeccab|le ɪm'pek.ə.b|l̩ **-ly** -li
impecunious ,ɪm.pɪ'kjuː.ni.əs, -pə'- **-ly** -li **-ness** -nəs, -nɪs
impedanc|e ɪm'piː.dᵊn*t*s **-es** -ɪz
imped|e ɪm'piːd **-es** -z **-ing** -ɪŋ **-ed** -ɪd
impediment ɪm'ped.ɪ.mənt, '-ə- **-s** -s
impedimenta ɪm,ped.ɪ'men.tə, ,ɪm.ped-
impel ɪm'pel **-s** -z **-ling** -ɪŋ **-led** -d **-ler/s** -əʳ/z (US) -ɚ/z **-lent** -ənt
impend ɪm'pend **-s** -z **-ing** -ɪŋ **-ed** -ɪd
impenetrability ɪm,pen.ɪ.trə'bɪl.ə.ti, ,ɪm.pen-, ,-ə-, -ɪ.ti (US) ɪm,pen.ɪ.trə'bɪl.ə.t̬i, ,-ə-

impenetrab|le ɪmˈpen.ɪ.trə.bl̩, ˌɪm-, ˈ-ə- **-ly** -li **-leness** -l̩.nəs, -nɪs

impenitence ɪmˈpen.ɪ.tᵊnts, ˌɪm- (US) ˈ-ə-

impenitent ɪmˈpen.ɪ.tᵊnt, ˌɪm- (US) ˈ-ə- **-ly** -li

imperative ɪmˈper.ə.tɪv (US) -t̬ɪv **-s** -z **-ly** -li **-ness** -nəs, -nɪs

imperator ˌɪm.pəˈrɑː.tɔːʳ, -ˈreɪ-, -təʳ (US) -ˈreɪ.tɔːr, -ˈrɑː-, -t̬ɚ **-s** -z

imperatorial ɪmˌper.əˈtɔː.ri.əl; ˌɪm.per-, -pᵊr- (US) ˌɪm.pɚ.əˈtɔːr.i.əl

imperceptibility ˌɪm.pəˌsep.təˈbɪl.ə.ti, -tɪˈ-, -ɪ.ti (US) -pɚˌsep.təˈbɪl.ə.t̬i

imperceptib|le ˌɪm.pəˈsep.tə.bl̩, -tɪ- (US) -pɚˈsep.tə- **-ly** -li **-leness** -l̩.nəs, -nɪs

imperceptive ˌɪm.pəˈsep.tɪv (US) -pɚˈ- **-ness** -nəs, -nɪs

imperfect ɪmˈpɜː.fɪkt, ˌɪm-, -fekt (US) -ˈpɜːr- **-s** -s **-ly** -li **-ness** -nəs, -nɪs

imperfection ˌɪm.pəˈfek.ʃᵊn (US) -pɚˈ- **-s** -z

imperfective ˌɪm.pəˈfek.tɪv (US) -pɚˈ-

imperforat|e ɪmˈpɜː.fᵊr.ət, ˌɪm-, -ɪt (US) -ˈpɜːr- **-ed** -ɪd **-s** -s

imperial ɪmˈpɪə.ri.əl (US) -ˈpɪr- **-s** -z **-ly** -i

imperial|ism ɪmˈpɪə.ri.ə.l|ɪ.zᵊm (US) -ˈpɪr.i- **-ist/s** -ɪst/s

imperialist ɪmˈpɪə.ri.ə.lɪst (US) -ˈpɪr.i-

imperialistic ɪmˌpɪə.ri.əˈlɪs.tɪk (US) -ˈpɪr.i-

imperil ɪmˈper.ᵊl, -ɪl (US) -ᵊl **-s** -z **-(l)ing** -ɪŋ **-(l)ed** -d

imperious ɪmˈpɪə.ri.əs (US) -ˈpɪr.i- **-ly** -li **-ness** -nəs, -nɪs

imperishab|le ɪmˈper.ɪ.ʃə.bl̩, ˌɪm- **-ly** -li **-leness** -l̩.nəs, -nɪs

impermanence ɪmˈpɜː.mə.nənts, ˌɪm- (US) -ˈpɜːr-

impermanent ɪmˈpɜː.mə.nənt, ˌɪm- (US) -ˈpɜːr- **-ly** -li

impermeability ɪmˌpɜː.mi.əˈbɪl.ə.ti, ˌɪm-, -ɪ.ti (US) -ˌpɜːr.mi.əˈbɪl.ə.t̬i

impermeable ɪmˈpɜː.mi.ə.bl|, ˌɪm- (US) -ˈpɜːr- **-ly** -li **-leness** -l̩.nəs, -nɪs

impermissibility ˌɪm.pəˌmɪs.əˈbɪl.ə.ti, -ɪˈ-, -ɪ.ti (US) -pɚˌmɪs.əˈbɪl.ə.t̬i, -ɪˈ-

impermissib|le ˌɪm.pəˈmɪs.ə.bl|, ˈ-ɪ- (US) -pɚˈ- **-ly** -li

impers|onal ɪmˈpɜː.s|ᵊn.ᵊl, ˌɪm- (US) -ˈpɜːr- **-onally** -nə.li, -ᵊn.ᵊl.i

impersonality ɪmˌpɜː.sᵊnˈæl.ə.ti, ˌɪm-, -ɪ.ti (US) -ˌpɜːr.sᵊnˈæl.ə.t̬i

imperson|ate ɪmˈpɜː.sᵊn|.eɪt (US) -ˈpɜːr- **-ates** -eɪts **-ating** -eɪ.tɪŋ (US) -eɪ.t̬ɪŋ **-ated** -eɪ.tɪd (US) -eɪ.t̬ɪd **-ator/s** -eɪ.təʳ/z (US) -eɪ.t̬ɚ/z

impersonation ɪmˌpɜː.sᵊnˈeɪ.ʃᵊn (US) -ˌpɜːr- **-s** -z

impertinence ɪmˈpɜː.tɪ.nənts, ˌɪm-, -tᵊn.ənts (US) -ˈpɜːr.t̬ᵊn-

impertinent ɪmˈpɜː.tɪ.nənt, ˌɪm-, -tᵊn.ənt (US) -ˈpɜːr.t̬ᵊn- **-ly** -li

imperturbability ˌɪm.pəˌtɜː.bəˈbɪl.ə.ti, -ɪ.ti (US) -pɚˌtɜːr.bəˈbɪl.ə.t̬i

imperturbab|le ˌɪm.pəˈtɜː.bə.bl̩ (US) -pɚˈtɜːr- **-ly** -li **-leness** -l̩.nəs, -nɪs

impervious ɪmˈpɜː.vi.əs, ˌɪm- (US) -ˈpɜːr- **-ly** -li **-ness** -nəs, -nɪs

impetigo ˌɪm.pɪˈtaɪ.gəʊ, -pəˈ-, -petˈaɪ- (US) -pəˈtaɪ.goʊ

impetuosity ɪmˌpet.juˈɒs.ə.ti (US) ˌɪm-, -ˌpetʃ.uˈ-, -ɪ.ti (US) ɪmˌpetʃ.uˈɑː.sə.t̬i

impetuous ɪmˈpetʃ.u.əs, ˌɪm-, -ˈpet.ju- (US) -ˈpetʃ.u- **-ly** -li **-ness** -nəs, -nɪs

impetus ˈɪm.pɪ.təs, -pə- (US) -t̬əs

Impey ˈɪm.pi

impiet|y ɪmˈpaɪ.ə.t|i, ˌɪm-, -ɪ.t|i (US) -ə.t̬|i **-ies** -iz

imping|e ɪmˈpɪndʒ **-es** -ɪz **-ing** -ɪŋ **-ed** -d **-ement/s** -mənt/s

impious ˈɪm.piː.əs; ɪmˈpaɪ-, ˌɪm- (US) ˈɪm.pi-; ɪmˈpaɪ- **-ly** -li **-ness** -nəs, -nɪs

impish ˈɪm.pɪʃ **-ly** -li **-ness** -nəs, -nɪs

implacability ɪmˌplæk.əˈbɪl.ə.ti, ˌɪm-, -ɪ.ti (US) -ə.t̬i

implacab|le ɪmˈplæk.ə.bl̩ **-ly** -li **-leness** -l̩.nəs, -nɪs

implant *(n.)* ˈɪm.plɑːnt (US) -plænt **-s** -s

implan|t *(v.)* ɪmˈplɑːn|t (US) -ˈplæn|t **-ts** -ts **-ting** -tɪŋ (US) -t̬ɪŋ **-ted** -tɪd (US) -t̬ɪd **-ter/s** -təʳ/z (US) -t̬ɚ/z

implantation ˌɪm.plɑːnˈteɪ.ʃᵊn, -plænˈ- (US) -plænˈ-

implausibilit|y ɪmˌplɔː.zəˈbɪl.ə.t|i, ˌɪm.plɔː-, ˌɪmˌplɔː-, -zɪˈ-, -ɪ.t|i (US) ɪmˌplɑː.zəˈbɪl.ə.t̬|i, ˌɪm-, -ˌplɔː- **-ies** -iz

implausib|le ɪmˈplɔː.zə.bl̩, ˌɪm-, -zɪ- (US) -ˈplɑː-, -ˈplɔː- **-ly** -li **-leness** -l̩.nəs, -nɪs

impleader ɪmˈpliː.dəʳ (US) -dɚ **-s** -z

implement *(n.)* ˈɪm.plɪ.mənt, -plə- **-s** -s

implemen|t *(v.)* ˈɪm.plɪ.men|t, -plə-, -mən|t (US) -men|t **-ts** -ts **-ting** -tɪŋ (US) -t̬ɪŋ **-ted** -tɪd (US) -t̬ɪd

implementation ˌɪm.plɪ.menˈteɪ.ʃᵊn, -plə-, -mənˈ- **-s** -z

impli|cate ˈɪm.plɪ|.keɪt, -plə- **-cates** -keɪts **-cating** -keɪ.tɪŋ (US) -keɪ.t̬ɪŋ **-cated** -keɪ.tɪd (US) -keɪ.t̬ɪd

implication ˌɪm.plɪˈkeɪ.ʃᵊn, -pləˈ- **-s** -z

implicative ɪmˈplɪk.ə.tɪv; ˈɪm.plɪ.keɪ.tɪv, -plə- (US) ˈɪm.plɪ.keɪ.t̬ɪv; ɪmˈplɪk.ə- **-ly** -li

implicature ɪmˈplɪk.ə.tʃəʳ, -tjʊəʳ (US) -tʃɚ **-s** -z

implicit ɪmˈplɪs.ɪt **-ly** -li **-ness** -nəs, -nɪs

implod|e ɪmˈpləʊd (US) -ˈploʊd **-es** -z **-ing** -ɪŋ **-ed** -ɪd

implor|e ɪmˈplɔːʳ (US) -ˈplɔːr **-es** -z **-ing/ly** -ɪŋ/li **-ed** -d **-er/s** -əʳ/z (US) -ɚ/z

implosion ɪmˈpləʊ.ʒᵊn (US) -ˈploʊ- **-s** -z

implosive ɪmˈpləʊ.sɪv, ˌɪm-, -zɪv (US) -ˈploʊ.sɪv **-s** -z

impl|y ɪmˈpl|aɪ **-ies** -aɪz **-ying** -aɪ.ɪŋ **-ied** -aɪd

impolic|y ɪmˈpɒl.ə.s|i, ˌɪm-, ˈ-ɪ- (US) -ˈpɑː.lə- **-ies** -iz

impolite ˌɪm.pᵊlˈaɪt (US) -pəˈlaɪt **-ly** -li **-ness** -nəs, -nɪs

impolitic ɪmˈpɒl.ə.tɪk, ˌɪm-, ˈ-ɪ- (US) -ˈpɑː.lə-

imponderab|le ɪmˈpɒn.dᵊr.ə.bl̩, ˌɪm- (US) -ˈpɑːn- **-les** -l̩z **-ly** -li **-leness** -l̩.nəs, -nɪs

import *(n.)* ˈɪm.pɔːt (US) -pɔːrt **-s** -s

impor|t *(v.)* ɪmˈpɔː|t, ˌɪm-, ˈ-- (US) ɪmˈpɔːr|t, ˈ-- **-ts** -ts **-ting** -tɪŋ (US) -t̬ɪŋ **-ted** -tɪd (US) -t̬ɪd **-ter/s** -təʳ/z (US) -t̬ɚ/z

importable ɪmˈpɔː.tə.bl̩, ˌɪm- (US) -ˈpɔːr.t̬ə-

importance ɪmˈpɔː.tᵊnts (US) -ˈpɔːr-

important ɪmˈpɔː.tᵊnt (US) -ˈpɔːr- **-ly** -li

importation ˌɪm.pɔːˈteɪ.ʃᵊn (US) -pɔːrˈ- **-s** -z

importunate ɪmˈpɔː.tjʊ.nət, -tʃʊ-, -tʃə-, -ɪt (US) -ˈpɔːr.tʃə.nɪt **-ly** -li **-ness** -nəs, -nɪs

importun|e ˌɪm.pəˈtjuːn, -ˈtʃuːn; ɪmˈpɔː.tjuːn, -tʃuːn (US) ˌɪm.pɔːrˈtuːn, -ˈtjuːn, ɪmˈpɔːr.tʃən **-es** -z **-ing** -ɪŋ **-ed** -d

importunit|y ˌɪm.pɔːˈtjuː.nə.t|i, -nɪ- (US) -pɔːrˈtuː.nə.t̬|i, -ˈtjuː- **-ies** -iz

impos|e ɪmˈpəʊz (US) -ˈpoʊz **-es** -ɪz **-ing** -ɪŋ **-ed** -d **-er/s** -əʳ/z (US) -ɚ/z **-able** -ə.bl̩

imposing ɪmˈpəʊ.zɪŋ (US) -ˈpoʊ- **-ly** -li **-ness** -nəs, -nɪs

imposition ˌɪm.pəˈzɪʃ.ᵊn **-s** -z

impossibilit|y ɪmˌpɒs.əˈbɪl.ə.t|i, ˌɪm.pɒs-, ˌɪmˌpɒs-, -ɪˈ-, -ɪ.t|i (US) ɪmˌpɑː.səˈbɪl.ə.t̬|i, ˌɪm- **-ies** -iz

impossib|le ɪmˈpɒs.ə.bl̩, ˌɪm-, ˈ-ɪ- (US) -ˈpɑː.sə- **-ly** -li

impost ˈɪm.pəʊst, -pɒst (US) -poʊst **-s** -s

impostor, imposter ɪmˈpɒs.təʳ (US) -ˈpɑː.stɚ **-s** -z

imposture ɪmˈpɒs.tjəʳ, -tʃəʳ (US) -ˈpɑːs.tʃɚ **-s** -z

impoten|ce ˈɪm.pə.tən|ts (US) -t̬ən|ts **-cy** -si

impotent ˈɪm.pə.tənt (US) -t̬ənt **-ly** -li

impound ɪmˈpaʊnd **-s** -z **-ing** -ɪŋ **-ed** -ɪd

impoverish ɪmˈpɒv.ᵊr.ɪʃ (US) -ˈpɑː.vɚ-, -ˈpɑːv.rɪʃ **-es** -ɪz **-ing** -ɪŋ **-ed** -t **-ment** -mənt

impracticabilit|y ɪmˌpræk.tɪ.kəˈbɪl.ə.t|i, ˌɪm-, -ɪ.t|i US -ə.t̬|i **-ies** -iz
impracticab|le ɪmˈpræk.tɪ.kə.b|l̩, ˌɪm- **-ly** -li **-leness** -l̩.nəs, -nɪs
impractic|al ɪmˈpræk.tɪ.k|ᵊl, ˌɪm- **-ally** -ᵊl.i US -li **-alness** -ᵊl.nəs, -nɪs
impracticalit|y ɪmˌpræk.tɪˈkæl.ə.t|i, ˌɪm.præk-, ˌɪmˌpræk-, -ɪ.t|i US ɪmˌpræk.tɪˈkæl.ə.t̬|i, ˌɪm- **-ies** -iz
impre|cate ˈɪm.prɪ|.keɪt, -prə- **-cates** -keɪts **-cating** -keɪ.tɪŋ US -keɪ.t̬ɪŋ **-cated** -keɪ.tɪd US -keɪ.t̬ɪd **-cator/s** -keɪ.tər/z US -keɪ.t̬ɚ/z
imprecation ˌɪm.prɪˈkeɪ.ʃᵊn, -prəˈ-, -prekˈeɪ- US -prɪˈkeɪ- **-s** -z
imprecatory ˈɪm.prɪ.keɪ.tᵊr.i, ˌɪm.prɪˈkeɪ-; ɪmˈprek.ə- US ˈɪm.prɪ.kə.tɔːr.i
imprecise ˌɪm.prɪˈsaɪs, -prəˈ- **-ly** -li **-ness** -nəs, -nɪs
imprecision ˌɪm.prɪˈsɪʒ.ᵊn, -prəˈ-
impregnability ɪmˌpreg.nəˈbɪl.ə.ti, ˌɪm-, -ɪ.ti US -ə.t̬i
impregnab|le ɪmˈpreg.nə.b|l̩ **-ly** -li
impregnate (*adj.*) ɪmˈpreg.nɪt, -nət, -neɪt
impregna|te (*v.*) ˈɪm.preg.neɪ|t, -ˈ-- US ɪmˈpreg.neɪ|t **-tes** -ts **-ting** -tɪŋ US -t̬ɪŋ **-ted** -tɪd US -t̬ɪd
impregnation ˌɪm.pregˈneɪ.ʃᵊn, -prɪgˈ- US -pregˈ- **-s** -z
impresario ˌɪm.prɪˈsɑː.ri.əʊ, -prəˈ-, -presˈɑː-, -ˈɑː- US ˌɪm.prəˈsɑːr.i.oʊ, -ˈser- **-s** -z
imprescriptible ˌɪm.prɪˈskrɪp.tə.bl̩
impress (*n.*) ˈɪm.pres **-es** -ɪz
impress (*v.*) ɪmˈpres **-es** -ɪz **-ing** -ɪŋ **-ed** -t
impressibility ɪmˌpres.ɪˈbɪl.ə.ti, -əˈ-, -ɪ.ti US -ə.t̬i
impressib|le ɪmˈpres.ə.b|l̩, ˈ-ɪ- **-ly** -li **-leness** -l̩.nəs, -nɪs
impression ɪmˈpreʃ.ᵊn **-s** -z
impressionability ɪmˌpreʃ.ᵊn.əˈbɪl.ə.ti, -ˌpreʃ.nəˈ-, -ɪ.ti US -ə.t̬i
impressionab|le ɪmˈpreʃ.ᵊn.ə.b|l̩, -ˈpreʃ.nə- **-ly** -li
impression|ism (I) ɪmˈpreʃ.ᵊn|.ɪ.zᵊm **-ist/s** -ɪst/s
impressionistic ɪmˌpreʃ.ᵊnˈɪs.tɪk **-ally** -ᵊl.i, -li
impressive ɪmˈpres.ɪv **-ly** -li **-ness** -nəs, -nɪs
impressment ɪmˈpres.mənt **-s** -s
imprest ˈɪm.prest, -ˈ- **-s** -s
imprimatur ˌɪm.prɪˈmeɪ.təʳ, -praɪˈ-, -ˈmɑː-, -tʊəʳ, -tɜːʳ US -prɪˈmɑː.t̬ɚ, -ˈmeɪ-, -tʊr **-s** -z
imprint (*n.*) ˈɪm.prɪnt **-s** -s
im|print (*v.*) ɪm|ˈprɪnt, ˌɪm- **-prints** -ˈprɪnts **-printing** -ˈprɪn.tɪŋ US -ˈprɪn.t̬ɪŋ **-printed** -ˈprɪn.tɪd US -ˈprɪn.t̬ɪd
imprison ɪmˈprɪz.ᵊn, ˌɪm- **-s** -z **-ing** -ɪŋ, -ˈprɪz.nɪŋ **-ed** -d
imprisonment ɪmˈprɪz.ᵊn.mənt, -ᵊm- US -ᵊn-
improbabilit|y ɪmˌprɒb.əˈbɪl.ə.t|i, ˌɪm.prɒb-, ˌɪmˌprɒb-, -ɪ.ti US ˌɪm.prɑː.bəˈbɪl.ə.t̬|i **-ies** -iz
improbab|le ɪmˈprɒb.ə.b|l̩, ˌɪm- US -ˈprɑː.bə- **-ly** -li
improbity ɪmˈprəʊ.bə.ti, ˌɪm-, -bɪ- US -ˈproʊ.bə.t̬i
impromptu ɪmˈprɒm*p*.tjuː, -tʃuː US -ˈprɑːm*p*.tuː, -tjuː **-s** -z
improper ɪmˈprɒp.əʳ, ˌɪm- US -ˈprɑː.pɚ **-ly** -li ˌ**improper ˈfraction, imˌproper ˈfraction**
impropri|ate ɪmˈprəʊ.pri|.eɪt US -ˈproʊ- **-ates** -eɪts **-ating** -eɪ.tɪŋ US -eɪ.t̬ɪŋ **-ated** -eɪ.tɪd US -eɪ.t̬ɪd **-ator/s** -eɪ.tər/z US -eɪ.t̬ɚ/z
impropriation ɪmˌprəʊ.priˈeɪ.ʃᵊn, ˌɪm.prəʊ-, ˌɪmˌprəʊ- US ɪmˌproʊ-, ˌɪm- **-s** -z
impropriet|y ˌɪm.prəˈpraɪ.ə.t|i US -t̬|i **-ies** -iz
improvability ɪmˌpruː.vəˈbɪl.ə.ti, -ɪ.ti US -ə.t̬i
improvab|le ɪmˈpruː.və.b|l̩ **-ly** -li **-leness** -l̩.nəs, -nɪs
improv|e ɪmˈpruːv **-es** -z **-ing** -ɪŋ **-ed** -d **-er/s** -ər/z US -ɚ/z
improvement ɪmˈpruːv.mənt **-s** -s
improvidence ɪmˈprɒv.ɪ.dᵊn*t*s, ˌɪm-, ˈ-ə- US -ˈprɑː.və-
improvident ɪmˈprɒv.ɪ.dᵊnt, ˌɪm- US -ˈprɑː.və- **-ly** -li
improvisation ˌɪm.prə.vaɪˈzeɪ.ʃᵊn US ɪmˌprɑː.vɪˈ-; ˌɪm.prə- **-s** -z
improvisatory ˌɪm.prə.vaɪˈzeɪ.tᵊr.i; -ˈvaɪ.zə- US ɪmˈprɑː.və.zə.tɔːr-; ˌɪm.prəˈvaɪ-
improvis|e ˈɪm.prə.vaɪz **-es** -ɪz **-ing** -ɪŋ **-ed** -d **-er/s** -ər/z US -ɚ/z **-or/s** -ər/z US -ɚ/z
imprudence ɪmˈpruː.dᵊn*t*s, ˌɪm-
imprudent ɪmˈpruː.dᵊnt, ˌɪm- **-ly** -li
impudence ˈɪm.pjə.dᵊn*t*s, -pjʊ-
impudent ˈɪm.pjə.dᵊnt, -pjʊ- **-ly** -li
impugn ɪmˈpjuːn **-s** -z **-ing** -ɪŋ **-ed** -d **-er/s** -ə/ʳz US -ɚ/z **-able** -ə.bl̩ **-ment** -mənt
impuissan|ce ɪmˈpjuː.ɪ.sᵊn|*t*s US -ˈpjuː.ɪ-, -ˈpwɪ.sᵊn*t*s; ˌɪm.pjuːˈɪs.ᵊn*t*s **-t** -t
impuls|e ˈɪm.pʌls **-es** -ɪz ˈ**impulse ˌbuying**
impulsion ɪmˈpʌl.ʃᵊn **-s** -z
impulsive ɪmˈpʌl.sɪv **-ly** -li **-ness** -nəs, -nɪs
impunit|y ɪmˈpjuː.nə.t|i, -nɪ- US -t̬|i **-ies** -iz
impure ɪmˈpjʊəʳ, ˌɪm-, -ˈpjɔːʳ US -ˈpjʊr **-ly** -li **-ness** -nəs, -nɪs
impurit|y ɪmˈpjʊə.rə.t|i, ˌɪm-, -ˈpjɔː-, -rɪ- US -ˈpjʊr.ə.t̬|i **-ies** -iz
imputability ɪmˌpjuː.təˈbɪl.ə.ti, ˌɪm.pjuː-, ˌɪmˌpjuː-, -ɪ.ti US ɪmˌpjuː.t̬əˈbɪl.ə.t̬i, ˌɪm-
imputation ˌɪm.pjʊˈteɪ.ʃᵊn **-s** -z
im|pute ɪm|ˈpjuːt **-putes** -ˈpjuːts **-puting** -ˈpjuː.tɪŋ US -ˈpjuː.t̬ɪŋ **-puted** -ˈpjuː.tɪd US -ˈpjuː.t̬ɪd **-putable** -ˈpjuː.tə.bl̩ US -ˈpjuː.t̬ə.bl̩
Imray ˈɪm.reɪ
Imrie ˈɪm.ri
IMRO ˈɪm.rəʊ US -roʊ
in- ɪn-
Note: Prefix. When the meaning of the prefix is "in", it often carries secondary stress, e.g. **inbuilt** /ˌɪnˈbɪlt/. The resulting compounds may undergo stress-shift (see entry for **inbuilt**). As a negative prefix, **in-** does not normally affect the stress pattern of the stem to which it is added, e.g. **active** /ˈæk.tɪv/, **inactive** /ɪnˈæk.tɪv/. In other cases, the prefix is normally stressed in nouns but not in verbs, e.g. **increase** noun /ˈɪn.kriːs /, verb /ɪnˈkriːs/.
in ɪn ˌ**ins and ˈouts**
in. (*abbrev. for* **inch/es**) *singular:* ɪntʃ *plural:* -ɪz
Ina ˈiː.nə, ˈaɪ- US ˈaɪ-
inabilit|y ˌɪn.əˈbɪl.ə.t|i, -ɪ.t|i US -ə.t̬|i **-ies** -iz
in absentia ˌɪn.æbˈsen.ti.ə, -*t*ʃi-, -ɑː US -ˈsen.*t*ʃə, -*t*ʃi.ə
inaccessibility ˌɪn.əkˌses.əˈbɪl.ə.ti, -ækˌ-, -ɪˈ-, -ɪ.ti US -ə.t̬i
inaccessib|le ˌɪn.əkˈses.ə.b|l̩, -ækˈ-, ˈ-ɪ- **-ly** -li **-leness** -l̩.nəs, -nɪs
inaccurac|y ɪnˈæk.jə.rə.s|i, ˌɪn-, -jʊ-, -rɪ.s|i US -jɚ.ə- **-ies** -iz
inaccurate ɪnˈæk.jə.rət, ˌɪn-, -jʊ-, -rɪt US -jɚ.ət **-ly** -li
inaction ɪnˈæk.ʃᵊn, ˌɪn-
inacti|vate ɪnˈæk.tɪ|.veɪt, ˌɪn-, -tə- **-vates** -veɪts **-vating** -veɪ.tɪŋ US -veɪ.t̬ɪŋ **-vated** -veɪ.tɪd US -veɪ.t̬ɪd
inactive ɪnˈæk.tɪv, ˌɪn- **-ly** -li
inactivity ˌɪn.ækˈtɪv.ə.ti, -ɪ.ti US -ə.t̬i
inadequac|y ɪˈnæd.ɪ.kwə.s|i, ˌɪnˈæd-, ˈ-ə- **-ies** -iz
inadequate ɪˈnæd.ɪ.kwət, ˌɪnˈæd-, -kwɪt **-ly** -li **-ness** -nəs, -nɪs
inadmissibility ˌɪn.ədˌmɪs.əˈbɪl.ə.ti, -ɪˈ-, -ɪ.ti US -ə.t̬i
inadmissib|le ˌɪn.ədˈmɪs.ə.b|l̩, ˈ-ɪ- **-ly** -li
inadverten|ce ˌɪn.ədˈvɜː.tᵊn*t*|s US -ˈvɜːr- **-cy** -si

inadvertent ˌɪn.əd'vɜː.tᵊnt US -'vɜːr- **-ly** -li

inadvisability ˌɪn.ədˌvaɪ.zə'bɪl.ə.ti, -ɪ.ti US -ə.t̬i

inadvisable ˌɪn.əd'vaɪ.zə.bl̩

inalienability ɪˌneɪ.li.ə.nə'bɪl.ə.ti, ˌɪnˌeɪ-, -ɪ.ti US -ə.t̬i

inalienab|le ɪ'neɪ.li.ə.nə.b|l̩, ˌɪn'eɪ- **-ly** -li **-leness** -l̩.nəs, -nɪs

inane ɪ'neɪn **-ly** -li **-ness** -nəs, -nɪs

inanimate ɪ'næn.ɪ.mət, ˌɪn'æn-, -mɪt **-ly** -li **-ness** -nəs, -nɪs

inanition ˌɪn.ə'nɪʃ.ᵊn, -æn'ɪʃ-

inanit|y ɪ'næn.ə.t|i, -ɪ.t|i US -ə.t̬|i **-ies** -iz

inappeasable ˌɪn.ə'piː.zə.bl̩

inapplicability ɪˌnæp.lɪ.kə'bɪl.ə.ti, ˌɪnˌæp-, -ɪ.ti; ˌɪn.əˌplɪk.ə'- US ɪˌnæp.lɪ.kə'bɪl.ə.t̬i, ˌɪnˌæp-; ˌɪn.ə.plɪ.kə'bɪl.ə.ti

inapplicable ˌɪn.ə'plɪk.ə.bl̩; ɪ'næp.lɪ.kə-, ˌɪn'æp- US ɪ'næp-, ˌɪn'æp-; ˌɪn.ə'plɪk.ə- **-ness** -nəs, -nɪs

inapposite ɪ'næp.ə.zɪt, ˌɪn'æp- **-ly** -li **-ness** -nəs, -nɪs

inappreciab|le ˌɪn.ə'priː.ʃi.ə.b|l̩, -ʃə- **-ly** -li

inapprehensible ɪnˌæp.rɪ'hen*t*.sə.bl̩, '-sɪ-

inapproachab|le ˌɪn.ə'prəʊ.tʃə.b|l̩ US -'proʊ- **-ly** -li

inappropriate ˌɪn.ə'prəʊ.pri.ət, -ɪt US -'proʊ- **-ly** -li **-ness** -nəs, -nɪs

inapt ɪ'næpt, ˌɪn'æpt **-ly** -li **-ness** -nəs, -nɪs

inaptitude ɪ'næp.tɪ.tjuːd, ˌɪn'æp- US -tə.tuːd, -tjuːd

inarguab|le ɪ'nɑː.gju.ə.b|l̩, ˌɪn'ɑː- US ˌɪn'ɑːr- **-ly** -li

inarticulate ˌɪn.ɑː'tɪk.jə.lət, -jʊ-, -lɪt US -ɑːr'- **-ly** -li **-ness** -nəs, -nɪs

inartistic ˌɪn.ɑː'tɪs.tɪk US -ɑːr'- **-al** -ᵊl **-ally** -ᵊl.i, -li

inasmuch ˌɪn.əz'mʌtʃ

inattention ˌɪn.ə'ten.*t*ʃᵊn

inattentive ˌɪn.ə'ten.tɪv US -t̬ɪv **-ly** -li **-ness** -nəs, -nɪs

inaudibility ɪˌnɔː.də'bɪl.ə.ti, ˌɪn.ɔː-, -dɪ'-, -ɪ.ti US ɪˌnɑː.dɪ'bɪl.ə.t̬i, ˌɪnˌɑː-, ɪˌnɔː-, ˌɪnˌɔː-

inaudib|le ɪ'nɔː.də.b|l̩, ˌɪn.ɔː-, -dɪ- US ɪ'nɑː-, ˌɪn'ɑː-, ɪ'nɔː-, ˌɪn'ɔː- **-ly** -li **-leness** -l̩.nəs, -nɪs

inaugural ɪ'nɔːg.jə.rᵊl, -jʊ- US ɪ'nɑːg.jʊr.ᵊl, -'nɔːg-, -jɚ-, '-ɚ-

inaugu|rate ɪ'nɔːg.jə|.reɪt, -jʊ- US ɪ'nɑːg.jʊ|.reɪt, ɪ'nɔːg-, -jə-, '-ə- **-rates** -reɪts **-rating** -reɪ.tɪŋ US -reɪ.t̬ɪŋ **-rated** -reɪ.tɪd US -reɪ.t̬ɪd **-rator/s** -reɪ.təʳ/z US -reɪ.t̬ɚ/z

inauguration ɪˌnɔːg.jə'reɪ.ʃᵊn, -jʊ'- US ɪˌnɑːg.jʊ'-, -ˌnɔːg-, -jə'-, -ə'- **-s** -z

inauspicious ˌɪn.ɔː'spɪʃ.əs, -ɒs'pɪʃ- US -ɑː'spɪʃ-, -ɔː'- **-ly** -li **-ness** -nəs, -nɪs

inboard ˌɪn'bɔːd, ˌɪm- US 'ɪn.bɔːrd *stress shift, British only:* ˌinboard 'motor

inborn ˌɪn'bɔːn, ˌɪm- US 'ɪn.bɔːrn *stress shift, British only:* ˌinborn 'talent

inbreath|e ˌɪn'briːð, ˌɪm- US ˌɪn- **-es** -z **-ing** -ɪŋ **-ed** -d

inbreed ˌɪn'briːd, ˌɪm- US 'ɪn.briːd **-s** -z **-ing** -ɪŋ **inbred** ˌɪn'bred, ˌɪm- US 'ɪn.bred *stress shift, British only:* ˌinbred 'trait

inbuilt ˌɪn'bɪlt, ˌɪm-, '-- US 'ɪn.bɪlt *stress shift, British only:* ˌinbuilt 'hazard

inc. (*abbrev. for* **incorporated**) ɪŋ'kɔː.pᵊr.eɪ.tɪd, ɪŋk US ɪn'kɔːr.pə.reɪ.t̬ɪd, ɪŋk

Inca 'ɪŋ.kə **-s** -z

incalculability ɪnˌkæl.kjə.lə'bɪl.ə.ti, ˌɪn-, ɪŋ-, ˌɪŋ-, -kjʊ-, -ɪ.ti US ɪnˌkæl.kjə.lə'bɪl.ə.t̬i, ˌɪn-, -kjʊ-

incalculab|le ɪn'kæl.kjə.lə.b|l̩, ˌɪn-, ɪŋ-, ˌɪŋ-, -kjʊ- US ɪn'kæl-, ˌɪn- **-ly** -li **-leness** -l̩.nəs, -nɪs

in camera ˌɪn'kæm.ᵊr.ə, ˌɪŋ-, '-rə US ˌɪn-

incandescence ˌɪn.kæn'des.ᵊn*t*s, ˌɪŋ-, -kən'- US ˌɪn.kən'-

incandescent ˌɪn.kæn'des.ᵊnt, ˌɪŋ-, -kən'- US ˌɪn.kən'- **-ly** -li

incantation ˌɪn.kæn'teɪ.ʃᵊn, ˌɪŋ- US ˌɪn- **-s** -z

incapabilit|y ɪnˌkeɪ.pə'bɪl.ə.t|i, ˌɪn-, ɪŋ-, ˌɪŋ-, -ɪ.t|i US ɪnˌkeɪ.pə'bɪl.ə.t̬|i, ˌɪn- **-ies** -iz

incapab|le ɪn'keɪ.pə.b|l̩, ˌɪn-, ɪŋ-, ˌɪŋ- US ɪn'keɪ-, ˌɪn- **-ly** -li **-leness** -l̩.nəs, -nɪs

incapaci|tate ˌɪn.kə'pæs.ɪ|.teɪt, ˌɪŋ-, '-ə- US ˌɪn- **-tates** -teɪts **-tating** -teɪ.tɪŋ US -teɪ.t̬ɪŋ **-tated** -teɪ.tɪd US -teɪ.t̬ɪd

incapacitation ˌɪn.kəˌpæs.ɪ'teɪ.ʃᵊn, ˌɪŋ-, -ə'- US ˌɪn- **-s** -z

incapacit|y ˌɪn.kə'pæs.ə.t|i, ˌɪŋ-, -ɪ.t|i US ˌɪn.kə'pæs.ə.t̬|i **-ies** -iz

in capite ˌɪn'kæp.ɪ.teɪ US -teɪ, -ti

incarcer|ate ɪn'kɑː.sᵊr|.eɪt, ɪŋ- US ɪn'kɑːr.sə.r|eɪt **-ates** -eɪts **-ating** -eɪ.tɪŋ US -eɪ.t̬ɪŋ **-ated** -eɪ.tɪd US -eɪ.t̬ɪd

incarceration ɪnˌkɑː.sᵊr'eɪ.ʃᵊn, ˌɪn.kɑː-, ˌɪnˌkɑː-, ɪŋˌkɑː-, ˌɪŋ.kɑː- US ɪnˌkɑːr.sə'reɪ-, ˌɪn- **-s** -z

incarnadine ɪn'kɑː.nə.daɪn, ɪŋ- US ɪn'kɑːr-, -diːn, -dɪn

incarnate (*adj.*) ɪn'kɑː.nət, ɪŋ-, -neɪt, -nɪt US ɪn'kɑːr-

incar|nate (*v.*) 'ɪn.kɑː|.neɪt, 'ɪŋ-, -'-- US ɪn'kɑːr- **-nates** -neɪts **-nating** -neɪ.tɪŋ US -neɪ.t̬ɪŋ **-nated** -neɪ.tɪd US -neɪ.t̬ɪd

incarnation (I) ˌɪn.kɑː'neɪ.ʃᵊn, ˌɪŋ- US ˌɪn.kɑːr'- **-s** -z

incautious ɪn'kɔː.ʃəs, ˌɪn-, ɪŋ-, ˌɪŋ- US ɪn'kɑː-, ˌɪn-, -'kɔː- **-ly** -li **-ness** -nəs, -nɪs

Ince ɪn*t*s

Ince-in-Makerfield ˌɪn*t*s.ɪn'meɪ.kə.fiːld US -kɚ-

incendiar|y ɪn'sen.di.ᵊr|.i, -djᵊr- US -di.er|.i, -ɚ.i **-ies** -iz **-ism** -ɪ.zᵊm

incense (*n.*) 'ɪn.sen*t*s

incens|e (*v.*) *enrage:* ɪn'sen*t*s **-es** -ɪz **-ing** -ɪŋ **-ed** -t

incens|e (*v.*) *burn incense:* 'ɪn.sen*t*s **-es** -ɪz **-ing** -ɪŋ **-ed** -t

incentive ɪn'sen.tɪv US -t̬ɪv **-s** -z

incept ɪn'sept **-s** -s **-ing** -ɪŋ **-ed** -ɪd **-or/s** -əʳ/z US -ɚ/z **-ive** -ɪv

inception ɪn'sep.ʃᵊn **-s** -z

incertitude ɪn'sɜː.tɪ.tjuːd, ˌɪn- US -'sɜːr.t̬ɪ.tuːd, -tjuːd **-s** -z

incessant ɪn'ses.ᵊnt **-ly** -li

incest 'ɪn.sest

incestuous ɪn'ses.tju.əs, -tʃu- US -tʃu- **-ly** -li **-ness** -nəs, -nɪs

inch (I) ɪn*t*ʃ **-es** -ɪz **-ing** -ɪŋ **-ed** -t **ˌgive him an ˌinch and he'll ˌtake a 'mile ; not ˌbudge an 'inch**

Inchcape 'ɪn*t*ʃ.keɪp, ˌ-'-

Inchinnan ɪn'ʃɪn.ən

inchoate (*adj.*) ɪn'kəʊ.eɪt, ɪŋ-, -ɪt, '--- US ɪn'koʊ- **-ly** -li

incho|ate (*v.*) 'ɪn.kəʊ|.eɪt, 'ɪŋ- US 'ɪn.koʊ- **-ates** -eɪts **-ating** -eɪ.tɪŋ US -eɪ.t̬ɪŋ **-ated** -eɪ.tɪd US -eɪ.t̬ɪd

inchoation ˌɪn.kəʊ'eɪ.ʃᵊn, ˌɪŋ- US ˌɪn.koʊ'-

inchoative 'ɪn.kəʊ.eɪ.tɪv, 'ɪŋ-; ɪn'kəʊ.ə.tɪv, ɪŋ- US ɪn'koʊ.ə.t̬ɪv

Inchon ˌɪn'tʃɒn US 'ɪn.tʃɑːn

inchworm 'ɪn*t*ʃ.wɜːm US -wɜːrm **-s** -z

incidence 'ɪn*t*.sɪ.dᵊn*t*s

incident 'ɪn*t*.sɪ.dᵊnt **-s** -s

incident|al ˌɪn*t*.sɪ'den.t|ᵊl US -t̬|ᵊl **-ly** -ᵊl.i, -li **-ness** -nəs, -nɪs **-s** -z ˌ**inciˌdental 'music**

inciner|ate ɪn'sɪn.ᵊr|.eɪt US -ə.r|eɪt **-ates** -eɪts **-ating** -eɪ.tɪŋ US -eɪ.t̬ɪŋ **-ated** -eɪ.tɪd US -eɪ.t̬ɪd

incineration ɪnˌsɪn.ᵊr'eɪ.ʃᵊn US -ə'reɪ-

incinerator ɪn'sɪn.ᵊr.eɪ.təʳ US -ə.reɪ.t̬ɚ **-s** -z

incipien|ce ɪn'sɪp.i.ən*t*|s **-cy** -si

incipient ɪn'sɪp.i.ənt **-ly** -li

incis|e ɪn'saɪz **-es** -ɪz **-ing** -ɪŋ **-ed** -d

incision ɪn'sɪʒ.ᵊn **-s** -z

incisive ɪn'saɪ.sɪv **-ly** -li **-ness** -nəs, -nɪs

incisor ɪn'saɪ.zəʳ US -zɚ **-s** -z

incitation ˌɪnt.saɪˈteɪ.ʃᵊn, -sɪˈ- (US) -səˈ- **-s** -z
in|cite ɪnˈsaɪt **-cites** -ˈsaɪts **-citing** -ˈsaɪ.tɪŋ (US) -ˈsaɪ.t̬ɪŋ **-cited** -ˈsaɪ.tɪd (US) -ˈsaɪ.t̬ɪd
incitement ɪnˈsaɪt.mənt **-s** -s
incivilit|y ˌɪn.sɪˈvɪl.ə.t|i, -səˈ-, -ɪ.t|i (US) -ə.t̬|i **-ies** -iz
incl. (*abbrev. for* **including**) ɪnˈkluː.dɪŋ, ɪŋ- (US) ɪn- (*abbrev. for* **inclusive**) ɪnˈkluː.sɪv, ɪŋ- (US) ɪn-
Incledon ˈɪŋ.kl̩.dən
inclemency ɪnˈklem.ənt.si, ˌɪn-, ɪŋ-, ˌɪŋ- (US) ɪnˈklem-, ˌɪn-
inclement ɪnˈklem.ənt, ˌɪn-, ɪŋ-, ˌɪŋ- (US) ɪnˈklem-, ˌɪn- **-ly** -li
inclination ˌɪn.klɪˈneɪ.ʃᵊn, ˌɪŋ-, -kləˈ- (US) ˌɪn- **-s** -z
incline (*n.*) ˈɪn.klaɪn, ˈɪŋ-, ˌ-ˈ- (US) ˈɪn.klaɪn, ˌ-ˈ- **-s** -z
inclin|e (*v.*) ɪnˈklaɪn, ɪŋ- (US) ɪn- **-es** -z **-ing** -ɪŋ **-ed** -d **-able** -ə.bl̩
inclos|e ɪnˈkləʊz, ɪŋ- (US) ɪnˈkloʊz **-es** -ɪz **-ing** -ɪŋ **-ed** -d
inclosure ɪnˈkləʊ.ʒəʳ, ɪŋ- (US) ɪnˈkloʊ.ʒɚ **-s** -z
includ|e ɪnˈkluːd, ɪŋ- (US) ɪn- **-es** -z **-ing** -ɪŋ **-ed** -ɪd
inclusion ɪnˈkluː.ʒᵊn, ɪŋ- (US) ɪn- **-s** -z
inclusive ɪnˈkluː.sɪv, ɪŋ- (US) ɪn- **-ly** -li
incognito ˌɪn.kɒgˈniː.təʊ, ˌɪŋ-; ɪnˈkɒg.nɪ.təʊ, ɪŋ-, -nə- (US) ˌɪn.kɑːgˈniː.toʊ; ɪnˈkɑːg.nɪ-, -t̬oʊ **-s** -z
incognizan|ce ɪnˈkɒg.nɪ.zᵊn|*t*s, ɪŋ- (US) ɪnˈkɑːg- **-t** -t
incoherence ˌɪn.kə*ʊ*ˈhɪə.rᵊn*t*s, ˌɪŋ- (US) ˌɪn.koʊˈhɪr.ᵊn*t*s, -ˈher-
incoherent ˌɪn.kə*ʊ*ˈhɪə.rᵊnt, ˌɪŋ- (US) ˌɪn.koʊˈhɪr.ᵊnt, -ˈher- **-ly** -li
incombustibility ˌɪn.kəmˌbʌs.təˈbɪl.ə.ti, ˌɪŋ-, -tɪˈ-, -ɪ.ti (US) ˌɪn.kəmˌbʌs.təˈbɪl.ə.t̬i, -tɪˈ-
incombustible ˌɪn.kəmˈbʌs.tə.bl̩, ˌɪŋ-, -tɪ- (US) ˌɪn- **-ness** -nəs, -nɪs
income ˈɪŋ.kʌm, ˈɪn-, -kəm (US) ˈɪn- **-s** -z ˌ**income sup'port**, ˈ**income sup**ˌ**port** ; ˈ**income** ˌ**tax**
incomer ˈɪnˌkʌm.əʳ, ˈɪŋ- (US) ˈɪnˌkʌm.ɚ **-s** -z
incoming ˈɪnˌkʌm.ɪŋ, ˈɪŋ- (US) ˈɪnˌkʌm- **-s** -z
incommensurability ˌɪn.kəˌmen.*t*ʃᵊr.əˈbɪl.ə.ti, ˌɪŋ-, -*t*ʃʊr-, -ɪ.ti (US) ˌɪn.kəˌmen*t*.sɚ.əˈbɪl.ə.t̬i, -ʃɚ-
incommensurab|le ˌɪn.kəˈmen.*t*ʃᵊr.ə.bl|, ˌɪŋ-, -*t*ʃʊr- (US) ˌɪn.kəˈmen*t*.sɚ-, -ʃɚ- **-les** -l̩z **-ly** -li **-leness** -l̩.nəs, -nɪs
incommensurate ˌɪn.kəˈmen.*t*ʃᵊr.ət, ˌɪŋ-, -*t*ʃʊr-, -ɪt (US) ˌɪn.kəˈmen*t*.sɚ-, -ʃɚ- **-ly** -li **-ness** -nəs, -nɪs
incommod|e ˌɪn.kəˈməʊd, ˌɪŋ- (US) ˌɪn.kəˈmoʊd **-es** -z **-ing** -ɪŋ **-ed** -ɪd
incommodious ˌɪn.kəˈməʊ.di.əs, ˌɪŋ- (US) ˌɪn.kəˈmoʊ- **-ly** -li **-ness** -nəs, -nɪs
incommunicab|le ˌɪn.kəˈmjuː.nɪ.kə.bl|, ˌɪŋ- (US) ˌɪn- **-ly** -li **-leness** -l̩.nəs, -nɪs
incommunicado ˌɪn.kəˌmjuː.nɪˈkɑː.dəʊ, ˌɪŋ-, -nəˈ- (US) ˌɪn.kəˌmjuː.nɪˈkɑː.doʊ, -nəˈ-
incommutab|le ˌɪn.kəˈmjuː.tə.bl|, ˌɪŋ- (US) ˌɪn.kəˈmjuː.t̬ə.bl| **-ly** -li **-leness** -l̩.nəs, -nɪs
incomparability ɪnˌkɒm.pᵊr.əˈbɪl.ə.ti, ɪŋ-, -ɪ.ti (US) ɪnˌkɑːm.pɚ.əˈbɪl.ə.t̬i
incomparab|le ɪnˈkɒm.pᵊr.ə.bl|, ɪŋ- (US) ɪnˈkɑːm- **-ly** -li **-leness** -l̩.nəs, -nɪs
incompatibilit|y ˌɪn.kəmˌpæt.əˈbɪl.ə.t|i, ˌɪŋ-, -ɪˈ-, -ɪ.t|i (US) ˌɪn.kəmˌpæt̬.əˈbɪl.ə.t̬|i **-ies** -iz
incompatib|le ˌɪn.kəmˈpæt.ə.bl|, ˌɪŋ-, ˈ-ɪ- (US) ˌɪn.kəmˈpæt̬- **-ly** -li **-leness** -l̩.nəs, -nɪs
incompeten|ce ɪnˈkɒm.pɪ.tᵊn*t*|s, ˌɪn-, ɪŋ-, ˌɪŋ-, -pə- (US) ɪnˈkɑːm.pə.t̬ən*t*|s, ˌɪn- **-cy** -si
incompetent ɪnˈkɒm.pɪ.tᵊnt, ˌɪn-, ɪŋ-, ˌɪŋ-, -pə- (US) ɪnˈkɑːm.pə.t̬ənt, ˌɪn- **-ly** -li
incomplete ˌɪn.kəmˈpliːt, ˌɪŋ- (US) ˌɪn- **-ly** -li **-ness** -nəs, -nɪs
incompletion ˌɪn.kəmˈpliː.ʃᵊn, ˌɪŋ- (US) ˌɪn-
incomprehensibility ɪnˌkɒm.prɪˌhen*t*.səˈbɪl.ə.ti, ˌɪn-, ɪŋ-, ˌɪŋ-, -prəˌ-, -sɪˈ-, -ɪ.ti (US) ˌɪn.kɑːm.prɪ.hen*t*.səˈbɪl.ə.t̬i
incomprehensib|le ɪnˌkɒm.prɪˈhen*t*.sə.bl|, ˌɪn-, ɪŋ-, ˌɪŋ-, -sɪ- (US) ˌɪn.kɑːm- **-ly** -li **-leness** -l̩.nəs, -nɪs
incomprehension ɪnˌkɒm.prɪˈhen.*t*ʃᵊn, ˌɪn-, ɪŋ-, ˌɪŋ-, -prəˈ- (US) ˌɪn.kɑːm-
incompressibility ˌɪn.kəmˌpres.əˈbɪl.ə.ti, ˌɪŋ-, -ɪˈ-, -ɪ.ti (US) ˌɪn.kəmˌpres.əˈbɪl.ə.t̬i
incompressible ˌɪn.kəmˈpres.ə.bl̩, ˌɪŋ-, ˈ-ɪ- (US) ˌɪn- **-ness** -nəs, -nɪs
incomputab|le ˌɪn.kəmˈpjuː.tə.bl|, ˌɪŋ-; ɪnˈkɒm.pjə.tə.bl|, ˌɪn-, ɪŋ-, ˌɪŋ-, -pjʊ- (US) ˌɪn.kəmˈpjuː.t̬ə- **-ly** -li
inconceivability ˌɪn.kənˌsiː.vəˈbɪl.ə.ti, ˌɪŋ-, -ɪ.ti (US) ˌɪn.kənˌsiː.vəˈbɪl.ə.t̬i
inconceivab|le ˌɪn.kənˈsiː.və.bl|, ˌɪŋ- (US) ˌɪn- **-ly** -li **-leness** -l̩.nəs, -nɪs
inconclusive ˌɪn.kənˈkluː.sɪv, ˌɪŋ-, -kəŋˈ- (US) ˌɪn.kənˈ- **-ly** -li **-ness** -nəs, -nɪs
incondite ɪnˈkɒn.dɪt, ɪŋ-, -daɪt (US) ɪnˈkɑːn-
incongruent ɪnˈkɒŋ.gru.ənt, ɪŋ- (US) ɪnˈkɑːŋ-; ˌɪn.kənˈgruː- **-ly** -li
incongruit|y ˌɪn.kɒŋˈgruː.ə.t|i, ˌɪŋ-, -ɪ.t|i (US) ˌɪn.kənˈgruː.ə.t̬|i **-ies** -iz
incongruous ɪnˈkɒŋ.gru.əs, ɪŋ- (US) ɪnˈkɑːŋ- **-ly** -li **-ness** -nəs, -nɪs
inconsequenc|e ɪnˈkɒn*t*.sɪ.kwən*t*s, ɪŋ-, -sə- (US) ɪnˈkɑːn*t*- **-es** -ɪz
inconsequent ɪnˈkɒn*t*.sɪ.kwənt, ɪŋ-, -sə- (US) ɪnˈkɑːn*t*- **-ly** -li
inconsequential ɪnˌkɒn*t*.sɪˈkwen.*t*ʃᵊl, ˌɪn-, ɪŋ-, ˌɪŋ-, -səˈ- (US) ɪnˌkɑːn*t*- **-ly** -i
inconsiderab|le ˌɪn.kənˈsɪd.ᵊr.ə.bl|, ˌɪŋ- (US) ˌɪn- **-ly** -li **-leness** -l̩.nəs, -nɪs
inconsiderate ˌɪn.kənˈsɪd.ᵊr.ət, ˌɪŋ-, -ɪt (US) ˌɪn- **-ly** -li **-ness** -nəs, -nɪs
inconsideration ˌɪn.kənˌsɪd.əˈreɪ.ʃᵊn, ˌɪŋ- (US) ˌɪn-
inconsistenc|y ˌɪn.kənˈsɪs.tᵊnt.s|i, ˌɪŋ- (US) ˌɪn- **-ies** -iz
inconsistent ˌɪn.kənˈsɪs.tənt, ˌɪŋ- (US) ˌɪn- **-ly** -li
inconsolab|le ˌɪn.kənˈsəʊ.lə.bl|, ˌɪŋ- (US) ˌɪn.kənˈsoʊ- **-ly** -li **-leness** -l̩.nəs, -nɪs
inconsonant ɪnˈkɒn*t*.sə.nənt, ɪŋ- (US) ɪnˈkɑːn*t*-
inconspicuous ˌɪn.kənˈspɪk.ju.əs, ˌɪŋ- (US) ˌɪn- **-ly** -li **-ness** -nəs, -nɪs
inconstanc|y ɪnˈkɒn*t*.stᵊnt.s|i, ˌɪn-, ɪŋ-, ˌɪŋ- (US) ɪnˈkɑːn*t*-, ˌɪn- **-ies** -iz
inconstant ɪnˈkɒn*t*.stənt, ˌɪn-, ɪŋ-, ˌɪŋ- (US) ɪnˈkɑːn*t*-, ˌɪn- **-ly** -li
incontestability ˌɪn.kənˌtes.təˈbɪl.ə.ti, ˌɪŋ-, -ɪ.ti (US) ˌɪn.kənˌtes.təˈbɪl.ə.t̬i
incontestab|le ˌɪn.kənˈtes.tə.bl|, ˌɪŋ- (US) ˌɪn- **-ly** -li
incontinence ɪnˈkɒn.tɪ.nən*t*s, ˌɪn-, ɪŋ-, ˌɪŋ-, -tə- (US) ɪnˈkɑːn.tᵊn.ᵊn*t*s, ˌɪn-
incontinent ɪnˈkɒn.tɪ.nənt, ˌɪn-, ɪŋ-, ˌɪŋ-, -tə- (US) ɪnˈkɑːn.tᵊn.ᵊnt, ˌɪn- **-ly** -li
incontrollab|le ˌɪn.kənˈtrəʊ.lə.bl|, ˌɪŋ- (US) ˌɪn.kənˈtroʊ- **-ly** -li
incontrovertibility ˌɪnˌkɒn.trəˌvɜː.təˈbɪl.ə.ti, ˌɪŋ-, -tɪˈ-, -ɪ.ti (US) ˌɪn.kɑːn.trəˌvɜːr.t̬əˈbɪl.ə.t̬i
incontrovertib|le ˌɪnˌkɒn.trəˈvɜː.tə.bl|, ˌɪŋ-, -tɪ- (US) ˌɪnˌkɑːn.trəˈvɜːr.t̬ə- **-ly** -li
inconvenienc|e ˌɪn.kənˈviː.ni.ən*t*s, ˌɪŋ- (US) ˌɪn-, ˈ-njən*t*s **-es** -ɪz **-ing** -ɪŋ **-ed** -t
inconvenient ˌɪn.kənˈviː.ni.ənt, ˌɪŋ- (US) ˌɪn-, ˈ-njənt **-ly** -li
inconvertibility ˌɪn.kənˌvɜː.təˈbɪl.ə.ti, ˌɪŋ-, -tɪˈ-, -ɪ.ti (US) ˌɪn.kənˌvɜːr.t̬əˈbɪl.ə.t̬i
inconvertib|le ˌɪn.kənˈvɜː.tə.bl|, ˌɪŋ-, -tɪ- (US) ˌɪn.kənˈvɜːr.t̬ə- **-ly** -li

incorporate (*adj.*) ɪnˈkɔː.pᵊr.ət, ˌɪn-, ɪŋ-, ˌɪŋ-, -ɪt (US) ɪnˈkɔːr-, ˌɪn-

incorpor|ate (*v.*) ɪnˈkɔː.pᵊr|.eɪt, ɪŋ- (US) ɪnˈkɔːr.pə.r|eɪt **-ates** -eɪts **-ating** -eɪ.tɪŋ (US) -eɪ.t̬ɪŋ **-ated** -eɪ.tɪd (US) -eɪ.t̬ɪd

incorporation ɪnˌkɔː.pᵊrˈeɪ.ʃᵊn, ɪŋ- (US) ɪnˌkɔːr.pəˈreɪ- **-s** -z

incorporeal ˌɪn.kɔːˈpɔː.ri.əl, ˌɪŋ- (US) ˌɪn.kɔːrˈpɔːr.i- **-ly** -i

incorrect ˌɪn.kᵊrˈekt, ˌɪŋ- (US) ˌɪn.kəˈrekt **-ly** -li **-ness** -nəs, -nɪs

incorrigibility ɪnˌkɒr.ɪ.dʒəˈbɪl.ə.ti, ɪŋ-, -dʒɪˈ-, -ɪ.ti (US) ɪnˌkɔːr.ə.dʒəˈbɪl.ə.t̬i

incorrigib|le ɪnˈkɒr.ɪ.dʒə.b|l̩, ɪŋ-, -dʒɪ- (US) ɪnˈkɔːr.ə.dʒə- **-ly** -li **-leness** -l̩.nəs, -nɪs

incorruptibility ˌɪn.kəˌrʌp.təˈbɪl.ə.ti, ˌɪŋ-, -tɪˈ-, -ɪ.ti (US) ˌɪn.kəˌrʌp.təˈbɪl.ə.t̬i

incorruptib|le ˌɪn.kəˈrʌp.tə.b|l̩, ˌɪŋ-, -tɪ- (US) ˌɪn- **-ly** -li **-leness** -l̩.nəs, -nɪs

incorruption ˌɪn.kəˈrʌp.ʃᵊn, ˌɪŋ- (US) ˌɪn-

increas|e (*n.*) ˈɪn.kriːs, ˈɪŋ-, -ˈ- (US) ˈɪn.kriːs, -ˈ- **-es** -ɪz

increas|e (*v.*) ɪnˈkriːs, ɪŋ-, ˈ-- (US) ɪnˈkriːs, ˈ-- **-es** -ɪz **-ing/ly** -ɪŋ/li **-ed** -t

incredibility ɪnˌkred.ɪˈbɪl.ə.ti, ɪŋ-, -əˈ-, -ɪ.ti (US) ɪnˌkred.ɪˈbɪl.ə.t̬i, -əˈ-

incredib|le ɪnˈkred.ɪ.b|l̩, ɪŋ-, ˈ-ə- (US) ˌɪn- **-ly** -li **-leness** -l̩.nəs, -nɪs

incredulity ˌɪn.krəˈdjuː.lə.ti, ˌɪŋ-, -krɪˈ-, -kredˈjuː-, -ɪ.ti (US) ˌɪn.krəˈduː.lə.t̬i, -ˈdjuː-

incredulous ɪnˈkred.jə.ləs, ɪŋ-, -jʊ-, -ˈkredʒ.ə-, ˈ-ʊ- (US) ɪnˈkredʒ.ʊ- **-ly** -li **-ness** -nəs, -nɪs

increment ˈɪn.krə.mənt, ˈɪŋ-, -krɪ- (US) ˈɪn- **-s** -s

incremental ˌɪn.krəˈmen.tᵊl, ˌɪŋ-, -krɪˈ- (US) ˌɪn.krəˈmen.t̬ᵊl **-ly** -i

incrimi|nate ɪnˈkrɪm.ɪ|.neɪt, ɪŋ-, ˈ-ə- (US) ɪn- **-nates** -neɪts **-nating** -neɪ.tɪŋ (US) -neɪ.t̬ɪŋ **-nated** -neɪ.tɪd (US) -neɪ.t̬ɪd

incrimination ɪnˌkrɪm.ɪˈneɪ.ʃᵊn, ɪŋ-, -əˈ- (US) ɪn-

incriminatory ɪnˈkrɪm.ɪ.nə.tᵊr.i, ɪŋ-, -ᵊn.ə-, -neɪ.tᵊr-; ɪnˌkrɪm.ɪˈneɪ-, ˌɪn-, ɪŋ-, ˌɪŋ- (US) ɪnˈkrɪm.ɪ.nə.tɔːr.i

incrust ɪnˈkrʌst, ɪŋ- (US) ɪn- **-s** -s **-ing** -ɪŋ **-ed** -ɪd

incrustation ˌɪn.krʌsˈteɪ.ʃᵊn, ˌɪŋ- (US) ˌɪn- **-s** -z

incu|bate ˈɪŋ.kjʊ|.beɪt, ˈɪn-, -kjə- **-bates** -beɪts **-bating** -beɪ.tɪŋ (US) -beɪ.t̬ɪŋ **-bated** -beɪ.tɪd (US) -beɪ.t̬ɪd **-bative** -beɪ.tɪv (US) -beɪ.t̬ɪv

incubation ˌɪŋ.kjʊˈbeɪ.ʃᵊn, ˌɪn-, -kjəˈ- **-s** -z

incubator ˈɪŋ.kjʊ.beɪ.təʳ, ˈɪn-, -kjə- (US) -t̬ɚ **-s** -z

incubatory ˈɪŋ.kjʊ.beɪ.tᵊr.i, ˈɪn-, -kjə- (US) -bə.tɔːr-, ˌɪŋ.kjʊˈbeɪ.tɚ-, ˌɪn-, -kjəˈ-

incub|us ˈɪŋ.kjʊ.bl|əs, ˈɪn-, -kjə- **-uses** -ə.sɪz **-i** -aɪ

incul|cate ˈɪn.kʌl|.keɪt, ˈɪŋ-, -kəl-; ɪnˈkʌl-, ɪŋ- (US) ˈɪn.kʌl-, -kəl-; ɪnˈkʌl- **-cates** -keɪts **-cating** -keɪ.tɪŋ (US) -keɪ.t̬ɪŋ **-cated** -keɪ.tɪd (US) -keɪ.t̬ɪd **-cator/s** -keɪ.təʳ/z (US) -keɪ.t̬ɚ/z

inculcation ˌɪn.kʌlˈkeɪ.ʃᵊn, ˌɪŋ-, -kəlˈ- (US) ˌɪn-

incul|pate ˈɪn.kʌl|.peɪt, ˈɪŋ-, -kəl-; ɪnˈkʌl-, ɪŋ- (US) ˈɪn.kʌl-, -kəl-; ɪnˈkʌl- **-pates** -peɪts **-pating** -peɪ.tɪŋ (US) -peɪ.t̬ɪŋ **-pated** -peɪ.tɪd (US) -peɪ.t̬ɪd

inculpation ˌɪn.kʌlˈpeɪ.ʃᵊn, ˌɪŋ-, -kəlˈ- (US) ˌɪn-

inculpatory ɪnˈkʌl.pə.tᵊr.i, ɪŋ-; ˈɪn.kʌl.peɪ-, ˈɪŋ-, -kəl-, ˌɪn.kʌlˈpeɪ-, ˌɪŋ-, -kəlˈ- (US) ɪnˈkʌl.pə.tɔːr.i

incumbenc|y ɪnˈkʌm.bənt.s|i, ɪŋ- (US) ɪn- **-ies** -iz

incumbent ɪnˈkʌm.bənt, ɪŋ- (US) ɪn- **-s** -s **-ly** -li

incumbranc|e ɪnˈkʌm.brənts, ɪŋ- (US) ɪn- **-es** -ɪz

incunabul|um ˌɪn.kjuːˈnæb.jə.l|əm, ˌɪŋ-, -jʊ- (US) -kjəˈ-, -kjʊˈ- **-a** -ə

incur ɪnˈkɜːʳ, ɪŋ- (US) ɪnˈkɜːr **-s** -z **-ring** -ɪŋ **-red** -d **-rable** -ə.bl̩

incurability ɪnˌkjʊə.rəˈbɪl.ə.ti, ˌɪn-, ɪŋ-, ˌɪŋ-, -ˌkjɔː-, -ɪ.ti (US) ɪnˌkjʊr.əˈbɪl.ə.t̬i

incurab|le ɪnˈkjʊə.rə.b|l̩, ˌɪn-, ɪŋ-, ˌɪŋ-, -ˈkjɔː- (US) ɪnˈkjʊr.ə- **-ly** -li **-leness** -l̩.nəs, -nɪs

incurious ɪnˈkjʊə.ri.əs, ˌɪn-, ɪŋ-, ˌɪŋ-, -ˈkjɔː- (US) ɪnˈkjʊr.i- **-ly** -li **-ness** -nəs, -nɪs

incursion ɪnˈkɜː.ʃᵊn, ɪŋ-, -ʒᵊn (US) ɪnˈkɜːr- **-s** -z

incursive ɪnˈkɜː.sɪv, ɪŋ- (US) ɪnˈkɜːr-

incurvate (*adj.*) ɪnˈkɜː.veɪt, ɪŋ-, -vət, -vɪt (US) ɪnˈkɜːr-

incur|vate (*v.*) ˈɪn.kɜː|.veɪt, ˈɪŋ- (US) ɪnˈkɜːr-, ˈɪn.kɜːr- **-vates** -veɪts **-vating** -veɪ.tɪŋ (US) -veɪ.t̬ɪŋ **-vated** -veɪ.tɪd (US) -veɪ.t̬ɪd

incurvation ˌɪn.kɜːˈveɪ.ʃᵊn, ˌɪŋ- (US) ˌɪn.kɜːrˈ-

incurv|e ˌɪnˈkɜːv, ˌɪŋ- (US) ˌɪnˈkɜːrv **-es** -z **-ing** -ɪŋ **-ed** -d *stress shift:* ˌincurved ˈsurface

incus|e ɪnˈkjuːz, ɪŋ- (US) ɪnˈkjuːz, -ˈkjuːs **-es** -ɪz **-ing** -ɪŋ **-ed** -d

Ind *surname:* ɪnd *India:* ɪnd, aɪnd

Ind. (*abbrev. for* **Indiana**) ˌɪn.diˈæn.ə, -ˈɑː.nə (US) -ˈæn.ə

ind. (*abbrev. for* **independent**) ˌɪn.dɪˈpen.dənt, -dəˈ- (*abbrev. for* **indicative**) ɪnˈdɪk.ə.tɪv (US) -t̬ɪv (*abbrev. for* **industrial**) ɪnˈdʌs.tri.əl

Indaur ɪnˈdɔːʳ (US) -ˈdɔːr

Ind Coope® ˌɪndˈkuːp

indebted ɪnˈdet.ɪd (US) -ˈdet̬- **-ness** -nəs, -nɪs

indecenc|y ɪnˈdiː.sᵊnt.s|i, ˌɪn- **-ies** -iz

indecent ɪnˈdiː.sᵊnt, ˌɪn- **-ly** -li **inˌdecent asˈsault**; **inˌdecent exˈposure**

indecipherable ˌɪn.dɪˈsaɪ.fᵊr.ə.bl̩, -dəˈ-

indecision ˌɪn.dɪˈsɪʒ.ᵊn, -dəˈ-

indecisive ˌɪn.dɪˈsaɪ.sɪv, -dəˈ- **-ly** -li **-ness** -nəs, -nɪs

indeclinable ˌɪn.dɪˈklaɪ.nə.bl̩, -dəˈ- **-s** -z

indecomposable ɪnˌdiː.kəmˈpəʊ.zə.bl̩, ˌɪn- (US) -ˈpoʊ-

indecorous ɪnˈdek.ᵊr.əs, ˌɪn- **-ly** -li **-ness** -nəs, -nəs

indecorum ˌɪn.dɪˈkɔː.rəm, -dəˈ- (US) -ˈkɔːr.əm

indeed (*adv.*) ɪnˈdiːd (*interj.*) ɪnˈdiːd, ˌɪn.diːd

indefatigab|le ˌɪn.dɪˈfæt.ɪ.gə.b|l̩, -dəˈ- (US) -ˈfæt̬- **-ly** -li **-leness** -l̩.nəs, -nɪs

indefeasibility ˌɪn.dɪˌfiː.zəˈbɪl.ə.ti, -dəˌ-, -zɪˈ-, -ɪ.ti (US) -ə.t̬i

indefeasib|le ˌɪn.dɪˈfiː.zə.b|l̩, -dəˈ-, -zɪ- **-ly** -li

indefensibility ˌɪn.dɪˌfent.səˈbɪl.ə.ti, -dəˌ-, -sɪˈ-, -ɪ.ti (US) -ə.t̬i

indefensib|le ˌɪn.dɪˈfent.sə.b|l̩, -dəˈ-, -sɪ- **-ly** -li

indefinab|le ˌɪn.dɪˈfaɪ.nə.b|l̩, -dəˈ- **-ly** -li

indefinite ɪnˈdef.ɪ.nət, ˌɪn-, -ᵊn.ət, ˈ-nət, -nɪt (US) -ə.nət, ˈ-nət **-ly** -li **-ness** -nəs, -nɪs **inˌdefinite ˈarticle**

indelibility ɪnˌdel.ɪˈbɪl.ə.ti, ˌɪn-, -əˈ-, -ɪ.ti (US) -ə.t̬i

indelib|le ɪnˈdel.ə.b|l̩, ˌɪn-, ˈ-ɪ- **-ly** -li

indelicac|y ɪnˈdel.ɪ.kə.s|i, ˌɪn-, ˈ-ə- **-ies** -iz

indelicate ɪnˈdel.ɪ.kət, ˌɪn-, ˈ-ə-, -kɪt **-ly** -li

in delicto ˌɪn.delˈɪk.təʊ, -dɪˈlɪk- (US) -dəˈlɪk.toʊ

indemnification ɪnˌdem.nɪ.fɪˈkeɪ.ʃᵊn, -nə- **-s** -z

indemni|fy ɪnˈdem.nɪ|.faɪ, -nə- **-fies** -faɪz **-fying** -faɪ.ɪŋ **-fied** -faɪd

indemnit|y ɪnˈdem.nə.t|i, -nɪ- (US) -t̬|i **-ies** -iz

indemonstrab|le ɪnˈdem.ənt.strə.b|l̩, ˌɪn-; ˌɪn.dɪˈmɒnt.strə-, -dəˈ- (US) ˌɪn.dɪˈmɑːnt.strə-; ɪnˈdem.ənt-, ˌɪn- **-ly** -li

indent (*n.*) ˈɪn.dent, -ˈ- **-s** -s

in|dent (*v.*) ɪn|ˈdent, ˌɪn- **-dents** -ˈdents **-denting** -ˈden.tɪŋ (US) -ˈden.t̬ɪŋ **-dented** -ˈden.tɪd (US) -ˈden.t̬ɪd

indentation ˌɪn.denˈteɪ.ʃᵊn **-s** -z
indenture ɪnˈden.tʃəʳ ⓊⓈ -tʃɚ **-s** -z **-d** -d
independen|ce ˌɪn.dɪˈpen.dənt|s, -dəˈ- **-cy** -si **Indeˈpendence ˌDay**
independent (I) ˌɪn.dɪˈpen.dənt, -dəˈ- **-s** -s **-ly** -li
in-depth ˌɪnˈdepθ *stress shift:* ˌin-depth ˈtreatment
indescribab|le ˌɪn.dɪˈskraɪ.bə.b|l̩, -dəˈ- **-ly** -li
indestructibility ˌɪn.dɪˌstrʌk.təˈbɪl.ə.ti, -tɪˈ-, -ɪ.ti ⓊⓈ -ə.t̬i
indestructib|le ˌɪn.dɪˈstrʌk.tə.b|l̩, -tɪ- **-ly** -li **-leness** -l̩.nəs, -l̩.nɪs
indetectab|le, -ib|le ˌɪn.dɪˈtek.tə.b|l̩, -dəˈ- **-ly** -li
indeterminab|le ˌɪn.dɪˈtɜː.mɪ.nə.b|l̩, -dəˈ- ⓊⓈ -ˈtɜːr- **-ly** -li **-leness** -l̩.nəs, -l̩.nɪs
indeterminacy ˌɪn.dɪˈtɜː.mɪ.nə.si, -dəˈ-, -mᵊn.ə- ⓊⓈ -ˈtɜːr-
indeterminate ˌɪn.dɪˈtɜː.mɪ.nət, -dəˈ-, -nɪt ⓊⓈ -ˈtɜːr- **-ly** -li **-ness** -nəs, -nɪs
indetermination ˌɪn.dɪˌtɜː.mɪˈneɪ.ʃᵊn, -dəˌ-, -məˈ- ⓊⓈ -ˌtɜːr-
ind|ex ˈɪn.d|eks **-exes** -ek.sɪz **-ices** -ɪ.siːz, -ə- **ˈindex ˌcard** ; ˌ**index ˈfinger**, **ˈindex ˌfinger** ; **ˈindex ˌnumber**
indexer ˈɪn.dek.səʳ ⓊⓈ -sɚ **-s** -z
index-linked ˌɪn.deksˈlɪŋ*k*t
Indi|a ˈɪn.di|.ə **-an/s** -ən/z ˌ**Indian ˈOcean** ; ˌ**India ˈrubber** ; ˌ**Indian ˈsummer**
Indiana ˌɪn.diˈæn.ə, -ˈɑː.nə ⓊⓈ -ˈæn.ə
Indianapolis ˌɪn.di.əˈnæp.ᵊl.ɪs ⓊⓈ -ə.lɪs
Indic ˈɪn.dɪk
indi|cate ˈɪn.dɪ|.keɪt, -də- **-cates** -keɪts **-cating** -keɪ.tɪŋ ⓊⓈ -keɪ.t̬ɪŋ **-cated** -keɪ.tɪd ⓊⓈ -keɪ.t̬ɪd
indication ˌɪn.dɪˈkeɪ.ʃᵊn, -dəˈ- **-s** -z
indicative (*n. adj.*) *in grammar:* ɪnˈdɪk.ə.tɪv ⓊⓈ -t̬ɪv **-s** -z **-ly** -li
indicative (*adj.*) *indicating:* ɪnˈdɪk.ə.tɪv; ˈɪn.dɪ.keɪ- ⓊⓈ ɪnˈdɪk.ə.t̬ɪv **-ly** -li
indicator ˈɪn.dɪ.keɪ.təʳ, -də- ⓊⓈ -t̬ɚ **-s** -z
indicatory ɪnˈdɪk.ə.tᵊr.i; ˈɪn.dɪ.keɪ-, ˌɪn.dɪˈkeɪ- ⓊⓈ ˈɪn.dɪ.kə.tɔːr-; ɪnˈdɪk.ə-
indices (*plur. of* **index**) ˈɪn.dɪ.siːz, -də-
indicia ɪnˈdɪʃ.i.ə ⓊⓈ -ˈdɪʃ.ə, -i.ə
in|dict ɪn|ˈdaɪt **-dicts** -ˈdaɪts **-dicting** -ˈdaɪ.tɪŋ ⓊⓈ -ˈdaɪ.t̬ɪŋ **-dicted** -ˈdaɪ.tɪd ⓊⓈ -ˈdaɪ.t̬ɪd **-dicter/s** -ˈdaɪ.təʳ/z ⓊⓈ -ˈdaɪ.t̬ɚ/z **-dictable** -ˈdaɪ.tə.bl̩ ⓊⓈ -ˈdaɪ.t̬ə.bl̩
indiction ɪnˈdɪk.ʃᵊn **-s** -z
indictment ɪnˈdaɪt.mənt **-s** -s
indie ˈɪn.di **-s** -z
Indies ˈɪn.diz
indifference ɪnˈdɪf.ᵊr.ᵊnts, ˈ-rᵊnts
indifferent ɪnˈdɪf.ᵊr.ᵊnt, ˈ-rᵊnt **-ly** -li
indigen ˈɪn.dɪ.dʒən, -də- **-s** -z
indigence ˈɪn.dɪ.dʒən*t*s
indigene ˈɪn.dɪ.dʒiːn **-s** -z
indigenous ɪnˈdɪdʒ.ɪ.nəs, -ᵊn.əs **-ly** -li **-ness** -nəs, -nɪs
indigent ˈɪn.dɪ.dʒənt **-s** -s **-ly** -li
indigestibility ˌɪn.dɪˌdʒes.təˈbɪl.ə.ti, -tɪˈ-, -ɪ.ti ⓊⓈ -dɪˌdʒes.təˈbɪl.ə.t̬i, -daɪˌ-
indigestib|le ˌɪn.dɪˈdʒes.tə.b|l̩, -dəˈ-, -tɪ- ⓊⓈ -dɪˈ-, -daɪˈ- **-leness** -l̩.nəs, -nɪs **-ly** -li
indigestion ˌɪn.dɪˈdʒes.tʃᵊn, -dəˈ-, -ˈdʒeʃ- ⓊⓈ -dɪˈdʒes-, -daɪˈ-
indignant ɪnˈdɪg.nənt **-ly** -li
indignation ˌɪn.dɪgˈneɪ.ʃᵊn
indignit|y ɪnˈdɪg.nə.t|i, -nɪ- ⓊⓈ -nə.t̬|i **-ies** -iz
indigo ˈɪn.dɪ.gəʊ ⓊⓈ -goʊ **-(e)s** -z
Indira ˈɪn.dɪ.rə, -dᵊr.ə; ɪnˈdɪə.rə ⓊⓈ ɪnˈdɪr.ə
indirect ˌɪn.dɪˈrekt, -daɪˈ-, -dəˈ- **-ly** -li **-ness** -nəs, -nɪs ˌ**indirect ˈobject** ; ˌ**indirect ˈspeech**
indiscernib|le ˌɪn.dɪˈsɜː.nə.b|l̩, -ˈzɜː-, -nɪ- ⓊⓈ -ˈsɜːr-, -ˈzɜːr- **-ly** -li
indisciplin|e ɪnˈdɪs.ə.plɪn, ˌɪn-, ˈ-ɪ- **-ed** -d **-able** -ə.bl̩
indiscreet ˌɪn.dɪˈskriːt, -dəˈ- **-ly** -li **-ness** -nəs, -nɪs
indiscrete ˌɪn.dɪˈskriːt, -dəˈ-
indiscretion ˌɪn.dɪˈskreʃ.ᵊn, -dəˈ- **-s** -z
indiscriminate ˌɪn.dɪˈskrɪm.ɪ.nət, -dəˈ-, ˈ-ə-, -nɪt **-ly** -li **-ness** -nəs, -nɪs
indiscrimination ˌɪn.dɪˌskrɪm.ɪˈneɪ.ʃᵊn, -dəˌ-, -əˈ-
indispensability ˌɪn.dɪˌspen*t*.səˈbɪl.ə.ti, -dəˌ-, -ɪ.ti ⓊⓈ -ə.t̬i
indispensab|le, -ib|le ˌɪn.dɪˈspen*t*.sə.b|l̩, -dəˈ- **-ly** -li **-leness** -nəs, -nɪs
indispos|e ˌɪn.dɪˈspəʊz, -dəˈ- ⓊⓈ -ˈspoʊz **-es** -ɪz **-ing** -ɪŋ **-ed** -d
indisposition ˌɪn.dɪ.spəˈzɪʃ.ᵊn; ɪnˌdɪs.pəˈ- ⓊⓈ ˌɪn.dɪ.spəˈ- **-s** -z
indisputability ˌɪn.dɪˌspjuː.təˈbɪl.ə.ti; ɪnˌdɪs.pjuː-, -ɪ.ti ⓊⓈ ˌɪn.dɪˌspjuː.təˈbɪl.ə.t̬i
indisputab|le ˌɪn.dɪˈspjuː.tə.b|l̩; ɪnˈdɪs.pjuː- ⓊⓈ ˌɪn.dɪˈspjuː.t̬ə-; ɪnˈdɪs.pjuː-, -pjə- **-ly** -li **-leness** -l̩.nəs, -nɪs
indissociable ˌɪn.dɪˈsəʊ.ʃi.ə.bl̩, -ʃə.bl̩ ⓊⓈ -ˈsoʊ-
indissolubility ˌɪn.dɪˌsɒl.jəˈbɪl.ə.ti, -dəˌ-, -jʊˈ-, -ɪ.ti ⓊⓈ -ˌsɑːl.jəˈbɪl.ə.t̬i
indissolub|le ˌɪn.dɪˈsɒl.jə.b|l̩, -dəˈ-, -jʊ- ⓊⓈ -ˈsɑːl- **-ly** -li **-leness** -l̩.nəs, -nɪs
indistinct ˌɪn.dɪˈstɪŋkt, -dəˈ- **-ly** -li **-ness** -nəs, -nɪs
indistinctive ˌɪn.dɪˈstɪŋ*k*.tɪv, -dəˈ- **-ly** -li **-ness** -nəs, -nɪs
indistinguishab|le ˌɪn.dɪˈstɪŋ.gwɪ.ʃə.b|l̩, -dəˈ- **-ly** -li **-leness** -l̩.nəs, -nɪs
in|dite ɪn|ˈdaɪt **-dites** -ˈdaɪts **-diting** -ˈdaɪ.tɪŋ ⓊⓈ -ˈdaɪ.t̬ɪŋ **-dited** -ˈdaɪ.tɪd ⓊⓈ -ˈdaɪ.t̬ɪd **-diter/s** -ˈdaɪ.təʳ/z ⓊⓈ -ˈdaɪ.t̬ɚ/z
indium ˈɪn.di.əm
individual ˌɪn.dɪˈvɪdʒ.u.əl, -dəˈ-, -ˈvɪd.ju- ⓊⓈ -ˈvɪdʒ.u-, -ˈvɪdʒ.ᵊl **-s** -z **-ly** -i
individual|ism ˌɪn.dɪˈvɪdʒ.u.ə.l|ɪ.zᵊm, -dəˈ-, -ˈvɪd.ju.ə.l|ɪz- ⓊⓈ -ˈvɪdʒ.u-, -ˈvɪdʒ.ᵊl|.ɪ- **-ist/s** -ɪst/s
individualistic ˌɪn.dɪˌvɪdʒ.u.əˈlɪs.tɪk, -dəˌ-, -ˌvɪd.ju- ⓊⓈ -ˌvɪdʒ.u-, -ˌvɪdʒ.ᵊlˈɪs- **-ally** -ᵊl.i, -li
individualit|y ˌɪn.dɪˌvɪdʒ.uˈæl.ə.t|i, -dəˌ-, -ˌvɪd.juˈ-, -ɪ.t|i ⓊⓈ -ˌvɪdʒ.uˈæl.ə.t̬|i **-ies** -iz
individualization, -isa- ˌɪn.dɪˌvɪdʒ.u.ᵊl.aɪˈzeɪ.ʃᵊn, -dəˌ-, -ˌvɪd.ju-, -ɪˈ- ⓊⓈ -ˌvɪdʒ.u.ᵊl.ɪˈ-, -ˌvɪdʒ.ᵊl-
individualiz|e, is|e ˌɪn.dɪˈvɪdʒ.u.ə.laɪz, -dəˈ-, -ˈvɪd.ju- ⓊⓈ -ˈvɪdʒ.u-, -ˈvɪdʒ.ᵊl.aɪz **-es** -ɪz **-ing** -ɪŋ **-ed** -d
individu|ate ˌɪn.dɪˈvɪdʒ.u|.eɪt, -dəˈ-, -ˈvɪd.ju- ⓊⓈ -ˈvɪdʒ.u- **-ates** -eɪts **-ating** -eɪ.tɪŋ ⓊⓈ -eɪ.t̬ɪŋ **-ated** -eɪ.tɪd ⓊⓈ -eɪ.t̬ɪd
individuation ˌɪn.dɪˌvɪdʒ.uˈeɪ.ʃᵊn, -dəˌ-, -ˌvɪd.juˈ- ⓊⓈ -ˌvɪdʒ.uˈ- **-s** -s
indivisibility ˌɪn.dɪˌvɪz.ɪˈbɪl.ə.ti, -əˈ-, -ɪ.ti ⓊⓈ -ə.t̬i
indivisib|le ˌɪn.dɪˈvɪz.ə.b|l̩, ˈ-ɪ- **-ly** -li **-leness** -l̩.nəs, -nɪs
Indo-China ˌɪn.dəʊˈtʃaɪ.nə ⓊⓈ -doʊˈ-
Indo-Chinese ˌɪn.dəʊ.tʃaɪˈniːz ⓊⓈ -doʊ-
indocile ɪnˈdəʊ.saɪl, ˌɪn- ⓊⓈ -ˈdɑː.səl
indocility ˌɪn.dəʊˈsɪl.ə.ti, -ɪ.ti ⓊⓈ -dɑːˈsɪl.ə.t̬i, -doʊˈ-
indoctri|nate ɪnˈdɒk.trɪ|.neɪt, -trə- ⓊⓈ -ˈdɑːk- **-nates** -neɪts **-nating** -neɪ.tɪŋ ⓊⓈ -neɪ.t̬ɪŋ **-nated** -neɪ.tɪd ⓊⓈ -neɪ.t̬ɪd **-nator/s** -neɪ.təʳ/z ⓊⓈ -neɪ.t̬ɚ/z
indoctrination ɪnˌdɒk.trɪˈneɪ.ʃᵊn, ˌɪn-, -trəˈ- ⓊⓈ -ˌdɑːk- **-s** -z
Indo-European ˌɪn.dəʊˌjʊə.rəˈpiː.ən, -ˌjɔː- ⓊⓈ -doʊ.jʊr.əˈ- **-s** -z
Indo-Germanic ˌɪn.dəʊ.dʒɜːˈmæn.ɪk, -dʒəˈ- ⓊⓈ -doʊ.dʒɜːrˈ-
indolence ˈɪn.dᵊl.ən*t*s
indolent ˈɪn.dᵊl.ən*t* **-ly** -li
indomitab|le ɪnˈdɒm.ɪ.tə.b|l̩, ˈ-ə- ⓊⓈ -ˈdɑː.mə.t̬ə- **-ly** -li **-leness** -l̩.nəs, -nɪs

Indonesi|a ˌɪn.dəʊ'niː.ʒ|ə, -zi|.ə, -si|.ə, -'niː.ʃ|ə (US) -də'niː.ʒ|ə, -ʃ|ə **-an/s** -ən/z
indoor ˌɪn'dɔːʳ (US) -'dɔːr *stress shift:* ˌindoor 'games
indoors ˌɪn'dɔːz (US) -'dɔːrz
Indore ˌɪn'dɔːʳ (US) -'dɔːr
indors|e ɪn'dɔːs (US) -'dɔːrs **-es** -ɪz **-ing** -ɪŋ **-ed** -t
indorsement ɪn'dɔːs.mənt (US) -'dɔːrs- **-s** -s
Indra 'ɪn.drə
indrawn ˌɪn'drɔːn (US) 'ɪn.drɑːn, -drɔːn *stress shift, British only:* ˌindrawn 'breath
indubitab|le ɪn'djuː.bɪ.tə.b|l̩, ˌɪn- (US) -'duː.bɪ.t̬ə-, -'djuː- **-ly** -li **-leness** -l̩.nəs, -nɪs
induc|e ɪn'djuːs (US) -'duːs, -'djuːs **-es** -ɪz **-ing** -ɪŋ **-ed** -t **-er/s** -əʳ/z (US) -ɚ/z
inducement ɪn'djuːs.mənt (US) -'duːs-, -'djuːs- **-s** -s
induct ɪn'dʌkt **-s** -s **-ing** -ɪŋ **-ed** -ɪd **-or/s** -əʳ/z (US) -ɚ/z
inductanc|e ɪn'dʌk.tᵊnts **-es** -ɪz
inductile ɪn'dʌk.taɪl, ˌɪn- (US) -tɪl
inductility ˌɪn.dʌk'tɪl.ə.ti, -ɪ.ti (US) -ə.t̬i
induction ɪn'dʌk.ʃᵊn **-s** -z **in'duction ˌcoil**
inductive ɪn'dʌk.tɪv **-ly** -li
indulg|e ɪn'dʌldʒ **-es** -ɪz **-ing** -ɪŋ **-ed** -d **-er/s** -əʳ/z (US) -ɚ/z
indulgenc|e ɪn'dʌl.dʒənts **-es** -ɪz
indulgent ɪn'dʌl.dʒənt **-ly** -li
indur|ate 'ɪn.djʊə.r|eɪt, -djʊr|.eɪt (US) -dʊ.r|eɪt, -djʊ-, -də- -djə- **-ates** -eɪts **-ating** -eɪ.tɪŋ (US) -eɪ.t̬ɪŋ **-ated** -eɪ.tɪd (US) -eɪ.t̬ɪd **-ative** -ə.tɪv (US) -t̬ɪv
induration ɪn.djʊə'reɪ.ʃᵊn, -djʊ'- (US) -dʊ'-, -djʊ'-, -də'-, -djə'-
Indus 'ɪn.dəs
industrial ɪn'dʌs.tri.əl **-ly** -i **inˌdustrial 'action ; inˌdustrial dis'pute, inˌdustrial 'dispute; inˌdustrial 'espionage; inˌdustrial es'tate; in'dustrial ˌpark; inˌdustrial re'lations; Inˌdustrial Revo'lution; inˌdustrial tri'bunal**
industrial|ism ɪn'dʌs.tri.əl|.ɪ.zᵊm **-ist/s** -ɪst/z
industrialization ɪnˌdʌs.tri.ə.laɪ'zeɪ.ʃᵊn, -lɪ'- (US) -lɪ'-
industrializ|e, -is|e ɪn'dʌs.tri.ə.laɪz **-es** -ɪz **-ing** -ɪŋ **-ed** -d
industrious ɪn'dʌs.tri.əs **-ly** -li **-ness** -nəs, -nɪs
industr|y 'ɪn.də.str|i **-ies** -iz
industrywide ˌɪn.də.stri'waɪd *stress shift:* ˌindustrywide 'slump
indwel|l ˌɪn'dwel, '-- **-ls** -z **-ling** -ɪŋ **-t** -t
indweller 'ɪnˌdwel.əʳ (US) -ɚ **-s** -z
-ine -aɪn, -iːn, -ɪn
inebriate (*n. adj.*) ɪ'niː.bri.ət, -ɪt, -eɪt **-s** -s
inebri|ate (*v.*) ɪ'niː.bri|.eɪt **-ates** -eɪts **-ating** -eɪ.tɪŋ (US) -eɪ.t̬ɪŋ **-ated** -eɪ.tɪd (US) -eɪ.t̬ɪd
inebriation ɪˌniː.bri'eɪ.ʃᵊn
inebriety ˌɪn.iː'braɪ.ə.ti, -ɪ'-, -ɪ.ti (US) -ə.t̬i
inedible ɪ'ned.ɪ.bl̩, ˌɪn'ed-, '-ə- (US) ˌɪn'ed-, ɪ'ned-
inedited ɪ'ned.ɪ.tɪd, ˌɪn'ed-, '-ə- (US) ˌɪn'ed.ɪ.t̬ɪd, ɪ'ned-, '-ə-
ineducable ɪ'ned.jə.kə.bl̩, ˌɪn'ed-, -'edʒ.ə-, '-ʊ- (US) ˌɪn'edʒ.ʊ-, ɪ'nedʒ-, '-ə-
ineffab|le ɪ'nef.ə.b|l̩, ˌɪn'ef- (US) ˌɪn'ef-, ɪ'nef- **-ly** -li **-leness** -l̩.nəs, -nɪs
ineffaceab|le ˌɪn.ɪ'feɪ.sə.b|l̩, -ef'eɪ-, -ə'feɪ- **-ly** -li
ineffective ˌɪn.ɪ'fek.tɪv, -ə'- **-ly** -li **-ness** -nəs, -nɪs
ineffectual ˌɪn.ɪ'fek.tʃu.ᵊl, -ə'-, -tju- (US) -tʃu- **-ly** -i **-ness** -nəs, -nɪs
inefficacious ˌɪn.ef.ɪ'keɪ.ʃəs, ɪˌnef- **-ly** -li
inefficacy ɪ'nef.ɪ.kə.si, ˌɪn'ef- (US) ˌɪn'ef-, ɪ'nef-
inefficiency ˌɪn.ɪ'fɪʃ.ᵊnt.si, -ə'-
inefficient ˌɪn.ɪ'fɪʃ.ᵊnt, -ə'- **-ly** -li
inelastic ˌɪn.ɪ'læs.tɪk, -ə'-, -'lɑː.stɪk (US) -iː'læs-, -ɪ'-
inelasticity ˌɪn.ɪ.læs'tɪs.ə.ti, ˌ-ə-, -ˌiː.læs'-, -lɑː'stɪs-, -ɪ.ti (US) -iː.læs'tɪs.ə.t̬i, ˌ-ɪ-
inelegance ɪ'nel.ɪ.gənts, ˌɪn'el-, '-ə- (US) ˌɪn'el-, ɪ'nel-
inelegant ɪ'nel.ɪ.gənt, ˌɪn'el-, '-ə- (US) ˌɪn'el-, ɪ'nel- **-ly** -li
ineligibility ɪˌnel.ɪ.dʒə'bɪl.ə.ti, ˌɪn.el-, -dʒɪ'-, -ɪ.ti (US) ˌɪn.el.ɪ.dʒə'bɪl.ə.t̬i, iˌnel-, -dʒɪ'-
ineligib|le ɪ'nel.ɪ.dʒə.b|l̩, ˌɪn'el-, -dʒɪ- (US) ˌɪn'el-, ɪ'nel- **-ly** -li
ineluctab|le ˌɪn.ɪ'lʌk.tə.b|l̩, -ə'- **-ly** -li
inept ɪ'nept, ˌɪn'ept (US) ˌɪn'ept, ɪ'nept **-ly** -li **-ness** -nəs, -nɪs
ineptitude ɪ'nep.tɪ.tjuːd, ˌɪn'ep-, -tə- (US) ˌɪn'ep.tɪ.tuːd, ɪ'nep-, -tə-, -tjuːd
inequab|le ɪ'nek.wə.b|l̩, ˌɪn'ek- (US) ˌɪn'ek-, ɪ'nek- **-ly** -li
inequalit|y ˌɪn.ɪ'kwɒl.ə.t|i, -ɪː'-, -ə'-, -ɪ.t|i (US) -'kwɑː.lə.t̬|i **-ies** -iz
inequitab|le ɪ'nek.wɪ.tə.b|l̩, ˌɪn'ek- (US) ˌɪn'ek.wə.t̬ə-, ɪ'nek- **-ly** -li
inequit|y ɪ'nek.wə.t|i, ˌɪn'ek-, -wɪ- (US) ˌɪn'ek.wə.t̬|i, ɪ'nek- **-ies** -iz
ineradicab|le ˌɪn.ɪ'ræd.ɪ.kə.b|l̩, -ə'- **-ly** -li
inert ɪ'nɜːt (US) ˌɪn'ɜːrt, ɪ'nɜːrt **-ly** -li **-ness** -nəs, -nɪs
inertia ɪ'nɜː.ʃə, -ʃi.ə (US) ˌɪn'ɜːr-, ɪ'nɜːr-
inescapab|le ˌɪn.ɪ'skeɪ.pə.b|l̩, -ə'- **-ly** -li
inessential ˌɪn.ɪ'sen.tʃᵊl, -ə'-
inessive ɪ'nes.ɪv, ˌɪn'es- (US) ˌɪn'es-, ɪ'nes-
inestimab|le ɪ'nes.tɪ.mə.b|l̩, ˌɪn'es-, -tə- (US) ˌɪn'es-, ɪ'nes- **-ly** -li
inevitability ɪˌnev.ɪ.tə'bɪl.ə.ti, ˌɪnˌev-, ˌ-ə-, -ɪ.ti (US) ˌɪnˌev.ɪ.t̬ə'bɪl.ə.t̬i, ɪˌnev-, ˌ-ə-
inevitab|le ɪ'nev.ɪ.tə.b|l̩, ˌɪn'ev-, '-ə- (US) ˌɪn'ev.ɪ.t̬ə-, ɪ'nev-, '-ə- **-ly** -li **-leness** -l̩.nəs, -nɪs
inexact ˌɪn.ɪg'zækt, -eg'-; -ɪk'sækt, -ek'- (US) -ɪg'zækt, -eg'- **-ly** -li **-ness** -nəs, -nɪs
inexactitude ˌɪn.ɪg'zæk.tɪ.tjuːd, -eg'-, -tə-; -ɪk'sæk-, -ek'- (US) -ɪg'zæk.tə.tuːd, -eg'- **-s** -z
inexcusab|le ˌɪn.ɪk'skjuː.zə.b|l̩, -ek'- **-ly** -li **-leness** -l̩.nəs, -nɪs
inexhaustibility ˌɪn.ɪgˌzɔː.stə'bɪl.ə.ti, -egˌ-, -stɪ'-, -ɪ.ti; -ɪkˌsɔː-, -ekˌ- (US) -ɪgˌzɑː.stə'bɪl.ə.t̬i, -egˌ-, -ˌzɔː-
inexhaustib|le ˌɪn.ɪg'zɔː.stə.b|l̩, -eg'-, -stɪ-; -ɪk'sɔː-, -ek'- (US) -ɪg'zɑː.stə-, -eg'-, -'zɔː- **-ly** -li **-leness** -l̩.nəs, -nɪs
inexisten|t ˌɪn.ɪg'zɪs.tᵊn|t, -ek'-; -ɪk'sɪs-, -ek'- (US) -ɪg'zɪs-, -eg'- **-ce** -ts
inexorability ɪˌnek.sᵊr.ə'bɪl.ə.ti, ˌɪnˌek-, -ɪ.ti (US) ˌɪnˌek.sɚ.ə'bɪl.ə.t̬i, ɪˌnek-
inexorab|le ɪ'nek.sᵊr.ə.b|l̩, ˌɪn'ek- (US) ˌɪn'ek-, ɪ'nek- **-ly** -li **-leness** -l̩.nəs, -nɪs
inexpedien|ce ˌɪn.ɪk'spiː.di.ən|ts, -ek'- **-cy** -si
inexpediency ˌɪn.ɪk'spiː.di.ənt.si, -ek'-
inexpedient ˌɪn.ɪk'spiː.di.ənt, -ek'- **-ly** -li
inexpensive ˌɪn.ɪk'spent.sɪv, -ek'- **-ly** -li **-ness** -nəs, -nɪs
inexperience ˌɪn.ɪk'spɪə.ri.ənts, -ek'- (US) -'spɪr.i- **-d** -t
inexpert ɪ'nek.spɜːt, ˌɪn'ek- (US) ˌɪn'ek.spɜːrt, ɪ'nek-; ˌɪn.ɪk'spɜːrt, -ek'- **-ly** -li **-ness** -nəs, -nɪs
inexpiab|le ɪ'nek.spi.ə.b|l̩, ˌɪn'ek- (US) ˌɪn'ek-, ɪ'nek- **-ly** -li **-leness** -l̩.nəs, -nɪs
inexplicability ˌɪn.ɪkˌsplɪk.ə'bɪl.ə.ti, -ekˌ-, -ɪ.ti; ɪnˌek.splɪk.ə'-, ˌɪn- (US) ɪˌnek.splɪ.kə'bɪl.ə.t̬i, ˌɪn.ek-
inexplicab|le ˌɪn.ɪk'splɪk.ə.b|l̩, -ek'-; ɪ'nek.splɪ.kə-, ˌɪn'ek-, -splə- (US) ˌɪn'ek.splɪ.kə-, ɪ'nek-, -splə-; ˌɪn.ɪk'splɪk.ə- **-ly** -li **-leness** -l̩.nəs, -nɪs

inexplicit ˌɪn.ɪk'splɪs.ɪt, -ek'- **-ly** -li **-ness** -nəs, -nɪs

inexplorable ˌɪn.ɪk'splɔː.rə.bl̩, -ek'- (US) -'splɔːr.ə-

inexpressib|le ˌɪn.ɪk'spres.ə.b|l̩, -ek'-, '-ɪ- **-ly** -li

inexpressive ˌɪn.ɪk'spres.ɪv, -ek'- **-ly** -li **-ness** -nəs, -nɪs

inexpugnab|le ˌɪn.ɪk'spʌg.nə.b|l̩, -ek'- (US) -'spʌg-, -'spjuː- **-ly** -li **-leness** -l̩.nəs, -nɪs

inextensible ˌɪn.ɪk'stent.sə.bl̩, -ek'-, -sɪ-

inextinguishab|le ˌɪn.ɪk'stɪŋ.gwɪ.ʃə.b|l̩, -ek'-, -wɪ- **-ly** -li

in extremis ˌɪn.ɪk'striː.mɪs (US) -ɪk'-, -ek'-

inextricab|le ˌɪn.ɪk'strɪk.ə.b|l̩, -ek'-; ɪ'nek.strɪ.kə-, ˌɪn'ek- **-ly** -li **-leness** -l̩.nəs, -nɪs

Inez 'iː.nez, 'aɪ- (US) iː'nez, ɪ-, aɪ-, 'iː.nez, 'aɪ-, -nes

infallibility ɪnˌfæl.ə'bɪl.ə.ti, ˌɪn-, -ɪ'-, -ɪ.ti (US) -ə.t̬i

infallib|le ɪn'fæl.ə.b|l̩, '-ɪ- **-ly** -li

infamous 'ɪn.fə.məs **-ly** -li **-ness** -nəs, -nɪs

infam|y 'ɪn.fə.m|i **-ies** -iz

infanc|y 'ɪn.fənt.s|i **-ies** -iz

infant 'ɪn.fənt **-s** -s 'infant ˌschool ; ˌinfant mor'tality ˌrate

infanta ɪn'fæn.tə (US) -t̬ə, -'fɑːn- **-s** -z

infante ɪn'fæn.ti (US) -teɪ, -'fɑːn- **-s** -z

infanticide ɪn'fæn.tɪ.saɪd, -tə- (US) -t̬ə- **-s** -z

infant|ile 'ɪn.fən.t|aɪl (US) -t|aɪl, -t|ɪl **-ine** -aɪn ˌinfantile pa'ralysis

infantilism ɪn'fæn.tɪ.lɪ.zəm, -tə- (US) 'ɪn.fən.t̬ə-, -taɪ-; ɪn'fæn.t̬ə-

infantry 'ɪn.fən.tri **-man** -mən, -mæn **-men** -mən, -men

infarct 'ɪn.fɑːkt, ˌ-'- (US) 'ɪn.fɑːrkt, ˌ-'- **-s** -s

infarction ɪn'fɑːk.ʃən (US) -'fɑːrk- **-s** -z

infatu|ate ɪn'fæt.ju|.eɪt, -'fætʃ.u- (US) -'fætʃ.u- **-ates** -eɪts **-ating** -eɪ.tɪŋ (US) -eɪ.t̬ɪŋ **-ated** -eɪ.tɪd (US) -eɪ.t̬ɪd

infatuation ɪnˌfæt.ju'eɪ.ʃən, -ˌfætʃ.u'- (US) -ˌfætʃ.u'- **-s** -z

infect ɪn'fekt **-s** -s **-ing** -ɪŋ **-ed** -ɪd

infection ɪn'fek.ʃən **-s** -z

infectious ɪn'fek.ʃəs **-ly** -li **-ness** -nəs, -nɪs

infecundity ˌɪn.fɪ'kʌn.də.ti, -fiː'-, -fek'ʌn-, -dɪ- (US) -fiː'kʌn.də.t̬i, -fɪ'-

infelicitous ˌɪn.fə'lɪs.ɪ.təs, -fɪ'-, -fel'ɪs-, '-ə- (US) -fə'lɪs.ə.t̬əs **-ly** -li

infelicit|y ˌɪn.fə'lɪs.ə.t|i, -fɪ'-, -fel'ɪs-, -ɪ- (US) -ə.t̬|i **-ies** -iz

infer ɪn'fɜːr (US) -'fɜːr **-s** -z **-ring** -ɪŋ **-red** -d **-able** -ə.bl̩

inferenc|e 'ɪn.fər.ənts, '-frənts **-es** -ɪz

inferential ˌɪn.fər'en.tʃəl (US) -fə'ren- **-ly** -i

inferior ɪn'fɪə.ri.ər, ˌɪn- (US) -'fɪr.i.ɚ **-s** -z

inferiority ɪnˌfɪə.ri'ɒr.ə.ti, ˌɪn-, -ɪ.ti (US) -ˌfɪr.i'ɔːr.ə.t̬i inferi'ority ˌcomplex

infernal ɪn'fɜː.nəl (US) -'fɜːr- **-ly** -i

inferno (I) ɪn'fɜː.nəʊ (US) -'fɜːr.noʊ **-s** -z

infertile ɪn'fɜː.taɪl, ˌɪn- (US) -'fɜːr.t̬əl

infertility ˌɪn.fə'tɪl.ə.ti, -fɜː'-, -ɪ.ti (US) -fɚ'tɪl.ə.t̬i

infest ɪn'fest **-s** -s **-ing** -ɪŋ **-ed** -ɪd

infestation ˌɪn.fes'teɪ.ʃən **-s** -z

infibu|late ɪn'fɪb.jə|.leɪt, -jʊ- **-lates** -leɪts **-lating** -leɪ.tɪŋ (US) -leɪ.t̬ɪŋ **-lated** -leɪ.tɪd (US) -leɪ.t̬ɪd

infibulation ɪnˌfɪb.jə'leɪ.ʃən, -jʊ'-

infidel 'ɪn.fɪ.dəl, -fə-, -del (US) -fə.del, -dəl **-s** -z

infidelit|y ˌɪn.fɪ'del.ə.t|i, -fə'-, -ɪ.t|i (US) -fə'del.ə.t̬|i **-ies** -iz

infield 'ɪn.fiːld **-s** -z

infielder 'ɪnˌfiːl.dər (US) -dɚ **-s** -z

infighting 'ɪnˌfaɪ.tɪŋ

infill 'ɪn.fɪl **-s** -s **-ing** -ɪŋ **-ed** -d

infilling 'ɪnˌfɪl.ɪŋ

infil|trate 'ɪn.fɪl|.treɪt, -fəl- (US) ɪn'fɪl|.treɪt, 'ɪn.fɪl- **-trates** -treɪts **-trating** -treɪ.tɪŋ (US) -treɪ.t̬ɪŋ **-trated** -treɪ.tɪd (US) -treɪ.t̬ɪd **-trator/s** -treɪ.tər/z (US) -treɪ.t̬ɚ/z

infiltration ˌɪn.fɪl'treɪ.ʃən, -fəl'- **-s** -z

in fine ˌɪn'faɪ.ni, -'fiː-, -neɪ

infinite *in non-technical sense:* 'ɪn.fɪ.nət, -fən.ət, -ɪt *in church music:* 'ɪn.fɪ.naɪt, -faɪ- (US) 'ɪn.fə.nɪt **-ly** -li **-ness** -nəs, -nɪs *in grammar:* ˌɪn'faɪ.naɪt *in mathematics:* 'ɪn.fɪ.nət, -fən.ət, -ɪt, -ˌfaɪ.naɪt

infinitesimal ˌɪn.fɪ.nɪ'tes.ɪ.məl, -fən.ɪ'-, -ə'-, -əm.əl (US) -'tes-, -'tez- **-ly** -i

infinitival ɪnˌfɪn.ɪ'taɪ.vəl, -ə'-; ˌɪn.fɪ.nɪ'-, -nə'- (US) ɪnˌfɪn.ɪ'taɪ-

infinitive ɪn'fɪn.ə.tɪv, '-ɪ- (US) -t̬ɪv **-s** -z **-ly** -li

infinitude ɪn'fɪn.ɪ.tjuːd, '-ə- (US) -tuːd, -tjuːd **-s** -z

infinit|y ɪn'fɪn.ə.t|i, -ɪ.t|i (US) -ə.t̬|i **-ies** -iz

infirm ɪn'fɜːm, ˌɪn- (US) -'fɜːrm **-ly** -li

infirmar|y ɪn'fɜː.mər|.i (US) -'fɜːr- **-ies** -iz

infirmit|y ɪn'fɜː.mə.t|i, -mɪ- (US) -'fɜːr.mə.t̬|i **-ies** -iz

infix *(n.)* 'ɪn.fɪks **-es** -ɪz

infix *(v.)* 'ɪn.fɪks, ˌ-'- **-es** -ɪz **-ing** -ɪŋ **-ed** -t

in flagrante delicto ɪn.fləˌgræn.teɪ.dɪ'lɪk.təʊ, -ti-, -də'-, -diː'-, -deɪ'- (US) -ˌgrɑːn.teɪ.dɪ'lɪk.toʊ, -ˌgræn-, -ti-, -də'-, -diː'-, -deɪ'-

inflam|e ɪn'fleɪm **-es** -z **-ing** -ɪŋ **-ed** -d

inflammability ɪnˌflæm.ə'bɪl.ə.ti, -ɪ.ti (US) -ə.t̬i

inflammable ɪn'flæm.ə.bl̩ **-ness** -nəs, -nɪs

inflammation ˌɪn.flə'meɪ.ʃən **-s** -z

inflammatory ɪn'flæm.ə.tər.i (US) -tɔːr-

inflatable ɪn'fleɪ.tə.bl̩ (US) -t̬ə- **-s** -z

in|flate ɪn|'fleɪt **-flates** -'fleɪts **-flating** -'fleɪ.tɪŋ (US) -'fleɪ.t̬ɪŋ **-flated** -'fleɪ.tɪd (US) -'fleɪ.t̬ɪd **-flator/s** -'fleɪ.tər/z (US) -'fleɪ.t̬ɚ/z

inflation ɪn'fleɪ.ʃən **-s** -z **-ary** -ər.i

inflationism ɪn'fleɪ.ʃən.ɪ.zəm

inflect ɪn'flekt **-s** -s **-ing** -ɪŋ **-ed** -ɪd

inflection ɪn'flek.ʃən **-s** -z

inflectional ɪn'flek.ʃən.əl

inflective ɪn'flek.tɪv

inflexibility ɪnˌflek.sə'bɪl.ə.ti, ˌɪn-, -sɪ'-, -ɪ.ti (US) -ə.t̬i

inflexib|le ɪn'flek.sə.b|l̩, -sɪ- **-ly** -li **-leness** -l̩.nəs, -nɪs

inflexion ɪn'flek.ʃən **-s** -z

inflexional ɪn'flek.ʃən.əl

inflict ɪn'flɪkt **-s** -s **-ing** -ɪŋ **-ed** -ɪd

infliction ɪn'flɪk.ʃən **-s** -z

in-flight ˌɪn'flaɪt (US) '--, ˌ-'- *stress shift, British only:* ˌin-flight 'service

inflorescence ˌɪn.flɔː'res.ənts, -flɒr'es-, -flə'res- (US) -flə'res-, -flɔː-, -floʊ-

inflow 'ɪn.fləʊ (US) -floʊ **-s** -z

influenc|e 'ɪn.flu.ənts, -flʊənts (US) -flu.ənts **-es** -ɪz **-ing** -ɪŋ **-ed** -t

influent 'ɪn.flu.ənt, -flʊənt (US) -flu.ənt **-s** -s

influential ˌɪn.flu'en.tʃəl **-ly** -i

influenza ˌɪn.flu'en.zə

influx 'ɪn.flʌks **-es** -ɪz

influxion ɪn'flʌk.ʃən

info 'ɪn.fəʊ (US) -foʊ

infomercial ˌɪn.fəʊ'mɜː.ʃəl (US) 'ɪn.foʊ.mɜːr- **-s** -z

inform ɪn'fɔːm (US) -'fɔːrm **-s** -z **-ing** -ɪŋ **-ed** -d inˌformed o'pinion

informal ɪn'fɔː.məl, ˌɪn- (US) -'fɔːr- **-ly** -i

informalit|y ˌɪn.fɔː'mæl.ə.t|i, -ɪ.t|i (US) -fɔːr'mæl.ə.t̬|i **-ies** -iz

informant ɪn'fɔː.mənt (US) -'fɔːr- **-s** -s

in forma pauperis ɪnˌfɔː.mə'paʊ.pər.ɪs (US) ɪnˌfɔːr.mə'pɑː.pɚ-, -'pɔː-

informatics ˌɪn.fə'mæt.ɪks, -fɔː'- (US) -fɚ'mæt̬-

information ˌɪn.fə'meɪ.ʃən, -fɔː'- (US) -fɚ'- **-s** -z inforˌmation tech'nology (US) inforˌmation tech'nology, infor'mation techˌnology

informa|tive ɪn'fɔː.mə|.tɪv (US) -'fɔːr.mə|.t̬ɪv **-tory** -tər.i (US) -tɔːr.i

informer ɪnˈfɔː.məʳ ⓤⓢ -ˈfɔːr.mɚ **-s** -z
infotainment ˌɪn.fəʊˈteɪn.mənt ⓤⓢ ˈɪn.foʊ.teɪn-, ˌɪn.foʊˈteɪn-
infra ˈɪn.frə ˌ**infra** ˈ**dig**
infract ɪnˈfrækt **-s** -s **-ing** -ɪŋ **-ed** -ɪd
infraction ɪnˈfræk.ʃᵊn **-s** -z
infralapsarian ˌɪn.frə.læpˈseə.ri.ən ⓤⓢ -ˈser.i- **-s** -z
infrangibility ɪnˌfræn.dʒɪˈbɪl.ə.ti, ˌɪn-, -dʒəˈ-, -ɪ.ti ⓤⓢ -ə.t̬i
infrangib|le ɪnˈfræn.dʒɪ.b|l̩, ˌɪn-, -dʒə- **-ly** -li **-leness** -l̩.nəs, -nɪs
infrared ˌɪn.frəˈred *stress shift:* ˌinfrared ˈcamera
infrastructure ˈɪn.frəˌstrʌk.tʃəʳ ⓤⓢ -tʃɚ **-s** -z
infrequency ɪnˈfriː.kwən*t*.si, ˌɪn-
infrequent ɪnˈfriː.kwənt, ˌɪn- **-ly** -li
infring|e ɪnˈfrɪndʒ **-es** -ɪz **-ing** -ɪŋ **-ed** -d **-er/s** -əʳ/z ⓤⓢ -ɚ/z
infringement ɪnˈfrɪndʒ.mənt **-s** -s
infuri|ate ɪnˈfjʊə.ri|.eɪt, -ˈfjɔː- ⓤⓢ -ˈfjʊr.i- **-ates** -eɪts **-ating/ly** -eɪ.tɪŋ/li ⓤⓢ -eɪ.t̬ɪŋ/li **-ated** -eɪ.tɪd ⓤⓢ -eɪ.t̬ɪd
infus|e ɪnˈfjuːz **-es** -ɪz **-ing** -ɪŋ **-ed** -d **-er/s** -əʳ/z ⓤⓢ -ɚ/z
infusible *capable of being infused:* ɪnˈfjuː.zə.bl̩, -zɪ- *not fusible:* ɪnˈfjuː.zə.bl̩, ˌɪn-, -zɪ-
infusion ɪnˈfjuː.ʒᵊn **-s** -z
infusori|an ˌɪn.fjʊˈzɔː.ri|.ən, -ˈsɔː- ⓤⓢ -ˈsɔːr.i- **-al** -əl
infusory ɪnˈfjuː.zᵊr.i, -sᵊr- ⓤⓢ -sɚ-, -zɚ-
in futuro ˌɪn.fjuːˈtjʊə.rəʊ ⓤⓢ -ˈtʊr.oʊ, -ˈtjʊr-
-ing -ɪŋ
Note: Suffix. Normally unstressed, e.g. **shopping** /ˈʃɒp.ɪŋ ⓤⓢ ˈʃɑː.pɪŋ/.
Inga ˈɪŋ.ə, -gə ⓤⓢ -gə
Ingall ˈɪŋ.gɔːl ⓤⓢ -gəl
Ingalls ˈɪŋ.gɔːlz ⓤⓢ -gəlz
Ingatestone ˈɪn.gət.stəʊn, ˈɪŋ- ⓤⓢ -stoʊn
ingathering ˈɪnˌgæð.ᵊr.ɪŋ **-s** -z
Inge *surname:* ɪŋ, ɪndʒ
Note: The American playwright is pronounced /ɪndʒ/. *girl's name:* ˈɪŋ.ə, -gə ⓤⓢ -gə
Ingelow ˈɪn.dʒɪ.ləʊ ⓤⓢ -loʊ
in genere ˌɪnˈdʒen.ᵊr.eɪ ⓤⓢ -ɚ.i
ingenious ɪnˈdʒiː.ni.əs, ˌɪn- ⓤⓢ ˈ-njəs, -ni.əs **-ly** -li **-ness** -nəs, -nɪs
ingénue, ingenue ˈæ̃n.ʒeɪ.njuː, ˈæn-, -ʒə-, -ʒen.juː, ˌ--ˈ- ⓤⓢ ˈæn.ʒə.nuː, ˈɑːn-, -dʒə-, -njuː **-s** -z
ingenuit|y ˌɪn.dʒɪˈnjuː.ə.t|i, -dʒəˈ-, -ɪ.t|i ⓤⓢ -ə.t̬|i **-ies** -iz
ingenuous ɪnˈdʒen.ju.əs **-ly** -li **-ness** -nəs, -nɪs
Ingersoll® ˈɪŋ.gə.sɒl ⓤⓢ -gɚ.sɑːl, -sɔːl **-s** -z
ingest ɪnˈdʒest **-s** -s **-ing** -ɪŋ **-ed** -ɪd **-ible** -ə.bl̩, -ɪ-
inges|tion ɪnˈdʒes|.tʃᵊn **-tive** -tɪv
Ingham ˈɪŋ.əm
ingle (I) ˈɪŋ.gl̩ **-s** -z
Ingleborough ˈɪŋ.gl̩.bᵊr.ə ⓤⓢ -oʊ
Ingleby ˈɪŋ.gl̩.bi
inglenook ˈɪŋ.gl̩.nʊk **-s** -s
Inglewood ˈɪŋ.gl̩.wʊd
Inglis ˈɪŋ.gᵊlz, -glɪs
inglorious ɪnˈglɔː.ri.əs, ˌɪn-, ɪŋ-, ˌɪŋ- ⓤⓢ -ˈglɔːr.i- **-ly** -li **-ness** -nəs, -nɪs
Ingmar ˈɪŋ.mɑːʳ ⓤⓢ -mɑːr
ingoing ˈɪnˌgəʊ.ɪŋ, ˈɪŋ- ⓤⓢ ˈɪnˌgoʊ-
Ingold ˈɪŋ.gəʊld ⓤⓢ -goʊld
Ingoldsby ˈɪŋ.gᵊldz.bi
ingot ˈɪŋ.gət, -gɒt ⓤⓢ -gət **-s** -s
Ingraham ˈɪŋ.grə.həm, -grɪəm ⓤⓢ ˈɪŋ.grəm
ingrain ɪnˈgreɪn, ˌɪn-, ɪŋ-, ˌɪŋ- ⓤⓢ ɪn-, ˌɪn- **-s** -z **-ing** -ɪŋ **-ed** -d *stress shift:* ˌingrained ˈhabits
Ingram ˈɪŋ.grəm
Ingrams ˈɪŋ.grəmz
ingrate ˈɪn.greɪt, ˈɪŋ-, -ˈ- ⓤⓢ ˈɪn.greɪt, -ˈ- **-s** -s **-ly** -li
ingrati|ate ɪnˈgreɪ.ʃi|.eɪt, ɪŋ- ⓤⓢ ɪn- **-ates** -eɪts **-ating** -eɪ.tɪŋ ⓤⓢ -eɪ.t̬ɪŋ **-ated** -eɪ.tɪd ⓤⓢ -eɪ.t̬ɪd
ingratitude ɪnˈgræt.ɪ.tjuːd, ˌɪn-, ɪŋ-, ˌɪŋ-, ˈ-ə- ⓤⓢ ɪnˈgræt̬.ə.tuːd, ˌɪn-, -tjuːd
Ingrebourne ˈɪŋ.grɪ.bɔːn ⓤⓢ -bɔːrn
ingredient ɪnˈgriː.di.ənt, ɪŋ- ⓤⓢ ɪn- **-s** -s
Ingres ˈæŋ.grə, ˈæ̃ŋ- ⓤⓢ ˈæŋ-, ˈæ̃ŋ, ˈæn-
ingress ˈɪn.gres, ˈɪŋ- ⓤⓢ ˈɪn-
ingressive ɪnˈgres.ɪv, ɪŋ- ⓤⓢ ɪn-
Ingrey ˈɪŋ.gri
Ingrid ˈɪŋ.grɪd
in-group ˈɪn.gruːp, ˈɪŋ- ⓤⓢ ˈɪn- **-s** -s
ingrow|ing ɪnˈgrəʊ|.ɪŋ, ˌɪn-, ɪŋ-, ˌɪŋ-, ˈ-ˌ-- ⓤⓢ ˈɪn.groʊ- ˌ**ingrowing** ˈ**toenail**
ingrown ɪnˈgrəʊn, ˌɪn-, ɪŋ-, ˌɪŋ ⓤⓢ ˈɪn.groʊn *stress shift, British only:* ˌingrown ˈtoenail
ingrowth ˈɪn.grəʊθ, -ˈɪŋ- ⓤⓢ -groʊθ **-s** -s
inguinal ˈɪŋ.gwɪ.nᵊl, -gwə-
inhab|it ɪnˈhæb|.ɪt **-its** -ɪts **-iting** -ɪ.tɪŋ ⓤⓢ -ɪ.t̬ɪŋ **-ited** -ɪ.tɪd ⓤⓢ -ɪ.t̬ɪd **-iter/s** -ɪ.təʳ/z ⓤⓢ -ɪ.t̬ɚ/z **-itable** -ɪ.tə.bl̩ ⓤⓢ -ɪ.t̬ə.bl̩
inhabitant ɪnˈhæb.ɪ.tᵊnt **-s** -s
inhabitation ɪnˌhæb.ɪˈteɪ.ʃᵊn
inhalation ˌɪn.*h*əˈleɪ.ʃᵊn **-s** -z
inhal|e ɪnˈheɪl **-es** -z **-ing** -ɪŋ **-ed** -d **-ant/s** -ənt/s **-er/s** -əʳ/z ⓤⓢ -ɚ/z
inharmonious ˌɪn.hɑːˈməʊ.ni.əs ⓤⓢ -hɑːrˈmoʊ- **-ly** -li **-ness** -nəs, -nɪs
inher|e ɪnˈhɪəʳ ⓤⓢ -ˈhɪr **-es** -z **-ing** -ɪŋ **-ed** -d
inheren|ce ɪnˈher.ᵊn*t*|s, -ˈhɪə.rᵊn*t*|s ⓤⓢ -ˈhɪr.ᵊn*t*|s, -ˈher- **-cy** -si
inherent ɪnˈher.ᵊnt, -ˈhɪə.rᵊnt ⓤⓢ -ˈhɪr.ᵊnt, -ˈher- **-ly** -li
inher|it ɪnˈher|.ɪt **-its** -ɪts **-iting** -ɪ.tɪŋ ⓤⓢ -ɪ.t̬ɪŋ **-ited** -ɪ.tɪd ⓤⓢ -ɪ.t̬ɪd **-itor/s** -ɪ.təʳ/z ⓤⓢ -ɪ.t̬ɚ/z **-itable** -ɪ.tə.bl̩ ⓤⓢ -ɪ.t̬ə.bl̩
inheritanc|e ɪnˈher.ɪ.tᵊn*t*s **-es** -ɪz
inheritrix ɪnˈher.ɪ.trɪks **-es** -ɪz
inhib|it ɪnˈhɪb|.ɪt **-its** -ɪts **-iting** -ɪ.tɪŋ ⓤⓢ -ɪ.t̬ɪŋ **-ited** -ɪ.tɪd ⓤⓢ -ɪ.t̬ɪd **-itor/s** -ɪ.təʳ/z ⓤⓢ -ɪ.t̬ɚ/z **-itory** -ɪ.tᵊr.i ⓤⓢ -ɪ.tɔːr.i
inhibition ˌɪn.*h*ɪˈbɪʃ.ᵊn **-s** -z
inhospitab|le ˌɪn.hɒsˈpɪt.ə.b|l̩; ɪnˈhɒs.pɪ.tə-, ˌɪn-, -pə- ⓤⓢ ɪnˈhɑː.spɪ.t̬ə-, ˌɪn-; ˌɪn.hɑːˈspɪt̬.ə- **-ly** -li **-leness** -l̩.nəs, -nɪs
inhospitality ɪnˌhɒs.pɪˈtæl.ə.ti, ˌɪn-, -ɪ.ti ⓤⓢ -ˌhɑː.spəˈtæl.ə.t̬i
in-house ˌɪnˈhaʊs *stress shift:* ˌin-house proˈduction
inhuman ɪnˈhjuː.mən, ˌɪn- **-ly** -li
inhumane ˌɪn.hjuːˈmeɪn, -hjʊˈ- **-ly** -li
inhumanit|y ˌɪn.hjuːˈmæn.ə.t|i, -hjʊˈ-, -ɪ.t|i ⓤⓢ -ə.t̬|i **-ies** -iz
inhumation ˌɪn.hjuːˈmeɪ.ʃᵊn, -hjʊˈ- **-s** -z
inhum|e ɪnˈhjuːm **-es** -z **-ing** -ɪŋ **-ed** -d
Inigo ˈɪn.ɪ.gəʊ ⓤⓢ -goʊ
inimic|al ɪˈnɪm.ɪ.k|ᵊl **-ally** -ᵊl.i, -li
inimitability ɪˌnɪm.ɪ.təˈbɪl.ə.ti, ˌ-ə-, -ɪ.ti ⓤⓢ -t̬əˈbɪl.ə.t̬i
inimitab|le ɪˈnɪm.ɪ.tə.b|l̩, ˈ-ə- ⓤⓢ -t̬ə- **-ly** -li **-leness** -l̩.nəs, -nɪs
iniquitous ɪˈnɪk.wɪ.təs, -wə- ⓤⓢ -t̬əs **-ly** -li
iniquit|y ɪˈnɪk.wə.t|i, -wɪ- ⓤⓢ -t̬|i **-ies** -iz
initial ɪˈnɪʃ|.ᵊl **-s** -ᵊlz **-ly** -ᵊl.i, -li **-(l)ing** -ᵊl.ɪŋ, -lɪŋ **-(l)ed** -ᵊld
initialization, -isa- ɪˌnɪʃ.ᵊl.aɪˈzeɪ.ʃᵊn, -ɪˈ- ⓤⓢ -ɪˈ-
initializ|e, -is|e ɪˈnɪʃ.ᵊl.aɪz **-es** -ɪz **-ing** -ɪŋ **-ed** -d
initiate (*n.*) ɪˈnɪʃ.i.ət, -eɪt, -ɪt **-s** -s
initi|ate (*v.*) ɪˈnɪʃ.i|.eɪt **-ates** -eɪts **-ating** -eɪ.tɪŋ ⓤⓢ -eɪ.t̬ɪŋ **-ated** -eɪ.tɪd ⓤⓢ -eɪ.t̬ɪd **-ator/s** -eɪ.təʳ/z ⓤⓢ -eɪ.t̬ɚ/z
initiation ɪˌnɪʃ.iˈeɪ.ʃᵊn **-s** -z
initiative ɪˈnɪʃ.ə.tɪv, -i.ə- ⓤⓢ -t̬ɪv **-s** -z
initiatory ɪˈnɪʃ.ə.tᵊr.i, -i.ə-, -eɪ- ⓤⓢ -ə.tɔːr.i
initio ɪˈnɪʃ.i.əʊ, -ˈnɪt-, -ˈnɪs- ⓤⓢ -oʊ
inject ɪnˈdʒekt **-s** -s **-ing** -ɪŋ **-ed** -ɪd **-or/s** -əʳ/z ⓤⓢ -ɚ/z **-able** -ə.bl̩
injection ɪnˈdʒek.ʃᵊn **-s** -z
injudicious ˌɪn.dʒuːˈdɪʃ.əs **-ly** -li **-ness** -nəs, -nɪs

Injun ˈɪn.dʒən **-s** -z

injunction ɪnˈdʒʌŋ*k*.ʃᵊn **-s** -z

injurant ˈɪn.dʒʊ.rənt, -dʒə.rənt **-s** -s

inj|ure ˈɪn.dʒ|əʳ (US) -dʒ|ɚ **-ures** -əz (US) -ɚz **-uring** -ᵊr.ɪŋ **-ured** -əd (US) -ɚd **-urer/s** -ᵊr.əʳ/z (US) -ɚ.ɚ/z

injuria absque damno ɪnˌdʒʊə.ri.əˌæb.skweɪˈdæm.nəʊ (US) -ˌdʒʊr.i.əˌæb.skweɪˈdæm.noʊ

injurious ɪnˈdʒʊə.ri.əs, -ˈdʒɔː- (US) -ˈdʒʊr.i- **-ly** -li **-ness** -nəs, -nɪs

injur|y ˈɪn.dʒᵊr|.i **-ies** -iz ˈ**injury ˌtime**

injustic|e ɪnˈdʒʌs.tɪs, ˌɪn- **-es** -ɪz

ink ɪŋk **-s** -s **-ing** -ɪŋ **-ed** -t **-er/s** -əʳ/z (US) -ɚ/z

Inkatha ɪnˈkɑː.tə, ɪŋ-

inkblot ˈɪŋk.blɒt (US) -blɑːt **-s** -s

Inkerman ˈɪŋ.kə.mən (US) -kɚ-

inkhorn ˈɪŋk.hɔːn (US) -hɔːrn **-s** -z

inkjet ˈɪŋk.dʒet **-s** -s

inkling ˈɪŋk.lɪŋ **-s** -z

Inkpen ˈɪŋk.pen

inkpot ˈɪŋk.pɒt (US) -pɑːt **-s** -s

ink-stain ˈɪŋk.steɪn **-s** -z

inkstand ˈɪŋk.stænd **-s** -z

inkwell ˈɪŋk.wel **-s** -z

ink|y ˈɪŋ.k|i **-ier** -i.əʳ (US) -i.ɚ **-iest** -i.ɪst, -i.əst **-iness** -ɪ.nəs, -ɪ.nɪs

INLA ˌaɪ.en.elˈeɪ

inlaid (*from* **inlay**) ɪnˈleɪd (US) ˈ-- *stress shift, British only:* ˌinlaid ˈgold

inland (*n. adj.*) ˈɪn.lənd, -lænd **-s** -z ˌ**Inland ˈRevenue**

inland (*adv.*) ˈɪn.lænd, -ˈ-

inlander ˈɪn.lən.dəʳ (US) -dɚ, -læn- **-s** -z

in-law ˈɪn.lɔː (US) -lɑː, -lɔː **-s** -z

inlay (*n.*) ˈɪn.leɪ

in|lay (*v.*) ɪn|ˈleɪ, ˌɪn- (US) ɪn|ˈleɪ, ˌɪn-, ˈɪn|.leɪ **-lays** -ˈleɪz (US) -ˈleɪz, -leɪz **-laying** -ˈleɪ.ɪŋ (US) -ˈleɪ-, -ˌleɪ-

inlet ˈɪn.let, -lət, -lɪt **-s** -s

in loco parentis ɪnˌləʊ.kəʊ.pəˈren.tɪs, -ˌlɒk.əʊ- (US) -ˌloʊ.koʊ.pəˈren.t̬ɪs

inly ˈɪn.li

Inman ˈɪn.mən, ˈɪm- (US) ˈɪn-

inmate ˈɪn.meɪt, ˈɪm- (US) ˈɪn- **-s** -s

in medias res ɪnˌmiː.di.æsˈreɪs, ɪm-, -ˌmeɪ-, -ˌmed.i-, -ɑːsˈ-, -əsˈ-, -ˈreɪz (US) ɪnˌmiː.di.əsˈreɪs, -ˌmed.i-, -ˈreɪz

in memoriam ˌɪn.mɪˈmɔː.ri.əm, ˌɪm-, -məˈ-, -æm (US) ˌɪn.mɪˈmɔːr.i-, -məˈ-

inmost ˈɪn.məʊst, ˈɪm- (US) ˈɪn.moʊst

inn ɪn **-s** -z

innards ˈɪn.ədz (US) -ɚdz

innate ɪˈneɪt, ˌɪnˈeɪt **-ly** -li **-ness** -nəs, -nɪs

innavigable *ɪn*ˈnæv.ɪ.gə.bl̩, ˌɪnˈnæv-, ˈ-ə-

inner ˈɪn.əʳ (US) -ɚ ˌ**inner ˈcity**; ˈ**inner ˌtube**

inner-city ˈɪn.əˌsɪt.i (US) -ɚˌsɪt̬-

innermost ˈɪn.ə.məʊst (US) -ɚ.moʊst

inner|vate ˈɪn.ə|.veɪt; ɪˈnɜː-, ˌɪnˈɜː- (US) ɪˈnɜːr-, ˌɪnˈɜːr-; ˈɪn.ɚ- **-vates** -veɪts **-vating** -veɪ.tɪŋ (US) -veɪ.t̬ɪŋ **-vated** -veɪ.tɪd (US) -veɪ.t̬ɪd

innervation ˌɪn.əˈveɪ.ʃᵊn (US) -ɚˈ-

Innes(s) ˈɪn.ɪs

inning ˈɪn.ɪŋ **-s** -z **-ses** -zɪz

innings ˈɪn.ɪŋz **-es** -ɪz

Innisfail ˌɪn.ɪsˈfeɪl, -əsˈ-

Innisfree ˌɪn.ɪsˈfriː, -əsˈ-

innit ˈɪn.ɪt

innkeeper ˈɪnˌkiː.pəʳ, ˈɪŋ- (US) -pɚ **-s** -z

innocen|ce ˈɪn.ə.sᵊn*t*|s **-cy** -si

innocent (I) ˈɪn.ə.sᵊnt **-s** -s **-ly** -li

innocuous ɪˈnɒk.ju.əs (US) -ˈnɑːk- **-ly** -li **-ness** -nəs, -nɪs

innominate ɪˈnɒm.ɪ.nət, ˈ-ə-, -nɪt, -neɪt (US) -ˈnɑːm.ə-

inno|vate ˈɪn.əʊ|.veɪt (US) ˈ-ə- **-vates** -veɪts **-vating** -veɪ.tɪŋ (US) -veɪ.t̬ɪŋ **-vated** -veɪ.tɪd (US) -veɪ.t̬ɪd **-vator/s** -veɪ.təʳ/z (US) -veɪ.t̬ɚ/z

innovation ˌɪn.əʊˈveɪ.ʃᵊn (US) -əˈ- **-s** -z

innovative ˈɪn.ə.və.tɪv, -veɪ-; ɪˈnəʊ.və.tɪv (US) ˈɪn.ə.veɪ.t̬ɪv

innovatory ˈɪn.əʊ.veɪ.tᵊr.i, -və- (US) ˈɪn.ə.və.tɔːr.i

innoxious ɪˈnɒk.ʃəs (US) -ˈnɑːk- **-ly** -li **-ness** -nəs, -nɪs

Innsbruck ˈɪnz.brʊk

Innsworth ˈɪnz.wəθ, -wɜːθ (US) -wɚθ, -wɜːrθ

innuendo ˌɪn.juˈen.dəʊ (US) -doʊ **-(e)s** -z

innumerability ɪˌnjuː.mᵊr.əˈbɪl.ə.ti, ˌɪnˌjuː-, -ɪ.ti (US) ɪˌnuː.mɚ.əˈbɪl.ə.t̬i, ˌɪnˌuː-, -ˌjuː-

innumerab|le ɪˈnjuː.mᵊr.ə.b|l̩, ˌɪnˈjuː- (US) ɪˈnuː-, ˌɪnˈuː-, -ˈjuː- **-ly** -li **-leness** -l̩.nəs, -nɪs

innumeracy ɪˈnjuː.mᵊr.ə.si, ˌɪnˈjuː- (US) ɪˈnuː-, ˌɪnˈuː-, -ˈjuː-

innumerate ɪˈnjuː.mᵊr.ət, ˌɪnˈjuː- (US) ɪˈnuː.mɚ-, ˌɪnˈuː-, -ˈjuː- **-s** -s

innutriti|on ˌɪn.*n*juːˈtrɪʃ|.ᵊn (US) -*n*uːˈ-, -*n*juːˈ- **-ous** -əs

inobservan|ce ˌɪn.əbˈzɜː.vᵊn|*t*s (US) -ˈzɜːr- **-t** -t

inoccupation ɪˌnɒk.jʊˈpeɪ.ʃᵊn, ˌɪnˌɒk- (US) ɪˌnɑː.kjəˈ-, ˌɪnˌɑː-

inocu|late ɪˈnɒk.jə|.leɪt, -jʊ- (US) -ˈnɑː.kjə- **-lates** -leɪts **-lating** -leɪ.tɪŋ (US) -leɪ.t̬ɪŋ **-lated** -leɪ.tɪd (US) -leɪ.t̬ɪd **-lator/s** -leɪ.təʳ/z (US) -leɪ.t̬ɚ/z

inoculation ɪˌnɒk.jəˈleɪ.ʃᵊn, -jʊˈ- (US) -ˌnɑː.kjəˈ- **-s** -z

inodorous ɪˈnəʊ.dᵊr.əs, ˌɪnˈəʊ- (US) ˌɪnˈoʊ-, ɪˈnoʊ-

inoffensive ˌɪn.əˈfen*t*.sɪv **-ly** -li **-ness** -nəs, -nɪs

inofficious ˌɪn.əˈfɪʃ.əs

in omnibus ˌɪnˈɒm.nɪ.bəs, -bʊs (US) -ˈɑːm.nɪ-, -niː-

inoperable ɪˈnɒp.ᵊr.ə.bl̩, ˌɪnˈɒp- (US) ˌɪnˈɑː.pɚ-, ɪˈnɑː-

inoperative ɪˈnɒp.ᵊr.ə.tɪv, ˌɪnˈɒp- (US) ˌɪnˈɑː.pɚ.ə.t̬ɪv, ɪˈnɑː-

inopportune ɪˈnɒp.ə.tjuːn, ˌɪnˈɒp-, -tʃuːn; ˌɪn.ɒp.əˈtjuːn, -ˈtʃuːn (US) ˌɪnˌɑː.pɚˈtuːn, ɪˌnɑː-, -ˈtjuːn **-ly** -li **-ness** -nəs, -nɪs

inordinate ɪˈnɔː.dɪ.nət, ˌɪnˈɔː-, -dᵊn.ət, -ɪt (US) ˌɪnˈɔːr.dᵊn.ɪt, ɪˈnɔːr- **-ly** -li **-ness** -nəs, -nɪs

inorganic ˌɪn.ɔːˈgæn.ɪk (US) -ɔːrˈ- **-ally** -ᵊl.i, -li

inoscu|late ɪˈnɒs.kjə|.leɪt, -kjʊ- (US) -ˈnɑː.skjuː-, ˌɪnˈɑː- **-lates** -leɪts **-lating** -leɪ.tɪŋ (US) -leɪ.t̬ɪŋ **-lated** -leɪ.tɪd (US) -leɪ.t̬ɪd

inosculation ɪˌnɒs.kjəˈleɪ.ʃᵊn (US) -ˌnɑː.skjuːˈ-, ˌɪnˌɑː-

in pais ˌɪnˈpeɪs (US) ˌɪnˈpeɪ

in pari delicto ɪnˌpær.i.dɪˈlɪk.təʊ (US) -dəˈlɪk.toʊ, -ˌpɑːr-

in pari materia ɪnˌpær.i.məˈtɪə.ri.ə (US) -ˈtɪr.i.ə, -ˌpɑːr-

inpatient ˈɪnˌpeɪ.ʃᵊnt **-s** -s

in personam ˌɪn.pɜːˈsəʊ.næm, ˌɪm-, -pəˈ-, -nəm (US) ˌɪn.pɚˈsoʊ.næm

in praesenti ˌɪn.praɪˈsen.tiː (US) -prɪˈzen.tiː

in|put ˈɪn|.pʊt, ˈɪm- **-puts** -pʊts **-putting** -ˌpʊt.ɪŋ (US) -ˌpʊt̬.ɪŋ **-putted** -ˌpʊt.ɪd (US) -ˌpʊt̬.ɪd **-putter/s** -ˌpʊt.əʳ/z (US) -ˌpʊt̬.ɚ/z

input-output ˌɪn.pʊtˈaʊt.pʊt, ˌɪm-

inquest ˈɪŋ.kwest, ˈɪn- (US) ˈɪn- **-s** -s

inquietude ɪnˈkwaɪə.tjuːd, ɪŋ-, -ˈkwaɪ.ɪ- (US) ɪnˈkwaɪə.tuːd, -ˈkwaɪ.ɪ-, -tjuːd

inquiline ˈɪŋ.kwɪ.laɪn, ˈɪn- (US) ˈɪn.kwɪ.laɪn, -lɪn **-s** -z

inquir|e ɪnˈkwaɪəʳ, ɪŋ- (US) ɪnˈkwaɪr **-es** -z **-ing/ly** -ɪŋ/li **-ed** -d **-er/s** -əʳ/z (US) -ɚ/z

inquir|y ɪnˈkwaɪə.r|i, ɪŋ- (US) ɪnˈkwaɪ-; ˈɪn.kwɚ|.i **-ies** -iz

inquisition (I) ˌɪŋ.kwɪˈzɪʃ.ᵊn, ˌɪn- (US) ˌɪn- **-s** -z

inquisitional ˌɪŋ.kwɪˈzɪʃ.ᵊn.ᵊl, ˌɪn- (US) ˌɪn-

inquisitive ɪnˈkwɪz.ə.tɪv, ɪŋ-, ˈ-ɪ- (US) ɪnˈkwɪz.ə.t̬ɪv, ˈ-ɪ- **-ly** -li **-ness** -nəs, -nɪs

inquisitor ɪnˈkwɪz.ɪ.təʳ, ɪŋ- (US) ɪnˈkwɪz.ɪ.t̬ɚ **-s** -z

inquisitorial ɪnˌkwɪz.ɪˈtɔː.ri.əl, ɪŋ-; ˌɪn.kwɪ.zɪˈ-, ˌɪŋ- (US) ɪnˌkwɪz.ɪˈtɔːr.i- **-ly** -i

inquorate ˌɪnˈkwɔː.reɪt, ˌɪŋ-, -rət, -rɪt (US) ɪnˈkwɔːr.eɪt, -ət, -ɪt

in re ˌɪn'reɪ
in rem ˌɪn'rem
inroad 'ɪn.rəʊd (US) -roʊd **-s** -z
inrush 'ɪn.rʌʃ **-es** -ɪz
INS ˌaɪ.en'es
insalubr|ious ˌɪn.sə'luː.br|i.əs, -'ljuː- (US) -'luː- **-ity** -ə.ti, -ɪ.ti (US) -ə.ţi
insane ɪn'seɪn, ˌɪn- **-ly** -li **-ness** -nəs, -nɪs
insanitar|y ɪn'sæn.ɪ.tᵊr|.i, ˌɪn-, '-ə-, -tr|i (US) -ter|.i **-iness** -ɪ.nəs, -nɪs
insanity ɪn'sæn.ə.ti, ˌɪn-, -ɪ.ti (US) -ə.ţi
insatiability ɪnˌseɪ.ʃə'bɪl.ə.ti, -ʃi.ə'-, -ɪ.ti (US) -ə.ţi
insatiab|le ɪn'seɪ.ʃə.bl|, -ʃi.ə- **-ly** -li **-leness** -l̩.nəs, -nɪs
insatiate ɪn'seɪ.ʃi.ət, -ɪt, -eɪt
inscape 'ɪn.skeɪp
inscrib|e ɪn'skraɪb **-es** -z **-ing** -ɪŋ **-ed** -d **-er/s** -əʳ/z (US) -ɚ/z
inscription ɪn'skrɪp.ʃᵊn **-s** -z
inscrutability ɪnˌskruː.tə'bɪl.ə.ti, ˌɪn-, -ɪ.ti (US) -ˌskruː.ţə'bɪl.ə.ţi
inscrutab|le ɪn'skruː.tə.bl|, ˌɪn- (US) -ţə- **-ly** -li **-leness** -l̩.nəs, -nɪs
insect 'ɪn.sekt **-s** -s
insectari|um ˌɪn.sek'teə.ri|.əm (US) -'ter.i- **-ums** -əmz **-a** -ə
insecticidal ɪnˌsek.tɪ'saɪ.dᵊl, -tə'- **-ly** -i
insecticide ɪn'sek.tɪ.saɪd, -tə- **-s** -z
insectivore ɪn'sek.tɪ.vɔːʳ, -tə- (US) -vɔːr **-s** -z
insectivorous ˌɪn.sek'tɪv.ᵊr.əs
insecure ˌɪn.sɪ'kjʊəʳ, -sə'-, -'kjɔːʳ (US) -'kjʊr **-ly** -li
insecurit|y ˌɪn.sɪ'kjʊə.rə.t|i, -sə'-, -'kjɔː-, -rɪ- (US) -'kjʊr.ə.ţ|i **-ies** -iz
insemi|nate ɪn'sem.ɪ|.neɪt, '-ə- **-nates** -neɪts **-nating** -neɪ.tɪŋ (US) -neɪ.ţɪŋ **-nated** -neɪ.tɪd (US) -neɪ.ţɪd **-nator/s** -neɪ.təʳ/z (US) -neɪ.ţɚ/z
insemination ɪnˌsem.ɪ'neɪ.ʃᵊn, ˌɪn-, -ə'-
insensate ɪn'sent.seɪt, ˌɪn-, -sət, -sɪt **-ly** -li **-ness** -nəs, -nɪs
insensibility ɪnˌsent.sə'bɪl.ə.ti, ˌɪn-, -sɪ'-, -ɪ.ti (US) -ə.ţi
insensib|le ɪn'sent.sə.bl|, ˌɪn-, -sɪ- **-ly** -li **-leness** -l̩.nəs, -nɪs
insensitive ɪn'sent.sə.tɪv, ˌɪn-, -sɪ- (US) -ţɪv **-ness** -nəs, -nɪs
insensitivity ɪnˌsent.sə'tɪv.ə.ti, ˌɪn-, -sɪ'-, -ɪ.ti (US) -ə.ţi
insentien|t ˌɪn'sen.*t*ʃᵊn|t, -*t*ʃi.ən|t **-ce** -*t*s
inseparability ɪnˌsep.ᵊr.ə'bɪl.ə.ti, ˌɪn-, ˌ-rə'-, -ɪ.ti (US) -ə.ţi
inseparab|le ɪn'sep.ᵊr.ə.bl|, ˌɪn-, '-rə- **-ly** -li **-leness** -l̩.nəs, -nɪs
insert (*n.*) 'ɪn.sɜːt (US) -sɜːrt **-s** -s
in|sert (*v.*) ɪn|'sɜːt (US) -'sɜːrt **-serts** -'sɜːts (US) -'sɜːrts **-serting** -'sɜː.tɪŋ (US) -'sɜːr.ţɪŋ **-serted** -'sɜː.tɪd (US) -'sɜːr.ţɪd
insertion ɪn'sɜː.ʃᵊn (US) -'sɜːr- **-s** -z
in-service ˌɪn'sɜː.vɪs (US) 'ɪnˌsɜːr- *stress shift, British only:* ˌin-service 'training
inset (*n.*) 'ɪn.set **-s** -s
inse|t (*v.*) ˌɪn'se|t (US) ɪn'se|t, '-- **-ts** -ts **-tting** -tɪŋ (US) -ţɪŋ
inseverable ɪn'sev.ᵊr.ə.bl̩, ˌɪn-
inshore ˌɪn'ʃɔːʳ (US) -'ʃɔːr *stress shift:* ˌinshore 'rescue
inside ˌɪn'saɪd, '-- **-s** -z ˌ**inside 'job** (US) '**inside ˌjob**; ˌ**inside 'out**
insider ɪn'saɪ.dəʳ, ˌɪn- (US) 'ɪnˌsaɪ.dɚ, -'-- **-s** -z **inˌsider 'dealing** (US) ˌ**insider 'dealing**; **inˌsider 'trading** (US) ˌ**insider 'trading**
insidious ɪn'sɪd.i.əs **-ly** -li **-ness** -nəs, -nɪs
insight 'ɪn.saɪt **-s** -s
insightful 'ɪn.saɪt.fᵊl, -fʊl (US) 'ɪnˌsaɪt.fᵊl, -'-- **-ly** -li
insignia ɪn'sɪg.ni.ə **-s** -z
insignifican|ce ˌɪn.sɪg'nɪf.ɪ.kᵊnt|s **-cy** -si
insignificant ˌɪn.sɪg'nɪf.ɪ.kᵊnt **-ly** -li
insincere ˌɪn.sɪn'sɪəʳ, -sᵊn'- (US) -'sɪr **-ly** -li
insincerit|y ˌɪn.sɪn'ser.ə.t|i, -sᵊn'-, -ɪ.t|i (US) -ə.ţ|i **-ies** -iz
insinu|ate ɪn'sɪn.ju|.eɪt **-ates** -eɪts **-ating/ly** -eɪ.tɪŋ/li (US) -eɪ.ţɪŋ/li **-ated** -eɪ.tɪd (US) -eɪ.ţɪd **-ator/s** -eɪ.təʳ/z (US) -eɪ.ţɚ/z
insinuation ɪnˌsɪn.ju'eɪ.ʃᵊn, ˌɪn- **-s** -z
insipid ɪn'sɪp.ɪd **-ly** -li **-ness** -nəs, -nɪs
insipidity ˌɪn.sɪ'pɪd.ə.ti, -ɪ.ti (US) -ɪ.ţi
insipien|ce ɪn'sɪp.i.ən|*t*s **-t** -t
insist ɪn'sɪst **-s** -s **-ing** -ɪŋ **-ed** -ɪd
insisten|ce ɪn'sɪs.tᵊnt|s **-cy** -si
insistent ɪn'sɪs.tᵊnt **-ly** -li
in situ ˌɪn'sɪt.juː, -'sɪtʃ.uː, -'saɪ.tjuː, -tʃuː (US) -'saɪ.tuː, -'siː-, -'sɪt.uː, -juː
Inskip 'ɪn.skɪp
insobriety ˌɪn.səʊ'braɪ.ə.ti, -'braɪ.ɪ- (US) -soʊ'braɪ.ə.ţi
insofar ˌɪn.səʊ'fɑːʳ (US) -soʊ'fɑːr
insolation ˌɪn.səʊ'leɪ.ʃᵊn (US) -soʊ'-
insole 'ɪn.səʊl (US) -soʊl **-s** -z
insolence 'ɪn*t*.sᵊl.ən*t*s
insolent 'ɪn*t*.sᵊl.ənt **-ly** -li
insolubility ɪnˌsɒl.jə'bɪl.ə.ti, ˌɪn-, -jʊ'-, -ɪ.ti (US) -ˌsɑːl.jə'bɪl.ə.ţi
insolub|le ɪn'sɒl.jə.bl|, ˌɪn-, -jʊ- (US) -'sɑːl.jə- **-ly** -li **-leness** -l̩.nəs, -nɪs
insolvable ɪn'sɒl.və.bl̩, ˌɪn- (US) -'sɑːl-
insolven|cy ɪn'sɒl.vᵊn|*t*.si, ˌɪn- (US) -'sɑːl- **-t** -t
insomnia ɪn'sɒm.ni.ə (US) -'sɑːm-
insomniac ɪn'sɒm.ni.æk (US) -'sɑːm- **-s** -s
insomuch ˌɪn.səʊ'mʌtʃ (US) -soʊ'-
insouciance ɪn'suː.si.ən*t*s (US) -si.ən*t*s, -ʃən*t*s
insouciant ɪn'suː.si.ənt (US) -si.ənt, -ʃənt **-ly** -li
in specie ˌɪn'spes.i.eɪ (US) ˌɪn'spiː.ʃi, -si
inspect ɪn'spekt **-s** -s **-ing** -ɪŋ **-ed** -ɪd
inspection ɪn'spek.ʃᵊn **-s** -z
inspector ɪn'spek.təʳ **-s** -z
inspectorate ɪn'spek.tᵊr.ət, -ɪt **-s** -s
inspectorship ɪn'spek.tə.ʃɪp (US) -tɚ- **-s** -s
inspiration ˌɪn*t*.spᵊr'eɪ.ʃᵊn, -spɪ'reɪ- (US) -spə'reɪ- **-s** -z
inspirational ˌɪn*t*.spᵊr'eɪ.ʃᵊn.əl, -spɪ'reɪ- (US) -spə'reɪ- **-ly** -i
inspirator 'ɪn*t*.spᵊr.eɪ.təʳ, -spɪ.reɪ- (US) -spə.reɪ.ţɚ **-s** -z
inspiratory ɪn'spaɪə.rə.tᵊr.i, -'spɪr.ə- (US) -'spaɪ.rə.tɔːr-
inspir|e ɪn'spaɪəʳ (US) -'spaɪr **-es** -z **-ing/ly** -ɪŋ/li **-ed** -d **-er/s** -əʳ/z (US) -ɚ/z
inspir|it ɪn'spɪr|.ɪt **-its** -ɪts **-iting** -ɪ.tɪŋ (US) -ɪ.ţɪŋ **-ited** -ɪ.tɪd (US) -ɪ.ţɪd
inspiss|ate ɪn'spɪs|.eɪt; 'ɪn.spɪ.s|eɪt (US) ɪn'spɪs|.eɪt **-ates** -eɪts **-ating** -eɪ.tɪŋ (US) -eɪ.ţɪŋ **-ated** -eɪ.tɪd (US) -eɪ.ţɪd
inst. (*abbrev. for* **instant**) ɪntst, 'ɪn*t*.stᵊnt
inst. (**I**) (*abbrev. for* **institute**) ɪntst, 'ɪn*t*.stɪ.tjuːt, -stə-, -tʃuːt (US) -tuːt, -tjuːt
instabilit|y ˌɪn.stə'bɪl.ə.t|i, -ɪ.t|i (US) -ə.ţ|i **-ies** -iz
instal ɪn'stɔːl (US) -'stɔːl, -'stɑːl **-s** -z **-ling** -ɪŋ **-led** -d
install ɪn'stɔːl (US) -'stɔːl, -'stɑːl **-s** -z **-ing** -ɪŋ **-ed** -d **-able** -ə.bl̩
installation ˌɪn.stə'leɪ.ʃᵊn **-s** -z
installer ɪn'stɔː.ləʳ (US) -'stɔː.lɚ, -'stɑː- **-s** -z
instal(l)ment ɪn'stɔːl.mənt (US) -'stɔːl-, -'stɑːl- **-s** -s **in'stallment ˌplan**
instanc|e 'ɪn*t*.stən*t*s **-es** -ɪz **-ing** -ɪŋ **-ed** -t
instant 'ɪn*t*.stənt **-s** -s **-ly** -li
instantaneous ˌɪn*t*.stən'teɪ.ni.əs **-ly** -li **-ness** -nəs, -nɪs
instanter ɪn'stæn.təʳ (US) -ţɚ
in statu quo ɪnˌstæt.juː'kwəʊ (US) -ˌsteɪ.tuː'kwoʊ, -ˌstɑː-
instead ɪn'sted
instep 'ɪn.step **-s** -s
insti|gate 'ɪn*t*.stɪ|.geɪt, -stə- **-gates** -geɪts **-gating** -geɪ.tɪŋ (US) -geɪ.ţɪŋ **-gated** -geɪ.tɪd (US) -geɪ.ţɪd **-gator/s** -geɪ.təʳ/z (US) -geɪ.ţɚ/z
instigation ˌɪn*t*.stɪ'geɪ.ʃᵊn, -stə'- **-s** -z
instil ɪn'stɪl **-s** -z **-ling** -ɪŋ **-led** -d **-ment** -mənt
instill ɪn'stɪl **-s** -z **-ing** -ɪŋ **-ed** -d **-ment** -mənt
instillation ˌɪn*t*.stɪ'leɪ.ʃᵊn, -stə'-
instinct 'ɪn*t*.stɪŋ*k*t **-s** -s

instinctive ɪn'stɪŋ*k*.tɪv **-ly** -li
institu|te 'ɪn*t*.stɪ.tjuːlt, -stə-, -tʃuːlt (US) -tuːlt, -tjuːlt **-tes** -ts **-ting** -tɪŋ (US) -t̬ɪŋ **-ted** -tɪd (US) -t̬ɪd **-tor/s** -təʳ/z (US) -t̬ɚ/z
institution ˌɪn*t*.stɪ'tjuː.ʃᵊn, -stə'-, -'tʃuː- (US) -'tuː-, -'tjuː- **-s** -z
institutional ˌɪn*t*.stɪ'tjuː.ʃᵊn.ᵊl, -stə'-, -'tʃuː- (US) -'tuː-, -'tjuː- **-ly** -li
institutionalization, -isa- ˌɪn*t*.stɪˌtjuː.ʃᵊn.ᵊl.aɪ'zeɪ.ʃᵊn, -stəˌ-, -ˌtʃuː-, -ɪ'- (US) -ˌtuː.ʃᵊn.ᵊl.ɪ'-, -ˌtjuː-
institutionaliz|e, -is|e ˌɪn*t*.stɪ'tjuː.ʃᵊn.ə.laɪz, -stə'-, -'tʃuː- (US) -'tuː-, -'tjuː- **-es** -ɪz **-ing** -ɪŋ **-ed** -d
in-store ˌɪn'stɔːʳ (US) -'stɔːr *stress shift:* ˌin-store 'restaurant
instress ˌɪn'stres
instruct ɪn'strʌkt **-s** -s **-ing** -ɪŋ **-ed** -ɪd
instruction ɪn'strʌk.ʃᵊn **-s** -z
instructional ɪn'strʌk.ʃᵊn.ᵊl **-ly** -i
instructive ɪn'strʌk.tɪv **-ly** -li **-ness** -nəs, -nɪs
instructor ɪn'strʌk.təʳ (US) -tɚ **-s** -z
instrument 'ɪn*t*.strə.mənt, -strʊ- (US) -strə- **-s** -s
instrumental ˌɪn*t*.strə'men.tᵊl, -strʊ'- (US) -strə'men.t̬ᵊl **-ly** -i **-ist/s** -ɪst/s
instrumentality ˌɪn*t*.strə.men'tæl.ə.ti, -strʊ-, -mən'-, -ɪ.ti (US) -strə.men'tæl.ə.t̬i, -mən'-
instrumentation ˌɪn*t*.strə.men'teɪ.ʃᵊn, -strʊ-, -mən'- (US) -strə-
insubordinate ˌɪn.sə'bɔː.dᵊn.ət, -dɪ.nət, -nɪt (US) -'bɔːr.dᵊn.ɪt **-s** -s
insubordination ˌɪn.səˌbɔː.dɪ'neɪ.ʃᵊn, -də'- (US) -ˌbɔːr-
insubstantial ˌɪn.səb'stæn.*t*ʃᵊl, -'stɑːn- (US) -'stæn- **-ly** -i
insufferab|le ɪn'sʌf.ᵊr.ə.bl̩ **-ly** -li
insufficien|ce ˌɪn.sə'fɪʃ.ᵊnt|s **-cy** -si
insufficient ˌɪn.sə'fɪʃ.ᵊnt **-ly** -li
insular 'ɪn*t*.sjə.ləʳ, -sjʊ- (US) -sə.lɚ, -sjə- **-ly** -li **-ism** -ɪ.zᵊm
insularity ˌɪn*t*.sjə'lær.ə.ti, -sjʊ'-, -ɪ.ti (US) -sə'ler.ə.t̬i, -sjə'-, -'lær-
insu|late 'ɪn*t*.sjəl.leɪt, -sjʊ- (US) -sə-, -sjə- **-lates** -leɪts **-lating** -leɪ.tɪŋ (US) -leɪ.t̬ɪŋ **-lated** -leɪ.tɪd (US) -leɪ.t̬ɪd **-lator/s** -leɪ.təʳ/z (US) -leɪ.t̬ɚ/z 'insulating ˌtape
insulation ˌɪn*t*.sjə'leɪ.ʃᵊn, -sjʊ'- (US) -sə'-, -sjə'-
insulin 'ɪn*t*.sjə.lɪn, -sjʊ- (US) -sə-
insult (*n.*) 'ɪn.sʌlt **-s** -s **add ˌinsult to 'injury**
in|sult (*v.*) ɪnl'sʌlt **-sults** -'sʌlts **-sulting/ly** -'sʌl.tɪŋ/li (US) -'sʌl.t̬ɪŋ/li **-sulted** -'sʌl.tɪd (US) -'sʌl.t̬ɪd **-sulter/s** -'sʌl.təʳ/z (US) -'sʌl.t̬ɚ/z
insuperability ɪnˌsuː.pᵊr.ə'bɪl.ə.ti, ˌɪn-, -ˌsjuː-, -ɪ.ti (US) -ˌsuː.pɚ.ə'bɪl.ə.t̬i
insuperab|le ɪn'suː.pᵊr.ə.bl̩|, ˌɪn-, -'sjuː- (US) -'suː- **-ly** -li
insupportab|le ˌɪn.sə'pɔː.tə.bl̩| (US) -'pɔːr.t̬ə- **-ly** -li **-leness** -l̩.nəs, -nɪs
insuppressib|le ˌɪn.sə'pres.ə.bl̩|, '-ɪ- **-ly** -li
insuranc|e ɪn'ʃʊə.rᵊn*t*s, -'ʃɔː- (US) -'ʃʊr.ᵊn*t*s **-es** -ɪz **in'surance ˌbroker ; in'surance ˌpolicy**
insur|e ɪn'ʃʊəʳ, -ʃɔːʳ (US) -'ʃʊr **-es** -z **-ing** -ɪŋ **-ed** -d **-er/s** -əʳ/z (US) -ɚ/z **-able** -ə.bl̩
insurgen|ce ɪn'sɜː.dʒᵊnt|s (US) -'sɜːr- **-cy** -si
insurgent ɪn'sɜː.dʒᵊnt (US) -'sɜːr- **-s** -s
insurmountability ˌɪn.səˌmaʊn.tə'bɪl.ə.ti, -ɪ.ti (US) -sɚˌmaʊn.t̬ə'bɪl.ə.t̬i
insurmountab|le ˌɪn.sə'maʊn.tə.bl̩| (US) -sɚ'maʊn.t̬ə- **-ly** -li
insurrection ˌɪn.sᵊr'ek.ʃᵊn (US) -sə'rek- **-s** -z
insurrectional ˌɪn.sᵊr'ek.ʃᵊn.ᵊl (US) -sə'rek-
insurrectionar|y ˌɪn.sᵊr'ek.ʃᵊn.ᵊr|.i (US) -sə'rek.ʃᵊn.er- **-ies** -iz
insurrection|ism ˌɪn.sᵊr'ek.ʃᵊn|.ɪ.zᵊm (US) -sə'rek- **-ist/s** -ɪst/s
insusceptibility ˌɪn.səˌsep.tə'bɪl.ə.ti, -tɪ'-, -ɪ.ti (US) -ə.t̬i
insusceptib|le ˌɪn.sə'sep.tə.bl̩|, -tɪ- **-ly** -li
intact ɪn'tækt, ˌɪn- **-ness** -nəs, -nɪs
intaglio ɪn'tɑː.li.əʊ, -'tæl.i- (US) -'tæl.joʊ, -'tɑːl- **-s** -z
intake 'ɪn.teɪk **-s** -s
intangibility ɪnˌtæn.dʒə'bɪl.ə.ti, ˌɪn-, -dʒɪ'-, -ɪ.ti (US) -ə.t̬i
intangib|le ɪn'tæn.dʒə.bl̩|, ˌɪn-, -dʒɪ- **-ly** -li **-leness** -l̩.nəs, -nɪs
integer 'ɪn.tɪ.dʒəʳ, -tə- (US) -dʒɚ, -t̬ə- **-s** -z
integral (*n.*) 'ɪn.tɪ.grəl, -tə- (US) -t̬ə- **-s** -z
integral (*adj.*) 'ɪn.tɪ.grəl, -tə-; ɪn'teg.rəl (US) 'ɪn.t̬ə.grəl; ɪn'teg.rəl **-ly** -i
Note: As a mathematical term always /'ɪn.tɪ.grəl (US) -t̬ə-/.
inte|grate 'ɪn.tɪl.greɪt, -tə- (US) -t̬ə- **-grates** -greɪts **-grating** -greɪ.tɪŋ (US) -greɪ.t̬ɪŋ **-grated** -greɪ.tɪd (US) -greɪ.t̬ɪd **-grator/s** -greɪ.təʳ/z (US) -greɪ.t̬ɚ/z **ˌintegrated 'circuit**
integration ˌɪn.tɪ'greɪ.ʃᵊn, -tə'- (US) -t̬ə'- **-s** -z
integrity ɪn'teg.rə.ti, -rɪ- (US) -t̬i
integument ɪn'teg.jə.mənt, -jʊ- **-s** -s
intellect 'ɪn.tᵊl.ekt, -tɪ.lekt (US) -t̬ə.lekt **-s** -s
intellection ˌɪn.tᵊl'ek.ʃᵊn, -tɪ'lek- (US) -t̬ə'lek-
intellective ˌɪn.tᵊl'ek.tɪv, -tɪ'lek- (US) -t̬ə'lek-
intellectual ˌɪn.tᵊl'ek.tju.əl, -tɪ'lek-, -tʃu- (US) -t̬ᵊl'ek.tʃu- **-s** -z **-ly** -i
intellectual|ism ˌɪn.tᵊl'ek.tju.ə.l|ɪ.zᵊm, -tɪ'lek-, -tʃu- (US) -t̬ᵊl'ek.tʃu- **-ist/s** -ɪst/s
intellectuality ˌɪn.tᵊlˌek.tju'æl.ə.ti, -tɪˌlek-, -tʃu'-, -ɪ.ti (US) -tʃu'æl.ə.t̬i
intellectualiz|e, -is|e ˌɪn.tᵊl'ek.tju.ə.laɪz, -tɪ'lek-, -tʃu- (US) -t̬ᵊl'ek.tʃu- **-es** -ɪz **-ing** -ɪŋ **-ed** -d
intelligence ɪn'tel.ɪ.dʒᵊn*t*s, '-ə- **-es** -ɪz **-er/s** -əʳ/z (US) -ɚ/z **in'telligence ˌtest**
intelligent ɪn'tel.ɪ.dʒᵊnt, '-ə- **-ly** -li
intelligentsia ɪnˌtel.ɪ'dʒent.si.ə, ˌɪn- (US) -'dʒent-, -'gent-
intelligibility ɪnˌtel.ɪ.dʒə'bɪl.ə.ti, ˌ-ə-, -dʒɪ'-, -ɪ.ti (US) -ə.t̬i
intelligib|le ɪn'tel.ɪ.dʒə.bl̩|, '-ə-, -dʒɪ- **-ly** -li **-leness** -l̩.nəs, -nɪs
intemperance ɪn'tem.pᵊr.ᵊn*t*s, ˌɪn-, '-prᵊn*t*s
intemperate ɪn'tem.pᵊr.ət, ˌɪn-, -ɪt, '-prət (US) -prɪt **-ly** -li **-ness** -nəs, -nɪs
intend ɪn'tend **-s** -z **-ing** -ɪŋ **-ed** -ɪd
intendan|ce ɪn'ten.dən|*t*s **-cy** -*t*si **-t/s** -t/s
intens|e ɪn'ten*t*s **-er** -əʳ **-est** -ɪst, -əst **-ely** -li **-eness** -nəs, -nɪs
intensification ɪnˌten*t*.sɪ.fɪ'keɪ.ʃᵊn, -sə- **-s** -z
intensi|fy ɪn'ten*t*.sɪl.faɪ, -sə- **-fies** -faɪz **-fying** -faɪ.ɪŋ **-fied** -faɪd **-fier/s** -faɪ.əʳ/z (US) -faɪ.ɚ/z
intension ɪn'ten.*t*ʃᵊn
intensit|y ɪn'ten*t*.sə.t|i, -sɪ- (US) -sə.t̬|i **-ies** -iz
intensive ɪn'ten*t*.sɪv **-ly** -li **-ness** -nəs, -nɪs **inˌtensive 'care**
in|tent ɪnl'tent **-tents** -'tents **-tenter** -'ten.təʳ (US) -'ten.t̬ɚ **-tentest** -'ten.tɪst, -'ten.təst (US) -'ten.t̬ɪst, -'ten.t̬əst **-tently** -'tent.li **-tentness** -'tent.nəs, -'tent.nɪs
intention ɪn'ten.*t*ʃᵊn **-s** -z **-ed** -d
intentional ɪn'ten.*t*ʃᵊn.ᵊl **-ly** -i
inter- ɪn.təʳ- (US) ɪn.t̬ɚ-
Note: Prefix. Normally takes either primary stress or secondary stress on the first syllable, with nouns often receiving front stress, e.g. **intercom** (noun) /'ɪn.tə.kɒm (US) -t̬ɚ.kɑːm/, **interact** (verb) /ˌɪn.təʳ'ækt (US) -t̬ɚ'ækt/. Exceptions exist; see individual entries. Note also that, although /r/ is normally assigned to a following strong syllable in US transcriptions, in **inter-** it is perceived to be morphemically linked to that morpheme and is retained in the prefix as /ɚ/.
inter (*v.*) ɪn'tɜːʳ (US) -'tɜːr **-s** -z **-ring** -ɪŋ **-red** -d

inter (*Latin prep., in such phrases as* **inter alia, inter se**) ˈɪn.təʳ ⓤⓢ -t̬ɚ
interact (*n.*) ˈɪn.təʳ.ækt ⓤⓢ -t̬ɚ.ækt **-s** -s
interact (*v.*) ˌɪn.təʳˈækt ⓤⓢ -t̬ɚˈækt **-s** -s **-ing** -ɪŋ **-ed** -ɪd
interaction ˌɪn.təʳˈæk.ʃən ⓤⓢ -t̬ɚˈæk- **-s** -z
interactive ˌɪn.təʳˈæk.tɪv ⓤⓢ -t̬ɚˈæk- **-ly** -li
inter alia ˌɪn.təʳˈeɪ.li.ə, -ˈæl.i- ⓤⓢ -t̬ɚˈɑː-, -ˈeɪ-, -ɑː
interblend ˌɪn.təˈblend ⓤⓢ -t̬ɚˈ- **-s** -z **-ing** -ɪŋ **-ed** -ɪd
inter|breed ˌɪn.tə|ˈbriːd ⓤⓢ -t̬ɚˈ- **-breeds** -ˈbriːdz **-breeding** -ˈbriː.dɪŋ **-bred** -ˈbred
intercalary ɪnˈtɜː.kəl.əʳ.i; ˌɪn.təˈkæl- ⓤⓢ ɪnˈtɝː.kə.ler-, ˌɪn.t̬ɚˈkæl.ɚ.i
interca|late ɪnˈtɜː.kə|.leɪt, ˈɪn.tə.kə- ⓤⓢ -ˈtɝː- **-lates** -leɪts **-lating** -leɪ.tɪŋ ⓤⓢ -leɪ.t̬ɪŋ **-lated** -leɪ.tɪd ⓤⓢ -leɪ.t̬ɪd
intercalation ɪnˌtɜː.kəˈleɪ.ʃən ⓤⓢ -ˌtɝː- **-s** -z
interced|e ˌɪn.təˈsiːd ⓤⓢ -t̬ɚˈ- **-es** -z **-ing** -ɪŋ **-ed** -ɪd **-er/s** -əʳ/z ⓤⓢ -ɚ/z
intercept (*n.*) ˈɪn.tə.sept ⓤⓢ -t̬ɚ- **-s** -s
intercept (*v.*) ˌɪn.təˈsept ⓤⓢ -t̬ɚˈ- **-s** -s **-ing** -ɪŋ **-ed** -ɪd **-er/s** -əʳ/z ⓤⓢ -ɚ/z **-or/s** -əʳ/z ⓤⓢ -ɚ/z
interception ˌɪn.təˈsep.ʃən ⓤⓢ -t̬ɚˈ- **-s** -z
interceptive ˌɪn.təˈsep.tɪv ⓤⓢ -t̬ɚˈ-
intercession ˌɪn.təˈseʃ.ən ⓤⓢ -t̬ɚˈ- **-s** -z
intercessional ˌɪn.təˈseʃ.ən.əl ⓤⓢ -t̬ɚˈ-
intercessor ˌɪn.təˈses.əʳ, ˈɪn.tə.ses- ⓤⓢ ˌɪn.t̬ɚˈses.ɚ, ˈɪn.t̬ɚ.ses- **-s** -z
intercessory ˌɪn.təˈses.əʳ.i ⓤⓢ -t̬ɚˈ-
interchang|e (*n.*) ˈɪn.tə.tʃeɪndʒ ⓤⓢ -t̬ɚ- **-es** -ɪz
interchang|e (*v.*) ˌɪn.təˈtʃeɪndʒ ⓤⓢ -t̬ɚˈ- **-es** -ɪz **-ing** -ɪŋ **-ed** -d
interchangeability ˌɪn.təˌtʃeɪn.dʒəˈbɪl.ə.ti, -ɪ.ti ⓤⓢ -t̬ɚˌtʃeɪn.dʒəˈbɪl.ə.t̬i
interchangeab|le ˌɪn.təˈtʃeɪn.dʒə.b|l̩ ⓤⓢ -t̬ɚˈ- **-ly** -li **-leness** -l̩.nəs, -nɪs
intercity (I) ˌɪn.təˈsɪt.i ⓤⓢ -t̬ɚˈsɪt̬- *stress shift:* ˌintercity ˈtrain
intercollegiate ˌɪn.tə.kəˈliː.dʒət, -kɒlˈiː-, -dʒi.ət, -ɪt ⓤⓢ -t̬ɚ.kəˈliː.dʒɪt
intercolonial ˌɪn.tə.kəˈləʊ.ni.əl ⓤⓢ -t̬ɚ.kəˈloʊ-
intercom ˈɪn.tə.kɒm ⓤⓢ -t̬ɚ.kɑːm **-s** -z
intercommuni|cate ˌɪn.tə.kəˈmjuː.nɪ|.keɪt, -nə- ⓤⓢ -t̬ɚ- **-cates** -keɪts **-cating** -keɪ.tɪŋ ⓤⓢ -keɪ.t̬ɪŋ **-cated** -keɪ.tɪd ⓤⓢ -keɪ.t̬ɪd **-cator/s** -keɪ.təʳ/z ⓤⓢ -keɪ.t̬ɚ/z
intercommunication ˌɪn.tə.kəˌmjuː.nɪˈkeɪ.ʃən, -nəˈ- ⓤⓢ -t̬ɚ-
intercommunion ˌɪn.tə.kəˈmjuː.ni.ən ⓤⓢ -t̬ɚ.kəˈmjuː.njən
intercommunity ˌɪn.tə.kəˈmjuː.nə.ti, -nɪ- ⓤⓢ -t̬ɚ.kəˈmjuː.nə.t̬i
interconnect ˌɪn.tə.kəˈnekt ⓤⓢ -t̬ɚ- **-s** -s **-ing** -ɪŋ **-ed** -ɪd
interconnection ˌɪn.tə.kəˈnek.ʃən ⓤⓢ -t̬ɚ- **-s** -z
intercontinental ˌɪn.təˌkɒn.tɪˈnen.təl, -təˈ- ⓤⓢ -t̬ɚˌkɑːn.təˈnen.t̬əl
intercostal ˌɪn.təˈkɒs.təl ⓤⓢ -t̬ɚˈkɑː.stəl
intercourse ˈɪn.tə.kɔːs ⓤⓢ -t̬ɚ.kɔːrs
intercurrent ˌɪn.təˈkʌr.ənt ⓤⓢ -t̬ɚˈkɝː- **-ly** -li
interdenominational ˌɪn.tə.dɪˌnɒm.ɪˈneɪ.ʃən.əl, -dəˌ-, -əˈ- ⓤⓢ -t̬ɚ.dɪˌnɑː.məˈ-, -diˌ- **-ism** -ɪ.zəm **-ly** -i
interdental ˌɪn.təˈden.təl ⓤⓢ -t̬ɚˈden.t̬əl
interdepartmental ˌɪn.təˌdiː.pɑːtˈmen.təl; ˌɪn.tə.dɪˌpɑːtˈ-, -dəˌ- ⓤⓢ -t̬ɚˌdiː.pɑːrtˈmen.t̬əl, -dɪ-
interdependence ˌɪn.tə.dɪˈpen.dənts, -dəˈ- ⓤⓢ -t̬ɚ.diːˈ-, -dɪˈ-
interdependent ˌɪn.tə.dɪˈpen.dənt, -dəˈ- ⓤⓢ -t̬ɚ.diːˈ-, -dɪˈ- **-ly** -li
interdict (*n.*) ˈɪn.tə.dɪkt, -daɪt ⓤⓢ -t̬ɚ.dɪkt **-s** -s
interdict (*v.*) ˌɪn.təˈdɪkt, -ˈdaɪt ⓤⓢ -t̬ɚˈdɪkt **-s** -s **-ing** -ɪŋ **-ed** -ɪd
interdiction ˌɪn.təˈdɪk.ʃən ⓤⓢ -t̬ɚˈ- **-s** -z
interdigi|tate ˌɪn.təˈdɪdʒ.ɪ|.teɪt, ˈ-ə- ⓤⓢ -t̬ɚˈ- **-tates** -teɪts **-tating** -teɪ.tɪŋ ⓤⓢ -teɪ.t̬ɪŋ **-tated** -teɪ.tɪd ⓤⓢ -teɪ.t̬ɪd
interdisciplinary ˌɪn.təˈdɪs.ɪ.plɪ.nəʳ.i, ˈ-ə-; ˌɪn.təˌdɪs.ɪˈplɪn.əʳ-, -əˈ- ⓤⓢ -t̬ɚˈdɪs.ə.plɪ.ner-
interest ˈɪn.trəst, -trest, -trɪst; -təʳ.əst, -est, -ɪst ⓤⓢ ˈɪn.trɪst, -trəst, -trest; -t̬ɚ.ɪst, -əst, -est **-s** -s **-ing** -ɪŋ **-ed/ly** -ɪd/li ˈinterest ˌrate
interesting ˈɪn.trə.stɪŋ, -tres.tɪŋ, -trɪ.stɪŋ, -təʳ.ə-, -es.tɪŋ, -ɪ.stɪŋ ⓤⓢ ˈɪn.trɪ.stɪŋ, -trə-, -tres.tɪŋ, -t̬ɚ.ɪ.stɪŋ, -es.tɪŋ **-ly** -li
interfac|e (*n.*) ˈɪn.tə.feɪs ⓤⓢ -t̬ɚ- **-es** -ɪz
interfac|e (*v.*) ˌɪn.təˈfeɪs, ˈ--- ⓤⓢ ˈɪn.t̬ɚ.feɪs **-es** -ɪz **-ing** -ɪŋ **-ed** -t
Note: The computer world uses first-syllable stress for both noun and verb.
interfaith ˌɪn.təˈfeɪθ ⓤⓢ ˈɪn.t̬ɚ.feɪθ *stress shift, British only:* ˌinterfaith ˈservice
interfer|e ˌɪn.təˈfɪəʳ ⓤⓢ -t̬ɚˈfɪr **-es** -z **-ing** -ɪŋ **-ed** -d **-er/s** -əʳ/z ⓤⓢ -ɚ/z
interferenc|e ˌɪn.təˈfɪə.rənts ⓤⓢ -t̬ɚˈfɪr.ənts **-es** -ɪz
interferon ˌɪn.təˈfɪə.rɒn ⓤⓢ -t̬ɚˈfɪr.ɑːn **-s** -z
Interflora® ˌɪn.təˈflɔː.rə ⓤⓢ -t̬ɚˈflɔːr.ə
interfus|e ˌɪn.təˈfjuːz ⓤⓢ -t̬ɚˈ- **-es** -ɪz **-ing** -ɪŋ **-ed** -d
interfusion ˌɪn.təˈfjuː.ʒən ⓤⓢ -t̬ɚˈ-
intergalactic ˌɪn.tə.gəˈlæk.tɪk ⓤⓢ -t̬ɚ-
interglacial ˌɪn.təˈgleɪ.si.əl, -ʃi-, -ʃəl ⓤⓢ -t̬ɚˈgleɪ.ʃəl
intergovernmental ˌɪn.tə.gʌv.ənˈmen.təl, -əmˈ- ⓤⓢ -t̬ɚˌgʌv.ɚnˈmen.t̬əl
interim ˈɪn.təʳ.ɪm ⓤⓢ -t̬ɚ-
interior ɪnˈtɪə.ri.əʳ ⓤⓢ -ˈtɪr.i.ɚ **-s** -z inˌterior ˈdecorator ; inˌterior deˈsigner
interioriz|e, -is|e ɪnˈtɪə.ri.ə.raɪz ⓤⓢ -ˈtɪr.i- **-es** -ɪz **-ing** -ɪŋ **-ed** -d
interject ˌɪn.təˈdʒekt ⓤⓢ -t̬ɚˈ- **-s** -s **-ing** -ɪŋ **-ed** -ɪd **-or/s** -əʳ/z ⓤⓢ -ɚ/z
interjection ˌɪn.təˈdʒek.ʃən ⓤⓢ -t̬ɚˈ- **-s** -z **-al/ly** -əl/i
inter|knit ˌɪn.tə|ˈnɪt ⓤⓢ -t̬ɚˈ- **-knits** -ˈnɪts **-knitting** -ˈnɪt.ɪŋ ⓤⓢ -ˈnɪt̬.ɪŋ **-knitted** -ˈnɪt.ɪd ⓤⓢ -ˈnɪt̬.ɪd
interlac|e ˌɪn.təˈleɪs ⓤⓢ -t̬ɚˈ- **-es** -ɪz **-ing** -ɪŋ **-ed** -t **-ement** -mənt
Interlaken ˈɪn.tə.lɑː.kən, ˌɪn.təˈlɑː- ⓤⓢ ˈɪn.t̬ɚ.lɑː-, ˌɪn.t̬ɚˈlɑː-, -t̬ɚ-
interlanguage ˈɪn.təˌlæŋ.gwɪdʒ ⓤⓢ -t̬ɚ-
interlard ˌɪn.təˈlɑːd ⓤⓢ -t̬ɚˈlɑːrd **-s** -z **-ing** -ɪŋ **-ed** -ɪd
interlea|f ˈɪn.tə.liː|f ⓤⓢ -t̬ɚ- **-ves** -vz
interleav|e ˌɪn.təˈliːv ⓤⓢ -t̬ɚˈ- **-es** -z **-ing** -ɪŋ **-ed** -d
interlin|e ˌɪn.təˈlaɪn ⓤⓢ -t̬ɚˈ- **-es** -z **-ing** -ɪŋ **-ed** -d
interlinear ˌɪn.təˈlɪn.i.əʳ ⓤⓢ -t̬ɚˈlɪn.i.ɚ
interlineation ˌɪn.təˌlɪn.iˈeɪ.ʃən ⓤⓢ -t̬ɚ- **-s** -z
interlink ˌɪn.təˈlɪŋk ⓤⓢ -t̬ɚˈ- **-s** -s **-ing** -ɪŋ **-ed** -t
interlock ˌɪn.təˈlɒk ⓤⓢ -t̬ɚˈlɑːk **-s** -s **-ing** -ɪŋ **-ed** -t
interlocution ˌɪn.tə.ləˈkjuː.ʃən, -lɒkˈjuː- ⓤⓢ -t̬ɚ.loʊˈkjuː- **-s** -z
interlocutor ˌɪn.təˈlɒk.jə.təʳ, -jʊ- ⓤⓢ -t̬ɚˈlɑː.kjə.t̬ɚ, -kjʊ- **-s** -z **-y** -i
interlocu|tress ˌɪn.təˈlɒk.jə.|trəs, -jʊ-, -trɪs ⓤⓢ -t̬ɚˈlɑː.kjʊ|.trɪs, -kjə- **-trice** -trɪs **-trix** -trɪks
interlop|e ˌɪn.təˈləʊp ⓤⓢ ˈɪn.t̬ɚ.loʊp **-es** -s **-ing** -ɪŋ **-ed** -t
interloper ˈɪn.təˌləʊ.pəʳ, ˌɪn.təˈləʊ.pəʳ ⓤⓢ ˈɪn.t̬ɚˌloʊ.pɚ **-s** -z

interlude ˈɪn.tə.luːd, -ljuːd (US) -t̬ɚ.luːd **-s** -z

intermarriag|e ˌɪn.təˈmær.ɪdʒ (US) -t̬ɚˈmer-, -ˈmær- **-es** -ɪz

intermarr|y ˌɪn.təˈmær|.i (US) ˈɪn.t̬ɚˌmer-, -ˈmær- **-ies** -iz **-ying** -i.ɪŋ **-ied** -id

intermeddl|e ˌɪn.təˈmed.l̩ (US) -t̬ɚˈ- **-es** -z **-ing** -ɪŋ, -ˈmed.lɪŋ **-ed** -d **-er/s** -əʳ/z, -ˈmed.ləʳ/z (US) -lɚ/z

intermediar|y ˌɪn.təˈmiː.di.ə.r|i (US) -t̬ɚˈmiː.di.er-, -ɚ- **-ies** -iz

intermediate ˌɪn.təˈmiː.di.ət, -ɪt (US) -t̬ɚˈ- **-s** -s **-ly** -li

interment ɪnˈtɜː.mənt (US) -ˈtɜːr- **-s** -s

intermezz|o ˌɪn.təˈmet.s|əʊ, -ˈmed.z|əʊ (US) -t̬ɚˈmet.s|oʊ, -ˈmed.z|oʊ **-os** -əʊz (US) -oʊz **-i** -i, -iː

interminab|le ɪnˈtɜː.mɪ.nə.b|l̩, ˌɪn-, -mᵊn.ə- (US) -ˈtɜːr- **-ly** -li **-leness** -l̩.nəs, -nɪs

intermingl|e ˌɪn.təˈmɪŋ.gl̩ (US) -t̬ɚˈ- **-es** -z **-ing** -ɪŋ, -ˈmɪŋ.glɪŋ **-ed** -d

intermission ˌɪn.təˈmɪʃ.ᵊn (US) -t̬ɚˈ- **-s** -z

inter|mit ˌɪn.tə|ˈmɪt (US) -t̬ɚˈ- **-mits** -ˈmɪts **-mitting/ly** -ˈmɪt.ɪŋ/li (US) -ˈmɪt̬.ɪŋ/li **-mitted** -ˈmɪt.ɪd (US) -ˈmɪt̬.ɪd

intermittent ˌɪn.təˈmɪt.ᵊnt (US) -t̬ɚˈmɪt- **-ly** -li

intermix ˌɪn.təˈmɪks (US) -t̬ɚˈ- **-es** -ɪz **-ing** -ɪŋ **-ed** -t

intermixture ˌɪn.təˈmɪks.tʃəʳ (US) -t̬ɚˈmɪks.tʃɚ **-s** -z

intermodal ˌɪn.təˈməʊ.dᵊl (US) -t̬ɚˈmoʊ-

intern (*n.*) ˈɪn.tɜːn, -ˈ- (US) ˈɪn.tɜːrn **-s** -z

intern (*v.*) ɪnˈtɜːn (US) ɪnˈtɜːrn, ˈ-- **-s** -z **-ing** -ɪŋ **-ed** -d

internal ɪnˈtɜː.nᵊl, ˌɪn- (US) -ˈtɜːr- **-ly** -i **inˌternal comˈbustion ; inˌternal comˈbustion ˌengine** (US) **inˌternal comˌbustion ˈengine ; Inˌternal ˈRevenue ˌService**

internalization ɪnˌtɜː.nᵊl.aɪˈzeɪ.ʃᵊn, ˌɪn-, -ɪˈ- (US) -ˌtɜːr.nᵊl.ɪˈ-

internaliz|e, -is|e ɪnˈtɜː.nᵊl.aɪz (US) -ˈtɜːr- **-es** -ɪz **-ing** -ɪŋ **-ed** -d

international ˌɪn.təˈnæʃ.ᵊn.ᵊl, -təˈnæʃ.nᵊl (US) -t̬ɚˈ- **-ly** -i

Internationale ˌɪn.təˌnæʃ.əˈnɑːl, -ˌnæʃ.i.əˈnɑːl (US) -t̬ɚˌnæʃ.əˈnæl, -ˈnɑːl

internationall|ism ˌɪn.təˈnæʃ.ᵊn.ᵊl|.ɪ.zᵊm, -ˈnæʃ.nᵊl- (US) -t̬ɚˈ- **-ist/s** -ɪst/s

internationalization, -isa- ˌɪn.təˌnæʃ.ᵊn.ᵊl.aɪˈzeɪ.ʃᵊn, ˌ-nᵊl-, -ɪˈ- (US) -t̬ɚˌnæʃ.ᵊn.ᵊl.ɪˈ-, ˌ-nᵊl-

internationaliz|e, -is|e ˌɪn.təˈnæʃ.ᵊn.ᵊl.aɪz, -ˈnæʃ.nᵊl- (US) -t̬ɚˈ- **-es** -ɪz **-ing** -ɪŋ **-ed** -d

interne ˈɪn.tɜːn (US) -tɜːrn **-s** -z

internecine ˌɪn.təˈniː.saɪn, -tɜːˈ- (US) -t̬ɚˈniː.sɪn, -siːn, -ˈnes.ɪn, -iːn

internee ˌɪn.tɜːˈniː (US) -tɜːrˈ- **-s** -z

Internet ˈɪn.tə.net (US) -t̬ɚ-

internist ˈɪn.tɜː.nɪst, -ˈ-- (US) ˈɪn.tɜːr-, -ˈ-- **-s** -s

internment ɪnˈtɜːn.mənt, -ˈtɜːm- (US) -ˈtɜːrn- **-s** -s

internodal ˌɪn.təˈnəʊ.dᵊl (US) -t̬ɚˈnoʊ-

internode ˈɪn.tə.nəʊd (US) -t̬ɚ.noʊd **-s** -z

internship ˈɪn.tɜːn.ʃɪp, -ˈ-- (US) ˈɪn.tɜːrn-, -ˈ-- **-s** -s

interoceanic ˌɪn.təʳ.əʊ.ʃiˈæn.ɪk (US) -t̬ɚˌoʊ-

inter pares ˌɪn.təˈpɑː.riːz, -ˈpeə-, -reɪs (US) -t̬ɚˈpɑː.res

inter partes ˌɪn.təˈpɑː.tiːz, -teɪs (US) ˌɪn.t̬ɚˈpɑːr.tes

interpellant ˌɪn.təˈpel.ənt (US) -t̬ɚˈ- **-s** -s

interpell|ate ɪnˈtɜː.pə.l|eɪt, -pɪ-, -pel|.eɪt; ˌɪn.təˈpel|.eɪt (US) ˌɪn.t̬ɚˈpel-; ɪnˈtɜː.pə.l|eɪt **-ates** -eɪts **-ating** -eɪ.tɪŋ (US) -eɪ.t̬ɪŋ **-ated** -eɪ.tɪd (US) -eɪ.t̬ɪd

interpellation ɪnˌtɜː.pəˈleɪ.ʃᵊn, -pɪˈ-, -pelˈeɪ-; ˌɪn.tə.pəˈleɪ- (US) ˌɪn.t̬ɚ.pəˈleɪ-; ɪnˌtɜːr- **-s** -z

interpene|trate ˌɪn.təˈpen.ɪ|.treɪt, ˈ-ə- (US) -t̬ɚˈ- **-trates** -treɪts **-trating** -treɪ.tɪŋ (US) -treɪ.t̬ɪŋ **-trated** -treɪ.tɪd (US) -treɪ.t̬ɪd

interpenetration ˌɪn.təˌpen.ɪˈtreɪ.ʃᵊn, -əˈ- (US) -t̬ɚˌ-

interpersonal ˌɪn.təˈpɜː.sᵊn.ᵊl (US) -t̬ɚˈpɜːr- **-ly** -i

interplanetary ˌɪn.təˈplæn.ɪ.tᵊr.i, ˈ-ə- (US) -t̬ɚˈplæn.ə.ter-

interplay ˈɪn.tə.pleɪ (US) -t̬ɚ-

interpleader ˌɪn.təˈpliː.dəʳ (US) -t̬ɚˈpliː.dɚ **-s** -z

Interpol ˈɪn.tə.pɒl (US) -t̬ɚ.pɑːl, -poʊl

interpo|late ɪnˈtɜː.pə|.leɪt (US) -ˈtɜːr- **-lates** -leɪts **-lating** -leɪ.tɪŋ (US) -leɪ.t̬ɪŋ **-lated** -leɪ.tɪd (US) -leɪ.t̬ɪd **-lator/s** -leɪ.təʳ/z (US) -leɪ.t̬ɚ/z

interpolation ɪnˌtɜː.pəˈleɪ.ʃᵊn (US) -ˌtɜːr- **-s** -z

interposal ˌɪn.təˈpəʊ.zᵊl (US) -t̬ɚˈpoʊ- **-s** -z

interpos|e ˌɪn.təˈpəʊz (US) -t̬ɚˈpoʊz **-es** -ɪz **-ing** -ɪŋ **-ed** -d **-er/s** -əʳ/z (US) -ɚ/z

interposition ˌɪn.tə.pəˈzɪʃ.ᵊn; ɪnˌtɜː- (US) ˌɪn.t̬ɚ.pəˈ- **-s** -z

interpre|t ɪnˈtɜː.prɪ|t, -prə|t (US) -ˈtɜːr.prə|t **-ts** -ts **-ting** -tɪŋ (US) -t̬ɪŋ **-ted** -tɪd (US) -t̬ɪd **-table** -tə.bl̩ (US) -t̬ə.bl̩

interpretation ɪnˌtɜː.prɪˈteɪ.ʃᵊn, -prəˈ- (US) -ˌtɜːr.prəˈ- **-s** -z **-al** -ᵊl

interpretative ɪnˈtɜː.prɪ.tə.tɪv, -prə-, -teɪ- (US) -ˈtɜːr.prə.teɪ.t̬ɪv, -t̬ə- **-ly** -li

interpreter ɪnˈtɜː.prɪ.təʳ, -prə- (US) -ˈtɜːr.prə.t̬ɚ **-s** -z

interpretive ɪnˈtɜː.prɪ.tɪv, -prə- (US) -ˈtɜːr.prə.t̬ɪv **-ly** -li

interquartile ˌɪn.təˈkwɔː.taɪl (US) -t̬ɚˈkwɔːr-, -tɪl, -t̬ᵊl

interracial ˌɪn.təˈreɪ.ʃᵊl, -ʃi.əl (US) -t̬ɚˈreɪ.ʃᵊl

interregn|um ˌɪn.təˈreg.n|əm (US) -t̬ɚˈ- **-ums** -əmz **-a** -ə

interre|late ˌɪn.tə.rɪ|ˈleɪt, -rəˈ- (US) -t̬ɚ.riˈ-, -rɪˈ- **-lates** -ˈleɪts **-lating** -ˈleɪ.tɪŋ (US) -ˈleɪ.t̬ɪŋ **-lated** -ˈleɪ.tɪd (US) -ˈleɪ.t̬ɪd

interrelation ˌɪn.tə.rɪˈleɪ.ʃᵊn, -rəˈ- (US) -t̬ɚ.riˈ-, -rɪˈ- **-s** -z

interrelationship ˌɪn.tə.rɪˈleɪ.ʃᵊn.ʃɪp

interro|gate ɪnˈter.ə|.geɪt **-gates** -geɪts **-gating** -geɪ.tɪŋ (US) -geɪ.t̬ɪŋ **-gated** -geɪ.tɪd (US) -geɪ.t̬ɪd **-gator/s** -geɪ.təʳ/z (US) -geɪ.t̬ɚ/z

interrogation ɪnˌter.əˈgeɪ.ʃᵊn **-s** -z

interrogative ˌɪn.təˈrɒg.ə.tɪv (US) -t̬ɚˈrɑː.gə.t̬ɪv **-s** -z **-ly** -li

interrogator|y ˌɪn.təˈrɒg.ə.tᵊr|.i (US) -t̬ɚˈrɑː.gə.tɔːr- **-ies** -iz

interrupt (*v.*) ˌɪn.təˈrʌpt (US) -t̬ɚˈ- **-s** -s **-ing** -ɪŋ **-ed** -ɪd **-er/s** -əʳ/z (US) -ɚ/z

interrupt (*n.*) ˈɪn.tə.rʌpt (US) -t̬ɚ-

interruption ˌɪn.təˈrʌp.ʃᵊn (US) -t̬ɚˈ- **-s** -z

intersect ˌɪn.təˈsekt (US) -t̬ɚˈ- **-s** -s **-ing** -ɪŋ **-ed** -ɪd **-or/s** -əʳ/z (US) -ɚ/z

intersection ˌɪn.təˈsek.ʃᵊn, ˈɪn.təˌsek- (US) ˌɪn.t̬ɚˈsek-, ˈɪn.t̬ɚˌsek- **-s** -z

Note: /ˈɪn.t̬ɚˌsek.ʃᵊn/ is the common US pronunciation for a place where streets meet.

interspac|e (*n.*) ˈɪn.tə.speɪs, ˌ--ˈ- (US) ˈɪn.t̬ɚ.speɪs **-es** -ɪz

interspac|e (*v.*) ˌɪn.təˈspeɪs (US) -t̬ɚˈ-, ˈ--- **-es** -ɪz **-ing** -ɪŋ **-ed** -t

interspers|e ˌɪn.təˈspɜːs (US) -t̬ɚˈspɜːrs **-es** -ɪz **-ing** -ɪŋ **-ed** -t

interspersion ˌɪn.təˈspɜː.ʃᵊn, -ʒᵊn (US) -t̬ɚˈspɜːr-

interstate (I) ˌɪn.təˈsteɪt (US) ˈɪn.t̬ɚ.steɪt *stress shift, British only:* ˌinterstate ˈhighway

interstellar ˌɪn.təˈstel.əʳ (US) -t̬ɚˈstel.ɚ *stress shift:* ˌinterstellar ˈtravel

interstic|e ɪnˈtɜː.stɪs (US) -ˈtɜːr- **-es** -ɪz, -iːz

interstitial ˌɪn.təˈstɪʃ.ᵊl (US) -t̬ɚˈ-

intertribal ˌɪn.təˈtraɪ.bᵊl (US) -t̬ɚˈ-

intertwin|e ˌɪn.təˈtwaɪn (US) -t̬ɚˈ- **-es** -z **-ing** -ɪŋ **-ed** -d
intertwist ˌɪn.təˈtwɪst (US) -t̬ɚˈ- **-s** -s **-ing** -ɪŋ **-ed** -ɪd
interurban ˌɪn.təʳˈɜː.bᵊn (US) -t̬ɚˈɝː-
interval ˈɪn.tə.vᵊl (US) -t̬ɚ- **-s** -z
interven|e ˌɪn.təˈviːn (US) -t̬ɚˈ- **-es** -z **-ing** -ɪŋ **-ed** -d **-er/s** -əʳ/z (US) -ɚ/z
intervention ˌɪn.təˈven.*t*ʃᵊn (US) -t̬ɚˈ- **-s** -z
intervention|ism ˌɪn.təˈven.*t*ʃᵊn|.ɪ.zᵊm (US) -t̬ɚˈ- **-ist/s** -ɪst/s
interventionist ˌɪn.təˈven.tʃᵊn.ɪst (US) -t̬ɚˈ-
interview ˈɪn.tə.vjuː (US) -t̬ɚ- **-s** -z **-ing** -ɪŋ **-ed** -d **-er/s** -əʳ/z (US) -ɚ/z
interviewee ˌɪn.tə.vjuˈiː (US) -t̬ɚ- **-s** -z
inter vivos ˌɪn.təˈviː.vəʊs (US) -tɚˈviː.voʊs, -ˈvaɪ-
intervocalic ˌɪn.tə.vəʊˈkæl.ɪk (US) -t̬ɚ.voʊˈ-
interweav|e ˌɪn.təˈwiːv (US) -t̬ɚˈ-, ˈ--- **-es** -z **-ing** -ɪŋ **-ed** -d **interwove** ˌɪn.təˈwəʊv (US) -t̬ɚˈwoʊv, ˈ--- **interwoven** ˌɪn.təˈwəʊ.vᵊn (US) -t̬ɚˈwoʊ.vᵊn, ˈɪn.t̬ɚˌwoʊ-
intestac|y ɪnˈtes.tə.s|i **-ies** -iz
intestate ɪnˈtes.teɪt, -tɪt, -tət **-s** -s
intestinal ɪnˈtes.tɪ.nᵊl, -tᵊn.ᵊl, ˌɪn.tesˈtaɪ.nᵊl (US) ɪnˈtes.tɪ-
intestine ɪnˈtes.tɪn, -tiːn (US) -tɪn, -tən **-s** -z
inthral(l) ɪnˈθrɔːl (US) -ˈθrɑːl, -ˈθrɔːl **-s** -z **-ing** -ɪŋ **-ed** -d
intifada ˌɪn.tɪˈfɑː.də **-s** -z
intimac|y ˈɪn.tɪ.mə.s|i, -tə- (US) -t̬ə-, -t̬ɪ- **-ies** -iz
intimate (*n. adj.*) ˈɪn.tɪ.mət, -tə-, -mɪt (US) -t̬ə.mət, -t̬ɪ- **-s** -s **-ly** -li
inti|mate (*v.*) ˈɪn.tɪ|.meɪt, -tə- (US) -t̬ə-, -t̬ɪ- **-mates** -meɪts **-mating** -meɪ.tɪŋ (US) -meɪ.t̬ɪŋ **-mated** -meɪ.tɪd (US) -meɪ.t̬ɪd **-mater/s** -meɪ.təʳ/z (US) -meɪ.t̬ɚ/z
intimation ˌɪn.tɪˈmeɪ.ʃᵊn, -təˈ- (US) -t̬əˈ- , -t̬ɪˈ- **-s** -z
intimi|date ɪnˈtɪm.ɪ|.deɪt, ˈ-ə- **-dates** -deɪts **-dating** -deɪ.tɪŋ (US) -deɪ.t̬ɪŋ **-dated** -deɪ.tɪd (US) -deɪ.t̬ɪd **-dator/s** -deɪ.təʳ/z (US) -deɪ.t̬ɚ/z
intimidation ɪnˌtɪm.ɪˈdeɪ.ʃᵊn, -əˈ-
intituled ɪnˈtɪt.juːld
into ˈɪn.tə -tu, -tuː (US) -tə, -tu
Note: In British English, the pronunciation /ˈɪn.tuː/ is sometimes used in final position (e.g. 'That's the wall he walked into'), though the /u/ vowel is more usual. Elsewhere, the pronunciation /ˈɪn.tə/ is used before consonants (e.g. 'into debt' /ˌɪn.təˈdet/) and /ˈɪn.tu/ before vowels (e.g. 'into each' /ɪn.tuˈiːtʃ/). In American English the schwa form is usual before consonants and also vowels (e.g. 'into each' /ˌɪn.təˈiːtʃ/).
intolerab|le ɪnˈtɒl.ᵊr.ə.b|l̩, ˌɪn- (US) -ˈtɑː.lɚ- **-ly** -li **-leness** -l̩.nəs, -nɪs
intolerance ɪnˈtɒl.ᵊr.ᵊn*t*s, ˌɪn- (US) -ˈtɑː.lɚ-
intolerant ɪnˈtɒl.ᵊr.ᵊnt, ˌɪn- (US) -ˈtɑː.lɚ- **-ly** -li
into|nate ˈɪn.təʊ|.neɪt (US) -toʊ-, -tə- **-nates** -neɪts **-nating** -neɪ.tɪŋ (US) -neɪ.t̬ɪŋ **-nated** -neɪ.tɪd (US) -neɪ.t̬ɪd
intonation ˌɪn.təʊˈneɪ.ʃᵊn (US) -toʊˈ-, -təˈ- **-s** -z
intonational ˌɪn.təʊˈneɪ.ʃᵊn.ᵊl (US) -toʊˈ-, -təˈ-
inton|e ɪnˈtəʊn (US) -ˈtoʊn **-es** -z **-ing** -ɪŋ **-ed** -d **-er/s** -əʳ/z (US) -ɚ/z
in toto ɪnˈtəʊ.təʊ (US) -ˈtoʊ.toʊ
Intourist® ˈɪnˌtʊə.rɪst, -ˌtɔː- (US) -ˌtʊr.ɪst
intoxicant ɪnˈtɒk.sɪ.kᵊnt, -sə- (US) -ˈtɑːk.sɪ- **-s** -s
intoxi|cate ɪnˈtɒk.sɪ|.keɪt, -sə- (US) -ˈtɑːk.sɪ- **-cates** -keɪts **-cating** -keɪ.tɪŋ (US) -keɪ.t̬ɪŋ **-cated** -keɪ.tɪd (US) -keɪ.t̬ɪd **-cator/s** -keɪ.təʳ/z (US) -keɪ.t̬ɚ/z
intoxication ɪnˌtɒk.sɪˈkeɪ.ʃᵊn, -səˈ- (US) -ˌtɑːk.sɪˈ-
intra- ˌɪn.trə-
Note: Prefix. Normally takes secondary stress on the first syllable, e.g. **intravenous** /ˌɪn.trəˈviː.nəs/.
intractability ɪnˌtræk.təˈbɪl.ə.ti, ˌɪn-, -ɪ.ti (US) -ə.t̬i
intractab|le ɪnˈtræk.tə.b|l̩, ˌɪn- **-ly** -li **-leness** -l̩.nəs, -nɪs
intrados ɪnˈtreɪ.dɒs (US) -dɑːs; ˈɪn.trə.dɑːs, -doʊs **-es** -ɪz
intramural ˌɪn.trəˈmjʊə.rᵊl, -ˈmjɔː- (US) -ˈmjʊr.ᵊl
intramuscular ˌɪn.trəˈmʌs.kjə.ləʳ, -kjʊ- (US) -lɚ **-ly** -li
intransigence ɪnˈtræn*t*.sɪ.dʒᵊn*t*s, -ˈtrɑːn*t*-, -sə-; -ˈtræn.zɪ-, -ˈtrɑːn-, -zə- (US) -ˈtræn*t*.sə-
intransigent ɪnˈtræn*t*.sɪ.dʒᵊnt, -ˈtrɑːn*t*-, -sə-; -ˈtræn.zɪ-, -ˈtrɑːn-, -zə- (US) -ˈtræn*t*.sə- **-s** -s **-ly** -li
intransitive ɪnˈtræn*t*.sə.tɪv, ˌɪn-, -ˈtrɑːn*t*-, -sɪ-; -ˈtræn.zə-, -ˈtrɑːn-, -zɪ- (US) -ˈtræn*t*.sə.t̬ɪv **-s** -z **-ly** -li
intransitivity ɪnˌtræn*t*.səˈtɪv.ə.ti, ˌɪn-, -ˌtrɑːn*t*-, -sɪˈ-; -ˌtræn.zəˈ-, -ˌtrɑːn-, -zɪˈ-, -ɪ.ti (US) -ˌtræn*t*.səˈtɪv.ə.t̬i
intrapersonal ˌɪn.trəˈpɜː.sᵊn.ᵊl (US) -ˈpɝː-
intrauterine ˌɪn.trəˈjuː.tᵊr.aɪn (US) -t̬ɚ.ɪn, -t̬ə.raɪn ˌ**intra**ˌ**uterine de**ˈ**vice**
intravenous ˌɪn.trəˈviː.nəs **-ly** -li
in-tray ˈɪn.treɪ **-s** -z
intrench ɪnˈtren*t*ʃ **-es** -ɪz **-ing** -ɪŋ **-ed** -t **-ment/s** -mənt/s
intrepid ɪnˈtrep.ɪd **-ly** -li
intrepidity ˌɪn.trəˈpɪd.ə.ti, -trɪˈ-, -trepˈɪd-, -ɪ.ti (US) ˌɪn.trəˈpɪd.ə.t̬i, -trɪˈ-
intricac|y ˈɪn.trɪ.kə.s|i, -trə- **-ies** -iz
intricate ˈɪn.trɪ.kət, -trə-, -kɪt **-ly** -li **-ness** -nəs, -nɪs
intrigue (*n.*) ˈɪn.triːg, ˌ-ˈ-
intrigu|e (*v.*) ɪnˈtriːg **-es** -z **-ing/ly** -ɪŋ **-ed** -d **-er/s** -əʳ/z (US) -ɚ/z
intrinsic ɪnˈtrɪn*t*.sɪk; -ˈtrɪn.zɪk **-ally** -ᵊl.i, -li
intro- ɪn.trəʊ- (US) ɪn.troʊ-, -trə-
Note: Prefix. Normally takes either primary or secondary stress on the first syllable, e.g. **introvert** (noun), /ˈɪn.trəʊ.vɜːt (US) -troʊ.vɝːt/, **introspect** /ˌɪn.trəʊˈspekt (US) -troʊˈ-/.
introduc|e ˌɪn.trəˈdjuːs, -ˈdʒuːs (US) -ˈduːs, -ˈdjuːs **-es** -ɪz **-ing** -ɪŋ **-ed** -t **-er/s** -əʳ/z (US) -ɚ/z
introduction ˌɪn.trəˈdʌk.ʃᵊn **-s** -z
introductor|y ˌɪn.trəˈdʌk.tᵊr|.i **-ily** -ᵊl.i, -ɪ.li **-iness** -ɪ.nəs, -nɪs
introit ˈɪn.trɔɪt, -trəʊ.ɪt; ɪnˈtrəʊ.ɪt (US) ɪnˈtroʊ.ɪt; ˈɪn.trɔɪt **-s** -s
intromission ˌɪn.trəʊˈmɪʃ.ᵊn (US) -troʊˈ-, -trəˈ- **-s** -z
intro|mit ˌɪn.trəʊ|ˈmɪt (US) -troʊˈ-, -trəˈ- **-mits** -ˈmɪts **-mitting** -ˈmɪt.ɪŋ (US) -ˈmɪt̬.ɪŋ **-mitted** -ˈmɪt.ɪd (US) -ˈmɪt̬.ɪd
introspect ˌɪn.trəʊˈspekt (US) -troʊˈ-, -trəˈ- **-s** -s **-ing** -ɪŋ **-ed** -ɪd
introspection ˌɪn.trəʊˈspek.ʃᵊn (US) -troʊˈ-, -trəˈ- **-ist/s** -ɪsts/s **-al** -ᵊl
introspective ˌɪn.trəʊˈspek.tɪv (US) -troʊˈ-, -trəˈ- **-ly** -li **-ness** -nəs, -nɪs
introversion ˌɪn.trəʊˈvɜː.ʃᵊn, -ʒᵊn (US) -troʊˈvɝː-, -trəˈ-
introvert (*n.*) ˈɪn.trəʊ.vɜːt (US) -troʊ.vɝːt, -trə- **-s** -s
introver|t (*v.*) ˌɪn.trəʊˈvɜː|t (US) -troʊˈvɝː|t, -trəˈ-, ˈ--- **-ts** -ts **-ting** -tɪŋ (US) -t̬ɪŋ **-ted** -tɪd (US) -t̬ɪd
intrud|e ɪnˈtruːd **-es** -z **-ing** -ɪŋ **-ed** -ɪd **-er/s** -əʳ/z (US) -ɚ/z
intrusion ɪnˈtruː.ʒᵊn **-s** -z
intrusive ɪnˈtruː.sɪv **-ly** -li **-ness** -nəs, -nɪs
intu|it ɪnˈtjuː|.ɪt (US) ɪnˈtuː-, -ˈtjuː-, ˈɪn.tu|.ɪt **-its** -ɪts **-iting** -ɪ.tɪŋ (US) -ɪ.t̬ɪŋ **-ited** -ɪ.tɪd (US) -ɪ.t̬ɪd **-itable** -ɪ.tə.bl̩

intuition ˌɪn.tjuˈɪʃ.ᵊn US -tuˈ-, -tjuˈ- **-s** -z **-al** -ᵊl
intuitive ɪnˈtjuː.ɪ.tɪv, ˈ-ə- US -ˈtuː.ɪ.t̬ɪv, -ˈtjuː- **-ly** -li **-ness** -nəs, -nɪs
intumescen|ce ˌɪn.tjuːˈmes.ᵊn|ts US -tuːˈ-, -tjuːˈ- **-t** -t
In(n)uit ˈɪn.u.ɪt, -ju- US ˈ-u- **-s** -s
inun|date ˈɪn.ʌn|.deɪt, -ən- US -ən- **-dates** -deɪts **-dating** -deɪ.tɪŋ US -deɪ.t̬ɪŋ **-dated** -deɪ.tɪd US -deɪ.t̬ɪd
inundation ˌɪn.ʌnˈdeɪ.ʃᵊn, -ənˈ- US -ənˈ- **-s** -z
inur|e ɪˈnjʊəʳ, -ˈnjɔːʳ US -ˈnjʊr, -ˈnʊr **-es** -z **-ing** -ɪŋ **-ed** -d **-ement** -mənt
in utero ɪnˈjuː.tᵊr.əʊ US -t̬ɚ.oʊ
inutility ˌɪn.juːˈtɪl.ə.ti, -ɪ.ti US -ə.t̬i
invad|e ɪnˈveɪd **-es** -z **-ing** -ɪŋ **-ed** -ɪd **-er/s** -əʳ/z US -ɚ/z
invalid (*n. v. adj.*) *infirm through illness, etc.:* ˈɪn.və.lɪd, -liːd US -lɪd **-s** -z **-ing** -ɪŋ **-ed** -ɪd
invalid (*adj.*) *not valid:* ɪnˈvæl.ɪd, ˌɪn-
invali|date ɪnˈvæl.ɪ|.deɪt, ˌɪn-, ˈ-ə- **-dates** -deɪts **-dating** -deɪ.tɪŋ US -deɪ.t̬ɪŋ **-dated** -deɪ.tɪd US -deɪ.t̬ɪd
invalidation ɪnˌvæl.ɪˈdeɪ.ʃᵊn, ˌɪn-, -əˈ-
invalidity ˌɪn.vəˈlɪd.ə.ti, -ɪ.ti US -ə.t̬i **invaˈlidity ˌbenefit**
invaluab|le ɪnˈvæl.ju.ə.b|l̩, -jə.b|l̩, -jʊ- US -ju.ə- **-ly** -li
Invar® ɪnˈvɑːʳ, ˈ--, ˈɪn.vəʳ US ˈɪn.vɑːr
invariability ɪnˌveə.ri.əˈbɪl.ə.ti, ˌɪn-, -ɪ.ti US -ˌver.i.əˈbɪl.ə.t̬i
invariab|le ɪnˈveə.ri.ə.b|l̩, ˌɪn- US -ˈver.i- **-ly** -li **-leness** -l̩.nəs, -nɪs
invariance ɪnˈveə.ri.ən*t*s, ˌɪn- US -ˈver.i-
invasion ɪnˈveɪ.ʒᵊn **-s** -z
invasive ɪnˈveɪ.sɪv, -zɪv US -zɪv, -sɪv **-ly** -li **-ness** -nəs, -nɪs
invective ɪnˈvek.tɪv **-s** -z
inveigh ɪnˈveɪ **-s** -z **-ing** -ɪŋ **-ed** -d
inveig|le ɪnˈveɪ.gl̩, -ˈviː- **-es** -z **-ing** -ɪŋ, -ˈveɪ.glɪŋ, -ˈviː- **-ed** -d **-ement/s** -mənt/s
in|vent ɪn|ˈvent **-vents** -ˈvents **-venting** -ˈven.tɪŋ US -ˈven.t̬ɪŋ **-vented** -ˈven.tɪd US -ˈven.t̬ɪd
invention ɪnˈven.*t*ʃᵊn **-s** -z
inventive ɪnˈven.tɪv US -t̬ɪv **-ly** -li **-ness** -nəs, -nɪs
inventor ɪnˈven.təʳ US -t̬ɚ **-s** -z
inventor|y ˈɪn.vᵊn.tr|i, -tᵊr|.i, ɪnˈven.tᵊr|.i US -tɔːr- **-ies** -iz
Inverary ˌɪn.vᵊrˈeə.ri, -rə US -vəˈrer.i
Invercargill *in Scotland:* ˌɪn.vəˈkɑː.gɪl, -gᵊl; -kɑːˈgɪl US -vɚˈkɑːr.gɪl *in New Zealand:* ˌɪn.vəˈkɑː.gɪl US -vɚˈkɑːr-
Invergordon ˌɪn.vəˈgɔː.dᵊn US -vɚˈgɔːr-
Inverkeithing ˌɪn.vəˈkiː.ðɪŋ US -vɚˈ-
Inverness, inverness ˌɪn.vəˈnes US -vɚˈ- **-es** -ɪz *stress shift:* ˌInverness ˈtrain
Inverness-shire ˌɪn.vəˈnes.ʃəʳ, -ˈneʃ-, -ˌʃɪəʳ US -vɚˈnes.ʃɚ, -ˌʃɪr
inverse ɪnˈvɜːs, ˈ-- US -ˈvɜːrs, ˈ-- **-s** -ɪz **-ly** -li **ˌinverse ˈfilter**
inversion ɪnˈvɜː.ʃᵊn, -ʒᵊn US -ˈvɜːr.ʒᵊn, -ʃᵊn **-s** -z
invert (*n. adj.*) ˈɪn.vɜːt US -vɜːrt **-s** -s
in|vert (*v.*) ɪn|ˈvɜːt US -ˈvɜːrt **-verts** -ˈvɜːts US -ˈvɜːrts **-verting** -ˈvɜː.tɪŋ US -ˈvɜːr.t̬ɪŋ **-verted** -ˈvɜː.tɪd US -ˈvɜːr.t̬ɪd **inˌverted ˈcomma** ; **inˌverted ˈsnob** ; **inˌverted ˈsnobbery**
invertase ɪnˈvɜː.teɪz US -ˈvɜːr.teɪs, -teɪz, ˈ---
invertebrate ɪnˈvɜː.tɪ.breɪt, ˌɪn-, ˈ-tə-, -brət, -brɪt US -ˈvɜːr.t̬ə.brɪt, -breɪt **-s** -s
Inverurie ˌɪn.vᵊrˈʊə.ri US -vəˈrʊr.i
invest ɪnˈvest **-s** -s **-ing** -ɪŋ **-ed** -ɪd
investi|gate ɪnˈves.tɪ|.geɪt, -tə- **-gates** -geɪts **-gating** -geɪ.tɪŋ US -geɪ.t̬ɪŋ **-gated** -geɪ.tɪd US -geɪ.t̬ɪd **-gator/s** -geɪ.təʳ/z US -geɪ.t̬ɚ/z
investigation ɪnˌves.tɪˈgeɪ.ʃᵊn, -təˈ- **-s** -z
investigative ɪnˈves.tɪ.gə.tɪv, -tə-, -geɪ- US -geɪ.t̬ɪv
investigatory ɪnˈves.tɪ.gə.tᵊr.i, -tə-, -geɪ-; ɪnˌves.tɪˈgeɪ-, -təˈ- US ɪnˈves.tɪ.gə.tɔːr-, -tə-
investiture ɪnˈves.tɪ.tʃəʳ, -tə-, -tjʊəʳ US -tʃɚ **-s** -z
investment ɪnˈves*t*.mənt **-s** -s **inˈvestment ˌbond**
investor ɪnˈves.təʳ US -tɚ **-s** -z
inveteracy ɪnˈvet.ᵊr.ə.si US -ˈvet̬-
inveterate ɪnˈvet.ᵊr.ət, -ɪt US -ˈvet̬- **-ly** -li **-ness** -nəs, -nɪs
invidious ɪnˈvɪd.i.əs **-ly** -li **-ness** -nəs, -nɪs
invigi|late ɪnˈvɪdʒ.ə|.leɪt, ˈ-ɪ- **-lates** -leɪts **-lating** -leɪ.tɪŋ US -leɪ.t̬ɪŋ **-lated** -leɪ.tɪd US -leɪ.t̬ɪd **-lator/s** -leɪ.təʳ/z US -leɪ.t̬ɚ/z
invigilation ɪnˌvɪdʒ.əˈleɪ.ʃᵊn, -ɪˈ- **-s** -z
invigor|ate ɪnˈvɪg.ᵊr|.eɪt US -ə.r|eɪt **-ates** -eɪts **-ating** -eɪ.tɪŋ US -eɪ.t̬ɪŋ **-ated** -eɪ.tɪd US -eɪ.t̬ɪd **-ator/s** -eɪ.təʳ/z US -eɪ.t̬ɚ/z
invigoration ɪnˌvɪg.ᵊrˈeɪ.ʃᵊn US -əˈreɪ-
invincibility ɪnˌvɪn*t*.səˈbɪl.ə.ti, -sɪˈ-, -ɪ.ti US -ə.t̬i
invincib|le ɪnˈvɪn*t*.sə.b|l̩, -sɪ- **-ly** -li **-leness** -l̩.nəs, -nɪs
inviolability ɪnˌvaɪə.ləˈbɪl.ə.ti, ˌɪn-, -ɪ.ti US -ə.t̬i
inviolab|le ɪnˈvaɪə.lə.b|l̩ **-ly** -li **-leness** -l̩.nəs, -nɪs
inviolate ɪnˈvaɪə.lət, -lɪt, -leɪt **-ly** -li **-ness** -nəs, -nɪs
invisibility ɪnˌvɪz.əˈbɪl.ə.ti, ˌɪn-, -ɪˈ-, -ɪ.ti US -ə.t̬i
invisib|le ɪnˈvɪz.ə.b|l̩, ˌɪn-, ˈ-ɪ- **-ly** -li **-leness** -l̩.nəs, -nɪs
invitation ˌɪn.vɪˈteɪ.ʃᵊn, -vəˈ- **-s** -z **-al/s** -ᵊl/z
in|vite (*v.*) ɪn|ˈvaɪt **-vites** -ˈvaɪts **-viting/ly** -ˈvaɪ.tɪŋ/li US -ˈvaɪ.t̬ɪŋ/li **-vited** -ˈvaɪ.tɪd US -ˈvaɪ.t̬ɪd **-viter/s** -ˈvaɪ.təʳ/z US -ˈvaɪ.t̬ɚ/z
invite (*n.*) ˈɪn.vaɪt **-s** -s
invitee ˌɪn.vaɪˈtiː, -vɪˈ- US -vaɪˈ-, -vəˈ-
in vitro ˌɪnˈviː.trəʊ, -ˈvɪt.rəʊ US -ˈviː.troʊ, -ˈvɪt.roʊ **in ˌvitro fertiliˈzation**
in vivo ˌɪnˈviː.vəʊ US -voʊ
invo|cate ˈɪn.vəʊ|.keɪt US -və- **-cates** -keɪts **-cating** -keɪ.tɪŋ US -keɪ.t̬ɪŋ **-cated** -keɪ.tɪd US -keɪ.t̬ɪd
invocation ˌɪn.vəʊˈkeɪ.ʃᵊn US -vəˈ- **-s** -z **-al** -ᵊl
invoic|e ˈɪn.vɔɪs **-es** -ɪz **-ing** -ɪŋ **-ed** -t
invok|e ɪnˈvəʊk US -ˈvoʊk **-es** -s **-ing** -ɪŋ **-ed** -t
involucre ˈɪn.və.luː.kəʳ, -ljuː-, ˌɪn.vəˈluː.kəʳ, -ˈljuː- US ˌɪn.voʊˈluː.kɚ, -vəˈ- **-s** -z
involuntar|y ɪnˈvɒl.ən.tᵊr|.i, ˌɪn-, -ᵊn-, -tr|i US -ˈvɑː.lən.ter|.i **-ily** -ᵊl.i, -ɪ.li **-iness** -ɪ.nəs, -ɪ.nɪs
involu|te ˈɪn.və.luː|t, -ljuː|t, ˌ--ˈ- US ˈɪn.və.luː|t **-tes** -ts **-ting** -tɪŋ US -t̬ɪŋ **-ted** -tɪd US -t̬ɪd
involution ˌɪn.vəˈluː.ʃᵊn, -ˈljuː- US -ˈluː- **-s** -z
involv|e ɪnˈvɒlv US -ˈvɑːlv, -ˈvɔːlv **-es** -z **-ing** -ɪŋ **-ed** -d
involvement ɪnˈvɒlv.mənt US -ˈvɑːlv-, -ˈvɔːlv- **-s** -s
invulnerability ɪnˌvʌl.nᵊr.əˈbɪl.ə.ti, ˌɪn-, -ˌvʌn.ᵊr-, -ɪ.ti US -ˌvʌl.nɚ.əˈbɪl.ə.t̬i
invulnerab|le ɪnˈvʌl.nᵊr.ə.b|l̩, ˌɪn-, -ˈvʌn.ᵊr- US -ˈvʌl.nɚ- **-ly** -li **-leness** -l̩.nəs, -nɪs
inward ˈɪn.wəd US -wɚd **-s** -z **-ly** -li **-ness** -nəs, -nɪs
Inwards ˈɪn.wədz US -wɚds
inweav|e ɪnˈwiːv **-es** -z **-ing** -ɪŋ **-ed** -d **inwove** ɪnˈwəʊv US -ˈwoʊv **inwoven** ɪnˈwəʊ.vᵊn US -ˈwoʊ-
Inwood ˈɪn.wʊd
inwov|e (*from* **inweave**) ɪnˈwəʊv US -ˈwoʊv **-en** -ᵊn
inwrought ɪnˈrɔːt US -ˈrɑːt, -ˈrɔːt
io (**I**) ˈaɪ.əʊ US -oʊ **-s** -z
io|date ˈaɪ.əʊ|.deɪt US ˈ-ə- **-dates** -deɪts **-dating** -deɪ.tɪŋ US -deɪ.t̬ɪŋ **-dated** -deɪ.tɪd US -deɪ.t̬ɪd

iodic aɪˈɒd.ɪk (US) -ˈɑː.dɪk
iodide ˈaɪ.əʊ.daɪd (US) ˈ-ə- **-s** -z
iodine ˈaɪ.ə.diːn, -daɪn (US) -daɪn, -dɪn, -diːn
iodiz|e, -is|e ˈaɪ.ə.daɪz **-es** -ɪz **-ing** -ɪŋ **-ed** -d
iodoform aɪˈɒd.ə.fɔːm (US) -ˈoʊ.də.fɔːrm, -ˈɑː-
Iolanthe ˌaɪ.əʊˈlænt.θi (US) ˌaɪəˈ-, ˌaɪ.oʊˈ-
iolite ˈaɪ.əʊ.laɪt (US) ˈ-oʊ-
Iolo ˈjəʊ.ləʊ (US) ˈjoʊ.loʊ
ion ˈaɪ.ən, -ɒn (US) -ən, -ɑːn **-s** -z
Iona aɪˈəʊ.nə (US) -ˈoʊ-
Ione aɪˈəʊ.ni (US) -ˈoʊ-
Ionesco jɒnˈes.kəʊ, ˌiː.ɒnˈ-, ˌiː.əˈnes-, -kuː (US) jəˈnes.koʊ, ˌiː.əˈ-
Ioni|a aɪˈəʊ.ni|.ə (US) -ˈoʊ- **-an/s** -ən/z
ionic (I) aɪˈɒn.ɪk (US) -ˈɑː.nɪk **-s** -s
ionization, -isa- ˌaɪə.naɪˈzeɪ.ʃᵊn, -nɪˈ- (US) -nɪˈ- **-s** -z
ioniz|e, -is|e ˈaɪə.naɪz **-es** -ɪz **-ing** -ɪŋ **-ed** -d **-er/s** -əʳ/z (US) -ɚ/z **-able** -ə.bl̩
ionosphere aɪˈɒn.ə.sfɪəʳ (US) -ˈɑː.nə.sfɪr **-s** -z
iota aɪˈəʊ.tə (US) -ˈoʊ.t̬ə **-s** -z
iotacism aɪˈəʊ.tə.sɪ.zᵊm (US) -ˈoʊ.t̬ə- **-s** -z
IOU ˌaɪ.əʊˈjuː (US) -oʊˈ- **-s** -z
Iowa ˈaɪ.əʊə, ˈaɪə.wə (US) ˈaɪə.wə **ˌIowa ˈCity**
IPA ˌaɪ.piːˈeɪ
ipecac ˈɪp.ɪ.kæk, ˈ-ə-
ipecacuanha ˌɪp.ɪˌkæk.juˈæn.ə, -əˌ-, -ˈɑː.nə (US) -juˈæn.ə
Iphicrates ɪˈfɪk.rə.tiːz
Iphigenia ˌɪf.ɪ.dʒɪˈnaɪə, ˌaɪ.fɪ-, -dʒəˈ-; ɪˌfɪdʒ.ɪˈ-, -əˈ- (US) ˌɪf.ə.dʒəˈ-
Ipoh ˈiː.pəʊ (US) -poʊ
ipse dixit ˌɪp.siˈdɪk.sɪt, -seɪˈ- (US) -siˈ-
ipso facto ˌɪp.səʊˈfæk.təʊ (US) -soʊˈfæk.toʊ
ipso jure ˌɪp.səʊˈjʊə.reɪ, -ri (US) -soʊˈdʒʊr.i
Ipswich ˈɪp.swɪtʃ
IQ ˌaɪˈkjuː **IˈQ ˌtest**
Iqbal ˈɪk.bæl, ˈɪg-, -bɑːl (US) ɪkˈbɑːl
Iquique ɪˈkiː.ki, -keɪ (US) iːˈkiː.keɪ
Iquitos ɪˈkiː.tɒs (US) iːˈkiː.toʊs, -tɔːs
Ira ˈaɪə.rə (US) ˈaɪ-
IRA ˌaɪ.ɑːʳˈeɪ (US) -ɑːrˈ-
Irak ɪˈrɑːk, -ˈræk (US) ɪ-, iː- **-i/s** -i/z
Iran ɪˈrɑːn, -ˈræn (US) -ˈræn, iːˈrɑːn
Iranian ɪˈreɪ.ni.ən, -ˈrɑː- (US) ɪ- **-s** -z
Iraq ɪˈrɑːk, -ˈræk (US) ɪ-, iː- **-i/s** -i/z
irascibility ɪˌræs.əˈbɪl.ə.ti, -ɪˈ-, -ɪ.ti (US) -ə.t̬i
irascib|le ɪˈræs.ə.b|l̩, ˈ-ɪ- **-ly** -li **-leness** -l̩.nəs, -nɪs
irate aɪˈreɪt, ˌaɪ- (US) aɪˈreɪt, ˈ-- **-ly** -li
Irbid ˈɪə.bɪd (US) ˈɪr-
ire aɪəʳ (US) aɪr
Iredell ˈaɪə.del (US) ˈaɪr-
ireful ˈaɪə.fᵊl, -fʊl (US) ˈaɪr **-ly** -i **-ness** -nəs, -nɪs
Ireland ˈaɪə.lənd (US) ˈaɪr-
Iremonger ˈaɪəˌmʌŋ.gəʳ (US) ˈaɪrˌmʌŋ.gɚ, -ˌmɑːŋ-
Irene ˈaɪ.riːn, -ˈ-; -ˈriː.ni (US) -ˈriːn; -ˈriː.ni
irenic aɪˈriː.nɪk, -ˈren.ɪk (US) -ˈren-, -ˈriː.nɪk **-al** -ᵊl
Ireton ˈaɪə.tᵊn (US) ˈaɪr-
Irian ˈɪr.i.ən, -ɑːn (US) -ɑːn, -ən
Irian Jaya ˌɪr.i.ɑːnˈdʒɑː.jə, -ənˈ-, -jɑː
irides (*plur. of* **iris**) ˈaɪə.rɪ.diːz, ˈɪr.ɪ- (US) ˈaɪ.rɪ-, ˈɪr.ɪ-
iridescence ˌɪr.ɪˈdes.ᵊnts, -əˈ-
iridescent ˌɪr.ɪˈdes.ᵊnt, -əˈ- **-ly** -li
iridium ɪˈrɪd.i.əm, aɪ-
iridolog|y ˌɪr.ɪˈdɒl.ə.dʒ|i (US) -ˈdɑː.lə- **-ist/s** -ɪst/s
Irion ˈɪr.i.ən, -ɒn (US) -ɑːn, -ən
iris (I) ˈaɪə.rɪs (US) ˈaɪ- **irises** ˈaɪə.rɪ.sɪz (US) ˈaɪ- **irides** ˈaɪə.rɪ.diːz, ˈɪr.ɪ- (US) ˈaɪ.rɪ-, ˈɪr.ɪ-
Irish ˈaɪə.rɪʃ (US) ˈaɪ- **-ism/s** -ɪ.zᵊm/z **ˌIrish ˈcoffee ; ˌIrish ReˈpublicV ; ˌIrish ReˌpublicanˈArmy ; ˌIrish ˈSea ; ˌIrish ˈstew**
Irish|man ˈaɪə.rɪʃ|.mən (US) ˈaɪ- **-men** -mən, -men
Irishry ˈaɪə.rɪʃ.ri (US) ˈaɪ-
Irish|woman ˈaɪə.rɪʃ|ˌwʊm.ən (US) ˈaɪ- **-women** -ˌwɪm.ɪn
irk ɜːk (US) ɜːrk **-s** -s **-ing** -ɪŋ **-ed** -t
irksome ˈɜːk.səm (US) ˈɜːrk- **-ly** -li **-ness** -nəs, -nɪs
Irkutsk ɜːˈkʊtsk, ɪə- (US) ɪr-
Irlam ˈɜː.ləm (US) ˈɜːr-
Irma ˈɜː.mə (US) ˈɜːr-
iron (I) aɪən (US) ˈaɪ.ɚn, aɪrn **-s** -z **-ing** -ɪŋ **-ed** -d **ˈIron ˌAge ; ˈironing ˌboard ; ˌIron ˈCurtain ; ˌiron ˈlung ; ˈiron ˌmould ; ˌstrike while the ˌiron's ˈhot**
ironbound ˈaɪən.baʊnd (US) ˈaɪ.ɚn-, ˈaɪrn-
Ironbridge ˈaɪən.brɪdʒ, -ˈ- (US) ˈaɪ.ɚn-, ˈaɪrn-
ironclad ˈaɪən.klæd (US) ˈaɪ.ɚn-, ˈaɪrn- **-s** -z
irongray, irongrey ˌaɪənˈgreɪ, ˌaɪəŋ- (US) ˌaɪ.ɚnˈ-, ˌaɪrn- *stress shift:* ˌirongray ˈbattleship
ironic aɪəˈrɒn.ɪk (US) aɪˈrɑː.nɪk **-al** -ᵊl **-ally** -ᵊl.i, -li
ironmonger ˈaɪənˌmʌŋ.gəʳ, ˈaɪəm- (US) ˈaɪ.ɚnˌmʌŋ.gɚ, ˈaɪrn-, -ˌmɑːŋ- **-s** -z
ironmongery ˈaɪənˌmʌŋ.gᵊr.i, ˈaɪəm- (US) ˈaɪ.ɚnˌ-, ˈaɪrn-, -ˌmɑːŋ-
ironside (I) ˈaɪən.saɪd (US) ˈaɪ.ɚn-, ˈaɪrn- **-s** -z
ironstone ˈaɪən.stəʊn (US) ˈaɪ.ɚn.stoʊn, ˈaɪrn-
Ironton ˈaɪən.tən (US) ˈaɪ.ɚn-, ˈaɪrn-
ironware ˈaɪən.weəʳ (US) ˈaɪ.ɚn.wer, ˈaɪrn-
ironwood (I) ˈaɪən.wʊd (US) ˈaɪ.ɚn-, ˈaɪrn-
ironwork ˈaɪən.wɜːk (US) ˈaɪ.ɚn.wɜːrk, ˈaɪrn- **-s** -s
iron|y (*n.*) *sarcasm, etc.:* ˈaɪə.rᵊn|.i (US) ˈaɪ- **-ies** -iz
irony (*adj.*) *like iron:* ˈaɪə.ni (US) ˈaɪ.ɚ-, ˈaɪr-
Iroquoian ˌɪr.əʊˈkwɔɪ.ən (US) -əˈ-
Iroquois (*sing.*) ˈɪr.ə.kwɔɪ, -kwɔɪ (*plur.*) ˈɪr.ə.kwɔɪz, -kwɔɪ
irradian|ce ɪˈreɪ.di.ənt|s (US) ɪrˈ- **-cy** -si
irradi|ate ɪˈreɪ.di|.eɪt (US) ɪrˈ- **-ates** -eɪts **-ating** -eɪ.tɪŋ (US) -eɪ.t̬ɪŋ **-ated** -eɪ.tɪd (US) -eɪ.t̬ɪd
irradiation ɪˌreɪ.diˈeɪ.ʃᵊn, ˌɪr.eɪ- (US) ɪrˈ- (US) ɪˌreɪ- **-s** -z
irradicab|le ɪˈræd.ɪ.kə.b|l̩ (US) ɪrˈ- **-ly** -li
irrational ɪˈræʃ.ᵊn.ᵊl, ˌɪrˈæʃ-, -ˈræʃ.nᵊl **-ly** -i
irrationality ɪˌræʃ.ᵊnˈæl.ə.ti, ˌɪrˌæʃ-, -ɪ.ti (US) -ə.t̬i
Irrawaddy ˌɪr.əˈwɒd.i (US) -ˈwɑː.di, -ˈwɔː-
irrebuttable ˌɪr.ɪˈbʌt.ə.bl̩ (US) -ˈbʌt̬-
irreceptive ˌɪr.ɪˈsep.tɪv
irreclaimab|le ˌɪr.ɪˈkleɪ.mə.b|l̩ **-ly** -li
irrecognizable, -isa- ɪˌrek.əgˈnaɪ.zə.bl̩, ˌɪrˌek-
irreconcilability ɪˌrek.ᵊnˌsaɪ.ləˈbɪl.ə.ti, ˌɪrˌek-, -ɪ.ti (US) -ə.t̬i
irreconcilab|le ˌɪr.ek.ᵊnˈsaɪ.lə.b|l̩, ɪˌrek- **-ly** -li **-leness** -l̩.nəs, -nɪs
irrecoverab|le ˌɪr.ɪˈkʌv.ᵊr.ə.b|l̩, -əˈ- **-ly** -li **-leness** -l̩.nəs, -nɪs
irredeemab|le ˌɪr.ɪˈdiː.mə.b|l̩, -əˈ- **-ly** -li **-leness** -l̩.nəs, -nɪs
irredent|ism ˌɪr.ɪˈden.t|ɪ.zᵊm, -əˈ- **-ist/s** -ɪst/s
irreducib|le ˌɪr.ɪˈdjuː.sə.b|l̩, -əˈ-, -sɪ- (US) -ˈduː-, -ˈdjuː- **-ly** -li **-leness** -l̩.nəs, -nɪs
irrefutability ɪˌref.jə.təˈbɪl.ə.ti, -jʊ-, -ɪ.ti; ˌɪr.ɪˌfjuː.təˈ-, -əˌ- (US) -t̬əˈbɪl.ə.t̬i
irrefutab|le ˌɪr.ɪˈfjuː.tə.b|l̩, -əˈ-; ɪˈref.jə-, -jʊ- (US) ɪˈref.jə.t̬ə-; ˌɪr.ɪˈfjuː-, -əˈ- **-ly** -li **-leness** -l̩.nəs, -nɪs
irregular ɪˈreg.jə.ləʳ, -jʊ- (US) -lɚ **-ly** -li
irregularit|y ɪˌreg.jəˈlær.ə.t|i, ˌɪrˌeg-, -jʊˈ-, -ɪ.t|i (US) ɪˌreg.jəˈler.ə.t̬|i, -ˈlær- **-ies** -iz
irrelevan|ce ɪˈrel.ə.vᵊnt|s, ˈ-ɪ- (US) ɪrˈ- **-cy** -si **-cies** -siz
irrelevant ɪˈrel.ə.vᵊnt, ˈ-ɪ- (US) ɪrˈ- **-ly** -li
irreligion ˌɪr.ɪˈlɪdʒ.ᵊn, -əˈ-

irreligious ˌɪr.ɪˈlɪdʒ.əs, -əˈ- **-ly** -li **-ness** -nəs, -nɪs
irremediab|le ˌɪr.ɪˈmiː.di.ə.b|l̩ **-ly** -li
irremovability ˌɪr.ɪˌmuː.vəˈbɪl.ə.ti, -əˌ-, -ɪ.ti (US) -ə.t̬i
irremovab|le ˌɪr.ɪˈmuː.və.b|l̩, -əˈ- **-ly** -li
irreparability ɪˌrep.ər.əˈbɪl.ə.ti, ˌɪrˌep-, -ɪ.ti (US) -ə.t̬i
irreparab|le ɪˈrep.ər.ə.b|l̩ **-ly** -li **-leness** -l̩.nəs, -nɪs
irreplaceable ˌɪr.ɪˈpleɪ.sə.bl̩
irrepressib|le ˌɪr.ɪˈpres.ə.b|l̩, -əˈ-, ˈ-ɪ- **-ly** -li **-leness** -l̩.nəs, -nɪs
irreproachability ˌɪr.ɪˌprəʊ.tʃəˈbɪl.ə.ti, -əˌ-, -ɪ.ti (US) -ˌproʊ.tʃəˈbɪl.ə.t̬i
irreproachab|le ˌɪr.ɪˈprəʊ.tʃə.b|l̩, -əˈ- (US) -ˈproʊ- **-ly** -li **-leness** -l̩.nəs, -nɪs
irresistibility ˌɪr.ɪˌzɪs.təˈbɪl.ə.ti, -əˌ-, -tɪˈ-, -ɪ.ti (US) -ə.t̬i
irresistib|le ˌɪr.ɪˈzɪs.tə.b|l̩, -əˈ-, -tɪ- **-ly** -li **-leness** -l̩.nəs, -nɪs
irresoluble ɪˈrez.əl.jə.bl̩, -jʊ- (US) ˌɪr.ɪˈzɑːl.jə-
irresolute ɪˈrez.əl.uːt, ˌɪrˈez-, -juːt (US) -uːt **-ly** -li **-ness** -nəs, -nɪs
irresolution ɪˌrez.əlˈuː.ʃən, -ˈljuː- (US) -ˈuː-
irresolvability ˌɪr.ɪˌzɒl.vəˈbɪl.ə.ti, -əˌ-, -ɪ.ti (US) -ˌzɑːl.vəˈbɪl.ə.t̬i
irresolvab|le ˌɪr.ɪˈzɒl.və.b|l̩ (US) -ˈzɑːl.və- **-ly** -li **-leness** -l̩.nəs, -nɪs
irrespective ˌɪr.ɪˈspek.tɪv, -əˈ- **-ly** -li
irresponsibility ˌɪr.ɪˌspɒnt.səˈbɪl.ə.ti, -əˌ-, -sɪˈ-, -ɪ.ti (US) -ˌspɑːnt.səˈbɪl.ə.t̬i
irresponsib|le ˌɪr.ɪˈspɒnt.sə.b|l̩, -əˈ-, -sɪ- (US) -ˈspɑːnt- **-ly** -li **-leness** -l̩.nəs, -nɪs
irresponsive ˌɪr.ɪˈspɒnt.sɪv, -əˈ- (US) -ˈspɑːnt- **-ly** -li **-ness** -nəs, -nɪs
irretentive ˌɪr.ɪˈten.tɪv, -əˈ- (US) -t̬ɪv
irretrievability ˌɪr.ɪˌtriː.vəˈbɪl.ə.ti, -əˌ-, -ɪ.ti (US) -ə.t̬i
irretrievab|le ˌɪr.ɪˈtriː.və.b|l̩, -əˈ- **-ly** -li **-leness** -l̩.nəs, -nɪs
irreverence ɪˈrev.ər.ənts, ˌɪrˈev-
irreverent ɪˈrev.ər.ənt, ˌɪrˈev- **-ly** -li
irreversibility ˌɪr.ɪˌvɜː.səˈbɪl.ə.ti, -əˌ-, -sɪˈ-, -ɪ.ti (US) -ˌvɜːr.səˈbɪl.ə.t̬i, -sɪˈ-
irreversib|le ˌɪr.ɪˈvɜː.sə.b|l̩, -əˈ-, -sɪ- (US) -ˈvɜːr- **-ly** -li **-leness** -l̩.nəs, -nɪs
irrevocability ɪˌrev.ə.kəˈbɪl.ə.ti, -ɪ.ti (US) -ə.t̬i
irrevocab|le ɪˈrev.ə.kə.b|l̩ **-ly** -li *when applied to letters of credit:* ˌɪr.ɪˈvəʊ.kə.bl̩, -əˈ- (US) ɪˈrev.ə.kə-; ˌɪr.ɪˈvoʊ-
irrigable ˈɪr.ɪ.gə.bl̩, ˈ-ə-
irri|gate ˈɪr.ɪ|.geɪt, ˈ-ə- **-gates** -geɪts **-gating** -geɪ.tɪŋ (US) -geɪ.t̬ɪŋ **-gated** -geɪ.tɪd (US) -geɪ.t̬ɪd **-gator/s** -geɪ.təʳ/z (US) -geɪ.t̬ɚ/z
irrigation ˌɪr.ɪˈgeɪ.ʃən, -əˈ- **-s** -z
irritability ˌɪr.ɪ.təˈbɪl.ə.ti, ˈ-ə-, -ɪ.ti (US) -t̬əˈbɪl.ə.t̬i
irritab|le ˈɪr.ɪ.tə.b|l̩, ˈ-ə- (US) -t̬ə- **-ly** -li **-leness** -l̩.nəs, -nɪs ˌ**irritable** ˈ**bowel** ˌ**syndrome**
irritant ˈɪr.ɪ.tənt, ˈ-ə- (US) -t̬ənt **-s** -s
irri|tate ˈɪr.ɪ|.teɪt, ˈ-ə- **-tates** -teɪts **-tating/ly** -teɪ.tɪŋ/li (US) -teɪ.t̬ɪŋ/li **-tated** -teɪ.tɪd (US) -teɪ.t̬ɪd **-tative** -teɪ.tɪv (US) -teɪ.t̬ɪv **-tator/s** -teɪ.təʳ/z (US) -teɪ.t̬ɚ/z
irritation ˌɪr.ɪˈteɪ.ʃən, -əˈ- **-s** -z
irrupt ɪˈrʌpt **-s** -s **-ing** -ɪŋ **-ed** -ɪd **-ive/ly** -ɪv/li
irruption ɪˈrʌp.ʃən **-s** -z
Irvine *name:* ˈɜː.vɪn, -vaɪn (US) ˈɜːr- *US city:* ˈɜː.vaɪn (US) ˈɜːr-
Irvinestown ˈɜː.vɪnz.taʊn (US) ˈɜːr-
Irving ˈɜː.vɪŋ (US) ˈɜːr-
Irwin ˈɜː.wɪn (US) ˈɜːr-
is (*from* **be**) *strong form:* ɪz *weak forms:* z, s
Note: /z/ is used only when the preceding word ends in a vowel or a voiced consonant other than /z/ or /ʒ/. /s/ is used only when the preceding word ends in a voiceless consonant other than /s/ or /ʃ/.
Isaac ˈaɪ.zək **-s** -s
Isaacson ˈaɪ.zək.sən
Isabel ˈɪz.ə.bel
Isabella ˌɪz.əˈbel.ə
Isabelle ˈɪz.ə.bel
Isaiah aɪˈzaɪə (US) aɪˈzeɪə, -ˈzaɪə
Isambard ˈɪz.əm.bɑːd (US) -bɑːrd
Isard ˈɪz.ɑːd (US) -ɑːrd
-isation -aɪˈzeɪ.ʃən, -ɪˈ- (US) -ɪˈ-
Note: Suffix. Words containing **-isation** alway carry primary stress as shown above, e.g. **decimalisation** /ˌdes.ɪ.məl.aɪˈzeɪ.ʃən (US) -ɪˈ-/.
ISBN ˌaɪ.es.biːˈen
Iscariot ɪsˈkær.i.ət (US) -ˈker-, -ˈkær-
Ischia ˈɪs.ki.ə
-ise -aɪz, -iːz
Note: Suffix. Where **-ise** forms a verb, the pronunciation is /-aɪz/. See note for **-ize**. Where **-ise** forms a noun, it usually carries primary stress (e.g. **experˈtise**) and is pronounced /-iːz/.
Iseult iˈzuːlt, -ˈsuːlt (US) -ˈsuːlt
-ish -ɪʃ
Note: Suffix. When forming an adjective, **-ish** does not affect the stress pattern of the word, e.g. **yellowish** /ˈjel.əʊ.ɪʃ (US) -oʊ-/. When forming a verb, the antepenultimate syllable is stressed, e.g. **demolish** /dɪˈmɒl.ɪʃ (US) -ˈmɑː.lɪʃ/.
Isham ˈaɪ.ʃəm
Isherwood ˈɪʃ.ə.wʊd (US) ˈ-ɚ-
Ishmael ˈɪʃ.meɪəl, -mi.əl
Ishmae|lite ˈɪʃ.mi.ə|.laɪt, -meɪə|.laɪt, -mə|.laɪt **-lites** -laɪts **-litish** -laɪ.tɪʃ (US) -laɪ.t̬ɪʃ
Ishtar ˈɪʃ.tɑːʳ (US) -tɑːr
Isidore ˈɪz.ɪ.dɔːʳ, ˈ-ə- (US) -ə.dɔːr
Isidorian ˌɪz.ɪˈdɔː.ri.ən, -əˈ- (US) -ɪˈdɔːr.i-
isinglass ˈaɪ.zɪŋ.glɑːs (US) -zɪn.glæs, -zɪŋ-
Isis ˈaɪ.sɪs
Isla ˈaɪ.lə
Islam ˈɪz.lɑːm, ˈɪs-, -læm, -ləm; ɪzˈlɑːm, ɪs-
Islamabad ɪzˈlɑː.mə.bæd, ɪs-, -ˈlæm.ə-, -bɑːd (US) -ˈlɑː.mə.bɑːd
Islamic ɪzˈlæm.ɪk, ɪs-, -ˈlɑː.mɪk (US) -ˈlɑː-, -ˈlæm.ɪk **-s** -s
Islam|ism ˈɪz.lə.m|ɪ.zəm, ˈɪs- **-ist/s** -ɪst/s
island ˈaɪ.lənd **-s** -z **-er/s** -əʳ/z (US) -ɚ/z
Islay ˈaɪ.leɪ *locally:* ˈaɪ.lə
isle aɪl **-s** -z
Isle of Dogs ˌaɪl.əvˈdɒgz (US) -ˈdɑːgz, -ˈdɔːgz
Isle of Man ˌaɪl.əvˈmæn
Isle of Wight ˌaɪl.əvˈwaɪt
islet ˈaɪ.lət, -lɪt, -let (US) -lɪt **-s** -s
Isleworth ˈaɪ.zəl.wəθ, -wɜːθ (US) -wɜːrθ, -wɚθ
Islington ˈɪz.lɪŋ.tən
Islip *archbishop:* ˈɪz.lɪp *in Oxfordshire:* ˈaɪ.slɪp
Islwyn ˈɪs.lu.ɪn; ɪzˈluː.ɪn, ɪs-
-ism -ɪ.zəm **-s** -z
Note: Suffix. When added to a free stem, **-ism** does not normally affect the stress pattern of the word, e.g. **absentee** /ˌæb.sənˈtiː/, **absenteeism** /ˌæb.sənˈtiː.ɪ.zəm/. When added to a bound stem, the word is normally stressed two syllables before the suffix, e.g. **exorcism** /ˈek.sɔː.sɪ.zəm (US) -sɔːr-/. Exceptions exist; see individual entries.
Ismail ˌɪz.mɑːˈiːl, ˌɪs-, ˈɪz.maɪl, -meɪl
Ismailiya ˌɪz.maɪˈliː.ə, ˌɪs- (US) ˌɪs.meɪ.əˈ-, ˌɪz-
Ismay ˈɪz.meɪ
isn't ˈɪz.ənt
iso- aɪ.səʊ-; aɪˈsɒ- (US) aɪ.soʊ-, -sə-; aɪˈsɑː-
Note: Prefix. Normally takes either primary or secondary stress on the first syllable, e.g. **isotope** /ˈaɪ.sə.təʊp (US) -toʊp/, **isotopic** /ˌaɪ.səˈtɒp.ɪk (US) -ˈtɑː.pɪk/, or primary stress on the second syllable, e.g. **isotropy** /aɪˈsɒt.rə.pi (US) -ˈsɑː.trə-/.
ISO ˌaɪ.esˈəʊ (US) -ˈoʊ
isobar ˈaɪ.səʊ.bɑːʳ (US) -soʊ.bɑːr, -sə- **-s** -z
Isobel ˈɪz.ə.bel

isochromatic ˌaɪ.səʊ.krəʊˈmæt.ɪk US -soʊ.kroʊˈmæţ.ɪk, -sə-
isochronal aɪˈsɒk.rə.nᵊl US -ˈsɑː.krə- **-ly** -i
isochronous aɪˈsɒk.rə.nəs US -ˈsɑː.krə- **-ly** -li
Isocrates aɪˈsɒk.rə.tiːz US -ˈsɑː.krə-
isogloss ˈaɪ.səʊ.glɒs US -soʊ.glɑːs, -sə- **-es** -ɪz
isolate (*n.*) ˈaɪ.sᵊl.ət, -ɪt, -eɪt US -sə.lɪt **-s** -s
iso|late (*v.*) ˈaɪ.sə|.leɪt **-lates** -leɪts **-lating** -leɪ.tɪŋ US -leɪ.ţɪŋ **-lated** -leɪ.tɪd US -leɪ.ţɪd **-lator/s** -leɪ.təʳ/z US -leɪ.ţɚ/z
isolation ˌaɪ.sᵊlˈeɪ.ʃᵊn
isolation|ism ˌaɪ.sᵊlˈeɪ.ʃᵊn|.ɪ.zᵊm **-ist/s** -ɪst/s
isolative ˈaɪ.sᵊl.ə.tɪv, -eɪ.tɪv US -sə.leɪ.ţɪv, -soʊ- **-ly** -li
Isolda ɪˈzɒl.də US -ˈsoʊl-, -ˈzoʊl-
Isolde ɪˈzɒl.də US -ˈsoʊl-, -ˈzoʊl-; -ˈsoʊld, -ˈzoʊld
isomer ˈaɪ.sə.məʳ US -soʊ.mɚ, -sə- **-s** -z
isomeric ˌaɪ.səʊˈmer.ɪk US -soʊˈ-, -səˈ-
isomer|ism aɪˈsɒm.ᵊr|.ɪ.zᵊm US -ˈsɑː.mɚ- **-ous** -əs
isometric ˌaɪ.səʊˈmet.rɪk US -soʊˈ-, -səˈ- **-al** -ᵊl **-ally** -ᵊl.i, -li
isomorph ˈaɪ.səʊ.mɔːf US -soʊ.mɔːrf, -sə- **-s** -s
isomorph|ism ˌaɪ.səʊˈmɔː.f|ɪ.zᵊm US -soʊˈmɔːr- **-ic** -ɪk **-ous** -əs
Ison ˈaɪ.sᵊn
isophone ˈaɪ.səʊ.fəʊn US -soʊ.foʊn, -sə- **-s** -z
isosceles aɪˈsɒs.ᵊl.iːz, -ɪ.liːz US -ˈsɑː.sᵊl.iːz
isotherm ˈaɪ.səʊ.θɜːm US -soʊ.θɜːrm, -sə- **-s** -z
isothermal ˌaɪ.səˈθɜː.mᵊl US -ˈθɜːr- **-ly** -i
isotonic ˌaɪ.səˈtɒn.ɪk US -ˈtɑː.nɪk
isotope ˈaɪ.sə.təʊp US -toʊp **-s** -s
isotopic ˌaɪ.səˈtɒp.ɪk US -ˈtɑː.pɪk **-ally** -ᵊl.i, -li
isotropic ˌaɪ.səˈtrɒp.ɪk US -ˈtrɑː.pɪk **-ally** -ᵊl.i, -li
isotropy aɪˈsɒt.rə.pi US -ˈsɑː.trə-
I-spy ˌaɪˈspaɪ
Israel ˈɪz.reɪəl, -ri.əl, -reɪ.el US -ri.əl, -reɪ-, -rᵊl
Israeli ɪzˈreɪ.li **-s** -z
Israelite ˈɪz.ri.ə.laɪt, -reɪ-, -rə.laɪt, -rɪ- US -ri.ə-, -reɪ- **-s** -s
Issachar ˈɪs.ə.kəʳ, -kɑːʳ US -kɑːr
iss|ue ˈɪʃ|.uː, ˈɪs.j|uː US ˈɪʃ|.uː **-ues** -uːz **-uing** -uː.ɪŋ **-ued** -uːd **-uer/s** -uː.əʳ/z US -uː.ɚ/z **-uable** -u.ə.bl̩ **-uance** -u.ᵊnts

-ist -ɪst
Note: Suffix. When attached to a free stem, **-ist** does not normally affect the stress pattern of the stem, e.g. **modern** /ˈmɒd.ᵊn US ˈmɑː.dɚn/, **modernist** /ˈmɒd.ᵊn.ɪst US ˈmɑː.dɚ.nɪst/. When attached to a bound stem, the word is normally stressed on the penultimate syllable, e.g. **Baptist** /ˈbæp.tɪst/. Exceptions exist; see individual entries.
Istanbul ˌɪs.tænˈbʊl, -tɑːnˈ-, -tæmˈ-, -tɑːmˈ- US -tɑːnˈ-, -tænˈ-, -ˈbuːl
isthmi (*plur. of* **isthmus**) ˈɪs.maɪ, ˈɪsθ-, ˈɪst- US ˈɪs-
isthmian (I) ˈɪsθ.mi.ən, ˈɪst-, ˈɪs- US ˈɪs-
isthmus ˈɪs.məs, ˈɪsθ-, ˈɪst- US ˈɪs- **-es** -ɪz
-istic -ˈɪs.tɪk
Note: Suffix. Normally takes primary stress as shown, e.g. **impressionistic** /ɪmˌpreʃ.ᵊnˈɪs.tɪk/.
istle ˈɪst.li
Istria ˈɪs.tri.ə
it ɪt
IT ˌaɪˈtiː
Italian ɪˈtæl.i.ən US ˈ-jən **-s** -z
italianate ɪˈtæl.i.ə.neɪt, -nət, -nɪt US ˈ-jə.nɪt
italianism ɪˈtæl.i.ə.nɪ.zᵊm US ˈ-jə- **-s** -z
italianiz|e, -is|e ɪˈtæl.i.ə.naɪz US ˈ-jə- **-es** -ɪz **-ing** -ɪŋ **-ed** -d
italic (I) ɪˈtæl.ɪk **-s** -s
italicization, -isa- ɪˌtæl.ɪ.saɪˈzeɪ.ʃᵊn, ˌ-ə-, -sɪˈ- US -sɪˈ-
italiciz|e, -is|e ɪˈtæl.ɪ.saɪz, ˈ-ə- **-es** -ɪz **-ing** -ɪŋ **-ed** -d
Italy ˈɪt.ᵊl.i US ˈɪţ-
itch ɪtʃ **-es** -ɪz **-ing** -ɪŋ **-ed** -t
Itchen ˈɪtʃ.ɪn, -ᵊn
itch|y ˈɪtʃ|.i **-ier** -i.əʳ US -i.ɚ **-iest** -i.ɪst, -i.əst **-iness** -ɪ.nəs, -ɪ.nɪs
it'd ˈɪt.əd US ˈɪţ-
item ˈaɪ.təm, -tɪm, -tem US -ţəm **-s** -z
itemiz|e, -is|e ˈaɪ.tə.maɪz, -tɪ- US -ţə- **-es** -ɪz **-ing** -ɪŋ **-ed** -d
iter|ate ˈɪt.ᵊr|.eɪt US ˈɪţ.ə.r|eɪt **-ates** -eɪts **-ating** -eɪ.tɪŋ US -eɪ.ţɪŋ **-ated** -eɪ.tɪd US -eɪ.ţɪd
iteration ˌɪt.ᵊrˈeɪ.ʃᵊn US ˌɪţ.əˈreɪ- **-s** -z
iterative ˈɪt.ᵊr.ə.tɪv, -eɪ- US ˈɪţ.ə.reɪ.ţɪv, -ɚ.ə- **-ly** -li **-ness** -nəs, -nɪs
Ithaca ˈɪθ.ə.kə
itinerancy aɪˈtɪn.ᵊr.ᵊnt.si, ɪ-
itinerant aɪˈtɪn.ᵊr.ᵊnt, ɪ- **-s** -s
itinerar|y aɪˈtɪn.ᵊr.ᵊr|.i, ɪ- US -ə.rer- **-ies** -iz
itiner|ate aɪˈtɪn.ᵊr|.eɪt, ɪ- US -ə.r|eɪt **-ates** -eɪts **-ating** -eɪ.tɪŋ US -eɪ.ţɪŋ **-ated** -eɪ.tɪd US -eɪ.ţɪd

-ition -ˈɪʃ.ᵊn
Note: Suffix. Always stressed as shown, e.g. **edition** /ɪˈdɪʃ.ᵊn/.
-itious -ˈɪʃ.əs
Note: Suffix. Always stressed as shown, e.g. **surreptitious** /ˌsʌr.əpˈtɪʃ.əs US ˌsɜːr.əpˈ-/.
-itis -ˈaɪ.tɪs US -ˈaɪ.ţɪs, -ţəs
Note: Suffix. Always stressed as shown, e.g. **tonsilitis** /ˌtɒnt.sᵊlˈaɪ.tɪs US ˌtɑːnt.səˈlaɪ.ţɪs/.
-itive -ɪ.tɪv, -ə- US -ə.ţɪv, -ɪ-
Note: Suffix. Words containing **-itive** are normally stressed on the antepenultimate syllable, e.g. **competitive** /kəmˈpet.ɪ.tɪv US -ə.ţɪv/. Exceptions exist; see individual entries.
it'll (= *it will, it shall*) ˈɪt.ᵊl US ˈɪţ-
-itory -ə.tᵊr.i, -ɪ-, -tri US -ə.tɔːr.i, -ɪ-
Note: Suffix. Words containing **-itory** are normally stressed on the syllable preceding the prefix, e.g. **territory** /ˈter.ɪ.tᵊr.i US ˈter.ɪ.tɔːr.i/. Exceptions exist; see individual entries.
its ɪts
it's (= *it is, it has*) ɪts
itself ɪtˈself
itsy-bitsy ˌɪt.siˈbɪt.si
itty-bitty ˌɪt.iˈbɪt.i US ˌɪţ.iˈbɪţ-
ITV ˌaɪ.tiːˈviː
-ity -ə.ti, -ɪ.ti US -ə.ţi
Note: Suffix. Words containing **-ity** are normally stressed on the antepenultimate syllable, e.g. **conformity** /kənˈfɔː.mə.ti US -ˈfɔːr.mə.ţi/.
IUD ˌaɪ.juːˈdiː
Ivan ˈaɪ.vᵊn US ˈaɪ.vən *foreign name:* iːˈvæn, ɪ-, -ˈvɑːn US -ˈvɑːn
Ivanhoe ˈaɪ.vᵊn.həʊ US -hoʊ
Ivanoff ɪˈvɑː.nəf, iː-, -nɒf US ˈiː.və.nɑːf; iːˈvɑː-
Ivatt ˈaɪ.vət, -væt **-s** -s
I've (= *I have*) aɪv
-ive -ɪv
Note: Suffix. Words containing **-ive** are either stressed on the penultimate syllable, e.g. **expensive** /ɪkˈspent.sɪv/, or on the antepenultimate syllable, e.g. **executive** /ɪgˈzek.jə tɪv US -ţɪv/.
Iveagh ˈaɪ.və, -veɪ
Iveco® ɪˈveɪ.kəʊ, aɪˈ-, -ˈviː- US -ˈveɪ.koʊ
Ivens ˈaɪ.vᵊnz
Iver ˈaɪ.vəʳ US -vɚ
Ives *surname, and towns* **St. Ives** *in Cornwall and Cambridgeshire:* aɪvz *in Stevenson's 'St. Ives':* iːvz
Ivey ˈaɪ.vi
IVF ˌaɪ.viːˈef
Ivor ˈaɪ.vəʳ US -vɚ, ˈiː-

ivor|y (I) ˈaɪ.vᵊr|.i **-ies** -iz ˌ**Ivory ˈCoast** ; ˌ**ivory ˈtower**
ivory-black ˌaɪ.vᵊr.iˈblæk
iv|y (I) ˈaɪ.v|i **-ies** -iz **-ied** -id ˈ**Ivy** ˌ**League**
Ivybridge ˈaɪ.vi.brɪdʒ
ixia ˈɪk.si.ə **-s** -z
Ixion ɪkˈsaɪən (US) -ˈsaɪən, -ˈsaɪ.ɑːn
Iza ˈaɪ.zə
Izaby ˈɪz.ə.bi
Izal® ˈaɪ.zᵊl
izard ˈɪz.əd (US) -ɚd **-s** -z
Izard ˈaɪ.zɑːd, -zəd; ˈɪz.əd (US) ˈaɪ.zɑːrd, -zɚd; ˈɪz.ɚd
-ization -aɪˈzeɪ.ʃᵊn, -ɪˈ- (US) -ɪˈ-
Note: Suffix. Words containing **-ization** always carry primary stress as shown above, e.g. **decimalization** /ˌdes.ɪ.mᵊl.aɪˈzeɪ.ʃᵊn (US) -ɪˈ-/.
-ize, **-ise** -aɪz
Note: Suffix. When attached to a free stem, **-ize** does not normally affect the stress pattern of the stem, e.g. **decimal** /ˈdes.ɪ.mᵊl/, **decimalize** /ˈdes.ɪ.mᵊl.aɪz (US) -mə.laɪz/. When attached to a bound stem, the word is normally stressed on the antepenultimate syllable, e.g. **recognize** /ˈrek.əg.naɪz/. Exceptions exist; see individual entries.
Izmir ˈɪz.mɪəʳ, -ˈ- (US) ɪzˈmɪr
Izzard ˈɪz.əd, -ɑːd (US) -ɚd, -ɑːrd

J

j (J) dʒeɪ **-'s** -z
jab dʒæb **-s** -z **-bing** -ɪŋ **-bed** -d
jabb|er 'dʒæb|.əʳ (US) -ɚ **-ers** -əz (US) -ɚz **-ering** -ᵊr.ɪŋ **-ered** -əd (US) -ɚd **-erer/s** -ᵊr.əʳ/z (US) -ɚ.ɚ/z
Jabberwock 'dʒæb.ə.wɒk (US) -ɚ.wɑːk **-y** -i
jabberwocky (J) 'dʒæb.ə.wɒk.i (US) -ɚ.wɑː.ki, -wɔːk
Jabez 'dʒeɪ.bez, -bɪz
jabiru ˌdʒæb.ə'ruː, -ɪ'-, '--- (US) 'dʒæb.ə.ruː, ˌ--'- **-s** -z
jaborandi ˌdʒæb.ə'ræn.di, ˌʒæb-, -ɔː'-; -ræn'diː (US) ˌdʒæb.ə'ræn.di; -ræn'diː
jabot 'ʒæb.əʊ (US) ʒæb'oʊ **-s** -z
jacamar 'dʒæk.ə.mɑːʳ, 'ʒæk- (US) 'dʒæk.ə.mɑːr **-s** -z
jacaranda ˌdʒæk.ə'ræn.də **-s** -z
Jacinta dʒə'sɪn.tə, hə-
jacinth (J) 'dʒæs.ɪn*t*θ, 'dʒeɪ.sɪn*t*θ **-s** -s
Jacintha dʒə'sɪn*t*.θə, dʒæs'ɪn*t*-
jack (J) dʒæk **-s** -s **-ing** -ɪŋ **-ed** -t ˌ**Jack 'Frost** ; ˌ**Jack 'Robinson** ; ˌ**Jack 'Russell** ; ˌ**jack 'tar** ; ˌ**Jack the 'lad**
jackal 'dʒæk.ɔːl, -ᵊl (US) -ᵊl **-s** -z
jackanapes 'dʒæk.ə.neɪps **-es** -ɪz
jackaroo ˌdʒæk.ᵊr'uː (US) -ə'ruː **-s** -z
jackass 'dʒæk.æs **-es** -ɪz
jackboot 'dʒæk.buːt **-s** -s **-ed** -ɪd
jackdaw 'dʒæk.dɔː (US) -dɑː, -dɔː **-s** -z
jackeroo ˌdʒæk.ᵊr'uː (US) -ə'ruː **-s** -z
jack|et 'dʒæk|.ɪt **-ets** -ɪts **-eting** -ɪ.tɪŋ (US) -ɪ.t̬ɪŋ **-eted** -ɪ.tɪd (US) -ɪ.t̬ɪd
jackhammer 'dʒækˌhæm.əʳ (US) -ɚ **-s** -z
Jackie 'dʒæk.i
jack-in-office 'dʒæk.ɪnˌɒf.ɪs (US) -ˌɑː.fɪs **jacks-in-office** 'dʒæks-
jack-in-the-box 'dʒæk.ɪn.ðə.bɒks (US) -bɑːks **-es** -ɪz
jack-kni|fe (*n*) 'dʒæk.naɪ|f **-ves** -vz
jackknif|e (*v*) 'dʒæk.naɪf **-es** -s **-ing** -ɪŋ **-ed** -t
Jacklin 'dʒæk.lɪn
Jackman 'dʒæk.mən
jack-of-all-trades ˌdʒæk.əv'ɔːl.treɪdz, -ɔːl'treɪdz (US) -'ɔːl-, -'ɑːl- **jacks-of-all-trades** ˌdʒæks-
jack-o'-lantern ˌdʒæk.əʊ'læn.tən, 'dʒæk.əʊˌlæn.tən (US) 'dʒæk.əˌlæn.tɚn **-s** -z
jackpot 'dʒæk.pɒt (US) -pɑːt **-s** -s ˌ**hit the 'jackpot**
jackrabbit 'dʒækˌræb.ɪt **-s** -s
Jackson 'dʒæk.sᵊn
Jacksonian ˌdʒæk'səʊ.ni.ən (US) -'soʊ-
Jacksonville 'dʒæk.sᵊn.vɪl
jack-tar ˌdʒæk'tɑːʳ, '-- (US) ˌdʒæk'tɑːr, '-- **-s** -z
Jacklyn 'dʒæk.lɪn
Jacob 'dʒeɪ.kəb ˌ**Jacob's 'ladder**
jacobean (J) ˌdʒæk.əʊ'biː.ən (US) -ə'-, -oʊ'- **-s** -z
Jacobi 'dʒæk.ə.bi; dʒə'kəʊ- (US) -'koʊ-
jacobian (J) dʒə'kəʊ.bi.ən (US) -'koʊ- **-s** -z
Jacobin 'dʒæk.əʊ.bɪn (US) '-ə- **-s** -z **-ism** -ɪ.zᵊm
Jacobit|e 'dʒæk.əʊ.baɪt (US) '-ə- **-es** -s **-ism** -ɪ.zᵊm
Jacobs 'dʒeɪ.kəbz
Jacobson 'dʒæk.əb.sᵊn, 'jæk- (US) 'dʒeɪ.kəb-
jacobus (J) dʒə'kəʊ.bəs (US) -'koʊ- **-es** -ɪz
Jacoby dʒə'kəʊ.bi; 'dʒæk.ə- (US) dʒə'koʊ-; 'dʒæk.ə-
Jacquard 'dʒæk.ɑːd, dʒə'kɑːd (US) dʒə'kɑːrd
Jacqueline 'dʒæk.ə.liːn, 'ʒæk-, -lɪn; 'dʒæk.liːn, -lɪn (US) 'dʒæk.ə.lɪn, -liːn; '-wə.lɪn
Jacques *English surname:* dʒeɪks, dʒæks *French name:* ʒæk (US) ʒɑːk
Jacqui 'dʒæk.i
jactitation ˌdʒæk.tɪ'teɪ.ʃᵊn **-s** -z
jacuzzi (J®) dʒə'kuː.zi, dʒæk'uː- (US) dʒə'kuː- **-s** -z
jad|e (J) dʒeɪd **-es** -z **-ing** -ɪŋ **-ed** -ɪd
jaeger (J®) 'jeɪ.gəʳ, 'dʒeɪ- (US) -gɚ **-s** -z
Jael dʒeɪəl, dʒeɪl, 'dʒeɪ.el (US) dʒeɪəl
Jaffa 'dʒæf.ə (US) 'dʒæf-, 'dʒɑː.fə, 'jɑː- **-s** -z
Jaffna 'dʒæf.nə
jag dʒæg **-s** -z **-ging** -ɪŋ **-ged** -d
Jaggard 'dʒæg.əd (US) -ɚd
jagged 'dʒæg.ɪd **-ly** -li **-ness** -nəs, -nɪs
jagger (J) 'dʒæg.əʳ (US) -ɚ **-s** -z
jagg|y 'dʒæg|.i **-ier** -i.əʳ (US) -i.ɚ **-iest** -i.ɪst, -i.əst **-iness** -ɪ.nəs, -ɪ.nɪs
Jago 'dʒeɪ.gəʊ (US) -goʊ
jaguar (J) 'dʒæg.ju.əʳ (US) 'dʒæg.wɑːr, '-ju.ɑːr **-s** -z
Jah dʒɑː, jɑː
Jahveh 'jɑː.veɪ, ˌjɑː'veɪ, 'dʒɑː.veɪ, 'jɑː.və (US) 'jɑː.veɪ
jai alai ˌhaɪ.ə'laɪ, '---, ˌhaɪ'laɪ, '-- (US) 'haɪˌlaɪ, -əˌlaɪ; ˌhaɪ.ə'laɪ
jail dʒeɪl **-s** -z **-ing** -ɪŋ **-ed** -d
jailbait 'dʒeɪl.beɪt
jailbird 'dʒeɪl.bɜːd (US) -bɝːd **-s** -z
jailbreak 'dʒeɪl.breɪk **-s** -s
jailer, jailor 'dʒeɪ.ləʳ (US) -lɚ **-s** -z
jailhou|se 'dʒeɪl.haʊ|s **-ses** -zɪz
Jaime *English name:* 'dʒeɪ.mi *Spanish name:* 'haɪ.mi
Jain dʒaɪn, dʒeɪn (US) dʒaɪn **-s** -z **-ism** -ɪ.zᵊm
Jaipur ˌdʒaɪ'pʊəʳ, -'pɔːʳ (US) -'pʊr
Jairus 'dʒaɪə.rəs, dʒeɪ'aɪə- (US) 'dʒaɪ-, dʒeɪ'aɪ-
Jakarta dʒə'kɑː.tə (US) -'kɑːr.t̬ə
Jake dʒeɪk
Jakes dʒeɪks
Jalalabad dʒə'lɑː.lə.bɑːd, -'læl.ə-, -bæd; dʒəˌlɑː.lə'bɑːd, -ˌlæl.ə'-, -'bæd
jalap 'dʒæl.əp
jalapeño ˌhæl.ə'peɪ.njəʊ (US) ˌhɑː.lə'peɪ.njoʊ, ˌhæl.ə'- **-s** -z
Jalisco hɑː'les.kəʊ (US) -'liːs.koʊ
jalop|y dʒə'lɒp|.i (US) -'lɑː.p|i **-ies** -iz
jalousie 'ʒæl.u.ziː, ˌ--'-, dʒə'luː.si (US) 'dʒæl.ə.si **-s** -z
jam dʒæm **-s** -z **-ming** -ɪŋ **-med** -d **'jam ˌjar** ; ˌ**jam 'tart** ; **'jam ˌsession**
Jam *Indian title:* dʒɑːm **-s** -z
Jamaic|a dʒə'meɪ.k|ə **-an/s** -ən/z
Jamal dʒə'mɑːl
jamb dʒæm*b* **-s** -z
jambalaya ˌdʒæm.bə'laɪ.ə, ˌdʒʌm- **-s** -z
jamboree ˌdʒæm.bᵊr'iː, '--- (US) ˌdʒæm.bə'riː **-s** -z
James dʒeɪmz
Jameson 'dʒeɪm.sᵊn, 'dʒɪm-, 'dʒem-, 'dʒæm-; 'dʒeɪ.mɪ.sᵊn, 'dʒɪm.ɪ-, 'dʒem-, 'dʒæm-, '-ə- (US) 'dʒeɪm.sᵊn; 'dʒeɪ.mɪ-
James's 'dʒeɪm.zɪz
Jamestown 'dʒeɪmz.taʊn
Jamia 'dʒʌm.i.ə, 'dʒæm-
Jamie 'dʒeɪ.mi
Jamieson 'dʒeɪ.mɪ.sᵊn, 'dʒæm.ɪ-, 'dʒem-, 'dʒɪm-, '-ə- (US) 'dʒeɪ.mɪ-
jam-jar 'dʒæm.dʒɑːʳ (US) -dʒɑːr
Jammu 'dʒæm.uː, 'dʒʌm- (US) 'dʒʌm-
jamm|y 'dʒæm|.i **-ier** -i.əʳ (US) -i.ɚ **-iest** -i.ɪst, -i.əst **-iness** -ɪ.nəs, -ɪ.nɪs
jam-pot 'dʒæm.pɒt (US) -pɑːt **-s** -s
Jamy 'dʒeɪ.mi
Jan *female first name:* dʒæn *male first name:* jæn
Jan. (*abbrev. for* **January**) dʒæn, 'dʒæn.ju.ᵊr.i, -jʊə.ri, -jʊ- (US) -ju.er.i
Jana 'dʒæn.ə, 'dʒeɪ.nə *as if Czech or Polish:* 'jɑː.nə (US) 'dʒæn.ə
Janácek 'jæn.ə.tʃek, '-ɑː- (US) 'jɑː.nə-
Jane dʒeɪn ˌ**Jane 'Doe**
Janeiro dʒə'nɪə.rəʊ, -'neə- (US) ʒə'ner.oʊ, dʒə-, -'nɪr-
Janet 'dʒæn.ɪt, -ət
jangl|e 'dʒæŋ.gḷ **-es** -z **-ing** -ɪŋ, 'dʒæŋ.glɪŋ **-ed** -d **-er/s** -əʳ/z (US) -ɚ/z, 'dʒæŋ.gləʳ/z (US) -glɚ/z
Janice 'dʒæn.ɪs
Janine dʒə'niːn
janissar|y 'dʒæn.ɪ.sᵊr|.i (US) -ə.ser- **-ies** -iz

janitor ˈdʒæn.ɪ.təʳ (US) -ə.t̬ɚ **-s** -z
Jan(n)ette dʒəˈnet, dzænˈet
Jansen ˈdʒænt.sᵊn
Jansen|ism ˈdʒænt.sᵊn|.ɪ.zᵊm **-ist/s** -ɪst/s
Jantzen® ˈjænt.sᵊn, ˈdʒænt- (US) ˈdʒænt-
Januarius ˌdʒæn.juˈeə.ri.əs (US) -ˈer.i-
Januar|y ˈdʒæn.ju.ᵊr|.i, -jʊə.r|i, -jʊ- (US) -ju.er|.i **-ies** -iz
Janus ˈdʒeɪ.nəs
Jap dʒæp **-s** -s
Japan, japan dʒəˈpæn **-s** -z **-ning** -ɪŋ **-ned** -d **-ner/s** -əʳ/z (US) -ɚ/z
Japanese ˌdʒæp.ᵊnˈiːz (US) -ˈiːz, -ˈiːs
jap|e dʒeɪp **-es** -s **-ing** -ɪŋ **-ed** -t
Japhet ˈdʒeɪ.fet, -fɪt
Japheth ˈdʒeɪ.feθ, -fɪθ
japhetic dʒeɪˈfet.ɪk, dʒə- (US) dʒəˈfet̬-
japonica dʒəˈpɒn.ɪ.kə (US) -ˈpɑː.nɪ- **-s** -z
Jaques *name:* dʒeɪks, dʒæks *Shakespearian character:* ˈdʒeɪ.kwɪz (US) -kwɪz, -kiːz; dʒeɪks, dʒæks
jar dʒɑːʳ (US) dʒɑːr **-s** -z **-ring/ly** -ɪŋ/li **-red** -d
Jardine ˈdʒɑː.diːn, -ˈ- (US) ˈdʒɑːr.diːn, -ˈ-
jardinière ˌʒɑː.dɪ.niˈeəʳ, ˌdʒɑː-, -dɪˈnjeəʳ (US) ˌdʒɑːr.dᵊnˈɪr, ˌʒɑːr-, -ˈjer **-s** -z
Jared ˈdʒær.əd (US) ˈdʒer-, ˈdʒær-
jarful ˈdʒɑː.fʊl (US) ˈdʒɑːr- **-s** -z
jargon ˈdʒɑː.gən (US) ˈdʒɑːr- **-s** -z
jargonelle ˌdʒɑː.gəˈnel (US) ˌdʒɑːr- **-s** -z
Jarley ˈdʒɑː.li (US) ˈdʒɑːr-
Jarlsberg® ˈjɑːlz.bɜːg (US) ˈjɑːrlz.bɜːrg
Jarlshof ˈjɑːlz.hɒf (US) ˈjɑːrlz.hɑːf
Jarmaine dʒɑːˈmeɪn (US) dʒɑːr-
Jarman ˈdʒɑː.mən (US) ˈdʒɑːr-
Jarndyce ˈdʒɑːn.daɪs (US) ˈdʒɑːrn-
Jarratt ˈdʒær.ət (US) ˈdʒer-, ˈdʒær-
Jarrell dʒəˈrel (US) dʒəˈrel; ˈdʒer.ᵊl, ˈdʒær-
Jarrett ˈdʒær.ət (US) ˈdʒer-, ˈdʒær-
Jarrod ˈdʒær.əd (US) ˈdʒer-, ˈdʒær-
Jarrold ˈdʒær.ᵊld (US) ˈdʒer-, ˈdʒær-
Jarrow ˈdʒær.əʊ (US) ˈdʒer.oʊ, ˈdʒær-
Jarry ˈʒær.i (US) ʒɑːˈriː
Jaruzelski ˌjær.uˈzel.ski (US) ˌjɑː.ruːˈ-
jarvey ˈdʒɑː.vi (US) ˈdʒɑːr- **-s** -z
Jarvie ˈdʒɑː.vi (US) ˈdʒɑːr-
Jarvis ˈdʒɑː.vɪs (US) ˈdʒɑːr-
Jas. (*abbrev. for* **James**) dʒeɪmz, dʒæs (US) dʒeɪmz
jasey ˈdʒeɪ.zi **-s** -z
Jasher ˈdʒæʃ.əʳ (US) -ɚ
jasmine (J) ˈdʒæz.mɪn, ˈdʒæs-
Jason ˈdʒeɪ.sᵊn
jasper (J) ˈdʒæs.pəʳ (US) ˈdʒæs.pɚ **-s** -z
Jaspers ˈjæs.pəz (US) ˈjɑː.spɚz
Jassy ˈdʒæs.i
jaundice ˈdʒɔːn.dɪs (US) ˈdʒɑːn-, ˈdʒɔːn- **-d** -t
jaun|t dʒɔːn|t (US) dʒɑːn|t, dʒɔːn|t **-ts** -ts **-ting/ly** -tɪŋ/li (US) -t̬ɪŋ/li **-ted** -tɪd (US) -t̬ɪd
jaunt|y ˈdʒɔːn.t|i (US) ˈdʒɑːn.t̬|i, ˈdʒɔːn- **-ier** -i.əʳ (US) -i.ɚ **-iest** -i.ɪst, -i.əst **-ily** -ɪ.li, -ᵊl.i **-iness** -ɪ.nəs, -ɪ.nɪs
Java ˈdʒɑː.və (US) ˈdʒɑː-, ˈdʒæv.ə
Note: **Java coffee** is more likely to be /ˈdʒæv.ə/ in the US.
Javan *of Java:* ˈdʒɑː.vᵊn (US) ˈdʒɑː-, ˈdʒæv.ᵊn *biblical name:* ˈdʒeɪ.væn
Javanese ˌdʒɑː.vᵊnˈiːz (US) -ˈiːz, -ˈiːs *stress shift:* ˌJavanese ˈpeople
javelin (J) ˈdʒæv.ᵊl.ɪn, -lɪn **-s** -z
jaw dʒɔː (US) dʒɑː, dʒɔː **-s** -z **-ing** -ɪŋ **-ed** -d
jawbone ˈdʒɔː.bəʊn (US) ˈdʒɑː.boʊn, ˈdʒɔː- **-s** -z
jawboning ˈdʒɔːˌbəʊ.nɪŋ (US) ˈdʒɑːˌboʊ-, ˈdʒɔː-
jawbreak|er ˈdʒɔːˌbreɪ.k|ə (US) ˈdʒɑːˌbreɪ.k|ɚ, ˈdʒɔː- **-ers** -əz (US) -ɚz **-ing** -ɪŋ
jay (J) dʒeɪ **-s** -z
Jayne dʒeɪn
jaywalk ˈdʒeɪ.wɔːk (US) -wɑːk, -wɔːk **-s** -s **-ing** -ɪŋ **-ed** -t **-er/s** -əʳ/z (US) -ɚ/z
jazz dʒæz **ˈjazz ˌband**
jazz|y ˈdʒæz|.i **-ier** -i.əʳ (US) -i.ɚ **-iest** -i.ɪst, -i.əst **-ily** -ɪ.li, -ᵊl.i **-iness** -ɪ.nəs, -ɪ.nɪs
JCB ˌdʒeɪ.siːˈbiː
JD ˌdʒeɪˈdiː
Jeakes dʒeɪks
jealous ˈdʒel.əs **-ly** -li **-ness** -nəs, -nɪs
jealous|y ˈdʒel.ə.s|i **-ies** -iz
Jean *girl's name:* dʒiːn *French name:* ʒɑ̃ːn (US) ʒɑ̃ːn
jean *cotton fabric:* dʒeɪn (US) dʒiːn
Jeanette dʒəˈnet, dʒɪ-
Jeanne *English name:* dʒiːn *French name:* ʒæn (US) ʒɑ̃ːn
Jeannie ˈdʒiː.ni
jeans dʒiːnz
Jeavons ˈdʒev.ᵊnz
Jebb dʒeb
Jebusite ˈdʒeb.ju.zaɪt (US) -jə.saɪt **-s** -s
Jed dʒed
Jedburgh ˈdʒed.bᵊr.ə (US) -bɜːrg
Jeddah ˈdʒed.ə
Jedediah ˌdʒed.ɪˈdaɪ.ə
Jeep® dʒiːp **-s** -s
jeepers ˈdʒiː.pəz (US) -pɚz
jeer dʒɪəʳ (US) dʒɪr **-s** -z **-ing/ly** -ɪŋ/li **-ed** -d **-er/s** -əʳ/z (US) -ɚ/z
Jeeves dʒiːvz
jeez dʒiːz
Jeff dʒef
Jefferies ˈdʒef.riz
Jeffers ˈdʒef.əz (US) -ɚz
Jefferson ˈdʒef.ə.sᵊn (US) ˈ-ɚ-
Jeffersonian ˌdʒef.əˈsəʊ.ni.ən (US) -ɚˈsoʊ-
Jeffery ˈdʒef.ri **-s** -z
Jeffrey ˈdʒef.ri **-s** -z
Jeffries ˈdʒef.riz
Jehoiachin dʒɪˈhɔɪ.ə.kɪn, dʒə-
Jehoiakim dʒɪˈhɔɪ.ə.kɪm, dʒə-
Jehoram dʒɪˈhɔː.rəm, dʒə-, -ræm (US) -ˈhɔːr.əm, -æm
Jehoshaphat dʒɪˈhɒʃ.ə.fæt, dʒə-, -ˈhɒs- (US) -ˈhɑː.ʃə-, -sə-
Jehovah dʒɪˈhəʊ.və, dʒə- (US) -ˈhoʊ- **Jeˌhovahˈs ˈwitness**
jehu (J) ˈdʒiː.hjuː (US) -hjuː, -huː **-s** -z
jejune dʒɪˈdʒuːn, dʒə- **-ly** -li **-ness** -nəs, -nɪs
jejunum dʒɪˈdʒuː.nəm, dʒə- **-s** -z
Jekyll ˈdʒek.ᵊl, -ɪl, ˈdʒiː.kɪl
jell dʒel **-s** -z **-ing** -ɪŋ **-ed** -d
jellaba(h) ˈdʒel.ə.bə **-s** -z
Jellicoe ˈdʒel.ɪ.kəʊ (US) -koʊ
jello ˈdʒel.əʊ (US) -oʊ **-s** -z
Jell-O® ˈdʒel.əʊ (US) -oʊ
jell|y ˈdʒel|.i **-ies** -iz **-ying** -i.ɪŋ **-ied** -id **ˈjelly ˌbag**; **ˈjelly ˌbaby, ˌjelly ˈbaby**; **ˈjelly ˌbean**
jellyfish ˈdʒel.i.fɪʃ **-es** -ɪz
jellygraph ˈdʒel.i.grɑːf, -græf (US) -græf **-s** -s **-ing** -ɪŋ **-ed** -t
jellyroll ˈdʒel.i.rəʊl (US) -roʊl **-s** -z
Jemima dʒɪˈmaɪ.mə, dʒə-
Jemma ˈdʒem.ə
jemm|y ˈdʒem|.i **-ies** -iz
Jena ˈjeɪ.nə (US) -nɑː
je ne sais quoi ˌʒə.nə.seɪˈkwɑː (US) -seɪˈ-, -seˈ-
Jenkin ˈdʒeŋ.kɪn **-s** -z
Jenkinson ˈdʒeŋ.kɪn.sᵊn
Jenna ˈdʒen.ə
Jenner ˈdʒen.əʳ (US) -ɚ
jennet ˈdʒen.ɪt **-s** -s
Jennifer ˈdʒen.ɪ.fəʳ, ˈ-ə- (US) -fɚ
Jennings ˈdʒen.ɪŋz
Jenny *girl's name:* ˈdʒen.i, ˈdʒɪn- (US) ˈdʒen-
jenn|y *in machinery:* ˈdʒen|.i *in billiards:* ˈdʒɪn|.i, ˈdʒen- **-ies** -iz
Jensen ˈdʒent.sᵊn **-s** -z
jeopardiz|e, -is|e ˈdʒep.ə.daɪz (US) ˈ-ɚ- **-es** -ɪz **-ing** -ɪŋ **-ed** -d
jeopardy ˈdʒep.ə.di (US) ˈ-ɚ-
Jephthah ˈdʒef.θə
jerboa dʒɜːˈbəʊ.ə, dʒə- (US) dʒɚˈboʊ- **-s** -z
jeremiad ˌdʒer.ɪˈmaɪ.əd, -əˈ-, -æd (US) -əˈ- **-s** -z
Jeremiah ˌdʒer.ɪˈmaɪ.ə, -əˈ- (US) -əˈ-
Jeremy ˈdʒer.ə.mi, ˈ-ɪ-
Jerez həˈrez *as if Spanish:* herˈeθ (US) -ˈres, -ˈreθ

Jericho 'dʒer.ɪ.kəʊ US -koʊ
jerk dʒɜːk US dʒɜːrk **-s** -s **-ing** -ɪŋ **-ed** -t
jerkin 'dʒɜː.kɪn US 'dʒɜːr- **-s** -z
jerkwater 'dʒɜːkˌwɔː.tər US 'dʒɜːrkˌwɑː.t̬ɚ, -ˌwɔː- **'jerkwater ˌtown**
jerk|y 'dʒɜː.k|i US 'dʒɜːr- **-ier** -i.ər US -i.ɚ **-iest** -i.ɪst, -i.əst **-ily** -ɪ.li, -əl.i **-iness** -ɪ.nəs, -ɪ.nɪs
Jermaine dʒɜː'meɪn, dʒə-, dʒɜːr- US dʒɚ-
Jermyn 'dʒɜː.mɪn US 'dʒɜːr-
jeroboam (J) ˌdʒer.ə'bəʊ.əm US -'boʊ- **-s** -z
Jerome *Saint:* dʒə'rəʊm, dʒer'əʊm, dʒɪ'rəʊm US dʒə'roʊm, dʒer'oʊm, dʒɪ'roʊm *surname:* dʒə'rəʊm, dʒer'əʊm, dʒɪ'rəʊm, 'dʒer.əm US dʒə'roʊm, dʒer'oʊm, dʒɪ'roʊm, 'dʒer.əm
Note: Jerome K. Jerome, the author, is pronounced /dʒə'rəʊm US -'roʊm/.
Jerram 'dʒer.əm
Jerrold 'dʒer.əld
jerr|y (J) 'dʒer|.i **-ies** -iz **'jerry ˌcan**
jerry-build 'dʒer.i.bɪld **-s** -z **-ing** -ɪŋ **jerry-built** 'dʒer.i.bɪlt **jerry-builder/s** 'dʒer.iˌbɪl.dər/z US -dɚ/z
jersey (J) 'dʒɜː.zi US 'dʒɜːr- **-s** -z
Jerusalem dʒə'ruː.səl.əm, dʒɪ-, -lem **Jeˌrusalem 'artichoke**
Jervaulx 'dʒɜː.vəʊ, 'dʒɑː-, -vɪs, -vəs US 'dʒɜːr.voʊ, -vɪs, -vəs
Jervis 'dʒɑː.vɪs, 'dʒɜː.vɪs US 'dʒɜːr-
Jervois 'dʒɜː.vɪs US 'dʒɜːr-
Jespersen 'jes.pə.sən US -pɚ-
jess (J) dʒes **-es** -ɪz **-ing** -ɪŋ **-ed** -t
jessamine (J) 'dʒes.ə.mɪn
Jesse 'dʒes.i
Jessel 'dʒes.əl
Jessica 'dʒes.ɪ.kə
Jessie 'dʒes.i
Jessop 'dʒes.əp
jest dʒest **-s** -s **-ing/ly** -ɪŋ/li **-ed** -ɪd
jester 'dʒes.tər US -tɚ **-s** -z
Jesu 'dʒiː.zjuː US 'dʒiː.zjuː, 'dʒeɪ-, 'jeɪ-, -suː, -zuː
Jesu|it 'dʒez.ju|.ɪt, '-u-, 'dʒeʒ.u|.ɪt **-its** -ɪts **-itism** -ɪ.tɪ.zəm US -ɪ.t̬ɪ-
jesuitic ˌdʒez.ju'ɪt.ɪk, -u'-, ˌdʒeʒ.u'- US -'ɪt- **-al** -əl **-ally** -əl.i, -li
Jesus 'dʒiː.zəs **ˌJesus 'Christ**
jet dʒet **-s** -s **-ting** -ɪŋ US 'dʒet̬.ɪŋ **-ted** -ɪd US 'dʒet̬.ɪd **ˌjet 'engine** ; **'jet ˌlag** ; **'jet ˌset** ; **'jet ˌsetter** ; **'jet ˌstream**
jeté ʒə'teɪ **-s** -z
jetfoil 'dʒet.fɔɪl **-s** -z
Jethro 'dʒeθ.rəʊ US -roʊ
jetliner 'dʒetˌlaɪ.nər US -nɚ **-s** -z
jetsam 'dʒet.səm, -sæm US -səm
jettison 'dʒet.ɪ.sən, -zən US 'dʒet̬.ə- **-s** -z **-ing** -ɪŋ **-ed** -d
jett|y 'dʒet|.i US 'dʒet̬- **-ies** -iz
Jetway® 'dʒet.weɪ
jeu ʒɜː **-s** -z
jeunesse dorée ˌʒɜː.nes.dɔː'reɪ US ʒɜːˌnes.dɔː'-
Jevons 'dʒev.ənz
Jew dʒuː **-s** -z **ˌJew's 'harp** US **'Jew's ˌharp**
jewel (J) 'dʒuː.əl, dʒʊəl US 'dʒuː.əl **-s** -z **-(l)ing** -ɪŋ **-(l)ed** -d
jewel(l)er 'dʒuː.ə.lər, 'dʒʊə.lər US 'dʒuː.ə.lɚ, 'dʒuː.lɚ **-s** -z
jewellery, jewelry 'dʒuː.əl.ri, 'dʒʊəl- US 'dʒuː.əl-
Jewess 'dʒuː.es, -ɪs, -əs; dʒuː'es US 'dʒuː.ɪs **-es** -ɪz
Jewett 'dʒuː.ɪt
Jewish 'dʒuː.ɪʃ **-ness** -nəs, -nɪs
Jewry 'dʒʊə.ri, 'dʒuː- US 'dʒuː.ri
Jewsbury 'dʒuːz.bər.i US -ˌber-
Jeyes dʒeɪz
Jezebel 'dʒez.ə.bel, '-ɪ-, -bəl
Jezreel 'dʒez.ri.əl, ˌdʒez'riːl
Jhabvala ˌdʒɑːb'vɑː.lə
Jiang Qing ˌdʒæŋ'tʃɪŋ
jiao dʒaʊ
jib dʒɪb **-s** -z **-bing** -ɪŋ **-bed** -d
jib-boom dʒɪ*b*'buːm, '-- **-s** -z
jib|e dʒaɪb **-es** -z **-ing** -ɪŋ **-ed** -d **-er/s** -ər/z US -ɚ/z
Jif® dʒɪf
jiff dʒɪf
jiff|y 'dʒɪf|.i **-ies** -iz **'Jiffy ˌbag ®**
jig dʒɪg **-s** -z **-ging** -ɪŋ **-ged** -d
jigger 'dʒɪg.ər US -ɚ **-s** -z
jiggered 'dʒɪg.əd US -ɚd
jiggery-pokery ˌdʒɪg.ər.i'pəʊ.kər.i US -'poʊ-
jiggl|e 'dʒɪg.l̩ **-es** -z **-ing** -ɪŋ, 'dʒɪg.lɪŋ **-ed** -d
jigsaw 'dʒɪg.sɔː US -sɑː, -sɔː **-s** -z **'jigsaw ˌpuzzle**
jihad dʒɪ'hɑːd, dʒə-, -'hæd US dʒɪ'hɑːd, dʒiː-
Jill dʒɪl
Jillian 'dʒɪl.i.ən
jilt dʒɪlt **-s** -s **-ing** -ɪŋ US 'dʒɪl.t̬ɪŋ **-ed** -ɪd US 'dʒɪl.t̬ɪd
Jim dʒɪm **-my** -i
jim-dandy ˌdʒɪm'dæn.di
jimjams 'dʒɪm.dʒæmz
Jimmy 'dʒɪm.i
jimsonweed 'dʒɪm*p*.sən.wiːd
jingl|e (J) 'dʒɪŋ.gl̩ **-es** -z **-ing** -ɪŋ, 'dʒɪŋ.glɪŋ **-ed** -d **-y** -i **-er/s** -ər/z US -ɚ/z
jingo (J) 'dʒɪŋ.gəʊ US -goʊ **-es** -z
jingo|ism 'dʒɪŋ.gəʊ|.ɪ.zəm US -goʊ- **-ist/s** -ɪst/s
jingoistic ˌdʒɪŋ.gəʊ'ɪs.tɪk US -goʊ'- **-ally** -əl.i, -li
jink dʒɪŋk **-s** -s **-ing** -ɪŋ **-ed** -t
jinks (J) dʒɪnks
jinn dʒɪn **-s** -z
Jinnah 'dʒɪn.ə
jinrick|sha ˌdʒɪn'rɪk|.ʃə US -ʃɑː, -ʃɔː **-shas** -ʃəz US -ʃɑːz, -ʃɔːz **-shaw/s** -ʃɔː/z US -ʃɑː/z, -ʃɔː/z
jinx dʒɪŋks **-es** -ɪz **-ing** -ɪŋ **-ed** -t
jitney 'dʒɪt.ni **-s** -z
jitter 'dʒɪt.ər US 'dʒɪt̬.ɚ **-s** -z **-ing** -ɪŋ **-ed** -d
jitterbug 'dʒɪt.ə.bʌg US 'dʒɪt̬.ɚ- **-s** -z **-ging** -ɪŋ **-ged** -d
jitters 'dʒɪt.əz US 'dʒɪt̬.ɚz
jitter|y 'dʒɪt.ər|.i US 'dʒɪt̬- **-iness** -ɪ.nəs, -ɪ.nɪs
jiujitsu ˌdʒjuː'dʒɪt.suː
jiv|e dʒaɪv **-es** -z **-ing** -ɪŋ **-ed** -d
jnr (J) (*abbrev. for* **junior**) 'dʒuː.ni.ər US '-njɚ
jo (J) dʒəʊ US dʒoʊ **-es** -z
Joab 'dʒəʊ.æb US 'dʒoʊ-
Joachim 'jəʊ.ə.kɪm US 'joʊ-
Joan dʒəʊn US dʒoʊn
Joanna dʒəʊ'æn.ə US dʒoʊ-
Joanne dʒəʊ'æn US dʒoʊ-
Joash 'dʒəʊ.æʃ US 'dʒoʊ-
job dʒɒb US dʒɑːb **-s** -z **-bing** -ɪŋ **-bed** -d **'Job ˌCentre** ; **'job desˌcription**, **ˌjob des'cription** ; **ˌjob 'lot** US **'job ˌlot** ; **'job ˌshare** ; **ˌgive something ˌup as a ˌbad 'job**
Job dʒəʊb US dʒoʊb
jobber 'dʒɒb.ər US 'dʒɑː.bɚ **-s** -z
jobbery 'dʒɒb.ər.i US 'dʒɑː.bɚ-
job-hop 'dʒɒb.hɒp US 'dʒɑːb.hɑːp **-s** -s **-ping** -ɪŋ **-ped** -t **-per/s** -ər/z US -ɚ/z
jobhunting 'dʒɒbˌhʌn.tɪŋ US 'dʒɑːbˌhʌn.t̬ɪŋ
jobless 'dʒɒb.ləs, -lɪs US 'dʒɑːb- **-ness** -nəs, -nɪs
jobmaster 'dʒɒbˌmɑː.stər US 'dʒɑːbˌmæs.tɚ **-s** -z
jobseeker 'dʒɒbˌ siː.kər US 'dʒɑːbˌsiː.kɚ
jobsharing 'dʒɒbˌʃeə.rɪŋ US 'dʒɑːbˌʃer.ɪŋ
Jobson 'dʒɒb.sən, 'dʒəʊb- US 'dʒɑːb-, 'dʒoʊb-
Jocasta dʒəʊ'kæs.tə US dʒoʊ-
Jocelyn 'dʒɒs.lɪn, '-əl.ɪn US 'dʒɑː.səl.ɪn, '-slɪn
jock (J) dʒɒk US dʒɑːk **-s**
jockey 'dʒɒk.i US 'dʒɑː.ki **-s** -z **-ing** -ɪŋ **-ed** -d **-ship** -ʃɪp **'Jockey ˌClub**
jockstrap 'dʒɒk.stræp US 'dʒɑːk- **-s** -s
jocose dʒəʊ'kəʊs US dʒoʊ'koʊs **-ly** -li **-ness** -nəs, -nɪs
jocosity dʒəʊ'kɒs.ə.ti, -ɪ.ti US dʒoʊ'kɑː.sə.t̬i

jocular 'dʒɒk.jə.ləʳ, -jʊ- Ⓤⓢ 'dʒɑː.kjə.lɚ **-ly** -li
jocularity ˌdʒɒk.jə'lær.ə.ti, -jʊ'-, -ɪ.ti Ⓤⓢ ˌdʒɑː.kjə'ler.ə.t̬i, -'lær-
jocund 'dʒɒk.ənd, 'dʒəʊ.kənd, -kʌnd Ⓤⓢ 'dʒɑː.kənd, 'dʒoʊ- **-ly** -li **-ness** -nəs, -nɪs
jocundity dʒəʊ'kʌn.də.ti, dʒɒk'ʌn-, -dɪ- Ⓤⓢ dʒoʊ'kʌn.də.t̬i
jod jɒd Ⓤⓢ jɑːd *as if Hebrew:* jʊd **-s** -z
jodhpurs 'dʒɒd.pəz, -pɜːz Ⓤⓢ 'dʒɑːd.pɚz
Jodi 'dʒəʊ.di Ⓤⓢ 'dʒoʊ-
Jodrell 'dʒɒd.rəl Ⓤⓢ 'dʒɑː.drəl ˌ**Jodrell 'Bank**
Jody 'dʒəʊ.di Ⓤⓢ 'dʒoʊ-
Joe dʒəʊ Ⓤⓢ dʒoʊ ˌ**Joe 'Bloggs** ; ˌ**Joe 'Blow** ; ˌ**Joe 'Public**
Joel 'dʒəʊ.əl, -el Ⓤⓢ 'dʒoʊ-
joey (J) 'dʒəʊ.i Ⓤⓢ 'dʒoʊ- **-s** -z
jog dʒɒg Ⓤⓢ dʒɑːg **-s** -z **-ging** -ɪŋ **-ged** -d **-ger/s** -əʳ/z Ⓤⓢ -ɚ/z '**jog** ˌ**trot**
joggl|e 'dʒɒg.l̩ Ⓤⓢ 'dʒɑː.gl̩ **-es** -z **-ing** -ɪŋ, 'dʒɒg.lɪŋ Ⓤⓢ 'dʒɑː.glɪŋ **-ed** -d **-er/s** -əʳ/z Ⓤⓢ -ɚ/z
johannes *coin:* dʒəʊ'æn.ɪs Ⓤⓢ dʒoʊ'hæn.iːz **-es** -ɪz
Johannes *personal name:* jəʊ'hæn.ɪs Ⓤⓢ joʊ'hɑː.nɪs
Johannesburg dʒəʊ'hæn.ɪs.bɜːg, -ɪz-, -əs-, -əz- Ⓤⓢ dʒoʊ'hæn.ɪs.bɝːg, joʊ'hɑː.nɪs-
Note: There exists also a local pronunciation /dʒə'hɒn.ɪs.bɜːg/, which is used by many English-speaking South Africans.
Johannine dʒəʊ'hæn.aɪn Ⓤⓢ dʒoʊ'hæn.ɪn, -aɪn
Johannisburger jəʊ'hæn.ɪsˌbɜː.gəʳ, -ɪz-, -əs-, -əz- Ⓤⓢ dʒoʊ'hæn.ɪsˌbɝː.gɚ, joʊ'hɑː.nɪs-
john (J) dʒɒn Ⓤⓢ dʒɑːn **-s** ˌ**John 'Bull** ; ˌ**John 'Doe** ; ˌ**John 'Dory**
Johnes dʒəʊnz, dʒɒnz Ⓤⓢ dʒoʊnz, dʒɑːnz
Johnian 'dʒəʊ.ni.ən Ⓤⓢ 'dʒoʊ- **-s** -z
johnn|y (J) 'dʒɒn|.i Ⓤⓢ 'dʒɑː.n|i **-ies** -iz
Johnny-come-latel|y ˌdʒɒn.i.kʌm'leɪt.l|i Ⓤⓢ ˌdʒɑː.ni- **-ies** -z
John o' Groat's ˌdʒɒn.ə'grəʊts Ⓤⓢ ˌdʒɑːn.ə'groʊts
Johns dʒɒnz Ⓤⓢ dʒɑːnz
Johnson 'dʒɒnt.sən Ⓤⓢ 'dʒɑːnt-
Johnsonese ˌdʒɒnt.sən'iːz Ⓤⓢ ˌdʒɑːnt-
Johnsonian dʒɒn'səʊ.ni.ən Ⓤⓢ dʒɑːn'soʊ-
Johnston(e) 'dʒɒnt.stən, -sən Ⓤⓢ 'dʒɑːnt-
Johore dʒəʊ'hɔːʳ Ⓤⓢ dʒə'hɔːr
Johor(e) Baharu ˌdʒəʊ.hɔː'bɑː.ruː Ⓤⓢ dʒəˌhɔːr'bɑːr.uː
joie de vivre ˌʒwɑː.də'viː.vrə, -'viːv
join dʒɔɪn **-s** -z **-ing** -ɪŋ **-ed** -d
joinder 'dʒɔɪn.dəʳ Ⓤⓢ -dɚ
joiner 'dʒɔɪ.nəʳ Ⓤⓢ -nɚ **-s** -z
joinery 'dʒɔɪ.nər.i
joint dʒɔɪnt **-s** -s **-ly** -li **-ing** -ɪŋ Ⓤⓢ 'dʒɔɪn.t̬ɪŋ **-ed** -ɪd Ⓤⓢ 'dʒɔɪn.t̬ɪd **-er/s** -əʳ/z Ⓤⓢ 'dʒɔɪn.t̬ɚ/z
joint-stock ˌdʒɔɪnt'stɒk Ⓤⓢ -'stɑːk *stress shift:* ˌjoint-stock 'bank
jointure 'dʒɔɪn.tʃəʳ Ⓤⓢ -tʃɚ **-s** -z
Joinville 'ʒwæ̃ːn.viːl Ⓤⓢ -'-
joist dʒɔɪst **-s** -s
jojoba həʊ'həʊ.bə Ⓤⓢ hoʊ'hoʊ-, hə-
jok|e dʒəʊk Ⓤⓢ dʒoʊk **-es** -s **-ing/ly** -ɪŋ/li **-ed** -t **-(e)y** -i
joker 'dʒəʊ.kəʳ Ⓤⓢ 'dʒoʊ.kɚ **-s** -z
Jolley 'dʒɒl.i Ⓤⓢ 'dʒɑː.li
Jolliffe 'dʒɒl.ɪf Ⓤⓢ 'dʒɑː.lɪf
jollification ˌdʒɒl.ɪ.fɪ'keɪ.ʃən, ˌ-ə- Ⓤⓢ ˌdʒɑː.lə- **-s** -z
jolli|fy 'dʒɒl.ɪ|.faɪ Ⓤⓢ 'dʒɑː.lɪ- **-fies** -faɪz **-fying** -faɪ.ɪŋ **-fied** -faɪd
jollit|y 'dʒɒl.ə.t|i, -ɪ.t|i Ⓤⓢ 'dʒɑː.lə.t̬|i **-ies** -iz
joll|y (J) 'dʒɒl|.i Ⓤⓢ 'dʒɑː.l|i **-ier** -i.əʳ Ⓤⓢ -i.ɚ **-iest** -i.ɪst, -i.əst **-ily** -ɪ.li, -əl.i **-iness** -ɪ.nəs, -ɪ.nɪs ˌ**Jolly 'Roger**
jollyboat 'dʒɒl.i.bəʊt Ⓤⓢ 'dʒɑː.li.boʊt **-s** -s
Jolson 'dʒɒl.sən, 'dʒəʊl- Ⓤⓢ 'dʒoʊl-
jolt dʒəʊlt Ⓤⓢ dʒoʊlt **-s** -s **-ing/ly** -ɪŋ/li Ⓤⓢ 'dʒoʊl.t̬ɪŋ/li **-ed** -ɪd Ⓤⓢ 'dʒoʊl.t̬ɪd
jolt|y 'dʒəʊl.t|i Ⓤⓢ 'dʒoʊl.t̬|i **-ier** -i.əʳ Ⓤⓢ -i.ɚ **-iest** -i.ɪst, -i.əst **-ily** -ɪ.li, -əl.i **-iness** -ɪ.nəs, -ɪ.nɪs
Jolyon 'dʒəʊ.li.ən, 'dʒɒl.i- Ⓤⓢ 'dʒoʊ.li-, 'dʒɑː-
Jon dʒɒn Ⓤⓢ dʒɑːn
Jonah 'dʒəʊ.nə Ⓤⓢ 'dʒoʊ-
Jonas 'dʒəʊ.nəs, -næs Ⓤⓢ 'dʒoʊ.nəs
Jonathan, Jonathon 'dʒɒn.ə.θən Ⓤⓢ 'dʒɑː.nə-
Jones dʒəʊnz Ⓤⓢ dʒoʊnz
Jonesboro 'dʒəʊnz.bər.ə Ⓤⓢ 'dʒoʊnz.bɚ.oʊ
jongleur ʒɔ̃ːŋ'glɜːʳ, ʒɔːŋ-, ʒɒŋ- Ⓤⓢ 'dʒɑːŋ.glɚ **-s** -z
jonquil 'dʒɒŋ.kwɪl, -kwəl Ⓤⓢ 'dʒɑːŋ.kwɪl, 'dʒɑːn- **-s** -z
Jonson 'dʒɒnt.sən Ⓤⓢ 'dʒɑːnt-
Joplin 'dʒɒp.lɪn Ⓤⓢ 'dʒɑːp-
Joppa 'dʒɒp.ə Ⓤⓢ 'dʒɑː.pə
Jopson 'dʒɒp.sən Ⓤⓢ 'dʒɑːp-
Joram 'dʒɔː.rəm, -ræm Ⓤⓢ 'dʒɔːr.əm
Jordan 'dʒɔː.dən Ⓤⓢ 'dʒɔːr- **-s** -z
Jordanian dʒɔː'deɪ.ni.ən Ⓤⓢ dʒɔːr- **-s** -z
Jorge dʒɔːdʒ *as if Spanish:* 'hɔː.heɪ, 'xɔː.xeɪ Ⓤⓢ 'hɔːr.heɪ
jorum 'dʒɔː.rəm Ⓤⓢ 'dʒɔːr.əm, 'dʒoʊ.rəm **-s** -z
Josceline 'dʒɒs.lɪn, '-əl.ɪn Ⓤⓢ 'dʒɑː.səl.ɪn, '-slɪn
José, Jose həʊ'zeɪ, -'seɪ Ⓤⓢ hoʊ-
joseph (J) 'dʒəʊ.zɪf, -zəf Ⓤⓢ 'dʒoʊ- **-s** -s
Josephine 'dʒəʊ.zə.fiːn, -zɪ- Ⓤⓢ 'dʒoʊ-
Josephus dʒəʊ'siː.fəs Ⓤⓢ dʒoʊ-
josh (J) dʒɒʃ Ⓤⓢ dʒɑːʃ **-es** -ɪz **-ing/ly** -ɪŋ/li **-ed** -t **-er/s** -əʳ/z Ⓤⓢ -ɚ/z
Joshua 'dʒɒʃ.ju.ə, '-u- Ⓤⓢ 'dʒɑːʃ-
Josiah dʒəʊ'saɪ.ə, -'zaɪ- Ⓤⓢ dʒoʊ-
Josias dʒəʊ'saɪ.əs, -'zaɪ- Ⓤⓢ dʒoʊ-
Josie 'dʒəʊ.zi, -si Ⓤⓢ 'dʒoʊ-
joss dʒɒs Ⓤⓢ dʒɑːs **-es** -ɪz '**joss** ˌ**house** ; '**joss** ˌ**stick**
Jost jəʊst Ⓤⓢ joʊst
jostl|e 'dʒɒs.l̩ Ⓤⓢ 'dʒɑː.sl̩ **-es** -z **-ing** -ɪŋ, 'dʒɒs.lɪŋ Ⓤⓢ 'dʒɑː.slɪŋ **-ed** -d **-er/s** -əʳ/z Ⓤⓢ -ɚ/z
jot dʒɒt Ⓤⓢ dʒɑːt **-s** -s **-ting/s** -ɪŋ/z Ⓤⓢ 'dʒɑː.t̬ɪŋ/z **-ted** -ɪd Ⓤⓢ 'dʒɑː.t̬ɪd
jotter 'dʒɒt.əʳ Ⓤⓢ 'dʒɑː.t̬ɚ **-s** -z
joule *unit of energy:* dʒuːl, dʒaʊl **-s** -z
Joule *English surname:* dʒuːl, dʒəʊl, dʒaʊl Ⓤⓢ dʒuːl, dʒoʊl, dʒaʊl
jounc|e dʒaʊnts **-es** -ɪz **-ing** -ɪŋ **-ed** -t
journal 'dʒɜː.nəl Ⓤⓢ 'dʒɝː- **-s** -z
journalese ˌdʒɜː.nəl'iːz Ⓤⓢ ˌdʒɝː-
journal|ism 'dʒɜː.nəl|.ɪ.zəm Ⓤⓢ 'dʒɝː- **-ist/s** -ɪst/s
journalistic ˌdʒɜː.nəl'ɪs.tɪk Ⓤⓢ ˌdʒɝː- **-ally** -əl.i, -li
journaliz|e, -is|e 'dʒɜː.nəl.aɪz Ⓤⓢ 'dʒɝː- **-es** -ɪz **-ing** -ɪŋ **-ed** -d
journey 'dʒɜː.ni Ⓤⓢ 'dʒɝː- **-s** -z **-ing/s** -ɪŋ/z **-ed** -d
journey|man 'dʒɜː.ni|.mən Ⓤⓢ 'dʒɝː- **-men** -mən
joust dʒaʊst **-s** -s **-ing** -ɪŋ **-ed** -ɪd **-er/s** -əʳ/z Ⓤⓢ -ɚ/z
Jove dʒəʊv Ⓤⓢ dʒoʊv
jovial 'dʒəʊ.vi.əl Ⓤⓢ 'dʒoʊ- **-ly** -i **-ness** -nəs, -nɪs
joviality ˌdʒəʊ.vi'æl.ə.ti, -ɪ.ti Ⓤⓢ ˌdʒoʊ.vi'æl.ə.t̬i
Jowett, Jowitt 'dʒaʊ.ɪt, 'dʒəʊ- Ⓤⓢ 'dʒaʊ-, 'dʒoʊ-
jowl dʒaʊl **-s** -z
joy (J) dʒɔɪ **-s** -z **-ing** -ɪŋ **-ed** -d
Joyce dʒɔɪs
joyful 'dʒɔɪ.fəl, -fʊl **-lest** -ɪst, -əst **-ly** -i **-ness** -nəs, -nɪs
joyless 'dʒɔɪ.ləs, -lɪs **-ly** -li **-ness** -nəs, -nɪs
joyous 'dʒɔɪ.əs **-ly** -li **-ness** -nəs, -nɪs
joy|ride 'dʒɔɪ|.raɪd **-rides** -raɪdz **-riding** -ˌraɪ.dɪŋ **-rode** -rəʊd Ⓤⓢ -roʊd **-ridden** -rɪd.ən **-rider/s** -ˌraɪ.dəʳ/z Ⓤⓢ -dɚ/z

joystick 'dʒɔɪ.stɪk **-s** -s
jr (J) (*abbrev. for* **junior**) 'dʒuː.ni.əʳ (US) '-njɚ
Juan *h*wɑːn; 'dʒuː.ən *as if Spanish:* xwɑːn, xwæn (US) *h*wɑːn
Note: In Byron's Don Juan, the pronunciation is /'dʒuː.ən/ in both British and American English.
Juan Carlos ˌ*h*wɑːn'kɑː.lɒs, ˌ*h*wɑːŋ- *as if Spanish:* ˌxwɑːn-, ˌxwæn- (US) ˌ*h*wɑːn'kɑːr.lous
Juan Fernandez ˌ*h*wɑːn.fə'næn.dez, -des *as if Spanish:* ˌxwɑːn.fə'næn.dez, ˌxwæn- (US) ˌ*h*wɑːn.fɚ'nɑːn.des
Juanita ˌdʒuː.ə'niː.tə; hwɑː'niː.tə, hwæn'iː (US) *h*wɑː'niː.t̬ə, *h*wə-
jubilant 'dʒuː.bɪ.lənt, -bəl.ənt **-ly** -li
jubi|late (*v.*) 'dʒuː.bɪ|.leɪt, -bə- **-lates** -leɪts **-lating** -leɪ.tɪŋ (US) -leɪ.t̬ɪŋ **-lated** -leɪ.tɪd (US) -leɪ.t̬ɪd
Jubilate (*n.*) ˌdʒuː.bɪ'lɑː.teɪ, ˌjuː-, -bə'-, -ti *old-fashioned:* ˌdʒuː.bɪ'leɪ.ti (US) ˌjuː.biː'lɑː.teɪ **-s** -z
jubilation ˌdʒuː.bɪ'leɪ.ʃən, -bə'- **-s** -z
jubilee 'dʒuː.bɪ.liː, -bə-, ˌ--'- **-s** -z
Judae|a dʒuː'diː|.ə **-an/s** -ən/z
Juda(h) 'dʒuː.də
Judaic dʒuː'deɪ.ɪk **-al** -əl **-ally** -əl.i, -li
Juda|ism 'dʒuː.deɪ|.ɪ.zəm, -di- (US) -deɪ-, -di-, -də- **-ist/s** -ɪst/s
judaiz|e, -is|e 'dʒuː.deɪ.aɪz (US) -deɪ-, -di-, -də- **-es** -ɪz **-ing** -ɪŋ **-ed** -d **-er/s** -əʳ/z (US) -ɚ/z
Judas 'dʒuː.dəs **-es** -ɪz **'Judas ˌtree**
Judd dʒʌd
judder 'dʒʌd.əʳ (US) -ɚ **-s** -z **-ing** -ɪŋ **-ed** -d
Jude dʒuːd
Jude|a dʒuː'diː|.ə **-an/s** -ən/z
judg|e (J) dʒʌdʒ **-es** -ɪz **-ing** -ɪŋ **-ed** -d
judg(e)ment 'dʒʌdʒ.mənt **-s** -s **'Judgement ˌDay**
judgeship 'dʒʌdʒ.ʃɪp, 'dʒʌd- **-s** -s
judgmental dʒʌdʒ'men.təl (US) -t̬əl **-ly** -i
judicator|y 'dʒuː.dɪ.kə.tər|.i (US) -tɔːr- **-ies** -iz
judicature 'dʒuː.dɪ.kə.tʃəʳ, -tjʊəʳ (US) -tʃɚ
judicial dʒuː'dɪʃ.əl **-ly** -i **juˌdicial re'view**
judiciar|y dʒuː'dɪʃ.ər|.i, -i.ər- (US) -i.er-, -'dɪʃ.ɚ-, -i.ɚ- **-ies** -iz
judicious dʒuː'dɪʃ.əs **-ly** -li **-ness** -nəs, -nɪs
Judith 'dʒuː.dɪθ
judo 'dʒuː.dəʊ (US) -doʊ
Judson 'dʒʌd.sən
Judy 'dʒuː.di
jug dʒʌg **-s** -z **-ging** -ɪŋ **-ged** -d
jugful 'dʒʌg.fʊl **-s** -z
juggernaut (J) 'dʒʌg.ə.nɔːt (US) -ɚ.nɑːt, -nɔːt **-s** -s
juggins (J) 'dʒʌg.ɪnz **-es** -ɪz
juggl|e 'dʒʌg.l̩ **-es** -z **-ing** -ɪŋ, 'dʒʌg.lɪŋ **-ed** -d **-er/s** -əʳ/z, 'dʒʌg.ləʳ/z (US) -ɚ/z, 'dʒʌg.lɚ/z
jugglery 'dʒʌg.lər.i
Jugoslav 'juː.gəʊ.slɑːv, ˌ--'- (US) 'juː.goʊ.slɑːv **-s** -z
Jugoslavi|a ˌjuː.gəʊ'slɑː.vi|.ə (US) -goʊ'- **-an** -ən
jugular 'dʒʌg.jə.ləʳ, -jʊ- (US) -lɚ ˌ**jugular 'vein, 'jugular ˌvein** (US) **'jugular ˌvein**
Jugurtha dʒʊ'gɜː.θə, jʊ- (US) dʒuː'gɜːr-
juic|e dʒuːs **-es** -ɪz **-ing** -ɪŋ **-ed** -t **-er/s** -əʳ/z (US) -ɚ/z
juic|y 'dʒuː.s|i **-ier** -i.əʳ (US) -i.ɚ **-iest** -i.ɪst, -i.əst **-ily** -ɪ.li, -əl.i **-iness** -ɪ.nəs, -ɪ.nɪs
jujitsu dʒuː'dʒɪt.suː
jujube 'dʒuː.dʒuːb **-s** -z
jukebox 'dʒuːk.bɒks (US) -bɑːks **-es** -ɪz
Jukes dʒuːks
Jul. (*abbrev. for* **July**) dʒʊ'laɪ, dʒə-, dʒuː-
julep 'dʒuː.lɪp, -lep, -ləp (US) -ləp **-s** -s
Julia 'dʒuː.li.ə (US) 'dʒuːl.jə
Julian 'dʒuː.li.ən (US) 'dʒuːl.jən
Juliana ˌdʒuː.li'ɑː.nə (US) -'æn.ə, -'ɑː.nə
Julie 'dʒuː.li
julienne ˌdʒuː.li'en, ˌʒuː- (US) ˌdʒuː-
Juliet 'dʒuː.li.ət; ˌdʒuː.li'et (US) 'dʒuː.li.et, -ɪt; ˌdʒuː.li'et; 'dʒuːl.jɪt
Julius 'dʒuː.li.əs (US) 'dʒuːl.jəs
Julius Caesar ˌdʒuː.li.əs'siː.zəʳ (US) ˌdʒuːl.jəs'siː.zɚ
Jul|y dʒʊ'l|aɪ, dʒə-, ˌdʒuː- **-ies** -aɪz
Julyan 'dʒuː.li.ən (US) 'dʒuːl.jən
jumbl|e 'dʒʌm.bl̩ **-es** -z **-ing** -ɪŋ, 'dʒʌm.blɪŋ **-ed** -d **'jumble ˌsale**
Jumbl|y 'dʒʌm.bl|i **-ies** -iz
jumbo (J) 'dʒʌm.bəʊ (US) -boʊ **-s** -z ˌ**jumbo 'jet, 'jumbo ˌjet**
Jumna 'dʒʌm.nə
jump dʒʌmp **-s** -s **-ing** -ɪŋ **-ed** -t **-er/s** -əʳ/z (US) -ɚ/z **'jumper ˌcables**; ˌ**jumping 'jack** (US) **'jumping ˌjack**; **'jump ˌleads**; **'jump ˌrope**; ˌ**jump the 'gun**
jumped-up ˌdʒʌm*p*t'ʌp *stress shift:* ˌjumped-up 'tyrant
jumper 'dʒʌm.pəʳ (US) -pɚ **-s** -z
jump-jet 'dʒʌmp.dʒet **-s** -s
jump-off 'dʒʌmp.ɒf (US) -ɑːf **-s** -s
jump|-start 'dʒʌmp|.stɑːt (US) -stɑːrt **-starts** -stɑːts (US) -stɑːrts **-starting** -ˌstɑː.tɪŋ (US) -ˌstɑːr.t̬ɪŋ **-started** -ˌstɑː.tɪd (US) -ˌstɑːr.t̬ɪd
jumpsuit 'dʒʌmp.suːt, -sjuːt (US) -suːt **-s** -s
jump|y 'dʒʌm.p|i **-ier** -i.əʳ (US) -i.ɚ **-iest** -i.ɪst, -i.əst **-ily** -ɪ.li, -əl.i **-iness** -ɪ.nəs, -ɪ.nɪs
jun. (*abbrev. for* **junior**) 'dʒuː.ni.əʳ (US) '-njɚ
Jun. (*abbrev. for* **June**) dʒuːn
junction 'dʒʌŋ*k*.ʃən **-s** -z **'junction ˌbox**
juncture 'dʒʌŋ*k*.*t*ʃəʳ (US) -tʃɚ **-s** -z
June dʒuːn **-s** -z
Juneau 'dʒuː.nəʊ, -'- (US) 'dʒuː.noʊ
Jung jʊŋ
Jungfrau 'jʊŋ.fraʊ
Jungian 'jʊŋ.i.ən **-s** -z
jungl|e 'dʒʌŋ.gl̩ **-es** -z **-y** -i **'jungle ˌfowl**; **'jungle ˌgym**, ˌ**jungle 'gym**
junior 'dʒuː.ni.əʳ (US) '-njɚ **-s** -z
juniority ˌdʒuː.ni'ɒr.ə.ti, -ɪ.ti (US) -'ɔːr.ə.t̬i
juniper 'dʒuː.nɪ.pəʳ, -nə- (US) -pɚ **-s** -z
Junius 'dʒuː.ni.əs (US) -njəs
junk dʒʌŋk **-s** -s **-ing** -ɪŋ **-ed** -t **'junk ˌbond**; **'junk ˌfood**, ˌ**junk 'food**; **'junk ˌmail**, ˌ**junk 'mail**; **'junk ˌshop**
junker (J) 'jʊŋ.kəʳ (US) -kɚ *old car:* 'dʒʌŋ.kəʳ (US) -kɚ **-s** -z
jun|ket 'dʒʌŋ|.kɪt **-kets** -kɪts **-keting** -kɪ.tɪŋ (US) -kɪ.t̬ɪŋ **-keted** -kɪ.tɪd (US) -t̬ɪd
junkie 'dʒʌŋ.ki **-s** -z
junkyard 'dʒʌŋk.jɑːd (US) -jɑːrd **-s** -z
Juno 'dʒuː.nəʊ (US) -noʊ
Junoesque ˌdʒuː.nəʊ'esk (US) -noʊ'-
junta 'dʒʌn.tə, 'dʒʊn-, 'hʊn- (US) 'hʊn-, 'dʒʊn-, 'dʒʌn-, 'hʌn- **-s** -z
junto 'dʒʌn.təʊ, 'dʒʊn-, 'hʊn (US) -toʊ **-s** -z
jupe ʒuːp (US) dʒuːp **-s** -s
Jupiter 'dʒuː.pɪ.təʳ, -pə- (US) -t̬ɚ
jupon 'ʒuː.pɒn, 'dʒuː-, -pɔ̃ːŋ, -pɒŋ (US) 'dʒuː.pɑːn, -'- **-s** -z
Jura 'dʒʊə.rə (US) 'dʒʊr.ə
Jurassic dʒʊə'ræs.ɪk (US) dʒʊ-, dʒə-
jurat 'dʒʊə.ræt (US) 'dʒʊr.æt **-s** -s
Jürgen 'jɜː.gən, 'jʊə- (US) 'jɜːr-
juridic|al dʒʊə'rɪd.ɪ.k|əl (US) dʒʊ- **-ally** -əl.i, -li
jurisdiction ˌdʒʊə.rɪs'dɪk.ʃən, -rəs'-, -rɪz'-, -rəz'- (US) ˌdʒʊr.ɪs'- **-s** -z **-al** -əl
jurisprudence ˌdʒʊə.rɪs'pruː.dən*t*s, -rəs-; 'dʒʊə.rɪsˌpruː-, -rəs- (US) ˌdʒʊr.ɪs'pruː-
jurist 'dʒʊə.rɪst (US) 'dʒʊr.ɪst **-s** -s
juror 'dʒʊə.rəʳ (US) 'dʒʊr.ɚ, -ɔːr **-s** -z
jur|y 'dʒʊə.r|i (US) 'dʒʊr.|i **-ies** -iz **'jury ˌbox**; **'jury ˌservice**
jury|man 'dʒʊə.ri|.mən (US) 'dʒʊr.i- **-men** -mən, -men
jury-mast 'dʒʊə.ri.mɑːst (US) 'dʒʊr.i.mæst *nautical pronunciation:* -məst **-s** -s

just (J) *(adj.)* dʒʌst **-er** -əʳ Ⓤⓢ -ɚ **-est** -ɪst, -əst **-ly** -li **-ness** -nəs, -nɪs
just *(adv.) strong form:* dʒʌst *weak form:* dʒəst
jus tertii ˌjʊs'tɜː.ti.iː Ⓤⓢ ˌdʒʌs'tertiː, ˌjuːs-
justic|e 'dʒʌs.tɪs **-es** -ɪz **ˌjustice of the 'peace**
justiciable dʒʌs'tɪʃ.i.ə.bl̩, -'tɪʃ.ə- Ⓤⓢ -i.ə-
justiciar dʒʌs'tɪʃ.i.ɑːʳ, -'tɪs- Ⓤⓢ -'tɪʃ.i.ɚ **-s** -z
justiciar|y dʒʌs'tɪʃ.i.ᵊr|.i, -'tɪʃ.ᵊr-, -'tɪs.i- Ⓤⓢ -'tɪʃ.i.er- **-ies** -iz
justifiab|le 'dʒʌs.tɪ.faɪ.ə.b|l̩, -tə'-; ˌdʒʌs.tɪ'faɪ-, -tə'- Ⓤⓢ 'dʒʌs.tə.faɪ-, -tɪ- **-ly** -li **-leness** -l̩.nəs, -nɪs
justification ˌdʒʌs.tɪ.fɪ'keɪ.ʃᵊn, -tə- Ⓤⓢ -tə-, -tɪ- **-s** -z
justificatory 'dʒʌs.tɪ.fɪ.keɪ.tᵊr.i, -tə-; ˌdʒʌs.tɪ.fɪ'keɪ-; ˌdʒʌs.tɪ'fɪk.ə- Ⓤⓢ dʒə'stɪf.ɪ.kə.tɔːr-; 'dʒʌs.tə.fɪ.keɪ.tɚ-
justi|fy 'dʒʌs.tɪ|.faɪ, -tə- **-fies** -faɪz **-fying** -faɪ.ɪŋ **-fied** -faɪd **-fier/s** -faɪ.əʳ/z Ⓤⓢ -faɪ.ɚ/z
Justin 'dʒʌs.tɪn
Justine dʒʌs'tiːn, '--
Justinian dʒʌs'tɪn.i.ən
Justus 'dʒʌs.təs
jut dʒʌt **-s** -s **-ting** -ɪŋ Ⓤⓢ 'dʒʌt̬.ɪŋ **-ted** -ɪd Ⓤⓢ 'dʒʌt̬.ɪd
Juta 'dʒuː.tə
jute (J) dʒuːt **-s** -s
Jutland 'dʒʌt.lənd
Juvenal 'dʒuː.vᵊn.ᵊl, -vɪ.nᵊl
juvenescen|ce ˌdʒuː.vᵊn'es.ᵊn|ts, -vɪ'nes- **-t** -t
juvenile 'dʒuː.vᵊn.aɪl, -vɪ.naɪl Ⓤⓢ -və.nᵊl, -naɪl **-s** -z **ˌjuvenile de'linquent**
juvenilia ˌdʒuː.və'nɪl.i.ə, -vɪ'-, -'niː.li- Ⓤⓢ -və'nɪl.i-, '-jə
juvenility ˌdʒuː.və'nɪl.ə.ti, -vɪ'-, -ɪ.ti Ⓤⓢ -ə.t̬i
Juventus juː'ven.təs
juxtapos|e ˌdʒʌk.stə'pəʊz, '--- Ⓤⓢ 'dʒʌk.stə.poʊz, ˌ--'- **-es** -ɪz **-ing** -ɪŋ **-ed** -d
juxtaposition ˌdʒʌk.stə.pə'zɪʃ.ᵊn **-s** -z **-al** -ᵊl

K

k (K) keɪ -'s -z
K2 ˌkeɪ'tuː
Kaaba 'kɑː.bə, 'kɑː.ə.bɑː US -bə
kabaka (K) kə'bɑː.kə -s -z
kabbadi kɑː'bɑː.di
Kab(b)ala kə'bɑː.lə, kæb'ɑː- US 'kæb.ə-; kə'bɑː-
kabob kə'bɒb US -'bɑːb
kabuki kə'buː.ki, kæb'uː- US kə-, kɑː-
Kabul 'kɑː.bᵊl, 'kɔː-, -bʊl; kə'bʊl US 'kɑː.bʊl; kə'bʊl
Kabwe 'kæb.weɪ US 'kɑːb-
Kabyle kə'baɪl, kæb'aɪl, -iːl -s -z
kachina (K) kə'tʃiː.nə -s -z
Kaddish 'kæd.ɪʃ US 'kɑː.dɪʃ -im -ɪm, -iːm
kaf(f)ir (K) 'kæf.əʳ -s -z
Kafka 'kæf.kə US 'kɑːf-
Kafkaesque ˌkæf.kə'esk US ˌkɑːf-
kaftan 'kæf.tæn US -tən, -tæn -s -z
kagoule kə'guːl -s -z
Kahn kɑːn
kailyard 'keɪl.jɑːd US -jɑːrd -s -z
Kaiser 'kaɪ.zəʳ US -zɚ -s -z
Kaiserslautern 'kaɪ.zəzˌlaʊ.tɜːn, -tən US ˌkaɪ.zɚz'laʊ.tɚn
Kaitlin, Kaitlyn 'keɪt.lɪn
Kakadu 'kæk.ə.duː, --'-
kakemono ˌkæk.i'məʊ.nəʊ US ˌkɑː.kə'moʊ.noʊ -s -z
Kalahari ˌkæl.ə'hɑː.ri US ˌkɑː.lɑː'hɑːr.i, ˌkæl-
Kalamazoo ˌkæl.ə.mə'zuː
Kalashnikov® kə'læʃ.nɪ.kɒf, -nə- US -'lɑːʃ.nɪ.kɑːf -s -s
Kalat kə'lɑːt
kale keɪl
kaleidoscope kə'laɪ.də.skəʊp US -skoʊp -s -s
kaleidoscopic kəˌlaɪ.də'skɒp.ɪk US -'skɑː.pɪk
kalends 'kæl.endz, -ɪndz, -əndz US -əndz, 'keɪ.ləndz
Kalevala ˌkɑː.lə'vɑː.lə US -lə, -lɑː
Kalgoorlie kæl'gʊə.li US -'gʊr-
Kali 'kɑː.li
Kalimantan ˌkæl.ɪ'mæn.tən US ˌkɑː.liː'mɑːn.tɑːn
Kam|a *Hindu god:* 'kɑː.m|ə -ic -ɪk *Russian river:* 'kɑː.mə
Kamasutra ˌkɑː.mə'suː.trə
Kamchatka kæm'tʃæt.kə US kæm'tʃæt-, kɑːm'tʃɑːt-
kamikaze ˌkæm.ɪ'kɑː.zi US ˌkɑː.mə'kɑː.zi -s -z
Kampala kæm'pɑː.lə US kɑːm-
kampong 'kæm.pɒŋ, -'- US 'kɑːm.pɔːŋ, -pɑːŋ
Kampuche|a ˌkæm.pʊ'tʃiː|.ə US -puː'- -an/s -ən/z
kana 'kɑː.nə US -nə, -nɑː
Kananga kə'næŋ.gə US -'nɑːŋ-
Kanarese ˌkæn.ᵊr'iːz US ˌkɑː.nə'riːz, -'riːs
Kanchenjunga ˌkæn.tʃən'dʒʊŋ.gə, -'dʒʌŋ- US ˌkɑːn.tʃən'dʒʊŋ-
Kandahar ˌkæn.də'hɑːʳ US ˌkɑːn.də'hɑːr
Kandinsky kæn'dɪn*t*.ski
Kandy 'kæn.di US 'kæn-, 'kɑːn-
Kane keɪn
Kanga 'kæŋ.gə
kangaroo ˌkæŋ.gᵊr'uː *sometimes in Australia:* '--- US ˌkæŋ.gə'ruː -s -z *stress shift, see compound:* **ˌkangaroo 'court**
Kangchenjunga ˌkæn.tʃən'dʒʊŋ.gə, -'dʒʌŋ- US ˌkɑːn.tʃən'dʒʊŋ-
kanji 'kæn.dʒi, 'kɑːn- US 'kɑːn.*d*ʒi -s -z
Kano 'kɑː.nəʊ, 'keɪ- US 'kɑː.noʊ
Kanpur kɑːn'pʊəʳ US 'kɑːn.pʊr
Kans. (*abbrev. for* **Kansas**) 'kæn.zəs
Kansas 'kæn.zəs **ˌKansas 'City** ; **ˌKansas ˌCity 'steak**
Kant kænt US kænt, kɑːnt
Kantian 'kæn.ti.ən US 'kæn.t̬i-, 'kɑːn-
Kant|ism 'kæn.t|ɪ.zᵊm US 'kæn.t|ɪ-, 'kɑːn- -ist/s -ɪst/s
Kaohsiung ˌkaʊ.ʃi'ʊŋ US -'ʃʊŋ
Kaolak 'kɑː.əʊ.læk, 'kaʊ.læk US 'kɑː.oʊ-, 'kaʊ.læk
kaolin 'keɪ.ə.lɪn
kapellmeister kə'pel.maɪ.stəʳ, kæp'el- US kɑː'pel.maɪ.stɚ, kə- -s -z
Kaplan 'kæp.lən
kapok 'keɪ.pɒk US -pɑːk
Kaposi kə'pəʊ.zi, kæp'əʊ-, -si; 'kɑː.pə.ʃi, 'kæp.ə- US kə'poʊ.zi, -si; 'kæp.ə- **Kaˌposi's sar'coma**
kappa 'kæp.ə
kaput(t) kə'pʊt, kæp'ʊt US kə'pʊt, -'puːt
Kara 'kɑː.rə US 'kɑːr.ə
Karachi kə'rɑː.tʃi
Karadzic 'kær.ə.*d*ʒɪtʃ, -dɪtʃ US kə'rɑː.dʒɪtʃ
Karaganda ˌkær.ə'gæn.də US ˌkɑːr.ə'gɑːn-
Karajan 'kær.ə.jɑːn US 'kɑːr-, -jən
karaoke ˌkær.i'əʊ.ki US ˌker.i'oʊ.ki, ˌkær- -s -z
karat 'kær.ət US 'ker-, 'kær- -s -z
karate kə'rɑː.ti, ker'ɑː- US kæ'rɑː.t̬i
Kareli|a kə'reɪ.li|.ə, -'riː- US -li|.ə, -lj|ə -ans -ənz
Karen *girl's name:* 'kær.ən US 'ker-, 'kær- *of Burma:* kə'ren -s -z
Karenina kə'ren.ɪ.nə
Karl kɑːl US kɑːrl
Karla 'kɑː.lə US 'kɑːr-
Karl-Marx-Stadt ˌkɑːl'mɑːksˌʃtæt US ˌkɑːr'mɑːrksˌʃtɑːt
Karloff 'kɑː.lɒf US 'kɑːr.lɑːf
Karlsbad 'kɑːlz.bæd US 'kɑːrlz-
Karlsruhe 'kɑːlz.ruː.ə US 'kɑːrlz-
karm|a 'kɑː.m|ə, 'kɜː- US 'kɑːr-, 'kɜːr- -ic -ɪk
Karnak 'kɑː.næk US 'kɑːr-
Karnataka kə'nɑː.tə.kə US kɑːr'nɑː.t̬ə-
Karpov 'kɑː.pɒf US 'kɑːr.pɑːf
karroo kə'ruː -s -z
Kars kɑːz US kɑːrz
Karsh kɑːʃ US kɑːrʃ
kart kɑːt US kɑːrt -s -s -ing -ɪŋ US 'kɑːr.t̬ɪŋ
Kasakhstan ˌkæz.æk'stɑːn, ˌkɑː.zæk'-, -zɑːk'-, -'stæn US ˌkɑː.zɑːk'stɑːn
kasbah (K) 'kæz.bɑː, -bə US -bɑː, 'kɑːz- -s -z
Kasey 'keɪ.si
kasha 'kæʃ.ə, 'kɑː.ʃə US 'kɑː.ʃə
Kashgar 'kæʃ.gɑːʳ US 'kɑːʃ.gɑːr
Kashmir ˌkæʃ'mɪəʳ US 'kæʃ.mɪr, -'- -i/s -i/z *stress shift, British only:* ˌKashmir 'border
Kaspar 'kæs.pəʳ, -pɑːʳ US -pɚ, -pɑːr
Kasparov kæs'pɑː.rɒf; 'kæs.pə- US kæs'pɑːr.ɔːf, kə'spɑːr-; 'kæs.pə.rɔːf
Kassala kə'sɑː.lə US kə-, kɑː-
Kassel 'kæs.əl US 'kɑː.səl, 'kæs.əl
Kasur kʌs'ɔːʳ US -'ʊr
katakana ˌkæt.ə'kɑː.nə US ˌkɑː.t̬ə'-
Kate keɪt
Katelyn 'keɪt.lɪn
Kater 'keɪ.təʳ US -t̬ɚ
Katerina ˌkæt.ᵊr'iː.nə US ˌkæt̬.ə'riː-
Kath kæθ
Katharina ˌkæθ.ᵊr'iː.nə US -ə'riː-
Katharine, Katherine 'kæθ.rɪn, -ᵊr.ɪn
Kathie 'kæθ.i
Kathleen 'kæθ.liːn, ˌ-'-
Kathmandu ˌkæt.mæn'duː, ˌkɑːt-, -mən'-, -mɑːn'- US ˌkɑːt.mɑːn'-, ˌkæt-
Kathryn 'kæθ.rɪn
Kathy 'kæθ.i
Katie 'keɪ.ti US -t̬i
Katin 'keɪ.tɪn US -t̬ɪn
Katmandu ˌkæt.mæn'duː, ˌkɑːt-, -mən'-, -mɑːn'- US ˌkɑːt.mɑːn'-, ˌkæt-
Katowice ˌkæt.əʊ'vɪt.seɪ, -'viːt- US -tə'viːt.sə, -tɔː'viːt.seɪ
Katrina kə'triː.nə
Katrine 'kæt.rɪn
Kattegat ˌkæt.ɪ'gæt, '--- US 'kæt̬-
Katty 'kæt.i US 'kæt̬-
Katy 'keɪ.ti US -t̬i

katydid ˈkeɪ.ti.dɪd ⓤⓢ -t̬i- **-s** -z
Katz kæts, keɪts
katzenjammer ˈkæt.sᵊnˌdʒæm.əʳ ⓤⓢ -ɚ
Kaufman ˈkɔːf.mən, ˈkaʊf- ⓤⓢ ˈkɑːf-, ˈkɔːf-
Kaunas ˈkaʊ.nəs ⓤⓢ -nɑːs
Kaunda kɑːˈʊn.də, -ˈuːn-
Kaur kaʊəʳ ⓤⓢ kaʊr
Kavanagh ˈkæv.ᵊn.ə; kəˈvæn.ə ⓤⓢ ˈkæv.ə.nɑː, -nɔː
Note: In Ireland always /ˈkæv.ᵊn.ə/.
Kawasaki® ˌkaʊ.əˈsɑː.ki, ˌkɑː.wəˈ-, -ˈsæk.i ⓤⓢ ˌkɑː.wəˈsɑː.ki
Kay keɪ
kayak ˈkaɪ.æk **-s** -s
Kaye keɪ **-s** -z
Kayla ˈkeɪ.lə
Kayleigh ˈkeɪ.li
Kayseri ˈkeɪ.sᵊr.i
Kazakh kəˈzæk, -ˈzɑːk; ˈkæz.æk ⓤⓢ kəˈzɑːk, kɑː-, -ˈzæk **-s** -s
Kazakhstan, **Kazakstan** ˌkæz.ækˈstɑːn, ˌkɑː.zækˈ-, -zɑːkˈ-, -ˈstæn ⓤⓢ kəˈzɑːk.stɑːn, kɑː-, -ˈzæk-, -stæn
Kazan kəˈzæn, -ˈzɑːn ⓤⓢ kəˈzæn, kɑː-, -ˈzɑːn
kazi ˈkɑː.zi **-s**
kazoo kəˈzuː **-s** -z
kcal (*abbrev. for* **kilocalorie**) ˈkɪl.əʊˌkæl.ᵊr.i ⓤⓢ ˈ-oʊ-, ˈ-ə-
kea ˈkeɪ.ə, ˈkiː- **-s** -z
Keady ˈkiː.di ⓤⓢ ˈkeɪ-
Kean(e) kiːn
Kearn(e)y ˈkɜː.ni, ˈkɑː- ⓤⓢ ˈkɑːr-, ˈkɜːr-
Kearsley ˈkɪəz.li *locally:* ˈkɜːz- ⓤⓢ ˈkɪrz-
Kearsney ˈkɜːz.ni ⓤⓢ ˈkɜːrz-
Kearton ˈkɪə.tᵊn, ˈkɜː- ⓤⓢ ˈkɪr-, ˈkɜːr-
Keary ˈkɪə.ri ⓤⓢ ˈkɪr.i
Keating(e) ˈkiː.tɪŋ ⓤⓢ -t̬ɪŋ
Keaton ˈkiː.tᵊn
Keats kiːts
kebab kɪˈbæb, kə- ⓤⓢ -ˈbɑːb **-s** -z
Keble ˈkiː.bl̩
kebob kəˈbɒb ⓤⓢ -ˈbɑːb **-s** -z
kedg|e kedʒ **-es** -ɪz **-ing** -ɪŋ **-ed** -d
kedgeree ˌkedʒ.ᵊrˈiː; ˈkedʒ.ᵊr.i ⓤⓢ ˈkedʒ.ᵊr-; ˌkedʒ.əˈriː **-s** -z
Kedleston ˈked.l̩.stᵊn
Kedron ˈked.rɒn, ˈkiː.drɒn ⓤⓢ ˈkiː.drɑːn, -drən
Keeble ˈkiː.bl̩
Keegan ˈkiː.gən
keel kiːl **-s** -z **-ing** -ɪŋ **-ed** -d **on an ˌeven ˈkeel**
Keele kiːl
Keeler ˈkiː.ləʳ ⓤⓢ -lɚ
keelhaul ˈkiːl.hɔːl ⓤⓢ -hɑːl, -hɔːl **-s** -z **-ing** -ɪŋ **-ed** -d
Keeling ˈkiː.lɪŋ
keelson ˈkel.sᵊn, ˈkiːl- **-s** -z
keen kiːn **-er** -əʳ ⓤⓢ -ɚ **-est** -ɪst, -əst **-ly** -li **-ness** -nəs, -nɪs **as ˌkeen as ˈmustard**
Keenan ˈkiː.nən
Keen(e) kiːn
keep kiːp **-s** -s **-ing** -ɪŋ **kept** kept **keeper/s** ˈkiː.pəʳ/z ⓤⓢ -pɚ/z
keepsake ˈkiːp.seɪk **-s** -s
Kefauver ˈkiːˌfɔː.vəʳ, -ˌfəʊ- ⓤⓢ -ˌfɑː.vɚ, -ˌfɔː-
Keflavik ˈkef.lə.vɪk
keg keg **-s** -z
Kegan ˈkiː.gən
Keig kiːg
Keighley *in West Yorkshire:* ˈkiːθ.li *surname:* ˈkiːθ.li, ˈkiː-, ˈkaɪ-
Keightley ˈkiːt.li, ˈkaɪt-
Keigwin ˈkeg.wɪn
Keiller, **Keillor** ˈkiː.ləʳ ⓤⓢ -lɚ
Keir kɪəʳ ⓤⓢ kɪr
Keisha ˈkiː.ʃə
Keith kiːθ
Kelland ˈkel.ənd
Kellas ˈkel.æs
Keller ˈkel.əʳ ⓤⓢ -ɚ
Kelley, **Kellie** ˈkel.i
Kellogg ˈkel.ɒg ⓤⓢ -ɑːg, -ɔːg
Kelly ˈkel.i
kelly-green ˌkel.iˈgriːn *stress shift:* ˌkelly-green ˈfabric
kelp kelp
kelpie ˈkel.pi **-s** -z
Kelsey ˈkel.si, -zi
Kelso ˈkel.səʊ ⓤⓢ -soʊ
kelson ˈkel.sᵊn **-s** -z
Kelt kelt **-s** -s **-ic** -ɪk
Kelty ˈkel.ti ⓤⓢ -t̬i
kelvin (K) ˈkel.vɪn
Kelway ˈkel.wi, -weɪ
Kemal kemˈɑːl, kəˈmɑːl ⓤⓢ kəˈmɑːl
Kemble ˈkem.bl̩
kemp kemp **-y** -i
Kemp(e) kemp
Kempenfelt ˈkem.pən.felt
Kempis ˈkem.pɪs
Kempson ˈkemp.sᵊn
Kempston ˈkemp.stᵊn
kempt kem*p*t
Kemsing ˈkem.zɪŋ
ken (K) ken **-s** -z **-ning** -ɪŋ **-ned** -d
Ken. (*abbrev. for* **Kentucky**) kenˈtʌk.i, kən- ⓤⓢ kən-
Kendal(l) ˈken.dᵊl
kendo ˈken.dəʊ ⓤⓢ -doʊ
Kendra ˈken.drə
Kendrick ˈken.drɪk
Keneal(l)y kɪˈniː.li, kə-, kenˈiː-
Kenelm ˈken.elm
Kenilworth ˈken.ᵊl.wəθ, -ɪl-, -wɜːθ ⓤⓢ -wɚθ, -wɜːrθ
Kenite ˈkiː.naɪt **-s** -s
Kénitra ˈkeɪ.niː.trə; kenˈiː-
Kenmare kenˈmeəʳ ⓤⓢ -ˈmer
Kenmore ˈken.mɔːʳ ⓤⓢ -mɔːr
Kennaird kəˈneəd, kenˈeəd ⓤⓢ kenˈerd, kəˈnerd
Kennan ˈken.ən
Kennard ˈken.ɑːd; kɪˈnɑːd ⓤⓢ ˈken.ɑːrd, kɪˈnɑːrd
Kennedy ˈken.ə.di, ˈ-ɪ-
kennel (K) ˈken.ᵊl **-s** -z **-(l)ing** -ɪŋ **-(l)ed** -d
Kennerley ˈken.ᵊl.i ⓤⓢ -ɚ.li
Kennet ˈken.ɪt, -ət
Kenneth ˈken.ɪθ, -əθ
Kenney ˈken.i
Kennicot ˈken.ɪ.kət ⓤⓢ -kət, -kɑːt
Kennington ˈken.ɪŋ.tən
Kennish ˈken.ɪʃ
Kennoway ˈken.ə.weɪ
Kenny ˈken.i
keno ˈkiː.nəʊ ⓤⓢ -noʊ
Kenosha kiːˈnəʊ.ʃə, kə- ⓤⓢ kəˈnoʊ-
Kenrick ˈken.rɪk
Kensal ˈken.sᵊl
Kensington ˈken.zɪŋ.tən
Kensit ˈken.zɪt, -sɪt
Kent kent **-s** -s **-ish** -ɪʃ
Kentucky kenˈtʌk.i, kən- ⓤⓢ kən- **KenˌtuckyˈDerby** ; **KenˌtuckyˌFried ˈChicken**
Kenwood® ˈken.wʊd
Kenya ˈken.jə, ˈkiː.njə
Note: Both pronunciations are heard locally.
Kenyatta kenˈjæt.ə ⓤⓢ -ˈjɑː.t̬ə
Kenyon ˈken.jən
Keogh kjəʊ; ˈkiː.əʊ ⓤⓢ ˈkiː.oʊ
Keown kjəʊn; kiˈəʊn; ˈkiː.əʊn; ⓤⓢ kjoʊn; kiˈoʊn; ˈkiː.oʊn;
kepi ˈkeɪ.pi ⓤⓢ ˈkeɪ-, ˈkep.i **-s** -z
Kepler ˈkep.ləʳ ⓤⓢ -lɚ
Keppel ˈkep.ᵊl
kept (*from* **keep**) kept
Ker kɑːʳ, keəʳ, kɜːʳ *in Scotland* kɛr ⓤⓢ kɜːr
Kerala ˈker.ᵊl.ə, kəˈrɑː.lə ⓤⓢ ˈker.ə.lə
Kerans ˈker.ənz
keratin ˈker.ə.tɪn ⓤⓢ -t̬ɪn
keratitis ˌker.əˈtaɪ.tɪs ⓤⓢ -t̬ɪs
kerb kɜːb ⓤⓢ kɜːrb **-s** -z
kerbside ˈkɜːb.saɪd ⓤⓢ ˈkɜːrb-
kerbstone ˈkɜːb.stəʊn ⓤⓢ ˈkɜːrb.stoʊn **-s** -z
ker|chief ˈkɜː|.tʃɪf, -tʃiːf, -tʃəf ⓤⓢ ˈkɜːr|.tʃɪf, -tʃiːf **-chiefs** -tʃɪfs, -tʃiːfs **-chieves** -tʃɪvz, -tʃiːvz **-chiefed** -tʃɪft **-chieft** -tʃiːft
Kerensky kəˈren*t*.ski
kerfuffl|e kəˈfʌf.l̩ ⓤⓢ kɚ- **-es** -z **-ing** -ɪŋ **-ed** -d
Kerguelen ˈkɜː.gɪ.lɪn, -gᵊl.ɪn, -ən ⓤⓢ ˈkɜːr.gᵊl.ən

Keri 'ker.i
Kerith 'kɪə.rɪθ, 'ker.ɪθ ⓊⓈ 'kɪr-, 'ker-
kermes 'kɜː.mɪz, -miːz ⓊⓈ 'kɜːr.miːz
Kermit 'kɜː.mɪt ⓊⓈ 'kɜːr-
Kermode 'kɜː.məʊd, -'-
ⓊⓈ 'kɜːr.moʊd, -'-
kern (K) kɜːn ⓊⓈ kɜːrn **-s** -z **-ing** -ɪŋ **-ed** -d
Kernahan 'kɜː.nə.hən, -ni.ən
ⓊⓈ 'kɜːr-, -nə.hæn
kernel 'kɜː.nᵊl ⓊⓈ 'kɜːr- **-s** -z
Kernohan 'kɜː.nə.hən ⓊⓈ 'kɜːr-, -hæn
kerosene 'ker.ə.siːn, ˌ--'-
Kerouac 'ker.u.æk ⓊⓈ 'ker.u.æk, '-ə-
Kerr kɜːʳ, keəʳ, kɑːʳ ⓊⓈ kɜːr, kɑːr
Kerri 'ker.i
kerria 'ker.i.ə **-s** -z
Kerridge 'ker.ɪdʒ
Kerry 'ker.i
Kerse kɜːs ⓊⓈ kɜːrs
kersey (K) 'kɜː.zi ⓊⓈ 'kɜːr- **-s** -z
kerseymere (K) 'kɜː.zi.mɪəʳ
ⓊⓈ 'kɜːr.zi.mɪr
Kes kes, kez
Kesey 'kes.i, 'kiː.si, -zi ⓊⓈ 'kiː.si, -zi
Kesteven *Barony:* 'kes.tɪ.vᵊn
Lincolnshire: kes'tiː.vᵊn, kə'stiː-
Keston 'kes.tᵊn
kestrel 'kes.trᵊl **-s** -z
Keswick 'kez.ɪk
ketch (K) ketʃ **-es** -ɪz
ketchup 'ketʃ.ʌp, -əp ⓊⓈ -əp **-s** -s
Ketteridge 'ket.ᵊr.ɪdʒ ⓊⓈ 'keţ-
Kettering 'ket.ᵊr.ɪŋ ⓊⓈ 'keţ-
kettle (K) 'ket.ļ ⓊⓈ 'keţ- **-s** -z **a 'pretty ˌkettle of ˌfish**
kettledrum 'ket.ļ.drʌm ⓊⓈ 'keţ- **-s** -z
Kevin 'kev.ɪn
Kevlar® 'kev.lɑːʳ ⓊⓈ -lɑːr
Kew kjuː **ˌKew 'Gardens**
kewpie 'kjuː.pi **-s** -z
key (K) kiː **-s** -z **-ing** -ɪŋ **-ed** -d **'key ˌring** ; **'key ˌsignature** ; **ˌKey 'West**
keyboard 'kiː.bɔːd ⓊⓈ -bɔːrd **-s** -z **-ing** -ɪŋ **-ed** -ɪd **-er/s** -əʳ/z ⓊⓈ -ɚ/z
Keyes kiːz, kaɪz
keyhole 'kiː.həʊl ⓊⓈ -hoʊl **-s** -z **ˌkeyhole 'surgery**
Key Largo ˌkiː'lɑː.gəʊ ⓊⓈ -'lɑːr.goʊ
Keymer 'kiː.məʳ, 'kaɪ- ⓊⓈ -mɚ
Keymour 'kiː.məʳ ⓊⓈ -mɚ
Keyne kiːn
Keynes *in Milton Keynes:* kiːnz
surname, other places: keɪnz
Keynesian 'keɪn.zi.ən **-ism** -ɪ.zᵊm
keynote 'kiː.nəʊt, ˌ-'- ⓊⓈ 'kiː.noʊt **-s** -s
Keynsham 'keɪn.ʃᵊm
keypad 'kiː.pæd **-s** -z
keypunch 'kiː.pʌntʃ **-es** -ɪz
Keyser 'kiː.zəʳ, 'kaɪ.zəʳ ⓊⓈ 'kaɪ.zɚ
keystone (K) 'kiː.stəʊn ⓊⓈ -stoʊn **-s** -z
keystroke 'kiː.strəʊk ⓊⓈ -stroʊk **-s** -s
keyword 'kiː.wɜːd ⓊⓈ -wɜːrd **-s** -z
Keyworth 'kiː.wəθ, -wɜːθ ⓊⓈ -wɚθ, -wɜːrθ
kg (*abbrev. for* **kilogram/s**) *singular:* 'kɪl.ə.græm *plural:* 'kɪl.ə.græmz
KGB ˌkeɪ.dʒiː'biː
Khabarovsk kɑː'bɑː.rɒfsk ⓊⓈ -rɔːfsk
Khachaturian ˌkætʃ.ə'tʊə.ri.ən, ˌkɑː.tʃə'-, -'tjʊə- ⓊⓈ -'tʊr.i-
khaki 'kɑː.ki ⓊⓈ 'kæk.i, 'kɑː.ki **-s** -z
khalif 'keɪ.lɪf, 'kæl.ɪf, 'kɑː.lɪf; kæl'ɪf ⓊⓈ 'keɪ.lɪf, 'kæl.ɪf **-s** -s
Khalifa kɑː'liː.fə, kə'liː- **-s** -z
khalifate 'kæl.ɪ.feɪt, 'keɪ.lɪ-, -lə-
ⓊⓈ 'kæl.ɪ-, '-ə- **-s** -s
Khan kɑːn ⓊⓈ kɑːn, kæn
Khanpur ˌkɑːn'pʊəʳ, ˌkɑːm'-, '--
ⓊⓈ ˌkɑːn'pʊr
Kharkov 'kɑː.kɒf ⓊⓈ 'kɑːr.kɔːf
Khartoum ˌkɑː'tuːm, kɑː- ⓊⓈ kɑːr-
Khayyam kaɪ'æm, -'ɑːm ⓊⓈ -'jɑːm, -'jæm
khazi 'kɑː.zi **-s** -z
khedival kɪ'diː.vᵊl, ked'iː-, kə'diː-
ⓊⓈ kə'diː-
khedive kɪ'diːv, ked'iːv, kə'diːv
ⓊⓈ kə'diːv **-s** -z
khedivial kɪ'diː.vi.əl, ked'iː-, kə'diː-
ⓊⓈ kə'diː-
Khmer kmeəʳ, kə'meəʳ ⓊⓈ kə'mer **Khˌmer 'Rouge**
Khomeini kɒm'eɪ.ni, kəʊ'meɪ-
ⓊⓈ koʊ-, kə-
khoums kuːmz
Khrus(h)chev 'krʊs.tʃɒf, 'krʊʃ-, ˌ-'-
ⓊⓈ 'kruː.tʃef, -tʃɔːf; kruːʃ'tʃɔːf
Khyber 'kaɪ.bəʳ ⓊⓈ -bɚ **ˌKhyber 'Pass**
kHz (*abbrev. for* **kilohertz**) 'kɪl.əʊ.hɜːts
ⓊⓈ -ə.hɜːrts
Kia Ora® ˌkɪə'ɔː.rə, ˌkiː.ə'-
ⓊⓈ ˌkiː.ə'ɔːr.ə
kibbl|e 'kɪb.ļ **-es** -z **-ing** -ɪŋ, 'kɪb.lɪŋ **-ed** -d
kibbutz kɪ'bʊts ⓊⓈ -'bʊts, -'buːts **-nik/s** -nɪk **-es** -ɪz **kibbutzim** ˌkɪb.ʊt'siːm; kɪ'bʊt.siːm
ⓊⓈ ˌkiː.buːt'siːm
kibe kaɪb **-s** -z
kibitz 'kɪb.ɪts **-es** -ɪz **-ing** -ɪŋ **-ed** -t **-er/s** -əʳ/z ⓊⓈ -ɚ/z
kibosh 'kaɪ.bɒʃ ⓊⓈ 'kaɪ.bɑːʃ; kɪ'bɑːʃ **-es** -ɪz **-ing** -ɪŋ **-ed** -t
kick kɪk **-s** -s **-ing** -ɪŋ **-ed** -t **-er/s** -əʳ/z ⓊⓈ -ɚ/z
kickabout 'kɪk.ə.baʊt **-s** -s
kickback 'kɪk.bæk **-s** -s
Kickham 'kɪk.əm
kick-off 'kɪk.ɒf ⓊⓈ -ɑːf **-s** -s
kickshaw 'kɪk.ʃɔː ⓊⓈ -ʃɑː, -ʃɔː **-s** -z
kick|-start 'kɪk|.stɑːt ⓊⓈ -stɑːrt **-starts** -stɑːts ⓊⓈ -stɑːrts **-starting** -ˌstɑː.tɪŋ ⓊⓈ -ˌstɑːr.ţɪŋ **-started** -ˌstɑː.tɪd ⓊⓈ -ˌstɑːr.ţɪd **-starter/s** -ˌstɑː.təʳ/z ⓊⓈ -ˌstɑːr.ţɚ/z
kid kɪd **-s** -z **-ding** -ɪŋ **-ded** -ɪd **ˌkid 'glove**
Kidd kɪd
Kidderminster 'kɪd.ə.mɪnt.stəʳ
ⓊⓈ -ɚ.mɪnt.stɚ
kiddie 'kɪd.i **-s** -z
kiddle (K) 'kɪd.ļ **-s** -z
kidd|y 'kɪd|.i **-ies** -iz
Kidlington 'kɪd.lɪŋ.tən
Kidman 'kɪd.mən
kidnap 'kɪd.næp **-s** -s **-(p)ing** -ɪŋ **-(p)ed** -t **-(p)er/s** -əʳ/z ⓊⓈ -ɚ/z
kidney 'kɪd.ni **-s** -z **'kidney ˌbean** ; **'kidney maˌchine**
Kidsgrove 'kɪdz.grəʊv ⓊⓈ -groʊv
Kiel kiːl
kielbassa kiːl'bæs.ə ⓊⓈ -'bɑː.sə, kɪl-
Kielder 'kiːl.dəʳ ⓊⓈ -dɚ
kier (K) kɪəʳ ⓊⓈ kɪr **-s** -z
Kieran 'kɪə.rᵊn ⓊⓈ 'kɪr.ᵊn
Kierkegaard 'kɪə.kə.gɑːd, -gɔːd
ⓊⓈ 'kɪr.kə.gɑːrd, -gɔːrd
Kiev 'kiː.ev, -ef, ˌ-'-
Kigali kɪ'gɑː.li ⓊⓈ kə-
Kikuyu kɪ'kuː.juː ⓊⓈ kiː-
Kilbirnie kɪl'bɜː.ni ⓊⓈ -'bɜːr-
Kilbride kɪl'braɪd ⓊⓈ 'kɪl.braɪd, -'-
Kilburn 'kɪl.bən, -bɜːn ⓊⓈ -bɚn, -bɜːrn
Kilby 'kɪl.bi
Kildale 'kɪl.deɪl
Kildare kɪl'deəʳ ⓊⓈ -'der
kilderkin 'kɪl.də.kɪn ⓊⓈ -dɚ- **-s** -z
Kilen 'kaɪ.lən
Kilham 'kɪl.əm
kilim (K) kɪ'liːm **-s** -z
Kilimanjaro ˌkɪl.ɪ.mən'dʒɑː.rəʊ, ˌ-ə-, -mæn'- ⓊⓈ -ə.mən'dʒɑːr.oʊ
Kilkeel kɪl'kiːl
Kilkenny kɪl'ken.i
kill kɪl **-s** -z **-ing** -ɪŋ **-ed** -d **ˌdressed to 'kill**
Killaloe ˌkɪl.ə'luː ⓊⓈ kɪ'læl.oʊ
Killamarsh 'kɪl.ə.mɑːʃ ⓊⓈ -mɑːrʃ
Killarney kɪ'lɑː.ni ⓊⓈ -'lɑːr-
Killearn kɪ'lɜːn ⓊⓈ -'lɜːrn
killer 'kɪl.əʳ ⓊⓈ -ɚ **-s** -z **'killer ˌinstinct** ; **'killer ˌwhale**
Killick 'kɪl.ɪk
Killiecrankie ˌkɪl.ɪ'kræŋ.ki
Killigrew 'kɪl.ɪ.gruː
Killin 'kɪl.ɪn
Killingworth 'kɪl.ɪŋ.wəθ, -wɜːθ
ⓊⓈ -wɚθ, -wɜːrθ
killjoy 'kɪl.dʒɔɪ **-s** -z
Killwick 'kɪl.wɪk
Kilmainham kɪl'meɪ.nəm
Kilmarnock kɪl'mɑː.nək, -nɒk
ⓊⓈ -'mɑːr.nək, -nɑːk
kiln kɪln, kɪl **-s** -z

Note: The pronunciation /kɪl/ appears to be used only by those concerned with the working of kilns.

Kilnsey ˈkɪln.zi

kilo- kɪl.əʊ-; kɪˈlɒ- ⓊⓈ kɪl.oʊ-, -ə-; kɪˈlɑː-

Note: Prefix. Normally carries primary stress on the first syllable, e.g. **kilometre** /ˈkɪl.əʊˌmiː.təʳ ⓊⓈ -əˌmiː.t̬ɚ/.

kilo ˈkiː.ləʊ ⓊⓈ -loʊ **-s** -z

kilobyte ˈkɪl.əʊ.baɪt ⓊⓈ ˈ-oʊ-, ˈ-ə- **-s** -s

kilocalorie ˈkɪl.əʊˌkæl.ᵊr.i ⓊⓈ ˈ-oʊ-, ˈ-ə- **-s** -z

kilocycle ˈkɪl.əʊˌsaɪ.kl̩ ⓊⓈ -oʊˌ-, -əˌ- **-s** -z

kilogram, kilogramme ˈkɪl.əʊ.græm ⓊⓈ ˈ-oʊ-, ˈ-ə- **-s** -z

kilohertz ˈkɪl.əʊ.hɜːts, -heəts ⓊⓈ -oʊ.herts, ˈ-ə-, -hɜːrts

kilojoule ˈkɪl.əʊ.dʒuːl ⓊⓈ ˈ-oʊ-, ˈ-ə- **-s** -z

kilolitre, kiloliter ˈkɪl.əʊˌliː.təʳ ⓊⓈ -oʊˌliː.t̬ɚ, -əˌ- **-s** -z

kilometre, kilometer kɪˈlɒm.ɪ.təʳ, ˈ-ə-; ˈkɪl.əʊˌmiː- ⓊⓈ kɪˈlɑː.mə.t̬ɚ; ˈkɪl.əˌmiː- **-s** -z

kiloton ˈkɪl.əʊ.tʌn ⓊⓈ ˈ-oʊ-, ˈ-ə- **-s** -z

kilovolt ˈkɪl.əʊ.vəʊlt ⓊⓈ -oʊ.voʊlt, ˈ-ə- **-s** -s

kilowatt ˈkɪl.əʊ.wɒt ⓊⓈ -oʊ.wɑːt, ˈ-ə- **-s** -s

Kilpatrick kɪlˈpæt.rɪk

Kilrush kɪlˈrʌʃ

Kilsyth kɪlˈsaɪθ

kilt kɪlt **-s** -s **-ing** -ɪŋ ⓊⓈ ˈkɪl.t̬ɪŋ **-ed** -ɪd ⓊⓈ ˈkɪl.t̬ɪd

kilter ˈkɪl.təʳ ⓊⓈ -t̬ɚ

Kilvert ˈkɪl.vət ⓊⓈ -vɚt

Kilwarden kɪlˈwɔː.dᵊn ⓊⓈ -ˈwɔːr-

Kilwinning kɪlˈwɪn.ɪŋ

Kim kɪm

Kimball ˈkɪm.bᵊl

Kimberly ˈkɪm.bᵊl.i ⓊⓈ -bɚ.li

Kimbolton kɪmˈbəʊl.tᵊn ⓊⓈ -ˈboʊl-

Kimmeridge ˈkɪm.ᵊr.ɪdʒ

Kimmins ˈkɪm.ɪnz

kimono kɪˈməʊ.nəʊ ⓊⓈ kəˈmoʊ.nə, -noʊ **-s** -z

kin kɪn

kina ˈkiː.nə

kinaesthetic ˌkɪn.iːsˈθet.ɪk, ˌkaɪ.niːsˈ-, -nɪsˈ- ⓊⓈ ˌkɪn.esˈθet̬.ɪk

Kincardine kɪnˈkɑː.dɪn, kɪŋ-, -dᵊn ⓊⓈ kɪnˈkɑːr- **-shire** -ʃəʳ, -ˌʃɪəʳ ⓊⓈ -ʃɚ, -ˌʃɪr

Kinchinjunga ˌkɪn.*t*ʃɪnˈdʒʌŋ.gə ⓊⓈ -tʃɪnˈdʒʊŋ-

kind kaɪnd **-s** -z **-er** -əʳ ⓊⓈ -ɚ **-est** -ɪst, -əst **-ly** -li **-ness/es** -nəs/ɪz, -nɪs/ɪz

kinda ˈkaɪn.də

kindergarten ˈkɪn.dəˌgɑː.tᵊn ⓊⓈ -dɚˌgɑːr- **-s** -z

Kinder Scout ˌkɪn.dəˈskaʊt ⓊⓈ -dɚ-

kind-hearted ˌkaɪndˈhɑː.tɪd ⓊⓈ -ˈhɑːr.t̬ɪd **-ly** -li **-ness** -nəs, -nɪs *stress shift:* ˌkindhearted ˈperson

kindl|e ˈkɪn.dl̩ **-es** -z **-ing** -ɪŋ, ˈkɪnd.lɪŋ **-ed** -d **-er/s** -əʳ/z, ˈkɪnd.ləʳ/z ⓊⓈ -ɚ/z, ˈkɪnd.lɚ/z

kindling ˈkɪnd.lɪŋ, ˈkɪn.dl̩.ɪŋ

kindl|y ˈkaɪnd.l|i **-ier** -i.əʳ ⓊⓈ -i.ɚ **-iest** -i.ɪst, -i.əst **-iness** -ɪ.nəs, -ɪ.nɪs

kindred ˈkɪn.drəd, -drɪd ˌ**kindred** ˈ**spirit**

kine kaɪn

kinema ˈkɪn.ɪ.mə, ˈ-ə- **-s** -z

kinematic ˌkɪn.ɪˈmæt.ɪk, ˌkaɪ.nɪˈ-, -nəˈ- ⓊⓈ ˌkɪn.əˈmæt̬- **-al** -ᵊl **-ally** -ᵊl.i, -li **-s** -s

kinematograph ˌkɪn.ɪˈmæt.ə.grɑːf, ˌkaɪ.nɪˈ-, -nəˈ-, -græf ⓊⓈ ˌkɪn.əˈmæt̬.ə.græf **-s** -s

kinesics kɪˈniː.sɪks, kaɪ- ⓊⓈ -sɪks, -zɪks

kinesis kɪˈniː.sɪs, kaɪ- ⓊⓈ -sɪs, -zɪs

kinesthetic ˌkɪn.iːsˈθet.ɪk, ˌkaɪ.niːsˈ-, -nɪsˈ- ⓊⓈ ˌkɪn.ɪsˈθet̬-

kinetic kɪˈnet.ɪk, kaɪ- ⓊⓈ kɪˈnet̬- **-ally** -ᵊl.i, -li **-s** -s

kinfolk ˈkɪn.fəʊk ⓊⓈ -foʊk **-s** -s

king (K) kɪŋ **-s** -z ˌ**King's** ˈ**Bench** ; ˌ**King Charles** ˈ**spaniel** ; ˌ**King's** ˈ**Counsel** ; ˌ**King's** ˈ**English** ; ˌ**king's** ˈ**evidence** ; ˌ**King's** ˈ**Lynn** ; ˌ**king** ˈ**prawn** ; ˈ**king-**ˌ**size**

king-at-arms ˌkɪŋ.ətˈɑːmz ⓊⓈ -ˈɑːrms **kings-at-arms** ˌkɪŋz-

kingcraft ˈkɪŋ.krɑːft ⓊⓈ -kræft

kingcup ˈkɪŋ.kʌp **-s** -s

kingdom (K) ˈkɪŋ.dəm **-s** -z ˌ**kingdom** ˈ**come**; ˌ**Kingdom** ˈ**Hall**

Kingdon ˈkɪŋ.dən

kingfisher ˈkɪŋˌfɪʃ.əʳ ⓊⓈ -ɚ **-s** -z

Kinghorn ˈkɪŋ.hɔːn ⓊⓈ -hɔːrn

Kinglake ˈkɪŋ.leɪk

kingless ˈkɪŋ.ləs, -lɪs

kinglet ˈkɪŋ.lət, -lɪt **-s** -s

kinglike ˈkɪŋ.laɪk

kingl|y ˈkɪŋ.l|i **-ier** -i.əʳ ⓊⓈ -i.ɚ **-iest** -i.ɪst, -i.əst **-iness** -ɪ.nəs, -ɪ.nɪs

kingmaker (K) ˈkɪŋˌmeɪ.kəʳ ⓊⓈ -kɚ **-s** -z

kingpin ˈkɪŋ.pɪn, ˌ-ˈ- ⓊⓈ ˈkɪŋ.pɪn **-s** -z

Kingsborough ˈkɪŋz.bᵊr.ə ⓊⓈ -oʊ

Kingsbury ˈkɪŋz.bᵊr.i ⓊⓈ -ˌber-

Kingscote -kəʊt ⓊⓈ -kət, -koʊt

Kings Cross ˌkɪŋzˈkrɒs ⓊⓈ -ˈkrɑːs *stress shift:* ˌKings Cross ˈStation

kingship ˈkɪŋ.ʃɪp

king-size ˈkɪŋ.saɪz **-d** -d

Kingsley ˈkɪŋz.li

Kings|man ˈkɪŋz|.mən, -mæn **-men** -mən, -men

Kingsteignton kɪŋˈsteɪn.tən ⓊⓈ -tᵊn

Kingston(e) ˈkɪŋ.stən, ˈkɪŋk-, ˈkɪŋz.tən

Kingstown ˈkɪŋz.taʊn, ˈkɪŋ.stən, ˈkɪŋk-

Kingsway ˈkɪŋz.weɪ

Kingswinford kɪŋˈswɪn.fəd ⓊⓈ -fɚd

Kingswood ˈkɪŋz.wʊd

Kington ˈkɪŋ.tən, ˈkɪŋk-

Kingussie kɪŋˈjuː.si

kink kɪŋk **-s** -s **-ing** -ɪŋ **-ed** -t

kinkajou ˈkɪŋ.kə.dʒuː **-s** -z

kink|y ˈkɪŋ.k|i **-ier** -i.əʳ ⓊⓈ -i.ɚ **-iest** -i.ɪst, -i.əst **-iness** -ɪ.nəs, -ɪ.nɪs

kinless ˈkɪn.ləs, -lɪs

Kinnaird kɪˈneəd ⓊⓈ -ˈnerd

Kinnear kɪˈnɪəʳ, -ˈneəʳ ⓊⓈ -ˈnɪr, -ˈner

Kinnock ˈkɪn.ək

Kinnoull kɪˈnuːl

kino ˈkiː.nəʊ ⓊⓈ -noʊ

Kinros|s kɪnˈrɒs ⓊⓈ -ˈrɑːs **-shire** -ʃəʳ, -ˌʃɪəʳ ⓊⓈ -ʃɚ, -ˌʃɪr

Kinsale kɪnˈseɪl

Kinsella kɪnˈsel.ə, ˈkɪn*t*.sel.ə

Kinsey ˈkɪn.zi

kinsfolk ˈkɪnz.fəʊk ⓊⓈ -foʊk

Kinshasa kɪnˈʃɑː.sə, -ˈʃæs.ə ⓊⓈ -ˈʃɑː.sə, -sɑː

kinship ˈkɪn.ʃɪp

kins|man ˈkɪnz|.mən **-men** -mən, -men

kins|woman ˈkɪnz|ˌwʊm.ən **-women** -ˌwɪm.ɪn

Kintore kɪnˈtɔːʳ ⓊⓈ -ˈtɔːr

Kintyre kɪnˈtaɪəʳ ⓊⓈ -ˈtaɪr

kiosk ˈkiː.ɒsk ⓊⓈ -ɑːsk, kiˈɑːsk **-s** -s

kip kɪp **-s** -s **-ping** -ɪŋ **-ped** -t

Kipling ˈkɪp.lɪŋ

Kippax ˈkɪp.æks, -əks

kipp|er ˈkɪp|.əʳ ⓊⓈ -ɚ **-ers** -əz ⓊⓈ -ɚz **-ering** -ᵊr.ɪŋ **-ered** -əd ⓊⓈ -ɚd

Kipps kɪps

kir kɪəʳ ⓊⓈ kɪr **-s** -z

Kirby ˈkɜː.bi ⓊⓈ ˈkɜːr-

Kircaldie kɜːˈkɔːl.di, kə- ⓊⓈ kɜːr-, kɚ-

Kirchner ˈkɜːk.nəʳ ⓊⓈ ˈkɪrk.nɚ *US family name:* ˈkɜːtʃ.nəʳ, ˈkɜːʃ- ⓊⓈ ˈkɜːrtʃ.nɚ, ˈkɜːrʃ-

Kirghiz ˈkɜː.gɪz, ˈkɪə- ⓊⓈ kɪrˈgiːz

Kirghizia kɜːˈgɪz.i.ə, kɪə- ⓊⓈ kɪrˈgiː.ʒə, -ʒi.ə

Kiribati ˌkɪr.əˈbæs, ˌkɪə.rəˈ-, -rɪˈ-; ˌkɪr.iˈbɑː.ti ⓊⓈ ˌkɪr.iˈbɑː.ti; ˈkɪr.ə.bæs

Kiri Te Kanawa ˌkɪr.i.tɪˈkæn.ə.wə, ˌkɪə.ri-, -ˈkɑː.nə-, -teɪ- ⓊⓈ ˌkɪr.i.təˈkɑː.nə.wɑː

kirk kɜːk ⓊⓈ kɜːrk **-s** -s

Kirkby *surname:* ˈkɜː.bi, ˈkɜːk.bi ⓊⓈ ˈkɜːr-, ˈkɜːrk- *place:* ˈkɜː.bi ⓊⓈ ˈkɜːr-

Kirkcaldy *place:* kɜːˈkɔː.di, kəˈkɒd.i, -ˈkɔː.di ⓤⓢ kɜːr-, kɚ- *surname:* kɜːˈkɔː.di, kə- ⓤⓢ kɜːr-, kɚ-
Kirkcudbright kɜːˈkuː.bri, kə- ⓤⓢ kɜːr-, kɚ- **-shire** -ʃəʳ, -ˌʃɪəʳ ⓤⓢ -ʃɚ, -ˌʃɪr
Kirkdale ˈkɜːk.deɪl ⓤⓢ ˈkɜːrk-
Kirk(e) kɜːk ⓤⓢ kɜːrk
Kirkham ˈkɜː.kəm ⓤⓢ ˈkɜːr-
Kirkintilloch ˌkɜː.kɪnˈtɪl.ək *as if Scots:* -əx ⓤⓢ ˌkɜːr.kɪnˈtɪl.ək
Kirkland ˈkɜːk.lənd ⓤⓢ ˈkɜːrk-
Kirklees ˌkɜːkˈliːz ⓤⓢ ˌkɜːrk-
Kirkman ˈkɜːk.mən ⓤⓢ ˈkɜːrk-
Kirkness ˌkɜːkˈnes ⓤⓢ ˌkɜːrk-
Kirkpatrick ˌkɜːkˈpæt.rɪk ⓤⓢ ˌkɜːrk-
Kirkstall ˈkɜːk.stɔːl *locally also:* -stᵊl ⓤⓢ ˈkɜːrk-
Kirkuk kɜːˈkʊk, ˈ-- ⓤⓢ kɪrˈkuːk
Kirkwall ˈkɜːk.wɔːl ⓤⓢ ˈkɜːrk-
Kirkwood ˈkɜːk.wʊd ⓤⓢ ˈkɜːrk-
Kirov ˈkɪə.rɒf, -rɒv ⓤⓢ ˈkiː.rɔːf
Kirovabad kɪəˈrɒv.ə.bæd, kɪ- ⓤⓢ kiːˈroʊ.və-, kɪ-
Kirriemuir ˌkɪr.iˈmjʊəʳ, -ˈmjɔːʳ ⓤⓢ -ˈmjʊɚ
kirsch kɪəʃ, kɜːʃ ⓤⓢ kɪrʃ
kirschwasser ˈkɪəʃˌvæs.əʳ, -ˌvɑː.səʳ ⓤⓢ ˈkɪrʃˌvɑː.sɚ
Kirsten ˈkɜː.stɪn, ˈkɪə-, -stᵊn ⓤⓢ ˈkɜːr-, ˈkɪr-
Kirstie, **Kirsty** ˈkɜː.sti ⓤⓢ ˈkɜːr-
kirtle ˈkɜː.tl̩ ⓤⓢ ˈkɜːr.t̬l̩ **-s** -z
Kisangani ˌkɪs.æŋˈgɑː.ni ⓤⓢ ˌkiː.sɑːnˈgɑː-
kish kɪʃ
Kishinev ˈkɪʃ.ɪ.nɒf, -nef ⓤⓢ -nev, -nef, -nɔːf
Kishon ˈkaɪ.ʃɒn *with some Jews:* ˈkiː.ʃɒn ⓤⓢ ˈkaɪ.ʃɑːn, -ʃᵊn
kismet ˈkɪz.met, ˈkɪs-, -mɪt, -mət ⓤⓢ -met, -mɪt
kiss kɪs **-es** -ɪz **-ing** -ɪŋ **-ed** -t **-er/s** -əʳ/z ⓤⓢ -ɚ/z ˌ**kiss of** ˈ**death** ; ˌ**kiss of** ˈ**life**
kissagram, **kiss-a-gram**, **kissogram** ˈkɪs.ə.græm **-s** -z
kiss-and-tell ˌkɪs.ᵊ*n*dˈtel
Kissinger ˈkɪs.ɪn.dʒəʳ, -ɪŋ.əʳ ⓤⓢ -ən.dʒɚ, -ɪn-
kiss-off ˈkɪs.ɒf ⓤⓢ -ɑːf
Kisumu kɪˈsuː.muː ⓤⓢ kiː-
kit (K) kɪt **-s** -s **-ting** -ɪŋ ⓤⓢ ˈkɪt̬.ɪŋ **-ted** -ɪd ⓤⓢ ˈkɪt̬.ɪd ˌ**kit and caˈboodle** ; ˈ**kit** ˌ**bag** ; ˈ**kit** ˌ**car**
kitbag ˈkɪt.bæg **-s** -z
kit-cat (K) ˈkɪt.kæt **-s** -s
kitchen (K) ˈkɪtʃ.ɪn, -ᵊn **-s** -z ˌ**kitchen** ˈ**cabinet** ; ˌ**kitchen** ˈ**garden** ; ˌ**kitchen** ˈ**sink** ; ˌ**kitchen** ˈ**unit**
kitchener (K) ˈkɪtʃ.ɪ.nəʳ, -ᵊn.əʳ ⓤⓢ -ə.nɚ **-s** -z
kitchenette ˌkɪtʃ.ɪˈnet, -əˈ- **-s** -s
kitchenmaid ˈkɪtʃ.ɪn.meɪd, -ᵊn- **-s** -z
kitchenware ˈkɪtʃ.ɪn.weəʳ, -ᵊn- ⓤⓢ -wer
Kitchin ˈkɪtʃ.ɪn
Kitching ˈkɪtʃ.ɪŋ
kit|e kaɪt **-es** -s **-ing** -ɪŋ **-ed** -əd
Kit-E-Kat® ˈkɪt.i.kæt
kitemark ˈkaɪt.mɑːk ⓤⓢ -mɑːrk
kith kɪθ
Kithnos ˈkɪθ.nɒs ⓤⓢ -nɑːs
Kit-Kat® ˈkɪt.kæt
kitsch kɪtʃ **-y** -i
Kitson ˈkɪt.sᵊn
kitten ˈkɪt.ᵊn **-s** -z
kittenish ˈkɪt.ᵊn.ɪʃ **-ly** -li
kittiwake ˈkɪt.ɪ.weɪk ⓤⓢ ˈkɪt̬- **-s** -s
Kitto ˈkɪt.əʊ ⓤⓢ ˈkɪt̬.oʊ
Kittredge ˈkɪt.rɪdʒ
Kitts kɪts
Kittson ˈkɪt.sᵊn
kitt|y (K) ˈkɪt|.i ⓤⓢ ˈkɪt̬- **-ies** -iz ˈ**Kitty** ˌ**Hawk**
Kitwe ˈkɪt.weɪ
Kitzbuhel, **Kitzbühel** ˈkɪts.bjuː.əl, -buː-, -bjuːl, -buːl
kiwi (K®) ˈkiː.wiː, -wi **-s** -z ˈ**kiwi** ˌ**fruit**
kJ (*abbrev. for* **kilojoule**) ˈkɪl.əʊˌdʒuːl ⓤⓢ ˈ-oʊ, ˈ-ə-
KKK (*abbrev. for* **Ku Klux Klan**) ˌkeɪ.keɪˈkeɪ
kl (*abbrev. for* **kilolitre/s**) *singular:* ˈkɪl.əʊˌliː.təʳ ⓤⓢ -oʊˌliː.t̬ɚ, ˈ-ə- *plural:* ˈkɪl.əʊˌliː.təz ⓤⓢ -oʊˌliː.t̬ɚz, ˈ-ə-
Klagenfurt ˈklɑː.gᵊn.fɜːt ⓤⓢ -fɜːrt
Klan klæn
Klans|man ˈklænz|.mən, -mæn **-men** -mən, -men
klatch klætʃ ⓤⓢ klætʃ, klɑːtʃ **-es** -ɪz
klaxon ˈklæk.sᵊn **-s** -z
Klee kleɪ
Kleenex® ˈkliː.neks
Klein klaɪn
Kleist klaɪst
Klemperer ˈklem.pᵊr.əʳ ⓤⓢ -ɚ
kleptomani|a ˌklep.təʊˈmeɪ.ni|.ə ⓤⓢ -toʊˈ-, -təˈ- **-ac/s** -æk/s
Kline klaɪn
Klondike ˈklɒn.daɪk ⓤⓢ ˈklɑːn-
Kluge *English name:* kluːdʒ *German name:* ˈkluː.gə
klutz klʌts **-es** -ɪz
klutz|y ˈklʌt.s|i **-iness** -ɪ.nəs, -ɪ.nɪs
km (*abbrev. for* **kilometre/s**) *singular:* kɪˈlɒm.ɪ.təʳ, ˈ-ə-; ˈkɪl.əʊˌmiː- ⓤⓢ kɪˈlɑː.mə.t̬ɚ; ˈkɪl.əˌmiː- *plural:* kɪˈlɒm.ɪ.təz, ˈ-ə-; ˈkɪl.əʊˌmiː.təz ⓤⓢ kɪˈlɑː.mɪ.t̬ɚz; ˈkɪl.əˌmiː.t̬ɚz
K Mart® ˈkeɪˌmɑːt ⓤⓢ -ˌmɑːrt
knack næk **-s** -s
knack|er ˈnæk|.əʳ ⓤⓢ -ɚ **-ers** -əz ⓤⓢ -ɚz **-ering** -ᵊr.ɪŋ **-ered** -əd ⓤⓢ -ɚd
knacker|y ˈnæk.ᵊr|.i **-ies** -iz
knag næg **-s** -z **-gy** -i
knap næp **-s** -s **-ping** -ɪŋ **-ped** -t
Knapp næp
knapsack ˈnæp.sæk **-s** -s
knar nɑːʳ ⓤⓢ nɑːr **-s** -z
Knaresborough ˈneəz.bᵊr.ə, ˈ-brə ⓤⓢ ˈnerz.bɚ.oʊ, ˈ-brə
knave neɪv **-s** -z
knaver|y ˈneɪ.vᵊr|.i **-ies** -iz
knavish ˈneɪ.vɪʃ **-ly** -li **-ness** -nəs, -nɪs
knead niːd **-s** -z **-ing** -ɪŋ **-ed** -ɪd
Knebworth ˈneb.wəθ, -wɜːθ ⓤⓢ -wɚθ, -wɜːrθ
knee niː **-s** -z **-ing** -ɪŋ **-d** -d ˌ**knee-**ˈ**deep** ; ˌ**weak at the** ˈ**knees**
knee-breeches ˈniːˌbrɪtʃ.ɪz
kneecap ˈniː.kæp **-s** -s **-ping** -ɪŋ **-ped** -t
knee-high (*adj.*) ˌniːˈhaɪ *stress shift:* ˌ**knee-high** ˈ**socks**
knee high (*n.*) ˈniː.haɪ **-s** -z
knee-jerk ˈniː.dʒɜːk ⓤⓢ -dʒɜːrk
knee-joint ˈniː.dʒɔɪnt **-s** -s
kneel niːl **-s** -z **-ing** -ɪŋ **-ed** -d **knelt** nelt
knees-up ˈniːz.ʌp
knell nel **-s** -z **-ing** -ɪŋ **-ed** -d
Kneller ˈnel.əʳ ⓤⓢ -ɚ **-s** -z
knelt (*from* **kneel**) nelt
Knesset ˈknes.et, kəˈnes-, -ɪt
knew (*from* **know**) njuː, nuː ⓤⓢ nuː, njuː
knicker ˈnɪk.əʳ ⓤⓢ -ɚ **-s** -z
knickerbocker (K) ˈnɪk.əˌbɒk.əʳ ⓤⓢ -ɚˌbɑː.kɚ **-s** -z ˌ**knickerbocker** ˈ**glory**
knick-knack ˈnɪk.næk **-s** -s **-ery** -ᵊr.i
kni|fe (*n.*) naɪ|f **-ves** -vz
knif|e (*v.*) naɪf **-es** -s **-ing** -ɪŋ **-ed** -t
knight (K) naɪt **-s** -s **-ing** -ɪŋ ⓤⓢ ˈnaɪ.t̬ɪŋ **-ed** -ɪd ⓤⓢ ˈnaɪ.t̬ɪd
knight-errant ˌnaɪtˈer.ᵊnt **knights-errant** ˌnaɪtsˈer.ᵊnt
knighthood ˈnaɪt.hʊd **-s** -z
Knightley ˈnaɪt.li
knightl|y ˈnaɪt.l|i **-ier** -i.əʳ ⓤⓢ -i.ɚ **-iest** -i.ɪst, -i.əst **-iness** -ɪ.nəs, -ɪ.nɪs
Knighton ˈnaɪ.tᵊn
Knightsbridge ˈnaɪts.brɪdʒ
knish kəˈnɪʃ **-es** -ɪz
knit nɪt **-s** -s **-ting** -ɪŋ ⓤⓢ ˈnɪt̬.ɪŋ **-ted** -ɪd ⓤⓢ ˈnɪt̬.ɪd **-ter/s** -əʳ/z ⓤⓢ ˈnɪt̬.ɚ/z ˈ**knitting ma**ˌ**chine** ; ˈ**knitting** ˌ**needle**
knitwear ˈnɪt.weəʳ ⓤⓢ -wer
knob nɒb ⓤⓢ nɑːb **-s** -z
knobbly ˈnɒb.l̩.i, ˈ-li ⓤⓢ ˈnɑː.bl̩.i, ˈ-bli
knobb|y ˈnɒb|.i ⓤⓢ ˈnɑː.b|i **-ier** -i.əʳ ⓤⓢ -i.ɚ **-iest** -i.ɪst, -i.əst **-iness** -ɪ.nəs, -ɪ.nɪs
knock nɒk ⓤⓢ nɑːk **-s** -s **-ing/s** -ɪŋ/z **-ed** -t **-er/s** -əʳ/z ⓤⓢ -ɚ/z
knockabout ˈnɒk.əˌbaʊt ⓤⓢ ˈnɑːk- **-s** -s

Knockbreda nɒk'breɪ.də (US) nɑːk-
knock-down 'nɒk.daʊn (US) 'nɑːk.daʊn
knock-down-drag-out ˌnɒk.daʊn'dræg.aʊt (US) ˌnɑːk- *stress shift:* ˌknock-down-ˌdrag-out 'fight
knock-kneed ˌnɒk'niːd (US) 'nɑːk.niːd *stress shift:* ˌknock-kneed 'child
knockoff 'nɒk.ɒf (US) 'nɑːk.ɑːf **-s** -s
knock-on (*adj.*) ˌnɒk'ɒn (US) ˌnɑːk'ɑːn *stress shift, see compound:* **'knock-on efˌfect**
knock-on (*n.*) (*in rugby*) ˌnɒk'ɒn, '-- (US) ˌnɑːk'ɑːn, '--
knock-out 'nɒk.aʊt (US) 'nɑːk- **-s** -s **'knockout ˌdrops**
knock-up 'nɒk.ʌp (US) 'nɑːk- **-s** -s
knockwurst 'nɒk.wɜːst (US) 'nɑːk.wɜːrst, -wʊrst
Knole nəʊl (US) noʊl
knoll nəʊl (US) noʊl **-s** -z
Knolles, Knollys nəʊlz (US) noʊlz
knop nɒp (US) nɑːp **-s** -s
Knossos 'knɒs.ɒs, 'knəʊ.sɒs, -səs (US) 'nɑː.səs
knot nɒt (US) nɑːt **-s** -s **-ting** -ɪŋ (US) 'nɑː.t̬ɪŋ **-ted** -ɪd (US) 'nɑː.t̬ɪd **at a ˌrate of 'knots**
knotgrass 'nɒt.grɑːs (US) 'nɑːt.græs
knothole 'nɒt.həʊl (US) 'nɑːt.hoʊl **-s** -z
Knott nɒt (US) nɑːt
Knottingley 'nɒt.ɪŋ.li (US) 'nɑː.t̬ɪŋ-
knott|y 'nɒt|.i (US) 'nɑː.t̬|i **-ier** -i.əʳ (US) -i.ɚ **-iest** -i.ɪst, -i.əst **-ily** -ɪ.li, -əl.i **-iness** -ɪ.nəs, -ɪ.nɪs
Knotty Ash ˌnɒt.i'æʃ (US) ˌnɑː.t̬i-
knout naʊt **-s** -s **-ing** -ɪŋ (US) 'naʊ.t̬ɪŋ **-ed** -ɪd (US) 'naʊ.t̬ɪd
know nəʊ (US) noʊ **-s** -z **-ing** -ɪŋ **knew** njuː (US) nuː **known** nəʊn (US) noʊn **knower/s** 'nəʊ.əʳ/z (US) 'noʊ.ɚ/z **knowable** 'nəʊ.ə.bl̩ (US) 'noʊ-
know-all 'nəʊ.ɔːl (US) 'noʊ-, -ɑːl **-s** -z
know-how 'nəʊ.haʊ (US) 'noʊ-
knowing 'nəʊ.ɪŋ (US) 'noʊ- **-ly** -li **-ness** -nəs, -nɪs
know-it-all 'nəʊ.ɪt.ɔːl (US) 'noʊ.ɪt̬-, -ɑːl **-s** -z
Knowle nəʊl (US) noʊl
knowledg|e 'nɒl.ɪdʒ (US) 'nɑː.lɪdʒ **-es** -ɪz
knowledgeab|le 'nɒl.ɪ.dʒə.b|l̩ (US) 'nɑː.lɪ- **-ly** -li
Knowles nəʊlz (US) noʊlz
known (*from* **know**) nəʊn (US) noʊn
know-nothing 'nəʊˌnʌθ.ɪŋ (US) 'noʊ- **-s** -z
Knox nɒks (US) nɑːks
Knoxville 'nɒks.vɪl (US) 'nɑːks-, -vəl
knuckl|e 'nʌk.l̩ **-es** -z **-ing** -ɪŋ, '-lɪŋ **-ed** -d **-y** -i, '-li ˌ**knuckle 'sandwich**
knuckleball 'nʌk.l̩.bɔːl (US) -bɔːl, -bɑːl
knucklebone 'nʌk.l̩.bəʊn (US) -boʊn **-s** -z
knuckle-duster 'nʌk.l̩ˌdʌs.təʳ (US) -tɚ **-s** -z
knucklehead 'nʌk.l̩.hed **-ed** -ɪd
knurled nɜːld (US) nɜːrld
Knutsford 'nʌts.fəd (US) -fɚd
KO, k.o. ˌkeɪ'əʊ (US) -'oʊ **-'s** -z **-'ing** -ɪŋ **-'d** -d
koala kəʊ'ɑː.lə (US) koʊ- **-s** -z
Kobe 'kəʊ.beɪ, -bi (US) ˌkoʊ'beɪ, 'koʊ.bi
Koblenz kəʊ'blents (US) 'koʊ.blents
kobo 'kɒb.əʊ (US) 'kɑː.boʊ, 'koʊ-; 'kɔː.bɔː
kobold 'kɒb.əʊld, 'kəʊ.bəʊld, -bəld (US) 'koʊ.bɔːld, -bɑːld **-s** -z
Koch kəʊk, kɒtʃ *as if German:* kɒx (US) koʊk, kɑːk, kɑːtʃ *as if German:* kɔːx, koʊx
Köchel 'kɜː.kəl *as if German:* -xəl (US) 'kɜːr- **'Köchel ˌnumber**
Kodak® 'kəʊ.dæk (US) 'koʊ- **-s** -s
Kodály 'kəʊ.daɪ, -dɑː.i (US) 'koʊ-; koʊ'dɑː.i
Kodiak 'kəʊ.di.æk (US) 'koʊ-
Koestler 'kɜːst.ləʳ (US) 'kest.lɚ
Koh-i-noor ˌkəʊ.i'nʊəʳ, -'nɔəʳ, -'nɔːʳ, '--- (US) 'koʊ.ɪ.nʊr
kohl kəʊl (US) koʊl
Kohl kəʊl (US) koʊl
kohlrab|i ˌkəʊl'rɑː.b|i (US) ˌkoʊl-, '--- **-ies** -iz
koine (K) 'kɔɪ.neɪ, -niː, -ni (US) kɔɪ'neɪ; 'kɔɪ.neɪ, -niː
Kojak 'kəʊ.dʒæk (US) 'koʊ-
kola (K) 'kəʊ.lə (US) 'koʊ-
kolkhoz ˌkɒl'kɒz, -'kɔːz, -'hɔːz (US) ˌkɑːl'kɔːz **-es** -ɪz
Kolnai 'kɒl.naɪ (US) 'kɑːl-
Komodo kə'məʊ.dəʊ (US) -'moʊ.doʊ
Kongo 'kɒŋ.gəʊ (US) 'kɑːŋ.goʊ
Konica® 'kɒn.ɪ.kə, 'kəʊ.nɪ- (US) 'kɑː.nɪ-
Königsberg 'kɜː.nɪgz.bɜːg, -beəg (US) 'kɜːr.nɪgz.bɜːrg, -berg
Konrad 'kɒn.ræd (US) 'kɑːn-
Konya 'kɔː.njɑː
koodoo 'kuː.duː **-s** -z
kook kuːk **-s** -s
kookaburra 'kʊk.əˌbʌr.ə (US) -ˌbɜːr-, -ˌbʌr- **-s** -z
kook|y 'kuː.k|i **-ier** -i.əʳ (US) -i.ɚ **-iest** -i.ɪst, -i.əst **-iness** -ɪ.nəs, -ɪ.nɪs
Kool-Aide® 'kuːl.eɪd
Koori(e) 'kʊə.ri, 'kɔː- (US) 'kʊr.i
Kop kɒp (US) kɑːp
kope(c)k 'kəʊ.pek, 'kɒp.ek (US) 'koʊ.pek **-s** -s
kopje 'kɒp.i (US) 'kɑː.pi **-s** -z
Kops kɒps (US) kɑːps
Korah 'kɔː.rə (US) 'kɔːr.ə
Koran kɒr'ɑːn, kɔː'rɑːn, kʊ-, kə- (US) kə'ræn, -'rɑːn; 'kɔːr.æn, -ɑːn
Koranic kɒr'æn.ɪk, kɔː'ræn-, kʊ-, kə- (US) kə'ræn.ɪk, -'rɑː.nɪk; 'kɔːr.æn.ɪk, -ɑː.nɪk
Kore|a kə'riː|.ə, kɒr'iː- (US) kə'riː-, kɔː- **-an/s** -ən/z
korma 'kɔː.mə (US) 'kɔːr-
koruna kɒr'uː.nə, kə'ruː- (US) 'kɔːr.uː- **-s** -z
koruny (*plur. of* **koruna**) kɒr'uː.ni, kə'ruː- (US) 'kɔːr.uː-
kosher 'kəʊ.ʃəʳ *occasionally, by non-Jews:* 'kɒʃ.əʳ (US) 'koʊ.ʃɚ
Kosice kɒʃ'ɪt.sə (US) 'kɔː.ʃiːt.seɪ, -ʃɪt-
Kosygin kə'siː.gɪn (US) kə-, koʊ-
Kotex® 'kəʊ.teks (US) 'koʊ-
kotow ˌkəʊ'taʊ (US) ˌkoʊ- **-s** -z **-ing** -ɪŋ **-ed** -d **-er/s** -əʳ/z (US) -ɚ/z
Kough kjəʊ, kəʊ (US) kjoʊ, koʊ
koumiss 'kuː.mɪs, -məs
Kowasaki kəʊ.ə'sɑː.ki, -'sæk.i (US) koʊ-
Kowloon ˌkaʊ'luːn
kowtow ˌkaʊ'taʊ (US) ˌkaʊ'taʊ, '-- **-s** -z **-ing** -ɪŋ **-ed** -d **-er/s** -əʳ/z (US) -ɚ/z
kraal krɑːl, krɔːl **-s** -z

Note: Usually pronounced /krɑːl/ in England, but /krɔːl/ in South Africa.

Kraft® krɑːft (US) kræft
Kragujevac kræg'uː.jə.væts (US) 'krɑː.guː.jə.vɑːts
krait kraɪt **-s** -s
Krakatoa ˌkræk.ə'təʊ.ə (US) -'toʊ-
kraken 'krɑː.kən, 'kreɪ- (US) 'krɑː- **-s** -z
Krakow 'kræk.ɒv, -ɒf, -aʊ (US) 'krɑː.kaʊ, 'kræk.aʊ, 'kreɪ.kaʊ; 'krɑː.kʊf
Kramer 'kreɪ.məʳ (US) -mɚ
krantz (K) krænts
Krasnodar ˌkrɑːs.nəʊ'dɑːʳ (US) -noʊ'dɑːr
Krasnoyarsk ˌkrɑːs.nəʊ'jɑːsk (US) -noʊ'jɑːrsk
Kravchuk kræv'tʃʊk
Kray kreɪ
kremlin (K) 'krem.lɪn **-s** -z
Kremlinolog|y ˌkrem.lɪ'nɒl.ə.dʒ|i (US) -'nɑː.lə- **-ist/s** -ɪst/s
kreu(t)zer (K) 'krɔɪt.səʳ (US) -sɚ **-s** -z
krill krɪl
kris kriːs **-es** -ɪz
Krishna 'krɪʃ.nə
Kris Kringle, Kriss Kringle ˌkrɪs'krɪŋ.gl̩
Krista 'krɪs.tə
Kristen 'krɪs.tən, -tɪn
Kristi 'krɪs.ti
Kristiansand 'krɪs.tʃən.sænd
Kristie 'krɪs.ti
Kristin 'krɪs.tɪn
Kristina krɪ'stiː.nə
Kristine krɪ'stiːn

Kristopher ˈkrɪs.tə.fəʳ Ⓤⓢ -fɚ
kro|na ˈkrəʊl.nə Ⓤⓢ ˈkroʊ- **-nor** -nɔːʳ Ⓤⓢ -nɔːr
kró|na ˈkrəʊl.nə Ⓤⓢ ˈkroʊ- **-nur** -nʊəʳ Ⓤⓢ -nɚ
kro|ne ˈkrəʊl.nə Ⓤⓢ ˈkroʊ- **-nes** -nəz **-ner** -nəʳ **-nen** -nən
Kronin ˈkrəʊ.nɪn Ⓤⓢ ˈkroʊ-
Krons(h)tadt ˈkrɒn*t*.ʃtæt Ⓤⓢ ˈkrɔːn*t*.ʃtɑːt
kroon kruːn
Kruger ˈkruː.gəʳ Ⓤⓢ -gɚ
krugerrand (K) ˈkruː.gᵊr.ænd Ⓤⓢ -gɚ- **-s** -z
Krupp krʊp, krʌp
Krushchev ˈkrʊs.tʃɒf, ˈkrʊʃ-, ˌ-ˈ- Ⓤⓢ ˈkruː.tʃef, -tʃɔːf, -tʃev, kruːʃˈtʃɔːf
krypton ˈkrɪp.tɒn, -tən Ⓤⓢ -tɑːn
kryptonite ˈkrɪp.tᵊn.aɪt Ⓤⓢ -tə.naɪt
Krystal ˈkrɪs.tᵊl
Krystle ˈkrɪs.tl̩
Kuala Lumpur ˌkwɑː.ləˈlʊm.pʊəʳ, ˌkwɒl-, -ˈlʌm-, -pəʳ Ⓤⓢ ˌkwɑː.ləˈlʊm.pʊr
Kubla Khan ˌkuː.bləˈkɑːn, ˌkʊb.ləˈ- Ⓤⓢ ˌkuː.bləˈ-
kudos ˈkjuː.dɒs Ⓤⓢ ˈkuː.doʊz, ˈkjuː-, -doʊs, -dɑːs
kudu ˈkuː.duː **-s** -z
Ku Klux Klan ˌkuː.klʌksˈklæn, ˌkjuː-
kulak ˈkuː.læk Ⓤⓢ kuːˈlɑːk, ˈ-- **-s** -s
kultur (K) kʊlˈtʊəʳ Ⓤⓢ -ˈtʊr
Kumanovo ˌkuː.məˈnəʊ.vəʊ Ⓤⓢ ˈkʊm.əˌnoʊ.voʊ
Kumar kuːˈmɑːʳ Ⓤⓢ ˈkuː.mɑːr
Kumasi kʊˈmæs.i, -ˈmɑː.si Ⓤⓢ -ˈmɑː.si
Kumin ˈkjuː.mɪn, ˈkuː- Ⓤⓢ ˈkuː-
kümmel ˈkʊm.ᵊl, ˈkɪm- Ⓤⓢ ˈkɪm-
kumquat ˈkʌm.kwɒt, -kwæt Ⓤⓢ -kwɑːt **-s** -s
kung fu ˌkʊŋˈfuː, ˌkʌŋ- Ⓤⓢ ˌkʌŋ-, ˌkʊŋ-, ˌgʊn-
Kunitz ˈkjuː.nɪts, ˈkuː- Ⓤⓢ ˈkuː-
Kuomintang ˌkwəʊ.mɪnˈtæŋ, ˌgwəʊ- Ⓤⓢ ˌkwoʊ-
Kurath ˈkjʊə.ræθ Ⓤⓢ ˈkʊr.ɑːt, ˈkjʊr- Ⓤⓢ -ɑːθ
Kurd kɜːd Ⓤⓢ kɜːrd, kʊrd **-s** -z **-ish** -ɪʃ
Kurdistan ˌkɜː.dɪˈstɑːn, -dəˈ-, -ˈstæn Ⓤⓢ ˌkɜːr.dɪˈstæn, ˌkʊr-, -dəˈ-, -ˈstɑːn
Kuril(e) kʊˈriːl, kjuː- Ⓤⓢ ˈkuː.rɪl; kuːˈriːl **-s** -z
kursaal ˈkʊə.zɑːl, ˈkɜː-, -sɑːl, -sᵊl Ⓤⓢ ˈkʊr-, ˈkɜːr- **-s** -z
Kurt kɜːt Ⓤⓢ kɜːrt
Kurtis ˈkɜː.tɪs Ⓤⓢ ˈkɜːr.t̬ɪs
Kurtz kɜːts Ⓤⓢ kɜːrts
kurus kʊˈrʊʃ, -ˈruːʃ Ⓤⓢ -ˈruːʃ
Kutaisi kʊˈtaɪ.si Ⓤⓢ kʊˈtaɪ.si, ˌkuː.təˈjiː.si
Ku|wait kuːˈweɪt, kjuː-, kə- Ⓤⓢ kuːˈweɪt, -ˈwaɪt **-waiti/s** -ˈweɪ.ti/z Ⓤⓢ -ˈweɪ.t̬i/z, -ˈwaɪ.t̬i/z
Kuyper ˈkaɪ.pəʳ Ⓤⓢ -pɚ
kvas(s) kvɑːs, kvæs Ⓤⓢ kvɑːs, kəˈvɑːs
kvetch kvetʃ, kəˈvetʃ **-es** -ɪz **-ing** -ɪŋ **-ed** -t
kW (*abbrev. for* **kilowatt**) ˈkɪl.əʊ.wɒt Ⓤⓢ -oʊ.wɑːt, ˈ-ə-
kwacha ˈkwɑː.tʃɑː
Kwangtung ˌkwænˈtʌŋ, ˌkwæŋ- Ⓤⓢ ˌkwɑːŋˈtʊŋ, ˌgwɑːŋ-
Kwantung ˌkwænˈtʌŋ Ⓤⓢ ˌkwɑːŋˈtʊŋ, ˌgwɑːŋ-
kwanza ˈkwæn.zə Ⓤⓢ ˈkwɑːn.zɑː, -zə **-s** -z
kwashiorcor ˌkwæʃ.iˈɔː.kɔːʳ, -kəʳ Ⓤⓢ ˌkwɑː.ʃiːˈɔːr.kɔːr
KwaZulu kwɑːˈzuː.luː
kwela ˈkweɪ.lə
KWIC kwɪk
Ky. (*abbrev. for* **Kentucky**) kenˈtʌk.i, kən- Ⓤⓢ kən-
kyat kiˈɑːt Ⓤⓢ tʃɑːt, kjɑːt
Kyd kɪd
Kyla ˈkaɪ.lə
kyle (K) kaɪl **-s** -z
Kylie ˈkaɪ.li
kylin ˈkaɪ.lɪn **-s** -z
Kyllachy ˈkaɪ.lə.ki, -xi Ⓤⓢ -ki
kyloe ˈkaɪ.ləʊ Ⓤⓢ -loʊ **-s** -z
kymogram ˈkaɪ.məʊ.græm Ⓤⓢ -moʊ-, -mə-
kymograph ˈkaɪ.məʊ.grɑːf, -græf Ⓤⓢ -moʊ.græf, -mə- **-s** -s
kymographic ˌkaɪ.məʊˈgræf.ɪk Ⓤⓢ -moʊˈ-, -məˈ-
Kynance ˈkaɪ.næn*t*s
Kynaston ˈkɪn.ə.stᵊn
Kyoto ˈkjəʊ.təʊ, kiˈəʊ.təʊ Ⓤⓢ kiːˈoʊ.toʊ, ˈkjoʊ-
Kyrgyzstan ˌkɜː.gɪˈstɑːn Ⓤⓢ ˈkɪr.gɪ.stɑːn, -stæn, ˌ--ˈ-
kyrie ˈkɪr.i.eɪ, ˈkɪə.ri-, -iː Ⓤⓢ ˈkɪr.i.eɪ **-s** -z
Kyrle kɜːl Ⓤⓢ kɜːrl
Kythe ˈkaɪ.θi
Kyushu ˈkjuː.ʃuː, kiˈuː-
Kyzyl-Kum kəˌzɪlˈkuːm, -ˈkʊm

L

l (L) el -'s -z

l (*abbrev. for* **litre/s**) *singular:* 'liː.təʳ US -t̬ɚ *plural:* 'liː.təz US -t̬ɚz

la lɑː -s -z

La. (*abbrev. for* **Louisiana**) luˌiː.zi'æn.ə, -'ɑː.nə; ˌluː.i.zi'- US luˌiː.zi'æn.ə; ˌluː.zi'-

LA ˌel'eɪ *stress shift:* ˌLA 'Law

laager 'lɑː.gəʳ US -gɚ -s -z

laari 'lɑː.ri US 'lɑːr.i -s -z

lab læb -s -z

Laban *biblical character:* 'leɪ.bən, -bæn US -bən *US family name:* lə'bæn

label 'leɪ.bᵊl -s -z -(l)ing -ɪŋ, 'leɪ.blɪŋ -(l)ed -d

labia (*from* **labium**) 'leɪ.bi.ə

labial 'leɪ.bi.əl -s -z -ly -i

labialization, -isa- ˌleɪ.bi.ᵊl.aɪ'zeɪ.ʃᵊn, -ɪ'- US -ɪ'-

labializ|e, -is|e 'leɪ.bi.ᵊl.aɪz -es -ɪz -ing -ɪŋ -ed -d

labia majora ˌleɪ.bi.ə.mə'dʒɔː.rə, -maɪ'ɔː- US -mə'dʒɔːr.ə

labia minora ˌleɪ.bi.ə.mɪ'nɔː.rə US -'nɔːr.ə

labiate 'leɪ.bi.eɪt, -ət, -ɪt -s -s

Labienus ˌlæb.i'iː.nəs, -'eɪ-

labile 'leɪ.baɪl US -baɪl, -bᵊl

labiodental ˌleɪ.bi.əʊ'den.tᵊl US -oʊ'den.t̬ᵊl -s -z

labiopalatal ˌleɪ.bi.əʊ'pæl.ə.tᵊl US -oʊ'pæl.ə.t̬ᵊl -s -z -ly -li

labiovelar ˌleɪ.bi.əʊ'viː.ləʳ US -oʊ'viː.lɚ -s -z

labiovelariz|e, -is|e ˌleɪ.bi.əʊ'viː.lᵊr.aɪz US -oʊ'viː.lə.raɪz -es -ɪz -ing -ɪŋ -ed -d

labi|um 'leɪ.bi|.əm -a -ə

La Bohème ˌlɑː.bəʊ'em, ˌlæ-, -'eɪm US ˌlɑː.boʊ'-

lab|or (L) 'leɪ.b|əʳ US -b|ɚ -ors -əz US -ɚz -oring -ᵊr.ɪŋ -ored -əd US -ɚd -orer/s -ᵊr.əʳ/z US -ɚ.ɚ/z ˌ**labor of 'love ; 'labor ˌunion**

laborator|y lə'bɒr.ə.tᵊr|.i, -tr|i US 'læb.rə.tɔːr.i, 'læb.ɚ.ə- -ies -iz

labor-intensive ˌleɪ.bᵊr.ɪn'ten*t*.sɪv US -bɚ- *stress shift:* ˌlabor-intensive 'work

laborious lə'bɔː.ri.əs US -'bɔːr.i- -ly -li -ness -nəs, -nɪs

laborite (L) 'leɪ.bᵊr.aɪt US -bə.raɪt -s -s

labor-saving 'leɪ.bəˌseɪ.vɪŋ US -bɚˌ- *stress shift:* ˌlabor-saving 'gadget

Labouchere ˌlæb.uː'ʃeəʳ, -ʊ'-, '--- US ˌlæb.uː'ʃer

lab|our (L) 'leɪ.b|əʳ US -b|ɚ -ours -əz US -ɚz -ouring -ᵊr.ɪŋ -oured -əd US -ɚd -ourer/s '-bᵊr.əʳ/-əz **'labour exˌchange; ˌlabour of 'love; 'Labour ˌParty**

labour-intensive ˌleɪ.bᵊr.ɪn'ten*t*.sɪv US -bɚ- *stress shift:* ˌlabour-intensive 'work

labourite (L) 'leɪ.bᵊr.aɪt US -bə.raɪt -s -s

labour-saving 'leɪ.bəˌseɪ.vɪŋ US -bɚˌ- *stress shift:* ˌlabour-saving 'gadget

Labrador 'læb.rə.dɔːʳ US -dɔːr -s -z

Labuan lə'buː.ən US ˌlɑː.buː'ɑːn, lə'buː.ən

laburnum lə'bɜː.nəm US -'bɜːr- -s -z

labyrinth 'læb.ᵊr.ɪn*t*θ, -ɪ.rɪn*t*θ US -ɚ.ɪn*t*θ, '-rən*t*θ -s -s

labyrinth|ian ˌlæb.ə'rɪn*t*.θ|i.ən, -ɪ'- US -ə'rɪn*t*- -ine -aɪn US -ɪn, -iːn, -aɪn

lac læk -s -s

Lacan læ'kɑ̃ː US lə'kɑːn, ˌlɑː'kɑːn

Laccadive 'læk.ə.dɪv, 'lɑː.kə-, -diːv, -daɪv US 'læk.ə.daɪv; 'lɑː.kə.diːv -s -z

laccolith 'læk.ə.lɪθ

lac|e leɪs -es -ɪz -ing -ɪŋ -ed -t -er/s -əʳ/z US -ɚ/z

Lacedaemon ˌlæs.ə'diː.mən, -ɪ'- US -ə'-

Lacedaemonian ˌlæs.ə.dɪ'məʊ.ni.ən, ˌ-ɪ-, -də'- US -ə.dɪ'moʊ.ni- -s -z

lacer|ate 'læs.ᵊr|.eɪt US -ə.r|eɪt -ates -eɪts -ating -eɪ.tɪŋ US -eɪ.t̬ɪŋ -ated -eɪ.tɪd US -eɪ.t̬ɪd

laceration ˌlæs.ᵊr'eɪ.ʃᵊn US -ə'reɪ- -s -z

Lacert|a lə'sɜː.t|ə US -'sɜːr.t̬|ə -ae -iː

Lacey 'leɪ.si

laches 'lætʃ.ɪz, 'leɪ.tʃɪz, -tʃəz US 'lætʃ.ɪz, 'leɪ.tʃɪz

Lachesis 'læk.ə.sɪs, -ɪ- US 'læk-, 'lætʃ-

Lachish 'leɪ.kɪʃ

Lachlan 'læk.lən, 'lɒk.lən US 'lɑːk-

lachrymal 'læk.rɪ.mᵊl

lachrymatory ˌlæk.rɪ'meɪ.tᵊr.i; 'læk.rɪ.mə-, -meɪ- US 'læk.rɪ.mə.tɔːr-

lachrymose 'læk.rɪ.məʊs, -rə-, -məʊz US -rɪ.moʊs -ly -li

lack læk -s -s -ing -ɪŋ -ed -t

lackadaisic|al ˌlæk.ə'deɪ.zɪ.k|ᵊl -ally -ᵊl.i, -li -alness -nəs, -nɪs

lackaday 'læk.ə.deɪ, ˌ--'-

lackey 'læk.i -s -z -ing -ɪŋ -ed -d

lacklustre, lackluster 'lækˌlʌs.təʳ, ˌ-'-- US 'lækˌlʌs.tɚ

Lacon 'leɪ.kən

Laconi|a lə'kəʊ.ni|.ə US -'koʊ- -an/s -ən/z

laconic (L) lə'kɒn.ɪk US -'kɑː.nɪk -al -ᵊl -ally -ᵊl.i, -li

lacqu|er 'læk|.əʳ US -ɚ -ers -əz US -ɚz -ering -ᵊr.ɪŋ -ered -əd US -ɚd -erer/s -ᵊr.əʳ/z US -ɚ.ɚ/z

lacquey 'læk.i -s -z -ing -ɪŋ -ed -d

lacrosse lə'krɒs US -'krɑːs

lactase 'læk.teɪs, -teɪz US -teɪs

lactate (*n.*) 'læk.teɪt

lacta|te (*v.*) læk'teɪ|t US '-- -tes -ts -ting -tɪŋ US -t̬ɪŋ -ted -tɪd US -t̬ɪd

lactation læk'teɪ.ʃᵊn

lacteal 'læk.ti.əl

lactic 'læk.tɪk ˌ**lactic 'acid**

lactometer læk'tɒm.ɪ.təʳ, -ə.təʳ US -'tɑː.mə.t̬ɚ -s -z

lactose 'læk.təʊs, -təʊz US -toʊs

lacun|a lə'kjuː.n|ə, læk'juː- US lə'kjuː- -ae -iː -as -əz

lacy (L) 'leɪ.si

lad læd -s -z

Lada® 'lɑː.də -s -z

Ladakh lə'dɑːk, -'dɔːk US -'dɑːk

Ladbroke 'læd.brʊk, -brəʊk US -brʊk, -broʊk

Ladbrokes 'læd.brəʊks, -brʊks US -broʊks, -brʊks

ladd|er 'læd|.əʳ US -ɚ -ers -əz US -ɚz -ering -ᵊr.ɪŋ -ered -əd US -ɚd

ladderback 'læd.ə.bæk US '-ɚ-

laddie 'læd.i -s -z

laddish 'læd.ɪʃ -ly -li -ness -nəs, -nɪs

lad|e leɪd -es -z -ing -ɪŋ -ed -ɪd -en -ᵊn

Ladefoged 'læd.ɪ.fəʊ.gɪd, '-ə-, -gəd US -ə.foʊ.gəd

laden (*from* **lade**) 'leɪ.dᵊn

la-di-da, lah-di-dah ˌlɑː.dɪ'dɑː US -diː'- *stress shift:* ˌla-di-da 'voice

ladies 'leɪ.diz **'ladies' ˌman ; 'ladies' ˌroom**

ladieswear 'leɪ.diz.weəʳ US -wer

Ladislaus 'læd.ɪ.slɔːs US -slɔːs, -slɑːs

Ladislaw 'læd.ɪ.slɔː US -slɔː, -slɑː

ladl|e 'leɪ.dl̩ -es -z -ing -ɪŋ, 'leɪd.lɪŋ -ed -d

ladleful 'leɪ.dl̩.fʊl -s -z

Ladoga 'læd.əʊ.gə, 'lɑː.dəʊ-; lə'dəʊ- US 'lɑː.dɔː.gɑː, -də.gə

la dolce vita lɑːˌdɒl.tʃeɪ'viː.tə US -ˌdoʊl.tʃeɪ'-, -tʃə'-, -t̬ə

Ladrone lə'drəʊn US -'droʊn

lad|y (L) 'leɪ.d|i -ies -iz ˌ**Lady 'Bountiful ; 'lady ˌchapel ; 'Lady ˌDay ; 'lady ˌfriend**

ladybird (L®) 'leɪ.di.bɜːd US -bɜːrd -s -z

ladybug 'leɪ.di.bʌg -s -z

ladyfinger 'leɪ.diˌfɪŋ.gəʳ US -gɚ -s -z

lady-in-waiting ˌleɪ.di.ɪn'weɪ.tɪŋ US -t̬ɪŋ **ladies-in-waiting** ˌleɪ.diz-

lady-killer 'leɪ.diˌkɪl.əʳ US -ɚ -s -z

ladylike 'leɪ.di.laɪk

ladylove 'leɪ.di.lʌv -s -z

ladyship 'leɪ.di.ʃɪp -s -s

Ladysmith ˈleɪ.di.smɪθ
Laertes leɪˈɜː.tiːz ⓊⓈ -ˈɜːr-, -ˈer-
Laestrygones liːˈstraɪ.ɡə.niːz ⓊⓈ lesˈtrɪɡ.ə-
Laetitia lɪˈtɪʃ.i.ə, liː-, lə-, -ˈtiː.ʃi-, ˈ-ʃə ⓊⓈ ləˈtɪʃ.ə, -ˈtiː.ʃə
Lafayette *French name:* ˌlɑː.faɪˈet, ˌlæf-, -feɪˈ- ⓊⓈ ˌlæf.iːˈ-, ˌlɑː.fiːˈ-, -faɪˈ- *in Louisiana:* ˌlɑːˈfeɪt, lə-
Lafcadio læfˈkɑː.di.əʊ ⓊⓈ lɑːfˈkɑː.di.oʊ
Laffan ˈlæf.ən; ləˈfæn
Laf(f)itte læfˈiːt, lɑːˈfiːt, lə- ⓊⓈ lɑːˈfiːt, lə-
lag læɡ **-s** -z **-ging** -ɪŋ **-ged** -d **-ger/s** -əʳ/z ⓊⓈ -ɚ/z
Lagan ˈlæɡ.ᵊn
lager *beer:* ˈlɑː.ɡəʳ ⓊⓈ -ɡɚ **-s** -z ˈ**lager** ˌ**lout**
Lager *English surname:* ˈleɪ.ɡəʳ ⓊⓈ -ɡɚ
Lagerfeld ˈlɑː.ɡə.felt ⓊⓈ -ɡɚ-
laggard ˈlæɡ.əd ⓊⓈ -ɚd **-s** -z **-ly** -li
lagn(i)appe ˈlæn.jæp, ˌ-ˈ-
lagoon ləˈɡuːn **-s** -z
Lagos ˈleɪ.ɡɒs ⓊⓈ -ɡɑːs; ˈlɑː.ɡoʊs
Lagrange læɡˈrɑ̃ːnʒ, ləˈ-, -ˈɡreɪndʒ ⓊⓈ lɑːˈɡrɑ̃ːndʒ, lə-
La Guardia ləˈɡwɑː.di.ə ⓊⓈ -ˈɡwɑːr-
Laguna Beach ləˌɡuː.nəˈbiːtʃ
lah lɑː **-s** -z
Lahore ləˈhɔːʳ, lɑː- ⓊⓈ -ˈhɔːr
laic ˈleɪ.ɪk **-al** -ᵊl
laid (*from* **lay**) leɪd
laid-back ˌleɪdˈbæk *stress shift:* ˌlaid-back ˈattitude
Laidlaw ˈleɪd.lɔː ⓊⓈ -lɑː, -lɔː
lain (*from* **lie**) leɪn
Laindon ˈleɪn.dən
Laing læŋ, leɪŋ
lair leəʳ ⓊⓈ ler **-s** -z
laird (L) leəd ⓊⓈ lerd **-s** -z **-ship** -ʃɪp
laissez-faire, laisser-faire ˌleɪ.seɪˈfeəʳ, ˌles.eɪˈ- ⓊⓈ ˌles.eɪˈfer, ˌleɪ.seɪˈ- *stress shift:* ˌlaissez-faire ˈattitude
laity ˈleɪ.ə.ti, -ɪ.ti ⓊⓈ -ti, -t̬i
Laius ˈlaɪ.əs, ˈleɪ- ⓊⓈ ˈleɪ-, ˈlaɪ-
lake (L) leɪk **-s** -s
Lakeland ˈleɪk.lənd, -lænd
Lakenheath ˈleɪ.kᵊn.hiːθ
Lake Placid ˌleɪkˈplæs.ɪd
Laker ˈleɪ.kəʳ ⓊⓈ -kɚ
lakeside (L) ˈleɪk.saɪd **-s** -z
lakh lɑːk, læk **-s** -s
Lakin ˈleɪ.kɪn
Lalage ˈlæl.ə.ɡi, -dʒi
Lalique® lælˈiːk, ləˈliːk ⓊⓈ lɑːˈliːk, lə-
lam læm **-s** -z **-ming** -ɪŋ **-med** -d
lama (L) ˈlɑː.mə **-s** -z
lamaser|y ˈlɑː.mə.sᵊr|.i, ˈlæm.ə- ⓊⓈ ˈlɑː.mə.ser- **-ies** -iz
Lamaze ləˈmɑːz **Laˈmaze** ˌ**method**
lamb (L) læm **-s** -z **-ing** -ɪŋ **-ed** -d ˌ**lamb's** ˈ**lettuce**; ˈ**lamb's** ˌ**wool**; ˌ**mutton dressed as** ˈ**lamb**
lambada læmˈbɑː.də ⓊⓈ lɑːm- **-s** -z **-ing** -ɪŋ **-ed** -d
lambast læmˈbæst ⓊⓈ -ˈbeɪst, -ˈbæst **-s** -s **-ing** -ɪŋ **-ed** -ɪd
lambast|e læmˈbeɪst ⓊⓈ -ˈbeɪst, -ˈbæst **-es** -s **-ing** -ɪŋ **-ed** -ɪd
lambda ˈlæm.də **-s** -z
lambdacism ˈlæm.də.sɪ.zᵊm **-s** -z
Lambe læm
lamben|cy ˈlæm.bən|*t*.si **-t** -t
Lambert ˈlæm.bət ⓊⓈ -bɚt
Lambeth ˈlæm.bəθ
lambkin ˈlæm.kɪn **-s** -z
lamblike ˈlæm.laɪk
Lamborghini® ˌlæm.bɔːˈɡiː.ni, -bəˈ- ⓊⓈ ˌlɑːm.bɔːrˈ-, ˌlæm-, -bɚˈ-
Lambretta® læmˈbret.ə ⓊⓈ -ˈbret̬
lambrusco (L) læmˈbrʊs.kəʊ ⓊⓈ -ˈbruː.skoʊ, lɑːm-, -ˈbrʊs.koʊ
lambskin ˈlæm.skɪn **-s** -z
Lambton ˈlæm*p*.tən
lam|e leɪm **-er** -əʳ ⓊⓈ -ɚ **-est** -ɪst, -əst **-ely** -li **-eness** -nəs, -nɪs **-es** -z **-ing** -ɪŋ **-ed** -d ˌ**lame** ˈ**duck**
lamé ˈlɑː.meɪ ⓊⓈ læmˈeɪ, lɑːˈmeɪ
lamebrain ˈleɪm.breɪn **-s** -z
Lamech ˈleɪ.mek, ˈlɑː-, -mex ⓊⓈ ˈleɪ.mek
lamell|a ləˈmel|.ə **-ae** -iː **-as** -əz **-ar** -əʳ ⓊⓈ -ɚ
la|ment lə|ˈment **-ments** -ˈments **-menting** -ˈmen.tɪŋ ⓊⓈ -ˈmen.t̬ɪŋ **-mented** -ˈmen.tɪd ⓊⓈ -ˈmen.t̬ɪd
lamentab|le ˈlæm.ən.tə.b|l̩, -ɪn-; ləˈmen- ⓊⓈ ləˈmen.t̬ə-; ˈlæm.ən.t̬ə- **-ly** -li
lamentation (L) ˌlæm.enˈteɪ.ʃᵊn, -ənˈ-, -ɪnˈ- ⓊⓈ -ənˈ- **-s** -z
Lamia *Greek town:* læmˈiː.ə ⓊⓈ ləˈmiː- *literary title, Keats:* ˈlɑː.mi.ə, ˈleɪ- ⓊⓈ ˈleɪ-
lamin|a ˈlæm.ɪ.n|ə, ˈ-ə- **-al** -ᵊl **-ae** -iː **-as** -əz **-ar** -əʳ ⓊⓈ -ɚ
lami|nate (*v.*) ˈlæm.ɪ|.neɪt, ˈ-ə- **-nates** -neɪts **-nating** -neɪ.tɪŋ ⓊⓈ -neɪ.t̬ɪŋ **-nated** -neɪ.tɪd ⓊⓈ -neɪ.t̬ɪd
laminate (*n.*) ˈlæm.ɪ.nət, ˈ-ə-, -nɪt, -neɪt ⓊⓈ -nɪt
lamination ˌlæm.ɪˈneɪ.ʃᵊn, -əˈ-
lamington (L) ˈlæm.ɪŋ.tən
Lammas ˈlæm.əs **-tide** -taɪd
lammergeier, lammergeyer ˈlæm.ə.ɡaɪəʳ ⓊⓈ -ɚ.ɡaɪɚ **-s** -z
Lammermoor ˈlæm.ə.mʊəʳ, -mɔːʳ, ˌ--ˈ- ⓊⓈ ˈlæm.ɚ.mʊr, -mɔːr, ˌ--ˈ-
Lammermuir ˈlæm.ə.mjʊəʳ, -mjɔːʳ ⓊⓈ -ɚ.mjʊr, -mjʊɚ
Lamond ˈlæm.ənd
Lamont *surname:* ləˈmɒnt; ˈlæm.ənt ⓊⓈ ləˈmɑːnt *in US:* ləˈmɒnt ⓊⓈ -ˈmɑːnt
lamp læmp **-s** -s
lampas *silk material:* ˈlæm.pəs *swelling in horse's mouth:* ˈlæm.pəz
lampblack ˈlæmp.blæk
Lampedusa ˌlæm.pɪˈdjuː.zə ⓊⓈ -pəˈduː.sə, -zə
Lampet ˈlæm.pɪt
Lampeter ˈlæm.pɪ.təʳ, -pə- ⓊⓈ -t̬ɚ
lampion ˈlæm.pi.ən **-s** -z
lamp|light ˈlæmp|.laɪt **-lighter/s** -ˌlaɪ.təʳ/z ⓊⓈ -ˌlaɪ.t̬ɚ/s
Lamplough ˈlæm.pluː, -plʌf
Lamplugh ˈlæm.pluː, -plə
lampoon læmˈpuːn **-s** -z **-ing** -ɪŋ **-ed** -d **-er/s** -əʳ/z ⓊⓈ -ɚ/z
lamp-post ˈlæmp.pəʊst ⓊⓈ -poʊst **-s** -s
lamprey ˈlæm.pri **-s** -z
lampshade ˈlæmp.ʃeɪd **-s** -z
Lampson ˈlæm*p*.sᵊn
lampstand ˈlæmp.stænd **-s** -z
LAN læn **-s** -z
Lana ˈlɑː.nə ⓊⓈ ˈlæn.ə, ˈlɑː.nə
Lanagan ˈlæn.ə.ɡᵊn
Lanark ˈlæn.ək ⓊⓈ -ɚk **-shire** -ʃəʳ, -ˌʃɪəʳ ⓊⓈ -ʃɚ, -ˌʃɪr
Lancashire ˈlæŋ.kə.ʃəʳ, -ˌʃɪəʳ ⓊⓈ -ʃɚ, -ˌʃɪr
Lancaster ˈlæŋ.kə.stəʳ, -kæs.təʳ ⓊⓈ ˈlæŋ.kə.stɚ, ˈlæn-, -kæs.tɚ
Lancasterian ˌlæŋ.kæsˈtɪə.ri.ən, -kəˈstɪə- ⓊⓈ ˌlæŋ.kæsˈtɪr.i-, ˌlæn-, -kəˈstɪr- **-s** -z
Lancastrian læŋˈkæs.tri.ən ⓊⓈ læŋ-, læn- **-s** -z
lanc|e (L) lɑːn*t*s ⓊⓈ læn*t*s **-es** -ɪz **-ing** -ɪŋ **-ed** -t ˌ**lance** ˈ**corporal**
Lancelot ˈlɑːn*t*.sə.lɒt, -sᵊl.ɒt, -ət ⓊⓈ ˈlæn*t*.sə.lɑːt, ˈlɑːn*t*-, -lət
lancer ˈlɑːn*t*.səʳ ⓊⓈ ˈlæn*t*.sɚ **-s** -z
lancet (L) ˈlɑːn*t*.sɪt ⓊⓈ ˈlæn*t*- **-s** -s
Lancia® ˈlɑːn*t*.si.ə, ˈlæn*t*- **-s** -z
Lancing ˈlɑːn*t*.sɪŋ ⓊⓈ ˈlæn*t*-
Lancôme®, Lancome ˈlɑ̃ː*ŋ*.kəʊm, -ˈ- ⓊⓈ ˈlæn.koʊm, -kəm, ˌlænˈkoʊm
Lancs. (*abbrev. for* **Lancashire**) læŋks
land (L) lænd **-s** -z **-ing** -ɪŋ **-ed** -ɪd
landau ˈlæn.dɔː, -daʊ **-s** -z
Lander ˈlæn.dəʳ ⓊⓈ -dɚ
landfall ˈlæn*d*.fɔːl ⓊⓈ -fɔːl, -fɑːl **-s** -z
landfill ˈlæn*d*.fɪl **-s** -z
landforc|e ˈlæn*d*.fɔːs ⓊⓈ -fɔːrs **-es** -ɪz
landgrabb|er ˈlæn*d*ˌɡræb|.əʳ, ˈlæŋ- ⓊⓈ ˈlæn*d*ˌɡræb|.ɚ **-ers** -əz ⓊⓈ -ɚz **-ing** -ɪŋ
landgrave ˈlæn*d*.ɡreɪv, ˈlæŋ- ⓊⓈ ˈlæn*d*- **-s** -z
landholder ˈlændˌhəʊl.dəʳ ⓊⓈ -ˌhoʊl.dɚ **-s** -z

landing 'læn.dɪŋ **-s** -z **'landing ˌgear ; 'landing ˌnet ; 'landing ˌstage ; 'landing ˌstrip**
landlad|y 'lænd̩ˌleɪ.d|i **-ies** -iz
landlocked 'lænd.lɒkt ⓤⓢ -lɑːkt
landlord 'lænd.lɔːd ⓤⓢ -lɔːrd **-s** -z **-ism** -ɪ.zᵊm
landlubber 'lænd̩ˌlʌb.əʳ ⓤⓢ -ɚ **-s** -z
landmark 'lænd.mɑːk, 'læm- ⓤⓢ 'lænd.mɑːrk **-s** -s
landmass 'lænd.mæs, 'læm- ⓤⓢ 'lænd- **-es** -ɪz
landmine 'lænd.maɪn, 'læm- ⓤⓢ 'lænd- **-s** -z
Landon 'læn.dən
Landor 'læn.dɔːʳ, -dəʳ ⓤⓢ -dɚ, -dɔːr
land-own|er 'lændˌəʊ.n|əʳ ⓤⓢ -ˌoʊ.n|ɚ **-ers** -əz ⓤⓢ -ɚz **-ing** -ɪŋ
landrail 'lænd.reɪl **-s** -z
Land Rover® 'lændˌrəʊ.vəʳ ⓤⓢ -ˌroʊ.vɚ **-s** -z
landscap|e 'lænd.skeɪp **-es** -s **-ing** -ɪŋ **-ed** -t **-er/s** -əʳ/z ⓤⓢ -ɚ/z **ˌlandscape 'gardener** ⓤⓢ **'landscape ˌgardener ; 'landscape ˌmode**
Landseer 'lændˌsiː.əʳ, -sɪəʳ ⓤⓢ -ˌsiː.ɚ, -ˌsɪr
Land's End ˌlændz'end
landslide 'lænd.slaɪd **-s** -z
landslip 'lænd.slɪp **-s** -s
lands|man 'lændz|.mən **-men** -mən
landward 'lænd.wəd ⓤⓢ -wɚd
landwehr 'lænd.veəʳ ⓤⓢ -veɪr
landwind 'lænd.wɪnd **-s** -z
lane (L) leɪn **-s** -z **in the 'fast ˌlane**
Lanfranc 'læn.fræŋk
Lang læŋ
Langbaine 'læŋ.beɪn
Langbourne 'læŋ.bɔːn ⓤⓢ -bɔːrn
Langdale 'læŋ.deɪl
Langerhans 'læŋ.ə.hænz, -hænts ⓤⓢ 'læŋ.ɚ.hænz, 'lɑːŋ.ɚ.hɑːnz
Langford 'læŋ.fəd ⓤⓢ -fɚd
Langham, Langholm(e) 'læŋ.əm
Langhorne 'læŋ.hɔːn ⓤⓢ -hɔːrn
Langland 'læŋ.lənd
langlauf 'lɑːŋ.laʊf **-s** -s
Langley 'læŋ.li
Langmere 'læŋ.mɪəʳ ⓤⓢ -mɪr
langoustine ˌlɑ̃ŋ.gʊ'stiːn, ˌlæn- ⓤⓢ ˌlæŋ.gə'- **-s** -z
Langridge 'læŋ.grɪdʒ
Langside 'læŋ.saɪd, ˌ-'-
lang syne ˌlæŋ'saɪn ⓤⓢ -'zaɪn, -'saɪn
Langton 'læŋk.tən
Langtry 'læŋk.tri
languag|e 'læŋ.gwɪdʒ **-es** -ɪz
langue lɑ̃ːŋg ⓤⓢ lɑ̃ːŋg, lɑːŋ
langue de chat ˌlɑ̃ːŋ.də'ʃɑː ⓤⓢ ˌlɑ̃ːŋg-, ˌlɑːŋ-
Languedoc 'lɑ̃ːŋ.gə.dɒk, ˌ--'- ⓤⓢ lɑ̃ːŋg'dɔːk, lɑːŋ-
languid 'læŋ.gwɪd **-ly** -li **-ness** -nəs, -nɪs
languish (L) 'læŋ.gwɪʃ **-es** -ɪz **-ing/ly** -ɪŋ/li **-ed** -t **-ment** -mənt
languor 'læŋ.gəʳ ⓤⓢ -gɚ **-ous/ly** -əs/li
langur 'læŋ.gəʳ, 'lʌŋ-, -gʊəʳ ⓤⓢ lɑːŋ'gʊr **-s** -z
Lanier 'læn.jəʳ; lə'nɪəʳ ⓤⓢ lə'nɪr
Lanigan 'læn.ɪ.gᵊn, '-ə-
lank læŋk **-er** -əʳ ⓤⓢ -ɚ **-est** -ɪst, -əst **-ly** -li **-ness** -nəs, -nɪs
Lankester 'læŋ.kɪ.stəʳ, -kə- ⓤⓢ -stɚ
lank|y 'læŋ.k|i **-ier** -i.əʳ ⓤⓢ -i.ɚ **-iest** -i.ɪst, -i.əst **-ily** -ɪ.li, -ᵊl.i **-iness** -ɪ.nəs, -ɪ.nɪs
lanolin(e) 'læn.ᵊl.ɪn, -ə.liːn ⓤⓢ -ə.lɪn
Lansbury 'lænz.bᵊr.i ⓤⓢ -ber.i
Lansdown(e) 'lænz.daʊn
Lansing 'lɑːnt.sɪŋ, 'lænt- ⓤⓢ 'lænt-
lantern 'læn.tən ⓤⓢ -t̬ɚn **-s** -z
lanthanum 'lænt.θə.nəm
lanyard 'læn.jəd, -jɑːd ⓤⓢ -jɚd, -jɑːrd **-s** -z
Lanzarote ˌlæn.zə'rɒt.i ⓤⓢ ˌlɑːnt.sə'roʊ.t̬i, -teɪ
Laocoön leɪ'ɒk.əʊ.ɒn, -ən ⓤⓢ -'ɑː.koʊ.ɑːn
Laodamia ˌleɪ.əʊ.də'maɪə, -'miː.ə ⓤⓢ leɪˌɑː.də'maɪ.ə
Laodice|a ˌleɪ.əʊ.dɪ'siː|.ə, -də'- ⓤⓢ leɪˌɑː.dɪ'-; ˌleɪ.ə.də'- **-an/s** -ən/z
Laois liːʃ
Laomedon leɪ'ɒm.ɪ.dən, '-ə- ⓤⓢ -'ɑː.mə.dɑːn
Laos 'leɪ.ɒs, 'lɑː-; laʊs, laʊz ⓤⓢ laʊs; 'leɪ.ɑːs, -oʊs
Laotian leɪ'aʊ.ʃᵊn; 'laʊ.ʃi.ən, -ʃᵊn; lɑː'ɒʃ.ᵊn ⓤⓢ leɪ'oʊ.ʃᵊn; 'laʊ.ʃᵊn
Lao-tsze ˌlɑː.əʊ'tseɪ, ˌlaʊ'tseɪ, -'tsiː ⓤⓢ ˌlaʊ'dzuː, -'tseɪ
lap læp **-s** -s **-ping** -ɪŋ **-ped** -t **-per/s** -əʳ/z ⓤⓢ -ɚ/z **in the ˌlap of 'luxury**
laparotom|y ˌlæp.ᵊr'ɒt.ə.m|i ⓤⓢ -ə'rɑː.t̬ə- **-ies** -iz
La Paz lɑː'pæz, læ- ⓤⓢ lə'pɑːz, lɑː-, -'pɑːs
lapdog 'læp.dɒg ⓤⓢ -dɑːg, -dɔːg **-s** -z
lapel lə'pel **-s** -z
lapful 'læp.fʊl **-s** -z
lapidar|y 'læp.ɪ.dᵊr|.i, '-ə- ⓤⓢ -ə.der- **-ies** -iz
lapis lazuli ˌlæp.ɪs'læz.jʊ.li, -jə-, -laɪ ⓤⓢ -'læz.ə.li, -'læʒ-, -jʊ-
Lapithae 'læp.ɪ.θiː
Lapland 'læp.lænd **-er/s** -əʳ/z ⓤⓢ -ɚ/z
La Porte lə'pɔːt ⓤⓢ -'pɔːrt
Lapp læp **-s** -s **-ish** -ɪʃ
lapp|et 'læp|.ɪt **-ets** -ɪts **-eted** -ɪ.tɪd ⓤⓢ -ɪ.t̬ɪd
Lappin 'læp.ɪn
Lapsang 'læp.sæŋ
Lapsang Souchong ˌlæp.sæŋ.suː'ʃɒŋ, -'tʃɒŋ ⓤⓢ -tʃɔːŋ, -ʃɔːŋ
laps|e læps **-es** -ɪz **-ing** -ɪŋ **-ed** -t
lapsus linguae ˌlæp.səs'lɪŋ.gwaɪ, -sʊs'-, -gweɪ ⓤⓢ -səs'lɪŋ.gwiː, -gwaɪ
laptop 'læp.tɒp ⓤⓢ -tɑːp **-s** -s
Laput|a lə'pjuː.t|ə ⓤⓢ -t̬|ə **-an/s** -ᵊn/z
lapwing 'læp.wɪŋ **-s** -z
lar (L) lɑːʳ ⓤⓢ lɑːr **lares** 'leə.riːz, 'lɑː.reɪz ⓤⓢ 'ler.iːz, 'lɑːr.iːz
Lara 'lɑː.rə ⓤⓢ 'lɑːr.ə, 'ler.ə
Laramie 'lær.ə.mi ⓤⓢ 'ler-, 'lær-
Larbert 'lɑː.bət, -bɜːt ⓤⓢ 'lɑːr.bɚt, -bɜːrt
larboard 'lɑː.bəd, -bɔːd ⓤⓢ -bɚd, -bɔːrd
larcenous 'lɑː.sᵊn.əs, -sɪ.nəs ⓤⓢ 'lɑːr.sə- **-ly** -li
larcen|y 'lɑː.sᵊn|.i, -sɪ.n|i ⓤⓢ 'lɑːr.sə- **-ies** -iz
larch lɑːtʃ ⓤⓢ lɑːrtʃ **-es** -ɪz
lard lɑːd ⓤⓢ lɑːrd **-s** -z **-ing** -ɪŋ **-ed** -ɪd
larder 'lɑː.dəʳ ⓤⓢ 'lɑːr.dɚ **-s** -z
Lardner 'lɑːd.nəʳ ⓤⓢ 'lɑːrd.nɚ
lardon 'lɑː.dᵊn ⓤⓢ 'lɑːr- **-s** -z
Laredo lə'reɪ.dəʊ ⓤⓢ -doʊ
lares (*plur. of* **lar**) 'leə.riːz, 'lɑː.reɪz ⓤⓢ 'ler.iːz, 'lɑːr.iːz
Largactil® lɑː'gæk.tɪl, -tᵊl ⓤⓢ lɑːr-
larg|e lɑːdʒ ⓤⓢ lɑːrdʒ **-er** -əʳ ⓤⓢ -ɚ **-est** -ɪst, -əst **-ely** -li **-eness** -nəs, -nɪs **as ˌlarge as 'life**
largehearted ˌlɑːdʒ'hɑː.tɪd ⓤⓢ ˌlɑːrʒ'hɑːr.t̬ɪd **-ness** -nəs, -nɪs
stress shift: ˌlargehearted 'person
large-scale ˌlɑːdʒ'skeɪl ⓤⓢ ˌlɑːrdʒ-
stress shift: ˌlarge-scale 'changes
largess|(e) lɑː'ʒes, -'dʒes; '-- ⓤⓢ lɑːr'dʒes, -'ʒes; 'lɑːr.dʒəs **-es** -ɪz
larghetto lɑː'get.əʊ ⓤⓢ lɑːr'get̬.oʊ **-s** -z
largish 'lɑː.dʒɪʃ ⓤⓢ 'lɑːr-
largo 'lɑː.gəʊ ⓤⓢ 'lɑːr.goʊ **-s** -z
Largs lɑːgz ⓤⓢ lɑːrgz
Larham 'lɑː.rəm ⓤⓢ 'lɑːr-
lari|at 'lær.i|.ət ⓤⓢ 'ler-, 'lær- **-ats** -əts **-ating** -ə.tɪŋ ⓤⓢ -ə.t̬ɪŋ **-ated** -ə.tɪd ⓤⓢ -ə.t̬ɪd
Larisa, Larissa lə'rɪs.ə
lark lɑːk ⓤⓢ lɑːrk **-s** -s **-ing** -ɪŋ **-ed** -t
Larkhall 'lɑːk.hɔːl ⓤⓢ 'lɑːrk-, -hɑːl
Larkin 'lɑː.kɪn ⓤⓢ 'lɑːr-
larkspur 'lɑːk.spɜːʳ, -spəʳ ⓤⓢ 'lɑːrk.spɜːr, -spɚ **-s** -z
lark|y 'lɑː.k|i ⓤⓢ 'lɑːr- **-ier** -i.əʳ ⓤⓢ -i.ɚ **-iest** -i.ɪst, -i.əst **-iness** -ɪ.nəs, -ɪ.nɪs
Larmor, Larmour 'lɑː.məʳ ⓤⓢ 'lɑːr.mɚ, -mɔːr
Larne lɑːn ⓤⓢ lɑːrn
Larousse lær'uːs ⓤⓢ lɑː'ruːs
larrikin 'lær.ɪ.kɪn, '-ə- ⓤⓢ 'ler-, 'lær- **-s** -z

larrup 'lær.əp (US) 'ler-, 'lær- **-s** -s **-ping** -ɪŋ **-ped** -t
Larry 'lær.i (US) 'ler-, 'lær-
Larsen, Larson 'lɑː.sᵊn (US) 'lɑːr-
Lars Porsena ˌlɑːz'pɔː.sɪ.nə, -sə- (US) ˌlɑːrz'pɔːr-
larum 'lær.əm (US) 'ler-, 'lær-; 'lɑːr.ʊm **-s** -z
larv|a 'lɑː.v|ə (US) 'lɑːr- **-ae** -iː **-al** -ᵊl
laryngal lə'rɪŋ.gᵊl, lær'ɪŋ- (US) lə'rɪŋ-, ler'ɪŋ-, lær-
laryngeal lə'rɪn.dʒi.əl, lær'ɪn-, -dʒᵊl; ˌlær.ɪn'dʒiː.əl, -ən'- (US) lə'rɪn.dʒi.əl, -dʒᵊl
laryngectom|y ˌlær.ɪn'dʒek.tə.m|i, -ən'- (US) ˌler-, ˌlær- **-ies** -iz
larynges (*plur. of* **larynx**) lær'ɪn.dʒiːz, lə'rɪn- (US) lə-, ler'ɪn-, lær-
laryngitis ˌlær.ɪn'dʒaɪ.tɪs, -ən'- (US) ˌler.ɪn'dʒaɪ.t̬ɪs, ˌlær-
laryngolog|y ˌlær.ɪŋ'gɒl.ə.dʒ|i, -əŋ'- (US) ˌler.ɪŋ'gɑː.lə-, ˌlær-, -ɪn'dʒɑː- **-ist/s** -ɪst/s
laryngoscope lə'rɪŋ.gə.skəʊp, lær'ɪŋ-; 'lær.ɪŋ- (US) lə'rɪŋ.goʊ.skoʊp, -gə-, -'rɪn.dʒə- **-s** -s
laryngoscopic ləˌrɪŋ.gə'skɒp.ɪk, lærˌɪŋ-; ˌlær.ɪŋ- (US) ləˌrɪŋ.goʊ'skɑː.pɪk, -gə'-, -ˌrɪn.dʒə'-
laryngoscop|y ˌlær.ɪŋ'gɒs.kə.p|i, -əŋ'- (US) ˌler.ɪŋ'gɑː.skə-, ˌlær-, -ɪn'dʒɑː- **-ist/s** -ɪst/s
larynx 'lær.ɪŋks (US) 'ler-, 'lær- **-es** -ɪz **larynges** lær'ɪn.dʒiːz, lə'rɪn- (US) lə-, ler'ɪn, lær-
lasagne, lasagna lə'zæn.jə, -'sæn-, -'zɑː.njə, -'sɑː- (US) -'zɑː.njə, -'sɑː-
Lascar 'læs.kəʳ (US) -kɚ **-s** -z
Lascaux 'læs.kəʊ, -'- (US) læs'koʊ
Lascelles 'læs.ᵊlz, lə'selz
lascivious lə'sɪv.i.əs **-ly** -li **-ness** -nəs, -nɪs
laser 'leɪ.zəʳ (US) -zɚ **-s** -z **'laser ˌdisk; 'laser ˌprinter**
laserjet 'leɪ.zə.dʒet (US) -zɚ- **-s** -s
lash læʃ **-es** -ɪz **-ing/s** -ɪŋ/z **-ed** -t **-er/s** -əʳ/z (US) -ɚ/z
Lasham 'læʃ.əm *locally also:* 'læs.əm
Las Palmas ˌlæs'pæl.məs, -'pɑːl- (US) ˌlɑːs'pɑːl-, -mɑːs
lass læs **-es** -ɪz
Lassa 'læs.ə, 'lɑː.sə (US) 'lɑː.sə, 'læs.ə **ˌLassa 'fever**
Lassalle lə'sæl
Lassell læs'el, lə'sel
lassie (L) 'læs.i **-s** -z
lassitude 'læs.ɪ.tjuːd, '-ə- (US) -tuːd, -tjuːd
lasso (*n.*) læs'uː; 'læs.əʊ (US) 'læs.oʊ, -uː **-(e)s** -z
lasso (*v.*) læs'uː, lə'suː (US) 'læs.oʊ, -uː **-(e)s** -z **-ing** -ɪŋ **-ed** -d

last (L) lɑːst (US) læst **-s** -s **-ing/ly** -ɪŋ/li **-ed** -ɪd **-ly** 'lɑːs*t*.li (US) 'læs*t*.li **ˌLast 'Judgment ; ˌlast 'straw ; ˌLast 'Supper ; ˌlast 'word ; at the ˌlast 'minute**
last-ditch ˌlɑːs*t*'dɪtʃ (US) ˌlæs*t*- *stress shift, see compound:* **ˌlast-ditch at'tempt**
last-minute ˌlɑːs*t*'mɪn.ɪt (US) ˌlæs*t*- *stress shift:* ˌlast-minute 'plans
Las Vegas ˌlæs'veɪ.gəs, ˌlɑːs- (US) ˌlɑːs-
lat læt **-s** -s
Latakia ˌlæt.ə'kiː.ə (US) ˌlɑː.t̬ə'-, ˌlæt̬.ə'-
latch lætʃ **-es** -ɪz **-ing** -ɪŋ **-ed** -t
latchet 'lætʃ.ɪt, -ət **-s** -s
latchkey 'lætʃ.kiː **-s** -z **'latchkey ˌchild, ˌlatchkey 'child**
lat|e leɪt **-er** -əʳ (US) 'leɪ.t̬ɚ **-est** -ɪst, -əst (US) 'leɪ.t̬ɪst, -t̬əst **-ely** -li **-eness** -nəs, -nɪs
latecomer 'leɪtˌkʌm.əʳ (US) -ɚ **-s** -z
lateen lə'tiːn (US) læt'iːn, lə'tiːn **-s** -z
latency 'leɪ.tᵊn*t*.si
late-night 'leɪtˌnaɪt **ˌlate-ˌnight 'shopping**
latent 'leɪ.tᵊnt **-ly** -li
lateral 'læt.ᵊr.ᵊl, '-rᵊl (US) 'læt̬.ɚ.ᵊl **-s** -z **-ly** -i **ˌlateral 'thinking**
Lateran 'læt.ᵊr.ᵊn (US) 'læt̬-
laterite 'læt.ᵊr.aɪt (US) 'læt̬.ə.raɪt
latex 'leɪ.teks **-es** -ɪz **latices** 'læt.ɪ.siːz, 'leɪ.tɪ- (US) 'læt̬.ɪ-, 'leɪ.t̬ɪ-
lath læθ, lɑːθ (US) læθ **-s** -s, lɑːðz (US) -s, læðz
Latham 'leɪ.θəm, -ðəm
Note: Generally /'leɪ.θəm/ in S. of England; always /'leɪ.ðəm/ in N.
Lathbury 'læθ.bᵊr.i (US) -ber-
lath|e leɪð **-es** -z **-ing** -ɪŋ **-ed** -d
lath|er 'lɑː.ð|əʳ, 'læð|.əʳ (US) 'læð|.ɚ **-ers** -əz (US) -ɚz **-ering** -ᵊr.ɪŋ **-ered** -əd (US) -ɚd
lathi 'lɑː.ti **-s** -z
Lathom 'leɪ.θəm, -ðəm
Lathrop 'leɪ.θrəp
latices (*plur. of* **latex**) 'læt.ɪ.siːz, 'leɪ.tɪ- (US) 'læt̬.ɪ-, 'leɪ.t̬ɪ-
Latimer 'læt.ɪ.məʳ, '-ə- (US) 'læt̬.ə.mɚ
Latin 'læt.ɪn (US) -ᵊn **-ate** -eɪt **ˌLatin A'merica**
latin|ism 'læt.ɪ.n|ɪ.zᵊm (US) -ᵊn|.ɪ- **-isms** -ɪ.zᵊmz **-ist/s** -ɪst/s
latinity lə'tɪn.ə.ti, læt'ɪn-, -ɪ.ti (US) læt'ɪn.ə.t̬i
latiniz|e, -is|e 'læt.ɪ.naɪz (US) -ᵊn.aɪz **-es** -ɪz **-ing** -ɪŋ **-ed** -d
latin|o (L) lə'tiː.n|əʊ, læt'iː- (US) -n|oʊ **-os** -əʊz (US) -oʊz **-a/s** -ə/z (US) -ɑː/z
Latinus lə'taɪ.nəs
latish 'leɪ.tɪʃ (US) -t̬ɪʃ
latitude 'læt.ɪ.tjuːd, '-ə-, -tʃuːd (US) 'læt̬.ə.tuːd, -tjuːd **-s** -z

latitudinal ˌlæt.ɪ'tjuː.dɪ.nᵊl, -ə'-, -'tʃuː-, -dᵊn.ᵊl (US) ˌlæt̬.ə'tuː-, -'tjuː-
latitudinarian ˌlæt.ɪˌtjuː.dɪ'neə.ri.ən, -əˌ-, -ˌtʃuː- (US) ˌlæt̬.əˌtuː.dɪ'ner.i-, -ˌtjuː- **-s** -z **-ism** -ɪ.zᵊm
Latium 'leɪ.ʃi.əm, 'læt.i- (US) 'leɪ.ʃᵊm, -ʃi.əm
latke 'lɑːt.kə **-s** -z
Latoya lə'tɔɪ.ə
latria lə'traɪə
latrine lə'triːn **-s** -z
Lattakia ˌlæt.ə'kiː.ə (US) ˌlɑː.t̬ə'-, ˌlæt̬.ə'-
latter 'læt.əʳ (US) 'læt̬.ɚ **-ly** -li
latter-day 'læt.ə.deɪ (US) 'læt̬.ɚ- **ˌLatter-Day 'Saint**
lattic|e 'læt.ɪs (US) 'læt̬- **-es** -ɪz **-ed** -t
latticework 'læt.ɪs.wɜːk (US) 'læt̬.ɪs.wɝːk
Latvi|a 'læt.vi|.ə **-an/s** -ən/z
laud (L) lɔːd (US) lɑːd, lɔːd **-s** -z **-ing** -ɪŋ **-ed** -ɪd
laudab|le 'lɔː.də.b|l̩ (US) 'lɑː-, 'lɔː- **-ly** -li **-leness** -l̩.nəs, -nɪs
laudanum 'lɔː.dᵊn.əm (US) 'lɑː-, 'lɔː-
laudatory 'lɔː.də.tᵊr.i (US) 'lɑː.də.tɔːr-, 'lɔː-
Lauder 'lɔː.dəʳ (US) 'lɑː.dɚ, 'lɔː-
Lauderdale 'lɔː.də.deɪl (US) 'lɑː.dɚ-, 'lɔː-
laugh lɑːf (US) læf **-s** -s **-ing/ly** -ɪŋ/li **-ed** -t **-er/s** -əʳ/z (US) -ɚ/z **'laughing ˌgas ; ˌlaughing 'jackass; no ˌlaughing 'matter, no 'laughing ˌmatter; have the ˌlast 'laugh**
laughab|le 'lɑː.fə.b|l̩ (US) 'læf.ə- **-ly** -li **-leness** -l̩.nəs, -nɪs
Laugharne lɑːn (US) lɑːrn
laughingstock 'lɑː.fɪŋ.stɒk (US) 'læf.ɪŋ.stɑːk **-s** -s
Laughland 'lɒk.lənd (US) 'lɑːk-
Laughlin 'lɒk.lɪn, 'lɒx-, 'lɒf-, 'lɑː.flɪn (US) 'lɑː-, 'lɔː-
laughter 'lɑːf.təʳ (US) 'læf.tɚ
Laughton 'lɔː.tᵊn (US) 'lɑː-, 'lɔː-
launc|e lɑːn*t*s (US) læn*t*s, lɑːn*t*s, lɔːn*t*s **-es** -ɪz
Launce lɑːn*t*s, lɔːn*t*s (US) læn*t*s, lɑːn*t*s, lɔːn*t*s
Launcelot 'lɑːn*t*.sᵊl.ɒt, 'lɔːn*t*-, -ət (US) 'læn*t*.sə.lɑːt, 'lɑːn*t*-, 'lɔːn*t*-, -lət
Launceston *in Cornwall:* 'lɔːn*t*.stən, -sᵊn, *locally:* 'lɑːn*t*- *in Tasmania:* 'lɔːn*t*.səs.tᵊn, *locally:* 'lɒn*t*- (US) 'lɑːn*t*-, 'lɔːn*t*-
launch lɔːn*t*ʃ (US) lɑːn*t*ʃ, lɔːn*t*ʃ **-es** -ɪz **-ing** -ɪŋ **-ed** -t **-er/s** -əʳ/z (US) -ɚ/z
launchpad 'lɔːn*t*ʃ.pæd (US) 'lɑːn*t*ʃ-, 'lɔːn*t*ʃ- **-s** -z
laund|er 'lɔːn.d|əʳ (US) 'lɑːn.d|ɚ, 'lɔːn- **-ers** -əz (US) -ɚz **-ering** -ᵊr.ɪŋ **-ered** -əd (US) -ɚd

launderette ˌlɔːn.dᵊrˈet, ˌ-ˈdret (US) ˌlɑːn.dəˈret, ˌlɔːn-, ˌ-ˈdret **-s** -s

laundress ˈlɔːn.dres, -drəs, -drɪs (US) ˈlɑːn.drɪs, ˈlɔːn- **-es** -ɪz

laundrette ˌlɔːnˈdret (US) ˌlɑːn-, ˌlɔːn- **-s** -s

Laundromat® ˈlɔːn.drə.mæt (US) ˈlɔːn.droʊ-, ˈlɑːn-, -drə- **-s** -s

laundr|y ˈlɔːn.dr|i (US) ˈlɑːn-, ˈlɔːn- **-ies** -iz ˈ**laundry** ˌ**basket**; ˈ**laundry** ˌ**list**

laundry|man ˈlɔːn.dri|.mæn, -mən (US) ˈlɑːn-, ˈlɔːn- **-men** -mən, -men **-woman** -ˌwʊm.ən **-women** -ˌwɪm.ɪn

Laundy ˈlɔːn.di (US) ˈlɑːn-, ˈlɔːn-

Laura ˈlɔː.rə (US) ˈlɔːr.ə

laureate (*n. adj.*) ˈlɔː.ri.ət, ˈlɒr.i-, -ɪt (US) ˈlɔːr.i.ɪt, ˈlɑːr- **-s** -s **-ship/s** -ʃɪp/s

laure|ate (*v.*) ˈlɔː.ri|.eɪt, ˈlɒr.i- (US) ˈlɔːr.i-, ˈlɑːr- **-ates** -eɪts **-ating** -eɪ.tɪŋ (US) -eɪ.t̬ɪŋ **-ated** -eɪ.tɪd (US) -eɪ.t̬ɪd

laurel (L) ˈlɒr.ᵊl (US) ˈlɔːr-, ˈlɑːr- **-s** -z

Lauren ˈlɔː.rən, ˈlɒr.ən (US) ˈlɔːr.ən, ˈlɑːr-

Laurence ˈlɒr.ᵊn*t*s (US) ˈlɔːr-, ˈlɑːr-

Laurent lɔːˈrɑ̃ː*ŋ*, lə- (US) lɑːˈrɑːn*t*, lə-

Laurie ˈlɒr.i, ˈlɔː.ri (US) ˈlɔːr.i, ˈlɑːr-

Laurier *English name:* ˈlɒr.i.əʳ (US) ˈlɔːr.i.ɚ, ˈlɑːr- *Canadian name:* ˈlɒr.i.eɪ (US) ˈlɔːr.i.eɪ

Lauriston ˈlɒr.ɪ.stᵊn, ˈ-ə- (US) ˈlɔːr-, ˈlɑːr-

laurustinus ˌlɒr.əˈstaɪ.nəs, ˌlɔː.rəˈ- (US) ˌlɑːr-, ˌlɔːr- **-es** -ɪz

Lausanne ləʊˈzæn (US) loʊ-, -ˈzɑːn

Lauterbrunnen ˈlaʊ.tə.brʊn.ən (US) -t̬ɚ-

Lautrec ləʊˈtrek (US) loʊ-, lə-

lav læv **-s** -z

lava ˈlɑː.və (US) ˈlɑː-, ˈlæv.ə

lavabo *ritual:* ləˈvɑː.bəʊ, lævˈɑː-, -ˈeɪ- (US) ləˈvɑː.boʊ, -ˈveɪ- **-s** -z *basin:* ləˈveɪ.bəʊ; ˈlæv.ə.bəʊ (US) ləˈvɑː.boʊ, -ˈveɪ- **-s** -z

lavage lævˈɑːʒ, ləˈvɑːʒ, -ˈvɑːdʒ; ˈlæv.ɪdʒ, -ɑːʒ (US) ləˈvɑːʒ; ˈlæv.ɪdʒ

Lavater lɑːˈvɑː.təʳ, ˈ--- (US) -t̬ɚ

lavatorial ˌlæv.əˈtɔː.ri.əl (US) -ˈtɔːr.i-

lavator|y ˈlæv.ə.tᵊr|.i, -tr|i (US) -tɔːr.i **-ies** -iz

lav|e leɪv **-es** -z **-ing** -ɪŋ **-ed** -d

lavender (L) ˈlæv.ᵊn.dəʳ, -ɪn- (US) -dɚ ˈ**lavender** ˌ**water**

Lavengro ləˈveŋ.grəʊ, lævˈeŋ- (US) -groʊ

Lavenham ˈlæv.ᵊn.əm

laver *seaweed:* ˈlɑː.vəʳ (US) ˈleɪ.vɚ, ˈlɑː- **-s** -z *all other senses:* ˈleɪ.vəʳ (US) -vɚ **-s** -z

Laver *name:* ˈleɪ.vəʳ (US) -vɚ

Laverty ˈlæv.ə.ti (US) -ɚ.t̬i

Lavery ˈleɪ.vᵊr.i, ˈlæv.ᵊr-

Lavin ˈlæv.ɪn

Lavington ˈlæv.ɪŋ.tən

Lavini|a ləˈvɪn.i|.ə **-an** -ən

lavish ˈlæv.ɪʃ **-ly** -li **-ness** -nəs, -nɪs **-es** -ɪz **-ing** -ɪŋ **-ed** -t

Lavoisier ləˈvwɑː.zi.eɪ, lævˈwɑː-, -ˈwæz.i- (US) ləˈvwɑː.zi-

law (L) lɔː (US) lɑː, lɔː **-s** -z ˈ**law** ˌ**lord**; **be a** ˌ**law unto one**ˈ**self**; **take the** ˌ**law into one's** ˌ**own** ˈ**hands**

law-abiding ˈlɔː.əˌbaɪ.dɪŋ (US) ˈlɑː-, ˈlɔː-

lawbreak|er ˈlɔːˌbreɪ.k|əʳ (US) ˈlɑːˌbreɪ.k|ɚ, ˈlɔː- **-ers** -əz (US) -ɚz **-ing** -ɪŋ

Lawes lɔːz (US) lɑːz, lɔːz

Lawesford ˈlɔːz.fəd (US) ˈlɑːz.fɚd, ˈlɔːz-

lawful ˈlɔː.fᵊl, -fʊl (US) ˈlɑː-, ˈlɔː- **-ly** -i **-ness** -nəs, -nɪs

lawgiv|er ˈlɔːˌɡɪv|.əʳ (US) ˈlɑːˌɡɪv|.ɚ, ˈlɔː- **-ers** -əz (US) -ɚz **-ing** -ɪŋ

lawks lɔːks (US) lɑːks, lɔːks

lawless (L) ˈlɔː.ləs, -lɪs (US) ˈlɑː-, ˈlɔː- **-ly** -li **-ness** -nəs, -nɪs

Lawley, Lawly ˈlɔː.li (US) ˈlɑː-, ˈlɔː-

lawmak|er ˈlɔːˌmeɪ.k|əʳ (US) ˈlɑːˌmeɪ.k|ɚ, ˈlɔː- **-ers** -əz (US) -ɚz **-ing** -ɪŋ

lawn lɔːn (US) lɑːn, lɔːn **-s** -z ˈ**lawn** ˌ**mower**; ˌ**lawn** ˈ**tennis** (US) ˈ**lawn** ˌ**tennis**

Lawrence, Lawrance ˈlɒr.ᵊn*t*s (US) ˈlɔːr-, ˈlɑːr-

lawrencium ləˈren*t*.si.əm, lɔː-, lɒrˈen*t*- (US) lɔːˈren*t*-, lɑː-

Lawrenson ˈlɒr.ᵊn*t*.sᵊn (US) ˈlɔːr.ᵊn*t*-, ˈlɑːr-

Lawrentian ləˈren.ʃi.ən, lɒrˈen-, -ʃᵊn (US) ləˈren*t*-, lɔː-, lɑː-

Lawson ˈlɔː.sᵊn (US) ˈlɑː-, ˈlɔː-

lawsuit ˈlɔː.suːt, -sjuːt (US) ˈlɑː.suːt, ˈlɔː- **-s** -s

Lawton ˈlɔː.tᵊn (US) ˈlɑː-, ˈlɔː-

lawyer ˈlɔɪ.əʳ, ˈlɔː.jəʳ (US) ˈlɑː.jɚ, ˈlɔː-, ˈlɔɪ- **-s** -z

lax læks **-er** -əʳ (US) -ɚ **-est** -ɪst, -əst **-ly** -li **-ness** -nəs, -nɪs

laxative ˈlæk.sə.tɪv (US) -t̬ɪv **-s** -z

laxity ˈlæk.sə.ti, -sɪ- (US) -sə.t̬i

lay leɪ **-s** -z **-ing** -ɪŋ **laid** leɪd ˌ**lay** ˈ**reader** (US) ˈ**lay** ˌ**reader**; ˌ**lay of the** ˈ**land**

layabout ˈleɪ.əˌbaʊt **-s** -s

Layamon ˈlaɪ.ə.mən, -mɒn (US) ˈleɪ.ə.mən, ˈlaɪ-

Layard ˈleɪ.ɑːd, leəd (US) ˈleɪ.ɑːrd, lerd

layaway ˈleɪ.ə.weɪ

lay-by ˈleɪ.baɪ **-s** -z

Laycock ˈleɪ.kɒk (US) -kɑːk

layer leɪəʳ, leəʳ (US) ˈleɪ.ɚ **-s** -z **-ing** -ɪŋ **-ed** -d

layette leɪˈet **-s** -s

lay|man ˈleɪ|.mən **-men** -mən

layoff ˈleɪ.ɒf (US) -ɑːf **-s** -s

layout ˈleɪ.aʊt **-s** -s

layover ˈleɪˌəʊ.vəʳ (US) -ˌoʊ.vɚ

lay|person ˈleɪˌpɜː.sᵊn (US) -ˌpɜːr- **-people** -ˌpiː.pl̩

Layton ˈleɪ.tᵊn

lay|woman ˈleɪ|ˌwʊm.ən **-women** -ˌwɪm.ɪn

lazar ˈlæz.əʳ (US) ˈleɪ.zɚ, ˈlæz.ɚ **-s** -z

lazaretto ˌlæz.əˈret.əʊ, -ᵊrˈet- (US) -ˈret̬.oʊ **-s** -z

Lazarus ˈlæz.ᵊr.əs

laz|e leɪz **-es** -ɪz **-ing** -ɪŋ **-ed** -d

Lazenby ˈleɪ.zᵊn.bi, -zᵊm- (US) -zᵊn-

Lazio ˈlæt.si.əʊ (US) ˈlɑːt.si.oʊ

lazuli ˈlæz.jə.liː, -jʊ-, ˈlæʒ.ə-, ˈ-ʊ-, -laɪ (US) ˈlæʒ.juː-, ˈlæz-, ˈ-ə-

lazulite ˈlæz.jə.laɪt, -jʊ-, ˈlæʒ.ə-, -ˈʊ- (US) ˈlæʒ.juː-, ˈlæz-, ˈ-ə-

laz|y ˈleɪ.z|i **-ier** -i.əʳ (US) -i.ɚ **-iest** -i.ɪst, -i.əst **-ily** -ɪ.li, -ᵊl.i **-iness** -ɪ.nəs, -ɪ.nɪs

lazybones ˈleɪ.ziˌbəʊnz (US) -ˌboʊnz

lb (*abbrev. for* **pound/s**) *singular:* paʊnd *plural:* paʊn*dz*

lbw ˌel.biːˈdʌb.l̩.juː

LCD ˌel.siːˈdiː

L-dopa ˌelˈdəʊ.pə (US) -ˈdoʊ-

lea (L) liː **-s** -z

LEA ˌel.iːˈeɪ

leach (L) liːtʃ **-es** -ɪz **-ing** -ɪŋ **-ed** -t

Leachman ˈliːtʃ.mən

Leacock ˈliː.kɒk, ˈleɪ- (US) -kɑːk

lead *metal:* led **-s** -z **-ing** -ɪŋ **-ed** -ɪd ˌ**lead** ˈ**pencil** (US) ˈ**lead** ˌ**pencil**; ˌ**lead** ˈ**poisoning**

lead *cable, flex:* liːd **-s** -z

lead *guide:* liːd **-s** -z **-ing** -ɪŋ **led** led ˌ**leading** ˈ**light**; ˈ**leading** ˌ**rein**; ˈ**lead** ˌ**time**

Lead *surname:* liːd

Leadbetter ˈledˌbet.əʳ, -ˈ-- (US) ˈledˌbet̬.ɚ, -ˈ--

leaden ˈled.ᵊn **-ly** -li **-ness** -nəs, -nɪs

Leadenhall ˈled.ᵊn.hɔːl (US) -hɔːl, -hɑːl

leader (L) ˈliː.dəʳ (US) -dɚ **-s** -z ˌ**leader of the** ˌ**oppo**ˈ**sition**

leaderette ˌliː.dᵊrˈet **-s** -s

leadership ˈliː.də.ʃɪp (US) -dɚ- **-s** -s

lead-in ˈliːd.ɪn **-s** -z

lead-off ˈliːd.ɒf (US) -ɑːf **-s** -s

leads (*n.*) *roofing:* ledz

lea|f (*n.*) liː|f **-ves** -vz ˈ**leaf** ˌ**mould**; **take a** ˌ**leaf out of** ˌ**someone's** ˈ**book**; ˌ**turn over a** ˌ**new** ˈ**leaf**

leaf (*v.*) liːf **-s** -s **-ing** -ɪŋ **-ed** -t

leafless ˈliːf.ləs, -lɪs

leafle|t ˈliː.flə|t, -flɪ|t **-ts** -ts **-(t)ting** -tɪŋ (US) -t̬ɪŋ **-(t)ted** -tɪd (US) -t̬ɪd

leaf|y ˈliː.f|i **-ier** -i.əʳ (US) -i.ɚ **-iest** -i.ɪst, -i.əst **-iness** -ɪ.nəs, -ɪ.nɪs

leagu|e liːg **-es** -z **-ing** -ɪŋ **-ed** -d
'**league** ˌ**table**
leaguer (L) 'liː.gəʳ (US) -gɚ **-s** -z
Leah 'liː.ə; lɪə (US) 'liː.ə
Leahy 'liː.hi (US) 'leɪ-
leak liːk **-s** -s **-ing** -ɪŋ **-ed** -t
leakag|e 'liː.kɪdʒ **-es** -ɪz
Leake liːk
Leakey 'liː.ki
leak|y 'liː.k|i **-ier** -i.əʳ (US) -i.ɚ **-iest** -i.ɪst, -i.əst **-iness** -ɪ.nəs, -ɪ.nɪs
Leamington 'lem.ɪŋ.tən ˌ**Leamington** '**Spa**
lean liːn **-er** -əʳ (US) -ɚ **-est** -ɪst, -əst **-ly** -li **-ness** -nəs, -nəs **-s** -z **-ing** -ɪŋ **leaned** -d, lent **leant** lent
Leander li'æn.dəʳ (US) -dɚ
Leanne li'æn
lean-to 'liːn.tuː **-s** -z
leap liːp **-s** -s **-ing** -ɪŋ **-ed** lept, liːpt **-t** lept **-er/s** -əʳ/z (US) -ɚ/z '**leap** ˌ**year** ; **by** ˌ**leaps and** '**bounds**
leapfrog 'liːp.frɒg (US) -frɑːg, -frɔːg **-s** -z **-ging** -ɪŋ **-ged** -d
Lear lɪəʳ (US) lɪr
learn lɜːn (US) lɜːrn **-s** -z **-ing** -ɪŋ **-ed** -d, -t **-t** -t **-er/s** -əʳ/z (US) -ɚ/z '**learning** ˌ**curve** ; '**learning disa**ˌ**bility**
learned *scholarly:* 'lɜː.nɪd (US) 'lɜːr- **-ly** -li **-ness** -nəs, -nɪs
Learney 'leə.ni (US) 'ler-
leas|e liːs **-es** -ɪz **-ing** -ɪŋ **-ed** -t **a** ˌ**new** ˌ**lease of** '**life** ; **a** ˌ**new** ˌ**lease on** '**life**
leaseback 'liːs.bæk
leasehold 'liːs.*h*əʊld (US) -hoʊld **-s** -z **-er/s** -əʳ/z (US) -ɚ/z
lease-|lend ˌliːs|'lend **-lends** -'len*d*z **-lending** -'len.dɪŋ **-lent** -'lent
leash liːʃ **-es** -ɪz **-ing** -ɪŋ **-ed** -t
least liːst
leastways 'liːst.weɪz
leastwise 'liːst.waɪz
leat liːt **-s** -s
Leatham 'liː.θᵊm, -ðᵊm
Leathart 'liː.θɑːt (US) -θɑːrt
leath|er 'leð|.əʳ (US) -ɚ **-ers** -əz (US) -ɚz **-ering** -ᵊr.ɪŋ **-ered** -əd (US) -ɚd
leatherback 'leð.ə.bæk (US) '-ɚ-
Leatherette® ˌleð.ᵊr'et
Leatherhead 'leð.ə.hed (US) '-ɚ-
leatherjacket 'leð.əˌdʒæk.ɪt (US) -ɚˌ- **-s** -s
leathern 'leð.ən (US) -ɚn
leatherneck 'leð.ə.nek (US) '-ɚ- **-s** -s
leather|y 'leð.ᵊr|.i **-iness** -ɪ.nəs, -ɪ.nɪs
Leathes liːðz
leave (*n.*) liːv **-s** -z
Note: Formerly, the pronunciation /liːf/ was used in the British army (plural: /liːfs/).
leav|e (*v.*) liːv **-es** -z **-ing/s** -ɪŋ/z **left** left **-er/s** -əʳ/z (US) -ɚ/z

leaved liːvd
leaven 'lev.ᵊn **-s** -z **-ing** -ɪŋ, 'lev.nɪŋ **-ed** -d
Leavenworth 'lev.ᵊn.wəθ, -wɜːθ (US) -wɚθ, -wɜːrθ
leaves (*plur. of* **leaf**) liːvz
leave-taking 'liːvˌteɪ.kɪŋ
Leavis 'liː.vɪs
Leavisite 'liː.vɪ.saɪt **-s** -s
Leavitt 'lev.ɪt
Lebanese ˌleb.ə'niːz *stress shift:* ˌLebanese 'capital
Lebanon 'leb.ə.nən, -nɒn (US) -nɑːn, -nən
Le Beau lə'bəʊ (US) -'boʊ
lebensraum (L) 'leɪ.bᵊnz.raʊm, -bᵊmz- (US) -bᵊnz-
Le Bon lə'bɒn (US) -'bɔːn
Lebowa lə'bəʊ.ə (US) -'boʊ-
Lebrun lə'brɜ̃ː*ŋ* (US) -'brɜ̃n
Leburn 'liː.bɜːn (US) -bɜːrn
Lec® lek
Le Carré, le Carré lə'kær.eɪ (US) -'kær.eɪ; -kɑː'reɪ
lech letʃ **-es** -ɪz **-ing** -ɪŋ **-ed** -t
Lech lek *as if Polish:* lex
lecher 'letʃ.əʳ (US) -ɚ **-s** -z
lecherous 'letʃ.ᵊr.əs **-ly** -li **-ness** -nəs, -nɪs
lechery 'letʃ.ᵊr.i
Lechlade 'letʃ.leɪd
Lechmere 'leʃ.mɪəʳ, 'letʃ- (US) -mɪr
lecithin 'les.ɪ.θɪn, '-ə-, -θən (US) -ɪ.θɪn
Leckhampton 'lekˌhæm*p*.tən
Leckie 'lek.i
Lecky 'lek.i
Leclanché lə'klɑ̃ː*n*.ʃeɪ
Leconfield 'lek.ᵊn.fiːld
Le Corbusier lə.kɔː'buː.zi.eɪ, -'bjuː- (US) -kɔːr.buː'zjeɪ, -zi'eɪ
lect lekt **-al** -ᵊl
lectern 'lek.tən, -tɜːn (US) -tɚn, -tɜːrn **-s** -z
lection 'lek.ʃᵊn **-s** -z
lectionar|y 'lek.ʃᵊn.ᵊr|.i (US) -er- **-ies** -iz
lector 'lek.tɔːʳ (US) -tɚ, -tɔːr **-s** -z
lect|ure 'lek.tʃ|əʳ (US) -tʃ|ɚ **-ures** -əz (US) -ɚz **-uring** -ᵊr.ɪŋ **-ured** -əd (US) -ɚd
lecturer 'lek.tʃᵊr.əʳ (US) -ɚ **-s** -z
lectureship 'lek.tʃə.ʃɪp (US) -tʃɚ- **-s** -s
led (*from* **lead**) led
LED ˌel.iː'diː
Leda 'liː.də
Ledbury 'led.bᵊr.i (US) 'led.ber-
lederhosen 'leɪ.dəˌhəʊ.zᵊn (US) -dɚˌhoʊ-
ledg|e ledʒ **-es** -ɪz
ledger 'ledʒ.əʳ (US) -ɚ **-s** -z '**ledger** ˌ**line**
Ledi 'led.i
Lediard 'led.i.əd, -ɑːd, '-jəd (US) 'led.jɚd, '-i.ɚd, -ɑːrd

Ledward 'led.wəd (US) -wɚd
Ledyard 'led.jəd (US) -jɚd
lee (L) liː **-s** -z
leech (L) liːtʃ **-es** -ɪz
Leeds liːdz
Lee-Enfield ˌliː'en.fiːld
leek (L) liːk **-s** -s
leer lɪəʳ (US) lɪr **-s** -z **-ing/ly** -ɪŋ/li **-ed** -d
leer|y 'lɪə.r|i (US) 'lɪr|.i **-ier** -i.əʳ (US) -i.ɚ **-iest** -i.ɪst, -i.əst **-ily** -ɪ.li, -ᵊl.i **-iness** -ɪ.nəs, -ɪ.nɪs
lees (L) liːz
Leeson liː.sᵊn
leet liːt **-s** -s
leeward 'liː.wəd (US) -wɚd *nautical pronunciation:* 'luː.əd, 'ljuː.əd (US) 'luː.ɚd
Leeward *islands:* 'liː.wəd (US) -wɚd
leeway 'liː.weɪ
Lefanu, Le Fanu 'lef.ə.njuː, -nuː; lə'fɑː.nuː (US) 'lef.ə.nuː, lə'fɑː-
Lefevre lə'fiː.vəʳ, -'feɪ-, -'fɛːv.rə (US) -'fiː.vɚ
Note: /lə'fiː.vəʳ (US) -vɚ/ in Sterne's 'Sentimental Journey'.
Lefroy lə'frɔɪ
left left ˌ**Left** '**Bank** *stress shift:* ˌLeft Bank 'artist
left-hand ˌleft'hænd, '--
left-hand|ed ˌleft'hæn.d|ɪd **-edness** -ɪd.nəs, -nɪs **-er/s** -əʳ/z (US) -ɚ/z *stress shift:* ˌleft-handed 'scissors
leftist 'lef.tɪst **-s** -s
left-luggage office ˌleft'lʌg.ɪdʒˌɒf.ɪs (US) -ˌɑː.fɪs
leftover 'leftˌəʊ.vəʳ (US) -ˌoʊ.vɚ **-s** -z
leftward 'left.wəd (US) -wɚd **-s** -z
left-wing ˌleft'wɪŋ **-er/s** -əʳ/z (US) -ɚ/z *stress shift:* ˌleft-wing 'tendencies
left|y 'lef.t|i **-ies** -iz
leg leg **-s** -z **-ging** -ɪŋ **-ged** -d ˌ**leg before** '**wicket** ; ˌ**leg** '**bye** ; **on one's** ˌ**last** '**legs** ; **not have a** ˌ**leg to** '**stand on**
legac|y 'leg.ə.s|i **-ies** -iz
legal 'liː.gᵊl **-ly** -i ˌ**legal** '**aid** ; ˌ**legal** '**tender**
legalese ˌliː.gᵊl'iːz
legal|ism 'liː.gᵊl|.ɪ.zᵊm **-ist/s** -ɪst/s
legalistic ˌliː.gᵊl'ɪs.tɪk **-ally** -əl.i, -li
legalit|y liː'gæl.ə.t|i, lɪ-, -ɪ.t|i (US) -ə.ţ|i **-ies** -iz
legalization, -isa- ˌliː.gᵊl.aɪ'zeɪ.ʃᵊn, -ɪ'- (US) -ɪ'-
legaliz|e, -is|e 'liː.gᵊl.aɪz **-es** -ɪz **-ing** -ɪŋ **-ed** -d
legal-size 'liː.gᵊlˌsaɪz
legate 'leg.ət, -ɪt, -eɪt (US) -ɪt **-s** -s
legatee ˌleg.ə'tiː **-s** -z
legation lɪ'geɪ.ʃᵊn, lə-, leg'eɪ- (US) lɪ'geɪ- **-s** -z
legatissimo ˌleg.ɑː'tɪs.ɪ.məʊ, -ə'- (US) -ɪ.moʊ

legato lɪ'gɑː.təʊ, lə-, leg'ɑː- ⓊⓈ -toʊ -s -z
legend 'ledʒ.ənd -s -z
legendary 'ledʒ.ən.dər.i, -ɪn- ⓊⓈ -der-
Leger 'ledʒ.əʳ ⓊⓈ -ɚ
Léger leɪ'ʒeɪ
legerdemain ˌledʒ.ə.də'meɪn *as if French:* ˌleʒ.ə.də'mæ̃ŋ ⓊⓈ ˌ-ɚ-
Leggatt 'leg.ət
Legge leg
-legged -'leg.ɪd, -'legd
Note: Suffix. Normally carries primary stress on the penultimate syllable, e.g. **three-legged** /ˌθriː'leg.ɪd/, but when a strong stress follows closely it undergoes stress shift, e.g. **ˌthree-legged 'stool**. However, the phrase "three-legged race" is usually **ˌthree-'legged ˌrace**.
Leggett 'leg.ɪt, -ət
Leggetter 'leg.ɪ.təʳ, '-ə- ⓊⓈ -t̬ɚ
legging 'leg.ɪŋ -s -z
leggy 'leg.i
Legh liː
leghorn *fowl:* leg'ɔːn, lɪ'gɔːn; 'leg.ɔːn, 'lɪg- ⓊⓈ 'leg.hɔːrn, -ɚn -s -z
leghorn *straw hat:* 'leg.hɔːn; leg'ɔːn, lɪ'gɔːn, lə- ⓊⓈ 'leg.hɔːrn, -ɚn -s -z
Leghorn *place:* 'leg.hɔːn, -'- ⓊⓈ -hɔːrn, ˌ-'-
legibility ˌledʒ.ə'bɪl.ə.ti, -ɪ'-, -ɪ.ti ⓊⓈ -ə.t̬i
legib|le 'ledʒ.ə.b|l̩, '-ɪ- **-ly** -li **-leness** -l̩.nəs, -nɪs
legion (L) 'liː.dʒən **-s** -z ˌ**Legion of 'Honour**
legionar|y 'liː.dʒə.nər|.i ⓊⓈ -er- **-ies** -iz
legionnaire (L) ˌliː.dʒə'neəʳ ⓊⓈ -'ner **-s** -z **Legion'naire's diˌsease**
legi|slate 'ledʒ.ɪ|.sleɪt, '-ə- **-slates** -sleɪts **-slating** -sleɪ.tɪŋ ⓊⓈ -sleɪ.t̬ɪŋ **-slated** -sleɪ.tɪd ⓊⓈ -sleɪ.t̬ɪd
legislation ˌledʒ.ɪ'sleɪ.ʃən, -ə'-
legislative 'ledʒ.ɪ.slə.tɪv, '-ə-, -sleɪ- ⓊⓈ -sleɪ.t̬ɪv
legislator 'ledʒ.ɪ.sleɪ.təʳ, '-ə- ⓊⓈ -t̬ɚ -s -z
legislature 'ledʒ.ɪ.slə.tʃəʳ, -sleɪ-, -tjʊəʳ, -tʃʊəʳ ⓊⓈ -sleɪ.tʃɚ -s -z
legit lə'dʒɪt, lɪ-
legitimacy lɪ'dʒɪt.ə.mə.si, lə-, '-ɪ- ⓊⓈ lə'dʒɪt̬.ə-
legitimate (*adj.*) lɪ'dʒɪt.ə.mət, lə-, '-ɪ-, -mɪt ⓊⓈ lə'dʒɪt̬.ə- **-ly** -li **-ness** -nəs, -nɪs
legiti|mate (*v.*) lɪ'dʒɪt.ə|.meɪt, lə-, '-ɪ- ⓊⓈ lə'dʒɪt̬.ə- **-mates** -meɪts **-mating** -meɪ.tɪŋ ⓊⓈ -meɪ.t̬ɪŋ **-mated** -meɪ.tɪd ⓊⓈ -meɪ.t̬ɪd
legitimation lɪˌdʒɪt.ə'meɪ.ʃən, lə-, -ɪ'- ⓊⓈ ləˌdʒɪt̬.ə'-
legitimatiz|e, -is|e lɪ'dʒɪt.ə.mə.taɪz, lə-, '-ɪ- ⓊⓈ lə'dʒɪt̬.ə- **-es** -ɪz **-ing** -ɪŋ **-ed** -d
legitimist lɪ'dʒɪt.ə.mɪst, lə-, '-ɪ- ⓊⓈ lə'dʒɪt̬.ə- **-s** -s
legitimiz|e, -is|e lɪ'dʒɪt.ə.maɪz, lə-, '-ɪ- ⓊⓈ lə'dʒɪt̬.ə- **-es** -ɪz **-ing** -ɪŋ **-ed** -d
legless 'leg.ləs, -lɪs
Lego® 'leg.əʊ ⓊⓈ -oʊ
leg-pull 'leg.pʊl **-s** -z **-ing** -ɪŋ **-ed** -d
Legree lɪ'griː, lə-
legroom 'leg.rʊm, -ruːm ⓊⓈ -ruːm, -rʊm
Legros lə'grəʊ ⓊⓈ -'groʊ
legume 'leg.juːm; lɪ'gjuːm, lə- **-s** -z
leguminous lɪ'gjuː.mɪ.nəs, lə-, leg'juː-, -mə- ⓊⓈ lə'gjuː-
leg-warmer 'legˌwɔː.məʳ ⓊⓈ -ˌwɔːr.mɚ **-s** -z
legwork 'leg.wɜːk ⓊⓈ -wɜːrk
Lehar, Lehàr leɪ'hɑːʳ, lɪ-, lə-; 'leɪ.hɑːʳ ⓊⓈ 'leɪ.hɑːr
Le Havre lə'*h*ɑː.vrə, -vəʳ ⓊⓈ -'hɑː.vrə, -vɚ
Lehigh 'liː.haɪ
Lehmann 'leɪ.mən, 'liː-
lehr lɪəʳ, leəʳ ⓊⓈ lɪr, ler **-s** -z
lei 'leɪ.iː **-s** -z
lei (*plur. of* **leu**) leɪ
Leibni(t)z 'laɪb.nɪts, 'liːb-
Leica® 'laɪ.kə
Leicester 'les.təʳ ⓊⓈ -tɚ **-shire** -ʃəʳ, -ˌʃɪəʳ ⓊⓈ -ʃɚ, -ˌʃɪr
Leics. (*abbrev. for* **Leicestershire**) 'les.tə.ʃəʳ, -ˌʃɪəʳ ⓊⓈ -ʃɚ, -ˌʃɪr
Leiden 'laɪ.dən, 'leɪ- ⓊⓈ 'laɪ-
Leigh *surname:* liː *place name:* liː, laɪ
Note: The places in Essex and Greater Manchester are /liː/; those in Surrey, Kent and Dorset are /laɪ/.
Leighton 'leɪ.tən
Leila 'liː.lə, 'leɪ-
Leinster *Irish province:* 'len*t*.stəʳ ⓊⓈ -stɚ *Duke of:* 'lɪn*t*.stəʳ ⓊⓈ -stɚ *square in London:* 'len*t*.stəʳ, 'lɪn*t*- ⓊⓈ -stɚ
Leipzig 'laɪp.sɪg, -sɪk
Leishman 'liːʃ.mən, 'lɪʃ-
leishmania ˌliːʃ'meɪ.ni.ə
leishmaniasis ˌliːʃ.mə'naɪ.ə.sɪs
leishmaniosis ˌleɪʃ.mə.ni'əʊ.sɪs, -meɪ- ⓊⓈ -meɪ.ni'oʊ-
leister 'liː.stəʳ ⓊⓈ -stɚ **-s** -z
Leister 'les.təʳ ⓊⓈ -tɚ
Leiston 'leɪ.stən
leisure 'leʒ.əʳ ⓊⓈ 'liː.ʒɚ, 'leʒ.ɚ **-d** -d **-ly** -li **-liness** -lɪ.nəs, -nɪs
Leith liːθ
leitmotif, leitmotiv 'laɪt.məʊˌtiːf, -ˌməʊ.tɪv ⓊⓈ -moʊˌtiːf **-s** -s, -z ⓊⓈ -s
Leitrim 'liː.trɪm
Leix liːʃ
lek lek **-s** -s **-king** -ɪŋ **-ked** -t
lekker 'lek.əʳ ⓊⓈ -ɚ
Leland 'liː.lənd
Lelean lə'liːn
Lely 'liː.li, 'lɪl.i
leman 'lem.ən, 'liː.mən **-s** -z
Leman *lake:* 'lem.ən, 'liː.mən; lɪ'mæn, lə'mæn, lə'mɑ̃ːŋ ⓊⓈ 'liː.mən; lə'mæn *surname:* 'le.mən, 'liː.mən *street in London:* 'lem.ən *formerly:* 'lɪm.æn
Le Mans lə'mɑ̃ːŋ ⓊⓈ -'mɑːn, -'mɑ̃ːn
Le Marchant lə'mɑː.tʃənt ⓊⓈ -'mɑːr-
Lemare lə'meəʳ ⓊⓈ -'mer
Lemberg 'lem.bɜːg ⓊⓈ -bɜːrg
Lemesurier, Le Mesurier lə'meʒ.ər.əʳ; lə.mə'ʒʊə.ri.eɪ ⓊⓈ lə'meʒ.ɚ.ɚ; lə.mə'ʒʊr.i.eɪ
lemma 'lem.ə **-s** -z
lemmatization, -isa- ˌlem.ə.taɪ'zeɪ.ʃən, -tɪ'- ⓊⓈ -t̬ɪ'-
lemmatiz|e, -is|e 'lem.ə.taɪz **-es** -ɪz **-ing** -ɪŋ **-ed** -d **-er/s** -əʳ/z ⓊⓈ -ɚ/z
lemme 'lem.i
lemming 'lem.ɪŋ **-s** -z
Lemmon 'lem.ən
lemnis|cus lem'nɪs|.kəs **-ci** -aɪ, -kaɪ, -iː, -kiː ⓊⓈ -aɪ, -kaɪ
Lemnos 'lem.nɒs ⓊⓈ -nɑːs, -noʊs
Lemoine lə'mɔɪn
lemon (L) 'lem.ən **-s** -z **'lemon ˌgrass** ; **'lemon ˌjuice** ; **ˌlemon 'sole** ; **ˌlemon 'squash** ; **ˌlemon meˌringue 'pie**
lemonade ˌlem.ə'neɪd **-s** -z
Le Morte D'Arthur ləˌmɔːt'dɑː.θəʳ ⓊⓈ -ˌmɔːrt'dɑːr.θɚ
lempira lem'pɪə.rə ⓊⓈ -'pɪr.ə **-s** -z
Lempriere 'lem.pri.eəʳ ⓊⓈ -er
Lemsip® 'lem.sɪp
Lemuel 'lem.juəl, -ju.əl ⓊⓈ -ju.əl, -jʊl
lemur 'liː.məʳ ⓊⓈ -mɚ **-s** -z
Len len
Lena *first name:* 'liː.nə *Siberian river:* 'leɪ.nə
lend lend **-s** -z **-ing** -ɪŋ **lent** lent **lender/s** 'len.dəʳ/z ⓊⓈ -dɚ/z **'lending ˌlibrary**
lenes (*plur. of* **lenis**) 'liː.neɪz, 'leɪ- ⓊⓈ 'liː.niːz, 'leɪ-
length leŋ*k*θ **-s** -s
lengthen 'leŋ*k*.θən **-s** -z **-ing** -ɪŋ, 'leŋ*k*θ.nɪŋ **-ed** -d
length|man 'leŋ*k*θ|.mən **-men** -mən
lengthways 'leŋ*k*θ.weɪz
lengthwise 'leŋ*k*θ.waɪz
length|y 'leŋ*k*.θ|i **-ier** -i.əʳ ⓊⓈ -i.ɚ **-iest** -i.ɪst, -i.əst **-ily** -ɪ.li, -əl.i **-iness** -ɪ.nəs, -ɪ.nɪs
lenien|ce 'liː.ni.ən*t*|s **-cy** -si
lenient 'liː.ni.ənt **-ly** -li
Lenin 'len.ɪn **-ism** -ɪ.zəm **-ist/s** -ɪst/s **-ite/s** -aɪt/s

Leningrad 'len.ɪn.græd, -ɪŋ-, -grɑːd (US) -græd
lenis 'liː.nɪs, 'leɪ- (US) 'liː.nɪs, 'leɪ- **lenes** 'liː.niːz, 'leɪ-, -neɪz
lenition lɪ'nɪʃ.ᵊn, lə-
lenitive 'len.ɪ.tɪv (US) -ə.t̬ɪv **-s** -z
lenity 'len.ə.ti, 'liː.nə-, -nɪ- (US) 'len.ə.t̬i
Lennie 'len.i
Lennon 'len.ən
Lennox 'len.əks
Lenny 'len.i
leno 'liː.nəʊ (US) -noʊ, 'len.əʊ, 'liː.nəʊ (US) 'len.oʊ, 'liː.noʊ
Note: The US television personality Jay Leno pronounces /'len.oʊ/.
Lenoir *surname:* lə'nwɑːʳ (US) -'nwɑːr *town in US:* lə'nɔːʳ (US) -'nɔːr
Lenor® lɪ'nɔːʳ, lə- (US) -'nɔːr
Lenore lɪ'nɔːʳ, lə- (US) -'nɔːr
Lenox 'len.əks
lens lenz **-es** -ɪz
lent (*from* **lend**) lent
Lent lent **-en** -ən
Lenthall *surname:* 'len.tɔːl *place in Yorkshire:* 'len.θɔːl, -θᵊl
Lenthéric®, Lentheric 'lɒn*t*.θᵊr.ɪk, 'lɑ̃ːn- (US) 'lɑːn*t*-
lenticel 'len.tɪ.sel (US) -t̬ɪ- **-s** -z
lenticular len'tɪk.jə.ləʳ, -jʊ- (US) -jə.lɚ
lentil 'len.tᵊl, -tɪl (US) -t̬ᵊl **-s** -z
lentivirus 'len.tɪ.vaɪə.rəs (US) -t̬ɪ.vaɪ- **-es** -ɪz
lento 'len.təʊ (US) -toʊ
Lenton 'len.tən
Lentulus 'len.tjə.ləs, -tjʊ- (US) -tuː-, -tə-
Lenz lents
Leo 'liː.əʊ (US) -oʊ
Leofric 'leɪ.əʊ.frɪk, 'lef.rɪk (US) leɪ'ɑː.frɪk, -'oʊ-
Leominster *place in Britain:* 'lem*p*.stəʳ (US) -stɚ *place in US:* 'lem.ɪn*t*.stəʳ (US) -stɚ
Leon 'liː.ɒn, 'leɪ-, -ən (US) -ɑːn
León leɪ'ɒn (US) -'oʊn
Leonard 'len.əd (US) -ɚd **-s** -z
Leonardo ˌliː.ə'nɑː.dəʊ, ˌleɪ- (US) ˌliː.ə'nɑːr.doʊ **-s** -z
leone (L) li'əʊ.ni (US) -'oʊ- **-s** -z
Leonid 'liː.əʊ.nɪd, 'leɪ- (US) '-ə- **-s** -z
Leonidas li'ɒn.ɪ.dæs, '-ə- (US) -'ɑː.nə.dəs
Leonie li'əʊ.ni (US) -'oʊ-
leonine 'liː.əʊ.naɪn (US) '-ə-
Leonora ˌliː.ə'nɔː.rə (US) -'nɔːr.ə
Leontes li'ɒn.tiːz, leɪ- (US) li'ɑːn-
leopard 'lep.əd (US) -ɚd **-s** -z **-ess/es** -es/ɪz, -ɪs/ɪz, -əs/ɪz
Leopold 'liː.ə.pəʊld, 'lɪə.pəʊld (US) 'liː.ə.poʊld
leotard 'liː.ə.tɑːd (US) -tɑːrd **-s** -z

Lepanto lɪ'pæn.təʊ, lə- (US) lɪ'pæn.toʊ, -'pɑːn-
leper 'lep.əʳ (US) -ɚ **-s** -z
lepidopter|an ˌlep.ɪ'dɒp.tᵊr|.ən (US) -'dɑːp- **-ans** -ənz **-a** -ə
lepidopterist ˌlep.ɪ'dɒp.tᵊr.ɪst (US) -'dɑːp- **-s** -s
lepidopterology ˌlep.ɪˌdɒp.tᵊr'ɒl.ə.dʒi (US) -ˌdɑːp.tə'rɑː.lə-
lepidopter|on ˌlep.ɪ'dɒp.tᵊr|.ən (US) -'dɑːp- **-ons** -ənz **-a** -ə
Lepidus 'lep.ɪ.dəs
Le Play lə'pleɪ
leprechaun 'lep.rə.kɔːn, -rɪ-, -hɔːn (US) -rə.kɑːn, -kɔːn **-s** -z
leprosy 'lep.rə.si
leprous 'lep.rəs **-ly** -li **-ness** -nəs, -nɪs
Lepsius 'lep.si.əs
lept|on 'lep.t|ɒn, -t|ən (US) -t|ɑːn **-a** -ə
Lepus 'liː.pəs, 'lep.əs (US) 'liː.pəs
Lermontov 'leə.mɒn.tɒf, -mən-, -təf (US) 'ler.mɑːn.tɔːf
Lerner 'lɜː.nəʳ (US) 'lɜːr.nɚ
Leroy 'liː.rɔɪ, lə'rɔɪ
Lerwick 'lɜː.wɪk (US) 'lɜːr-
les *in French phrases:* leɪ, leɪz
Note: The form /leɪz/ only occurs when the following word begins with a vowel.
Les *first name:* lez (US) les
Lesbi|a 'lez.bi|.ə **-an** -ən
lesbian 'lez.bi.ən **-s** -z **-ism** -ɪ.zᵊm
Lesbos 'lez.bɒs (US) -bɑːs, -boʊs
lèse-majesté, lese-majesty ˌleɪz'mæ*d*ʒ.ə.steɪ, ˌliːz-, '-ɪ-, -sti (US) ˌliːzˌmæʒ.es'teɪ; -'mædʒ.ɪ.sti
lesion 'liː.ʒᵊn **-s** -z
Leskovac 'les.kəʊ.vɑːts, -væts (US) -kɔː-
Leslie, Lesley 'lez.li (US) 'les-, 'lez-
Lesmahagow ˌles.mə'heɪ.gəʊ (US) -goʊ
Lesotho lə'suː.tuː, lɪ-, leɪ-, -'səʊ-, -təʊ (US) lə'soʊ.toʊ, -'suː.tuː
less les **-er** -əʳ (US) -ɚ
lessee les'iː **-s** -z
lessen 'les.ᵊn **-s** -z **-ing** -ɪŋ, 'les.nɪŋ **-ed** -d
Lesseps 'les.əps, -eps; les'eps (US) 'les.əps
Lessing 'les.ɪŋ
lesson 'les.ᵊn **-s** -z ˌ**learn one's 'lesson**
lessor les'ɔːʳ, '-- (US) 'les.ɔːr, -'- **-s** -z
lest lest
Lester 'les.təʳ (US) -tɚ
L'Estrange lə'streɪn*d*ʒ, lɪ-
Le Sueur lə'suː.əʳ (US) -'sʊr
let let **-s** -s **-ting** -ɪŋ (US) 'let̬.ɪŋ
letch letʃ **-es** -ɪz **-ing** -ɪŋ **-ed** -t
Letchworth 'letʃ.wəθ, -wɜːθ (US) -wɚθ, -wɜːrθ
let-down 'let.daʊn **-s** -z
lethal 'liː.θᵊl **-li** -i

lethargic lə'θɑː.dʒɪk, lɪ-, leθ'ɑː- (US) lɪ'θɑːr-, lə- **-ally** -ᵊl.i, -li
lethargy 'leθ.ə.dʒi (US) '-ɚ-
Lethe 'liː.θi, -θiː
Letheby 'leθ.ə.bi
Lethem 'leθ.ᵊm
Letitia lɪ'tɪʃ.i.ə, liː-, lə-, -'tiː.ʃi-, '-ʃə (US) lə'tɪʃ.ə, -'tiː.ʃə
Letraset® 'let.rə.set
Lett let **-s** -s
lett|er 'let|.əʳ (US) 'let̬|.ɚ **-ers** -əz (US) -ɚz **-ering** -ᵊr.ɪŋ **-ered** -əd (US) -ɚd '**letter** ˌ**bomb**; '**letter** ˌ**box**; '**letter** ˌ**carrier**; '**letter** ˌ**opener**
letterhead 'let.ə.hed (US) 'let̬.ɚ- **-s** -z
Letterman 'let.ə.mən (US) 'let̬.ɚ-
letter-perfect ˌlet.ə'pɜː.fɪkt, -fekt (US) ˌlet̬.ɚ'pɜːr.fɪkt
letterpress 'let.ə.pres (US) 'let̬.ɚ-
letter-quality 'let.əˌkwɒl.ə.ti, -ɪ.ti (US) 'let̬.ɚˌkwɑː.lə.t̬i
letter-size 'let.ə.saɪz (US) 'let̬.ɚ-
Lettice 'let.ɪs (US) 'let̬-
Lettish 'let.ɪʃ (US) 'let̬-
lettuc|e 'let.ɪs, -əs (US) 'let̬- **-es** -ɪz
Letty 'let.i (US) 'let̬-
letup 'let.ʌp (US) 'let̬- **-s** -s
leu 'leɪ.uː **lei** leɪ
Leuchars *place in Scotland:* 'luː.kəz, 'ljuː-, -xəz (US) 'luː.kɚz *surname:* 'luː.kəs, 'ljuː- (US) 'luː.kɚs
leucine 'ljuː.siːn, 'luː-, -saɪn (US) 'luː-
leucite 'ljuː.saɪt, 'luː- (US) 'luː-
leucocyte 'ljuː.kəʊ.saɪt, 'luː- (US) 'luː.koʊ-, -kə- **-s** -s
leucotom|y ljuː'kɒt.ə.m|i, luː- (US) luː'kɑː.t̬ə- **-ies** -iz
Leuctra 'ljuːk.trə (US) 'luːk-
leuk(a)emia ljuː'kiː.mi.ə, luː- (US) luː-
lev lev (US) lef **leva** 'lev.ə
le|vant (L) (*n.v.*) lə|'vænt, lɪ- (US) lə- **-vants** -'vænts **-vanting** -'væn.tɪŋ (US) -'væn.t̬ɪŋ **-vanted** -'væn.tɪd (US) -'væn.t̬ɪd
levant (*adj.*) 'lev.ənt
levanter (L) lə'væn.təʳ, lɪ- (US) lə'væn.t̬ɚ **-s** -z
Levantine 'lev.ᵊn.taɪn, -tiːn (US) 'lev.ᵊn.tiːn, -taɪn; lɪ'væn-
levee *royal reception:* 'lev.i, -eɪ (US) 'lev.i; lə'viː, -'veɪ **-s** -z
levee *embankment:* 'lev.i **-s** -z
level 'lev.ᵊl **-s** -z **-(l)ing** -ɪŋ, 'lev.lɪŋ **-(l)ed** -d **-(l)er/s** -əʳ/z (US) -ɚ/z **-ness** -nəs, -nɪs **-ly** -li ˌ**level 'crossing**
level-headed ˌlev.ᵊl'hed.ɪd (US) 'lev.ᵊl'hed.ɪd *stress shift, British only:* ˌlevel-headed 'person
Leven *loch:* 'liː.vᵊn *surname:* 'lev.ᵊn, 'liː.vᵊn
Note: The Earl pronounces /'liː.vᵊn/.

lev|er (*n. v.*) *on machine:* 'liː.vlər (US) 'lev.lɚ, 'liː.vlɚ **-ers** -əz (US) -ɚz **-ering** -ᵊr.ɪŋ **-ered** -əd (US) -ɚd
Lever *surname:* 'liː.vər (US) -vɚ
leverag|e 'liː.vᵊr.ɪdʒ (US) 'lev.ɚ-, 'liː.vɚ- **-ed** -d
leveret 'lev.ᵊr.ɪt, -ət **-s** -s
Leverett 'lev.ᵊr.ɪt
Leverhulme 'liː.və.hjuːm (US) -vɚ-
Levertov 'lev.ə.tɒf (US) -ɚ.tɑːf
Leveson 'lev.ɪ.sᵊn
Leveson-Gower ˌluː.sᵊn'gɔːr, ˌljuː-, -sᵊŋ'- (US) ˌluː.sᵊn'gɔːr
Levett 'lev.ɪt
Levey 'liː.vi, 'lev.i
Levi 'liː.vaɪ, 'lev.i, 'liː.vi
leviable 'lev.i.ə.bl̩
leviathan (L) lɪ'vaɪə.θᵊn, lə- **-s** -z
Levin 'lev.ɪn
Levine lə'viːn, -'vaɪn
levirate 'liː.vɪ.rət, 'lev.ɪ-, -rɪt (US) 'lev.ə.rɪt, 'liː.və-, -reɪt
Levis *in Quebec:* 'lev.i
Levis *trademark, jeans brand:* 'liː.vaɪz
Lévi-Strauss ˌlev.i'straʊs (US) ˌleɪ.vi-, ˌlev.i'-
levi|tate 'lev.ɪ|.teɪt, '-ə- **-tates** -teɪts **-tating** -teɪ.tɪŋ (US) -teɪ.t̬ɪŋ **-tated** -teɪ.tɪd (US) -teɪ.t̬ɪd
levitation ˌlev.ɪ'teɪ.ʃᵊn, -ə'- **-s** -z
Levite 'liː.vaɪt **-s** -s
levitic lə'vɪt.ɪk, lɪ- (US) lə'vɪt̬- **-al** -ᵊl **-ally** -ᵊl.i, -li
Leviticus lə'vɪt.ɪ.kəs, lɪ- (US) lə'vɪt̬-
Levitt 'lev.ɪt
levit|y 'lev.ə.t|i, -ɪ.t|i (US) -ə.t̬|i **-ies** -iz
lev|y (*n. v.*) 'lev|.i **-ies** -iz **-ying** -i.ɪŋ **-ied** -id **-ier/s** -i.ər/z (US) -i.ɚ/z
Levy *surname:* 'liː.vi, 'lev.i
lewd ljuːd, luːd (US) luːd **-er** -ər (US) -ɚ **-est** -ɪst, -əst **-ly** -li **-ness** -nəs, -nɪs
Lewes 'luː.ɪs
Lewin 'luː.ɪn
lewis (L) 'luː.ɪs **-es** -ɪz
Lewisham 'luː.ɪ.ʃəm
Lewison 'luː.ɪ.sᵊn
Lewsey 'ljuː.si (US) 'luː-
lexeme 'lek.siːm **-s** -z
lexic|al 'lek.sɪ.k|ᵊl **-ally** -ᵊl.i, -li
lexicographic ˌlek.sɪ.kəʊ'græf.ɪk (US) -koʊ'-, -kə'- **-al** -ᵊl **-ally** -ᵊl.i, -li
lexicograph|y ˌlek.sɪ'kɒg.rə.f|i (US) -kɑː'grə- **-er/s** -ər/z (US) -ɚ/z
lexicological ˌlek.sɪ.kə'lɒdʒ.ɪ.kᵊl (US) -'lɑː.dʒɪ-
lexicolog|y ˌlek.sɪ'kɒl.ə.dʒ|i (US) -'kɑː.lə- **-ist/s** -ɪst/s
lexicon 'lek.sɪ.kən, -kɒn (US) -kɑːn, -kən **-s** -z
Lexington 'lek.sɪŋ.tən
lexis 'lek.sɪs
lex loci contractus ˌleks,ləʊ.saɪ.kɒn'træk.təs, -ˌləʊ.kiː- (US) -ˌloʊ.saɪ.kɑːn'-, -kiː-, -siː-
lex loci delicti ˌleks,ləʊ.saɪ.del'ɪk.tiː, -ˌləʊ.kiː-, -taɪ (US) -ˌloʊ.saɪ.də'lɪk-, -kiː-, -siː-
ley (L) leɪ, liː **'ley ˌline**
Leybourne 'leɪ.bɔːn (US) -bɔːrn
Leyburn 'leɪ.bɜːn (US) -bɜːrn
Leyden jar ˌleɪ.dᵊn'dʒɑːr (US) 'laɪ.dᵊn,dʒɑːr **-s** -z
Leyland 'leɪ.lənd
Leys liːz
Leyton 'leɪ.tᵊn
Lhasa 'lɑː.sə, 'læs.ə
li liː **-s** -z
liabilit|y ˌlaɪ.ə'bɪl.ə.t|i, -ɪ.t|i (US) -ə.t̬|i **-ies** -iz
liable 'laɪ.ə.bl̩
liais|e li'eɪz **-es** -ɪz **-ing** -ɪŋ **-ed** -d
liaison li'eɪ.zᵊn, -zɒn *as if French:* -zɔ̃ːŋ (US) 'liː.ə.zɑːn; li'eɪ-, -zᵊn **-s** -z
Note: In military use always /li'eɪ.zᵊn (US) -zɑːn, -zᵊn/.
Liam 'liː.əm
liana li'ɑː.nə, -'æn.ə
liar 'laɪ.ər (US) -ɚ **-s** -z
Lias 'laɪ.əs
Liassic laɪ'æs.ɪk, li-
lib lɪb **ˌwomen's 'lib**
Libanus 'lɪb.ə.nəs
libation laɪ'beɪ.ʃᵊn, lɪ- (US) laɪ- **-s** -z
libber 'lɪb.ər (US) -ɚ **-s** -z **ˌwomen's 'libber**
Libby 'lɪb.i
Libdem ˌlɪb'dem **-s** -z *stress shift:* ˌLibdem 'vote
libel 'laɪ.bᵊl **-s** -z **-(l)ing** -ɪŋ **-(l)ed** -d **-(l)er/s** -ər/z (US) -ɚ/z
libel(l)ous 'laɪ.bᵊl.əs **-ly** -li
Liber 'laɪ.bər (US) -bɚ
Liberace ˌlɪb.ᵊr'ɑː.tʃi (US) -ə'rɑː-
liberal (L) 'lɪb.ᵊr.ᵊl, '-rᵊl **-s** -z **-ly** -i
Liberal Democrat ˌlɪb.ᵊr.ᵊl'dem.ə.kræt, -rᵊl'- **-s** -s
liberalism (L) 'lɪb.ᵊr.ᵊl.ɪ.zᵊm, '-rᵊl-
liberality ˌlɪb.ə'ræl.ə.ti, lɪ'bræl- (US) ˌlɪb.ə'ræl-, -ɪ.ti (US) -ə.t̬i
liberalization ˌlɪb.ᵊr.ᵊl.aɪ'zeɪ.ʃᵊn, ˌ-rᵊl-, -ɪ'- (US) -ɪ'-
liberaliz|e, -is|e 'lɪb.ᵊr.ᵊl.aɪz, '-rᵊl- **-es** -ɪz **-ing** -ɪŋ **-ed** -d
liber|ate 'lɪb.ᵊr|.eɪt (US) -ə.r|eɪt **-ates** -eɪts **-ating** -eɪ.tɪŋ (US) -eɪ.t̬ɪŋ **-ated** -eɪ.tɪd (US) -eɪ.t̬ɪd **-ator/s** -eɪ.tər/z (US) -eɪ.t̬ɚ/z
liberation ˌlɪb.ᵊr'eɪ.ʃᵊn (US) -ə'reɪ-
Liberi|a laɪ'bɪə.ri|.ə (US) -'bɪr.i- **-an/s** -ən/z
libertarian ˌlɪb.ə'teə.ri.ən (US) -ɚ'ter.i- **-s** -z **-ism** -ɪ.zᵊm
libertine 'lɪb.ə.tiːn, -taɪn (US) -ɚ.tiːn, -tɪn **-s** -z
Liberton 'lɪb.ə.tᵊn (US) '-ɚ-
libert|y (L) 'lɪb.ə.t|i (US) -ɚ.t̬|i **-ies** -iz **ˌLiberty 'Island**
libidinous lɪ'bɪd.ɪ.nəs, lə-, -ᵊn.əs (US) lə'bɪd.ᵊn.əs **-ly** -li **-ness** -nəs, -nɪs
libido lɪ'biː.dəʊ, lə- (US) -doʊ **-s** -z
libr|a *pound:* 'liː.br|ə, 'laɪ- (US) 'liː- **-ae** -iː, -eɪ, -aɪ
Libr|a *constellation:* 'liː.br|ə, 'lɪb.r|ə, 'laɪ.br|ə (US) 'liː-, 'laɪ- **-an/s** -ən/z
librarian laɪ'breə.ri.ən (US) -'brer.i- **-s** -z **-ship** -ʃɪp
librar|y 'laɪ.brᵊr|.i, -br|i (US) -brer|.i **-ies** -iz
libration laɪ'breɪ.ʃᵊn **-s** -z
librettist lɪ'bret.ɪst, lə- (US) lɪ'bret̬|- **-s** -s
librett|o lɪ'bret|.əʊ, lə- (US) lɪ'bret̬|.oʊ **-os** -əʊz (US) -oʊz **-i** -iː
Libreville 'liː.brə.vɪl (US) -viːl, -vɪl
Librium® 'lɪb.ri.əm
Liby|a 'lɪb.i|.ə **-an/s** -ən/z
lice (*plur. of* **louse**) laɪs
licenc|e 'laɪ.sᵊnts **-es** -ɪz **-ed** -t
licens|e 'laɪ.sᵊnts **-es** -ɪz **-ing** -ɪŋ **-ed** -t **-er/s** -ər/z (US) -ɚ/z **-or/s** -ər/z (US) -ɚ/z **'license ˌplate**
licensee ˌlaɪ.sᵊnt'siː **-s** -z
licentiate laɪ'sen.*t*ʃi.ət, lɪ-, -*t*ʃət, -*t*ʃi.ɪt (US) -ʃi.ɪt, -ʃi.eɪt, -ʃət **-s** -s
licentious laɪ'sen.*t*ʃəs **-ly** -li **-ness** -nəs, -nɪs
lichee ˌlaɪ'tʃiː; 'laɪ.tʃiː, 'liː- (US) 'liː.tʃiː **-s** -z
lichen 'laɪ.kən, -kɪn, 'lɪtʃ.ən, -ɪn (US) 'laɪ.kən **-s** -z **-ed** -d
lichenous 'laɪ.kə.nəs, -kɪ-, 'lɪtʃ.ə-, '-ɪ- (US) 'laɪ.kə-
Lichfield 'lɪtʃ.fiːld
lichgate 'lɪtʃ.geɪt **-s** -s
Licini|an laɪ'sɪn.i|.ən, lɪ- **-us** -əs
licit 'lɪs.ɪt **-ly** -li **-ness** -nəs, -nɪs
lick lɪk **-s** -s **-ing** -ɪŋ/z **-ed** -t
lickety-split ˌlɪk.ə.ti'splɪt, ˌ-ɪ- (US) -ə.t̬i'-
licorice 'lɪk.ᵊr.ɪs, -ɪʃ, 'lɪk.rɪs, -rɪʃ (US) 'lɪk.ɚ.ɪʃ, '-rɪʃ, 'lɪk.ɚ.ɪs
lictor 'lɪk.tər, -tɔːr (US) -tɚ **-s** -z
lid lɪd **-s** -z **-ded** -ɪd
Liddell 'lɪd.ᵊl, lɪ'del
Liddesdale 'lɪdz.deɪl
Liddle 'lɪd.l̩
Liddon 'lɪd.ᵊn
Lidell lɪ'del
Lidgate 'lɪd.geɪt, -gɪt
lido (L) 'liː.dəʊ, 'laɪ- (US) 'liː.doʊ **-s** -z
lie (*n. v.*) *falsehood:* laɪ **-s** -z **lying/ly** 'laɪ.ɪŋ/li **lied** laɪd **ˌlie through one's 'teeth**
lie (*v.*) *recline:* laɪ **-s** -z **lying** 'laɪ.ɪŋ **lay** leɪ **lain** leɪn

lie-abed ˈlaɪ.ə.bed **-s** -z
liebfraumilch (L) ˈliːb.fraʊ.mɪtʃ *as if German:* -mɪlx ⓤⓢ -mɪlk, ˈliːp-
Liebig ˈliː.bɪg *as if German:* -bɪx ⓤⓢ -bɪg *as if German:* -bɪx
Liebknecht ˈliːb.knekt *as if German:* -knext
Liechtenstein ˈlɪk.tᵊn.staɪn *as if German:* ˈlɪx-
lied *German song:* liːd *as if German:* liːt **lieder** ˈliː.dəʳ ⓤⓢ -dɚ
lief liːf **-er** -əʳ ⓤⓢ -ɚ
lieg|e liːdʒ **-es** -ɪz
Liège liˈeɪʒ, -ˈeʒ
lie-in ˌlaɪˈɪn, ˈ-- **-s** -z
lien ˈliː.ən, liːn ⓤⓢ liːn, ˈliː.ən **-s** -z
Liepaja lɪˈpɑː.jə ⓤⓢ liˈep.ə-, lɪˈpɑː-
lieu ljuː, luː ⓤⓢ luː
lieutenanc|y lefˈten.ən*t*.s|i, ləf- ⓤⓢ luː- **-ies** -iz
lieutenant lefˈten.ənt, ləf- ⓤⓢ luː- **-s** -s **lieuˌtenant ˈcolonel** ; **lieuˌtenant comˈmander** ; **lieuˌtenant ˈgeneral** ; **lieuˌtenant ˈgovernor**
li|fe laɪ|f **-ves** -vz **ˈlife ˌcycle** ; **ˈlife exˌpectancy** ; **ˈlife inˌsurance** ; **ˌlife ˈsavings** ; **ˌlife ˈsentence**
life-and-death ˌlaɪf.ənˈdeθ *stress shift:* ˌlife-and-death ˈissue
lifebelt ˈlaɪf.belt **-s** -s
lifeblood ˈlaɪf.blʌd
lifeboat ˈlaɪf.bəʊt ⓤⓢ -boʊt **-s** -s
life-buoy ˈlaɪf.bɔɪ ⓤⓢ -bɔɪ, -ˌbuː.i **-s** -z
life-giving ˈlaɪfˌgɪv.ɪŋ
lifeguard ˈlaɪf.gɑːd ⓤⓢ -gɑːrd **-s** -z
lifejacket ˈlaɪfˌdʒæk.ɪt **-s** -s
lifeless ˈlaɪf.ləs, -lɪs **-ly** -li **-ness** -nəs, -nɪs
lifelike ˈlaɪf.laɪk
lifeline ˈlaɪf.laɪn **-s** -z
lifelong ˌlaɪfˈlɒŋ ⓤⓢ ˌlaɪfˈlɑːŋ, -ˈlɔːŋ *stress shift:* ˌlifelong ˈdream
life of Riley ˌlaɪf.əvˈraɪ.li
life-or-death ˌlaɪf.ɔːˈdeθ ⓤⓢ -ɔːrˈ- *stress shift:* ˌlife-or-death ˈissue
life-preserver ˈlaɪf.prɪˌzɜː.vəʳ, -prəˌ- ⓤⓢ -priːˌzɜːr.vɚ, -prɪˌ- **-s** -z
lifer ˈlaɪ.fəʳ ⓤⓢ -fɚ **-s** -z
lifesaver ˈlaɪfˌseɪ.vəʳ ⓤⓢ -vɚ **-s** -z
life-saving ˈlaɪfˌseɪ.vɪŋ *stress shift:* ˌlife-saving ˈmedicine
life-size ˈlaɪf.saɪz, ˌ-ˈ-
lifespan ˈlaɪf.spæn **-s** -z
lifestyle ˈlaɪf.staɪl **-s** -z
life-support ˈlaɪf.səˌpɔːt, ˌ--ˈ- ⓤⓢ ˈlaɪf.səˌpɔːrt **ˌlife-supˈport ˌsystem**, **ˈlife-supˌport ˌsystem**
lifetime ˈlaɪf.taɪm **-s** -z
lifework ˌlaɪfˈwɜːk, ˈ-- ⓤⓢ ˌlaɪfˈwɜːrk, ˈ-- **-s** -s
Liffey ˈlɪf.i
Lifford ˈlɪf.əd ⓤⓢ -ɚd
lift lɪft **-s** -s **-ing** -ɪŋ **-ed** -ɪd **-er/s** -əʳ/z ⓤⓢ -ɚ/z
lift-off ˈlɪft.ɒf ⓤⓢ -ɑːf
ligament ˈlɪg.ə.mənt **-s** -s
ligament|al ˌlɪg.əˈmen.t|ᵊl ⓤⓢ -t̬|ᵊl **-ous** -əs
ligature ˈlɪg.ə.tʃəʳ, -tjʊəʳ, -tʃʊəʳ ⓤⓢ -tʃɚ **-s** -z **-d** -d
liger ˈlaɪ.gəʳ ⓤⓢ -gɚ **-s** -z
Liggett ˈlɪg.ɪt, -ət
light laɪt **-s** -s **-er** -əʳ ⓤⓢ ˈlaɪ.t̬ɚ **-est** -ɪst, -əst ⓤⓢ ˈlaɪ.t̬ɪst, -t̬əst **-ly** -li **-ness** -nəs, -nɪs **-ing** -ɪŋ ⓤⓢ ˈlaɪ.t̬ɪŋ **-ed** -ɪd ⓤⓢ ˈlaɪ.t̬ɪd **lit** lɪt **ˌlight ˈaircraft** ; **ˈlight ˌbulb** ; **ˈlight ˌmeter**
lighten ˈlaɪ.tᵊn **-s** -z **-ing** -ɪŋ, ˈlaɪt.nɪŋ **-ed** -d
lighter ˈlaɪ.təʳ ⓤⓢ -t̬ɚ **-s** -z
lighterage ˈlaɪ.tᵊr.ɪdʒ ⓤⓢ -t̬ɚ-
light-fingered ˌlaɪtˈfɪŋ.gəd ⓤⓢ -gɚd *stress shift:* ˌlight-fingered ˈthief
lightfoot (L) ˈlaɪt.fʊt
light-headed ˌlaɪtˈhed.ɪd **-ly** -li **-ness** -nəs, -nɪs *stress shift:* ˌlight-headed ˈdaze
light-hearted ˌlaɪtˈhɑː.tɪd ⓤⓢ -ˈhɑːr.t̬ɪd **-ly** -li **-ness** -nəs, -nɪs *stress shift:* ˌlight-hearted ˈcomment
lighthou|se ˈlaɪt.haʊ|s **-ses** -zɪz
lighthousekeeper ˈlaɪt.haʊsˌkiː.pəʳ ⓤⓢ -pɚ **-s** -z
lighting-up time ˌlaɪ.tɪŋˈʌpˌtaɪm ⓤⓢ -t̬ɪŋˈ-
lightning ˈlaɪt.nɪŋ **-s** -z
lightning-conductor ˈlaɪt.nɪŋ.kənˌdʌk.təʳ ⓤⓢ -t̬ɚ **-s** -z
lightship ˈlaɪt.ʃɪp **-s** -s
lightweight ˈlaɪt.weɪt **-s** -s
light-year ˈlaɪt.jɪəʳ ⓤⓢ -jɪr **-s** -z
ligneous ˈlɪg.ni.əs
lignite ˈlɪg.naɪt
lignum ˈlɪg.nəm
Liguri|a lɪgˈjʊə.ri|.ə, -ˈjɔː- ⓤⓢ -ˈjʊr.i- **-an/s** -ən/z
likable ˈlaɪ.kə.bl̩ **-ness** -nəs, -nɪs
lik|e laɪk **-es** -s **-ing** -ɪŋ **-ed** -t
likeable ˈlaɪ.kə.bl̩ **-ness** -nəs, -nɪs
likelihood ˈlaɪ.kli.hʊd
likel|y ˈlaɪ.kl|i **-ier** -i.əʳ ⓤⓢ -i.ɚ **-iest** -i.ɪst, -i.əst **-iness** -ɪ.nəs, -ɪ.nɪs
likeminded ˌlaɪkˈmaɪn.dɪd ⓤⓢ ˈ-ˌ--, ˌ-ˈ-- *stress shift, British only:* ˌlikeminded ˈfriend
liken ˈlaɪ.kᵊn **-s** -z **-ing** -ɪŋ **-ed** -d
likeness ˈlaɪk.nəs, -nɪs **-es** -ɪz
likewise ˈlaɪk.waɪz
liking ˈlaɪ.kɪŋ **-s** -z
Likud lɪˈkʊd, -ˈkuːd ⓤⓢ -ˈkuːd
likuta liːˈkuː.tɑː **makuta** *(plur.)* mɑːˈkuː.tɑː
lilac ˈlaɪ.lək ⓤⓢ -lək, -læk, -lɑːk **-s** -s
liliaceous ˌlɪl.iˈeɪ.ʃəs
Lilian ˈlɪl.i.ən
Lilias ˈlɪl.i.əs
Liliburlero ˌlɪl.i.bəˈleə.rəʊ ⓤⓢ -bɚˈler.oʊ
Lilith ˈlɪl.ɪθ
Lilla ˈlɪl.ə
Lille liːl
Lillehammer ˈlɪl.ɪ.hæm.əʳ, -əˌ- ⓤⓢ -ə.hɑː.mɚ, -hæm.ɚ
Lil-lets® lɪˈlets
Lilley ˈlɪl.i
Lillian ˈlɪl.i.ən
Lilliput ˈlɪl.ɪ.pʌt, ˈ-ə-, -pʊt, -pət ⓤⓢ -ə.pʌt, -pət, -pʊt
lilliputian (L) ˌlɪl.ɪˈpjuː.ʃᵊn, -əˈ-, -ʃi.ən ⓤⓢ -əˈpjuː.ʃᵊn **-s** -z
Lilly ˈlɪl.i
Lillywhite ˈlɪl.i.*h*waɪt
Lilo® ˈlaɪ.ləʊ ⓤⓢ -loʊ **-s** -z
Lilongwe lɪˈlɒŋ.weɪ ⓤⓢ -ˈlɔːŋ-, -ˈlɑːŋ-
lilt lɪlt **-s** -s **-ing** -ɪŋ ⓤⓢ ˈlɪl.t̬ɪŋ **-ed** -ɪd ⓤⓢ ˈlɪl.t̬ɪd
lil|y (L) ˈlɪl|.i **-ies** -iz **ˌlily of the ˈvalley**
lily-livered ˌlɪl.iˈlɪv.əd ⓤⓢ -ɚd *stress shift:* ˌlily-livered ˈscoundrel
lily-white ˌlɪl.iˈ*h*waɪt *stress shift:* ˌlily-white ˈhands
Lima *in Peru:* ˈliː.mə *in US:* ˈlaɪ.mə
lima *bean:* ˈliː.mə ⓤⓢ ˈlaɪ-
Limavady ˌlɪm.əˈvæd.i
limb lɪm **-s** -z **-ed** -d **ˌout on a ˈlimb**
limber *(n. adj.)* ˈlɪm.bəʳ ⓤⓢ -bɚ **-s** -z
limbo (L) ˈlɪm.bəʊ ⓤⓢ -boʊ **-s** -z **-ing** -ɪŋ **-ed** -d
Limburg ˈlɪm.bɜːg ⓤⓢ -bɜːrg
lim|e *(n. v.)* laɪm **-es** -z **-ing** -ɪŋ **-ed** -d **ˌlime ˈgreen**
limeade ˌlaɪˈmeɪd ⓤⓢ ˌ-ˈ-, ˈlaɪ.meɪd
Limehouse ˈlaɪm.haʊs
limekiln ˈlaɪm.kɪln, -kɪl **-s** -z
limelight ˈlaɪm.laɪt **-s** -s
limen ˈlaɪ.men, -mən ⓤⓢ -mən
limerick (L) ˈlɪm.ᵊr.ɪk ⓤⓢ -ɚ.ɪk, ˈ-rɪk **-s** -s
limescale ˈlaɪm.skeɪl
limestone ˈlaɪm.stəʊn ⓤⓢ -stoʊn
limewash ˈlaɪm.wɒʃ ⓤⓢ -wɑːʃ, -wɔːʃ **-es** -ɪz **-ing** -ɪŋ **-ed** -t
limewater ˈlaɪmˌwɔː.təʳ ⓤⓢ -ˌwɑː.t̬ɚ, -ˌwɔː-
limey ˈlaɪ.mi **-s** -z
liminal ˈlɪm.ɪ.nᵊl
lim|it *(n. v.)* ˈlɪm|.ɪt **-its** -ɪts **-iting** -ɪ.tɪŋ ⓤⓢ -ɪ.t̬ɪŋ **-ited/ness** -ɪ.tɪd/nəs, -nɪs ⓤⓢ -ɪ.t̬ɪd/nəs, -nɪs **-itable** -ɪ.tə.bl̩ ⓤⓢ -ɪ.t̬ə.bl̩
limitation ˌlɪm.ɪˈteɪ.ʃᵊn, -əˈ- **-s** -z
limitless ˈlɪm.ɪt.ləs, -lɪs
limn lɪm **-s** -z **-ing** -ɪŋ, -nɪŋ **-ed** -d **-er/s** -nəʳ/z ⓤⓢ -ɚ/z, -nɚ/z
limo ˈlɪm.əʊ ⓤⓢ -oʊ **-s** -z
Limoges lɪˈməʊʒ ⓤⓢ liːˈmoʊʒ

Limousin ˌlɪm.uː'zæn *as if French:* -'zæ̃ŋ (US) ˌliː.muː'zæn
limousine ˌlɪm.ə'ziːn, -ʊ'-, '--- (US) 'lɪm.ə.ziːn, ˌ--'- **-s** -z
limp lɪmp **-s** -s **-er** -əʳ (US) -ɚ **-est** -ɪst, -əst **-ly** -li **-ness** -nəs, -nɪs **-ing/ly** -ɪŋ/li **-ed** -t
limpet 'lɪm.pɪt **-s** -s
limpid 'lɪm.pɪd **-ly** -li **-ness** -nəs, -nɪs
limpidity lɪm'pɪd.ə.ti, -ɪ.ti (US) -ə.t̬i
Limpopo lɪm'pəʊ.pəʊ (US) -'poʊ.poʊ
limp-wristed ˌlɪmp'rɪs.tɪd (US) ˌ-'--, 'lɪmpˌrɪs-
limy 'laɪ.mi
Linacre 'lɪn.ə.kəʳ, '-ɪ- (US) -kɚ
linag|e 'laɪ.nɪdʒ **-es** -ɪz
linchpin 'lɪntʃ.pɪn **-s** -z
Lincoln 'lɪŋ.kən **-shire** -ʃəʳ, -ˌʃɪəʳ (US) -ʃɚ, -ˌʃɪr
Lincs. (*abbrev. for* **Lincolnshire**) lɪŋks, 'lɪŋ.kən.ʃəʳ, -ʃɪəʳ (US) -ʃɚ, -ˌʃɪr
linctus 'lɪŋk.təs **-es** -ɪz
Lind lɪnd
Linda 'lɪn.də
Lindbergh 'lɪn*d*.bɜːg (US) -bɜːrg
linden (L) 'lɪn.dən **-s** -z
Lindisfarne 'lɪn.dɪs.fɑːn, -dəs- (US) -fɑːrn
Lindley 'lɪn*d*.li
Lindon 'lɪn.dən
Lindsay, Lindsey 'lɪn*d*.zi
lin|e (L) laɪn **-es** -z **-ing** -ɪŋ **-ed** -d **'line ˌdrawing**; **ˌread beˌtween the 'lines**
lineag|e *family:* 'lɪn.i.ɪdʒ (US) '-ɪdʒ, -i.ɪdʒ **-es** -ɪz
lineag|e *alternative spelling of* **linage**: 'laɪ.nɪdʒ **-es** -ɪz
lineal 'lɪn.i.əl **-ly** -i
lineament 'lɪn.i.ə.mənt **-s** -s
linear 'lɪn.i.əʳ (US) -ɚ **-ly** -li
lineation ˌlɪn.i'eɪ.ʃən **-s** -z
linebacker 'laɪnˌbæk.əʳ, 'laɪm- (US) 'laɪnˌbæk.ɚ **-s** -z
line-engraving 'laɪn.ɪnˌgreɪ.vɪŋ, -ɪŋˌ- (US) -ɪnˌ- **-s** -z
Lineker 'lɪn.ɪ.kəʳ, '-ə- (US) -kɚ
line|man 'laɪn|.mən, 'laɪm- (US) 'laɪn- **-men** -mən, -men
linen 'lɪn.ɪn, -ən **-s** -z
line-out 'laɪn.aʊt **-s** -s
liner 'laɪ.nəʳ (US) -nɚ **-s** -z
lines|man 'laɪnz|.mən **-men** -mən, -men
line-up 'laɪn.ʌp **-s** -s
Linford 'lɪn.fəd (US) -fɚd
ling (L) lɪŋ **-s** -z
lingam 'lɪŋ.gəm, -æm
Lingay 'lɪŋ.gi
Lingen 'lɪŋ.ən
ling|er 'lɪŋ.g|əʳ (US) -g|ɚ **-ers** -əz (US) -ɚz **-ering/ly** -ᵊr.ɪŋ/li **-ered** -əd (US) -ɚd **-erer/s** -ᵊr.əʳ/z (US) -ɚ.ɚ/z
lingerie 'læ̃n.ʒᵊr.i, 'lɒn-, -dʒᵊr-, -ri, -reɪ (US) ˌlɑːn.ʒə'reɪ; ˌlæn.ʒə'riː, -dʒə'-
lingo 'lɪŋ.gəʊ (US) -goʊ **-s** -z
lingua franca ˌlɪŋ.gwə'fræŋ.kə
lingual 'lɪŋ.gwəl **-ly** -i
Linguaphone® 'lɪŋ.gwə.fəʊn (US) -foʊn
Linguarama® ˌlɪŋ.gwə'rɑː.mə (US) -'ræm.ə, -'rɑː.mə
linguine, linguini lɪŋ'gwiː.ni
linguist 'lɪŋ.gwɪst **-s** -s
linguistic lɪŋ'gwɪs.tɪk **-s** -s **-al** -ᵊl **-ally** -ᵊl.i, -li
linguistician ˌlɪŋ.gwɪ'stɪʃ.ᵊn **-s** -z
liniment 'lɪn.ɪ.mənt, '-ə- **-s** -s
lining 'laɪ.nɪŋ **-s** -z
link (*n. v.*) lɪŋk **-s** -s **-ing** -ɪŋ **-ed** -t
linkag|e 'lɪŋ.kɪdʒ **-es** -ɪz
Linklater 'lɪŋkˌleɪ.təʳ (US) -t̬ɚ
links lɪŋks
linkup 'lɪŋk.ʌp
Linley 'lɪn.li
Linlithgow lɪn'lɪθ.gəʊ (US) -goʊ **-shire** -ʃəʳ, -ˌʃɪəʳ (US) -ʃɚ, -ˌʃɪr
Linnaean lɪ'niː.ən, -'neɪ-
Linnaeus lɪ'niː.əs, -'neɪ-
Linnean lɪ'niː.ən, -'neɪ-
linnet (L) 'lɪn.ɪt **-s** -s
lino 'laɪ.nəʊ (US) -noʊ **-s** -z
linocut 'laɪ.nəʊ.kʌt (US) -noʊ-, -nə- **-s** -s
linoleum lɪ'nəʊ.li.əm (US) -'noʊ- **-s** -z
Linotype® 'laɪ.nəʊ.taɪp (US) -nə- **-s** -s
linseed 'lɪn.siːd **'linseed ˌoil, ˌlinseed 'oil**
linsey (L) 'lɪn.zi
linsey-woolsey (L) ˌlɪn.zi'wʊl.zi
lint lɪnt
lintel 'lɪn.tᵊl (US) -t̬ᵊl **-s** -z
Linthwaite 'lɪn.θweɪt
Linton 'lɪn.tən
Lintot(t) 'lɪn.tɒt (US) -tɑːt
Linus 'laɪ.nəs
Linz lɪn*ts*
lion laɪən **-s** -z **'lion ˌtamer**
Lionel 'laɪə.nᵊl
lioness 'laɪə.nes, -nɪs; ˌlaɪə'nes (US) 'laɪə.nes, -nɪs **-es** -ɪz
Lionheart 'laɪən.hɑːt (US) -hɑːrt
lion-hearted ˌlaɪən'hɑː.tɪd (US) 'laɪənˌhɑːr.t̬ɪd *stress shift, British only:* ˌlion-hearted 'warrior
lioniz|e, -is|e 'laɪə.naɪz **-es** -ɪz **-ing** -ɪŋ **-ed** -d
lip lɪp **-s** -s **-ping** -ɪŋ **-ped** -t **'lip ˌservice**
Lipari 'lɪp.ᵊr.i, 'liː.pær-
lipas|e 'laɪ.peɪz, 'lɪp.eɪz, -eɪs (US) 'lɪp.eɪs, 'laɪ.peɪs **-es** -ɪz
lipbrush 'lɪp.brʌʃ **-es** -ɪz
lipid(e) 'lɪp.ɪd, 'laɪ.pɪd (US) 'lɪp.ɪd **-s** -z
Lipman 'lɪp.mən
lipoid 'lɪp.ɔɪd, 'laɪ.pɔɪd
lipoprotein ˌlɪp.əʊ'prəʊ.tiːn, ˌlaɪ.pəʊ'- (US) ˌlɪp.oʊ'pro.tiːn, ˌlaɪ.poʊ'-, -pə'-, -tiː.ɪn **-s** -z
liposome 'lɪp.əʊ.səʊm (US) -ə.soʊm, 'laɪ.pə- **-s** -z
liposuction 'lɪp.əʊˌsʌk.ʃᵊn (US) 'lɪp.oʊˌ-, 'laɪ.poʊˌ-, -pəˌ-
Lippi 'lɪp.i
Lippincott 'lɪp.ɪŋ.kət, -kɒt (US) -ɪn.kɑːt, -kət
Lippizaner ˌlɪp.ɪt'sɑː.nəʳ, -ət'- (US) -nɚ **-s** -z
Lippmann 'lɪp.mən
lipp|y 'lɪp|.i **-ier** -i.əʳ (US) -i.ɚ **-iest** -i.ɪst, -i.əst **-iness** -ɪ.nəs, -ɪ.nɪs
lip|-read 'lɪp|.riːd **-reads** -riːdz **-reading** -ˌriː.dɪŋ **-read** *past tense:* -red **-readers** -ˌriː.dəʳ/z (US) -ˌriː.dɚ/z
lip-salve 'lɪp.sælv, -sɑːlv (US) -sæv, -sɑːv **-s** -z
Lipscomb(e) 'lɪp.skəm
lipstick 'lɪp.stɪk **-s** -s
lip-synch 'lɪp.sɪŋk **-s** -s **-ing** -ɪŋ **-ed** -t
Lipton 'lɪp.tən
liquefaction ˌlɪk.wɪ'fæk.ʃᵊn, -wə'-
lique|fy 'lɪk.wɪ|.faɪ, -wə- **-fies** -faɪz **-fying** -faɪ.ɪŋ **-fied** -faɪd **-fier/s** -faɪ.əʳ/z (US) -faɪ.ɚ/z **-fiable** -faɪ.ə.bl̩
liqueur lɪ'kjʊəʳ, lə-, -'kjɔːʳ, -'kjɜːʳ (US) lɪ'kɜːr, -'kʊr, -'kjʊr **-s** -z
liquid 'lɪk.wɪd **-s** -z **-ly** -li **-ness** -nəs, -nɪs
liqui|date 'lɪk.wɪ|.deɪt, -wə- **-dates** -deɪts **-dating** -deɪ.tɪŋ (US) -deɪ.t̬ɪŋ **-dated** -deɪ.tɪd (US) -deɪ.t̬ɪd **-dator/s** -deɪ.təʳ/z (US) -deɪ.t̬ɚ/z
liquidation ˌlɪk.wɪ'deɪ.ʃᵊn, -wə'- **-s** -z
liquidity lɪ'kwɪd.ə.ti, lə-, -ɪ.ti (US) -ə.t̬i
liquidiz|e, -is|e 'lɪk.wɪ.daɪz, -wə- **-es** -ɪz **-ing** -ɪŋ **-ed** -d
liquidizer, -iser 'lɪk.wɪ.daɪ.zəʳ, -wə- (US) -zɚ **-s** -z
liqu|or 'lɪk|.əʳ (US) -ɚ **-ors** -əz (US) -ɚz **-oring** -ᵊr.ɪŋ **-ored** -əd (US) -ɚd
liquorice 'lɪk.ᵊr.ɪs, -ɪʃ, 'lɪk.rɪs, -rɪʃ (US) 'lɪk.ɚ.ɪʃ, '-rɪʃ, 'lɪk.ɚ.ɪs
lir|a 'lɪə.r|ə (US) 'lɪr|.ə **-as** -əz **-e** -i, -eɪ
Lisa 'liː.sə, -zə
Lisbet 'lɪz.bət, -bet, -bɪt
Lisbeth 'lɪz.bəθ, -beθ, -bɪθ
Lisbon 'lɪz.bən
Lisburn 'lɪz.bɜːn (US) -bɜːrn
lisente lɪ'sen.teɪ (US) -ti
Lisette lɪ'zet, 'liː.zet
Liskeard 'lɪs.kɑːd (US) -kɑːrd
lisle *thread:* laɪl
Lisle laɪl, liːl
Note: Baron Lisle pronounces /laɪl/.
Lismore *in Scotland and Ireland:* lɪz'mɔːʳ (US) -'mɔːr *in Australia:* 'lɪz.mɔːʳ (US) -mɔːr
lisp, LISP lɪsp **-s** -s **-ing/ly** -ɪŋ/li **-ed** -t **-er/s** -əʳ/z (US) -ɚ/z

lis pendens ˌlɪsˈpen.denz
Liss lɪs
lissome ˈlɪs.əm **-ness** -nəs, -nɪs
Lisson ˈlɪs.ᵊn
list lɪst **-s** -s **-ing** -ɪŋ **-ed** -ɪd
listen ˈlɪs.ᵊn **-s** -z **-ing** -ɪŋ, ˈlɪs.nɪŋ **-ed** -d **-er/s** -əʳ/z, ˈlɪs.nəʳ/z ⓤⓢ **-er/z** ˈlɪs.ᵊn.ɚ/z **-er/s** ˈlɪs.nɚ/z
Lister ˈlɪs.təʳ ⓤⓢ -tɚ
listeria lɪˈstɪə.ri.ə ⓤⓢ -ˈstɪr.i-
listeriasis ˌlɪs.təˈriː.ə.sɪs
Listerine® ˈlɪs.tᵊr.iːn ⓤⓢ ˌlɪs.təˈriːn
listeriosis lɪˌstɪə.riˈəʊ.sɪs, ˌlɪs.tɪə- ⓤⓢ lɪˌstɪr.iˈoʊ-
listless ˈlɪs*t*.ləs, -lɪs **-ly** -li **-ness** -nəs, -nɪs
Liston ˈlɪs.tᵊn
Listowel lɪˈstəʊəl ⓤⓢ -ˈstoʊəl, -ˈstaʊl
Liszt lɪst
lit (*from* **light**) lɪt
litan|y ˈlɪt.ᵊn|.i **-ies** -iz
Litchfield ˈlɪtʃ.fiːld
litchi ˌlaɪˈtʃiː; ˈlaɪ.tʃiː, ˈliː- ⓤⓢ ˈliː.tʃiː **-s** -z
lite laɪt
liter ˈliː.təʳ ⓤⓢ -t̬ɚ **-s** -z
literacy ˈlɪt.ᵊr.ə.si, ˈ-rə.si ⓤⓢ ˈlɪt̬.ɚ.ə-
literal ˈlɪt.ᵊr.ᵊl, ˈ-rᵊl ⓤⓢ ˈlɪt̬.ɚ.ᵊl **-ly** -i **-ness** -nəs, -nɪs
literal|ism ˈlɪt.ᵊr.ᵊl|.ɪ.zᵊm, ˈ-rᵊl- ⓤⓢ ˈlɪt̬.ɚ.ᵊl- **-ist/s** -ɪst/s
literality ˌlɪt.ᵊrˈæl.ə.ti, -ɪ.ti ⓤⓢ -əˈræl.ə.t̬i
literar|y ˈlɪt.ᵊr.ᵊr|.i, ˈ-ᵊr|.i ⓤⓢ ˈlɪt̬.ə.rer- **-ily** -ᵊl.i, -ɪ.li **-iness** -ɪ.nəs, -ɪ.nɪs
literate ˈlɪt.ᵊr.ət, -ɪt, ˈ-rət, -rɪt ⓤⓢ ˈlɪt̬.ɚ.ət **-s** -s
literati ˌlɪt.ᵊrˈɑː.tiː ⓤⓢ ˌlɪt̬.əˈrɑː.t̬iː
literatim ˌlɪt.ᵊrˈɑː.tɪm ⓤⓢ ˌlɪt̬.əˈreɪ.t̬ɪm, -ˈrɑː-
literature ˈlɪt.rə.tʃəʳ, -rɪ-, ˈ-ᵊr.ə-, -ɪ- ⓤⓢ ˈlɪt̬.ɚ.ə.tʃɚ, -tʃʊr **-s** -z
litharge ˈlɪθ.ɑːdʒ ⓤⓢ -ɑːrdʒ; lɪˈθɑːrdʒ
lith|e laɪð **-er** -əʳ ⓤⓢ -ɚ **-est** -ɪst, -əst **-ely** -li **-eness** -nəs, -nɪs
Litheby ˈlɪð.ɪ.bi, ˈ-ə-
Litherland ˈlɪð.ə.lænd ⓤⓢ ˈ-ɚ-
lithesome ˈlaɪð.səm **-ness** -nəs, -nɪs
Lithgow ˈlɪθ.gəʊ ⓤⓢ -goʊ
lithia ˈlɪθ.i.ə
lithic ˈlɪθ.ɪk
lithium ˈlɪθ.i.əm
litho ˈlɪθ.əʊ, ˈlaɪ.θəʊ ⓤⓢ ˈlɪθ.oʊ **-s** -z
lithograph ˈlɪθ.ə*ʊ*.grɑːf, -græf ⓤⓢ -ə.græf, ˈ-oʊ- **-s** -s **-ing** -ɪŋ **-ed** -t
Note: In British printers' usage /ˈlaɪ.θə*ʊ*-/. So also with derived words (**lithographer,** etc.).
lithographer lɪˈθɒg.rə.fəʳ ⓤⓢ -ˈθɑː.grə.fɚ **-s** -z
lithographic ˌlɪθ.ə*ʊ*ˈgræf.ɪk ⓤⓢ -oʊˈ-, -əˈ- **-al** -ᵊl **-ally** -ᵊl.i, -li
lithography lɪˈθɒg.rə.fi ⓤⓢ -ˈθɑː.grə-
lithosphere ˈlɪθ.ə*ʊ*ˌsfɪəʳ ⓤⓢ -oʊˌsfɪr, -əˌ- **-s** -z
Lithuani|a ˌlɪθ.juˈeɪ.ni|.ə, -uˈ- ⓤⓢ -uˈeɪ-, -əˈweɪ- **-an/s** -ən/z
litigant ˈlɪt.ɪ.gənt, ˈ-ə- ⓤⓢ ˈlɪt̬- **-s** -s
liti|gate ˈlɪt.ɪ|.geɪt, ˈ-ə- ⓤⓢ ˈlɪt̬- **-gates** -geɪts **-gating** -geɪ.tɪŋ ⓤⓢ -geɪ.t̬ɪŋ **-gated** -geɪ.tɪd ⓤⓢ -geɪ.t̬ɪd
litigation ˌlɪt.ɪˈgeɪ.ʃᵊn, -əˈ- ⓤⓢ ˌlɪt̬- **-s** -z
litigious lɪˈtɪdʒ.əs, lə- ⓤⓢ lɪ- **-ly** -li **-ness** -nəs, -nɪs
litmus ˈlɪt.məs ˈ**litmus** ˌ**paper** ; ˈ**litmus** ˌ**test**
litotes laɪˈtəʊ.tiːz; ˈlaɪ.tə*ʊ*- ⓤⓢ ˈlaɪ.tə.tiːz; laɪˈtoʊ-; ˈlɪt.oʊ-
litre ˈliː.təʳ ⓤⓢ -t̬ɚ **-s** -z
Littel lɪˈtel
litt|er ˈlɪt|.əʳ ⓤⓢ ˈlɪt̬|.ɚ **-ers** -əz ⓤⓢ -ɚz **-ering** -ᵊr.ɪŋ **-ered** -əd ⓤⓢ -ɚd
litterbug ˈlɪt.ə.bʌg ⓤⓢ ˈlɪt̬.ɚ- **-s** -z
littl|e (L) ˈlɪt|.l̩ **-er** -əʳ ⓤⓢ -ɚ **-est** -ɪst, -əst **-eness** -nəs, -nɪs
Littleborough ˈlɪt.l̩.bᵊr.ə, -ˌbʌr.ə ⓤⓢ ˈlɪt̬.l̩.bɚ.oʊ
Littlechild ˈlɪt.l̩.tʃaɪld
little-englander ˌlɪt.l̩ˈɪŋ.glən.dəʳ ⓤⓢ ˌlɪt̬.l̩ˈɪŋ.glən.dɚ **-s** -z
little-go ˈlɪt.l̩.gəʊ ⓤⓢ ˈlɪt̬.l̩.goʊ **-es** -z
Littlehampton ˈlɪt.l̩ˌhæm*p*.tən, ˌlɪt.l̩ˈhæm*p*- ⓤⓢ ˌlɪt̬.l̩ˈ-, ˈlɪt̬.l̩ˌ-
Littlejohn ˈlɪt.l̩.dʒɒn ⓤⓢ ˈlɪt̬.l̩.dʒɑːn
littleneck ˈlɪt.l̩.nek ⓤⓢ ˈlɪt̬- **-s** -s
Littler ˈlɪt.l̩.əʳ, ˈ-ləʳ ⓤⓢ ˈlɪt.lɚ, ˈlɪt̬.l̩.ɚ
Littleton ˈlɪt.l̩.tᵊn ⓤⓢ ˈlɪt̬-
Litton ˈlɪt.ᵊn
littoral ˈlɪt.ᵊr.ᵊl ⓤⓢ ˈlɪt̬- **-s** -z
liturgic lɪˈtɜː.dʒɪk, lə- ⓤⓢ lɪˈtɜːr- **-s** -s **-al** -ᵊl **-ally** -ᵊl.i, -li
liturgist ˈlɪt.ə.dʒɪst, ˈ-ɜː- ⓤⓢ ˈlɪt̬.ɚ- **-s** -s
liturg|y ˈlɪt.ə.dʒ|i, ˈ-ɜː- ⓤⓢ ˈlɪt̬.ɚ- **-ies** -iz
livable ˈlɪv.ə.bl̩
live (*adj.*) laɪv
liv|e (*v.*) lɪv **-es** -z **-ing** -ɪŋ **-ed** -d **-er/s** -əʳ/z ⓤⓢ -ɚ/z ˌ**living** ˈ**will**
live-circuit ˌlaɪvˈsɜː.kɪt ⓤⓢ -ˈsɜːr- **-s** -s
live-in ˌlɪvˈɪn, ˈ-- ˌ**live-in** ˈ**lover**
livelihood ˈlaɪv.li.hʊd **-s** -z
livelong ˈlɪv.lɒŋ, ˈlaɪv- ⓤⓢ ˈlɪv.lɑːŋ, -lɔːŋ
livel|y (L) ˈlaɪv.l|i **-ier** -i.əʳ ⓤⓢ -i.ɚ **-iest** -i.ɪst, -i.əst **-iness** -ɪ.nəs, -ɪ.nɪs
liven ˈlaɪ.vᵊn **-s** -z **-ing** -ɪŋ, ˈlaɪv.nɪŋ **-ed** -d
Livens ˈlɪv.ᵊnz
liv|er ˈlɪv|.əʳ ⓤⓢ -ɚ **-ers** -əz ⓤⓢ -ɚz **-erish** -ᵊr.ɪʃ
Livermore ˈlɪv.ə.mɔːʳ ⓤⓢ -ɚ.mɔːr
Liverpool ˈlɪv.ə.puːl ⓤⓢ ˈ-ɚ-
Liverpudlian ˌlɪv.əˈpʌd.li.ən ⓤⓢ -ɚˈ- **-s** -z
Liversedge ˈlɪv.ə.sedʒ ⓤⓢ ˈ-ɚ-
liverwort ˈlɪv.ə.wɜːt ⓤⓢ -ɚ.wɜːrt, -wɔːrt **-s** -s
liverwurst ˈlɪv.ə.wɜːst ⓤⓢ -ɚ.wɜːrst
liver|y ˈlɪv.ᵊr|.i, ˈ-r|i **-ies** -iz **-ied** -id
livery|man ˈlɪv.ᵊr.i|.mən ⓤⓢ ˈ-ri-, -mæn **-men** -mən, -men
livery-stable ˈlɪv.ᵊr.iˌsteɪ.bl̩ ⓤⓢ ˈ-riˌ- **-s** -z
lives (*plur. of* **life**) laɪvz (*from* **live** *v.*) lɪvz
Livesey ˈlɪv.si, -zi
livestock ˈlaɪv.stɒk ⓤⓢ -stɑːk
live wire ˌlaɪvˈwaɪəʳ ⓤⓢ -ˈwaɪr, ˈ-- **-s** -z
Livia ˈlɪv.i.ə
livid ˈlɪv.ɪd **-ly** -li **-ness** -nəs, -nɪs
lividity lɪˈvɪd.ə.ti, -ɪ.ti ⓤⓢ -ə.t̬i
living ˈlɪv.ɪŋ **-s** -z
living-room ˈlɪv.ɪŋ.rʊm, -ruːm ⓤⓢ -ruːm, -rʊm **-s** -z
Livingston(e) ˈlɪv.ɪŋ.stᵊn
Livoni|a lɪˈvəʊ.ni|.ə ⓤⓢ -ˈvoʊ-, ˈ-njə **-an/s** -ən/z
Livorno lɪˈvɔː.nəʊ ⓤⓢ ləˈvɔːr.noʊ
Livy ˈlɪv.i
lixivi|ate lɪkˈsɪv.i|.eɪt **-ates** -eɪts **-ating** -eɪ.tɪŋ ⓤⓢ -eɪ.t̬ɪŋ **-ated** -eɪ.tɪd ⓤⓢ -eɪ.t̬ɪd
Liz lɪz
Liza ˈlaɪ.zə, ˈliː- ⓤⓢ ˈlaɪ-
lizard (L) ˈlɪz.əd ⓤⓢ -ɚd **-s** -z
Lizzie ˈlɪz.i
Ljubljana ˌlʊb. liˈɑː.nə *as if Slovene:* ˌljuːbˈljɑː.nə ⓤⓢ ˌluː.bliˈɑː.nə
llama (L) ˈlɑː.mə ⓤⓢ ˈlɑː-, ˈjɑː- **-s** -z
Llanberis *h*lænˈber.ɪs, θlæn- ⓤⓢ *h*læn-
Llandaff ˈ*h*læn.dəf, ˈθlæn-; lænˈdæf, θlæn- ⓤⓢ *h*lænˈdɑːf
Llandeilo *h*lænˈdaɪ.ləʊ, θlæn- ⓤⓢ *h*lænˈdaɪ.loʊ
Llandovery *h*lænˈdʌv.ᵊr.i, θlæn- ⓤⓢ *h*læn-
Llandrindod Wells *h*lænˌdrɪn.dɒdˈwelz, θlæn- ⓤⓢ *h*lænˌdrɪn.dɑːdˈ-
Llandudno *h*lænˈdɪd.nəʊ, θlæn-, -ˈdʌd- ⓤⓢ *h*lænˈdɪd.noʊ, -ˈdʌd-
Llanelli *h*lænˈeθ.li, ləˈneθ-, θlænˈeθ-, θləˈneθ- ⓤⓢ *h*lænˈel.i
Llanfair *h*lænˈfeəʳ, θlæn-, -ˈvaɪəʳ ⓤⓢ *h*lænˈfer
Llanfairfechan ˌ*h*læn.feəˈfek.ən, ˌθlæn-, -vaɪəˈ-, -ˈvek-, -ˈvex- ⓤⓢ ˌ*h*læn.ferˈfek-
Llanfair PG ˌ*h*læn.feəˌpiːˈdʒiː, ˌθlæn-, -vaɪəˌ- ⓤⓢ ˌ*h*læn.fer-
Note: This is the accepted abbreviation of the following entry.

Llanfairpwllgwyngyllgogerychwyrnd robwllllantysiliogogogoch ˌhlæn.feə.pʊl.ɡwɪŋ.ɡɪl.ɡəʊˌɡer.əˌkwɜːnˌdrəʊ.bʊlˌhlæn.dəˌsɪl.i.əʊˌɡəʊ.ɡəʊˈɡɒf, ˌθlæn-, ˌ-vaɪə-, -ˌθlæn- *as if Welsh:* -xwɜːn-, -ˈɡɒx (US) ˌhlæn.fer.pʊlˌɡwɪn.ɡɪl.ɡoʊˌɡer.ə.kwɜːrnˌdroʊ.bʊlˌhlæn.dəˌsɪl.i.oʊˌɡoʊ.ɡoʊˈɡɑːf
Llangattock hlænˈɡæt.ək, θlæn-, læŋ-, θlæŋ- (US) hlænˈɡæt̬.ək
Llangollen hlænˈɡɒθ.lən, θlæn-, læŋ-, θlæŋ-, -len (US) hlænˈɡɑː.lən
Llanharan hlænˈhær.ən, θlæn- (US) hlænˈhɑːr.ən
Llanrwst hlænˈruːst, θlæn- (US) hlæn-
Llantrisant hlænˈtrɪs.ənt
Llantwit Major ˌhlæn.twɪtˈmeɪ.dʒəʳ (US) -dʒɚ
Llanuwchllyn hlænˈjuː.klɪn, θlæn-, -ˈjuːx.lɪn (US) hlænˈjuː.klɪn
Llechwedd hlekˈwed
Llewel(l)yn *English name:* luːˈel.ɪn, ləˈwel- *Welsh name:* hluːˈel.ɪn, θluː- (US) hluː-
Lleyn hliːn, θliːn, hleɪn, θleɪn (US) hliːn, hleɪn
Lliw hluː
Lloyd lɔɪd
Lloyd Webber ˌlɔɪdˈweb.əʳ (US) -ɚ
Llyn Tegid ˌhlɪnˈteɡ.ɪd, ˌθlɪn- (US) ˌhlɪn-
Llywelyn hləˈwel.ɪn, θlə- (US) hlə-
lo ləʊ (US) loʊ
load ləʊd (US) loʊd **-s** -z **-ing** -ɪŋ **-ed** -ɪd **-er/s** -əʳ/z (US) -ɚ/z
loadstone ˈləʊd.stəʊn (US) ˈloʊd.stoʊn **-s** -z
loa|f (*n.*) ləʊ|f (US) loʊ|f **-ves** -vz
loaf (*v.*) ləʊf (US) loʊf **-s** -s **-ing** -ɪŋ **-ed** -t
loafer ˈləʊ.fəʳ (US) ˈloʊ.fɚ **-s** -z
loam ləʊm (US) loʊm
loam|y ˈləʊ.m|i (US) ˈloʊ.m|i **-ier** -i.əʳ (US) -i.ɚ **-iest** -i.ɪst, -i.əst **-iness** -ɪ.nəs, -ɪ.nɪs
loan ləʊn (US) loʊn **-s** -z **-ing** -ɪŋ **-ed** -d **-er/s** -əʳ/z (US) -ɚ/z ˈ**loan** ˌ**shark**
Loanhead ˌləʊnˈhed (US) ˌloʊn-
loanword ˈləʊn.wɜːd (US) ˈloʊn.wɜːrd **-s** -z
loath ləʊθ (US) loʊθ, loʊð **-ness** -nəs, -nɪs
loath|e ləʊð (US) loʊð **-es** -z **-ing/ly** -ɪŋ/li **-ed** -d
loathsome ˈləʊð.səm, ˈləʊθ- (US) ˈloʊð-, ˈloʊθ- **-ly** -li **-ness** -nəs, -nɪs
loaves (*plur. of* **loaf**) ləʊvz (US) loʊvz
lob (L) lɒb (US) lɑːb **-s** -z **-bing** -ɪŋ **-bed** -d **-ber/s** -əʳ/z (US) -ɚ/z
lobb|y ˈlɒb|.i (US) ˈlɑː.b|i **-ies** -iz **-ying** -i.ɪŋ **-ied** -id
lobbyist ˈlɒb.i.ɪst (US) ˈlɑː.bi- **-s** -s
lobe ləʊb (US) loʊb **-s** -z **-d** -d
lobelia ləʊˈbiː.li.ə (US) loʊˈbiːl.jə, -ˈbiː.li.ə **-s** -z
lobotomiz|e, -is|e ləʊˈbɒt.ə.maɪz (US) loʊˈbɑː.t̬ə-, lə- **-es** -ɪz **-ing** -ɪŋ **-ed** -d
lobotom|y ləʊˈbɒt.ə.m|i (US) loʊˈbɑː.t̬ə-, lə- **-ies** -iz
lobster ˈlɒb.stəʳ (US) ˈlɑːb.stɚ **-s** -z
lobular ˈlɒb.jə.ləʳ, -jʊ- (US) ˈlɑː.bjə.lɚ
lobule ˈlɒb.juːl (US) ˈlɑː.bjuːl **-s** -z
local ˈləʊ.kᵊl (US) ˈloʊ- **-s** -z **-ly** -i ˌ**local** ˈ**colo(u)r** ; ˈ**local** ˌ**time**, ˌ**local** ˈ**time**
locale ləʊˈkɑːl (US) loʊˈkæl **-s** -z
localism ˈləʊ.kᵊl.ɪ.zᵊm (US) ˈloʊ-
localit|y ləʊˈkæl.ə.t|i, -ɪ.t|i (US) loʊˈkæl.ə.t̬|i **-ies** -iz
localization, -isa- ˌləʊ.kᵊl.aɪˈzeɪ.ʃᵊn, -ɪˈ- (US) ˌloʊ.kᵊl.ɪˈ-
localiz|e, -is|e ˈləʊ.kᵊl.aɪz (US) ˈloʊ- **-es** -ɪz **-ing** -ɪŋ **-ed** -d **-er/s** -əʳ/z (US) -ɚ/z
Locarno ləʊˈkɑː.nəʊ, lɒkˈɑː- (US) loʊˈkɑːr.noʊ
loca|te ləʊˈkeɪ|t (US) ˈloʊ.keɪ|t, -ˈ- **-tes** -ts **-ting** -tɪŋ (US) -t̬ɪŋ **-ted** -tɪd (US) -t̬ɪd
location ləʊˈkeɪ.ʃᵊn (US) loʊ- **-s** -z
locative ˈlɒk.ə.tɪv (US) ˈlɑː.kə.t̬ɪv **-s** -z
loc. cit. ˌlɒkˈsɪt, ˌlɒk.əʊ.sɪˈtɑː.təʊ *old-fashioned:* ˌləʊ.kəʊ.sɪˈteɪ.təʊ (US) ˌlɑːkˈsɪt
loch (L) lɒk *as if Scots:* lɒx (US) lɑːk *as if Scots:* lɑːx **-s** -s
Lochaber lɒkˈɑː.bəʳ, -ˈæb.əʳ *as if Scots:* lɒx- (US) lɑːˈkɑː.bɚ *as if Scots:* -ˈxɑː-
Lochgelly lɒkˈɡel.i *as if Scots:* lɒx- (US) lɑːk- *as if Scots:* lɑːx-
Lochhead ˈlɒk.hed *as if Scots:* ˈlɒx- (US) ˈlɑːk- *as if Scots:* ˈlɑːx-
Lochiel lɒkˈiːl *as if Scots:* lɒx- (US) lɑːˈkiːl *as if Scots:* -ˈxiːl
Lochinvar ˌlɒk.ɪnˈvɑːʳ *as if Scots:* ˌlɒx- (US) ˌlɑː.kɪnˈvɑːr *as if Scots:* -xɪnˈ-
Lochleven lɒkˈliː.vᵊn *as if Scots:* lɒx- (US) lɑːk- *as if Scots:* lɑːx-
Lochnagar ˌlɒk.nəˈɡɑːʳ *as if Scots:* ˌlɒx- (US) ˌlɑːk.nəˈɡɑːr *as if Scots:* ˌlɑːx-
loci (*plur. of* **locus**) ˈləʊ.saɪ, -kaɪ, -kiː; ˈlɒk.aɪ, ˈlɒs- (US) ˈloʊ.saɪ, -kaɪ, -ki
lock (L) lɒk (US) lɑːk **-s** -s **-ing** -ɪŋ **-ed** -t ˌ**lock**, ˌ**stock, and** ˈ**barrel** ; **under** ˌ**lock and** ˈ**key**
Locke lɒk (US) lɑːk
locker (L) ˈlɒk.əʳ (US) ˈlɑː.kɚ **-s** -z ˈ**locker** ˌ**room**
Lockerbie ˈlɒk.ə.bi (US) ˈlɑː.kɚ-
locket ˈlɒk.ɪt (US) ˈlɑː.kɪt **-s** -s
Lockhart ˈlɒk.ət, -hɑːt (US) ˈlɑːk.hɑːrt, ˈlɑː.kɚt

Note: The Bruce-Lockhart family pronounce /ˈlɒk.ət/ (or in the Scottish manner /ˈlɒk.ərt/).

Lockheed ˈlɒk.hiːd (US) ˈlɑːk-
Lockie ˈlɒk.i (US) ˈlɑː.ki
lockjaw ˈlɒk.dʒɔː (US) ˈlɑːk.dʒɑː, -dʒɔː
lock-keeper ˈlɒkˌkiː.pəʳ (US) ˈlɑːkˌkiː.pɚ **-s** -z
locknut ˈlɒk.nʌt (US) ˈlɑːk- **-s** -s
lockout ˈlɒk.aʊt (US) ˈlɑːk- **-s** -s
Locksley ˈlɒk.sli (US) ˈlɑːk-
locksmith ˈlɒk.smɪθ (US) ˈlɑːk- **-s** -s
lockstep ˈlɒk.step (US) ˈlɑːk-
lockstitch ˈlɒk.stɪtʃ (US) ˈlɑːk- **-es** -ɪz
lock-up ˈlɒk.ʌp (US) ˈlɑːk- **-s** -s
Lockwood ˈlɒk.wʊd (US) ˈlɑːk-
Lockyer ˈlɒk.jəʳ (US) ˈlɑː.kjɚ
loco ˈləʊ.kəʊ (US) ˈloʊ.koʊ **-s** -z
locomotion ˌləʊ.kəˈməʊ.ʃᵊn (US) ˌloʊ.kəˈmoʊ-
locomotive ˌləʊ.kəˈməʊ.tɪv, ˈləʊ.kəˌməʊ- (US) ˌloʊ.kəˈmoʊ.t̬ɪv **-s** -z
locomotor ˌləʊ.kəˈməʊ.təʳ, ˈləʊ.kəˌməʊ- (US) ˌloʊ.kəˈmoʊ.t̬ɚ *stress shift, see compound:* ˌ**locomotor a**ˈ**taxia**
Locri|a ˈləʊ.kri|.ə (US) ˈloʊ- **-an/s** -ən/z
Locrine ˈlɒk.raɪn (US) ˈlɑː.kraɪn
Locris ˈləʊ.krɪs (US) ˈloʊ-
Loctite® ˈlɒk.taɪt (US) ˈlɑːk-
locum ˈləʊ.kəm (US) ˈloʊ- **-s** -z
locum-tenens ˌləʊ.kəmˈten.enz, -ˈtiː.nenz (US) ˌloʊ.kəmˈtiː.nenz, -ˈten.enz
locus ˈləʊ.kəs, ˈlɒk.əs (US) ˈloʊ.kəs **-es** -ɪz **loci** ˈləʊ.saɪ, -kaɪ, -kiː; ˈlɒk.aɪ, ˈlɒs- (US) ˈloʊ.saɪ
locus delicti ˌləʊ.kəs.delˈɪk.taɪ (US) ˌloʊ.kəs.dəˈlɪk.ti, -taɪ
locus in quo ˌləʊ.kəsˌɪnˈkwəʊ, -ˌɪŋˈ- (US) ˌloʊ.kəs.ɪnˈkwoʊ
locust ˈləʊ.kəst (US) ˈloʊ- **-s** -s
locution ləʊˈkjuː.ʃᵊn, lɒkˈjuː- (US) loʊˈkjuː- **-s** -z
locutionary ləʊˈkjuː.ʃᵊn.ᵊr.i, lɒkˈjuː- (US) loʊˈkjuː-
locutor|y ˈlɒk.jə.tᵊr|.i, -jʊ- (US) ˈlɑː.kjə.tɔːr- **-ies** -iz
lode ləʊd (US) loʊd **-s** -z
loden ˈləʊ.dᵊn (US) ˈloʊ-
lodestar ˈləʊd.stɑːʳ (US) ˈloʊd.stɑːr **-s** -z
lodestone ˈləʊd.stəʊn (US) ˈloʊd.stoʊn **-s** -z
lodg|e (L) lɒdʒ (US) lɑːdʒ **-es** -ɪz **-ing/s** -ɪŋ/z **-ed** -d
lodg(e)ment ˈlɒdʒ.mənt (US) ˈlɑːdʒ- **-s** -s
lodger ˈlɒdʒ.əʳ (US) ˈlɑː.dʒɚ **-s** -z
lodging-hou|se ˈlɒdʒ.ɪŋ.haʊ|s (US) ˈlɑː.dʒɪŋ- **-ses** -zɪz
Lodore ləʊˈdɔːʳ (US) loʊˈdɔːr
Łódź wʊdʒ, wuːdʒ (US) luːdʒ, lɑːdʒ, loʊdz, wuːdʒ
Loe luː

Loeb lɜːb, ləub (US) loub
loess 'ləu.es, -ɪs, -əs; lɜːs (US) 'lou.es, less, lɜːs
Loewe 'ləu.i (US) lou
Lofoten ləʊ'fəu.tᵊn; 'ləu.fəu- (US) 'lou.fu-, -fou-
loft lɒft (US) lɑːft **-s** -s **-ing** -ɪŋ **-ed** -ɪd **-er/s** -əʳ/z (US) -ɚ/z
Lofthouse 'lɒf.təs, 'lɒft.haus (US) 'lɑːf.təs, 'lɑːft.haus
Lofting 'lɒf.tɪŋ (US) 'lɑːf-
Loftus 'lɒf.təs (US) 'lɑːf-
loft|y 'lɒf.t|i (US) 'lɑːf- **-ier** -i.əʳ (US) -i.ɚ **-iest** -i.ɪst, -i.əst **-ily** -ɪ.li, -ᵊl.i **-iness** -ɪ.nəs, -ɪ.nɪs
log lɒg (US) lɑːg, lɔːg **-s** -z **-ging** -ɪŋ **-ged** -d **-ger/s** -əʳ/z (US) -ɚ/z **ˌlog 'cabin** ; **ˌsleep like a 'log**
-log -lɒg (US) -lɑːg, -lɔːg
Logan 'ləu.gən (US) 'lou-
loganberr|y 'ləu.gᵊn.bᵊr.|i, -gəm-, -ˌber- (US) 'lou.gənˌber- **-ies** -iz
logarithm 'lɒg.ᵊr.ɪ.ðᵊm, -θᵊm (US) 'lɑː.gɚ.ɪ.ðᵊm, 'lɔː- **-s** -z
logarithmic ˌlɒg.ᵊr'ɪð.mɪk, -'rɪθ- (US) ˌlɑː.gə'rɪθ-, ˌlɔː- **-al** -ᵊl **-ally** -ᵊl.i, -li
logbook 'lɒg.buk (US) 'lɑːg-, 'lɔːg- **-s** -s
logger 'lɒg.əʳ (US) 'lɑː.gɚ, 'lɔː- **-s** -z
loggerhead 'lɒg.ə.hed (US) 'lɑː.gɚ-, 'lɔː- **-s** -z
loggia 'ləu.dʒə, 'lɒdʒ.ə, -i.ə (US) 'lɑː.dʒə, -dʒi.ə **-s** -z
Logia 'lɒg.i.ə (US) 'lou.gi-, 'lɑː-
logic 'lɒdʒ.ɪk (US) 'lɑː.dʒɪk **-al** -ᵊl **-ally** -ᵊl.i, -li
logician lɒdʒ'ɪʃ.ᵊn (US) lou'dʒɪ- **-s** -z
Logie 'ləu.gi (US) 'lou-
-logist -lə.dʒɪst
Note: Suffix. Words containing **-logist** are normally stressed on the syllable preceding the suffix, e.g. **sociologist** /ˌsəu.ʃi'ɒl.ə.dʒɪst (US) ˌsou.si'ɑː.lə-/.
logistic lə'dʒɪs.tɪk, lɒdʒ'ɪs- (US) lou'dʒɪs- **-s** -s **-al** -ᵊl **-ally** -ᵊl.i, -li
logjam 'lɒg.dʒæm (US) 'lɑːg-, 'lɔːg- **-s** -z
logo 'ləu.gəu, 'lɒg.əu (US) 'lou.gou **-s** -z
logogram 'lɒg.əu.græm (US) 'lɑː.gou-, 'lɔː-, 'lou-, -gə- **-s** -z
logograph 'lɒg.əu.grɑːf, -græf (US) 'lɑː.gou.græf, 'lɔː-, 'lou-, -gə- **-s** -s
logographic ˌlɒg.əu'græf.ɪk (US) ˌlɑː.gou-, ˌlɔː-, ˌlou-, -gə- **-al** -ᵊl **-ally** -ᵊl.i, -li
Logos 'lɒg.ɒs, 'ləu.gɒs (US) 'lou.gous, 'lɔː-, 'lɑː-, -gɔːs, -gɑːs
logotype 'lɒg.əu.taɪp (US) 'lɑː.gə-, 'lɔː- **-s** -s
logroll 'lɒg.rəul (US) 'lɑːg.roul, 'lɔːg- **-s** -z **-ing** -ɪŋ **-ed** -d **-er/s** -əʳ/z (US) -ɚ/z

Logue ləug (US) loug
-logue -lɒg (US) -lɑːg, -lɔːg
-logy -lə.dʒi
Note: Suffix. Words containing **-logy** are normally stressed on the syllable preceding the suffix, e.g. **biology** /baɪ'ɒl.ə.dʒi (US) -'ɑː.lə-/.
Lohengrin 'ləu.ən.grɪn, -ɪn-, -əŋ-, -ɪŋ- (US) 'lou.ən-
loin lɔɪn **-s** -z
loin|cloth 'lɔɪn|.klɒθ (US) -klɑːθ **-cloths** -klɒθs (US) -klɑːθs
Loire lwɑːʳ (US) lwɑːr
Lois 'ləu.ɪs (US) 'lou-
loit|er 'lɔɪ.t|əʳ (US) -ţ|ɚ **-ers** -əz (US) -ɚz **-ering** -ᵊr.ɪŋ **-ered** -əd (US) -ɚd **-erer/s** -ᵊr.əʳ/z (US) -ɚ.ɚ/z
Loki 'ləu.ki (US) 'lou-
Lola 'ləu.lə (US) 'lou-
Lolita lɒl'iː.tə, ləu'liː- (US) lou'liː.ţə
loll lɒl (US) lɑːl **-s** -z **-ing** -ɪŋ **-ed** -d
Lollard 'lɒl.əd, -ɑːd (US) 'lɑː.lɚd **-s** -z
lollipop 'lɒl.i.pɒp (US) 'lɑː.li.pɑːp **-s** -s
lollop 'lɒl.əp (US) 'lɑː.ləp **-s** -s **-ing** -ɪŋ **-ed** -t
lollo rosso ˌlɒl.əu'rɒs.əu (US) ˌlɑː.lou'rɑː.sou, ˌlou-, '-rou-
loll|y 'lɒl|.i (US) 'lɑː.l|i **-ies** -iz
lollypop 'lɒl.i.pɒp (US) 'lɑː.li.pɑːp **-s** -s
Loman 'ləu.mən (US) 'lou-
Lomas 'ləu.mæs, -məs (US) 'lou.mæs
Lomax 'ləu.mæks, -məks (US) 'lou.mæks
Lombard 'lɒm.bəd, -bɑːd (US) 'lɑːm.bɑːrd, -bɚd, 'lʌm- **-s** -z
Lombardy 'lɒm.bə.di (US) 'lɑːm.bɚ-, 'lʌm-
Lombok 'lɒm.bɒk (US) 'lɑːm.bɑːk
Lomé 'ləu.meɪ (US) lou'meɪ
Lomond 'ləu.mənd (US) 'lou-
Londesborough 'lɒnz.bᵊr.ə (US) 'lɑːndz.bɚ.ou
London 'lʌn.dən **-er/s** -əʳ/z (US) -ɚ/z **ˌLondon 'Bridge** ; **ˌLondon 'pride** ; **ˌLondon 'weighting**
Londonderry *place:* 'lʌn.dən.der.i, ˌlʌn.dən'der- (US) 'lʌn.dən.der- *Lord:* 'lʌn.dən.dᵊr.i (US) -der-
lone ləun (US) loun
lonel|y 'ləun.l|i (US) 'loun- **-ier** -i.əʳ (US) -i.ɚ **-iest** -i.ɪst, -i.əst **-iness** -ɪ.nəs, -ɪ.nɪs **ˌlonely 'hearts**
loner 'ləu.nəʳ (US) 'lou.nɚ **-s** -z
lonesome 'ləun.səm (US) 'loun- **-ness** -nəs, -nɪs
long **(L)** *(n. adj.)* lɒŋ (US) lɑːŋ, lɔːŋ **-er** -gəʳ (US) -gɚ **-est** -gɪst, -gəst **ˌLong 'Island** ; **'long ˌjump**; **'long ˌshot**; **'long ˌwave**; **ˌlong week'end** (US) **ˌlong 'weekend**; **the ˌlong and the 'short of it**; **in the 'long ˌrun**

long *(v.)* lɒŋ (US) lɑːŋ, lɔːŋ **-s** -z **-ing/ly** -ɪŋ/li **-ed** -d **-er/s** -əʳ/z (US) -ɚ/z
Longannet lɒŋ'æn.ɪt, -ət (US) lɑːŋ-, lɔːŋ-
longboat 'lɒŋ.bəut (US) 'lɑːŋ.bout, 'lɔːŋ- **-s** -s
longbow **(L)** 'lɒŋ.bəu (US) 'lɑːŋ.bou, 'lɔːŋ- **-s** -z
Longdendale 'lɒŋ.ən.deɪl (US) 'lɑːŋ-, 'lɔːŋ-
long-distance ˌlɒŋ'dɪs.tᵊnts (US) ˌlɑːŋ-, ˌlɔːŋ- *stress shift:* ˌlong-distance 'driver
long-drawn-out ˌlɒŋ.drɔːn'aut (US) ˌlɑːŋ.drɑːn'-, ˌlɔːŋ-, -drɔːn'- *stress shift:* ˌlong-drawn-out 'sigh
longeron 'lɒn.dʒᵊr.ᵊn (US) 'lɑːn.dʒə.rɑːn, -dʒɚ.ən **-s** -z
longevity lɒn'dʒev.ə.ti, 'lɒŋ-, -ɪ.ti (US) lɑːn'dʒev.ə.ţi, lɑːŋ-, lɔːŋ-
Longfellow 'lɒŋˌfel.əu (US) 'lɑːŋˌfel.ou, 'lɔːŋ-
Longfield 'lɒŋ.fiːld (US) 'lɑːŋ-, 'lɔːŋ-
Longford 'lɒŋ.fəd (US) 'lɑːŋ.fɚd, 'lɔːŋ-
longhand 'lɒŋ.hænd (US) 'lɑːŋ-, 'lɔːŋ-
long-haul ˌlɒŋ'hɔːl, '-- (US) ˌlɑːŋ'hɑːl, ˌlɔːŋ-, -hɔːl, '-- *stress shift:* ˌlong-haul 'jet
longheaded ˌlɒŋ'hed.ɪd (US) ˌlɑːŋ-, ˌlɔːŋ- *stress shift:* ˌlongheaded 'elder
longhorn 'lɒŋ.hɔːn (US) 'lɑːŋ.hɔːrn, 'lɔːŋ- **-s** -z
Longines® 'lɒn.*dʒ*iːn, -'- (US) ˌlɑːn'dʒiːn
longing 'lɒŋ.ɪŋ (US) 'lɑːŋ-, 'lɔːŋ- **-s** -z
Longinus lɒn'dʒaɪ.nəs, lɒŋ'giː- (US) lɑːn'dʒaɪ-
longish 'lɒŋ.ɪʃ (US) 'lɑːŋ-, 'lɔːŋ-
longitude 'lɒn.dʒɪ.tjuːd, 'lɒŋ.gɪ- (US) 'lɑːn.dʒə.tuːd, -tjuːd **-s** -z
longitudinal ˌlɒn.dʒɪ'tjuː.dɪ.nᵊl, -dʒə'-, ˌlɒŋ.gɪ'-, -gə'-, -də- (US) ˌlɑːn.dʒə'tuː-, -'tjuː- **-ly** -i
long johns 'lɒŋ.dʒɒnz, ˌ-'- (US) 'lɑːŋ.dʒɑːnz, 'lɔːŋ-, ˌ-'-
Longland 'lɒŋ.lənd (US) 'lɑːŋ-, 'lɔːŋ-
Longleat 'lɒŋ.liːt (US) 'lɑːŋ-, 'lɔːŋ-
long-lived ˌlɒŋ'lɪvd (US) ˌlɑːŋ-, ˌlɔːŋ-, -laɪvd *stress shift:* ˌlong-lived 'person
Longman 'lɒŋ.mən (US) 'lɑːŋ-, 'lɔːŋ-
long-range ˌlɒŋ'reɪndʒ (US) ˌlɑːŋ-, ˌlɔːŋ- *stress shift:* ˌlong-range 'missile
Longridge 'lɒŋ.rɪdʒ (US) 'lɑːŋ-, 'lɔːŋ-
longshore|man 'lɒŋ.ʃɔː|.mən (US) 'lɑːŋ.ʃɔːr-, 'lɔːŋ- **-men** -mən, -men
long-sighted ˌlɒŋ'saɪ.tɪd (US) ˌlɑːŋ'saɪ.ţɪd, ˌlɔːŋ-, '-ˌ-- **-ness** -nəs, -nɪs *stress shift, British only:* ˌlong-sighted 'person
Longstaff 'lɒŋ.stɑːf (US) 'lɑːŋ.stæf, 'lɔːŋ-
Longstreet 'lɒŋ.striːt (US) 'lɑːŋ-, 'lɔːŋ-
long-suffering ˌlɒŋ'sʌf.ᵊr.ɪŋ (US) ˌlɑːŋ-, ˌlɔːŋ- *stress shift:* ˌlong-suffering 'family

Longton 'lɒŋ*k*.tən ⓊⓈ 'lɑːŋ-, 'lɔːŋ-
Longtown 'lɒŋ.taʊn ⓊⓈ 'lɑːŋ-, 'lɔːŋ-
longueur lɔ̃ːŋ'gɜːr, lɔːŋ-, lɒŋ- ⓊⓈ lɔːŋ'gɜːr **-s** -z
Longus 'lɒŋ.gəs ⓊⓈ 'lɑːŋ-, 'lɔːŋ-
longways 'lɒŋ.weɪz ⓊⓈ 'lɑːŋ-, 'lɔːŋ-
long-winded ˌlɒŋ'wɪn.dɪd ⓊⓈ ˌlɑːŋ-, ˌlɔːŋ- **-ness** -nəs, -nɪs *stress shift:* ˌlong-winded 'story
longwise 'lɒŋ.waɪz ⓊⓈ 'lɑːŋ-, 'lɔːŋ-
lonicera lɒn'ɪs.ər.ə, lə'nɪs- ⓊⓈ loʊ-; ˌlɑː.nɪ'sɪr.ə **-s** -z
Lonrho® 'lɒn.rəʊ, 'lʌn- ⓊⓈ 'lɑːn.roʊ
Lonsdale 'lɒnz.deɪl ⓊⓈ 'lɑːnz-
loo luː **-s** -z
loob|y 'luː.b|i **-ies** -iz
Looe luː
loofah 'luː.fə **-s** -z
look lʊk **-s** -s **-ing** -ɪŋ **-ed** -t **-er/s** -ər/z ⓊⓈ -ɚ/z
lookalike 'lʊk.ə.laɪk **-s** -s
looker-on ˌlʊk.ər'ɒn ⓊⓈ -kɚ'ɑːn **lookers-on** ˌlʊk.əz'ɒn ⓊⓈ -kɚz'ɑːn
looking-glass 'lʊk.ɪŋ.glɑːs ⓊⓈ -glæs **-es** -ɪz
lookout 'lʊk.aʊt **-s** -s
look-see 'lʊk.siː
loom luːm **-s** -z **-ing** -ɪŋ **-ed** -d
loon luːn **-s** -z
loon|y 'luː.n|i **-ies** -iz **'loony ˌbin** ; ˌ**loony 'left**
loop luːp **-s** -s **-ing** -ɪŋ **-ed** -t
loophol|e 'luːp.həʊl ⓊⓈ -hoʊl **-es** -z **-ing** -ɪŋ **-ed** -d
loop|y 'luː.p|i **-ier** -i.ər ⓊⓈ -i.ɚ **-iest** -i.ɪst, -i.əst
Loos ləʊs, luːs ⓊⓈ luːs
loos|e luːs **-er** -ər ⓊⓈ -ɚ **-est** -ɪst, -əst **-eness** -nəs, -nɪs **-es** -ɪz **-ing** -ɪŋ **-ed** -t ˌ**let someone 'loose on**
looseleaf ˌluːs'liːf *stress shift:* ˌlooseleaf 'folder
loosely 'luː.sli
loosen 'luː.sən **-s** -z **-ing** -ɪŋ, 'luːs.nɪŋ **-ed** -d
loosestrife 'luːs.straɪf
loot luːt **-s** -s **-ing** -ɪŋ ⓊⓈ 'luː.t̬ɪŋ **-ed** -ɪd ⓊⓈ 'luː.t̬ɪd **-er/s** -ər/z ⓊⓈ 'luː.t̬ɚ/z
lop lɒp ⓊⓈ lɑːp **-s** -s **-ping** -ɪŋ **-ped** -t
lop|e ləʊp ⓊⓈ loʊp **-es** -s **-ing** -ɪŋ **-ed** -t
lop-eared ˌlɒp'ɪəd ⓊⓈ 'lɑːp.ɪrd *stress shift, British only:* ˌlop-eared 'rabbit
Lopez 'ləʊ.pez ⓊⓈ 'loʊ-
lopping 'lɒp.ɪŋ ⓊⓈ 'lɑː.pɪŋ **-s** -z
lop-sided ˌlɒp'saɪ.dɪd ⓊⓈ ˌlɑːp- **-ness** -nəs, -nɪs *stress shift:* ˌlop-sided 'smile
loquacious ləʊ'kweɪ.ʃəs, lɒk'weɪ- ⓊⓈ loʊ'kweɪ- **-ly** -li **-ness** -nəs, -nɪs
loquacity ləʊ'kwæs.ə.ti, lɒk'wæs-, -ɪ.ti ⓊⓈ loʊ'kwæs.ə.t̬i
loquat 'ləʊ.kwɒt, 'lɒk.wɒt, -wæt ⓊⓈ 'loʊ.kwɑːt, -kwæt **-s** -s
lor lɔːr ⓊⓈ lɔːr
Loraine lə'reɪn, lɒr'eɪn ⓊⓈ lə'reɪn
Loram 'lɔː.rəm ⓊⓈ 'lɔːr.əm
Lorca 'lɔː.kə ⓊⓈ 'lɔːr-
lord (L) lɔːd ⓊⓈ lɔːrd **-s** -z **-ing** -ɪŋ **-ed** -ɪd
Note: British lawyers addressing a judge in court sometimes pronounce **my lord** as /mɪ'lʌd/ instead of the normal /mɪ'lɔːd/. ˌ**Lord's 'Prayer**
lordling 'lɔːd.lɪŋ ⓊⓈ 'lɔːrd- **-s** -z
lordl|y 'lɔːd.l|i ⓊⓈ 'lɔːrd- **-ier** -i.ər ⓊⓈ -i.ɚ **-iest** -i.ɪst, -i.əst **-iness** -ɪ.nəs, -ɪ.nɪs
lordship (L) 'lɔːd.ʃɪp ⓊⓈ 'lɔːrd- **-s** -s
lore lɔːr ⓊⓈ lɔːr
L'Oréal® 'lɒr.i.æl ⓊⓈ ˌlɔːr.i'æl
Lorelei 'lɔː.rə.laɪ, 'lɒr.ə- ⓊⓈ 'lɔːr-
Loren 'lɔː.ren, -rən; lɔː'ren ⓊⓈ 'lɔːr.ən
Lorenzo lə'ren.zəʊ, lɒr'en- ⓊⓈ lə'ren.zoʊ, lɔː-
Loretto lə'ret.əʊ, lɔː- ⓊⓈ lə'ret̬.oʊ, lɔː-
lorgnette lɔː'njet ⓊⓈ lɔːr- **-s** -s
Lori(e) 'lɒr.i ⓊⓈ 'lɔːr-
lorikeet 'lɒr.ɪ.kiːt, '-ə- ⓊⓈ 'lɔːr.ɪ- **-s** -s
lorimer (L) 'lɒr.ɪ.mər ⓊⓈ 'lɔːr.ɪ.mɚ **-s** -z
loris 'lɔː.rɪs ⓊⓈ 'lɔːr.ɪs **-es** -ɪz
lorn lɔːn ⓊⓈ lɔːrn
Lorna 'lɔː.nə ⓊⓈ 'lɔːr-
Lorne lɔːn ⓊⓈ lɔːrn
Lorraine lə'reɪn, lɒr'eɪn ⓊⓈ lə'reɪn, lɔː-
lorr|y 'lɒr|.i ⓊⓈ 'lɔːr- **-ies** -iz
lor|y 'lɔː.r|i ⓊⓈ 'lɔːr|.i **-ies** -iz
losable 'luː.zə.bl̩
Los Alamos ˌlɒs'æl.ə.mɒs, -məʊs ⓊⓈ ˌlɑːs'æl.ə.moʊs, ˌlɔːs-
Los Angeles lɒs'æn.*dʒ*ɪ.liːz, -*dʒ*ə-, -lɪz, -lɪs ⓊⓈ lɑːs'æn.dʒə.ləs, lɔːs-, -gə-, -liːz
los|e luːz **-es** -ɪz **-ing** -ɪŋ **lost** lɒst ⓊⓈ lɑːst
loser 'luː.zər ⓊⓈ -zɚ **-s** -z
Losey 'ləʊ.zi ⓊⓈ 'loʊ-
loss lɒs ⓊⓈ lɑːs **-es** -ɪz **'loss ˌleader**
Lossiemouth ˌlɒs.i'maʊθ, 'lɒs.i.maʊθ ⓊⓈ ˌlɑː.si'-
lost (*from* **lose**) lɒst ⓊⓈ lɑːst ˌ**lost 'property**
Lostwithiel lɒs*t*'wɪθ.i.əl, -'wɪð- ⓊⓈ lɑːs*t*-
lot (L) lɒt ⓊⓈ lɑːt **-s** -s **-ting** -ɪŋ ⓊⓈ 'lɑː.t̬ɪŋ **-ted** -ɪd ⓊⓈ 'lɑː.t̬ɪd
loth ləʊθ ⓊⓈ loʊθ, loʊð
Lothair ləʊ'θeər ⓊⓈ loʊ'θer
Lothario ləʊ'θɑː.ri.əʊ, lɒθ'ɑː-, -'eə- ⓊⓈ loʊ'θer.i.oʊ, -'θɑːr-
Lothbury 'ləʊθ.bər.i, 'lɒθ- ⓊⓈ 'loʊθ.ber-, 'lɑːθ-, -bɚ-
Lothian 'ləʊ.ði.ən ⓊⓈ 'loʊ-
loti 'ləʊ.ti ⓊⓈ 'loʊ-
lotion 'ləʊ.ʃən ⓊⓈ 'loʊ- **-s** -z
lotta 'lɒt.ə ⓊⓈ 'lɑː.t̬ə
lotter|y 'lɒt.ər|.i ⓊⓈ 'lɑː.t̬ɚ- **-ies** -iz
Lottie 'lɒt.i ⓊⓈ 'lɑː.t̬i
lotto (L) 'lɒt.əʊ ⓊⓈ 'lɑː.t̬oʊ
lotus 'ləʊ.təs ⓊⓈ 'loʊ.t̬əs **-es** -ɪz **'lotus poˌsition**
Lou luː
louche luːʃ **-ly** -li **-ness** -nəs, -nɪs
loud laʊd **-er** -ər ⓊⓈ -ɚ **-est** -ɪst, -əst **-ly** -li **-ness** -nəs, -nɪs
loud-hailer ˌlaʊd'heɪ.lər ⓊⓈ -lɚ **-s** -z
loud|mouth 'laʊd|.maʊθ **-mouths** -maʊðz **-mouthed** -maʊθt
Loudo(u)n 'laʊ.dən
loudspeaker ˌlaʊd'spiː.kər ⓊⓈ 'laʊdˌspiː.kɚ **-s** -z
Loudwater 'laʊdˌwɔː.tər ⓊⓈ -ˌwɑː.t̬ɚ, -ˌwɔː-
lough *lake:* lɒk *as if Irish:* lɒx ⓊⓈ lɑːk *as if Irish:* lɑːx **-s** -s
Lough *surname:* lʌf, ləʊ ⓊⓈ lʌf, loʊ
Loughborough 'lʌf.bər.ə ⓊⓈ -bɚ.oʊ, -ə
Loughlin 'lɒk.lɪn, -lən *as if Irish:* 'lɒx- ⓊⓈ 'lɑːk-, lɑːf- *as if Irish:* 'lɑːx-
Loughman 'lʌf.mən
Loughran *as if Irish:* 'lɒx.rən ⓊⓈ *as if Irish:* 'lɑːx-
Loughrea lɒk'reɪ *as if Irish:* lɒx- ⓊⓈ lɑːk- *as if Irish:* lɑːx-
Loughrey *as if Irish:* 'lɒx.ri ⓊⓈ 'lɑːk-, 'lɑːf- *as if Irish:* 'lɑːx-
Loughton 'laʊ.tən
Louie 'luː.i
Louis *English name:* 'luː.i, -ɪs *French name:* 'luː.i, -iː, lu'i
Louisa lu'iː.zə
Louisburg 'luː.ɪs.bɜːg ⓊⓈ -bɜːrg
louis-d'or ˌluː.i'dɔːr ⓊⓈ -'dɔːr **-s** -z
Louise lu'iːz
Louisiana luˌiː.zi'æn.ə, -'ɑː.nə; ˌluː.ɪ.zi'- ⓊⓈ luˌiː.zi'æn.ə; ˌluː.zi'-
Louis Quatorze ˌluː.i.kæt'ɔːz ⓊⓈ -'ɔːrz
Louis Quinze ˌluː.i'kæ̃nz
Louisville 'luː.i.vɪl ⓊⓈ -ɪ.vɪl *locally:* 'luː.ə.vəl
loung|e laʊndʒ **-es** -ɪz **-ing** -ɪŋ **-ed** -d **-er/s** -ər/z ⓊⓈ -ɚ/z **'lounge ˌbar** ; **'lounge ˌlizard** ; **'lounge ˌsuit**
lounge lizard 'laʊndʒˌlɪz.əd ⓊⓈ -ɚd **-s** -z
Lounsbury 'laʊnz.bər.i ⓊⓈ -ber-, -bɚ-
lour laʊər ⓊⓈ laʊr **-s** -z **-ing** -ɪŋ **-ed** -d
Lourdes lʊəd, lʊədz, lɔːdz ⓊⓈ lʊrd, lʊrdz
Lourenço Marques ləˌren*t*.səʊ'mɑː.kez, -kes ⓊⓈ -soʊ'mɑːr.kes
louse (*n.*) laʊs **lice** laɪs

lous|e (*v.*) laʊz, laʊs (US) laʊs, laʊz **-es** -ɪz **-ing** -ɪŋ **-ed** -d, laʊst
lous|y 'laʊ.z|i **-ier** -i.əʳ (US) -i.ɚ **-iest** -i.ɪst, -i.əst **-ily** -ɪ.li, -əl.i **-iness** -ɪ.nəs, -ɪ.nɪs
lout laʊt **-s** -s
Louth *in Ireland:* laʊð *in Lincolnshire:* laʊθ
loutish 'laʊ.tɪʃ (US) -t̬ɪʃ **-ly** -li **-ness** -nəs, -nɪs
Louvain 'luː.væ̃ŋ, -veɪn; lʊ'væ̃ŋ, -'væn (US) luː'væn, -'væ̃n
louver, louvre 'luː.vəʳ (US) -vɚ **-s** -z
Louvre 'luː.vrə, 'luː.vəʳ (US) -vrə, -vɚ; luːv
lovab|le 'lʌv.ə.b|l **-ly** -li **-leness** -l.nəs, -nɪs
lovage 'lʌv.ɪdʒ
Lovat 'lʌv.ət
lov|e (L) lʌv **-es** -z **-ing/ly** -ɪŋ/li **-ed** -d **'love af,fair ; 'love ,letter ; ,make 'love ; 'love song ; 'love ,story ; not for ,love nor 'money**
loveab|le 'lʌv.ə.b|l **-ly** -li **-leness** -l.nəs, -nɪs
lovebird 'lʌv.bɜːd (US) -bɜːrd **-s** -z
lovebite 'lʌv.baɪt **-s** -s
love|-child 'lʌv|.tʃaɪld **-children** -,tʃɪl.drən
Loveday 'lʌv.deɪ
Lovejoy 'lʌv.dʒɔɪ
Lovel 'lʌv.əl
Lovelace 'lʌv.leɪs
loveless 'lʌv.ləs, -lɪs **-ly** -li **-ness** -nəs, -nɪs
Lovell 'lʌv.əl
lovelorn 'lʌv.lɔːn (US) -lɔːrn
lovel|y 'lʌv.l|i **-ies** -i.z **-ier** -i.əʳ (US) -i.ɚ **-iest** -i.ɪst, -i.əst **-iness** -ɪ.nəs, -ɪ.nɪs
lovemaking 'lʌv,meɪ.kɪŋ
love-match 'lʌv.mætʃ **-es** -ɪz
love-potion 'lʌv,pəʊ.ʃən (US) -,poʊ- **-s** -z
lover 'lʌv.əʳ (US) -ɚ **-s** -z
Loveridge 'lʌv.rɪdʒ, -ər.ɪdʒ
lovesick 'lʌv.sɪk **-ness** -nəs, -nɪs
love-stor|y 'lʌv,stɔː.r|i (US) -,stɔːr|.i **-ies** -ɪz
Lovett 'lʌv.ɪt
lovey-dovey ,lʌv.i'dʌv.i, 'lʌv.i,dʌv-
Loveys 'lʌv.ɪs
Lovibond 'lʌv.ɪ.bɒnd (US) -bɑːnd
Lovick 'lʌv.ɪk
loving-cup 'lʌv.ɪŋ.kʌp **-s** -s
low (L) ləʊ (US) loʊ **-er** -əʳ (US) -ɚ **-est** -ɪst, -əst **-ness** -nəs, -nɪs **-s** -z **-ing** -ɪŋ **-ed** -d **,Low 'Church ; ,low 'profile ; 'low ,season**
lowborn ,ləʊ'bɔːn (US) 'loʊ.bɔːrn *stress shift, British only:* ,lowborn 'person
lowbred ,ləʊ'bred (US) 'loʊ.bred *stress shift, British only:* ,lowbred 'person
lowbrow 'ləʊ.braʊ (US) 'loʊ-
lowdown (*n.*) 'ləʊ.daʊn (US) 'loʊ-
low-down (*adj.*) ,ləʊ'daʊn (US) ,loʊ- *stress shift:* ,low-down 'scoundrel
Lowe ləʊ (US) loʊ
Lowell 'ləʊ.əl (US) 'loʊ-
low|er (*v. adj.*) *cause to descend:* 'ləʊ|.əʳ (US) 'loʊ|.ɚ **-ers** -əz, -ɚs **-ering** -ər.ɪŋ **-ered** -əd (US) -ɚd
lower (*v.*) *look threatening:* laʊəʳ (US) laʊr, laʊɚ **-s** -z **-ing/ly** -ɪŋ/li **-ed** -d
lower-case ,ləʊ.ə'keɪs (US) ,loʊ.ɚ'- *stress shift:* ,lower-case 'letter
lowermost 'ləʊ.ə.məʊst, -məst (US) 'loʊ.ɚ.moʊst
Lowery 'laʊə.ri (US) 'laʊ.ri
Lowes ləʊz (US) loʊz
Lowestoft 'ləʊ.stɒft, 'ləʊ.ɪ-, -stəft (US) 'loʊ.stɑːft, 'loʊ.ɪ- *locally:* 'ləʊ.stəf (US) 'loʊ-
Lowick 'ləʊ.ɪk (US) 'loʊ-
Lowis 'laʊ.ɪs
lowkey ,ləʊ'kiː (US) ,loʊ-
lowland (L) 'ləʊ.lənd (US) 'loʊ- **-s** -z **-er/s** -əʳ/z (US) -ɚ/z
low-life 'ləʊ.laɪf, ,-'- (US) 'loʊ-, ,-'- **-s** -s
low-loader ,ləʊ'ləʊ.dəʳ (US) 'loʊ,loʊ.dɚ **-s** -z
lowl|y 'ləʊ.l|i (US) 'loʊ- **-ier** -i.əʳ (US) -i.ɚ **-iest** -i.ɪst, -i.əst **-iness** -ɪ.nəs, -ɪ.nɪs
low-lying ,ləʊ'laɪ.ɪŋ (US) ,loʊ- *stress shift:* ,low-lying 'cloud
Lowndes laʊndz
low-necked ,ləʊ'nekt (US) ,loʊ- *stress shift:* ,low-necked 'sweater
Lowood 'ləʊ.wʊd (US) 'loʊ-
Lowries 'laʊə.rɪz, 'laʊ- (US) 'laʊ-
Lowry 'laʊə.ri, 'laʊ- (US) 'laʊ-
Lowsley 'ləʊz.li (US) 'loʊz-
Lowson 'ləʊ.sən, 'laʊ- (US) 'loʊ-, 'laʊ-
Lowth laʊθ
Lowther 'laʊ.ðəʳ (US) -ðɚ
Lowton 'ləʊ.tən (US) 'loʊ-
Lowville 'laʊ.vɪl
lox lɒks (US) lɑːks
Loxley 'lɒk.sli (US) 'lɑːk-
loyal lɔɪəl (US) 'lɔɪ.əl **-ly** -i
loyalist 'lɔɪə.lɪst (US) 'lɔɪ.ə.lɪst **-s** -s
loyalt|y 'lɔɪəl.t|i (US) 'lɔɪ.əl.t̬|i **-ies** -iz
Loyd lɔɪd
Loyola 'lɔɪ.əʊ.lə; lɔɪ'əʊ- (US) lɔɪ'oʊ-
lozeng|e 'lɒz.ɪndʒ, -əndʒ (US) 'lɑː.zəndʒ **-es** -ɪz
LP ,el'piː
L-plate 'el.pleɪt **-s** -s
LPN ,el.piː'en
LSD ,el.es'diː
LSE ,el.es'iː
Ltd. 'lɪm.ɪ.tɪd, '-ə- (US) -ə.t̬ɪd
Luanda lu'æn.də (US) -'æn-, -'ɑːn-
luau 'luː.aʊ
Lubavitcher 'luː.bə.vɪ.tʃəʳ (US) -tʃɚ **-s** -z
lubber 'lʌb.əʳ (US) -ɚ **-s** -z
Lubbock 'lʌb.ək
lube luːb **-s** -z
Lübeck 'luː.bek, 'ljuː- (US) 'luː-
Lubin 'luː.bɪn
Lublin 'luː.blɪn
lubricant 'luː.brɪ.kənt, 'ljuː-, -brə- (US) 'luː- **-s** -s
lubri|cate 'luː.brɪ|.keɪt, 'ljuː-, -brə- (US) 'luː- **-cates** -keɪts **-cating** -keɪ.tɪŋ (US) -keɪ.t̬ɪŋ **-cated** -keɪ.tɪd (US) -keɪ.t̬ɪd **-cator/s** -keɪ.təʳ/z (US) -keɪ.t̬ɚ/z
lubrication ,luː.brɪ'keɪ.ʃən, ,ljuː-, -brə'- (US) ,luː- **-s** -z
lubricious luː'brɪʃ.əs, ljuː- (US) luː- **-ly** -li **-ness** -nəs, -nɪs
lubricity luː'brɪs.ə.ti, ljuː-, -ɪ.ti (US) luː'brɪs.ə.t̬i
Lubumbashi ,luː.bʊm'bæʃ.i (US) -'bɑː.ʃi
Luca 'luː.kə
Lucan 'luː.kən, 'ljuː- (US) 'luː-
Lucania luː'keɪ.ni.ə, ljuː- (US) luː-
lucarne luː'kɑːn, ljuː- (US) luː'kɑːrn **-s** -z
Lucas 'luː.kəs
Luce luːs
lucen|t 'luː.sən|t, 'ljuː- (US) 'luː- **-cy** -*t*.si
lucern(e) luː'sɜːn, ljuː-, '-- (US) luː'sɜːrn
Lucerne luː'sɜːn, ljuː- (US) luː'sɜːrn
luces (*plur. of* **lux**) 'luː.siːz
Lucia 'luː.si.ə, '-ʃə; luː'tʃiː.ə
Lucian 'luː.si.ən, '-ʃən, -ʃi.ən (US) 'luː.ʃən
Luciana ,luː.si'ɑː.nə, ,ljuː- (US) ,luː-, -'æn.ə
Lucianus ,luː.si'ɑː.nəs, ,ljuː-, -'eɪ- (US) ,luː.si'ɑː-
lucid 'luː.sɪd, 'ljuː- (US) 'luː- **-ly** -li **-ness** -nəs, -nɪs
lucidity luː'sɪd.ə.ti, ljuː-, -ɪ.ti (US) luː'sɪd.ə.t̬i
Lucie 'luː.si, 'ljuː- (US) 'luː-
Lucien 'luː.si.ən, 'ljuː- (US) 'luː-
Lucie-Smith ,luː.si'smɪθ, ,ljuː- (US) ,luː-
lucifer (L) 'luː.sɪ.fəʳ, 'ljuː-, -sə- (US) 'luː.sə.fɚ **-s** -z
Lucilius luː'sɪl.i.əs, ljuː- (US) luː-
Lucille luː'siːl
Lucina luː'siː.nə, ljuː-, -'saɪ-, -'tʃiː- (US) luː'saɪ-, -'siː-
Lucinda luː'sɪn.də, ljuː- (US) luː-
Lucite® 'luː.saɪt, 'ljuː- (US) 'luː-
Lucius 'luː.si.əs, 'ljuː-, '-ʃəs, -ʃi.əs (US) 'luː.ʃəs
luck (L) lʌk **to be ,down on one's 'luck**
luckless 'lʌk.ləs, -lɪs **-ly** -li **-ness** -nəs, -nɪs
Lucknow 'lʌk.naʊ, ,-'- (US) 'lʌk.naʊ

luck|y ˈlʌk|.i **-ier** -i.əʳ (US) -i.ɚ **-iest** -i.ɪst, -i.əst **-ily** -ɪ.li, -ᵊl.i **-iness** -ɪ.nəs, -ɪ.nɪs
Lucock ˈluː.kɒk, ˈljuː- (US) ˈluː.kɑːk
Lucozade® ˈluː.kə.zeɪd
lucrative ˈluː.krə.tɪv, ˈljuː- (US) ˈluː.krə.t̬ɪv **-ly** -li **-ness** -nəs, -nɪs
lucre ˈluː.kəʳ, ˈljuː- (US) ˈluː.kɚ
Lucrece luːˈkriːs, ljuː- (US) luː-
Lucretia luːˈkriː.ʃə, ljuː-, -ʃi.ə (US) luːˈkriː.ʃə
Lucretius luːˈkriː.ʃəs, ljuː-, -ʃi.əs (US) luːˈkriː.ʃəs
lucu|brate ˈluː.kjə|.breɪt, -kjʊ-, ˈljuː- (US) ˈluː- **-brates** -breɪts **-brating** -breɪ.tɪŋ (US) -breɪ.t̬ɪŋ **-brated** -breɪ.tɪd (US) -breɪ.t̬ɪd
lucubration ˌluː.kjəˈbreɪ.ʃᵊn, -kjʊˈ-, ˌljuː- (US) ˌluː- **-s** -z
Lucullus luːˈkʌl.əs, ljuː-, -ˈsʌl- (US) luːˈkʌl-
Lucy ˈluː.si
Lud lʌd
Luddite ˈlʌd.aɪt **-s** -s
Ludgate ˈlʌd.gət, -gɪt, -geɪt
ludicrous ˈluː.dɪ.krəs, ˈljuː-, -də- (US) ˈluː- **-ly** -li **-ness** -nəs, -nɪs
Ludlow ˈlʌd.ləʊ (US) -loʊ
Ludmilla lʊdˈmɪl.ə, lʌd-
ludo ˈluː.dəʊ (US) -doʊ
Ludovic ˈluː.də.vɪk
Ludwig ˈlʊd.vɪg, ˈluːd- (US) ˈlʊd-, ˈluːd-, ˈlʌd-, -wɪg
luff (L) lʌf **-s** -s **-ing** -ɪŋ **-ed** -t
Lufthansa® ˈlʊftˌhænt.sə, -ˌhæn.zə (US) lʊfˈtɑːn.zə
Luftwaffe ˈlʊftˌwæf.ə, -ˌvæf-, -ˌwɑː.fə, -ˌvɑː- (US) -ˌvɑː-, -ˌwɑː-
lug lʌg **-s** -z **-ging** -ɪŋ **-ged** -d
Lugano luːˈgɑː.nəʊ, lə- (US) luːˈgɑː.noʊ
Lugard ˈluː.gɑːd, -ˈ- (US) ˈluː.gɑːrd, -ˈ-
lug|e luːʒ, luːdʒ (US) luːʒ **-es** -ɪz **-(e)ing** -ɪŋ **-ed** -d
Luger® ˈluː.gəʳ (US) -gɚ
luggable ˈlʌg.ə.bl̩
luggage ˈlʌg.ɪdʒ **ˈluggage ˌlabel** ; **ˈluggage ˌrack**
lugger ˈlʌg.əʳ (US) -ɚ **-s** -z
lughole ˈlʌg.həʊl, -əʊl (US) -hoʊl **-s** -z
Lugosi luːˈgəʊ.si (US) -ˈgoʊ-
lugsail ˈlʌg.seɪl *nautical pronunciation:* -sᵊl **-s** -z
lugubrious luːˈguː.bri.əs, ljuː-, lə- (US) ləˈguː-, luː- **-ly** -li **-ness** -nəs, -nɪs
lugworm ˈlʌg.wɜːm (US) -wɜːrm **-s** -z
Luis ˈluː.ɪs
Luka ˈluː.kə
Lukacs, Lukács ˈluː.kætʃ (US) -kɑːtʃ
Luke luːk
lukewarm ˌluːkˈwɔːm, ˈ-- (US) ˈluːk.wɔːrm, ˌ-ˈ- **-ly** -li **-ness** -nəs, -nɪs

lull lʌl **-s** -z **-ing** -ɪŋ **-ed** -d
lullab|y ˈlʌl.ə.b|aɪ **-ies** -aɪz
Lully ˈlʊl.i; *as if French:* luːˈliː (US) luːˈliː
Lulu ˈluː.luː
lumbago lʌmˈbeɪ.gəʊ (US) -goʊ
lumbar ˈlʌm.bəʳ, -bɑːʳ (US) -bɑːr, -bɚ
lumb|er ˈlʌm.b|əʳ (US) -b|ɚ **-ers** -əz (US) -ɚz **-ering** -ᵊr.ɪŋ **-ered** -əd (US) -ɚd **-erer/s** -ᵊr.əʳ/z (US) -ɚ.ɚ/z **-erman** -ə.mən (US) -ɚ.mən **-ermen** -ə.mən, -ə.men (US) -ɚ.mən, -ɚ.men
lumberjack ˈlʌm.bə.dʒæk (US) -bɚ- **-s** -s
lumberyard ˈlʌm.bə.jɑːd (US) -bɚ.jɑːrd **-s** -z
lumiere, lumière ˈluː.mi.eəʳ, ˌ--ˈ- (US) ˌluː.miˈer
luminar|y ˈluː.mɪ.nᵊr|.i, ˈljuː-, -mə- (US) ˈluː.mə.ner- **-ies** -iz
luminesc|e ˌluː.mɪˈnes, ˌljuː-, -məˈ- (US) ˌluː.məˈ- **-es** -ɪz **-ing** -ɪŋ **-ed** -t
luminescen|ce ˌluː.mɪˈnes.ᵊn|*t*s, ˌljuː-, -məˈ- (US) ˌluː.məˈ- **-t** -t
luminiferous ˌluː.mɪˈnɪf.ᵊr.əs, ˌljuː-, -məˈ- (US) ˌluː.məˈ-
luminosity ˌluː.mɪˈnɒs.ə.ti, ˌljuː-, -məˈ-, -ɪ.ti (US) ˌluː.məˈnɑː.sə.t̬i
luminous ˈluː.mɪ.nəs, ˈljuː-, -mə- (US) ˈluː.mə- **-ly** -li **-ness** -nəs, -nɪs
Lumley ˈlʌm.li
lumme ˈlʌm.i
lummox ˈlʌm.əks **-es** -ɪz
lump lʌmp **-s** -s **-ing** -ɪŋ **-ed** -t
lumpectom|y lʌmˈpek.tə.m|i **-ies** -iz
lumpen ˈlʌm.pən, ˈlʊm-
lumpenproletariat ˌlʌm.pənˌprəʊ.ləˈteə.ri.ət, ˌlʊm-, -pəmˌ-, -lɪˈ-, -æt (US) -pənˌproʊ.ləˈter.i.ət
lumpfish ˈlʌmp.fɪʃ **-es** -ɪz
lumpish ˈlʌm.pɪʃ **-ly** -li **-ness** -nəs, -nɪs
Lumpkin ˈlʌmp.kɪn
lump|y ˈlʌm.p|i **-ier** -i.əʳ (US) -i.ɚ **-iest** -i.ɪst, -i.əst **-iness** -ɪ.nəs, -ɪ.nɪs
Lumsden ˈlʌmz.dən
Luna ˈluː.nə, ˈljuː- (US) ˈluː-
lunacy ˈluː.nə.si, ˈljuː- (US) ˈluː-
lunar ˈluː.nəʳ, ˈljuː- (US) ˈluː.nɚ
lunate ˈluː.neɪt, ˈljuː-, -nət, -nɪt (US) ˈluː.neɪt, -nɪt
lunatic ˈluː.nə.tɪk, ˈljuː- (US) ˈluː- **-s** -s **ˈlunatic aˌsylum** ; **ˌlunatic ˈfringe**
lunation luːˈneɪ.ʃᵊn, ljuː- (US) luː- **-s** -z
Luncarty ˈlʌŋ.kə.ti (US) -kɚ.t̬i
lunch lʌn*t*ʃ **-es** -ɪz **-ing** -ɪŋ **-ed** -t
lunchbox ˈlʌn*t*ʃ.bɒks (US) -bɑːks **-es** -ɪz
luncheon ˈlʌn.*t*ʃən **-s** -z **ˈluncheon ˌmeat**; **ˈluncheon ˌvoucher**
luncheonette ˌlʌn.*t*ʃəˈnet **-s** -s
lunchroom ˈlʌn*t*ʃ.ruːm, -rʊm **-s** -z
Lund *place in Sweden:* lʊnd (US) lʊnd, lʌnd *family name:* lʌnd

Lundy ˈlʌn.di
lune (L) luːn, ljuːn (US) luːn **-s** -z
Lüneburg ˈluː.nə.bɜːg (US) -bɜːrg
lunette luːˈnet, ljuː- (US) luː- **-s** -s
lung lʌŋ **-s** -z
lung|e lʌndʒ **-es** -ɪz **-ing** -ɪŋ **-ed** -d **-er/s** -əʳ/z (US) -ɚ/z
lungfish ˈlʌŋ.fɪʃ **-es** -ɪz
lunkhead ˈlʌŋk.hed **-s** -z
Lunn lʌn
lunul|a ˈluː.njə.l|ə, ˈljuː- (US) -njʊ-, ˈluː.njə- **-ae** -iː
lunule ˈluː.njuːl, ˈljuː- (US) ˈluː- **-s** -z
Lupercal ˈluː.pə.kæl, ˈljuː-, -pɜː- (US) ˈluː.pɚ.kæl
Lupercalia ˌluː.pəˈkeɪ.li.ə, ˌljuː-, -pɜːˈ- (US) ˌluː.pɚˈkeɪl.jə
lupin(e) *flower*: ˈluː.pɪn **-s** -z
lupine *(adj.) wolfish:* ˈluː.paɪn, ˈljuː- (US) ˈluː-
lupus (L) ˈluː.pəs, ˈljuː- (US) ˈluː-
lurch lɜːtʃ (US) lɜːrtʃ **-es** -ɪz **-ing** -ɪŋ **-ed** -t **-er/s** -əʳ/z (US) -ɚ/z **ˌleave someone in the ˈlurch**
lur|e lʊəʳ, ljʊəʳ, ljɔːʳ (US) lʊr **-es** -z **-ing** -ɪŋ **-ed** -d
Lurex® ˈljʊə.reks, ˈlʊə-, ˈljɔː- (US) ˈlʊr.eks
Lurgan ˈlɜː.gᵊn (US) ˈlɜːr-
lurg|y ˈlɜː.g|i (US) ˈlɜːr- **-ies** -iz
lurid ˈlʊə.rɪd, ˈljʊə-, ˈljɔː- (US) ˈlʊr.ɪd **-ly** -li **-ness** -nəs, -nɪs
lurk lɜːk (US) lɜːrk **-s** -s **-ing** -ɪŋ **-ed** -t **-er/s** -əʳ/z (US) -ɚ/z
Lurpak® ˈlɜː.pæk (US) ˈlɜːr-
Lusaka luːˈsɑː.kə, lʊ-, -ˈzɑː- (US) luːˈsɑː.kɑː
Lusardi luːˈsɑː.di (US) -ˈsɑːr-
Lusati|a luːˈseɪ.ʃ|ə, -ʃi|.ə **-an/s** -ən/z
luscious ˈlʌʃ.əs **-ly** -li **-ness** -nəs, -nɪs
lush (L) lʌʃ **-es** -ɪz **-er** -əʳ (US) -ɚ **-est** -ɪst, -əst **-ing** -ɪŋ **-ed** -t **-ness** -nəs, -nɪs
Lushington ˈlʌʃ.ɪŋ.tən
Lusiad ˈluː.si.æd, ˈljuː- (US) ˈluː- **-s** -z
Lusitania ˌluː.sɪˈteɪ.ni.ə, ˌljuː-, -səˈ- (US) ˌluː-
lust lʌst **-s** -s **-ing** -ɪŋ **-ed** -ɪd
luster ˈlʌs.təʳ (US) -tɚ **-s** -z **-less** -ləs, -lɪs
lustful ˈlʌst.fᵊl, -fʊl **-ly** -i **-ness** -nəs, -nɪs
lustral ˈlʌs.trᵊl
lustration lʌsˈtreɪ.ʃᵊn **-s** -z
lustre ˈlʌs.təʳ (US) -tɚ **-s** -z **-less** -ləs, -lɪs
lustrous ˈlʌs.trəs **-ly** -li **-ness** -nəs, -nɪs
lustr|um ˈlʌs.tr|əm **-ums** -əmz **-a** -ə
lust|y ˈlʌs.t|i **-ier** -i.əʳ (US) -i.ɚ **-iest** -i.ɪst, -i.əst **-ily** -ɪ.li, -ᵊl.i **-iness** -ɪ.nəs, -ɪ.nɪs
lutanist ˈluː.tᵊn.ɪst, ˈljuː- (US) ˈluː-
lute luːt, ljuːt (US) luːt **-s** -s

lutein 'luː.ti.ɪn, 'ljuː-, -tiːn, 'luː.ti.ɪn
luteiniz|e, -is|e 'luː.ti.ɪ.naɪz, 'ljuː-, -ə-; -tɪ.naɪz, -tə-, -tiː-, -tᵊn.aɪz (US) 'luː.ti.ə.naɪz, -ə- **-es** -ɪz **-ing** -ɪŋ **-ed** -d
lutenist 'luː.tᵊn.ɪst, 'ljuː- (US) 'luː- **-s** -s
lutetium luː'tiː.ʃəm, ljuː-, -ʃi.əm (US) luː'tiː.ʃi.əm
Luth|er 'luː.θ|əʳ (US) 'luː.θ|ɚ **-eran/s** -ᵊr.ᵊn/z **-eranism** -ᵊr.ᵊn.ɪ.zᵊm **-erism** -ᵊr.ɪ.zᵊm
Lutine luː'tiːn, '--
lutist 'luː.tɪst, 'ljuː- (US) 'luː.t̬ɪst **-s** -s
Luton 'luː.tᵊn
Lutterworth 'lʌt.ə.wəθ, -wɜːθ (US) 'lʌt̬.ɚ.wɚθ, -wɜːrθ
Lutton 'lʌt.ᵊn
Luttrell 'lʌt.rəl
Lutyens 'lʌt.jənz, 'lʌtʃ.ənz
luvv|ie, luvv|y 'lʌv|.i **-ies** -ɪz
lux lʌks **luxes** 'lʌk.sɪz
Lux® lʌks
luxe lʌks, luːks, lʊks
Luxemb(o)urg 'lʌk.sᵊm.bɜːg (US) -bɜːrg
Luxor 'lʌk.sɔːʳ (US) -sɔːr, 'lʊk-
luxuriance lʌg'ʒʊə.ri.ənts, ləg-, -'ʒɔː-, -'zjʊə-, -'zjɔː-; lʌk'sjʊə-, lək-, -'sjɔː- (US) lʌg'ʒʊr.i-, -'zjʊr-; lʌk'ʃʊr-, -'sjʊr-
luxuriant lʌg'ʒʊə.ri.ənt, ləg-, -'ʒɔː-, -'zjʊə-, -'zjɔː-; lʌk'sjʊə-, lək-, -'sjɔː- (US) lʌg'ʒʊr.i-, -'zjʊr-; lʌk'ʃʊr-, -'sjʊr- **-ly** -li
luxuri|ate lʌg'ʒʊə.ri|.eɪt, ləg-, -'ʒjɔː-, -'zjʊə-, -'zjɔː-; lʌk'sjʊə-, lək-, -'sjɔː- (US) lʌg'ʒʊr.i-, -'ʒjʊr-; lʌk'ʃʊr-, -'sjʊr- **-ates** -eɪts **-ating** -eɪ.tɪŋ (US) -eɪ.t̬ɪŋ **-ated** -eɪ.tɪd (US) -eɪ.t̬ɪd
luxurious lʌg'ʒʊə.ri.əs, ləg-, -'ʒɔː-, -'zjʊə-, -'zjɔː-; lʌk'sjʊə-, lək-, -'sjɔː- (US) lʌg'ʒʊr.i-, -'zjʊr-; lʌk'ʃʊr-, -'sjʊr- **-ly** -li **-ness** -nəs, -nɪs
luxur|y 'lʌk.ʃᵊr|.i (US) 'lʌk.ʃɚ|.i, -ʃʊr-; 'lʌg.ʒɚ-, -ʒʊr- **-ies** -iz **in the ˌlap of 'luxury**
Luzon luː'zɒn (US) -'zɑːn
Lvov lə'vɒf (US) -'vɑːf
lwei lə'weɪ **-s** -z
-ly -li
Note: Suffix. Does not alter the stress pattern of the stem to which it is added, e.g. **rapid** /'ræp.ɪd/, **rapidly** /'ræp.ɪd.li/.
Lyall 'laɪ.əl, laɪəl
lycanthrope 'laɪ.kᵊn.θrəʊp; laɪ'kænt.θrəʊp (US) -θroʊp **-s** -s
lycanthropic ˌlaɪ.kᵊn'θrɒp.ɪk (US) -'θrɑː.pɪk
lycanthropy laɪ'kænt.θrə.pi
lycée 'liː.seɪ (US) liː'seɪ **-s** -z
Lycett 'laɪ.sɪt, -set
lyceum (L) laɪ'siː.əm, 'laɪ- **-s** -z
lychee ˌlaɪ'tʃiː; 'laɪ.tʃiː, 'liː- (US) 'liː.tʃiː **-s** -z
lychgate 'lɪtʃ.geɪt **-s** -s
lychnis 'lɪk.nɪs
Lyci|a 'lɪs.i|.ə, 'lɪʃ-, 'lɪʃ|.ə (US) 'lɪʃ|.ə, -i|.ə **-an/s** -ən/z
Lycidas 'lɪs.ɪ.dæs (US) -dæs, -dəs
Lycoming laɪ'kɒm.ɪŋ (US) -'kʌm-
lycopodium ˌlaɪ.kəʊ'pəʊ.di.əm (US) -koʊ'poʊ- **-s** -z
Lycra® 'laɪ.krə
Lycurgus laɪ'kɜː.gəs (US) -'kɜːr-
Lydall 'laɪ.dᵊl
Lydd lɪd
lyddite 'lɪd.aɪt
Lydekker laɪ'dek.əʳ (US) -ɚ
Lydgate *fifteenth century poet, place in Greater Manchester:* 'lɪd.geɪt, -gɪt *place in Yorkshire:* 'lɪd.gɪt, 'lɪ.gɪt *lane in Sheffield:* 'lɪdʒ.ɪt
Lydi|a 'lɪd.i|.ə **-an/s** -ən/z
Lydiate 'lɪd.i.ət
Lydney 'lɪd.ni
Lydon 'laɪ.dᵊn
lye (L) laɪ
Lyell 'laɪ.əl; laɪəl
Lygon 'lɪg.ən
lying (*from* **lie**) 'laɪ.ɪŋ **ˌtake something ˌlying 'down**
Lyle laɪl
Lyly 'lɪl.i
Lyme laɪm **'Lyme diˌsease**
Lyme Regis ˌlaɪm'riː.dʒɪs
Lymeswold® 'laɪmz.wəʊld (US) -woʊld
Lymington 'lɪm.ɪŋ.tən
Lymm lɪm
Lympany 'lɪm.pə.ni
lymph lɪmpf **-s** -s
lymphatic lɪm'fæt.ɪk (US) -'fæt̬- **-s** -s **-ally** -ᵊl.i, -li
lymphocyte 'lɪmp.fəʊ.saɪt (US) -foʊ-, -fə- **-s** -s
lymphoid 'lɪmp.fɔɪd
lymphoma lɪm'fəʊ.mə (US) -'foʊ- **-s** -z
Lympne lɪm
Lyn lɪn
Lynam 'laɪ.nəm
Lynas 'laɪ.nəs
lynch (L) lɪntʃ (US) lɪntʃ **-es** -ɪz **-ing** -ɪŋ **-ed** -t
Lynchburg 'lɪntʃ.bɜːg (US) -bɜːrg
Lyndhurst 'lɪnd.hɜːst (US) -hɜːrst
Lyndon 'lɪn.dən
Lyndsay, Lyndsey 'lɪnd.zi
Lyness 'laɪ.nɪs, -nəs, -nes
Lynette lɪ'net
Lynmouth 'lɪn.məθ
Lynn lɪn
Lynton 'lɪn.tən
lynx lɪŋks **-es** -ɪz
Lyon laɪən
lyonnaise ˌlaɪə'neɪz, ˌliː.ə'-
Lyons laɪənz *French city:* 'liː.ɔ̃ːŋ, -ɒn; laɪənz *as if French:* li'ɔ̃ŋ (US) li'õʊn
Lyr|a 'laɪə.r|ə (US) 'laɪ- **-ae** -iː
lyrate 'laɪə.rɪt, -reɪt, -rət (US) 'laɪ.reɪt
lyre laɪəʳ (US) laɪr **-s** -z
lyrebird 'laɪə.bɜːd (US) 'laɪr.bɜːrd **-s** -z
lyric (L) 'lɪr.ɪk **-s** -s **-al** -ᵊl **-ally** -ᵊl.i, -li
lyricism 'lɪr.ɪ.sɪ.zᵊm, '-ə-
lyricist 'lɪr.ɪ.sɪst, '-ə- **-s** -s
lyrist *player on the lyre:* 'laɪə.rɪst, 'lɪr.ɪst (US) 'laɪr.ɪst **-s** -s
lyrist *lyric poet:* 'lɪr.ɪst **-s** -s
Lysander laɪ'sæn.dəʳ (US) -dɚ
lysergic laɪ'sɜː.dʒɪk, lɪ- (US) laɪ'sɜːr-
Lysias 'lɪs.i.æs
Lysicrates laɪ'sɪk.rə.tiːz
Lysippus laɪ'sɪp.əs
-lysis -lə.sɪs, -lɪ-
Note: Suffix. Words containing **-lysis** are normally stressed on the syllable preceding the suffix, e.g. **paralysis** /pə'ræl.ə.sɪs/.
Lysistrata laɪ'sɪs.trə.tə (US) ˌlɪs.ɪ'strɑː-; laɪ'sɪs.trə-
Lysol® 'laɪ.sɒl (US) -sɑːl
Lystra 'lɪs.trə
Lyte laɪt
Lytham 'lɪð.əm
Lythe laɪð
Lyttelton 'lɪt.ᵊl.tən (US) 'lɪt̬-
Lyttle 'lɪt.l̩ (US) 'lɪt̬-
Lytton 'lɪt.ᵊn

M

m (M) em **-'s** -z
m (*abbrev. for* **metre/s**) *singular:* 'miː.təʳ (US) -t̬ɚ *plural:* -z
ma (*mother*) mɑː **-s** -z
MA ˌem'eɪ
ma'am (*abbrev. for* **madam**) mæm, mɑːm, məm, m (US) mæm
Note: /mɑːm/, or alternatively /mæm/, is used in addressing members of the royal family.
Maas mɑːs
Maastricht 'mɑː.strikt, -strɪxt; *as if Dutch*: mɑː'strɪxt (US) 'mɑː.strɪkt, -strɪxt
Mab mæb
Mabel 'meɪ.bᵊl
Mabinogion ˌmæb.ɪ'nɒg.i.ɒn, -ə'-, -ən (US) -'nɔː.gi.ɑːn, -'nɑː-, -ən
Mablethorpe 'meɪ.bl̩.θɔːp (US) -θɔːrp
Mabley 'mæb.li (US) 'mæb-, 'meɪb-
Mabs mæbz
Mac mæk
mac, mack mæk **-s** -s
macabre mə'kɑː.brə, mæk'ɑː-, -bəʳ (US) mə'kɑː.brə, -'kɑːb, -'kɑː.bɚ
macadam mə'kæd.əm
MacAdam mə'kæd.əm
macadamia ˌmæk.ə'deɪ.mi.ə **-s** -z
ˌ**maca'damia** ˌ**nut**
macadamization, -isa- məˌkæd.ə.maɪ'zeɪ.ʃᵊn, -mɪ'- (US) -mə'-
macadamiz|e, -is|e mə'kæd.ə.maɪz **-es** -ɪz **-ing** -ɪŋ **-ed** -d
Macalister mə'kæl.ɪ.stəʳ (US) -stɚ
Macan mə'kæn
Macao mə'kaʊ, mæk'aʊ (US) mə'kaʊ
macaque mə'kɑːk, -'kæk; 'mæk.æk (US) mə'kɑːk **-s** -s
macaroni ˌmæk.ᵊr'əʊ.ni (US) -ə'roʊ- **-(e)s** -z *stress shift, see compound:* ˌ**macaroni** '**cheese**
macaroon ˌmæk.ᵊr'uːn (US) -ə'ruːn **-s** -z
MacArthur mə'kɑː.θəʳ (US) -'kɑːr.θɚ
MacCarthy mə'kɑː.θi (US) -'kɑːr-
macassar (M) mə'kæs.əʳ (US) -ɚ
ma'cassar ˌ**oil**
Macau mə'kaʊ, mæk'aʊ (US) mə'kaʊ
Macaulay mə'kɔː.li (US) -'kɑː.li, -'kɔː-
Macavity mə'kæv.ə.ti, -ɪ.ti (US) -ə.t̬i
MacAvoy 'mæk.ə.vɔɪ
macaw mə'kɔː (US) -'kɑː, -'kɔː **-s** -z
MacBain mək'beɪn
Macbeth mək'beθ, mæk-
Note: In Scotland always /mək-/.
Maccabaeus ˌmæk.ə'biː.əs, -'beɪ- (US) -'biː-
Maccabean ˌmæk.ə'biː.ən, -'beɪ- (US) -'biː-
Maccabees 'mæk.ə.biːz
Maccabeus ˌmæk.ə'biː.əs, -'beɪ- (US) -'biː-
MacCaig mə'keɪg
MacCall mə'kɔːl (US) -'kɔːl, -'kɑːl
MacCallum mə'kæl.əm
Macclesfield 'mæk.l̩z.fiːld, -l̩s-
MacCunn mə'kʌn
MacDaire mək'dɑː.rə (US) mək'der
MacDiarmid mək'dɜː.mɪd, -'deə- (US) -'dɜːr-
Macdonald, MacDonald mək'dɒn.ᵊld, mæk- (US) -'dɑː.nᵊld
MacDonaugh mək'dɒn.ə (US) -'dɑː.nə
MacDon(n)ell mək'dɒn.ᵊl (US) -'dɑː.nᵊl
MacDougal mək'duː.gᵊl
MacDuff mək'dʌf, mæk-
Note:In Scotland always /mək-/.
mace® meɪs **-s** -ɪz
macedoine, macédoine ˌmæs.ɪ'dwɑːn, -ə'-, '--- (US) ˌmæs.ɪ'dwɑːn **-s** -z
Macedon 'mæs.ɪ.dᵊn, '-ə- (US) -ə.dɑːn, -dən
Macedoni|a ˌmæs.ɪ'dəʊ.ni|.ə (US) -ə'doʊ.ni-, '-nj|ə **-an/s** -ən/z
MacElder(r)y ˌmæk.ᵊl'der.i, mə'kel.dᵊr- (US) mə'kel.dɚ-
MacElwain 'mæk.ᵊl.weɪn; mə'kel.weɪn
MacElwin 'mæk.ᵊl.wɪn
macer|ate 'mæs.ᵊr|.eɪt (US) -ə.r|eɪt **-ates** -eɪts **-ating** -eɪ.tɪŋ (US) -eɪ.t̬ɪŋ **-ated** -eɪ.tɪd (US) -eɪ.t̬ɪd
maceration ˌmæs.ᵊr'eɪ.ʃᵊn (US) -ə'reɪ- **-s** -z
macerator 'mæs.ᵊr.eɪ.təʳ (US) -ə.reɪ.t̬ɚ **-s** -z
MacFarlane mək'fɑː.lən (US) -'fɑːr-
Macfarren mək'fær.ᵊn (US) -'fer-, -'fær-
Macgillicuddy, MacGillicuddy mə'gɪl.i.kʌd.i; 'mæg.li-, 'mæk.ɪl- (US) mə'gɪl.i-
Note: **Macgillicuddy's Reeks** is pronounced /məˌgɪl.i.kʌd.iz'riːks/.
Macgregor, MacGregor mə'greg.əʳ (US) -ɚ
Mach mæk, mɑːk (US) mɑːk, mæk
Machakos mə'tʃɑː.kɒs (US) -kɑːs
Macheath mək'hiːθ (US) mæk-, mək-
Machen 'meɪ.tʃɪn, -tʃən; 'mæk.ɪn *as if Welsh:* 'mæx- (US) 'mæk.ɪn
machete mə'*t*ʃet.i, mæ*t*ʃ'et-, -'eɪ.ti (US) mə'*t*ʃet̬.i **-s** -z
Machiavelli ˌmæk.i.ə'vel.i, ˌ-jə'-
Machiavellian ˌmæk.i.ə'vel.i.ən, ˌmæk.jə- **-s** -z **-ism** -ɪ.zᵊm
machico|late mə'tʃɪk.əʊ|.leɪt, mætʃ'ɪk- (US) mə'tʃɪk.oʊ-, '-ə- **-lates** -leɪts **-lating** -leɪ.tɪŋ (US) -leɪ.t̬ɪŋ **-lated** -leɪ.tɪd (US) -leɪ.t̬ɪd
machicolation məˌtʃɪk.əʊ'leɪ.ʃᵊn, mætʃˌɪk- (US) məˌtʃɪk.oʊ'-, -ə'- **-s** -z
Machin 'meɪ.tʃɪn
machi|nate 'mæk.ɪ|.neɪt, 'mæʃ-, '-ə- (US) -ə|.neɪt **-nates** -neɪts **-nating** -neɪ.tɪŋ (US) -neɪ.t̬ɪŋ **-nated** -neɪ.tɪd (US) -neɪ.t̬ɪd **-nator/s** -neɪ.təʳ/z (US) -neɪ.t̬ɚ/s
machination ˌmæk.ɪ'neɪ.ʃᵊn, ˌmæʃ-, -ə'- (US) -ə'- **-s** -z
machin|e mə'ʃiːn **-es** -z **-ing** -ɪŋ **-ed** -d
ma'chine ˌ**code**; **ma'chine** ˌ**tool**
machine-gun mə'ʃiːn,gʌn, -'ʃiːŋ,- (US) -'ʃiːn,- **-s** -z **-ning** -ɪŋ **-ned** -d **-ner/s** -əʳ/z (US) -ɚ/z
machine-made mə'ʃiːn.meɪd
machine-readable məˌʃiːn'riː.də.bl̩ *stress shift:* maˌchine-readable 'dictionary
machiner|y mə'ʃiː.nᵊr.i **-ies** -ɪz
machine-washable məˌʃiːn'wɒʃ.ə.bl̩ (US) -'wɑː.ʃə- *stress shift:* maˌchine-washable 'wool
machinist mə'ʃiː.nɪst **-s** -s
machismo mætʃ'ɪz.məʊ, mə'tʃɪz-, -'kɪz- (US) mɑː'tʃiːz.moʊ, mə'kɪz-
macho 'mætʃ.əʊ (US) 'mɑː.tʃoʊ **-s** -z
macho-|man 'mætʃ.əʊ|ˌmæn (US) 'mɑː.tʃoʊ- **-men** -men
Machu Picchu ˌmɑː.tʃuː'piːk.tʃuː
Machynlleth mə'kʌn.*h*ləθ
MacIlwain 'mæk.ᵊl.weɪn, -ɪl-
MacIlwraith 'mæk.ɪl.reɪθ, -ɪt
Macindoe, MacIndoe 'mæk.ɪn.dəʊ, -ᵊn- (US) -doʊ
MacInnes, MacInnis mə'kɪn.ɪs
macintosh® 'mæk.ɪn.tɒʃ (US) -tɑːʃ **-es** -ɪz
MacIntyre 'mæk.ɪn.taɪəʳ, -ᵊn- (US) -taɪɚ
MacIver mə'kaɪ.vəʳ, -'kɪv.əʳ (US) -vɚ
MacIvor mə'kaɪ.vəʳ (US) -vɚ
Mack mæk
Mackay(e), MacKay(e) mə'kaɪ, mə'keɪ
Note: /mə'keɪ/ mainly in U.S.A.
Mackenzie mə'ken.zi
mackerel 'mæk.rᵊl, 'mæk.ᵊr.ᵊl **-s** -z
Mackeson 'mæk.ɪ.sᵊn, '-ə-
Mackie 'mæk.i
Mackin 'mæk.ɪn
mackinaw 'mæk.ɪ.nɔː (US) -nɑː, -nɔː **-s** -z
Mackinlay, Mackinley mə'kɪn.li
mackintosh (M) 'mæk.ɪn.tɒʃ (US) -tɑːʃ **-es** -ɪz
Mackowie, MacKowie mə'kaʊ.i
MacLachlan mə'klɒk.lən, -'klɒx-, -'klæk-, -'klæx- (US) -'klɑː.klən
MacLagan mə'klæg.ᵊn (US) -mək'lɑː.kən, -'glɑː.kən
MacLaglan mə'klæg.lən (US) -'klæg-, -'klɑːg-

Maclaren mə'klær.ən ⓊⓈ -'kler-, -'klær-
MacLaverty mə'klæv.ə.ti ⓊⓈ -ɚ.ţi
Maclean mə'kleɪn, -'kliːn ⓊⓈ -'kliːn
Macleans® mə'kliːnz
MacLeish mə'kliːʃ
MacLeod mə'klaʊd
Maclise mə'kliːs
MacManus mək'mæn.əs, -meɪ.nəs
Macmillan mək'mɪl.ən, mæk-
Macmorran mək'mɒr.ən, mæk- ⓊⓈ -'mɔːr-
MacNab mək'næb
Macnamara ˌmæk.nə'mɑː.rə ⓊⓈ 'mæk.nə.mer.ə, -mær-
MacNaught mək'nɔːt ⓊⓈ -nɑːt, -nɔːt
MacNeice mək.niːs
Mâcon 'mɑː.kɔ̃ːŋ, 'mæk.ɔ̃ːŋ, -ɒn, -ən ⓊⓈ mɑː'koʊn
Macon 'meɪ.kən
Maconchy mə'kɒŋ.ki ⓊⓈ -'kɑːŋ-, -'kɔːŋ-
Maconochie mə'kɒn.ə.ki, -xi ⓊⓈ -'kɑː.nə-
MacPhee mək'fiː
MacPherson, Macpherson mək'fɜː.sən, mæk-, -'fɪə- ⓊⓈ -'fɜːr-, -'fɪr-
Macquarie mə'kwɒr.i ⓊⓈ -'kwɑːr-, -'kwɔːr-
macrame, macramé mə'krɑː.meɪ, -mi ⓊⓈ 'mæk.rə.meɪ
Macready mə'kriː.di
macro- 'mæk.rəʊ- ⓊⓈ 'mæk.roʊ-, -rə-
macro 'mæk.rəʊ ⓊⓈ -roʊ **-s** -z
macrobiotic ˌmæk.rəʊ.baɪ'ɒt.ɪk ⓊⓈ -roʊ.baɪ'ɑː.ţɪk, -rə- **-s** -s
macroclimate 'mæk.rəʊˌklaɪ.mɪt, -mət ⓊⓈ -roʊˌ- **-s** -s
macroclimatic ˌmæk.rəʊ.klaɪ'mæt.ɪk ⓊⓈ -roʊ.klaɪ'mæţ-, -rə-
macrocosm 'mæk.rəʊˌkɒz.əm ⓊⓈ -roʊˌkɑː.zəm, -rə- **-s** -z
macroeconomic ˌmæk.rəʊ.iː.kə'nɒm.ɪk, -ek.ə'- ⓊⓈ -roʊˌek.ə'nɑː.mɪk, -ˌiː.kə'- **-s** -s
macron 'mæk.rɒn ⓊⓈ 'meɪ.krɑːn, 'mæk.rɑːn, -rən **-s** -z
macrophag|e 'mæk.rəʊ.feɪdʒ ⓊⓈ -roʊ- **-es** -ɪz
macrophagic ˌmæk.rəʊ'feɪ.dʒɪk ⓊⓈ -roʊ'fædʒ.ɪk
macroscopic ˌmæk.rəʊ'skɒp.ɪk ⓊⓈ -roʊ'skɑː.pɪk **-al** -əl
Macrow mə'krəʊ ⓊⓈ -'kroʊ
MacSwiney mək'swiː.ni, -'swɪn-
MacTavish mək'tæv.ɪʃ
macul|a 'mæk.jʊ.l|ə, -jə- ⓊⓈ -jə-, -juː- **-as** -əz **-ae** -iː
Macy® 'meɪ.si **Macy's** 'meɪ.siz
mad mæd **-der** -əʳ ⓊⓈ -ɚ **-dest** -ɪst, -əst **-ly** -li **-ness** -nəs, -nɪs **as ˌmad as a 'hatter**; **ˌmad 'cow diˌsease**

Madagasc|ar ˌmæd.ə'gæs.k|əʳ ⓊⓈ -k|ɚ **-an/s** -ən/z
madam 'mæd.əm **-s** -z
madame (M) 'mæd.əm, mə'dæm, -'dɑːm; **-s** -z
Madan 'mæd.ən, 'meɪ.dən
madcap 'mæd.kæp **-s** -s
Maddalo 'mæd.əl.əʊ ⓊⓈ -oʊ
madden (M) 'mæd.ən **-s** -z **-ing** -ɪŋ **-ed** -d
madder 'mæd.əʳ ⓊⓈ -ɚ **-s** -z
Maddie 'mæd.i
madding 'mæd.ɪŋ
Maddison 'mæd.ɪ.sən, '-ə-
Maddox 'mæd.əks
made (*from* **make**) meɪd
Madeira mə'dɪə.rə ⓊⓈ -'dɪr.ə **-s** -z **Ma'deira ˌcake**
Madeleine 'mæd.əl.ɪn, -eɪn
Madeley 'meɪd.li
Madeline 'mæd.əl.ɪn, -eɪn
mademoiselle (M) ˌmæd.ə.m*w*ə'zel, ˌmæm.*w*ə'-, ˌmæm'zel ⓊⓈ ˌmæd.ə.mə'-, ˌmæm'- **-s** -z
made-to-measure ˌmeɪd.tə'meʒ.əʳ ⓊⓈ -ɚ *stress shift:* ˌmade-to-measure 'suit
made-to-order ˌmeɪd.tu'ɔː.dəʳ ⓊⓈ -'ɔːr.dɚ *stress shift:* ˌmade-to-order 'suit
Madge mædʒ
madhou|se 'mæd.haʊ|s **-ses** -zɪz
Madhya Pradesh ˌmʌd.jə.prɑː'deʃ, ˌmɑːd- ⓊⓈ -'prɑː.deʃ
Madingley 'mæd.ɪŋ.li
Madison 'mæd.ɪ.sən, '-ə- **ˌMadison 'Avenue**
mad|man 'mæd|.mən ⓊⓈ -mən, -mæn **-men** -mən, -men **-woman** -ˌwʊm.ən **-women** -ˌwɪm.ɪn
Madoc 'mæd.ək
madonna (M) mə'dɒn.ə ⓊⓈ -'dɑː.nə **-s** -z
Madras *in India:* mə'drɑːs, -dræs
madras *fabric:* 'mæd.rəs ⓊⓈ 'mæd.rəs, mə'dræs, -'drɑːs
madrepore ˌmæd.rɪ'pɔːʳ, -rə'-, '--- ⓊⓈ 'mæd.rə.pɔːr **-s** -z
Madrid mə'drɪd
madrigal 'mæd.rɪ.gəl, -rə- **-s** -z
madrigalist 'mæd.rɪ.gəl.ɪst, -rə- **-s** -s
Madura mə'djʊə.rə, -'dʒʊə-, -'dʊə- ⓊⓈ mɑː'dʊr.ə
madwort 'mæd.wɜːt ⓊⓈ -wɜːrt, -wɔːrt
Mae meɪ
Maecenas maɪ'siː.næs, miː'-, -nəs ⓊⓈ miː'-, mɪ-
maelstrom (M) 'meɪl.strɒm, -strəʊm ⓊⓈ -strəm
maenad 'miː.næd **-s** -z
Maerdy 'mɑː.di, 'meə- ⓊⓈ 'mɑːr-, 'mer-

Maesteg ˌmaɪ'steɪg
maestoso ˌmɑː.es'təʊ.zəʊ, maɪ'stəʊ-, -səʊ ⓊⓈ maɪ'stoʊ.zoʊ
maestr|o (M®) 'maɪ.strəʊ ⓊⓈ -stroʊ **-os** -əʊz ⓊⓈ -oʊz **-i** -i
Maeterlinck 'meɪ.tə.lɪŋk ⓊⓈ 'meɪ.tɚ-, 'met.ɚ-
Maev(e) meɪv
Mae West ˌmeɪ'west **-s** -s
Mafeking 'mæf.ɪ.kɪŋ, '-ə-
maffick 'mæf.ɪk **-s** -s **-ing** -ɪŋ **-ed** -t **-er/s** -əʳ/z ⓊⓈ -ɚ/z
mafia (M) 'mæf.i.ə, 'mɑː.fi- ⓊⓈ 'mɑː-
Mafikeng 'mæf.ɪ.keŋ, '-ə-
mafios|o (M) ˌmæf.i'əʊ.s|əʊ, ˌmɑː.fi'-, -z|əʊ ⓊⓈ ˌmɑː.fi'oʊ.s|oʊ **-os** -əʊz ⓊⓈ -oʊz **-i** -iː
mag (M) mæg **-s** -z
magalog 'mæg.ə.lɒg ⓊⓈ -lɑːg **-s** -z
Magan 'meɪ.gən, mə'gæn
magazine ˌmæg.ə'ziːn, '--- ⓊⓈ 'mæg.ə.ziːn, ˌ--'- **-s** -z
Note: The stressing /'---/ is usual in the north of England, but uncommon in the south.
Magdala 'mæg.dəl.ə, ˌmæg'dɑː.lə ⓊⓈ 'mæg.dəl.ə
Magdalen *biblical name, modern first name, Canadian islands:* 'mæg.dəl.ɪn, -ən ⓊⓈ -ən, -ɪn *Oxford college and bridge:* 'mɔːd.lɪn ⓊⓈ 'mɑːd-, 'mɔːd- *Oxford street:* 'mæg.dəl.ɪn, -ən ⓊⓈ -ən, -ɪn
Magdalene *biblical name:* ˌmæg.də'liː.ni; 'mæg.dəl.iːn, -ɪn ⓊⓈ 'mæg.dəl.iːn, -ən, -ɪn; ˌmæg.də'liː.nə *modern first name:* 'mæg.dəl.iːn, -ɪn ⓊⓈ -iːn, -ən, -ɪn *Cambridge college and street:* 'mɔːd.lɪn ⓊⓈ 'mɑːd-, 'mɔːd-
Magdalenian ˌmæg.dəl'iː.ni.ən
Magdeburg 'mæg.də.bɜːg, '-dɪ- ⓊⓈ 'mæg.də.bɜːrg, 'mɑːg.də.bʊrg
mag|e meɪdʒ **-es** -ɪz
Magee mə'giː
Magellan mə'gel.ən ⓊⓈ -'dʒel-
magenta (M) mə'dʒen.tə ⓊⓈ -ţə
Maggie 'mæg.i
Maggiore ˌmædʒ'ɔː.reɪ, -ri; ˌ-i'-, mə'dʒɔː- ⓊⓈ mə'dʒɔːr.i
magg|ot 'mæg|.ət **-ots** -əts **-oty** -ə.ti ⓊⓈ -ə.ţi
Maghera ˌmæk.ə'rɑː, ˌmæ.hə'-
Magherafelt ˌmæk.ər.ə'felt, ˌmæ.hər-
Maghreb, Maghrib 'mɑː.greb, 'mʌg.reb, 'mæg.reb, -rɪb, -rəb; mə'greb, mɑː- ⓊⓈ 'mʌg.rəb
Maghull mə'gʌl
Magi (*plur. of* **Magus**) 'meɪ.dʒaɪ, -gaɪ ⓊⓈ -dʒaɪ
magic 'mædʒ.ɪk **-al** -əl **-ally** -əl.i, -li ˌ**magic 'carpet**; ˌ**magic 'eye**; ˌ**magic**

ˈlantern; ˌmagic ˈmushroom; ˌmagic ˈwand

magician məˈdʒɪʃ.ᵊn **-s** -z

Maginot ˈmæʒ.ɪ.nəʊ, ˈmædʒ-, ˈ-ə- (US) -ə.noʊ **ˈMaginot ˌLine**

magisterial ˌmædʒ.ɪˈstɪə.ri.əl, -əˈ- (US) -ɪˈstɪr.i- **-ly** -i

magistrac|y ˈmædʒ.ɪ.strə.s|i, ˈ-ə- (US) ˈ-ɪ- **-ies** -iz

magistral məˈdʒɪs.trᵊl, mædʒˈɪs-; ˈmædʒ.ɪ.strᵊl, ˈ-ə- (US) ˈmædʒ.ɪ.strᵊl

magistrate ˈmædʒ.ɪ.streɪt, ˈ-ə-, -strɪt, -strət (US) -ɪ.streɪt, -strɪt **-s** -s

magistrature ˈmædʒ.ɪ.strə.tʃəʳ, ˈ-ə-, -ˌtjʊəʳ, -ˌtʃʊəʳ (US) -ɪ.streɪ.tʃɚ, -strə.tʃʊr **-s** -z

magma ˈmæg.mə

magmatic mægˈmæt.ɪk (US) -ˈmæt̬-

Magna Carta ˌmæg.nəˈkɑː.tə (US) -ˈkɑːr.t̬ə

magna cum laude ˌmæg.nɑː.kʊmˈlaʊ.deɪ

magnanimity ˌmæg.nəˈnɪm.ə.ti, -nænˈɪm-, -ɪ.ti (US) -nəˈnɪm.ə.t̬i

magnanimous mægˈnæn.ɪ.məs, məg- (US) mægˈnæn.ə- **-ly** -li

magnate ˈmæg.neɪt, -nɪt **-s** -s

magnesia *substance:* mægˈniː.ʃə, məg-, ˈ-si.ə, -zi.ə, -ʒi.ə, -ʒə (US) mægˈniː.ʒə, -ʃə

Magnesia *city:* mægˈniː.zi.ə, -ʒi.ə, -ʒə (US) -zi.ə, -ʒi.ə, -ʒə, -ʃə

magnesium mægˈniː.zi.əm, məg-, -si-, -ʒi- (US) mægˈniː.zi-, -ʒi-, ˈ-ʒᵊm

magnet ˈmæg.nət, -nɪt **-s** -s

magnetic mægˈnet.ɪk, məg- (US) mægˈnet̬- **-al** -ᵊl **-ally** -ᵊl.i, -li magˌnetic ˈ**field**; magˌnetic ˈ**north**; magˌnetic ˈ**storm**; magˌnetic ˈ**tape**

magnetism ˈmæg.nə.tɪ.zᵊm, -nɪ- (US) -t̬ɪ-

magnetiz|e, -is|e ˈmæg.nə.taɪz, -nɪ- **-es** -ɪz **-ing** -ɪŋ **-ed** -d **-er/s** -əʳ/z (US) -ɚ/z

magneto mægˈniː.təʊ, məg- (US) mægˈniː.t̬oʊ **-s** -z

magnetron ˈmæg.nə.trɒn, -nɪ- (US) -trɑːn **-s** -z

Magnificat mægˈnɪf.ɪ.kæt, məg-, ˈ-ə- (US) mægˈnɪf-; mɑːˈnjɪ.fɪ.kɑːt **-s** -s

magnification ˌmæg.nɪ.fɪˈkeɪ.ʃᵊn, -nə- **-s** -z

magnificence mægˈnɪf.ɪ.sᵊn*t*s, məg-, ˈ-ə- (US) mæg-

magnificent mægˈnɪf.ɪ.sᵊnt, məg-, ˈ-ə- (US) mæg- **-ly** -li

magnifico mægˈnɪf.ɪ.kəʊ, ˈ-ə- (US) -koʊ **-(e)s** -z

magni|fy ˈmæg.nɪ|.faɪ, -nə- **-fies** -faɪz **-fying** -faɪ.ɪŋ **-fied** -faɪd **-fier/s** -faɪ.əʳ/z (US) -faɪ.ɚ/z **-fiable** -faɪ.ə.bl̩ **ˈmagnifying ˌglass**

magniloquen|ce mægˈnɪl.ə.kwən|*t*s **-t** -t

magnitude ˈmæg.nɪ.tjuːd, -nə-, -tʃuːd (US) -tuːd, -tjuːd **-s** -z

magnolia mægˈnəʊ.li.ə, məg- (US) mægˈnoʊl.jə, -ˈnoʊ.li.ə **-s** -z

magnum ˈmæg.nəm **-s** -z

magnum bonum ˌmæg.nəmˈbəʊ.nəm, -ˈbɒn.əm (US) -ˈboʊ.nəm **-s** -z

magnum opus ˌmæg.nəmˈəʊ.pəs, -ˈɒp.əs (US) -ˈoʊ.pəs

Magnus ˈmæg.nəs

Magnyficence mægˈnɪf.ɪ.sᵊn*t*s, ˈ-ə-

Magog ˈmeɪ.gɒg (US) -gɑːg, -gɔːg

magpie ˈmæg.paɪ **-s** -z

Magrath məˈgrɑː, -ˈgrɑːθ, -ˈgræθ (US) -ˈgræθ

Magritte mægˈriːt, məˈgriːt (US) mɑː-

Magruder məˈgruː.dəʳ (US) -dɚ

Maguiness məˈgɪn.ɪs, -əs

Maguire məˈgwaɪəʳ (US) -ˈgwaɪɚ

ma|gus (M) ˈmeɪ|.gəs **-gi** -dʒaɪ, -gaɪ (US) -dʒaɪ

Magwitch ˈmæg.wɪtʃ

Magyar ˈmæg.jɑːʳ (US) -jɑːr **-s** -z

Mahabharata məˌhɑːˈbɑː.rə.tə, ˌmɑː.həˈ- (US) məˌhɑːˈbɑːr.ə-, ˌmɑː-, -ˈrɑː.tɑː

Mahaffy məˈhæf.i

Mahan məˈhæn; mɑːn (US) məˈhæn

Mahany ˈmɑː.ni

maharaja(h) ˌmɑː.*h*əˈrɑː.dʒə (US) -həˈ- **-s** -z

maharani, maharanee ˌmɑː.*h*əˈrɑː.ni (US) -həˈ- **-s** -z

Maharashtra ˌmɑː.*h*əˈræʃ.trə, -ˈrɑːʃ- (US) -hɑːˈrɑːʃ-

maharishi (M) ˌmɑː.*h*əˈriː.ʃi (US) -həˈ- **-s** -z

mahatma (M) məˈhɑːt.mə, -ˈhæt- **-s** -z

Mahayana məˌhɑːˈjɑː.nə, ˌmɑː.həˈ- (US) ˌmɑː.həˈ-

Mahdi ˈmɑː.diː, -di **-s** -z

Mahé ˈmɑː.*h*eɪ (US) mɑːˈheɪ

Mahican məˈ*h*iː.kᵊn, mɑː- **-s** -z

mah-jong(g) ˌmɑːˈdʒɒŋ (US) -ˈdʒɔːŋ, -ˈdʒɑːŋ, -ˈʒɔːŋ, -ˈʒɑːŋ

Mahler ˈmɑː.ləʳ (US) -lɚ

mahlstick ˈmɔːl.stɪk (US) ˈmɑːl-, ˈmɔːl- **-s** -s

Mahmud mɑːˈmuːd

mahogany məˈhɒg.ᵊn.i (US) -ˈhɑː.gᵊn-

Mahomet, Mahomed məˈhɒm.ɪt, -et (US) məˈhɑː.mɪt

Mahometan məˈhɒm.ɪ.tᵊn, ˈ-ə- (US) -ˈhɑː.mə.t̬ən **-s** -z

Mahommed məˈhɒm.ɪd, -ed (US) -ˈhɑː.mɪd

Mahommedan məˈhɒm.ɪ.dᵊn (US) -ˈhɑː.mə- **-s** -z

Mahon mɑːn; ˈmæ.hən; məˈhuːn, -ˈhəʊn (US) mæn, məˈhoʊn, -ˈhuːn

Mahon(e)y ˈmɑː.ə.nɪ, ˈmɑː.ni, məˈhəʊ.ni (US) məˈhoʊ-

mahonia məˈhəʊ.ni.ə, mɑː- (US) məˈhoʊ- **-s** -z

mahout məˈhaʊt, mɑː-, -ˈhuːt (US) məˈhoʊt **-s** -s

Mahratta məˈræt.ə (US) -ˈrɑː.t̬ə **-s** -z

Maia ˈmaɪ.ə, ˈmeɪ-

maid meɪd **-s** -z

Maida ˈmeɪ.də

maidan (M) maɪˈdɑːn, mædˈɑːn **-s** -z

maiden ˈmeɪ.dᵊn **-s** -z **-ly** -li ˌ**maiden** ˈ**name**

maidenhair ˈmeɪ.dᵊn.heəʳ (US) -her **-s** -z

maidenhead (M) ˈmeɪ.dᵊn.hed

maidenhood ˈmeɪ.dᵊn.hʊd

Maidens ˈmeɪ.dᵊnz

maid-servant ˈmeɪdˌsɜː.vᵊnt (US) -ˌsɜːr- **-s** -s

Maidstone ˈmeɪd.stᵊn, -stəʊn (US) -stoʊn, -stᵊn

maieutic meɪˈuː.tɪk, maɪ- (US) -ˈjuː.t̬ɪk

Maigret ˈmeɪ.greɪ (US) ˌ-ˈ-

mail meɪl **-s** -z **-ing** -ɪŋ **-ed** -d **-er/s** -əʳ/z (US) -ɚ/z **ˈmail ˌdrop**; **ˈmailing ˌlist**

mailbag ˈmeɪl.bæg **-s** -z

mailbox ˈmeɪl.bɒks (US) -bɑːks **-es** -ɪz

Mailer ˈmeɪ.ləʳ (US) -lɚ

Mailgram® ˈmeɪl.græm

Maillard ˈmeɪ.ləd (US) -lɚd

mail|man ˈmeɪl|.mæn **-men** -men, -mən

mail-order ˌmeɪlˈɔː.dəʳ (US) ˈmeɪlˌɔːr.dɚ *stress shift, British English:* ˌmail-order ˈcatalogue

mailroom ˈmeɪl.rʊm, -ruːm (US) -ruːm, -rʊm **-s** -z

mailshot ˈmeɪl.ʃɒt (US) -ʃɑːt **-s** -s

maim meɪm **-s** -z **-ing** -ɪŋ **-ed** -d

main meɪn **-s** -z ˌ**main** ˈ**drag**; ˌ**main** ˈ**line**; ˈ**Main** ˌ**Street**

Main *German river:* maɪn, meɪn

mainbrac|e ˈmeɪn.breɪs, ˈmeɪm- (US) ˈmeɪn- **-es** -ɪz

Maine meɪn

mainframe ˈmeɪn.freɪm **-s** -z

mainland ˈmeɪn.lənd, -lænd

Mainland ˈmeɪn.lænd

mainlin|e ˈmeɪn.laɪn, ˌ-ˈ- (US) ˈ-- **-es** -z **-ing** -ɪŋ **-ed** -d **-er/s** -əʳ/z (US) -ɚ/z

mainly ˈmeɪn.li

mainmast ˈmeɪn.mɑːst, ˈmeɪm- (US) ˈmeɪn.mæst *nautical pronunciation:* -məst **-s** -s

mainsail ˈmeɪn.seɪl *nautical pronunciation:* -sᵊl **-s** -z

mainspring ˈmeɪn.sprɪŋ **-s** -z

mainstay ˈmeɪn.steɪ **-s** -z

mainstream ˈmeɪn.striːm, ˌ-ˈ- (US) ˈ--

mainstreaming ˈmeɪnˌstriː.mɪŋ

maintain meɪnˈteɪn, mən-, men- (US) meɪn- **-s** -z **-ing** -ɪŋ **-ed** -d **-able** -ə.bl̩ **-er/s** -əʳ/z (US) -ɚ/z

maintenance ˈmeɪn.tᵊn.ən*t*s, -tɪ.nən*t*s (US) -tᵊn.ən*t*s

Mainwaring *surname:* 'mæn.ᵊr.ɪŋ *in Wales:* 'meɪn.wə.rɪŋ, -weə-; ˌmeɪn'weə- Ⓤⓢ 'meɪn.wɚ.ɪŋ, -wer-; ˌmeɪn'wer-
Mainz maɪnts
Maisie 'meɪ.zi
maisonette ˌmeɪ.zᵊn'et, -sᵊn'- **-s** -s
Maitland 'meɪt.lənd
maître d', maitre d' ˌmeɪ.trə'diː, ˌmet.rə'- Ⓤⓢ ˌmeɪ.trə'-, -t̬ɚ'- **-s** -z
maître(s) d'hôtel ˌmeɪ.trə.dəʊ'tel, ˌmet.rə- Ⓤⓢ ˌmeɪ.trə.doʊ'-, -t̬ɚ-
maize meɪz
majestic (M) mə'dʒes.tɪk **-al** -ᵊl **-ally** -ᵊl.i, -li
majest|y (M) 'mædʒ.ə.st|i, '-ɪ- **-ies** -iz
majolica mə'jɒl.ɪ.kə, -'dʒɒl- Ⓤⓢ -'dʒɑː.lɪ-
maj|or (M) 'meɪ.dʒ|əʳ Ⓤⓢ -dʒ|ɚ **-ors** -əz Ⓤⓢ -ɚz **-oring** -ᵊr.ɪŋ **-ored** -əd Ⓤⓢ -ɚd
Majorca mə'jɔː.kə, maɪ'ɔː-, -'dʒɔː- Ⓤⓢ -'jɔːr-, -'dʒɔːr-
major-domo ˌmeɪ.dʒə'dəʊ.məʊ Ⓤⓢ -dʒɚ'doʊ.moʊ **-s** -z
majorette ˌmeɪ.dʒᵊr'et **-s** -s
major-general ˌmeɪ.dʒə'dʒen.ᵊr.ᵊl, '-rᵊl Ⓤⓢ -dʒɚ'- **-s** -z
majorit|y mə'dʒɒr.ə.t|i, -ɪ.t|i Ⓤⓢ -'dʒɔːr.ə.t̬|i **-ies** -iz
majuscule 'mædʒ.ə.skjuːl Ⓤⓢ mə'dʒʌs.kjuːl; 'mædʒ.ə.skjuːl **-s** -z
Makarios mə'kɑː.ri.ɒs, -'kær.i- Ⓤⓢ mə'kɑːr.i.oʊs, -'kær.i-, -ɑːs, -əs
mak|e meɪk **-es** -s **-ing** -ɪŋ **made** meɪd **maker/s** 'meɪ.kəʳ/z Ⓤⓢ -kɚ/z
make-believe 'meɪk.bɪˌliːv, -bəˌ-, ˌ--'-
Makeham 'meɪ.kəm
make-or-break ˌmeɪk.ɔː'breɪk Ⓤⓢ -ɔːr'-, -ɚ'- *stress shift:* ˌmake-or-break 'deal
makeover 'meɪkˌəʊ.vəʳ Ⓤⓢ -ˌoʊ.vɚ **-s** -z
Makepeace 'meɪk.piːs
Makerere mə'ker.ᵊr.i
makeshift 'meɪk.ʃɪft
make-up 'meɪk.ʌp **-s** -s
makeweight 'meɪk.weɪt **-s** -s
makings 'meɪ.kɪŋz
Makins 'meɪ.kɪnz
Makower mə'kaʊəʳ Ⓤⓢ -'kaʊɚ
makuta (*plur. of* **likuta**) mɑː'kuː.tɑː
mal- mæl-
Note: Prefix. In verbs or adjectives, **mal-** usually carries secondary stress, e.g. **malfunction** /ˌmæl'fʌnk.ʃᵊn/, **malajusted** /ˌmæl.ə'dʒʌs.tɪd/. Nouns containing **mal-** normally carry stress on the first syllable, e.g. **malcontent** /'mæl.kən.tent/. Exceptions exist: see individual entries.
Malabar 'mæl.ə.bɑːʳ, ˌ--'- Ⓤⓢ 'mæl.ə.bɑːr
Malabo mə'lɑː.bəʊ Ⓤⓢ -boʊ; 'mæl.ə-
malabsorption ˌmæl.əb'zɔːp.ʃᵊn, -'sɔːp- Ⓤⓢ -'sɔːrp-, -'zɔːrp-
Malacca mə'læk.ə Ⓤⓢ -'læk-, -'lɑː.kə
Malachi 'mæl.ə.kaɪ
malachite 'mæl.ə.kaɪt
maladjusted ˌmæl.ə'dʒʌs.tɪd *stress shift:* ˌmaladjusted 'person
maladjustment ˌmæl.ə'dʒʌst.mənt **-s** -s
maladministration ˌmæl.ədˌmɪn.ɪ'streɪ.ʃᵊn Ⓤⓢ -ə'-
maladroit ˌmæl.ə'drɔɪt, '--- **-ly** -li **-ness** -nəs, -nɪs *stress shift:* ˌmaladroit 'tactics
malad|y 'mæl.ə.d|i **-ies** -iz
mala fide ˌmeɪ.lə'faɪ.di, ˌmæl.ə'fɪd.i, -eɪ Ⓤⓢ ˌmeɪ.lə'fiː.di, ˌmæl.ə'fiː.deɪ
Malaga, Málaga 'mæl.ə.gə Ⓤⓢ 'mɑː.lɑː.gɑː, 'mæl.ə.gə
Malagasy ˌmæl.ə'gæs.i, -'gɑː.zi Ⓤⓢ -'gæs.i
Malahide 'mæl.ə.haɪd
malaise mə'leɪz, mæl'eɪz
Malamud 'mæl.ə.mʊd Ⓤⓢ -məd, -mʊd
Malan *English surname:* 'mæl.ən *South African name:* mə'læn, -'lɑːn
malaprop (M) 'mæl.ə.prɒp Ⓤⓢ -prɑːp **-s** -s
malapropism 'mæl.ə.prɒp.ɪ.zᵊm Ⓤⓢ -prɑː.pɪ- **-s** -z
malapropos ˌmælˌæp.rə'pəʊ, ˌ-'--- Ⓤⓢ ˌmæl.æp.rə'poʊ
malari|a mə'leə.ri|.ə Ⓤⓢ -'ler.i- **-al** -əl **-an** -ən
malark(e)y mə'lɑː.ki Ⓤⓢ -'lɑːr-
Malawi mə'lɑː.wi Ⓤⓢ mɑː-, mə- **-an/s** -ən/z
Malay mə'leɪ Ⓤⓢ 'meɪ.leɪ, mə'leɪ **-s** -z
Malay|a mə'leɪ|.ə **-an/s** -ən/z
Malayalam ˌmæl.i'ɑː.ləm, -eɪ'-; -ə'jɑː- Ⓤⓢ ˌmæl.ə'jɑː.ləm
Malaysi|a mə'leɪ.zi|.ə, -ʒi-, '-ʒ|ə Ⓤⓢ -ʒ|ə, -ʃ|ə **-an/s** -ən/z
Malchus 'mæl.kəs
Malcolm 'mæl.kəm
malcontent 'mæl.kənˌtent **-s** -s
Malden 'mɔːl.dᵊn, 'mɒl- Ⓤⓢ 'mɔːl-, 'mɑːl-
Maldive 'mɔːl.diːv, 'mɒl-, -dɪv, -daɪv Ⓤⓢ 'mæl.daɪv, 'mɑːl-, -diːv **-s** -z
Maldivian mɔːl'dɪv.i.ən, mɒl-, mɑːl- Ⓤⓢ mæl'daɪ.vi-, mɑːl-, -'diː- **-s** -z
Maldon 'mɔːl.dᵊn, 'mɒl- Ⓤⓢ 'mɔːl-, 'mɑːl-
male meɪl **-s** -z **-ness** -nəs, -nɪs ˌ**male** '**chauvinist**; ˌ**male** ˌ**chauvinist** '**pig**
Malé 'mɑː.liː, -leɪ Ⓤⓢ -liː
malediction ˌmæl.ɪ'dɪk.ʃᵊn, -ə'- Ⓤⓢ -ə'- **-s** -z
maledictory ˌmæl.ɪ'dɪk.tᵊr.i, -ə'- Ⓤⓢ -ə'-
malefaction ˌmæl.ɪ'fæk.ʃᵊn, -ə'- Ⓤⓢ -ə'- **-s** -z
malefactor 'mæl.ɪ.fæk.təʳ, '-ə- Ⓤⓢ -ə.fæk.tɚ **-s** -z
malefic mə'lef.ɪk
maleficen|ce mə'lef.ɪ.sᵊn|ts, mæl'ef- Ⓤⓢ mə'lef.ə- **-t** -t
Malet 'mæl.ɪt
malevolence mə'lev.ᵊl.ənts, mæl'ev- Ⓤⓢ mə'lev-
malevolent mə'lev.ᵊl.ənt, mæl'ev- Ⓤⓢ mə'lev- **-ly** -li
malfeasance mæl'fiː.zᵊnts
Malfi 'mæl.fi
malformation ˌmæl.fɔː'meɪ.ʃᵊn, -fə'- Ⓤⓢ -fɔːr'- **-s** -z
malformed ˌmæl'fɔːmd Ⓤⓢ -'fɔːrmd
malfunction ˌmæl'fʌŋk.ʃᵊn **-s** -z **-ing** -ɪŋ **-ed** -d
Malham 'mæl.əm
Mali 'mɑː.li
Malibu 'mæl.ɪ.buː, '-ə-
malic 'mæl.ɪk, 'meɪ-
malice 'mæl.ɪs
malicious mə'lɪʃ.əs **-ly** -li **-ness** -nəs, -nɪs
malign mə'laɪn **-ly** -li **-s** -z **-ing** -ɪŋ **-ed** -d **-er/s** -əʳ/z Ⓤⓢ -ɚ/z
malignancy mə'lɪg.nənt.si
malignant mə'lɪg.nənt **-ly** -li
malignity mə'lɪg.nə.ti, -nɪ- Ⓤⓢ -nə.t̬i
Malin 'mæl.ɪn, 'meɪ.lɪn
Malines mæl'iːn
maling|er mə'lɪŋ.g|əʳ Ⓤⓢ -g|ɚ **-ers** -əz Ⓤⓢ -ɚz **-ering** -ᵊr.ɪŋ **-ered** -əd Ⓤⓢ -ɚd **-erer/s** -ᵊr.əʳ/z Ⓤⓢ -ɚ.ɚ/z
Malins 'meɪ.lɪnz, 'mæl.ɪnz
malkin 'mɔː.kɪn, 'mɔːl-, 'mɒl- Ⓤⓢ 'mɔː-, 'mɔːl- **-s** -z
Malkin 'mæl.kɪn
mall mɔːl, mæl Ⓤⓢ mɔːl, mɑːl **-s** -z
Mall (*in* **The Mall, Chiswick Mall, Pall Mall**) mæl
mallard (M) 'mæl.ɑːd, -ləd Ⓤⓢ -ɚd **-s** -z
Mallarmé 'mæl.ɑː.meɪ Ⓤⓢ ˌmæl.ɑːr'meɪ
Malle mæl, mɑːl Ⓤⓢ mɑːl
malleability ˌmæl.i.ə'bɪl.ə.ti, ˌmæl.ə'bɪl-, -ɪ.ti Ⓤⓢ ˌmæl.i.ə'bɪl.ə.t̬i
malleable 'mæl.i.ə.bl̩, '-ə.bl̩ Ⓤⓢ '-i.ə- **-ness** -nəs, -nɪs
mallee 'mæl.i
malleolar mə'liː.ə.ləʳ Ⓤⓢ -lɚ
malleo|lus mə'liː.ə|.ləs **-li** -laɪ
mallet (M) 'mæl.ɪt, -ət **-s** -s
malle|us 'mæl.i|.əs **-i** -aɪ
Malling 'mɔː.lɪŋ Ⓤⓢ 'mɔː-, 'mɑː-
Mallon 'mæl.ən
Mallorca mə'jɔː.kə, -'ljɔː-, -'lɔː- Ⓤⓢ mɑː'jɔːr.kɑː, mɑːl-, mə-, -kə
Mallory 'mæl.ᵊr.i
mallow (M) 'mæl.əʊ Ⓤⓢ -oʊ **-s** -z

Malmaison ˌmælˈmeɪ.zɔ̃ːŋ, -zɒn, ˌ--ˈ- (US) -ˈzɑːn, -ˈzɔ̃ːn -s -z
Malmesbury ˈmɑːmz.bᵊr.i (US) -ber-, -bɚ-
Malmö ˈmæl.məʊ, -mɜː (US) -moʊ
malmsey (M) ˈmɑːm.zi
malnourished ˌmælˈnʌr.ɪʃt (US) -ˈnɜːr-
malnutrition ˌmæl.njuːˈtrɪ.ʃᵊn (US) -nuːˈ-
malodor ˌmælˈəʊ.dəʳ (US) -ˈoʊ.dɚ **-s** -z
malodorous ˌmælˈəʊ.dᵊr.əs (US) -ˈoʊ- **-ly** -li **-ness** -nəs, -nɪs
Malone məˈləʊn (US) -ˈloʊn
Maloney məˈləʊ.ni (US) -ˈloʊ-
Malory ˈmæl.ᵊr.i
Malpas *near Truro:* ˈməʊ.pəs (US) ˈmoʊ- *in Gwent:* ˈmæl.pəs *in Cheshire:* ˈmɔːl.pəs, ˈmɔː-, ˈmæl-
Note: Viscount Malpas pronounces /ˈmɔːl.pəs/.
Malpighi mælˈpiː.gi (US) mɑːl-, mæl-
Malpighian mælˈpɪg.i.ən, -ˈpiː.gi- (US) mɑːlˈpɪg.i-, mæl- **Malˌpighian ˈlayer**
Malplaquet ˈmæl.plə.keɪ, ˌ--ˈ- (US) ˌmæl.plækˈeɪ, -pləˈkeɪ
malpractic|e ˌmælˈpræk.tɪs **-es** -ɪz
Malraux ˈmæl.rəʊ (US) ˈmæl.roʊ; mɑːlˈroʊ
mal|t mɔːl|t, mɒl|t (US) mɔːl|t, mɑːl|t **-ts** -ts **-ting** -tɪŋ (US) -t̬ɪŋ **-ted** -tɪd (US) -t̬ɪd **ˌmalted ˈmilk**
Malta ˈmɔːl.tə, ˈmɒl- (US) ˈmɔːl.t̬ə, ˈmɑːl-
maltase ˈmɔːl.teɪz, ˈmɒl- (US) ˈmɔːl.teɪs, ˈmɑːl-
Maltby ˈmɔːlt.bi, ˈmɒlt- (US) ˈmɔːlt-, ˈmɑːlt-
Maltese ˌmɔːlˈtiːz, ˌmɒl- (US) ˌmɔːlˈtiːz, ˌmɑːl-, -ˈtiːs *stress shift, see compounds:* **ˌMaltese ˈcross**; **ˌMaltese ˈfalcon**
Maltesers® mɔːlˈtiː.zəz, mɒl- (US) mɔːlˈtiː.zɚz, mɑːl-
Malthus ˈmæl.θəs
Malthusian mælˈθjuː.zi.ən, mɔːl-, mɒl-, -ˈθuː- (US) mælˈθuː.ʒᵊn, -zi.ən **-s** -z **-ism** -ɪ.zᵊm
maltings ˈmɔːl.tɪŋz, ˈmɒl- (US) ˈmɔːl.t̬ɪŋz, ˈmɑːl-
Malton ˈmɔːl.tᵊn, ˈmɒl- (US) ˈmɔːl-, ˈmɑːl-
maltose ˈmɔːl.təʊz, ˈmɒl- (US) ˈmɔːl.toʊz, ˈmɑːl-, -toʊs
Maltravers mælˈtræv.əz (US) -ɚz
mal|treat ˌmælˈtriːt **-treats** -ˈtriːts **-treating** -ˈtriː.tɪŋ (US) -ˈtriː.t̬ɪŋ **-treated** -ˈtriː.tɪd (US) -ˈtriː.t̬ɪd **-treatment** -ˈtriːt.mənt **-treater/s** -ˈtriː.təʳ/z (US) -ˈtriː.t̬ɚ/z
maltster ˈmɔːlt.stəʳ, ˈmɒlt- (US) ˈmɔːlt.stɚ, ˈmɑːlt- **-s** -z
Maltz mɔːlts, mɒlts (US) mɔːlts, mɑːlts
malum in se ˌmɑː.lʊm.ɪnˈseɪ (US) ˌmɑː.ləm.ɪnˈseɪ
malum prohibitum ˌmɑː.lʊm.prəʊˈhɪb.ɪ.tʊm (US) ˌmɑː.ləm.proʊˈhɪb.ɪ.təm
Malvasia ˌmæl.vəˈsiː.ə
Malvern *in UK:* ˈmɔːl.vᵊn, ˈmɒl-, -vɜːn *locally also:* ˈmɔː.vᵊn (US) ˈmɔːl.vɚn *in US:* ˈmæl.vən (US) -vɚn
malversation ˌmæl.vɜːˈseɪ.ʃᵊn, -vəˈ- (US) -vɚˈ-
Malvinas mælˈviː.nəs
Malvolio mælˈvəʊ.li.əʊ (US) -ˈvoʊ.li.oʊ, -ˈvoʊl.joʊ
Malyon ˈmæl.jən
mama məˈmɑː; ˈmæm.ə (US) ˈmɑː.mə; məˈmɑː **-s** -z
mamba ˈmæm.bə (US) ˈmɑːm- **-s** -z
mambo ˈmæm.bəʊ (US) ˈmɑːm.boʊ **-es** -z **-ing** -ɪŋ **-ed** -d
Mameluke ˈmæm.ɪ.luːk, ˈ-ə-, -ljuːk (US) -ə.luːk **-s** -s
Mamet ˈmæm.ɪt (US) -ət
Mamie ˈmeɪ.mi
Mamilius məˈmɪl.i.əs, mæmˈɪl-
mamma *mother:* məˈmɑː (US) ˈmɑː.mə, məˈmɑː **-s** -z
mamm|a *milk-secreting organ:* ˈmæm|.ə **-ae** -iː
mammal ˈmæm.ᵊl **-s** -z
mammalian mæmˈeɪ.li.ən, məˈmeɪ-
mammary ˈmæm.ᵊr.i **ˈmammary ˌgland**
mammogram ˈmæm.ə.græm **-s** -z
mammograph ˈmæm.əʊ.grɑːf, -græf (US) -græf, -ə-, -oʊ- **-s** -s
mammography mæmˈɒg.rə.fi, məˈmɒg- (US) məˈmɑː.grə-, mæmˈɑːg-
mammon (M) ˈmæm.ən
mammoth ˈmæm.əθ **-s** -s
mamm|y ˈmæm|.i **-ies** -iz
man (M) (*n.*) mæn **men** men **ˌman ˈFriday**; **ˌman of the ˈworld**
man (*v.*) mæn **-s** -z **-ning** -ɪŋ **-ned** -d
manacl|e ˈmæn.ə.kl̩ **-es** -z **-ing** -ɪŋ, ˈmæn.ə.klɪŋ **-ed** -d
manag|e ˈmæn.ɪdʒ, -ədʒ **-es** -ɪz **-ing** -ɪŋ **-ed** -d **ˌmanaging diˈrector**
manageability ˌmæn.ɪ.dʒəˈbɪl.ə.ti, ˌ-ə-, -ɪ.ti (US) -ə.t̬i
manageab|le ˈmæn.ɪ.dʒə.bl|̩, ˈ-ə- **-ly** -li **-leness** -l̩.nəs, -nɪs
management ˈmæn.ɪdʒ.mənt, -ədʒ- **-s** -s
manager ˈmæn.ɪ.dʒəʳ, ˈ-ə- (US) -dʒɚ **-s** -z
manageress ˌmæn.ɪ.dʒᵊrˈes, ˌ-ə-; ˈmæn.ɪ.dʒᵊr.es, ˈ-ə- (US) ˈmæn- **-es** -ɪz
managerial ˌmæn.əˈdʒɪə.ri.əl (US) -ˈdʒɪr.i- **-ly** -i
Managua məˈnæg.wə, mænˈæg-, -ˈɑː.gwə (US) məˈnɑː.gwɑː, mɑː-, -gwə
Manama məˈnɑː.mə (US) -ˈnæm.ə
mañana mænˈjɑː.nə, məˈnjɑː- (US) məˈnjɑː-, mɑː-
Manassas məˈnæs.əs
Manasseh məˈnæs.i, -ə (US) -ə
Manasses məˈnæs.ɪz, -iːz
manatee (M) ˌmæn.əˈtiː (US) ˈmæn.ə.ti, ˌmæn.əˈtiː **-s** -z
Manáus məˈnaʊs (US) mə-, mɑː-
Manchester ˈmæn.tʃɪs.təʳ, -tʃes-, -tʃəs- (US) -tʃes.tɚ, -tʃɪ.stɚ
Manchu ˌmænˈtʃuː *stress shift:* ˌManchu ˈdynasty **-s** -z
Manchukuo ˌmænˌtʃuːˈkwəʊ (US) -ˈkwoʊ
Manchuri|a mænˈtʃʊə.ri|.ə, -ˈtʃɔː- (US) -ˈtʃʊr.i- **-an/s** -ən/z
manciple ˈmænt.sɪ.pl̩, -sə- **-s** -z
Mancunian mæŋˈkjuː.ni.ən, mæn- (US) mæn- **-s** -z
mandala ˈmæn.dᵊl.ə, ˈmʌn-; mənˈdɑː.lə, mæn- (US) ˈmʌn.də- **-s** -z
Mandalay ˌmæn.dᵊlˈeɪ, ˈ---
mandamus mænˈdeɪ.məs **-es** -ɪz
mandarin (M) ˈmæn.dᵊr.ɪn, ˌ--ˈ- (US) ˈmæn.dɚ.ɪn **-s** -z
mandate (*n.*) ˈmæn.deɪt, -dɪt, -dət (US) -deɪt **-s** -s
manda|te (*v.*) mænˈdeɪ|t, ˈ-- (US) ˈ-- **-tes** -ts **-ting** -tɪŋ (US) -t̬ɪŋ **-ted** -tɪd (US) -t̬ɪd **-tor/s** -təʳ/z (US) -t̬ɚ/z
mandator|y ˈmæn.də.tᵊr|.i, -tr|i; mænˈdeɪ- (US) ˈmæn.də.tɔːr|.i **-ies** -iz
Mandela mænˈdel.ə, -ˈdeɪ.lə (US) -ˈdel.ə
Mandelson ˈmæn.dᵊl.sᵊn (US) -sᵊn, -soʊn
Mandelstam ˈmæn.dᵊl.stæm, -stəm
Mander ˈmɑːn.dəʳ, ˈmæn- (US) -dɚ
Mandeville ˈmæn.də.vɪl, -dɪ-
mandible ˈmæn.dɪ.bl̩, -də- **-s** -z
Mandingo mænˈdɪŋ.gəʊ (US) -goʊ **-(e)s** -z
mandolin ˌmæn.dᵊlˈɪn, ˈ--- **-s** -z
mandoline ˌmæn.dᵊlˈiːn **-s** -z
mandragora mænˈdræg.ᵊr.ə, mən- (US) mæn-
mandrake ˈmæn.dreɪk **-s** -s
mandrax (M®) ˈmæn.dræks **-es** -ɪz
mandrill ˈmæn.drɪl, -drᵊl (US) -drɪl **-s** -z
Mandy ˈmæn.di
mane meɪn **-s** -z **-d** -d
man-eater ˈmænˌiː.təʳ (US) -t̬ɚ **-s** -z
manège, manege mænˈeɪʒ, -ˈeʒ, ˈ-- (US) mænˈeʒ, məˈneʒ, -ˈneɪʒ **-s** -ɪz
manes (M) ˈmɑː.neɪz, -neɪs, ˈmeɪ.niːz (US) ˈmeɪ.niːz, ˈmɑː.neɪs
Manet ˈmæn.eɪ (US) mænˈeɪ, məˈneɪ
Manette mænˈet

maneuv|er mə'nuː.v|əʳ (US) -v|ɚ **-ers** -əz (US) -ɚz **-ering** -ᵊr.ɪŋ **-ered** -əd (US) -ɚd **-erer/s** -ᵊr.əʳ/z (US) -ɚ.ɚ/z
maneuverability məˌnuː.vᵊr.ə'bɪl.ə.ti, -ɪ.ti (US) -ə.t̬i
maneuverable mə'nuː.vᵊr.ə.bl̩
Manfred 'mæn.fred, -frɪd
manful 'mæn.fᵊl, -fʊl **-ly** -i **-ness** -nəs, -nɪs
Mangan 'mæŋ.gən
manganate 'mæŋ.gə.neɪt **-s** -s
manganese 'mæŋ.gə.niːz, ˌ--'- (US) '---, -niːs
manganic mæŋ'gæn.ɪk, mæn- (US) mæn-
mange meɪndʒ
mangel-wurzel 'mæŋ.gᵊlˌwɜː.zᵊl, ˌmæŋ.gᵊl'wɜː- (US) 'mæŋ.gᵊlˌwɜːr-, -ˌwɜːrt.sᵊl **-s** -z
manger 'meɪn.dʒəʳ (US) -dʒɚ **-s** -z
mangetout ˌmɑ̃ːnʒ'tuː (US) ˌmɑ̃ːndʒ- **-s** -z
mangl|e 'mæŋ.gl̩ **-es** -z **-ing** -ɪŋ, 'mæŋ.glɪŋ **-ed** -d **-er/s** -əʳ/z (US) -ɚ/z
mango 'mæŋ.gəʊ (US) -goʊ **-(e)s** -z
mangold (M) 'mæŋ.gəʊld (US) -goʊld **-s** -z
mangosteen 'mæŋ.gəʊ.stiːn (US) -gə- **-s** -z
Mangotsfield 'mæŋ.gəts.fiːld
mangrove 'mæŋ.grəʊv (US) 'mæn.groʊv, 'mæŋ- **-s** -z
mang|y 'meɪn.dʒ|i **-ier** -i.əʳ (US) -i.ɚ **-iest** -i.ɪst, -i.əst **-ily** -ɪ.li, -ᵊl.i **-iness** -ɪ.nəs, -ɪ.nɪs
manhandl|e 'mænˌhæn.dl̩, ˌ-'-- (US) '--- **-es** -z **-ing** -ɪŋ, -ˌhænd.lɪŋ **-ed** -d
manhattan (M) mæn'hæt.ᵊn (US) mæn-, mən-
manhole 'mæn.həʊl (US) -hoʊl **-s** -z
manhood (M) 'mæn.hʊd
manhunt 'mæn.hʌnt **-s** -s
mania 'meɪ.ni.ə (US) -ni.ə, '-njə **-s** -z
maniac 'meɪ.ni.æk **-s** -s
maniac|al mə'naɪə.k|ᵊl **-ally** -ᵊl.i (US) -li
manic 'mæn.ɪk **-s** -s ˌ**manic de'pression**
manic-depressive ˌmæn.ɪk.dɪ'pres.ɪv, -də'- **-s** -z
Manich(a)ean ˌmæn.ɪ'kiː.ən, -ə'- **-s** -z
manicur|e 'mæn.ɪ.kjʊəʳ, '-ə-, -kjɔːʳ (US) -kjʊr **-es** -z **-ing** -ɪŋ **-ed** -d **-ist/s** -ɪst/s
manifest 'mæn.ɪ.fest, '-ə- **-ly** -li **-s** -s **-ing** -ɪŋ **-ed** -ɪd **-ness** -nəs, -nɪs
manifestation ˌmæn.ɪ.fes'teɪ.ʃᵊn, ˌ-ə-, -fə'steɪ- **-s** -z
manifesto ˌmæn.ɪ'fes.təʊ, -ə'- (US) -toʊ **-(e)s** -z
manifold 'mæn.ɪ.fəʊld, '-ə- (US) -foʊld **-ness** -nəs, -nɪs
manikin 'mæn.ɪ.kɪn, '-ə- **-s** z
manila (M) mə'nɪl.ə **-s** -z
manilla mə'nɪl.ə **-s** -z
Manilow 'mæn.ɪ.ləʊ, '-ə- (US) -loʊ
manioc 'mæn.i.ɒk (US) -ɑːk
maniple 'mæn.ɪ.pl̩, '-ə- **-s** -z
manipu|late mə'nɪp.jə|.leɪt, -jʊ- (US) -jə-, -juː- **-lates** -leɪts **-lating** -leɪ.tɪŋ (US) -leɪ.t̬ɪŋ **-lated** -leɪ.tɪd (US) -leɪ.t̬ɪd **-lator/s** -leɪ.təʳ/z (US) -leɪ.t̬ɚ/z
manipulation məˌnɪp.jə'leɪ.ʃᵊn, -jʊ'- (US) -jə'-, -juː'- **-s** -z
manipulative mə'nɪp.jə.lə.tɪv, -jʊ- (US) -jə.leɪ.t̬ɪv, -juː-, -lə- **-ly** -li **-ness** -nəs, -nɪs
Manitoba ˌmæn.ɪ'təʊ.bə, -ə'- (US) -ə'toʊ-
manit(o)u 'mæn.ɪ.tuː (US) '-ə- **-s** -z
mankind *general use:* mæn'kaɪnd, mæŋ- (US) mæn-
mank|y 'mæŋ.k|i **-ier** -i.əʳ (US) -i.ɚ **-iest** -i.ɪst, -i.əst
Manley 'mæn.li
manlike 'mæn.laɪk
Manlius 'mæn.li.əs
manl|y (M) 'mæn.l|i **-ier** -i.əʳ (US) -i.ɚ **-iest** -i.ɪst, -i.əst **-iness** -ɪ.nəs, -ɪ.nɪs
man-made ˌmæn'meɪd, ˌmæm- (US) ˌmæn- *stress shift:* ˌman-made 'fibre
Mann mæn
manna 'mæn.ə
mannequin 'mæn.ɪ.kɪn, '-ə- **-s** -z
manner 'mæn.əʳ (US) -ɚ **-s** -z **-ed** -d
mannerism (M) 'mæn.ᵊr.ɪ.zᵊm **-s** -z
mannerist (M) 'mæn.ᵊr.ɪst
mannerl|y 'mæn.ᵊl|.i (US) -ɚ.l|i **-iness** -ɪ.nəs, -ɪ.nɪs
Manners 'mæn.əz (US) -ɚz
Mannheim 'mæn.haɪm
mannikin 'mæn.ɪ.kɪn, '-ə- **-s** -z
Manning 'mæn.ɪŋ
mannish 'mæn.ɪʃ **-ly** -li **-ness** -nəs, -nɪs
Manns mænz
Manny 'mæn.i
Mannyng of Brunne ˌmæn.ɪŋ.əv'brʊn
manoeuvrability məˌnuː.vᵊr.ə'bɪl.ə.tɪ, -ɪ.ti (US) -ə.t̬i
manoeuvrable mə'nuː.vᵊr.ə.bl̩
manoeuv|re mə'nuː.v|əʳ (US) -v|ɚ **-res** -əz (US) -ɚz **-ring** -ᵊr.ɪŋ **-red** -əd (US) -ɚd **-rer/s** -ᵊr.əʳ/z (US) -ɚ.ɚ/z
man-of-war ˌmæn.əv'wɔːʳ (US) -'wɔːr **men-of-war** ˌmen-
manometer mə'nɒm.ɪ.təʳ, mæn'ɒm-, '-ə- (US) mə'nɑː.mə.t̬ɚ **-s** -z
manometric ˌmæn.əʊ'met.rɪk (US) -ə'- **-al** -ᵊl **-ally** -ᵊl.i, -li
manor 'mæn.əʳ (US) -ɚ **-s** -z
manor-hou|se 'mæn.ə.haʊ|s (US) '-ɚ- **-ses** -zɪz
manorial mə'nɔː.ri.əl, mæn'ɔː- (US) mə'nɔːr.i-
manpower 'mænˌpaʊəʳ, 'mæm- (US) 'mænˌpaʊɚ
manqué 'mɑ̃ːŋ.keɪ (US) mɑ̃ːŋ'keɪ
Manresa mæn'reɪ.sə, -zə (US) mɑːn'reɪ.sə, mæn-
Mansa 'mænt.sə
mansard 'mænt.sɑːd (US) -sɑːrd **-s** -z
mans|e mænts **-es** -ɪz
Mansel(l) 'mænt.sᵊl
Mansergh *surname:* 'mæn.zəʳ, 'mænt.səʳ, -sɜːdʒ (US) 'mæn.zɚ, 'mænt.sɚ, -sɜːrdʒ *place in Cumbria:* 'mæn.zəʳ (US) -zɚ
manservant 'mænˌsɜː.vᵊnt (US) -ˌsɜːr- **menservants** 'menˌsɜː.vᵊnts (US) -ˌsɜːr-
Mansfield 'mænts.fiːld (US) 'mænz-
-manship -mən.ʃɪp
mansion (M) 'mæn.tʃᵊn **-s** -z
mansion-hou|se (M) 'mæn.tʃᵊn.haʊ|s **-ses** -zɪz
manslaughter 'mænˌslɔː.təʳ (US) -ˌslɑː.t̬ɚ, -ˌslɔː-
Manson 'mænt.sᵊn
Manston 'mænt.stᵊn
mansuetude 'mæn.swɪ.tjuːd (US) -tuːd, -tjuːd
Manta 'mæn.tə
Mantegna mæn'ten.jə (US) mɑːn'ten.jɑː, -jə
mantel 'mæn.tᵊl **-s** -z
mantelpiec|e 'mæn.tᵊl.piːs **-es** -ɪz
mantelshel|f 'mæn.tᵊl.ʃel|f **-ves** -vz
-mantic -'mæn.tɪk
mantilla mæn'tɪl.ə (US) -'tɪl-, -'tiː.jə **-s** -z
mantis 'mæn.tɪs (US) -t̬ɪs **-es** -ɪz
mantissa mæn'tɪs.ə **-s** -z
mantl|e 'mæn.tl̩ **-es** -z **-ing** -ɪŋ, 'mænt.lɪŋ **-ed** -d
Mantovani ˌmæn.tə'vɑː.ni (US) ˌmɑːn-
mantra 'mæn.trə, 'mʌn- (US) 'mæn-, 'mɑːn-, 'mʌn- **-s** -z
mantrap 'mæn.træp **-s** -s
Mantu|a (M) 'mæn.tju|.ə, -tu-, -tʃu- (US) -tʃu.w|ə, -tu- **-an/s** -ənz
manual 'mæn.ju.əl **-s** -z **-ly** -i
Manuel *surname:* 'mæn.ju.el, -əl
Manuel *first name:* mæn'wel; ˌmæn.u'el, -ju'- (US) mæn'wel, mɑːn-
manufact|ure ˌmæn.jə'fæk.tʃ|əʳ, -jʊ'-, -ə'- (US) -jə'fæk.tʃ|ɚ, -juː'- **-ures** -əz (US) -ɚz **-uring** -ᵊr.ɪŋ **-ured** -əd (US) -ɚd **-urer/s** -ᵊr.əʳ/z (US) -ɚ.ɚ/z
manumission ˌmæn.jə'mɪʃ.ᵊn, -jʊ'- (US) -jə'-, -juː- **-s** -z
manu|mit ˌmæn.jə|'mɪt, -jʊ'- (US) -jə'-, -juː'- **-mits** -'mɪts **-mitting** -'mɪt.ɪŋ (US) -'mɪt̬.ɪŋ **-mitted** -'mɪt.ɪd (US) -'mɪt̬.ɪd

manur|e mə'njʊəʳ, -njɔːʳ (US) -'nʊr, -'njʊr **-es** -z **-ing** -ɪŋ **-ed** -d
manuscript 'mæn.jə.skrɪpt, -jʊ- **-s** -s
Manutius mə'njuː.ʃi.əs, '-ʃəs (US) -'nuː.ʃi.əs, -'njuː-
Manwaring 'mæn.ᵊr.ɪŋ
Manx mæŋks ˌ**Manx** '**cat**
Manx|man 'mæŋks|.mæn, -mən **-men** -men, -mən **-woman** -ˌwʊm.ən **-women** -ˌwɪm.ɪn
many 'men.i
manyfold 'men.i.fəʊld (US) -foʊld
many-sided ˌmen.i'saɪ.dɪd **-ness** -nəs, -nɪs *stress shift:* ˌmany-sided 'shape
manzanilla (M) ˌmæn.zə'nɪl.ə, -jə (US) -'niːl.jə, -'niː-, -'nɪl.ə
Manzoni mæn'zəʊ.ni (US) mɑːn'zoʊ-
Mao maʊ
Mao|ism 'maʊ|.ɪ.zᵊm **-ist/s** -ɪst/s
Maori 'maʊə.ri (US) 'maʊ.ri; 'mɑː.oʊ.ri **-s** -z
Mao Tse-tung ˌmaʊ.tseɪ'tʊŋ, ˌmaʊ.dʒeɪ'dʊŋ (US) -tsə'dʊŋ
Mao Zedong ˌmaʊ.dʒeɪ'dʊŋ, maʊ.tseɪ'tʊŋ (US) -dʒə'-, -'dɑːŋ
map mæp **-s** -s **-ping** -ɪŋ **-ped** -t
maple (M) 'meɪ.pl̩ **-s** -z '**Maple** ˌ**Leaf** ; ˌ**maple** '**syrup**
Maplin Sands ˌmæp.lɪn'sændz, -lən'-
mapmak|er/s 'mæp.meɪ.k|əʳ/z, -k|ɚ/z **-ing** -ɪŋ
Mappin 'mæp.ɪn
Mapplethorpe 'mæp.l̩.θɔːp (US) 'meɪ.pl̩.θɔːrp
Maputo mə'puː.təʊ (US) -toʊ
maquillage ˌmæk.iː'ɑːʒ, -'jɑːʒ (US) ˌmɑː.ki'ɑːʒ
maquis mæk'iː, '-- (US) mɑː'kiː, mæk'iː
mar (M) mɑːʳ (US) mɑːr **-s** -z **-ring** -ɪŋ **-red** -d
Mar. (*abbrev. for* **March**) mɑːtʃ (US) mɑːrtʃ
marabou 'mær.ə.buː (US) 'mer-, 'mær- **-s** -z
maraca mə'ræk.ə (US) -'rɑː.kə **-s** -z
Maracaibo ˌmær.ə'kaɪ.bəʊ (US) ˌmer.ə'kaɪ.boʊ, ˌmær-
Maradona ˌmær.ə'dɒn.ə (US) ˌmer.ə'dɑː.nə, ˌmær-
maraschino (M) ˌmær.ə'ʃiː.nəʊ, -'skiː- (US) ˌmer.ə'ʃiː.noʊ, ˌmær-, -'skiː- **-s** -z ˌ**mara**ˌ**schino** '**cherry**
Marat 'mær.ɑː (US) mɑː'rɑː, mə-
Marathi mə'rɑː.ti **-s** -z
marathon (M) 'mær.ə.θᵊn (US) 'mer.ə.θɑːn, 'mær- **-s** -z
maraud mə'rɔːd (US) -'rɑːd, -'rɔːd **-s** -z **-ing** -ɪŋ **-ed** -ɪd **-er/s** -əʳ/z (US) -ɚ/z
Marazion ˌmær.ə'zaɪən (US) ˌmer-, ˌmær-
Marbella mɑː'beɪ.ə, -jə (US) mɑːr-
marbl|e 'mɑː.bl̩ (US) 'mɑːr- **-es** -z **-ing** -ɪŋ, 'mɑː.blɪŋ (US) 'mɑːr- **-ed** -d
Marburg 'mɑː.bʊəg, -bɜːg (US) 'mɑːr.bɜːrg, -bʊrg
Marc mɑːk (US) mɑːrk
marcasite 'mɑː.kə.saɪt (US) 'mɑːr-
Marceau ˌmɑː'səʊ, '-- (US) mɑːr'soʊ
Marcel mɑː'sel (US) mɑːr-
Marcella mɑː'sel.ə (US) mɑːr-
Marcelle mɑː'sel (US) mɑːr-
Marcellus mɑː'sel.əs (US) mɑːr-
march (M) mɑːtʃ (US) mɑːrtʃ **-es** -ɪz **-ing** -ɪŋ **-ed** -t **-er/s** -əʳ/z (US) -ɚ/z
Marchant 'mɑː.tʃᵊnt (US) 'mɑːr-
Marchbank 'mɑːtʃ.bæŋk (US) 'mɑːrtʃ- **-s** -s
marchioness ˌmɑː.ʃᵊn'es, -'ɪs; 'mɑː.ʃᵊn.əs (US) 'mɑːr.ʃᵊn.ɪs; ˌmɑːr.ʃᵊn'es **-es** -ɪz
Marchmain 'mɑːtʃ.meɪn (US) 'mɑːrtʃ-
Marchmont 'mɑːtʃ.mənt (US) 'mɑːrtʃ-
Marcia 'mɑː.si.ə, '-ʃə (US) 'mɑːr.ʃə
Marciano ˌmɑː.si'ɑː.nəʊ, -ʃi'- (US) ˌmɑːr.si'æn.oʊ, -ʃi'-, -'ɑː.noʊ
Marco 'mɑː.kəʊ (US) 'mɑːr.koʊ
Marconi mɑː'kəʊ.ni (US) mɑːr'koʊ-
marconigram mɑː'kəʊ.ni.græm (US) mɑːr'koʊ- **-s** -z
Marcos 'mɑː.kɒs (US) 'mɑːr.koʊs
Marcus 'mɑː.kəs (US) 'mɑːr-
Marcuse mɑː'kuː.zə; mɑː'kjuːz (US) mɑːr'kuː.zə
Mar del Plata ˌmɑː.del'plɑː.tə (US) ˌmɑːr.del'plɑː.tə
Marden *in Kent:* 'mɑː.dᵊn; mɑː'den (US) 'mɑːr.dᵊn; mɑːr'den *other places:* 'mɑː.dᵊn (US) 'mɑːr-
Mardi Gras ˌmɑː.di'grɑː (US) 'mɑːr.diˌgrɑː, ˌ--'-
Marduk 'mɑː.dʊk (US) 'mɑːr-
mare *female horse:* meəʳ (US) mer **-s** -z
mare *lunar plain:* 'mɑː.reɪ (US) 'mɑːr.eɪ **maria** 'mɑː.ri.ə (US) 'mɑːr.i-
Marengo mə'reŋ.gəʊ (US) -goʊ
mare's-nest 'meəz.nest, ˌ-'- (US) 'merz.nest **-s** -s
mare's-tail 'meəz.teɪl, ˌ-'- (US) 'merz- **-s** -z
Margaret 'mɑː.gᵊr.ət, -ɪt, '-grət, -grɪt (US) 'mɑːr.grət
margarine ˌmɑː.dʒə'riːn, -gə'-, '--- (US) 'mɑːr.dʒɚ.ɪn
margarita (M) ˌmɑː.gᵊr'iː.tə (US) -gə'riː.t̬ə **-s** -z
Margate 'mɑː.geɪt, -gɪt (US) 'mɑːr-
marge mɑːdʒ (US) mɑːrdʒ
Margerison mɑː'dʒer.ɪ.sᵊn, '-ə-; 'mɑː.dʒᵊr- (US) mɑːr'dʒer-; 'mɑːr.dʒə.rɪ-, -rə-
Margery 'mɑː.dʒᵊr.i (US) 'mɑːr-
Margetts 'mɑː.gɪts (US) 'mɑːr-
margin 'mɑː.dʒɪn (US) 'mɑːr- **-s** -z
marginal 'mɑː.dʒɪ.nᵊl, -dʒᵊn.ᵊl (US) 'mɑːr- **-ly** -i
marginalia ˌmɑː.dʒɪ'neɪ.li.ə, -dʒə'- (US) ˌmɑːr-, -'neɪl.jə
marginalization, -isa- ˌmɑː.dʒɪ.nᵊl.aɪ'zeɪ.ʃᵊn, -dʒᵊn.ᵊl-, -ɪ'- (US) ˌmɑːr.dʒɪ.nᵊl.ɪ'-, -dʒᵊn.ᵊl-
marginaliz|e, -is|e 'mɑː.dʒɪ.nᵊl.aɪz, -dʒᵊn.ᵊl- (US) 'mɑːr- **-es** -ɪz **-ing** -ɪŋ **-ed** -d
Margolis mɑː'gəʊ.lɪs (US) mɑːr'goʊ-
Margot 'mɑː.gəʊ (US) 'mɑːr.goʊ
margrave (M) 'mɑː.greɪv (US) 'mɑːr- **-s** -z
margravine 'mɑː.grə.viːn (US) 'mɑːr- **-s** -z
marguerite (M) ˌmɑː.gᵊr'iːt (US) ˌmɑːr.gə'riːt **-s** -s
Margulies 'mɑː.gʊ.lɪs (US) 'mɑːr'guː.lɪz
Marham *in Norfolk:* 'mær.əm, 'mɑː.rəm (US) 'mær.əm, 'mɑːr-
Note: The pronunciation of the local residents is /'mær.əm/.
Marhamchurch 'mær.əm.tʃɜːtʃ (US) -tʃɜːrtʃ
Maria *first name:* mə'riː.ə, mə'raɪ.ə
maria (*plur. of* **mare**) 'mɑː.ri.ə (US) 'mɑːr.i-
Marian *first name:* 'mær.i.ən (US) 'mer-, 'mær-
Marian (*n. adj.*) *of Mary, or person devoted to Mary:* 'meə.ri.ən (US) 'mer.i-, 'mær-
Mariana *English name:* ˌmær.i'æn.ə, ˌmeə.ri'-, -'ɑː.nə (US) ˌmer.i'æn.ə, ˌmær- *Spanish historian:* ˌmɑː.ri'ɑː.nə (US) ˌmɑːr.i'ɑː-
Marianne ˌmær.i'æn (US) ˌmer.i'æn, ˌmær-
Maribor 'mær.i.bɔːʳ (US) 'mɑːr.i.bɔːr
Marie mə'riː, 'mɑː.ri, 'mær.i (US) mə'riː
Marie Antoinette ˌmær.iˌæn.twə'net, -ˌɑ̃ːn- (US) məˌriː.æn-
Marienbad 'mær.i.ən.bæd, -əm-; mə'riː- (US) 'mer.i.ən-, 'mær-
marigold (M) 'mær.ɪ.gəʊld (US) 'mer.ɪ.goʊld, 'mær- **-s** -z
marijuana, **marihuana** ˌmær.ɪ'wɑː.nə, -ə'-, -'hwɑː- (US) ˌmer.ɪ'-, ˌmær-
Marilla mə'rɪl.ə
Marilyn 'mær.ɪ.lɪn, '-ə- (US) 'mer-, 'mær-
marimba mə'rɪm.bə **-s** -z
marina (M) mə'riː.nə **-s** -z
marinad|e ˌmær.ɪ'neɪd, '--- (US) ˌmer.ɪ'neɪd, ˌmær-, '--- **-es** -z **-ing** -ɪŋ **-ed** -ɪd
marinara ˌmær.ɪ'nɑː.rə, -ə'- (US) ˌmer.ɪ'ner.ə, -nær.ə, -nɑː.rə
marinat|e 'mær.ɪ.neɪt, '-ə- (US) 'mer-, 'mær- **-es** -s **-ing** -ɪŋ **-ed** -ɪd

marination ˌmær.ɪˈneɪ.ʃᵊn, -əˈ- Ⓤⓢ ˌmer-, ˌmær-
marine məˈriːn **-s** -z
mariner ˈmær.ɪ.nəʳ, ˈ-ə- Ⓤⓢ ˈmer.ɪ.nɚ, ˈmær-, ˈ-ə- **-s** -z
Marino Faliero məˌriː.nəʊ.fəˈlɪə.rəʊ Ⓤⓢ -noʊ.fəˈlɪr.oʊ
Mario ˈmær.i.əʊ, ˈmɑː.ri- Ⓤⓢ ˈmɑːr.i.oʊ, ˈmer-, ˈmær-
Marion ˈmær.i.ən, ˈmeə.ri- Ⓤⓢ ˈmer.i-, ˈmær-
marionette ˌmær.i.əˈnet Ⓤⓢ ˌmer-, ˌmær- **-s** -s
Marisa məˈrɪs.ə
Marischal ˈmɑː.ʃᵊl Ⓤⓢ ˈmɑːr.ɪ.ʃɑːl, ˈ-ʃɑːl, ˈ-ʃəl
Marissa məˈrɪs.ə
marital ˈmær.ɪ.tᵊl, ˈ-ə- Ⓤⓢ ˈmer.ɪ.t̬ᵊl, ˈmær- **-ly** -i
maritime (M) ˈmær.ɪ.taɪm, ˈ-ə- Ⓤⓢ ˈmer-, ˈmær-
Marius ˈmær.i.əs, ˈmeə.ri-, ˈmɑː- Ⓤⓢ ˈmer.i-, ˈmær-
marjoram ˈmɑː.dʒᵊr.əm Ⓤⓢ ˈmɑːr.dʒɚ.əm
Marjoribanks ˈmɑːtʃ.bæŋks Ⓤⓢ ˈmɑːrtʃ-
Marjorie, Marjory ˈmɑː.dʒᵊr.i Ⓤⓢ ˈmɑːr-
mark (M) mɑːk Ⓤⓢ mɑːrk **-s** -s **-ing/s** -ɪŋ/z **-ed** -t **-edly** -ɪd.li **-er/s** -əʳ/z Ⓤⓢ -ɚ/z ˌ**Mark ˈAntony**
Markby ˈmɑːk.bi Ⓤⓢ ˈmɑːrk-
markdown ˈmɑːk.daʊn Ⓤⓢ ˈmɑːrk-
mar|ket (M) ˈmɑː|.kɪt Ⓤⓢ ˈmɑːr- **-kets** -kɪts **-keting** -kɪ.tɪŋ Ⓤⓢ -kɪ.t̬ɪŋ **-keted** -kɪ.tɪd **-keter/s** -kɪ.təʳ/z Ⓤⓢ -kɪ.t̬ɚ/z **-keted** -kɪ.t̬ɪd **-ketable** -kɪ.tə.bl̩ Ⓤⓢ -kɪ.t̬ə.bl̩ ˌ**market eˈconomy** ; ˌ**market ˈgardening**; ˌ**market reˈsearch** Ⓤⓢ ˈ**market** ˌ**research**, ˈ**market re**ˌ**search**; ˈ**market** ˌ**town**, ˌ**market ˈtown**
marketability ˌmɑː.kɪ.təˈbɪl.ə.ti, -ɪ.ti Ⓤⓢ ˌmɑːr.kɪ.t̬əˈbɪl.ə.t̬i
Market Deeping ˌmɑː.kɪtˈdiː.pɪŋ Ⓤⓢ ˌmɑːr-
marketeer ˌmɑː.kɪˈtɪəʳ, -kəˈ- Ⓤⓢ ˌmɑːr.kəˈtɪr **-s** -z
market-plac|e ˈmɑː.kɪt.pleɪs Ⓤⓢ ˈmɑːr- **-es** -ɪz
Market Rasen ˌmɑː.kɪtˈreɪ.zᵊn Ⓤⓢ ˌmɑːr-
Markham ˈmɑː.kəm Ⓤⓢ ˈmɑːr-
markk|a ˈmɑː.k|ɑː, -k|ə Ⓤⓢ ˈmɑːr- **-aa** -ɑː
Markov ˈmɑː.kɒf, -kɒv Ⓤⓢ ˈmɑːr.kɔːf
Markova mɑːˈkəʊ.və Ⓤⓢ mɑːrˈkoʊ-
Marks mɑːks Ⓤⓢ mɑːrks
Marks and Spencer® ˌmɑːks.ᵊndˈspent.səʳ Ⓤⓢ ˌmɑːrks.ᵊndˈspent.sɚ
marks|man ˈmɑːks|.mən Ⓤⓢ ˈmɑːrks- **-men** -mən, -men **-woman** -ˌwʊm.ən **-women** -ˌwɪm.ɪn
marksmanship ˈmɑːks.mən.ʃɪp Ⓤⓢ ˈmɑːrks-
markup ˈmɑːk.ʌp Ⓤⓢ ˈmɑːrk- **-s** -s
marl mɑːl Ⓤⓢ mɑːrl
Marlboro® ˈmɑːl.bᵊr.ə, ˈmɔːl- Ⓤⓢ ˈmɑːrl-
Marlborough *town in Wiltshire, family name:* ˈmɔːl.bᵊr.ə Ⓤⓢ ˈmɑːrl.bə.roʊ *London streets, town in US, New Zealand district:* ˈmɑːl.bᵊr.ə Ⓤⓢ ˈmɑːrl.bɚ-
Marlene *English name:* ˈmɑː.liːn, -ˈ- Ⓤⓢ mɑːrˈ- *German name:* mɑːˈleɪ.nə Ⓤⓢ mɑːr-
Marler ˈmɑː.ləʳ Ⓤⓢ ˈmɑːr.lɚ
Marley ˈmɑː.li Ⓤⓢ ˈmɑːr-
marlin ˈmɑː.lɪn Ⓤⓢ ˈmɑːr- **-s** -z
Marling ˈmɑː.lɪŋ Ⓤⓢ ˈmɑːr-
Marlovian mɑːˈləʊ.vi.ən Ⓤⓢ mɑːrˈloʊ-
Marlow(e) ˈmɑː.ləʊ Ⓤⓢ ˈmɑːr.loʊ
Marmaduke ˈmɑː.mə.djuːk Ⓤⓢ ˈmɑːr.mə.duːk, -djuːk
marmalade ˈmɑː.mᵊl.eɪd Ⓤⓢ ˈmɑːr- **-s** -z
Marmion ˈmɑː.mi.ən Ⓤⓢ ˈmɑːr-
marmite (M®) ˈmɑː.maɪt Ⓤⓢ ˈmɑːr-
Marmora ˈmɑː.mᵊr.ə Ⓤⓢ ˈmɑːr-
marmoreal mɑːˈmɔː.ri.əl Ⓤⓢ mɑːrˈmɔːr.i- **-ly** -i
marmoset ˈmɑː.mə.zet, -set, ˌ--ˈ- Ⓤⓢ ˈmɑːr.mə- **-s** -s
marmot ˈmɑː.mət Ⓤⓢ ˈmɑːr- **-s** -s
Marne mɑːn Ⓤⓢ mɑːrn
Marner ˈmɑː.nəʳ Ⓤⓢ ˈmɑːr.nɚ
marocain ˈmær.ə.keɪn, ˌ--ˈ- Ⓤⓢ ˈmer-, ˈmær-
maroon məˈruːn **-s** -z **-ing** -ɪŋ **-ed** -d
Marple ˈmɑː.pl̩ Ⓤⓢ ˈmɑːr-
Marprelate ˈmɑː.prel.ət, -ɪt Ⓤⓢ ˈmɑːr-
Marquand ˈmɑː.kwənd Ⓤⓢ ˈmɑːr-
marque mɑːk Ⓤⓢ mɑːrk **-s** -s
marquee mɑːˈkiː Ⓤⓢ mɑːr- **-s** -z
Marquesas mɑːˈkeɪ.səs, -zəs, -sæs, -zæs Ⓤⓢ mɑːrˈkeɪ.zəs, -səs
marquess ˈmɑː.kwɪs, -kwəs Ⓤⓢ ˈmɑːr- **-es** -ɪz
marquetr|y ˈmɑː.kɪ.tr|i, -kə- Ⓤⓢ ˈmɑːr- **-ies** -iz
marquis (M) ˈmɑː.kwɪs, -kwəs; mɑːˈkiː Ⓤⓢ ˈmɑːr.kwɪs, -kwəs; mɑːrˈkiː **marquises** ˈmɑː.kwɪ.sɪz, -kwə- Ⓤⓢ ˈmɑːr.kwɪ- (*alternative plur. of* **marquis**) mɑːˈkiːz Ⓤⓢ mɑːr-
marquis|e mɑːˈkiːz Ⓤⓢ mɑːr- **-es** -ɪz
Marrakesh, Marrakech ˌmær.əˈkeʃ, məˈræk.eʃ Ⓤⓢ ˈmer.ə.keʃ, ˈmær-; ˌməˈrɑː.keʃ
marram grass ˈmær.əmˌɡrɑːs Ⓤⓢ ˈmer.əm.ɡræs, ˈmær-
marriag|e ˈmær.ɪdʒ Ⓤⓢ ˈmer-, ˈmær- **-es** -ɪz **-eable** -ə.bl̩
Marriner ˈmær.ɪ.nəʳ Ⓤⓢ ˈmer.ɪ.nɚ, ˈmær-
marron ˈmær.ᵊn, -ɔ̃ːŋ Ⓤⓢ ˈmer.ᵊn, ˈmær-; məˈroʊn **-s** -z
marrons glacés ˌmær.ᵊnˈɡlæs.eɪ, -ᵊŋˈ-, -ɔ̃ːŋˈ- Ⓤⓢ məˌroʊn.ɡlɑːˈseɪ
marrow ˈmær.əʊ Ⓤⓢ ˈmer.oʊ, ˈmær- **-s** -z **-y** -i
marrowbone ˈmær.əʊ.bəʊn Ⓤⓢ ˈmer.oʊ.boʊn, ˈmær- **-s** -z
marrowfat ˈmær.əʊ.fæt Ⓤⓢ ˈmer.oʊ-, ˈmær- **-s** -s
marr|y ˈmær|.i Ⓤⓢ ˈmer-, ˈmær- **-ies** -iz **-ying** -i.ɪŋ **-ied** -id **-ier/s** -i.əʳ/z Ⓤⓢ -i.ɚ/z
Marryat ˈmær.i.ət Ⓤⓢ ˈmer-, ˈmær-
Mars mɑːz Ⓤⓢ mɑːrz ˈ**Mars** ˌ**bar®**
Marsala mɑːˈsɑː.lə Ⓤⓢ mɑːrˈsɑː.lɑː
Marsden ˈmɑːz.dᵊn Ⓤⓢ ˈmɑːrz-
Marseillaise ˌmɑː.seɪˈjeɪz, -ˈeɪz, -sᵊlˈeɪz Ⓤⓢ ˌmɑːr.sᵊlˈeɪz, -seɪˈez
Marseilles, Marseille ˌmɑːˈseɪ Ⓤⓢ ˌmɑːr-
marsh (M) mɑːʃ Ⓤⓢ mɑːrʃ **-es** -ɪz
Marsha ˈmɑː.ʃə Ⓤⓢ ˈmɑːr-
marshal ˈmɑː.ʃᵊl Ⓤⓢ ˈmɑːr- **-s** -z **-(l)ing** -ɪŋ **-(l)ed** -d **-(l)er/s** -əʳ/z Ⓤⓢ -ɚ/z
Marshall ˈmɑː.ʃᵊl Ⓤⓢ ˈmɑːr-
marshmallow ˌmɑːʃˈmæl.əʊ Ⓤⓢ ˈmɑːrʃ.mel.oʊ, -mæl- **-s** -z
marsh|y ˈmɑː.ʃ|i Ⓤⓢ ˈmɑːr- **-ier** -i.əʳ Ⓤⓢ -i.ɚ **-iest** -i.ɪst, -i.əst **-iness** -ɪ.nəs, -ɪ.nɪs
Marske mɑːsk Ⓤⓢ mɑːrsk
Marsland ˈmɑːz.lənd Ⓤⓢ ˈmɑːrz-
Marston ˈmɑː.stᵊn Ⓤⓢ ˈmɑːr-
marsupial mɑːˈsuː.pi.əl, -ˈsjuː- Ⓤⓢ mɑːrˈsuː- **-s** -z
mart mɑːt Ⓤⓢ mɑːrt **-s** -s
Martel(l) mɑːˈtel Ⓤⓢ mɑːr-
Martello tower mɑːˌtel.əʊˈtaʊəʳ Ⓤⓢ mɑːrˌtel.oʊˈtaʊɚ **-s** -z
marten ˈmɑː.tɪn Ⓤⓢ ˈmɑːr.tᵊn **-s** -z
Martens ˈmɑː.tɪnz; mɑːˈtenz Ⓤⓢ ˈmɑːr.tᵊnz; mɑːrˈtenz
Martha ˈmɑː.θə Ⓤⓢ ˈmɑːr- ˌ**Martha's ˈVineyard**
martial (M) ˈmɑː.ʃᵊl Ⓤⓢ ˈmɑːr- **-ly** -i ˌ**martial ˈlaw**
Martian ˈmɑː.ʃᵊn Ⓤⓢ ˈmɑːr- **-s** -z
martin (M) ˈmɑː.tɪn Ⓤⓢ ˈmɑːr.tᵊn **-s** -z
Martina mɑːˈtiː.nə Ⓤⓢ mɑːr-
Martineau ˈmɑː.tɪ.nəʊ, -tə- Ⓤⓢ ˈmɑːr.tə.noʊ
martinet (M) ˌmɑː.tɪˈnet, -təˈ-, -ˈneɪ Ⓤⓢ ˌmɑːr.tᵊnˈet, -ˈeɪ, ˈ--- **-s** -s
Martinez mɑːˈtiː.nez Ⓤⓢ mɑːr-, -nəs

martingale 'mɑː.tɪŋ.geɪl (US) 'mɑːr.tᵊn- **-s** -z
martini (M®) mɑː'tiː.ni (US) mɑːr- **-s** -z
Martinique ˌmɑː.tɪ'niːk, -tə'- (US) ˌmɑːr.tᵊn'iːk
Martinmas 'mɑː.tɪn.məs, -tɪm-, -mæs (US) 'mɑːr.tᵊn.məs
mart|yr (M) 'mɑː.t|əʳ (US) 'mɑːr.t̬|ɚ **-yrs** -əz (US) -ɚz **-yring** -ᵊr.ɪŋ **-yred** -əd (US) -ɚd
martyrdom 'mɑː.tə.dəm (US) 'mɑːr.t̬ɚ- **-s** -z
martyriz|e, -is|e 'mɑː.tᵊr.aɪz, -tɪ.raɪz (US) 'mɑːr.t̬ə.raɪz **-es** -ɪz **-ing** -ɪŋ **-ed** -d
marvel 'mɑː.vᵊl (US) 'mɑːr- **-s** -z **-(l)ing** -ɪŋ, 'mɑːv.lɪŋ **-(l)ed** -d
Marvell 'mɑː.vᵊl (US) 'mɑːr-
marvel(l)ous 'mɑː.vᵊl.əs; 'mɑːv.ləs (US) 'mɑːr.vᵊl.əs; 'mɑːrv.ləs **-ly** -li **-ness** -nəs, -nɪs
Marvin 'mɑː.vɪn (US) 'mɑːr-
Marx mɑːks (US) mɑːrks 'Marx ˌBrothers
Marxian 'mɑːk.si.ən (US) 'mɑːrk-
Marx|ism 'mɑːk.s|ɪ.zᵊm (US) 'mɑːrk- **-ist/s** -ɪst/s
Marxism-Leninism ˌmɑːk.sɪ.zᵊm'len.ɪ.nɪ.zᵊm (US) ˌmɑːrk-
Marxist-Leninist ˌmɑːk.sɪst'len.ɪ.nɪst (US) ˌmɑːrk- **-s** -s
Mary 'meə.ri (US) 'mer.i
Maryborough 'meə.ri.bᵊr.ə, -ˌbʌr.ə (US) 'mer.i.bə.roʊ
Maryland 'meə.ri.lænd, 'mer.ɪ-, -lənd (US) 'mer.ə.lənd
Marylebone *road, district:* 'mær.ᵊl.ə.bən, -bəʊn; '-ə.bən, '-ɪ-; 'mɑː.lɪ- (US) 'mer.ᵊl.ə.bən, -boʊn; '-ə.bən, '-ɪ-; 'mɑːr.lɪ-
Mary-le-Bone *preceded by 'St.':* 'mær.ɪ.lə.bən, -ᵊl.ə- (US) 'mer-
Maryport 'meə.ri.pɔːt (US) 'mer.i.pɔːrt
marzipan 'mɑː.zɪ.pæn, -zə-, ˌ--'- (US) 'mɑːr.zɪ.pæn, 'mɑːrt.sɪ-, -pɑːn
Masaccio mə'zɑː.tʃəʊ, -'zætʃ.əʊ, -tʃi.əʊ (US) -'sɑː.tʃi.oʊ
Masada mə'sɑː.də, mæs'ɑː- (US) mə'sɑː.də; ˌmɑː.sɑː'dɑː
Masai 'mɑː.saɪ; -'-, mə'- (US) mɑː'saɪ, mə'-
masala mə'sɑː.lə, mɑː-
Masaryk 'mæs.ə.rɪk, 'mæz- (US) 'mæs.ɚ.ɪk
Mascagni mæs'kɑː.nji, -'kæn.ji (US) mɑːs-
mascara mə'skɑː.rə, mæs'kɑː- (US) mæs'ker.ə, -'kær- **-s** -z
mascarpone ˌmæs.kɑː'pəʊ.neɪ (US) ˌmɑːs.kɑːr'poʊ-, ˌmæs-
mascot 'mæs.kɒt, -kət (US) -kɑːt, -kət **-s** -s
masculine 'mæs.kjə.lɪn, -kjʊ- (US) 'mæs.kjə-, -kjuː- **-s** -z
masculinity ˌmæs.kjə'lɪn.ə.ti, -kjʊ'-, -ɪ.ti (US) ˌmæs.kjə'lɪn.ə.t̬i, -kjuː'-
Masefield 'meɪs.fiːld
maser 'meɪ.zəʳ (US) -zɚ **-s** -z
Maserati® ˌmæz.ᵊr'ɑː.ti (US) ˌmɑː.sə'rɑː.t̬i, ˌmæz.ə'- **-s** -z
Maseru mə'sɪə.ruː, -'seə- (US) 'mæz.ə.ruː, ˌmɑː.sə'ruː
mash (M) mæʃ **-es** -ɪz **-ing** -ɪŋ **-ed** -t
MASH mæʃ
Masham *in North Yorkshire:* 'mæs.əm *surname:* 'mæs.əm, 'mæʃ-
masher 'mæʃ.əʳ (US) -ɚ **-s** -z
mashie 'mæʃ.i **-s** -z
Mashona mə'ʃɒn.ə, -'ʃəʊ.nə (US) -'ʃɑː-, -'ʃoʊ- **-s** -z **-land** -lænd
mash|y 'mæʃ|.i **-ies** -iz
Masie 'meɪ.zi
mask mɑːsk (US) mæsk **-s** -s **-ing** -ɪŋ **-ed** -t 'masking ˌtape
Maskell 'mæs.kᵊl
Maskelyne 'mæs.kɪ.lɪn, -kᵊl.ɪn (US) -ɪn, -aɪn
masoch|ism 'mæs.ə.k|ɪ.zᵊm, 'mæz- **-ist/s** -ɪst/s
masochistic ˌmæs.ə'kɪs.tɪk, ˌmæz- **-ally** -ᵊl.i, -li
mason (M) 'meɪ.sᵊn **-s** -z 'mason ˌjar
Mason-Dixon ˌmeɪ.sᵊn'dɪk.sᵊn ˌMason-'Dixon ˌline
masonic (M) mə'sɒn.ɪk (US) -'sɑː.nɪk
Masonite® 'meɪ.sᵊn.aɪt
masonr|y (M) 'meɪ.sᵊn.r|i **-ies** -iz
masque mɑːsk, mæsk (US) mæsk **-s** -s
masquerad|e ˌmæs.kᵊr'eɪd, ˌmɑː.skᵊr'- (US) ˌmæs.kə'reɪd **-es** -z **-ing** -ɪŋ **-ed** -ɪd **-er/s** -əʳ/z (US) -ɚ/z
mass mæs **-es** -ɪz **-ing** -ɪŋ **-ed** -t ˌmass 'media ; ˌmass pro'duction
mass (M) (*n.*) *religious service:* mæs, mɑːs (US) mæs **-es** -ɪz
Mass. (*abbrev. for* **Massachusetts**) mæs
Massachusetts ˌmæs.ə'tʃuː.sɪts, -səts (US) -sɪts
massac|re 'mæs.ə.k|əʳ, '-ɪ- (US) -k|ɚ **-res** -əz (US) -ɚz **-ring** -ᵊr.ɪŋ **-red** -əd (US) -ɚd
massag|e 'mæs.ɑːdʒ (US) mə'sɑːdʒ **-es** -ɪz **-ing** -ɪŋ **-ed** -d **-er/s** -əʳ/z (US) **-er/z** -ɚ/z **-ist/s** -ɪst/s 'massage ˌparlour (US) mas'sage ˌparlor
Massawa mə'sɑː.wə (US) mɑː'sɑː.wɑː, mə'sɑː.wə
Massenet 'mæs.ᵊn.eɪ (US) ˌ--'-
masseur mæs'ɜːʳ, mə'sɜːʳ (US) -'sɜːr, -'suːr, -'sʊr **-s** -z
masseus|e mæs'ɜːz, mə'sɜːz (US) -'sɜːz, -'suːz, -'sʊz **-es** -ɪz
Massey 'mæs.i
massif mæs'iːf, '-- (US) mæs'iːf **-s** -s
Massif Central ˌmæs.iːf.sɑ̃ːn'trɑːl
Massinger 'mæs.ɪn.dʒəʳ (US) -dʒɚ
massive 'mæs.ɪv **-ly** -li **-ness** -nəs, -nɪs
mass-market ˌmæs'mɑː.kɪt (US) -'mɑːr- **-s** -s **-ing** -ɪŋ **-ed** -ɪd
mass-meeting ˌmæs'miː.tɪŋ, '-ˌ-- (US) -t̬ɪŋ **-s** -z
Masson 'mæs.ᵊn (US) 'mæs.ɑːn, -'-
mass-produc|e ˌmæs.prə'djuːs, -'dʒuːs (US) ˌmæs.prə'duːs, -proʊ'-, -'djuːs **-es** -ɪz **-ing** -ɪŋ **-ed** -t **-er/s** -əʳ/z (US) -ɚ/z *stress shift:* ˌmass-produced 'goods
mass-production ˌmæs.prə'dʌk.ʃᵊn, 'mæs.prəˌ- (US) ˌmæs.prə'dʌk-, -proʊ'-
mass|y 'mæs|.i **-iness** -ɪ.nəs, -ɪ.nɪs
mast mɑːst (US) mæst **-s** -s
mastectom|y mæs'tek.tə.m|i (US) mə'stek-, mæs'tek- **-ies** -iz
mast|er 'mɑː.st|əʳ (US) 'mæs.t|ɚ **-ers** -əz (US) -ɚz **-ering** -ᵊr.ɪŋ **-ered** -əd (US) -ɚd ˌmaster 'bedroom ; 'master ˌclass; ˌmaster of 'ceremonies; 'master ˌkey; 'master ˌrace
master-at-arms ˌmɑː.stᵊr.ət'ɑːms (US) ˌmæs.tɚ.ət'ɑːrms
masters-at-arms ˌmɑː.stəz- (US) ˌmæs.tɚz-
Mastercard® 'mɑː.stə.kɑːd (US) 'mæs.tɚ.kɑːrd
masterful 'mɑː.stə.fᵊl, -fʊl (US) 'mæs.tɚ- **-ly** -i **-ness** -nəs, -nɪs
masterl|y 'mɑː.stə.l|i (US) 'mæs.tɚ- **-iness** -ɪ.nəs, -ɪ.nɪs
Masterman 'mɑː.stə.mən (US) 'mæs.tɚ-
mastermind 'mɑː.stə.maɪnd (US) 'mæs.tɚ- **-s** -z **-ing** -ɪŋ **-ed** -ɪd
masterpiec|e 'mɑː.stə.piːs (US) 'mæs.tɚ- **-es** -ɪz
Masters 'mɑː.stəz (US) 'mæs.tɚz
mastership 'mɑː.stə.ʃɪp (US) 'mæs.tɚ-
master-stroke 'mɑː.stə.strəʊk (US) 'mæs.tɚ.stroʊk **-s** -s
masterwork 'mɑː.stə.wɜːk (US) 'mæs.tɚ.wɜːrk **-s** -s
master|y 'mɑː.stᵊr|.i (US) 'mæs.tɚ- **-ies** -iz
masthead 'mɑːst.hed (US) 'mæst- **-s** -z
mastic 'mæs.tɪk
masti|cate 'mæs.tɪ|.keɪt, -tə- **-cates** -keɪts **-cating** -keɪ.tɪŋ (US) -keɪ.t̬ɪŋ **-cated** -keɪ.tɪd (US) -keɪ.t̬ɪd **-cator/s** -keɪ.təʳ/z (US) -keɪ.t̬ɚ/z
mastication ˌmæs.tɪ'keɪ.ʃᵊn, -tə'-
masticatory 'mæs.tɪ.kə.tᵊr.i, -keɪ-; ˌmæs.tɪ'keɪ-, -tə'- (US) 'mæs.tɪ.kə.tɔːr-, -tə-

mastiff ˈmæs.tɪf, ˈmɑː.stɪf US ˈmæs.tɪf **-s** -s
mastitis mæsˈtaɪ.tɪs, məˈstaɪ- US mæsˈtaɪ.t̬ɪs, məˈstaɪ- **mastitides** mæsˈtɪt.ə.diːz, məˈstɪt- US mæsˈtɪt̬.ə-, məˈstɪt̬-
mastodon ˈmæs.tə.dɒn, -dən US -dɑːn **-s** -z
mastoid ˈmæs.tɔɪd **-s** -z
mastur|bate ˈmæs.tə|.beɪt US -tɚ- **-bates** -beɪts **-bating** -beɪ.tɪŋ US -beɪ.t̬ɪŋ **-bated** -beɪ.tɪd US -beɪ.t̬ɪd **-bator/s** -beɪ.təʳ/z US -beɪ.t̬ɚ/z
masturbation ˌmæs.təˈbeɪ.ʃən US -tɚ- **-s** -z
masturbatory ˌmæs.təˈbeɪ.tər.i, ˈmæs.tə.beɪ- US ˈmæs.tɚ.bə.tɔːr-
mat mæt **-s** -s **-ting** -ɪŋ US ˈmæt̬.ɪŋ **-ted** -ɪd US ˈmæt̬.ɪd
Matabel|e ˌmæt.əˈbiː.li US ˌmæt̬- **-ies** -iz **-ie** -i
Matabeleland ˌmæt.əˈbiː.li.lænd US ˌmæt̬-
matador ˈmæt.ə.dɔːʳ US ˈmæt̬.ə.dɔːr **-s** -z
Mata Hari ˌmɑː.təˈhɑː.ri US ˌmɑː.t̬əˈhɑːr.i, ˌmæt̬.əˈher-, -ˈhær-
match mætʃ **-es** -ɪz **-ing** -ɪŋ **-ed** -t **-er/s** -əʳ/z US -ɚ/z ˌ**match** ˈ**point**
matchboard ˈmætʃ.bɔːd US -bɔːrd
matchbook ˈmætʃ.bʊk **-s** -s
matchbox ˈmætʃ.bɒks US -bɑːks **-es** -ɪz
matchless ˈmætʃ.ləs, -lɪs **-ly** -li **-ness** -nəs, -nɪs
matchlock ˈmætʃ.lɒk US -lɑːk **-s** -s
matchmaker ˈmætʃˌmeɪ.kəʳ US -kɚ **-s** -z
matchmaking ˈmætʃˌmeɪ.kɪŋ
matchplay ˈmætʃ.pleɪ
matchstick ˈmætʃ.stɪk **-s** -s
matchwood ˈmætʃ.wʊd
mat|e meɪt **-es** -s **-ing** -ɪŋ US ˈmeɪ.t̬ɪŋ **-ed** -ɪd US ˈmeɪ.t̬ɪd
matelot ˈmæt.ləʊ, ˈ-əl.əʊ US -əl.oʊ **-s** -z
mater ˈmeɪ.təʳ, ˈmɑː- US -t̬ɚ **-s** -z
materfamilias ˌmæt.ə.fəˈmɪl.i.æs US ˌmeɪ.t̬ɚ.fəˈmɪl.i.əs, ˌmɑː-
material məˈtɪə.ri.əl US -ˈtɪr.i- **-s** -z **-ly** -i
material|ism məˈtɪə.ri.ə.l|ɪ.zəm US -ˈtɪr.i- **-ist/s** -ɪst/s
materialistic məˌtɪə.ri.əˈlɪs.tɪk US -ˌtɪr.i-
materialization, -isa- məˌtɪə.ri.əl.aɪˈzeɪ.ʃən, -ɪˈ- US -ˌtɪr.i.əl.ɪˈ- **-s** -z
materializ|e, -is|e məˈtɪə.ri.ə.laɪz US -ˈtɪr.i- **-es** -ɪz **-ing** -ɪŋ **-ed** -d
matériel, materiel məˌtɪə.riˈel, mætˌɪə-; məˈtɪə.ri.əl US məˌtɪr.iˈel; məˈtɪr.i.əl
maternal məˈtɜː.nəl US -ˈtɜːr- **-ly** -i
maternit|y məˈtɜː.nə.t|i, -ɪ.t|i US -ˈtɜːr.nə.t̬|i **-ies** -iz **maˈternity** ˌ**leave** ; **maˈternity** ˌ**ward**
matey ˈmeɪ.ti US -t̬i **-ness** -ɪ.nəs, -ɪ.nɪs
math mæθ
mathematic ˌmæθ.əmˈæt.ɪk, -ɪˈmæt-, mæθˈmæt- US ˌmæθ.əˈmæt̬-, mæθˈmæt̬-
mathematic|al ˌmæθ.əmˈæt.ɪ.k|əl, -ɪˈmæt, mæθˈmæt- US ˌmæθ.əˈmæt̬-, mæθˈmæt̬- **-ally** -əl.i, -li
mathematician ˌmæθ.əm.əˈtɪʃ.ən, -ɪ.məˈ-, ˌmæθ.məˈ- US ˌmæθ.ə.məˈ-, ˌmæθ.məˈ- **-s** -z
mathematics mæθ.əmˈæt.ɪks, -ɪˈmæt-, mæθˈmæt- US ˌmæθ.əˈmæt̬-, mæθˈmæt̬-
Mather ˈmeɪ.ðəʳ, -θəʳ; ˈmæð.əʳ US ˈmæð.ɚ **-s** -z
Matheson ˈmæθ.ɪ.sən, ˈ-ə-
Mathew ˈmæθ.juː, ˈmeɪ.θjuː
Mathews ˈmæθ.juːz, ˈmeɪ.θjuːz
Mathias məˈθaɪəs
Mathilda məˈtɪl.də
Mathis ˈmæθ.ɪs
maths mæθs
Matilda məˈtɪl.də
matinée, matinee ˈmæt.ɪ.neɪ, -ən.eɪ US ˌmæt.ənˈeɪ **-s** -z ˈ**matinée** ˌ**idol** US **matinˈee** ˌ**idol**
matins ˈmæt.ɪnz US -ənz
Matisse məˈtiːs US mə-, mɑː-
Matlock ˈmæt.lɒk US -lɑːk
Mato Grosso ˌmæt.əʊˈgrəʊ.səʊ, ˌmɑː.təʊˈ- US ˌmæt̬.əˈgroʊ.soʊ, ˌmɑː.tuːˈgroʊ.suː, -ˈgrɔː-
Maton ˈmeɪ.tən
Matravers məˈtræv.əz US -ɚz
matriarch ˈmeɪ.tri.ɑːk, ˈmæt.ri- US ˈmeɪ.tri.ɑːrk **-y** -i
matriarchal ˌmeɪ.triˈɑː.kəl, ˌmæt.riˈ- US ˌmeɪ.triˈɑːr-
matric məˈtrɪk
matrices (*plur. of* **matrix**) ˈmeɪ.trɪ.siːz, -trə, ˈmæt.rɪ-, -rə- US ˈmeɪ.trɪ-
matricidal ˌmæt.rɪˈsaɪ.dəl, ˌmeɪ.trɪˈ-, -trəˈ-
matricide ˈmæt.rɪ.saɪd, ˈmeɪ.trɪ-, -trə- **-s** -z
matricu|late məˈtrɪk.jə|.leɪt, -jʊ- US -jə-, -juː- **-lates** -leɪts **-lating** -leɪ.tɪŋ US -leɪ.t̬ɪŋ **-lated** -leɪ.tɪd US -leɪ.t̬ɪd **-lator/s** -leɪ.təʳ/z US -leɪ.t̬ɚ/z
matriculation məˌtrɪk.jəˈleɪ.ʃən, -jʊˈ- US -jəˈ-, -juːˈ- **-s** -z
matrilineal ˌmæt.rɪˈlɪn.i.əl, ˌmeɪ.trɪˈ-, -trəˈ- US -trəˈ- **-ly** -i
matrimonial ˌmæt.rɪˈməʊ.ni.əl, -rəˈ- US -rəˈmoʊ- **-ly** -i
matrimon|y ˈmæt.rɪ.mə.n|i, -rə- US -rə.moʊ- **-ies** -iz
mat|rix ˈmeɪ.t|rɪks, ˈmæt|.rɪks US ˈmeɪ.t|rɪks **-rixes** -rɪk.sɪz **-rices** -rɪ.siːz, -rə-
Note: British doctors generally pronounce /ˈmeɪ.trɪks/ when talking about the cell type. Those connected with the printing trade pronounce /ˈmæt.rɪks/.
matron ˈmeɪ.trən **-s** -z **-ly** -li ˌ**matron of** ˈ**honour**
Matrûh mætˈruː
Matsui® mætˈsuː.i
Matsushita® ˌmæt.suˈʃiː.tə US -t̬ə
matt(e) mæt
matt|er ˈmæt|.əʳ US ˈmæt̬|.ɚ **-ers** -əz US -ɚz **-ering** -ər.ɪŋ **-ered** -əd US -ɚd as a ˌ**matter of** ˈ**fact**
Matterhorn ˈmæt.ə.hɔːn US ˈmæt̬.ɚ.hɔːrn
matter-of-fact ˌmæt.ər.əvˈfækt US ˌmæt̬.ɚ-
Matthau ˈmæθ.aʊ, ˈmæt-
Matthes ˈmæθ.əs
Matthew ˈmæθ.juː
Matthews ˈmæθ.juːz
Matthias məˈθaɪəs
Matthiessen ˈmæθ.ɪ.sən
matting ˈmæt.ɪŋ US ˈmæt̬-
mattins ˈmæt.ɪnz US -ənz
mattock ˈmæt.ək US ˈmæt̬- **-s** -s
mattress ˈmæt.rəs, -trɪs **-es** -ɪz
matur|ate ˈmæt.jər|.eɪt, -jʊ.r|eɪt; ˈmætʃ.ər|.eɪt US ˈmætʃ.ə.r|eɪt, -ʊ- **-ates** -eɪts **-ating** -eɪ.tɪŋ US -eɪ.t̬ɪŋ **-ated** -eɪ.tɪd US -eɪ.t̬ɪd
maturation ˌmæt.jərˈeɪ.ʃən, -jʊˈreɪ-; ˌmætʃ.ərˈeɪ- US ˌmætʃ.əˈreɪ-, -ʊˈ-
matur|e (M) məˈtjʊəʳ, -ˈtjɔːʳ, -ˈtʃʊəʳ, -ˈtʃɔːʳ US -ˈtʊr, -ˈtjʊr, -ˈtʃʊr **-ely** -li **-eness** -nəs, -nɪs **-es** -z **-ing** -ɪŋ **-ed** -d
Maturin *surname:* ˈmæt.jʊə.rɪn, -jəˈ- US ˌmɑː.tuːˈriːn, -təˈ-
Maturín *in Venezuela:* ˌmæt.jʊəˈrɪn, -jəˈ- US ˌmɑː.tuːˈriːn, -t̬əˈ-
maturity məˈtjʊə.rə.ti, -ˈtjɔː-, -ˈtʃʊə-, -ˈtʃɔː-, -rɪ- US -ˈtʊr.ə.t̬i, -ˈtjʊr-, -ˈtʃʊr-
matutinal ˌmæt.jʊˈtaɪ.nəl; məˈtjuː.tɪ-, -tə- US məˈtuː.tən.əl, -ˈtjuː-
matzo(h) ˈmɒt.sə, ˈmæt-, ˈmɑːt-, -səʊ US ˈmɑːt.sə, -soʊ **-s** -z **matzoth** ˈmɒt.sət, ˈmæt-, ˈmɑːt-, -səʊθ US -soʊt
maté ˈmɑː.teɪ, ˈmæt.eɪ
maud (M) mɔːd US mɑːd, mɔːd **-s** -z
Maude mɔːd US mɑːd, mɔːd
maudlin ˈmɔːd.lɪn US ˈmɑːd-, ˈmɔːd-

Mauger 'meɪ.dʒəʳ, 'mɔː.gəʳ (US) 'mɑː.gɚ, 'mɔː-, 'meɪ.dʒɚ
Maugham mɔːm; 'mɒf.əm (US) mɑːm, mɔːm
Note: The author Somerset Maugham is pronounced /mɔːm/.
Maughan mɔːn (US) mɑːn, mɔːn
maugre 'mɔː.gəʳ (US) 'mɑː.gɚ, 'mɔː-
Maui 'maʊ.i
maul mɔːl (US) mɑːl, mɔːl **-s** -z **-ing** -ɪŋ **-ed** -d **-er/s** -əʳ/z (US) -ɚ/z
Mauleverer mɔː'lev.ᵊr.əʳ, mə- (US) mɑː'lev.ɚ.ɚ, mɔː-, mə-
maulstick 'mɔːl.stɪk (US) 'mɑːl-, 'mɔːl- **-s** -s
Mau Mau 'maʊˌmaʊ, ˌ-'-
Mauna Kea ˌmaʊ.nə'keɪ.ə (US) ˌmaʊ-, ˌmɑː-, ˌmɔː-
Mauna Loa ˌmaʊ.nə'ləʊ.ə (US) -'loʊ-, ˌmɑː-, ˌmɔː-
maunder 'mɔːn.dəʳ (US) 'mɑːn.dɚ, 'mɔːn- **-s** -z **-ing** -ɪŋ **-ed** -d
maundy (M) 'mɔːn.di (US) 'mɑːn-, 'mɔːn- ˌ**Maundy 'Thursday**
Maunsell 'mæn*t*.sᵊl
Maupassant 'məʊ.pæs.ɑ̃ːŋ (US) 'moʊ.pə.sɑːnt
Maureen 'mɔː.riːn, -'- (US) mɔː'riːn, mə-
Mauretani|a ˌmɒr.ɪ'teɪ.ni|.ə, ˌmɔː.rɪ'- (US) ˌmɔːr.ɪ'-, ˌmɑːr-, '-nj|ə **-an/s** -ən/z
Mauriac 'mɒr.i.æk, mɔː.ri- (US) 'mɔːr-, 'mɑːr-
Maurice 'mɒr.ɪs, mɒr'iːs (US) mɔː'riːs, mɑː-, mə-; 'mɑːr.ɪs, 'mɔːr-
Mauritani|a ˌmɒr.ɪ'teɪ.ni|.ə, ˌmɔː.rɪ'- (US) ˌmɔːr.ɪ'-, ˌmɑːr-, -'nj|ə **-an/s** -ən/z
Maurit|ius mə'rɪʃ|.əs, mɔː-, mɒr'ɪʃ- (US) mɔː'rɪʃ.i|.əs, mɑː-, '-əs **-ian/s** -ən/z
Mauser 'maʊ.zəʳ (US) -zɚ **-s** -z
mausoleum ˌmɔː.sə'liː.əm, ˌmaʊ-, -zə'-, -'leɪ- (US) ˌmɑː.sə'liː-, ˌmɔː-, -zə'- **-s** -z
mauve məʊv (US) moʊv, mɑːv, mɔːv **-s** -z
maven 'meɪ.vən **-s** -z
maverick 'mæv.ᵊr.ɪk (US) 'mæv.ɚ-, '-rɪk **-s** -s
mavis (M) 'meɪ.vɪs
maw (M) mɔː (US) mɑː, mɔː **-s** -z
Mawer 'mɔː.əʳ, mɔːʳ (US) 'mɔː.ɚ
Mawhinney, Mawhinny mə'*h*wɪn.i
mawkish 'mɔː.kɪʃ (US) 'mɑː-, 'mɔː- **-ly** -li **-ness** -nəs, -nɪs
max (M) mæks
Maxey 'mæk.si
Max Factor® ˌmæks'fæk.təʳ (US) -tɚ
maxi 'mæk.si **-s** -z
maxill|a mæk'sɪl|.ə **-ae** -iː **-as** -əz **-ary** -ᵊr.i
maxim (M) 'mæk.sɪm **-s** -z
maximal 'mæk.sɪ.mᵊl, -sə- **-ly** -i
maximalist 'mæk.sɪ.mᵊl.ɪst, -sə- **-s** -s
Maximilian ˌmæk.sɪ'mɪl.i.ən, -sə'- (US) '-jən, '-i.ən
maximization, -isa- ˌmæk.sɪ.maɪ'zeɪ.ʃᵊn, -sə-, -mɪ'- (US) -mɪ'- **-s** -z
maximiz|e, -is|e 'mæk.sɪ.maɪz, -sə- **-es** -ɪz **-ing** -ɪŋ **-ed** -d **-er/s** -əʳ/z (US) -ɚ/z
maxim|um 'mæk.sɪ.m|əm, -sə- **-ums** -əmz **-a** -ə
Maximus 'mæk.sɪ.məs, -sə-
Maxine mæk'siːn, '-- (US) mæk'siːn
Maxse 'mæk.si
Maxwell 'mæk.swəl, -swel
may (*auxil. v.*) meɪ
May meɪ **-s** **'May ˌDay**
May|a 'maɪ|.ə (US) 'mɑː.j|ə, 'maɪ|.ə **-as** -əz **-an/s** -ən/z
Mayall 'meɪ.ɔːl, -əl (US) -ɔːl, -ɑːl, -əl
mayapple 'meɪˌæp.l̩ **-s** -z
maybe 'meɪ.bi, -biː, ˌ-'-
maybug 'meɪ.bʌg **-s** -z
mayday (M) 'meɪ.deɪ **-s** -z
Mayer 'meɪ.əʳ (US) -ɚ
mayest 'meɪ.ɪst, -əst; meɪst
Mayfair 'meɪ.feəʳ (US) -fer
Mayfield 'meɪ.fiːld
mayflower (M) 'meɪ.flaʊəʳ (US) -flaʊɚ **-s** -z
mayfl|y 'meɪ.fl|aɪ **-ies** -aɪz
mayhap 'meɪ.hæp
mayhem 'meɪ.hem
Mayhew 'meɪ.hjuː
maying 'meɪ.ɪŋ
Maynard 'meɪ.nɑːd, -nəd (US) -nɚd
Maynooth mə'nuːθ, meɪ-
mayn't meɪnt; 'meɪ.ᵊnt
Maynwaring 'mæn.ᵊr.ɪŋ
Mayo *in Ireland, surname:* 'meɪ.əʊ, -'- (US) -oʊ, -'- **-s** -z *American Indian:* 'maɪ.əʊ (US) -oʊ **-s** -z
mayo (*abbrev. for* **mayonnaise**) 'meɪ.əʊ (US) -oʊ
mayonnaise 'meɪ.ə'neɪz (US) 'meɪ.ə.neɪz, ˌ--'-
mayor (M) meəʳ (US) meɪɚ, mer **-s** -z
mayoral 'meə.rᵊl (US) 'meɪ.ɔːr.ᵊl
mayoralt|y 'meə.rᵊl.t|i (US) 'meɪɚ.ᵊl.t̬|i, 'mer- **-ies** -iz
mayoress (M) ˌmeə'res; 'meə.res, -rɪs, -rəs (US) 'meɪɚ.ɪs, 'mer-, -əs **-es** -ɪz
mayorship 'meə.ʃɪp (US) 'meɪɚ-, 'mer- **-s** -s
Mayotte maɪ'jɒt (US) mɑː'jɑːt
Mayou 'meɪ.uː
maypole 'meɪ.pəʊl (US) -poʊl **-s** -z
mayst meɪst
Mazda® 'mæz.də (US) 'mɑːz- **-s** -z
maz|e meɪz **-es** -ɪz
Mazeppa mə'zep.ə
Mazo de la Roche ˌmæz.əʊ.də.lɑː'rɒʃ, ˌmeɪ.zəʊ- (US) ˌmɑː.zoʊ.də.lɑː'roʊʃ
mazourka mə'zɜː.kə (US) -'zɜːr-, -'zʊr- **-s** -z
mazuma mə'zuː.mə
mazurka mə'zɜː.kə (US) -'zɜːr-, -'zʊr- **-s** -z
mazuzah mə'zuː.zə
maz|y 'meɪ.z|i **-ier** -i.əʳ (US) -i.ɚ **-iest** -i.ɪst, -i.əst **-ily** -ɪ.li, -ᵊl.i **-iness** -ɪ.nəs, -ɪ.nɪs
MBA ˌem.biː'eɪ
Mbabane ᵊm.bɑː'bɑː.neɪ (US) ˌem-
MBE ˌem.biː'iː
Mbuji-Mayi ᵊm'buː.dʒi.maɪ.i (US) emˌbuː.dʒi'maɪ.ji, -'mɑː-
Mc mək, mæk
MC ˌem'siː
McAdam mə'kæd.əm
McAfee mə'kæf.i; ˌmæk.ə'fiː (US) 'mæk.ə.fiː; mə'kæf.i
McAiley mə'keɪ.li
McAleer ˌmæk.ə'lɪəʳ (US) -'lɪr
McAleese ˌmæk.ə'liːs
McAlinden ˌmæk.ə'lɪn.dən
McAlister mə'kæl.ɪ.stəʳ (US) -stɚ
McAll mə'kɔːl (US) -'kɔːl, -'kɑːl
McAl(l)ister mə'kæl.ɪ.stəʳ, '-ə- (US) -stɚ
McAlpine mə'kæl.pɪn, -paɪn
McAnally ˌmæk.ə'næl.i (US) 'mæk.ᵊn.æl.i
McArdle mə'kɑː.dl̩ (US) -'kɑːr-
McArthur mə'kɑː.θəʳ (US) -'kɑːr.θɚ
McAteer ˌmæk.ə'tɪəʳ, '--- (US) ˌmæk.ə'tɪr, '---
McAulay mə'kɔː.li (US) -'kɔː-, -'kɑː-
McAvoy 'mæk.ə.vɔɪ
McBain mək'beɪn
McBean mək'beɪn, -'biːn
McBeth mək'beθ
McBrain mək'breɪn
McBride mək'braɪd
MCC ˌem.siː'siː
McCabe mə'keɪb
McCaffrey mə'kæf.ri
McCain® mə'keɪn
McCall mə'kɔːl (US) -'kɔːl, -'kɑːl
McCallie mə'kɔː.li (US) -'kɑː.li, -'kɔː-
McCallion mə'kæl.i.ən
McCallum mə'kæl.əm
McCann mə'kæn
McCartan, McCarten mə'kɑː.tᵊn (US) -'kɑːr-
McCarthy mə'kɑː.θi (US) -'kɑːr- **-ism** -ɪ.zᵊm **-ite/s** -aɪt/s
McCartney mə'kɑːt.ni (US) -'kɑːrt-
McCaughey mə'kæx.i, -'kæ.hi, -'kɒf.i (US) -'kæ.hi, -'kɑː.fi
McCausland mə'kɔːz.lənd (US) -'kɑːz-, -'kɔːz-
McClain mə'kleɪn
McClean mə'kleɪn, -'kliːn

McClear mə'klɪəʳ (US) -'klɪr
McClellan mə'klel.ən
McClelland mə'klel.ənd
McClintock mə'klɪn.tək, -tɒk (US) -ṭək, -tɑːk
McCloskey mə'klɒs.ki (US) -'klɑː.ski, -'klʌs.ki
McClure mə'klʊəʳ, -'klɔːʳ (US) -'klʊr
McCollum mə'kɒl.əm (US) -'kɑː.ləm
McComb mə'kəʊm (US) -'koʊm
McConnell mə'kɒn.əl (US) -'kɑː.nəl
McConochie mə'kɒn.ə.ki, -xi (US) -'kɑː.nə-
McConville mə'kɒn.vɪl (US) -'kɑːn-
McCormack mə'kɔː.mək (US) -'kɔːr-
McCormick mə'kɔː.mɪk (US) -'kɔːr-
McCorquodale mə'kɔː.kə.deɪl (US) -'kɔːr-
McCorry mə'kɒr.i (US) -'kɔːr-
McCourt mə'kɔːt (US) -'kɔːrt
McCoy mə'kɔɪ
McCrae, **McCrea** mə'kreɪ
McCready mə'kriː.di
McCrory mə'krɔː.ri (US) -'krɔːr.i
McCullagh mə'kʌl.ə
McCullam mə'kʌl.əm
McCullers mə'kʌl.əz (US) -ɚz
McCulloch mə'kʌl.ək, -əx
McCusker mə'kʌs.kəʳ (US) -kɚ
McDade mək'deɪd
McDaniels mək'dæn.jəlz
McDermot(t) mək'dɜː.mət (US) -'dɜːr-
McDiarmid mək'dɜː.mɪd, -'deə- (US) -'dɜːr-
McDonald mək'dɒn.əld, mæk- (US) -'dɑː.nəld
McDonaugh mək'dɒn.ə (US) -'dɑː.nə
McDon(n)ell mək'dɒn.əl, ˌmæk.də'nel (US) -'dɑː.nəl
McDono(u)gh mək'dʌn.ə, -'dɒn- (US) -'dɑː.nə, -'dʌn-
McDougal mək'duː.gəl
McDougall mək'duː.gəl
McDougall's® mək'duː.gəlz, mæk-
McDowell, **McDowall** mək'daʊəl, -'dəʊəl (US) -'daʊəl, -'doʊəl
McDuff mək'dʌf, mæk-
Note: In Scotland always /mək-/.
McElder(r)y 'mæk.əlˌder.i, ˌmæk.əl'der-
McEldowney ˌmæk.əl'daʊ.ni, 'mæk.əlˌdaʊ-
McElroy 'mæk.əl.rɔɪ
McElwain mə'kel.weɪn; 'mæk.əl.weɪn
McElwin mə'kel.wɪn
McEnroe 'mæk.ɪn.rəʊ, -ən- (US) -roʊ
McEwen, **McEwan** mə'kjuː.ən, -ɪn
McFadzean mək'fæd.i.ən
McFarland mək'fɑː.lənd (US) -'fɑːr-
McFarlane mək'fɑː.lɪn, -lən (US) -'fɑːr-
McGahey mə'gæx.i, -'gæ.hi (US) -'geɪ.hi
McGee mə'giː
McGillicuddy 'mæg.li.kʌd.i, 'mæk.ɪl-; mə'gɪl.i- (US) mə'gɪl.i-
McGillivray mə'gɪl.ɪ.vri, -'gɪl.vri, -'glɪv.ri, -reɪ
McGoldrick mə'gəʊl.drɪk (US) -goʊl-
McGough mə'gɒf (US) -'gɑːf
McGovern mə'gʌv.ən (US) -ɚn
McGowan mə'gaʊən
McGrath mə'grɑː, -'grɑːθ, -'græθ (US) -'græθ
McGraw mə'grɔː (US) -'grɑː, -'grɔː
McGregor mə'greg.əʳ (US) -ɚ
McGuane mə'gweɪn
McGuigan mə'gwɪg.ən
McGuire mə'gwaɪəʳ (US) -'gwaɪɚ
McIlrath 'mæk.əl.rɑːθ, -ɪl- (US) -ræθ
McIlroy 'mæk.əl.rɔɪ, -ɪl-, ˌ--'-
McIlvanney ˌmæk.əl'væn.i, -ɪl'-
McIlwraith 'mæk.əl.reɪθ, -ɪl-
McInlay, **McInley** mə'kɪn.li (US) mək'ɪn.li
McInroy 'mæk.ɪn.rɔɪ, -ən-
McIntosh 'mæk.ɪn.tɒʃ, -ən- (US) -tɑːʃ
McIntyre 'mæk.ɪn.taɪəʳ, -ən- (US) -taɪɚ
McIver mə'kaɪ.vəʳ, -'kɪv.əʳ (US) -vɚ
McIvor mə'kiː.vəʳ, -'kaɪ.vəʳ (US) -vɚ
McKee mə'kiː
McKellen mə'kel.ən
McKenna mə'ken.ə
McKenzie mə'ken.zi
McKeown mə'kjəʊn, -'kjʊən (US) -'kjoʊn
McKerras mə'ker.əs
McKie mə'kaɪ, -'kiː
McKinlay, **McKinley** mə'kɪn.li
McKinnon mə'kɪn.ən
McKinny mə'kɪn.i
McKnight mək'naɪt
McLachlan mə'klɒk.lən, -'klɒx-, -'klæk-, -'klæx- (US) -'klɑː.klən
McLagan mə'klæg.ən
McLaine mə'kleɪn
McLaren mə'klær.ən (US) -'kler-, -klær-, -ən
McLaughlin mə'klɒk.lɪn, -'klɒx- (US) -'klɑː.klɪn, -'klɑːf-, -'klɔːf-
McLay mə'kleɪ
McLean mə'kleɪn, -'kliːn (US) -'kliːn
McLeish mə'kliːʃ
McLeod mə'klaʊd
McMahon mək'mɑːn (US) -'mæn, -'meɪən, -'mɑːn
McManus mək'mæn.əs, -'meɪ.nəs
McMaster mək'mɑː.stəʳ (US) -'mæs.tɚ
McMenem(e)y mək'men.ə.mi
McMichael mək'maɪ.kəl
McMillan mək'mɪl.ən
McMullen mək'mʌl.ən
McMurdo mək'mɜː.dəʊ (US) -'mɜːr.doʊ
McNab mək'næb
McNaghten, **McNachton** mək'nɔː.tən (US) -'nɑː-, -'nɔː-
McNally mək'næl.i
McNamara ˌmæk.nə'mɑː.rə (US) 'mæk.nə.mer.ə, -mær-
McNaught mək'nɔːt (US) -'nɑːt, -'nɔːt -**on** -ən -**en** -ən
McNeice mək'niːs
McNeil mək'niːl
McPhee mək'fiː
McQuarie mə'kwɒr.i, -'kwaɪr-, -'kwɔːr- (US) mə'kwaː.ri
McQueen mə'kwiːn
McReady mə'kriː.di
McShane mək'ʃeɪn
McShea mək'ʃeɪ
McSwiney mək'swiː.ni, -'swɪn-
McTaggart mək'tæg.ət (US) -ɚt
McTavish mək'tæv.ɪʃ
McTeague mək'tiːg
McVay mək'veɪ
McVeagh mək'veɪ
McVean mək'veɪn, -viːn
McVeigh mək'veɪ
McVey mək'veɪ
McVicar mək'vɪk.əʳ (US) -ɚ
McVitie's® mək'vɪt.iz (US) -'vɪṭ-
McVit(t)ie mək'vɪt.i (US) -'vɪṭ-
McWhirter mək'*h*wɜː.təʳ (US) -'*h*wɜːr.ṭɚ
McWilliams mək'wɪl.jəmz, -i.əmz (US) '-jəmz
MD ˌem'di
Md. (*abbrev. for* **Maryland**) 'meə.rɪ.lænd, 'mer.ɪ-, -lənd (US) 'mer.ə.lənd
me *note in Tonic Sol-fa:* miː -**s** -z
me (*pron.*) *normal form:* miː *freq. weak form:* mɪ
Me. (*abbrev. for* **Maine**) meɪn
ME ˌem'iː
mea culpa ˌmeɪ.ə'kʊl.pə, -ɑː'-, -'kʌl-, -pɑː (US) -ɑː'kʊl.pɑː, miː-, -ə'kʌl.pə
mead (M) miːd -**s** -z
Meaden 'miː.dən
meadow 'med.əʊ (US) -oʊ -**s** -z -**y** -i
meadowlark 'med.əʊ.lɑːk (US) -oʊ.lɑːrk -**s** -s
Meadows 'med.əʊz (US) -oʊz
meadowsweet 'med.əʊ.swiːt (US) -oʊ-
Meagan 'miː.gən
meag|er 'miː.g|əʳ (US) -g|ɚ -**erer** -ər.əʳ (US) -ɚ.ɚ -**erest** -ər.ɪst, -əst -**erly** -əl.i (US) -ɚ.li -**erness** -ə.nəs, -nɪs (US) -ɚ-
Meagher mɑːʳ (US) mɑːr
meag|re 'miː.g|əʳ (US) -gɚ -**rer** -ər.əʳ (US) -ɚ.ɚ -**rest** -ər.ɪst, -əst -**rely** -əl.i (US) -ɚ.li -**reness** -ə.nəs, -nɪs (US) -ɚ-
Meaker 'miː.kəʳ (US) -kɚ
meal miːl -**s** -z ˌ**meals on 'wheels**; '**meal** ˌ**ticket**

mealie 'miː.li **-s** -z
mealtime 'miːl.taɪm **-s** -z
meal|y 'miː.l|i **-ier** -i.əʳ (US) -i.ɚ **-iest** -i.ɪst, -i.əst **-iness** -ɪ.nəs, -ɪ.nɪs
mealybug 'miː.li.bʌg
mealy-mouthed ˌmiː.li'maʊðd (US) 'miː.li.maʊðd, -maʊθt, ˌ--'- *stress shift, British only:* ˌmealy-mouthed 'person
mean miːn **-s** -z **-er** -əʳ (US) -ɚ **-est** -ɪst, -əst **-ly** -li **-ness** -nəs, -nɪs **-ing** -ɪŋ **meant** ment 'means ˌtest
meand|er (M) mi'æn.d|əʳ (US) -d|ɚ **-ers** -əz (US) -ɚz **-ering/s** -ᵊr.ɪŋ **-ered** -əd (US) -ɚd
meanie 'miː.ni **-s** -z
meaning 'miː.nɪŋ **-s** -z **-ly** -li
meaningful 'miː.nɪŋ.fᵊl, -fʊl **-ly** -i **-ness** -nəs, -nɪs
meaningless 'miː.nɪŋ.ləs, -lɪs **-ly** -li **-ness** -nəs, -nɪs
means-test 'miːnz.test **-s** -s **-ing** -ɪŋ **-ed** -ɪd
meant (*from* **mean**) ment
meantime ˌmiːn'taɪm, '-- (US) 'miːn-
meanwhile ˌmiːn'*h*waɪl, '-- (US) 'miːn-
mean|y 'miː.n|i **-ies** -iz
Meany 'miː.ni
Mearns mɜːnz, meənz, mɪənz (US) mɜːrnz, mernz, mɪrnz
Mears mɪəz (US) mɪrz
measles 'miː.zl̩z
measly 'miːz.li
measurab|le 'meʒ.ᵊr.ə.b|l̩ **-ly** -li **-leness** -l̩.nəs, -nɪs
meas|ure 'meʒ|.əʳ (US) -ɚ **-ures** -əz (US) -ɚz **-uring** -ᵊr.ɪŋ **-ured** -əd (US) -ɚd **-urer/s** -ᵊr.əʳ/z (US) -ɚ.ɚ/z
measureless 'meʒ.ə.ləs, -lɪs (US) '-ɚ- **-ly** -li **-ness** -nəs, -nɪs
measurement 'meʒ.ə.mənt (US) '-ɚ- **-s** -s
meat miːt **-s** -s
meat-and-potatoes ˌmiːt.ᵊn*d*.pə'teɪ.təʊz, -ᵊm- (US) -ᵊn*d*.pə'teɪ.t̬oʊz
meatball 'miːt.bɔːl (US) -bɔːl, -bɑːl **-s** -z
Meates miːts
Meath *Irish county:* miːð
Note: Often pronounced /miːθ/ by English people.
meathead 'miːt.hed **-s** -z
meatless 'miːt.ləs, -lɪs
meatloa|f 'miːt.ləʊ|f (US) -loʊ|f **-ves** -vz
meatpacking 'miːtˌpæk.ɪŋ
meatus mi'eɪ.təs (US) -t̬əs **-es** -ɪz
meat|y 'miː.t|i (US) -t̬|i **-ier** -i.əʳ (US) -i.ɚ **-iest** -i.ɪst, -i.əst **-iness** -ɪ.nəs, -ɪ.nɪs
mecca (M) 'mek.ə
Meccano® mɪ'kɑː.nəʊ, mek'ɑː-, mə'kɑː- (US) -noʊ
mechanic mɪ'kæn.ɪk, mə- **-s** -s **-al** -ᵊl **-ally** -ᵊl.i, -li
mechanician ˌmek.ə'nɪʃ.ᵊn **-s** -z
mechanism 'mek.ə.nɪ.zᵊm **-s** -z
mechanistic ˌmek.ə'nɪs.tɪk **-ally** -ᵊl.i, -li
mechanization, -isa- ˌmek.ə.naɪ'zeɪ.ʃᵊn, -nɪ'- (US) -nɪ'-
mechaniz|e, -is|e 'mek.ə.naɪz **-es** -ɪz **-ing** -ɪŋ **-ed** -d
Mecklenburg 'mek.lɪn.bɜːg, -lən-, -lɪm-, -ləm- (US) -lɪn.bɜːrg, -lən-
MEd ˌem'ed
Med med
medal 'med.ᵊl **-s** -z
medalist 'med.ᵊl.ɪst **-s** -s
medallion mɪ'dæl.i.ən, med'æl-, mə'dæl- (US) mə'dæl.jən **-s** -z
medallist 'med.ᵊl.ɪst **-s** -s
Medan 'med.ɑːn, 'meɪ.dɑːn, -'- (US) meɪ'dɑːn, '--
Medawar 'med.ə.wəʳ (US) -wɚ
meddl|e 'med.l̩ **-es** -z **-ing** -ɪŋ, '-lɪŋ **-ed** -d **-er/s** -əʳ/z (US) -ɚ/z, '-ləʳ/z (US) '-l̩.ɚ/z, '-lɚ/z
meddlesome 'med.l̩.səm **-ness** -nəs, -nɪs
Mede miːd **-s** -z
Medea mɪ'dɪə, mə-, -'diː.ə (US) mɪ'diː-, mə-
Medellín ˌmed.ᵊl'ɪn, -'iːn *as if Spanish:* ˌmed.eɪ'jin (US) -'iːn
medfl|y 'med.fl|aɪ **-ies** -aɪz
media (*plur. of* **medium**) 'miː.di.ə
mediaeval (M) ˌmed.i'iː.vᵊl, med'iː- (US) ˌmiː.di'-, ˌmed.i'; mə'diː- **-ism** -ɪ.zᵊm **-ist/s** -ɪst/s
medial 'miː.di.əl
median 'miː.di.ən **-s** -z 'median ˌstrip
mediant 'miː.di.ənt **-s** -s
mediastin|um ˌmiː.di.ə'staɪ.n|əm (US) -æs'taɪ- **-a** -ə
mediate (*adj.*) 'miː.di.ət, -ɪt **-ly** -li **-ness** -nəs, -nɪs
medi|ate (*v.*) 'miː.di|.eɪt **-ates** -eɪts **-ating** -eɪ.tɪŋ (US) -eɪ.t̬ɪŋ **-ated** -eɪ.tɪd (US) -eɪ.t̬ɪd
mediation ˌmiː.di'eɪ.ʃᵊn **-s** -z
mediative 'miː.di.ə.tɪv (US) -t̬ɪv
mediator 'miː.di.eɪ.təʳ (US) -t̬ɚ **-s** -z
mediatorial ˌmiː.di.ə'tɔː.ri.əl (US) -'tɔːr.i- **-ly** -i
mediatory 'miː.di.ə.tᵊr.i, -tri (US) -tɔːr.i
medic 'med.ɪk **-s** -s
Medicaid 'med.ɪ.keɪd
medic|al 'med.ɪ.k|ᵊl **-als** -ᵊlz **-ally** -ᵊl.i, -li
medicament mə'dɪk.ə.mənt, mɪ-, med'ɪk-; 'med.ɪ.kə- (US) mə'dɪk.ə-; 'med.ɪ.kə- **-s** -s
Medicare 'med.ɪ.keəʳ (US) -ker
medi|cate 'med.ɪ|.keɪt **-cates** -keɪts **-cating** -keɪ.tɪŋ (US) -keɪ.t̬ɪŋ **-cated** -keɪ.tɪd (US) -keɪ.t̬ɪd
medication ˌmed.ɪ'keɪ.ʃᵊn **-s** -z
Medici 'med.ɪ.tʃiː, -tʃi; med'iː.tʃi, mə'diː-, mɪ- (US) 'med.ə.tʃiː
medicinal mə'dɪs.ɪ.nᵊl, mɪ-, med'ɪs-, -ᵊn.ᵊl (US) mə'dɪs- **-ly** -i
medicine 'med.sᵊn, -sɪn, '-ɪ.sᵊn, '-ə-, -sɪn (US) 'med.ɪ.sən **-s** -z 'medicine ˌball; 'medicine ˌchest; ˌgive someone a ˌtaste of their ˌown 'medicine
medico 'med.ɪ.kəʊ (US) -koʊ **-s** -z
medico- ˌmed.ɪ.kəʊ- (US) -koʊ-
medieval (M) ˌmed.i'iː.vᵊl, med'iː- (US) ˌmiː.di'-, ˌmed.i'-; mə'diː- **-ism** -ɪ.zᵊm **-ist/s** -ɪst/s
Medill mə'dɪl
Medina *in Saudi Arabia:* med'iː.nə, mɪ'diː-, mə- (US) mə- *in US:* med'aɪ.nə, mɪ'daɪ-, mə- (US) mə-
mediocre ˌmiː.di'əʊ.kəʳ, 'miː.di.əʊ- (US) ˌmiː.di'oʊ.kɚ, 'miː.di.oʊ-
mediocrit|y ˌmiː.di'ɒk.rə.t|i, ˌmed.i'-, -ɪ.t|i (US) ˌmiː.di'ɑː.krə.t̬|i **-ies** -iz
medi|tate 'med.ɪ|.teɪt, '-ə- **-tates** -teɪts **-tating** -teɪ.tɪŋ (US) -teɪ.t̬ɪŋ **-tated** -teɪ.tɪd (US) -teɪ.t̬ɪd **-tator/s** -teɪ.təʳ/z (US) -teɪ.t̬ɚ/z
meditation ˌmed.ɪ'teɪ.ʃᵊn, -ə'- **-s** -z
meditative 'med.ɪ.tə.tɪv, '-ə-, -teɪ- (US) -teɪ.t̬ɪv **-ly** -li **-ness** -nəs, -nɪs
Mediterranean ˌmed.ɪ.tᵊr'eɪ.ni.ən, ˌ-ə- (US) -tə'reɪ-
medi|um 'miː.di|.əm **-a** -ə **-ums** -əmz 'medium ˌwave
Medjugorje 'met.jʊ.gɔː.tʃə (US) -gɔːr-
medlar 'med.ləʳ (US) -lɚ **-s** -z
medley (M) 'med.li **-s** -z
Medlock 'med.lɒk (US) -lɑːk
Médoc 'meɪ.dɒk, 'med.ɒk, -'- (US) 'meɪ.dɑːk, -'- **-s** -s
medulla med'ʌl.ə, mɪ'dʌl-, mə- (US) mɪ- **-s** -z
medus|a (M) mɪ'djuː.z|ə, mə-, med'juː-, -s|ə (US) mə'duː-, -'djuː- **-as** -əz **-ae** -iː
Medway 'med.weɪ
Mee miː
meed miːd **-s** -z
meek (M) miːk **-er** -əʳ (US) -ɚ **-est** -ɪst, -əst **-ly** -li **-ness** -nəs, -nɪs
meerkat 'mɪə.kæt (US) 'mɪr- **-s** -s
meerschaum 'mɪə.ʃəm, -ʃaʊm (US) 'mɪr-, -ʃɑːm, -ʃɔːm **-s** -z
Meerut 'mɪə.rət (US) 'miː-
meet miːt **-s** -s **-ness** -nəs, -nɪs **-ing** -ɪŋ, 'miː.t̬ɪŋ **met** met
meeting 'miː.tɪŋ (US) -t̬ɪŋ **-s** -z
Meg meg
mega- 'meg.ə-, ˌmeg.ə'-
Note: Prefix. May carry primary or secondary stress on the first syllable, e.g. **megalith** /'meg.ə.lɪθ/, **megalithic** /ˌmeg.ə'lɪθ.ɪk/.

megabit 'meg.ə.bɪt **-s** -s
megabucks 'meg.ə.bʌks
megabyte 'meg.ə.baɪt **-s** -s
megacycle 'meg.əˌsaɪ.kl̩ **-s** -z
megadeath 'meg.ə.deθ **-s** -s
megahertz 'meg.ə.hɜːts Ⓤⓢ -hɜːrts, -herts
megalith 'meg.ə.lɪθ **-s** -s
megalithic ˌmeg.ə'lɪθ.ɪk
megalomania ˌmeg.əl.əʊ'meɪ.ni.ə Ⓤⓢ -oʊ'meɪ-, -ə'-, '-njə
megalomaniac ˌmeg.əl.əʊ'meɪ.ni.æk Ⓤⓢ -oʊ'-, -ə'- **-s** -s
megalomaniacal ˌmeg.əl.əʊ.mə'naɪ.ə.kəl
megalopolis ˌmeg.əl'ɒp.ə.lɪs Ⓤⓢ -'ɑː.pə-
Megan 'meg.ən Ⓤⓢ 'meg-, 'miː.gən
megaphone 'meg.ə.fəʊn Ⓤⓢ -foʊn **-s** -z
megastar 'meg.ə.stɑːr Ⓤⓢ -stɑːr **-s** -z
megastore 'meg.ə.stɔːr Ⓤⓢ -stɔːr **-s** -z
megatheri|um ˌmeg.ə'θɪə.ri|.əm Ⓤⓢ -'θɪr.i- **-a** -ə
megaton 'meg.ə.tʌn **-s** -z
megavolt 'meg.ə.vəʊlt, -vɒlt Ⓤⓢ -voʊlt **-s** -s
megawatt 'meg.ə.wɒt Ⓤⓢ -wɑːt **-s** -s
Meghan 'meg.ən Ⓤⓢ 'meg-, 'miː.gən
megilp mə'gɪlp, mɪ- Ⓤⓢ mə-
megrim 'miː.grɪm, -grəm Ⓤⓢ -grɪm **-s** -z
Mehta 'meɪ.tə
Meier 'maɪ.ər Ⓤⓢ -ɚ
Meikle 'miː.kl̩
Meiklejohn 'mɪk.l̩.dʒɒn, 'miː.kl̩- Ⓤⓢ -dʒɑːn
meios|is maɪ'əʊ.s|ɪs Ⓤⓢ -'oʊ- **-es** -iːz
Meir *English surname:* mɪər Ⓤⓢ mɪr *Israeli surname:* meɪ'ɪər Ⓤⓢ meɪ'ɪr, maɪ.ər
Meirionnydd mer.i.ɒn.ɪð Ⓤⓢ -ɑː.nɪθ
Meissen 'maɪ.sən
Meistersinger 'maɪ.stəˌsɪŋ.ər, -ˌzɪŋ- Ⓤⓢ -stɚˌsɪŋ.ɚ, -ˌzɪŋ- **-s** -z
Mekka 'mek.ə
Meknès mek'nes
Mekong ˌmiː'kɒŋ, ˌmeɪ- Ⓤⓢ ˌmeɪ'kɑːŋ, -kɔːŋ *stress shift:* ˌMekong 'River
Mel mel
melamine 'mel.ə.miːn, -mɪn Ⓤⓢ -miːn
melancholia ˌmel.ən'kəʊ.li.ə, -əŋ'- Ⓤⓢ -ən'koʊ-
melancholic ˌmel.ən'kɒl.ɪk, -əŋ'- Ⓤⓢ -ən'kɑː.lɪk *stress shift:* ˌmelancholic 'mood
melancholy 'mel.ən.kəl.i, -əŋ-, -kɒl- Ⓤⓢ -ən.kɑː.li
Melanchthon mə'læŋk.θɒn, mɪ-, mel'æŋk-, -θən Ⓤⓢ mə'læŋk.θən
Melanesi|a ˌmel.ə'niː.zi|.ə, -ʒi-, '-ʒ|ə Ⓤⓢ -ʒ|ə, -ʃ|ə **-an/s** -ən/z
mélang|e meɪ'lɑ̃ːnʒ, '-- Ⓤⓢ meɪ'lɑ̃ːʒ, -'lɔ̃ːʒ, -'lɑːndʒ, -'lɔːndʒ **-es** -ɪz
Melanie 'mel.ə.ni
mela|nin 'mel.ə|.nɪn **-nism** -nɪ.zəm
melanom|a ˌmel.ə'nəʊ.m|ə Ⓤⓢ -'noʊ- **-as** -əz **-ata** -ə.tə Ⓤⓢ -t̬ə
Melanthius mə'lænt.θi.əs, mɪ-, mel'ænt-, -ɒs Ⓤⓢ mə'lænt.θi.əs
Melba 'mel.bə ˌ**Melba 'toast**
Melbourne 'mel.bən, -bɔːn Ⓤⓢ -bɚn, -bɔːrn
Note: In Australia always /'mel.bən/.
Melchett 'mel.tʃɪt
Melchior 'mel.ki.ɔːr Ⓤⓢ -ɔːr
Melchizedek mel'kɪz.ə.dek
Melcombe 'mel.kəm
meld meld **-s** -s **-ing** -ɪŋ **-ed** -ɪd
Meleager ˌmel.i'eɪ.gər Ⓤⓢ -dʒɚ
mêlée, melee 'mel.eɪ, 'meɪ.leɪ, -'- Ⓤⓢ 'meɪ.leɪ, -'- **-s** -z
Melhuish 'mel.ɪʃ, 'mel.ju.ɪʃ, -hju-; mel'juː.ɪʃ, -'hjuː-
Melibeus ˌmel.ɪ'biː.əs, -ə'- Ⓤⓢ -ə'-
Melincourt 'mel.ɪn.kɔːt, -ɪŋ- Ⓤⓢ -ɪn.kɔːrt
Melinda mə'lɪn.də, mɪ-, mel'ɪn- Ⓤⓢ mə'lɪn-
melinite 'mel.ɪ.naɪt
meliorable 'miː.li.ər.ə.bl̩ Ⓤⓢ 'miːl.jɚ.ə-
melior|ate 'miː.li.ər|.eɪt Ⓤⓢ 'miːl.jə.r|eɪt, 'miː.li.ə- **-ates** -eɪts **-ating** -eɪ.tɪŋ Ⓤⓢ -eɪ.t̬ɪŋ **-ated** -eɪ.tɪd Ⓤⓢ -eɪ.t̬ɪd
melioration ˌmiː.li.ər'eɪ.ʃən Ⓤⓢ ˌmiːl.jə'reɪ-, ˌmiː.li.ə'- **-s** -z
meliorative 'miː.li.ər.ə.tɪv Ⓤⓢ 'miːl.jɚ-
meliorator 'miː.li.ər.eɪ.tər Ⓤⓢ 'miːl.jə.reɪ.t̬ɚ **-s** -z
Melissa mə'lɪs.ə, mɪ-, mel'ɪs- Ⓤⓢ mə'lɪs-
Melita mə'liː.tə, 'mel.ɪ- Ⓤⓢ 'mel.ɪ.t̬ə; mə'liː-, -'lɪt̬.ə
Melksham 'melk.ʃəm
mellifluen|t mɪ'lɪf.lu.ən|t, mə-, mel'ɪf- Ⓤⓢ mə'lɪf- **-ce** -*t*s
mellifluous mɪ'lɪf.lu.əs, mə-, mel'ɪf- Ⓤⓢ mə'lɪf- **-ly** -li **-ness** -nəs, -nɪs
Mellin 'mel.ɪn
Mellor 'mel.ər, -ɔːr Ⓤⓢ -ɚ, -ɔːr
Mellors 'mel.əz, -ɔːz Ⓤⓢ -ɚz, -ɔːrz
mellow 'mel.əʊ Ⓤⓢ -oʊ **-er** -ər Ⓤⓢ -ɚ **-est** -ɪst, -əst **-ness** -nəs, -nɪs **-s** -z **-ing** -ɪŋ **-ed** -d
Melmoth 'mel.məθ
Melmotte 'mel.mɒt, -'- Ⓤⓢ 'mel.mɑːt
melodic mə'lɒd.ɪk, mɪ-, mel'ɒd- Ⓤⓢ mə'lɑː.dɪk **-ally** -əl.i, -li
melodious mə'ləʊ.di.əs, mɪ-, mel'əʊ- Ⓤⓢ mə'loʊ- **-ly** -li **-ness** -nəs, -nɪs
melodist 'mel.ə.dɪst **-s** -s
melodrama 'mel.əʊˌdrɑː.mə Ⓤⓢ -oʊˌdrɑː.mə, -əˌ-, -ˌdræm.ə **-s** -z
melodramatic ˌmel.əʊ.drə'mæt.ɪk Ⓤⓢ -oʊ.drə'mæt̬-, ˌ-ə- **-s** -s **-ally** -əl.i, -li
melodramatist ˌmel.əʊ'dræm.ə.tɪst Ⓤⓢ -oʊ'drɑː.mə.t̬ɪst, -ə'-, -'dræm.ə- **-s** -s
melod|y (M) 'mel.ə.d|i **-ies** -iz
Meloids® 'mel.ɔɪdz
melon 'mel.ən **-s** -z
Melos 'miː.lɒs, 'mel.ɒs Ⓤⓢ 'miː.lɑːs
Melpomene mel'pɒm.ə.ni, '-ɪ-, -niː Ⓤⓢ -'pɑː.mə-
Melrose 'mel.rəʊz Ⓤⓢ -roʊz
melt melt **-s** -s **-ing/ly** -ɪŋ/li Ⓤⓢ 'mel.t̬ɪŋ/li **-ed** -ɪd Ⓤⓢ 'mel.t̬ɪd **'melting ˌpot**
meltdown 'melt.daʊn **-s** -z
Meltham 'mel.θəm
Melton 'mel.tən
Meltonian® mel'təʊ.ni.ən Ⓤⓢ -'toʊ-
Melton Mowbray ˌmel.tən'məʊ.breɪ, -təm'-, -bri Ⓤⓢ -tən'moʊ-
meltwater 'meltˌwɔː.tər Ⓤⓢ -ˌwɑː.t̬ɚ, -ˌwɔː- **-s** -z
Melville 'mel.vɪl
Melvin, Melvyn 'mel.vɪn
member 'mem.bər Ⓤⓢ -bɚ **-s** -z **-ship/s** -ʃɪp/s ˌ**Member of 'Parliament**
membrane 'mem.breɪn **-s** -z
membraneous mem'breɪ.ni.əs
membranous 'mem.brə.nəs
Memel 'meɪ.məl
memento mɪ'men.təʊ, mem'en-, mə'men- Ⓤⓢ mə'men.toʊ **-(e)s** -z
memento mori mɪˌmen.təʊ'mɒr.i, memˌen-, məˌmen-, -'mɔː.raɪ Ⓤⓢ məˌmen.toʊ'mɔːr.iː, -aɪ
Memnon 'mem.nɒn, -nən Ⓤⓢ -nɑːn
memo 'mem.əʊ Ⓤⓢ -oʊ **-s** -z
memoir 'mem.wɑːr Ⓤⓢ -wɑːr, -wɔːr **-s** -z
memorabilia ˌmem.ər.ə'bɪl.i.ə, -'biː.li- Ⓤⓢ -'bɪl.i-, '-jə, -'biː.li-, -'biːl.jə
memorab|le 'mem.ər.ə.b|l̩ **-ly** -li
memorand|um ˌmem.ər'æn.d|əm Ⓤⓢ -ə'ræn- **-a** -ə **-ums** -əmz
memorial mə'mɔː.ri.əl, mɪ'-, mem'ɔː- Ⓤⓢ mə'mɔːr.i- **-s** -z
memorializ|e, -is|e mə'mɔː.ri.ə.laɪz, mɪ'-, mem'ɔː- Ⓤⓢ mə'mɔːr.i- **-es** -ɪz **-ing** -ɪŋ **-ed** -d
memoriz|e, -is|e 'mem.ər.aɪz Ⓤⓢ -ə.raɪz **-es** -ɪz **-ing** -ɪŋ **-ed** -d
memor|y 'mem.ər|.i, '-r|i **-ies** -iz
Memphis 'mem*p*.fɪs
memsahib 'memˌsɑː.*h*ɪb, '-sɑːb Ⓤⓢ 'memˌsɑː.*h*ɪb, '-sɑːb; ˌmem.sɑː'hiːb, -'ɪb **-s** -z
men (*plur. of* **man**) men **'men's ˌroom**

menac|e ˈmen.ɪs, -əs ⓊⓈ -əs **-es** -ɪz **-ing/ly** -ɪŋ/li **-ed** -t
ménag|e menˈɑːʒ, meɪˈnɑːʒ, mə-, mɪ-, -ˈnæʒ, ˈ-- ⓊⓈ meɪˈnɑːʒ, mə- **-es** -ɪz
ménage à trois men,ɑːʒ.ɑːˈtrwɑː, meɪ,nɑːz-, mə-, mɪ-, -,næʒ, ,men.ɑːz-, ,meɪ.nɑːʒ-, -,næʒ ⓊⓈ meɪ,nɑːʒ-, mə-
menagerie məˈnædʒ.ᵊr.i, mɪ-, menˈædʒ-, -ˈæʒ- ⓊⓈ məˈnædʒ-, -ˈnæʒ- **-s** -z
Menai ˈmen.aɪ
Menander məˈnæn.dəʳ, mɪ-, menˈæn- ⓊⓈ məˈnæn.dɚ
menarche menˈɑː.ki, mɪˈnɑː-, mə-; ˈmen.ɑːk ⓊⓈ məˈnɑːr.ki, men-
Mencken ˈmeŋ.kən
mend mend **-s** -z **-ing** -ɪŋ **-ed** -ɪd **-er/s** -əʳ/z ⓊⓈ -ɚ/z
mendacious menˈdeɪ.ʃəs **-ly** -li **-ness** -nəs, -nɪs
mendacity menˈdæs.ə.ti, -ɪ.ti ⓊⓈ -ə.t̬i
Mendel ˈmen.dᵊl
Mendeleev ,men.dᵊlˈeɪ.ev, -dɪˈleɪ-, -ef, -əf ⓊⓈ -dəˈleɪ.əf
mendelevium ,men.dᵊlˈiː.vi.əm, -dɪˈliː- ⓊⓈ -dəˈliː-
Mendeleyev ,men.dᵊlˈeɪ.ev, -dɪˈleɪ-, -ef, -əf ⓊⓈ -dəˈleɪ.əf
Mendelian menˈdiː.li.ən
Mendelssohn *English surname:* ˈmen.dᵊl.sᵊn *German composer:* ˈmen.dᵊl.sᵊn, -səʊn ⓊⓈ -sᵊn, -soʊn, -zoʊn
mendican|cy ˈmen.dɪ.kən|t.si **-t/s** -t/s
mendicity menˈdɪs.ə.ti, -ɪ.ti ⓊⓈ -ə.t̬i
Mendip ˈmen.dɪp **-s** -s
Mendoza menˈdəʊ.zə ⓊⓈ -ˈdoʊ-, -sɑː
mene ˈmiː.ni
Menelaus ,men.ɪˈleɪ.əs, -ᵊlˈeɪ-
menfolk ˈmen.fəʊk ⓊⓈ -foʊk **-s** -s
menhir ˈmen.hɪəʳ ⓊⓈ -hɪr **-s** -z
menial ˈmiː.ni.əl, ˈ-njəl **-s** -z **-ly** -i
Ménière ˈmen.i.eəʳ, ˈmeɪ.ni-, ,--ˈ-; ˈmeɪ.njeəʳ, -ˈ- ⓊⓈ meɪˈnjer
meningeal menˈɪn.dʒi.əl, məˈnɪn-, mɪ-; ,men.ɪnˈdʒiː.əl, -ənˈ- ⓊⓈ məˈnɪn.dʒi-
meninges (*plur. of* **meninx**) məˈnɪn.dʒiːz, mɪ-, menˈɪn- ⓊⓈ məˈnɪn-
meningitis ,men.ɪnˈdʒaɪ.tɪs, -ənˈ- ⓊⓈ -t̬ɪs
meningococcal mə,nɪn.dʒəʊˈkɒk.ᵊl, -,nɪŋ.gəʊˈ- ⓊⓈ -,nɪŋ.goʊˈkɑː.kᵊl
meningo|coccus mə,nɪn.dʒəʊ|ˈkɒk.əs, -,nɪŋ.gəʊˈ- ⓊⓈ -,nɪŋ.goʊ|ˈkɑː.kəs **-cocci** -ˈkɒk.saɪ, -aɪ, -iː ⓊⓈ -ˈkɑːk.saɪ, -ˈkɑː.kaɪ, -kiː
meninx ˈmen.ɪnks ⓊⓈ ˈmiː.nɪŋks, ˈmen.ɪŋks **meninges** məˈnɪn.dʒiːz, mɪ-, menˈɪn- ⓊⓈ məˈnɪn-
menisc|us məˈnɪs.kləs, mɪ-, menˈɪs- ⓊⓈ məˈnɪs- **-uses** -ə.sɪz **-i** -aɪ, -iː
Menlo Park ,men.ləʊˈpɑːk ⓊⓈ -loʊˈpɑːrk
Mennonite ˈmen.ə.naɪt **-s** -s
Meno ˈmiː.nəʊ ⓊⓈ -noʊ
men-of-war (*plur. of* **man-of-war**) ,men.əvˈwɔːʳ ⓊⓈ -ˈwɔːr
menopausal ,men.əʊˈpɔː.zᵊl, ,miː.nəʊˈ- ⓊⓈ ˈmen.ə.pɑː.zᵊl, -pɔː-
menopause ˈmen.əʊ.pɔːz, ˈmiː.nəʊ- ⓊⓈ ˈmen.ə.pɑːz, -pɔːz
menorah mɪˈnɔː.rə, mə- ⓊⓈ -ˈnɔːr.ə **-s** -z
Menorca menˈɔː.kə, məˈnɔː-, mɪ- ⓊⓈ məˈnɔːr.kə
Mensa ˈment.sə
menservants (*plur. of* **manservant**) ˈmen,sɜː.vᵊnts ⓊⓈ -,sɜːr-
menses ˈment.siːz
Menshevik ˈmen.ʃə.vɪk, -ʃɪ- ⓊⓈ -ʃə.vɪk **-s** -s
mens rea ,menzˈreɪ.ə ⓊⓈ -ˈriː.ə
menstrual ˈment.struəl, -stru.əl ⓊⓈ -strəl, -stru.əl
menstru|ate ˈment.stru|.eɪt ⓊⓈ -stru-, -str|eɪt **-ates** -eɪts **-ating** -eɪ.tɪŋ ⓊⓈ -eɪ.t̬ɪŋ **-ated** -eɪ.tɪd ⓊⓈ -eɪ.t̬ɪd
menstruation ,ment.struˈeɪ.ʃᵊn ⓊⓈ -struˈeɪ-, -ˈstreɪ-
mensual ˈment.sju.əl, sjʊəl ⓊⓈ -ʃu.əl
mensurability ,ment.ʃᵊr.əˈbɪl.ə.ti, -ʃʊ.rəˈ-, -sjᵊr.əˈ-, -sjʊ.rəˈ-, -ɪ.ti ⓊⓈ -ʃɚ.əˈbɪl.ə.t̬i, -sɚ-
mensurable ˈment.ʃᵊr.ə.bl̩, -ʃʊ.rə-, -sjᵊr.ə-, -sjʊ.rə- ⓊⓈ -ʃɚ.ə-, -sɚ-
mensuration ,ment.ʃᵊrˈeɪ.ʃᵊn, -ʃʊˈreɪ-, -sjᵊrˈeɪ-, -sjʊˈreɪ- ⓊⓈ -ʃəˈreɪ-, -səˈ-
menswear ˈmenz.weəʳ ⓊⓈ -wer
-ment -mənt
mental ˈmen.tᵊl ⓊⓈ -t̬ᵊl **-ly** -i ,**mental ˈage** ; ˈ**mental** ,**hospital**
mentalism ˈmen.tᵊl.ɪ.zᵊm ⓊⓈ -t̬ᵊl-
mentalistic ,men.tᵊlˈɪs.tɪk ⓊⓈ -t̬ᵊlˈ- **-ally** -ᵊl.i, -li
mentalit|y menˈtæl.ə.t|i, -ɪ.t|i ⓊⓈ -ə.t̬|i **-ies** -iz
Menteith menˈtiːθ, mən-
menthol ˈment.θɒl, -θᵊl ⓊⓈ -θɔːl, -θɑːl, -θᵊl, -θoʊl
mentholated ˈment.θᵊl.eɪ.tɪd ⓊⓈ -t̬ɪd
mention ˈmen.tʃᵊn **-s** -z **-ing** -ɪŋ **-ed** -d **-able** -ə.bl̩, ˈmentʃ.nə-
Mentone menˈtəʊ.neɪ, -ni ⓊⓈ -ˈtoʊ.ni
mentor ˈmen.tɔːʳ, -təʳ ⓊⓈ -tɚ, -tɔːr **-s** -z
menu ˈmen.juː **-s** -z
menu-driven ˈmen.juː,drɪv.ᵊn, ,men.juːˈdrɪv- ⓊⓈ ˈmen.juː,drɪv-
Menuhin ˈmen.ju.ɪn, -hɪn ⓊⓈ -ɪn
Menzies ˈmen.zɪz, ˈmeŋ.ɪs, ˈmɪŋ- ⓊⓈ ˈmen.ziːz
Meopham ˈmep.əm
meow miːˈaʊ **-s** -z **-ing** -ɪŋ **-ed** -d
MEP ,em.iːˈpiː
Mepham ˈmef.əm
Mephisto məˈfɪs.təʊ, mɪ-, mefˈɪs- ⓊⓈ məˈfɪs.toʊ
Mephistophelean, **-lian** ,mef.ɪ.stəˈfiː.li.ən, ,-ə-, -stɒfˈɪl-; mə,fɪs.təˈ-, mɪ-, mef,ɪs-; ,mef.ɪ,stɒf.əˈliː- ⓊⓈ ,mef.ɪ.stəˈfiː.li-; mə,fɪs.təˈ-; ,mef.ə,stɑː.fəˈliː-, -,stoʊ-
Mephistopheles ,mef.ɪˈstɒf.ɪ.liːz, -ᵊl.iːz ⓊⓈ -əˈstɑː.fə.liːz
mephitic mɪˈfɪt.ɪk, mefˈɪt- ⓊⓈ məˈfɪt̬-
mephitis mɪˈfaɪ.tɪs, mefˈaɪ- ⓊⓈ məˈfaɪ.t̬ɪs
Merc mɜːk ⓊⓈ mɜːrk **-s** -s
mercantile ˈmɜː.kᵊn.taɪl ⓊⓈ ˈmɜːr-, -tiːl, -taɪl, -tɪl
mercantilism ˈmɜː.kᵊn.tɪ.lɪ.zᵊm, -taɪ-, -tᵊl.ɪ- ⓊⓈ ˈmɜːr.kən.tiː-, -tɪ-, -taɪ-
Mercator mɜːˈkeɪ.təʳ, -tɔːʳ ⓊⓈ mɚˈkeɪ.t̬ɚ
Mercedes *English female name:* ˈmɜː.sɪ.diːz ⓊⓈ ˈmɜːr-; mɚˈseɪ.diːz *trademark:* məˈseɪ.diːz, mɜː- ⓊⓈ mɚ-, mɜːr-
Mercedes-Benz mə,seɪ.diːzˈbents, mɜː-, -ˈbenz ⓊⓈ mɚ,seɪ.diːzˈbenz, mɜːr-, -ˈbents
mercenar|y ˈmɜː.sᵊn.ᵊr|.i, -sɪ.nᵊr-, -sᵊn.r|i ⓊⓈ ˈmɜːr.sə.ner.i **-ies** -iz
mercer (M) ˈmɜː.səʳ ⓊⓈ ˈmɜːr.sɚ **-s** -z
merceriz|e, -is|e ˈmɜː.sᵊr.aɪz ⓊⓈ ˈmɜːr- **-es** -ɪz **-ing** -ɪŋ **-ed** -d
merchandise (*n.*) ˈmɜː.tʃᵊn.daɪz, -daɪs ⓊⓈ ˈmɜːr-
merchandiz|e, -ise (*v.*) ˈmɜː.tʃᵊn.daɪz ⓊⓈ ˈmɜːr- **-es** -ɪz **-ing** -ɪŋ **-ed** -d **-er/s** -əʳ/z ⓊⓈ -ɚ/z
merchant ˈmɜː.tʃᵊnt ⓊⓈ ˈmɜːr- **-s** -s **-able** -ə.bl̩ ,**merchant ˈbank** ; ,**merchant ˈnavy**
merchant|man ˈmɜː.tʃᵊnt|.mən ⓊⓈ ˈmɜːr- **-men** -mən, -men
Merchison ˈmɜː.kɪ.sᵊn ⓊⓈ ˈmɜːr-
Merchiston ˈmɜː.tʃɪ.stᵊn ⓊⓈ ˈmɜːr-
Merci|a ˈmɜː.si|.ə, -ʃi|.ə ⓊⓈ ˈmɜːr.ʃ|ə, ˈ-ʃi|.ə, -si- **-an** -ən
merciful ˈmɜː.sɪ.fᵊl, -fʊl ⓊⓈ ˈmɜːr- **-ly** -i **-ness** -nəs, -nɪs
merciless ˈmɜː.sɪ.ləs, -lɪs ⓊⓈ ˈmɜːr- **-ly** -li **-ness** -nəs, -nɪs
mercurial mɜːˈkjʊə.ri.əl, -ˈkjɔː- ⓊⓈ mɜːrˈkjʊr.i- **-s** -z **-ly** -i
mercuric mɜːˈkjʊə.rɪk, -ˈkjɔː- ⓊⓈ mɜːrˈkjʊr.ɪk
Mercurochrome® mɜːˈkjʊə.rə.krəʊm, -ˈkjɔː- ⓊⓈ mɜːrˈkjʊr.ə.kroʊm

mercurous 'mɜː.kjᵊr.əs, -kjʊ.rəs (US) 'mɜːr.kjʊr.əs, -kjɚ-
mercury (M) 'mɜː.kjᵊr.i, -kjʊ.ri (US) 'mɜːr.kjə.ri, -kjɚ-
Mercutio mɜː'kjuː.ʃi.əʊ (US) mɜːr'kjuː.ʃi.oʊ
merc|y (M) 'mɜː.s|i (US) 'mɜːr- **-ies** -iz 'mercy ˌkilling
mere mɪəʳ (US) mɪr **-s** -z
Meredith 'mer.ə.dɪθ, '-ɪ- *as if Welsh:* mer'ed.ɪθ
merely 'mɪə.li (US) 'mɪr-
merest 'mɪə.rɪst, -rəst (US) 'mɪr.ɪst, -əst
meretricious ˌmer.ɪ'trɪʃ.əs, -ə'- (US) -ə'- **-ly** -li **-ness** -nəs, -nɪs
merganser mɜː'gænt.səʳ, -'gæn.zəʳ (US) mɜːr'gænt.sɚ **-s** -z
merg|e mɜːdʒ (US) mɜːrdʒ **-es** -ɪz **-ing** -ɪŋ **-ed** -d
merger 'mɜː.dʒəʳ (US) 'mɜːr.dʒɚ **-s** -z
Mérida 'mer.ɪ.də (US) -iː.dɑː
meridian mə'rɪd.i.ən, mɪ- (US) mə'rɪd- **-s** -z
meridional mə'rɪd.i.ə.nᵊl, mɪ- (US) mə'rɪd- **-ly** -i
Mérimée 'mer.ɪ.meɪ (US) ˌmeɪ.riː'meɪ
meringue mə'ræŋ **-s** -z
merino mə'riː.nəʊ (US) -noʊ **-s** -z
Merioneth ˌmer.i'ɒn.ɪθ, -neθ, -nəθ (US) -'ɑː.nɪθ **-shire** -ʃəʳ, -ʃɪəʳ (US) -ʃɚ, -ˌʃɪr
meristem 'mer.i.stem, '-ə- (US) '-ə- **-s** -z
meristematic ˌmer.i.stɪ'mæt.ɪk, ˌ-ə-, -stə'- (US) -ə.stə'mæţ- **-ally** -ᵊl.i, -li
mer|it 'mer|.ɪt **-its** -ɪts **-iting** -ɪ.tɪŋ (US) -ɪ.ţɪŋ **-ited** -ɪ.tɪd (US) -ɪ.ţɪd
meritocrac|y ˌmer.ɪ'tɒk.rə.s|i, -ə'- (US) -ə'tɑː.krə- **-ies** -iz
meritocratic ˌmer.ɪ.tə'kræt.ɪk
meritorious ˌmer.ɪ'tɔː.ri.əs, -ə'- (US) -ə'tɔːr.i- **-ly** -li **-ness** -nəs, -nɪs
Merivale 'mer.ɪ.veɪl
merl mɜːl (US) mɜːrl **-s** -z
merle (M) mɜːl (US) mɜːrl **-s** -z
merlin (M) 'mɜː.lɪn (US) 'mɜːr- **-s** -z
merlot (M) 'meə.ləʊ, -'- (US) mɜːr'loʊ, mer- **-s** -s
mermaid 'mɜː.meɪd (US) 'mɜːr- **-s** -z
mer|man (M) 'mɜː|.mæn (US) 'mɜːr- **-men** -men
Meroe 'mer.əʊ.i (US) -oʊ-
Merope 'mer.ə.pi
Merovingian ˌmer.əʊ'vɪn.dʒi.ən, '-dʒᵊn (US) -oʊ'-, -ə'-
Merrick 'mer.ɪk
Merrilies 'mer.ɪ.liz, -ᵊl.iz
Merrill 'mer.ᵊl, -ɪl
Merrimac 'mer.ɪ.mæk, '-ə-
Merriman 'mer.i.mən
merriment 'mer.i.mənt
Merritt 'mer.ɪt
Merrivale 'mer.i.veɪl
merr|y (M) 'mer|.i **-ier** -i.əʳ (US) -i.ɚ **-iest** -i.ɪst, -i.əst **-ily** -ᵊl.i, -ɪ.li **-iness** -ɪ.nəs, -ɪ.nɪs
merry-andrew ˌmer.i'æn.druː **-s** -z
Merrydown® 'mer.i.daʊn
merry-go-round 'mer.i.gəʊˌraʊnd (US) -goʊˌ- **-s** -z
merrymak|er 'mer.iˌmeɪ.k|əʳ (US) -k|ɚ **-ers** -əz (US) -ɚz **-ing** -ɪŋ
Merryweather 'mer.iˌweð.əʳ (US) -ɚ
Mersey 'mɜː.zi (US) 'mɜːr- **-side** -saɪd **-sider/s** -ˌsaɪ.dəʳ/z
Merthyr 'mɜː.θəʳ (US) 'mɜːr.θɚ
Merthyr Tydfil ˌmɜː.θə'tɪd.vɪl (US) ˌmɜːr.θɚ'-
Merton 'mɜː.tᵊn (US) 'mɜːr-
Mervyn 'mɜː.vɪn (US) 'mɜːr-
Meryl 'mer.ᵊl, -ɪl
mesa 'meɪ.sə **-s** -z
mésallianc|e mez'æl.i.ənts, meɪ'zæl-, -ɑ̃ːns *as if French:* ˌmez.æl.i.ɑ̃ːns (US) meɪ'zæl.i.ᵊnts; ˌmeɪ.zə'liː- **-es** -ɪz
mescal 'mes.kæl, -'- (US) -'- **-s** -z
mescalin(e) 'mes.kᵊl.ɪn, -iːn
mesdames (M) (*plur. of* **madame**) meɪ'dæm, -dæmz, '-- (US) -'dɑːm, -'dæm
mesdemoiselles (M) (*plur. of* **mademoiselle**) ˌmeɪ.dᵊm.wə'zel, -'zelz (US) ˌmeɪd.mwɑː'zel
meseems mɪ'siːmz
mesembryanthemum məˌzem.bri'ænt.θɪ.məm, mɪ-, -θᵊm.əm (US) mesˌem-, mez- **-s** -z
mesh meʃ **-es** -ɪz **-ing** -ɪŋ **-ed** -t
Meshach, Meschak 'miː.ʃæk
Meshed 'meʃ.ed
mesial 'miː.zi.əl (US) 'miː-, 'mez.i-, 'mes-
Mesmer 'mez.məʳ (US) -mɚ
mesmeric mez'mer.ɪk
mesmer|ism 'mez.mᵊr|.ɪ.zᵊm **-ist/s** -ɪst/s
mesmeriz|e, -is|e 'mez.mᵊr.aɪz **-es** -ɪz **-ing** -ɪŋ **-ed** -d **-er/s** -əʳ/z (US) -ɚ/z
mesne miːn
meso- mes.əʊ-, mez-, miː.səʊ-, -zəʊ- (US) mez.oʊ-, mes-, -ə-, miː.soʊ-, -sə-

Note: Prefix. May carry either primary or secondary stress on the first syllable, e.g. **mesoderm** /'mes.əʊ.dɜːm (US) 'mez.oʊ.dɜːrm/, **mesodermal** /ˌmes.əʊ'dɜː.mᵊl (US)ˌmez.oʊ'dɜːr-/.

mesoderm 'mes.əʊ.dɜːm, 'mez-, 'miː.səʊ-, -zəʊ- (US) 'mez.oʊ.dɜːrm, 'mes-, '-ə-
mesodermal ˌmes.əʊ'dɜː.mᵊl, ˌmez-, ˌmiː.səʊ'-, -zəʊ'- (US) ˌmez.oʊ'dɜːr-, ˌmes-, -ə'-
mesodermic ˌmes.əʊ'dɜː.mɪk, ˌmez-, ˌmiː.səʊ'-, -zəʊ'- (US) ˌmez.oʊ'dɜːr-, ˌmes-, -ə'-
mesolect 'mes.əʊ.lekt, 'mez-, 'miː.səʊ-, -zəʊ- (US) 'mez.oʊ-, 'mes-, -ə- **-s** -s
mesolectal ˌmes.əʊ'lek.tᵊl, ˌmez-, ˌmiː.səʊ'-, -zəʊ'- (US) ˌmez.oʊ'-, ˌmes-, -ə-
mesomorph 'mes.əʊ.mɔːf, 'mez-, 'miː.səʊ-, -zəʊ- (US) 'mez.oʊ.mɔːrf, 'mes-, '-ə- **-s** -s
meson 'miː.zɒn, 'meɪ-, -sɒn, 'mes.ɒn, 'mez- (US) 'mez.ɑːn, 'mes-, 'meɪ.sɑːn, 'miː-, -zɑːn **-s** -z
Mesopotami|a ˌmes.ə.pə'teɪ.mi|.ə **-an/s** -ən/z
mesotron 'mes.əʊ.trɒn, 'mez-, 'miː.səʊ-, -zəʊ- (US) 'mez.oʊ.trɑːn, 'mes-, '-ə- **-s** -z
Mesozoic ˌmes.əʊ'zəʊ.ɪk, ˌmiː.səʊ'- (US) ˌmez.oʊ'zoʊ-, ˌmes-, -ə'-
mesquite (M) mes'kiːt, mə'skiːt, mɪ-; 'mes.kɪt (US) mə'skiːt, mes'kiːt
mess mes **-es** -ɪz **-ing** -ɪŋ **-ed** -t
messag|e 'mes.ɪdʒ **-es** -ɪz **-ing** -ɪŋ **-ed** -d
messeigneurs (*plur. of* **monseigneur**) ˌmes.eɪ'njɜː
messenger 'mes.ɪn.dʒəʳ, -ᵊn- (US) -dʒɚ **-s** -z
Messerschmitt® 'mes.ə.ʃmɪt (US) '-ɚ-
Messiaen 'mes.jɑ̃ːŋ, -i.ɑ̃ːŋ *as if French:* mes'jɑ̃ːŋ (US) mes'jɑ̃ːn
messiah (M) mə'saɪ.ə, mɪ-, mes'aɪ- (US) mə'saɪ- **-s** -z
messianic ˌmes.i'æn.ɪk
messieurs meɪ'sjɜːz, mes'jɜːz, 'mes.əz *as if French:* mes'jɜː (US) -ɚz
Messina mes'iː.nə, mə'siː-, mɪ- (US) mə-, mes'iː-
messmate 'mes.meɪt **-s** -s
Messrs. (*plur. of* **Mr**) 'mes.əz (US) -ɚz
messuag|e 'mes.wɪdʒ, -ju.ɪdʒ (US) '-wɪdʒ **-es** -ɪz
mess|y 'mes|.i **-ier** -i.əʳ (US) -i.ɚ **-iest** -i.ɪst, -i.əst **-ily** -ɪ.li, -ᵊl.i **-iness** -ɪ.nəs, -ɪ.nɪs
mestiz|o mes'tiː.z|əʊ, mə'stiː-, mɪ- (US) mes'tiː.z|oʊ **-a** -ə **-os** -əʊz (US) -oʊz **-as** -əz
Mestre 'mes.treɪ
met (*from* **meet**) met
meta- met.ə-; mə'tæ-, met'æ-, mɪ'tæ- (US) meţ.ə-; mə'tæ-, met'æ-

Note: Prefix. Normally carries primary or secondary stress on the first syllable, e.g. **metaplasm** /'met.əˌplæz.ᵊm (US) 'meţ-/, **metabolic** /ˌmet.ə'bɒl.ɪk (US) ˌmeţ.ə'bɑː.lɪk/, or primary stress on the second syllable, e.g. **metabolism** /mə'tæb.ᵊl.ɪ.zᵊm/.

metabolic ˌmet.ə'bɒl.ɪk (US) ˌmeţ.ə'bɑː.lɪk **-ally** -ᵊl.i, -li
metabolism mə'tæb.ᵊl.ɪ.zᵊm, mɪ-, met'æb- (US) mə'tæb- **-s** -z

metaboliz|e, -is|e mə'tæb.ᵊl.aɪz, mɪ-, met'æb- ⓤⓢ mə'- **-es** -ɪz **-ing** -ɪŋ **-ed** -d
metacarp|al ˌmet.ə'kɑː.p|ᵊl ⓤⓢ ˌmeţ.ə'kɑːr- **-us** -əs
metacentre, -center 'met.əˌsen.təʳ ⓤⓢ 'meţ.əˌsen.ţɚ **-s** -z
metagalax|y 'met.əˌgæl.ək.s|i ⓤⓢ 'meţ- **-ies** -iz
metal 'met.ᵊl ⓤⓢ 'meţ- **-s** -z **-ling** -ɪŋ **-led** -d ˈ**metal deˌtector**
metalanguage 'met.ᵊlˌæŋ.gwɪdʒ ⓤⓢ 'meţ-
metallic mə'tæl.ɪk, mɪ-, met'æl- ⓤⓢ mə'tæl- **-ally** -ᵊl.i, -li
metalliferous ˌmet.ᵊl'ɪf.ᵊr.əs ⓤⓢ ˌmeţ-
metallography ˌmet.ᵊl'ɒg.rə.fi ⓤⓢ ˌmeţ.ᵊl'ɑː.grə-
metalloid 'met.ᵊl.ɔɪd ⓤⓢ 'meţ-
metallurgic|al ˌmet.ᵊl'ɜː.dʒɪ.k|ᵊl ⓤⓢ ˌmeţ.ᵊl'ɜːr- **-ally** -ᵊl.i, -li
metallurgist met'æl.ə.dʒɪst, mə'tæl-, mɪ-; 'met.ᵊl.ɜː- ⓤⓢ 'meţ.ᵊl.ɜːr- **-s** -s
metallurgy met'æl.ə.dʒi, mə'tæl, mɪ-; 'met.ᵊl.ɜː- ⓤⓢ 'meţ.ᵊl.ɜːr-
metalwork 'met.ᵊl.wɜːk ⓤⓢ 'meţ.ᵊl.wɜːrk **-er/s** -əʳ/z ⓤⓢ -ɚ/z
metamorphic ˌmet.ə'mɔː.fɪk ⓤⓢ ˌmeţ.ə'mɔːr-
metamorphism ˌmet.ə'mɔː.fɪ.zᵊm ⓤⓢ ˌmeţ.ə'mɔːr- **-s** -z
metamorphos|e ˌmet.ə'mɔː.fəʊz ⓤⓢ ˌmeţ.ə'mɔːr.foʊz **-es** -ɪz **-ing** -ɪŋ **-ed** -d
metamorphos|is ˌmet.ə'mɔː.fə.s|ɪs; -mɔː'fəʊ- ⓤⓢ ˌmeţ.ə'mɔːr.fə-; -mɔːr'foʊ- **-es** -iːz
metaphor 'met.ə.fəʳ, -fɔːʳ ⓤⓢ 'meţ.ə.fɔːr, -fɚ **-s** -z
metaphoric ˌmet.ə'fɒr.ɪk ⓤⓢ ˌmeţ.ə'fɔːr.ɪk **-al** -ᵊl **-ally** -ᵊl.i, -li
metaphysic|al ˌmet.ə'fɪz.ɪ.k|ᵊl ⓤⓢ ˌmeţ- **-ally** -ᵊl.i, -li
metaphysician ˌmet.ə.fɪ'zɪʃ.ᵊn ⓤⓢ ˌmeţ- **-s** -z
metaphysics ˌmet.ə'fɪz.ɪks ⓤⓢ ˌmeţ-, 'meţ.əˌfɪz-
metaplasm 'met.əˌplæz.ᵊm ⓤⓢ 'meţ-
metastas|is met'æs.tə.s|ɪs, mɪ'tæs- mə'tæs- ⓤⓢ mə'tæs- **-es** -iːz
metatarsal ˌmet.ə'tɑː.sᵊl ⓤⓢ ˌmeţ.ə'tɑːr- **-s** -z
metatars|us ˌmet.ə'tɑː.s|əs ⓤⓢ ˌmeţ.ə'tɑːr- **-i** -aɪ
metathes|is met'æθ.ə.s|ɪs, mɪ'tæθ-, mə-, '-ɪ- ⓤⓢ mə'tæθ.ə- **-es** -iːz
Metaxa® met'æk.sə, mɪ'tæk-, mə- ⓤⓢ mə-
Metayers mɪ'teɪəz, mə- ⓤⓢ -'teɪɚz
Metcalfe 'met.kɑːf, -kəf ⓤⓢ -kæf
met|e miːt **-es** -s **-ing** -ɪŋ ⓤⓢ 'miː.ţɪŋ **-ed** -ɪd ⓤⓢ 'miː.ţɪd
Metellus mɪ'tel.əs, met'el- ⓤⓢ mɪ'tel-
metempsychosis ˌmet.emp.saɪ'kəʊ.sɪs, -əmp-, -sɪ'-; met,emp- ⓤⓢ mɪˌtemp.sɪ'koʊ-; ˌmet.əmp.saɪ'-
meteor 'miː.ti.əʳ, -ɔːʳ ⓤⓢ -ţi.ɚ, -ɔːr **-s** -z
meteoric ˌmiː.ti'ɒr.ɪk ⓤⓢ -ţi'ɔːr- **-ally** -ᵊl.i, -li
meteorite 'miː.ti.ᵊr.aɪt ⓤⓢ -ţi.ə.raɪt **-s** -s
meteorologic ˌmiː.ti.ᵊr.ə'lɒdʒ.ɪk ⓤⓢ -ţi.ɚ.ə'lɑː.dʒɪ- **-al** -ᵊl **-ally** -ᵊl.i, -li
meteorologist ˌmiː.ti.ᵊr'ɒl.ə.dʒɪst ⓤⓢ -ţi.ə'rɑːl- **-s** -s
meteorology ˌmiː.ti.ᵊr'ɒl.ə.dʒi ⓤⓢ -ə'rɑː.lə-
met|er 'miː.t|əʳ ⓤⓢ -ţ|ɚ **-ers** -əz ⓤⓢ -ɚz **-ering** -ᵊr.ɪŋ **-ered** -əd ⓤⓢ -ɚd
methadone 'meθ.ə.dəʊn ⓤⓢ -doʊn
methane 'miː.θeɪn ⓤⓢ 'meθ.eɪn
methanol 'meθ.ə.nɒl, 'miː.θə- ⓤⓢ 'meθ.ə.nɑːl, -noʊl
metheglin meθ'eg.lɪn, mɪ'θeg-, mə- ⓤⓢ mə'θeg-
methinks mɪ'θɪŋks
method 'meθ.əd **-s** -z
méthode champenoise meɪˌtɒd.ʃɑ̃ːm.pᵊn'wɑːz ⓤⓢ -toʊd.ʃɑːm-
methodic mə'θɒd.ɪk, mɪ-, meθ'ɒd- ⓤⓢ mə'θɑː.dɪk **-al** -ᵊl **-ally** -ᵊl.i, -li
Method|ism 'meθ.ə.d|ɪ.zᵊm **-ist/s** -ɪst/s
methodologi|cal ˌmeθ.ə.dᵊl'ɒdʒ.ɪ|kᵊl ⓤⓢ -dᵊl'ɑː.dʒɪ- **-ally** -kᵊl.i, -kli
methodolog|y ˌmeθ.ə'dɒl.ə.dʒ|i ⓤⓢ -'dɑː.lə- **-ies** -iz
methought mɪ'θɔːt ⓤⓢ -'θɑːt, -'θɔːt
meths meθs
Methuen *surname:* 'meθ.ju.ən, -ɪn ⓤⓢ mɪ'θjuː.ɪn, mə-, -'θuː-, -ən; 'meθ.juː-, -uː- *US town:* mɪ'θjuː.ɪn, mə-, -'θuː-, -ən
Methuselah mə'θjuː.zᵊl.ə, mɪ-, -'θuː- ⓤⓢ mə'θuː-, -'θjuː-
Methven 'meθ.vən, -ven
methyl *commercial and general pronunciation:* 'meθ.ᵊl, -ɪl ⓤⓢ -aɪl *chemists' pronunciation:* 'miː.θaɪl ⓤⓢ 'meθ.aɪl
methylated 'meθ.ᵊl.eɪ.tɪd, -ɪ.leɪ- ⓤⓢ -ɪ.leɪ.ţɪd ˌ**methylated 'spirits**
methylene 'meθ.ᵊl.iːn, -ɪ.liːn ⓤⓢ '-ɪ-
meti|cal ˌmet.ɪ|'kæl ⓤⓢ ˌmeţ- **-cais** -'kaɪʃ
meticulous mə'tɪk.jə.ləs, mɪ-, met'ɪk-, -jʊ- ⓤⓢ mə'tɪk.jə-, -juː- **-ly** -li **-ness** -nəs, -nɪs
métier 'meɪ.ti.eɪ, 'met.i- ⓤⓢ meɪ'tjeɪ **-s** -z
metonym 'met.ə.nɪm ⓤⓢ 'meţ- **-s** -z
metonymy met'ɒn.ə.mi, mɪ'tɒn-, mə-, '-ɪ- ⓤⓢ mə'tɑː.nə-
me-too ˌmiː'tuː **-ism** -ɪ.zᵊm
metope 'met.əʊp; -əʊ.pi ⓤⓢ 'meţ.ə.pi; '-oʊp **-s** -s
metre 'miː.təʳ ⓤⓢ -ţɚ **-s** -z
metric 'met.rɪk **-al** -ᵊl **-ally** -ᵊl.i, -li
metrication ˌmet.rɪ'keɪ.ʃᵊn, -rə'-
metrics 'met.rɪks
metro (M) 'met.rəʊ ⓤⓢ -roʊ **-s** -z
metro- 'met.rəʊ-, met'rɒ- ⓤⓢ 'met.roʊ-, -rə-; mə'trɑː-
Metro-Goldwyn-Mayer ˌmet.rəʊˌgəʊld.wɪn'meɪ.əʳ ⓤⓢ -roʊˌgoʊld.wɪn'meɪ.ɚ
Metroland 'met.rəʊ.lænd ⓤⓢ -roʊ-
metronome 'met.rə.nəʊm ⓤⓢ -noʊm **-s** -z
metronomic ˌmet.rə'nɒm.ɪk ⓤⓢ -'nɑː.mɪk **-al** -ᵊl **-ally** -ᵊl.i, -li
Metropole 'met.rə.pəʊl ⓤⓢ -poʊl
metropolis mə'trɒp.ə.lɪs, mɪ-, met'rɒp-, -ᵊl.ɪs ⓤⓢ mə'trɑː.pᵊl- **-es** -ɪz
metropolitan ˌmet.rə'pɒl.ɪ.tᵊn, '-ə- ⓤⓢ -'pɑː.lə- **-s** -z
-metry -mə.tri
mettle 'met.l̩ ⓤⓢ 'meţ- **-some** -səm
Metz mets *as if French:* mes
meunière, meuniere ˌmɜː.ni'eəʳ, -'njeəʳ, mə'-, '--- ⓤⓢ mə'njer
Meursault 'mɜː.səʊ ⓤⓢ mɚ'soʊ
Meuse mɜːz ⓤⓢ mjuːz, mɜːz
Meux mjuːz, mjuːks, mjuː
Mevagissey ˌmev.ə'gɪs.i
mew (M) mjuː **-s** -z **-ing** -ɪŋ **-ed** -d
mewl mjuːl **-s** -z **-ing** -ɪŋ **-ed** -d
mews mjuːz
Mexborough 'meks.bᵊr.ə ⓤⓢ -oʊ
Mexicali ˌmek.sɪ'kɑː.li, -'kæl.i ⓤⓢ -'kæl.i
Mexican 'mek.sɪ.kᵊn ˌ**Mexican 'wave**
Mexico 'mek.sɪ.kəʊ ⓤⓢ -koʊ ˌ**Mexico 'City**
Mey meɪ
Meyer 'maɪ.əʳ, 'meɪ-, meəʳ ⓤⓢ 'maɪ.ɚ
Meyerbeer 'maɪ.ə.bɪəʳ, -beəʳ ⓤⓢ -ɚ.bɪr, -ber
Meyers 'maɪ.əz, 'meɪ.əz, meəz ⓤⓢ 'maɪ.ɚz
Meynell 'men.ᵊl, 'meɪ.nᵊl; meɪ'nel
Meyrick 'mer.ɪk, 'meɪ.rɪk
mezzanine 'met.sə.niːn, 'mez.ə- ⓤⓢ 'mez-, ˌ--'- **-s** -z
mezzo 'met.səʊ, 'med.zəʊ ⓤⓢ 'met.soʊ, 'med.zoʊ, 'mez.oʊ **-s** -z
mezzo-soprano ˌmet.səʊ.sə'prɑː.nəʊ, ˌmed.zəʊ- ⓤⓢ ˌmet.soʊ.sə'præn.oʊ, -'prɑː.noʊ, ˌmed.zoʊ-, ˌmez.oʊ- **-s** -z
mezzotint 'met.səʊ.tɪnt, 'med.zəʊ- ⓤⓢ 'met.soʊ-, 'med.zoʊ-, 'mez.oʊ- **-s** -s

mg (*abbrev. for* **milligram/s**) *singular:* ˈmɪl.ɪ.græm *plural:* ˈmɪl.ɪ.græmz
MGM® ˌem.dʒiːˈem
Mgr. (*abbrev. for* **Monseigneur, Monsignor**) mɒnˈsiː.njəʳ, -njɔːʳ ⓤⓢ mɑːnˈsiː.njɚ **-s.** -z
MHz (*abbrev. for* **megahertz**) ˈmeg.ə.hɜːts ⓤⓢ -hɜːrts
mi miː **-s** -z
MI5 ˌem.aɪˈfaɪv
Mia ˈmiː.ə
MIA ˌem.aɪˈeɪ
Miami maɪˈæm.i ⓤⓢ -i, -ə
miaow ˌmiːˈaʊ, miˈaʊ ⓤⓢ miˈaʊ, mjaʊ **-s** -z **-ing** -ɪŋ **-ed** -d
miasm|a miˈæz.m|ə, maɪ- ⓤⓢ maɪ-, mi- **-as** -əz **-ata** -ə.tə ⓤⓢ -ə.t̬ə **-al** -əl
mica ˈmaɪ.kə
micaceous maɪˈkeɪ.ʃəs
Micah ˈmaɪ.kə
Micawber mɪˈkɔː.bəʳ, mə- ⓤⓢ -ˈkɑː.bɚ, -ˈkɔː-
mice (*plur. of* **mouse**) maɪs
Mich. (*abbrev. for* **Michigan**) ˈmɪʃ.ɪ.gən, ˈ-ə- ⓤⓢ ˈ-ɪ-
Michael ˈmaɪ.kəl
Michaela mɪˈkaɪ.lə
Michaelmas ˈmɪk.əl.məs
Michelangelo ˌmaɪ.kəlˈæn.dʒə.ləʊ, -dʒɪ- ⓤⓢ -loʊ, ˌmɪk.əl-
Micheldever ˈmɪtʃ.əl.dev.əʳ ⓤⓢ -ɚ
Michele, Michèle mɪˈʃel, miː-
Michelin® ˈmɪtʃ.əl.ɪn, ˈmɪʃ- *as if French:* miːʃˈlæ̃ŋ ⓤⓢ ˈmɪʃ.ə.lɪn, ˈmɪtʃ- **-s** -z
Note: In the UK, /miːʃˈlæ̃ŋ/ is used for the Guide, but not the tyres.
Michelle mɪˈʃel, miː-
Michelmore ˈmɪtʃ.əl.mɔːʳ ⓤⓢ -mɔːr
Michelson ˈmɪtʃ.əl.sən, ˈmɪk.əl-, ˈmaɪ.kəl- ⓤⓢ ˈmaɪ-, ˈmɪk.əl-
Michie ˈmɪx.i, ˈmiː.xi, ˈmɪk.i ⓤⓢ ˈmɪk.i
Michigan ˈmɪʃ.ɪ.gən, ˈ-ə- ⓤⓢ ˈ-ɪ-
Michmash ˈmɪk.mæʃ
Michoacán ˌmɪtʃ.əʊ.əˈkæn ⓤⓢ -ə.wɑːˈkɑːn
mick (M) mɪk
mickey (M) ˈmɪk.i **ˌMickey ˈFinn** ; ⓤⓢ **ˈMickey ˌMouse ˌMickey ˈMouse**
mickey-mouse (*adj.*) ˌmɪk.iˈmaʊs ⓤⓢ ˈ--ˌ- *stress shift, British only:* ˌmickey-mouse ˈjob
micra (*plur. of* **micron**) ˈmaɪ.krə
Micra® ˈmaɪ.krə
micro- maɪ.krəʊ- ⓤⓢ maɪ.kroʊ-, maɪ.krə-
Note: Prefix. May carry primary or secondary stress, e.g. **microfiche** /ˈmaɪ.krəʊ.fiːʃ ⓤⓢ -kroʊ-/, **microbiology** /ˌmaɪ.krəʊ.baɪˈɒl.ə.dʒi ⓤⓢ -kroʊ.baɪˈɑː.lə-/.
micro ˈmaɪ.krəʊ ⓤⓢ -kroʊ **-s** -z
microbe ˈmaɪ.krəʊb ⓤⓢ -kroʊb **-s** -z
microbiologic|al ˌmaɪ.krəʊˌbaɪ.əˈlɒdʒ.ɪ.k|əl ⓤⓢ -kroʊˌbaɪ.əˈlɑː.dʒɪ- **-ally** -əl.i ⓤⓢ -li
microbiologist ˌmaɪ.krəʊ.baɪˈɒl.ə.dʒɪst ⓤⓢ -kroʊ.baɪˈɑː.lə- **-s** -s
microbiolog|y ˌmaɪ.krəʊ.baɪˈɒl.ə.dʒ|i ⓤⓢ -kroʊ.baɪˈɑː.lə- **-ist/s** -ɪst/s
microcephalic ˌmaɪ.krəʊ.sefˈæl.ɪk, -sɪˈfæl-, -kefˈæl-, -kɪˈfæl- ⓤⓢ -kroʊ.səˈfæl-
microcephalous ˌmaɪ.krəʊˈsef.əl.əs, -ˈkef- ⓤⓢ -kroʊˈsef-
microchip ˈmaɪ.krəʊ.tʃɪp ⓤⓢ -kroʊ-, -krə- **-s** -s
microcircuit ˈmaɪ.krəʊˌsɜː.kɪt ⓤⓢ -kroʊˌsɜːr- **-s** -s
microclimate ˈmaɪ.krəʊˌklaɪ.mɪt, -mət ⓤⓢ -mɪt, -kroʊ- **-s** -s
microcomputer ˈmaɪ.krəʊ.kəmˌpjuː.təʳ ⓤⓢ -kroʊ.kəmˌpjuː.t̬ɚ **-s** -z
microcop|y ˈmaɪ.krəʊˌkɒp|.i ⓤⓢ -kroʊˌkɑː.p|i **-ies** -iz
microcosm ˈmaɪ.krəʊˌkɒz.əm ⓤⓢ -kroʊˌkɑː.zəm, -krəˌ- **-s** -z
microdot ˈmaɪ.krəʊ.dɒt ⓤⓢ -kroʊ.dɑːt, -krə- **-s** -s
microeconomic ˌmaɪ.krəʊ.iː.kəˈnɒm.ɪk, -ek.əˈ- ⓤⓢ -kroʊˌek.əˈnɑː.mɪk, -krəˌ-, -ˌiː.kəˈ- **-s** -s
microelectronics ˌmaɪ.krəʊˌɪl.ekˈtrɒn.ɪks, -ˌel-, -ˌel.ɪkˈ-, -ˌiː.lekˈ- ⓤⓢ -kroʊ.ɪˌlekˈtrɑː.nɪks, -ˌiː.lekˈ-
microfich|e ˈmaɪ.krəʊ.fiːʃ ⓤⓢ -kroʊ-, -krə- **-es** -ɪz
microfilm ˈmaɪ.krəʊ.fɪlm ⓤⓢ -kroʊ-, -krə- **-s** -z
microgram, microgramme ˈmaɪ.krəʊ.græm ⓤⓢ -kroʊ- **-s** -z
microgroove ˈmaɪ.krəʊ.gruːv ⓤⓢ -kroʊ- **-s** -z
microlight ˈmaɪ.krəʊ.laɪt ⓤⓢ -kroʊ- **-s** -s
micromesh ˈmaɪ.krəʊ.meʃ ⓤⓢ -kroʊ-
micrometer *measuring device:* maɪˈkrɒm.ɪ.təʳ, ˈ-ə- ⓤⓢ -ˈkrɑː.mə.t̬ɚ
micrometre, micrometer *unit of measurement:* ˈmaɪ.krəʊˌmiː.təʳ ⓤⓢ -kroʊˌmiː.t̬ɚ **-s** -z
micr|on ˈmaɪ.kr|ɒn, -kr|ən ⓤⓢ -kr|ɑːn **-ons** -ɒnz, -ənz ⓤⓢ -ɑːnz **-a** -ə
Micronesi|a ˌmaɪ.krəʊˈniː.zi|.ə, -ʒi|.ə, -ʒ|ə, -si|.ə, -ʃi|.ə, -ʃ|ə ⓤⓢ -kroʊˈniː.ʒ|ə, -ʃ|ə **-an/s** -ən/z
microorganism ˌmaɪ.krəʊˈɔː.gən.ɪ.zəm, ˈmaɪ.krəʊˌɔː- ⓤⓢ ˌmaɪ.kroʊˈɔːr- **-s** -z
microphone ˈmaɪ.krə.fəʊn ⓤⓢ -foʊn **-s** -z
microprocessor ˌmaɪ.krəʊˈprəʊ.ses.əʳ, ˈmaɪ.krəʊˌprəʊ- ⓤⓢ ˈmaɪ.kroʊˌprɑː.ses.ɚ **-s** -z
micropyle ˈmaɪ.krəʊ.paɪl ⓤⓢ -kroʊ-
microscope ˈmaɪ.krə.skəʊp ⓤⓢ -skoʊp **-s** -s
microscopic ˌmaɪ.krəˈskɒp.ɪk ⓤⓢ -ˈskɑː.pɪk **-al** -əl **-ally** -əl.i ⓤⓢ -li
microscopy maɪˈkrɒs.kə.pi ⓤⓢ -ˈkrɑː.skə-
microsecond ˈmaɪ.krəʊˌsek.ənd ⓤⓢ -kroʊˌ-, -krəˌ- **-s** -z
Microsoft® ˈmaɪ.krəʊ.sɒft ⓤⓢ -kroʊ.sɑːft, -krə-
microsurgery ˌmaɪ.krəʊˈsɜː.dʒər.i ⓤⓢ -kroʊˈsɜːr-, ˈmaɪ.kroʊˌsɜːr-
microsurgical ˌmaɪ.krəʊˈsɜː.dʒɪ.kəl ⓤⓢ -kroʊˈsɜːr- *stress shift:* ˌmicrosurgical ˈgraft
microwav|e ˈmaɪ.krəʊ.weɪv ⓤⓢ -kroʊ-, -krə- **-es** -z **-ing** -ɪŋ **-ed** -d **-eable** -ə.bl̩ **ˌmicrowave ˈoven**
mictur|ate ˈmɪk.tjər|.eɪt, -tjʊ.reɪt ⓤⓢ -tʃuː-, -tʃə-, -tə- **-ates** -eɪts **-ating** -eɪ.tɪŋ ⓤⓢ -eɪ.t̬ɪŋ **-ated** -eɪ.tɪd ⓤⓢ -eɪ.t̬ɪd
micturation ˌmɪk.tjərˈeɪ.ʃən, -tjʊˈreɪ- ⓤⓢ -tʃuːˈreɪ-, -tʃəˈ-, -təˈ- **-s** -z
micturition ˌmɪk.tjərˈɪʃ.ən, -tjʊˈrɪʃ- ⓤⓢ -tʃuːˈ-, -tʃəˈ-, -təˈ-
mid mɪd
midair ˌmɪdˈeəʳ, mɪˈdeəʳ ⓤⓢ ˌmɪdˈer *stress shift:* ˌmidair ˈcrash
Midas ˈmaɪ.dəs, -dæs ⓤⓢ -dəs
midday ˌmɪdˈdeɪ **-s** -z *stress shift:* ˌmidday ˈsun
midden ˈmɪd.ən **-s** -z
middle ˈmɪd.l̩ **-s** -z **ˌmiddle ˈage** ; **ˌMiddle ˈAges**; **ˌmiddle ˈclass**; **ˌMiddle ˈEast**; **ˌmiddle ˈmanagement**; **ˌmiddle ˈname**; **ˌmiddle of ˈnowhere**; **ˈmiddle ˌschool**
middle-aged ˌmɪd.l̩ˈeɪdʒd *stress shift, see compound:* **ˌmiddle-aged ˈspread**
middlebrow ˈmɪd.l̩.braʊ **-s** -z
middle-class ˌmɪd.l̩ˈklɑːs ⓤⓢ -ˈklæs *stress shift:* ˌmiddle-class ˈvalues
middle distance (*n.*) ˌmɪd.l̩ˈdɪs.tənts
middle-distance (*adj.*) ˈmɪd.l̩ˌdɪs.tənts
Middle-Earth ˌmɪd.l̩ˈɜːθ ⓤⓢ -ˈɜːrθ
Middle East ˌmɪd.l̩ˈiːst **-ern** -ən *stress shift:* ˌMiddle Eastern ˈcustoms
Middleham ˈmɪd.l̩.əm
middle|man ˈmɪd.l̩|.mæn **-men** -men
Middlemarch ˈmɪd.l̩.mɑːtʃ ⓤⓢ -mɑːrtʃ
Middlemast ˈmɪd.l̩.mɑːst, -mæst ⓤⓢ -mæst
middlemost ˈmɪd.l̩.məʊst ⓤⓢ -moʊst
middle-of-the-road ˌmɪd.l̩.əv.ðəˈrəʊd ⓤⓢ -ˈroʊd

Middlesbrough 'mɪd.l̩z.brə
Middlesex 'mɪd.l̩.seks
Middleton 'mɪd.l̩.tən
middleweight 'mɪd.l̩.weɪt **-s** -s
Middlewich 'mɪd.l̩.wɪtʃ
middling 'mɪd.l̩.ɪŋ, 'mɪd.lɪŋ
Middx. (*abbrev. for* **Middlesex**) 'mɪd.l̩.seks
midd|y 'mɪd|.i **-ies** -iz
midfield 'mɪd.fiːld, -'-
midfielder 'mɪdˌfiːl.dəʳ, ˌ-'-- Ⓤⓢ 'mɪdˌfiːl.dɚ, ˌ-'-- **-s** -z
Midgard 'mɪd.gɑːd Ⓤⓢ -gɑːrd
midg|e mɪdʒ **-es** -ɪz
midget 'mɪdʒ.ɪt **-s** -s
Midhurst 'mɪd.hɜːst Ⓤⓢ -hɜːrst
MIDI *computer interface:* 'mɪd.i
midi *style of clothes:* 'mɪd.i **-s** -z
Midi *in France:* miː'di, mɪd'iː Ⓤⓢ miː'di
Midian 'mɪd.i.ən **-ite/s** -aɪt/s
midland (M) 'mɪd.lənd **-s** -z
mid-life ˌmɪd'laɪf *stress shift, see compound:* ˌ**mid-life 'crisis**
Midlothian ˌmɪd'ləʊ.ði.ən Ⓤⓢ -'loʊ-
midmorning ˌmɪd'mɔː.nɪŋ Ⓤⓢ -'mɔːr-
midnight 'mɪd.naɪt
mid-off ˌmɪd'ɒf Ⓤⓢ -'ɑːf **-s** -s
mid-on ˌmɪd'ɒn Ⓤⓢ -'ɑːn **-s** -z
midpoint 'mɪd.pɔɪnt **-s** -s
midriff 'mɪd.rɪf **-s** -s
midsection 'mɪd.sek.ʃᵊn **-s**
midship|man 'mɪdˌʃɪp|.mən Ⓤⓢ 'mɪdˌ-, ˌmɪd'ʃɪp- **-men** -mən
midships 'mɪd.ʃɪps
midst mɪdst, mɪtst
midstream ˌmɪd'striːm
midsummer (M) ˌmɪd'sʌm.əʳ, '--- Ⓤⓢ -ɚ **-'s** -z *stress shift, see compounds:* ˌ**Midsummer 'Day** ; ˌ**midsummer 'madness** ; ˌ**Midsummer ˌNight's 'Dream**
midterm (*n.*) 'mɪd.tɜːm Ⓤⓢ -tɜːrm
mid-term (*adj.*) ˌmɪd'tɜːm Ⓤⓢ -'tɜːrm *stress shift:* ˌmidterm 'crisis
midway ˌmɪd'weɪ, '--
Midway *island:* 'mɪd.weɪ
midweek ˌmɪd'wiːk *stress shift:* ˌmidweek 'news
Midwest ˌmɪd'west *stress shift:* ˌMidwest 'town
midwi|fe 'mɪd.waɪ|f **-ves** -vz
midwifery mɪd'wɪf.ᵊr.i, 'mɪdˌwɪf.ᵊr- Ⓤⓢ ˌmɪd'wɪf.ɚ-; 'mɪdˌwaɪf.ɚ-
midwinter ˌmɪd'wɪn.təʳ Ⓤⓢ -t̬ɚ *stress shift:* ˌmidwinter 'holiday
mien miːn **-s** -z
Miers maɪəz Ⓤⓢ maɪɚz
Mies van der Rohe ˌmiːz.væn.də'rəʊ.ə, ˌmiːs- Ⓤⓢ -dɚ'roʊ.ə
miff mɪf **-s** -s **-ing** -ɪŋ **-ed** -t

MiG, MIG mɪg **-s** -z
might maɪt
mightn't 'maɪ.tᵊnt
might|y 'maɪ.t|i Ⓤⓢ -t̬|i **-ier** -i.əʳ Ⓤⓢ -i.ɚ **-iest** -i.ɪst, -i.əst **-ily** -ɪ.li, -ᵊl.i **-iness** -ɪ.nəs, -ɪ.nɪs
mignon 'miː.njɒn, ˌ-'- *as if French:* mɪ'njɔ̃ːŋ Ⓤⓢ ˌmiː'njɑːn, -'njɔ̃ːn
mignonette (M) ˌmɪn.jə'net, '--- Ⓤⓢ ˌ--'- **-s** -s
mignonne 'miː.njɒn, ˌ-'- *as if French:* mɪ'njɔːn Ⓤⓢ ˌmiː'njɑːn, -njɔːn
migraine 'miː.greɪn, 'maɪ-, 'mɪg.reɪn Ⓤⓢ 'maɪ.greɪn **-s** -z
migrant 'maɪ.grᵊnt **-s** -s
migra|te maɪ'greɪ|t, '-- Ⓤⓢ 'maɪ.greɪ|t **-tes** -ts **-ting** -tɪŋ Ⓤⓢ -t̬ɪŋ **-ted** -tɪd Ⓤⓢ -t̬ɪd **-tor/s** -təʳ/z Ⓤⓢ -t̬ɚ/z
migration maɪ'greɪ.ʃᵊn **-s** -z
migratory 'maɪ.grə.tᵊr.i; maɪ'greɪ- Ⓤⓢ 'maɪ.grə.tɔːr-
Miguel mɪ'gel, miː-
mikado (M) mɪ'kɑː.dəʊ, mə- Ⓤⓢ mɪ'kɑː.doʊ **-s** -z
Mikardo mɪ'kɑː.dəʊ, mə- Ⓤⓢ mɪ'kɑːr.doʊ
mike (M) maɪk **-s** -s
Mikonos 'mɪk.ə.nɒs, -ɒn.ɒs Ⓤⓢ 'miː.kɑː.nɑːs
mil mɪl **-s**
milady mɪ'leɪ.di, mə-
Milan *in Italy:* mɪ'læn, mə-, -'lɑːn, 'mɪl.ən Ⓤⓢ mɪ'læn, -'lɑːn
Note: /'mɪl.ən/ is used for rhythm in Shakespeare's 'The Tempest'. *in US:* 'maɪ.lən *Serbian king:* 'miː.lən, -læn
Milanese *from Milan:* ˌmɪl.ə'niːz, -'neɪz Ⓤⓢ -'niːz, -'niːs
Milanese *cookery term: as if Italian:* ˌmɪl.ə'neɪ.zeɪ, -æn'eɪ-, -zi Ⓤⓢ -ə'neɪz
milch mɪltʃ Ⓤⓢ mɪltʃ
mild maɪld **-er** -əʳ Ⓤⓢ -ɚ **-est** -ɪst, -əst **-ly** -li **-ness** -nəs, -nɪs
Mildenhall 'mɪl.dᵊn.hɔːl Ⓤⓢ 'mɪl.dᵊn.hɔːl, -hɑːl
mildew 'mɪl.djuː Ⓤⓢ -duː, -djuː **-s** -z **-ing** -ɪŋ **-ed** -d
Mildmay 'maɪld.meɪ
Mildred 'mɪl.drəd, -drɪd, -dred
mile maɪl **-s** -z
mileag|e 'maɪ.lɪdʒ **-es** -ɪz
mileometer maɪ'lɒm.ɪ.təʳ, '-ə- Ⓤⓢ -'lɑː.mə.t̬ɚ **-s** -z
Miles maɪlz
Milesian maɪ'liː.zi.ən, mɪ-, -ʒi.ən, -ʒᵊn Ⓤⓢ -ʒᵊn, -ʃᵊn **-s** -z
milestone 'maɪl.stəʊn Ⓤⓢ -stoʊn **-s** -z
Miletus maɪ'liː.təs, mɪ- Ⓤⓢ maɪ-
milfoil 'mɪl.fɔɪl **-s** -z
Milford 'mɪl.fəd Ⓤⓢ -fɚd

Milhaud 'miː.jəʊ, -əʊ *as if French:* miː'jəʊ Ⓤⓢ miː'joʊ
milieu 'miː.ljɜː, -'- Ⓤⓢ miːl'jɜː, mɪl-, -'juː, '-- **-s** -z
milieux (*alternative plur. of* **milieu**) 'miː.ljɜː, -ljɜːz, -'- Ⓤⓢ miːl'jɜː, mɪl-, -'juː, -'jɜːz, -'juːz, '--
militancy 'mɪl.ɪ.tᵊn*t*.si, '-ə- Ⓤⓢ -tən*t*-
militant 'mɪl.ɪ.tᵊnt, '-ə- Ⓤⓢ -tənt **-s** -s **-ly** -li
militar|ism 'mɪl.ɪ.tᵊr|.ɪ.zᵊm, '-ə- Ⓤⓢ -tɚ- **-ist/s** -ɪst/s
militaristic ˌmɪl.ɪ.tᵊr'ɪs.tɪk, ˌ-ə- Ⓤⓢ -tə'rɪs- **-ally** -ᵊl.i, -li
militarization, -isa- ˌmɪl.ɪ.tᵊr.aɪ'zeɪ.ʃᵊn, ˌ-ə-, -ɪ'- Ⓤⓢ -tɚ.ɪ'-
militariz|e, -is|e 'mɪl.ɪ.tᵊr.aɪz, '-ə- Ⓤⓢ -tə.raɪz **-es** -ɪz **-ing** -ɪŋ **-ed** -d
military 'mɪl.ɪ.tri, '-ə-, -tᵊr.i Ⓤⓢ -ter- ˌ**military po'lice**
mili|tate 'mɪl.ɪ|.teɪt, '-ə- **-tates** -teɪts **-tating** -teɪ.tɪŋ Ⓤⓢ -teɪ.t̬ɪŋ **-tated** -teɪ.tɪd Ⓤⓢ -teɪ.t̬ɪd
militia mɪ'lɪʃ.ə, mə- **-man** -mən **-men** -mən, -men
milk mɪlk **-s** -s **-ing** -ɪŋ **-ed** -t **-er/s** -əʳ/z Ⓤⓢ -ɚ/z ˌ**milk 'chocolate** Ⓤⓢ **'milk ˌchocolate** ; **'milk ˌfloat**; ˌ**milk of mag'nesia**; **'milk ˌround**; **'milk ˌrun**; **'milk ˌshake**; **'milk ˌtooth**; **'milking maˌchine**; **it's ˌno good ˌcrying over ˌspilt 'milk**
milkfish 'mɪlk.fɪʃ **-es** -ɪz
milkmaid 'mɪlk.meɪd **-s** -z
milk|man 'mɪlk|.mən Ⓤⓢ -mæn, -mən **-men** -mən, -men
milksop 'mɪlk.sɒp Ⓤⓢ -sɑːp **-s** -s
milkwort 'mɪlk.wɜːt Ⓤⓢ -wɜːrt, -wɔːrt **-s** -s
milk|y 'mɪl.k|i **-ier** -i.əʳ Ⓤⓢ -i.ɚ **-iest** -i.ɪst, -i.əst **-ily** -ɪ.li, -ᵊl.i **-iness** -ɪ.nəs, -ɪ.nɪs ˌ**Milky 'Way**
mill (M) mɪl **-s** -z **-ing** -ɪŋ **-ed** -d
Millais 'mɪl.eɪ, -'- Ⓤⓢ mɪ'leɪ
Millard 'mɪl.əd, -ɑːd Ⓤⓢ -ɚd
Millay mɪ'leɪ
Millbank 'mɪl.bæŋk
millboard 'mɪl.bɔːd Ⓤⓢ -bɔːrd
millefeuille(s) ˌmiːl'fɔɪ, -'fɜː.jə Ⓤⓢ -'fɜː.jə
millenarian ˌmɪl.ə'neə.ri.ən, -ɪ'- Ⓤⓢ -ə'ner.i- **-s** -z
millenarianism ˌmɪl.ə'neə.ri.ə.nɪ.zᵊm, -ɪ'- Ⓤⓢ -ə'ner.i-
millenary mɪ'len.ᵊr.i, mə- Ⓤⓢ 'mɪl.ə.ner-
millenni|um mɪ'len.i|.əm, mə- Ⓤⓢ mɪ- **-ums** -əmz **-a** -ə **-al** -əl
millepede 'mɪl.ɪ.piːd, '-ə- **-s** -z
miller (M) 'mɪl.əʳ Ⓤⓢ -ɚ **-s** -z
millesimal mɪ'les.ɪ.mᵊl, mə-, '-ə- Ⓤⓢ mɪ'les.ə- **-ly** -i

millet (M) ˈmɪl.ɪt
milliard ˌmɪl.iˈɑːd; mɪlˈjɑːd
ⓊⓈ ˈmɪl.jɚd, -jɑːrd **-s** -z
millibar ˈmɪl.ɪ.bɑːʳ ⓊⓈ -bɑːr **-s** -z
Millicent ˈmɪl.ɪ.sᵊnt, ˈ-ə-
milligram(me) ˈmɪl.ɪ.græm **-s** -z
millilitre, milliliter ˈmɪl.ɪˌliː.təʳ, ˈ-ə-
ⓊⓈ -t̬ɚ **-s** -z
millimetre, millimeter ˈmɪl.ɪˌmiː.təʳ, ˈ-ə- ⓊⓈ -t̬ɚ **-s** -z
milliner ˈmɪl.ɪ.nəʳ, ˈ-ə- ⓊⓈ -nɚ **-s** -z
millinery ˈmɪl.ɪ.nᵊr.i, ˈ-ə- ⓊⓈ -ner-
Millington ˈmɪl.ɪŋ.tən
million ˈmɪl.jən, -i.ən ⓊⓈ ˈ-jən **-s** -z
a ˌchance in a ˈmillion
millionaire ˌmɪl.jəˈneəʳ, -i.əˈ-
ⓊⓈ ˌ-jəˈner, ˈmɪl.jə.ner **-s** -z
millionairess ˌmɪl.jə.neəˈres, ˌ-i.ə-; -ˈneə.rɪs, -res ⓊⓈ -jəˈner.ɪs **-es** -ɪz
millionfold ˈmɪl.jən.fəʊld, -i.ən-
ⓊⓈ -jən.foʊld
millionth ˈmɪl.jən*t*θ, -i.ən*t*θ
ⓊⓈ ˈ-jən*t*θ **-s** -s
millipede ˈmɪl.ɪ.piːd, ˈ-ə- **-s** -z
millisecond ˈmɪl.ɪˌsek.ənd, ˈ-ə- **-s** -z
Millom ˈmɪl.əm
millpond ˈmɪl.pɒnd ⓊⓈ -pɑːnd **-s** -z
millrac|e ˈmɪl.reɪs **-es** -ɪz
Mills mɪlz
millstone ˈmɪl.stəʊn ⓊⓈ -stoʊn **-s** -z
Milltimber ˈmɪlˌtɪm.bəʳ ⓊⓈ -bɚ
Millwall ˈmɪl.wɔːl, -wəl; mɪlˈwɔːl
Millward ˈmɪl.wɔːd, -wəd ⓊⓈ -wɚd
Milman ˈmɪl.mən
Milne mɪln, mɪl
Milner ˈmɪl.nəʳ ⓊⓈ -nɚ
Milnes mɪlz, mɪlnz
Milngavie mɪlˈgaɪ, mʌl-
Milnrow ˈmɪln.rəʊ ⓊⓈ -roʊ
Milo ˈmaɪ.ləʊ, ˈmiː- ⓊⓈ ˈmaɪ.loʊ
milometer maɪˈlɒm.ɪ.təʳ, ˈ-ə-
ⓊⓈ -ˈlɑː.mə.t̬ɚ **-s** -z
milord mɪˈlɔːd, mə- ⓊⓈ -ˈlɔːrd **-s** -z
Milos ˈmiː.lɒs ⓊⓈ -lɑːs
Milosevic mɪˈlɒs.ə.vɪtʃ ⓊⓈ -ˈlɑː.sə-
Milosz ˈmiː.lɒʃ ⓊⓈ -lɑːʃ
milquetoast ˈmɪlk.təʊst ⓊⓈ -toʊst **-s** -s
Milton ˈmɪl.tᵊn
Miltonic mɪlˈtɒn.ɪk ⓊⓈ -ˈtɑː.nɪk
Milton Keynes ˌmɪl.tᵊnˈkiːnz
Milwaukee mɪlˈwɔː.ki, -iː ⓊⓈ -ˈwɑː-, -ˈwɔː-
mim|e maɪm **-es** -z **-ing** -ɪŋ **-ed** -d **-er/s** -əʳ/z ⓊⓈ -ɚ/z
mimeo ˈmɪm.i.əʊ ⓊⓈ -oʊ **-s** -z **-ing** -ɪŋ **-ed** -d
mimeograph ˈmɪm.i.əʊ.grɑːf, -græf
ⓊⓈ -ə.græf **-s** -s **-ing** -ɪŋ **-ed** -t
mimesis mɪˈmiː.sɪs, maɪ-
mimetic mɪˈmet.ɪk, maɪ-
mimic ˈmɪm.ɪk **-s** -s **-king** -ɪŋ **-ked** -t **-ker/s** -əʳ/z ⓊⓈ -ɚ/z

mimicry ˈmɪm.ɪ.kri
mimosa mɪˈməʊ.zə, -sə
ⓊⓈ -ˈmoʊ.sə, -zə **-s** -z
mimulus ˈmɪm.jə.ləs, -jʊ- ⓊⓈ -jə-, -juː- **-es** -ɪz
mina ˈmaɪ.nə **-s** -z
minaret ˌmɪn.əˈret, ˈ--- **-s** -s
minatory ˈmɪn.ə.tᵊr.i, ˈmaɪ-
ⓊⓈ ˈmɪn.ə.tɔːr-
minc|e mɪn*t*s **-es** -ɪz **-ing/ly** -ɪŋ/li **-ed** -t **-er/s** -əʳ/z ⓊⓈ -ɚ/z ˌ**mince ˈpie**
mincemeat ˈmɪn*t*s.miːt **make ˈmincemeat of ˌsomeone**
Minch mɪn*t*ʃ **-es** -ɪz
mind maɪnd **-s** -z **-ing** -ɪŋ **-ed** -ɪd **ˈmind ˌreader** ; **ˌmind's ˈeye** ; **ˌgive someone a ˌpiece of one's ˈmind**
Mindanao ˌmɪn.dəˈnaʊ ⓊⓈ -ˈnaʊ, -ˈnɑː.oʊ
mind-blowing ˈmaɪn*d*ˌbləʊ.ɪŋ
ⓊⓈ -ˌbloʊ- **-ly** -li
mind-boggling ˈmaɪn*d*ˌbɒg.l̩.ɪŋ, ˈmaɪm-, -ˌbɒg.lɪŋ
ⓊⓈ ˈmaɪn*d*ˌbɑː.glɪŋ, -ˌbɑː.gl̩.ɪŋ **-ly** -li
minder ˈmaɪn.dəʳ ⓊⓈ -dɚ **-s** -z
mind-expanding ˈmaɪnd.ɪkˌspæn.dɪŋ, -ekˌ- ⓊⓈ -ekˌ-, -ɪkˌ-
mindful ˈmaɪn*d*.fᵊl, -fʊl **-ly** -i **-ness** -nəs, -nɪs
mindless ˈmaɪn*d*.ləs, -lɪs **-ly** -li **-ness** -nəs, -nɪs
mind-set ˈmaɪn*d*.set
Mindy ˈmɪn.di
min|e maɪn **-es** -z **-ing** -ɪŋ **-ed** -d
minefield ˈmaɪn.fiːld **-s** -z
Minehead ˈmaɪn.hed, ˌ-ˈ-
Minelli mɪˈnel.i, mə-
miner ˈmaɪ.nəʳ ⓊⓈ -nɚ **-s** -z
mineral ˈmɪn.ᵊr.ᵊl **-s** -z **ˈmineral ˌwater**
mineraliz|e, -is|e ˈmɪn.ᵊr.ᵊl.aɪz **-es** -ɪz **-ing** -ɪŋ **-ed** -d
mineralogical ˌmɪn.ᵊr.əˈlɒdʒ.ɪ.kᵊl
ⓊⓈ -ˈlɑː.dʒɪ- **-ly** -i
mineralog|y ˌmɪn.ᵊrˈæl.ə.dʒ|i
ⓊⓈ -əˈrɑː.lə-, -ˈræl.ə- **-ist/s** -ɪst/s
Minerva mɪˈnɜː.və ⓊⓈ məˈnɜːr-
minestrone ˌmɪn.ɪˈstrəʊ.ni, -əˈ-
ⓊⓈ -əˈstroʊ-
minesweep|er ˈmaɪnˌswiː.p|əʳ ⓊⓈ -p|ɚ **-ers** -əz ⓊⓈ -ɚz **-ing** -ɪŋ
Ming mɪŋ
mingl|e ˈmɪŋ.gl̩ **-es** -z **-ing** -ɪŋ, ˈmɪŋ.glɪŋ **-ed** -d
mingogram ˈmɪŋ.gəʊ.græm, -əʊ-
ⓊⓈ -gə- **-s** -z
mingograph® ˈmɪŋ.gəʊ.grɑːf, -əʊ-, -græf ⓊⓈ -gə.græf **-s** -s
Mingus ˈmɪŋ.gəs
ming|y ˈmɪn.dʒ|i **-ier** -i.əʳ ⓊⓈ -i.ɚ **-iest** -i.ɪst, -i.əst
mini (M®) ˈmɪn.i **-s** -z

miniature ˈmɪn.ə.tʃəʳ, ˈ-ɪ-
ⓊⓈ ˈ-i.ə.tʃɚ, ˈ-ə.tʃɚ **-s** -z
miniaturist ˈmɪn.ə.tʃᵊr.ɪst, ˈ-ɪ-, -tjʊə.rɪst ⓊⓈ ˈ-i.ə.tʃɚ.ɪst, ˈ-ə.tʃɚ- **-s** -s
miniaturization, -isa- ˌmɪn.ə.tʃᵊr.aɪˈzeɪ.ʃᵊn, ˌ-ɪ-
ⓊⓈ -i.ə.tʃɚ.ɪˈ-, -ə.tʃɚ- **-s** -z
miniaturiz|e, -is|e ˈmɪn.ə.tʃᵊr.aɪz, ˈ-ɪ-
ⓊⓈ ˈ-i.ə.tʃɚ-, ˈ-ə.tʃɚ- **-es** -ɪz **-ing** -ɪŋ **-ed** -d
minibus ˈmɪn.ɪ.bʌs ⓊⓈ mɪn.i- **-es** -ɪz
minicab ˈmɪn.ɪ.kæb ⓊⓈ mɪn.i- **-s** -z
minicam ˈmɪn.ɪ.kæm ⓊⓈ mɪn.i- **-s** -z
minicomputer ˈmɪn.ɪ.kəmˌpjuː.təʳ, ˌmɪn.ɪ.kəmˈpjuː- ⓊⓈ mɪn.i-, -ˈpjuː.t̬ɚ **-s** -z
minim (M) ˈmɪn.ɪm **-s** -z
minimal ˈmɪn.ɪ.mᵊl, ˈ-ə- **-ly** -i
minimal|ism ˈmɪn.ɪ.mᵊl|.ɪ.zᵊm, ˈ-ə- **-ist/s** -ɪst/s
minimization ˌmɪn.ɪ.maɪˈzeɪ.ʃᵊn, ˌ-ə-, -mɪˈ- ⓊⓈ -mɪˈ-
minimiz|e, -is|e ˈmɪn.ɪ.maɪz, ˈ-ə- **-es** -ɪz **-ing** -ɪŋ **-ed** -d
minim|um ˈmɪn.ɪ.m|əm **-a** -ə
ˌminimum ˈwage
mining ˈmaɪ.nɪŋ
minion ˈmɪn.jən **-s** -z
minipill ˈmɪn.ɪ.pɪl
miniseries ˈmɪn.ɪˌsɪə.rɪz, -riːz
ⓊⓈ mɪn.i-, -ˌsɪr.iːz
minish ˈmɪn.ɪʃ **-es** -ɪz **-ing** -ɪŋ **-ed** -t
mini-skirt ˈmɪn.ɪ.skɜːt ⓊⓈ mɪn.i-, -skɜːrt **-s** -s **-ed** -ɪd
minist|er ˈmɪn.ɪ.st|əʳ, ˈ-ə- ⓊⓈ -st|ɚ **-ers** -əz ⓊⓈ -ɚz **-ering** -ᵊr.ɪŋ **-ered** -əd ⓊⓈ -ɚd
ministerial ˌmɪn.ɪˈstɪə.ri.əl, -əˈ-
ⓊⓈ -ˈstɪr.i- **-ly** -i
ministration ˌmɪn.ɪˈstreɪ.ʃᵊn, -əˈ- **-s** -z
ministr|y ˈmɪn.ɪ.str|i, ˈ-ə- **-ies** -iz
miniver (M) ˈmɪn.ɪ.vəʳ, ˈ-ə- ⓊⓈ -vɚ
mink mɪŋk **-s** -s
minke ˈmɪŋ.ki, -kə ⓊⓈ -kə **-s** -z
Minn. (*abbrev. for* **Minnesota**) ˌmɪn.ɪˈsəʊ.tə, -əˈ- ⓊⓈ -ˈsoʊ.t̬ə
Minneapolis ˌmɪn.iˈæp.ᵊl.ɪs
Minnehaha ˌmɪn.iˈhɑː.hɑː
Minnelli mɪˈnel.i, mə-
minneola ˌmɪn.iˈəʊ.lə ⓊⓈ -ˈoʊ- **-s** -z
minnesinger ˈmɪn.ɪˌsɪŋ.əʳ, -əˌ-, -gəʳ
ⓊⓈ -ɚ **-s** -z
Minnesot|a ˌmɪn.ɪˈsəʊ.t|ə, -əˈ-
ⓊⓈ -ˈsoʊ.t̬|ə **-an/s** -ən/z
Minnie ˈmɪn.i
minnow ˈmɪn.əʊ ⓊⓈ -oʊ **-s** -z
Minoan mɪˈnəʊ.ən, mə-, maɪ- ⓊⓈ mɪ-
Minogue mɪˈnəʊg, mə- ⓊⓈ -ˈnoʊg
Minolta® mɪˈnɒl·tə, mə-, -ˈnəʊl-
ⓊⓈ -ˈnoʊl-, -ˈnɑːl-
minor ˈmaɪ·nəʳ ⓊⓈ -nɚ **-s** -z

Minorca mɪˈnɔː.kə, mə- (US) -ˈnɔːr-

Minories ˈmɪn.ᵊr.iz

minorit|y maɪˈnɒr.ə.t|i, mɪ-, mə-, -ɪ.t|i (US) maɪˈnɔːr.ə.t̬|i, mɪ- **-ies** -iz

Minos ˈmaɪ.nɒs (US) -nɑːs, -nəs

Minotaur ˈmaɪ.nə.tɔːʳ (US) ˈmɪn.ə.tɔːr **-s** -z

Minsk mɪn*t*sk

Minsmere ˈmɪnz.mɪəʳ (US) -mɪr

minster (M) ˈmɪn.stəʳ (US) -stɚ **-s** -z

minstrel ˈmɪn*t*.strᵊl **-s** -z

minstrel|sy ˈmɪn*t*.strᵊl|.si **-sies** -siz

mint mɪnt **-s** -s **-ing** -ɪŋ (US) ˈmɪn.t̬ɪŋ **-ed** -ɪd (US) ˈmɪn.t̬ɪd **-age** -ɪdʒ (US) ˈmɪn.t̬ɪdʒ ˌ**mint conˈdition** ; ˌ**mint ˈjulep** ; ˌ**mint ˈsauce** (US) ˈ**mint ˌsauce**

Minto ˈmɪn.təʊ (US) -toʊ

Mintoff ˈmɪn.tɒf (US) -tɑːf

minuet ˌmɪn.juˈet **-s** -s

minus ˈmaɪ.nəs **-es** -ɪz

minuscule ˈmɪn.ə.skjuːl, ˈ-ɪ- (US) ˈ-ɪ-; mɪˈnʌs.kjuːl **-s** -z

minu|te *very small:* maɪˈnjuː|t (US) -ˈnuː|t, -ˈnjuː|t **-test** -tɪst, -təst (US) -t̬ɪst, -t̬əst **-tely** -t.li **-teness** -t.nəs, -t.nɪs

minute *(n.) division of time, angle, memorandum:* ˈmɪn.ɪt **-s** -s

min|ute *(v.)* ˈmɪn|.ɪt **-utes** -ɪts **-uting** -ɪ.tɪŋ (US) -ɪ.t̬ɪŋ **-uted** -ɪ.tɪd (US) -ɪ.t̬ɪd

minute-gun ˈmɪn.ɪt.gʌn **-s** -z

minute-hand ˈmɪn.ɪt.hænd **-s** -z

minute|man (M) ˈmɪn.ɪt|.mæn **-men** -men

minuti|a maɪˈnjuː.ʃi|.ə, mɪ-, mə-, -ˈnuː-, -ti- (US) mɪˈnuː.ʃi-, -ˈnjuː-, ˈ-ʃ|ə **-ae** -iː, -aɪ

minx mɪŋks **-es** -ɪz

Miocene ˈmaɪ.əʊ.siːn (US) ˈ-oʊ-, ˈ-ə-

mios|is maɪˈəʊ.s|ɪs (US) -ˈoʊ- **-es** -iːz

miotic maɪˈɒt.ɪk (US) -ˈɑː.t̬ɪk **-s** -s

mips, MIPS mɪps

Mira ˈmaɪə.rə, ˈmɪr.ə (US) ˈmaɪ.rə

Mirabell ˈmɪr.ə.bel

miracle ˈmɪr.ə.kl̩, ˈ-ɪ- **-s** -z

miraculous mɪˈræk.jə.ləs, mə-, -jʊ- (US) mɪˈræk.jə.ləs, -juː- **-ly** -li **-ness** -nəs, -nɪs

mirag|e ˈmɪr.ɑːʒ; məˈrɑːʒ, mɪˈ- (US) mɪˈrɑːʒ, mə- **-es** -ɪz

Miranda mɪˈræn.də (US) mə-, mɪ-

MIRAS ˈmaɪə.rəs, -ræs (US) ˈmaɪ-

mire maɪəʳ (US) maɪr

Mirfield ˈmɜː.fiːld (US) ˈmɜːr-

Miriam ˈmɪr.i.əm

mirk|y ˈmɜː.k|i (US) ˈmɜːr- **-ier** -i.əʳ (US) -i.ɚ **-iest** -i.ɪst, -i.əst **-ily** -ɪ.li, -ᵊl.i **-iness** -ɪ.nəs, -ɪ.nɪs

Miró mɪˈrəʊ (US) miːˈroʊ

Mirren ˈmɪr.ən

mirr|or ˈmɪr|.əʳ (US) -ɚ **-ors** -əz (US) -ɚz **-oring** -ᵊr.ɪŋ **-ored** -əd (US) -ɚd ˌ**mirror ˈimage**

mirth mɜːθ (US) mɜːrθ

mirthful ˈmɜːθ.fᵊl, -fʊl (US) ˈmɜːrθ- **-ly** -i **-ness** -nəs, -nɪs

mirthless ˈmɜːθ.ləs, -lɪs (US) ˈmɜːrθ- **-ly** -li **-ness** -nəs, -nɪs

MIRV mɜːv (US) mɜːrv **-s** -z **-ing** -ɪŋ **-ed** -d

mir|y ˈmaɪə.r|i **-ier** -i.əʳ (US) -i.ɚ **-iest** -i.ɪst, -i.əst **-iness** -ɪ.nəs, -ɪ.nɪs

mis- mɪs-

Note: Prefix. In words containing **mis-**, the prefix may either be unstressed, e.g. **misdeal** /mɪsˈdiːl/, or receive secondary stress, especially if the stem is stressed on its second syllable, e.g. **align** /əˈlaɪn/, **misalign** /ˌmɪs.əˈlaɪn/. There is sometimes a difference between nouns and verbs, e.g. **miscount**, noun /ˈmɪs.kaʊnt/, verb /mɪˈskaʊnt/. There are exceptions; see individual entries.

misadventure ˌmɪs.ədˈven.tʃəʳ (US) -tʃɚ **-s** -z

misalign ˌmɪs.əˈlaɪn **-s** -z

misaligned ˌmɪs.əˈlaɪnd

misalignment ˌmɪs.əˈlaɪn.mənt, -ˈlaɪm- (US) -ˈlaɪn- **-s** -s

misallianc|e ˌmɪs.əˈlaɪ.ən*t*s **-es** -ɪz

misandry mɪˈsæn.dri; ˈmɪs.ᵊn- (US) ˈmɪs.æn-

misanthrope ˈmɪs.ᵊn.θrəʊp, ˈmɪz-, -æn- (US) -ən.θroʊp **-s** -s

misanthropic ˌmɪs.ᵊnˈθrɒp.ɪk, ˌmɪz-, -ænˈ- (US) -ənˈθrɑː.pɪk **-al** -ᵊl **-ally** -ᵊl.i, -li

misanthrop|y mɪˈsæn.θrə.p|i, -ˈzæn- **-ist/s** -ɪst/s

misapplication ˌmɪs.æp.lɪˈkeɪ.ʃᵊn, -ləˈ- **-s** -z

misappl|y ˌmɪs.əˈpl|aɪ **-ies** -aɪz **-ying** -aɪ.ɪŋ **-ied** -aɪd

misapprehend ˌmɪs.æp.rɪˈhend, -rəˈ- **-s** -z **-ing** -ɪŋ **-ed** -ɪd

misapprehension ˌmɪs.æp.rɪˈhen.*t*ʃᵊn, -rəˈ- **-s** -z

misappropri|ate ˌmɪs.əˈprəʊ.pri|.eɪt (US) -ˈproʊ- **-ates** -eɪts **-ating** -eɪ.tɪŋ (US) -eɪ.t̬ɪŋ **-ated** -eɪ.tɪd (US) -eɪ.t̬ɪd

misappropriation ˌmɪs.əˌprəʊ.priˈeɪ.ʃᵊn (US) -ˌproʊ- **-s** -z

misbecoming ˌmɪs.bɪˈkʌm.ɪŋ, -bəˈ-

misbegotten ˌmɪs.bɪˈgɒt.ᵊn, -bəˈ-, ˈmɪs.bɪˌgɒt-, -bəˌ- (US) ˌmɪs.bɪˈgɑː.tᵊn

misbehav|e ˌmɪs.bɪˈheɪv, -bəˈ- **-es** -z **-ing** -ɪŋ **-ed** -d

misbehavio(u)r ˌmɪs.bɪˈheɪ.vjəʳ, -bəˈ- (US) -vjɚ **-s** -z

misbelief ˌmɪs.bɪˈliːf, -bəˈ-, ˈ--- (US) ˌ--ˈ- **-s**

misbeliev|e ˌmɪs.bɪˈliːv, -bəˈ-, ˈ--- (US) ˌ--ˈ- **-es** -z **-ing** -ɪŋ **-ed** -d **-er/s** -əʳ/z (US) -ɚ/z

misc. *(abbrev. for* **miscellaneous***)* ˌmɪs.ᵊlˈeɪ.ni.əs

miscalcu|late mɪsˈkæl.kjə|.leɪt, -kjʊ-; ˌmɪsˈkæl- (US) -kjə-, -kjuː- **-lates** -leɪts **-lating** -leɪ.tɪŋ (US) -leɪ.t̬ɪŋ **-lated** -leɪ.tɪd (US) -leɪ.t̬ɪd

miscalculation ˌmɪs.kæl.kjəˈleɪ.ʃᵊn, -kjʊˈ- (US) -kjəˈ-, -kjuːˈ- **-s** -z

miscall mɪˈskɔːl; ˌmɪsˈkɔːl (US) mɪsˈkɔːl, -ˈkɑːl; ˌmɪsˈkɔːl, -ˈkɑːl **-s** -z **-ing** -ɪŋ **-ed** -d

miscarriag|e mɪˈskær.ɪdʒ; ˌmɪsˈkær-, ˈ-ˌ-- (US) ˈmɪsˌker-, -ˌkær-; mɪˈsker-, -ˈskær-; ˌmɪsˈker-, -ˈkær- **-es** -ɪz

miscarr|y mɪˈskær|.i; ˌmɪsˈkær- (US) ˈmɪsˌker-, -ˌkær-; mɪˈsker-, -ˈskær-; ˌmɪsˈker-, -ˈkær- **-ies** -iz **-ying** -i.ɪŋ **-ied** -id

miscast mɪˈskɑːst; ˌmɪsˈkɑːst (US) mɪˈskæst; ˌmɪsˈkæst **-s** -s **-ing** -ɪŋ

miscegenation ˌmɪs.ɪ.dʒɪˈneɪ.ʃᵊn, ˌ-ə-, ˌ-e-, -dʒəˈ- (US) -edʒ.əˈ-; -ɪ.dʒəˈ- **-al** -ᵊl

miscellanea ˌmɪs.ᵊlˈeɪ.ni.ə

miscellaneous ˌmɪs.ᵊlˈeɪ.ni.əs, -ɪˈleɪ- **-ly** -li **-ness** -nəs, -nɪs

miscellan|y mɪˈsel.ə.n|i (US) ˈmɪs.ə.leɪ- **-ies** -iz

mischanc|e mɪsˈtʃɑːn*t*s, ˌmɪs-, ˈ-- (US) mɪsˈtʃæn*t*s, ˌmɪs-, ˈ-- **-es** -ɪz

mischief ˈmɪs.tʃɪf, -tʃiːf (US) -tʃɪf **-s** -s

mischief-mak|er ˈmɪs.tʃɪfˌmeɪ.k|əʳ (US) -k|ɚ **-ers** -əz (US) -ɚz **-ing** -ɪŋ

mischievous ˈmɪs.tʃɪ.vəs, -tʃə- (US) -tʃə- **-ly** -li **-ness** -nəs, -nɪs

miscibility ˌmɪs.ɪˈbɪl.ɪ.ti, -əˈ-, ˈ-ə- (US) -əˈbɪl.ə.t̬i

miscible ˈmɪs.ɪ.bl̩, ˈ-ə- (US) ˈ-ə-

misconceiv|e ˌmɪs.kənˈsiːv **-es** -z **-ing** -ɪŋ **-ed** -d

misconception ˌmɪs.kənˈsep.ʃᵊn **-s** -z

misconduct *(n.)* mɪˈskɒn.dʌkt; ˌmɪsˈkɒn-, -dəkt (US) mɪˈskɑːn.dʌkt; ˌmɪsˈkɑːn-

misconduct *(v.)* ˌmɪs.kənˈdʌkt **-s** -s **-ing** -ɪŋ **-ed** -ɪd

misconstruction ˌmɪs.kənˈstrʌk.ʃᵊn **-s** -z

misconstru|e ˌmɪs.kənˈstruː, -kɒnˈ- (US) -kənˈ- **-es** -z **-ing** -ɪŋ **-ed** -d

miscount *(n.)* ˈmɪs.kaʊnt **-s** -s

miscoun|t *(v.)* mɪˈskaʊn|t; **-ts** -ts **-ting** -tɪŋ (US) -t̬ɪŋ **-ted** -tɪd (US) -t̬ɪd

miscreant ˈmɪs.kri.ənt **-s** -s

miscu|e mɪˈskjuː; ˌmɪsˈkjuː (US) mɪˈskjuː; ˌmɪsˈkjuː, ˈ-- **-es** -z **-ing** -ɪŋ **-ed** -d

misdeal mɪsˈdiːl, ˌ-ˈ- (US) mɪsˈdiːl, ˌ-ˈ-, ˈ-- **-s** -z **-ing** -ɪŋ **misdealt** -ˈdelt, ˌ-ˈ- (US) -ˈ-, ˌ-ˈ-, ˈ--

misdeed mɪsˈdiːd, ˌ-ˈ-, ˈ-- **-s** -z

misdemeano(u)r ˌmɪs.dɪˈmiː.nəʳ, -dəˈ- (US) -nɚ, ˈ-ˌ--- **-s** -z

misdiagnos|e mɪsˈdaɪəg.nəʊz, ˌ-ˈ--- (US) ˌmɪs.daɪ.əgˈnoʊs, -ˈnoʊz; -ˈ---, ˌ-ˈ---, -noʊz **-es** -ɪz **-ing** -ɪŋ **-ed** -d

misdiagnos|is ˌmɪs.daɪəgˈnəʊ.s|ɪs (US) -ˈnoʊ- **-es**

misdirect ˌmɪs.dɪˈrekt, -dəˈ-, -daɪəˈ- (US) -dəˈ-, -daɪˈ- **-s** -s **-ing** -ɪŋ **-ed** -ɪd

misdirection ˌmɪs.dɪˈrek.ʃᵊn, -dəˈ-, -daɪəˈ- (US) -dəˈ-, -daɪˈ-

misdoing mɪsˈduː.ɪŋ, ˌmɪs- **-s** -z

mise-en-scène ˌmiːz.ɑ̃ːnˈseɪn, -ˈsen (US) -ɑ̃ːnˈsen **mise-en-scènes** ˌmiːz.ɑ̃ːnˈseɪn, -ˈsen, -z (US) -ɑ̃ːnˈsen, -z

miser ˈmaɪ.zəʳ (US) -zɚ **-s** -z

miserab|le ˈmɪz.ᵊr.ə.b|l̩, ˈmɪz.rə- **-ly** -li **-leness** -l̩.nəs, -nɪs

miserere ˌmɪz.ᵊrˈeə.ri, -ˈɪə-, -reɪ (US) -ˈrer.eɪ **-s** -z

misericord mɪˈzer.ɪ.kɔːd, mə-, ˈ-ə-; ˈmɪz.ᵊr.ɪ- (US) -kɔːrd **-s** -z

miserl|y ˈmaɪ.zᵊl|.i (US) -zɚ.l|i **-iness** -ɪ.nəs, -ɪ.nɪs

miser|y ˈmɪz.ᵊr|.i (US) ˈ-r|i, ˈ-ɚ|.i **-ies** -iz

misfeasance mɪsˈfiː.zᵊnts (US) ˌmɪs-

misfire (*n.*) mɪsˈfaɪəʳ, ˌmɪs-, ˈ-- (US) ˈmɪs.faɪɚ

misfir|e (*v.*) mɪsˈfaɪəʳ, ˌmɪs- (US) -ˈfaɪɚ **-es** -z **-ing** -ɪŋ **-ed** -d

misfit (*n.*) ˈmɪs.fɪt **-s** -s

misfortune mɪsˈfɔː.tʃuːn, ˌmɪs-, -tʃən, -tjuːn (US) -ˈfɔːr.tʃən **-s** -z

misgiving mɪsˈgɪv.ɪŋ, ˌmɪs- **-s** -z

misgovern mɪsˈgʌv.ᵊn, ˌmɪs- (US) -ɚn **-s** -z **-ing** -ɪŋ **-ed** -d **-ment** -mənt

misguided mɪsˈgaɪ.dɪd, ˌmɪs- **-ly** -li **-ness** -nəs, -nɪs

mishandl|e mɪsˈhæn.dl̩, ˌmɪs- **-es** -z **-ing** -ɪŋ, -ˈhænd.lɪŋ **-ed** -d

mishap ˈmɪs.hæp, -ˈ-, ˌ-ˈ- (US) ˈmɪs.hæp **-s** -s

mis|hear mɪs|ˈhɪəʳ, ˌmɪs- (US) -ˈhɪr **-hears** -ˈhɪəz (US) -ˈhɪrz **-hearing** -ˈhɪə.rɪŋ (US) -ˈhɪr.ɪŋ **-heard** -ˈhɜːd (US) -ˈhɜːrd

Mishima ˈmɪʃ.ɪ.mə; mɪˈʃiː- (US) ˈmɪʃ.ɪ-, ˈmiː.ʃɪ-

mis|hit mɪs|ˈhɪt, ˌmɪs- **-hits** -ˈhɪts **-hitting** -ˈhɪt.ɪŋ (US) -ˈhɪt̬.ɪŋ

mishmash ˈmɪʃ.mæʃ

misinform ˌmɪs.ɪnˈfɔːm (US) -ˈfɔːrm **-s** -z **-ing** -ɪŋ **-ed** -d **-ant/s** -ənt/s **-er/s** -əʳ/z (US) -ɚ/z

misinformation ˌmɪs.ɪn.fəˈmeɪ.ʃᵊn (US) -fɚˈ-

misinter|pret ˌmɪs.ɪnˈtɜː|.prɪt (US) -ˈtɜːr- **-prets** -prɪts **-preting** -prɪ.tɪŋ (US) -prɪ.t̬ɪŋ **-preted** -prɪ.tɪd (US) -prɪ.t̬ɪd

misinterpretation ˌmɪs.ɪnˌtɜː.prɪˈteɪ.ʃᵊn, -prəˈ- (US) -ˌtɜːr.prɪˈ- **-s** -z

misjoinder mɪsˈdʒɔɪn.dəʳ, ˌmɪs- (US) -dɚ

misjudg|e mɪsˈdʒʌdʒ, ˌmɪs- **-es** -ɪz **-ing** -ɪŋ **-ed** -d

misjudg(e)ment mɪsˈdʒʌdʒ.mənt, ˌmɪs- **-s** -s

Miskolc ˈmɪʃ.kəʊlts (US) -kɔːlts

mislay mɪˈsleɪ, ˌmɪsˈleɪ **-lays** -ɪz **-laying** -ɪŋ **mislaid** mɪˈsleɪd, ˌmɪsˈleɪd

mislead mɪˈsliːd, ˌmɪsˈliːd **-s** -z **-ing/ly** -ɪŋ/li **misled** mɪˈsled, ˌmɪsˈled

mismanag|e ˌmɪsˈmæn.ɪdʒ **-es** -ɪz **-ing** -ɪŋ **-ed** -d **-ement** -mənt

mismatch (*n.*) ˈmɪs.mætʃ; -ˈ-, ˌ-ˈ- **-es** -ɪz

mismatch (*v.*) mɪˈsmætʃ; ˌmɪsˈmætʃ, ˈ-- (US) mɪˈsmætʃ; ˌmɪsˈmætʃ **-es** -ɪs **-ing** -ɪŋ **-ed** -t

misnomer mɪˈsnəʊ.məʳ; ˌmɪsˈnəʊ- (US) mɪˈsnoʊ.mɚ, ˌmɪsˈnoʊ- **-s** -z

miso ˈmiː.səʊ (US) -soʊ

misogynistic mɪˌsɒdʒ.ᵊnˈɪs.tɪk, maɪ-, mə-, -dʒɪˈnɪs- (US) -ˌsɑː.dʒɪˈ-

misogyn|y mɪˈsɒdʒ.ɪ.n|i, maɪ-, mə- (US) -sɑːdʒ-

misogynist mɪˈsɒdʒ.ᵊn.ɪst, maɪ-, mə- (US) -ˈsɑːdʒ- **-s** -s

misplac|e mɪˈspleɪs, ˌmɪsˈpleɪs **-es** -ɪz **-ing** -ɪŋ **-ed** -t **-ement** -mənt *stress shift:* ˌmisplaced ˈtrust

misprint (*n.*) ˈmɪs.prɪnt **-s** -s

misprin|t (*v.*) mɪˈsprɪn|t; ˌmɪsˈprɪn|t **-ts** -ts **-ting** -tɪŋ (US) -t̬ɪŋ **-ted** -tɪd (US) -t̬ɪd

misprision mɪˈsprɪʒ.ᵊn

mispronounc|e ˌmɪs.prəˈnaʊnts (US) -prəˈ-, -proʊˈ- **-es** -ɪz **-ing** -ɪŋ **-ed** -t

mispronunciation ˌmɪs.prəˌnʌnt.siˈeɪ.ʃən (US) -prəˌ-, -proʊˌ- **-s** -z

misquotation ˌmɪs.kwəʊˈteɪ.ʃᵊn (US) -kwoʊˈ- **-s** -z

misquo|te mɪˈskwəʊ|t; ˌmɪsˈkwəʊ|t (US) mɪˈskwoʊ|t; ˌmɪsˈkwoʊ|t **-tes** -ts **-ting** -tɪŋ (US) -t̬ɪŋ **-ted** -tɪd (US) -t̬ɪd

Misratah ˈmɪs.ræt.ɑː

misread mɪsˈriːd, ˌmɪs- **-s** -z **-ing** -ɪŋ *past tense:* mɪsˈred, ˌmɪs-

misrememb|er ˌmɪs.rɪˈmem.b|əʳ, -rəˈ- (US) -b|ɚ **-ers** -əz (US) -ɚz **-ering** -ᵊr.ɪŋ **-ered** -əd (US) -ɚd

misre|port ˌmɪs.rɪ|ˈpɔːt (US) -ˈpɔːrt **-ports** -ˈpɔːts (US) -ˈpɔːrts **-porting** -ˈpɔː.tɪŋ (US) -ˈpɔːr.t̬ɪŋ **-ported** -ˈpɔː.tɪd (US) -ˈpɔːr.t̬ɪd

misrepre|sent ˌmɪs.rep.rɪ|ˈzent **-sents** -ˈzents **-senting** -ˈzen.tɪŋ (US) -ˈzen.t̬ɪŋ **-sented** -ˈzen.tɪd (US) -ˈzen.t̬ɪd

misrepresentation ˌmɪs.rep.rɪ.zenˈteɪ.ʃᵊn, -zᵊnˈ- (US) -zenˈ- **-s** -z

misrule mɪsˈruːl, ˌmɪs-

miss (M) mɪs **-es** -ɪz **-ing** -ɪŋ **-ed** -t

Miss. (*abbrev. for* **Mississippi**) ˌmɪs.ɪˈsɪp.i (US) -əˈ-, -ɪˈ-

missal ˈmɪs.ᵊl **-s** -z

missel thrush ˈmɪz.ᵊlˌθrʌʃ, ˈmɪs-

Missenden ˈmɪs.ᵊn.dən

misshapen mɪsˈʃeɪ.pᵊn, ˌmɪs-, mɪʃ-, ˌmɪʃ- **-ly** -li

missile ˈmɪs.aɪl (US) -ᵊl **-s** -z

missing ˈmɪs.ɪŋ

mission ˈmɪʃ.ᵊn **-s** -z

missionar|y ˈmɪʃ.ᵊn.ᵊr|.i, ˈmɪʃ.nᵊr- (US) ˈ-ᵊn.er- **-ies** -iz ˈ**missionary poˌsition**

missioner ˈmɪʃ.ᵊn.əʳ (US) -ɚ **-s** -z

missis ˈmɪs.ɪz

Mississippi ˌmɪs.ɪˈsɪp.i (US) -əˈ-, -ɪˈ- **-an/s** -ən/z

missive ˈmɪs.ɪv **-s** -z

Missoula mɪˈzuː.lə

Missouri mɪˈzʊə.ri, -ˈsʊə- (US) -ˈzʊr.i *locally:* -ə

misspell mɪsˈspel, ˌmɪs- **-s** -z **-ing/s** -ɪŋ/z **-ed** -t, -d **misspelt** mɪsˈspelt (US) ˌmɪs-

misspend mɪsˈspend, ˌmɪs **-s** -z **-ing** -ɪŋ **misspent** mɪsˈspent, ˌmɪs- ˌ**misspent** ˈ**youth**

mis|state mɪs|ˈsteɪt, ˌmɪs- **-states** -ˈsteɪts **-stating** -ˈsteɪ.tɪŋ (US) -ˈsteɪ.t̬ɪŋ **-stated** -ˈsteɪ.tɪd (US) -ˈsteɪ.t̬ɪd **-statement/s** -ˈsteɪt.mənt/s

missus ˈmɪs.ɪz, -ɪs

miss|y ˈmɪs|.i **-ies** -iz

mist mɪst **-s** -s **-ing** -ɪŋ **-ed** -ɪd **-er/s** -əʳ/z, -ɚ/z

mistak|e mɪˈsteɪk **-es** -s **-ing** -ɪŋ **mistook** mɪˈstʊk

mistak(e)able mɪˈsteɪ.kə.bl̩

mistaken mɪˈsteɪ.kᵊn **-ly** -li

mister (M) ˈmɪs.təʳ (US) -tɚ

mistim|e mɪsˈtaɪm; ˌmɪs- **-es** -z **-ing** -ɪŋ **-ed** -d

mistle thrush ˈmɪs.l̩ˌθrʌʃ, ˈmɪz- (US) ˈmɪs-

mistletoe ˈmɪs.l̩.təʊ, ˈmɪz- (US) ˈmɪs.l̩.toʊ

mistook (*from* **mistake**) mɪˈstʊk

mistral (M) ˈmɪs.trᵊl, -trɑːl; mɪˈstrɑːl (US) mɪˈstrɑːl; ˈmɪs.trᵊl **-s** -z

mistransla|te ˌmɪs.trænˈsleɪ|t, -trɑːn-, -trᵊn-; -trænzˈleɪ|t, -trɑːnzˈ-, -trᵊnzˈ- (US) ˌmɪsˈtræn.sleɪ|t,

-'trænz.leɪ|t; mɪs.træn'sleɪ|t; -trænz'leɪ|t **-tes** -ts **-ting** -tɪŋ Ⓤⓢ -t̬ɪŋ **-ted** -tɪd Ⓤⓢ -t̬ɪd
mistranslation ˌmɪs.træn'sleɪ.ʃᵊn, -trɑːn'-, -trᵊn'-; -trænz'leɪ-, -trænz'-, -trᵊnz'- Ⓤⓢ -træn'sleɪ-; -trænz'leɪ- **-s** -z
mistrea|t mɪs'triː|t; ˌmɪs- **-ts** -ts **-ting** -tɪŋ Ⓤⓢ -t̬ɪŋ **-ted** -tɪd Ⓤⓢ -t̬ɪd
mistreatment mɪs'triːt.mənt; ˌmɪs-
mistress 'mɪs.trəs, -trɪs Ⓤⓢ -trɪs **-es** -ɪz
mistrial mɪ'straɪəl; ˌmɪs'traɪ- Ⓤⓢ 'mɪsˌtraɪ-; mɪ'straɪ-; ˌmɪs'traɪ- **-s** -z
mistrust mɪ'strʌst; ˌmɪs'trʌst Ⓤⓢ ˌmɪs'trʌst; mɪ'strʌst; 'mɪs.trʌst; **-s** -s **-ing** -ɪŋ **-ed** -ɪd
mistrustful mɪ'strʌst.fᵊl, ˌmɪs'trʌst- **-ly** -li
mist|y (M) 'mɪs.t|i **-ier** -i.əʳ Ⓤⓢ -i.ɚ **-iest** -i.ɪst, -i.əst **-ily** -ɪ.li, -ᵊl.i **-iness** -ɪ.nəs, -ɪ.nɪs
misunder|stand ˌmɪs.ʌn.də|'stænd Ⓤⓢ -dɚ'- **-stands** -'stændz **-standing/s** -'stæn.dɪŋ/z **-stood** -'stʊd
misuse (*n.*) ˌmɪs'juːs
misus|e (*v.*) ˌmɪs'juːz **-es** -ɪz **-ing** -ɪŋ **-ed** -d
MIT ˌem.aɪ'tiː *stress shift:* ˌMIT 'graduate
Mitcham 'mɪtʃ.əm
Mitchel(l) 'mɪtʃ.ᵊl
Mitchison 'mɪtʃ.ɪ.sᵊn
Mitchum 'mɪtʃ.əm
mite maɪt **-s** -s
mit|er 'maɪ.t|əʳ Ⓤⓢ -t̬|ɚ **-ers** -əz Ⓤⓢ -ɚz **-ering** -ᵊr.ɪŋ **-ered** -əd Ⓤⓢ -ɚd **'miter ˌbox**; **'miter ˌjoint**
Mitford 'mɪt.fəd Ⓤⓢ -fɚd
Mithr|a 'mɪθ.r|ə **-as** -æs Ⓤⓢ -əs, -æs
Mithraic mɪ'θreɪ.ɪk
Mithra|ism 'mɪθ.reɪ|.ɪ.zᵊm; mɪ'θreɪ- Ⓤⓢ 'mɪθ.reɪ-, -rə- **-ist/s** -ɪst/s
Mithridates ˌmɪθ.rɪ'deɪ.tiːz Ⓤⓢ -rə'-
mitigable 'mɪt.ɪ.gə.bl̩ Ⓤⓢ 'mɪt̬-
miti|gate 'mɪt.ɪ|.geɪt Ⓤⓢ 'mɪt̬- **-gates** -geɪts **-gating** -geɪ.tɪŋ Ⓤⓢ -geɪ.t̬ɪŋ **-gated** -geɪ.tɪd Ⓤⓢ -geɪ.t̬ɪd **-gator/s** -geɪ.təʳ/z Ⓤⓢ -geɪ.t̬ɚ/z
mitigation ˌmɪt.ɪ'geɪ.ʃᵊn Ⓤⓢ ˌmɪt̬-
mitigatory 'mɪt.ɪ.geɪ.tᵊr.i Ⓤⓢ 'mɪt̬.ɪ.gə.tɔːr-
mitochondrial ˌmaɪ.təʊ'kɒn.dri.əl Ⓤⓢ -toʊ'kɑːn-, -t̬ə'-
mitochondri|on ˌmaɪ.təʊ'kɒn.dri|.ən Ⓤⓢ -toʊ'kɑːn-, -t̬ə'- **-a** -ə
mitosis maɪ'təʊ.sɪs Ⓤⓢ -'toʊ-
mitrailleus|e ˌmɪt.raɪ'ɜːz Ⓤⓢ ˌmiː.treɪ'jɜːz **-es** -ɪz
mitral 'maɪ.trᵊl
mit|re 'maɪ.t|əʳ Ⓤⓢ -t̬|ɚ **-res** -əz Ⓤⓢ -ɚz **-ring** -ᵊr.ɪŋ **-red** -əd Ⓤⓢ -ɚd **'mitre ˌbox**; **'mitre ˌjoint**
Mitsubishi® ˌmɪt.sʊ'bɪʃ.i, -suː'- Ⓤⓢ -suː'-
mitt mɪt **-s** -s
mitten 'mɪt.ᵊn **-s** -z
Mitterand, **Mitterrand** 'miː.tə.rɑ̃ːŋ Ⓤⓢ 'miː.t̬ə.rɑːnd, 'mɪt-
Mitylene ˌmɪt.ᵊl'iː.ni, -ɪ'liː- Ⓤⓢ ˌmɪt̬.ə'liː-
mitz|vah 'mɪts|.və Ⓤⓢ 'mɪts-; mɪts'vɑː **-vahs** -əz Ⓤⓢ 'mɪts.vəs; mɪts'vɑːz **-voth** -vɒt Ⓤⓢ 'mɪts.voʊt, -voʊs
Mivart 'maɪ.vət, -vɑːt Ⓤⓢ -vɚt, -vɑːrt
mix (*n. v.*) mɪks **-es** -ɪz **-ing** -ɪŋ **-ed** -t ˌ**mixed 'bag**; ˌ**mixed 'blessing**; ˌ**mixed 'doubles**; ˌ**mixed 'farming**; ˌ**mixed 'grill**; ˌ**mixed 'marriage**; ˌ**mixed 'metaphor**
mix-and-match ˌmɪks.ᵊnd'mætʃ, -ᵊm'- Ⓤⓢ -ᵊnd'- *stress shift:* ˌmix-and-match 'clothes
mixed-ability ˌmɪkst.ə'bɪl.ə.ti, -ɪ.ti Ⓤⓢ -ə.t̬i *stress shift:* ˌmixed-ability 'students
mixed blessing ˌmɪkst'bles.ɪŋ
mixed-up ˌmɪkst'ʌp *stress shift:* ˌmixed-up 'kid
mixer 'mɪk.səʳ Ⓤⓢ -sɚ **-s** -z
mixture 'mɪks.tʃəʳ Ⓤⓢ -tʃɚ **-s** -z
mix-up 'mɪks.ʌp **-s** -s
Mizpah 'mɪz.pə
mizzen 'mɪz.ᵊn **-s** -z
mizzen-mast 'mɪz.ᵊnˌmɑːst, -ᵊmˌ-, -ᵊnˌmæst *nautical pronunciation:* -məst Ⓤⓢ -ᵊn.mæst **-s** -s
mizzl|e 'mɪz.l̩ **-es** -z **-ing** -ɪŋ, 'mɪz.lɪŋ **-ed** -d **-y** -i
ml (*abbrev. for* **millilitre/s**) *singular:* 'mɪl.ɪˌliː.təʳ, '-ə- Ⓤⓢ -t̬ɚ *plural:* -z
mm (*abbrev. for* **millimetre/s**) *singular:* 'mɪl.ɪˌmiː.təʳ, '-ə- Ⓤⓢ -t̬ɚ *plural:* -z
mnemonic nɪ'mɒn.ɪk, nə-, niː-, mnɪ-, mnə-, mniː- Ⓤⓢ nɪ'mɑː.nɪk, niː- **-s** -s **-ally** -ᵊl.i, -li
Mnemosyne nɪ'mɒz.ɪ.ni, nə-, niː-, mnɪ-, mnə-, mniː-, -'mɒs-, -ᵊn.i Ⓤⓢ nɪ'mɑː.sɪ-, niː-, -zɪ-
mo, mo' məʊ Ⓤⓢ moʊ
Mo. (*abbrev. for* **Missouri**) mɪ'zʊə.ri, -'sʊə- Ⓤⓢ -'zʊr.i *locally:* -ə
Mo məʊ Ⓤⓢ moʊ
moa məʊə Ⓤⓢ moʊə **-s** -z
Moab 'məʊ.æb Ⓤⓢ 'moʊ-
Moabite 'məʊ.ə.baɪt Ⓤⓢ 'moʊ- **-s** -s
moan məʊn Ⓤⓢ moʊn **-s** -z **-ing/s** -ɪŋ/z **-ed** -d
moat (M) məʊt Ⓤⓢ moʊt **-s** -s **-ing** -ɪŋ Ⓤⓢ 'moʊ.t̬ɪŋ **-ed** -ɪd Ⓤⓢ 'moʊ.t̬ɪd
mob mɒb Ⓤⓢ mɑːb **-s** -z **-bing** -ɪŋ **-bed** -d
mobcap 'mɒb.kæp Ⓤⓢ 'mɑːb- **-s** -s
Moberly 'məʊ.bᵊl.i Ⓤⓢ 'moʊ.bɚ.li
Mobil® 'məʊ.bɪl, -bᵊl Ⓤⓢ 'moʊ.bᵊl, -bɪl
mobile (*adj.*) 'məʊ.baɪl Ⓤⓢ 'moʊ.bᵊl, -bɪl, -baɪl ˌ**mobile 'phone**; ˌ**mobile 'home**
mobile (*n.*) 'məʊ.baɪl Ⓤⓢ 'moʊ.biːl **-s** -z
mobility məʊ'bɪl.ə.ti, -ɪ.ti Ⓤⓢ moʊ'bɪl.ə.t̬i
mobilization, **-isa-** ˌməʊ.bɪ.laɪ'zeɪ.ʃᵊn, -bᵊl.aɪ'-, -ɪ'- Ⓤⓢ -bᵊl.ɪ'- **-s** -z
mobiliz|e, **-is|e** 'məʊ.bɪ.laɪz, -bᵊl.aɪz Ⓤⓢ -bə.laɪz **-es** -ɪz **-ing** -ɪŋ **-ed** -d
mobius, **möbius** (M) 'məʊ.bi.əs *as if German:* 'mɜː- Ⓤⓢ 'meɪ.bi.əs, 'moʊ-, 'miː- *as if German:* 'mɜː- ˌ**Mobius 'strip**
mobster 'mɒb.stəʳ Ⓤⓢ 'mɑːb.stɚ **-s** -z
Mobutu mə'buː.tuː
Moby Dick ˌməʊ.bi'dɪk Ⓤⓢ ˌmoʊ-
moccasin 'mɒk.ə.sɪn Ⓤⓢ 'mɑː.kə.sən, -sɪn **-s** -z
mocha *coffee, leather, etc.:* 'mɒk.ə, 'məʊ.kə Ⓤⓢ 'moʊ.kə
Mocha *Arabian seaport:* 'məʊ.kə, 'mɒk.ə Ⓤⓢ 'moʊ.kə
mock mɒk Ⓤⓢ mɑːk **-s** -s **-ing/ly** -ɪŋ/li **-ed** -t **-er/s** -əʳ/z Ⓤⓢ -ɚ/z
mockers 'mɒk.əz Ⓤⓢ 'mɑː.kɚz **put the 'mockers on ˌsomething**
mocker|y 'mɒk.ᵊr|.i Ⓤⓢ 'mɑː.kɚ- **-ies** -iz
Mockett 'mɒk.ɪt Ⓤⓢ 'mɑː.kɪt
mocking-bird 'mɒk.ɪŋˌbɜːd Ⓤⓢ 'mɑː.kɪŋˌbɜːrd **-s** -z
mock-turtle ˌmɒk'tɜː.tl̩ Ⓤⓢ ˌmɑːk'tɜːr.t̬l̩ *stress shift:* ˌmock-turtle 'soup
mock-up 'mɒk.ʌp Ⓤⓢ 'mɑːk- **-s** -s
mod (M) mɒd Ⓤⓢ mɑːd **-s** -z
MoD ˌem.əʊ'diː Ⓤⓢ -oʊ'- *stress shift:* ˌMoD 'cuts
modal 'məʊ.dᵊl Ⓤⓢ 'moʊ- **-ly** -i ˌ**modal 'verb**
modality məʊ'dæl.ə.ti, -ɪ.ti Ⓤⓢ moʊ'dæl.ət̬.i
mod con ˌmɒd'kɒn Ⓤⓢ ˌmɑːd'kɑːn, '-- **-s** -z
mode məʊd Ⓤⓢ moʊd **-s** -z
model 'mɒd.ᵊl Ⓤⓢ 'mɑː.dᵊl **-s** -z **-(l)ing** -ɪŋ, 'mɒd.lɪŋ Ⓤⓢ 'mɑːd- **-(l)ed** -d **-(l)er/s** -əʳ/z Ⓤⓢ -ɚ/z, 'mɒd.ləʳ/z Ⓤⓢ 'mɑːd.lɚ/z
modem 'məʊ.dem, -dəm Ⓤⓢ 'moʊ.dəm, -dem **-s** -z
Modena 'mɒd.ɪ.nə; mɒd'eɪ.nə, mə'deɪ- Ⓤⓢ 'moʊ.dᵊn.ə, 'mɔː-, -ɑː
moderate (*n. adj.*) 'mɒd.ᵊr.ət, -ɪt Ⓤⓢ 'mɑː.dɚ- **-s** -s **-ly** -li **-ness** -nəs, -nɪs

moder|ate (*v.*) ˈmɒd.ᵊr|.eɪt (US) ˈmɑː.də.r|eɪt **-ates** -eɪts **-ating** -eɪ.tɪŋ (US) -eɪ.t̬ɪŋ **-ated** -eɪ.tɪd (US) -eɪ.t̬ɪd **-ator/s** -eɪ.təʳ/z (US) -eɪ.t̬ɚ/z

moderation ˌmɒd.ᵊrˈeɪ.ʃᵊn (US) ˌmɑː.dəˈreɪ- **-s** -z

moderato ˌmɒd.ᵊrˈɑː.təʊ (US) ˌmɑː.dəˈrɑː.toʊ **-s** -z

modern ˈmɒd.ᵊn (US) ˈmɑː.dɚn **-s** -z **-ly** -li **-ness** -nəs, -nɪs ˌ**modern** ˈ**languages**

modern|ism (M) ˈmɒd.ᵊn|.ɪ.zᵊm (US) ˈmɑːd.ɚ.n|ɪ- **-ist/s** -ɪst/s

modernistic ˌmɒd.ᵊnˈɪs.tɪk (US) ˌmɑː.dɚˈnɪs- **-ally** -ᵊl.i, -li

modernity mɒdˈɜː.nə.ti, məˈdɜː-, -ɪ.ti (US) mɑːˈdɜːr.nə.t̬i, mə-, moʊ-

modernization, -isa- ˌmɒd.ᵊn.aɪˈzeɪ.ʃᵊn, -ɪˈ- (US) ˌmɑː.dɚ.nɪˈ- **-s** -z

moderniz|e, -is|e ˈmɒd.ᵊn.aɪz (US) ˈmɑː.dɚ.naɪz **-es** -ɪz **-ing** -ɪŋ **-ed** -d

modest ˈmɒd.ɪst (US) ˈmɑː.dɪst **-ly** -li **-y** -i

modicum ˈmɒd.ɪ.kəm, ˈ-ə- (US) ˈmɑː.dɪ- **-s** -z

modification ˌmɒd.ɪ.fɪˈkeɪ.ʃᵊn, ˌ-ə- (US) ˌmɑː.dɪ- **-s** -z

modi|fy ˈmɒd.ɪ|.faɪ (US) ˈmɑː.dɪ- **-fies** -faɪz **-fying** -faɪ.ɪŋ **-fied** -faɪd **-fier/s** -faɪ.əʳ/z (US) -faɪ.ɚ/z **-fiable** -faɪ.ə.bl̩

Modigliani ˌmɒd.ɪˈljɑː.ni (US) ˌmoʊ.diːlˈjɑː-

modish ˈməʊ.dɪʃ (US) ˈmoʊ- **-ly** -li **-ness** -nəs, -nɪs

modiste məʊˈdiːst (US) moʊ- **-s** -s

Modred ˈməʊ.drɪd (US) ˈmoʊ-

modular ˈmɒd.jə.ləʳ, ˈmɒdʒ-, -jʊ- (US) ˈmɑː.dʒə.lɚ

modularity ˌmɒd.jəˈlær.ə.ti, ˌmɒdʒ-, -jʊˈ-, -ɪ.ti (US) ˌmɑː.dʒəˈler.ə.t̬i, -ˈlær-

modu|late ˈmɒd.jə|.leɪt, ˈmɒdʒ-, -jʊ- (US) ˈmɑː.dʒə- **-lates** -leɪts **-lating** -leɪ.tɪŋ (US) -leɪ.t̬ɪŋ **-lated** -leɪ.tɪd (US) -leɪ.t̬ɪd **-lator/s** -leɪ.təʳ/z (US) -leɪ.t̬ɚ/z

modulation ˌmɒd.jəˈleɪ.ʃᵊn, ˌmɒdʒ-, -jʊˈ- (US) ˌmɑː.dʒəˈ- **-s** -z

module ˈmɒd.juːl, ˈmɒdʒ-, (US) ˈmɑː.dʒuːl **-s** -z

modul|us ˈmɒd.jə.l|əs, -jʊ- (US) ˈmɑː.dʒə- **-uses** -ə.sɪz **-i** -aɪ

modus ˈməʊ.dəs (US) ˈmoʊ-

modus operandi ˌməʊ.dəsˌɒp.əˈræn.diː, ˌmɒd.əs-, -daɪ (US) ˌmoʊ.dəsˌoʊ.pəˈrɑːn.di, -ɑː-, -ˈræn-

modus vivendi ˌməʊ.dəs.vɪˈven.diː, ˌmɒd.əs-, -viːˈ-, -daɪ (US) ˌmoʊ.dəs.viːˈven.di

Moesia ˈmiː.si.ə, -ʃə, -zi.ə, -ʒə (US) -ʃi.ə, -ʃə

Moffat ˈmɒf.ət (US) ˈmɑː.fət

Moffett ˈmɒf.ət, -ɪt (US) ˈmɑː.fət

Mogadishu ˌmɒg.əˈdɪʃ.uː (US) ˌmoʊ.gɑːˈdiː.ʃuː, ˌmɑː-, -gəˈ-, -ˈdɪʃ.uː

Mogadon® ˈmɒg.ə.dɒn (US) ˈmɑː.gə.dɑːn

Mogador ˌmɒg.əˈdɔːʳ, ˈ--- (US) ˈmɑː.gə.dɔːr, ˌ--ˈ-

Moggach ˈmɒg.ək, -əx (US) ˈmɑː.gək

mogg|y, mogg|ie ˈmɒg|.i (US) ˈmɑː.g|i **-ies** -z

mogul (M) ˈməʊ.gᵊl, -gʊl, -gʌl (US) ˈmoʊ.gʌl, -gᵊl; moʊˈgʌl **-s** -z

mohair ˈməʊ.heəʳ (US) ˈmoʊ.her

Moham(m)ed məʊˈhæm.ɪd, -əd, -ed (US) moʊ-

Mohammedan məʊˈhæm.ɪ.dᵊn, ˈ-ə- (US) moʊ- **-s** -z **-ism** -ɪ.zᵊm

Mohave məʊˈhɑː.vi (US) moʊ-

Mohawk ˈməʊ.hɔːk (US) ˈmoʊ.hɑːk, -hɔːk **-s** -s

Mohegan məʊˈhiː.gᵊn, mə- (US) moʊ- **-s** -z

Mohican məʊˈhiː.kᵊn; ˈməʊ.ɪ- (US) moʊˈhiː- **-s** -z

Mohun məʊən; ˈməʊ.hən; muːn (US) muːn, ˈmoʊ.hᵊn

moidore ˌmɔɪˈdɔːʳ, ˌməʊ.ɪˈ-; ˈmɔɪ.dɔːʳ (US) ˈmɔɪ.dɔːr **-s** -z

Note: In John Masefield's poem 'Cargoes' the stress is on the last syllable.

moiet|y ˈmɔɪ.ə.t|i, ˈ-ɪ- (US) -ə.t̬|i **-ies** -iz

moil mɔɪl **-s** -z **-ing** -ɪŋ **-ed** -d

Moir mɔɪəʳ (US) mɔɪɚ

Moira ˈmɔɪə.rə (US) ˈmɔɪ-

moire mwɑːʳ, mwɔːʳ (US) mwɑːr, mɔːr **-s** -z

moiré ˈmwɑː.reɪ, ˈmwɔː- (US) mwɑːˈreɪ, mɔː-; ˈmɔː.reɪ

moist mɔɪst **-er** -əʳ (US) -ɚ **-est** -ɪst, -əst **-ly** -li **-ness** -nəs, -nɪs

moisten ˈmɔɪ.sᵊn **-s** -z **-ing** -ɪŋ, ˈmɔɪs.nɪŋ **-ed** -d

moisture ˈmɔɪs.tʃəʳ (US) -tʃɚ

moisturiz|e, -is|e ˈmɔɪs.tʃᵊr.aɪz (US) -tʃə.raɪz **-es** -ɪz **-ing** -ɪŋ **-ed** -d **-er/s** -əʳ/z (US) -ɚ/z

Moivre ˈmɔɪ.vəʳ (US) -vɚ

Mojave məʊˈhɑː.vi (US) moʊ-

moke məʊk (US) moʊk **-s** -s

molar ˈməʊ.ləʳ (US) ˈmoʊ.lɚ **-s** -z

molasses məʊˈlæs.ɪz, -əz (US) mə-

molassine ˈmɒl.ə.siːn, ˈməʊ.lə- (US) ˈmɑː.lə-, ˈmoʊ-

Mold məʊld (US) moʊld

mold məʊld (US) moʊld **-s** -z **-ing/s** -ɪŋ **-ed** -ɪd

Moldavi|a mɒlˈdeɪ.vi|.ə (US) mɑːl-, ˈ-vj|ə **-an/s** -ən

mold|er ˈməʊl.d|əʳ (US) ˈmoʊl.d|ɚ **-ers** -əz (US) -ɚz **-ering** -ᵊr.ɪŋ **-ered** -əd (US) -ɚd

Moldova mɒlˈdəʊ.və (US) mɑːlˈdoʊ-

mold|y ˈməʊl.d|i (US) ˈmoʊl- **-ier** -i.əʳ (US) -i.ɚ **-iest** -i.ɪst, -i.əst **-iness** -ɪ.nəs, -ɪ.nɪs

mole (M) məʊl (US) moʊl **-s** -z

Molech ˈməʊ.lek (US) ˈmoʊ-

molecular məʊˈlek.jə.ləʳ, mɒlˈek-, -jʊ- (US) məˈlek.jə.lɚ, moʊ-, -juː-

molecule ˈmɒl.ɪ.kjuːl, ˈməʊ.lɪ-, -lə- (US) ˈmɑː.lɪ.kjuːl **-s** -z

molehill ˈməʊl.hɪl (US) ˈmoʊl- **-s** -z **make a** ˌ**mountain out of a** ˈ**mole-hill**

Molesey ˈməʊl.zi (US) ˈmoʊl-

moleskin ˈməʊl.skɪn (US) ˈmoʊl- **-s** -z

molest məʊˈlest (US) mə-, moʊ- **-s** -s **-ing** -ɪŋ **-ed** -ɪd **-er/s** -əʳ/z (US) -ɚ/z

molestation ˌməʊ.lesˈteɪ.ʃən, ˌmɒl.esˈ- (US) ˌmoʊ.lesˈ-, ˌmɑː- **-s** -z

molester məʊˈles.təʳ (US) məˈles.tɚ, moʊ- **-s** -z

Molesworth ˈməʊlz.wəθ, -wɜːθ (US) ˈmoʊlz.wɚθ, -wɜːrθ

Molière ˈmɒl.i.eəʳ, ˈməʊ.li- (US) ˌmoʊlˈjer

Moline məʊˈliːn (US) moʊ-

moll (M) mɒl (US) mɑːl

mollification ˌmɒl.ɪ.fɪˈkeɪ.ʃᵊn, ˌ-ə- (US) ˌmɑː.lə-

molli|fy ˈmɒl.ɪ|.faɪ, ˈ-ə- (US) ˈmɑː.lə- **-fies** -faɪz **-fying** -faɪ.ɪŋ **-fied** -faɪd

mollusc ˈmɒl.əsk, -ʌsk (US) ˈmɑː.ləsk **-s** -s

molluscan mɒlˈʌs.kᵊn, məˈlʌs- (US) mə-

molluscoid mɒlˈʌs.kɔɪd, məˈlʌs- (US) mə-

moll|y (M) ˈmɒl|.i (US) ˈmɑː.l|i **-ies** -iz

mollycoddl|e ˈmɒl.iˌkɒd.l̩ (US) ˈmɑː.liˌkɑː.dl̩ **-es** -z **-ing** -ɪŋ, -ˌkɒd.lɪŋ (US) -ˌkɑːd.lɪŋ **-ed** -d

Moloch ˈməʊ.lɒk (US) ˈmoʊ.lɑːk, ˈmɑː.lək

Molony məˈləʊ.ni (US) -ˈloʊ-

Molotov ˈmɒl.ə.tɒf (US) ˈmɑː.lə.tɔːf, ˈmoʊ-, -tɔːv ˌ**Molotov** ˈ**cocktail**

molt məʊlt (US) moʊlt **-s** -s **-ing** -ɪŋ (US) ˈmoʊl.t̬ɪŋ **-ed** -ɪd (US) ˈmoʊl.t̬ɪd **-er/s** -əʳ/z (US) ˈmoʊl.t̬ɚ/z

molten ˈməʊl.tᵊn (US) ˈmoʊl-

molto ˈmɒl.təʊ (US) ˈmoʊl.toʊ

Molton ˈməʊl.tᵊn (US) ˈmoʊl-

Moluccas məʊˈlʌk.əz (US) moʊ-, mə-

moly ˈməʊ.li (US) ˈmoʊ-

molybdenum məˈlɪb.də.nəm, -dɪ-, mɒlˈɪb-, məʊˈlɪb-; ˌmɒl.ɪbˈdiː.nəm (US) məˈlɪb.də-

Molyneux ˈmɒl.ɪ.njuːks, ˈmʌl-, ˈ-ə-, -njuː (US) ˈmʌl.ɪ.nuːks, -njuː, -nuː

mom (M) mɒm US mɑːm **-s** -z
Mombasa mɒm'bæs.ə, -'bɑː.sə US mɑːm'bɑː.sə, -'bæs.ə
moment 'məʊ.mənt US 'moʊ- **-s** -s ˌ**moment of 'truth**
momenta (*plur. of* **momentum**) məʊ'men.tə US moʊ'men.t̬ə, mə-
momentarily 'məʊ.mən.tᵊr.ᵊl.i, -ɪ.li; ˌməʊ.mən'ter- US ˌmoʊ.mən'ter-, 'moʊ.mən.ter-
momentar|y 'məʊ.mən.tᵊr|.i US 'moʊ.mən.ter- **-iness** -ɪ.nəs, -ɪ.nɪs
momentous məʊ'men.təs US moʊ'men.t̬əs, mə- **-ly** -li **-ness** -nəs, -nɪs
moment|um məʊ'men.t|əm US moʊ'men.t̬|əm, mə- **-ums** -əmz **-a** -ə
momma (M) 'mɒm.ə US 'mɑː.mə **-s** -z
momm|y 'mɒm|.i US 'mɑː.m|i **-ies** -iz
Mon *language:* məʊn, mɒn US moʊn
Mon. (*abbrev. for* **Monday**) 'mʌn.deɪ, -di
Note: Can be pronounced /mʌn/ in British English.
mona (M) 'məʊ.nə US 'moʊ- **-s** -z ˌ**Mona 'Lisa**
Monaco 'mɒn.ə.kəʊ, mə'nɑː- US 'mɑː.nə.koʊ, mə'nɑː-
monad 'mɒn.æd, 'məʊ.næd US 'moʊ-, 'mɑː.næd **-s** -z
Monadhliath ˌməʊ.nə'liː.ə US ˌmoʊ-
monadic mɒn'æd.ɪk, məʊ'næd- US mə-, moʊ-
Monaghan 'mɒn.ə.hən, -kən *as if Irish:* -xən US 'mɑː.nə.gən
monarch 'mɒn.ək US 'mɑː.nɚk, -nɑːrk **-s** -s
monarch|al mɒn'ɑː.k|ᵊl, mə'nɑː- US mə'nɑːr-, moʊ- **-ic** -ɪk **-ical** -ɪ.kᵊl
monarch|ism 'mɒn.ə.k|ɪ.zᵊm US 'mɑː.nɚ-, -nɑːr- **-ist/s** -ɪst/s
monarchiz|e, -is|e 'mɒn.ə.kaɪz US 'mɑː.nɚ-, -nɑːr- **-es** -ɪz **-ing** -ɪŋ **-ed** -d
monarch|y 'mɒn.ə.k|i US 'mɑː.nɚ-, -nɑːr- **-ies** -iz
Monash 'mɒn.æʃ US 'mɑː.næʃ
monaster|y 'mɒn.ə.stᵊr|.i, -str|i US 'mɑː.nə.ster|.i **-ies** -iz
monastic mə'næs.tɪk, mɒn'æs- US mə-, moʊ- **-al** -ᵊl **-ally** -ᵊl.i, -li
monasticism mə'næs.tɪ.sɪ.zᵊm, mɒn'æs- US mə'næs-, moʊ-
monatomic ˌmɒn.ə'tɒm.ɪk US ˌmɑː.nə'tɑː.mɪk
monaural mɒn'ɔː.rᵊl US mɑː'nɔːr.ᵊl
Monchen-Gladbach, Mönchen-Gladbach ˌmɜːn.ʃən'glæd.bæk, ˌmʊn-, -kəŋ'- US -kən'glɑːt.bɑːk
Monck mʌŋk
Monckton 'mʌŋk.tən
Moncrieff mən'kriːf, məŋ-, mɒn-, mɒŋ- US mɑːn-, mən-; 'mɑːn.kriːf
Mond mɒnd US mɑːnd
Mondale 'mɒn.deɪl US 'mɑːn-
Monday 'mʌn.deɪ, -di **-s** -z
Mondeo® ˌmɒn'deɪ.əʊ US ˌmɑːn'deɪ.oʊ
Mondrian 'mɒn.dri.æn, -ən US 'mɑːn.dri.ɑːn, -ən
Monegasque ˌmɒn.ɪ'gæsk, -ə'- US ˌmɑː.neɪ'-
Monet 'mɒn.eɪ *as if French:* -'- US moʊ'neɪ, mə-
monetar|ism 'mʌn.ɪ.tᵊr|.ɪ.zᵊm, '-ə- US 'mɑː.nə-, 'mʌn.ə- **-ist/s** -ɪst/s
monetary 'mʌn.ɪ.tᵊr.i, '-ə-, -tri US 'mɑː.nə.ter.i, 'mʌn.ə-
monetiz|e, -is|e 'mʌn.ɪ.taɪz, '-ə- US 'mɑː.nə-, 'mʌn.ə- **-es** -ɪz **-ing** -ɪŋ **-ed** -d
mon|ey (M) 'mʌn|.i **-eys** -z **-ies** -iz **-eyed** -id **-ied** -id **'money ˌbox**; **'money ˌchanger**; **'money ˌmarket**; **'money ˌorder**; **'money ˌsupply**; ˌ**throw good ˌmoney after 'bad**
moneybag 'mʌn.i.bæg **-s** -z
moneygrabb|ing 'mʌn.iˌgræb|.ɪŋ **-er/s** -ər/z US -ɚ/z
money-grubb|er 'mʌn.iˌgrʌb|.əʳ US -ɚ **-ers** -əz US -ɚz **-ing** -ɪŋ
moneylend|er 'mʌn.iˌlen.d|əʳ US -d|ɚ **-ers** -əz US -ɚz **-ing** -ɪŋ
money-market 'mʌn.iˌmɑː.kɪt US -ˌmɑːr- **-s** -s
money-off ˌmʌn.i'ɒf US -'ɑːf
Moneypenny 'mʌn.iˌpen.i
money-spinner 'mʌn.iˌspɪn.əʳ US -ɚ **-s** -z
monger 'mʌŋ.gəʳ US -gɚ, 'mɑːŋ- **-s** -z
mongo 'mɒŋ.gəʊ US 'mɑːŋ.goʊ **-s** -z
mongol (M) 'mɒŋ.gəl, -gɒl US 'mɑːŋ-, 'mɑːn-, -gəl, -goʊl **-s** -z **-oid** -ɔɪd
Mongoli|a mɒŋ'gəʊ.li|.ə US mɑːŋ'goʊ-, mɑːn-, -'goʊl.j|ə **-an/s** -ən/z
mongolism (M) 'mɒŋ.gᵊl.ɪ.zᵊm, -gɒl- US 'mɑːŋ.gᵊl-, 'mɑːn-
mongoos|e 'mɒŋ.guːs, 'mʌŋ- US 'mɑːŋ-, 'mɑːn- **-es** -ɪz
mongrel 'mʌŋ.grᵊl US 'mɑːŋ-, 'mʌŋ- **-s** -z
Monica 'mɒn.ɪ.kə US 'mɑː.nɪ-
monicker 'mɒn.ɪ.kəʳ US 'mɑː.nɪ.kɚ **-s** -z
Monier 'mʌn.i.əʳ, 'mɒn- US 'mɑː.ni.ɚ, 'mʌn.i-
moniker 'mɒn.ɪ.kəʳ US 'mɑː.nɪ.kɚ **-s** -z
Monique mɒn'iːk US moʊ-, mə-
mon|ism 'mɒn|.ɪ.zᵊm, 'məʊ.n|ɪ- US 'moʊ-, 'mɑː- **-ist/s** -ɪst/s
monistic mɒn'ɪs.tɪk, mə'nɪs- US moʊ-, mə- **-al** -ᵊl
monition məʊ'nɪʃ.ᵊn, mɒn'ɪʃ- US moʊ'nɪʃ-, mə- **-s** -z
monitor 'mɒn.ɪ.təʳ, '-ə- US 'mɑː.nɪ.t̬ɚ **-s** -z **-ship/s** -ʃɪp/s
monitorial ˌmɒn.ɪ'tɔː.ri.əl, -ə'- US ˌmɑː.nɪ'tɔːr.i-
monitory 'mɒn.ɪ.tᵊr.i, '-ə- US 'mɑː.nɪ.tɔːr-
monk (M) mʌŋk **-s** -s **-ish** -ɪʃ
monkey 'mʌŋ.ki **-s** -z **'monkey ˌbars**; **'monkey ˌbusiness**; **'monkey ˌwrench**
monkey-puzzle 'mʌŋ.kiˌpʌz.l̩ **-s** -z
monkfish 'mʌŋk.fɪʃ **-es** -ɪz
Monkhouse 'mʌŋk.haʊs
Monkton 'mʌŋk.tən
Monmouth 'mɒn.məθ, *rarely* 'mʌn- US 'mɑːn- **-shire** -ʃəʳ, -ˌʃɪəʳ US -ʃɚ, -ˌʃɪr
mono- mɒn.əʊ-; mə'nɒ- US mɑː.noʊ-, -nə-; mə'nɑː-
Note: Prefix. Normally either takes primary or secondary stress on the first syllable, e.g. **monotone** /'mɒn.ə.təʊn US 'mɑː.nə.toʊn/, **monotonic** /ˌmɒn.ə'tɒ.nɪk US ˌmɑː.nə'tɑː.nɪk/, or primary stress on the second syllable, e.g. **monotony** /mə'nɒt.ᵊn.i US -'nɑː.tᵊn-/.
mono *monotype:* 'məʊ.nəʊ, 'mɒn.əʊ US 'mɑː.noʊ **-s** -z *in sound recording:* 'mɒn.əʊ US 'mɑː.noʊ **-s** -z
monobasic ˌmɒn.əʊ'beɪ.sɪk US ˌmɑː.nə'-
monoceros mə'nɒs.ᵊr.ɒs, mɒn'ɒs- US mə'nɑː.sɚ-
monochloride ˌmɒn.əʊ'klɔː.raɪd US ˌmɑː.noʊ'klɔːr.aɪd, -ə'- **-s** -z
monochord 'mɒn.əʊ.kɔːd US 'mɑː.nə.kɔːrd **-s** -z
monochromatic ˌmɒn.ə.krəʊ'mæt.ɪk US ˌmɑː.nə.kroʊ'mæt̬-, -krə-
monochrome 'mɒn.ə.krəʊm US 'mɑː.nə.kroʊm **-s** -z
monocle 'mɒn.ə.kl̩ US 'mɑː.nə- **-s** -z
monoclonal ˌmɒn.əʊ'kləʊ.nᵊl US ˌmɑː.nə'kloʊ-, -noʊ'-
monocotyledon ˌmɒn.əʊˌkɒt.ɪ'liː.dᵊn, -ᵊl'iː- US ˌmɑː.nəˌkɑː.tᵊl'iː-, -noʊˌ- **-s** -z
monoculture 'mɒn.əʊˌkʌl.tʃəʳ US 'mɑː.nəˌkʌl.tʃɚ, -noʊˌ-
monod|y 'mɒn.ə.d|i US 'mɑː.nə- **-ies** -iz
monogamist mə'nɒg.ə.mɪst, mɒn'ɒg- US mə'nɑː.gə- **-s** -s
monogamous mə'nɒg.ə.məs, mɒn'ɒg- US mə'nɑː.gə-
monogamy mə'nɒg.ə.mi, mɒn'ɒg- US mə'nɑː.gə-

monoglot 'mɒn.ə.glɒt
(US) 'mɑː.nə.glɑːt **-s** -s
monogram 'mɒn.ə.græm (US) 'mɑː.nə- **-s** -z **-ming** -ɪŋ **-med** -d
monograph 'mɒn.ə.grɑːf, -græf
(US) 'mɑː.nə.græf **-s** -s
monographic ˌmɒn.əʊ'græf.ɪk
(US) ˌmɑː.nə'-
monolingual ˌmɒn.əʊ'lɪŋ.gwəl
(US) ˌmɑː.nə'-, -noʊ'- **-s** -z **-ly** -i
monolinguist ˌmɒn.əʊ'lɪŋ.gwɪst
(US) ˌmɑː.nə'- -noʊ'- **-s** -s
monolith 'mɒn.əʊ.lɪθ (US) 'mɑː.nə- **-s** -s
monolithic ˌmɒn.əʊ'lɪθ.ɪk
(US) ˌmɑː.nə'-
monologue, **monolog** 'mɒn.əl.ɒg
(US) 'mɑː.nə.lɑːg, -lɔːg **-s** -z
monolog(u)ist 'mɒn.əl.ɒg.ɪst, -ɒdʒ-; mə'nɒl.ə.gɪst, -dʒɪst
(US) 'mɑː.nə.lɑːg.ɪst, -lɔːg.ɪst, mə'nɑː.lə.dʒɪst **-s** -s
monomani|a ˌmɒn.əʊ'meɪ.ni|.ə
(US) ˌmɑː.noʊ'-, -nə'- **-ac/s** -æk/s
mononuclear ˌmɒn.əʊ'njuː.kli.əʳ
(US) ˌmɑː.noʊ'nuː.kli.ɚ, -'njuː-
mononucleosis
ˌmɒn.əʊˌnjuː.kli'əʊ.sɪs
(US) ˌmɑː.noʊˌnuː.kli'oʊ-, -ˌnjuː-
monophonic ˌmɒn.əʊ'fɒn.ɪk
(US) ˌmɑː.nə'fɑː.nɪk, -noʊ-
monophthong 'mɒn.əf.θɒŋ, '-ə-
(US) 'mɑː.nəf.θɑːŋ, -θɔːŋ **-s** -z
monophthong|al ˌmɒn.əf'θɒŋ.g|əl, -ə'-
(US) ˌmɑː.nəf'θɑːŋ|.əl, -'θɔːŋ-, -g|əl **-ic** -ɪk
monophthongiz|e, **-is|e** 'mɒn.əf.θɒŋ.gaɪz, '-ə-, -aɪz
(US) 'mɑː.nəf.θɑːŋ-, -θɔːŋ- **-es** -ɪz **-ing** -ɪŋ **-ed** -d
monoplane 'mɒn.əʊ.pleɪn
(US) 'mɑː.nə- **-s** -z
monopole 'mɒn.ə.pəʊl
(US) 'mɑː.nə.poʊl
monopolism mə'nɒp.əl.ɪ.zəm
(US) mə'nɑː.pə.lɪ-
monopolist mə'nɒp.əl.ɪst
(US) -'nɑː.pə.lɪst **-s** -s
monopolistic məˌnɒp.əl'ɪs.tɪk
(US) -ˌnɑː.pə'lɪs- **-ally** -əl.i, -li
monopoliz|e, **-is|e** mə'nɒp.əl.aɪz
(US) -'nɑː.pə.laɪz **-es** -ɪz **-ing** -ɪŋ **-ed** -d **-er/s** -əʳ/z
monopol|y mə'nɒp.əl|.i (US) -'nɑː.pəl- **-ies** -iz
monorail 'mɒn.əʊ.reɪl (US) 'mɑː.nə-, -noʊ- **-s** -z
monosaccharide ˌmɒn.əʊ'sæk.ər.aɪd
(US) ˌmɑː.noʊ'sæk.ə.raɪd, -nə'- **-s** -z
monosodium ˌmɒn.əʊ'səʊ.di.əm
(US) ˌmɑː.noʊ'soʊ-, -nə'- *stress shift, see compound:* **ˌmonosodium 'glutamate**
monosyllabic ˌmɒn.əʊ.sɪ'læb.ɪk
(US) ˌmɑː.nə-, -noʊ- *stress shift:* ˌmonosyllabic 'word **-ally** -əl.i, -li
monosyllable 'mɒn.əʊˌsɪl.ə.bl̩
(US) 'mɑː.nəˌ-, -noʊˌ- **-s** -z
monothe|ism 'mɒn.əʊ.θiː|.ɪ.zəm, ˌmɒn.əʊ'θiː- (US) 'mɑː.noʊˌθiː-, -nəˌ- **-ist/s** -ɪst/s
monotheistic ˌmɒn.əʊ.θi'ɪs.tɪk
(US) ˌmɑː.noʊ- *stress shift:* ˌmonotheistic 'culture
monoton|e 'mɒn.ə.təʊn
(US) 'mɑː.nə.toʊn **-es** -z **-ing** -ɪŋ **-ed** -d
monotonic ˌmɒn.ə'tɒn.ɪk
(US) ˌmɑː.nə'tɑː.nɪk *stress shift:* ˌmonotonic 'function
monotonous mə'nɒt.ən.əs
(US) -'nɑː.tən- **-ly** -li **-ness** -nəs, -nɪs
monotony mə'nɒt.ən.i (US) -'nɑː.tən-
monotype (M®) 'mɒn.əʊ.taɪp, 'məʊ.nəʊ- (US) 'mɑː.noʊ-, -nə- **-s** -s
monovalen|ce ˌmɒn.əʊ'veɪ.lən|ts, 'mɒn.əʊˌveɪ- (US) ˌmɑː.noʊ'veɪ-, 'mɑː.noʊˌveɪ-, -nə'- **-t** -t
monoxide mə'nɒk.saɪd, mɒn'ɒk-
(US) mə'nɑːk- **-s** -z
Monro(e) mən'rəʊ, mʌn'rəʊ, 'mʌn.rəʊ
(US) mən'roʊ
Monrovia mɒn'rəʊ.vi.ə, mən-
(US) mən'roʊ-
Mons mɒnz *as if French:* mɔ̃ːns
(US) mõʊns
Monsarrat 'mɒnt.sər.æt, ˌ--'-
(US) ˌmɑːnt.sə'rɑːt, -'ræt
monseigneur ˌmɒn.sen'jɜːʳ
(US) ˌmɑːn.sən'jɜːr **-s** -z **messeigneurs** ˌmes.eɪ'njɜː (US) -'jɜːr
monsieur (M) mə'sjɜːʳ, -'sjəʳ
(US) -'sjɜːr, -'sjɜː
Note: /mə'sjɜːʳ/ is the form of address in isolation. When attached to the surname /mə'sjəʳ/ is unstressed.
monsignor (M) mɒn'siː.njəʳ
(US) mɑːn'siː.njɚ
Monson 'mʌnt.sən
monsoon mɒn'suːn, mən- (US) mɑːn- **-s** -z
monster 'mɒnt.stəʳ (US) 'mɑːnt.stɚ **-s** -z
monstranc|e 'mɒnt.strənts
(US) 'mɑːnt- **-es** -ɪz
monstrosit|y mɒn'strɒs.ə.t|i, mən-, -ɪ.t|i (US) mɑːn'strɑː.sə.t̬|i **-ies** -iz
monstrous 'mɒnt.strəs (US) 'mɑːnt- **-ly** -li **-ness** -nəs, -nɪs
Mont. (*abbrev. for* **Montana**)
mɒn'tæn.ə, -'tɑː.nə (US) mɑːn'tæn.ə
montag|e mɒn'tɑːʒ; '--, -tɪdʒ
(US) 'mɑːn.tɑːʒ; moʊn'tɑːʒ
Montagu(e) 'mɒn.tə.gjuː, -tɪ-, 'mʌn-
(US) 'mɑːn-
Montaigne mɒn'teɪn (US) mɑːn-
Montana mɒn'tæn.ə, -'tɑː.nə
(US) mɑːn'tæn.ə
Mont Blanc *as if French:* ˌmɔ̃ːm'blɑ̃ːŋ
(US) *as if French:* mõʊm'blɑ̃ːŋ
montbretia mɒn'briː.ʃə, mɒm-, -ʃi.ə
(US) mɑːnt'- **-s** -z
Mont Cenis ˌmɔ̃ːn.sə'niː (US) ˌmõʊn-
monte (M) 'mɒn.teɪ, -ti (US) 'mɑːn.t̬i
Monte Carlo ˌmɒnt.i'kɑː.ləʊ
(US) ˌmɑːn.t̬i'kɑːr.loʊ
Montefiore ˌmɒn.ti.fi'ɔː.reɪ, -ri, -tə-, -'fjɔː- (US) ˌmɑːn.t̬i.fi'ɔːr.i
Montego® mɒn'tiː.gəʊ
(US) mɑːn'tiː.goʊ
Montego Bay mɒnˌtiː.gəʊ'beɪ
(US) mɑːnˌtiː.goʊ'-
monteith mɒn'tiːθ (US) mɑːn- **-s** -s
Monteith mən'tiːθ, mɒn- (US) mɑːn-
Montenegr|o ˌmɒn.tɪ'niː.gr|əʊ, -tə'-, -'neɪ- (US) ˌmɑːn.t̬ə'niː.gr|oʊ, -'neg.r|oʊ **-an/s** -ən/z
Monte Rosa ˌmɒn.tɪ'rəʊ.zə, -tə'-
(US) ˌmɑːn.t̬ə'roʊ-
Monterrey ˌmɒn.tər.eɪ, -tɪ'reɪ
(US) ˌmɑːn.t̬ə'reɪ
Montesquieu ˌmɒn.tes'kjuː, -'kjɜː, '---
(US) 'mɑːn.t̬ə.skjuː
Montessori ˌmɒn.tes'ɔː.ri, -tɪ'sɔː-
(US) ˌmɑːn.t̬ə'sɔːr.i
Monteverdi ˌmɒn.tɪ'vɜː.di, -tə'-, -'veə- (US) ˌmɑːn.t̬ə'ver
Montevideo ˌmɒn.tɪ.vɪ'deɪ.əʊ, -tə- (US) ˌmɑːn.t̬ə.və'deɪ.oʊ, -'vɪd.i.oʊ
Montezuma ˌmɒn.tɪ'zuː.mə, -tə'-, -'zjuː- (US) ˌmɑːn.t̬ə'zuː-
Montfort 'mɒnt.fət, -fɔːt
(US) 'mɑːnt.fɚt, -fɔːrt
Montgomerie mənt'gʌm.ər.i, mɒnt-, -'gɒm-, '-ri (US) mɑːnt'gʌm.ri, mənt-, '-ɚ.i
Montgomery mənt'gʌm.ər.i, mɒnt-, -'gɒm-, -'ri (US) mɑːnt'gʌm.ri, mənt-, '-ɚ.i **-shire** -ʃəʳ, -ˌʃɪəʳ (US) -ʃɚ, -ˌʃɪr
month mʌntθ **-s** -s **-ly** -li **in a ˌmonth of 'Sundays**
Monticello ˌmɒn.tɪ'tʃel.əʊ
(US) ˌmɑːn.tɪ'tʃel.oʊ, -'sel-
Montmorency ˌmɒnt.mər'ent.si
(US) ˌmɑːnt-
Montpelier *in US, London street:* mɒnt'piː.li.əʳ (US) mɑːnt'piːl.jɚ
Montpellier *in France:* mɔ̃ːm'pel.i.eɪ
(US) ˌmõʊn.pəl'jeɪ *in names of streets, etc.:* mɒnt'pel.i.əʳ, mənt-
(US) mɑːnt'pel.i.ɚ
Montreal ˌmɒn.tri'ɔːl (US) ˌmɑːn.tri'ɔːl, ˌmʌn-, -'ɑːl
Montreux mɒn'trɜː *as if French:* mɔ̃ːn-
(US) mɑːn-
Montrose mɒn'trəʊz, mən-
(US) mɑːn'troʊz

Mont-Saint-Michel ˌmɒntˌsæn.mɪˈʃel, -ˌsæm- *as if French:* ˌmɔ̃ːn- ⓤⓢ *as if French:* ˌmoʊ̃nˌsæn.miːˈʃel
Montserrat *island in West Indies:* ˌmɒnt.səˈræt, -serˈæt ⓤⓢ ˌmɑːnt.səˈræt *monastery in Spain:* ˌmɒnt.səˈrɑːt, -serˈɑːt ⓤⓢ ˌmɑːnt.səˈrɑːt
Monty ˈmɒn.ti ⓤⓢ ˈmɑːn.t̬i, -ti
monument ˈmɒn.jə.mənt, -jʊ- ⓤⓢ ˈmɑːn.jə-, -juː- **-s** -s
monumental ˌmɒn.jəˈmen.tᵊl, -jʊˈ- ⓤⓢ ˌmɑːn.jəˈmen.t̬ᵊl, -juːˈ- **-ly** -i
Monza ˈmɒn.zə ⓤⓢ ˈmɔːnt.sɑː, ˈmoʊnt-, ˈmɑː-
Monzie məˈniː, mɒnˈiː ⓤⓢ mɔːnˈziː, mɑːn-, ˈ--
moo muː **-s** -z **-ing** -ɪŋ **-ed** -d
mooch muːtʃ **-es** -ɪz **-ing** -ɪŋ **-ed** -t **-er/s** -əʳ/z ⓤⓢ -ɚ/z
moo-cow ˈmuː.kaʊ **-s** -z
mood muːd **-s** -z
mood|y (M) ˈmuː.d|i **-ier** -i.əʳ ⓤⓢ -i.ɚ **-iest** -i.ɪst, -i.əst **-ily** -ɪ.li, -ᵊl.i **-iness** -ɪ.nəs, -ɪ.nɪs
Moog® məʊg, muːg ⓤⓢ moʊg, muːg
moola(h) ˈmuː.lə
mooli ˈmuː.li
moon (M) muːn **-s** -z **-ing** -ɪŋ **-ed** -d ˌ**over the** ˈ**moon**
moonbeam ˈmuːn.biːm, ˈmuːm- ⓤⓢ ˈmuːn- **-s** -z
mooncal|f ˈmuːn.kɑː|f, ˈmuːŋ- ⓤⓢ ˈmuːn.kæ|f **-ves** -vz
Mooney ˈmuː.ni
moonie (M) ˈmuː.ni **-s** -z
moon|light ˈmuːn|.laɪt **-lit** -lɪt **-lights** -laɪts **-lighting** -ˌlaɪ.tɪŋ ⓤⓢ -ˌlaɪ.t̬ɪŋ **-lighted** -ˌlaɪ.tɪd ⓤⓢ -ˌlaɪ.t̬ɪd
moonscape ˈmuːn.skeɪp **-s** -s
moonshine ˈmuːn.ʃaɪn
moonstone ˈmuːn.stəʊn ⓤⓢ -stoʊn **-s** -z
moonstruck ˈmuːn.strʌk
moony ˈmuː.ni
moor (M) mɔːʳ, mʊəʳ ⓤⓢ mʊr **-s** -z **-ing** -ɪŋ/z **-ed** -d
Moorall ˈmɔː.rɔːl ⓤⓢ ˈmɔːr.ɔːl, -ᵊl
moorcock (M) ˈmɔː.kɒk, ˈmʊə- ⓤⓢ ˈmʊr.kɑːk **-s** -z
Moorcroft ˈmɔː.krɒft, ˈmʊə- ⓤⓢ ˈmʊr.krɑːft
Moore mɔːʳ, mʊəʳ ⓤⓢ mʊr, mɔːr
Moorends ˈmɔː.rendz, ˈmʊə- ⓤⓢ ˈmʊr.endz
Moorfoot ˈmɔː.fʊt, ˈmʊə- ⓤⓢ ˈmʊr-
Moorgate ˈmɔː.geɪt, ˈmʊə-, -gɪt ⓤⓢ ˈmʊr-
Moorhead ˈmɔː.hed, ˈmʊə- ⓤⓢ ˈmʊr-, ˈmɔːr-
moorhen ˈmɔː.hen, ˈmʊə- ⓤⓢ ˈmʊr- **-s** -z
Moorhouse ˈmɔː.haʊs, ˈmʊə- ⓤⓢ ˈmʊr-, ˈmɔːr-
mooring ˈmɔː.rɪŋ, ˈmʊə- ⓤⓢ ˈmʊr.ɪŋ **-s** -z
Moorish ˈmʊə.rɪʃ, ˈmɔː- ⓤⓢ ˈmʊr.ɪʃ
moorland ˈmɔː.lənd, ˈmʊə-, -lænd ⓤⓢ ˈmʊr- **-s** -z
Note: The variant /-lænd/ is not used when the word is attributive.
moos|e muːs **-es** -ɪz
moot muːt **-s** -s **-ing** -ɪŋ ⓤⓢ ˈmuː.t̬ɪŋ **-ed** -ɪd ⓤⓢ ˈmuː.t̬ɪd
mop mɒp ⓤⓢ mɑːp **-s** -s **-ping** -ɪŋ **-ped** -t
mop|e məʊp ⓤⓢ moʊp **-es** -s **-ing/ly** -ɪŋ/li **-ed** -t
moped (*n.*) ˈməʊ.ped ⓤⓢ ˈmoʊ- **-s** -z
moppet (M) ˈmɒp.ɪt ⓤⓢ ˈmɑː.pɪt **-s** -s
Mopsy ˈmɒp.si ⓤⓢ ˈmɑːp-
moquette mɒkˈet, məʊˈket ⓤⓢ moʊ-
mor|a ˈmɔː.r|ə ⓤⓢ ˈmɔːr|.ə, ˈmoʊ.r|ə **-ae** -iː, -aɪ **-as** -əz
Morag ˈmɔː.ræg ⓤⓢ ˈmɔːr.æg
moraine mɒrˈeɪn, məˈreɪn ⓤⓢ mə-, mɔː- **-s** -z
moral ˈmɒr.ᵊl ⓤⓢ ˈmɔːr- **-s** -z **-ly** -i
morale məˈrɑːl, mɒrˈɑːl ⓤⓢ məˈræl, mɔː-
Morales mɒrˈɑː.lez, -les ⓤⓢ məˈræl.ɪs, mɔːˈrɑː.lɪs
moralist ˈmɒr.ᵊl.ɪst ⓤⓢ ˈmɔːr- **-s** -s
moralistic ˌmɒr.ᵊlˈɪs.tɪk ⓤⓢ ˌmɔːr- **-ally** -ᵊl.i, -li
morality məˈræl.ə.ti, mɒrˈæl-, -ɪ.ti ⓤⓢ mɔːˈræl.ə.t̬i, mə- **moˈrality ˌplay**
moraliz|e, -is|e ˈmɒr.ᵊl.aɪz ⓤⓢ ˈmɔːr- **-es** -ɪz **-ing** -ɪŋ **-ed** -d **-er/s** -əʳ/z ⓤⓢ -ɚ/z
Moran ˈmɔː.rən, ˈmɒr.ən; məˈræn, mɒrˈæn ⓤⓢ mɔːˈræn, mə-; ˈmɔːr.ən
Morant məˈrænt, mɒrˈænt ⓤⓢ mɔːˈrænt, mə-
Morar ˈmɔː.rəʳ ⓤⓢ ˈmɔːr.ɚ
morass məˈræs, mɒrˈæs ⓤⓢ məˈræs, mɔː- **-es** -ɪz
moratori|um ˌmɒr.əˈtɔː.ri|.əm, ˌmɔː.rəˈ- ⓤⓢ ˌmɔːr.əˈtɔːr.i- **-ums** -əmz **-a** -ə
Moravi|a məˈreɪ.vi|.ə, mɒrˈeɪ- ⓤⓢ mɔːˈreɪ-, mə- **-an/s** -ən/z
moray *eel:* ˈmɒr.eɪ, ˈmɔː.reɪ; məˈreɪ ⓤⓢ ˈmɔːr.eɪ; mɔːˈreɪ, mə- **-s** -z
Moray ˈmʌr.i ⓤⓢ ˈmɜːr-
morbid ˈmɔː.bɪd ⓤⓢ ˈmɔːr- **-ly** -li **-ness** -nəs, -nɪs
morbidity mɔːˈbɪd.ə.ti, -ɪ.ti ⓤⓢ mɔːrˈbɪd.ə.t̬i
mordant ˈmɔː.dᵊnt ⓤⓢ ˈmɔːr- **-s** -s **-ly** -li
Mordaunt ˈmɔː.dᵊnt, -daʊnt ⓤⓢ ˈmɔːr-
Mordecai ˌmɔː.dɪˈkeɪ.aɪ, -dəˈ-, -ˈkaɪ.iː; ˈmɔː.dɪ.kaɪ, -də- ⓤⓢ ˈmɔːr.də.kaɪ, -ˈkeɪ.əɪ
Morden ˈmɔː.dᵊn ⓤⓢ ˈmɔːr-
mordent ˈmɔː.dᵊnt ⓤⓢ ˈmɔːr- **-s** -s
Mordor ˈmɔː.dɔːʳ ⓤⓢ ˈmɔːr.dɔːr
Mordred ˈmɔː.drɪd, -drəd, -dred ⓤⓢ ˈmɔːr.dred, -drəd
more (M) mɔːʳ ⓤⓢ mɔːr
Morea mɒrˈiː.ə, məˈriː.ə, mɔː- ⓤⓢ mɔːˈriː.ə
Morecambe ˈmɔː.kəm ⓤⓢ ˈmɔːr-
moreish ˈmɔː.rɪʃ ⓤⓢ ˈmɔːr.ɪʃ
morel (M) mɒrˈel, məˈrel ⓤⓢ mɔː-, mə- **-s** -z
morello məˈrel.əʊ, mɒrˈel- ⓤⓢ məˈrel.oʊ **-s** -z
Morelos məˈrel.ɒs, mɔː- ⓤⓢ mɔːˈrel.ɑːs
Moreno məˈriː.nəʊ, mɒrˈiː- ⓤⓢ məˈriː.noʊ, mɔː-, -ˈren.oʊ
moreover mɔːrˈəʊ.vəʳ, məʳ- ⓤⓢ mɔːrˈoʊ.vɚ, ˈ-ˌ--
mores ˈmɔː.reɪz, -riːz ⓤⓢ ˈmɔːr.eɪz, -iːz
Moresby *surname:* ˈmɔːz.bi ⓤⓢ ˈmɔːrz- *in Cumbria:* ˈmɒr.ɪs.by ⓤⓢ ˈmɔːr.ɪs-
Moreton ˈmɔː.tᵊn ⓤⓢ ˈmɔːr-
Morgan ˈmɔː.gᵊn ⓤⓢ ˈmɔːr-
morganatic ˌmɔː.gəˈnæt.ɪk ⓤⓢ ˌmɔːr.gəˈnæt̬- **-ally** -ᵊl.i ⓤⓢ -li
Morgan le Fay ˌmɔː.gᵊn.ləˈfeɪ ⓤⓢ ˌmɔːr-
morgue mɔːg ⓤⓢ mɔːrg **-s** -z
MORI ˈmɔː.ri, ˈmɒr.i ⓤⓢ ˈmɔːr.i
Moriah mɒrˈaɪ.ə, mɔːˈraɪ.ə, mə- ⓤⓢ mə-, mɔː-, moʊ-
Moriarty ˌmɒr.iˈɑː.ti ⓤⓢ ˌmɔːr.iˈɑːr.t̬i
moribund ˈmɒr.ɪ.bʌnd, ˈmɔː.rɪ-, -bənd ⓤⓢ ˈmɔːr.ɪ.bʌnd
Morison ˈmɒr.ɪ.sᵊn, ˈ-ə- ⓤⓢ ˈmɔːr.ɪ-
Morley ˈmɔː.li ⓤⓢ ˈmɔːr-
Morlock ˈmɔː.lɒk ⓤⓢ ˈmɔːr.lɑːk **-s** -s
Mormon ˈmɔː.mən ⓤⓢ ˈmɔːr- **-s** -z **-ism** -ɪ.zᵊm
morn mɔːn ⓤⓢ mɔːrn **-s** -z
mornay ˈmɔː.neɪ ⓤⓢ mɔːrˈneɪ
morning ˈmɔː.nɪŋ ⓤⓢ ˈmɔːr- **-s** -z ˈ**morning** ˌ**coat** ; ˈ**morning** ˌ**dress**, ˌ**morning** ˈ**dress** ; ˈ**morning** ˌ**room** ; ˈ**morning** ˌ**sickness** ; ˌ**morning** ˈ**star**
morning-after ˌmɔː.nɪŋˈɑːf.təʳ ⓤⓢ ˌmɔːr.nɪŋˈæf.tɚ ˌ**morning-**ˈ**after** ˌ**pill**
Mornington ˈmɔː.nɪŋ.tən ⓤⓢ ˈmɔːr-
Moroccan məˈrɒk.ən ⓤⓢ -ˈrɑː.kən **-s** -z
Morocco, **morocco** məˈrɒk.əʊ ⓤⓢ -ˈrɑː.koʊ **-s** -z
moron ˈmɔː.rɒn ⓤⓢ ˈmɔːr.ɑːn **-s** -z
Moroni məˈrəʊ.ni ⓤⓢ -ˈroʊ-, mɔː-
moronic mɔːˈrɒn.ɪk, mə-, mɒrˈɒn- ⓤⓢ mɔːˈrɑː.nɪk, mə- **-ally** -ᵊl.i, -li
morose məˈrəʊs, mɒrˈəʊs ⓤⓢ məˈroʊs, mɔː- **-ly** -li **-ness** -nəs, -nɪs

Morpeth 'mɔː.peθ, -pəθ ⓤⓢ 'mɔːr-
-morph -mɔːf ⓤⓢ -mɔːrf
Note: Suffix. Normally not stressed, e.g. **ectomorph** /'ek.təʊ.mɔːf ⓤⓢ -tə.mɔːrf/.
morpheme 'mɔː.fiːm ⓤⓢ 'mɔːr- **-s** -z
morphemic mɔː'fiː.mɪk ⓤⓢ mɔːr- **-ally** -ᵊl.i, -li
morphemics mɔː'fiː.mɪks ⓤⓢ mɔːr-
Morpheus 'mɔː.fi.əs, '-fjəs ⓤⓢ 'mɔːr.fi.əs, '-fjuːs
morphia 'mɔː.fi.ə ⓤⓢ 'mɔːr-
morphine 'mɔː.fiːn ⓤⓢ 'mɔːr-
morpho- mɔː.fəʊ-; mɔː'fɒ- ⓤⓢ mɔːr.foʊ-, -fə-; mɔːr'fɑː-
Note: Prefix. Normally takes secondary stress on the first syllable, e.g. **morphologic** /ˌmɔː.fə'lɒdʒ.ɪk ⓤⓢ ˌmɔːr.fə'lɑː.dʒɪk/, or primary stress on the second syllable, e.g **morphology** /mɔː'fɒl.ə.dʒi ⓤⓢ mɔːr'fɑː.lə-/.
morphologic ˌmɔː.fə'lɒdʒ.ɪk ⓤⓢ ˌmɔːr.fə'lɑː.dʒɪk **-al** -ᵊl **-ally** -ᵊl.i, -li
morpholog|y mɔː'fɒl.ə.dʒ|i ⓤⓢ mɔːr'fɑː.lə- **-ies** -iz **-ist/s** -ɪst/s
morphophoneme ˌmɔː.fəʊ'fəʊ.niːm ⓤⓢ ˌmɔːr.foʊ'foʊ- **-s** -z
morphophonemic ˌmɔː.fəʊ.fə'niː.mɪk ⓤⓢ ˌmɔːr.foʊ- **-s** -s
morphophonology ˌmɔː.fəʊ.fə'nɒl.ə.dʒi ⓤⓢ ˌmɔːr.foʊ.fə'nɑː.lə-
morphosyntactic ˌmɔː.fəʊ.sɪn'tæk.tɪk ⓤⓢ ˌmɔːr.foʊ- **-ally** -ᵊl.i, -li
morphosyntax ˌmɔː.fəʊ'sɪn.tæks ⓤⓢ ˌmɔːr.foʊ-
Morphy 'mɔː.fi ⓤⓢ 'mɔːr-
Morrell 'mʌr.ᵊl, mə'rel
Morrill 'mɒr.ɪl, -ᵊl ⓤⓢ 'mɔːr-
morris (M) 'mɒr.ɪs ⓤⓢ 'mɔːr- **-es** -ɪz **'morris ˌdancing**; **'morris ˌman**
Morrison 'mɒr.ɪ.sᵊn, '-ə- ⓤⓢ 'mɔːr-
Morristown 'mɒr.ɪs.taʊn ⓤⓢ 'mɔːr-
morrow (M) 'mɒr.əʊ ⓤⓢ 'mɑːr.oʊ, 'mɔːr- **-s** -z
mors|e (M) mɔːs ⓤⓢ mɔːrs **-es** -ɪz **ˌMorse 'code**, **'Morse ˌcode**
morsel 'mɔː.sᵊl ⓤⓢ 'mɔːr- **-s** -z
Morshead 'mɔːz.hed ⓤⓢ 'mɔːrz-
mort (M) mɔːt ⓤⓢ mɔːrt **-s** -s
mortadella ˌmɔː.tə'del.ə ⓤⓢ ˌmɔːr-
mortal 'mɔː.tᵊl ⓤⓢ 'mɔːr.t̬ᵊl **-s** -z **-ly** -i **ˌmortal 'sin**
mortalit|y (M) mɔː'tæl.ə.t|i, -ɪ.t|i ⓤⓢ mɔːr'tæl.ə.t̬|i **-ies** -iz
mort|ar 'mɔː.t|əʳ ⓤⓢ 'mɔːr.t̬|ɚ **-ars** -əz ⓤⓢ -ɚz **-aring** -ᵊr.ɪŋ **-ared** -əd ⓤⓢ -ɚd
mortarboard 'mɔː.tə.bɔːd ⓤⓢ 'mɔːr.t̬ɚ.bɔːrd **-s** -z

Morte d'Arthur(e) ˌmɔːt'dɑː.θəʳ ⓤⓢ ˌmɔːrt'dɑːr.θɚ
mortgag|e 'mɔː.gɪdʒ ⓤⓢ 'mɔːr- **-es** -ɪz **-ing** -ɪŋ **-ed** -d
mortgagee ˌmɔː.gɪ'dʒiː, -gə'- ⓤⓢ ˌmɔːr- **-s** -z
mortgagor ˌmɔː.gɪ'dʒɔːʳ, -gə'-; 'mɔː.gɪ.dʒəʳ, -gə- ⓤⓢ 'mɔːr.gɪ.dʒɚ **-s** -z
mortic|e 'mɔː.tɪs ⓤⓢ 'mɔːr.t̬ɪs **-es** -ɪz **-ing** -ɪŋ **-ed** -t
mortician mɔː'tɪʃ.ᵊn ⓤⓢ mɔːr- **-s** -z
mortification ˌmɔː.tɪ.fɪ'keɪ.ʃᵊn, -tə- ⓤⓢ ˌmɔːr.t̬ə.fɪ'-
morti|fy 'mɔː.tɪ|.faɪ, -tə- ⓤⓢ 'mɔːr.t̬ə- **-fies** -faɪz **-fying** -faɪ.ɪŋ **-fied** -faɪd
Mortimer 'mɔː.tɪ.məʳ, -tə- ⓤⓢ 'mɔːr.t̬ə.mɚ
mortis|e 'mɔː.tɪs ⓤⓢ 'mɔːr.t̬ɪs **-es** -ɪz **-ing** -ɪŋ **-ed** -t **'mortise ˌlock**
Mortlake 'mɔːt.leɪk ⓤⓢ 'mɔːrt-
Mortlock 'mɔːt.lɒk ⓤⓢ 'mɔːrt.lɑːk
mortmain 'mɔːt.meɪn ⓤⓢ 'mɔːrt-
Morton 'mɔː.tᵊn ⓤⓢ 'mɔːr-
mortuar|y 'mɔː.tʃu.ᵊr|.i, -tjʊ-, -tjʊ.r|i, -tʃᵊr|.i ⓤⓢ 'mɔːr.tʃu.er|.i **-ies** -iz
Morwenna mɔː'wen.ə ⓤⓢ mɔːr-
mosaic (M) məʊ'zeɪ.ɪk ⓤⓢ moʊ- **-s** -s
Mosborough 'mɒz.brə, -bᵊr.ə ⓤⓢ 'mɑːz.bɚ.oʊ, -bᵊr.ə
Mosby 'mɒz.bi ⓤⓢ 'moʊz-
Mosca 'mɒs.kə ⓤⓢ 'mɑːs-
Moscow 'mɒs.kəʊ ⓤⓢ 'mɑː.skaʊ, -skoʊ
Moseley 'məʊz.li ⓤⓢ 'moʊz-
moselle (M) məʊ'zel ⓤⓢ moʊ- **-s** -z
Moses 'məʊ.zɪz ⓤⓢ 'moʊ- **'Moses ˌbasket**
mosey 'məʊ.zi ⓤⓢ 'moʊ- **-s** -z **-ing** -ɪŋ **-ed** -d
Mosimann 'mɒs.ɪ.mən ⓤⓢ 'mɑː.sɪ-
Moslem 'mɒz.ləm, 'mʊz-, -lem, -lɪm ⓤⓢ 'mɑːz.lem, 'mɑːs- **-s** -z
Mosley 'məʊz.li, 'mɒz- ⓤⓢ 'moʊz-
mosque mɒsk ⓤⓢ mɑːsk **-s** -s
mosquito (M) mɒs'kiː.təʊ, mə'skiː- ⓤⓢ mə'skiː.t̬oʊ **-(e)s** -z **mos'quito ˌnet**
moss (M) mɒs ⓤⓢ mɑːs **-es** -ɪz
moss-grown 'mɒs.grəʊn ⓤⓢ 'mɑːs.groʊn
Mossley 'mɒs.li ⓤⓢ 'mɑːs-
Mossman *area of Sydney:* 'mɒz.mən ⓤⓢ 'mɑːz- *other senses:* 'mɒs.mən ⓤⓢ 'mɑːs-
Mossmorran mɒs'mɒr.ən ⓤⓢ mɑːs'mɔːr-
moss|y 'mɒs|.i ⓤⓢ 'mɑː.s|i **-ier** -i.əʳ ⓤⓢ -i.ɚ **-iest** -i.ɪst, -i.əst **-iness** -ɪ.nəs, -ɪ.nɪs
mos|t məʊs|t ⓤⓢ moʊs|t **-tly** -*t*li
Mostar 'mɒs.tɑːʳ ⓤⓢ 'mɑː.stɑːr
Mostyn 'mɒs.tɪn ⓤⓢ 'mɑː.stɪn

Mosul 'məʊ.sᵊl ⓤⓢ moʊ'suːl; 'moʊ.səl
mot məʊ ⓤⓢ moʊ **-s** -z
MoT, MOT ˌem.əʊ'tiː ⓤⓢ -oʊ'- **-s** -z **-'s** -z **-'d** -d **-'ing** -ɪŋ **ˌMoT cer'tificate**, **ˌMo'T cerˌtificate** ; **ˌMoT 'test**, **ˌMo'T ˌtest**
mote məʊt ⓤⓢ moʊt **-s** -s
motel məʊ'tel ⓤⓢ moʊ- **-s** -z
motet məʊ'tet ⓤⓢ moʊ- **-s** -s
moth mɒθ ⓤⓢ mɑːθ **-s** -s
Mothaks® 'mɒθ.æks ⓤⓢ 'mɑː.θæks
mothball 'mɒθ.bɔːl ⓤⓢ 'mɑːθ-, -bɑːl **-s** -z **-ing** -ɪŋ **-ed** -d
moth-eaten 'mɒθˌiː.tᵊn ⓤⓢ 'mɑːθˌiː-
moth|er (M) 'mʌð|.əʳ ⓤⓢ -ɚ **-ers** -əz ⓤⓢ -ɚz **-ering** -ᵊr.ɪŋ **-ered** -əd ⓤⓢ -ɚd **-erless** -ə.ləs, -les, -lɪs ⓤⓢ -ɚ- **'mother ˌcountry** ; **ˌmother 'hen** ; **ˌmother 'nature** ; **ˌmother su'perior** ; **'Mother's ˌDay** ; **ˌmother 'tongue**
motherboard 'mʌð.ə.bɔːd ⓤⓢ -ɚ.bɔːrd **-s** -z
Mothercare® 'mʌð.ə.keəʳ ⓤⓢ -ɚ.ker
motherfucker 'mʌð.əˌfʌk.əʳ ⓤⓢ -ɚˌfʌk.ɚ **-s** -z
mother-fucking 'mʌð.əˌfʌk.ɪŋ ⓤⓢ -ɚˌ-
motherhood 'mʌð.ə.hʊd ⓤⓢ '-ɚ-
mother-in-law 'mʌð.ᵊr.ɪnˌlɔː ⓤⓢ -ɚ.ɪnˌlɑː, -ˌlɔː **mothers-in-law** 'mʌð.əz- ⓤⓢ -ɚz-
motherland 'mʌð.ə.lænd ⓤⓢ '-ɚ- **-s** -z
motherl|y 'mʌð.ᵊl|.i ⓤⓢ -ɚ.l|i **-iness** -ɪ.nəs, -ɪ.nɪs
mother-of-pearl ˌmʌð.ᵊr.əv'pɜːl ⓤⓢ -ɚ.əv'pɜːrl
mothersill 'mʌð.ə.sɪl ⓤⓢ '-ɚ-
Motherwell 'mʌð.ə.wel ⓤⓢ '-ɚ-
motif məʊ'tiːf ⓤⓢ moʊ- **-s** -s
motile 'məʊ.taɪl ⓤⓢ 'moʊ.t̬ᵊl, -taɪl
motion (M) 'məʊ.ʃᵊn ⓤⓢ 'moʊ- **-s** -z **-ing** -ɪŋ, 'məʊʃ.nɪŋ ⓤⓢ 'moʊʃ- **-ed** -d **-less** -ləs, -lɪs **ˌmotion 'picture** ; **'motion ˌsickness**
moti|vate 'məʊ.tɪ|.veɪt, -tə- ⓤⓢ 'moʊ.t̬ə- **-vates** -veɪts **-vating** -veɪ.tɪŋ ⓤⓢ -veɪ.t̬ɪŋ **-vated** -veɪ.tɪd ⓤⓢ -veɪ.t̬ɪd **-vator/s** -veɪ.təʳ/z ⓤⓢ -veɪ.t̬ɚ/z
motivation ˌməʊ.tɪ'veɪ.ʃᵊn, -tə'- ⓤⓢ ˌmoʊ.t̬ə'-
motive 'məʊ.tɪv ⓤⓢ 'moʊ.t̬ɪv **-s** -z **-less** -ləs, -lɪs
mot juste ˌməʊ'ʒuːst ⓤⓢ ˌmoʊ-
motley (M) 'mɒt.li ⓤⓢ 'mɑːt-
motocross 'məʊ.təʊ.krɒs ⓤⓢ 'moʊ.t̬oʊ.krɑːs
mot|or 'məʊ.t|əʳ ⓤⓢ 'moʊ.t̬|ɚ **-ors** -əz ⓤⓢ -ɚz **-oring** -ᵊr.ɪŋ **-ored** -əd ⓤⓢ -ɚd **'motor ˌcar** ; **'motor ˌhome** ; **'motor ˌlodge** ; **'motor ˌscooter** ; **'motor ˌvehicle**

Motorail® 'məʊ.tᵊr.eɪl (US) 'moʊ.t̬ə.reɪl
motorbike 'məʊ.tə.baɪk (US) 'moʊ.t̬ɚ- **-s** -s
motorboat 'məʊ.tə.bəʊt (US) 'moʊ.t̬ɚ.boʊt **-s** -s
motorcade 'məʊ.tə.keɪd (US) 'moʊ.t̬ɚ- **-s** -z
motorcycle 'məʊ.tə,saɪ.kl̩ (US) 'moʊ.t̬ɚ- **-s** -z
motorcyclist 'məʊ.tə,saɪ.klɪst, -kl̩.ɪst (US) 'moʊ.t̬ɚ- **-s** -s
motorist 'məʊ.tᵊr.ɪst (US) 'moʊ.t̬ɚ- **-s** -s
motoriz|e, -is|e 'məʊ.tᵊr.aɪz (US) 'moʊ.t̬ə.raɪz **-es** -ɪz **-ing** -ɪŋ **-ed** -d
motormou|th 'məʊ.tə.maʊ|θ (US) 'moʊ.t̬ɚ- **-ths** -ðz
motor-scooter 'məʊ.tə,skuː.təʳ (US) 'moʊ.t̬ɚ,skuː.t̬ɚ **-s** -z
motorway 'məʊ.tə.weɪ (US) 'moʊ.t̬ɚ- **-s** -z
Motown® 'məʊ.taʊn (US) 'moʊ-
Mott mɒt (US) mɑːt
motte mɒt (US) mɑːt **-s** -s
Mottistone 'mɒt.ɪ.stᵊn, -stəʊn (US) 'mɑː.t̬ɪ.stᵊn, -stoʊn
mottl|e 'mɒt.l̩ (US) 'mɑː.t̬l̩ **-es** -z **-ing** -ɪŋ **-ed** -d
motto 'mɒt.əʊ (US) 'mɑː.t̬oʊ **-(e)s** -z
Mottram 'mɒt.rəm (US) 'mɑː.trəm
moue muː **-s** -z
moues (*alternative plur. of* **moue**) muː
mouf(f)lon 'muː.flɒn (US) -flɑːn **-s** -z
Moughton 'məʊ.tᵊn (US) 'moʊ-
Mouland 'muː.lænd, mʊ'lænd
mould məʊld (US) moʊld **-s** -z **-ing/s** -ɪŋ/z **-ed** -ɪd
mould|er 'məʊl.d|əʳ (US) 'moʊl.d|ɚ **-ers** -əz (US) -ɚz **-ering** -ᵊr.ɪŋ **-ered** -əd (US) -ɚd
mould|y 'məʊl.d|i (US) 'moʊl- **-ier** -i.əʳ (US) -i.ɚ **-iest** -i.ɪst, -i.əst **-iness** -ɪ.nəs, -ɪ.nɪs
Moule məʊl, muːl (US) moʊl, muːl
Moulinex® 'muː.lɪ.neks, -lə-
Moulin Rouge ,muː.læ̃n'ruːʒ
Moulmein 'maʊl.meɪn (US) mʊl'meɪn, moʊl-
Moulsford 'məʊls.fəd, 'məʊlz- (US) 'moʊls.fɚd, 'moʊlz-
moult məʊlt (US) moʊlt **-s** -s **-ing** -ɪŋ (US) 'moʊl.t̬ɪŋ **-ed** -ɪd (US) 'moʊl.t̬ɪd
Moulton 'məʊl.tᵊn (US) 'moʊl-
Moultrie 'mɔːl.tri, 'muː-
mound (M) maʊnd **-s** -z
Mounsey 'maʊn.zi
mount (M) maʊnt **-s** -s **-ing** -ɪŋ (US) 'maʊn.t̬ɪŋ **-ed** -ɪd (US) 'maʊn.t̬ɪd
Mount Everest ,maʊnt'ev.ᵊr.ɪst, -est
mountain 'maʊn.tɪn, -tən (US) -tᵊn **-s** -z **'mountain ,bike ; 'mountain ,lion; make a ,mountain out of a 'mole-hill**
mountain-ash ,maʊn.tɪn'æʃ, -tən'- (US) -tᵊn'- **-es** -ɪz
mountaineer ,maʊn.tɪ'nɪəʳ, -tə'- (US) -tᵊn'ɪr **-s** -z **-ing** -ɪŋ
mountainous 'maʊn.tɪ.nəs, -tə- (US) -tᵊn.əs
mountainside 'maʊn.tɪn.saɪd, -tən- (US) -tᵊn- **-s** -z
mountaintop 'maʊn.tɪn.tɒp, -tən- (US) -tᵊn.tɑːp **-s** -s
mountant 'maʊn.tənt **-s** -s
Mountbatten maʊnt'bæt.ᵊn (US) -'bæt̬-
mountebank 'maʊn.tɪ.bæŋk, -tə- (US) -t̬ə- **-s** -s
Mountford 'maʊnt.fəd (US) -fɚd
Mountie 'maʊn.ti (US) -t̬i **-s** -z
Mountjoy ,maʊnt'dʒɔɪ, '--
Mountsorrel ,maʊnt'sɒr.əl (US) -'sɔːr-
Mount Vernon ,maʊnt'vɜː.nən (US) -'vɜːr-
Mount|y 'maʊn.t|i (US) -t̬|i **-ies** -iz
Moura 'mʊə.rə (US) 'mʊr.ə
mourn mɔːn (US) mɔːrn **-s** -z **-ing** -ɪŋ **-ed** -d **-er/s** -əʳ/z (US) -ɚ/z
Mourne mɔːn (US) mɔːrn
mournful 'mɔːn.fᵊl, -fʊl (US) 'mɔːrn- **-ly** -i **-ness** -nəs, -nɪs
Mousa 'muː.zə
mouse (*n.*) maʊs **mice** maɪs
mous|e (*v.*) maʊs, maʊz (US) maʊz **-es** -ɪz **-ing** -ɪŋ **-ed** -d
Mousehole 'maʊ.zᵊl
mouser 'maʊ.səʳ, -zəʳ (US) -zɚ **-s** -z
mouse-trap 'maʊs.træp **-s** -s
mous|ey 'maʊ.s|i **-ier** -i.əʳ (US) -i.ɚ **-iest** -i.ɪst, -i.əst
moussaka mʊ'sɑː.kə, 'muː.sæk.ə (US) ,mu'sɑː.kə; ,muː.sɑː'kɑː
mousse muːs
Moussec® ,muː'sek
mousseline 'muː.slɪn, ,muː'sliːn (US) ,muː'sliːn
Moussorgsky mʊ'sɔːg.ski, muː- (US) muː'sɔːrg-, mə-, -'zɔːrg-, -'sɔːrk-, -'zɔːrk-
moustach|e mə'stɑːʃ, mʊ- (US) 'mʌs.tæʃ; mə'stæʃ **-es** -ɪz
mous|y 'maʊ.s|i **-ier** -i.əʳ (US) -i.ɚ **-iest** -i.ɪst, -i.əst
mou|th (*n.*) maʊ|θ **-ths** -ðz **'mouth ,organ ; from the ,horse's 'mouth ; ,down in the 'mouth**
mouth (*v.*) maʊð **-s** -z **-ing** -ɪŋ **-ed** -d
mouthful 'maʊθ.fʊl **-s** -z
mouthpiec|e 'maʊθ.piːs **-es** -ɪz
mouth-to-mouth ,maʊθ.tə'maʊθ *stress shift, see compound:* **,mouth-to-mouth re,susci'tation**
mouthwash 'maʊθ.wɒʃ (US) -wɑːʃ, -wɔːʃ **-es** -ɪz
mouthwatering 'maʊθ,wɔː.tᵊr.ɪŋ (US) -,wɑː.t̬ɚ-, -,wɔː- **-ly** -li
mouth|y 'maʊ.ð|i, -θ|i **-ier** -i.əʳ (US) -i.ɚ **-iest** -i.ɪst, -i.əst
movability ,muː.və'bɪl.ə.ti, -ɪ.ti (US) -ə.t̬i
movable 'muː.və.bl̩ **-s** -z **-ness** -nəs, -nɪs
movant 'muː.vənt **-s** -s
mov|e muːv **-es** -z **-ing/ly** -ɪŋ/li **-ed** -d **-er/s** -əʳ/z (US) -ɚ/z **-eable** -ə.bl̩
movement 'muːv.mənt **-s** -s
movie 'muː.vi **-s** -z
moviegoer 'muː.vi,gəʊ.əʳ (US) -,goʊ.ɚ **-s** -z
moviegoing 'muː.vi,gəʊ.ɪŋ (US) -,goʊ-
moviemak|er 'muː.vi,meɪ.k|əʳ (US) -ɚ **-ers** -əz (US) -ɚz **-ing** -ɪŋ
mow (*v.*) *cut down and stack:* məʊ (US) moʊ **-s** -z **-ing** -ɪŋ **-ed** -d **-n** -n **-er/s** -əʳ/z (US) -ɚ/z
mow (*n.*) *stack:* maʊ **-s** -z
mow (*n.*) *grimace:* maʊ (US) moʊ, maʊ **-s** -z
Mowat, Mowatt maʊət, məʊət (US) maʊət, moʊət
Mowbray 'məʊ.breɪ, -bri (US) 'moʊ-
Mowgli 'maʊ.gli
mown (*from* **mow** *v.*) məʊn (US) moʊn
Moxon 'mɒk.sᵊn (US) 'mɑːk-
moya (M) 'mɔɪ.ə **-s** -z
Moyes mɔɪz
Moygashel *place:* mɔɪ'gæʃ.ᵊl *linen:* 'mɔɪ.gə.ʃᵊl
Moynahan 'mɔɪ.nə.hæn, -hən (US) 'mɔɪ.nə.hæn
Moynihan 'mɔɪ.ni.ən, -hæn; -nə.hæn (US) 'mɔɪ.nɪ.hæn, -nə-
Mozambique ,məʊ.zæm'biːk, -zəm'- (US) ,moʊ-
Mozart 'məʊt.sɑːt (US) 'moʊt.sɑːrt
Mozartian ,məʊt'sɑː.ti.ən (US) ,moʊt'sɑːr.t̬i- **-s** -z
mozzarella ,mɒt.sə'rel.ə (US) ,mɑːt-, ,moʊt-
MP ,em'piː
mph ,em.piː'eɪtʃ
MPhil ,em'fɪl
Mr 'mɪs.təʳ (US) -tɚ
Mrs 'mɪs.ɪz
ms, MS (*abbrev. for* **manuscript**) ,em'es, 'mæn.jə.skrɪpt, -jʊ-
MS (*abbrev. for* **multiple sclerosis**) ,em'es
Ms mɪz, məz (US) mɪz
Note: Used to avoid indicating a woman's marital status. The pronunciation is unstable in Britain.
MSc ,em.es'siː
MS-DOS® ,em.es'dɒs (US) -'dɑːs
MSS (*abbrev. for* **manuscripts**) ,em.es'es, 'mæn.jə.skrɪpts, -jʊ-
MTV ,em.tiː'viː
mu mjuː (US) mjuː, muː

Mubarak mʊ'bɑː.rək, -'bær.æk, -ək
(US) muː'bɑːr.ək
much mʌtʃ **-ly** -li
Muchalls 'mʌk.əlz, 'mʌx-
muchness 'mʌtʃ.nəs, -nɪs
mucilag|e 'mjuː.sɪ.lɪdʒ, -səl.ɪdʒ
(US) -sə.lɪdʒ **-es** -ɪz
mucilaginous ˌmjuː.sɪ'lædʒ.ɪ.nəs, -səl'ædʒ-, '-ə- (US) -sɪ'lædʒ.ə-
muck mʌk **-s** -s **-ing** -ɪŋ **-ed** -t
muck|er 'mʌk|.ər (US) -ɚ **-ers** -əz
(US) -ɚz **-ering** -ər.ɪŋ **-ered** -əd (US) -ɚd
Muckle Flugga ˌmʌk.l̩'flʌg.ə
muckrak|e 'mʌk.reɪk **-es** -s **-ing** -ɪŋ **-ed** -t **-er/s** -ər/z (US) -ɚ/z
muck|y 'mʌk|.i **-ier** -i.ər (US) -i.ɚ **-iest** -i.ɪst, -i.əst **-iness** -ɪ.nəs, -ɪ.nɪs
muc(o)us 'mjuː.kəs ˌ**mucous 'membrane**
mud mʌd **-s** -z
mudba|th 'mʌd.bɑː|θ (US) -bæ|θ **-ths** -ðz
Mud(d)eford 'mʌd.ɪ.fəd (US) -fɚd
muddl|e 'mʌd.l̩ **-es** -z **-ing** -ɪŋ, 'mʌd.lɪŋ **-ed** -d **-er/s** -ər/z (US) -ɚ/z, 'mʌd.lər/z (US) -lɚ/z
muddleheaded ˌmʌd.l̩'hed.ɪd, 'mʌd.l̩ˌhed- (US) 'mʌd.l̩ˌhed- **-ness** -nəs, -nɪs
mudd|y 'mʌd|.i **-ier** -i.ər (US) -i.ɚ **-iest** -i.ɪst, -i.əst **-ily** -ɪ.li, -əl.i **-iness** -ɪ.nəs, -ɪ.nɪs **-ies** -iz **-ying** -i.ɪŋ **-ied** -id
mudflap 'mʌd.flæp **-s** -s
mudguard 'mʌd.gɑːd (US) -gɑːrd **-s** -z
Mudie 'mjuː.di
mudlark 'mʌd.lɑːk (US) -lɑːrk **-s** -s
mudpack 'mʌd.pæk **-s** -s
mudslide 'mʌd.slaɪd **-s** -z
Mueller 'mjuː.lər, 'mʊl.ər (US) -ɚ
muesli 'mjuːz.li, 'muːz- (US) 'mjuːz-, 'mjuːs- **-s** -z
muezzin mu'ez.ɪn, mju- (US) mju-, mu- **-s** -z
muff mʌf **-s** -s **-ing** -ɪŋ **-ed** -t
muffin 'mʌf.ɪn **-s** -z
muffl|e 'mʌf.l̩ **-es** -z **-ing** -ɪŋ, 'mʌf.lɪŋ **-ed** -d
muffler 'mʌf.lər (US) -lɚ **-s** -z
mufti 'mʌf.ti
mug mʌg **-s** -z **-ging** -ɪŋ **-ged** -d **'mug ˌshot**
Mugabe mʊ'gɑː.beɪ, -bi
mugger 'mʌg.ər (US) -ɚ **-s** -z
muggins (M) 'mʌg.ɪnz **-es** -ɪz
Muggins 'mʌg.ɪnz, 'mjuː.gɪnz
Muggleton 'mʌg.l̩.tən (US) -tən
Muggletonian ˌmʌg.l̩'təʊ.ni.ən (US) -'toʊ- **-s** -z
mugg|y 'mʌg|.i **-ier** -i.ər (US) -i.ɚ **-iest** -i.ɪst, -i.əst **-iness** -ɪ.nəs, -ɪ.nɪs
mugwump 'mʌg.wʌmp **-s** -s

Muir mjʊər, mjɔːr (US) mjʊr
Muirhead 'mjʊə.hed, 'mjɔː- (US) 'mjʊr-
Mukden 'mʊk.dən
Mukle 'mjuː.kli
mukluk 'mʌk.lʌk **-s** -s
mulatto mjuː'læt.əʊ, mjə-, mjʊ-, mə- (US) mə'læt̬.oʊ, mjuː-, -'lɑː.t̬oʊ **-(e)s** -z
mulberr|y 'mʌl.bər|.i (US) -ˌber- **-ies** -iz
Mulcaster 'mʌl.kæs.tər (US) -tɚ
mulch mʌltʃ **-es** -ɪz **-ing** -ɪŋ **-ed** -t
Mulciber 'mʌl.sɪ.bər (US) -bɚ
mulct mʌlkt **-s** -s **-ing** -ɪŋ **-ed** -ɪd
mule mjuːl **-s** -z
muleteer ˌmjuː.lɪ'tɪər, -lə'- (US) -lə'tɪr **-s** -z
mulga 'mʊl.gə **-s** -z
Mulgrave 'mʌl.greɪv
Mulholland mʌl'hɒl.ənd (US) -'hɑː.lənd
mulish 'mjuː.lɪʃ **-ly** -li **-ness** -nəs, -nɪs
mull (M) mʌl **-s** -z **-ing** -ɪŋ **-ed** -d
mullah (M) 'mʌl.ə, 'mʊl.ə **-s** -z
Mullan, Mullen 'mʌl.ən
mullein 'mʌl.ɪn, -eɪn (US) -ɪn
mullet (M) 'mʌl.ɪt, -ət **-s** -s
Mulligan 'mʌl.ɪ.gən, '-ə-
mulligatawny ˌmʌl.ɪ.gə'tɔː.ni, ˌ-ə- (US) -'tɑː.ni, -'tɔː-
Mullinar, Mulliner 'mʌl.ɪ.nər (US) -nɚ
Mullinger 'mʌl.ɪn.dʒər, -ən- (US) -dʒɚ
Mullins 'mʌl.ɪnz
mullion (M) 'mʌl.jən, '-i.ən (US) '-jən **-s** -z **-ed** -d
mullock 'mʌl.ək
Mulready mʌl'red.i
Mulroney mʌl'rəʊ.ni (US) -'roʊ-
Multan ˌmʌl'tɑːn (US) ˌmʊl-
multi- mʌl.ti-, -tɪ-, -tə- (US) mʌl.t̬i-, -t̬ə-, -taɪ
Note: Prefix. Normally carries primary or secondary stress on the first syllable, e.g. **multiform** /'mʌl.ti.fɔːm (US) -t̬i.fɔːrm/, **multilingual** /ˌmʌl.ti'lɪŋ.gwəl (US) -t̬i'-/.
multicolo(u)red ˌmʌl.ti'kʌl.əd, 'mʌl.tiˌkʌl- (US) ˌmʌl.t̬ɪ'kʌl.ɚd, 'mʌl.t̬iˌkʌl-
multicultural ˌmʌl.ti'kʌl.tʃər.əl (US) -t̬i'-, -taɪ- **-ly** -i *stress shift:* ˌmulticultural 'festival
multiethnic ˌmʌl.ti'eθ.nɪk (US) -t̬i'- *stress shift:* ˌmultiethnic 'background
multifarious ˌmʌl.tɪ'feə.ri.əs (US) -t̬ə'fer.i- **-ly** -li **-ness** -nəs, -nɪs *stress shift:* ˌmultifarious 'influences
multiform 'mʌl.ti.fɔːm (US) -t̬i.fɔːrm
multilateral ˌmʌl.ti'læt.ər.əl (US) -t̬i'læt̬-, -taɪ- **-ly** -i *stress shift:* ˌmultilateral 'talks
multilingual ˌmʌl.ti'lɪŋ.gwəl (US) -t̬i'- **-ly** -i *stress shift:* ˌmultilingual 'people
multimedia ˌmʌl.ti'miː.di.ə (US) -t̬i'-

multimillionaire ˌmʌl.tiˌmɪl.jə'neər, -i.ə'- (US) -t̬iˌmɪl.jə'ner, -taɪˌ-, ˌmʌl.t̬i'mɪl.jə.ner, -taɪ'- **-s** -z
multinational ˌmʌl.ti'næʃ.ən.əl, -'næʃ.nəl (US) -t̬i'-, -taɪ- **-s** -z *stress shift:* ˌmultinational 'company
multipartite ˌmʌl.ti'pɑː.taɪt (US) -t̬i'pɑːr- *stress shift:* ˌmultipartite 'treaty
multiple 'mʌl.tɪ.pl̩, -tə- (US) -t̬ə- **-s** -z ˌ**multiple scle'rosis**
multiple-choice ˌmʌl.tɪ.pl̩'tʃɔɪs, -tə- (US) -t̬ə- *stress shift:* ˌmultiple-choice 'paper
multiplex 'mʌl.tɪ.pleks, -tə- (US) -t̬ə- **-es** -ɪz
multiplicand ˌmʌl.tɪ.plɪ'kænd, -tə- (US) -t̬ə- **-s** -z
multiplication ˌmʌl.tɪ.plɪ'keɪ.ʃən, -tə- (US) -t̬ə- **-s** -z
multiplicative ˌmʌl.tɪ'plɪk.ə.tɪv, -tə'-; 'mʌl.tɪ.plɪ.keɪ.tɪv (US) 'mʌl.t̬ə.plɪ.keɪ.t̬ɪv; ˌmʌl.tə'plɪk.ə-
multiplicator 'mʌl.tɪ.plɪ.keɪ.tər (US) -t̬ɚ **-s** -z
multiplicit|y ˌmʌl.tɪ'plɪs.ə.t|i, -tə'-, -ɪ.t|i (US) -t̬ə'plɪs.ə.t̬|i **-ies** -iz
multipl|y 'mʌl.tɪ.pl|aɪ, -tə- (US) -t̬ə- **-ies** -aɪz **-ying** -aɪ.ɪŋ **-ied** -aɪd **-ier/s** -aɪ.ər/z (US) -aɪ.ɚ/z
multiprocessing ˌmʌl.ti'prəʊ.ses.ɪŋ (US) -t̬i'prɑː-
multiprocessor ˌmʌl.ti'prəʊ.ses.ər (US) -t̬i'prɑː.ses.ɚ **-s** -z
multipurpose ˌmʌl.ti'pɜː.pəs (US) -t̬i'pɜːr- *stress shift:* ˌmultipurpose 'tool
multiracial ˌmʌl.ti'reɪ.ʃəl, -ʃi.əl (US) -t̬i'reɪ.ʃəl, -taɪ- *stress shift:* ˌmultiracial 'area
multiscreen ˌmʌl.ti'skriːn *stress shift:* ˌmultiscreen 'cinema
multi-storey ˌmʌl.ti'stɔː.ri (US) -t̬i'stɔːr.i *stress shift, see compound:* ˌ**multi-storey 'car park**
multi-tasking ˌmʌl.ti'tɑː.skɪŋ, 'mʌl.tiˌtɑː- (US) 'mʌl.t̬iˌtæs.kɪŋ
multitude 'mʌl.tɪ.tjuːd, -tə-, -tʃuːd (US) -t̬ə.tuːd, -tjuːd **-s** -z
multitudinous ˌmʌl.tɪ'tjuː.dɪ.nəs, -tə'-, -'tʃuː-, -dən.əs (US) -t̬ə'tuː.dən-, -'tjuː- **-ly** -li **-ness** -nəs, -nɪs
multivalen|t ˌmʌl.ti'veɪ.lən|t (US) -t̬i'- **-ce** -*t*s
multivitamin ˌmʌl.ti'vɪt.ə.mɪn, -'vaɪ.tə- (US) -'vaɪ.t̬ə- **-s** -z
multum in parvo ˌmʊl.təm.ɪn'pɑː.vəʊ, ˌmʌl- (US) -'pɑːr.voʊ
mum (M) mʌm **-s** -z
Mum and the Sothsegger ˌmʌm.ən*d*.ðə'sɒθ.seg.ər, -'səʊθ- (US) -æn*d*.ðə'sɑːθ.seg.ɚ

mumbl|e ˈmʌm.bl̩ **-es** -z **-ing/ly** -ɪŋ/li, ˈ-blɪŋ/li **-ed** -d **-er/s** -əʳ/z Ⓤⓢ ˈ-bləʳ/z, ˈ-bl̩.ɚ/z Ⓤⓢ ˈ-blɚ/z
Mumbles ˈmʌm.bl̩z
mumbo-jumbo ˌmʌm.bəʊˈdʒʌm.bəʊ Ⓤⓢ -boʊˈdʒʌm.boʊ
Mumm mʌm *as if French:* mʊm
mumm|er ˈmʌm|.əʳ Ⓤⓢ -ɚ **-ers** -əz, -ɚz **-ery** -ᵊr.i
mummification ˌmʌm.ɪ.fɪˈkeɪ.ʃᵊn, ˌ-ə-
mummi|fy ˈmʌm.ɪ|.faɪ Ⓤⓢ ˈ-ə- **-fies** -faɪz **-fying** -faɪ.ɪŋ **-fied** -faɪd
mumm|y (M) ˈmʌm|.i **-ies** -iz
mump mʌmp **-s** -s **-ing** -ɪŋ **-ed** -t
mumpish ˈmʌm.pɪʃ **-ly** -li **-ness** -nəs, -nɪs
mumps mʌmps
mums|y ˈmʌm.z|i **-ily** -ɪ.li, -ᵊl.i **-iness** -ɪ.nəs, -ɪ.nɪs
Munby ˈmʌn.bi, ˈmʌm- Ⓤⓢ ˈmʌn-
munch mʌnʧ **-es** -ɪz **-ing** -ɪŋ **-ed** -t **-er/s** -əʳ/z Ⓤⓢ -ɚ/z
Munch mʊŋk **-s** -s
Munchausen, **Münchausen**, **Münchhausen** ˈmʌn.ʧaʊ.zᵊn, ˈmʊnʧ-, -haʊ-; mʌnˈʧɔː.zᵊn Ⓤⓢ ˈmʌn.ʧaʊ.zᵊn, ˈmʊn-, -ʧɔː-
munchies (M®) ˈmʌn.ʧiz
munchkin ˈmʌnʧ.kɪn **-s** -z
Muncie ˈmʌn.tsi
mundane mʌnˈdeɪn, ˈ-- **-ly** -li
Munera Pulveris ˌmjuː.nᵊr.əˈpʊl.vᵊr.ɪs
mung mʌŋ ˈ**mung** ˌ**bean**
mungo (M) ˈmʌŋ.gəʊ Ⓤⓢ -goʊ **-s** -z
Munich ˈmjuː.nɪk
municipal mjuːˈnɪs.ɪ.pᵊl, ˈ-ə- Ⓤⓢ ˈ-ə-
municipalit|y mjuːˌnɪs.ɪˈpæl.ə.t|i, -əˈ-, -ɪ.t|i; ˌmjuː.nɪ.sɪˈ-, -səˈ- Ⓤⓢ mjuːˌnɪs.əˈpæl.ə.t̬|i **-ies** -iz
municipaliz|e, **-is|e** mjuːˈnɪs.ɪ.pᵊl.aɪz, ˈ-ə- Ⓤⓢ ˈ-ə.pə.laɪz **-es** -ɪz **-ing** -ɪŋ **-ed** -d
munificen|ce mjuːˈnɪf.ɪ.sᵊn|ts, ˈ-ə- Ⓤⓢ ˈ-ə- **-t/ly** -t/li
muniment ˈmjuː.nɪ.mənt, -nə- Ⓤⓢ -nə- **-s** -s
munition mjuːˈnɪʃ.ᵊn **-s** -z
Munro mʌnˈrəʊ, mənˈ-; ˈmʌn.rəʊ Ⓤⓢ mənˈroʊ
Munsey ˈmʌn.zi
Munster *in Ireland:* ˈmʌnt.stəʳ Ⓤⓢ -stɚ
Münster *in Germany:* ˈmʊnt.stəʳ Ⓤⓢ -stɚ, ˈmʌnt-
muntjak, **muntjac** ˈmʌnt.dʒæk, ˈmʌnt.ʃæk Ⓤⓢ ˈmʌnt.dʒæk **-s** -s
Muppet ˈmʌp.ɪt **-s** -s
mural ˈmjʊə.rᵊl, ˈmjɔː- Ⓤⓢ ˈmjʊr.ᵊl **-s** -z
Murchie ˈmɜː.ki *in S. England also:* -tʃi Ⓤⓢ ˈmɜːr-
Murchison ˈmɜː.tʃɪ.sᵊn, -kɪ- Ⓤⓢ ˈmɜːr.tʃɪ-
Murcia ˈmɜː.ʃi.ə *as if Spanish:* ˈmʊə.θi.ə Ⓤⓢ ˈmɜːr.ʃə, -ʃi.ə
Murcott ˈmɜː.kət Ⓤⓢ ˈmɜːr-
murd|er ˈmɜː.d|əʳ Ⓤⓢ ˈmɜːr.d|ɚ **-ers** -əz Ⓤⓢ -ɚz **-ering** -ᵊr.ɪŋ **-ered** -əd Ⓤⓢ -ɚd
murderer ˈmɜː.dᵊr.əʳ Ⓤⓢ ˈmɜːr.dɚ.ɚ **-s** -z
murderess ˈmɜː.dᵊr.ɪs, -es, -əs; ˌmɜː.dəˈres Ⓤⓢ ˈmɜːr.dɚ.əs; ˌmɜːr.dɚˈes **-es** -ɪz
murderous ˈmɜː.dᵊr.əs Ⓤⓢ ˈmɜːr- **-ly** -li
Murdo ˈmɜː.dəʊ Ⓤⓢ ˈmɜːr.doʊ
Murdoch, **Murdock** ˈmɜː.dɒk Ⓤⓢ ˈmɜːr.dɑːk
Murdstone ˈmɜːd.stᵊn Ⓤⓢ ˈmɜːrd-
Mure mjʊəʳ, mjɔːʳ Ⓤⓢ mjʊr
muriate ˈmjʊə.ri.ət, ˈmjɔː-, -ɪt, -eɪt Ⓤⓢ ˈmjʊr.i.eɪt, -ɪt
muriatic ˌmjʊə.riˈæt.ɪk, ˌmjɔː-, ˈmjʊə.ri.æt-, ˈmjɔː- Ⓤⓢ ˌmjʊr.iˈæt̬-
Muriel ˈmjʊə.ri.əl, ˈmjɔː- Ⓤⓢ ˈmjʊr.i-
Murillo mjʊˈrɪl.əʊ, mjʊə-, -jəʊ *as if Spanish:* mʊˈriː.jəʊ Ⓤⓢ mjʊˈrɪl.oʊ, mə- **-s** -z
Murison ˈmjʊə.rɪ.sᵊn, ˈmjɔː- Ⓤⓢ ˈmjʊr.ɪ-
murk mɜːk Ⓤⓢ mɜːrk
murk|y ˈmɜː.k|i Ⓤⓢ ˈmɜːr- **-ier** -i.əʳ Ⓤⓢ -i.ɚ **-iest** -i.ɪst, -i.əst **-ily** -ɪ.li, -ᵊl.i **-iness** -ɪ.nəs, -ɪ.nɪs
Murmansk mɜːˈmæntsk, mə- Ⓤⓢ mʊrˈmɑːntsk; ˈmɜːr.mæntsk
murm|ur ˈmɜː.m|əʳ Ⓤⓢ ˈmɜːr.m|ɚ **-urs** -əz Ⓤⓢ -ɚz **-uring/ly** -ᵊr.ɪŋ/li **-ured** -əd Ⓤⓢ -ɚd **-urer/s** -ᵊr.əʳ/z Ⓤⓢ -ɚ.ɚ/z
murph|y (M) ˈmɜː.f|i Ⓤⓢ ˈmɜːr- **-ies** -iz ˈ**Murphy's** ˌ**law**
murrain ˈmʌr.ɪn, -eɪn Ⓤⓢ ˈmɜːr.ɪn
Murray ˈmʌr.i Ⓤⓢ ˈmɜːr-, ˈmʌr-
Murree ˈmʌr.i Ⓤⓢ ˈmɜːr-
Murrell ˈmʌr.ᵊl; mʌrˈel, məˈrel Ⓤⓢ ˈmɜːr.ᵊl; məˈrel
Murrie ˈmjʊə.ri Ⓤⓢ ˈmjʊr.i
Murrumbidgee ˌmʌr.əmˈbɪdʒ.i Ⓤⓢ ˌmɜːr-
Murry ˈmʌr.i Ⓤⓢ ˈmɜːr-
Murtagh ˈmɜː.tə Ⓤⓢ ˈmɜːr.tɑː
Murtle ˈmɜː.tl̩ Ⓤⓢ ˈmɜːr.t̬l̩
Murton ˈmɜː.tᵊn Ⓤⓢ ˈmɜːr-
Mururoa mʊ.rʊˈrəʊ.ə Ⓤⓢ ˌmuː.ruːˈroʊ-
muscadet (M) ˈmʌs.kə.deɪ, ˌ--ˈ- Ⓤⓢ ˈmʌs.kə.deɪ **-s** -z
muscat (M) ˈmʌs.kət, -kæt **-s** -s
muscatel ˌmʌs.kəˈtel **-s** -z
muscl|e ˈmʌs.l̩ **-es** -z **-ing** -ɪŋ, ˈmʌs.lɪŋ **-ed** -d
muscle-bound ˈmʌs.l̩ˌbaʊnd
muscle|man ˈmʌs.l̩|.mæn **-men** -men
muscl|y ˈmʌs.l|i, ˈmʌs.l̩|.i **-ier** -i.əʳ Ⓤⓢ -i.ɚ **-iest** -i.ɪst, -i.əst
muscovado ˌmʌs.kəˈvɑː.dəʊ, -ˈveɪ- Ⓤⓢ -doʊ
Muscovite ˈmʌs.kə.vaɪt **-s** -s
Muscovy ˈmʌs.kə.vi
muscular ˈmʌs.kjə.ləʳ, -kjʊ- Ⓤⓢ -kjə.lɚ, -kjuː- **-ly** -li ˌ**muscular** ˈ**dystrophy**
muscularity ˌmʌs.kjəˈlær.ə.ti, -kjʊˈ-, -ɪ.ti Ⓤⓢ -kjəˈler.ə.t̬i, -kjuːˈ-, -ˈlær-
musculature ˈmʌs.kjə.lə.tʃəʳ, -kjʊ-, -tjʊəʳ, -tʃʊəʳ Ⓤⓢ -kjə.lə.tʃɚ, -kjuː- **-s** -z
mus|e (M) mjuːz **-es** -ɪz **-ing/ly** -ɪŋ/li **-ed** -d
musette mjuːˈzet **-s** -s
museum mjuːˈziː.əm, mjʊ- **-s** -z
Museveni ˌmuː.səˈveɪ.ni
Musgrave ˈmʌz.greɪv
mush mʌʃ **-es** -ɪz **-ing** -ɪŋ **-ed** -t
mushroom ˈmʌʃ.rʊm, -ruːm Ⓤⓢ -ruːm, -rʊm **-s** -z **-ing** -ɪŋ **-ed** -d
mush|y ˈmʌʃ|.i **-ier** -i.əʳ Ⓤⓢ -i.ɚ **-iest** -i.ɪst, -i.əst **-iness** -ɪ.nəs, -ɪ.nɪs
music ˈmjuː.zɪk ˈ**music** ˌ**centre** ; ˈ**music** ˌ**hall** ; ˈ**music** ˌ**stand** ; ˈ**music** ˌ**stool** ; ˈ**music** ˌ**video** ; ˌ**face the** ˈ**music**
music|al ˈmjuː.zɪ.k|ᵊl, -zə- **-als** -ᵊlz **-ally** -ᵊl.i, -li **-alness** -ᵊl.nəs, -nɪs ˈ**musical** ˌ**box** ; ˌ**musical** ˈ**chairs**
musicale ˌmjuː.zɪˈkɑːl, -ˈkæl Ⓤⓢ -ˈkæl **-s** -z
musicality ˌmjuː.zɪˈkæl.ə.ti, -ɪ.ti Ⓤⓢ -ə.t̬i
musician mjuːˈzɪʃ.ᵊn **-s** -z **-ly** -li **-ship** -ʃɪp
musicolog|y ˌmjuː.zɪˈkɒl.ə.dʒ|i Ⓤⓢ -ˈkɑː.lə- **-ist/s** -ɪst/s
Musil ˈmuː.zɪl, -sɪl
musk mʌsk **-y** -i ˈ**musk** ˌ**deer**; ˈ**musk** ˌ**rose**
musket ˈmʌs.kɪt **-s** -s **-ry** -ri
musketeer ˌmʌs.kɪˈtɪəʳ, -kəˈ- Ⓤⓢ -kəˈtɪr **-s** -z
Muskett ˈmʌs.kɪt
Muskie ˈmʌs.ki
musk-ox ˈmʌsk.ɒks, ˌ-ˈ- Ⓤⓢ ˈmʌsk.ɑːks **-en** -ᵊn
muskrat ˈmʌsk.ræt, ˌ-ˈ- Ⓤⓢ ˈ-- **-s** -s
Muslim ˈmʊz.lɪm, ˈmʊs-, -ləm Ⓤⓢ ˈmʌz.ləm, ˈmʌs-, ˈmʊz-, ˈmʊs-, ˈmuːz-, ˈmuːz-, -lɪm **-s** -z
muslin ˈmʌz.lɪn **-s** -z
musquash ˈmʌs.kwɒʃ Ⓤⓢ -kwɑːʃ
muss mʌs **-es** -ɪz **-ing** -ɪŋ **-ed** -t
mussel ˈmʌs.ᵊl **-s** -z
Musselburgh ˈmʌs.l.bᵊr.ə, -ˌbʌr.ə
Mussolini ˌmʊs.əˈliː.ni, ˌmʌs- Ⓤⓢ ˌmuː.səˈ-
Mussorgsky mʊˈsɔːg.ski, mə-, -ˈzɔːg- Ⓤⓢ məˈsɔːrg-, -ˈsɔːrk-, -ˈzɔːrg-, -ˈzɔːrk-
Mussulman ˈmʌs.ᵊl.mən, -mæn **-s** -z
must (*n. adj.*) mʌst
must (*v.*) *strong form:* mʌst *weak forms:* məst, məs

Note: Weak form word. There are two senses of **must**: one is concerned with supposition, or making deductions, and in this sense it is usual for the strong form to be used (e.g. 'If he's late, he must be ill'). The other sense is related to obligation: the word may be stressed, in which case it has the strong form (e.g. 'You must try harder'), or unstressed, in which case the pronunciation is either /məs/ before a consonant, or /məst/ before a vowel (e.g. 'Each of us must buy some' /ˈiːtʃ.əv.əs.məsˌbaɪ.sʌm/; 'You must always look first' /jʊ.məstˌɔːl.wɪz.lʊkˈfɜːst Ⓤⓢ -ˌɑːl.weɪz.lʊkˈfɜːrst/).

mustach|e məˈstɑːʃ, mʊ- Ⓤⓢ ˈmʌs.tæʃ; məˈstæʃ **-es** -ɪz **-ed** -t

mustachio məˈstɑː.ʃi.əʊ, -ˈstæʃ.i- Ⓤⓢ -ˈstæʃ.i.oʊ, -ˈstɑː.ʃi- **-s** -z **-ed** -d

mustang ˈmʌs.tæŋ **-s** -z

Mustapha ˈmʊs.tə.fə, ˈmʌs-, -fɑː; mʊˈstɑː.fə, mə- Ⓤⓢ ˈmʊs.tɑː.fɑː *Egyptian:* mʊˈstɑː.fə, mə- Ⓤⓢ ˈmʊs.tɑː.fɑː

Mustapha Kemal ˌmʊs.tə.fə.kemˈɑːl, -kɪˈmɑːl Ⓤⓢ ˌmʊs.tɑː.fɑː.kemˈɑːl

mustard (M) ˈmʌs.təd Ⓤⓢ -tɚd **-s** **ˈmustard ˌgas ; ˈmustard ˌplaster ; as ˌkeen as ˈmustard**

Mustel ˈmʌs.tᵊl

must|er ˈmʌs.t|əʳ Ⓤⓢ -t|ɚ **-ers** -əz Ⓤⓢ -ɚz **-ering** -ᵊr.ɪŋ **-ered** -əd Ⓤⓢ -ɚd

musth mʌst

Mustique muːˈstiːk

mustn't ˈmʌs.ᵊnt

must|y ˈmʌs.t|i **-ier** -i.əʳ Ⓤⓢ -i.ɚ **-iest** -i.ɪst, -i.əst **-ily** -ɪ.li, -ᵊl.i **-iness** -ɪ.nəs, -ɪ.nɪs

Mut muːt

mutability ˌmjuː.təˈbɪl.ə.ti, -ɪ.ti Ⓤⓢ -t̬əˈbɪl.ə.t̬i

mutable ˈmjuː.tə.bl̩ Ⓤⓢ -t̬ə-

mutant ˈmjuː.tᵊnt **-s** -s

muta|te mjuːˈteɪ|t Ⓤⓢ ˈ-- **-tes** -ts **-ting** -tɪŋ Ⓤⓢ -t̬ɪŋ **-ted** -tɪd Ⓤⓢ -t̬ɪd

mutation mjuːˈteɪ.ʃᵊn **-s** -z

mutatis mutandis muːˌtɑː.tiːs.muˈtæn.diːs, mjuːˌteɪ.tiːs.mjuˈ- Ⓤⓢ muːˌtɑː.t̬ɪs.muːˈtɑːn.dɪs, mjuːˌteɪ.t̬ɪs.mjuːˈtæn.dɪs

mut|e mjuːt **-es** -s **-ely** -li **-eness** -nəs, -nɪs **-ing** -ɪŋ Ⓤⓢ ˈmjuː.t̬ɪŋ **-ed** -ɪd Ⓤⓢ ˈmjuː.t̬ɪd

mutil|ate ˈmjuː.tɪ.l|eɪt, -tᵊl|.eɪt Ⓤⓢ -t̬ᵊl- **-ates** -eɪts **-ating** -eɪ.tɪŋ Ⓤⓢ -eɪ.t̬ɪŋ **-ated** -eɪ.tɪd Ⓤⓢ -eɪ.t̬ɪd **-ator/s** -eɪ.təʳ/z Ⓤⓢ -eɪ.t̬ɚ/z

mutilation ˌmjuː.tɪˈleɪ.ʃᵊn, -tᵊlˈeɪ- Ⓤⓢ -t̬ᵊlˈ- **-s** -z

mutineer ˌmjuː.tɪˈnɪəʳ, -tᵊn.ɪəʳ Ⓤⓢ -tᵊnˈɪr **-s** -z

mutinous ˈmjuː.tɪ.nəs, -tᵊn.əs Ⓤⓢ -tᵊn- **-ly** -li **-ness** -nəs, -nɪs

mutin|y ˈmjuː.tɪ.n|i, -tᵊl|n.i **-ies** -iz **-ying** -i.ɪŋ **-ied** -id

mutism ˈmjuː.tɪ.zᵊm

mutt mʌt **-s** -s

mutt|er ˈmʌt|.əʳ Ⓤⓢ ˈmʌt̬|.ɚ **-ers** -əz Ⓤⓢ -ɚz **-ering/ly** -ᵊr.ɪŋ/li **-ered** -əd Ⓤⓢ -ɚd **-erer/s** -ᵊr.əʳ/z Ⓤⓢ -ɚ.ɚ/z **-erings** -ᵊr.ɪŋz Ⓤⓢ -ɚ.ɪŋz

mutton (M) ˈmʌt.ᵊn **ˌmutton ˌdressed as ˈlamb**

muttonhead ˈmʌt.ᵊn.hed **-s** -z

mutual ˈmjuː.tʃu.əl, -tʃəl, -tju.əl Ⓤⓢ -tʃu.əl **-ly** -i **ˈmutual ˌfund**

mutuality ˌmjuː.tjuˈæl.ə.ti, -ɪ.ti Ⓤⓢ -tʃuˈæl.ə.t̬i

Muzak® ˈmjuː.zæk

muzzl|e ˈmʌz.l̩ **-es** -z **-ing** -ɪŋ, ˈmʌz.l.ɪŋ **-ed** -d

muzzle-load|er ˈmʌz.l̩ˌləʊ.d|əʳ Ⓤⓢ -ˌloʊ.d|ɚ **-ers** -əz Ⓤⓢ -ɚz **-ing** -ɪŋ

muzz|y ˈmʌz|.i **-ier** -i.əʳ Ⓤⓢ -i.ɚ **-iest** -i.ɪst, -i.əst **-iness** -ɪ.nəs, -ɪ.nɪs

Mwanza məˈwæn.zə Ⓤⓢ ˈmwɑːn.zɑː

my *normal form:* maɪ *occasional weak form:* mɪ

Note: Occasional weak form word. The strong form is used contrastively (e.g. 'My friends and your friends') or for emphasis (e.g. 'It's *my* turn'). Many speakers do not have a special weak form, and simply produce a brief, weakened pronunciation of /maɪ/. However, some speakers do use a weak form of **my** in common phrases. British English speakers may have the pronunciation /mi/ before a vowel (e.g. 'On my own' /ˌɒn.miˈəʊn/), and /mə/ before a consonant (e.g. 'On my back' /ˌɒn.məˈbæk/). For American English, the variant /mə/ may be used before a consonant, but /mi/ is not acceptable. In British English, there is also a special form of my used by lawyers in court, in phrases such as 'my Lord' or My Learned Friend', pronounced /mɪ/ or /mə/.

myalg|ia maɪˈæl.dʒ|ə, -i.ə **-ic** -ɪk

Myanmar ˈmjæn.mɑːʳ Ⓤⓢ mjɑːnˈmɑːr

Myatt maɪət

myceli|um maɪˈsiː.li|.əm **-a** -ə

Mycenae maɪˈsiː.ni, -niː

Mycenaean ˌmaɪ.sɪˈniː.ən, -sᵊnˈiː- Ⓤⓢ -səˈniː-

mycolog|ist maɪˈkɒl.ə.dʒ|ɪst Ⓤⓢ -ˈkɑː.lə- **-ists** -ɪsts **-y** -i

mycolog|y maɪˈkɒl.ə.dʒ|i Ⓤⓢ -ˈkɑː.lə- **-ist/s** -ɪsts

myelitis ˌmaɪəˈlaɪ.tɪs, ˌmaɪ.ɪˈ-, maɪˈ- Ⓤⓢ ˌmaɪ.əˈ-

Myers maɪəz Ⓤⓢ maɪɚz

Myerscough ˈmaɪə.skəʊ Ⓤⓢ ˈmaɪɚ.skoʊ

Myfanwy məˈvæn.wi, mɪ-, -ˈfæn-

Myingyan mjɪŋˈjɑːn

Mylar® ˈmaɪ.lɑːʳ Ⓤⓢ -lɑːr

myna(h) ˈmaɪ.nə **-s** -z **ˈmyna(h) ˌbird**

mynheer maɪnˈhɪəʳ, -ˈheəʳ Ⓤⓢ mɪˈner, -ˈnɪr; maɪnˈher, -hɪr **-s** -z

Mynheer *form of address in S Africa:* məˈnɪəʳ Ⓤⓢ -ˈner, -ˈnɪr

Mynott ˈmaɪ.nət

myoelastic ˌmaɪ.əʊ.ɪˈlæs.tɪk, -ˈlɑː.stɪk Ⓤⓢ -oʊ.ɪˈlæs.tɪk

myope ˈmaɪ.əʊp Ⓤⓢ -oʊp **-s** -s

myopia maɪˈəʊ.pi.ə Ⓤⓢ -ˈoʊ-

myopic maɪˈɒp.ɪk Ⓤⓢ -ˈɑː.pɪk

myosin ˈmaɪ.əʊ.sɪn Ⓤⓢ -oʊ-

myosis maɪˈəʊ.sɪs Ⓤⓢ -ˈoʊ-

myosotis ˌmaɪ.əʊˈsəʊ.tɪs Ⓤⓢ -oʊˈsoʊ.t̬ɪs

Myra ˈmaɪə.rə Ⓤⓢ ˈmaɪ-

myriad ˈmɪr.i.əd **-s** -z

myrmidon (M) ˈmɜː.mɪ.dᵊn, -dɒn Ⓤⓢ ˈmɜːr.mə.dɑːn, -dᵊn **-s** -z

myrrh mɜːʳ Ⓤⓢ mɜːr

Myrrha ˈmɪr.ə

myrrhic ˈmɜː.rɪk, ˈmɪr.ɪk Ⓤⓢ ˈmɜːr-

myrrhine ˈmɜː.raɪn, ˈmɪr.aɪn Ⓤⓢ ˈmɜːr.iːn, -ɪn

myrtle (M) ˈmɜː.tl̩ Ⓤⓢ ˈmɜːr.t̬l̩ **-s** -z

myself maɪˈself, mɪ- Ⓤⓢ maɪ-, mə-

Mysia ˈmɪs.i.ə, ˈmɪʃ.ə

Mysore ˈmaɪ.sɔːʳ Ⓤⓢ -sɔːr

mysterious mɪˈstɪə.ri.əs Ⓤⓢ -ˈstɪr.i- **-ly** -li **-ness** -nəs, -nɪs

myster|y ˈmɪs.tᵊr|.i, ˈ-tr|i **-ies** -iz **ˈmystery ˌplay**

mystic ˈmɪs.tɪk **-s** -s

mystic|al ˈmɪs.tɪ.k|ᵊl **-ally** -ᵊl.i, -li **-alness** -ᵊl.nəs, -nɪs

mysticism ˈmɪs.tɪ.sɪ.zᵊm, -tə-

mystification ˌmɪs.tɪ.fɪˈkeɪ.ʃᵊn, -tə-

mysti|fy ˈmɪs.tɪ|.faɪ **-fies** -faɪz **-fying/ly** -faɪ.ɪŋ/li **-fied** -faɪd

mystique mɪˈstiːk

myth mɪθ **-s** -s

mythic ˈmɪθ.ɪk **-al** -ᵊl **-ally** -ᵊl.i, -li

Mytholmroyd ˌmaɪ.ðᵊmˈrɔɪd

mythologic ˌmɪθ.ᵊlˈɒdʒ.ɪk, ˌmaɪ.θᵊlˈ- Ⓤⓢ ˌmɪθ.əˈlɑː.dʒɪk **-al** -ᵊl **-ally** -ᵊl.i, -li

mythologist mɪˈθɒl.ə.dʒɪst, maɪ- Ⓤⓢ mɪˈθɑː.lə- **-s** -s

mythologiz|e, -is|e mɪˈθɒl.ə.dʒaɪz, maɪ- Ⓤⓢ mɪˈθɑː.lə- **-es** -ɪz **-ing** -ɪŋ **-ed** -d

mytholog|y mɪˈθɒl.ə.dʒ|i, maɪ- Ⓤⓢ -ˈθɑː.lə- **-ies** -iz

Mytilene ˌmɪt.ɪˈliː.ni, ˌmaɪ.tɪˈ-, -tᵊlˈiː-, -niː Ⓤⓢ ˌmɪt.ᵊlˈiː-

myxomatosis ˌmɪk.sə.məˈtəʊ.sɪs Ⓤⓢ -ˈtoʊ-

N

n (N) en **-'s** -z

N (*abbrev. for* **North**) nɔːθ ⓊⓈ nɔːrθ (*abbrev. for* **Northerly**) ˈnɔː.ðᵊl.i ⓊⓈ ˈnɔːr.ðɚ.li (*abbrev. for* **Northern**) ˈnɔː.ðᵊn ⓊⓈ ˈnɔːr.ðɚn

'n', 'n ᵊn ˌ**fish 'n' 'chips**; ˌ**rock 'n' 'roll**

NAACP ˌen.dʌb.l̩ˌeɪ.siːˈpiː

NAAFI, Naafi ˈnæf.i

Naaman ˈneɪə.mən

naan nɑːn, næn ⓊⓈ nɑːn **-s** -z

Naas neɪs ⓊⓈ neɪs, nɑːs

nab næb **-s** -z **-bing** -ɪŋ **-bed** -d

Nabisco® nəˈbɪs.kəʊ, næbˈɪs- ⓊⓈ -koʊ

nablab ˈnæb.læb **-s** -z

Nablus ˈnɑː.bləs, ˈnæb.ləs ⓊⓈ ˈnɑː.bləs, ˈnæb.ləs ⓊⓈ -lʊs

nabob ˈneɪ.bɒb ⓊⓈ -bɑːb **-s** -z

nabobess ˌneɪ.bɒbˈes ⓊⓈ -bɑːˈbes **-es** -ɪz

Nabokov ˈnæb.ə.kɒf; nəˈbəʊ- ⓊⓈ nəˈbɑː.kɑːf; ˈnɑː.bə-, ˈnæb.ə-

Naboth ˈneɪ.bɒθ ⓊⓈ -bɑːθ

nacelle nəˈsel, næsˈel ⓊⓈ nəˈsel **-s** -z

nacho ˈnɑː.tʃəʊ, ˈnætʃ.əʊ ⓊⓈ ˈnɑː.tʃoʊ **-s** -z

NACNE ˈnæk.niː

NACODS ˈneɪ.kɒdz ⓊⓈ -kɑːdz

nacre ˈneɪ.kəʳ ⓊⓈ -kɚ

nacreous ˈneɪ.kri.əs

nacrite ˈneɪ.kraɪt

NACRO, Nacro ˈnæk.rəʊ ⓊⓈ -roʊ

Nadia ˈnɑː.di.ə, ˈneɪ- ⓊⓈ ˈnɑː-, ˈ-djə

Nadine neɪˈdiːn, nə-; ˈneɪ.diːn ⓊⓈ nəˈdiːn, neɪ-

nadir ˈneɪ.dɪəʳ, -dəʳ; ˈnæd.ɪəʳ ⓊⓈ ˈneɪ.dɚ, -dɪr **-s** -z

Nadir nædˈɪəʳ ⓊⓈ -ɪr

naev|us ˈniː.v|əs **-uses** -ə.sɪz **-i** -aɪ

naff næf

NAFTA ˈnæf.tə

nag næg **-s** -z **-ging** -ɪŋ **-ged** -d **-ger/s** -əʳ/z ⓊⓈ -ɚ/z

Naga ˈnɑː.gə **-s** -z

Nagasaki ˌnæg.əˈsɑː.ki, -ˈsæk.i ⓊⓈ ˌnɑː.gəˈsɑː.ki

Nagorno-Karabakh nəˌgɔː.nəʊˌkær.əˈbæk ⓊⓈ -ˌgɔːr.noʊ.kɑː.rɑːˈbɑːk

Nagoya nəˈgɔɪ.ə ⓊⓈ nɑːˈgɔː.jɑː, -ˈgɔɪ.ə

Nagpur ˌnægˈpʊəʳ ⓊⓈ ˌnɑːgˈpʊr

nah næː ⓊⓈ næː, nɑː

Note: This is an informal pronunciation of **no**; in the British accent described, its usage is often semi-comical.

Nahuatl ˈnɑː.wɑː.tl̩, -ˈ-- ⓊⓈ ˈnɑː.wɑː.t̬l̩ **-s** -z

Nahuatlan ˈnɑː.wɑː.t.lən, nɑːˈwɑː- ⓊⓈ ˈnɑː.wɑː.t̬lən- **-s** -z

Nahum ˈneɪ.həm, -hʌm ⓊⓈ -həm, -əm

naiad ˈnaɪ.æd ⓊⓈ ˈneɪ-, ˈnaɪ-, -əd **-s** -z

naif, naïf naɪˈiːf, nɑː- ⓊⓈ nɑː- **-s** -s

nail neɪl **-s** -z **-ing** -ɪŋ **-ed** -d ˈ**nail** ˌ**file**; ˈ**nail** ˌ**polish**; ˈ**nail** ˌ**scissors**; ˈ**nail** ˌ**varnish**; ˌ**hit the** ˌ**nail on the** ˈ**head**

nailbiting ˈneɪlˌbaɪ.tɪŋ ⓊⓈ -t̬ɪŋ **-ly** -li

nailbrush ˈneɪl.brʌʃ **-es** -ɪz

nailclipper ˈneɪlˌklɪp.əʳ ⓊⓈ -ɚ **-s** -z

Nailsea ˈneɪl.siː

Nailsworth ˈneɪlz.wəθ, -wɜːθ ⓊⓈ -wɚθ, -wɜːrθ

Nain ˈneɪ.ɪn; neɪn

Naipaul ˈnaɪ.pɔːl ⓊⓈ -pɑːl, -pɔːl

naira ˈnaɪ.rə **-s** -z

Nairn(e) neən ⓊⓈ nern

Nairnshire ˈneən.ʃəʳ, -ˌʃɪəʳ ⓊⓈ ˈnern.ʃɚ, -ˌʃɪr

Nairobi naɪˈrəʊ.bi ⓊⓈ -ˈroʊ-

Naish næʃ, neɪʃ

naiv|e, naïv|e naɪˈiːv, nɑː- ⓊⓈ nɑː-, naɪ- **-ely** -li **-eness** -nəs, -nɪs

naiveté, naïveté nɑːˈiː.və.teɪ, naɪ-, -ˈiː.v.teɪ ⓊⓈ ˌnɑː.iːvˈteɪ, ˌnaɪ-, -ˈ--

naivety, naïvety naɪˈiː.və.ti, nɑː- ⓊⓈ nɑːˈiː.və.t̬i, naɪ-

naked ˈneɪ.kɪd **-ly** -li **-ness** -nəs, -nɪs **the** ˌ**naked** ˈ**eye**

naker ˈneɪ.kəʳ, ˈnæk.əʳ ⓊⓈ ˈneɪ.kɚ **-s** -z

Nakhon Ratchasima nəˌkɒn.rɑː.tʃɑːˈsiː.mə ⓊⓈ -ˌkɑːn-

NALGO ˈnæl.gəʊ ⓊⓈ -goʊ

Nam, 'Nam (*abbrev. for* **Vietnam**) nɑːm, næm

Namangan ˌnæm.æŋˈgɑːn ⓊⓈ ˌnɑː.mən-, nə-

namby-pamby ˌnæm.biˈpæm.bi **-ism** -ɪ.zᵊm

nam|e neɪm **-es** -z **-ing** -ɪŋ **-ed** -d **-eless** -ləs, -lɪs

name-brand ˈneɪm.brænd **-s** -z

namedrop ˈneɪm.drɒp ⓊⓈ -drɑːp **-s** -s **-ping** -ɪŋ **-ped** -t **-per/s** -əʳ/z ⓊⓈ -ɚ/z

namely ˈneɪm.li

nameplate ˈneɪm.pleɪt **-s** -s

namesake ˈneɪm.seɪk **-s** -s

nametag ˈneɪm.tæg **-s** -z

Namibi|a nəˈmɪb.i|.ə, næmˈɪb- ⓊⓈ nəˈmɪb- **-an/s** -ən/z

Namier ˈneɪ.mɪəʳ, -mi.əʳ ⓊⓈ -mi.ɚ

Nampula næmˈpuː.lə

Namur næmˈʊəʳ ⓊⓈ -ˈʊr, nɑːˈmʊr

nan *bread:* nɑːn, næn ⓊⓈ næn, nɑːn **-s** -z

Nan *name:* næn

nana ˈnæn.ə ⓊⓈ ˈnæn.ə, ˈnɑː.nə, -nɑː **-s** -z

Nanaimo nəˈnaɪ.məʊ, nænˈaɪ- ⓊⓈ nəˈnaɪ.moʊ

Nanak ˈnɑː.nək

nance (N) nænts

nancy (N) *female name or effeminate man:* ˈnænt.si ˈ**nancy** ˌ**boy**

Nancy *in France:* ˈnɑ̃ːn.si; *as if French:* nɑ̃ːnˈsiː ⓊⓈ ˈnɑ̃ːn.si, ˈnænt-

NAND nænd

Nanette nænˈet, nəˈnet

Nanjing nænˈdʒɪŋ

nankeen næŋˈkiːn, næn- ⓊⓈ næn-

Nank|in ˌnænˈk|ɪn, ˌnæŋ- ⓊⓈ ˌnæn-, ˌnɑːn- **-ing** -ɪŋ *stress shift:* ˌNankin ˈhighway

Nannie ˈnæn.i

nann|y (N) ˈnæn|.i **-ies** -iz ˈ**nanny** ˌ**goat**

nanometre, nanometer ˈnæn.əʊˌmiː.təʳ; nænˈɒm.ɪ- ⓊⓈ ˈnæn.oʊˌmiː.t̬ɚ; nænˈɑː.mɪ-

Nanook ˈnæn.uːk ⓊⓈ -ʊk

nanosecond ˈnæn.əʊˌsek.ᵊnd ⓊⓈ -oʊˌ-, -əˌ- **-s** -z

nanotechnology ˌnæn.əʊ.tekˈnɒl.ə.dʒi ⓊⓈ -oʊ.tekˈnɑː.lə-

Nansen ˈnænt.sᵊn

Nantes nɑ̃ːnt ⓊⓈ nɑ̃ːnt, nænts

Nantucket nænˈtʌk.ɪt

Nantwich ˈnænt.wɪtʃ *locally also:* -waɪtʃ

Naoise ˈniː.ʃə ⓊⓈ -si, ˈneɪ-

Naomi ˈneɪ.ə.mi; neɪˈəʊ- ⓊⓈ -ˈoʊ-; ˈneɪ.oʊ-

nap næp **-s** -s **-ping** -ɪŋ **-ped** -t

napalm ˈneɪ.pɑːm, ˈnæp.ɑːm ⓊⓈ ˈneɪ.pɑːm **-s** -z **-ing** -ɪŋ **-ed** -d

Napa Valley ˌnæp.əˈvæl.i

nape neɪp **-s** -s

napery ˈneɪ.pᵊr.i

Naphtali ˈnæf.tə.laɪ

naphtha ˈnæf.θə, ˈnæp-

naphthalene ˈnæf.θə.liːn, ˈnæp-

naphthol ˈnæf.θɒl, ˈnæp- ⓊⓈ -θɑːl

Napier ˈneɪ.pi.əʳ, nəˈpɪəʳ ⓊⓈ ˈneɪ.pi.ɚ, nəˈpɪr

Napierian nəˈpɪə.ri.ən, neɪ- ⓊⓈ -ˈpɪr.i-

napkin ˈnæp.kɪn **-s** -z ˈ**napkin** ˌ**ring**

Naples ˈneɪ.pl̩z

napoleon (N) nəˈpəʊ.li.ən ⓊⓈ -ˈpoʊ- **-s** -z

Napoleonic nəˌpəʊ.liˈɒn.ɪk ⓊⓈ -ˌpoʊ.liˈɑː.nɪk

napp|y ˈnæp|.i **-ies** -iz ˈ**nappy** ˌ**rash**

Narayan nəˈraɪ.ən ⓊⓈ nɑːˈrɑː.jən

Narbonne nɑːˈbɒn ⓊⓈ nɑːrˈbɑːn

Narborough ˈnɑː.bᵊr.ə ⓊⓈ ˈnɑːr.bə.roʊ

narc nɑːk ⓊⓈ nɑːrk **-s** -s

narcissi (*plur. of* **narcissus**) nɑːˈsɪs.aɪ ⓊⓈ nɑːr-

narcissism ˈnɑː.sɪ.sɪ.zᵊm; nɑːˈsɪs.ɪ- ⓊⓈ ˈnɑːr.sə.sɪ-

narcissist ˈnɑː.sɪ.sɪst; nɑːˈsɪs.ɪst ⓊⓈ ˈnɑːr.sɪ- **-s** -s

narcissistic ˌnɑː.sɪˈsɪs.tɪk (US) ˌnɑːr-
narciss|us (N) nɑːˈsɪs|.əs (US) nɑːr- **-uses** -ə.sɪz **-i** -aɪ
narcolepsy ˈnɑː.kəʊ.lep.si (US) ˈnɑːr.kə-, -koʊ-
narcoleptic ˌnɑː.kəʊˈlep.tɪk (US) ˌnɑːr.kəˈ-, -koʊ- **-s** -s
narcos|is nɑːˈkəʊ.s|ɪs (US) nɑːrˈkoʊ- **-es** -iːz
narcotic nɑːˈkɒt.ɪk (US) nɑːrˈkɑːt̬- **-s** -s
nard nɑːd (US) nɑːrd
nares ˈneə.riːz (US) ˈner.iːz
Nares neəz (US) nerz
narghile, nargileh ˈnɑː.gɪ.leɪ, -gə-, -li (US) ˈnɑːr.gə- **-s** -z
nark nɑːk (US) nɑːrk **-s** -s **-ing** -ɪŋ **-ed** -t
nark|y ˈnɑː.k|i (US) ˈnɑːr- **-ier** -i.əʳ (US) -i.ɚ **-iest** -i.ɪst, -i.əst
Narnia ˈnɑː.ni.ə (US) ˈnɑːr-
Narragansett ˌnær.əˈgæn.sɪt (US) ˌnær-, ˌner-
narra|te nəˈreɪ|t, nærˈeɪ|t (US) ˈner.eɪ|t, ˈnær-; nəˈreɪ|t, nærˈeɪ|t **-tes** -ts **-ting** -tɪŋ (US) -t̬ɪŋ **-ted** -tɪd (US) -t̬ɪd
narration nəˈreɪ.ʃən, nærˈeɪ- (US) nerˈeɪ-, nær- **-s** -z
narrative ˈnær.ə.tɪv (US) ˈner.ə.t̬ɪv, ˈnær- **-s** -z
narrator nəˈreɪ.təʳ, nærˈeɪ- (US) ˈner.eɪ.t̬ɚ, ˈnær-; nəˈreɪ-, nærˈeɪ- **-s** -z
narrow ˈnær.əʊ (US) ˈner.oʊ, ˈnær- **-s** -z **-er** -əʳ (US) -ɚ **-est** -ɪst, -əst **-ly** -li **-ness** -nəs, -nɪs **-ing** -ɪŋ **-ed** -d **ˈnarrow ˌboat**; **ˌnarrow ˈgauge** *stress shift:* ˌnarrow gauge ˈrailway
narrowcast ˈnær.əʊˌkɑːst (US) ˈner.oʊˌkæst, ˈnær- **-s** -s **-ing** -ɪŋ **-ed** -ɪd **-er/s** -əʳ/z (US) -ɚ/z
narrow-minded ˌnær.əʊˈmaɪn.dɪd (US) ˌner.oʊˈ-, ˌnær- **-ly** -li **-ness** -nəs, -nɪs *stress shift:* ˌnarrow-minded ˈperson
narw(h)al ˈnɑː.wəl (US) ˈnɑːr- **-s** -z
nary ˈneə.ri (US) ˈner.i
NASA ˈnæs.ə
nasal ˈneɪ.zəl **-s** -z **-ly** -i
nasalism ˈneɪ.zəl.ɪ.zəm
nasality neɪˈzæl.ə.ti, nə-, -ɪ.ti (US) neɪˈzæl.ə.t̬i
nasalization, -isa- ˌneɪ.zəl.aɪˈzeɪ.ʃən, -ɪˈ- (US) -ɪˈ- **-s** -z
nasaliz|e, -is|e ˈneɪ.zəl.aɪz **-es** -ɪz **-ing** -ɪŋ **-ed** -d
Nasby ˈnæz.bi
nascen|t ˈnæs.ən|t, ˈneɪ.sən|t **-ce** -*t*s **-cy** -*t*.si
Naseby ˈneɪz.bi
Nash(e) næʃ
Nashville ˈnæʃ.vɪl *locally:* -vəl
nasi goreng ˌnɑː.si.gəˈreŋ, -zi-, ˌnæs.i-
Nasmyth *name:* ˈneɪz.mɪθ, ˈneɪ.smɪθ, ˈnæz.mɪθ, ˈnæs- *in US:* ˈneɪ.smɪθ
nasopharyngeal ˌneɪ.zəʊ.fær.ɪnˈdʒiː.əl, -ən-; -fərˈɪn.dʒi.əl, -færˈ- (US) -zoʊ.fəˈrɪn- *stress shift:* ˌnasopharyngeal ˈport
nasopharynx ˌneɪ.zəʊˈfær.ɪŋks (US) -zoʊˈfer-, -ˈfær-
Nassau *in Bahamas and US:* ˈnæs.ɔː (US) -ɑː, -ɑː *German province:* ˈnæs.aʊ (US) ˈnɑː.saʊ *princely family:* ˈnæs.ɔː, -aʊ (US) ˈnɑː.saʊ
Nasser ˈnæs.əʳ, ˈnɑː.səʳ (US) ˈnæs.ɚ, ˈnɑː.sɚ
Nastase næsˈtɑː.zi, nəˈstɑː-, -zeɪ
nasturtium nəˈstɜː.ʃəm (US) -ˈstɜːr-, næsˈtɜːr- **-s** -z
nast|y ˈnɑː.st|i (US) ˈnæs.t|i **-ies** -iz **-ier** -i.əʳ (US) -i.ɚ **-iest** -i.ɪst, -i.əst **-ily** -ɪ.li, -əl.i **-iness** -ɪ.nəs, -ɪ.nɪs
natal *(adj.)* ˈneɪ.təl (US) -t̬əl
Natal nəˈtæl, -tɑːl
Natalie ˈnæt.əl.i (US) ˈnæt̬-
Natasha nəˈtæʃ.ə
natation nəˈteɪ.ʃən, neɪ- (US) neɪ-, nætˈeɪ-
natch nætʃ
NATFHE ˈnæt.fiː
Nathan ˈneɪ.θən, -θæn (US) -θən
Nathaniel nəˈθæn.jəl
nation ˈneɪ.ʃən **-s** -z
national ˈnæʃ.ən.əl, ˈnæʃ.nəl **-ly** -i **ˌnational ˈanthem**; **ˌnational curˈriculum**; **ˌnational ˈdebt**; **ˌNational ˈFront**; **ˌNational ˈGuard**; **ˌNational ˈHealth ˌService**; **ˌnational ˈpark**; **ˌnational seˈcurity**; **ˌnational ˈservice**; **ˌNational ˈTrust**
national|ism ˈnæʃ.ən.əl|.ɪ.zəm, ˈnæʃ.nəl- **-ist/s** -ɪst/s
nationalistic ˌnæʃ.ən.əlˈɪs.tɪk, ˌnæʃ.nəlˈ- **-ally** -əl.i, -li
nationalit|y ˌnæʃ.ənˈæl.ə.t|i, ˌnæʃˈnæl-, -ɪ.t|i **-ies** -iz
nationalization, -isa- ˌnæʃ.ən.əl.aɪˈzeɪ.ʃən, ˌnæʃ.nəl-, -ɪˈ- (US) -ɪˈ-
nationaliz|e, -is|e ˈnæʃ.ən.əl.aɪz, ˈnæʃ.nəl- **-es** -ɪz **-ing** -ɪŋ **-ed** -d
nation-state ˌneɪ.ʃənˈsteɪt (US) ˈ--- **-s** -s
nationwide® ˌneɪ.ʃənˈwaɪd *stress shift:* ˌnationwide ˈsearch
native ˈneɪ.tɪv (US) -t̬ɪv **-s** -z **-ly** -li **ˌNative Aˈmerican**; **ˌnative ˈspeaker**
nativit|y (N) nəˈtɪv.ə.t|i, -ɪ.t|i (US) -ə.t̬|i **-ies** -iz **naˈtivity ˌplay**
NATO, Nato ˈneɪ.təʊ (US) -t̬oʊ
natron ˈneɪ.trən, -trɒn (US) -trɑːn
NATSOPA nætˈsəʊ.pə (US) -ˈsoʊ-
natt|er ˈnæt|.əʳ (US) ˈnæt̬|.ɚ **-ers** -əz (US) -ɚz **-ering** -ər.ɪŋ (US) -ɚ.ɪŋ **-ered** -əd (US) -ɚd **-erer/s** -ər.əʳ/z, -ɚ.ɚ/z
natterjack ˈnæt.ə.dʒæk (US) ˈnæt̬.ɚ- **-s** -s
natt|y ˈnæt|.i (US) ˈnæt̬|.i **-ier** -i.əʳ (US) -i.ɚ **-iest** -i.ɪst, -i.əst **-ily** -ɪ.li, -əl.i **-iness** -ɪ.nəs, -ɪ.nɪs
natural ˈnætʃ.ər.əl, -ʊ.rəl (US) -ɚ.əl, ˈ-rəl **-s** -z **-ly** -i **-ness** -nəs, -nɪs **ˌnatural ˈchildbirth**; **ˌnatural ˈgas**; **ˌnatural ˈhistory**; **ˌnatural reˈsources** (US) **ˌnatural ˈresources**; **ˌnatural seˈlection**
natural|ism ˈnætʃ.ər.əl|.ɪ.zəm, -ʊr- (US) -ɚ.əl-, ˈ-rəl- **-ist/s** -ɪst/s
naturalistic ˌnætʃ.ər.əlˈɪs.tɪk, -ʊr- (US) -ɚ.əlˈ-, ˌ-rəlˈ- **-ally** -əl.i, -li
naturalization, -isa- ˌnætʃ.ər.əl.aɪˈzeɪ.ʃən, -ʊr-, -ɪˈ- (US) -ɚ.əl.ɪˈ-, ˌ-rəl-
naturaliz|e, -is|e ˈnætʃ.ər.əl.aɪz, -ʊr- (US) -ɚ.əl-, ˈ-rəl- **-es** -ɪz **-ing** -ɪŋ **-ed** -d
nature ˈneɪ.tʃəʳ (US) -tʃɚ **-s** -z **-d** -d **ˈnature reˌserve**
natur|ism ˈneɪ.tʃər|.ɪ.zəm **-ist/s** -ɪst/s
naturopath ˈneɪ.tʃər.əʊ.pæθ, -tʃʊr-, ˈnætʃ.ər-, -ʊr- (US) ˈneɪ.tʃɚ.ə- **-s** -s
naturopathic ˌneɪ.tʃər.əʊˈpæθ.ɪk, -tʃʊr-, ˌnætʃ.ər- (US) ˌneɪ.tʃɚ.əˈ- **-ally** -əl.i, -li
naturopathy ˌneɪ.tʃərˈɒp.ə.θi, -tʃʊr-, ˌnætʃ.ərˈ-, -ʊrˈ- (US) ˌneɪ.tʃəˈrɑː.pə-
NatWest® ˌnætˈwest *stress shift:* ˌNatWestˈ Bank
Naugahyde® ˈnɔː.gə.haɪd (US) ˈnɑː.gə-, ˈnɔː-
naught nɔːt (US) nɑːt, nɔːt **-s** -s
Naughtie ˈnɒx.ti (US) ˈnɑːk-, ˈnɑːx-
naught|y ˈnɔː.t|i (US) ˈnɑː.t̬|i, ˈnɔː- **-ier** -i.əʳ (US) -i.ɚ **-iest** -i.ɪst, -i.əst **-ily** -ɪ.li, -əl.i **-iness** -ɪ.nəs, -ɪ.nɪs
Nauru nɑːˈuː.ruː; naʊˈruː, nɑː-, ˈ-- (US) nɑːˈuː.ruː
Nauruan nɑːˈuː.ruː.ən; naʊˈruː-, nɑː- (US) nɑːˈuː.ruː- **-s** -z
nausea ˈnɔː.si.ə, -zi-, ˈ-ʒə (US) ˈnɑː.zi.ə, ˈnɔː-, ˈ-ʒə, ˈ-ʃə, ˈ-si.ə
nause|ate ˈnɔː.si|.eɪt, -zi-, ˈ-ʒ|eɪt (US) ˈnɑː.zi-, ˈnɔː-, -ʒi-, -ʃi-, -si- **-ates** -eɪts **-ating** -eɪ.tɪŋ (US) -eɪ.t̬ɪŋ **-ated** -eɪ.tɪd (US) -eɪ.t̬ɪd
nauseating ˈnɔː.si.eɪ.tɪŋ, -zi- (US) ˈnɑː.zi-, ˈnɔː-, -ʒi-, -ʃi-, -si- **-ly** -li
nauseous ˈnɔː.si.əs, -zi-, ˈ-ʃəs, ˈ-ʒəs (US) ˈnɑː.ʃəs, ˈnɔː-, ˈ-zi.əs **-ly** -li **-ness** -nəs, -nɪs
Nausicaa, Nausicaä nɔːˈsɪk.i.ə, -eɪ.ə (US) nɑː-, nɔː-
nautch nɔːtʃ (US) nɑːtʃ, nɔːtʃ **-es** -ɪz
nautic|al ˈnɔː.tɪ.k|əl (US) ˈnɑː.t̬i-, ˈnɔː- **-ally** -əl.i **ˌnautical ˈmile**

nautil|us 'nɔː.tɪ.l|əs, '-tᵊl- ⓊⓈ 'nɑː.t̬ɪ-, 'nɔː- **-uses** -ə.sɪz **-i** -aɪ, -iː
Navajo, Navaho 'næv.ə.həʊ ⓊⓈ -hoʊ, 'nɑː.və- **-s** -z
naval 'neɪ.vᵊl
Navan 'neɪ.vᵊn
navarin 'næv.ᵊr.ɪn **-s** -z
Navarino ˌnæv.ᵊr'iː.nəʊ ⓊⓈ -ə'riː.noʊ
Navarre nə'vɑːʳ ⓊⓈ -'vɑːr
nave neɪv **-s** -z
navel 'neɪ.vᵊl **-s** -z
navicular nə'vɪk.jə.ləʳ, -jʊ- ⓊⓈ -lɚ
navigability ˌnæv.ɪ.gə'bɪl.ə.ti, -ɪ.ti ⓊⓈ -ə.t̬i
navigable 'næv.ɪ.gə.bl̩ **-ness** -nəs, -nɪs
navi|gate 'næv.ɪ|.geɪt **-gates** -geɪts **-gating** -geɪ.tɪŋ ⓊⓈ -geɪ.t̬ɪŋ **-gated** -geɪ.tɪd ⓊⓈ -geɪ.t̬ɪd
navigation ˌnæv.ɪ'geɪ.ʃᵊn **-al** -ᵊl **-ally**
navigator 'næv.ɪ.geɪ.təʳ ⓊⓈ -t̬ɚ **-s** -z
Navratilova næv.ræt.ɪ'ləʊ.və, ˌnæv.rə- ⓊⓈ ˌnæv.rə.tɪ'loʊ.və, ˌnɑːv-
navv|y 'næv|.i **-ies** -iz
nav|y 'neɪ.v|i **-ies** -iz ˌ**navy 'blue**
nawab (N) nə'wɑːb ⓊⓈ -'wɑːb, -'wɔːb **-s** -z
Nawanagar nə'wɑː.nə.gəʳ ⓊⓈ ˌnɑː.wə'nʌg.ɚ; nə'wɑː.nə.gɚ
Naxos 'næk.sɒs ⓊⓈ -sɑːs, -soʊs
nay neɪ **-s**
Nayarit 'nɑː.jɑː.rɪt
Naylor 'neɪ.ləʳ ⓊⓈ -lɚ
naysayer 'neɪˌseɪ.əʳ ⓊⓈ -ɚ **-s** -z
Nazarene ˌnæz.ᵊr'iːn, '--- ⓊⓈ ˌnæz.ə'riːn, '--- **-s** -z
Nazareth 'næz.ᵊr.əθ, -ɪθ
Nazarite 'næz.ᵊr.aɪt ⓊⓈ -ə.raɪt **-s** -s
Naze neɪz
Nazeing 'neɪ.zɪŋ
nazi (N) 'nɑːt.si ⓊⓈ 'nɑːt-, 'næt- **-s** -z
nazism (N) 'nɑːt.sɪ.zᵊm ⓊⓈ 'nɑːt-, 'næt-
NB ˌen'biː; ˌnəʊ.tə'biː.ni, -tɑː'ben.eɪ ⓊⓈ ˌen'biː; ˌnoʊ.t̬ə'ben.eɪ, -tɑː'-, -'biː.ni
NBA ˌen.biː'eɪ, ˌem- ⓊⓈ ˌen-
NBC ˌen.biː'siː, ˌem- ⓊⓈ ˌen-
N.C. ˌen'siː
NCO ˌen.siː'əʊ ⓊⓈ -'oʊ **-s** -z
NCT ˌen.siː'tiː
N.D. ˌen'diː
Ndebele ᵊn.dɪ'bel.i, -də'-, -'beɪ.li, -'biː-, -leɪ ⓊⓈ ᵊn.də'bel.eɪ, -'biː.li **-s** -z
N'Djamena ᵊn.dʒɑː'meɪ.nə, -dʒæm'eɪ- ⓊⓈ -'dʒɑː.mə-
Ndola ᵊn'dəʊ.lə ⓊⓈ -'doʊ-
NE (*abbrev. for* **northeast**) ˌen'iː, ˌnɔːθ'iːst ⓊⓈ ˌen'iː, ˌnɔːrθ'iːst
Neagh neɪ
Neagle 'niː.gl̩
Neal(e) niːl
Neanderthal ni'æn.də.tɑːl, -θɔːl, -tᵊl ⓊⓈ -dɚ.θɔːl, -tɑːl
neap niːp **-s** -s
Neapolis ni'æp.ə.lɪs
neapolitan (N) ˌniː.ə'pɒl.ɪ.tᵊn, nɪə'-, '-ə- ⓊⓈ ˌniː.ə'pɑː.lə- **-s** -z
near nɪəʳ ⓊⓈ nɪr **-er** -əʳ ⓊⓈ -ɚ **-est** -ɪst, -əst **-ness** -nəs, -nɪs **-s** -z **-ing** -ɪŋ **-ed** -d ˌ**Near 'East** ; ˌ**near 'miss** ; ˌ**nearest and 'dearest**
nearby ˌnɪə'baɪ ⓊⓈ ˌnɪr- *stress shift:* ˌnearby 'town
nearly 'nɪə.li ⓊⓈ 'nɪr-
nearside ˌnɪə'saɪd ⓊⓈ ˌnɪr- *stress shift:* ˌnearside 'lane
nearsighted ˌnɪə'saɪ.tɪd ⓊⓈ ˌnɪr'saɪ.t̬ɪd **-ness** -nəs, -nɪs *stress shift:* ˌnearsighted 'vision
Neasden 'niːz.dən
neat niːt **-er** -əʳ ⓊⓈ 'niː.t̬ɚ **-est** -ɪst, -əst ⓊⓈ 'niː.t̬ɪst, -t̬əst **-ly** -li **-ness** -nəs, -nɪs
neaten 'niː.tᵊn **-s** -z **-ing** -ɪŋ **-ed** -d
'neath niːθ
Neath niːθ
Nebo 'niː.bəʊ ⓊⓈ -boʊ
Nebr. (*abbrev. for* **Nebraska**) nɪ'bræs.kə, neb'ræs-, nə'bræs- ⓊⓈ nə'bræs-
Nebrask|a nɪ'bræs.k|ə, neb'ræs-, nə'bræs- ⓊⓈ nə'bræs- **-an** -ən
Nebuchadnezzar ˌneb.jə.kəd'nez.əʳ, -jʊ- ⓊⓈ -ə.kəd'nez.ɚ, ˌneb.jə-
nebul|a 'neb.jə.l|ə, -jʊ- ⓊⓈ -jə- **-ae** -iː **-as** -əz **-ar** -əʳ ⓊⓈ -ɚ **-ous** -əs
nebuliz|e, -is|e 'neb.jə.laɪz, -jʊ- ⓊⓈ -jə- **-es** -ɪs **-ing** -ɪŋ **-ed** -d **-er/s** -əʳ/z ⓊⓈ -ɚ/z
nebulosity ˌneb.jə'lɒs.ə.ti, -jʊ'-, -ɪ.ti ⓊⓈ -jə'lɑː.sə.t̬i
nebulous 'neb.jə.ləs, -jʊ- **-ly** -li **-ness** -nəs, -nɪs
NEC ˌen.iː'siː
necessarily 'nes.ə.sᵊr.ᵊl.i, '-ɪ-, -ɪ.li; ˌnes.ə'ser-, -ɪ'- ⓊⓈ ˌnes.ə'ser-; 'nes.ə.ser-
necessar|y 'nes.ə.sᵊr|.i, '-ɪ-, -ser- ⓊⓈ -ser- **-ies** -iz **-iness** -ɪ.nəs, -ɪ.nɪs
necessi|tate nə'ses.ɪ|.teɪt, nɪ-, '-ə- ⓊⓈ nə- **-tates** -teɪts **-tating** -teɪ.tɪŋ ⓊⓈ -teɪ.t̬ɪŋ **-tated** -teɪ.tɪd ⓊⓈ -teɪ.t̬ɪd
necessitous nə'ses.ɪ.təs, nɪ-, '-ə- ⓊⓈ nə'ses.ə.t̬əs **-ly** -li **-ness** -nəs, -nɪs
necessit|y nə'ses.ə.t|i, nɪ-, -ɪ.t|i ⓊⓈ nə'ses.ə.t̬|i **-ies** -iz
neck nek **-s** -s **-ing** -ɪŋ **-ed** -t ˌ**neck and 'neck** ; ˌ**neck of the 'woods**; ˌ**pain in the 'neck**; ˌ**up to one's 'neck**
Neckar 'nek.əʳ *as if German:* -ɑːʳ ⓊⓈ -ɚ *as if German:* -ɑːr
neckband 'nek.bænd **-s** -z
neck|cloth 'nek|.klɒθ ⓊⓈ -klɑːθ **-cloths** -klɒθs, -klɒðz ⓊⓈ -klɑːθs, -klɑːðz
necker|chief 'nek.ə|.tʃɪf, -tʃiːf ⓊⓈ '-ɚ- **-chiefs** -tʃɪfs **-chieves** -tʃiːvz
necklac|e 'nek.ləs, -lɪs **-es** -ɪz **-ing** -ɪŋ **-ed** -t
necklet 'nek.lət, -lɪt **-s** -s
neckline 'nek.laɪn **-s** -z
necktie 'nek.taɪ **-s** -z
neckwear 'nek.weəʳ ⓊⓈ -wer
necro- nek.rəʊ-; nek'rɒ- ⓊⓈ nek.roʊ-, -rə-; nek'rɑː-, nə'krɑː-
Note: Prefix. Normally takes either primary or secondary stress on the first syllable, e.g. **necrophile** /'nek.rəʊ.faɪl ⓊⓈ -rə-/, **necrophilia** /ˌnek.rəʊ'fɪl.i.ə ⓊⓈ -ə'-/, or primary stress on the second syllable, e.g. **necrology** /nek'rɒl.ə.dʒi ⓊⓈ -'rɑː.lə-/.
necrolatry nek'rɒl.ə.tri ⓊⓈ -'rɑː.lə-, nə'krɑː-
necrological ˌnek.rə'lɒdʒ.ɪ.kᵊl ⓊⓈ -'lɑː.dʒɪ-
necrolog|y nek'rɒl.ə.dʒ|i ⓊⓈ -'rɑː.lə-, nə'krɑː- **-ies** -iz **-ist/s** -ɪst/s
necromanc|er 'nek.rəʊ.mænt.s|əʳ ⓊⓈ -rə.mænt.s|ɚ **-ers** -əz ⓊⓈ -ɚz **-y** -i
necromantic ˌnek.rəʊ'mæn.tɪk ⓊⓈ -rə- **-ally** -ᵊl.i, -li
necrophile 'nek.rəʊ.faɪl ⓊⓈ -rə- **-s** -z
necrophili|a ˌnek.rəʊ'fɪl.i|.ə ⓊⓈ -ə'-, -'fɪl.i|.ə, -'fiːl.j|ə **-ac/s** -æk/s
necrophilism nek'rɒf.ɪ.lɪ.zᵊm, nɪ'krɒf-, '-ə- ⓊⓈ nek'rɑː.fə-, nə'krɑː-
necropol|is nek'rɒp.ᵊl|.ɪs, nɪ'krɒp- ⓊⓈ nek'rɑː-, nə'krɑː- **-ises** -ɪ.sɪz **-i** -aɪ
necrops|y 'nek.rɒp.s|i ⓊⓈ -rɑːp- **-ies** -iz
necrosis nek'rəʊ.sɪs, nɪ'krəʊ- ⓊⓈ nek'roʊ-, nə'kroʊ- **-es**
nectar 'nek.təʳ ⓊⓈ -tɚ **-ous** -əs
nectarial nek'teə.ri.ᵊl ⓊⓈ -'ter.i-
nectarine 'nek.tᵊr.iːn, -ɪn ⓊⓈ ˌnek.tə'riːn, '--- **-s** -z
nectar|y 'nek.tᵊr|.i **-ies** -iz
Ned ned
Nedd|y 'ned|.i **-ies** -iz
Neden 'niː.dᵊn
née, nee neɪ
need niːd **-s** -z **-ing** -ɪŋ **-ed** -ɪd
needful 'niːd.fᵊl, -fʊl **-ly** -i **-ness** -nəs, -nɪs
Needham 'niː.dəm
needl|e (N) 'niː.dl̩ **-es** -z **-ing** -ɪŋ, 'niːd.lɪŋ **-ed** -d
needlecord 'niː.dl̩.kɔːd ⓊⓈ -kɔːrd
needlecraft 'niː.dl̩.krɑːft ⓊⓈ -kræft **-s** -s
needlepoint 'niː.dl̩.pɔɪnt

needless 'niːd.ləs, -lɪs **-ly** -li **-ness** -nəs, -nɪs
needle|woman 'niː.dl̩ˌwʊm.ən **-women** -ˌwɪm.ɪn
needlework 'niː.dl̩.wɜːk (US) -wɜːrk
needn't 'niː.dᵊnt
needs (N) niːdz
need|y 'niː.d|i **-ier** -i.əʳ (US) -i.ɚ **-iest** -i.ɪst, -i.əst **-ily** -ɪ.li, -ᵊl.i **-iness** -ɪ.nəs, -ɪ.nɪs
neep niːp **-s** -s
ne'er neəʳ (US) ner
ne'er-do-well 'neə.duˌwel (US) 'ner- **-s** -z
Neeson 'niː.sᵊn
nefarious nɪ'feə.ri.əs, nə-, nef'eə- (US) nə'fer.i- **-ly** -li **-ness** -nəs, -nɪs
Nefertiti ˌnef.ə'tiː.ti (US) -ɚ'-
Neff® nef
neg. (*abbrev. for* **negative**) neg, 'neg.ə.tɪv (US) neg, 'neg.ə.t̬ɪv
nega|te nɪ'geɪ|t, nə-, neg'eɪ|t (US) nɪ'geɪ|t **-tes** -ts **-ting** -tɪŋ (US) -t̬ɪŋ **-ted** -tɪd (US) -t̬ɪd
negation nɪ'geɪ.ʃᵊn, nə-, neg'eɪ- (US) nɪ'geɪ- **-s** -z
negativ|e 'neg.ə.tɪv (US) -t̬ɪv **-es** -z **-ely** -li **-eness** -nəs, -nɪs **-ing** -ɪŋ **-ed** -d ˌ**negative 'feedback**
negativ|ism 'neg.ə.tɪ.v|ɪ.zᵊm (US) -t̬ɪ- **-ist/s** -ɪst/s
negativity ˌneg.ə'tɪv.ə.ti, -ɪ.ti (US) -ə.t̬i
Negeb 'neg.eb
Negev 'neg.ev
neglect nɪ'glekt, nə- (US) nɪ- **-s** -s **-ing** -ɪŋ **-ed** -ɪd
neglectful nɪ'glekt.fᵊl, nə-, -fʊl (US) nɪ- **-ly** -i **-ness** -nəs, -nɪs
negligé(s), negligee(s) 'neg.lɪ.ʒeɪ, -lə-, -liː-, ˌ--'- (US) ˌneg.lə'ʒeɪ, '---
negligenc|e 'neg.lɪ.dʒənts, -lə- **-es** -ɪz
negligent 'neg.lɪ.dʒənt, -lə- **-ly** -li
negligibility ˌneg.lɪ.dʒə'bɪl.ə.ti, -lə-, -ɪ.ti (US) -t̬i
negligi|ble 'neg.lɪ.dʒə|bl̩, -lə-, -dʒɪ- (US) -dʒə- **-bly** -bli
negotiability nɪˌgəʊ.ʃi.ə'bɪl.ə.ti, nə-, ˌ-ʃə'-, -ɪ.ti (US) nɪˌgoʊ.ʃi.ə'bɪl.ə.t̬i, ˌ-ʃə'-
negotiable nɪ'gəʊ.ʃi.ə.bl̩, nə-, '-ʃə- (US) nɪ'goʊ.ʃi.ə-, '-ʃə-
negoti|ate nɪ'gəʊ.ʃi|.eɪt, nə-, -si- (US) nɪ'goʊ- **-ates** -eɪts **-ating** -eɪ.tɪŋ (US) -eɪ.t̬ɪŋ **-ated** -eɪ.tɪd (US) -eɪ.t̬ɪd **ne'gotiating ˌtable**
negotiation nɪˌgəʊ.ʃi'eɪ.ʃᵊn, nə-, -si'- (US) nɪˌgoʊ- **-s** -z
negotiator nɪ'gəʊ.ʃi.eɪ.təʳ, nə-, -si- (US) nɪ'goʊ.ʃi.eɪ.t̬ɚ, -si- **-s** -z
negotiatory nɪ'gəʊ.ʃi.eɪ.tᵊr.i, nə-, -si- (US) nɪ'goʊ.ʃi.eɪ.t̬ɚ-

negress (N) 'niː.grəs, -grɪs, -gres (US) -grɪs **-es** -ɪz
Negrillo nɪ'grɪl.əʊ, nə-, neg'rɪl- (US) nə'grɪl.oʊ **-(e)s** -z
Negrito nɪ'griː.təʊ, nə-, neg'riː- (US) nə'griː.t̬oʊ **-(e)s** -z
negritude 'neg.rɪ.tjuːd, 'niː.grɪ-, -grə- (US) -tuːd, -tjuːd
negro (N) *person:* 'niː.grəʊ (US) -groʊ **-es** -z
Negro *river:* 'neɪ.grəʊ, 'neg.rəʊ (US) 'neɪ.groʊ
negroid 'niː.grɔɪd
negus (N) 'niː.gəs **-es** -ɪz
Nehemiah ˌniː.*h*ɪ'maɪ.ə, ˌneɪ-, -*h*ə'- (US) ˌniː.ə'-, -hɪ'-
Nehru 'neə.ruː (US) 'neɪ-
neigh neɪ **-s** -z **-ing** -ɪŋ **-ed** -d
neighb|o(u)r 'neɪ.b|əʳ (US) -bɚ **-o(u)rs** -əz (US) -ɚz **-o(u)ring** -ᵊr.ɪŋ
neighbo(u)rhood 'neɪ.bə.hʊd (US) -bɚ- **-s** -z ˌ**neighbourhood 'watch**
neighbo(u)ring 'neɪ.bᵊr.ɪŋ
neighbo(u)rl|y 'neɪ.bᵊl|.i (US) -bɚ.l|i **-iness** -ɪ.nəs, -ɪ.nɪs
Neil(l) niːl
Neilson 'niːl.sᵊn
Neisse 'naɪ.sə
neither 'naɪ.ðəʳ, 'niː- (US) 'niː.ðɚ, 'naɪ-
nekton 'nek.tən (US) -tɑːn, -tən
Nell nel
Nellie 'nel.i
nelly (N) 'nel.i
Nelson 'nel.sᵊn
Nelsonian nel'səʊ.ni.ən (US) -'soʊ-
nematode 'nem.ə.təʊd (US) -toʊd **-s** -z
Nembutal® 'nem.bjə.tæl, -bjʊ-, -tɑːl (US) -bjə.tɑːl, -bjʊ-, -tɔːl
nem. con. ˌnem'kɒn (US) -'kɑːn
Neme|a nɪ'miː|.ə, nə-, nem'iː-; 'nem.i-, 'niː.mi- (US) 'niː.mi- **-an** -ən
nemesis (N) 'nem.ə.sɪs, '-ɪ- (US) '-ə- **nemeses** 'nem.ə.siːz
Nemo 'niː.məʊ (US) -moʊ
nemophila nə'mɒf.ɪ.lə, nɪ-, -ᵊl.ə (US) niː'mɑː.fᵊl.ə, nə- **-s** -z
Nen nen
Nene *river:* niːn, nen
nene *goose:* 'neɪ.neɪ
Nennius 'nen.i.əs
neo-, Neo- niː.*əʊ*-; ni'ɒ- (US) ni.oʊ-, -ə-; ni'ɑː-
Note: Prefix. Normally either takes primary or secondary stress on the first syllable, e.g. **neonate** /'niː.*əʊ*.neɪt (US) -oʊ-/, **neonatal** /ˌniː.*əʊ*'neɪ.tᵊl (US) -oʊ'neɪ.t̬ᵊl/, or primary stress on the second syllable, e.g. **neologize** /ni'ɒl.ə.dʒaɪz (US) -'ɑː.lə-/.
neoclassic ˌniː.əʊ'klæs.ɪk (US) -oʊ'- **-al** -ᵊl

neoclassic|ism ˌniː.əʊ'klæs.ɪ.s|ɪ.zᵊm (US) -oʊ'- **-ist/s** -ɪst/s
neocolonial|ism ˌniː.əʊ.kə'ləʊ.ni.ᵊl|.ɪ.zᵊm, '-njᵊl- (US) -oʊ.kə'loʊ- **-ist/s** -ɪst/s
neodymium ˌniː.əʊ'dɪm.i.əm (US) -oʊ'-
neoimpressionism ˌniː.əʊ.ɪm'preʃ.ᵊnɪ.zᵊm (US) -oʊ-
neoimpressionist ˌniː.əʊ.ɪm'preʃ.ᵊn.ɪst (US) -oʊ- **-s** -s
Neo-Latin ˌniː.əʊ'læt.ɪn (US) -oʊ'læt.ᵊn
neolithic (N) ˌniː.*əʊ*'lɪθ.ɪk (US) -oʊ'-, -ə'-
neolog|ism ni'ɒl.ə.dʒ|ɪ.zᵊm (US) -'ɑː.lə- **-isms** -ɪ.zᵊmz **-y** -i
neologiz|e, -is|e ni'ɒl.ə.dʒaɪz (US) -'ɑː.lə- **-es** -ɪz **-ing** -ɪŋ **-ed** -d
neon 'niː.ɒn (US) -ɑːn ˌ**neon 'light**
neonatal ˌniː.*əʊ*'neɪ.tᵊl (US) -oʊ'neɪ.t̬ᵊl, -ə'- **-ly** -i
neonate 'niː.*əʊ*.neɪt (US) -oʊ-, '-ə- **-s** -s
neophyte 'niː.*əʊ*.faɪt (US) -oʊ-, '-ə- **-s** -s
neoprene 'niː.*əʊ*.priːn (US) -oʊ-, '-ə-
Nepal nɪ'pɔːl, nə-, nep'ɔːl, -ɑːl (US) nə'pɔːl, -'pɑːl
Nepalese ˌnep.ᵊl'iːz, -ɔː'liːz (US) -ə'liːz, -'liːs
Nepali nɪ'pɔː.li, nə-, nep'ɔː-, -'ɑː- (US) nɪ'pɔː-, nep'ɔː-, -'ɑː- **-s** -z
nepenthe nɪ'pen*t*.θi, nə-, nep'en*t*- (US) nɪ'pen*t*-
nephew 'nef.juː, 'nev- (US) 'nef- **-s** -z
nephrite 'nef.raɪt
nephritic nɪ'frɪt.ɪk, nə-, nef'rɪt- (US) nɪ'frɪt̬-, nef'rɪt̬-
nephritis nɪ'fraɪ.tɪs, nə-, nef'raɪ- (US) nɪ'fraɪ.t̬əs, nef'raɪ-
Nephthys 'nef.tɪs (US) -θɪs
ne plus ultra ˌneɪ.plʊs'ʊl.trɑː, ˌniː-, -plʌs'-, -'ʌl-, -trə (US) -plʌs'ʌl.trə, -plʊs'-, -'ʊl-
Nepos 'niː.pɒs, 'nep.ɒs (US) 'niː.pɑːs, 'nep.ɑːs
nepotism 'nep.ə.tɪ.zᵊm, -ɒt.ɪ- (US) -ə.tɪ- **-ist/s** -ɪst/s
nepotistic nep.ə'tis.tik
Neptune 'nep.tjuːn, -tʃuːn (US) -tuːn, -tjuːn
neptunian (N) nep'tjuː.ni.ən, -'tʃuː- (US) -'tuː-, -'tjuː-
neptunium nep'tjuː.ni.əm, -'tʃuː- (US) -'tuː-, -'tjuː-
nerd nɜːd (US) nɜːrd **-s** -z **-y** -i
nereid (N) 'nɪə.ri.ɪd (US) 'nɪr.i- **-s** -z
Nereus 'nɪə.ri.uːs, -əs (US) 'nɪr.i.əs, '-juːs
Neri 'nɪə.ri (US) 'nɪr.i, 'ner-, 'neɪ.ri
Nero 'nɪə.rəʊ (US) 'nɪr.oʊ, 'niː.roʊ
nerv|e nɜːv (US) nɜːrv **-es** -z **-ing** -ɪŋ **-ed** -d **'nerve ˌcell** ; **'nerve ˌcentre** ; **'nerve ˌgas** ; ˌ**get on ˌsomeone's 'nerves**

nerveless 'nɜːv.ləs, -lɪs (US) 'nɜːrv- **-ly** -li **-ness** -nəs, -nɪs
nerve-racking, nerve-wracking 'nɜːvˌræk.ɪŋ (US) 'nɜːrv-
nerves nɜːvz (US) nɜːrvz
nervine 'nɜː.viːn (US) 'nɜːr-, -vaɪn
nervous 'nɜː.vəs (US) 'nɜːr- **-ly** -li **-ness** -nəs, -nɪs ˌ**nervous 'breakdown**; '**nervous ˌsystem**
nerv|y 'nɜː.v|i (US) 'nɜːr- **-ier** -i.əʳ (US) -i.ɚ **-iest** -i.ɪst, -i.əst **-ily** -ɪ.li, -əl.i **-iness** -ɪ.nəs, -ɪ.nɪs
Nesbit(t) 'nez.bɪt
Nescafé® 'nes.kə.feɪ, -kæf.eɪ (US) 'nes.kə.feɪ, -kæf.eɪ, ˌ--'-
nescien|ce 'nes.i.ən|*t*s (US) 'neʃ.ən|*t*s, '-i.ən|*t*s **-t** -t
Nesfield 'nes.fiːld
Nesquik® 'nes.kwɪk
ness (N) nes **-es** -ɪz
-ness *noun-forming suffix:* -nəs, -nɪs
Note: Suffix. When added to a stem to form a noun, **-ness** does not change the existing stress pattern, e.g. **happy** /'hæp.i/, **happiness** /'hæp.ɪ.nəs/.
-ness *in place names:* -'ness
Note: In place names, the suffix **-ness** normally takes primary stress, e.g. **Inverness** /ˌɪn.və'nes (US) -vɚ'-/. However, placenames containing **-ness** are subject to stress shift; see individual entries.
Nessie 'nes.i
nest nest **-s** -s **-ing** -ɪŋ **-ed** -ɪd '**nest ˌegg**
Nesta 'nes.tə
nestl|e 'nes.l̩ **-es** -z **-ing** -ɪŋ, 'nes.lɪŋ **-ed** -d
Nestlé® 'nes.leɪ, -li, -l̩ (US) 'nes.li
nestling 'nes*t*.lɪŋ **-s** -z
Neston 'nes.tən
Nestor 'nes.tɔːʳ, -təʳ (US) -tɚ, -tɔːr
Nestorian nes'tɔː.ri.ən (US) -'tɔːr.i- **-s** -z
net (N) net **-s** -s **-ting** -ɪŋ (US) 'neţ.ɪŋ **-ted** -ɪd (US) 'neţ.ɪd
Netanyahu ˌnet.ən'jɑː.hu, -æn'- (US) ˌnet.ɑːn'jɑː.hu, -ən'-
netball 'net.bɔːl (US) -bɔːl, -bɑːl
nether 'neð.əʳ (US) -ɚ **-most** -məʊst (US) -moʊst
Nether|land 'neð.ə|lənd, -əl|l.ənd (US) -ɚ|lənd **-lands** -ləndz **-lander/s** -lən.dəʳ/z (US) -lən.dɚ/z ˌNetherlands An'tilles
netherworld 'neð.ə.wɜːld (US) -ɚ.wɜːrld **-s** -z
Netley 'net.li
netsuke 'net.skeɪ, -ski, '-sʊ.ki, -keɪ (US) -sʊ.ki, -sə.keɪ **-s** -z
Nettie, Netty 'net.i (US) 'neţ-
netting 'net.ɪŋ (US) 'neţ-
nettl|e 'net.l̩ (US) 'neţ- **-es** -z **-ing** -ɪŋ, 'net.lɪŋ **-ed** -d '**nettle ˌrash**; ˌ**grasp the 'nettle**
Nettlefold 'net.l̩.fəʊld (US) 'neţ.l̩.foʊld
nettlerash 'net.l̩.ræʃ (US) 'neţ-
Nettleship 'net.l̩.ʃɪp (US) 'neţ-
nettlesome 'net.l̩.səm (US) 'neţ-
network 'net.wɜːk (US) -wɜːrk **-s** -s **-ing** -ɪŋ **-ed** -t
Neuchâtel ˌnɜː.ʃæt'el, -ʃə'tel; (US) ˌnuː.ʃə'tel, ˌnɜː-
Neufchâtel ˌnɜː.ʃæt'el, -ʃə'tel (US) ˌnuː.ʃə'tel, ˌnɜː-
neum(e) njuːm (US) nuːm, njuːm **-s** -z
neural 'njʊə.rəl, 'njɔː- (US) 'nʊr.əl, 'njʊr-, 'nɜːr- ˌ**neural 'network**
neuralg|ia njʊə'ræl.dʒ|ə, njɔː-, njər'æl-, njʊ'ræl- (US) nʊ'ræl-, njʊ-, nə- **-ic** -ɪk
neurasthenia ˌnjʊə.rəs'θiː.ni.ə, ˌnjɔː- (US) ˌnʊr.æs'-, ˌnjʊr-
neurasthenic ˌnjʊə.rəs'θen.ɪk, ˌnjɔː- (US) ˌnʊr.æs'-, ˌnjʊr- **-s** -s
neuritis njʊə'raɪ.tɪs, njɔː-, njər'aɪ-, njʊ'raɪ- (US) nʊ'raɪ.ţəs, njʊ-
neuro- ˌnjʊə.rəʊ-, ˌnjɔː-, njʊə'rɒ-, njɔː'- (US) ˌnʊr.oʊ-, ˌnjʊr-, ˌ-ə-
Note: Prefix. Normally either takes primary or secondary stress on the first syllable, e.g. **neuron** /'njʊə.rɒn (US) 'nʊr.ɑːn/, **neurological** /ˌnjʊə.rə'lɒdʒ.ɪk.əl (US) ˌnʊr.ə'lɑː.dʒɪ-/, or primary stress on the second syllable, e.g. **neurologist** /njʊə'rɒl.ə.dʒɪst (US) nʊ'rɑː.lə-/.
neurologi|cal ˌnjʊə.rə'lɒdʒ.ɪ.kəl, ˌnjɔː- (US) ˌnʊr.ə'lɑː.dʒɪ-, ˌnjʊr- **-cally** -kəl.i, -kli
neurolog|ist njʊə'rɒl.ə.dʒ|ɪst, njɔː-, njər'ɒl-, njʊ'rɒl- (US) nʊ'rɑː.lə-, njʊ- **-ists** -ɪst/s **-y** -i
neuron 'njʊə.rɒn, 'njɔː- (US) 'nʊr.ɑːn, 'njʊr- **-s** -z
neurone 'njʊə.rəʊn, 'njɔː- (US) 'nʊr.oʊn, 'njʊr- **-s** -z
neuroscien|ce ˌnjʊə.rəʊ'saɪ.ən|*t*s, ˌnjɔː-, 'njʊə.rəʊˌ-, 'njɔː- (US) ˌnʊr.oʊ'saɪ-, ˌnjʊr-, 'nʊr.oʊˌsaɪ-, 'njʊr- **-ces** -tsɪz **-tist/s** -tɪst/s
neuros|is njʊə'rəʊ.s|ɪs, njɔː-, njər'əʊ-, njʊ'rəʊ- (US) nʊ'roʊ-, njʊ-, nə- **-es** -iːz
neurosurgeon ˌnjʊə.rəʊ'sɜː.dʒən, ˌnjɔː-, 'njʊə.rəʊˌ-, 'njɔː- (US) ˌnʊr.oʊ'sɜːr-, ˌnjʊr- **-s** -z
neurosurg|ery ˌnjʊə.rəʊ'sɜː.dʒ|ər.i, ˌnjɔː- (US) ˌnʊr.oʊ'sɜːr-, ˌnjʊr- **-ical** -ɪ.kəl
neurotic njʊə'rɒt.ɪk, njɔː-, njər'ɒt-, njʊ'rɒt- (US) nʊ'rɑː.ţɪk, njʊ-, nə- **-s** -s **-ally** -əl.i, -li
neurotransmitter ˌnjʊə.rəʊ.trænz'mɪt.əʳ, '---ˌ--, ˌnjɔː- (US) ˌnʊr.oʊ.træn'smɪţ.ɚ, ˌnjʊr-, -trænz'mɪţ- **-s** -z
neut|er 'njuː.t|əʳ (US) 'nuː.ţ|ɚ, 'njuː- **-ers** -əz (US) -ɚz **-ering** -ər.ɪŋ **-ered** -əd (US) -ɚd
neutral 'njuː.trəl (US) 'nuː-, 'njuː- **-s** -z **-ly** -i **-ness** -nəs, -nɪs
neutralism 'njuː.trəl.ɪ.zəm (US) 'nuː-, 'njuː-
neutralist 'njuː.trəl.ɪst (US) 'nuː-, 'njuː- **-s** -s
neutrality njuː'træl.ə.ti, -ɪ.ti (US) nuː'træl.ə.ţi, njuː-
neutralization, -isa- ˌnjuː.trəl.aɪ'zeɪ.ʃən, -ɪ'- (US) ˌnuː.trəl.ɪ'-, ˌnjuː-
neutraliz|e, -is|e 'njuː.trəl.aɪz (US) 'nuː-, 'njuː- **-es** -ɪŋ **-ing** -ɪz **-ed** -d
neutrino njuː'triː.nəʊ (US) nuː'triː.noʊ, njuː- **-s** -z
neutron 'njuː.trɒn (US) 'nuː.trɑːn, 'njuː- **-s** -z '**neutron ˌbomb**
Nev. (*abbrev. for* **Nevada**) nə'vɑː.də, nɪ-, nev'ɑː- (US) nə'væd.ə, -'vɑː.də
Neva 'neɪ.və, 'niː- (US) 'niː-
Nevada nə'vɑː.də, nɪ-, nev'ɑː- (US) nə'væd.ə, -'vɑː.də
Neve niːv
névé 'nev.eɪ (US) neɪ'veɪ, '--
never 'nev.əʳ (US) -ɚ
never-ending ˌnev.ər'en.dɪŋ (US) '-ɚ-
nevermore ˌnev.ə'mɔːʳ (US) -ɚ'mɔːr
never-never ˌnev.ə'nev.əʳ (US) ˌ-ɚ'nev.ɚ **on the** ˌ**never-'never**; ˌ**never-'never ˌland**
nevertheless ˌnev.ə.ðə'les (US) ˌ-ɚ-
Nevey 'nev.i
Nevil 'nev.əl, -ɪl (US) -əl
Nevill(e) 'nev.əl, -ɪl (US) -əl
Nevin 'nev.ɪn
Nevinson 'nev.ɪn.sən
Nevis *in Scotland:* 'nev.ɪs *in West Indies:* 'niː.vɪs
nev|us 'niː.v|əs **-uses** -ə.sɪz **-i** -aɪ
new njuː (US) nuː, njuː **-er** -əʳ (US) -ɚ **-est** -ɪst, -əst **-ish** -ɪʃ **-ly** -li **-ness** -nəs, -nɪs ˌ**New 'Age** *stress shift:* ˌNew Age 'traveller; ˌ**new 'broom**; ˌ**New 'Brunswick**; ˌ**New Cale'donia**; ˌ**New 'Deal**; ˌ**New 'Delhi**; ˌ**New 'England** *stress shift:* ˌNew England 'coast; ˌ**New 'Forest** *stress shift:* ˌNew Forest 'ponies; ˌ**New 'Hampshire** *stress shift:* ˌNew Hampshire 'primary; ˌ**New 'Jersey** *stress shift:* ˌNew Jersey 'turnpike; ˌ**new 'man**; ˌ**New 'Mexico**; ˌ**New 'Quay** *stress shift:* ˌNew Quay 'harbour; ˌ**New ˌSouth 'Wales**; ˌ**New 'Testament**; ˌ**New 'Wave** *stress shift:* ˌNew Wave 'band; ˌ**New 'World** *stress shift:* ˌNew World

'Symphony; ˌ**New 'Year** *stress shift:* ˌNew Year 'party; ˌ**New ˌYear's 'Day**; ˌ**New ˌYear's 'Eve**
Newark 'njuː.ək (US) 'nuː.ɚk, 'njuː-
Newbery 'njuː.bᵊr.i (US) 'nuː.ber-, 'njuː-
Newbiggin *place:* 'njuː.bɪ.gɪn (US) 'nuː-, 'njuː- *surname:* 'njuː.bɪ.gɪn, -'bɪg.ɪn (US) 'nuː-, 'njuː-, -'bɪg.ɪn
Newbold 'njuː.bəʊld (US) 'nuː.boʊld, 'njuː-
Newbolt 'njuː.bəʊlt (US) 'nuː.boʊlt, 'njuː-
newborn ˌnjuː'bɔːn (US) 'nuː.bɔːrn, 'njuː- *stress shift, British only:* ˌnewborn 'baby
Newbridge 'njuː.brɪdʒ (US) 'nuː-, 'njuː-
Newburg(h) *in the UK:* 'njuː.bᵊr.ə (US) 'nuː-, 'njuː- *in the US:* 'njuː.bɜːg (US) 'nuː.bɜːrg, 'njuː-
Newburn 'njuː.bɜːn (US) 'nuː.bɜːrn, 'njuː-
Newbury 'njuː.bᵊr.i (US) 'nuː.ber-, 'njuː-, -bɚ-
Newby 'njuː.bi (US) 'nuː-, 'njuː-
Newcastle 'njuːˌkɑː.sl̩ (US) 'nuːˌkæs.l̩, 'njuː-
Newcastle-under-Lyme ˌnjuː.kɑː.sl̩ˌʌn.də'laɪm (US) ˌnuː.kæs.l̩ˌʌn.dɚ'-, ˌnjuː-
Newcastle upon Tyne ˌnjuː.kɑː.sl̩.ə.pɒn'taɪn (US) ˌnuː.kæs.l̩.ə.pɑːn-, ˌnjuː-
Note: /njuː'kæs.l̩/ is the local form.
Newcome 'njuː.kəm (US) 'nuː-, 'njuː- **-s** -z
newcomer 'njuːˌkʌm.əʳ (US) 'nuːˌkʌm.ɚ, 'njuː- **-s** -z
Newdigate 'njuː.dɪ.geɪt, -gɪt, -gət (US) 'nuː.dɪ.geɪt, 'njuː-, -gət
Newe njuː (US) nuː, njuː
newel 'njuː.əl (US) 'nuː.əl, 'njuː- **-s** -z **'newel ˌpost**
Newell 'njuː.əl (US) 'nuː.əl, 'njuː-
Newey 'njuː.i (US) 'nuː-, 'njuː-
newfangled ˌnjuː'fæŋ.gl̩d (US) ˌnuː-, ˌnjuː- *stress shift:* ˌnewfangled 'ways
new-fashioned ˌnjuː'fæʃ.ᵊnd (US) 'nuːˌfæʃ-, 'njuː-
new-found ˌnjuː'faʊnd (US) ˌnuː-, ˌnjuː- *stress shift:* ˌnew-found 'love
Newfoundland *place:* 'njuː.fᵊnd.lənd, -lænd; njuː'faʊnd-; ˌnjuː.fᵊnd'lænd (US) 'nuː.fənd.lənd, 'njuː-, -lænd; ˌnuː.faʊnd'lænd, ˌnjuː-; nuː'faʊnd.lənd, njuː-, -lænd **-er/s** -əʳ/z (US) -ɚ/z
Note: /ˌnjuː.fᵊnd'lænd/ is the local form; it is also the nautical pronunciation in England.
Newfoundland *dog:* njuː'faʊnd.lənd (US) 'nuː.fənd.lənd, 'njuː-, -lænd; nuː'faʊnd-, njuː- **-s** -z
Newgate 'njuː.geɪt, -gɪt, -gət (US) 'nuː.geɪt, 'njuː-
Newham 'njuː.əm; njuː'hæm (US) 'nuː.əm, 'njuː-; nuː'hæm, njuː-
Newhaven 'njuː.heɪ.vᵊn, -'-- (US) 'nuː.heɪ-, 'njuː-, -'--
Newington 'njuː.ɪŋ.tən (US) 'nuː-, 'njuː-
new-laid ˌnjuː'leɪd (US) ˌnuː-, ˌnjuː- *stress shift:* ˌnew-laid 'eggs
Newlands 'njuː.ləndz (US) 'nuː-, 'njuː-
newlywed 'njuː.li.wed (US) 'nuː-, 'njuː- **-s** -z
Newman 'njuː.mən (US) 'nuː-, 'njuː-
Newmarket 'njuː.mɑː.kɪt (US) 'nuː.mɑːr-, 'njuː-
Newnes njuːnz (US) nuːnz, njuːnz
Newnham 'njuː.nəm (US) 'nuː-, 'njuː-
New Orleans ˌnjuː'ɔː.li.ənz, '-lɪənz, '-lənz; -ɔː'liːnz (US) ˌnuː'ɔːr.li.ənz, ˌnjuː-, '-lənz; -ɔːr'liːnz
Newport 'njuː.pɔːt (US) 'nuː.pɔːrt, 'njuː-
Newport Pagnell ˌnjuː.pɔːt'pæg.nᵊl (US) ˌnuː.pɔːrt'-, ˌnjuː-
Newquay 'njuː.ki (US) 'nuː-, 'njuː-
New Rossington ˌnjuː'rɒs.ɪŋ.tən (US) ˌnuː'rɑː.sɪŋ-, ˌnjuː-
Newry 'njʊə.ri (US) 'nʊr.i, 'njʊr-
news njuːz (US) nuːz, njuːz **'news ˌagency**; **'news ˌconference**
newsagent 'njuːzˌeɪ.dʒᵊnt (US) 'nuːz-, 'njuːz- **-s** -s
newsboy 'njuːz.bɔɪ (US) 'nuːz-, 'njuːz- **-s** -z
newsbreak 'njuːz.breɪk (US) 'nuːz-, 'njuːz- **-s** -s
newscast 'njuːz.kɑːst (US) 'nuːz.kæst, 'njuːz- **-s** -s **-ing** -ɪŋ **-er/s** -əʳ/z (US) -ɚ/z
newscopy 'njuːzˌkɒp.i (US) 'nuːzˌkɑː.pi, 'njuːz-
newsflash 'njuːz.flæʃ (US) 'nuːz-, 'njuːz- **-es** -ɪz
newshound 'njuːz.haʊnd (US) 'nuːz-, 'njuːz- **-s** -z
newsletter 'njuːzˌlet.əʳ (US) 'nuːzˌlet̬.ɚ, 'njuːz- **-s** -z
news|man 'njuːz|.mən, -mæn (US) 'nuːz-, 'njuːz- **-men** -men, -mən
newsmonger 'njuːzˌmʌŋ.gəʳ (US) 'nuːzˌmʌŋ.gɚ, 'njuːz-, -ˌmɑːŋ- **-s** -z
newspaper 'njuːsˌpeɪ.pəʳ, 'njuːz- (US) 'nuːzˌpeɪ.pɚ, 'njuːz- **-s** -z
newspeak (N) 'njuː.spiːk (US) 'nuː-, 'njuː-
news|person 'njuːz|ˌpɜː.sᵊn (US) 'nuːz|ˌpɜːr-, 'njuːz- **-people** -ˌpiː.pl̩
newsprint 'njuːz.prɪnt (US) 'nuːz-, 'njuːz-
newsreader 'njuːzˌriː.dəʳ (US) 'nuːzˌriː.dɚ, 'njuːz- **-s** -z
newsreel 'njuːz.riːl (US) 'nuːz-, 'njuːz- **-s** -z
newsroom 'njuːz.rʊm, -ruːm (US) 'nuːz.ruːm, 'njuːz-, -rʊm **-s** -z
news-sheet 'njuːz.ʃiːt, 'njuːʒ- (US) 'nuːz-, 'njuːz- **-s** -z
newsstand 'njuːz.stænd (US) 'nuːz-, 'njuːz- **-s** -z
Newstead 'njuː.stɪd, -sted (US) 'nuː-, 'njuː-
newsvendor 'njuːzˌven.dəʳ (US) 'nuːzˌven.dɚ, 'njuːz- **-s** -z
news|woman 'njuːz|ˌwʊm.ən (US) 'nuːz-, 'njuːz- **-women** -ˌwɪm.ɪn
newsworthy 'njuːzˌwɜː.ði (US) 'nuːzˌwɜːr-, 'njuːz-
news|y 'njuː.z|i (US) 'nuː-, 'njuː- **-iness** -ɪ.nəs, -ɪ.nɪs
newt njuːt (US) nuːt, njuːt **-s** -s
New Testament ˌnjuː'tes.tə.mənt (US) ˌnuː-, ˌnjuː-
newton (N) 'njuː.tᵊn (US) 'nuː-, 'njuː-
Newtonian njuː'təʊ.ni.ən (US) nuː'toʊ-, njuː-
Newton-le-Willows ˌnjuː.tᵊn.li'wɪl.əʊz (US) ˌnuː.tᵊn.li'wɪl.oʊz, ˌnjuː-
Newtown 'njuː.taʊn (US) 'nuː-, 'njuː-
Newtownabbey ˌnjuː.tᵊn'æb.i (US) ˌnuː-, ˌnjuː-
Newtownards ˌnjuː.tᵊn'ɑːdz (US) ˌnuː.tᵊn'ɑːrdz, ˌnjuː-
Newtown St Boswells ˌnjuː.tᵊn.sᵊnt'bɒz.welz (US) ˌnuː.tᵊn.sᵊnt'bɑːz-, ˌnjuː-
New York ˌnjuː'jɔːk (US) ˌnuː'jɔːrk, ˌnjuː- **-er/s** -əʳ/z (US) -ɚ/z *stress shift, see compound:* ˌ**New York 'City**
New Zealand ˌnjuː'ziː.lənd (US) ˌnuː-, ˌnjuː- **-er/s** -əʳ/z (US) -ɚ/z
next nekst ˌ**next 'door** *stress shift:* ˌnext door 'neighbours; ˌ**next of 'kin**
nexus 'nek.səs **-es** -ɪz
Ngaio 'naɪ.əʊ *as if Maori:* 'ŋaɪ- (US) -oʊ
Ngami ᵊŋ'gɑː.mi (US) ᵊn-, ᵊŋ-
ngultrum ᵊŋ'guːl.trəm (US) -'ʊl.trʊm; ən'gʌl.trəm, əŋ- **-s** -z
ngwee ᵊŋ'gweɪ (US) -'gwiː
N.H. ˌen'eɪtʃ
NHS ˌen.eɪtʃ'es
NI ˌen'aɪ
niacin 'naɪə.sɪn
Niagara naɪ'æg.ᵊr.ə (US) '-rə, '-ɚ.ə Niˌagara 'Falls
Niall 'naɪ.əl, naɪl, niːl
Niamey ni'ɑː.meɪ; nɪə'meɪ (US) ni'ɑː.meɪ; njɑː'meɪ
Niamh niːv, nɪəv

nib nɪb **-s** -z
nibbl|e ˈnɪb.l̩ **-es** -z **-ing** -ɪŋ, ˈnɪb.lɪŋ **-ed** -d **-er/s** -əʳ/z ⓊⓈ -ɚ/z
Nibelung ˈniː.bə.lʊŋ, -bɪ- ⓊⓈ -bə- **-s** -z **-en** -ən
Nibelungenlied ˌniː.bəˈlʊŋ.ən.liːt, -ˌliːd
niblick ˈnɪb.lɪk **-s** -s
NiCad® ˈnaɪ.kæd
Nicaea naɪˈsiː.ə
NICAM ˈnaɪ.kæm
Nicaragu|a ˌnɪk.əˈræg.ju|.ə, -ˈɑː.gju-; -ˈɑː.gw|ə, -ˈæg.w|ə ⓊⓈ -əˈrɑː.gw|ə **-an/s** -ən/z
nic|e *(adj.)* naɪs **-er** -əʳ ⓊⓈ -ɚ **-est** -ɪst, -əst **-ely** -li **-eness** -nəs, -nɪs
Nice *in France:* niːs
nicely ˈnaɪs.li
Nicene ˈnaɪ.siːn, -ˈ- ˌ**Nicene ˈCreed**
nicet|y ˈnaɪ.sə.t|i, -sɪ- ⓊⓈ -sə.t̬|i **-ies** -iz
nich|e niːʃ ⓊⓈ nɪtʃ, niːʃ **-es** -ɪz **-ed** -t
Nicholas ˈnɪk.əl.əs
Nichol(l) ˈnɪk.əl **-s** -z
Nicholson ˈnɪk.əl.sən
nick (N) nɪk **-s** -s **-ing** -ɪŋ **-ed** -t **in the ˌnick of ˈtime**
nickel ˈnɪk.l̩ **-s** -z **-(l)ing** -ɪŋ **-(l)ed** -d
nickel-and-dime ˌnɪk.əl.ənˈdaɪm **-s** -z **-ing** -ɪŋ **-ed** -d
nickelodeon ˌnɪk.l̩ˈəʊ.di.ən ⓊⓈ -ˈoʊ- **-s** -z
nicker ˈnɪk.əʳ ⓊⓈ -ɚ
Nicklaus ˈnɪk.laʊs, -ləs ⓊⓈ -ləs
Nickleby ˈnɪk.l̩.bi
Nicklin ˈnɪk.lɪn
nicknack ˈnɪk.næk **-s** -s
nicknam|e ˈnɪk.neɪm **-es** -z **-ing** -ɪŋ **-ed** -d
Nicobar ˈnɪk.əʊ.bɑːʳ ⓊⓈ -oʊ.bɑːr, ˌ--ˈ-
Nicodemus ˌnɪk.əʊˈdiː.məs ⓊⓈ -əˈ-
nicoise, niçoise niːˈswɑːz, nɪ-
Nicol(l) ˈnɪk.əl **-s** -z
Nicola ˈnɪk.əl.ə
Nicolas ˈnɪk.əl.əs
Nicole nɪˈkəʊl, niː- ⓊⓈ -ˈkoʊl
Nicolson ˈnɪk.əl.sən
Nicomachean ˌnaɪ.kɒm.əˈkiː.ən, naɪˌkɒm- ⓊⓈ ˌnɪk.oʊ.məˈ-; ˌnaɪ.kɑː.məˈ-
Nicomachus naɪˈkɒm.ə.kəs ⓊⓈ nɪˈkɑː.mə.kəs; ˌnaɪ.koʊˈmæk.əs
Nicosia ˌnɪk.əʊˈsiː.ə ⓊⓈ -əˈ-, -oʊˈ-
nicotine ˈnɪk.ə.tiːn, ˌ--ˈ-
nic|tate ˈnɪk|.teɪt **-tates** -teɪts **-tating** -teɪ.tɪŋ ⓊⓈ -teɪ.t̬ɪŋ **-tated** -teɪ.tɪd ⓊⓈ -teɪ.t̬ɪd
nictation nɪkˈteɪ.ʃən
nicti|tate ˈnɪk.tɪ|.teɪt ⓊⓈ -tə- **-tates** -teɪts **-tating** -teɪ.tɪŋ ⓊⓈ -teɪ.t̬ɪŋ **-tated** -teɪ.tɪd ⓊⓈ -teɪ.t̬ɪd
nictitation ˌnɪk.tɪˈteɪ.ʃən ⓊⓈ -təˈ-
niec|e niːs **-es** -ɪz
Niedersachsen ˈniː.dəˌzæk.sən *as if German:* -ˌzæx- ⓊⓈ -dɚˌzɑːk-
Nielsen ˈniːl.sən
Niersteiner ˈnɪə.staɪ.nəʳ *as if German:* -ʃtaɪ- ⓊⓈ ˈnɪr.staɪ.nɚ *as if German:* -ʃtaɪ-
Nietzsche ˈniː.tʃə ⓊⓈ -tʃə, -tʃi
niff nɪf **-s** -s **-ing** -ɪŋ **-ed** -t **-y** -i
nift|y ˈnɪf.t|i **-ier** -i.əʳ ⓊⓈ -i.ɚ **-iest** -i.ɪst, -i.əst **-ies** -iz **-ily** -ɪ.li
Nige naɪdʒ
Nigel ˈnaɪ.dʒəl
Nigella naɪˈdʒel.ə
Niger *river:* ˈnaɪ.dʒəʳ ⓊⓈ -dʒɚ *country:* niːˈʒeəʳ ⓊⓈ ˈnaɪ.dʒɚ **-ien/s** -i.ən/z
Nigeri|a naɪˈdʒɪə.ri|.ə ⓊⓈ -ˈdʒɪr.i- **-an/s** -ən/z
niggard ˈnɪg.əd ⓊⓈ -ɚd **-s** -z
niggardl|y ˈnɪg.əd.l|i ⓊⓈ -ɚd- **-iness** -ɪ.nəs, -ɪ.nɪs
nigger ˈnɪg.əʳ ⓊⓈ -ɚ **-s** -z
niggl|e ˈnɪg.l̩ **-es** -z **-ing** -ɪŋ, ˈnɪg.lɪŋ **-ed** -d
niggl|y ˈnɪg.l|i, ˈnɪg.l̩|.i **-iness** -ɪ.nəs, -ɪ.nɪs
nigh naɪ
night naɪt **-s** -s ˌ**night ˈblindness** ⓊⓈ ˈ**night ˌblindness**; ˈ**night ˌowl**; ˌ**night ˈporter** ⓊⓈ ˈ**night ˌporter**; ˈ**night ˌschool**; ˈ**night ˌshift**; ˌ**night ˈwatchman**
nightcap ˈnaɪt.kæp **-s** -s
nightclothes ˈnaɪt.kləʊðz ⓊⓈ -kloʊðz
nightclub ˈnaɪt.klʌb **-s** -z **-bing** -ɪŋ **-ber/s** -əʳ/z ⓊⓈ -ɚ/z
nightdress ˈnaɪt.dres **-es** -ɪz
nightfall ˈnaɪt.fɔːl ⓊⓈ -fɔːl, -fɑːl
nightgown ˈnaɪt.gaʊn **-s** -z
nighthawk ˈnaɪt.hɔːk ⓊⓈ -hɑːk, -hɔːk
nightie ˈnaɪ.ti ⓊⓈ -t̬i **-s** -z
nightingale (N) ˈnaɪ.tɪŋ.geɪl ⓊⓈ -tən-, -t̬ɪŋ- **-s** -z
nightjar ˈnaɪt.dʒɑːʳ ⓊⓈ -dʒɑːr **-s** -z
nightlife ˈnaɪt.laɪf
night-light ˈnaɪt.laɪt **-s** -s
nightlong ˌnaɪtˈlɒŋ ⓊⓈ -ˈlɑːŋ, -ˈlɔːŋ *stress shift:* ˌnightlong ˈvigil
nightly ˈnaɪt.li
nightmar|e ˈnaɪt.meəʳ ⓊⓈ -mer **-es** -z **-ish** -ɪʃ **-ishly** -ɪʃ.li **-ishness** -ɪʃ.nəs, -ɪʃ.nɪs
nightshade ˈnaɪt.ʃeɪd **-s**
nightshirt ˈnaɪt.ʃɜːt ⓊⓈ -ʃɝːt **-s** -s
nightspot ˈnaɪt.spɒt ⓊⓈ -spɑːt **-s** -s
nightstick ˈnaɪt.stɪk **-s** -s
nighttime ˈnaɪt.taɪm
nightwatch ˈnaɪt.wɒtʃ, ˌ-ˈ- ⓊⓈ ˈnaɪt.wɑːtʃ, -wɔːtʃ **-es** -ɪz
nightwear ˈnaɪt.weəʳ ⓊⓈ -wer
nihil ˈniː.hɪl, ˈnaɪ-, -həl ⓊⓈ ˈnaɪ.hɪl, ˈniː-
nihil|ism ˈniː.ɪ.l|ɪ.zəm, ˈnaɪ-, ˈ-hɪ-, -əl|.ɪ-, -həl- ⓊⓈ ˈnaɪ.ə.l|ɪ-, ˈniː- **-ist/s** -ɪst/s **-istic** ˌ--ˈɪs.tɪk
Nijinsky nɪˈdʒɪnt.ski, nə-, -ˈʒɪnt- ⓊⓈ nəˈdʒɪnt-
Nijmegen ˈnaɪ.meɪ.gən, -ˈ-- ⓊⓈ ˈ---
Nike *goddess:* ˈnaɪ.kiː *trademark:* ˈnaɪ.ki; naɪk ⓊⓈ ˈnaɪ.ki
Nikita nɪˈkiː.tə ⓊⓈ -t̬ə
Nikkei nɪˈkeɪ ⓊⓈ ˈniː.keɪ *stress shift, see compound:* ˌ**Nikkei ˈindex**
Nikki ˈnɪk.i
Nikon® ˈnɪk.ɒn ⓊⓈ ˈnaɪ.kɑːn, ˈniː-
nil nɪl
nil desperandum ˌnɪl.des.pəˈræn.dəm, -pəˈræn-, -dʊm ⓊⓈ -pəˈræn.dəm; -ˈrɑːn.dʊm
Nile naɪl
Nilgiri ˈnɪl.gɪ.ri **-s** -z
nilometer naɪˈlɒm.ɪ.təʳ, -ə.təʳ ⓊⓈ -ˈlɑː.mə.t̬ɚ **-s** -z
Nilotic naɪˈlɒt.ɪk ⓊⓈ -ˈlɑː.t̬ɪk
Nilsen ˈniːl.sən, ˈnɪl-
Nilsson ˈniːl.sən, ˈnɪl-
nimbi *(plur. of* **nimbus**) ˈnɪm.baɪ
nimb|le ˈnɪm.b|l̩ **-ler** -ləʳ, -l̩.əʳ ⓊⓈ -lɚ, -l̩.ɚ **-lest** -lɪst, -ləst, -l̩.ɪst, -l̩.əst **-ly** -li **-leness** -l̩.nəs, -l̩.nɪs
nimb|us ˈnɪm.b|əs **-uses** -ə.sɪz **-i** -aɪ
nimb|y, NIMB|Y ˈnɪm.b|i **-ies** -iz
Nîmes niːm
nimiety nɪˈmaɪə.ti, -ˈmaɪ.ɪ.ti ⓊⓈ -t̬i
nimini-piminy, niminy-piminy ˌnɪm.ɪ.niˈpɪm.ɪ.ni, ˌ-ə-, ˈ-ə- ⓊⓈ -ə.niˈpɪm.ə-
Nimmo ˈnɪm.əʊ ⓊⓈ -oʊ
Nimrod ˈnɪm.rɒd ⓊⓈ -rɑːd
Nin nɪn ⓊⓈ nɪn, niːn
Nina ˈniː.nə ⓊⓈ ˈniː-, ˈnaɪ-
nincompoop ˈnɪŋ.kəm.puːp, ˈnɪn- ⓊⓈ ˈnɪn-, ˈnɪŋ- **-s** -s
nine naɪn **-s** -z **-fold** -fəʊld ⓊⓈ -foʊld ˌ**dressed ˌup to the ˈnines**; ˌ**nine-to-ˈfive**; ˌ**nine days' ˈwonder**
ninepenc|e ˈnaɪn.pənts, ˈnaɪm- ⓊⓈ ˈnaɪn- **-es** -ɪz
Note: See note under **penny**.
ninepenny ˈnaɪn.pən.i, ˈnaɪm- ⓊⓈ ˈnaɪn-
ninepin ˈnaɪn.pɪn, ˈnaɪm- ⓊⓈ ˈnaɪn- **-s** -z
nineteen ˌnaɪnˈtiːn **-s** -z **-th/s** -tθ/s *stress shift:* ˌnineteen ˈyears ˌ**nineteen to the ˈdozen**
ninetieth ˈnaɪn.ti.əθ, -ɪθ ⓊⓈ -t̬i- **-s** -s
Ninette nɪˈnet, niː-
ninet|y ˈnaɪn.t|i ⓊⓈ -t̬|i **-ies** -iz
ninetyfold ˈnaɪn.ti.fəʊld ⓊⓈ -t̬i.foʊld
ninety-nine ˌnaɪn.tiˈnaɪn ⓊⓈ -t̬iˈ- *stress shift:* ˌninety-nine ˈdays
Nineveh ˈnɪn.ɪ.və, ˈ-ə- ⓊⓈ ˈ-ə-
ninish ˈnaɪ.nɪʃ

ninja 'nɪn.dʒə -s -z ˌ**Ninja** '**warriors**
ninn|y 'nɪn|.i -**ies** -iz
Nintendo® nɪn'ten.dəʊ Ⓤⓢ -doʊ
ninth naɪntθ -**s** -s -**ly** -li
Ninus 'naɪ.nəs
Niobe 'naɪ.əʊ.bi Ⓤⓢ -oʊ-, '-ə-
niobium naɪ'əʊ.bi.əm Ⓤⓢ -'oʊ-
nip (N) nɪp -**s** -s -**ping** -ɪŋ -**ped** -t ˌ**nip and** '**tuck**
nipper 'nɪp.əʳ Ⓤⓢ -ɚ -**s** -z
nipple 'nɪp.l̩ -**s** -z
Nippon 'nɪp.ɒn Ⓤⓢ -ɑːn; nɪ'pɑːn -**ese** --'iːz
nipp|y 'nɪp|.i -**ier** -i.əʳ Ⓤⓢ -i.ɚ -**iest** -i.ɪst, -i.əst -**ily** -ɪ.li, -ᵊl.i -**iness** -ɪ.nəs, -ɪ.nɪs
NIREX 'naɪə.reks Ⓤⓢ 'naɪ-
nirvana (N) nɪə'vɑː.nə, nɜː- Ⓤⓢ nɪr-, nɚ- -**s** -z
Nis, **Nish** niːʃ
Nisan 'naɪ.sæn *Jewish pronunciation:* 'nɪs.ɑːn Ⓤⓢ niː'sɑːn; 'nɪs.ən
Nisbet(t) 'nɪz.bɪt, -bət
nisei niː'seɪ Ⓤⓢ niː'seɪ, '-- -**s** -z
Nish nɪʃ
nisi 'naɪ.saɪ, 'niː-, -si Ⓤⓢ 'naɪ.saɪ
nisi prius ˌnaɪ.saɪ'praɪ.əs, ˌniː-, -si'-, -'priː- Ⓤⓢ ˌnaɪ.saɪ'praɪ-
Nissan® 'nɪs.æn Ⓤⓢ 'niː.sɑːn
Nissen 'nɪs.ᵊn '**Nissen** ˌ**hut**
nisus 'naɪ.səs
nit nɪt -**s** -s
niter 'naɪ.təʳ Ⓤⓢ -t̬ɚ
Nith nɪθ
nit-pick 'nɪt.pɪk -**s** -s -**ing** -ɪŋ -**ed** -t -**er/s** -əʳ/z Ⓤⓢ -ɚ/z
nitrate 'naɪ.treɪt, -trɪt Ⓤⓢ -treɪt -**s** -s
nitre 'naɪ.təʳ Ⓤⓢ -t̬ɚ
nitric 'naɪ.trɪk ˌ**nitric** '**acid**
nitrite 'naɪ.traɪt
nitro- ˌnaɪ.trəʊ- Ⓤⓢ ˌnaɪ.troʊ-, -trə-
nitrochalk 'naɪ.trəʊ.tʃɔːk, ˌ--'- Ⓤⓢ 'naɪ.troʊ.tʃɔːk, -tʃɑːk
nitrogen 'naɪ.trə.dʒən, -trɪ- Ⓤⓢ -trə-
nitrogenous naɪ'trɒdʒ.ɪ.nəs, -ᵊn.əs Ⓤⓢ -'trɑː.dʒə.nəs
nitroglycerine, **nitroglycerin** ˌnaɪ.trəʊ'glɪs.ᵊr.iːn, -ɪn Ⓤⓢ -troʊ'-, -trə'-
nitrous 'naɪ.trəs
nitty-gritty ˌnɪt.i'grɪt.i Ⓤⓢ ˌnɪt̬.i'grɪt̬-
nitwit 'nɪt.wɪt -**s** -s
Niue 'njuː.eɪ, ni'uː- Ⓤⓢ ni'uː- -**an/s** -ᵊn/z
Nivea® 'nɪv.i.ə
Niven 'nɪv.ᵊn
nix nɪks -**es** -ɪz -**ing** -ɪŋ -**ed** -t
Nixdorf® 'nɪks.dɔːf Ⓤⓢ -dɔːrf
nixie 'nɪk.si -**s** -z
Nixon 'nɪk.sᵊn
nizam (N) naɪ'zæm, nɪ-, -'zɑːm Ⓤⓢ nɪ'zɑːm; naɪ'zæm -**ate** -eɪt -**s** -z

Nizhni Novgorod ˌnɪʒ.ni'nɒv.gᵊr.ɒd Ⓤⓢ -'nɑːv.gə.rɑːd
N.J. ˌen'dʒeɪ
Nkomo ᵊŋ'kəʊ.məʊ Ⓤⓢ -'koʊ.moʊ, ᵊn-
Nkrumah ᵊŋ'kruː.mə Ⓤⓢ ᵊŋ-, ᵊn-
N.M. (*abbrev. for* **New Mexico**) ˌen'em
NME ˌen.em'iː
N.Mex. (*abbrev. for* **New Mexico**) ˌen'meks
NNE (*abbrev. for* **north-northeast**) ˌnɔːθ.nɔːθ'iːst Ⓤⓢ ˌnɔːrθ.nɔːrθ'- *nautical pronunciation:* ˌnɔː.nɔː'riːst Ⓤⓢ ˌnɔːr.nɔːr'iːst
NNW (*abbrev. for* **north-northwest**) ˌnɔːθ.nɔːθ'west Ⓤⓢ ˌnɔːrθ.nɔːrθ'- *nautical pronunciation:* ˌnɔː.nɔː'- Ⓤⓢ ˌnɔːr.nɔːr'-
no (*n. interj.*) nəʊ Ⓤⓢ noʊ -**es** -z
no (*adj.*) *normal form:* nəʊ Ⓤⓢ noʊ *weak form:* nə
Note: Occasional weak form word. The pronunciation of **no** is nearly always /nəʊ Ⓤⓢ noʊ/, but, particularly in British English, there is a weak form /nə/ in a few common expressions such as "no more do I" /nə,mɔː.duː'aɪ Ⓤⓢ -ˌmɔːr-/.
no. (N) (*abbrev. for* **number**) 'nʌm.bəʳ Ⓤⓢ -bɚ **nos.** -z
no-account 'nəʊ.ə,kaʊnt Ⓤⓢ 'noʊ-
Noah 'nəʊ.ə Ⓤⓢ 'noʊ- ˌ**Noah's** '**ark**
Noakes nəʊks Ⓤⓢ noʊks
Noam 'nəʊ.əm, nəʊm Ⓤⓢ 'noʊ.əm, noʊm
nob nɒb Ⓤⓢ nɑːb -**s** -z
no-ball ˌnəʊ'bɔːl Ⓤⓢ 'noʊ-, -bɑːl -**s** -z -**ing** -ɪŋ -**ed** -d
nobbl|e 'nɒb.l̩ Ⓤⓢ 'nɑː.bl̩ -**es** -z -**ing** -ɪŋ, 'nɒb.lɪŋ Ⓤⓢ 'nɑː.blɪŋ -**ed** -d
nobb|y 'nɒb|.i Ⓤⓢ 'nɑː.b|i -**ier** -i.əʳ Ⓤⓢ -i.ɚ -**iest** -i.ɪst, -i.əst -**ily** -ɪ.li, -ᵊl.i -**iness** -ɪ.nəs, -ɪ.nɪs
Nobel nəʊ'bel Ⓤⓢ noʊ- *stress shift, see compound:* ˌ**Nobel** '**prize**
nobelium nəʊ'biː.li.əm Ⓤⓢ noʊ'bel.i-
nobilit|y nəʊ'bɪl.ə.t|i, -ɪ.t|i Ⓤⓢ noʊ'bɪl.ə.t̬|i -**ies** -iz
nob|le (N) 'nəʊ.bl| Ⓤⓢ 'noʊ- -**les** -l̩z -**ler** -ləʳ, -l̩.əʳ -**lest** -lɪst, -ləst, -l̩.ɪst, -l̩.əst -**ly** -li -**leness** -l̩.nəs, -l̩.nɪs
noble|man 'nəʊ.bl̩|.mən Ⓤⓢ 'noʊ- -**men** -mən
noble-minded ˌnəʊ.bl̩'maɪn.dɪd Ⓤⓢ ˌnoʊ- -**ness** -nəs, -nɪs *stress shift:* ˌnoble-minded 'person
noblesse nəʊ'bles Ⓤⓢ noʊ-
noblesse oblige nəʊˌbles.əʊ'bliːʒ, ˌnəʊ.bles- Ⓤⓢ noʊˌbles.oʊ'-
noble|woman 'nəʊ.bl̩|ˌwʊm.ən Ⓤⓢ 'noʊ- -**women** -ˌwɪm.ɪn

nobod|y 'nəʊ.bə.d|i, -bɒd|.i Ⓤⓢ 'noʊ.bɑː.d|i, -bʌd|.i, -bə.d|i -**ies** -iz
nock (N) nɒk Ⓤⓢ nɑːk
no-claim bonus ˌnəʊ'kleɪmˌbəʊ.nəs, ˌnəʊˌkleɪm'bəʊ- Ⓤⓢ ˌnoʊ'kleɪmˌboʊ-, ˌnoʊˌkleɪm'boʊ- -**es** -ɪz
no-claims bonus ˌnəʊ'kleɪmzˌbəʊ.nəs, ˌnəʊˌkleɪmz'bəʊ- Ⓤⓢ ˌnoʊ'kleɪmzˌboʊ-, ˌnoʊˌkleɪmz'boʊ- -**es** -ɪz
no-confidence ˌnəʊ'kɒn.fɪ.dᵊnts Ⓤⓢ ˌnoʊ'kɑːn-
noctambul|ism nɒk'tæm.bjə.l|ɪ.zᵊm, -bjʊ- Ⓤⓢ nɑːk'tæm.bjuː-, -bjə- -**ist/s** -ɪst/s
Noctes Ambrosianae ˌnɒk.teɪsˌæm.brəʊ.zi'ɑː.naɪ, -brɒs.i'- Ⓤⓢ ˌnɑːk.tiːz.æm.broʊ.si'eɪ.ni
nocturnal nɒk'tɜː.nᵊl Ⓤⓢ nɑːk'tɜːr- -**ly** -i
nocturn(e) 'nɒk.tɜːn, ˌ-'- Ⓤⓢ 'nɑːk.tɜːrn -**s** -z
nocuous 'nɒk.ju.əs Ⓤⓢ 'nɑːk- -**ly** -li
nod (N) nɒd Ⓤⓢ nɑːd -**s** -z -**ding** -ɪŋ -**ded** -ɪd
nodal 'nəʊ.dᵊl Ⓤⓢ 'noʊ- -**ly** -i
nodding 'nɒd.ɪŋ Ⓤⓢ 'nɑː.dɪŋ
noddle 'nɒd.l̩ Ⓤⓢ 'nɑː.dl̩ -**s** -z
nodd|y (N) 'nɒd|.i Ⓤⓢ 'nɑː.d|i -**ies** -iz
node nəʊd Ⓤⓢ noʊd -**s** -z
nodul|ar 'nɒd.jə.l|əʳ, -jʊ- Ⓤⓢ 'nɑː.djuː.l|ɚ, -djə- -**ous** -əs
nodule 'nɒd.juːl Ⓤⓢ 'nɑː.djuːl -**s** -z
Noel, **Noël** *personal name:* nəʊəl Ⓤⓢ noʊəl *Christmas:* nəʊ'el Ⓤⓢ noʊ-
no-fault 'nəʊ.fɔːlt, -fɒlt Ⓤⓢ 'noʊ.fɔːlt, -fɑːlt
no-fly ˌnəʊ'flaɪ Ⓤⓢ ˌnoʊ- *stress shift:* ˌno-fly 'zone
no-frills ˌnəʊ'frɪlz Ⓤⓢ ˌnoʊ- *stress shift:* ˌno-frills 'service
noggin 'nɒg.ɪn Ⓤⓢ 'nɑː.gɪn -**s** -z
no-go ˌnəʊ'gəʊ Ⓤⓢ ˌnoʊ'goʊ *stress shift, see compound:* ˌ**no-go** '**area**
no-good ˌnəʊ'gʊd Ⓤⓢ ˌnoʊ- *stress shift:* ˌno-good 'cheat
Noh nəʊ Ⓤⓢ noʊ
no-holds-barred ˌnəʊˌhəʊldz'bɑːd Ⓤⓢ ˌnoʊˌhoʊldz'bɑːrd *stress shift:* ˌno-holds-barred 'contest
no-hoper ˌnəʊ'həʊ.pəʳ Ⓤⓢ ˌnoʊ'hoʊ.pɚ -**s** -z
nohow 'nəʊ.haʊ Ⓤⓢ 'noʊ-
noir nwɑːʳ Ⓤⓢ nwɑːr
nois|e nɔɪz -**es** -ɪz -**ing** -ɪŋ -**ed** -d
noiseless 'nɔɪz.ləs, -lɪs -**ly** -li -**ness** -nəs, -nɪs
noisemaker 'nɔɪzˌmeɪ.kəʳ Ⓤⓢ -kɚ -**s** -z
noisette nwɑː'zet -**s** -s

noisettes (*alternative plur. of* **noisette**) nwɑː'zet
noisome 'nɔɪ.səm **-ly** -li **-ness** -nəs, -nɪs
nois|y 'nɔɪ.z|i **-ier** -i.əʳ (US) -i.ɚ **-iest** -i.ɪst, -i.əst **-ily** -ɪ.li, -əl.i **-iness** -ɪ.nəs, -ɪ.nɪs
Nokes nəʊks (US) noʊks
Nokomis nəʊ'kəʊ.mɪs (US) noʊ'koʊ-
Nolan 'nəʊ.lən (US) 'noʊ-
noli me tangere ˌnəʊ.liˌmeɪ'tæŋ.gə.reɪ, '-dʒə- (US) ˌnoʊ-
Noll nɒl (US) nɑːl
nolo contendere ˌnəʊ.ləʊ.kɒn'ten.dər.i, -eɪ (US) ˌnoʊ.loʊ.kən'-
noma 'nəʊ.mə (US) 'noʊ- **-s** -z
nomad 'nəʊ.mæd (US) 'noʊ- **-s** -z **-ism** -ɪ.zəm
nomadic nəʊ'mæd.ɪk (US) noʊ- **-ally** -əl.i, -li
no-man's-land 'nəʊ.mænz.lænd (US) 'noʊ-
nom(s) de guerre ˌnɔ̃ːn.də'geəʳ, ˌnɒm- (US) ˌnɑːm.də'ger
nom(s) de plume ˌnɔ̃ːn.də'pluːm, ˌnɒm- (US) ˌnɑːm.də'-
-nome -nəʊm, -noʊm
Note: Suffix. Normally unstressed, e.g. **metronome** /'met.rə.nəʊm (US) -noʊm/.
nomenclature nəʊ'meŋ.klə.tʃəʳ; 'nəʊ.men.kleɪ-, -mən- (US) 'noʊ.men.kleɪ.tʃɚ, -mən-; noʊ'men.klə- **-s** -z
-nomic -'nɒm.ɪk, -'nəʊ.mɪk (US) -'nɑː.mɪk, -'noʊ- **-s** -s
Note: Suffix. Words containing **-nomic** normally carry primary stress on the penultimate syllable, e.g. **ergonomic** /ˌɜː.gə'nɒm.ɪk (US) ˌɜːr.gə'nɑː.mɪk/.
nominal 'nɒm.ɪ.nəl, -ən.əl (US) 'nɑː.mə.nəl **-ly** -i
nomi|nate 'nɒm.ɪ|.neɪt, '-ə- (US) 'nɑː.mə- **-nates** -neɪts **-nating** -neɪ.tɪŋ (US) -neɪ.t̬ɪŋ **-nated** -neɪ.tɪd (US) -neɪ.t̬ɪd **-nator/s** -neɪ.təʳ/z (US) -neɪ.t̬ɚ/z
nomination ˌnɒm.ɪ'neɪ.ʃən, -ə'- (US) ˌnɑː.mə'- **-s** -z
nominative 'nɒm.ɪ.nə.tɪv, -ən.ə- (US) 'nɑː.mə.nə.t̬ɪv **-s** -z
nominee ˌnɒm.ɪ'niː, -ə'- (US) ˌnɑː.mə'- **-s** -z
-nomy -nə.mi
Note: Suffix. Words containing **-nomy** normally carry stress on the syllable preceding the suffix, e.g. **astronomy** /ə'strɒn.ə.mi (US) -'strɑː.nə-/.
non- ˌnɒn- (US) ˌnɑːn-
Note: Prefix. In words containing **non-**, the stress pattern of the stem to which it is added does not normally change, e.g. **verbal** /'vɜː.bəl (US) 'vɜːr-/, **nonverbal** /ˌnɒn'vɜː.bəl (US) ˌnɑːn'vɜːr-/.
non nɒn (US) nɑːn
non-acceptance ˌnɒn.ək'sep.tənts, -æk'- (US) ˌnɑː.nək'-
nonage 'nəʊ.nɪdʒ, 'nɒn.ɪdʒ (US) 'nɑː.nɪdʒ, 'noʊ-, -neɪdʒ
nonagenarian ˌnəʊ.nə.dʒə'neə.ri.ən, ˌnɒn.ə-, -dʒɪ'- (US) ˌnɑː.nə.dʒə'ner.i-, ˌnoʊ- **-s** -z
nonaggression ˌnɒn.ə'greʃ.ən (US) ˌnɑː.nə'-
nonagon 'nɒn.ə.gɒn, 'nəʊ.nə- (US) 'nɑː.nə.gɑːn, 'noʊ- **-s** -z
nonalcoholic ˌnɒn.æl.kə'hɒl.ɪk (US) ˌnɑː.næl.kə'hɑː.lɪk
nonalign|ed ˌnɒn.əl'aɪn|d (US) ˌnɑː.nə'laɪn|d **-ment** -mənt
non-appearance ˌnɒn.ə'pɪə.rənts (US) ˌnɑː.nə'pɪr.ənts
nonary 'nəʊ.nər.i, 'nɒn.ər- (US) 'noʊ.nɚ-, 'nɑː-
non-attendance ˌnɒn.ə'ten.dənts (US) ˌnɑː.nə'-
nonbeliever ˌnɒn.bɪ'liː.vəʳ, ˌnɒm-, -bə'- (US) ˌnɑːn.bɪ'liː.vɚ, -bə'- **-s** -z
non-biological ˌnɒnˌbaɪə'lɒdʒ.ɪ.kəl (US) ˌnɑːn.baɪə'lɑː.dʒɪ-
nonc|e nɒnts (US) nɑːnts **-es** -ɪz 'nonce ˌword
non-certifiable ˌnɒnˌsɜː.tɪ'faɪ.ə.bl̩, -tə'- (US) ˌnɑːnˌsɜːr.t̬ə'-
nonchalance 'nɒn.tʃəl.ənts (US) ˌnɑːn.ʃə'lɑːnts
nonchalant 'nɒn.tʃəl.ənt (US) ˌnɑːn.ʃə'lɑːnt **-ly** -li
non-collegiate ˌnɒn.kəl'iː.dʒi.ət, ˌnɒŋ-, -kɒl'-, '-dʒət (US) ˌnɑːn.kə'liː.dʒɪt, -dʒi.ɪt **-s** -s
non-combatant ˌnɒn'kɒm.bə.tənt, ˌnɒŋ-, -'kʌm-; -kəm'bæt.ənt (US) ˌnɑːn.kəm'bæt.ənt; ˌnɑːn'kɑːm.bə.tənt **-s** -s
noncommercial ˌnɒn.kə'mɜː.ʃəl, ˌnɒŋ- (US) ˌnɑːn.kə'mɜːr-
non-commissioned ˌnɒn.kə'mɪʃ.ənd, ˌnɒŋ- (US) ˌnɑːn- *stress shift, see compound:* **ˌnon-commissioned 'officer**
noncommitt|al ˌnɒn.kə'mɪt|.əl, ˌnɒŋ- (US) ˌnɑːn.kə'mɪt̬- **-ally** -əli *stress shift:* ˌnoncommittal 'answer
noncompetitive ˌnɒn.kəm'pet.ə.tɪv, 'nɒŋ-, '-ɪ- (US) ˌnɑːn.kəm'pet̬.ə.t̬ɪv **-ly** -li *stress shift:* ˌnoncompetitive 'games
non-compliance ˌnɒn.kəm'plaɪ.ənts, ˌnɒŋ- (US) ˌnɑːn-
non compos mentis ˌnɒnˌkɒm.pəs'men.tɪs, ˌnɒŋ-, -pɒs'- (US) ˌnɑːnˌkɑːm.poʊs'men.t̬ɪs, -pəs'-
non-conducting ˌnɒn.kən'dʌk.tɪŋ, ˌnɒŋ- (US) ˌnɑːn- *stress shift:* ˌnon-conducting 'substance
nonconductor ˌnɒn.kən'dʌk.təʳ, ˌnɒŋ- (US) ˌnɑːn.kən'dʌk.tɚ **-s** -z
nonconform|ist ˌnɒn.kən'fɔː.m|ɪst, ˌnɒŋ- (US) ˌnɑːn.kən'fɔːr- **-ists** -ɪsts **-ism** -ɪ.zəm *stress shift:* ˌnonconformist 'stance
nonconformity ˌnɒn.kən'fɔː.mə.ti, ˌnɒŋ-, -mɪ- (US) ˌnɑːn.kən'fɔːr.mə.t̬i
noncontiguous ˌnɒn.kən'tɪg.ju.əs, ˌnɒŋ-, -kɒn'- (US) ˌnɑːn.kən'- **-ly** -li *stress shift:* ˌnoncontiguous 'boundaries
noncontributory ˌnɒn.kən'trɪb.jə.tər.i, ˌnɒŋ-, -jʊ- (US) ˌnɑːn.kən'trɪb.juː.tɔːr-, -jə- *stress shift:* ˌnoncontributory 'action
noncooperation ˌnɒn.kəʊˌɒp.ər'eɪ.ʃən, ˌnɒŋ- (US) ˌnɑːn.koʊˌɑː.pə'reɪ-
noncooperationist ˌnɒn.kəʊˌɒp.ər'eɪ.ʃən.ɪst, ˌnɒŋ- (US) ˌnɑːn.koʊˌɑː.pə'reɪ- **-s** -s *stress shift:* ˌnon-cooperationist 'stance
noncorrosive ˌnɒn.kər'əʊ.sɪv, ˌnɒŋ-, -zɪv (US) ˌnɑːn.kə'roʊ- *stress shift:* ˌnoncorrosive 'acid
non-custodial ˌnɒn.kʌs'təʊ.di.əl, ˌnɒŋ- (US) ˌnɑːn.kʌs'toʊ- *stress shift:* ˌnon-custodial 'sentence
nondairy ˌnɒn'deə.ri (US) ˌnɑːn'der.i *stress shift:* ˌnondairy 'product
non-delivery ˌnɒn.dɪ'lɪv.ər.i, -də'- (US) ˌnɑːn.də'-, '-ri
nondenominational ˌnɒn.dɪˌnɒm.ɪ'neɪ.ʃən.əl, -dəˌ-, -'neɪʃ.nəl (US) ˌnɑːn.dəˌnɑː.mə'- *stress shift:* ˌnondenominational 'policy
nondescript 'nɒn.dɪ.skrɪpt, -də- (US) 'nɑːn.dɪ-, ˌ--'- **-s** -s
nondriver ˌnɒn'draɪ.vəʳ (US) ˌnɑːn'draɪ.vɚ **-s** -z
none (*adj. pron. adv.*) *not any:* nʌn
none (N) (*n.*) *church service:* nəʊn (US) noʊn **-s** -z
nonentit|y ˌnɒn'en.tə.t|i, nə'nen-, -ɪ.t|i (US) ˌnɑː'nen.t̬ə.t̬|i **-ies** -iz
nones (N) nəʊnz (US) noʊnz
non-essential ˌnɒn.ɪ'sen.tʃəl (US) ˌnɑː.nɪ'- **-s** -z *stress shift:* ˌnon-essential 'item
nonesuch 'nʌn.sʌtʃ **-es** -ɪz
nonet nəʊ'net, nɒn'et (US) noʊ'net **-s** -s
nonetheless ˌnʌn.ðə'les
non-event ˌnɒn.ɪ'vent, '--- (US) ˌnɑː.nɪ'vent **-s** -s
non-existen|t ˌnɒn.ɪg'zɪs.tən|t, -eg'-, -ɪk'sɪs-, -ek'- (US) ˌnɑː.nɪg'zɪs-, -neg'- **-ce** -ts *stress shift:* ˌnonexistent 'means

nonfat ˌnɒnˈfæt (US) ˌnɑːn- *stress shift:* ˌnonfat ˈsubstance
non-feasance ˌnɒnˈfiː.zᵊnts (US) ˌnɑːn-
nonfiction ˌnɒnˈfɪk.ʃᵊn (US) ˌnɑːn-
nonflammab|le ˌnɒnˈflæm.ə.bl̩ (US) ˌnɑːn- **-ility** *stress shift:* ˌnonflammable ˈclothing
nonillion nəʊˈnɪl.jən, nɒnˈɪl-, ˈ-i.ən (US) noʊˈnɪl.jən **-s** -z
non-intervention ˌnɒn.ɪn.təˈven.*t*ʃᵊn (US) ˌnɑː.nɪn.t̬ɚˈven*t*.ʃᵊn
non-interventionist ˌnɒn.ɪn.təˈven.*t*ʃᵊn.ɪst (US) ˌnɑː.nɪn.t̬ɚˈven*t*.ʃᵊn- **-s** -s *stress shift:* ˌnon-interventionist ˈpolicy
nonjudgmental ˌnɒn.dʒʌdʒˈmen.tᵊl (US) ˌnɑːn.dʒʌdʒˈmen.t̬ᵊl **-ly** -i *stress shift:* ˌnonjudgmental ˈview
nonjuror ˌnɒnˈdʒʊə.rəʳ (US) ˌnɑːnˈdʒʊr.ɚ, -ɔːr **-s** -z
nonlinear ˌnɒnˈlɪn.i.əʳ (US) ˌnɑːnˈlɪn.i.ɚ *stress shift:* ˌnonlinear ˈtheory
non-member ˌnɒnˈmem.bəʳ, ˈ--- (US) ˌnɑːnˈmem.bɚ, ˈ--- **-s** -z
non-nuclear ˌnɒnˈnjuː.kli.əʳ (US) ˌnɑːnˈnuː.kli.ɚ, -ˈnjuː- *stress shift:* ˌnon-nuclear ˈpower
no-no ˈnəʊ.nəʊ (US) ˈnoʊ.noʊ **-s** -z
non-observance ˌnɒn.əbˈzɜː.vᵊn*t*s (US) ˌnɑː.nəbˈzɜːr-
non obstante ˌnɒn.ɒbˈstæn.teɪ (US) ˌnɑːn.əbˈstæn.ti, -ˈstɑːn-
non obstante verdicto ˌnɒn.ɒbˌstæn.teɪ.vəˈdɪk.təʊ (US) ˌnɑːn.əbˌstæn.ti.verˈdɪk.toʊ, -ˌstɑːn-
nonoccurrence ˌnɒn.əˈkʌr.ᵊn*t*s (US) ˌnɑː.nəˈkɜːr-
no-nonsense ˌnəʊˈnɒn*t*.sᵊn*t*s (US) ˌnoʊˈnɑːn*t*.sen*t*s *stress shift:* ˌno-nonsense ˈattitude
nonoperational ˌnɒn.ɒp.əˈreɪ.ʃᵊn.ᵊl, -ˈreɪʃ.nᵊl (US) ˌnɑː.nɑː.pəˈreɪ.ʃᵊn.ᵊl, -ˈreɪʃ.nᵊl *stress shift:* ˌnonoperational ˈforces
nonpareil ˈnɒn.pᵊr.ᵊl, ˈnɒm-; ˌnɒn.pəˈreɪl, ˌnɒm-, -ˈeɪ (US) ˌnɑːn.pəˈrel
non-payment ˌnɒnˈpeɪ.mənt, ˌnɒm- (US) ˌnɑːn-
nonplaying ˌnɒnˈpleɪ.ɪŋ, ˌnɒm- (US) ˌnɑːn- *stress shift:* ˌnonplaying ˈteam
nonplus ˌnɒnˈplʌs, ˌnɒm- (US) ˌnɑːn- **-ses** -ɪz **-sing** -ɪŋ **-sed** -t
non-profit-making ˌnɒnˈprɒf.ɪtˌmeɪ.kɪŋ, ˌnɒm- (US) ˌnɑːnˈprɑː.fɪt- *stress shift, see compound:* **ˌnon-profit-making ˌorganiˈsation**
nonproliferation ˌnɒn.prəˌlɪf.əˈreɪ.ʃᵊn, ˌnɒm- (US) ˌnɑːn-
nonrefundable ˌnɒn.rɪˈfʌnd.ə.bl̩, -riːˈ- (US) ˌnɑːn- *stress shift:* ˌnonrefundable ˈmoney
nonresident ˌnɒnˈrez.ɪ.dᵊnt, ˈ-ə- (US) ˌnɑːn- **-s** -s
nonrestrictive ˌnɒn.rɪˈstrɪk.tɪv, -rəˈ- (US) ˌnɑːn- *stress shift:* ˌnonrestrictive ˈclause
nonreturnable ˌnɒn.rɪˈtɜː.nə.bl̩, -rəˈ- (US) ˌnɑːn.rɪˈtɜːr- *stress shift:* ˌnonreturnable ˈgoods
nonsectarian ˌnɒn.sekˈteə.ri.ən (US) ˌnɑːn.sekˈter.i- *stress shift:* ˌnonsectarian ˈviolence
nonsense ˈnɒn.sᵊn*t*s (US) ˈnɑːn.sen*t*s, -sən*t*s **ˈnonsense ˌverse**
nonsensical ˌnɒnˈsen*t*.sɪ.kl̩ (US) ˌnɑːn- **-ly** -i **-ness** -nəs, -nɪs
non sequitur ˌnɒnˈsek.wɪ.təʳ, ˌnəʊn-, -wə- (US) ˌnɑːnˈsek.wɪ.t̬ɚ **-s** -z
nonskid ˌnɒnˈskɪd (US) ˌnɑːn- *stress shift:* ˌnonskid ˈsurface
nonslip ˌnɒnˈslɪp (US) ˌnɑːn- *stress shift:* ˌnonslip ˈsurface
nonsmok|er ˌnɒnˈsməʊ.k|əʳ (US) ˌnɑːnˈsmoʊ.k|ɚ **-ers** -əz (US) -ɚz **-ing** -ɪŋ
nonspecific ˌnɒn.spəˈsɪf.ɪk, -spɪˈ- (US) ˌnɑːn- *stress shift:* ˌnonspecific ˈorder
nonstandard ˌnɒnˈstæn.dəd (US) ˌnɑːnˈstæn.dɚd *stress shift:* ˌnonstandard ˈfitting
nonstarter ˌnɒnˈstɑː.təʳ (US) ˌnɑːnˈstɑːr.t̬ɚ **-s** -z
nonstick ˌnɒnˈstɪk (US) ˌnɑːn- *stress shift:* ˌnonstick ˈcoating
non-stop ˌnɒnˈstɒp (US) ˌnɑːnˈstɑːp *stress shift:* ˌnon-stop ˈmusic
nonsuch (N) ˈnʌn.sʌtʃ
nonsui|t ˌnɒnˈsuː|t, -ˈsjuː|t (US) ˌnɑːnˈsuː|t **-ts** -ts **-ting** -tɪŋ (US) -t̬ɪŋ **-ted** -tɪd (US) -t̬ɪd
nonswimmer ˌnɒnˈswɪm.əʳ (US) ˌnɑːnˈswɪm.ɚ **-s** -z
nontrivial ˌnɒnˈtrɪv.i.əl (US) ˌnɑːn- *stress shift:* ˌnontrivial ˈproblem
non-U ˌnɒnˈjuː (US) ˌnɑːn- *stress shift:* ˌnon-U ˈaccent
nonunion ˌnɒnˈjuː.njən, ˈ-ni.ən (US) ˌnɑːnˈjuː.njən *stress shift:* ˌnonunion ˈmembers
non-user ˌnɒnˈjuː.zəʳ (US) ˌnɑːnˈjuː.zɚ *stress shift:* ˌnon-user ˈguide
nonverbal ˌnɒnˈvɜː.bᵊl (US) ˌnɑːnˈvɜːr- *stress shift:* ˌnonverbal ˈmessage
non-violen|t ˌnɒnˈvaɪə.lən|t (US) ˌnɑːn- **-ly** -li **-ce** -*t*s *stress shift:* ˌnon-violent ˈpolicy
nonvoter ˌnɒnˈvəʊ.təʳ (US) ˌnɑːnˈvoʊ.t̬ɚ **-s** -z
nonwhite ˌnɒnˈwaɪt (US) ˌnɑːn- *stress shift:* ˌnonwhite ˈprejudice
noodle ˈnuː.dl̩ **-s** -z
nook nʊk **-s** -s **ˌnook and ˈcranny**
nooky, nookie ˈnʊk.i
noon nuːn **-s** -z
Noonan ˈnuː.nən
noonday ˈnuːn.deɪ
no one ˈnəʊ.wʌn (US) ˈnoʊ-
noontide ˈnuːn.taɪd
noos|e nuːs **-es** -ɪz **-ing** -ɪŋ **-ed** -t
nope nəʊp (US) noʊp
noplace ˈnəʊ.pleɪs (US) ˈnoʊ-
nor *normal form:* nɔːʳ (US) nɔːr *weak form:* nəʳ (US) nɚ
Note: Occasional weak form word. The pronunciation is normally /nɔːʳ (US) nɔːr/, but, particularly in British English, there is a weak form /nəʳ (US) nɚ/, as in "no use to man nor beast" /nəʊˌjuːs.təˌmæn.nəˈbiːst (US) noʊˌjuːs.təˌmæn.nɚˈ-/.
NORAD ˈnɔː.ræd (US) ˈnɔːr.æd
noradrenalin(e) ˌnɔː.rəˈdren.ᵊl.ɪn, ˌnɒr.əˈ-, -iːn (US) ˌnɔːr.əˈdren.ə.lɪn
Nora(h) ˈnɔː.rə (US) ˈnɔːr.ə
Noraid ˈnɔː.reɪd (US) ˈnɔːr.eɪd
Norden ˈnɔː.dᵊn (US) ˈnɔːr-
Nordenfelt ˈnɔː.dᵊn.felt (US) ˈnɔːr-
Nordic ˈnɔː.dɪk (US) ˈnɔːr-
Nore nɔːʳ (US) nɔːr
Norf. (*abbrev. for* **Norfolk**) ˈnɔː.fək (US) ˈnɔːr-, -fɔːk, -foʊk
Norfolk ˈnɔː.fək (US) ˈnɔːr-, -fɔːk, -foʊk **ˌNorfolk ˈBroads**
Norgate ˈnɔː.geɪt, -gɪt (US) ˈnɔːr-
Norham ˈnɒr.əm, ˈnɔː.rəm (US) ˈnɔːr.əm
nori ˈnɒr.i, ˈnɔː.ri (US) ˈnɔːr.i
Norland ˈnɔː.lənd (US) ˈnɔːr-
norm nɔːm (US) nɔːrm **-s** -z
Norma ˈnɔː.mə (US) ˈnɔːr-
normal ˈnɔː.mᵊl (US) ˈnɔːr- **-ly** -i
normalcy ˈnɔː.mᵊl.si (US) ˈnɔːr-
normality nɔːˈmæl.ə.ti, -ɪ.ti (US) nɔːrˈmæl.ə.t̬i
normalization, -isa- ˌnɔː.mᵊl.aɪˈzeɪ.ʃᵊn, -ɪˈ- (US) ˌnɔːr.mᵊl.ɪˈ-
normaliz|e, -is|e ˈnɔː.mᵊl.aɪz (US) ˈnɔːr- **-es** -ɪz **-ing** -ɪŋ **-ed** -d
normally ˈnɔː.mᵊl.i (US) ˈnɔːr-
Norman ˈnɔː.mən (US) ˈnɔːr- **-s** -z **ˌNorman ˈconquest**
Normanby ˈnɔː.mən.bi, -məm- (US) ˈnɔːr-
Normandy *in France:* ˈnɔː.mən.di (US) ˈnɔːr- *in Surrey:* ˈnɔː.mən.di (US) ˈnɔːr- *also locally:* nɔːˈmæn.di (US) nɔːr-

Normanton 'nɔː.mən.tən (US) 'nɔːr-
normative 'nɔː.mə.tɪv (US) 'nɔːr.mə.t̬ɪv **-ly** -li
Norn nɔːn (US) nɔːrn **-s** -z
Norodom Sihanouk ˌnɒr.ə.dɒm'siː.jæn.ʊk (US) ˌnɔːr.ə.dɑːm-, -jɑː.nʊk
Norris 'nɒr.ɪs (US) 'nɔːr-
Norrköping 'nɔː.tʃɜː.pɪŋ (US) 'nɔːr-
Norroy 'nɒr.ɔɪ (US) 'nɔːr- **-s** -z
Norse nɔːs (US) nɔːrs **-man** -mən **-men** -mən, -men
north (N) nɔːθ (US) nɔːrθ **ˌNorth A'merica ; ˌNorth At'lantic ; ˌNorth Caro'lina; ˌNorth Da'kota ; 'North ˌIsland ; ˌNorth Ko'rea ; ˌnorth 'pole ; ˌNorth 'Sea**
Northallerton ˌnɔː'θæl.ə.t^{ə}n (US) ˌnɔːrθ'æl.ɚ.t̬ən
Northampton ˌnɔː'θæmp.tən, ˌnɔːθ'hæmp- *locally:* nə'θæmp- (US) ˌnɔːr'θæmp-, ˌnɔːrθ'hæmp- **-shire** -ʃə^{r} (US) -ʃɚ, -ˌʃɪə^{r} (US) -ˌʃɪr
Northanger nɔː'θæŋ.gə^{r}, -ə^{r}; 'nɔː.θæŋ-, 'nɔːθ.hæŋ- (US) nɔːr'θæŋ.gɚ, -ɚ; 'nɔːr.θæŋ-, 'nɔːrθ.hæŋ-
Northants. (*abbrev. for* **Northamptonshire**) 'nɔː.θænts, -'- (US) 'nɔːr.θænts, -'-
North Baddesley ˌnɔːθ'bædz.li (US) ˌnɔːrθ-
northbound 'nɔːθ.baʊnd (US) 'nɔːrθ-
Northbrook 'nɔːθ.brʊk (US) 'nɔːrθ-
Northcliffe 'nɔːθ.klɪf (US) 'nɔːrθ-
Northcote 'nɔːθ.kət, -kəʊt (US) 'nɔːrθ.kət, -koʊt
northeast (N) ˌnɔːθ'iːst (US) ˌnɔːrθ- *nautical pronunciation:* ˌnɔː'riːst (US) ˌnɔːr'iːst **-wards** -wədz (US) -wɚdz *stress shift:* ˌnortheast 'wind
northeaster ˌnɔːθ'iː.stə^{r} (US) ˌnɔːrθ'iː.stɚ *in nautical usage also:* ˌnɔː'riː- (US) ˌnɔːr'iː- **-s** -z
northeasterl|y ˌnɔːθ'iː.st^{ə}l.|i (US) ˌnɔːrθ'iː.stɚ.l|i *in nautical usage also:* ˌnɔː'riː- (US) ˌnɔːr'iː- **-ies** -iz
northeastern (N) ˌnɔːθ'iː.stən (US) ˌnɔːrθ'iː.stɚn *in nautical usage also:* ˌnɔː'riː- (US) ˌnɔːr'iː- **-er/s** -ə^{r}/z (US) -ɚ/z
northeastward ˌnɔːθ'iːst.wəd (US) ˌnɔːrθ'iːst.wɚd *in nautical usage also:* ˌnɔː'riː- (US) ˌnɔːr'iː- **-s** -z
Northen 'nɔː.ð^{ə}n (US) 'nɔːr-
northerl|y 'nɔː.ð^{ə}l.|i (US) 'nɔːr.ðɚ.l|i **-ies** -iz
northern (N) 'nɔː.ð^{ə}n (US) 'nɔːr.θɚn **-most** -məʊst, -məst (US) -moʊst, -məst **ˌNorthern 'Ireland ; ˌnorthern 'lights ; ˌNorthern 'Territory**
northerner (N) 'nɔː.ð^{ə}n.ə^{r} (US) 'nɔːr.θɚ.nɚ **-s** -z
Northfield 'nɔːθ.fiːld (US) 'nɔːrθ-
Northfleet 'nɔːθ.fliːt (US) 'nɔːrθ-
northing 'nɔː.θɪŋ (US) 'nɔːr-
Northland 'nɔːθ.lənd (US) 'nɔːrθ.lænd, -lənd
North|man 'nɔːθ|.mən (US) 'nɔːrθ- **-men** -mən, -men
north-northeast ˌnɔːθ.nɔːθ'iːst (US) ˌnɔːrθ.nɔːrθ'- *in nautical usage also:* ˌnɔː.nɔː'riːst (US) ˌnɔːr.nɔːr'iːst
north-northwest ˌnɔːθ.nɔːθ'west (US) ˌnɔːrθ.nɔːrθ'- *in nautical usage also:* ˌnɔː.nɔː'- (US) ˌnɔːr.nɔːr'-
Northolt 'nɔː.θəʊlt (US) 'nɔːr.θoʊlt
North-South ˌnɔːθ'saʊθ (US) ˌnɔːrθ- **ˌNorth-ˌSouth di'vide**
Northumberland nɔː'θʌmb.^{ə}l.ənd, nə- (US) nɔːr'θʌm.bɚ.lənd
Northumbri|a nɔː'θʌm.bri|.ə (US) nɔːr- **-an/s** -ən/z
northward 'nɔːθ.wəd (US) 'nɔːrθ.wɚd **-s** -z **-ly** -li
northwest (N) ˌnɔːθ'west (US) ˌnɔːrθ- *nautical pronunciation:* ˌnɔː'west (US) ˌnɔːr- **-wards** -wədz (US) -wɚdz *stress shift, see compound:* **ˌNorthwest 'Territories**
northwesterl|y ˌnɔːθ'wes.t^{ə}l.|i (US) ˌnɔːrθ'wes.tɚ.l|i *in nautical usage also:* ˌnɔː- (US) ˌnɔːr- **-ies** -iz
northwestern (N) ˌnɔːθ'wes.tən (US) ˌnɔːrθ'wes.tɚn *in nautical usage also:* ˌnɔː- (US) ˌnɔːr- **-er/s** -ə^{r}/z (US) -ɚ/z
northwestward ˌnɔːθ'west.wəd (US) ˌnɔːrθ'west.wɚd *in nautical usage also:* ˌnɔː- (US) ˌnɔːr-
Northwich 'nɔːθ.wɪtʃ (US) 'nɔːrθ-
Northwood 'nɔːθ.wʊd (US) 'nɔːrθ-
Norton 'nɔː.t^{ə}n (US) 'nɔːr-
Norton Radstock ˌnɔː.t^{ə}n'ræd.stɒk (US) ˌnɔːr.t^{ə}n'ræd.stɑːk
Norway 'nɔː.weɪ (US) 'nɔːr-
Norwegian nɔː'wiː.dʒ^{ə}n (US) nɔːr- **-s** -z
Norwich *in England:* 'nɒr.ɪdʒ, -ɪtʃ (US) 'nɔːr.ɪtʃ, -wɪtʃ *in US:* 'nɔː.wɪtʃ (US) 'nɔːr-
Norwood 'nɔː.wʊd (US) 'nɔːr-
nos. (N) (*abbrev. for* **numbers**) 'nʌm.bəz (US) -bɚz
nos|e nəʊz (US) noʊz **-es** -ɪz **-ing** -ɪŋ **-ed** -d **'nose ˌbag ; 'nose ˌring ; ˌcut off one's ˌnose to ˌspite one's 'face ; ˌkeep one's ˌnose to the 'grindstone ; ˌlook down one's 'nose at ; ˌpay through the 'nose (for) ; ˌpoke one's 'nose (into)**
nosebleed 'nəʊz.bliːd (US) 'noʊz- **-s** -z
nose-div|e 'nəʊz.daɪv (US) 'noʊz- **-es** -z **-ing** -ɪŋ **-ed** -d
no-see-um ˌnəʊ'siː.əm (US) ˌnoʊ- **-s** -z
nosegay 'nəʊz.geɪ (US) 'noʊz- **-s** -z
nos|ey 'nəʊ.z|i (US) 'noʊ- **-ier** -i.ə^{r} (US) -i.ɚ **-iest** -i.ɪst, -i.əst **-ily** -ɪ.li, -^{ə}l.i **-iness** -ɪ.nəs, -ɪ.nɪs
Nosferatu ˌnɒs.fə'rɑː.tuː (US) ˌnɑːs-
nosh nɒʃ (US) nɑːʃ **-es** -ɪz **-ing** -ɪŋ **-ed** -t
no-show ˌnəʊ'ʃəʊ (US) 'noʊˌʃoʊ *stress shift, British only:* ˌno-show 'passenger
nosh-up 'nɒʃ.ʌp (US) 'nɑːʃ- **-s** -s
nostalg|ia nɒs'tæl.dʒ|ə, -dʒ|i.ə (US) nɑː'stæl.dʒ|ə, nə-, nɔː-, -dʒ|i.ə **-ic** -ɪk **-ically** -ɪ.k^{ə}l.i, -ɪ.kli
Nostradamus ˌnɒs.trə'deɪ.məs, -'dɑː- (US) ˌnoʊ.strə'dɑː-, ˌnɑː.strə'deɪ-
nostril 'nɒs.tr^{ə}l, -trɪl (US) 'nɑː.str^{ə}l **-s** -z
Nostromo nɒs'trəʊ.məʊ (US) nɑː'stroʊ.moʊ
nostrum 'nɒs.trəm (US) 'nɑː.strəm **-s** -z
nos|y 'nəʊ.z|i (US) 'noʊ- **-ier** -i.ə^{r} (US) -i.ɚ **-iest** -i.ɪst, -i.əst **-ily** -ɪ.li, -^{ə}l.i **-iness** -ɪ.nəs, -ɪ.nɪs
nosy parker ˌnəʊ.zi'pɑː.kə^{r} (US) ˌnoʊ.zi'pɑːr.kɚ **-s** -z
not nɒt (US) nɑːt
nota bene ˌnəʊ.tɑː'ben.eɪ, -tə'biː.ni (US) ˌnoʊ.t̬ə'ben.eɪ, -tɑː'-, -'biː.ni
notabilit|y ˌnəʊ.tə'bɪl.ə.t|i, -ɪ.t|i (US) ˌnoʊ.t̬ə'bɪl.ə.t̬|i **-ies** -iz
notab|le 'nəʊ.tə.b|l̩ (US) 'noʊ.t̬ə- **-ly** -li **-leness** -l̩.nəs, -nɪs
notarial nəʊ'teə.ri.əl (US) noʊ'ter.i- **-ly** -i
notariz|e, -is|e 'nəʊ.t^{ə}r.aɪz (US) 'noʊ.t̬ə.raɪz **-es** -ɪz **-ing** -ɪŋ **-ed** -d
notar|y 'nəʊ.t^{ə}r|.i (US) 'noʊ.t̬ɚ- **-ies** -iz
nota|te nəʊ'teɪ|t (US) 'noʊ.teɪ|t **-tes** -ts **-ting** -tɪŋ (US) -t̬ɪŋ **-ted** -tɪd (US) -t̬ɪd
notation nəʊ'teɪ.ʃ^{ə}n (US) noʊ- **-s** -z
notch nɒtʃ (US) nɑːtʃ **-es** -ɪz **-ing** -ɪŋ **-ed** -t
not|e nəʊt (US) noʊt **-es** -s **-ing** -ɪŋ (US) 'noʊ.t̬ɪŋ **-ed** -ɪd (US) 'noʊ.t̬ɪd
notebook 'nəʊt.bʊk (US) 'noʊt- **-s** -s
notelet 'nəʊt.lət, -lɪt (US) 'noʊt- **-s** -s
notepad 'nəʊt.pæd (US) 'noʊt- **-s** -z
notepaper 'nəʊtˌpeɪ.pə^{r} (US) 'noʊtˌpeɪ.pɚ
noteworth|y 'nəʊtˌwɜː.ð|i (US) 'noʊtˌwɜːr- **-ily** -ɪ.li, -^{ə}.li **-iness** -ɪ.nəs, -ɪ.nɪs
not-for-profit ˌnɒt.fə'prɒf.ɪt (US) ˌnɑːt.fɚ'prɑː.fɪt
nothing 'nʌθ.ɪŋ **-s** -z **-ness** -nəs, -nɪs
notic|e 'nəʊ.tɪs (US) 'noʊ.t̬ɪs **-es** -ɪz **-ing** -ɪŋ **-ed** -t
noticeab|le 'nəʊ.tɪ.sə.b|l̩ (US) 'noʊ.t̬ɪ- **-ly** -li
notice-board 'nəʊ.tɪs.bɔːd (US) 'noʊ.t̬ɪs.bɔːrd **-s** -z
notifiable 'nəʊ.tɪ.faɪ.ə.bl̩, -tə-, ˌnəʊ.tɪ'faɪ-, -tə'- (US) 'noʊ.t̬ə.faɪ-
notification ˌnəʊ.tɪ.fɪ'keɪ.ʃ^{ə}n, -tə- (US) ˌnoʊ.t̬ə- **-s** -z

noti|fy 'nəʊ.tɪ|.faɪ, -tə- US 'noʊ.t̬ə- **-fies** -faɪz **-fying** -faɪ.ɪŋ **-fied** -faɪd
notion 'nəʊ.ʃən US 'noʊ- **-s** -z
notional 'nəʊ.ʃən.əl, 'nəʊʃ.nəl US 'noʊ.ʃən.əl, 'noʊʃ.nəl **-ly** -i
notoriety ˌnəʊ.tər'aɪ.ə.ti US ˌnoʊ.t̬ə'raɪ.ə.t̬i
notorious nəʊ'tɔː.ri.əs US noʊ'tɔːr.i- **-ly** -li **-ness** -nəs, -nɪs
Notre Dame *in France:* ˌnəʊ.trə'dɑːm, ˌnɒt.rə'- US ˌnoʊ.trə'-, ˌnoʊ.t̬ɚ'-, -'deɪm *in the US:* ˌnəʊ.trə'deɪm US ˌnoʊ.t̬ɚ'-
Nottingham 'nɒt.ɪŋ.əm US 'nɑː.t̬ɪŋ- **-shire** -ʃəʳ, -ˌʃɪəʳ US -ʃɚ, -ˌʃɪr
Notting Hill ˌnɒt.ɪŋ'hɪl US ˌnɑː.t̬ɪŋ'- *stress shift, see compound:* ˌ**Notting Hill 'Gate**
Notts. (*abbrev. for* **Nottinghamshire**) nɒts US nɑːts
notwithstanding ˌnɒt.wɪθ'stæn.dɪŋ, -wɪð'- US ˌnɑːt-
Nouakchott nu'ɑːk.ʃɒt US 'nwɑːk.ʃɑːt, -'-
nougat 'nuː.gɑː, 'nʌg.ət US 'nuː.gət **nougats** 'nuː.gɑːz, 'nʌg.əts US 'nuː.gəts
nought nɔːt US nɑːt, nɔːt **-s** -s ˌ**noughts and 'crosses**
noumen|on 'nuː.mə.n|ən, 'naʊ-, -mɪ-, -n|ɒn US 'nuː.mə.n|ɑːn **-a** -ə **-al** -əl
noun naʊn **-s** -z
nourish 'nʌr.ɪʃ US 'nɜːr- **-es** -ɪz **-ing** -ɪŋ **-ed** -t **-ment** -mənt
nourishing 'nʌr.ɪ.ʃɪŋ US 'nɜːr-
nous naʊs US nuːs, naʊs
nouveau(x) 'nuː.vəʊ, -'- US nuː'voʊ, '--
nouveau(x) riche(s) ˌnuː.vəʊ'riːʃ US -voʊ'-
nouveau roman ˌnuː.vəʊ.rəʊ'mɑ̃ːŋ US -voʊ.roʊ'mɑːn
nouvelle cuisine ˌnuː.vel.kwɪ'ziːn, nuːˌvel-, -kwə'-, -kwiː- US nuːˌvel-
nouvelle vague (N) ˌnuː.vel'vɑːg
Nov. (*abbrev. for* **November**) nɒv, nəʊ'vem.bəʳ US noʊ'vem.bɚ
nov|a (N) 'nəʊ.v|ə US 'noʊ- **-ae** -iː **-as** -əz
Nova Scotia ˌnəʊ.və'skəʊ.ʃə US ˌnoʊ.və'skoʊ-
novation nəʊ'veɪ.ʃən US noʊ- **-s**
Novaya Zemlya ˌnɒv.ə.jə.zem'ljɑː, ˌ-ɑː- US ˌnɔː.vɑː.jɑː-, ˌnoʊ-
novel 'nɒv.əl US 'nɑː.vəl **-istic** --'ɪs.tɪk **-s** -z
novelette ˌnɒv.əl'et US ˌnɑː.vəl'- **-s** -s
novelist 'nɒv.əl.ɪst US 'nɑː.və- **-s** -s
novelization, -isation ˌnɒv.əl.aɪ'zeɪ.ʃən, -ɪ'- US ˌnɑː.vəl.ɪ'- **-s** -z
noveliz|e, -is|e 'nɒv.əl.aɪz US 'nɑː.və.laɪz **-es** -ɪz **-ing** -ɪŋ **-ed** -d
novel|la nəʊ'vel|.ə US noʊ- **-las** -z **-le** -eɪ
Novello nə'vel.əʊ US -oʊ
novelt|y 'nɒv.əl.t|i US 'nɑː.vəl.t̬|i **-ies** -iz
November nəʊ'vem.bəʳ US noʊ'vem.bɚ **-s** -z
novena nəʊ'viː.nə US noʊ- **-s** -z
Novgorod 'nɒv.gə.rɒd US 'nɔːv.gə.rɑːd, 'nɑːv-, -rɑːt
Novial 'nəʊ.vi.əl US 'noʊ-
novic|e 'nɒv.ɪs US 'nɑː.vɪs **-es** -ɪz
novitiate nəʊ'vɪʃ.i.ət, nɒv'ɪʃ-, -eɪt, -ɪt US noʊ'vɪʃ.ɪt, '-i.ɪt, -eɪt **-s** -s
Novocaine® 'nəʊ.vəʊ.keɪn, 'nɒv.əʊ- US 'noʊ.və-
Novosibirsk ˌnəʊ.vəʊ.sɪ'bɪəsk, ˌnɒv.əʊ-, -sə'- US ˌnoʊ.və.sɪ'bɪrsk, -sə'-
Novum Organum ˌnəʊ.vəm.'ɔː.gə.nəm, ɔː'gɑː.nəm US ˌnoʊ.vəm'ɔːr.gə.nəm; -ɔːr'gæn-
now naʊ
NOW naʊ
nowadays 'naʊ.ə.deɪz, 'naʊə-
Nowell *personal name:* nəʊəl; 'nəʊ.el US noʊəl; 'noʊ.el *Christmas:* nəʊ'el US noʊ-
nowhere 'nəʊ.*h*weəʳ US 'noʊ.*h*wer
no-win ˌnəʊ'wɪn US ˌnoʊ- *stress shift, see compound:* ˌ**no-win situ'ation**
nowise 'nəʊ.waɪz US 'noʊ-
nowt naʊt
noxious 'nɒk.ʃəs US 'nɑːk- **-ly** -li **-ness** -nəs, -nɪs
Noyes nɔɪz
nozzle 'nɒz.l̩ US 'nɑː.zl̩ **-s** -z
nr (*abbrev. for* **near**) nɪəʳ US nɪr
NSPCC ˌen.esˌpiː.siː'siː
-n't -ənt
Note: Weak form suffix. This spelling represents a weak form of **not** which occurs after auxiliary verbs.
nth enθ
nu njuː US nuː, njuː
nuanc|e 'njuː.ɑːnts, -ɑ̃ːns, -'- US 'nuː.ɑːnts, 'njuː-, -'- **-es** -ɪz
nub nʌb
nubble 'nʌb.l̩ **-s** -z
nubbly 'nʌb.li, -l̩.i
Nubi|a 'njuː.bi|.ə US 'nuː-, 'njuː- **-an/s** -ən/z
nubile 'njuː.baɪl US 'nuː.bɪl, 'njuː-, -baɪl, -bəl
nubility njuː'bɪl.ə.ti, -ɪ.ti US nuː'bɪl.ə.t̬i, njuː-
nuclear 'njuː.kli.əʳ US 'nuː.kli.ɚ, 'njuː- ˌ**nuclear dis'armament**; ˌ**nuclear 'energy**; ˌ**nuclear 'family**; ˌ**nuclear 'fusion**; ˌ**nuclear 'industry**; ˌ**nuclear re'actor**; ˌ**nuclear 'winter**
nuclear-free ˌnjuː.kli.ə'friː US ˌnuː.kli.ɚ'-, ˌnjuː- *stress shift, British only, see compound:* ˌ**nuclear-free 'zone** US ˌ**nuclear-'free** ˌ**zone**
nucleic njuː'kliː.ɪk, -'kleɪ- US nuː'kliː-, njuː-, -'kleɪ- **nuˌcleic 'acid**
nucleo- ˌnjuː.kli.əʊ- US ˌnuː.kli.oʊ-, ˌnjuː-, -ə-
nucleol|us njuː'kliː.əl|.əs; ˌnjuː.kli'əʊ.l|əs US nuː'kliː.əl|.əs, njuː- **-i** -aɪ
nucleotide 'njuː.kli.əʊ.taɪd US 'nuː.kli.oʊ-, 'njuː- **-s** -z
nucle|us 'njuː.kli|.əs US 'nuː-, 'njuː- **-uses** -ə.sɪz **-i** -aɪ
nuclide 'njuː.klaɪd US 'nuː-, 'njuː- **-s** -z
nude njuːd US nuːd, njuːd **-s** -z
nudg|e nʌdʒ **-es** -ɪz **-ing** -ɪŋ **-ed** -d
nud|ism 'njuː.dɪ|.zəm US 'nuː-, 'njuː- **-ist/s** -ɪst/s
nudit|y 'njuː.də.t|i, -ɪ.t|i US 'nuː.də.t̬|i, 'njuː-
Nuevo Leon nweɪ.vəʊ.leɪ'ɒn US nuː'eɪ.voʊ.leɪ'ɑːn
Nuffield 'nʌf.iːld
nugatory 'njuː.gə.tər.i; njuː'geɪ- US 'nuː.gə.tɔːr-, 'njuː-
Nugent 'njuː.dʒənt US 'nuː-, 'njuː-
nugg|et 'nʌg|.ɪt **-ets** -ɪts **-ety** -ɪ.ti US -ɪ.t̬i
nuisanc|e 'njuː.sənts US 'nuː-, 'njuː- **-es** -ɪz
Nuit nʌt US nʌt, nuːt
NUJ ˌen.juː'dʒeɪ
nuk|e njuːk US nuːk, njuːk **-es** -s **-ing** -ɪŋ **-ed** -t
Nuku'alofa ˌnuː.kuː.ə'lɔː.fə
null nʌl ˌ**null and 'void**
nullah 'nʌl.ə **-s** -z
Nullarbor 'nʌl.ə.bɔːʳ US -ɚ.bɔːr ˌ**Nullarbor 'Plains**
nullification ˌnʌl.ɪ.fɪ'keɪ.ʃən, ˌ-ə-
nulli|fy 'nʌl.ɪ|.faɪ, '-ə- **-fies** -faɪz **-fying** -faɪ.ɪŋ **-fied** -faɪd
nullipar|a nʌl'ɪp.ər|.ə US nʌl-, nə'lɪp- **-ae** -iː **-as** -əz **-ous** -əs
nullit|y 'nʌl.ə.t|i, -ɪ.t|i US -ə.t̬|i **-ies** -iz
NUM ˌen.juː'em
Numa Pompilius ˌnjuː.mə.pɒm'pɪl.i.əs US ˌnuː.mə.pɑːm'-, ˌnjuː-
numb nʌm **-ly** -li **-ness** -nəs, -nɪs **-s** -z **-ing** -ɪŋ **-ed** -d
numbat 'nʌm.bæt **-s** -s
numb|er 'nʌm.b|əʳ US -b|ɚ **-ers** -əz US -ɚz **-ering** -ər.ɪŋ **-ered** -əd US -ɚd **-erless** -əl.əs, -ɪs US -ɚ.ləs, -lɪs ˌ**number 'one** *stress shift:* ˌnumber one 'fan; ˌ**Number '10/Ten** *stress*

shift: ˌNumber 10/Ten 'Downing Street
number-crunch 'nʌm.bə.krʌntʃ (US) -bɚ- **-es** -ɪz **-ing** -ɪŋ **-ed** -t **-er/s** -əʳ/z (US) -ɚ/z
numberplate 'nʌm.bə.pleɪt (US) -bɚ- **-s** -s
Numbers 'nʌm.bəz (US) -bɚz
numbing 'nʌm.ɪŋ **-ly** -li
numbskull 'nʌm.skʌl **-s** -z
numerable 'njuː.mᵊr.ə.bl̩ (US) 'nuː-, 'njuː-
numeracy 'njuː.mᵊr.ə.si (US) 'nuː-, 'njuː-
numeral 'njuː.mᵊr.ᵊl (US) 'nuː-, 'njuː- **-s** -z
numerate (*adj.*) 'njuː.mᵊr.ət, -ɪt (US) 'nuː-, 'njuː-
numer|ate (*v.*) 'njuː.mᵊr|.eɪt (US) 'nuː.mə.r|eɪt, 'njuː- **-ates** -eɪts **-ating** -eɪ.tɪŋ (US) -eɪ.t̬ɪŋ **-ated** -eɪ.tɪd (US) -eɪ.t̬ɪd
numeration ˌnjuː.mᵊr'eɪ.ʃᵊn (US) ˌnuː.mə'reɪ-, ˌnjuː-
numerative 'njuː.mᵊr.ə.tɪv (US) 'nuː.mɚ.ə.t̬ɪv, 'njuː- **-s** -z
numerator 'njuː.mᵊr.eɪ.təʳ (US) 'nuː.mə.reɪ.t̬ɚ, 'njuː- **-s** -z
numeric njuː'mer.ɪk (US) nuː-, njuː- **-s** -s
numerical njuː'mer.ɪ.kl̩ (US) nuː-, njuː- **-ly** -i
numerologic|al ˌnjuː.mᵊr.ə'lɒdʒ.ɪ.k|ᵊl (US) ˌnuː.mɚ.ə'lɑː.dʒɪ-, ˌnjuː- **-ally** -ᵊl.i, -li
numerolog|y ˌnjuː.mᵊr'ɒl.ə.dʒ|i (US) ˌnuː.mə'rɑː.lə-, ˌnjuː- **-ist** -ɪst/s
numero uno ˌnuː.mᵊr.əʊ'uː.nəʊ (US) ˌnuː.mə.roʊ'uː.noʊ, ˌnjuː-
numerous 'njuː.mᵊr.əs (US) 'nuː-, 'njuː- **-ly** -li **-ness** -nəs, -nɪs
Numidi|a njuː'mɪd.i|.ə (US) nuː-, njuː- **-an/s** -ən/z
numinous 'njuː.mɪ.nəs (US) 'nuː-, 'njuː-
numismatic ˌnjuː.mɪz'mæt.ɪk (US) ˌnuː.mɪz'mæt̬.ɪk, ˌnjuː- **-s** -s **-ally** -ᵊl.i, -li
numismatist njuː'mɪz.mə.tɪst (US) nuː-, njuː- **-s** -s
numnah 'nʌm.nə **-s** -z
numskull 'nʌm.skʌl **-s** -z
nun (N) nʌn **-s** -z
Nunc Dimittis ˌnʊŋk.dɪ'mɪt.ɪs, ˌnʌŋk-, -daɪ'-, -də'- (US) ˌnʊŋk.dɪ'mɪt̬- **-es** -ɪz
nunciature 'nʌnt.si.ə.tjʊəʳ, -tʃəʳ (US) -tjʊr, -tʃɚ
nuncio 'nʌn.ʃi.əʊ, -ʃəʊ, 'nʌnt.si- (US) 'nʌnt.si.oʊ, 'nʊnt- **-s** -z
Nuneaton nʌn'iː.tᵊn
Nuneham 'njuː.nəm (US) 'nuː-, 'njuː-
Nunn nʌn
nunner|y 'nʌn.ᵊr|.i **-ies** -iz
NUPE *trades union:* 'njuː.pi (US) 'nuː-, 'njuː-
Nupe *language and people:* 'nuː.peɪ **-s** -z
nuptial 'nʌp.ʃᵊl, -tʃᵊl **-s** -z
Nuremberg 'njʊə.rəm.bɜːg, 'njɔː- (US) 'nʊr.əm.bɜːrg, 'njʊr-
Nureyev 'njʊə.ri.ef; -reɪ-, njʊə'reɪ-, -ev (US) 'nʊr.i.ef, nʊ'reɪ.jef
Nurofen® 'njʊə.rəʊ.fen, 'njɔː- (US) nuː'roʊ.fən, njʊ'-
nurs|e nɜːs (US) nɜːrs **-es** -ɪz **-ing** -ɪŋ **-ed** -t
nurs(e)ling 'nɜːs.lɪŋ (US) 'nɜːrs- **-s** -z
nursemaid 'nɜːs.meɪd (US) 'nɜːrs- **-s** -z
nurser|y 'nɜː.sᵊr|.i (US) 'nɜːr- **-ies** -iz 'nursery ˌrhyme ; 'nursery ˌschool ; 'nursery ˌslope
nurserymaid 'nɜː.sᵊr.i.meɪd (US) 'nɜːr- **-s** -z
nursery|man 'nɜː.sᵊr.i|.mən (US) 'nɜːr- **-men** -mən
nursing 'nɜː.sɪŋ (US) 'nɜːr- 'nursing ˌhome ; ˌnursing 'mother
nurt|ure 'nɜː.tʃ|əʳ (US) 'nɜːr.tʃ|ɚ **-ures** -əz (US) -ɚz **-uring** -ᵊr.ɪŋ **-ured** -əd (US) -ɚd
NUS ˌen.juː'es
nut *food:* nʌt **-s** -s **-ting** -ɪŋ **-ted** -ɪd
Nut *Egyptian goddess:* nʌt (US) nʌt, nuːt
NUT *trades union:* ˌen.juː'tiː
nu|tate njuː|'teɪt (US) nuː-, njuː- **-tates** -'teɪts **-tating** -'teɪ.tɪŋ (US) -'teɪ.t̬ɪŋ **-tated** -'teɪ.tɪd (US) -'teɪ.t̬ɪd
nutation njuː'teɪ.ʃᵊn (US) nuː-, njuː- **-al** **-s** -z
nut-brown ˌnʌt'braʊn *stress shift:* ˌnut-brown 'hair
nutcracker 'nʌtˌkræk.əʳ (US) -ɚ **-s** -z
nuthatch 'nʌt.hætʃ **-es** -ɪz
nuthou|se 'nʌt.haʊ|s **-ses** -zɪz
Nutkin 'nʌt.kɪn
nutmeg 'nʌt.meg **-s** -z
Nutrasweet® 'njuː.trəˌswiːt (US) 'nuː-, 'njuː
nutria 'njuː.tri.ə (US) 'nuː-, 'njuː-
nutrient 'njuː.tri.ənt (US) 'nuː-, 'njuː- **-s**
nutriment 'njuː.trə.mənt, -trɪ- (US) 'nuː-, 'njuː- **-s** -s
nutrition njuː'trɪʃ.ᵊn (US) nuː-, njuː- **-al** -ᵊl **-ally** -ᵊl.i
nutritionist njuː'trɪʃ.ᵊn.ɪst, -'trɪʃ.nɪst (US) nuː-, njuː- **-s** -s
nutritious njuː'trɪʃ.əs (US) nuː-, njuː- **-ly** -li **-ness** -nəs, -nɪs
nutritive 'njuː.trə.tɪv, -trɪ- (US) 'nuː.trə.t̬ɪv, 'njuː-
nuts nʌts ˌ**nuts and 'bolts**
nutshell 'nʌt.ʃel **-s** -z
Nutt nʌt
Nuttall 'nʌt.ɔːl
nutter (N) 'nʌt.əʳ (US) 'nʌt̬.ɚ **-s**
nutt|y 'nʌt|.i (US) 'nʌt̬|.i **-ily** -ɪ.li **-iness** -ɪ.nəs, -ɪ.nɪs
nux vomica ˌnʌks'vɒm.ɪ.kə (US) -'vɑː.mɪ-
nuzzl|e 'nʌz.l̩ **-es** -z **-ing** -ɪŋ, 'nʌz.lɪŋ **-ed** -d
NVQ ˌen.viː'kjuː
NW (*abbrev. for* **northwest**) ˌen'dʌb.l̩.juː; ˌnɔːθ'west (US) ˌen'dʌb.l̩.juː; ˌnɔːrθ-
NY (*abbrev. for* **New York**) ˌen'waɪ
Nyanja 'njæn.dʒə
Nyanza ni'æn.zə, naɪ-; 'njæn- (US) 'njæn-, ni'æn-, naɪ-
Nyasa naɪ'æs.ə, ni-; 'njæs- (US) naɪ'æs.ə; 'njɑː.sɑː
Nyasaland naɪ'æs.ə.lænd, ni-; 'njæs- (US) naɪ'æs-; 'njɑː.sɑː.lænd
Nyerere njə'reə.ri, nɪə-, -'rer.i (US) njə'rer-, ˌni.ə'-
nylon 'naɪ.lɒn (US) -lɑːn **-s** -z
Nyman 'naɪ.mən
nymph nɪmpf **-s** -s **-al** -ᵊl
nymphet, **nymphette** nɪmp'fet; 'nɪmp.fɪt, -fət, -fet (US) 'nɪmp.fət; nɪmp'fet
nympho 'nɪmp.fəʊ (US) -foʊ **-s** -z
nymphomani|a ˌnɪmp.fəʊ'meɪ.ni|.ə (US) -foʊ'-, -fə'-, '-nj|ə **-ac/s** -æk
Nyree 'naɪə.riː, -ri (US) 'naɪ-
nystagmus nɪ'stæg.məs
NZ (*abbrev. for* **New Zealand**) ˌen'zed (US) -'ziː

O

o *the letter:* əʊ ⓊⓈ oʊ **-'s** -z **-es** -z
O (*interjection*) əʊ ⓊⓈ oʊ
o' (*abbrev. for* **of**) *weak form only:* ə
Note: This spelling is used to represent a weak form of **of** in archaic and slang expressions and names, for example "pint o' bitter" /ˌpaɪnt.ə'bɪt.əʳ ⓊⓈ -'bɪṭ.ɚ/, "will-o'-the-wisp" /ˌwɪl.ə.ðə'wɪsp/.
O. (*abbrev. of* **Ohio**) əʊ; əʊ'haɪ.əʊ ⓊⓈ oʊ; oʊ'haɪ.oʊ, ə-
Oadby 'əʊd.bi ⓊⓈ 'oʊd-
oaf əʊf ⓊⓈ oʊf **-s** -s
oafish 'əʊ.fɪʃ ⓊⓈ 'oʊ- **-ly** -li **-ness** -nəs, -nɪs
Oahu əʊ'ɑː.huː ⓊⓈ oʊ-
oak əʊk ⓊⓈ oʊk **-s** -s **-en** -ᵊn **-y** -i
oak-apple 'əʊkˌæp.l̩ ⓊⓈ 'oʊk- **-s** -z
Oakdale 'əʊk.deɪl ⓊⓈ 'oʊk-
Oakeley 'əʊk.li ⓊⓈ 'oʊk-
Oakengates 'əʊ.kᵊn.geɪts, -kᵊŋ-, ˌ--'- ⓊⓈ 'oʊk.ᵊn.geɪts, ˌ--'-
Oakes əʊks ⓊⓈ oʊks
Oakey 'əʊ.ki ⓊⓈ 'oʊ-
Oakham 'əʊ.kəm ⓊⓈ 'oʊ-
Oakhampton ˌəʊk'hæmp.tən ⓊⓈ 'oʊkˌhæmp- *stress shift, British only:* ˌOakhampton 'centre
Oakland 'əʊk.lənd ⓊⓈ 'oʊk- **-s** -z
Oakleigh, Oakley 'əʊk.li ⓊⓈ 'oʊk-
Oaks əʊks ⓊⓈ oʊks
oakum 'əʊ.kəm ⓊⓈ 'oʊ-
Oakworth 'əʊk.wəθ, -wɜːθ ⓊⓈ 'oʊk.wɚθ, -wɜːrθ
OAP ˌəʊ.eɪ'piː ⓊⓈ ˌoʊ- **-s** -z
OAPEC ˌəʊ'eɪ.pek ⓊⓈ ˌoʊ-
oar ɔːʳ ⓊⓈ ɔːr **-s** -z **-ing** -ɪŋ **-ed** -d ˌ**stick one's 'oar in**
oarlock 'ɔː.lɒk ⓊⓈ 'ɔːr.lɑːk **-s** -s
oars|man 'ɔːz|.mən ⓊⓈ 'ɔːrz- **-men** -mən **-woman** -ˌwʊm.ən **-women** -ˌwɪm.ɪn
OAS ˌəʊ.eɪ.'es ⓊⓈ ˌoʊ-
oas|is (**O**) əʊ'eɪ.s|ɪs ⓊⓈ oʊ- **-es** -iːz
oast əʊst ⓊⓈ oʊst **-s** -s
oasthou|se 'əʊst.haʊ|s ⓊⓈ 'oʊst- **-ses** -zɪz
oat əʊt ⓊⓈ oʊt **-s** -s
oatcake 'əʊt.keɪk ⓊⓈ 'oʊt- **-s** -s
oaten 'əʊ.tᵊn ⓊⓈ 'oʊ-
Oates əʊts ⓊⓈ oʊts
oa|th əʊ|θ ⓊⓈ oʊ|θ **-ths** -ðz, -θs
Oatlands 'əʊt.ləndz ⓊⓈ 'oʊt-
oatmeal 'əʊt.miːl ⓊⓈ 'oʊt-
oats əʊts ⓊⓈ oʊts
Oaxaca wə'hɑː.kə, wɑː- ⓊⓈ wɑː'hɑː.kɑː, wə-, -kə
Ob ɒb ⓊⓈ ɑːb, ɑːp
Obadiah ˌəʊ.bə'daɪə ⓊⓈ ˌoʊ-
Oban 'əʊ.bᵊn ⓊⓈ 'oʊ-
obbligat|o ˌɒb.lɪ'gɑː.t|əʊ, -lə'- ⓊⓈ ˌɑː.blɪ'gɑː.ṭ|oʊ **-os** -əʊz ⓊⓈ -oʊz **-i** -iː
obduracy 'ɒb.djᵊr.ə.si, -djʊ.rə- ⓊⓈ 'ɑːb.dʊr.ə-, -djʊr-
obdurate 'ɒb.djᵊr.ət, -djʊ.rət, -rɪt, -reɪt ⓊⓈ 'ɑːb.dʊr.ɪt, -djʊr- **-ly** -li **-ness** -nəs, -nɪs
obduration ˌɒb.djᵊr'eɪ.ʃᵊn, -djʊ'reɪ- ⓊⓈ ˌɑːb.dʊr'eɪ, -djʊr'-
OBE ˌəʊ.biː'iː ⓊⓈ ˌoʊ- **-s** -z
obeah (**O**) 'əʊ.bi.ə ⓊⓈ 'oʊ-
obedience əʊ'biː.di.ən*t*s ⓊⓈ oʊ-, ə-, '-djən*t*s
obedient əʊ'biː.di.ənt ⓊⓈ oʊ-, ə-, '-djənt **-ly** -li
obeisanc|e əʊ'beɪ.sᵊn*t*s ⓊⓈ oʊ-, -'biː- **-es** -ɪz
obelisk 'ɒb.ᵊl.ɪsk, -ɪ.lɪsk ⓊⓈ 'ɑː.bᵊl.ɪsk **-s** -s
obel|us 'ɒb.ᵊl|.əs, -ɪ.l|əs ⓊⓈ 'ɑː.bᵊl.|əs, 'oʊ- **-i** -aɪ
Oberammergau ˌəʊ.bə'ræm.ə.gaʊ ⓊⓈ ˌoʊ.bɚ'ɑː.mɚ-
Oberland 'əʊ.bə.lænd ⓊⓈ 'oʊ.bɚ-
Oberlin 'əʊ.bə.lɪn ⓊⓈ 'oʊ.bɚ-
Oberon 'əʊ.bᵊr.ɒn, -ᵊn ⓊⓈ 'oʊ.bə.rɑːn, -bɚ.ən
obese əʊ'biːs ⓊⓈ oʊ- **-ness** -nəs, -nɪs
obesity əʊ'biː.sə.ti, -sɪ- ⓊⓈ oʊ'biː.sə.ṭi
obey əʊ'beɪ ⓊⓈ oʊ-, ə- **-s** -z **-ing** -ɪŋ **-ed** -d **-er/s** -əʳ/z ⓊⓈ -ɚ/z
obfus|cate 'ɒb.fʌs|.keɪt, -fə.s|keɪt ⓊⓈ 'ɑːb.fə-; ɑːb'fʌs|.keɪt **-cates** -keɪts **-cating** -keɪ.tɪŋ ⓊⓈ -keɪ.ṭɪŋ **-cated** -keɪ.tɪd ⓊⓈ -keɪ.ṭɪd
obfuscation ˌɒb.fʌs'keɪ.ʃᵊn, -fə'skeɪ- ⓊⓈ ˌɑːb.fə'skeɪ- **-s** -z
obfuscatory ˌɒb.fʌs'keɪ.tᵊr.i, -fə'skeɪ- ⓊⓈ ɑːb'fʌs.kə.tɔːr-, əb-
obi 'əʊ.bi ⓊⓈ 'oʊ- **-s** -z
Obi *river in Siberia:* 'əʊ.bi ⓊⓈ 'oʊ-
Obie 'əʊ.bi ⓊⓈ 'oʊ- **-s** -z
obit 'ɒb.ɪt; əʊ'bɪt ⓊⓈ 'oʊ-, -'- **-s** -s
obiter dict|um ˌɒb.ɪ.tə'dɪk.t|əm, ˌəʊ.bɪ-, -təm ⓊⓈ ˌoʊ.bɪ.ṭɚ'dɪk-, ˌɑː- **-a** -ə
obituarist əʊ'bɪtʃ.ʊə.rɪst, ɒb'ɪtʃ-, -'ɪt.jʊə-, -jə-, -jʊ- ⓊⓈ oʊ'bɪtʃ.u.ɚ.ɪst, ə- **-s** -s
obituar|y əʊ'bɪtʃ.ʊə.r|i, ɒb'ɪtʃ-, -'ɪt.jʊə-, -jə-, -jʊ- ⓊⓈ oʊ'bɪtʃ.u.er|.i, ə- **-ies** -iz
object (*n.*) 'ɒb.dʒɪkt, -dʒekt ⓊⓈ 'ɑːb- **-s** -s **'object ˌlesson**
object (*v.*) əb'dʒekt **-s** -s **-ing** -ɪŋ **-ed** -ɪd **-or/s** -əʳ/z ⓊⓈ -ɚ/z
objecti|fy əb'dʒek.tɪ|.faɪ, ɒb-, -tə- ⓊⓈ əb'dʒek.tə- **-fies** -faɪz **-fying** -faɪ.ɪŋ **-fied** -faɪd
objection əb'dʒek.ʃᵊn **-s** -z
objectionab|le əb'dʒek.ʃᵊn.ə.b|l̩, -'dʒekʃ.nə- **-ly** -li
objective əb'dʒek.tɪv, ɒb- ⓊⓈ əb- **-s** -z **-ly** -li **-ness** -nəs, -nɪs
objectivism əb'dʒek.tɪ.vɪ.zᵊm, ɒb- ⓊⓈ əb'dʒek.tə-
objectivity ˌɒb.dʒɪk'tɪv.ə.ti, -dʒek-, -ɪ.ti ⓊⓈ ˌɑːb.dʒek'tɪv.ə.ṭi
objectless 'ɒb.dʒɪkt.ləs, -dʒekt-, -lɪs ⓊⓈ 'ɑːb.dʒɪkt-
objet(s) d'art ˌɒb.ʒeɪ'dɑːʳ ⓊⓈ ˌɑːb.ʒeɪ'dɑːr
objet(s) trouvé(s) ˌɒb.ʒeɪ.truː'veɪ ⓊⓈ ˌɑːb-
objur|gate 'ɒb.dʒə|.geɪt, -dʒɜː- ⓊⓈ 'ɑːb.dʒɚ-, əb'dʒɜːr- **-gates** -geɪts **-gating** -geɪ.tɪŋ ⓊⓈ -geɪ.ṭɪŋ **-gated** -geɪ.tɪd ⓊⓈ -geɪ.ṭɪd
objurgation ˌɒb.dʒə'geɪ.ʃᵊn, -dʒɜː'- ⓊⓈ ˌɑːb.dʒɚ'- **-s** -z
objurgatory ɒb'dʒɜː.gə.tᵊr.i, əb-; ˌɒb.dʒə'geɪ-, -dʒɜː'- ⓊⓈ əb'dʒɜːr.gə.tɔːr-
oblate (*adj.*) 'ɒb.leɪt; -'-, əʊ'bleɪt ⓊⓈ 'ɑː.bleɪt, -'- **-ly** -li **-ness** -nəs, -nɪs
oblate (*n.*) 'ɒb.leɪt ⓊⓈ 'ɑː.bleɪt **-s** -s
oblation əʊ'bleɪ.ʃᵊn, ɒb'leɪ- ⓊⓈ ə'bleɪ-, oʊ-, ɑː- **-s** -z
obligat|e 'ɒb.lɪ.geɪt ⓊⓈ 'ɑː.blɪ- **-es** -s **-ing** -ɪŋ **-ed** -ɪd
obligation ˌɒb.lɪ'geɪ.ʃᵊn, -lə'- ⓊⓈ ˌɑː.blə'- **-s** -z
obligat|o ˌɒb.lɪ'gɑː.t|əʊ, -lə'- ⓊⓈ ˌɑː.blɪ'gɑː.ṭ|oʊ **-os** -əʊz ⓊⓈ -oʊz **-i** -iː
obligator|y ə'blɪg.ə.tᵊr|.i, ɒb'lɪg-; ˌɒb.lɪ'geɪ-, -lə'- ⓊⓈ ə'blɪg.ə.tɔːr-; 'ɑː.blə.gə- **-ily** -ᵊl.i, -ɪ.li **-iness** -ɪ.nəs, -ɪ.nɪs
oblig|e ə'blaɪdʒ ⓊⓈ ə-, oʊ- **-es** -ɪz **-ing/ly** -ɪŋ/li **-ingness** -ɪŋ.nəs, -nɪs **-ed** -d
obliged ə'blaɪdʒd ⓊⓈ ə-, oʊ-
obligee ˌɒb.lɪ'dʒiː, -lə'- ⓊⓈ ˌɑː.blə'- **-s** -z
obliging ə'blaɪ.dʒɪŋ ⓊⓈ ə-, oʊ-
obligor ˌɒb.lɪ'gɔːʳ, -lə'- ⓊⓈ ˌɑː.blə'gɔːr, '--- **-s** -z
oblique əʊ'bliːk ⓊⓈ oʊ-, ə-, -'blaɪk **-ly** -li **-ness** -nəs, -nɪs
Note: The US form /-'blaɪk/ is associated with military usage.
obliquit|y əʊ'blɪk.wə.t|i, -wɪ- ⓊⓈ ə'blɪk.wə.ṭ|i **-ies** -iz
obliter|ate ə'blɪt.ᵊr|.eɪt ⓊⓈ -'blɪṭ.ə.r|eɪt, oʊ- **-ates** -eɪts **-ating** -eɪ.tɪŋ ⓊⓈ -eɪ.ṭɪŋ **-ated** -eɪ.tɪd ⓊⓈ -eɪ.ṭɪd
obliteration əˌblɪt.ᵊr'eɪ.ʃᵊn ⓊⓈ -ˌblɪṭ.ə'reɪ-, oʊ- **-s** -z

oblivion ə'blɪv.i.ən

oblivious ə'blɪv.i.əs **-ly** -li **-ness** -nəs, -nɪs

oblong 'ɒb.lɒŋ (US) 'ɑːb.lɑːŋ, -lɔːŋ **-s** -z

obloquy 'ɒb.lə.kwi (US) 'ɑːb-

obnoxious əb'nɒk.ʃəs, ɒb- (US) əb'nɑːk-, ɑːb- **-ly** -li **-ness** -nəs, -nɪs

oboe 'əʊ.bəʊ (US) 'oʊ.boʊ **-s** -z

oboe d'amore ˌəʊ.bəʊ.dæm'ɔː.reɪ, -də'mɔː-, -riː (US) ˌoʊ.boʊ.də'mɔːr.eɪ

oboist 'əʊ.bəʊ.ɪst (US) 'oʊ.boʊ- **-s** -s

obol 'ɒb.ɒl, 'əʊ.bɒl, -bᵊl (US) 'ɑː.bᵊl, 'oʊ- **-s** -z

Obote əʊ'bəʊ.teɪ, ɒb'əʊ-, -ti (US) oʊ'boʊ-

O'Boyle əʊ'bɔɪl (US) oʊ-

O'Brady əʊ'breɪ.di, -'brɔː- (US) oʊ'breɪ-

O'Brien, **O'Bryan** əʊ'braɪən (US) oʊ-

obscene əb'siːn, ɒb- (US) əb-, ɑːb- **-ly** -li **-ness** -nəs, -nɪs

obscenit|y əb'sen.ə.t|i, ɒb-, -ɪ.t|i (US) əb'sen.ə.t̬|i, ɑːb- **-ies** -iz

obscurant ɒb'skjʊə.rᵊnt, əb- (US) ɑːb'skjʊr.ᵊnt, əb-

obscurant|ism ˌɒb.skjʊə'ræn.t|ɪ.zᵊm; ɒb'skjʊə.rən-, əb- (US) ɑːb'skjʊr.ən-, əb- **-ist/s** -ɪst/s

obscuration ˌɒb.skjʊə'reɪ.ʃᵊn, -skjə'- (US) ˌɑːb.skjʊ'- **-s** -z

obscur|e əb'skjʊəʳ, -'skjɔːʳ (US) əb'skjʊr, ɑːb- **-er** -əʳ (US) -ɚ **-est** -ɪst, -əst **-ely** -li **-eness** -nəs, -nɪs **-es** -z **-ing** -ɪŋ **-ed** -d

obscurit|y əb'skjʊə.rə.t|i, -'skjɔː-, -rɪ- (US) əb'skjʊr.ə.t̬|i, ɑːb- **-ies** -iz

obse|crate 'ɒb.sɪ|.kreɪt, -sə- (US) 'ɑːb.sɪ- **-crates** -kreɪts **-crating** -kreɪ.tɪŋ (US) -kreɪ.t̬ɪŋ **-crated** -kreɪ.tɪd (US) -kreɪ.t̬ɪd

obsecration ˌɒb.sɪ'kreɪ.ʃᵊn, -sə'- (US) ˌɑːb.sə'- **-s** -z

obsequies 'ɒb.sɪ.kwiz, -sə-; ɒb'siː- (US) 'ɑːb.sɪ-

obsequious əb'siː.kwi.əs, ɒb- (US) əb-, ɑːb- **-ly** -li **-ness** -nəs, -nɪs

observab|le əb'zɜː.və.b|l̩ (US) -'zɝː- **-ly** -li **-leness** -l̩.nəs, -nɪs

observanc|e əb'zɜː.vᵊnts (US) -'zɝː- **-es** -ɪz

observant əb'zɜː.vᵊnt (US) -'zɝː- **-ly** -li

observation ˌɒb.zə'veɪ.ʃᵊn (US) ˌɑːb.zɚ'-, -sɚ'- **-s** -z

observational ˌɒb.zə'veɪ.ʃᵊn.ᵊl, -veɪʃ.nᵊl (US) ˌɑːb.zɚ'-, -sɚ'- **-ly** -i

observator|y əb'zɜː.və.tr|i, -tᵊr|.i (US) -'zɝː.və.tɔːr- **-ies** -iz

observ|e əb'zɜːv (US) -'zɝːv **-es** -z **-ing/ly** -ɪŋ/li **-ed** -d

observer (O) əb'zɜː.vəʳ (US) -'zɝː.vɚ **-s** -z

obsess əb'ses, ɒb- (US) əb- **-es** -ɪz **-ing** -ɪŋ **-ed** -t

obsession əb'seʃ.ᵊn, ɒb- (US) əb- **-s** -s **-al** -ᵊl

obsessive əb'ses.ɪv, ɒb- (US) əb- **-ly** -li **-ness** -nəs, -nɪs

obsidian ɒb'sɪd.i.ən, əb- (US) əb-, ɑːb-

obsolescence ˌɒb.sə'les.ᵊnts, -sᵊl'es- (US) ˌɑːb-

obsolescent ˌɒb.sə'les.ᵊnt, -sᵊl'es- (US) ˌɑːb- **-ly** -li

obsolete 'ɒb.sᵊl.iːt (US) ˌɑːb.sᵊl'iːt **-ly** -li **-ness** -nəs, -nɪs

obstacle 'ɒb.stə.kl̩, -stɪ- (US) 'ɑːb.stə- **-s** -z **'obstacle ˌcourse**

obstetric ɒb'stet.rɪk, əb- (US) əb-, ɑːb- **-al** -ᵊl **-s** -s

obstetrician ˌɒb.stə'trɪʃ.ᵊn, -stɪ'-, -stet'rɪʃ- (US) ˌɑːb.stə'trɪʃ- **-s** -z

obstinac|y 'ɒb.stɪ.nə.s|i, -stᵊn.ə- (US) 'ɑːb.stə.nə- **-ies** -iz

obstinate 'ɒb.stɪ.nət, -stᵊn.ət, -ɪt (US) 'ɑːb.stə.nət **-ly** -li **-ness** -nəs, -nɪs

obstreperous əb'strep.ᵊr.əs, ɒb- (US) əb-, ɑːb- **-ly** -li **-ness** -nəs, -nɪs

obstruct əb'strʌkt **-s** -s **-ing** -ɪŋ **-ed** -ɪd **-or/s** -əʳ/z (US) -ɚ/z

obstruction əb'strʌk.ʃᵊn **-s** -z

obstructionism əb'strʌk.ʃᵊn.ɪ.zᵊm

obstructionist əb'strʌk.ʃᵊn.ɪst **-s** -s

obstructive əb'strʌk.tɪv **-ly** -li **-ness** -nəs, -nɪs

obstruent 'ɒb.stru.ənt (US) 'ɑːb- **-s** -s

obtain əb'teɪn **-s** -z **-ing** -ɪŋ **-ed** -d **-er/s** -əʳ/z (US) -ɚ/z **-able** -ə.bl̩

obtrud|e əb'truːd, ɒb- (US) əb-, ɑːb- **-es** -z **-ing** -ɪŋ **-ed** -ɪd **-er/s** -əʳ/z (US) -ɚ/z

obtrusion əb'truː.ʒᵊn, ɒb- (US) əb-, ɑːb- **-s** -z

obtrusive əb'truː.sɪv, ɒb-, -zɪv (US) əb-, ɑːb- **-ly** -li **-ness** -nəs, -nɪs

obtu|rate 'ɒb.tjʊə|.reɪt, -tjə- (US) 'ɑːb.tə-, -tjə-, -tʊ-, -tjʊ- **-rates** -reɪts **-rating** -reɪ.tɪŋ (US) -reɪ.t̬ɪŋ **-rated** -reɪ.tɪd (US) -reɪ.t̬ɪd **-rator/s** -reɪ.təʳ/z (US) -reɪ.t̬ɚ/z

obturation ˌɒb.tjʊə'reɪ.ʃᵊn, -tjə'- (US) ˌɑːb.tə'-, -tjə'-, -tʊ'-, -tjʊ'- **-s** -z

obtuse əb'tjuːs, ɒb- (US) ɑːb'tuːs, əb-, -'tjuːs **-ly** -li **-ness** -nəs, -nɪs

obvers|e (*adj.*) 'ɒb.vɜːs (US) ɑːb'vɝːs, əb-; 'ɑːb.vɝːs

obvers|e (*n.*) 'ɒb.vɜːs (US) 'ɑːb.vɝːs **-es** -ɪz

obversely 'ɒb.vɜː.sli (US) ɑːb'vɝː-

ob|vert ɒb|'vɜːt, əb- (US) ɑːb|'vɝːt, əb- **-verts** -'vɜːts (US) -'vɝːts **-verting** -'vɜː.tɪŋ (US) -'vɝː.t̬ɪŋ **-verted** -'vɜː.tɪd (US) -'vɝː.t̬ɪd

obvi|ate 'ɒb.vi|.eɪt (US) 'ɑːb- **-ates** -eɪts **-ating** -eɪ.tɪŋ (US) -eɪ.t̬ɪŋ **-ated** -eɪ.tɪd (US) -eɪ.t̬ɪd

obviative 'ɒb.vi.ə.tɪv (US) 'ɑːb.vi.eɪ.t̬ɪv

obvious 'ɒb.vi.əs (US) 'ɑːb- **-ly** -li **-ness** -nəs, -nɪs

O'Byrne əʊ'bɜːn (US) oʊ'bɝːn

O'Callaghan əʊ'kæl.ə.hən, -gən, -hæn (US) oʊ'kæl.ə.hən, -hæn

ocarina ˌɒk.ᵊr'iː.nə (US) ˌɑː.kə'riː- **-s** -z

O'Casey əʊ'keɪ.si (US) oʊ-

occam (O) 'ɒk.əm (US) 'ɑː.kəm

occasion ə'keɪ.ʒᵊn **-s** -z **-ing** -ɪŋ **-ed** -d **ˌrise to the oc'casion**

occasional ə'keɪ.ʒᵊn.ᵊl, -'keɪʒ.nᵊl **-ly** -i

occasional|ism ə'keɪ.ʒᵊn.ᵊl|.ɪ.zᵊm, -'keɪʒ.nᵊl- **-ist/s** -ɪst/s

occident (O) 'ɒk.sɪ.dᵊnt, -sə- (US) 'ɑːk.sə.dənt, -sɪ-, -dent

occidental (O) ˌɒk.sɪ'den.tᵊl, -sə'- (US) ˌɑːk.sə'den.t̬ᵊl, -sɪ'- **-s** -z

occidental|ism (O) ˌɒk.sɪ'den.tᵊl|.ɪ.zᵊm, -sə'- (US) ˌɑːk.sə'den.t̬ᵊl-, -sɪ'- **-ist/s** -ɪst/s

occidentaliz|e, -is|e ˌɒk.sɪ'den.tᵊl.aɪz, -sə'- (US) ˌɑːk.sə'den.t̬ᵊl-, -sɪ'- **-es** -ɪz **-ing** -ɪŋ **-ed** -d

occipita (*from* **occiput**) ɒk'sɪp.ɪ.tə (US) ɑːk'sɪp.ɪ.t̬ə

occipital ɒk'sɪp.ɪ.tᵊl, '-ə- (US) ɑːk'sɪp.ɪ.t̬ᵊl **-ly** -i

occiput 'ɒk.sɪ.pʌt, -pət (US) ɑːk- **-s** -s **occipita** ɒk'sɪp.ɪ.tə (US) ɑːk'sɪp.ɪ.t̬ə

Occleve 'ɒk.liːv (US) 'ɑːk-

occlud|e ə'kluːd, ɒk'luːd (US) ə'kluːd, ɑː- **-es** -z **-ing** -ɪŋ **-ed** -ɪd

occlusal ə'kluː.zᵊl, ɒk'luː- (US) ə'kluː-, ɑː-

occlusion ə'kluː.ʒᵊn, ɒk'luː- (US) ə'kluː-, ɑː- **-s** -z

occlusive ə'kluː.sɪv, ɒk'luː- (US) ə'kluː-, ɑː- **-s** -z

occult (*adj.*) 'ɒk.ʌlt; ə'kʌlt, ɒk'ʌlt (US) ə'kʌlt; 'ɑː.kʌlt **-ly** -li **-ness** -nəs, -nɪs

occul|t (*v.*) ɒk'ʌl|t, ə'kʌl|t (US) ə- **-ts** -ts **-ting** -tɪŋ (US) -t̬ɪŋ **-ted** -tɪd (US) -t̬ɪd

occultation ˌɒk.ᵊl'teɪ.ʃᵊn, -ʌl'- (US) ˌɑː.kʌl'- **-s** -z

occult|ism 'ɒk.ᵊl.t|ɪ.zᵊm, -ʌl-; ɒk'ʌl-, ə'kʌl- (US) ə'kʌl-; 'ɑː.kʌl- **-ist/s** -ɪst/s

occupancy 'ɒk.jə.pənt.si, -jʊ- (US) 'ɑː.kjə-, -kjʊ-

occupant 'ɒk.jə.pənt, -jʊ- (US) 'ɑː.kjə-, -kjʊ- **-s** -s

occupation ˌɒk.jə'peɪ.ʃᵊn, -jʊ'- (US) ˌɑː.kjə'-, -kjʊ'- **-s** -z

occupational ˌɒk.jə'peɪ.ʃᵊn.ᵊl, -jʊ'-, -'peɪʃ.nᵊl (US) ˌɑː.kjə'-, -kjʊ'- **-ly** -i *stress shift, see compound:* **ˌoccupational 'therapy**

occupier 'ɒk.jə.paɪ.əʳ, -jʊ- (US) 'ɑː.kjə.paɪ.ɚ, -kjʊ- **-s** -z

occup|y 'ɒk.jə.pl|aɪ, -jʊ- US 'ɑː.kjuː-, -kjə- **-ies** -aɪz **-ying** -aɪ.ɪŋ **-ied** -aɪd

occur ə'kɜːʳ US -'kɜːr **-s** -z **-ring** -ɪŋ **-red** -d

occurrenc|e ə'kʌr.ᵊnts US -'kɜːr- **-es** -ɪz

ocean 'əʊ.ʃᵊn US 'oʊ- **-s** -z **a ˌdrop in the 'ocean**

oceanfront 'əʊ.ʃᵊn.frʌnt US 'oʊ- **-s** -s

ocean-going 'əʊ.ʃᵊnˌgəʊ.ɪŋ US 'oʊ.ʃᵊnˌgoʊ-

Oceani|a ˌəʊ.ʃi'eɪ.ni|.ə, -si'-, -'ɑː- US ˌoʊ.ʃi'æn.i-, -'ɑː.ni-, -'eɪ- **-an/s** -ən/z

oceanic (O) ˌəʊ.ʃi'æn.ɪk, -si'- US ˌoʊ.ʃi'-

oceanographic ˌəʊ.ʃᵊn.əʊ'græf.ɪk, -ʃi.ᵊn- US ˌoʊ.ʃə.noʊ'-, -ʃi.ə- **-ally** -ᵊl.i, -li

oceanograph|y ˌəʊ.ʃᵊn'ɒg.rə.f|i, -ʃi.ᵊn'- US ˌoʊ.ʃə'nɑː.grə-, -ʃi.ə'- **-er/s** -əʳ/z US -ɚ/z

oceanolog|y ˌəʊ.ʃᵊn'ɒl.ə.dʒ|i, -ʃi.ᵊn'- US ˌoʊ.ʃə'nɑː.lə-, -ʃi.ə'- **-ist/s** -ɪst/s

Oceanus əʊ'siː.ə.nəs, -'ʃiː- US oʊ'siː-

ocell|us əʊ'sel|.əs US oʊ- **-i** -aɪ, -iː

ocelot 'ɒs.ᵊl.ɒt, 'əʊ.sᵊl-, -sɪ.lɒt US 'ɑː.sə.lɑːt, 'oʊ-, -lət **-s** -s

och ɒx US ɑːk *as if Scots:* ɑːx

oche 'ɒk.i US 'ɑː.ki **-s** -z

ocher 'əʊ.kəʳ US 'oʊ.kɚ **-ous** -əs

Ochil(l) 'əʊ.kᵊl, -xᵊl US 'oʊ.tʃɪl, 'ɑː-, -kᵊl

Ochiltree *in Scott's 'Antiquary':* 'əʊ.kɪl.triː, -xɪl-, 'ɒk.ɪl-, 'ɒx-, -ᵊl- US 'oʊ.kɪl-, 'ɑː-, -tʃɪl- *in US:* 'əʊ.kɪl.triː US 'oʊ-

och|re 'əʊ.k|əʳ US 'oʊ.k|ɚ **-res** -əz US -ɚz **-reing** -ᵊr.ɪŋ **-red** -əd US -ɚd

ochreous 'əʊ.kri.əs, -kᵊr- US 'oʊ-

ochry 'əʊ.kᵊr.i US 'oʊ-

Ochterlony ˌɒk.tə'ləʊ.ni, ˌɒx- US ˌɑːk.tɚ'loʊ-

ocker, okker 'ɒk.əʳ US 'ɑː.kɚ **-s** -z

Ockham 'ɒk.əm US 'ɑː.kəm

Ockley 'ɒk.li US 'ɑːk-

O'Clery əʊ'klɪə.ri US oʊ'klɪr.i

o'clock ə'klɒk US -'klɑːk

O'Connell əʊ'kɒn.ᵊl US oʊ'kɑː.nᵊl

O'Connor əʊ'kɒn.əʳ US oʊ'kɑː.nɚ

Ocracoke 'əʊ.krə.kəʊk US 'oʊ.krə.koʊk

Oct. (*abbrev. for* **October**) ɒkt; ɒk'təʊ.bəʳ US ɑːk'toʊ.bɚ

octa- ɒk.tə-; ɒk'tæ- US ɑːk-; ɑːk'tæ-

Note: Prefix. Normally either takes primary or secondary stress on the first syllable, e.g. **octagon** /'ɒk.tə.gən US 'ɑːk.tə.gɑːn/, **octahedron** /ˌɒk.tə'hiː.drən US ˌɑːk.tə'hiː.drən/, or primary stress on the second syllable, e.g. **octagonal** /ɒk'tæg.ᵊn.ᵊl US ɑːk-/.

octagon 'ɒk.tə.gən US 'ɑːk.tə.gɑːn **-s** -z

octagonal ɒk'tæg.ᵊn.ᵊl US ɑːk- **-ly** -i

octahedr|on ˌɒk.tə'hiː.dr|ᵊn, -'hed.r|ᵊn US 'ɑːk.tə'hiː.dr|ᵊn **-ons** -ᵊnz **-a** -ə **-al** -ᵊl

octal 'ɒk.tᵊl US 'ɑːk-

octane 'ɒk.teɪn US 'ɑːk-

octant 'ɒk.tənt US 'ɑːk- **-s** -s

Octateuch 'ɒk.tə.tjuːk US 'ɑːk.tə.tuːk, -tjuːk

octave *musical term:* 'ɒk.tɪv, -teɪv US 'ɑːk- **-s** -z

octave *ecclesiastical term:* 'ɒk.teɪv, -tɪv US 'ɑːk.tɪv, -teɪv **-s** -z

Octavi|a ɒk'teɪ.vi|.ə, -'tɑː- US ɑːk'teɪ- **-an** -ən

Octavius ɒk'teɪ.vi.əs, -'tɑː- US ɑːk'teɪ-

octavo ɒk'tɑː.vəʊ, -'teɪ- US ɑːk'teɪ.voʊ, -'tɑː- **-s** -z

octennial ɒk'ten.i.əl US ɑːk- **-ly** -i

octet(te) ɒk'tet US ɑːk- **-s** -s

octillion ɒk'tɪl.jən, -i.ən US ɑːk'tɪl.jən **-s** -z

octo- ɒk.təʊ- US ɑːk.toʊ-, -tə-

Note: Prefix. Normally takes primary or secondary stress on the first syllable, e.g. **octosyllable** /'ɒk.təʊˌsɪl.ə.bl̩ US 'ɑːk.toʊ-/, **octosyllabic** /ˌɒk.təʊ.sɪ'læb.ɪk US ˌɑːk.toʊ-/.

October ɒk'təʊ.bəʳ US ɑːk'toʊ.bɚ **-s** -z

octodecimo ˌɒk.təʊ'des.ɪ.məʊ US ˌɑːk.toʊ'des.ɪ.moʊ **-s** -z

octogenarian ˌɒk.təʊ.dʒə'neə.ri.ən, -dʒɪ'- US ˌɑːk.toʊ.dʒɪ'ner.i-, -tə- **-s** -z

octop|us 'ɒk.tə.p|əs, -p|ʊs US 'ɑːk.tə.p|əs **-uses** -ə.sɪz, -ʊ.sɪz US -ə.sɪz **-i** -aɪ

octoroon ˌɒk.tə'ruːn US ˌɑːk- **-s** -z

octosyllabic ˌɒk.təʊ.sɪ'læb.ɪk, -sə'- US ˌɑːk.toʊ-, -tə- *stress shift:* ˌoctosyllabic 'meter

octosyllable 'ɒk.təʊˌsɪl.ə.bl̩ US 'ɑːk.toʊˌ-, -təˌ- **-s** -z

octroi 'ɒk.trwɑː, -trɔɪ US 'ɑːk.trɔɪ **-s** -z

octuple 'ɒk.tjə.pl̩, -tjʊ-; ɒk'tjuː- US 'ɑːk.tə-; ɑːk'tuː-

ocular 'ɒk.jə.ləʳ, -jʊ- US 'ɑː.kjə.lɚ, -kjʊ- **-ly** -li

oculist 'ɒk.jə.lɪst, -jʊ- US 'ɑː.kjə-, -kjʊ- **-s** -s

O'Curry əʊ'kʌr.i US oʊ'kɜːr-

od (O) ɒd US ɑːd **-s** -z

OD ˌəʊ'diː US ˌoʊ- **-'s** -z **-'ing** -ɪŋ **-'d** -d

odalisque, odalisk 'əʊ.dᵊl.ɪsk, 'əʊ.dᵊl- US 'oʊ.dᵊl- **-s** -s

O'Daly əʊ'deɪ.li US oʊ-

Odam 'əʊ.dəm US 'oʊ-

odd ɒd US ɑːd **-er** -əʳ US -ɚ **-est** -ɪst, -əst **-ly** -li **-ness** -nəs, -nɪs **ˌodd man 'out**

oddball 'ɒd.bɔːl US 'ɑːd-, -bɑːl **-s** -z

Oddbins® 'ɒd.bɪnz US 'ɑːd-

odd bod 'ɒd.bɒd US 'ɑːd.bɑːd **-s** -z

Oddfellow 'ɒdˌfel.əʊ US 'ɑːdˌfel.oʊ **-s** -z

Oddie 'ɒd.i US 'ɑː.di

oddish 'ɒd.ɪʃ US 'ɑː.dɪʃ

oddit|y 'ɒd.ɪ.t|i, -ə.t|i US 'ɑː.də.t̬|i **-ies** -iz

odd-job |man ˌɒd'dʒɒb|.mæn US 'ɑːd.dʒɑːb- **-men** -men

oddment 'ɒd.mənt US 'ɑːd- **-s** -s

odds ɒdz US ɑːdz **ˌodds and 'ends**

odds-on ˌɒdz'ɒn US ˌɑːdz'ɑːn *stress shift:* ˌodds-on 'favourite

ode əʊd US oʊd **-s** -z

O'Dea əʊ'deɪ US oʊ-

Odell əʊ'del; 'əʊ.dᵊl US oʊ'del

Odense 'əʊ.dᵊnt.sə US 'oʊ.dənt-, -θənt-

Odeon® 'əʊ.di.ən US 'oʊ-

Oder 'əʊ.dəʳ US 'oʊ.dɚ

Oder-Neisse Line ˌəʊ.də'naɪ.səˌlaɪn US ˌoʊ.dɚ'-

Odessa əʊ'des.ə US oʊ-

Odets əʊ'dets US oʊ-

Odette əʊ'det US oʊ-

ode|um əʊ'diː|.əm; 'əʊ.di- US oʊ'diː-; 'oʊ.di- **-a** -ə **-ums** -əmz

Odgers 'ɒdʒ.əz US 'ɑː.dʒɚz

Odham 'ɒd.əm US 'ɑː.dəm

Odiham 'əʊ.dɪ.əm, -həm US 'oʊ-

Odile əʊ'diːl US oʊ-

Odin 'əʊ.dɪn US 'oʊ-

odious 'əʊ.di.əs US 'oʊ- **-ly** -li **-ness** -nəs, -nɪs

odium 'əʊ.di.əm US 'oʊ-

Odling 'ɒd.lɪŋ US 'ɑːd-

Odlum 'ɒd.ləm US 'ɑːd-

Odo 'əʊ.dəʊ US 'oʊ.doʊ

Odoacer ˌɒd.əʊ'eɪ.səʳ, ˌəʊ.dəʊ'- US ˌoʊ.doʊ'eɪ.sɚ

O'Doherty əʊ'dəʊ.ə.ti, -'dɒ.hə.ti, -'dɒx.ə- US oʊ'dɔːr.t̬i, -'dɑː.hɚ-

odometer əʊ'dɒm.ɪ.təʳ, ɒd'ɒm-, -ə.təʳ US oʊ'dɑː.mə.t̬ɚ **-s** -z

O'Donnell əʊ'dɒn.ᵊl US oʊ'dɑː.nᵊl

odontolog|y ˌɒd.ɒn'tɒl.ə.dʒ|i, ˌəʊ.dɒn'- US ˌoʊ.dɑːn'tɑː.lə- **-ist/s** -ɪst/s

odor 'əʊ.dəʳ US 'oʊ.dɚ **-s** -z **-ed** -d **-less** -ləs, -lɪs

odoriferous ˌəʊ.dᵊr'ɪf.ᵊr.əs, ˌɒd.ᵊr'- US ˌoʊ.də'rɪf.ɚ.əs **-ly** -li **-ness** -nəs, -nɪs

odorous 'əʊ.dᵊr.əs US 'oʊ- **-ly** -li **-ness** -nəs, -nɪs

odour 'əʊ.dəʳ US 'oʊ.dɚ **-s** -z **-ed** -d **-less** -ləs, -lɪs

O'Dowd əʊˈdaʊd (US) oʊ-

odsbodikins ˌɒdzˈbɒd.ɪ.kɪnz (US) ˌɑːdzˈbɑːd-

O'Dwyer əʊˈdwaɪəʳ (US) oʊˈdwaɪɚ

Ody ˈəʊ.di (US) ˈoʊ-

Odysseus əˈdɪs.juːs, ɒdˈɪs-, əʊˈdɪs-, ˈ-i.əs (US) oʊˈdɪs.i.əs, ˈ-juːs

odyssey (O) ˈɒd.ɪ.si, ˈ-ə- (US) ˈɑː.dɪ-

OECD ˌəʊ.iː.siːˈdiː (US) ˌoʊ-

oecumenic ˌiː.kjʊˈmen.ɪk (US) ˌek.jəˈ-, -jʊˈ- **-al** -ᵊl *stress shift:* ˌoecumenic ˈservice

oedema ɪˈdiː.mə, iː- (US) ɪ- **-ta** -tə (US) -t̬ə

oedematous ɪˈdiː.mə.təs, iː-, -ˈdem.ə- (US) ɪˈdem.ə.t̬əs

oedipal (O) ˈiː.dɪ.pᵊl, -də- (US) ˈed.ɪ-, ˈiː.dɪ-

Oedipus ˈiː.dɪ.pəs, -də- (US) ˈed.ɪ-, ˈiː.dɪ- **ˈOedipus ˌcomplex**

OEEC ˌəʊ.iː.iːˈsiː (US) ˌoʊ-

Oenomaus ˌiː.nəʊˈmeɪ.əs (US) -nəˈ-, -noʊˈ-

Oenone iːˈnəʊ.niː, ɪ-, -ni (US) iːˈnoʊ-

o'er (*contracted form of* **over**) ɔəʳ, ɔːʳ, əʊəʳ (US) ɔːr, oʊɚ

oes (*plur. of* **O**) əʊz (US) oʊz

oesophageal ɪˌsɒf.əˈdʒiː.əl, iː-, ə-, ˌiː.sɒf- (US) ɪˌsɑː.fəˈ-; ˌiː.sɑː-

oesopha|gus iːˈsɒf.ə|.gəs, ɪ-, ə- (US) ɪˈsɑː.fə-, iː- **-guses** -gə.sɪz **-gi** -gaɪ, -dʒaɪ

oestrogen ˈiː.strəʊ.dʒᵊn, ˈes.trəʊ- (US) ˈes.trə-, -dʒen

oestrus ˈiː.strəs (US) ˈes.trəs **-es** -ɪz

oeuvre ˈɜː.vrə **-s** -z

of *strong form:* ɒv (US) ɑːv *weak form:* əv

Note: Weak form word. The strong form is usually found only in final position (e.g. "She's the one I'm fond of"), though it can occur initially in some forms such as "Of the ten who set out, only three returned". Elsewhere the weak form /əv/ is used.

O'Faolain, O'Faoláin əʊˈfeɪ.lən, -ˈfæl.ən (US) oʊ-

off ɒf (US) ɑːf

Offa ˈɒf.ə (US) ˈɑː.fə **ˌOffa's ˈDyke**

offal ˈɒf.ᵊl (US) ˈɑː.fᵊl

Offaly ˈɒf.ᵊl.i (US) ˈɑː.fᵊl.i

off-bail ˌɒfˈbeɪl (US) ˌɑːf- **-s** -z

Note: Also ˈ-- when in contrast with **leg-bail**.

offbeat (*adj.*) ˌɒfˈbiːt (US) ˌɑːfˈbiːt

offbeat (*n.*) ˈɒf.biːt (US) ˈɑːf- **-s** -s

off-bye ˌɒfˈbaɪ (US) ˌɑːf- **-s** -z

Note: Also ˈ-- when in contrast with **leg-bye**.

off-chance ˈɒf.tʃɑːn*t*s (US) ˈɑːf.tʃæn*t*s **ˌon the ˈoff-ˌchance**

off-colo(u)r ˌɒfˈkʌl.əʳ (US) ˌɑːfˈkʌl.ɚ

offcut ˈɒf.kʌt (US) ˈɑːf- **-s** -s

off-drive ˈɒf.draɪv (US) ˈɑːf- **-s** -z

Offenbach ˈɒf.ᵊn.bɑːk, -ᵊm- (US) ˈɑː.fᵊn.bɑːk, ˈɔː-

offenc|e əˈfen*t*s **-es** -ɪz **-eless** -ləs, -lɪs

offend əˈfend **-s** -z **-ing** -ɪŋ **-ed** -ɪd **-er/s** -əʳ/z (US) -ɚ/z

offens|e əˈfen*t*s (US) ə-; *especially in sport:* ˈɑː.fen*t*s **-es** -ɪz **-eless** -ləs, -lɪs

offensive əˈfen*t*.sɪv (US) ə-; *especially in sport:* ˈɑː-, ˈʌf.en*t*- **-s** -z **-ly** -li **-ness** -nəs, -nɪs

off|er ˈɒf|.əʳ (US) ˈɑː.f|ɚ **-ers** -əz (US) -ɚz **-ering/s** -ᵊr.ɪŋ/z **-ered** -əd (US) -ɚd **-erer/s** -ᵊr.əʳ/z (US) -ɚ.ɚ/z **-erable** -ᵊr.ə.bl̩

offertor|y ˈɒf.ə.tᵊr|.i (US) ˈɑː.fɚ.tɔːr-, ˈɔː- **-ies** -iz

off-hand ˌɒfˈhænd (US) ˌɑːf-

off-handed ˌɒfˈhæn.dɪd (US) ˌɑːf- **-ly** -li **-ness** -nəs, -nɪs

offic|e ˈɒf.ɪs (US) ˈɑː.fɪs **-es** -ɪz **ˈoffice ˌblock**; **ˈoffice ˌhours**, **ˌoffice ˈhours**

office-bearer ˈɒf.ɪsˌbeə.rəʳ (US) ˈɑː.fɪsˌber.ɚ **-s** -z

office-boy ˈɒf.ɪsˌbɔɪ (US) ˈɑː.fɪs- **-s** -z

officer ˈɒf.ɪ.səʳ (US) ˈɑː.fɪ.sɚ **-s** -z

official əˈfɪʃ|.ᵊl (US) ə-, oʊ- **-s** -z **-ly** -i **-ism** -ɪ.zᵊm **ofˌficial reˈceiver**; **Ofˌficial ˈSecrets ˌAct**

officialdom əˈfɪʃ.ᵊl.dəm (US) ə-

officialese əˌfɪʃ.ᵊlˈiːz, əˈfɪʃ.ᵊl.iːz (US) əˌfɪʃ.ᵊlˈiːz

officiant əˈfɪʃ.i.ənt, ɒfˈɪʃ- (US) əˈfɪʃ.ᵊnt, -i.ənt **-s** -s

offici|ate əˈfɪʃ.i|.eɪt **-ates** -eɪts **-ating** -eɪ.tɪŋ (US) -eɪ.t̬ɪŋ **-ated** -eɪ.tɪd (US) -eɪ.t̬ɪd

officinal ˌɒf.ɪˈsaɪ.nᵊl; ɒfˈɪs.ɪ.nᵊl (US) əˈfɪs.ɪ-; ˌɑː.fɪˈsaɪ-

officious əˈfɪʃ.əs **-ly** -li **-ness** -nəs, -nɪs

offing ˈɒf.ɪŋ (US) ˈɑː.fɪŋ **-s** -z

offish ˈɒf.ɪʃ (US) ˈɑː.fɪʃ

off-key ˌɒfˈkiː (US) ˌɑːf- *stress shift:* ˌoff-key ˈsinging

off-licenc|e ˈɒfˌlaɪ.sᵊn*t*s (US) ˌɑːfˈlaɪ- **-es** -ɪz

off-line ˌɒfˈlaɪn (US) ˌɑːf- *stress shift:* ˌoff-line ˈprinter

off-load ˌɒfˈləʊd (US) ˈɑːf.loʊd **-s** -z **-ing** -ɪŋ **-ed** -ɪd

Offor ˈɒf.əʳ (US) ˈɑː.fɚ

off-peak ˌɒfˈpiːk (US) ˌɑːf- *stress shift:* ˌoff-peak ˈtravel

off-piste ˌɒfˈpiːst (US) ˌɑːf- *stress shift:* ˌoff-piste ˈskiing

off-print ˈɒf.prɪnt (US) ˈɑːf- **-s** -s

off-putting ˌɒfˈpʊt.ɪŋ (US) ˈɑːfˌpʊt̬- *stress shift, British only:* ˌoff-putting ˈhabit

offscreen ˌɒfˈskriːn (US) ˌɑːf- *stress shift:* ˌoffscreen ˈlife

off|set (*v.*) *compensate:* ˌɒf|ˈset (US) ˌɑːf- **-sets** -ˈsets **-setting** -ˈset.ɪŋ (US) -ˈset̬.ɪŋ

offse|t (*n. v.*) ˈɒf.se|t (US) ˈɑːf-, -ˈ- **-ts** -ts **-tting** -tɪŋ (US) -t̬ɪŋ

offshoot ˈɒf.ʃuːt (US) ˈɑːf- **-s** -s

offshore ˌɒfˈʃɔːʳ (US) ˌɑːfˈʃɔːr *stress shift:* ˌoffshore ˈsavings

offside ˌɒfˈsaɪd (US) ˌɑːf- *stress shift:* ˌoffside ˈrule

offspring ˈɒf.sprɪŋ (US) ˈɑːf- **-s** -z

offstage ˌɒfˈsteɪdʒ (US) ˌɑːf- *stress shift:* ˌoffstage ˈwhisper

off-street ˌɒfˈstriːt (US) ˌɑːf- *stress shift:* ˌoff-street ˈshops

off-the-cuff ˌɒf.ðəˈkʌf (US) ˌɑːf- *stress shift:* ˌoff-the-cuff ˈcomment

off-the-peg ˌɒf.ðəˈpeg (US) ˌɑːf- *stress shift:* ˌoff-the-peg ˈsuit

off-the-rack ˌɒf.ðəˈræk (US) ˌɑːf- *stress shift:* ˌoff-the-rack ˈsuit

off-the-record ˌɒf.ðəˈrek.ɔːd (US) ˌɑːf.ðəˈrek.ɔːrd, -ˈrek.ɚd *stress shift:* ˌoff-the-record ˈquote

off-the-shelf ˌɒf.ðəˈʃelf (US) ˌɑːf- *stress shift:* ˌoff-the-shelf ˈgoods

off-the-wall ˌɒf.ðəˈwɔːl (US) ˌɑːf.ðəˈwɔːl, -ˈwɔːl *stress shift:* ˌoff-the-wall ˈcomedy

off-white ˌɒfˈ*h*waɪt (US) ˌɑːf- *stress shift:* ˌoff-white ˈdrapes

Ofgas, OFGAS ˈɒf.gæs (US) ˈɑːf-

O'Flaherty əʊˈfleə.ti, -ˈflæ.hə-, -ˈflɑː.ə-, -ˈflɑː- (US) oʊˈfler.t̬i, -ˈflæ.hɚ-

O'Flynn əʊˈflɪn (US) oʊ-

oft ɒft (US) ɑːft

Oftel, OFTEL ˈɒf.tel (US) ˈɑːf-

often ˈɒf.ᵊn, -tᵊn (US) ˈɑː.fᵊn, ˈɑːf.tᵊn **-times** -taɪmz **as ˌoften as ˈnot**

often|er ˈɒf.ᵊn|.əʳ, -tᵊn-, ˈɒf.n|əʳ (US) ˈɑː.fᵊn|.ɚ, ˈɑːf.tᵊn-, ˈɑːf.n|ɚ **-est** -ɪst

ofttimes ˈɒf*t*.taɪmz (US) ˈɑːf*t*-

Ofwat, OFWAT ˈɒf.wɒt (US) ˈɑːf.wɑːt

Og ɒg (US) ɑːg, ɔːg

ogam ˈɒg.əm (US) ˈɑː.gəm

ogamic ɒgˈæm.ɪk (US) ɑːˈgæm-, ɔː-, oʊ-

Ogbomosho ˌɒg.bəˈməʊ.ʃəʊ (US) ˌɑːg.bəˈmoʊ.ʃoʊ

Ogden ˈɒg.dən (US) ˈɑːg-, ˈɔːg-

ogee ˈəʊ.dʒiː, -ˈ- (US) ˈoʊ.dʒiː, -ˈ- **-s** -z

ogham ˈɒg.əm (US) ˈɑː.gəm, ˈɔː-

oghamic ɒgˈæm.ɪk (US) ɑːˈgæm-, ɔː-, oʊ-

Ogilby ˈəʊ.gᵊl.bi (US) ˈoʊ-

Ogilvie, Ogilvy ˈəʊ.gᵊl.vi (US) ˈoʊ-

ogival əʊˈdʒaɪ.vᵊl, -ˈgaɪ- (US) oʊˈdʒaɪ-

ogive ˈəʊ.dʒaɪv, -gaɪv, -ˈ- (US) ˈoʊ.dʒaɪv, -gaɪv, -ˈ- **-s** -z

ogl|e (O) ˈəʊ.gl̩ (US) ˈoʊ-, ˈɑː- **-es** -z **-ing** -ɪŋ, ˈəʊ.glɪŋ (US) ˈoʊ-, ˈɑː- **-ed** -d

-er/s -əʳ/z (US) -ɚ/z, 'əʊ.gləʳ/z (US) 'oʊ.glɚ/z, 'ɑː-
Ogleby 'əʊ.gl̩.bi (US) 'oʊ-
Oglethorpe 'əʊ.gl̩.θɔːp (US) 'oʊ.gl̩.θɔːrp
Ogmore 'ɒg.mɔːʳ (US) 'ɑːg.mɔːr, 'ɔːg-
Ogoni ə'gəʊ.ni, ɒg'- (US) oʊ'- **-land** -lænd
Ogpu 'ɒg.puː (US) 'ɑːg-, 'ɔːg-
O'Grady əʊ'greɪ.di (US) oʊ-
og|re 'əʊ.g|əʳ (US) 'oʊ.g|ɚ **-res** -əz (US) -ɚz **-reish** -ᵊr.ɪʃ
ogress 'əʊ.grəs, -rɪs (US) 'oʊ- **-es** -ɪz
Ogwr 'ɒg.ʊəʳ (US) 'ɑː.gʊr
oh əʊ (US) oʊ
O'Hagan əʊ'heɪ.gᵊn (US) oʊ-
O'Halloran əʊ'hæl.ᵊr.ən (US) oʊ-
O'Hanlon əʊ'hæn.lən (US) oʊ-
O'Hara əʊ'hɑː.rə (US) oʊ'her.ə, -'hær-
O'Hare əʊ'heəʳ (US) oʊ'her
O'Hea əʊ'heɪ (US) oʊ-
Ohio əʊ'haɪ.əʊ (US) oʊ'haɪ.oʊ, ə- **-an/s** -ən/z
ohm (O) əʊm (US) oʊm **-s** -z
OHMS ˌəʊ.eɪtʃ.em'es (US) ˌoʊ-
oho əʊ'həʊ (US) oʊ'hoʊ
oick ɔɪk **-s** -s
-oid -ɔɪd
Note: Suffix. Does not normally change the stress pattern of the stem, e.g. **human** /'hjuː.mən/, **humanoid** /'hjuː.mə.nɔɪd/.
oik ɔɪk **-s** -s
oil ɔɪl **-s** -z **-ing** -ɪŋ **-ed** -d **-er/s** -əʳ/z (US) -ɚ/z **'oil ˌcan**; **'oil ˌfield**; **'oil ˌpaint**; **'oil ˌpainting**; **'oil ˌslick**; **'oil ˌwell**; **ˌpour ˌoil on ˌtroubled 'waters**; **ˌburn the ˌmidnight 'oil**
oil|cloth 'ɔɪl|.klɒθ (US) -klɑːθ **-cloths** -klɒθs, -klɒðz (US) -klɑːθs, -klɑːðz
oil-rig 'ɔɪl.rɪg **-s** -z
oilseed 'ɔɪl.siːd
oilskin 'ɔɪl.skɪn **-s** -z
oil|y 'ɔɪ.l|i **-ier** -i.əʳ (US) -i.ɚ **-iest** -i.ɪst, -i.əst **-iness** -ɪ.nəs, -ɪ.nɪs
oink ɔɪŋk **-s** -s
ointment 'ɔɪnt.mənt **-s** -s
Oisin 'ɔɪ.zɪn (US) 'ɑː.ʃən, -ə.ʃiːn
Oistrakh 'ɔɪ.strɑːk *as if Russian:* -strɑːx
Ojai 'əʊ.haɪ (US) 'oʊ-
Ojibwa(y) əʊ'dʒɪb.weɪ, ɒdʒ'ɪb-, -wə (US) oʊ'dʒɪb.weɪ, -wə **-s** -z
OK əʊ'keɪ (US) oʊ-, ə- **-s** -z **-ing** -ɪŋ **-ed** -d *stress shift:* ˌOK 'person
O'Kane əʊ'keɪn (US) oʊ-
okapi əʊ'kɑː.pi (US) oʊ- **-s** -z
Okara ɒk'ɑː.rə (US) ə'kɑːr.ə
Okavango, **Okovango** ˌɒk.ə'væŋ.gəʊ (US) ˌoʊ.kə'væŋ.goʊ
okay əʊ'keɪ (US) oʊ-, ə- **-s** -z **-ing** -ɪŋ **-ed** -d *stress shift:* ˌokay 'person
Okeechobee ˌəʊ.kɪ'tʃəʊ.bi, -kiː'- (US) ˌoʊ.kɪ'tʃoʊ-, -kiː'-
O'Keef(f)e əʊ'kiːf (US) oʊ-
Okehampton ˌəʊk'hæmp.tᵊn (US) 'oʊkˌhæmp- *stress shift, British only:* ˌOkehampton 'centre
O'Kelly əʊ'kel.i (US) oʊ-
okeydoke ˌəʊ.ki'dəʊk (US) ˌoʊ.ki'doʊk **-y** -i
Okhotsk əʊ'kɒtsk, ɒk'ɒtsk (US) oʊ'kɑːtsk
Okie 'əʊ.ki (US) 'oʊ- **-s** -z
Okinawa ˌɒk.ɪ'nɑː.wə, ˌəʊ.kɪ'- (US) ˌoʊ.kə'nɑː.wə, -kɪ-
okker, **ocker** 'ɒk.əʳ (US) 'ɑː.kɚ **-s** -z
Okla. (*abbrev. for* **Oklahoma**) ˌəʊ.klə'həʊ.mə (US) ˌoʊ.klə'hoʊ-
Oklahom|a ˌəʊ.klə'həʊ.m|ə (US) ˌoʊ.klə'hoʊ- **-an/s** -ən/z
Okovango, **Okavango** ˌɒk.ə'væŋ.gəʊ (US) ˌoʊ.kə'væŋ.goʊ
okra 'ɒk.rə, 'əʊ.krə (US) 'oʊ-
Okri 'ɒk.ri (US) 'ɑː.kri
Olaf, **Olav** 'əʊ.læf, -ləf (US) 'oʊ.ləf, -lɑːf
Olave 'ɒl.ɪv, -əv, -eɪv (US) 'oʊ.ləf, -lɑːf, -ləv
Olcott 'ɒl.kət (US) 'ɑːl-
old əʊld (US) oʊld **-er** -əʳ (US) -ɚ **-est** -ɪst **-ness** -nəs, -nɪs **ˌOld 'Bailey**; **'old boy**; **ˌOld 'English**; **ˌOld ˌEnglish 'sheepdog**; **ˌOld 'Faithful**; **ˌOld 'Glory**; **ˌold 'guard**; **ˌold 'hand**; **ˌold 'hat**; **ˌold 'lady**; **ˌold 'maid**; **ˌold 'man**; **ˌold 'master**; **'old ˌschool**; **ˌOld 'Testament**; **as ˌold as the 'hills**
old-age (*adj.*) 'əʊldˌeɪdʒ (US) 'oʊld- (*n.*) **old age** ˌəʊld'eɪdʒ (US) ˌoʊld-
old-age pension ˌəʊld.eɪdʒ'pen.*t*ʃᵊn (US) ˌoʊld- **-s** -z **-er/s** -əʳ/z (US) -ɚ/z
Oldbuck 'əʊl*d*.bʌk (US) 'oʊl*d*-
Oldbury 'əʊl*d*.bᵊr.i (US) 'oʊl*d*ˌber-, -bɚ.i
Oldcastle 'əʊl*d*ˌkɑː.sl̩ (US) 'oʊl*d*ˌkæs.l̩
olden 'əʊl.dᵊn (US) 'oʊl-
Oldenburg 'əʊl.dᵊn.bɜːg, -dᵊm- (US) 'oʊl.dᵊn.bɜːrg
olde worlde ˌəʊl.di'wɜːl.di (US) ˌoʊl.di'wɜːrl-
Note: Joking imitation of spelling.
old-fashioned ˌəʊl*d*'fæʃ.ᵊnd (US) ˌoʊl*d*- *stress shift:* ˌold-fashioned 'ways
Oldfield 'əʊl*d*.fiːld (US) 'oʊl*d*-
old-fog(e)yish ˌəʊl*d*'fəʊ.gi.ɪʃ (US) ˌoʊl*d*'foʊ-
Oldham 'əʊl.dəm (US) 'oʊl-
oldie 'əʊl.di (US) 'oʊl- **-s** -z
oldish 'əʊl.dɪʃ (US) 'oʊl-
Oldrey 'əʊl.dri (US) 'oʊl-
Oldsmobile® 'əʊldz.mə.biːl (US) 'oʊldz-
oldster 'əʊld.stəʳ (US) 'oʊld.stɚ **-s** -z
old-time ˌəʊl*d*'taɪm (US) ˌoʊl*d*- *stress shift:* ˌold-time 'dancing
old-timer ˌəʊl*d*'taɪ.məʳ (US) 'oʊl*d*ˌtaɪ.mɚ **-s** -z
old wives' tale ˌəʊld'waɪvzˌteɪl (US) ˌoʊld-
old-world ˌəʊld'wɜːld (US) ˌoʊld'wɜːrld *stress shift:* ˌold-world 'values
olé əʊ'leɪ (US) oʊ-
oleaginous ˌəʊ.li'ædʒ.ɪ.nəs, '-ə- (US) ˌoʊ- **-ly** -li **-ness** -nəs, -nɪs
oleander (O) ˌəʊ.li'æn.dəʳ (US) ˌoʊ.li'æn.dɚ, 'oʊ.liˌæn- **-s** -z
O'Leary əʊ'lɪə.ri (US) oʊ'lɪr.i
oleaster ˌəʊ.li'æs.təʳ (US) ˌoʊ.li'æs.tɚ **-s** -z
oleograph 'əʊ.li.əʊ.grɑːf, 'ɒl.i-, -græf (US) 'oʊ.li.oʊ.græf, -ə- **-s** -s
O level 'əʊˌlev.ᵊl (US) 'oʊ- **-s** -z
olfactory ɒl'fæk.tᵊr.i (US) ɑːl-, oʊl-
Olga 'ɒl.gə (US) 'ɑːl-, 'ɔːl-, 'oʊl-
Oliffe 'ɒl.ɪf (US) 'ɑː.lɪf
oligarch 'ɒl.ɪ.gɑːk (US) 'ɑː.lɪ.gɑːrk, 'oʊ- **-s** -s
oligarchal ˌɒl.ɪ'gɑː.kᵊl (US) ˌɑː.lɪ'gɑːr-, ˌoʊ- *stress shift:* ˌoligarchal 'state
oligarchic ˌɒl.ɪ'gɑː.kɪk (US) ˌɑː.lɪ'gɑːr-, ˌoʊ- *stress shift:* ˌoligarchic 'state
oligarch|y 'ɒl.ɪ.gɑː.k|i (US) 'ɑː.lɪ.gɑːr-, 'oʊ- **-ies** -iz
Oligocene 'ɒl.ɪ.gəʊ.siːn; ɒl'ɪg.əʊ- (US) 'ɑː.lɪ.goʊ-, 'oʊ-
oligopol|y ˌɒl.ɪ'gɒp.ᵊl|.i (US) ˌɑː.lɪ'gɑː.pᵊl-, ˌoʊ- **-ies** -iz
olio 'əʊ.li.əʊ (US) 'oʊ.li.oʊ **-s** -z
Oliphant 'ɒl.ɪ.fənt, '-ə- (US) 'ɑː.lɪ-
olivaceous ˌɒl.ɪ'veɪ.ʃəs (US) ˌɑː.lɪ'-
olive (O) 'ɒl.ɪv (US) 'ɑː.lɪv **-s** -z **'olive ˌbranch**; **ˌolive 'green**; **ˌolive 'oil**, **'olive ˌoil**
oliver (O) 'ɒl.ɪ.vəʳ, '-ə- (US) 'ɑː.lɪ.vɚ **-s** -z
Oliverian ˌɒl.ɪ'vɪə.ri.ən, -ə'- (US) ˌɑː.lɪ'ver.i-
Olivet 'ɒl.ɪ.vet, '-ə-, -vɪt, -vət (US) 'ɑː.lɪ.vet, -lə-
Olivetti® ˌɒl.ɪ'vet.i, -ə'- (US) ˌɑː.lə'veṭ.i
Olivia ɒl'ɪv.i.ə, ə'lɪv-, əʊ- (US) oʊ-, ə-
Olivier ə'lɪv.i.eɪ, ɒl'ɪv-, -ə (US) oʊ'lɪv.i.eɪ
olivine 'ɒl.ɪ.viːn, '-ə-, ˌ--'- (US) 'ɑː.lə.viːn **-s** -z
olla podrida ˌɒl.jə.pɒd'riː.də, -pə'driː- (US) ˌɑː.lə.poʊ'-, -pə'- **-s** -z
Ollendorf 'ɒl.ən.dɔːf, -ɪn- (US) 'ɑː.lən.dɔːrf
Ollerton 'ɒl.ə.tᵊn (US) 'ɑː.lɚ-
Olley, **Ollie** 'ɒl.i (US) 'ɑː.li
Olliffe 'ɒl.ɪf (US) 'ɑː.lɪf
Ollivant 'ɒl.ɪ.vənt, -vænt (US) 'ɑː.lɪ-
Olmstead 'ɒm.sted (US) 'oʊm-, 'ɑːm-, -stəd

Olney 'əʊl.ni, 'əʊ- ⓤⓢ 'oʊl-, 'oʊ-, 'ɑːl-
-olog|y -'ɒl.ə.dʒ|i ⓤⓢ -'ɑː.lə.dʒ|i
-ies -iz
Note: Suffix. Normally takes primary stress as shown, e.g. **biology** /baɪ'ɒl.ə.dʒi ⓤⓢ -'ɑː.lə-/, **pharmacology** /ˌfɑː.mə'kɒl.ə.dʒi ⓤⓢ ˌfɑːr.mə'kɑː.lə-/.
oloroso ˌɒl.ə'rəʊ.səʊ, ˌəʊ.lə'-, -zəʊ ⓤⓢ ˌoʊ.loʊ'roʊ.soʊ, -lə'- **-s** -z
Olsen, Olson 'əʊl.sᵊn ⓤⓢ 'oʊl-
Olver 'ɒl.vəʳ, 'əʊl- ⓤⓢ 'ɑː.lvɚ
Olwen 'ɒl.wen, -wɪn ⓤⓢ 'ɑːl-
Olympi|a əʊ'lɪm.pi|.ə ⓤⓢ oʊ-, ə- **-an** -ən
Olympiad əʊ'lɪm.pi.æd ⓤⓢ oʊ-, ə- **-s** -z
Olympic əʊ'lɪm.pɪk ⓤⓢ oʊ-, ə- **-s** -s
O,lympic 'Games
Olympus əʊ'lɪm.pəs ⓤⓢ oʊ-, ə-
Olynthus əʊ'lɪnt.θəs ⓤⓢ oʊ-, ə-
om (O) əʊm, ɒm ⓤⓢ oʊm
Omagh 'əʊ.mə, -mɑː ⓤⓢ 'oʊ-
Omaha 'əʊ.mə.hɑː ⓤⓢ 'oʊ-, -hɔː
O'Malley əʊ'mæl.i, -'meɪ.li ⓤⓢ oʊ-
Oman əʊ'mɑːn ⓤⓢ oʊ-
Omar 'əʊ.mɑːʳ ⓤⓢ 'oʊ.mɑːr
Omar Khayyám ˌəʊ.mɑː.kaɪ'æm, -'ɑːm ⓤⓢ ˌoʊ.mɑːr.kaɪ'jɑːm, -'æm
ombre 'ɒm.bəʳ ⓤⓢ 'ɑːm.bɚ
ombuds|man 'ɒm.bʊdz|.mən, -bʌdz-, -bədz-, -mæn ⓤⓢ 'ɑːm.bədz-, -bʌdz-; ɑːm'bʌdz- **-men** -mən, -men
Omdurman ˌɒm.dɜː'mɑːn, -də'-, -'mæn; 'ɒm.də.mən ⓤⓢ ˌɑːm.dʊr'mɑːn
O'Meara əʊ'mɑː.rə, -'mɪə- ⓤⓢ oʊ'mɪr.ə, -'mɑːr-
omega (O) 'əʊ.mɪ.gə, -meg.ə ⓤⓢ oʊ'meɪ.gə, -'meg.ə, -'miː.gə; 'oʊ.meg- **-s** -z
omelet, omelette 'ɒm.lət, -lɪt, -let, ⓤⓢ 'ɑːm.lət, -lɪt; 'ɑː.mə- **-s** -s
omen 'əʊ.mən, -men ⓤⓢ 'oʊ- **-s** -z **-ed** -d
omer (O) 'əʊ.məʳ ⓤⓢ 'oʊ.mɚ **-s** -z
omertà ˌəʊ.mə'tɑː ⓤⓢ ˌoʊ.mer'tɑː
omicron əʊ'maɪ.krɒn, -krᵊn; 'ɒm.ɪ- ⓤⓢ 'oʊ.mɪ.krɑːn, 'ɑː- **-s** -z
ominous 'ɒm.ɪ.nəs, 'əʊ.mɪ-, -mə- ⓤⓢ 'ɑː.mə- **-ly** -li **-ness** -nəs, -nɪs
omissible əʊ'mɪs.ɪ.bl̩, '-ə- ⓤⓢ oʊ-
omission əʊ'mɪʃ.ᵊn ⓤⓢ oʊ- **-s** -z
o|mit əʊ|'mɪt ⓤⓢ oʊ- **-mits** -'mɪts **-mitting** -'mɪt.ɪŋ ⓤⓢ -'mɪţ.ɪŋ **-mitted** -'mɪt.ɪd ⓤⓢ -'mɪţ.ɪd
ommatidi|um ˌɒm.ə'tɪd.i|.əm ⓤⓢ ˌɑː.mə'- **-a** -ə **-al** -əl
omni- ɒm.nɪ-, -nə-, -ni-; ɒm'nɪ- ⓤⓢ ɑːm.nɪ-, -nə-, -ni-; ɑːm'nɪ-
Note: Prefix. Normally takes either primary or secondary stress on the first syllable, e.g. **omnibus** /'ɒm.nɪ.bəs ⓤⓢ 'ɑːm-/, **omnipresent** /ˌɒm.nɪ'pres.ᵊnt ⓤⓢ ˌɑːm-/, or primary stress on the second syllable, e.g. **omnipotent** /ɒm'nɪp.ə.tᵊnt ⓤⓢ ɑːm'nɪ.pə.ţənt/.
omnibus 'ɒm.nɪ.bəs, -nə-, -bʌs ⓤⓢ 'ɑːm- **-es** -ɪz
omnifarious ˌɒm.nɪ'feə.ri.əs ⓤⓢ ˌɑːm.nɪ'fer.i-
omnificent ɒm'nɪf.ɪ.sᵊnt ⓤⓢ ɑːm-
omnipotence ɒm'nɪp.ə.tᵊnts ⓤⓢ ɑːm'nɪp.ə.ţənts
omnipotent ɒm'nɪp.ə.tᵊnt ⓤⓢ ɑːm'nɪp.ə.ţənt **-ly** -li
omnipresen|t ˌɒm.nɪ'prez.ᵊn|t, -nə'- ⓤⓢ ˌɑːm.nɪ'- **-ce** -ts
omniscience ɒm'nɪs.i.ənts, -'nɪʃ-, -'nɪʃ.ᵊnts ⓤⓢ ɑːm'nɪʃ.ᵊnts
omniscient ɒm'nɪs.i.ənt, -'nɪʃ-, -'nɪʃ.ᵊnt ⓤⓢ ɑːm'nɪʃ.ᵊnt **-ly** -li
omnium (O) 'ɒm.ni.əm ⓤⓢ 'ɑːm- **-s** -z
omnium gatherum ˌɒm.ni.əm'gæð.ᵊr.əm ⓤⓢ ˌɑːm- **-s** -z
omnivore 'ɒm.nɪ.vɔːʳ, -nə- ⓤⓢ 'ɑːm.nɪ.vɔːr **-s** -z
omnivorous ɒm'nɪv.ᵊr.əs ⓤⓢ ɑːm- **-ly** -li
Omond 'əʊ.mənd ⓤⓢ 'oʊ-
omphalos 'ɒmp.fᵊl.ɒs ⓤⓢ 'ɑːmp.fᵊl.əs, -ɑːs
Omri 'ɒm.raɪ ⓤⓢ 'ɑːm-
Omsk ɒmsk ⓤⓢ ɔːmsk, ɑːmsk
on (*n. adj. adv. prep.*) ɒn ⓤⓢ ɑːn, ɔːn
onager 'ɒn.ə.gəʳ ⓤⓢ 'ɑː.nə.gɚ **-s** -z
Onan 'əʊ.næn, -nən ⓤⓢ 'oʊ-
onan|ism 'əʊ.nə.n|ɪ.zᵊm, -næn|.ɪ- ⓤⓢ 'oʊ- **-ist/s** -ɪst/s
onanistic ˌəʊ.nə'nɪs.tɪk, -næn'ɪst- ⓤⓢ ˌoʊ-
Onassis əʊ'næs.ɪs ⓤⓢ oʊ-, -'nɑː.sɪs
on-board (*adj.*) 'ɒn.bɔːd ⓤⓢ 'ɑːn.bɔːrd
once wʌnts **ˌonce and for 'all**
once-over 'wʌnts,əʊ.vəʳ, ˌ-'-- ⓤⓢ 'wʌnts,oʊ.vɚ
oncer 'wʌnt.səʳ ⓤⓢ -sɚ **-s** -z
onco- ɒŋ.kəʊ-; ɒŋ'kɒ- ⓤⓢ ɑːn.koʊ-, ɑːŋ-, -kə-; ɑːn'kɑː-, ɑːŋ-
Note: Prefix. Normally either takes primary or secondary stress on the first syllable, e.g. **oncogene** /'ɒŋ.kəʊ.dʒiːn ⓤⓢ 'ɑːŋ.kə-/, **oncogenic** /ˌɒŋ.kəʊ'dʒen.ɪk ⓤⓢ ˌɑːŋ.kə-/, or primary stress on the second syllable, e.g. **oncology** /ɒŋ'kɒl.ə.dʒi ⓤⓢ ɑːŋ'kɑː.lə-/.
oncogene 'ɒŋ.kəʊ.dʒiːn ⓤⓢ 'ɑːn.kə-, 'ɑːŋ- **-s** -z
oncogenic ˌɒŋ.kəʊ'dʒen.ɪk ⓤⓢ ˌɑːn.kə'-, ˌɑːŋ-
oncologic ˌɒŋ.kəʊ'lɒdʒ.ɪk ⓤⓢ ˌɑːn.kə'lɑː.dʒɪk, ˌɑːŋ-
oncological ˌɒŋ.kəʊ'lɒdʒ.ɪ.kᵊl ⓤⓢ ˌɑːn.kə'lɑː.dʒɪ-, ˌɑːŋ-
oncologist ɒŋ'kɒl.ə.dʒɪst ⓤⓢ ɑːn'kɑː.lə-, ɑːŋ- **-s** -s
oncology ɒŋ'kɒl.ə.dʒi ⓤⓢ ɑːn'kɑː.lə-, ɑːŋ-
oncoming 'ɒn,kʌm.ɪŋ, 'ɒŋ- ⓤⓢ 'ɑːn-, 'ɔːn-
Ondaatje ɒn'dɑː.tʃə ⓤⓢ ɑːn'dɑː.tʃe
on-drive 'ɒn.draɪv ⓤⓢ 'ɑːn-, 'ɔːn- **-s** -z
one wʌn **-s** -z
O'Neal əʊ'niːl ⓤⓢ oʊ-
one-armed ˌwʌn'ɑːmd ⓤⓢ -'ɑːrmd **ˌone-armed 'bandit**
one-eyed ˌwʌn'aɪd *stress shift:* ˌone-eyed 'pirate
Onega ɒn'eɪ.gə, əʊ'neɪ-, -'njeg.ə; *old fashioned:* 'əʊ.nɪ.gə ⓤⓢ oʊn'jeg.ə, -neɪ-
Onegin ɒn'jeɪ.gɪn ⓤⓢ ɑːn-
one-horse ˌwʌn'hɔːs ⓤⓢ -'hɔːrs *stress shift, see compound:* **ˌone-horse 'town**
O'Neil(l) əʊ'niːl ⓤⓢ oʊ-
one-legged ˌwʌn'leg.ɪd, -'legd *stress shift:* ˌone-legged 'table
one-liner ˌwʌn'laɪ.nəʳ ⓤⓢ -nɚ **-s** -z
one-man ˌwʌn'mæn, ˌwʌm- ⓤⓢ ˌwʌn- *stress shift, see compound:* **ˌone-man 'band**
oneness 'wʌn.nəs, -nɪs
one-night stand ˌwʌn.naɪt'stænd
one-off ˌwʌn'ɒf, '-- ⓤⓢ 'wʌn.ɑːf **-s** -s
one-parent family ˌwʌn.peə.rᵊnt'fæm.ᵊl.i, ˌwʌm-, -ɪ.li ⓤⓢ ˌwʌn.per.ᵊnt'-, -pær-
one-piece 'wʌn.piːs, 'wʌm- ⓤⓢ 'wʌn-
oner 'wʌn.əʳ ⓤⓢ -ɚ **-s** -z
onerous 'əʊ.nᵊr.əs, 'ɒn.ᵊr- ⓤⓢ 'ɑː.nɚ-, 'oʊ- **-ly** -li **-ness** -nəs, -nɪs
oneself wʌn'self **ˌkeep oneˌself to one'self**
onesided ˌwʌn'saɪ.dɪd **-ly** -li **-ness** -nəs, -nɪs *stress shift:* ˌonesided 'argument
Onesimus əʊ'nes.ɪ.məs, -'niː.sɪ-, -sə- ⓤⓢ oʊ-
onetime 'wʌn.taɪm
one-to-one ˌwʌn.tə'wʌn, -tu'- ⓤⓢ -ţə'-
one-track mind ˌwʌn.træk'maɪnd **-s** -z
one-upmanship ˌwʌn'ʌp.mən.ʃɪp
one-way ˌwʌn'weɪ *stress shift, see compound:* **ˌone-way 'street**
ongoing 'ɒn,gəʊ.ɪŋ, 'ɒŋ-, ˌ-'-- ⓤⓢ 'ɑːn,goʊ- **-s** -z
Onians ə'naɪənz, əʊ- ⓤⓢ oʊ-
Onich 'əʊ.nɪk, -nɪx ⓤⓢ 'oʊ-
onion 'ʌn.jən **-s** -z **-y** -i
Onions 'ʌn.jənz, əʊ'naɪənz ⓤⓢ 'ʌn.jənz
on-line ˌɒn'laɪn ⓤⓢ ˌɑːn-, ˌɔːn- *stress shift:* ˌon-line 'chat
onlook|er 'ɒn,lʊk|.əʳ ⓤⓢ 'ɑːn,lʊk|.ɚ, 'ɔːn- **-ers** -əz ⓤⓢ -ɚz **-ing** -ɪŋ

only 'əʊn.li (US) 'oʊn-
Ono 'əʊ.nəʊ (US) 'oʊ.noʊ
onomasiological ˌɒn.əʊˌmeɪ.si.ə'lɒdʒ.ɪ.kəl, -zi- (US) ˌɑː.noʊˌmeɪ.si.ə'lɑː.dʒɪ-, -nəˌ-
onomasiology ˌɒn.əʊˌmeɪ.si'ɒl.ə.dʒi, -zi'- (US) ˌɑː.noʊˌmeɪ.si'ɑː.lə, -nəˌ-
onomastic ˌɒn.əʊ'mæs.tɪk (US) ˌɑː.noʊ'-, -nə'- **-s** -s
onomatopoe|ia ˌɒn.əʊˌmæt.ə'piː|.ə (US) ˌɑː.noʊˌmæt̬.oʊ'-, -nəˌ- **-ias** -əz **-ic** -ɪk
onrush 'ɒn.rʌʃ (US) 'ɑːn-, 'ɔːn- **-ing** -ɪŋ
onset 'ɒn.set (US) 'ɑːn-, 'ɔːn- **-s** -s
onshore ˌɒn'ʃɔːr (US) 'ɑːn.ʃɔːr, 'ɔːn- *stress shift, British only:* ˌonshore 'wind
onside ˌɒn'saɪd (US) 'ɑːn.saɪd, 'ɔːn- *stress shift, British only:* ˌonside 'player
onslaught 'ɒn.slɔːt (US) 'ɑːn.slɑːt, 'ɔːn-, -slɔːt **-s** -s
Onslow 'ɒnz.ləʊ (US) 'ɑːnz.loʊ
onstream ˌɒn'striːm (US) ˌɑːn-, ˌɔːn- *stress shift:* ˌonstream 'oilfield
Ontario ɒn'teə.ri.əʊ (US) ɑːn'ter.i.oʊ
onto 'ɒn.tuː, -tə, -tu (US) 'ɑːn.tuː, 'ɔːn-, -tə, -tu
Note: The pronunciation /'ɒn.tuː (US) 'ɑːn-/ is only rarely heard. The usual pronunciation is /'ɒn.tə (US) ɑːn.tə/ before consonants, e.g. "onto ships" /ˌɒn.tə'ʃɪps (US) ˌɑːn.tə'-/, and /'ɒn.tu (US) 'ɑːn-/ before vowels, e.g. "onto aircraft" /ˌɒn.tu'eə.krɑːft (US) ˌɑːn.tu'er.kræft/.
ontogenesis ˌɒn.təʊ'dʒen.ə.sɪs, '-ɪ- (US) ˌɑːn.toʊ'dʒen.ə-
ontogenetic ˌɒn.təʊ.dʒə'net.ɪk, -dʒɪ'- (US) ˌɑːn.toʊ.dʒə'net̬- **-ally** -əl.i, -li
ontogeny ɒn'tɒdʒ.ə.ni, '-ɪ- (US) ɑːn'tɑː.dʒə-
ontologic ˌɒn.tə'lɒdʒ.ɪk (US) ˌɑːn.toʊ'lɑː.dʒɪk **-al** -əl **-ally** -əl.i, -li
ontolog|y ɒn'tɒl.ə.dʒ|i (US) ɑːn'tɑː.lə- **-ist/s** -ɪst/s
onus 'əʊ.nəs (US) 'oʊ-
onward 'ɒn.wəd (US) 'ɑːn.wɚd, 'ɔːn- **-s** -z
onyx 'ɒn.ɪks (US) 'ɑː.nɪks **-es** -ɪz
oodles 'uː.dl̩z
oof uːf
ooh uː
oolite 'əʊ.əʊ.laɪt (US) 'oʊ.ə- **-s** -s
oolitic ˌəʊ.əʊ'lɪt.ɪk (US) ˌoʊ.ə'lɪt̬-
oolog|y əʊ'ɒl.ə.dʒ|i (US) oʊ'ɑː.lə- **-ist/s** -ɪst/s
Oolong 'uː.lɒŋ, ˌ-'- (US) 'uː.lɑːŋ, -lɔːŋ
oompah 'ʊm.pɑː, 'uːm-
oomph ʊm*p*f, uːm*p*f
oops uːps, ʊps
oops-a-daisy ˌʊps.ə'deɪ.zi, ˌuːps-, ˌwʊps-, 'ʊps.əˌdeɪ-, 'uːps-, 'wʊps-
ooz|e uːz **-es** -ɪz **-ing** -ɪŋ **-ed** -d
ooz|y 'uː.z|i **-ier** -i.ər (US) -i.ɚ **-iest** -i.ɪst, -i.əst **-ily** -ɪ.li, -əl.i **-iness** -ɪ.nəs, -ɪ.nɪs
op ɒp (US) ɑːp **-s** -s
opacity əʊ'pæs.ə.ti, -ɪ.ti (US) oʊ'pæs.ə.t̬i
opal 'əʊ.pəl (US) 'oʊ- **-s** -z
opalescen|t ˌəʊ.pəl'es.ən|t (US) ˌoʊ- **-ce** -*t*s
opaline (*adj.*) 'əʊ.pəl.aɪn (US) 'oʊ.pəl.iːn, -aɪn, -ɪn
opaline (*n.*) 'əʊ.pəl.iːn, -aɪn (US) 'oʊ- **-s** -z
opaque əʊ'peɪk (US) oʊ- **-ly** -li **-ness** -nəs, -nɪs
op art 'ɒpˌɑːt (US) 'ɑːpˌɑːrt
op. cit. ˌɒp'sɪt (US) ˌɑːp-
op|e əʊp (US) oʊp **-es** -s **-ing** -ɪŋ **-ed** -t
OPEC, Opec 'əʊ.pek (US) 'oʊ-
Opel® 'əʊ.pəl (US) 'oʊ-
open 'əʊ.pən (US) 'oʊ- **-er** -ər (US) -ɚ **-est** -ɪst (US) -əst **-s** -z **-ing** -ɪŋ, 'əʊp.nɪŋ (US) 'oʊp- **-ed** -d **ˌopen 'book** ; **ˌopen 'day** ; **ˌopen 'house** ; **ˌopen 'market** ; **ˌopen 'prison** ; **ˌopen 'sesame** ; **ˌOpen Uni'versity** ; **ˌopen 'verdict**
open-air (*adj.*) ˌəʊ.pən'eər (US) ˌoʊ.pən'er *stress shift:* ˌopen-air 'concert (*n.*) **open air** ˌəʊ.pən'eər (US) ˌoʊ.pən'er
open-and-shut ˌəʊ.pən.ənd'ʃʌt (US) ˌoʊ- *stress shift:* ˌopen-and-shut 'case
opencast 'əʊ.pən.kɑːst, -pəŋ- (US) 'oʊ.pən.kæst
open-ended ˌəʊ.pən'end.ɪd (US) ˌoʊ- *stress shift:* ˌopen-ended 'verdict
opener 'əʊ.pən.ər (US) 'oʊ.pən.ɚ **-s** -z
open-eyed ˌəʊ.pən'aɪd (US) ˌoʊ- *stress shift:* ˌopen-eyed 'onlooker
open-handed ˌəʊ.pən'hæn.dɪd, 'əʊ.pənˌhæn- (US) 'oʊ.pənˌhæn-, ˌoʊ.pən'hæn- **-ness** -nəs, -nɪs *stress shift, British only:* ˌopen-handed 'benefactor
open-heart ˌəʊ.pən'hɑːt (US) ˌoʊ.pən'hɑːrt *stress shift, see compound:* **ˌopen-heart 'surgery**
open-hearted ˌəʊ.pən'hɑː.tɪd, 'əʊ.pənˌhɑː- (US) 'oʊ.pənˌhɑːr.t̬ɪd, ˌoʊ.pən'hɑːr- **-ly** -li **-ness** -nəs, -nɪs *stress shift, British only:* ˌopen-hearted 'person
opening 'əʊp.nɪŋ, 'əʊ.pən.ɪŋ (US) 'oʊp.nɪŋ, 'oʊ.pən.ɪŋ **-s** -z
opening time 'əʊp.nɪŋˌtaɪm, 'əʊ.pən.ɪŋˌ- (US) 'oʊp.nɪŋˌ-, 'oʊ.pən.ɪŋˌ-
openly 'əʊ.pən.li (US) 'oʊ-
open-minded ˌəʊ.pən'maɪn.dɪd, -pəm'-, 'əʊ.pənˌmaɪn-, -pəmˌ- (US) ˌoʊ.pən'maɪn-, 'oʊ.pənˌmaɪn- **-ly** -li **-ness** -nəs, -nɪs *stress shift, British only:* ˌopen-minded 'person
open-mouthed ˌəʊ.pən'maʊðd, -pəm'-, 'əʊ.pənˌmaʊðd (US) 'oʊ.pənˌmaʊðd, -ˌmaʊθt, ˌ--'- *stress shift, British only:* ˌopen-mouthed 'children
openness 'əʊ.pən.nəs, -nɪs (US) 'oʊ-
open-plan ˌəʊ.pən'plæn, -pəm'- (US) ˌoʊ.pən- *stress shift:* ˌopen-plan 'offices
open sesame ˌəʊ.pən'ses.ə.mi (US) ˌoʊ-
Openshaw 'əʊ.pən.ʃɔː (US) 'oʊ.pən.ʃɑː, -ʃɔː
open-work 'əʊ.pən.wɜːk (US) 'oʊ.pən.wɜːrk
opera 'ɒp.ər.ə, 'ɒp.rə (US) 'ɑː.pər.ə, 'ɑː.prə **-s** -z **'opera ˌhouse**
operability ˌɒp.ər.ə'bɪl.ɪ.ti, -ə.ti (US) ˌɑː.pər.ə'bɪl.ə.t̬i, ˌɑː.prə'-
operab|le 'ɒp.ər.ə.b|l̩ (US) 'ɑː.pər.ə-, 'ɑː.prə- **-ly** -ly
opéra bouffe ˌɒp.ər.ə'buːf (US) ˌɑː.pər-, ˌɑː.prə'-
opera buffa ˌɒp.ər.ə'buː.fə (US) ˌɑː.pər.ə'-, ˌɑː.prə'-
opéra comique ˌɒp.ər.ə.kɒm'iːk (US) ˌɑː.pər.ə.kɑː'miːk, ˌɑː.prə-
operant 'ɒp.ər.ənt (US) 'ɑː.pər- **-s** -s
oper|ate 'ɒp.ər|.eɪt (US) 'ɑː.pər- **-ates** -eɪts **-ating** -eɪ.tɪŋ (US) -eɪ.t̬ɪŋ **-ated** -eɪ.tɪd (US) -eɪ.t̬ɪd **-ator/s** -eɪ.tər/z (US) -eɪ.t̬ɚ/z **'operating ˌsystem** ; **'operating ˌtable**
operatic ˌɒp.ər'æt.ɪk (US) ˌɑː.pə'ræt̬- **-s** -s **-ally** -əl.i, -li
operation ˌɒp.ər'eɪ.ʃən (US) ˌɑː.pə'reɪ- **-s** -z
operational ˌɒp.ər'eɪ.ʃən.əl, -'eɪʃ.nəl (US) ˌɑː.pə'reɪ.ʃən.əl, -'reɪʃ.nəl **-ly** -i
operative 'ɒp.ər.ə.tɪv, -eɪ- (US) 'ɑː.pɚ.ə.t̬ɪv, -pə.reɪ- **-ly** -li **-ness** -nəs, -nɪs
operetta ˌɒp.ər'et.ə (US) ˌɑː.pə'ret̬- **-s** -z
operettist ˌɒp.ər'et.ɪst (US) ˌɑː.pə'ret̬- **-s** -s
Ophelia əʊ'fiː.li.ə, ɒf'iː- (US) oʊ'fiːl.jə
ophicleide 'ɒf.ɪ.klaɪd (US) 'ɑː.fɪ- **-s** -z
ophidian ɒf'ɪd.i.ən, əʊ'fɪd- (US) oʊ-
Ophir 'əʊ.fər (US) 'oʊ.fɚ
Ophiuchus ɒf'juː.kəs, ˌɒf.i'uː- (US) ˌɑː.fi'juː.kəs, ˌoʊ-
ophthalmia ɒf'θæl.mi.ə, ɒp- (US) ɑːf-, ɑːp-
ophthalmic ɒf'θæl.mɪk, ɒp- (US) ɑːf-, ɑːp-
ophthalmo- ɒfˌθæl.məʊ-, ɒp- (US) ɑːfˌθæl.moʊ-, ɑːp-, -mə-

ophthalmolog|y ˌɒf.θælˈmɒl.ə.dʒ|i, ɒp- ⓤⓢ ˌɑːf.θælˈmɑː.lə-, ˌɑːp- **-ist/s** -ɪst/s
ophthalmoscope ɒfˈθæl.mə.skəʊp, ɒp- ⓤⓢ ɑːfˈθæl.mə.skoʊp, ɑːp- **-s** -s
ophthalmoscopy ˌɒf.θælˈmɒs.kə.pi, ɒp- ⓤⓢ ˌɑːf.θælˈmɑː.skə-, ˌɑːp-
opiate ˈəʊ.pi.ət, -ɪt, -eɪt ⓤⓢ ˈoʊ.pi.ɪt, -eɪt **-s** -s
opiated ˈəʊ.pi.eɪ.tɪd ⓤⓢ ˈoʊ.pi.eɪ.t̬ɪd
Opie ˈəʊ.pi ⓤⓢ ˈoʊ-
opin|e əʊˈpaɪn ⓤⓢ oʊ- **-es** -z **-ing** -ɪŋ **-ed** -d
opinion əˈpɪn.jən ⓤⓢ ə-, oʊ- **-s** -z **oˈpinion ˌpoll**
opinionated əˈpɪn.jə.neɪ.tɪd ⓤⓢ -t̬ɪd, oʊ-
opium ˈəʊ.pi.əm ⓤⓢ ˈoʊ- **ˈopium ˌden**
Oporto əʊˈpɔː.təʊ ⓤⓢ oʊˈpɔːr.toʊ
opossum əˈpɒs.əm ⓤⓢ -ˈpɑː.səm **-s** -z
Oppenheim ˈɒp.ən.haɪm ⓤⓢ ˈɑː.pən- **-er** -əʳ ⓤⓢ -ɚ
oppidan ˈɒp.ɪ.dən ⓤⓢ ˈɑː.pɪ- **-s** -z
opponent əˈpəʊ.nənt ⓤⓢ -ˈpoʊ- **-s** -s
opportune ˈɒp.ə.tjuːn, -tʃuːn, ˌ--ˈ- ⓤⓢ ˌɑː.pɚˈtuːn, -ˈtjuːn **-ly** -li **-ness** -nəs, -nɪs
opportun|ism ˌɒp.əˈtjuː.n|ɪ.zəm, -ˈtʃuː-, ˈɒp.ə.tjuː-, -tʃuː- ⓤⓢ ˌɑː.pɚˈtuː-, -ˈtjuː- **-ist/s** -ɪst/s
opportunistic ˌɒp.ə.tjuːˈnɪs.tɪk, -tʃuːˈ- ⓤⓢ ˌɑː.pɚ.tuːˈ-, -tjuːˈ- **-ally** -əl.i, -li
opportunit|y ˌɒp.əˈtjuː.nə.t|i, -ˈtʃuː-, -nɪ- ⓤⓢ ˌɑː.pɚˈtuː.nə.t̬|i, -ˈtjuː- **-ies** -iz
oppos|e əˈpəʊz ⓤⓢ -ˈpoʊz **-es** -ɪz **-ing** -ɪŋ **-ed** -d **-er/s** -əʳ/z ⓤⓢ -ɚ/z **-able** -ə.bl̩
opposite ˈɒp.ə.zɪt, -sɪt ⓤⓢ ˈɑː.pə- **-ly** -li **-ness** -nəs, -nɪs ˌ**opposite ˈnumber**
opposition ˌɒp.əˈzɪʃ.ən ⓤⓢ ˌɑː.pəˈ- **-s** -z
oppress əˈpres **-es** -ɪz **-ing** -ɪŋ **-ed** -t
oppression əˈpreʃ.ən **-s** -z
oppressive əˈpres.ɪv **-ly** -li **-ness** -nəs, -nɪs
oppressor əˈpres.əʳ ⓤⓢ -ɚ **-s** -z
opprobrious əˈprəʊ.bri.əs ⓤⓢ -ˈproʊ- **-ly** -li **-ness** -nəs, -nɪs
opprobrium əˈprəʊ.bri.əm ⓤⓢ -ˈproʊ-
oppugn əˈpjuːn **-s** -z **-ing** -ɪŋ **-ed** -d **-er/s** -əʳ/z ⓤⓢ -ɚ/z
Oprah ˈəʊ.prə ⓤⓢ ˈoʊ-
Opren® ˈɒp.rən, -ren ⓤⓢ ˈɑː.prən, -pren
opt ɒpt ⓤⓢ ɑːpt **-s** -s **-ing** -ɪŋ **-ed** -ɪd
optative ˈɒp.tə.tɪv; ɒpˈteɪ- ⓤⓢ ˈɑːp.tə.t̬ɪv **-s** -z
optic ˈɒp.tɪk ⓤⓢ ˈɑːp- **-s** -s
optical ˈɒp.tɪ.kəl ⓤⓢ ˈɑːp- **-ly** -i ˌ**optical ˈfibre** ; ˌ**optical ilˈlusion**
optician ɒpˈtɪʃ.ən ⓤⓢ ɑːp- **-s** -z
optimal ˈɒp.tɪ.məl ⓤⓢ ˈɑːp- **-ly** -i
optime ˈɒp.tɪ.meɪ ⓤⓢ ˈɑːp- **-s** -z
optim|ism ˈɒp.tɪ.m|ɪ.zəm, -tə- ⓤⓢ ˈɑːp.tə- **-ist/s** -ɪst/s
optimistic ˌɒp.tɪˈmɪs.tɪk, -təˈ- ⓤⓢ ˌɑːp.təˈ- **-al** -əl **-ally** -əl.i, -li
optimization ˌɒp.tɪ.maɪˈzeɪ.ʃən, -tə-, -mɪˈ- ⓤⓢ ˌɑːp.tə.mɪˈzeɪ- **-s** -z
optimiz|e, -is|e ˈɒp.tɪ.maɪz, -tə- ⓤⓢ ˈɑːp.tə- **-es** -ɪz **-ing** -ɪŋ **-ed** -d
optim|um ˈɒp.tɪ.m|əm, -tə- ⓤⓢ ˈɑːp.tə- **-ums** -əmz **-a** -ə
option ˈɒp.ʃən ⓤⓢ ˈɑːp- **-s** -z
optional ˈɒp.ʃən.əl ⓤⓢ ˈɑːp.ʃən.əl **-ly** -i
optometric ˌɒp.təʊˈmet.rɪk ⓤⓢ ˌɑːp.təˈmet- **-s** -s
optometrist ɒpˈtɒm.ə.trɪst, ˈ-ɪ- ⓤⓢ ɑːpˈtɑː.mə- **-s** -s
optometry ɒpˈtɒm.ɪ.tri, ˈ-ə- ⓤⓢ ɑːpˈtɑː.mə-
Optrex® ˈɒp.treks ⓤⓢ ˈɑːp-
opulence ˈɒp.jə.lənts, -jʊ- ⓤⓢ ˈɑːp-
opulent ˈɒp.jə.lənt, -jʊ- ⓤⓢ ˈɑːp- **-ly** -li
opus ˈəʊ.pəs, ˈɒp.əs ⓤⓢ ˈoʊ.pəs **-es** -ɪz **opera** ˈɒp.ər.ə ⓤⓢ ˈoʊ.pɚ.ə, ˈɑː-, ˈ-prə
opuscule ɒpˈʌs.kjuːl, əʊˈpʌs- ⓤⓢ oʊˈpʌs.kjuːl **-s** -z
or (*n.*) ɔːʳ ⓤⓢ ɔːr
or (*conj.*) *normal form:* ɔːʳ ⓤⓢ ɔːr *weak form:* əʳ ⓤⓢ ɚ
Note: Occasional weak form word. The weak form /əʳ ⓤⓢ ɚ/ is used in phrases such as "two or three pounds" /ˌtuː.əˌθriːˈpaʊndz ⓤⓢ -ɚˌ-/.
orach|(e) ˈɒr.ɪtʃ ⓤⓢ ˈɔːr.ətʃ **-es** -ɪz
oracle ˈɒr.ə.kl̩, ˈ-ɪ- ⓤⓢ ˈɔːr.ə- **-s** -z
oracular ɒrˈæk.jə.ləʳ, ɔːˈræk-, ə-, -jʊ- ⓤⓢ ɔːˈræk.juː.lɚ, ə-, -jə- **-ly** -li **-ness** -nəs, -nɪs
oracy ˈɔː.rə.si ⓤⓢ ˈɔːr.ə-
Oradea ɒrˈɑː.di.ə ⓤⓢ ɔːˈrɑː.djɑː
oral ˈɔː.rəl ⓤⓢ ˈɔːr.əl **-s** -z **-ly** -i ˌ**oral ˈsex**
Oran ɔːˈrɑːn, ə-, ɒrˈɑːn, -ˈæn ⓤⓢ oʊˈrɑːn, -ˈræn
orang|e (O) ˈɒr.ɪndʒ, -əndʒ ⓤⓢ ˈɔːr.ɪndʒ **-es** -ɪz ˌ**Orange ˈFree ˌState** ; ˈ**orange ˌjuice**
orangeade ˌɒr.ɪndʒˈeɪd, -əndʒˈ- ⓤⓢ ˌɔːr.ɪndʒˈ-
orange-blossom ˈɒr.ɪndʒˌblɒs.əm, -əndʒˌ- ⓤⓢ ˈɔːr.ɪndʒˌblɑː.səm **-s** -z
Orange|man ˈɒr.ɪndʒ|.mən, -əndʒ-, -mæn ⓤⓢ ˈɔːr.ɪndʒ **-men** -mən, -men
oranger|y ˈɒr.ɪn.dʒər|.i, -ən-, ˈ-ɪndʒ.r|i ⓤⓢ ˈɔːr.ɪndʒ.ri **-ies** -iz
orangoutan, orangutan, orangutang ɔːˌræŋ.uːˈtæn, ɒrˌæŋ-, əˌræŋ-, -əˈ-, -juːˈ-, -ˈtɑːn, -ˈtæŋ, ɔːˈræŋ.uː.tæn, ɒrˈæŋ-, əˈræŋ-, ˈ-ə-, ˈ-juː-, -tɑːn, -tæŋ ⓤⓢ ɔːˈræŋ.ə.tæn, ə-, oʊ-, -tæŋ **-s** -s
ora|te ɔːˈreɪt, ɒrˈeɪt, əˈreɪt ⓤⓢ ˈɔːr.eɪt; ɔːˈreɪt **-tes** -ts **-ting** -tɪŋ ⓤⓢ -t̬ɪŋ **-ted** -tɪd ⓤⓢ -t̬ɪd
oration ɔːˈreɪ.ʃən, ɒrˈeɪ-, əˈreɪ- ⓤⓢ ɔː- **-s** -z
orator ˈɒr.ə.təʳ ⓤⓢ ˈɔːr.ə.t̬ɚ **-s** -z
oratorical ˌɒr.əˈtɒr.ɪ.kəl ⓤⓢ ˌɔːr.əˈtɔːr- **-ly** -i
oratorio ˌɒr.əˈtɔː.ri.əʊ ⓤⓢ ˌɔːr.əˈtɔːr.i.oʊ **-s** -z
orator|y (O) ˈɒr.ə.tər|.i ⓤⓢ ˈɔːr.ə.tɔːr- **-ies** -iz
orb ɔːb ⓤⓢ ɔːrb **-s** -z **-ing** -ɪŋ **-ed** -d
Orbach ˈɔː.bæk ⓤⓢ ˈɔːr-
orbed ɔːbd ⓤⓢ ɔːrbd *in poetry generally:* ˈɔː.bɪd ⓤⓢ ˈɔːr.bɪd
orbicular ɔːˈbɪk.jə.ləʳ, -jʊ- ⓤⓢ ɔːrˈbɪk.juː.lɚ, -jə- **-ly** -li
Orbison ˈɔː.bɪ.sən, -bə- ⓤⓢ ˈɔːr-
or|bit ˈɔː|.bɪt ⓤⓢ ˈɔːr- **-bits** -bɪts **-bital** -bɪ.təl ⓤⓢ -t̬əl
orc ɔːk ⓤⓢ ɔːrk **-s** -s
Orcadian ɔːˈkeɪ.di.ən ⓤⓢ ɔːr- **-s** -z
orchard (O) ˈɔː.tʃəd ⓤⓢ ˈɔːr.tʃɚd **-s** -z
Orchardson ˈɔː.tʃəd.sən ⓤⓢ ˈɔːr.tʃɚd-
Orchehill ˈɔː.tʃɪl ⓤⓢ ˈɔːr-
orchestra ˈɔː.kɪ.strə, -kə-, -kes.trə ⓤⓢ ˈɔːr.kɪ.strə, -kes.trə **-s** -z
orchestral ɔːˈkes.trəl ⓤⓢ ɔːr-
orchest|rate ˈɔː.kɪ.st|reɪt, -kə-, -kes.t|reɪt ⓤⓢ ˈɔːr.kɪ.st|reɪt, -kes.t|reɪt **-rates** -reɪts **-rating** -reɪ.tɪŋ ⓤⓢ -reɪ.t̬ɪŋ **-rated** -reɪ.tɪd ⓤⓢ -reɪ.t̬ɪd
orchestration ˌɔː.kɪˈstreɪ.ʃən, -kəˈ-, -kesˈtreɪ- ⓤⓢ ˌɔːr.kɪˈstreɪ-, -kesˈtreɪ- **-s** -z
orchestrion ɔːˈkes.tri.ən ⓤⓢ ɔːr- **-s** -z
orchid ˈɔː.kɪd ⓤⓢ ˈɔːr- **-s** -z
orchidaceous ˌɔː.kɪˈdeɪ.ʃəs ⓤⓢ ˌɔːr-
orchil ˈɔː.tʃɪl, -kɪl ⓤⓢ ˈɔːr-
orchis ˈɔː.kɪs ⓤⓢ ˈɔːr- **-es** -ɪz
Orczy ˈɔːk.si, ˈɔːt- ⓤⓢ ˈɔːrk-, ˈɔːrt-
Ord ɔːd ⓤⓢ ɔːrd
ordain ɔːˈdeɪn ⓤⓢ ɔːr- **-s** -z **-ing** -ɪŋ **-ed** -d **-er/s** -əʳ/z ⓤⓢ -ɚ/z
Orde ɔːd ⓤⓢ ɔːrd
ordeal ɔːˈdiːl, ˈ-- ⓤⓢ ɔːrˈdiːl, ˈ-- **-s** -z
ord|er ˈɔː.d|əʳ ⓤⓢ ˈɔːr.d|ɚ **-ers** -əz ⓤⓢ -ɚz **-ering** -ər.ɪŋ **-ered** -əd ⓤⓢ -ɚd **-erless** -əl.əs, -ɪs ⓤⓢ -ɚ.ləs, -lɪs
orderl|y ˈɔː.dəl|.i ⓤⓢ ˈɔːr.dɚ.l|i **-ies** -iz **-iness** -ɪ.nəs, -ɪ.nɪs
ordinaire ˌɔː.dɪˈneəʳ, -dən.eəʳ, ˈ--- ⓤⓢ ˌɔːr.dɪˈner
ordinal ˈɔː.dɪ.nəl, -dən.əl ⓤⓢ ˈɔːr.dən-, ˈɔːrd.nəl **-s** -z ˌ**ordinal ˈnumber**
ordinanc|e ˈɔː.dɪ.nənts, -dən.ənts ⓤⓢ ˈɔːr.dən-, ˈɔːrd.nənts **-es** -ɪz

ordinand 'ɔː.dɪ.nænd, -dᵊn.ænd, ˌ--'- US 'ɔːr.dᵊn.ænd **-s** -z

ordinarily 'ɔː.dᵊn.ᵊr.ᵊl.i, -dɪ.nᵊr-, -ɪ.li; ˌɔː.dᵊn'er.ɪ- US 'ɔːr.dᵊn.er.ᵊl.i, ˌɔːr.dᵊn'er-

ordinariness 'ɔː.dᵊn.ᵊr.ɪ.nəs, -dɪ.nᵊr-, -nɪs US ˌɔːr.dᵊn'er-

ordinar|y 'ɔː.dᵊn.ᵊr|.i, -dɪ.nᵊr- US 'ɔːr.dᵊn.er- **-ies** -iz

ordinate 'ɔː.dᵊn.ət, -dɪ.nət, -nɪt US 'ɔːr.dᵊn.ɪt, -eɪt **-s** -s

ordination ˌɔː.dɪ'neɪ.ʃᵊn, -dᵊn'eɪ- US ˌɔːr.dᵊn'eɪ- **-s** -z

ordnance 'ɔːd.nən*t*s US 'ɔːrd- ˌ**Ordnance 'Survey**

ordure 'ɔː.djʊəʳ, -djəʳ US 'ɔːr.dʒɚ, -djʊr

Ore. (*abbrev. for* **Oregon**) 'ɒr.ɪ.gən, '-ə-, -gɒn US 'ɔːr.ɪ.gən, -gɑːn

ore (**O**) ɔːʳ US ɔːr **-s** -z

öre, ore 'ɜː.rə US 'ɜːr.ə

oread 'ɔː.ri.æd US 'ɔːr.i- **-s** -z

Örebro 'ɜː.rə.bruː US 'ɜːr.ə-

O'Regan əʊ'riː.gən US oʊ-

oregano ˌɒr.ɪ'gɑː.nəʊ, -ə'- US ɔː'reg.ə.noʊ, ə-

Oregon 'ɒr.ɪ.gən, '-ə-, -gɒn US 'ɔːr.ɪ.gən, -gɑːn

O'Reilly əʊ'raɪ.li US oʊ-

Oreo® 'ɔː.ri.əʊ US 'ɔːr.i.oʊ **-s** -z

Oresteia ˌɒr.ɪ'staɪə, ˌɔː.rɪ'-, -rə'-, -'steɪə US ˌɔːr.es'tiː.ə, -ə'stiː-

Orestes ɒr'es.tiːz, ɔː'res-, ə- US ɔː-

orfe ɔːf US ɔːrf

Orfeo 'ɔː.fi.əʊ *as if Italian:* ɔː'feɪ.əʊ US 'ɔːr.fi.oʊ, -feɪ-

Orff ɔːf US ɔːrf

Orford 'ɔː.fəd US 'ɔːr.fɚd

organ 'ɔː.gən US 'ɔːr- **-s** -z

organd|y, -|ie 'ɔː.gᵊn.d|i, ɔː'gæn- US 'ɔːr.gən- **-ies** -iz

organelle ˌɔː.gᵊn'el US ˌɔːr- **-s** -z

organ-grinder 'ɔː.gᵊnˌgraɪn.dəʳ, -gᵊŋˌ- US 'ɔːr.gᵊnˌgraɪn.dɚ **-s** -z

organic ɔː'gæn.ɪk US ɔːr- **-al** -ᵊl **-ally** -ᵊl.i, -li

organism 'ɔː.gᵊn.ɪ.zᵊm US 'ɔːr- **-s** -z

organist 'ɔː.gᵊn.ɪst US 'ɔːr- **-s** -s

organizability, -isa- ˌɔː.gᵊnˌaɪ.zə'bɪl.ə.ti, -ɪ.ti US ˌɔːr.gᵊnˌaɪ.zə'bɪl.ə.t̬i

organization, -isa- ˌɔː.gᵊn.aɪ'zeɪ.ʃᵊn, -ɪ'- US ˌɔːr.gᵊn.ɪ'- **-s** -z

organizational ˌɔː.gᵊn.aɪ'zeɪ.ʃᵊn.ᵊl, -ɪ'- US ˌɔːr.gᵊn.ɪ'- **-ly** -i

organiz|e, -is|e 'ɔː.gᵊn.aɪz US 'ɔːr- **-es** -ɪz **-ing** -ɪŋ **-ed** -d **-er/s** -əʳ/z US -ɚ/z **-able** -ə.bl̩

organ|on 'ɔː.gə.n|ɒn US 'ɔːr.gə.n|ɑːn **-ons** -ɒnz US -ɑːnz **-a** -ə

organum 'ɔː.gə.nəm US 'ɔːr- **-s** -z

organza ɔː'gæn.zə US ɔːr-

orgasm 'ɔː.gæz.ᵊm US 'ɔːr- **-s** -z

orgasmic ɔː'gæz.mɪk US ɔːr- **-ally** -ᵊl.i, -li

orgiastic ˌɔː.dʒi'æs.tɪk US ˌɔːr- **-ally** -ᵊl.i, -li

org|y 'ɔː.dʒ|i US 'ɔːr- **-ies** -iz

Oriana ˌɒr.i'ɑː.nə, ˌɔː.ri'- US ˌɔːr.i'æn.ə

oriel (**O**) 'ɔː.ri.əl US 'ɔːr.i- **-s** -z

orient (**O**) (*n. adj.*) 'ɔː.ri.ənt, 'ɒr.i- US 'ɔːr.i- ˌ**Orient Ex'press**

ori|ent (*v.*) 'ɔː.ri|.ent, 'ɒr.i- US 'ɔːr.i- **-ents** -ents **-enting** -en.tɪŋ US -en.t̬ɪŋ **-ented** -en.tɪd US -en.t̬ɪd

oriental (**O**) ˌɔː.ri'en.tᵊl, ˌɒr.i'- US ˌɔːr.i'- **-s** -z

oriental|ism ˌɔː.ri'en.tᵊl|.ɪ.zᵊm, ˌɒr.i'- US ˌɔːr.i'en.t̬ᵊl- **-ist/s** -ɪst/s

orientaliz|e, -is|e ˌɔː.ri'en.tᵊl.aɪz, ˌɒr.i'- US ˌɔːr.i'en.t̬ᵊl- **-es** -ɪz **-ing** -ɪŋ **-ed** -d

orien|tate 'ɔː.ri.ən|.teɪt, 'ɒr.i-, -en- US 'ɔːr.i.en-, ˌɔːr.i'en- **-tates** -teɪts **-tating** -teɪ.tɪŋ US -teɪ.t̬ɪŋ **-tated** -teɪ.tɪd US -teɪ.t̬ɪd

orientation ˌɔː.ri.en'teɪ.ʃᵊn, ˌɒr.i- US ˌɔːr.i.en'- **-s** -z

orienteer ˌɔː.ri.ən'tɪəʳ, ˌɒr.i-, -en'- US ˌɔːr.i.en'tɪr **-s** -z

orienteering ˌɔː.ri.ən'tɪə.rɪŋ, ˌɒr.i-, -en'- US ˌɔːr.i.en'tɪr.ɪŋ

orific|e 'ɒr.ɪ.fɪs, '-ə- US 'ɔːr.ə- **-es** -ɪz

oriflamme 'ɒr.ɪ.flæm, '-ə- US 'ɔːr.ɪ- **-s** -z

origami ˌɒr.ɪ'gɑː.mi, -'gæm.i US ˌɔːr.ɪ'gɑː.mi

Origen 'ɒr.ɪ.dʒen, '-ə- US 'ɔːr.ɪ.dʒən, -dʒen

origin 'ɒr.ɪ.dʒɪn, '-ə-, -dʒən US 'ɔːr.ə.dʒɪn **-s** -z

original ə'rɪdʒ.ᵊn.ᵊl, ɒr'ɪdʒ-, -ɪ.nᵊl US ə'rɪdʒ.ɪ- **-s** -z **-ness** -nəs, -nɪs **oˌriginal 'sin**

originalit|y əˌrɪdʒ.ᵊn'æl.ə.t|i, ɒrˌɪdʒ-, -ɪ'næl-, -ɪ.t|i US əˌrɪdʒ.ɪ'næl.ə.t̬|i **-ies** -iz

originally ə'rɪdʒ.ᵊn.ᵊl.i, ɒr'ɪdʒ-, -ɪ.nᵊl- US ə'rɪdʒ.ɪ-

origi|nate ə'rɪdʒ.ᵊn|.eɪt, ɒr'ɪdʒ-, -ɪ.n|eɪt US ə'rɪdʒ.ɪ- **-nates** -neɪts **-nating** -neɪ.tɪŋ US -neɪ.t̬ɪŋ **-nated** -neɪ.tɪd US -neɪ.t̬ɪd **-nator/s** -neɪ.təʳ/z US -neɪ.t̬ɚ/z **-native** -neɪ.tɪv US -neɪ.t̬ɪv

origination əˌrɪdʒ.ᵊn'eɪ.ʃᵊn, ɒrˌɪdʒ-, -ɪ'neɪ- US əˌrɪdʒ.ɪ'-

Orinoco ˌɒr.ɪ'nəʊ.kəʊ, -ə'- US ˌɔːr.ə'noʊ.koʊ

oriole 'ɔː.ri.əʊl US 'ɔːr.i.oʊl **-s** -z

Orion ə'raɪən, ɒr'aɪən-, ɔː'raɪən US oʊ-, ə-

O'Riordan əʊ'rɪə.dᵊn, -'raɪə- US oʊ'rɪr-

orison 'ɒr.ɪ.zᵊn, -ə- US 'ɔːr.ɪ.zᵊn, -sᵊn **-s** -z

Orissa ɒr'ɪs.ə, ɔː'rɪs-, ə- US oʊ-, ɔː-

Oriya ɒr'iː.ə US ɔː'riː.ə

ork ɔːk US ɔːrk **-s** -s

Orkney 'ɔːk.ni US 'ɔːrk- **-s** -z

Orlan® 'ɔː.lᵊn, -læn US 'ɔːr.lɑːn

Orlando ɔː'læn.dəʊ US ɔːr'læn.doʊ

Orléans *in France:* ɔː'lɪənz, '-- *as if French:* ˌɔː.leɪ'ɑ̃ːŋ US -'liː.ənz *as if French:* ˌɔːr.leɪ'ɑ̃ːn

Orleans *in US:* 'ɔː.li.ənz, '-lɪənz, '-lənz; ɔː'liːnz US 'ɔːr.li.ənz, '-lənz; ɔːr'liːnz

Orlon® 'ɔː.lɒn US 'ɔːr.lɑːn

Orly 'ɔː.li US 'ɔːr-

Orm(e) ɔːm US ɔːrm

ormer 'ɔː.məʳ US 'ɔːr.mɚ **-s** -z

Ormes ɔːmz US ɔːrmz

Ormiston 'ɔː.mɪ.stᵊn US 'ɔːr-

ormolu 'ɔː.mə.luː, -ljuː, ˌ--'- US 'ɔːr.mə.luː

Ormond(e) 'ɔː.mənd US 'ɔːr-

Ormsby 'ɔːmz.bi US 'ɔːrmz-

Ormulum 'ɔː.mjə.ləm, -mjʊ- US 'ɔːr.mjuː-, -mjə-

ornament (*n.*) 'ɔː.nə.mənt US 'ɔːr- **-s** -s

orna|ment 'ɔː.nə|.ment US 'ɔːr- **-ments** -ments **-menting** -men.tɪŋ US -men.t̬ɪŋ **-mented** -men.tɪd US -men.t̬ɪd

ornamental ˌɔː.nə'men.tᵊl US ˌɔːr.nə'men.t̬ᵊl **-ly** -i

ornamentation ˌɔː.nə.men'teɪ.ʃᵊn US ˌɔːr- **-s** -z

ornate ɔː'neɪt US ɔːr- **-ly** -li **-ness** -nəs, -nɪs

ornery 'ɔː.nᵊr.i US 'ɔːr.nɚ-

ornithologic|al ˌɔː.nɪ.θə'lɒdʒ.ɪ.k|ᵊl, -θᵊl'ɒdʒ-, -nə- US ˌɔːr.nə.θə'lɑː.dʒɪ- **-ally** -ᵊl.i, -li

ornitholog|y ˌɔː.nɪ'θɒl.ə.dʒ|i, -nə'- US ˌɔːr.nə'θɑː.lə- **-ist/s** -ɪst/s

orographic ˌɒr.əʊ'græf.ɪk, ˌɔː.rəʊ'- US ˌɔːr.oʊ'- **-al** -ᵊl

orography ɒr'ɒg.rə.fi, ɔː'rɒg- US ɔː'rɑː.grə-

orological ˌɒr.ə'lɒdʒ.ɪ.kᵊl, ˌɔː.rə'- US ˌɔːr.ə'lɑː.dʒɪ-

orology ɒr'ɒl.ə.dʒi, ɔː'rɒl- US ɔː'rɑː.lə-

Oronsay 'ɒr.ᵊn.seɪ, -zeɪ US 'ɔːr-, -ɑːn-

Orontes ɒr'ɒn.tiːz, ə'rɒn- US oʊ'rɑːn-

Oroonoko ˌɒr.ʊ'nəʊ.kəʊ US ˌɔːr.ʊ'noʊ.koʊ

Orosius ə'rəʊ.si.əs, ɒr'əʊ- US ɔː'roʊ.ʒi.əs

orotund 'ɒr.əʊ.tʌnd, 'ɔː.rəʊ- US 'ɔːr.ə-, -oʊ-, '-ə-

O'Rourke əʊ'rɔːk ⓤⓢ oʊ'rɔːrk
orphan 'ɔː.fᵊn ⓤⓢ 'ɔːr- **-s** -z **-ing** -ɪŋ **-ed** -d
orphanag|e 'ɔː.fᵊn.ɪdʒ ⓤⓢ 'ɔːr- **-es** -ɪz
Orphean ɔː'fiː.ən; 'ɔː.fi- ⓤⓢ 'ɔːr.fi.ən
Orpheus 'ɔː.fi.əs, -fjuːs ⓤⓢ 'ɔːr.fi.əs, '-fjuːs
orpiment 'ɔː.pɪ.mənt ⓤⓢ 'ɔːr-
Orpington 'ɔː.pɪŋ.tən ⓤⓢ 'ɔːr- **-s** -z
Orr ɔːʳ ⓤⓢ ɔːr
Orrell 'ɒr.ᵊl ⓤⓢ 'ɔːr-
orrer|y (O) 'ɒr.ᵊr|.i ⓤⓢ 'ɔːr- **-ies** -iz
orris 'ɒr.ɪs ⓤⓢ 'ɔːr-
Orsino ɔː'siː.nəʊ ⓤⓢ ɔːr'siː.noʊ
Orson 'ɔː.sᵊn ⓤⓢ 'ɔːr-
Ortega ɔː'teɪ.gə ⓤⓢ ɔːr-; ˌɔːr.t̬ə'gɑː
ortho- ɔː.θəʊ-; ɔː'θɒ- ⓤⓢ ɔːr.θoʊ-, -θə-; ɔːr'θɑː-

Note: Prefix. Normally either takes primary or secondary stress on the first syllable, e.g. **orthodox** /'ɔː.θə.dɒks ⓤⓢ 'ɔːr.θə.dɑːks/, **orthogenic** /ˌɔː.θəʊ'dʒen.ɪk ⓤⓢ ˌɔːr.θoʊ-/, or primary stress on the second syllable, e.g. **orthography** /ɔː'θɒg.rə.fi ⓤⓢ ɔːr'θɑː.grə-/.

orthochromatic ˌɔː.θəʊ.krəʊ'mæt.ɪk ⓤⓢ ˌɔːr.θoʊ.kroʊ'mæt̬-, -θə-
orthodontic ˌɔː.θəʊ'dɒn.tɪk ⓤⓢ ˌɔːr.θoʊ'dɑːn.t̬ɪk, -θə'- **-s**
orthodontist ˌɔː.θəʊ'dɒn.tɪst ⓤⓢ ˌɔːr.θoʊ'dɑːn.t̬ɪst, -θə'- **-s** -s
orthodox 'ɔː.θə.dɒks ⓤⓢ 'ɔːr.θə.dɑːks
orthodox|y 'ɔː.θə.dɒk.s|i ⓤⓢ 'ɔːr.θə.dɑːk- **-ies** -iz
orthoep|y 'ɔː.θəʊ.ep|.i; ɔː'θəʊ.ɪ.p|i; ˌɔː.θəʊ'ep|.i; ⓤⓢ ɔːr'θoʊ.ə.p|i, 'ɔːr.θoʊ-, -ep|.i **-ist/s** -ɪst/s
orthogenic ˌɔː.θəʊ'dʒen.ɪk ⓤⓢ ˌɔːr.θoʊ'-, -θə'-
orthogonal ɔː'θɒg.ᵊn.ᵊl ⓤⓢ ɔːr'θɑː.gᵊn-
orthographer ɔː'θɒg.rə.fəʳ ⓤⓢ ɔːr'θɑː.grə.fɚ **-s** -z
orthographic ˌɔː.θəʊ'græf.ɪk ⓤⓢ ˌɔːr.θoʊ'-, -θə'- **-al** -ᵊl **-ally** -ᵊl.i, -li
orthograph|y ɔː'θɒg.rə.f|i ⓤⓢ ɔː'θɑː.grə- **-ist/s** -ɪst/s
orthop(a)edic ˌɔː.θəʊ'piː.dɪk ⓤⓢ ˌɔːr.θoʊ'-, -θə'- **-s** -s **-ally** -ᵊl.i, -li
orthop(a)ed|y ˌɔː.θəʊ'piː.d|i ⓤⓢ ˌɔːr.θoʊ'-, -θə'- **-ist/s** -ɪst/s
orthopterous ɔː'θɒp.tᵊr.əs ⓤⓢ ɔːr'θɑːp-
orthoptic ɔː'θɒp.tɪk ⓤⓢ ɔːr'θɑːp-
Ortiz 'ɔː.tɪz, ɔː'tɪz, -'tiːz, -'tiːs ⓤⓢ ɔːr'tiːz, -'tiːs
Ortler 'ɔːt.ləʳ ⓤⓢ 'ɔːrt.lɚ
ortolan 'ɔː.tᵊl.ən, -æn ⓤⓢ 'ɔːr.t̬ə.lən **-s** -z
Orton 'ɔː.tᵊn ⓤⓢ 'ɔːr-
Oruro ɒr'ʊə.rəʊ ⓤⓢ ɔː'rʊr.oʊ, -'ruː.roʊ
Orville 'ɔː.vɪl ⓤⓢ 'ɔːr-
Orwell 'ɔː.wel, -wəl ⓤⓢ 'ɔːr-
Orwellian ɔː'wel.i.ən ⓤⓢ ɔːr-
-ory -ᵊr.i, -ri ⓤⓢ -ɔːr.i, -ᵊr.i

Note: Suffix. When added to a free stem, **-ory** does not change the stress pattern of the word, e.g. **promise** /'prɒ.mɪs ⓤⓢ 'prɑː.mɪs/, **promissory** /'prɒm.ɪs.ᵊr.i ⓤⓢ 'prɑː.mɪ.sɔːr.i/. When added to a bound stem, stress may be one or two syllables before the suffix, e.g. **olfactory** /ɒl'fæk.tᵊr.i ⓤⓢ ɑːl-/.

oryx 'ɒr.ɪks ⓤⓢ 'oʊ.rɪks, 'ɔːr.ɪks **-es** -ɪz
Osage ˌəʊ'seɪdʒ, '-- ⓤⓢ ˌoʊ'seɪdʒ, '--
Osaka əʊ'sɑː.kə, 'ɔː.sə.kə ⓤⓢ 'oʊ.sɑː.kɑː, oʊ'sɑː.kɑː
Osbaldiston(e) ˌɒz.bᵊl'dɪs.tᵊn ⓤⓢ ˌɑːz-
Osbert 'ɒz.bət, -bɜːt ⓤⓢ 'ɑːz.bɚt, -bɜːrt
Osborn(e), **Osbourne** 'ɒz.bɔːn, -bən ⓤⓢ 'ɑːz.bɔːrn, -bɚn
Oscan 'ɒs.kən ⓤⓢ 'ɑːs- **-s** -z
Oscar 'ɒs.kəʳ ⓤⓢ 'ɑː.skɚ **-s** -z
oscill|ate 'ɒs.ɪ.l|eɪt, -ᵊl|.eɪt ⓤⓢ 'ɑː.sᵊl- **-ates** -eɪts **-ating** -eɪ.tɪŋ ⓤⓢ -eɪ.t̬ɪŋ **-ated** -eɪ.tɪd ⓤⓢ -eɪ.t̬ɪd **-ator/s** -eɪ.təʳ/z ⓤⓢ -eɪ.t̬ɚ/z
oscillation ˌɒs.ɪ'leɪ.ʃᵊn, -ᵊl'eɪ- ⓤⓢ ˌɑː.sᵊl'- **-s** -z
oscillatory 'ɒs.ɪ.lə.tᵊr.i, -ᵊl.eɪ-, -leɪ-; ˌɒs.ɪ'leɪ-, -ᵊl'eɪ- ⓤⓢ 'ɑː.sᵊl.ə.tɔːr-
oscillogram ə'sɪl.ə.græm, ɒs'ɪl- ⓤⓢ ə'sɪl- **-s** -z
oscillograph ə'sɪl.ə.grɑːf, ɒs'ɪl-, -græf ⓤⓢ ə'sɪl.ə.græf **-s** -s
oscilloscope ə'sɪl.ə.skəʊp, ɒs'ɪl- ⓤⓢ ə'sɪl.ə.skoʊp **-s** -s
osculant 'ɒs.kjə.lənt, -kjʊ- ⓤⓢ 'ɑː.skjuː-, -skjə-
oscular 'ɒs.kjə.ləʳ, -kjʊ- ⓤⓢ 'ɑː.skjuː.lɚ, -skjə-
oscu|late 'ɒs.kjə|.leɪt, -kjʊ- ⓤⓢ 'ɑː.skjuː-, -skjə- **-lates** -leɪts **-lating** -leɪ.tɪŋ ⓤⓢ -leɪ.t̬ɪŋ **-lated** -leɪ.tɪd ⓤⓢ -leɪ.t̬ɪd
osculation ˌɒs.kjə'leɪ.ʃᵊn, -kjʊ'- ⓤⓢ ˌɑː.skjuː'-, -skjə'- **-s** -z
osculator|y 'ɒs.kjə.lə.tᵊr|.i, -kjʊ-; ˌɒs.kjə'leɪ-, -kjʊ'- ⓤⓢ 'ɑː.skjuː.lə.tɔːr-, -skjə- **-ies** -iz
Osgood 'ɒz.gʊd ⓤⓢ 'ɑːz-
O'Shaughnessy əʊ'ʃɔː.nɪ.si, -nə- ⓤⓢ oʊ'ʃɑː.nə-, -'ʃɔː-
O'Shea əʊ'ʃeɪ ⓤⓢ oʊ-
Oshkosh 'ɒʃ.kɒʃ ⓤⓢ 'ɑːʃ.kɑːʃ
Oshogbo ə'ʃɒg.bəʊ ⓤⓢ oʊ'ʃɑːg.boʊ
osier 'əʊ.zi.əʳ, -ʒəʳ ⓤⓢ 'oʊ.ʒɚ **-s** -z
Osijek 'ɒs.i.ek ⓤⓢ ɔː'siː.ek
Osirian əʊ'saɪə.ri.ən, ɒs'aɪə- ⓤⓢ oʊ'saɪ- **-s** -z
Osiris əʊ'saɪə.rɪs, ɒs'aɪə- ⓤⓢ oʊ'saɪ-
-osis -ə.sɪs; -'əʊ.sɪs ⓤⓢ -ə.sɪs; -'oʊ.sɪs

Note: Suffix. Words containing **-osis** either carry primary stress on the syllable preceeding the suffix, or on the suffix itself e.g. **metamorphosis** /ˌmet.ə'mɔː.fə.sɪs; -mɔː'fəʊ- ⓤⓢ ˌmet̬.ə'mɔːr.fə-; -mɔːr'foʊ-/. See individual entries.

-osity -'ɒs.ə.ti, -ɪ.ti ⓤⓢ -'ɑː.sə.t̬i

Note: Suffix. Normally takes primary stress as shown, e.g. **curious** /'kjʊə.ri.əs ⓤⓢ 'kjʊr.i-/, **curiosity** /ˌkjʊə.ri'ɒs.ə.ti ⓤⓢ ˌkjʊr.i'ɑː.sə.t̬i/.

Osler 'əʊz.ləʳ, 'əʊ.sləʳ ⓤⓢ 'oʊz.lɚ, 'oʊ.slɚ
Oslo 'ɒz.ləʊ, 'ɒs- ⓤⓢ 'ɑː.sloʊ, 'ɑːz-
Osman ɒz'mɑːn, ɒs-; '--, -mən ⓤⓢ 'ɑːz.mən, 'ɑːs-
Osmanli ɒz'mæn.li, ɒs-, -'mɑːn- ⓤⓢ ɑːs'mæn-, ɑːz- **-s** -z
osmium 'ɒz.mi.əm ⓤⓢ 'ɑːz-
Osmond 'ɒz.mənd ⓤⓢ 'ɑːz-
osmosis ɒz'məʊ.sɪs ⓤⓢ ɑːz'moʊ-, ɑːs-
osmotic ɒz'mɒt.ɪk ⓤⓢ ɑːz'mɑː.t̬ɪk, ɑːs- **-ally** -ᵊl.i, -li
osmund (O) 'ɒz.mənd ⓤⓢ 'ɑːz-, 'ɑːs- **-s** -z
osmunda ɒz'mʌn.də ⓤⓢ ɑːz-, ɑːs- **-s** -z
Osnaburg(h) 'ɒz.nə.bɜːg ⓤⓢ 'ɑːz.nə.bɜːrg
osprey 'ɒs.preɪ, -pri ⓤⓢ 'ɑː.spri, -spreɪ **-s** -z
Ossa 'ɒs.ə ⓤⓢ 'ɑː.sə
osseous 'ɒs.i.əs ⓤⓢ 'ɑː.si-
Ossett 'ɒs.ɪt ⓤⓢ 'ɑː.sɪt
Ossian 'ɒs.i.ən ⓤⓢ 'ɑː.si-
ossicle 'ɒs.ɪ.kl̩ ⓤⓢ 'ɑː.sɪ- **-s** -z
ossicular ɒs'ɪk.jə.ləʳ, -jʊ- ⓤⓢ ɑː'sɪk.jə.lɚ, -jʊ-
ossification ˌɒs.ɪ.fɪ'keɪ.ʃᵊn, ˌ-ə- ⓤⓢ ˌɑː.sə.fɪ'-
ossifrag|e 'ɒs.ɪ.frɪdʒ, '-ə-, -freɪdʒ ⓤⓢ 'ɑː.sə- **-es** -ɪz
ossi|fy 'ɒs.ɪ|.faɪ, '-ə- ⓤⓢ 'ɑː.sə- **-fies** -faɪz **-fying** -faɪ.ɪŋ **-fied** -faɪd
Ossining 'ɒs.ɪn.ɪŋ ⓤⓢ 'ɑː.sɪn-
osso buc(c)o ˌɒs.əʊ'buː.kəʊ ⓤⓢ ˌɑː.soʊ'buː.koʊ, ˌoʊ-
Ossory 'ɒs.ᵊr.i ⓤⓢ 'ɑː.sɚ-
ossuar|y 'ɒs.jʊə.r|i ⓤⓢ 'ɑː.sjuː.er|.i **-ies** -iz
osteitis ˌɒs.ti'aɪ.tɪs ⓤⓢ ˌɑː.sti'-
Ostend ɒs'tend ⓤⓢ ɑː'stend, '--
ostensibility ɒsˌtent.sɪ'bɪl.ə.ti, -sə'-, -ɪ.ti ⓤⓢ ɑːˌstent.sə'bɪl.ə.t̬i
ostensib|le ɒs'tent.sɪ.b|l̩, -sə- ⓤⓢ ɑː'stent.sə- **-ly** -li
ostentation ˌɒs.ten'teɪ.ʃᵊn, -tən'- ⓤⓢ ˌɑː.stən'-
ostentatious ˌɒs.ten'teɪ.ʃəs, -tən'- ⓤⓢ ˌɑː.stən'- **-ly** -li **-ness** -nəs, -nɪs

osteo- ˌɒs.ti.əʊ- Ⓤⓢ ˌɑː.sti.oʊ-, -ə-
osteoarthritis ˌɒs.ti.əʊ.ɑːˈθraɪ.tɪs Ⓤⓢ ˌɑː.sti.oʊ.ɑːrˈθraɪ.t̬ɪs
osteologic|al ˌɒs.ti.əˈlɒdʒ.ɪ.k|əl Ⓤⓢ ˌɑː.sti.oʊˈlɑː.dʒɪ- **-ally** -əl.i, -li
osteolog|y ˌɒs.tiˈɒl.ə.dʒ|i Ⓤⓢ ˌɑː.stiˈɑː.lə- **-ist/s** -ɪst/s
osteomyelitis ˌɒs.ti.əʊ.maɪ.əlˈaɪ.tɪs Ⓤⓢ ˌɑː.sti.oʊ.maɪ.əˈlaɪ.t̬ɪs
osteopath ˈɒs.ti.əʊ.pæθ Ⓤⓢ ˈɑː.sti.oʊ-, -ə- **-s** -s
osteopathic ˌɒs.ti.əʊˈpæθ.ɪk Ⓤⓢ ˌɑː.sti.oʊˈ-
osteopathy ˌɒs.tiˈɒp.ə.θi Ⓤⓢ ˌɑː.stiˈɑː.pə-
osteoporosis ˌɒs.ti.əʊ.pəˈrəʊ.sɪs, -pɔːˈ- Ⓤⓢ ˌɑː.sti.oʊ.pəˈroʊ-
Osterley ˈɒs.təl.i Ⓤⓢ ˈɑː.stɚ.li
Ostia ˈɒs.ti.ə Ⓤⓢ ˈɑː.sti-
ostiar|y ˈɒs.ti.ər|.i Ⓤⓢ ˈɑː.sti.er- **-ies** -iz
osti|um (O) ˈɒs.ti|.əm Ⓤⓢ ˈɑː.sti- **-a** -ə
ostler ˈɒs.ləʳ Ⓤⓢ ˈɑː.slɚ **-s** -z
ostracism ˈɒs.trə.sɪ.zəm Ⓤⓢ ˈɑː.strə-
ostraciz|e, -is|e ˈɒs.trə.saɪz Ⓤⓢ ˈɑː.strə- **-es** -ɪz **-ing** -ɪŋ **-ed** -d
Ostrava ˈɒs.trə.və Ⓤⓢ ˈɔː.strɑː.vɑː, ˈɑː-
ostrich ˈɒs.trɪtʃ Ⓤⓢ ˈɑː.strɪtʃ **-es** -ɪz
Ostrogoth ˈɒs.trəʊ.gɒθ Ⓤⓢ ˈɑː.strə.gɑːθ **-s** -s
O'Sullivan əʊˈsʌl.ɪ.vən, ˈ-ə- Ⓤⓢ oʊ-
Oswald ˈɒz.wəld Ⓤⓢ ˈɑːz-, -wɔːld
Oswaldtwistle ˈɒz.wəldˌtwɪs.l̩ Ⓤⓢ ˈɑːz.wɔːld-
Oswego ɒzˈwiː.gəʊ, ɒs- Ⓤⓢ ɑːˈswiː.goʊ **-s** -z
Oswestry ˈɒz.wə.stri, -wɪ- Ⓤⓢ ˈɑːz-
Otago əʊˈtɑː.gəʊ, ɒtˈɑː- Ⓤⓢ əˈtɑː.go, oʊ-
Otaheite ˌəʊ.tɑːˈheɪ.ti, -təˈ- Ⓤⓢ ˌoʊ.t̬əˈhiː.t̬i, -ˈheɪ-
otar|y ˈəʊ.tər|.i Ⓤⓢ ˈoʊ.t̬ɚ- **-ies** -iz
OTB ˌəʊ.tiːˈbiː Ⓤⓢ ˌoʊ-
Otford ˈɒt.fəd Ⓤⓢ ˈɑːt.fɚd
Otfried ˈɒt.friːd Ⓤⓢ ˈɑːt-
Othello əʊˈθel.əʊ, ɒθˈel- Ⓤⓢ oʊˈθel.oʊ, ə-
other ˈʌð.əʳ Ⓤⓢ -ɚ **-s** -z **-ness** -nəs, -nɪs
otherwise ˈʌð.ə.waɪz Ⓤⓢ ˈ-ɚ-
otherworld|ly ˌʌð.əˈwɜːld|.li Ⓤⓢ -ɚˈwɜːrld- **-liness** -lɪ.nəs, -nɪs
Othman ɒθˈmɑːn, ˈ-- Ⓤⓢ ˈɑːθ.mən, ʊθˈmɑːn
Othniel ˈɒθ.ni.əl Ⓤⓢ ˈɑːθ-
Otho ˈəʊ.θəʊ Ⓤⓢ ˈoʊ.θoʊ
-otic -ˈɒt.ɪk Ⓤⓢ -ˈɑː.t̬ɪk
Note: Suffix. Normally takes primary stress as shown, e.g **idiot** /ˈɪd.i.ət/, **idiotic** /ˌɪd.iˈɒt.ɪk Ⓤⓢ -ˈɑː.t̬ɪk/.
otiose ˈəʊ.ti.əʊz, -ʃi-, -əʊs Ⓤⓢ ˈoʊ.ʃi.oʊs, -t̬i- **-ly** -li **-ness** -nəs, -nɪs
otiosity ˌəʊ.tiˈɒs.ə.ti, -ʃiˈ-, -ɪ.ti Ⓤⓢ ˌoʊ.ʃiˈɑː.sə.t̬i, -t̬iˈ-
Otis ˈəʊ.tɪs Ⓤⓢ ˈoʊ.t̬ɪs
otitis əʊˈtaɪ.tɪs Ⓤⓢ oʊˈtaɪ.t̬ɪs
Otley ˈɒt.li Ⓤⓢ ˈɑːt-
otolaryngolog|y ˌəʊ.təʊˌlær.ɪŋˈgɒl.ə.dʒ|i, -ˌleə.rɪŋˈ- Ⓤⓢ ˌoʊ.t̬oʊˌler.ɪŋˈgɑː.lə-, -ˌlær- **-ist/s** -ɪst/s
otological ˌəʊ.təˈlɒdʒ.ɪ.kəl Ⓤⓢ ˌoʊ.t̬əˈlɑː.dʒɪ-
otolog|y əʊˈtɒl.ə.dʒ|i Ⓤⓢ oʊˈtɑː.lə- **-ist/s** -ɪst/s
otoscope ˈəʊ.tə.skəʊp Ⓤⓢ ˈoʊ.t̬oʊ.skoʊp, -t̬ə- **-s** -s
Otranto ɒtˈræn.təʊ, ˈɒt.rən- Ⓤⓢ oʊˈtrɑːn.toʊ
O'Trigger əʊˈtrɪg.əʳ Ⓤⓢ oʊˈtrɪg.ɚ
OTT ˌəʊ.tiːˈtiː Ⓤⓢ ˌoʊ- *stress shift:* ˌOTT ˈspeech
Note: The letters OTT stand for "over-the-top"; see also that entry.
ottava rima ɒtˈɑː.vəˌriː.mə Ⓤⓢ oʊˈtɑː-
Ottaw|a ˈɒt.ə.w|ə Ⓤⓢ ˈɑː.t̬ə.wə, -w|ɑː, -w|ɔː **-as** -əz Ⓤⓢ -əz, -ɑːz, -ɔːz **-an/s** -ən/z
Ottaway ˈɒt.ə.weɪ Ⓤⓢ ˈɑː.t̬ə-
otter ˈɒt.əʳ Ⓤⓢ ˈɑː.t̬ɚ **-s** -z
Otterburn ˈɒt.ə.bɜːn Ⓤⓢ ˈɑː.t̬ɚ.bɜːrn
Ottery ˈɒt.ər.i Ⓤⓢ ˈɑː.t̬ɚ-
Ottley ˈɒt.li Ⓤⓢ ˈɑːt-
otto (O) ˈɒt.əʊ Ⓤⓢ ˈɑː.t̬oʊ
ottoman (O) ˈɒt.əʊ.mən Ⓤⓢ ˈɑː.t̬ə.mən **-s** -z
Ottoway ˈɒt.ə.weɪ Ⓤⓢ ˈɑː.t̬ə-
Otuel ˈɒt.juəl Ⓤⓢ ɔːˈtʊl, -ˈtuː.əl
Otway ˈɒt.weɪ Ⓤⓢ ˈɑːt-
Ouagadougou ˌwɑː.gəˈduː.guː, ˌwæg.əˈ- Ⓤⓢ ˌwɑː.gəˈ-
oubliette ˌuː.bliˈet **-s** -s
ouch aʊtʃ
Oudenarde ˈuː.də.nɑːd, -dɪ- Ⓤⓢ -dən.ɑːrd; ˌuː.dəˈnɑːr.də
Oudh aʊd
Ougham ˈɔː.əm
ought ɔːt Ⓤⓢ ɑːt, ɔːt **-n't** -ənt
Oughtershaw ˈaʊ.tə.ʃɔː Ⓤⓢ -t̬ɚ.ʃɑː, -ʃɔː
Oughterside ˈaʊ.tə.saɪd Ⓤⓢ -t̬ɚ-
Oughton ˈaʊ.tən, ˈɔː.tən
Oughtred ˈɔː.tred, -trɪd Ⓤⓢ ˈɔː-, ˈɑː-
ouguiya uːˈgwiː.ə, -ˈgiː-
Ouida ˈwiː.də
Ouija® ˈwiː.dʒə, -dʒɑː, -dʒi Ⓤⓢ -dʒə, -dʒi
Oujda uːdʒˈdɑː
Ould əʊld Ⓤⓢ oʊld
ounc|e aʊnts **-es** -ɪz
Oundle ˈaʊn.dl̩
our aʊəʳ, ɑːʳ Ⓤⓢ aʊɚ, aʊr, ɑːr **-s** -z
oursel|f ˌaʊəˈsel|f, ˌɑː- Ⓤⓢ ˌaʊɚ-, ˌaʊr-, ˌɑːr- **-ves** -vz
Ouse uːz
ousel ˈuː.zl̩ **-s** -z
Ouseley ˈuːz.li
Ousey ˈuː.zi
Ousley ˈaʊ.sli
oust aʊst **-s** -s **-ing** -ɪŋ **-ed** -ɪd **-er/s** -əʳ/z Ⓤⓢ -ɚ/z
Ouston ˈaʊ.stən
out- aʊt-
Note: Prefix. Many compounds with beginning with **out-** have the stress pattern ˌ**out**ˈ-; these are likely to undergo stress shift when a stressed syllable follows closely, especially in adjectives derived from verbs.
out aʊt **-s** -s **-ing** -ɪŋ Ⓤⓢ ˈaʊ.t̬ɪŋ **-ed** -ɪd Ⓤⓢ ˈaʊ.t̬ɪd
out-and-out ˌaʊt.əndˈaʊt *stress shift:* ˌout-and-out ˈscoundrel
outback ˈaʊt.bæk
outbalanc|e ˌaʊtˈbæl.ənts, aʊt- **-es** -ɪz **-ing** -ɪŋ **-ed** -t
outbid ˌaʊtˈbɪd, aʊt- **-s** -z **-ding** -ɪŋ
outboard ˈaʊt.bɔːd Ⓤⓢ -bɔːrd
outbound ˈaʊt.baʊnd
outbrav|e ˌaʊtˈbreɪv, aʊt- **-es** -z **-ing** -ɪŋ **-ed** -d
outbreak ˈaʊt.breɪk **-s** -s
outbuilding ˈaʊtˌbɪl.dɪŋ **-s** -z
outburst ˈaʊt.bɜːst Ⓤⓢ -bɜːrst **-s** -s
outcast ˈaʊt.kɑːst Ⓤⓢ -kæst **-s** -s
outcast|e ˈaʊt.kɑːst Ⓤⓢ -kæst **-es** -s **-ing** -ɪŋ **-ed** -ɪd
outclass ˌaʊtˈklɑːs, aʊt- Ⓤⓢ -ˈklæs **-es** -ɪz **-ing** -ɪŋ **-ed** -t
outcome ˈaʊt.kʌm **-s** -z
outcrop ˈaʊt.krɒp Ⓤⓢ -krɑːp **-s** -s **-ping** -ɪŋ **-ped** -t
outcr|y ˈaʊt.kr|aɪ **-ies** -aɪz
out|date ˌaʊt|ˈdeɪt, aʊt- **-dates** -ˈdeɪts **-dating** -ˈdeɪ.tɪŋ Ⓤⓢ -ˈdeɪ.t̬ɪŋ **-dated** -ˈdeɪ.tɪd Ⓤⓢ -ˈdeɪ.t̬ɪd
outdated ˌaʊtˈdeɪ.tɪd, aʊt- Ⓤⓢ -t̬ɪd *stress shift:* ˌoutdated ˈclothes
outdistanc|e ˌaʊtˈdɪs.tənts, aʊt- **-es** -ɪz **-ing** -ɪŋ **-ed** -t
out|do ˌaʊt|ˈduː, aʊt- **-does** -ˈdʌz **-doing** -ˈduː.ɪŋ **-did** -ˈdɪd **-done** -ˈdʌn
outdoor ˌaʊtˈdɔːʳ, aʊt- Ⓤⓢ -ˈdɔːr **-s** -z *stress shift:* ˌoutdoor ˈsports
outer ˈaʊ.təʳ Ⓤⓢ -t̬ɚ **-most** -məʊst Ⓤⓢ -məst, -moʊst ˌ**outer** ˈ**space**
outerwear ˈaʊ.tə.weəʳ Ⓤⓢ -t̬ɚ.wer
outfac|e ˌaʊtˈfeɪs, aʊt- **-s** -ɪz **-ing** -ɪŋ **-ed** -t
outfall ˈaʊt.fɔːl **-s** -z
outfield ˈaʊt.fiːld **-s** -z **-er/s** -əʳ/z Ⓤⓢ -ɚ/z
out|fit ˈaʊt|.fɪt **-fits** -fɪts **-fitting** -ˌfɪt.ɪŋ Ⓤⓢ -ˌfɪt̬.ɪŋ **-fitted** -ˌfɪt.ɪd Ⓤⓢ -ˌfɪt̬.ɪd **-fitter/s** -ˌfɪt.ər/z Ⓤⓢ -ˌfɪt̬.ɚ/z

outflank ˌaʊtˈflæŋk, aʊt- **-s** -s **-ing** -ɪŋ **-ed** -t
outflow (*n.*) ˈaʊt.fləʊ (US) -floʊ **-s** -z
outflow (*v.*) ˌaʊtˈfləʊ, aʊt- (US) -ˈfloʊ **-s** -z **-ing** -ɪŋ **-ed** -d
outfox ˌaʊtˈfɒks, aʊt- (US) -ˈfɑːks **-es** -ɪz **-ing** -ɪŋ **-ed** -t
outgeneral ˌaʊtˈdʒen.ər.əl, aʊt- **-s** -z **-(l)ing** -ɪŋ **-(l)ed** -d
outgo (*n.*) ˈaʊt.gəʊ (US) -goʊ **-es** -z
out|go (*v.*) ˌaʊt|ˈgəʊ, aʊt- (US) -ˈgoʊ **-goes** -ˈgəʊz (US) -ˈgoʊz **-going** -ˈgəʊ.ɪŋ (US) -ˈgoʊ.ɪŋ **-went** -ˈwent **-gone** -ˈgɒn (US) -ˈgɑːn
outgoer ˈaʊtˌgəʊ.əʳ (US) -ˌgoʊ.ɚ **-s** -z
outgoing ˌaʊtˈgəʊ.ɪŋ, aʊt-, ˈ--- (US) ˈaʊt.goʊ- **-s** -z
out|grow (*v.*) ˌaʊt|ˈgrəʊ, aʊt- (US) -ˈgroʊ **-grows** -ˈgrəʊz (US) -ˈgroʊz **-growing** -ˈgrəʊ.ɪŋ (US) -ˈgroʊ.ɪŋ **-grew** -ˈgruː **-grown** -ˈgrəʊn (US) -ˈgroʊn
outgrowth ˈaʊt.grəʊθ (US) -groʊθ **-s** -s
outguess ˌaʊtˈges, aʊt- **-es** -ɪz **-ing** -ɪŋ **-ed** -t
outgun ˌaʊtˈgʌn, aʊt- **-s** -z **-ning** -ɪŋ **-ned** -d
out-Herod ˌaʊtˈher.əd, aʊt- **-s** -z **-ing** -ɪŋ **-ed** -ɪd
outhou|se ˈaʊt.haʊ|s **-ses** -zɪz
Outhwaite ˈuː.θweɪt, ˈəʊ-, ˈaʊ- (US) ˈuː-, ˈoʊ-, ˈaʊ-
outing ˈaʊ.tɪŋ (US) -t̬ɪŋ **-s** -z
Outlander ˈaʊtˌlæn.dəʳ (US) -dɚ **-s** -z
outlandish ˌaʊtˈlæn.dɪʃ, aʊt- **-ly** -li **-ness** -nəs, -nɪs
outlast ˌaʊtˈlɑːst, aʊt- (US) -ˈlæst **-s** -s **-ing** -ɪŋ **-ed** -ɪd
outlaw ˈaʊt.lɔː (US) -lɑː, -lɔː **-s** -z **-ing** -ɪŋ **-ed** -d **-ry** -ri
outlay (*n.*) ˈaʊt.leɪ **-s** -z
out|lay (*v.*) ˌaʊt|ˈleɪ, aʊt- **-lays** -ˈleɪz **-laying** -ˈleɪ.ɪŋ **-laid** -ˈleɪd
outlet ˈaʊt.let, -lət, -lɪt (US) -let, -lət **-s** -s
outlier ˈaʊtˌlaɪ.əʳ (US) -ɚ **-s** -z
outline (*n.*) ˈaʊt.laɪn **-s** -z
outlin|e (*v.*) ˈaʊt.laɪn, ˌ-ˈ-, aʊt- (US) ˈ-- **-es** -z **-ing** -ɪŋ **-ed** -d
outliv|e ˌaʊtˈlɪv, aʊt- **-es** -z **-ing** -ɪŋ **-ed** -d
outlook ˈaʊt.lʊk **-s** -s
outlying ˈaʊtˌlaɪ.ɪŋ, ˌ-ˈ--, aʊt- (US) ˈ-ˌ--
outmanoeuv|re, outmaneuv|er ˌaʊt.məˈnuː.v|əʳ (US) -v|ɚ **-res** -əz (US) -ɚz **-ring** -ər.ɪŋ **-red** -əd (US) -ɚd
outmarch ˌaʊtˈmɑːtʃ, aʊt- (US) -ˈmɑːrtʃ **-es** -ɪz **-ing** -ɪŋ **-ed** -t
outmatch ˌaʊtˈmætʃ, aʊt- **-es** -ɪz **-ing** -ɪŋ **-ed** -t
outmoded ˌaʊtˈməʊ.dɪd, aʊt- (US) -ˈmoʊ- *stress shift:* ˌoutmoded ˈclothes
outmost ˈaʊt.məʊst (US) -moʊst
outnumb|er ˌaʊtˈnʌm.b|əʳ, aʊt- (US) -bɚ **-ers** -əz (US) -ɚz **-ering** -ər.ɪŋ **-ered** -əd (US) -ɚd
out-of-date ˌaʊt.əvˈdeɪt (US) ˌaʊt̬- *stress shift:* ˌout-of-date ˈfoodstuffs
out-of-door ˌaʊt.əvˈdɔːʳ (US) ˌaʊt̬.əvˈdɔːr **-s** -z *stress shift:* ˌout-of-door ˈsports
out-of-pocket ˌaʊt.əvˈpɒk.ɪt (US) ˌaʊt̬.əvˈpɑː.kɪt *stress shift:* ˌout-of-pocket ˈpayment
out-of-state ˌaʊt.əvˈsteɪt (US) ˌaʊt̬- *stress shift:* ˌout-of-state ˈvisitors
out-of-the-way ˌaʊt.əv.ðəˈweɪ (US) ˌaʊt̬.əv.ðəˈ- *stress shift:* ˌout-of-the-way ˈplaces
outpac|e ˌaʊtˈpeɪs, aʊt- **-es** -ɪz **-ing** -ɪŋ **-ed** -t
outpatient ˈaʊtˌpeɪ.ʃənt **-s** -s
outplacement ˈaʊtˌpleɪs.mənt
outplay ˌaʊtˈpleɪ, aʊt- **-s** -z **-ing** -ɪŋ **-ed** -d
outport ˈaʊt.pɔːt (US) -pɔːrt **-s** -s
outpost ˈaʊt.pəʊst (US) -poʊst **-s** -s
outpour (*n.*) ˈaʊt.pɔːʳ (US) -pɔːr **-s** -z
outpour (*v.*) ˌaʊtˈpɔːʳ, aʊt- (US) -ˈpɔːr **-s** -z **-ing** -ɪŋ **-ed** -d
outpouring ˈaʊtˌpɔː.rɪŋ, ˌ-ˈ--, aʊt- (US) ˈaʊtˌpɔːr.ɪŋ **-s** -z
out|put ˈaʊt|.pʊt **-puts** -pʊts **-putting** -ˌpʊt.ɪŋ (US) -ˌpʊt̬.ɪŋ **-putted** -ˌpʊt.ɪd (US) -ˌpʊt̬.ɪd
outrage (O) (*n.*) ˈaʊt.reɪdʒ
outrag|e (*v.*) ˈaʊt.reɪdʒ, ˌ-ˈ-, aʊt- (US) ˈ-- **-es** -ɪz **-ing** -ɪŋ **-ed** -d
outrageous ˌaʊtˈreɪ.dʒəs, aʊt- **-ly** -li **-ness** -nəs, -nɪs
Outram ˈuː.trəm
outrang|e ˌaʊtˈreɪndʒ, aʊt- **-es** -ɪz **-ing** -ɪŋ **-ed** -d
outrank ˌaʊtˈræŋk, aʊt- **-s** -s **-ing** -ɪŋ **-ed** -t
outré ˈuː.treɪ (US) -ˈ-
outreach (*n.*) ˈaʊt.riːtʃ **-es** -ɪz
outreach (*v.*) ˌaʊtˈriːtʃ, aʊt- **-es** -ɪz **-ing** -ɪŋ **-ed** -t
out|ride ˌaʊt|ˈraɪd, aʊt- **-rides** -ˈraɪdz **-riding** -ˈraɪ.dɪŋ **-rode** -ˈrəʊd (US) -ˈroʊd **-ridden** -ˈrɪd.ən
outrider ˈaʊtˌraɪ.dəʳ (US) -dɚ **-s** -z
outrigger ˈaʊtˌrɪg.əʳ (US) -ɚ **-s** -z
outright (*adj.*) ˈaʊt.raɪt (*adv.*) ˌaʊtˈraɪt, aʊt-
outrival ˌaʊtˈraɪ.vəl, aʊt- **-s** -z **-ling** -ɪŋ **-led** -d
out|run ˌaʊt|ˈrʌn, aʊt- **-runs** -ˈrʌnz **-running** -ˈrʌn.ɪŋ **-ran** -ˈræn
outrush ˈaʊt.rʌʃ **-es** -ɪz
out|sell ˌaʊt|ˈsel, aʊt- **-sells** -ˈselz **-selling** -ˈsel.ɪŋ **-sold** -ˈsəʊld (US) -ˈsoʊld
outset ˈaʊt.set **-s** -s
out|shine ˌaʊt|ˈʃaɪn, aʊt- **-shines** -ˈʃaɪnz **-shining** -ˈʃaɪ.nɪŋ **-shined** -ˈʃaɪnd **-shone** -ˈʃɒn (US) -ˈʃoʊn
outside ˌaʊtˈsaɪd, aʊt- **-s** -z *stress shift:* ˌoutside ˈtoilet
outsider ˌaʊtˈsaɪ.dəʳ, aʊt- (US) aʊtˈsaɪ.dɚ, ˈ--- **-s** -z *stress shift, British only:* ˌoutsider ˈdealing
outsiz|e ˌaʊtˈsaɪz, aʊt- **-es** -ɪz **-ed** -d *stress shift:* ˌoutsize ˈclothes
outskirts ˈaʊt.skɜːts (US) -skɜːrts
out|smart ˌaʊt|ˈsmɑːt, aʊt- (US) -ˈsmɑːrt **-smarts** -ˈsmɑːts (US) -ˈsmɑːrts **-smarting** -ˈsmɑː.tɪŋ (US) -ˈsmɑːr.t̬ɪŋ **-smarted** -ˈsmɑː.tɪd (US) -ˈsmɑːr.t̬ɪd
outsourc|e ˈaʊt.sɔːs (US) -sɔːrs **-es** -ɪz **-ing** -ɪŋ **-ed** -t
Outspan® ˈaʊt.spæn **-s** -z
outspan ˌaʊtˈspæn, aʊt- **-s** -z **-ning** -ɪŋ **-ned** -d
outspend ˌaʊtˈspend, aʊt- **-s** -z **-ing** -ɪŋ **outspent** ˌaʊtˈspent, aʊt-
outspoken ˌaʊtˈspəʊ.kən, aʊt- (US) -ˈspoʊ- **-ly** -li **-ness** -nəs, -nɪs *stress shift:* ˌoutspoken ˈperson
outspread ˌaʊtˈspred (US) aʊt- **-s** -z **-ing** -ɪŋ *stress shift:* ˌoutspread ˈarms
outstanding *very good:* ˌaʊtˈstæn.dɪŋ, aʊt- **-ly** -li *sticking out:* ˈaʊtˌstæn.dɪŋ
outstar|e ˌaʊtˈsteəʳ, aʊt- (US) -ˈster **-es** -z **-ing** -ɪŋ **-ed** -d
outstation ˈaʊt.steɪ.ʃən **-s** -z **-ed** -d
outstay ˌaʊtˈsteɪ, aʊt- **-s** -z **-ing** -ɪŋ **-ed** -d
outstretch ˌaʊtˈstretʃ, aʊt- **-es** -ɪz **-ing** -ɪŋ **-ed** -t *stress shift:* ˌoutstretched ˈarms
outstrip ˌaʊtˈstrɪp, aʊt- **-s** -s **-ping** -ɪŋ **-ped** -t
outta ˈaʊ.t̬ə
Note: This is a form of **out of**, and is only used by British speakers when imitating American speakers.
outtake ˈaʊt.teɪk **-s** -s
out|vote ˌaʊt|ˈvəʊt, aʊt- (US) -ˈvoʊt **-votes** -ˈvəʊts (US) -ˈvoʊts **-voting** -ˈvəʊ.tɪŋ (US) -ˈvoʊ.t̬ɪŋ **-voted** -ˈvəʊ.tɪd (US) -ˈvoʊ.t̬ɪd
outward ˈaʊt.wəd (US) -wɚd **-s** -z **-ly** -li **-ness** -nəs, -nɪs
outward-bound ˌaʊt.wədˈbaʊnd (US) -wɚdˈ- ˌ**Outward** ˈ**Bound** ˌ**course**
out|wear ˌaʊt|ˈweəʳ, aʊt- (US) -ˈwer **-wears** -ˈweəz (US) -ˈwers **-wearing** -ˈweə.rɪŋ (US) -ˈwer.ɪŋ **-worn** -ˈwɔːn (US) -ˈwɔːrn
outweigh ˌaʊtˈweɪ, aʊt- **-s** -z **-ing** -ɪŋ **-ed** -d
outwent (*from* **outgo**) ˌaʊtˈwent, aʊt-
out|wit ˌaʊt|ˈwɪt, aʊt- **-wits** -ˈwɪts **-witting** -ˈwɪt.ɪŋ (US) -ˈwɪt̬.ɪŋ **-witted** -ˈwɪt.ɪd (US) -ˈwɪt̬.ɪd

outwith ˌaʊtˈwɪθ, aʊt, -ˈwɪð
outwork (*n.*) ˈaʊt.wɜːk (US) -wɜːrk **-s** -s
outwork (*v.*) ˌaʊtˈwɜːk, aʊt- (US) -ˈwɜːrk **-s** -s **-ing** -ɪŋ **-ed** -t
out-worker ˈaʊtˌwɜː.kəʳ (US) -ˌwɜːr.kɚ **-s** -z
outworn ˌaʊtˈwɔːn, aʊt- (US) -ˈwɔːrn *stress shift:* ˌoutworn ˈtheories
ouzel ˈuː.zəl **-s** -z
ouzo ˈuː.zəʊ (US) -zoʊ **-s**
ova (*plur. of* **ovum**) ˈəʊ.və (US) ˈoʊ-
oval (O) ˈəʊ.vəl (US) ˈoʊ- **-s** -z **-ly** -i **ˈOval ˌOffice, ˌOval ˈOffice**
Ovaltine® ˈəʊ.vəl.tiːn (US) ˈoʊ-
ovari|an əʊˈveə.ri|.ən (US) oʊˈver.i- **-al** -əl
ovariectomy əʊˌveə.riˈek.tə.mi (US) oʊˌver.iˈ-
ovariotomy əʊˌveə.riˈɒt.ə.mi (US) oʊˌver.iˈɑː.t̬ə-
ovar|y ˈəʊ.vər|.i (US) ˈoʊ- **-ies** -iz
ovate (*n.*) *Welsh title:* ˈɒv.ət, -ɪt; ˈəʊ.veɪt (US) ˈoʊ.veɪt; ˈɑː.vət **-s** -s
ovate (*adj.*) *egg-shaped:* ˈəʊ.veɪt, -vɪt, -vət (US) ˈoʊ.veɪt
ovation əʊˈveɪ.ʃən (US) oʊ- **-s** -z **ˌstanding oˈvation**
oven ˈʌv.ən **-s** -z **ˈoven ˌglove**
ovenbird ˈʌv.ən.bɜːd, -əm- (US) -ən.bɜːrd **-s** -s
ovenproof ˈʌv.ən.pruːf, -əm- (US) -ən-
oven-ready ˌʌv.ənˈred.i *stress shift:* ˌoven-ready ˈchicken
ovenware ˈʌv.ən.weəʳ (US) -wer
over- əʊ.vəʳ-, oʊ.vɚ-
Note: Prefix. Many compounds with **over-** have the stress pattern **ˌoverˈ-**; these are likely to undergo stress shift when a stressed syllable follows, especially in adjectives derived from verbs.
over ˈəʊ.vəʳ (US) ˈoʊ.vɚ **-s** -z **ˌover and ˈdone ˌwith**
over-abundan|ce ˌəʊ.vər.əˈbʌn.dən|ts (US) ˌoʊ.vɚ- **-t** -t
over-achiever ˌəʊ.vər.əˈtʃiː.vəʳ (US) ˌoʊ.vɚ.əˈtʃiː.vɚ, ˈoʊ.vɚ.əˌtʃiː- **-s** -z
overact ˌəʊ.vərˈækt (US) ˌoʊ.vɚˈ- **-s** -s **-ing** -ɪŋ **-ed** -ɪd
overactive ˌəʊ.vərˈæk.tɪv (US) ˌoʊ.vɚˈ- *stress shift:* ˌoveractive ˈgland
over-age ˌəʊ.vərˈeɪdʒ (US) ˌoʊ.vɚˈ- *stress shift:* ˌover-age ˈapplicant
overall (O) (*n. adj.*) ˈəʊ.vər.ɔːl (US) ˈoʊ- **-s** -z
overall (*adv.*) ˌəʊ.vərˈɔːl (US) ˌoʊ.vɚˈ-, -ˈɑːl
over-ambitious ˌəʊ.vər.æmˈbɪʃ.əs (US) ˌoʊ.vɚ- *stress shift:* ˌover-ambitious ˈpartner
over-anxiety ˌəʊ.vər.æŋˈzaɪ.ə.ti (US) ˌoʊ.vɚ.æŋˈzaɪ.ə.t̬i
over-anxious ˌəʊ.vərˈæŋk.ʃəs (US) ˌoʊ.vɚˈ- **-ly** -li *stress shift:* ˌover-anxious ˈparent
overarm ˈəʊ.vər.ɑːm (US) ˈoʊ.vɚ.ɑːrm
overaw|e ˌəʊ.vərˈɔː (US) ˌoʊ.vɚˈɑː, -ˈɔː **-es** -z **-ing** -ɪŋ **-ed** -d
overbalanc|e ˌəʊ.vəˈbæl.ənts (US) ˌoʊ.vɚˈ- **-es** -ɪz **-ing** -ɪŋ **-ed** -t
overbear ˌəʊ.vəˈbeəʳ (US) ˌoʊ.vɚˈber **-s** -z **-ing** -ɪŋ **over|bore** ˌəʊ.və|ˈbɔːʳ (US) ˌoʊ.vɚ|ˈbɔːr **-borne** -ˈbɔːn (US) -ˈbɔːrn
overbearing ˌəʊ.vəˈbeə.rɪŋ (US) ˌoʊ.vɚˈber.ɪŋ **-ly** -li **-ness** -nəs, -nɪs *stress shift:* ˌoverbearing ˈrelatives
overbite ˈəʊ.və.baɪt (US) ˈoʊ.vɚ-
over|blow ˌəʊ.və|ˈbləʊ (US) ˌoʊ.vɚ|ˈbloʊ, ˈ--|- **-blows** -ˈbləʊz (US) -ˈbloʊz, -bloʊz **-blowing** -ˈbləʊ.ɪŋ (US) -ˈbloʊ.ɪŋ, -ˌbloʊ.ɪŋ **-blew** -ˈbluː (US) -ˈbluː, -bluː **-blown** -ˈbləʊn (US) -ˈbloʊn, -bloʊn
overboard ˈəʊ.və.bɔːd, ˌ--ˈ- (US) ˈoʊ.vɚ.bɔːrd
overbook ˌəʊ.vəˈbʊk (US) ˌoʊ.vɚˈ- **-s** -s **-ing** -ɪŋ **-ed** -t
overbreadth ˌəʊ.vəˈbredθ, -ˈbretθ (US) ˌoʊ.vɚˈ-
overbrim ˌəʊ.vəˈbrɪm (US) ˌoʊ.vɚˈ- **-s** -z **-ming** -ɪŋ **-med** -d
overbuild ˌəʊ.vəˈbɪld (US) ˌoʊ.vɚˈ-, ˈ--- **-s** -z **-ing** -ɪŋ **overbuilt** ˌəʊ.vəˈbɪlt (US) ˌoʊ.vɚˈ-, ˈ---
overburden ˌəʊ.vəˈbɜː.dən (US) ˌoʊ.vɚˈbɜːr- **-s** -z **-ing** -ɪŋ **-ed** -d
Overbury ˈəʊ.və.bər.i (US) ˈoʊ.vɚˌber-, -bɚ-
over-careful ˌəʊ.vəˈkeə.fəl, -fʊl (US) ˌoʊ.vɚˈker- **-ly** -i **-ness** -nəs, -nɪs
overcast ˈəʊ.və.kɑːst, ˌ--ˈ- (US) ˈoʊ.vɚ.kæst, ˌoʊ.vɚˈkæst
over-cautious ˌəʊ.vəˈkɔː.ʃəs (US) ˌoʊ.vɚˈkɑː-, -ˈkɔː- *stress shift:* ˌover-cautious ˈperson
overcharg|e (*v.*) ˌəʊ.vəˈtʃɑːdʒ (US) ˌoʊ.vɚˈtʃɑːrdʒ, ˈ--- **-es** -ɪz **-ing** -ɪŋ **-ed** -d
overcloud ˌəʊ.vəˈklaʊd (US) ˌoʊ.vɚˈklaʊd **-s** -z **-ing** -ɪŋ **-ed** -ɪd
overcoat ˈəʊ.və.kəʊt (US) ˈoʊ.vɚ.koʊt **-s** -s
over|come ˌəʊ.və|ˈkʌm (US) ˌoʊ.vɚˈ- **-comes** -ˈkʌmz **-coming** -ˈkʌm.ɪŋ **-came** -ˈkeɪm
overcompen|sate ˌəʊ.vəˈkɒm.pən|.seɪt, -pen- (US) ˌoʊ.vɚˈkɑːm.pən- **-sates** -seɪts **-sating** -seɪ.tɪŋ (US) -seɪ.t̬ɪŋ **-sated** -seɪ.tɪd (US) -seɪ.t̬ɪd
overcompensation ˌəʊ.vəˌkɒm.pənˈseɪ.ʃən, -penˈ- (US) ˌoʊ.vɚˌkɑːm.pənˈ-
over-confidence ˌəʊ.vəˈkɒn.fɪ.dənts, -fə- (US) ˌoʊ.vɚˈkɑːn.fə-
over-confident ˌəʊ.vəˈkɒn.fɪ.dənt, -fə- (US) ˌoʊ.vɚˈkɑːn.fə- **-ly** -li *stress shift:* ˌover-confident ˈcandidate
over-cook ˌəʊ.vəˈkʊk (US) ˌoʊ.vɚˈ- **-s** -s **-ing** -ɪŋ **-ed** -t
overcrowd ˌəʊ.vəˈkraʊd (US) ˌoʊ.vɚˈ- **-s** -z **-ing** -ɪŋ **-ed** -ɪd *stress shift:* ˌovercrowded ˈroom
over-develop ˌəʊ.və.dɪˈvel.əp, -dəˈ- (US) ˌoʊ.vɚ.dɪˈ- **-s** -s **-ing** -ɪŋ **-ed** -t **-ment** -mənt *stress shift:* ˌoverdeveloped ˈmuscles
over|do ˌəʊ.və|ˈduː (US) ˌoʊ.vɚˈ- **-does** -ˈdʌz **-doing** -ˈduː.ɪŋ **-did** -ˈdɪd **-done** -ˈdʌn
overdone *over-cooked:* ˌəʊ.vəˈdʌn (US) ˌoʊ.vɚˈ- *stress shift:* ˌoverdone ˈchicken
overdos|e (*n.*) ˈəʊ.və.dəʊs (US) ˈoʊ.vɚ.doʊs **-es** -ɪz
overdos|e (*v.*) ˌəʊ.vəˈdəʊs (US) ˌoʊ.vɚˈdoʊs, ˈ--- **-es** -ɪz **-ing** -ɪŋ **-ed** -t
overdraft ˈəʊ.və.drɑːft (US) ˈoʊ.vɚ.dræft **-s** -s
overdraught ˈəʊ.və.drɑːft (US) ˈoʊ.vɚ.dræft **-s** -s
overdraw ˌəʊ.vəˈdrɔː (US) ˌoʊ.vɚˈdrɑː, -ˈdrɔː, ˈ--- **-s** -z **-ing** -ɪŋ **over|drew** ˌəʊ.və|ˈdruː (US) ˌoʊ.vɚ-, ˈ--- **-drawn** -ˈdrɔːn (US) -ˈdrɑːn, -ˈdrɔːn, -drɑːn, -drɔːn
overdress (*v.*) ˌəʊ.vəˈdres (US) ˌoʊ.vɚˈ-, ˈ--- **-es** -ɪz **-ing** -ɪŋ **-ed** -t
overdress (*n.*) ˈəʊ.və.dres (US) ˈoʊ.vɚ- **-es** -ɪz
overdrive (*n.*) ˈəʊ.və.draɪv (US) ˈoʊ.vɚ-
over|drive (*v.*) ˌəʊ.və|ˈdraɪv (US) ˌoʊ.vɚˈ- **-drives** -ˈdraɪvz **-driving** -ˈdraɪ.vɪŋ **-drove** -ˈdrəʊv (US) -ˈdroʊv **-driven** -ˈdrɪv.ən
overdue ˌəʊ.vəˈdjuː (US) ˌoʊ.vɚˈduː, -ˈdjuː *stress shift:* ˌoverdue ˈpayment
over|eat ˌəʊ.vər|ˈiːt (US) ˌoʊ.vɚˈ- **-eats** -ˈiːts **-eating** -ˈiː.tɪŋ (US) -ˈiː.t̬ɪŋ **-eaten** -ˈiː.tən **-ate** -ˈet, -ˈeɪt (US) -ˈeɪt
over-emphasis ˌəʊ.vərˈemp.fə.sɪs (US) ˌoʊ.vɚˈ-
over-emphasiz|e, -is|e ˌəʊ.vərˈemp.fə.saɪz (US) ˌoʊ.vɚˈ- **-es** -ɪz **-ing** -ɪŋ **-ed** -d
overestimate (*n.*) ˌəʊ.vərˈes.tɪ.mət, -tə-, -mɪt, -meɪt (US) ˌoʊ.vɚˈes.tɪ.mɪt **-s** -s
overesti|mate (*v.*) ˌəʊ.vərˈes.tɪ|.meɪt, -tə- (US) ˌoʊ.vɚˈes.tə- **-mates** -meɪts **-mating** -meɪ.tɪŋ (US) -meɪ.t̬ɪŋ **-mated** -meɪ.tɪd (US) -meɪ.t̬ɪd
over-estimation ˌəʊ.vərˌes.tɪˈmeɪ.ʃən, -təˈ- (US) ˌoʊ.vɚˌes.təˈ-

overex|cite ˌəʊ.vᵊr.ɪk|ˈsaɪt, -ek'- Ⓤⓢ ˌoʊ.vɚ- **-cites** -ˈsaɪts **-citing** -ˈsaɪ.tɪŋ Ⓤⓢ -ˈsaɪ.t̬ɪŋ **-cited** -ˈsaɪ.tɪd Ⓤⓢ -ˈsaɪ.t̬ɪd **-citement** -ˈsaɪt.mənt

overexer|t ˌəʊ.vᵊr.ɪɡˈzɜː|t, -eɡ'- Ⓤⓢ ˌoʊ.vɚ.ɪɡˈzɜːr|t, -eɡ'- **-ts** -ts **-ting** -tɪŋ Ⓤⓢ -t̬ɪŋ **-ted** -tɪd Ⓤⓢ -t̬ɪd

overexertion ˌəʊ.vᵊr.ɪɡˈzɜː.ʃᵊn, -eɡ'- Ⓤⓢ ˌoʊ.vɚ.ɪɡˈzɜːr-, -eɡ'-

overexpos|e ˌəʊ.vᵊr.ɪkˈspəʊz, -ek'- Ⓤⓢ ˌoʊ.vɚ.ɪkˈspoʊz, -ek'- **-es** -ɪz **-ing** -ɪŋ **-ed** -d

over-exposure ˌəʊ.vᵊr.ɪkˈspəʊ.ʒəʳ, -ek'- Ⓤⓢ ˌoʊ.vɚ.ɪkˈspoʊ.ʒɚ, -ek'-

overfatigu|e ˌəʊ.və.fəˈtiːɡ Ⓤⓢ ˌoʊ.vɚ- **-es** -z **-ing** -ɪŋ **-ed** -d

overfeed ˌəʊ.vəˈfiːd Ⓤⓢ ˌoʊ.vɚˈ- **-s** -z **-ing** -ɪŋ **overfed** ˌəʊ.vəˈfed Ⓤⓢ ˌoʊ.vɚˈ- *stress shift:* ˌoverfed ˈpets

overflow (*n.*) ˈəʊ.və.fləʊ Ⓤⓢ ˈoʊ.vɚ.floʊ **-s** -z

overflow (*v.*) ˌəʊ.vəˈfləʊ Ⓤⓢ ˌoʊ.vɚˈfloʊ **-s** -z **-ing** -ɪŋ **-ed** -d

over|fly ˌəʊ.və|ˈflaɪ Ⓤⓢ ˌoʊ.vɚˈ-, ˈ--- **-flies** -ˈflaɪz Ⓤⓢ -ˈflaɪz, -flaɪz **-flying** -ˈflaɪ.ɪŋ Ⓤⓢ -ˈflaɪ.ɪŋ, -flaɪ.ɪŋ **-flew** -ˈfluː Ⓤⓢ -ˈfluː, -fluː **-flown** -ˈfləʊn Ⓤⓢ -ˈfloʊn, -floʊn

over-fond ˌəʊ.vəˈfɒnd Ⓤⓢ ˌoʊ.vɚˈfɑːnd

over-generalization, -isa- ˌəʊ.vəˌdʒen.ᵊr.ᵊl.aɪˈzeɪ.ʃᵊn, -ɪ'- Ⓤⓢ ˌoʊ.vɚˌdʒen.ɚ.ᵊl.ɪ'-

overground ˈəʊ.və.ɡraʊnd, ˌ--'- Ⓤⓢ ˈoʊ.vɚ.ɡraʊnd, ˌ--'-

over|grow ˌəʊ.və|ˈɡrəʊ Ⓤⓢ ˌoʊ.vɚˈɡroʊ **-grows** -ˈɡrəʊz Ⓤⓢ -ˈɡroʊz **-growing** -ˈɡrəʊ.ɪŋ Ⓤⓢ -ˈɡroʊ.ɪŋ **-grew** -ˈɡruː **-grown** -ˈɡrəʊn Ⓤⓢ -ˈɡroʊn

overgrowth ˈəʊ.və.ɡrəʊθ Ⓤⓢ ˈoʊ.vɚ.ɡroʊθ **-s** -s

overhand (*n. adj.*) ˈəʊ.və.hænd Ⓤⓢ ˈoʊ.vɚ- **-s** -z

overhang (*n.*) ˈəʊ.və.hæŋ Ⓤⓢ ˈoʊ.vɚ- **-s** -z

overhang (*v.*) ˌəʊ.vəˈhæŋ Ⓤⓢ ˌoʊ.vɚˈ-, ˈ--- **-s** -z **-ing** -ɪŋ **overhung** ˌəʊ.vəˈhʌŋ Ⓤⓢ ˌoʊ.vɚˈ-, ˈ---

over-hasty ˌəʊ.vəˈheɪ.sti Ⓤⓢ ˌoʊ.vɚˈ- *stress shift:* ˌover-hasty ˈchoice

overhaul (*n.*) ˈəʊ.və.hɔːl Ⓤⓢ ˈoʊ.vɚ.hɑːl, -hɔːl **-s** -z

overhaul (*v.*) ˌəʊ.vəˈhɔːl Ⓤⓢ ˌoʊ.vɚˈhɑːl, -ˈhɔːl, ˈ--- **-s** -z **-ing** -ɪŋ **-ed** -d

overhead (*n. adj.*) ˈəʊ.və.hed Ⓤⓢ ˈoʊ.vɚ- **-s** -z ˌ**overhead proˈjector**

overhead (*adv.*) ˌəʊ.vəˈhed Ⓤⓢ ˌoʊ.vɚˈ-

overhear ˌəʊ.vəˈhɪəʳ Ⓤⓢ ˌoʊ.vɚˈhɪr **-s** -z **-ing** -ɪŋ **overheard** ˌəʊ.vəˈhɜːd Ⓤⓢ ˌoʊ.vɚˈhɜːrd

over|heat ˌəʊ.və|ˈhiːt Ⓤⓢ ˌoʊ.vɚˈ- **-heats** -ˈhiːts **-heating** -ˈhiː.tɪŋ Ⓤⓢ -ˈhiː.t̬ɪŋ **-heated** -ˈhiː.tɪd Ⓤⓢ -ˈhiː.t̬ɪd

over-impress|ed ˌəʊ.vᵊr.ɪmˈpres|t Ⓤⓢ ˌoʊ.vɚ- **-ive** -ɪv

over-indulg|e ˌəʊ.vᵊr.ɪnˈdʌldʒ Ⓤⓢ ˌoʊ.vɚ- **-es** -ɪz **-ing** -ɪŋ **-ed** -d **-ence** -ᵊnts

overjoyed ˌəʊ.vəˈdʒɔɪd Ⓤⓢ ˌoʊ.vɚˈ- *stress shift:* ˌoverjoyed ˈwinner

overkill ˈəʊ.və.kɪl Ⓤⓢ ˈoʊ.vɚ-

overladen ˌəʊ.vəˈleɪ.dᵊn Ⓤⓢ ˌoʊ.vɚˈ- *stress shift:* ˌoverladen ˈbasket

overlaid ˌəʊ.vəˈleɪd Ⓤⓢ ˌoʊ.vɚˈ-

overland (*adj.*) ˈəʊ.və.lænd Ⓤⓢ ˈoʊ.vɚ-

overland (*adv.*) ˌəʊ.vəˈlænd, ˈ--- Ⓤⓢ ˌoʊ.vɚˈlænd, ˈ---

overlap (*n.*) ˈəʊ.və.læp Ⓤⓢ ˈoʊ.vɚ- **-s** -s

overlap (*v.*) ˌəʊ.vəˈlæp Ⓤⓢ ˌoʊ.vɚˈ- **-s** -s **-ping** -ɪŋ **-ped** -t

overlay (*n.*) ˈəʊ.vᵊl.eɪ Ⓤⓢ ˈoʊ.vɚ.leɪ **-s** -z

overlay (*v.*) ˌəʊ.vᵊlˈeɪ Ⓤⓢ ˌoʊ.vɚˈleɪ **-s** -z **-ing** -ɪŋ **overlaid** ˌəʊ.vᵊlˈeɪd Ⓤⓢ ˌoʊ.vɚˈleɪd

overleaf ˌəʊ.vᵊlˈiːf Ⓤⓢ ˈoʊ.vɚ.liːf

overload (*n.*) ˈəʊ.vᵊl.əʊd Ⓤⓢ ˈoʊ.vɚ.loʊd **-s** -z

overload (*v.*) ˌəʊ.vᵊlˈəʊd Ⓤⓢ ˌoʊ.vɚˈloʊd, ˈ--- **-s** -z **-ing** -ɪŋ **-ed** -ɪd

overlock ˈəʊ.vᵊl.ɒk Ⓤⓢ ˈoʊ.vɚ.lɑːk **-s** -s **-ing** -ɪŋ **-ed** -t

overlong ˌəʊ.vəˈlɒŋ Ⓤⓢ ˌoʊ.vɚˈlɑːŋ, -ˈlɔːŋ

overlook (*v.*) ˌəʊ.vəˈlʊk Ⓤⓢ ˌoʊ.vɚˈ- **-s** -s **-ing** -ɪŋ **-ed** -t

overlook (*n.*) ˈəʊ.və.lʊk Ⓤⓢ ˈoʊ.vɚ- **-s** -s

overlord ˈəʊ.və.lɔːd Ⓤⓢ ˈoʊ.vɚ.lɔːrd **-s** -z

overly ˈəʊ.vᵊl.i Ⓤⓢ ˈoʊ.vɚ.li

overlying ˌəʊ.vᵊlˈaɪ.ɪŋ Ⓤⓢ ˌoʊ.vɚˈlaɪ- *stress shift:* ˌoverlying ˈstructure

overman (*v.*) ˌəʊ.vəˈmæn Ⓤⓢ ˌoʊ.vɚˈ- **-s** -z **-ning** -ɪŋ **-ned** -d

over|man (*n.*) ˈəʊ.və|.mæn Ⓤⓢ ˈoʊ.vɚ- **-men** -men

overmantel ˈəʊ.vəˌmæn.tᵊl Ⓤⓢ ˈoʊ.vɚˌmæn.t̬ᵊl **-s** -z

overmast|er ˌəʊ.vəˈmɑː.st|əʳ Ⓤⓢ ˌoʊ.vɚˈmæs.tɚ **-ers** -əz Ⓤⓢ -ɚz **-ering** -ᵊr.ɪŋ **-ered** -əd Ⓤⓢ -ɚd

overmatch ˌəʊ.vəˈmætʃ Ⓤⓢ ˌoʊ.vɚ-, ˈ--- **-es** -ɪz **-ing** -ɪŋ **-ed** -t

overmuch ˌəʊ.vəˈmʌtʃ, ˈ--- Ⓤⓢ ˌoʊ.vɚˈ-, ˈ---

overnight ˌəʊ.vəˈnaɪt Ⓤⓢ ˌoʊ.vɚˈ- *stress shift:* ˌovernight ˈsleeper

overoptimistic ˌəʊ.vᵊrˌɒp.tɪˈmɪs.tɪk, -tə'- Ⓤⓢ ˌoʊ.vɚˌɑːp.tə'- **-ally** -ᵊl.i, -li *stress shift:* ˌoveroptimistic ˈoutlook

overpass (*n.*) ˈəʊ.və.pɑːs Ⓤⓢ ˈoʊ.vɚ.pæs **-es** -ɪz

over|pay ˌəʊ.və|ˈpeɪ Ⓤⓢ ˌoʊ.vɚˈ-, ˈ--|- **-pays** -ˈpeɪz **-paying** -ˈpeɪ.ɪŋ **-paid** -ˈpeɪd **-payment/s** -ˈpeɪ.mənt/s

overplus ˈəʊ.və.plʌs Ⓤⓢ ˈoʊ.vɚ- **-es** -ɪz

overpopu|late ˌəʊ.vəˈpɒp.jə|.leɪt, -jʊ- Ⓤⓢ ˌoʊ.vɚˈpɑː.pjə-, -pjʊ- **-lates** -leɪts **-lating** -leɪ.tɪŋ Ⓤⓢ -leɪ.t̬ɪŋ **-lated** -leɪ.tɪd Ⓤⓢ -leɪ.t̬ɪd

overpopulation ˌəʊ.vəˌpɒp.jəˈleɪ.ʃᵊn, -jʊ'- Ⓤⓢ ˌoʊ.vɚˌpɑː.pjə'-, -pjʊ'-

overpower ˌəʊ.vəˈpaʊəʳ Ⓤⓢ ˌoʊ.vɚˈpaʊɚ **-s** -z **-ing/ly** -ɪŋ/li **-ed** -d

overpriced ˌəʊ.vəˈpraɪst Ⓤⓢ ˌoʊ.vɚ- *stress shift:* ˌoverpriced ˈgoods

overprint (*n.*) ˈəʊ.və.prɪnt Ⓤⓢ ˈoʊ.vɚ- **-s** -s

overprin|t (*v.*) ˌəʊ.vəˈprɪn|t, ˈ--- Ⓤⓢ ˌoʊ.vɚˈ-, ˈ--- **-ts** -ts **-ting** -tɪŋ Ⓤⓢ -t̬ɪŋ **-ted** -tɪd Ⓤⓢ -t̬ɪd

overproduc|e ˌəʊ.və.prəˈdjuːs Ⓤⓢ ˌoʊ.vɚ.proʊˈduːs, -ˈdjuːs, ˈoʊ.vɚ.proʊˌduːs, -ˌdjuːs **-es** -ɪz **-ing** -ɪŋ **-ed** -t

overproduction ˌəʊ.və.prəˈdʌk.ʃᵊn Ⓤⓢ ˌoʊ.vɚ-

overprotect ˌəʊ.və.prəˈtekt Ⓤⓢ ˌoʊ.vɚ- **-s** -s **-ing** -ɪŋ **-ed** -ɪd

overprotective ˌəʊ.və.prəˈtek.tɪv Ⓤⓢ ˌoʊ.vɚ- *stress shift:* ˌoverprotective ˈparent

overqualified ˌəʊ.vəˈkwɒl.ɪ.faɪd, ˈ-ə- Ⓤⓢ ˌoʊ.vɚˈkwɑː.lɪ-, ˈoʊ.vɚˌkwɑː.lɪ- *stress shift, British only:* ˌoverqualified ˈapplicant

overra|te ˌəʊ.vᵊrˈeɪ|t Ⓤⓢ ˌoʊ.vɚˈreɪ|t, ˈ--- **-tes** -ts **-ting** -tɪŋ Ⓤⓢ -t̬ɪŋ **-ted** -tɪd Ⓤⓢ -t̬ɪd

overreach (*n.*) ˈəʊ.vᵊrˈiːtʃ Ⓤⓢ ˈoʊ.vɚ.riːtʃ **-es** -ɪz

overreach (*v.*) ˌəʊ.vᵊrˈiːtʃ Ⓤⓢ ˌoʊ.vɚˈriːtʃ, ˈ--- **-es** -ɪz **-ing** -ɪŋ **-ed** -t

overreact ˌəʊ.vᵊr.iˈækt Ⓤⓢ ˌoʊ.vɚ.ri'- **-s** -s **-ing** -ɪŋ **-ed** -ɪd

overreaction ˌəʊ.vᵊr.iˈæk.ʃᵊn Ⓤⓢ -oʊ.vɚ.ri'-

overrid|e ˌəʊ.vᵊrˈaɪd Ⓤⓢ ˌoʊ.vɚˈraɪd **-es** -z **-ing** -ɪŋ **overrode** ˌəʊ.vᵊrˈəʊd Ⓤⓢ ˌoʊ.vɚˈroʊd **overridden** ˌəʊ.vᵊrˈɪd.ᵊn Ⓤⓢ ˌoʊ.vɚˈrɪd-

overrider ˈəʊ.vᵊrˌaɪ.dəʳ Ⓤⓢ ˈoʊ.vɚˌraɪ.dɚ **-s** -z

overripe ˌəʊ.vᵊr'aɪp (US) ˌoʊ.vɚ'raɪp **-ness** -nəs, -nɪs *stress shift:* ˌoverripe 'fruit

overripen ˌəʊ.vᵊr'aɪ.pᵊn (US) ˌoʊ.vɚ'raɪ- **-s** -z **-ing** -ɪŋ, -vᵊr'aɪp.nɪŋ (US) -vɚ'raɪp- **-ed** -d

overrul|e ˌəʊ.vᵊr'uːl (US) ˌoʊ.vɚ'ruːl **-es** -z **-ing** -ɪŋ **-ed** -d

overrun (*v.*) ˌəʊ.vᵊr'ʌn (US) ˌoʊ.vɚ'rʌn **-s** -z **-ning** -ɪŋ **overran** ˌəʊ.vᵊr'æn (US) ˌoʊ.vɚ'ræn

overrun (*n.*) 'əʊ.vᵊr.ʌn (US) 'oʊ.vɚ- **-s** -z

over-scrupulous ˌəʊ.və'skruː.pjə.ləs, -pjʊ- (US) ˌoʊ.vɚ'skruː.pjə- **-ly** -li **-ness** -nəs, -nɪs *stress shift:* ˌover-scrupulous 'person

oversea ˌəʊ.və'siː (US) ˌoʊ.vɚ'-, 'oʊ.vɚ.siː **-s** -z *stress shift:* ˌoverseas 'applicant

over|see ˌəʊ.və|'siː (US) ˌoʊ.vɚ'- **-sees** -'siːz **-seeing** -'siː.ɪŋ **-saw** -'sɔː (US) -'sɑː, -'sɔː **-seen** -'siːn

overseer 'əʊ.vəˌsiː.əʳ (US) 'oʊ.vɚˌsiː.ɚ, -ˌsɪr **-s** -z

over|sell ˌəʊ.və|'sel (US) -vɚ- **-sells** -selz **-selling** -sel.ɪŋ **-sold** -səʊld (US) -soʊld

oversensitive ˌəʊ.və'sen*t*.sɪ.tɪv, -sə- (US) ˌoʊ.vɚ'sen*t*.sə.t̬ɪv *stress shift:* ˌoversensitive 'person

oversensitivity ˌəʊ.vəˌsen*t*.sɪ'tɪv.ə.ti, -sə'-, -ɪ.ti (US) ˌoʊ.vɚˌsen*t*.sə'tɪv.ə.t̬i

oversew 'əʊ.və.səʊ, ˌ--'- (US) 'oʊ.vɚ.soʊ, ˌ--'- **-s** -z **-ing** -ɪŋ **-ed** -d **-n** -n

oversexed ˌəʊ.və'sekst (US) ˌoʊ.vɚ'- *stress shift:* ˌoversexed 'person

overshadow ˌəʊ.və'ʃæd.əʊ (US) ˌoʊ.vɚ'ʃæd.oʊ **-s** -z **-ing** -ɪŋ **-ed** -d

overshoe 'əʊ.və.ʃuː (US) 'oʊ.vɚ- **-s** -z

overshoot (*n.*) 'əʊ.və.ʃuːt (US) 'oʊ.vɚ-

overshoot (*v.*) ˌəʊ.və'ʃuːt (US) ˌoʊ.vɚ'- **-s** -s **-ing** -ɪŋ **overshot** ˌəʊ.və'ʃɒt (US) ˌoʊ.vɚ'ʃɑːt

overside (*adv.*) 'əʊ.və.saɪd (US) 'oʊ.vɚ-

oversight 'əʊ.və.saɪt (US) 'oʊ.vɚ- **-s** -s

oversimplification ˌəʊ.vəˌsɪm.plɪ.fɪ'keɪ.ʃᵊn, -plə- (US) ˌoʊ.vɚˌsɪm.plə- **-s** -z

oversimpli|fy ˌəʊ.və'sɪm.plɪ|.faɪ, -plə- (US) ˌoʊ.vɚ'sɪm.plə-, 'ˌ--ˌ--- **-fies** -faɪz **-fying** -faɪ.ɪŋ **-fied** -faɪd

oversize ˌəʊ.və'saɪz (US) ˌoʊ.vɚ'-, '--- **-d** -d *stress shift:* ˌoversize 'clothes

oversleep ˌəʊ.və'sliːp (US) ˌoʊ.vɚ'- **-s** -s **-ing** -ɪŋ **overslept** ˌəʊ.və'slept (US) ˌoʊ.vɚ'-

oversold (*from* **oversell**) ˌəʊ.və'səʊld (US) ˌoʊ.vɚ'soʊld *stress shift:* ˌoversold 'concept

overspend ˌəʊ.və'spend (US) ˌoʊ.vɚ'-, '--- **-s** -z **-ing** -ɪŋ **overspent** ˌəʊ.və'spent (US) ˌoʊ.vɚ'-, '---

overspill 'əʊ.və.spɪl (US) 'oʊ.vɚ-

overspread ˌəʊ.və'spred (US) ˌoʊ.vɚ'-, '--- **-s** -z **-ing** -ɪŋ

overstaff ˌəʊ.və'stɑːf (US) ˌoʊ.vɚ'stæf **-s** -s **-ing** -ɪŋ **-ed** -t

over|state ˌəʊ.və|'steɪt (US) ˌoʊ.vɚ'- **-states** -'steɪts **-stating** -'steɪ.tɪŋ (US) -'steɪ.t̬ɪŋ **-stated** -'steɪ.tɪd (US) -'steɪ.t̬ɪd *stress shift:* ˌoverstated 'argument

overstatement ˌəʊ.və'steɪt.mənt, 'əʊ.vəˌsteɪt- (US) ˌoʊ.vɚ'steɪt, 'oʊ.vɚˌsteɪt **-s** -s

overstay ˌəʊ.və'steɪ (US) ˌoʊ.vɚ'-, '--- **-s** -z **-ing** -ɪŋ **-ed** -d

overstep ˌəʊ.və'step (US) ˌoʊ.vɚ'- **-s** -s **-ping** -ɪŋ **-ped** -t

overstimu|late ˌəʊ.və'stɪm.jə|.leɪt, -jʊ- (US) ˌoʊ.vɚ'stɪm.jə-, -jʊ- **-lates** -leɪts **-lating** -leɪ.tɪŋ (US) -leɪ.t̬ɪŋ **-lated** -leɪ.tɪd (US) -leɪ.t̬ɪd

overstock ˌəʊ.və'stɒk (US) ˌoʊ.vɚ'stɑːk **-s** -s **-ing** -ɪŋ **-ed** -t

overstrain (*n.*) 'əʊ.və.streɪn, ˌ--'- (US) ˌoʊ.vɚ'-, '---

overstrain (*v.*) ˌəʊ.və'streɪn (US) ˌoʊ.vɚ'- **-s** -z **-ing** -ɪŋ **-ed** -d

Overstrand 'əʊ.və.strænd (US) 'oʊ.vɚ-

overstretch ˌəʊ.və'stretʃ (US) ˌoʊ.vɚ'- **-es** -ɪz **-ing** -ɪŋ **-ed** -t

overstrung *in state of nervous tension:* ˌəʊ.və'strʌŋ (US) ˌoʊ.vɚ'- *of piano:* 'əʊ.və.strʌŋ (US) 'oʊ.vɚ-

oversubscrib|e ˌəʊ.və.səb'skraɪb (US) ˌoʊ.vɚ- **-es** -z **-ing** -ɪŋ **-ed** -d

oversubscription ˌəʊ.və.səb'skrɪp.ʃᵊn (US) ˌoʊ.vɚ-

oversupp|ly ˌəʊ.və.sə'pl|aɪ (US) ˌoʊ.vɚ- **-ies** -aɪz

overt əʊ'vɜːt; 'əʊ.vɜːt (US) oʊ'vɜːrt, '-- **-ly** -li **-ness** -nəs, -nɪs

over|take ˌəʊ.və|'teɪk (US) ˌoʊ.vɚ'- **-takes** -'teɪks **-taking** -'teɪ.kɪŋ **-took** -'tʊk **-taken** -'teɪ.kᵊn, -kᵊŋ (US) -kᵊn

overtask ˌəʊ.və'tɑːsk (US) ˌoʊ.vɚ'tæsk **-s** -s **-ing** -ɪŋ **-ed** -t

overtax ˌəʊ.və'tæks (US) ˌoʊ.vɚ'- **-es** -ɪz **-ing** -ɪŋ **-ed** -t

over-the-counter ˌəʊ.və.ðə'kaʊn.təʳ (US) ˌoʊ.vɚ.ðə'kaʊn.t̬ɚ *stress shift:* ˌover-the-counter 'sales

over-the-top ˌəʊ.və.ðə'tɒp (US) ˌoʊ.vɚ.ðə'tɑːp *stress shift:* ˌover-the-top 'speech

Note: See also **OTT**.

overthrow (*n.*) 'əʊ.və.θrəʊ (US) 'oʊ.vɚ.θroʊ **-s** -z

overthrow (*v.*) ˌəʊ.və'θrəʊ (US) ˌoʊ.vɚ'θroʊ, '--- **-s** -z **-ing** -ɪŋ

overthrew ˌəʊ.və'θruː (US) ˌoʊ.vɚ'-, '--- **overthrown** ˌəʊ.və'θrəʊn (US) ˌoʊ.vɚ'θroʊn, '---

overthrust 'əʊ.və.θrʌst (US) 'oʊ.vɚ- **-s** -s

overtime 'əʊ.və.taɪm (US) 'oʊ.vɚ-

overtir|e ˌəʊ.və'taɪəʳ (US) ˌoʊ.vɚ'taɪɚ **-es** -z **-ing** -ɪŋ **-ed** -d

overtone 'əʊ.və.təʊn (US) 'oʊ.vɚ.toʊn **-s** -z

overtop ˌəʊ.və'tɒp (US) ˌoʊ.vɚ'tɑːp **-s** -s **-ping** -ɪŋ **-ped** -t

Overtoun 'əʊ.və.tᵊn (US) 'oʊ.vɚ-

Overtown 'əʊ.və.tᵊn (US) 'oʊ.vɚ-

over-trump ˌəʊ.və'trʌmp (US) ˌoʊ.vɚ'- **-s** -s **-ing** -ɪŋ **-ed** -t

overture 'əʊ.və.tjʊəʳ, -tjəʳ, -tʃʊəʳ, -tʃəʳ (US) 'oʊ.vɚ.tʃɚ, -tʃʊr **-s** -z

overturn (*n.*) 'əʊ.və.tɜːn (US) 'oʊ.vɚ.tɜːrn **-s** -z

overturn (*v.*) ˌəʊ.və'tɜːn (US) ˌoʊ.vɚ'tɜːrn **-s** -z **-ing** -ɪŋ **-ed** -d

overus|e (*v*) ˌəʊ.və'juːz (US) ˌoʊ.vɚ'- **-es** -ɪz **-ing** -ɪŋ **-ed** -d

overuse (*n*) ˌəʊ.və'juːs (US) ˌoʊ.vɚ'-

overval|ue ˌəʊ.və'væl|.juː (US) ˌoʊ.vɚ'- **-ues** -juːz **-uing** -juː.ɪŋ **-ued** -juːd

overview 'əʊ.və.vjuː (US) 'oʊ.vɚ- **-s** -z

overweening ˌəʊ.və'wiː.nɪŋ (US) ˌoʊ.vɚ'-, 'oʊ.vɚˌwiː- **-ly** -li *stress shift:* ˌoverweening 'pride

overweight (*n.*) 'əʊ.və.weɪt (US) 'oʊ.vɚ- **-s** -s

overweight (*adj.*) ˌəʊ.və'weɪt (US) ˌoʊ.vɚ'-, '--- *stress shift, British only:* ˌoverweight 'person

overweigh|t (*v.*) ˌəʊ.və'weɪ|t (US) ˌoʊ.vɚ'-, '--- **-ts** -ts **-ting** -tɪŋ (US) -t̬ɪŋ **-ted** -tɪd (US) -t̬ɪd

overwhelm ˌəʊ.və'*h*welm (US) ˌoʊ.vɚ'- **-s** -z **-ing/ly** -ɪŋ/li **-ed** -d

overwind ˌəʊ.və'waɪnd (US) ˌoʊ.vɚ'-, '--- **-s** -z **-ing** -ɪŋ **overwound** ˌəʊ.və'waʊnd (US) ˌoʊ.vɚ'-, '---

overwint|er ˌəʊ.və'wɪn.t|əʳ (US) ˌoʊ.vɚ'wɪn.t̬|ɚ **-ers** -əz (US) -ɚz **-ering** -ᵊr.ɪŋ **-ered** -əd (US) -ɚd

overwork (*n.*) 'əʊ.və.wɜːk (US) 'oʊ.vɚ.wɜːrk

overwork (*v.*) ˌəʊ.və'wɜːk (US) ˌoʊ.vɚ'wɜːrk, '--- **-s** -s **-ing** -ɪŋ **-ed** -t **-er/s** -əʳ/z (US) -ɚ/z *stress shift:* ˌoverworked 'editor

overwrit|e ˌəʊ.vᵊr'aɪt (US) ˌoʊ.vɚ'raɪt **-es** -s **-ing** -ɪŋ **overwrote** ˌəʊ.vᵊr'əʊt (US) ˌoʊ.vɚ'roʊt **overwritten** ˌəʊ.vᵊr'ɪt.ᵊn (US) ˌoʊ.vɚ'rɪt-

overwrought ˌəʊ.vᵊr'ɔːt (US) ˌoʊ.vɚ'rɑːt, -'rɔːt *stress shift:* ˌoverwrought 'person

overzealous ˌəʊ.vəˈzel.əs (US) ˌoʊ.vɚˈ- *stress shift:* ˌoverzealous ˈfollower

Ovett ˈəʊ.vet, -ˈ- (US) ˈoʊ.vet, -ˈ-

Ovid *Latin poet:* ˈɒv.ɪd (US) ˈɑː.vɪd *US surname:* ˈəʊ.vɪd (US) ˈoʊ-

Ovidian əʊˈvɪd.i.ən, ɒvˈɪd- (US) oʊˈvɪd-

Oviedo ˌɒv.iˈeɪ.dəʊ (US) oʊˈvjeɪ.doʊ, -ðoʊ

oviform ˈəʊ.vɪ.fɔːm (US) ˈoʊ.vɪ.fɔːrm

ovine ˈəʊ.vaɪn (US) ˈoʊ-

Ovingdean ˈɒv.ɪŋ.diːn (US) ˈɑː.vɪŋ-

Ovingham ˈɒv.ɪn.dʒəm (US) ˈɑː.vɪn-

Ovington *in North Yorkshire, street in London:* ˈɒv.ɪŋ.tən (US) ˈɑː.vɪŋ- *in Norfolk, surname:* ˈəʊ.vɪŋ.tən (US) ˈoʊ-

oviparous əʊˈvɪp.ər.əs (US) oʊ- **-ly** -li **-ness** -nəs, -nɪs

ovoid ˈəʊ.vɔɪd (US) ˈoʊ- **-s** -z

ovular ˈɒv.jə.ləʳ, ˈəʊ.vjə-, -vjʊ- (US) ˈɑː.vjuː.lɚ, ˈoʊ-, -vjə-

ovu|late ˈɒv.jə|.leɪt, ˈəʊ.vjə- (US) ˈɑː.vjuː-, ˈoʊ-, -vjə- **-lates** -leɪts **-lating** -leɪ.tɪŋ (US) -leɪ.t̬ɪŋ **-lated** -leɪ.tɪd (US) -leɪ.t̬ɪd

ovulation ˌɒv.jəˈleɪ.ʃən, ˌəʊ.vjəˈ-, -vjʊˈ- (US) ˌɑː.vjuːˈ-, ˌoʊ-, -vjəˈ-

ovule ˈɒv.juːl, ˈəʊ.vjuːl (US) ˈɑː-, ˈoʊ- **-s** -z

ov|um ˈəʊ.v|əm (US) ˈoʊ- **-a** -ə

Owbridge ˈəʊ.brɪdʒ (US) ˈoʊ-

ow|e əʊ (US) oʊ **-es** -z **-ing** -ɪŋ **-ed** -d

Owen ˈəʊ.ɪn (US) ˈoʊ- **-s** -z

Ower aʊəʳ (US) aʊɚ

Owers əʊəz, aʊəz (US) oʊɚz, aʊɚz

owing (*from* **owe**) ˈəʊ.ɪŋ (US) ˈoʊ-

owl aʊl **-s** -z

owler|y ˈaʊ.lər|.i **-ies** -iz

Owles əʊlz, aʊlz, uːlz (US) oʊlz, aʊlz, uːlz

owlet ˈaʊ.lət, -lɪt, -let (US) -lɪt **-s** -s

Owlett ˈaʊ.lɪt, -let (US) -lɪt

owlish ˈaʊ.lɪʃ **-ly** -li **-ness** -nəs, -nɪs

own əʊn (US) oʊn **-s** -z **-ing** -ɪŋ **-ed** -d **-er/s** -əʳ/z (US) -ɚ/z ˌ**own** ˈ**goal**

own-brand ˌəʊnˈbrænd, ˌəʊm-, ˈ-- (US) ˌoʊnˈ-, ˈ-- **-s** -z **-ing** -ɪŋ

owner-driver ˌəʊ.nəˈdraɪ.vəʳ (US) ˌoʊ.nɚˈdraɪ.vɚ **-s** -z *stress shift:* ˌowner-driver ˈtaxi

owner-occup|ier ˌəʊ.nərˈɒk.jə.p|aɪ.əʳ, -jʊ- (US) ˌoʊ.nɚˈɑː.kjuː.p|aɪ.ɚ, -kjə- **-iers** -aɪ.əz (US) -aɪ.ɚz **-ied** -aɪd

ownership ˈəʊ.nə.ʃɪp (US) ˈoʊ.nɚ-

own-label ˌəʊnˈleɪ.bəl (US) ˌoʊn-

Owsley ˈaʊz.li

owt aʊt, əʊt (US) aʊt, oʊt

ox ɒks (US) ɑːks **-en** -ən

oxalate ˈɒk.sə.leɪt, -lɪt, -lət (US) ˈɑːk.sə.leɪt **-s** -s

oxalic ɒkˈsæl.ɪk (US) ɑːkˈ-

oxalis ɒkˈsɑː.lɪs, -ˈsæl.ɪs, -ˈseɪ.lɪs; ˈɒk.sə.lɪs (US) ˈɑːk.sə.lɪs; ɑːkˈsæl.ɪs

oxbow ˈɒks.bəʊ (US) ˈɑːks.boʊ **-s** -z

Oxbridge ˈɒks.brɪdʒ (US) ˈɑːks-

Oxbrow ˈɒks.braʊ (US) ˈɑːks-

oxen (*plur. of* **ox**) ˈɒk.sən (US) ˈɑːk-

Oxenden ˈɒk.sən.dən (US) ˈɑːk-

Oxenford ˈɒk.sən.fɔːd, -fəd (US) ˈɑːk.sən.fɔːrd, -fɚd

Oxenham ˈɒk.sən.əm (US) ˈɑːk-

Oxenhope ˈɒk.sən.həʊp (US) ˈɑːk.sən.hoʊp

oxer ˈɒk.səʳ (US) ˈɑːk.sɚ **-s** -z

oxeye ˈɒks.aɪ (US) ˈɑːk.saɪ **-s** -z **-d** -d

Oxfam ˈɒks.fæm (US) ˈɑːks-

Oxford ˈɒks.fəd (US) ˈɑːks.fɚd **-shire** -ʃəʳ, -ˌʃɪəʳ (US) -ʃɚ, -ˌʃɪr

oxidant ˈɒk.sɪ.dənt, -sə- (US) ˈɑːk.sɪ- **-s** -s

oxi|date ˈɒk.sɪ|.deɪt, -sə- (US) ˈɑːk.sɪ- **-dates** -deɪts **-dating** -deɪ.tɪŋ (US) -deɪ.t̬ɪŋ **-dated** -deɪ.tɪd (US) -deɪ.t̬ɪd

oxidation ˌɒk.sɪˈdeɪ.ʃən, -səˈ- (US) ˌɑːk.sɪˈ-

oxide ˈɒk.saɪd (US) ˈɑːk- **-s** -z

oxidization, -isa- ˌɒk.sɪ.daɪˈzeɪ.ʃən, -sə-, -dɪˈ- (US) ˌɑːk.sɪ.dɪˈ-

oxidiz|e, -is|e ˈɒk.sɪ.daɪz, -sə- (US) ˈɑːk.sɪ- **-es** -ɪz **-ing** -ɪŋ **-ed** -d **-er/s** -əʳ/z (US) -ɚ/z **-able** -ə.bl̩

Oxley ˈɒk.sli (US) ˈɑːk-

oxlip ˈɒk.slɪp (US) ˈɑːk- **-s** -s

oxo (O®) ˈɒk.səʊ (US) ˈɑːk.soʊ

Oxon. ˈɒk.sən, -sɒn (US) ˈɑːk.sən, -sɑːn

Oxonian ɒkˈsəʊ.ni.ən (US) ɑːkˈsoʊ- **-s** -z

Oxshott ˈɒk.ʃɒt (US) ˈɑːk.ʃɑːt

oxtail ˈɒks.teɪl (US) ˈɑːks- **-s** -z ˌ**oxtail** ˈ**soup**

Oxted ˈɒk.stɪd (US) ˈɑːk-

ox-tongue ˈɒks.tʌŋ (US) ˈɑːks- **-s** -z

Oxus ˈɒk.səs (US) ˈɑːk-

oxy- ɒk.sɪ-, -si-; ɒkˈsɪ (US) ɑːk.sɪ-, -si-; ɑːkˈsɪ-

Note: Prefix. Normally either takes primary or secondary stress on the first syllable, e.g. **oxygen** /ˈɒk.sɪ.dʒən (US) ˈɑːk-/, **oxychloride** /ˌɒk.sɪˈklɔː.raɪd (US) ˌɑːk.sɪˈklɔːr.aɪd/, or primary stress on the second syllable, e.g. **oxygenous** /ɒkˈsɪdʒ.ən.əs (US) ɑːk-/.

oxyacetylene ˌɒk.si.əˈset.əl.iːn, -ɪ.liːn, -lɪn (US) ˌɑːk.si.əˈset̬.əl.iːn, -ɪn

oxychloride ˌɒk.sɪˈklɔː.raɪd (US) ˌɑːk.sɪˈklɔːr.aɪd **-s** -z

oxygen ˈɒk.sɪ.dʒən, -sə- (US) ˈɑːk.sɪ-

oxyge|nate ˈɒk.sɪ.dʒə|.neɪt, -sə-, -dʒɪ-; (US) ˈɑːk.sɪ.dʒə- **-nates** -neɪts **-nating** -neɪ.tɪŋ (US) -neɪ.t̬ɪŋ **-nated** -neɪ.tɪd (US) -neɪ.t̬ɪd

oxygenation ˌɒk.sɪ.dʒəˈneɪ.ʃən, -sə-, -dʒɪˈ-; (US) ˌɑːk.sɪ.dʒəˈ-

oxygeniz|e, -is|e ˈɒk.sɪ.dʒə.naɪz, -sə- (US) ˈɑːk.sɪ- **-es** -ɪz **-ing** -ɪŋ **-ed** -d

oxygenous ɒkˈsɪdʒ.ən.əs, -ɪ.nəs (US) ɑːk-

oxyhaemoglobin ˌɒk.siˌhiː.məʊˈgləʊ.bɪn (US) ˌɑːk.siˌhiː.məˈgloʊ-, -moʊˈ-

oxyhydrogen ˌɒk.siˈhaɪ.drə.dʒən, -drɪ- (US) ˌɑːk.siˈhaɪ.drə-

oxymoron ˌɒk.sɪˈmɔː.rɒn, -rən (US) ˌɑːk.sɪˈmɔːr.ɑːn **-s** -z

oxytone ˈɒk.sɪ.təʊn (US) ˈɑːk.sɪ.toʊn **-s** -z

oyer ˈɔɪ.əʳ (US) -ɚ ˌ**oyer and** ˈ**terminer**

oyes, oyez əʊˈjes, -ˈjez, -ˈjeɪ, ˈ-- (US) ˈoʊ.jes, -jez, -jeɪ

oyster (O) ˈɔɪ.stəʳ (US) -stɚ **-s** -z

oyster-catcher ˈɔɪ.stəˌkætʃ.əʳ (US) -stɚˌkætʃ.ɚ **-s** -z

Oystermouth ˈɔɪ.stə.maʊθ (US) -stɚ-

oz. (*abbrev. for* **ounce/s**) *singular:* aʊnts *plural:* ˈaʊnt.sɪz

Oz ɒz (US) ɑːz

Ozalid® ˈəʊ.zəl.ɪd, ˈɒz.əl- (US) ˈɑː.zəl- **-s** -z

Ozanne əʊˈzæn (US) oʊ-

Ozarks ˈəʊ.zɑːks (US) ˈoʊ.zɑːrks

ozokerite əʊˈzəʊ.kər.ɪt, ɒzˈəʊ-, əˈzəʊ- (US) oʊˈzoʊ.kə.raɪt; ˌoʊ.zoʊˈkɪr.aɪt

ozone ˈəʊ.zəʊn (US) ˈoʊ.zoʊn ˈ**ozone** ˌ**layer**

ozone-friendly ˌəʊ.zəʊnˈfrend.li (US) ˌoʊ.zoʊnˈ- *stress shift:* ˌozone-friendly ˈchemicals

ozonic əʊˈzɒn.ɪk (US) oʊˈzɑː.nɪk

ozoniferous ˌəʊ.zəʊˈnɪf.ər.əs (US) ˌoʊ.zəˈ-

ozonosphere əʊˈzɒn.ə.sfɪəʳ, -ˈzəʊ.nə- (US) oʊˈzoʊ.nə.sfɪr

Ozymandias ˌɒz.ɪˈmæn.di.əs, -æs (US) ˌɑː.zi-

Ozzie ˈɒz.i (US) ˈɑː.zi

P

p (P) piː **-'s** -z ˌ**p's and 'q's**
pa pɑː **-s** -z
PA ˌpiːˈeɪ
Pa. (*abbrev. for* **Pennsylvania**) ˌpent.sɪlˈveɪ.ni.ə, -sᵊlˈ-, ˈ-njə (US) -sᵊlˈveɪ.njə, ˈ-ni.ə
pa'anga pɑːˈæŋ.gə, -ə (US) -ˈɑːŋ.gə, ˈpɑːŋ-
pabulum ˈpæb.jə.ləm, -jʊ-
pac|e (*n. v.*) peɪs **-es** -ɪz **-ing** -ɪŋ **-ed** -t **-er/s** -əʳ/z (US) -ɚ/z ˌ**put someone** ˌ**through their 'paces**
pace (*prep.*) ˈpeɪ.si, ˈpɑː.tʃeɪ, -keɪ
pacemaker ˈpeɪsˌmeɪ.kəʳ (US) -kɚ **-s** -z
pace-setter ˈpeɪsˌset.əʳ (US) -ˌset̬.ɚ **-s** -z
Pachmann ˈpɑːk.mən, -mɑːn
pachyderm ˈpæk.ɪ.dɜːm (US) -ə.dɜːrm **-s** -z
pachydermatous ˌpæk.ɪˈdɜː.mə.təs (US) -əˈdɜːr.mə.t̬əs
pacific (P) pəˈsɪf.ɪk **-ally** -ᵊl.i, -li
pacification ˌpæs.ɪ.fɪˈkeɪ.ʃᵊn, ˌ-ə- (US) ˌ-ə- **-s** -z
pacificatory pəˈsɪf.ɪ.kə.tᵊr.i, pæsˈɪf-, ˌpæs.ɪ.fɪˈkeɪ-, ˌ-ə-; ˈ-ə- (US) pəˈsɪf.ɪ.kə.tɔːr-
pacificist pəˈsɪf.ɪ.sɪst, pæsˈɪf- (US) pəˈsɪf- **-s** -s
pacifism ˈpæs.ɪ.fɪ.zᵊm, ˈ-ə- (US) ˈ-ə-
pacifist ˈpæs.ɪ.fɪst, ˈ-ə- (US) ˈ-ə- **-s** -s
paci|fy ˈpæs.ɪ|.faɪ, ˈ-ə- (US) ˈ-ə- **-fies** -faɪz **-fying** -faɪ.ɪŋ **-fied** -faɪd **-fier/s** -faɪ.əʳ/z (US) -faɪ.ɚ/z
Pacino pəˈtʃiː.nəʊ (US) -noʊ
pack pæk **-s** -s **-ing** -ɪŋ **-ed** -t **-er/s** -əʳ/z (US) -ɚ/z ˈ**pack** ˌ**ice** ; ˈ**packing** ˌ**case**
packag|e ˈpæk.ɪdʒ **-es** -ɪz **-ing** -ɪŋ **-ed** -d ˌ**package 'holiday** ; ˈ**package** ˌ**store**
Packard ˈpæk.ɑːd (US) -ɚd
packed pækt
Packer ˈpæk.əʳ (US) -ɚ
packet ˈpæk.ɪt **-s** -s
packhors|e ˈpæk.hɔːs (US) -hɔːrs **-es** -ɪz
packing|house ˈpæk.ɪŋ|.haʊs **-houses** -haʊ.zɪz
pack|man ˈpæk|.mən, -mæn **-men** -mən (US) -mən, -men
Pac-man® ˈpæk.mæn
pact pækt **-s** -s
pactum ˈpæk.təm
pac|y ˈpeɪ.s|i **-ier** -i.əʳ (US) -i.ɚ **-iest** -i.ɪst
pad pæd **-s** -z **-ding** -ɪŋ **-ded** -ɪd ˌ**padded 'cell**
Padang ˈpɑː.dɑːŋ (US) pɑːˈdɑːŋ
Paddington ˈpæd.ɪŋ.tən
paddl|e ˈpæd.l̩ **-es** -z **-ing** -ɪŋ, ˈpæd.lɪŋ **-ed** -d **-er/s** -əʳ/z, ˈpæd.ləʳ/z (US) ˈpæd.l̩.ɚ/z, ˈpæd.lɚ/z ˈ**paddle** ˌ**steamer** ; ˈ**paddle** ˌ**wheel**
paddleboard ˈpæd.l̩.bɔːd (US) -bɔːrd **-s** -z
paddling-pool ˈpæd.l̩.ɪŋ.puːl, ˈ-lɪŋ-
paddock (P) ˈpæd.ək **-s** -s
padd|y (P) ˈpæd|.i **-ies** -iz
paddyfield ˈpæd.i.fiːld **-s** -z
paddywagon ˈpæd.iˌwæg.ᵊn
Paderewski ˌpæd.ᵊrˈef.ski, -ᵊrˈev- (US) ˌpæd.əˈ-, ˌpɑː.dəˈ-
Padiham ˈpæd.i.əm
padlock ˈpæd.lɒk (US) -lɑːk **-s** -s **-ing** -ɪŋ **-ed** -t
Padraic ˈpɑː.drɪk, ˈpæt.rɪk (US) ˈpɑː.drɪk, -drɪg
Padraic Colum ˌpɑː.drɪkˈkɒl.əm, ˌpæt.rɪk- (US) ˌpɑː.drɪkˈkɑː.ləm, -drɪgˈ-
padre ˈpɑː.dreɪ, -dri **-s** -z
padrone pædˈrəʊ.neɪ, pəˈdrəʊ-, -ni (US) pəˈdroʊ- **-s** -z
Padstow ˈpæd.stəʊ (US) -stoʊ
Padu|a ˈpæd.ju|.ə (US) ˈpædʒ.uː-, ˈpæd.juː- **-an/s** -ən/z
paean ˈpiː.ən **-s** -z
paederast ˈpiː.dᵊr.æst, ˈped.ᵊr- (US) ˈped.ə.ræst **-s** -s **-y** -i
paediatric ˌpiː.diˈæt.rɪk **-s** -s
paediatrician ˌpiː.di.əˈtrɪʃ.ᵊn **-s** -z
paedophile ˈpiː.dəʊ.faɪl (US) ˈped.oʊ-, ˈpiː.doʊ-, -də- **-s** -z
paedophili|a ˌpiː.dəʊˈfɪl.i|.ə (US) ˌped.oʊˈfiː.li-, ˌpiː.doʊˈ-, -dəˈ-, -ˈfiːl.j|ə **-ac/s** -æk/s
paella paɪˈel.ə (US) pɑːˈjel-, -ˈeɪ.jɑː **-s** -z
paeon ˈpiː.ən **-s** -z
paeonic piːˈɒn.ɪk (US) -ˈɑː.nɪk
paeon|y ˈpiː.ə.n|i **-ies** -iz
pagan ˈpeɪ.gᵊn **-s** -z
Pagani pəˈgɑː.ni (US) pə-, pɑː-
Paganini ˌpæg.əˈniː.ni
paganism ˈpeɪ.gᵊn.ɪ.zᵊm
paganiz|e, -is|e ˈpeɪ.gᵊn.aɪz **-es** -ɪz **-ing** -ɪŋ **-ed** -d
pag|e (P) peɪdʒ **-es** -ɪz **-ing** -ɪŋ **-ed** -d
pageant ˈpædʒ.ənt **-s** -s
pageantry ˈpædʒ.ən.tri
pageboy ˈpeɪdʒ.bɔɪ
pager ˈpeɪ.dʒəʳ (US) -dʒɚ **-s**
Paget ˈpædʒ.ɪt
paginal ˈpædʒ.ɪ.nᵊl, ˈpeɪ.dʒɪ- (US) ˈpædʒ.ə-
pagin|ate ˈpædʒ.ɪ.n|eɪt, ˈpeɪ.dʒɪ-, -dʒᵊn|.eɪt (US) ˈpædʒ.ᵊn- **-ates** -eɪts **-ating** -eɪ.tɪŋ (US) -eɪ.t̬ɪŋ **-ated** -eɪ.tɪd (US) -eɪ.t̬ɪd
pagination ˌpædʒ.ɪˈneɪ.ʃᵊn, ˌpeɪ.dʒɪ-, -dʒᵊnˈeɪ- (US) ˌpædʒ.ᵊnˈeɪ- **-s** -z
Pagliacci ˌpæl.iˈɑː.tʃi, -ˈætʃ.i (US) pɑːˈjɑː.tʃi
Pagnell ˈpæg.nəl
pagoda pəˈgəʊ.də (US) -ˈgoʊ- **-s** -z
pah pɑː
Pahang pəˈhʌŋ, -ˈhæŋ (US) -ˈhɑːŋ, pɑː-
Note: Usually pronounced /pəˈhʌŋ/ in Malaya.
paid (*from* **pay**) peɪd
Paige peɪdʒ
Paignton ˈpeɪn.tən (US) -tᵊn
pail peɪl **-s** -z **-ful/s** -fʊl/z
paillass|e ˈpæl.i.æs, ˌ--ˈ- (US) pælˈjæs, ˈ-- **-es** -ɪz
paillette pælˈjet, ˌpæl.iˈet (US) ˌpælˈjet, ˈpɑː.jet **-s** -s
pain peɪn **-s** -z **-ing** -ɪŋ **-ed** -d ˌ**pain in the 'neck** ; **be at** ˌ**pains to 'do something**
Pain(e) peɪn
painful ˈpeɪn.fᵊl, -fʊl **-ly** -i **-ness** -nəs, -nɪs
painkill|er ˈpeɪnˌkɪl|.əʳ, ˈpeɪŋ- (US) ˈpeɪnˌkɪl|.ɚ **-ers** -əz (US) -ɚz **-ing** -ɪŋ
painless ˈpeɪn.ləs, -lɪs **-ly** -li **-ness** -nəs, -nɪs
painstaking ˈpeɪnzˌteɪ.kɪŋ, ˈpeɪns- (US) ˈpeɪnz- **-ly** -li
Painswick ˈpeɪnz.wɪk
paint peɪnt **-s** -s **-ing/s** -ɪŋ/z (US) ˈpeɪn.t̬ɪŋ **-ed** -ɪd (US) ˈpeɪn.t̬ɪd **-er/s** -əʳ/z (US) ˈpeɪn.t̬ɚ/z ˌ**painted 'lady**
paintball ˈpeɪnt.bɔːl (US) -bɔːl, -bɑːl **-ing** -ɪŋ **-er/s** -əʳ/z (US) -ɚ/z
paintbox ˈpeɪnt.bɒks (US) -bɑːks **-es** -ɪz
paintbrush ˈpeɪnt.brʌʃ **-es** -ɪz
Painter ˈpeɪn.təʳ (US) -t̬ɚ
painterly ˈpeɪn.tᵊl.i (US) -t̬ɚ.li
paintwork ˈpeɪnt.wɜːk (US) -wɜːrk
paint|y ˈpeɪn.t|i (US) -t̬|i **-ier** -i.əʳ (US) -i.ɚ **-iest** -i.ɪst, -i.əst
pair peəʳ (US) per **-s** -z **-ing** -ɪŋ **-ed** -d
pais|a ˈpaɪ.s|ɑː **-e** -eɪ **-as** -ɑːz
paisley (P) ˈpeɪz.li
pajama pəˈdʒɑː.mə (US) -ˈdʒɑː-, -ˈdʒæm.ə **-s** -z
pak-choi ˌpækˈtʃɔɪ, ˌbɒk-, ˌpɑːk- (US) ˌbɑːkˈtʃɔɪ
Pakeman ˈpeɪk.mən
Pakenham ˈpæk.ᵊn.əm
Paki ˈpæk.i **-s** -z
Pakistan ˌpɑː.kɪˈstɑːn, ˌpæk.ɪˈ-, -ˈstæn (US) ˈpæk.ɪ.stæn, ˈpɑː.kɪ.stɑːn; ˌpæk.ɪˈstæn, ˌpɑː.kɪˈstɑːn
Pakistani ˌpɑː.kɪˈstɑː.ni, ˌpæk.ɪˈ- **-s** -z
pakora pəˈkɔː.rə (US) -ˈkɔːr.ə
pal pæl **-s** -z
palac|e ˈpæl.ɪs, -əs (US) -əs **-es** -ɪz
paladin ˈpæl.ə.dɪn **-s** -z

palaeo- ˌpæl.i.əʊ-, ˌpeɪ.li.əʊ- US ˌpeɪ.li.oʊ-, -ə-
palaeobotany ˌpæl.i.əʊˈbɒt.ᵊn.i, ˌpeɪ.li- US ˌpeɪ.li.oʊˈbɑː.tᵊn-
Palaeocene ˈpæl.i.əʊ.siːn, ˈpeɪ.li- US ˈpeɪ.li.oʊ-, -ə-
palaeographic ˌpæl.i.əʊˈgræf.ɪk, ˌpeɪ.li- US ˌpeɪ.li.oʊˈ-, -əˈ-
palaeograph|y ˌpæl.iˈɒg.rə.f|i, ˌpeɪ.li- US ˌpeɪ.liˈɑː.grə- **-er/s** -əʳ/z US -ɚ/z
palaeolithic (P) ˌpæl.i.əʊˈlɪθ.ɪk, ˌpeɪ.li- US ˌpeɪ.li.oʊˈ-, -əˈ-
palaeontological ˌpæl.iˌɒn.təˈlɒdʒ.ɪ.kᵊl, ˌpeɪ.li- US ˌpeɪ.liˌɑːn.təˈlɑː.dʒɪ-
palaeontolog|y ˌpæl.i.ɒnˈtɒl.ə.dʒ|i, ˌpeɪ.li- US ˌpeɪ.li.ɑːnˈtɑː.lə- **-ist/s** -ɪsts
palaeotype ˈpæl.i.əʊ.taɪp, ˈpeɪ.li- US ˈpeɪ.li.oʊ-, -ə-
Palaeozoic ˌpæl.i.əʊˈzəʊ.ɪk, ˌpeɪ.li- US ˌpeɪ.li.oʊˈzoʊ-, -ə-
Palamedes ˌpæl.əˈmiː.diːz
Palamon ˈpæl.ə.mən, -mɒn US -mən, -mɑːn
palanquin ˌpæl.əŋˈkiːn US -ənˈ- **-s** -z
palatab|le ˈpæl.ə.tə.b|l̩, ˈ-ɪ- US -ə.t̬ə- **-ly** -li **-leness** -l̩.nəs, -nɪs
palatal ˈpæl.ə.tᵊl US -t̬ᵊl **-s** -z
palatalization, -isa- ˌpæl.ə.tᵊl.aɪˈzeɪ.ʃᵊn, pəˌlæt.ᵊl-, -ɪˈ- US ˌpæl.ə.t̬ᵊl.ɪˈ- **-s** -z
palataliz|e, -is|e ˈpæl.ə.tᵊl.aɪz, pəˈlæt.ᵊl- US ˈpæl.ə.t̬ə.laɪz **-es** -ɪz **-ing** -ɪŋ **-ed** -d
palate ˈpæl.ət, -ɪt US -ət **-s** -s
palatial pəˈleɪ.ʃᵊl US -ʃᵊl **-ly** -i
palatinate (P) pəˈlæt.ɪ.nət, -ᵊn.ət, -ɪt US -ᵊn.eɪt, -ɪt **-s** -s
palatine (P) ˈpæl.ə.taɪn US -taɪn, -tɪn **-s** -z
palatogram ˈpæl.ə.təʊ.græm, pəˈlæt.əʊ- US ˈpæl.ə.toʊ-, -t̬ə- **-s** -z
palatography ˌpæl.əˈtɒg.rə.fi US -ˈtɑː.grə-
palav|er pəˈlɑː.v|əʳ US -ˈlæv|.ɚ, -ˈlɑː.v|ɚ **-ers** -əz US -ɚz **-ering** -ᵊr.ɪŋ **-ered** -əd US -ɚd
palazzo pəˈlæt.səʊ, -sə; -ˈlæd.zəʊ, -zə US pəˈlɑːt.soʊ, pɑː- **paˌlazzo ˈpants**
pal|e peɪl **-er** -əʳ US -ɚ **-est** -ɪst, -əst **-ely** -li **-eness** -nəs, -nɪs **-es** -z **-ing** -ɪŋ **-ed** -d **ˌpale ˈale** ; **beˌyond the ˈpale**
palefac|e ˈpeɪl.feɪs **-es** -ɪz
paleo- ˌpæl.i.əʊ-, ˌpeɪ.li.əʊ- US ˈpeɪ.li.oʊ-, -ə-
paleobotany ˌpæl.i.əʊˈbɒt.ᵊn.i, ˌpeɪ.li- US ˌpeɪ.li.oʊˈbɑː.tᵊn-
Paleocene ˈpæl.i.əʊ.siːn, ˈpeɪ.li- US ˈpeɪ.li.oʊ-, -ə-
paleographic ˌpæl.i.əʊˈgræf.ɪk, ˌpeɪ.li- US ˌpeɪ.li.oʊˈ-, -əˈ-
paleograph|y ˌpæl.iˈɒg.rə.f|i, ˌpeɪ.li- US ˌpeɪ.liˈɑː.grə- **-er/s** -əʳ/z US -ɚ/z
paleolithic (P) ˌpæl.i.əʊˈlɪθ.ɪk, ˌpeɪ.li- US ˌpeɪ.li.oʊˈ-, -əˈ-
paleontological ˌpæl.iˌɒn.təˈlɒdʒ.ɪ.kᵊl, ˌpeɪ.li- US ˌpeɪ.liˌɑːn.təˈlɑː.dʒɪ-
paleontolog|y ˌpæl.i.ɒnˈtɒl.ə.dʒ|i, ˌpeɪ.li- US ˌpeɪ.li.ɑːnˈtɑː.lə- **-ist/s** -ɪst/s
paleotype ˈpæl.i.əʊ.taɪp, ˈpeɪ.li- US ˈpeɪ.li.oʊ-, -ə-
Palermo pəˈlɜː.məʊ, -ˈleə- US -ˈler.moʊ
Palestine ˈpæl.ə.staɪn, ˈ-ɪ- US -ə.staɪn
Palestinian ˌpæl.əˈstɪn.i.ən, -ɪˈ- US -əˈstɪn- **-s** -z
Palestrina ˌpæl.əˈstriː.nə, -ɪˈ- US -əˈstriː-
palette ˈpæl.ət, -ɪt, -et US -ɪt **-s** -s **ˈpalette ˌknife**
Paley ˈpeɪ.li
palfrey (P) ˈpɔːl.fri, ˈpɒl- US ˈpɔːl-, ˈpɑːl- **-s** -z
Palgrave ˈpɔːl.greɪv, ˈpæl- US ˈpæl-, ˈpɔːl-
Pali ˈpɑː.li
palimony ˈpæl.ɪ.mə.ni, ˈ-ə- US -ə.moʊ-
palimpsest ˈpæl.ɪm*p*.sest, -əm*p*- US -ɪm*p*- **-s** -s
Palin ˈpeɪ.lɪn
palindrome ˈpæl.ɪn.drəʊm, -ən- US -ɪn.droʊm **-s** -z
palindromic ˌpæl.ɪnˈdrɒm.ɪk, -ənˈ- US -ɪnˈdrɑː.mɪk, -ˈdroʊ-
paling ˈpeɪ.lɪŋ **-s** -z
palingenesis ˌpæl.ɪnˈdʒen.ə.sɪs, ˈ-ɪ- US ˈ-ə-
palinode ˈpæl.ɪ.nəʊd, ˈ-ə- US -ə.noʊd **-s** -z
palisad|e (P) ˌpæl.ɪˈseɪd, -əˈ- US -əˈ-, ˈ--- **-es** -z **-ing** -ɪŋ **-ed** -ɪd
palish ˈpeɪ.lɪʃ
Palk pɔːlk, pɒlk US pɔːlk, pɔːk
pall pɔːl **-s** -z **-ing** -ɪŋ **-ed** -d
palladi|an (P) pəˈleɪ.di|.ən **-um/s** -əm/z
Pallas ˈpæl.əs, -æs
pall-bearer ˈpɔːlˌbeə.rəʳ US -ˌber.ɚ, ˈpɑːl- **-s** -z
pallet ˈpæl.ɪt, -ət US -ɪt **-s** -s
palliass|e ˈpæl.i.æs, ˌ--ˈ- US pælˈjæs, ˈ-- **-es** -ɪz
palli|ate ˈpæl.i|.eɪt **-ates** -eɪts **-ating** -eɪ.tɪŋ US -eɪ.t̬ɪŋ **-ated** -eɪ.tɪd US -eɪ.t̬ɪd
palliation ˌpæl.iˈeɪ.ʃᵊn
palliative ˈpæl.i.ə.tɪv US -t̬ɪv **-s** -z
pallid ˈpæl.ɪd **-est** -ɪst, -əst **-ly** -li **-ness** -nəs, -nɪs
Palliser ˈpæl.ɪ.səʳ US -sɚ
palli|um ˈpæl.i|.əm **-ums** -əmz **-a** -ə
Pall Mall ˌpælˈmæl, ˌpelˈmel US ˌpælˈmæl, ˌpelˈmel, ˌpɔːlˈmɔːl *stress shift:* ˌPall Mall ˈClub
pall-mall ˌpælˈmæl US ˌpælˈmæl, ˌpelˈmel, ˌpɑːlˈmɑːl
pallor ˈpæl.əʳ US -ɚ
pally ˈpæl.i
palm pɑːm **-s** -z **-ing** -ɪŋ **-ed** -d **ˌPalm ˈBeach** ; **ˌPalm ˈSprings** ; **ˌPalm ˈSunday** ; **ˌgrease one's ˈpalm**
Palma ˈpæl.mə, ˈpɑː-, ˈpɑːl- US ˈpɑːl.mɑː
palmar ˈpæl.məʳ, -mɑːʳ US -mɚ, ˈpɑː*l*-
palma|te ˈpæl.meɪ|t, ˈpɑː-, -mɪ|t US ˈpæl.meɪ|t, ˈpɑːl-, ˈpɑː- **-ted** -tɪd US -t̬ɪd
palmer (P) ˈpɑː.məʳ US -mɚ **-s** -z
Palmerston ˈpɑː.mə.stᵊn US -mɚ-
palmist ˈpɑː.mɪst **-s** -s
palmistry ˈpɑː.mɪ.stri
palm-oil ˈpɑːm.ɔɪl, ˌ-ˈ- US ˈpɑːm.ɔɪl
Palmolive® pɑːˈmɒl.ɪv US -ˈmɑː.lɪv
palmtop ˈpɑːm.tɒp US -tɑːp **-s** -s
palm|y ˈpɑː.m|i **-ier** -i.əʳ US -i.ɚ **-iest** -i.ɪst, -i.əst
palmyra (P) pælˈmaɪə.rə US -ˈmaɪ- **-s** -z
Palo Alto ˌpæl.əʊˈæl.təʊ US -oʊˈæl.t̬oʊ
Palomar ˈpæl.əʊ.mɑːʳ US -ə.mɑːr
palomino ˌpæl.əˈmiː.nəʊ US -noʊ, -oʊˈ- **-s** -z
palooka pəˈluː.kə **-s** -z
palpability ˌpæl.pəˈbɪl.ə.ti, ˈ-ɪ- US -ə.t̬i
palpab|le ˈpæl.pə.b|l̩ **-ly** -li **-leness** -l̩.nəs, -nɪs
palpa|te (*v.*) pælˈpeɪ|t US ˈ-- **-tes** -ts **-ting** -tɪŋ US -t̬ɪŋ **-ted** -tɪd US -t̬ɪd
palpate (*adj.*) ˈpæl.peɪt US -peɪt, -pɪt
palpation pælˈpeɪ.ʃᵊn
palpi|tate ˈpæl.pɪ|.teɪt US -pə- **-tates** -teɪts **-tating** -teɪ.tɪŋ US -teɪ.t̬ɪŋ **-tated** -teɪ.tɪd US -teɪ.t̬ɪd
palpitation ˌpæl.pɪˈteɪ.ʃᵊn US -pəˈ- **-s** -z
palsgrave (P) ˈpɔːlz.greɪv US ˈpɔːlz-, ˈpælz- **-s** -z
pals|y ˈpɔːl.z|i, ˈpɒl- US ˈpɔːl-, ˈpɑːl- **-ies** -iz **-ied** -id
palt|er ˈpɔːl.t|əʳ, ˈpɒl- US ˈpɔːl.t̬|ɚ, ˈpɑːl- **-ers** -əz US -ɚz **-ering** -ᵊr.ɪŋ **-ered** -əd US -ɚd **-erer/s** -ᵊr.əʳ/z US -ɚ.ɚ/z
paltr|y ˈpɔːl.tr|i, ˈpɒl- US ˈpɔːl-, ˈpɑːl- **-ier** -i.əʳ US -i.ɚ **-iest** -i.ɪst, -i.əst **-ily** -ɪ.li, -ᵊl.i **-iness** -ɪ.nəs, -ɪ.nɪs
Pam pæm
Pamela ˈpæm.ᵊl.ə, -ɪ.lə US -ᵊl.ə
Pamir pəˈmɪəʳ US pɑːˈmɪr **-s** -z
Pampa ˈpæm.pə **-s** -z
pampas ˈpæm.pəs US ˈpæm.pəz, ˈpɑːm-, -pəs **ˈpampas ˌgrass**

pamp|er 'pæm.p|ləʳ US -p|ɚ **-ers** -əz US -ɚz **-ering** -ᵊr.ɪŋ **-ered** -əd US -ɚd **-erer/s** -ᵊr.əʳ/z US -ɚ.ɚ/z

Pampers® 'pæm.pəz US -pɚz

pamphlet 'pæm.flɪt, -flət US -flɪt **-s** -s

pamphleteer ˌpæm.flə'tɪəʳ, -flɪ'- US -flɪ'tɪr **-s** -z **-ing** -ɪŋ

Pamphyli|a pæm'fɪl.i|.ə **-an/s** -ən/z

Pamplona pæm'pləʊ.nə US pæm'ploʊ.nə, pɑːm-, -nɑː

pan (P) pæn **-s** -z **-ning** -ɪŋ **-ned** -d

panacea ˌpæn.ə'siː.ə **-s** -z

panach|e pə'næʃ, pæn'æʃ-, -'ɑːʃ US pə'næʃ, -'nɑːʃ **-es** -ɪz

Panadol® 'pæn.ə.dɒl US -dɑːl

panama (P) ˌpæn.ə'mɑː, '--- US '---, -mɔː **-s** -z ˌ**Panama Ca'nal** ; ˌ**Panama 'City** ; ˌ**panama 'hat**

Panamanian ˌpæn.ə'meɪ.ni.ən **-s** -z

Pan-American ˌpæn.ə'mer.ɪ.kən **-ism** -ɪ.zᵊm

Panasonic ˌpæn.ə'sɒn.ɪk US -'sɑː.nɪk

panatel(l)a ˌpæn.ə'tel.ə **-s** -z

pancake 'pæn.keɪk, 'pæŋ- US 'pæn- **-s** -s '**Pancake** ˌ**Day**

panchromatic ˌpæn.krəʊ'mæt.ɪk, ˌpæŋ- US ˌpæn.kroʊ'mæt̬-

Pancras 'pæŋ.krəs

pancreas 'pæŋ.kri.əs, -æs US 'pæn.kri.əs, 'pæŋ- **-es** -ɪz

pancreatic ˌpæŋ.kri'æt.ɪk US ˌpæn.kri'æt̬-, ˌpæŋ-

panda 'pæn.də **-s** -z '**panda** ˌ**car**

pandanus pæn'deɪ.nəs, -'dæn.əs **-es** -ɪz

pandect 'pæn.dekt **-s** -s

pandemic pæn'dem.ɪk **-s** -s

pandemonium (P) ˌpæn.də'məʊ.ni.əm, -dɪ'- US -də'moʊ- **-s** -z

pand|er 'pæn.d|əʳ US -ɚ **-ers** -əz US -ɚz **-ering** -ᵊr.ɪŋ **-ered** -əd US -ɚd

pandialectal ˌpæn,daɪə'lek.tᵊl

pandit (P) 'pæn.dɪt **-s** -s

pandora (P) pæn'dɔː.rə US -'dɔːr.ə **-s** -z **Panˌdora's 'box**

pandowd|y pæn'daʊ.d|i **-ies** -iz

pane peɪn **-s** -z

panegyric ˌpæn.ə'dʒɪr.ɪk, -ɪ'- US -ə'-, -'dʒaɪ.rɪk **-s** -s **-al** -ᵊl

panegyrist ˌpæn.ə'dʒɪr.ɪst, -ɪ'-, 'pæn.ə.dʒɪr-, -'ɪ- US ˌpæn.ə'dʒɪr-, -'dʒaɪ.rɪst **-s** -s

panegyriz|e, -is|e 'pæn.ə.dʒɪ.raɪz, '-ɪ-, -dʒᵊr.aɪz US -dʒə.raɪz **-es** -ɪz **-ing** -ɪŋ **-ed** -d

panel 'pæn.ᵊl **-s** -z **-(l)ing/s** -ɪŋ/z **-(l)ed** -d '**panel** ˌ**beater**

panel(l)ist 'pæn.ᵊl.ɪst **-s** -s

panettone ˌpæn.ə'təʊ.neɪ, -ni US -ɪ'toʊ- **-s** -z

pan-|fry 'pæn|.fry **-fries** -fraɪz **-frying** -fraɪ.ɪŋ **-fried** -fraɪd

panful 'pæn.fʊl **-s** -z

pang pæŋ **-s** -z

panga 'pæŋ.gə **-s** -z

Pangbourne 'pæŋ.bɔːn, -bən US -bɔːrn

Pangloss 'pæŋ.glɒs, 'pæn- US 'pæn.glɑːs

panglossian (P) pæŋ'glɒs.i.ən, pæn- US pæn'glɑː.si-

pangolin 'pæŋ.gəʊ.lɪn; pæŋ'gəʊ- US 'pæn.goʊ-, 'pæŋ-, -gə-; pæn'goʊ-, pæŋ- **-s** -z

panhandl|e 'pænˌhæn.dl̩ **-es** -z **-ing** -ɪŋ, -ˌhænd.lɪŋ **-ed** -d **-er/s** -əʳ/z US -ɚ/z, -ˌhænd.ləʳ/z US -lɚ/z

panic 'pæn.ɪk **-s** -s **-king** -ɪŋ **-ked** -t '**panic** ˌ**button** ; '**panic** ˌ**stations**

panicky 'pæn.ɪ.ki

panicle 'pæn.ɪ.kl̩ **-s** -z

panic-stricken 'pæn.ɪkˌstrɪk.ᵊn

Panini 'pɑː.nɪ.niː, -ni US pɑː'niː.ni

panjandr|um pæn'dʒæn.dr|əm, pən- US pæn- **-ums** -əmz **-a** -ə

Pankhurst 'pæŋk.hɜːst US -hɜːrst

panlectal ˌpæn'lek.tᵊl

panne pæn

pannier 'pæn.i.əʳ US '-jɚ, '-i.ɚ **-s** -z

pannikin 'pæn.ɪ.kɪn, '-ə- US '-ɪ- **-s** -z

Pannill 'pæn.ɪl

panopl|y 'pæn.ə.pl|i **-ies** -iz **-ied** -id

panorama ˌpæn.ᵊr'ɑː.mə US -ə'ræm.ə, -'rɑː.mə **-s** -z

panoramic ˌpæn.ᵊr'æm.ɪk, -'ɑː.mɪk US -ə'ræm.ɪk, -'rɑː.mɪk **-ally** -ᵊl.i US -li

panpipe 'pæn.paɪp, 'pæm- US 'pæn- **-s** -s

Pan-Slavism ˌpæn'slɑː.vɪ.zᵊm, -'slæv.ɪ-

pans|y 'pæn.z|i **-ies** -iz

pant pænt **-s** -s **-ing/ly** -ɪŋ/li US 'pæn.t̬ɪŋ/li **-ed** -ɪd US 'pæn.t̬ɪd

Pantagruel ˌpæn.tə.gru'el; 'pæn.tə.gru.əl, pæn'tæg.ru.əl US ˌpæn.t̬ə.gru'el; -'gruː.əl; pæn'tæg.ru.el

pantaloon ˌpæn.tᵊl'uːn, '--- US ˌpæn.t̬ᵊl'uːn, '- -- **-s** -z

pantechnicon pæn'tek.nɪ.kən **-s** -z

panthe|ism 'pænt.θi|.ɪ.zᵊm **-ist/s** -ɪst/s

pantheistic ˌpænt.θi'ɪs.tɪk **-al** -ᵊl

pantheon (P) 'pænt.θi.ən US -ɑːn, -ən **-s** -z

panther 'pænt.θəʳ US -θɚ **-s** -z

pantie girdle 'pæn.tiˌgɜː.dl̩ US -t̬iˌgɜːr- **-s** -z

panties 'pæn.tiz US -t̬iz

pantihose 'pæn.ti.həʊz US -t̬i.hoʊz

pantile 'pæn.taɪl **-s** -z

panto 'pæn.təʊ US -toʊ **-s** -z

pantograph 'pæn.təʊ.grɑːf, -græf US -t̬ə.græf **-s** -s

pantographic ˌpæn.təʊ'græf.ɪk US -t̬ə'- **-al** -ᵊl

pantomim|e 'pæn.tə.maɪm US -t̬ə- **-s** -z **-ist/s** -ɪst/s

pantomimic ˌpæn.təʊ'mɪm.ɪk US -t̬ə'- **-al** -ᵊl **-ally** -ᵊl.i, -li

pantr|y 'pæn.tr|i **-ies** -iz

pants pænts

pantsuit 'pænt.suːt, -sjuːt US -suːt **-s** -s

pantyhose 'pæn.ti.həʊz US -t̬i.hoʊz

pantyliner 'pæn.tiˌlaɪ.nəʳ US -t̬iˌlaɪ.nɚ **-s**

Panza 'pæn.zə

panzer 'pænt.səʳ, 'pæn.zəʳ US 'pæn.zɚ, 'pɑːnt.sɚ **-s** -z

pap pæp **-s** -s

papa pə'pɑː US 'pɑː.pə; pə'pɑː **-s** -z

papac|y (P) 'peɪ.pə.s|i **-ies** -iz

papal 'peɪ.pᵊl

papal|ism 'peɪ.pᵊl|.ɪ.zᵊm **-ist/s** -ɪst/s

Papandreou ˌpæp.æn'dreɪ.uː

paparazz|o ˌpæp.ᵊr'æt.s|əʊ US ˌpɑː.pɑː'rɑːt.s|oʊ **-i** -i

papaw 'pɔː.pɔː, pə'pɔː US pɔː'pɑː, -'ɔː, 'pɑː-, 'pɔː- **-s** -z

papaya pə'paɪ.ə US -'paɪ.ə, -'pɑː.jə **-s** -z

Papeete ˌpɑː.pi'eɪ.ti, -'iː-; pə'piː.ti US ˌpɑː.pi'eɪ.teɪ; pə'piː.ti

pap|er 'peɪ.p|əʳ US -ɚ **-ers** -əz US -ɚz **-ering** -ᵊr.ɪŋ **-ered** -əd US -ɚ **-erer/s** -ᵊr.əʳ/z US -ɚ.ɚ/z **-ery** -ᵊr.i ˌ**paper 'bag** ; '**paper** ˌ**boy** ; '**paper** ˌ**chase** ; '**paper** ˌ**clip** ; '**paper** ˌ**knife** ; ˌ**paper 'money** ; '**paper** ˌ**round** ; ˌ**paper 'tiger** ; '**paper** ˌ**trail**

paperback 'peɪ.pə.bæk US -pɚ- **-s** -s

paperbark 'peɪ.pə.bɑːk US -pɚ.bɑːrk **-s** -s

paperhang|er 'peɪ.pəˌhæŋ|.əʳ US -pɚˌhæŋ|.ɚ **-ers** -əz US -ɚz **-ing** -ɪŋ

paperweight 'peɪ.pə.weɪt US -pɚ- **-s** -s

paperwork 'peɪ.pə.wɜːk US -pɚ.wɜːrk

Paphlagoni|a ˌpæf.lə'gəʊ.ni|.ə US -'goʊ- **-an/s** -ən/z

Paphos *in Cyprus, ancient city:* 'peɪ.fɒs, 'pæf.ɒs US 'peɪ.fɑːs *modern town:* 'pæf.ɒs US 'peɪ.fɑːs

papier-mâché ˌpæp.i.eɪ'mæʃ.eɪ, ˌpeɪ.pə'- US ˌpeɪ.pɚ.mə'ʃeɪ, ˌpæp.jeɪ-

papill|a pə'pɪl|.ə **-ae** -iː

papillary pə'pɪl.ᵊr.i US 'pæp.ə.ler-; pə'pɪl.ɚ-

papillote 'pæp.ɪ.lɒt, -ləʊt, -jɒt US -ə.loʊt, 'pɑː.pə-, -joʊt **-s** -s

papist (P) 'peɪ.pɪst **-s** -s
papistry 'peɪ.pɪ.stri
papoos|e pə'puːs Ⓤⓢ pæp'uːs, pə'puːs **-es** -ɪz
Papp pæp
papp|us (P) 'pæp|.əs **-i** -aɪ
pappy 'pæp.i
paprika 'pæp.rɪ.kə; pə'priː- Ⓤⓢ pæp'riː-, pə'priː-
Papu|a 'pæp.u|.ə, 'pɑː.pu-, -pju- Ⓤⓢ 'pæp.ju|.ə, pɑː'puː- **-an/s** -ən/z ˌPapua New 'Guinea
Papworth 'pæp.wəθ, -wɜːθ Ⓤⓢ -wɚθ, -wɜːrθ
papyr|us pə'paɪə.r|əs Ⓤⓢ -'paɪ- **-i** -aɪ **-uses** -ə.sɪz
par (P) pɑːʳ Ⓤⓢ pɑːr
para- pær.ə-; pə'ræ- Ⓤⓢ per.ə-, pær.ə-; pə'ræ-
Note: Prefix. Normally either carries primary or secondary stress on the first syllable, e.g. **parachute** /'pær.ə.ʃuːt Ⓤⓢ 'per-/, **parabolic** /ˌpær.ə'bɒl.ɪk Ⓤⓢ ˌper.ə'bɑː.lɪk/, or primary stress on the second syllable, e.g. **paraboloid** /pə'ræb.əl.ɔɪd Ⓤⓢ -ə.lɔɪd/.
para *paratrooper, paramilitary:* 'pær.ə Ⓤⓢ 'per.ə, 'pær- **-s** -z
para *Turk or Yugoslav monetary unit:* 'pɑː.rə Ⓤⓢ 'pɑː.rɑː, -'- **-s** -z
Pará *Brazilian river:* pə'rɑː
parable 'pær.ə.bl̩ Ⓤⓢ 'per-, 'pær- **-s** -z
parabola pə'ræb.əl.ə **-s** -z
parabolic ˌpær.ə'bɒl.ɪk Ⓤⓢ ˌper.ə'bɑː.lɪk, ˌpær- **-al** -əl **-ally** -əl.i, -li
paraboloid pə'ræb.əl.ɔɪd Ⓤⓢ -ə.lɔɪd **-s** -z
Paracelsus ˌpær.ə'sel.səs Ⓤⓢ ˌper-, ˌpær-
paracetamol ˌpær.ə'siː.tə.mɒl, -'set.ə- Ⓤⓢ ˌper.ə'siː.t̬ə.mɑːl, ˌpær-, -'set̬.ə-, -moʊl **-s**
para|chute 'pær.ə|.ʃuːt Ⓤⓢ 'per-, 'pær- **-chutes** -ʃuːts **-chuting** -ˌʃuː.tɪŋ Ⓤⓢ -ˌʃuː.t̬ɪŋ **-chuted** -ˌʃuː.tɪd Ⓤⓢ -ˌʃuː.t̬ɪd
parachutist 'pær.əˌʃuː.tɪst Ⓤⓢ 'per.əˌʃuː.t̬ɪst, 'pær- **-s** -s
Paraclete 'pær.ə.kliːt Ⓤⓢ 'per-, 'pær-
parad|e pə'reɪd **-es** -z **-ing** -ɪŋ **-ed** -ɪd pa'rade ˌground
paradigm 'pær.ə.daɪm Ⓤⓢ 'per-, 'pær-, -dɪm **-s** -z
paradigmatic ˌpær.ə.dɪg'mæt.ɪk Ⓤⓢ ˌper.ə.dɪg'mæt̬-, ˌpær- **-al** -əl **-ally** -əl.i, -li
paradisal ˌpær.ə'daɪ.səl, -zəl Ⓤⓢ ˌper.ə'daɪ-, ˌpær-
paradis|e (P) 'pær.ə.daɪs Ⓤⓢ 'per-, 'pær-, -daɪz **-es** -ɪz
paradisiac ˌpær.ə'dɪs.i.æk, -'dɪz- Ⓤⓢ ˌper.ə'dɪs-, ˌpær-
paradisiacal ˌpær.ə.dɪ'saɪ.ə.kəl, -də'-, -'zaɪ- Ⓤⓢ ˌper.ə.dɪ'-, ˌpær-
Paradiso ˌpær.ə'diː.səʊ Ⓤⓢ ˌper.ə'diː.soʊ, ˌpær-
parador 'pær.ə.dɔːʳ Ⓤⓢ 'per.ə.dɔːr, 'pær- **paradores** ˌpær.ə'dɔː.reɪs, -rɪs Ⓤⓢ ˌper.ə'dɔːr.əs, ˌpær-, -'dɔːrz
parados 'pær.ə.dɒs Ⓤⓢ 'per.ə.dɑːs, 'pær- **-es** -ɪz
paradox 'pær.ə.dɒks Ⓤⓢ 'per.ə.dɑːks, 'pær- **-es** -ɪz
paradoxic|al ˌpær.ə'dɒk.sɪ.k|əl Ⓤⓢ ˌper.ə'dɑːk-, ˌpær- **-ally** -əl.i, -li **-alness** -əl.nəs, -nɪs
paraffin 'pær.ə.fɪn, -fiːn, ˌ--'- Ⓤⓢ 'per.ə.fɪn, 'pær-
paraffine ˌpær.ə'fiːn Ⓤⓢ 'per.ə.fɪn, 'pær-, -fiːn
paragliding 'pær.əˌglaɪ.dɪŋ Ⓤⓢ 'per.ə-, 'pær-
paragoge ˌpær.ə'gəʊ.dʒi Ⓤⓢ 'per.ə.goʊ-, 'pær- **-s** -z
paragogic ˌpær.ə'gɒdʒ.ɪk Ⓤⓢ ˌper.ə'gɑː.dʒɪk, ˌpær-
paragon 'pær.ə.gən Ⓤⓢ 'per.ə.gɑːn, 'pær-, -gən **-s** -z
paragraph 'pær.ə.grɑːf, -græf Ⓤⓢ 'per.ə.græf, 'pær- **-s** -s **-ing** -ɪŋ **-ed** -t
Paraguay 'pær.ə.gwaɪ, -gweɪ, ˌ--'- Ⓤⓢ 'per.ə.gweɪ, 'pær-, -gwaɪ
Paraguayan ˌpær.ə'gwaɪ.ən, -'gweɪ- Ⓤⓢ ˌper.ə'gweɪ-, ˌpær-, -'gwaɪ-
parakeet ˌpær.ə'kiːt, '--- Ⓤⓢ 'per.ə.kiːt, 'pær- **-s** -s
paraldehyde pə'ræl.dɪ.haɪd, pær'æl-, -də- Ⓤⓢ pə'ræl.də-
paralexia ˌpær.ə'lek.si.ə Ⓤⓢ ˌper-, ˌpær-
paralinguistic ˌpær.ə.lɪŋ'gwɪs.tɪk Ⓤⓢ ˌper-, ˌpær- **-s** -s **-ally** -əl.i, -li
parallax 'pær.ə.læks Ⓤⓢ 'per-, 'pær- **-es** -ɪz
parallel 'pær.ə.lel, -əl.əl Ⓤⓢ 'per-, 'pær- **-s** -z **-ing** -ɪŋ **-ed** -d **-ism** -ɪ.zəm ˌparallel 'bars
parallelepiped ˌpær.ə.lel'ep.ɪ.ped, -əl.ə'lep-; ˌpær.əˌlel.ə'paɪ- Ⓤⓢ ˌper.əˌlel.ə'paɪ-, ˌpær-, -'pɪp.əd, -ed **-s** -z
parallelogram ˌpær.ə'lel.ə.græm Ⓤⓢ ˌper-, ˌpær- **-s** -z
Paralympics ˌpær.ə'lɪm.pɪks Ⓤⓢ ˌper-, ˌpær-
paralys|e, -lyz|e 'pær.əl.aɪz Ⓤⓢ 'per-, 'pær- **-es** -ɪz **-ing** -ɪŋ **-ed** -d **-er/s** -əʳ/z Ⓤⓢ -ɚ/z
paralys|is pə'ræl.ə.s|ɪs, pər'æl-, '-ɪ- Ⓤⓢ '-ə- **-es** -iːz
paralytic ˌpær.ə'lɪt.ɪk Ⓤⓢ ˌper.ə'lɪt̬-, ˌpær- **-s** -s
paralyzation ˌpær.əl.aɪ'zeɪ.ʃən Ⓤⓢ ˌper.ə.lɪ'-, ˌpær-
Paramaribo ˌpær.ə'mær.ɪ.bəʊ Ⓤⓢ ˌper.ə'mer.ɪ.boʊ, ˌpær-, -'mær-
paramatta (P) ˌpær.ə'mæt.ə Ⓤⓢ ˌper.ə'mæt̬-, ˌpær-
paramecium ˌpær.ə'miː.si.əm Ⓤⓢ ˌper-, ˌpær-, -ʃi-
paramedic ˌpær.ə'med.ɪk Ⓤⓢ ˌper.ə'med-, ˌpær-, 'per.əˌmed-, 'pær- **-s** -s **-al** -əl
parameter pə'ræm.ɪ.təʳ, pər'æm-, '-ə- Ⓤⓢ -ə.t̬ɚ **-s** -z
parametric ˌpær.ə'met.rɪk Ⓤⓢ ˌper-, ˌpær- **-ally** -əl.i, -li
paramilitary ˌpær.ə'mɪl.ɪ.tər.i, '-ə- Ⓤⓢ ˌper.ə'mɪl.ə.ter-, ˌpær-
paramount (P) 'pær.ə.maʊnt Ⓤⓢ 'per-, 'pær- **-ly** -li
paramour 'pær.ə.mʊəʳ, -mɔːʳ Ⓤⓢ 'per.ə.mʊr, 'pær- **-s** -z
Paraná pær.æn'ɑː
paranoi|a ˌpær.ə'nɔɪ.ə Ⓤⓢ ˌper-, ˌpær- **-ac** -æk
paranoid 'pær.ən.ɔɪd Ⓤⓢ 'per.ə.nɔɪd, 'pær-
paranormal ˌpær.ə'nɔː.məl Ⓤⓢ ˌper.ə'nɔːr-, ˌpær- **-ly** -i
parape|t 'pær.ə.pɪ|t, -pe|t, -pə|t Ⓤⓢ 'per.ə.pe|t, 'pær-, -pə|t **-ts** -ts **-ted** -tɪd Ⓤⓢ -t̬ɪd
paraphernalia ˌpær.ə.fə'neɪ.li.ə Ⓤⓢ ˌper.ə.fɚ'neɪl.jə, ˌpær-, -'neɪ.li.ə
paraphras|e 'pær.ə.freɪz Ⓤⓢ 'per-, 'pær- **-es** -ɪz **-ing** -ɪŋ **-ed** -d
paraphrastic ˌpær.ə'fræs.tɪk Ⓤⓢ ˌper-, ˌpær- **-ally** -əl.i, -li
parapleg|ia ˌpær.ə'pliː.dʒ|ə, -dʒi|.ə Ⓤⓢ ˌper-, ˌpær- **-ic/s** -ɪk
paraprax|is ˌpær.ə'præk.s|ɪs Ⓤⓢ ˌper-, ˌpær- **-es** -ɪz
parapsychologic ˌpær.əˌsaɪ.kə'lɒdʒ.ɪk, -kəl'ɒdʒ- Ⓤⓢ ˌper.ə.saɪ.kə'lɑː.dʒɪ-, ˌpær- **-al** -əl **-ally** -əl.i, -li
parapsycholog|y ˌpær.ə.saɪ'kɒl.ə.dʒ|i, -psaɪ'- Ⓤⓢ ˌper.ə.saɪ'kɑː.lə-, ˌpær- **-ist/s** -ɪst/s
Paraquat® 'pær.ə.kwɒt, -kwæt Ⓤⓢ 'per.ə.kwɑːt, 'pær-
parasang 'pær.ə.sæŋ Ⓤⓢ 'per-, 'pær- **-s** -z
parascend|ing 'pær.əˌsen.d|ɪŋ Ⓤⓢ 'per-, 'pær- **-er/s** -əʳ/z Ⓤⓢ -ɚ/z
parasite 'pær.ə.saɪt Ⓤⓢ 'per-, 'pær- **-s** -s
parasitic ˌpær.ə'sɪt.ɪk Ⓤⓢ ˌper.ə'sɪt̬-, ˌpær- **-al** -əl **-ally** -əl.i, -li **-alness** -əl.nəs, -nɪs
parasitolog|y ˌpær.ə.saɪ'tɒl.ə.dʒ|i, -sɪ'- Ⓤⓢ ˌper.ə.saɪ'tɑː.lə-, ˌpær-, -sɪ'- **-ist/s** -ɪst/s
parasol 'pær.ə.sɒl, ˌ--'- Ⓤⓢ 'per.ə.sɔːl, 'pær-, -sɑːl **-s** -z

paratactic ˌpær.əˈtæk.tɪk US ˌper-, ˌpær-
parataxis ˌpær.əˈtæk.sɪs US ˌper-, ˌpær-
parathyroid ˌpær.əˈθaɪə.rɔɪd US ˌper.əˈθaɪ-, ˌpær-
paratone ˈpær.ə.təʊn US ˈper.ə.toʊn, ˈpær- **-s** -z
paratroop ˈpær.ə.truːp US ˈper-, ˈpær- **-s** -s **-er/s** -əʳ/z US -ɚ/z
paratyphoid ˌpær.əˈtaɪ.fɔɪd US ˌper-, ˌpær-
paravane ˈpær.ə.veɪn US ˈper-, ˈpær- **-s** -z
parboil ˈpɑː.bɔɪl US ˈpɑːr **-s** -z **-ing** -ɪŋ **-ed** -d
parcel ˈpɑː.sᵊl US ˈpɑːr- **-s** -z **-(l)ing** -ɪŋ **-(l)ed** -d **ˈparcel ˌpost**
parch pɑːtʃ US pɑːrtʃ **-es** -ɪz **-ing** -ɪŋ **-ed** -t **-edness** -t.nəs, -nɪs
Parcheesi® pɑːˈtʃiː.zi US pɑːr-
parchment (P) ˈpɑːtʃ.mənt US ˈpɑːrtʃ- **-s** -s
pard pɑːd US pɑːrd **-s** -z
Pardoe ˈpɑː.dəʊ US ˈpɑːr.doʊ
pardon ˈpɑː.dᵊn US ˈpɑːr- **-s** -z **-ing** -ɪŋ **-ed** -d **-er/s** -əʳ/z US -ɚ/z
pardonab|le ˈpɑː.dᵊn.ə.b|l̩ US ˈpɑːr- **-ly** -li **-leness** -l̩.nəs, -nɪs
par|e peəʳ US per **-es** -z **-ing** -ɪŋ **-ed** -d
paregoric ˌpær.ɪˈɡɒr.ɪk, -əˈ- US ˌper.əˈɡɔːr.ɪk, ˌpær-
paren|t ˈpeə.rᵊn|t US ˈper.ᵊn|t, ˈpær- **-ts** -ts **-tage** -tɪdʒ US -t̬ɪdʒ
parental pəˈren.tᵊl **-ly** -i
parenthes|is pəˈren*t*.θə.s|ɪs, -θɪ- US -θə- **-es** -iːz
parenthesiz|e, -is|e pəˈren*t*.θə.saɪz, -θɪ- US -θə- **-es** -ɪz **-ing** -ɪŋ **-ed** -d
parenthetic ˌpær.ᵊnˈθet.ɪk, -enˈ- US ˌper.ᵊnˈθet̬-, ˌpær- **-al** -ᵊl **-ally** -ᵊl.i, -li
parenthood ˈpeə.rᵊnt.hʊd US ˈper.ᵊnt-, ˈpær-
parenting ˈpeə.rᵊn.tɪŋ US ˈper.ᵊn.t̬ɪŋ, ˈpær-
parentless ˈpeə.rᵊnt.ləs, -lɪs US ˈper.ᵊnt-, ˈpær-
parent-teacher ˌpeə.rᵊntˈtiː.tʃəʳ US ˌper.ᵊn*t*ˈtiː.tʃɚ, ˌpær- **ˌparent-ˈteacher associˌation**
pareo pɑːˈreɪ.əʊ US -oʊ **-s** -z
paresis pəˈriː.sɪs; ˈpær.ə- US pəˈriː-; ˈper.ə-, ˈpær-
paretic pəˈret.ɪk US -ˈret̬-, -ˈriː.t̬ɪk
pareu pɑːˈreɪ.uː **-s** -z
par excellence ˌpɑːrˈek.sᵊl.ɑ̃ːns, -sel-, -ɑːn*t*s, ˌpɑːr.ek.sᵊlˈɑ̃ːns, -selˈ-, -ˈɑːn*t*s US ˌpɑːrˌek.səˈlɑːn*t*s
parfait ˌpɑːˈfeɪ, ˈ-- US pɑːrˈfeɪ **-s** -z
Parfitt ˈpɑː.fɪt US ˈpɑːr-
parfum ˈpɑː.fʌm US pɑːrˈfʌm
par|get ˈpɑː|.dʒɪt US ˈpɑːr- **-gets** -dʒɪts **-get(t)ing** -dʒɪ.tɪŋ US -dʒɪ.t̬ɪŋ **-get(t)ed** -dʒɪ.tɪd US -dʒɪ.t̬ɪd
Pargiter ˈpɑː.dʒɪ.təʳ US ˈpɑːr.dʒɪ.t̬ɚ
parheli|on pɑːˈhiː.li|.ən, -ɒn US pɑːrˈhiː-, -ˈhiːl.j|ən **-a** -ə
pariah pəˈraɪə, ˈpær.i.ə US pəˈraɪə **-s** -z
Parian ˈpeə.ri.ən US ˈper.i-, ˈpær- **-s** -z
parietal pəˈraɪə.tᵊl, -ˈraɪ.ɪ- US -ˈraɪə-
paring ˈpeə.rɪŋ US ˈper.ɪŋ, ˈpær- **-s** -z
Paris ˈpær.ɪs US ˈper-, ˈpær-
parish (P) ˈpær.ɪʃ US ˈper-, ˈpær- **-es** -ɪz **ˌparish ˈpriest**
parishioner pəˈrɪʃ.ᵊn.əʳ US -ɚ **-s** -z
Parisian pəˈrɪz.i.ən, -ˈrɪʒ.ᵊn US -ˈrɪʒ-, -ˈriː.ʒᵊn **-s** -z
parisyllabic ˌpær.ɪ.sɪˈlæb.ɪk, ˌ-ə-, -sᵊlˈæb- US ˌper-, ˌpær-
parity ˈpær.ə.ti, -ɪ.ti US ˈper.ə.t̬i, ˈpær-
park (P) pɑːk US pɑːrk **-s** -s **-ing** -ɪŋ **-ed** -t **ˈparking ˌlot** ; **ˈparking ˌmeter** ; **ˈparking ˌspace** ; **ˈparking ˌticket** ; **ˌpark-and-ˈride**
parka ˈpɑː.kə US ˈpɑːr- **-s** -z
Parke pɑːk US pɑːrk **-s** -s
Parker ˈpɑː.kəʳ US ˈpɑːr.kɚ
Parkestone ˈpɑːk.stən US ˈpɑːrk-
Parkhurst ˈpɑːk.hɜːst US ˈpɑːrk.hɜːrst
parkin (P) ˈpɑː.kɪn US ˈpɑːr-
parking meter ˈpɑː.kɪŋˌmiː.təʳ US ˈpɑːr.kɪŋˌmiː.t̬ɚ **-s** -z
Parkinson ˈpɑː.kɪn.sᵊn US ˈpɑːr- **-ism** -ɪ.zᵊm **ˈParkinson's diˌsease**
parkland ˈpɑːk.lænd US ˈpɑːrk-
Parkman ˈpɑːk.mən US ˈpɑːrk-
Parks pɑːks US pɑːrks
Parkstone ˈpɑːk.stən US ˈpɑːrk-
parkway ˈpɑːk.weɪ US ˈpɑːrk- **-s** -z
park|y ˈpɑː.k|i US ˈpɑːr- **-ier** -i.əʳ US -i.ɚ **-iest** -i.ɪst, -i.əst
parlance ˈpɑː.lən*t*s US ˈpɑːr-
parlay (*v.*) ˈpɑː.li US ˈpɑːr.leɪ, -li; pɑːrˈleɪ **-s** -z **-ing** -ɪŋ **-ed** -d
parlay (*n.*) ˈpɑː.li US ˈpɑːr.leɪ, -li **-s** -z
Parlement of Foules ˌpɑː.lə.mənt.əvˈfuːlz US ˌpɑːr-
parley (P) ˈpɑː.li US ˈpɑːr- **-s** -z **-ing** -ɪŋ **-ed** -d
parliament (P) ˈpɑː.lə.mənt, -lɪ-, -li.ə- US ˈpɑːr.lə- **-s** -s
parliamentarian (P) ˌpɑː.lə.menˈteə.ri.ən, -lɪ-, -li.ə-, -mənˈ- US ˌpɑːr.lə.menˈter.i- **-s** -z
parliamentary ˌpɑː.ləˈmen.tᵊr.i, -lɪˈ-, -li.əˈ- US ˌpɑːr.ləˈmen.t̬ɚ-, ˈ-tri
parlo(u)r ˈpɑː.ləʳ US ˈpɑːr.lɚ **-s** -z **ˈparlo(u)r ˌcar** ; **ˈparlo(u)r ˌgame** ; **ˈparlo(u)r ˌmaid**
parlous ˈpɑː.ləs US ˈpɑːr- **-ly** -li
Parma ˈpɑː.mə US ˈpɑːr- **ˌParma ˈham**
Parmar ˈpɑː.məʳ US ˈpɑːr.mɚ
Parmenter ˈpɑː.mɪn.təʳ, -mən- US ˈpɑːr.mən.t̬ɚ
Parmesan ˈpɑː.mɪˌzæn, ˌ--ˈ-, -əˈ- US ˈpɑːr.mə.zɑːn, -zən, -zæn, -ʒɑːn
Parminter ˈpɑː.mɪn.təʳ US ˈpɑːr.mɪn.t̬ɚ
Parmiter ˈpɑː.mɪ.təʳ US ˈpɑːr.mɪ.t̬ɚ
Parnassian pɑːˈnæs.i.ən US pɑːr-
Parnassus pɑːˈnæs.əs US pɑːr-
Parnell pɑːˈnel; ˈpɑː.nᵊl US pɑːrˈnel; ˈpɑːr.nᵊl
parochial pəˈrəʊ.ki.əl US -ˈroʊ- **-ly** -i **-ism** -ɪ.zᵊm
parodist ˈpær.ə.dɪst US ˈper-, ˈpær- **-s** -s
parod|y ˈpær.ə.d|i US ˈper-, ˈpær- **-ies** -iz **-ying** -i.ɪŋ **-ied** -id
parol ˈpær.əl; pəˈrəʊl US -ˈroʊl, ˈper.ᵊl, ˈpær-
parol|e pəˈrəʊl US -ˈroʊl **-es** -z **-ing** -ɪŋ **-ed** -d
Parolles pəˈrɒl.ɪz, -ɪs, -iːz, -es, -ez US pəˈrɑː.ləs
paronomazia, -sia ˌpær.ə.nəˈmeɪ.zi.ə, -si.ə, ˈ-ʒə US ˌper.ə.noʊˈmeɪ.ʒə, ˌpær-, ˈ-ʒi.ə
paronym ˈpær.ə.nɪm US ˈper-, ˈpær- **-s** -z
paronymy pəˈrɒn.ɪ.mi, pærˈɒn-, ˈ-ə- US pəˈrɑːn-
Paros ˈpær.ɒs US ˈper.ɑːs, ˈpær-, ˈpɑːr-
parotid pəˈrɒt.ɪd US -ˈrɑː.t̬ɪd **-s** -z
paroxysm ˈpær.ək.sɪ.zᵊm, -ɒk-; pəˈrɒk- US ˈper.ək-, ˈpær- **-s** -z
paroxysmal ˌpær.əkˈsɪz.mᵊl, -ɒkˈ- US ˌper.əkˈ-, ˌpær-
paroxytone pəˈrɒk.sɪ.təʊn, pærˈɒk- US perˈɑːk.sɪ.toʊn, pær- **-s** -z
parquet ˈpɑː.keɪ, -ki US pɑːrˈkeɪ **-s** -z
parquetry ˈpɑː.kɪ.tri, -kə- US ˈpɑːr.kə-
parr (P) pɑːʳ US pɑːr
parrakeet ˌpær.əˈkiːt, ˈ--- US ˈper.ə.kiːt, ˈpær- **-s** -s
Parramatta ˌpær.əˈmæt.ə US ˌper.əˈmæt̬-, ˌpær-
Parratt ˈpær.ət US ˈper-, ˈpær-
Parret ˈpær.ɪt US ˈper-, ˈpær-
parricidal ˌpær.ɪˈsaɪ.dᵊl, -əˈ- US ˌper.əˈ-, ˌpær-
parricide ˈpær.ɪ.saɪd, ˈ-ə- US ˈper.ə-, ˈpær- **-s** -z
Parrish ˈpær.ɪʃ US ˈper-, ˈpær-
parrot (P) ˈpær.ət US ˈper-, ˈpær- **-s** -s **-ing** -ɪŋ **-ed** -ɪd
parrot-fashion ˈpær.ətˌfæʃ.ᵊn US ˈper-, ˈpær-
parr|y (P) ˈpær|.i US ˈper-, ˈpær- **-ies** -iz **-ying** -i.ɪŋ **-ied** -id

pars|e pɑːz ⓊⓈ pɑːrs **-es** -ɪz **-ing** -ɪŋ **-ed** -d **-er/s** -əʳ/z ⓊⓈ -ɚ/z
Parsi, Parsee ˌpɑːˈsiː, ˈ-- ⓊⓈ ˈpɑːr.siː, -ˈ- **-s** -z
Parsifal ˈpɑː.sɪ.fəl, -sə-, -fɑːl, -fæl ⓊⓈ ˈpɑːr.sə.fəl, -fɑːl
parsimonious ˌpɑː.sɪˈməʊ.ni.əs, -səˈ- ⓊⓈ ˌpɑːr.səˈmoʊ- **-ly** -li **-ness** -nəs, -nɪs
parsimony ˈpɑː.sɪ.mə.ni, -sə- ⓊⓈ ˈpɑːr.sə.moʊ-
parsley ˈpɑː.sli ⓊⓈ ˈpɑːr-
parsnip ˈpɑː.snɪp ⓊⓈ ˈpɑːr- **-s** -z
parson ˈpɑː.sən ⓊⓈ ˈpɑːr- **-s** -z ˌ**parson's** ˈ**nose**
parsonag|e ˈpɑː.sən.ɪdʒ ⓊⓈ ˈpɑːr- **-es** -ɪz
Parsons ˈpɑː.sənz ⓊⓈ ˈpɑːr-
part pɑːt ⓊⓈ pɑːrt **-s** -s **-ing** -ɪŋ ⓊⓈ ˈpɑːr.t̬ɪŋ **-ed** -ɪd ⓊⓈ ˈpɑːr.t̬ɪd ˌ**part and** ˈ**parcel** ; ˌ**part ex**ˈ**change**; ˌ**parting** ˈ**shot** ⓊⓈ ˈ**parting** ˌ**shot**; ˌ**part of** ˈ**speech**
partak|e pɑːˈteɪk ⓊⓈ pɑːr- **-es** -s **-ing** -ɪŋ **partook** pɑːˈtʊk ⓊⓈ pɑːr- **partak|en** pɑːˈteɪ.kən ⓊⓈ pɑːr- **-er/s** -əʳ/z ⓊⓈ -ɚ/z
parterre pɑːˈteəʳ ⓊⓈ pɑːrˈter **-s** -z
Parthenia pɑːˈθiː.ni.ə ⓊⓈ pɑːr-
parthenogenesis ˌpɑː.θə.nəʊˈdʒen.ɪ.sɪs, -θɪ-, ˈ-ə- ⓊⓈ ˌpɑːr.θə.noʊˈdʒen.ə-
Parthenon ˈpɑː.θən.ən, -θɪ.nən, -nɒn ⓊⓈ ˈpɑːr.θə.nɑːn, -nən **-s** -z
Parthenope pɑːˈθen.ə.pi ⓊⓈ pɑːr-
Parthi|a ˈpɑː.θi|.ə ⓊⓈ ˈpɑːr- **-an/s** -ən/z
partial ˈpɑː.ʃəl ⓊⓈ ˈpɑːr- **-ly** -i
partiality ˌpɑː.ʃiˈæl.ə.ti, -ɪ.ti ⓊⓈ ˌpɑːr.ʃiˈæl.ə.t̬i
participant pɑːˈtɪs.ɪ.pənt, ˈ-ə- ⓊⓈ pɑːrˈtɪs.ə-, pɚ- **-s** -s
partici|pate pɑːˈtɪs.ɪ|.peɪt, ˈ-ə- ⓊⓈ pɑːrˈtɪs.ə-, pɚ- **-pates** -peɪts **-pating** -peɪ.tɪŋ ⓊⓈ -peɪ.t̬ɪŋ **-pated** -peɪ.tɪd ⓊⓈ -peɪ.t̬ɪd **-pator/s** -peɪ.təʳ/z ⓊⓈ -peɪ.t̬ɚ/z
participation pɑːˌtɪs.ɪˈpeɪ.ʃən, ˌpɑː.tɪ.sɪˈ-, -səˈ- ⓊⓈ pɑːrˌtɪs.əˈ-, pɚ- **-s** -z
participatory pɑːˈtɪs.ɪ.pə.tər.i, ˈ-ə-; ˌpɑː.tɪ.sɪˈpeɪ-, -səˈ- ⓊⓈ pɑːrˈtɪs.ə.pəˌtɔːr-, pɚ-
participial ˌpɑː.tɪˈsɪp.i.əl, -təˈ- ⓊⓈ ˌpɑːr.tɪˈ- **-ly** -i
participle pɑːˈtɪs.ɪ.pl̩, ˈ-ə- ⓊⓈ ˈpɑːr.tɪ.sɪ- **-s** -z
particle ˈpɑː.tɪ.kl̩, -tə- ⓊⓈ ˈpɑːr.t̬ə- **-s** -z
particleboard ˈpɑː.tɪ.kl̩ˌbɔːd ⓊⓈ ˈpɑːr.t̬ɪ.kl̩ˌbɔːrd
particolo(u)red ˈpɑː.tiˌkʌl.əd, ˌpɑː.tiˈkʌl- ⓊⓈ ˈpɑːr.t̬iˌkʌl.ɚd
particular pəˈtɪk.jə.ləʳ, -jʊ- ⓊⓈ pɚˈtɪk.jə.lɚ, -juː- **-s** -z **-ly** -li
particularit|y pəˌtɪk.jəˈlær.ə.t|i, -jʊˈ-, -ɪ.t|i ⓊⓈ pɚˌtɪk.jəˈler.ə.t̬|i, -juːˈ-, -ˈlær- **-ies** -iz
particulariz|e, -is|e pəˈtɪk.jə.lər.aɪz, -jʊ- ⓊⓈ pɚˈtɪk.jə.lə.raɪz, -juː- **-es** -ɪz **-ing** -ɪŋ **-ed** -d
parting ˈpɑː.tɪŋ ⓊⓈ ˈpɑːr.t̬ɪŋ **-s** -z
Partington ˈpɑː.tɪŋ.tən ⓊⓈ ˈpɑːr.t̬ɪŋ-
partisan ˌpɑː.tɪˈzæn, -təˈ-, ˈ--- ⓊⓈ ˈpɑːr.t̬ɪ.zən, -zæn **-s** -z **-ship/s** -ʃɪp/s
partita pɑːˈtiː.tə ⓊⓈ pɑːrˈtiː.t̬ə
partite ˈpɑː.taɪt ⓊⓈ ˈpɑːr-
partition pɑːˈtɪʃ.ən, pə- ⓊⓈ pɑːr- **-s** -z **-ing** -ɪŋ **-ed** -d
partitive ˈpɑː.tɪ.tɪv, -tə- ⓊⓈ ˈpɑːr.t̬ə.t̬ɪv **-ly** -li
partly ˈpɑːt.li ⓊⓈ ˈpɑːrt-
partn|er ˈpɑːt.n|əʳ ⓊⓈ ˈpɑːrt.n|ɚ **-ers** -əz ⓊⓈ -ɚz **-ering** -ər.ɪŋ **-ered** -əd ⓊⓈ -ɚd
partnership ˈpɑːt.nə.ʃɪp ⓊⓈ ˈpɑːrt.nɚ- **-s** -s
Parton ˈpɑː.tən ⓊⓈ ˈpɑːr-
partook (*from* **partake**) pɑːˈtʊk ⓊⓈ pɑːr-
partridg|e (P) ˈpɑː.trɪdʒ ⓊⓈ ˈpɑːr- **-es** -ɪz
part-singing ˈpɑːtˌsɪŋ.ɪŋ ⓊⓈ ˈpɑːrt-
part-song ˈpɑːt.sɒŋ ⓊⓈ ˈpɑːrt.sɑːŋ, -sɔːŋ **-s** -z
part-tim|e ˌpɑːtˈtaɪm ⓊⓈ ˌpɑːrt-, ˈ-- **-er/s** -əʳ/z ⓊⓈ -ɚ/z *stress shift, British only:* ˌpart-time ˈjob
parturition ˌpɑː.tjʊəˈrɪʃ.ən, -tjəʳˈɪʃ- ⓊⓈ ˌpɑːr.tuːˈrɪʃ-, -tjuːˈ-, -t̬əˈ-, -tʃəˈ- **-s** -z
partway ˌpɑːtˈweɪ ⓊⓈ ˌpɑːrt- *stress shift:* ˌpartway ˈthere
part|y ˈpɑː.t|i ⓊⓈ ˈpɑːr.t̬|i **-ies** -iz **-ying** -i.ɪŋ **-ied** -id ˈ**party** ˌ**piece** ; ˌ**party** ˈ**wall**
partygoer ˈpɑː.tiˌgəʊ.əʳ ⓊⓈ ˈpɑːr.t̬iˌgoʊ.ɚ **-s** -z
party line *in politics:* ˌpɑː.tiˈlaɪn ⓊⓈ ˌpɑː.t̬iˈ-
party line *telephone:* ˈpɑː.ti.laɪn ⓊⓈ ˈpɑːr.t̬i-
party poop|er ˈpɑː.tiˌpuː.p|əʳ ⓊⓈ ˈpɑːr.t̬iˌpuː.p|ɚ **-ers** -əz ⓊⓈ -ɚz **-ing** -ɪŋ
party-spirit ˌpɑː.tiˈspɪr.ɪt ⓊⓈ ˌpɑːr.t̬iˈ-
parvenu(e) ˈpɑː.və.njuː, -nuː ⓊⓈ ˈpɑːr.və.nuː, -njuː **-s** -z
Parzival ˈpɑːt.sɪ.fɑːl ⓊⓈ ˈpɑːrt-
pas *singular:* pɑː *plural:* pɑːz, pɑː
Pasadena ˌpæs.əˈdiː.nə
Pascal, PASCAL pæsˈkæl, -ˈkɑːl ⓊⓈ pæsˈkæl, pɑːˈskæl, ˈ--
paschal ˈpæs.kəl, ˈpɑː.skəl ⓊⓈ ˈpæs.kəl
pas de deux ˌpɑː.dəˈdɜː
pasha (P) ˈpɑː.ʃə, ˈpæʃ.ə; pəˈʃɑː **-s** -z
Pasiphae pəˈsɪf.i.iː, -eɪ ⓊⓈ ˈ-ə.i
paso doble ˌpæs.əʊˈdəʊ.bleɪ ⓊⓈ ˌpɑː.soʊˈdoʊ-
Pasolini ˌpæs.əʊˈliː.ni ⓊⓈ -oʊˈ-
pasquinade ˌpæs.kwɪˈneɪd, -kwəˈ- ⓊⓈ -kwɪˈ- **-s** -z
pass pɑːs ⓊⓈ pæs **-es** -ɪz **-ing** -ɪŋ **-ed** -t **-er/s** -əʳ/z ⓊⓈ -ɚ/z ˈ**pass de**ˌ**gree** ; ˈ**pass** ˌ**law**
passab|le ˈpɑː.sə.bl̩ ⓊⓈ ˈpæs.ə- **-ly** -li **-leness** -l̩.nəs, -nɪs
passacaglia ˌpæs.əˈkɑː.li.ə, -ˈkæl.jə ⓊⓈ ˌpɑː.səˈkɑːl.jə, ˌpæs.əˈ-, -ˈkæl- **-s** -z
passag|e ˈpæs.ɪdʒ **-es** -ɪz **-ing** -ɪŋ **-ed** -d
passageway ˈpæs.ɪdʒ.weɪ
passant *in heraldry:* ˈpæs.ənt *in chess:* pæsˈɑ̃ːŋ, pɑːˈsɑːŋ ⓊⓈ ˈpæs.ənt
Passat® pæsˈæt, -ɑːt ⓊⓈ pəˈsɑːt, pæsˈɑːt
passbook ˈpɑːs.bʊk ⓊⓈ ˈpæs- **-s** -s
Passe pæs
passé(e) pæsˈeɪ, pɑːˈseɪ, ˈ-- ⓊⓈ pæsˈeɪ, ˈ--; pɑːˈseɪ
passenger ˈpæs.ən.dʒəʳ, -ɪn- ⓊⓈ -ən.dʒɚ **-s** -z
passe-partout ˌpæs.pəˈtuː, ˌpɑːs-, -pɑːˈ-, ˈ--- ⓊⓈ ˌpæs.pɑːrˈ-, ˌpɑːs- **-s** -z
passer-by ˌpɑː.səˈbaɪ ⓊⓈ ˌpæs.ɚˈ- **passers-by** ˌpɑː.səzˈbaɪ ⓊⓈ ˌpæs.ɚzˈ-
passerine ˈpæs.ə.raɪn, -riːn ⓊⓈ -ə.raɪn, -ɚ.ɪn
Passfield ˈpæs.fiːld, ˈpɑːs- ⓊⓈ ˈpæs-
passibility ˌpæs.ɪˈbɪl.ə.ti, -əˈ-, -ɪ.ti ⓊⓈ -ɪˈbɪl.ə.t̬i
passible ˈpæs.ɪ.bl̩, ˈ-ə- ⓊⓈ ˈ-ɪ-
passim ˈpæs.ɪm
passing note ˈpɑː.sɪŋˌnəʊt ⓊⓈ ˈpæs.ɪŋˌnoʊt **-s** -s
passion (P) ˈpæʃ.ən **-s** -z ˈ**passion** ˌ**play**
passionate ˈpæʃ.ən.ət, -ɪt ⓊⓈ -ə.nɪt **-ly** -li **-ness** -nəs, -nɪs
passionflower ˈpæʃ.ənˌflaʊəʳ ⓊⓈ -ˌflaʊɚ **-s** -z
passionfruit ˈpæʃ.ən.fruːt **-s** -s
Passiontide ˈpæʃ.ən.taɪd
passive ˈpæs.ɪv **-ly** -li **-ness** -nəs, -nɪs ˌ**passive** ˈ**smoking**
passivity pæsˈɪv.ə.ti, pəˈsɪv-, -ɪ.ti ⓊⓈ pæsˈɪv.ə.t̬i
passivization, -isa- ˌpæs.ɪ.vaɪˈzeɪ.ʃən, ˌ-ə-, -vɪˈ- ⓊⓈ -ɪ.vɪˈ-
passiviz|e, -is|e ˈpæs.ɪ.vaɪz, ˈ-ə- ⓊⓈ ˈ-ɪ- **-es** -ɪz **-ing** -ɪŋ **-ed** -d
pass-key ˈpɑːs.kiː ⓊⓈ ˈpæs- **-s** -z
Passmore ˈpɑːs.mɔːʳ, ˈpæs- ⓊⓈ ˈpæs.mɔːr
Passover ˈpɑːsˌəʊ.vəʳ ⓊⓈ ˈpæsˌoʊ.vɚ **-s** -z

passport 'pɑːs.pɔːt (US) 'pæs.pɔːrt **-s** -s
password 'pɑːs.wɜːd (US) 'pæs.wɜːrd **-s** -z
past pɑːst (US) pæst ,**past par'ticiple** (US) ,**past 'participle**; ,**past 'perfect**; ,**past 'tense**
pasta 'pæs.tə, 'pɑː.stə (US) 'pɑː.stə
past|e peɪst **-es** -s **-ing** -ɪŋ **-ed** -ɪd
pasteboard 'peɪst.bɔːd (US) -bɔːrd
pastel 'pæs.tᵊl, -tel; pæs'tel (US) pæs'tel **-s** -z
pastelist 'pæs.tᵊl.ɪst (US) pæs'tel-; 'pæs.tᵊl- **-s** -s
pastern 'pæs.tɜːn, -tən (US) -tɚn **-s** -z
Pasternak 'pæs.tə.næk (US) -tɚ-
paste-up 'peɪst.ʌp **-s** -s
Pasteur pæs'tɜːʳ, pɑː'stɜːʳ (US) pæs'tɜːr, pɑː'stɜːr
pasteurization, -isa- ,pæs.tʃᵊr.aɪ'zeɪ.ʃᵊn, ,pɑːs-, -tjᵊr-, -tᵊr-, -ɪ'- (US) ,pæs.tʃɚ.ɪ'-, -tɚ-
pasteuriz|e, -is|e 'pæs.tʃᵊr.aɪz, 'pɑːs-, -tjᵊr-, -tᵊr- (US) 'pæs.tʃə.raɪz, -tə- **-es** -ɪz **-ing** -ɪŋ **-ed** -d
pastich|e pæs'tiːʃ, '-- (US) pæs'tiːʃ, pɑː'stiːʃ **-es** -ɪz
pastille 'pæs.tᵊl, -tɪl, -tiːl; pæs'tiːl (US) pæs'tiːl **-s** -z
pastime 'pɑːs.taɪm (US) 'pæs- **-s** -z
pastis pæs'tiːs
past-master ,pɑːst'mɑː.stəʳ, '-,-- (US) 'pæst,mæs.tɚ, ,-'-- **-s** -z
Paston 'pæs.tᵊn
pastor 'pɑː.stəʳ (US) 'pæs.tɚ **-s** -z
pastoral 'pɑː.stᵊr.ᵊl, 'pæs.tᵊr- (US) 'pæs- **-s** -z
pastorale ,pæs.tᵊr'ɑːl, -'æl, -'ɑː.leɪ (US) -tə'rɑːl, -'ræl, -'rɑː.leɪ **-s** -z
pastoralism 'pɑː.stᵊr.ᵊl.ɪ.zᵊm, 'pæs.tᵊr- (US) 'pæs-
pastorate 'pɑː.stᵊr.ət, -ɪt (US) 'pæs.tɚ.ɪt **-s** -s
pastrami pæs'trɑː.mi, pə'strɑː- (US) pə-
pastr|y 'peɪ.str|i **-ies** -iz
pastrycook 'peɪ.stri.kʊk **-s** -s
pasturage 'pɑː.stjʊ.rɪdʒ, -tjᵊr.ɪdʒ, -tʃᵊr- (US) 'pæs.tʃɚ.ɪdʒ, -tjɚ-
past|ure 'pɑːs.tʃ|əʳ (US) 'pæs.tʃ|ɚ, -tj|ɚ **-ures** -əz (US) -ɚz **-uring** -ᵊr.ɪŋ **-ured** -əd (US) -ɚd
pastureland 'pɑː.stʃə.lænd (US) 'pæs.tʃɚ-, -tjɚ-
past|y (*n.*) 'pæs.t|i *for the Cornish kind also:* 'pɑː.st|i (US) 'pæs.t|i **-ies** -iz
past|y (*adj.*) 'peɪ.st|i **-ier** -i.əʳ (US) -i.ɚ **-iest** -i.ɪst, -i.əst **-ily** -ɪ.li, -ᵊl.i **-iness** -ɪ.nəs, -ɪ.nɪs
pat (P) pæt **-s** -s **-ting** -ɪŋ (US) 'pæţ.ɪŋ **-ted** -ɪd (US) 'pæţ.ɪd
pat-a-cake 'pæt.ə.keɪk (US) 'pæţ- **-s** -s
Patagoni|a ,pæt.ə'gəʊ.ni|.ə (US) ,pæţ.ə'goʊ-, '-nj|ə **-an/s** -ən/z
Patara 'pæt.ᵊr.ə
patch pætʃ **-es** -ɪz **-ing** -ɪŋ **-ed** -t
patchouli, patchouly pə'tʃuː.li; 'pætʃ.ʊ.li, -ᵊl.i (US) 'pætʃ.uː.li; pə'tʃuː-
patchwork 'pætʃ.wɜːk (US) -wɜːrk **-s** -s ,**patchwork 'quilt**
patch|y 'pætʃ|.i **-ier** -i.əʳ (US) -i.ɚ **-iest** -i.ɪst, -i.əst **-ily** -ɪ.li, -ᵊl.i **-iness** -ɪ.nəs, -ɪ.nɪs
pate peɪt **-s** -s
pâté 'pæt.eɪ, -'- (US) pɑː'teɪ, pæt'eɪ
pâté de foie ,pæt.eɪ.də'fwɑː (US) pɑː,teɪ-, pæt,eɪ-
pâté de foie gras ,pæt.eɪ.də,fwɑː'grɑː (US) pɑː,teɪ- pæt,eɪ-
Patel pə'tel, -'teɪl
Pateley 'peɪt.li
patell|a pə'tel|.ə **-as** -əz **-ae** -iː **-ar** -əʳ (US) -ɚ
paten 'pæt.ᵊn **-s** -z
paten|t 'peɪ.tᵊn|t, 'pæt.ᵊn|t (US) 'pæt-, 'peɪ.tᵊn|t **-ts** -ts **-ting** -tɪŋ (US) -ţɪŋ **-ted** -tɪd (US) -ţɪd **-table** -tə.bl̩ (US) -ţə.bl̩
Note: For British English, /'pæt.ᵊnt/ in **letters patent**; otherwise /'peɪ.tᵊnt/ seems the more usual. For American English, the usual pronunciation is /'pæt.ᵊnt/, except for the meanings **open, obvious**, where /'peɪ.tᵊnt/ is the normal form. ,**patent 'leather**
patentee ,peɪ.tᵊn'tiː, ,pæt.ᵊn'- (US) ,pæt.ᵊn'tiː **-s** -z
patently 'peɪ.tᵊnt.li (US) 'peɪ-, 'pæt.ᵊnt-
pater (P) 'peɪ.təʳ, 'pɑː- (US) 'pɑː.ţɚ **-s** -z
Note: This word is never used to mean **father** in the U.S..
paterfamilias ,peɪ.tə.fə'mɪl.i.æs, ,pæt.ə-, -əs (US) ,peɪ.ţɚ.fə'mɪl.i.əs, ,pɑː.ţɚ-, ,pæţ.ɚ-
paternal pə'tɜː.nᵊl (US) -'tɜːr- **-ly** -li
paternal|ism pə'tɜː.nᵊl|.ɪ.zᵊm (US) -'tɜːr- **-ist/s** -ɪst/s
paternalistic pə,tɜː.nᵊl'ɪs.tɪk (US) -,tɜːr- **-ally** -ᵊl.i, -li
paternity pə'tɜː.nə.ti, -nɪ- (US) -'tɜːr.nə.ţi **pa'ternity ,leave**; **pa'ternity ,suit**; **pa'ternity ,test**
Paternoster *Lord's prayer:* ,pæt.ə'nɒs.təʳ (US) ,pɑː.ţɚ'nɑː.stɚ, -'noʊ- **-s** -z
Paternoster *Square:* 'pæt.ə,nɒs.təʳ (US) ,pɑː.ţɚ'nɑː.stɚ, ,pæt.ɚ'-, ,peɪ.tɚ'-, -'nɑː-
Paterson 'pæt.ə.sᵊn (US) 'pæţ.ɚ-
Pateshall 'pæt.ə.ʃᵊl, '-ɪ- (US) 'pæţ-
Patey 'peɪ.ti (US) -ţi
pa|th pɑː|θ (US) pæ|θ **-ths** -ðz (US) -θs, -ðz ,**lead someone ,up/,down the ,garden 'path**
path. pæθ
-path -pæθ
Note: Suffix. Normally unstressed, e.g. **psychopath** /'saɪ.kəʊ.pæθ (US) -kə-/.
Pathan pə'tɑːn (US) pə'tɑːn, pət'hɑːn **-s** -z
Pathé 'pæθ.eɪ
pathetic pə'θet.ɪk (US) -'θeţ- **-ally** -ᵊl.i, -li
pathfinder (P) 'pɑːθ,faɪn.dəʳ (US) 'pæθ,faɪn.dɚ **-s** -z
-pathic -'pæθ.ɪk
Note: Suffix. Words containing **-pathic** normally carry primary stress on the penultimate syllable, e.g. **psychopathic** /,saɪ.kəʊ'pæθ.ɪk (US) -kə'-/.
pathless 'pɑːθ.ləs, -lɪs (US) 'pæθ-
patho- pæθ.əʊ-; pə'θɒ-, pæθ'ɒ- (US) pæθ.ə-; pə'θɑː-, pæθ'ɑː-
Note: Prefix. Normally either carries primary or secondary stress on the first syllable, e.g. **pathogen** /'pæθ.əʊ.dʒen (US) -ə-/, **pathogenic** /,pæθ.əʊ'dʒen.ɪk (US) -ə'-/, or primary stress on the second syllable, e.g. **pathology** /pə'θɒl.ə.dʒi (US) -'θɑː.lə-/.
pathogen 'pæθ.əʊ.dʒən, -dʒen (US) -ə.dʒən **-s** -z
pathogenesis ,pæθ.əʊ'dʒen.ə.sɪs, '-ɪ- (US) '-ə-
pathogenic ,pæθ.əʊ'dʒen.ɪk (US) -ə'- **-ally** -ᵊl.i, -li
pathologic ,pæθ.ə'lɒdʒ.ɪk (US) -'lɑː.dʒɪk **-al** -ᵊl **-ally** -ᵊl.i, -li
patholog|y pə'θɒl.ə.dʒ|i, pæθ'ɒl- (US) pə'θɑː.lə- **-ist/s** -ɪst/s
pathos 'peɪ.θɒs (US) -θɑːs
pathway 'pɑːθ.weɪ (US) 'pæθ- **-s** -z
-pathy -pə.θi
Note: Suffix. Normally unstressed, e.g. **telepathy** /tə'lep.ə.θi/.
patience (P) 'peɪ.ʃᵊnts
patient 'peɪ.ʃᵊnt **-s** -s **-ly** -li
patina 'pæt.ɪ.nə, -ᵊn.ə; pə'tiː.nə (US) 'pæt.ᵊn.ə; pə'tiː.nə
patio 'pæt.i.əʊ (US) 'pæţ.i.oʊ, 'pɑː.ţi- **-s** -z
pâtisserie pə'tiː.sᵊr.i, pæt'ɪs- **-s** -z
Patman 'pæt.mən
Patmore 'pæt.mɔːʳ (US) -mɔːr
Patmos 'pæt.mɒs (US) -məs, 'pɑːt-, -mɑːs
Patna 'pæt.nə, 'pʌt- (US) 'pʌt-, 'pæt-
patois *singular:* 'pæt.wɑː *plural:* -z
Paton 'peɪ.tᵊn
Patou 'pæt.uː *as if French:* -'-
Patras pə'træs; 'pæt.rəs
patrial 'peɪ.tri.əl, 'pæt.ri- (US) 'peɪ.tri-
patriarch 'peɪ.tri.ɑːk, 'pæt.ri- (US) 'peɪ.tri.ɑːrk **-s** -s **-y** -i **-ies** -iz
patriarch|al ,peɪ.tri'ɑː.k|ᵊl, ,pæt.ri'- (US) ,peɪ.tri'ɑːr- **-ic** -ɪk

patriarchate ˈpeɪ.tri.ɑː.kɪt, ˈpæt.ri-, -keɪt, -kət (US) ˈpeɪ.tri.ɑːr.kɪt, -keɪt **-s** -s
Patricia pəˈtrɪʃ.ə (US) -ˈtrɪʃ-, -ˈtriː.ʃə
patrician pəˈtrɪʃ.ᵊn **-s** -z
patriciate pəˈtrɪʃ.i.ət, -ˈtrɪʃ.ət (US) -ˈtrɪs.i-, -ɪt, -eɪt (US) -trɪʃ.i.ɪt, -eɪt; -ˈtrɪʃ.ɪt
patricide ˈpæt.rɪ.saɪd, ˈpeɪ.trɪ-, -trə- (US) ˈpæt.rə- **-s** -z
Patrick ˈpæt.rɪk
patrilineal ˌpæt.rɪˈlɪn.i.əl, -rəˈ- (US) ˌpæt.rəˈ-
patrimonial ˌpæt.rɪˈməʊ.ni.əl, -rəˈ- (US) ˌpæt.rəˈmoʊ- **-ly** -i
patrimon|y ˈpæt.rɪ.mə.n|i, -rə- (US) -rə.moʊ- **-ies** -iz
patriot ˈpæt.ri.ət, ˈpeɪ.tri- (US) ˈpeɪ-, -ɑːt **-s** -s
patriotic ˌpæt.riˈɒt.ɪk, ˌpeɪ.triˈ- (US) ˌpeɪ.triˈɑː.t̬ɪk **-ally** -ᵊl.i, -li
patriotism ˈpæt.ri.ə.tɪ.zᵊm, ˈpeɪ.tri- (US) ˈpeɪ.tri-
patristic pəˈtrɪs.tɪk **-s** -s **-al** -ᵊl
Patroclus pəˈtrɒk.ləs (US) -ˈtroʊ.kləs; ˈpæt.roʊ-
patrol pəˈtrəʊl (US) -ˈtroʊl **-s** -z **-ling** -ɪŋ **-led** -d
patrolcar pəˈtrəʊl.kɑːʳ (US) -ˈtroʊl.kɑːr **-s** -z
patrol|man pəˈtrəʊl|.mən, -mæn (US) -ˈtroʊl- **-men** -mən, -men
patron ˈpeɪ.trᵊn, ˈpæt.rᵊn (US) ˈpeɪ.trᵊn **-s** -z
patronage ˈpæt.rᵊn.ɪdʒ, ˈpeɪ.trᵊn- (US) ˈpeɪ.trᵊn-, ˈpæt.rᵊn-
patronal pəˈtrəʊ.nᵊl, pætˈrəʊ- (US) ˈpeɪ.trᵊn.ᵊl, ˈpæt.rᵊn-; pəˈtroʊ.nᵊl
patroness ˌpeɪ.trəˈnes, ˌpæt.rəˈ-; ˈpeɪ.trᵊn.es, ˈpæt.rᵊn-, -ɪs, -əs (US) ˈpeɪ.trə.nɪs **-es** -ɪz
patroniz|e, -is|e ˈpæt.rᵊn.aɪz (US) ˈpeɪ.trᵊn-, ˈpæt.rᵊn- **-es** -ɪz **-ing/ly** -ɪŋ/li **-ed** -d
patronymic ˌpæt.rəˈnɪm.ɪk (US) -rəˈ-, -roʊˈ- **-s** -s
patroon pəˈtruːn **-s** -z
pats|y (P) ˈpæt.s|i **-ies** -iz
patten (P) ˈpæt.ᵊn **-s** -z
patt|er ˈpæt|.əʳ (US) ˈpæt̬|.ɚ **-ers** -əz (US) -ɚz **-ering** -ᵊr.ɪŋ **-ered** -əd (US) -ɚd
Patterdale ˈpæt.ə.deɪl (US) ˈpæt̬.ɚ-
pattern ˈpæt.ᵊn (US) ˈpæt̬.ɚn **-s** -z **-ing** -ɪŋ **-ed** -d
Patterson ˈpæt.ə.sᵊn (US) ˈpæt̬.ɚ-
Patteson ˈpæt.ɪ.sᵊn, ˈ-ə- (US) ˈpæt̬-
Patti(e) ˈpæt.i (US) ˈpæt̬-
Pattison ˈpæt.ɪ.sᵊn (US) ˈpæt̬-
Patton ˈpæt.ᵊn
patt|y ˈpæt|.i (US) ˈpæt̬- **-ies** -iz

paucity ˈpɔː.sə.ti, -sɪ- (US) ˈpɑː.sə.t̬i, ˈpɔː-
Paul pɔːl (US) pɔːl, pɑːl **-'s** -z ˌ**Paul ˈJones**
Paula ˈpɔː.lə (US) ˈpɑː-, ˈpɔː-
Paulding ˈpɔːl.dɪŋ (US) ˈpɑːl-, ˈpɔːl-
Paulette pɔːˈlet (US) pɑː-, pɔː-
Pauley ˈpɔː.li (US) ˈpɑː-, ˈpɔː-
Pauli ˈpɔː.li, ˈpaʊ- (US) ˈpaʊ-, ˈpɔː-
Paulin ˈpɔː.lɪn (US) ˈpɑː-, ˈpɔː-
Pauline *scholar of St Paul's school, relating to St Paul:* ˈpɔː.laɪn (US) ˈpɑː.laɪn, ˈpɔː-, -liːn **-s** -z
Pauline *female name:* ˈpɔː.liːn, -ˈ- (US) pɑːˈliːn, pɔː-
Pauling ˈpɔː.lɪŋ (US) ˈpɑː-, ˈpɔː-
Paulinus pɔːˈlaɪ.nəs (US) pɑː-, pɔː-
Paulus ˈpɔː.ləs (US) ˈpɑː-, ˈpɔː-
Pauncefote ˈpɔːnts.fʊt, -fət (US) ˈpɑːnts-, ˈpɔːnts-
paunch pɔːntʃ (US) pɑːntʃ, pɔːntʃ **-es** -ɪz **-y** -i **-iness** -ɪ.nəs, -ɪ.nɪs
pauper ˈpɔː.pəʳ (US) ˈpɑː.pɚ, ˈpɔː- **-s** -z
pauperism ˈpɔː.pᵊr.ɪ.zᵊm (US) ˈpɑː-, ˈpɔː-
pauperization, -isa- ˌpɔː.pᵊr.aɪˈzeɪ.ʃᵊn, -ɪˈ- (US) ˌpɑː.pɚ.ɪˈ-, ˌpɔː-
pauperiz|e, -is|e ˈpɔː.pᵊr.aɪz (US) ˈpɑː-, ˈpɔː- **-es** -ɪz **-ing** -ɪŋ **-ed** -d
Pausanias pɔːˈseɪ.ni.æs, -əs (US) pɑːˈseɪ.ni.əs, pɔː-
paus|e pɔːz (US) pɑːz, pɔːz **-es** -ɪz **-ing** -ɪŋ **-ed** -d
pavan(e) ˈpæv.ᵊn; pəˈvæn, -ˈvɑːn (US) pəˈvɑːn, -ˈvæn **-s** -z
Pavarotti ˌpæv.əˈrɒt.i (US) -ˈrɔː.t̬i, ˌpɑː.vəˈ-
pav|e peɪv **-es** -z **-ing** -ɪŋ **-ed** -d **-er/s** -əʳ/z (US) -ɚ/z ˈ**paving** ˌ**stone**
pavé ˈpæv.eɪ, -ˈ- (US) pævˈeɪ, ˈ-- **-s** -z
pavement ˈpeɪv.mənt **-s** -s
Pavia pəˈviː.ə, pɑː-, pɑːˈviː.ɑː
pavid ˈpæv.ɪd
pavilion pəˈvɪl.jən, ˈ-i.ən (US) ˈ-jən **-s** -z **-ing** -ɪŋ **-ed** -d
pavio(u)r ˈpeɪ.vjəʳ (US) -vjɚ **-s** -s
Pavitt ˈpæv.ɪt
Pavlov ˈpæv.lɒf, -lɒv (US) -lɔːv, -lɔːf
pavlova pævˈləʊ.və (US) pɑːvˈloʊ-, pæv- **-s** -z
Pavlova ˈpæv.lə.və, ˈpɑːv-; pævˈləʊ- (US) pɑːvˈloʊ-, pæv-
Pavlovian pævˈləʊ.vi.ən (US) pɑːvˈloʊ-, pæv-
paw (*n. v.*) pɔː (US) pɑː, pɔː **-s** -z **-ing** -ɪŋ **-ed** -d
pawk|y ˈpɔː.k|i (US) ˈpɑː-, ˈpɔː- **-ier** -i.əʳ (US) -i.ɚ **-iest** -i.ɪst, -i.əst **-ily** -ɪ.li, -ᵊl.i **-iness** -ɪ.nəs, -ɪ.nɪs
pawl pɔːl (US) pɑːl, pɔːl **-s** -z
pawn pɔːn (US) pɑːn, pɔːn **-s** -z **-ing** -ɪŋ **-ed** -d

pawnbrok|er ˈpɔːnˌbrəʊ.k|əʳ, ˈpɔːm- (US) ˈpɑːnˌbroʊ.k|ɚ, ˈpɔːn- **-ers** -əz (US) -ɚz **-ing** -ɪŋ
Pawnee ˌpɔːˈniː (US) ˌpɑː-, ˌpɔː- **-s** -z
pawnshop ˈpɔːn.ʃɒp (US) ˈpɑːn.ʃɑːp, ˈpɔːn- **-s** -s
pawpaw ˈpɔː.pɔː (US) ˈpɑː.pɑː; ˈpɔː.pɔː **-s** -z
Pawtucket pɔːˈtʌk.ɪt (US) pɑː-, pɔː-
pax pæks
Paxo® ˈpæk.səʊ (US) -soʊ
Paxos ˈpæk.sɒs (US) -sɑːs
Paxton ˈpæk.stᵊn
pay peɪ **-s** -z **-ing** -ɪŋ **paid** peɪd **payer/s** ˈpeɪ.əʳ/z (US) -ɚ/z ˈ**pay** ˌ**packet**
payable ˈpeɪ.ə.bl̩
payback ˈpeɪ.bæk
paybed ˈpeɪ.bed
paycheck, -cheque ˈpeɪ.tʃek
payday ˈpeɪ.deɪ **-s** -z
PAYE ˌpiː.eɪ.waɪˈiː
payee peɪˈiː **-s** -z
payload ˈpeɪ.ləʊd (US) -loʊd **-s** -z
paymaster ˈpeɪˌmɑː.stəʳ (US) -ˌmæs.tɚ **-s** -z ˌ**paymaster** ˈ**general**
payment ˈpeɪ.mənt **-s** -s
Payne peɪn
paynim (P) ˈpeɪ.nɪm
Paynter ˈpeɪn.təʳ (US) -t̬ɚ
payoff ˈpeɪ.ɒf (US) -ɑːf **-s** -s
payola peɪˈəʊ.lə (US) -ˈoʊ-
payphone ˈpeɪ.fəʊn (US) -foʊn
payroll ˈpeɪ.rəʊl (US) -roʊl **-s** -z
payslip ˈpeɪ.slɪp
paytrain ˈpeɪ.treɪn **-s** -z
Paz pæz (US) pɑːz, pɑːs
pazazz pəˈzæz
PBS ˌpiː.biːˈes
PC ˌpiːˈsiː
PE ˌpiːˈiː
pea piː **-s** -z
Peabody ˈpiːˌbɒd.i (US) -ˌbɑː.di
peac|e (P) piːs **-es** -ɪz ˈ**Peace** ˌ**Corps**; ˈ**peace** ˌ**offering**; ˈ**peace** ˌ**pipe**
peaceab|le ˈpiː.sə.bl̩| **-ly** -li **-leness** -l̩.nəs, -nɪs
peaceful ˈpiːs.fᵊl, -fʊl **-ly** -i **-ness** -nəs, -nɪs
Peacehaven ˈpiːsˌheɪ.vᵊn
peacekeep|er ˈpiːsˌkiː.p|əʳ (US) -ɚ **-ers** -əz (US) -ɚz **-ing** -ɪŋ
peacekeeping ˈpiːsˌkiː.pɪŋ
peacemaker ˈpiːsˌmeɪ.kəʳ (US) -kɚ **-s** -z
peacenik ˈpiːs.nɪk **-s** -s
peacetime ˈpiːs.taɪm
Peacey ˈpiː.si
peach piːtʃ **-es** -ɪz **-ing** -ɪŋ **-ed** -t **-er/s** -əʳ/z (US) -ɚ/z
Peachey ˈpiː.tʃi
Peachum ˈpiː.tʃəm
peach|y ˈpiː.tʃ|i **-ier** -i.əʳ (US) -i.ɚ **-iest** -i.ɪst, -i.əst **-iness** -ɪ.nəs, -ɪ.nɪs

peacock (P) 'piː.kɒk (US) -kɑːk **-s** -s

peacetime 'piːs.taɪm

pea-green ˌpiː'griːn *stress shift:* ˌpea-green 'boat

peahen 'piː.hen, ˌ-'- (US) '-- **-s** -z

pea-jacket 'piːˌdʒæk.ɪt **-s** -s

peak (P) piːk **-s** -s **-ing** -ɪŋ **-ed** -t **'Peak ˌDistrict** ; **ˌpeak 'time** *stress shift:* ˌpeak time 'traffic

Peake piːk

peaky 'piː.ki

peal piːl **-s** -z **-ing** -ɪŋ **-ed** -d

Peall piːl

pean *alternative spelling of* **paean***:* 'piː.ən **-s** -z

pean *in heraldry:* piːn

peanut 'piː.nʌt **-s** -s **ˌpeanut 'butter** (US) **'peanut ˌbutter**

pear peəʳ (US) per **-s** -z

Pear *surname:* pɪəʳ (US) pɪr

Pearce pɪəs (US) pɪrs

Peard pɪəd (US) pɪrd

pearl (P) pɜːl (US) pɜːrl **-s** -z **-ing** -ɪŋ **-ed** -d **ˌPearl 'Harbor**

pearlite 'pɜː.laɪt (US) 'pɜːr-

pearly 'pɜː.li (US) 'pɜːr- **ˌpearly 'gates** ; **ˌpearly 'king** ; **ˌpearly 'queen**

pearmain 'pɜː.meɪn, 'peə- (US) 'per- **-s** -z

Pearman 'pɪə.mən (US) 'pɪr-

Pears pɪəz, peəz (US) pɪrs, perz

Note: /peəz (US) perz/ in **Pears' soap**; /pɪəz (US) pɪrz/ for the singer.

Pearsall 'pɪə.sɔːl, -səl (US) 'pɪr-, -sɑːl

Pearse pɪəs (US) pɪrs

pear-shaped 'peə.ʃeɪpt (US) 'per-

Pearson 'pɪə.sən (US) 'pɪr-

Peart pɪət (US) pɪrt

Peary 'pɪə.ri (US) 'pɪr.i

peasant 'pez.ənt **-s** -s

peasantry 'pez.ən.tri

Peascod 'pes.kəd (US) -kəd, -kɑːd

pease (P) piːz

Peaseblossom 'piːzˌblɒs.əm (US) -ˌblɑː.səm

peasecod 'piːz.kɒd (US) -kɑːd **-s** -z

pease-pudding ˌpiːz'pʊd.ɪŋ, ˌpiːs-

peashooter 'piːˌʃuː.təʳ (US) -t̬ɚ **-s** -z

pea-souper ˌpiː'suː.pəʳ (US) 'piːˌsuː.pɚ, ˌ-'-- **-s** -z

peat piːt **'peat ˌbog**

peat|y 'piː.t|i (US) -t̬|i **-ier** -i.əʳ (US) -i.ɚ **-iest** -i.ɪst, -i.əst **-iness** -ɪ.nəs, -ɪ.nɪs

pebble 'peb.l̩ **-s** -z

pebbledash 'peb.l̩.dæʃ **-es** -ɪz **-ing** -ɪŋ **-ed** -t

pebbly 'peb.l̩.i, 'peb.li

pecan 'piː.kæn, -kən; pɪ'kæn (US) pɪ'kɑːn, piː-, -'kæn; 'piː.kɑːn, -kæn **-s** -z **ˌpecan 'pie**

peccability ˌpek.ə'bɪl.ə.ti, -ɪ.ti (US) -ə.t̬i

peccable 'pek.ə.bl̩

peccadillo ˌpek.ə'dɪl.əʊ (US) -oʊ **-(e)s** -z

peccant 'pek.ənt **-ly** -li

peccar|y 'pek.ər|.i **-ies** -iz

peccavi pek'ɑː.viː *old-fashioned:* -'keɪ.vaɪ (US) peɪ'kɑː.vi **-s** -z

Pechey 'piː.tʃi

Pechili 'petʃ.ɪ.li

peck (P) pek **-s** -s **-ing** -ɪŋ **-ed** -t **-er/s** -əʳ/z (US) -ɚ/z **'pecking ˌorder**

Peckham 'pek.əm

Peckinpah 'pek.ɪn.pɑː

peckish 'pek.ɪʃ **-ly** -li **-ness** -nəs, -nɪs

Peckitt 'pek.ɪt

Pecksniff 'pek.snɪf

Pecock 'pek.ɒk (US) -ɑːk

pecorino (P) ˌpek.ər'iː.nəʊ (US) -ə'riː.noʊ

Pecos 'peɪ.kəs, -kɒs (US) -kəs, -koʊs

Pécs petʃ (US) peɪtʃ

pect|in 'pek.t|ɪn **-ic** -ɪk **-inous** -ɪ.nəs

pectoral 'pek.tər.əl **-s** -z **'pectoral ˌmuscle**

pecu|late 'pek.jə|.leɪt **-lates** -leɪts **-lating** -leɪ.tɪŋ (US) -leɪ.t̬ɪŋ **-lated** -leɪ.tɪd (US) -leɪ.t̬ɪd **-lator/s** -leɪ.təʳ/z (US) -leɪ.t̬ɚ/z

peculation ˌpek.jə'leɪ.ʃən, -jʊ'- **-s** -z

peculiar pɪ'kjuː.li.əʳ, pə- (US) pɪ'kjuːl.jɚ, piː- **-s** -z **-ly** -li

peculiarit|y pɪˌkjuː.li'ær.ə.t|i, pə-, -ɪ.t|i (US) pɪˌkjuː.li'er.ə.t̬|i, piː-, -'ær- **-ies** -iz

pecuniar|y pɪ'kjuː.njər|.i, -ni.ə.r|i (US) pɪ'kjuː.ni.er-, piː- **-ily** -əl.i, -ɪ.li

pedagogic ˌped.ə'gɒdʒ.ɪk, -'gɒg-, -'gəʊ.dʒɪk (US) -'gɑː-, -'goʊ- **-s** -s **-al** -əl **-ally** -əl.i, -li *stress shift:* ˌpedagogic 'function

pedagogue 'ped.ə.gɒg (US) -gɑːg, -gɔːg **-s** -z

pedagogy 'ped.ə.gɒdʒ.i, -gɒg-, -gəʊ.dʒi (US) -gɑː.dʒi, -goʊ-

pedal *(n. v.)* 'ped.əl **-s** -z **-(l)ing** -ɪŋ **-(l)ed** -d **'pedal ˌpushers**

pedal *(adj.) of the foot:* 'piː.dəl, 'ped.əl *in geometry:* 'ped.əl

pedalo 'ped.əl.əʊ (US) -oʊ **-(e)s** -z

pedant 'ped.ənt **-s** -s

pedantic pɪ'dæn.tɪk, pə-, ped'æn-, pə'dæn- (US) ped'æn- **-al** -əl **-ally** -əl.i, -li

pedantism 'ped.ən.tɪ.zəm, pɪ'dæn-, ped'æn-

pedantr|y 'ped.ən.tr|i **-ies** -iz

peddl|e 'ped.l̩ **-es** -z **-ing** -ɪn, 'ped.lɪŋ **-ed** -d **-er/s** -əʳ/z (US) -ɚ/z, 'ped.ləʳ/z (US) **-er/z** -ɚ/z

Peden 'piː.dən (US) 'piː.dən, 'peɪ-

pederast 'ped.ər.æst, 'piː.dər- (US) 'ped.ə.ræst **-s** -s **-y** -i

pedestal 'ped.ɪ.stəl, '-ə- **-s** -z

pedestrian pɪ'des.tri.ən, pə- (US) pə- **-s** -z **-ism** -ɪ.zəm **peˌdestrian 'crossing**

pedestrianiz|e, -is|e pɪ'des.tri.ə.naɪz, pə- (US) pə- **-es** -ɪz **-ing** -ɪŋ **-ed** -d

pediatric ˌpiː.di'æt.rɪk **-s** -s

pediatrician ˌpiː.di.ə'trɪʃ.ən **-s** -z

pedicel 'ped.ɪ.sel, '-ə- **-s** -z

pedicle 'ped.ɪ.kl̩, '-ə- **-s** -z

pedicure 'ped.ɪ.kjʊəʳ, '-ə-, -kjɔːʳ (US) -ɪ.kjʊr **-s** -z

pedigree 'ped.ɪ.griː, '-ə- **-s** -z **-d** -d

pediment 'ped.ɪ.mənt, '-ə- **-s** -s

pedimental ˌped.ɪ'men.təl, -ə'-

pedimented 'ped.ɪ.men.tɪd, '-ə-, -mən- (US) -men.t̬ɪd

pedlar 'ped.ləʳ (US) -lɚ **-s** -z

pedometer pɪ'dɒm.ɪ.təʳ, pə-, ped'ɒm-, '-ə- (US) pɪ'dɑː.mə.t̬ɚ, pə- **-s** -z

pedophile 'piː.dəʊ.faɪl (US) 'ped.oʊ-, 'piː.doʊ-, -də- **-s** -z

pedophili|a ˌpiː.dəʊ'fɪl.i|.ə (US) ˌped.oʊ'fiː.li-, ˌpiː.doʊ'-, -də'-, -'fiːl.j|ə **-ac/s** -æk

Pedro 'ped.rəʊ, 'piː.drəʊ (US) 'peɪ.droʊ, 'ped.roʊ

Note: The pronunciation /'piː.drəʊ/ is generally used in Shakespeare's 'Much Ado.'

peduncle pɪ'dʌŋ.kl̩, pə-, ped'ʌŋ- (US) pɪ'dʌŋ-; 'piː.dʌŋ- **-s** -z

pee piː **-s** -z **-ing** -ɪŋ **-d** -d

Peeb|les 'piː.bl̩|z **-les-shire** -l̩z.ʃəʳ, -l̩ʒ.ʃəʳ, -l̩.ʃəʳ, -ˌʃɪəʳ (US) -ʃɚ, -ˌʃɪr

peek (P) piːk **-s** -s **-ing** -ɪŋ **-ed** -t

peekaboo 'piː.kə.buː

peel (P) piːl **-s** -z **-ing/s** -ɪŋ/z **-ed** -d

Peele piːl

peeler 'piː.ləʳ (US) -lɚ **-s** -z

peep (P) piːp **-s** -s **-ing** -ɪŋ **-ed** -t **-er/s** -əʳ/z (US) -ɚ/z

peepal 'piː.pəl **-s** -z

peep-bo 'piːp.bəʊ, -əʊ, ˌ-'- (US) 'piːp.boʊ, -oʊ, ˌ-'-

peep-hole 'piːp.həʊl (US) -hoʊl **-s** -z

peeping Tom ˌpiː.pɪŋ'tɒm (US) -'tɑːm **-s** -z

peepshow 'piːp.ʃəʊ (US) -ʃoʊ **-s** -z

peep-toe 'piːp.təʊ (US) -toʊ **-d** -d

peepul 'piː.pəl **-s** -z

peer pɪəʳ (US) pɪr **-s** -z **-ing** -ɪŋ **-ed** -d

peerag|e 'pɪə.rɪdʒ (US) 'pɪr.ɪdʒ **-es** -ɪz

peeress pɪə'res; 'pɪə.rəs, -rɪs, -res (US) 'pɪr.ɪs **-es** -ɪz

peergroup 'pɪə.gruːp (US) 'pɪr- **-s** -s

peerless (P) 'pɪə.ləs, -lɪs (US) 'pɪr- **-ly** -li **-ness** -nəs, -nɪs

peev|e piːv **-es** -z **-ing** -ɪŋ **-ed** -d

peevish 'piː.vɪʃ **-ly** -li **-ness** -nəs, -nɪs

peewee 'piː.wiː **-s** -z

peewit 'piː.wɪt **-s** -s

peg (P) peg **-s** -z **-ging** -ɪŋ **-ged** -d
Pegasus 'peg.ə.səs
Pegeen peg'iːn
Pegge peg
Peggotty 'peg.ə.ti ⓤⓢ -t̬i
Peggy 'peg.i
Pegram, Pegrum 'piː.grəm
Pegu peg'uː
Pei peɪ
peignoir 'peɪ.nwɑːr, -nwɔːr ⓤⓢ peɪn'wɑːr, pen-, '-- **-s** -z
Peile piːl
Peiping ˌpeɪ'pɪŋ
Peirce pɪəs ⓤⓢ pɪrs, pɜːrs
pejoration ˌpiː.dʒər'eɪ.ʃən, ˌpedʒ.ər'- ⓤⓢ ˌpedʒ.ə'reɪ-, ˌpiː.dʒə'-
pejorative pɪ'dʒɒr.ə.tɪv, pə-, 'piː.dʒər- ⓤⓢ pɪ'dʒɔːr.ə.t̬ɪv; 'pedʒ.ə.reɪ-, 'piː.dʒə- **-s** -z **-ly** -li
peke piːk **-s** -s
Pekin ˌpiː'kɪn ⓤⓢ '--
pekines|e (P) ˌpiː.kɪ'niːz, -kən'iːz ⓤⓢ ˌpiː.kə'niːz, -'niːs **-es** -ɪz
Peking ˌpiː'kɪŋ *stress shift, see compound:* ˌ**Peking 'duck**
pekinges|e (P) ˌpiː.kɪŋ'iːz, -kɪ'niːz, -kən'iːz ⓤⓢ -kɪŋ'iːz, -'iːs **-es** -ɪz
pekoe 'piː.kəʊ ⓤⓢ -koʊ
pelagic pə'lædʒ.ɪk, pɪ-, pel'ædʒ- ⓤⓢ pə'lædʒ-, pɪ-
pelargonium ˌpel.ə'gəʊ.ni.əm, -ɑː'- ⓤⓢ -ɑːr'goʊ- **-s** -z
Pelasgian pel'æz.gi.ən, pɪ'læz-, pə-, -dʒi- ⓤⓢ pə'læz.dʒi- **-s** -z
Pelé 'pel.eɪ, -'- ⓤⓢ 'pel.eɪ
pelerine 'pel.ər.iːn ⓤⓢ -ə.riːn **-s** -z
Peleus 'piː.ljuːs, 'pel.juːs, -jəs, -i.əs ⓤⓢ 'piː.li.əs, 'piːl.juːs
pelf pelf
pelham (P) 'pel.əm
Pelias 'piː.li.æs, 'pel.i-, -əs ⓤⓢ -əs
pelican 'pel.ɪ.kən, '-ə- **-s** -z ˌ**pelican 'crossing**
peliss|e pel'iːs, pɪ'liːs, pə- ⓤⓢ pə'liːs **-es** -ɪz
pellagr|a pə'læg.r|ə, pel'æg- ⓤⓢ pə'leɪ.gr|ə, -'læg.r|ə **-ous** -əs
Pelleas, Pelléas 'pel.eɪ.æs, '-i- ⓤⓢ '-i-
Pelles 'pel.iːz
pellet 'pel.ɪt, -ət **-s** -s
Pelley 'pel.i
pellicle 'pel.ɪ.kl̩, '-ə- **-s** -z
pellitory 'pel.ɪ.tər.i, '-ə- ⓤⓢ -tɔːr-
pell-mell ˌpel'mel
pellucid pɪ'luː.sɪd, pə-, pel'uː-, -'juː- ⓤⓢ pə'luː.sɪd **-ly** -li **-ness** -nəs, -nɪs
Pelman 'pel.mən **-ism** -ɪ.zəm
pelmet 'pel.mɪt, -mət **-s** -s
Peloponnese 'pel.ə.pə.niːz, -niːs, ˌpel.ə.pə'niːs, -'niːz ⓤⓢ ˌpel.ə.pə'niːz, -'niːs
Peloponnesian ˌpel.ə.pə'niː.ʃən, -ʃi.ən, '-ʒən ⓤⓢ -ʒən, -ʃən **-s** -z
Peloponnesus ˌpel.ə.pə'niː.səs
Pelops 'piː.lɒps ⓤⓢ -lɑːps
pelota pə'lɒt.ə, pɪ-, pel'ɒt-, -'əʊ.tə ⓤⓢ pə'loʊ.t̬ə
Pelsall 'pel.sɔːl
pelt pelt **-s** -s **-ing** -ɪŋ ⓤⓢ 'pel.t̬ɪŋ **-ed** -ɪd ⓤⓢ 'pel.t̬ɪd
Peltier effect 'pel.ti.eɪ.ɪˌfekt ⓤⓢ 'pel.tjeɪ.ɪˌ-, -əˌ-, -iːˌ-
pelv|is 'pel.v|ɪs **-ises** -ɪ.sɪz **-es** -iːz **-ic** -ɪk
Pemba 'pem.bə
Pemberton 'pem.bə.tən ⓤⓢ -bɚ-
Pembridge 'pem.brɪdʒ
Pembroke 'pem.brʊk, -brək ⓤⓢ -brʊk, -broʊk **-shire** -ʃər, -ˌʃɪər ⓤⓢ -ʃɚ, -ˌʃɪr
Pembury 'pem.bər.i
pemmican 'pem.ɪ.kən
pen (P) pen **-s** -z **-ning** -ɪŋ **-ned** -d **'pen ˌfriend** ; **'pen ˌname** ; **'pen ˌpal** ; **'pen ˌpusher**
penal 'piː.nəl **-ly** -i **'penal ˌcolony**
penaliz|e, -is|e 'piː.nəl.aɪz ⓤⓢ 'piː-, 'pen.əl- **-es** -ɪz **-ing** -ɪŋ **-ed** -d
penalt|y 'pen.əl.t|i ⓤⓢ -t̬|i **-ies** -iz **'penalty ˌbox**
penanc|e 'pen.ənts **-es** -ɪz
pen-and-ink ˌpen.ənd'ɪŋk *stress shift:* ˌpen-and-ink 'drawing
Penang pen'æŋ, pɪ'næŋ, pə- ⓤⓢ pɪ'næŋ, pen'æŋ
Penarth pen'ɑːθ, pə'nɑːθ ⓤⓢ pen'ɑːrθ
penates pen'ɑː.teɪz, pɪ'nɑː-, pə-, -'neɪ-, -tiːz ⓤⓢ pə'neɪ.t̬iːz, -'nɑː-
pence (*plur. of* **penny**) pents
Note: See **penny**.
penchant 'pɑ̃ːŋ.ʃɑ̃ːŋ ⓤⓢ 'pen.tʃənt **-s** -z
pencil 'pent.səl **-s** -z **-(l)ing** -ɪŋ **-(l)ed** -d **'pencil ˌcase** ; **'pencil ˌsharpener**
Pencoed pen'kɔɪd, peŋ- ⓤⓢ pen-
pendant 'pen.dənt **-s** -s
penden|cy 'pen.dən|t.si **-t** -t
Pendennis pen'den.ɪs
pendente lite penˌden.ti'laɪ.ti
Pender 'pen.dər ⓤⓢ -dɚ
Pendine pen'daɪn
pending 'pen.dɪŋ
Pendle 'pen.dl̩
Pendlebury 'pen.dl̩.bər.i ⓤⓢ -ˌber-, -bɚ-
Pendleton 'pen.dl̩.tən
pendragon (P) pen'dræg.ən **-s** -z
pendulous 'pen.djəl.əs, -dʒʊ.ləs, -dʒəl.əs ⓤⓢ -dʒə.ləs, -djə-, -də-, -dʒʊ- **-ly** -li **-ness** -nəs, -nɪs
pendulum 'pen.djəl.əm, -djʊ.ləm, -dʒəl.əm ⓤⓢ -dʒə.ləm, -djə-, -də-, -dʒʊ- **-s** -z
Penelope pə'nel.ə.pi, pɪ- ⓤⓢ pə-
penetrability ˌpen.ɪ.trə'bɪl.ə.ti, ˌ-ə-, -ɪ.ti ⓤⓢ -ə.t̬i
penetrab|le 'pen.ɪ.trə.b|l̩, '-ə- **-ly** -li **-leness** -l̩.nəs, -nɪs
penetralia ˌpen.ɪ'treɪ.li.ə, -ə'-
pene|trate 'pen.ɪ|.treɪt, '-ə- **-trates** -treɪts **-trating/ly** -treɪ.tɪŋ/li ⓤⓢ -treɪ.t̬ɪŋ/li **-trated** -treɪ.tɪd ⓤⓢ -treɪ.t̬ɪd
penetration ˌpen.ɪ'treɪ.ʃən, -ə'- **-s** -z
penetrative 'pen.ɪ.trə.tɪv, '-ə-, -treɪ- ⓤⓢ -treɪ.t̬ɪv **-ly** -li **-ness** -nəs, -nɪs
Penfold 'pen.fəʊld ⓤⓢ -foʊld
penful 'pen.fʊl **-s** -z
Penge pendʒ
penguin 'peŋ.gwɪn ⓤⓢ 'peŋ-, 'pen- **-s** -z
Penhaligon pen'hæl.ɪ.gən
penholder 'penˌhəʊl.dər ⓤⓢ -ˌhoʊl.dɚ **-s** -z
penicillin ˌpen.ɪ'sɪl.ɪn, -ə'-
penicillium ˌpen.ɪ'sɪl.i.əm, -ə'-
Penicuik 'pen.ɪ.kʊk
penile 'piː.naɪl ⓤⓢ -naɪl, -nɪl
peninsul|a (P) pə'nɪnt.sjə.l|ə, pɪ-, pen'ɪnt-, -sjʊ-, -ʃə-, -ʃʊ- ⓤⓢ pə'nɪnt.sə-, -sjə-, -'nɪn.tʃə- **-as** -əz **-ar** -ər ⓤⓢ -ɚ
penis 'piː.nɪs **-es** -ɪz **'penis ˌenvy**
Penistone 'pen.ɪ.stən
penitence 'pen.ɪ.tənts, '-ə-
penitent 'pen.ɪ.tənt, '-ə- **-s** -s **-ly** -li
penitential ˌpen.ɪ'ten.tʃəl, -ə'- ⓤⓢ -ʃəl **-ly** -i
penitentiar|y ˌpen.ɪ'ten.tʃər|.i, -ə'- ⓤⓢ -tʃə.ri **-ies** -iz
penkni|fe 'pen.naɪ|f **-ves** -vz
Penkridge 'peŋ.krɪdʒ
penlight 'pen.laɪt **-s** -s
Penmaenmawr ˌpen.mən'maʊər, -'mɔːr ⓤⓢ -'maʊɚ, -'mɔːr
pen|man 'pen|.mən, 'pem- ⓤⓢ 'pen- **-men** -mən
Penman 'pen.mən, 'pem- ⓤⓢ 'pen-
penmanship 'pen.mən.ʃɪp, 'pem- ⓤⓢ 'pen-
Penn pen
Penn. (*abbrev. for* **Pennsylvania**) pen, ˌpent.sɪl'veɪ.ni.ə, -səl'-, '-njə ⓤⓢ ˌpent.səl'veɪ.njə, '-ni.ə, pen
Note: The form /pen/ is especially used when referring to university names.
pennant (P) 'pen.ənt **-s** -s
penne 'pen.eɪ, -i ⓤⓢ -i, -eɪ
penn|i 'pen|.i **-is** -ɪs **-ia** -i.ə
penniless 'pen.i.ləs, -lɪs
Pennine 'pen.aɪn **-s** -z
Pennington 'pen.ɪŋ.tən
pennon 'pen.ən **-s** -z
Pennsylvani|a ˌpent.sɪl'veɪ.ni|.ə, -səl'-, '-nj|ə ⓤⓢ -səl'veɪ.nj|ə, '-ni.ə **-an/s** -ən/z ˌ**Pennsylˌvania 'Dutch**

penn|y (P) 'pen|.i **-ies** -iz **pence** pen*t*s
Note: After decimalization of the currency in Britain, the pronunciation of compounds with **penny**, **pence** (now abbreviated to **p**) changed. Formerly, compounds from **1/2d** to **11d** invariably had /-pᵊn.i, -pᵊn*t*s/, e.g. see entries under **half-penny**, **fourpence**, etc.. With the extension of **-pence** compounds beyond **11p**, e.g. **12p**, the reduced forms have more or less disappeared. Instead, the full forms /'pen.i/ and /pen*t*s/, or commonly /piː/, are used, e.g. **4p** (/'fɔː.pᵊn*t*s/) is /ˌfɔː'pen*t*s/ or /-'piː/; **12p** is /ˌtwelv'pen*t*s/ or /-'piː/. **ˌpenny ar'cade** ; **ˌpenny 'black** ; **ˌpenny 'dreadful** ; **ˌpenny 'farthing**
penny-pinch|ing 'pen.iˌpɪn.*t*ʃ|ɪŋ **-er/s** -əʳ/z (US) -ɚ/z
pennyroyal ˌpen.i'rɔɪəl (US) 'pen.iˌrɔɪ.əl, ˌpen.i'rɔɪ-
pennyweight 'pen.i.weɪt **-s** -s
pennywort 'pen.i.wɜːt (US) -wɜːrt, -wɔːrt
pennyworth 'pen.i.wəθ, -wɜːθ, 'pen.əθ (US) 'pen.i.wɚθ, -wɜːrθ **-s** -s
Penobscot pen'ɒb.skɒt, pə'nɒb- (US) pə'nɑːb.skɑːt, pen'ɑːb-, -skət
penological ˌpiː.nə'lɒdʒ.ɪ.kᵊl (US) -'lɑː.dʒɪ-
penolog|y piː'nɒl.ə.dʒ|i, pɪ- (US) piː'nɑː.lə- **-ist/s** -ɪst/s
Penrhyn pen'rɪn
Penrith *town in Cumbria:* pen'rɪθ, '-- *surname:* 'pen.rɪθ
Penrose *surname:* 'pen.rəʊz, -'- (US) 'pen.roʊz, -'- *place in Cornwall:* pen'rəʊz (US) -'roʊz
Penryn pen'rɪn
Pensacola ˌpen*t*.sə'kəʊ.lə (US) -'koʊ-
Pensarn pen'sɑːn (US) -'sɑːrn
penseroso ˌpen*t*.sə'rəʊ.zəʊ, -səʊ (US) -'roʊ.soʊ
Penshurst 'penz.hɜːst (US) -hɜːrst
pension (*n. v.*) *monetary allowance, etc.:* 'pen.*t*ʃᵊn **-s** -z **-ing** -ɪŋ **-ed** -d
pension (*n.*) *boarding house, board:* 'pɑ̃ːn.sjɔ̃ːŋ, -'- (US) pɑ̃ːn'sjõʊŋ, ˌpɑːn'sjoʊn **-s** -z
pensionable 'pen.*t*ʃᵊn.ə.bl̩ (US) -ʃᵊn-
pensioner 'pen.*t*ʃᵊn.əʳ (US) -ʃᵊn.ɚ **-s** -z
pensive 'pen*t*.sɪv **-ly** -li **-ness** -nəs, -nɪs
penta- pen.tə-; pen'tæ- (US) pen.t̬ə-; pen'tæ-
Note: Prefix. Normally either takes primary or secondary stress on the first syllable, e.g. **pentagon** /'pen.tə.gᵊn (US) -t̬ə.gɑːn/, **pentatonic** /ˌpen.tə'tɒn.ɪk (US) -t̬ə'tɑː.nɪk/, or primary stress on the second syllable, e.g. **pentagonal** /pen'tæg.ᵊn.ᵊl/.

pentad 'pen.tæd **-s** -z
pentagon (P) 'pen.tə.gᵊn, -gɒn (US) -t̬ə.gɑːn **-s** -z
pentagonal pen'tæg.ᵊn.ᵊl **-ly** -i
pentagram 'pen.tə.græm (US) -t̬ə- **-s** -z
pentahedr|on ˌpen.tə'hiː.dr|ən, -dr|ɒn (US) -t̬ə'hiː.dr|ən **-ons** -ənz, -ɒnz (US) -ənz **-a** -ə **-al** -ᵊl
pentameter pen'tæm.ɪ.təʳ, '-ə- (US) -ə.t̬ɚ **-s** -z
pentangle 'pen.tæŋ.gl̩ **-s** -z
Pentateuch 'pen.tə.tjuːk (US) -t̬ə.tuːk, -tjuːk
pentathlete pen'tæθ.liːt **-s** -s
pentathlon pen'tæθ.lɒn, -lən (US) -lɑːn, -lən
pentatonic ˌpen.tə'tɒn.ɪk (US) -t̬ə'tɑː.nɪk *stress shift:* ˌpentatonic 'scale
Pentax® 'pen.tæks
Pentecost 'pen.tɪ.kɒst, -tə- (US) -t̬ɪ.kɑːst **-s** -s
Pentecostal ˌpen.tɪ'kɒs.tᵊl, -tə'- (US) -t̬ɪ'kɑː.stᵊl **-ism** -ɪ.zᵊm **-ist/s** -ɪst/s *stress shift:* ˌPentecostal 'feast
Pentel® 'pen.tel
Penthesilea ˌpen*t*.θes.ɪ'liː.ə, -θə.sɪ'-, -sə'-, -'leɪ- (US) -θə.sə'liː-
penthou|se (P) 'pent.haʊ|s **-ses** -zɪz
pentiment|o ˌpen.tɪ'men.t|əʊ (US) -t̬ɪ'men.t|oʊ **-i** -iː
Pentland 'pent.lənd **-s** -z
Pentonville 'pen.tən.vɪl
Pentothal® 'pen.tə.θæl, -θɔːl (US) -t̬ə.θɔːl, -θɑːl
pentstemon pent'stem.ən, pen-, -'stiː.mən; 'pen*t*.stɪ.mən, -stə- (US) pent'stiː-; 'pent.stə-
pent-up ˌpent'ʌp *stress shift:* ˌpent-up 'anger
pentyl 'pen.taɪl, -tɪl (US) -tɪl, -t̬ᵊl
penult pə'nʌlt, pɪ-, pen'ʌlt (US) 'piː.nʌlt; pɪ'nʌlt **-s** -s
penultimate pə'nʌl.tɪ.mət, pɪ-, pen'ʌl-, -tə-, -mɪt (US) pɪ'nʌl.t̬ə.mət **-s** -s **-ly** -li
penumbr|a pə'nʌm.br|ə, pɪ-, pen'ʌm- (US) pɪ'nʌm- **-as** -əz **-ae** -iː **-al** -ᵊl
penurious pə'njʊə.ri.əs, pɪ-, pen'jʊə-, -'jɔː- (US) pə'nʊr.i-, pen'ʊr-, -'jʊr- **-ly** -li **-ness** -nəs, -nɪs
penury 'pen.jə.ri, -jʊ- (US) -jʊ.ri, -jɚ.i
Pen-y-Ghent ˌpen.i'gent
Penzance pen'zænts, pən- *locally:* pən'zɑːn*t*s (US) pen'zæn*t*s
peon *Indian servant:* pjuːn; 'piː.ən; peɪ'ɒn (US) 'piː.ɑːn, 'peɪ-, -ən **-s** -z *in US:* 'piː.ən (US) -ɑːn, -ən **-s** -z
peon|y 'piː.ə.n|i **-ies** -iz
peopl|e 'piː.pl̩ **-es** -z **-ing** -ɪŋ, 'piːp.lɪŋ **-ed** -d
Peoria piː'ɔː.ri.ə (US) -'ɔːr.i-

Peover 'piː.vəʳ (US) -vɚ
pep pep **-s** -s **-ping** -ɪŋ **-ped** -t **'pep ˌpill** ; **'pep ˌtalk**
PEP pep, ˌpiː.iː'piː
Pepin 'pep.ɪn
peplum 'pep.ləm **-s** -z
pepp|er (P) 'pep|.əʳ (US) -ɚ **-ers** -əz (US) -ɚz **-ering** -ᵊr.ɪŋ **-ered** -əd (US) -ɚd **'pepper ˌpot**
pepperbox 'pep.ə.bɒks (US) -ɚ.bɑːks **-es** -ɪz
peppercorn 'pep.ə.kɔːn (US) -ɚ.kɔːrn **-s** -z
peppermint 'pep.ə.mɪnt (US) -ɚ-, -mənt **-s** -s
pepperoni ˌpep.ə'rəʊ.ni (US) -'roʊ-
pepper|y 'pep.ᵊr|.i **-iness** -ɪ.nəs, -ɪ.nɪs
pepp|y 'pep|.i **-ier** -i.əʳ (US) -i.ɚ **-iest** -i.ɪst, -i.əst **-iness** -ɪ.nəs, -ɪ.nɪs **-ily** -ɪ.li, -ᵊl.i
Pepsi® 'pep.si
Pepsi-Cola® ˌpep.si'kəʊ.lə (US) -'koʊ-
pepsin 'pep.sɪn
Pepsodent® 'pep.səʊ.dent, -sə.dᵊnt (US) -soʊ.dent, -sə-
peptic 'pep.tɪk
Pepto-Bismol® ˌpep.təʊ'bɪz.mɒl (US) -toʊ'bɪz.mɑːl, -tə-
peptone 'pep.təʊn (US) -toʊn **-s** -z
Pepys 'pep.ɪs; piːps, peps
Note: The pronunciation in the family of the present Lord Cottenham is /'pep.ɪs/. Samuel Pepys is generally referred to as /piːps/.
per *strong form:* pɜːʳ (US) pɜːr *weak form:* pəʳ (US) pɚ
Note: This word has a weak form /pəʳ (US) pɚ/, which is almost always used in the phrases **per cent**, **per annum**. It is also used in phrases such as **per capita**, **per centimetre**, **per head**, but the strong form /pɜːʳ (US) pɜːr/ is more usual.
peradventure pə.rəd'ven.tʃəʳ, ˌpɜː.rəd'-, ˌper.əd'- (US) ˌpɜːr.əd'ven.tʃɚ, ˌper-
Perak 'peə.rə, 'pɪə.rə; pə'ræk, pɪ-, per'æk (US) 'peɪ.ræk, -rɑːk; 'per.ə, 'pɪr-
Note: English speakers who have lived in Malaysia pronounce /'peə.rə (US) 'per.ə/ or /'pɪə.rə (US) 'pɪr.ə/.
perambu|late pə'ræm.bjə|.leɪt, -bjʊ- **-lates** -leɪts **-lating** -leɪ.tɪŋ (US) -leɪ.t̬ɪŋ **-lated** -leɪ.tɪd (US) -leɪ.t̬ɪd
perambulation pəˌræm.bjə'leɪ.ʃᵊn, -bjʊ'- **-s** -z
perambulator pə'ræm.bjə.leɪ.təʳ, -bjʊ- (US) -t̬ɚ **-s** -z
per annum pəʳ'æn.əm (US) pɚ-
percale pə'keɪl, -'kɑːl (US) pɚ'keɪl
per capita pə'kæp.ɪ.tə, ˌpɜː- (US) pɚ'kæp.ɪ.t̬ə

perceivab|le pə'siː.və.bl̩, pɜː- ⓤⓢ pɚ- **-ly** -li
perceiv|e pə'siːv ⓤⓢ pɚ- **-es** -z **-ing** -ɪŋ **-ed** -d
percener 'pɜː.sᵊn.əʳ ⓤⓢ 'pɝː.sᵊn.ɚ **-s** -z
per cent pə'sent ⓤⓢ pɚ-
percentag|e pə'sen.tɪdʒ ⓤⓢ pɚ'sen.t̬ɪdʒ **-es** -ɪz
percentile pə'sen.taɪl ⓤⓢ pɚ'sen-, -t̬ᵊl **-s** -z
percept 'pɜː.sept ⓤⓢ 'pɝː- **-s** -s
perceptibility pəˌsep.tə'bɪl.ə.ti, -tɪ'-, -ɪ.ti ⓤⓢ pɚˌsep.tə'bɪl.ə.t̬i
perceptib|le pə'sep.tə.bl̩, -tɪ- ⓤⓢ pɚ'sep.tə- **-ly** -li **-leness** -l̩.nəs, -nɪs
perception pə'sep.ʃᵊn ⓤⓢ pɚ- **-s** -z
perceptive pə'sep.tɪv ⓤⓢ pɚ- **-ly** -li **-ness** -nəs, -nɪs
perceptual pə'sep.tʃu.əl, -tju- ⓤⓢ -tʃu-, pɚ'sep.tju- **-ly** -i
Perceval 'pɜː.sɪ.vᵊl, -sə- ⓤⓢ 'pɝː-
perch pɜːtʃ ⓤⓢ pɝːtʃ **-es** -ɪz **-ing** -ɪŋ **-ed** -t
perchance pə'tʃɑːnts, ˌpɜː- ⓤⓢ pɚ'tʃænts
Percheron 'pɜː.ʃə.rɒn ⓤⓢ 'pɝː.tʃə.rɑːn **-s** -z
percipien|t pə'sɪp.i.ən|t ⓤⓢ pɚ- **-ce** -ts
Percival(e) 'pɜː.sɪ.vᵊl, -sə- ⓤⓢ 'pɝː-
percol|ate 'pɜː.kᵊl|.eɪt ⓤⓢ 'pɝː- **-ates** -eɪts **-ating** -eɪ.tɪŋ ⓤⓢ -eɪ.t̬ɪŋ **-ated** -eɪ.tɪd ⓤⓢ -eɪ.t̬ɪd
percolation ˌpɜː.kᵊl'eɪ.ʃᵊn ⓤⓢ ˌpɝː- **-s** -z
percolator 'pɜː.kᵊl.eɪ.təʳ ⓤⓢ 'pɝː.kᵊl.eɪ.t̬ɚ **-s** -z
per contra ˌpɜː'kɒn.trə ⓤⓢ pɚ'kɑːn-
per curiam ˌpɜː'kjʊə.ri.æm, -'kjɔː- ⓤⓢ pɚ'kjʊr.i-
percuss pə'kʌs, pɜː- ⓤⓢ pɚ- **-es** -ɪz **-ing** -ɪŋ **-ed** -t
percussion pə'kʌʃ.ᵊn, pɜː- ⓤⓢ pɚ- **-s** -z **-ist/s** -ɪst/s
percussive pə'kʌs.ɪv, pɜː- ⓤⓢ pɚ-
percutaneous ˌpɜː.kjuː'teɪ.ni.əs, -kjʊ'- ⓤⓢ ˌpɝː.kjuː'- **-ly** -li
Percy 'pɜː.si ⓤⓢ 'pɝː-
per diem ˌpɜː'diː.em, -'daɪ- ⓤⓢ ˌpɝː-
Perdita 'pɜː.dɪ.tə ⓤⓢ 'pɝː.dɪ.t̬ə; pɚ'diː-
perdition pə'dɪʃ.ᵊn, pɜː- ⓤⓢ pɚ-
perdu(e) 'pɜː.djuː ⓤⓢ pɚ'duː, -'djuː
père, pere peəʳ ⓤⓢ per
peregrin 'per.ɪ.grɪn, '-ə- **-s** -z
peregri|nate 'per.ɪ.grɪ|.neɪt, '-ə-, -grə- ⓤⓢ -ə.grɪ- **-nates** -neɪts **-nating** -neɪ.tɪŋ ⓤⓢ -neɪ.t̬ɪŋ **-nated** -neɪ.tɪd ⓤⓢ -neɪ.t̬ɪd
peregrination ˌper.ɪ.grɪ'neɪ.ʃᵊn, ˌ-ə-, -grə'- ⓤⓢ -ə.grɪ'- **-s** -z
peregrine (P) (*n. adj.*) 'per.ɪ.grɪn, '-ə-, -griːn ⓤⓢ -grɪn, -griːn, -graɪn **-s** -z ˌ**peregrine 'falcon**
Perelman 'per.ᵊl.mən, 'pɜːl- ⓤⓢ 'pɝːrl-
peremptor|y pə'rem*p*.tᵊr|.i, pɪ-; 'per.ᵊm*p*- ⓤⓢ pə'rem*p*- **-ily** -ᵊl.i, -ɪ.li **-iness** -ɪ.nəs, -ɪ.nɪs
Note: /'per.ᵊm*p*-/ is more usual in British English when the word is used as a legal term. Otherwise /pə'rem*p*-/ and /pɪ-/ are commoner.
perennial pᵊr'en.i.əl, pɪ'ren- ⓤⓢ pə'ren- **-s** -z **-ly** -i
Peres 'per.ez
perestroika ˌper.ə'strɔɪ.kə, -ɪ'-
Perez 'per.es ⓤⓢ 'per.ez, -es, -əz, -əs
Pérez de Cuéllar ˌper.es.də'kweɪ.jɑː ⓤⓢ ˌper.ez.deɪ'kweɪ.jɑːr, ˌ-əz-, ˌ-es-
perfec|t (*n. adj.*) 'pɜː.fɪk|t ⓤⓢ 'pɝː- **-ts** -ts **-tly** -*t*.li **-tness** -*t*.nəs, -nɪs ˌ**perfect 'pitch** ; ˌ**perfect 'tense**
perfect (*v.*) pə'fekt, pɜː- ⓤⓢ pɝː-, pɚ- **-s** -s **-ing** -ɪŋ **-ed** -ɪd
perfectibility pəˌfek.tɪ'bɪl.ə.ti, pɜː-, -tə'-, -ɪ.ti ⓤⓢ pɚˌfek.tə'bɪl.ə.t̬i
perfectible pə'fek.tə.bᵊl, pɜː-, -tɪ- ⓤⓢ pɚ-
perfection pə'fek.ʃᵊn ⓤⓢ pɚ- **-s** -z **-ist/s** -ɪst/s **-ism** -ɪ.zᵊm
perfective pə'fek.tɪv ⓤⓢ pɚ- **-ly** -li **-ness** -nəs, -nɪs
perfervid pɜː'fɜː.vɪd, pə- ⓤⓢ pɚ'fɝː-
perfidious pə'fɪd.i.əs, pɜː- ⓤⓢ pɚ- **-ly** -li **-ness** -nəs, -nɪs
perfid|y 'pɜː.fɪ.d|i, -fə- ⓤⓢ 'pɝː.fə- **-ies** -iz
perforable 'pɜː.fᵊr.ə.bl̩ ⓤⓢ 'pɝː-
perforate (*adj.*) 'pɜː.fᵊr.ɪt, -ət, -eɪt ⓤⓢ 'pɝː.fɚ.ɪt, -fə.reɪt
perfor|ate (*v.*) 'pɜː.fᵊr|.eɪt ⓤⓢ 'pɝː.fə.r|eɪt **-ates** -eɪts **-ating** -eɪ.tɪŋ ⓤⓢ -eɪ.t̬ɪŋ **-ated** -eɪ.tɪd ⓤⓢ -eɪ.t̬ɪd **-ator/s** -eɪ.təʳ/z ⓤⓢ -eɪ.t̬ɚ/z
perforation ˌpɜː.fᵊr'eɪ.ʃᵊn ⓤⓢ ˌpɝː.fə'reɪ- **-s** -z
perforce pə'fɔːs, pɜː- ⓤⓢ pɚ'fɔːrs
perform pə'fɔːm ⓤⓢ pɚ'fɔːrm **-s** -z **-ing** -ɪŋ **-ed** -d **-er/s** -əʳ/z ⓤⓢ -ɚ/z **-able** -ə.bl̩
performanc|e pə'fɔː.mənts ⓤⓢ pɚ'fɔːr- **-es** -ɪz **per'formance ˌart**, **perˌformance 'art** ; **perˌformance re'lated**; **perˌformance reˌlated 'pay**
performative pə'fɔː.mə.tɪv ⓤⓢ pɚ'fɔːr.mə.t̬ɪv **-s** -z
perfume (*n.*) 'pɜː.fjuːm ⓤⓢ 'pɝː-, -'- **-s** -z
perfum|e (*v.*) pə'fjuːm, pɜː-; 'pɜː.fjuːm ⓤⓢ pɚ'fjuːm **-es** -z **-ing** -ɪŋ **-ed** -d
perfumed 'pɜː.fjuːmd ⓤⓢ pɚ'fjuːmd
perfum|er pə'fjuː.m|əʳ, pɜː- ⓤⓢ pɚ'fjuː.m|ɚ **-ers** -əz ⓤⓢ -ɚz **-ery** -ᵊr.i
perfunctor|y pə'fʌŋ*k*.tᵊr|.i, pɜː- ⓤⓢ pɚ- **-ily** -ᵊl.i, -ɪ.li **-iness** -ɪ.nəs, -ɪ.nɪs
Pergam|um 'pɜː.gə.m|əm ⓤⓢ 'pɝː- **-us** -əs
pergola 'pɜː.gᵊl.ə ⓤⓢ 'pɝː- **-s** -z
Pergolese ˌpɜː.gəʊ'leɪ.zi, ˌpeə-, -zeɪ ⓤⓢ ˌper.goʊ'leɪ.zi, -si
Perham 'per.əm
perhaps pə'hæps; præps ⓤⓢ pɚ'hæps, -'æps
Note: In British English, /pə'hæps/ is more usual in formal speech, and colloquially when the word is said in isolation or used parenthetically (as in **You know, perhaps, ...**). /præps/ is common in other situations, especially initially (e.g. in **Perhaps we shall, perhaps it is a mistake**).
peri- per.ɪ-, -i-; pə'rɪ-, per'ɪ-
Note: Prefix. Normally either takes primary or secondary stress on the first syllable, e.g. **periscope** /'per.ɪ.skəʊp ⓤⓢ -skoʊp/, **periscopic** /ˌper.ɪ'skɒp.ɪk ⓤⓢ -'skɑː.pɪk/, or primary stress on the second syllable, e.g. **peripheral** /pə'rɪf.ᵊr.ᵊl/.
peri 'pɪə.ri ⓤⓢ 'piː-, 'pɪr.i **-s** -z
perianth 'per.i.ænʈθ **-s** -s
pericarditis ˌper.ɪ.kɑː'daɪ.tɪs ⓤⓢ -kɑːr'daɪ.t̬ɪs
pericardi|um ˌper.ɪ'kɑː.di|.əm ⓤⓢ -'kɑːr- **-a** -ə
pericarp 'per.ɪ.kɑːp, '-ə- ⓤⓢ -ɪ.kɑːrp **-s** -s
Pericles 'per.ɪ.kliːz, '-ə- ⓤⓢ -ɪ.kliːz
peridot 'per.ɪ.dɒt ⓤⓢ -dɑːt **-s** -s
perigee 'per.ɪ.dʒiː, '-ə- ⓤⓢ '-ɪ- **-s** -z
periheli|on ˌper.ɪ'hiː.li|.ən ⓤⓢ -'hiː.li.ən, -'hiːl.jən **-a** -ə
peril 'per.ᵊl, -ɪl ⓤⓢ -ᵊl **-s** -z
perilous 'per.ᵊl.əs, -ɪ.ləs ⓤⓢ -ᵊl.əs **-ly** -li **-ness** -nəs, -nɪs
perilune 'per.ɪ.luːn, -ljuːn ⓤⓢ -luːn **-s** -z
Perim 'per.ɪm ⓤⓢ pə'rɪm
perimeter pə'rɪm.ɪ.təʳ, pɪ-, per'ɪm-, '-ə- ⓤⓢ pə'rɪm.ə.t̬ɚ **-s** -z
perinatal ˌper.ɪ'neɪ.tᵊl ⓤⓢ -t̬ᵊl
perine|um ˌper.ɪ'niː|.əm **-a** -ə **-al** -ᵊl
period 'pɪə.ri.əd ⓤⓢ 'pɪr.i- **-s** -z **'period ˌpiece**
periodic ˌpɪə.ri'ɒd.ɪk ⓤⓢ ˌpɪr.i'ɑː.dɪk *stress shift, see compound:* ˌ**periodic 'table**
periodic|al ˌpɪə.ri'ɒd.ɪ.k|ᵊl ⓤⓢ ˌpɪr.i'ɑː.dɪ- **-als** -ᵊlz **-ally** -ᵊl.i, -li

periodicit|y ˌpɪə.ri.əˈdɪs.ə.t|i, -ɒdˈɪs-, -ɪ.t|i (US) ˌpɪr.i.oʊˈdɪs.ə.t̬|i, -əˈ- **-ies** -iz
periodontal ˌper.i.əʊˈdɒn.tᵊl (US) -oʊˈdɑːn.t̬ᵊl, -əˈ- **-ly** -i
periodont|ic ˌper.i.əʊˈdɒn.t|ɪk (US) -oʊˈdɑːn.t̬|ɪk, -əˈ- **-ics** -ɪks **-ist/s** -ɪst/s
peripatetic ˌper.ɪ.pəˈtet.ɪk, ˌ-ə- (US) -ˈtet̬- **-ally** -ᵊl.i, -li *stress shift:* ˌperipatetic ˈteacher
peripheral pəˈrɪf.ᵊr.ᵊl, pɪ-, perˈɪf- (US) pəˈrɪf- **-s** -z **-ly** -i
peripher|y pəˈrɪf.ᵊr|.i, pɪ-, perˈɪf- (US) pəˈrɪf- **-ies** -iz
periphras|is pəˈrɪf.rə.s|ɪs, pɪ-, perˈɪf- (US) pəˈrɪf **-es** -iːz
periphrastic ˌper.ɪˈfræs.tɪk, -əˈ- **-ally** -ᵊl.i, -li
periscope ˈper.ɪ.skəʊp, ˈ-ə- (US) -ɪ.skoʊp **-s** -s
periscopic ˌper.ɪˈskɒp.ɪk, -əˈ- (US) -ɪˈskɑː.pɪk
perish ˈper.ɪʃ **-es** -ɪz **-ing/ly** -ɪŋ/li **-ed** -t **-er/s** -əʳ/z (US) -ɚ/z
perishability ˌper.ɪ.ʃəˈbɪl.ə.ti, -ɪ.ti (US) -ə.t̬i
perishab|le ˈper.ɪ.ʃə.b|l̩ **-ly** -li **-leness** -l̩.nəs, -nɪs
perispomenon ˌper.ɪˈspəʊ.mɪ.nən, -mə-, -nɒn (US) -ˈspoʊ.mɪ.nɑːn
peristalsis ˌper.ɪˈstæl.sɪs, -əˈ- (US) -ɪˈstɑːl-, -ˈstæl-
peristaltic ˌper.ɪˈstæl.tɪk, -əˈ- (US) -ɪˈstɑːl.t̬ɪk, -ˈstæl-
peristyle ˈper.ɪ.staɪl, ˈ-ə- (US) ˈ-ɪ- **-s** -z
peritone|um ˌper.ɪ.təʊˈniː|.əm, ˌ-ə- (US) -ˈtoʊ.ni-; -tə- **-ums** -əmz **-a** -ə
peritonitis ˌper.ɪ.təʊˈnaɪ.tɪs, ˌ-ə- (US) -ɪ.toʊˈnaɪ.t̬ɪs
Perivale ˈper.ɪ.veɪl, ˈ-ə- (US) ˈ-ɪ-
periwig ˈper.ɪ.wɪɡ, ˈ-ə- (US) ˈ-ɪ- **-s** -z
periwinkle ˈper.ɪˌwɪŋ.kl̩, ˈ-ə- (US) -ɪˌ- **-s** -z
perj|ure ˈpɜː.dʒ|əʳ (US) ˈpɜːr.dʒ|ɚ **-ures** -əz (US) -ɚz **-uring** -ᵊr.ɪŋ **-ured** -əd (US) -ɚd **-urer/s** -ᵊr.əʳ/z (US) -ɚ.ɚ/z
perjur|y ˈpɜː.dʒᵊr|.i (US) ˈpɜːr- **-ies** -iz
perk pɜːk (US) pɜːrk **-s** -s **-ing** -ɪŋ **-ed** -t
Perkin ˈpɜː.kɪn (US) ˈpɜːr- **-s** -z
Perks pɜːks (US) pɜːrks
perk|y ˈpɜː.k|i (US) ˈpɜːr- **-ier** -i.əʳ (US) -i.ɚ **-iest** -i.ɪst, -i.əst **-ily** -ɪ.li, -ᵊl.i **-iness** -ɪ.nəs, -ɪ.nɪs
Perlis ˈpɜː.lɪs (US) ˈpɜːr-
perlite ˈpɜː.laɪt (US) ˈpɜːr-
Perlman ˈpɜːl.mən (US) ˈpɜːrl-
perlocutionary ˌpɜː.ləˈkjuː.ʃᵊn.ᵊr.i, -lɒkˈjuː- (US) ˌpɜːr.loʊˈkjuː-
perm pɜːm (US) pɜːrm **-s** -z
Perm *city in Eastern Europe:* pɜːm, peəm (US) perm
permafrost ˈpɜː.mə.frɒst (US) ˈpɜːr.mə.frɑːst
permanenc|e ˈpɜː.mᵊn.ənts (US) ˈpɜːr- **-es** -ɪz **-y** -i **-ies** -iz
permanent ˈpɜː.mᵊn.ənt (US) ˈpɜːr- **-ly** -li
permanganate pɜːˈmæŋ.ɡə.neɪt, pə-, -nɪt, -nət (US) pɚˈmæŋ.ɡə.neɪt
permeability ˌpɜː.mi.əˈbɪl.ə.ti, -ɪ.ti (US) ˌpɜːr.mi.əˈbɪl.ə.t̬i
permeab|le ˈpɜː.mi.ə.b|l̩ (US) ˈpɜːr- **-ly** -li **-leness** -l̩.nəs, -nɪs
perme|ate ˈpɜː.mi|.eɪt (US) ˈpɜːr- **-ates** -eɪts **-ating** -eɪ.tɪŋ (US) -eɪ.t̬ɪŋ **-ated** -eɪ.tɪd (US) -eɪ.t̬ɪd
permeation ˌpɜː.miˈeɪ.ʃᵊn (US) ˌpɜːr-
permissib|le pəˈmɪs.ə.b|l̩, ˈ-ɪ- (US) pɚˈmɪs.ə- **-ly** -li **-leness** -l̩.nəs, -nɪs
permission pəˈmɪʃ.ᵊn (US) pɚ- **-s** -z
permissive pəˈmɪs.ɪv (US) pɚ- **-ly** -li **-ness** -nəs, -nɪs **perˌmissive soˈciety**
permit *(n.)* ˈpɜː.mɪt (US) ˈpɜːr-; pɚˈmɪt **-s** -s
per|mit *(v.)* pə|ˈmɪt (US) pɚ- **-mits** -ˈmɪts **-mitting** -ˈmɪt.ɪŋ (US) -ˈmɪt̬.ɪŋ **-mitted** -ˈmɪt.ɪd (US) -ˈmɪt̬.ɪd
permutation ˌpɜː.mjʊˈteɪ.ʃᵊn, -mjuːˈ-, -mjəˈ- (US) ˌpɜːr.mjuːˈ- **-s** -z
per|mute pə|ˈmjuːt (US) pɚ- **-mutes** -ˈmjuːts **-muting** -ˈmjuː.tɪŋ (US) -ˈmjuː.t̬ɪŋ **-muted** -ˈmjuː.tɪd (US) -ˈmjuː.t̬ɪd **-mutable** -ˈmjuː.tə.bl̩ (US) -ˈmjuː.t̬ə.bl̩
Pernambuco ˌpɜː.næmˈbuː.kəʊ, -nəmˈ-, -ˈbjuː- (US) ˌpɜːr.nəmˈbuː.koʊ
pernicious pəˈnɪʃ.əs, pɜː- (US) pɚ- **-ly** -li **-ness** -nəs, -nɪs
pernicket|y pəˈnɪk.ə.t|i, -ɪ.t|i (US) pɚˈnɪk.ə.t̬|i **-iness** -ɪ.nəs, -ɪ.nɪs
Pernod® ˈpɜː.nəʊ, ˈpeə- (US) perˈnoʊ
Perón, Peron pəˈrɒn, perˈɒn, pɪˈrɒn (US) perˈoʊn, pəˈroʊn
peror|ate ˈper.ᵊr|.eɪt, -ɒr- (US) -ə.r|eɪt, -oʊ- **-ates** -eɪts **-ating** -eɪ.tɪŋ (US) -eɪ.t̬ɪŋ **-ated** -eɪ.tɪd (US) -eɪ.t̬ɪd
peroration ˌper.ᵊrˈeɪ.ʃᵊn, -ɒrˈ- (US) ˌper.əˈreɪ-, -oʊˈ- **-s** -z
Perowne pəˈrəʊn, pɪ-, perˈəʊn (US) pəˈroʊn
peroxide pəˈrɒk.saɪd (US) pəˈrɑːk- **-s** -z
perpend *(v.)* pəˈpend, pɜː- (US) pɚ- **-s** -z **-ing** -ɪŋ **-ed** -ɪd
perpend *(n.)* ˈpɜː.pənd (US) ˈpɜːr- **-s** -z
perpendicular ˌpɜː.pᵊnˈdɪk.jʊ.ləʳ, -kjə- (US) ˌpɜːr.pənˈdɪk.juː.lɚ, -jə- **-s** -z **-ly** -li
perpendicularity ˌpɜː.pᵊnˌdɪk.jəˈlær.ə.ti, -jʊˈ-, -ɪ.ti (US) ˌpɜːr.pənˌdɪk.juːˈler.ə.t̬i, -jəˈ-, -ˈlær-
perpe|trate ˈpɜː.pɪ|.treɪt, -pə- (US) ˈpɜːr.pə|.treɪt **-trates** -treɪts **-trating** -treɪ.tɪŋ (US) -treɪ.t̬ɪŋ **-trated** -treɪ.tɪd (US) -treɪ.t̬ɪd **-trator/s** -treɪ.təʳ/z (US) -treɪ.t̬ɚ/z
perpetration ˌpɜː.pɪˈtreɪ.ʃᵊn, -pəˈ- (US) ˌpɜːr.pəˈ- **-s** -z
perpetual pəˈpetʃ.u.əl, -ˈpet.ju- (US) pɚˈpetʃ.u- **-ly** -i
perpetu|ate pəˈpetʃ.u|.eɪt, pɜː-, -ˈpet.ju- (US) pɚˈpetʃ.u- **-ates** -eɪts **-ating** -eɪ.tɪŋ (US) -eɪ.t̬ɪŋ **-ated** -eɪ.tɪd (US) -eɪ.t̬ɪd
perpetuation pəˌpetʃ.uˈeɪ.ʃᵊn, pɜː-, -ˌpet.juˈ- (US) ˌpɚ.petʃ.uˈ- **-s** -z
perpetuit|y ˌpɜː.pɪˈtjuː.ə.t|i, -pəˈ-, -ɪ.t|i (US) ˌpɜːr.pəˈtuː.ə.t̬|i, -ˈtjuː- **-ies** -iz
perpetuum mobile pəˌpetʃ.u.ʊmˈməʊ.bɪ.leɪ, pɜː-, -ˌpet.ju-, -əmˈ- (US) pɚˌpetʃ.ə.wəmˈmoʊ-
Perpignan ˈpɜː.piː.njɑ̃ŋ, ˈpeə-, ˌ--ˈ- (US) ˌper.piːˈnjɑ̃ːŋ
perplex pəˈpleks (US) pɚ- **-es** -ɪz **-ing/ly** -ɪŋ/li **-ed** -t **-edly** -ɪd.li, -t.li **-edness** -ɪd.nəs, -t.nəs, -nɪs
perplexit|y pəˈplek.sə.t|i, -ɪ.t|i (US) pɚˈplek.sə.t̬|i **-ies** -iz
perquisite ˈpɜː.kwɪ.zɪt, -kwə- (US) ˈpɜːr.kwɪ- **-s** -s
per quod ˌpɜːˈkwɒd (US) ˌpɜːrˈkwɑːd
Perrault ˈper.əʊ, -ˈ- (US) perˈoʊ
Perrett ˈper.ɪt
Perrier® ˈper.i.eɪ (US) -eɪ, ˌ--ˈ-
perrin (P) ˈper.ɪn
perr|y (P) ˈper|.i **-ies** -iz
Perse pɜːs (US) pɜːrs
per se ˌpɜːˈseɪ (US) ˌpɜːr-
perse|cute ˈpɜː.sɪ|.kjuːt, -sə- (US) ˈpɜːr.sɪ- **-cutes** -kjuːts **-cuting** -kjuː.tɪŋ (US) -kjuː.t̬ɪŋ **-cuted** -kjuː.tɪd (US) -kjuː.t̬ɪd **-cutor/s** -kjuː.təʳ/z (US) -kjuː.t̬ɚ/z
persecution ˌpɜː.sɪˈkjuː.ʃᵊn, -səˈ- (US) ˌpɜːr.sɪˈ- **-s** -z
Persephone pɜːˈsef.ᵊn.i, pə- (US) pɚ-
Persepolis pɜːˈsep.ᵊl.ɪs, pə- (US) pɚ-
Perseus ˈpɜː.si.əs, ˈ-sjuːs (US) ˈpɜːr-
persever|ate pəˈsev.ᵊr|.eɪt, pɜː- (US) pɚˈsev.ə.r|eɪt **-ates** -eɪts **-ating** -eɪ.tɪŋ (US) -eɪ.t̬ɪŋ **-ated** -eɪ.tɪd (US) -eɪ.t̬ɪd
perseveration pəˌsev.ᵊrˈeɪ.ʃᵊn, pɜː- (US) pɚˌsev.əˈreɪ-
persever|e ˌpɜː.sɪˈvɪəʳ, -səˈ- (US) ˌpɜːr.səˈvɪr **-es** -z **-ing/ly** -ɪŋ/li **-ed** -d **-ance** -ᵊnts
Pershing ˈpɜː.ʃɪŋ (US) ˈpɜːr-
Pershore ˈpɜː.ʃɔːʳ (US) ˈpɜːr.ʃɔːr

Persi|a ˈpɜː.ʃ|ə, -ʒ|ə ⓊⓈ ˈpɝː.ʒ|ə, -ʃ|ə **-an/s** -ən/z
persiflage ˈpɜː.sɪ.flɑːʒ, ˈpeə-, -sə-, ˌ--ˈ- ⓊⓈ ˈpɝː.sɪ-
Persil® ˈpɜː.sɪl, -sᵊl ⓊⓈ ˈpɝː-
persimmon (P) pəˈsɪm.ən, pɜː- ⓊⓈ pɚ- **-s** -z
persist pəˈsɪst ⓊⓈ pɚ- **-s** -s **-ing/ly** -ɪŋ/li **-ed** -ɪd
persisten|ce pəˈsɪs.tᵊnt|s ⓊⓈ pɚ- **-cy** -si
persistent pəˈsɪs.tᵊnt ⓊⓈ pɚ- **-ly** -li
persnickety pəˈsnɪk.ə.ti, -ɪ.ti ⓊⓈ pɚˈsnɪk.ə.t̬i
person ˈpɜː.sᵊn ⓊⓈ ˈpɝː- **-s** -z
person|a pəˈsəʊ.n|ə, pɜː- ⓊⓈ pɚˈsoʊ- **-ae** -iː, -aɪ **-s**
personable ˈpɜː.sᵊn.ə.bl̩ ⓊⓈ ˈpɝː-
personag|e ˈpɜː.sᵊn.ɪdʒ ⓊⓈ ˈpɝː- **-es** -ɪz
personal ˈpɜː.sᵊn.ᵊl, ˈpɜːs.nᵊl ⓊⓈ ˈpɝː.sᵊn.ᵊl, ˈpɝːrs.nᵊl **-ly** -i **ˌpersonal asˈsistant ; ˈpersonal ˌcolumn ; ˌpersonal comˈputer ; ˌpersonal ˈhygiene ; ˌpersonal ˈstereo**
personalit|y ˌpɜː.sᵊnˈæl.ə.t|i, -ɪ.t|i ⓊⓈ ˌpɝː.sᵊnˈæl.ə- **-ies** -iz
personalization, -isa- ˌpɜː.sᵊn.ᵊl.aɪˈzeɪ.ʃᵊn, -ɪˈ- ⓊⓈ ˌpɝː.sᵊn.ᵊlˈɪ-
personaliz|e, is|e ˈpɜː.sᵊn.ᵊl.aɪz ⓊⓈ ˈpɝː- **-es** -ɪz **-ing** -ɪŋ **-ed** -d
personalt|y ˈpɜː.sᵊn.ᵊl.t|i ⓊⓈ ˈpɝː.sᵊn.ᵊl.t̬|i **-ies** -iz
persona non grata pəˌsəʊ.nə.nɒnˈgrɑː.tə, pɜː-, -nəʊnˈ- ⓊⓈ pɚˌsoʊ.nə.nɑːnˈgrɑː.t̬ə, -ˈgræt̬.ə
person|ate ˈpɜː.sᵊn|.eɪt ⓊⓈ ˈpɝː- **-ates** -eɪts **-ating** -eɪ.tɪŋ ⓊⓈ -eɪ.t̬ɪŋ **-ated** -eɪ.tɪd ⓊⓈ -eɪ.t̬ɪd **-ator/s** -eɪ.təʳ/z ⓊⓈ -eɪ.t̬ɚ/z
personation ˌpɜː.sᵊnˈeɪ.ʃᵊn ⓊⓈ ˌpɝː- **-s** -s
personification pəˌsɒn.ɪ.fɪˈkeɪ.ʃᵊn, pɜː-, ˌ-ə- ⓊⓈ pɚˌsɑː.nɪ- **-s** -z
personi|fy pəˈsɒn.ɪ|.faɪ, pɜː-, ˈ-ə- ⓊⓈ pɚˈsɑː.nɪ- **-fies** -faɪz **-fying** -faɪ.ɪŋ **-fied** -faɪd
personnel ˌpɜː.sᵊnˈel ⓊⓈ ˌpɝː- **-s** -z **personˈnel ˌmanager**
perspective pəˈspek.tɪv, pɜː- ⓊⓈ pɚ- **-s** -z **-ly** -li
Perspex® ˈpɜː.speks ⓊⓈ ˈpɝː-
perspicacious ˌpɜː.spɪˈkeɪ.ʃəs, -spəˈ- ⓊⓈ ˌpɝː.spɪˈ- **-ly** -li **-ness** -nəs, -nɪs
perspicacity ˌpɜː.spɪˈkæs.ə.ti, -spəˈ-, -ɪ.ti ⓊⓈ ˌpɝː.spɪˈkæs.ə.t̬i
perspicuity ˌpɜː.spɪˈkjuː.ə.ti, -ɪ.ti ⓊⓈ ˌpɝː.spɪˈkjuː.ə.t̬i
perspicuous pəˈspɪk.ju.əs, pɜː- ⓊⓈ pɚ- **-ly** -li **-ness** -nəs, -nɪs
perspiration ˌpɜː.spᵊrˈeɪ.ʃᵊn ⓊⓈ ˌpɝː.spəˈreɪ-
perspir|e pəˈspaɪəʳ ⓊⓈ pɚˈspaɪɚ **-es** -z **-ing** -ɪŋ **-ed** -d
per stirpes ˌpɜːˈstɜː.piːz ⓊⓈ pɚˈstɝː-
persuad|e pəˈsweɪd ⓊⓈ pɚ- **-es** -z **-ing** -ɪŋ **-ed** -ɪd **-er/s** -əʳ/z ⓊⓈ -ɚ/z
persuasion pəˈsweɪ.ʒᵊn ⓊⓈ pɚ- **-s** -z
persuasive pəˈsweɪ.sɪv, -zɪv ⓊⓈ pɚˈsweɪ.sɪv **-ly** -li **-ness** -nəs, -nɪs
pert pɜːt ⓊⓈ pɝːt **-er** -əʳ ⓊⓈ ˈpɝː.t̬ɚ **-est** -ɪst, -əst ⓊⓈ ˈpɝː.t̬ɪst, -t̬əst **-ly** -li **-ness** -nəs, -nɪs
pertain pəˈteɪn, pɜː- ⓊⓈ pɚ- **-s** -z **-ing** -ɪŋ **-ed** -d
Perth pɜːθ ⓊⓈ pɝːθ **-shire** -ʃəʳ, -ˌʃɪəʳ ⓊⓈ -ʃɚ, -ˌʃɪr
pertinacious ˌpɜː.tɪˈneɪ.ʃəs, -təˈ- ⓊⓈ ˌpɝː.tᵊnˈeɪ- **-ly** -li **-ness** -nəs, -nɪs
pertinacity ˌpɜː.tɪˈnæs.ə.ti, -təˈ-, -ɪ.ti ⓊⓈ ˌpɝː.tᵊnˈæs.ə.t̬i
pertinen|ce ˈpɜː.tɪ.nənt|s, -tə- ⓊⓈ ˈpɝː.tᵊn.ᵊnt|s **-cy** -si
pertinent ˈpɜː.tɪ.nənt, -tə- ⓊⓈ ˈpɝː.tᵊn.ᵊnt **-ly** -li
perturb pəˈtɜːb, pɜː- ⓊⓈ pɚˈtɝːb **-s** -z **-ing** -ɪŋ **-ed** -d **-er/s** -əʳ/z **-able** -ə.bl̩
perturbation ˌpɜː.təˈbeɪ.ʃᵊn, -tɜːˈ- ⓊⓈ ˌpɝː.t̬ɚˈ- **-s** -z
pertussis pəˈtʌs.ɪs, pɜː- ⓊⓈ pɚ-
Pertwee ˈpɜː.twiː ⓊⓈ ˈpɝː-
Peru pəˈruː, pɪ- ⓊⓈ pə-
Perugia pəˈruː.dʒə, pɪ-, perˈuː-, -dʒi.ə ⓊⓈ perˈuː.dʒɑː, -dʒi.ə
Perugino ˌper.uˈdʒiː.nəʊ ⓊⓈ -noʊ
peruke pəˈruːk, pɪ-, perˈuːk ⓊⓈ pəˈruːk **-s** -s
perusal pəˈruː.zᵊl, pɪ- ⓊⓈ pəˈruː- **-s** -z
perus|e pəˈruːz, pɪ- ⓊⓈ pəˈruːz **-es** -ɪz **-ing** -ɪŋ **-ed** -d **-er/s** -əʳ/z ⓊⓈ -ɚ/z
Peruvian pəˈruː.vi.ən, pɪ-, perˈuː- ⓊⓈ pəˈruː- **-s** -z
pervad|e pəˈveɪd, pɜː- ⓊⓈ pɚ- **-es** -z **-ing** -ɪŋ **-ed** -ɪd
pervasion pəˈveɪ.ʒᵊn, pɜː- ⓊⓈ pɚ-
pervasive pəˈveɪ.sɪv, pɜː-, -zɪv ⓊⓈ pɚˈveɪ.sɪv **-ly** -li **-ness** -nəs, -nɪs
perverse pəˈvɜːs, pɜː- ⓊⓈ pɚˈvɝːs **-ly** -li **-ness** -nəs, -nɪs
perversion pəˈvɜː.ʃᵊn, pɜː-, -ʒᵊn ⓊⓈ pɚˈvɝː.ʒᵊn, -ʃᵊn **-s** -z
perversit|y pəˈvɜː.sə.t|i, pɜː-, -ɪ.t|i ⓊⓈ pɚˈvɝː.sə.t̬|i **-ies** -iz
pervert (*n.*) ˈpɜː.vɜːt ⓊⓈ ˈpɝː.vɝːt **-s** -s
per|vert (*v.*) pə|ˈvɜːt, pɜː- ⓊⓈ pɚ|ˈvɝːt **-verts** -ˈvɜːts ⓊⓈ -ˈvɝːts **-verting** -ˈvɜː.tɪŋ ⓊⓈ -ˈvɝː.t̬ɪŋ **-verted** -ˈvɜː.tɪd ⓊⓈ -ˈvɝː.t̬ɪd **-verter/s** -ˈvɜː.təʳ/z ⓊⓈ -ˈvɝː.t̬ɚ/z
pervious ˈpɜː.vi.əs ⓊⓈ ˈpɝː- **-ly** -li **-ness** -nəs, -nɪs
pesante pezˈæn.teɪ ⓊⓈ pesˈɑːn-
Pescadores ˌpes.kəˈdɔː.rɪz ⓊⓈ -ˈdɔːr.iːz, -ɪs
peseta pəˈseɪ.tə, pɪ-, pesˈeɪ- ⓊⓈ pəˈseɪ.t̬ə **-s** -z
pesewa pɪˈseɪ.wɑː ⓊⓈ ˈpes.ə.wɑː; peɪˈseɪ- **-s** -z
Peshawar pəˈʃɔː.əʳ, peʃˈɔː-, -ˈɑː-, -wə ⓊⓈ peʃˈɑː.wɚ, pəˈʃɑː-
peshwari peʃˈwɑː.ri
pesk|y ˈpes.k|i **-ier** -i.əʳ ⓊⓈ -i.ɚ **-iest** -i.ɪst, -i.əst **-ily** -ɪ.li, -ᵊl.i **-iness** -ɪ.nəs, -ɪ.nɪs
peso ˈpeɪ.səʊ ⓊⓈ -soʊ **-s** -z
pessar|y ˈpes.ᵊr|.i **-ies** -iz
pessim|ism ˈpes.ɪ.m|ɪ.zᵊm, ˈ-ə- ⓊⓈ ˈ-ə- **-ist/s** -ɪst/s
pessimistic ˌpes.ɪˈmɪs.tɪk, -əˈ- ⓊⓈ -əˈ- **-al** -ᵊl **-ally** -ᵊl.i, -li
pest (P) pest **-s** -s
Pestalozzi ˌpes.təˈlɒt.si ⓊⓈ -ˈlɑːt-
pest|er ˈpes.t|əʳ ⓊⓈ -t|ɚ **-ers** -əz ⓊⓈ -ɚz **-ering/ly** -ᵊr.ɪŋ/li **-ered** -əd ⓊⓈ -ɚd **-erer/s** -ᵊr.əʳ/z ⓊⓈ -ɚ.ɚ/z
pesticide ˈpes.tɪ.saɪd ⓊⓈ -tə- **-s** -z
pestiferous pesˈtɪf.ᵊr.əs **-ly** -li **-ness** -nəs, -nɪs
pestilenc|e ˈpes.tɪ.lənts, -tᵊl.ənts ⓊⓈ -tᵊl- **-es** -ɪz
pestilent ˈpes.tɪ.lənt, -tᵊl.ənt ⓊⓈ -tᵊl- **-ly** -li
pestilential ˌpes.tɪˈlen.tʃᵊl, -təˈ- ⓊⓈ -təˈlent.ʃᵊl **-ly** -i
pestl|e ˈpes.l̩, -tl̩ **-es** -z **-ing** -ɪŋ, ˈpes.lɪŋ, ˈpest.lɪŋ **-ed** -d
pesto ˈpes.təʊ ⓊⓈ -toʊ
pestolog|y pesˈtɒl.ə.dʒ|i ⓊⓈ -ˈtɑː.lə- **-ist/s** -ɪst/s
pet pet **-s** -s **-ting** -ɪŋ ⓊⓈ ˈpet̬.ɪŋ **-ted** -ɪd ⓊⓈ ˈpet̬.ɪd
petal ˈpet.ᵊl ⓊⓈ ˈpet̬- **-s** -z **-(l)ed** -d
pétanque peɪˈtɑ̃ːŋk
petard petˈɑːd, pɪˈtɑːd, pə-; ˈpet.ɑːd ⓊⓈ pɪˈtɑːrd **-s** -z **ˌhoist by one's ˌown peˈtard**
Pete piːt
pet|er (P) ˈpiː.t|əʳ ⓊⓈ -t̬|ɚ **-ers** -əz ⓊⓈ -ɚz **-ering** -ᵊr.ɪŋ **-ered** -əd ⓊⓈ -ɚd **ˌPeter ˈPan**
Peterborough, -boro' ˈpiː.tə.bᵊr.ə, -ˌbʌr.ə ⓊⓈ -t̬ɚˌbɚ.oʊ, -ə
Peterhead ˌpiː.təˈhed ⓊⓈ -t̬ɚˈ- *stress shift:* ˌPeterhead ˈresident
Peterlee ˌpiː.təˈliː, ˈ--- ⓊⓈ ˌpiː.t̬ɚˈliː, ˈ---
Peters ˈpiː.təz ⓊⓈ -t̬ɚz
Petersburg ˈpiː.təz.bɜːg ⓊⓈ -t̬ɚz.bɝːg
Petersfield ˈpiː.təz.fiːld ⓊⓈ -t̬ɚz-
petersham (P) ˈpiː.tə.ʃᵊm ⓊⓈ -t̬ɚ- **-s** -z
Peterson, Petersen ˈpiː.tə.sᵊn ⓊⓈ -t̬ɚ-
Pethick ˈpeθ.ɪk

petiole 'pet.i.əʊl, 'piː.ti- ⓊⓈ 'pet̬.i.oʊl **-s** -z
petit(s) bourgeois ˌpet.i'bɔː.ʒwɑː, -'bʊə- ⓊⓈ pəˌtiː.bʊr'ʒwɑː; ˌpet̬.i-
petit bourgeoisie ˌpet.iˌbɔː.ʒwɑː'ziː, -ˌbʊə- ⓊⓈ pəˌtiː.bʊr-; ˌpet̬.i-
petite pə'tiːt
petite bourgeoisie pəˌtiːtˌbɔː.ʒwɑː'zi, -ˌbʊə- ⓊⓈ -ˌbʊr-
petit four ˌpet.i'fɔːʳ, -fʊəʳ ⓊⓈ ˌpet̬.i'fɔːr **-s** -z
petition pə'tɪʃ.ᵊn, pɪ- ⓊⓈ pə- **-s** -z **-ing** -ɪŋ **-ed** -d **-er/s** -əʳ/z
petit mal ˌpet.i'mæl ⓊⓈ pəˌtiː'mɑːl, -'mæl; ˌpet̬.i'-
petit point ˌpet.i'pɔɪnt ⓊⓈ 'pet̬.iˌpɔɪnt
petit(s) pois ˌpet.i'pwɑː ⓊⓈ pəˌtiː'-, ˌpet̬.i'-
Peto 'piː.təʊ ⓊⓈ -toʊ
Petra 'pet.rə ⓊⓈ 'piː.trə, 'pet.rə
Petrarch 'pet.rɑːk ⓊⓈ 'piː.trɑːrk, 'pet.rɑːrk
Petrarchan pet'rɑː.kᵊn, pə'trɑː-, pɪ- ⓊⓈ pɪ'trɑːr-
Petre 'piː.təʳ ⓊⓈ -t̬ɚ
petrel 'pet.rᵊl **-s** -z
petri dish 'pet.riˌdɪʃ ⓊⓈ 'piː.tri- **-es** -ɪz
Petrie 'piː.tri
petrifaction ˌpet.rɪ'fæk.ʃᵊn, -rə'-
petrification ˌpet.rɪ.fɪ'keɪ.ʃᵊn, -rə-
petri|fy 'pet.rɪ|.faɪ, -rə- **-fies** -faɪz **-fying** -faɪ.ɪŋ **-fied** -faɪd
petrochem|ical ˌpet.rəʊ'kem|.ɪ.kᵊl ⓊⓈ -toʊ'- **-istry** -ɪ.stri
petrodollar 'pet.rəʊˌdɒl.əʳ ⓊⓈ -roʊˌdɑː.lɚ **-s** -z
Petrograd 'pet.rəʊ.græd, -grɑːd ⓊⓈ -rə.græd
petrol 'pet.rᵊl **'petrol ˌpump** ; **'petrol ˌstation**
petrolatum ˌpet.rə'leɪ.təm ⓊⓈ -t̬əm
petrol-bomb 'pet.rᵊl.bɒm ⓊⓈ -bɑːm **-s** -z **-ing** -ɪŋ **-ed** -d
petroleum pə'trəʊ.li.əm, pɪ- ⓊⓈ pə'troʊ- **peˌtroleum 'jelly**
petrolog|y pet'rɒl.ə.dʒ|i, pə'trɒl-, pɪ- ⓊⓈ pə'trɑː.lə- **-ist/s** -ɪst/s
Petruchio pɪ'truː.ki.əʊ, pə-, pet'ruː-, -tʃi- ⓊⓈ pɪ'truː.ki.oʊ, pə-, -tʃi-
Pett pet
petticoat 'pet.ɪ.kəʊt ⓊⓈ 'pet̬.ɪ.koʊt **-s** -s
pettifogg|ing 'pet.ɪˌfɒg|.ɪŋ ⓊⓈ 'pet̬.ɪˌfɑː.g|ɪŋ, -ˌfɔː- **-er/s** -əʳ/z ⓊⓈ -ɚ/z
Pettigrew 'pet.ɪ.gruː ⓊⓈ 'pet̬-
pettish 'pet.ɪʃ ⓊⓈ 'pet̬- **-ly** -li **-ness** -nəs, -nɪs
Pettit 'pet.ɪt ⓊⓈ 'pet̬-
pettitoes 'pet.ɪ.təʊz ⓊⓈ 'pet̬.ɪ.toʊz
pett|y 'pet|.i ⓊⓈ 'pet̬- **-ier** -i.əʳ ⓊⓈ -i.ɚ **-iest** -i.ɪst, -i.əst **-ily** -ɪ.li, -ᵊl.i **-iness/es** -ɪ.nəs/ɪz, -ɪ.nɪs/ɪz ˌ**petty 'cash** ; ˌ**petty 'officer**
petty bourgeois ˌpet.i'bɔː.ʒwɑː, -'bʊə- ⓊⓈ ˌpet̬.i.bʊr'ʒwɑː
petty bourgeoisie ˌpet.iˌbɔː.ʒwɑː'zi, -ˌbʊə- ⓊⓈ ˌpet̬.iˌbʊr-
Petula pɪ'tjuː.lə, pə-, pet'juː- ⓊⓈ pə'tuː-, -'tjuː-
petulan|ce 'pet.jə.lənt|s, -jʊ-, 'petʃ.ə-, '-ʊ- ⓊⓈ 'petʃ.ə- **-cy** -si
petulant 'pet.jə.lənt, -jʊ-, 'petʃ.ə-, '-ʊ- ⓊⓈ 'petʃ.ə- **-ly** -li
petunia pɪ'tjuː.ni.ə, pə- ⓊⓈ pə'tuː.njə, -'tjuː-, '-ni.ə **-s** -z
Petworth 'pet.wəθ, -wɜːθ ⓊⓈ -wɚθ, -wɜːrθ
Peugeot® 'pɜː.ʒəʊ ⓊⓈ pɜː'ʒoʊ, puː-, pjuː- **-s** -z
Pevensey 'pev.ᵊn.zi
Peveril 'pev.ᵊr.ɪl
pew pjuː **-s** -z
pewit 'piː.wɪt ⓊⓈ 'piː-, 'pjuː.ɪt **-s** -s
pewter 'pjuː.təʳ ⓊⓈ -t̬ɚ
Peynell 'peɪ.nᵊl, -nel
peyote peɪ'əʊ.ti ⓊⓈ -'oʊ.t̬i **-s** -z
Peyton 'peɪ.tᵊn
pfennig '*p*fen.ɪg ⓊⓈ 'fen- **-s** -z
pH ˌpiː'eɪtʃ
Phaedo 'fiː.dəʊ, 'faɪ- ⓊⓈ 'fiː.doʊ
Phaedra 'fiː.drə, 'faɪ- ⓊⓈ 'fiː-, 'fed.rə
Phaedrus 'fiː.drəs, 'faɪ- ⓊⓈ 'fiː-
Phaer feɪəʳ ⓊⓈ feɪɚ, fer
Phaethon 'feɪ.ə.θən, '-ɪ- ⓊⓈ -ə.θɑːn, -θən
phaeton *carriage:* 'feɪ.tᵊn, -tɒn ⓊⓈ 'feɪ.ə.t̬ən, 'feɪ.tᵊn **-s** -z
Phaeton *Greek mythology:* 'feɪ.ə.tᵊn, '-ɪ- ⓊⓈ -ə.tɑːn
phagocyte 'fæg.əʊ.saɪt ⓊⓈ -oʊ-, -ə- **-s** -s
phagocytosis ˌfæg.əʊ.saɪ'təʊ.sɪs ⓊⓈ -oʊ.saɪ'toʊ-, ˌ-ə-
phalang|e 'fæl.ændʒ; fə'lændʒ ⓊⓈ feɪ'lændʒ, fə-; 'fæl.əndʒ **-es** -ɪz
phalanges (*alternative plur. of* **phalanx**) fæl'æn.dʒiːz, fə'læn- ⓊⓈ fə-, feɪ-
phalangist (P) fæl'æn.dʒɪst, fə'læn- ⓊⓈ fə-, feɪ- **-s** -s
phalanster|y 'fæl.ən.stᵊr|.i ⓊⓈ -ster- **-ies** -iz
phalanx 'fæl.æŋ*k*s ⓊⓈ 'feɪ.læŋks, 'fæl.æŋks **-es** -ɪz **phalanges** fæl'æn.dʒiːz, fə'læn- ⓊⓈ fə-, feɪ-
Phalaris 'fæl.ə.rɪs
phalarope 'fæl.ə.rəʊp ⓊⓈ -roʊp **-s** -s
phallic 'fæl.ɪk
phallicism 'fæl.ɪ.sɪ.zᵊm
phall|us 'fæl|.əs **-uses** -ə.sɪz **-i** -aɪ
phanerogam 'fæn.ᵊr.əʊ.gæm, fə'ner- ⓊⓈ 'fæn.ə.roʊ-, -ɚ.ə-; fə'ner.oʊ-, '-ə- **-s** -z
phanerogamic ˌfæn.ᵊr.əʊ'gæm.ɪk, fəˌner- ⓊⓈ ˌfæn.ə.roʊ'-, -ɚ.ə'-, fəˌner.oʊ'-, -ə'-
phanerogamous ˌfæn.ᵊr'ɒg.ə.məs ⓊⓈ -ə'rɑː.gə-
phantasm 'fæn.tæz.ᵊm **-s** -z
phantasmagoria ˌfæn.tæz.mə'gɔː.ri.ə, -təz-, -'gɒr.i- ⓊⓈ -'gɔːr.i-
phantasmagoric ˌfæn.tæz.mə'gɒr.ɪk, -təz- ⓊⓈ -'gɔːr.ɪk **-al** -ᵊl
phantasm|al fæn'tæz.m|ᵊl **-ally** -ᵊl.i **-ic** -ɪk
phantas|y 'fæn.tə.s|i ⓊⓈ -t̬ə- **-ies** -iz
phantom 'fæn.təm ⓊⓈ -t̬əm **-s** -z
pharaoh (P) 'feə.rəʊ ⓊⓈ 'fer.oʊ, 'fær-, 'feɪ.roʊ **-s** -z
pharisaic (P) ˌfær.ɪ'seɪ.ɪk, -ə'- ⓊⓈ ˌfer.ɪ'-, ˌfær- **-al** -ᵊl **-ally** -ᵊl.i, -li **-alness** -ᵊl.nəs, -nɪs
pharisaism (P) 'fær.ɪ.seɪ.ɪ.zᵊm, '-ə- ⓊⓈ 'fer.ɪ-, 'fær-
pharisee (P) 'fær.ɪ.siː, '-ə- ⓊⓈ 'fer.ɪ-, 'fær- **-s** -z
pharmaceutic ˌfɑː.mə'sjuː.tɪk, -'suː-, -'kjuː- ⓊⓈ ˌfɑːr.mə'suː.t̬ɪ-, -'sjuː- **-al/s** -ᵊl/z **-ally** -ᵊl.i, -li **-s** -s
pharmacist 'fɑː.mə.sɪst ⓊⓈ 'fɑːr- **-s** -s
pharmacolog|y ˌfɑː.mə'kɒl.ə.dʒ|i ⓊⓈ ˌfɑːr.mə'kɑː.lə- **-ist/s** -ɪst/s
pharmacop(o)ei|a ˌfɑː.mə.kə'piː|.ə, -kəʊ'- ⓊⓈ ˌfɑːr.mə'koʊ- **-as** -əz **-al** -ᵊl
pharmac|y 'fɑː.mə.s|i ⓊⓈ 'fɑːr- **-ies** -iz
Pharos 'feə.rɒs, 'fær.ɒs ⓊⓈ 'fer.ɑːs
pharyngal fə'rɪŋ.gᵊl, fær'ɪŋ- ⓊⓈ fə'rɪŋ-
pharyngeal ˌfær.ɪn'dʒiː.əl; fə'rɪn.dʒi.əl, fær'ɪn- ⓊⓈ fə'rɪn.dʒi-; ˌfer.ɪn'dʒiː-, ˌfær-
pharynges (*plur. of* **pharynx**) fær'ɪn.dʒiːz, fə'rɪn- ⓊⓈ fə-
pharyngitis ˌfær.ɪn'dʒaɪ.tɪs ⓊⓈ ˌfer.ɪn'dʒaɪ.t̬ɪs, ˌfær-
pharynx 'fær.ɪŋks **-es** -ɪz **pharynges** fær'ɪn.dʒiːz, fə'rɪn- ⓊⓈ fə-
phas|e feɪz **-es** -ɪz **-ing** -ɪŋ **-ed** -d
phas|is 'feɪ.s|ɪs ⓊⓈ -s|ɪs, -z|ɪs **-es** -iːz
phatic 'fæt.ɪk ⓊⓈ 'fæt̬-
PhD ˌpiː.eɪtʃ'diː **-'s** -z
pheasant 'fez.ᵊnt **-s** -s
Phebe 'fiː.bi
Phelps felps
phenacetin fɪ'næs.ɪ.tɪn, fə-, fen'æs-, '-ə- ⓊⓈ fɪ'næs.ə-, -tən
Phenic|ia fɪ'nɪʃ|.ə, fə-, fiː-, -'niː.ʃ|ə, -i|.ə ⓊⓈ fə'nɪʃ|.ə, -'niː.ʃ|ə **-ian/s** -ᵊn/z
pheno- ˌfiː.nəʊ- ⓊⓈ ˌfiː.noʊ-, -nə-
phenobarbitone ˌfiː.nəʊ'bɑː.bɪ.təʊn, -bə- ⓊⓈ -noʊ'bɑːr.bɪ.toʊn, -nə'-
phenol 'fiː.nɒl ⓊⓈ -noʊl, -nɔːl, -nɑːl

phenolphthalein ˌfiː.nɒlf'θæl.iːn, -nɒl'-, -'θeɪ.li-, -i.ɪn Ⓤⓢ -noʊl'θæl.iːn, -noʊlf'-, -iː.ɪn
phenom fɪ'nɒm, fə- Ⓤⓢ -'nɑːm **-s** -z
phenomenologic|al fɪˌnɒm.ɪ.nə'lɒdʒ.ɪ.k|ᵊl, fə-, ˌ-ə- Ⓤⓢ fəˌnɑː.mə.nə'lɑː.dʒɪ- **-ally** -ᵊl.i, -li
phenomenology fɪˌnɒm.ɪ'nɒl.ə.dʒi, fə-, -ə'- Ⓤⓢ fəˌnɑː.mə'nɑː.lə-
phenomen|on fɪ'nɒm.ɪ.n|ən, fə-, '-ə- Ⓤⓢ fə'nɑː.mə.n|ɑːn, -n|ən **-a** -ə **-al** -ᵊl **-ally** -ᵊl.i
phenotype 'fiː.nəʊ.taɪp Ⓤⓢ -noʊ-, -nə-
pheromonal 'fer.ə.məʊ.nᵊl Ⓤⓢ ˌfer.ə'moʊ-
pheromon|e 'fer.ə.məʊn Ⓤⓢ -moʊn **-es** -s
phew ɸ, pɸ, fjuː
Note: Expression of surprise, or exclamation indicating that the speaker is hot. It may be a non-verbal exclamation, or have a spelling-based pronunciation /fjuː/.
phi faɪ **-s** -z
phial faɪəl **-s** -z
Phi Beta Kappa ˌfaɪˌbiː.tə'kæp.ə Ⓤⓢ -ˌbeɪ.t̬ə'-, -ˌbiː-
Phidias 'faɪ.di.æs, 'fɪd.i- Ⓤⓢ 'fɪd.i.əs
Phidippides faɪ'dɪp.ɪ.diːz
Phil fɪl
Philadelphi|a ˌfɪl.ə'del.fi|.ə Ⓤⓢ -fi|.ə, -fj|ə **-an/s** -ən/z
philand|er fɪ'læn.d|əʳ, fə- Ⓤⓢ fɪ'læn.d|ɚ **-ers** -əz Ⓤⓢ -ɚz **-ering** -ᵊr.ɪŋ **-ered** -əd Ⓤⓢ -ɚd **-erer/s** -ᵊr.əʳ/z Ⓤⓢ -ɚ.ɚ/z
philanthrope 'fɪl.ən.θrəʊp, -æn- Ⓤⓢ -ən.θroʊp **-s** -s
philanthropic ˌfɪl.ən'θrɒp.ɪk Ⓤⓢ -æn'-, -ən'θrɑː.pɪk **-al** -ᵊl **-ally** -ᵊl.i, -li
philanthrop|y fɪ'lænt.θrə.p|i, fə- Ⓤⓢ fə-, fɪ-, -θroʊ- **-ist/s** -ɪst/s
Philaster fɪ'læs.təʳ Ⓤⓢ -tɚ
philatelic ˌfɪl.ə'tel.ɪk *stress shift:* ˌphilatelic 'club
philatel|y fɪ'læt.ᵊl|.i, fə- Ⓤⓢ -'læt̬- **-ist/s** -ɪst/s
Philbrick 'fɪl.brɪk
Philby 'fɪl.bi
-phile, -phil -faɪl Ⓤⓢ -faɪl, -fɪl
Note: Suffix. Normally unstressed, e.g. **francophile** /'fræŋ.kəʊ.faɪl Ⓤⓢ -koʊ-/.
Philemon fɪ'liː.mɒn, faɪ-, fə-, -mən Ⓤⓢ fɪ'liː.mən, faɪ-
Philharmonia ˌfɪl.hɑː'məʊ.ni.ə, -ə'- Ⓤⓢ -hɑːr'moʊ-, -ɚ'-
philharmonic (P) ˌfɪl.hɑː'mɒn.ɪk, -ə'- Ⓤⓢ -hɑːr'mɑː.nɪk, -ɚ'- **-s** -s *stress shift:* ˌphilharmonic 'orchestra

philhellene fɪl'hel.iːn, '--- Ⓤⓢ fɪl'hel- **-s** -z
philhellenic ˌfɪl.hel'iː.nɪk, -hə'liː-, -'len.ɪk Ⓤⓢ -hə'len-
philhellenism fɪl'hel.ɪ.nɪ.zᵊm, '-ə- Ⓤⓢ '-ə-
-philia -'fɪl.i.ə Ⓤⓢ -'fɪl.i.ə, '-jə
Note: Suffix. Words containing **-philia** are normally stressed on /-'fɪl-/, e.g. **haemophilia** /ˌhiː.mə'fɪl.i.ə Ⓤⓢ -moʊ'-/.
-philiac -'fɪl.i.æk
Note: Suffix. Words containing **-philiac** are normally stressed on the antepenultimate syllable, e.g. **haemophiliac** /ˌhiː.mə'fɪl.i.æk Ⓤⓢ -moʊ'-/.
Philip 'fɪl.ɪp **-s** -s
Philippa 'fɪl.ɪ.pə, '-ə-
Philippi fɪ'lɪp.aɪ, fə-; 'fɪl.ɪ.paɪ, '-ə- Ⓤⓢ fɪ'lɪp.aɪ
Philippian fɪ'lɪp.i.ən, fə- **-s** -z
philippic fɪ'lɪp.ɪk, fə- **-s** -s
Philippine 'fɪl.ɪ.piːn, '-ə-, -paɪn, ˌ--'- Ⓤⓢ 'fɪl.ə.piːn **-s** -z
Philipps 'fɪl.ɪps
Philistia fɪ'lɪs.ti.ə, fə- Ⓤⓢ fə-
philistine (P) 'fɪl.ɪ.staɪn, '-ə- Ⓤⓢ 'fɪl.ɪ.stiːn, -staɪn; fɪ'lɪs.tɪn, -tiːn **-s** -z
philistinism 'fɪl.ɪ.stɪ.nɪ.zᵊm, '-ə- Ⓤⓢ 'fɪl.ɪ.stiː-, -staɪ-; fɪ'lɪs.tɪ-
Phillimore 'fɪl.ɪ.mɔːʳ Ⓤⓢ -mɔːr
Phillip(p)s 'fɪl.ɪps
Phillpot 'fɪl.pɒt Ⓤⓢ -pɑːt **-s** -s
phillumenist fɪ'luː.mə.nɪst, fə-, -'ljuː-, -mɪ- Ⓤⓢ -'luː.mə- **-s** -s
philo- fɪl.əʊ-; fɪ'lɒ-, fə- Ⓤⓢ fɪl.oʊ-, -ə-; fɪ'lɑː-, fə-
Note: Prefix. Normally either takes primary or secondary stress on the first syllable, e.g. **philosophic** /ˌfɪl.ə'sɒf.ɪk Ⓤⓢ -'sɑː.fɪk/, or primary stress on the second syllable, e.g. **philosophy** /fɪ'lɒs.ə.fi Ⓤⓢ -'lɑː.sə-/.
Philoctetes ˌfɪl.ək'tiː.tiːz, -ɒk'- Ⓤⓢ -ək'-, -ɑːk'-
philodendron ˌfɪl.ə'den.drən **-s** -z
philologic ˌfɪl.ə'lɒdʒ.ɪk Ⓤⓢ -'lɑː.dʒɪk **-al** -ᵊl **-ally** -ᵊl.i, -li
philolog|y fɪ'lɒl.ə.dʒ|i, fə- Ⓤⓢ fɪ'lɑː.lə- **-ist/s** -ɪst/s
Philomel 'fɪl.əʊ.mel Ⓤⓢ -oʊ- **-s** -z
Philomela ˌfɪl.əʊ'miː.lə Ⓤⓢ -oʊ'-
Philomena ˌfɪl.əʊ'miː.nə Ⓤⓢ -oʊ'-
philosopher fɪ'lɒs.ə.fəʳ, fə- Ⓤⓢ -'lɑː.sə.fɚ **-s** -z
philosophic ˌfɪl.ə'sɒf.ɪk Ⓤⓢ -ə'sɑː.fɪk, -oʊ'- **-al** -ᵊl **-ally** -ᵊl.i, -li *stress shift:* ˌphilosophic 'view
philosoph|ism fɪ'lɒs.ə.f|ɪ.zᵊm, fə- Ⓤⓢ -'lɑː.sə- **-ist/s** -ɪst/s

philosophiz|e, -is|e fɪ'lɒs.ə.faɪz, fə- Ⓤⓢ -'lɑː.sə- **-es** -ɪz **-ing** -ɪŋ **-ed** -d
philosoph|y fɪ'lɒs.ə.f|i, fə- Ⓤⓢ -'lɑː.sə- **-ies** -iz
Philostratus fɪ'lɒs.trə.təs, fə- Ⓤⓢ fɪ'lɑː.strə.t̬əs
Philotas 'fɪl.ə.tæs
Philpot 'fɪl.pɒt Ⓤⓢ -pɑːt
Philpotts 'fɪl.pɒts Ⓤⓢ -pɑːts
philtre, philter 'fɪl.təʳ Ⓤⓢ -t̬ɚ **-s** -z
Phineas 'fɪn.i.əs, -æs Ⓤⓢ -əs
Phipps fɪps
phiz (P) fɪz
Phizackerley fɪ'zæk.ᵊl.i, fə- Ⓤⓢ -ɚ.li
phizog 'fɪz.ɒg Ⓤⓢ -ɑːg
phlebitic flɪ'bɪt.ɪk, fleb'ɪt- Ⓤⓢ fliː'bɪt̬.ɪk, flɪ-
phlebitis flɪ'baɪ.tɪs, fleb'aɪ- Ⓤⓢ fliː'baɪ.t̬ɪs, flɪ-
phlebotomy flɪ'bɒt.ə.mi, fleb'ɒt- Ⓤⓢ fliː'bɑː.t̬ə-, flɪ-
Phlegethon 'fleg.ɪ.θɒn, '-ə-, -θən Ⓤⓢ -ɪ.θɑːn, 'fledʒ-
phlegm flem **-s** -z
phlegmatic fleg'mæt.ɪk Ⓤⓢ -'mæt̬- **-al** -ᵊl **-ally** -ᵊl.i, -li
phloem 'fləʊ.em, -ɪm Ⓤⓢ 'floʊ.em
phlogistic flɒdʒ'ɪs.tɪk, flɒg-, flə'dʒɪs-, flə'gɪs- Ⓤⓢ floʊ'dʒɪs-
phlogiston flɒdʒ'ɪs.tən, flɒg-, flə'dʒɪs-, flə'gɪs-, -tɒn Ⓤⓢ floʊ'dʒɪs.tɑːn, -tən
phlox flɒks Ⓤⓢ flɑːks **-es** -ɪz
Phnom Penh ˌnɒm'pen, pəˌnɒm- Ⓤⓢ ˌnɑːm-
-phobe -fəʊb Ⓤⓢ -foʊb
Note: Suffix. Normally unstressed, e.g. **technophobe** /'tek.nəʊ.fəʊb Ⓤⓢ -nə.foʊb/.
phob|ia 'fəʊ.b|i.ə Ⓤⓢ 'foʊ- **-ias** -i.əz **-ic** -ɪk
-phobia -'fəʊ.bi.ə Ⓤⓢ -'foʊ.bi.ə
Note: Suffix. Words containing **-phobia** are normally stressed on the antepenultimate syllable, e.g. **arachnophobia** /əˌræk.nəʊ'fəʊ.bi.ə Ⓤⓢ -'foʊ-/.
-phobic -'fəʊ.bɪk Ⓤⓢ -'foʊ.bɪk
Note: Suffix. Words containing **-phobic** are normally stressed on the penultimate syllable, e.g. **claustrophobic** /ˌklɔː.strə'fəʊ.bɪk Ⓤⓢ ˌklɑː.strə'foʊ-/.
Phocian 'fəʊ.ʃi.ən, -si- Ⓤⓢ 'foʊ.si- **-s** -z
Phocion 'fəʊ.si.ən, -ɒn Ⓤⓢ 'foʊ.si.ɑːn
Phocis 'fəʊ.sɪs Ⓤⓢ 'foʊ-
Phoebe 'fiː.bi
Phoebus 'fiː.bəs
Phoenic|ia fɪ'nɪʃ|.ə, fə-, fiː-, -'niː.ʃ|ə, -i|.ə Ⓤⓢ fə'nɪʃ|.ə, -'niː.ʃ|ə **-ian/s** -ᵊn/z

phoenix (P) ˈfiː.nɪks **-es** -ɪz
phon fɒn Ⓤ faːn **-s** -z
phonaesthesia ˌfəʊ.nɪsˈθiː.zi.ə, -niːsˈ-, -nəsˈ-, -ʒi.ə, -ʒə Ⓤ ˌfoʊ.nɪsˈθiː.ʒə, -niːsˈ-, -nəsˈ-
pho|nate fəʊ|ˈneɪt Ⓤ ˈfoʊ|.neɪt **-nates** -ˈneɪts Ⓤ -neɪt **-nating** -ˈneɪ.tɪŋ Ⓤ -neɪ.t̬ɪŋ **-nated** -ˈneɪ.tɪd Ⓤ -neɪ.t̬ɪd
phonation fəʊˈneɪ.ʃən Ⓤ foʊ-
phonatory ˈfəʊ.nə.tər.i, fəʊˈneɪ- Ⓤ ˈfoʊ.nə.tɔːr-
phon|e fəʊn Ⓤ foʊn **-es** -z **-ing** -ɪŋ **-ed** -d **ˈphone ˌbook ; ˈphone ˌbooth ; ˈphone ˌbox ; ˈphone ˌcall**
phonecard ˈfəʊn.kaːd, ˈfəʊŋ- Ⓤ ˈfoʊn.kaːrd **-s** -z
phone-in ˈfəʊn.ɪn Ⓤ ˈfoʊn- **-s** -z
phonematic ˌfəʊ.nɪˈmæt.ɪk, -niːˈ- Ⓤ ˌfoʊ.nɪˈmæt̬- **-s** -s **-ally** -əl.i, -li
phoneme ˈfəʊ.niːm Ⓤ ˈfoʊ- **-s** -z
phonemic fəʊˈniː.mɪk Ⓤ foʊ-, fə- **-s** -s **-ally** -əl.i, -li
phonemicist fəʊˈniː.mɪ.sɪst, -mə- Ⓤ foʊ-, fə- **-s** -s
phone-tapping ˈfəʊnˌtæp.ɪŋ Ⓤ ˈfoʊn-
phonetic fəʊˈnet.ɪk Ⓤ foʊˈnet̬-, fə- **-ally** -əl.i, -li **-s** -s
phonetician ˌfəʊ.nɪˈtɪʃ.ən, ˌfɒn.ɪˈ-, -əˈ- Ⓤ ˌfoʊ.nəˈ- **-s** -z
phoneticiz|e, -is|e fəʊˈnet.ɪ.saɪz, ˈ-ə- Ⓤ foʊˈnet̬-, fə- **-es** -ɪz **-ing** -ɪŋ **-ed** -d
phonetist ˈfəʊ.nɪ.tɪst, -nə-, -net.ɪst Ⓤ ˈfoʊ.nə.t̬ɪst **-s** -s
phon|ey ˈfəʊ.n|i Ⓤ ˈfoʊ- **-ier** -i.əʳ Ⓤ -i.ɚ **-iest** -i.ɪst, -i.əst **-ily** -ɪ.li, -əl.i **-eys** -iz **-iness** -ɪ.nəs, -ɪ.nɪs
phonic ˈfɒn.ɪk Ⓤ ˈfaː.nɪk
phonics ˈfɒn.ɪks Ⓤ ˈfaː.nɪks
phono- fəʊ.nəʊ-, fɒn.əʊ-; fəʊˈnɒ- Ⓤ foʊ.nə-, faː-, -noʊ-; foʊˈnaː-, fə-
Note: Prefix. Normally either takes primary or secondary stress on the first syllable, e.g. **phonogram** /ˈfəʊ.nə.græm Ⓤ ˈfoʊ.nə-/, **phonographic** /ˌfəʊ.nəˈgræf.ɪk Ⓤ ˌfoʊ.nəˈ-/, or primary stress on the second syllable, e.g. **phonology** /fəʊˈnɒl.ə.dʒi Ⓤ fəˈnaː.lə-/.
phonogram ˈfəʊ.nə.græm Ⓤ ˈfoʊ- **-s** -z
phonograph ˈfəʊ.nə.graːf, -græf Ⓤ ˈfoʊ.nə.græf **-s** -s
phonographer fəʊˈnɒg.rə.fəʳ Ⓤ foʊˈnaː.grə.fɚ, fə- **-s** -z
phonographic ˌfəʊ.nəˈgræf.ɪk Ⓤ ˌfoʊˈ- **-al** -əl **-ally** -əl.i, -li *stress shift:* ˌphonographic ˈsystem
phonographist fəʊˈnɒg.rə.fɪst Ⓤ foʊˈnaː.grə-, fə- **-s** -s
phonography fəʊˈnɒg.rə.fi Ⓤ foʊˈnaː.grə-, fə-
phonological ˌfəʊ.nəˈlɒdʒ.ɪ.kəl, ˌfɒn.əˈ-, -əlˈɒdʒ- Ⓤ ˌfoʊ.nəˈlaː.dʒɪ-, -noʊˈ- **-ly** -i *stress shift:* ˌphonological ˈtheory
phonologist fəʊˈnɒl.ə.dʒɪst Ⓤ fəˈnaː.lə-, foʊ- **-s** -s
phonolog|y fəʊˈnɒl.ə.dʒ|i Ⓤ fəˈnaː.lə-, foʊ- **-ies** -iz
phonotactic ˌfəʊ.nəʊˈtæk.tɪk, ˌfɒn.əʊˈ- Ⓤ ˌfoʊ.nəˈ-, -noʊˈ- **-s** -s **-ally** -əl.i, -li *stress shift:* ˌphonotactic ˈrules
phonotype ˈfəʊ.nəʊ.taɪp Ⓤ ˈfoʊ.nə-, -noʊ- **-s** -s
phon|y ˈfəʊ.n|i Ⓤ ˈfoʊ- **-ier** -i.əʳ Ⓤ -i.ɚ **-iest** -i.ɪst, -i.əst **-ily** -ɪ.li, -əl.i **-ies** -iz **-iness** -ɪ.nəs, -ɪ.nɪs
phosgene ˈfɒz.dʒiːn, ˈfɒs- Ⓤ ˈfaːs-, ˈfaːz-
phosphate ˈfɒs.feɪt, -fɪt, -fət Ⓤ ˈfaːs.feɪt **-s** -s
phosphene ˈfɒs.fiːn Ⓤ ˈfaːs-, ˈfaːz- **-s** -z
phosphide ˈfɒs.faɪd Ⓤ ˈfaːs- **-s** -z
phosphite ˈfɒs.faɪt Ⓤ ˈfaːs- **-s** -s
phospho- ˌfɒs.fəʊ- Ⓤ ˌfaːs.foʊ-, -fə-
phosphor ˈfɒs.fəʳ Ⓤ ˈfaːs.fɚ, -fɔːr **-s** -z
phosphoresc|e ˌfɒs.fərˈes Ⓤ ˌfaːs.fəˈres **-es** -ɪz **-ing** -ɪŋ **-ed** -t
phosphorescence ˌfɒs.fərˈes.ənts Ⓤ ˌfaːs.fəˈres-
phosphorescent ˌfɒs.fərˈes.ənt Ⓤ ˌfaːs.fəˈres- *stress shift:* ˌphosphorescent ˈink
phosphoric fɒsˈfɒr.ɪk Ⓤ faːsˈfɔːr-
phosphorous ˈfɒs.fər.əs Ⓤ ˈfaːs-; faːsˈfɔːr-
phosphorus ˈfɒs.fər.əs Ⓤ ˈfaːs-
phossy ˈfɒs.i Ⓤ ˈfaː.si
photic ˈfəʊ.tɪk Ⓤ ˈfoʊ.t̬ɪk
photo ˈfəʊ.təʊ Ⓤ ˈfoʊ.t̬oʊ **-s** -z ˌ**photo ˈfinish**
photocall ˈfəʊ.təʊ.kɔːl Ⓤ ˈfoʊ.t̬oʊ- **-s** -z
photocell ˈfəʊ.təʊ.sel Ⓤ ˈfoʊ.t̬oʊ- **-s** -z
photochemical ˌfəʊ.təʊˈkem.ɪ.kəl Ⓤ ˌfoʊ.t̬oʊ-
photochrome ˈfəʊ.təʊ.krəʊm Ⓤ ˈfoʊ.t̬oʊ.kroʊm **-s** -z
photocompos|e ˌfəʊ.təʊ.kəmˈpəʊz Ⓤ ˌfoʊ.t̬oʊ.kəmˈpoʊz **-es** -ɪz **-ing** -ɪŋ **-ed** -d
photocomposition ˌfəʊ.təʊˌkɒm.pəˈzɪʃ.ən Ⓤ ˌfoʊ.t̬oʊˌkaːm.pəˈ- **-s** -z
photocopier ˈfəʊ.təʊˌkɒp.i.əʳ, ˌfəʊ.təʊˈkɒp.i.əʳ Ⓤ ˈfoʊ.t̬oʊˌkaː.pi.ɚ, -t̬əˌ- **-s** -z
photocop|y ˈfəʊ.təʊˌkɒp|.i Ⓤ ˈfoʊ.t̬oʊˌkaː.p|i, -t̬əˌ- **-ies** -iz **-ying** -i.ɪŋ **-ied** -id
photoelectric ˌfəʊ.təʊ.ɪˈlek.trɪk Ⓤ ˌfoʊ.t̬oʊ- *stress shift:* ˌphotoelectric ˈcell
photo-essay ˈfəʊ.təʊˌes.eɪ Ⓤ ˌfoʊ.toʊ- **-s** -z
Photofit® ˈfəʊ.təʊ.fɪt Ⓤ ˈfoʊ.t̬oʊ-
photogenic ˌfəʊ.təʊˈdʒen.ɪk, -ˈdʒiː.nɪk Ⓤ ˌfoʊ.t̬oʊˈdʒen.ɪk, -t̬əˈ- *stress shift:* ˌphotogenic ˈperson
photogrammetr|ist ˌfəʊ.təʊˈgræm.ə.tr|ɪst, ˈ-ɪ- Ⓤ ˌfoʊ.t̬oʊ- **-ists** -ɪsts **-y** -i
photograph ˈfəʊ.tə.graːf, -græf Ⓤ ˈfoʊ.t̬oʊ.græf, -t̬ə- **-s** -s **-ing** -ɪŋ **-ed** -t
photographer fəˈtɒg.rə.fəʳ Ⓤ -ˈtaː.grə.fɚ **-s** -z
photographic ˌfəʊ.təˈgræf.ɪk Ⓤ ˌfoʊ.t̬əˈ- **-al** -əl **-ally** -əl.i, -li *stress shift:* ˌphotographic ˈmodel
photography fəˈtɒg.rə.fi Ⓤ -ˈtaː.grə-
photogravure ˌfəʊ.təʊ.grəˈvjʊəʳ, -ˈvjɔːʳ Ⓤ ˌfoʊ.t̬oʊ.grəˈvjʊr, -t̬ə- **-s** -z
photojournal|ism ˌfəʊ.təʊˈdʒɜː.nəl|.ɪ.zəm Ⓤ ˌfoʊ.t̬oʊˈdʒɜːr- **-ist/s** -ɪst/s
photomontag|e ˌfəʊ.təʊ.mɒnˈtaːʒ Ⓤ ˌfoʊ.t̬oʊ.maːnˈ- **-es** -ɪz
photon ˈfəʊ.tɒn Ⓤ ˈfoʊ.taːn **-s** -z
photo-opportunit|y ˌfəʊ.təʊˌɒp.əˈtjuː.nə.t|i, -ˈtʃuː-, -nɪ- Ⓤ ˌfoʊ.t̬oʊˌaː.pɚˈtuː.nə.t̬|i, -ˈtjuː- **-ies** -iz
photosensitive ˌfəʊ.təʊˈsent.sɪ.tɪv, -sə- Ⓤ ˌfoʊ.t̬oʊˈsent.sə-
photosensitivity ˌfəʊ.təʊˌsent.sɪˈtɪv.ə.ti, -səˈ-, -ə.ti Ⓤ ˌfoʊ.t̬oʊˌsent.səˈt̬ɪv.ə.t̬i
photosensitiz|e, -is|e ˌfəʊ.təʊˈsent.sɪ.taɪz Ⓤ ˌfoʊ.t̬oʊˈsent.sə- **-es** -ɪz **-ing** -ɪŋ **-ed** -d
photosphere ˈfəʊ.təʊ.sfɪəʳ Ⓤ ˈfoʊ.t̬oʊ.sfɪr **-s** -z
photo|stat® ˈfəʊ.təʊ|.stæt Ⓤ ˈfoʊ.t̬oʊ-, -t̬ə- **-stats** -stæts **-statting** -stæt.ɪŋ Ⓤ -stæt̬.ɪŋ **-statted** -stæt.ɪd Ⓤ -stæt̬.ɪd
photostatic ˌfəʊ.təʊˈstæt.ɪk Ⓤ ˌfoʊ.t̬oʊˈstæt̬.ɪk, -t̬əˈ- *stress shift:* ˌphotostatic ˈcopy
photosynthesis ˌfəʊ.təʊˈsɪnt.θə.sɪs, -θɪ- Ⓤ ˌfoʊ.t̬oʊˈ-, -t̬əˈ-
photosynthesiz|e, -is|e ˌfəʊ.təʊˈsɪnt.θə.saɪz, -θɪ- Ⓤ ˌfoʊ.t̬oʊˈ-, -t̬əˈ- **-es** -ɪz **-ing** -ɪŋ **-ed** -d
photosynthetic ˌfəʊ.təʊ.sɪnˈθet.ɪk Ⓤ ˌfoʊ.t̬oʊ.sɪnˈθet̬-, -t̬ə- **-ally** -əl.i, -li

phototropic ˌfəʊ.təʊˈtrɒp.ɪk Ⓤⓢ ˌfoʊ.t̬oʊˈtrɑː.pɪk, -t̬əˈ-, -ˈtroʊ- **-ally** -ᵊl.i Ⓤⓢ -li
phototropism fəʊˈtɒt.rə.pɪ.zᵊm; ˌfəʊ.təʊˈtrəʊ- Ⓤⓢ foʊˈtɑː.trə- **-s** -z
phrasal ˈfreɪ.zᵊl **-s** -z ˌ**phrasal ˈverb**
phras|e freɪz **-es** -ɪz **-ing** -ɪŋ **-ed** -d ˈ**phrase** ˌ**book**
phraseologic ˌfreɪ.zi.əˈlɒdʒ.ɪk Ⓤⓢ -ˈlɑː.dʒɪk **-al** -ᵊl **-ally** -ᵊl.i, -li
phraseolog|y ˌfreɪ.ziˈɒl.ə.dʒ|i Ⓤⓢ -ˈɑː.lə- **-ies** -iz
phrenetic frəˈnet.ɪk, frɪ-, frenˈet- Ⓤⓢ frɪˈnet̬-, frə- **-al** -ᵊl **-ally** -ᵊl.i, -li
phrenic ˈfren.ɪk
phrenologic|al ˌfren.ᵊlˈɒdʒ.ɪ.k|ᵊl Ⓤⓢ -əˈlɑː.dʒɪ- **-ally** -ᵊl.i, -li
phrenolog|y frɪˈnɒl.ə.dʒ|i, frə-, frenˈɒl- Ⓤⓢ frɪˈnɑː.lə-, frə- **-ist/s** -ɪst/s
Phryg|ia ˈfrɪdʒ|.i.ə **-ian/s** -i.ən/z Ⓤⓢ -i.ən/z, -jən/z
Phryne ˈfraɪ.ni
phthalic ˈθæl.ɪk, ˈfθæl-, ˈθeɪ.lɪk Ⓤⓢ ˈθæl-, ˈfθæl-
phthisis ˈθaɪ.sɪs, ˈfθaɪ- Ⓤⓢ ˈθaɪ-, ˈtaɪ-, ˈfθaɪ-
Phuket ˌpuːˈket
phut fʌt
phylacter|y fɪˈlæk.tᵊr|.i **-ies** -iz
Phyllis ˈfɪl.ɪs
phyllo ˈfaɪ.ləʊ, ˈfiː-, ˈfɪl.əʊ Ⓤⓢ ˈfiː.loʊ, ˈfaɪ- ˌphyllo ˈpastry Ⓤⓢ ˈphyllo ˌpastry
phylloxer|a fɪˈlɒk.sᵊr|.ə; ˌfɪl.ɒkˈsɪə.r|ə Ⓤⓢ fɪˈlɑːk.sɚ|.ə; ˌfɪl.ɑːkˈsɪr- **-ae** -iː **-as** -əz
phyl|um ˈfaɪ.l|əm **-a** -ə
physiatric ˌfɪz.iˈæt.rɪk **-s** -s **-al** -ᵊl
physiatricist ˌfɪz.iˈæt.rɪ.sɪst, -rə- **-s** -s
physic ˈfɪz.ɪk **-s** -s **-king** -ɪŋ **-ked** -t
physic|al ˈfɪz.ɪ.k|ᵊl **-als** -ᵊlz **-ally** -ᵊl.i, -li ˌ**physical eduˈcation** ; ˌ**physical ˈtherapy**
physicality ˌfɪz.ɪˈkæl.ə.ti, -ɪ.ti Ⓤⓢ -ə.t̬i
physician fɪˈzɪʃ.ᵊn, fə- Ⓤⓢ fɪ- **-s** -z
physicist ˈfɪz.ɪ.sɪst, ˈ-ə- Ⓤⓢ ˈ-ɪ- **-s** -s
physio- fɪz.i.əʊ-; ˌfɪz.iˈɒ- Ⓤⓢ fɪz.i.oʊ-, -ə-; ˌfɪz.iˈɑː-
Note: Prefix. Normally either takes primary or secondary stress on the first syllable, e.g. **physiologic** /ˌfɪz.i.əˈlɒdʒ.ɪk Ⓤⓢ -ˈlɑː.dʒɪk/, or secondary stress on the first syllable with primary stress on the third syllable, e.g. **physiology** /ˌfɪz.iˈɒl.ə.dʒi Ⓤⓢ -ˈɑː.lə-/.
physio ˈfɪz.i.əʊ Ⓤⓢ -oʊ **-s** -z
physiognomic ˌfɪz.i.əˈnɒm.ɪk Ⓤⓢ -ɑːgˈnɑː.mɪk, -əˈ- **-al** -ᵊl **-ally** -ᵊl.i, -li
physiognomist ˌfɪz.iˈɒn.ə.mɪst Ⓤⓢ -ˈɑːg.nə- **-s** -s
physiognom|y ˌfɪz.iˈɒn.ə.m|i Ⓤⓢ -ˈɑːg.nə- **-ies** -iz
physiographic ˌfɪz.i.əʊˈgræf.ɪk Ⓤⓢ -oʊˈ-, -əˈ- **-al** -ᵊl
physiograph|y ˌfɪz.iˈɒg.rə.f|i Ⓤⓢ -ˈɑː.grə- **-er/s** -əʳ/z Ⓤⓢ -ɚ/z
physiologic ˌfɪz.i.əˈlɒdʒ.ɪk Ⓤⓢ -ˈlɑː.dʒɪk **-al** -ᵊl **-ally** -ᵊl.i, -li
physiolog|y ˌfɪz.iˈɒl.ə.dʒ|i Ⓤⓢ -ˈɑː.lə- **-ist/s** -ɪst/s
physiotherap|y ˌfɪz.i.əʊˈθer.ə.p|i Ⓤⓢ -oʊˈ-, -əˈ- **-ist/s** -ɪst/s
physique fɪˈziːk, fə- Ⓤⓢ fɪ-
phytoplankton ˌfaɪ.təʊˈplæŋk.tən, -tɒn Ⓤⓢ -t̬oʊˈplæŋk.tən
pi paɪ **-s** -z
Piaf ˈpiː.æf, -ˈ- Ⓤⓢ ˈpiː.ɑːf, -ˈ-
piaff|e piˈæf, pjæf Ⓤⓢ pjæf **-es** -s **-ing** -ɪŋ **-ed** -t
Piaget piˈæʒ.eɪ, -ˈɑː.ʒeɪ Ⓤⓢ ˌpiː.əˈʒeɪ, pjɑːˈ-
pia mater ˌpaɪ.əˈmeɪ.təʳ, ˌpiː- Ⓤⓢ -ˈmeɪ.t̬ɚ, -ˈmɑː-
pianissimo ˌpiː.əˈnɪs.ɪ.məʊ, -ænˈɪs-, pjɑːˈnɪs-, ˌpiː.ɑːˈ-, pjænˈɪs-, pjəˈnɪs- Ⓤⓢ ˌpiː.əˈnɪs.ɪ.moʊ **-s** -z
Note: Among British professional musicians, /pjɑːˈnɪs-, ˌpɪ.ɑːˈ-, ˌpiː.əˈ-/ appear to be the most frequently used forms.
pianist ˈpiː.ə.nɪst, ˈpjɑː.nɪst, ˈpjæn.ɪst, piˈæn- Ⓤⓢ ˈpiː.ᵊn.ɪst; piˈæn-, ˈpjæn- **-s** -s
Note: British professional musicians generally pronounce /ˈpiː.ə.nɪst/.
piano *instrument:* piˈæn.əʊ, ˈpjæn-, ˈpjɑː.nəʊ, piˈɑː- Ⓤⓢ piˈæn.oʊ, ˈpjæn- **-s** -z
Note: The forms /ˈpjɑː.nəʊ, piˈɑː-/ are frequent among British professional musicians. **piˌano acˈcordion** ; **piˈano ˌbar** ; **piˈano ˌstool**
piano *softly:* ˈpjɑː.nəʊ, piˈɑː- Ⓤⓢ -noʊ **-s** -z
pianoforte piˌæn.əʊˈfɔː.teɪ, ˌpjæn-, ˌpjɑː.nəʊˈ-, piˌɑː-, -ti Ⓤⓢ piˌæn.oʊˈfɔːr.teɪ, -ti; -ˈæn.oʊ.fɔːrt **-s** -z
Pianola® ˌpiː.əˈnəʊ.lə, pjænˈəʊ-, ˌpiː.ænˈ- Ⓤⓢ ˌpiː.əˈnoʊ-, -ænˈoʊ- **-s** -z
piastre, **piaster** piˈæs.təʳ, -ˈɑː.stəʳ Ⓤⓢ -ˈæs.tɚ **-s** -z
piazza piˈæt.sə, -ˈɑːt- Ⓤⓢ -ˈɑːt.sə, -sɑː, -ˈɑː.zə, -ˈæt.sə, -ˈæz.ə **-s** -z
pibroch ˈpiː.brɒk, -brɒx Ⓤⓢ -brɑːk **-s** -s
pica ˈpaɪ.kə
picador ˈpɪk.ə.dɔːʳ Ⓤⓢ -dɔːr **-s** -z
picadores (*alternative plur. of* **picador**) ˌpɪk.əˈdɔː.riːz Ⓤⓢ -ˈdɔːr.iːz
picaninn|y ˌpɪk.əˈnɪn|.i, ˈpɪk.ə.nɪ.n|i Ⓤⓢ ˈpɪk- **-ies** -iz
Picardy ˈpɪk.ə.di, -ɑː- Ⓤⓢ ˈ-ɚ-, ˈ-ɑːr-
picaresque ˌpɪk.ᵊrˈesk Ⓤⓢ -ɚˈ-
picaroon ˌpɪk.əˈruːn **-s** -z **-ing** -ɪŋ **-ed** -d
Picasso pɪˈkæs.əʊ Ⓤⓢ -ˈkɑː.soʊ, -ˈkæs.oʊ
picayun|e ˌpɪk.əˈjuːn, -eɪˈ-, -iˈ- Ⓤⓢ ˈpɪk.ə.juːn, ˌ--ˈ- **-es** -z **-ish** -ɪʃ
Piccadilly ˌpɪk.əˈdɪl.i *stress shift, see compound:* ˌ**Piccadilly ˈCircus**
piccalilli ˌpɪk.əˈlɪl.i Ⓤⓢ ˈpɪk.ə.lɪl-
piccaninn|y ˌpɪk.əˈnɪn|.i, ˈpɪk.ə.nɪ.n|i Ⓤⓢ ˈpɪk- **-ies** -iz
piccolo ˈpɪk.ə.ləʊ Ⓤⓢ -loʊ **-s** -z
pick pɪk **-s** -s **-ing** -ɪŋ **-ed** -t **-er/s** -əʳ/z Ⓤⓢ -ɚ/z
pickaback ˈpɪk.ə.bæk **-s**
pickaninn|y ˌpɪk.əˈnɪn|.i, ˈpɪk.ə.nɪ.n|i Ⓤⓢ ˈpɪk- **-ies** -iz
pickax|(e) ˈpɪk.æks **-es** -ɪz **-ing** -ɪŋ **-ed** -t
pickerel ˈpɪk.ᵊr.ᵊl **-s** -z
Pickering ˈpɪk.ᵊr.ɪŋ
pick|et ˈpɪk|.ɪt **-ets** -ɪts **-eting** -ɪ.tɪŋ Ⓤⓢ -ɪ.t̬ɪŋ **-eted** -ɪ.tɪd Ⓤⓢ -ɪ.t̬ɪd **-er/s** -ɪ.təʳ/z Ⓤⓢ -ɪ.t̬ɚ/z ˈ**picket** ˌ**line**
Pickford ˈpɪk.fəd Ⓤⓢ -fɚd
pickings ˈpɪk.ɪŋz
pickl|e ˈpɪk.l̩ **-es** -z **-ing** -ɪŋ, ˈpɪk.lɪŋ **-ed** -d
Pickles ˈpɪk.l̩z
picklock ˈpɪk.lɒk Ⓤⓢ -lɑːk **-s** -s
pick-me-up ˈpɪk.mi.ʌp **-s** -s
pickpocket ˈpɪkˌpɒk.ɪt Ⓤⓢ -ˌpɑː.kɪt **-s** -s
pick-up ˈpɪk.ʌp **-s** -s ˈ**pick-up** ˌ**truck**
Pickwick ˈpɪk.wɪk ˌ**Pickwick ˈPapers** Ⓤⓢ ˈ**Pickwick** ˌ**Papers**
Pickwickian pɪkˈwɪk.i.ən
pick|y ˈpɪk|.i **-ier** -i.əʳ Ⓤⓢ -i.ɚ **-iest** -i.ɪst, -i.əst **-iness** -ɪ.nəs, -ɪ.nɪs
picnic ˈpɪk.nɪk **-s** -s **-king** -ɪŋ **-ked** -t **-ker/s** -əʳ/z Ⓤⓢ -ɚ/z
picot ˈpiː.kəʊ, -ˈ-, pɪˈkəʊ Ⓤⓢ ˈpiː.koʊ, -ˈ-
picotee ˌpɪk.əˈtiː Ⓤⓢ ˌpɪk.əˈtiː, ˈ--- **-s** -z
picric ˈpɪk.rɪk
Pict pɪkt **-s** -s
Pictish ˈpɪk.tɪʃ
pictograph ˈpɪk.təʊ.grɑːf, -græf Ⓤⓢ -toʊ.græf, -tə- **-s** -s
Picton ˈpɪk.tən
pictorial pɪkˈtɔː.ri.əl Ⓤⓢ -ˈtɔːr.i- **-ly** -i
pict|ure ˈpɪk.tʃ|əʳ Ⓤⓢ -tʃ|ɚ **-ures** -əz Ⓤⓢ -ɚz **-uring** -ᵊr.ɪŋ **-ured** -əd Ⓤⓢ -ɚd ˈ**picture** ˌ**book** ; ˌ**picture ˈpostcard** ; ˌ**picture ˈwindow**
picturesque ˌpɪk.tʃᵊrˈesk **-ly** -li **-ness** -nəs, -nɪs

piddl|e ˈpɪd.l̩ **-es** -z **-ing** -ɪŋ, ˈpɪd.lɪŋ **-ed** -d **-er/s** -əʳ/z Ⓤⓢ -ɚ/z, ˈpɪd.ləʳ/z Ⓤⓢ -lɚ/z
piddling *(adj.)* ˈpɪd.l̩.ɪŋ, ˈpɪd.lɪŋ
pidgin (P) ˈpɪdʒ.ɪn **-s** -z
Pidsley ˈpɪdz.li
pie paɪ **-s** -z ˈ**pie** ˌ**chart** ; **as** ˌ**easy as** ˈ**pie** ; **have a** ˌ**finger in** ˌ**every** ˈ**pie** ; **to** ˌ**eat** ˌ**humble** ˈ**pie** ; ˌ**pie in the** ˈ**sky**
piebald ˈpaɪ.bɔːld Ⓤⓢ -bɔːld, -bɑːld **-s** -z
piec|e piːs **-es** -ɪz **-ing** -ɪŋ **-ed** -t ˈ**piece** ˌ**rate** ; ˌ**piece of** ˈ**cake**
pièce(s) de résistance piˌes.də.rez.ɪˈstɑ̃ns, ˌpjes-, -rɪ.zɪˈ-, -rə- Ⓤⓢ ˌpjes.dəˌreɪ.ziːˈstɑ̃ːns
piecemeal ˈpiːs.miːl
piecework ˈpiːs.wɜːk Ⓤⓢ -wɜːrk
piecrust ˈpaɪ.krʌst **-s** -s
pied paɪd ˌ**pied** ˈ**piper**
pied(s)-à-terre ˌpjeɪd.ɑːˈteəʳ, ˌpjed- Ⓤⓢ -ˈter
piedmont (P) ˈpiːd.mənt, -mɒnt Ⓤⓢ -mɑːnt
piedmontese (P) ˌpiːd.mənˈtiːz, -mɒnˈ- Ⓤⓢ -mɑːnˈ-
pie-eyed ˌpaɪˈaɪd *stress shift:* ˌpie-eyed ˈreveller
pier pɪəʳ Ⓤⓢ pɪr **-s** -z
pierc|e (P) pɪəs Ⓤⓢ pɪrs **-es** -ɪz **-ing/ly** -ɪŋ/li **-ed** -t **-er/s** -əʳ/z Ⓤⓢ -ɚ/z **-eable** -ə.bl̩
Piercy ˈpɪə.si Ⓤⓢ ˈpɪr-
pierglass ˈpɪə.glɑːs Ⓤⓢ ˈpɪr.glæs **-es** -ɪz
pierhead ˈpɪə.hed Ⓤⓢ ˈpɪr- **-s** -z
Pierian paɪˈer.i.ən, -ˈɪə.ri-, pi- Ⓤⓢ paɪˈɪr.i-
Pierpoint ˈpɪə.pɔɪnt Ⓤⓢ ˈpɪr-
Pierpont ˈpɪə.pɒnt, -pənt Ⓤⓢ ˈpɪr.pɑːnt
Pierre *name:* piˈeəʳ Ⓤⓢ piːˈer
Pierre *place in US:* pɪəʳ Ⓤⓢ pɪr
Pierrepont ˈpɪə.pɒnt, -pənt Ⓤⓢ ˈpɪr.pɑːnt
pierrot (P) ˈpɪə.rəʊ, ˈpjer.əʊ Ⓤⓢ ˌpiː.əˈroʊ **-s** -z
Piers pɪəz Ⓤⓢ pɪrz
Pierson ˈpɪə.sᵊn Ⓤⓢ ˈpɪr-
Piesporter ˈpiːz.pɔː.təʳ Ⓤⓢ -pɔːr.t̬ɚ
pietà ˌpiː.etˈɑː, -erˈtɑː, ˈ--- Ⓤⓢ ˌpiː.eɪˈtɑː, ˌpjeɪˈ- **-s** -z
Pietermaritzburg ˌpiː.təˈmær.ɪts.bɜːg Ⓤⓢ -t̬ɚˈmer.ɪts.bɜːrg
piet|ism ˈpaɪə.t|ɪ.zᵊm, ˈpaɪ.ɪ- Ⓤⓢ ˈpaɪə- **-ist/s** -ɪst/s
pietistic ˌpaɪəˈtɪs.tɪk
piet|y ˈpaɪə.t|i, ˈpaɪ.ɪ- Ⓤⓢ ˈpaɪə.t̬|i **-ies** -iz
piezoelectric piˌet.səʊ.ɪˈlek.trɪk; ˌpiː.zəʊ-; paɪˌiː.zəʊ-; ˌpaɪ.ɪ- Ⓤⓢ paɪˌiː.zoʊ-; piːˌeɪ- **-al** -ᵊl
piezoelectricity piˌet.səʊˌel.ɪkˈtrɪs.ə.ti; ˌpiː.zəʊ-; paɪˌiː.zəʊ-; ˌpaɪ.ɪ-; -ˌiː.lekˈ-; -ɪˌlekˈ-; -ɪ.ti; Ⓤⓢ paɪˌiː.zoʊˌiː.lekˈtrɪs.ə.t̬i, -iːˌlekˈ-; piˌeɪ-
piffl|e ˈpɪf.l̩ **-es** -z **-ing** -ɪŋ, ˈpɪf.lɪŋ **-ed** -d
pig pɪg **-s** -z **-ging** -ɪŋ **-ged** -d ˈ**pig** ˌ**iron** ; ˌ**make a** ˌ**pig's** ˈ**ear of**
pigeon ˈpɪdʒ.ən, -ɪn Ⓤⓢ -ən **-s** -z
pigeonhol|e *(n. v.)* ˈpɪdʒ.ən.həʊl, -ɪn- Ⓤⓢ -ən.hoʊl **-es** -z **-ing** -ɪŋ **-ed** -d
pigeon-toed ˌpɪdʒ.ənˈtəʊd, -ɪn- Ⓤⓢ ˈpɪdʒ.ən.toʊd *stress shift, British only:* ˌpigeon-toed ˈwalk
pigger|y ˈpɪg.ᵊr|.i **-ies** -iz
piggish ˈpɪg.ɪʃ **-ly** -li **-ness** -nəs, -nɪs
Piggott ˈpɪg.ət
pigg|y ˈpɪg|.i **-ies** -iz **-ier** -i.əʳ Ⓤⓢ -i.ɚ **-iest** -i.ɪst, -i.əst
piggyback ˈpɪg.i.bæk
piggybank ˈpɪg.i.bæŋk **-s** -s
pigheaded ˌpɪgˈhed.ɪd **-ly** -li **-ness** -nəs, -nɪs *stress shift:* ˌpigheaded ˈperson
piglet ˈpɪg.lət, -lɪt Ⓤⓢ -lɪt **-s** -s
pigment *(n.)* ˈpɪg.mənt **-s**
pigmen|t *(v.)* pɪgˈmen|t, ˈpɪg.mən|t Ⓤⓢ ˈpɪg.mən|t **-ts** -ts **-ting** -tɪŋ Ⓤⓢ -t̬ɪŋ **-ted** -tɪd Ⓤⓢ -t̬ɪd
pigmentation ˌpɪg.mənˈteɪ.ʃᵊn, -menˈ- **-s** -z
pigm|y ˈpɪg.m|i **-ies** -iz
pignut ˈpɪg.nʌt **-s** -s
Pigott ˈpɪg.ət
pigpen ˈpɪg.pen **-s** -z
pigskin ˈpɪg.skɪn **-s** -z
pig-sticking ˈpɪgˌstɪk.ɪŋ
pigst|y ˈpɪg.st|aɪ **-ies** -aɪz
pigswill ˈpɪg.swɪl
pigtail ˈpɪg.teɪl **-s** -z
pike (P) paɪk **-s** -s ˌ**Pike's** ˈ**Peak**
pikelet ˈpaɪ.klət, -klɪt Ⓤⓢ -lɪt **-s** -s
pikestaff ˈpaɪk.stɑːf Ⓤⓢ -stæf **-s** -s
pilaf(f) ˈpɪl.æf, ˈpiː.læf, -ˈ- Ⓤⓢ piːˈlɑːf, ˈ-- **-s** -s
pilaster pɪˈlæs.təʳ, pə- Ⓤⓢ pɪˈlæs.tɚ **-s** -z
Pilate ˈpaɪ.lət
Pilatus pɪˈlɑː.təs Ⓤⓢ pɪ-; piːˈlɑː.tʊs
pilau ˈpɪl.aʊ, ˈpiː.laʊ, -ˈ- Ⓤⓢ pɪˈlɔː, piː-, -ˈlaʊ, -ˈlɑː **-s** -z
pilchard ˈpɪl.tʃəd Ⓤⓢ -tʃɚd **-s** -z
pil|e paɪl **-es** -z **-ing** -ɪŋ **-ed** -d
pile-driv|er ˈpaɪlˌdraɪ.v|əʳ Ⓤⓢ -v|ɚ **-ers** -əz Ⓤⓢ -ɚz **-ing** -ɪŋ
pile-up ˈpaɪl.ʌp **-s** -s
pilf|er ˈpɪl.f|əʳ Ⓤⓢ -f|ɚ **-ers** -əz Ⓤⓢ -ɚz **-ering** -ᵊr.ɪŋ **-ered** -əd Ⓤⓢ -ɚd **-erer/s** -ᵊr.əʳ/z Ⓤⓢ -ɚ.ɚ/z
pilferage ˈpɪl.fᵊr.ɪdʒ
pilferous ˈpɪl.fᵊr.əs
pilgrim ˈpɪl.grɪm **-s** -z ˌ**Pilgrim** ˈ**Father**
pilgrimag|e ˈpɪl.grɪ.mɪdʒ, -grə- **-es** -ɪz
piling ˈpaɪ.lɪŋ **-s** -z
Pilkington ˈpɪl.kɪŋ.tən
pill pɪl **-s** -z **-ing** -ɪŋ **-ed** -d
pillag|e ˈpɪl.ɪdʒ **-es** -ɪz **-ing** -ɪŋ **-ed** -d **-er/s** -əʳ/z Ⓤⓢ -ɚ/z
pillar ˈpɪl.əʳ Ⓤⓢ -ɚ **-s** -z **-ed** -d **from** ˌ**pillar to** ˈ**post**
pillar-box ˈpɪl.ə.bɒks Ⓤⓢ -ɚ.bɑːks **-es** -ɪz
pillbox ˈpɪl.bɒks Ⓤⓢ -bɑːks **-es** -ɪz
pillion ˈpɪl.i.ən Ⓤⓢ ˈ-jən **-s** -z
pillock ˈpɪl.ək **-s** -s
pillor|y ˈpɪl.ᵊr|.i **-ies** -iz **-ying** -i.ɪŋ **-ied** -id
pillow ˈpɪl.əʊ Ⓤⓢ -oʊ **-s** -z **-ing** -ɪŋ **-ed** -d ˈ**pillow** ˌ**slip** ; ˈ**pillow** ˌ**talk**
pillowcas|e ˈpɪl.əʊ.keɪs Ⓤⓢ -oʊ- **-es** -ɪz
Pillsbury ˈpɪlz.bᵊr.i Ⓤⓢ -ˌber-
pilocarpine ˌpaɪ.ləʊˈkɑː.pɪn, -paɪn Ⓤⓢ ˌpaɪ.loʊˈkɑːr.piːn, ˌpɪl.oʊˈ-, -pɪn
pi|lot ˈpaɪ|.lət **-lots** -ləts **-loting** -lə.tɪŋ Ⓤⓢ -lə.t̬ɪŋ **-loted** -lə.tɪd Ⓤⓢ -lə.t̬ɪd **-lotage** -lə.tɪdʒ Ⓤⓢ -lə.t̬ɪdʒ ˈ**pilot** ˌ**light**
Pilsen ˈpɪl.zᵊn, -sᵊn
pilsener (P) ˈpɪlz.nəʳ, ˈpɪl.snəʳ, -sᵊn.əʳ Ⓤⓢ ˈpɪlz.nɚ, ˈpɪl.snɚ
Pilsworth ˈpɪlz.wəθ, -wɜːθ Ⓤⓢ -wəθ, -wɜːrθ
Piltdown ˈpɪlt.daʊn
pilule ˈpɪl.juːl **-s** -z
pimento pɪˈmen.təʊ Ⓤⓢ -toʊ **-s** -z
pimiento pɪˈmjen.təʊ, -ˈmen- Ⓤⓢ -toʊ **-s** -z
Pimlico ˈpɪm.lɪ.kəʊ Ⓤⓢ -koʊ
Pimm pɪm **-'s** -z
pimp pɪmp **-s** -s **-ing** -ɪŋ **-ed** -t
pimpernel ˈpɪm.pə.nel, -nᵊl Ⓤⓢ -pɚ- **-s** -z
pimple ˈpɪm.pl̩ **-s** -z **-d** -d
pimpl|y ˈpɪm.pl̩|.i, ˈ-pl|i Ⓤⓢ ˈ-pl|i **-iness** -ɪ.nəs, -ɪ.nɪs
pin pɪn **-s** -z **-ning** -ɪŋ **-ned** -d ˈ**pin** ˌ**money** ; ˈ**pin** ˌ**tuck** ; ˌ**pins and** ˈ**needles**
PIN pɪn ˈ**PIN** ˌ**number**
piña colada ˌpiː.nə.kəʊˈlɑː.də, -njə- Ⓤⓢ -njə.koʊˈ- **-s** -z
pinafore (P) ˈpɪn.ə.fɔːʳ Ⓤⓢ -fɔːr **-s** -z ˈ**pinafore** ˌ**dress**
piñata pɪnˈjɑː.tə Ⓤⓢ -t̬ə **-s** -z
pinball ˈpɪn.bɔːl, ˈpɪm- Ⓤⓢ ˈpɪn-, -bɑːl **-s** -z ˈ**pinball ma**ˌ**chine**
pince-nez *singular:* ˌpæ̃nsˈneɪ, ˌpænts-, ˌpɪnts-, ˈ-ˌ- *plural:* -ˈneɪz
pincer ˈpɪnt.səʳ Ⓤⓢ -sɚ **-s** -z
pinch pɪntʃ **-es** -ɪz **-ing** -ɪŋ **-ed** -t **-er/s** -əʳ/z Ⓤⓢ -ɚ/z ˌ**take something with a** ˌ**pinch of** ˈ**salt**

pinchbeck ˈpɪn*t*ʃ.bek **-s** -s
Pinches ˈpɪn.*t*ʃɪz
pinch-hit ˈpɪn*t*ʃ.hɪt **-s** -s **-ting** -ɪŋ (US) -ˌhɪt̬.ɪŋ
Pinckney ˈpɪŋk.ni
pincushion ˈpɪnˌkʊʃ.ᵊn, ˈpɪŋ- (US) ˈpɪn- **-s** -z
Pindar ˈpɪn.dəʳ (US) -dɚ
Pindaric pɪnˈdær.ɪk (US) -ˈdær-, -ˈder- **-s** -s
Pindus ˈpɪn.dəs
pin|e paɪn **-es** -z **-ing** -ɪŋ **-ed** -d **ˈpine ˌcone**; **ˈpine ˌkernel**; **ˈpine ˌmarten**; **ˈpine ˌneedle**; **ˈpine ˌnut**
pineal ˈpɪn.i.əl; paɪˈniː- (US) ˈpɪn.i-
pineapple ˈpaɪ.næp.l̩ **-s** -z
Pinel pɪˈnel (US) pɪ-, ˌpiː-
Pinero pɪˈnɪə.rəʊ, -ˈneə- (US) -ˈnɪr.oʊ
piner|y ˈpaɪ.nᵊr|.i **-ies** -iz
pinetum paɪˈniː.təm (US) -t̬əm
pinewood (P) ˈpaɪn.wʊd **-s** -z
ping pɪŋ **-s** -z **-ing** -ɪŋ **-ed** -d **-er/s** -əʳ/z (US) -ɚ/z
ping-pong ˈpɪŋˌpɒŋ (US) -ˌpɑːŋ, -ˌpɔːŋ
pinhead ˈpɪn.hed **-s** -z **-ed** -ɪd
pinhole ˈpɪn.həʊl (US) -hoʊl **-s** -z ˌ**pinhole ˈcamera**
pinion ˈpɪn.jən **-s** -z **-ing** -ɪŋ **-ed** -d
pink (P) pɪŋk **-s** -s **-ing** -ɪŋ **-ed** -t ˌ**pink ˈgin**; ˌ**pink ˈslip**; **ˈpinking ˌshears**
Pinkerton ˈpɪŋ.kə.tən (US) -kɚ.t̬ən
pink-eye ˈpɪŋk.aɪ **-d** -d
pinkie ˈpɪŋ.ki **-s** -z
pinkish ˈpɪŋ.kɪʃ
pinko ˈpɪŋ.kəʊ (US) -koʊ **-(e)s** -z
pink|y ˈpɪŋ.k|i **-ies** -iz
pinnac|e ˈpɪn.ɪs, -əs **-es** -ɪz
pinnacl|e ˈpɪn.ə.kl̩, ˈ-ɪ- **-es** -z **-ing** -ɪŋ, ˈpɪn.ə.klɪŋ, ˈ-ɪ- **-ed** -d
pinnate ˈpɪn.eɪt, -ɪt, -ət (US) -eɪt, -ɪt
pinner (P) ˈpɪn.əʳ (US) -ɚ **-s** -z
pinn|y ˈpɪn|.i **-ies** -iz
Pinocchio pɪˈnəʊ.ki.əʊ, -ˈnɒk.i- (US) pəˈnoʊ.ki.oʊ, pɪ-
Pinochet ˈpɪn.əʊ.ʃeɪ (US) ˈpiː.noʊ.ʃet, -ʃeɪ
pinoc(h)le ˈpiː.nʌk.l̩, -nɒk- (US) -nʌk-, -nɑː.kl̩
pinot ˈpiː.nəʊ, -ˈ- (US) piːˈnoʊ **-s** -z
Pinot Blanc ˌpiː.nəʊˈblɑ̃ːŋ (US) -noʊˈ-
Pinot Noir ˌpiː.nəʊˈnwɑːʳ (US) -noʊˈnwɑːr
pin|point ˈpɪn|.pɔɪnt, ˈpɪm- (US) ˈpɪn- **-points** -pɔɪnts **-pointing** -ˌpɔɪn.tɪŋ (US) -ˌpɔɪn.t̬ɪŋ **-pointed** -ˌpɔɪn.tɪd (US) -ˌpɔɪn.t̬ɪd
pinprick ˈpɪn.prɪk, ˈpɪm- (US) ˈpɪn- **-s** -s
pinstripe ˈpɪn.straɪp **-s** -s **-d** -t
pint paɪnt **-s** -s
pinta *pint of milk:* ˈpaɪn.tə (US) -t̬ə **-s** -z
pinta (P) *disease:* ˈpɪn.tə, ˈpiːn- (US) ˈpɪn.t̬ə, -tɑː
pintado pɪnˈtɑː.dəʊ (US) -doʊ **-(e)s** -z
pintail ˈpɪn.teɪl **-s** -z
Pinter ˈpɪn.təʳ (US) -t̬ɚ
Pinteresque ˌpɪn.tᵊrˈesk (US) -t̬ɚˈ-
pinto ˈpɪn.təʊ (US) -t̬oʊ **-(e)s** -z **pinto bean**
pint-pot ˈpaɪnt.pɒt, ˌ-ˈ- (US) ˈpaɪnt.pɑːt **-s** -s
pint-size ˈpaɪnt.saɪz **-d** -d
pin-up ˈpɪn.ʌp **-s** -s
pinwheel ˈpɪn.*h*wiːl **-s** -z
pinxit ˈpɪŋk.sɪt
Pinxton ˈpɪŋk.stᵊn
pioneer (P) ˌpaɪəˈnɪəʳ (US) -ˈnɪr **-s** -z **-ing** -ɪŋ **-ed** -d
pious ˈpaɪ.əs **-ly** -li **-ness** -nəs, -nɪs
pip (P) pɪp **-s** -s **-ping** -ɪŋ **-ped** -t
pipal ˈpiː.pᵊl **-s** -z
pip|e (P) paɪp **-es** -s **-ing** -ɪŋ **-ed** -t **-er/s** -əʳ/z (US) -ɚ/z **ˈpipe ˌcleaner**; **ˈpipe ˌdream**; ˌ**pipe of ˈpeace**
pipeclay ˈpaɪp.kleɪ
pipeline ˈpaɪp.laɪn **-s** -z
Piper ˈpaɪ.pəʳ (US) -pɚ
pipette pɪˈpet (US) paɪ-, pɪ- **-s** -s
piping ˈpaɪ.pɪŋ
pipistrel(le) ˌpɪp.ɪˈstrel, -əˈ-, ˈ--- (US) ˌpɪp.ɪˈstrel **-s** -z
pipit ˈpɪp.ɪt **-s** -s
pipkin ˈpɪp.kɪn **-s** -z
Pippa ˈpɪp.ə
pippin ˈpɪp.ɪn **-s** -z
pipsqueak ˈpɪp.skwiːk **-s** -s
piquancy ˈpiː.kən*t*.si
piquant ˈpiː.kənt, -kɑːnt **-ly** -li
piqu|e piːk **-es** -s **-ing** -ɪŋ **-ed** -t
piqué ˈpiː.keɪ (US) -ˈ-
piquet *card game:* piːˈket, -ˈkeɪ; ˈpɪk.et, -eɪ (US) piːˈkeɪ, -ˈket
piquet *soldiers:* ˈpɪk.ɪt **-s** -s
Piquet *racing driver:* ˈpiː.keɪ
piracy|y ˈpaɪə.rə.s|i (US) ˈpaɪ- **-ies** -iz
Piraeus paɪˈriː.əs, pɪˈreɪ-, pə- (US) paɪˈriː-
Pirandello ˌpɪr.ᵊnˈdel.əʊ (US) -oʊ
piranha pɪˈrɑː.nə, pə-, -njə (US) pəˈrɑː.njə, pɪ-, -nə **-s** -z
pira|te ˈpaɪə.rə|t, -rɪ|t (US) ˈpaɪ.rə|t **-tes** -ts **-ting** -tɪŋ (US) -t̬ɪŋ **-ted** -tɪd (US) -t̬ɪd
piratical paɪəˈræt.ɪ.kᵊl, pə-, pɪ- (US) paɪˈræt̬- **-ly** -i
Pirbright ˈpɜː.braɪt (US) ˈpɜːr-
Pirie ˈpɪr.i
pirogue pɪˈrəʊg, pə- (US) -ˈroʊg **-s** -z
pirou|ette ˌpɪr.uˈ|et **-ettes** -ˈets **-etting** -ˈet.ɪŋ (US) -ˈet̬.ɪŋ **-etted** -ˈet.ɪd (US) -ˈet̬.ɪd *stress shift:* ˌpirouetting ˈdancer
Pisa ˈpiː.zə
pis aller ˌpiːzˈæl.eɪ, ˌ--ˈ- (US) -ælˈeɪ **-s** -z
Piscator pɪˈskeɪ.təʳ (US) -ˈskɑː.tɔːr
piscatorial ˌpɪs.kəˈtɔː.ri.əl (US) -ˈtɔːr.i-
piscatory ˈpɪs.kə.tᵊr.i (US) -tɔːr-
Piscean ˈpaɪ.si.ən, ˈpɪs.i-, ˈpɪs.ki-; pɪˈsiː- (US) ˈpaɪ.si-, ˈpɪs.i-
Pisces ˈpaɪ.siːz, ˈpɪs.iːz, ˈpɪs.kiːz (US) ˈpaɪ.siːz, ˈpɪs.iːz
pisciculture ˈpɪs.ɪˌkʌl.tʃəʳ (US) -tʃɚ
piscin|a pɪˈsiː.n|ə **-as** -əz **-ae** -iː
piscine ˈpɪs.aɪn, ˈpɪsk-, ˈpaɪ.saɪn (US) ˈpaɪ.siːn, ˈpɪs.iːn-, -aɪn, -ɪn
Piscis| Austrinus ˌpɪs.ɪs|.ɒsˈtraɪ.nəs, ˌ-kɪs-, -ɔːˈstraɪ- (US) ˌpaɪ.sɪs|.ɔːˈ-, ˌpɪs.ɪs-, -ɑːˈ- **-Australis** -ɒsˈtrɑː.lɪs, -ɔːˈstrɑː- (US) -ɔːˈstreɪ-, -ɑːˈ-
Pisgah ˈpɪz.gə, -gɑː (US) -gə
pish pɪʃ
Pisidia paɪˈsɪd.i.ə (US) pɪ-
Pisistratus paɪˈsɪs.trə.təs, pɪ-
pismire ˈpɪs.maɪəʳ (US) -maɪɚ, ˈpɪz- **-s** -z
piss pɪs **-es** -ɪz **-ing** -ɪŋ **-ed** -t **ˈpiss ˌartist**
pissant ˈpɪs.ᵊnt (US) -ænt **-s** -s
Pissarro pɪˈsɑː.rəʊ (US) -ˈsɑːr.oʊ
pissed pɪst ˌ**pissed as a ˈnewt**; ˌ**pissed as a ˈfart**
pissoir ˈpɪs.wɑːʳ, ˈpiː.swɑːʳ (US) piːˈswɑːr **-s** -z
piss-take ˈpɪs.teɪk **-s** -s
piss-up ˈpɪs.ʌp **-s** -s
pistachio pɪˈstɑː.ʃi.əʊ, -ˈstæʃ.i- (US) -ˈstæʃ.i.oʊ, -ˈstɑː.ʃi- **-s** -z
piste piːst **-s** -s
pistil ˈpɪs.tɪl, -tᵊl **-s** -z
pistol ˈpɪs.tᵊl **-s** -z
pistole pɪˈstəʊl; ˈpɪs.təʊl (US) pɪˈstoʊl **-s** -z
pistol-whip ˈpɪs.tᵊl.*h*wɪp **-s** -s **-ping** -ɪŋ **-ped** -t
piston ˈpɪs.tᵊn **-s** -z **ˈpiston ˌrod**
pit pɪt **-s** -s **-ting** -ɪŋ (US) ˈpɪt̬.ɪŋ **-ted** -ɪd (US) ˈpɪt̬.ɪd ˌ**pit bull ˈterrier**; **ˈpit ˌpony**; **ˈpit ˌstop**
pita ˈpɪt.ə (US) ˈpiː.t̬ə **ˈpita ˌbread**
pit-a-pat ˌpɪt.əˈpæt, ˈ--- (US) ˈpɪt̬.ə.pæt
Pitcairn *surname:* pɪtˈkeən (US) -ˈkern *island:* pɪtˈkeən, ˈ-- (US) pɪtˈkern, ˈ--
pitch pɪtʃ **-es** -ɪz **-ing** -ɪŋ **-ed** -t **ˈpitch ˌpipe**
pitch-and-putt ˌpɪtʃ.ᵊndˈpʌt
pitch-and-toss ˌpɪtʃ.ᵊndˈtɒs (US) -ˈtɑːs
pitch-black ˌpɪtʃˈblæk *stress shift:* ˌpitch-black ˈnight
pitchblende ˈpɪtʃ.blend
pitch-dark ˌpɪtʃˈdɑːk (US) -ˈdɑːrk *stress shift:* ˌpitch-dark ˈnight
pitcher (P) ˈpɪtʃ.əʳ (US) -ɚ **-s** -z **ˈpitcher ˌplant**
pitchfork ˈpɪtʃ.fɔːk (US) -fɔːrk **-s** -s **-ing** -ɪŋ **-ed** -t
pitch|man ˈpɪtʃ|.mən, -mæn **-men** -mən, -men

pitchpine 'pɪtʃ.paɪn **-s** -z
pitchy 'pɪtʃ.i
piteous 'pɪt.i.əs (US) 'pɪt̬- **-ly** -li **-ness** -nəs, -nɪs
pitfall 'pɪt.fɔːl (US) -fɔːl, -fɑːl **-s** -z
pith pɪθ **-s** -s **-ing** -ɪŋ **-ed** -t **-less** -ləs, -lɪs ˌ**pith 'helmet** (US) '**pith ˌhelmet**
pithead 'pɪt.hed **-s** -z
pithecanthrop|us ˌpɪθ.ɪ.kæn'θrəʊ.pləs; -'kænt.θrə- (US) -'kænt.θroʊ-, -θrə-; -kæn'θroʊ- **-i** -aɪ
Pither 'paɪ.θəʳ, -ðəʳ (US) -θɚ, -ðɚ
pith|y 'pɪθ|.i **-ier** -i.əʳ (US) -i.ɚ **-iest** -i.ɪst, -i.əst **-ily** -ɪ.li, -ᵊl.i **-iness** -ɪ.nəs, -ɪ.nɪs
pitiab|le 'pɪt.i.ə.b|l̩ (US) 'pɪt̬- **-ly** -li **-leness** -l̩.nəs, -nɪs
pitiful 'pɪt.i.fᵊl, -fʊl (US) 'pɪt̬- **-ly** -i **-ness** -nəs, -nɪs
pitiless 'pɪt.i.ləs, -lɪs (US) 'pɪt̬- **-ly** -li **-ness** -nəs, -nɪs
Pitlochry pɪt'lɒk.ri, -'lɒx- (US) -'lɑː.kri
pit|man (P) 'pɪt|.mən **-men** -mən, -men
piton 'piː.tɒn, -tɔ̃ːŋ (US) -tɑːn **-s** -z
Pitsea 'pɪt.siː, -si
Pitt pɪt
pitta 'pɪt.ə (US) 'pɪt̬- '**pitta ˌbread**
pittanc|e 'pɪt.ᵊnts (US) 'pɪt- **-es** -ɪz
Pittaway 'pɪt.ə.weɪ (US) 'pɪt̬-
pitted 'pɪt.ɪd (US) 'pɪt̬-
pitter-patter 'pɪt.əˌpæt.əʳ, ˌpɪt.ə'pæt- (US) 'pɪt̬.ɚˌpæt̬.ɚ
Pittman 'pɪt.mən
Pitts pɪts
Pittsburgh 'pɪts.bɜːg (US) -bɜːrg
pituitary pɪ'tjuː.ɪ.tᵊr.i, '-ə- (US) -'tuː.ə.ter-, pə-, -'tjuː- **pi'tuitary ˌgland**
pit|y 'pɪt|.i (US) 'pɪt̬- **-ies** -iz **-ying/ly** -i.ɪŋ/li **-ied** -id
pityriasis ˌpɪt.ɪ'raɪə.sɪs, -ə'- (US) ˌpɪt̬.ɪ'-
Pius paɪəs
piv|ot 'pɪv|.ət **-ots** -əts **-oting** -ə.tɪŋ (US) -ə.t̬ɪŋ **-oted** -ə.tɪd (US) -ə.t̬ɪd
pivotal 'pɪv.ə.tᵊl (US) -t̬ᵊl **-ly** -i
pix pɪks
pixel 'pɪk.sᵊl, -sel **-s** -z
pix|ie, -|y 'pɪk.s|i **-ies** -iz
pixilated 'pɪk.sɪ.leɪ.tɪd, -sə- (US) -t̬ɪd
Pizarro pɪ'zɑː.rəʊ (US) -'zɑːr.oʊ
pizazz pɪ'zæz, pə- (US) pɪ-
pizza 'piːt.sə, 'pɪt- (US) 'piːt- **-s** -z
pizzazz pɪ'zæz, pə- (US) pɪ-
pizzeria ˌpiːt.sə'riː.ə, ˌpɪt- (US) ˌpiːt- **-s** -z
pizzicat|o ˌpɪt.sɪ'kɑː.t|əʊ (US) -t|oʊ **-os** -əʊz (US) -oʊz **-i** -iː
placability ˌplæk.ə'bɪl.ə.ti, -ə.ti (US) -ə.t̬i, ˌpleɪ.kə'-
placab|le 'plæk.ə.b|l̩ (US) 'plæk.ə-, 'pleɪ.kə- **-ly** -li **-leness** -l̩.nəs, -nɪs
placard (*n.*) 'plæk.ɑːd (US) -ɑːrd, -ɚd
placard (*v.*) 'plæk.ɑːd (US) -ɑːrd, -ɚd; plə'kɑːrd, plæk'ɑːrd **-s** -z **-ing** -ɪŋ **-ed** -ɪd
placa|te plə'keɪ|t, pleɪ- (US) 'pleɪ.keɪ|t, 'plæk.eɪ|t; pleɪ'keɪ|t **-tes** -ts **-ting** -tɪŋ (US) -t̬ɪŋ **-ted** -tɪd (US) -t̬ɪd
placatory plə'keɪ.tᵊr.i, pleɪ'- (US) 'pleɪ.kə.tɔːr-, 'plæk.ə-
plac|e pleɪs **-es** -ɪz **-ing** -ɪŋ **-ed** -t **-er/s** -əʳ/z (US) -ɚ/z '**place ˌsetting**
placebo plə'siː.bəʊ, plæs'iː- (US) plə'siː.boʊ **-s** -z **pla'cebo efˌfect**
placekick 'pleɪs.kɪk **-s** -s **-ing** -ɪŋ **-ed** -t
place|man 'pleɪs|.mən **-men** -mən
placement 'pleɪs.mənt **-s** -s
placent|a plə'sen.t|ə, plæs'en- (US) plə'sen.t̬|ə **-as** -əz **-ae** -iː
placet 'pleɪ.set, -sɪt
placid (P) 'plæs.ɪd **-ly** -li **-ness** -nəs, -nɪs
placidity plə'sɪd.ə.ti, plæs'ɪd-, -ɪ.ti (US) plə'sɪd.ə.t̬i
placket 'plæk.ɪt **-s** -s
plagal 'pleɪ.gᵊl
plag|e plɑːʒ **-es** -ɪz
plagiarism 'pleɪ.dʒᵊr.ɪ.zᵊm, -dʒi.ə.rɪ- (US) -dʒɚ.ɪ-, -dʒi.ɚ- **-s** -z
plagiarist 'pleɪ.dʒᵊr.ɪst, -dʒi.ə.rɪst (US) -dʒɚ.ɪst, -dʒi.ɚ- **-s** -s
plagiaristic ˌpleɪ.dʒᵊr'ɪs.tɪk, -dʒi.ə'rɪs- (US) -dʒə'rɪs-, -dʒi.ə'-
plagiariz|e, -is|e 'pleɪ.dʒᵊr.aɪz, -dʒi.ə.raɪz (US) -dʒə.raɪz, -dʒi.ə- **-es** -ɪz **-ing** -ɪŋ **-ed** -d
plagiar|y 'pleɪ.dʒᵊr|.i, -dʒi.ə.r|i (US) -dʒɚ|.i, -dʒi.ɚ- **-ies** -iz
plagu|e pleɪg **-es** -z **-ing** -ɪŋ **-ed** -d **-er/s** -əʳ/z (US) -ɚ/z
plagu|y 'pleɪ.g|i **-ily** -ɪ.li, -ᵊl.i **-iness** -ɪ.nəs, -ɪ.nɪs
plaice pleɪs
plaid plæd **-s** -z **-ed** -ɪd
Plaid Cymru ˌplaɪd'kʌm.ri
plain pleɪn **-s** -z **-er** -əʳ (US) -ɚ **-est** -ɪst, -əst **-ly** -li **-ness** -nəs, -nɪs ˌ**plain 'clothes** ; ˌ**plain 'sailing**
plainchant 'pleɪn.tʃɑːnt (US) -tʃænt **-s** -s **-ing** -ɪŋ **-ed** -ɪd
plainsong 'pleɪn.sɒŋ (US) -sɑːŋ, -sɔːŋ
plain-spoken ˌpleɪn'spəʊ.kᵊn (US) -'spoʊ-, '-ˌ-- **-ness** -nəs, -nɪs *stress shift:* ˌplain-spoken 'person
plaint pleɪnt **-s** -s
plaintiff 'pleɪn.tɪf (US) -t̬ɪf **-s** -s
plaintive 'pleɪn.tɪv (US) -t̬ɪv **-ly** -li **-ness** -nəs, -nɪs
Plaistow 'plæs.təʊ, 'plɑː.stəʊ (US) 'plæs.toʊ, 'plɑː.stoʊ
Note: The local pronunciation is /'plɑː.stəʊ/.
plait plæt **-s** -s **-ing** -ɪŋ (US) 'plæt̬.ɪŋ **-ed** -ɪd (US) 'plæt̬.ɪd
plan plæn **-s** -z **-ning** -ɪŋ **-ned** -d **-ner/s** -əʳ/z (US) -ɚ/z '**planning perˌmission**
planchet 'plɑːn.tʃɪt (US) 'plæn-, -tʃet **-s** -s
planchette plɑ̃ːn'ʃet, plɑːn- (US) plæn'ʃet **-s** -s
Planck plæŋk
plan|e pleɪn **-es** -z **-ing** -ɪŋ **-ed** -d '**plane ˌtree**
planer (P) 'pleɪ.nəʳ (US) -nɚ **-s** -z
planet 'plæn.ɪt **-s** -s
planetari|um ˌplæn.ɪ'teə.ri|.əm, -ə'- (US) -ɪ'ter.i- **-ums** -əmz **-a** -ə
planetary 'plæn.ɪ.tᵊr.i, '-ə- (US) -ɪ.ter-
plangent 'plæn.dʒᵊnt **-ly** -li
planimeter plæn'ɪm.ɪ.təʳ, plə'nɪm-, '-ə- (US) plə'nɪm.ə.t̬ɚ, pleɪ- **-s** -z
planimetric ˌplæn.ɪ'met.rɪk (US) ˌpleɪ.nɪ'-, ˌplæn.ɪ'-
planimetry plæn'ɪm.ɪ.tri, plə'nɪm-, '-ə- (US) plə'nɪm-, pleɪ-
plank plæŋk **-s** -s **-ing** -ɪŋ **-ed** -t
plankton 'plæŋk.tən, -tɒn (US) -tən
plant (P) (*n. v.*) plɑːnt (US) plænt **-s** -s **-ing** -ɪŋ (US) 'plæn.t̬ɪŋ **-ed** -ɪd (US) 'plæn.t̬ɪd **-er/s** -əʳ/z (US) 'plæn.t̬ɚ/z
Plantagenet plæn'tædʒ.ᵊn.ɪt, -ɪn-, -ət, -et (US) -ə.nɪt **-s** -s
plantain 'plæn.tɪn, 'plɑːn-, -teɪn (US) 'plæn.tɪn, -tᵊn **-s** -z
plantation plæn'teɪ.ʃᵊn, plɑːn- (US) plæn- **-s** -z
Plantin 'plæn.tɪn, 'plɑːn- (US) 'plɑːn.tæn, 'plæn-
plantocrac|y plɑːn'tɒk.rə.s|i (US) plæn'tɑː.krə- **-ies** -iz
plaque plɑːk, plæk (US) plæk **-s** -s
plash plæʃ **-es** -ɪz **-ing** -ɪŋ **-ed** -t **-y** -i
plasm 'plæz.ᵊm
plasm|a 'plæz.m|ə **-ic** -ɪk
plasmolysis plæz'mɒl.ə.sɪs, '-ɪ- (US) -'mɑː.lɪ-
Plassey 'plæs.i
plast|er 'plɑː.st|əʳ (US) 'plæs.t|ɚ **-ers** -əz (US) -ɚz **-ering** -ᵊr.ɪŋ **-ered** -əd (US) -ɚz **-erer/s** -ᵊr.əʳ/z (US) -ɚ.ɚ/z ˌ**plaster 'cast** ; ˌ**plaster of 'Paris**
plasterboard 'plɑː.stə.bɔːd (US) 'plæs.tɚ.bɔːrd
plastic 'plæs.tɪk, 'plɑː.stɪk (US) 'plæs.tɪk **-s** -s ˌ**plastic 'bullet** ; ˌ**plastic 'money** ; ˌ**plastic 'surgeon** ; ˌ**plastic 'surgery**
Plasticine® 'plæs.tə.siːn, 'plɑː.stə-, -stɪ- (US) 'plæs.tɪ-
plasticity plæs'tɪs.ə.ti, plɑː'stɪs-, -ɪ.ti (US) plæs'tɪs.ə.t̬i
plasticiz|e, -is|e 'plæs.tɪ.saɪz, 'plɑː.stɪ-, -stə- (US) 'plæs.tɪ- **-es** -ɪs **-ing** -ɪŋ **-ed** -d **-er/s** -əʳ/z (US) -ɚ/z

plastid 'plæs.tɪd **-s** -z
Plata 'plɑː.tə ⓊⓈ -tɑː
Plataea plə'tiː.ə
platan 'plæt.ᵊn **-s** -z
plat(s) du jour ˌplɑː.dju'ʒʊəʳ, -dʊ'-, -də'- ⓊⓈ -'ʒʊr
plat|e (P) (*n. v.*) pleɪt **-es** -s **-ing** -ɪŋ ⓊⓈ 'pleɪ.t̬ɪŋ **-ed** -ɪd ⓊⓈ 'pleɪ.t̬ɪd ˌ**plate tec'tonics**
plateau 'plæt.əʊ; -'-, plə'təʊ ⓊⓈ plæt'oʊ **-s** -z **-x** -z
plateful 'pleɪt.fʊl **-s** -z
plate-glass ˌpleɪt'glɑːs ⓊⓈ -'glæs ˌ**plate-glass 'window**
platelayer 'pleɪtˌleɪ.əʳ ⓊⓈ -ɚ **-s** -z
platelet 'pleɪt.lət, -lɪt **-s** -s
platen 'plæt.ᵊn **-s** -z
platform 'plæt.fɔːm ⓊⓈ -fɔːrm **-s** -z **-ing** -ɪŋ **-ed** -d ˌ**platform 'shoes**
Plath plæθ
Platignum® plæt'ɪg.nəm, plə'tɪg- ⓊⓈ plə-
platiniz|e, -is|e 'plæt.ɪ.naɪz, -ᵊn.aɪz ⓊⓈ -ᵊn- **-es** -ɪz **-ing** -ɪŋ **-ed** -d
platinum 'plæt.ɪ.nəm, -ᵊn.əm ⓊⓈ 'plæt.nəm ˌ**platinum 'blond(e)**
platitude 'plæt.ɪ.tjuːd, '-ə-, -tʃuːd ⓊⓈ 'plæt̬.ə.tuːd, -tjuːd **-s** -z
platitudinarian ˌplæt.ɪˌtjuː.dɪ'neə.ri.ən, -əˌ-, -ˌtʃuː-, -də'- ⓊⓈ ˌplæt̬.əˌtuː.dɪ'ner.i-, -ˌtjuː- **-s** -z
platitudinous ˌplæt.ɪ'tjuː.dɪ.nəs, -ə'-, -'tʃuː-, -dᵊn.əs ⓊⓈ ˌplæt̬.ə'tuː.dᵊn-, -'tjuː- **-ly** -li
Plato 'pleɪ.təʊ ⓊⓈ -t̬oʊ
platonic plə'tɒn.ɪk, plæt'ɒn- ⓊⓈ plə'tɑː.nɪk, pleɪ- **-al** -ᵊl **-ally** -ᵊl.i, -li
Platon|ism 'pleɪ.tᵊn|.ɪ.zᵊm **-ist/s** -ɪst/s
platoon plə'tuːn **-s** -z
Platt plæt **-s** -s
platter 'plæt.əʳ ⓊⓈ 'plæt̬.ɚ **-s** -z
platyp|us 'plæt.ɪ.pl|əs, '-ə- ⓊⓈ 'plæt̬.ɪ- **-uses** -ə.sɪz **-i** -aɪ
plaudit 'plɔː.dɪt ⓊⓈ 'plɑː-, 'plɔː- **-s** -s
plausibility ˌplɔː.zɪ'bɪl.ə.ti, -zə'-, -ɪ.ti ⓊⓈ ˌplɑː.zə'bɪl.ə.t̬i, ˌplɔː-
plausib|le 'plɔː.zɪ.bl̩, -zə- ⓊⓈ 'plɑː.zə-, 'plɔː- **-ly** -li **-leness** -l̩.nəs, -nɪs
Plautus 'plɔː.təs ⓊⓈ 'plɑː.t̬əs, 'plɔː-
play pleɪ **-s** -z **-ing** -ɪŋ **-ed** -d **-er/s** -əʳ/z ⓊⓈ -ɚ/z ˌ**play on 'words** ; ˌ**play the 'field** ; '**playing** ˌ**card** ; '**playing** ˌ**field**
playable 'pleɪ.ə.bl̩
play-act 'pleɪ.ækt **-s** -z **-ing** -ɪŋ **-ed** -ɪd **-or/s** -əʳ/z ⓊⓈ -ɚ/z
playback 'pleɪ.bæk
playboy 'pleɪ.bɔɪ **-s** -z
Play-Doh® 'pleɪ.dəʊ ⓊⓈ -doʊ
player (P) 'pleɪ.əʳ ⓊⓈ -ɚ **-s** -z
Playfair 'pleɪ.feəʳ ⓊⓈ -fer
playfellow 'pleɪˌfel.əʊ ⓊⓈ -oʊ **-s** -z
playful 'pleɪ.fᵊl, -fʊl **-ly** -i **-ness** -nəs, -nɪs
playgoer 'pleɪˌgəʊ.əʳ ⓊⓈ -ˌgoʊ.ɚ **-s** -z
playground 'pleɪ.graʊnd **-s** -z
playgroup 'pleɪ.gruːp **-s** -s
playhou|se 'pleɪ.haʊ|s **-ses** -zɪz
playlet 'pleɪ.lət, -lɪt **-s** -s
playlist 'pleɪ.lɪst **-s** -s
playmate 'pleɪ.meɪt **-s** -s
play-off 'pleɪ.ɒf ⓊⓈ -ɑːf **-s** -s
playpen 'pleɪ.pen **-s** -z
playroom 'pleɪ.rʊm, -ruːm ⓊⓈ -ruːm, -rʊm **-s** -z
playschool 'pleɪ.skuːl **-s**
playsuit 'pleɪ.suːt, -sjuːt ⓊⓈ -suːt **-s** -s
Playtex® 'pleɪ.teks
plaything 'pleɪ.θɪŋ **-s** -z
playtime 'pleɪ.taɪm **-s** -z
playwright 'pleɪ.raɪt **-s** -s
plaza (P) 'plɑː.zə ⓊⓈ 'plɑː-, 'plæz.ə **-s** -z
plc ˌpiː.el'siː
plea pliː **-s** -z
plea-bargain 'pliːˌbɑː.gɪn, -gən ⓊⓈ -ˌbɑːr.gən **-s** -z **-ing** -ɪŋ **-ed** -d
plead pliːd **-s** -z **-ing/ly** -ɪŋ/li **-ed** -ɪd **pled** pled **pleader/s** 'pliː.dəʳ/z ⓊⓈ -dɚ/z
pleading 'pliː.dɪŋ **-s** -z
pleasance (P) 'plez.ᵊnts
pleas|ant 'plez|.ᵊnt **-anter** -ᵊn.təʳ ⓊⓈ -ᵊn.t̬ɚ **-antest** -ᵊn.tɪst, -ᵊn.təst ⓊⓈ -ᵊn.t̬ɪst, -ᵊn.t̬əst **-antly** -ᵊnt.li **-antness** -ᵊnt.nəs, -ᵊnt.nɪs
pleasantr|y 'plez.ᵊn.tr|i **-ies** -iz
pleas|e pliːz **-es** -ɪz **-ing/ly** -ɪŋ/li **-ed** -d
pleasurab|le 'pleʒ.ᵊr.ə.bl|̩ **-ly** -li **-leness** -l̩.nəs, -nɪs
pleasure 'pleʒ.əʳ ⓊⓈ -ɚ **-s** -z **-ing** -ɪŋ **-ed** -d '**pleasure** ˌ**principle**
pleat pliːt **-s** -s **-ing** -ɪŋ ⓊⓈ 'pliː.t̬ɪŋ **-ed** -ɪd ⓊⓈ 'pliː.t̬ɪd
pleb pleb **-s** -z
plebe pliːb **-s** -z
plebeian plə'biː.ən, plɪ- ⓊⓈ plɪ-, plə- **-s** -z
plebiscite 'pleb.ɪ.sɪt, '-ə-, -saɪt ⓊⓈ -ə.saɪt, -sɪt **-s** -s
plectr|um 'plek.tr|əm **-ums** -əmz **-a** -ə
pled (*past of* **plead**) pled
pledg|e pledʒ **-es** -ɪz **-ing** -ɪŋ **-ed** -d **-er/s** -əʳ/z ⓊⓈ -ɚ/z
Pledger 'pledʒ.əʳ ⓊⓈ -ɚ
-plegia -'pliː.dʒi.ə, -dʒə
Note: Suffix. Words containing **-plegia** are always stressed on the syllable **-ple-**, e.g. **paraplegia** /ˌpær.ə'pliː.dʒə ⓊⓈ ˌper-/.
-plegic -'pliː.dʒɪk
Note: Suffix. Words containing **-plegic** are always stressed on the penultimate syllable, e.g. **paraplegic** /ˌpær.ə'pliː.dʒɪk ⓊⓈ ˌper-/.
Pleiad 'plaɪ.æd, -əd, 'pliː-, 'pleɪ- ⓊⓈ 'pliː.æd, 'plaɪ-, -jæd, -əd **-s** -z **-es** -iːz
Pléiade 'pleɪ.ɑːd, -æd, -'- **-s** -z
Pleistocene 'plaɪ.stəʊ.siːn ⓊⓈ -stoʊ-, -stə-
plenar|y 'pliː.nᵊr|.i ⓊⓈ 'pliː-, 'plen.ɚ- **-ily** -ᵊl.i, -ɪ.li
plenipotentiar|y ˌplen.ɪ.pəʊ'ten*t*.ʃᵊr|.i, -ʃi.ᵊr- ⓊⓈ ˌplen.ɪ.poʊ'ten*t*.ʃi.er-, -pə'-, '-ʃɚ- **-ies** -iz
plenitude 'plen.ɪ.tjuːd ⓊⓈ -tuːd, -tjuːd
plenteous 'plen.ti.əs ⓊⓈ -t̬i- **-ly** -li **-ness** -nəs, -nɪs
plentiful 'plen.tɪ.fᵊl, -fʊl ⓊⓈ -t̬ɪ- **-ly** -i **-ness** -nəs, -nɪs
plenty 'plen.ti ⓊⓈ -t̬i
plen|um 'pliː.n|əm ⓊⓈ 'pliː-, 'plen|.əm **-ums** -əmz **-a** -ə
pleonasm 'pliː.əʊ.næz.ᵊm ⓊⓈ -oʊ-, '-ə- **-s** -z
pleonastic ˌpliː.əʊ'næs.tɪk ⓊⓈ -oʊ'-, -ə'- **-al** -ᵊl **-ally** -ᵊl.i, -li
plesiosaur 'pliː.si.əʊ.sɔːʳ ⓊⓈ -oʊ.sɔːr, -ə- **-s** -z
Plessey® 'ples.i
plethora 'pleθ.ᵊr.ə; pleθ'ɔː.rə, plə'θɔː-, plɪ- ⓊⓈ 'pleθ.ɚ.ə
plethoric pleθ'ɒr.ɪk, plə-, plɪ- ⓊⓈ plə'θɔːr-
pleur|a 'plʊə.r|ə, 'plɔː- ⓊⓈ 'plʊr|.ə **-ae** -iː **-as** -əz **-al** -ᵊl
pleurisy 'plʊə.rə.si, 'plɔː-, -rɪ- ⓊⓈ 'plʊr.ə-
pleuritic plʊə'rɪt.ɪk, plɔː- ⓊⓈ plʊ'rɪt̬-
pleuro-pneumonia ˌplʊə.rəʊ.njuː'məʊ.ni.ə, ˌplɔː- ⓊⓈ ˌplʊr.oʊ.nuː'moʊ.njə, -njuː'-
Plexiglas® 'plek.si.glɑːs ⓊⓈ -sɪ.glæs
plexiglass 'plek.si.glɑːs ⓊⓈ -sɪ.glæs
plexus 'plek.səs **-es** -ɪz
Pleyel 'pleɪ.el, 'plaɪ- ⓊⓈ 'plaɪ- **-s** -z
pliability ˌplaɪ.ə'bɪl.ə.ti, -ɪ.ti ⓊⓈ -ə.t̬i
pliab|le 'plaɪ.ə.bl|̩ **-ly** -li **-leness** -l̩.nəs, -nɪs
pliancy 'plaɪ.ᵊn*t*.si
pliant 'plaɪ.ᵊnt **-ly** -li **-ness** -nəs, -nɪs
plié 'pliː.eɪ, -'- ⓊⓈ -'- **-s** -z
pliers plaɪəz ⓊⓈ plaɪɚz
plight plaɪt **-s** -s **-ing** -ɪŋ ⓊⓈ 'plaɪ.t̬ɪŋ **-ed** -ɪd ⓊⓈ 'plaɪ.t̬ɪd
plimsoll (P) 'plɪm*p*.sᵊl, -sɒl ⓊⓈ -səl, -sɑːl, -sɔːl **-s** -z '**Plimsoll** ˌ**line**
Plinlimmon plɪn'lɪm.ən
plinth plɪn*t*θ **-s** -s
Pliny 'plɪn.i
Pliocene 'plaɪ.əʊ.siːn ⓊⓈ -oʊ-, '-ə-
PLO ˌpiː.el'əʊ ⓊⓈ -'oʊ

plod plɒd Ⓤⓢ plɑːd **-s** -z **-ding** -ɪŋ **-ded** -ɪd **-der/s** -ər/z Ⓤⓢ -ɚ/z
Ploesti, Ploiesti pləʊˈjeʃ.ti Ⓤⓢ plɔː-, -ˈjeʃt
Plomer ˈpluː.məʳ, ˈplʌm.əʳ Ⓤⓢ -ɚ
Plomley ˈplʌm.li
plonk (*n. v.*) plɒŋk Ⓤⓢ plʌŋk, plɑːŋk **-s** -s **-ing** -ɪŋ **-ed** -t
plonker ˈplɒŋ.kəʳ Ⓤⓢ ˈplʌŋ.kɚ **-s** -z
plop plɒp Ⓤⓢ plɑːp **-s** -s **-ping** -ɪŋ **-ped** -t
plosion ˈpləʊ.ʒᵊn Ⓤⓢ ˈploʊ- **-s** -z
plosive ˈpləʊ.sɪv, -zɪv Ⓤⓢ ˈploʊ.sɪv **-s** -z
plot plɒt Ⓤⓢ plɑːt **-s** -s **-ting** -ɪŋ Ⓤⓢ ˈplɑː.t̬ɪŋ **-ted** -ɪd Ⓤⓢ ˈplɑː.t̬ɪd **-ter/s** -ər/z Ⓤⓢ ˈplɑː.t̬ɚ/z
plough (P) plaʊ **-s** -z **-ing** -ɪŋ **-ed** -d **-er/s** -ər/z Ⓤⓢ -ɚ/z **-able** -ə.bl̩
ploughboy ˈplaʊ.bɔɪ **-s** -z
plough|man ˈplaʊ|.mən **-men** -mən, -men ˌ**Ploughman's** ˈ**Lunch**
ploughshare ˈplaʊ.ʃeəʳ Ⓤⓢ -ʃer **-s** -z
Plovdiv ˈplɒv.dɪv, -dɪf Ⓤⓢ ˈplɔːv.dɪf
plover ˈplʌv.əʳ Ⓤⓢ -ɚ **-s** -z
plow plaʊ **-s** -z **-ing** -ɪŋ **-ed** -d **-er/s** -ər/z Ⓤⓢ -ɚ/z **-able** -ə.bl̩
plowboy ˈplaʊ.bɔɪ **-s** -z
Plowden ˈplaʊ.dᵊn
plow|man (P) ˈplaʊ|.mən **-men** -mən, -men
Plowright ˈplaʊ.raɪt
plowshare ˈplaʊ.ʃeəʳ Ⓤⓢ -ʃer **-s** -z
ploy plɔɪ **-s** -z
pluck (P) plʌk **-s** -s **-ing** -ɪŋ **-ed** -t
pluck|y ˈplʌk|.i **-ier** -i.əʳ Ⓤⓢ -i.ɚ **-iest** -i.ɪst, -i.əst **-ily** -ɪ.li, -ᵊl.i **-iness** -ɪ.nəs, -ɪ.nɪs
plug plʌg **-s** -z **-ging** -ɪŋ **-ged** -d
plughole ˈplʌg.həʊl Ⓤⓢ -hoʊl **-s** -z
plum plʌm **-s** -z ˌ**plum** ˈ**pudding**
plumag|e ˈpluː.mɪdʒ **-es** -ɪz
plumb (P) plʌm **-s** -z **-ing** -ɪŋ **-ed** -d
plumbago plʌmˈbeɪ.gəʊ Ⓤⓢ -goʊ **-s** -z
Plumbe plʌm
plumber ˈplʌm.əʳ Ⓤⓢ -ɚ **-s** -z
plumbic ˈplʌm.bɪk
plumbing ˈplʌm.ɪŋ
plumb-line ˈplʌm.laɪn **-s** -z
plumbous ˈplʌm.bəs
plum|e pluːm **-es** -z **-ing** -ɪŋ **-ed** -d
Plummer ˈplʌm.əʳ Ⓤⓢ -ɚ
plumm|et ˈplʌm|.ɪt **-ets** -ɪts **-eting** -ɪ.tɪŋ Ⓤⓢ -ɪ.t̬ɪŋ **-eted** -ɪ.tɪd Ⓤⓢ -ɪ.t̬ɪd
plummy ˈplʌm.i
plump plʌmp **-er** -əʳ Ⓤⓢ -ɚ **-est** -ɪst, -əst **-ly** -li **-ness** -nəs, -nɪs **-s** -z **-ing** -ɪŋ **-ed** -t
Plumpton ˈplʌm*p*.tən
Plum(p)tre ˈplʌm*p*.triː
Plumridge ˈplʌm.rɪdʒ
Plumstead ˈplʌm*p*.stɪd, -sted
plumule ˈpluː.mjuːl **-s** -z
plund|er ˈplʌn.d|əʳ Ⓤⓢ -d|ɚ **-ers** -əz Ⓤⓢ -ɚz **-ering** -ᵊr.ɪŋ **-ered** -əd Ⓤⓢ -ɚd **-erer/s** -ᵊr.əʳ/z Ⓤⓢ -ɚ.ɚ/z **-erous** -ᵊr.əs
plung|e plʌndʒ **-es** -ɪz **-ing** -ɪŋ **-ed** -d
plunger ˈplʌn.dʒəʳ Ⓤⓢ -dʒɚ **-s** -z
Plunket(t) ˈplʌŋ.kɪt
pluperfect ˌpluːˈpɜː.fɪkt, -fekt Ⓤⓢ ˈpluːˌpɜːr.fɪkt, ˌ-ˈ-- **-s** -s *stress shift, British only:* ˌpluperfect ˈtense
plural ˈplʊə.rᵊl, ˈplɔː- Ⓤⓢ ˈplʊr.ᵊl **-s** -z **-ly** -i
plural|ism ˈplʊə.rᵊl|.ɪ.zᵊm, ˈplɔː- Ⓤⓢ ˈplʊr.ᵊl- **-ist/s** -ɪst/s
pluralistic ˌplʊə.rᵊlˈɪs.tɪk Ⓤⓢ ˌplʊr.ᵊlˈ- **-ally** -ᵊl.i, -li *stress shift:* ˌpluralistic ˈsystem
pluralit|y plʊəˈræl.ə.t|i, plɔː-, -ɪ.t|i Ⓤⓢ plʊˈræl.ə.t̬|i **-ies** -iz
pluraliz|e, -is|e ˈplʊə.rᵊl.aɪz, ˈplɔː- Ⓤⓢ ˈplʊr.ᵊl- **-es** -ɪz **-ing** -ɪŋ **-ed** -d
plurisegmental ˌplʊə.rɪ.segˈmen.tᵊl, ˌplɔː- Ⓤⓢ ˌplʊr.ɪ.segˈmen.t̬ᵊl *stress shift:* ˌplurisegmental ˈitem
plus plʌs **-(s)es** -ɪz
plus-fours ˌplʌsˈfɔːz Ⓤⓢ -ˈfɔːrz
plush plʌʃ **-es** -ɪz **-y** -i
Plutarch ˈpluː.tɑːk Ⓤⓢ -tɑːrk
Pluto ˈpluː.təʊ Ⓤⓢ -t̬oʊ
plutocracy pluːˈtɒk.rə.si Ⓤⓢ -ˈtɑː.krə-
plutocrat ˈpluː.tə*ʊ*.kræt Ⓤⓢ -t̬ə-, -toʊ- **-s** -s
plutocratic ˌpluː.tə*ʊ*ˈkræt.ɪk Ⓤⓢ -toʊˈkræt̬-, -t̬əˈ- **-ally** -ᵊl.i, -li *stress shift:* ˌplutocratic ˈgovernment
plutonian (P) pluːˈtəʊ.ni.ən Ⓤⓢ -ˈtoʊ-
plutonic (P) pluːˈtɒn.ɪk Ⓤⓢ -ˈtɑː.nɪk
plutonium pluːˈtəʊ.ni.əm Ⓤⓢ -ˈtoʊ-
pluvi|al ˈpluː.vi|.əl **-ous** -əs
pluviometer ˌpluː.viˈɒm.ɪ.təʳ, ˈ-ə- Ⓤⓢ -ˈɑː.mə.t̬ɚ **-s** -z
pl|y pl|aɪ **-ies** -aɪz **-ying** -aɪ.ɪŋ **-ied** -aɪd
Plymouth ˈplɪm.əθ ˌ**Plymouth** ˈ**Brethren** ; ˌ**Plymouth** ˈ**Rock**
Plynlimon Fawr plɪnˌlɪm.ənˈvaʊəʳ Ⓤⓢ -ˈvaʊr
plywood ˈplaɪ.wʊd
p.m. ˌpiːˈem
PM ˌpiːˈem
PMS ˌpiː.emˈes
PMT ˌpiː.emˈtiː
pneumatic njuːˈmæt.ɪk Ⓤⓢ nuːˈmæt̬-, njuː- **-s** -s **-al** -ᵊl **-ally** -ᵊl.i, -li pneuˌmatic ˈdrill
pneumatolog|y ˌnjuː.məˈtɒl.ə.dʒ|i Ⓤⓢ ˌnuː.məˈtɑː.lə-, ˌnjuː- **-ist/s** -ɪst/s
pneumoconios|is ˌnjuː.mə*ʊ*ˌkəʊ.niˈəʊ.s|ɪs, -ˌkɒn.iˈ- Ⓤⓢ ˌnuː.moʊˌkoʊ.niˈoʊ-, ˌnjuː-, -məˌ- **-es** -iːz
pneumonia njuːˈməʊ.ni.ə Ⓤⓢ nuːˈmoʊ.njə, njuː-
pneumonic njuːˈmɒn.ɪk Ⓤⓢ nuːˈmɑː.nɪk, njuː-
Pnom Penh ˌnɒmˈpen, pəˌnɒm- Ⓤⓢ ˌnɑːm-
po (P) pəʊ Ⓤⓢ poʊ **-es** -z
PO ˌpiːˈəʊ Ⓤⓢ -ˈoʊ ˈ**PO** ˌ**box**
poach pəʊtʃ Ⓤⓢ poʊtʃ **-es** -ɪz **-ing** -ɪŋ **-ed** -t **-er/s** -ər/z Ⓤⓢ -ɚ/z
Pocahontas ˌpɒk.əˈhɒn.təs, -tæs Ⓤⓢ ˌpoʊ.kəˈhɑːn.t̬əs
pochard ˈpəʊ.tʃəd, ˈpɒtʃ.əd Ⓤⓢ ˈpoʊ.tʃɚd, -kɚd **-s** -z
pochette pɒʃˈet Ⓤⓢ poʊˈʃet **-s** -s
pock pɒk Ⓤⓢ pɑːk **-s** -s **-ed** -t
pock|et ˈpɒk|.ɪt Ⓤⓢ ˈpɑː.k|ɪt **-ets** -ɪts **-eting** -ɪ.tɪŋ Ⓤⓢ -ɪ.t̬ɪŋ **-eted** -ɪ.tɪd Ⓤⓢ -ɪ.t̬ɪd **-etable** -ɪ.tə.bl̩ Ⓤⓢ -ɪ.t̬ə.bl̩ **-etful/s** -ɪt.fʊl/z ˈ**pocket** ˌ**money**
pocketbook ˈpɒk.ɪt.bʊk Ⓤⓢ ˈpɑː.kɪt- **-s** -s
pocket-handkerchie|f ˌpɒk.ɪtˈhæŋ.kə.tʃiː|f, -tʃɪ|f Ⓤⓢ ˌpɑː.kɪtˈhæŋ.kɚ- **-fs** -fs **-ves** -vz
pocketknif|e ˈpɒk.ɪt.naɪ|f Ⓤⓢ ˈpɑː.kɪt- **-ves** -vz
pocket-size ˈpɒk.ɪt.saɪz Ⓤⓢ ˈpɑː.kɪt- **-d** -d
Pocklington ˈpɒk.lɪŋ.tən Ⓤⓢ ˈpɑː.klɪŋ-
pockmark ˈpɒk.mɑːk Ⓤⓢ ˈpɑːk.mɑːrk **-s** -s **-ing** -ɪŋ **-ed** -t
poco ˈpəʊ.kəʊ Ⓤⓢ ˈpoʊ.koʊ
Pocock ˈpəʊ.kɒk Ⓤⓢ ˈpoʊ.kɑːk
pococurante ˌpəʊ.kəʊ.kjʊəˈræn.teɪ, -ti Ⓤⓢ ˌpoʊ.koʊ.kuːˈræn.t̬i, -kjuːˈ-, -ˈrɑːn- **-s** -z
pod pɒd Ⓤⓢ pɑːd **-s** -z **-ding** -ɪŋ **-ded** -ɪd
podagra pə*ʊ*ˈdæg.rə, pɒdˈæg-, ˈpɒd.ə.grə Ⓤⓢ pəˈdæg.rə; ˈpɑː.də.grə
podg|y ˈpɒdʒ|.i Ⓤⓢ ˈpɑː.dʒ|i **-ier** -i.əʳ Ⓤⓢ -i.ɚ **-iest** -i.ɪst, -i.əst **-ily** -ɪ.li, -ᵊl.i **-iness** -ɪ.nəs, -ɪ.nɪs
podiatric ˌpəʊ.diˈæt.rɪk, ˌpɒd.iˈ- Ⓤⓢ ˌpoʊ-
podiatr|y pə*ʊ*ˈdaɪ.ə.tr|i, pɒdˈaɪ- Ⓤⓢ pəˈdaɪ-, poʊ- **-ist/s** -ɪst/s
podi|um ˈpəʊ.di|.əm Ⓤⓢ ˈpoʊ- **-ums** -əmz **-a** -ə
Podunk ˈpəʊ.dʌŋk Ⓤⓢ ˈpoʊ-
Poe pəʊ Ⓤⓢ poʊ
Poel pəʊəl; ˈpəʊ.el, -ɪl Ⓤⓢ poʊəl; ˈpoʊ.el, -ɪl
poem ˈpəʊ.ɪm, -em; pəʊəm Ⓤⓢ poʊəm **-s** -z
Poema Morale pəʊˌeɪ.mə.mɒrˈɑː.leɪ, -mɔːˈrɑː- Ⓤⓢ poʊˌeɪ.mə.mɔːrˈɑː-
poesy ˈpəʊ.ɪ.zi, -ez.i; ˈpəʊə.zi Ⓤⓢ ˈpoʊə.si, -zi

poet 'pəʊ.ɪt, -et; pəʊət (US) poʊət **-s** -s ˌpoet 'laureate

poetaster ˌpəʊ.ɪ'tæs.təʳ, ˌpəʊə'- (US) 'poʊə.tæs.tɚ **-s** -z

poetess ˌpəʊ.ɪ'tes, ˌpəʊə'-; 'pəʊ.ɪ.tɪs, 'pəʊə.tɪs, -tes (US) 'poʊ.ɪ.t̬ɪs **-es** -ɪz

poetic pəʊ'et.ɪk (US) poʊ'et̬- **-al** -əl **-ally** -əl.i, -li **poˌetic 'justice**

poeticism pəʊ'et.ɪ.sɪ.zəm, '-ə- (US) poʊ'et̬.ə-

poeticiz|e, -is|e pəʊ'et.ɪ.saɪz, '-ə- (US) poʊ'et̬.ə- **-es** -ɪz **-ing** -ɪŋ **-ed** -d **-er/s** -əʳ/z (US) -ɚ/z

poetiz|e, -is|e 'pəʊ.ɪ.taɪz, 'pəʊə.taɪz (US) 'poʊə- **-es** -ɪz **-ing** -ɪŋ **-ed** -d **-er/s** -əʳ/z (US) -ɚ/z

poetry 'pəʊ.ɪ.tri, 'pəʊə.tri (US) 'poʊə-

po-faced ˌpəʊ'feɪst (US) ˌpoʊ- *stress shift:* ˌpo-faced 'person

Pogner 'pəʊg.nəʳ (US) 'poʊg.nɚ

pogo 'pəʊ.gəʊ (US) 'poʊ.goʊ **-s** -z **-ing** -ɪŋ **-ed** -d **'pogo ˌstick**

pogrom 'pɒg.rəm, -rɒm (US) 'poʊ.grəm, -grɑːm; pə'grɑːm **-s** -z

poignancy 'pɔɪ.njənt.si, -nənt- (US) -njənt.si

poignant 'pɔɪ.njənt, -nənt (US) -njənt **-ly** -li

poikilotherm pɔɪ'kɪl.əʊ.θɜːm (US) -ə.θɜːrm, '-oʊ-

poikilotherm|ic ˌpɔɪ.kɪ.ləʊ'θɜː.m|ɪk (US) -lə'θɜːr-, -loʊ'- **-al** -əl **-ism** -ɪ.zəm

Poindexter 'pɔɪn.dek.stəʳ (US) -stɚ

poinsettia ˌpɔɪnt'set.i.ə (US) -'set̬-, '-ə **-s** -z

point pɔɪnt **-s** -s **-ing** -ɪŋ (US) 'pɔɪn.t̬ɪŋ **-ed** -ɪd (US) 'pɔɪn.t̬ɪd **-er/s** -əʳ/z (US) 'pɔɪn.t̬ɚ/z ˌ**point of ˌno re'turn** ; ˌ**point of 'order** ; ˌ**point of 'view**

point-blank ˌpɔɪnt'blæŋk *stress shift:* ˌpoint-blank 'range

point-duty 'pɔɪntˌdjuː.ti (US) -ˌduː.t̬i, -ˌdjuː-

pointed 'pɔɪn.tɪd (US) -t̬ɪd **-ly** -li **-ness** -nəs, -nɪs

Pointe-Noire ˌpwæ̃ːnt'nwɑːʳ (US) -'nwɑːr

pointill|ism 'pɔɪn.tɪ.l|ɪ.zəm, 'pwæ̃n.tiː.j|ɪ.zəm (US) 'pwæn.tə.l|ɪ-, -tiː.j|ɪ- **-ist/s** -ɪst/s

pointless 'pɔɪnt.ləs, -lɪs **-ly** -li **-ness** -nəs, -nɪs

point-of-sale ˌpɔɪnt.əv'seɪl

Pointon 'pɔɪn.tən (US) -tən

point-to-point ˌpɔɪnt.tə'pɔɪnt *stress shift:* ˌpoint-to-point 'champion

points|man 'pɔɪnts|.mən **-men** -mən, -men

Poirot 'pwɑː.rəʊ, -'- (US) pwɑː'roʊ

pois|e pɔɪz **-es** -ɪz **-ing** -ɪŋ **-ed** -d

poison 'pɔɪ.zən **-s** -z **-ing** -ɪŋ **-ed** -d **-er/s** -əʳ/z (US) -ɚ/z ˌ**poison 'ivy** ; ˌ**poison 'oak** ; **'poison ˌpill**

poisonous 'pɔɪ.zən.əs **-ly** -li **-ness** -nəs, -nɪs

poison-pen letter ˌpɔɪ.zən'penˌlet.əʳ (US) -ˌlet̬.ɚ **-s** -z

Poitier 'pwɒt.i.eɪ, 'pwæt-, 'pwɑː.ti- (US) 'pwɑː.ti.eɪ, -tjeɪ

Poitiers 'pwɑː.ti.eɪ, 'pwɒt.i-, 'pwæt.i-, ˌ--'- (US) pwɑː'tjeɪ, -ti'eɪ

pok|e pəʊk (US) poʊk **-es** -s **-ing** -ɪŋ **-ed** -t

poker 'pəʊ.kəʳ (US) 'poʊ.kɚ **-s** -z **'poker ˌface**

pok|ey 'pəʊ.k|i (US) 'poʊ- **-eys** -iz **-ies** -iz

pokie 'pəʊ.ki (US) 'poʊ- **-s** -z

pok|y 'pəʊ.k|i (US) 'poʊ- **-ier** -i.əʳ (US) -i.ɚ **-iest** -i.ɪst, -i.əst **-ily** -ɪ.li, -əl.i **-iness** -ɪ.nəs, -ɪ.nɪs

Pola(c)k 'pəʊ.læk (US) 'poʊ- **-s** -s

Poland 'pəʊ.lənd (US) 'poʊ-

Polanski pəʊ'lænt.ski, pɒl'ænt- (US) pə'lænt-, poʊ-

polar 'pəʊ.ləʳ (US) 'poʊ.lɚ **-s** -z ˌ**polar 'bear**, **'polar ˌbear**

Polaris pəʊ'lɑː.rɪs, -'lær.ɪs, -'leə.rɪs (US) pə'ler.ɪs, poʊ-, -'lær-

Note: In British English, the rocket and submarine are usually pronounced with /-'lɑː-/.

polariscope pəʊ'lær.ɪ.skəʊp, '-ə- (US) poʊ'ler.ɪ.skoʊp, -'lær- **-s** -s

polarity pəʊ'lær.ə.ti, -ɪ.ti (US) poʊ'ler.ə.t̬i, -'lær-

polarization, -isa- ˌpəʊ.lər.aɪ'zeɪ.ʃən, -ɪ'- (US) ˌpoʊ.lɚ.ɪ'-

polariz|e, -is|e 'pəʊ.lər.aɪz (US) 'poʊ.lə.raɪz **-es** -ɪz **-ing** -ɪŋ **-ed** -d **-er/s** -əʳ/z (US) -ɚ/z

Polaroid® 'pəʊ.lər.ɔɪd (US) 'poʊ.lə.rɔɪd **-s** -z

polder 'pɒl.dəʳ, 'pəʊl- (US) 'poʊl.dɚ **-s** -z

pole pəʊl (US) poʊl **-s** -z **'Pole ˌStar**; **'pole ˌvault**

Pole *inhabitant of Poland:* pəʊl (US) poʊl **-s** -z

Pole *surname:* pəʊl, puːl (US) poʊl, puːl

poleax|(e) 'pəʊl.æks (US) 'poʊl- **-es** -ɪz **-ing** -ɪŋ **-ed** -t

polecat 'pəʊl.kæt (US) 'poʊl- **-s** -s

polemic pə'lem.ɪk, pɒl'em- (US) pə'lem- **-s** -s **-al** -əl **-ally** -əl.i, -li

polemicist pə'lem.ɪ.sɪst, pɒl'em- (US) pə'lem- **-s** -s

polemiciz|e, -is|e pə'lem.ɪ.saɪz, pɒl'em- (US) pə'lem.ɪ.saɪz **-es** -ɪz **-ing** -ɪŋ **-ed** -d

polenta pəʊ'len.tə (US) poʊ'len.t̬ə, pə-

polestar 'pəʊl.stɑːʳ (US) 'poʊl.stɑːr **-s** -z

Polesworth 'pəʊlz.wəθ, -wɜːθ (US) 'poʊlz.wɚθ, -wɜːrθ

pole-vaul|t 'pəʊl.vɔː|lt, -vɒ|lt (US) 'poʊl.vɑː|lt, -vɔː|lt **-ts** -ts **-ting** -tɪŋ (US) -t̬ɪŋ **-ted** -tɪd (US) -t̬ɪd **-ter/s** -təʳ/z (US) -t̬ɚ/z

polic|e pə'liːs, pliːs (US) pə'liːs, poʊ-, pliːs **-es** -ɪz **-ing** -ɪŋ **-ed** -t **po'lice ˌcar** ; **poˌlice 'constable**; **po'lice ˌforce**; **po'lice ˌofficer**, **poˌlice 'officer**; **poˌlice 'state** (US) **po'lice ˌstate**; **po'lice ˌstation**

police|man pə'liːs|.mən, 'pliːs- (US) pə'liːs-, poʊ-, pliːs- **-men** -mən

police|woman pə'liːs|ˌwʊm.ən, 'pliːs- (US) pə'liːs-, poʊ-, pliːs- **-women** -ˌwɪm.ɪn

polic|y 'pɒl.ə.s|i, '-ɪ- (US) 'pɑː.lə- **-ies** -iz

policyholder 'pɒl.ə.siˌhəʊl.dəʳ, '-ɪ- (US) 'pɑː.lə.siˌhoʊl.dɚ **-s** -z

polio 'pəʊ.li.əʊ (US) 'poʊ.li.oʊ

poliomyelitis ˌpəʊl.i.əʊ.maɪə'laɪ.tɪs, -maɪ.ɪ'-, -el'aɪ- (US) ˌpoʊ.li.oʊˌmaɪə'laɪ.t̬əs

polish (*n. v.*) 'pɒl.ɪʃ (US) 'pɑː.lɪʃ **-es** -ɪz **-ing** -ɪŋ **-ed** -t **-er/s** -əʳ/z (US) -ɚ/z

Polish (*adj.*) *of Poland:* 'pəʊ.lɪʃ (US) 'poʊ-

politburo (P) 'pɒl.ɪtˌbjʊə.rəʊ, pɒl'ɪt-, -ˌbjɔː-; -bjəˌrəʊ, -bjʊˌ- (US) 'pɑː.lɪtˌbjʊr.oʊ, 'poʊ-; poʊ'lɪt-, pə- **-s** -z

po|lite pəl'aɪt (US) pə-, poʊ- **-litest** -'laɪ.tɪst, -'laɪ.təst (US) -'laɪ.t̬ɪst, -'laɪ.t̬əst **-litely** -'laɪt.li **-liteness** -'laɪt.nəs, -'laɪt.nɪs

politic 'pɒl.ə.tɪk, '-ɪ- (US) 'pɑː.lə- **-s** -s

politic|al pə'lɪt.ɪ.k|əl, '-ə- (US) -'lɪt̬.ə-, poʊ- **-ally** -əl.i, -li **poˌlitical 'prisoner** ; **poˌlitical 'science**

politician ˌpɒl.ɪ'tɪʃ.ən, -ə'- (US) ˌpɑː.lə'- **-s** -z

politiciz|e, -cis|e pə'lɪt.ɪ.saɪz, '-ə- (US) -'lɪt̬.ə-, poʊ- **-es** -ɪz **-ing** -ɪŋ **-ed** -d

politick 'pɒl.ə.tɪk, '-ɪ- (US) 'pɑː.lə- **-s** -s **-ing** -ɪŋ **-ed** -t **-er/s** -əʳ/z (US) -ɚ/z

politico- pəˌlɪt.ɪ.kəʊ- (US) pəˌlɪt̬.ɪ.koʊ-, poʊ-, -kə-

politico pə'lɪt.ɪ.kəʊ (US) -'lɪt̬.ɪ.koʊ, poʊ- **-s** -z

polity 'pɒl.ə.ti, -ɪ.ti (US) 'pɑː.lə.t̬i

Polixenes pɒl'ɪk.sə.niːz, pə'lɪk-, -sɪ- (US) pə'lɪk.sə-

Polk pəʊk (US) poʊk

polka 'pɒl.kə (US) 'poʊl- **-s** -z **'polka ˌdot**

poll (*n. v.*) pəʊl (US) poʊl **-s** -z **-ing** -ɪŋ **-ed** -d **'poll ˌtax** ; **'polling ˌbooth** ; **'polling ˌstation**

pollard 'pɒl.əd, -ɑːd (US) 'pɑː.lɚd **-s** -z **-ing** -ɪŋ **-ed** -ɪd

Pollard 'pɒl.ɑːd (US) 'pɑː.lɚd

pollen (P) ˈpɒl.ən, -ɪn (US) ˈpɑː.lən **-s** -z ˈ**pollen** ˌ**count**

polli|nate ˈpɒl.ə|.neɪt, ˈ-ɪ- (US) ˈpɑː.lə- **-nates** -neɪts **-nating** -neɪ.tɪŋ (US) -neɪ.t̬ɪŋ **-nated** -neɪ.tɪd (US) -neɪ.t̬ɪd

pollination ˌpɒl.əˈneɪ.ʃᵊn, -ɪˈ- (US) ˌpɑː.ləˈ-

Pollock ˈpɒl.ək (US) ˈpɑː.lək

pollster ˈpəʊl.stəʳ (US) ˈpoʊl.stɚ **-s** -z

pollutant pəˈluː.tᵊnt, -ˈljuː- (US) -ˈluː- **-s** -s

pollu|te pəˈluː|t, -ˈljuː|t (US) -luː|t **-tes** -ts **-ting** -tɪŋ (US) -t̬ɪŋ **-ted** -tɪd (US) -t̬ɪd **-ter/s** -təʳ/z (US) -t̬ɚ/z

pollution pəˈluː.ʃᵊn, -ˈljuː- (US) -ˈluː- **-s** -z

Pollux ˈpɒl.əks (US) ˈpɑː.ləks

Polly ˈpɒl.i (US) ˈpɑː.li

pollyanna (P) ˌpɒl.iˈæn.ə (US) ˌpɑː.liˈ- **-s** -z

Polmont ˈpəʊl.mənt (US) ˈpoʊl.mɑːnt

polo (P) ˈpəʊ.ləʊ (US) ˈpoʊ.loʊ ˈ**polo** ˌ**neck**

polonais|e ˌpɒl.əˈneɪz (US) ˌpɑː.ləˈ-, ˌpoʊ- **-es** -ɪz

polonium pəˈləʊ.ni.əm (US) -ˈloʊ-

Polonius pəˈləʊ.ni.əs, pɒlˈəʊ- (US) pəˈloʊ-

polon|y pəˈləʊ.n|i (US) -ˈloʊ- **-ies** -iz

Pol Pot ˌpɒlˈpɒt (US) ˌpɑːlˈpɑːt

Polson ˈpəʊl.sᵊn (US) ˈpoʊl-

poltergeist ˈpɒl.tə.gaɪst, ˈpəʊl- (US) ˈpoʊl.t̬ɚ- **-s** -s

poltroon pɒlˈtruːn (US) pɑːl- **-s** -z **-ery** -ᵊr.i

Polwarth *in Scotland:* ˈpəʊl.wəθ (US) ˈpoʊl.wɚθ *surname:* ˈpɒl.wəθ (US) ˈpɑːl.wɚθ

poly- pɒl.i-, -ɪ-; pəˈlɪ- (US) pɑː.li-, -lɪ-, -lə-; pəˈlɪ-

Note: Prefix. Many compounds with **poly-** have the stress pattern ˌ**poly**ˈ-; these are likely to undergo stress shift when a stressed syllable follows. The prefix may also be stressed on the second syllable, e.g. **polygonal** /pəˈlɪg.ᵊn.ᵊl/.

poly ˈpɒl.i (US) ˈpɑː.li **-s** -z

polyamide ˌpɒl.iˈæm.aɪd, -ˈeɪ.maɪd (US) ˌpɑː.liˈ- **-s** -z

polyandrous ˌpɒl.iˈæn.drəs (US) ˌpɑː.liˈ-

polyandry ˈpɒl.i.æn.dri, ˌpɒl.iˈæn- (US) ˈpɑː.liˌæn-, ˌpɑː.liˈæn-

polyanth|us ˌpɒl.iˈænt.θ|əs (US) ˌpɑː.liˈ- **-uses** -ə.sɪz **-i** -aɪ

polybag ˈpɒl.i.bæg, ˌ--ˈ- (US) ˈpɑː.li.bæg **-s** -z

Polybius pəˈlɪb.i.əs, pɒlˈɪb- (US) pəˈlɪb-, poʊ-

polycarbonate ˌpɒl.ɪˈkɑː.bə.neɪt, -iˈ-, -nət, -nɪt (US) ˌpɑː.lɪˈkɑːr.bə.nɪt, -liˈ-, -neɪt **-s** -s

Polycarp ˈpɒl.ɪ.kɑːp, -i- (US) ˈpɑː.lɪ.kɑːrp, -li-

Polycell® ˈpɒl.ɪ.sel, -i- (US) ˈpɑː.lɪ-, -li-

polyclinic ˌpɒl.ɪˈklɪn.ɪk (US) ˌpɑː.lɪˈ- **-s** -s

polycotton ˌpɒl.ɪˈkɒt.ᵊn, -iˈ- (US) ˌpɑː.lɪˈkɑː.tᵊn, -liˈ-

Polycrates pəˈlɪk.rə.tiːz, pɒlˈɪk- (US) pəˈlɪk-

polyester ˌpɒl.iˈes.təʳ (US) ˌpɑː.liˈes.tɚ, ˈpɑː.li.es-

polyethylene ˌpɒl.iˈeθ.ɪ.liːn, ˈ-ə- (US) ˌpɑː.liˈeθ.ə-

Polyfilla® ˈpɒl.ɪˌfɪl.ə, -i- (US) ˈpɑː.lɪˌ-, -liˌ-

polygam|y pəˈlɪg.ə.m|i, pɒlˈɪg- (US) pəˈlɪg- **-ist/s** -ɪst/s **-ous** -əs

polyglot ˈpɒl.ɪ.glɒt, -i- (US) ˈpɑː.lɪ.glɑːt, -li- **-s** -s

polygon ˈpɒl.ɪ.gən, -gɑːn (US) ˈpɑː.lɪ.gɑːn **-s** -z

polygonal pəˈlɪg.ᵊn.ᵊl, pɒlˈɪg- (US) pəˈlɪg- **-ly** -i

polygonum pəˈlɪg.ᵊn.əm, pɒlˈɪg- (US) pəˈlɪg-

polygraph ˈpɒl.ɪ.grɑːf, -i-, -græf (US) ˈpɑː.lɪ.græf, -li- **-s** -s

polyhedr|on ˌpɒl.ɪˈhiː.dr|ᵊn, -iˈ-, -ˈhed.r|ᵊn (US) ˌpɑː.lɪˈhiː-, -li- **-ons** -ᵊnz **-a** -ə **-al** -ᵊl

polylectal ˌpɒl.ɪˈlek.tᵊl, -iˈ- (US) ˌpɑː.lɪˈ-, -liˈ-

polymath ˈpɒl.ɪ.mæθ, -i- (US) ˈpɑː.lɪ-, -li- **-s** -s

polymer ˈpɒl.ɪ.məʳ (US) ˈpɑː.lɪ.mɚ **-s** -z

polymeras|e ˈpɒl.ɪ.mᵊr.eɪs, -eɪz (US) ˈpɑː.lɪ.mə.reɪz, -reɪs **-es** -ɪz

polymeric ˌpɒl.ɪˈmer.ɪk (US) ˌpɑː.lɪ- **-ally** -ᵊl.i, -li

polymerism pəˈlɪm.ᵊr.ɪ.zᵊm, pɒlˈɪm-; ˈpɒl.ɪ.mᵊr- (US) pəˈlɪm.ɚ-; ˈpɑː.lɪ.mɚ-

polymerization, -isa- ˌpɒl.ɪ.mᵊr.aɪˈzeɪ.ʃᵊn, -lə-, -ɪˈ- (US) ˌpɑː.lɪ.mɚ.ɪˈ-

polymeriz|e, -is|e ˈpɒl.ɪ.mᵊr.aɪz, ˈ-ə- (US) ˈpɑː.lɪ.mə.raɪz **-es** -ɪz **-ing** -ɪŋ **-ed** -d

polymerous pəˈlɪm.ᵊr.əs, pɒlˈɪm- (US) pəˈlɪm-

polymorph|ic ˌpɒl.ɪˈmɔː.f|ɪk, -i- (US) ˌpɑː.lɪˈmɔːr-, -iˈ- **-ism** -ɪ.zᵊm **-ous** -əs

Polynesi|a ˌpɒl.ɪˈniː.ʒ|ə, -zi|.ə, -ʒi|.ə, -si|.ə, -ʃi|.ə, -ʃ|ə (US) ˌpɑː.ləˈniː.ʒ|ə, -ʃ|ə **-an/s** -ən/z

polynomial ˌpɒl.ɪˈnəʊ.mi.əl (US) ˌpɑː.liˈnoʊ- **-s** -z

Poly-Olbion ˌpɒl.iˈɒl.bi.ən (US) ˌpɑː.liˈɑːl-

polyp ˈpɒl.ɪp (US) ˈpɑː.lɪp **-s** -s **-ous** -əs

polypeptide ˌpɒl.ɪˈpep.taɪd, -i- (US) ˌpɑː.lɪˈ-, -liˈ- **-s** -z

Polyphemus ˌpɒl.ɪˈfiː.məs, -əˈ- (US) ˌpɑː.lɪˈ-

polyphon|ic ˌpɒl.ɪˈfɒn|.ɪk, -əˈ-, -iˈ- (US) ˌpɑː.lɪˈfɑː.n|ɪk, -liˈ- **-ous** -əs

polyphony pəˈlɪf.ᵊn.i, pɒlˈɪf- (US) pəˈlɪf-

polypody ˈpɒl.ɪ.pəʊ.di, -i- (US) ˈpɑː.lɪ.poʊ-, -li-

polyp|us ˈpɒl.ɪ.p|əs, ˈ-ə- (US) ˈpɑː.lɪ- **-i** -aɪ

polysaccharide ˌpɒl.ɪˈsæk.ᵊr.aɪd, -ɪ-, -ɪd (US) ˌpɑː.lɪˈsæk.ə.raɪd, -liˈ-

polysemous pəˈlɪs.ɪ.məs, pɒlˈɪs-; ˌpɒl.ɪˈsiː- (US) ˌpɑː.lɪˈsiː-; pəˈlɪs.ə-

polysemy pəˈlɪs.ɪ.mi; ˌpɒl.ɪˈsiː.mi, ˈpɒl.ɪ.siː- (US) ˈpɑː.lɪ.siː-; pəˈlɪs.ə-

polystyrene ˌpɒl.ɪˈstaɪə.riːn, -iˈ- (US) ˌpɑː.lɪˈstaɪ-, -liˈ-

polysyllabic ˌpɒl.ɪ.sɪˈlæb.ɪk, -ɪ-, -səˈ- (US) ˌpɑː.lɪ.sɪˈ-, -liˈ- **-al** -ᵊl **-ally** -ᵊl.i, -li

polysyllable ˌpɒl.ɪˈsɪl.ə.bl̩, ˈpɒl.ɪˌsɪl-, -i- (US) ˈpɑː.lɪˌsɪl-, -liˌ- **-s** -z

polysyndeton ˌpɒl.ɪˈsɪn.də.tən, -iˈ-, -dɪ- (US) ˌpɑː.lɪˈsɪn.də.tɑːn, -liˈ-, -tən

polysynthesis ˌpɒl.ɪˈsɪnt.θə.sɪs, -iˈ-, -θɪ- (US) ˌpɑː.lɪˈ-, -liˈ-

polysynthetic ˌpɒl.ɪ.sɪnˈθet.ɪk, -i- (US) ˌpɑː.lɪ.sɪnˈθet̬.ɪk, -li-

polysystemic ˌpɒl.ɪ.sɪˈstiː.mɪk, -ɪ-, -səˈ- (US) ˌpɑː.lɪ-, -li-

polytechnic ˌpɒl.ɪˈtek.nɪk, -iˈ- (US) ˌpɑː.lɪˈ-, -liˈ- **-s** -s

polythe|ism ˈpɒl.ɪ.θiː|.ɪ.zᵊm, ˌpɒl.ɪˈθiː-, -i- (US) ˈpɑː.lɪ.θiː-, ˌpɑː.liˈθiː, -li- **-ist/s** -ɪst/s

polytheistic ˌpɒl.ɪ.θiˈɪs.tɪk; -ˈθiː.ɪ.stɪk, -i- (US) ˌpɑː.lɪ.θiˈɪs.tɪk, -li-

polythene ˈpɒl.ɪ.θiːn, ˈ-ə- (US) ˈpɑː.lɪ-

polyunsaturate ˌpɒl.i.ʌnˈsætʃ.ᵊr.eɪt, -ˈsæt.jᵊr-, -ət (US) ˌpɑː.li.ʌnˈsætʃ.ə.reɪt **-s** -s

polyunsaturated ˌpɒl.i.ʌnˈsætʃ.ᵊr.eɪ.tɪd, -ˈsæt.jᵊr- (US) ˌpɑː.li.ʌnˈsætʃ.ə.reɪ.t̬ɪd

polyurethane ˌpɒl.ɪˈjʊə.rə.θeɪn, -ˈjɔː-, -iˈ-, -rɪ- (US) ˌpɑː.lɪˈjʊr.ə-, -liˈ-

polyvalent ˌpɒl.ɪˈveɪ.lənt, -iˈ- (US) ˌpɑː.lɪˈ-, ˈpɑː.lɪ.veɪ-, -liˈ-

polyvinyl ˌpɒl.ɪˈvaɪ.nᵊl, -iˈ-, -nɪl (US) ˌpɑː.lɪˈvaɪ.nəl, -liˈ-

Polyxen|a pəˈlɪk.sɪ.n|ə, pɒlˈɪk-, -sə- (US) pəˈlɪk-; ˌpoʊ.lɪkˈsiː- **-us** -əs

Polzeath pɒlˈzeθ (US) pɑːl-

pom (P) pɒm (US) pɑːm **-s** -z

pomace ˈpʌm.ɪs (US) ˈpʌm-, ˈpɑː.mɪs

pomade pəʊˈmeɪd, pɒmˈeɪd, -ˈɑːd (US) pɑːˈmeɪd, poʊ-, ˈpɑː.meɪd, -mɑːd **-s** -z

Pomagne® pəˈmeɪn, pɒmˈeɪn (US) pɑːˈmeɪn, pə-

pomander pəˈmæn.dəʳ, pɒmˈæn- (US) ˈpoʊ.mæn.dɚ; -ˈ--, pə- **-s** -z

pomatum pə'meɪ.təm, -'mɑː- ⓤⓢ -ţəm, poʊ- **-s** -z
pome pəʊm ⓤⓢ poʊm **-s** -z
pomegranate 'pɒm.ɪˌgræn.ɪt, -əˌ- ⓤⓢ 'pɑːmˌgræn-, 'pʌmˌ-, 'pɑː.məˌ-, 'pʌm.əˌ- **-s** -s
pomelo 'pɒm.ɪ.ləʊ, '-ə-; pə'mel.oʊ ⓤⓢ 'pɑː.mə.loʊ **-s** -z
Pomerania ˌpɒm.ə'reɪ.ni.ə ⓤⓢ ˌpɑː.mə'-
Pomeranian ˌpɒm.ə'reɪ.ni.ən ⓤⓢ ˌpɑː.mə'- *stress shift:* ˌPomeranian 'dog
Pomeroy 'pɒm.ə.rɔɪ, 'pəʊm.rɔɪ ⓤⓢ 'pɑː.mə.rɔɪ, 'pɑːm.rɔɪ
pomfret *fish:* 'pɒm.frɪt ⓤⓢ 'pɑːm-, 'pʌm- **-s** -s
Pomfret 'pʌm.frɪt, 'pɒm- ⓤⓢ 'pʌm-, 'pɑːm- **'Pomfret ˌcake**
pommel (*n.*) 'pɒm.əl ⓤⓢ 'pʌm.əl, 'pɑː.məl **-s** -z
pommel (*v.*) 'pʌm.əl, 'pɒm- ⓤⓢ 'pʌm-, 'pɑː.məl **-s** -z **-(l)ing** -ɪŋ **-(l)ed** -d
pomm|ie, pomm|y (P) 'pɒm|.i ⓤⓢ 'pɑː.m|i **-ies** -iz
Pomona pə'məʊ.nə, pɒm'əʊ- ⓤⓢ pə'moʊ-
pomp pɒmp ⓤⓢ pɑːmp **-s** -s
pompadour (P) 'pɒm.pə.dʊəʳ, 'pɔ̃ːm-, -dɔːʳ ⓤⓢ 'pɑːm.pə.dɔːr, -dʊr **-s** -z
Pompeian pɒm'peɪ.ən, -'piː- ⓤⓢ pɑːm'peɪ-
Pompeii pɒm'peɪ.i, -'peɪ ⓤⓢ pɑːm-
Pompey 'pɒm.pi ⓤⓢ 'pɑːm-, -peɪ
Pompidou 'pɒm.pɪ.duː ⓤⓢ 'pɑːm- **'Pompidou ˌCentre**
pompom 'pɒm.pɒm ⓤⓢ 'pɑːm.pɑːm **-s** -z
pompon 'pɒm.pɒn, -pɒŋ, 'pɔ̃ːm.pɔ̃ːŋ ⓤⓢ 'pɑːm.pɑːn **-s** -z
pomposity pɒm'pɒs.ə.ti, -ɪ.ti ⓤⓢ pɑːm'pɑː.sə.ţi
pompous 'pɒm.pəs ⓤⓢ 'pɑːm- **-ly** -li **-ness** -nəs, -nɪs
ponc|e pɒnts ⓤⓢ pɑːnts **-es** -ɪz **-(e)y** -i
poncho 'pɒn.tʃəʊ ⓤⓢ 'pɑːn.tʃoʊ **-s** -z
pond (P) pɒnd ⓤⓢ pɑːnd **-s** -z
pond|er 'pɒn.d|əʳ ⓤⓢ 'pɑːn.d|ɚ **-ers** -əz ⓤⓢ -ɚz **-ering/ly** -ər.ɪŋ/li **-ered** -əd ⓤⓢ -ɚd
ponderability ˌpɒn.dər.ə'bɪl.ə.ti, -ɪ.ti ⓤⓢ ˌpɑːn.dɚ.ə'bɪl.ə.ţi
ponderable 'pɒn.dər.ə.bl̩ ⓤⓢ 'pɑːn.dɚ- **-ness** -nəs, -nɪs
ponderous 'pɒn.dər.əs ⓤⓢ 'pɑːn- **-ly** -li **-ness** -nəs, -nɪs
Ponders 'pɒn.dəz ⓤⓢ 'pɑːn.dɚz
Pondicherry ˌpɒn.dɪ'tʃer.i, -'ʃer- ⓤⓢ ˌpɑːn.dɪ'tʃer-
pondweed 'pɒnd.wiːd ⓤⓢ 'pɑːnd-
pong pɒŋ ⓤⓢ pɑːŋ, pɔːŋ **-s** -z **-ing** -ɪŋ **-ed** -d
pongee ˌpɒn'dʒiː, ˌpʌn- ⓤⓢ ˌpɑːn'dʒiː; 'pɑːn.dʒi
poniard 'pɒn.jəd, -jɑːd ⓤⓢ 'pɑː.njɚd **-s** -z **-ing** -ɪŋ **-ed** -ɪd
pons asinorum ˌpɒnzˌæs.ɪ'nɔː.rəm, -rʊm ⓤⓢ ˌpɑːnzˌæs.ɪ'nɔːr.əm
Ponsonby 'pʌnt.sən.bi, 'pɒnt-, -səm- ⓤⓢ 'pɑːnt.sən-, 'pʌnt-
Pontardawe ˌpɒn.tə'daʊ.i, -eɪ ⓤⓢ ˌpɑːn.ţɚ'-
Pontardulais ˌpɒn.tə'dɪl.əs, -'dʌl-, -aɪs ⓤⓢ ˌpɑːn.ţɚ'-
Pontefract 'pɒn.tɪ.frækt ⓤⓢ 'pɑːn.ţɪ- **'Pontefract ˌcake**
Ponteland pɒn'tiː.lənd ⓤⓢ pɑːn-
Pontiac 'pɒn.ti.æk ⓤⓢ 'pɑːn.ţi- **-s** -s
pontifex (P) 'pɒn.tɪ.feks ⓤⓢ 'pɑːn.ţɪ- **pontifices** pɒn'tɪf.ɪ.siːz ⓤⓢ pɑːn-
pontiff 'pɒn.tɪf ⓤⓢ 'pɑːn.ţɪf **-s** -s
pontific pɒn'tɪf.ɪk ⓤⓢ pɑːn- **-al/s** -əl/z **-ally** -əl.i, -li
pontificate (*n*) *pope:* pɒn'tɪf.ɪ.kət, '-ə-, -kɪt, -keɪt ⓤⓢ pɑːn'tɪf.ɪ.kət, -keɪt **-s** -s
pontifi|cate (*v.*) *give opinions:* pɒn'tɪf.ɪ|.keɪt, '-ə- ⓤⓢ pɑːn- **-cates** -keɪts **-cating** -keɪ.tɪŋ, -keɪ.ţɪŋ **-cated** -keɪ.tɪd ⓤⓢ -keɪ.ţɪd
pontification ˌpɒn.tɪ.fɪ'keɪ.ʃən, -tə- ⓤⓢ ˌpɑːn.tɪ-, -ţə- **-s** -z
Pontine 'pɒn.taɪn ⓤⓢ 'pɑːn.tiːn, -taɪn
Ponting 'pɒn.tɪŋ ⓤⓢ 'pɑːn.ţɪŋ
Pontins® 'pɒn.tɪnz ⓤⓢ 'pɑːn-
Pontius 'pɒn.ti.əs, -tʃi.əs, '-ʃəs ⓤⓢ 'pɑːn.tʃəs, '-ţi.əs **ˌPontius 'Pilate**
Pont l'Évêque ˌpɔ̃ːn.leɪ'vek ⓤⓢ ˌpɑ̃ːnt.lə'vek
Pontllanfraith ˌpɒnt.hlæn'vraɪθ, -θlæn'- ⓤⓢ ˌpɑːnt.θlæn'-
pontoon pɒn'tuːn ⓤⓢ pɑːn- **-s** -z
Pont|us 'pɒn.t|əs ⓤⓢ 'pɑːn.ţ|əs **-ic** -ɪk
Pontyclun ˌpɒn.tɪ'klɪn, -tə'- ⓤⓢ ˌpɑːn.ţɪ'-
Pontypool ˌpɒn.tɪ'puːl, -tə'- ⓤⓢ ˌpɑːn.ţɪ'-
Pontypridd ˌpɒn.tɪ'priːð, -tə'- ⓤⓢ ˌpɑːn.ţɪ'-
pon|y 'pəʊ.n|i ⓤⓢ 'poʊ- **-ies** -iz **'pony ˌtrekking**
ponytail 'pəʊ.ni.teɪl ⓤⓢ 'poʊ- **-s** -z
pooch puːtʃ **-es** -ɪz
pood puːd **-s** -z
poodle 'puː.dl̩ **-s** -z
poof pʊf, puːf ⓤⓢ puːf, pʊf **-s** -s
poofter 'pʊf.təʳ, 'puːf- ⓤⓢ 'puːf.tɚ **-s** -z
poofy 'pʊf.i, 'puː.fi ⓤⓢ 'puː.fi
poo(h) (P) *exclamation:* pɸu, phuː, puː *other senses:* puː
Note:/puː/ is the pronunciation for A. A. Milne's character "Winnie the Pooh".
Pooh-Bah ˌpuː'bɑː, '-- ⓤⓢ '--
pooh-pooh ˌpuː'puː **-s** -z **-ing** -ɪŋ **-ed** -d
Pook puːk
pool puːl **-s** -z **-ing** -ɪŋ **-ed** -d
Poole puːl
Pooley 'puː.li
poolroom 'puːl.rʊm, -ruːm ⓤⓢ -ruːm, -rʊm **-s** -z
poon puːn **-s** -z
Poona 'puː.nə, -nɑː ⓤⓢ -nə
poontang 'puːn.tæŋ
poop puːp **-s** -s **-ing** -ɪŋ **-ed** -t **'poop ˌdeck**
pooper 'puː.pəʳ ⓤⓢ -pɚ **-s** -z
pooper-scooper 'puː.pəˌskuː.pəʳ ⓤⓢ -pɚˌskuː.pɚ **-s** -z
poop-scoop 'puːp.skuːp **-s** -s
poor (P) pɔːʳ, pʊəʳ ⓤⓢ pʊr **-er** -əʳ ⓤⓢ -ɚ **-est** -ɪst, -əst **-ly** -li **-ness** -nəs, -nɪs **'poor ˌbox**; **'poor ˌlaw**; **ˌpoor re'lation**; **ˌpoor 'white**
Poore pɔːʳ, pʊəʳ ⓤⓢ pʊr
poorhou|se 'pɔː.haʊ|s, 'pʊə- ⓤⓢ 'pʊr- **-ses** -zɪz
poorly 'pɔː.li, 'pʊə- ⓤⓢ 'pʊr-
Pooter 'puː.təʳ ⓤⓢ -ţɚ **-ish** -ɪʃ
poove puːv **-s** -z
pop pɒp ⓤⓢ pɑːp **-s** -s **-ping** -ɪŋ **-ped** -t **-per/s** -əʳ/z ⓤⓢ -ɚ/z **'pop ˌart**; **'pop ˌmusic** ⓤⓢ **ˌpop 'music**; **'pop ˌstar**
popadom, -dum 'pɒp.ə.dəm ⓤⓢ 'pɑː.pə- **-s** -z
popcorn 'pɒp.kɔːn ⓤⓢ 'pɑːp.kɔːrn
pop-down 'pɒp.daʊn ⓤⓢ 'pɑːp-
pope (P) pəʊp ⓤⓢ poʊp **-s** -s **-dom/s** -dəm/z
popery 'pəʊ.pər.i ⓤⓢ 'poʊ-
Popeye 'pɒp.aɪ ⓤⓢ 'pɑː.paɪ
pop-eyed ˌpɒp'aɪd ⓤⓢ 'pɑːpˌaɪd *stress shift, British only:* ˌpop-eyed 'monster
pop-gun 'pɒp.gʌn ⓤⓢ 'pɑːp- **-s** -z
Popham 'pɒp.əm ⓤⓢ 'pɑː.pəm
popinjay 'pɒp.ɪn.dʒeɪ ⓤⓢ 'pɑː.pɪn- **-s** -z
popish 'pəʊ.pɪʃ ⓤⓢ 'poʊ- **-ly** -li **-ness** -nəs, -nɪs
poplar (P) 'pɒp.ləʳ ⓤⓢ 'pɑː.plɚ **-s** -z
poplin 'pɒp.lɪn ⓤⓢ 'pɑː.plɪn **-s** -z
Popocatépetl ˌpɒp.əʊˌkæt.ɪ'pet.l̩, ˌpəʊ.pəʊ-, -ə'-, ˌpəʊ.pəʊ'kæt.ɪ.pet-, ˌpɒp.əʊ'-, '-ə- ⓤⓢ ˌpoʊ.pə'kæt.ə.peţ.l̩; ˌpɑː.pɑː.kɑː'teɪ-
popover 'pɒpˌəʊ.vəʳ ⓤⓢ 'pɑːˌpoʊ.vɚ **-s** -z
poppa 'pɒp.ə ⓤⓢ 'pɑː.pə **-s** -z
poppadom, -dum 'pɒp.ə.dəm ⓤⓢ 'pɑː.pə- **-s** -z
popper (P) 'pɒp.əʳ ⓤⓢ 'pɑː.pɚ **-s** -z
Popperian pɒp'ɪə.ri.ən ⓤⓢ pɑː'pɪr.i-
poppet 'pɒp.ɪt ⓤⓢ 'pɑː.pɪt **-s** -s
popping creas|e 'pɒp.ɪŋˌkriːs ⓤⓢ 'pɑː.pɪŋˌ- **-es** -ɪz

poppl|e 'pɒp.l̩ (US) 'pɑː.pl̩ **-es** -z **-ing** -ɪŋ, 'pɒp.lɪŋ (US) 'pɑː.plɪŋ **-ed** -d

Popplewell 'pɒp.l̩.wel (US) 'pɑː.pl̩-

popp|y (P) 'pɒp|.i (US) 'pɑː.p|i **-ies** -iz **'Poppy ˌDay**

poppycock 'pɒp.ɪ.kɒk (US) 'pɑː.pɪ.kɑːk

popsicle (P®) 'pɒp.sɪ.kl̩ (US) 'pɑːp- **-s** -z

pop|sy, pop|sie 'pɒp|.si (US) 'pɑːp- **-sies** -siz

populace 'pɒp.jə.ləs, -jʊ-, -lɪs (US) 'pɑː.pjə.lɪs, -pjʊ-, -ləs

popular 'pɒp.jə.ləʳ, -jʊ- (US) 'pɑː.pjə.lɚ, -pjʊ- **-ly** -li

popularity ˌpɒp.jə'lær.ə.ti, -jʊ'-, -ɪ.ti (US) ˌpɑː.pjə'ler.ə.t̬i, -pjʊ'-, -'lær-

popularization, -isa- ˌpɒp.jə.lᵊr.aɪ'zeɪ.ʃᵊn, -jə-, -ɪ'- (US) ˌpɑː.pjə.lɚ.ɪ'-, -pjʊ-

populariz|e, -is|e 'pɒp.jə.lᵊr.aɪz, -jʊ- (US) 'pɑː.pjə.lə.raɪz, -pjʊ- **-es** -ɪz **-ing** -ɪŋ **-ed** -d

popu|late 'pɒp.jə|.leɪt, -jʊ- (US) 'pɑː.pjə-, -pjʊ- **-lates** -leɪts **-lating** -leɪ.tɪŋ (US) -leɪ.t̬ɪŋ **-lated** -leɪ.tɪd (US) -leɪ.t̬ɪd

population ˌpɒp.jə'leɪ.ʃᵊn, -jʊ'- (US) ˌpɑː.pjə'-, -pjʊ'- **-s** -z **popu'lation exˌplosion**

popul|ism 'pɒp.jə.l|ɪ.zᵊm, -jʊ- (US) 'pɑː.pjə-, -pjʊ- **-ist/s** -ɪst/s

populous 'pɒp.jə.ləs, -jʊ- (US) 'pɑː.pjə-, -pjʊ- **-ly** -li **-ness** -nəs, -nɪs

pop-up 'pɒp.ʌp (US) 'pɑːp-

porcelain 'pɔː.sᵊl.ɪn (US) 'pɔːr-, '-slɪn **-s** -z

porch pɔːtʃ (US) pɔːrtʃ **-es** -ɪz

Porchester 'pɔː.tʃɪ.stəʳ, -tʃə- (US) 'pɔːr.tʃɪ.stɚ, -tʃə-

porcine 'pɔː.saɪn (US) 'pɔːr-, -sɪn

porcin|o pɔː'tʃiː.n|əʊ (US) pɔːr'tʃiː.n|oʊ **-i** -iː

porcupine 'pɔː.kjə.paɪn, -kjʊ- (US) 'pɔːr- **-s** -z

por|e pɔːʳ (US) pɔːr **-es** -z **-ing** -ɪŋ **-ed** -d

porg|y *fish:* 'pɔː.dʒ|i (US) 'pɔːr.g|i **-ies** -iz

Porgy *name:* 'pɔː.gi (US) 'pɔːr-

pork pɔːk (US) pɔːrk **-er/s** -əʳ/z (US) -ɚ/z **-y** -i ˌ**pork 'pie**

porkpie hat ˌpɔːk.paɪ'hæt (US) ˌpɔːrk- **-s** -s

Porlock 'pɔː.lɒk (US) 'pɔːr.lɑːk

porn pɔːn (US) pɔːrn

porno 'pɔː.nəʊ (US) 'pɔːr.noʊ

pornographic ˌpɔː.nə'græf.ɪk (US) ˌpɔːr-

pornograph|y pɔː'nɒg.rə.f|i (US) pɔːr'nɑː.grə- **-er/s** -əʳ/z (US) -ɚ/z

porosity pɔː'rɒs.ə.ti, -ɪ.ti (US) pɔː'rɑː.sə.t̬i, pə-

porous 'pɔː.rəs (US) 'pɔːr.əs **-ly** -li **-ness** -nəs, -nɪs

porphyria pɔː'fɪr.i.ə, -'faɪ.ri- (US) pɔːr'fɪr.i-

porphyrin 'pɔː.fᵊr.ɪn, -fɪ.rɪn (US) 'pɔːr.fɚ.ɪn

porphyry (P) 'pɔː.fᵊr.i, -fɪ.ri (US) 'pɔːr.fɚ.i

porpois|e 'pɔː.pəs (US) 'pɔːr- **-es** -ɪz

porridge 'pɒr.ɪdʒ (US) 'pɔːr-

porringer 'pɒr.ɪn.dʒəʳ (US) 'pɔːr.ɪn.dʒɚ **-s** -z

Porsch|e® pɔːʃ, 'pɔː.ʃ|ə (US) pɔːrʃ, 'pɔːr.ʃ|ə **-es** -iz, -əz

Porsena 'pɔː.sɪ.nə, -sᵊn.ə (US) 'pɔːr-

Porson 'pɔː.sᵊn (US) 'pɔːr-

port pɔːt (US) pɔːrt **-s** -s **-ing** -ɪŋ (US) 'pɔːr.t̬ɪŋ **-ed** -ɪd (US) 'pɔːr.t̬ɪd ˌ**Port 'Moresby** ; ˌ**port of 'call** ; ˌ**port of 'entry** ; ˌ**Port 'Stanley** ; ˌ**Port 'Talbot**

portability ˌpɔː.tə'bɪl.ə.ti, -ɪ.ti (US) ˌpɔːr.t̬ə'bɪl.ə.t̬i

portable 'pɔː.tə.bl̩ (US) 'pɔːr.t̬ə- **-ness** -nəs, -nɪs

Portadown ˌpɔː.tə'daʊn (US) ˌpɔːr.t̬ə'-

portage 'pɔː.tɪdʒ (US) 'pɔːr.t̬ɪdʒ

Portakabin® 'pɔː.təˌkæb.ɪn (US) 'pɔːr.t̬əˌ- **-s** -z

portal (P) 'pɔː.tᵊl (US) 'pɔːr.t̬ᵊl **-s** -z

portament|o ˌpɔː.tə'men.t|əʊ (US) ˌpɔːr.t̬ə'men.t|oʊ **-i** -iː

Port-au-Prince ˌpɔː.təʊ'prɪn*t*s (US) ˌpɔːr.toʊ'-

Portchester 'pɔː.tʃɪ.stəʳ, -tʃə- (US) 'pɔːr.tʃə.stɚ, -tʃɪ-

portcullis ˌpɔːt'kʌl.ɪs (US) ˌpɔːrt- **-es** -ɪz

Porte pɔːt (US) pɔːrt

portend pɔː'tend (US) pɔːr- **-s** -z **-ing** -ɪŋ **-ed** -ɪd

portent 'pɔː.tent, -tᵊnt (US) 'pɔːr.tent **-s** -s

portentous pɔː'ten.təs (US) pɔːr'ten.t̬əs **-ly** -li **-ness** -nəs, -nɪs

Porteous 'pɔː.ti.əs (US) 'pɔːr.t̬i-

porter (P) 'pɔː.təʳ (US) 'pɔːr.t̬ɚ **-s** -z **-age** -ɪdʒ

porterhou|se 'pɔː.tə.haʊ|s (US) 'pɔːr.t̬ɚ- **-ses** -zɪz

Porteus 'pɔː.ti.əs (US) 'pɔːr.t̬i-

portfolio ˌpɔːt'fəʊ.li.əʊ (US) ˌpɔːrt'foʊ.li.oʊ **-s** -z

Porthcawl ˌpɔːθ'kɔːl, -'kaʊl (US) ˌpɔːrθ'kɑːl, -'kɔːl, -'kaʊl

porthole 'pɔːt.həʊl (US) 'pɔːrt.hoʊl **-s** -z

Portia 'pɔː.ʃə, -ʃi.ə (US) 'pɔːr.ʃə

portico 'pɔː.tɪ.kəʊ (US) 'pɔːr.t̬ɪ.koʊ **-(e)s** -z

portière ˌpɔː.ti'eəʳ (US) ˌpɔːr'tjer, -ti'er, ˌ-'tɪr **-s** -z

Portillo pɔː'tɪl.əʊ (US) pɔːr'tɪl.oʊ

portion 'pɔː.ʃᵊn (US) 'pɔːr- **-s** -z **-ing** -ɪŋ **-ed** -d

Portishead 'pɔː.tɪs.hed (US) 'pɔːr.t̬ɪs-

Portland 'pɔːt.lənd (US) 'pɔːrt- ˌ**Portland ce'ment** ; ˌ**Portland 'stone**

portl|y 'pɔːt.l|i (US) 'pɔːrt- **-ier** -i.əʳ (US) -i.ɚ **-iest** -i.ɪst, -i.əst **-iness** -ɪ.nəs, -ɪ.nɪs

Portmadoc ˌpɔːt'mæd.ək (US) ˌpɔːrt-

Portman 'pɔːt.mən (US) 'pɔːrt-

portmanteau pɔːt'mæn.təʊ (US) pɔːrt'mæn.toʊ, ˌ--'- **-s** -z **-x** -z

Portmeirion ˌpɔːt'mer.i.ən (US) ˌpɔːrt-

Pôrto Alegre ˌpɔː.təʊ.ə'leg.ri (US) ˌpɔːr.tu.ə'leg.rə

Portobello ˌpɔː.tə'bel.əʊ (US) ˌpɔːr.t̬ə'bel.oʊ, -t̬oʊ'- *stress shift, see compound:* ˌ**Portobello 'Road**

Porto-Novo ˌpɔː.təʊ'nəʊ.vəʊ (US) ˌpɔːr.toʊ'noʊ.voʊ

Porto Rico ˌpɔː.təʊ'riː.kəʊ (US) ˌpɔːr.t̬oʊ'riː.koʊ, -t̬ə'-

portrai|t 'pɔː.trɪ|t, -trə|t, -treɪ|t (US) 'pɔːr.trɪ|t, -treɪ|t **-ts** -ts **-tist/s** -tɪst/s (US) -t̬ɪst/s

portraiture 'pɔː.trɪ.tʃə, -trə-, -tjʊəʳ (US) 'pɔːr.trɪ.tʃɚ

portray pɔː'treɪ, pə- (US) pɔːr- **-s** -z **-ing** -ɪŋ **-ed** -d **-er/s** -əʳ/z (US) -ɚ/z

portrayal pɔː'treɪ.əl, pə- (US) pɔːr- **-s** -z

Portrush ˌpɔːt'rʌʃ (US) ˌpɔːrt-

Port Said ˌpɔːt'saɪd, -sɑː'iːd (US) ˌpɔːrt.sɑː'iːd, -ɪd

Port Salut ˌpɔː.sə'luː, -sæl'uː (US) ˌpɔːr.sæl'uː

Portsea 'pɔːt.si, -siː (US) 'pɔːrt-

Portslade ˌpɔːt'sleɪd (US) ˌpɔːrt-

Portsmouth 'pɔːt.sməθ (US) 'pɔːrt-

Portstewart ˌpɔːt'stjuː.ət (US) ˌpɔːrt'stuː.ɚt, -'stjuː-

Portugal 'pɔː.tʃə.gᵊl, -tʃʊ-, -tjə-, -tjʊ- (US) 'pɔːr.tʃə-

Portuguese ˌpɔː.tʃə'giːz, -tʃʊ'-, -tjə'-, -tjʊ'- (US) ˌpɔːr.tʃə'-, -'giːs, '--- *stress shift, British only, see compound:* ˌ**Portuguese ˌman-of-'war**

pos|e pəʊz (US) poʊz **-es** -ɪz **-ing** -ɪŋ **-ed** -d

Poseidon pə'saɪ.dᵊn, pɒs'aɪ- (US) poʊ'saɪ-, pə-

poser 'pəʊ.zəʳ (US) 'poʊ.zɚ **-s** -z

poseur pəʊ'zɜːʳ (US) poʊ'zɜːr **-s** -z

posh pɒʃ (US) pɑːʃ

pos|it 'pɒz|.ɪt (US) 'pɑː.z|ɪt **-its** -ɪts **-iting** -ɪ.tɪŋ (US) -ɪ.t̬ɪŋ **-ited** -ɪ.tɪd (US) -ɪ.t̬ɪd

position pə'zɪʃ.ᵊn **-s** -z **-ing** -ɪŋ **-ed** -d

positional pə'zɪʃ.ᵊn.ᵊl

positive 'pɒz.ə.tɪv, '-ɪ- (US) 'pɑː.zə.t̬ɪv **-s** -z **-ly** -li **-ness** -nəs, -nɪs ˌ**positive discrimi'nation**

positiv|ism 'pɒz.ɪ.tɪ.v|ɪ.zᵊm, '-ə- (US) 'pɑː.zɪ.t̬ɪ- **-ist/s** -ɪst/s

positron ˈpɒz.ɪ.trɒn, -trən (US) ˈpɑː.zɪ.trɑːn **-s** -z
posse ˈpɒs.i (US) ˈpɑː.si **-s** -z
possess pəˈzes **-es** -ɪz **-ing** -ɪŋ **-ed** -t **-or/s** -əʳ/z (US) -ɚ/z
possession pəˈzeʃ.ən **-s** -z
possessive pəˈzes.ɪv **-s** -z **-ly** -li **-ness** -nəs, -nɪs **pos,sessive ˈadjective** ; **pos,sessive ˈpronoun**
possessory pəˈzes.ər.i
posset ˈpɒs.ɪt (US) ˈpɑː.sɪt **-s** -s
possibilit|y ˌpɒs.əˈbɪl.ə.t|i, -ɪˈ-, -ɪ.t|i (US) ˌpɑː.səˈbɪl.ə.t̬|i **-ies** -iz
possib|le ˈpɒs.ə.b|l̩, ˈ-ɪ- (US) ˈpɑː.sə- **-ly** -li
possum ˈpɒs.əm (US) ˈpɑː.səm **-s** -z
post pəʊst (US) poʊst **-s** -s **-ing** -ɪŋ **-ed** -ɪd **ˈpost ˌoffice**
postag|e ˈpəʊ.stɪdʒ (US) ˈpoʊ- **-es** -ɪz **ˈpostage ˌstamp** ; **ˌpostage and ˈpacking**
postal ˈpəʊ.stəl (US) ˈpoʊ- **ˈpostal ˌorder**
postbag ˈpəʊst.bæg (US) ˈpoʊst- **-s** -z
postbellum ˌpəʊstˈbel.əm (US) ˌpoʊst- *stress shift:* ˌpostbellum ˈbuilding
postbox ˈpəʊst.bɒks (US) ˈpoʊst.bɑːks **-es** -ɪz
postcard ˈpəʊst.kɑːd (US) ˈpoʊst.kɑːrd **-s** -z
post-chaise ˈpəʊst.ʃeɪz, ˌ-ˈ- (US) ˈpoʊst.ʃeɪz, ˌ-ˈ- **-s** -ɪz
postcode ˈpəʊst.kəʊd (US) ˈpoʊst.koʊd **-s** -z
postda|te ˌpəʊstˈdeɪ|t, ˈ-- (US) ˌpoʊstˈdeɪ|t, ˈ-- **-tes** -ts **-ting** -tɪŋ (US) -t̬ɪŋ **-ted** -tɪd (US) -t̬ɪd
post-diluvian ˌpəʊst.dɪˈluː.vi.ən, -daɪˈ-, -ˈljuː- (US) ˌpoʊst.dɪˈluː-
postdoctoral ˌpəʊstˈdɒk.tər.əl (US) ˌpoʊstˈdɑːk- *stress shift:* ˌpostdoctoral ˈcontract
poster ˈpəʊ.stəʳ (US) ˈpoʊ.stɚ **-s** -z **ˈposter ˌpaint**
poste restante ˌpəʊstˈres.tɑːnt, -tɑ̃ːnt, ˌ--ˈ- (US) ˌpoʊst.resˈtɑːnt
posterior pɒsˈtɪə.ri.əʳ (US) pɑːˈstɪr.i.ɚ, poʊ-, pə- **-ly** -li
posteriority pɒsˌtɪə.riˈɒr.ə.ti, ˌpɒs.tɪə-, -ɪ.ti (US) pɑːˌstɪr.iˈɔːr.ə.t̬i, poʊ-
posterit|y pɒsˈter.ə.t|i, -ɪ.t|i (US) pɑːˈster.ə- **-ies** -iz
postern ˈpɒs.tən, ˈpəʊ.stən, -stɜːn (US) ˈpoʊ.stɚn, ˈpɑː- **-s** -z
post-free ˌpəʊstˈfriː (US) ˌpoʊst- *stress shift:* ˌpost-free ˈsystem
Postgate ˈpəʊst.geɪt, -gɪt (US) ˈpoʊst.geɪt
postglacial ˌpəʊstˈgleɪ.si.əl, -ʃəl, -ˈglæs.i.əl (US) ˌpoʊstˈgleɪ.ʃəl *stress shift:* ˌpostglacial ˈperiod

postgraduate ˌpəʊstˈgrædʒ.u.ət, -ˈgræd.ju-, -ɪt (US) ˌpoʊstˈgrædʒ.u.wɪt, ˈ-ə-; ˈ-u.eɪt **-s** -s *stress shift:* ˌpostgraduate ˈstudent
posthaste ˌpəʊstˈheɪst (US) ˌpoʊst-
post hoc ˌpəʊstˈhɒk (US) ˌpoʊstˈhɑːk, -ˈhoʊk
posthumous ˈpɒs.tjə.məs, -tjʊ- (US) ˈpɑːs.tʃə.məs, -tʃʊ- **-ly** -li
Posthumus ˈpɒs.tjʊ.məs, ˈpɒst.hjʊ- (US) ˈpɑːs.tjuː-, -tʃuː-
postich|e pɒsˈtiːʃ (US) pɑːˈstiːʃ, pɔː- **-es** -ɪz
postie ˈpəʊ.sti (US) ˈpoʊ- **-s** -z
postil ˈpɒs.tɪl (US) ˈpɑː.stɪl **-s** -z
postil(l)ion pəˈstɪl.i.ən, pɒsˈtɪl-, ˈ-jən (US) poʊˈstɪl.jən, pɑː- **-s** -z
Post-impression|ism ˌpəʊst.ɪmˈpreʃ.ən|.ɪ.zəm (US) ˌpoʊst- **-ist/s** -ɪst/s
posting ˈpəʊ.stɪŋ (US) ˈpoʊ- **-s** -z
Post-it® ˈpəʊst.ɪt (US) ˈpoʊst-
Postlethwaite ˈpɒs.l̩.θweɪt (US) ˈpɑː.sl̩-
post|man ˈpəʊst|.mən (US) ˈpoʊst- **-men** -mən **-woman** -ˌwʊm.ən **-women** -ˌwɪm.ɪn **ˌpostman's ˈknock**
postmark ˈpəʊst.mɑːk (US) ˈpoʊst.mɑːrk **-s** -s **-ing** -ɪŋ **-ed** -t
postmaster ˈpəʊstˌmɑː.stəʳ (US) ˈpoʊstˌmæs.tɚ **-s** -z **ˌPostmaster ˈGeneral**
post-meridian ˌpəʊst.məˈrɪd.i.ən (US) ˌpoʊst-
postmistress ˈpəʊst.mɪs.trəs, -trɪs (US) ˈpoʊst- **-es** -ɪz
postmodern ˌpəʊstˈmɒd.ən (US) ˌpoʊstˈmɑː.dɚn **-ism** -ɪ.zəm **-ist/s** -ɪst/s *stress shift:* ˌpostmodern ˈartists
postmortem ˌpəʊstˈmɔː.tem, -təm (US) ˌpoʊstˈmɔːr.t̬əm **-s** -z
postnatal ˌpəʊstˈneɪ.təl (US) ˌpoʊstˈneɪ.t̬əl *stress shift, see compound:* **ˌpostnatal deˈpression**
postoperative ˌpəʊstˈɒp.ər.ə.tɪv (US) ˌpoʊstˈɑː.pɚ.ə.t̬ɪv
postpaid ˌpəʊstˈpeɪd (US) ˌpoʊst- *stress shift:* ˌpostpaid ˈenvelope
post partum ˌpəʊstˈpɑː.təm (US) ˌpoʊstˈpɑːr.t̬əm
postpon|e pəʊstˈpəʊn, pəs- (US) poʊstˈpoʊn **-es** -z **-ing** -ɪŋ **-ed** -d **-ement/s** -mənt/s
postposition ˌpəʊst.pəˈzɪʃ.ən, ˈpəʊst.pəˌzɪʃ- (US) ˌpoʊst.pəˈzɪʃ- **-s** -z
postpositional ˌpəʊst.pəˈzɪʃ.ən.əl (US) ˌpoʊst- *stress shift:* ˌpostpositional ˈparticle
postpositive ˌpəʊstˈpɒz.ə.tɪv, ˈ-ɪ- (US) ˌpoʊstˈpɑː.zə.t̬ɪv *stress shift:* ˌpostpositive ˈadjective

postscript ˈpəʊst.skrɪpt (US) ˈpoʊst- **-s** -s
post-structuralism ˌpəʊstˈstrʌk.tʃər.əl.ɪ.zəm, -tʃʊ.rəl- (US) ˌpoʊstˈstrʌk.tʃɚ-
post-traumatic stress disorder ˌpəʊst.trɔːˌmæt.ɪkˈstres.dɪˌsɔː.dəʳ, -ˌzɔː- (US) ˌpoʊst.trɑːˌmæt̬.ɪkˈstres.dɪˌsɔːr.dɚ, -trɔːˌ-
postulant ˈpɒs.tjə.lənt, -tjʊ- (US) ˈpɑːs.tʃə-, ˈpɑː.stjə- **-s** -s
postulate (*n.*) ˈpɒs.tjə.lət, -tjʊ-, -lɪt, -leɪt (US) ˈpɑːs.tʃə.lɪt, -tʃʊ-, ˈpɑː.stjə-, -stjʊ-, -leɪt **-s** -s
postu|late (*v.*) ˈpɒs.tjə|.leɪt, -tjʊ- (US) ˈpɑːs.tʃə-, ˈpɑː.stjə- **-lates** -leɪts **-lating** -leɪ.tɪŋ (US) -leɪ.t̬ɪŋ **-lated** -leɪ.tɪd (US) -leɪ.t̬ɪd
postulation ˌpɒs.tjəˈleɪ.ʃən, -tjʊˈ- (US) ˌpɑːs.tʃəˈ-, ˌpɑː.stjəˈ- **-s** -z
post|ure ˈpɒs.tʃ|əʳ (US) ˈpɑːs.tʃ|ɚ **-ures** -əz (US) -ɚz **-uring** -ər.ɪŋ **-ured** -əd (US) -ɚd
postviral ˌpəʊstˈvaɪə.rəl (US) ˌpoʊstˈvaɪ- *stress shift, see compound:* **ˌpostviral faˈtigue ˌsyndrome**
post-war ˌpəʊstˈwɔːʳ (US) ˌpoʊstˈwɔːr *stress shift:* ˌpost-war ˈpolitics
pos|y ˈpəʊ.z|i (US) ˈpoʊ- **-ies** -iz
pot pɒt (US) pɑːt **-s** -s **-ting** -ɪŋ (US) ˈpɑː.t̬ɪŋ **-ted** -ɪd (US) ˈpɑː.t̬ɪd **-er/s** -əʳ/z (US) ˈpɑː.t̬ɚ/z **ˌpot ˈluck** ; **ˈpot ˌplant** ; **ˌpotted ˈplant** ; **ˈpotting ˌshed**
potable ˈpəʊ.tə.bl̩ (US) ˈpoʊ.t̬ə- **-s** -z
potag|e pɒtˈɑːʒ, pəʊˈtɑːʒ, ˈ-- (US) poʊˈtɑːʒ **-es** -ɪz
potash ˈpɒt.æʃ (US) ˈpɑːt-
potassium pəˈtæs.i.əm (US) pə-, poʊ-
potation pəʊˈteɪ.ʃən (US) poʊ- **-s** -z
potato pəˈteɪ.təʊ (US) -t̬oʊ **-es** -z **poˈtato ˌchip** ; **poˌtato ˈcrisp**
pot-au-feu ˌpɒt.əʊˈfɜː (US) ˌpɑːt.oʊˈ-
pot-bell|y pɒtˈbel|.i, ˈ-ˌ-- (US) ˈpɑːtˌbel- **-ied** -id
potboiler ˈpɒtˌbɔɪ.ləʳ (US) ˈpɑːtˌbɔɪ.lɚ **-s** -z
potbound (*adj.*) ˈpɒt.baʊnd (US) ˈpɑːt-
poteen pɒtˈiːn, pəʊˈtiːn, -ˈtʃiːn (US) poʊˈtiːn
Potemkin pəˈtemp.kɪn, pɒtˈemp-, pəˈtjɒm.kɪn (US) poʊˈtemp-, pə-
potency ˈpəʊ.tənt.si (US) ˈpoʊ-
potent ˈpəʊ.tənt (US) ˈpoʊ- **-ly** -li
potentate ˈpəʊ.tən.teɪt (US) ˈpoʊ- **-s** -s
potential pəʊˈten.tʃəl (US) poʊ-, pə- **-s** -z **-ly** -i
potentialit|y pəʊˌten.tʃiˈæl.ə.t|i, -ɪ.t|i (US) poʊˌten.tʃiˈæl.ə.t̬|i, pə- **-ies** -iz
potentilla ˌpəʊ.tənˈtɪl.ə (US) ˌpoʊ- **-s** -z

potentiometer pəʊˌten.tʃiˈɒm.ɪ.təʳ, ˈ-ə- (US) poʊˌten.tʃiˈɑː.mə.t̬ɚ, pə- **-s** -z
potheen pɒtˈiːn, pəʊˈtiːn, -tʃiːn, -θiːn, ˈpɒθ.iːn (US) poʊˈθiːn, -ˈtiːn
poth|er ˈpɒð.əʳ (US) ˈpɑː.ð|ɚ **-ers** -əz (US) -ɚz **-ering** -ᵊr.ɪŋ **-ered** -əd (US) -ɚd
pot-herb ˈpɒt.hɜːb (US) ˈpɑːt.hɜːrb **-s** -z
pothole ˈpɒt.həʊl (US) ˈpɑːt.hoʊl **-s** -z
potholl|ing ˈpɒtˌhəʊ.l|ɪŋ (US) ˈpɑːtˌhoʊ- **-er/s** -əʳ/z (US) -ɚ/z
pothook ˈpɒt.hʊk (US) ˈpɑːt- **-s** -s
pothou|se ˈpɒt.haʊ|s (US) ˈpɑːt- **-ses** -zɪz
pot-hunter ˈpɒtˌhʌn.təʳ (US) ˈpɑːtˌhʌn.t̬ɚ **-s** -z
potion ˈpəʊ.ʃᵊn (US) ˈpoʊ- **-s** -z
Potiphar ˈpɒt.ɪ.fɑːʳ, ˈ-ə-, -fəʳ (US) ˈpɑː.t̬ə.fɚ
Potomac pəˈtəʊ.mæk, -mək (US) -ˈtoʊ.mək
potometer pəʊˈtɒm.ɪ.təʳ, ˈ-ə- (US) pəˈtɑː.mə.tɚ
Potosí *in Bolivia:* ˌpɒt.əʊˈsiː (US) ˌpɔː.tɔːˈ-
Potosi *in US:* pəˈtəʊ.si (US) -ˈtoʊ-
pot-pourri ˌpəʊˈpʊə.ri, ˌpɒt-, -ˈpʊr.i, -iː; ˌpəʊ.pəˈriː, -pʊˈ- (US) ˌpoʊ.pʊˈriː, -pəˈ-; ˈpoʊ.pʊr.i, -pɚ- **-s** -z
pot-roast ˈpɒt.rəʊst (US) ˈpɑːt.roʊst **-s** -s **-ing** -ɪŋ **-ed** -ɪd
Potsdam ˈpɒts.dæm (US) ˈpɑːts-
potsherd ˈpɒt.ʃɜːd (US) ˈpɑːt.ʃɜːrd **-s** -z
potshot ˈpɒt.ʃɒt, ˌ-ˈ- (US) ˈpɑːt.ʃɑːt **-s** -s
Pott pɒt (US) pɑːt
pottage ˈpɒt.ɪdʒ (US) ˈpɑː.t̬ɪdʒ
potted ˈpɒt.ɪd (US) ˈpɑː.t̬ɪd
pott|er (P) ˈpɒt|.əʳ (US) ˈpɑː.t̬|ɚ **-ers** -əz (US) -ɚz **-ering** -ᵊr.ɪŋ **-ered** -əd (US) -ɚd **-erer/s** -ᵊr.əʳ/z (US) -ɚ.ɚ/z
potter|y (P) ˈpɒt.ᵊr|.i (US) ˈpɑː.t̬ɚ- **-ies** -iz
pottle ˈpɒt.l̩ (US) ˈpɑː.t̬l̩ **-s** -z
Potts pɒts (US) pɑːts
pott|y ˈpɒt|.i (US) ˈpɑː.t̬|i **-ier** -i.əʳ (US) -i.ɚ **-iest** -i.ɪst, -i.əst **-iness** -ɪ.nəs, -ɪ.nɪs
pouch paʊtʃ **-es** -ɪz **-ing** -ɪŋ **-ed** -t
pouf *(derog. for homosexual)* pʊf, puːf (US) puːf **-s** -s
pouffe, pouf, pouff *(seat, headdress)* puːf **-s** -s
Poughill ˈpɒf.ɪl, ˈpʌf-, ˈpaʊ- (US) ˈpɑː.fɪl, ˈpʌf.ɪl, ˈpaʊ-
Poughkeepsie pəˈkɪp.si (US) pə-, poʊ-
Poulenc ˈpuː.læ̃ŋk (US) puːˈlæ̃ŋk
Poulson ˈpəʊl.sᵊn, ˈpuːl- (US) ˈpoʊl-, ˈpuːl-
poult *chicken:* pəʊlt (US) poʊlt **-s** -s
poult *silk material:* puːlt (US) puːlt, puː
Poulter ˈpəʊl.təʳ (US) ˈpoʊl.t̬ɚ
poulterer ˈpəʊl.tᵊr.əʳ (US) ˈpoʊl.t̬ɚ.ɚ **-s** -z
poultic|e ˈpəʊl.tɪs (US) ˈpoʊl.t̬ɪs **-es** -ɪz **-ing** -ɪŋ **-ed** -t
Poultney ˈpəʊlt.ni (US) ˈpoʊlt-
Poulton ˈpəʊl.tᵊn (US) ˈpoʊl-
Poulton-le-Fylde ˌpəʊl.tᵊn.ləˈfaɪld, -lɪˈ- (US) ˌpoʊl-
poultry ˈpəʊl.tri (US) ˈpoʊl-
poultry|man ˈpəʊl.tri|.mən, -mæn (US) ˈpoʊl- **-men** -mən, -men
pounc|e paʊnts **-es** -ɪz **-ing** -ɪŋ **-ed** -t
Pouncefoot ˈpaʊnts.fʊt
pound (P) paʊnd **-s** -z **-ing** -ɪŋ **-ed** -ɪd **-er/s** -əʳ/z (US) -ɚ/z ˌ**pound** ˈ**sterling**
poundag|e ˈpaʊn.dɪdʒ **-es** -ɪz
Pounds paʊndz
Pount(e)ney ˈpaʊnt.ni
Poupart ˈpəʊ.pɑːt, ˈpuː- (US) ˌpuːˈpɑːrt
Pouparts ˈpuː.pɑːts (US) ˌpuːˈpɑːrts
pour pɔːʳ (US) pɔːr **-s** -z **-ing** -ɪŋ **-ed** -d **-er/s** -əʳ/z (US) -ɚ/z
pourboire ˈpʊə.bwɑːʳ, ˈpɔː- (US) pʊrˈbwɑːr **-s** -z
pourparler ˌpʊəˈpɑː.leɪ, ˌpɔː- (US) ˌpʊr.pɑːrˈleɪ **-s** -z
poussin (P) ˈpuː.sæ̃ŋ (US) puːˈsæ̃n **-s** -z
pout paʊt **-s** -s **-ing** -ɪŋ (US) ˈpaʊ.t̬ɪŋ **-ed** -ɪd (US) ˈpaʊ.t̬ɪd
poverty ˈpɒv.ə.ti (US) ˈpɑː.vɚ.t̬i ˈ**poverty** ˌ**trap**
poverty-stricken ˈpɒv.ə.tiˌstrɪk.ᵊn (US) ˈpɑː.vɚ.t̬iˌ-
Povey ˈpəʊ.vi; pəˈveɪ (US) ˈpoʊ.vi; pəˈveɪ
Pow paʊ
POW ˌpiː.əʊˈdʌb.l̩.juː (US) -oʊˈ- **-'s** -z
powd|er ˈpaʊ.d|əʳ (US) -d|ɚ **-ers** -əz (US) -ɚz **-ering** -ᵊr.ɪŋ **-ered** -əd (US) -ɚd ˌ**powder** ˈ**blue** ; ˈ**powder** ˌ**keg** ; ˈ**powder** ˌ**puff** ; ˈ**powder** ˌ**room**
powder|y ˈpaʊ.dᵊr|.i **-iness** -ɪ.nəs, -ɪ.nɪs
Powell paʊəl, pəʊəl; ˈpaʊ.ɪl, ˈpəʊ-, -el (US) paʊəl, poʊəl
power (P) paʊəʳ (US) paʊɚ **-s** -z ˈ**power** ˌ**base** ; ˈ**power** ˌ**cut** ; ˌ**power of at**ˈ**torney** ; ˌ**power** ˈ**politics** ; ˈ**power** ˌ**station** ; ˌ**power** ˈ**steering**
powerboat ˈpaʊə.bəʊt (US) ˈpaʊɚ.boʊt **-s** -s
powerful ˈpaʊə.fᵊl, -fʊl (US) ˈpaʊɚ- **-ly** -i **-ness** -nəs, -nɪs
powerhou|se ˈpaʊə.haʊ|s (US) ˈpaʊɚ- **-ses** -zɪz
powerless ˈpaʊə.ləs, -lɪs (US) ˈpaʊɚ- **-ly** -li **-ness** -nəs, -nɪs
powerpack ˈpaʊə.pæk (US) ˈpaʊɚ- **-s** -s
powerpoint ˈpaʊə.pɔɪnt (US) ˈpaʊɚ- **-s** -s
Powerscourt ˈpɔːz.kɔːt, ˈpaʊəz- (US) ˈpaʊɚz.kɔːrt
Powicke ˈpəʊ.ɪk (US) ˈpoʊ-
Powis *place in Scotland, square in London:* ˈpaʊ.ɪs *surname:* ˈpəʊ.ɪs, ˈpaʊ- (US) ˈpoʊ-, ˈpaʊ-
Powles pəʊlz (US) poʊlz
Powlett ˈpɔː.lɪt (US) ˈpɑː-, ˈpɔː-
Pownall ˈpaʊ.nᵊl
pow-wow *(n. v.)* ˈpaʊ.waʊ **-s** -z **-ing** -ɪŋ **-ed** -d
Powys ˈpəʊ.ɪs, ˈpaʊ.ɪs (US) ˈpoʊ-, ˈpaʊ-
pox pɒks (US) pɑːks
poxy ˈpɒk.si (US) ˈpɑːk-
Poyner ˈpɔɪ.nəʳ (US) -nɚ
Poynings ˈpɔɪ.nɪŋz
Poynter ˈpɔɪn.təʳ (US) -t̬ɚ
Poynton ˈpɔɪn.tən
Poznań ˈpɒz.næn (US) ˈpoʊz-, -nɑːn
PR ˌpiːˈɑːʳ (US) -ˈɑːr
practicability ˌpræk.tɪ.kəˈbɪl.ə.ti, -ɪ.ti (US) -ə.t̬i
practicab|le ˈpræk.tɪ.kə.bl̩ **-ly** -li **-leness** -l̩.nəs, -nɪs
practical ˈpræk.tɪ.kᵊl **-ness** -nəs, -nɪs ˌ**practical** ˈ**joke**
practicality ˌpræk.tɪˈkæl.ə.ti, -ɪ.ti (US) -ə.t̬i
practically ˈpræk.tɪ.kᵊl.i (US) -tɪ.kli
practic|e ˈpræk.tɪs **-es** -ɪz **-ing** -ɪŋ **-ed** -t
practician prækˈtɪʃ.ᵊn **-s** -z
practis|e ˈpræk.tɪs **-es** -ɪz **-ing** -ɪŋ **-ed** -t ˌ**practise what one** ˈ**preaches**
practitioner prækˈtɪʃ.ᵊn.əʳ (US) -ɚ **-s** -z
Prado ˈprɑː.dəʊ (US) -doʊ
praecox ˈpriː.kɒks, ˈpraɪ- (US) ˈpriː.kɑːks
Praed preɪd
prae|nomen ˌpriː|ˈnəʊ.men, ˌpraɪ- (US) ˌpriː|ˈnoʊ- **-nomens** -ˈnəʊ.mənz (US) -ˈnoʊ- **-nomina** -ˈnɒm.ɪ.nə, -ˈnəʊ.mɪ- (US) -ˈnɑː-, -ˈnoʊ-
praepostor ˌpriːˈpɒs.təʳ (US) -ˈpɑː.stɚ **-s** -z
praesidi|um prɪˈsɪd.i|.əm, prə-, praɪ- **-ums** -əmz **-a** -ə
Praeterita ˌpriːˈter.ɪ.tə, prɪ-, praɪ- (US) prɪˈter.ɪ.t̬ə
praetor ˈpriː.təʳ, ˈpraɪ-, -tɔːʳ (US) ˈpriː.t̬ɚ **-s** -z **-ship/s** -ʃɪp/s
praetori|al priːˈtɔː.ri|.əl, praɪˈ- (US) -ˈtɔːr- **-an** -ən
pragmatic prægˈmæt.ɪk (US) -ˈmæt̬- **-s** -s **-al** -ᵊl **-ally** -ᵊl.i, -li
pragmat|ism ˈpræg.mə.t|ɪ.zᵊm **-ist/s** -ɪst/s
Prague prɑːg
Praia ˈpraɪ.ə (US) ˈprɑː.jə
prairie (P) ˈpreə.ri (US) ˈprer.i **-s** -z ˈ**prairie** ˌ**dog** ; ˌ**prairie** ˈ**oyster**
prais|e preɪz **-es** -ɪz **-ing** -ɪŋ **-ed** -d **-er/s** -əʳ/z
praiseworth|y ˈpreɪzˌwɜː.ð|i (US) -ˌwɜːr- **-iness** -ɪ.nəs, -ɪ.nɪs

Prakrit 'prɑː.krɪt
praline 'prɑː.liːn ⓤⓢ 'prɑː-, 'preɪ- **-s** -z
Prall prɔːl ⓤⓢ prɔːl, prɑːl
pram *baby carriage:* præm **-s** -z
pram *flat-bottomed boat:* prɑːm **-s** -z
pranc|e (P) prɑːnts ⓤⓢ prænts **-es** -ɪz **-ing** -ɪŋ **-ed** -t **-er/s** -əʳ/z ⓤⓢ -ɚ/z
prandial 'præn.di.əl
prang præŋ **-s** -z **-ing** -ɪŋ **-ed** -d
prank præŋk **-s** -s **-ing** -ɪŋ **-ed** -t
prank|ish 'præŋ.k|ɪʃ **-some** -səm
prankster 'præŋk.stəʳ ⓤⓢ -stɚ **-s** -z
praseodymium ˌpreɪ.zi.əʊ'dɪm.i.əm, ˌpraɪ.zəʊ'- ⓤⓢ ˌpreɪ.zi.oʊ'-, -si-
prat præt **-s** -s
Pratchett 'prætʃ.ɪt
prat|e preɪt **-es** -s **-ing** -ɪŋ **-ed** -ɪd **-er/s** -əʳ/z ⓤⓢ -ɚ/z
pratfall 'præt.fɔːl **-s** -z
pratincole 'præt.ɪŋ.kəʊl, 'preɪ.tɪŋ- ⓤⓢ 'præt.ɪn.koʊl, 'preɪ.tɪn-, -tən-, -ɪŋ- **-s** -z
pratique 'præt.iːk, -ɪk, præt'iːk ⓤⓢ præt'iːk; 'præt̬.ɪk **-s** -s
Pratt præt
prattl|e 'præt.l̩ ⓤⓢ 'præt̬- **-es** -z **-ing** -ɪŋ, 'præt.lɪŋ **-ed** -d **-er/s** -əʳ/z, 'præt.ləʳ/z ⓤⓢ 'præt̬.l̩.ɚ/z, 'præt.lɚ/z
Pravda 'prɑːv.də
prawn prɔːn ⓤⓢ prɑːn, prɔːn **-s** -z
ˌprawn 'cocktail ; **ˌprawn 'cracker**
prax|is 'præk.s|ɪs **-es** -iːz
Praxiteles præk'sɪt.əl.iːz, -tɪ.liːz ⓤⓢ -'sɪt̬.əl.iːz
pray (P) preɪ **-s** -z **-ing** -ɪŋ **-ed** -d
prayer *person who prays:* 'preɪ.əʳ ⓤⓢ -ɚ **-s** -z
prayer *supplication:* preəʳ ⓤⓢ prer **-s** -z **'prayer ˌmat** ; **'prayer ˌmeeting** ; **'prayer ˌrug** ; **'prayer ˌwheel**
prayer-book 'preə.bʊk ⓤⓢ 'prer- **-s** -s
prayerful 'preə.fəl, -fʊl ⓤⓢ 'prer- **-ly** -i **-ness** -nəs, -nɪs
prayerless 'preə.ləs, -lɪs ⓤⓢ 'prer- **-ly** -li **-ness** -nəs, -nɪs
praying mant|is ˌpreɪ.ɪŋ'mæn.t|ɪs ⓤⓢ -t̬|ɪs **-ises** -ɪ.sɪz **-es** -iːz
pre- priː-, prɪ-, pri-, prə-
Note: Prefix. In words containing **pre-** where the stem is free, and the meaning is **beforehand**, it generally takes secondary stress, e.g. **pre-eminence** /ˌpriː'em.ɪ.nənts/. Attached to bound stems the pronunciation is normally /prɪ-/ or /prə-/ for British English and /prɪ-/ or /priː-/ for American English, e.g. **prefer** /prɪ'fɜː ⓤⓢ priː'fɜːr/. There are exceptions; see individual entries.
preach priːtʃ **-es** -ɪz **-ing** -ɪŋ **-ed** -t **-er/s** -əʳ/z ⓤⓢ -ɚ/z **ˌpreach to the con'verted**

preachi|fy 'priː.tʃɪ|.faɪ **-fies** -faɪz **-fying** -faɪ.ɪŋ **-fied** -faɪd
preach|y 'priː.tʃ|i **-ily** -ɪ.li, -əl.i **-iness** -ɪ.nəs, -ɪ.nɪs
Preager 'preɪ.gəʳ ⓤⓢ -gɚ
preamble 'priː.æm.bl̩, pri'æm- **-s** -z
preamplifier pri'æm.plɪ.faɪ.əʳ ⓤⓢ -plə.faɪ.ɚ **-s** -z
prearrang|e ˌpriː.ə'reɪndʒ **-es** -ɪz **-ing** -ɪŋ **-ed** -d
Prebble 'preb.l̩
prebend 'preb.ənd **-s** -z
prebendar|y 'preb.ən.dər|.i, -əm-, -ən.der- **-ies** -ɪz
Precambrian ˌpriː'kæm.bri.ən
precancerous ˌpriː'kænt.sər.əs *stress shift:* ˌprecancerous 'tissue
precarious prɪ'keə.ri.əs, prə- ⓤⓢ prɪ'ker.i-, priː- **-ly** -li **-ness** -nəs, -nɪs
precast ˌpriː'kɑːst ⓤⓢ 'priː.kæst, ˌ-'- *stress shift, British only:* ˌprecast 'concrete
preca|tory 'prek.ə|.tər.i ⓤⓢ -tɔːr- **-tive** -tɪv ⓤⓢ -t̬ɪv
precaution prɪ'kɔː.ʃən, prə- ⓤⓢ prɪ'kɑː-, priː-, -'kɔː- **-s** -z
precautionary prɪ'kɔː.ʃən.ər.i, prə- ⓤⓢ prɪ'kɑː.ʃən.er-, priː-, -'kɔː-
preced|e priː'siːd, prɪ- ⓤⓢ prɪ-, priː- **-es** -z **-ing** -ɪŋ **-ed** -ɪd
precedenc|e 'pres.ɪ.dənts, 'priː.sɪ- ⓤⓢ 'pres.ə.dents; prɪ'siː.dənts, priː- **-y** -i
precedent (*n.*) 'pres.ɪ.dənt ⓤⓢ '-ə- **-s** -s **-ed** -ɪd
precedent (*adj.*) prɪ'siː.dənt, 'pres.ɪ.dənt ⓤⓢ prɪ'siː.dənt, priː-, 'pres.ə.dənt **-ly** -li
precentor ˌpriː'sen.təʳ, prɪ- ⓤⓢ priː'sen.t̬ɚ **-s** -z
precept 'priː.sept **-s** -s
preceptor prɪ'sep.təʳ ⓤⓢ priː'sep.tɚ, prɪ- **-s** -z
preceptor|y prɪ'sep.tər|.i ⓤⓢ prɪ-, priː- **-ies** -iz
precession prɪ'seʃ.ən, prə- ⓤⓢ prɪ-, priː- **-s** -z
precinct 'priː.sɪŋkt **-s** -s
preciosity ˌpres.i'ɒs.ə.ti, ˌpreʃ-, -ɪ.ti ⓤⓢ ˌpreʃ.i'ɑː.sə.t̬i, ˌpres-
precious (P) 'preʃ.əs **-ly** -li **-ness** -nəs, -nɪs **ˌprecious 'metal** ; **ˌprecious 'stone**
precipic|e 'pres.ɪ.pɪs, '-ə- ⓤⓢ '-ə- **-es** -ɪz
precipitanc|e prɪ'sɪp.ɪ.tənts, prə-, '-ə- ⓤⓢ prɪ-, priː- **-y** -i
precipitate (*n.*) prɪ'sɪp.ɪ.teɪt, prə-, '-ə-, -tət, -tɪt ⓤⓢ prɪ'sɪp.ɪ.tɪt, priː-, -teɪt **-s** -s
precipitate (*adj.*) prɪ'sɪp.ɪ.tət, prə-, '-ə-, -tɪt ⓤⓢ prɪ'sɪp.ɪ.tɪt, priː-, -teɪt **-ly** -li **-ness** -nəs, -nɪs

precipi|tate (*v.*) prɪ'sɪp.ɪ|.teɪt, prə-, '-ə- ⓤⓢ prɪ'sɪp.ɪ-, priː- **-tates** -teɪts **-tating** -teɪ.tɪŋ ⓤⓢ -teɪ.t̬ɪŋ **-tated** -teɪ.tɪd ⓤⓢ -teɪ.t̬ɪd
precipitation prɪˌsɪp.ɪ'teɪ.ʃən, prə-, -ə'- ⓤⓢ prɪˌsɪp.ɪ'-, priː- **-s** -z
precipitous prɪ'sɪp.ɪ.təs, prə-, '-ə- ⓤⓢ prɪ'sɪp.ɪ.t̬əs, priː- **-ly** -li **-ness** -nəs, -nɪs
précis *singular:* 'preɪ.siː ⓤⓢ 'preɪ.siː, -'- *plural:* -z
precise prɪ'saɪs, prə- ⓤⓢ prɪ-, priː- **-ly** -li **-ness** -nəs, -nɪs
precision prɪ'sɪʒ.ən, prə- ⓤⓢ prɪ-, priː-
preclassical ˌpriː'klæs.ɪ.kəl *stress shift:* ˌpreclassical 'music
preclud|e prɪ'kluːd ⓤⓢ prɪ-, priː- **-es** -z **-ing** -ɪŋ **-ed** -ɪd
preclu|sion prɪ'kluː|.ʒən ⓤⓢ prɪ-, priː- **-sive** -sɪv
precocious prɪ'kəʊ.ʃəs, prə- ⓤⓢ prɪ'koʊ-, priː- **-ly** -li **-ness** -nəs, -nɪs
precocity prɪ'kɒs.ə.ti, prə-, -ɪ.ti ⓤⓢ prɪ'kɑː.sə.t̬i, priː-
precognition ˌpriː.kɒg'nɪʃ.ən ⓤⓢ -kɑːg'-
preconceiv|e ˌpriː.kən'siːv **-es** -z **-ing** -ɪŋ **-ed** -d
preconception ˌpriː.kən'sep.ʃən **-s** -z
precon|cert ˌpriː.kən|'sɜːt ⓤⓢ -'sɜːrt **-certs** -'sɜːts ⓤⓢ -'sɜːrts **-certing** -'sɜː.tɪŋ ⓤⓢ -'sɜːr.t̬ɪŋ **-certed** -'sɜː.tɪd ⓤⓢ -'sɜːr.t̬ɪd
precondition ˌpriː.kən'dɪʃ.ən **-s** -z **-ing** -ɪŋ **-ed** -d
precook ˌpriː'kʊk **-s** -s **-ing** -ɪŋ **-ed** -t
precursor ˌpriː'kɜː.səʳ, prɪ- ⓤⓢ prɪ'kɜːr.sɚ, priː- **-s** -z **-y** -i
preda|te ˌpriː'deɪ|t ⓤⓢ ˌpriː'deɪ|t, '-- **-tes** -ts **-ting** -tɪŋ ⓤⓢ -t̬ɪŋ **-ted** -tɪd ⓤⓢ -t̬ɪd *stress shift:* ˌpredated 'cheque
predation prɪ'deɪ.ʃən, prə- ⓤⓢ prɪ-, priː- **-s** -z
predator 'pred.ə.təʳ, '-ɪ- ⓤⓢ -də.t̬ɚ **-s**
predator|y 'pred.ə.tər|.i ⓤⓢ -tɔːr- **-ily** -əl.i, -ɪ.li **-iness** -ɪ.nəs, -ɪ.nɪs
predeceas|e ˌpriː.dɪ'siːs, -də'- ⓤⓢ -diː'-, -dɪ'- **-es** -ɪz **-ing** -ɪŋ **-ed** -t
predecessor 'priː.dɪˌses.əʳ, -də-, ˌpriː.dɪ'ses-, -də'- ⓤⓢ 'pred.ə.ses.ɚ, 'priː.də-; ˌpred.ə'ses- **-s** -z
predesti|nate (*v.*) ˌpriː'des.tɪ|.neɪt, prɪ-, -tə- ⓤⓢ ˌpriː'des.tə- **-nates** -neɪts **-nating** -neɪ.tɪŋ ⓤⓢ -neɪ.t̬ɪŋ **-nated** -neɪ.tɪd ⓤⓢ -neɪ.t̬ɪd
predestinate (*adj.*) ˌpriː'des.tɪ.nət, prɪ-, -tə- ⓤⓢ ˌpriː'des.tə.nɪt
predestination ˌpriː.des.tɪ'neɪ.ʃən, prɪˌdes- ⓤⓢ priː-, -tə'-, priːˌdes.tə'-
predestin|e ˌpriː'des.tɪn, prɪ- ⓤⓢ ˌpriː- **-es** -z **-ing** -ɪŋ **-ed** -d

predetermination ˌpriː.dɪˌtɜː.mɪˈneɪ.ʃᵊn, -dəˌ-, -məˈ- (US) -dɪˌtɜːr.məˈ-
predetermin|e ˌpriː.dɪˈtɜː.mɪn, -dəˈ-, -mən (US) -dɪˈtɜːr.mən **-es** -z **-ing** -ɪŋ **-ed** -d *stress shift:* ˌpredetermined ˈpath
predeterminer ˌpriː.dɪˈtɜː.mɪ.nəʳ, -dəˈ-, -mə- (US) -dɪˈtɜːr.mə.nɚ
predicability ˌpred.ɪ.kəˈbɪl.ə.ti, -ɪ.ti (US) -ə.t̬i
predicable ˈpred.ɪ.kə.bl̩
predicament prɪˈdɪk.ə.mənt, prə- (US) prɪ-, priː- **-s** -s
predicate (*n.*) ˈpred.ɪ.kət, ˈpriː.dɪ-, -də-, -kɪt, -keɪt (US) ˈpred.ɪ.kɪt, ˈ-ə- **-s** -s
predi|cate (*v.*) ˈpred.ɪ|.keɪt, ˈ-ə- (US) ˈ-ɪ- **-cates** -keɪts **-cating** -keɪ.tɪŋ (US) -keɪ.t̬ɪŋ **-cated** -keɪ.tɪd (US) -keɪ.t̬ɪd
predication ˌpred.ɪˈkeɪ.ʃᵊn, -əˈ- (US) -ɪˈ- **-s** -z
predicative prɪˈdɪk.ə.tɪv, prə- (US) prɪˈdɪk.ə.t̬ɪv, priː- **-ly** -li
predicatory ˈpred.ɪ.keɪ.tᵊr.i, ˈ-ə-, ˌpred.ɪˈkeɪ-, -əˈ- (US) ˈpred.ɪ.kə.tɔːr-
predict prɪˈdɪkt, prə- (US) prɪ-, priː- **-s** -s **-ing** -ɪŋ **-ed** -ɪd **-or/s** -əʳ/z (US) -ɚ/z
predictability prɪˌdɪk.təˈbɪl.ɪ.ti, prə- (US) prɪˌdɪk.təˈbɪl.ə.t̬i, priː-
predictab|le prɪˈdɪk.tə.b|l̩, prə- (US) prɪ-, priː- **-ly** -li
prediction prɪˈdɪk.ʃᵊn, prə- (US) prɪ-, priː- **-s** -z
predictive prɪˈdɪk.tɪv **-ly** -li
predilection ˌpriː.dɪˈlek.ʃᵊn, -dəˈ- (US) ˌpred.ᵊlˈek-, ˌpriː.dᵊlˈ- **-s** -z
predispos|e ˌpriː.dɪˈspəʊz, -dəˈ- (US) -dɪˈspoʊz **-es** -ɪz **-ing** -ɪŋ **-ed** -d
predisposition ˌpriː.dɪ.spəˈzɪʃ.ᵊn, priːˌdɪs.pəˈ- **-s** -z
predominance prɪˈdɒm.ɪ.nənts, prə-, ˈ-ə- (US) prɪˈdɑː.mə-, priː-
predominant prɪˈdɒm.ɪ.nənt, prə-, ˈ-ə- (US) prɪˈdɑː.mə-, priː- **-ly** -li
predomi|nate prɪˈdɒm.ɪ|.neɪt, prə-, ˈ-ə- (US) prɪˈdɑː.mə-, priː- **-nates** -neɪts **-nating** -neɪ.tɪŋ (US) -neɪ.t̬ɪŋ **-nated** -neɪ.tɪd (US) -neɪ.t̬ɪd
predomination prɪˌdɒm.ɪˈneɪ.ʃᵊn, prə-, -əˈ- (US) prɪˌdɑː.məˈ-, priː-
Preece priːs
pre-eclampsia ˌpriː.ɪˈklæm*p*.si.ə
pre-eminence ˌpriːˈem.ɪ.nən*t*s, pri-, ˈ-ə-
pre-eminent ˌpriːˈem.ɪ.nənt, pri-, ˈ-ə- **-ly** -li
pre-empt ˌpriːˈem*p*t, pri- **-s** -s **-ing** -ɪŋ **-ed** -ɪd
pre-emption ˌpriːˈem*p*.ʃᵊn, pri-
pre-emptive ˌpriːˈem*p*.tɪv, pri- **pre-ˌemptive ˈstrike**
preen priːn **-s** -z **-ing** -ɪŋ **-ed** -d
pre-exist ˌpriː.ɪgˈzɪst, -egˈ-; -ɪkˈsɪst, -ekˈ- (US) -ɪgˈzɪst, -egˈ- **-s** -s **-ing** -ɪŋ **-ed** -ɪd **-ence** -ᵊn*t*s **-ent** -ᵊnt *stress shift:* ˌpre-existing ˈrule
prefab ˈpriː.fæb **-s** -z
prefabri|cate ˌpriːˈfæb.rɪ|.keɪt, -rə- **-cates** -keɪts **-cating** -keɪ.tɪŋ (US) -keɪ.t̬ɪŋ **-cated** -keɪ.tɪd (US) -keɪ.t̬ɪd
pre-fabrication ˌpriː.fæb.rɪˈkeɪ.ʃᵊn, priːˌfæb-, -rəˈ- (US) ˌpriː.fæb-
prefac|e ˈpref.ɪs, -əs (US) -ɪs **-es** -ɪz **-ing** -ɪŋ **-ed** -t
prefatorial ˌpref.əˈtɔː.ri.əl (US) -ˈtɔːr.i- **-ly** -i
prefatory ˈpref.ə.tᵊr.i (US) -tɔːr-
prefect ˈpriː.fekt **-s** -s
prefecture ˈpriː.fek.tʃəʳ, -tʃʊəʳ, -tjʊəʳ (US) -tʃɚ **-s** -z
prefer prɪˈfɜːʳ, prə- (US) priːˈfɜːr, prɪ- **-s** -z **-ring** -ɪŋ **-red** -d
preferability ˌpref.ᵊr.əˈbɪl.ə.ti, -ɪ.ti (US) -ə.t̬i
preferab|le ˈpref.ᵊr.ə.b|l̩ **-ly** -li **-leness** -l̩.nəs, -nɪs
preferenc|e ˈpref.ᵊr.ᵊn*t*s **-es** -ɪz
preferential ˌpref.ᵊrˈen.*t*ʃᵊl **-ly** -i
preferment prɪˈfɜː.mənt, prə- (US) priːˈfɜːr-, prɪ- **-s** -s
prefigurative priːˈfɪg.ᵊr.ə.tɪv (US) -jɚ- **-ly** -li **-ness** -nəs, -nɪs
prefig|ure priːˈfɪg|.əʳ (US) -j|ɚ **-ures** -əz (US) -ɚz **-uring** -ᵊr.ɪŋ **-ured** -əd (US) -ɚd
prefigurement priːˈfɪg.ə.mənt (US) -jɚ-, -jʊr- **-s** -s
prefix (*n.*) ˈpriː.fɪks **-es** -ɪz
prefix (*v.*) ˌpriːˈfɪks, ˈ-- (US) ˈpriː.fɪks, ˌ-ˈ- **-es** -ɪz **-ing** -ɪŋ **-ed** -t
preggers ˈpreg.əz (US) -ɚz
pregnable ˈpreg.nə.bl̩
pregnancy ˈpreg.nən*t*.si
pregnant ˈpreg.nənt **-ly** -li
pre|heat ˌpriː|ˈhiːt **-heats** -ˈhiːts **-heating** -ˈhiː.tɪŋ (US) -ˈhiː.t̬ɪŋ **-heated** -ˈhiː.tɪd (US) -ˈhiː.t̬ɪd *stress shift:* ˌpreheated ˈmeal
prehensible prɪˈhen*t*.sə.bl̩, -sɪ- (US) priː-
prehensile prɪˈhen*t*.saɪl, ˌpriː- (US) priːˈhen*t*.sɪl, -sᵊl
prehistoric ˌpriː.*h*ɪˈstɒr.ɪk (US) -hɪˈstɔːr- **-ally** -ᵊl.i, -li *stress shift:* ˌprehistoric ˈmonster
prehistory ˌpriːˈhɪs.tᵊr.i
prejudg|e ˌpriːˈdʒʌdʒ **-es** -ɪz **-ing** -ɪŋ **-ed** -d **-(e)ment** -mənt
prejudic|e ˈpredʒ.ə.dɪs, ˈ-ʊ- **-es** -ɪz **-ing** -ɪŋ **-ed** -t
prejudicial ˌpredʒ.əˈdɪʃ.ᵊl, -ʊˈ- **-ly** -i
prelac|y ˈprel.ə.s|i **-ies** -iz
prelate ˈprel.ɪt, -ət (US) -ɪt **-s** -s
preliminar|y prɪˈlɪm.ɪ.nᵊr|.i, prə-, -ᵊn.ᵊr- (US) prɪˈlɪm.ə.ner-, priː- **-ies** -iz **-ily** -ᵊl.i, -ɪ.li
prelims ˈpriː.lɪmz, ˌ-ˈ-; prɪ- (US) ˈpriː.lɪms; ˌpriːˈlɪmz, prɪ-
prelud|e ˈprel.juːd (US) ˈprel-, -uːd; ˈpreɪ.luːd, ˈpriː- **-es** -z **-ing** -ɪŋ **-ed** -ɪd
premarital ˌpriːˈmær.ɪ.tᵊl (US) -ˈmer.ə.t̬ᵊl, -ˈmær- **-ly** -i *stress shift, see compound:* **ˌpremarital ˈsex**
premature ˈprem.ə.tʃəʳ, ˈpriː.mə-, -tjʊəʳ, -tʃʊəʳ, -tjɔːʳ, -tʃɔːʳ; ˌ--ˈ- (US) ˌpriː.məˈtʊr, -ˈtjʊr, -ˈtʃʊr **-ly** -li **-ness** -nəs, -nɪs *stress shift, British only:* ˌpremature ˈaging
premed ˌpriːˈmed **-s** -z *stress shift:* ˌpremed ˈscience
premedical ˌpriːˈmed.ɪ.kᵊl, ˈ-ə- *stress shift:* ˌpremedical ˈscience
premedication ˌpriː.med.ɪˈkeɪ.ʃᵊn, -əˈ-
premedi|tate ˌpriːˈmed.ɪ|.teɪt, prɪ-, ˈ-ə- (US) priːˈmed.ɪ- **-tates** -teɪts **-tating** -teɪ.tɪŋ (US) -teɪ.t̬ɪŋ **-tated/ly** -teɪ.tɪd/li (US) -teɪ.t̬ɪd/li
premeditation ˌpriː.med.ɪˈteɪ.ʃᵊn, prɪˌmed-, priː-, -əˈ- (US) priː-
premenstrual ˌpriːˈmen*t*.stru.əl (US) -strəl **-ly** -i *stress shift, see compounds:* **ˌpremenstrual ˈtension**; **ˌpremenstrual ˈsyndrome**
premier ˈprem.i.əʳ, ˈpriː.mi- (US) prɪˈmɪr, -ˈmjɪr; ˈpriː.miː.ɚ **-s** -z **-ship/s** -ʃɪp/s
première ˈprem.i.eəʳ, ˌ--ˈ- (US) prɪˈmɪr, premˈɪr, -ˈjer, -ˈjɪr **-s** -z
Preminger ˈprem.ɪn.dʒəʳ, ˈpreɪ.mɪŋ.əʳ (US) ˈprem.ɪn.dʒɚ
premis|e (*n.*) ˈprem.ɪs **-s** -ɪz
premis|e (*v.*) prɪˈmaɪz, ˈprem.ɪs (US) ˈprem.ɪs **-es** -ɪz **-ing** -ɪŋ **-ed** prɪˈmaɪzd, ˈprem.ɪst (US) ˈprem.ɪst
premium ˈpriː.mi.əm **-s** -z **ˈpremium ˌbond**
premodification ˌpriː.mɒd.ɪ.fɪˈkeɪ.ʃᵊn, priːˌmɒd-, -ə- (US) ˌpriː.mɑː.dɪ.fɪˈ-
premodif|y priːˈmɒd.ɪ.f|aɪ (US) -ˈmɑː.dɪ- **-ies** -aɪz **-ying** -aɪ.ɪŋ **-ied** -aɪd
premolar ˌpriːˈməʊ.ləʳ (US) -ˈmoʊ.lɚ **-s** -z *stress shift:* ˌpremolar ˈteeth
premonition ˌprem.əˈnɪʃ.ᵊn, ˌpriː.məˈ- **-s** -z
premonitorily prɪˈmɒn.ɪ.tᵊr.ᵊl.i, -ɪ.li (US) priːˈmɑː.nə.tɔːr-, -ˌmɑː.nəˈtɔːr-
premonitory prɪˈmɒn.ɪ.tᵊr.i (US) priːˈmɑː.nə.tɔːr-
prenatal ˌpriːˈneɪ.tᵊl (US) -t̬ᵊl **-ly** -i *stress shift:* ˌprenatal ˈcare
Prendergast ˈpren.də.gɑːst, -gæst (US) -dɚ.gæst

prentic|e (P) ˈpren.tɪs ⓊⓈ -t̬ɪs **-es** -ɪz
Prentis(s) ˈpren.tɪs ⓊⓈ -t̬ɪs
prenuptial ˌpriːˈnʌp.tʃəl *stress shift, see compound:* ˌ**prenuptial aˈgreement**
preoccupation priːˌɒk.jəˈpeɪ.ʃən, prɪ-, ˌpriː.ɒk-, -jʊˈ- ⓊⓈ priːˌɑː.kjuːˈ-, -kjəˈ- **-s** -z
preoccup|y ˌpriːˈɒk.jə.p|aɪ, pri- ⓊⓈ priːˈɑː.kjuː-, -kjə- **-ies** -aɪz **-ying** -aɪ.ɪŋ **-ied** -aɪd
preordain ˌpriː.ɔːˈdeɪn ⓊⓈ -ɔːrˈ- **-s** -z **-ing** -ɪŋ **-ed** -d *stress shift:* ˌpreordained ˈdestiny
prep prep **-s** -s ˈ**prep** ˌ**school**
prepackag|e ˌpriːˈpæk.ɪdʒ **-es** -ɪz **-ing** -ɪŋ **-ed** -d *stress shift:* ˌprepackaged ˈgoods
prepaid (*from* **prepay**) ˌpriːˈpeɪd *stress shift:* ˌprepaid ˈpostage
preparation ˌprep.ərˈeɪ.ʃən ⓊⓈ -əˈreɪ- **-s** -z
preparative prɪˈpær.ə.tɪv, prə- ⓊⓈ prɪˈper.ə.t̬ɪv, priː-, -ˈpær- **-ly** -li
preparator|y prɪˈpær.ə.tər|.i, prə- ⓊⓈ prɪˈper.ə.tɔːr-, priː-, -ˈpær-; ˈprep.ɚ.ə- **-ily** -əl.i, -ɪ.li **preˈparatory** ˌ**school**
prepar|e prɪˈpeər, prə- ⓊⓈ prɪˈper, priː- **-es** -z **-ing** -ɪŋ **-ed** -d **-edly** -d.li, -ɪd.li **-edness** -d.nəs, -nɪs, -ɪd.nəs, -nɪs **-er/s** -ər/z ⓊⓈ -ɚ/z
prepay ˌpriːˈpeɪ **-s** -z **-ing** -ɪŋ **prepaid** ˌpriːˈpeɪd *stress shift:* ˌprepaid ˈpostage
prepayment ˌpriːˈpeɪ.mənt **-s** -s
prepense prɪˈpents **-ly** -li
preponderance prɪˈpɒn.dər.ənts, prə- ⓊⓈ prɪˈpɑːn-, priː-
preponderant prɪˈpɒn.dər.ənt, prə- ⓊⓈ prɪˈpɑːn-, priː- **-ly** -li
preponder|ate prɪˈpɒn.dər|.eɪt, prə- ⓊⓈ prɪˈpɑːn.də.r|eɪt, priː- **-ates** -eɪts **-ating/ly** -eɪ.tɪŋ/li ⓊⓈ -eɪ.t̬ɪŋ/li **-ated** -eɪ.tɪd ⓊⓈ -eɪ.t̬ɪd
preponderation prɪˌpɒn.dərˈeɪ.ʃən, prə-, priː- ⓊⓈ prɪˌpɑːn.dəˈreɪ-, priː-
preposition ˌprep.əˈzɪʃ.ən **-s** -z
prepositional ˌprep.əˈzɪʃ.ən.əl, ˈ-nəl ⓊⓈ -əˈ- **-ly** -i *stress shift, see compound:* ˌ**prepositional ˈphrase**
prepositive prɪˈpɒz.ə.tɪv, priː-, ˈ-ɪ- ⓊⓈ prɪˈpɑː.zə.t̬ɪv, priː- *stress shift:* ˌprepositive ˈadjective
prepossess ˌpriː.pəˈzes **-es** -ɪz **-ing/ly** -ɪŋ/li **-ed** -t
prepossession ˌpriː.pəˈzeʃ.ən **-s** -z
preposterous prɪˈpɒs.tər.əs, prə- ⓊⓈ prɪˈpɑː.stɚ-, priː- **-ly** -li **-ness** -nəs, -nɪs
prepp|y, prepp|ie ˈprep|.i **-ies** -iz **-ier** -i.ər ⓊⓈ -i.ɚ **-iest** -i.ɪst, -i.əst **-iness** -ɪ.nəs, -ɪ.nɪs
prepubescen|t ˌpriː.pjuːˈbes.ən|t **-ce** -ts
prepuc|e ˈpriː.pjuːs **-es** -ɪz
prequel ˈpriː.kwəl **-s** -z
Pre-Raphaelite ˌpriːˈræf.i.əl.aɪt, -eɪ-, -ˈræf.əl-, -ɪ.laɪt ⓊⓈ -ˈræf.i.əl-, -ˈreɪ.fi- **-s** -s ˌ**Pre-**ˌ**Raphaelite** ˈ**Brotherhood**
prerecord ˌpriː.rɪˈkɔːd, -rəˈ- ⓊⓈ -rɪˈkɔːrd **-s** -z **-ing** -ɪŋ **-ed** -ɪd
prerequisite ˌpriːˈrek.wɪ.zɪt, -wə- **-s** -s
prerogative prɪˈrɒg.ə.tɪv, prə- ⓊⓈ -ˈrɑː.gə.t̬ɪv **-s** -z
presag|e (*n.*) ˈpres.ɪdʒ **-es** -ɪz
presag|e (*v.*) ˈpres.ɪdʒ; prɪˈseɪdʒ, prə- ⓊⓈ prɪˈseɪdʒ; ˈpres.ɪdʒ **-es** -ɪz **-ing** -ɪŋ **-ed** -d
presbyopia ˌprez.biˈəʊ.pi.ə ⓊⓈ -ˈoʊ-, ˌpres-
presbyter ˈprez.bɪ.tər ⓊⓈ -t̬ɚ, ˈpres- **-s** -z
presbyterian (P) ˌprez.bɪˈtɪə.ri.ən, -bəˈ- ⓊⓈ -bɪˈtɪr.i-, ˌpres- **-s** -z **-ism** -ɪ.zəm
presbyter|y ˈprez.bɪ.tər|.i, -bə- ⓊⓈ -bɪ.ter-, ˈpres- **-ies** -iz
Prescel(l)y prɪˈsel.i, prə-, presˈel-
preschool ˈpriːˌskuːl, ˌ-ˈ- ⓊⓈ ˈ--
preschooler ˈpriːˌskuː.lər ⓊⓈ -lɚ **-s** -z
prescience ˈpres.i.ənts, ˈpreʃ- ⓊⓈ ˈpreʃ.ənts, ˈpriː.ʃənts, -ʃi.ənts
prescient ˈpres.i.ənt, ˈpreʃ- ⓊⓈ ˈpreʃ.ənt, ˈpriː.ʃənt, -ʃi.ənt **-ly** -li
prescind prɪˈsɪnd, prə-, priː- ⓊⓈ prɪ-, priː- **-s** -z **-ing** -ɪŋ **-ed** -ɪd
Prescot(t) ˈpres.kət, -kɒt ⓊⓈ -kət, -kɑːt
prescrib|e prɪˈskraɪb, prə- ⓊⓈ prɪ-, priː- **-es** -z **-ing** -ɪŋ **-ed** -d **-er/s** -ər/z ⓊⓈ -ɚ/z
prescript ˈpriː.skrɪpt **-s** -s
prescription prɪˈskrɪp.ʃən, prə- ⓊⓈ prɪ-, priː- **-s** -z
prescriptive prɪˈskrɪp.tɪv, prə-, priː- ⓊⓈ prɪ-, priː- **-ly** -li
prescriptiv|ism prɪˈskrɪp.tɪ.v|ɪ.zəm, prə-, priː- ⓊⓈ prɪ-, priː- **-ist/s** -ɪst/s
Preseli prɪˈsel.i, prə-, priː-
presenc|e ˈprez.ənts **-es** -ɪz ˌ**presence of ˈmind**
present (*n.*) *ordinary senses:* ˈprez.ənt **-s** -s
present (*n.*) *military term:* prɪˈzent, prə- **-s** -s
present (*adj.*) ˈprez.ənt **-ly** -li ˌ**present parˈticiple** ⓊⓈ ˌ**present ˈparticiple**; ˌ**present ˈperfect**; ˌ**present ˈtense**
pre|sent (*v.*) prɪ|ˈzent, prə- ⓊⓈ prɪ-, priː- **-sents** -ˈzents **-senting** -ˈzen.tɪŋ ⓊⓈ -ˈzen.t̬ɪŋ **-sented** -ˈzen.tɪd ⓊⓈ -ˈzen.t̬ɪd
presentab|le prɪˈzen.tə.b|l̩, prə- ⓊⓈ prɪˈzen.t̬ə-, priː- **-ly** -li **-leness** -l̩.nəs, -nɪs
presentation ˌprez.ənˈteɪ.ʃən, -enˈ- ⓊⓈ -ənˈ-, ˌpriː.zənˈ- **-s** -z
present-day ˌprez.əntˈdeɪ *stress shift:* ˌpresent-day ˈfashions
presenter prɪˈzen.tər, prə- ⓊⓈ prɪˈzen.t̬ɚ, priː- **-s** -z
presentient prɪˈsent.ʃi.ənt, -ʃənt ⓊⓈ priː-, prɪ-
presentiment prɪˈzen.tɪ.mənt ⓊⓈ prɪ-, priː- **-s** -s
presently ˈprez.ənt.li
preservation ˌprez.əˈveɪ.ʃən ⓊⓈ -ɚˈ- **-s** -z **preserˈvation** ˌ**order**
preservative prɪˈzɜː.və.tɪv, prə- ⓊⓈ prɪˈzɜːr.və.t̬ɪv, priː- **-s** -z
preserv|e prɪˈzɜːv, prə- ⓊⓈ prɪˈzɜːrv, priː- **-es** -z **-ing** -ɪŋ **-ed** -d **-er/s** -ər/z ⓊⓈ -ɚ/z **-able** -ə.bl̩
pre|set priː|ˈset **-sets** -ˈsets **-setting** -ˈset.ɪŋ ⓊⓈ -ˈset̬.ɪŋ *stress shift:* ˌpreset ˈchannel
pre|shrink ˌpriːˈʃrɪŋk **-shrinks** -ˈʃrɪŋks **-shrinking** -ˈʃrɪŋ.kɪŋ **-shrank** -ˈʃræŋk **-shrunk** -ˈʃrʌŋk **-shrunken** -ˈʃrʌŋ.kən *stress shift:* ˌpreshrunk ˈjeans
presid|e prɪˈzaɪd, prə- ⓊⓈ prɪ-, priː- **-es** -z **-ing** -ɪŋ **-ed** -ɪd
presidenc|y ˈprez.ɪ.dənt.s|i **-ies** -iz
president ˈprez.ɪ.dənt **-s** -s
presidential ˌprez.ɪˈden.tʃəl *stress shift:* ˌpresidential ˈsuite
presidi|um prɪˈsɪd.i|.əm, prə- **-ums** -əmz **-a** -ə
Presley ˈprez.li ⓊⓈ ˈpres-, ˈprez-
pre|sort ˌpriː|ˈsɔːt ⓊⓈ -ˈsɔːrt **-sorts** -ˈsɔːts ⓊⓈ -ˈsɔːrts **-sorting** -ˈsɔː.tɪŋ ⓊⓈ -ˈsɔːr.t̬ɪŋ **-sorted** -ˈsɔː.tɪd ⓊⓈ -ˈsɔːr.t̬ɪd
press pres **-es** -ɪz **-ing/ly** -ɪŋ/li **-ed** -t **-er/s** -ər/z ⓊⓈ -ɚ/z ˈ**press** ˌ**agent**; ˈ**press** ˌ**baron**; ˈ**press** ˌ**conference**; ˈ**press** ˌ**cutting**; ˈ**press** ˌ**office**; ˈ**press reˌlease**
pressgang ˈpres.gæŋ **-s** -z **-ing** -ɪŋ **-ed** -d
pressie ˈprez.i **-s** -z
pression ˈpreʃ.ən
press|man ˈpres|.mæn, -mən **-men** -mən, -men
pressrun ˈpres.rʌn
press-stud ˈpres.stʌd **-s** -s
press-up ˈpres.ʌp **-s** -s
pressur|e ˈpreʃ.ər ⓊⓈ -ɚ **-es** -z **-ing** -ɪŋ **-ed** -d ˈ**pressure** ˌ**cooker**; ˈ**pressure** ˌ**group**
pressuriz|e, -is|e ˈpreʃ.ər.aɪz ⓊⓈ -ə.raɪz **-es** -ɪz **-ing** -ɪŋ **-ed** -d
Prestage ˈpres.tɪdʒ
Prestatyn presˈtæt.ɪn, prɪˈstæt-

Presteign pres'tiːn

Prestel® 'pres.tel

prestidigitation ˌpres.tɪˌdɪdʒ.ɪ'teɪ.ʃᵊn Ⓤⓢ -təˌ-

prestidigitator ˌpres.tɪ'dɪdʒ.ɪ.teɪ.təʳ Ⓤⓢ -tə'dɪdʒ.ə.teɪ.t̬ɚ **-s** -z

prestige pres'tiːʒ Ⓤⓢ -'tiːdʒ

Prestige *surname:* 'pres.tɪdʒ

prestigious pres'tɪdʒ.əs, prɪ'stɪdʒ-, prə-, -i.əs Ⓤⓢ pres'tɪdʒ.əs, -'tiː.dʒəs **-ly** -li **-ness** -nəs, -nɪs

prestissimo pres'tɪs.ɪ.məʊ, '-ə- Ⓤⓢ -ə.moʊ

presto (P) 'pres.təʊ Ⓤⓢ -toʊ **-s** -z

Preston 'pres.tᵊn

Prestonpans ˌpres.tᵊn'pænz, -tᵊm'- Ⓤⓢ -tᵊn'-

prestressed ˌpriː'strest

Prestwich 'pres.twɪtʃ

Prestwick 'pres.twɪk

Prestwood 'pres.twʊd

presumab|ly prɪ'zjuː.mə.b|li, prə-, -'zuː- Ⓤⓢ prɪ'zuː.mə-, priː- **-le** -l̩

presum|e prɪ'zjuːm, prə-, -'zuːm Ⓤⓢ prɪ'zuːm, priː- **-es** -z **-ing/ly** -ɪŋ/li **-ed** -d

presumption prɪ'zʌmp.ʃᵊn, prə- Ⓤⓢ prɪ-, priː- **-s** -z

presumptive prɪ'zʌmp.tɪv, prə- Ⓤⓢ prɪ-, priː- **-ly** -li

presumptuous prɪ'zʌmp.tʃu.əs, prə-, -tju-, -tʃəs Ⓤⓢ prɪ'zʌmp.tʃuː.əs, priː-, -tʃə.wəs **-ly** -li **-ness** -nəs, -nɪs

presuppos|e ˌpriː.sə'pəʊz Ⓤⓢ -'poʊz **-es** -ɪz **-ing** -ɪŋ **-ed** -d

presupposition ˌpriː.sʌp.ə'zɪʃ.ᵊn **-s** -z

prêt-à-porter ˌpret.ɑː'pɔː.teɪ Ⓤⓢ -pɔːr'teɪ

pretax ˌpriː'tæks *stress shift:* ˌpretax 'profit

preteen ˌpriː'tiːn **-s** -z *stress shift:* ˌpreteen 'years

pretenc|e prɪ'tents, prə- Ⓤⓢ 'priː.tents; prɪ'tents **-es** -ɪz

pretend prɪ'tend, prə- Ⓤⓢ prɪ-, priː- **-s** -z **-ing** -ɪŋ **-ed** -ɪd **-er/s** -əʳ/z Ⓤⓢ -ɚ/z

pretens|e prɪ'tents, prə- Ⓤⓢ 'priː.tents; prɪ'tents **-es** -ɪz

pretension prɪ'ten.tʃᵊn, prə- Ⓤⓢ prɪ-, priː- **-s** -z

pretentious prɪ'ten.tʃəs, prə- Ⓤⓢ prɪ-, priː- **-ly** -li **-ness** -nəs, -nɪs

preterit(e) 'pret.ᵊr.ɪt, -ət Ⓤⓢ 'pret̬.ɚ.ɪt **-s** -s

pretermission ˌpriː.tə'mɪʃ.ᵊn Ⓤⓢ -t̬ɚ'-

preter|mit ˌpriː.tə'mɪt Ⓤⓢ -t̬ɚ'- **-mits** -'mɪts **-mitting** -'mɪt.ɪŋ Ⓤⓢ -'mɪt̬.ɪŋ **-mitted** -'mɪt.ɪd Ⓤⓢ -'mɪt̬.ɪd

preternatural ˌpriː.tə'nætʃ.ᵊr.ᵊl, -ʊ.rᵊl Ⓤⓢ -t̬ɚ'nætʃ.ɚ.ᵊl, '-rᵊl **-ly** -i **-ness** -nəs, -nɪs *stress shift:* ˌpreternatural 'happening

pretext 'priː.tekst **-s** -s

pretor 'priː.təʳ Ⓤⓢ -t̬ɚ **-s** -z **-ship/s** -ʃɪp/s

Pretori|a prɪ'tɔː.ri|.ə, prə- Ⓤⓢ prɪ'tɔːr.i.-, priː- **-us** -əs

pretori|al prɪ'tɔː.ri|.əl, prə- Ⓤⓢ prɪ'tɔːr.i.-, priː- **-an** -ən

prettification ˌprɪt.ɪ.fɪ'keɪ.ʃᵊn, ˌ-ə- Ⓤⓢ ˌprɪt̬-

prettif|y 'prɪt.ɪ.f|aɪ Ⓤⓢ 'prɪt̬- **-ies** -aɪz **-ying** -aɪ.ɪŋ **-ied** -aɪd

prett|y *(adj. adv.)* 'prɪt|.i Ⓤⓢ 'prɪt̬- **-ier** -i.əʳ Ⓤⓢ -i.ɚ **-iest** -i.ɪst, -i.əst **-ily** -ɪ.li, -ᵊl.i **-iness** -ɪ.nəs, -ɪ.nɪs

Pretty *surname:* 'prɪt.i, 'pret- Ⓤⓢ 'prɪt̬-, 'pret̬-

Pret(t)yman 'prɪt.ɪ.mən Ⓤⓢ 'prɪt̬-

pretty-pretty 'prɪt.iˌprɪt.i Ⓤⓢ 'prɪt̬.iˌprɪt̬.i

pretzel 'pret.sᵊl **-s** -z

prevail prɪ'veɪl, prə- Ⓤⓢ prɪ-, priː- **-s** -z **-ing** -ɪŋ **-ed** -d

prevalence 'prev.ᵊl.ənts Ⓤⓢ -ə.lənts

prevalent 'prev.ᵊl.ənt Ⓤⓢ -ə.lənt **-ly** -li

prevari|cate prɪ'vær.ɪ|.keɪt, prə-, '-ə- Ⓤⓢ prɪ'ver.ɪ-, -'vær- **-cates** -keɪts **-cating** -keɪ.tɪŋ Ⓤⓢ -keɪ.t̬ɪŋ **-cated** -keɪ.tɪd Ⓤⓢ -keɪ.t̬ɪd **-cator/s** -keɪ.təʳ/z Ⓤⓢ -keɪ.t̬ɚ/z

prevarication prɪˌvær.ɪ'keɪ.ʃᵊn, prə-, -ə'- Ⓤⓢ prɪˌver-, -ˌvær- **-s** -z

pre|vent *hinder:* prɪ|'vent, prə- Ⓤⓢ prɪ-, priː- **-vents** -'vents **-venting** -'ven.tɪŋ Ⓤⓢ -'ven.t̬ɪŋ **-vented** -'ven.tɪd Ⓤⓢ -'ven.t̬ɪd **-venter/s** -'ven.təʳ/z Ⓤⓢ -'ven.t̬ɚ/z **-ventable** -'ven.tə.bl̩ Ⓤⓢ -'ven.t̬ə.bl̩

pre|vent *go before:* ˌpriː|'vent, prɪ- Ⓤⓢ priː-, prɪ- **-vents** -'vents **-venting** -'ven.tɪŋ Ⓤⓢ -'ven.t̬ɪŋ **-vented** -'ven.tɪd Ⓤⓢ -'ven.t̬ɪd

preventability prɪˌven.tə'bɪl.ə.ti, prə-, -ɪ.ti Ⓤⓢ prɪˌven.t̬ə'bɪl.ə.t̬i, priː-

preventative prɪ'ven.tə.tɪv, prə- Ⓤⓢ prɪ'ven.t̬ə.t̬ɪv, priː- **-s** -z

prevention prɪ'ven.tʃᵊn, prə- Ⓤⓢ prɪ-, priː-

preventive prɪ'ven.tɪv, prə- Ⓤⓢ prɪ'ven.t̬ɪv, priː- **-ly** -li **-ness** -nəs, -nɪs

preverbal ˌpriː'vɜː.bᵊl Ⓤⓢ -'vɜːr- *stress shift:* ˌpreverbal 'state

preview 'priː.vjuː **-s** -z **-ing** -ɪŋ **-ed** -d

Previn 'prev.ɪn

previous 'priː.vi.əs, '-vjəs Ⓤⓢ -vi.əs **-ly** -li **-ness** -nəs, -nɪs

prevision ˌpriː'vɪʒ.ᵊn, prɪ- Ⓤⓢ priː-

prevocalic ˌpriː.vəʊ'kæl.ɪk Ⓤⓢ -voʊ'- **-ally** -ᵊl.i, -li *stress shift:* ˌprevocalic 'consonant

Prevost 'prev.əʊ, 'prev.əʊst, prev'əʊ Ⓤⓢ 'preɪ.voʊ, 'prev.oʊ

pre-war ˌpriː'wɔːʳ Ⓤⓢ -'wɔːr *stress shift:* ˌpre-war 'politics

Prewett 'pruː.ɪt

prey preɪ **-s** -z **-ing** -ɪŋ **-ed** -d

Priam praɪəm, 'praɪ.æm

priapic praɪ'æp.ɪk, -'eɪ.pɪk

priapism 'praɪ.ə.pɪ.zᵊm

priapus (P) praɪ'eɪ.pəs; 'praɪ.ə.pəs **-es** -ɪz

pric|e (P) praɪs **-es** -ɪz **-ing** -ɪŋ **-ed** -t **'price ˌtag**; **'price ˌwar**

price-cutting 'praɪsˌkʌt.ɪŋ Ⓤⓢ -ˌkʌt̬-

priceless 'praɪ.sləs, -slɪs **-ness** -nəs, -nɪs

pric|ey 'praɪ.s|i **-ier** -i.əʳ Ⓤⓢ -i.ɚ **-iest** -i.ɪst, -i.əst **-ily** -ɪ.li, -ᵊl.i **-iness** -ɪ.nəs, -ɪ.nɪs

prick prɪk **-s** -s **-ing/s** -ɪŋ/z **-ed** -t **-er/s** -əʳ/z Ⓤⓢ -ɚ/z

prickl|e 'prɪk.l̩ **-es** -z **-ing** -ɪŋ, 'prɪk.lɪŋ **-ed** -d

prickl|y 'prɪk.l|i, -l̩|.i Ⓤⓢ '-li **-ier** -i.əʳ Ⓤⓢ -i.ɚ **-iest** -ɪ.ɪst, -i.əst **-iness** -ɪ.nəs, -ɪ.nɪs **ˌprickly 'pear**

pride (P) praɪd **ˌpride of 'place**

Prideaux 'prɪd.əʊ, 'priː.dəʊ Ⓤⓢ 'prɪd.oʊ

Pridham 'prɪd.əm

prie-dieu ˌpriː'djɜː, '-- Ⓤⓢ 'priː.djɜː **prie-dieus** ˌpriː'djɜːz, -'djɜː, '-- Ⓤⓢ 'priː.djɜːz

prie-dieux (*alternative plur. of* **prie-dieu**) ˌpriː'djɜːz, -'djɜː, '-- Ⓤⓢ 'priː.djɜːz

priest (P) priːst **-s** -s

priestess ˌpriː'stes; 'priː.stəs, -stɪs Ⓤⓢ 'priː.stɪs **-es** -ɪz

priesthood 'priːst.hʊd

Priestland 'priːst.lənd

Priestley 'priːst.li

priestl|y 'priːst.l|i **-iness** -ɪ.nəs, -ɪ.nɪs

prig prɪg **-s** -z **-gery** -ᵊr.i

priggish 'prɪg.ɪʃ **-ly** -li **-ness** -nəs, -nɪs

prim (P) prɪm **-mer** -əʳ Ⓤⓢ -ɚ **-mest** -ɪst, -əst **-ly** -li **-ness** -nəs, -nɪs **-s** -z **-ming** -ɪŋ **-med** -d

prima ballerina ˌpriː.mə.bæl.ᵊr'iː.nə Ⓤⓢ -ə'riː- **-s** -z

primac|y 'praɪ.mə.s|i **-ies** -iz

prima donna ˌpriː.mə'dɒn.ə Ⓤⓢ -'dɑː.nə, ˌprɪm.ə'- **-s** -z

primaeval ˌpraɪ'miː.vᵊl

prima facie ˌpraɪ.mə'feɪ.ʃi, -ʃiː, '-ʃi.iː, '-si, -siː, '-si.iː Ⓤⓢ '-ʃi.ː, '-ʃiː, -ʃə

primal 'praɪ.mᵊl **ˌprimal 'therapy**

primarily praɪ'mer.ᵊl.i, -'meə.rᵊl-, -ɪ.li; 'praɪ.mᵊr.ᵊl-, -ɪ.li Ⓤⓢ praɪ'mer.ᵊl.i, 'praɪ.mer-

primar|y 'praɪ.mᵊr|.i Ⓤⓢ -mer-, -mɚ- **-ies** -iz **-iness** -ɪ.nəs, -ɪ.nɪs **ˌprimary 'colour** Ⓤⓢ **'primary ˌcolor**; **'primary ˌschool**; **ˌprimary 'stress**

primate *archbishop:* ˈpraɪ.meɪt, -mɪt, -mət (US) -mɪt **-s** -s

primate *higher mammal:* ˈpraɪ.meɪt **-s** -s

primateship ˈpraɪ.mət.ʃɪp, -mɪt-, -meɪt- (US) -mɪt- **-s** -s

prim|e (P) praɪm **-es** -z **-ing** -ɪŋ **-ed** -d ˌ**prime ˈminister** ; ˌ**prime ˈmover** ; ˈ**prime ˌtime,** ˌ**prime ˈtime**

primer *thing that primes:* ˈpraɪ.məʳ (US) -mɚ **-s** -z *elementary school book:* ˈpraɪ.məʳ, ˈprɪm.əʳ (US) ˈprɪm.ɚ **-s** -z

primer *printing type:* ˈprɪm.əʳ (US) -ɚ

primeval praɪˈmiː.vᵊl

primipar|a praɪˈmɪp.ᵊr|.ə **-as** -əz **-ae** -iː

primiparous praɪˈmɪp.ᵊr.əs

primitive ˈprɪm.ɪ.tɪv, ˈ-ə- (US) -ɪ.t̬ɪv **-ly** -li **-ness** -nəs, -nɪs

primitiv|ism ˈprɪm.ɪ.tɪ.v|ɪ.zᵊm, ˈ-ə- (US) -ɪ.t̬ɪ- **-ist/s** -ɪst/s

primo ˈpriː.məʊ (US) -moʊ

primogenitor ˌpraɪ.məʊˈdʒen.ɪ.təʳ, ˌpriː-, ˈ-ə- (US) ˌpraɪ.moʊˈdʒen.ɪ.t̬ɚ, -məˈ- **-s** -z

primogeniture ˌpraɪ.məʊˈdʒen.ɪ.tʃəʳ, ˈ-ə-, -tʃʊəʳ, -tjʊəʳ (US) ˌpraɪ.moʊˈdʒen.ɪ.tʃɚ, -məˈ-

primordial praɪˈmɔː.di.əl (US) -ˈmɔːr- **-s** -z **-ly** -i

primp prɪmp **-s** -s **-ing** -ɪŋ **-ed** -t, prɪmt

primros|e (P) ˈprɪm.rəʊz (US) -roʊz **-es** -ɪz ˌ**primrose ˈpath**

primula ˈprɪm.jə.lə, -jʊ- **-s** -z

primum mobile ˌpraɪ.məmˈməʊ.bɪ.li, ˌpriː-, -mʊmˈ-, -bᵊl.i, -eɪ (US) ˌpraɪ.məmˈmoʊ.bᵊl.i, ˌpriː-, -eɪ **-s** -z

primus (P®) ˈpraɪ.məs **-es** -ɪz

princ|e (P) prɪnts **-es** -ɪz ˌ**prince ˈcharming** ; ˌ**prince ˈconsort;** ˌ**Prince ˈEdward ˌIsland** (US) ˌ**Prince ˌEdward ˈIsland;** ˌ**Prince of ˈWales;** ˌ**prince ˈregent**

princedom ˈprɪnts.dəm **-s** -z

princeling ˈprɪnts.lɪŋ **-s** -z

princel|y ˈprɪnts.l|i **-ier** -i.əʳ (US) -i.ɚ **-iest** -i.ɪst, -i.əst **-iness** -ɪ.nəs, -ɪ.nɪs

Princes Risborough ˌprɪnt.sɪzˈrɪz.bᵊr.ə (US) -bɚ.oʊ

princess (P) prɪnˈses, ˈprɪn.ses, -ɪs, -əs (US) ˈprɪnt.sɪs, -ses **-es** -ɪz ˌ**princess ˈroyal**

Princeton ˈprɪnt.stən

Princetown ˈprɪnts.taʊn

princip|al (P) ˈprɪnt.sə.p|ᵊl, -sɪ- (US) -sə- **-als** -ᵊlz **-ally** -ᵊl.i, -li **-alness** -ᵊl.nəs, -nɪs ˌ**principal ˈboy**

principalit|y ˌprɪnt.sɪˈpæl.ə.t|i, -səˈ-, -ɪ.t|i (US) -səˈpæl.ə.t̬|i **-ies** -iz

principalship ˈprɪnt.sə.pᵊl.ʃɪp, -sɪ- (US) -sə- **-s** -s

principate ˈprɪnt.sɪ.pət, -sə-, -pɪt, -peɪt (US) -sə.peɪt, -pɪt **-s** -s

Principia prɪnˈsɪp.i.ə

principle ˈprɪnt.sə.pl̩, -sɪ- (US) -sə- **-s** -z **-d** -d

Pring prɪŋ

Pringle ˈprɪŋ.gl̩

Prinknash ˈprɪn.ɪdʒ

Prinsep ˈprɪnt.sep

print prɪnt **-s** -s **-ing/s** -ɪn/z (US) ˈprɪn.t̬ɪŋ/z **-ed** -ɪd (US) ˈprɪn.t̬ɪd ˈ**print ˌrun** ; ˈ**printing ˌpress**

printable ˈprɪn.tə.bl̩ (US) -t̬ə-

printer ˈprɪn.təʳ (US) -t̬ɚ **-s** -z

printmak|ing ˈprɪntˌmeɪ.k|ɪŋ **-er/s** -əʳ/z (US) -ɚ/z

printout ˈprɪnt.aʊt **-s** -s

printwheel ˈprɪnt.*h*wiːl **-s** -z

prior (P) praɪəʳ (US) praɪɚ **-s** -z

prioress ˈpraɪə.rəs, -rɪs, -res; ˌpraɪəˈres (US) ˈpraɪɚ.ɪs **-es** -ɪz

prioritiz|e, -is|e praɪˈɒr.ɪ.taɪz, ˈ-ə- (US) -ˈɔːr.ə- **-es** -ɪz **-ing** -ɪŋ **-ed** -d

priorit|y praɪˈɒr.ə.t|i, -ɪ.t|i (US) -ˈɔːr.ə.t̬|i **-ies** -iz

prior|y ˈpraɪə.r|i **-ies** -iz

Priscian ˈprɪʃ.i.ən (US) ˈ-ən, -i.ən

Priscilla prɪˈsɪl.ə, prə- (US) prɪ-

pris|e praɪz **-es** -ɪz **-ing** -ɪŋ **-ed** -d

prism ˈprɪz.ᵊm **-s** -z

prismatic prɪzˈmæt.ɪk (US) -ˈmæt̬- **-al** -ᵊl **-ally** -ᵊl.i, -li

prison ˈprɪz.ᵊn **-s** -z ˈ**prison ˌcamp** ; ˌ**prison ˈvisitor**

prisoner ˈprɪz.ᵊn.əʳ, ˈ-nəʳ (US) ˈprɪz.ᵊn.ɚ, ˈ-nɚ **-s** -z ˌ**prisoner of ˈconscience** ; ˌ**prisoner of ˈwar**

priss|y ˈprɪs|.i **-ier** -i.əʳ (US) -i.ɚ **-iest** -i.ɪst, -i.əst **-ily** -ɪ.li, -ᵊl.i **-iness** -ɪ.nəs, -ɪ.nɪs

Pristina ˈprɪʃ.tɪ.nə

pristine ˈprɪs.tiːn, -taɪn (US) -tiːn; prɪˈstiːn

Pritchard ˈprɪtʃ.əd, -ɑːd (US) -ɚd

Pritchett ˈprɪtʃ.ɪt, -ət

prithee ˈprɪð.i, -iː

privacy ˈprɪv.ə.si, ˈpraɪ.və- (US) ˈpraɪ-

private ˈpraɪ.vɪt, -vət (US) -vət **-s** -s **-ly** -li **-ness** -nəs, -nɪs ˌ**private deˈtective** ; ˌ**private ˈenterprise;** ˌ**private ˈeye;** ˌ**private ˈmember's ˌbill;** ˌ**private ˈsector** (US) ˈ**private ˌsector;** ˌ**private ˈschool**

privateer ˌpraɪ.vəˈtɪəʳ, -vɪˈ- (US) -vəˈtɪr **-s** -z

privation praɪˈveɪ.ʃᵊn **-s** -z

privative ˈprɪv.ə.tɪv **-ly** -li

privatization, -isa- ˌpraɪ.vɪ.taɪˈzeɪ.ʃᵊn, -və-, -tɪˈ- (US) -və.tɪˈ- **-s** -z

privatiz|e, -is|e ˈpraɪ.vɪ.taɪz, -və- (US) -və- **-es** -ɪz **-ing** -ɪŋ **-ed** -d

privet ˈprɪv.ɪt **-s** -s ˈ**privet ˌhedge,** ˌ**privet ˈhedge**

privileg|e ˈprɪv.ᵊl.ɪdʒ, -ɪ.lɪdʒ (US) -ᵊl.ɪdʒ, ˈ-lɪdʒ **-es** -ɪz **-ed** -d

privity ˈprɪv.ə.ti, -ɪ.ti (US) -ə.t̬i

priv|y ˈprɪv|.i **-ies** -iz **-ily** -ɪ.li, -ᵊl.i ˌ**Privy ˈCouncil** ; ˌ**Privy ˈPurse** ; ˌ**Privy ˈSeal**

priz|e praɪz **-es** -ɪz **-ing** -ɪŋ **-ed** -d ˈ**prize ˌday**

prize|-fight ˈpraɪz|.faɪt **-fights** -faɪts **-fighter/s** -ˌfaɪ.təʳ/z (US) -ˌfaɪ.t̬ɚ/z

prizewinn|er ˈpraɪzˌwɪn|.əʳ (US) -ɚ **-ers** -əz (US) -ɚz **-ing** -ɪŋ

Prizren ˈprɪz.rɪn (US) ˈpriːz.rən

pro- prəʊ- (US) proʊ-, prə-

Note: Prefix. In words containing **pro-** where the stem is free and the meaning is **in favour of**, it generally takes secondary stress, e.g. **pro-choice** /ˌprəʊˈtʃɔɪs (US) ˌproʊ-/. Attached to bound stems, the pron is normally /prəʊ- (US) proʊ-, prə-/, e.g. **probation** /prəʊˈbeɪ.ʃᵊn (US) proʊ-/. There are exceptions; see individual entries.

PRO ˌpiː.ɑːˈrəʊ (US) -ɑːrˈoʊ

pro prəʊ (US) proʊ **-s** -z ˌ**pros and ˈcons**

proactive ˌprəʊˈæk.tɪv (US) ˌproʊ- **-ly** -li

pro-am ˌprəʊˈæm (US) ˌproʊ-

probabilistic ˌprɒb.ə.bᵊlˈɪs.tɪk, -bɪˈlɪs- (US) ˌprɑː.bə.bᵊlˈɪs-

probabilit|y ˌprɒb.əˈbɪl.ə.t|i, -ɪ.t|i (US) ˌprɑː.bəˈbɪl.ə.t̬|i **-ies** -iz

probab|le ˈprɒb.ə.b|l̩ (US) ˈprɑː.bə- **-ly** -li

proba|te ˈprəʊ.beɪ|t, -bɪt (US) ˈproʊ.beɪ|t **-tes** -ts **-ting** -tɪŋ (US) -t̬ɪŋ **-ted** -tɪd (US) -t̬ɪd

probation prəʊˈbeɪ.ʃᵊn (US) proʊ- **-s** -z proˈ**bation ˌofficer**

probationary prəʊˈbeɪ.ʃᵊn.ᵊr.i, -ˈbeɪʃ.nᵊr- (US) proʊˈbeɪ.ʃᵊn.er-

probationer prəʊˈbeɪ.ʃᵊn.əʳ, -ˈbeɪʃ.nəʳ (US) proʊˈbeɪ.ʃᵊn.ɚ, -ˈbeɪʃ.nɚ **-s** -z

probative ˈprəʊ.bə.tɪv (US) ˈproʊ.bə.t̬ɪv

prob|e prəʊb (US) proʊb **-es** -z **-ing** -ɪŋ **-ed** -d

Probert ˈprəʊ.bət, ˈprɒb.ət (US) ˈproʊ.bɚt, ˈprɑː.bɚt

probity ˈprəʊ.bə.ti, -ɪ.ti (US) ˈproʊ.bə.t̬i

problem ˈprɒb.ləm, -lem, -lɪm (US) ˈprɑː.bləm **-s** -z ˈ**problem ˌchild** ; ˈ**problem ˌpage**

problematic ˌprɒb.ləˈmæt.ɪk, -lɪˈ-, -lemˈæt- (US) ˌprɑː.bləˈmæt̬- **-al** -ᵊl **-ally** -ᵊl.i, -li *stress shift:* ˌproblematic ˈstate

pro bono ˌprəʊˈbəʊ.nəʊ (US) ˌproʊˈboʊ.noʊ

proboscis prəʊˈbɒs.ɪs (US) proʊˈbɑː.sɪs **-es** -iːz

Probus ˈprəʊ.bəs (US) ˈproʊ-

Probyn ˈprəʊ.bɪn (US) ˈproʊ-

procedural prəˈsiː.dʒər.əl, prəʊ-, -djʊ.rəl, -djər.əl US prəˈsiː.dʒɚ.əl, proʊ-
procedure prəʊˈsiː.dʒər, -djər US prəˈsiː.dʒɚ, proʊ- **-s** -z
proceed (*v.*) prəʊˈsiːd US proʊ-, prə- **-s** -z **-ing/s** -ɪŋ/z **-ed** -ɪd
proceeds (*n.*) ˈprəʊ.siːdz US ˈproʊ-
pro-celebrity ˌprəʊ.səˈleb.rɪ.ti, -sɪˈ-, -rə- US ˌproʊ.səˈleb.rə.t̬i *stress shift:* ˌpro-celebrity ˈgolf
proc|ess (*n.*) ˈprəʊ.s|es, -s|ɪs US ˈprɑː.s|es, -s|əs **-esses** -es.ɪz, -ɪ.sɪz US -es.ɪz, -ə.sɪz
process (*v.*) *go in a procession:* prəʊˈses US prə-, proʊ- **-es** -ɪz **-ing** -ɪŋ **-ed** -t
process (*v.*) *treat by a process:* ˈprəʊ.ses, -sɪs US ˈprɑː.ses, -səs **-es** -ɪz **-ing** -ɪŋ **-ed** -t **-or/s** -ər/z US -ɚ/z
procession prəˈseʃ.ən US prə-, proʊ- **-s** -z
processional prəˈseʃ.ən.əl US prə-, proʊ- **-s** -z
pro-choice ˌprəʊˈtʃɔɪs US ˌproʊ-
proclaim prəʊˈkleɪm US proʊ-, prə- **-s** -z **-ing** -ɪŋ **-ed** -d **-er/s** -ər/z US -ɚ/z
proclamation ˌprɒk.ləˈmeɪ.ʃən US ˌprɑː.kləˈ- **-s** -z
proclitic prəʊˈklɪt.ɪk US proʊˈklɪt̬- **-s** -s
proclivit|y prəʊˈklɪv.ə.t|i, -ɪ.t|i US proʊˈklɪv.ə.t̬|i **-ies** -iz
proconsul prəʊˈkɒnt.səl US proʊˈkɑːnt- **-s** -z
proconsul|ar prəʊˈkɒnt.sjə.l|ər, -sjʊ- US proʊˈkɑːnt.səl|.ɚ **-ate/s** -ət/s, -ɪt/s, -eɪt/s US -ɪt/s
proconsulship prəʊˈkɒnt.səl.ʃɪp US proʊˈkɑːnt- **-s** -s
procrasti|nate prəʊˈkræs.tɪ|.neɪt US proʊˈkræs.tə-, prə- **-nates** -neɪts **-nating** -neɪ.tɪŋ US -neɪ.t̬ɪŋ **-nated** -neɪ.tɪd US -neɪ.t̬ɪd **-nator/s** -neɪ.tər/z US -neɪ.t̬ɚ/z
procrastination prəʊˌkræs.tɪˈneɪ.ʃən US proʊˌkræs.təˈ-, prə- **-s** -z
procreant ˈprəʊ.kri.ənt US ˈproʊ-
procrea|te ˈprəʊ.kri.eɪ|t, ˌ--ˈ- US ˈproʊ.kri.eɪ|t **-tes** -ts **-ting** -tɪŋ US -t̬ɪŋ **-ted** -tɪd US -t̬ɪd
procreation ˌprəʊ.kriˈeɪ.ʃən US ˌproʊ-
procreative ˈprəʊ.kri.eɪ.tɪv, -ə-, ˌprəʊ.kriˈeɪ- US ˈproʊ.kri.eɪ.t̬ɪv
Procrust|es prəʊˈkrʌs.t|iːz US proʊ- **-ean** -i.ən
Procter ˈprɒk.tər US ˈprɑːk.tɚ
proctor (P) ˈprɒk.tər US ˈprɑːk.tɚ **-s** -z
proctorial prɒkˈtɔː.ri.əl US prɑːkˈtɔːr.i-
procumbent prəʊˈkʌm.bənt US proʊ-
procuration ˌprɒk.jʊəˈreɪ.ʃən, -jəˈ- US ˌprɑːk.juːˈ-, -jəˈ- **-s** -z
procurator ˈprɒk.jʊə.reɪ.tər, -jə- US ˈprɑː.kjə.reɪ.t̬ɚ, -kjʊ- **-s** -z
procurator-fiscal (PF) ˌprɒk.jʊə.reɪ.təˈfɪs.kəl, -jə- US ˌprɑː.kjə.reɪ.t̬ɚˈ-, -kjʊ- **-s** -z
procur|e prəˈkjʊər, -kjɔːr US proʊˈkjʊr, prə- **-es** -z **-ing** -ɪŋ **-ed** -d **-er/s** -ər/z US -ɚ/z **-able** -ə.bl̩
procurement prəˈkjʊə.mənt, -ˈkjɔː- US proʊˈkjʊr-, prə-
procuress prəˈkjʊə.res, -ˈkjɔː-, -rɪs; ˈprɒk.jə-, -jʊ- US proʊˈkjʊr.ɪs, prə- **-es** -ɪz
Procyon ˈprəʊ.si.ən US ˈproʊ.si.ɑːn
prod prɒd US prɑːd **-s** -z **-ding** -ɪŋ **-ded** -ɪd
prodigal ˈprɒd.ɪ.gəl US ˈprɑː.dɪ- **-s** -z **-ly** -i **-ness** -nəs, -nɪs ˌ**prodigal ˈson**
prodigality ˌprɒd.ɪˈgæl.ə.ti, -ɪ.ti US ˌprɑː.dɪˈgæl.ə.t̬i
prodigaliz|e, -is|e ˈprɒd.ɪ.gəl.aɪz US ˈprɑː.dɪ- **-es** -ɪz **-ing** -ɪŋ **-ed** -d
prodigious prəˈdɪdʒ.əs US prə-, proʊ- **-ly** -li **-ness** -nəs, -nɪs
prodig|y ˈprɒd.ɪ.dʒ|i, ˈ-ə- US ˈprɑː.də- **-ies** -iz
produce (*n.*) ˈprɒd.juːs, ˈprɒdʒ.uːs US ˈprɑː.duːs, ˈproʊ-, -djuːs
produc|e (*v.*) prəˈdjuːs, -ˈdʒuːs US -ˈduːs, proʊ-, -ˈdjuːs **-es** -ɪz **-ing** -ɪŋ **-ed** -t **-er/s** -ər/z US -ɚ/z
producible prəˈdjuː.sə.bl̩, -sɪ- US -ˈduː.sə-, proʊ-, -ˈdjuː-
product ˈprɒd.ʌkt, -əkt US ˈprɑː.dʌkt, -dəkt **-s** -s
production prəˈdʌk.ʃən US prə-, proʊ- **-s** -z **proˈduction ˌline**
productional prəˈdʌk.ʃən.əl US prə-, proʊ-
productive prəˈdʌk.tɪv US prə-, proʊ- **-ly** -li **-ness** -nəs, -nɪs
productivity ˌprɒd.ʌkˈtɪv.ə.ti, -əkˈ-, -ɪ.ti US ˌproʊ.dəkˈtɪv.ə.t̬i, ˌprɑː-; proʊˌdʌkˈ-, prə-
proem ˈprəʊ.em US ˈproʊ- **-s** -z
prof prɒf US prɑːf **-s** -s
profanation ˌprɒf.əˈneɪ.ʃən US ˌprɑː.fəˈ- **-s** -z
profan|e prəˈfeɪn US proʊ-, prə- **-est** -ɪst, -əst **-ely** -li **-eness** -nəs, -nɪs **-es** -z **-ing** -ɪŋ **-ed** -d **-er/s** -ər/z US -ɚ/z
profanit|y prəˈfæn.ə.t|i, -ɪ.t|i US proʊˈfæn.ə.t̬|i, prə- **-ies** -iz
profess prəˈfes US prə-, proʊ- **-es** -ɪz **-ing** -ɪŋ **-ed** -t **-edly** -ɪd.li
profession prəˈfeʃ.ən US prə-, proʊ- **-s** -z
professional prəˈfeʃ.ən.əl US prə-, proʊ- **-s** -z
professionalism prəˈfeʃ.ən.əl.ɪ.zəm US prə-, proʊ-
professionally prəˈfeʃ.ən.əl.i, ˈ-nəl.i US prə-, proʊ-
professor prəˈfes.ər US -ɚ, proʊ- **-s** -z
professorate prəˈfes.ər.ət, -eɪt US -ɚ.ət, proʊ- **-s** -s
professorial ˌprɒf.ɪˈsɔː.ri.əl, -əˈ-, -esˈɔː- US ˌproʊ.fəˈsɔːr.i-, ˌprɑː- **-ly** -i *stress shift:* ˌprofessorial ˈduties
professoriat(e) ˌprɒf.ɪˈsɔː.ri.ət, -əˈ-, -esˈɔː-, -ɪt US ˌproʊ.fəˈsɔːr.i.ət, ˌprɑː- **-s** -s
professorship prəˈfes.ə.ʃɪp US ˈ-ɚ-, proʊ- **-s** -s
proff|er ˈprɒf|.ər US ˈprɑː.f|ɚ **-ers** -əz US -ɚz **-ering** -ər.ɪŋ **-ered** -əd US -ɚd
proficiency prəˈfɪʃ.ənt.si US prə-, proʊ-
proficient prəˈfɪʃ.ənt US prə-, proʊ- **-ly** -li
profil|e ˈprəʊ.faɪl US ˈproʊ- **-es** -z **-ing** -ɪŋ **-ed** -d
prof|it (*n. v.*) ˈprɒf|.ɪt US ˈprɑː.f|ɪt **-its** -ɪts **-iting** -ɪ.tɪŋ US -ɪ.t̬ɪŋ **-ited** -ɪ.tɪd US -ɪ.t̬ɪd ˌ**profit and ˈloss** ; ˈ**profit ˌmargin**
profitability ˌprɒf.ɪ.təˈbɪl.ɪ.ti, ˌ-ə-, -ə.ti US ˌprɑː.fɪ.t̬əˈbɪl.ə.t̬i
profitab|le ˈprɒf.ɪ.tə.b|l̩, ˈ-ə- US ˈprɑː.fɪ.t̬ə- **-ly** -li **-leness** -l̩.nəs, -nɪs
profiteer ˌprɒf.ɪˈtɪər, -əˈ- US ˌprɑː.fɪˈtɪr **-s** -z **-ing** -ɪŋ **-ed** -d
profiterole prɒfˈɪt.ər.əʊl, prəˈfɪt-; ˈprɒf.ɪ.tər-, ˌprɒf.ɪ.tərˈəʊl US prəˈfɪt.ə.roʊl **-s** -z
profitless ˈprɒf.ɪt.ləs, -lɪs US ˈprɑː.fɪt-
profitmaking ˈprɒf.ɪtˌmeɪ.kɪŋ US ˈprɑː.fɪt-
profit-sharing ˈprɒf.ɪtˌʃeə.rɪŋ US ˈprɑː.fɪtˌʃer.ɪŋ
profligacy ˈprɒf.lɪ.gə.si US ˈprɑː.flɪ-
profligate ˈprɒf.lɪ.gət, -gɪt US ˈprɑː.flɪ.gɪt **-s** -s **-ly** -li **-ness** -nəs, -nɪs
pro forma ˌprəʊˈfɔː.mə US ˌproʊˈfɔːr-
profound prəˈfaʊnd US prə-, proʊ- **-er** -ər US -ɚ **-est** -ɪst, -əst **-ly** -li **-ness** -nəs, -nɪs
Profumo prəˈfjuː.məʊ US -moʊ
profundit|y prəˈfʌn.də.t|i, -ɪ.t|i US proʊ-, prə- **-ies** -iz
profus|e prəˈfjuːs US prə-, proʊ- **-est** -ɪst, -əst **-ely** -li **-eness** -nəs, -nɪs
profusion prəˈfjuː.ʒən US prə-, proʊ- **-s** -z
prog prɒg US prɑːg, prɔːg **-s** -z **-ging** -ɪŋ **-ged** -d
progenitor prəʊˈdʒen.ɪ.tər, ˈ-ə- US proʊˈdʒen.ə.t̬ɚ, prə- **-s** -z
progeniture prəʊˈdʒen.ɪ.tʃər, ˈ-ə-, -tjʊər, -tjər US proʊˈdʒen.ə.tʃɚ, prə-

progen|y 'prɒdʒ.ə.n|i, '-ɪ- ⓊⓈ 'prɑː.dʒə- **-ies** -iz
progesterone prəʊ'dʒes.tᵊr.əʊn ⓊⓈ proʊ'dʒes.tə.roʊn
progestogen prəʊ'dʒes.tə.dʒɪn, -dʒən ⓊⓈ proʊ'dʒes.tə.dʒən, -dʒen **-s** -z
prognathic prɒg'næθ.ɪk ⓊⓈ prɑːg-, -'neɪ.θɪk
prognathism 'prɒg.nə.θɪ.zᵊm; prɒg'næθ.ɪ- ⓊⓈ 'prɑːg.nə.θɪ-; prɑːg'neɪ-
prognathous prɒg'neɪ.θəs; 'prɒg.nə.θəs ⓊⓈ 'prɑːg.nə-; prɑːg'neɪ-
prognos|is prɒg'nəʊ.s|ɪs ⓊⓈ prɑːg'noʊ- **-es** -iːz
prognostic prɒg'nɒs.tɪk, prəg- ⓊⓈ prɑːg'nɑː.stɪk
prognosti|cate prɒg'nɒs.tɪ|.keɪt, prəg- ⓊⓈ prɑːg'nɑː.stɪ- **-cates** -keɪts **-cating** -keɪ.tɪŋ ⓊⓈ -keɪ.t̬ɪŋ **-cated** -keɪ.tɪd ⓊⓈ -keɪ.t̬ɪd **-cator/s** -keɪ.təʳ/z ⓊⓈ -keɪ.t̬ɚ/z
prognostication prəg,nɒs.tɪ'keɪ.ʃᵊn, prɒg- ⓊⓈ prɑːg,nɑː.stɪ'- **-s** -z
program 'prəʊ.græm ⓊⓈ 'proʊ-, -grəm **-s** -z **-ing** -ɪŋ **-ed** -d **-er/s** -əʳ/z ⓊⓈ -ɚ/z
programmable prəʊ'græm.ə.bl̩; 'prəʊ.græm- ⓊⓈ 'proʊ.græm.ə-, -grə.mə-
programmatic ,prəʊ.grə'mæt.ɪk ⓊⓈ ,proʊ.grə'mæt̬-
programm|e 'prəʊ.græm ⓊⓈ 'proʊ-, -grəm **-es** -z **-ing** -ɪŋ **-ed** -d **-er/s** -əʳ/z ⓊⓈ -ɚ/z
progress (*n.*) 'prəʊ.gres ⓊⓈ 'prɑː- **'progress re,port**
progress (*v.*) prəʊ'gres ⓊⓈ prə-, proʊ- **-es** -ɪz **-ing** -ɪŋ **-ed** -t
progression prəʊ'greʃ.ᵊn ⓊⓈ prə-, proʊ- **-s** -z
progressional prəʊ'greʃ.ᵊn.ᵊl, '-nᵊl ⓊⓈ prə-, proʊ-
progressionist prəʊ'greʃ.ᵊn.ɪst ⓊⓈ prə-, proʊ- **-s** -s
progressist prəʊ'gres.ɪst ⓊⓈ 'prɑː.gres-, 'proʊ-; prə'gres- **-s** -s
progressive prəʊ'gres.ɪv ⓊⓈ prə-, proʊ- **-s** -z **-ly** -li **-ness** -nəs, -nɪs
progressiv|ism prəʊ'gres.ɪ.v|ɪ.zᵊm ⓊⓈ prə-, proʊ- **-ist/s** -ɪst/s
prohib|it prəʊ'hɪb|.ɪt ⓊⓈ proʊ-, prə- **-its** -ɪts **-iting** -ɪ.tɪŋ ⓊⓈ -ɪ.t̬ɪŋ **-ited** -ɪ.tɪd ⓊⓈ -ɪ.t̬ɪd
prohibition (P) ,prəʊ.*h*ɪ'bɪʃ.ᵊn ⓊⓈ ,proʊ- **-s** -z
prohibition|ism ,prəʊ.*h*ɪ'bɪʃ.ᵊn|.ɪ.zᵊm ⓊⓈ ,proʊ- **-ist/s** -ɪst/s
prohibitive prəʊ'hɪb.ə.tɪv ⓊⓈ proʊ'hɪb.ə.t̬ɪv, prə- **-ly** -li
prohibitory prəʊ'hɪb.ɪ.tᵊr.i ⓊⓈ proʊ'hɪb.ə.tɔːr-, prə-
project (*n.*) 'prɒdʒ.ekt, -ɪkt ⓊⓈ 'prɑː.dʒekt, -dʒɪkt **-s** -s
project (*v.*) prəʊ'dʒekt ⓊⓈ prə-, proʊ- **-s** -s **-ing** -ɪŋ **-ed** -ɪd
projectile prəʊ'dʒek.taɪl ⓊⓈ prə'dʒek.tᵊl, proʊ- **-s** -z
projection prəʊ'dʒek.ʃᵊn ⓊⓈ prə-, proʊ- **-s** -z **-ist/s** -ɪst/s
projective prəʊ'dʒek.tɪv ⓊⓈ prə-, proʊ- **-ly** -li
projector prəʊ'dʒek.təʳ ⓊⓈ prə'dʒek.tɚ, proʊ- **-s** -z
Prokofiev prə'kɒf.i.ef ⓊⓈ proʊ'kɔː.fi.ef, prə-, -'koʊ-
prolactin prəʊ'læk.tɪn ⓊⓈ proʊ-
prolaps|e 'prəʊ.læps, -'- ⓊⓈ 'proʊ- **-es** -ɪz **-ing** -ɪŋ **-ed** -t
prolate 'prəʊ.leɪt, ,-'- ⓊⓈ 'proʊ.leɪt
prole prəʊl ⓊⓈ proʊl **-s** -z
prolegomen|on ,prəʊ.lɪ'gɒm.ɪ.n|ən, -lə'-, -leg'ɒm-, '-ə-, -ɒn ⓊⓈ ,proʊ.lɪ'gɑː.mə.n|ɑːn, -n|ən **-a** -ə
proleps|is prəʊ'lep.s|ɪs, -'liːp- ⓊⓈ proʊ'lep- **-es** -iːz
proleptic prəʊ'lep.tɪk, -'liːp- ⓊⓈ proʊ'lep- **-ally** -ᵊl.i, -li
proletarian ,prəʊ.lɪ'teə.ri.ən, -lə'-, -let'eə- ⓊⓈ ,proʊ.lə'ter.i-, -'tær- **-s** -z **-ism** -ɪ.zᵊm
proletariat ,prəʊ.lɪ'teə.ri.ət, -lə'-, -let'eə-, -æt ⓊⓈ ,proʊ.lə'ter.i.ət, -'tær-
pro-life ,prəʊ'laɪf ⓊⓈ ,proʊ-
prolifer|ate prəʊ'lɪf.ᵊr|.eɪt ⓊⓈ proʊ'lɪf.ə.r|eɪt, prə- **-ates** -eɪts **-ating** -eɪ.tɪŋ ⓊⓈ -eɪ.t̬ɪŋ **-ated** -eɪ.tɪd ⓊⓈ -eɪ.t̬ɪd
proliferation prəʊ,lɪf.ᵊr'eɪ.ʃᵊn ⓊⓈ proʊ,lɪf.ə'reɪ-, prə- **-s** -z
prolific prəʊ'lɪf.ɪk ⓊⓈ proʊ-, prə- **-ally** -ᵊl.i, -li **-ness** -nəs, -nɪs
prolix 'prəʊ.lɪks ⓊⓈ proʊ'lɪks, '--
prolixity prəʊ'lɪk.sə-, -sɪ- ⓊⓈ proʊ'lɪk.sə.t̬i, prə-
prolix|ly prəʊ'lɪk.s|li, '--- ⓊⓈ proʊ'lɪk.s|li, prə- **-ness** -nəs, -nɪs
prolocutor prəʊ'lɒk.jə.təʳ, -jʊ- ⓊⓈ proʊ'lɑː.kjə.t̬ɚ, -kjʊ- **-s** -z
prolog, PROLOG 'prəʊ.lɒg ⓊⓈ 'proʊ.lɑːg, -lɔːg **-s** -z
prologu|e 'prəʊ.lɒg ⓊⓈ 'proʊ.lɑːg, -lɔːg **-es** -z **-ing** -ɪŋ **-ed** -d
prolong prəʊ'lɒŋ ⓊⓈ proʊ'lɑːŋ, prə-, -'lɔːŋ **-s** -z **-ing** -ɪŋ **-ed** -d
prolongation ,prəʊ.lɒŋ'geɪ.ʃᵊn, ,prɒl.ɒŋ'- ⓊⓈ ,proʊ.lɑːŋ'-, -lɔːŋ'- **-s** -z
prom (P) prɒm ⓊⓈ prɑːm **-s** -z
promenad|e ,prɒm.ə'nɑːd, -ɪ'- ⓊⓈ ,prɑː.mə'neɪd, -'nɑːd **-es** -z **-ing** -ɪŋ **-ed** -ɪd **-er/s** -əʳ/z ⓊⓈ -ɚ/z *stress shift:* ,promenade 'concert
Note: A British pronunciation /,prɒm.ə'neɪd, -ɪ'-/ also exists, used chiefly in square dancing.
Promethean prəʊ'miː.θi.ən ⓊⓈ proʊ-, prə-
Prometheus prəʊ'miː.θi.uːs, -əs ⓊⓈ proʊ'miː.θi.əs, prə-, -uːs
promethium prəʊ'miː.θi.əm ⓊⓈ proʊ-
prominenc|e 'prɒm.ɪ.nənts, '-ə- ⓊⓈ 'prɑː.mə- **-es** -ɪz
prominent 'prɒm.ɪ.nənt, '-ə- ⓊⓈ 'prɑː.mə- **-ly** -li
promiscuity ,prɒm.ɪ'skjuː.ə.ti, -ə'-, -ɪ.ti ⓊⓈ ,prɑː.mɪ'skjuː.ə.t̬i, ,proʊ-
promiscuous prə'mɪs.kju.əs, prɒm'ɪs- ⓊⓈ prə'mɪs-, proʊ- **-ly** -li **-ness** -nəs, -nɪs
promis|e 'prɒm.ɪs ⓊⓈ 'prɑː.mɪs **-es** -ɪz **-ing/ly** -ɪŋ/li **-ed** -t **,promised 'land** ⓊⓈ **'promised ,land**
promissory 'prɒm.ɪ.sᵊr.i; prə'mɪs.ᵊr- ⓊⓈ 'prɑː.mɪ.sɔːr- **,promissory 'note** ⓊⓈ **'promissory ,note**
promo 'prəʊ.məʊ ⓊⓈ 'proʊ.moʊ **-s** -z
promontor|y 'prɒm.ən.tᵊr|.i ⓊⓈ 'prɑː.mən.tɔːr- **-ies** -iz
pro|mote prə|'məʊt ⓊⓈ -'moʊt **-motes** -'məʊts ⓊⓈ -'moʊts **-moting** -'məʊ.tɪŋ ⓊⓈ -'moʊ.t̬ɪŋ **-moted** -'məʊ.tɪd ⓊⓈ -'moʊ.t̬ɪd **-moter/s** -'məʊ.təʳ/z ⓊⓈ -'moʊ.t̬ɚ/z
promotion prə'məʊ.ʃᵊn ⓊⓈ -'moʊ-, proʊ- **-s** -z
promotional prə'məʊ.ʃᵊn.ᵊl ⓊⓈ -'moʊ-, proʊ- **-ly** -i
promotive prə'məʊ.tɪv ⓊⓈ -'moʊ.t̬ɪv, proʊ-
prompt prɒm*p*t ⓊⓈ prɑːm*p*t **-s** -s **-est** -ɪst, -əst **-ly** -li **-ness** -nəs, -nɪs **-ing/s** -ɪŋ/z **-ed** -ɪd **-er/s** -əʳ/z ⓊⓈ -ɚ/z
promptitude 'prɒm*p*.tɪ.tjuːd ⓊⓈ 'prɑːm*p*.tɪ.tuːd
promul|gate 'prɒm.ᵊl|.geɪt, -ʌl- ⓊⓈ 'prɑː.mᵊl-; proʊ'mʌl- **-gates** -geɪts **-gating** -geɪ.tɪŋ ⓊⓈ -geɪ.t̬ɪŋ **-gated** -geɪ.tɪd ⓊⓈ -geɪ.t̬ɪd **-gator/s** -geɪ.təʳ/z ⓊⓈ -geɪ.t̬ɚ/z
promulgation ,prɒm.ᵊl'geɪ.ʃᵊn, -ʌl'- ⓊⓈ ,prɑː.məl'- **-s** -z
prone prəʊn ⓊⓈ proʊn **-ly** -li **-ness** -nəs, -nɪs
prong prɒŋ ⓊⓈ prɑːŋ, prɔːŋ **-s** -z **-ing** -ɪŋ **-ed** -d
pronghorn 'prɒŋ.hɔːn ⓊⓈ 'prɑːŋ.hɔːrn, 'prɔːŋ- **-s** -z
pronominal prəʊ'nɒm.ɪ.nᵊl, -ᵊn.ᵊl ⓊⓈ proʊ'nɑː.mə- **-ly** -i
pronominalization prəʊ,nɒm.ɪ.nᵊl.aɪ'zeɪ.ʃᵊn, -ᵊn.ᵊl-, -ɪ'- ⓊⓈ proʊ,nɑː.mɪ.nᵊl.ɪ'- **-s** -z

pronominaliz|e, -is|e prəʊˈnɒm.ɪ.nəl.aɪz, -ən.əl- (US) proʊˈnɑː.mɪ.nəl- **-es** -ɪz **-ing** -ɪŋ **-ed** -d
pronoun ˈprəʊ.naʊn (US) ˈproʊ- **-s** -z
pronounc|e prəˈnaʊnts (US) prə-, proʊ- **-es** -ɪz **-ing** -ɪŋ **-ed** -t **-edly** -t.li, -ɪd.li **-er/s** -əʳ/z (US) -ɚ/z **-eable/ness** -ə.bl̩/nəs, -nɪs
pronouncement prəʊˈnaʊnt.smənt (US) prə-, proʊ- **-s** -s
pronto ˈprɒn.təʊ (US) ˈprɑːn.t̬oʊ
pronunciamento prəʊˌnʌnt.si.əˈmen.təʊ, -ʃi- (US) proʊˌnʌnt.si.əˈmen.toʊ, prə- **-(e)s** -z
pronunciation prəˌnʌnt.siˈeɪ.ʃən (US) prə-, proʊ- **-s** -z
proof pruːf **-s** -s
proofread ˈpruːf.riːd **-s** -z **-ing** -ɪŋ **-er/s** -əʳ/z (US) -ɚ/z *past tense:* ˈpruːf.red
Proops pruːps
prop prɒp (US) prɑːp **-s** -s **-ping** -ɪŋ **-ped** -t
propaedeutic ˌprəʊ.piːˈdjuː.tɪk (US) ˌproʊ.pɪˈduː.t̬ɪk, -ˈdjuː- **-al** -əl **-s** -s
propaganda ˌprɒp.əˈgæn.də (US) ˌprɑː.pəˈ-
propagand|ism ˌprɒp.əˈgæn.d|ɪ.zəm (US) ˌprɑː.pəˈ- **-ist/s** -ɪst/s
propa|gate ˈprɒp.ə|.geɪt (US) ˈprɑː.pə- **-gates** -geɪts **-gating** -geɪ.tɪŋ (US) -geɪ.t̬ɪŋ **-gated** -geɪ.tɪd (US) -geɪ.t̬ɪd **-gator/s** -geɪ.təʳ/z (US) -geɪ.t̬ɚ/z
propagation ˌprɒp.əˈgeɪ.ʃən (US) ˌprɑː.pəˈ-
propane ˈprəʊ.peɪn (US) ˈproʊ-
proparoxytone ˌprəʊ.pəʳˈɒk.sɪ.təʊn, -pærˈ-, ˈ-ə-, -tən (US) ˌproʊ.pəˈrɑːk.sɪ.toʊn, -pærˈ- **-s** -z
propel prəˈpel **-s** -z **-ling** -ɪŋ **-led** -d **proˌpelling ˈpencil**
propellant, propellent prəˈpel.ənt **-s** -s
propeller, propellor prəˈpel.əʳ (US) -ɚ **-s** -z
propene ˈprəʊ.piːn (US) ˈproʊ-
propensit|y prəʊˈpent.sə.t|i, -ɪ.t|i (US) prəˈpent.sə.t̬|i, proʊ- **-ies** -iz
proper ˈprɒp.əʳ (US) ˈprɑː.pɚ **ˌproper ˈnoun**
properly ˈprɒp.əl.i, ˈ-li (US) ˈprɑː.pɚ.li
Propertius prəʊˈpɜː.ʃəs, -ʃi.əs (US) proʊˈpɝː-
propert|y ˈprɒp.ə.t|i (US) ˈprɑː.pɚ.t̬|i **-ies** -iz **-ied** -id
prophec|y (*n.*) ˈprɒf.ə.s|i, ˈ-ɪ- (US) ˈprɑː.fə- **-ies** -iz
prophes|y (*v.*) ˈprɒf.ə.s|aɪ, ˈ-ɪ- (US) ˈprɑː.fə- **-ies** -aɪz **-ying** -aɪ.ɪŋ **-ied** -aɪd **-ier/s** -aɪ.əʳ/z (US) -aɪ.ɚ/z
prophet ˈprɒf.ɪt (US) ˈprɑː.fɪt **-s** -s
prophetess ˌprɒf.ɪˈtes; ˈprɒf.ɪ.tɪs, -tes (US) ˈprɑː.fɪ.t̬əs **-es** -ɪz
prophetic prəʊˈfet.ɪk (US) prə-, proʊ- **-al** -əl **-ally** -əl.i, -li
prophylactic ˌprɒf.ɪˈlæk.tɪk, -əˈ- (US) ˌproʊ.fəˈ-, ˌprɑː- **-s** -s **-ally** -əl.i, -li *stress shift:* ˌprophylactic ˈmedicine
prophylax|is ˌprɒf.ɪˈlæk.s|ɪs, -əˈ- (US) ˌproʊ.fəˈ-, ˌprɑː- **-es** -iːz
propinquity prəʊˈpɪŋ.kwə.ti, prɒpˈɪŋ-, -kwɪ- (US) proʊˈpɪŋ.kwə.t̬i, -ˈpɪn-
propiti|ate prəˈpɪʃ.i|.eɪt (US) proʊ-, prə- **-ates** -eɪts **-ating** -eɪ.tɪŋ (US) -eɪ.t̬ɪŋ **-ated** -eɪ.tɪd (US) -eɪ.t̬ɪd **-ator/s** -eɪ.təʳ/z (US) -eɪ.t̬ɚ/z
propitiation prəˌpɪʃ.iˈeɪ.ʃən (US) proʊ-, prə- **-s** -z
propitiatory prəˈpɪʃ.i.ə.tər.i, -ˈpɪʃ.ə-, -eɪ.tər-; prəʊˌpɪʃ.iˈeɪ- (US) proʊˈpɪʃ.i.ə.tɔːr-, prə-
propitious prəˈpɪʃ.əs (US) prə-, proʊ- **-ly** -li **-ness** -nəs, -nɪs
propjet ˈprɒp.dʒet (US) ˈprɑːp- **-s** -s
Pro-Plus® ˌprəʊˈplʌs (US) ˌproʊ-
proponent prəʊˈpəʊ.nənt (US) prəˈpoʊ-, proʊ- **-s** -s
proportion prəˈpɔː.ʃən (US) -ˈpɔːr- **-s** -z **-ing** -ɪŋ **-ed** -d
proportionab|le prəˈpɔː.ʃən.ə.b|l̩ (US) -ˈpɔːr- **-ly** -li **-leness** -l̩.nəs, -nɪs
proportional prəˈpɔː.ʃən.əl, -ˈpɔːʃ.nəl (US) -ˈpɔːr.ʃən.əl, -ˈpɔːrʃ.nəl **-ly** -i **proˌportional ˌrepresenˈtation**
proportionality prəˌpɔː.ʃənˈæl.ə.ti, -ɪ.ti (US) -ˌpɔːr.ʃənˈæl.ə.t̬i
proportionate prəˈpɔː.ʃən.ət, -ˈpɔːʃ.nət, -nɪt (US) -ˈpɔːr.ʃən.ɪt, -ˈpɔːrʃ.nɪt **-ly** -li **-ness** -nəs, -nɪs
proposal prəˈpəʊ.zəl (US) -ˈpoʊ- **-s** -z
propos|e prəˈpəʊz (US) -ˈpoʊz **-es** -ɪz **-ing** -ɪŋ **-ed** -d **-er/s** -əʳ/z (US) -ɚ/z
proposition ˌprɒp.əˈzɪʃ.ən (US) ˌprɑː.pəˈ- **-s** -z
propound prəˈpaʊnd (US) prə-, proʊ- **-s** -z **-ing** -ɪŋ **-ed** -ɪd **-er/s** -əʳ/z (US) -ɚ/z
propranolol prəʊˈpræn.ə.lɒl (US) proʊˈpræn.oʊ.lɔːl, ˈ-ə-, -loʊl
proprietary prəˈpraɪə.tər.i (US) -ter-
proprietor prəˈpraɪə.təʳ (US) proʊˈpraɪə.t̬ɚ, prə- **-s** -z **-ship/s** -ʃɪp/s
proprietorial prəˌpraɪəˈtɔː.ri.əl (US) -ˈtɔːr.i-, proʊ- **-ly** -i
proprietress prəˈpraɪə.trɪs, -tres (US) proʊ-, -trɪs, -trəs **-es** -ɪz
propriet|y prəˈpraɪə.t|i (US) -t̬|i, proʊ- **-ies** -iz
propriocep|tion ˌprəʊ.pri.əʊˈsep|.ʃən, ˌprɒp.ri- (US) ˌproʊ.pri.oʊˈ-, -əˈ- **-tive** -tɪv
propul|sion prəˈpʌl|.ʃən (US) prə-, proʊ- **-sive** -sɪv
propylae|um (P) ˌprɒp.ɪˈliː|.əm, -əˈ- (US) ˌprɑː.pəˈ- **-a** -ə
propylene ˈprɒp.ɪ.liːn, ˈ-ə- (US) ˈproʊ.pə-
pro rata ˌprəʊˈrɑː.tə, -ˈreɪ- (US) ˌproʊˈreɪ.t̬ə, -ˈrɑː-
prorogation ˌprəʊ.rəʊˈgeɪ.ʃən, ˌprɒr.əʊˈ- (US) ˌproʊ.roʊˈ- **-s** -z
prorogu|e prəʊˈrəʊg (US) proʊˈroʊg **-es** -z **-ing** -ɪŋ **-ed** -d
prosaic prəʊˈzeɪ.ɪk (US) proʊ- **-al** -əl **-ally** -əl.i, -li **-ness** -nəs, -nɪs
prosceni|um prəʊˈsiː.ni|.əm (US) proʊ- **-ums** -əmz **-a** -ə **proˌscenium ˈarch**
prosciutto prəʊˈʃuː.təʊ (US) proʊˈʃuː.t̬oʊ
proscrib|e prəʊˈskraɪb (US) proʊ- **-es** -z **-ing** -ɪŋ **-ed** -d **-er/s** -əʳ/z (US) -ɚ/z
proscription prəʊˈskrɪp.ʃən (US) proʊ- **-s** -z
proscriptive prəʊˈskrɪp.tɪv (US) proʊ-
pro se ˌprəʊˈseɪ (US) ˌproʊ-
pros|e prəʊz (US) proʊz **-es** -ɪz **-ing** -ɪŋ **-ed** -d **-er/s** -əʳ/z (US) -ɚ/z
prose|cute ˈprɒs.ɪ|.kjuːt, ˈ-ə- (US) ˈprɑː.sɪ- **-cutes** -kjuːts **-cuting** -kjuː.tɪŋ (US) -kjuː.t̬ɪŋ **-cuted** -kjuː.tɪd (US) -kjuː.t̬ɪd **ˌprosecuting atˈtorney**
prosecution ˌprɒs.ɪˈkjuː.ʃən, -əˈ- (US) ˌprɑː.sɪˈ- **-s** -z *stress shift:* ˌprosecution ˈwitness
prosecutor ˈprɒs.ɪ.kjuː.təʳ, ˈ-ə- (US) ˈprɑː.sɪ.kjuː.t̬ɚ **-s** -z
prosecutorial ˌprɒs.ɪ.kjuːˈtɔː.ri.əl (US) ˌprɑː.sɪ.kjuːˈtɔːr.i-
prosecutrix ˈprɒs.ɪ.kjuː.trɪks, ˈ-ə-; ˌprɒs.ɪˈkjuː-, -əˈ- (US) ˈprɑː.sɪ.kjuː-, ˌprɑː.sɪˈkjuː- **-es** -ɪz
proselyte ˈprɒs.ə.laɪt, ˈ-ɪ- (US) ˈprɑː.sə- **-s** -s
proselytism ˈprɒs.əl.ɪ.tɪ.zəm, -ɪ.lɪ-, -lə- (US) ˈprɑː.sə.lɪ-, -laɪ-
proselytiz|e, -is|e ˈprɒs.əl.ɪ.taɪz, -ɪ.lɪ-, -lə- (US) ˈprɑː.sə.lɪ- **-es** -ɪz **-ing** -ɪŋ **-ed** -d
Proserpina prəˈsɜː.pɪ.nə, prɒsˈɜː- (US) proʊˈsɝːr-
Proserpine ˈprɒs.ə.paɪn (US) ˈprɑː.sɚ-; proʊˈsɝːr.pɪ.niː
prosit ˈprəʊ.zɪt, -sɪt; prəʊst (US) ˈproʊ.sɪt, -zɪt; proʊst
prosodic prəˈsɒd.ɪk (US) proʊˈsɑː.dɪk, prə- **-al** -əl **-ally** -əl.i, -li
prosodist ˈprɒs.ə.dɪst, ˈprɒz- (US) ˈprɑː.sə-, -zə- **-s** -s
prosod|y ˈprɒs.ə.d|i, ˈprɒz- (US) ˈprɑː.sə-, -zə- **-ies** -iz

prospect (**P**) (*n.*) ˈprɒs.pekt ⓤⓢ ˈprɑː.spekt **-s** -s
prospect (*v.*) prəˈspekt, prɒsˈpekt; ˈprɒs.pekt ⓤⓢ ˈprɑː.spekt **-s** -s **-ing** -ɪŋ **-ed** -ɪd
prospective prəˈspek.tɪv, prɒsˈpek- ⓤⓢ prəˈspek-, proʊ-, prɑː- **-ly** -li **-ness** -nəs, -nɪs
prospector prəˈspek.təʳ, prɒsˈpek- ⓤⓢ ˈprɑː.spek.tɚ **-s** -z
prospectus prəˈspek.təs ⓤⓢ prə-, proʊ-, prɑː- **-es** -ɪz
prosp|er ˈprɒs.p|əʳ ⓤⓢ ˈprɑː.sp|ɚ **-ers** -əz ⓤⓢ -ɚz **-ering** -ᵊr.ɪŋ **-ered** -əd ⓤⓢ -ɚd
prosperity prɒsˈper.ə.ti, prəˈsper-, -ɪ.ti ⓤⓢ prɑːˈsper.ə.t̬i
Prospero ˈprɒs.pᵊr.əʊ ⓤⓢ ˈprɑː.spə.roʊ
prosperous ˈprɒs.pᵊr.əs ⓤⓢ ˈprɑː.spɚ- **-ly** -li **-ness** -nəs, -nɪs
Prosser ˈprɒs.əʳ ⓤⓢ ˈprɑː.sɚ
prostaglandin ˌprɒs.təˈglæn.dɪn ⓤⓢ ˌprɑː.stəˈ- **-s** -z
prostate ˈprɒs.teɪt ⓤⓢ ˈprɑː.steɪt **-s** -s **ˈprostate ˌgland**
prostatic prɒsˈtæt.ɪk, prəˈstæt- ⓤⓢ proʊˈstæt̬.ɪk, prɑː-
prosthes|is *grammatical term:* ˈprɒs.θɪ.s|ɪs, -θə-; ˈprɑːs.θə- **-es** -iːz *medical term:* ˈprɒs.θə.s|ɪs, -θɪ-; prɒsˈθiː- ⓤⓢ ˈprɑːs.θə.s|ɪs; prɑːsˈθiː- **-es** -iːz
prosthetic prɒsˈθet.ɪk ⓤⓢ prɑːsˈθet̬- **-s** -s
prosthetist prɒsˈθiː.tɪst, prəs- ⓤⓢ ˈprɑːs.θɪ.tɪst **-s** -s
prostitu|te ˈprɒs.tɪ.tjuː|t, -tə-, -tʃuː|t ⓤⓢ ˈprɑː.stə.tuː|t, -tjuː|t **-tes** -ts **-ting** -tɪŋ ⓤⓢ -t̬ɪŋ **-ted** -tɪd ⓤⓢ -t̬ɪd
prostitution ˌprɒs.tɪˈtjuː.ʃᵊn, -təˈ-, -ˈtʃuː.ʃᵊn ⓤⓢ -ˈtʃuː-, ˌprɑː.stəˈtuː- **-s** -z
prostrate (*adj.*) ˈprɒs.treɪt, -ˈ- ⓤⓢ ˈprɑː.streɪt
prostra|te (*v.*) prɒsˈtreɪ|t, prəˈstreɪ|t ⓤⓢ ˈprɑː.streɪ|t **-tes** -ts **-ting** -tɪŋ ⓤⓢ -t̬ɪŋ **-ted** -tɪd ⓤⓢ -t̬ɪd
prostration prɒsˈtreɪ.ʃᵊn, prəˈstreɪ- ⓤⓢ prɑːˈstreɪ- **-s** -z
pros|y ˈprəʊ.z|i ⓤⓢ ˈproʊ- **-ier** -i.əʳ ⓤⓢ -i.ɚ **-iest** -i.ɪst, -i.əst **-ily** -ɪ.li, -ᵊl.i **-iness** -ɪ.nəs, -ɪ.nɪs
protactinium ˌprəʊ.tækˈtɪn.i.əm ⓤⓢ ˌproʊ-
protagonist prəʊˈtæg.ᵊn.ɪst ⓤⓢ proʊ- **-s** -s
Protagoras prəʊˈtæg.ᵊr.æs, -ɒr-, -əs ⓤⓢ proʊˈtæg.ɚ.əs
pro tanto ˌprəʊˈtæn.təʊ ⓤⓢ ˌproʊˈtæn.toʊ, -ˈtɑːn-

protas|is ˈprɒt.ə.s|ɪs ⓤⓢ ˈprɑː.t̬ə- **-es** -iːz
protean prəʊˈtiː.ən; ˈprəʊ.ti- ⓤⓢ ˈproʊ-; proʊˈtiː-
protect prəˈtekt ⓤⓢ prə-, proʊ- **-s** -s **-ing/ly** -ɪŋ/li **-ed** -ɪd **-or/s** -əʳ/z ⓤⓢ -ɚ/z
protection prəˈtek.ʃᵊn ⓤⓢ prə-, proʊ- **-s** -z
protection|ism prəˈtek.ʃᵊn|.ɪ.zᵊm ⓤⓢ prə-, proʊ- **-ist/s** -ɪst/s
protective prəˈtek.tɪv ⓤⓢ prə-, proʊ- **-ly** -li **-ness** -nəs, -nɪs
protectorate prəˈtek.tᵊr.ət, -ɪt ⓤⓢ -ɪt, proʊ- **-s** -s
protectress prəˈtek.trəs, -trɪs ⓤⓢ -trɪs, proʊ- **-es** -ɪz
protégé(e), **protege(e)** ˈprɒt.ɪ.ʒeɪ, ˈprəʊ.tɪ-, -tə-, -teʒ.eɪ, -teɪ.ʒeɪ ⓤⓢ ˈproʊ.t̬ə.ʒeɪ, ˌ--ˈ- **-s** -z
protein ˈprəʊ.tiːn, -ti.ɪn ⓤⓢ ˈproʊ-
pro tem ˌprəʊˈtem ⓤⓢ ˌproʊˈtem
protest (*n.*) ˈprəʊ.test ⓤⓢ ˈproʊ.test **-s** -s
protest (*v.*) prəʊˈtest ⓤⓢ proʊˈtest, prə-; ˈproʊ.test **-s** -s **-ing/ly** -ɪŋ/li **-ed** -ɪd **-er/s** -əʳ/z ⓤⓢ -ɚ/z
protestant (**P**) ˈprɒt.ɪ.stᵊnt, ˈ-ə- ⓤⓢ ˈprɑː.t̬ə- **-s** -s **-ism** -ɪ.zᵊm
protestantiz|e, -is|e ˈprɒt.ɪ.stən.taɪz, ˈ-ə- ⓤⓢ ˈprɑː.t̬ə- **-es** -ɪz **-ing** -ɪŋ **-ed** -d
protestation ˌprɒt.esˈteɪ.ʃᵊn; ˌprəʊ.tesˈ-, -tɪˈsteɪ-, -təˈ- ⓤⓢ ˌprɑː.t̬esˈteɪ-, ˌproʊ-, -t̬əˈsteɪ- **-s** -z
Proteus ˈprəʊ.ti.uːs, -əs ⓤⓢ ˈproʊ.t̬i.əs
prothalami|on ˌprəʊ.θᵊlˈeɪ.mi|.ən ⓤⓢ ˌproʊ.θəˈleɪ-, -ɑːn **-um** -əm **-a** -ə
Protheroe ˈprɒð.ᵊr.əʊ ⓤⓢ ˈprɑː.ðə.roʊ
prothes|is ˈprɒθ.ɪ.s|ɪs, ˈ-ə- ⓤⓢ ˈprɑː.θə- **-es** -iːz
protium ˈprəʊ.ti.əm ⓤⓢ ˈproʊ.t̬i-
proto- prəʊ.təʊ- ⓤⓢ proʊ.t̬oʊ-, -t̬ə-
Note: Prefix. Normally takes primary or secondary stress on the first syllable, e.g. **prototype** /ˈprəʊ.təʊ.taɪp ⓤⓢ ˈproʊ.tə-/, **prototypic** /ˌprəʊ.təʊˈtɪp.ɪk ⓤⓢ ˌproʊ.t̬əˈ-/.
protocol ˈprəʊ.tə.kɒl ⓤⓢ ˈproʊ.t̬ə.kɔːl, -t̬oʊ-, -kɑːl **-s** -z
proton (**P®**) ˈprəʊ.tɒn ⓤⓢ ˈproʊ.tɑːn **-s** -z
protoplasm ˈprəʊ.təʊ.plæz.ᵊm ⓤⓢ ˈproʊ.t̬ə-, -t̬oʊ-
prototype ˈprəʊ.təʊ.taɪp ⓤⓢ ˈproʊ.t̬ə-, -t̬oʊ- **-s** -s
prototypic ˌprəʊ.təʊˈtɪp.ɪk ⓤⓢ ˌproʊ.t̬əˈ-, -t̬oʊˈ- **-al** -ᵊl
protozo|a ˌprəʊ.təʊˈzəʊ|.ə ⓤⓢ ˌproʊ.t̬əˈzoʊ-, -t̬oʊˈ- **-an/s** -ən/z **-on** -ɒn ⓤⓢ -ɑːn **-ic** -ɪk

protract prəʊˈtrækt ⓤⓢ proʊ-, prə- **-s** -s **-ing** -ɪŋ **-ed/ly** -ɪd/li **-ile** -aɪl ⓤⓢ -ᵊl
protraction prəʊˈtræk.ʃᵊn ⓤⓢ proʊ-, prə- **-s** -z
protractor prəʊˈtræk.təʳ ⓤⓢ proʊ-, prə- **-s** -z
protrud|e prəʊˈtruːd ⓤⓢ proʊ-, prə- **-es** -z **-ing** -ɪŋ **-ed** -ɪd
protrusion prəʊˈtruː.ʒᵊn ⓤⓢ proʊ-, prə- **-s** -z
protrusive prəʊˈtruː.sɪv ⓤⓢ proʊ-, prə- **-ly** -li **-ness** -nəs, -nɪs
protuberanc|e prəʊˈtjuː.bᵊr.ᵊnts ⓤⓢ proʊˈtuː-, prə-, -ˈtjuː- **-es** -ɪz
protuberant prəʊˈtjuː.bᵊr.ᵊnt ⓤⓢ proʊˈtuː-, prə-, -ˈtjuː- **-ly** -li
proud praʊd **-er** -əʳ ⓤⓢ -ɚ **-est** -ɪst, -əst **-ly** -li **-ness** -nəs, -nɪs
Proudfoot ˈpraʊd.fʊt
Proudhon ˈpruː.dɒn ⓤⓢ -dɑːn, -doʊn
Proudie ˈpraʊ.di
Proust pruːst
Proustian ˈpruː.sti.ən
Prout praʊt
provab|le ˈpruː.və.b|l̩ **-ly** -li **-leness** -l̩.nəs, -nɪs
prov|e pruːv **-es** -z **-ing** -ɪŋ **-ed** -d **-er/s** -əʳ/z ⓤⓢ -ɚ/z
proven ˈpruː.vᵊn, ˈprəʊ- ⓤⓢ ˈpruː-
provenance ˈprɒv.ᵊn.ənts, -ɪ.nənts ⓤⓢ ˈprɑː.vᵊn.ᵊnts
Provençal(e), **Provencal(e)** ˌprɒv.ɑ̃ːnˈsɑːl, -ɔ̃ːn-, -vəntˈ- ⓤⓢ ˌproʊ.vɑːnˈ-, ˌprɑː-, -vənˈ-
Provence prɒvˈɑ̃ːns, prəˈvɑ̃ːns, -ˈvɔ̃ːns, -ˈvɑːnts ⓤⓢ prɑːˈvɑ̃ːnts, proʊ-
provender ˈprɒv.ɪn.dəʳ, -ᵊn- ⓤⓢ ˈprɑː.vᵊn.dɚ
proverb (**P**) ˈprɒv.ɜːb ⓤⓢ ˈprɑː.vɜːrb **-s** -z
proverbial prəʊˈvɜː.bi.əl ⓤⓢ prəˈvɜːr-, proʊ- **-ly** -i
provid|e prəʊˈvaɪd ⓤⓢ prə-, proʊ- **-es** -z **-ing** -ɪŋ **-ed** -ɪd **-er/s** -əʳ/z ⓤⓢ -ɚ/z
providen|ce (**P**) ˈprɒv.ɪ.dᵊn|ts ⓤⓢ ˈprɑː.və- **-t/ly** -t/li
providential ˌprɒv.ɪˈden.tʃᵊl ⓤⓢ ˌprɑː.vəˈ- **-ly** -i
provinc|e ˈprɒv.ɪnts ⓤⓢ ˈprɑː.vɪnts **-es** -ɪz
provincial prəʊˈvɪn.tʃᵊl ⓤⓢ prəˈvɪnt.ʃᵊl, proʊ- **-s** -z **-ly** -i
provincialism prəʊˈvɪn.tʃᵊl.ɪ.zᵊm ⓤⓢ prəˈvɪnt.ʃᵊl-, proʊ- **-s** -z
provinciality prəʊˌvɪn.tʃiˈæl.ə.ti, -ɪ.ti ⓤⓢ prəˌvɪnt.ʃiˈæl.ə.t̬i, proʊ-
provincializ|e, -is|e prəʊˈvɪn.tʃᵊl.aɪz ⓤⓢ prəˈvɪnt.ʃᵊl-, proʊ- **-es** -ɪz **-ing** -ɪŋ **-ed** -d

provision prəʊ'vɪʒ.ᵊn Ⓤⓢ prə-, proʊ- **-s** -z **-ing** -ɪŋ **-ed** -d
provisional prəʊ'vɪʒ.ᵊn.ᵊl, '-nᵊl Ⓤⓢ prə-, proʊ- **-ly** -i
proviso prəʊ'vaɪ.zəʊ Ⓤⓢ prə'vaɪ.zoʊ, proʊ- **-(e)s** -z
provisor prəʊ'vaɪ.zəʳ Ⓤⓢ prə'vaɪ.zɚ, proʊ- **-s** -z
provisor|y prəʊ'vaɪ.zᵊr|.i Ⓤⓢ prə-, proʊ- **-ily** -ᵊl.i, -ɪ.li
Provo 'prəʊ.vəʊ Ⓤⓢ 'proʊ.voʊ **-s** -z
provocation ˌprɒv.ə'keɪ.ʃᵊn Ⓤⓢ ˌprɑː.və'- **-s** -z
provocative prə'vɒk.ə.tɪv Ⓤⓢ -'vɑː.kə.t̬ɪv, proʊ- **-ly** -li
provok|e prə'vəʊk Ⓤⓢ -'voʊk, proʊ- **-es** -s **-ing/ly** -ɪŋ/li **-ed** -t
provost 'prɒv.əst Ⓤⓢ 'proʊ.voʊst, -vəst; 'prɑː.vəst; *also in the US military:* 'proʊ.voʊ **-s** -s ˌ**provost 'marshal**
provostship 'prɒv.əst.ʃɪp Ⓤⓢ 'proʊ.voʊst-, -vəst-; 'prɑː.vəst- **-s** -s
prow praʊ **-s** -z
prowess 'praʊ.ɪs, -es; praʊ'es Ⓤⓢ 'praʊ.ɪs
prowl praʊl **-s** -z **-ing** -ɪŋ **-ed** -d **-er/s** -əʳ/z Ⓤⓢ -ɚ/z
Prowse praʊs, praʊz
prox. prɒks, 'prɒk.sɪ.məʊ, -sə- Ⓤⓢ 'prɑːk.sə.moʊ
proximal 'prɒk.sɪ.mᵊl, -sə- Ⓤⓢ 'prɑːk.sə- **-ly** -i
proximate 'prɒk.sɪ.mət, -sə-, -mɪt Ⓤⓢ 'prɑːk.sə.mət **-ly** -li
proxime access|it ˌprɒk.sɪ.meɪ.æk'sesl.ɪt, -ək'-, -ə'kes- Ⓤⓢ ˌprɑːk.səm.æk'ses.ət, -sɪm- **-erunt** -ə.rʊnt
proximit|y prɒk'sɪm.ə.t|i, -ɪ.t|i Ⓤⓢ prɑːk'sɪm.ə.t̬|i **-ies** -iz
proximo 'prɒk.sɪ.məʊ, -sə- Ⓤⓢ 'prɑːk.sə.moʊ
prox|y 'prɒk.s|i Ⓤⓢ 'prɑːk- **-ies** -iz
prud|e pruːd **-es** -z **-ery** -ᵊr.i
prudence (P) 'pruː.dᵊnts
prudent 'pruː.dᵊnt **-ly** -li
prudential pruː'den.*t*ʃᵊl Ⓤⓢ -'den*t*.ʃᵊl **-ly** -i
Prudhoe 'prʌd.*h*əʊ, 'pruː.dəʊ, 'pruːd.həʊ Ⓤⓢ 'pruːd.hoʊ, 'pruː.doʊ, 'prʌd.*h*oʊ
prudish 'pruː.dɪʃ **-ly** -li **-ness** -nəs, -nɪs
Prufrock 'pruː.frɒk Ⓤⓢ -frɑːk
prun|e pruːn **-es** -z **-ing** -ɪŋ **-ed** -d
prunella (P) pruː'nel.ə **-s** -z
prurience 'prʊə.ri.ən*t*s Ⓤⓢ 'prʊr.i-
prurient 'prʊə.ri.ənt Ⓤⓢ 'prʊr.i- **-ly** -li
prurigo prʊə'raɪ.gəʊ Ⓤⓢ prʊ'raɪ.goʊ
pru|ritus prʊə|'raɪ.təs Ⓤⓢ prʊ|'raɪ.t̬əs **-ritic** -'rɪt.ɪk Ⓤⓢ -'rɪt̬-
Prussia 'prʌʃ.ə
Prussian 'prʌʃ.ᵊn **-s** -z ˌ**Prussian 'blue**
prussiate 'prʌʃ.i.ət, 'prʌʃ.ət, -ɪt Ⓤⓢ 'prʌs.i.eɪt, 'prʌʃ-, -ɪt **-s** -s
prussic acid ˌprʌs.ɪk'æs.ɪd
Pruth pruːt
pr|y pr|aɪ **-ies** -aɪz **-ying/ly** -aɪ.ɪŋ/li **-ied** -aɪd **-yer/s** -aɪ.əʳ/z Ⓤⓢ -aɪ.ɚ/z
Pryce praɪs
Pryde praɪd
Pryke praɪk
Prynne prɪn
Pryor praɪəʳ Ⓤⓢ praɪɚ
Przewalski pʃə'væl.ski, -'vɑːl- Ⓤⓢ pʃə'vɑːl- **Prze**ˌ**walski's 'horse**
PS ˌpiː'es **-'s** -ɪz
psalm (P) sɑːm **-s** -z **-ist/s** -ɪst/s
psalmodic sæl'mɒd.ɪk Ⓤⓢ sɑː'mɑː.dɪk, sæl-
psalmod|y 'sæl.mə.d|i, 'sɑː.mə- Ⓤⓢ 'sɑː-, 'sæl- **-ist/s** -ɪst/s
psalter 'sɔːl.təʳ, 'sɒl- Ⓤⓢ 'sɔːl.t̬ɚ, 'sɑːl- **-s** -z
psalt(e)r|y 'sɔːl.tᵊr|.i, 'sɒl- Ⓤⓢ 'sɔːl.tɚ-, 'sɑːl- **-ies** -iz
Note: In the following words beginning with **ps-**, the form with /p/ is rare.
psepholog|y *p*sɪ'fɒl.ə.dʒ|i, *p*sə-, *p*sef'ɒl- Ⓤⓢ siː'fɑː.lə- **-ist/s** -ɪst/s
pseud sjuːd, suːd Ⓤⓢ suːd **-s** -z **-y**
pseudo- ˌsjuː.dəʊ-, ˌsuː- Ⓤⓢ ˌsuː.doʊ-
pseudo 'sjuː.dəʊ, 'suː- Ⓤⓢ 'suː.doʊ **-s** -z
pseudonym 'sjuː.də.nɪm, 'suː- Ⓤⓢ 'suː.dᵊn.ɪm **-s** -z
pseudonymity ˌsjuː.də'nɪm.ə.ti, ˌsuː-, -ɪ.ti Ⓤⓢ ˌsuː.dᵊn'ɪm.ə.t̬i
pseudonymous sjuː'dɒn.ɪ.məs, suː- Ⓤⓢ suː'dɑː.nɪ-
pseudopodi|um ˌsjuː.də'pəʊ.di|.əm, ˌsuː- Ⓤⓢ ˌsuː.doʊ'poʊ- **-a** -ə
Pseudoxia Epidemica sjuːˌdɒk.si.ə.ep.ɪ'dem.ɪ.kə, suː- Ⓤⓢ suːˌdɑːk.si-
pshaw (*interj.*) pɸ, pʃɔː Ⓤⓢ *p*ʃɔː, *p*ʃɑː
Note: Sound of derision or protest: the spelling was probably originally intended to represent a voiceless bilabial affricate (a more polite version of the bilabial trill known as a "raspberry" in British English and also as a "Bronx Cheer" in American English), but it is usually now given a spelling-based pronunciation.
psi psaɪ, saɪ Ⓤⓢ saɪ, psiː
psittacosis ˌ*p*sɪt.ə'kəʊ.sɪs Ⓤⓢ ˌsɪt.ə'koʊ-
Psmith smɪθ
psoriasis *p*sə'raɪə.sɪs, *p*sɒr'aɪə-, *p*sɔː'raɪə-, *p*sʊ- Ⓤⓢ sə'raɪə-, soʊ-
psych saɪk **-s** -s **-ing** -ɪŋ **-ed** -t
psych|e (*v.*) saɪk **-es** -s **-ing** -ɪŋ **-ed** -t
psyche (*n.*) 'saɪ.ki, -kiː **-s** -s
psychedelia ˌsaɪ.kɪ'diː.li.ə, -kə'- Ⓤⓢ -kə'diː.li.ə, -'diːl.jə
psychedelic ˌsaɪ.kɪ'del.ɪk, -kə'- Ⓤⓢ -kə'- **-ally** -ᵊl.i, -li *stress shift:* ˌpsychedelic 'colours
psychiatric ˌsaɪ.ki'æt.rɪk **-al** -ᵊl **-ally** -ᵊl.i, -li *stress shift:* ˌpsychiatric 'nurse
psychiatr|y saɪ'kaɪə.tr|i, sɪ-, sə- Ⓤⓢ saɪ-, sɪ- **-ist/s** -ɪst/s
psychic 'saɪ.kɪk **-al** -ᵊl **-ally** -ᵊl.i, -li
psycho- saɪ.kəʊ-; saɪ'kɒ- Ⓤⓢ saɪ.koʊ-, -kə-; saɪ'kɑː-
Note: Prefix. Normally either takes primary or secondary stress on the first syllable, e.g. **psychodrama** /'saɪ.kəʊˌdrɑː.mə Ⓤⓢ -koʊˌ-/, **psychodramatic** /ˌsaɪ.kəʊ.drə'mæt.ɪk Ⓤⓢ -koʊ.drə'mæt̬.ɪk/, or primary stress on the second syllable, e.g. **psychotic** /saɪ'kɒt.ɪk Ⓤⓢ -'kɑː.t̬ɪk/.
psycho 'saɪ.kəʊ Ⓤⓢ -koʊ **-s** -z
psychoanalys|e ˌsaɪ.kəʊ'æn.ᵊl.aɪz Ⓤⓢ -koʊ'æn.ə.laɪz **-es** -ɪz **-ing** -ɪŋ **-ed** -d
psychoanalysis ˌsaɪ.kəʊ.ə'næl.ə.sɪs, '-ɪ- Ⓤⓢ -koʊ-
psychoanalyst ˌsaɪ.kəʊ'æn.ᵊl.ɪst Ⓤⓢ -koʊ'æn.ə.lɪst **-s** -s
psychoanalytic ˌsaɪ.kəʊˌæn.ᵊl'ɪt.ɪk Ⓤⓢ -koʊˌæn.ə'lɪt̬.ɪk **-al** -ᵊl **-ally** -ᵊl.i, -li *stress shift:* ˌpsychoanalytic 'counselling
psychoanalyz|e ˌsaɪ.kəʊ'æn.ᵊl.aɪz Ⓤⓢ -koʊ'æn.ə.laɪz **-es** -ɪz **-ing** -ɪŋ **-ed** -d
psychobabble 'saɪ.kəʊˌbæb.l̩ Ⓤⓢ -koʊˌ-
psychodrama 'saɪ.kəʊˌdrɑː.mə Ⓤⓢ -koʊˌ-, -ˌdræm.ə **-s** -z
psychodramatic ˌsaɪ.kəʊ.drə'mæt.ɪk Ⓤⓢ -koʊ.drə'mæt̬-
psychokinesis ˌsaɪ.kəʊ.kaɪ'niː.sɪs, -kɪ'- Ⓤⓢ -koʊ.kɪ'-, -kaɪ'-
psychokinetic ˌsaɪ.kəʊ.kɪ'net.ɪk, -kaɪ'- Ⓤⓢ -koʊ- *stress shift:* ˌpsychokinetic 'powers
psycholinguist ˌsaɪ.kəʊ'lɪŋ.gwɪst Ⓤⓢ -koʊ'- **-s** -s
psycholinguistic ˌsaɪ.kəʊ.lɪŋ'gwɪs.tɪk Ⓤⓢ -koʊ- **-s** -s **-ally** -ᵊl.i, -li *stress shift:* ˌpsycholinguistic 'process
psychologic ˌsaɪ.kə'lɒdʒ.ɪk Ⓤⓢ -'lɑː.dʒɪk *stress shift:* ˌpsychologic 'warfare
psychological ˌsaɪ.kᵊl'ɒdʒ.ɪ.kᵊl Ⓤⓢ -kə'lɑː.dʒɪ- **-ly** -i *stress shift, see compound:* ˌ**psychological 'warfare**
psychologiz|e, -is|e saɪ'kɒl.ə.dʒaɪz Ⓤⓢ -'kɑː.lə- **-es** -ɪz **-ing** -ɪŋ **-ed** -d
psycholog|y saɪ'kɒl.ə.dʒ|i Ⓤⓢ -'kɑː.lə- **-ist/s** -ɪst/s

psychometric ˌsaɪ.kəʊˈmet.rɪk (US) -koʊ'- **-s** -s *stress shift:* ˌpsychometric ˈmeasurement
psychometr|y saɪˈkɒm.ɪ.tr|i, ˈ-ə- (US) -ˈkɑː.mə- **-ist/s** -ɪst/s
psychopath ˈsaɪ.kəʊ.pæθ (US) -kə-, -koʊ- **-s** -s
psychopathic ˌsaɪ.kəʊˈpæθ.ɪk (US) -kəˈ-, -koʊˈ- **-ally** -əl.i, -li *stress shift:* ˌpsychopathic ˈtendencies
psychopatholog|y ˌsaɪ.kəʊ.pæθˈɒl.ə.dʒ|i (US) -koʊ.pæθˈɑː.lə- **-ist/s** -ɪst/s
psychophysical ˌsaɪ.kəʊˈfɪz.ɪ.kəl, ˈ-ə- (US) -koʊˈ- **-ly** -li *stress shift:* ˌpsychophysical ˈstimulus
psychosexual ˌsaɪ.kəʊˈsek.ʃʊəl, -sjʊəl (US) -ʃu.əl **-ly** -i *stress shift:* ˌpsychosexual ˈaspects
psychos|is saɪˈkəʊ.s|ɪs (US) -ˈkoʊ- **-es** -iːz
psychosocial ˌsaɪ.kəʊˈsəʊ.ʃəl (US) -koʊˈsoʊ- *stress shift:* ˌpsychosocial ˈproblems
psychosomatic ˌsaɪ.kəʊ.səʊˈmæt.ɪk (US) -koʊ.soʊˈmæt̬- **-ally** -əl.i, -li *stress shift:* ˌpsychosomatic ˈsymptoms
psychotherap|y ˌsaɪ.kəʊˈθer.ə.p|i (US) -koʊˈ- **-ist/s** -ɪst/s
psychotic saɪˈkɒt.ɪk (US) -ˈkɑː.t̬ɪk **-ally** -əl.i, -li
pt (*abbrev. for* **pint**) paɪnt
PTA ˌpiː.tiːˈeɪ
Ptah tɑː, ptɑː, pəˈtɑː (US) pəˈtɑː
ptarmigan ˈtɑː.mɪ.gən, -mə- (US) ˈtɑːr-
pterodactyl ˌter.əʊˈdæk.tɪl, -təl (US) -əˈdæk.təl, -oʊˈ- **-s** -z
pterosaur ˈter.əʊ.sɔːʳ (US) -ə.sɑːr, -oʊ-, -sɔːr **-s** -z
PTO ˌpiː.tiːˈəʊ (US) -ˈoʊ
Ptolemaeus ˌtɒl.əˈmiː.əs, -ɪˈ-, -ˈmeɪ- (US) ˌtɑː.ləˈmeɪ-, -ˈmiː-
Ptolema|ic ˌtɒl.əˈmeɪ|.ɪk, -ɪˈ- (US) ˌtɑː.ləˈ- **-ist** -ɪst
Ptolemy ˈtɒl.ə.mi, ˈ-ɪ- (US) ˈtɑː.lə-
ptomaine ˈtəʊ.meɪn; təʊˈmeɪn (US) ˈtoʊ.meɪn
Pty (*abbrev. for* **Proprietary**) prəˈpraɪə.tər.i (US) proʊ-, prə-
ptyalin ˈtaɪə.lɪn
pub pʌb **-s** -z **-by** -i
pub-crawl ˈpʌb.krɔːl (US) -krɑːl, -krɔːl **-s** -z **-ing** -ɪŋ **-ed** -d **-er/s** -əʳ/z (US) -ɚ/z
puberty ˈpjuː.bə.ti (US) -bɚ.t̬i
pubes *slang for pubic hair:* pjuːbz
pubes *plural of* **pubis**: ˈpjuː.biːz
pubescen|ce pjuːˈbes.ən|ts, pjʊ- **-t** -t
pubic ˈpjuː.bɪk ˌ**pubic ˈhair** (US) ˈ**pubic** ˌ**hair**
pub|is ˈpjuː.b|ɪs **-es** -iːz
public ˈpʌb.lɪk **-ly** -li ˌ**public conˈvenience**; ˌ**public ˈenemy**; ˌ**public ˈhouse**; ˌ**public oˈpinion**; ˌ**public reˈlations**; ˌ**public ˈschool**; ˌ**public ˈsector** (US) ˈ**public** ˌ**sector** *stress shift, British only:* ˌpublic sector ˈservices; ˌ**public ˈspeaking**; ˌ**public ˈtransport**
public-address system ˌpʌb.lɪk.əˈdres.ˌsɪs.təm **-s** -z
publican ˈpʌb.lɪ.kən **-s** -z
publication ˌpʌb.lɪˈkeɪ.ʃən, -ləˈ- **-s** -z
publicist ˈpʌb.lɪ.sɪst, -lə- **-s** -s
publicity pʌbˈlɪs.ə.ti, pəˈblɪs-, -ɪ.ti (US) -ə.t̬i
publiciz|e, -is|e ˈpʌb.lɪ.saɪz, -lə- **-es** -ɪz **-ing** -ɪŋ **-ed** -d
public-spirited ˌpʌb.lɪkˈspɪr.ɪ.tɪd, ˈ-ə- (US) -ə.t̬ɪd **-ness** -nəs, -nɪs *stress shift:* ˌpublic-spirited ˈpolicies
publish ˈpʌb.lɪʃ **-es** -ɪz **-ing** -ɪŋ **-ed** -t **-er/s** -əʳ/z (US) -ɚ/z
Publius ˈpʌb.li.əs
Puccini pʊˈtʃiː.ni (US) puː-
puce pjuːs
puck (P) pʌk **-s** -s
puck|er ˈpʌk|.əʳ (US) -ɚ **-ers** -əz (US) -ɚz **-ering** -ər.ɪŋ **-ered** -d (US) -ɚd
puckish ˈpʌk.ɪʃ **-ly** -li **-ness** -nəs, -nɪs
pud pʊd **-s** -z
pudding ˈpʊd.ɪŋ **-s** -z **the** ˌ**proof of the** ˌ**pudding is** ˌ**in the ˈeating**
puddl|e ˈpʌd.l̩ **-es** -z **-ing** -ɪŋ, ˈpʌd.lɪŋ **-ed** -d **-er/s** -əʳ/z (US) -ɚ/z, ˈpʌd.ləʳ/z (US) -lɚ/z
pudend|um pjuːˈden.d|əm, pjʊ- (US) pjuː- **-a** -ə
pudg|y ˈpʌdʒ|.i **-ier** -i.əʳ (US) -i.ɚ **-iest** -i.ɪst, -i.əst **-iness** -ɪ.nəs, -ɪ.nɪs
Pudsey ˈpʌd.zi *locally:* ˈpʊt.si
Puebla ˈpweb.lə, puˈeb- (US) ˈpweb.lɑː
pueblo (P) ˈpweb.ləʊ, puˈeb- (US) ˈpweb.loʊ **-s** -z
puerile ˈpjʊə.raɪl, ˈpjɔː- (US) ˈpjuː.ɚ.ɪl, ˈpjʊr.ɪl, -aɪl **-ly** -li
puerilit|y pjʊəˈrɪl.ə.t|i, pjɔː-, -ɪ.t|i (US) ˌpjuː.əˈrɪl.ə.t̬|i, pjʊˈ- **-ies** -iz
puerperal pjuˈɜː.pər.əl (US) -ˈɜːr-
Puerto Ric|o ˌpwɜː.təʊˈriː.k|əʊ, ˌpweə- (US) ˌpwer.t̬əˈriː.koʊ, -toʊˈ-, ˌpɔːr.t̬əˈ- **-an/s** -ən/z
Puerto Vallarta ˌpwɜː.təʊ.vælˈɑː.tə *as if Spanish:* ˌpweə.təʊ.vaɪˈ- (US) ˌpwer.toʊ.vɑːˈjɑːr.t̬ə, -tɑː
puff pʌf **-s** -s **-ing** -ɪŋ **-ed** -t **-er/s** -əʳ/z (US) -ɚ/z ˈ**puff** ˌ**adder**; ˌ**puff ˈpastry**
puffball ˈpʌf.bɔːl (US) -bɔːl, -bɑːl **-s** -z ˌ**puffball ˈskirt**
puffed sleeve ˌpʌftˈsliːv **-s** -z
puffery ˈpʌf.ər.i (US) -ɚ-
puffin (P) ˈpʌf.ɪn **-s** -z
puff|y ˈpʌf|.i **-ier** -i.əʳ (US) -i.ɚ **-iest** -i.ɪst, -i.əst **-ily** -ɪ.li, -əl.i **-iness** -ɪ.nəs, -ɪ.nɪs
pug pʌg **-s** -z
pug(g)aree ˈpʌg.ər.i **-s** -z
puggree ˈpʌg.ri **-s** -z
Pugh pjuː
pugil|ism ˈpjuː.dʒɪ.l|ɪ.zəm, -dʒə- **-ist/s** -ɪst/s
pugilistic ˌpjuː.dʒɪˈlɪs.tɪk, -dʒəˈ- **-ally** -əl.i, -li *stress shift:* ˌpugilistic ˈattitude
Pugin ˈpjuː.dʒɪn
pugnacious pʌgˈneɪ.ʃəs **-ly** -li **-ness** -nəs, -nɪs
pugnacity pʌgˈnæs.ə.ti, -ɪ.ti (US) -ə.t̬i
pug-nos|e ˌpʌgˈnəʊz (US) ˈpʌg.noʊz **-es** -ɪz **-ed** -d *stress shift, British only:* ˌpug-nose ˈface
puisne ˈpjuː.ni
puissan|ce *power:* ˈpjuː.ɪ.sən|ts, ˈpwɪs.ən|ts *sometimes in poetry:* pjuˈɪ.sən|ts **-t** -t
puissance *in show-jumping:* ˈpwiː.sɑ̃ːns, -sɑːnts, -sənts
puk|e pjuːk **-es** -s **-ing** -ɪŋ **-ed** -t
pukka ˈpʌk.ə
pul puːl **-s** -z **-i** -iː
pula ˈpjuː.lə, ˈpuː- (US) ˈpuː.lɑː
Pulaski pəˈlæs.ki, pjuː- (US) pə-, pʊlˈæs-
pulchritude ˈpʌl.krɪ.tjuːd, -krə- (US) -tuːd, -tjuːd
pulchritudinous ˌpʌl.krɪˈtjuː.dɪ.nəs, -krəˈ-, -dən.əs (US) -ˈtuː.dən-, -ˈtjuː-
pul|e pjuːl **-es** -z **-ing** -ɪŋ **-ed** -d
Puleston ˈpʊl.ɪ.stən *locally also:* ˈpɪl.sən
Pulham ˈpʊl.əm
Pulitzer *US publisher:* ˈpʊl.ɪt.səʳ (US) ˈpʊl.ɪt.sɚ, ˈpjuː.lɪt- *prize at Columbia University:* ˈpjuː.lɪt.səʳ (US) ˈpʊl.ɪt.sɚ, ˈpjuː.lɪt- ˈ**Pulitzer** ˌ**prize**, ˌ**Pulitzer ˈprize**
pull pʊl **-s** -z **-ing** -ɪŋ **-ed** -d **-er/s** -əʳ/z (US) -ɚ/z
pull-down ˈpʊl.daʊn
pullet ˈpʊl.ɪt, -ət **-s** -s
pulley ˈpʊl.i **-s** -z
pullman (P) ˈpʊl.mən **-s** -z
pullover ˈpʊl.əʊ.vəʳ (US) -oʊ.vɚ **-s** -z
pullu|late ˈpʌl.jə|.leɪt, -jʊ- **-lates** -leɪts **-lating** -leɪ.tɪŋ (US) -leɪ.t̬ɪŋ **-lated** -leɪ.tɪd (US) -leɪ.t̬ɪd
pullulation ˌpʌl.jəˈleɪ.ʃən, -jʊˈ-
pull-up ˈpʊl.ʌp **-s** -s
pulmonary ˈpʌl.mə.nər.i, ˈpʊl- (US) -ner-
pulmonic pʌlˈmɒn.ɪk, pʊl- (US) -ˈmɑː.nɪk
pulp pʌlp **-s** -s **-ing** -ɪŋ **-ed** -t
pulpi|fy ˈpʌl.pɪ|.faɪ **-fies** -faɪz **-fying** -faɪ.ɪŋ **-fied** -faɪd
pulpit ˈpʊl.pɪt (US) ˈpʊl-, ˈpʌl- **-s** -s
pulp|y ˈpʌl.p|i **-ier** -i.əʳ (US) -i.ɚ **-iest** -i.ɪst, -i.əst **-iness** -ɪ.nəs, -ɪ.nɪs

pulsar ˈpʌl.sɑːʳ, -səʳ US -sɑːr, -sɚ **-s** -z

pul|sate pʌlˈseɪt US ˈ-- **-sates** -ˈseɪts US -seɪts **-sating** -ˈseɪ.tɪŋ US -seɪ.t̬ɪŋ **-sated** -ˈseɪ.tɪd US -seɪ.t̬ɪd

pulsatile ˈpʌl.sə.taɪl US -tɪl, -taɪl

pulsation pʌlˈseɪ.ʃᵊn **-s** -z

pulsative ˈpʌl.sə.tɪv US -t̬ɪv

pulsatory ˈpʌl.sə.tᵊr.i, pʌlˈseɪ- US ˈpʌl.sə.tɔːr-

puls|e pʌls **-es** -ɪz **-ing** -ɪŋ **-ed** -t

Pulteney *surname:* ˈpʌlt.ni, ˈpəʊlt-, ˈpʊlt- US ˈpʌlt-, ˈpoʊlt-, ˈpʊlt-

Pulteney *bridge in Bath:* ˈpʌlt.ni

pulverization, -isa- ˌpʌl.vᵊr.aɪˈzeɪ.ʃᵊn, -ɪˈ- US -ɪˈ- **-s** -z

pulveriz|e, -is|e ˈpʌl.vᵊr.aɪz US -və.raɪz **-es** -ɪz **-ing** -ɪŋ **-ed** -d

puma ˈpjuː.mə US ˈpjuː-, ˈpuː- **-s** -z

Pumblechook ˈpʌm.bl̩.tʃʊk

pumic|e ˈpʌm.ɪs **-es** -ɪz **-ing** -ɪŋ **-ed** -t **ˈpumice ˌstone**

pummel ˈpʌm.ᵊl **-s** -z **-(l)ing** -ɪŋ **-(l)ed** -d

pump pʌmp **-s** -s **-ing** -ɪŋ **-ed** -t **-er/s** -əʳ/z US -ɚ/z **ˈpump ˌroom**

pumpernickel ˈpʌm.pəˌnɪk.l̩ US -pɚˌ-

pumpkin ˈpʌmp.kɪn **-s** -z **ˌpumpkin ˈpie**

pun pʌn **-s** -z **-ning** -ɪŋ **-ned** -d **-ner/s** -əʳ/z US -ɚ/z

punch (P) pʌntʃ US pʌntʃ **-es** -ɪz **-ing** -ɪŋ **-ed** -t **-er/s** -əʳ/z US -ɚ/z

Punch-and-Judy ˌpʌntʃ.ᵊndˈdʒuː.di US ˌpʌntʃ- **ˌPunch-and-ˈJudy ˌshow**

punchbag ˈpʌntʃ.bæg US ˈpʌntʃ- **-s** -z

punchball ˈpʌntʃ.bɔːl US ˈpʌntʃ.bɔːl, -bɑːl **-s** -z

punchbowl ˈpʌntʃ.bəʊl US ˈpʌntʃ.boʊl **-s** -z

punch-drunk ˈpʌntʃ.drʌŋk US ˈpʌntʃ-

puncheon ˈpʌn.tʃᵊn US -tʃᵊn **-s** -z

punchinello (P) ˌpʌn.tʃɪˈnel.əʊ, -tʃəˈ- US -tʃəˈnel.oʊ

punchline ˈpʌntʃ.laɪn US ˈpʌntʃ- **-s** -z

punch-up ˈpʌntʃ.ʌp US ˈpʌntʃ- **-s** -s

punch|y ˈpʌn.tʃ|i US -tʃ|i **-ier** -i.əʳ US -i.ɚ **-iest** -i.ɪst, -i.əst **-ily** -ɪ.li, -ᵊl.i **-iness** -ɪ.nəs, -ɪ.nɪs

punctilio pʌŋkˈtɪl.i.əʊ US -oʊ **-s** -z

punctilious pʌŋkˈtɪl.i.əs **-ly** -li **-ness** -nəs, -nɪs

punctual ˈpʌŋk.tʃu.əl, -tʃʊəl, -tju.əl, -tjʊəl US ˈpʌŋk.tʃu.əl **-ly** -i

punctuality ˌpʌŋk.tʃuˈæl.ə.ti, -tjuˈ-, -ɪ.ti US -ə.t̬i

punctu|ate ˈpʌŋk.tʃu|.eɪt, -tju- US -tʃu- **-ates** -eɪts **-ating** -eɪ.tɪŋ US -eɪ.t̬ɪŋ **-ated** -eɪ.tɪd US -eɪ.t̬ɪd **-ator/s** -eɪ.təʳ/z US -eɪ.t̬ɚ/z

punctuation ˌpʌŋk.tʃuˈeɪ.ʃᵊn, -tjuˈ- US -tʃuˈ- **-s** -z

punct|ure ˈpʌŋk.tʃ|əʳ US -tʃ|ɚ **-ures** -əz US -ɚz **-uring** -ᵊr.ɪŋ **-ured** -əd US -ɚd

pundit ˈpʌn.dɪt **-s** -s

Pune pjuːn

pungency ˈpʌn.dʒᵊnt.si

pungent ˈpʌn.dʒᵊnt **-ly** -li

Punic ˈpjuː.nɪk

puniness ˈpjuː.nɪ.nəs, -nɪs US -ni-

punish ˈpʌn.ɪʃ **-es** -ɪz **-ing/ly** -ɪŋ/li **-ed** -t **-er/s** -əʳ/z US -ɚ/z **-able/ness** -ə.bl̩/nəs, -nɪs

punishment ˈpʌn.ɪʃ.mənt **-s** -s

puni|tive ˈpjuː.nə|.tɪv, -nɪ- US -nə|.t̬ɪv **-tively** -tɪv.li US -t̬ɪv.li **-tory** -tᵊr.i US -tɔːr.i

Punjab ˌpʌnˈdʒɑːb, ˌpʊn-, ˈ-- US pʌnˈdʒɑːb; ˈpʌn.dʒɑːb, -dʒæb **-i** -iː, -i

Punjabi pʌnˈdʒɑː.biː, pʊn-, -bi US pʌn-

punk pʌŋk **-s** -s **-y** -i **-ier** -i.əʳ US -i.ɚ **-iest** -i.ɪst, -i.əst **ˌpunk ˈrock** ; **ˌpunk ˈrocker**

punkah ˈpʌŋ.kə **-s** -z

punnet ˈpʌn.ɪt **-s** -s

Punshon ˈpʌn.ʃᵊn

punster ˈpʌn.stəʳ US -stɚ **-s** -z

punt *boat:* pʌnt **-s** -s **-ing** -ɪŋ US ˈpʌn.t̬ɪŋ **-ed** -ɪd US ˈpʌn.t̬ɪd

punt *currency:* pʊnt **-s** -s

punter ˈpʌn.təʳ US -t̬ɚ **-s** -z

Punto® ˈpʊn.təʊ, ˈpʌn- US -toʊ

pun|y ˈpjuː.n|i **-ier** -i.əʳ US -i.ɚ **-iest** -i.ɪst, -i.əst **-iness** -ɪ.nəs, -ɪ.nɪs

pup pʌp **-s** -s **-ping** -ɪŋ **-ped** -t

pup|a ˈpjuː.p|ə **-ae** -iː **-as** -əz **-al** -ᵊl

pupil ˈpjuː.pᵊl, -pɪl US -pᵊl **-s** -z

pupil(l)age ˈpjuː.pɪ.lɪdʒ, -pᵊl.ɪdʒ US -pᵊl.ɪdʒ

pupillary ˈpjuː.pɪ.lᵊr.i, -pᵊl.ᵊr- US -pᵊl.er-

puppet ˈpʌp.ɪt **-s** -s **ˌpuppet ˈgovernment**

puppeteer ˌpʌp.ɪˈtɪəʳ, -əˈ- US -əˈtɪr **-s** -z

pupp|y ˈpʌp|.i **-ies** -iz **ˈpuppy ˌdog** ; **ˈpuppy ˌfat** ; **ˈpuppy ˌlove**

Purbeck ˈpɜː.bek US ˈpɜːr-

purblind ˈpɜː.blaɪnd US ˈpɜːr- **-ness** -nəs, -nɪs

Purcell ˈpɜː.sel, -sᵊl; pɜːˈsel US ˈpɜːr.sᵊl, -ˈ-

purchas|e ˈpɜː.tʃəs, -tʃɪs US ˈpɜːr.tʃəs **-es** -ɪz **-ing** -ɪŋ **-ed** -t **-er/s** -əʳ/z US -ɚ/z **-able** -ə.bl̩

purdah ˈpɜː.də, -dɑː US ˈpɜːr.də

Purdie, Purdy ˈpɜː.di US ˈpɜːr-

pur|e pjʊəʳ, pjɔːʳ US pjʊr **-er** -əʳ US -ɚ **-est** -ɪst, -əst **-ely** -li **-eness** -nəs, -nɪs

purebred ˈpjʊə.bred, ˈpjɔː- US ˈpjʊr- **-s** -z

purée, puree ˈpjʊə.reɪ, ˈpjɔː- US pjʊˈreɪ; ˈpjʊr.eɪ **-s** -z **-ing** -ɪŋ **-d** -d

purfl|e ˈpɜː.fl̩ US ˈpɜːr- **-es** -z **-ing** -ɪŋ, ˈ-flɪŋ **-ed** -d

purfling ˈpɜː.flɪŋ US ˈpɜːr- **-s** -z

purgation pɜːˈgeɪ.ʃᵊn US pɜːr- **-s** -z

purgative ˈpɜː.gə.tɪv US ˈpɜːr.gə.t̬ɪv **-s** -z

purgatorial ˌpɜː.gəˈtɔː.ri.əl US ˌpɜːr.gəˈtɔːr.i-

Purgatorio ˌpɜː.gəˈtɔː.ri.əʊ US ˌpɜːr.gəˈtɔːr.i.oʊ

purgator|y (P) ˈpɜː.gə.tᵊr|.i, -tr|i US ˈpɜːr.gə.tɔːr- **-ies** -iz

purg|e pɜːdʒ US pɜːrdʒ **-es** -ɪz **-ing** -ɪŋ **-ed** -d

purification ˌpjʊə.rɪ.fɪˈkeɪ.ʃᵊn, ˌpjɔː-, -rə- US ˌpjʊr.ə- **-s** -z

purificatory ˌpjʊə.rɪ.fɪˈkeɪ.tᵊr.i, ˌpjɔː-, -rə-; US pjʊˈrɪf.ɪ.kəˌtɔːr-

puri|fy ˈpjʊə.rɪ|.faɪ, ˈpjɔː-, -rə- US ˈpjʊr.ə- **-fies** -faɪz **-fying** -faɪ.ɪŋ **-fied** -faɪd **-fier/s** -faɪ.əʳ/z US -faɪ.ɚ/z

Purim ˈpʊə.rɪm, ˈpjʊə- US ˈpʊr.ɪm; puːˈriːm

purism ˈpjʊə.rɪ.zᵊm, ˈpjɔː- US ˈpjʊr.ɪ-

purist ˈpjʊə.rɪst, ˈpjɔː- US ˈpjʊr.ɪst **-s** -s

puristic pjʊəˈrɪs.tɪk, pjɔː- US pjʊ- **-al** -ᵊl

puritan (P) ˈpjʊə.rɪ.tᵊn, ˈpjɔː- US ˈpjʊr.ɪ- **-s** -z **-ism** -ɪ.zᵊm

puritanic ˌpjʊə.rɪˈtæn.ɪk, ˌpjɔː- US ˌpjʊr.ɪˈ- **-al** -ᵊl **-ally** -ᵊl.i, -li

purity ˈpjʊə.rə.ti, ˈpjɔː-, -rɪ- US ˈpjʊr.ɪ.t̬i, ˈ-ə-

Purkinje pɜːˈkɪn.ji US pɜːr-

Purkiss ˈpɜː.kɪs US ˈpɜːr-

purl pɜːl US pɜːrl **-s** -z **-ing** -ɪŋ **-ed** -d

Purley ˈpɜː.li US ˈpɜːr-

purlieu ˈpɜː.ljuː US ˈpɜːrl.juː, ˈpɜːr.luː **-s** -z

purlin(e) ˈpɜː.lɪn US ˈpɜːr- **-s** -z

purloin pɜːˈlɔɪn, ˈ-- US pɚˈlɔɪn; ˈpɜːr.lɔɪn **-s** -z **-ing** -ɪŋ **-ed** -d

purloiner pɜːˈlɔɪ.nəʳ US pɚˈlɔɪ.nɚ **-s** -z

Purnell pɜːˈnel US pɜːr-

purpl|e ˈpɜː.pl̩ US ˈpɜːr- **-er** -əʳ, ˈpɜː.pləʳ US ˈpɜːr.plɚ **-est** -ɪst, -əst, ˈpɜː.plɪst, -pləst, -pləst US ˈpɜːr- **-es** -z **-ing** -ɪŋ, ˈpɜː.plɪŋ US ˈpɜːr- **-ed** -d **ˌPurple ˈHeart**

purplish ˈpɜː.pl̩.ɪʃ, -plɪʃ US ˈpɜːr-

purpor|t pəˈpɔː|t, pɜː-; ˈpɜː.pə|t, -pɔː|t US pɜːrˈpɔːr|t, ˈ-- **-ts** -ts **-ting** -tɪŋ US -t̬ɪŋ **-ted** -tɪd US -t̬ɪd

purpos|e ˈpɜː.pəs US ˈpɜːr- **-es** -ɪz **-ing** -ɪŋ **-ed** -t

purpose-built ˌpɜː.pəsˈbɪlt US ˌpɜːr- *stress shift:* ˌpurpose-built ˈresidence

purposeful 'pɜː.pəs|.fᵊl, -fʊl (US) 'pɜːr- **-ly** -i **-ness** -nəs, -nɪs
purposeless 'pɜː.pəs.ləs, -lɪs (US) 'pɜːr- **-ly** -li **-ness** -nəs, -nɪs
purposely 'pɜː.pə.sli (US) 'pɜːr-
purposive 'pɜː.pə.sɪv (US) 'pɜːr- **-ly** -li **-ness** -nəs, -nɪs
purpura 'pɜː.pjʊ.rə, -pjə- (US) 'pɜːr.pɚ.ə, -pjɚ-, -pʊ.rə
purr pɜːʳ (US) pɜːr **-s** -z **-ing** -ɪŋ **-ed** -d
purs|e pɜːs (US) pɜːrs **-es** -ɪz **-ing** -ɪŋ **-ed** -t
purser 'pɜː.səʳ (US) 'pɜːr.sɚ **-s** -z
purse-string 'pɜːs.strɪŋ (US) 'pɜːrs- **-s** -z
purslane 'pɜː.slɪn, -slən, -sleɪn (US) 'pɜːr.slɪn, -sleɪn
pursuance pə'sjuː.ən*t*s, pɜː-, -'su- (US) pɚ'suː-
pursuant pə'sjuː.ənt, pɜː-, -'su- (US) pɚ'suː- **-ly** -li
pursu|e pə'sjuː, pɜː-, -'suː (US) pɚ'suː **-es** -z **-ing** -ɪŋ **-ed** -d **-er/z** -əʳ/z (US) -ɚ/z
pursuit pə'sjuːt, pɜː-, -'suːt (US) pɚ'suːt **-s** -s
pursuivant 'pɜː.sɪ.vənt, -sə- *old fashioned:* -swɪ- (US) 'pɜːr.sɪ-, -swɪ- **-s** -s
Purton 'pɜː.tᵊn (US) 'pɜːr-
purulency 'pjʊə.rʊ.lən*t*.si, -rjʊ-, -rə- (US) 'pjʊr.ə-, -jə-
purulent 'pjʊə.rʊ.lənt, -rjʊ-, -rə- (US) 'pjʊr.ə-, -rjə- **-ly** -li
Purver 'pɜː.vəʳ (US) 'pɜːr.vɚ
Purves 'pɜː.vɪs (US) 'pɜːr-
purvey pə'veɪ, pɜː- (US) pɚ- **-s** -z **-ing** -ɪŋ **-ed** -d
purvey|ance pə'veɪ|.ən*t*s, pɜː- (US) pɚ- **-or/s** -əʳ/z (US) -ɚ/z
purview 'pɜː.vjuː (US) 'pɜːr- **-s** -z
pus pʌs
Pusan ˌpuː'sæn (US) -'sɑːn
Pusey 'pjuː.zi **-ism** -ɪ.zᵊm **-ite/s** -aɪt/s
push pʊʃ **-es** -ɪz **-ing** -ɪŋ/li **-ed** -t **-er/s** -əʳ/z (US) -ɚ/z
pushball 'pʊʃ.bɔːl (US) -bɔːl, -bɑːl
push-bike 'pʊʃ.baɪk **-s** -s
push-button 'pʊʃˌbʌt.ᵊn **-s** -z
push-cart 'pʊʃ.kɑːt (US) -kɑːrt **-s** -s
pushchair 'pʊʃ.tʃeəʳ (US) -tʃer **-s** -z
pushdown 'pʊʃ.daʊn
pushful 'pʊʃ.fᵊl, -fʊl **-ness** -nəs, -nɪs
Pushkin 'pʊʃ.kɪn
pushover 'pʊʃˌəʊ.vəʳ (US) -ˌoʊ.vɚ **-s** -z
pushpin 'pʊʃ.pɪn **-s** -z
push|-start 'pʊʃ|.stɑːt (US) -stɑːrt **-starts** -stɑːts (US) -stɑːrts **-starting** -ˌstɑː.tɪŋ (US) -ˌstɑːr.t̬ɪŋ **-started** -ˌstɑː.tɪd (US) -ˌstɑːr.t̬ɪd
Pushtu 'pʌʃ.tuː, ˌ-'- (US) 'pʌʃ.tuː
pushup 'pʊʃ.ʌp **-s** -s
push|y 'pʊʃ|.i **-ier** -i.əʳ (US) -i.ɚ **-iest** -i.ɪst, -i.ɪst **-iness** -ɪ.nəs, -ɪ.nɪs
pusillanimity ˌpjuː.sɪ.lə'nɪm.ə.ti, -zɪ-, -læn'ɪm-, -ɪ.ti (US) -sɪ.lə'nɪm.ə.t̬i
pusillanimous ˌpjuː.sɪ'læn.ɪ.məs, -zɪ'-, '-ə- (US) -sɪ'læn.ə- **-ly** -li **-ness** -nəs, -nɪs
puss pʊs **-es** -ɪz
puss|y 'pʊs|.i **-ies** -iz ˌ**pussy 'willow**
pussycat 'pʊs.i.kæt **-s** -s
pussy|foot 'pʊs.i|.fʊt **-foots** -fʊts **-footing** -ˌfʊt.ɪŋ (US) -ˌfʊt̬.ɪŋ **-footed** -ˌfʊt.ɪd (US) -ˌfʊt̬.ɪd **-footer/s** -ˌfʊt.əʳ/z (US) -ˌfʊt̬.ɚ/z
pustular 'pʌs.tjə.ləʳ, -tjʊ- (US) -tʃə.lɚ, -tjə-, -tjʊ-
pustu|late 'pʌs.tjə|.leɪt, -tjʊ- (US) -tjuː-, -tjə-, -tʃə- **-lated** -leɪ.tɪd (US) -leɪ.t̬ɪd
pustulation ˌpʌs.tjə'leɪ.ʃᵊn, -tjʊ'- (US) -tʃə'-, -tjə'-, -tjʊ'- **-s** -z
pustule 'pʌs.tjuːl (US) -tʃuːl, -tjuːl **-s** -z
pustulous 'pʌs.tjə.ləs, -tjʊ- (US) -tʃə-, -tjə-, -tjʊ-
put pʊt **-s** -s **-ting** -ɪŋ (US) 'pʊt̬.ɪŋ
putative 'pjuː.tə.tɪv (US) -t̬ə.t̬ɪv **-ly** -li
put-down 'pʊt.daʊn **-s** -z
Putnam 'pʌt.nəm
Putney 'pʌt.ni
put-on 'pʊt.ɒn (US) -ɑːn **-s** -z
putrefaction ˌpjuː.trɪ'fæk.ʃᵊn, -trə'- (US) -trə'-
putre|fy 'pjuː.trɪ|.faɪ, -trə- (US) -trə- **-fies** -faɪz **-fying** -faɪ.ɪŋ **-fied** -faɪd
putrescenc|e pjuː'tres.ᵊn|*t*s **-t** -t
putrid 'pjuː.trɪd **-ly** -li **-ness** -nəs, -nɪs
putridity pjuː'trɪd.ə.ti, -ɪ.ti (US) -ə.t̬i
putsch pʊtʃ **-es** -ɪz
putt (P) pʌt **-s** -s **-ing** -ɪŋ (US) 'pʌt̬.ɪŋ **-ed** -ɪd (US) 'pʌt̬.ɪd **-er/s** -əʳ/z (US) 'pʌt̬.ɚ/z **'putting ˌgreen**
puttee 'pʌt.i, -iː; pʌt'iː (US) pʌt'iː, '-- **-s** -z
Puttenham 'pʌt.ᵊn.əm
putter (*from* **putt**) 'pʌt.əʳ (US) 'pʌt̬.ɚ **-s** -z
putter (*from* **put**) 'pʊt.əʳ (US) 'pʊt̬.ɚ **-z** -z
putti (*plur. of* **putto**) 'pʊt.i, -iː (US) 'puː.ti, -tiː
Puttick 'pʌt.ɪk (US) 'pʌt̬-
Puttnam 'pʌt.nəm
putt|o 'pʊt|.əʊ (US) 'puː.t|oʊ **-i** -i, -iː
putt|y 'pʌt|.i (US) 'pʌt̬- **-ies** -iz **-ying** -i.ɪŋ **-ied** -id
putz pʌts **-es** -ɪz
puzzl|e 'pʌz.l̩ **-es** -z **-ing/ly** -ɪŋ/li, '-lɪŋ/li **-ed** -d
puzzlement 'pʌz.l̩.mənt
puzzler 'pʌz.ləʳ, -l̩.əʳ (US) '-lɚ, -l̩.ɚ **-s** -z
PVC ˌpiː.viː'siː
Pwllheli pʊθ'lel.i *as if Welsh:* pʊ'*h*lel.i
PWR ˌpiːˌdʌb.l̩.ju'ɑːʳ (US) -'ɑːr
pya pjɑː, pi'ɑː (US) pjɑː **-s** -z
pyaemia paɪ'iː.mi.ə
Pybus 'paɪ.bəs
Pye paɪ
pygmaean pɪg'miː.ən
Pygmalion pɪg'meɪ.li.ən (US) -'meɪl.jən, -'meɪ.li.ən
pygm|y 'pɪg.m|i **-ies** -iz
pyjama pɪ'dʒɑː.mə, pə- (US) pə'dʒɑː-, -'dʒæm.ə **-s** -z
Pyke paɪk
Pylades 'pɪl.ə.diːz, 'paɪ.lə-
Pyle paɪl
pylon 'paɪ.lɒn, -lən (US) -lɑːn, -lən **-s** -z
pylor|us paɪ'lɔː.rləs (US) -'lɔːr|.əs, pɪ- **-i** -aɪ **-ic** -ɪk
Pym pɪm
Pynchon 'pɪn.*t*ʃən (US) 'pɪn.tʃən
Pyongyang ˌpjɒŋ'jæŋ (US) ˌpjʌŋ'jɑːŋ, ˌpjɑːŋ-, -'jæŋ
pyorrhoea ˌpaɪə'rɪə (US) -'riː.ə
pyracantha ˌpaɪə.rə'kæn*t*.θə (US) ˌpaɪ-, ˌpɪr.ə'- **-s** -z
pyramid 'pɪr.ə.mɪd **-s** -z **'pyramid ˌselling, ˌpyramid 'selling**
pyramidal pɪ'ræm.ɪ.dᵊl, pə-, '-ə- (US) pɪ'ræm.ɪ-, pə-, '-ə-; ˌpɪr.ə'mɪd.ᵊl **-ly** -i
Pyramus 'pɪr.ə.məs
pyre paɪəʳ (US) paɪɚ **-s** -z
Pyrene paɪə'riː.ni (US) paɪ'riːn
Pyren|ees ˌpɪr.ə'n|iːz, -ɪ'- (US) -ə'- **-ean** -iː.ən
pyrethrin paɪə'riː.θrɪn (US) paɪ-, -'reθ.rɪn
pyrethrum paɪə'riː.θrəm (US) paɪ-, -'reθ.rəm **-s** -z
pyretic paɪə'ret.ɪk, pɪ- (US) paɪ'ret̬-
Pyrex® 'paɪə.reks (US) 'paɪ-
pyriform 'pɪr.ɪ.fɔːm (US) -fɔːrm
pyrite 'paɪə.raɪt (US) 'paɪ-
pyrites paɪə'raɪ.tiːz, pɪ-, pə- (US) paɪ'raɪ.tiːz, pɪ-; 'paɪ.raɪts
pyritic paɪə'rɪt.ɪk (US) paɪ'rɪt̬-
pyro- paɪə.rəʊ-; paɪə'rɒ-; (US) paɪ.roʊ-, -rə-; paɪ'rɑː-
Note: Prefix. Normally either takes primary or secondary stress on the first syllable, e.g. **pyromania** /ˌpaɪə.rəʊ'meɪ.ni.ə (US) ˌpaɪ.roʊ'-/, or primary stress on the second syllable, e.g. **pyrolysis** /paɪə'rɒl.ə.sɪs (US) paɪ'rɑː.lə-/.
pyrocanthus ˌpaɪə.rəʊ'kæn.θəs (US) ˌpaɪ.roʊ-
pyrogallic ˌpaɪə.rəʊ'gæl.ɪk (US) ˌpaɪ.roʊ'-, -'gɑː.lɪk
pyrolysis (P) paɪə'rɒl.ə.sɪs, '-ə- (US) paɪ'rɑː.lə-
pyromani|a ˌpaɪə.rəʊ'meɪ.ni|.ə (US) ˌpaɪ.roʊ'-, '-nj|ə **-ac** -æk

pyromet|er paɪə'rɒm.ɪ.t|əʳ, '-ə- (US) paɪ'rɑː.mə.t̬|ɚ **-ers** -əz (US) -ɚz **-ry** -ri

pyrometric ˌpaɪə.rəʊ'met.rɪk (US) ˌpaɪ.roʊ'-, -rə'- **-ally** -ᵊl.i, -li *stress shift:* ˌpyrometric 'measurement

pyrotechnic ˌpaɪə.rəʊ'tek.nɪk (US) ˌpaɪ.roʊ'-, -rə'- **-al** -ᵊl **-ally** -ᵊl.i, -li **-s** -s *stress shift:* ˌpyrotechnic 'substance

Pyrrh|a 'pɪr|.ə **-us** -əs

pyrrhic (P) 'pɪr.ɪk **-s** -s ˌ**Pyrrhic 'victory**

Pytchley 'paɪtʃ.li

Pythagoras paɪ'θæg.ᵊr.əs, -ɒr-, -æs (US) pɪ'θæg.ɚ.əs **Pyˌthagoras' 'theorem**

Pythagorean paɪˌθæg.ᵊr'iː.ən, ˌpaɪ.θæg-, -ɒr'- (US) pɪˌθæg.ə'riː- **-s** -z

Pythian 'pɪθ.i.ən

Pythias 'pɪθ.i.æs (US) -əs

python 'paɪ.θᵊn (US) -θɑːn, -θən **-s** -z

Pythonesque ˌpaɪ.θᵊn'esk

pythoness 'paɪ.θᵊn.es, -ɪs (US) 'paɪ-, 'pɪθ.ᵊn-, -ɪs **-es** -ɪz

pythonic paɪ'θɒn.ɪk (US) -'θɑː.nɪk, pɪ-

pyx pɪks **-es** -ɪz

Q

q (Q) kjuː **-'s** -z
Qaddafi, **Qadhafi** gəˈdɑː.fi, -ˈdæf.i (US) kə ˈdɑː-
Qantas® ˈkwɒn.təs, -tæs (US) ˈkwɑːn.təs
Qatar ˈkʌt.ɑːʳ, ˈkæt-, ˈgæt-; kəˈtɑːʳ, gætˈɑːʳ, kæt- (US) ˈkɑː.tɑːr; kəˈtɑːr
QC ˌkjuːˈsiː **-'s** -z
q.e.d., **QED** ˌkjuː.iːˈdiː
qintar kɪnˈtɑːʳ, ˈ-- (US) kɪnˈtɑːr **-s** -z
qt ˌkjuːˈtiː
Q-Tip® ˈkjuː.tɪp **-s** -s
qua kweɪ, kwɑː
quack kwæk **-s** -s **-ing** -ɪŋ **-ed** -t **-ery** -ᵊr.i **-ish** -ɪʃ
quad kwɒd (US) kwɑːd **-s** -z
Quadragesim|a ˌkwɒd.rəˈdʒes.ɪ.m|ə, ˈ-ə- (US) ˌkwɑː.drəˈ-, -ˈdʒeɪ.zɪ- **-al** -ᵊl
quadrangle ˈkwɒd.ræŋ.gl̩, kwɒdˈræŋ- (US) ˈkwɑː.dræŋ- **-s** -z
quadrangular kwɒdˈræŋ.gjə.ləʳ, kwəˈdræŋ-, -gjʊ- (US) kwɑːˈdræŋ.gjə.lɚ, -gjʊ-
quadrant ˈkwɒd.rᵊnt (US) ˈkwɑː.drᵊnt **-s** -s
quadraphonic ˌkwɒd.rəˈfɒn.ɪk (US) ˌkwɑː.drəˈfɑː.nɪk **-ally** -ᵊl.i, -li **-s** -s *stress shift:* ˌquadraphonic ˈsound
quadraphony kwɒdˈrɒf.ᵊn.i, kwəˈdrɒf-, -ˈdræf-; ˈkwɒd.rə.fɒn- (US) kwɑːˈdræf.ᵊn-
quadrate (*n. adj.*) ˈkwɒd.rət, -rɪt, -reɪt (US) ˈkwɑː.drɪt, -dreɪt **-s** -s
quadra|te (*v.*) kwɒdˈreɪ|t, kwəˈdreɪ|t (US) kwɑːˈdreɪ|t **-tes** -ts **-ting** -tɪŋ (US) -t̬ɪŋ **-ted** -tɪd (US) -t̬ɪd
quadratic kwɒdˈræt.ɪk, kwəˈdræt- (US) kwɑːˈdræt̬- **-s** -s **quadˌratic eˈquation**
quadrature ˈkwɒd.rə.tʃəʳ, -rɪ-, -tjʊəʳ (US) ˈkwɑː.drə.tʃɚ
quadric ˈkwɒd.rɪk (US) ˈkwɑː.drɪk **-s** -s
quadri|ga kwɒdˈriː|.gə, kwəˈdriː-, -ˈdraɪ- (US) kwɑːˈdraɪ- **-gae** -dʒiː (US) -giː, -dʒiː **-gas** -gəz
quadrilateral ˌkwɒd.rɪˈlæt.ᵊr.ᵊl, -rəˈ-, ˈ-rᵊl (US) ˌkwɑː.drɪˈlæt̬- **-s** -z *stress shift:* ˌquadrilateral ˈshape
quadrilingual ˌkwɒd.rɪˈlɪŋ.gwəl, -rəˈ- (US) ˌkwɑː.drɪˈ- *stress shift:* ˌquadrilingual ˈnation
quadrille kwəˈdrɪl, kwɒdˈrɪl (US) kwəˈdrɪl, kwɑː- **-s** -z
quadrillion kwɒdˈrɪl.jən, kwəˈdrɪl-, ˈ-i.ən (US) kwɑːˈdrɪl.jən **-s** -z
quadriplegia ˌkwɒd.rɪˈpliː.dʒə, -rəˈ-, ˈ-dʒi.ə (US) ˌkwɑː.drɪˈpliː-
quadriplegic ˌkwɒd.rɪˈpliː.dʒɪk, -rəˈ- (US) ˌkwɑː.drɪˈ- **-s** -s *stress shift:* ˌquadriplegic ˈstate
quadrisyllabic ˌkwɒd.rɪ.sɪˈlæb.ɪk, -rə-, -səˈ- (US) ˌkwɑː.drɪ- *stress shift:* ˌquadrisyllabic ˈword
quadrisyllable ˌkwɒd.rɪˈsɪl.ə.bl̩ (US) ˈkwɑː.drɪˌsɪl- **-s** -z
quadroon kwɒdˈruːn, kwəˈdruːn (US) kwɑːˈdruːn **-s** -z
quadrophonic ˌkwɒd.rəˈfɒn.ɪk (US) ˌkwɑː.drəˈfɑː.nɪk **-ally** -ᵊl.i, -li **-s** -s *stress shift:* ˌquadrophonic ˈsound
quadrophony kwɒdˈrɒf.ᵊn.i, kwəˈdrɒf-; ˈkwɒd.rə.fɒn- (US) kwɑːˈdræf.ᵊn-
quadrumana kwɒdˈruː.mə.nə, kwəˈdruː- (US) kwɑːˈdruː-
quadrumanous kwɒdˈruː.mə.nəs, kwəˈdruː- (US) kwɑːˈdruː-
quadruped ˈkwɒd.rə.ped, -rʊ- (US) ˈkwɑː.drʊ-, -drə- **-s** -z
quadrupl|e ˈkwɒd.rʊp.l̩, -ruː.pl̩; kwɒdˈruː.pl̩, kwəˈdruː- (US) kwɑːˈdruː.pl̩, kwə-, -ˈdrʊp.l̩; ˈkwɑː.druː.pl̩, -drʊ-, -drə- **-es** -z **-y** -i **-ing** -ɪŋ **-ed** -d
quadruplet ˈkwɒd.rʊ.plət, -plɪt, -plet; kwɒdˈruː- (US) kwɑːˈdruː.plɪt; ˈkwɑː.druː-, -drə-; kwɑːˈdrʌp.lɪt **-s** -s
quadruplicate (*n. adj.*) kwɒdˈruː.plɪ.kət, kwəˈdruː-, -plə-, -kɪt, -keɪt (US) kwɑːˈdruː.plɪ.kɪt, -keɪt **-s** -s
quadrupli|cate (*v.*) kwɒdˈruː.plɪ|.keɪt, kwəˈdruː- (US) kwɑːˈdruː- **-cates** -keɪts **-cating** -keɪ.tɪŋ (US) -keɪ.t̬ɪŋ **-cated** -keɪ.tɪd (US) -keɪ.t̬ɪd
quaestor ˈkwiː.stəʳ, ˈkwaɪ-, -stɔːʳ (US) ˈkwes.tɚ, ˈkwiː.stɚ **-s** -z
quaff kwɒf, kwɑːf (US) kwɑːf, kwæf, kwɔːf **-s** -s **-ing** -ɪŋ **-ed** -t **-er/s** -əʳ/z (US) -ɚ/z
quag kwɒg, kwæg (US) kwæg, kwɑːg **-s** -z
quagga ˈkwæg.ə, ˈkwɒg- (US) ˈkwæg-, ˈkwɑː.gə **-s** -z
Quaglino's® kwægˈliː.nəʊz (US) -noʊz
quagmire ˈkwɒg.maɪəʳ, ˈkwæg- (US) ˈkwæg.maɪɚ, ˈkwɑːg- **-s** -z
quail (Q) kweɪl **-s** -z **-ing** -ɪŋ **-ed** -d
Quain kweɪn
quaint kweɪnt **-er** -əʳ (US) ˈkweɪn.t̬ɚ **-est** -ɪst, -əst (US) ˈkweɪn.t̬ɪst, -t̬əst **-ly** -li **-ness** -nəs, -nɪs
quak|e kweɪk **-es** -s **-ing** -ɪŋ **-ed** -t
Quaker ˈkweɪ.kəʳ (US) -kɚ **-s** -z
qualification ˌkwɒl.ɪ.fɪˈkeɪ.ʃᵊn, ˌ-ə- (US) ˌkwɑː.lɪ- **-s** -z
qualificative ˈkwɒl.ɪ.fɪ.kə.tɪv, ˈ-ə- (US) ˈkwɑː.lɪ.fɪ.keɪ.t̬ɪv **-s** -z
qualificatory ˌkwɒl.ɪ.fɪˈkeɪ.tᵊr.i, ˌ-ə- (US) ˈkwɑː.lɪ.fə.kə.tɔːr-
quali|fy ˈkwɒl.ɪ|.faɪ, ˈ-ə- (US) ˈkwɑː.lɪ- **-fies** -faɪz **-fying** -faɪ.ɪŋ **-fied** -faɪd **-fier/s** -faɪ.əʳ/z (US) -faɪ.ɚ/z
qualitative ˈkwɒl.ɪ.tə.tɪv, -teɪ- (US) ˈkwɑː.lɪ.teɪ.t̬ɪv **-ly** -li
qualit|y ˈkwɒl.ə.t|i, -ɪ.t|i (US) ˈkwɑː.lə.t̬|i **-ies** -iz ˈ**quality conˌtrol**; ˈ**quality ˌtime**
qualm kwɑːm, kwɔːm (US) kwɑːm **-s** -z
qualmish ˈkwɑː.mɪʃ, ˈkwɔː- (US) ˈkwɑː- **-ly** -li **-ness** -nəs, -nɪs
quandar|y (Q) ˈkwɒn.dᵊr|.i, -dr|i (US) ˈkwɑːn- **-ies** -iz
quango ˈkwæŋ.gəʊ (US) -goʊ **-s** -z
Quant kwɒnt (US) kwɑːnt
quanta (*plur. of* **quantum**) ˈkwɒn.tə (US) ˈkwɑːn.t̬ə
quantal ˈkwɒn.tᵊl (US) ˈkwɑːn.t̬ᵊl
quantic ˈkwɒn.tɪk (US) ˈkwɑːn.t̬ɪk **-s** -s
quantifiable ˈkwɒn.tɪ.faɪ.ə.bl̩, -tə-, ˌkwɒn.tɪˈfaɪ-, -təˈ- (US) ˈkwɑːn.t̬ə.faɪ-
quantification ˌkwɒn.tɪ.fɪˈkeɪ.ʃᵊn, -tə- (US) ˌkwɑːn.t̬ə-
quanti|fy ˈkwɒn.tɪ|.faɪ, -tə- (US) ˈkwɑːn.t̬ə- **-fies** -faɪz **-fying** -faɪ.ɪŋ **-fied** -faɪd **-fier/s** -faɪ.əʳ/z (US) -faɪ.ɚ/z
quantitative ˈkwɒn.tɪ.tə.tɪv, -teɪ- (US) ˈkwɑːn.t̬ə.teɪ.t̬ɪv **-ly** -li
quantit|y ˈkwɒn.tə.t|i, -tɪ- (US) ˈkwɑːn.t̬ə.t̬|i **-ies** -iz ˌ**quantity surˈveyor**; ˈ**quantity surˌveyor**
quantiz|e, -is|e ˈkwɒn.taɪz (US) ˈkwɑːn- **-es** -ɪz **-ing** -ɪŋ **-ed** -d
Quantock ˈkwɒn.tək, -tɒk (US) ˈkwɑːn.t̬ək, -tɑːk
quant|um *amount:* ˈkwɒn.t|əm (US) ˈkwɑːn.t̬|əm **-a** -ə ˌ**quantum ˈjump**; ˌ**quantum ˈleap**; ˌ**quantum meˈchanics**; ˈ**quantum ˌtheory**
quantum *in Latin phrases:* ˈkwæn.tʊm, ˈkwɒn-, -təm (US) ˈkwɑːn.t̬əm, -tʊm
quantum meruit ˌkwæn.tʊmˈmer.u.ɪt, ˌkwɒn-, -təmˈ- (US) ˌkwɑːn.tʊmˈ-, -t̬əmˈ-
quarantin|e ˈkwɒr.ᵊn.tiːn, -taɪn (US) ˈkwɔːr.ᵊn.tiːn, ˈkwɑːr- **-es** -z **-ing** -ɪŋ **-ed** -d
quare clausim fregit ˌkwɑː.reɪˌklaʊ.səmˈfreɪ.gɪt (US) ˌkwɑːr.iˌklaʊ.səmˈfreɪ.gət, -gɪt
Quaritch ˈkwɒr.ɪtʃ (US) ˈkwɑːr-
quark *in physics:* kwɑːk, kwɔːk (US) kwɑːrk, kwɔːrk **-s** -s
quark *soft cheese:* kwɑːk (US) kwɑːrk, kwɔːrk
Quarles kwɔːlz (US) kwɔːrlz, kwɑːrlz
Quarmby ˈkwɔːm.bi (US) ˈkwɔːrm-

quarrel ˈkwɒr.ᵊl (US) ˈkwɔːr-, ˈkwɑːr- **-s** -z **-(l)ing** -ɪŋ **-(l)ed** -d **-(l)er/s** -əʳ/z (US) -ɚ/z

quarrelsome ˈkwɒr.ᵊl.səm (US) ˈkwɔːr-, ˈkwɑːr- **-ly** -li **-ness** -nəs, -nɪs

quarr|y ˈkwɒr|.i (US) ˈkwɔːr-, ˈkwɑːr- **-ies** -iz **-ying** -i.ɪŋ **-ied** -id ˈ**quarry** ˌ**tile**, ˌ**quarry** ˈ**tile**

quarry|man ˈkwɒr.i|.mən, -mæn (US) ˈkwɔːr-, ˈkwɑːr- **-men** -mən, -men

quart *measurement:* kwɔːt (US) kwɔːrt **-s** -s

quart *in card games, fencing:* kɑːt (US) kɑːrt **-s** -s **-ing** -ɪŋ (US) ˈkɑːr.t̬ɪŋ **-ed** -ɪd (US) ˈkɑːr.t̬ɪd

quartan ˈkwɔː.tᵊn (US) ˈkwɔːr-

quarte (*n. v.*) *in card games, fencing:* kɑːt (US) kɑːrt **-s** -s **-ing** -ɪŋ (US) ˈkɑːr.t̬ɪŋ **-ed** -ɪd (US) ˈkɑːr.t̬ɪd

quart|er ˈkwɔː.t|əʳ (US) ˈkwɔːr.t̬|ɚ **-ers** -əz (US) -ɚz **-ering/s** -ᵊr.ɪŋ/z **-ered** -əd (US) -ɚd **-erage** -ᵊr.ɪdʒ ˈ**quarter** ˌ**day** ; ˈ**quarter** ˌ**note** ; ˈ**Quarter** ˌ**Sessions** ; ˈ**quarter** ˌ**tone**

quarterback ˈkwɔː.tə.bæk (US) ˈkwɔːr.t̬ɚ- **-s** -s

quarterdeck ˈkwɔː.tə.dek (US) ˈkwɔːr.t̬ɚ- **-s** -s

quarterfinal ˌkwɔː.təˈfaɪ.nᵊl (US) ˌkwɔːr.t̬ɚˈ- **-s** -z

quarterfinalist ˌkwɔː.təˈfaɪ.nᵊl.ɪst (US) ˌkwɔːr.t̬ɚˈ- **-s** -s

quarterl|y ˈkwɔː.tᵊl|.i (US) ˈkwɔːr.t̬ɚ.l|i **-ies** -iz

Quartermain(e) ˈkwɔː.tə.meɪn (US) ˈkwɔːr.t̬ɚ-

quartermaster ˈkwɔː.təˌmɑː.stəʳ (US) ˈkwɔːr.t̬ɚˌmæs.tɚ **-s** -z

quartern ˈkwɔː.tᵊn (US) ˈkwɔːr.t̬ɚn **-s** -z

quarter|staff ˈkwɔː.tə|.stɑːf (US) ˈkwɔːr.t̬ɚ|.stæf **-aves** -steɪvz

quartet(te) kwɔːˈtet (US) kwɔːr- **-s** -s

quartic ˈkwɔː.tɪk (US) ˈkwɔːr.t̬ɪk **-s** -s

quartile ˈkwɔː.taɪl (US) ˈkwɔːr-, -t̬ɪl, -t̬ᵊl **-s** -z

quarto ˈkwɔː.təʊ (US) ˈkwɔːr.t̬oʊ **-s** -z

quartus (Q) ˈkwɔː.təs (US) ˈkwɔːr.t̬əs

quartz ˈkwɔːts (US) ˈkwɔːrts

quasar ˈkweɪ.zɑːʳ, -sɑːʳ (US) -zɑːr, -sɑːr

quash kwɒʃ (US) kwɑːʃ, kwɔːʃ **-es** -ɪz **-ing** -ɪŋ **-ed** -t

quasi- kweɪ.zaɪ-, kwɑː-, -saɪ-, -zi- (US) kweɪ.saɪ-, -zaɪ-; kwɑː.zi-, -si-

Note: Prefix. Words beginning with **quasi-** are normally hyphenated, with **quasi-** taking secondary stress on the first syllable, e.g. **quasi-stellar** /ˌkweɪ.zaɪˈstel.əʳ (US) -saɪˈstel.ɚ/.

quasi ˈkweɪ.zaɪ, ˈkwɑː-, -saɪ, -zi (US) ˈkweɪ.saɪ, -zaɪ; ˈkwɑː.zi, -si

quasi in rem ˌkweɪ.zi.ɪnˈrem (US) ˌkwɑː-, -ənˈ-

Quasimodo ˌkwɑː.ziˈməʊ.dəʊ, ˌkwɒz.iˈ-, ˌkwæz- (US) ˌkwɑː.ziˈmoʊ.doʊ

quassia ˈkwɒʃ.ə, -i.ə (US) ˈkwɑː.ʃə, ˈ-ʃi.ə

quatercentenar|y ˌkwæt.ə.senˈtiː.nᵊr|.i, ˌkwɔː.tə-, ˌkwɒt.ə-, ˌkweɪ.tə-, -ˈten.ᵊr- (US) ˌkwɑː.t̬ɚ.senˈten.ɚ|.i; -ˈsen.tᵊn.er- **-ies** -iz

Quatermain ˈkwɔː.tə.meɪn (US) ˈkwɑː.t̬ɚ-

quaternar|y (Q) kwəˈtɜː.nᵊr|.i, kwɒtˈɜː- (US) ˈkwɑː.t̬ɚ.ner-; kwəˈtɜːr.nɚ- **-ies** -iz

quaternion kwəˈtɜː.ni.ən, kwɒtˈɜː- (US) kwəˈtɜːr-, kwɑː- **-s** -z

quatorzain kəˈtɔː.zeɪn, kætˈɔː-; ˈkæt.ə- (US) kəˈtɔːr-, kætˈɔːr-; ˈkæt̬.ɚ- **-s** -z

quatrain ˈkwɒt.reɪn, -rᵊn (US) ˈkwɑː.treɪn, -ˈ- **-s** -z

quatrefoil ˈkæt.rə.fɔɪl, ˈ-ə- (US) ˈkæt̬.ɚ.fɔɪl, -rə- **-s** -z

quatrillion kwɒtˈrɪl.jən, kwəˈtrɪl-, ˈ-i.ən (US) kwɑːˈtrɪl-, kwə- **-s** -z

quattrocento (Q) ˌkwæt.rəʊˈtʃen.təʊ, ˌkwɒt- (US) ˌkwɑː.troʊˈtʃen.toʊ

quav|er ˈkweɪ.v|əʳ (US) -v|ɚ **-ers** -əz (US) -ɚz **-ering/ly** -ᵊr.ɪŋ/li **-ered** -əd (US) -ɚd

quay kiː (US) kiː, keɪ, kweɪ **-s** -z **-age** -ɪdʒ

Quay *place name:* kiː *surname:* kweɪ

Quayle kweɪl

quayside ˈkiː.saɪd

quean kwiːn **-s** -z

queas|y ˈkwiː.z|i **-ily** -ɪ.li **-iness** -ɪ.nəs, -ɪ.nɪs

Quebec kwɪˈbek, kwə-, kɪ-, kə- *as if French:* kebˈek (US) kwiːˈbek, kwɪ-, kɪ- *as if French:* kebˈek

Quebecois, Québecois ˌkeɪ.bekˈwɑː, ˌkeb.ekˈ-, -ɪˈkwɑː, -əˈ- (US) ˌkeɪ.bekˈwɑː

Quechu|a ˈketʃ.u|.ə, -w|ə (US) -w|ɑː, -w|ə **-an/s** -ən/z

queen kwiːn **-s** -z **-ing** -ɪŋ **-ed** -d ˌ**Queen's** ˈ**Counsel** ; ˌ**Queen's** ˈ**English** ; ˌ**queen's** ˈ**evidence** ; ˌ**Queen** ˈ**Mother**

Queenborough ˈkwiːn.bᵊr.ə, ˈkwiːm- (US) ˈkwiːn.bɚ.oʊ

Queenie ˈkwiː.ni

queenlike ˈkwiːn.laɪk

queenl|y ˈkwiːn.l|i **-ier** -i.əʳ (US) -i.ɚ **-iest** -i.ɪst, -i.əst **-iness** -ɪ.nəs, -ɪ.nɪs

Queens kwiːnz

Queensberry ˈkwiːnz.bᵊr.i (US) -ˌber.i, -bɚ- ˌ**Queensberry** ˈ**rules**

Queensbury ˈkwiːnz.bᵊr.i

Queensferry ˈkwiːnzˌfer.i

Queensland ˈkwiːnz.lənd, -lænd

Queenstown ˈkwiːnz.taʊn

Queensway ˈkwiːnz.weɪ

queer kwɪəʳ (US) kwɪr **-s** -z **-er** -əʳ (US) -ɚ **-est** -ɪst (US) -əst **-ly** -li **-ness** -nəs, -nɪs **-ish** -ɪʃ ˈ**queer** ˌ**street**

quell kwel **-s** -z **-ing** -ɪŋ **-ed** -d **-er/s** -əʳ/z (US) -ɚ/z

quench kwentʃ **-es** -ɪz **-ing** -ɪŋ **-ed** -t **-er/s** -əʳ/z (US) -ɚ/z **-able** -ə.bl̩

quenelle kəˈnel, kɪ- (US) kə- **-s** -z

Quen(n)ell kwɪˈnel, kwə-, ˈkwen.ᵊl (US) kwəˈnel, ˈkwen.ᵊl

Quentin ˈkwen.tɪn (US) -tᵊn

Querétaro kəˈreɪ.tᵊr.əʊ (US) -ˈret.ə.roʊ; kɚ.əˈtɑːr.oʊ

quern kwɜːn (US) kwɜːrn **-s** -z

querulous ˈkwer.ʊ.ləs, -jʊ-, ˈ-ə- (US) ˈkwer.jə.ləs, -jʊ-, ˈ-ə-, ˈ-ʊ- **-ly** -li **-ness** -nəs, -nɪs

quer|y ˈkwɪə.r|i (US) ˈkwɪr|.i **-ies** -iz **-ying** -i.ɪŋ **-ied** -id

quesadilla ˌkeɪ.səˈdiː.jə, -ljə (US) -jə **-s** -z

Quesnel ˈkeɪ.nᵊl

quest kwest **-s** -s **-ing** -ɪŋ **-ed** -ɪd

Quested ˈkwes.tɪd

question ˈkwes.tʃən, ˈkweʃ- (US) ˈkwes.tʃən, -tjən **-s** -z **-ing/ly** -ɪŋ/li **-ed** -d **-er/s** -əʳ/z (US) -ɚ/z ˈ**question** ˌ**mark** ; ˈ**question** ˌ**time** ; ˌ**out of the** ˈ**question**

questionab|le ˈkwes.tʃə.nə.bl|̩, ˈkweʃ- (US) ˈkwes.tʃə-, -tjə- **-ly** -li **-leness** -l̩.nəs, -nɪs

questionar|y ˈkwes.tʃə.nᵊr|.i, ˈkweʃ- (US) ˈkwes.tʃə.ner-, -tjə- **-ies** -iz

question-master ˈkwes.tʃənˌmɑː.stəʳ, ˈkweʃ-, -tʃəmˌ- (US) ˈkwes.tʃənˌmæs.tɚ, -tjənˌ- **-s** -z

questionnaire ˌkwes.tʃəˈneəʳ, ˌkweʃ-, ˌkes-, ˈ--- (US) ˌkwes.tʃəˈner, -tjəˈ- **-s** -z

Quetta ˈkwet.ə (US) ˈkwet̬-

quetzal ˈkwet.sᵊl (US) ketˈsɑːl **-s** -z **quetzales** kwetˈsɑː.les (US) ket-

Quetzalcoatl ˌket.sᵊl.kəʊˈæt.ᵊl (US) -sɑːl.koʊˈɑː.t̬ᵊl

queue kjuː **-s** -z **-ing** -ɪŋ **-d** -d

queue-jump ˈkjuː.dʒʌmp **-s** -s **-ing** -ɪŋ **-ed** -t **-er/s** -əʳ/z (US) -ɚ/z

Quex kweks

Quezon City ˌkeɪ.zɒnˈsɪt.i, -sɒnˈ- (US) ˌkeɪ.sɑːnˈsɪt̬-

quibbl|e ˈkwɪb.l̩ **-es** -z **-ing** -ɪŋ, ˈkwɪb.lɪŋ **-ed** -d **-er/s** -əʳ/z, ˈkwɪb.ləʳ/z (US) ˈkwɪb.l̩.ɚ/z, ˈ-lɚ/z

Quibell ˈkwaɪ.bᵊl, ˈkwɪb.ᵊl; kwɪˈbel, kwaɪˈbel

Note: Baron Quibell of Scunthorpe pronounced /ˈkwaɪ.bᵊl/.

quich|e kiːʃ **-es** -ɪz

quick (Q) kwɪk **-er** -əʳ (US) -ɚ **-est** -ɪst, -əst **-ly** -li **-ness** -nəs, -nɪs ˌ**quick** ˈ**march** ; ˈ**quick** ˌ**time**

quick-change ˌkwɪk'tʃeɪndʒ *stress shift:* ˌquick-change 'tyres
Quicke kwɪk
quicken 'kwɪk.ᵊn **-s** -z **-ing** -ɪŋ **-ed** -d
quickfire 'kwɪk.faɪəʳ US -faɪɚ
quick-freez|e ˌkwɪk'friːz, '-- US 'kwɪk.friːz **-es** -ɪz **-ing** -ɪŋ **quick-froze** ˌkwɪk'frəʊz, '-- US 'kwɪk.froʊz **quick frozen** -ən **quick-freezer/s** ˌkwɪk'friː.zəʳ/z, '-ˌ-- US 'kwɪkˌfriː.zɚ/z
quickie 'kwɪk.i **-s** -z
quicklime 'kwɪk.laɪm
Quickly 'kwɪk.li
quicksand 'kwɪk.sænd **-s** -z
quickset 'kwɪk.set
quicksilver 'kwɪkˌsɪl.vəʳ US -vɚ
quickstep 'kwɪk.step **-s** -s
quick-tempered ˌkwɪk'tem.pəd US -pɚd, '-ˌ-- *stress shift, British only:* ˌquick-tempered 'person
quick-witted ˌkwɪk'wɪt.ɪd US -'wɪt̬-, '-ˌ-- **-ly** -li **-ness** -nəs, -nɪs *stress shift, British only:* ˌquick-witted 'person
quid kwɪd **-s** -z
quiddit|y 'kwɪd.ɪ.t|i, -ə.t|i US -ə.t̬|i **-ies** -iz
quid pro quo ˌkwɪd.prəʊ'kwəʊ US -proʊ'kwoʊ **-s** -z
quiescence kwi'es.ᵊnts US kwaɪ-, kwi-
quiescent kwi'es.ᵊnt US kwaɪ-, kwi- **-ly** -li
quiet kwaɪət **-er** -əʳ US 'kwaɪə.t̬ɚ **-est** -ɪst, -əst US 'kwaɪə.t̬ɪst, -əst **-ly** -li **-ness** -nəs, -nɪs **-s** -s **-ing** -ɪŋ US 'kwaɪə.t̬ɪŋ **-ed** -ɪd US 'kwaɪə.t̬ɪd
quieten 'kwaɪə.tᵊn **-s** -z **-ing** -ɪŋ **-ed** -d
quiet|ism 'kwaɪə.t|ɪ.zᵊm, 'kwaɪ.ɪ- US 'kwaɪə.t|ɪ- **-ist/s** -ɪst/s
quietude 'kwaɪə.tjuːd, 'kwaɪ.ɪ- US 'kwaɪə.tuːd, -tjuːd
quietus kwaɪ'iː.təs, -'eɪ- US -'iː.t̬əs
quiff kwɪf **-s** -s
Quigg kwɪg
Quiggin 'kwɪg.ɪn
Quigley 'kwɪg.li
quill kwɪl **-s** -z **-ing** -ɪŋ **-ed** -d
Quiller-Couch ˌkwɪl.ə'kuːtʃ US -ɚ'-
Quilliam 'kwɪl.i.əm
Quilp kwɪlp
quilt kwɪlt **-s** -s **-ing** -ɪŋ US 'kwɪl.t̬ɪŋ **-ed** -ɪd US 'kwɪl.t̬ɪd
Quilter 'kwɪl.təʳ US -t̬ɚ
quin (Q) kwɪn **-s** -z
Quinault *North American people:* 'kwɪn.ᵊlt, -ɔːlt US kwɪ'nɑːlt *French dramatist:* 'kiː.nəʊ US kɪ'noʊ
quinc|e (Q) kwɪn*t*s **-es** -ɪz
quincentenar|y ˌkwɪn.sen'tiː.nᵊr|.i, -'ten.ᵊr-, -'tɪn- US kwɪn'sen.tə.ner|.i; ˌkwɪn.sen'ten.ɚ- **-ies** -iz
Quincey 'kwɪn*t*.si
quincunx 'kwɪn.kʌŋks, 'kwɪŋ- US 'kwɪn- **-es** -ɪz
Quincy 'kwɪn*t*.si
quindecagon kwɪn'dek.ə.gᵊn US -gɑːn **-s** -z
quinella kwɪ'nel.ə
quingentenar|y ˌkwɪn.dʒen'tiː.nᵊr|.i, -'ten.ᵊr-, -'tɪn- **-ies** -iz
quinine 'kwɪn.iːn, -'-; kwə- US 'kwaɪ.naɪn
Quink® kwɪŋk
Quinn kwɪn
Quinney 'kwɪn.i
quinquagenarian ˌkwɪŋ.kwə.dʒə'neə.ri.ən, -kwɪ-, -dʒɪ'- US ˌkwɪn.kwə.dʒə'ner.i-, ˌkwɪŋ- **-s** -z
Quinquagesima ˌkwɪŋ.kwə'dʒes.ɪ.mə, -kwɪ'-, '-ə- US ˌkwɪn.kwə'dʒeɪ.zɪ-, ˌkwɪŋ-, -'dʒes.ɪ-
quinquennial kwɪŋ'kwen.i.əl US kwɪn-, kwɪŋ-
quinquennium kwɪŋ'kwen.i.əm US kwɪn-, kwɪŋ- **-s** -z
quinsy 'kwɪn.zi
quint *organ stop:* kwɪnt **-s** -s *in piquet:* kɪnt, kwɪnt *old fashioned:* kent **-s** -s *US for quintuplet:* kwɪnt **-s** -s
quintain 'kwɪn.tɪn **-s** -z
quintal 'kwɪn.tᵊl US -t̬ᵊl **-s** -z
Quintana Roo kɪnˌtɑː.nə'rəʊ.əʊ US -'roʊ.oʊ
quintessence kwɪn'tes.ᵊn*t*s
quintessential ˌkwɪn.tɪ'sen.*t*ʃᵊl, -tə'- US -te'sen*t*.ʃəl **-ly** -i
quintet, quintette kwɪn'tet **-s** -s
quintic 'kwɪn.tɪk US -t̬ɪk **-s** -s
Quintilian kwɪn'tɪl.i.ən US '-jən, -i.ən
quintillion kwɪn'tɪl.jən, '-i.ən US '-jən **-s** -z
Quintin 'kwɪn.tɪn US -tɪn, -tᵊn
Quinton 'kwɪn.tən US -tᵊn
quintupl|e 'kwɪn.tjʊ.pl̩, -tjuː-; kwɪn'tjuː- US kwɪn'tuː-, -'tjuː-; 'kwɪn.t̬ə- **-es** -z **-ing** -ɪŋ **-ed** -d
quintuplet 'kwɪn.tjʊ.plət, -plɪt, -plet; kwɪn'tjuː- US kwɪn'tʌp.lɪt, -'tuː.plɪt, -'tjuː-; 'kwɪn.tə.plet **-s** -s
quintus (Q) 'kwɪn.təs US -t̬əs
quip kwɪp **-s** -s **-ping** -ɪŋ **-ped** -t
quire kwaɪəʳ US kwaɪɚ **-s** -z
Quirey *in England, surname:* 'kwaɪə.ri US 'kwaɪ- *in Ireland:* 'kwɪə.ri US 'kwɪr.i
Quirinal 'kwɪr.ɪ.nᵊl, -ᵊn.ᵊl US 'kwɪr.ɪ.nᵊl; kwɪ'raɪ-
Quirinus kwɪ'raɪ.nəs
quirk (Q) kwɜːk US kwɜːrk **-s** -s
quirk|y 'kwɜː.k|i US 'kwɜːr- **-ier** -i.əʳ US -i.ɚ **-iest** -i.ɪst, -i.əst **-ily** -ɪ.li, -ᵊl.i **-iness** -ɪ.nəs, -ɪ.nɪs
quisling 'kwɪz.lɪŋ **-s** -z
quit kwɪt **-s** -s **-ting** -ɪŋ US 'kwɪt̬.ɪŋ **-ted** -ɪd US 'kwɪt̬.ɪd
quitclaim 'kwɪt.kleɪm **-s** -s
quite kwaɪt
Quito 'kiː.təʊ US -t̬oʊ, -toʊ
quit-rent 'kwɪt.rent **-s** -s
quits kwɪts
quittanc|e 'kwɪt.ᵊn*t*s **-es** -ɪz
quitter 'kwɪt.əʳ US 'kwɪt̬.ɚ **-s** -z
quiv|er 'kwɪv|.əʳ US -ɚ **-ers** -əz US -ɚz **-ering/ly** -ᵊr.ɪŋ/li **-ered** -əd US -ɚd
Quiverful 'kwɪv.ə.fʊl US '-ɚ-
qui vive ˌkiː'viːv
Quixote 'kwɪk.sət, -səʊt; kɪ'həʊ.ti, -teɪ US kɪ'hoʊ.t̬i, -teɪ; 'kwɪk.sət
quixotic kwɪk'sɒt.ɪk US -'sɑː.t̬ɪk **-ally** -ᵊl.i, -li
quiz kwɪz **-zes** -ɪz **-zing** -ɪŋ **-zed** -d
quiz-master 'kwɪzˌmɑː.stəʳ US -ˌmæs.tɚ **-s** -z
quizzic|al 'kwɪz.ɪ.k|ᵊl **-ally** -ᵊl.i, -li
quod kwɒd US kwɑːd **-s** -z **-ding** -ɪŋ **-ded** -ɪd
quod erat demonstrandum ˌkwɒdˌer.ætˌdem.ən'stræn.dəm US ˌkwɑːd-, -'strɑːn-
quodlibet 'kwɒd.lɪ.bet US 'kwɑːd.lə- **-s** -s
quoin kɔɪn, kwɔɪn **-s** -z **-ing** -ɪŋ **-ed** -d
quoit kɔɪt, kwɔɪt **-s** -s
quokka 'kwɒk.ə US 'kwɑː.kə **-s** -z
quondam 'kwɒn.dæm, -dəm US 'kwɑːn.dəm, -dæm
Quonset® 'kwɒn*t*.sɪt, -sət, -set US 'kwɑːn*t*- **'Quonset ˌhut**
quorate 'kwɔː.reɪt, -rət, -rɪt US 'kwɔːr.ɪt, -eɪt
Quorn® kwɔːn US kwɔːrn
quorum 'kwɔː.rəm US 'kwɔːr.əm **-s** -z
quota 'kwəʊ.tə US 'kwoʊ.t̬ə **-s** -z **-ing** -ɪŋ **-ed** -d
quotable 'kwəʊ.tə.bl̩ US 'kwoʊ.t̬ə-
quotation kwəʊ'teɪ.ʃᵊn US kwoʊ- **-s** -z **quo'tation ˌmark**
quot|e kwəʊt US kwoʊt **-es** -s **-ing** -ɪŋ US 'kwoʊ.t̬ɪŋ **-ed** -ɪd US 'kwoʊ.t̬ɪd
quoth kwəʊθ US kwoʊθ **-a** -ə
quotidian kwəʊ'tɪd.i.ən, kwɒt'ɪd- US kwoʊ'tɪd-
quotient 'kwəʊ.ʃᵊnt US 'kwoʊ- **-s** -s
quo warranto ˌkwəʊ.wɒr'æn.təʊ US ˌkwoʊ.wə'ræn.toʊ, -'rɑːn-, -wɔː'-
Qur'an, Quran kɒr'ɑːn, kɔː'rɑːn, kʊ-, kə- US kə'rɑːn, kɔː-, kʊ-, -'ræn
qursh 'kuː.əʃ; kʊəʃ US 'kuː.ɚʃ; kʊrʃ
Quy kwaɪ
q.v. ˌkjuː'viː, ˌwɪtʃ'siː, ˌkwɒd'vɪd.eɪ US ˌkjuː'viː, ˌwɪtʃ'siː, ˌkwɑːd'vɪd.eɪ
qwerty, QWERTY 'kwɜː.ti US 'kwɜːr.t̬i

R

r (R) ɑːʳ (US) ɑːr **-'s** -z

Ra rɑː

Rabat rə'bɑːt, rɑː-, -'bæt (US) rə'bɑːt, rɑː-

rabbet 'ræb.ɪt **-s** -s **-ing** -ɪŋ **-ed** -ɪd

rabbi 'ræb.aɪ **-s** -z

rabbinate 'ræb.ɪ.nət, '-ə-, -nɪt, -neɪt (US) -ɪ.nɪt, -neɪt **-s** -s

rabbinic rə'bɪn.ɪk, ræb'ɪn- (US) rə'bɪn- **-al** -əl **-ally** -əl.i, -li

rabb|it 'ræb|.ɪt **-its** -ɪts **-iting** -ɪ.tɪŋ (US) -ɪ.t̬ɪŋ **-ited** -ɪ.tɪd (US) -ɪ.t̬ɪd **'rabbit ˌhole ; 'rabbit ˌhutch ; 'rabbit ˌwarren**

rabble 'ræb.l̩ **-s** -z

rabble-rous|er 'ræb.l̩ˌraʊ.z|əʳ (US) -z|ɚ **-ers** -əz (US) -ɚz **-ing** -ɪŋ

Rabelais 'ræb.əl.eɪ (US) ˌræb.ə'leɪ, '---

Rabelaisian ˌræb.əl'eɪ.zi.ən, -ʒən (US) -ə'leɪ.ʒən, '-zi.ən

rabid 'ræb.ɪd, 'reɪ.bɪd (US) 'ræb.ɪd **-ly** -li **-ness** -nəs, -nɪs

rabies 'reɪ.biːz, -biz

Rabin 'reɪ.bɪn *Israeli politician:* ræb'iːn (US) rɑː'biːn

Rabindranath Tagore rəˌbɪn.drə.nɑːt.tə'gɔːʳ, -nɑːθ- (US) -ˌben.drə.nɑːt.tə'gɔːr, -nɑːθ-

Rabinowitz rə'bɪn.ə.wɪts, ræb'ɪn-, -vɪts

Raby 'reɪ.bi

RAC ˌɑːʳ.eɪ'siː (US) ˌɑːr-

Racal® 'reɪ.kəl, -kɔːl

raccoon rə'kuːn, ræk'uːn (US) ræk'uːn, rə'kuːn **-s** -z

rac|e reɪs **-es** -ɪz **-ing** -ɪŋ **-ed** -t **-er/s** -əʳ/z (US) -ɚ/z **ˌrace re'lations**

racecar 'reɪs.kɑːʳ (US) -kɑːr **-s** -z

racecours|e 'reɪs.kɔːs (US) -kɔːrs **-es** -ɪz

racegoer 'reɪsˌgəʊ.əʳ (US) -ˌgoʊ.ɚ **-s** -z

racehors|e 'reɪs.hɔːs (US) -ˌhɔːrs **-es** -ɪz

raceme 'ræs.iːm, 'reɪ.siːm; rə'siːm, ræs'iːm (US) reɪ'siːm, rə- **-s** -z

race-meeting 'reɪsˌmiː.tɪŋ (US) -t̬ɪŋ **-s** -z

racemic rə'siː.mɪk, ræs'iː-, reɪ'siː-, -'sem.ɪk (US) reɪ'siː-, rə-

racetrack 'reɪs.træk **-s** -s

Rachael, Rachel 'reɪ.tʃəl

Rachelle rə'ʃel; 'reɪ.tʃəl

rachitis rə'kaɪ.tɪs, ræk'aɪ- (US) -t̬əs

Rachman 'ræk.mən

Rachmaninoff, Rachmaninov ræk'mæn.ɪ.nɒf, ræx'- (US) rɑːk'mɑːn.ɪ.nɔːf

rachmanism (R) 'ræk.mə.nɪ.zəm

racial 'reɪ.ʃəl, -ʃi.əl (US) '-ʃəl **-ly** -i

racial|ism 'reɪ.ʃəl|.ɪ.zəm, -ʃi.əl- (US) '-ʃəl- **-ist/s** -ɪst/s

Racine *English personal name, city in US:* rə'siːn (US) rə-, reɪ- *French author:* ræs'iːn, rə'siːn (US) rɑː'siːn, rə-

rac|ism 'reɪ.s|ɪ.zəm **-ist/s** -ɪst/s

rack ræk **-s** -s **-ing** -ɪŋ **-ed** -t

rack|et 'ræk|.ɪt **-ets** -ɪts **-eting** -ɪ.tɪŋ (US) -ɪ.t̬ɪŋ **-eted** -ɪ.tɪd (US) -ɪ.t̬ɪd **-ety** -ə.ti, -ɪ.ti (US) -ə.t̬i

racketball 'ræk.ɪt.bɔːl (US) -bɔːl, -bɑːl

racketeer ˌræk.ɪ'tɪəʳ, -ə'- (US) -ə'tɪr **-s** -z **-ing** -ɪŋ **-ed** -d

Rackham 'ræk.əm

rack|-rent 'ræk|.rent **-rents** -rents **-renter/s** -ˌren.təʳ/z (US) -ˌren.t̬ɚ/z

raclette ræk'let

raconteur ˌræk.ɒn'tɜːʳ, -ɔ̃ːn'- (US) -ɑːn'tɜːr, -ən'- **-s** -z

racoon rə'kuːn, ræk'uːn (US) ræk'uːn, rə'kuːn **-s** -z

racquet 'ræk.ɪt **-s** -s

racquetball 'ræk.ɪt.bɔːl (US) -bɔːl, -bɑːl

rac|y 'reɪ.s|i **-ier** -i.əʳ (US) -i.ɚ **-iest** -i.ɪst, -i.əst **-ily** -ɪ.li, -əl.i **-iness** -ɪ.nəs, -ɪ.nɪs

rad ræd **-s** -z

RADA 'rɑː.də

radar 'reɪ.dɑːʳ (US) -dɑːr

Radcliffe 'ræd.klɪf

raddled 'ræd.l̩d

Radetzky rə'det.ski, ræd'et- (US) rɑː'det-, rə-

Radford 'ræd.fəd (US) -fɚd

radial 'reɪ.di.əl **-ly** -i

radian 'reɪ.di.ən **-s** -z

radianc|e 'reɪ.di.ən*t*s **-es** -ɪz

radiant 'reɪ.di.ənt **-s** -s **-ly** -li

radi|ate 'reɪ.di|.eɪt **-ates** -eɪts **-ating** -eɪ.tɪŋ (US) -eɪ.t̬ɪŋ **-ated** -eɪ.tɪd (US) -eɪ.t̬ɪd

radiation ˌreɪ.di'eɪ.ʃən **-s** -z **radi'ation ˌsickness**

radiator 'reɪ.di.eɪ.təʳ (US) -t̬ɚ **-s** -z

radic|al 'ræd.ɪ.k|əl **-als** -əlz **-ally** -əl.i, -li **-alness** -əl.nəs, -əl.nɪs **-alism** -əl.ɪ.zəm **ˌradical 'chic ; ˌradical 'sign**

radicaliz|e, -is|e 'ræd.ɪ.kəl.aɪz **-es** -ɪz **-ing** -ɪŋ **-ed** -d

radicchio rə'dɪk.i.əʊ, ræd'ɪk- (US) rə'diː.ki.oʊ, rɑː-, '-kjoʊ **-s** -z

Radice rə'diː.tʃi, -tʃeɪ

radicle 'ræd.ɪ.kl̩ **-s** -z

radii (*plur. of* **radius**) 'reɪ.di.aɪ

radio (*n.v.*) 'reɪ.di.əʊ (US) -oʊ **-s** -z **-ing** -ɪŋ **-ed** -d **ˌradio a'larm ; 'radio ˌcar ; ˌradio 'telescope ; 'radio ˌwave**

radioactive ˌreɪ.di.əʊ'æk.tɪv (US) -oʊ'- **-ly** -li *stress shift:* ˌradioactive 'waste

radioactivity ˌreɪ.di.əʊ.æk'tɪv.ə.ti, -ɪ.ti (US) -oʊ.æk'tɪv.ə.t̬i

radiocarbon ˌreɪ.di.əʊ'kɑː.bən (US) -oʊ'kɑːr-

radiogenic ˌreɪ.di.əʊ'dʒen.ɪk (US) -oʊ'- *stress shift:* ˌradiogenic 'output

radiogram 'reɪ.di.əʊ.græm (US) -oʊ- **-s** -z

radiograph 'reɪ.di.əʊ.grɑːf, -græf (US) -oʊ.græf **-s** -s

radiograph|y ˌreɪ.di'ɒg.rə.f|i (US) -'ɑː.grə- **-er/s** -əʳ/z (US) -ɚ/z

radioisotope ˌreɪ.di.əʊ'aɪ.sə.təʊp (US) -oʊ'aɪ.sə.toʊp **-s** -s

radiolo|cate ˌreɪ.di.əʊ.ləʊ|'keɪt (US) -oʊ.loʊ'- **-cates** -'keɪts **-cating** -'keɪ.tɪŋ (US) -'keɪ.t̬ɪŋ **-cated** -'keɪ.tɪd (US) -'keɪ.t̬ɪd

radiolocation ˌreɪ.di.əʊ.ləʊ'keɪ.ʃən (US) -oʊ.loʊ'-

radiolog|y ˌreɪ.di'ɒl.ə.dʒ|i (US) -'ɑː.lə- **-ist/s** -ɪst/s

radiometer ˌreɪ.di'ɒm.ɪ.təʳ, '-ə- (US) -'ɑː.mə.t̬ɚ **-s** -z

radionics ˌreɪ.di'ɒn.ɪks (US) -'ɑː.nɪks

radiopag|e ˌreɪ.di.əʊ'peɪdʒ, 'reɪ.di.əʊ.peɪdʒ (US) 'reɪ.di.oʊ- **-es** -ɪz **-ing** -ɪŋ **-ed** -d **-er/s** -əʳ/z (US) -ɚ/z

radiophone 'reɪ.di.əʊ.fəʊn (US) -oʊ.foʊn **-s** -z

radiophonic ˌreɪ.di.əʊ'fɒn.ɪk (US) -oʊ'fɑː.nɪk

radiotelegram ˌreɪ.di.əʊ'tel.ɪ.græm, '-ə- (US) -oʊ'tel.ə- **-s** -z

radiotelegraph ˌreɪ.di.əʊ'tel.ɪ.grɑːf, '-ə-, -græf (US) -oʊ'tel.ə.græf **-s** -s

radiotelephone ˌreɪ.di.əʊ'tel.ɪ.fəʊn, '-ə- (US) -oʊ'tel.ə.foʊn **-s** -z

radiotherap|y ˌreɪ.di.əʊ'θer.ə.p|i (US) -oʊ'- **-ist/s** -ɪst/s

radish 'ræd.ɪʃ **-es** -ɪz

radium 'reɪ.di.əm

radi|us 'reɪ.di|.əs **-i** -aɪ

rad|ix 'reɪ.d|ɪks, 'ræd- **-ixes** -ɪk.sɪz **-ices** -ɪ.siːz (US) 'ræd.ə.siːz, 'reɪ.də-

Radlett 'ræd.lɪt, -lət

Radley 'ræd.li

Radnor 'ræd.nəʳ, -nɔːʳ (US) -nɚ, -nɔːr **-shire** -ʃəʳ, -ˌʃɪəʳ (US) -ʃɚ, -ˌʃɪr

radon 'reɪ.dɒn (US) -dɑːn

Radovan 'ræd.ə.væn

Radox® 'reɪ.dɒks (US) -dɑːks

Rae reɪ

Raeburn 'reɪ.bɜːn (US) -bɜːrn **-s** -z

Raf ræf

RAF ˌɑːʳ.eɪ'ef; ræf (US) ˌɑːr-

Rafferty 'ræf.ə.ti (US) -ɚ.t̬i

raffia 'ræf.i.ə

raffish 'ræf.ɪʃ **-ly** -li **-ness** -nəs, -nɪs

raffl|e 'ræf.l̩ **-es** -z **-ing** -ɪŋ, 'ræf.lɪŋ **-ed** -d **'raffle ˌticket**

Raffles 'ræf.l̩z
Rafsanjani ˌræf.sɑːn'dʒɑː.ni, -sæn'-, -'dʒæn.i; -dʒɑː'niː ⓤⓢ ˌrɑːf.sɑːn'dʒɑː.ni; ˌrʌf.sən'dʒæn.i
raft rɑːft ⓤⓢ ræft **-s** -s **-ing** -ɪŋ **-ed** -ɪd
rafter 'rɑːf.təʳ ⓤⓢ 'ræf.tɚ **-s** -z **-ed** -d
rag ræg **-s** -z **-ging** -ɪŋ **-ged** -d ˌ**rag 'doll** ; '**rag ˌtrade**
raga 'rɑː.gə; rɑːg ⓤⓢ 'rɑː.gə **-s** -z
ragamuffin 'ræg.əˌmʌf.ɪn **-s** -z
rag-and-bone|-man ˌræg.ᵊnd'bəʊn|.mæn, -ᵊm'- ⓤⓢ -ᵊnd'boʊn- **-men** -men
ragbag 'ræg.bæg **-s** -z
rag|e reɪdʒ **-es** -ɪz **-ing/ly** -ɪŋ/li **-ed** -d
ragga 'ræg.ə
ragged 'ræg.ɪd **-er** -əʳ ⓤⓢ -ɚ **-est** -ɪst, -əst **-ly** -li **-ness** -nəs, -nɪs **-y** -i
raggle-taggle 'ræg.l̩ˌtæg.l̩, ˌræg.l̩'tæg-
raglan (R) 'ræg.lən ˌ**raglan 'sleeve**
ragout ræg'uː, '-- ⓤⓢ ræg'uː **-s** -z
ragtag 'ræg.tæg
ragtime 'ræg.taɪm
ragweed 'ræg.wiːd
ragwort 'ræg.wɜːt ⓤⓢ -wɜːrt, -wɔːrt **-s** -s
Rahman 'rɑː.mən
rah-rah 'rɑː.rɑː
raid reɪd **-s** -z **-ing** -ɪŋ **-ed** -ɪd **-er/s** -əʳ/z ⓤⓢ -ɚ/z
Raikes reɪks
rail reɪl **-s** -z **-ing** -ɪŋ **-ed** -d
railcard 'reɪl.kɑːd ⓤⓢ -kɑːrd **-s** -z
railhead 'reɪl.hed **-s** -z
railing 'reɪ.lɪŋ **-s** -z
railler|y 'reɪ.lᵊr|.i **-ies** -iz
railroad 'reɪl.rəʊd ⓤⓢ -roʊd **-s** -z **-ing** -ɪŋ **-ed** -ɪd
railway 'reɪl.weɪ **-s** -z
railway|man 'reɪl.weɪ|.mən, -mæn **-men** -mən, -men
raiment 'reɪ.mənt
rain reɪn **-s** -z **-ing** -ɪŋ **-ed** -d **-less** -ləs, -lɪs '**rain ˌforest** ; ˌ**take a 'rain ˌcheck** ; **come ˌrain or 'shine**
rainbow 'reɪn.bəʊ, 'reɪm- ⓤⓢ 'reɪn.boʊ **-s** -z ˌ**rainbow 'trout**
rainbow-colo(u)red 'reɪn.bəʊˌkʌl.əd, 'reɪm- ⓤⓢ 'reɪn.boʊˌkʌl.ɚd
raincoat 'reɪn.kəʊt, 'reɪŋ- ⓤⓢ 'reɪn.koʊt **-s** -s
raindrop 'reɪn.drɒp ⓤⓢ -drɑːp **-s** -s
Raine reɪn
Rainey 'reɪ.ni
rainfall 'reɪn.fɔːl ⓤⓢ -fɔːl, -fɑːl
Rainford 'reɪn.fəd ⓤⓢ -fɚd
rain-gaug|e 'reɪn.geɪdʒ, 'reɪŋ- ⓤⓢ 'reɪn- **-es** -ɪz
Rainier *prince of Monaco:* 'reɪ.ni.eɪ ⓤⓢ reɪ'nɪr, rə-; ren'jeɪ
Rainier *Mount:* 'reɪ.ni.əʳ; reɪ'nɪəʳ, rə- ⓤⓢ rə'nɪr, reɪ-
rainmak|ing 'reɪnˌmeɪ.k|ɪŋ, 'reɪm- ⓤⓢ 'reɪn- **-er/s** -əʳ/z ⓤⓢ -ɚ/z
rainproof 'reɪn.pruːf, 'reɪm- ⓤⓢ 'reɪn-
rainstorm 'reɪn.stɔːm ⓤⓢ -stɔːrm **-s** -z
rainwater 'reɪnˌwɔː.təʳ ⓤⓢ -ˌwɑː.t̬ɚ, -ˌwɔː-
Rainworth 'reɪn.wəθ, -wɜːθ ⓤⓢ -wɜːrθ, -wɚθ
rain|y 'reɪ.n|i **-ier** -i.əʳ ⓤⓢ -i.ɚ **-iest** -i.ɪst, -i.əst **-iness** -ɪ.nəs, -ɪ.nɪs ˌ**save something for a ˌrainy 'day**
Raisa raɪ'iː.sə, rɑː- ⓤⓢ rɑː-
rais|e reɪz **-es** -ɪz **-ing** -ɪŋ **-ed** -d
raisin 'reɪ.zᵊn **-s** -z
raison d'être ˌreɪ.zɔ̃ːn'deɪ.trə, -zɒn'-, -'det.rə ⓤⓢ ˌreɪ.zoʊn'det, ˌrez.ɑːn'-, -'det.rə
raj (R) rɑːdʒ, rɑːʒ ⓤⓢ rɑːdʒ
raja(h) (R) 'rɑː.dʒə ⓤⓢ -dʒə, -dʒɑː **-s** -z
Rajasthan ˌrɑː.dʒə'stɑːn ⓤⓢ -dʒɑː'-
Rajasthani ˌrɑː.dʒə'stɑː.ni ⓤⓢ -dʒɑː'-
Rajiv rɑː'dʒiːv *stress shift:* ˌRajiv 'Ghandi
Rajput 'rɑːdʒ.pʊt ⓤⓢ -puːt
Rajputana ˌrɑːdʒ.pʊ'tɑː.nə ⓤⓢ -puː'-
rak|e reɪk **-es** -s **-ing** -ɪŋ **-ed** -t
rakee 'rɑː.ki, 'ræk.i; rɑː'kiː
rake-off 'reɪk.ɒf ⓤⓢ -ɑːf **-s** -s
raki 'rɑː.ki, 'ræk.i; rɑː'kiː
rakish 'reɪ.kɪʃ **-ly** -li **-ness** -nəs, -nɪs
rale rɑːl, ræl ⓤⓢ rɑːl **-s** -z
Rale(i)gh 'rɔː.li, 'rɑː-, 'ræl.i ⓤⓢ 'rɑː.li, 'rɔː-

Note: The family of the late Sir Walter Raleigh pronounced /'rɔː.li ⓤⓢ 'rɑː-, rɔː-/. Raleigh bicycles are generally called /'ræl.i/ in Britain and /'rɑː.li/ in the United States. When used as the name of a ship, the British English pronunciation is /'ræl.i/.

rallentand|o ˌræl.en'tæn.d|əʊ, -ən'-, -ɪn'- ⓤⓢ ˌrɑː.lən'tɑːn.d|oʊ **-os** -əʊz ⓤⓢ -oʊz **-i** -i
rall|y 'ræl|.i **-ies** -iz **-ying** -i.ɪŋ **-ied** -id '**rally ˌdriver**
rallycross 'ræl.i.krɒs ⓤⓢ -krɑːs
Ralph rælf
Ralph Cross ˌrɑːlf'krɒs, ˌrælf- ⓤⓢ ˌrælf'krɑːs
Ralston 'rɔːl.stᵊn
ram (R) ræm **-s** -z **-ming** -ɪŋ **-med** -d **-mer/s** -əʳ/z ⓤⓢ -ɚ/z
RAM ræm
Ramad(h)an ˌræm.ə'dæn, ˌrɑː.mə'-, -'dɑːn, '--- ⓤⓢ ˌræm.ə'dɑːn, ˌrɑː.mə'-
Ramage 'ræm.ɪdʒ
Rama(h) 'rɑː.mə
Ramaphosa ˌræm.ə'pəʊ.zə ⓤⓢ -'poʊ-
Ramayana rɑː'maɪ.ə.nə, rə-, -'mɑː- ⓤⓢ rɑː'mɑː.jə-
Rambert 'rɑ̃ːm.beə, -'- ⓤⓢ rɑːm'ber
rambl|e 'ræm.bl̩ **-es** -z **-ing** -ɪŋ, 'ræm.blɪŋ **-ed** -d
rambler (R) 'ræm.bləʳ ⓤⓢ -blɚ **-s** -z
rambling 'ræm.blɪŋ, -bl̩.ɪŋ **-ly** -li
Rambo 'ræm.bəʊ ⓤⓢ -boʊ
Ramboesque ˌræm.bəʊ'esk ⓤⓢ -boʊ'-
rambunctious ræm'bʌŋ*k*.ʃəs **-ly** -li **-ness** -nəs, -nɪs
rambutan ræm'buː.tᵊn; ˌræm.bʊ'tæn, -'tɑːn ⓤⓢ ræm'buː.tᵊn **-s** -z
ramekin, ramequin 'ræm.ɪ.kɪn, '-ə-, '-kɪn ⓤⓢ '-ə.kɪn **-s** -z
Rameses 'ræm.ɪ.siːz, '-ə-
ramification ˌræm.ɪ.fɪ'keɪ.ʃᵊn, ˌ-ə- **-s** -z
rami|fy 'ræm.ɪ|.faɪ, '-ə- **-fies** -faɪz **-fying** -faɪ.ɪŋ **-fied** -faɪd
Ramillies 'ræm.ɪ.liz
Ramirez rə'mɪə.rez ⓤⓢ -'mɪr.ez, -'miː.reɪs, rɑː'mɪr.ez, -'miː.reθ
ramjet 'ræm.dʒet **-s** -s
Ramos 'rɑː.mɒs ⓤⓢ 'reɪ.moʊs, rɑː'moʊs
ramp ræmp **-s** -s **-ing** -ɪŋ **-ed** -t
rampag|e (*n.*) 'ræm.peɪdʒ, -'- ⓤⓢ 'ræm.peɪdʒ **-es** -ɪz (*v.*) ræm'peɪdʒ, '-- **-es** -ɪz **-ing** -ɪŋ **-ed** -d
rampageous ræm'peɪ.dʒəs **-ly** -li **-ness** -nəs, -nɪs
rampant 'ræm.pənt **-ly** -li
rampart 'ræm.pɑːt, -pət ⓤⓢ -pɑːrt, -pɚt **-s** -s
rampion 'ræm.pi.ən **-s** -z
Ramprakash 'ræm.prə.kæʃ
Rampton 'ræm*p*.tən
ram-raid 'ræm.reɪd **-s** -z **-er/s** -əʳ/z ⓤⓢ -ɚ/z **-ing** -ɪŋ
ramrod 'ræm.rɒd ⓤⓢ -rɑːd **-s** -z
Ramsaran 'rɑːm*p*.sᵊr.ən
Ramsay 'ræm.zi
Ramsbottom 'ræmzˌbɒt.əm ⓤⓢ -ˌbɑː.t̬əm
Ramsden 'ræmz.dən
Ramses 'ræm.siːz
Ramsey 'ræm.zi
Ramsgate 'ræmz.geɪt, -gɪt
ramshackle 'ræmˌʃæk.l̩
ran (*from* **run**) ræn
rance ræn*t*s
Rance *surname:* rɑːn*t*s ⓤⓢ ræn*t*s
ranch rɑːn*t*ʃ, ræn*t*ʃ ⓤⓢ ræn*t*ʃ **-es** -ɪz **-ing** -ɪŋ **-ed** -t **-er/s** -əʳ/z ⓤⓢ -ɚ/z '**ranch ˌhouse**
ranchero rɑːn'tʃeə.rəʊ, ræn- ⓤⓢ ræn'tʃer.oʊ **-s** -z
rancid 'ræn*t*.sɪd **-ness** -nəs, -nɪs
rancidity ræn'sɪd.ə.ti, -ɪ.ti ⓤⓢ -ə.t̬i
rancorous 'ræŋ.kᵊr.əs **-ly** -li
ranco(u)r 'ræŋ.kəʳ ⓤⓢ -kɚ

rand (R) *South African money and region:* rænd, rɑːnd, rɑːnt, rɒnt (US) rænd, rɑːnd, rɑːnt *strip, border:* rænd **-s** -z
Randall, Randell 'ræn.dᵊl
Randalstown 'ræn.dᵊlz.taʊn
R and B ˌɑːʳ.ᵊnd'biː, -ᵊm'- (US) ˌɑːr-
R and D ˌɑːʳ.ᵊnd'diː (US) ˌɑːr-
Randi 'ræn.di
Randle 'ræn.dl̩
Randolph 'ræn.dɒlf, -dᵊlf (US) -dɑːlf, -dᵊlf
random 'ræn.dəm **-ly** -li **-ness** -nəs, -nɪs
random-access ˌræn.dəm'æk.ses *stress shift:* ˌrandom-access 'memory
randomization, -isa- ˌræn.dəm.aɪ'zeɪ.ʃᵊn, -ɪ'- (US) -ɪ'-
randomiz|e, -is|e 'ræn.də.maɪz **-es** -ɪz **-ing** -ɪŋ **-ed** -d
R and R ˌɑːʳ.ᵊnd'ɑːʳ (US) ˌɑːr.ᵊnd'ɑːr
rand|y (R) 'ræn.d|i **-ier** -i.əʳ (US) -i.ɚ **-iest** -i.ɪst, -i.əst **-ily** -ɪ.li, -ᵊl.i **-iness** -ɪ.nəs, -ɪ.nɪs
ranee (R) 'rɑː.niː, ˌ-'- (US) 'rɑː.niː **-s** -z
Ranelagh 'ræn.ɪ.lə, -ᵊl.ə, -ɔː (US) -ᵊl.ə
rang (*from* **ring**) ræŋ
rang|e reɪndʒ **-es** -ɪz **-ing** -ɪŋ **-ed** -d
range-finder 'reɪndʒˌfaɪn.dəʳ (US) -dɚ **-s** -z
ranger (R) 'reɪn.dʒəʳ (US) -dʒɚ **-s** -z
Rangoon ˌræŋ'guːn (US) ˌræn-, ˌræŋ- *stress shift:* ˌRangoon 'streets
rang|y 'reɪn.dʒ|i **-ier** -i.əʳ (US) -i.ɚ **-iest** -i.ɪst, -i.əst **-iness** -ɪ.nəs, -ɪ.nɪs
rani 'rɑː.niː, ˌ-'- (US) 'rɑː.niː **-s** -z
rank (R) ræŋk **-s** -s **-ing** -ɪŋ **-ed** -t **-ly** -li **-ness** -nəs, -nɪs ˌ**rank and 'file**
Rankin(e) 'ræŋ.kɪn
rankl|e 'ræŋ.kl̩ **-es** -z **-ing** -ɪŋ, 'ræŋ.klɪŋ **-ed** -d
Rannoch 'ræn.ək, -əx (US) -ək
Ranoe 'rɑː.nəʊ (US) -noʊ
ransack 'ræn.sæk **-s** -s **-ing** -ɪŋ **-ed** -t **-er/s** -əʳ/z (US) -ɚ/z
ransom (R) 'ræn*t*.sᵊm **-s** -z **-ing** -ɪŋ **-ed** -d **-er/s** -əʳ/z (US) -ɚ/z
Ransome 'ræn*t*.səm
rant rænt **-s** -s **-ing/ly** -ɪŋ/li (US) 'ræn.t̬ɪŋ/li **-ed** -ɪd (US) 'ræn.t̬ɪd **-er/s** -əʳ/z (US) 'ræn.t̬ɚ/z
Rantzen 'rænt.sᵊn
Ranulph 'ræn.ʌlf, -ᵊlf
ranuncul|us rə'nʌŋ.kjə.l|əs, ræn'ʌŋ-, -kjʊ- (US) rə'nʌŋ- **-uses** -ə.sɪz **-i** -aɪ
Ranworth 'ræn.wəθ, -wɜːθ (US) -wɚθ, -wɜːrθ
rap ræp **-s** -s **-ping** -ɪŋ **-ped** -t **-per/s** -əʳ/z (US) -ɚ/z
rapacious rə'peɪ.ʃəs **-ly** -li **-ness** -nəs, -nɪs
rapacity rə'pæs.ə.ti, -ɪ.ti (US) -ə.t̬i
rap|e reɪp **-es** -s **-ing** -ɪŋ **-ed** -t **-ist/s** -ɪst/s
Raphael *angel:* 'ræf.eɪ.əl; ˌræf.ɑː'el; 'ræf.eɪl; 'reɪ.fi.əl; *and in Jewish usage:* 'reɪ.fᵊl (US) 'ræf.i.əl; ˌrɑː.fi'el; 'reɪ.fi.el *modern name:* 'reɪ.fᵊl, 'ræf.eɪl *Italian artist:* 'ræf.eɪ.əl, -fi.əl, -feɪl (US) 'ræf.i.əl; ˌrɑː.fi'el; 'reɪ.fi.el
rapid 'ræp.ɪd **-est** -ɪst, -əst **-ly** -li **-ness** -nəs, -nɪs **-s** -z ˌ**rapid 'eye** ˌ**movement**; ˌ**rapid 'transit**
rapid-fire ˌræp.ɪd'faɪəʳ (US) -'faɪɚ *stress shift:* ˌrapid-fire 'shooting
rapidity rə'pɪd.ə.ti, ræp'ɪd-, -ɪ.ti (US) rə'pɪd.ə.t̬i
rapier 'reɪ.pi.əʳ (US) -pi.ɚ, '-pjɚ **-s** -z
rapine 'ræp.aɪn, -ɪn (US) -ɪn
rapparee ˌræp.ᵊr'iː (US) -ə'riː **-s** -z
rappel (US) ræp'el **-s** -z **-ling** -ɪŋ **-led** -d
rapport ræp'ɔːʳ, rə'pɔːʳ; 'ræp.ɔːʳ (US) ræp'ɔːr, rə'pɔːr
rapporteur ˌræp.ɔː'tɜːʳ (US) -ɔːr'tɜːr **-s** -z
rapprochement ræp'rɒʃ.mɑ̃ːŋ, -'rəʊʃ- (US) ˌræp.roːʃ'mɑ̃ːŋ, -roʊʃ'- **-s** -z
rapscallion ræp'skæl.jən, '-i.ən (US) '-jən **-s** -z
rapt ræpt
rapture 'ræp.tʃəʳ (US) -tʃɚ **-s** -z **-d** -d
rapturous 'ræp.tʃᵊr.əs **-ly** -li
Rapunzel rə'pʌn.zᵊl
Raquel rə'kel, ræk'el
rara avis ˌrɑː.rə'æv.ɪs, ˌreə-, -'eɪ.vɪs (US) ˌrer.ə'eɪ.vɪs
rare reəʳ (US) rer **-r** -əʳ (US) -ɚ **-st** -ɪst, -əst **-ly** -li **-ness** -nəs, -nɪs ˌ**rare 'earth**
rarebit 'reə.bɪt (US) 'rer- **-s** -s
Note: The pronunciation /'ræb.ɪt/ is very often used in British English in the phrase **Welsh rarebit**.
rarefaction ˌreə.rɪ'fæk.ʃᵊn, -rə'- (US) ˌrer.ə'-
rarefication ˌreə.rɪ.fɪ'keɪ.ʃᵊn, -rə- (US) ˌrer.ə-
rare|fy 'reə.rɪ|.faɪ, -rə- (US) 'rer.ə- **-fies** -faɪz **-fying** -faɪ.ɪŋ **-fied** -faɪd
raring (*adj.*) 'reə.rɪŋ (US) 'rer.ɪŋ
rarit|y 'reə.rə.t|i, -ɪ.t|i (US) 'rer.ə.t̬|i **-ies** -iz
Rarotonga ˌreə.rəʊ'tɒŋ.gə, ˌrær.əʊ'- (US) ˌrɑːr.oʊ'tɔːŋ.gə, ˌrer.ə'-
Ras al Khaimah ˌrɑːs.æl'kaɪ.mə
rascal 'rɑː.skᵊl (US) 'ræs.kᵊl **-s** -z
rascalit|y rɑː'skæl.ə.t|i, -ɪ.t|i (US) ræs'kæl.ə.t̬|i **-ies** -iz
rascally 'rɑː.skᵊl.i (US) 'ræs.kᵊl-
ras|e reɪz **-es** -ɪz **-ing** -ɪŋ **-ed** -d
rash ræʃ **-es** -ɪz **-er** -əʳ (US) -ɚ **-est** -ɪst, -əst **-ly** -li **-ness** -nəs, -nɪs
rasher 'ræʃ.əʳ (US) -ɚ **-s** -z
Rashid ræʃ'iːd (US) ræʃ-, rɑː'ʃiːd
rasp rɑːsp (US) ræsp **-s** -s **-ing** -ɪŋ **-ed** -t
raspberr|y 'rɑːz.bᵊr|.i, 'rɑːs- (US) 'ræzˌber|.i, -bɚ- **-ies** -iz
Rasputin ræs'pjuː.tɪn, -'puː- (US) -'pjuː-
rasp|y 'rɑː.sp|i (US) 'ræsp|.i **-iness** -ɪ.nəs, -ɪ.nɪs
Rasselas 'ræs.ɪ.ləs (US) '-ə-, -læs
Rasta 'ræs.tə (US) 'rɑː.stə, 'ræs.tə **-s** -z
Rastafarian ˌræs.tə'feə.ri.ən (US) ˌrɑː.stə'fer.i-, ˌræs.tə'-, -'fɑːr- **-s** -z **-ism** -ɪ.zᵊm
Rasta|man 'ræs.tə|.mæn (US) 'rɑː.stə-, 'ræs.tə- **-men** -men
rat ræt **-s** -s **-ting** -ɪŋ (US) 'ræt̬.ɪŋ **-ted** -ɪd (US) 'ræt̬.ɪd **'rat ˌrace**; **'rat ˌtrap**
rata 'reɪ.tə (US) 'rɑː.t̬ə **-s** -z
rata (*in* **pro rata**) 'rɑː.tə, 'reɪ- (US) -t̬ə
ratability ˌreɪ.tə'bɪl.ə.ti, -ɪ.ti (US) -t̬ə'bɪl.ə.t̬i
ratab|le 'reɪ.tə.b|l̩ (US) -t̬ə- **-ly** -li
ratafia ˌræt.ə'fiː.ə **-s** -z
rataplan ˌræt.ə'plæn (US) 'ræt̬.ə.plæn
rat-a-tat ˌræt.ə'tæt, '--- (US) ˌræt̬-, '---
ratatouille ˌræt.ə'twiː, -'tuː.i (US) -'tuː.i, ˌrɑː.tɑː'-
ratbag 'ræt.bæg **-s** -z
rat-catcher 'rætˌkætʃ.əʳ (US) -ɚ **-s** -z
ratchet 'rætʃ.ɪt **-s** -s
Ratcliff(e) 'ræt.klɪf
rat|e reɪt **-es** -s **-ing** -ɪŋ (US) 'reɪ.t̬ɪŋ **-ed** -ɪd (US) 'reɪ.t̬ɪd ˌ**rate of ex'change**
rateab|le 'reɪ.tə.b|l̩ (US) -t̬ə- **-ly** -li ˌ**rateable 'value**
rate-cap 'reɪt.kæp **-s** -s **-ping** -ɪŋ **-ped** -t
ratel 'reɪ.tᵊl, 'rɑː-, -tel (US) 'reɪ.t̬ᵊl, 'rɑː- **-s** -z
ratepayer 'reɪtˌpeɪ.əʳ (US) -ɚ **-s** -z
Rath ræθ
Rathbone 'ræθ.bəʊn, -bən (US) -boʊn, -bən
rather (*adv.*) 'rɑː.ðəʳ (US) 'ræð.ɚ (*interj.*) *British only, old-fashioned:* ˌrɑː'ðɜːʳ
Rather 'ræð.əʳ (US) 'ræð.ɚ
Rathfarnham ræθ'fɑː.nəm (US) -'fɑːr-
Rathlin 'ræθ.lɪn
ratification ˌræt.ɪ.fɪ'keɪ.ʃᵊn, ˌ-ə- (US) ˌræt̬.ə- **-s** -z
rati|fy 'ræt.ɪ|.faɪ, '-ə- (US) 'ræt̬.ə- **-fies** -faɪz **-fying** -faɪ.ɪŋ **-fied** -faɪd **-fier/s** -faɪ.əʳ/z (US) -faɪ.ɚ/z
rating 'reɪ.tɪŋ (US) -t̬ɪŋ **-s** -z
ratio 'reɪ.ʃi.əʊ (US) -oʊ, '-ʃoʊ **-s** -z
ratioci|nate ˌræt.i'ɒs.ɪ|.neɪt, ˌræʃ-, -'əʊ.sɪ-, -sə- (US) ˌræʃ.i'ɑː.sə- **-nates** -neɪts **-nating** -neɪ.tɪŋ (US) -neɪ.t̬ɪŋ **-nated** -neɪ.tɪd (US) -neɪ.t̬ɪd

ratiocination ˌræt.i.ɒs.ɪˈneɪ.ʃᵊn, ˌræʃ-, -əʊ.sɪˈ-, -səˈ- (US) ˌræʃ.i.ɑː.səˈ- **-s** -z
ratio decidendi ˌræt.i.əʊˌdeɪ.sɪˈden.di (US) ˌræt̬.i.oʊˌ-, ˌrɑː.t̬i-
ratio legis ˌræt.i.əʊˈleɪ.gɪs (US) ˌræt̬.i.oʊˈleg.ɪs, ˌrɑː.t̬i-
ration ˈræʃ.ᵊn (US) ˈræʃ.ᵊn, ˈreɪ- **-s** -z **-ing** -ɪŋ **-ed** -d
rational ˈræʃ.ᵊn.ᵊl, ˈ-nᵊl **-ly** -i
rationale ˌræʃ.əˈnɑːl, -ˈnæl, -ˈnɑː.leɪ (US) -əˈnæl **-s** -z
rational|ism ˈræʃ.ᵊn.ᵊl|.ɪ.zᵊm, ˈ-nᵊl- **-ist/s** -ɪst/s
rationalistic ˌræʃ.ᵊn.ᵊlˈɪs.tɪk, ˌ-nᵊlˈ- **-ally** -ᵊl.i, -li
rationality ˌræʃ.ᵊnˈæl.ə.ti, -ɪ.ti (US) -ə.t̬i
rationalization, -isa- ˌræʃ.ᵊn.ᵊl.aɪˈzeɪ.ʃᵊn, ˌ-nᵊl-, -ɪˈ- (US) -ɪˈ-
rationaliz|e, -is|e ˈræʃ.ᵊn.ᵊl.aɪz, ˈ-nᵊl- (US) -ᵊn.ᵊ.laɪz, ˈ-nə- **-es** -ɪz **-ing** -ɪŋ **-ed** -d
Ratisbon ˈræt.ɪz.bɒn, -ɪs-, -əz-, -əs- (US) -ɪz.bɑːn, -ɪs-
ratline ˈræt.lɪn **-s** -z
Ratner ˈræt.nəʳ (US) -nɚ **-'s** -z
rat-race ˈræt.reɪs
rat-tail ˈræt.teɪl **-s** -z **-ed** -d
rattan rəˈtæn, rætˈæn **-s** -z
Rattigan ˈræt.ɪ.gən, ˈ-ə- (US) ˈræt̬-
rattl|e (R) ˈræt.l̩ (US) ˈræt̬- **-es** -z **-ing** -ɪŋ, ˈræt.lɪŋ **-ed** -d **-er/s** -əʳ/z (US) -ɚ/z, ˈræt.ləʳ/z (US) -lɚ/z
rattlesnake ˈræt.l̩.sneɪk (US) ˈræt̬- **-s** -s
rattling ˈræt.lɪŋ, -l̩.ɪŋ (US) ˈræt.lɪŋ, ˈræt̬.l̩.ɪŋ
ratt|y (R) ˈræt|.i (US) ˈræt̬- **-ier** -i.əʳ (US) -i.ɚ **-iest** -i.ɪst, -i.əst **-ily** -ɪ.li, -ᵊl.i **-iness** -ɪ.nəs, -ɪ.nɪs
raucous ˈrɔː.kəs (US) ˈrɑː-, ˈrɔː- **-ly** -li **-ness** -nəs, -nɪs
raunch|y ˈrɔːn.*t*ʃ|i (US) ˈrɑːn.tʃ|i, ˈrɔːn- **-ier** -i.əʳ (US) -i.ɚ **-iest** -i.ɪst, -i.əst **-ily** -ɪ.li, -ᵊl.i **-iness** -ɪ.nəs, -ɪ.nɪs
Raunds rɔːn*dz* (US) rɑːn*dz*, rɔːn*dz*
Rauschenberg ˈraʊ.ʃᵊn.bɜːg (US) -bɜːrg
ravag|e ˈræv.ɪdʒ **-es** -ɪz **-ing** -ɪŋ **-ed** -d **-er/s** -əʳ/z (US) -ɚ/z
Ravana rəˈvɑː.nə (US) ˈrɑː.və-; rəˈvɑː-
rav|e reɪv **-es** -z **-ing/s** -ɪŋ/z **-ed** -d
ravel ˈræv.ᵊl **-s** -z **-(l)ing** -ɪŋ **-(l)ed** -d
Ravel *French composer:* rævˈel (US) rəˈvel, rɑː-
ravelin ˈræv.ᵊl.ɪn **-s** -z
raven (R) *(n.)* ˈreɪ.vᵊn **-s** -z
raven *(v.)* ˈræv.ᵊn **-s** -z **-ing** -ɪŋ **-ed** -d
Ravening ˈreɪ.vᵊn.ɪŋ, ˈræv.ᵊn-
Ravenna rəˈven.ə, rævˈen- (US) rə-, rɑː-
ravenous ˈræv.ᵊn.əs, -ɪ.nəs (US) -ᵊn.əs **-ly** -li **-ness** -nəs, -nɪs
Ravensbourne ˈreɪ.vᵊnz.bɔːn (US) -bɔːrn
Ravenshead ˈreɪ.vᵊnz.hed
Ravenshoe ˈreɪ.vᵊnz.həʊ (US) -hoʊ
raver ˈreɪ.vəʳ (US) -vɚ **-s** -z
Raverat ˈrɑː.vᵊr.ɑː (US) -və.rɑː
rave-up ˈreɪv.ʌp **-s** -s
ravin ˈræv.ɪn
ravine rəˈviːn **-s** -z
raving ˈreɪ.vɪŋ **-s** -z
ravioli ˌræv.iˈəʊ.li (US) -ˈoʊ-
ravish ˈræv.ɪʃ **-es** -ɪz **-ing/ly** -ɪŋ/li **-ed** -t **-er/s** -əʳ/z (US) -ɚ/z **-ment** -mənt
raw rɔː (US) rɑː, rɔː **-er** -əʳ (US) -ɚ **-est** -ɪst, -əst **-ly** -li **-ness** -nəs, -nɪs ˌ**raw** ˈ**deal** ; ˌ**raw ma**ˈ**terial**
Rawalpindi ˌrɑː.wəlˈpɪn.di, ˌrɔːlˈpɪn- (US) ˌrɑː.wəlˈ-
Rawdon ˈrɔː.dᵊn (US) ˈrɑː-, ˈrɔː-
rawhid|e ˈrɔː.haɪd (US) ˈrɑː-, ˈrɔː- **-es** -z **-ing** -ɪŋ **-ed** -ɪd
Rawlings ˈrɔː.lɪŋz (US) ˈrɑː-, ˈrɔː-
Rawlins ˈrɔː.lɪnz (US) ˈrɑː-, ˈrɔː-
Rawlinson ˈrɔː.lɪn.sᵊn (US) ˈrɑː-, ˈrɔː-
Rawlplug® ˈrɔːl.plʌg (US) ˈrɑːl-, ˈrɔːl-
Rawmarsh ˈrɔː.mɑːʃ (US) ˈrɑː.mɑːrʃ, ˈrɔː-
Rawtenstall ˈrɒt.ᵊn.stɔːl, ˈrɔː.tᵊn- (US) ˈrɑː.tᵊn-, ˈrɔː-
ray (R) reɪ **-s** -z
Ray-Bans® ˈreɪ.bænz
Raybould ˈreɪ.bəʊld (US) -boʊld
Rayburn ˈreɪ.bɜːn (US) -bɜːrn
Rayleigh ˈreɪ.li
Rayment ˈreɪ.mənt
Raymond ˈreɪ.mənd
Rayner ˈreɪ.nəʳ (US) -nɚ
Raynes reɪnz
rayon ˈreɪ.ɒn, -ən (US) -ɑːn
raz|e reɪz **-es** -ɪz **-ing** -ɪŋ **-ed** -d
razoo rəˈzuː (US) rə-, rɑː-
razor ˈreɪ.zəʳ (US) -zɚ **-s** -z ˈ**razor** ˌ**blade**
razorback ˈreɪ.zə.bæk (US) -zɚ- **-s** -s
razorbill ˈreɪ.zə.bɪl (US) -zɚ- **-s** -z
razor-blade ˈreɪ.zə.bleɪd (US) -zɚ- **-s** -z
razor-shell ˈreɪ.zə.ʃel (US) -zɚ- **-s** -z
razzamat(t)azz ˌræz.ə.məˈtæz, ˈræz.ə.mə.tæz (US) ˈræz.ə.mə.tæz
razzia ˈræz.i.ə **-s** -z
razzle ˈræz.l̩ ˌ**on the** ˈ**razzle**
razzle-dazzle ˌræz.l̩ˈdæz.l̩, ˈræz.l̩ˌdæz- (US) ˌræz.l̩ˈdæz-
razzmatazz ˌræz.məˈtæz, ˈ--- (US) ˈræz.mə.tæz
RC (*abbrev. for* **Roman Catholic**) ˌɑːˈsiː; ˌrəʊ.mənˈkæθ.ᵊl.ɪk, -məŋˈ-, ˈ-lɪk (US) ˌɑːr-; ˌroʊ.mənˈkæθ.ᵊl.ɪk, ˈ-lɪk
Rd (*abbrev. for* **Road**) rəʊd (US) roʊd
re- *prefix denoting repetition:* ˌriː-, rɪ-, ri-, rə-
Note: Prefix. In compounds containing **re-** where the stem is free and the meaning is "again", it is normally pronounced /ˌriː-/, e.g. **re-read** /ˌriːˈriːd/. Many such compounds are likely to undergo stress shift, especially in adjectives derived from verbs, e.g. ˌ**rear**ˈ**range**, ˌ**rearranged** ˈ**furniture**. Attached to bound stems the pronunciation is normally /rɪ-, ri-/ or /rə-/, e.g. **refer** /rɪˈfɜːʳ (US) -ˈfɜːr/. There are exceptions; see individual entries.
re *note in Tonic Sol-fa:* reɪ **-s** -z
re (*prep.*) *with regard to:* riː
RE (*abbrev. for* **Religious Education**) ˌɑːʳˈiː (US) ˌɑːr-
Rea reɪ, rɪə, riː
reach riːtʃ **-es** -ɪz **-ing** -ɪŋ **-ed** -t
reach-me-down ˈriːtʃ.mi.daʊn **-s** -z
react riˈækt **-s** -s **-ing** -ɪŋ **-ed** -ɪd
reactant riˈæk.tᵊnt (US) -tənt **-s** -s
reaction riˈæk.ʃᵊn **-s** -z
reactionar|y riˈæk.ʃᵊn.ᵊr|.i (US) -er- **-ies** -iz
reacti|vate riˈæk.tɪ|.veɪt, ˌriː-, -tə- (US) -tə- **-vates** -veɪts **-vating** -veɪ.tɪŋ (US) -veɪ.t̬ɪŋ **-vated** -veɪ.tɪd (US) -veɪ.t̬ɪd
reactivation ˌriː.æk.tɪˈveɪ.ʃᵊn, riˌæk-, -təˈ- (US) riˌæk-
reactive riˈæk.tɪv **-ly** -li
reactor riˈæk.təʳ (US) -tɚ **-s** -z
read (R) *present tense:* riːd **-s** -z **-ing** -ɪŋ *past tense:* red
readability ˌriː.dəˈbɪl.ə.ti, -ɪ.ti (US) -ə.t̬i
readab|le ˈriː.də.b|l̩ **-ly** -li **-leness** -l̩.nəs, -nɪs
re-address ˌriː.əˈdres **-es** -ɪz **-ing** -ɪŋ **-ed** -t
Reade riːd
reader (R) ˈriː.dəʳ (US) -dɚ **-s** -z
readership ˈriː.də.ʃɪp (US) -dɚ- **-s** -s
readies ˈred.iz
reading (*n.*) ˈriː.dɪŋ **-s** -z
Reading ˈred.ɪŋ
readjust ˌriː.əˈdʒʌst **-s** -s **-ing** -ɪŋ **-ed** -ɪd
readjustment ˌriː.əˈdʒʌs*t*.mənt **-s** -s
readmission ˌriː.ədˈmɪʃ.ᵊn **-s** -z
read|mit ˌriː.əd|ˈmɪt **-mits** -ˈmɪts **-mitting** -ˈmɪt.ɪŋ (US) -ˈmɪt̬.ɪŋ **-mitted** -ˈmɪt.ɪd (US) -ˈmɪt̬.ɪd **-mittance** -ˈmɪt.ᵊn*t*s
read|y ˈred|.i **-ier** -i.əʳ (US) -i.ɚ **-iest** -i.ɪst, -i.əst **-ily** -ɪ.li, -ᵊl.i **-iness** -ɪ.nəs, -ɪ.nɪs **-ies** -iz **-ying** -i.ɪŋ **-ied** -id ˌ**ready** ˈ**money**
ready-made ˌred.iˈmeɪd *stress shift:* ˌready-made ˈmeal
ready-to-wear ˌred.i.təˈweəʳ (US) -ˈwer, ˈred.i.təˌwer *stress shift, British only:* ˌready-to-wear ˈsuit

reaffirm ˌriː.əˈfɜːm (US) -ˈfɜːrm **-s** -z **-ing** -ɪŋ **-ed** -d

reafforest ˌriː.əˈfɒr.ɪst (US) -ˈfɔːr.ɪst **-s** -s **-ing** -ɪŋ **-ed** -ɪd

reafforestation ˌriː.əˌfɒr.ɪˈsteɪ.ʃən, -əˈ- (US) -ˌfɔːr.ɪˈ-

Reagan ˈreɪ.gən, ˈriː-

Note: The former US president is normally /ˈreɪ-/.

Reaganomics ˌreɪ.gənˈɒm.ɪks (US) -ˈɑː.mɪks

reagent ˌriːˈeɪ.dʒənt **-s** -s

real (*adj.*) rɪəl (US) riːl, ˈriː.əl **ˈreal eˌstate** ; **ˌreal ˈlife**

real *monetary unit:* reɪˈɑːl (US) reɪˈɑːl; ˈreɪ.əl **-s** -z

realia riˈeɪ.li.ə, -ˈɑː- (US) riˈeɪ-; reɪˈɑː-

realign ˌriː.əˈlaɪn **-s** -z **-ing** -ɪŋ **-ed** -d **-ment/s** -mənt/s

real|ism ˈrɪə.l|ɪ.zəm (US) ˈriː-, ˈriː.ə- **-ist/s** -ɪst/s

realistic ˌrɪəˈlɪs.tɪk (US) ˌriː.əˈ- **-ally** -əl.i, -li

realit|y riˈæl.ə.t|i, -ɪ.t|i (US) -ə.ţ|i **-ies** -iz

realization, -isa- ˌrɪə.laɪˈzeɪ.ʃən, -lɪˈ- (US) ˌriː.ə.lɪˈ- **-s** -z

realiz|e, -is|e ˈrɪə.laɪz (US) ˈriː.ə- **-es** -ɪz **-ing** -ɪŋ **-ed** -d **-able** -ə.bl̩

real-life ˌrɪəlˈlaɪf (US) ˌriː.əlˈ- *stress shift:* ˌreal-life ˈdrama

reallo|cate riˈæl.ə|.keɪt **-cates** -keɪts **-cating** -keɪ.tɪŋ (US) -keɪ.ţɪŋ **-cated** -keɪ.tɪd (US) -keɪ.ţɪd

reallocation ˌriː.æl.əˈkeɪ.ʃən, riˌæl- (US) ˌriː.æl-

really ˈrɪə.li (US) ˈriː.ə-, ˈriː.li

realm relm **-s** -z

realpolitik reɪˈɑːl.pɒl.ɪˌtiːk, -ə- (US) -poʊ.lɪˌ- **-s** -s

real-time ˈrɪəl.taɪm (US) ˈriː.əl-

realtor (R®) ˈriːl.tər, ˈrɪəl-, -tɔːr (US) ˈriː.əl.ţɚ, -tɔːr **-s** -z

realty ˈrɪəl.ti (US) ˈriː.əl.ţi

ream riːm **-s** -z **-ing** -ɪŋ **-ed** -d

reamer ˈriː.mər (US) -mɚ **-s** -z

reap riːp **-s** -s **-ing** -ɪŋ **-ed** -t **-er/s** -ər/z (US) -ɚ/z

reappear ˌriː.əˈpɪər (US) -ˈpɪr **-s** -z **-ing** -ɪŋ **-ed** -d

reappearanc|e ˌriː.əˈpɪə.rənts (US) -ˈpɪr.ənts **-es** -ɪz

reapplication ˌriː.æp.lɪˈkeɪ.ʃən, riˌæp-, -ləˈ- (US) ˌriː.æp- **-s** -z

reappl|y ˌriː.əˈpl|aɪ **-ies** -aɪz **-ying** -aɪ.ɪŋ **-ied** -aɪd

reap|point ˌriː.ə|ˈpɔɪnt **-points** -ˈpɔɪnts **-pointing** -ˈpɔɪn.tɪŋ (US) -ˈpɔɪn.ţɪŋ **-pointed** -ˈpɔɪn.tɪd (US) -ˈpɔɪn.ţɪd **-pointment/s** -ˈpɔɪnt.mənt/s

reappraisal ˌriː.əˈpreɪ.zəl **-s** -z

reapprais|e ˌriː.əˈpreɪz **-es** -ɪz **-ing** -ɪŋ **-ed** -d

rear rɪər (US) rɪr **-s** -z **-ing** -ɪŋ **-ed** -d **ˌbring up the ˈrear**

rear-admiral ˌrɪərˈæd.mər.əl, -mɪ.rəl (US) ˌrɪr- **-s** -z

rearguard ˈrɪə.gɑːd (US) ˈrɪr.gɑːrd **-s** -z **ˌrearguard ˈaction**

rearm ˌriːˈɑːm (US) -ˈɑːrm **-s** -z **-ing** -ɪŋ **-ed** -d

rearmament riˈɑː.mə.mənt, ˌriː- (US) -ˈɑːr-

rearmost ˈrɪə.məʊst (US) ˈrɪr.moʊst

rearrang|e ˌriː.əˈreɪndʒ **-es** -ɪz **-ing** -ɪŋ **-ed** -d **-ement/s** -mənt/s

rearview ˌrɪəˈvjuː (US) ˌrɪr- *stress shift, see compound:* **ˌrearview ˈmirror**

rearward ˈrɪə.wəd (US) ˈrɪr.wɚd **-s** -z

reason ˈriː.zən **-s** -z **-ing/s** -ɪŋ/z **-ed** -d **-er/s** -ər/z (US) -ɚ/z

reasonab|le ˈriː.zən.ə.b|l̩ **-ly** -li **-leness** -l̩.nəs, -nɪs

reassembl|e ˌriː.əˈsem.bl̩ **-es** -z **-ing** -ɪŋ, ˌriː.əˈsem.blɪŋ **-ed** -d

reas|sert ˌriː.ə|ˈsɜːt (US) -ˈsɜːrt **-serts** -ˈsɜːts (US) -ˈsɜːrts **-serting** -ˈsɜː.tɪŋ (US) -ˈsɜːr.ţɪŋ **-serted** -ˈsɜː.tɪd (US) -ˈsɜːr.ţɪd

reassess ˌriː.əˈses **-es** -ɪz **-ing** -ɪŋ **-ed** -t **-ment/s** -mənt/s

reassign ˌriː.əˈsaɪn **-s** -z **-ing** -ɪŋ **-ed** -d

reassuranc|e ˌriː.əˈʃʊə.rənts, -ˈʃɔː- (US) -ˈʃʊr.ənts, -ˈʃɜːr- **-es** -ɪz

reassur|e ˌriː.əˈʃʊər, -ˈʃɔːr (US) -ˈʃʊr, -ˈʃɜːr **-es** -z **-ing/ly** -ɪŋ/li **-ed** -d

Réaumur ˈreɪ.əʊ.mjʊər, -mər (US) -ə.mjʊr, ˈ-oʊ-

reawaken ˌriː.əˈweɪ.kən **-s** -z **-ing** -ɪŋ **-ed** -d

Reay reɪ

rebarbative rɪˈbɑː.bə.tɪv, rə- (US) rɪˈbɑːr.bə.ţɪv **-ly** -li

rebate (*n.*) *discount:* ˈriː.beɪt; rɪˈbeɪt, rə- (US) ˈriː.beɪt **-s** -s

reba|te (*v.*) *deduct:* rɪˈbeɪ|t, rə-; ˈriː.beɪ|t (US) ˈriː.beɪ|t, rɪˈbeɪ|t **-tes** -ts **-ting** -tɪŋ (US) -ţɪŋ **-ted** -tɪd (US) -ţɪd

reba|te (*v.*) *in masonry and woodworking:* ˈræb.ɪ|t, ˈriː.beɪ|t (US) ˈriː.beɪ|t, ˈræb.ɪ|t **-tes** -ts **-ting** -tɪŋ (US) -ţɪŋ **-ted** -tɪd (US) -ţɪd

Rebecca rɪˈbek.ə, rə-

rebec(k) ˈriː.bek, ˈreb.ek **-s** -s

Rebekah rɪˈbek.ə, rə-

rebel (*n.*) ˈreb.əl **-s** -z

rebel (*v.*) rɪˈbel, rə- **-s** -z **-ling** -ɪŋ **-led** -d

rebellion rɪˈbel.i.ən, rə-, ˈ-jən (US) ˈ-jən **-s** -z

rebellious rɪˈbel.i.əs, rə- (US) rɪˈbel.jəs **-ly** -li **-ness** -nəs, -nɪs

rebirth ˌriːˈbɜːθ (US) -ˈbɜːrθ **-s** -s

rebirthing ˌriːˈbɜː.θɪŋ (US) -ˈbɜːr-

reborn ˌriːˈbɔːn (US) -ˈbɔːrn

rebound (*n.*) ˈriː.baʊnd **-s** -z **ˌon the ˈrebound**

rebound (*adj.*) *of books, etc.:* ˌriːˈbaʊnd

rebound (*v.*) rɪˈbaʊnd, ˌriː- (US) ˈriː.baʊnd-; ˌriːˈbaʊnd, rɪ- **-s** -z **-ing** -ɪŋ **-ed** -ɪd

rebuff rɪˈbʌf, rə- **-s** -s **-ing** -ɪŋ **-ed** -t

rebuild ˌriːˈbɪld **-s** -z **-ing** -ɪŋ **rebuilt** ˌriːˈbɪlt

rebuk|e rɪˈbjuːk, rə- **-es** -s **-ing/ly** -ɪŋ/li **-ed** -t

rebus ˈriː.bəs **-es** -ɪz

re|but rɪ|ˈbʌt **-buts** -ˈbʌts **-butting** -ˈbʌt.ɪŋ (US) -ˈbʌţ.ɪŋ **-butted** -ˈbʌt.ɪd (US) -ˈbʌţ.ɪd

rebuttable rɪˈbʌt|.ə.bl̩ (US) -ˈbʌţ-

rebutt|al rɪˈbʌt|.əl (US) -ˈbʌţ- **-er/s** -ər/z (US) -ɚ/z

recalcitran|t rɪˈkæl.sɪ.trən|t, rə-, -sə- (US) -sɪ- **-ts** -ts **-ce** -ts

recall (*v.*) rɪˈkɔːl, rə- (US) rɪ-, rə-; ˈriː.kɔːl, -kɑːl **-s** -z **-ing** -ɪŋ **-ed** -d

recall (*n.*) rɪˈkɔːl, rə-; ˈriː.kɔːl (US) ˈriː.kɔːl, -kɑːl **-s** -z

re|cant rɪ|ˈkænt **-cants** -ˈkænts **-canting** -ˈkæn.tɪŋ (US) -ˈkæn.ţɪŋ **-canted** -ˈkæn.tɪd (US) -ˈkæn.ţɪd

recantation ˌriː.kænˈteɪ.ʃən **-s** -z

recap (*n.*) *recapitulation:* ˈriː.kæp **-s** -s

recap (*v.*) *recapitulate:* ˈriː.kæp; ˌriːˈkæp, rɪ-, rə- (US) ˈriː.kæp **-s** -s **-ping** -ɪŋ **-ped** -t

recap (*n.*) *a recapped tyre:* ˈriː.kæp **-s** -s

recap (*v.*) *retread a tyre:* ˌriːˈkæp (US) ˌriːˈkæp, ˈ-- **-s** -s **-ping** -ɪŋ **-ped** -t

recapitu|late ˌriː.kəˈpɪt.jə|.leɪt, -jʊ-, -ˈpɪtʃ.ə-, ˈ-ʊ- (US) -ˈpɪtʃ.ə- **-lates** -leɪts **-lating** -leɪ.tɪŋ (US) -leɪ.ţɪŋ **-lated** -leɪ.tɪd (US) -leɪ.ţɪd

recapitulation ˌriː.kəˌpɪt.jəˈleɪ.ʃən, -jʊˈ-, -ˌpɪtʃ.əˈ-, -ʊˈ- (US) -ˌpɪtʃ.əˈ- **-s** -z

recapitulatory ˌriː.kəˈpɪt.jə.lə.tər.i, -jʊ-, -ˈpɪtʃ.ə-, ˈ-ʊ-, -leɪ- (US) -ˈpɪtʃ.ə.lə.tɔːr-

recapt|ure ˌriːˈkæp.tʃ|ər (US) -tʃ|ɚ **-ures** -əz (US) -ɚz **-uring** -ər.ɪŋ **-ured** -əd (US) -ɚd

recast ˌriːˈkɑːst (US) -ˈkæst **-s** -s **-ing** -ɪŋ

recce (R) ˈrek.i **-s** -z **-ing** -ɪŋ **-(e)d** -d

reced|e rɪˈsiːd, rə-, ˌriː- **-es** -z **-ing** -ɪŋ **-ed** -ɪd

re|ceipt rɪ|ˈsiːt, rə- **-ceipts** -ˈsiːts **-ceipting** -ˈsiː.tɪŋ (US) -ˈsiː.ţɪŋ **-ceipted** -ˈsiː.tɪd (US) -ˈsiː.ţɪd

receiv|e rɪˈsiːv, rə- **-es** -z **-ing** -ɪŋ **-ed** -d **-er/s** -ər/z (US) -ɚ/z **-able** -ə.bl̩ **ReˌceivedpronunciˈAtion** ; **ˌon the reˈceiving ˌend (of)**

receivership rɪˈsɪː.və.ʃɪp, rə- (US) -vɚ-

recency ˈriː.sənt.si

recension rɪˈsent.ʃən, rə- **-s** -z
recent ˈriː.sənt **-ly** -li **-ness** -nəs, -nɪs
receptacle rɪˈsep.tə.kl̩, rə- **-s** -z
reception rɪˈsep.ʃən, rə- **-s** -z
receptionist rɪˈsep.ʃən.ɪst, rə- **-s** -s
receptive rɪˈsep.tɪv, rə- **-ly** -li **-ness** -nəs, -nɪs
receptivity ˌriː.sepˈtɪv.ə.ti, ˌrɪs.epˈ-, ˌres.epˈ-, -ɪ.ti (US) riːˌsepˈtɪv.ə.ţi, rɪ-
receptor rɪˈsep.təʳ, rə- (US) -tɚ **-s** -z
recess rɪˈses, rə-; ˈriː.ses (US) ˈriː.ses; rɪˈses **-es** -ɪz
recession rɪˈseʃ.ən, rə- **-s** -z
recessional rɪˈseʃ.ən.əl, rə- **-s** -z
recessive rɪˈses.ɪv, rə- **-ly** -li **-ness** -nəs, -nɪs
Rechabite ˈrek.ə.baɪt
recharg|e (*v.*) ˌriːˈtʃɑːdʒ, rɪ- (US) ˌriːˈtʃɑːrdʒ **-es** -ɪz **-ing** -ɪŋ **-ed** -d **-able** -ə.bl̩ **-er/s** -əʳ/z (US) -ɚ/z
recharge (*n.*) ˈriː.tʃɑːdʒ (US) -tʃɑːrdʒ
recherché rəˈʃeə.ʃeɪ (US) -ˈʃer-, --ˈ-
rechristen ˌriːˈkrɪs.ən **-s** -z **-ing** -ɪŋ **-ed** -d
recidivism rɪˈsɪd.ɪ.vɪ.zəm, rə-, ˈ-ə- (US) ˈ-ə-
recidivist rɪˈsɪd.ɪ.vɪst, rə-, ˈ-ə- (US) ˈ-ə- **-s** -s
Recife resˈiː.fə (US) rəˈsiː-, resˈiː
recipe ˈres.ɪ.pi, ˈ-ə-, -piː **-s** -z
recipient rɪˈsɪp.i.ənt, rə- **-s** -s
reciproc|al rɪˈsɪp.rə.k|əl, rə- **-als** -əlz **-ally** -əl.i, -li **-alness** -əl.nəs, -nɪs
recipro|cate rɪˈsɪp.rə|.keɪt, rə- **-cates** -keɪts **-cating** -keɪ.tɪŋ (US) -keɪ.ţɪŋ **-cated** -keɪ.tɪd (US) -keɪ.ţɪd
reciprocation rɪˌsɪp.rəˈkeɪ.ʃən, rə-
reciprocity ˌres.ɪˈprɒs.ə.ti, -ɪ.ti (US) -ˈprɑː.sə.ţi
recis(s)ion rɪˈsɪʒ.ən, rə-
recital rɪˈsaɪ.təl, rə- (US) -ţəl **-s** -z
recitation ˌres.ɪˈteɪ.ʃən **-s** -z
recitative (*adj.*) *relating to recital:* rɪˈsaɪ.tə.tɪv (US) ˈres.ɪ.teɪ.ţɪv; rɪˈsaɪ.ţə-
recitative (*n. adj.*) *in music:* ˌres.ɪ.təˈtiːv (US) -təˈ- **-s** -z
re|cite rɪ|ˈsaɪt, rə- **-cites** -ˈsaɪts **-citing** -ˈsaɪ.tɪŋ (US) -ˈsaɪ.ţɪŋ **-cited** -ˈsaɪ.tɪd (US) -ˈsaɪ.ţɪd **-citer/s** -ˈsaɪ.təʳ/z (US) -ˈsaɪ.ţɚ/z
reck rek **-s** -s **-ing** -ɪŋ **-ed** -t
reckless ˈrek.ləs, -lɪs **-ly** -li **-ness** -nəs, -nɪs
reckon ˈrek.ən **-s** -z **-ing/s** -ɪŋ/z **-ed** -d **-er/s** -əʳ/z (US) -ɚ/z
reclaim rɪˈkleɪm, ˌriː- **-s** -z **-ing** -ɪŋ **-ed** -d
reclaimable rɪˈkleɪ.mə.bl̩, ˌriː-
reclamation ˌrek.ləˈmeɪ.ʃən **-s** -z
reclin|e rɪˈklaɪn, rə- **-es** -z **-ing** -ɪŋ **-ed** -d
recliner rɪˈklaɪ.nəʳ, rə- (US) -nɚ **-s** -z
reclus|e rɪˈkluːs, rə- (US) ˈrek.luːs; rɪˈkluːs **-es** -ɪz **-ive** -ɪv
recognition ˌrek.əgˈnɪʃ.ən **-s** -z
recognizab|le, -isa- ˈrek.əg.naɪ.zə.b|l̩, ˌrek.əgˈnaɪ- (US) ˈrek.əg.naɪ- **-ly** -li
recognizanc|e, -isa- rɪˈkɒg.nɪ.zənts, rə-, -ˈkɒn.ɪ- (US) -ˈkɑːg.nɪ-, -ˈkɑː- **-es** -ɪz
recogniz|e, -is|e ˈrek.əg.naɪz **-es** -ɪz **-ing** -ɪŋ **-ed** -d
recoil (*n.*) ˈriː.kɔɪl; rɪˈkɔɪl, rə- **-s** -z
recoil (*v.*) rɪˈkɔɪl, rə- **-s** -z **-ing** -ɪŋ **-ed** -d
recollect ˌrek.əlˈekt, ˈ--- (US) ˌrek.əˈlekt **-s** -s **-ing** -ɪŋ **-ed** -ɪd
recollection ˌrek.əlˈek.ʃən (US) -əˈlek- **-s** -z
recombinant ˌriːˈkɒm.bɪ.nənt, rɪ-, rə-, -bə- (US) -ˈkɑːm.bə-
recommenc|e ˌriː.kəˈments, ˌrek.əˈ- **-es** -ɪz **-ing** -ɪŋ **-ed** -t
recommend ˌrek.əˈmend **-s** -z **-ing** -ɪŋ **-ed** -ɪd **-able** -ə.bl̩
recommendation ˌrek.ə.menˈdeɪ.ʃən, -mənˈ- (US) -mənˈ- **-s** -z
recompens|e ˈrek.əm.pents **-es** -ɪz **-ing** -ɪŋ **-ed** -t
recompos|e ˌriː.kəmˈpəʊz (US) -ˈpoʊz **-es** -ɪz **-ing** -ɪŋ **-ed** -d
reconcilab|le ˈrek.ən.saɪ.lə.b|l̩, ˌrek.ənˈsaɪ- (US) ˌrek.ənˈsaɪ- **-ly** -li
reconcil|e ˈrek.ən.saɪl **-es** -z **-ing** -ɪŋ **-ed** -d **-er/s** -əʳ/z (US) -ɚ/z
reconciliation ˌrek.ənˌsɪl.iˈeɪ.ʃən **-s** -z
recondite ˈrek.ən.daɪt; rɪˈkɒn-, rə- (US) ˈrek.ən-; rɪˈkɑːn-, rə-
recondition ˌriː.kənˈdɪʃ.ən **-s** -z **-ing** -ɪŋ **-ed** -d
reconduct ˌriː.kənˈdʌkt **-s** -s **-ing** -ɪŋ **-ed** -ɪd
reconnaissanc|e rɪˈkɒn.ɪ.sənts, rə-, ˈ-ə- (US) -ˈkɑː.nə-, -zənts **-es** -ɪz
reconnoit|er ˌrek.əˈnɔɪ.t|əʳ (US) ˌriː.kəˈnɔɪ.ţ|ɚ, ˌrek.əˈ- **-ers** -əz (US) -ɚz **-ering** -ər.ɪŋ **-ered** -əd (US) -ɚd
reconnoit|re ˌrek.əˈnɔɪ.t|əʳ (US) ˌriː.kəˈnɔɪ.ţ|ɚ, ˌrek.əˈ- **-res** -əz (US) -ɚz **-ring** -ər.ɪŋ **-red** -əd (US) -ɚd
reconqu|er ˌriːˈkɒŋ.k|əʳ (US) -ˈkɑːŋ.k|ɚ **-ers** -əz (US) -ɚz **-ering** -ər.ɪŋ **-ered** -əd (US) -ɚd
reconquest ˌriːˈkɒŋ.kwest (US) -ˈkɑːŋ- **-s** -s
reconsid|er ˌriː.kənˈsɪd|.əʳ (US) -ɚ **-ers** -əz (US) -ɚz **-ering** -ər.ɪŋ **-ered** -əd (US) -ɚz
reconsideration ˌriː.kənˌsɪd.ərˈeɪ.ʃən (US) -əˈreɪ-
reconstitu|te ˌriːˈkɒn.stɪ.tjuː|t, -stə-, -tʃuː|t (US) -ˈkɑːn.stə.tuː|t, -tjuː|t **-tes** -ts **-ting** -tɪŋ (US) -ţɪŋ **-ted** -tɪd (US) -ţɪd
reconstitution ˌriːˌkɒnt.stɪˈtjuː.ʃən, -stəˈ-, -ˈtʃuː- (US) -ˌkɑːnt.stəˈtuː-, -ˈtjuː- **-s** -z
reconstruct ˌriː.kənˈstrʌkt **-s** -s **-ing** -ɪŋ **-ed** -ɪd **-ive** -ɪv
reconstruction ˌriː.kənˈstrʌk.ʃən **-s** -z
reconversion ˌriː.kənˈvɜː.ʃən, -ʒən (US) -ˈvɜːr.ʒən, -ʃən **-s** -z
recon|vert ˌriː.kən|ˈvɜːt (US) -ˈvɜːrt **-verts** -ˈvɜːts (US) -ˈvɜːrts **-verting** -ˈvɜː.tɪŋ (US) -ˈvɜːr.ţɪŋ **-verted** -ˈvɜː.tɪd (US) -ˈvɜːr.ţɪd
reconvey ˌriː.kənˈveɪ **-s** -z **-ing** -ɪŋ **-ed** -d
record (*n.*) ˈrek.ɔːd (US) -ɚd **-s** -z ˈ**record** ˌ**player**
record (*v.*) rɪˈkɔːd, rə- (US) -ˈkɔːrd **-s** -z **-ing** -ɪŋ **-ed** -ɪd **-able** -ə.bl̩ **re**ˌ**corded de**ˈ**livery**
record-break|ing ˈrek.ɔːdˌbreɪ.k|ɪŋ (US) -ɚdˌ- **-er/s** -əʳ/z (US) -ɚ/z
recorder rɪˈkɔː.dəʳ, rə- (US) -ˈkɔːr.dɚ **-s** -z
recordist rɪˈkɔː.dɪst, rə- (US) -ˈkɔːr- **-s** -s
recount (*n.*) ˈriː.kaʊnt, ˌ-ˈ- (US) ˈriː.kaʊnt **-s** -s
re|count (*v.*) *count again:* ˌriː|ˈkaʊnt **-counts** -ˈkaʊnts **-counting** -ˈkaʊn.tɪŋ (US) -ˈkaʊn.ţɪŋ **-counted** -ˈkaʊn.tɪd (US) -ˈkaʊn.ţɪd
re|count (*v.*) *narrate:* rɪ|ˈkaʊnt, rə- **-counts** -ˈkaʊnts **-counting** -ˈkaʊn.tɪŋ (US) -ˈkaʊn.ţɪŋ **-counted** -ˈkaʊn.tɪd (US) -ˈkaʊn.ţɪd
recoup rɪˈkuːp, rə-, ˌriː- (US) rɪ-, rə- **-s** -s **-ing** -ɪŋ **-ed** -t **-ment** -mənt
recourse rɪˈkɔːs, rə- (US) ˈriː.kɔːrs; rɪˈkɔːrs
recov|er *get back, come back to health, etc.:* rɪˈkʌv|.əʳ, rə- (US) -ɚ **-ers** -əz (US) -ɚz **-ering** -ər.ɪŋ **-ered** -əd (US) -ɚd **-erable** -ər.ə.bl̩
recov|er *cover again:* ˌriːˈkʌv|.əʳ (US) -ɚ **-ers** -əz (US) -ɚz **-ering** -ər.ɪŋ **-ered** -əd (US) -ɚd
recover|y rɪˈkʌv.ər|.i, rə- (US) -ɚ|.i ˈ-r|i **-ies** -iz
recreant ˈrek.ri.ənt **-s** -s **-ly** -li
recre|ate *create anew:* ˌriː.kri|ˈeɪt **-ates** -ˈeɪts **-ating** -ˈeɪ.tɪŋ (US) -ˈeɪ.ţɪŋ **-ated** -ˈeɪ.tɪd (US) -ˈeɪ.ţɪd
recre|ate *refresh:* ˈrek.ri.|eɪt **-ates** -eɪts **-ating** -eɪ.tɪŋ (US) -eɪ.ţɪŋ **-ated** -eɪ.tɪd (US) -eɪ.ţɪd **-ative** -eɪ.tɪv (US) -eɪ.ţɪv
recreation *creating anew:* ˌriː.kriˈeɪ.ʃən **-s** -z
recreation *refreshment, amusement:* ˌrek.riˈeɪ.ʃən **-s** -z **-al** -əl

recrimi|nate rɪˈkrɪm.ɪ|.neɪt, rə-, ˈ-ə- (US) ˈ-ə- **-nates** -neɪts **-nating** -neɪ.tɪŋ (US) -neɪ.t̬ɪŋ **-nated** -neɪ.tɪd (US) -neɪ.t̬ɪd **-nator/s** -neɪ.təʳ/z (US) -neɪ.t̬ɚ/z

recrimination rɪˌkrɪm.ɪˈneɪ.ʃən, rə-, -əˈ- (US) -əˈ- **-s** -z

recriminatory rɪˈkrɪm.ɪ.nə.tər.i, rə-, ˈ-ə- (US) -ə.nə.tɔːr-

recross ˌriːˈkrɒs (US) -ˈkrɑːs **-es** -ɪz **-ing** -ɪŋ **-ed** -t

recrudesc|e ˌriː.kruːˈdes, ˌrek.ruːˈ- (US) ˌriː.kruːˈ- **-es** -ɪz **-ing** -ɪŋ **-ed** -t

recrudescen|ce ˌriː.kruːˈdes.ən|ts, ˌrek.ruːˈ- (US) ˌriː.kruːˈ- **-t** -t

re|cruit rɪ|ˈkruːt, rə- **-cruits** -ˈkruːts **-cruiting** -ˈkruː.tɪŋ (US) -ˈkruː.t̬ɪŋ **-cruited** -ˈkruː.tɪd (US) -ˈkruː.t̬ɪd **-cruiter/s** -ˈkruː.təʳ/z (US) -ˈkruː.t̬ɚ/z **-cruitment** -ˈkruːt.mənt

rectal ˈrek.təl **-ly** -i

rectangle ˈrek.tæŋ.gl̩ **-s** -z

rectangular rekˈtæŋ.gjə.ləʳ, -gjʊ- (US) -gjə.lɚ **-ly** -li

rectification ˌrek.tɪ.fɪˈkeɪ.ʃən, -tə- (US) -tə- **-s** -z

recti|fy ˈrek.tɪ|.faɪ, -tə- (US) -tə- **-fies** -faɪz **-fying** -faɪ.ɪŋ **-fied** -faɪd **-fier/s** -faɪ.əʳ/z (US) -faɪ.ɚ/z **-fiable** -faɪ.ə.bl̩

rectiline|al ˌrek.tɪˈlɪn.i|.əl, -təˈ- (US) -təˈ- **-ar** -əʳ (US) -ɚ

rectitude ˈrek.tɪ.tjuːd, -tə-, -tʃuːd (US) -tə.tuːd, -tjuːd

recto ˈrek.təʊ (US) -toʊ

rector ˈrek.təʳ (US) -tɚ **-s** -z

rectorate ˈrek.tər.ət, -ɪt, -eɪt (US) -ɪt **-s** -s

rectorial rekˈtɔː.ri.əl (US) -ˈtɔːr.i-

rectorship ˈrek.tə.ʃɪp (US) -tɚ- **-s** -s

rector|y ˈrek.tər|.i **-ies** -ɪz

rect|um ˈrek.t|əm **-ums** -əmz **-a** -ə

rect|us ˈrek.t|əs **-i** -aɪ

Reculver rɪˈkʌl.vəʳ, rə- (US) -vɚ **-s** -z

recumben|ce rɪˈkʌm.bən|ts, rə- **-cy** -si

recumbent rɪˈkʌm.bənt, rə- **-ly** -li

recuper|ate rɪˈkjuː.pər|.eɪt, rə-, -ˈkuː- (US) -ˈkuː.pə.r|eɪt, -ˈkjuː- **-ates** -eɪts **-ating** -eɪ.tɪŋ (US) -eɪ.t̬ɪŋ **-ated** -eɪ.tɪd (US) -eɪ.t̬ɪd

recuperation rɪˌkjuː.pərˈeɪ.ʃən, rə-, -ˌkuː- (US) -ˌkuː.pəˈreɪ-, -ˌkjuː-

recuperative rɪˈkjuː.pər.ə.tɪv, rə-, -ˈkjuː- (US) -ˈkuː.pɚ.ə.t̬ɪv, -ˈkjuː-

recur rɪˈkɜːʳ, rə- (US) -ˈkɜːr **-s** -z **-ring** -ɪŋ **-red** -d

recurrenc|e rɪˈkʌr.ənts, rə- (US) -ˈkɜːr- **-es** -ɪz

recurrent rɪˈkʌr.ənt, rə- (US) -ˈkɜːr- **-ly** -li

recursive rɪˈkɜː.sɪv, ˌriː- (US) -ˈkɜːr- **-s** -z **-ly** -li

recurved ˌriːˈkɜːvd, rɪ-, rə- (US) -ˈkɜːrvd

recusan|cy ˈrek.jʊ.zən|t.si, -jə-; rɪˈkjuː-, rə- (US) ˈrek.jʊ-; rɪˈkjuː-, rə- **-ce** -s

recusant ˈrek.jʊ.zənt, -jə-; rɪˈkjuː-, rə- (US) ˈrek.jʊ-; rɪˈkjuː-, rə- **-s** -s

recycl|e ˌriːˈsaɪ.kl̩ **-es** -z **-ing** -ɪŋ, ˈ-klɪŋ **-ed** -d **-able** -ə.bl̩, ˈ-klə.bl̩

red (R) red **-s** -z **-der** -əʳ (US) -ɚ **-dest** -ɪst, -əst **-ness** -nəs, -nɪs **ˌred aˈlert** ; **ˌred ˈcard** ; **ˌred ˈcarpet** ; **ˌRed ˈCrescent** ; **ˌRed ˈCross** ; **ˌred ˈherring** ; **ˌRed ˈIndian** ; **ˌRed ˈSea** ; **ˌred ˈtape** ; **in the ˈred** ; **ˌsee ˈred** ; **ˌnot worth a ˌred ˈcent** ; **ˌreds under the ˈbed**

redact rɪˈdækt, rə- **-s** -s **-ing** -ɪŋ **-ed** -ɪd **-or/s** -əʳ/z (US) -ɚ/z

redaction rɪˈdæk.ʃən, rə- **-s** -z

red-blooded ˌredˈblʌd.ɪd **-ness** -nəs, -nɪs *stress shift:* ˌred-blooded ˈmale

Redbourn ˈred.bɔːn (US) ˈred.bɔːrn

redbreast ˈred.brest **-s** -s

redbrick ˈred.brɪk, ˌ-ˈ- (US) ˈred.brɪk **ˌredbrick uniˈversity**

Redbridge ˈred.brɪdʒ

redbud ˈred.bʌd **-s** -z

redcap ˈred.kæp **-s** -s

Redcar ˈred.kɑːʳ (US) ˈred.kɑːr

Redcliffe, Redclyffe ˈred.klɪf

redcoat ˈred.kəʊt (US) -koʊt **-s** -s

redcurrant ˈred,kʌr.ənt **-s** -s

Reddaway ˈred.ə.weɪ

redden ˈred.ən **-s** -z **-ing** -ɪŋ **-ed** -d

Redding ˈred.ɪŋ

reddish ˈred.ɪʃ **-ness** -nəs, -nɪs

Redditch ˈred.ɪtʃ

reddle ˈred.l̩

redecor|ate ˌriːˈdek.ər|.eɪt (US) -ə.r|eɪt **-ates** -eɪts **-ating** -eɪ.tɪŋ (US) -eɪ.t̬ɪŋ **-ated** -eɪ.tɪd (US) -eɪ.t̬ɪd

redeem rɪˈdiːm, rə- **-s** -z **-ing** -ɪŋ **-ed** -d **-able** -ə.bl̩

redeemer (R) rɪˈdiː.məʳ, rə- (US) -mɚ **-s** -z

redefin|e ˌriː.dɪˈfaɪn, -dəˈ- **-es** -z **-ing** -ɪŋ **-ed** -d

redeliv|er ˌriː.dɪˈlɪv|.əʳ, -dəˈ- (US) -ɚ **-ers** -əz (US) -ɚz **-ering** -ər.ɪŋ **-ered** -əd (US) -ɚd **-ery** -ər.i

redemption (R) rɪˈdemp.ʃən, rə- **-s** -z

redemptive rɪˈdemp.tɪv, rə-

re-deploy ˌriː.dɪˈplɔɪ, -dəˈ- **-s** -z **-ing** -ɪŋ **-ed** -d **-ment/s** -mənt/s

redesign ˌriː.dɪˈzaɪn, -dəˈ- **-s** -z **-ing** -ɪŋ **-ed** -d

redevelop ˌriː.dɪˈvel.əp, -dəˈ- **-s** -s **-ing** -ɪŋ **-ed** -t **-ment/s** -mənt/s

red-eye ˈred.aɪ **-s** -z

Redfern ˈred.fɜːn (US) -fɜːrn

Redfield ˈred.fiːld

Redford ˈred.fəd (US) -fɚd

Redgrave ˈred.greɪv, ˈreg- (US) ˈred-

red-handed ˌredˈhæn.dɪd

redhead (R) ˈred.hed **-s** -z

Redheugh ˈred.hjuːf, -juːf, -jəf

Redhill ˌredˈhɪl, ˈ--

red-hot ˌredˈhɒt (US) -ˈhɑːt *stress shift:* ˌred-hot ˈpoker

re-dial ˌriːˈdaɪəl (US) -ˈdaɪəl **-s** -z **-ling** -ɪŋ **-led** -d

Rediffusion® ˌriː.dɪˈfjuː.ʒən, -dəˈ-

redintegration rɪˌdɪn.tɪˈgreɪ.ʃən, redˌɪn-, -təˈ- (US) redˌɪn.t̬əˈ-, rɪˌdɪn-

redirect ˌriː.dɪˈrekt, -daɪ-, -də- (US) -dɪˈ-, -daɪˈ- **-s** -s **-ing** -ɪŋ **-ed** -ɪd

rediscov|er ˌriː.dɪˈskʌv|.əʳ (US) -ɚ **-ers** -əz (US) -ɚz **-ering** -ər.ɪŋ **-ered** -əd (US) -ɚd **-ery** -ər.i

redistribu|te ˌriː.dɪˈstrɪb.juː|t, -jʊ|t, -dəˈ-; -strɪˈbjuː|t, -stəˈ- (US) ˌriː.dɪˈstrɪb.juː|t, -jʊ|t **-tes** -ts **-ting** -tɪŋ (US) -t̬ɪŋ **-ted** -tɪd (US) -t̬ɪd

redistribution ˌriː.dɪ.strɪˈbjuː.ʃən, -strəˈ- **-s** -z

redivid|e ˌriː.dɪˈvaɪd, -dəˈ- **-es** -z **-ing** -ɪŋ **-ed** -ɪd

redivivus ˌred.ɪˈvaɪ.vəs, -əˈ-, -ˈviː-

red-letter day ˌredˈlet.əˌdeɪ (US) -ˈlet̬.ɚˌ- **-s** -z

red-light district ˌredˈlaɪtˌdɪs.trɪkt (US) ˈred.laɪtˌ- **-s** -s

Redmond ˈred.mənd

redneck ˈred.nek **-s** -s

re|-do ˌriː|ˈduː **-does** -ˈdʌz **-doing** -ˈduː.ɪŋ **-did** -ˈdɪd **-done** -ˈdʌn

redolen|t ˈred.əl.ən|t, -əʊ.lən|t (US) -əl.ən|t **-ce** -ts

redoubl|e ˌriːˈdʌb.l̩, rɪ- **-es** -z **-ing** -ɪŋ, ˌriːˈdʌb.lɪŋ, rɪˈdʌb- **-ed** -d

redoubt rɪˈdaʊt, rə- **-s** -s

redoubtab|le rɪˈdaʊ.tə.bl|l̩, rə- (US) -t̬ə- **-ly** -li

redound rɪˈdaʊnd, rə- **-s** -z **-ing** -ɪŋ **-ed** -ɪd

Redpath ˈred.pɑːθ, ˈreb- (US) ˈred.pæθ

redraft ˌriːˈdrɑːft (US) -ˈdræft **-s** -s **-ing** -ɪŋ **-ed** -ɪd

re-draw ˌriːˈdrɔː (US) -ˈdrɑː, -ˈdrɔː **-s** -z **-ing** -ɪŋ **re-drew** ˌriːˈdruː **re-drawn** ˌriːˈdrɔːn (US) -ˈdrɑːn, -ˈdrɔːn

redress (*v.*) rɪˈdres, rə- **-es** -ɪz **-ing** -ɪŋ **-ed** -t

redress (*n.*) rɪˈdres, rə-; ˈriː.dres (US) ˈriː.dres

Redriff ˈred.rɪf

Redruth ˌredˈruːθ, ˈ--

redshank ˈred.ʃæŋk **-s** -s

redskin (R) ˈred.skɪn **-s** -z

redstart ˈred.stɑːt (US) -stɑːrt **-s** -s

reduc|e rɪˈdjuːs, rə- (US) -ˈduːs, -ˈdjuːs **-es** -ɪz **-ing** -ɪŋ **-ed** -t **-er/s** -əʳ/z (US) -ɚ/z

reducibility rɪˌdjuː.səˈbɪl.ə.ti, rə-, -sɪˈ-, -ɪ.ti ⓊⓈ -ˌduː.səˈbɪl.ə.t̬i, -ˌdjuː-
reducible rɪˈdjuː.sə.bl̩, rə-, -sɪ- ⓊⓈ -ˈduː.sə-, -ˈdjuː-
reductio ad absurdum rɪˌdʌk.ti.əʊ.æd.æbˈsɜː.dəm, rə-, -ʃi-, -əbˈ- ⓊⓈ -ti.oʊ.æd.æbˈsɝː-, ˈ-ʃi-
reduction rɪˈdʌk.ʃən, rə- **-s** -z
reduction|ism rɪˈdʌk.ʃən|.ɪ.zəm **-ist/s** -ɪst/s
reductionistic rɪˌdʌk.ʃənˈɪs.tɪk, rə-
redundan|cy rɪˈdʌn.dənt|.si, rə- **-cies** -siz **-ce** -s
redundant rɪˈdʌn.dənt, rə- **-ly** -li
redupli|cate rɪˈdjuː.plɪ|.keɪt, rə-, ˌriː-, -ˈdʒuː-, -plə- ⓊⓈ -ˈduː.plə-, -ˈdjuː- **-cates** -keɪts **-cating** -keɪ.tɪŋ ⓊⓈ -keɪ.t̬ɪŋ **-cated** -keɪ.tɪd ⓊⓈ -keɪ.t̬ɪd
reduplication rɪˌdjuː.plɪˈkeɪ.ʃən, rə-, ˌriː-, -ˌdʒuː-, -pləˈ- ⓊⓈ -ˌduː.pləˈ-, -ˌdjuː- **-s** -z
reduplicative rɪˈdjuː.plɪ.kə.tɪv, rə-, -ˈdʒuː-, -plə-, -keɪ- ⓊⓈ -ˈduː.plə.keɪ.t̬ɪv, -ˈdju-
redwing ˈred.wɪŋ **-s** -z
redwood (R) ˈred.wʊd **-s** -z
Reebok® ˈriː.bɒk ⓊⓈ -bɑːk **-s** -s
Reece riːs
re-echo ˌriːˈek.əʊ, ri- ⓊⓈ -oʊ **-es** -z **-ing** -ɪŋ **-ed** -d
reed (R) riːd **-s** -z
re-ed|it ˌriːˈed|.ɪt **-its** -ɪts **-iting** -ɪ.tɪŋ ⓊⓈ -ɪ.t̬ɪŋ **-ited** -ɪ.tɪd ⓊⓈ -ɪ.t̬ɪd
re-edition ˌriː.ɪˈdɪʃ.ən, -əˈ- **-s** -z
re-edu|cate ˌriːˈedʒ.ʊ|.keɪt, ˈ-ə-, -ˈed.jʊ-, -jə- ⓊⓈ -ˈedʒ.ʊ-, ˈ-ə- **-cates** -keɪts **-cating** -keɪ.tɪŋ ⓊⓈ -keɪ.t̬ɪŋ **-cated** -keɪ.tɪd ⓊⓈ -keɪ.t̬ɪd
re-education ˌriː.edʒ.ʊˈkeɪ.ʃən, -əˈ-, -ˌed.jʊˈ-, -jəˈ- ⓊⓈ -ˌedʒ.ʊˈ-, -əˈ-
reed-warbler ˈriːdˌwɔː.bləʳ, ˌ-ˈ-- ⓊⓈ ˈriːdˌwɔːr.blɚ **-s** -z
reed|y ˈriː.d|i **-ier** -i.əʳ ⓊⓈ -i.ɚ **-iest** -i.ɪst, -i.əst **-iness** -ɪ.nəs, -ɪ.nɪs
reef riːf **-s** -s **-ing** -ɪŋ **-ed** -t ˈ**reef** ˌ**knot**
reefer ˈriː.fəʳ ⓊⓈ -fɚ **-s** -z
reek riːk **-s** -s **-ing** -ɪŋ **-ed** -t
Reekie ˈriː.ki
reel riːl **-s** -z **-ing** -ɪŋ **-ed** -d
re-elect ˌriː.ɪˈlekt, -əˈ- **-s** -s **-ing** -ɪŋ **-ed** -ɪd
re-election ˌriː.ɪˈlek.ʃən, -əˈ- **-s** -z
reel-to-reel ˌriːl.təˈriːl, -tʊˈ-
re-embark ˌriː.ɪmˈbɑːk, -emˈ- ⓊⓈ -ˈbɑːrk **-s** -s **-ing** -ɪŋ **-ed** -t
re-embarkation ˌriː.ɪm.bɑːˈkeɪ.ʃən, -em-; riˌem- ⓊⓈ ˌriː.ɪm.bɑːrˈ-, -em- **-s** -z
re-enact ˌriː.ɪˈnækt, -əˈ-, -enˈækt **-s** -s **-ing** -ɪŋ **-ed** -ɪd **-ment/s** -mənt/s
reenforc|e ˌriː.ɪnˈfɔːs, -ənˈ- ⓊⓈ -ˈfɔːrs **-es** -ɪz **-ing** -ɪŋ **-ed** -t
re-engag|e ˌriː.ɪŋˈgeɪdʒ, -eŋˈ-, -ɪnˈ-, -enˈ- ⓊⓈ -ɪnˈ-, -enˈ- **-es** -ɪz **-ing** -ɪŋ **-ed** -d **-ement/s** -mənt/s
re-enlist ˌriː.ɪnˈlɪst, -enˈ- **-s** -s **-ing** -ɪŋ **-ed** -ɪd
re-ent|er ˌriːˈen.t|əʳ, ri- ⓊⓈ -t̬|ɚ **-ers** -əz ⓊⓈ -ɚz **-ering** -ər.ɪŋ **-ered** -əd ⓊⓈ -ɚd
re-entr|y ˌriːˈen.tr|i, ri- **-ies** -iz
Rees(e) riːs
re-establish ˌriː.ɪˈstæb.lɪʃ, -esˈtæb- **-es** -ɪz **-ing** -ɪŋ **-ed** -t **-ment** -mənt
reeve (R) riːv **-s** -z
Reeves riːvz
re-examination ˌriː.ɪgˌzæm.ɪˈneɪ.ʃən, -egˌ-, -əˈ- **-s** -z
re-examin|e ˌriː.ɪgˈzæm.ɪn, -egˈ- **-es** -z **-ing** -ɪŋ **-ed** -d
re-expor|t (*v.*) ˌriː.ɪkˈspɔː|t, -ekˈ- ⓊⓈ -ˈspɔːr|t; -ˈek.spɔːr|t **-ts** -ts **-ting** -tɪŋ ⓊⓈ -t̬ɪŋ **-ted** -tɪd ⓊⓈ -t̬ɪd
ref (R) ref **-s** -s
refac|e ˌriːˈfeɪs **-es** -ɪz **-ing** -ɪŋ **-ed** -t
refashion ˌriːˈfæʃ.ən **-s** -z **-ing** -ɪŋ **-ed** -d
refection rɪˈfek.ʃən, rə-
refector|y rɪˈfek.tər|.i, rə-, ˈref.ɪk- ⓊⓈ rɪˈfek-, rə- **-ies** -iz
refer rɪˈfɜːʳ, rə- ⓊⓈ -ˈfɝː **-s** -z **-ring** -ɪŋ **-red** -d
referable rɪˈfɜː.rə.bl̩, rə-; ˈref.ər- ⓊⓈ rɪˈfɝː.ə-, rə-; ˈref.ɚ-
referee ˌref.ərˈiː ⓊⓈ -əˈriː **-s** -z
referenc|e ˈref.ər.ənts, ˈ-rənts **-es** -ɪz ˈ**reference** ˌ**book** ; ˈ**reference** ˌ**library**
referend|um ˌref.ərˈen.d|əm ⓊⓈ -əˈren- **-ums** -əmz **-a** -ə
referent ˈref.ər.ənt, ˈ-rənt **-s** -s
referential ˌref.ərˈen.tʃəl ⓊⓈ -əˈrent.ʃəl **-ly** -i
referral rɪˈfɜː.rəl, rə- ⓊⓈ -ˈfɝː.əl **-s** -z
refill (*n.*) ˈriː.fɪl **-s** -z
refill (*v.*) ˌriːˈfɪl **-s** -z **-ing** -ɪŋ **-ed** -d
refin|e rɪˈfaɪn, rə- **-es** -z **-ing** -ɪŋ **-ed** -d **-er/s** -əʳ/z ⓊⓈ -ɚ/z **-ement/s** -mənt/s
refiner|y rɪˈfaɪ.nər|.i, rə- **-ies** -iz
refit (*n.*) ˈriː.fɪt, ˌ-ˈ-
re|fit (*v.*) ˌriː|ˈfɪt **-fits** -ˈfɪts **-fitting** -ˈfɪt.ɪŋ ⓊⓈ -ˈfɪt̬.ɪŋ **-fitted** -ˈfɪt.ɪd ⓊⓈ -ˈfɪt̬.ɪd
re|flate ˌriː|ˈfleɪt **-flates** -ˈfleɪts **-flating** -ˈfleɪ.tɪŋ ⓊⓈ -ˈfleɪ.t̬ɪŋ **-flated** -ˈfleɪ.tɪd ⓊⓈ -ˈfleɪ.t̬ɪd
reflation ˌriːˈfleɪ.ʃən
reflationary ˌriːˈfleɪ.ʃən.ər.i ⓊⓈ -er-
reflect rɪˈflekt, rə- **-s** -s **-ing** -ɪŋ **-ed** -ɪd **-or/s** -əʳ/z ⓊⓈ -ɚ/z
reflection rɪˈflek.ʃən, rə- **-s** -z
reflective rɪˈflek.tɪv, rə- **-ly** -li **-ness** -nəs, -nɪs
reflex ˈriː.fleks **-es** -ɪz
reflexed rɪˈflekst, ˌriː-; ˈriː.flekst
reflexive rɪˈflek.sɪv, rə- **-ly** -li **-ness** -nəs, -nɪs
reflexolog|y ˌriː.flekˈsɒl.ə.dʒ|i ⓊⓈ -ˈsɑː.lə- **-ist/s** -ɪst/s
re|float ˌriː|ˈfləʊt ⓊⓈ -ˈfloʊt **-floats** -ˈfləʊts ⓊⓈ -ˈfloʊts **-floating** -ˈfləʊ.tɪŋ ⓊⓈ -ˈfloʊ.t̬ɪŋ **-floated** -ˈfləʊ.tɪd ⓊⓈ -ˈfloʊ.t̬ɪd
refluent ˈref.lu.ənt
reflux ˈriː.flʌks **-es** -ɪz
reforest ˌriːˈfɒr.ɪst ⓊⓈ -ˈfɔːr.ɪst **-s** -s **-ing** -ɪŋ **-ed** -ɪd
reforestation ˌriː.fɒr.ɪˈsteɪ.ʃən, -əˈ- ⓊⓈ -fɔːr.ɪˈ-
reform (*n. v.*) *make better, become better, etc.:* rɪˈfɔːm, rə- ⓊⓈ -ˈfɔːrm **-s** -z **-ing** -ɪŋ **-ed** -d **-er/s** -əʳ/z ⓊⓈ -ɚ/z **-able** -ə.bl̩ **reˈform** ˌ**school**
re-form (*v.*) *form again:* ˌriːˈfɔːm ⓊⓈ -ˈfɔːrm **-s** -z **-ing** -ɪŋ **-ed** -d
reformation (R) ˌref.əˈmeɪ.ʃən, -ɔːˈ- ⓊⓈ -ɚˈ- **-s** -z
reformative rɪˈfɔː.mə.tɪv, rə- ⓊⓈ -ˈfɔːr.mə.t̬ɪv
reformator|y rɪˈfɔː.mə.tər|.i, rə- ⓊⓈ -ˈfɔːr.mə.tɔːr- **-ies** -iz
reformist rɪˈfɔː.mɪst, rə- ⓊⓈ -ˈfɔːr-
refract rɪˈfrækt, rə- **-s** -s **-ing** -ɪŋ **-ed** -ɪd **-or/s** -əʳ/z ⓊⓈ -ɚ/z **-ive** -ɪv
refraction rɪˈfræk.ʃən, rə- **-s** -z
refractor|y rɪˈfræk.tər|.i, rə- **-ily** -əl.i, -ɪ.li **-iness** -ɪ.nəs, -ɪ.nɪs
refrain rɪˈfreɪn, rə- **-s** -z **-ing** -ɪŋ **-ed** -d
refresh rɪˈfreʃ, rə- **-es** -ɪz **-ing/ly** -ɪŋ/li **-ed** -t **-er/s** -əʳ/z ⓊⓈ -ɚ/z **reˈfresher** ˌ**course**
refreshment rɪˈfreʃ.mənt, rə- **-s** -s
refried ˌriːˈfraɪd *stress shift, see compound:* ˌ**refried** ˈ**beans**
refriger|ate rɪˈfrɪdʒ.ər|.eɪt, rə- ⓊⓈ -ə.r|eɪt **-ates** -eɪts **-ating** -eɪ.tɪŋ ⓊⓈ -eɪ.t̬ɪŋ **-ated** -eɪ.tɪd ⓊⓈ -eɪ.t̬ɪd
refrigeration rɪˌfrɪdʒ.ərˈeɪ.ʃən, rə- ⓊⓈ -əˈreɪ-
refrigerator rɪˈfrɪdʒ.ər.eɪ.təʳ, rə- ⓊⓈ -ə.reɪ.t̬ɚ **-s** -z
reft reft
re-fuel ˌriːˈfjuː.əl, -ˈfjʊəl ⓊⓈ -ˈfjuː.əl, -ˈfjuːl **-s** -z **-ling** -ɪŋ **-led** -d
refug|e ˈref.juːdʒ **-es** -ɪz
refugee ˌref.jʊˈdʒiː, -jəˈ- ⓊⓈ ˌref.jʊˈdʒiː, -jəˈ-; ˈref.jʊ.dʒi, -jə- **-s** -z
refulgen|ce rɪˈfʌl.dʒən|ts, rə- ⓊⓈ -ˈfʌl-, -ˈfʊl- **-t/ly** -t/li
refund (*n.*) ˈriː.fʌnd **-s** -z
refund (*v.*) ˌriːˈfʌnd, rɪ-, rə-; ˈriː.fʌnd ⓊⓈ ˌriːˈfʌnd, rɪ-, rə- **-s** -z **-ing** -ɪŋ **-ed** -ɪd
refurbish ˌriːˈfɜː.bɪʃ ⓊⓈ -ˈfɝː- **-es** -ɪz **-ing** -ɪŋ **-ed** -t **-ment/s** -mənt/s

refurnish ˌriːˈfɜː.nɪʃ (US) -ˈfɜːr- **-es** -ɪz **-ing** -ɪŋ **-ed** -t
refusal rɪˈfjuː.zᵊl, rə- **-s** -z
refuse (*n. adj.*) ˈref.juːs
refus|e (*v.*) rɪˈfjuːz, rə- **-es** -ɪz **-ing** -ɪŋ **-ed** -d **-able** -ə.bl̩
refusenik rɪˈfjuːz.nɪk, rə- **-s** -s
refutability ˌref.jʊ.təˈbɪl.ə.ti, -jə-, -ɪ.ti; rɪˌfjuː-, rə- (US) rɪˌfjuː.t̬əˈbɪl.ə.t̬i; ˌref.jə.t̬əˈ-
refutab|le ˈref.jʊ.tə.b|l̩, -jə-; rɪˈfjuː-, rə- (US) rɪˈfjuː.t̬ə-, rə-; ˈref.jə- **-ly** -li
refutation ˌref.jʊˈteɪ.ʃᵊn, -jəˈ- **-s** -z
re|fute rɪ|ˈfjuːt, rə- **-futes** -ˈfjuːts **-futing** -ˈfjuː.tɪŋ (US) -ˈfjuː.t̬ɪŋ **-futed** -ˈfjuː.tɪd (US) -ˈfjuː.t̬ɪd
Reg redʒ
-reg *car numberplate:* -ˌredʒ
Note: Used in the UK to refer to the year of registration of a car, which is indicated on the numberplate by a letter, e.g. **an F-reg**.
regain rɪˈgeɪn, ˌriː- **-s** -z **-ing** -ɪŋ **-ed** -d
regal ˈriː.gᵊl **-ly** -i
regal|e rɪˈgeɪl, rə- **-es** -z **-ing** -ɪŋ **-ed** -d
regalia rɪˈgeɪ.li.ə, rə- (US) -ˈgeɪl.jə, -ˈgeɪ.li.ə
Regan ˈriː.gᵊn
regard rɪˈgɑːd, rə- (US) -ˈgɑːrd **-s** -z **-ing** -ɪŋ **-ed** -ɪd **-ant** -ᵊnt
regardful rɪˈgɑːd.fᵊl, rə-, -fʊl (US) -ˈgɑːrd- **-ly** -i **-ness** -nəs, -nɪs
regardless rɪˈgɑːd.ləs, rə-, -lɪs (US) -ˈgɑːrd- **-ly** -li **-ness** -nəs, -nɪs
regatta rɪˈgæt.ə, rə- (US) -ˈgɑː.t̬ə, -ˈgæt̬.ə **-s** -z
regenc|y (R) ˈriː.dʒᵊnt.s|i **-ies** -iz
regeneratl|e (*adj.*) rɪˈdʒen.ᵊr.ət, rə-, -ɪt, -eɪt (US) -ɪt **-ive** -ɪv
regener|ate (*v.*) rɪˈdʒen.ᵊr|.eɪt, rə-, ˌriː- (US) -ə.r|eɪt **-ates** -eɪts **-ating** -eɪ.tɪŋ (US) -eɪ.t̬ɪŋ **-ated** -eɪ.tɪd (US) -eɪ.t̬ɪd
regeneration rɪˌdʒen.ᵊrˈeɪ.ʃᵊn, rə-, ˌriː.dʒen- (US) -əˈreɪ- **-s** -z
Regensburg ˈreɪ.gᵊnz.bɜːg (US) -bɜːrg
regent (R) ˈriː.dʒᵊnt **-s** -s
regentship ˈriː.dʒᵊnt.ʃɪp **-s** -s
reggae ˈreg.eɪ
Reggie ˈredʒ.i
Reggio ˈredʒ.i.əʊ (US) ˈ-oʊ
regicidal ˌredʒ.ɪˈsaɪ.dᵊl, -əˈ-
regicide ˈredʒ.ɪ.saɪd, ˈ-ə- **-s** -z
regime, régime reɪˈʒiːm, rɪ-, rə-, reʒˈiːm; ˈreɪ.ʒiːm (US) rəˈʒiːm, rɪ-, reɪ- **-s** -z
regimen ˈredʒ.ɪ.mən, ˈ-ə-, -men (US) ˈ-ə- **-s** -z
regiment (*n.*) ˈredʒ.ɪ.mənt, ˈ-ə- (US) ˈ-ə- **-s** -s
regimen|t (*v.*) ˈredʒ.ɪ.men|t, ˈ-ə-, ˌ--ˈ- (US) ˈredʒ.ə.men|t **-ts** -ts **-ting** -tɪŋ (US) -t̬ɪŋ **-ted** -tɪd (US) -t̬ɪd
regimental ˌredʒ.ɪˈmen.tᵊl, -əˈ- (US) -əˈmen.t̬ᵊl **-s** -z *stress shift:* ˌregimental ˈcolours
regimentation ˌredʒ.ɪ.menˈteɪ.ʃᵊn, -ə-, -mənˈ- (US) -ə.mənˈ-, -menˈ-
Regina rɪˈdʒaɪ.nə, rə- (US) -ˈdʒaɪ-, -ˈdʒiː-
Note: In the US, /-ˈdʒiː-/ is especially suitable for the female name.
Reginald ˈredʒ.ɪ.nᵊld
region ˈriː.dʒᵊn **-s** -z
regional ˈriː.dʒᵊn.ᵊl **-ly** -i
regional|ism ˈriː.dʒᵊn.ᵊl|.ɪ.zᵊm **-ist/s** -ɪst/s
regionalistic ˌriː.dʒᵊn.ᵊlˈɪs.tɪk
Regis ˈriː.dʒɪs
regist|er ˈredʒ.ɪ.st|əʳ, ˈ-ə- (US) -st|ɚ **-ers** -əz (US) -ɚz **-ering** -ᵊr.ɪŋ **-ered** -əd (US) -ɚd ˌ**registered ˈmail**
registrant ˈredʒ.ɪ.strənt, ˈ-ə- **-s** -s
registrar ˌredʒ.ɪˈstrɑːʳ, -əˈ-, ˈ--- (US) ˈredʒ.ɪ.strɑːr, ˌ--ˈ- **-s** -z
registrar|y ˈredʒ.ɪ.strᵊr|.i, ˈ-ə- (US) -ɪ.strer- **-ies** -iz
registration ˌredʒ.ɪˈstreɪ.ʃᵊn, -əˈ- **-s** -z **regiˈstration ˌnumber**
registr|y ˈredʒ.ɪ.str|i, ˈ-ə- **-ies** -iz **ˈregistry ˌoffice**
Regius ˈriː.dʒi.əs, -dʒəs
regn|al ˈreg.n|ᵊl **-ant** -ənt
regress (*n.*) ˈriː.gres
regress (*v.*) rɪˈgres, ˌriː-, rə- **-es** -ɪz **-ing** -ɪŋ **-ed** -t
regression rɪˈgreʃ.ᵊn, ˌriː-, rə- **-s** -z
regressive rɪˈgres.ɪv, ˌriː-, rə- **-ly** -li **-ness** -nəs, -nɪs
re|gret rɪ|ˈgret, rə- **-grets** -ˈgrets **-gretting** -ˈgret.ɪŋ (US) -ˈgret̬.ɪŋ **-gretted** -ˈgret.ɪd (US) -ˈgret̬.ɪd
regretful rɪˈgret.fᵊl, rə-, -fʊl **-ly** -i
regrettab|le rɪˈgret.ə.b|l̩, rə- (US) -ˈgret̬- **-ly** -li
regroup ˌriːˈgruːp **-s** -s **-ing** -ɪŋ **-ed** -t
regular ˈreg.jə.ləʳ, -jʊ- (US) -lɚ **-s** -z **-ly** -li
regularity ˌreg.jəˈlær.ə.ti, -jʊˈ-, -ɪ.ti (US) -ˈler.ə.t̬i, -ˈlær-
regularization, -isa- ˌreg.jə.lᵊr.aɪˈzeɪ.ʃᵊn, -jʊ-, -ɪˈ- (US) -ɪˈ-
regulariz|e, -is|e ˈreg.jə.lᵊr.aɪz, -jʊ- (US) -lə.raɪz **-es** -ɪz **-ing** -ɪŋ **-ed** -d
regu|late ˈreg.jə|.leɪt, -jʊ- **-lates** -leɪts **-lating** -leɪ.tɪŋ (US) -leɪ.t̬ɪŋ **-lated** -leɪ.tɪd (US) -leɪ.t̬ɪd **-lator/s** -leɪ.təʳ/z (US) -leɪ.t̬ɚ/z
regulation ˌreg.jəˈleɪ.ʃᵊn, -jʊˈ- **-s** -z
regulative ˈreg.jə.lə.tɪv, -jʊ-, -leɪ- (US) -leɪ.t̬ɪv, -lə-
regulatory ˈreg.jə.lə.tᵊr.i, -jʊ-, ˌreg.jəˈleɪ-, -jəˈ- (US) ˈreg.jə.lə.tɔːr-, -jʊ-
regul|us (R) ˈreg.jə.l|əs, -jʊ- **-uses** -ə.sɪz **-i** -aɪ
regurgi|tate rɪˈgɜː.dʒɪ|.teɪt, rə-, ˌriː-, -dʒə- (US) -ˈgɜːr.dʒə- **-tates** -teɪts **-tating** -teɪ.tɪŋ (US) -teɪ.t̬ɪŋ **-tated** -teɪ.tɪd (US) -teɪ.t̬ɪd
regurgitation rɪˌgɜː.dʒɪˈteɪ.ʃᵊn, rə-, ˌriː-, -dʒəˈ- (US) -ˌgɜːr.dʒəˈ-
rehab ˈriː.hæb **-s** -z **-bing** -ɪŋ **-bed** -d
rehabili|tate ˌriː.həˈbɪl.ɪ|.teɪt, -əˈ-, ˈ-ə- (US) ˈ-ə- **-tates** -teɪts **-tating** -teɪ.tɪŋ (US) -teɪ.t̬ɪŋ **-tated** -teɪ.tɪd (US) -teɪ.t̬ɪd
rehabilitation ˌriː.həˌbɪl.ɪˈteɪ.ʃᵊn, -əˌ-, -əˈ- (US) -əˈ- **-s** -z
Rehan ˈriː.ən, ˈreɪ- (US) ˈriː-
rehash (*n.*) ˈriː.hæʃ, ˌ-ˈ- **-es** -ɪz
rehash (*v.*) ˌriːˈhæʃ **-es** -ɪz **-ing** -ɪŋ **-ed** -t
rehear ˌriːˈhɪəʳ (US) -ˈhɪr **-s** -z **-ing** -ɪŋ **reheard** ˌriːˈhɜːd (US) -ˈhɜːrd
rehearsal rɪˈhɜː.sᵊl, rə- (US) -ˈhɜːr- **-s** -z
rehears|e rɪˈhɜːs, rə- (US) -ˈhɜːrs **-es** -ɪz **-ing** -ɪŋ **-ed** -t
re|heat ˌriː|ˈhiːt **-heats** -ˈhiːts **-heating** -ˈhiː.tɪŋ (US) -ˈhiː.t̬ɪŋ **-heated** -ˈhiː.tɪd (US) -ˈhiː.t̬ɪd **-heater/s** -ˈhiː.təʳ/z (US) -ˈhiː.t̬ɚ/z
Rehnquist ˈren.kwɪst, ˈreŋ-
rehoboam (R) ˌriː.əˈbəʊ.əm, -həˈ- (US) -həˈboʊ- **-s** -z
re-hous|e ˌriːˈhaʊz **-es** -ɪz **-ing** -ɪŋ **-ed** -d
rehy|drate ˌriː.haɪ|ˈdreɪt (US) -ˈhaɪ|.dreɪt **-drates** -ˈdreɪts (US) -dreɪts **-drating** -ˈdreɪ.tɪŋ (US) -dreɪ.t̬ɪŋ **-drated** -ˈdreɪ.tɪd (US) -dreɪ.t̬ɪd
rehydration ˌriː.haɪˈdreɪ.ʃᵊn
Reich raɪk *as if German:* raɪx
Reichstag ˈraɪk.stɑːg *as if German:* ˈraɪx-, -tɑːk (US) ˈraɪk.stɑːg *as if German:* ˈraɪx-
Reid riːd
reification ˌreɪ.ɪ.fɪˈkeɪ.ʃᵊn, ˌriː-, ˌ-ə- (US) ˌ-ə-
rei|fy ˈreɪ.ɪ|.faɪ, ˈriː-, ˈ-ə- (US) ˈriː.ə- **-fies** -faɪz **-fying** -faɪ.ɪŋ **-fied** -faɪd
Reigate ˈraɪ.geɪt, -gɪt
reign (*n. v.*) reɪn **-s** -z **-ing** -ɪŋ **-ed** -d ˌ**reign of ˈterror**
Reigny ˈreɪ.ni
Reill(e)y ˈraɪ.li
reimburs|e ˌriː.ɪmˈbɜːs, -əmˈ- (US) -ˈbɜːrs **-es** -ɪz **-ing** -ɪŋ **-ed** -t **-ement/s** -mənt/s
re-im|port ˌriː.ɪm|ˈpɔːt (US) -ˈpɔːrt, -ˈ-- **-ports** -ˈpɔːts (US) -ˈpɔːrts **-porting** -ˈpɔː.tɪŋ (US) -ˈpɔːr.t̬ɪŋ **-ported** -ˈpɔː.tɪd (US) -ˈpɔːr.t̬ɪd

reimpos|e ˌriː.ɪmˈpəʊz Ⓤ -ˈpoʊz **-es** -ɪz **-ing** -ɪŋ **-ed** -d
reimpression ˌriː.ɪmˈpreʃ.ᵊn **-s** -z
Reims riːmz
rein reɪn **-s** -z **-ing** -ɪŋ **-ed** -d
reincarnate (*adj.*) ˌriː.ɪnˈkɑː.nət, -ɪŋˈ-, -nɪt, -neɪt Ⓤ -ɪnˈkɑːr.nɪt, -neɪt
reincarna|te (*v.*) ˌriː.ɪn.kɑːˈneɪ|t, -ɪŋ-, ˌriːˈɪn.kɑː.neɪ|t, -ˈɪŋ- Ⓤ ˌriː.ɪnˈkɑːr.neɪ|t **-tes** -ts **-ting** -tɪŋ Ⓤ -t̬ɪŋ **-ted** -tɪd Ⓤ -t̬ɪd
reincarnation ˌriː.ɪn.kɑːˈneɪ.ʃᵊn, -ɪŋ- Ⓤ -ɪn.kɑːrˈ- **-s** -z
reindeer ˈreɪn.dɪəʳ Ⓤ -dɪr
reinforc|e ˌriː.ɪnˈfɔːs Ⓤ -ˈfɔːrs **-es** -ɪz **-ing** -ɪŋ **-ed** -t **-ement/s** -mənt/s
Reinhard(t) ˈraɪn.hɑːt Ⓤ -hɑːrt
reinstal|l ˌriː.ɪnˈstɔːl Ⓤ -stɔːl, -stɑːl **-(l)s** -z **-(l)ing** -ɪŋ **-(l)ed** -d **-ment** -mənt
rein|state ˌriː.ɪn|ˈsteɪt **-states** -ˈsteɪts **-stating** -ˈsteɪ.tɪŋ Ⓤ -ˈsteɪ.t̬ɪŋ **-stated** -ˈsteɪ.tɪd Ⓤ -ˈsteɪ.t̬ɪd **-statement** -ˈsteɪt.mənt
reinsur|e ˌriː.ɪnˈʃʊəʳ, -ˈʃɔːʳ Ⓤ -ˈʃʊr **-es** -z **-ing** -ɪŋ **-ed** -d **-ance/s** -ᵊnts/ɪz
reintroduc|e ˌriː.ɪn.trəˈdjuːs, -ˈdʒuːs Ⓤ -ˈduːs, -ˈdjuːs **-es** -ɪz **-ing** -ɪŋ **-ed** -t
reintroduction ˌriː.ɪn.trəˈdʌk.ʃᵊn **-s** -z
rein|vent ˌriː.ɪn|ˈvent **-vents** -ˈvents **-venting** -ˈven.tɪŋ Ⓤ -ˈven.t̬ɪŋ **-vented** -ˈven.tɪd Ⓤ -ˈven.t̬ɪd
reinvention ˌriː.ɪnˈven.*t*ʃᵊn Ⓤ -ˈvent.ʃᵊn
reinvest ˌriː.ɪnˈvest **-s** -s **-ing** -ɪŋ **-ed** -ɪd
reinvigor|ate ˌriː.ɪnˈvɪg.ᵊr|.eɪt Ⓤ -ə.r|eɪt **-ates** -eɪts **-ating** -eɪ.tɪŋ Ⓤ -eɪ.t̬ɪŋ **-ated** -eɪ.tɪd Ⓤ -eɪ.t̬ɪd
reinvigoration ˌriː.ɪn.vɪ.gᵊrˈeɪ.ʃᵊn Ⓤ -gəˈreɪ-
reissu|e ˌriːˈɪʃ.uː, -ˈɪs.juː Ⓤ -ˈɪʃ.juː, -uː **-es** -z **-ing** -ɪŋ **-ed** -d
reiter|ate riˈɪt.ᵊr|.eɪt Ⓤ -ˈɪt̬.ə.r|eɪt **-ates** -eɪts **-ating** -eɪ.tɪŋ Ⓤ -eɪ.t̬ɪŋ **-ated** -eɪ.tɪd Ⓤ -eɪ.t̬ɪd
reiteration riˌɪt.ᵊrˈeɪ.ʃᵊn Ⓤ -ˌɪt̬.əˈreɪ- **-s** -z
reiterative riˈɪt.ᵊr.ə.tɪv, -eɪ- Ⓤ -ˈɪt̬.ə.reɪ.t̬ɪv, ˈ-ɚ.ə- **-ly** -li **-ness** -nəs, -nɪs
Reith riːθ
reject (*n.*) ˈriː.dʒekt **-s** -s
reject (*v.*) rɪˈdʒekt, rə- **-s** -s **-ing** -ɪŋ **-ed** -ɪd **-or/s** -əʳ/z Ⓤ -ɚ/z
rejection rɪˈdʒek.ʃᵊn, rə- **-s** -z
rejig ˌriːˈdʒɪg **-s** -z **-ging** -ɪŋ **-ged** -d
rejoic|e rɪˈdʒɔɪs, rə- **-es** -ɪz **-ing/ly** -ɪŋ/li **-ed** -t
rejoin *answer:* rɪˈdʒɔɪn, rə- **-s** -z **-ing** -ɪŋ **-ed** -d
rejoin *join again:* ˌriːˈdʒɔɪn, rɪ- **-s** -z **-ing** -ɪŋ **-ed** -d
rejoinder rɪˈdʒɔɪn.dəʳ, rə- Ⓤ -dɚ **-s** -z
rejuven|ate rɪˈdʒuː.vᵊn|.eɪt, -vɪ.n|eɪt Ⓤ -və- **-ates** -eɪts **-ating** -eɪ.tɪŋ Ⓤ -eɪ.t̬ɪŋ **-ated** -eɪ.tɪd Ⓤ -eɪ.t̬ɪd
rejuvenation rɪˌdʒuː.vᵊnˈeɪ.ʃᵊn, rə-, -vɪˈneɪ- Ⓤ -vəˈ-
rejuvenescen|ce ˌriː.dʒuː.vᵊnˈes.ᵊn|*t*s, rɪˌdʒuː-, -vɪˈnes- Ⓤ rɪˌdʒuː.vəˈ- **-t** -t
rekindl|e ˌriːˈkɪn.dl̩ **-es** -z **-ing** -ɪŋ, ˌriːˈkɪnd.lɪŋ **-ed** -d
re-label ˌriːˈleɪ.bᵊl **-s** -z **-ling** -ɪŋ, -ˈleɪ.blɪŋ **-led** -d
relaid (*past of* **relay** = *lay again*) riːˈleɪd, rɪ-, rə-
relapse (*n.*) rɪˈlæps, rə-; ˈriː.læps
relaps|e (*v.*) rɪˈlæps, rə- **-es** -ɪz **-ing** -ɪŋ **-ed** -t
re|late (R) rɪ|ˈleɪt, rə- **-lates** -ˈleɪts **-lating** -ˈleɪ.tɪŋ Ⓤ -ˈleɪ.t̬ɪŋ **-lated** -ˈleɪ.tɪd Ⓤ -ˈleɪ.t̬ɪd **-later/s** -ˈleɪ.təʳ/z Ⓤ -ˈleɪ.t̬ɚ/z
relation rɪˈleɪ.ʃᵊn, rə- **-s** -z
relational rɪˈleɪ.ʃᵊn.ᵊl, rə-
relationship rɪˈleɪ.ʃᵊn.ʃɪp, rə- **-s** -s
relatival ˌrel.əˈtaɪ.vᵊl
relative ˈrel.ə.tɪv Ⓤ -t̬ɪv **-s** -z **-ly** -li ˌ**relative ˈclause** ; ˌ**relative ˈpronoun**
relativ|ism ˈrel.ə.tɪ.v|ɪ.zᵊm Ⓤ -t̬ɪ- **-ist/s** -ɪst/s
relativistic ˌrel.ə.tɪˈvɪs.tɪk Ⓤ -t̬ɪˈ-
relativity ˌrel.əˈtɪv.ə.ti, -ɪ.ti Ⓤ -ə.t̬i
relax rɪˈlæks, rə- **-es** -ɪz **-ing** -ɪŋ **-ed** -t **-ant/s** -ᵊnt/s
relaxation ˌriː.lækˈseɪ.ʃᵊn **-s** -z
relay (*n.*) ˈriː.leɪ, rɪˈleɪ, rə- Ⓤ ˈriː.leɪ **-s** -z ˈ**relay** ˌ**race**
relay (*v.*) *lay again:* ˌriːˈleɪ **-s** -z **-ing** -ɪŋ **relaid** ˌriːˈleɪd
relay (*v.*) *send, broadcast:* ˈriː.leɪ, rɪˈleɪ, rə-, riː- **-s** -z **-ing** -ɪŋ **-ed** -d
releas|e rɪˈliːs, rə- **-es** -ɪz **-ing** -ɪŋ **-ed** -t
rele|gate ˈrel.ɪ|.geɪt, ˈ-ə- Ⓤ ˈ-ə- **-gates** -geɪts **-gating** -geɪ.tɪŋ Ⓤ -geɪ.t̬ɪŋ **-gated** -geɪ.tɪd Ⓤ -geɪ.t̬ɪd
relegation ˌrel.ɪˈgeɪ.ʃᵊn, -əˈ- Ⓤ -əˈ-
re|lent rɪ|ˈlent, rə- **-lents** -ˈlents **-lenting** -ˈlen.tɪŋ Ⓤ -ˈlen.t̬ɪŋ **-lented** -ˈlen.tɪd Ⓤ -ˈlen.t̬ɪd
relentless rɪˈlent.ləs, rə-, -lɪs **-ly** -li **-ness** -nəs, -nɪs
re|-let ˌriː|ˈlet **-lets** -ˈlets **-letting** -ˈlet.ɪŋ Ⓤ -ˈlet̬.ɪŋ
relevan|ce ˈrel.ə.vən*t*|s, ˈ-ɪ- Ⓤ ˈ-ə- **-cy** -si
relevant ˈrel.ə.vənt, ˈ-ɪ- Ⓤ ˈ-ə- **-ly** -li
reliability rɪˌlaɪ.əˈbɪl.ə.ti, rə-, -ɪ.ti Ⓤ -ə.t̬i
reliab|le rɪˈlaɪ.ə.bl|̩, rə- **-ly** -li **-leness** -l̩.nəs, -nɪs
relian|ce rɪˈlaɪ.ən|*t*s, rə- **-t** -t
reliant rɪˈlaɪ.ənt, rə-
relic ˈrel.ɪk **-s** -s
relict ˈrel.ɪkt **-s** -s
reliction rɪˈlɪk.ʃᵊn
relief rɪˈliːf, rə- **-s** -s **reˈlief** ˌ**map**
reliev|e rɪˈliːv, rə- **-es** -z **-ing** -ɪŋ **-ed** -d **-able** -ə.bl̩
relievo rɪˈliː.vəʊ Ⓤ -voʊ
Religio Laici rɪˌlɪg.i.əʊˈlɑː.ɪ.siː, rə-, -kiː Ⓤ rɪˌlɪdʒ.i.oʊˈleɪ.ə-
religion rɪˈlɪdʒ.ᵊn, rə- **-s** -z
religion|ism rɪˈlɪdʒ.ᵊn|.ɪ.zᵊm, rə- **-ist/s** -ɪst/s
religiosity rɪˌlɪdʒ.iˈɒs.ə.ti, rə-, -ɪ.ti Ⓤ -ˈɑː.sə.t̬i
religious rɪˈlɪdʒ.əs, rə- **-ly** -li **-ness** -nəs, -nɪs
relin|e ˌriːˈlaɪn **-es** -z **-ing** -ɪŋ **-ed** -d
relinquish rɪˈlɪŋ.kwɪʃ, rə- **-es** -ɪz **-ing** -ɪŋ **-ed** -t **-ment** -mənt
reliquar|y ˈrel.ɪ.kwᵊr|.i Ⓤ -ə.kwer- **-ies** -ɪz
relish ˈrel.ɪʃ **-es** -ɪz **-ing** -ɪŋ **-ed** -t
reliv|e ˌriːˈlɪv **-es** -z **-ing** -ɪŋ **-ed** -d
reload ˌriːˈləʊd Ⓤ -ˈloʊd **-s** -z **-ing** -ɪŋ **-ed** -ɪd
relo|cate ˌriː.ləʊ|ˈkeɪt Ⓤ -ˈloʊ|.keɪt **-cates** -ˈkeɪts Ⓤ -keɪts **-cating** -ˈkeɪ.tɪŋ Ⓤ -keɪ.t̬ɪŋ **-cated** -ˈkeɪ.tɪd Ⓤ -keɪ.t̬ɪd
relocation ˌriː.ləʊˈkeɪ.ʃᵊn Ⓤ -loʊˈ-
reluctance rɪˈlʌk.tᵊn*t*s, rə-
reluctant rɪˈlʌk.tᵊnt, rə- **-ly** -li
reluctivity ˌrel.ʌkˈtɪv.ə.ti, ˌriː.lʌkˈ-; rɪˌlʌkˈ-, rə-, -ɪ.ti Ⓤ ˌrel.əkˈtɪv.ə.t̬i
re|ly rɪ|ˈlaɪ, rə- **-lies** -ˈlaɪz **-lying** -ˈlaɪ.ɪŋ **-lied** -ˈlaɪd
REM, rem ˌɑːʳ.iːˈem; rem Ⓤ ˌɑːr.iːˈem; rem
remain rɪˈmeɪn, rə- **-s** -z **-ing** -ɪŋ **-ed** -d
remainder rɪˈmeɪn.dəʳ, rə- Ⓤ -dɚ **-s** -z **-ing** -ɪŋ **-ed** -d
remak|e (*v.*) ˌriːˈmeɪk **-es** -s **-ing** -ɪŋ **remade** ˌriːˈmeɪd
re-make (*n.*) ˈriː.meɪk **-s** -s
remand rɪˈmɑːnd, rə- Ⓤ -ˈmænd **-s** -z **-ing** -ɪŋ **-ed** -ɪd **reˈmand** ˌ**home**
remanence ˈrem.ə.nən*t*s
remark rɪˈmɑːk, rə- Ⓤ -ˈmɑːrk **-s** -s **-ing** -ɪŋ **-ed** -t
remarkab|le rɪˈmɑː.kə.bl|̩, rə- Ⓤ -ˈmɑːr- **-ly** -li **-leness** -l̩.nəs, -nɪs
Remarque rɪˈmɑːk, rə- Ⓤ -ˈmɑːrk
remarriag|e ˌriːˈmær.ɪdʒ Ⓤ -ˈmer-, -ˈmær- **-es** -ɪz
remarr|y ˌriːˈmær|.i Ⓤ -ˈmer-, -ˈmær- **-ies** -iz **-ying** -i.ɪŋ **-ied** -id
Rembrandt ˈrem.brænt, -brənt Ⓤ -brænt, -brɑːnt **-s** -s
REME ˈriː.mi
remediable rɪˈmiː.di.ə.bl̩, rə-
remedial rɪˈmiː.di.əl, rə- **-ly** -i
remediation rɪˌmiː.diˈeɪ.ʃᵊn, rə-

remed|y 'rem.ə.d|i, '-ɪ- **-ies** -iz **-ying** -i.ɪŋ **-ied** -id
rememb|er rɪ'mem.b|əʳ, rə- Ⓤⓢ -b|ɚ **-ers** -əz Ⓤⓢ -ɚz **-ering** -ᵊr.ɪŋ **-ered** -əd Ⓤⓢ -ɚd
remembranc|e rɪ'mem.brᵊnts, rə- **-es** -ɪz **-er/s** -əʳ/z Ⓤⓢ -ɚ/z **Re'membrance ˌDay**
re-militariz|e, -is|e ˌriː'mɪl.ɪ.tᵊr.aɪz, '-ə- Ⓤⓢ -t̬ə.raɪz **-es** -ɪz **-ing** -ɪŋ **-ed** -d
remind rɪ'maɪnd, rə- **-s** -z **-ing** -ɪŋ **-ed** -ɪd **-er/s** -əʳ/z Ⓤⓢ -ɚ/z
Remington 'rem.ɪŋ.tən **-s** -z
reminisc|e ˌrem.ɪ'nɪs, -ə'- Ⓤⓢ -ə'- **-es** -ɪz **-ing** -ɪŋ **-ed** -t
reminiscenc|e ˌrem.ɪ'nɪs.ᵊnts, -ə'- Ⓤⓢ -ə'- **-es** -ɪz
reminiscent ˌrem.ɪ'nɪs.ᵊnt, -ə'- Ⓤⓢ -ə'-
remiss rɪ'mɪs, rə- **-ly** -li **-ness** -nəs, -nɪs
remission rɪ'mɪʃ.ᵊn, rə- **-s** -z
remit (*n.*) 'riː.mɪt; rɪ'mɪt, rə-, riː- Ⓤⓢ rɪ'mɪt, rə- **-s** -s
re|mit (*v.*) rɪ|'mɪt, rə- **-mits** -'mɪts **-mitting** -'mɪt.ɪŋ Ⓤⓢ -'mɪt̬.ɪŋ **-mitted** -'mɪt.ɪd Ⓤⓢ -'mɪt̬.ɪd **-mitter/s** -'mɪt.əʳ/z Ⓤⓢ -'mɪt̬.ɚ/z
remittal rɪ'mɪt.ᵊl, rə- Ⓤⓢ -'mɪt̬- **-s** -z
remittanc|e rɪ'mɪt.ᵊnts, rə- **-es** -ɪz
remittitur rɪ'mɪt.ɪ.tʊəʳ, rə-, -tɜːʳ Ⓤⓢ rə'mɪt̬.ə.t̬ɚ
remnant 'rem.nənt **-s** -s
remodel ˌriː'mɒd.ᵊl Ⓤⓢ -'mɑː.dᵊl **-s** -z **-(l)ing** -ɪŋ **-(l)ed** -d
remold (*v.*) ˌriː'məʊld Ⓤⓢ -'moʊld **-s** -z **-ing** -ɪŋ **-ed** -ɪd
remold (*n.*) 'riː.məʊld Ⓤⓢ -moʊld **-s** -z
remonetiz|e, -is|e ˌriː'mʌn.ɪ.taɪz, '-ə- Ⓤⓢ -'mɑː.nə-, -'mʌn.ə- **-es** -ɪz **-ing** -ɪŋ **-ed** -d
remonstranc|e rɪ'mɒnt.strᵊnts, rə- Ⓤⓢ -'mɑːnt- **-es** -ɪz
remonstrant rɪ'mɒnt.strᵊnt, rə- Ⓤⓢ -'mɑːnt- **-ly** -li
remon|strate 'rem.ən|.streɪt; rɪ'mɒnt-, rə- Ⓤⓢ rɪ'mɑːnt-, rə-; 'rem.ənt- **-strates** -streɪts **-strating** -streɪ.tɪŋ Ⓤⓢ -streɪ.t̬ɪŋ **-strated** -streɪ.tɪd Ⓤⓢ -streɪ.t̬ɪd
remonstrative rɪ'mɒnt.strə.tɪv, rə- Ⓤⓢ -'mɑːnt.strə.t̬ɪv **-ly** -li
remorse rɪ'mɔːs, rə- Ⓤⓢ -'mɔːrs
remorseful rɪ'mɔːs.fᵊl, rə-, -fʊl Ⓤⓢ -'mɔːrs- **-ly** -i
remorseless rɪ'mɔː.sləs, rə-, -lɪs Ⓤⓢ -'mɔːrs- **-ly** -li **-ness** -nəs, -nɪs
remortgage ˌriː'mɔː.gɪdʒ Ⓤⓢ -'mɔːr- **-s** -ɪz **-ing** -ɪŋ **-ed** -d
remote rɪ'məʊt, rə- Ⓤⓢ -'moʊt **-ly** -li **-ness** -nəs, -nɪs **reˌmote con'trol**
remould (*v.*) ˌriː'məʊld Ⓤⓢ -'moʊld **-s** -z **-ing** -ɪŋ **-ed** -ɪd
remould (*n.*) 'riː.məʊld Ⓤⓢ -moʊld **-s** -z
remount (*n.*) 'riː.maʊnt, ˌ-'- Ⓤⓢ 'riː.maʊnt **-s** -s
re|mount (*v.*) ˌriː|'maʊnt **-mounts** -'maʊnts **-mounting** -'maʊn.tɪŋ Ⓤⓢ -'maʊn.t̬ɪŋ **-mounted** -'maʊn.tɪd Ⓤⓢ -'maʊn.t̬ɪd
removability rɪˌmuː.və'bɪl.ə.ti, rə-, -ɪ.ti Ⓤⓢ -ə.t̬i
removal rɪ'muː.vᵊl, rə- **-s** -z **re'moval ˌvan**
remov|e rɪ'muːv, rə- **-es** -z **-ing** -ɪŋ **-ed** -d **-er/s** -əʳ/z Ⓤⓢ -ɚ/z **-able** -ə.bl̩
Remploy® 'rem.plɔɪ
remuner|ate rɪ'mjuː.nᵊr|.eɪt, rə- Ⓤⓢ -nə.r|eɪt **-ates** -eɪts **-ating** -eɪ.tɪŋ Ⓤⓢ -eɪ.t̬ɪŋ **-ated** -eɪ.tɪd Ⓤⓢ -eɪ.t̬ɪd
remuneration rɪˌmjuː.nᵊr'eɪ.ʃᵊn, rə- Ⓤⓢ -nə'reɪ- **-s** -z
remunerative rɪ'mjuː.nᵊr.ə.tɪv, rə- Ⓤⓢ -nə.reɪ.t̬ɪv, -nɚ.ə-
Remus 'riː.məs
renaissance (R) rə'neɪ.sᵊnts, rɪ-, ˌren.eɪ'sɑ̃ːns, -'sɑːnts Ⓤⓢ ˌren.ə'sɑːnts, -'zɑːnts, '--- **Reˌnaissance 'man**
renal 'riː.nᵊl
renam|e ˌriː'neɪm **-es** -z **-ing** -ɪŋ **-ed** -d
renascen|t rɪ'neɪ.sᵊn|t, rə-, -'næs.ᵊn|t Ⓤⓢ -'næs.ᵊn|t, -'neɪ.sᵊn|t **-ce** -ts
Renault® 'ren.əʊ Ⓤⓢ rə'noʊ, -'nɔːlt **-s** -z
rend rend **-s** -z **-ing** -ɪŋ **-ed** -ɪd **rent** rent
Rendell 'ren.dᵊl
rend|er 'ren.d|əʳ Ⓤⓢ -d|ɚ **-ers** -əz Ⓤⓢ -ɚz **-ering/s** -ᵊr.ɪŋ/z **-ered** -əd Ⓤⓢ -ɚd
rendezvous *singular:* 'rɒn.dɪ.vuː, -deɪ- Ⓤⓢ 'rɑːn.deɪ-, -diː-, -dɪ- *plural:* -z
rendition ren'dɪʃ.ᵊn **-s** -z
Renee, Renée 'ren.eɪ; rə'neɪ; 'riː.ni Ⓤⓢ rə'neɪ
renegade 'ren.ɪ.geɪd, '-ə- Ⓤⓢ '-ə- **-s** -z
renegoti|ate ˌriː.nɪ'gəʊ.ʃi|.eɪt, -nə'- Ⓤⓢ -nə'goʊ- **-ates** -eɪts **-ating** -eɪ.tɪŋ Ⓤⓢ -eɪ.t̬ɪŋ **-ated** -eɪ.tɪd Ⓤⓢ -eɪ.t̬ɪd
renegotiation ˌriː.nɪˌgəʊ.ʃi'eɪ.ʃᵊn, -nəˌ- Ⓤⓢ -nəˌgoʊ- **-s** -z
reneg(u)|e rɪ'niːg, rə-, -'neɪg, -'neg Ⓤⓢ -'nɪg, -'neg, -'niːg **-es** -z **-ing** -ɪŋ **-ed** -d
renew rɪ'njuː, rə- Ⓤⓢ rɪ'nuː, -'njuː **-s** -z **-ing** -ɪŋ **-ed** -d **-able** -ə.bl̩
renewal rɪ'njuː.əl, rə-, -'njʊəl Ⓤⓢ -'nuː.əl, -'njuː- **-s** -z
Renfrew 'ren.fruː **-shire** -ʃəʳ, -ˌʃɪəʳ Ⓤⓢ -ʃɚ, -ˌʃɪr
renin 'riː.nɪn Ⓤⓢ 'riː.nɪn, 'ren.ən
renminbi ren'mɪn.bi Ⓤⓢ 'ren.mɪn-
Rennes ren
rennet 'ren.ɪt
Rennie 'ren.i
Rennies® 'ren.iz
rennin 'ren.ɪn
Reno 'riː.nəʊ Ⓤⓢ -noʊ
Renoir rən'wɑːʳ; 'ren.wɑːʳ, ˌ-'- Ⓤⓢ rən'wɑːr, 'ren.wɑːr
renounc|e rɪ'naʊnts, rə- **-es** -ɪz **-ing** -ɪŋ **-ed** -t **-ement** -mənt
reno|vate 'ren.ə|.veɪt **-vates** -veɪts **-vating** -veɪ.tɪŋ Ⓤⓢ -veɪ.t̬ɪŋ **-vated** -veɪ.tɪd Ⓤⓢ -veɪ.t̬ɪd **-vator/s** -veɪ.təʳ/z Ⓤⓢ -veɪ.t̬ɚ/z
renovation ˌren.ə'veɪ.ʃᵊn **-s** -z
renown rɪ'naʊn, rə- **-ed** -d
Renshaw 'ren.ʃɔː Ⓤⓢ -ʃɑː, -ʃɔː
rent rent **-s** -s **-ing** -ɪŋ Ⓤⓢ 'ren.t̬ɪŋ **-ed** -ɪd Ⓤⓢ 'ren.t̬ɪd **-er/s** -əʳ/z Ⓤⓢ 'ren.t̬ɚ/z
rent-a-crowd 'rent.ə.kraʊd Ⓤⓢ 'rent̬-
rental 'ren.tᵊl Ⓤⓢ -t̬ᵊl **-s** -z
rent-free ˌrent'friː *stress shift:* ˌrent-free 'flat
rentier 'rɑːn.ti.eɪ Ⓤⓢ -'tjeɪ **-s** -z
Rentokil® 'ren.təʊ.kɪl Ⓤⓢ -t̬ə-, -toʊ-
Renton 'ren.tən Ⓤⓢ -tᵊn
rent-roll 'rent.rəʊl Ⓤⓢ -roʊl **-s** -z
renunciation rɪˌnʌnt.si'eɪ.ʃᵊn, rə- **-s** -z
renvoi ren'vɔɪ
Renwick 'ren.ɪk, -wɪk
Note: For US names, /'ren.wɪk/ is the likely pronunciation.
reoccupation riːˌɒk.jə'peɪ.ʃᵊn, ri-, -jʊ'- Ⓤⓢ -ˌɑː.kjə'-, -kjʊ'- **-s** -z
reoccup|y ˌriː'ɒk.jə.p|aɪ, ri-, -jʊ- Ⓤⓢ -'ɑː.kjə-, -kjʊ- **-ies** -aɪz **-ying** -aɪ.ɪŋ **-ied** -aɪd
reopen ˌriː'əʊ.pᵊn, ri-, -pᵊm Ⓤⓢ -'oʊ.pᵊn **-s** -z **-ing** -ɪŋ **-ed** -d
reorganization, -isa- riːˌɔː.gᵊn.aɪ'zeɪ.ʃᵊn, ri-, -ɪ'- Ⓤⓢ -ˌɔːr.gᵊn.ɪ'-; ˌriː.ɔːr- **-s** -z
reorganiz|e, -is|e ˌriː'ɔː.gᵊn.aɪz, ri- Ⓤⓢ -'ɔːr- **-es** -ɪz **-ing** -ɪŋ **-ed** -d
reori|ent ˌriː'ɔː.ri|.ənt, ri- Ⓤⓢ -'ɔːr.i- **-ents** -ənts **-enting** -ən.tɪŋ Ⓤⓢ -ən.t̬ɪŋ **-ented** -ən.tɪd Ⓤⓢ -ən.t̬ɪd
reorien|tate ˌriː'ɔː.ri.ən|.teɪt, -'ɒr.i-, -en- Ⓤⓢ ˌriː'ɔːr.i.en-, -ən- **-tates** -teɪts **-tating** -teɪ.tɪŋ Ⓤⓢ -teɪ.t̬ɪŋ **-tated** -teɪ.tɪd Ⓤⓢ -teɪ.t̬ɪd
reorientation riːˌɔː.ri.ən'teɪ.ʃᵊn, -ˌɒr.i-, -en'- Ⓤⓢ -ˌɔːr.i.en'-, -ən'-
rep rep **-s** -s
repackag|e ˌriː'pæk.ɪdʒ **-s** -ɪz **-ing** -ɪŋ **-ed** -d
repaid (*from* **repay**, *pay back*) rɪ'peɪd, rə-, ˌriː- (*from* **repay**, *pay a second time*) ˌriː'peɪd
repair rɪ'peəʳ, rə- Ⓤⓢ -'per **-s** -z **-ing** -ɪŋ **-ed** -d **-er/s** -əʳ/z Ⓤⓢ -ɚ/z
repairable rɪ'peə.rə.bl̩, rə- Ⓤⓢ -'per.ə-

reparability ˌrep.ᵊr.əˈbɪl.ə.ti, -ɪ.ti (US) -ə.t̬i

reparable ˈrep.ᵊr.ə.bl̩

reparation ˌrep.ᵊrˈeɪ.ʃᵊn (US) -əˈreɪ- **-s** -z

repartee ˌrep.ɑːˈtiː (US) -ɑːrˈ-, -ɚˈ-, -ˈteɪ

repass ˌriːˈpɑːs (US) -ˈpæs **-es** -ɪz **-ing** -ɪŋ **-ed** -t

repast rɪˈpɑːst, rə- (US) -ˈpæst **-s** -s

repatri|ate riːˈpæt.ri|.eɪt, rɪ- (US) -ˈpeɪ.tri- **-ates** -eɪts **-ating** -eɪ.tɪŋ (US) -eɪ.t̬ɪŋ **-ated** -eɪ.tɪd (US) -eɪ.t̬ɪd

repatriation ˌriː.pæt.riˈeɪ.ʃᵊn; rɪˌpæt- (US) rɪˌpeɪ.triˈ-

repay *pay back:* rɪˈpeɪ, rə-, ˌriː- **-s** -z **-ing** -ɪŋ **repaid** rɪˈpeɪd, rə-, ˌriː-

repay *pay again:* ˌriːˈpeɪ **-s** -z **-ing** -ɪŋ **repaid** ˌriːˈpeɪd

repayable rɪˈpeɪ.ə.bl̩, ˌriː-

repayment rɪˈpeɪ.mənt, ˌriː- **-s** -s

repeal rɪˈpiːl, rə- **-s** -z **-ing** -ɪŋ **-ed** -d

re|peat rɪ|ˈpiːt, rə- **-peats** -ˈpiːts **-peating** -ˈpiː.tɪŋ (US) -ˈpiː.t̬ɪŋ **-peated/ly** -ˈpiː.tɪd/li (US) -ˈpiː.t̬ɪd/li **-peater/s** -ˈpiː.təʳ/z (US) -ˈpiː.t̬ɚ/z

repeatability rɪˌpiː.təˈbɪl.ɪ.ti, rə-, -ə.ti (US) -t̬əˈbɪl.ə.t̬i

repêchage, repechage ˈrep.ə.ʃɑːʒ, ˈ-ɪ-, ˌ--ˈ- (US) ˌrep.əˈʃɑːʒ; rəˌpeʃˈ-

repel rɪˈpel, rə- **-s** -z **-ling** -ɪŋ **-led** -d

repellent, repellant rɪˈpel.ᵊnt, rə- **-s** -s

re|pent rɪ|ˈpent, rə- **-pents** -ˈpents **-penting** -ˈpen.tɪŋ (US) -ˈpen.t̬ɪŋ **-pented** -ˈpen.tɪd (US) -ˈpen.t̬ɪd

repentanc|e rɪˈpen.tən*t*s, rə- (US) -tᵊnts **-es** -ɪz

repentant rɪˈpen.tənt, rə- (US) -tᵊnt **-ly** -li

repercussion ˌriː.pəˈkʌʃ.ᵊn (US) -pɚˈ-, ˌrep.ɚˈ- **-s** -z

repertoire ˈrep.ə.twɑːʳ (US) -ɚ.twɑːr, ˈ-ə- **-s** -z

repertor|y ˈrep.ə.tᵊr|.i (US) -ɚ.tɔːr-, ˈ-ə- **-ies** -iz

répétiteur rɪˌpet.ɪˈtɜːʳ, rə- (US) ˌreɪ.peɪˈtiː.tɚ **-s** -z

repetition ˌrep.ɪˈtɪʃ.ᵊn, -əˈ- (US) -əˈ- **-s** -z

repetitious ˌrep.ɪˈtɪʃ.əs, -əˈ- (US) -əˈ- **-ly** -li **-ness** -nəs, -nɪs

repetitive rɪˈpet.ə.tɪv, rə-, ˈ-ɪ- (US) -ˈpet̬.ə.t̬ɪv **-ly** -li **-ness** -nəs, -nɪs **reˌpetitive ˈstrain ˌinjury** ; **reˌpetitive ˈmotion ˌinjury**

rephras|e ˌriːˈfreɪz **-es** -ɪz **-ing** -ɪŋ **-ed** -d

repin|e rɪˈpaɪn, rə- **-es** -z **-ing** -ɪŋ **-ed** -d

replac|e rɪˈpleɪs, rə-, ˌriː- **-es** -ɪz **-ing** -ɪŋ **-ed** -t

replaceable rɪˈpleɪ.sə.bl̩, rə-, ˌriː-

replacement rɪˈpleɪs.mənt, rə-, ˌriː- **-s** -s

re|plant ˌriː|ˈplɑːnt (US) -ˈplænt **-plants** -ˈplɑːnts (US) -ˈplænts **-planting** -ˈplɑːn.tɪŋ (US) -ˈplæn.t̬ɪŋ **-planted** -ˈplɑːn.tɪd (US) -ˈplæn.t̬ɪd

replay (*n.*) ˈriː.pleɪ **-s** -z

replay (*v.*) ˌriːˈpleɪ **-s** -z **-ing** -ɪŋ **-ed** -d

replenish rɪˈplen.ɪʃ, rə- **-es** -ɪz **-ing** -ɪŋ **-ed** -t **-ment** -mənt

replete rɪˈpliːt **-ness** -nəs, -nɪs

repletion rɪˈpliː.ʃᵊn

replevin rɪˈplev.ɪn, rə-

replevy rɪˈplev.i, rə-

replica ˈrep.lɪ.kə, -lə- (US) -lɪ- **-s** -z

replicable ˈrep.lɪ.kə.bl̩, -lə- (US) -lɪ-

repli|cate ˈrep.lɪ|.keɪt, -lə- (US) -lɪ- **-cates** -keɪts **-cating** -keɪ.tɪŋ (US) -keɪ.t̬ɪŋ **-cated** -keɪ.tɪd (US) -keɪ.t̬ɪd

replication ˌrep.lɪˈkeɪ.ʃᵊn, -ləˈ- (US) -ləˈ- **-s** -z

repl|y rɪˈpl|aɪ, rə- **-ies** -aɪz **-ying** -aɪ.ɪŋ **-ied** -aɪd

repo ˈriː.pəʊ (US) -poʊ **-s** -z

re|point ˌriː|ˈpɔɪnt **-points** -ˈpɔɪnts **-pointing** -ˈpɔɪn.tɪŋ (US) -ˈpɔɪn.t̬ɪŋ **-pointed** -ˈpɔɪn.tɪd (US) -ˈpɔɪn.t̬ɪd

repolish ˌriːˈpɒl.ɪʃ (US) -ˈpɑː.lɪʃ **-es** -ɪz **-ing** -ɪŋ **-ed** -t

repopu|late ˌriːˈpɒp.jə|.leɪt, rɪˈ-, -jʊ- (US) -ˈpɑː.pjə-, -pjʊ- **-lates** -leɪts **-lating** -leɪ.tɪŋ (US) -leɪ.t̬ɪŋ **-lated** -leɪ.tɪd (US) -leɪ.t̬ɪd

re|port rɪ|ˈpɔːt, rə- (US) -ˈpɔːrt **-ports** -ˈpɔːts (US) -ˈpɔːrts **-porting** -ˈpɔː.tɪŋ (US) -ˈpɔːr.t̬ɪŋ **-ported/ly** -ˈpɔː.tɪd/li (US) -ˈpɔːr.t̬ɪd/li **reˌported ˈspeech**

reportage ˌrep.ɔːˈtɑːʒ; rɪˈpɔː.tɪdʒ, rə- (US) rɪˈpɔːr.t̬ɪdʒ, rə-; ˌrep.ɚˈtɑːʒ

reporter rɪˈpɔː.təʳ, rə- (US) -ˈpɔːr.t̬ɚ **-s** -z

repos|e rɪˈpəʊz, rə- (US) -ˈpoʊz **-es** -ɪz **-ing** -ɪŋ **-ed** -d

reposeful rɪˈpəʊz.fᵊl, rə-, -fʊl (US) -ˈpoʊz- **-ly** -i

repositor|y rɪˈpɒz.ɪ.tᵊr|.i, rə- (US) -ˈpɑː.zɪ.tɔːr- **-ies** -iz

repossess ˌriː.pəˈzes **-es** -ɪz **-ing** -ɪŋ **-ed** -t

repossession ˌriː.pəˈzeʃ.ᵊn **-s** -z

repoussé rəˈpuː.seɪ, rɪ- (US) rəˌpuːˈseɪ

reprehend ˌrep.rɪˈhend, -rəˈ- (US) -rɪˈ- **-s** -z **-ing** -ɪŋ **-ed** -ɪd

reprehensib|le ˌrep.rɪˈhen*t*.sə.b|l̩, -rəˈ-, -sɪ- (US) -sə- **-ly** -li

reprehension ˌrep.rɪˈhen.*t*ʃᵊn, -rəˈ-

repre|sent ˌrep.rɪ|ˈzent, -rəˈ- (US) -rɪˈ- **-sents** -ˈzents **-senting** -ˈzen.tɪŋ (US) -ˈzen.t̬ɪŋ **-sented** -ˈzen.tɪd (US) -ˈzen.t̬ɪd

representation ˌrep.rɪ.zenˈteɪ.ʃᵊn, -rə-, -zᵊnˈ- (US) -rɪ.zenˈ- **-s** -z

representational ˌrep.rɪ.zenˈteɪ.ʃᵊn.ᵊl, -rə-, -zᵊnˈ- (US) -rɪ.zenˈ- **-ly** -i

representative ˌrep.rɪˈzen.tə.tɪv, -rəˈ- (US) -rɪˈzen.t̬ə.t̬ɪv **-s** -z **-ly** -li

repress rɪˈpres, rə- **-es** -ɪz **-ing** -ɪŋ **-ed** -t **-ible** -ə.bl̩, -ɪ.bl̩

repression rɪˈpreʃ.ᵊn, rə- **-s** -z

repressive rɪˈpres.ɪv, rə- **-ly** -li **-ness** -nəs, -nɪs

repriev|e rɪˈpriːv, rə- **-es** -z **-ing** -ɪŋ **-ed** -d

reprimand (*n.*) ˈrep.rɪ.mɑːnd, -rə- (US) -rə.mænd **-s** -z

reprimand (*v.*) ˈrep.rɪ.mɑːnd, -rə-, ˌ--ˈ- (US) ˈrep.rə.mænd, ˌ--ˈ- **-s** -z **-ing** -ɪŋ **-ed** -ɪd

reprint (*n.*) ˈriː.prɪnt, ˌ-ˈ- (US) ˈriː.prɪnt **-s** -s

re|print (*v.*) ˌriː|ˈprɪnt **-prints** -ˈprɪnts **-printing** -ˈprɪn.tɪŋ (US) -ˈprɪn.t̬ɪŋ **-printed** -ˈprɪn.tɪd (US) -ˈprɪn.t̬ɪd

reprisal rɪˈpraɪ.zᵊl, rə- **-s** -z

repris|e (*n. v.*) *in music:* rɪˈpriːz, rə- **-es** -ɪz **-ing** -ɪŋ **-ed** -d *legal term:* rɪˈpraɪz, rə-, -ˈpriːz (US) -ˈpraɪz **-es** -ɪz **-ing** -ɪŋ **-ed** -d

repro ˈriː.prəʊ (US) -proʊ **-s** -z

reproach rɪˈprəʊtʃ, rə- (US) -ˈproʊtʃ **-es** -ɪz **-ing** -ɪŋ **-ed** -t **-able** -ə.bl̩

reproachful rɪˈprəʊtʃ.fᵊl, rə-, -fʊl (US) -ˈproʊtʃ- **-ly** -i **-ness** -nəs, -nɪs

reprobate (*n. adj.*) ˈrep.rəʊ.beɪt, -bɪt (US) -rə.beɪt, -bɪt **-s** -s

repro|bate (*v.*) ˈrep.rəʊ|.beɪt (US) -rə- **-bates** -beɪts **-bating** -beɪ.tɪŋ (US) -beɪ.t̬ɪŋ **-bated** -beɪ.tɪd (US) -beɪ.t̬ɪd

reprobation ˌrep.rəʊˈbeɪ.ʃᵊn (US) -rəˈ-

reprocess ˌriːˈprəʊ.ses, -sɪs (US) -ˈprɑː.ses, -səs **-es** -ɪz **-ing** -ɪŋ **-ed** -t

reproduc|e ˌriː.prəˈdjuːs, -ˈdʒuːs (US) -ˈduːs, -ˈdjuːs **-es** -ɪz **-ing** -ɪŋ **-ed** -t **-er/s** -əʳ/z (US) -ɚ/z

reproduction ˌriː.prəˈdʌk.ʃᵊn **-s** -z

reproductive ˌriː.prəˈdʌk.tɪv **-ness** -nəs, -nɪs

reprogram ˌriːˈprəʊ.græm (US) -ˈproʊ- **-s** -z **-(m)ing** -ɪŋ **-(m)ed** -d

reprographic ˌriː.prəʊˈgræf.ɪk, ˌrep.rəʊˈ- (US) ˌriː.proʊˈ-, -prəˈ- **-s** -s

reprograph|y rɪˈprɒg.rə.f|i, riː- (US) -ˈprɑː.grə- **-er/s** -əʳ/z (US) -ɚ/z

reproof rɪˈpruːf, rə- **-s** -s

re-proof (*v.*) ˌriːˈpruːf **-s** -s **-ing** -ɪŋ **-ed** -t

reproval rɪˈpruː.vᵊl, rə- **-s** -z

reprov|e rɪˈpruːv, rə- **-es** -z **-ing/ly** -ɪŋ/li **-ed** -d **-er/s** -əʳ/z (US) -ɚ/z

reptile ˈrep.taɪl (US) -taɪl, -tᵊl **-s** -z

reptilian repˈtɪl.i.ən (US) -i.ən, ˈ-jən **-s** -z

Repton ˈrep.tən

republic (R) rɪˈpʌb.lɪk, rə- **-s** -s

republican (R) rɪˈpʌb.lɪ.kən, rə- **-s** -z **-ism** -ɪ.zᵊm

republication ˌriːˌpʌb.lɪˈkeɪ.ʃᵊn, -ləˈ- (US) ˌriː.pʌb.lɪˈ- **-s** -z

republish ˌriːˈpʌb.lɪʃ **-es** -ɪz **-ing** -ɪŋ **-ed** -t

repudi|ate rɪˈpjuː.di|.eɪt, rə- **-ates** -eɪts **-ating** -eɪ.tɪŋ (US) -eɪ.t̬ɪŋ **-ated** -eɪ.tɪd (US) -eɪ.t̬ɪd **-ater/s** -eɪ.təʳ/z (US) -eɪ.t̬ɚ/z

repudiation rɪˌpjuː.diˈeɪ.ʃᵊn, rə-

repugnance rɪˈpʌg.nən*t*s, rə-

repugnant rɪˈpʌg.nənt, rə- **-ly** -li

repuls|e rɪˈpʌls, rə- **-es** -ɪz **-ing** -ɪŋ **-ed** -t

repulsion rɪˈpʌl.ʃᵊn, rə-

repulsive rɪˈpʌl.sɪv, rə- **-ly** -li **-ness** -nəs, -nɪs

reputability ˌrep.jə.təˈbɪl.ə.ti, -jʊ-, -ɪ.ti (US) -t̬əˈbɪl.ə.t̬i

reputab|le ˈrep.jə.tə.b|l̩, -jʊ- (US) -t̬ə- **-ly** -li

reputation ˌrep.jəˈteɪ.ʃᵊn, -jʊˈ- **-s** -z

re|pute rɪ|ˈpjuːt, rə- **-puted/ly** -ˈpjuː.tɪd/li (US) -ˈpjuː.t̬ɪd/li

request rɪˈkwest, rə- **-s** -s **-ing** -ɪŋ **-ed** -ɪd

requiem ˈrek.wi.əm, -em **-s** -z ˌ**requiem** ˈ**mass**

requiescat ˌrek.wiˈes.kæt (US) ˌreɪ.kwiˈ-, ˌrek.wiˈ-, -kɑːt

requir|e rɪˈkwaɪəʳ, rə- (US) -ˈkwaɪɚ **-es** -z **-ing** -ɪŋ **-ed** -d

requirement rɪˈkwaɪə.mənt, rə- (US) -ˈkwaɪɚ- **-s** -s

requisite ˈrek.wɪ.zɪt, -wə- **-s** -s **-ly** -li **-ness** -nəs, -nɪs

requisition ˌrek.wɪˈzɪʃ.ᵊn, -wəˈ- **-s** -z **-ing** -ɪŋ **-ed** -d

re|quite rɪ|ˈkwaɪt, rə- **-quites** -ˈkwaɪts **-quiting** -ˈkwaɪ.tɪŋ (US) -ˈkwaɪ.t̬ɪŋ **-quited** -ˈkwaɪ.tɪd (US) -ˈkwaɪ.t̬ɪd **-quital** -ˈkwaɪ.tᵊl (US) -ˈkwaɪ.t̬ᵊl

re-read *present tense:* ˌriːˈriːd **-s** -z **-ing** -ɪŋ *past tense:* ˌriːˈred

reredos ˈrɪə.dɒs (US) ˈrɪr.dɑːs **-es** -ɪz

rereleas|e (*v.*) ˌriː.rɪˈliːs **-es** -ɪz **-ing** -ɪŋ **-ed** -t

rereleas|e (*n.*) ˈriː.rɪ.liːs **-s** -es

rerou|te ˌriːˈruː|t (US) -ˈruː|t, -ˈraʊ|t **-tes** -ts **-ting** -tɪŋ (US) -t̬ɪŋ **-ted** -tɪd (US) -t̬ɪd

rerun (*v*) ˌriːˈrʌn **-s** -z **-ning** -ɪŋ **reran** ˌriːˈræn

rerun (*n*) ˈriː.rʌn **-s** -z

res reɪz, reɪs, riːz (US) reɪs, riːz

resale ˈriː.seɪl, ˌ-ˈ- (US) ˈriː.seɪl **-s** -z

reschedul|e ˌriːˈʃed.juːl, -ˈʃedʒ.uːl (US) -ˈskedʒ.uːl, -əl **-es** -z **-ing** -ɪŋ **-ed** -d

rescind rɪˈsɪnd, rə- **-s** -z **-ing** -ɪŋ **-ed** -ɪd

rescission rɪˈsɪʒ.ᵊn, rə-

rescript ˈriː.skrɪpt **-s** -s

rescu|e ˈres.kjuː **-es** -z **-ing** -ɪŋ **-ed** -d **-er/s** -əʳ/z (US) -ɚ/z

research (*n.*) rɪˈsɜːtʃ, rə-, ˈriː.sɜːtʃ (US) ˈriː.sɝːtʃ; rɪˈsɝːtʃ, rə- **-es** -ɪz

research (*v.*) rɪˈsɜːtʃ, rə- (US) -ˈsɝːtʃ; ˈriː.sɝːtʃ **-es** -ɪz **-ing** -ɪŋ **-ed** -t **-er/s** -əʳ/z (US) -ɚ/z

re|seat ˌriː|ˈsiːt **-seats** -ˈsiːts **-seating** -ˈsiː.tɪŋ (US) -ˈsiː.t̬ɪŋ **-seated** -ˈsiː.tɪd (US) -ˈsiː.t̬ɪd

resection ˌriːˈsek.ʃᵊn, rɪ- **-s** -z

reseda ˈres.ɪ.də, ˈrez-, ˈ-ə-; rɪˈsiː.də, rə- (US) rɪˈsiː.də, rə-, -ˈsed.ə **-s** -z

reselect ˌriː.sɪˈlekt, -səˈ- **-s** -s **-ing** -ɪŋ **-ed** -ɪd

reselection ˌriː.sɪˈlek.ʃᵊn, -səˈ-

resell ˌriːˈsel **-s** -z **-ing** -ɪŋ **resold** ˌriːˈsəʊld (US) -ˈsoʊld

resemblanc|e rɪˈzem.blən*t*s, rə- **-es** -ɪz

resembl|e rɪˈzem.bl̩, rə- **-es** -z **-ing** -ɪŋ, -ˈzem.blɪŋ **-ed** -d

re|sent rɪ|ˈzent, rə- **-sents** -ˈzents **-senting** -ˈzen.tɪŋ (US) -ˈzen.t̬ɪŋ **-sented** -ˈzen.tɪd (US) -ˈzen.t̬ɪd

resentful rɪˈzent.fᵊl, rə-, -fʊl **-ly** -li

resentment rɪˈzent.mənt, rə-

reservation ˌrez.əˈveɪ.ʃᵊn (US) -ɚˈ- **-s** -z

reserv|e rɪˈzɜːv, rə- (US) -ˈzɝːv **-es** -z **-ing** -ɪŋ **-ed** -d

reservedly rɪˈzɜː.vɪd.li, rə- (US) -ˈzɝː-

reservist rɪˈzɜː.vɪst, rə- (US) -ˈzɝː- **-s** -s

reservoir ˈrez.əv.wɑːʳ (US) -ɚv.wɑːr, -wɔːr, ˈ-ɚ.vɔːr, ˈ-ə- **-s** -z

re|set ˌriː|ˈset **-sets** -ˈsets **-setting/s** -ˈset.ɪŋ/z (US) -ˈset̬.ɪŋ/z

resettle ˌriːˈset.l̩ **-s** -z **-ing** -ɪŋ **-ed** -d **-ment** -mənt

res gestae ˌreɪsˈges.taɪ, ˌreɪz-, ˌriːz-, -ˈdʒes-, -tiː

reshap|e ˌriːˈʃeɪp **-es** -s **-ing** -ɪŋ **-ed** -t

reship ˌriːˈʃɪp **-s** -s **-ping** -ɪŋ **-ped** -t **-ment/s** -mənt/s

reshuffle (*n.*) ˌriːˈʃʌf.l̩, ˈ-ˌ-- (US) ˌriːˈʃʌf- **-s** -z

reshuffl|e (*v.*) ˌriːˈʃʌf.l̩ **-es** -z **-ing** -ɪŋ, -ˈʃʌf.lɪŋ **-ed** -d

resid|e rɪˈzaɪd, rə- **-es** -z **-ing** -ɪŋ **-ed** -ɪd

residenc|e ˈrez.ɪ.dᵊn*t*s **-es** -ɪz

residenc|y ˈrez.ɪ.dᵊn*t*.s|i **-ies** -iz

resident ˈrez.ɪ.dᵊnt **-s** -s

residential ˌrez.ɪˈden.*t*ʃᵊl

residual rɪˈzɪd.ju.əl, rə-, -ˈzɪdʒ.u- (US) -ˈzɪdʒ- **-ly** -i

residuary rɪˈzɪd.ju.əri, rə-, -ˈzɪdʒ.ʊə- (US) -ˈzɪdʒ.u.er-

residue ˈrez.ɪ.djuː, ˈ-ə-, -dʒuː (US) -ə.duː, -djuː **-s** -z

residu|um rɪˈzɪd.ju|.əm, rə-, -ˈzɪdʒ.u- (US) -ˈzɪdʒ- **-a** -ə

resign rɪˈzaɪn, rə- **-s** -z **-ing** -ɪŋ **-ed** -d **-edly** -ɪd.li

resignation ˌrez.ɪgˈneɪ.ʃᵊn, -əgˈ- (US) -ɪgˈ- **-s** -z

resilien|ce rɪˈzɪl.i.ən*t*|s, rə-, -ˈsɪl- (US) -ˈzɪl.jən*t*|s, ˈ-i.ən*t*|s **-cy** -si

resilient rɪˈzɪl.i.ənt, rə-, -ˈsɪl- (US) -ˈzɪl.jənt, ˈ-i.ənt **-ly** -li

resin ˈrez.ɪn **-s** -z **-ous** -əs

res ipsa loquitur ˌreɪsˌɪp.sɑːˈlɒk.wɪ.tʊəʳ, ˌreɪz-, ˌriːz-, -səˈ-, -təʳ (US) ˌreɪsˌɪp.səˈlɑː.wɪ.tʊr

resist rɪˈzɪst, rə- **-s** -s **-ing** -ɪŋ **-ed** -ɪd **-or/s** -əʳ/z (US) -ɚ/z

resistanc|e rɪˈzɪs.tᵊn*t*s, rə- **-es** -ɪz

resistant rɪˈzɪs.tᵊnt, rə- **-ly** -li

resistivity ˌriː.zɪˈstɪv.ə.ti, ˌrez.ɪˈ-, -ɪ.ti (US) ˌriː.zɪˈstɪv.ə.t̬i; rɪˌzɪsˈtɪv-

resistless rɪˈzɪst.ləs, rə-, -lɪs

resistor rɪˈzɪs.təʳ, rə- (US) -tɚ **-s** -z

resit (*n.*) ˈriː.sɪt **-s** -s

re|sit (*v.*) ˌriː|ˈsɪt **-sits** -ˈsɪts **-sitting** -ˈsɪt.ɪŋ (US) -ˈsɪt̬.ɪŋ **resat** ˌriːˈsæt

res judicata ˌreɪsˌdʒuː.dɪˈkɑː.tə, ˌreɪz-, ˌriːz-, -dəˈ- (US) ˌreɪs-, ˌreɪz-, ˌriːz-, ˌriːs-

resnoid ˈrez.nɔɪd **-s** -z

resol|e ˌriːˈsəʊl (US) -ˈsoʊl **-es** -z **-ing** -ɪŋ **-ed** -d

resoluble rɪˈzɒl.jə.bl̩, rə-, -jʊ-; ˈrez.ᵊl- (US) rɪˈzɑːl.jə-, rə-, -jʊ-; ˈrez.ᵊl-

resolute ˈrez.ᵊl.uːt, -juːt (US) -ə.luːt **-ly** -li **-ness** -nəs, -nɪs

resolution ˌrez.ᵊlˈuː.ʃᵊn, -ˈjuː- (US) -əˈluː- **-s** -z

resolvability rɪˌzɒl.vəˈbɪl.ə.ti, rə-, -ɪ.ti (US) -ˌzɑːl.vəˈbɪl.ə.t̬i

resolv|e rɪˈzɒlv, rə- (US) -ˈzɑːlv **-es** -z **-ing** -ɪŋ **-ed** -d **-able** -ə.bl̩

resonanc|e ˈrez.ᵊn.ən*t*s **-es** -ɪz

resonant ˈrez.ᵊn.ənt **-ly** -li

reson|ate ˈrez.ᵊn|.eɪt **-ates** -eɪts **-ating** -eɪ.tɪŋ (US) -eɪ.t̬ɪŋ **-ated** -eɪ.tɪd (US) -eɪ.t̬ɪd

resonator ˈrez.ᵊn.eɪ.təʳ (US) -t̬ɚ **-s** -z

resorb rɪˈzɔːb, rə-, -ˈsɔːb (US) -ˈsɔːrb, -ˈzɔːrb **-s** -z **-ing** -ɪŋ **-ed** -d

resorp|tion rɪˈsɔːp|.ʃᵊn, rə-, -ˈzɔːp- (US) -ˈsɔːrp-, -ˈzɔːrp- **-tive** -tɪv

re|sort (*n. v.*) rɪ|ˈzɔːt, rə- (US) -ˈzɔːrt **-sorts** -ˈzɔːts (US) -ˈzɔːrts **-sorting** -ˈzɔː.tɪŋ (US) -ˈzɔːr.t̬ɪŋ **-sorted** -ˈzɔː.tɪd (US) -ˈzɔːr.t̬ɪd

re|-sort (*v.*) *sort again:* ˌriː|ˈsɔːt (US) -ˈsɔːrt **-sorts** -ˈsɔːts (US) -ˈsɔːrts **-sorting** -ˈsɔː.tɪŋ (US) -ˈsɔːr.t̬ɪŋ **-sorted** -ˈsɔː.tɪd (US) -ˈsɔːr.t̬ɪd

resound rɪˈzaʊnd, rə- **-s** -z **-ing** -ɪŋ **-ed** -ɪd

resourc|e rɪˈzɔːs, rə-, -ˈsɔːs; ˈriː.sɔːs (US) ˈriː.sɔːrs, -zɔːrs; rɪˈsɔːrs, rə-, -ˈzɔːrs **-es** -ɪz **-ed** -t

resourceful rɪˈzɔːs.fᵊl, rə-, -ˈsɔːs-, -fʊl (US) -ˈsɔːrs-, -ˈzɔːrs- **-ly** -i **-ness** -nəs, -nɪs

respect rɪˈspekt, rə- **-s** -s **-ing** -ɪŋ **-ed** -ɪd **-er/s** -əʳ/z (US) -ɚ/z
respectability rɪˌspek.təˈbɪl.ə.ti, rə-, -ɪ.ti (US) -ə.t̬i
respectab|le rɪˈspek.tə.b|l̩, rə- **-ly** -li **-leness** -l̩.nəs, -nɪs
respectful rɪˈspekt.fəl, rə-, -fʊl **-ly** -i **-ness** -nəs, -nɪs
respective rɪˈspek.tɪv, rə- **-ly** -li
Respighi resˈpiː.gi, rɪˈspiː-, rə-
respirable ˈres.pɪ.rə.bl̩, rɪˈspaɪə-, rə- (US) ˈres.pɚ.ə.bl̩; rɪˈspaɪ-, rə-
respiration ˌres.pəˈreɪ.ʃən, -pɪˈreɪ- (US) -pəˈreɪ- **-s** -z
respirator ˈres.pər.eɪ.təʳ, -pɪ.reɪ- (US) -pə.reɪ.t̬ɚ **-s** -z
respiratory rɪˈspɪr.ə.tər.i, -ˈspaɪə.rə-, rə-, resˈpaɪə-, ˈres.pɪ.rə-, -reɪ- (US) ˈres.pɚ.ə.tɔːr-; rɪˈspaɪ.rə-, rə-
respir|e rɪˈspaɪəʳ, rə- (US) -ˈspaɪɚ **-es** -z **-ing** -ɪŋ **-ed** -d
respi|te ˈres.paɪ|t, -pɪ|t (US) -pɪ|t **-tes** -ts **-ting** -tɪŋ (US) -t̬ɪŋ **-ted** -tɪd (US) -t̬ɪd
resplenden|ce rɪˈsplen.dənt|s, rə- **-cy** -si
resplendent rɪˈsplen.dənt, rə- **-ly** -li
respond rɪˈspɒnd, rə- (US) -ˈspɑːnd **-s** -z **-ing** -ɪŋ **-ed** -ɪd **-er/s** -əʳ/z (US) -ɚ/z
respondeat resˈpɒn.deɪ.æt, rɪs-, -di- (US) resˈpɑːn.di.ət
respondent rɪˈspɒn.dənt, rə- (US) -ˈspɑːn- **-s** -s
respons|e rɪˈspɒnts, rə- (US) -ˈspɑːnts **-es** -ɪz
responsibilit|y rɪˌspɒnt.səˈbɪl.ə.t|i, rə-, -sɪˈ-, -ɪ.t|i (US) -ˌspɑːnt.səˈbɪl.ə.t̬|i **-ies** -iz
responsib|le rɪˈspɒnt.sə.b|l̩, rə-, -sɪ- (US) -ˈspɑːnt.sə- **-ly** -li **-leness** -l̩.nəs, -nɪs
responsive rɪˈspɒnt.sɪv, rə- (US) -ˈspɑːnt- **-ly** -li **-ness** -nəs, -nɪs
respray (*n.*) ˈriː.spreɪ **-s** -z
respray (*v.*) ˌriːˈspreɪ **-s** -z **-ing** -ɪŋ **-ed** -d
rest rest **-s** -s **-ing** -ɪŋ **-ed** -ɪd **ˈrest ˌhome** ; **ˈrest ˌroom** ; **ˈresting ˌplace**
re|start ˌriː|ˈstɑːt (US) -ˈstɑːrt **-starts** -ˈstɑːts (US) -ˈstɑːrts **-starting** -ˈstɑː.tɪŋ (US) -ˈstɑːr.t̬ɪŋ **-started** -ˈstɑː.tɪd (US) -ˈstɑːr.t̬ɪd
re|state ˌriː|ˈsteɪt **-states** -ˈsteɪts **-stating** -ˈsteɪ.tɪŋ (US) -ˈsteɪ.t̬ɪŋ **-stated** -ˈsteɪ.tɪd (US) -ˈsteɪ.t̬ɪd
re-statement ˌriːˈsteɪt.mənt **-s** -s
restaur|ant ˈres.tər|.ɔ̃ːŋ, -ɑ̃ːŋ, -ɑːŋ, -ɒnt, -ənt, ˈ-tr|ɔ̃ːŋ, -tr|ɑ̃ːŋ, -tr|ɑːŋ, -tr|ɒnt, -tr|ənt (US) -tə.r|ɑːnt, -tɚ|.ənt, ˈ-tr|ɑːnt, -tr|ənt **-ants** -ɔ̃ːŋz, -ɑ̃ːŋz, -ɑːŋz, -ɒŋz, -ɒnts, -ənts (US) -ɑːnts, -ənts **ˈrestaurant ˌcar**
restaurateur ˌres.tɒr.əˈtɜːʳ, -tər-, -tɔː.rəˈ- (US) -tɚ.əˈtɜːr, -ˈtʊr **-s** -z
restful ˈrest.fəl, -fʊl **-ly** -i **-ness** -nəs, -nɪs
restitution ˌres.tɪˈtjuː.ʃən (US) -ˈtuː-, -ˈtjuː-
restive ˈres.tɪv **-ly** -li **-ness** -nəs, -nɪs
restless ˈrest.ləs, -lɪs **-ly** -li **-ness** -nəs, -nɪs
restock ˌriːˈstɒk (US) -ˈstɑːk **-s** -s **-ing** -ɪŋ **-ed** -t
restoration (R) ˌres.tərˈeɪ.ʃən (US) -təˈreɪ- **-s** -z
restorative rɪˈstɒr.ə.tɪv, rə-, resˈtɒr-, -ˈtɔː.rə- (US) rɪˈstɔːr.ə.t̬ɪv, rə- **-s** -z
restor|e rɪˈstɔːʳ, rə- (US) -ˈstɔːr **-es** -z **-ing** -ɪŋ **-ed** -d **-er/s** -əʳ/z (US) -ɚ/z **-able** -ə.bl̩
restrain rɪˈstreɪn, rə- **-s** -z **-ing** -ɪŋ **-ed** -d **-er/s** -əʳ/z (US) -ɚ/z
restraint rɪˈstreɪnt, rə- **-s** -s
restrict rɪˈstrɪkt, rə- **-s** -s **-ing** -ɪŋ **-ed** -ɪd
restriction rɪˈstrɪk.ʃən, rə- **-s** -z
restrictionism rɪˈstrɪk.ʃən.ɪ.zəm, rə-
restrictive rɪˈstrɪk.tɪv, rə- **-ly** -li **-ness** -nəs, -nɪs **reˌstrictive ˈpractice**
restruct|ure ˌriːˈstrʌk.tʃ|əʳ (US) -tʃ|ɚ **-ures** -əz (US) -ɚz **-uring** -ər.ɪŋ **-ured** -əd (US) -ɚd
re|sult rɪ|ˈzʌlt, rə- **-sults** -ˈzʌlts **-sulting** -ˈzʌl.tɪŋ (US) -ˈzʌl.t̬ɪŋ **-sulted** -ˈzʌl.tɪd (US) -ˈzʌl.t̬ɪd **-sultant/s** -ˈzʌl.tənt/s
resultative rɪˈzʌl.tə.tɪv, rə- (US) -t̬ə.t̬ɪv
resum|e rɪˈzjuːm, rə-, -ˈzuːm (US) -ˈzuːm **-es** -z **-ing** -ɪŋ **-ed** -d
résumé, resumé ˈrez.juː.meɪ, ˈreɪ.zuː-, -zjʊ-, -zʊ-; rɪˈzjuː-, rə- (US) ˈrez.ʊ.meɪ, ˈ-ə-, ˌ--ˈ- **-s** -z
resumption rɪˈzʌmp.ʃən, rə- **-s** -z
resumptive rɪˈzʌmp.tɪv, rə-
re-surfac|e ˌriːˈsɜː.fɪs, -fəs (US) -ˈsɜːr- **-es** -ɪz **-ing** -ɪŋ **-ed** -t
resurgenc|e rɪˈsɜː.dʒənts, rə- (US) -ˈsɜːr- **-es** -ɪz
resurgent rɪˈsɜː.dʒənt, rə- (US) -ˈsɜːr-
resurrect ˌrez.ərˈekt (US) -əˈrekt **-s** -s **-ing** -ɪŋ **-ed** -ɪd
resurrection (R) ˌrez.ərˈek.ʃən (US) -əˈrek- **-s** -z
resusci|tate rɪˈsʌs.ɪ|.teɪt, rə-, ˈ-ə- (US) ˈ-ə- **-tates** -teɪts **-tating** -teɪ.tɪŋ (US) -teɪ.t̬ɪŋ **-tated** -teɪ.tɪd (US) -teɪ.t̬ɪd **-tator/s** -teɪ.təʳ/z (US) -teɪ.t̬ɚ/z
resuscitation rɪˌsʌs.ɪˈteɪ.ʃən, rə-, -əˈ- (US) -əˈ- **-s** -z
retail (*n. adj.*) ˈriː.teɪl, ˌ-ˈ- (US) ˈriː.teɪl **ˌretail ˈprice**
retail (*v.*) *sell:* ˈriː.teɪl, ˌ-ˈ- (US) ˈriː.teɪl; rɪˈteɪl **-s** -z **-ing** -ɪŋ **-ed** -d **-er/s** -əʳ/z (US) -ɚ/z
retail (*v.*) *tell:* rɪˈteɪl, rə-, ˌriː- **-s** -z **-ing** -ɪŋ **-ed** -d
retain rɪˈteɪn, rə- **-s** -z **-ing** -ɪŋ **-ed** -d **-er/s** -əʳ/z (US) -ɚ/z
retake (*n.*) ˈriː.teɪk **-s** -s
re|take (*v.*) ˌriː|ˈteɪk **-takes** -ˈteɪks **-taking** -ˈteɪ.kɪŋ **-took** -ˈtʊk **-taken** -ˈteɪ.kən
retali|ate rɪˈtæl.i|.eɪt, rə- **-ates** -eɪts **-ating** -eɪ.tɪŋ (US) -eɪ.t̬ɪŋ **-ated** -eɪ.tɪd (US) -eɪ.t̬ɪd
retaliation rɪˌtæl.iˈeɪ.ʃən, rə-
retaliatory rɪˈtæl.i.ə.tər.i, rə-, -eɪ-; rɪˌtæl.iˈeɪ-, rə- (US) rɪˈtæl.i.ə.tɔːr-, rə-, ˈ-jə-
retard (*v.*) rɪˈtɑːd, rə- (US) -ˈtɑːrd **-s** -z **-ing** -ɪŋ **-ed** -ɪd
retard (*n.*) ˈriː.tɑːd (US) -tɑːrd **-s** -z
retardant rɪˈtɑː.dənt, rə- (US) -ˈtɑːr- **-s** -s
retardation ˌriː.tɑːˈdeɪ.ʃən (US) -tɑːrˈ- **-s** -z
retch retʃ, riːtʃ (US) retʃ **-es** -ɪz **-ing** -ɪŋ **-ed** -t
retell ˌriːˈtel **-s** -z **-ing** -ɪŋ **retold** ˌriːˈtəʊld (US) -ˈtoʊld
retention rɪˈten.tʃən, rə-
retentive rɪˈten.tɪv, rə- (US) -t̬ɪv **-ly** -li **-ness** -nəs, -nɪs
Retford ˈret.fəd (US) -fɚd
rethink (*v.*) ˌriːˈθɪŋk **-s** -s **-ing** -ɪŋ **rethought** ˌriːˈθɔːt (US) -ˈθɑːt, -ˈθɔːt
rethink (*n.*) ˈriː.θɪŋk **-s** -s
reticence ˈret.ɪ.sənts, ˈ-ə- (US) ˈret̬.ə-
reticent ˈret.ɪ.sənt, ˈ-ə- (US) ˈret̬.ə- **-ly** -li
reticle ˈret.ɪ.kl̩ (US) ˈret̬.ɪ- **-s** -z
reticulate (*adj.*) rɪˈtɪk.jə.lət, rə-, retˈɪk-, -jʊ-, -lɪt, -leɪt (US) rɪˈtɪk.jə.lɪt, rə-, -jʊ-, -leɪt
reticu|late (*v.*) rɪˈtɪk.jə|.leɪt, rə-, retˈɪk-, -jʊ- (US) rɪˈtɪk-, rə- **-lates** -leɪts **-lating** -leɪ.tɪŋ (US) -leɪ.t̬ɪŋ **-lated** -leɪ.tɪd (US) -leɪ.t̬ɪd
reticulation rɪˌtɪk.jəˈleɪ.ʃən, rə-, retˌɪk-, -jʊˈ- (US) rɪˌtɪk-, rə- **-s** -z
reticule ˈret.ɪ.kjuːl, ˈ-ə- (US) ˈret̬.ə- **-s** -z
retin|a ˈret.ɪ.n|ə (US) -ən|.ə **-as** -əz **-ae** -iː **-al** -əl
retinue ˈret.ɪ.njuː (US) -ən.uː, -juː **-s** -z
retir|e rɪˈtaɪəʳ, rə- (US) -ˈtaɪɚ **-es** -z **-ing** -ɪŋ **-ed** -d **-ant/s** -ənts
retiree rɪˌtaɪəˈriː, rə- (US) rɪˈtaɪ.riː, rə- **-s** -z
retirement rɪˈtaɪə.mənt, rə- (US) -ˈtaɪɚ- **reˈtirement ˌage** ; **reˈtirement ˌhome**
retold (*from* **retell**) ˌriːˈtəʊld (US) -ˈtoʊld
re|tort rɪ|ˈtɔːt, rə- (US) -ˈtɔːrt **-torts** -ˈtɔːts (US) -ˈtɔːrts **-torting** -ˈtɔː.tɪŋ (US) -ˈtɔːr.t̬ɪŋ **-torted** -ˈtɔː.tɪd (US) -ˈtɔːr.t̬ɪd

retouch ˌriːˈtʌtʃ **-es** -ɪz **-ing** -ɪŋ **-ed** -t
retrac|e rɪˈtreɪs, ˌriː- **-es** -ɪz **-ing** -ɪŋ **-ed** -t
retract rɪˈtrækt, rə- **-s** -s **-ing** -ɪŋ **-ed** -ɪd **-or/s** -əʳ/z (US) -ɚ/z
retractable rɪˈtræk.tə.bl̩, rə-
retractation ˌriː.trækˈteɪ.ʃᵊn
retraction rɪˈtræk.ʃᵊn, rə- **-s** -z
retransla|te ˌriː.trænˈsleɪ|t, -trɑːnˈ-, -trænzˈleɪ|t, -trɑːnzˈ-, -trᵊnˈsleɪ|t, -trᵊnzˈleɪ|t (US) ˌriːˈtræn.sleɪ|t, -ˈtrænz.leɪ|t, ˌ--ˈ- **-tes** -ts **-ting** -tɪŋ (US) -t̬ɪŋ **-ted** -tɪd (US) -t̬ɪd
retranslation ˌriː.trænˈsleɪ.ʃᵊn, -trɑːnˈ-, -trænzˈleɪ-, -trɑːnzˈ-, -trᵊnˈsleɪ-, -trᵊnzˈleɪ- (US) -trænˈsleɪ-, -trænzˈleɪ- **-s** -z
retread (*n.*) ˈriː.tred **-s** -z
retread (*v.*) ˌriːˈtred **-s** -z **-ing** -ɪŋ **retrod** ˌriːˈtrɒd (US) -ˈtrɑːd
re|treat rɪ|ˈtriːt, rə- **-treats** -ˈtriːts **-treating** -ˈtriː.tɪŋ (US) -ˈtriː.t̬ɪŋ **-treated** -ˈtriː.tɪd (US) -ˈtriː.t̬ɪd
retrench rɪˈtrentʃ, rə- (US) -ˈtrentʃ **-es** -ɪz **-ing** -ɪŋ **-ed** -t **-ment/s** -mənt/s
retrial ˌriːˈtraɪəl, ˈ-- (US) ˈriː.traɪəl, ˌ-ˈ- **-s** -z
retribution ˌret.rɪˈbjuː.ʃᵊn, -rəˈ- (US) -rəˈ-
retribu|tive rɪˈtrɪb.jə|.tɪv, rə-, -jʊ-, -t̬ɪv **-tory** -tᵊr.i (US) -tɔːr-
retrievab|le rɪˈtriː.və.b|l̩, rə- **-ly** -li **-leness** -l̩.nəs, -nɪs
retrieval rɪˈtriː.vᵊl, rə-
retriev|e rɪˈtriːv, rə- **-es** -z **-ing** -ɪŋ **-ed** -d **-er/s** -əʳ/z (US) -ɚ/z
retrim ˌriːˈtrɪm **-s** -z **-ming** -ɪŋ **-med** -d
retro- ret.rəʊ- (US) ret.roʊ-, -rə-
Note: Prefix. Normally takes primary or secondary stress on the first syllable, e.g. **retrograde** /ˈret.rəʊ.greɪd (US) -rə-/, **retroact** /ˌret.rəʊˈækt (US) -roʊˈ-/.
retro ˈret.rəʊ (US) -roʊ
retroact ˌret.rəʊˈækt (US) -roʊˈ- **-s** -s **-ing** -ɪŋ **-ed** -ɪd
retroaction ˌret.rəʊˈæk.ʃᵊn (US) -roʊˈ-
retroactive ˌret.rəʊˈæk.tɪv (US) -roʊˈ- **-ly** -li *stress shift:* ˌretroactive ˈlaws
retroced|e ˌret.rəʊˈsiːd (US) -roʊˈ-, -rəˈ- **-es** -z **-ing** -ɪŋ **-ed** -ɪd
retrocession ˌret.rəʊˈseʃ.ᵊn (US) -roʊˈ-, -rəˈ- **-s** -z
retroflex ˈret.rəʊ.fleks (US) -rə- **-ed** -t
retroflexion ˌret.rəʊˈflek.ʃᵊn (US) -rəˈ-
retrograde ˈret.rəʊ.greɪd (US) -rə-, -roʊ-
retrogress ˌret.rəʊˈgres (US) ˈret.rə.gres, -roʊ-, ˌ--ˈ- **-es** -ɪz **-ing** -ɪŋ **-ed** -t **-ive/ly** -ɪv/li
retrogression ˌret.rəʊˈgreʃ.ᵊn (US) -rəˈ-, -roʊˈ-
retro-rocket ˈret.rəʊˌrɒk.ɪt (US) -roʊˌrɑː.kɪt **-s** -s
retrospect ˈret.rəʊ.spekt (US) -rə- **-s** -s
retrospection ˌret.rəʊˈspek.ʃᵊn (US) -rəˈ- **-s** -z
retrospective ˌret.rəʊˈspek.tɪv (US) -rəˈ- **-s** -z **-ly** -li *stress shift:* ˌretrospective ˈview
retroussé rəˈtruː.seɪ, rɪ- (US) rəˌtruːˈseɪ, retˌruː-
retroversion ˌret.rəʊˈvɜː.ʃᵊn, -ʒən (US) -roʊˈvɜːr.ʒᵊn, -rəˈ-, -ʃᵊn **-s** -z
retrovert (*n.*) ˈret.rəʊ.vɜːt (US) -roʊ.vɜːrt, -rə- **-s** -s
retro|vert (*v.*) ˌret.rəʊ|ˈvɜːt (US) -roʊ|ˈvɜːrt, -rə- **-verts** -ˈvɜːts (US) -ˈvɜːrts **-verting** -ˈvɜː.tɪŋ (US) -ˈvɜːr.t̬ɪŋ **-verted** -ˈvɜː.tɪd (US) -ˈvɜːr.t̬ɪd
retrovirus ˈret.rəʊ.vaɪə.rəs, ˌret.rəʊˈvaɪə- (US) ˈret.roʊˌvaɪ- **-es** -ɪz
retr|y ˌriːˈtr|aɪ **-ies** -aɪz **-ying** -aɪ.ɪŋ **-ied** -aɪd
retsina retˈsiː.nə, ˈret.sɪ.nə
returf ˌriːˈtɜːf (US) -ˈtɜːrf **-s** -s **-ing** -ɪŋ **-ed** -t
return rɪˈtɜːn, rə- (US) -ˈtɜːrn **-s** -z **-ing** -ɪŋ **-ed** -d **-able** -ə.bl̩ **-er/s** -əʳ/z (US) -ɚ/z
returnee rɪˌtɜːˈniː, rə-, -ˈtɜː.niː (US) rɪˌtɜːrˈniː, rə- **-s** -z
Reuben ˈruː.bən, -bɪn (US) -bən
reunification ˌriː.juː.nɪ.fɪˈkeɪ.ʃᵊn, riːˌjuː-, -nə- (US) riːˌjuː.nə- **-s** -z
reuni|fy ˌriːˈjuː.nɪ|.faɪ, -nə- (US) -nə- **-fies** -faɪ **-fying** -faɪ.ɪŋ **-fied** -faɪd
reunion ˌriːˈjuː.ni.ən (US) ˈ-njən **-s** -z
Réunion ˌriːˈjuː.ni.ən; *as if French:* ˌreɪ.uːˈnjɔ̃ːŋ (US) ˌriːˈjuːn.jən
reu|nite ˌriː.juː|ˈnaɪt **-nites** -ˈnaɪts **-niting** -ˈnaɪ.tɪŋ (US) -ˈnaɪ.t̬ɪŋ **-nited** -ˈnaɪ.tɪd (US) -ˈnaɪ.t̬ɪd
reusable ˌriːˈjuː.zə.bl̩
re-use (*n.*) ˌriːˈjuːs, ˈ-- (US) ˌriːˈjuːs
re-us|e (*v.*) ˌriːˈjuːz **-es** -ɪz **-ing** -ɪŋ **-ed** -d
Reuter ˈrɔɪ.təʳ (US) -t̬ɚ **-s** -z
Rev. (*abbrev. for* **Reverend**) ˈrev.ᵊr.ᵊnd, rev
rev (*n. v.*) rev **-s** -z **-ving** -ɪŋ **-ved** -d ˈ**rev** ˌ**counter**
revamp (*v.*) ˌriːˈvæmp **-s** -s **-ing** -ɪŋ **-ed** -t
revamp (*n.*) ˈriː.væmp **-s** -s
revanch|ist rɪˈvæntʃ|.ɪst **-ists** -ɪsts **-ism** -ɪ.zᵊm
Revd (*abbrev. for* **Reverend**) ˈrev.ᵊr.ᵊnd
reveal rɪˈviːl, rə- **-s** -z **-ing** -ɪŋ **-ed** -d **-er/s** -əʳ/z (US) -ɚ/z **-able** -ə.bl̩
revealing rɪˈviː.lɪŋ **-ly** -li
reveille rɪˈvæl.i, rə-, -ˈvel- (US) ˈrev.ᵊl.i **-s** -z
revel ˈrev.ᵊl **-s** -z **-(l)ing** -ɪŋ **-(l)ed** -d **-(l)er/s** -əʳ/z (US) -ɚ/z
revelation (R) ˌrev.ᵊlˈeɪ.ʃᵊn **-s** -z
Revell ˈrev.ᵊl
revelr|y ˈrev.ᵊl.r|i **-ies** -iz
Revelstoke ˈrev.ᵊl.stəʊk (US) -stoʊk
revendication rɪˌven.dɪˈkeɪ.ʃᵊn, rə-, -dəˈ- (US) -dəˈ- **-s** -z
reveng|e rɪˈvendʒ, rə- **-es** -ɪz **-ing** -ɪŋ **-ed** -d
revengeful rɪˈvendʒ.fᵊl, rə-, -fʊl **-ly** -i **-ness** -nəs, -nɪs
revenue ˈrev.ᵊn.juː, -ɪ.njuː (US) ˈrev.ə.nuː, -njuː **-s** -z
reverber|ate rɪˈvɜː.bᵊr|.eɪt, rə- (US) -ˈvɜːr.bə.r|eɪt **-ates** -eɪts **-ating** -eɪ.tɪŋ (US) -eɪ.t̬ɪŋ **-ated** -eɪ.tɪd (US) -eɪ.t̬ɪd **-ator/s** -eɪ.təʳ/z (US) -eɪ.t̬ɚ/z
reverberation rɪˌvɜː.bᵊrˈeɪ.ʃᵊn, rə- (US) -ˌvɜːr.bəˈreɪ- **-s** -z
reverberatory rɪˈvɜː.bᵊr.ə.tᵊr.i, rə-, -reɪ- (US) -ˈvɜːr.bɚ.ə.tɔːr-
rever|e (R) rɪˈvɪəʳ, rə- (US) -ˈvɪr **-es** -z **-ing** -ɪŋ **-ed** -d
reverenc|e ˈrev.ᵊr.ᵊnts, ˈ-rᵊnts **-es** -ɪz **-ing** -ɪŋ **-ed** -t
reverend (R) ˈrev.ᵊr.ᵊnd, ˈ-rᵊnd **-s** -z
reverent ˈrev.ᵊr.ᵊnt, ˈ-rᵊnt **-ly** -li
reverential ˌrev.ᵊrˈen.tʃᵊl (US) -əˈrent.ʃᵊl **-ly** -i
reverie ˈrev.ᵊr.i (US) -ə.ri **-s** -z
revers *singular:* rɪˈvɪəʳ, rə-, -ˈveəʳ (US) -ˈvɪr, -ˈver *plural:* -z
reversal rɪˈvɜː.sᵊl, rə- (US) -ˈvɜːr- **-s** -z
revers|e rɪˈvɜːs, rə- (US) -ˈvɜːrs **-es** -ɪz **-ing** -ɪŋ **-ed** -t
reversibility rɪˌvɜː.səˈbɪl.ə.ti, rə-, -sɪˈ-, -ɪ.ti (US) -ˌvɜːr.səˈbɪl.ə.t̬i
reversible rɪˈvɜː.sə.bl̩, rə-, -sɪ- (US) -ˈvɜːr.sə-
reversion rɪˈvɜː.ʃᵊn, rə- (US) -ˈvɜːr.ʒᵊn, -ʃᵊn **-s** -z
reversionary rɪˈvɜː.ʃᵊn.ᵊr.i, rə-, -ʒᵊn- (US) -ˈvɜːr.ʒᵊn.er-, -ʃᵊn-
re|vert rɪ|ˈvɜːt, rə- (US) -ˈvɜːrt **-verts** -ˈvɜːts (US) -ˈvɜːrts **-verting** -ˈvɜː.tɪŋ (US) -ˈvɜːr.t̬ɪŋ **-verted** -ˈvɜː.tɪd (US) -ˈvɜːr.t̬ɪd
reverter rɪˈvɜː.təʳ, rə- (US) -ˈvɜːr.t̬ɚ
re|vet rɪ|ˈvet, rə- **-vets** -ˈvets **-vetting** -ˈvet.ɪŋ (US) -ˈvet̬.ɪŋ **-vetted** -ˈvet.ɪd (US) -ˈvet̬.ɪd **-vetment/s** -ˈvet.mənt/s
review rɪˈvjuː, rə- **-s** -z **-ing** -ɪŋ **-ed** -d **-er/s** -əʳ/z (US) -ɚ/z
revil|e rɪˈvaɪl, rə- **-es** -z **-ing** -ɪŋ **-ed** -d **-er/s** -əʳ/z (US) -ɚ/z
revis|e rɪˈvaɪz, rə- **-es** -ɪz **-ing** -ɪŋ **-ed** -d **-er/s** -əʳ/z (US) -ɚ/z **Reˌvised ˈVersion, Reˈvised ˌVersion**
revision rɪˈvɪʒ.ᵊn, rə- **-s** -z

revision|ism rɪ'vɪʒ.ᵊn|.ɪ.zᵊm, rə- **-ist/s** -ɪst/s
revis|it ˌriː'vɪz|.ɪt **-its** -ɪts **-iting** -ɪ.tɪŋ (US) -ɪ.t̬ɪŋ **-ited** -ɪ.tɪd (US) -ɪ.t̬ɪd
revisualiz|e, -is|e ˌriː'vɪz.ju.ᵊl.aɪz, -'vɪʒ-, -u- (US) -'vɪʒ.u- **-es** -ɪz **-ing** -ɪŋ **-ed** -d
revitaliz|e, is|e ˌriː'vaɪ.tᵊl.aɪz (US) -t̬ᵊl- **-es** -ɪz **-ing** -ɪŋ **-ed** -d
revival rɪ'vaɪ.vᵊl, rə- **-s** -z
revival|ism rɪ'vaɪ.vᵊl|.ɪ.zᵊm, rə- **-ist/s** -ɪst/s
reviv|e rɪ'vaɪv, rə- **-es** -z **-ing** -ɪŋ **-ed** -d
revivi|fy ˌriː'vɪv.ɪ|.faɪ, rɪ- **-fies** -faɪz **-fying** -faɪ.ɪŋ **-fied** -faɪd
reviviscence ˌrev.ɪ'vɪs.ᵊnts, ˌriː.vaɪ'- (US) ˌrev.ə'-
Revlon® 'rev.lɒn (US) -lɑːn
revocability ˌrev.ə.kə'bɪl.ə.ti, -ɪ.ti (US) -ə.t̬i
revocable 'rev.ə.kə.bl̩ *when applied to letters of credit:* rɪ'vəʊ.kə.bl̩, rə- (US) -'voʊ-
revocation ˌrev.əʊ'keɪ.ʃᵊn (US) -ə'- **-s** -z
revok|e rɪ'vəʊk, rə- (US) -'voʊk **-es** -s **-ing** -ɪŋ **-ed** -t
re|volt rɪ|'vəʊlt, rə- (US) -'voʊlt **-volts** -'vəʊlts (US) -'voʊlts **-volting** -'vəʊl.tɪŋ (US) -'voʊl.t̬ɪŋ **-volted** -'vəʊl.tɪd (US) -'voʊl.t̬ɪd
revolution ˌrev.ᵊl'uː.ʃᵊn, -'juː- (US) -ə'luː- **-s** -z
revolutionar|y ˌrev.ᵊl'uː.ʃᵊn.ᵊr|.i, -'juː- (US) -ə'luː.ʃᵊn.er- **-ies** -iz
revolutionist ˌrev.ᵊl'uː.ʃᵊn.ɪst, -'juː- (US) -ə'luː- **-s** -s
revolutioniz|e, -is|e ˌrev.ᵊl'uː.ʃᵊn.aɪz, -'juː- (US) -ə'luː- **-es** -ɪz **-ing** -ɪŋ **-ed** -d
revolv|e rɪ'vɒlv, rə- (US) -'vɑːlv **-es** -z **-ing** -ɪŋ **-ed** -d **reˌvolving 'door** ; **reˌvolving 'credit** ; **reˌvolving 'fund**
revolver rɪ'vɒl.vəʳ, rə- (US) -'vɑːl.vɚ **-s** -z
revue rɪ'vjuː, rə- **-s** -z
revulsion rɪ'vʌl.ʃᵊn, rə- **-s** -z
reward rɪ'wɔːd, rə- (US) -'wɔːrd **-s** -z **-ing** -ɪŋ **-ed** -ɪd
rewind ˌriː'waɪnd **-s** -z **-ing** -ɪŋ **rewound** ˌriː'waʊnd
rewir|e ˌriː'waɪəʳ (US) -'waɪɚ **-es** -z **-ing** -ɪŋ **-ed** -d
reword ˌriː'wɜːd (US) -'wɜːrd **-s** -z **-ing** -ɪŋ **-ed** -ɪd
rework ˌriː'wɜːk **-s** -s **-ing** -ɪŋ **-ed** -t
rewrite (*n.*) 'riː.raɪt **-s** -s
re|write (*v.*) ˌriː|'raɪt **-writes** -'raɪts **-writing** -'raɪ.tɪŋ (US) -'raɪ.t̬ɪŋ **-wrote** ˌriː'rəʊt (US) -'roʊt **-written** ˌriː'rɪt.ᵊn
Rex reks
Reyes raɪz, reɪz
Reykjavik 'reɪ.kjə.vɪk, 'rek.jə-, -viːk (US) 'reɪ.kjə.viːk, -vɪk
reynard 'ren.ɑːd, 'reɪ.nɑːd, -nəd (US) 'ren.ɚd, 'reɪ.nɚd, -nɑːrd **-s** -z
Reynard 'ren.əd, -ɑːd, 'reɪ.nɑːd (US) -nɑːrd, 'reɪ.nɚd,'ren.ɚd
Reynold 'ren.ᵊld **-s** -z
rezon|e ˌriː'zəʊn (US) -'zoʊn **-es** -z **-ing** -ɪŋ **-ed** -d
Rh (*abbrev. for* **rhesus**) 'riː.səs
Rhadamanthus ˌræd.ə'mænt.θəs
Rhaeti|a 'riː.ʃi|.ə, '-ʃ|ə (US) -ʃ|ə, '-ʃi|.ə **-an** -ən
Rhaetic 'riː.tɪk (US) -t̬ɪk
Rhaeto-Roman|ce ˌriː.təʊ.rəʊ'mæn|ts (US) -t̬oʊ.roʊ'- **-ic** -ɪk
rhapsodic ræp'sɒd.ɪk (US) -'sɑː.dɪk **-al** -ᵊl **-ally** -ᵊl.i, -li
rhapsodiz|e, -is|e 'ræp.sə.daɪz **-es** -ɪz **-ing** -ɪŋ **-ed** -d
rhapsod|y 'ræp.sə.d|i **-ies** -iz
rhea (R) 'riː.ə, rɪə (US) 'riː.ə **-s** -z
Rhea Silvia ˌriː.ə'sɪl.vi.ə, ˌrɪə'- (US) ˌriː.ə'-
Rheims riːmz
Rhenish 'ren.ɪʃ
rhenium 'riː.ni.əm
rheostat 'riː.əʊ.stæt (US) -oʊ-, '-ə- **-s** -s
rhesus 'riː.səs **-es** -ɪz **'rhesus ˌfactor** ; **ˌrhesus 'monkey, 'rhesus ˌmonkey**
rhetoric 'ret.ᵊr.ɪk (US) 'ret̬-
rhetoric|al rɪ'tɒr.ɪ.k|ᵊl, rə- (US) -'tɔːr.ɪ- **-ally** -ᵊl.i, -li **rheˌtorical 'question**
rhetorician ˌret.ᵊr'ɪʃ.ᵊn, -ɒr'- (US) ˌret̬.ə'rɪʃ- **-s** -z
Rhett ret
rheum ruːm
rheumatic ruː'mæt.ɪk (US) -'mæt̬- **-s** -s **-ky** -i
rheumatism 'ruː.mə.tɪ.zᵊm
rheumatoid 'ruː.mə.tɔɪd **ˌrheumatoid arth'ritis**
rheumatolog|y ˌruː.mə'tɒl.ə.dʒ|i (US) -'tɑː.lə- **-ist/s** -ɪst/s
rheumy 'ruː.mi
Rhiannon ri'æn.ən
Rhine raɪn **-land** -lænd, -lənd
Rhineland-Palatinate ˌraɪn.lænd.pə'læt.ɪ.nɪt, -lənd-, -nət, -neɪt (US) -lænd.pə'læt.ᵊn.eɪt, -lənd-, -ɪt
rhinestone 'raɪn.stəʊn (US) -stoʊn **-s** -z
rhinitis ˌraɪ'naɪ.tɪs (US) -t̬əs
rhino- raɪ.nəʊ-; raɪ'nɒ- (US) raɪ.noʊ-, -nə-; raɪ'nɑː-
Note: Prefix. Normally either takes primary or secondary stress on the first syllable, e.g. **rhinoplasty** /'raɪ.nəʊ.plæs.ti (US) -noʊ-/, or primary stress on the second syllable, e.g. **rhinoceros** /raɪ'nɒs.ᵊr.əs (US) -'nɑː.sɚ-/.
rhino 'raɪ.nəʊ (US) -noʊ **-s** -z
rhinoceri (*alternative plur. of* **rhinoceros**) raɪ'nɒs.ᵊr.aɪ (US) -'nɑː.sə.raɪ
rhinoceros raɪ'nɒs.ᵊr.əs (US) -'nɑː.sɚ- **-es** -ɪz
rhinolog|y raɪ'nɒl.ə.dʒ|i (US) -'nɑː.lə- **-ist/s** -ɪst/s
rhinoplasty 'raɪ.nəʊ.plæs.ti (US) -noʊ-, -nə-
rhinoscope 'raɪ.nəʊ.skəʊp (US) -skoʊp **-s** -s
rhinoscopy raɪ'nɒs.kə.pi (US) -'nɑː.skə-
rhizome 'raɪ.zəʊm (US) -zoʊm **-s** -z
rho rəʊ (US) roʊ
Rhoads rəʊdz (US) roʊdz
Rhoda 'rəʊ.də (US) 'roʊ-
Rhode Island *state in US:* ˌrəʊd'aɪ.lənd (US) ˌroʊd- **-er/s** -əʳ/z (US) -ɚ/z *stress shift, see compound:* **ˌRhode Island 'Red**
Rhodes rəʊdz (US) roʊdz **ˌRhodes 'scholar**
Rhodesi|a rəʊ'diː.ʒ|ə, -ʃ|ə (US) roʊ-, '-ʒi|.ə **-an** -ən
Rhodian 'rəʊ.di.ən (US) 'roʊ- **-s** -z
rhodium 'rəʊ.di.əm (US) 'roʊ-
rhododendron ˌrəʊ.də'den.drən, -dɪ'- (US) ˌroʊ.də'- **-s** -z
rhomb rɒm (US) rɑːmb **-s** -z
rhomboid 'rɒm.bɔɪd (US) 'rɑːm- **-s** -z
rhomb|us 'rɒm.b|əs (US) 'rɑːm- **-uses** -ə.sɪz **-i** -aɪ
Rhona 'rəʊ.nə (US) 'roʊ-
Rhonda 'rɒn.də (US) 'rɑːn-
Rhondda 'rɒn.də, -ðə (US) 'rɑːn-
Rhone rəʊn (US) roʊn
Rhosllanerchrugog ˌrəʊs.ɬæn.ə'krɪg.ɒg, -θlæn- (US) ˌroʊs.ɬæn.ə'kriː.gɑːg
rhotacism 'rəʊ.tə.sɪ.zᵊm (US) 'roʊ.t̬ə-
rhotacization, -isa- ˌrəʊ.tə.saɪ'zeɪ.ʃᵊn, -tɪ- (US) ˌroʊ.t̬ə.sɪ'- **-s** -z
rhotaciz|e, -is|e 'rəʊ.tə.saɪz (US) 'roʊ.t̬ə- **-es** -ɪz **-ing** -ɪŋ **-ed** -d
rhotic 'rəʊ.tɪk (US) 'roʊ.t̬ɪk **-s** -s
rhoticity rəʊ'tɪs.ɪ.ti, -ə.ti (US) roʊ'tɪs.ə.t̬i
rhubarb 'ruː.bɑːb (US) -bɑːrb
Rhuddlan 'rɪð.lən, -læn
rhumb rʌm (US) rʌmb **-s** -z
Rhyl rɪl
rhym|e raɪm **-es** -z **-ing** -ɪŋ **-ed** -d **-er/s** -əʳ/z (US) -ɚ/z
rhymester 'raɪm.stəʳ (US) -stɚ **-s** -z
Rhymney 'rʌm.ni
Rhys *Welsh name:* riːs *family name of Baron Dynevor:* raɪs
rhythm 'rɪð.ᵊm, 'rɪθ- (US) 'rɪð- **-s** -z **ˌrhythm and 'blues** ; **'rhythm ˌmethod**
rhythmic 'rɪð.mɪk, 'rɪθ- (US) 'rɪð- **-al** -ᵊl **-ally** -ᵊl.i (US) -li

RI ˌɑːrˈaɪ (US) ˌɑːr-
ria ˈriː.ə, rɪə (US) ˈriː.ə **-s** -z
rial riˈɑːl; ˈraɪ.əl, ˈraɪ.əl; (US) ˈriː.ɔːl, -ɑːl **-s** -z
Note: The usual pronunciation for the Saudi Arabian currency is /riˈɑːl (US) ˈriː.ɔːl/.
rialto (R) riˈæl.təʊ (US) -toʊ **-s** -z
rib rɪb **-s** -z **-bing** -ɪŋ **-bed** -d **ˈrib ˌcage**
ribald ˈrɪb.əld, ˈraɪ.bəld, -bɔːld (US) ˈrɪb.əld, ˈraɪ.bɔːld **-s** -z **-ry** -ri
riband ˈrɪb.ənd **-s** -z
Ribbentrop ˈrɪb.ən.trɒp (US) -trɑːp
Ribble ˈrɪb.l̩
ribbon ˈrɪb.ən **-s** -z
Ribena® raɪˈbiː.nə
riboflavin ˌraɪ.bəʊˈfleɪ.vɪn, ˈraɪ.bəʊ.fleɪ- (US) ˈraɪ.bə.fleɪ.vɪn, ˌraɪ.bəˈfleɪ-, -boʊˈ-
ribosomal ˌraɪ.bəʊˈsəʊ.məl (US) -bəˈsoʊ-
ribosome ˈraɪ.bəʊ.səʊm (US) -bə.soʊm **-s** -z
Rica ˈriː.kə
Ricardo rɪˈkɑː.dəʊ (US) -ˈkɑːr.doʊ
Ricci ˈriː.tʃi
Riccio ˈrɪtʃ.i.əʊ, ˈrɪt.si- (US) ˈrɪt.ʃi.oʊ; ˈriːt.ʃoʊ
ric|e (R) raɪs **-es** -ɪz **-ing** -ɪŋ **-ed** -t **ˈrice ˌpaper** ; **ˌrice ˈpudding**
Rice Krispies® ˌraɪsˈkrɪs.piz
rich (R) rɪtʃ **-es** -ɪz **-er** -ər (US) -ɚ **-est** -ɪst, -əst **-ly** -li **-ness** -nəs, -nɪs
Richard ˈrɪtʃ.əd (US) -ɚd **-s** -z
Richardson ˈrɪtʃ.əd.sən (US) -ɚd-
Richelieu ˈriː.ʃəl.jɜː, ˈrɪʃ.əl-, -juː (US) ˈrɪʃ.luː, ˈriːʃ-, ˈ-ə.luː
Riches ˈrɪtʃ.ɪz
Richey, Richie ˈrɪtʃ.i
Richler ˈrɪtʃ.lər (US) -lɚ
Richmond ˈrɪtʃ.mənd
Richter ˈrɪk.tə, ˈrɪx- (US) ˈrɪk.tɚ- **ˈRichter ˌscale**
Richthofen ˈrɪk.təʊ.fən, ˈrɪx- (US) -toʊ-
rick rɪk **-s** -s
Rickard ˈrɪk.ɑːd (US) -ɑːrd **-s** -z
rickets ˈrɪk.ɪts
Rickett ˈrɪk.ɪt
Ricketts ˈrɪk.ɪts
rickettsi|a rɪˈket.si|.ə **-ae** -iː **-as** -əz
rickety ˈrɪk.ə.t|i, -ɪ.t|i (US) -ə.t̬|i **-ier** -i.ər (US) -i.ɚ **-iest** -i.ɪst, -i.əst **-ily** -ɪ.li, -əl.i **-iness** -ɪ.nəs, -ɪ.nɪs
Rickmansworth ˈrɪk.mənz.wəθ, -wɜːθ (US) -wɚθ, -wɜːrθ
rickshaw ˈrɪk.ʃɔː (US) -ʃɑː, -ʃɔː **-s** -z
Ricky ˈrɪk.i
Rico ˈriː.kəʊ (US) -koʊ
ricoch|et ˈrɪk.ə.ʃ|eɪ, -ɒʃ|.eɪ, -et, ˌ--ˈ- (US) ˈrɪk.ə.ʃ|eɪ, ˌ--ˈ- **-ets** -eɪz, -ets (US) -eɪz **-eting** -eɪ.ɪŋ, -et.ɪŋ (US) -eɪ.ɪŋ **-eted** -eɪd, -et.ɪd (US) -eɪd
ricotta rɪˈkɒt.ə, rə- (US) -ˈkɑː.t̬ə
rictus ˈrɪk.təs
rid rɪd **-s** -z **-ding** -ɪŋ
Ridd rɪd
riddance ˈrɪd.ənts
Riddell ˈrɪd.əl; rɪˈdel
-ridden -ˌrɪd.ən
Ridding ˈrɪd.ɪŋ
riddl|e ˈrɪd.l̩ **-es** -z **-ing** -ɪŋ, ˈrɪd.lɪŋ **-ed** -d
rid|e (R) raɪd **-es** -z **-ing** -ɪŋ **rode** rəʊd (US) roʊd **ridden** ˈrɪd.ən
rid|er (R) ˈraɪ.d|ər (US) -d|ɚ **-ers** -əz (US) -ɚz **-erless** -əl.əs, -ɪs, -es (US) -ɚ.ləs, -lɪs, -les
ridg|e (R) rɪdʒ **-es** -ɪz **-ed** -d
ridgepole ˈrɪdʒ.pəʊl (US) -poʊl **-s** -z
Ridg(e)way ˈrɪdʒ.weɪ
ridicul|e ˈrɪd.ɪ.kjuːl, ˈ-ə- **-es** -z **-ing** -ɪŋ **-ed** -d
ridiculous rɪˈdɪk.jə.ləs, rə-, -jʊ- **-ly** -li **-ness** -nəs, -nɪs
Riding ˈraɪ.dɪŋ **-s** -z
Ridley ˈrɪd.li
Ridout ˈrɪd.aʊt, ˈraɪ.daʊt
Ridpath ˈrɪd.pɑːθ (US) -pæθ
riel ˈriː.əl (US) riˈel
Rienzi riˈen.zi, -ˈent.si (US) -ˈen.zi
Riesling ˈriː.slɪŋ, ˈriːz.lɪŋ (US) ˈriːz-, ˈriː.slɪŋ
Rievaulx ˈriː.vəʊ, -vəʊz; ˈrɪv.əz (US) ˈriː.voʊ, -voʊz; ˈrɪv.əz
Note: /ˈriː.vəʊ (US) -voʊ/ is the usual local pronunciation.
rife raɪf
riff rɪf **-s** -s
riffl|e ˈrɪf.l̩ **-es** -z **-ing** -ɪŋ, ˈrɪf.lɪŋ **-ed** -d
riff-raff ˈrɪf.ræf
Rifkind ˈrɪf.kɪnd
rifl|e ˈraɪ.fl̩ **-es** -z **-ing** -ɪŋ, ˈraɪ.flɪŋ **-ed** -d **ˈrifle ˌrange**
rift rɪft **-s** -s **-ing** -ɪŋ **-ed** -ɪd **ˌrift ˈvalley, ˈrift ˌvalley**
rig rɪg **-s** -z **-ging** -ɪŋ **-ged** -d
Riga ˈriː.gə
rigatoni ˌrɪg.əˈtəʊ.ni (US) -ˈtoʊ-
Rigby ˈrɪg.bi
Rigel ˈraɪ.gəl, -dʒəl (US) -dʒəl, -gəl
Rigg rɪg
rigger ˈrɪg.ər (US) -ɚ **-s** -z
rigging (*n.*) ˈrɪg.ɪŋ **-s** -z
right (R) raɪt **-s** -s **-ly** -li **-ness** -nəs, -nɪs **-ing** -ɪŋ (US) ˈraɪ.t̬ɪŋ **-ed** -ɪd (US) ˈraɪ.t̬ɪd **ˈright ˌangle** ; **ˌright ˈwing**
rightabout ˈraɪt.əˌbaʊt (US) ˈraɪt̬-
right angle (*n.*) ˈraɪtˌæŋ.gl̩ (US) ˈraɪt- **-s** -z
right-angled (*adj.*) ˈraɪtˌæŋ.gl̩*d* (US) ˈraɪt-, ˌ-ˈ--
righteous ˈraɪ.tʃəs, -ti.əs (US) -tʃəs **-ly** -li **-ness** -nəs, -nɪs
rightful ˈraɪt.fəl, -fʊl **-ly** -i **-ness** -nəs, -nɪs
right-hand ˌraɪtˈhænd (US) ˌraɪtˈhænd, ˈ-- *stress shift, British only, see compound:* **ˌright-hand ˈman**
right-handed ˌraɪtˈhæn.dɪd *stress shift:* ˌright-handed ˈplayer
right(h)o ˌraɪtˈəʊ (US) -ˈoʊ
rightism (R) ˈraɪ.t|ɪ.zəm (US) -t̬|ɪ- **-ist/s** -ɪst/s
rightist ˈraɪ.tɪst **-s** -s
right-minded ˌraɪtˈmaɪn.dɪd **-ly** -li **-ness** -nəs, -nɪs *stress shift:* ˌright-minded ˈperson
right-of-way ˌraɪt.əvˈweɪ (US) ˌraɪt.əvˈweɪ, ˈ--ˌ- **rights-of-way** ˌraɪts- (US) ˌraɪts-, ˈ--ˌ-
right-on ˌraɪtˈɒn (US) -ˈɑːn *stress shift:* ˌright-on ˈspeaker
right-wing (*adj.*) ˌraɪtˈwɪŋ **-er/s** -ər/s (US) -ɚ/z *stress shift:* ˌright-wing ˈpolicies
righty-ho ˌraɪ.tiˈhəʊ (US) -t̬iˈhoʊ
rigid ˈrɪdʒ.ɪd **-ly** -li **-ness** -nəs, -nɪs
rigidity rɪˈdʒɪd.ə.ti, -ɪ.ti (US) -ə.t̬i
rigmarole ˈrɪg.mər.əʊl (US) -mə.roʊl **-s** -z
Rigoletto ˌrɪg.əʊˈlet.əʊ (US) -əˈlet.oʊ
rigor ˈrɪg.ər (US) -ɚ
rigor mortis ˌrɪg.əˈmɔː.tɪs, ˌraɪ.gɔːˈ- (US) ˌrɪg.ɚˈmɔːr.t̬ɪs, ˌraɪ.gɔːrˈ-
rigorous ˈrɪg.ər.əs **-ly** -li **-ness** -nəs, -nɪs
rigour ˈrɪg.ər (US) -ɚ **-s** -z
rig-out ˈrɪg.aʊt
Rig-Veda ˌrɪgˈveɪ.də (US) -ˈveɪ-, -ˈviː-
Rijeka riˈek.ə (US) -ˈjek-, -ˈek-
Rikki-Tiki-Tavi ˌrɪk.iˌtɪk.iˈtɑː.vi, -ˈteɪ- (US) -ˈtɑː-, -ˈtæv.i
ril|e raɪl **-es** -z **-ing** -ɪŋ **-ed** -d
Riley ˈraɪ.li
rilievo ˌrɪl.iˈeɪ.vəʊ (US) -voʊ, -ˈjeɪ-
Rilke ˈrɪl.kə
rill rɪl **-s** -z
rim rɪm **-s** -z **-ming** -ɪŋ **-med** -d **-less** -ləs, -lɪs
Rimbaud ˈræ̃*m*.bəʊ (US) ræmˈboʊ
rime raɪm **-s** -z
Rimington ˈrɪm.ɪŋ.tən
Rimini ˈrɪm.ɪ.ni, ˈ-ə- (US) ˈ-ə-
Rimsky-Korsakov ˌrɪm*p*.skiˈkɔː.sə.kɒf, -kɒv (US) -ˈkɔːr.sə.kɔːf
Rinaldo rɪˈnæl.dəʊ (US) rɪˈnɑːl.doʊ, -næl-
rind raɪnd **-s** -z
Rind rɪnd
rinderpest ˈrɪn.də.pest (US) -dɚ-
ring (*n. v.*) *encircle, put a ring on, etc.:* rɪŋ **-s** -z **-ing** -ɪŋ **-ed** -d **ˈring ˌbinder, ˌring ˈbinder** ; **ˈring ˌfinger** ;

'**ring ˌroad** ; ˌ**run 'rings round ˌsomeone**
ring (*n. v.*) *sound, etc.*: rɪŋ **-s** -z **-ing** -ɪŋ **rang** ræŋ **rung** rʌŋ **-er/s** -əʳ/z Ⓤⓢ -ɚ/z
ringgit 'rɪŋ.gɪt **-s** -s
ringleader 'rɪŋˌliː.dəʳ Ⓤⓢ -dɚ **-s** -z
ring|let 'rɪŋ|.lɪt, -lət Ⓤⓢ -lɪt **-lets** -lɪts, -ləts Ⓤⓢ -lɪts **-leted** -lɪ.tɪd, -lə.tɪd Ⓤⓢ -lɪ.t̬ɪd
ringmaster 'rɪŋˌmɑː.stəʳ Ⓤⓢ -ˌmæs.tɚ **-s** -z
Ringshall 'rɪŋ.ʃᵊl
ringside 'rɪŋ.saɪd ˌ**ringside 'seat**
ring-tailed 'rɪŋ.teɪld
Ringwood 'rɪŋ.wʊd
ringworm 'rɪŋ.wɜːm Ⓤⓢ -wɜːrm
rink rɪŋk **-s** -s
rinky-dink 'rɪŋ.ki.dɪŋk
rins|e rɪn*t*s **-es** -ɪz **-ing** -ɪŋ **-ed** -t
Rintoul 'rɪn.tuːl, -'-
Rio 'riː.əʊ Ⓤⓢ -oʊ
Rio de Janeiro ˌriː.əʊ.də.dʒə'nɪə.rəʊ, -deɪ-, -dɪ-, -ʒə'-, -'neə- Ⓤⓢ -oʊ.deɪ.ʒə'ner.oʊ, -diː-, -də-, -dʒə'-, -'nɪr-
Rio Grande ˌriː.əʊ'grænd, -'græn.di, -deɪ Ⓤⓢ -oʊ'grænd, -'græn.di, -'grɑːn.deɪ
rioja (R) ri'ɒk.ə, -'ɒx-, -'əʊ.kə Ⓤⓢ -'ɔː.hɑː, -'oʊ-
riot raɪət **-s** -s **-ing** -ɪŋ Ⓤⓢ 'raɪə.t̬ɪŋ **-ed** -ɪd Ⓤⓢ 'raɪə.t̬ɪd **-er/s** -əʳ/z Ⓤⓢ 'raɪə.t̬ɚ/z '**riot poˌlice** ; ˌ**read someone the 'riot act**
riotous 'raɪə.təs Ⓤⓢ -t̬əs **-ly** -li **-ness** -nəs, -nɪs
rip rɪp **-s** -s **-ping** -ɪŋ **-ped** -t
RIP ˌɑːʳ.aɪ'piː Ⓤⓢ ˌɑːr-
riparian raɪ'peə.ri.ən, rɪ- Ⓤⓢ rɪ'per.i-, raɪ-
ripcord 'rɪp.kɔːd Ⓤⓢ -kɔːrd **-s** -z
rip|e raɪp **-er** -əʳ Ⓤⓢ -ɚ **-est** -ɪst, -əst **-ely** -li **-eness** -nəs, -nɪs
ripen 'raɪ.pᵊn **-s** -z **-ing** -ɪŋ **-ed** -d
ripien|o ˌrɪp.i'eɪ.n|əʊ Ⓤⓢ rɪ'pjeɪ.n|oʊ **-os** -əʊz Ⓤⓢ -oʊz **-i** -iː
Ripley 'rɪp.li
Ripman 'rɪp.mən
rip-off 'rɪp.ɒf Ⓤⓢ -ɑːf **-s** -s
Ripon 'rɪp.ən
ripost|e, ripost rɪ'pɒst, -'pəʊst Ⓤⓢ -'poʊst **-(e)s** -s **-ing** -ɪŋ **-ed** -ɪd
ripper 'rɪp.əʳ Ⓤⓢ -ɚ **-s** -z
ripping 'rɪp.ɪŋ **-ly** -li
rippl|e 'rɪp.l̩ **-es** -z **-ing** -ɪŋ, 'rɪp.lɪŋ **-ed** -d
rip-roaring ˌrɪp'rɔː.rɪŋ Ⓤⓢ -'rɔːr.ɪŋ
stress shift: ˌrip-roaring 'wave
ripsnort|ing ˌrɪp'snɔː.t|ɪŋ Ⓤⓢ -'snɔːr.t̬|ɪŋ **-er/s** -əʳ/z Ⓤⓢ -ɚ/z
stress shift: ˌripsnorting 'finish
riptide 'rɪp.taɪd **-s** -z
Ripuarian ˌrɪp.ju'eə.ri.ən Ⓤⓢ -'er.i-
Rip van Winkle ˌrɪp.væn'wɪŋ.kl̩
Risborough, -boro' 'rɪz.bᵊr.ə Ⓤⓢ -bɚ.oʊ
Risca 'rɪs.kə
ris|e raɪz **-es** -ɪz **-ing** -ɪŋ **rose** rəʊz Ⓤⓢ roʊz **risen** 'rɪz.ᵊn
riser 'raɪ.zəʳ Ⓤⓢ -zɚ **-s** -z
Rishton 'rɪʃ.tᵊn
risibility ˌrɪz.ə'bɪl.ə.ti, ˌraɪ.zə'-, -zɪ'-, -ɪ.ti Ⓤⓢ ˌrɪz.ə'bɪl.ə.t̬i
risib|le 'rɪz.ə.b|l̩, 'raɪ.zə-, -zɪ- Ⓤⓢ 'rɪz.ə- **-ly** -li
rising 'raɪ.zɪŋ **-s** -z
risk rɪsk **-s** -s **-ing** -ɪŋ **-ed** -t
risk|y 'rɪs.k|i **-ier** -i.əʳ Ⓤⓢ -i.ɚ **-iest** -i.ɪst, -i.əst **-iness** -ɪ.nəs, -ɪ.nɪs
Risley 'rɪz.li
risotto rɪ'zɒt.əʊ, -'sɒt- Ⓤⓢ -'zɑː.t̬oʊ, -'sɑː- **-s** -z
risqué 'rɪs.keɪ, 'riː.skeɪ Ⓤⓢ rɪ'skeɪ
rissole 'rɪs.əʊl Ⓤⓢ -oʊl **-s** -z
Rita 'riː.tə Ⓤⓢ -t̬ə
ritardando ˌrɪt.ɑː'dæn.dəʊ Ⓤⓢ ˌriː.tɑːr'dɑːn.doʊ **-s** -z
Ritchie 'rɪtʃ.i
rite raɪt **-s** -s ˌ**rite of 'passage**
ritornell|o ˌrɪt.ɔː'nel|.əʊ, -ᵊn'el- Ⓤⓢ -ɚ'nel|.oʊ, -ɔːr'- **-os** -əʊz Ⓤⓢ -oʊz **-i** -iː
Ritson 'rɪt.sᵊn
ritual 'rɪt.ju.əl, 'rɪtʃ.u- Ⓤⓢ 'rɪtʃ- **-s** -z
ritual|ism 'rɪt.ju.ᵊl|.ɪ.zᵊm, 'rɪtʃ.u- Ⓤⓢ 'rɪtʃ- **-ist/s** -ɪst/s
ritualistic ˌrɪt.ju.ᵊl'ɪs.tɪk, ˌrɪtʃ.u- Ⓤⓢ ˌrɪtʃ- **-ally** -ᵊl.i, -li
ritualiz|e, -is|e 'rɪt.ju.ᵊl.aɪz, 'rɪtʃ.u- Ⓤⓢ 'rɪtʃ- **-es** -ɪz **-ing** -ɪŋ **-ed** -d
Ritz rɪts
ritz|y 'rɪt.s|i **-ier** -i.əʳ Ⓤⓢ -i.ɚ **-iest** -i.ɪst, -i.əst **-iness** -ɪ.nəs, -ɪ.nɪs
rival 'raɪ.vᵊl **-s** -z **-(l)ing** -ɪŋ **-(l)ed** -d
rivalr|y 'raɪ.vᵊl.r|i **-ies** -iz
riv|e raɪv **-es** -z **-ing** -ɪŋ **-ed** -d
riven 'rɪv.ᵊn
river (R) 'rɪv.əʳ Ⓤⓢ -ɚ **-s** -z '**river ˌbank**, ˌ**river 'bank** ; '**river ˌbed**, ˌ**river 'bed** ; ˌ**sell someone ˌdown the 'river**
Rivera rɪ'veə.rə Ⓤⓢ -'ver.ə
riverboat 'rɪv.ə.bəʊt Ⓤⓢ -ɚ.boʊt **-s** -s
Rivers 'rɪv.əz Ⓤⓢ -ɚz
riverside (R) 'rɪv.ə.saɪd Ⓤⓢ '-ɚ-
riv|et 'rɪv|.ɪt, -ət Ⓤⓢ -ɪt **-ets** -ɪts, -əts Ⓤⓢ -ɪts **-eting** -ɪ.tɪŋ, -ə.tɪŋ Ⓤⓢ -ɪ.t̬ɪŋ **-eted** -ɪ.tɪd, -ə.tɪd Ⓤⓢ -ɪ.t̬ɪd **-eter/s** -ɪ.təʳ/z, -ə.təʳ/z Ⓤⓢ -ɪ.t̬ɚ/z
Riviera ˌrɪv.i'eə.rə Ⓤⓢ -'er.ə
Rivington 'rɪv.ɪŋ.tən **-s** -z
rivulet 'rɪv.jə.lət, -jʊ-, -lɪt, -let Ⓤⓢ -lɪt **-s** -s
Rix rɪks
Riyadh 'riː.æd; -ɑːd, -'- Ⓤⓢ riː'jɑːd
riyal ri'ɑːl, -'æl; 'riː.ɑːl, -æl Ⓤⓢ riː'jɑːl, -'jɔːl, -'ɑːl, -'ɔːl **-s** -z
Rizla® 'rɪz.lə
Rizzio 'rɪt.si.əʊ Ⓤⓢ -oʊ
RN (*abbrev. for* **Royal Navy**) ˌɑːʳ'en; ˌrɔɪəl'neɪ.vi Ⓤⓢ ˌɑːr'en; ˌrɔɪəl'neɪ.vi
roach (R) rəʊtʃ Ⓤⓢ roʊtʃ **-es** -ɪz
road rəʊd Ⓤⓢ roʊd **-s** -z '**road ˌhog** ; '**road ˌrage** ; '**road ˌtax**
roadblock 'rəʊd.blɒk Ⓤⓢ 'roʊd.blɑːk **-s** -s
roadhou|se 'rəʊd.haʊ|s Ⓤⓢ 'roʊd- **-ses** -zɪz
roadie 'rəʊ.di Ⓤⓢ 'roʊ- **-s** -z
roadrunner 'rəʊdˌrʌn.əʳ Ⓤⓢ 'roʊdˌrʌn.ɚ **-s** -z
roadshow 'rəʊd.ʃəʊ Ⓤⓢ 'roʊd.ʃoʊ **-s** -z
roadside 'rəʊd.saɪd Ⓤⓢ 'roʊd-
roadstead 'rəʊd.sted Ⓤⓢ 'roʊd- **-s** -z
roadster 'rəʊd.stəʳ Ⓤⓢ 'roʊd.stɚ **-s** -z
road-test 'rəʊd.test Ⓤⓢ 'roʊd- **-s** -s **-ing** -ɪŋ **-ed** -ɪd
roadway 'rəʊd.weɪ Ⓤⓢ 'roʊd- **-s** -z
roadworks 'rəʊd.wɜːks Ⓤⓢ 'roʊd.wɜːrks
roadworth|y 'rəʊdˌwɜː.ð|i Ⓤⓢ 'roʊdˌwɜːr- **-iness** -ɪ.nəs, -ɪ.nɪs
Roald rəʊəld Ⓤⓢ roʊəld
roam rəʊm Ⓤⓢ roʊm **-s** -z **-ing** -ɪŋ **-ed** -d
roan (R) rəʊn Ⓤⓢ roʊn **-s** -z
Roanoke 'rəʊə.nəʊk, 'rəʊ-, ˌrəʊə'nəʊk Ⓤⓢ 'roʊə.noʊk
roar rɔːʳ Ⓤⓢ rɔːr **-s** -z **-ing** -ɪŋ **-ed** -d
roast rəʊst Ⓤⓢ roʊst **-s** -s **-ing** -ɪŋ **-ed** -ɪd **-er/s** -əʳ/z Ⓤⓢ -ɚ/z
rob (R) rɒb Ⓤⓢ rɑːb **-s** -z **-bing** -ɪŋ **-bed** -d
Robb rɒb Ⓤⓢ rɑːb
robber 'rɒb.əʳ Ⓤⓢ 'rɑː.bɚ **-s** -z
robber|y 'rɒb.ᵊr|.i Ⓤⓢ 'rɑː.bɚ|.i, '-br|i **-ies** -iz
Robbins 'rɒb.ɪnz Ⓤⓢ 'rɑː.bɪnz
rob|e rəʊb Ⓤⓢ roʊb **-es** -z **-ing** -ɪŋ **-ed** -d
Robens 'rəʊ.bɪnz Ⓤⓢ 'roʊ-
Roberson 'rəʊ.bə.sᵊn, 'rɒb.ə- Ⓤⓢ 'roʊ.bɚ-, 'rɑː-
Note: In **Roberson's medium** the usual pronunciation is /'rɒb.ə- Ⓤⓢ 'rɑː.bɚ-/.
Robert 'rɒb.ət Ⓤⓢ 'rɑː.bɚt **-s** -s
Roberta rəʊ'bɜː.tə, rɒb'ɜː- Ⓤⓢ rə'bɜːr.t̬ə, roʊ-
Roberto rəʊ'bɜː.təʊ, rɒb'ɜː- Ⓤⓢ rə'bɜːr.t̬oʊ, roʊ-, -toʊ
Robertson 'rɒb.ət.sᵊn Ⓤⓢ 'rɑːb.ɚt-
Robeson 'rəʊb.sᵊn Ⓤⓢ 'roʊb-
Robespierre 'rəʊbz.pjeəʳ, -pɪəʳ, 'rəʊb.spjeəʳ, -spɪəʳ Ⓤⓢ ˌroʊbz'pjer, -'pɪr, -pi'er

robin (R) 'rɒb.ɪn (US) 'rɑː.bɪn **-s** -z **ˌRobin 'Hood,** (US) **'Robin ˌHood** ; **ˌRobin Hood's 'Bay**
Robina rɒb'iː.nə, rəʊ'biː- (US) rə'biː-, roʊ-
Robins 'rəʊ.bɪnz, 'rɒb.ɪnz (US) 'rɑː.bɪnz, 'roʊ-
Robinson 'rɒb.ɪn.sᵊn (US) 'rɑː.bɪn- **ˌRobinson 'Crusoe**
robot 'rəʊ.bɒt (US) 'roʊ.bɑːt, -bət **-s** -s
Robotham 'rəʊ.bɒθ.əm, -bɒt- (US) 'roʊ.bɑː.θəm, -bɑː.t̬əm
robotic rəʊ'bɒt.ɪk (US) roʊ'bɑː.t̬ɪk **-s** -s
Rob Roy ˌrɒb'rɔɪ (US) ˌrɑːb-
Robsart 'rɒb.sɑːt (US) 'rɑːb.sɑːrt
Robson 'rɒb.sᵊn (US) 'rɑːb-
robust rəʊ'bʌst (US) roʊ-, '-- **-ly** -li **-ness** -nəs, -nɪs
Roby 'rəʊ.bi (US) 'roʊ-
Robyn 'rɒb.ɪn (US) 'rɑː.bɪn
Rochdale 'rɒtʃ.deɪl (US) 'rɑːtʃ-
Roche rəʊtʃ, rəʊʃ, rɒʃ (US) roʊtʃ, roʊʃ, rɑːʃ
Rochester 'rɒtʃ.ɪ.stəʳ, '-ə- (US) 'rɑː.tʃə.stɚ, -tʃes.tɚ
rochet 'rɒtʃ.ɪt (US) 'rɑː.tʃɪt **-s** -s
Rochford 'rɒtʃ.fəd (US) 'rɑːtʃ.fɚd
rock (R) rɒk (US) rɑːk **-s** -s **-ing** -ɪŋ **-ed** -t **-er/s** -əʳ/z (US) -ɚ/z **'rock ˌcake** ; **'rock ˌclimbing** ; **'rock ˌgarden** ; **'rock ˌsalmon** ; **'rock ˌsalt** ; **'rocking ˌchair** ; **'rocking ˌhorse**
rockabilly 'rɒk.əˌbɪl.i (US) 'rɑː.kəˌ-
rock-and-roll ˌrɒk.ᵊnd'rəʊl (US) ˌrɑːk.ᵊnd'roʊl **-er/s** -əʳ/z (US) -ɚ/z *stress shift:* ˌrock-and-roll 'music
rock-bottom ˌrɒk'bɒt.əm (US) ˌrɑːk'bɑː.t̬əm *stress shift:* ˌrock-bottom 'level
rockbound 'rɒk.baʊnd (US) 'rɑːk-
Rockefeller 'rɒk.əˌfel.əʳ, -ɪˌ- (US) 'rɑː.kəˌfel.ɚ **'Rockefeller ˌCenter** (US) **ˌRockefeller 'Center**
rocker|y 'rɒk.ᵊr|.i (US) 'rɑː.kɚ- **-ies** -iz
rock|et 'rɒk|.ɪt (US) 'rɑː.k|ɪt **-ets** -ɪts **-eting** -ɪ.tɪŋ (US) -ɪ.t̬ɪŋ **-eted** -ɪ.tɪd (US) -ɪ.t̬ɪd **'rocket ˌbase** ; **'rocket ˌrange**
rocketry 'rɒk.ɪ.tri, '-ə- (US) 'rɑː.kɪ-, -kə-
rockfall 'rɒk.fɔːl (US) 'rɑːk-, -fɑːl **-s** -z
Rockhampton rɒk'hæmp.tən (US) rɑːk-
Rockies 'rɒk.iz (US) 'rɑː.kiz
Rockingham 'rɒk.ɪŋ.əm (US) 'rɑː.kɪŋ-
Rockne 'rɒk.ni (US) 'rɑːk-
rock 'n' roll ˌrɒk.ᵊnd'rəʊl (US) ˌrɑːk.ᵊnd'roʊl **-er/s** -əʳ/z (US) -ɚ/z *stress shift:* ˌrock 'n' roll 'music
rockros|e 'rɒk.rəʊz (US) 'rɑːk.roʊz **-es** -ɪz
Rockwell 'rɒk.wel, -wəl (US) 'rɑː.kwel, -kwəl

rock|y (R) 'rɒk|.i (US) 'rɑː.k|i **-ier** -i.əʳ (US) -i.ɚ **-iest** -i.ɪst, -i.əst **-iness** -ɪ.nəs, -ɪ.nɪs **ˌRocky 'Mountains**
rococo rəʊ'kəʊ.kəʊ (US) rə'koʊ.koʊ; ˌroʊ.kə'koʊ
rod (R) rɒd (US) rɑːd **-s** -z **make a ˌrod for one's ˌown 'back** ; **ˌrule someone with a ˌrod of 'iron**
Roddick 'rɒd.ɪk (US) 'rɑː.dɪk
rode (*from* **ride**) rəʊd (US) roʊd
Roden 'rəʊ.dᵊn (US) 'roʊ-
rodent 'rəʊ.dᵊnt (US) 'roʊ- **-s** -s
rodeo rəʊ'deɪ.əʊ; 'rəʊ.di- (US) 'roʊ.di.oʊ; roʊ'deɪ.oʊ **-s** -z
Roderic(k) 'rɒd.ᵊr.ɪk (US) 'rɑː.dɚ-
Rodger 'rɒdʒ.əʳ (US) 'rɑː.dʒɚ **-s** -z
Rodgers 'rɒdʒ.əz (US) 'rɑː.dʒɚz
Rodin 'rəʊ.dæ̃ŋ (US) roʊ'dæ̃n
Roding 'rəʊ.dɪŋ *locally sometimes:* 'ruː.dɪŋ, -ðɪŋ (US) 'roʊ.dɪŋ, 'ruː-, -ðɪŋ
Rodmell 'rɒd.mᵊl (US) 'rɑːd-
Rodney 'rɒd.ni (US) 'rɑːd-
rodomontad|e ˌrɒd.ə.mɒn'teɪd, ˌrəʊ.də-, -'tɑːd (US) ˌrɑː.də.mən'teɪd, ˌroʊ-, -'tɑːd **-es** -z **-ing** -ɪŋ **-ed** -ɪd
Rodriguez rɒd'riː.gez (US) rɑː'driː.ges, -geɪs, -geɪz, -gəz
Rodway 'rɒd.weɪ (US) 'rɑːd-
roe (R) rəʊ (US) roʊ **-s** -z
Roebling 'rəʊ.blɪŋ (US) 'roʊ-
roebuck (R) 'rəʊ.bʌk (US) 'roʊ- **-s** -s
Roedean 'rəʊ.diːn (US) 'roʊ-
Roehampton rəʊ'hæmp.tən (US) roʊ- *stress shift:* ˌRoehampton 'College
roentgen (R) 'rɒn.tjən, 'rɜːn-, 'rɒnt.gən, 'rɜːn- (US) 'rent.gən, 'rɜːnt-, 'rʌnt-, 'ren.tʃən, 'rɜːn-, 'rʌn- **-s** -z
Roethke 'ret.kə (US) 'ret-, 'reθ-, -ki
rogation (R) rəʊ'geɪ.ʃᵊn (US) roʊ- **-s** -z
rogatory 'rɒg.ə.tᵊr.i, -tri (US) 'rɑː.gə.tɔːr-
rog|er (R) 'rɒdʒ|.əʳ (US) 'rɑː.dʒ|ɚ **-ers** -əz (US) -ɚz **-ering** -ᵊr.ɪŋ **-ered** -əd (US) -ɚd
Roget 'rɒʒ.eɪ, 'rəʊ.ʒeɪ (US) ˌroʊ'ʒeɪ, '-- **ˌRoget's The'saurus**
rogue rəʊg (US) roʊg **-s** -z **ˌrogue's 'gallery**
roguer|y 'rəʊ.gᵊr|.i (US) 'roʊ- **-ies** -iz
roguish 'rəʊ.gɪʃ (US) 'roʊ- **-ly** -li **-ness** -nəs, -nɪs
roil rɔɪl **-s** -z **-ing** -ɪŋ **-ed** -d
roist|er 'rɔɪ.st|əʳ (US) -st|ɚ **-ers** -əz (US) -ɚz **-ering** -ᵊr.ɪŋ **-ered** -əd (US) -ɚd **-erer/s** -ᵊr.əʳ/z (US) -ɚ.ɚ/z
Rokeby 'rəʊk.bi (US) 'roʊk-
Roker 'rəʊ.kəʳ (US) 'roʊ.kɚ
Roland 'rəʊ.lənd (US) 'roʊ-
role, rôle rəʊl (US) roʊl **-s** -z **'role ˌmodel**

roleplay 'rəʊl.pleɪ (US) 'roʊl- **-s** -z **-ing** -ɪŋ **-ed** -d
Rolex® 'rəʊ.leks (US) 'roʊ-
Rolf(e) rɒlf, rəʊf (US) rɑːlf
roll rəʊl (US) roʊl **-s** -z **-ing** -ɪŋ **-ed** -d **'roll ˌbar** ; **'roll ˌcall** ; **'rolling ˌpin** ; **'rolling ˌstock** ; **ˌrolling 'stone** ; **ˌRolling 'Stones**
Rollason 'rɒl.ə.sᵊn (US) 'rɑː.lə-
roller 'rəʊ.ləʳ (US) 'roʊ.lɚ **-s** -z **'roller ˌblind** ; **'roller ˌcoaster,** **ˌroller 'coaster**
Rollerblade® 'rəʊ.lə.bleɪd (US) 'roʊ.lɚ- **-s** -z
roller|-skate 'rəʊ.lə|.skeɪt (US) 'roʊ.lɚ- **-skates** -skeɪts **-skating** -skeɪ.tɪŋ (US) -skeɪ.t̬ɪŋ **-skated** -skeɪ.tɪd (US) -skeɪ.t̬ɪd
Rolleston 'rəʊl.stᵊn (US) 'roʊl-
rollicking 'rɒl.ɪ.kɪŋ (US) 'rɑː.lɪ- **-ly** -li
Rollins 'rɒl.ɪnz (US) 'rɑː.lɪnz
rollmop 'rəʊl.mɒp (US) 'roʊl.mɑːp **-s** -s
rollneck 'rəʊl.nek (US) 'roʊl- **-s** -s
Rollo 'rɒl.əʊ (US) 'rɑː.loʊ
roll-on 'rəʊl.ɒn (US) 'roʊl.ɑːn **-s** -z
Rolls rəʊlz (US) roʊlz
Rolls-Royc|e® ˌrəʊlz'rɔɪs (US) ˌroʊlz- **-es** -ɪz *stress shift:* ˌRolls-Royce 'engine
roll-top 'rəʊl.tɒp (US) 'roʊl.tɑːp **-s** -s
Rolo® 'rəʊ.ləʊ (US) 'roʊ.loʊ
Rolodex® 'rəʊ.lə.deks (US) 'roʊ-
Rolph rɒlf (US) rɑːlf
roly-pol|y ˌrəʊ.li'pəʊ.l|i (US) ˌroʊ.li'poʊ- **-ies** -iz *stress shift:* ˌroly-poly 'pudding
ROM rɒm (US) rɑːm
Romagna rəʊ'mɑː.njə (US) roʊ'-
Romaic rəʊ'meɪ.ɪk (US) roʊ-
romaine rəʊ'meɪn (US) rə-, roʊ- **roˌmaine 'lettuce,** **ˌromaine 'lettuce**
Roman 'rəʊ.mən (US) 'roʊ- **-s** -z **ˌRoman 'candle** ; **ˌRoman 'Catholic** ; **ˌRoman Ca'tholicism** ; **ˌRoman 'Empire** ; **ˌRoman 'holiday** ; **ˌRoman 'nose** ; **ˌRoman 'numeral**
roman(s) à clef rəʊˌmɑ̃ːn.ɑː'kleɪ (US) roʊ-
roman à thèse rəʊˌmɑ̃ːn.ɑː'teɪz (US) roʊ-
romanc|e (R) rəʊ'mænts; 'rəʊ.mænts (US) roʊ'mænts, '-- **-es** -ɪz **-ing** -ɪŋ **-ed** -t **-er/s** -əʳ/z (US) -ɚ/z
Romanes *surname:* rəʊ'mɑː.nɪz, -nɪs, -nes (US) roʊ'mɑː.nɪz *gypsy language:* 'rɒm.ə.nes, -nɪs (US) 'rɑː.mə-
Romanesque ˌrəʊ.mᵊn'esk (US) ˌroʊ- *stress shift:* ˌRomanesque 'church
roman fleuve rəʊˌmɑ̃ːŋ'flɜːv (US) roʊ-
Romani|a ruː'meɪ.ni|.ə, rəʊ-, ruː- (US) roʊ-, ruː-, '-nj|ə **-an/s** -ən/z

Romanic rəʊ'mæn.ɪk ⓤⓢ roʊ-
Roman|ism 'rəʊ.mᵊn|.ɪ.zᵊm ⓤⓢ 'roʊ- **-ist/s** -ɪst/s
romanization, -isa- ˌrəʊ.mᵊn.aɪ'zeɪ.ʃᵊn, -ɪ'- ⓤⓢ ˌroʊ.mᵊn.ɪ'- **-s** -z
romaniz|e, -is|e 'rəʊ.mᵊn.aɪz ⓤⓢ 'roʊ- **-es** -ɪz **-ing** -ɪŋ **-ed** -d
Romanov 'rəʊ.mᵊn.ɒf, -nɒv ⓤⓢ 'roʊ.mə.nɔːf; roʊ'mɑː-
Romans(c)h rəʊ'mænʃ, rʊ- ⓤⓢ roʊ'mɑːnʃ, -'mænʃ
romantic (R) rəʊ'mæn.tɪk ⓤⓢ roʊ'mæn.t̬ɪk **-ally** -ᵊl.i, -li
romantic|ism (R) rəʊ'mæn.tɪ.s|ɪ.zᵊm, -tə- ⓤⓢ roʊ'mæn.t̬ə- **-ist/s** -ɪst/s
romanticization, -isa- rəʊˌmæn.tɪ.saɪ'zeɪ.ʃᵊn, -tə-, -sɪ'- ⓤⓢ roʊˌmæn.t̬ə.sɪ'-
romanticiz|e, -is|e rəʊ'mæn.tɪ.saɪz, -tə- ⓤⓢ roʊ'mæn.t̬ə- **-es** -ɪz **-ing** -ɪŋ **-ed** -d
Roman|y 'rɒm.ə.n|i, 'rəʊ.mə- ⓤⓢ 'rɑː.mə-, 'roʊ- **-ies** -iz
romaunt rəʊ'mɔːnt ⓤⓢ roʊ'mɑːnt, -'mɔːnt **-s** -s
Rombauer 'rɒm.baʊəʳ ⓤⓢ 'rɑːm.baʊɚ
Rome rəʊm ⓤⓢ roʊm
Romeo 'rəʊ.mi.əʊ; rəʊ'meɪ- ⓤⓢ 'roʊ.mi.oʊ **-s**
Romero rəʊ'meə.roʊ ⓤⓢ roʊ'mer.oʊ, rə-
Romford 'rɒm.fəd, 'rʌm- ⓤⓢ 'rɑːm.fɚd
romic (R) 'rəʊ.mɪk ⓤⓢ 'roʊ-
Romiley 'rɒm.ᵊl.i, -ɪ.li ⓤⓢ 'rɑː.mᵊl.i
Romilly 'rɒm.ᵊl.i, -ɪ.li ⓤⓢ 'rɑː.mᵊl.i
Romish 'rəʊ.mɪʃ ⓤⓢ 'roʊ-
Rommel 'rɒm.ᵊl ⓤⓢ 'rɑː.mᵊl
Romney 'rɒm.ni, 'rʌm- ⓤⓢ 'rɑːm-, 'rʌm- **-s** -z
Romola 'rɒm.ᵊl.ə ⓤⓢ 'rɑː.mᵊl-
romp rɒmp ⓤⓢ rɑːmp **-s** -s **-ing** -ɪŋ **-ed** -t
romper 'rɒm.pəʳ ⓤⓢ 'rɑːm.pɚ **-s** -z **'romper ˌsuit**
Romsey 'rʌm.zi, 'rɒm- ⓤⓢ 'rɑːm-
Romulus 'rɒm.jʊ.ləs, -jə- ⓤⓢ 'rɑː.mjə-, -mjʊ-
Ronald 'rɒn.ᵊld ⓤⓢ 'rɑː.nᵊld
Ronaldshay 'rɒn.ᵊld.ʃeɪ ⓤⓢ 'rɑː.nᵊld-
Ronaldsway 'rɒn.ᵊldz.weɪ ⓤⓢ 'rɑː.nᵊldz-
Ronan 'rəʊ.nən ⓤⓢ 'roʊ-
Ronay 'rəʊ.neɪ ⓤⓢ 'roʊ-
ron|deau 'rɒn|.dəʊ ⓤⓢ 'rɑːn|.doʊ **-deaus** -dəʊz, -dəʊ ⓤⓢ -doʊz **-deaux** -dəʊ ⓤⓢ -doʊ
rondel 'rɒn.dᵊl ⓤⓢ 'rɑːn-, -del **-s** -z
rondo 'rɒn.dəʊ ⓤⓢ 'rɑːn.doʊ **-s** -z
roneo (R®) 'rəʊ.ni.əʊ ⓤⓢ 'roʊ.ni.oʊ **-s** -z **-ing** -ɪŋ **-ed** -d
Ronnie 'rɒn.i ⓤⓢ 'rɑː.ni
Ronson 'rɒnt.sᵊn ⓤⓢ 'rɑːnt-
Ronstadt 'rɒn.stæt ⓤⓢ 'rɑːn-
röntgen, rontgen (R) 'rɒn.tjən, 'rɜːn-, 'rɒnt.gən, 'rɜːnt- ⓤⓢ 'rent.gən, 'rɜːnt-, 'rʌnt-, 'ren.tʃən, 'rɜːn-, 'rʌn- **-s** -z
röntgenogram 'rɒn.tʃən.ə.græm, 'rɜːn-, 'rɒnt.gən-, 'rɜːnt- ⓤⓢ 'rent.gə.nə-, 'rɜːnt-, 'rʌnt-, 'ren.tʃə-, 'rɜːn-, 'rʌn-, -dʒə- **-s** -z
Ronuk 'rɒn.ək ⓤⓢ 'rɑː.nək
rood ruːd **-s** -z **'rood ˌscreen**
roo|f (*n.*) ruː|f ⓤⓢ ruː|f, rʊ|f **-fs** -fs **-ves** -vz **'roof ˌgarden** ; **'roof ˌrack**
roof (*v.*) ruːf ⓤⓢ ruːf, rʊf **-s** -s **-ing** -ɪŋ **-ed** -t
roofer 'ruː.fəʳ ⓤⓢ -fɚ, 'rʊf.ɚ **-s** -z
rooftop 'ruːf.tɒp ⓤⓢ -tɑːp, 'rʊf- **-s** -s
rook rʊk **-s** -s **-ing** -ɪŋ **-ed** -t
Rooke rʊk **-s** -s
rooker|y 'rʊk.ᵊr|.i **-ies** -iz
rookie 'rʊk.i **-s** -z
room (R) ruːm, rʊm **-s** -z **-er/s** -əʳ/z ⓤⓢ -ɚ/z **'room ˌservice** ; **'rooming ˌhouse**
roomful 'ruːm.fʊl, 'rʊm- **-s** -z
roommate 'ruːm.meɪt, 'rʊm- **-s** -s
Rooms ruːmz
room|y 'ruː.m|i, 'rʊm|.i **-ier** -i.əʳ ⓤⓢ -i.ɚ **-iest** -i.ɪst, -i.əst **-ily** -ɪ.li, -ᵊl.i **-iness** -ɪ.nəs, -ɪ.nɪs
Rooney 'ruː.ni
Roosevelt 'rəʊ.zə.velt, 'ruː-, -sə-; 'ruːs.velt ⓤⓢ 'roʊ.zə.velt, 'ruː-, -vəlt; 'roʊz.velt
Note: /'rəʊ.zə.velt ⓤⓢ 'roʊ-/ is the pronunciation used in the families of the late presidents of the U.S.A..
roost (R) ruːst **-s** -s **-ing** -ɪŋ **-ed** -ɪd
rooster 'ruː.stəʳ ⓤⓢ -stɚ **-s** -z
root (R) ruːt **-s** -s **-ing** -ɪŋ ⓤⓢ 'ruː.t̬ɪŋ **-ed** -ɪd ⓤⓢ 'ruː.t̬ɪd **-less/ness** -ləs/nəs, -lɪs/nɪs **'root ˌbeer, ˌroot 'beer** ; **'root caˌnal** ; **'root ˌvegetable, ˌroot 'vegetable**
Rootham 'ruː.təm ⓤⓢ -t̬əm
rootstock 'ruːt.stɒk ⓤⓢ -stɑːk **-s** -s
rop|e rəʊp ⓤⓢ roʊp **-es** -s **-ing** -ɪŋ **-ed** -t **ˌrope 'ladder**
Roper 'rəʊ.pəʳ ⓤⓢ 'roʊ.pɚ
rop|ey, rop|y 'rəʊ.p|i ⓤⓢ 'roʊ- **-ier** -i.əʳ ⓤⓢ -i.ɚ **-iest** -i.ɪst, -i.əst **-iness** -ɪ.nəs, -ɪ.nɪs
Roquefort® 'rɒk.fɔːʳ ⓤⓢ 'roʊk.fɚt
roquet 'rəʊ.ki, -keɪ ⓤⓢ roʊ'keɪ **-s** -z **-ing** -ɪŋ **-ed** -d
Rorke rɔːk ⓤⓢ rɔːrk
Rorqual 'rɔː.kwᵊl, -kᵊl ⓤⓢ 'rɔːr.kwᵊl **-s** -z
Rorschach 'rɔː.ʃɑːk, -ʃæk ⓤⓢ 'rɔːr.ʃɑːk
Rory 'rɔː.ri ⓤⓢ 'rɔːr.i
Ros (*abbrev. for* **Rosalind**) rɒz ⓤⓢ rɑːz
Ros *surname:* rɒs ⓤⓢ rɑːs
Rosa 'rəʊ.zə ⓤⓢ 'roʊ-
rosaceous rəʊ'zeɪ.ʃəs ⓤⓢ roʊ-
Rosalba rəʊ'zæl.bə, rɒz'æl- ⓤⓢ roʊ'zɑːl-, -bɑː
Rosalie 'rəʊ.zᵊl.i, 'rɒz.ᵊl- ⓤⓢ 'roʊ.zə.li, 'rɑː-
Rosalind 'rɒz.ᵊl.ɪnd ⓤⓢ 'rɑː.zə.lɪnd
Rosaline 'rɒz.ᵊl.aɪn, -iːn ⓤⓢ 'rɑː.zə.lɪn, -laɪn
Rosalynde 'rɒz.ᵊl.ɪnd ⓤⓢ 'rɑː.zə.lɪnd
Rosamond 'rɒz.ə.mənd ⓤⓢ 'rɑː.zə-, 'roʊ-
Rosario rəʊ'sɑː.ri.əʊ ⓤⓢ roʊ'zɑːr.i.oʊ, -sɑːr-
rosarium rəʊ'zeə.ri.əm ⓤⓢ roʊ'zer.i- **-s** -z
rosar|y 'rəʊ.zᵊr|.i ⓤⓢ 'roʊ- **-ies** -iz
Roscius 'rɒʃ.i.əs, 'rɒs-; 'rɒs.ki.əs ⓤⓢ 'rɑː.ʃi-, '-ʃəs
Roscoe 'rɒs.kəʊ ⓤⓢ 'rɑː.skoʊ
Roscommon rɒs'kɒm.ən ⓤⓢ rɑː'skɑː.mən
ros|e (R) rəʊz ⓤⓢ roʊz **-es** -ɪz **'rose ˌbush** ; **'rose ˌgarden** ; **'rose ˌwater** ; **ˌrose 'window**
rose (*from* **rise**) rəʊz ⓤⓢ roʊz
rosé 'rəʊ.zeɪ, -'- ⓤⓢ roʊ'zeɪ
Roseanne rəʊ'zæn ⓤⓢ roʊ-
roseate 'rəʊ.zi.ət, -ɪt, -eɪt ⓤⓢ 'roʊ.zi.ɪt, -eɪt
Roseau rəʊ'zəʊ ⓤⓢ roʊ'zoʊ
Rosebery 'rəʊz.bᵊr.i ⓤⓢ 'roʊzˌber-
rosebud 'rəʊz.bʌd ⓤⓢ 'roʊz- **-s** -z
rose-colo(u)red 'rəʊzˌkʌl.əd ⓤⓢ 'roʊzˌkʌl.ɚd
rosehip 'rəʊz.hɪp ⓤⓢ 'roʊz- **-s** -s
rosemary (R) 'rəʊz.mᵊr.i ⓤⓢ 'roʊz.mer-
Rosenberg 'rəʊ.zᵊn.bɜːg, -zᵊm- ⓤⓢ 'roʊ.zᵊn.bɜːrg
Rosencrantz 'rəʊ.zᵊn.krænts, -zᵊŋ- ⓤⓢ 'roʊ-
roseola rəʊ'ziː.ᵊl.ə; ˌrəʊ.zi'əʊ.lə ⓤⓢ roʊ'ziː.ᵊl.ə; ˌroʊ.zi'oʊ.lə
Rosetta rəʊ'zet.ə ⓤⓢ roʊ'zet̬- **Roˌsetta 'Stone** ⓤⓢ **Ro'setta ˌStone**
rosette rəʊ'zet ⓤⓢ roʊ- **-s** -s
rosewood 'rəʊz.wʊd ⓤⓢ 'roʊz-
Rosh Hashana ˌrɒʃ.hæʃ'ɑː.nə, -hə'ʃɑː- ⓤⓢ ˌroʊʃ.hə'ʃɔː.nə, ˌrɑːʃ-, -'ʃɑː-
Rosicrucian ˌrəʊ.zɪ'kruː.ʃᵊn, ˌrɒz.ɪ'-, -ʃi.ən ⓤⓢ ˌroʊ.zə'kruː.ʃən, ˌrɑː- **-s** -z
Rosie 'rəʊ.zi ⓤⓢ 'roʊ-
Rosier 'rəʊ.zɪəʳ, -zi.əʳ ⓤⓢ 'roʊ.ʒɚ; roʊ'zɪr
rosin 'rɒz.ɪn ⓤⓢ 'rɑː.zən
Rosina rəʊ'ziː.nə ⓤⓢ roʊ-
Roslin 'rɒz.lɪn ⓤⓢ 'rɑːz-
Ross rɒs ⓤⓢ rɑːs
Rossall 'rɒs.ᵊl ⓤⓢ 'rɑː.sᵊl

Ross|e rɒs (US) rɑːs **-er** -əʳ (US) -ɚ
Rossetti rəˈzet.i, rɒzˈet-, rəˈset-, rɒsˈet- (US) roʊˈzet̬-, rə-, -ˈset̬-
Rossini rɒsˈiː.ni, rəˈsiː- (US) roʊˈsiː-, rɑː-
Rossiter ˈrɒs.ɪ.təʳ, ˈ-ə- (US) ˈrɑː.sə.t̬ɚ
Rosslare ˌrɒsˈleəʳ (US) rɑːˈsler *stress shift:* ˌRosslare ˈstreets
Rosslyn ˈrɒs.lɪn (US) ˈrɑː.slɪn
Ross-on-Wye ˌrɒs.ɒnˈwaɪ (US) ˌrɑːs.ɑːnˈ- *stress shift:* ˌRoss-on-Wye ˈstreets
rost|er ˈrɒs.t|əʳ (US) ˈrɑː.st|ɚ **-ers** -əz (US) -ɚz **-ering** -ᵊr.ɪŋ **-ered** -əd (US) -ɚd
Rostock ˈrɒs.tɒk (US) ˈrɑː.stɑːk
Rostov ˈrɒs.tɒv (US) ˈrɑː.stɑːf; rəˈstɔːf
Rostrevor rɒsˈtrev.əʳ (US) rɑːˈstrev.ɚ
Rostropovich ˌrɒs.trəˈpəʊ.vɪtʃ (US) ˌrɑː.strəˈpoʊ.viːtʃ, -strɑːˈpɔː-
rostr|um ˈrɒs.tr|əm (US) ˈrɑː.str|əm **-ums** -əmz **-a** -ə
ros|y (R) ˈrəʊ.zli (US) ˈroʊ- **-ier** -i.əʳ (US) -i.ɚ **-iest** -i.ɪst, -i.əst **-ily** -ɪ.li, -ᵊl.i **-iness** -ɪ.nəs, -ɪ.nɪs
Rosyth rɒsˈaɪθ, rəˈsaɪθ (US) rɑːˈsaɪθ, rə-
rot rɒt (US) rɑːt **-s** -s **-ting** -ɪŋ (US) ˈrɑː.t̬ɪŋ **-ted** -ɪd (US) ˈrɑː.t̬ɪd
rota ˈrəʊ.tə (US) ˈroʊ.t̬ə **-s** -z
Rotarian rəʊˈteə.ri.ən (US) roʊˈter.i- **-s** -z
rotar|y ˈrəʊ.tᵊr|.i (US) ˈroʊ.t̬ɚ- **-ies** -iz ˈRotary ˌClub
rotatable rəʊˈteɪ.tə.bl̩ (US) ˈroʊ.teɪ.t̬ə-
rota|te rəʊˈteɪ|t (US) ˈroʊ.teɪ|t, -ˈ- **-tes** -ts **-ting** -tɪŋ (US) -t̬ɪŋ **-ted** -tɪd (US) -t̬ɪd **-tor/s** -təʳ/z (US) -t̬ɚ/z
rotation rəʊˈteɪ.ʃᵊn (US) roʊ- **-s** -z
rotatory ˈrəʊ.tə.tᵊr.i; rəʊˈteɪ- (US) ˈroʊ.tə.tɔːr-
ROTC ˌɑːʳ.əʊ.tiːˈsiː; ˌrɒtˈsiː (US) ˌɑːr.oʊ.tiːˈsiː; ˈrɑːt.si
rote rəʊt (US) roʊt
rotgut ˈrɒt.gʌt (US) ˈrɑːt-
Roth rɒθ, rəʊθ (US) rɑːθ
Rothamsted ˈrɒθ.ᵊm.sted (US) ˈrɑː.θəm-
Rothenstein ˈrəʊ.θᵊn.staɪn, -tᵊn-; ˈrɒθ.ᵊn- (US) ˈrɑː.θən-, ˈroʊ-
Rother ˈrɒð.əʳ (US) ˈrɑː.ðɚ
Rotherfield ˈrɒð.ə.fiːld (US) ˈrɑː.ðɚ-
Rotherham ˈrɒð.ᵊr.əm (US) ˈrɑː.ðɚ-
Rotherhithe ˈrɒð.ə.haɪð (US) ˈrɑː.ðɚ-
Rothermere ˈrɒð.ə.mɪəʳ (US) ˈrɑː.ðɚ.mɪr
Rotherston ˈrɒð.ə.stᵊn (US) ˈrɑː.ðɚ-
Rotherwick ˈrɒð.ᵊr.ɪk, -ə.wɪk (US) ˈrɑː.ðɚ.ɪk, -wɪk
Rothes ˈrɒθ.ɪs (US) ˈrɑː.θɪs
Rothesay ˈrɒθ.si, -seɪ (US) ˈrɑːθ-
Rothko ˈrɒθ.kəʊ (US) ˈrɑːθ.koʊ
Rothman ˈrɒθ.mən (US) ˈrɑːθ-
Rothschild ˈrɒθ.tʃaɪld, ˈrɒs-, ˈrɒθs- (US) ˈrɑːθ-, ˈrɔːθ-, ˈrɑːθs-, ˈrɔːθs-
Rothwell ˈrɒθ.wel, -wəl (US) ˈrɑːθ.wel, -wəl
roti ˈrəʊ.ti (US) roʊˈtiː **-s** -z
rotisserie rəʊˈtɪs.ᵊr.i, -ˈtiː.sᵊr- (US) roʊˈtɪs.ɚ- **-s** -z
rotogravure ˌrəʊ.təʊ.grəˈvjʊəʳ (US) ˌroʊ.t̬ə.grəˈvjʊr; ˈroʊ.t̬əˌgreɪ.vjɚ
rotor ˈrəʊ.təʳ (US) ˈroʊ.t̬ɚ **-s** -z
Rotorua ˌrəʊ.təˈruː.ə (US) ˌroʊ.t̬əˈ-
roto|vate ˈrəʊ.tə|.veɪt (US) ˈroʊ.t̬ə- **-vates** -veɪts **-vating** -veɪ.tɪŋ (US) -veɪ.t̬ɪŋ **-vated** -veɪ.tɪd (US) -veɪ.t̬ɪd
rotovator (R®) ˈrəʊ.tə.veɪ.təʳ (US) ˈroʊ.t̬ə.veɪ.t̬ɚ **-s** -z
rotten ˈrɒt.ᵊn (US) ˈrɑː.tᵊn **-est** -ɪst **-ly** -li **-ness** -nəs, -nɪs **ˌrotten ˈborough**
rottenstone ˈrɒt.ᵊn.stəʊn (US) ˈrɑː.tᵊn.stoʊn
rotter ˈrɒt.əʳ (US) ˈrɑː.t̬ɚ **-s** -z
Rotterdam ˈrɒt.ə.dæm, ˌ--ˈ- (US) ˈrɑː.t̬ɚ.dæm
Rottingdean ˈrɒt.ɪŋ.diːn, ˌ--ˈ- (US) ˈrɑː.t̬ɪŋ.diːn
rottweiler (R) ˈrɒt.waɪ.ləʳ, -vaɪ- (US) ˈrɑːt.waɪ.lɚ, ˈrɔːt.vaɪ- **-s** -z
rotund rəʊˈtʌnd; ˈrəʊ.tʌnd (US) roʊ- **-ity** -ə.ti, -ɪ.ti (US) -ə.t̬i **-ness** -nəs, -nɪs
rotunda (R) rəʊˈtʌn.də (US) roʊ- **-s** -z
rouble ˈruː.bl̩ **-s** -z
Rouch raʊtʃ
roué ˈruː.eɪ, -ˈ- (US) ruˈeɪ; ˈruː.eɪ **-s** -z
Rouen ˈruː.ɑ̃ːŋ, -ɑːŋ, -ˈ- (US) ruˈɑ̃ːŋ, -ˈɑːn
roug|e ruːʒ **-es** -ɪz **-ing** -ɪŋ **-ed** -d
rough rʌf **-s** -s **-er** -əʳ (US) -ɚ **-est** -ɪst, -əst **-ly** -li **-ness** -nəs, -nɪs **-ing** -ɪŋ **-ed** -t **ˌrough ˈdiamond ; ˈrough ˌstuff ; ˌrough ˈtrade ; take the ˌrough with the ˈsmooth**
roughage ˈrʌf.ɪdʒ
rough-and-ready ˌrʌf.ᵊndˈred.i *stress shift:* ˌrough-and-ready ˈtreatment
rough-and-tumble ˌrʌf.ᵊndˈtʌm.bl̩ *stress shift:* ˌrough-and-tumble ˈgames
roughcast ˈrʌf.kɑːst (US) -kæst
roughen ˈrʌf.ᵊn **-s** -z **-ing** -ɪŋ, ˈrʌf.nɪŋ **-ed** -d
rough-hew ˌrʌfˈhjuː **-s** -z **-ing** -ɪŋ **-ed** -d **-n** -n *stress shift:* ˌrough-hewn ˈstone
roughhous|e ˈrʌf.haʊs **-es** -ɪz **-ing** -ɪŋ **-ed** -t
roughish ˈrʌf.ɪʃ
roughneck ˈrʌf.nek **-s** -s
roughrider ˈrʌfˌraɪ.dəʳ (US) -dɚ **-s** -z
roughshod ˈrʌf.ʃɒd (US) -ʃɑːd **ˌride ˈroughshod over**
rough-spoken ˌrʌfˈspəʊ.kᵊn (US) -ˈspoʊ- *stress shift:* ˌrough-spoken ˈperson
Rough Tor ˌraʊˈtɔːʳ (US) -ˈtɔːr
roulade ruːˈlɑːd **-s** -z
roulette ruːˈlet
Roulston ˈrəʊl.stᵊn (US) ˈroʊl-
Roumani|a rʊˈmeɪ.ni|.ə, rʊ-, rəʊ- (US) ruː-, roʊ-, ˈ-nj|ə **-an/s** -ən/z
round (R) raʊnd **-s** -z **-er** -əʳ (US) -ɚ **-est** -ɪst, -əst **-ly** -li **-ness** -nəs, ˈraʊn.nəs, -nɪs **-ish** -ɪʃ **-ing** -ɪŋ **-ed** -ɪd **ˌround ˈrobin ; ˌRound ˈTable** (US) **ˈRound ˌTable ; ˌround ˈtrip**
roundabout ˈraʊnd.əˌbaʊt **-s** -s
roundel ˈraʊn.dᵊl **-s** -z
roundelay ˈraʊn.dɪ.leɪ, -dᵊl.eɪ (US) -də.leɪ **-s** -z
rounders ˈraʊn.dəz (US) -dɚz
roundhand ˈraʊnd.hænd
Roundhay ˈraʊn.deɪ, ˈraʊnd.heɪ
Roundhead ˈraʊnd.hed **-s** -z
roundhou|se ˈraʊnd.haʊ|s **-ses** -zɪz
round-shouldered ˌraʊndˈʃəʊl.dəd (US) -ˈʃoʊl.dɚd *stress shift:* ˌround-shouldered ˈperson
rounds|man ˈraʊndz|.mən **-men** -mən
round-table ˌraʊndˈteɪ.bl̩ (US) ˈ-ˌ-- *stress shift:* ˌround-table ˈconference
round-the-clock ˌraʊnd.ðəˈklɒk (US) -ˈklɑːk *stress shift:* ˌround-the-clock ˈvigil
round-up ˈraʊnd.ʌp **-s** -s
roundworm ˈraʊnd.wɜːm (US) -wɜːrm **-s** -z
Rourke rɔːk (US) rɔːrk
Rous raʊs
rous|e raʊz **-es** -ɪz **-ing/ly** -ɪŋ/li **-ed** -d
Rouse raʊs, ruːs
Rousseau ˈruː.səʊ, -ˈ- (US) ruːˈsoʊ
Roussillon ˌruː.siːˈjɒ̃ŋ, ˈ--- (US) -ˈjõʊn
roustabout ˈraʊst.əˌbaʊt **-s** -s
rout raʊt **-s** -s **-ing** -ɪŋ (US) ˈraʊ.t̬ɪŋ **-ed** -ɪd (US) ˈraʊ.t̬ɪd
rout|e ruːt (US) ruːt, raʊt **-es** -s **-(e)ing/s** -ɪŋ/z (US) ˈruː.t̬ɪŋ, ˈraʊ- **-ed** -ɪd (US) ˈruː.t̬ɪd, ˈraʊ- **ˈroute ˌmarch**
Routh raʊθ
routine ruːˈtiːn **-s** -z **-ly**
Routledge ˈraʊt.lɪdʒ, -ledʒ, ˈrʌt-
Routley ˈraʊt.li
roux (R) ruː
rov|e rəʊv (US) roʊv **-es** -z **-ing** -ɪŋ **-ed** -d **-er/s** -əʳ/z (US) -ɚ/z
Rover® ˈrəʊ.vəʳ (US) ˈroʊ.vɚ **-s** -z
row (*n.v.*) *quarrel:* raʊ **-s** -z **-ing** -ɪŋ **-ed** -d
row (*n.v.*) *all other senses:* rəʊ (US) roʊ **-s** -z **-ing** -ɪŋ **-ed** -d **ˈrow ˌhouse ; ˈrowing ˌboat**
Rowallan rəʊˈæl.ən (US) roʊ-
rowan *tree:* rəʊən, raʊən; ˈrəʊ.æn (US) roʊən, raʊən **-s** -z

Note: More commonly /raʊən/ in Scotland.
Rowan *name:* rəʊən, raʊən (US) roʊən, raʊən
rowanberr|y 'rəʊən,ber|.i, 'rəʊəm- (US) 'roʊən- **-ies** -iz
Rowant raʊənt
row-boat 'rəʊ.bəʊt (US) 'roʊ.boʊt **-s** -s
Rowbottom, Rowbotham 'rəʊ,bɒt.ᵊm (US) 'roʊ,bɑː.t̬əm
Rowden 'raʊ.dᵊn
rowd|y 'raʊ.d|i **-ies** -iz **-ier** -i.əʳ (US) -i.ɚ **-iest** -i.ɪst, -i.əst **-ily** -ɪ.li, -ᵊl.i **-iness** -ɪ.nəs, -ɪ.nɪs **-yism** -i.ɪ.zᵊm
Rowe rəʊ (US) roʊ
rowel raʊəl **-s** -z
Rowell raʊəl
Rowena rəʊ'iː.nə (US) roʊ-, -'wiː-
Rowenta® rəʊ'en.tə (US) roʊ'en.t̬ə
rower 'rəʊ.əʳ (US) 'roʊ.ɚ **-s** -z
Rowland 'rəʊ.lənd (US) 'roʊ- **-s** -z
Rowlandson 'rəʊ.lənd.sən (US) 'roʊ-
Rowles rəʊlz (US) roʊlz
Rowley 'rəʊ.li, 'raʊ- (US) 'roʊ-, 'raʊ-
Rowlinson 'rəʊ.lɪn.sᵊn (US) 'roʊ-
rowlock 'rɒl.ək, 'rəʊ.lɒk, 'rʌl.ək (US) 'rɑː.lək, 'rʌl.ək, 'roʊ.lɑːk **-s** -s
Rowney 'rəʊ.ni, 'raʊ- (US) 'roʊ-, 'raʊ-
Rowntree 'raʊn.triː ,**Rowntree 'Mackintosh®**
Rowridge 'raʊ.rɪdʒ
Rowse raʊs
Rowton 'raʊ.tᵊn, 'rɔː-
Roxana rɒk'sɑː.nə, -'sæn.ə (US) rɑːk'sæn-
Roxanne rɒk'sæn (US) rɑːk-
Roxburgh(e) 'rɒks.bᵊr.ə (US) 'rɑːks- **-shire** -ʃəʳ, -,ʃɪəʳ (US) -ʃɚ, -,ʃɪr
Roxy 'rɒk.si (US) 'rɑːk-
Roy rɔɪ
royal 'rɔɪəl **-ly** -i ,**Royal 'Air** ,**Force** ; ,**royal 'blue** ; ,**royal 'family** ; ,**Royal 'Highness** ; ,**royal 'jelly** ; ,**Royal 'Mail** ; ,**Royal 'Navy**
royal|ism 'rɔɪə.l|ɪ.zᵊm **-ist/s** -ɪst/s
royalt|y 'rɔɪəl.t|i (US) -t̬|i **-ies** -iz
Royce rɔɪs
Royston 'rɔɪ.stᵊn
Royton 'rɔɪ.tᵊn
RP ,ɑː'piː (US) ,ɑːr-
rpm (R) ,ɑː.piː'em (US) ,ɑːr-
RSA ,ɑːʳ.es'eɪ (US) ,ɑːr-
RSC ,ɑːʳ.es'siː (US) ,ɑːr-
RSPB ,ɑːʳ.es,piː'biː (US) ,ɑːr-
RSPCA ,ɑːʳ.es,piː.siː'eɪ (US) ,ɑːr-
RSVP ,ɑːʳ.es.viː'piː (US) ,ɑːr-
Rt. Hon. (*abbrev. for* **Right Honourable**) ,raɪt'ɒn.ᵊr.ə.bl̩ (US) -'ɑː.nɚ.ə- *stress shift:* ,Rt. Hon. 'member
Ruabon ru'æb.ᵊn
Ruanda ru'æn.də (US) -'ɑːn-
rub rʌb **-s** -z **-bing** -ɪŋ **-bed** -d
Rubáiyát 'ruː.baɪ.jæt, -beɪ- (US) ,ruː.baɪ'jɑːt, -biː'-, '---
rubato ruː'bɑː.təʊ, rʊ- (US) ruː'bɑː.toʊ **-s** -z
rubb|er 'rʌb|.əʳ (US) -ɚ **-ers** -əz (US) -ɚz **-ery** -ᵊr.i ,**rubber 'band** ; **'rubber ,plant**
rubberiz|e, -is|e 'rʌb.ᵊr.aɪz (US) -ə.raɪz **-es** -ɪz **-ing** -ɪŋ **-ed** -d
rubberneck 'rʌb.ə.nek (US) '-ɚ- **-s** -s **-ing** -ɪŋ **-ed** -t **-er/s** -əʳ/z (US) -ɚ/z
rubber-stamp ,rʌb.ə'stæmp (US) -ɚ'- **-s** -s **-ing** -ɪŋ **-ed** -t *stress shift:* ,rubber-stamped 'document
rubbish 'rʌb.ɪʃ **-es** -ɪz **-ing** -ɪŋ **-ed** -t **-y** -i
rubble 'rʌb.l̩
Rubbra 'rʌb.rə
rubefacient ,ruː.bɪ'feɪ.ʃi.ənt, '-ʃᵊnt (US) -bə'feɪ.ʃᵊnt
Rube Goldberg ,ruːb'gəʊl*d*.bɜːg (US) -'goʊld.bɜːrg
rubella ruː'bel.ə, rʊ- (US) ruː-
Ruben 'ruː.bɪn, -bən (US) -bən
Rubenesque ,ruː.bɪ'nesk, -bᵊn'esk (US) -bə'nesk
Rubens 'ruː.bənz, -bɪnz (US) -bənz
rubeola ruː'biː.əʊ.lə, rʊ-; ,ruː.bi'əʊ.lə (US) ruː'bi.ᵊl.ə; ,ruː.bi'oʊ.lə
Rubicon 'ruː.bɪ.kᵊn, -kɒn (US) -kɑːn
rubicund 'ruː.bɪ.kənd, -kʌnd (US) -bə.kʌnd, -bɪ-, -kənd
rubidium ruː'bɪd.i.əm, rʊ- (US) ruː-
Rubik 'ruː.bɪk ,**Rubik's 'Cube**
Rubinstein 'ruː.bɪn.staɪn, -bən- (US) -bɪn-
ruble 'ruː.bl̩ **-s** -z
rubric 'ruː.brɪk **-s** -s
rub|y (R) 'ruː.b|i **-ies** -iz
RUC ,ɑː.juː'siː (US) ,ɑːr-
ruch|e ruːʃ **-es** -ɪz **-ing** -ɪŋ **-ed** -t
ruck rʌk **-s** -s **-ing** -ɪŋ **-ed** -t
rucksack 'rʌk.sæk, 'rʊk- **-s** -s
ruckus 'rʌk.əs
ruction 'rʌk.ʃᵊn **-s** -z
rudd (R) rʌd **-s** -z
rudd|er 'rʌd|.əʳ (US) -ɚ **-ers** -əz (US) -ɚz **-erless** -ᵊl.əs, -ɪs (US) -ɚ.ləs, -lɪs
Rudderham 'rʌd.ᵊr.əm
Ruddigore 'rʌd.ɪ.gɔːʳ (US) -gɔːr
ruddl|e 'rʌd.l̩ **-es** -z **-ing** -ɪŋ, 'rʌd.lɪŋ **-ed** -d
Ruddlington 'rʌd.lɪŋ.tən
Ruddock 'rʌd.ək
rudd|y 'rʌd|.i **-ier** -i.əʳ (US) -i.ɚ **-iest** -i.ɪst, -i.əst **-ily** -ɪ.li, -ᵊl.i **-iness** -ɪ.nəs, -ɪ.nɪs
rud|e ruːd **-er** -əʳ (US) -ɚ **-est** -ɪst, -əst **-ely** -li **-eness** -nəs, -nɪs
Rudge rʌdʒ
Rudi 'ruː.di
rudiment 'ruː.dɪ.mənt, -də- (US) -də- **-s** -s
rudimentary ,ruː.dɪ'men.tᵊr.i, -də'-, '-tri (US) -də'- *stress shift:* ,rudimentary 'knowledge
Rudolf, Rudolph 'ruː.dɒlf (US) -dɑːlf
Rudy 'ruː.di
Rudyard *first name:* 'rʌd.jəd, -jɑːd (US) -jɚd, -jɑːrd
Rudyard *in Staffordshire:* 'rʌdʒ.əd (US) -ɚd
rue ruː **-s** -z **-ing** -ɪŋ **-d** -d
rueful 'ruː.fᵊl, -fʊl **-ly** -i **-ness** -nəs, -nɪs
ruff rʌf **-s** -s **-ing** -ɪŋ **-ed** -t
ruffian 'rʌf.i.ən **-s** -z **-ly** -li **-ism** -ɪ.zᵊm
ruffl|e 'rʌf.l̩ **-es** -z **-ing** -ɪŋ, 'rʌf.lɪŋ **-ed** -d
rufiyaa 'ruː.fi.jɑː
rufous 'ruː.fəs
Rufus 'ruː.fəs
rug rʌg **-s** -z
Rugbeian rʌg'biː.ən **-s** -z
rugby (R) 'rʌg.bi ,**Rugby 'League** ; ,**Rugby 'Union**
Rugeley 'ruːdʒ.li, 'ruːʒ-
rugged 'rʌg.ɪd **-ly** -li **-ness** -nəs, -nɪs
rugger 'rʌg.əʳ (US) -ɚ
Ruhr rʊəʳ (US) rʊr
ruin 'ruː.ɪn **-s** -z **-ing** -ɪŋ **-ed** -d
ruination ,ruː.ɪ'neɪ.ʃᵊn, rʊɪ'- (US) ,ruː.ə'-
ruinous 'ruː.ɪ.nəs (US) 'ruː.ə- **-ly** -li **-ness** -nəs, -nɪs
Ruislip 'raɪ.slɪp, 'raɪz.lɪp
Ruiz ru'iːθ (US) ru'iːθ, ruː'iːs
rul|e (R) ruːl **-es** -z **-ing** -ɪŋ **-ed** -d **-er/s** -əʳ/z (US) -ɚ/z
rulebook 'ruːl.bʊk **-s** -s
ruling 'ruː.lɪŋ **-s** -z ,**ruling 'class** (US) **'ruling ,class**
rum rʌm **-mer** -əʳ (US) -ɚ **-mest** -ɪst, -əst
Rumani|a rʊ'meɪ.ni|.ə, rəʊ-, ruː- (US) roʊ-, ruː-, '-nj|ə **-an/s** -ənz
rumba 'rʌm.bə **-s** -z
Rumbelow 'rʌm.bə.ləʊ, -bɪ- (US) -loʊ
rumbl|e 'rʌm.bl̩ **-es** -z **-ing/s** -ɪŋ/z, 'rʌm.blɪŋ/z **-ed** -d
Rumbold 'rʌm.bəʊld (US) -boʊld
rumbustious rʌm'bʌs.ti.əs, '-tʃəs (US) -tʃəs **-ness** -nəs, -nɪs
Rumelia ruː'miː.li.ə (US) -li.ə, -'miːl.jə
rumen 'ruː.men, -mɪn, -mən (US) -mən **-s** -z **rumina** 'ruː.mɪ.nə, -mə- (US) -mə-
Rumford 'rʌm.fəd (US) -fɚd
ruminant 'ruː.mɪ.nənt, -mə- (US) -mə- **-s** -s
rumi|nate 'ruː.mɪ|.neɪt, -mə- (US) -mə- **-nates** -neɪts **-nating** -neɪ.tɪŋ (US) -neɪ.t̬ɪŋ **-nated** -neɪ.tɪd (US) -neɪ.t̬ɪd
rumination ,ruː.mɪ'neɪ.ʃᵊn, -mə'- (US) -mə'- **-s** -z
ruminative 'ruː.mɪ.nə.tɪv, -mə-, -neɪ- (US) -mə,neɪ.t̬ɪv

rummag|e 'rʌm.ɪdʒ **-es** -ɪz **-ing** -ɪŋ **-ed** -d **'rummage ˌsale**
rumm|y 'rʌm|.i **-ier** -i.əʳ (US) -i.ɚ **-iest** -i.ɪst, -i.əst **-ily** -ɪ.li, -ᵊl.i **-iness** -ɪ.nəs, -ɪ.nɪs
rumo(u)r 'ruː.məʳ (US) -mɚ **-s** -z **-ed** -d
rumo(u)r-mong|er 'ruː.məˌmʌŋ.g|əʳ (US) -mɚˌmʌŋ.g|ɚ, -ˌmɑːŋ- **-ers** -əz (US) -ɚz **-ering** -ᵊr.ɪŋ
rump rʌmp **-s** -s **ˌrump 'steak**
Rumpelstiltskin ˌrʌm.pᵊl'stɪlt.skɪn
rumpl|e 'rʌm.pl̩ **-es** -z **-ing** -ɪŋ, 'rʌm.plɪŋ **-ed** -d
Rumpole 'rʌm.pəʊl (US) -poʊl
rumpus 'rʌm.pəs **-es** -ɪz
rum-runner 'rʌmˌrʌn.əʳ (US) -ɚ **-s** -z
run rʌn **-s** -z **-ning** -ɪŋ **ran** ræn **ˌrunning 'water** ; **ˌtake a ˌrunning 'jump** ; **'running ˌshoe**
runabout 'rʌn.əˌbaʊt **-s** -s
runagate 'rʌn.əˌgeɪt **-s** -s
runaround 'rʌn.ᵊrˌaʊnd
runaway 'rʌn.əˌweɪ **-s** -z
runcible 'rʌn*t*.sɪ.bl̩, -sə- (US) -sə-
Runcie 'rʌn*t*.si
Runciman 'rʌn*t*.sɪ.mən
Runcorn 'rʌŋ.kɔːn (US) -kɔːrn
run-down *(adj)* ˌrʌn'daʊn *stress shift:* ˌrun-down 'area
rundown *(n)* 'rʌn.daʊn **-s** -z
rune (R) ruːn **-s** -z
rung rʌŋ **-s** -z
rung *(from* **ring***)* rʌŋ
Runham 'rʌn.əm
runic (R) 'ruː.nɪk
run-in 'rʌn.ɪn **-s** -z
runnel 'rʌn.ᵊl **-s** -z
runner 'rʌn.əʳ (US) -ɚ **-s** -z **ˌrunner 'bean, 'runner ˌbean**
runner-up ˌrʌn.əʳ'ʌp (US) -ɚ'- **runners-up** ˌrʌn.əz'- (US) -ɚz'- *stress shift:* ˌrunner-up 'prizes
running-board 'rʌn.ɪŋ.bɔːd (US) -bɔːrd **-s** -z
runn|y 'rʌn|.i **-ier** -i.əʳ (US) -i.ɚ **-iest** -i.ɪst, -i.əst **-iness** -ɪ.nəs, -ɪ.nɪs
Runnymede 'rʌn.i.miːd
run-of-the-mill ˌrʌn.əv.ðə'mɪl *stress shift:* ˌrun-of-the-mill 'job
runt rʌnt **-s** -s **-y** -i (US) 'rʌn.t̬i
Runton 'rʌn.tən (US) -tᵊn
runway 'rʌn.weɪ **-s** -z
Runyon 'rʌn.jən
rupee ruː'piː (US) 'ruː.piː, -'- **-s** -z
Rupert 'ruː.pət (US) -pɚt
rupiah ruː'piː.ə **-s** -z
rupt|ure 'rʌp.tʃ|əʳ (US) -tʃ|ɚ **-ures** -əz (US) -ɚz **-uring** -ᵊr.ɪŋ **-ured** -əd (US) -ɚd
rural 'rʊə.rᵊl (US) 'rʊr.ᵊl **-ly** -i
ruridecanal ˌrʊə.rɪ.dɪ'keɪ.nᵊl, -rə- (US) ˌrʊr.ɪ.də'-; -'dek.ə.næl
Ruritani|a ˌrʊə.rɪ'teɪ.ni|.ə, -rə'- (US) ˌrʊr.ɪ'- **-an** -ən
rus|e ruːz (US) ruːz, ruːs **-es** -ɪz
rusé 'ruː.zeɪ (US) ruː'zeɪ
rush (R) rʌʃ **-es** -ɪz **-ing** -ɪŋ **-ed** -t **-er/s** -əʳ/z (US) -ɚ/z **'rush ˌhour**
Rushall 'rʌʃ.ᵊl
Rushden 'rʌʃ.dən
Rushdie 'rʊʃ.di, 'rʌʃ-
Rushforth 'rʌʃ.fɔːθ, -fəθ (US) -fɔːrθ, -fɚθ
rushlight 'rʌʃ.laɪt **-s** -s
Rushmere 'rʌʃ.mɪəʳ (US) -mɪr
Rushmore 'rʌʃ.mɔːʳ (US) -mɔːr
Rusholme 'rʌʃ.əm, -həʊm (US) -əm, -hoʊm
Rushton 'rʌʃ.tən
Rushworth 'rʌʃ.wəθ, -wɜːθ (US) -wɚθ, -wɜːrθ
rushy 'rʌʃ.i
rusk (R) rʌsk **-s** -s
Ruskin 'rʌs.kɪn
Rusper 'rʌs.pəʳ (US) -pɚ
Russell 'rʌs.ᵊl
russet 'rʌs.ɪt **-s** -s
Russia 'rʌʃ.ə
Russian 'rʌʃ.ᵊn **-s** -z **ˌRussian rou'lette**
russianism (R) 'rʌʃ.ᵊn.ɪ.zᵊm **-s** -z
russianiz|e, -is|e (R) 'rʌʃ.ᵊn.aɪz **-es** -ɪz **-ing** -ɪŋ **-ed** -d
Russo- ˌrʌs.əʊ- (US) ˌrʌs.oʊ-, ˌ-ə-
Russo 'rʌs.əʊ (US) -oʊ
rust (R) rʌst **-s** -s **-ing** -ɪŋ **-ed** -ɪd
rustbelt 'rʌs*t*.belt
rustbucket 'rʌs*t*ˌbʌk.ɪt **-s** -s
rustic 'rʌs.tɪk **-s** -s **-ally** -ᵊl.i, -li
rusti|cate 'rʌs.tɪ|.keɪt (US) -tə- **-cates** -keɪts **-cating** -keɪ.tɪŋ (US) -keɪ.t̬ɪŋ **-cated** -keɪ.tɪd (US) -keɪ.t̬ɪd
rustication ˌrʌs.tɪ'keɪ.ʃᵊn (US) -tə'-
rusticity rʌs'tɪs.ə.ti, -ɪ.ti (US) -ə.t̬i
rustl|e 'rʌs.l̩ **-es** -z **-ing** -ɪŋ, 'rʌs.lɪŋ **-ed** -d **-er/s** -əʳ/z (US) -ɚ/z, 'rʌs.ləʳ/z (US) -lɚ/z
rustproof 'rʌs*t*.pruːf
Rustum 'rʌs.tᵊm
rust|y (R) 'rʌs.t|i **-ier** -i.əʳ (US) -i.ɚ **-iest** -i.ɪst, -i.əst **-iness** -ɪ.nəs, -ɪ.nɪs
Ruswarp 'rʌs.əp, 'rʌz- (US) -ɚp
rut rʌt **-s** -s **-ting** -ɪŋ (US) 'rʌt̬.ɪŋ **-ted** -ɪd (US) 'rʌt̬.ɪd
rutabaga ˌruː.tə'beɪ.gə, ˌrʊt.ə'-, 'ruː.təˌbeɪ-, 'rʊt.əˌ- (US) ˌruː.t̬ə'beɪ-, 'ruː.t̬əˌbeɪ- **-s** -z
Rutgers 'rʌt.gəz (US) -gɚz
Ruth, ruth ruːθ
Ruthenia ruː'θiː.ni.ə (US) -ni.ə, '-njə
Ruthenian ruː'θiː.ni.ən (US) -ni.ən, '-njən **-s** -z
ruthenium ruː'θiː.ni.əm
Rutherford 'rʌð.ə.fəd (US) -ɚ.fɚd, 'rʌθ-
rutherfordium ˌrʌð.ə'fɔː.di.əm (US) -ɚ'fɔːr-
Rutherglen 'rʌð.ə.glen (US) '-ɚ-
ruthful 'ruːθ.fᵊl, -fʊl **-ly** -li **-ness** -nəs, -nɪs
Ruthin 'rɪθ.ɪn, 'ruː.θɪn
ruthless 'ruːθ.ləs, -lɪs **-ly** -li **-ness** -nəs, -nɪs
Ruthven *personal name:* 'ruːθ.vən, 'rɪv.ən *Baron, place in Tayside region:* 'rɪv.ən *place in Grampian region, loch in Highland region:* 'rʌθ.vən
Ruthwell 'rʌθ.wᵊl *locally:* 'rɪð.ᵊl
rutilant 'ruː.tɪ.lənt (US) -tᵊl.ənt
rutile 'ruː.taɪl (US) -tiːl, -taɪl
rutin 'ruː.tɪn, -tᵊn (US) -tᵊn
Rutland 'rʌt.lənd
Rutledge 'rʌt.lɪdʒ
Rutskoi ˌrʊt'skɔɪ, ˌruːt-
Rutter 'rʌt.əʳ (US) 'rʌt̬.ɚ
Rutterford 'rʌt.ə.fəd (US) 'rʌt̬.ɚ.fɚd
rutt|y 'rʌt|.i (US) 'rʌt̬- **-ier** -i.əʳ (US) -i.ɚ **-iest** -i.ɪst, -i.əst **-iness** -ɪ.nəs, -ɪ.nɪs
Ruysdael 'raɪz.dɑːl, 'riːz-, -deɪl (US) 'raɪs.dɑːl, 'raɪz-, 'rɔɪs-
Ruyter 'raɪ.təʳ (US) 'rɔɪ.t̬ɚ, 'raɪ-
RV ˌɑː'viː (US) ˌɑːr-
Rwanda ru'æn.də (US) -'ɑːn- **-n/s** -n/z
Ryan raɪən
Rydal 'raɪ.dᵊl
Ryde raɪd
Ryder 'raɪ.dəʳ (US) -dɚ **ˌRyder 'Cup**
rye (R) raɪ **'rye ˌbread** ; **'rye ˌgrass**
Ryecroft 'raɪ.krɒft (US) -krɑːft
Ryle raɪl
Rylstone 'rɪl.stən, -stəʊn (US) -stən, -stoʊn
Ryman 'raɪ.mən
Rymer 'raɪ.məʳ (US) -mɚ
ryot raɪət **-s** -s
Ryswick 'rɪz.wɪk
Ryton 'raɪ.tᵊn
Ryukyu ri'uː.kjuː (US) -'juː-, -'uː-
Ryvita® raɪ'viː.tə (US) -t̬ə

S

s (S) es **-'s** -ɪz
S (*abbrev. for* **south**) saʊθ
Saab® sɑːb
Saarbrücken ˌsɑːˈbrʊk.ᵊn *as if German:* ˌzɑː- (US) ˈsɑːrˌbrʊk- *as if German:* ˈzɑːr-
Saarland ˈsɑː.lænd *as if German:* ˈzɑː- (US) ˈsɑːr- *as if German:* ˈzɑːr-
Saatchi ˈsɑː.tʃi
Saba *in Arabia:* ˈsɑː.bə, ˈseɪ- (US) ˈseɪ.bə, ˈsɑː- *in West Indies:* ˈseɪ.bə, ˈsɑː- (US) ˈsɑː.bə
Sabaean səˈbiː.ən, sæbˈiː- (US) səˈbiː-
Sabah ˈsɑː.bɑː
Sabaoth sæbˈeɪ.ɒθ, səˈbeɪ-, ˈsæb.eɪ.ɒθ, -əθ (US) ˈsæb.eɪ.ɑːθ, -ə.ɔːθ; səˈbeɪ.ɔːθ
Sabatini ˌsæb.əˈtiː.ni
Sabbatarian ˌsæb.əˈteə.ri.ən (US) -ˈter.i- **-s** -z **-ism** -ɪ.zᵊm
Sabbath ˈsæb.əθ **-s** -s
sabbatical səˈbæt.ɪ.kᵊl (US) -ˈbæt̬-
Sabena® səˈbiː.nə, sæbˈiː-
sab|er ˈseɪ.b|əʳ (US) -b|ɚ **-ers** -əz (US) -ɚz **-ering** -ᵊr.ɪŋ **-ered** -əd (US) -ɚd
Sabin ˈseɪ.bɪn, ˈsæb.ɪn (US) ˈseɪ.bɪn
Sabine *Italian people:* ˈsæb.aɪn, ˈseɪ.baɪn (US) ˈseɪ.baɪn **-s** -z *surname:* ˈsæb.aɪn, ˈseɪ.baɪn, -bɪn (US) ˈseɪ- *river, lake, pass in US:* səˈbiːn, sæbˈiːn (US) səˈbiːn
sable ˈseɪ.bl̩ **-s** -z
sabot ˈsæb.əʊ, -ˈ- (US) sæbˈoʊ, ˈ-- **-s** -z
sabotag|e ˈsæb.ə.tɑːdʒ (US) -tɑːʒ, ˌ--ˈ- **-es** -ɪz **-ing** -ɪŋ **-ed** -d
saboteur ˌsæb.əˈtɜːʳ, ˈ--- (US) ˌsæb.əˈtɜːr, -ˈtʊr **-s** -z
sabra (S) ˈsɑː.brə
sab|re ˈseɪ.b|əʳ (US) -b|ɚ **-res** -əz (US) -ɚz **-ring** -ᵊr.ɪŋ **-red** -əd (US) -ɚd **ˈsabre ˌrattling**
sabretach|e ˈsæb.ə.tæʃ (US) ˈseɪ.bɚ-, ˈsæb.ɚ- **-es** -ɪz
sabre-toothed ˌseɪ.bəˈtuːθt (US) ˈseɪ.bɚ.tuːθt *stress shift, British only, see compound:* **ˌsabre-toothed ˈtiger**
Sabrina səˈbriː.nə
sabulous ˈsæb.jə.ləs, -jʊ-
sac sæk **-s** -s
saccade sækˈɑːd, səˈkɑːd, -ˈkeɪd (US) sækˈɑːd, səˈkɑːd **-s** -z
Note: In British psychology, /sækˈeɪd, səˈkeɪd/ is the usual pronunciation.
saccharide ˈsæk.ᵊr.aɪd, -ɪd (US) -ə.raɪd **-s** -z
saccharin(e) (*n.*) ˈsæk.ᵊr.ɪn, -iːn (US) -ɪn, -ən
saccharine (*adj.*) ˈsæk.ᵊr.aɪn, -iːn (US) -ɚ.ɪn, -ə.raɪn
sacerdotal ˌsæs.əˈdəʊ.tᵊl (US) -ɚˈdoʊ.tᵊl, ˌsæk- **-ly** -i
sachem ˈseɪ.tʃəm, -tʃem (US) -tʃəm **-s** -z
sachet ˈsæʃ.eɪ (US) -ˈ- **-s** -z
Sacheverell səˈʃev.ᵊr.ᵊl, sæʃˈev-
Sachs sæks
sack sæk **-s** -s **-ing** -ɪŋ **-ed** -t
sackbut ˈsæk.bʌt, -bət (US) -bʌt **-s** -s
sackcloth ˈsæk.klɒθ (US) -klɑːθ **ˌsackcloth and ˈashes**
sackful ˈsæk.fʊl **-s** -z **sacksful** ˈsæks.fʊl
sacking ˈsæk.ɪŋ
sackload ˈsæk.ləʊd (US) -loʊd
Sackville-West ˌsæk.vɪlˈwest
sacral ˈseɪ.krᵊl
sacrament (S) ˈsæk.rə.mənt **-s** -s
sacramental ˌsæk.rəˈmen.tᵊl (US) -t̬ᵊl **-ly** -i **-ism** -ɪ.zᵊm
Sacramento ˌsæk.rəˈmen.təʊ (US) -t̬oʊ
sacred ˈseɪ.krɪd **-ly** -li **-ness** -nəs, -nɪs **ˌsacred ˈcow**
sacrific|e ˈsæk.rɪ.faɪs, -rə- (US) -rə- **-es** -ɪz **-ing** -ɪŋ **-ed** -t
sacrificial ˌsæk.rɪˈfɪʃ.ᵊl, -rəˈ- (US) -rəˈ- **-ly** -i
sacrilege ˈsæk.rɪ.lɪdʒ, -rə- (US) -rə-
sacrilegious ˌsæk.rɪˈlɪdʒ.əs, -rəˈ- (US) -rəˈ- **-ly** -li **-ness** -nəs, -nɪs
sacristan ˈsæk.rɪ.stᵊn, -rə- (US) -rɪ- **-s** -z
Sacriston ˈsæk.rɪ.stᵊn, -rə- (US) -rɪ-
sacrist|y ˈsæk.rɪ.st|i, -rə- (US) -rɪ- **-ies** -iz
sacrosanct ˈsæk.rəʊ.sæŋ*k*t (US) -roʊ- **-ity** -ə.ti, -ɪ.ti (US) -ə.t̬i
sacr|um ˈseɪ.kr|əm, ˈsæk.r|əm **-a** -ə
sad sæd **-der** -əʳ (US) -ɚ **-dest** -ɪst, -əst **-ly** -li **-ness** -nəs, -nɪs
Sadat səˈdæt, sædˈæt (US) səˈdɑːt, sɑː-, -ˈdæt
Saddam səˈdæm, sædˈæm; ˈsæd.əm (US) sɑːˈdɑːm, sə-, sædˈæm, səˈdæm
sadden ˈsæd.ᵊn **-s** -z **-ing** -ɪŋ **-ed** -d
saddhu ˈsɑː.duː **-s** -z
saddl|e ˈsæd.l̩ **-es** -z **-ing** -ɪŋ, ˈsæd.lɪŋ **-ed** -d **ˈsaddle ˌhorse**; **ˈsaddle ˌsore**
saddleback ˈsæd.l̩.bæk **-s**
saddlebag ˈsæd.l̩.bæg **-s** -z
saddle|cloth ˈsæd.l̩|.klɒθ (US) -klɑːθ **-cloths** -klɒθs, -klɒðz (US) -klɑːθs, -klɑːðz
saddler ˈsæd.ləʳ, -l̩.əʳ (US) ˈ-lɚ, -l̩.ɚ **-s** -z **-y** -i
Sadducee ˈsæd.jʊ.siː, -jə- (US) ˈsædʒ.ʊ-, ˈsæd.jʊ- **-s** -z
Sade sɑːd (US) sɑːd, sæd
sadhu ˈsɑː.duː **-s** -z
Sadie ˈseɪ.di
sad|ism ˈseɪ.d|ɪ.zᵊm (US) ˈsæd|.ɪ-, ˈseɪ.d|ɪ- **-ist/s** -ɪst/s
sadistic səˈdɪs.tɪk, sædˈɪs- (US) səˈdɪs-, seɪ-, sædˈɪs- **-ally** -ᵊl.i, -li
Sadleir ˈsæd.ləʳ (US) -lɚ
Sadler ˈsæd.ləʳ (US) -lɚ
sadomasoch|ism ˌseɪ.dəʊˈmæs.ə.k|ɪ.zᵊm, -ˈmæz- (US) ˌsæd.oʊˈ-, ˌseɪ.doʊˈ- **-ist/s** -ɪst/s
sadomasochistic ˌseɪ.dəʊˌmæs.əˈkɪs.tɪk, -ˌmæz- (US) ˌsæd.oʊˌ-, ˌseɪ.doʊˌ-
Sadova ˈsɑː.dəʊ.ə, -və (US) -dɔː.vɑː, sɑːˈdɔː-
sae, **SAE** ˌes.eɪˈiː
safari səˈfɑː.ri (US) -ˈfɑːr.i **-s** -z **saˈfari ˌpark**; **saˈfari ˌsuit**
saf|e seɪf **-es** -s **-er** -əʳ (US) -ɚ **-est** -ɪst, -əst **-ely** -li **-eness** -nəs, -nɪs **ˈsafe ˌhouse**, **ˌsafe ˈhouse** (US) **ˈsafe ˌhouse**; **ˌsafe ˈsex**
safe-break|er ˈseɪfˌbreɪ.k|əʳ (US) -k|ɚ **-s** -z **-ing** -ɪŋ
safe-conduct ˌseɪfˈkɒn.dʌkt, -dəkt (US) -ˈkɑːn.dʌkt **-s** -s
safe-crack|er ˈseɪfˌkræk|.əʳ (US) -ɚ **-s** -z **-ing** -ɪŋ
safe-deposit ˈseɪf.dɪˌpɒz.ɪt, -dəˌ- (US) -dɪˈpɑː.zɪt **-s** -s **ˈsafe-deˌposit ˌbox**, **ˌsafe-deˈposit ˌbox** (US) **ˈsafe-deˌposit ˌbox**
safeguard ˈseɪf.gɑːd (US) -gɑːrd **-s** -z **-ing** -ɪŋ **-ed** -ɪd
safekeeping ˌseɪfˈkiː.pɪŋ
safety ˈseɪf.ti **ˈsafety ˌbelt**; **ˈsafety ˌcurtain**; **ˈsafety ˌlamp**; **ˈsafety ˌmatch**; **ˈsafety ˌnet**; **ˈsafety ˌpin**; **ˈsafety ˌrazor**; **ˈsafety ˌvalve**
Saffell səˈfel
safflower ˈsæf.laʊəʳ (US) -laʊɚ **-s** -z
saffron (S) ˈsæf.rən, -rɒn (US) -rən
sag sæg **-s** -z **-ging** -ɪŋ **-ged** -d
saga ˈsɑː.gə **-s** -z
sagacious səˈgeɪ.ʃəs **-ly** -li **-ness** -nəs, -nɪs
sagacity səˈgæs.ə.ti, -ɪ.ti (US) -ə.t̬i
Sagan *English name:* ˈseɪ.gən *French name:* səˈgɑ̃ːŋ, sægˈɑ̃ːŋ (US) ˈseɪ.gᵊn; sɑːˈgɑ̃ːn
sag|e (S) seɪdʒ **-es** -ɪz **-ely** -li **-eness** -nəs, -nɪs
sagg|y ˈsæg|.i **-ier** -i.əʳ (US) -i.ɚ **-iest** -i.ɪst, -i.əst **-iness** -i.nəs, -i.nɪs
sagitt|a (S) səˈdʒɪt|.ə, -ˈgɪt- (US) -ˈdʒɪt̬- **-ae** -iː, -aɪ
sagittal ˈsædʒ.ɪ.tᵊl (US) -ə.t̬ᵊl **-ly** -i
Sagittarian ˌsædʒ.ɪˈteə.ri.ən, ˌsæg-, -əˈ-, -ˈtɑː- (US) ˌsædʒ.əˈter.i- **-s** -z
Sagittarius ˌsædʒ.ɪˈteə.ri.əs, ˌsæg-, -əˈ-, -ˈtɑː- (US) ˌsædʒ.əˈter.i-
sago ˈseɪ.gəʊ (US) -goʊ

Sahara səˈhɑː.rə ⓤⓢ -ˈher.ə, -ˈhær-, -ˈhɑːr-
Sahel sɑːˈhel, sə- ⓤⓢ sɑː-
sahib (S) sɑːb; ˈsɑː.*h*ɪb ⓤⓢ ˈsɑː.*h*ɪb, -*h*iːb, -ˈ- **-s** -z
said (*from* **say**) sed
Said (*in* **Port Said**) saɪd, seɪd, sɑːˈiːd ⓤⓢ sɑːˈiːd
Saigon saɪˈɡɒn ⓤⓢ -ˈɡɑːn, ˈ--
Saigonese ˌsaɪ.ɡɒnˈiːz, -ɡᵊnˈ- ⓤⓢ -ɡɑːˈniːz, -ɡəˈ- *stress shift:* ˌSaigonese ˈexports
sail seɪl **-s** -z **-ing/s** -ɪŋ/z **-ed** -d **ˈsailing ˌboat** ; **ˈsailing ˌship**
sailboard ˈseɪl.bɔːd ⓤⓢ -bɔːrd **-s** -z **-ing** -ɪŋ **-er/s** -əʳ/z ⓤⓢ -ɚ/z
sailboat ˈseɪl.bəʊt ⓤⓢ -boʊt **-s** -s
sailcloth ˈseɪl.klɒθ ⓤⓢ -klɑːθ
sailor ˈseɪ.ləʳ ⓤⓢ -lɚ **-s** -z **ˈsailor ˌsuit**
sailplane ˈseɪl.pleɪn **-s** -z
sainfoin ˈsæn.fɔɪn, ˈseɪn- ⓤⓢ ˈseɪn-, ˈsæn-
Sainsbury ˈseɪnz.bᵊr.i ⓤⓢ -bɚ-, -ber- **-ˈs** -z
saint (S) *strong form:* seɪnt **-s** -s **-ed** -ɪd **-hood** -hʊd *weak forms:* sᵊnt, sɪnt
Note: The weak forms are usual in British English for the names of saints (and places containing the word **Saint**), while the strong form is used when the word occurs on its own. For example, "This would try the patience of a saint" would have the strong form, while **St. John**, **St. Cecilia** (saints' names), **St. Alban's**, **St. Helen's** (placenames) have the weak forms. In American English, the strong form is usually used in all cases. When **Saint** occurs in British family names (e.g. **St. Clair**) the pronunciation is variable and individual names should be checked in their dictionary entries.
Saint-Etienne ˌsæ̃nt.eɪˈtjen
Saint Laurent ˌsæ̃n.lɔːˈrɑ̃ːŋ, -ləˈ- ⓤⓢ -lɑːˈrɑːnt, -ləˈ-
saintl|y ˈseɪnt.l|i **-ier** -i.əʳ ⓤⓢ -i.ɚ **-iest** -i.ɪst, -i.əst **-iness** -ɪ.nəs, -ɪ.nɪs
Saint-Saëns ˌsæ̃nˈsɑ̃ːŋ, -ˈsɑ̃ːns
Saintsbury ˈseɪnts.bᵊr.i
saith (*from* **say**) seθ, seɪθ
sake *cause, purpose:* seɪk **-s** -s
sake *drink:* ˈsɑː.ki, ˈsæk.i ⓤⓢ ˈsɑː.ki
Sakhalin ˈsæk.ə.liːn, ˈsɑː.kə-, -lɪn *as if Russian:* ˌsæx.əˈliːn ⓤⓢ ˈsæk.ə.liːn
Sakharov ˈsæk.ə.rɒf, -rɒv *as if Russian:* ˈsæx- ⓤⓢ ˈsɑː.kə.rɔːf, ˈsæk.ə-, -rɑːf
Saki ˈsɑː.ki
salaam səˈlɑːm, sælˈɑːm ⓤⓢ səˈlɑːm **-s** -z **-ing** -ɪŋ **-ed** -d
salability ˌseɪ.ləˈbɪl.ə.ti, -ɪ.ti ⓤⓢ -ə.t̬i
salable ˈseɪ.lə.bl̩

salacious səˈleɪ.ʃəs **-ly** -li **-ness** -nəs, -nɪs
salacity səˈlæs.ə.ti, -ɪ.ti ⓤⓢ -ə.t̬i
salad ˈsæl.əd **-s** -z **ˈsalad ˌbar** ; **ˈsalad ˌcream**, **ˌsalad ˈcream** ⓤⓢ **ˈsalad ˌcream**; **ˈsalad ˌdays**; **ˈsalad ˌdressing**; **ˈsalad ˌonion**
Saladin ˈsæl.ə.dɪn
Salamanca ˌsæl.əˈmæŋ.kə
salamander ˈsæl.ə.mæn.dəʳ ⓤⓢ -dɚ **-s** -z
salami səˈlɑː.mi **-s** -z
Salamis ˈsæl.ə.mɪs
sal ammoniac ˌsæl.əˈməʊ.ni.æk ⓤⓢ -ˈmoʊ-
salariat səˈleə.ri.æt
salar|y ˈsæl.ᵊr|.i **-ies** -iz **-ied** -id
Salcombe ˈsɔːl.kəm, ˈsɒl- ⓤⓢ ˈsɔːl-, ˈsɑːl-
sale (S) seɪl **-s** -z **ˌsale or reˈturn** ; **ˌsale of ˈwork** ; **ˈsales ˌtax**
saleability ˌseɪ.ləˈbɪl.ə.ti, -ɪ.ti ⓤⓢ -ə.t̬i
saleable ˈseɪ.lə.bl̩
Salem ˈseɪ.ləm, -lem ⓤⓢ -ləm
Salerno səˈlɜː.nəʊ, -ˈleə- ⓤⓢ -ˈlɜːr.noʊ; sɑːˈler-
Salesbury ˈseɪlz.bᵊr.i
salesclerk ˈseɪlz.klɑːk ⓤⓢ -klɜːrk **-s** -s
salesgirl ˈseɪlz.ɡɜːl ⓤⓢ -ɡɜːrl **-s** -z
sales|man ˈseɪlz|.mən **-men** -mən, -men
salesmanship ˈseɪlz.mən.ʃɪp
sales|person ˈseɪlz|ˌpɜː.sᵊn ⓤⓢ -ˌpɜːr- **-people** -ˌpiː.pl̩
salesroom ˈseɪlz.rʊm, -ruːm ⓤⓢ -ruːm, -rʊm **-s** -z
salestalk ˈseɪlz.tɔːk ⓤⓢ -tɑːk, -tɔːk
sales|woman ˈseɪlz|ˌwʊm.ən **-women** -ˌwɪm.ɪn
Salford ˈsɔːl.fəd, ˈsɒl- ⓤⓢ ˈsɔːl.fɚd, ˈsɑːl-
Salfords ˈsæl.fədz ⓤⓢ -fɚdz
Salian ˈseɪ.li.ən **-s** -z
Salic, **Salique** ˈsæl.ɪk, ˈseɪ.lɪk
salicylate səˈlɪs.ɪ.leɪt, sælˈɪs-, -ᵊl.eɪt ⓤⓢ səˈlɪs.ə.leɪt; ˌsæl.əˈsɪl.eɪt, -ɪt **-s** -s
salicylic ˌsæl.ɪˈsɪl.ɪk, -əˈ- ⓤⓢ -əˈ- *stress shift, see compound:* **ˌsalicylic ˈacid**
salienc|e ˈseɪ.li.ənts **-y** -i
salient ˈseɪ.li.ənt ⓤⓢ ˈseɪl.jənt, ˈseɪ.li.ənt **-s** -s **-ly** -li
Salieri ˌsæl.iˈeə.ri ⓤⓢ -ˈer.i
saline (*adj.*) ˈseɪ.laɪn, ˈsæl.aɪn ⓤⓢ ˈseɪ.liːn, -laɪn
saline (*n.*) ˈseɪ.laɪn, ˈsæl.aɪn ⓤⓢ ˈseɪ.liːn, -laɪn; səˈliːn
Saline *in Fife:* ˈsæl.ɪn *in US:* səˈliːn
Salinger ˈsæl.ɪn.dʒəʳ, ˈseɪ.lɪn- ⓤⓢ ˈsæl.ɪn.dʒɚ
salinity səˈlɪn.ə.ti, -ɪ.ti ⓤⓢ -ə.t̬i
Salisbury ˈsɔːlz.bᵊr.i, ˈsɒlz- ⓤⓢ ˈsɔːlz-, ˈsɑːlz-, -ber- **ˌSalisbury ˈPlain**

saliva səˈlaɪ.və
salivary ˈsæl.ɪ.vᵊr.i, ˈ-ə-; səˈlaɪ- ⓤⓢ ˈsæl.ə.ver- **saˈlivary ˌgland**, **ˈsalivary ˌgland**
sali|vate ˈsæl.ɪ|.veɪt, ˈ-ə- ⓤⓢ ˈ-ə- **-vates** -veɪts **-vating** -veɪ.tɪŋ ⓤⓢ -veɪ.t̬ɪŋ **-vated** -veɪ.tɪd ⓤⓢ -veɪ.t̬ɪd **-vation** ˌ--ˈveɪ.ʃᵊn
Salk sɔːlk **ˈSalk ˌvaccine**
sallet ˈsæl.ɪt, -ət ⓤⓢ -ɪt **-s** -s
Sallis ˈsæl.ɪs
sallow ˈsæl.əʊ ⓤⓢ -oʊ **-s** -z **-y** -i **-ness** -nəs, -nɪs
Sallust ˈsæl.əst
sall|y (S) ˈsæl|.i **-ies** -iz **-ying** -i.ɪŋ **-ied** -id **ˌSally ˈArmy**
Sally Lunn ˌsæl.iˈlʌn **-s** -z
salmagundi ˌsæl.məˈɡʌn.di
Salman ˈsæl.mæn, -mən
salmi ˈsæl.mi **-s** -z
salmon ˈsæm.ən
Salmon *surname:* ˈsæm.ən, ˈsæl.mən, ˈsɑː- *river, etc. in Canada & US:* ˈsæm.ən *biblical name:* ˈsæl.mɒn, -mən ⓤⓢ -mən
salmonberr|y ˈsæm.ən.bᵊr|.i, ˈ-əm- ⓤⓢ -ˌber- **-ies** -iz
salmonella ˌsæl.məˈnel.ə
Salome səˈləʊ.mi, -meɪ ⓤⓢ -ˈloʊ-; ˈsæl.ə.meɪ
salon ˈsæl.ɔ̃ːŋ, -lɒn ⓤⓢ səˈlɑːn; ˈsæl.ɑːn **-s** -z
Salonika, **Salonica** səˈlɒn.ɪ.kə, ˌsæl.əˈniː- ⓤⓢ səˈlɑː.nə-; ˌsæl.əˈnaɪ-, -ˈniː-
saloon səˈluːn **-s** -z **saˌloon ˈbar** ; **saˈloon ˌcar**
Salop ˈsæl.əp
Salopian səˈləʊ.pi.ən ⓤⓢ -ˈloʊ- **-s** -z
Salpeter ˈsæl.piː.təʳ ⓤⓢ -t̬ɚ
salpingitis ˌsæl.pɪnˈdʒaɪ.tɪs, -təs ⓤⓢ -t̬ɪs
salsa ˈsæl.sə ⓤⓢ ˈsɑːl-
salsify ˈsæl.sɪ.fi, -sə-, -faɪ ⓤⓢ -sə-
salt, SALT (S) sɔːlt, sɒlt ⓤⓢ sɔːlt, sɑːlt **-s** -s **-ing** -ɪŋ ⓤⓢ ˈsɔːl.t̬ɪŋ **-ed** -ɪd ⓤⓢ ˈsɔːl.t̬ɪd **-ness** -nəs, -nɪs **ˈsalt ˌcellar** ; **ˌSalt ˌLake ˈCity** ; **ˈsalt ˌmarsh** ; **ˈsalt ˌshaker** ; **rub ˌsalt into someone's ˈwounds** ; **ˌsalt of the ˈearth** ; **ˌtake something with a ˌpinch/grain of ˈsalt**
Saltaire sɔːlˈteəʳ, sɒl- ⓤⓢ sɑːlˈter
saltant ˈsæl.tənt, ˈsɔːl-, ˈsɒl- ⓤⓢ ˈsæl.tᵊnt
Saltash ˈsɔːl.tæʃ, ˈsɒl- ⓤⓢ ˈsɑːl-
saltation sælˈteɪ.ʃᵊn **-s** -z
Saltburn ˈsɔːlt.bɜːn, ˈsɒlt- ⓤⓢ ˈsɔːlt.bɜːrn, ˈsɑːlt-
Saltcoats ˈsɔːlt.kəʊts, ˈsɒlt- ⓤⓢ ˈsɔːlt.koʊts, ˈsɑːlt-
Saltdean ˈsɔːlt.diːn, ˈsɒlt- ⓤⓢ ˈsɔːlt-, ˈsɑːlt-

Salter 'sɔːl.təʳ, 'sɒl- (US) 'sɔːl.t̬ɚ, 'sɑːl-
Salterton 'sɔːl.tə.tᵊn, 'sɒl- (US) 'sɔːl.t̬ɚ.tən, 'sɑːl-
Saltfleetby 'sɔːltˌfliːt.bi, 'sɒlt- *locally also:* 'sɒl.ə.bi (US) 'sɔːltˌfliːt.bi, 'sɑːlt-
Salting 'sɔːl.tɪŋ, 'sɒl- (US) 'sɔːl.t̬ɪŋ, 'sɑːl-
saltire 'sɔːl.taɪəʳ, 'sɒl-, 'sæl- (US) 'sɔːl.tɪr, 'sɑːl-, 'sæl-, -taɪɚ **-s** -z
Saltmarsh 'sɔːlt.mɑːʃ, 'sɒlt- (US) 'sɔːlt.mɑːrʃ, 'sɑːlt-
Salto 'sæl.təʊ (US) 'sɑːl.toʊ
Saltoun 'sɔːl.tᵊn, 'sɒlt- (US) 'sɔːl.tən, 'sɑːl-
saltpan 'sɔːlt.pæn, 'sɒlt- (US) 'sɔːlt-, 'sɑːlt- **-s** -z
saltpetre, saltpeter ˌsɔːlt'piː.təʳ, ˌsɒlt-, '--- (US) 'sɔːltˌpiː.t̬ɚ, 'sɑːlt-
saltwater 'sɔːltˌwɔː.təʳ, 'sɒlt- (US) 'sɔːltˌwɑː.t̬ɚ, 'sɑːlt-, -ˌwɔː-
salt|y 'sɔːl.t|i, 'sɒl- (US) 'sɔːl.t̬|i, 'sɑːl- **-ier** -i.əʳ (US) -i.ɚ **-iest** -i.ɪst, -i.əst **-iness** -ɪ.nəs, -ɪ.nɪs
salubrious sə'luː.bri.əs, -'ljuː- (US) -'luː- **-ly** -li **-ness** -nəs, -nɪs
salubrity sə'luː.brə.ti, -'ljuː-, -brɪ- (US) -'luː.brə.t̬i
Salusbury 'sɔːlz.bᵊr.i
Salut (*in* **Port Salut**) sə'luː
salutar|y 'sæl.jə.tᵊr|.i, -jʊ- (US) -ter- **-ily** -ᵊl.i, -ɪ.li **-iness** -ɪ.nəs, -ɪ.nɪs
salutation ˌsæl.jə'teɪ.ʃᵊn, -jʊ'- **-s** -z
salu|te sə'luː|t, -'ljuː|t (US) -'luː|t **-tes** -ts **-ting** -tɪŋ (US) -t̬ɪŋ **-ted** -tɪd (US) -t̬ɪd
salvable 'sæl.və.bl̩
Salvador 'sæl.və.dɔːʳ, ˌ--'- (US) 'sæl.və.dɔːr **-an/s** -ən/z
Salvadorean, Salvadorian ˌsæl.və'dɔː.ri.ən (US) -'dɔːr.i- **-s** -z
salvag|e 'sæl.vɪdʒ **-es** -ɪz **-ing** -ɪŋ **-ed** -d **-eable** -ə.bl̩ **-er/s** -əʳ/z (US) -ɚ/z
Salvarsan® 'sæl.və.sən, -sæn (US) -vɚ-
salvation sæl'veɪ.ʃᵊn **-s** -z **Salˌvation 'Army**
salvation|ism sæl'veɪ.ʃᵊn|.ɪ.zᵊm **-ist/s** -ɪst/s
salv|e *anoint, soothe:* sælv, sɑːv (US) sæv, sɑːv **-es** -z **-ing** -ɪŋ **-ed** -d
salv|e *save ship, cargo:* sælv **-es** -z **-ing** -ɪŋ **-ed** -d
Salve *Catholic antiphon:* 'sæl.veɪ **-s** -z
salver 'sæl.vəʳ (US) -vɚ **-s** -z
salvia 'sæl.vi.ə **-s** -z
salvo 'sæl.vəʊ (US) -voʊ **-(e)s** -z **-ing** -ɪŋ **-ed** -d
sal volatile ˌsæl.vəʊ'læt.ᵊl.i, -vɒl'æt- (US) -voʊ'læt̬.ᵊl-
Salyut sə'ljuːt, sæl'juːt (US) 'sæl.juːt
Salzburg 'sælts.bɜːg, 'sɑːlts- (US) 'sɔːlz.bɜːrg, 'sɑːlz-
Sam sæm **ˌSam ˌBrowne 'belt**
Samantha sə'mænt.θə
Samara sə'mɑː.rə (US) -'mɑːr.ə, -'mær-
Samaria sə'meə.ri.ə (US) -'mer.i-, -'mær-
Samaritan sə'mær.ɪ.tᵊn (US) -'mer.ə-, -'mær- **-s** -z **ˌgood Sa'maritan**
samarium sə'meə.ri.əm (US) -'mer.i-, -'mær-
Samarkand ˌsæm.ɑː'kænd, -ə'-, '--- (US) 'sæm.ɚ.kænd, ˌ--'-
samarskite sə'mɑː.skaɪt (US) -'mɑːr-; 'sæm.ɚ-
samba 'sæm.bə (US) 'sɑːm-, 'sæm- **-s** -z **-ing** -ɪŋ **-ed** -d
sambo (S) 'sæm.bəʊ (US) -boʊ **-s** -z
same seɪm **-y** -i **-ness** -nəs, -nɪs
S. America (*abbrev. for* **South America**) ˌsaʊθ.ə'mer.ɪ.kə
samite 'seɪ.maɪt, 'sæm.aɪt (US) 'sæm.aɪt, 'seɪ.maɪt
samizdat ˌsæm.ɪz'dæt, '--- (US) 'sɑː.mɪz.dɑːt, ˌ--'-
Sammy 'sæm.i
Samnite 'sæm.naɪt **-s** -s
Samo|a sə'məʊ|ə, sɑː- (US) sə'moʊ|ə **-an/s** -ən/z
Samos 'seɪ.mɒs, 'sæm- (US) -mɑːs; 'sæm.oʊs
samosa sə'məʊ.sə, sæm'əʊ-, -zə (US) sə'moʊ.sə **-s** -z
Samothrace 'sæm.əʊ.θreɪs (US) '-ə-, -oʊ-
samovar 'sæm.ə.vɑːʳ, ˌ--'- (US) 'sæm.ə.vɑːr; ˌsɑː.mə'vɑːr **-s** -z
Samoyed *people:* ˌsæm.ɔɪ'ed; -'--, -ɪd (US) 'sæm.ə.jed; sə'mɔɪ.ed **-s** -z *dog:* sə'mɔɪ.ed, -ɪd (US) 'sæm.ə.jed; sə'mɔɪ.ed **-s** -z
sampan 'sæm.pæn **-s** -z
samphire 'sæmp.faɪəʳ (US) -faɪɚ
sampl|e 'sɑːm.pl̩ (US) 'sæm- **-es** -z **-ing** -ɪŋ, 'sɑːm.plɪŋ (US) 'sæm- **-ed** -d
sampler 'sɑːm.pləʳ (US) 'sæm.plɚ **-s** -z
Sampson 'sæmp.sᵊn
Samson 'sæmp.sᵊn
Samsonite® 'sæmp.sᵊn.aɪt
Samuel 'sæm.jʊəl, -ju.əl (US) -ju.əl, -jʊl **-s** -z
samurai (S) 'sæm.ʊ.raɪ, -jʊ- (US) -ə.raɪ **-s** -z
San Antonio ˌsæn.æn'təʊ.ni.əʊ (US) -'toʊ.ni.oʊ
sanatari|um ˌsæn.ə'teə.ri|.əm (US) -'ter.i- **-ums** -əmz **-a** -ə
Sanatogen® sə'næt.ə.dʒᵊn, -dʒen (US) -'næt̬-
sanatori|um ˌsæn.ə'tɔː.ri|.əm (US) -'tɔːr.i- **-ums** -əmz **-a** -ə
Sancerre sæn'seəʳ, sɑ̃ːn- (US) sɑːn'ser
Sanchez 'sæn.tʃez
Sancho Panza ˌsæn.tʃəʊ'pæn.zə (US) ˌsɑːn.tʃoʊ'pɑːn-
San Cristóbal ˌsæn.krɪ'stəʊ.bæl, ˌsæŋ- (US) ˌsæn.krɪ'stoʊ.bəl, -bɑːl
sanctification ˌsæŋk.tɪ.fɪ'keɪ.ʃᵊn, -tə-
sancti|fy 'sæŋk.tɪ|.faɪ, -tə- **-fies** -faɪz **-fying** -faɪ.ɪŋ **-fied** -faɪd
sanctimonious ˌsæŋk.tɪ'məʊ.ni.əs, -tə'- (US) -'moʊ- **-ly** -li **-ness** -nəs, -nɪs
sanction 'sæŋk.ʃᵊn **-s** -z **-ing** -ɪŋ **-ed** -d
sanctity 'sæŋk.tə.ti, -tɪ- (US) -tə.t̬i
sanctuar|y 'sæŋk.tʃʊə.r|i, -tʃᵊ.r|i, -tjʊə.r|i, -tjᵊr|.i (US) -tʃu.er|.i **-ies** -ɪz
sanct|um 'sæŋk.t|əm **-ums** -əmz **-a** -ə **ˌinner 'sanctum**
Sanctus 'sæŋk.təs **-es** -ɪz
sand *on beach:* sænd **-s** -z **-ing** -ɪŋ **-ed** -ɪd **-er/s** -əʳ/z (US) -ɚ/z **'sand ˌdollar ; 'sand ˌtrap ; ˌbury one's ˌhead in the 'sand, ˌbury one's 'head in the ˌsand (US) ˌbury one's ˌhead in the 'sand**
Sand *French novelist:* sɑ̃ːnd (US) sænd, sɑ̃ːnd
sandal 'sæn.dᵊl **-s** -z
sandalwood 'sæn.dᵊl.wʊd
Sanday 'sæn.deɪ, -di
Sandbach 'sænd.bætʃ, 'sæm- (US) 'sænd-
sandbag 'sænd.bæg, 'sæm- (US) 'sænd- **-s** -z **-ging** -ɪŋ **-ged** -d **-ger/s** -əʳ/z (US) -ɚ/z
sandbank 'sænd.bæŋk, 'sæm- (US) 'sænd- **-s** -s
sandbar 'sænd.bɑːʳ, 'sæm- (US) 'sænd.bɑːr **-s** -z
sandblast 'sænd.blɑːst, 'sæm- (US) 'sænd.blæst **-s** -s **-ing** -ɪŋ **-ed** -ɪd **-er/s** -əʳ/z (US) -ɚ/z
sandbox 'sænd.bɒks, 'sæm- (US) -bɑːks **-es** -ɪz
sandboy 'sænd.bɔɪ, 'sæm- (US) 'sænd- **-s** -z **ˌhappy as a 'sandboy**
Sandburg 'sænd.bɜːg (US) -bɜːrg
sandcastle 'sændˌkɑː.sl̩, 'sæŋ- (US) 'sændˌkæs.l̩ **-s** -z
sanderling 'sæn.dᵊl.ɪŋ (US) -dɚ.lɪŋ **-s** -z
Sanders 'sɑːn.dəz (US) 'sæn.dɚz
Sanderson 'sɑːn.də.sᵊn (US) 'sæn.dɚ-
Sanderstead 'sɑːn.də.sted, -stɪd (US) 'sæn.dɚ-
sandfl|y 'sænd.fl|aɪ **-ies** -aɪz
Sandford 'sænd.fəd, -fɔːd; 'sæn.əd (US) 'sænd.fɚd, -fɔːrd
Sandgate 'sænd.geɪt, 'sæŋ-, -gɪt (US) 'sænd-
sandhi 'sæn.diː, 'sʌn-; 'sænd.hiː, 'sʌnd- (US) 'sæn.di, 'sɑːn-, 'sʌn-
sandhopper 'sændˌhɒp.əʳ (US) -ˌhɑː.pɚ **-s** -z
Sandhurst 'sænd.hɜːst (US) -hɜːrst
San Diego ˌsæn.di'eɪ.gəʊ (US) -goʊ
Sandinista ˌsæn.də'nɪs.tə, -dɪ'- (US) -'niː.stə **-s** -z

Sanditon ˈsæn.dɪ.tən ⓤⓢ -t̬ən
Sandling ˈsænd.lɪŋ
sand|man ˈsænd|.mæn, ˈsæm- ⓤⓢ ˈsænd- **-men** -men
San Domingo ˌsæn.dəˈmɪŋ.gəʊ, -dəʊˈ-, -dɒmˈɪŋ- ⓤⓢ -dəˈmɪŋ.goʊ, -doʊˈ-
Sandown ˈsæn.daʊn
sandpap|er ˈsændˌpeɪ.p|əʳ, ˈsæm- ⓤⓢ ˈsændˌpeɪ.p|ɚ **-ers** -əz ⓤⓢ -ɚz **-ering** -ər.ɪŋ **-ered** -əd ⓤⓢ -ɚd
sandpiper ˈsændˌpaɪ.pəʳ, ˈsæm- ⓤⓢ ˈsændˌpaɪ.pɚ **-s** -z
sandpit ˈsænd.pɪt, ˈsæm- ⓤⓢ ˈsænd- **-s** -s
Sandra ˈsæn.drə, ˈsɑːn- ⓤⓢ ˈsæn-
Sandringham ˈsæn.drɪŋ.əm
Sands sændz
sandstone ˈsænd.stəʊn ⓤⓢ -stoʊn
sandstorm ˈsænd.stɔːm ⓤⓢ -stɔːrm **-s** -z
sand|wich ˈsæn|.wɪdʒ, ˈsæm-, -wɪtʃ ⓤⓢ ˈsænd|.wɪtʃ **-wiches** -wɪdʒ.ɪz, -wɪtʃ.ɪz ⓤⓢ -wɪtʃ.ɪz **-wiching** -wɪdʒ.ɪŋ, -wɪtʃ.ɪŋ ⓤⓢ -wɪtʃ.ɪŋ **-wiched** -wɪdʒd, -wɪtʃt ⓤⓢ -wɪtʃt
Note: Some British speakers use /-wɪtʃ/ in the uninflected form and /-wɪdʒ/ in the inflected forms of this word. **ˈsandwich ˌboard** ; **ˈsandwich ˌcourse**
Sandwich *in Kent:* ˈsænd.wɪtʃ, ˈsæm-, -wɪdʒ ⓤⓢ ˈsænd.wɪtʃ
sandwich|man ˈsænd.wɪdʒ|.mæn, ˈsæm-, -wɪtʃ- ⓤⓢ ˈsænd.wɪtʃ- **-men** -men
Sandwick ˈsænd.wɪk
sand|y (S) ˈsæn.d|i **-ier** -i.əʳ ⓤⓢ -i.ɚ **-iest** -i.ɪst, -i.əst **-iness** -ɪ.nəs, -ɪ.nɪs
Sandys sændz
san|e seɪn **-er** -əʳ ⓤⓢ -ɚ **-est** -ɪst, -əst **-ely** -li **-eness** -nəs, -nɪs
San Fernando ˌsæn.fəˈnæn.dəʊ ⓤⓢ -fɚˈnæn.doʊ
Sanford ˈsæn.fəd ⓤⓢ -fɚd
sanforiz|e, -is|e ˈsæn.fər.aɪz ⓤⓢ -fə.raɪz **-es** -ɪz **-ing** -ɪŋ **-ed** -d
San Francisco ˌsæn.frənˈsɪs.kəʊ, -frænˈ- ⓤⓢ -koʊ
sang (*from* **sing**) sæŋ
Sanger ˈsæŋ.gəʳ, -əʳ ⓤⓢ -ɚ
sang-froid ˌsɑ̃ːŋˈfrwɑː ⓤⓢ ˌsɑ̃ːŋ-, ˌsɑ̃ːn-
sangria ˈsæŋ.gri.ə, sæŋˈgriː- ⓤⓢ sænˈgriː-, sæŋ-
sanguinar|y ˈsæŋ.gwɪ.nər|.i, -gwə- ⓤⓢ -gwɪ.ner- **-ily** -əl.i, -ɪ.li **-iness** -ɪ.nəs, -ɪ.nɪs
sanguine ˈsæŋ.gwɪn **-ly** -li **-ness** -nəs, -nɪs
sanguineous sæŋˈgwɪn.i.əs
sanitari|um ˌsæn.ɪˈteə.ri|.əm, -əˈ- ⓤⓢ -ˈter.i- **-ums** -əmz **-a** -ə
sanitar|y ˈsæn.ɪ.tər|.i, -tr|i ⓤⓢ -ter|.i **-ily** -əl.i, -ɪ.li **-iness** -ɪ.nəs, -ɪ.nɪs **ˈsanitary ˌtowel** ; **ˈsanitary ˌnapkin**
sanitation ˌsæn.ɪˈteɪ.ʃən, -əˈ- **saniˈtation ˌworker**
sanitization, [-isa-] ˌsæn.ɪ.taɪˈzeɪ.ʃən, ˌ-ə-, -tɪˈ- ⓤⓢ -tɪˈ-
sanitiz|e, -is|e ˈsæn.ɪ.taɪz, ˈ-ə- **-es** -ɪz **-ing** -ɪŋ **-ed** -d
sanitori|um ˌsæn.əˈtɔː.ri|.əm, -ɪˈ- ⓤⓢ -ˈtɔːr.i- **-ums** -əmz **-a** -ə
sanity ˈsæn.ə.ti, -ɪ.ti ⓤⓢ -ə.t̬i
San José ˌsæn.həʊˈzeɪ, -əʊˈ- ⓤⓢ -hoʊˈ-, -əˈ-
San Juan ˌsænˈhwɑːn ⓤⓢ -ˈhwɑːn, -ˈwɔːn
sank (*from* **sink**) sæŋk
Sankey ˈsæŋ.ki
San Marino ˌsæn.məˈriː.nəʊ, ˌsæm- ⓤⓢ ˌsæn.məˈriː.noʊ
San Miguel ˌsæn.mɪˈgel, ˌsæm- ⓤⓢ ˌsæn-
San Pedro Sula sænˌped.rəʊˈsuː.lə, sæm- ⓤⓢ sænˌpiː.droʊˈ-, -ˌped.roʊˈ-
San Remo ˌsænˈreɪ.məʊ, -ˈriː- ⓤⓢ -ˈriː.moʊ, -ˈreɪ-
sans *English word:* sænz *in French phrases:* sɑ̃ːŋ ⓤⓢ sænz, sɑ̃ːn
San Salvador ˌsænˈsæl.və.dɔːʳ, -ˌsæl.vəˈdɔːʳ ⓤⓢ -ˈsæl.və.dɔːr
sans-culotte ˌsænz.kjʊˈlɒt ⓤⓢ -kuːˈlɑːt, -kjuːˈ- **-s** -s
San Sebastian ˌsæn.sɪˈbæs.ti.ən, -səˈ- ⓤⓢ -sɪˈbæs.tʃən
Sanskrit ˈsæn.skrɪt
sanskritic (S) sænˈskrɪt.ɪk ⓤⓢ -ˈskrɪt̬-
sans serif ˌsænˈser.ɪf
Santa ˈsæn.tə ⓤⓢ -t̬ə **-s** -z
Santa Ana ˌsæn.təˈæn.ə ⓤⓢ -t̬əˈ-
Santa Claus ˌsæn.təˈklɔːz, ˈ--ˌ- ⓤⓢ ˈsæn.t̬əˌklɑːz, -ˌklɔːz **-es** -ɪz
Santa Cruz ˌsæn.təˈkruːz ⓤⓢ ˈsæn.t̬ə.kruːz, ˌ--ˈ-
Santa Fe ˌsæn.təˈfeɪ ⓤⓢ ˈsæn.t̬ə.feɪ, ˌ--ˈ-
Santa Marta ˌsæn.təˈmɑː.tə ⓤⓢ -t̬əˈmɑːr.t̬ə
Santander ˌsæn.tənˈdeəʳ, -tænˈ-; ⓤⓢ ˌsɑːn.tɑːnˈder
Santayana ˌsæn.taɪˈɑː.nə ⓤⓢ -t̬iˈæn-, -ˈɑː.nə
Santiago ˌsæn.tiˈɑː.gəʊ ⓤⓢ -t̬iˈɑː.goʊ, ˌsɑːn-
Santley ˈsænt.li
Santo Domingo ˌsæn.təʊ.dəʊˈmɪŋ.gəʊ, -dɒmˈɪŋ- ⓤⓢ -toʊ.dəˈmɪŋ.goʊ, ˌsɑːn-, -doʊˈ-
Sanyo® ˈsæn.jəʊ ⓤⓢ -joʊ
Saône səʊn ⓤⓢ soʊn
São Paulo saʊmˈpaʊ.ləʊ, saʊ- ⓤⓢ sɑ̃ʊˈpaʊ.lu, -loʊ
São Tomé ˌsaʊn.təˈmeɪ, ˌsaʊ- ⓤⓢ ˌsɑ̃ʊ.toʊˈ-, -təˈ-
sap sæp **-s** -s **-ping** -ɪŋ **-ped** -t
sapele (S) sæpˈɪl.i, səˈpɪl-, -ˈpiː.li ⓤⓢ səˈpiː.li **saˌpele maˈhogany**
sapien|ce ˈseɪ.pi.ən|ts, ˈsæp.i- ⓤⓢ ˈseɪ.pi- **-t/ly** -t/li
sapiens ˈsæp.i.enz, -seɪ.pi-
Sapir səˈpɪəʳ, sæpˈɪəʳ; ˈseɪ.pɪəʳ ⓤⓢ sæpˈɪr, səˈpɪr
sapless ˈsæp.ləs, -lɪs **-ness** -nəs, -nɪs
sapling ˈsæp.lɪŋ **-s** -z
saponaceous ˌsæp.əʊˈneɪ.ʃəs ⓤⓢ -əˈ- **-ness** -nəs, -nɪs
saponification səˌpɒn.ɪ.fɪˈkeɪ.ʃən, sæpˌɒn-, ˌ-ə- ⓤⓢ səˌpɑː.nə-
saponi|fy səˈpɒn.ɪ|.faɪ, sæpˈɒn-, ˈ-ə- ⓤⓢ səˈpɑː.nə- **-fies** -faɪz **-fying** -faɪ.ɪŋ **-fied** -faɪd
sapper ˈsæp.əʳ ⓤⓢ -ɚ **-s** -z
sapphic (S) ˈsæf.ɪk **-s** -s
Sapphira səˈfaɪə.rə, sæfˈaɪə- ⓤⓢ səˈfaɪ-
sapphire ˈsæf.aɪəʳ ⓤⓢ -aɪɚ **-s** -z
sapph|ism (S) ˈsæf|.ɪ.zəm **-ist/s** -ɪst/s
Sappho ˈsæf.əʊ ⓤⓢ -oʊ
Sapporo səˈpɔː.rəʊ, sæpˈɔː-, -ˈɒr.əʊ ⓤⓢ səˈpɔːr.oʊ, sɑː-
sapp|y ˈsæp|.i **-iness** -ɪ.nəs, -ɪ.nɪs
saprogenic ˌsæp.rəʊˈdʒen.ɪk ⓤⓢ -rəˈ-
saprophyte ˈsæp.rəʊ.faɪt ⓤⓢ -rə- **-s** -s
sapwood ˈsæp.wʊd
Sara ˈsɑː.rə, ˈseə- ⓤⓢ ˈser.ə, ˈsær-
saraband(e) ˈsær.ə.bænd, ˌ--ˈ- ⓤⓢ ˈsær.ə.bænd, ˈser- **-s** -z
Saracen ˈsær.ə.sən, -sɪn, -sen ⓤⓢ -sən, ˈser-, ˈsær- **-s** -z
Saracenic ˌsær.əˈsen.ɪk ⓤⓢ ˌser-, ˌsær-
Saragossa ˌsær.əˈgɒs.ə ⓤⓢ -ˈgɑː.sə, ˌser-, ˌsær-
Sarah ˈseə.rə ⓤⓢ ˈser.ə, ˈsær-
Sarajevo ˌsær.əˈjeɪ.vəʊ ⓤⓢ -voʊ, ˌser-, ˌsær-
Saran® səˈræn **Saˈran ˌwrap**
Sarasate ˌsær.əˈsɑː.teɪ ⓤⓢ ˌsɑːr.ɑːˈsɑː.teɪ
Saratoga ˌsær.əˈtəʊ.gə ⓤⓢ ˌser.əˈtoʊ-, ˌsær-
Sarawak səˈrɑː.wæk, -wək, -wə ⓤⓢ -ˈrɑː.wɑːk
Sarawakian ˌsær.əˈwæk.i.ən ⓤⓢ ˌser.əˈwɑː.ki-, ˌsær- **-s** -z
sarcasm ˈsɑː.kæz.əm ⓤⓢ ˈsɑːr- **-s** -z
sarcastic sɑːˈkæs.tɪk ⓤⓢ sɑːr- **-ally** -əl.i, -li
sarcenet ˈsɑːs.net, -nət, -nɪt ⓤⓢ ˈsɑːr.snet
sarcoma sɑːˈkəʊ.mə ⓤⓢ sɑːrˈkoʊ- **-s** -z **-ta** -tə **-tous** -təs
sarcopha|gus sɑːˈkɒf.ə|.gəs ⓤⓢ sɑːrˈkɑː.fə- **-guses** -gə.sɪz **-gi** -gaɪ, -dʒaɪ
Sardanapalus ˌsɑː.dəˈnæp.əl.əs; -nəˈpɑː.ləs ⓤⓢ ˌsɑːr.dəˈnæp.əl.əs; -nəˈpeɪ.ləs

sardine *fish:* sɑːˈdiːn (US) sɑːr- **-s** -z

sardine *stone:* ˈsɑː.daɪn (US) ˈsɑːr.dɪn, -daɪn

Sardini|a sɑːˈdɪn.i|.ə (US) sɑːr-, ˈ-j|ə **-an/s** -ən/z

Sardis ˈsɑː.dɪs (US) ˈsɑːr-

sardius ˈsɑː.di.əs (US) ˈsɑːr- **-es** -ɪz

sardonic sɑːˈdɒn.ɪk (US) sɑːrˈdɑː.nɪk **-ally** -ᵊl.i, -li

sardonyx ˈsɑː.dᵊn.ɪks; sɑːˈdɒn- (US) sɑːrˈdɑː.nɪks; ˈsɑːr.də- **-es** -ɪz

Sargant ˈsɑː.dʒᵊnt (US) ˈsɑːr-

sargasso (S) sɑːˈgæs.əʊ (US) sɑːrˈgæs.oʊ **-(e)s** -z **Sarˌgasso ˈSea**

sarge sɑːdʒ (US) sɑːrdʒ

Sargeant, Sargent ˈsɑː.dʒᵊnt (US) ˈsɑːr-

Sargent ˈsɑː.dʒᵊnt (US) ˈsɑːr-

Sargeson ˈsɑː.dʒɪ.sᵊn (US) ˈsɑːr-

Sargon ˈsɑː.gɒn (US) ˈsɑːr.gɑːn

sari ˈsɑː.ri (US) ˈsɑːr.i **-s** -z

Sark sɑːk (US) sɑːrk

sark|y ˈsɑː.k|i (US) ˈsɑːr- **-ier** -i.əʳ (US) -i.ɚ **-iest** -i.ɪst, -i.əst

Sarmati|a sɑːˈmeɪ.ʃi|.ə, ˈ-ʃ|ə (US) sɑːrˈmeɪ.ʃ|ə, -ʃi|.ə **-an/s** -ən/z

sarnie ˈsɑː.ni (US) ˈsɑːr- **-s** -z

sarong səˈrɒŋ, sɑː-, særˈɒŋ (US) səˈrɔːŋ, -ˈrɑːŋ **-s** -z

Saro-Wiwa ˌsær.əʊˈwiː.wə, -wɑː (US) ˌsɑːr.oʊˈwiː.wə, ˈsær-

Saroyan səˈrɔɪən

sarsaparilla ˌsɑː.spᵊrˈɪl.ə, -sə.pᵊrˈ- (US) ˌsɑːr.sə.pəˈrɪl-, ˌsɑːr.spəˈ- *popularly:* ˌsæs.pəˈ-

sarsenet ˈsɑːs.net, -nət, -nɪt (US) ˈsɑːr.snet

Sarton ˈsɑː.tᵊn (US) ˈsɑːr-

Sartor ˈsɑː.tɔːʳ, -təʳ (US) ˈsɑːr.tɔːr, -t̬ɚ

sartorial sɑːˈtɔː.ri.əl (US) sɑːrˈtɔːr.i- **-ly**

Sartre ˈsɑː.trə (US) ˈsɑːr-; sɑːrt

Sarum ˈseə.rəm (US) ˈser.əm

SAS ˌes.eɪˈes

SASE ˌes.eɪ.esˈiː

sash sæʃ **-es** -ɪz **-ed** -t ˌ**sash ˈwindow**

Sasha ˈsæʃ.ə (US) ˈsɑː.ʃə, ˈsæʃ.ə

sashay ˈsæʃ.eɪ, -ˈ- (US) sæʃˈeɪ **-s** -z **-ing** -ɪŋ **-ed** -d

sashimi sæʃˈiː.mi, səˈʃiː- (US) sɑːˈʃiː.mi

Saskatchewan səˈskætʃ.ɪ.wən, sæsˈkætʃ-, ˈ-ə-, -wɒn (US) sæsˈkætʃ.ə.wɑːn, -wən **-er/s** -əʳ/z (US) -ɚ/z

saskatoon (S) ˌsæs.kəˈtuːn

Saskia ˈsæs.ki.ə

sasquatch (S) ˈsæs.kwɒtʃ, -kwætʃ (US) -kwɑːtʃ, -kwætʃ **-es** -ɪz

sass sæs

sassafras ˈsæs.ə.fræs **-es** -ɪz

Sassenach ˈsæs.ə.næk, -næx, -nək, -nəx (US) -næk **-s** -s

Sassoon səˈsuːn, sæsˈuːn (US) sæsˈuːn, səˈsuːn

sass|y ˈsæs|.i **-ier** -i.əʳ (US) -i.ɚ **-iest** -i.ɪst, -i.əst

sat (*from* **sit**) sæt

Sat. (*abbrev. for* **Saturday**) ˈsæt.ə.deɪ, -di (US) ˈsæt̬.ɚ-

Satan ˈseɪ.tᵊn **-ism** -ɪ.zᵊm **-ist/s** -ɪst/s

satang sætˈæŋ (US) sɑːˈtæŋ **-s** -z

satanic səˈtæn.ɪk, seɪˈtæn- **-ally** -ᵊl.i (US) -li

satay, saté ˈsæt.eɪ, ˈsɑː.teɪ (US) sɑːˈteɪ **-s** -z ˌ**satay ˈsauce** (US) ˈ**satay** ˌ**sauce**

satchel ˈsætʃ.ᵊl **-s** -z

Satchwell ˈsætʃ.wel

sateen sætˈiːn, səˈtiːn **-s** -z

satellite ˈsæt.ᵊl.aɪt, -ɪ.laɪt (US) ˈsæt̬.ᵊl.aɪt **-s** -s ˈ**satellite** ˌ**dish**; ˌ**satellite ˈtelevision** (US) ˈ**satellite** ˌ**television**

sati ˈsɑː.tiː **-s** -z

satiable ˈseɪ.ʃi.ə.bl̩, ˈ-ʃə.bl̩ (US) -ʃə-, -ʃi.ə-

sati|ate (*v.*) ˈseɪ.ʃi|.eɪt **-ates** -eɪts **-ating** -eɪ.tɪŋ (US) -eɪ.t̬ɪŋ **-ated** -eɪ.tɪd (US) -eɪ.t̬ɪd

satiate (*adj.*) ˈseɪ.ʃi.ət, -ɪt, -eɪt (US) -ɪt

satiation ˌseɪ.ʃiˈeɪ.ʃᵊn

Satie ˈsæt.i, ˈsɑː.ti, -ˈ- (US) sɑːˈtiː

satiety səˈtaɪ.ə.ti, -ˈtaɪ.ɪ-; ˈseɪ.ʃə.ti, -ʃi.ə- (US) səˈtaɪ.ə.t̬i

satin ˈsæt.ɪn (US) -ᵊn **-s** -z **-y** -i

satinette, satinet ˌsæt.ɪˈnet (US) -ᵊnˈet

satinwood ˈsæt.ɪn.wʊd (US) -ᵊn-

satire ˈsæt.aɪəʳ (US) -aɪɚ **-s** -z

satiric|al səˈtɪr.ɪ.k|ᵊl, ˈ-ə- (US) ˈ-ɪ- **-ally** -ᵊl.i, -li

satirist ˈsæt.ᵊr.ɪst, -ɪ.rɪst (US) ˈsæt̬.ɚ.ɪst **-s** -s

satiriz|e, -is|e ˈsæt.ᵊr.aɪz, -ɪ.raɪz (US) ˈsæt̬.ə.raɪz **-es** -ɪz **-ing** -ɪŋ **-ed** -d

satisfaction ˌsæt.ɪsˈfæk.ʃᵊn, -əsˈ- (US) ˌsæt̬-

satisfactor|y ˌsæt.ɪsˈfæk.tᵊr|.i, -əsˈ-, -tr|i (US) ˌsæt̬- **-ily** -ᵊl.i, -ɪ.li **-iness** -ɪ.nəs, -ɪ.nɪs

satis|fy ˈsæt.ɪs|.faɪ (US) -əs-, ˈsæt̬- **-fies** -faɪz **-fying** -faɪ.ɪŋ **-fied** -faɪd

satrap ˈsæt.ræp, -rəp (US) ˈseɪ.træp, ˈsæt.ræp **-s** -s **-y** -i **-ies** -iz

satsuma ˌsætˈsuː.mə, -sʊ- (US) ˈsæt.sə.mɑː; sɑːtˈsuː.mə **-s** -z

satur|ate (*v.*) ˈsætʃ.ᵊr|.eɪt, -ʊ.r|eɪt, -tjᵊr|.eɪt, -tjʊ.r|eɪt (US) ˈsætʃ.ə.r|eɪt **-ates** -eɪts **-ating** -eɪ.tɪŋ (US) -eɪ.t̬ɪŋ **-ated** -eɪ.tɪd (US) -eɪ.t̬ɪd ˌ**saturated ˈfat**

saturate (*adj.*) ˈsætʃ.ᵊr.eɪt, -ʊ.reɪt, ˈsæt.jᵊr.eɪt, -jʊ.reɪt (US) ˈsætʃ.ɚ.ɪt

saturation ˌsætʃ.ᵊrˈeɪ.ʃᵊn, -tʃʊˈreɪ-, -tjᵊrˈeɪ-, -tjʊˈreɪ- (US) ˌsætʃ.əˈreɪ- **satuˈration** ˌ**point**

Saturday ˈsæt.ə.deɪ, -di (US) ˈsæt̬.ɚ- **-s** -z

Saturn ˈsæt.ən, -ɜːn (US) ˈsæt̬.ɚn

saturnalia (S) ˌsæt.əˈneɪ.li.ə, -ɜːˈ- (US) ˌsæt̬.ɚˈ-, -ˈneɪl.jə **-n** -n **-s** -z

saturnian (S) sætˈɜː.ni.ən, səˈtɜː- (US) səˈtɜːr-

saturnine ˈsæt.ə.naɪn (US) ˈsæt̬.ɚ-

satyr ˈsæt.əʳ (US) ˈseɪ.t̬ɚ, ˈsæt̬.ɚ **-s** -z

satyriasis ˌsæt.ᵊrˈaɪə.sɪs (US) ˌseɪ.t̬əˈraɪə.sɪs, ˌsæt̬-

satyric səˈtɪr.ɪk (US) seɪ-, sə-

sauc|e sɔːs (US) sɑːs, sɔːs **-es** -ɪz **-ing** -ɪŋ **-ed** -d ˈ**sauce** ˌ**boat**

saucepan ˈsɔːs.pən (US) ˈsɑːs-, ˈsɔːs- **-s** -z

saucer ˈsɔː.səʳ (US) ˈsɑː.sɚ, ˈsɔː- **-s** -z

Sauchiehall ˌsɔː.kɪˈhɔːl, ˌsɒk.ɪˈ-, ˌ--ˈ- (US) ˌsɑː.kiˈ-, ˌsɔː-

sauc|y ˈsɔː.s|i (US) ˈsɑː-, ˈsɔː- **-ier** -i.əʳ (US) -i.ɚ **-iest** -i.ɪst, -i.əst **-ily** -ɪ.li, -ᵊl.i **-iness** -ɪ.nəs, -ɪ.nɪs

Saudi ˈsaʊ.di, ˈsɔː- (US) ˈsaʊ-, ˈsɔː-, ˈsɑː- **-s** -z ˌ**Saudi Aˈrabia**

sauerbraten ˈsaʊəˌbrɑː.tᵊn (US) ˈsaʊɚ-

sauerkraut ˈsaʊə.kraʊt (US) ˈsaʊɚ-

Saul sɔːl (US) sɔːl, sɑːl

Sault St. Marie ˌsuː.seɪnt.məˈriː

sauna ˈsɔː.nə, ˈsaʊ- (US) ˈsaʊ-, ˈsɔː-, ˈsɑː- **-s** -z

Saunders ˈsɔːn.dəz, ˈsɑːn- (US) ˈsɑːn-, ˈsɔːn-, -dɚz

Saunderson ˈsɔːn.də.sᵊn, ˈsɑːn- (US) ˈsɑːn-, ˈsɔːn-, -dɚ-

saunt|er ˈsɔːn.t|əʳ (US) ˈsɑːn.t̬|ɚ, ˈsɔːn- **-ers** -əz (US) -ɚz **-ering** -ᵊr.ɪŋ **-ered** -əd (US) -ɚd **-erer/s** -ə.rəʳ/z (US) -ɚ.ɚ/z

saurian ˈsɔː.ri.ən (US) ˈsɑːr.i-, ˈsɔːr- **-s** -z

sausag|e ˈsɒs.ɪdʒ (US) ˈsɑː.sɪdʒ, ˈsɔː- **-es** -ɪz ˈ**sausage** ˌ**dog**; ˈ**sausage maˌchine**; ˌ**sausage ˈroll** (US) ˈ**sausage** ˌ**roll**

Saussure səʊˈsjʊəʳ, -ˈsʊəʳ (US) soʊˈsʊr

sauté ˈsəʊ.teɪ, ˈsɔː- (US) sɔːˈteɪ, soʊ-, sɑː- **-s** -z **-ing** -ɪŋ **-(e)d** -d

Sauternes, Sauterne səʊˈtɜːn, -ˈteən (US) soʊˈtɜːrn, sɔː-, sɑː-

Sauvage ˈsæv.ɪdʒ; səʊˈvɑːʒ (US) ˈsæv.ɪdʒ; soʊˈvɑːʒ

Sauvignon ˈsəʊ.viː.njɔ̃ːŋ, -vɪ-, -njɒn, ˌ--ˈ- (US) ˌsoʊ.viːˈnjõʊn, ˈ--- ˌ**Sauvignon ˈBlanc**

savag|e (S) ˈsæv.ɪdʒ **-es** -ɪz **-est** -ɪst, -əst **-ely** -li **-eness** -nəs, -nɪs **-ery** -ᵊr.i, -ri **-ing** -ɪŋ **-ed** -d

savanna(h) (S) səˈvæn.ə **-s** -z

savant ˈsæv.ənt (US) sævˈɑːnt; səˈvænt; ˈsæv.ənt **-s** -s

sav|e seɪv **-es** -z **-ing/s** -ɪŋ **-ed** -d **-er/s** -əʳ/z (US) -ɚ/z **-(e)able** -ə.bl̩

saveloy ˈsæv.ə.lɔɪ, ˈ-ɪ-, ˌ--ˈ- (US) ˈsæv.ə.lɔɪ **-s** -z

Savels ˈsæv.əlz
Savernake ˈsæv.ə.næk (US) ˈ-ɚ-
Savery ˈseɪv.ər.i
Savile ˈsæv.ɪl, -əl ˌSavile ˈRow
Savill ˈsæv.ɪl, -əl
saving ˈseɪ.vɪŋ **-s** -z ˌ**saving** ˈ**grace** ; ˈ**savings ac**ˌ**count** ; ˈ**savings** ˌ**bank** ; ˈ**savings** ˌ**bond** ; ˈ**savings cer**ˌ**tificate** ; ˈ**savings** ˌ**stamp**
savio(u)r (S) ˈseɪ.vjəʳ (US) -vjɚ **-s** -z
Savlon® ˈsæv.lɒn (US) -lɑːn
savoir faire ˌsæv.wɑːˈfeəʳ (US) -wɑːrˈfer, -wɑːˈ-
savoir vivre ˌsæv.wɑːˈviː.vrə (US) -wɑːrˈ-, -wɑːˈ-
Savonarola ˌsæv.ən.əˈrəʊ.lə (US) -ˈroʊ-
sav|or ˈseɪ.v|əʳ (US) -v|ɚ **-ors** -əz (US) -ɚz **-oring** -ər.ɪŋ **-ored** -əd (US) -ɚd **-orless** -ə.ləs, -lɪs (US) -ɚ.ləs, -lɪs
savory (S) ˈseɪ.vər.i **-ies** -iz **-iness** -ɪ.nəs, -ɪ.nɪs
sav|our ˈseɪ.v|əʳ (US) -v|ɚ **-ours** -əz (US) -ɚz **-ouring** -ər.ɪŋ **-oured** -əd (US) -ɚd **-ourless** -ə.ləs, -lɪs (US) -ɚ.ləs, -lɪs
savour|y ˈseɪ.vər|.i **-ies** -iz **-iness** -ɪ.nəs, -ɪ.nɪs
savoy (S) səˈvɔɪ **-s** -z **sa**ˌ**voy** ˈ**cabbage**
Savoyard səˈvɔɪ.ɑːd; ˌsæv.ɔɪˈɑːd (US) səˈvɔɪ.ɚd; ˌsæv.ɔɪˈɑːrd **-s** -z
savvy ˈsæv.i
saw sɔː (US) sɑː, sɔː **-s** -z **-ing** -ɪŋ **-ed** -d **-n** -n
saw (*from* **see**) sɔː (US) sɑː, sɔː
saw|bones *singular:* ˈsɔː|.bəʊnz (US) ˈsɑː|.boʊnz, ˈsɔː- *plural:* ˈsɔː|.bəʊnz (US) ˈsɑː|.boʊnz, ˈsɔː- **-boneses** -ˌbəʊn.zɪz (US) -ˌboʊn-
Sawbridgeworth ˈsɔː.brɪdʒ.wɜːθ *old-fashioned:* ˈsæp.swəθ (US) ˈsɑː.brɪdʒ.wɝːθ, ˈsɔː-
sawbuck ˈsɔː.bʌk (US) ˈsɑː-, ˈsɔː- **-s** -s
sawd|er ˈsɔː.d|əʳ (US) ˈsɑː.d|ɚ, ˈsɔː- **-ers** -əz (US) -ɚz **-ering** -ər.ɪŋ **-ered** -əd (US) -ɚd
sawdust ˈsɔː.dʌst (US) ˈsɑː-, ˈsɔː-
sawfish ˈsɔː.fɪʃ (US) ˈsɑː-, ˈsɔː-
sawfl|y ˈsɔː.fl|aɪ (US) ˈsɑː-, ˈsɔː- **-ies** -aɪz
sawhors|e ˈsɔː.hɔːs (US) ˈsɑː.hɔːrs, ˈsɔː- **-es** -ɪz
sawmill ˈsɔː.mɪl (US) ˈsɑː-, ˈsɔː- **-s** -z
sawn (*from* **saw**) sɔːn (US) sɑːn, sɔːn
Sawney ˈsɔː.ni (US) ˈsɑː-, ˈsɔː- **-s** -z
sawn-off ˌsɔːnˈɒf (US) ˌsɑːnˈɑːf, ˌsɔːn- *stress shift, see compound:* ˌ**sawn-off** ˈ**shotgun**
Sawston ˈsɔːs.tən (US) ˈsɑːz-, ˈsɔːz-
sawtooth ˈsɔː.tuːθ (US) ˈsɑː-, ˈsɔː- **-ed** -t
Sawtry ˈsɔː.tri (US) ˈsɑː-, ˈsɔː-
sawyer (S) ˈsɔː.jəʳ, ˈsɔɪ.əʳ (US) ˈsɑː.jɚ, ˈsɔː-, ˈsɔɪ.ɚ **-s** -z

sax sæks **-es** -ɪz
Saxe-Coburg-Gotha ˌsæksˌkəʊ.bɜːgˈgəʊ.θə, -tə (US) -ˌkoʊ.bɝːgˈgoʊ-
saxhorn ˈsæks.hɔːn (US) -hɔːrn **-s** -z
saxifrag|e ˈsæk.sɪ.frɪdʒ, -sə-, -freɪdʒ (US) -sə.frɪdʒ **-es** -ɪz
Saxmundham sæksˈmʌn.dəm
Saxon ˈsæk.sən **-s** -z
Saxone® ˈsæk.səʊn, -ˈ- (US) -ˈsoʊn
saxony (S) ˈsæk.sən.i
saxophone ˈsæk.sə.fəʊn (US) -foʊn **-s** -z
saxophonist sækˈsɒf.ən.ɪst (US) ˈsæk.sə.foʊ.nɪst **-s** -s
say seɪ **says** sez **saying** ˈseɪ.ɪŋ **said** sed
Sayce seɪs
SAYE ˌes.eɪ.waɪˈiː
sayer (S) ˈseɪəʳ (US) ˈseɪɚ **-s** -z
saying ˈseɪ.ɪŋ **-s** -z
Sayle seɪl
say-so ˈseɪ.səʊ (US) -soʊ
SC (*abbrev. for* **South Carolina**) ˌsaʊθ.kær.əlˈaɪ.nə (US) -ker.əˈlaɪ-, -kær-
scab skæb **-s** -z **-by** -i **-biness** -ɪ.nəs, -ɪ.nɪs **-bing** -ɪŋ **-bed** -d
scabbard ˈskæb.əd (US) -ɚd **-s** -z
scabies ˈskeɪ.biːz, -biz
scabious ˈskeɪ.bi.əs **-es** -ɪz
scabrous ˈskeɪ.brəs (US) ˈskæb.rəs, ˈskeɪ.brəs **-ly** -li **-ness** -nəs, -nɪs
scad skæd **-s** -z
Scafell ˌskɔːˈfel *stress shift, see compound:* ˌ**Scafell** ˈ**Pike**
scaffold ˈskæf.əʊld, -əld (US) -əld, -oʊld **-s** -z
scaffolding ˈskæf.əl.dɪŋ **-s** -z
scag skæg
Scala ˈskɑː.lə
scalable ˈskeɪ.lə.bl̩
scalar ˈskeɪ.ləʳ, -lɑːʳ (US) -lɚ, -lɑːr
scalawag ˈskæl.ə.wæg, ˈ-ɪ- (US) ˈ-ə- **-s** -z
Scalby ˈskæl.bi
scald skɔːld (US) skɑːld, skɔːld **-s** -z **-ing** -ɪŋ **-ed** -ɪd
scal|e skeɪl **-es** -z **-ing** -ɪŋ **-ed** -d **-less** -ləs, -lɪs **-er/s** -əʳ/z (US) -ɚ/z
scalene ˈskeɪ.liːn; -ˈ-, skælˈiːn (US) ˈskeɪ.liːn, -ˈ-
scales (S) skeɪlz ˌ**tip the** ˈ**scales**
Scaliger ˈskæl.ɪ.dʒəʳ (US) -dʒɚ
scallion ˈskæl.i.ən, ˈ-jən (US) ˈ-jən **-s** -z
scallop ˈskæl.əp, ˈskɒl- (US) ˈskɑː.ləp, ˈskæl.əp **-s** -s **-ing** -ɪŋ **-ed** -t
scallywag ˈskæl.i.wæg **-s** -z
scalp skælp **-s** -s **-ing** -ɪŋ **-ed** -t **-er/s** -əʳ/z (US) -ɚ/z
scalpel ˈskæl.pəl **-s** -z
scal|y ˈskeɪ.l|i **-ier** -i.əʳ (US) -i.ɚ **-iest** -i.ɪst, -i.əst **-iness** -ɪ.nəs, -ɪ.nɪs

scam skæm **-s** -z
Scammell ˈskæm.əl
scamp skæmp **-s** -s **-ing** -ɪŋ **-ed** -t **-ish** -ɪʃ
scamp|er ˈskæm.p|əʳ (US) -p|ɚ **-ers** -əz (US) -ɚz **-ering** -ər.ɪŋ **-ered** -əd (US) -ɚd
scampi ˈskæm.pi
scan skæn **-s** -z **-ning** -ɪŋ **-ned** -d
scandal ˈskæn.dəl **-s** -z
scandalization, -isa- ˌskæn.dəl.aɪˈzeɪ.ʃən (US) -ɪˈ-
scandaliz|e, -is|e ˈskæn.dəl.aɪz (US) -də.laɪz **-es** -ɪz **-ing** -ɪŋ **-ed** -d
scandalmong|er ˈskæn.dəlˌmʌŋ.g|əʳ (US) -ˌmɑːŋ.g|ɚ, -ˌmʌŋ- **-ers** -əz (US) -ɚz **-ering** -ər.ɪŋ
scandalous ˈskæn.dəl.əs **-ly** -li **-ness** -nəs, -nɪs
scandent ˈskæn.dənt
Scandian ˈskæn.di.ən
Scandinavi|a ˌskæn.dɪˈneɪ.vi|.ə, -dəˈ- (US) -vi|.ə, ˈ-vj|ə **-an/s** -ən/z
scandium ˈskæn.di.əm
Scania® ˈskæn.i.ə, ˈ-jə
Scanlan, Scanlon ˈskæn.lən
Scannell ˈskæn.əl; skəˈnel
scanner ˈskæn.əʳ (US) -ɚ **-s** -z
scansion ˈskæn.ʃən **-s** -z
scant skænt **-ly** -li **-ness** -nəs, -nɪs
scant|y ˈskæn.t|i (US) -t̬|i **-ier** -i.əʳ (US) -i.ɚ **-iest** -i.ɪst, -i.əst **-ily** -ɪ.li, -əl.i **-iness** -ɪ.nəs, -ɪ.nɪs
Scapa Flow ˌskɑː.pəˈfləʊ, ˌskæp.əˈ- (US) -ˈfloʊ
scape skeɪp **-s** -s
-scape -skeɪp
Note: Suffix. Normally unstressed, e.g. **landscape** /ˈlænd.skeɪp/.
scapegoat ˈskeɪp.gəʊt (US) -goʊt **-s** -s **-ing** -ɪŋ **-ed** -ɪd
scapegrac|e ˈskeɪp.greɪs **-es** -ɪz
scapul|a ˈskæp.jə.l|ə, -jʊ- **-as** -əz **-ae** -iː **-ar/s** -əʳ
scar (S) skɑːʳ (US) skɑːr **-s** -z **-ring** -ɪŋ **-red** -d ˈ**scar** ˌ**tissue**
scarab ˈskær.əb (US) ˈsker-, ˈskær- **-s** -z
scarabae|us ˌskær.əˈbiː|.əs (US) ˌsker-, ˌskær- **-uses** -ə.sɪz **-i** -aɪ
scaramouch(e) (S) ˈskær.ə.muːtʃ, -muːʃ, -maʊtʃ, ˌ--ˈ- (US) ˈsker.ə.muːʃ, ˈskær-, -muːtʃ **-(e)s** -ɪz
Scarborough, Scarboro' ˈskɑː.bər.ə (US) ˈskɑːr.bɚ.oʊ, -ə
Scarbrough ˈskɑː.brə (US) ˈskɑːr-, -broʊ
scarc|e skeəs (US) skers **-er** -əʳ (US) -ɚ **-est** -ɪst, -əst **-ely** -li **-eness** -nəs, -nɪs
scarcity ˈskeə.sə.ti, -sɪ- (US) ˈsker.sə.t̬i
scar|e skeəʳ (US) sker **-es** -z **-ing** -ɪŋ **-ed** -d **-er/s** -əʳ/z (US) -ɚ/z ˈ**scare** ˌ**story**
scarecrow ˈskeə.krəʊ (US) ˈsker.kroʊ **-s** -z

scaredy-cat 'skeə.di.kæt Ⓤ 'sker- **-s** -s
scaremong|er 'skeəˌmʌŋ.g|əʳ Ⓤ 'skerˌmɑːŋ.g|ɚ, -ˌmʌŋ- **-ers** -əz Ⓤ -ɚz **-ering** -ᵊr.ɪŋ
scar|ey 'skeə.r|i Ⓤ 'sker|.i **-ier** -i.əʳ Ⓤ -i.ɚ **-iest** -i.ɪst, -i.əst **-ily** -ɪ.li **-iness** -ɪ.nəs, -ɪ.nɪs
scar|f (*n.*) skɑː|f Ⓤ skɑːr|f **-ves** -vz **-fs** -fs
scarf (*v.*) skɑːf Ⓤ skɑːrf **-s** -s **-ing** -ɪŋ **-ed** -t
Scarfe skɑːf Ⓤ skɑːrf
Scargill 'skɑː.gɪl Ⓤ 'skɑːr-
scarification ˌskær.ɪ.fɪ'keɪ.ʃᵊn, ˌskeə.rɪ-, -rə- Ⓤ ˌsker.ə.fɪ'-, ˌskær-
scari|fy 'skær.ɪ|.faɪ, 'skeə.rɪ-, -rə- Ⓤ 'sker.ə-, 'skær- **-fies** -faɪz **-fying** -faɪ.ɪŋ **-fied** -faɪd
scarlatina ˌskɑː.lə'tiː.nə, -lɪ'- Ⓤ ˌskɑːr.lə'-
Scarlatti skɑː'læt.i Ⓤ skɑːr'lɑː.t̬i
scarlet (S) 'skɑː.lət, -lɪt Ⓤ 'skɑːr- ˌ**scarlet 'fever** ; ˌ**scarlet 'pimpernel** ; ˌ**scarlet 'woman**
Scarlett 'skɑː.lət, -lɪt Ⓤ 'skɑːr-
Scarman 'skɑː.mən Ⓤ 'skɑːr-
scarp skɑːp Ⓤ skɑːrp **-s** -s **-ing** -ɪŋ **-ed** -t
scarper 'skɑː.pəʳ Ⓤ 'skɑːr.pɚ **-s** -z **-ing** -ɪŋ **-ed** -d
scarves (*plur. of* **scarf**) skɑːvz Ⓤ skɑːrvs
scar|y 'skeə.r|i Ⓤ 'sker|.i **-ier** -i.əʳ Ⓤ -i.ɚ **-iest** -i.ɪst, -i.əst **-ily** -ɪ.li, -ᵊl.i **-iness** -ɪ.nəs, -ɪ.nɪs
Scase skeɪs
scat skæt **-s** -s **-ting** -ɪŋ Ⓤ 'skæt̬.ɪŋ **-ted** -ɪd Ⓤ 'skæt̬.ɪd
scath|e skeɪð **-es** -z **-ing** -ɪŋ/li **-ed** -d **-eless** -ləs, -lɪs
scathing 'skeɪ.ðɪŋ **-ly** -li
scatological ˌskæt.ə'lɒdʒ.ɪ.kᵊl Ⓤ ˌskæt̬.ə'lɑː.dʒɪ-
scatolog|y skæt'ɒl.ə.dʒ|i Ⓤ -'ɑː.lə-, skə'tɑː- **-ist/s** -ɪst/s
scatt|er 'skæt|.əʳ Ⓤ 'skæt̬|.ɚ **-ers** -əz Ⓤ -ɚz **-ering** -ᵊr.ɪŋ **-ered** -əd Ⓤ -ɚd
scatterbrain 'skæt.ə.breɪn Ⓤ 'skæt̬.ɚ- **-s** -z **-ed** -d
scatt|y 'skæt|.i Ⓤ 'skæt̬|.i **-ier** -i.əʳ Ⓤ -i.ɚ **-iest** -i.ɪst, -i.əst **-iness** -ɪ.nəs, -ɪ.nɪs
scaup skɔːp Ⓤ skɑːp, skɔːp **-s** -s
scaveng|e 'skæv.ɪndʒ, -ᵊndʒ **-es** -ɪz **-ing** -ɪŋ **-ed** -d **-er/s** -əʳ/z Ⓤ -ɚ/z
Scawfell ˌskɔː'fel Ⓤ ˌskɑː-, ˌskɔː- *stress shift, see compound:* ˌ**Scawfell 'Pike**
scena 'ʃeɪ.nə Ⓤ **-s** -z
scenario sɪ'nɑː.ri.əʊ, sə-, sen'ɑː- Ⓤ sə'ner.i.oʊ, -'nær-, -'nɑːr- **-s** -z
scenarist 'siː.nᵊr.ɪst Ⓤ sə'ner-, -'nær-, -'nɑːr- **-s** -s
scene siːn **-s** -z
scenery 'siː.nᵊr.i
sceneshifter 'siːnˌʃɪf.təʳ Ⓤ -tɚ **-s** -z
scenic 'siː.nɪk, 'sen.ɪk Ⓤ 'siː- **-ally** -ᵊl.i, -li ˌ**scenic 'railway**
scent sent **-s** -s **-ing** -ɪŋ Ⓤ 'sen.t̬ɪŋ **-ed** -ɪd Ⓤ 'sen.t̬ɪd
scepter 'sep.təʳ Ⓤ -tɚ **-s** -z **-ed** -əd ˌ**scepter'd 'isle**
sceptic 'skep.tɪk **-s** -s **-al** -ᵊl **-ally** -ᵊl.i, -li
scepticism 'skep.tɪ.sɪ.zᵊm, -tə-
sceptre 'sep.təʳ Ⓤ -tɚ **-s** -z **-d** -d
schadenfreude 'ʃɑː.dᵊnˌfrɔɪ.də
Schaefer 'ʃeɪ.fəʳ Ⓤ -fɚ
schedul|e 'ʃed.juːl, 'ʃedʒ.uːl, -ᵊl; 'sked.juːl, 'skedʒ.uːl, -ᵊl Ⓤ 'skedʒ.uːl, -u.əl, -ᵊl **-es** -z **-ing** -ɪŋ **-ed** -d
Scheherazade ʃɪˌher.ə'zɑː.də, ʃə-, -ˌhɪə.rə'-, -'zɑːd Ⓤ ʃəˌher.ə'zɑːd, -'zɑː.də
Scheldt skelt, ʃelt Ⓤ skelt
schema 'skiː.mə **-s** -z **schemata** 'skiː.mə.tə; skɪ'mɑː.tə Ⓤ skiː'mɑː.t̬ə; 'skiː.mə.t̬ə
schematic skiː'mæt.ɪk, skɪ- Ⓤ skiː'mæt̬-, skə- **-ally** -ᵊl.i, -li
schematiz|e, -is|e 'skiː.mə.taɪz **-es** -ɪz **-ing** -ɪŋ **-ed** -d
schem|e skiːm **-es** -z **-ing/ly** -ɪŋ/li **-ed** -d **-er/s** -əʳ/z Ⓤ -ɚ/z
Schenectady skɪ'nek.tə.di, skə- Ⓤ skə-
scherzand|o skeət'sæn.d|əʊ, skɜːt- Ⓤ skert'sɑːn.d|oʊ, -'sæn- **-os** -əʊz Ⓤ -oʊz **-i** -i
scherz|o 'skeət.s|əʊ, 'skɜːt- Ⓤ 'skert.s|oʊ **-os** -əʊz Ⓤ -oʊz **-i** -i
Schiaparelli ˌskæp.ə'rel.i, ˌskjæp-, ˌʃæp- Ⓤ ˌskæp-, ˌʃæp-, ˌskjɑː.pɑː'-
Schiedam skɪ'dæm, 'skɪd.æm Ⓤ skɪ'dɑːm
Schiller 'ʃɪl.əʳ Ⓤ -ɚ
schilling (S) 'ʃɪl.ɪŋ **-s** -z
schipperke (S) 'ʃɪp.ə.ki, 'skɪ-; 'ʃɪp.ək Ⓤ 'skɪp.ɚ.ki **schipperkes** 'ʃɪp.ə.kiz, 'skɪ-; 'ʃɪp.əks Ⓤ 'skɪp.ɚ.kiz
schism 'skɪz.əm, 'sɪz- Ⓤ 'sɪz-, 'skɪz- **-s** -z
schismatic skɪz'mæt.ɪk, sɪz- Ⓤ sɪz'mæt̬-, skɪz- **-al** -ᵊl **-ally** -ᵊl.i, -li
schist ʃɪst **-s** -s **-ose** -əʊs Ⓤ -oʊs
schizo 'skɪt.səʊ Ⓤ -soʊ **-s** -z
schizoid 'skɪt.sɔɪd
schizophrenia ˌskɪt.səʊ'friː.ni.ə, ˌskɪd.zəʊ'- Ⓤ ˌskɪt.sə'-, -soʊ'-, -'fren.i-
schizophrenic ˌskɪt.səʊ'fren.ɪk, ˌskɪd.zəʊ'-, -'friː.nɪk Ⓤ ˌskɪt.sə'-, -soʊ'- **-ally** -ᵊl.i, -li **-s** -s
Schlegel 'ʃleɪ.gᵊl
schlemiel ʃlə'miːl **-s** -z
schlep(p) ʃlep **-s** -s **-ping** -ɪŋ **-ped** -t
Schlesinger 'ʃlez.ɪn.dʒəʳ, 'ʃles- Ⓤ 'ʃlees.ɪŋ.ɚ; 'ʃlez.ɪn.dʒɚ, 'ʃleɪ.zɪŋ-
Schleswig-Holstein ˌʃlez.vɪg'həʊl.staɪn, ˌʃles-, -wɪg'- Ⓤ -wɪg'hoʊl-, ˌʃles.vɪg'-, -'hɔːl.ʃtaɪn
schlock ʃlɒk Ⓤ ʃlɑːk **-s** -s
schlockmeister 'ʃlɒkˌmaɪ.stəʳ Ⓤ 'ʃlɑːkˌmaɪ.stɚ **-s** -z
schmal(t)z ʃmɔːlts, ʃmɒlts, ʃmælts Ⓤ ʃmɑːlts, ʃmɔːlts **-y** -i **-ier** -i.əʳ Ⓤ -i.ɚ **-iest** -i.ɪst, -i.əst
Schmidt ʃmɪt
schmo ʃməʊ Ⓤ ʃmoʊ **-es** -z
schmooz|e ʃmuːz **-es** -ɪz **-ing** -ɪŋ **-ed** -d
schmuck ʃmʌk **-s** -s
Schnabel ʃnɑː.bᵊl
schnap(p)s ʃnæps Ⓤ ʃnɑːps, ʃnæps
schnauzer 'ʃnaʊt.səʳ Ⓤ 'ʃnaʊ.zɚ **-s** -z
Schneider 'ʃnaɪ.dəʳ Ⓤ -dɚ
schnitzel 'ʃnɪt.sᵊl **-s** -z
Schnitzler 'ʃnɪt.sləʳ Ⓤ -slɚ
schnorkel 'ʃnɔː.kᵊl Ⓤ 'ʃnɔːr- **-s** -z
schnozzle 'ʃnɒz.l̩ Ⓤ 'ʃnɑː.zl̩ **-s** -z
Schoen ʃəʊn, ʃɜːn Ⓤ ʃoʊn, ʃɜːrn
Schoenberg 'ʃɜːn.bɜːg, -beəg Ⓤ 'ʃɜːrn.bɚg, 'ʃoʊn-
Schofield 'skəʊ.fiːld Ⓤ 'skoʊ-
scholar 'skɒl.əʳ Ⓤ 'skɑː.lɚ **-s** -z **-ly** -li
scholarship 'skɒl.ə.ʃɪp Ⓤ 'skɑː.lɚ- **-s** -s
scholastic skə'læs.tɪk, skɒl'æs- Ⓤ skə'læs- **-ally** -ᵊl.i, -li
scholasticism skə'læs.tɪ.sɪ.zᵊm, skɒl'æs- Ⓤ skə'læs.tə-
Scholes skəʊlz Ⓤ skoʊlz
scholiast 'skəʊ.li.æst Ⓤ 'skoʊ-, -əst **-s** -s
scholi|um 'skəʊ.li|.əm Ⓤ 'skoʊ- **-a** -ə
Scholl ʃɒl, ʃəʊl, skɒl Ⓤ ʃoʊl
Schönberg 'ʃɜːn.bɜːg, -beəg Ⓤ 'ʃɜːrn.bɚg, 'ʃoʊn-
school skuːl **-s** -z **-ing** -ɪŋ **-ed** -d ˌ**school 'leaver** ; ˌ**school 'tie**
schoolbag 'skuːl.bæg **-s** -z
schoolbook 'skuːl.bʊk **-s** -s
schoolboy 'skuːl.bɔɪ **-s** -z **-ish** -ɪʃ
school|child 'skuːl|.tʃaɪld **-children** -ˌtʃɪl.drᵊn
schooldays 'skuːl.deɪz
schoolgirl 'skuːl.gɜːl Ⓤ -gɜːrl **-s** -z **-ish** -ɪʃ
schoolhou|se 'skuːl.haʊ|s **-ses** -zɪz
schoolkid 'skuːl.kɪd **-s** -z
schoolmarm 'skuːl.mɑːm Ⓤ -mɑːrm **-s** -z **-ish** -ɪʃ
schoolmaster 'skuːlˌmɑː.stəʳ Ⓤ -ˌmæs.tɚ **-s** -z

schoolmate ˈskuːl.meɪt **-s** -s

schoolmistress ˈskuːlˌmɪs.trɪs, -trəs **-es** -ɪz

schoolroom ˈskuːl.rʊm, -ruːm (US) -ruːm, -rʊm **-s** -z

schoolteacher ˈskuːlˌtiː.tʃəʳ (US) -tʃɚ **-s** -z

schooltime ˈskuːl.taɪm

schoolwork ˈskuːl.wɜːk (US) -wɜːrk

schoolyard ˈskuːl.jɑːd (US) -jɑːrd

schooner ˈskuː.nəʳ (US) -nɚ **-s** -z

Schopenhauer ˈʃəʊ.pᵊn.haʊ.əʳ, ˈʃɒp.ᵊn- (US) ˈʃoʊ.pᵊn.haʊ.ɚ

schottisch|e ʃɒtˈiːʃ, ʃəˈtiːʃ (US) ˈʃɑː.t̬ɪʃ **-es** -ɪz

Schreiner ˈʃraɪ.nəʳ (US) -nɚ

Schrödinger ˈʃrɜː.dɪŋ.əʳ (US) ˈʃroʊ.dɪŋ.ɚ, ˈʃrɜːr-

Schroeder ˈʃrɜː.dəʳ (US) ˈʃroʊ.dɚ, ˈʃreɪ-

schtuck ʃtʊk

Schubert ˈʃuː.bət, -bɜːt (US) -bɚt

Schultz ʃʊlts

Schuman ˈʃuː.mən

Schumann ˈʃuː.mən, -mæn, -mɑːn (US) -mɑːn, -mən

schuss ʃʊs, ʃuːs **-es** -ɪz **-ing** -ɪŋ **-ed** -t

schwa ʃwɑː **-s** -z

Schwabe ʃwɑːb, ˈʃwɑː.bə

Schwann ʃwɒn *as if German:* ʃvæn (US) ʃvɑːn, ʃwɑːn

Schwartz ʃwɔːts *as if German:* ʃvaːts (US) ʃwɔːrts

Schwarzenegger ˈʃwɔːts.ᵊn.eg.əʳ (US) ˈʃwɔːrts.ᵊn.eg.ɚ

Schwarzkopf ˈʃvaːts.kɒpf, ˈʃwaːts-, ˈʃwɔːts- (US) ˈʃwɔːrts.kɑːpf

Schwarzwald ˈʃvaːts.væld, ˈʃwaːts-, -wæld (US) ˈʃvaːrts.vaːlt

Schweitzer ˈʃwaɪt.səʳ *as if German:* ˈʃvaɪt- (US) ˈʃwaɪt.sɚ *as if German:* ˈʃvaɪt-

Schweizer ˈʃwaɪt.səʳ *as if German:* ˈʃvaɪt- (US) ˈʃwaɪt.sɚ *as if German:* ˈʃvaɪt-

Schweppes® ʃweps

Schwerin ʃveəˈriːn, ʃweə- (US) ʃverˈiːn, ʃverˈriːn

sciatic saɪˈæt.ɪk (US) -ˈæt̬-

sciatica saɪˈæt.ɪ.kə (US) -ˈæt̬-

scienc|e saɪənts **-es** -ɪz ˌ**science ˈfiction** ; ˈ**science ˌpark**

scientific ˌsaɪənˈtɪf.ɪk **-ally** -ᵊl.i, -li

scientist ˈsaɪən.tɪst (US) -t̬ɪst **-s** -s

scientologist (S) ˌsaɪənˈtɒl.ə.dʒɪst (US) -ˈtɑː.lə- **-s** -s

Scientology® ˌsaɪənˈtɒl.ə.dʒi (US) -ˈtɑː.lə-

sci-fi ˈsaɪˌfaɪ

scilicet ˈsaɪ.lɪ.set, ˈsɪl.ɪ- (US) ˈsɪl.ɪ-

Scillonian sɪˈləʊ.ni.ən (US) -ˈloʊ- **-s** -z

Scill|y ˈsɪl|.i **-ies** -ɪz ˈ**Scilly ˌIsles**

scimitar ˈsɪm.ɪ.təʳ, ˈ-ə-, -tɑːʳ (US) -ə.t̬ɚ, -tɑːr **-s** -z

scintilla sɪnˈtɪl.ə

scintill|ate ˈsɪn.tɪ.l|eɪt, -tᵊl|.eɪt (US) -t̬ᵊl|.eɪt **-ates** -eɪts **-ating** -eɪ.tɪŋ (US) -eɪ.t̬ɪŋ **-ated** -eɪ.tɪd (US) -eɪ.t̬ɪd

scintillation ˌsɪn.tɪˈleɪ.ʃᵊn, -tᵊlˈeɪ- (US) -t̬ᵊlˈeɪ- **-s** -z

sciol|ism ˈsaɪ.əʊ.l|ɪ.zᵊm (US) ˈ-ə- **-ist/s** -ɪst/s

scion saɪən **-s** -z

Scipio ˈskɪp.i.əʊ, ˈsɪp- (US) ˈsɪp.i.oʊ

scire facias ˌsaɪə.riˈfeɪ.ʃi.æs, -əs (US) ˌsaɪ.riˈfeɪ.ʃi.æs

scirocco ʃɪˈrɒk.əʊ, sɪ-, sə- (US) ʃɪˈrɑː.koʊ, sə- **-s** -z

scission ˈsɪʒ.ᵊn, ˈsɪʃ- **-s** -z

sciss|or ˈsɪz|.əʳ (US) -ɚ **-ors** -əz (US) -ɚz **-oring** -ᵊr.ɪŋ **-ored** -əd (US) -ɚd

scissors ˈsɪz.əz (US) -ɚz

scissors-and-paste ˌsɪz.əz.ᵊndˈpeɪst (US) -ɚz-

scler|a ˈsklɪə.r|ə (US) ˈsklɪr|.ə **-as** -əz **-ae** -iː

scleros|is skləˈrəʊ.s|ɪs, sklɪ-, sklerˈəʊ-, sklɪəˈrəʊ- (US) sklɪˈroʊ- **-es** -iːz

sclerotic skləˈrɒt.ɪk, sklɪ-, sklerˈɒt-, sklɪəˈrɒt- (US) sklɪˈrɑː.t̬ɪk

scoff skɒf (US) skɑːf **-s** -s **-ing/ly** -ɪŋ/li **-ed** -t **-er/s** -əʳ/z (US) -ɚ/z

scofflaw ˈskɒf.lɔː (US) ˈskɑːf.lɑː, -lɔː **-s** -z

Scofield ˈskəʊ.fiːld (US) ˈskoʊ-

Scoggin ˈskɒg.ɪn (US) ˈskɑː.gɪn **-s** -z

scold skəʊld (US) skoʊld **-s** -z **-ing/s** -ɪŋ/z **-ed** -ɪd

scoliosis ˌskɒl.iˈəʊ.sɪs (US) ˌskoʊ.liˈoʊ-, ˌskɑː-

scollop ˈskɒl.əp (US) ˈskɑː.ləp **-s** -s **-ing** -ɪŋ **-ed** -t

sconc|e skɒn*t*s (US) skɑːn*t*s **-es** -ɪz **-ing** -ɪŋ **-ed** -t

scone skɒn, skəʊn (US) skoʊn, skɑːn **-s** -z

Scone skuːn ˌ**Stone of ˈScone**

scoop skuːp **-s** -s **-ing** -ɪŋ **-ed** -t

scoot skuːt **-s** -s **-ing** -ɪŋ (US) ˈskuː.t̬ɪŋ **-ed** -ɪd (US) ˈskuː.t̬ɪd

scooter ˈskuː.təʳ (US) -t̬ɚ **-s** -z

scope skəʊp (US) skoʊp **-s** -s

-scope -skəʊp (US) -skoʊp

Note: Suffix. Normally unstressed, e.g. **microscope** /ˈmaɪ.krə.skəʊp (US) -skoʊp/.

-scopic -ˈskɒp.ɪk (US) -ˈskɑː.pɪk

Note: Suffix. Words containing **-scopic** normally carry primary stress on the penultimate syllable, e.g. **microscopic** /ˌmaɪ.krəˈskɒp.ɪk (US) -ˈskɑː.pɪk/.

scopolamine skəˈpɒl.ə.miːn, -mɪn; ˌskəʊ.pəˈlæm.ɪn (US) skəˈpɑː.lə.miːn, skoʊ-, -mɪn

-scopy -skə.pi

Note: Suffix. Words containing **-scopy** normally carry primary stress on the antepenultimate syllable, e.g. **microscopy** /maɪˈkrɒs.kə.pi (US) -ˈkrɑː.skə-/.

scorbutic skɔːˈbjuː.tɪk (US) skɔːrˈbjuː.t̬ɪk

scorch skɔːtʃ (US) skɔːrtʃ **-es** -ɪz **-ing/ly** -ɪŋ/li **-ed** -t **-er/s** -əʳ/z (US) -ɚ/z ˌ**scorched ˈearth**

scor|e skɔːʳ (US) skɔːr **-es** -z **-ing** -ɪŋ **-ed** -d **-er/s** -əʳ/z (US) -ɚ/z **-less** -ləs, -lɪs

scoreboard ˈskɔː.bɔːd (US) ˈskɔːr.bɔːrd **-s** -z

scorecard ˈskɔː.kɑːd (US) ˈskɔːr.kɑːrd **-s** -z

scorekeeper ˈskɔːˌkiː.pəʳ (US) ˈskɔːrˌkiː.pɚ **-s** -z

score-line ˈskɔː.laɪn (US) ˈskɔːr- **-s** -z

scoresheet ˈskɔː.ʃiːt (US) ˈskɔːr- **-s** -s

scoria ˈskɔː.ri.ə, ˈskɒr.i- (US) ˈskɔːr.i-

scoriaceous ˌskɔː.riˈeɪ.ʃəs, ˌskɒr.iˈ- (US) ˌskɔːr.iˈ-

scorn skɔːn (US) skɔːrn **-s** -z **-ing** -ɪŋ **-ed** -d

scornful ˈskɔːn.fᵊl, -fʊl (US) ˈskɔːrn- **-ly** -i **-ness** -nəs, -nɪs

Scorpi|o ˈskɔː.pi|.əʊ (US) ˈskɔːr.pi|.oʊ **-os** -əʊz (US) -oʊz **-an/s** -ən/z

scorpion ˈskɔː.pi.ən (US) ˈskɔːr- **-s** -z

Scorsese skɔːˈseɪ.zi, -zeɪ (US) skɔːrˈseɪ.zi

scot (S) skɒt (US) skɑːt **-s** -s

scotch (S) skɒtʃ (US) skɑːtʃ **-es** -ɪz **-ing** -ɪŋ **-ed** -t ˌ**Scotch ˈbroth** ; ˌ**Scotch ˈegg** ; ˌ**Scotch ˈmist** ; ˌ**Scotch ˈpine** ; ˌ**Scotch ˈtape**

Scotch|man ˈskɒtʃ|.mən (US) ˈskɑːtʃ- **-men** -mən

Scotch|woman ˈskɒtʃ|ˌwʊm.ən (US) ˈskɑːtʃ- **-women** -ˌwɪm.ɪn

scoter ˈskəʊ.təʳ (US) ˈskoʊ.t̬ɚ **-s** -z

scot-free ˌskɒtˈfriː (US) ˌskɑːt-

scotia (S) ˈskəʊ.ʃə (US) ˈskoʊ-

Scotland ˈskɒt.lənd (US) ˈskɑːt- ˌ**Scotland ˈYard**

Scots skɒts (US) skɑːts ˌ**Scots ˈpine**

Scots|man ˈskɒts|.mən (US) ˈskɑːts- **-men** -mən

Scots|woman ˈskɒts|ˌwʊm.ən (US) ˈskɑːts- **-women** -ˌwɪm.ɪn

Scott skɒt (US) skɑːt

Scotticism ˈskɒt.ɪ.sɪ.zᵊm (US) ˈskɑː.t̬ɪ- **-s** -z

Scotticiz|e, -is|e ˈskɒt.ɪ.saɪz (US) ˈskɑː.t̬ɪ- **-es** -ɪz **-ing** -ɪŋ **-ed** -d

scottie (S) ˈskɒt.i (US) ˈskɑː.t̬i

Scottish ˈskɒt.ɪʃ (US) ˈskɑː.t̬ɪʃ **-ness** -nəs, -nɪs ˌ**Scottish ˈterrier**

scoundrel ˈskaʊn.drəl **-s** -z **-ly** -i

scour skaʊəʳ (US) skaʊɚ **-s** -z **-ing** -ɪŋ **-ed** -d **-er/s** -əʳ/z (US) -ɚ/z **'scouring ˌpad**

scourg|e skɜːdʒ (US) skɜːrdʒ **-es** -ɪz **-ing** -ɪŋ **-ed** -d

Scous|e skaʊs **-er/s** -əʳ/z (US) -ɚ/z

scout skaʊt **-s** -s **-ing** -ɪŋ (US) 'skaʊ.t̬ɪŋ **-ed** -ɪd (US) 'skaʊ.t̬ɪd **-er/s** -əʳ/z (US) 'skaʊ.t̬ɚ/z **ˌscout's 'hono(u)r**

scoutmaster 'skaʊtˌmɑː.stəʳ (US) -ˌmæs.tɚ **-s** -z

scow skaʊ **-s** -z

scowl skaʊl **-s** -z **-ing/ly** -ɪŋ/li **-ed** -d

scrabbl|e® 'skræb.l̩ **-es** -z **-ing** -ɪŋ, 'skræb.lɪŋ **-ed** -d

scrag skræg **-s** -z **-ging** -ɪŋ **-ged** -d

scrag-end ˌskræg'end **-s** -z

scraggly 'skræg.l̩.i **-ier** -i.əʳ (US) -i.ɚ **-iest** -i.ɪst **-iness** -ɪ.nəs, -ɪ.nɪs

scragg|y 'skræg|.i **-ier** -i.əʳ (US) -i.ɚ **-iest** -i.ɪst, -i.əst **-iness** -ɪ.nəs, -ɪ.nɪs

scram skræm **-s** -z **-ming** -ɪŋ **-med** -d

scrambl|e 'skræm.bl̩ **-es** -z **-ing** -ɪŋ, 'skræm.blɪŋ **-ed** -d **-er/s** **ˌscrambled 'eggs**

scramjet 'skræm.dʒet **-s** -s

scran skræn **-s** -z

scrap skræp **-s** -s **-ping** -ɪŋ **-ped** -t **-per/s** -əʳ/z (US) -ɚ/z **'scrap ˌheap ; 'scrap ˌmerchant ; ˌscrap 'metal** (US) **'scrap ˌmetal**

scrapbook 'skræp.bʊk **-s** -s

scrap|e skreɪp **-es** -s **-ing/s** -ɪŋ/z **-ed** -t **-er/s** -əʳ/z (US) -ɚ/z

scraperboard 'skreɪ.pə.bɔːd (US) -pɚ.bɔːrd **-s** -z

scrapie 'skreɪ.pi (US) 'skreɪ-, 'skræp.i

scrapple 'skræp.l̩

scrapp|y 'skræp|.i **-ier** -i.əʳ (US) -i.ɚ **-iest** -i.ɪst, -i.əst **-ily** -ɪ.li, -ᵊl.i **-iness** -ɪ.nəs, -ɪ.nɪs

scrapyard 'skræp.jɑːd (US) -jɑːrd **-s** -z

scratch skrætʃ **-es** -ɪz **-ing** -ɪŋ **-ed** -t **-er/s** -əʳ/z (US) -ɚ/z **'scratch ˌpaper**

scratchcard 'skrætʃ.kɑːd (US) -kɑːrd **-s** -z

scratch|y 'skrætʃ|.i **-ier** -i.əʳ (US) -i.ɚ **-iest** -i.ɪst, -i.əst **-ily** -ɪ.li, -ᵊl.i **-iness** -ɪ.nəs, -ɪ.nɪs

scrawl skrɔːl (US) skrɑːl, skrɔːl **-s** -z **-ing** -ɪŋ **-ed** -d

scrawl|y 'skrɔː.l|i (US) 'skrɑː-, 'skrɔː- **-ier** -i.əʳ (US) -i.ɚ **-iest** -i.ɪst, -ɪ.əst **-iness** -ɪ.nəs, -ɪ.nɪs

scrawn|y 'skrɔː.n|i (US) 'skrɑː-, 'skrɔː- **-ier** -i.əʳ (US) -i.ɚ **-iest** -i.ɪst, -i.əst **-iness** -ɪ.nəs, -ɪ.nɪs

scray skreɪ **-s** -z

scream skriːm **-s** -z **-ing/ly** -ɪŋ **-ed** -d **-er/s** -əʳ/z (US) -ɚ/z

scree skriː **-s** -z

screech skriːtʃ **-es** -ɪz **-ing** -ɪŋ **-ed** -t **-er/s** -əʳ/z (US) -ɚ/z **'screech ˌowl**

screed skriːd **-s** -z

screen skriːn **-s** -z **-ing/s** -ɪŋ **-ed** -d **'screen ˌprinting ; 'screen ˌtest**

screenplay 'skriːn.pleɪ, 'skriːm- (US) 'skriːn- **-s** -z

screenwriter 'skriːnˌraɪ.təʳ (US) -t̬ɚ **-s** -z

screw skruː **-s** -z **-ing** -ɪŋ **-ed** -d **ˌscrew 'cap** (US) **'screw ˌcap ; ˌscrew 'top** (US) **'screw ˌtop ; ˌscrewed 'up**

screwball 'skruː.bɔːl (US) -bɔːl, -bɑːl **-s** -z

screwdriver 'skruːˌdraɪ.vəʳ (US) -vɚ **-s** -z

screw|y 'skruː|.i **-ier** -i.əʳ (US) -i.ɚ **-iest** -i.ɪst, -i.əst **-iness** -ɪ.nəs, -ɪ.nɪs

Scriabin 'skrɪə.bɪn, skri'æb.ɪn (US) skri'ɑː.bɪn

scribal 'skraɪ.bᵊl

scribbl|e 'skrɪb.l̩ **-es** -z **-ing** -ɪŋ, 'skrɪb.lɪŋ **-ed** -d **-er/s** -əʳ/z, 'skrɪb.ləʳ/z (US) '-l̩.ɚ/z, '-lɚ/z

scribe skraɪb **-s** -z

Scriblerus skrɪ'blɪə.rəs (US) -'bler.əs, -'blɪr-

Scribner 'skrɪb.nəʳ (US) -nɚ

scrim skrɪm

scrimmag|e 'skrɪm.ɪdʒ **-es** -ɪz **-ing** -ɪŋ **-ed** -d

scrimp skrɪmp **-s** -s **-ing** -ɪŋ **-ed** -t **-er/s** -əʳ/z (US) -ɚ/z

scrimshaw 'skrɪm.ʃɔː (US) -ʃɑː, -ʃɔː **-s** -z **-ing** -ɪŋ **-ed** -d

scrip skrɪp **-s** -s

script skrɪpt **-s** -s **-ing** -ɪŋ **-ed** -ɪd

scriptori|um skrɪp'tɔː.ri|.əm (US) -'tɔːr.i- **-ums** -əmz **-a** -ə

scriptural 'skrɪp.tʃᵊr.ᵊl, -tʃʊ.rᵊl (US) -tʃɚ.ᵊl **-ly** -i

scripture (S) 'skrɪp.tʃəʳ (US) -tʃɚ **-s** -z

scriptwriter 'skrɪptˌraɪ.təʳ (US) -t̬ɚ **-s** -z

Scriven 'skrɪv.ᵊn

scrivener (S) 'skrɪv.ᵊn.əʳ, '-nəʳ (US) '-ᵊn.ɚ, '-nɚ **-s** -z

scrofula 'skrɒf.jʊ.lə (US) 'skrɑː.fjə-

scrofulous 'skrɒf.jʊ.ləs (US) 'skrɑː.fjə- **-ly** -li **-ness** -nəs, -nɪs

scroll skrəʊl (US) skroʊl **-s** -z

scrooge (S) skruːdʒ **-s** -ɪz

Scroope skruːp

Scrope skruːp, skrəʊp (US) skruːp, skroʊp

scrot|um 'skrəʊ.t|əm (US) 'skroʊ.t̬|əm **-ums** -əmz **-a** -ə **-al** -ᵊl

scroung|e skraʊndʒ **-es** -ɪz **-ing** -ɪŋ **-ed** -d **-er/s** -əʳ/z (US) -ɚ/z

scrub skrʌb **-s** -z **-bing** -ɪŋ **-bed** -d **'scrubbing ˌbrush ; 'scrub ˌbrush**

scrubber 'skrʌb.əʳ (US) -ɚ **-s** -z

scrubb|y 'skrʌb|.i **-ier** -i.əʳ (US) -i.ɚ **-iest** -i.ɪst, -i.əst **-iness** -ɪ.nəs, -ɪ.nɪs

scrubland 'skrʌb.lənd, -lænd (US) -lænd **-s** -z

scruff skrʌf **-s** -s

scruff|y 'skrʌf|.i **-ier** -i.əʳ (US) -i.ɚ **-iest** -i.ɪst, -i.əst **-iness** -ɪ.nəs, -ɪ.nɪs **-ily** -ɪ.li, -ᵊl.i

scrum skrʌm **-s** -z

scrum-|half ˌskrʌm|'hɑːf (US) -'hæf **-halfs** -'hɑːfs (US) -'hæfs **-halves** -'hɑːvz (US) -'hævz

scrummag|e 'skrʌm.ɪdʒ **-es** -ɪz **-ing** -ɪŋ **-ed** -d **-er/s** -əʳ/z (US) -ɚ/z

scrummy 'skrʌm.i **-ier** -i.əʳ (US) -i.ɚ **-iest** -i.ɪst **-iness** -ɪ.nəs, -ɪ.nɪs

scrump skrʌmp **-s** -s **-ing** -ɪŋ **-ed** -t

scrumptious 'skrʌm*p*.ʃəs, -tʃəs

scrumpy 'skrʌm.pi

scrunch skrʌn*t*ʃ **-es** -ɪz **-ing** -ɪŋ **-ed** -t **-y** -i

scrupl|e 'skruː.pl̩ **-es** -z **-ing** -ɪŋ, 'skruː.plɪŋ **-ed** -d

scrupulosity ˌskruː.pjə'lɒs.ə.ti, -pjʊ'-, -ɪ.ti (US) -'lɑː.sə.t̬i

scrupulous 'skruː.pjə.ləs, -pjʊ- **-ly** -li **-ness** -nəs, -nɪs

scrutator skruː'teɪ.təʳ (US) -t̬ɚ **-s** -z

scrutineer ˌskruː.tɪ'nɪəʳ, -tᵊn'ɪəʳ (US) -tᵊn'ɪr **-s** -z

scrutiniz|e, -is|e 'skruː.tɪ.naɪz, -tᵊn.aɪz (US) -tᵊn.aɪz **-es** -ɪz **-ing** -ɪŋ **-ed** -d

scrutin|y 'skruː.tɪ.n|i, -tᵊn|.i (US) -tᵊn|.i **-ies** -iz

scr|y skr|aɪ **-ies** -aɪz **-ying** -aɪ.ɪŋ **-ied** -aɪd

Scrymgeour 'skrɪm.dʒəʳ (US) -dʒɚ

scuba 'skuː.bə, 'skjuː- (US) 'skuː- **'scuba ˌdiving**

scud (S) skʌd **-s** -z **-ding** -ɪŋ **-ded** -ɪd

Scudamore 'skjuː.də.mɔːʳ (US) 'skuː.də.mɔːr

scuff skʌf **-s** -s **-ing** -ɪŋ **-ed** -t

scuffl|e 'skʌf.l̩ **-es** -z **-ing** -ɪŋ, 'skʌf.lɪŋ **-ed** -d

scull skʌl **-s** -z **-ing** -ɪŋ **-ed** -d **-er/s** -əʳ/z (US) -ɚ/z

sculler|y 'skʌl.ᵊr|.i **-ies** -iz **'scullery ˌmaid**

scullion (S) 'skʌl.i.ən (US) '-jən **-s** -z

sculpsit 'skʌlp.sɪt

sculpt skʌlpt **-s** -s **-ing** -ɪŋ **-ed** -ɪd

sculptor 'skʌlp.təʳ (US) -tɚ **-s** -z

sculpt|ure 'skʌlp.tʃ|əʳ (US) -tʃ|ɚ **-ures** -əz (US) -ɚz **-uring** -ᵊr.ɪŋ **-ured** -əd (US) -ɚd **-ural** -ᵊr.ᵊl

scum skʌm **-s** -z **-ming** -ɪŋ **-med** -d **-my** -i

scumbag 'skʌm.bæg **-s** -z

Scunthorpe 'skʌn.θɔːp (US) -θɔːrp

scupper 'skʌp.əʳ (US) -ɚ **-s** -z **-ing** -ɪŋ **-ed** -d

scurf skɜːf (US) skɜːrf **-y** -i **-iness** -ɪ.nəs, -ɪ.nɪs
scurrility skʌr'ɪl.ə.ti, skə'rɪl-, -ɪ.ti (US) skə'rɪl.ə.ţi
scurrilous 'skʌr.ə.ləs, '-ɪ- (US) 'skɜːr- **-ly** -li **-ness** -nəs, -nɪs
scurr|y 'skʌr|.i (US) 'skɜːr- **-ies** -iz **-ying** -i.ɪŋ **-ied** -id
scurv|y 'skɜː.v|i (US) 'skɜːr- **-ier** -i.əʳ (US) -i.ɚ **-iest** -i.ɪst, -i.əst **-ily** -ɪ.li, -əl.i **-iness** -ɪ.nəs, -ɪ.nɪs
Scutari 'skuː.tər.i; skuː'tɑː.ri, skʊ- (US) 'skuː.ţɚ.i, -tɑː-
scutcheon 'skʌtʃ.ən **-s** -z
scutt|er 'skʌt|.əʳ (US) 'skʌţ|.ɚ **-ers** -əz (US) -ɚz **-ering** -ər.ɪŋ **-ered** -əd (US) -ɚd
scuttl|e 'skʌt.l̩ (US) 'skʌţ- **-es** -z **-ing** -ɪŋ, 'skʌt.lɪŋ **-ed** -d
scuttlebutt 'skʌt.l̩.bʌt **-s** -s
scut|um 'skjuː.t|əm (US) -ţ|əm **-ums** -əmz **-a** -ə
scuzz|y 'skʌz|.i **-ier** -i.əʳ (US) -i.ɚ **-iest** -i.ɪst, -i.əst **-iness** -ɪ.nəs, -ɪ.nɪs
Scylla 'sɪl.ə
scyth|e saɪð **-es** -z **-ing** -ɪŋ **-ed** -d
Scythi|a 'sɪð.i|.ə, 'sɪθ- (US) 'sɪθ-, 'sɪð- **-an/s** -ən/z
S.D. (*abbrev. for* **South Dakota**) ˌsaʊθ.də'kəʊ.tə (US) -'koʊ.ţə
S.D.I. ˌes.diː'aɪ
SDP ˌes.diː'piː
SE (*abbrev. for* **southeast**) ˌes'iː, ˌsaʊθ'iːst
sea siː **-s** -z ˌ**sea 'breeze** (US) **'sea ˌbreeze** ; **'sea ˌcaptain** ; **'sea ˌchange** ; **'sea ˌcow** ; **'sea ˌelephant** ; **'sea ˌfog** ; ˌ**sea 'green** ; **'sea ˌhorse** ; **'sea ˌlegs** ; **'sea ˌlevel** ; **'sea ˌlion** ; **'sea ˌpower** ; **'sea ˌserpent** ; **'sea ˌslug** ; **'sea ˌsnail** ; **'sea ˌurchin** ; **between the ˌdevil and the ˌdeep ˌblue 'sea**
seabed 'siː.bed, -'-
seabird 'siː.bɜːd (US) -bɜːrd **-s** -z
seaboard 'siː.bɔːd (US) -bɔːrd
seaborne 'siː.bɔːn (US) -bɔːrn
Seabright 'siː.braɪt
seadog 'siː.dɒg (US) -dɑːg, -dɔːg **-s** -z
seafar|er 'siːˌfeə.r|əʳ (US) -ˌfer|.ɚ **-ers** -əz (US) -ɚz **-ing** -ɪŋ
seafood 'siː.fuːd
Seaford 'siː.fəd, -fɔːd (US) -fɚd, -fɔːrd
Seaforth 'siː.fɔːθ (US) -fɔːrθ **-s** -s
seafront 'siː.frʌnt **-s** -s
Seager 'siː.gəʳ (US) -gɚ
seagoing 'siːˌgəʊ.ɪŋ (US) -ˌgoʊ-
seagull 'siː.gʌl **-s** -z
Seaham 'siː.əm
seakale 'siː.keɪl, ˌ-'- (US) 'siː.keɪl
seal siːl **-s** -z **-ing** -ɪŋ **-ed** -d **'sealing ˌwax**
sealant 'siː.lənt **-s** -s
sealer 'siː.ləʳ (US) -lɚ **-s** -z
sealskin 'siːl.skɪn **-s** -z
Sealyham 'siː.li.əm **-s** -z
seam siːm **-s** -z **-ing** -ɪŋ **-ed** -d **-less** -ləs, -lɪs
sea|man (S) 'siː|.mən **-men** -mən, -men **-manship** -mən.ʃɪp **-manlike** -mən.laɪk
Seamas 'ʃeɪ.məs
seamstress 'sem*p*.strɪs, 'siːm*p*-, -strəs (US) 'siːm*p*- **-es** -ɪz
Seamus 'ʃeɪ.məs
seamy 'siː.mi **-ier** -i.əʳ (US) -i.ɚ **-iest** -i.ɪst, -i.əst **-iness** -ɪ.nəs, -ɪ.nɪs
Sean ʃɔːn (US) ʃɑːn, ʃɔːn
seanc|e, séance 'seɪ.ɑ̃ː*n*ts (US) 'seɪ.ɑːn*t*s **-es** -ɪz
sea-pink 'siː.pɪŋk
seaplane 'siː.pleɪn **-s** -z
seaport 'siː.pɔːt (US) -pɔːrt **-s** -s
sear sɪəʳ (US) sɪr **-s** -z **-ing/ly** -ɪŋ **-ed** -d
search sɜːtʃ (US) sɜːrtʃ **-es** -ɪz **-ing/ly** -ɪŋ/li **-ed** -t **-er/s** -əʳ/z (US) -ɚ/z **'search ˌparty** ; **'search ˌwarrant**
searchlight 'sɜːtʃ.laɪt (US) 'sɜːrtʃ- **-s** -s
Searle sɜːl (US) sɜːrl
Sears sɪəz (US) sɪrz
Seascale 'siː.skeɪl
seascape 'siː.skeɪp **-s** -s
seashell 'siː.ʃel **-s** -z
seashore 'siː.ʃɔːʳ, ˌ-'- (US) 'siː.ʃɔːr **-s** -z
seasick 'siː.sɪk **-ness** -nəs, -nɪs
seaside 'siː.saɪd
season 'siː.zən **-s** -z **-ing** -ɪŋ **-ed** -d **-er/s** ˌ**Season's 'Greetings** ; **'season ˌticket** (US) ˌ**season 'ticket**
seasonab|le 'siː.zən.ə.b|l̩, 'siːz.nə- **-ly** -li **-leness** -l̩.nəs, -nɪs
seasonal 'siː.zən.əl **-ly** -i
seasoning 'siː.zən.ɪŋ **-s** -z
seat siːt **-s** -s **-ing** -ɪŋ (US) 'siː.ţɪŋ **-ed** -ɪd (US) 'siː.ţɪd **-er/s** -əʳ/z (US) -ɚ/z **'seat ˌbelt**
SEATO 'siː.təʊ (US) -ţoʊ
Seaton 'siː.tən
Seaton Delavel ˌsiː.tən'del.ə.vəl
Seattle si'æt.l̩ (US) -'æţ-
seawall ˌsiː'wɔːl, '-- (US) 'siː.wɔːl, -wɑːl **-s** -z
seaward 'siː.wəd (US) -wɚd **-s**
seawater 'siːˌwɔː.təʳ (US) -ˌwɑː.ţɚ, -ˌwɔː-
seaway 'siː.weɪ **-s** -z
seaweed 'siː.wiːd
seaworth|y 'siːˌwɜː.ð|i (US) -ˌwɜːr- **-iness** -ɪ.nəs, -ɪ.nɪs
sebaceous sɪ'beɪ.ʃəs, seb'eɪ- (US) sə'beɪ- **se'baceous ˌgland**
Sebastian sɪ'bæs.ti.ən, sə'bæs-, seb'æs- (US) sə'bæs.tʃən
Sebastopol sɪ'bæs.tə.pɒl, sə-, seb'æs-, -pəl (US) sɪ'bæs.tə.poʊl
seborrhea ˌseb.ə'riː.ə, -'rɪə (US) -'riː.ə
sebum 'siː.bəm
sec sek **-s** -s
secant 'siː.kənt, 'sek.ənt (US) 'siː.kənt, -kænt **-s** -s
secateurs ˌsek.ə'tɜːz; '---, -təz (US) 'sek.ə.tɚz
seced|e sɪ'siːd, siː-, sə- (US) sɪ- **-es** -z **-ing** -ɪŋ **-ed** -ɪd **-er/s** -əʳ/z (US) -ɚ/z
secession sɪ'seʃ.ən, sə- **-s** -z **-ist/s** -ɪst/s
seclud|e sɪ'kluːd, sə- **-es** -z **-ing** -ɪŋ **-ed** -ɪd
seclusion sɪ'kluː.ʒən, sə-
Secombe 'siː.kəm
second (*n. adj. v.*) *most senses:* 'sek.ənd **-s** -z **-ly** -li **-ing** -ɪŋ **-ed** -ɪd **-er/s** -əʳ/z (US) -ɚ/z ˌ**second 'best** ; ˌ**Second 'Coming** ; ˌ**second 'cousin** ; ˌ**second 'fiddle** ; ˌ**second 'nature** ; ˌ**second 'person** ; *stress shift:* ˌsecond person 'singular ˌ**second 'reading** ; ˌ**second 'sight** ; ˌ**second 'thoughts** ; ˌ**second 'wind** ; ˌ**Second ˌWorld 'War**
second (*v.*) *to release for temporary service:* sɪ'kɒnd, sə- (US) -'kɑːnd **-s** -z **-ing** -ɪŋ **-ed** -ɪd
secondar|y 'sek.ən.dər|.i, -dr|i (US) -der|.i **-ies** -iz **-ily** -əl.i, -ɪ.li ˌ**secondary 'modern** ; **'secondary ˌschool**
second-class ˌsek.ənd'klɑːs (US) -'klæs ˌ**second-class 'citizen**
second-generation ˌsek.ənˌdʒen.ər'eɪ.ʃən (US) -ə'reɪ-
second-guess ˌsek.ənd'ges **-es** -ɪz **-ing** -ɪŋ **-ed** -t
secondhand ˌsek.ənd'hænd *stress shift:* ˌsecondhand 'books
Secondi *town in Ghana:* ˌsek.ən'diː *surname:* sɪ'kɒn.di, sə- (US) -'kɑːn-
secondment sɪ'kɒnd.mənt, sə- (US) -'kɑːnd-
secondo sek'ɒn.dəʊ, sɪ'kɒn- (US) sɪ'kɑːn.doʊ **-s** -z
second|-rate ˌsek.ənd|'reɪt **-rater/s** -'reɪ.təʳ/z (US) -'reɪ.ţɚ/z
secrecy 'siː.krə.si, -krɪ-
secret 'siː.krət, -krɪt **-s** -s **-ly** -li ˌ**secret 'agent** ; ˌ**secret po'lice** ; ˌ**secret 'service**
secretarial ˌsek.rə'teə.ri.əl, -rɪ'- (US) -rə'ter.i-
secretariat ˌsek.rə'teə.ri.ət, -rɪ'-, -æt (US) -rə'ter.i.ət **-s** -s
secretar|y 'sek.rə.tər|.i, -r|i-, -tr|i (US) -rə.ter|.i **-ies** -iz **-yship/s** -i.ʃɪp/s ˌ**Secretary of 'State**
secretary-general, (S G) ˌsek.rə.tər.i'dʒen.ər.əl, -rɪ- (US) -rə.ter.i'- **-s** -z **secretaries-general** ˌsek.rə.tər.iz'-, -rɪ- (US) -rə.ter.iz'-

se|crete sɪ'kriːt, siː-, sə- ⓤⓢ sɪ- **-cretes** -'kriːts **-creting** -'kriː.tɪŋ ⓤⓢ -'kriː.t̬ɪŋ **-creted** -'kriː.tɪd ⓤⓢ -'kriː.t̬ɪd
secretion sɪ'kriː.ʃᵊn, siː-, sə- ⓤⓢ sɪ- **-s** -z
secretive *inclined to secrecy:* 'siː.krə.tɪv, -krɪ- ⓤⓢ -krə.t̬ɪv **-ly** -li **-ness** -nəs, -nɪs
secretive *of secretion:* sɪ'kriː.tɪv, sə- ⓤⓢ -t̬ɪv
sect sekt **-s** -s
sectarian sek'teə.ri.ən ⓤⓢ -'ter.i- **-s** -z **-ism** -ɪ.zᵊm
sectar|y 'sek.tᵊr|.i **-ies** -iz
section 'sek.ʃᵊn **-s** -z **-ing** -ɪŋ **-ed** -d
sectional 'sek.ʃᵊn.ᵊl **-ly** -i
sectional|ism 'sek.ʃᵊn.ᵊl|.ɪ.zᵊm **-ist/s** -ɪst/s
sectionaliz|e, -is|e 'sek.ʃᵊn.ᵊl.aɪz ⓤⓢ -ə.laɪz **-es** -ɪz **-ing** -ɪŋ **-ed** -d
sector 'sek.təʳ ⓤⓢ -tɚ **-s** -z
secular 'sek.jə.ləʳ, -jʊ- ⓤⓢ -lɚ **-ly** -li
secular|ism 'sek.jə.lᵊr|.ɪ.zᵊm, -jʊ- **-ist/s** -ɪst/s
secularity ˌsek.jə'lær.ə.ti, -jʊ'-, -ɪ.ti ⓤⓢ -'ler.ə.t̬i, -'lær-
secularization, -isa- ˌsek.jə.lᵊr.aɪ'zeɪ.ʃᵊn, -jʊ-, -ɪ'- ⓤⓢ -ɪ'-
searculariz|e, -is|e 'sek.jə.lᵊr.aɪz, -jʊ- ⓤⓢ -lə.raɪz **-es** -ɪz **-ing** -ɪŋ **-ed** -d
secur|e sɪ'kjʊəʳ, sə-, -'kjɔːʳ ⓤⓢ -'kjʊr **-er** -əʳ ⓤⓢ -ɚ **-est** -ɪst, -əst **-ely** -li **-es** -z **-ing** -ɪŋ **-ed** -d **-able** -rə.bl̩
Securicor® sɪ'kjʊə.rɪ.kɔːʳ, sə-, -'kjɔː-, -rə- ⓤⓢ -'kjʊr.ə.kɔːr
securit|y sɪ'kjʊə.rə.t|i, sə-, -'kjɔː-, -ɪ.t|i ⓤⓢ -'kjʊr.ə.t̬|i **-ies** -iz **se'curity ˌguard**; **Se'curity ˌCouncil**; **se'curity ˌrisk**
sedan (S) sɪ'dæn, sə- **seˌdan 'chair** ⓤⓢ **se'dan ˌchair**
se|date (*v.*) sɪ|'deɪt, sə- **-dates** -'deɪts **-dating** -'deɪ.tɪŋ ⓤⓢ -'deɪ.t̬ɪŋ **-dated** -'deɪ.tɪd ⓤⓢ -'deɪ.t̬ɪd
sedate (*adj*) sɪ'deɪt, sə- **-ly** -li **-ness** -nəs, -nɪs
sedation sɪ'deɪ.ʃᵊn, sə-
sedative 'sed.ə.tɪv ⓤⓢ -t̬ɪv **-s** -z
Sedbergh *public school:* 'sed.bəʳ, -bɜːg ⓤⓢ -bɜːrg, -bɚ *name of town:* 'sed.bəʳ ⓤⓢ -bɚ
Sedding 'sed.ɪŋ
Seddon 'sed.ᵊn
sedentar|y 'sed.ᵊn.tᵊr|.i, -tr|i ⓤⓢ -ter|.i **-ily** -ᵊl.i, -ɪ.li **-iness** -ɪ.nəs, -ɪ.nɪs
sedg|e sedʒ **-es** -ɪz **'sedge ˌwarbler, ˌsedge 'warbler** ⓤⓢ **'sedge ˌwarbler**
Sedgefield 'sedʒ.fiːld
Sedgemoor 'sedʒ.mɔːʳ, -mʊəʳ ⓤⓢ -mʊr, -mɔːr
Sedgley 'sedʒ.li
Sedgwick 'sedʒ.wɪk
sedilia sed'iː.li.ə, sɪ'diː-, sə-, -'daɪ- ⓤⓢ sɪ'dɪl.i.ə, '-jə
sediment 'sed.ɪ.mənt, '-ə- ⓤⓢ '-ə- **-s** -s **-ation** ˌ--men'teɪ.ʃᵊn
sedimentary ˌsed.ɪ'men.tᵊr.i, -ə'-, '-tri
sedition sɪ'dɪʃ.ᵊn, sə- **-s** -z
seditious sɪ'dɪʃ.əs, sə- **-ly** -li **-ness** -nəs, -nɪs
Sedlescombe 'sed.l̩z.kəm
Sedley 'sed.li
seduc|e sɪ'djuːs, sə-, -'dʒuːs ⓤⓢ -'duːs, -'djuːs **-es** -ɪz **-ing** -ɪŋ **-ed** -t **-er/s** -əʳ/z ⓤⓢ -ɚ/z
seduction sɪ'dʌk.ʃᵊn, sə- **-s** -z
seductive sɪ'dʌk.tɪv, sə- **-ly** -li **-ness** -nəs, -nɪs
seductress sɪ'dʌk.trɪs, -trəs **-es** -ɪz
sedulous 'sed.jʊ.ləs, -jə-, 'sedʒ.ʊ-, '-ə- ⓤⓢ 'sedʒ.ə-, '-ʊ- **-ly** -li **-ness** -nəs, -nɪs
sedum 'siː.dəm **-s** -z
see (S) siː **-s** -z **-ing** -ɪŋ **saw** sɔː ⓤⓢ sɑː, sɔː **seen** siːn
Seebeck 'siː.bek
seed siːd **-s** -z **-ing** -ɪŋ **-ed** -ɪd **-er/s** **ˌgo to 'seed**; **'seed poˌtato, ˌseed po'tato**
seedbed 'siːd.bed **-s** -z
seedcake 'siːd.keɪk **-s** -s
seedcas|e 'siːd.keɪs **-es** -ɪz
seedless 'siːd.ləs, -lɪs
seedling 'siːd.lɪŋ **-s** -z
seeds|man 'siːdz|.mən **-men** -mən, -men
seedtime 'siːd.taɪm **-s** -z
seed|y 'siː.d|i **-ier** -i.əʳ ⓤⓢ -i.ɚ **-iest** -i.ɪst, -i.əst **-ily** -ɪ.li, -ᵊl.i **-iness** -ɪ.nəs, -ɪ.nɪs
Seeger 'siː.gəʳ ⓤⓢ -gɚ
seek siːk **-s** -s **-ing** -ɪŋ **sought** sɔːt ⓤⓢ sɑːt, sɔːt **seeker/s** 'siː.kəʳ/z ⓤⓢ -kɚ/z
Seel(e)y 'siː.li
seem siːm **-s** -z **-ing/ly** -ɪŋ/li **-ed** -d
seeml|y 'siːm.l|i **-ier** -i.əʳ ⓤⓢ -i.ɚ **-iest** -i.ɪst, -i.əst **-iness** -ɪ.nəs, -ɪ.nɪs
seen (*from* **see**) siːn
seep siːp **-s** -s **-ing** -ɪŋ **-ed** -t
seepage 'siː.pɪdʒ
seer *prophet:* 'siː.əʳ, sɪəʳ ⓤⓢ sɪr, 'siː.ɚ **-s** -z
seer *Indian weight:* sɪəʳ ⓤⓢ siːr, sɪr **-s** -z
seersucker 'sɪəˌsʌk.əʳ ⓤⓢ 'sɪrˌsʌk.ɚ
seesaw 'siː.sɔː ⓤⓢ -sɑː, -sɔː **-s** -z **-ing** -ɪŋ **-ed** -d
seeth|e siːð **-es** -z **-ing** -ɪŋ **-ed** -d
see-through 'siː.θruː
Sefton 'sef.tᵊn ⓤⓢ -tən
Segal 'siː.gəl
segment (*n.*) 'seg.mənt **-s** -s
segmen|t (*v.*) seg'men|t, səg-, sɪg- ⓤⓢ 'seg.men|t, -'- **-ts** -ts **-ting** -tɪŋ ⓤⓢ -t̬ɪŋ **-ted** -tɪd ⓤⓢ -t̬ɪd
segmental seg'men.tᵊl, səg-, sɪg- ⓤⓢ seg'men.t̬ᵊl
segmentation ˌseg.men'teɪ.ʃᵊn, -mən'-
segn|o 'sen.j|əʊ, 'seɪ.nj|əʊ ⓤⓢ 'seɪ.nj|oʊ **-i** -i
Segovia sɪ'gəʊ.vi.ə, sə-, seg'əʊ- ⓤⓢ sɪ'goʊ-, sə-
segregate (*n.*) 'seg.rɪ.gət, -rə-, -geɪt, -gɪt ⓤⓢ -rə.gɪt
segre|gate (*v.*) 'seg.rɪ|.geɪt, -rə- ⓤⓢ -rə- **-gates** -geɪts **-gating** -geɪ.tɪŋ ⓤⓢ -geɪ.t̬ɪŋ **-gated** -geɪ.tɪd ⓤⓢ -geɪ.t̬ɪd
segregation ˌseg.rɪ'geɪ.ʃᵊn, -rə'- ⓤⓢ -rə'-
segu|e 'seg.weɪ, 'seɪ.gweɪ, -gwi **-es** -z **-ing** -ɪŋ **-d** -d
seguidilla ˌseg.ɪ'diː.jə, -li.ə ⓤⓢ -ə'diː.jə, ˌseɪ.gə'-, -'diːl- **-s** -z
seich|e seɪʃ ⓤⓢ seɪʃ, siːtʃ **-es** -ɪz
Seidlitz 'sed.lɪts
seigneur sen'jɜːʳ, seɪ'njɜːʳ; 'seɪ.njəʳ ⓤⓢ seɪ'njɜːr, sen'jɜːr **-s** -z **-ial** -i.əl
seignior *lord:* 'seɪ.njəʳ ⓤⓢ 'seɪ.njɚ; seɪ'njɔːr **-s** -z
Seignior *surname:* 'siː.njəʳ ⓤⓢ -njɚ
seignior|y 'seɪ.njᵊr|.i ⓤⓢ 'seɪ- **-ies** -iz
Seiko® 'seɪ.kəʊ ⓤⓢ -koʊ
sein|e *net:* seɪn **-es** -z **-ing** -ɪŋ **-ed** -d
Seine *river in France:* seɪn, sen
Seir 'siː.əʳ ⓤⓢ -ɚ
seis|e siːz **-es** -ɪz **-ing** -ɪŋ **-ed** -d
seisin 'siː.zɪn **-s** -z
seismic 'saɪz.mɪk ⓤⓢ 'saɪz-, 'saɪs-
seismo- saɪz.məʊ-; saɪz'mɒ- ⓤⓢ saɪz.moʊ-, saɪs-, -mə-; saɪz'mɑː-, saɪs-

Note: Prefix. Normally takes either primary or secondary stress on the first syllable, e.g. **seismograph** /'saɪz.məʊ.grɑːf ⓤⓢ -mə.græf/, **seismographic** /ˌsaɪz.məʊ'græf.ɪk ⓤⓢ -mə'-/, or primary stress on the second syllable, e.g. **seismographer** /saɪz'mɒg.rə.fəʳ ⓤⓢ -'mɑː.grə.fɚ/.

seismograph 'saɪz.məʊ.grɑːf, -græf ⓤⓢ -mə.græf, 'saɪs-, -moʊ- **-s** -s
seismograph|er saɪz'mɒg.rə.f|əʳ ⓤⓢ -'mɑː.grə.f|ɚ, saɪs- **-ers** -əz ⓤⓢ -ɚz **-y** -i
seismographic ˌsaɪz.məʊ'græf.ɪk ⓤⓢ -mə'-, saɪs-, -moʊ'-
seismologic|al ˌsaɪz.mə'lɒdʒ.ɪ.k|ᵊl ⓤⓢ -mə'lɑː.dʒɪ-, saɪs- **-ally** -ᵊl.i ⓤⓢ -li
seismolog|y saɪz'mɒl.ə.dʒ|i ⓤⓢ -'mɑː.lə-, seɪs- **-ist/s** -ɪst/s
seismometer saɪz'mɒm.ɪ.təʳ, '-ə- ⓤⓢ -'mɑː.mə.t̬ɚ, saɪs- **-s** -z

seizable ˈsiː.zə.bl̩
seiz|e siːz **-es** -ɪz **-ing** -ɪŋ **-ed** -d
seizin ˈsiː.zɪn **-s** -z
seizure ˈsiː.ʒəʳ (US) -ʒɚ **-s** -z
sejant ˈsiː.dʒənt
Sejanus sɪˈdʒeɪ.nəs, sə-, sedʒˈeɪ- (US) sɪˈdʒeɪ-
Sekhmet ˈsek.met
Sekondi-Takoradi ˌsek.ənˌdiː.tɑː.kəˈrɑː.di
selah ˈsiː.lə, -lɑː (US) ˈsiː.lə, ˈsel.ə, -ɑː **-s** -z
Selangor səˈlæŋ.əʳ, sɪ-, -ɔːʳ (US) selˈɑːŋ.gɔːr
Selassie səˈlæs.i (US) -ˈlæs-, -ˈlɑː.si
Selborne ˈsel.bɔːn, -bən (US) -bɔːrn, -bɚn
Selby ˈsel.bi
Selden ˈsel.dᵊn
seldom ˈsel.dəm
select sɪˈlekt, sə- (US) sə- **-ness** -nəs, -nɪs **-s** -s **-ing** -ɪŋ **-ed** -ɪd **seˌlect comˈmittee**
selection sɪˈlek.ʃᵊn, sə- (US) sə- **-s** -z
selective sɪˈlek.tɪv, sə- (US) sə- **-ly** -li **-ness** -nəs, -nɪs
selectivity ˌsɪl.ekˈtɪv.ə.ti, ˌsel-, ˌsiː.lekˈ-, -ɪ.ti; səˌlekˈ-, sɪ- (US) səˌlekˈtɪv.ə.t̬i, sɪ-; ˌsiː.lekˈ-
selector sɪˈlek.təʳ, sə- (US) səˈlek.tɚ **-s** -z
Selena sɪˈliː.nə, sə-
selenite *substance:* ˈsel.ɪ.naɪt, ˈ-ə- (US) ˈ-ə-
Selenite *inhabitant of moon:* sɪˈliː.naɪt, sə- (US) sɪˈliː-, sə-; ˈsel.ə- **-s** -s
selenium sɪˈliː.ni.əm, sə- (US) sə-
Seleuci|a sɪˈljuː.ʃi|.ə, sə-, -ˈluː-, -si- (US) səˈluː.ʃi-, ˈ-ʃə **-an/s** -ən/z
Seleucid sɪˈljuː.sɪd, sə-, -ˈluː- (US) səˈluː- **-s** -z
Seleucus sɪˈljuː.kəs, sə-, -ˈluː- (US) səˈluː-
self- self-

Note: Many compounds beginning with **self-** have the stress pattern **ˌselfˈ-**; these are likely to undergo stress shift when a stressed syllable follows closely, especially in adjectives or adjectives derived from verbs.

sel|f sel|f **-ves** -vz
self-abuse ˌself.əˈbjuːs
self-addressed ˌself.əˈdrest
self-appointed ˌself.əˈpɔɪn.tɪd (US) -t̬ɪd
self-assurance ˌself.əˈʃʊə.rᵊnts (US) -ˈʃʊr.ᵊnts
self-assured ˌself.əˈʃʊəd (US) -ˈʃʊrd
self-catering ˌselfˈkeɪ.tᵊr.ɪŋ (US) -t̬ɚ-
self-centred, self-centered ˌselfˈsen.təd (US) -t̬ɚd **-ly** -li **-ness** -nəs, -nɪs
self-command ˌself.kəˈmɑːnd (US) -ˈmænd
self-confessed ˌself.kənˈfest
self-conscious ˌselfˈkɒn.*t*ʃəs (US) -ˈkɑːn*t*.ʃəs **-ly** -li **-ness** -nəs, -nɪs
self-contained ˌself.kənˈteɪnd **-ly** -li **-ness** -nəs, -nɪs **-ment** -mənt
self-control ˌself.kənˈtrəʊl (US) -ˈtroʊl **-led** -d
self-critic|al ˌselfˈkrɪt.ɪ.k|ᵊl (US) -ˈkrɪt̬- **-ally** -ᵊl.i, -li
self-deception ˌself.dɪˈsep.ʃᵊn
self-defence, self-defense ˌself.dɪˈfen*t*s
self-denial ˌself.dɪˈnaɪ.əl
self-denying ˌself.dɪˈnaɪ.ɪŋ
self-destruct ˌself.dɪˈstrʌkt **-s** -s **-ing** -ɪŋ **-ed** -ɪd **-ive** -ɪv **-ion** -ʃᵊn
self-determination ˌself.dɪˌtɜː.mɪˈneɪ.ʃᵊn (US) -ˌtɜːr-
self-discipline ˌselfˈdɪs.ɪ.plɪn, ˈ-ə- **-d** -d
self-drive ˌselfˈdraɪv
self-effac|ing ˌself.ɪˈfeɪ.s|ɪŋ **-ingly** -ɪŋ.li **-ement** -mənt
self-employed ˌself.ɪmˈplɔɪd, -emˈ-
self-esteem ˌself.ɪˈstiːm, -əˈ-
self-evident ˌselfˈev.ɪ.dᵊnt
self-explanatory ˌself.ɪkˈsplæn.ə.tᵊr.i, -ekˈ-, ˈ-ɪ- (US) -tɔːr-
self-fulfilling ˌself.fʊlˈfɪl.ɪŋ
self-governing ˌselfˈgʌv.ᵊn.ɪŋ (US) -ɚ.nɪŋ
self-government ˌselfˈgʌv.ᵊn.mənt, -ᵊm-, -və.mənt (US) -ɚn.mənt
self-heal ˌselfˈhiːl
self-help ˌselfˈhelp
self-image ˌselfˈɪm.ɪdʒ **-s** -ɪz
self-importan|ce ˌself.ɪmˈpɔː.tᵊn|*t*s (US) -ˈpɔːr- **-t/ly** -t/li
self-imposed ˌself.ɪmˈpəʊzd (US) -ˈpoʊzd
self-indulgen|ce ˌself.ɪnˈdʌl.dʒᵊn|*t*s **-t/ly** -t/li
self-inflicted ˌself.ɪnˈflɪk.tɪd
self-interest ˌselfˈɪn.trəst, -trəst; -tᵊr.əst, -est, -ɪst (US) -ˈɪn.trɪst, -trəst, -trest; -t̬ɚ.ɪst, -əst, -est
selfish ˈsel.fɪʃ **-ly** -li **-ness** -nəs, -nɪs
selfless ˈsel.fləs, -flɪs **-ly** -li **-ness** -nəs, -nɪs
self-made ˌselfˈmeɪd
self-pity ˌselfˈpɪt.i (US) -ˈpɪt̬-
self-portrait ˌselfˈpɔː.trɪt, -trət, -treɪt (US) -ˈpɔːr.trɪt, -treɪt **-s** -s
self-possessed ˌself.pəˈzest
self-possession ˌself.pəˈzeʃ.ᵊn
self-preservation ˌselfˌprez.əˈveɪ.ʃᵊn (US) -ɚˈ-
self-proclaimed ˌself.prəʊˈkleɪmd (US) -proʊˈ-, -prəˈ-
self-raising ˌselfˈreɪ.zɪŋ **ˌself-raising ˈflour, selfˌ-raising ˈflour**
self-relian|ce ˌself.rɪˈlaɪ.ən|*t*s, -rəˈ- **-t** -t
self-respect ˌself.rɪˈspekt, -rəˈ-
self-respecting ˌself.rɪˈspek.tɪŋ, -rəˈ-
self-restraint ˌself.rɪˈstreɪnt, -rəˈ-
Selfridge ˈsel.frɪdʒ **-'s** -ɪz
Selfridges ˈsel.frɪdʒ.ɪz
self-righteous ˌselfˈraɪ.tʃəs, -tjəs (US) -tʃəs **-ly** -li **-ness** -nəs, -nɪs
self-rising ˌselfˈraɪ.zɪŋ **ˌself-rising ˈflour, selfˌ-rising ˈflour**
self-rul|e ˌselfˈruːl **-ing** -ɪŋ
self-sacrific|e ˌselfˈsæk.rɪ.faɪs, -rə- **-ing/ly** -ɪŋ/li
selfsame ˈself.seɪm
self-satisfaction ˌselfˌsæt.ɪsˈfæk.ʃᵊn (US) -ˌsæt̬-
self-satisfied ˌselfˈsæt.ɪs.faɪd (US) -ˈsæt̬-
self-service ˌselfˈsɜː.vɪs (US) -ˈsɜːr-
self-starter ˌselfˈstɑː.təʳ (US) -ˈstɑːr.t̬ɚ **-s** -z
self-styled ˌselfˈstaɪld
self-sufficien|cy ˌself.səˈfɪʃ.ᵊn|*t*.si **-t** -t
self-taught ˌselfˈtɔːt (US) -ˈtɑːt, -ˈtɔːt
self-will ˌselfˈwɪl **-ed** -d
self-winding ˌselfˈwaɪn.dɪŋ
Selhurst ˈsel.hɜːst (US) -hɜːrst
Selina səˈliː.nə
Selkirk ˈsel.kɜːk (US) -kɜːrk
sell (S) sel **-s** -z **-ing** -ɪŋ **sold** səʊld (US) soʊld **seller/s** ˈsel.əʳ/z (US) -ɚ/z
Sellafield ˈsel.ə.fiːld
Sellar ˈsel.əʳ (US) -ɚ
sell-by ˈsel.baɪ **ˈsell-by ˌdate**
Sellers ˈsel.əz (US) -ɚz
sellotap|e® ˈsel.əʊ.teɪp (US) -oʊ- **-es** -s **-ing** -ɪŋ **-ed** -t
sellout ˈsel.aʊt **-s** -s
Selous səˈluː
Selsey ˈsel.si
Selston ˈsel.stᵊn
seltzer (S) ˈselt.səʳ (US) -sɚ **-s** -z
selva ˈsel.və **-s** -z
selvag|e, selvedg|e ˈsel.vɪdʒ **-es** -ɪz
selves (*plur. of* **self**) selvz
Selwyn ˈsel.wɪn
Selznick ˈselz.nɪk
semantic sɪˈmæn.tɪk, sə-, semˈæn-, siːˈmæn- (US) səˈmæn.t̬ɪk, sɪ- **-s** -s **-ally** -ᵊl.i, -li
semanticism sɪˈmæn.tɪ.sɪ.zᵊm, sə-, semˈæn-, siːˈmæn- (US) səˈmæn.t̬ə-, sɪ-
semanticist sɪˈmæn.tɪ.sɪst, sə-, semˈæn-, siːˈmæn-, -tə- (US) səˈmæn.t̬ə-, sɪ- **-s** -s
semanticiz|e, -is|e sɪˈmæn.tɪ.saɪz, sə-, semˈæn-, siːˈmæn-, -tə- (US) səˈmæn.t̬ə-, sɪ- **-es** -ɪz **-ing** -ɪŋ **-ed** -d
semaphore ˈsem.ə.fɔːʳ (US) -fɔːr **-s** -z **-ing** -ɪŋ **-ed** -d

semaphoric ˌsem.əˈfɒr.ɪk (US) -ˈfɔːr- **-ally** -ᵊl.i, -li

semasiology sɪˌmeɪ.siˈɒl.ə.dʒi, sə-, semˌeɪ-, -ziˈ- (US) sɪˌmeɪ.siˈɑː.lə-

sematology ˌsem.əˈtɒl.ə.dʒi, ˌsiː.məˈ- (US) -ˈtɑː.lə-

semblanc|e ˈsem.blən*t*s **-es** -ɪz

seme siːm **-s** -z

Semele ˈsem.ɪ.li (US) ˈ-ə-

sememe ˈsiː.miːm (US) ˈsem.iːm **-s** -z

sememic sɪˈmiː.mɪk, sə- (US) sə-, sɪ- **-s** -s

semen ˈsiː.mən, -men (US) -mən

semester sɪˈmes.təʳ, sə- (US) səˈmes.tɚ **-s** -z

semi- sem.ɪ-, -i- (US) sem.ɪ-, -i-, -aɪ-, -ə-

Note: Many compounds beginning with **semi-** have the stress pattern ˌ**semiˈ-**; these are likely to undergo stress shift when a stressed syllable follows closely, especially in adjectives and adjectives derived from verbs.

semi *house:* ˈsem.i **-s** -z

semiautomatic ˌsem.i.ɔː.təˈmæt.ɪk (US) -ɑː.t̬əˈmæt̬.ɪk, ˌ-aɪ-, -ɔː- **-s** -s

semiautonomous ˌsem.i.ɔːˈtɒn.ə.məs (US) -ɑːˈtɑː.nə-, -aɪ-, -ɔːˈ-

semibreve ˈsem.ɪ.briːv, -i- **-s** -z

semicircle ˈsem.ɪˌsɜː.kl̩, -iˌ- (US) -ˌsɜːr-, -aɪˌ- **-s** -z

semicircular ˌsem.ɪˈsɜː.kjə.ləʳ, -iˈ- -kjʊ- (US) -ˈsɜːr.kjə.lɚ, -aɪˈ-

semicolon ˌsem.ɪˈkəʊ.lən, ˈsem.ɪˌkəʊ-, -lɒn (US) ˈsem.ɪˌkoʊ.lən **-s** -z

semiconductivity ˌsem.ɪˌkɒn.dʌkˈtɪv.ə.ti, -iˌ-, -ɪ.ti (US) -ˌkɑːn.dʌkˈtɪv.ə.t̬i, -aɪ-

semiconduc|tor ˌsem.ɪ.kənˈdʌk|.təʳ, -i- (US) -tɚ, -aɪ- **-tors** -təz (US) -tɚz **-ting** -tɪŋ

semiconscious ˌsem.ɪˈkɒn.*t*ʃəs, -iˈ- (US) -ˈkɑːn-, -aɪˈ- **-ness** -nəs, -nɪs

semidesert ˌsem.ɪˈdez.ət, -iˈ- (US) -ɚt, -aɪˈ- **-s** -s

semidetached ˌsem.ɪ.dɪˈtætʃt, -i- (US) -ɪ-, -i-, ˌ-aɪ-

semifinal ˌsem.ɪˈfaɪ.nᵊl, -iˈ- (US) -ɪˈ-, -iˈ-, -aɪˈ- **-s** -z

semifinalist ˌsem.ɪˈfaɪ.nᵊl.ɪst, -iˈ- (US) -ɪˈ-, -iˈ-, -aɪˈ- **-s** -s

semiformal ˌsem.ɪˈfɔː.mᵊl, -iˈ- (US) -ˈfɔːr-, -aɪˈ-

Sémillon ˌseɪ.miːˈjɔ̃ː*ŋ* (US) -ˈjõʊ*n*, ˌsem.iːˈ-

seminal ˈsem.ɪ.nᵊl, ˈsiː.mɪ-, -mə- (US) ˈsem.ə- **-ly** -i

seminar ˈsem.ɪ.nɑːʳ, ˈ-ə- (US) -ə.nɑːr **-s** -z

seminarist ˈsem.ɪ.nᵊr.ɪst (US) ˌsem.ɪˈner- **-s** -s

seminar|y ˈsem.ɪ.nᵊr|.i (US) -ner- **-ies** -iz

seminiferous ˌsem.ɪˈnɪf.ᵊr.əs

Seminole ˈsem.ɪ.nəʊl (US) -noʊl **-s** -z

semiolog|y ˌsem.iˈɒl.ə.dʒ|i, ˌsiː.miˈ- (US) ˌsiː.miˈɑː.lə-, ˌsem.iˈ- **-ist/s** -ɪst/s

semiotic ˌsem.iˈɒt.ɪk, ˌsiː.miˈ- (US) ˌsiː.miˈɑː.t̬ɪk, ˌsem.iˈ- **-s** -s

Semipalatinsk ˌsem.i.pælˈæt.ɪnsk (US) -pəˈlɑː-

semiprecious ˌsem.ɪˈpreʃ.əs, -iˈ- (US) -ɪˈ-, -iˈ-, -aɪˈ-

semiprofessional ˌsem.ɪ.prəˈfeʃ.ᵊn.ᵊl, -i- (US) -ɪ.prəˈ-, -i-, ˌ-aɪ-, -proʊˈ-

semiquaver ˈsem.ɪˌkweɪ.vəʳ, -iˌ- (US) -ɪˌ-, -iˌ-, -vɚ **-s** -z

Semiramide ˌsem.ɪˈrɑː.mɪ.deɪ, -ˈræm.ɪ-, ˈ-ə-, -di

Semiramis semˈɪr.ə.mɪs, sɪˈmɪr- (US) sɪˈmɪr-

semiretired ˌsem.ɪ.rɪˈtaɪəd, -i- (US) -taɪrd, ˌ-aɪ-

semiretirement ˌsem.ɪ.rɪˈtaɪə.mənt, -i- (US) -ˈtaɪr-, ˌ-aɪ-

semiskilled ˌsem.ɪˈskɪld, -iˈ- (US) -ɪˈ-, -iˈ-, -aɪˈ-

semiskimmed ˌsem.ɪˈskɪmd, -iˈ- (US) -ɪˈ-, -iˈ-, -aɪˈ-

Semite ˈsiː.maɪt, ˈsem.aɪt (US) ˈsem.aɪt **-s** -s

Semitic sɪˈmɪt.ɪk, sə-, semˈɪt- (US) səˈmɪt̬-

Semitism ˈsem.ɪ.tɪ.zᵊm, ˈ-ə- (US) ˈ-ə-

semitone ˈsem.ɪ.təʊn, -i- (US) -toʊn, -aɪ- **-s** -z

semitropical ˌsem.ɪˈtrɒp.ɪ.kᵊl, -iˈ- (US) -ˈtrɑː.pɪ-, -aɪˈ-

semivowel ˈsem.ɪˌvaʊəl **-s** -z

semolina ˌsem.ᵊlˈiː.nə (US) -əˈliː-

semology semˈɒl.ə.dʒi, siːˈmɒl- (US) semˈɑː.lə-, siːˈmɑː-

Semon ˈsiː.mən

Sempill ˈsem.pᵊl

sempiternal ˌsem.pɪˈtɜː.nᵊl (US) -ˈtɜːr- **-ly** -i

Semple ˈsem.pl̩

semplice ˈsem.plɪ.tʃeɪ

sempre ˈsem.preɪ

sempstress ˈsem*p*.strɪs, -strəs (US) -strɪs **-es** -ɪz

Semtex® ˈsem.teks

sen sen

senary ˈsiː.nᵊr.i

senate (S) ˈsen.ɪt, -ət (US) -ɪt **-s** -s

senator (S) ˈsen.ə.təʳ, ˈ-ɪ- (US) -ə.t̬ɚ **-s** -z

senatorial ˌsen.əˈtɔː.ri.əl (US) -ˈtɔːr.i- **-ly** -i

send send **-s** -z **-ing** -ɪŋ **sent** sent **sender/s** ˈsen.dəʳ/z (US) -dɚ/z

Sendai ˈsen.daɪ

Sendak ˈsen.dæk

send-off ˈsend.ɒf (US) -ɑːf **-s** -s

send-up ˈsend.ʌp **-s** -s

sene ˈseɪ.neɪ

Seneca ˈsen.ɪ.kə **-s** -z

Senegal ˌsen.ɪˈgɔːl (US) ˌsen.ɪˈgɔːl, -ˈgɑːl; ˈsen.ə.gᵊl

Senegalese ˌsen.ɪ.gəˈliːz, -gɔːˈ- (US) -gəˈ-

Senegambia ˌsen.ɪˈgæm.bi.ə

senescen|ce sɪˈnes.ᵊn|*t*s, sə-, senˈes- (US) səˈnes- **-t** -t

seneschal ˈsen.ɪ.ʃᵊl (US) ˈ-ə- **-s** -z

Senghenydd ˌseŋˈhen.ɪð

Senghor ˈseŋ.gɔːʳ *as if French:* ˈsæ̃*ŋ*- (US) sæ̃nˈgɔːr

senhor (S) senˈjɔːʳ (US) -ˈjɔːr, seɪˈnjɔːr **-s** -z **-es** -z *stress shift:* ˌSenhor Soˈares

senhora (S) senˈjɔː.rə (US) -ˈjɔːr.ə, seɪˈnjɔːr- **-s** -z

senhorita (S) ˌsen.jɔːˈriː.tə, -jəˈ- (US) ˌsen.jəˈriː.t̬ə, ˌseɪ.njəˈ-, -njɔːˈ- **-s** -z

senile ˈsiː.naɪl (US) ˈsiː-, ˈsen.aɪl

senility sɪˈnɪl.ə.ti, sə-, senˈɪl-, -ɪ.ti (US) səˈnɪl.ə.t̬i

senior (S) ˈsiː.ni.əʳ, ˈnjəʳ (US) -njɚ **-s** -z ˌ**senior ˈcitizen**

seniorit|y ˌsiː.niˈɒr.ə.t|i, -ɪ.t|i (US) siːˈnjɔːr.ə.t̬|i **-ies** -iz

seniti ˈsen.ɪ.ti (US) -ə.t̬i

Senlac ˈsen.læk

senna (S) ˈsen.ə

Sennacherib senˈæk.ə.rɪb, sɪˈnæk-, sə- (US) səˈnæk.ɚ.ɪb

sennet ˈsen.ɪt, -ət (US) -ɪt

sennight ˈsen.aɪt (US) -aɪt, -ɪt **-s** -s

señor, senor (S) senˈjɔːʳ (US) -ˈjɔːr, seɪˈnjɔːr **-s** -z *stress shift:* ˌSeñor ˈLopez

señora, senora (S) senˈjɔː.rə (US) -ˈjɔːr.ə, seɪˈnjɔːr- **-s** -z

señorita, senorita (S) ˌsen.jɔːˈriː.tə, -jəˈ- (US) ˌsen.jəˈriː.t̬ə, ˌseɪ.njəˈ-, -njɔːˈ- *stress shift:* ˌSeñorita ˈLopez

sensate ˈsen.seɪt (US) -seɪt, -sɪt **-ly** -li

sensation senˈseɪ.ʃᵊn, sᵊn- (US) sen- **-s** -z

sensational senˈseɪ.ʃᵊn.ᵊl, sᵊn-, -ˈseɪʃ.nᵊl (US) sen- **-ly** -i

sensational|ism senˈseɪ.ʃᵊn.ᵊl|.ɪ.zᵊm, sᵊn-, -ˈseɪʃ.nᵊl- (US) sen- **-ist/s** -ɪst/s

sensationaliz|e, -is|e ˌsenˈseɪ.ʃᵊn.ᵊl.aɪz **-es** -ɪz **-ing** -ɪŋ **-ed** -d

sens|e sen*t*s **-es** -ɪz **-ing** -ɪŋ **-ed** -d ˌ**sense of ˈhumo(u)r**

senseless ˈsen*t*.sləs, -slɪs **-ly** -li **-ness** -nəs, -nɪs

sensibilit|y ˌsen*t*.sɪˈbɪl.ə.t|i, -səˈ-, -ɪ.t|i (US) -səˈbɪl.ə.t̬|i **-ies** -iz

sensib|le ˈsen*t*.sɪ.bl̩, -sə- (US) -sə- **-ly** -li

sensitive ˈsen*t*.sɪ.tɪv, -sə- (US) -sə.t̬ɪv **-s** -z **-ly** -li **-ness** -nəs, -nɪs

sensitivit|y ˌsen*t*.sɪˈtɪv.ə.t|i, -səˈ-, -ɪ.t|i (US) -səˈtɪv.ə.t̬|i **-ies** -iz

sensitization, **-isa-** ˌsent.sɪ.taɪˈzeɪ.ʃᵊn, -sə-, -tɪˈ- (US) -sə.tɪˈ-
sensitiz|e, **-is|e** ˈsent.sɪ.taɪz, -sə- (US) -sə- **-es** -ɪz **-ing** -ɪŋ **-ed** -d
Sensodyne® ˈsent.səʊ.daɪn (US) -soʊ-, -sə-
sensor ˈsent.səʳ (US) -sɚ **-s** -z
sensorial sentˈsɔː.ri.əl (US) -ˈsɔːr.i- **-ly** -i
sensor|y ˈsent.sᵊr|.i **-ily** -ᵊl.i, -ɪ.li
sensual ˈsent.sjʊəl, -sju.əl, -ʃʊəl, -ʃu.əl (US) -ʃu.əl **-ly** -i **-ness** -nəs, -nɪs
sensual|ism ˈsent.sjʊə.l|ɪ.zᵊm, -sju.ᵊl|.ɪ-, -ʃʊə.l|ɪ-, -ʃu.ᵊl|.ɪ- (US) -ʃu.ə.l|ɪ- **-ist/s** -ɪst/s
sensuality ˌsent.sjuˈæl.ə.ti, -ʃuˈ-, -ɪ.ti (US) -ʃuˈæl.ə.t̬i
sensuous ˈsent.sjʊəs, -sju.əs, -ʃʊəs, -ʃu.əs (US) -ʃu.əs **-ly** -li **-ness** -nəs, -nɪs
Sensurround® ˈsent.sə.raʊnd
sent (*from* **send**) sent
sentenc|e ˈsen.tənts (US) -t̬ənts, -tᵊnts **-es** -ɪz **-ing** -ɪŋ **-ed** -t
sentential senˈten.tʃᵊl, sən- (US) senˈtent.ʃᵊl **-ly** -li
sententious senˈten.tʃəs, sən- (US) senˈtent.ʃəs **-ly** -li **-ness** -nəs, -nɪs
sentience ˈsen.tʃᵊnts, -tʃi.ənts (US) ˈsent.ʃᵊnts, -ʃi.ənts
sentient ˈsen.tʃᵊnt, -tʃi.ənt (US) ˈsent.ʃᵊnt, -ʃi.ənt **-ly** -li
sentiment ˈsen.tɪ.mənt, -tə- (US) -t̬ə- **-s** -s
sentimental ˌsen.tɪˈmen.tᵊl, -təˈ- (US) -t̬əˈmen.t̬ᵊl **-ly** -i **-ism** -ɪ.zᵊm **-ist/s** -ɪst/s
sentimentality ˌsen.tɪ.menˈtæl.ə.ti, -tə-, -mən-, -ɪ.ti (US) -t̬ə.menˈtæl.ə.t̬i
sentimentalization, **-isa-** ˌsen.tɪ.men.tᵊl.aɪˈzeɪ.ʃᵊn, -ˌmen-, -tə-, -ɪˈ- (US) -t̬əˌmen.t̬ᵊl.ɪˈ-
sentimentaliz|e, **-is|e** ˌsen.tɪˈmen.tᵊl.aɪz, -təˈ- (US) -t̬əˈmen.t̬ə.laɪz **-es** -ɪz **-ing** -ɪŋ **-ed** -d
sentinel ˈsen.tɪ.nᵊl, -tə- (US) -t̬ɪ-, -tᵊn.ᵊl **-s** -z
sentr|y ˈsen.tr|i **-ies** -iz ˈ**sentry** ˌ**box**
sentry-go ˈsen.tri.gəʊ (US) -goʊ
senza ˈsent.sə
Seoul səʊl (US) soʊl
sepal ˈsep.əl, ˈsiː.pəl (US) ˈsiː.pᵊl **-s** -z
separability ˌsep.ᵊr.əˈbɪl.ə.ti, -ɪ.ti (US) -ə.t̬i
separab|le ˈsep.ᵊr.ə.b|l̩ **-ly** -li **-leness** -l̩.nəs, -l̩.nɪs
separate (*adj.*) ˈsep.ᵊr.ət, -ɪt, ˈ-rət, -rɪt (US) -ɚ.ɪt, ˈ-rɪt **-ly** -li **-ness** -nəs, -nɪs
separ|ate (*v.*) ˈsep.ᵊr|.eɪt (US) -ə.r|eɪt **-ates** -eɪts **-ating** -eɪ.tɪŋ (US) -eɪ.t̬ɪŋ **-ated** -eɪ.tɪd (US) -eɪ.t̬ɪd **-ator/s** -eɪ.təʳ/z (US) -eɪ.t̬ɚ/z
separates ˈsep.ᵊr.əts, -ɪts, ˈ-rəts, ˈ-rɪts (US) -ɚ.ɪts, ˈ-rɪts
separation ˌsep.ᵊrˈeɪ.ʃᵊn (US) -əˈreɪ- **-s** -z
separat|ism ˈsep.ᵊr.ə.t|ɪ.zᵊm, ˈ-rə- **-ist/s** -ɪst/s
Sephardi səˈfɑː.di, sefˈɑː- (US) səˈfɑːr.di; -ˌfɑːrˈdiː **Sephardim** səˈfɑː.dɪm, sefˈɑː- (US) səˈfɑːr.dɪm; -ˌfɑːrˈdiːm
Sephardic səˈfɑː.dɪk, sefˈɑː- (US) səˈfɑːr-
sepia ˈsiː.pi.ə
sepoy ˈsiː.pɔɪ **-s** -z
seppuku sepˈuː.kuː
seps|is ˈsep.s|ɪs **-es** -iːz
Sept. (*abbrev. for* **September**) sepˈtem.bəʳ, səp-, sɪp- (US) sepˈtem.bɚ
September sepˈtem.bəʳ, səp-, sɪp- (US) sepˈtem.bɚ **-s** -z
Septembrist sepˈtem.brɪst, səp-, sɪp- (US) sep- **-s** -s
septennial sepˈten.i.əl
septet, **septette** sepˈtet **-s** -s
septic ˈsep.tɪk ˌ**septic** ˈ**tank**, ˈ**septic** ˌ**tank** (US) ˈ**septic** ˌ**tank**
septic(a)emia ˌsep.tɪˈsiː.mi.ə (US) -təˈ-
septillion sepˈtɪl.jən **-s** -z
Septimus ˈsep.tɪ.məs
septuagenarian ˌsep.tjʊə.dʒɪˈneə.ri.ən, -tʃʊə-, -dʒəˈ- (US) -tu.ə.dʒəˈner.i-, -tju- **-s** -z
Septuagesima ˌsep.tjʊəˈdʒes.ɪ.mə, -tʃʊəˈ-, ˈ-ə- (US) -tu.əˈdʒes.ɪ-, -tju-, -ˈdʒeɪ.zɪ-
Septuagint ˈsep.tjʊə.dʒɪnt, -tʃʊə- (US) -tu.ə-, -tju-
sept|um ˈsep.t|əm **-ums** -əmz **-a** -ə
septuple ˈsep.tjʊ.pl̩, -tjuː- (US) sepˈtuː-; ˈsep.tə-
sepulcher ˈsep.ᵊl.kə (US) -kɚ **-s** -z
sepulchral sɪˈpʌl.krᵊl, sə-, sepˈʌl- (US) səˈpʌl- **-ly** -i
sepulchre ˈsep.ᵊl.kəʳ (US) -kɚ **-s** -z
sepulture ˈsep.ᵊl.tʃəʳ, -ˌtjʊəʳ (US) -tʃɚ
sequel ˈsiː.kwᵊl **-s** -z
sequel|a sɪˈkwiː.l|ə, sə- (US) sɪˈkwiː-, -ˈkwel|.ə **-ae** -iː
sequenc|e ˈsiː.kwənts (US) -kwənts, -kwents **-es** -ɪz **-ing** -ɪŋ **-ed** -t
sequential sɪˈkwen.tʃᵊl (US) -ˈkwent.ʃᵊl **-ly** -i
sequest|er sɪˈkwes.t|əʳ, sə- (US) sɪˈkwes.t|ɚ **-ers** -əz (US) -ɚz **-ering** -ᵊr.ɪŋ **-ered** -əd (US) -ɚd
seques|trate sɪˈkwes|.treɪt, sə-; ˈsiː.kwə.s|treɪt (US) sɪˈkwes|.treɪt; ˈsiː.kwə.s|treɪt, ˈsek.wə- **-trates** -treɪts **-trating** -treɪ.tɪŋ (US) -treɪ.t̬ɪŋ **-trated** -treɪ.tɪd (US) -treɪ.t̬ɪd
sequestration ˌsiː.kwesˈtreɪ.ʃᵊn, ˌsek.wesˈ-, -wəˈstreɪ-, -wɪˈ- (US) ˌsiː.kwəˈstreɪ-, ˌsek.wəˈ-; sɪˌkwesˈtreɪ- **-s** -z
sequin ˈsiː.kwɪn **-s** -z **-(n)ed** -d
sequoia sɪˈkwɔɪə, sekˈwɔɪə (US) sɪˈkwɔɪə **-s** -z
seraglio serˈɑː.li.əʊ, sɪˈrɑː-, sə-, -ˈɑːl.jəʊ (US) sɪˈræl.joʊ, -ˈrɑːl- **-s** -z
serai serˈaɪ, səˈraɪ (US) sɪˈreɪ.i, sə- **-s** -z
seraph (**S**) ˈser.əf **-s** -s **-im** -ɪm
seraphic serˈæf.ɪk, sɪˈræf-, sə- (US) səˈræf- **-al** -ᵊl **-ally** -ᵊl.i, -li
Serapis ˈser.ə.pɪs, səˈreɪ-
Serb sɜːb (US) sɜːrb **-s** -z
Serbi|a ˈsɜː.bi|.ə (US) ˈsɜːr- **-an/s** -ən/z
Serbo-Croat ˌsɜː.bəʊˈkrəʊ.æt (US) ˌsɜːr.boʊˈkroʊ- **-s** -s
Serbo-Croatian ˌsɜː.bəʊ.krəʊˈeɪ.ʃᵊn (US) ˌsɜːr.boʊ.kroʊˈ- **-s** -z
sere sɪəʳ (US) sɪr **-s** -z
Serena səˈriː.nə, sɪ-, -ˈreɪ- (US) səˈriː-
serenad|e ˌser.əˈneɪd, -ɪˈ- (US) -əˈ- **-es** -z **-ing** -ɪŋ **-ed** -ɪd
serenata ˌser.ɪˈnɑː.tə, -əˈ- (US) -əˈnɑː.t̬ə **-s** -z
serendipit|y ˌser.ᵊnˈdɪp.ə.t|i, -enˈ-, -ɪ.t|i (US) -ənˈdɪp.ə.t̬|i **-ous** -əs
seren|e sɪˈriːn, sə- (US) sə- **-est** -ɪst, -əst **-ely** -li
Serengeti ˌser.ᵊnˈget.i, -ᵊŋˈ-, -ɪnˈ-, -ɪŋˈ- (US) -ᵊnˈget̬-
serenity sɪˈren.ɪ.ti, sə-, -ə.ti (US) səˈren.ə.t̬i
serf sɜːf (US) sɜːrf **-s** -s **-dom** -dəm
serg|e (**S**) sɜːdʒ (US) sɜːrdʒ **-es** -ɪz
sergeant (**S**) ˈsɑː.dʒᵊnt (US) ˈsɑːr- **-s** -s ˌ**sergeant** ˈ**major**
sergeant-at-arms, ˌsɑː.dʒᵊnt.ətˈɑːmz (US) ˌsɑːr.dʒᵊnt.ətˈɑːrmz **sergeants-at-arms** ˌsɑː.dʒᵊnts- (US) ˌsɑːr.dʒᵊnts-
Sergei ˈseə.geɪ, ˈsɜː-, -ˈ- (US) ˈser.geɪ, ˈsɜːr-
serial ˈsɪə.ri.əl (US) ˈsɪr.i- **-s** -z ˈ**serial** ˌ**killer**; ˈ**serial** ˌ**number**
serialization, **-isa-** ˌsɪə.ri.ᵊl.aɪˈzeɪ.ʃᵊn, -ɪˈ- (US) ˌsɪr.i.ᵊl.ɪˈ- **-s** -z
serializ|e, **-is|e** ˈsɪə.ri.ᵊl.aɪz (US) ˈsɪr.i.ə.laɪz **-es** -ɪz **-ing** -ɪŋ **-ed** -d
seriatim ˌsɪə.riˈeɪ.tɪm, ˌser.iˈ-, -ˈɑː- (US) ˌsɪr.iˈeɪ.t̬ɪm
series ˈsɪə.riːz, -rɪz (US) ˈsɪr.iːz, ˈsiː.riːz
serif ˈser.ɪf **-s** -s
Serifos ˈser.ɪ.fɒs (US) səˈraɪ.fəs; ˈser.ɪ.fɑːs
serin ˈser.ɪn **-s** -z
seringa sɪˈrɪŋ.gə, sə- (US) sə- **-s** -z

Seringapatam səˌrɪŋ.gə.pə'tɑːm, sɪ-, -'tæm
seriocomic ˌsɪə.ri.əʊ'kɒm.ɪk (US) ˌsɪr.i.oʊ'kɑː.mɪk **-ally** -əl.i, -li
serious 'sɪə.ri.əs (US) 'sɪr.i- **-ly** -li **-ness** -nəs, -nɪs
serjeant (S) 'sɑː.dʒənt (US) 'sɑːr- **-s** -s ˌ**serjeant-at-'arms**
Serjeantson 'sɑː.dʒənt.sən (US) 'sɑːr-
sermon 'sɜː.mən (US) 'sɜːr- **-s** -z
sermonette ˌsɜː.mə'net (US) ˌsɜːr- **-s** -s
sermoniz|e, -is|e 'sɜː.mə.naɪz (US) 'sɜːr- **-es** -ɪz **-ing** -ɪŋ **-ed** -d
serolog|y sɪ'rɒl.ə.dʒ|i, sɪə- (US) sɪ'rɑː.lə- **-ist/s** -ɪst/s
seronegative ˌsɪə.rəʊ'neg.ə.tɪv (US) ˌsɪr.oʊ'neg.ə.t̬ɪv
seropositive ˌsɪə.rəʊ'pɒs.ɪ.tɪv, '-ə- (US) ˌsɪr.oʊ'pɑː.zə.t̬ɪv
serotonin ˌser.ə'təʊ.nɪn, ˌsɪə.rə'- (US) ˌser.ə'toʊ-, ˌsɪr-
serous 'sɪə.rəs (US) 'sɪr.əs
Serpell 'sɜː.pəl (US) 'sɜːr-
Serpens 'sɜː.penz, -pənz (US) 'sɜːr-
serpent 'sɜː.pənt (US) 'sɜːr- **-s** -s
serpentine (S) 'sɜː.pən.taɪn (US) 'sɜːr-
SERPS sɜːps (US) sɜːrps
serrate 'ser.ɪt, -eɪt, -ət (US) -eɪt, -ɪt
serrated sɪ'reɪ.tɪd, sə-, ser'eɪ- (US) 'ser.eɪ.t̬ɪd
serration sɪ'reɪ.ʃən, sə-, ser'eɪ- (US) sə'reɪ-, ser'eɪ- **-s** -z
serried 'ser.id ˌ**serried 'ranks**
ser|um 'sɪə.r|əm (US) 'sɪr|.əm **-ums** -əmz **-a** -ə
servant 'sɜː.vənt (US) 'sɜːr- **-s** -s
serv|e sɜːv (US) sɜːrv **-es** -z **-ing** -ɪŋ **-ed** -d **-er/s** -ər/z (US) -ɚ/z
server|y 'sɜː.vər|.i (US) 'sɜːr- **-ies** -iz
servic|e (S) 'sɜː.vɪs (US) 'sɜːr- **-es** -ɪz **-ing** -ɪŋ **-ed** -t **'service ˌcharge**; **'service ˌstation**
serviceability ˌsɜː.vɪ.sə'bɪl.ə.ti, -ɪ.ti (US) ˌsɜːr.vɪ.sə'bɪl.ə.t̬i
serviceab|le 'sɜː.vɪ.sə.bl̩ (US) 'sɜːr- **-ly** -li **-leness** -l̩.nəs, -l̩.nɪs
service|man 'sɜː.vɪs|.mən, -mæn (US) 'sɜːr- **-men** -mən
service|woman 'sɜː.vɪs|ˌwʊm.ən (US) 'sɜːr- **-women** -wɪm.ɪn
serviette ˌsɜː.vi'et, -s (US) ˌsɜːr- **-s**
servile 'sɜː.vaɪl (US) 'sɜːr.vəl, -vaɪl **-ly** -li
servility sɜː'vɪl.ə.ti, -ɪ.ti (US) sɜːr'vɪl.ə.t̬i
serving 'sɜː.vɪŋ (US) 'sɜːr- **-s** -z
serving-spoon 'sɜː.vɪŋ.spuːn (US) 'sɜːr- **-s** -z
servitor 'sɜː.vɪ.tər (US) 'sɜːr.və.t̬ɚ **-s** -z
servitude 'sɜː.vɪ.tjuːd, -tʃuːd (US) 'sɜːr.və.tuːd, -tjuːd
servo 'sɜː.vəʊ (US) 'sɜːr.voʊ **-s** -z
servomechanism 'sɜː.vəʊˌmek.ə.nɪ.zəm, ˌsɜː.vəʊ'mek- (US) ˌsɜːr.voʊ'mek- **-s** -z
servomotor 'sɜː.vəʊˌməʊ.tər (US) 'sɜːr.voʊˌmoʊ.t̬ɚ **-s** -z
sesame (S) 'ses.ə.mi **-s** -z **'sesame ˌseed**
Sesotho ses'uː.tuː, sɪ'suː-, sə-, -'səʊ.θəʊ (US) ses'uː.tuː, sɪ'suː-, sə-, -'soʊ.θoʊ
sesqui- 'ses.kwɪ-
sesquicentennial ˌses.kwɪ.sen'ten.i.əl, -sən'- (US) -sen'-
sesquipedalian ˌses.kwɪ.pɪ'deɪ.li.ən, -pə'-, -ped'eɪ- (US) -pə'deɪ-, -'deɪl.jən
sessile 'ses.aɪl (US) -ɪl, -aɪl
session 'seʃ.ən **-s** -z
sessional 'seʃ.ən.əl **-s** -z
sesterc|e 'ses.tɜːs, -təs (US) -tɜːrs **-es** -ɪz
sesterti|um ses'tɜː.ti|.əm, -ʃi- (US) -'tɜːr.ʃi-, '-ʃ|əm **-a** -ə
sestet ses'tet (US) ses'tet, '-- **-s** -s
set set **-s** -s **-ting** -ɪŋ (US) 'set̬.ɪŋ ˌ**set 'book**; ˌ**set 'piece** (US) **'set ˌpiece**; ˌ**set 'point** (US) **'set ˌpoint**
setaceous sɪ'teɪ.ʃəs, sə- (US) sɪ- **-ly** -li
setback 'set.bæk **-s** -s
Setchell 'setʃ.əl
Setebos 'set.ɪ.bɒs (US) 'set̬.ə.bɑːs
Seth seθ
set-off 'set.ɒf (US) -ɑːf **-s** -s
seton (S) 'siː.tən **-s** -z
setsquare 'set.skweər (US) -skwer **-s** -z
sett set **-s** -s
settee set'iː **-s** -z
setter (S) 'set.ər (US) 'set̬.ɚ **-s** -z
setting 'set.ɪŋ (US) 'set̬.ɪŋ **-s** -z
settl|e (S) 'set.l̩ (US) 'set̬- **-es** -z **-ing** -ɪn, 'set.lɪŋ **-ed** -d
settlement 'set.l̩.mənt (US) 'set̬- **-s** -s
settler 'set.l̩.ər, '-lər (US) 'set.lɚ, 'set̬.l̩.ɚ **-s** -z
set-to 'set.tuː **-s**
Setúbal sə'tuː.bəl, set'uː-
set-up 'set.ʌp (US) 'set̬- **-s** -s
Seurat 'sɜː.rɑː, -'- (US) sɜː'rɑː
Seuss sjuːs (US) suːs
Sevastopol sə'væst.ə.pɒl (US) -poʊl
Seve 'sev.i
seven 'sev.ən **-s** -z **-fold** -fəʊld (US) -foʊld ˌ**seven 'seas**
sevenish 'sev.ən.ɪʃ
Sevenoaks 'sev.ən.əʊks (US) -oʊks
seven|pence 'sev.ən|.pənts, -əm- (US) -ən- **-penny** -pən.i
Note: See note under **penny**.
seventeen ˌsev.ən'tiːn **-s** -z **-th/s** -tθ/s
seventh 'sev.əntθ **-s** -s **-ly** -li ˌ**seventh 'heaven**
sevent|y 'sev.ən.t|i (US) -t̬|i **-ies** -iz **-ieth/s** -i.əθ/s, -i.ɪθ/s
seventy-eight, 78 ˌsev.ən.ti'eɪt (US) -t̬i'- **-s** -s
sev|er 'sev|.ər (US) -ɚ **-ers** -əz (US) -ɚz **-ering** -ər.ɪŋ **-ered** -əd (US) -ɚd
several 'sev.ər.əl, '-rəl **-ly** -i
severalty 'sev.ər.əl.ti, '-rəl-
severance 'sev.ər.ənts **'severance ˌpay**
sever|e sɪ'vɪər, sə- (US) sə'vɪr **-er** -ər (US) -ɚ **-est** -ɪst, -əst **-ely** -li **-eness** -nəs, -nɪs
severit|y sɪ'ver.ə.t|i, sə-, -ɪ.t|i (US) sə'ver.ə.t̬|i **-ies** -iz
Severn 'sev.ən (US) -ɚn
Severus sɪ'vɪə.rəs, sə- (US) sə'vɪr.əs
seviche sev'iːʃ
Sevier 'sev.i.ər (US) -ɚ; sə'vɪr
Seville sə'vɪl, sɪ-, sev'ɪl; 'sev.ɪl, -əl (US) sə'vɪl *stress shift, see compound:* ˌ**Seville 'orange**
Sèvres 'seɪ.vrə, -vər (US) -vrə
sew səʊ (US) soʊ **-s** -z **-ing** -ɪŋ **-ed** -d **-n** -n
sewage 'suː.ɪdʒ, 'sjuː- (US) 'suː-
Sewanee sə'wɒn.i (US) -'wɑː.ni, -'wɔː-
Seward 'siː.wəd (US) 'suː.ɚd; 'siː.wɚd
Sewell 'sjuː.əl, sjʊəl (US) 'suː.əl
sewer *one who sews:* 'səʊ.ər (US) 'soʊ.ɚ **-s** -z
sewer *drain:* sʊər, sjʊər (US) 'suː.ɚ **-s** -z
sewerage 'sʊə.rɪdʒ, 'sjʊə- (US) 'suː.ɚ.ɪdʒ
sewing 'səʊ.ɪŋ (US) 'soʊ- **'sewing maˌchine**
sewn (*from* **sew**) səʊn (US) soʊn
sex seks **-es** -ɪz **-ing** -ɪŋ **-ed** -t **'sex apˌpeal**; **'sex ˌchange**; **'sex ˌkitten**; **'sex ˌobject**
sexagenarian ˌsek.sə.dʒɪ'neə.ri.ən, -dʒə'- (US) -dʒɪ'ner.i- **-s** -z
Sexagesi|ma ˌsek.sə'dʒes.ɪ|.mə (US) -'dʒes.ɪ.mə, -'dʒeɪ.zɪ-
sexagesimal ˌsek.sə'dʒes.ɪ.məl, '-ə-
sex|ism 'sek.s|ɪ.zəm **-ist/s** -ɪst/s
sexless 'sek.sləs, -slɪs **-ness** -nəs, -nɪs
sexolog|y sek'sɒl.ə.dʒ|i (US) -'sɑː.lə- **-ist/s** -ɪst/s
sexploitation ˌsek.splɔɪ'teɪ.ʃən
sexpot 'seks.pɒt (US) -pɑːt **-s** -s
sext sekst
sextant 'sek.stənt **-s** -s
sextet, sextette sek'stet **-s** -s
sextillion sek'stɪl.jən, -i.ən (US) '-jən **-s** -z
sexto 'sek.stəʊ (US) -stoʊ **-s** -z
sexton (S) 'sek.stən **-s** -z
sextuple 'sek.stjʊ.pl̩, -stjə-; sek'stjuː- (US) sek'stuː-, -'stjuː-; 'sek.stə.pl̩
sextuplet 'sek.stjʊ.plet, -stjə-; -plət, -plɪt, sek'stjuː- (US) sek'stʌp.lɪt, -'stuː.plɪt, -'stjuː-; 'sek.stə- **-s** -s

sexual 'sek.ʃʊəl, -ʃu.əl, -sjʊəl, -sju.əl (US) -ʃu.əl **-ly** -i ˌ**sexual 'intercourse** ; ˌ**sexual re'lations** ; ˌ**sexual repro'duction**
sexuality ˌsek.ʃu'æl.ə.ti, -sju'-, -ɪ.ti (US) -ʃu'æl.ə.t̬i
sex|y 'sek.s|i **-ier** -i.əʳ (US) -i.ɚ **-iest** -i.ɪst, -i.əst **-ily** -ɪ.li, -əl.i **-iness** -ɪ.nəs, -ɪ.nɪs
Sey seɪ
Seychelles seɪ'ʃelz, '-- (US) seɪ'ʃelz, -'ʃel
Seymour 'siː.mɔːʳ, 'seɪ-, -məʳ (US) -mɔːr
Note: /'seɪ-/ chiefly in families of Scottish origin.
Sfax sfæks (US) sfɑːks
sferics 'sfer.ɪks (US) 'sfɪr-, 'sfer-
sforzando sfɔːt'sæn.dəʊ (US) sfɔːrt'sɑːn.doʊ
sgian-dhu ˌskiː.ən'duː, ˌskɪən'- (US) ˌskiː.ən'- **-s** -z
sgraffit|o sgræf'iː.t|əʊ (US) skræf'iː.t|oʊ, zgrɑː'fiː- **-i** -i
Sgt. (*abbrev. for* **Sergeant**) 'sɑː.dʒənt (US) 'sɑːr-
sh, shh, ssh ʃ
Note: Used to command silence.
Shabbat ʃə'bæt
shabb|y 'ʃæb|.i **-ier** -i.əʳ (US) -i.ɚ **-iest** -i.ɪst, -i.əst **-ily** -ɪ.li, -əl.i **-iness** -ɪ.nəs, -ɪ.nɪs
Shabuoth 'ʃæb.u.ɒt (US) ˌʃɑː.vuː'ɑːt; ʃə'vuː.oʊt, -oʊθ
shack ʃæk **-s** -s
shackl|e (S) 'ʃæk.l̩ **-es** -z **-ing** -ɪŋ, 'ʃæk.lɪŋ **-ed** -d
Shackleton 'ʃæk.l̩.tən
shad ʃæd **-s** -z
Shadbolt 'ʃæd.bəʊlt (US) -boʊlt
shaddock (S) 'ʃæd.ək
shad|e ʃeɪd **-es** -z **-ing** -ɪŋ **-ed** -ɪd
shadoof ʃæd'uːf, ʃə'duːf (US) ʃɑː- **-s** -s
shadow 'ʃæd.əʊ (US) -oʊ **-s** -z **-ing** -ɪŋ **-ed** -d **-y** -i **-iness** -ɪ.nəs, -ɪ.nɪs
shadowbox 'ʃæd.əʊ.bɒks (US) -oʊ.bɑːks **-es** -ɪz **-ing** -ɪŋ **-ed** -t
shadowless 'ʃæd.əʊ.ləs, -lɪs (US) -oʊ-
Shadrach, Shadrak 'ʃæd.ræk
Note: Some Jews pronounce /-rɑːx/.
Shadwell 'ʃæd.wel, -wəl
shad|y 'ʃeɪ.d|i **-ier** -i.əʳ (US) -i.ɚ **-iest** -i.ɪst, -i.əst **-ily** -ɪ.li, -əl.i **-iness** -ɪ.nəs, -ɪ.nɪs
Shaffer 'ʃæf.əʳ (US) 'ʃeɪ.fɚ, 'ʃæf.ɚ
shaft ʃɑːft (US) ʃæft **-s** -s **-ing** -ɪŋ **-ed** -ɪd
Shaftesbury 'ʃɑːfts.bər.i (US) 'ʃæftsˌber-, 'ʃɑːfts-, -bɚ-
shag ʃæg **-s** -z **-ging** -ɪŋ **-ged** -d
shagg|y 'ʃæg|.i **-ier** -i.əʳ (US) -i.ɚ **-iest** -i.ɪst, -i.əst **-ily** -ɪ.li, -əl.i **-iness** -ɪ.nəs, -ɪ.nɪs ˌ**shaggy 'dog** ˌ**story**
shagreen ʃæg'riːn, ʃə'griːn (US) ʃə-
shah (S) ʃɑː **-s** -z

Shairp ʃeəp, ʃɑːp (US) ʃerp, ʃɑːrp
shak|e ʃeɪk **-es** -s **-ing** -ɪŋ **shook** ʃʊk **shaken** 'ʃeɪ.kən
shakedown 'ʃeɪk.daʊn **-s** -z
shaken (*from* **shake**) 'ʃeɪ.kən
shakeout 'ʃeɪk.aʊt **-s** -s
shaker (S) 'ʃeɪ.kəʳ (US) -kɚ **-s** -z **-ism** -ɪ.zəm
Shakespear(e) 'ʃeɪk.spɪəʳ (US) -spɪr
Shakespearean ˌʃeɪk'spɪə.ri.ən (US) -'spɪr.i- **-s** -z
Shakespeareana ʃeɪkˌspɪə.ri'ɑː.nə, ˌʃeɪk- (US) ˌʃeɪk.spɪr.i.æn.ə, -'ɑː.nə
Shakespearian ʃeɪk'spɪə.ri.ən (US) -'spɪr.i- **-s** -z
Shakespeariana ʃeɪkˌspɪə.ri'ɑː.nə, ˌʃeɪk.spɪə- (US) ˌʃeɪk.spɪr.i'æn.ə, -'ɑː.nə
shake-up 'ʃeɪk.ʌp **-s** -s
shako 'ʃæk.əʊ, 'ʃeɪ.kəʊ, 'ʃɑː- (US) 'ʃæk.oʊ, 'ʃeɪ.koʊ, 'ʃɑː- **-(e)s** -z
shak|y 'ʃeɪ.k|i **-ier** -i.əʳ (US) -i.ɚ **-iest** -i.ɪst, -i.əst **-ily** -ɪ.li, -əl.i **-iness** -ɪ.nəs, -ɪ.nɪs
shale ʃeɪl
shall *strong form:* ʃæl *weak form:* ʃəl
Note: Weak form word. The strong form is used for strong insistence or prediction (e.g. "You **shall** go to the ball, Cinderella"), and in final position (e.g. "And so you **shall**"). The weak form is used elsewhere (e.g. "What shall we do today?" /ˌwɒt.ʃəl.wiˌduː.tə'deɪ (US) ˌwɑːt-/). American English uses 'shall' much less frequently than British English.
shallop 'ʃæl.əp **-s** -s
shallot (S) ʃə'lɒt (US) -'lɑːt; 'ʃæl.ət **-s** -s
shallow (S) 'ʃæl.əʊ (US) -oʊ **-s** -z **-er** -əʳ (US) -ɚ **-est** -ɪst, -əst **-ly** -li **-ness** -nəs, -nɪs
shalom ʃæl'ɒm, ʃə'lɒm, -'ləʊm (US) ʃɑː'loʊm, ʃə-
shalt (*from* **shall**) *strong form:* ʃælt *weak form:* ʃəlt
shal|y 'ʃeɪ.l|i **-iness** -ɪ.nəs, -ɪ.nɪs
sham ʃæm **-s** -z **-ming** -ɪŋ **-med** -d **-mer/s** -əʳ/z (US) -ɚ/z
shaman 'ʃæm.ən, 'ʃeɪ.mən, 'ʃɑː- (US) 'ʃɑː.mən, 'ʃeɪ-, 'ʃæm.ən **-s** -z **-ist/s** **-ism** -ɪ.zəm
shamateur ˌʃæm.ə'tɜːʳ (US) -'tɜːr **-s** -z **-ism** -ɪ.zəm
shambl|e 'ʃæm.bl̩ **-es** -z **-ing** -ɪŋ, '-blɪŋ **-ed** -d
shambles (*n.*) 'ʃæm.bl̩z
shambolic ʃæm'bɒl.ɪk (US) -'bɑː.lɪk
sham|e ʃeɪm **-es** -z **-ing** -ɪŋ **-ed** -d
shamefaced ˌʃeɪm'feɪst (US) '-- *stress shift, British only:* ˌshamefaced 'person

shamefaced|ness ˌʃeɪm'feɪst|.nəs, -'feɪ.sɪd-, -nɪs (US) 'ʃeɪm.feɪst-; ˌʃeɪm'feɪ.sɪd- **-ly** -li
shameful 'ʃeɪm.fəl, -fʊl **-ly** -i **-ness** -nəs, -nɪs
shameless 'ʃeɪm.ləs, -lɪs **-ly** -li **-ness** -nəs, -nɪs ˌ**shameless 'hussy**
Shamir ʃæm'ɪəʳ, ʃə'mɪəʳ (US) ʃə'mɪr, ʃæm'ɪr
shamm|y 'ʃæm.i **-ies** -iz
shampoo ʃæm'puː **-(e)s** -z **-ing** -ɪŋ **-ed** -d
shamrock (S) 'ʃæm.rɒk (US) -rɑːk **-s**
Shan ʃɑːn (US) ʃɑːn, ʃæn
Shana 'ʃɑː.nə (US) 'ʃeɪ-, 'ʃɑː-
shand|y (S) 'ʃæn.d|i **-ies** -iz
Shane ʃɑːn, ʃɔːn, ʃeɪn (US) ʃeɪn
shanghai (*v.*) ˌʃæŋ'haɪ (US) 'ʃæŋ.haɪ, -'- **-s** -z **-ing** -ɪŋ **-ed** -d
Shanghai ˌʃæŋ'haɪ (US) ˌʃæŋ-, ˌʃɑːŋ-, '-- *stress shift, British only:* ˌShanghai 'trader
Shangri-la ˌʃæŋ.gri'lɑː
shank ʃæŋk **-s** -s ˌ**shank's 'pony**, ˌ**shanks's 'pony**
Shankill 'ʃæŋ.kɪl
Shanklin 'ʃæŋ.klɪn
Shanks ʃæŋks
Shanna 'ʃæn.ə
Shannon 'ʃæn.ən
shan't ʃɑːnt (US) ʃænt
shantung *silk material:* ˌʃæn'tʌŋ
Shantung ˌʃæn'dʌŋ, -tʌŋ, -dʊŋ, -tʊŋ (US) ˌʃæn'-, ˌʃɑːn'-
shant|y 'ʃæn.t|i (US) -t̬|i **-ies** -iz
shantytown 'ʃæn.ti.taʊn (US) -t̬i- **-s** -z
shap|e ʃeɪp **-es** -s **-ing** -ɪŋ **-ed** -t
SHAPE ʃeɪp
shapeless 'ʃeɪp.ləs, -lɪs **-ly** -li **-ness** -nəs, -nɪs
shapel|y 'ʃeɪ.pl|i **-ier** -i.əʳ (US) -i.ɚ **-iest** -i.ɪst, -i.əst **-iness** -ɪ.nəs, -ɪ.nɪs
Shapiro ʃə'pɪə.rəʊ (US) -'pɪr.oʊ
shard ʃɑːd (US) ʃɑːrd **-s** -z
shar|e ʃeəʳ (US) ʃer **-es** -z **-ing** -ɪŋ **-ed** -d
sharecropp|er 'ʃeəˌkrɒp|.əʳ (US) 'ʃerˌkrɑː.p|ɚ **-ers** -əz (US) -ɚz **-ing** -ɪŋ
shareholder 'ʃeəˌhəʊl.dəʳ (US) 'ʃerˌhoʊl.dɚ **-s** -z
share-out 'ʃeəʳ.aʊt (US) 'ʃer- **-s** -s
shareware 'ʃeə.weəʳ (US) 'ʃer.wer
sharia(h) ʃə'riː.ə
Sharjah 'ʃɑː.dʒɑː, -ʒɑː, -dʒə (US) 'ʃɑːr.dʒɑː
shark ʃɑːk (US) ʃɑːrk **-s** -s
sharkskin 'ʃɑːk.skɪn (US) 'ʃɑːrk-
Sharman 'ʃɑː.mən (US) 'ʃɑːr-
Sharon *female name & fruit:* 'ʃær.ən, 'ʃɑː.rən, 'ʃeə-, -rɒn (US) 'ʃer.ən, 'ʃær- *Israeli politician:* ʃə'rəʊn, -'rɒn (US) -'roʊn

sharp (S) ʃɑːp ⓊⓈ ʃɑːrp **-s** -s **-er** -əʳ ⓊⓈ -ɚ **-est** -ɪst, -əst **-ly** -li **-ness** -nəs, -nɪs ˌsharp 'end, 'sharp ˌend ; ˌsharp 'practice
Sharpe ʃɑːp ⓊⓈ ʃɑːrp
sharpen 'ʃɑː.pᵊn ⓊⓈ 'ʃɑːr- **-s** -z **-ing** -ɪŋ, -ɪŋ **-ed** -d
sharpener 'ʃɑː.pᵊn.əʳ ⓊⓈ 'ʃɑːr.pᵊn.ɚ **-s** -z
sharper 'ʃɑː.pəʳ ⓊⓈ 'ʃɑːr.pɚ **-s** -z
Sharpeville 'ʃɑːp.vɪl ⓊⓈ 'ʃɑːrp-
sharp-eyed ˌʃɑːp'aɪd ⓊⓈ ˌʃɑːrp-
sharpish 'ʃɑː.pɪʃ ⓊⓈ 'ʃɑːr-
Sharples 'ʃɑː.p|z ⓊⓈ 'ʃɑːr-
sharp-set ˌʃɑːp'set ⓊⓈ 'ʃɑːrp.set *stress shift, British only:* ˌsharp-set 'features
sharpshooter 'ʃɑːpˌʃuː.təʳ ⓊⓈ 'ʃɑːrpˌʃuː.t̬ɚ **-s** -z
sharp-sighted ˌʃɑːp'saɪ.tɪd ⓊⓈ 'ʃɑːrpˌsaɪ.t̬ɪd *stress shift, British only:* ˌsharp-sighted 'person
sharp-witted ˌʃɑːp'wɪt.ɪd ⓊⓈ 'ʃɑːrpˌwɪt̬- *stress shift, British only:* ˌsharp-witted 'person
shashlik ʃɑːʃ'lɪk, ʃæʃ-, '-- ⓊⓈ 'ʃɑːʃ- **-s** -s
Shasta 'ʃæs.tə
Shastri 'ʃæs.tri ⓊⓈ 'ʃɑː.stri
shat *(from* **shit***)* ʃæt
Note: This past tense form is rarely used in American English.
Shatt-al-Arab ˌʃæt.æl'ær.əb ⓊⓈ -əl'er-, -'ær-
shatt|er 'ʃæt|.əʳ ⓊⓈ 'ʃæt̬|.ɚ **-ers** -əz ⓊⓈ -ɚz **-ering** -ᵊr.ɪŋ **-ered** -əd ⓊⓈ -ɚd
shatterproof 'ʃæt.ə.pruːf ⓊⓈ 'ʃæt̬.ɚ-
Shaughnessy 'ʃɔː.nə.si ⓊⓈ 'ʃɑː-, 'ʃɔː-
Shaula 'ʃəʊ.lə ⓊⓈ 'ʃoʊ-, 'ʃɔː-
Shaun ʃɔːn ⓊⓈ ʃɑːn, ʃɔːn
Shauna 'ʃɔː.nə ⓊⓈ 'ʃɑː-, 'ʃɔː-
shav|e ʃeɪv **-es** -z **-ing** -ɪŋ **-ed** -d **'shaving ˌbrush ; 'shaving ˌcream ; 'shaving ˌfoam**
shaven 'ʃeɪ.vᵊn
shaver 'ʃeɪ.vəʳ ⓊⓈ -vɚ **-s** -z
Shavian 'ʃeɪ.vi.ən
shaving 'ʃeɪ.vɪŋ **-s** -z
shaw (S) ʃɔː ⓊⓈ ʃɑː, ʃɔː **-s** -z
shawl ʃɔːl ⓊⓈ ʃɑːl, ʃɔːl **-s** -z
shawm ʃɔːm ⓊⓈ ʃɑːm, ʃɔːm **-s** -z
Shawn ʃɔːn ⓊⓈ ʃɑːn, ʃɔːn
Shawna 'ʃɔː.nə ⓊⓈ 'ʃɑː-, 'ʃɔː-
Shawnee ʃɔː'niː ⓊⓈ ʃɑː-, ʃɔː- **-s** -z
shay ʃeɪ **-s** -z
she *normal form:* ʃiː *freq. weak form:* ʃi
Note: Weak form word. The strong form, /ʃiː/ is used mainly contrastively (e.g. "I wouldn't go, so SHE went") or emphatically (e.g. "What does SHE want?"). The weak form is /ʃi/ (e.g. "off she went", /ˌɒf.ʃi'went ⓊⓈ ˌɑːf-/).
shea ʃɪə, 'ʃiː.ə, ʃiː ⓊⓈ ʃiː, ʃeɪ **-s** -z
Shea ʃeɪ
shea|f ʃiː|f **-ves** -vz
Sheaffer 'ʃeɪ.fəʳ ⓊⓈ -fɚ
shear ʃɪəʳ ⓊⓈ ʃɪr **-s** -z **-ing** -ɪŋ **-ed** -d shorn ʃɔːn ⓊⓈ ʃɔːrn
Sheard ʃeəd, ʃɪəd, ʃɜːd ⓊⓈ ʃerd, ʃɪrd, ʃɜːrd
shearer (S) 'ʃɪə.rəʳ ⓊⓈ 'ʃɪr.ɚ **-s** -z
Shearman 'ʃɪə.mən, 'ʃɜː.mən ⓊⓈ 'ʃɪr-, 'ʃɜːr-
Shearn ʃɪən, ʃɜːn ⓊⓈ ʃɪrn, ʃɜːrn
shears (S) ʃɪəz ⓊⓈ ʃɪrz
Shearson 'ʃɪə.sᵊn ⓊⓈ 'ʃɪr-
shearwater 'ʃɪəˌwɔː.təʳ ⓊⓈ 'ʃɪrˌwɑː.t̬ɚ, -ˌwɔː- **-s** -z
shea|th ʃiː|θ **-ths** -ðz, -θs
sheath|e ʃiːð **-es** -z **-ing** -ɪŋ **-ed** -d
sheaves *(plur. of* **sheaf***)* ʃiːvz
Sheba 'ʃiː.bə
shebang ʃɪ'bæŋ, ʃə-
she-bear 'ʃiː.beəʳ ⓊⓈ -ber **-s** -z
shebeen ʃɪ'biːn, ʃə-, ʃeb'iːn ⓊⓈ ʃɪ'biːn **-s** -z
she-cat 'ʃiː.kæt **-s** -s
Shechem 'ʃiː.kem, 'ʃek.em; *as if Jewish:* ʃə'xem ⓊⓈ 'ʃiː.kəm, 'ʃek.əm
shed ʃed **-s** -z **-ding** -ɪŋ
she-devil 'ʃiːˌdev.ᵊl **-s** -z
Shee ʃiː
sheen (S) ʃiːn
Sheena 'ʃiː.nə
sheen|y 'ʃiː.n|i **-ies** -iz
sheep ʃiːp **'sheep's ˌeyes ; ˌseparate the ˌsheep from the 'goats**
sheep-dip 'ʃiːp.dɪp
sheepdog 'ʃiːp.dɒg ⓊⓈ -dɑːg, -dɔːg **-s** -z
sheepfold 'ʃiːp.fəʊld ⓊⓈ -foʊld **-s** -z
sheepish 'ʃiː.pɪʃ **-ly** -li **-ness** -nəs, -nɪs
sheepshank 'ʃiːp.ʃæŋk **-s** -s
Sheepshanks 'ʃiːp.ʃæŋks
sheepshear|ing 'ʃiːpˌʃɪə.r|ɪŋ ⓊⓈ -ˌʃɪr|.ɪŋ **-er/s** -əʳ/z ⓊⓈ -ɚ/z
sheepskin 'ʃiːp.skɪn **-s** -z
sheer ʃɪəʳ ⓊⓈ ʃɪr **-s** -z **-ing** -ɪŋ **-ed** -d
Sheerness ˌʃɪə'nes ⓊⓈ 'ʃɪr.nes
sheet ʃiːt **-s** -s **-ing** -ɪŋ ⓊⓈ 'ʃiː.t̬ɪŋ **'sheet ˌanchor ; ˌsheet 'lightning** ⓊⓈ **'sheet ˌlightning ; ˌsheet 'metal ; 'sheet ˌmusic ; ˌwhite as a 'sheet**
Sheffield 'ʃef.iːld *locally:* -ɪld ⓊⓈ -iːld
Shefford 'ʃef.əd ⓊⓈ -ɚd
she-goat 'ʃiː.gəʊt ⓊⓈ -goʊt **-s** -s
sheik(h) ʃeɪk, ʃiːk, ʃek, ʃex ⓊⓈ ʃiːk, ʃeɪk **-s** -s **-dom/s** -dəm/z
sheila (S) 'ʃiː.lə
shekel 'ʃek.ᵊl **-s** -z
Shekinah ʃek'aɪ.nə, ʃɪ'kaɪ- ⓊⓈ ʃə'kiː-, -'kaɪ-
Shelagh 'ʃiː.lə
Shelby 'ʃel.bi
Sheldon 'ʃel.dᵊn
Sheldonian ʃel'dəʊ.ni.ən ⓊⓈ -'doʊ-
sheldrake 'ʃel.dreɪk **-s** -s
Sheldrick 'ʃel.drɪk
shelduck 'ʃel.dʌk **-s** -s
shel|f ʃel|f **-ves** -vz
Shelfield 'ʃel.fiːld
shelf-life 'ʃelf.laɪf **-lives** -laɪvz
Shelford 'ʃel.fəd ⓊⓈ -fɚd
shell (S) ʃel **-s** -z **-ing** -ɪŋ **-ed** -d **'shell ˌshock ; 'shell ˌsuit**
shellac ʃə'læk, ʃel'æk; 'ʃel.æk ⓊⓈ ʃə'læk **-s** -s **-king** -ɪŋ **-ked** -t
Shelley 'ʃel.i
shellfish 'ʃel.fɪʃ
Shelta 'ʃel.tə ⓊⓈ -t̬ə
shelt|er 'ʃel.t|əʳ ⓊⓈ -t̬|ɚ **-ers** -əz ⓊⓈ -ɚz **-ering** -ᵊr.ɪŋ **-ered** -əd ⓊⓈ -ɚd
shelt|ie, shelt|y 'ʃel.t|i ⓊⓈ -t̬|i **-ies** -iz
Shelton 'ʃel.tən ⓊⓈ -tᵊn
shelv|e ʃelv **-es** -z **-ing** -ɪŋ **-ed** -d
Shem ʃem
shemozzle ʃɪ'mɒz.l̩, ʃə- ⓊⓈ -'mɑː.zl̩ **-s** -z
Shenandoah ˌʃen.ən'dəʊə ⓊⓈ -'doʊə
shenanigan ʃɪ'næn.ɪ.gən, ʃə- **-s** -z
Shennan 'ʃen.ən
Shenstone 'ʃen.stən
Shenyang ˌʃen'jæŋ ⓊⓈ ˌʃʌn'jɑːŋ
Shepard 'ʃep.əd ⓊⓈ -ɚd
shepherd (S) 'ʃep.əd ⓊⓈ -ɚd **-s** -z **-ing** -ɪŋ **-ed** -ɪd ˌ**shepherd's 'pie**
shepherdess ˌʃep.ə'des; '---, -dɪs ⓊⓈ 'ʃep.ɚ.dɪs **-es** -ɪz
Sheppard 'ʃep.əd ⓊⓈ -ɚd
Shepperton 'ʃep.ə.tᵊn ⓊⓈ -ɚ.t̬ən
Sheppey 'ʃep.i
Shepreth 'ʃep.rəθ
Shepshed 'ʃep.ʃed
Shepton Mallet ˌʃep.tən'mæl.ɪt
Sheraton 'ʃer.ə.tᵊn ⓊⓈ -t̬ən, -tᵊn
sherbet, sherbert 'ʃɜː.bət ⓊⓈ 'ʃɜːr-, -bɚt
Note: Both pronunciations are possible for both variants in American English, even though only one is spelt with an **r**.
Sherborne 'ʃɜː.bən, -bɔːn ⓊⓈ 'ʃɜːr.bɔːrn, -bɚn
Sherbrooke 'ʃɜː.brʊk ⓊⓈ 'ʃɜːr-
sherd ʃɜːd ⓊⓈ ʃɜːrd **-s** -z
Shere ʃɪəʳ ⓊⓈ ʃɪr
Sheridan 'ʃer.ɪ.dᵊn
sheriff (S) 'ʃer.ɪf **-s** -s
Sheringham 'ʃer.ɪŋ.əm
sherlock (S) 'ʃɜː.lɒk ⓊⓈ 'ʃɜːr.lɑːk
Sherman 'ʃɜː.mən ⓊⓈ 'ʃɜːr-
Sherpa 'ʃɜː.pə ⓊⓈ 'ʃɜːr- **-s** -z
Sherrin 'ʃer.ɪn
sherr|y (S) 'ʃer|.i **-ies** -iz
Sherwood 'ʃɜː.wʊd ⓊⓈ 'ʃɜːr- ˌ**Sherwood 'Forest**
she's *(from* **she is** *or* **she has***) strong form:* ʃiːz *weak form:* ʃɪz

Note: The use of the strong form /ʃiːz/ and the weak form /ʃɪz/ is parallel to the two forms of **she**.
Shetland 'ʃet.lənd **-s** -z **-er/s** -əʳ/z (US) -ɚ/z **'Shetland ˌIslands** ; **ˌShetland 'pony**
Shevardnaze ˌʃev.əd'nɑːd.zeɪ (US) -ɚd'-
Shevington 'ʃev.ɪŋ.tən
shew ʃəʊ (US) ʃoʊ **-s** -z **-ing** -ɪŋ **-ed** -d **-n** -n
shewbread 'ʃəʊ.bred (US) 'ʃoʊ-
Shewell ʃʊəl, 'ʃuː.əl (US) 'ʃuː.əl
shewn (*from* **shew**) ʃəʊn (US) ʃoʊn
she-wol|f 'ʃiː.wʊl|f **-ves** -vz
shh, sh, ssh ʃ
Note: Used to command silence.
Shia(h) 'ʃiː.ə ˌ**Shia 'Muslim**
shiatsu ʃi'æt.su (US) -'ɑːt-
shibboleth (S) 'ʃɪb.əl.eθ, -əθ, -ɪθ (US) -ə.leθ, -ləθ **-s** -s
shickered 'ʃɪk.əd (US) -ɚd
shield (S) ʃiːld **-s** -z **-ing** -ɪŋ **-ed** -ɪd
shieling 'ʃiː.lɪŋ **-s** -z
Shiels ʃiːlz
Shifnal 'ʃɪf.nəl
shift ʃɪft **-s** -s **-ing** -ɪŋ **-ed** -ɪd **'shift ˌstick**
shiftless 'ʃɪft.ləs, -lɪs **-ly** -li **-ness** -nəs, -nɪs
shiftwork 'ʃɪft.wɜːk (US) -wɜːrk **-er/s** -əʳ/z (US) -ɚ/z
shift|y 'ʃɪf.t|i **-ier** -i.əʳ (US) -i.ɚ **-iest** -i.ɪst, -i.əst **-ily** -ɪ.li, -əl.i **-iness** -ɪ.nəs, -ɪ.nɪs
Shiism 'ʃiː.ɪ.zəm
Shiite 'ʃiː.aɪt **-s** -s
shikari ʃɪ'kɑː.ri, -'kær.i (US) -'kɑːr.i **-s** -z
Shikoku ʃɪ'kəʊ.kuː (US) -'kɑː-, ʃiː-, -'kɔː-
shiksa 'ʃɪk.sə **-s** -z
shikse 'ʃɪk.sə **-s** -z
Shildon 'ʃɪl.dən
Shillan ʃɪ'læn
shillela(g)h (S) ʃɪ'leɪ.lə, -li (US) -li, -lə **-s** -z
Shilleto, Shillito 'ʃɪl.ɪ.təʊ (US) -toʊ
shilling 'ʃɪl.ɪŋ **-s** -z
shilly-shall|y 'ʃɪl.iˌʃæl|.i, ˌʃɪl.i'ʃæl- (US) 'ʃɪl.iˌʃæl- **-ies** -iz **-ying** -i.ɪŋ **-ied** -id
Shiloh 'ʃaɪ.ləʊ (US) -loʊ
Shilton 'ʃɪl.tən
shimm|er 'ʃɪm|.əʳ (US) -ɚ **-ers** -əz (US) -ɚz **-ering** -ər.ɪŋ **-ered** -əd (US) -ɚd
shimm|y 'ʃɪm|.i **-ies** -iz **-ying** -i.ɪŋ **-ied** -id
shin ʃɪn **-s** -z **-ning** -ɪŋ **-ned** -d
shinbone 'ʃɪn.bəʊn, 'ʃɪm- (US) 'ʃɪn.boʊn **-s** -z
shindig 'ʃɪn.dɪg **-s** -z
shind|y 'ʃɪn.d|i **-ies** -iz
shin|e ʃaɪn **-es** -z **-ing** -ɪŋ **-ed** -d **shone** ʃɒn (US) ʃoʊn, ʃɑːn
shiner 'ʃaɪ.nəʳ (US) -nɚ **-s** -z
shingle 'ʃɪŋ.gl̩ **-s** -z
shingly 'ʃɪŋ.gli, -gl̩.i
shinn|y 'ʃɪn|.i **-ies** -iz **-ying** -i.ɪŋ **-ied** -id
shinsplints 'ʃɪn.splɪnts
Shinto 'ʃɪn.təʊ (US) -toʊ **-ism** -ɪ.zəm **-ist/s** -ɪst/s
Shinwell 'ʃɪn.wəl, -wel
shin|y 'ʃaɪ.n|i **-ier** -i.əʳ (US) -i.ɚ **-iest** -i.ɪst, -i.əst **-iness** -ɪ.nəs, -ɪ.nɪs
ship ʃɪp **-s** -s **-ping** -ɪŋ **-ped** -t **-per/s** -əʳ/z (US) -ɚ/z
-ship -ʃɪp
Note: Suffix. Normally unstressed, e.g. **kinship** /'kɪn.ʃɪp/.
shipboard 'ʃɪp.bɔːd (US) -bɔːrd
shipbroker 'ʃɪpˌbrəʊ.kəʳ (US) -ˌbroʊ.kɚ **-s** -z
shipbuild|er 'ʃɪpˌbɪl.d|əʳ (US) -d|ɚ **-ers** -əz (US) -ɚz **-ing** -ɪŋ
Shiplake 'ʃɪp.leɪk
Shipley 'ʃɪp.li
shipload 'ʃɪp.ləʊd (US) -loʊd **-s** -z
shipmaster 'ʃɪpˌmɑː.stəʳ (US) -ˌmæs.tɚ **-s** -z
shipmate 'ʃɪp.meɪt **-s** -s
shipment 'ʃɪp.mənt **-s** -s
Shipp ʃɪp
shipping 'ʃɪp.ɪŋ **'shipping ˌclerk**
shipshape 'ʃɪp.ʃeɪp
Shipston 'ʃɪp.stən
Shipton 'ʃɪp.tən
shipway 'ʃɪp.weɪ **-s** -z
shipwreck 'ʃɪp.rek **-s** -s **-ing** -ɪŋ **-ed** -t
shipwright (S) 'ʃɪp.raɪt **-s** -s
shipyard 'ʃɪp.jɑːd (US) -jɑːrd **-s** -z
Shiraz ʃɪə'rɑːz, ʃɪ-, -'ræz (US) ʃiː-
shire ʃaɪəʳ (US) ʃaɪɚ **-s** -z **'shire ˌhorse**
-shire -ʃəʳ, -ˌʃɪəʳ (US) -ʃɚ, -ˌʃɪr
Note: Suffix. Does not normally change the stress pattern of the stem to which it is added, e.g. **Lincoln** /'lɪŋ.kən/, **Lincolnshire** /'lɪŋ.kən.ʃəʳ (US) -ʃɚ/. There is a free choice between the unstressed variant and that with secondary stress in all names ending **-shire**.
Shirebrook 'ʃaɪə.brʊk (US) 'ʃaɪɚ-
Shiremoor 'ʃaɪə.mɔːʳ, -mʊəʳ (US) 'ʃaɪɚ.mɔːr, -mʊr
shirk ʃɜːk (US) ʃɜːrk **-s** -s **-ing** -ɪŋ **-ed** -t **-er/s** -əʳ/z (US) -ɚ/z
Shirley 'ʃɜː.li (US) 'ʃɜːr-
shirr ʃɜːʳ (US) ʃɜːr **-s** -z **-ing** -ɪŋ **-ed** -d
shirt (S) ʃɜːt (US) ʃɜːrt **-s** -s
shirtdress 'ʃɜːt.dres (US) 'ʃɜːrt- **-es** -ɪz
shirt-front 'ʃɜːt.frʌnt (US) 'ʃɜːrt- **-s** -s
shirting 'ʃɜː.tɪŋ (US) 'ʃɜːr.t̬ɪŋ
shirt-sleev|es 'ʃɜːt.sliːv|z, -'- (US) 'ʃɜːrt- **-ed** -d
shirt-tail 'ʃɜːt.teɪl (US) 'ʃɜːrt- **-s** -z
shirtwaist 'ʃɜːt.weɪst (US) 'ʃɜːrt- **-s** -s **-er/s** -əʳ/z (US) -ɚ/z
shirtwaister 'ʃɜːtˌweɪ.stəʳ, ˌ-'-- (US) 'ʃɜːrtˌweɪ.stɚ **-s** -z
shirt|y 'ʃɜː.t|i (US) 'ʃɜːr.t̬|i **-ier** -i.əʳ (US) -i.ɚ **-iest** -i.ɪst, -i.əst **-iness** -ɪ.nəs, -ɪ.nɪs
Shishak 'ʃaɪ.ʃæk, -ʃək *rarely:* 'ʃɪʃ.æk, -ək (US) 'ʃaɪ.ʃɑːk, -ʃæk
shish kebab 'ʃiːʃ.kɪˌbæb, -kəˌ-, ˌ--'- (US) 'ʃɪʃ.kəˌbɑːb **-s** -z
shit ʃɪt **-s** -s **-ting** -ɪŋ (US) 'ʃɪt̬.ɪŋ **shat** ʃæt
Note: The past tense form **shat** is rarely used in American English, the normal past tense being **shit**.
shitfaced 'ʃɪt.feɪst
shithouse 'ʃɪt.haʊs
shitless 'ʃɪt.ləs, -lɪs
shitt|y 'ʃɪt|.i (US) 'ʃɪt̬|.i **-ier** -i.əʳ (US) -i.ɚ **-iest** -i.ɪst, -i.əst **-iness** -ɪ.nəs, -ɪ.nɪs
Shiva 'ʃiː.və, 'ʃɪv.ə (US) 'ʃiː.və
shiv|er 'ʃɪv|.əʳ (US) -ɚ **-ers** -əz (US) -ɚz **-ering/ly** -ər.ɪŋ/li **-ered** -əd (US) -ɚd
shiver|y 'ʃɪv.ər|.i **-iness** -ɪ.nəs, -ɪ.nɪs
shlemiel ʃlə'miːl **-s** -z
shlep ʃlep **-s** -s **-ping** -ɪŋ **-ped** -t
shlock ʃlɒk (US) ʃlɑːk **-s** -s
shlockmeister 'ʃlɒkˌmaɪ.stəʳ (US) 'ʃlɑːkˌmaɪ.stɚ **-s** -z
Shloer® ʃlɜːʳ (US) ʃlɜːr
shmal(t)z ʃmɔːlts, ʃmɒlts, ʃmælts (US) ʃmɑːlts, ʃmɔːlts **-y** -i **-ier** -i.əʳ (US) -i.ɚ **-iest** -i.ɪst, -i.əst
shmuck ʃmʌk **-s** -s
shoal ʃəʊl (US) ʃoʊl **-s** -z
shock ʃɒk (US) ʃɑːk **-s** -s **-ing** -ɪŋ **-ed** -t **-er/s** -əʳ/z (US) -ɚ/z **'shock abˌsorber** ; **'shock ˌtreatment** ; **'shock ˌwave**
shocking 'ʃɒk.ɪŋ (US) 'ʃɑː.kɪŋ **-ly** -li
shockproof 'ʃɒk.pruːf (US) 'ʃɑːk-
shodd|y 'ʃɒd|.i (US) 'ʃɑː.d|i **-ier** -i.əʳ (US) -i.ɚ **-iest** -i.ɪst, -i.əst **-ily** -ɪ.li, -əl.i **-iness** -ɪ.nəs, -ɪ.nɪs
shoe ʃuː **-s** -z **-ing** -ɪŋ **shod** ʃɒd (US) ʃɑːd **'shoe ˌleather**
shoeblack 'ʃuː.blæk **-s** -s
Shoeburyness ˌʃuː.bər.i'nes
shoehorn 'ʃuː.hɔːn (US) -hɔːrn **-s** -z
shoe-horn 'ʃuː.hɔːn (US) -hɔːrn **-s** -z **-ing** -ɪŋ **-ed** -d
shoelac|e 'ʃuː.leɪs **-es** -ɪz
shoeless 'ʃuː.ləs, -lɪs
shoemaker (S) 'ʃuːˌmeɪ.kəʳ (US) -kɚ **-s** -z
shoeshine 'ʃuː.ʃaɪn **-s** -z
shoestring 'ʃuː.strɪŋ
shoetree 'ʃuː.triː **-s** -z
shogun 'ʃəʊ.gʌn, -guːn, -gən (US) 'ʃoʊ.gʌn, -gʊn, -guːn **-s** -s

Sholokhov 'ʃɒl.ə.kɒf US 'ʃɔː.lə.kɔːf
Shona *female name:* 'ʃəʊ.nə US 'ʃoʊ- *African language & people:* 'ʃɒ.nə, 'ʃɔː-, 'ʃəʊ- US 'ʃoʊ-
shone (*from* **shine**) ʃɒn US ʃoʊn
shoo ʃuː **-s** -z **-ing** -ɪŋ **-ed** -d
shoofl|y 'ʃuː.fl|aɪ **-ies** -aɪz
shook (*from* **shake**) ʃʊk
shook-up ˌʃʊk'ʌp
shoot ʃuːt **-s** -s **-ing** -ɪŋ US 'ʃuː.t̬ɪŋ **shot** ʃɒt US ʃɑːt **ˌshoot the 'breeze**
shooter (S) 'ʃuː.təʳ US -t̬ɚ **-s** -z
shooting 'ʃuː.tɪŋ US -t̬ɪŋ **-s** -z **'shooting ˌgallery ; ˌshooting 'star, 'shooting ˌstar** US **ˌshooting 'star ; 'shooting ˌstick**
shoot-out 'ʃuːt.aʊt **-s** -s
shop ʃɒp US ʃɑːp **-s** -s **-ping** -ɪŋ **-ped** -t **-per/s** -əʳ/z US -ɚ/z **'shop asˌsistant ; ˌshop 'steward** US **'shop ˌsteward; ˌshop 'window**
shopfloor ˌʃɒp'flɔːʳ US ˌʃɑːp'flɔːr
shopfront ˌʃɒp'frʌnt, '-- US 'ʃɑːp.frʌnt **-s** -s
shopgirl 'ʃɒp.gɜːl US 'ʃɑːp.gɜːrl **-s** -z
shopkeeper 'ʃɒpˌkiː.pəʳ US 'ʃɑːpˌkiː.pɚ **-s** -z
shoplift 'ʃɒp.lɪft US 'ʃɑːp- **-s** -s **-ing** -ɪŋ **-ed** -ɪd
shop-lifter 'ʃɒpˌlɪf.təʳ US 'ʃɑːpˌlɪf.tɚ **-s** -z
shopping 'ʃɒp.ɪŋ **'shopping ˌcentre/ˌcenter ; 'shopping ˌlist ; 'shopping ˌmall**
shop-soiled ˌʃɒp'sɔɪld US 'ʃɑːpˌsɔɪld *stress shift, British only:* ˌshop-soiled 'goods
shoptalk 'ʃɒp.tɔːk US 'ʃɑːp.tɑːk, -tɔːk
shopwalker 'ʃɒpˌwɔː.kəʳ US 'ʃɑːpˌwɔː.kɚ, -ˌwɑː- **-s** -z
shopworn 'ʃɒp.wɔːn US 'ʃɑːp.wɔːrn
shor|e ʃɔːʳ US ʃɔːr **-s** -z **-ing** -ɪŋ **-ed** -d
Shoreditch 'ʃɔː.dɪtʃ US 'ʃɔːr-
Shoreham 'ʃɔː.rəm US 'ʃɔːr.əm
shoreline 'ʃɔː.laɪn US 'ʃɔːr-
shoreward 'ʃɔː.wəd US 'ʃɔːr.wɚd
shorn (*from* **shear**) ʃɔːn US ʃɔːrn
Shorncliffe 'ʃɔːn.klɪf US 'ʃɔːrn-
short (S) ʃɔːt US ʃɔːrt **-s** -s **-er** -əʳ US 'ʃɔːr.t̬ɚ **-est** -ɪst, -əst US 'ʃɔːr.t̬ɪst, -t̬əst **-ly** -li **-ness** -nəs, -nɪs **-ing -ed ˌshort ˌback and 'sides ; ˌshort 'shrift ; ˌshort 'story ; the ˌshort ˌend of the 'stick ; the ˌlong and the 'short of it**
shortag|e 'ʃɔː.tɪdʒ US 'ʃɔːr.t̬ɪdʒ **-es** -ɪz
shortbread 'ʃɔːt.bred US 'ʃɔːrt- **-s** -z
shortcake 'ʃɔːt.keɪk US 'ʃɔːrt- **-s** -s
short-chang|e ˌʃɔːt'tʃeɪndʒ US ˌʃɔːrt- **-es** -ɪz **-ing** -ɪŋ **-ed** -d
short-cir|cuit ˌʃɔːt'sɜː.kɪt US ˌʃɔːrt'sɜːr- **-cuits** -kɪts **-cuiting** -kɪ.tɪŋ US -kɪ.t̬ɪŋ **-cuited** -kɪ.tɪd US -kɪ.t̬ɪd
shortcoming 'ʃɔːtˌkʌm.ɪŋ, ˌ-'-- US 'ʃɔːrtˌkʌm- **-s** -z
shortcrust 'ʃɔːt.krʌst US 'ʃɔːrt- **-s** -s **ˌshortcrust 'pastry**
shortcut 'ʃɔːt.kʌt US 'ʃɔːrt- **-s** -s
short-dated ˌʃɔːt'deɪ.tɪd US ˌʃɔːrt'deɪ.t̬ɪd
short-eared ˌʃɔːt'ɪəd US 'ʃɔːrt.ɪrd *stress shift, British only:* ˌshort-eared 'rabbit
shorten 'ʃɔː.tᵊn US 'ʃɔːr- **-s** -z **-ing** -ɪŋ, 'ʃɔːt.nɪŋ US 'ʃɔːr.tᵊn.ɪŋ, 'ʃɔːrt.nɪŋ **-ed** -d
shortening 'ʃɔːt.nɪŋ; 'ʃɔː.tᵊn.ɪŋ US 'ʃɔːrt.nɪŋ; 'ʃɔːr.tᵊn.ɪŋ
shortfall 'ʃɔːt.fɔːl US 'ʃɔːrt-, -fɑːl **-s** -z
shorthand 'ʃɔːt.hænd US 'ʃɔːrt- **ˌshorthand 'typist**
short-handed ˌʃɔːt'hæn.dɪd US ˌʃɔːrt- *stress shift:* ˌshort-handed 'vessel
short-haul 'ʃɔːt.hɔːl, ˌ-'- US 'ʃɔːrt.hɑːl, -hɔːl, ˌ-'-
shorthorn 'ʃɔːt.hɔːn US 'ʃɔːrt.hɔːrn **-s** -z
shortlist 'ʃɔːt.lɪst US 'ʃɔːrt- **-s** -s **-ing** -ɪŋ **-ed** -ɪd
short-lived ˌʃɔːt'lɪvd US 'ʃɔːrt.laɪvd, -lɪvd *stress shift, British only:* ˌshort-lived 'glory
short-order 'ʃɔːtˌɔː.dəʳ, ˌ-'-- US 'ʃɔːrtˌɔːr.dɚ
short-range ˌʃɔːt'reɪndʒ US ˌʃɔːrt- *stress shift:* ˌshort-range 'missile
shortsighted ˌʃɔːt'saɪ.tɪd US 'ʃɔːrtˌsaɪ.t̬ɪd **-ly** -li **-ness** -nəs, -nɪs *stress shift, British only:* ˌshort-sighted 'person
short-staffed ˌʃɔːt'stɑːft US ˌʃɔːrt'stæft *stress shift:* ˌshort-staffed 'bar
short-tempered ˌʃɔːt'tem.pəd US ˌʃɔːrt'tem.pɚd *stress shift:* ˌshort-tempered 'person
short-term ˌʃɔːt'tɜːm US 'ʃɔːrt.tɜːrm **-ism** -ɪ.zᵊm *stress shift, British only:* ˌshort-term 'plans
shortwave 'ʃɔːt.weɪv US 'ʃɔːrt- **-s** -z
short-winded ˌʃɔːt'wɪn.dɪd US 'ʃɔːrtˌwɪn-, ˌ-'-- *stress shift, British only:* ˌshort-winded 'story
short|y 'ʃɔː.t|i US 'ʃɔːr.t̬|i **-ies** -iz
Shostakovich ˌʃɒs.tə'kəʊ.vɪtʃ US ˌʃɑː.stə'koʊ-
shot ʃɒt US ʃɑːt **-s** -s **'shot ˌput ; 'shot ˌputter**
shotgun 'ʃɒt.gʌn US 'ʃɑːt- **-s** -z **ˌshotgun 'wedding**
Shotton 'ʃɒt.ᵊn US 'ʃɑː.tᵊn
Shotts ʃɒts US ʃɑːts
should *strong form:* ʃʊd *weak forms:* ʃəd, ʃd, ʃt
Note: Weak form word. The strong form is used for emphatic pronunciation (e.g. "He **should** have asked first"), or for contrast (e.g. "Don't tell me what I should or shouldn't do"). It is also used in final position (e.g. "We both should"). The most usual weak form is /ʃəd/, as in "When should it arrive?" /ˌwen.ʃəd.ɪt.ə'raɪv/, but in rapid speech we also find /ʃd/ before voiced sounds (e.g. "I should go now" /ˌaɪ.ʃd'gəʊ.naʊ US -'goʊ-/) and /ʃt/ before voiceless sounds (e.g. "You should try to finish" /ju.ʃtˌtraɪ.tə'fɪn.ɪʃ US -t̬ə'-/).
should|er 'ʃəʊl.d|əʳ US 'ʃoʊl.d|ɚ **-ers** -əz US -ɚz **-ering** -ᵊr.ɪŋ **-ered** -əd US -ɚd **'shoulder ˌbag ; 'shoulder ˌblade ; 'shoulder ˌpad ; 'shoulder ˌstrap ; a 'shoulder to ˌcry on, a ˌshoulder to 'cry on** US **a ˌshoulder to 'cry on**
shouldn't 'ʃʊd.ᵊnt
shout ʃaʊt **-s** -s **-ing** -ɪŋ US 'ʃaʊ.t̬ɪŋ **-ed** -ɪd US 'ʃaʊ.t̬ɪd
shov|e (*n. v.*) ʃʌv **-es** -z **-ing** -ɪŋ **-ed** -d
shove-halfpenny ˌʃʌv'heɪp.ni
shovel (S) 'ʃʌv.ᵊl **-s** -z **-(l)ing** -ɪŋ, 'ʃʌv.lɪŋ **-(l)ed** -d **-(l)er/s** -əʳ/z, 'ʃʌv.ləʳ/z US '-l̩.ɚ/z, '-lɚ/z **-ful/s** -fʊl/z
show ʃəʊ US ʃoʊ **-s** -z **-ing** -ɪŋ **-ed** -d **-n** -n **'show ˌbusiness ; ˌshow 'trial, 'show ˌtrial**
showbiz 'ʃəʊ.bɪz US 'ʃoʊ-
showboat 'ʃəʊ.bəʊt US 'ʃoʊ.boʊt **-s** -s **-ing** -ɪŋ
showbread 'ʃəʊ.bred US 'ʃoʊ-
showcas|e 'ʃəʊ.keɪs US 'ʃoʊ- **-es** -ɪz **-ing** -ɪŋ **-ed** -t
showdown 'ʃəʊ.daʊn US 'ʃoʊ- **-s** -z
shower *fall of rain, etc.:* ʃaʊəʳ US ʃaʊɚ **-s** -z **-ing** -ɪŋ **-ed** -d **-y** -i
shower *one who shows:* 'ʃəʊ.əʳ US 'ʃoʊ.ɚ **-s** -z
shower-ba|th 'ʃaʊə.bɑː|θ US 'ʃaʊɚ.bæ|θ **-ths** -ðz
showerproof 'ʃaʊə.pruːf US 'ʃaʊɚ-
showgirl 'ʃəʊ.gɜːl US 'ʃoʊ.gɜːrl **-s** -z
showjump 'ʃəʊ.dʒʌmp US 'ʃoʊ- **-s** -s **-ing** -ɪŋ **-er/s** -əʳ/z US -ɚ/z
show|man 'ʃəʊ|.mən US 'ʃoʊ- **-men** -mən, -men
showmanship 'ʃəʊ.mən.ʃɪp US 'ʃoʊ-
shown (*from* **show**) ʃəʊn US ʃoʊn
show-off 'ʃəʊ.ɒf US 'ʃoʊ.ɑːf **-s**
showpiec|e 'ʃəʊ.piːs US 'ʃoʊ- **-es** -ɪz
showplac|e 'ʃəʊ.pleɪs US 'ʃoʊ- **-es** -ɪz
showroom 'ʃəʊ.rʊm, -ruːm US 'ʃoʊ.ruːm, -rʊm **-s** -z

showstopp|er 'ʃəʊˌstɒp|.əʳ (US) 'ʃoʊˌstɑː.p|ɚ **-ers** -əz (US) ɚz **-ing** -ɪŋ
show|y 'ʃəʊ|.i (US) 'ʃoʊ- **-ier** -i.əʳ (US) -i.ɚ **-iest** -i.ɪst, -i.əst **-ily** -ɪ.li, -ᵊl.i **-iness** -ɪ.nəs, -ɪ.nɪs
shoyu 'ʃɔɪ.juː (US) 'ʃoʊ.juː
shrank (*from* **shrink**) ʃræŋk
shrapnel 'ʃræp.nᵊl
shred ʃred **-s** -z **-ding** -ɪŋ **-ded** -ɪd **-der/s** -əʳ/z (US) -ɚ/z
Shredded Wheat® ˌʃred.ɪd'*h*wiːt **-s** -s
shrew ʃruː **-s** -z
shrewd ʃruːd **-er** -əʳ (US) -ɚ **-est** -ɪst, -əst **-ly** -li **-ness** -nəs, -nɪs
shrewish 'ʃruː.ɪʃ **-ly** -li **-ness** -nəs, -nɪs
Shrewsbury *in the UK:* 'ʃrəʊz.bᵊr.i, 'ʃruːz-, '-bri (US) 'ʃruːzˌber.i, 'ʃroʊz-, -bɚ-
Note: /'ʃrəʊz-/ is the most widely used pronunciation, but /'ʃruːz-/ or /'ʃuːz-/ is more usually used by many local people.
Shrewsbury *in the US:* 'ʃruːz.bᵊr.i (US) -ˌber-, -bɚ-
shriek ʃriːk **-s** -s **-ing** -ɪŋ **-ed** -t
shrift ʃrɪft
shrike ʃraɪk **-s** -s
shrill ʃrɪl **-er** -əʳ (US) -ɚ **-est** -ɪst, -əst **-y** -i, -li **-ness** -nəs, -nɪs
shrimp ʃrɪmp **-s** -s **-ing** -ɪŋ **-er/s** -əʳ/z (US) -ɚ/z
Shrimpton 'ʃrɪmp.tən
shrine ʃraɪn **-s** -z
shriner (S) 'ʃraɪ.nəʳ (US) -nɚ **-s** -z
shrink ʃrɪŋk **-s** -s **-ing/ly** -ɪŋ/li **shrank** ʃræŋk **shrunk** ʃrʌŋk **shrunken** 'ʃrʌŋ.kən **ˌshrinking 'violet**
shrinkage 'ʃrɪŋ.kɪdʒ
shrink-wrap 'ʃrɪnk.ræp, -'- **-s** -s **-ping** -ɪŋ **-ped** -t
shriv|e (S) ʃraɪv **-es** -z **-ing** -ɪŋ **shrove** ʃrəʊv (US) ʃroʊv **shriven** 'ʃrɪv.ᵊn
shrivel 'ʃrɪv.ᵊl **-s** -z **-(l)ing** -ɪŋ, 'ʃrɪv.lɪŋ **-(l)ed** -d
shriven (*from* **shrive**) 'ʃrɪv.ᵊn
shroff ʃrɒf (US) ʃrɑːf **-s** -s **-ing** -ɪŋ **-ed** -t
Shropshire 'ʃrɒp.ʃəʳ, -ˌʃɪəʳ (US) 'ʃrɑːp.ʃɚ, -ˌʃɪr
shroud ʃraʊd **-s** -z **-ing** -ɪŋ **-ed** -ɪd **-less** -ləs, -lɪs
shrove (*from* **shrive**) ʃrəʊv (US) ʃroʊv
Shrove ʃrəʊv (US) ʃroʊv **ˌShrove 'Tuesday**
Shrovetide 'ʃrəʊv.taɪd (US) 'ʃroʊv-
shrub ʃrʌb **-s** -z
shrubber|y 'ʃrʌb.ᵊr|.i **-ies** -iz
shrubby 'ʃrʌb.i
shrug ʃrʌg **-s** -z **-ging** -ɪŋ **-ged** -d
shrunk (*from* **shrink**) ʃrʌŋk **-en** -ᵊn
shtick ʃtɪk
shuck ʃʌk **-s** -s
Shuckburgh 'ʃʌk.bᵊr.ə (US) -bɜːrg, -bɚ.ə
shudd|er 'ʃʌd|.əʳ (US) -ɚ **-ers** -əz (US) -ɚz **-ering** -ᵊr.ɪŋ **-ered** -əd (US) -ɚd
shuffl|e 'ʃʌf.l̩ **-es** -z **-ing** -ɪŋ, 'ʃʌf.lɪŋ **-ed** -d **-er/s** -əʳ/z, 'ʃʌf.ləʳ/z (US) '-l̩.ɚ/z, '-lɚ/z
shuffleboard 'ʃʌf.l̩.bɔːd (US) -bɔːrd **-s** -z
shufti 'ʃʊf.ti, 'ʃʌf- **-s** -z
Shulamite 'ʃuː.lə.maɪt
shun ʃʌn **-s** -z **-ning** -ɪŋ **-ned** -d
shunt ʃʌnt **-s** -s **-ing** -ɪŋ (US) 'ʃʌn.t̬ɪŋ **-ed** -ɪd (US) 'ʃʌn.t̬ɪd **-er/s** -əʳ/z (US) 'ʃʌn.t̬ɚ/z
shush ʃʊʃ, ʃʌʃ **-es** -ɪz **-ing** -ɪŋ **-ed** -t
shut ʃʌt **-s** -s **-ting** -ɪŋ (US) 'ʃʌt̬.ɪŋ
shutdown 'ʃʌt.daʊn **-s** -z
Shute ʃuːt
shut-eye 'ʃʌt.aɪ (US) 'ʃʌt̬-
shut-out 'ʃʌt.aʊt **-s** -z
shutt|er 'ʃʌt|.əʳ (US) 'ʃʌt̬|.ɚ **-ers** -əz (US) -ɚz **-ering** -ᵊr.ɪŋ **-ered** -əd (US) -ɚd
shuttle 'ʃʌt.l̩ (US) 'ʃʌt̬- **-s** -z **-ling** -ɪŋ **-ed** -d **ˌshuttle di'plomacy**
shuttlecock 'ʃʌt.l̩.kɒk (US) 'ʃʌt̬.l̩.kɑːk **-s** -s
Shuttleworth 'ʃʌt.l̩.wəθ, -wɜːθ (US) 'ʃʌt̬.l̩.wɚθ, -wɜːrθ
shwa ʃwɑː **-s** -z
sh|y ʃ|aɪ **-ies** -aɪz **-yer** -aɪ.əʳ (US) -aɪ.ɚ **-yest** -aɪ.ɪst, -aɪ.əst **-yly** -aɪ.li **-yness** -aɪ.nəs, -nɪs **-ying** -aɪ.ɪŋ **-ied** -aɪd
shylock (S) 'ʃaɪ.lɒk (US) -lɑːk
shyster 'ʃaɪ.stəʳ (US) -stɚ **-s** -z
si siː
Sialkot si'æl.kɒt (US) -'ɑːl.koʊt
Siam ˌsaɪ'æm, '-- (US) saɪ'æm
Siamese ˌsaɪ.ə'miːz (US) -'miːz, -'miːs *stress shift, see compounds:* **ˌSiamese 'cat** ; **ˌSiamese 'twins**
Sian, Siân ʃɑːn
Sibbald 'sɪb.əld
Sibelius sɪ'beɪ.li.əs (US) -li.əs, -'beɪl.jəs
Siberi|a saɪ'bɪə.ri|.ə (US) -'bɪr.i- **-an/s** -ən/z
sibilan|ce 'sɪb.ɪ.lᵊn|*t*s, -ᵊl.ᵊn|*t*s (US) -ᵊl.ᵊn|*t*s **-t/s** -t/s
sibilation ˌsɪb.ɪ'leɪ.ʃᵊn (US) -ᵊl'eɪ-, -ə'leɪ **-s** -z
Sibley 'sɪb.li
sibling 'sɪb.lɪŋ **-s** -z **ˌsibling 'rivalry**
sibyl (S) 'sɪb.ᵊl, -ɪl (US) -ᵊl **-s** -z
sibylline 'sɪb.ə.laɪn, '-ɪ-; sɪ'bɪl.aɪn (US) 'sɪb.ə.laɪn, -liːn, -lɪn
sic sɪk, siːk
Sichuan ˌsɪtʃ'wɑːn (US) '-ˌ-
Sicilian sɪ'sɪl.jən, sə-, -i.ən **-s** -z
Sicil|y 'sɪs.ɪ.l|i, -ᵊl|.i (US) -ᵊl|.i **-ies** -iz
sick sɪk **-er** -əʳ (US) -ɚ **-est** -ɪst, -əst **-ness** -nəs, -nɪs **'sick ˌbay** ; **ˌsick 'building ˌsyndrome** ; **'sick ˌleave** ; **'sick ˌpay**
sickbed 'sɪk.bed **-s** -z
sicken 'sɪk.ᵊn **-s** -z **-ing/ly** -ɪŋ, 'sɪk.nɪŋ **-ed** -d
Sickert 'sɪk.ət (US) -ɚt
sickle 'sɪk.l̩ **-s** -z **ˌsickle-cell a'n(a)emia**
sickl|y 'sɪk.l|i **-ier** -i.əʳ (US) -i.ɚ **-iest** -i.ɪst, -i.əst **-iness** -ɪ.nəs, -ɪ.nɪs
sickness 'sɪk.nəs, -nɪs
sicko 'sɪk.əʊ (US) -oʊ **-s** -z
sick-out 'sɪk.aʊt **-s** -s
sickroom 'sɪk.rʊm, -ruːm (US) -ruːm, -rʊm **-s** -z
sic transit gloria mundi ˌsɪkˌtræn.zɪtˌglɔː.ri.ə'mʊn.di, ˌsiːk-, -ˌtræn*t*.sɪt-, -ˌtrɑːn.zɪt-, -ˌtrɑːn*t*.sɪt- (US) ˌsɪkˌtræn.sɪtˌglɔːr.i.ə'mʌn.di
Sid sɪd
Sidcup 'sɪd.kʌp, -kəp
Siddeley 'sɪd.ᵊl.i
Siddharta sɪ'dɑː.tə (US) -'dɑːr.t̬ə
Siddons 'sɪd.ᵊnz
sid|e saɪd **-es** -z **-ing** -ɪŋ **-ed** -ɪd **'side ˌarm** ; **ˌside by 'side** ; **'side ˌdish** ; **'side ˌdrum** ; **'side efˌfect** ; **'side ˌissue** ; **'side ˌsalad** ; **'side ˌstreet** ; **ˌknow which ˌside one's ˌbread is 'buttered (on)**, **ˌknow which ˌside one's 'bread is ˌbuttered (on)** ; **ˌlaugh on the ˌother ˌside of one's 'face** ; **ˌlook on the 'bright ˌside (of things)**
sidebar 'saɪd.bɑːʳ (US) -bɑːr **-s** -z
sideboard 'saɪd.bɔːd (US) -bɔːrd **-s** -z
Sidebotham 'saɪdˌbɒt.əm (US) -ˌbɑː.t̬əm
Sidebottom 'saɪdˌbɒt.əm, 'siːd-, ˌsɪd.ɪ.bə'təʊm (US) 'saɪdˌbɑː.t̬əm, 'siːd-; ˌsɪd.ɪ.bə'toʊm
sideburn 'saɪd.bɜːn (US) -bɜːrn **-s** -z
sidecar 'saɪd.kɑːʳ (US) -kɑːr **-s** -z
sidedish 'saɪd.dɪʃ **-es** -ɪz
sidekick 'saɪd.kɪk **-s** -s
sidelight 'saɪd.laɪt **-s** -s
sidelin|e 'saɪd.laɪn **-es** -z **-ing** -ɪŋ **-ed** -d
sidelong 'saɪd.lɒŋ (US) -lɑːŋ, -lɔːŋ
sidereal saɪ'dɪə.ri.əl, sɪ- (US) saɪ'dɪr.i-
siderite 'saɪ.dᵊr.aɪt, 'sɪd.ᵊr- (US) 'sɪd.ə.raɪt
Sidery 'saɪ.dᵊr.i
sidesaddle 'saɪdˌsæd.l̩ **-s** -z
sideshow 'saɪd.ʃəʊ (US) -ʃoʊ **-s** -z
sideslip 'saɪd.slɪp **-s** -s **-ping** -ɪŋ **-ped** -t
sides|man 'saɪdz|.mən **-men** -mən, -men
sidespin 'saɪd.spɪn
sidesplitting 'saɪdˌsplɪt.ɪŋ (US) -ˌsplɪt̬-
sidestep 'saɪd.step **-s** -s **-ping** -ɪŋ **-ped** -t
sidestroke 'saɪd.strəʊk (US) -stroʊk **-s** -s
sideswip|e 'saɪd.swaɪp **-es** -s **-ing** -ɪŋ **-ed** -t
sidetrack 'saɪd.træk **-s** -s **-ing** -ɪŋ **-ed** -t

sidewalk 'saɪd.wɔːk (US) -wɑːk, -wɔːk **-s** -s
sideways 'saɪd.weɪz
sidewinder 'saɪdˌwaɪn.dəʳ (US) -dɚ **-s** -z
Sidgwick 'sɪdʒ.wɪk
siding 'saɪ.dɪŋ **-s** -z
Sidlaw 'sɪd.lɔː (US) -lɑː, -lɔː
sidl|e 'saɪ.dl̩ **-es** -z **-ing** -ɪŋ, 'saɪd.lɪŋ **-ed** -d
Sidmouth 'sɪd.məθ
Sidney 'sɪd.ni
Sidon 'saɪ.dᵊn, -dɒn (US) -dᵊn
Sidonian saɪ'dəʊ.ni.ən, sɪ- (US) saɪ'doʊ.ni.ən **-s** -z
Sidonie sɪ'dəʊ.ni (US) -'doʊ-
sieg|e siːdʒ **-es** -ɪz **'siege menˌtality**
Siegfried 'siːg.friːd *as if German:* 'ziːg (US) 'sɪg-, 'siːg-
sieg heil ˌsiːg'haɪl *as if German:* ˌziːk-
Sieglinde siː'glɪn.də *as if German:* ziː- (US) siː-, ziː-, sɪ-
Siegmund 'siːg.mʊnd *as if German:* 'ziːg-, -mənd (US) 'sɪg-, 'siːg-
Siemens 'siː.mənz *as if German:* 'ziː- **ˌSiemens-'Nixdorf**
Siena si'en.ə
Sienese ˌsi.en'iːz, -ə'niːz (US) -ə'niːz, -'niːs
sienna si'en.ə
sierra (S) si'er.ə, -'eə.rə; (US) si'er.ə **-s** -z
Sierra Leone siˌer.ə.li'əʊn, -ˌeə.rə-, -'əʊ.ni (US) siˌer.ə.li'oʊn
Sierra Madre siˌer.ə'mɑː.dreɪ, -ˌeə.rə'-; (US) siˌer.ə'-
Sierra Nevada siˌer.ə.nə'vɑː.də, -'eə.rə-; (US) siˌer.ə.nə'væd.ə, -'vɑː.də
siesta si'es.tə **-s** -z
siev|e sɪv **-es** -z **-ing** -ɪŋ **-ed** -d
sift sɪft **-s** -s **-ing** -ɪŋ **-ed** -ɪd **-er/s** -əʳ/z (US) -ɚ/z
sigh saɪ **-s** -z **-ing** -ɪŋ **-ed** -d
sight saɪt **-s** -s **-ing** -ɪŋ (US) 'saɪ.t̬ɪŋ **-ed** -ɪd (US) 'saɪ.t̬ɪd **-less/ness** -ləs, -lɪs **ˌsight un'seen**
sightl|y 'saɪt.l|i **-iness** -ɪ.nəs, -ɪ.nɪs
sightread *present tense:* 'saɪt.riːd **-s** -z **-ing** -ɪŋ *past tense:* 'saɪt.red
sightreader 'saɪtˌriː.dəʳ (US) -dɚ **-s** -z
sightscreen 'saɪt.skriːn **-s** -z
sightsee 'saɪt.siː **-s** -z **-ing** -ɪŋ
sight-seeing 'saɪtˌsiː.ɪŋ
sightseer 'saɪtˌsiː.əʳ (US) -ɚ **-s** -z
Sigismond, Sigismund 'sɪg.ɪs.mənd, 'sɪdʒ-, -ɪz- (US) -ɪs-
sigma (S) 'sɪg.mə **-s** -z
Sigmund 'sɪg.mənd *as if German:* 'zɪg-
sign saɪn **-s** -z **-ing** -ɪŋ **-ed** -d **-er/s** -əʳ/z (US) -ɚ/z **-age** -ɪdʒ **'sign ˌlanguage** ; **ˌsign of the 'times**
signal 'sɪg.nᵊl **-s** -z **-(l)y** -i **-(l)ing** -ɪŋ **-(l)ed** -d **-(l)er/s** -əʳ/z (US) -ɚ/z **'signal ˌbox**
signaliz|e, -is|e 'sɪg.nᵊl.aɪz (US) -nə.laɪz **-es** -ɪz **-ing** -ɪŋ **-ed** -d
signal|man 'sɪg.nᵊl|.mən, -mæn **-men** -mən, -men
signator|y 'sɪg.nə.tᵊr|.i (US) -tɔːr- **-ies** -iz
signature 'sɪg.nə.tʃəʳ, -nɪ- (US) -nə.tʃɚ **-s** -z **'signature ˌtune**
signboard 'saɪn.bɔːd, 'saɪm- (US) 'saɪn.bɔːrd **-s** -z
signer 'saɪ.nəʳ (US) -nɚ **-s** -z
signet 'sɪg.nɪt, -nət **-s** -s **'signet ˌring**
significance sɪg'nɪf.ɪ.kən*t*s, '-ə- (US) '-ə-
significant sɪg'nɪf.ɪ.kənt, '-ə- (US) '-ə- **-ly** -li **sigˌnificant 'other**
signification ˌsɪg.nɪ.fɪ'keɪ.ʃᵊn, -nə- (US) -nə-
significative sɪg'nɪf.ɪ.kə.tɪv, '-ə-, -keɪ- (US) -keɪ.t̬ɪv **-ly** -li **-ness** -nəs, -nɪs
signi|fy 'sɪg.nɪ|.faɪ, -nə- (US) -nə- **-fies** -faɪz **-fying** -faɪ.ɪŋ **-fied** -faɪd **-fier/s** -faɪ.əʳ/z (US) -faɪ.ɚ/z
signor (S) 'siː.njɔːʳ (US) siː'njɔːr **-s** -z
signora (S) siː'njɔː.r|ə (US) -'nɔːr|.ə **-az** -əz **-ez** -eɪz
signorina (S) ˌsiː.njɔː'riː.nə, -njə'-
signpost 'saɪn.pəʊst, 'saɪm- (US) 'saɪn.poʊst **-s** -s **-ing** -ɪŋ **-ed** -ɪd
Sigurd *English first name:* 'siː.gɜːd, 'sɪg.ɜːd (US) 'sɪg.ɚd *Scandinavian name:* 'sɪg.ʊəd, -ɜːd (US) 'sɪg.ɚd
Sikes saɪks
Sikh siːk **-s** -s **-ism** -ɪ.zᵊm
Sikkim 'sɪk.ɪm, sɪ'kɪm (US) 'sɪk.ɪm
Sikorsky sɪ'kɔː.ski (US) -'kɔːr-
silage 'saɪ.lɪdʒ
Silas 'saɪ.ləs, -læs (US) -ləs
Silchester 'sɪl.tʃɪ.stəʳ, -tʃə-, -tʃes.təʳ (US) -tʃes.tɚ
Sileby 'saɪl.bi
silenc|e 'saɪ.lən*t*s **-es** -ɪz **-ing** -ɪŋ **-ed** -t
silencer 'saɪ.lən*t*.səʳ (US) -sɚ **-s** -z
silent 'saɪ.lənt **-ly** -li **-ness** -nəs, -nɪs **ˌsilent ma'jority** ; **ˌsilent 'partner**
Silenus saɪ'liː.nəs, sɪ-, -'leɪ- (US) saɪ'liː-
Silesi|a saɪ'liː.zi|.ə, sɪ-, -ʒi|.ə, '-ʒ|ə, -si|.ə, -ʃi|.ə, '-ʃ|ə (US) saɪ'liː.ʃ|ə, sɪ-, -ʒ|ə **-an/s** -ən/z
silex 'saɪ.leks
silhouett|e ˌsɪl.u'et, '--- (US) ˌsɪl.u'et **-es** -s **-ing** -ɪŋ **-ed** -ɪd
silica 'sɪl.ɪ.kə **ˌsilica 'gel** (US) **'silica ˌgel**
silicate 'sɪl.ɪ.keɪt, '-ə-, -kət, -kɪt (US) -ɪ.keɪt, -kɪt
silicon 'sɪl.ɪ.kən, '-ə- (US) '-ɪ-, -kɑːn **ˌsilicon 'chip** (US) **'silicon ˌchip** ; **ˌSilicon 'Valley**
silicone 'sɪl.ɪ.kəʊn, '-ə- (US) -ɪ.koʊn
silicosis ˌsɪl.ɪ'kəʊ.sɪs, -ə'- (US) -ɪ'koʊ-
silicotic ˌsɪl.ɪ'kɒt.ɪk, -ə'- (US) -ɪ'kɑː.t̬ɪk **-s** -s
silk (S) sɪlk **-s** -s **-en** -ᵊn
Silkin 'sɪl.kɪn
silk-screen 'sɪlk.skriːn **-s** -z **-ing** -ɪŋ **-ed** -d **ˌsilk-screen 'printing**
silkworm 'sɪlk.wɜːm (US) -wɜːrm **-s** -z
silk|y 'sɪl.k|i **-ier** -i.əʳ (US) -i.ɚ **-iest** -i.ɪst, -i.əst **-iness** -ɪ.nəs, -ɪ.nɪs
sill (S) sɪl **-s** -z
sillabub 'sɪl.ə.bʌb, -bəb (US) -bʌb **-s** -z
Sillery 'sɪl.ᵊr.i
Sillitoe 'sɪl.ɪ.təʊ (US) -toʊ
Silloth 'sɪl.əθ
sill|y 'sɪl|.i **-ies** -iz **-ier** -i.əʳ (US) -i.ɚ **-iest** -i.ɪst, -i.əst **-ily** -ɪ.li, -ᵊl.i **-iness** -ɪ.nəs, -ɪ.nɪs
silly-bill|y ˌsɪl.i'bɪl|.i **-ies** -iz
silo 'saɪ.ləʊ (US) -loʊ **-s** -z
Siloam saɪ'ləʊ.əm, sɪ-, -æm (US) sɪ'loʊ.əm, saɪ-
Silsden 'sɪlz.dən
silt sɪlt **-s** -s **-ing** -ɪŋ (US) 'sɪl.t̬ɪŋ **-ed** -ɪd (US) 'sɪl.t̬ɪd **-y** -i (US) 'sɪl.t̬i
Silurian saɪ'lʊə.ri.ən, sɪ-, -'ljʊə-, -'ljɔː- (US) sɪ'lʊr.i-, saɪ-
Silva 'sɪl.və
silvan 'sɪl.vən
Silvanus sɪl'veɪ.nəs
silv|er (S) 'sɪl.v|əʳ (US) -v|ɚ **-ers** -əz (US) -ɚz **-ering** -ᵊr.ɪŋ **-ered** -əd (US) -ɚd **-ery** -ᵊr.i **-eriness** -ᵊr.ɪ.nəs, -nɪs **ˌsilver 'birch** ; **ˌsilver 'foil** (US) **'silver ˌfoil** ; **ˌsilver 'lining** ; **ˌsilver 'nitrate** ; **ˌsilver 'paper** ; **ˌsilver 'plate** (US) **'silver ˌplate** ; **ˌsilver 'screen** ; **ˌsilver 'spoon** ; **ˌsilver 'wedding**
silverfish 'sɪl.və.fɪʃ (US) -vɚ- **-es** -ɪz
Silverman 'sɪl.və.mən (US) -vɚ-
Silvers 'sɪl.vəz (US) -vɚz
silverside 'sɪl.və.saɪd (US) -vɚ- **-s** -z
silversmith 'sɪl.və.smɪθ (US) -vɚ- **-s** -s
Silverstone 'sɪl.və.stəʊn, -stən (US) -vɚ.stoʊn, -stən
silver-tongued ˌsɪl.və'tʌŋd (US) -vɚ'- *stress shift:* ˌsilver-tongued 'devil
Silvertown 'sɪl.və.taʊn (US) -vɚ- **-s** -z
silverware 'sɪl.və.weəʳ (US) -vɚ.wer
Silvester sɪl'ves.təʳ (US) -tɚ
Silvia 'sɪl.vi.ə
Silvikrin® 'sɪl.vɪ.krɪn, -və-
Sim sɪm
Simca® 'sɪm.kə **-s** -z
Simcox 'sɪm.kɒks (US) -kɑːks
Simenon 'siː.mə.nɔ̃ː*ŋ*, 'sɪm.ə-, -nɒn (US) 'siː.mə.noʊn, -nɔ̃ː*n*
Simeon 'sɪm.i.ən
simian 'sɪm.i.ən **-s** -z
similar 'sɪm.ɪ.ləʳ, '-ə- (US) -ə.lɚ **-ly** -li

similarit|y ˌsɪm.ɪˈlær.ə.t|i, -əˈ-, -ɪ.t|i (US) -əˈler.ə.t̬|i, -ˈlær- **-ies** -iz
simile ˈsɪm.ɪ.li, -ᵊl.i (US) -ə.li **-s** -z
similitude sɪˈmɪl.ɪ.tjuːd, ˈ-ə-, -tʃuːd (US) səˈmɪl.ə.tuːd, -tjuːd **-s** -z
Simla ˈsɪm.lə
simm|er ˈsɪm|.əʳ (US) -ɚ **-ers** -əz (US) -ɚz **-ering** -ᵊr.ɪŋ **-ered** -əd (US) -ɚd
Simmon(d)s ˈsɪm.ənd͡z
Simms sɪmz
simnel (S) ˈsɪm.nᵊl **-s** -z ˈ**simnel** ˌ**cake**
Simon ˈsaɪ.mən
Simond ˈsaɪ.mənd, ˈsɪm.ənd
Simonds ˈsɪm.ənd͡z
Simone sɪˈməʊn, sə- (US) -ˈmoʊn
simoniacal ˌsaɪ.məʊˈnaɪə.kᵊl (US) -məˈ-, ˌsɪm.əˈ-
Simons ˈsaɪ.mənz
simony ˈsaɪ.mə.ni, ˈsɪm.ə-
simoom sɪˈmuːm (US) sɪ-, saɪ- **-s** -z
simpatico sɪmˈpæt.ɪ.kəʊ (US) -ˈpæt̬.ɪ.koʊ
simp|er ˈsɪm.p|əʳ (US) -p|ɚ **-ers** -əz (US) -ɚz **-ering/ly** -ᵊr.ɪŋ **-ered** -əd (US) -ɚd
Simpkin ˈsɪmp.kɪn **-s** -z **-son** -sən
simp|le ˈsɪm.p|l̩ **-ler** -ləʳ (US) -lɚ **-lest** -lɪst, -ləst **-ly** -li **-leness** -l̩.nəs, -nɪs
simplehearted ˌsɪm.pl̩ˈhɑː.tɪd (US) -ˈhɑːr.t̬ɪd *stress shift:* ˌsimplehearted ˈperson
simple-minded ˌsɪm.pl̩ˈmaɪn.dɪd *stress shift:* ˌsimple-minded ˈperson
simpleton ˈsɪm.pl̩.tᵊn (US) -tən **-s** -z
simplex ˈsɪm.pleks **-es** -ɪz
simplicity sɪmˈplɪs.ə.ti, -ɪ.ti (US) -ə.t̬i
simplification ˌsɪm.plɪ.fɪˈkeɪ.ʃᵊn, -plə- (US) -plə- **-s** -z
simpli|fy ˈsɪm.plɪ|.faɪ (US) -plə- **-fies** -faɪz **-fying** -faɪ.ɪŋ **-fied** -faɪd
simplistic sɪmˈplɪs.tɪk **-ally** -ᵊl.i, -li
Simplon ˈsæ̃m.plɔ̃ːŋ, ˈsæm-, ˈsɪm-, -plən (US) ˈsɪm.plɑːn; ˈsæ̃m.plɔ̃ːn
simply ˈsɪm.pli
Simpson ˈsɪmp.sən
Sims sɪmz
Simson ˈsɪmp.sən
simulacr|um ˌsɪm.jəˈleɪ.kr|əm, -jʊˈ-, -ˈlæk.r|əm (US) -ˈleɪ-, -ˈlæk.r|əm **-ums** -əmz **-a** -ə
simu|late ˈsɪm.jə|.leɪt, -jʊ- **-lates** -leɪts **-lating** -leɪ.tɪŋ (US) -leɪ.t̬ɪŋ **-lated** -leɪ.tɪd (US) -leɪ.t̬ɪd
simulation ˌsɪm.jəˈleɪ.ʃᵊn, -jʊˈ- **-s** -z
simulator ˈsɪm.jə.leɪ.təʳ, -jʊ- (US) -t̬ɚ **-s** -z ˈ**flight** ˌ**simulator**
simulcast ˈsɪm.ᵊl.kɑːst (US) ˈsaɪ.mᵊl.kæst, ˈsɪm.ᵊl- **-s** -s **-ing** -ɪŋ
simultaneity ˌsɪm.ᵊl.təˈniː.ə.ti, ˌsaɪ.mᵊl-, -ˈneɪ-, -ɪ.ti (US) ˌsaɪ.mᵊl.təˈniː.ə.t̬i, ˌsɪm.ᵊl-
simultaneous ˌsɪm.ᵊlˈteɪ.ni.əs, ˌsaɪ.mᵊlˈ- (US) ˌsaɪ.mᵊlˈteɪ.njəs, ˌsɪm.ᵊlˈ-, -ni.əs **-ly** -li **-ness** -nəs, -nɪs
sin (*n. v.*) *do wrong:* sɪn **-s** -z **-ning** -ɪŋ **-ned** -d **-ner/s** -əʳ/z (US) -ɚ/z ˈ**sin** ˌ**bin**
sin *in trigonometry:* saɪn
Sinai ˈsaɪ.naɪ, -ni.aɪ, -neɪ- (US) ˈsaɪ.naɪ
sinapism ˈsɪn.ə.pɪ.zᵊm **-s** -z
Sinatra sɪˈnɑː.trə
Sinbad ˈsɪn.bæd, ˈsɪm- (US) ˈsɪn-
since sɪnts
sincer|e sɪnˈsɪəʳ, sᵊn- (US) sɪnˈsɪr **-er** -əʳ (US) -ɚ **-est** -ɪst, -əst **-ely** -li **-eness** -nəs, -nɪs
sincerity sɪnˈser.ə.ti, sᵊn-, -ɪ.ti (US) sɪnˈser.ə.t̬i
Sinclair ˈsɪŋ.kleəʳ, ˈsɪn-, -kləʳ; sɪŋˈkleəʳ, sɪn- (US) sɪnˈkler, ˈ--
Sind sɪnd
Sindbad ˈsɪnd.bæd
Sindh sɪnd
Sindhi ˈsɪn.diː, -di
Sindlesham ˈsɪn.dl̩.ʃəm
Sindy® ˈsɪn.di ˈ**Sindy** ˌ**doll**
sine saɪn **-s** -z
Sinead, Sinéad ʃɪˈneɪd, -ˈneəd (US) -ˈneɪd
sinecure ˈsaɪ.nɪ.kjʊəʳ, ˈsɪn.ɪ-, -kjɔːʳ (US) ˈsaɪ.nə.kjʊr, ˈsɪn.ə- **-s** -z
sine die ˌsaɪ.nɪˈdaɪ.iː, -ɪ; ˌsɪn.ɪˈdiː.eɪ (US) ˌsaɪ.niˈdaɪ.i, ˌsɪn.eɪˈdiː.eɪ
Sinel ˈsɪn.ᵊl
sine qua non ˌsɪn.i.kwɑːˈnəʊn, ˌsaɪ.ni.kweɪˈnɒn (US) ˌsɪn.eɪ.kwɑːˈnoʊn, ˌsaɪ.ni.kweɪˈnɑːn **-s** -z
sinew ˈsɪn.juː **-s** -z **-y** -i
sinfonia sɪnˈfəʊ.ni.ə; ˌsɪn.fəʊˈniː- (US) ˌsɪn.fəˈniː-; sɪnˈfoʊ.ni- **-s** -z
sinfonia concertante sɪn.fəʊ.ni.əˌkɒnt.ʃəˈtæn.teɪ (US) ˌsɪn.fəˌniː.əˌkɑːnt.sɚˈtɑːn.teɪ, -ˌkɑːn.tʃɚˈ-; sɪnˌfoʊ.ni-
sinfonietta ˌsɪn.fəʊ.niˈet.ə, -fɒn.iˈ- (US) -fəˈnjet̬-, -foʊˈ- **-s** -z
sinful ˈsɪn.fᵊl, -fʊl **-ly** -i **-ness** -nəs, -nɪs
sing sɪŋ **-s** -z **-ing** -ɪŋ **sang** sæŋ **sung** sʌŋ **singer/s** ˈsɪŋ.əʳ/z (US) -ɚ/z
singable ˈsɪŋ.ə.bl̩
sing-along ˈsɪŋ.ə.lɒŋ (US) -lɑːŋ **-s** -z
Singapore ˌsɪŋ.əˈpɔːʳ, -gəˈ-, ˈ--- (US) ˈsɪŋ.ə.pɔːr, -gə-
Singaporean ˌsɪŋ.ə.pɔːˈriː.ən, -gə-; -ˈpɔː.ri- (US) ˌsɪŋ.ə.pɔːˈriː-, -gə-; -ˈpɔːr.i- **-s** -z
sing|e sɪndʒ **-es** -ɪz **-eing** -ɪŋ **-ed** -d
Singer ˈsɪŋ.əʳ, -gəʳ (US) -ɚ, -gɚ
Singh sɪŋ
Singhalese ˌsɪŋ.həˈliːz, -gəˈ-, -ˈliːs (US) -gəˈliːz, -ˈliːs
sing|le (S) ˈsɪŋ.g|l̩ **-les** **-ly** -li **-leness** -l̩.nəs, -nɪs ˌ**single** ˈ**bed** (US) ˈ**single** ˌ**bed**; ˌ**single** ˈ**currency**; ˌ**single** ˈ**file**; ˌ**single** ˈ**figures**
single-breasted ˌsɪŋ.gl̩ˈbres.tɪd *stress shift:* ˌsingle-breasted ˈjacket
single-decker ˌsɪŋ.gl̩ˈdek.əʳ (US) -ɚ **-s** -z *stress shift:* ˌsingle-decker ˈbus
single-handed ˌsɪŋ.gl̩ˈhæn.dɪd **-ly** -li **-ness** -nəs, -nɪs *stress shift:* ˌsingle-handed ˈcrossing
single-hearted ˌsɪŋ.gl̩ˈhɑː.tɪd (US) ˈsɪŋ.gl̩ˌhɑːr.t̬ɪd **-ly** -li **-ness** -nəs, -nɪs *stress shift, British only:* ˌsingle-hearted ˈlove
single-minded ˌsɪŋ.gl̩ˈmaɪn.dɪd (US) ˈsɪŋ.gl̩ˌmaɪn- **-ly** -li **-ness** -nəs, -nɪs *stress shift, British only:* ˌsingle-minded ˈperson
singlestick ˈsɪŋ.gl̩.stɪk **-s** -s
singlet ˈsɪŋ.glɪt, -glət **-s** -s
singleton (S) ˈsɪŋ.gl̩.tən (US) -t̬ən, -tən **-s** -z
singly ˈsɪŋ.gli
singsong ˈsɪŋ.sɒŋ (US) -sɑːŋ, -sɔːŋ **-s** -z
singular ˈsɪŋ.gjə.ləʳ, -gjʊ- (US) -lɚ **-s** -z **-ly** -li
singularit|y ˌsɪŋ.gjəˈlær.ə.t|i, -gjʊˈ-, -ɪ.t|i (US) -ˈler.ə.t̬|i, -ˈlær- **-ies** -iz
Sinhalese ˌsɪŋ.həˈliːz, ˌsɪn- (US) ˌsɪn.həˈliːz, -ˈliːs
Sinim ˈsɪn.ɪm, ˈsaɪ.nɪm
sinister ˈsɪn.ɪ.stəʳ (US) -stɚ
sinistral ˈsɪn.ɪ.strᵊl **-ly** -i
Sinitic saɪˈnɪt.ɪk, sɪ- (US) -ˈnɪt̬-
sink sɪŋk **-s** -s **-ing** -ɪŋ **sank** sæŋk **sunk** sʌŋk **sunken** ˈsʌŋ.kᵊn
sinker ˈsɪŋ.kəʳ (US) -kɚ **-s** -z
sinless ˈsɪn.ləs, -lɪs **-ly** -li **-ness** -nəs, -nɪs
sinner ˈsɪn.əʳ (US) -ɚ **-s** -z
Sinn Fein ˌʃɪnˈfeɪn **-er/s** -əʳ/z (US) -ɚ/z
sinologue ˈsɪn.ə.lɒg, ˈsaɪ.nə-, -ləʊg (US) ˈsaɪ.nə.lɑːg, ˈsɪn.ə-, -lɔːg **-s** -z
sinolog|y saɪˈnɒl.ə.dʒ|i, sɪ- (US) -ˈnɑː.lə- **-ist/s** -ɪst/s
sinuosit|y ˌsɪn.juˈɒs.ə.t|i, -ɪ.t|i (US) -ˈɑː.sə.t̬|i **-ies** -iz
sinuous ˈsɪn.ju.əs **-ly** -li **-ness** -nəs, -nɪs
sinus ˈsaɪ.nəs **-es** -ɪz
sinusitis ˌsaɪ.nəˈsaɪ.tɪs (US) -t̬ɪs
sinusoid ˈsaɪ.nə.sɔɪd **-s** -z
Siobhan ʃɪˈvɔːn, ʃə- (US) -ˈvɑːn, -ˈvɔːn
Sion ˈsaɪ.ən, ˈzaɪ- (US) ˈsaɪ-
Sioux *singular:* suː, sjuː (US) suː *plural:* suːz, sjuːz, suː, sjuː (US) suːz, suː
sip sɪp **-s** -s **-ping** -ɪŋ **-ped** -t
siphon (*n. v.*) ˈsaɪ.fᵊn **-s** -z **-ing** -ɪŋ, ˈsaɪf.nɪŋ **-ed** -d
sir (S) *strong forms:* sɜːʳ (US) sɜːr *weak forms:* səʳ (US) sɚ **-s** -z
Note: Weak form word. The strong form is used in various social situations. In school, it is often used by children to address a male teacher (e.g. "Sir, can I

go now?"), and contrastively (e.g. "Dear Sir or Madam"). Similarly, in old-fashioned speech, the strong form would be used to begin addressing someone (e.g. "Sir, you are a scoundrel"). When it occurs utterance-finally in addressing someone, either form may be used, although the weak form is more common in military usage (e.g. "Ready to sail, sir"). In the title of a Knight (e.g. **Sir John Roberts**), the weak form is always used.

sirdar (S) ˈsɜː.dɑːʳ (US) sɚˈdɑːr; ˈsɜːr.dɑːr **-s** -z
sir|e saɪəʳ (US) saɪɚ **-es** -z **-ing** -ɪŋ **-ed** -d
siren ˈsaɪə.rən, -rɪn (US) ˈsaɪ.rən **-s** -z
Sirion ˈsɪr.i.ən
Sirius ˈsɪr.i.əs
sirloin ˈsɜː.lɔɪn (US) ˈsɜːr- **-s** -z
sirocco sɪˈrɒk.əʊ, sə- (US) səˈrɑː.koʊ, ʃə- **-s** -z
Siros ˈsɪə.rɒs (US) ˈsiː.rɑːs
sirrah ˈsɪr.ə
sirree, siree ˌsɜːˈriː, sə- (US) sə-
sis sɪs
sisal ˈsaɪ.sᵊl (US) ˈsaɪ-, ˈsɪs.ᵊl
Sisal *Mexican port:* sɪˈsɑːl (US) ˈsiː.səl, ˈsɪs.ɑːl
Sisera ˈsɪs.ᵊr.ə
siskin (S) ˈsɪs.kɪn **-s** -z
Sisley ˈsɪz.li
Sissinghurst ˈsɪs.ɪŋ.hɜːst (US) -hɜːrst
Sisson ˈsɪs.ᵊn **-s** -z
siss|y ˈsɪs|.i **-ies** -iz
sist|er ˈsɪs.t|əʳ (US) -t|ɚ **-ers** -əz (US) -ɚz **-erly** -ᵊl.i (US) -ɚ.li
sisterhood ˈsɪs.tə.hʊd (US) -tɚ- **-s** -z
sister-in-law ˈsɪs.tᵊr.ɪn.lɔː (US) -tɚ.ɪn.lɑː, -lɔː **sisters-in-law** -təz- (US) -tɚz-
Sistine ˈsɪs.tiːn, -taɪn (US) -tiːn, -ˈ- ˌSistine ˈChapel
sistrum ˈsɪs.trəm **-s** -z
Sisulu sɪˈsuː.luː
Sisyphean, Sisyphian ˌsɪs.ɪˈfiː.ən, -əˈ- (US) -əˈ-
Sisyphus ˈsɪs.ɪ.fəs, ˈ-ə- (US) ˈ-ə-
sit sɪt **-s** -s **-ting** -ɪŋ/z (US) ˈsɪt̬.ɪŋ/z **sat** sæt **ˌSitting ˈBull** ; **ˌsit on the ˈfence**
Sita ˈsɪt.ə, ˈsiː.tə (US) ˈsiː.tɑː
sitar sɪˈtɑːʳ; ˈsɪt.ɑːʳ (US) sɪˈtɑːr
sitcom ˈsɪt.kɒm (US) -kɑːm **-s** -z
sit-down ˈsɪt.daʊn
sit|e saɪt **-s** -s **-ing** -ɪŋ **-ed** -ɪd
sit-in ˈsɪt.ɪn (US) ˈsɪt̬- **-s** -z
sitting ˈsɪt.ɪŋ (US) ˈsɪt̬- **-s** -z **ˌsitting ˈduck** ; **ˈsitting ˌroom** ; **ˌsitting ˈtarget** ; **ˌsitting ˈtenant**
Sittingbourne ˈsɪt.ɪŋ.bɔːn (US) ˈsɪt̬.ɪŋ.bɔːrn
situate (*adj.*) ˈsɪt.ju.eɪt, ˈsɪtʃ.u-, -ɪt, -ət (US) ˈsɪtʃ.u.ɪt, -eɪt
situ|ate (*v.*) ˈsɪt.ju|.eɪt, ˈsɪtʃ.u- (US) ˈsɪtʃ.u- **-ates** -eɪts **-ating** -eɪ.tɪŋ (US) -eɪ.t̬ɪŋ **-ated** -eɪ.tɪd (US) -eɪ.t̬ɪd
situation ˌsɪt.juˈeɪ.ʃᵊn, ˌsɪtʃ.uˈ- (US) ˌsɪtʃ.uˈ- **-s** -z **ˌsituation ˈcomedy**
sit-up ˈsɪt.ʌp **-s** -s
Sitwell ˈsɪt.wəl, -wel
Siva ˈʃiː.və, ˈsiː-, ˈsɪv.ə, ˈʃɪv- (US) ˈʃiː.və, ˈsiː-
Siward ˈsjuː.əd (US) -ɚd, ˈsuː-
six sɪks **-es** -ɪz **-fold** -fəʊld (US) -foʊld
sixer ˈsɪk.səʳ (US) -sɚ **-s** -z
sixish ˈsɪk.sɪʃ
six-pack ˈsɪks.pæk **-s** -s
six|pence ˈsɪks|.pən*t*s **-pences** -pən*t*.sɪz **-penny** -pᵊn.i
Note: See note under **penny**.
six-shooter ˈsɪksˌʃuː.təʳ, ˈsɪkʃ-, ˌ-ˈ-- (US) ˈsɪksˌʃuː.t̬ɚ **-s** -z
sixte sɪkst
sixteen ˌsɪkˈstiːn **-s** -z **-th/s** -θ/s **-thly** -θ.li *stress shift, British only:* ˌsixteen ˈdays **sixˈteenth ˌnote**
sixteenmo, 16mo sɪkˈstiːn.məʊ (US) -moʊ **-s** -z
sixth sɪksθ (US) sɪkstθ **-s** -s **-ly** -li **ˈsixth ˌform** ; **ˌsixth form ˈcollege** ; **ˌsixth ˈsense**
Sixtus ˈsɪk.stəs
sixt|y ˈsɪk.st|i **-ies** -iz **-ieth/s** -i.əθs, -i.ɪθ/s
sixty-nine, 69 ˌsɪk.stiˈnaɪn
sizar ˈsaɪ.zəʳ (US) -zɚ **-s** -z **-ship/s** -ʃɪp/s
siz|e saɪz **-es** -ɪz **-ing** -ɪŋ **-ed** -d
sizeab|le, sizab|le ˈsaɪ.zə.b|l̩ **-ly** -li **-leness** -l̩.nəs, -nɪs
Sizer ˈsaɪ.zəʳ (US) -zɚ
Sizewell ˈsaɪz.wəl, -wel
sizzl|e ˈsɪz.l̩ **-es** -z **-ing** -ɪŋ, ˈsɪz.lɪŋ **-ed** -d
sizzler ˈsɪz.ləʳ, -l̩.əʳ (US) ˈ-lɚ, -l̩.ɚ **-s** -z
sjambok ˈʃæm.bɒk, -bʌk (US) -bɑːk, -bʌk **-s** -s **-ing** -ɪŋ **-ed** -t
ska skɑː
Skagerrak ˈskæg.ə.ræk
Skara Brae ˌskær.əˈbreɪ
skat skæt
skat|e skeɪt **-es** -s **-ing** -ɪŋ (US) ˈskeɪ.t̬ɪŋ **-ed** -ɪd (US) ˈskeɪ.t̬ɪd **-er/s** -əʳ/z (US) ˈskeɪ.t̬ɚ/z
skateboard ˈskeɪt.bɔːd (US) -bɔːrd **-er/s** -əʳ/z (US) -ɚ/z **-ing** -ɪŋ
skating-rink ˈskeɪ.tɪŋ.rɪŋk **-s** -s
skean dhu ˌskiː.ənˈduː, ˌskiːnˈ- (US) ˌskiːn-, ˌʃkiːn- **-s** -z
Skeat skiːt
skedaddl|e skɪˈdæd.l̩ **-es** -z **-ing** -ɪŋ, -ˈdæd.lɪŋ **-ed** -d
Skeels skiːlz
Skeggs skegz
Skegness ˌskegˈnes *stress shift:* ˌSkegness ˈbeach
skein skeɪn **-s** -z
skeletal ˈskel.ɪ.tᵊl, ˈ-ə-; skɪˈliː-, skə- (US) ˈskel.ə.t̬ᵊl **-ly** -i
skeleton ˈskel.ɪ.tᵊn, ˈ-ə- (US) ˈ-ə- **-s** -z **ˈskeleton ˌkey** ; **ˌskeleton in the ˈcupboard** ; **ˌskeleton in the ˈcloset**
Skelmanthorpe ˈskel.mən.θɔːp (US) -θɔːrp
Skelmersdale ˈskel.məz.deɪl (US) -mɚz-
skelter ˈskel.təʳ (US) -t̬ɚ
Skelton ˈskel.tᵊn
skeptic ˈskep.tɪk **-al** -ᵊl **-ally** -ᵊl.i, -li
skepticism ˈskep.tɪ.sɪ.zᵊm, -tə- (US) -tə-
sketch sketʃ **-es** -ɪz **-ing** -ɪŋ **-ed** -t **-able** -ə.bl̩ **-er/s** -əʳ/z (US) -ɚ/z
sketchbook ˈsketʃ.bʊk **-s** -s
Sketchley ˈsketʃ.li
sketchpad ˈsketʃ.pæd **-s** -z
sketch|y ˈsketʃ|.i **-ier** -i.əʳ (US) -i.ɚ **-iest** -i.ɪst, -i.əst **-ily** -ɪ.li, -ᵊl.i **-iness** -ɪ.nəs, -ɪ.nɪs
skew skjuː **-s** -z
skewbald ˈskjuː.bɔːld (US) -bɑːld, -bɔːld
skewer skjʊəʳ (US) ˈskjuː.ɚ, ˈskjuː.ɚ **-s** -z **-ing** -ɪŋ **-ed** -d
skew-whiff ˌskjuːˈ*h*wɪf
Skey skiː
ski skiː **-s** -z **-ing** -ɪŋ **-ed** -d **ˈski ˌlift** ; **ˈski ˌpants**
skibob ˈskiː.bɒb (US) -bɑːb **-s** -z **-bing** -ɪŋ **-bed** -d
skid skɪd **-s** -z **-ding** -ɪŋ **-ded** -ɪd **-dy** -i **ˌskid ˈrow**
Skiddaw ˈskɪd.ɔː, *locally:* -ə (US) ˈskɪd.ɑː, -ɔː
Skidmore ˈskɪd.mɔːʳ (US) -mɔːr
skidpan ˈskɪd.pæn **-s** -z
skier ˈskiː.əʳ (US) -ɚ **-s** -z
skiff skɪf **-s** -s
skiffle ˈskɪf.l̩
ski-jump ˈskiː.dʒʌmp **-s** -s **-ing** -ɪŋ **-ed** -t **-er/s** -əʳ/z (US) -ɚ/z
skilful ˈskɪl.fᵊl, -fʊl **-ly** -i **-ness** -nəs, -nɪs
skill skɪl **-s** -z **-ed** -d
skillet ˈskɪl.ɪt **-s** -s
skilly ˈskɪl.i
skim skɪm **-s** -z **-ming** -ɪŋ **-med** -d **-mer/s** -əʳ/z (US) -ɚ/z
skimp skɪmp **-s** -s **-ing** -ɪŋ/li **-ed** -t
skimp|y ˈskɪm.p|i **-ier** -i.əʳ (US) -i.ɚ **-iest** -i.ɪst, -i.əst **-ily** -ɪ.li, -ᵊl.i **-iness** -ɪ.nəs, -ɪ.nɪs
skin skɪn **-s** -z **-ning** -ɪŋ **-ned** -d **-less** -ləs, -lɪs **by the ˌskin of one's ˈteeth**
skincare ˈskɪn.keəʳ, ˈskɪŋ- (US) -ker

skin-deep ˌskɪnˈdiːp Ⓤⓢ ˌskɪnˈdiːp, ˈ-- *stress shift, British only:* ˌskin-deep ˈwound
skin-div|ing ˈskɪnˌdaɪ.v|ɪŋ **-er/s** -əʳ/z Ⓤⓢ -ɚ/z
skinflint ˈskɪn.flɪnt **-s** -s
skinful ˈskɪn.fʊl **-s** -z
skinhead ˈskɪn.hed **-s** -z
skink skɪŋk **-s** -s
skinner (S) ˈskɪn.əʳ Ⓤⓢ -ɚ **-s** -z
skinn|y ˈskɪn|.i **-ier** -i.əʳ Ⓤⓢ -i.ɚ **-iest** -i.ɪst, -i.əst **-iness** -ɪ.nəs, -ɪ.nɪs
skinny-dip ˈskɪn.i.dɪp **-s** -s **-ping** -ɪŋ **-ped** -t
skint skɪnt
skintight ˈskɪn.taɪt
skip skɪp **-s** -s **-ping** -ɪŋ **-ped** -t
skipjack ˈskɪp.dʒæk **-s** -s
skipper ˈskɪp.əʳ Ⓤⓢ -ɚ **-s** -z **-ing** -ɪŋ **-ed** -d
skipping-rope ˈskɪp.ɪŋ.rəʊp Ⓤⓢ -roʊp **-s** -s
Skipton ˈskɪp.tən
skirl skɜːl Ⓤⓢ skɜːrl **-s** -z
skirmish ˈskɜː.mɪʃ Ⓤⓢ ˈskɜːr- **-es** -ɪz **-ing** -ɪŋ **-ed** -t **-er/s** -əʳ/z Ⓤⓢ -ɚ/z
skirt skɜːt Ⓤⓢ skɜːrt **-s** -s **-ing** -ɪŋ/z Ⓤⓢ ˈskɜːr.t̬ɪŋ/s **-ed** -ɪd Ⓤⓢ ˈskɜːr.t̬ɪd
skirting ˈskɜː.tɪŋ Ⓤⓢ ˈskɜːr.t̬ɪŋ **-s** -z
skirting-board ˈskɜː.tɪŋ.bɔːd Ⓤⓢ ˈskɜːr.t̬ɪŋ.bɔːrd **-s** -z
skit skɪt **-s** -s
skitter ˈskɪt.əʳ Ⓤⓢ ˈskɪt̬.ɚ **-s** -z **-ing** -ɪŋ **-ed** -d
skittish ˈskɪt.ɪʃ Ⓤⓢ ˈskɪt̬- **-ly** -li **-ness** -nəs, -nɪs
skittle ˈskɪt.l̩ Ⓤⓢ ˈskɪt̬- **-s** -z
skiv|e skaɪv **-es** -z **-ing** -ɪŋ **-ed** -d **-er/s** -əʳ/z Ⓤⓢ -ɚ/z
skivv|y ˈskɪv|.i **-ies** -iz
Skoda® ˈskəʊ.də Ⓤⓢ ˈskoʊ-
Skol® skɒl, skəʊl Ⓤⓢ skoʊl, skɑːl
Skopje ˈskɔː.pjeɪ, ˈskɒp.jeɪ Ⓤⓢ ˈskɔː.pjeɪ, ˈskɑː-
Skrimshire ˈskrɪm.ʃəʳ, -ˌʃaɪəʳ Ⓤⓢ -ʃɚ, -ˌʃaɪɚ
Skrine skriːn
skua ˈskjuː.ə, skjʊə Ⓤⓢ ˈskjuː.ə **-s** -z
skul(l)duggery skʌlˈdʌg.ər.i
skulk skʌlk **-s** -s **-ing** -ɪŋ **-ed** -t
skull skʌl **-s** -z **ˌskull and ˈcrossbones**
skullcap ˈskʌl.kæp **-s** -s
skunk skʌŋk **-s** -s
sk|y® sk|aɪ **-ies** -aɪz **-ying** -aɪ.ɪŋ **-ied** -aɪd **-ier/s** -aɪ.əʳ/z Ⓤⓢ -aɪ.ɚ/z
sky-blue ˌskaɪˈbluː *stress shift:* ˌsky-blue ˈfabric
skycap (S) ˈskaɪ.kæp **-s** -s
skydiv|er ˈskaɪˌdaɪ.v|əʳ Ⓤⓢ -v|ɚ **-ers** -əz Ⓤⓢ -ɚz **-ing** -ɪŋ
Skye skaɪ
sky-high ˌskaɪˈhaɪ *stress shift:* ˌsky-high ˈprices
skyjack ˈskaɪ.dʒæk **-s** -s **-ing** -ɪŋ **-ed** -t **-er/s** -əʳ/z Ⓤⓢ -ɚ/z
skylark ˈskaɪ.lɑːk Ⓤⓢ -lɑːrk **-s** -s **-ing** -ɪŋ **-ed** -t **-er/s** -əʳ/z Ⓤⓢ -ɚ/z
skylight ˈskaɪ.laɪt **-s** -s
skyline ˈskaɪ.laɪn **-s** -z
skyrock|et ˈskaɪˌrɒk|.ɪt Ⓤⓢ -ˌrɑː.k|ɪt **-ets** -ɪts **-eting** -ɪ.tɪŋ Ⓤⓢ -ɪ.t̬ɪŋ **-eted** -ɪ.tɪd Ⓤⓢ -ɪ.t̬ɪd
skyscape ˈskaɪ.skeɪp **-s** -s
skyscraper ˈskaɪˌskreɪ.pəʳ Ⓤⓢ -pɚ **-s** -z
skyward ˈskaɪ.wəd Ⓤⓢ -wɚd **-s** -z
skywriting ˈskaɪˌraɪ.tɪŋ Ⓤⓢ -t̬ɪŋ
slab slæb **-s** -z **-bing** -ɪŋ **-bed** -d
slack slæk **-s** -s **-er** -əʳ Ⓤⓢ -ɚ **-est** -ɪst, -əst **-ly** -li **-ness** -nəs, -nɪs **-ing** -ɪŋ **-ed** -t **-er/s** -əʳ/z Ⓤⓢ -ɚ/z
slacken ˈslæk.ən **-s** -z **-ing** -ɪŋ, ˈslæk.nɪŋ **-ed** -d
Slade sleɪd
slag slæg **-s** -z **-ging** -ɪŋ **-ged** -d **-gy** -i
slagheap ˈslæg.hiːp **-s** -s
slain (*from* slay) sleɪn
slainte ˈslɑːn.tʃə, -tjə
Slaithwaite ˈslæθ.wət, -weɪt *locally also:* ˈslaʊ.ɪt
slak|e sleɪk **-es** -s **-ing** -ɪŋ **-ed** -t
slalom ˈslɑː.ləm **-s** -z
slam slæm **-s** -z **-ming** -ɪŋ **-med** -d
slam-bang ˌslæmˈbæŋ *stress shift:* ˌslam-bang ˈclatter
slam-dunk ˌslæmˈdʌŋk, ˈ-- **-s** -s **-ing** -ɪŋ **-ed** -t
slammer ˈslæm.əʳ Ⓤⓢ -ɚ **-s** -z
sland|er ˈslɑːn.d|əʳ Ⓤⓢ ˈslæn.d|ɚ **-ers** -əz Ⓤⓢ -ɚz **-ering** -ər.ɪŋ **-ered** -əd Ⓤⓢ -ɚd **-erer/s** -ər.əʳ/z Ⓤⓢ -ɚ.ɚ/z
slanderous ˈslɑːn.dər.əs, ˈ-drəs Ⓤⓢ ˈslæn.dɚ.əs, ˈ-drəs **-ly** -li **-ness** -nəs, -nɪs
slang slæŋ **-s** -z **-ing** -ɪŋ **-ed** -d **-y** -i **-ier** -i.əʳ Ⓤⓢ -i.ɚ **-iest** -i.ɪst, -i.əst **-ily** -ɪ.li, -əl.i **-iness** -ɪ.nəs, -ɪ.nɪs **ˈslanging ˌmatch**
slant slɑːnt Ⓤⓢ slænt **-s** -s **-ing/ly** -ɪŋ/li Ⓤⓢ ˈslæn.t̬ɪŋ/li **-ed** -ɪd Ⓤⓢ ˈslæn.t̬ɪd
slantways ˈslɑːnt.weɪz Ⓤⓢ ˈslænt-
slantwise ˈslɑːnt.waɪz Ⓤⓢ ˈslænt-
slap slæp **-s** -s **-ping** -ɪŋ **-ped** -t **ˌslap and ˈtickle**
slap-bang ˌslæpˈbæŋ *stress shift:* ˌslap-bang ˈcentral
slapdash ˈslæp.dæʃ, ˌ-ˈ-
slaphappy ˌslæpˈhæp.i Ⓤⓢ ˈ-ˌ-- *stress shift, British only:* ˌslaphappy ˈstate
slapstick ˈslæp.stɪk **-s** -s
slap-up ˌslæpˈʌp Ⓤⓢ ˈ-- *stress shift, British only:* ˌslap-up ˈmeal
slash slæʃ **-es** -ɪz **-ing** -ɪŋ **-ed** -t **-er/s** -əʳ/z Ⓤⓢ -ɚ/z
slash-and-burn ˌslæʃ.əndˈbɜːn, -əmˈ- Ⓤⓢ -əndˈbɜːrn *stress shift:* ˌslash-and-burn ˈfarming
slat slæt **-s** -s **-ted** -ɪd
slat|e sleɪt **-es** -s **-ing** -ɪŋ Ⓤⓢ ˈsleɪ.t̬ɪŋ **-ed** -ɪd Ⓤⓢ ˈsleɪ.t̬ɪd **-er/s** -əʳ/z Ⓤⓢ ˈsleɪ.t̬ɚ/z
Slater ˈsleɪ.təʳ Ⓤⓢ -t̬ɚ
slath|er ˈslæð|.əʳ Ⓤⓢ -ɚ **-ers** -əz Ⓤⓢ -ɚz **-ering** -ər.ɪŋ **-ered** -əd Ⓤⓢ -ɚd
slattern ˈslæt.ən, -ɜːn Ⓤⓢ ˈslæt̬.ɚn **-s** -z **-ly** -li **-liness** -lɪ.nəs, -nɪs
Slattery ˈslæt.ər.i Ⓤⓢ ˈslæt̬.ɚ-
slaty ˈsleɪ.ti Ⓤⓢ -t̬i
slaught|er (S) (*n. v.*) ˈslɔː.t|əʳ Ⓤⓢ ˈslɑː.t̬|ɚ, ˈslɔː- **-ers** -əz Ⓤⓢ -ɚz **-ering** -ər.ɪŋ **-ered** -əd Ⓤⓢ -ɚd **-erer/s** -ər.əʳ/z Ⓤⓢ -ɚ.ɚ/z **-erous/ly** -ər.əs/li
slaughterhou|se ˈslɔː.tə.haʊ|s Ⓤⓢ ˈslɑː.t̬ɚ-, ˈslɔː- **-ses** -zɪz
Slav slɑːv Ⓤⓢ slɑːv, slæv **-s** -z
slav|e sleɪv **-es** -z **-ing** -ɪŋ **-ed** -d **-er/s** -əʳ/z Ⓤⓢ -ɚ/z **ˈslave ˌdriver**; **ˌslave ˈlabour**; **ˈslave ˌtrade**
slave-owner ˈsleɪvˌəʊ.nəʳ Ⓤⓢ -ˌoʊ.nɚ **-s** -z
slaver *slave-trader:* ˈsleɪ.vəʳ Ⓤⓢ -vɚ **-s** -z
slav|er (*n. v.*) *slobber:* ˈslæv|.əʳ, ˈsleɪ.v|əʳ Ⓤⓢ ˈslæv|.ɚ **-ers** -əz Ⓤⓢ -ɚz **-ering** -ər.ɪŋ **-ered** -əd Ⓤⓢ -ɚd
slavery ˈsleɪ.vər.i
slavey ˈsleɪ.vi, ˈslæv.i **-s** -z
Slavic ˈslɑː.vɪk, ˈslæv.ɪk
slavish ˈsleɪ.vɪʃ **-ly** -li **-ness** -nəs, -nɪs
Slavonic sləˈvɒn.ɪk, slævˈɒn- Ⓤⓢ sləˈvɑː.nɪk
slaw slɔː Ⓤⓢ slɑː, slɔː **-s** -z
slay sleɪ **-s** -z **-ing** -ɪŋ **slew** sluː **slain** sleɪn **slayer/s** sleɪ.əʳ/z Ⓤⓢ -ɚ/z
Slazenger® ˈslæz.ən.dʒəʳ Ⓤⓢ -dʒɚ
Sleaford ˈsliː.fəd Ⓤⓢ -fɚd
sleaze sliːz
sleazebag ˈsliːz.bæg **-s** -z
sleazeball ˈsliːz.bɔːl Ⓤⓢ -bɔːl, -bɑːl **-s** -z
sleaz|y ˈsliː.z|i **-ier** -i.əʳ Ⓤⓢ -i.ɚ **-iest** -i.ɪst, -i.əst **-ily** -ɪ.li, -əl.i **-iness** -ɪ.nəs, -ɪ.nɪs
sled sled **-s** -z **-ding** -ɪŋ **-ded** -ɪd
sledg|e sledʒ **-es** -ɪz **-ing** -ɪŋ **-ed** -d
sledgehammer ˈsledʒˌhæm.əʳ Ⓤⓢ -ɚ **-s** -z **-ing** -ɪŋ **-ed** -d
sleek sliːk **-er** -əʳ Ⓤⓢ -ɚ **-est** -ɪst, -əst **-ly** -li **-ness** -nəs, -nɪs
sleep sliːp **-s** -s **-ing** -ɪŋ **slept** slept **ˈsleeping ˌbag**; **ˌSleeping ˈBeauty**; **ˈsleeping ˌcar**; **ˈsleeping ˌdraught**; **ˈsleeping ˌpill**; **ˈsleeping ˌpartner**; **ˌsleeping poˈliceman**; **ˈsleeping ˌsickness**

sleeper ˈsliː.pəʳ ⓊⓈ -pɚ **-s** -z
sleepless ˈsliː.pləs, -plɪs **-ly** -li **-ness** -nəs, -nɪs
sleepwalk|er ˈsliːpˌwɔː.k|əʳ ⓊⓈ -ˌwɑː.k|ɚ, -ˌwɔː- **-ers** -əz ⓊⓈ -ɚz **-ing** -ɪŋ
sleep|y ˈsliː.p|i **-ier** -i.əʳ ⓊⓈ -i.ɚ **-iest** -i.ɪst, -i.əst **-ily** -ɪ.li, -əl.i **-iness** -ɪ.nəs, -ɪ.nɪs
sleepyhead ˈsliː.pi.hed **-s** -z
sleet sliːt **-s** -s **-ing** -ɪŋ ⓊⓈ ˈsliː.t̬ɪŋ **-ed** -ɪd ⓊⓈ ˈsliː.t̬ɪd **-y** -i ⓊⓈ ˈsliː.t̬i **-iness** -ɪ.nəs, -ɪ.nɪs ⓊⓈ ˈsliː.t̬ɪ.nəs, -nɪs
sleeve sliːv **-s** -z **-d** -d **-less** -ləs, -lɪs
sleigh sleɪ **-s** -z **-ing** -ɪŋ **-ed** -d ˈ**sleigh** ˌ**bells**
sleight (S) slaɪt ˌ**sleight of** ˈ**hand**
Sleights slaɪts
slender ˈslen.dəʳ ⓊⓈ -dɚ **-er** -əʳ ⓊⓈ -ɚ **-est** -ɪst, -əst **-ly** -li **-ness** -nəs, -nɪs
slenderiz|e ˈslen.dər.aɪz ⓊⓈ -də.raɪz **-es** -ɪz **-ing** -ɪŋ **-ed** -d
slept (*from* **sleep**) slept
sleuth sluːθ, sljuːθ ⓊⓈ sluːθ **-s** -s **-ing** -ɪŋ **-ed** -t
sleuthhound ˈsluːθ.haʊnd, ˈsljuːθ- ⓊⓈ ˈsluːθ- **-s** -z
slew sluː **-s** -z **-ing** -ɪŋ **-ed** -d
slic|e slaɪs **-es** -ɪz **-ing** -ɪŋ **-ed** -t **-er/s** -əʳ/z ⓊⓈ -ɚ/z ˌ**sliced** ˈ**bread**
slick slɪk **-er** -əʳ ⓊⓈ -ɚ **-est** -ɪst, -əst **-ly** -li **-ness** -nəs, -nɪs
slicker ˈslɪk.əʳ ⓊⓈ -ɚ **-s** -z
slid (*from* **slide**) slɪd
slid|e slaɪd **-es** -z **-ing** -ɪŋ **slid** slɪd ˈ**slide** **proˌjector** ; ˈ**slide** ˌ**rule** ; ˈ**slide** ˌ**valve** ; ˌ**sliding** ˈ**door** ; ˌ**sliding** ˈ**scale**
slight slaɪt **-s** -s **-er** -əʳ ⓊⓈ ˈslaɪ.t̬ɚ **-est** -ɪst, -əst ⓊⓈ ˈslaɪ.t̬ɪst, -t̬əst **-ly** -li **-ness** -nəs, -nɪs **-ing/ly** -ɪŋ/li ⓊⓈ ˈslaɪ.t̬ɪŋ/li **-ed** -ɪd ⓊⓈ ˈslaɪ.t̬ɪd
Sligo ˈslaɪ.gəʊ ⓊⓈ -goʊ
slim (S) slɪm **-mer/s** -əʳ/z ⓊⓈ -ɚ/z **-mest** -ɪst **-est** -əst **-ly** -li **-ness** -nəs, -nɪs **-s** -z **-ming** -ɪŋ **-med** -d ˈ**Slim di**ˌ**sease**
Slimbridge ˈslɪm.brɪdʒ
slim|e slaɪm **-es** -z **-ing** -ɪŋ **-ed** -d
slimline ˈslɪm.laɪn
slim|y ˈslaɪ.m|i **-ier** -i.əʳ ⓊⓈ -i.ɚ **-iest** -i.ɪst, -i.əst **-ily** -ɪ.li, -əl.i **-iness** -ɪ.nəs, -ɪ.nɪs
sling slɪŋ **-s** -z **-ing** -ɪŋ **slung** slʌŋ
slingback ˈslɪŋ.bæk **-s** -s
slingshot ˈslɪŋ.ʃɒt ⓊⓈ -ʃɑːt **-s** -s
slink slɪŋk **-s** -s **-ing** -ɪŋ **slunk** slʌŋk
slink|y ˈslɪŋ.k|i **-ier** -i.əʳ ⓊⓈ -i.ɚ **-iest** -i.ɪst, -i.əst
slip slɪp **-s** -s **-ping** -ɪŋ **-ped** -t ˌ**slipped** ˈ**disc** ; ˈ**slip** ˌ**road** ; ˈ**slip** ˌ**stitch** ; ˌ**give someone the** ˈ**slip**
slipcas|e ˈslɪp.keɪs **-es** -ɪz
slipcover ˈslɪpˌkʌv.əʳ ⓊⓈ -ɚ **-s** -z
slipknot ˈslɪp.nɒt ⓊⓈ -nɑːt **-s** -s
slip-on ˈslɪp.ɒn ⓊⓈ -ɑːn **-s** -z
slipover ˈslɪpˌəʊ.vəʳ ⓊⓈ -ˌoʊ.vɚ **-s** -z
slippag|e ˈslɪp.ɪdʒ **-es** -ɪz
slipper ˈslɪp.əʳ ⓊⓈ -ɚ **-s** -z **-ing** -ɪŋ **-ed** -d
slipper|y ˈslɪp.ər|.i **-ier** -i.əʳ ⓊⓈ -i.ɚ **-iest** -i.ɪst, -i.əst **-ily** -ɪ.li, -əl.i **-iness** -ɪ.nəs, -ɪ.nɪs ˌ**slippery** ˈ**slope**
slipp|y ˈslɪp|.i **-ier** -i.əʳ ⓊⓈ -i.ɚ **-iest** -i.ɪst, -i.əst **-iness** -ɪ.nəs, -ɪ.nɪs
slipshod ˈslɪp.ʃɒd ⓊⓈ -ʃɑːd
slipstream ˈslɪp.striːm **-s** -z **-ing** -ɪŋ **-ed** -d
slip-up ˈslɪp.ʌp **-s** -s
slipway ˈslɪp.weɪ **-s** -z
slit slɪt **-s** -s **-ting** -ɪŋ ⓊⓈ ˈslɪt̬.ɪŋ
slith|er ˈslɪð|.əʳ ⓊⓈ -ɚ **-ers** -əz ⓊⓈ -ɚz **-ering** -ər.ɪŋ **-ered** -əd ⓊⓈ -ɚd **-ery** -ər.i
sliv|er ˈslɪv|.əʳ ⓊⓈ -ɚ **-ers** -əz ⓊⓈ -ɚz **-ering** -ər.ɪŋ **-ered** -əd ⓊⓈ -ɚd
slivovitz ˈslɪv.ə.vɪts, ˈsliː.və- ⓊⓈ ˈslɪv.ə-
Sloan sləʊn ⓊⓈ sloʊn
Sloan|e sləʊn ⓊⓈ sloʊn **-es** -z **-ey** -i **-ier** -i.əʳ ⓊⓈ -ɚ **-iest** -i.ɪst, -əst ˌ**Sloane** ˈ**Ranger** ; ˌ**Sloane** ˈ**Square**
slob slɒb ⓊⓈ slɑːb **-s** -z **-bing** -ɪŋ **-bed** -d **-bish** -ɪʃ
slobb|er ˈslɒb|.əʳ ⓊⓈ ˈslɑː.b|ɚ **-ers** -əz ⓊⓈ -ɚz **-ering** -ər.ɪŋ **-ered** -əd ⓊⓈ -ɚd **-erer/s** -ə.rəʳ/z ⓊⓈ -ɚ.ɚ/z
slobber|y ˈslɒb.ər|.i ⓊⓈ ˈslɑː.bɚ- **-iness** -ɪ.nəs, -ɪ.nɪs
Slocombe ˈsləʊ.kəm ⓊⓈ ˈsloʊ-
Slocum ˈsləʊ.kəm ⓊⓈ ˈsloʊ-
sloe sləʊ ⓊⓈ sloʊ **-s** -z ˌ**sloe** ˈ**gin**
slog slɒg ⓊⓈ slɑːg, slɔːg **-s** -z **-ging** -ɪŋ **-ged** -d **-ger/s** -əʳ/z ⓊⓈ -ɚ/z
slogan ˈsləʊ.gən ⓊⓈ ˈsloʊ- **-s** -z
sloganeer ˌsləʊ.gəˈnɪəʳ ⓊⓈ ˌsloʊ.gəˈnɪr **-s** -z **-ing/s** -ɪŋ/z **-ed** -d
sloganiz|e, -is|e ˈsləʊ.gə.naɪz ⓊⓈ ˈsloʊ- **-es** -ɪz **-ing** -ɪŋ **-ed** -d **-er/s** -əʳ/z ⓊⓈ -ɚ/z
sloop sluːp **-s** -s
slop slɒp ⓊⓈ slɑːp **-s** -s **-ping** -ɪŋ **-ped** -t
slop|e sləʊp ⓊⓈ sloʊp **-es** -s **-ing** -ɪŋ/li **-ed** -t **-er/s** -əʳ/z ⓊⓈ -ɚ/z
Sloper ˈsləʊ.pəʳ ⓊⓈ ˈsloʊ.pɚ
slopp|y ˈslɒp|.i ⓊⓈ ˈslɑː.p|i **-ier** -i.əʳ ⓊⓈ -i.ɚ **-iest** -i.ɪst, -i.əst **-ily** -ɪ.li, -əl.i **-iness** -ɪ.nəs, -ɪ.nɪs ˌ**sloppy** ˈ**joe**
slosh slɒʃ ⓊⓈ slɑːʃ **-es** -ɪz **-ing** -ɪŋ **-ed** -t
slosh|y ˈslɒʃ|.i ⓊⓈ ˈslɑː.ʃ|i **-ier** -i.əʳ ⓊⓈ -i.ɚ **-iest** -i.ɪst, -i.əst **-iness** -ɪ.nəs, -ɪ.nɪs
slot slɒt ⓊⓈ slɑːt **-s** -s **-ting** -ɪŋ ⓊⓈ ˈslɑː.t̬ɪŋ **-ted** -ɪd ⓊⓈ ˈslɑː.t̬ɪd
sloth sləʊθ ⓊⓈ slɑːθ, slɔːθ, sloʊθ **-s** -s
slothful ˈsləʊθ.fəl, -fʊl ⓊⓈ ˈslɑːθ-, ˈslɔːθ-, ˈsloʊθ- **-ly** -i **-ness** -nəs, -nɪs
slot-machine ˈslɒt.məˌʃiːn ⓊⓈ ˈslɑːt- **-s** -z
slouch slaʊtʃ **-es** -ɪz **-ing/ly** -ɪŋ/li **-ed** -t
slough (*n.*) *bog:* slaʊ ⓊⓈ sluː, slaʊ **-s** -z **-y** -i
slough (*v.*) *skin:* slʌf **-s** -s **-ing** -ɪŋ **-ed** -t
Slough slaʊ
Slovak ˈsləʊ.væk ⓊⓈ ˈsloʊ.vɑːk, -væk **-s** -s
Slovaki|a sləʊˈvæk.i|.ə, -ˈvɑː.ki- ⓊⓈ sloʊˈvɑː.ki-, -ˈvæk.i- **-an/s** -ən/z
sloven ˈslʌv.ən **-s** -z
Slovene sləʊˈviːn; ˈsləʊ.viːn ⓊⓈ ˈsloʊ.viːn **-s** -z
Sloveni|a sləʊˈviː.ni|.ə, ˈ-nj|ə ⓊⓈ sloʊ- **-an/s** -ən/z
slovenl|y ˈslʌv.ən.l|i **-iness** -ɪ.nəs, -ɪ.nɪs
slow sləʊ ⓊⓈ sloʊ **-er** -əʳ ⓊⓈ -ɚ **-est** -ɪst, -əst **-ly** -li **-ness** -nəs, -nɪs **-s** -z **-ing** -ɪŋ **-ed** -d ˌ**slow** ˈ**motion**
slowcoach ˈsləʊ.kəʊtʃ ⓊⓈ ˈsloʊ.koʊtʃ **-es** -ɪz
slowdown ˈsləʊ.daʊn ⓊⓈ ˈsloʊ- **-s** -z
slowpoke ˈsləʊ.pəʊk ⓊⓈ ˈsloʊ.poʊk **-s** -s
slow-witted ˌsləʊˈwɪt.ɪd ⓊⓈ ˌsloʊˈwɪt̬-
slowworm ˈsləʊ.wɜːm ⓊⓈ ˈsloʊ.wɜːrm **-s** -z
slub slʌb **-s** -z **-bing** -ɪŋ **-bed** -d
sludg|e slʌdʒ **-y** -i
slu|e sluː **-s** -z **-ing** -ɪŋ **-ed** -d
slug slʌg **-s** -z **-ging** -ɪŋ **-ged** -d
slugabed ˈslʌg.ə.bed **-s** -z
sluggard ˈslʌg.əd ⓊⓈ -ɚd **-s** -z **-ly** -li
sluggish ˈslʌg.ɪʃ **-ly** -li **-ness** -nəs, -nɪs
sluic|e sluːs **-es** -ɪz **-ing** -ɪŋ **-ed** -t ˈ**sluice** ˌ**gate**
sluiceway ˈsluːs.weɪ **-s** -z
slum slʌm **-s** -z **-ming** -ɪŋ **-med** -d **-mer/s** -əʳ/z ⓊⓈ -ɚ/z
slumb|er ˈslʌm.b|əʳ ⓊⓈ -b|ɚ **-ers** -əz ⓊⓈ -ɚz **-ering** -ər.ɪŋ **-ered** -əd ⓊⓈ -ɚd **-erer/s** -ər.əʳ/z ⓊⓈ -ɚ.ɚ/z ˈ**slumber** ˌ**party**
slumm|y ˈslʌm|.i **-ier** -i.əʳ ⓊⓈ -i.ɚ **-iest** -i.ɪst, -i.əst **-iness** -ɪ.nəs, -ɪ.nɪs
slump slʌmp **-s** -s **-ing** -ɪŋ **-ed** -t
slung (*from* **sling**) slʌŋ
slunk (*from* **slink**) slʌŋk
slur slɜːʳ ⓊⓈ slɜːr **-s** -z **-ring** -ɪŋ **-red** -d
slurp slɜːp ⓊⓈ slɜːrp **-s** -s **-ing** -ɪŋ **-ed** -t
slurr|y ˈslʌr|.i ⓊⓈ ˈslɜːr- **-ies** -iz
slush slʌʃ **-y** -i **-ier** -i.əʳ ⓊⓈ -i.ɚ **-iest** -i.ɪst, -i.əst **-iness** -ɪ.nəs, -ɪ.nɪs ˈ**slush** ˌ**fund**
slut slʌt **-s** -s **-ty** -i

sluttish ˈslʌt.ɪʃ ⓊⓈ ˈslʌt̬- **-ly** -li **-ness** -nəs, -nɪs
Sluys slɔɪs
sly slaɪ **-er** -əʳ ⓊⓈ -ɚ **-est** -ɪst, -əst **-ly** -li **-ness** -nəs, -nɪs
slyboots ˈslaɪ.buːts
SM ˌesˈem
smack smæk **-s** -s **-ing/s** -ɪŋ/z **-ed** -t **-er/s** -əʳ/z ⓊⓈ -ɚ/z
smacker ˈsmæk.əʳ ⓊⓈ -ɚ **-s** -z
smackeroo ˌsmæk.ᵊrˈuː ⓊⓈ -əˈruː **-s** -z
Smale smeɪl
small (S) smɔːl ⓊⓈ smɔːl, smɑːl **-s** -z **-er** -əʳ ⓊⓈ -ɚ **-est** -ɪst, -əst **-ness** -nəs, -nɪs **-ish** -ɪʃ **ˈsmall ˌad, ˌsmall ˈad** ; **ˌsmall ˈarm** ; **ˌsmall ˈbeer** ; **ˌsmall ˈchange** ; **ˈsmall ˌfry** ; **ˈsmall ˌhours** ⓊⓈ **ˌsmall ˈhours** ; **ˌsmall poˈtatoes** ; **ˌsmall ˈprint, ˈsmall ˌprint** ⓊⓈ **ˌsmall ˈprint** ; **ˌsmall ˈscreen** ; **ˈsmall ˌtalk**
small-claims ˌsmɔːlˈkleɪmz ⓊⓈ ˌsmɔːl-, ˌsmɑːl- **ˌsmall-ˈclaims ˌcourt, ˌsmall-claims ˈcourt**
Smalley ˈsmɔː.li ⓊⓈ ˈsmɔː-, ˈsmɑː-
small-hold|er ˈsmɔːlˌhəʊl.d|əʳ ⓊⓈ -ˌhoʊl.dɚ, ˈsmɑːl- **-ers** -əz ⓊⓈ -ɚz **-ing/s** -ɪŋ/z
smallish ˈsmɔː.lɪʃ ⓊⓈ ˈsmɔː-, ˈsmɑː-
small-minded ˌsmɔːlˈmaɪn.dɪd ⓊⓈ ˌsmɔːl-, ˌsmɑːl- **-ly** -li **-ness** -nəs, -nɪs *stress shift:* ˌsmall-minded ˈperson
smallpox ˈsmɔːl.pɒks ⓊⓈ -pɑːks, ˈsmɑːl-
small-scale ˌsmɔːlˈskeɪl ⓊⓈ ˈ--, ˈsmɑːl- *stress shift, British only:* ˌsmall-scale ˈproject
small-tim|e ˌsmɔːlˈtaɪm ⓊⓈ ˈ--, ˈsmɑːl- **-er/s** -əʳ/z ⓊⓈ -ɚ/z
small-town ˈsmɔːl.taʊn ⓊⓈ ˈsmɔːl-, ˈsmɑːl-
Smallwood ˈsmɔːl.wʊd ⓊⓈ ˈsmɔːl-, ˈsmɑːl-
smalt smɔːlt, smɒlt ⓊⓈ smɔːlt, smɑːlt
smarm smɑːm ⓊⓈ smɑːrm **-s** -z **-ing** -ɪŋ **-ed** -d
smarm|y ˈsmɑː.m|i ⓊⓈ ˈsmɑːr- **-ily** -ɪli, -ᵊli **-iness** -ɪ.nəs, -ɪ.nɪs
smart (S) smɑːt ⓊⓈ smɑːrt **-s** -s **-er** -əʳ ⓊⓈ ˈsmɑːr.t̬ɚ **-est** -ɪst, -əst ⓊⓈ ˈsmɑːr.t̬ɪst, -t̬əst **-ly** -li **-ness** -nəs, -nɪs **-ing** -ɪŋ ⓊⓈ ˈsmɑːr.t̬ɪŋ **-ed** -ɪd ⓊⓈ ˈsmɑːr.t̬ɪd **ˈsmart ˌalec(k)** ⓊⓈ **ˌsmart ˈalec(k)** ; **ˈsmart ˌcard** ; **ˌsmart ˈmoney** ; **ˈsmart ˌset**
smartarse ˈsmɑːt.ɑːs ⓊⓈ ˈsmɑːrt.ɑːrs
smartass ˈsmɑːt.ɑːs, -æs ⓊⓈ ˈsmɑːrt.æs
smarten ˈsmɑː.tᵊn ⓊⓈ ˈsmɑːr- **-s** -z **-ing** -ɪŋ, ˈsmɑːt.nɪŋ ⓊⓈ ˈsmɑːrt- **-ed** -d
Smarties® ˈsmɑː.tiz ⓊⓈ ˈsmɑːr.t̬iz
smartish ˈsmɑː.tɪʃ ⓊⓈ ˈsmɑːr.t̬ɪʃ
smarty-pants ˈsmɑː.ti.pænts ⓊⓈ ˈsmɑːr.t̬i-
smash smæʃ **-es** -ɪz **-ing** -ɪŋ **-ed** -t **-er/s** -əʳ/z ⓊⓈ -ɚ/z **ˌsmash ˈhit**
smash-and-grab ˌsmæʃ.ᵊndˈgræb, -ᵊŋ'- ⓊⓈ -ᵊnd'- **-s** -z *stress shift:* ˌsmash-and-grab ˈraid
smattering ˈsmæt.ᵊr.ɪŋ ⓊⓈ ˈsmæt̬- **-s** -z
smear smɪəʳ ⓊⓈ smɪr **-s** -z **-ing** -ɪŋ **-ed** -d **-y** -i **-iness** -ɪ.nəs, -ɪ.nɪs **ˈsmear camˌpaign** ; **ˈsmear ˌtest**
Smeaton ˈsmiː.tᵊn
Smeeth smiːð, smiːθ
smegma ˈsmeg.mə
smell smel **-s** -z **-ing** -ɪŋ **smelt** -t **smelled** -t, -d **ˈsmelling ˌsalts**
smell|y ˈsmel|.i **-ier** -i.əʳ ⓊⓈ -i.ɚ **-iest** -i.ɪst, -i.əst **-iness** -ɪ.nəs, -ɪ.nɪs
smelt smelt **-s** -s **-ing** -ɪŋ ⓊⓈ ˈsmel.t̬ɪŋ **-ed** -ɪd ⓊⓈ ˈsmel.t̬ɪd **-er/s** -əʳ/z ⓊⓈ -ɚ/z
Smetana ˈsmet.ᵊn.ə
Smethwick ˈsmeð.ɪk
smew smjuː **-s** -z
smidgen, smidgin, smidgeon ˈsmɪdʒ.ᵊn, -ɪn
Smieton ˈsmiː.tᵊn
Smike smaɪk
smilax ˈsmaɪ.læks **-es** -ɪz
smil|e smaɪl **-es** -z **-ing/ly** -ɪŋ/li **-ed** -d
Smiles smaɪlz
smil|ey (S) ˈsmaɪ.l|i **-ier** -i.əʳ ⓊⓈ -i.ɚ **-iest** -i.ɪst, -i.əst
Smillie ˈsmaɪ.li
smirch smɜːtʃ ⓊⓈ smɜːrtʃ **-es** -ɪz **-ing** -ɪŋ **-ed** -t
smirk smɜːk ⓊⓈ smɜːrk **-s** -s **-ing** -ɪŋ **-ed** -t **-er/s** -əʳ/z ⓊⓈ -ɚ/z
Smirke smɜːk ⓊⓈ smɜːrk
Smirnoff® ˈsmɜː.nɒf ⓊⓈ ˈsmɜːr.nɔːf, ˈsmɪr-, -nɑːf
smit (*from* **smite**) smɪt
smit|e smaɪt **-es** -s **-ing** -ɪŋ ⓊⓈ ˈsmaɪ.t̬ɪŋ **smote** sməʊt ⓊⓈ smoʊt **smit** smɪt **smitten** ˈsmɪt.ᵊn
smith (S) smɪθ **-s** -s
Smithells ˈsmɪð.ᵊlz
smithereens ˌsmɪð.ᵊrˈiːnz ⓊⓈ -əˈriːnz
Smithers ˈsmɪð.əz ⓊⓈ -ɚz
Smithfield ˈsmɪθ.fiːld
Smithson ˈsmɪθ.sᵊn
Smithsonian smɪθˈsəʊ.ni.ən ⓊⓈ -ˈsoʊ-
smith|y ˈsmɪð|.i, ˈsmɪθ- ⓊⓈ ˈsmɪθ-, ˈsmɪð- **-ies** -iz
smitten (*from* **smite**) ˈsmɪt.ᵊn
smock smɒk ⓊⓈ smɑːk **-s** -s **-ing** -ɪŋ **-ed** -t
smog smɒg ⓊⓈ smɑːg, smɔːg
smogg|y ˈsmɒg|.i ⓊⓈ ˈsmɑː.g|i, ˈsmɔː- **-ier** -i.əʳ ⓊⓈ -i.ɚ **-iest** -i.ɪst, -i.əst
smok|e sməʊk ⓊⓈ smoʊk **-es** -s **-ing** -ɪŋ **-ed** -t **-er/s** -əʳ/z ⓊⓈ -ɚ/z **ˈsmoke aˌlarm** ; **ˌsmoke and ˈmirrors** ; **ˈsmoke ˌscreen** ; **ˈsmoking comˌpartment** ; **ˈsmoking ˌjacket** ; **ˈsmoking ˌroom** ; **ˌgo up in ˈsmoke** ; **there's ˌno ˌsmoke without ˈfire**
smokehou|se ˈsməʊk.haʊ|s ⓊⓈ ˈsmoʊk- **-ses** -zɪz
smokeless ˈsməʊk.ləs, -lɪs ⓊⓈ ˈsmoʊk-
smokestack ˈsməʊk.stæk ⓊⓈ ˈsmoʊk- **-s** -s **ˈsmokestack ˌindustry**
Smokies ˈsməʊ.kiz ⓊⓈ ˈsmoʊ-
smoko ˈsməʊ.kəʊ ⓊⓈ ˈsmoʊ.koʊ **-s** -z
smok|y ˈsməʊ.k|i ⓊⓈ ˈsmoʊ- **-ier** -i.əʳ ⓊⓈ -i.ɚ **-iest** -i.ɪst, -i.əst **-ily** -ɪ.li, -ᵊl.i **-iness** -ɪ.nəs, -ɪ.nɪs
smold|er ˈsməʊl.d|əʳ ⓊⓈ ˈsmoʊl.d|ɚ **-ers** -əz ⓊⓈ -ɚz **-ering** -ᵊr.ɪŋ **-ered** -əd ⓊⓈ -ɚd
Smollett ˈsmɒl.ɪt ⓊⓈ ˈsmɑː.lɪt
smolt sməʊlt ⓊⓈ smoʊlt
smooch smuːtʃ **-es** -ɪz **-ing** -ɪŋ **-ed** -t **-y** -i
smooth (*adj.*) smuːð **-er** -əʳ ⓊⓈ -ɚ **-est** -ɪst, -əst **-ly** -li **-ness** -nəs, -nɪs
smoothbore ˈsmuːð.bɔːʳ ⓊⓈ -bɔːr **-s** -z
smooth|(e) (*v.*) smuːð **-(e)s** -z **-ing** -ɪŋ **-ed** -d
smooth|ie, smooth|y ˈsmuː.ð|i **-ies** -iz
smorgasbord ˈsmɔː.gəs.bɔːd ⓊⓈ ˈsmɔːr.gəs.bɔːrd **-s** -z
smote (*from* **smite**) sməʊt ⓊⓈ smoʊt
smoth|er ˈsmʌð|.əʳ ⓊⓈ -ɚ **-ers** -əz ⓊⓈ -ɚz **-ering** -ᵊr.ɪŋ **-ered** -əd ⓊⓈ -ɚd
smould|er ˈsməʊl.d|əʳ ⓊⓈ ˈsmoʊl.d|ɚ **-ers** -əz ⓊⓈ -ɚz **-ering** -ᵊr.ɪŋ **-ered** -əd ⓊⓈ -ɚd
smudg|e smʌdʒ **-es** -ɪz **-ing** -ɪŋ **-ed** -d **-y** -i **-ier** -i.əʳ ⓊⓈ -i.ɚ **-iest** -i.ɪst, -i.əst **-ily** -ɪ.li, -ᵊl.i **-iness** -ɪ.nəs, -ɪ.nɪs
smug smʌg **-ly** -li **-ness** -nəs, -nɪs
smuggl|e ˈsmʌg|.l̩ **-es** -z **-ing** -ɪŋ, ˈsmʌg.lɪŋ **-ed** -d
smuggler ˈsmʌg.ləʳ, ˈ-l̩.əʳ ⓊⓈ ˈ-lɚ, ˈ-l̩.ɚ **-s** -z
smut smʌt **-s** -s **-ty** -i ⓊⓈ ˈsmʌt̬.i **-tier** -i.əʳ ⓊⓈ ˈsmʌt̬.i.ɚ **-tiest** -i.ɪst, -i.əst ⓊⓈ ˈsmʌt̬.i.ɪst, -i.əst **-tily** -ɪ.li, -ᵊl.i ⓊⓈ ˈsmʌt̬.ɪ.li, -ᵊl.i **-tiness** -ɪ.nəs, -ɪ.nɪs ⓊⓈ ˈsmʌt̬.ɪ.nəs, -ɪ.nɪs
Smylie ˈsmaɪ.li
Smyrna ˈsmɜː.nə ⓊⓈ ˈsmɜːr-
Smyth smɪθ, smaɪθ
Smythe smaɪð, smaɪθ
snack snæk **-s** -s **-ing** -ɪŋ **-ed** -d **ˈsnack ˌbar**
Snaefell ˌsneɪˈfel
snaffl|e ˈsnæf.l̩ **-es** -z **-ing** -ɪŋ, ˈsnæf.lɪŋ **-ed** -d

snafu snæf'uː (US) snæf'uː, '-- **-es** -z **-ing** -ɪŋ **-ed** -d

snag snæg **-s** -z **-ging** -ɪŋ **-ged** -d

Snagge snæg

snail sneɪl **-s** -z **-like** -laɪk **'snail's ˌpace**

snak|e sneɪk **-es** -s **-ing** -ɪŋ **-ed** -t **'snake ˌcharmer ; ˌsnakes and 'ladders ; ˌsnake in the 'grass** (US) **'snake in the ˌgrass**

snakebite 'sneɪk.baɪt **-s** -s

snakeskin 'sneɪk.skɪn

snak|y 'sneɪ.k|i **-iness** -ɪ.nəs, -ɪ.nɪs

snap snæp **-s** -s **-ping** -ɪŋ **-ped** -t **'snap ˌfastener**

snapdragon 'snæpˌdræg.ən **-s** -z

Snape sneɪp

snapper 'snæp.əʳ (US) -ɚ **-s** -z

snappish 'snæp.ɪʃ **-ly** -li **-ness** -nəs, -nɪs

snapp|y 'snæp|.i **-ier** -i.əʳ (US) -i.ɚ **-iest** -i.ɪst, -i.əst **-ily** -ɪ.li, -ᵊl.i **-iness** -ɪ.nəs, -ɪ.nɪs

snapshot 'snæp|.ʃɒt (US) -ʃɑːt **-s**

snar|e sneəʳ (US) sner **-es** -z **-ing** -ɪŋ **-ed** -d **'snare ˌdrum**

snark snɑːk (US) snɑːrk **-s** -s

snarl snɑːl (US) snɑːrl **-s** -z **-ing** -ɪŋ **-ed** -d

snarl-up 'snɑːl.ʌp (US) 'snɑːrl- **-s** -s

snatch snætʃ **-es** -ɪz **-ing** -ɪŋ **-ed** -t **-er/s** -əʳ/z (US) -ɚ/z

snatch|y 'snætʃ|.i **-ier** -i.əʳ (US) -i.ɚ **-iest** -i.ɪst, -i.əst **-ily** -ɪ.li, -ᵊl.i

snazz|y 'snæz|.i **-ier** -i.əʳ (US) -i.ɚ **-iest** -i.ɪst, -i.əst **-ily** -ɪ.li, -ᵊl.i **-iness** -ɪ.nəs, -ɪ.nɪs

sneak sniːk **-s** -s **-ing/ly** -ɪŋ/li **-ed** -t **-y** -i **-ier** -i.əʳ (US) -i.ɚ **-iest** -i.ɪst, -i.əst **-ily** -ɪ.li, -ᵊl.i **-iness** -ɪ.nəs, -ɪ.nɪs **ˌsneak 'preview ; 'sneak ˌthief, ˌsneak 'thief** (US) **'sneak ˌthief**

sneaker 'sniː.kəʳ (US) -kɚ **-s** -z

sneakers 'sniː.kəz (US) -kɚz

sneaky 'sniː.ki **-ier** -i.əʳ (US) -i.ɚ **-iest** -i.ɪst, -i.əst **-iness** -ɪ.nəs, -ɪ.nɪs

Snedden 'sned.ᵊn

sneer snɪəʳ (US) snɪr **-s** -z **-ing/ly** -ɪŋ/li **-ed** -d

sneez|e sniːz **-es** -ɪz **-ing** -ɪŋ **-ed** -d

Snelgrove 'snel.grəʊv (US) -groʊv

snell (S) snel **-s** -z

Sneyd sniːd

snib snɪb **-s** -z

snick snɪk **-s** -s **-ing** -ɪŋ **-ed** -t

snick|er 'snɪk|.əʳ (US) -ɚ **-ers** -əz (US) -ɚz **-ering** -ᵊr.ɪŋ **-ered** -əd (US) -ɚd

Snickers® 'snɪk.əz (US) -ɚz

snickersnee ˌsnɪk.ə'sniː, '--- (US) 'snɪk.ɚ.sniː **-s** -z

snide snaɪd **-ly** -li **-ness** -nəs, -nɪs

sniff snɪf **-s** -s **-ing** -ɪŋ **-ed** -t **-y** -i **-ier** -i.əʳ (US) -i.ɚ **-iest** -i.ɪst, -i.əst **-ily** -ɪ.li, -ᵊl.i **-iness** -ɪ.nəs, -ɪ.nɪs

sniffer 'snɪf.əʳ (US) -ɚ **-s** -z **'sniffer ˌdog**

sniffl|e 'snɪf.l̩ **-es** -z **-ing** -ɪŋ, 'snɪf.lɪŋ **-ed** -d

snifter 'snɪf.təʳ (US) -tɚ **-s** -z

snigg|er 'snɪg|.əʳ (US) -ɚ **-ers** -əz (US) -ɚz **-ering** -ᵊr.ɪŋ **-ered** -əd (US) -ɚd **-erer/s** -ə.rəʳ/z (US) -ɚ.ɚ/z

snip snɪp **-s** -s **-ping** -ɪŋ **-ped** -t **-per/s** -əʳ/z (US) -ɚ/z

snip|e snaɪp **-es** -s **-ing** -ɪŋ **-ed** -t **-er/s** -əʳ/z (US) -ɚ/z

snipp|et 'snɪp|.ɪt **-ets** -ɪts **-ety** -ɪ.ti (US) -ɪ.t̬i

snit snɪt **-s** -s

snitch snɪtʃ **-es** -ɪz **-ing** -ɪŋ **-ed** -t

snivel 'snɪv.ᵊl **-s** -z **-(l)ing** -ɪŋ, 'snɪv.lɪŋ **-(l)ed** -d **-(l)er/s** -əʳ/z, 'snɪv.ləʳ/z (US) '-ᵊl.ɚ/z, '-lɚ/z

snob snɒb (US) snɑːb **-s** -z **-bism** -ɪ.zᵊm

snobbery 'snɒb.ᵊr.i (US) 'snɑː.bɚ-

snobbish 'snɒb.ɪʃ (US) 'snɑː.bɪʃ **-ly** -li **-ness** -nəs, -nɪs

snobb|y 'snɒb|.i (US) 'snɑː.b|i **-ier** -i.əʳ (US) -i.ɚ **-iest** -i.ɪst, -i.əst

SNOBOL 'snəʊ.bɒl (US) 'snoʊ.bɔːl, -bɑːl

Snodgrass 'snɒd.grɑːs (US) 'snɑːd.græs

Snodland 'snɒd.lənd (US) 'snɑːd-

snoek snʊk, snuːk **-s** -s

snog snɒg (US) snɑːg, snɔːg **-s** -z **-ging** -ɪŋ **-ged** -d

snood snuːd, snʊd (US) snuːd **-s** -z **-ed** -ɪd

Snoody 'snuː.di

snook snuːk (US) snʊk, snuːk **-s** -s

snooker 'snuː.kəʳ (US) 'snʊk.ɚ **-s** -z **-ing** -ɪŋ **-ed** -d

snoop snuːp **-s** -s **-ing** -ɪŋ **-ed** -t **-er/s** -əʳ/z (US) -ɚ/z

Snoopy® 'snuː.pi

snoot|y 'snuː.t|i (US) -t̬|i **-ily** -ɪ.li, -ᵊl.i **-iness** -ɪ.nəs, -ɪ.nɪs **-ier** -i.əʳ (US) -i.ɚ **-iest** -i.ɪst, -i.əst

snooz|e snuːz **-es** -ɪz **-ing** -ɪŋ **-ed** -d **-er/s** -əʳ/z (US) -ɚ/z

snor|e snɔːʳ (US) snɔːr **-es** -z **-ing** -ɪŋ **-ed** -d **-er/s** -əʳ/z (US) -ɚ/z

snorkel 'snɔː.kᵊl (US) 'snɔːr- **-s** -z **-(l)ing** -ɪŋ **-(l)ed** -d **-(l)er/s** -əʳ/z (US) -ɚ/z

snort snɔːt (US) snɔːrt **-s** -s **-ing** -ɪŋ (US) 'snɔːr.t̬ɪŋ **-ed** -ɪd (US) 'snɔːr.t̬ɪd

snorter 'snɔː.təʳ (US) 'snɔːr.t̬ɚ **-s** -z

snort|y 'snɔː.t|i (US) 'snɔːr.t̬|i **-ier** -i.əʳ (US) -i.ɚ **-iest** -i.ɪst, -i.əst **-ily** -ɪ.li, -ᵊl.i **-iness** -ɪ.nəs, -ɪ.nɪs

snot snɒt (US) snɑːt **-ty** -i (US) 'snɑː.t̬i

snout (S) snaʊt **-s** -s

snow (S) snəʊ (US) snoʊ **-s** -z **-ing** -ɪŋ **-ed** -d **'snow ˌblindness ; 'snow ˌgoose ; ˌSnow 'White**

snowball 'snəʊ.bɔːl (US) 'snoʊ.bɔːl, -bɑːl **-s** -z **-ing** -ɪŋ **-ed** -d

snowberr|y 'snəʊ.bᵊr|.i, -br|i (US) 'snoʊˌber|.i **-ies** -iz

snowblower 'snəʊˌbləʊ.əʳ (US) 'snoʊˌbloʊ.ɚ **-s** -z

snowbound 'snəʊ.baʊnd (US) 'snoʊ-

snowcap 'snəʊ.kæp (US) 'snoʊ- **-s** -s **-ped** -t

Snowden, Snowdon 'snəʊ.dᵊn (US) 'snoʊ-

Snowdonia snəʊ'dəʊ.ni.ə (US) snoʊ'doʊ-

snowdrift 'snəʊ.drɪft (US) 'snoʊ- **-s** -s

snowdrop 'snəʊ.drɒp (US) 'snoʊ.drɑːp **-s** -s

snowfall 'snəʊ.fɔːl (US) 'snoʊ-, -fɑːl **-s** -z

snowfield 'snəʊ.fiːld (US) 'snoʊ- **-s** -z

snowflake 'snəʊ.fleɪk (US) 'snoʊ- **-s** -s

snow|man 'snəʊ|.mæn (US) 'snoʊ- **-men** -men

snowmobile 'snəʊ.məˌbiːl (US) 'snoʊ.moʊˌ- **-s** -z

snowplough, snowplow 'snəʊ.plaʊ (US) 'snoʊ- **-s** -z **-ing** -ɪŋ **-ed** -d

snowshoe 'snəʊ.ʃuː (US) 'snoʊ- **-s** -z

snowstorm 'snəʊ.stɔːm (US) 'snoʊ.stɔːrm **-s** -z

snowsuit 'snəʊ.suːt, -sjuːt (US) 'snoʊ.suːt **-s** -s

snow-white ˌsnəʊ'*h*waɪt (US) ˌsnoʊ- *stress shift:* ˌsnow-white 'hair

snow|y 'snəʊ|.i (US) 'snoʊ- **-ier** -i.əʳ (US) -i.ɚ **-iest** -i.ɪst, -i.əst **-ily** -ɪ.li, -ᵊl.i **-iness** -ɪ.nəs, -ɪ.nɪs **ˌsnowy 'owl**

SNP ˌes.en'piː, -em'- (US) -en'-

snr (S) (*abbrev. for* **senior**) 'siː.ni.əʳ, -njəʳ (US) -njɚ

snub snʌb **-s** -z **-bing** -ɪŋ **-bed** -d

snub-nosed ˌsnʌb'nəʊzd (US) 'snʌb.noʊzd *stress shift, British only:* ˌsnub-nosed 'bullet

snuck snʌk

snuff snʌf **-s** -s **-ing** -ɪŋ **-ed** -t **-er/s** -əʳ/z (US) -ɚ/z **'snuff ˌbox**

snuffl|e 'snʌf.l̩ **-es** -z **-ing** -ɪŋ, 'snʌf.lɪŋ **-ed** -d **-er/s** -əʳ/z, 'snʌf.ləʳ/z (US) '-l̩.ɚ/z, '-lɚ/z **-y** -i

snug snʌg **-ger** -əʳ (US) -ɚ **-gest** -ɪst, -əst **-ly** -li **-ness** -nəs, -nɪs

snugger|y 'snʌg.ᵊr|.i **-ies** -iz

snuggl|e 'snʌg.l̩ **-es** -z **-ing** -ɪŋ, 'snʌg.lɪŋ **-ed** -d

Snyder 'snaɪ.dəʳ (US) -dɚ

so *normal forms:* səʊ (US) soʊ *occasional weak form:* sə

Note: Weak form word. The weak form is used only rarely, and only in casual speech before adjectives and adverbs (e.g. "Not so bad" /ˌnɒt.sə'bæd (US) ˌnɑːt-/, "Don't go so fast"

/ˌdəʊnt.gəʊ.sə'fɑːst (US) ˌdoʊnt.goʊ.sə'fæst/). ˌ**so 'long, 'so ˌlong**
soak səʊk (US) soʊk **-s** -s **-ing** -ɪŋ **-ed** -t
soakaway 'səʊk.əˌweɪ (US) 'soʊk- **-s** -z
Soames səʊmz (US) soʊmz
so-and-so 'səʊ.ənd.səʊ (US) 'soʊ.ənd.soʊ **-(')s** -z
Soane səʊn (US) soʊn **-s** -z
soap səʊp (US) soʊp **-s** -s **-ing** -ɪŋ **-ed** -t **-y** -i **-ier** -i.əʳ (US) -i.ɚ **-iest** -i.ɪst, -i.əst **-ily** -ɪ.li, -əl.i **-iness** -ɪ.nəs, -ɪ.nɪs
soapbox 'səʊp.bɒks (US) 'soʊp.bɑːks **-es** -ɪz
soap opera 'səʊpˌɒp.ər.ə, ˌ-rə (US) 'soʊpˌɑː.pɚ.ə, ˌ-prə **-s** -z
soapstone 'səʊp.stəʊn (US) 'soʊp.stoʊn
soapsuds 'səʊp.sʌdz (US) 'soʊp-
soar (S) sɔːʳ (US) sɔːr **-s** -z **-ing** -ɪŋ **-ed** -d
soaraway 'sɔː.rə.weɪ (US) 'sɔːr.ə-
Soares səʊ'ɑː.rɪz (US) soʊ'ɑːr.ɪz
sob sɒb (US) sɑːb **-s** -z **-bing** -ɪŋ **-bed** -d **'sob ˌstory**
SOB ˌes.əʊ'biː (US) -oʊ'-
sob|er 'səʊ.bləʳ (US) 'soʊ.blɚ **-erer** -ər.əʳ (US) -ɚ.ɚ **-erest** -ər.ɪst, -ər.əst **-erly** -əl.i (US) -ɚ.li **-erness** -ə.nəs, -ə.nɪs (US) -ɚ.nəs, -ɚ.nɪs **-ers** -əz (US) -ɚz **-ering/ly** -ər.ɪŋ/li **-ered** -əd (US) -ɚd
Sobers 'səʊ.bəz (US) 'soʊ.bɚz
sobersides 'səʊ.bə.saɪdz (US) 'soʊ.bɚ-
sobriety səʊ'braɪ.ɪ.ti, '-ə- (US) sə'braɪ.ə.ţi, soʊ-
sobriquet 'səʊ.brɪ.keɪ (US) 'soʊ-, -ket, ˌ--'- **-s** -z
soc(c)age 'sɒk.ɪdʒ (US) 'sɑː.kɪdʒ
so-called ˌsəʊ'kɔːld (US) ˌsoʊ'kɑːld, -'kɔːld *stress shift:* ˌso-called 'friend
soccer 'sɒk.əʳ (US) 'sɑː.kɚ
sociability ˌsəʊ.ʃə'bɪl.ə.ti, -ɪ.ti (US) ˌsoʊ.ʃə'bɪl.ə.ţi
sociab|le 'səʊ.ʃə.bl̩ (US) 'soʊ- **-ly** -li **-leness** -l̩.nəs, -nɪs
social 'səʊ.ʃəl (US) 'soʊ- **-ly** -i ˌ**social 'climber** (US) **'social ˌclimber** ; ˌ**social de'mocracy** ; ˌ**social 'democrat** ; **'social ˌlife** ; ˌ**social 'science** (US) **'social ˌscience** ; ˌ**social 'secretary** ; ˌ**social se'curity** ; ˌ**social 'service** (US) **'social ˌservice** ; **'social ˌwork**
social|ism 'səʊ.ʃəl|.ɪ.zəm (US) 'soʊ- **-ist/s** -ɪst/s
socialistic ˌsəʊ.ʃəl'ɪs.tɪk (US) ˌsoʊ.ʃə'lɪs-
socialite 'səʊ.ʃəl.aɪt (US) 'soʊ.ʃə.laɪt **-s** -s
socialization, -isa- ˌsəʊ.ʃəl.aɪ'zeɪ.ʃən (US) ˌsoʊ.ʃəl.ɪ'-
socializ|e, -is|e 'səʊ.ʃəl.aɪz (US) 'soʊ.ʃə.laɪz **-es** -ɪz **-ing** -ɪŋ **-ed** -d

societal sə'saɪ.ə.təl (US) -ţəl
societ|y (S) sə'saɪ.ə.t|i (US) -ţ|i **-ies** -iz
Socinian səʊ'sɪn.i.ən (US) soʊ- **-s** -z
Socinus səʊ'saɪ.nəs (US) soʊ-
socio- səʊ.ʃi.əʊ-, -si-; ˌsəʊ.ʃi'ɒ-, -si'- (US) soʊ.si.oʊ-, -ʃi-, -ə-; ˌsoʊ.si'ɑː-, -ʃi'-
Note: Prefix. Normally either takes primary or secondary stress on the first syllable, e.g. **sociopath** /'səʊ.ʃi.əʊ.pæθ (US) 'soʊ.si.ə-/, **sociopolitical** /ˌsəʊ.ʃi.əʊ.pə'lɪt.ɪ.kəl (US) ˌsoʊ.si.oʊ.pə'lɪţ-/, or secondary stress on the first syllable and primary stress on the third syllable, e.g. **sociology** /ˌsəʊ.ʃi'ɒl.ə.dʒi (US) ˌsoʊ.si'ɑː.lə-/.
sociobiolog|y ˌsəʊ.ʃi.əʊ.baɪ'ɒl.ə.dʒ|i, -si- (US) ˌsoʊ.si.oʊ.baɪ'ɑː.lə-, -ʃi- **-ist/s** -ɪst/s
sociocultural ˌsəʊ.ʃi.əʊ'kʌl.tʃər.əl, -si- (US) ˌsoʊ.si.oʊ-, -ʃi- **-ly** -i
socioeconomic ˌsəʊ.ʃi.əʊˌiː.kə'nɒm.ɪk, -si-, -ˌek.ə'- (US) ˌsoʊ.si.oʊˌek.ə'nɑː.mɪk, -ʃi-, -ˌiː.kə'-
sociolinguist ˌsəʊ.ʃi.əʊ'lɪŋ.gwɪst, -si- (US) ˌsoʊ.si.oʊ'-, -ʃi- **-s** -s
sociolinguistic ˌsəʊ.ʃi.əʊ.lɪŋ'gwɪs.tɪk, -si- (US) ˌsoʊ.si.oʊ-, -ʃi- **-s** -s
sociologic|al ˌsəʊ.ʃi.ə'lɒdʒ.ɪ.k|əl, -si- (US) ˌsoʊ.si.ə'lɑː.dʒɪ-, -ʃi- **-ally** -əl.i, -li
sociologist ˌsəʊ.ʃi'ɒl.ə.dʒɪst, -si'- (US) ˌsoʊ.si'ɑː.lə-, -ʃi'- **-s** -s
sociolog|y ˌsəʊ.ʃi'ɒl.ə.dʒ|i, -si'- (US) ˌsoʊ.si'ɑː.lə-, -ʃi'- **-ist/s** -ɪst/s
sociopath 'səʊ.ʃi.əʊ.pæθ, -si- (US) 'soʊ.si.ə-, -ʃi- **-s** -s
sociopolitical ˌsəʊ.ʃi.əʊ.pəl'ɪt.ɪ.kəl, -si- (US) ˌsoʊ.si.oʊ.pə'lɪţ-, -ʃi-
socioreligious ˌsəʊ.ʃi.əʊ.rɪ'lɪdʒ.əs, -si-, -rə'- (US) ˌsoʊ.si.oʊ-, -ʃi-
sock sɒk (US) sɑːk **-s** -s **-ing** -ɪŋ **-ed** -t
sockdolager, sockdologer sɒk'dɒl.ə.dʒəʳ (US) sɑːk'dɑː.lə.dʒɚ **-s** -z
sock|et 'sɒk|.ɪt (US) 'sɑː.k|ɪt **-ets** -ɪts **-eted** -ɪ.tɪd (US) -ɪ.ţɪd
Socotra səʊ'kəʊ.trə, sɒk'əʊ- (US) soʊ'koʊ-
Socrates 'sɒk.rə.tiːz (US) 'sɑː.krə-
socratic (S) sɒk'ræt.ɪk, səʊ'kræt- (US) sə'kræţ-, soʊ- **-ally** -əl.i, -li
sod sɒd (US) sɑːd **-s** -z **-ding** -ɪŋ **-ded** -ɪd ˌ**sod's 'law, 'sod's ˌlaw**
soda 'səʊ.də (US) 'soʊ- **-s** -z **'soda ˌbiscuit** ; **'soda ˌbread** ; **'soda ˌcracker** ; **'soda ˌfountain** ; **'soda ˌpop** ; **'soda ˌsiphon** ; **'soda ˌwater**
sodalit|y səʊ'dæl.ə.t|i, -ɪ.t|i (US) soʊ'dæl.ə.ţ|i **-ies** -iz
sodden 'sɒd.ən (US) 'sɑː.dən **-ness** -nəs, -nɪs **-s** -z **-ing** -ɪŋ **-ed** -d

sodding 'sɒd.ɪŋ (US) 'sɑː.dɪŋ
sodium 'səʊ.di.əm (US) 'soʊ-
Sodom 'sɒd.əm (US) 'sɑː.dəm
sodomiz|e, -is|e 'sɒd.ə.maɪz (US) 'sɑː.də- **-es** -ɪz **-ing** -ɪŋ **-ed** -d
sodom|y 'sɒd.ə.m|i (US) 'sɑː.də- **-ite/s** -aɪt/s
Sodor 'səʊ.dəʳ (US) 'soʊ.dɚ
soever səʊ'ev.əʳ (US) soʊ'ev.ɚ
sofa 'səʊ.fə (US) 'soʊ- **-s** -z
sofabed 'səʊ.fə.bed (US) 'soʊ- **-s** -z
Sofala səʊ'fɑː.lə (US) soʊ-, sə-
soffit 'sɒf.ɪt (US) 'sɑː.fɪt **-s** -s
Sofia 'sɒf.i.ə, 'səʊ.fi- (US) 'soʊ.fi-; soʊ'fiː-
soft sɒft (US) sɑːft **-s** -s **-er** -əʳ (US) -ɚ **-est** -ɪst, -əst **-ly** -li **-ness** -nəs, -nɪs ˌ**soft 'copy** ; ˌ**soft 'drink** (US) **'soft ˌdrink** ; ˌ**soft 'fruit** ; ˌ**soft 'furnishings** ; ˌ**soft 'landing** ; ˌ**soft 'option** ; ˌ**soft 'sell** ; **'soft ˌspot**, ˌ**soft 'spot** (US) **'soft ˌspot** ; ˌ**soft 'target** ; **'soft ˌtouch**, ˌ**soft 'touch**
softball 'sɒft.bɔːl (US) 'sɑːft-, -bɑːl
soft-boil ˌsɒft'bɔɪl (US) ˌsɑːft- **-s** -z **-ing** -ɪŋ **-ed** -d
soft-centred ˌsɒft'sen.təd (US) ˌsɑːft'sen.tɚd
soft-core 'sɒft.kɔːʳ (US) 'sɑːft.kɔːr
softcover ˌsɒft'kʌv.əʳ (US) 'sɑːft.kʌv.ɚ **-s** -z
soften 'sɒf.ən (US) 'sɑː.fən **-s** -z **-ing** -ɪŋ, 'sɒf.nɪŋ (US) 'sɑːf- **-ed** -d
softener 'sɒf.ən.əʳ, '-nəʳ (US) 'sɑː.fən.ɚ, 'sɑːf.nɚ **-s** -z
softhearted ˌsɒft'hɑː.tɪd (US) 'sɑːftˌhɑːr.ţɪd **-ly** -li **-ness** -nəs, -nɪs *stress shift, British only:* ˌsofthearted 'person
soft|ie 'sɒf.t|i (US) 'sɑːf- **-ies** -iz
softish 'sɒf.tɪʃ (US) 'sɑːf-
softly-softly ˌsɒft.li'sɒft.li (US) ˌsɑːft.li'sɑːft-
soft-pedal ˌsɒf*t*'ped.əl (US) ˌsɑːf*t*- **-s** -z **-(l)ing** -ɪŋ, -'ped.lɪŋ **-(l)ed** -d
soft-soap ˌsɒf*t*'səʊp (US) ˌsɑːf*t*'soʊp **-s** -s **-ing** -ɪŋ **-ed** -t
soft-spoken ˌsɒf*t*'spəʊ.kən (US) ˌsɑːft'spoʊ- *stress shift:* ˌsoft-spoken 'person
software 'sɒf*t*.weəʳ (US) 'sɑːf*t*.wer
softwood 'sɒf*t*.wʊd (US) 'sɑːf*t*- **-s** -z
soft|y 'sɒf.t|i (US) 'sɑːf- **-ies** -iz
SOGAT 'səʊ.gæt (US) 'soʊ-
sogg|y 'sɒg|.i (US) 'sɑː.g|i **-ily** -ɪ.li, -əl.i **-ier** -i.əʳ (US) -i.ɚ **-iest** -i.ɪst, -i.əst **-iness** -ɪ.nəs, -ɪ.nɪs
soh səʊ (US) soʊ **-s** -z
Soham 'səʊ.əm (US) 'soʊ-
Soho 'səʊ.həʊ; (US) 'soʊ.hoʊ
soi-disant ˌswɑː.diː'zɑ̃ː*ŋ*, ˌ-'-- (US) ˌswɑː.diː'zɑ̃ː*n*

soigné(e) 'swɑː.njeɪ, -'- ⓊⓈ swɑː'njeɪ
soil sɔɪl **-s** -z **-ing** -ɪŋ **-ed** -d **'soil ˌpipe**
soirée, soiree 'swɑː.reɪ, 'swɒr.eɪ, -'- ⓊⓈ swɑː'reɪ **-s** -z
soixante-neuf ˌswæs.ɑ̃ːnt'nɜːf, ˌswʌs- ⓊⓈ ˌswɑː.sɑ̃ːnt'nɜːf
sojourn 'sɒdʒ.ɜːn, 'sʌdʒ-, -ən ⓊⓈ 'soʊ.dʒɜːrn, -'- **-s** -z **-ing** -ɪŋ **-ed** -d **-er/s** -əʳ/z ⓊⓈ -ɚ/z
Sokoto 'səʊ.kə.təʊ, ˌ--'- ⓊⓈ 'soʊ.koʊ.toʊ, ˌ--'-; sə'koʊ-
sol (S) sɒl ⓊⓈ soʊl, sɑːl **-s** -z
sola 'səʊ.lə ⓊⓈ 'soʊ-
solac|e 'sɒl.əs, -ɪs ⓊⓈ 'sɑː.lɪs **-es** -ɪz **-ing** -ɪŋ **-ed** -t
solanum səʊ'leɪ.nəm, -'lɑː- ⓊⓈ soʊ'leɪ-
solar 'səʊ.ləʳ ⓊⓈ 'soʊ.lɚ ˌ**solar 'energy**; ˌ**solar 'panel**; ˌ**solar 'plexus**; **'solar ˌsystem**
solari|um səʊ'leə.ri.əm ⓊⓈ soʊ'ler.i-, sə- **-ums** -z **-a** -ə
solati|um səʊ'leɪ.ʃi|.əm ⓊⓈ soʊ- **-ums** -əmz **-a** -ə
sold (*from* **sell**) səʊld ⓊⓈ soʊld
sold|er 'səʊl.d|əʳ, 'sɒl- ⓊⓈ 'sɑː.d|ɚ **-ers** -əz ⓊⓈ -ɚz **-ering** -ᵊr.ɪŋ **-ered** -əd ⓊⓈ -ɚd **'soldering ˌiron**
soldi|er 'səʊl.dʒ|əʳ ⓊⓈ 'soʊl.dʒ|ɚ **-ers** -əz ⓊⓈ -ɚz **-ering** -ᵊr.ɪŋ **-ered** -əd ⓊⓈ -ɚd ˌ**soldier of 'fortune**
soldierly 'səʊl.dʒᵊl.i ⓊⓈ 'soʊl.dʒɚ.li
soldiery 'səʊl.dʒᵊr.i ⓊⓈ 'soʊl-
sol|e (S) səʊl ⓊⓈ soʊl **-es** -z **-ely** -li **-ing** -ɪŋ **-ed** -d
solecism 'sɒl.ɪ.sɪ.zᵊm, '-ə-, -es.ɪ- ⓊⓈ 'sɑː.lə- **-s** -z
solemn 'sɒl.əm ⓊⓈ 'sɑː.ləm **-ly** -li **-ness** -nəs, -nɪs
solemnif|y sə'lem.nɪ.f|aɪ, sɒl'em- ⓊⓈ sə'lem- **-ies** -z **-ying** -ɪŋ **-ied** -d
solemnit|y sə'lem.nə.t|i, sɒl'em-, -nɪ- ⓊⓈ sə'lem.nə.t̬|i **-ies** -z
solemnization, -isa- ˌsɒl.əm.naɪ'zeɪ.ʃᵊn, -nɪ'- ⓊⓈ ˌsɑː.ləm.nɪ'- **-s** -z
solemniz|e, -is|e 'sɒl.əm.naɪz ⓊⓈ 'sɑː.ləm- **-es** -ɪz **-ing** -ɪŋ **-ed** -d
solenoid 'səʊ.lə.nɔɪd, 'sɒl.ə-, '-ɪ- ⓊⓈ 'soʊ.lə-, 'sɑː- **-s** -z
Solent 'səʊ.lənt ⓊⓈ 'soʊ-
sol-fa (S) ˌsɒl'fɑː, '-- ⓊⓈ ˌsoʊl-
solfegg|io sɒl'fedʒ|.i.əʊ ⓊⓈ soʊl'fedʒ|.i.oʊ; sɑːl'fedʒ|.oʊ **-i** -iː
solferino (S) ˌsɒl.fᵊr'iː.nəʊ ⓊⓈ ˌsoʊl.fə'riː.noʊ, ˌsɑːl-
solic|it sə'lɪs|.ɪt **-its** -ɪts **-iting** -ɪ.tɪŋ ⓊⓈ -ɪ.t̬ɪŋ **-ited** -ɪ.tɪd ⓊⓈ -ɪ.t̬ɪd
solicitation səˌlɪs.ɪ'teɪ.ʃᵊn **-s** -z
solicitor sə'lɪs.ɪ.təʳ, '-ə- ⓊⓈ -t̬ɚ **-s** -z soˌ**licitor 'general**
solicitous sə'lɪs.ɪ.təs ⓊⓈ -t̬əs **-ly** -li **-ness** -nəs, -nɪs
solicitude sə'lɪs.ɪ.tjuːd, -tʃuːd ⓊⓈ -tuːd, -tjuːd
solid 'sɒl.ɪd ⓊⓈ 'sɑː.lɪd **-s** -z **-est** -ɪst, -əst **-ly** -li **-ness** -nəs, -nɪs
solidarity (S) ˌsɒl.ɪ'dær.ə.ti, -ɪ.ti ⓊⓈ ˌsɑː.lə'der.ə.t̬i, -'dær-
solidifiable sə'lɪd.ɪ.faɪ.ə.bl̩, sɒl'ɪd- ⓊⓈ sə'lɪd-
solidification səˌlɪd.ɪ.fɪ'keɪ.ʃᵊn, sɒlˌɪd- ⓊⓈ səˌlɪd.ə-
solidi|fy sə'lɪd.ɪ.|faɪ, sɒl'ɪd- ⓊⓈ sə'lɪd.ə- **-fies** -faɪz **-fying** -faɪ.ɪŋ **-fied** -faɪd
solidity sə'lɪd.ə.ti, sɒl'ɪd-, -ɪ.ti ⓊⓈ sə'lɪd.ə.t̬i
solid-state ˌsɒl.ɪd'steɪt ⓊⓈ ˌsɑː.lɪd'- *stress shift, see compound:* ˌ**solid-state 'physics**
solid|us 'sɒl.ɪ.d|əs ⓊⓈ 'sɑː.lɪ- **-i** -aɪ, -iː
Solihull ˌsəʊ.lɪ'hʌl, ˌsɒl.ɪ'- ⓊⓈ ˌsoʊ.lɪ'- *stress shift:* ˌSolihull 'residents
soliloquiz|e, -is|e sə'lɪl.ə.kwaɪz, sɒl'ɪl- ⓊⓈ sə'lɪl- **-es** -ɪz **-ing** -ɪŋ **-ed** -d
soliloqu|y sə'lɪl.ə.kw|i, sɒl'ɪl- ⓊⓈ sə'lɪl- **-ies** -iz
solipsism 'sɒl.ɪp.sɪ.zᵊm, 'səʊ.lɪp- ⓊⓈ 'sɑː.lɪp-, 'soʊ- **-s** -z
solipsist 'sɒl.ɪp.sɪst ⓊⓈ 'sɑː.lɪp- **-s** -s **-ic** -ɪk
solitaire ˌsɒl.ɪ'teəʳ, '--- ⓊⓈ 'sɑː.lə.ter **-s** -z
solitar|y 'sɒl.ɪ.tᵊr|.i, '-ə-, -tr|i ⓊⓈ 'sɑː.lə.ter|.i **-ies** -iz **-ily** -ᵊl.i, -ɪ.li **-iness** -ɪ.nəs, -ɪ.nɪs ˌ**solitary con'finement**
solitude 'sɒl.ɪ.tjuːd, '-ə-, -tʃuːd ⓊⓈ 'sɑː.lə.tuːd, -tjuːd **-s** -z
Solloway 'sɒl.ə.weɪ ⓊⓈ 'sɑː.lə-
solo 'səʊ.ləʊ ⓊⓈ 'soʊ.loʊ **-s** -z
soloist 'səʊ.ləʊ.ɪst ⓊⓈ 'soʊ.loʊ- **-s** -s
Solomon 'sɒl.ə.mən ⓊⓈ 'sɑː.lə- **'Solomon ˌIslands**
Solon 'səʊ.lɒn, -lən ⓊⓈ 'soʊ.lən, -lɑːn
so-long ˌsəʊ'lɒŋ; sə- ⓊⓈ ˌsoʊ'lɑːŋ, sə-, -'lɔːŋ
solstic|e 'sɒl.stɪs ⓊⓈ 'sɑːl- **-es** -ɪz
Solti 'ʃɒl.ti ⓊⓈ 'soʊl.tiː
solubility ˌsɒl.jə'bɪl.ə.ti, -jʊ'-, -ɪ.ti ⓊⓈ ˌsɑːl.jə'bɪl.ə.t̬i, -jʊ'-
soluble 'sɒl.jə.bl̩, -jʊ- ⓊⓈ 'sɑːl-
solus 'səʊ.ləs ⓊⓈ 'soʊ-
solution sə'luː.ʃᵊn, -'ljuː- ⓊⓈ -'luː- **-s** -z
solvability ˌsɒl.və'bɪl.ə.ti, -ɪ.ti ⓊⓈ ˌsɑːl.və'bɪl.ə.t̬i
solv|e sɒlv ⓊⓈ sɑːlv **-es** -z **-ing** -ɪŋ **-ed** -d **-able** -ə.bl̩
solvency 'sɒl.vᵊnt.si ⓊⓈ 'sɑːl-
solvent 'sɒl.vənt ⓊⓈ 'sɑːl- **'solvent aˌbuse**
Solway 'sɒl.weɪ ⓊⓈ 'sɑːl-
Solzhenitsyn ˌsɒl.ʒə'nɪt.sɪn ⓊⓈ ˌsoʊl.ʒə'niːt-
som|a 'səʊ.m|ə ⓊⓈ 'soʊ- **-ata** -ə.tə ⓊⓈ -ə.t̬ə
Somali sə'mɑː.li ⓊⓈ soʊ-, sə- **-s** -z
Somali|a sə'mɑː.li|.ə ⓊⓈ soʊ-, sə- **-an/s** -ən/z
somatic səʊ'mæt.ɪk ⓊⓈ soʊ'mæt̬-
somatostatin ˌsəʊ.mə.tə'stæt.ɪn ⓊⓈ səˌmæt̬.ə'stæt.ᵊn; ˌsoʊ.mə.t̬ə'-
somatotropin səʊˌmæt.ə'trəʊ.pɪn; ˌsəʊ.mə.tə'- ⓊⓈ səˌmæt̬.ə'troʊ.pən; ˌsoʊ.mə.t̬ə'-
somb|er 'sɒm.b|əʳ ⓊⓈ 'sɑːm.b|ɚ **-erest** -ᵊr.ɪst, -ᵊr.əst **-erly** -ə.li ⓊⓈ -ɚ.li **-erness** -ə.nəs, -ə.nɪs ⓊⓈ -ɚ.nəs, -ɚ.nɪs
sombr|e 'sɒm.b|əʳ ⓊⓈ 'sɑːm.b|ɚ **-est** -ᵊr.ɪst, -ᵊr.əst **-ely** -ə.li **-eli** -ɚ.li **-eness** -ə.nəs, -ə.nɪs ⓊⓈ -ɚ.nəs, -ɚ.nɪs
sombrero sɒm'breə.rəʊ ⓊⓈ sɑːm'brer.oʊ, səm- **-s** -z
some *strong form:* sʌm *weak form:* sᵊm
Note: Weak form word. There are two grammatical functions for this word, one being the determiner, as in "some apples, some bananas", etc., where a weak form is used, the other being a quantifier, as in "some were tired and some were hungry", where the strong form is usual. In final position, the strong form is used (e.g. "I want some").
-some -səm
Note: Suffix. Does not normally change the stress pattern of the word to which it is added, e.g. **trouble** /'trʌb.l̩/, **troublesome** /'trʌb.l̩.səm/.
somebody 'sʌm.bə.di, -ˌbɒd.i ⓊⓈ -ˌbɑː.di, -ˌbʌd.i, -bə.di
someday 'sʌm.deɪ
somehow 'sʌm.haʊ
someone 'sʌm.wʌn
someplace 'sʌm.pleɪs
Somers 'sʌm.əz ⓊⓈ -ɚz
somersault 'sʌm.ə.sɔːlt, -sɒlt ⓊⓈ -ɚ.sɑːlt, -sɔːlt **-s** -s **-ing** -ɪŋ **-ed** -ɪd
Somerset 'sʌm.ə.set, -sɪt ⓊⓈ '-ɚ- **-shire** -ʃəʳ, -ˌʃɪəʳ ⓊⓈ -ʃɚ, -ʃɪr
Somerton 'sʌm.ə.tᵊn ⓊⓈ -ɚ.t̬ən
Somervell 'sʌm.ə.vɪl, -vel ⓊⓈ '-ɚ-
Somerville 'sʌm.ə.vɪl ⓊⓈ '-ɚ-
something 'sʌmp.θɪŋ
sometime 'sʌm.taɪm
sometimes 'sʌm.taɪmz
someway 'sʌm.weɪ
somewhat 'sʌm.hwɒt ⓊⓈ -hwɑːt, -hwʌt, -hwət
somewhere 'sʌm.hweəʳ ⓊⓈ -hwer

Somme sɒm (US) sʌm

sommelier sɒm'el.i.əʳ, sʌm-, -eɪ; 'sʌm.ᵊl.jeɪ, 'sɒm- (US) ˌsʌm.ᵊl'jeɪ **-s** -z

somnambul|ism sɒm'næm.bjə.l|ɪ.zᵊm, -bjʊ- (US) sɑːm'næm- **-ist/s** -ɪst/s

somniferous sɒm'nɪf.ᵊr.əs (US) sɑːm-

somnolen|ce 'sɒm.nᵊl.ən|ts (US) 'sɑːm- **-t/ly** -t/li

Sompting 'sɒm*p*.tɪŋ, 'sʌm*p*-

son (S) sʌn **-s** -z ˌ**son of a 'bitch** ; ˌ**son of a 'gun**

sonagram 'səʊ.nə.græm, 'sɒn.ə- (US) 'sɑː.nə-, 'soʊ- **-s** -z

sonagraph (S®) 'səʊ.nə.grɑːf, 'sɒn.ə-, -græf (US) 'sɑː.nə.græf, 'soʊ- **-s** -s

sonant 'səʊ.nənt (US) 'soʊ- **-s** -s

sonar 'səʊ.nɑːʳ (US) 'soʊ.nɑːr

sonata sə'nɑː.tə (US) -t̬ə **-s** -z

sonatina ˌsɒn.ə'tiː.nə (US) ˌsɑː.nə'- **-s** -z

Sondheim 'sɒnd.haɪm (US) 'sɑːnd-

son et lumière ˌsɒn.eɪ'luː.mjeəʳ, ˌsɔːn-, -luː'mjeəʳ (US) ˌsɑːn.eɪ'luː.mjer, ˌsɔːn-

song sɒŋ (US) sɑːŋ, sɔːŋ **-s** -z ˌ**song and 'dance** ; '**song ˌthrush**

songbird 'sɒŋ.bɜːd (US) 'sɑːŋ.bɜːrd, 'sɔːŋ- **-s** -z

songbook 'sɒŋ.bʊk (US) 'sɑːŋ-, 'sɔːŋ- **-s** -s

songfest 'sɒŋ.fest (US) 'sɑːŋ-, 'sɔːŋ- **-s** -s

songster 'sɒŋ*k*.stəʳ (US) 'sɑːŋ*k*.stɚ, 'sɔːŋ*k*- **-s** -z

songwrit|er 'sɒŋˌraɪ.t|əʳ (US) 'sɑːŋˌraɪ.t̬|ɚ, 'sɔːŋ- **-ers** -əz (US) -ɚz **-ing** -ɪŋ

Sonia 'sɒn.jə, 'səʊ.njə (US) 'sɑː.njə, 'soʊ-

sonic 'sɒn.ɪk (US) 'sɑː.nɪk ˌ**sonic 'boom**

son-in-law 'sʌn.ɪn.lɔː (US) -lɑː, -lɔː **sons-in-law** 'sʌnz-

sonnet 'sɒn.ɪt (US) 'sɑː.nɪt **-s** -s

sonneteer ˌsɒn.ɪ'tɪəʳ, -ə'- (US) ˌsɑː.nə'tɪr **-s** -z

Sonning 'sɒn.ɪŋ, 'sʌn- (US) 'sɑː.nɪŋ, 'sʌn.ɪŋ

sonn|y 'sʌn|.i **-ies** -iz

sonogram 'səʊ.nə.græm, 'sɒn.ə- (US) 'sɑː.nə-, 'soʊ- **-s** -z

sonograph 'səʊ.nə.grɑːf, 'sɒn.ə-, -græf (US) 'sɑː.nə.græf, 'soʊ- **-s** -s

sonometer səʊ'nɒm.ɪ.təʳ, '-ə- (US) sə'nɑː.mə.t̬ɚ, soʊ- **-s** -z

Sonora sə'nɔː.rə (US) -'nɔːr.ə

sonorant 'sɒn.ᵊr.ənt, 'səʊ.nᵊr- (US) 'sɑː.nɚ-, 'soʊ-; sə'nɔːr-, soʊ- **-s** -s

sonorit|y səʊ'nɒr.ə.t|i, -ɪ.t|i (US) sə'nɔːr.ə.t̬|i, soʊ- **-ies** -iz

sonorous 'sɒn.ᵊr.əs; sə'nɔː.rəs (US) sə'nɔːr.əs, soʊ-; 'sɑː.nɚ-, 'soʊ- **-ly** -li

sonsie, sonsy 'sɒn*t*.si (US) 'sɑːn*t*-

Sontag 'sɒn.tæg (US) 'sɑːn-

Sony® 'səʊ.ni, 'sɒn.i (US) 'soʊ.ni

Sonya 'sɒn.jə, 'səʊ.njə (US) 'sɑː.njə, 'soʊ-

soon suːn **-er** -əʳ (US) -ɚ **-est** -ɪst, -əst ˌ**sooner or 'later**

soot sʊt (US) sʊt, suːt

sooth suːθ

sooth|e suːð **-es** -z **-ing/ly** -ɪŋ/li **-ed** -d

soothsayer 'suːθˌseɪ.əʳ (US) -ɚ **-s** -z

soot|y (S) 'sʊt|.i (US) 'sʊt̬-, 'suː.t̬|i **-ier** -i.əʳ (US) -i.ɚ **-iest** -i.ɪst, -i.əst **-iness** -ɪ.nəs, -ɪ.nɪs

sop sɒp (US) sɑːp **-s** -s **-ping** -ɪŋ **-ped** -t

Sophia səʊ'fiː.ə, -'faɪ- (US) soʊ-

Sophie 'səʊ.fi (US) 'soʊ-

soph|ism 'sɒf|.ɪ.zᵊm (US) 'sɑː.f|ɪ- **-isms** -ɪ.zᵊmz **-ist/s** -ɪst/s

sophister 'sɒf.ɪ.stəʳ (US) 'sɑː.fɪ.stɚ **-s** -z

sophistic səʊ'fɪs.tɪk (US) sə- **-al** -ᵊl **-ally** -ᵊl.i, -li

sophisti|cate (*v.*) sə'fɪs.tɪ|.keɪt (US) -tə- **-cates** -keɪts **-cating** -keɪ.tɪŋ (US) -keɪ.t̬ɪŋ **-cated** -keɪ.tɪd (US) -keɪ.t̬ɪd

sophisticate (*n.*) sə'fɪs.tɪ.kət, -kɪt, -keɪt (US) -tə.kɪt **-s** -s

sophistication səˌfɪs.tɪ'keɪ.ʃᵊn (US) -tə'-

sophistr|y 'sɒf.ɪ.str|i (US) 'sɑː.fɪ- **-ies** -iz

Sophoclean ˌsɒf.ə'kliː.ən (US) ˌsɑː.fə'-

Sophocles 'sɒf.ə.kliːz (US) 'sɑː.fə-

sophomore 'sɒf.ə.mɔːʳ (US) 'sɑː.fə.mɔːr **-s** -z

Sophy 'səʊ.fi (US) 'soʊ-

soporific ˌsɒp.ᵊr'ɪf.ɪk, ˌsəʊ.pᵊr'- (US) ˌsɑː.pə'rɪf-, ˌsoʊ- **-ally** -ᵊl.i, -li

sopping 'sɒp.ɪŋ (US) 'sɑː.pɪŋ ˌ**sopping 'wet**

sopp|y 'sɒp|.i (US) 'sɑː.p|i **-ier** -i.əʳ (US) -i.ɚ **-iest** -i.ɪst, -i.əst **-iness** -ɪ.nəs, -ɪ.nɪs **-ily** -ɪ.li

sopranino ˌsɒp.rə'niː.nəʊ (US) ˌsoʊ.prə'niː.noʊ **-s** -z

sopran|o sə'prɑː.n|əʊ (US) -'præn|.oʊ, -'prɑː.n|oʊ **-os** -əʊz (US) -oʊz **-i** -iː

Sopwith 'sɒp.wɪθ (US) 'sɑːp- **-s** -s

sorbet 'sɔː.beɪ (US) 'sɔːr.beɪ; sɔːr'bət **-s** -s

sorbic 'sɔː.bɪk (US) 'sɔːr- ˌ**sorbic 'acid**

sorbitol 'sɔː.bɪ.tɒl (US) 'sɔːr.bɪ.tɑːl, -tɔːl, -toʊl

Sorbonne sɔː'bɒn (US) sɔːr'bɑːn, -'bʌn

sorcer|y 'sɔː.sᵊr|.i (US) 'sɔːr- **-ies** -iz **-er/s** -əʳ/z (US) ɚz **-ess/es** -ɪs/ɪz, -es/ɪz

Sorcha 'sɔː.ʃə

Sordello sɔː'del.əʊ (US) sɔːr'del.oʊ

sordid 'sɔː.dɪd (US) 'sɔːr- **-ly** -li **-ness** -nəs, -nɪs

sordin|o sɔː'diː.n|əʊ (US) sɔːr'diː.n|oʊ **-i** -iː

sor|e sɔːʳ (US) sɔːr **-es** -z **-er** -əʳ (US) -ɚ **-est** -ɪst, -əst **-ely** -li **-eness** -nəs, -nɪs

sorghum 'sɔː.gəm (US) 'sɔːr-

Soroptimist sə'rɒp.tɪ.mɪst, -tə- (US) -'rɑːp.tɪ- **-s** -s

sororit|y sə'rɒr.ə.t|i, sɒr'ɒr-, -ɪ.t|i (US) sə'rɔːr.ə.t̬|i **-ies** -iz

sorrel 'sɒr.ᵊl (US) 'sɔːr-

Sorrento sə'ren.təʊ (US) -toʊ

sorrow 'sɒr.əʊ (US) 'sɑːr.oʊ **-s** -z **-ing/ly** -ɪŋ/li **-ed** -d **-er/s** -əʳ/z (US) -ɚ/z

sorrow|ful 'sɒr.əʊ|.fᵊl, -fʊl (US) 'sɑːr.ə- **-fully** -fᵊl.i, -fli, -fʊl.i **-fulness** -fᵊl.nəs, -fʊl.nəs, -nɪs

sorr|y 'sɒr|.i (US) 'sɑːr- **-ier** -i.əʳ (US) -i.ɚ **-iest** -i.ɪst, -i.əst **-ily** -ᵊl.i, -ɪ.li **-iness** -ɪ.nəs, -ɪ.nɪs

sort sɔːt (US) sɔːrt **-s** -s **-ing** -ɪŋ (US) 'sɔːr.t̬ɪŋ **-ed** -ɪd (US) 'sɔːr.t̬ɪd **-er/s** -əʳ/z (US) 'sɔːr.t̬ɚ/z

sortie 'sɔː.ti (US) 'sɔːr.tiː, ˌ-'- **-s** -z

sortilege 'sɔː.tɪ.lɪdʒ (US) 'sɔːr.t̬ᵊl.ɪdʒ, -edʒ

SOS ˌes.əʊ'es (US) -oʊ'-

so-so 'səʊ.səʊ, ˌ-'- (US) 'soʊ.soʊ, ˌ-'-

sostenuto ˌsɒs.tə'nuː.təʊ, -tɪ'-, -'njuː- (US) ˌsɑː.stə'nuː.t̬oʊ, ˌsoʊ-

sot sɒt (US) sɑːt **-s** -s

Sotheby 'sʌð.ə.bi **-'s** -z

Sothern 'sʌð.ᵊn (US) -ɚn

Sotho 'suː.tuː, 'səʊ.təʊ (US) 'soʊ.toʊ **-s** -z

sottish 'sɒt.ɪʃ (US) 'sɑː.t̬ɪʃ **-ly** -li **-ness** -nəs, -nɪs

sotto voce ˌsɒt.əʊ'vəʊ.tʃeɪ (US) ˌsɑː.t̬oʊ'voʊ-

sou suː **-s** -z

soubise suː'biːz

soubrette suː'bret, sʊ- (US) suː- **-s** -s

soubriquet 'suː.brɪ.keɪ, 'soʊ-, -brə- (US) 'suː.brə-, -ket **-s** -z

souchong ˌsuː'*t*ʃɒŋ, '-- (US) 'suː.tʃɑːŋ, -ʃɑːŋ

souffle 'suː.fl̩ **-s** -z

soufflé 'suː.fleɪ (US) suː'fleɪ, '-- **-s** -z **-ed** -d

sough saʊ, sʌf **-s** saʊz, sʌfs **-ing** 'saʊ.ɪŋ, 'sʌf.ɪŋ **-ed** saʊd, sʌft

sought (*from* seek) sɔːt (US) sɑːt, sɔːt

sought-after 'sɔːtˌɑːf.təʳ (US) 'sɑːtˌæf.tɚ, 'sɔːt-

souk suːk **-s** -s

soul səʊl (US) soʊl **-s** -z '**soul ˌfood** ; '**soul ˌmate**

Soulbury 'səʊl.bᵊr.i (US) 'soʊl-, -ber.i

soul-destroying 'səʊl.dɪˌstrɔɪ.ɪŋ (US) 'soʊl-

soulful ˈsəʊl.fəl, -fʊl ⓤⓢ ˈsoʊl- **-ly** -i **-ness** -nəs, -nɪs
soulless ˈsəʊl.ləs, -lɪs ⓤⓢ ˈsoʊl- **-ly** -li **-ness** -nəs, -nɪs
soul-searching ˈsəʊlˌsɜː.tʃɪŋ ⓤⓢ ˈsoʊlˌsɜːr-
sound saʊnd **-s** -z **-er** -əʳ ⓤⓢ -ɚ **-est** -ɪst, -əst **-ly** -li **-ness** -nəs, -nɪs **-ing/s** -ɪŋ/z **-ed** -ɪd **ˈsound ˌbarrier ; ˈsound ˌbite ; ˈsound ˌbox ; ˈsound efˌfect**
soundboard ˈsaʊnd.bɔːd, ˈsaʊm- ⓤⓢ ˈsaʊnd.bɔːrd **-s** -z
soundless ˈsaʊnd.ləs, -lɪs **-ly** -li
soundproof ˈsaʊnd.pruːf, ˈsaʊm- ⓤⓢ ˈsaʊnd- **-s** -s **-ing** -ɪŋ **-ed** -t
soundtrack ˈsaʊnd.træk **-s** -s
soundwave ˈsaʊnd.weɪv **-s** -z
soup suːp **-s** -s **-y** -i **-ed** -t **ˈsoup ˌkitchen ; ˌsouped ˈup**
soupçon ˈsuːp.sɔ̃ːŋ, -sɒŋ, -sɒn ⓤⓢ suːpˈsõʊn, suː-, -ˈsɑːn, ˈ-- **-s** -z
soupspoon ˈsuːp.spuːn **-s** -z
sour saʊəʳ ⓤⓢ saʊɚ **-er** -əʳ ⓤⓢ -ɚ **-est** -ɪst, -əst **-ly** -li **-ness** -nəs, -nɪs **-s** -z **-ing** -ɪŋ **-ed** -d **ˌsour ˈcream ; ˌsour ˈgrapes**
sourc|e sɔːs ⓤⓢ sɔːrs **-es** -ɪz **-ing** -ɪŋ **-ed** -t
sourdine sʊəˈdiːn ⓤⓢ sʊr- **-s** -z
sourdough ˈsaʊə.dəʊ ⓤⓢ ˈsaʊɚ.doʊ
sourpuss ˈsaʊə.pʊs ⓤⓢ ˈsaʊɚ- **-es** -ɪz
Sousa ˈsuː.zə ⓤⓢ -zə, -sə
sousaphone ˈsuː.zə.fəʊn ⓤⓢ -zə.foʊn, -sə- **-s** -z
sous-chef ˈsuː.ʃef **-s** -s
sous|e saʊs **-es** -ɪz **-ing** -ɪŋ **-ed** -t
Sousse suːs
soutane suːˈtɑːn ⓤⓢ -ˈtæn, -ˈtɑːn **-s** -z
Souter ˈsuː.təʳ ⓤⓢ -t̬ɚ
south (S) (*n. adj. adv.*) saʊθ **ˌSouth ˈAfrica ; ˌSouth AˈmerIca ; ˌSouth CaroˈlIna ; ˌSouth DaˈkOta ; ˌSouth ˈIsland** ⓤⓢ **ˈSouth ˌIsland ; ˌSouth KoˈrEa ; ˌsouth ˈpole ; ˌSouth ˈSeas**
Southall *place in London:* ˈsaʊ.θɔːl, -ðɔːl ⓤⓢ -θɔːl, -θɑːl, -ðɔːl, -ðɑːl *surname:* ˈsʌð.ɔːl, -əl ⓤⓢ -ɔːl, -ɑːl, -əl
Southam ˈsaʊ.θəm
Southampton saʊˈθæmp.tən, saʊθˈhæmp-
southbound ˈsaʊθ.baʊnd
Southbourne ˈsaʊθ.bɔːn ⓤⓢ -bɔːrn
Southdown ˈsaʊθ.daʊn
southeast (S) ˌsaʊθˈiːst *in nautical usage also:* ˌsaʊ- **-wards** -wədz ⓤⓢ -wɚdz *stress shift:* ˌsoutheast ˈwind
south-easter ˌsaʊθˈiː.stəʳ ⓤⓢ -stɚ *in nautical usage also:* ˌsaʊ- **-s** -z
southeasterl|y ˌsaʊθˈiː.stəl.i ⓤⓢ -stɚ.li *in nautical usage also:* ˌsaʊ- **-ies** -iz
southeastern (S) ˌsaʊθˈiː.stən ⓤⓢ -stɚn *in nautical usage also:* ˌsaʊ- **-er/s** -əʳ/z ⓤⓢ -ɚ/z *stress shift:* ˌsoutheastern ˈwind
southeastward ˌsaʊθˈiːst.wəd ⓤⓢ -wɚd **-s** -z
Southend ˌsaʊθˈend *stress shift:* ˌSouthend ˈpier
southerl|y ˈsʌð.əl|.i ⓤⓢ -ɚ.l|i **-ies** -iz
southern (S) ˈsʌð.ən ⓤⓢ -ɚn **-most** -ən.məʊst, -əm.məʊst ⓤⓢ -ɚn.moʊst **ˌSouthern ˈCross**
southerner (S) ˈsʌð.ən.əʳ ⓤⓢ -ɚ.nɚ **-s** -z
southernwood ˈsʌð.ən.wʊd ⓤⓢ -ɚn-
Southey ˈsaʊ.ði, ˈsʌð.i
Southgate ˈsaʊθ.geɪt, -gɪt
Southon ˈsaʊ.ðən
southpaw ˈsaʊθ.pɔː ⓤⓢ -pɑː, -pɔː **-s** -z
Southport ˈsaʊθ.pɔːt ⓤⓢ -pɔːrt
southron (S) ˈsʌð.rən **-s** -z
Southsea ˈsaʊθ.siː, -si
south-southeast ˌsaʊθ.saʊθˈiːst *in nautical usage also:* ˌsaʊ.saʊ-
south-southwest ˌsaʊθ.saʊθˈwest *in nautical usage also:* ˌsaʊ.saʊ-
southward ˈsaʊθ.wəd ⓤⓢ -wɚd **-s** -z **-ly** -li
Southwark ˈsʌð.ək ⓤⓢ -ɚk
Southwell *surname:* ˈsaʊθ.wəl, -wel; ˈsʌð.əl *town in Nottinghamshire:* ˈsaʊθ.wəl *locally:* ˈsʌð.əl
Note: Viscount Southwell is /ˈsʌð.əl/.
southwest (S) ˌsaʊθˈwest *in nautical usage also:* ˌsaʊ- **-wards** -wədz ⓤⓢ -wɚdz *stress shift:* ˌsouthwest ˈwind
south-wester ˌsaʊθˈwes.təʳ ⓤⓢ -tɚ *in nautical usage also:* ˌsaʊ- **-s** -z
south-westerl|y ˌsaʊθˈwes.təl|.i ⓤⓢ -tɚ.l|i *in nautical usage also:* ˌsaʊ- **-ies** -iz
southwestern (S) ˌsaʊθˈwes.tən ⓤⓢ -tɚn *in nautical usage also:* ˌsaʊ- **-er/s** -əʳ/z ⓤⓢ -ɚ/z *stress shift:* ˌsouthwestern ˈwind
south-westward ˌsaʊθˈwest.wəd ⓤⓢ -wɚd *in nautical usage also:* ˌsaʊ- **-s** -z
Southwick *in West Sussex:* ˈsaʊθ.wɪk *in Northamptonshire:* ˈsʌð.ɪk *in Hampshire:* ˈsʌð.ɪk, ˈsaʊθ.wɪk
Southwold ˈsaʊθ.wəʊld ⓤⓢ -woʊld
Soutter ˈsuː.təʳ ⓤⓢ -t̬ɚ
souvenir ˌsuː.vənˈɪəʳ, -vɪˈnɪəʳ, ˈ--- ⓤⓢ ˌsuː.vəˈnɪr, ˈ--- **-s** -z
sou'wester ˌsaʊˈwes.təʳ ⓤⓢ -tɚ **-s** -z
Souza ˈsuː.zə
sovereign ˈsɒv.ər.ɪn, ˈ-rɪn ⓤⓢ ˈsɑːv.rən, -ɚ.ən **-s** -z **-ly** -li
sovereignty ˈsɒv.rən.ti, -rɪn- ⓤⓢ ˈsɑːv.rən.t̬i, -ɚ.ən-
soviet (S) ˈsəʊ.vi.ət, ˈsɒv.i- ⓤⓢ ˈsoʊ.vi.et, -ɪt; ˌ--ˈ- **-s** -s **-ism** -ɪ.zəm **ˌSoviet ˈUnion**
sovran ˈsɒv.rən ⓤⓢ ˈsɑːv- **-s** -z
sow (*n.*) *pig, metal, channel for metal:* saʊ **-s** -z
sow (*v.*) *plant seed:* səʊ ⓤⓢ soʊ **-s** -z **-ing** -ɪŋ **-ed** -d **-n** -n **-er/s** -əʳ/z ⓤⓢ -ɚ/z
Sowerby *in North Yorkshire:* ˈsaʊə.bi ⓤⓢ ˈsaʊɚ- *in West Yorkshire, surname:* ˈsəʊə.bi, ˈsaʊə- ⓤⓢ ˈsoʊɚ-, ˈsaʊɚ-
Soweto səˈwet.əʊ, -ˈweɪ.təʊ ⓤⓢ -ˈwet̬.oʊ, -ˈweɪ.t̬oʊ
sox sɒks ⓤⓢ sɑːks
soy sɔɪ **ˌsoy ˈsauce** ⓤⓢ **ˈsoy ˌsauce**
soya ˈsɔɪ.ə **ˈsoya ˌbean**
soybean ˈsɔɪ.biːn **-s** -z
Soyinka sɔɪˈɪŋ.kə
Soyuz sɔːˈjuz, səˈjuːz ⓤⓢ ˈsɑː.juːz, ˈsɔɪ.jʊz
sozzled ˈsɒz.l̩d ⓤⓢ ˈsɑː.zl̩d
spa (S) spɑː **-s** -z
spac|e speɪs **-es** -ɪz **-ing** -ɪŋ **-ed** -t **ˈspace ˌage ; ˈspace ˌbar ; ˈspace ˌshuttle ; ˈspace ˌstation ; ˈspace ˌsuit ; ˈspace ˌwalk**
spacecraft ˈspeɪs.krɑːft ⓤⓢ -kræft **-s** -s
spaced-out ˌspeɪstˈaʊt *stress shift:* ˌspaced-out ˈperson
spacelab ˈspeɪs.læb **-s** -z
space|man ˈspeɪs|.mæn, -mən **-men** -men, -mən
spaceship ˈspeɪs.ʃɪp, ˈspeɪʃ- ⓤⓢ ˈspeɪs- **-s** -s
space-time ˌspeɪsˈtaɪm *stress shift:* ˌspace-time conˈtinuum
spacewalk ˈspeɪs.wɔːk ⓤⓢ -wɔːk, -wɑːk **-s** -s **-ing** -ɪŋ **-ed** -t **-er/s** -əʳ/z ⓤⓢ -ɚ/z
spac|ey ˈspeɪ.s|i **-ier** -i.əʳ ⓤⓢ -i.ɚ **-iest** -i.ɪst, -i.əst **-iness** -ɪ.nəs, -ɪ.nɪs
spacious ˈspeɪ.ʃəs **-ly** -li **-ness** -nəs, -nɪs
spade speɪd **-s** -z **-ful/s** -fʊl/z **ˌcall a ˌspade a ˈspade**
spadework ˈspeɪd.wɜːk ⓤⓢ -wɜːrk
spaghetti spəˈget.i ⓤⓢ -ˈget̬- **spaˌghetti bologˈnese**
spahi ˈspɑː.hiː, -iː ⓤⓢ -hiː **-s** -z
Spain speɪn
spake (*archaic past tense of* **speak**) speɪk
Spalding ˈspɔːl.dɪŋ, ˈspɒl- ⓤⓢ ˈspɔːl-, ˈspɑːl-
spall spɔːl ⓤⓢ spɔːl, spɑːl **-s** -z **-ing** -ɪŋ **-ed** -d
Spam® spæm
span spæn **-s** -z **-ning** -ɪŋ **-ned** -d
Spandau ˈspæn.daʊ
spandex ˈspæn.deks

spandrel 'spæn.drəl **-s** -z
spangl|e 'spæŋ.gl̩ **-es** -z **-ing** -ɪŋ, 'spæŋ.glɪŋ **-ed** -d
Spaniard 'spæn.jəd (US) -jɚd **-s** -z
spaniel 'spæn.jəl **-s** -z
Spanish 'spæn.ɪʃ ˌ**Spanish 'fly** ; ˌ**Spanish 'omelette** ; ˌ**Spanish 'onion** ; ˌ**Spanish Sa'hara**
spank spæŋk **-s** -s **-ing** -ɪŋ **-ed** -t **-er/s** -əʳ/z (US) -ɚ/z
spanking 'spæŋ.kɪŋ **-s** -z **-ly**
spanner 'spæn.əʳ (US) -ɚ **-s** -z
spar spɑːʳ (US) spɑːr **-s** -z **-ring** -ɪŋ **-red** -d **'sparring ˌmatch** ; **'sparring ˌpartner**
spar|e speəʳ (US) sper **-ely** -li **-eness** -nəs, -nɪs **-es** -z **-ing** -ɪŋ/li **-ed** -d ˌ**spare 'part** ; ˌ**spare 'rib** ; ˌ**spare 'tyre**
sparing 'speə.rɪŋ (US) 'sper.ɪŋ **-ly** -li
spark (S) spɑːk (US) spɑːrk **-s** -s **-ing** -ɪŋ **-ed** -t **'spark ˌplug** ; **'sparking ˌplug**
Sparkes spɑːks (US) spɑːrks
sparkl|e 'spɑː.kl̩ (US) 'spɑːr- **-es** -z **-ing** -ɪŋ, 'spɑː.klɪŋ (US) 'spɑːr- **-ed** -d ˌ**sparkling 'wine**
sparkler 'spɑː.kləʳ (US) 'spɑːr.klɚ **-s** -z
spark|y 'spɑː.k|i (US) 'spɑːr.k|i **-ier** -i.əʳ (US) -i.ɚ **-iest** -i.ɪst, -i.əst **-iness** -ɪ.nəs, -ɪ.nɪs **-ily** -ɪ.li
sparrow (S) 'spær.əʊ (US) 'sper.oʊ, 'spær- **-s** -z
sparrowhawk 'spær.əʊ.hɔːk (US) 'sper.oʊ.hɑːk, 'spær-, -hɔːk **-s** -s
spars|e spɑːs (US) spɑːrs **-er** -əʳ (US) -ɚ **-est** -ɪst, -əst **-ely** -li **-eness** -nəs, -nɪs **-ity** -ə.ti, -ɪ.ti (US) -ə.t̬i
Spar|ta 'spɑː|.tə (US) 'spɑːr|.t̬ə **-tan/s** -tən/z
Spartacus 'spɑː.tə.kəs (US) 'spɑːr.t̬ə-
spartan 'spɑː.tən (US) 'spɑːr-
spasm 'spæz.əm **-s** -z
spasmodic spæz'mɒd.ɪk (US) -'mɑː.dɪk **-ally** -əl.i, -li
spastic 'spæs.tɪk **-s** -s
spasticity spæs'tɪs.ə.ti, -ɪ.ti (US) -ə.t̬i
spat spæt **-s** -s **-ting** -ɪŋ **-ted** -ɪd
spatchcock 'spætʃ.kɒk (US) -kɑːk **-s** -s **-ing** -ɪŋ **-ed** -t
spate speɪt **-s** -s
spatial 'speɪ.ʃəl **-ly** -i
spatt|er 'spæt|.əʳ (US) 'spæt̬|.ɚ **-ers** -əz (US) -ɚz **-ering** -ər.ɪŋ **-ered** -əd (US) -ɚd
spatul|a 'spæt.jə.l|ə, -jʊ-, 'spætʃ.ə-, '-ʊ- (US) 'spætʃ.ə- **-ae** -iː **-as** -əz
spatulate 'spæt.jə.lət, -jʊ-, 'spætʃ.ə-, '-ʊ-, -lɪt, -leɪt (US) 'spætʃ.ə.lɪt, -leɪt
spavin 'spæv.ɪn **-ed** -d
spawn spɔːn (US) spɑːn, spɔːn **-s** -z **-ing** -ɪŋ **-ed** -d
spay speɪ **-s** -z **-ing** -ɪŋ **-ed** -d
Speaight speɪt
speak spiːk **-s** -s **-ing** -ɪŋ **spoke** spəʊk (US) spoʊk **spoken** 'spəʊ.kən (US) 'spoʊ- **speaker/s** 'spiː.kəʳ/z (US) -kɚ/z
speakeas|y 'spiːkˌiː.z|i **-ies** -iz
Spean spɪən, 'spiː.ən (US) 'spiː.ən
spear spɪəʳ (US) spɪr **-s** -z **-ing** -ɪŋ **-ed** -d
spearhead 'spɪə.hed (US) 'spɪr- **-s** -z **-ing** -ɪŋ **-ed** -ɪd
spear|man (S) 'spɪə|.mən (US) 'spɪr- **-men** -mən, -men
spearmint 'spɪə.mɪnt (US) 'spɪr-
spec spek
speci|al 'speʃ|.əl **-als** -əlz **-ally** -əl.i, -li **-alness** -əl.nəs, -əl.nɪs **'Special ˌBranch** ; ˌ**special de'livery** ; ˌ**special ef'fects**
special|ism 'speʃ.əl.ɪ|.zəm, '-lɪ- (US) '-əl.ɪ- **-s** -z
specialist 'speʃ.əl.ɪst **-s** -s
specialit|y ˌspeʃ.i'æl.ə.t|i, -ɪ.t|i (US) -ə.t̬|i **-ies** -iz
specialization, -isa- ˌspeʃ.əl.aɪ'zeɪ.ʃən, -ɪ'- (US) -ɪ'-
specializ|e, -is|e 'speʃ.əl.aɪz (US) -ə.laɪz **-es** -ɪz **-ing** -ɪŋ **-ed** -d
specialt|y 'speʃ.əl.t|i (US) -t̬|i **-ies** -iz
specie 'spiː.ʃiː, -ʃi (US) -ʃiː, -siː
species 'spiː.ʃiːz, -ʃɪz, -siːz, -sɪz (US) -ʃiːz, -siːz **-ism** -ɪ.zəm
specific spə'sɪf.ɪk, spɪ- (US) spə- **-s** -s **-ally** -əl.i, -li speˌ**cific 'gravity**
specification ˌspes.ɪ.fɪ'keɪ.ʃən, ˌ-ə- (US) ˌ-ə- **-s** -z
specificity ˌspes.ɪ'fɪs.ə.ti, -ɪ.ti (US) -ə'fɪs.ə.t̬i
speci|fy 'spes.ɪ|.faɪ, '-ə- (US) '-ə- **-fies** -faɪz **-fying** -faɪ.ɪŋ **-fied** -faɪd **-fiable** -faɪ.ə.bl̩
specimen 'spes.ə.mɪn, '-ɪ-, -mən (US) -ə.mən **-s** -z
specious 'spiː.ʃəs **-ly** -li **-ness** -nəs, -nɪs
speck spek **-s** -s **-ed** -t
speckle 'spek.l̩ **-s** -z **-d** -d
speckless 'spek.ləs, -lɪs
specs speks
spectacle 'spek.tə.kl̩, -tɪ- **-s** -z **-d** -d
spectacular spek'tæk.jə.ləʳ, -jʊ- (US) -lɚ **-ly** -li
spectat|e spek'teɪt **-es** -s **-ing** -ɪŋ **-ed** -ɪd
spectator (S) spek'teɪ.təʳ (US) -t̬ɚ **-s** -z specˌ**tator 'sport**, **spec'tator ˌsport**
specter 'spek.təʳ (US) -tɚ **-s** -z
spectral 'spek.trəl
spectre 'spek.təʳ (US) -tɚ **-s** -z
spectrogram 'spek.trəʊ.græm (US) -trə- **-s** -z
spectrograph 'spek.trəʊ.grɑːf, -græf (US) -trə.græf **-s** -s
spectrographic ˌspek.trəʊ'græf.ɪk (US) -trə'- *stress shift:* ˌspectrographic 'section
spectrography spek'trɒg.rə.fi (US) -'trɑː.grə-
spectrometer spek'trɒm.ɪ.təʳ, '-ə- (US) -'trɑː.mə.t̬ɚ **-s** -z
spectroscope 'spek.trə.skəʊp (US) -trə.skoʊp **-s** -s
spectroscopic ˌspek.trə'skɒp.ɪk (US) -'skɑː.pɪk **-al** -əl **-ally** -əl.i, -li *stress shift:* ˌspectroscopic 'picture
spectroscop|ist spek'trɒs.kə.p|ɪst (US) -'trɑː.skə- **-ists** -ɪsts **-y** -i
spectr|um 'spek.tr|əm **-a** -ə **-ums** -əmz
specu|late 'spek.jə|.leɪt, -jʊ- **-lates** -leɪts **-lating** -leɪ.tɪŋ (US) -leɪ.t̬ɪŋ **-lated** -leɪ.tɪd (US) -leɪ.t̬ɪd **-lator/s** -leɪ.təʳ/z (US) -leɪ.t̬ɚ/z
speculation ˌspek.jə'leɪ.ʃən, -jʊ'- **-s** -z
speculative 'spek.jə.lə.tɪv, -jʊ-, -leɪ- (US) -leɪ.t̬ɪv, -lə- **-ly** -li **-ness** -nəs, -nɪs
specul|um 'spek.jə.l|əm, -jʊ- **-a** -ə **-ar** -əʳ (US) -ɚ
sped (*from* **speed**) sped
speech spiːtʃ **-es** -ɪz **'speech ˌday** ; **'speech imˌpediment** ; ˌ**speech 'synthesiser**
speechification ˌspiː.tʃɪ.fɪ'keɪ.ʃən, -tʃə- (US) -tʃə- **-s** -z
speechi|fy 'spiː.tʃɪ|.faɪ, -tʃə- (US) -tʃə- **-fies** -faɪz **-fying** -faɪ.ɪŋ **-fied** -faɪd **-fier/s** -faɪ.əʳ/z (US) -faɪ.ɚ/z
speechless 'spiːtʃ.ləs, -lɪs **-ly** -li **-ness** -nəs, -nɪs
speed (S) spiːd **-s** -z **-ing** -ɪŋ **-ed** -ɪd **sped** sped **'speed ˌbump** ; **'speed ˌlimit** ; **'speed ˌtrap**
speedboat 'spiːd.bəʊt (US) -boʊt **-s** -s
speed-cop 'spiːd.kɒp (US) -kɑːp **-s** -s
speedo 'spiː.dəʊ (US) -doʊ **-s** -z
speedometer spiː'dɒm.ɪ.təʳ, spɪ-, -mə- (US) -'dɑː.mə.t̬ɚ **-s** -z
speed-read 'spiːd.riːd **-s** -z **-ing** -ɪŋ *past tense:* 'spiːd.red
speedway 'spiːd.weɪ **-s** -z
speedwell (S) 'spiːd.wel, -wəl **-s** -z
Speedwriting® 'spiːdˌraɪ.tɪŋ (US) -t̬ɪŋ
speed|y 'spiː.d|i **-ier** -i.əʳ (US) -i.ɚ **-iest** -i.ɪst, -i.əst **-ily** -əl.i, -ɪ.li **-iness** -ɪ.nəs, -ɪ.nɪs
Speen spiːn
Speer speəʳ *as if German:* ʃpeəʳ (US) spɪr *as if German:* ʃper
Speight speɪt
Speirs spɪəz (US) spɪrz
speiss spaɪs
Speke spiːk
speleological ˌspiː.li.ə'lɒdʒ.ɪ.kəl, ˌspel.i- (US) -'lɑː.dʒɪ-
speleolog|y ˌspiː.li'ɒl.ə.dʒ|i, ˌspel.i'- (US) ˌspiː.li'ɑː.lə- **-ist/s** -ɪst/s
spell spel **-s** -z **-ing/s** -ɪŋ/z **-ed** -t, -d **spelt** -t **speller/s** 'spel.əʳ/z (US) -ɚ/z **'spelling ˌbee**

spell|bind ˈspel|.baɪnd **-binds** -baɪndz **-binding** -baɪn.dɪŋ **-bound** -baʊnd **-binder/s** -ˌbaɪn.dəʳ/z (US) -ˌbaɪn.dɚ/z
spellbound ˈspel.baʊnd
spelt (*from* **spell**) spelt
spelt|er ˈspel.t|əʳ (US) -t̬|ɚ **-ers** -əz (US) -ɚz **-ering** -ᵊr.ɪŋ **-ered** -əd (US) -ɚd
spelunk|er spəˈlʌŋ.k|əʳ (US) -k|ɚ; ˈspiː.lʌŋ- **-er/s** -ᵊr.əʳ/z (US) -ɚ.ɚ/z **-ing** -ɪŋ
spenc|e (S) spents **-es** -ɪz
spencer (S) ˈspent.səʳ (US) -sɚ **-s** -z
spend spend **-s** -z **-ing** -ɪŋ **spent** -t **spender/s** ˈspen.dəʳ/z (US) -dɚ/z
Spender ˈspen.dəʳ (US) -dɚ
spendthrift ˈspend.θrɪft **-s** -s
Spengler ˈspeŋ.gləʳ (US) -glɚ
Spenlow ˈspen.ləʊ (US) -loʊ
Spennymoor ˈspen.i.mɔːʳ, -mʊəʳ (US) -mɔːr, -mʊr
Spens spenz
Spenser ˈspent.səʳ (US) -sɚ
Spenserian spenˈsɪə.ri.ən (US) -ˈsɪr.i-
spent (*from* **spend**) spent
sperm spɜːm (US) spɜːrm **-s** -z ˈ**sperm** ˌ**bank** ; ˈ**sperm** ˌ**whale**
spermaceti ˌspɜː.məˈset.i, -ˈsiː.ti (US) ˌspɜːr.məˈsiː.ti, -ˈset.i
spermatozo|on ˌspɜː.mə.təʊˈzəʊ|.ɒn, -ən (US) ˌspɜːr.mə.t̬əˈzoʊ|.ɑːn, -ən **-a** -ə
spermicidal ˌspɜː.mɪˈsaɪ.dᵊl (US) ˌspɜːr.məˈ-
spermicide ˈspɜː.mɪ.saɪd (US) ˈspɜːr.mə- **-s** -z
Sperrin ˈsper.ɪn
spew spjuː **-s** -z **-ing** -ɪŋ **-ed** -d
Spey speɪ
Spezia ˈspet.si.ə, ˈsped.zi- (US) ˈspet.si.ɑː
Spezzia ˈspet.si.ə
sphagnum ˈsfæg.nəm ˌ**sphagnum** ˈ**moss**
sphene spiːn, sfiːn (US) sfiːn **-s** -z
sphere sfɪəʳ (US) sfɪr **-s** -z
spheric ˈsfer.ɪk (US) ˈsfɪr-, ˈsfer- **-s** -s **-al** -ᵊl **-ally** -ᵊl.i, -li
spheroid ˈsfɪə.rɔɪd (US) ˈsfɪr.ɔɪd, ˈsfer- **-s** -z
spheroidal sfɪəˈrɔɪ.dᵊl, sferˈɔɪ- (US) sfɪˈrɔɪ-, sferˈɔɪ-
spherometer sfɪəˈrɒm.ɪ.təʳ, sferˈɒm-, ˈ-ə- (US) sfɪˈrɑː.mə.tɚ, sferˈɑː- **-s** -z
sphincter ˈsfɪŋk.təʳ (US) -tɚ **-s** -z
sphinx sfɪŋks **-es** -ɪz
sphragistics sfrəˈdʒɪs.tɪks
sphygmomanometer ˌsfɪg.məʊ.məˈnɒm.ɪ.təʳ, ˈ-ə- (US) -moʊ.məˈnɑː.mə.t̬ɚ **-s** -z
spic spɪk **-s** -s
spi|ca (S) ˈspaɪ|.kə **-cae** -siː **-cas** -kəz
spiccato spɪˈkɑː.təʊ (US) -t̬oʊ
spic|e (S) spaɪs **-es** -ɪz **-ing** -ɪŋ **-ed** -t
spiceberr|y ˈspaɪs.bᵊr|.i, -br|i (US) -ˌber|.i **-ies** -iz
Spicer ˈspaɪ.səʳ (US) -sɚ
spick spɪk ˌ**spick and** ˈ**span**
spicule ˈspɪk.juːl, ˈspaɪ.kjuːl (US) ˈspɪk.juːl **-s** -z
spic|y ˈspaɪ.s|i **-ier** -i.əʳ (US) -i.ɚ **-iest** -i.ɪst, -i.əst **-ily** -ɪ.li, -ᵊl.i **-iness** -ɪ.nəs, -ɪ.nɪs
spid|er ˈspaɪ.d|əʳ (US) -dɚ **-ers** -əz (US) -ɚz **-ery** -ᵊr.i ˈ**spider** ˌ**monkey** ; ˈ**spider** ˌ**plant**
spiderweb ˈspaɪ.də.web (US) -dɚ- **-s** -z
spiel ʃpiːl, spiːl (US) spiːl, ʃpiːl
Spielberg ˈspiːl.bɜːg (US) -bɜːrg
spiffing ˈspɪf.ɪŋ **-ly** -li
spiff|y ˈspɪf|.i **-ier** -i.əʳ (US) -i.ɚ **-iest** -i.ɪst, -i.əst
spigot ˈspɪg.ət **-s** -s
spik spɪk **-s** -s
spik|e spaɪk **-es** -s **-ing** -ɪŋ **-ed** -t
spikenard ˈspaɪk.nɑːd, ˈspaɪ.kə- (US) ˈspaɪk.nɑːrd, -nɚd
Spikins ˈspaɪ.kɪnz
spik|y ˈspaɪ.k|i **-ier** -i.əʳ (US) -i.ɚ **-iest** -i.ɪst, -i.əst **-iness** -ɪ.nəs, -ɪ.nɪs
spill spɪl **-s** -z **-ing** -ɪŋ **-ed** -d **spilt** -t
spillag|e ˈspɪl.ɪdʒ **-es** -ɪz
spiller (S) ˈspɪl.əʳ (US) -ɚ **-s** -z
spillikin ˈspɪl.ɪ.kɪn **-s** -z
Spilling ˈspɪl.ɪŋ
spillover ˈspɪl.əʊ.vəʳ (US) -oʊ.vɚ **-s** -z
spilt (*from* **spill**) spɪlt
spin spɪn **-s** -z **-ning** -ɪŋ **span** spæn **spun** spʌn **spinner/s** ˈspɪn.əʳ/z (US) -ɚ/z ˌ**spin** ˈ**bowling** (US) ˈ**spin** ˌ**bowling** ; ˈ**spin** ˌ**doctor** ; ˈ**spinning** ˌ**wheel**
spina bifida ˌspaɪ.nəˈbɪf.ɪ.də, -ˈbaɪ.fɪ- (US) -ˈbɪf.ɪ-
spinach ˈspɪn.ɪtʃ, -ɪdʒ (US) -ɪtʃ
spinal ˈspaɪ.nᵊl ˈ**spinal** ˌ**cord**, ˌ**spinal** ˈ**cord** (US) ˈ**spinal** ˌ**cord**
spindl|e ˈspɪn.dl̩ **-es** -z **-y** -i, ˈspɪnd.li
spindle-legged ˌspɪn.dl̩ˈlegd (US) ˈspɪn.dl̩.legd, -ˌleg.ɪd *stress shift, British only:* ˌspindle-legged ˈchair
spindrift ˈspɪn.drɪft
spin-dr|y ˌspɪnˈdr|aɪ, ˈ-- (US) ˈspɪn.dr|aɪ **-ies** -aɪz **-ying** -aɪ.ɪŋ **-ied** -aɪd **-ier/s** -aɪ.əʳ/z (US) -aɪ.ɚ/z
spine spaɪn **-s** -z **-d** -d
spine-chill|ing ˈspaɪnˌtʃɪl|.ɪŋ **-ingly** -ɪŋ.li **-er/s** -əʳ/z (US) -ɚ/z
spinel spɪˈnel (US) spɪˈnel; ˈspɪn.ᵊl
spineless ˈspaɪn.ləs, -lɪs **-ly** -li **-ness** -nəs, -nɪs
spinet spɪˈnet; ˈspɪn.et, -ɪt (US) ˈspɪn.ɪt **-s** -s
spinifex ˈspɪn.ɪ.feks, ˈ-ə-
Spink spɪŋk **-s** -s
spinnaker ˈspɪn.ə.kəʳ, ˈ-ɪ- (US) -ə.kɚ **-s** -z
spinney ˈspɪn.i **-s** -z
spin-off ˈspɪn.ɒf (US) -ɑːf **-s** -s
spinose ˈspaɪ.nəʊs, -ˈ- (US) ˈspaɪ.noʊs
spinous ˈspaɪ.nəs
Spinoza spɪˈnəʊ.zə (US) -ˈnoʊ-
spinster ˈspɪnt.stəʳ (US) -stɚ **-s** -z **-hood** -hʊd **-ish** -ɪʃ
spin|y ˈspaɪ.n|i **-iness** -ɪ.nəs, -ɪ.nɪs
Spion Kop ˌspaɪ.ənˈkɒp, -əŋˈ- (US) -ənˈkɑːp
spiraea spaɪˈriː.ə, -ˈrɪə (US) -ˈriː.ə **-s** -z
spiral ˈspaɪə.rᵊl (US) ˈspaɪ- **-s** -z **-ly** -i **-(l)ing** -ɪŋ **-(l)ed** -d ˌ**spiral** ˈ**staircase**
spirant ˈspaɪə.rᵊnt (US) ˈspaɪ- **-s** -s
spire spaɪəʳ (US) spaɪɚ **-s** -z **-d** -d
spirea spaɪˈrɪə, -ˈriː.ə (US) -ˈriː.ə **-s** -z
spir|it ˈspɪr|.ɪt **-its** -ɪts **-ited** -ɪ.tɪd/li (US) -ɪ.t̬ɪd/li **-itedness** -ɪ.tɪd.nəs, -nɪs (US) -ɪ.t̬ɪd.nəs, -nɪs ˈ**spirit** ˌ**lamp** ; ˈ**spirit** ˌ**level**
spiritism ˈspɪr.ɪ.tɪ.zᵊm (US) -t̬ɪ-
spiritless ˈspɪr.ɪt.ləs, -lɪs **-ly** -li **-ness** -nəs, -nɪs
spiritual ˈspɪr.ɪ.tʃu.əl, ˈ-ə-, -tju- (US) -tʃu- **-s** -z **-ly** -i
spiritual|ism ˈspɪr.ɪ.tʃu.ᵊl|.ɪ.zᵊm, ˈ-ə-, -tju- (US) -tʃu- **-ist/s** -ɪst/s
spiritualistic ˌspɪr.ɪ.tʃu.ᵊlˈɪs.tɪk, ˌ-ə-, -tju- (US) -tʃu-
spiritualit|y ˌspɪr.ɪ.tʃuˈæl.ə.t|i, ˌ-ə-, -tjuˈ-, -ɪ.t|i (US) -tʃuˈæl.ə.t̬|i **-ies** -iz
spirituous ˈspɪr.ɪ.tʃu.əs, -tju.əs (US) -tʃu-
spiritus ˈspɪr.ɪ.təs, ˈ-ə- (US) -t̬əs
spirogyra ˌspaɪə.rəʊˈdʒaɪə.rə (US) ˌspaɪ.roʊˈdʒaɪ-
spirt spɜːt (US) spɜːrt **-s** -s **-ing** -ɪŋ (US) ˈspɜːr.t̬ɪŋ **-ed** -ɪd (US) ˈspɜːr.t̬ɪd
spit (*n. v.*) spɪt **-s** -s **-ting** -ɪŋ (US) ˈspɪt̬.ɪŋ **-ted** -ɪd (US) ˈspɪt̬.ɪd **spat** spæt ˌ**spitting** ˈ**image** ; ˌ**spit and** ˈ**polish**
Spitalfields ˈspɪt.ᵊl.fiːldz (US) ˈspɪt̬-
spitball ˈspɪt.bɔːl (US) -bɔːl, -bɑːl **-s** -z
spit|e spaɪt **-es** -s **-ing** -ɪŋ (US) ˈspaɪ.t̬ɪŋ **-ed** -ɪd (US) ˈspaɪ.t̬ɪd
spiteful ˈspaɪt.fᵊl, -fʊl **-ly** -i **-ness** -nəs, -nɪs
spitfire (S) ˈspɪtˌfaɪəʳ (US) -ˌfaɪɚ **-s** -z
Spithead ˌspɪtˈhed *stress shift:* ˌSpithead ˈcoastline
Spitsbergen ˈspɪtsˌbɜː.gən, ˌ-ˈ-- (US) ˈspɪtsˌbɜːr-
spittle ˈspɪt.l̩ (US) ˈspɪt̬-
spittoon spɪˈtuːn **-s** -z
spiv spɪv **-s** -z **-vy** -i
splash splæʃ **-es** -ɪz **-ing** -ɪŋ **-ed** -t **-er/s** -əʳ/z (US) -ɚ/z ˈ**splash** ˌ**guard**
splashback ˈsplæʃ.bæk **-s** -s
splashboard ˈsplæʃ.bɔːd (US) -bɔːrd **-s** -z

splashdown 'splæʃ.daʊn **-s** -z
splash|y 'splæʃ|.i **-iness** -ɪ.nəs, -ɪ.nɪs
splat splæt **-s** -s **-ting** -ɪŋ **-ted** -ɪd
splatt|er 'splæt|.əʳ (US) 'splæt̬|.ɚ **-ers** -əz (US) -ɚz **-ering** -ᵊr.ɪŋ **-ered** -əd (US) -ɚd
splay spleɪ **-s** -z **-ing** -ɪŋ **-ed** -d
splayfooted ˌspleɪ'fʊt.ɪd (US) 'spleɪˌfʊt̬- *stress shift, British only:* ˌsplayfooted 'walk
spleen spliːn **-s** -z **-ful** -fᵊl, -fʊl **-fully** -fᵊl.i, -fʊ.li
splendid 'splen.dɪd **-ly** -li **-ness** -nəs, -nɪs
splendiferous splen'dɪf.ᵊr.əs **-ly** -li **-ness** -nəs, -nɪs
splendo(u)r 'splen.dəʳ (US) -dɚ **-s** -z
splenetic splə'net.ɪk, splɪ- (US) splɪ'net̬- **-s** -s **-ally** -ᵊl.i, -li
splic|e splaɪs **-es** -ɪz **-ing** -ɪŋ **-ed** -t
spliff splɪf **-s** -s
splint splɪnt **-s** -s **-ing** -ɪŋ (US) 'splɪn.t̬ɪŋ **-ed** -ɪd (US) 'splɪn.t̬ɪd
splint|er 'splɪn.t|əʳ (US) -t̬|ɚ **-ers** -əz (US) -ɚz **-ery** -ᵊr.i **'splinter ˌgroup**
split (S) splɪt **-s** -s **-ting** -ɪŋ (US) 'splɪt̬.ɪŋ **-ter/s** -əʳ/z (US) 'splɪt̬.ɚ/z **ˌsplit de'cision** ; **ˌsplit 'ends** ; **ˌsplit 'hairs** ; **ˌsplit in'finitive** ; **ˌsplit 'pea** ; **ˌsplit perso'nality** ; **ˌsplit 'screen** *stress shift:* ˌsplit screen 'picture; **ˌsplit 'second** *stress shift:* ˌsplit second 'timing
split-level ˌsplɪt'lev.ᵊl *stress shift:* ˌsplit-level 'flat
splodg|e splɒdʒ (US) splɑːdʒ **-es** -ɪz
splodg|y 'splɒdʒ|.i (US) 'splɑː.dʒ|i **-ier** -i.əʳ (US) -i.ɚ **-iest** -i.ɪst, -i.əst **-iness** -ɪ.nəs, -ɪ.nɪs
splosh splɒʃ (US) splɑːʃ **-es** -ɪz **-ing** -ɪŋ **-ed** -t
splotch splɒtʃ (US) splɑːtʃ **-es** -ɪz **-y** -i
splurg|e splɜːdʒ (US) splɜːrdʒ **-es** -ɪz **-ing** -ɪŋ **-ed** -d
splutt|er 'splʌt|.əʳ (US) 'splʌt̬|.ɚ **-ers** -əz (US) -ɚz **-ering** -ᵊr.ɪŋ **-ered** -əd (US) -ɚd
Spock spɒk (US) spɑːk
Spode spəʊd (US) spoʊd
Spofforth 'spɒf.əθ (US) 'spɑː.fɚθ
Spohr spɔːʳ *as if German:* ʃpɔːʳ (US) spɔːr *as if German:* ʃpɔːr
spoil spɔɪl **-s** -z **-ing** -ɪŋ **-ed** -t, -d **-t** -t **-er/s** -əʳ/z (US) -ɚ/z **-age** -ɪdʒ
spoilsport 'spɔɪl.spɔːt (US) -spɔːrt **-s** -s
spoke *of wheel:* spəʊk (US) spoʊk **-s** -s
spok|e (*from* **speak**) spəʊk (US) spoʊk **-en** -ᵊn
spokes|man 'spəʊks|.mən (US) 'spoʊks- **-men** -mən
spokes|person 'spəʊks|ˌpɜː.sᵊn (US) 'spoʊks|ˌpɜːr- **-persons** -ˌpɜː.sᵊnz (US) -ˌpɜːr- **-people** -ˌpiː.pl̩
spokes|woman 'spəʊks|ˌwʊm.ən (US) 'spoʊks- **-women** -ˌwɪm.ɪn
spoliation ˌspəʊ.li'eɪ.ʃᵊn (US) ˌspoʊ-
spoliator 'spəʊ.li.eɪ.təʳ (US) 'spoʊ.li.eɪ.t̬ɚ **-s** -z
spondee 'spɒn.diː, -di (US) 'spɑːn- **-s** -z
spondulicks spɒn'djuː.lɪks, -'duː- (US) spɑːn'duː-
spondylitis ˌspɒn.dɪ'laɪ.tɪs, -də'- (US) ˌspɑːn.də'laɪ.t̬əs
spong|e spʌndʒ **-es** -ɪz **-(e)ing** -ɪŋ **-ed** -d **-er/s** -əʳ/z (US) -ɚ/z **'sponge ˌbag** ; **'sponge ˌcake** ; **ˌsponge 'finger**
spongiform 'spʌn.dʒɪ.fɔːm (US) -fɔːrm
spong|y 'spʌn.dʒ|i **-ier** -i.əʳ (US) -i.ɚ **-iest** -i.ɪst, -i.əst **-iness** -ɪ.nəs, -ɪ.nɪs
sponson 'spɒnt.sən (US) 'spɑːnt- **-s** -z
spons|or 'spɒnt.s|əʳ (US) 'spɑːnt.s|ɚ **-ors** -əz (US) -ɚz **-oring** -ᵊr.ɪŋ **-ored** -əd (US) -ɚd **-orship** -ə.ʃɪp (US) -ɚ.ʃɪp
spontaneity ˌspɒn.tə'neɪ.ə.ti, -'niː.ə.ti, -ɪ.ti (US) ˌspɑːn.tᵊn'eɪ.ə.t̬i, -'iː-
spontaneous spɒn'teɪ.ni.əs, spən- (US) spɑːn- **-ly** -li **-ness** -nəs, -nɪs **sponˌtaneous com'bustion**
spoof spuːf **-s** -s **-ing** -ɪŋ **-ed** -t
spook spuːk **-s** -s **-ing** -ɪŋ **-ed** -t **-ish** -ɪʃ
spook|y 'spuː.k|i **-ier** -i.əʳ (US) -i.ɚ **-iest** -i.ɪst, -i.əst **-ily** -ɪ.li, -ᵊl.i **-iness** -ɪ.nəs, -ɪ.nɪs
spool spuːl **-s** -z **-ing** -ɪŋ **-ed** -d
spoon spuːn **-s** -z **-ing** -ɪŋ **-ed** -d
spoonbill 'spuːn.bɪl, 'spuːm- (US) 'spuːn- **-s** -z **-ed** -d
Spooner 'spuː.nəʳ (US) -nɚ
spoonerism 'spuː.nᵊr.ɪ.zᵊm **-s** -z
spoon|-feed 'spuːn|.fiːd **-feeds** -fiːdz **-feeding** -ˌfiː.dɪŋ **-fed** -fed
spoonful 'spuːn.fʊl, -fᵊl **-s** -z **spoonsful** 'spuːnz-
spoon|y 'spuː.n|i **-ier** -i.əʳ (US) -i.ɚ **-iest** -i.ɪst, -i.əst **-ily** -ɪ.li, -ᵊl.i **-iness** -ɪ.nəs, -ɪ.nɪs
spoor spɔːʳ, spʊəʳ (US) spʊr **-s** -z **-ing** -ɪŋ **-ed** -d
Sporades 'spɒr.ə.diːz (US) 'spɔːr-
sporadic spə'ræd.ɪk, spɒr'æd- (US) spə'ræd-, spɔː- **-ally** -ᵊl.i, -li
sporangi|um spə'ræn.dʒi|.əm (US) spə-, spoʊ- **-a** -ə
spore spɔːʳ (US) spɔːr **-s** -z
sporran 'spɒr.ən (US) 'spɔːr-, 'spɑːr- **-s** -z
sport spɔːt (US) spɔːrt **-s** -s **-ing** -ɪŋ (US) 'spɔːr.t̬ɪŋ **-ed** -ɪd (US) 'spɔːr.t̬ɪd **'sports ˌcar** ; **'sports ˌday** ; **'sports ˌjacket**
sportive 'spɔː.tɪv (US) 'spɔːr.t̬ɪv **-ly** -li **-ness** -nəs, -nɪs
sportscast 'spɔːts.kɑːst (US) 'spɔːrts.kæst **-s** -s **-ing** -ɪŋ **-er/s** -əʳ/z (US) -ɚ/z
sports|man 'spɔːts|.mən (US) 'spɔːrts- **-men** -mən
sportsman|like 'spɔːts.mən|.laɪk (US) 'spɔːrts- **-ship** -ʃɪp
sports|person 'spɔːts|ˌpɜː.sᵊn (US) 'spɔːrts|ˌpɜːr- **-persons** -ˌpɜː.sᵊnz (US) -ˌpɜːr- **-people** -ˌpiː.pl̩
sportswear 'spɔːts.weəʳ (US) 'spɔːrts.wer
sports|woman 'spɔːts|ˌwʊm.ən (US) 'spɔːrts- **-women** -ˌwɪm.ɪn
sport|y 'spɔː.t|i (US) 'spɔːr.t̬|i **-ier** -i.əʳ (US) -i.ɚ **-iest** -i.ɪst, -i.əst **-ily** -ɪ.li, -ᵊl.i **-iness** -ɪ.nəs, -ɪ.nɪs
spot spɒt (US) spɑːt **-s** -s **-ting** -ɪŋ (US) 'spɑː.t̬ɪŋ **-ted** -ɪd (US) 'spɑː.t̬ɪd **-ter/s** **ˌspotted 'dick** ; **ˌknock (the) 'spots off**
spot-check ˌspɒt'tʃek, '-- (US) 'spɑːt.tʃek **-s** -s **-ing** -ɪŋ **-ed** -t
spotless 'spɒt.ləs, -lɪs (US) 'spɑːt- **-ly** -li **-ness** -nəs, -nɪs
spotlight 'spɒt.laɪt (US) 'spɑːt- **-s** -s **-ing** -ɪŋ **-ed** -ɪd **spotlit** -lɪt
spot-on ˌspɒt'ɒn (US) spɑːt'ɑːn
Spottiswoode 'spɒt.ɪs.wʊd, -ɪz-; 'spɒt.swʊd (US) 'spɑː.tɪs-, 'spɑːt.swʊd
spott|y 'spɒt|.i (US) 'spɑː.t̬|i **-ier** -i.əʳ (US) -i.ɚ **-iest** -i.ɪst, -i.əst **-iness** -ɪ.nəs, -ɪ.nɪs
spous|e spaʊs **-s** -ɪz
spout spaʊt **-s** -s **-ing** -ɪŋ (US) 'spaʊ.t̬ɪŋ **-ed** -ɪd (US) 'spaʊ.t̬ɪd **-er/s** -əʳ/z (US) 'spaʊ.t̬ɚ/z
Spragge spræg
Sprague spreɪg
sprain spreɪn **-s** -z **-ing** -ɪŋ **-ed** -d
sprang (*from* **spring**) spræŋ
Sprange spreɪndʒ
Sprangle 'spræŋ.gl̩
sprat (S) spræt **-s** -s
Spratt spræt
sprawl sprɔːl (US) sprɑːl, sprɔːl **-s** -z **-ing** -ɪŋ **-ed** -d **-er/s** -əʳ/z (US) -ɚ/z
sprawl|y 'sprɔː.l|i (US) 'sprɑː-, 'sprɔː- **-ier** -i.əʳ (US) -i.ɚ **-iest** -i.ɪst, -i.əst **-iness** -ɪ.nəs, -ɪ.nɪs
spray spreɪ **-s** -z **-ing** -ɪŋ **-ed** -d **-er/s** -əʳ/z (US) -ɚ/z **'spray ˌgun**
spraycan 'spreɪ.kæn **-s** -z
spread spred **-s** -z **-ing** -ɪŋ **-er/s** -əʳ/z (US) -ɚ/z
spread-eagl|e ˌspred'iː.gl̩ (US) 'spredˌiː- **-es** -z **-ing** -ɪŋ, -'iː.glɪŋ (US) -ˌiː.glɪŋ **-ed** -d
spreadsheet 'spred.ʃiːt **-s** -s

sprechgesang (S) ˈʃprek.gə.sæŋ *as if German:* ˈʃprex.gə.zæŋ Ⓤⓢ ˈʃprek.gə.sɑːŋ

spree spriː **-s** -z

sprig sprɪg **-s** -z

Sprigg sprɪg **-s** -z

sprightl|y ˈspraɪt.l|i **-ier** -i.əʳ Ⓤⓢ -i.ɚ **-iest** -i.ɪst, -i.əst **-iness** -ɪ.nəs, -ɪ.nɪs

spring (S) sprɪŋ **-s** -z **-ing** -ɪŋ **sprang** spræŋ **sprung** sprʌŋ **springer/s** ˈsprɪŋ.əʳ/z Ⓤⓢ -ɚ/z ˌ**spring** ˈ**balance**, ˈ**spring** ˌ**balance** Ⓤⓢ ˈ**spring** ˌ**balance**; ˌ**spring** ˈ**chicken** ; ˌ**spring** ˈ**fever** ; ˌ**spring** ˈ**greens** ; ˌ**spring** ˈ**onion** ; ˌ**spring** ˈ**roll** Ⓤⓢ ˈ**spring** ˌ**roll**

springboard ˈsprɪŋ.bɔːd Ⓤⓢ -bɔːrd **-s** -z

springbok (S) ˈsprɪŋ.bɒk Ⓤⓢ -bɑːk **-s** -s

spring-clean ˌsprɪŋˈkliːn **-s** -z **-ing** -ɪŋ **-ed** -d

spring|e sprɪndʒ **-es** -ɪz

Springell ˈsprɪŋ.ᵊl, -gᵊl

springer (S) ˈsprɪŋ.əʳ Ⓤⓢ -ɚ ˌ**springer** ˈ**spaniel**

Springfield ˈsprɪŋ.fiːld

springlike ˈsprɪŋ.laɪk

Springsteen ˈsprɪŋ.stiːn

springtime ˈsprɪŋ.taɪm

spring|y ˈsprɪŋ|.i **-ier** -i.əʳ Ⓤⓢ -i.ɚ **-iest** -i.ɪst, -i.əst **-ily** -ɪ.li, -ᵊl.i **-iness** -ɪ.nəs, -ɪ.nɪs

sprinkl|e ˈsprɪŋ.kḷ **-es** -z **-ing** -ɪŋ, ˈsprɪŋ.klɪŋ **-ed** -d **-er/s** -əʳ/z, ˈsprɪŋ.kləʳ/z Ⓤⓢ ˈ-kḷ.ɚ/z, ˈ-klɚ/z

sprinkling ˈsprɪŋ.klɪŋ, ˈ-kḷ.ɪŋ **-s** -z

sprint sprɪnt **-s** -s **-ing** -ɪŋ Ⓤⓢ ˈsprɪn.t̬ɪŋ **-ed** -ɪd Ⓤⓢ ˈsprɪn.t̬ɪd **-er/s** -əʳ/z Ⓤⓢ ˈsprɪn.t̬ɚ/z

sprit sprɪt **-s** -s

sprite spraɪt **-s** -s

spritsail ˈsprɪt.sᵊl, -seɪl Ⓤⓢ -seɪl, -sᵊl **-s** -z

spritz sprɪts **-es** -ɪz **-ing** -ɪŋ **-ed** -t

spritzer ˈsprɪt.səʳ Ⓤⓢ -sɚ **-s** -z

sprocket ˈsprɒk.ɪt Ⓤⓢ ˈsprɑː.kɪt **-s** -s

sprog sprɒg Ⓤⓢ sprɑːg, sprɔːg **-s** -z

Sproule sprəʊl Ⓤⓢ spraʊl, sproʊl

sprout spraʊt **-s** -s **-ing** -ɪŋ Ⓤⓢ ˈspraʊ.t̬ɪŋ **-ed** -ɪd Ⓤⓢ ˈspraʊ.t̬ɪd

spruc|e spruːs **-es** -ɪz **-er** -əʳ Ⓤⓢ -ɚ **-est** -ɪst, -əst **-ely** -li **-eness** -nəs, -nɪs **-ing** -ɪŋ **-ed** -t

sprue spruː **-s** -z

sprung (*from* **spring**) sprʌŋ

spry (S) spraɪ **-er** -əʳ Ⓤⓢ -ɚ **-est** -ɪst, -əst **-ness** -nəs, -nɪs

spud spʌd **-s** -z

spu|e spjuː **-es** -z **-ing** -ɪŋ **-ed** -d

spum|e spjuːm **-es** -z **-ing** -ɪŋ **-ed** -d **-y** -i

spun (*from* **spin**) spʌn

spunk spʌŋk **-y** -i **-ier** -i.əʳ Ⓤⓢ -i.ɚ **-iest** -i.ɪst, -i.əst **-iness** -ɪ.nəs, -ɪ.nɪs

spur spɜːʳ Ⓤⓢ spɜːr **-s** -z **-ring** -ɪŋ **-red** -d **on the** ˌ**spur of the** ˈ**moment**

spurg|e spɜːdʒ Ⓤⓢ spɜːrdʒ **-es** -ɪz

Spurgeon ˈspɜː.dʒᵊn Ⓤⓢ ˈspɜːr-

spurious ˈspjʊə.ri.əs, ˈspjɔː- Ⓤⓢ ˈspjʊr.i- **-ly** -li **-ness** -nəs, -nɪs

spurn (S) spɜːn Ⓤⓢ spɜːrn **-s** -z **-ing** -ɪŋ **-ed** -d

Spurr spɜːʳ Ⓤⓢ spɜːr

Spurrier ˈspʌr.i.əʳ Ⓤⓢ ˈspɜːr.i.ɚ

spurt spɜːt Ⓤⓢ spɜːrt **-s** -s **-ing** -ɪŋ Ⓤⓢ ˈspɜːr.t̬ɪŋ **-ed** -ɪd Ⓤⓢ ˈspɜːr.t̬ɪd

sputnik (S) ˈspʌt.nɪk, ˈspʊt-

sputt|er ˈspʌt|.əʳ Ⓤⓢ ˈspʌt̬|.ɚ **-ers** -əz Ⓤⓢ -ɚz **-ering** -ᵊr.ɪŋ **-ered** -əd Ⓤⓢ -ɚd **-erer/s** -ᵊr.əʳ/z Ⓤⓢ -ɚ.ɚ/z

sput|um ˈspjuː|.təm Ⓤⓢ -t̬əm **-a** -ə

sp|y sp|aɪ **-ies** -aɪz **-ying** -aɪ.ɪŋ **-ied** -aɪd

spyglass ˈspaɪ.glɑːs Ⓤⓢ -glæs **-es** -ɪz

spyhole ˈspaɪ.həʊl Ⓤⓢ -hoʊl **-s** -z

spymaster ˈspaɪˌmɑː.stəʳ Ⓤⓢ -ˌmæs.tɚ **-s** -z

sq (*abbrev. for* **square**) skweəʳ Ⓤⓢ skwer

squab skwɒb Ⓤⓢ skwɑːb **-s** -z ˌ**squab** ˈ**pie**

squabbl|e ˈskwɒb.ḷ Ⓤⓢ ˈskwɑː.bḷ **-es** -z **-ing** -ɪŋ, ˈskwɒb.lɪŋ Ⓤⓢ ˈskwɑː.blɪŋ **-ed** -d **-er/s** -əʳ/z, ˈskwɒb.ləʳ/z Ⓤⓢ ˈskwɑː.bḷ.ɚ/z, ˈ-blɚ/z

squad skwɒd Ⓤⓢ skwɑːd **-s** -z ˈ**squad** ˌ**car**

squadd|y, squadd|ie ˈskwɒd|.i Ⓤⓢ ˈskwɑː.d|i **-ies** -iz

squadron ˈskwɒd.rᵊn Ⓤⓢ ˈskwɑː.drən **-s** -z

squalid ˈskwɒl.ɪd Ⓤⓢ ˈskwɑː.lɪd **-est** -ɪst, -əst **-ly** -li **-ness** -nəs, -nɪs

squall skwɔːl Ⓤⓢ skwɔːl, skwɑːl **-s** -z **-ing** -ɪŋ **-ed** -d **-y** -i

squalor ˈskwɒl.əʳ Ⓤⓢ ˈskwɑː.lɚ

squam|a ˈskweɪ.m|ə, ˈskwɑː- **-ae** -iː

squamate ˈskweɪ.meɪt, ˈskwɑː-

squam|ose ˈskweɪ.m|əʊs, ˈskwɑː- Ⓤⓢ -m|oʊs **-ous/ness** -əs/nəs, -nɪs

squand|er ˈskwɒn.d|əʳ Ⓤⓢ ˈskwɑːn.d|ɚ **-ers** -əz Ⓤⓢ -ɚz **-ering** -ᵊr.ɪŋ **-ered** -əd Ⓤⓢ -ɚd **-erer/s** -ᵊr.əʳ/z Ⓤⓢ -ɚ.ɚ/z

squar|e skweəʳ Ⓤⓢ skwer **-es** -z **-er** -əʳ Ⓤⓢ -ɚ **-est** -ɪst, -əst **-ely** -li **-eness** -nəs, -nɪs **-ing** -ɪŋ **-ed** -d ˈ**square** ˌ**dance** ; ˌ**square** ˈ**deal** ; ˌ**square** ˈ**foot** ; ˌ**square** ˈ**leg** ; ˌ**square** ˈ**meal** ; ˌ**Square** ˈ**Mile** ; ˌ**square** ˈ**one** ; ˌ**square** ˈ**root**

squarish ˈskweə.rɪʃ Ⓤⓢ ˈskwer.ɪʃ

squash skwɒʃ Ⓤⓢ skwɑːʃ **-es** -ɪz **-ing** -ɪŋ **-ed** -t

squash|y ˈskwɒʃ|.i Ⓤⓢ ˈskwɑː.ʃ|i **-ier** -i.əʳ Ⓤⓢ -i.ɚ **-iest** -i.ɪst, -i.əst **-iness** -ɪ.nəs, -ɪ.nɪs

squat skwɒt Ⓤⓢ skwɑːt **-ly** -li **-ness** -nəs, -nɪs **-s** -s **-ting** -ɪŋ Ⓤⓢ ˈskwɑː.t̬ɪŋ **-ted** -ɪd Ⓤⓢ ˈskwɑː.t̬ɪd **-ter/s** -əʳ/z Ⓤⓢ ˈskwɑː.t̬ɚ/z

squaw skwɔː Ⓤⓢ skwɑː, skwɔː **-s** -z

squawk skwɔːk Ⓤⓢ skwɑːk, skwɔːk **-s** -s **-ing** -ɪŋ **-ed** -t

squeak skwiːk **-s** -s **-ing** -ɪŋ **-ed** -t **-er/s** -əʳ/z Ⓤⓢ -ɚ/z

squeak|y ˈskwiː.k|i **-ier** -i.əʳ Ⓤⓢ -i.ɚ **-iest** -i.ɪst, -i.əst **-ily** -ɪ.li, -ᵊl.i **-iness** -ɪ.nəs, -ɪ.nɪs

squeaky-clean ˌskwiː.kiˈkliːn

squeal skwiːl **-s** -z **-ing** -ɪŋ **-ed** -d **-er/s** -əʳ/z Ⓤⓢ -ɚ/z

squeamish ˈskwiː.mɪʃ **-ly** -li **-ness** -nəs, -nɪs

squeegee ˈskwiː.dʒiː, ˌ-ˈ- Ⓤⓢ ˈskwiː.dʒiː **-s** -z **-ing** -ɪŋ **-d** -d

Squeers skwɪəz Ⓤⓢ skwɪrz

squeez|e skwiːz **-es** -ɪz **-ing** -ɪŋ **-ed** -d **-er/s** -əʳ/z Ⓤⓢ -ɚ/z **-able** -ə.bḷ **-y** -i

squeeze-box ˈskwiːz.bɒks Ⓤⓢ -bɑːks **-es** -ɪz

squelch skweltʃ **-es** -ɪz **-ing** -ɪŋ **-ed** -t **-y** -i

squib skwɪb **-s** -z

squid skwɪd **-s** -z

squidg|y ˈskwɪdʒ|.i **-ier** -i.əʳ Ⓤⓢ -i.ɚ **-iest** -i.ɪst, -i.əst **-iness** -ɪ.nəs, -ɪ.nɪs

squiff|y ˈskwɪf|.i **-ed** -t **-ier** -i.əʳ Ⓤⓢ -i.ɚ **-iest** -i.ɪst, -i.əst **-iness** -ɪ.nəs, -ɪ.nɪs

squiggl|e ˈskwɪg|.ḷ **-es** -z **-ing** -ɪŋ, ˈskwɪg.lɪŋ **-ed** -d **-y** -i

squilgee ˈskwɪl.dʒiː, ˌ-ˈ- Ⓤⓢ ˈskwɪl.dʒiː **-s** -z **-ing** -ɪŋ **-d** -d

squill skwɪl **-s** -z

squint skwɪnt **-s** -s **-ing** -ɪŋ Ⓤⓢ ˈskwɪn.t̬ɪŋ **-ed** -ɪd Ⓤⓢ ˈskwɪn.t̬ɪd **-y** -i

squirarch|y ˈskwaɪə.rɑː.k|i Ⓤⓢ ˈskwaɪɚ.ɑːr- **-ies** -iz

squir|e (S) skwaɪəʳ Ⓤⓢ skwaɪɚ **-s** -z **-ing** -ɪŋ **-ed** -d

squirearch|y ˈskwaɪə.rɑː.k|i Ⓤⓢ ˈskwaɪɚ.ɑːr- **-ies** -iz

Squires skwaɪəz Ⓤⓢ skwaɪɚz

squirm skwɜːm Ⓤⓢ skwɜːrm **-s** -z **-ing** -ɪŋ **-ed** -d **-y** -i

squirrel ˈskwɪr.ᵊl Ⓤⓢ ˈskwɜːr- **-s** -z **-(l)ing** -ɪŋ **-(l)ed** -d

squirt skwɜːt Ⓤⓢ skwɜːrt **-s** -s **-ing** -ɪŋ Ⓤⓢ ˈskwɜːr.t̬ɪŋ **-ed** -ɪd Ⓤⓢ ˈskwɜːr.t̬ɪd **-er/s** -əʳ/z Ⓤⓢ -ɚ/z

squish skwɪʃ **-es** -ɪz **-ing** -ɪŋ **-ed** -t **-y** -i

sr (S) (*abbrev. for* **senior**) ˈsiː.ni.əʳ, -njəʳ Ⓤⓢ -njɚ

Srebrenica ˌsreb.rəˈniːt.sə, ˌʃreb-, -tʃə

Sri Lank|a ˌsriːˈlæŋ.kə, ˌsrɪ-, ˌʃriː- Ⓤⓢ -ˈlɑːŋ- **-an/s** -ən/z

Srinagar srɪ'nʌg.əʳ, sriː-, ʃrɪ-, ʃriː-, -'nɑː.gəʳ ⓤⓢ ˌsriː'nʌg.ɚ
SS *Nazi unit:* ˌes'es *stress shift:* ˌSS 'officer
SS (*abbrev. for* **steamship**) ˌes'es *stress shift:* ˌSS ˌGreat 'Britian
SSE (*abbrev. for* **south-southeast**) ˌes.es'iː, ˌsaʊθ.saʊθ'iːst *in nautical usage also:* ˌsaʊ.saʊ-
ssh, sh, shh ʃ
Note: Used to command silence
SSW (*abbrev. for* **south-southwest**) ˌes.es'dʌb.l̩.juː, -ju, ˌsaʊθ.saʊθ'west ⓤⓢ ˌesˌes'dʌb.l̩.juː, -jə, ˌsaʊθ.saʊθ'west *in nautical usage also:* ˌsaʊ.saʊ-
St. (*abbrev. for* **Street**) striːt
St. (*abbrev. for* **Saint**) sᵊn*t*, sɪn*t*, seɪnt ⓤⓢ seɪnt
Note: See panel information at **Saint**.
st (*abbrev. for* **stone**) stəʊn ⓤⓢ stoʊn
stab stæb **-s** -z **-bing** -ɪŋ **-bed** -d
Stabat Mater ˌstɑː.bæt'mɑː.təʳ, -bət'- ⓤⓢ -bɑːt'mɑː.tɚ **-s** -z
St. Abb's sᵊnt'æbz, sɪnt- ⓤⓢ seɪnt-
stability stə'bɪl.ə.ti, -ɪ.ti ⓤⓢ -ə.t̬i
stabilization, -isa- ˌsteɪ.bᵊl.aɪ'zeɪ.ʃᵊn, -bɪ.laɪ-, -lɪ'- ⓤⓢ -bᵊl.ɪ'-
stabiliz|e, -is|e 'steɪ.bᵊl.aɪz, -bɪ.laɪz ⓤⓢ -bə.laɪz **-es** -ɪz **-ing** -ɪŋ **-ed** -d **-er/s** -əʳ/z ⓤⓢ -ɚ/z
stabl|e 'steɪ.bl̩ **-es** -z **-y** -i, 'steɪ.bli **-eness** -nəs, -nɪs **-ing** -ɪŋ, 'steɪ.blɪŋ **-ed** -d ˌ**stable 'door** ; '**stable** ˌ**lad**
stablemate 'steɪ.bl̩.meɪt **-s** -s
stabling 'steɪ.bl̩.ɪŋ, '-blɪŋ
stablish 'stæb.lɪʃ **-es** -ɪz **-ing** -ɪŋ **-ed** -t
staccato stə'kɑː.təʊ ⓤⓢ -t̬oʊ **-s** -z
Stacey, Stacie 'steɪ.si
stack stæk **-s** -s **-ing** -ɪŋ **-ed** -t
Stacpoole 'stæk.puːl
Stacy 'steɪ.si
stadi|um 'steɪ.di|.əm **-ums** -əmz **-a** -ə
staff stɑːf ⓤⓢ stæf **-s** -s **-ing** -ɪŋ **-ed** -t '**staff** ˌ**nurse** ; '**staff** ˌ**sergeant**
Staffa 'stæf.ə
Stafford 'stæf.əd ⓤⓢ -ɚd **-shire** -ʃəʳ, -ˌʃɪəʳ ⓤⓢ -ʃɚ, -ˌʃɪr
Staffs. (*abbrev. for* **Staffordshire**) stæfs
stag stæg **-s** -z '**stag** ˌ**night**
stag|e steɪdʒ **-es** -ɪz **-ing** -ɪŋ **-ed** -d ˌ**stage 'door** ; '**stage** ˌ**fright**
stagecoach 'steɪdʒ.kəʊtʃ ⓤⓢ -koʊtʃ **-es** -ɪz
stagecraft 'steɪdʒ.krɑːft ⓤⓢ -kræft
stagehand 'steɪdʒ.hænd **-s** -z
stage-manag|e ˌsteɪdʒ'mæn.ɪdʒ, '-ˌ-- ⓤⓢ 'steɪdʒˌmæn- **-es** -ɪz **-ing** -ɪŋ **-ed** -d **-ment** -mənt
stage-manager ˌsteɪdʒ'mæn.ə.dʒəʳ, '-ɪ- ⓤⓢ 'steɪdʒˌmæn.ə.dʒɚ
stager 'steɪ.dʒəʳ ⓤⓢ -dʒɚ **-s** -z
stage-struck 'steɪdʒ.strʌk
stag|ey 'steɪ.dʒ|i **-ier** -i.əʳ ⓤⓢ -i.ɚ **-iest** -i.ɪst, -i.əst **-iness** -ɪ.nəs, -ɪ.nɪs
stagflation stæg'fleɪ.ʃᵊn
stagg|er 'stæg|.əʳ ⓤⓢ -ɚ **-ers** -əz ⓤⓢ -ɚz **-ering/ly** -ᵊr.ɪŋ **-ered** -əd ⓤⓢ -ɚd **-erer/s** -ᵊr.əʳ/z ⓤⓢ -ɚ.ɚ/z
staghound 'stæg.haʊnd **-s** -z
staging 'steɪ.dʒɪŋ **-s** -z
Stagirite 'stædʒ.ɪ.raɪt ⓤⓢ '-ə- **-s** -s
stagnancy 'stæg.nən*t*.si
stagnant 'stæg.nənt **-ly** -li
stagna|te stæg'neɪ|t, '-- ⓤⓢ 'stæg.neɪ|t **-tes** -ts **-ting** -tɪŋ ⓤⓢ -t̬ɪŋ **-ted** -tɪd ⓤⓢ -t̬ɪd
stagnation stæg'neɪ.ʃᵊn
St. Agnes sᵊnt'æg.nɪs, sɪnt-, seɪnt- ⓤⓢ seɪnt-
stag|y 'steɪ.dʒ|i **-ier** -i.əʳ ⓤⓢ -i.ɚ **-iest** -i.ɪst, -i.əst **-ily** -ɪ.li, -ᵊl.i **-iness** -ɪ.nəs, -ɪ.nɪs
staid steɪd **-ly** -li **-ness** -nəs, -nɪs
stain steɪn **-s** -z **-ing** -ɪŋ **-ed** -d **-er/s** -əʳ/z ⓤⓢ -ɚ/z ˌ**stained 'glass**
Stainer *English name:* 'steɪ.nəʳ ⓤⓢ -nɚ *German name:* 'staɪ.nəʳ *as if German:* 'ʃtaɪ- ⓤⓢ -nɚ
Staines steɪnz
Stainforth 'steɪn.fəθ ⓤⓢ -fɚθ
stainless 'steɪn.ləs, -lɪs **-ly** -li **-ness** -nəs, -nɪs ˌ**stainless 'steel**
stair steəʳ ⓤⓢ ster **-s** -z
staircas|e 'steə.keɪs ⓤⓢ 'ster- **-es** -ɪz
stair-rod 'steə.rɒd ⓤⓢ 'ster.rɑːd **-s** -z
stairway 'steə.weɪ ⓤⓢ 'ster- **-s** -z
stairwell 'steə.wel ⓤⓢ 'ster- **-s** -z
Staithes steɪðz
stak|e steɪk **-es** -s **-ing** -ɪŋ **-ed** -t
stakeholder 'steɪkˌhəʊl.dəʳ ⓤⓢ -ˌhoʊl.dɚ **-s** -z
stakeout 'steɪk.aʊt **-s** -s
Stakhanov|ite stæk'æn.ə.v|aɪt ⓤⓢ stə'kɑː.nə- **-ites** -aɪts **-ism** -ɪ.zᵊm
stalactite 'stæl.ək.taɪt ⓤⓢ stə'læk-; 'stæl.ək- **-s** -s
stalag 'stæl.æg ⓤⓢ 'stɑː.lɑːg, 'stæl.æg **-s** -z
stalagmite 'stæl.əg.maɪt ⓤⓢ stə'læg-; 'stæl.əg- **-s** -s
St. Albans sᵊnt'ɔːl.bənz, sɪnt-, -'ɒl- ⓤⓢ seɪnt'ɔːl-, -'ɑːl-
Stalbridge 'stɔːl.brɪdʒ ⓤⓢ 'stɔːl-
St. Aldate's sᵊnt'ɔːl.deɪts, sɪnt-, -'ɒl-, -dɪts *old-fashioned:* -'əʊldz ⓤⓢ seɪnt'ɔːl.deɪts, -'ɑːl-
stal|e steɪl **-er** -əʳ ⓤⓢ -ɚ **-est** -ɪst, -əst **-ely** -li **-eness** -nəs, -nɪs
stale|mate 'steɪl|.meɪt **-mates** -meɪts **-mating** -meɪ.tɪŋ ⓤⓢ -meɪ.t̬ɪŋ **-mated** -meɪ.tɪd ⓤⓢ -meɪ.t̬ɪd
Stalin 'stɑː.lɪn, 'stæl.ɪn **-ism** -ɪ.zᵊm
Stalingrad 'stɑː.lɪn.græd, 'stæl.ɪn-, -grɑːd ⓤⓢ 'stɑː.lɪn.græd, 'stæl.ɪn-
stalin|ism (S) 'stɑː.lɪ.n|ɪ.zᵊm, 'stæl.ɪ- ⓤⓢ 'stɑː.lɪ- **-ist/s** -ɪsts
stalk stɔːk ⓤⓢ stɔːk, stɑːk **-s** -s **-ing** -ɪŋ **-ed** -t **-er/s** -əʳ/z ⓤⓢ -ɚ/z
stalking-hors|e 'stɔː.kɪŋ.hɔːs ⓤⓢ -hɔːrs, 'stɑː- **-es** -ɪz
Stalky 'stɔː.ki ⓤⓢ 'stɔː-, 'stɑː-
stall stɔːl ⓤⓢ stɔːl, stɑːl **-s** -z **-ing** -ɪŋ **-ed** -d
stallage 'stɔː.lɪdʒ
stallholder 'stɔːlˌhəʊl.dəʳ ⓤⓢ 'stɔːlˌhoʊl.dɚ, 'stɑːl- **-s** -z
stallion 'stæl.jən, -i.ən ⓤⓢ '-jən **-s** -z
Stallone stə'ləʊn, stæl'əʊn ⓤⓢ stə'loʊn
stalwart 'stɔːl.wət, 'stɒl- ⓤⓢ 'stɔːl.wɚt, 'stɑːl- **-s** -s **-ly** -li **-ness** -nəs, -nɪs
Stalybridge 'steɪ.lɪ.brɪdʒ
Stamboul stæm'buːl ⓤⓢ stɑːm-
St. Ambrose sᵊnt'æm.brəʊz, sɪnt-, -brəʊs ⓤⓢ seɪnt'æm.broʊz, -broʊs
stamen 'steɪ.men, -mən **-s** -z
Stamford 'stæm*p*.fəd ⓤⓢ -fɚd
stamina 'stæm.ɪ.nə, '-ə- ⓤⓢ '-ə-
stamm|er 'stæm|.əʳ ⓤⓢ -ɚ **-ers** -əz ⓤⓢ -ɚz **-ering** -ᵊr.ɪŋ **-ered** -əd ⓤⓢ -ɚd **-erer/s** -ᵊr.əʳ/z ⓤⓢ -ɚ.ɚ/z
stamp (S) stæmp **-s** -s **-ing** -ɪŋ **-ed** -t **-er/s** -əʳ/z ⓤⓢ -ɚ/z '**stamp** ˌ**album** ; '**stamp col**ˌ**lector** ; '**stamp** ˌ**duty** ; '**stamping** ˌ**ground**
stamped|e stæm'piːd **-es** -z **-ing** -ɪŋ **-ed** -ɪd
Stanbury 'stæn.bᵊr.i, 'stæm-, '-bri ⓤⓢ 'stæn.ber.i, -bɚ-
stanc|e stæn*t*s, stɑːn*t*s ⓤⓢ stæn*t*s **-es** -ɪz
stanch stɑːn*t*ʃ ⓤⓢ stɑːntʃ, stɔːntʃ, stæntʃ **-es** -ɪz **-ing** -ɪŋ **-ed** -t
stanchion 'stɑːn.*t*ʃᵊn, 'stæn- ⓤⓢ 'stæn- **-s** -z **-ing** -ɪŋ **-ed** -d
stand stænd **-s** -z **-ing** -ɪŋ **stood** stʊd
stand-alone 'stænd.əˌləʊn, -ᵊlˌəʊn ⓤⓢ -əˌloʊn
standard 'stæn.dəd ⓤⓢ -dɚd **-s** -z ˌ**standard devi'ation** ; '**standard** ˌ**lamp** ; ˌ**standard of 'living** ; '**standard** ˌ**time**
standard-bearer 'stæn.dədˌbeə.rəʳ ⓤⓢ -dɚdˌber.ɚ **-s** -z
standardization, -isa- ˌstæn.də.daɪ'zeɪ.ʃᵊn, -dɪ'- ⓤⓢ -dɚ.dɪ'-
standardiz|e, -is|e 'stæn.də.daɪz ⓤⓢ -dɚ- **-es** -ɪz **-ing** -ɪŋ **-ed** -d
standby 'stæn*d*.baɪ, 'stæm- ⓤⓢ 'stæn*d*- **-s** -z
stand-in 'stænd.ɪn **-s** -z

standing 'stæn.dɪŋ **-s** -z ˌ**standing 'joke** ; ˌ**standing 'order** ; '**standing ˌroom**
standish (S) 'stæn.dɪʃ **-es** -ɪz
standoff 'stænd.ɒf (US) -ɑːf **-s** -s
standoffish ˌstænd'ɒf.ɪʃ (US) -'ɑː.fɪʃ **-ly** -li **-ness** -nəs, -nɪs
standout 'stænd.aʊt **-s** -s
standpipe 'stæn*d*.paɪp, 'stæm- (US) 'stæn*d*- **-s** -s
standpoint 'stæn*d*.pɔɪnt, 'stæm- (US) 'stæn*d*- **-s** -s
St. Andrew sᵊnt'æn.druː, sɪnt- (US) seɪnt- **-(')s** -z **St. ˌAndrew's 'cross**
standstill 'stæn*d*.stɪl **-s** -z
stand-up 'stænd.ʌp
Staneydale 'steɪ.ni.deɪl
Stanfield 'stæn.fiːld
Stanford 'stæn.fəd (US) -fɚd
Stanford-Binet ˌstæn.fəd'biː.neɪ, ˌstæm-; -bɪ'neɪ (US) ˌstæn.fɚd.bɪ'neɪ
Stanford le Hope ˌstæn.fəd.lɪ'həʊp (US) -fɚd.lɪ'hoʊp
stanhope (S) 'stæn.əp, -həʊp (US) -hoʊp, -əp **-s** -s
staniel 'stæn.jəl, -i.əl (US) '-jəl **-s** -z
Stanis|las 'stæn.ɪ.s|læs, '-ə-, -sləs, -slɑːs (US) -slɑːs **-laus** -slɔːs
Stanislavski ˌstæn.ɪ'slæv.ski, -'slæf- (US) -ə'slɑːv-, -'slɑːf- **Stani'slavski ˌmethod**
stank (*from* **stink**) stæŋk
Stanley 'stæn.li '**Stanley ˌknife**
Stanmore 'stæn.mɔːʳ, 'stæm- (US) 'stæn.mɔːr
Stannard 'stæn.əd (US) -ɚd
stannar|y 'stæn.ᵊr|.i **-ies** -iz
St. Anne sᵊnt'æn, sɪnt- (US) seɪnt- **-'s** -z
stann|ic 'stæn|.ɪk **-ous** -əs
Stansfield 'stænz.fiːld, 'stæn*t*s-
Stansted 'stæn*t*.sted, -stɪd, -stəd ˌ**Stansted 'Airport**
Stansted Mountfitchet ˌstæn*t*.sted.maʊnt'fɪtʃ.ɪt, -stɪd-, -stəd
St. Anthony sᵊnt'æn.tə.ni, sɪnt- (US) seɪnt'æn.tᵊn.i, -θə.ni
Stanton 'stæn.tən, 'stɑːn- (US) 'stæn.tᵊn
stanza 'stæn.zə **-s** -z
stapes 'steɪ.piːz
staphylo|coccus ˌstæf.ɪ.ləʊ|'kɒk.əs, -ᵊl.əʊ'- (US) -ə.loʊ|'kɑː.kəs **-cocci** -'kɒk.saɪ, -aɪ, -iː (US) -'kɑːk.saɪ, -aɪ **-coccal** -'kɒk.ᵊl (US) -'kɑː.kᵊl **-coccic** -'kɒk.ɪk (US) -'kɑː.kɪk
stapl|e (S) 'steɪ.pl̩ **-es** -z **-ing** -ɪŋ, 'steɪ.plɪŋ **-ed** -d
Stapleford 'steɪ.pl̩.fəd (US) -fɚd
stapler 'steɪ.pləʳ (US) -plɚ **-s** -z
Stapleton 'steɪ.pl̩.tən (US) -t̬ən
Stapley 'stæp.li, 'steɪ.pli

star stɑːʳ (US) stɑːr **-s** -z **-ring** -ɪŋ **-red** -d ˌ**Stars and 'Bars** ; ˌ**star 'chamber** ; ˌ**Star of 'David** ; '**star ˌsign** ; ˌ**Stars and 'Stripes** ; '**star ˌwars**
starboard 'stɑː.bəd, -bɔːd (US) 'stɑːr.bɚd, -bɔːrd
Note: The nautical pronunciation is /'stɑː.bəd (US) -bɚd/.
Starbuck 'stɑː.bʌk (US) 'stɑːr-
starch stɑːtʃ (US) stɑːrtʃ **-es** -ɪz **-ing** -ɪŋ **-ed** -t **-y** -i **-ier** -i.əʳ (US) -i.ɚ **-iest** -i.ɪst, -i.əst **-iness** -ɪ.nəs, -ɪ.nɪs **-ily** -ɪ.li
starch-reduced ˌstɑːtʃ.rɪ'djuːst, -rə'-, -'dʒuːst, '--ˌ- (US) 'stɑːrtʃ.rɪˌduːst, -ˌdjuːst
star-crossed 'stɑː.krɒst (US) 'stɑːr.krɑːst ˌ**star-crossed 'lovers**
stardom 'stɑː.dəm (US) 'stɑːr-
stardust 'stɑː.dʌst (US) 'stɑːr-
star|e steəʳ (US) ster **-es** -z **-ing/ly** -ɪŋ/li **-ed** -d **-er/s** -əʳ/z (US) -ɚ/z
starfish 'stɑː.fɪʃ (US) 'stɑːr- **-es** -ɪz
stargaz|e 'stɑː.geɪz (US) 'stɑːr- **-es** -ɪz **-ing** -ɪŋ **-er/s** -əʳ/z (US) -ɚ/z
stark (S) stɑːk (US) stɑːrk **-ly** -li **-ness** -nəs, -nɪs ˌ**stark 'naked** ; ˌ**stark ˌraving 'mad**
starkers 'stɑː.kəz (US) 'stɑːr.kɚz
star|less 'stɑː|.ləs, -lɪs (US) 'stɑːr-
starlet 'stɑː.lət, -lɪt (US) 'stɑːr- **-s** -s
starlight 'stɑː.laɪt (US) 'stɑːr-
starling (S) 'stɑː.lɪŋ (US) 'stɑːr- **-s** -z
starlit 'stɑː.lɪt (US) 'stɑːr-
Starr stɑːʳ (US) stɑːr
starr|y 'stɑː.r|i (US) 'stɑːr|.i **-iness** -ɪ.nəs, -ɪ.nɪs
starry-eyed ˌstɑː.ri'aɪd (US) 'stɑː.riˌaɪd *stress shift, British only:* ˌstarry-eyed 'fan
star-spangled 'stɑːˌspæŋ.gl̩d (US) 'stɑːr- ˌ**star-ˌspangled 'banner**
starstruck 'stɑː.strʌk (US) 'stɑːr-
star-studded 'stɑːˌstʌd.ɪd (US) 'stɑːr-
start (S) stɑːt (US) stɑːrt **-s** -s **-ing** -ɪŋ (US) 'stɑːr.t̬ɪŋ **-ed** -ɪd (US) 'stɑːr.t̬ɪd **-er/s** -əʳ/z (US) 'stɑːr.t̬ɚ/z '**starting ˌblock** ; '**starting ˌpoint**
startl|e 'stɑː.tl̩ (US) 'stɑːr.t̬l̩ **-es** -z **-ing/ly** -ɪŋ, 'stɑːt.lɪŋ (US) 'stɑːrt- **-ed** -d **-er/s** -əʳ/z, 'stɑːt.ləʳ/z (US) 'stɑːr.t̬l̩.ɚ/z, 'stɑːrt.lɚ/z
Start-rite® 'stɑːt.raɪt (US) 'stɑːrt-
start-up 'stɑːt.ʌp (US) 'stɑːrt-
starvation stɑː'veɪ.ʃᵊn (US) stɑːr- **starˌvation 'wages**
starv|e stɑːv (US) stɑːrv **-es** -z **-ing** -ɪŋ **-ed** -d
starveling 'stɑːv.lɪŋ (US) 'stɑːrv- **-s** -z
St. Asaph sᵊnt'æs.əf, sɪnt- (US) seɪnt-
stash stæʃ **-es** -ɪz **-ing** -ɪŋ **-ed** -t

Stasi 'stɑː.zi *as if German:* 'ʃtɑː-
stas|is 'steɪ.s|ɪs (US) 'steɪ-, 'stæs|.ɪs **-es** -iːz
stat|e steɪt **-es** -s **-ing** -ɪŋ (US) 'steɪ.t̬ɪŋ **-ed/ly** -ɪd (US) 'steɪ.t̬ɪd '**State ˌDepartment** ; ˌ**state of e'mergency** ; '**state ˌschool** ; ˌ**state 'trooper**
statecraft 'steɪt.krɑːft (US) -kræft
statehood 'steɪt.hʊd
stateless 'steɪt.ləs, -lɪs **-ness** -nəs, -nɪs
statel|y 'steɪt.l|i **-ier** -i.əʳ (US) -i.ɚ **-iest** -i.ɪst, -i.əst **-iness** -ɪ.nəs, -ɪ.nɪs ˌ**stately 'home**
statement 'steɪt.mənt **-s** -s
Staten Island ˌstæt.ᵊn'aɪ.lənd
state-of-the-art ˌsteɪt.əv.ði'ɑːt (US) -'ɑːrt *stress shift:* ˌstate-of-the-art 'gadget
stateroom 'steɪt.rʊm, -ruːm (US) -ruːm, -rʊm **-s** -z
States steɪts
stateside 'steɪt.saɪd
states|man 'steɪts|.mən **-men** -mən
statesman|like 'steɪts.mən|.laɪk **-ly** -li **-ship** -ʃɪp
states|woman 'steɪts|ˌwʊm.ən **-women** -ˌwɪm.ɪn
statewide 'steɪt.waɪd
Statham 'steɪ.θəm, -ðəm (US) -ðəm, -θəm, -t̬əm; 'stæt̬.əm
St. Athan sᵊnt'æθ.ᵊn, sɪnt- (US) seɪnt-
static 'stæt.ɪk (US) 'stæt̬- **-s** -s **-al** -ᵊl **-ally** -ᵊl.i, -li
static|e 'stæt.ɪs, -ɪ.s|i (US) 'stæt̬.ə.s|i, '-ɪs **-es** -ɪz, -iz
station 'steɪ.ʃᵊn **-s** -z **-ing** -ɪŋ, 'steɪʃ.nɪŋ **-ed** -d '**station ˌwagon** ; ˌ**stations of the 'cross**
stationar|y 'steɪ.ʃᵊn.ᵊr|.i, 'steɪʃ.nᵊr- (US) 'steɪ.ʃə.ner- **-ily** -ᵊl.i, -ɪ.li **-iness** -ɪ.nəs, -ɪ.nɪs
stationer 'steɪ.ʃᵊn.əʳ, 'steɪʃ.nəʳ (US) -ʃᵊn.ɚ, 'steɪʃ.nɚ **-s** -z
stationery 'steɪ.ʃᵊn.ᵊr.i, 'steɪʃ.nᵊr- (US) 'steɪ.ʃə.ner-
stationmaster 'steɪ.ʃᵊnˌmɑː.stəʳ (US) -ˌmæs.tɚ **-s** -z
stat|ism 'steɪ.t|ɪ.zᵊm (US) -t̬|ɪ- **-ist/s** -ɪst/s
statistic stə'tɪs.tɪk, stæt'ɪs- (US) stə'tɪs- **-s** -s **-al** -ᵊl **-ally** -ᵊl.i, -li
statistician ˌstæt.ɪ'stɪʃ.ᵊn, -ə'- (US) -ɪ'- **-s** -z
Statius 'steɪ.ʃəs
stative 'steɪ.tɪv (US) -t̬ɪv
stator 'steɪ.təʳ (US) -t̬ɚ **-s** -z
statuary 'stætʃ.u.ᵊr.i, 'stæt.ju- (US) 'stætʃ.u.er-
statue 'stætʃ.uː, 'stæt.juː (US) 'stætʃ.uː **-s** -z
statuesque ˌstæt.ju'esk, ˌstætʃ.u'- (US) ˌstætʃ.u'-

statuette ˌstæt.ju'et, ˌstætʃ.u'- (US) ˌstætʃ.u'- **-s** -s

stature 'stætʃ.əʳ, 'stæt.jəʳ (US) 'stætʃ.ɚ **-s** -z

status 'steɪ.təs (US) -t̬əs **-es** -ɪz **'status ˌsymbol**

status quo ˌsteɪ.təs'kwəʊ, ˌstæt.əs'- (US) ˌstæt̬.əs'kwoʊ, ˌsteɪ.t̬əs'-

statute 'stæt.juːt, 'stætʃ.uːt (US) 'stætʃ.uːt **-s** -s **'statute ˌbook**

statutory 'stæt.jə.tᵊr.i, -jʊ-, 'stætʃ.ə-, '-ʊ- (US) 'stætʃ.ə.tɔːr-, '-ʊ- **ˌstatutory 'rape**

St. Augustine sᵊnt.ɔː'gʌs.tɪn, sɪnt-, ˌsent-, ˌseɪnt-, -ə'- (US) seɪnt'ɔː.gə.stiːn, -'ɑː-

staunch stɔːntʃ (US) stɔːntʃ, stɑːntʃ **-er** -əʳ (US) -ɚ **-est** -ɪst, -əst **-ly** -li **-ness** -nəs, -nɪs **-es** -ɪz **-ing** -ɪŋ **-ed** -t

Staunton *English surname:* 'stɔːn.tən (US) 'stɑːn.tᵊn, 'stɔːn- *towns in US:* 'stæn.tən (US) -tᵊn

St. Austell sᵊnt'ɔː.stᵊl, sɪnt- *locally:* -'ɔː.sᵊl (US) seɪnt'ɑː.stᵊl, -'ɔː-

Stavanger stə'væŋ.əʳ, stæv'æŋ- (US) stə'vɑːŋ.ɚ, stɑː-

stav|e steɪv **-es** -z **-ing** -ɪŋ **-ed** -d **stove** stəʊv (US) stoʊv

Staveley 'steɪv.li

stay steɪ **-s** -z **-ing** -ɪŋ **-ed** -d **-er/s** -əʳ/z (US) -ɚ/z

stay-at-home 'steɪ.ət.həʊm (US) -hoʊm

staysail 'steɪ.seɪl *nautical pronunciation:* -sᵊl **-s** -z

St. Bartholomew sᵊn*t*.bɑː'θɒl.ə.mjuː, sɪn*t*-, -bə'- (US) ˌseɪnt.bɑːr'θɑː.lə- **-'s** -z

St. Bees sᵊn*t*'biːz, sɪn*t*- (US) seɪnt-

St. Bernard sᵊn*t*'bɜː.nəd, sɪn*t*- (US) ˌseɪnt.bɚ'nɑːrd **-s** -z

St. Blaize sᵊn*t*'bleɪz, sɪn*t*- (US) seɪnt-

St. Blazey sᵊn*t*'bleɪ.zi, sɪn*t*- (US) seɪnt-

St. Bride's sᵊn*t*'braɪdz, sɪn*t*- (US) seɪnt-

St. Bruno sᵊn*t*'bruː.nəʊ, sɪn*t*- (US) seɪnt'bruː.noʊ

St. Catherine, St. Catharine sᵊn*t*'kæθ.ᵊr.ɪn, sɪn*t*-, sᵊŋ'-, '-rɪn (US) seɪnt- **-'s** -z

St. Cecilia sᵊnt.sɪ'sɪl.i.ə, sɪnt-, -'siː.li.ə, '-ljə (US) ˌseɪnt.sɪ'siːl.jə

St. Christopher sᵊn*t*'krɪs.tə.fəʳ, sɪn*t*-, sᵊŋ- (US) seɪnt'krɪs.tə.fɚ **-s** -z

St. Clair *surname:* 'sɪŋ.kleəʳ, 'sɪn- (US) seɪnt'kler *place in US:* sᵊn*t*'kleəʳ, sɪn*t*-, sᵊŋ- (US) seɪnt'kler

St. Columb sᵊn*t*'kɒl.əm, sɪn*t*- (US) seɪnt'kɑː.ləm

STD ˌes.tiː'diː **ST'D ˌcode**

St. David sᵊn*t*'deɪ.vɪd, sɪn*t*- (US) seɪnt- **-'s** -z

stead (S) sted

steadfast 'sted.fɑːst, -fəst (US) -fæst, -fəst **-ly** -li **-ness** -nəs, -nɪs

steading 'sted.ɪŋ **-s** -z

Steadman 'sted.mən

stead|y 'sted|.i **-ier** -i.əʳ (US) -i.ɚ **-iest** -i.ɪst, -i.əst **-ily** -ɪ.li, -ᵊl.i **-iness** -ɪ.nəs, -ɪ.nɪs **-ies** -iz **-ying** -i.ɪŋ **-ied** -id **ˌsteady 'state** ; **ˌsteady 'state ˌtheory**

steak steɪk **-s** -s **ˌsteak tar'tare** ; **ˌsteak and ˌkidney 'pie**

steakhou|se 'steɪk.haʊ|s **-ses** -zɪz

steal stiːl **-s** -z **-ing** -ɪŋ **stole** stəʊl (US) stoʊl **stolen** 'stəʊ.lᵊn (US) 'stoʊ- **stealer/s** 'stiː.ləʳ/z (US) -lɚ/z

stealth stelθ

stealth|y 'stel.θ|i **-ier** -i.əʳ (US) -i.ɚ **-iest** -i.ɪst, -i.əst **-ily** -ɪ.li, -ᵊl.i **-iness** -ɪ.nəs, -ɪ.nɪs

steam stiːm **-s** -z **-ing** -ɪŋ **-ed** -d **-er/s** -əʳ/z (US) -ɚ/z **'steam ˌengine** ; **'steam ˌiron** ; **'steam ˌpower**

steamboat 'stiːm.bəʊt (US) -boʊt **-s** -s

steam-hammer 'stiːmˌhæm.əʳ (US) -ɚ **-s** -z

steamroll 'stiːm.rəʊl (US) -roʊl **-s** -z **-ing** -ɪŋ **-ed** -d

steamroll|er 'stiːmˌrəʊ.l|əʳ (US) -ˌroʊ.l|ɚ **-ers** -əz (US) -ɚz **-ering** -ᵊr.ɪŋ **-ered** -əd (US) -ɚd

steamship 'stiːm.ʃɪp **-s** -s

steam|y 'stiː.m|i **-ier** -i.əʳ (US) -i.ɚ **-iest** -i.ɪst, -i.əst **-iness** -ɪ.nəs, -ɪ.nɪs

stearic sti'ær.ɪk (US) sti'ær-; 'stɪr-

stearin 'stɪə.rɪn (US) 'stiː.ɚ.ɪn; 'stɪr-

Stearn(e) stɜːn (US) stɜːrn **-s** -z

steatite 'stɪə.taɪt (US) 'stiː.ə-

steatolysis stɪə'tɒl.ə.sɪs, '-ɪ- (US) ˌstiː.ə'tɑː.lə-

steatopygia ˌstɪə.təʊ'pɪdʒ.i.ə, -'paɪ.dʒi-, '-dʒə (US) ˌstiː.æt.ə'paɪ.dʒi.ə, -'pɪdʒ.i-

steatopygous ˌstɪə.təʊ'paɪ.gəs; stɪə'tɒp.ɪ- (US) ˌstiː.æt.ə'paɪ-

Stedman 'sted.mən

St. Edmunds sᵊnt'ed.mənd*z*, sɪnt- (US) seɪnt-

steed stiːd **-s** -z

steel (S) stiːl **-s** -z **-ing** -ɪŋ **-ed** -d **ˌsteel 'wool**

Steele stiːl

steel-plated ˌstiːl'pleɪ.tɪd (US) '-ˌ-- *stress shift, British only:* ˌsteel-plated 'hull

steelworker 'stiːlˌwɜː.kəʳ (US) ˌwɜːr.kɚ **-s** -z

steelworks 'stiːl.wɜːks (US) -wɜːrks

steel|y 'stiː.l|i **-ier** -i.əʳ (US) -i.ɚ **-iest** -i.ɪst, -i.əst **-iness** -ɪ.nəs, -ɪ.nɪs

steelyard 'stiːl.jɑːd, 'stɪl.jəd (US) 'stiːl.jɑːrd, 'stɪl.jɚd **-s** -z

steenbok 'stiːn.bɒk, 'steɪn- (US) -bɑːk **-s** -s

Steenson 'stiːn*t*.sən

steep stiːp **-s** -s **-er** -əʳ (US) -ɚ **-est** -ɪst, -əst **-ly** -li **-ness** -nəs, -nɪs **-ing** -ɪŋ **-ed** -t

steepen 'stiː.pᵊn **-s** -z **-ing** -ɪŋ, 'stiːp.nɪŋ **-ed** -d

steeple 'stiː.pl̩ **-s** -z **-d** -d

steeplechas|e 'stiː.pl̩.tʃeɪs **-es** -ɪz **-ing** -ɪŋ **-er/s** -əʳ/z (US) -ɚ/z

steeplejack 'stiː.pl̩.dʒæk **-s** -s

steer stɪəʳ (US) stɪr **-s** -z **-ing** -ɪŋ **-ed** -d **-er/s** -əʳ/z (US) -ɚ/z **'steering ˌgear** ; **'steering comˌmittee** ; **'steering ˌwheel**

steerage 'stɪə.rɪdʒ (US) 'stɪr.ɪdʒ

steers|man 'stɪəz|.mən (US) 'stɪrz- **-men** -mən

steev|e stiːv **-es** -z **-ing** -ɪŋ **-ed** -d

Steevens 'stiː.vᵊnz

Stefanie 'stef.ᵊn.i

stein *beer mug:* staɪn *as if German:* ʃtaɪn **-s** -z

Stein *surname:* staɪn, stiːn *as if German:* ʃtaɪn

Steinbeck 'staɪn.bek, 'staɪm- (US) 'staɪn-

steinbock 'staɪn.bɒk, 'staɪm- (US) 'staɪn.bɑːk **-s** -s

Steinem 'staɪ.nəm

Steiner 'staɪ.nəʳ (US) -nɚ

Steinway® 'staɪn.weɪ **-s** -z

stel|e *monument:* 'stiː.l|i; stiːl (US) 'stiː.l|i **-ae** -iː **-es** 'stiː.liz; stiːlz (US) 'stiː.liz *in architecture or botany:* 'stiː.l|i; stiːl (US) stiːl; 'stiː.l|i **-ae** -iː **-es** 'stiː.liz; stiːlz (US) stiːlz; 'stiː.liz

St. Elian sᵊnt'iː.li.ən, sɪnt- (US) seɪnt-

St. Elias sᵊnt.ɪ'laɪ.əs, sɪnt-, -æs (US) ˌseɪnt.ɪ'laɪ.əs

Stella 'stel.ə **ˌStella 'Artois** *as if French:* **ˌStella Ar'tois**

stellar 'stel.əʳ (US) -ɚ

St. Elmo sᵊnt'el.məʊ, sɪnt- (US) seɪnt'el.moʊ **-'s** -z **St. ˌElmo's 'fire**

stem stem **-s** -z **-ming** -ɪŋ **-med** -d

stemple 'stem.pl̩ **-s** -z

Sten sten **'Sten ˌgun**

stench sten*t*ʃ (US) stentʃ **-es** -ɪz

stencil 'sten*t*.sᵊl, -ɪl (US) -sᵊl **-s** -z **-(l)ing** -ɪŋ **-(l)ed** -d

Stendhal 'stɑ̃ːn.dɑːl, -'- (US) 'sten-, 'stæn-

Stenhouse 'sten.haʊs

Stenhousemuir ˌsten.haʊs'mjʊəʳ, -əs'-, -'mjɔːʳ (US) -'mjʊɚ

Stenness 'sten.əs

steno 'sten.əʊ (US) -oʊ **-s** -z

stenograph 'sten.əʊ.grɑːf, -græf (US) -ə.græf **-s** -s

stenograph|er stə'nɒg.rə.f|əʳ, sten'ɒg- (US) stə'nɑː.grə.f|ɚ **-ers** -əz (US) -ɚ **-y** -i

stenotyp|e 'sten.əʊ.taɪp (US) '-ə- **-ing** -ɪŋ **-ist/s** -ɪst/s

stentorian sten'tɔː.ri.ən (US) -'tɔːr.i-
step step **-s** -s **-ping** -ɪŋ **-ped** -t **-per/s** -əʳ/z (US) -ɚ/z ˌ**step ae'robics** ; '**step** ˌ**dance** ; ˌ**step by 'step**
stepbrother 'stepˌbrʌ.ðəʳ (US) -ðɚ **-s** -z
step|child 'step|.tʃaɪld **-children** -ˌtʃɪl.drᵊn
stepdad 'step.dæd **-s** -z
stepdaughter 'stepˌdɔː.təʳ (US) -ˌdɑː.t̬ɚ, -ˌdɔː- **-s** -z
stepfather 'stepˌfɑː.ðəʳ (US) -ðɚ **-s** -z
Stephanie 'stef.ᵊn.i
Stephano 'stef.ᵊn.əʊ (US) -ə.noʊ
stephanotis ˌstef.ə'nəʊ.tɪs (US) -'noʊ.t̬ɪs
Stephen 'stiː.vᵊn **-s** -z
Stephenson 'stiː.vᵊn.sᵊn
stepladder 'stepˌlæd.əʳ (US) -ɚ **-s** -z
stepmother 'stepˌmʌð.əʳ (US) -ɚ **-s** -z
stepmum 'step.mʌm **-s** -z
Stepney 'step.ni
stepparent 'stepˌpeə.rᵊnt (US) -ˌper.ᵊnt, -ˌpær- **-s** -s
steppe step **-s** -s
stepping-stone 'step.ɪŋ.stəʊn (US) -stoʊn **-s** -z
stepsister 'stepˌsɪs.təʳ (US) -tɚ **-s** -z
stepsson 'step.sʌn **-s** -z
Steptoe 'step.təʊ (US) -toʊ
-ster -stəʳ (US) -stɚ
Note: Suffix. Does not normally change the stress pattern of the word to which it is added, e.g. **prank** /præŋk/, **prankster** /'præŋk.stəʳ (US) -stɚ/.
stereo- ster.i.əʊ-, stɪə.ri-; ˌster.i'ɒ-, ˌstɪə.ri'- (US) ster.i.oʊ-, stɪr-, -ə-; ˌster.i'ɑː-, ˌstɪr-
Note: Prefix. Normally either takes primary or secondary stress on the first syllable, e.g. **stereoscope** /'ster.i.əʊ.skəʊp (US) -ə.skoʊp/, **stereophonic** /ˌster.i.əʊ'fɒn.ɪk (US) -ə'fɑː.nɪk/, or secondary stress on the first syllable and primary stress on the third syllable, e.g. **stereophony** /ˌster.i'ɒf.ᵊn.i (US) -'ɑː.fᵊn-/.
stereo 'ster.i.əʊ, 'stɪə.ri- (US) 'ster.i.oʊ, 'stɪr- **-s** -z
stereophonic ˌster.i.əʊ'fɒn.ɪk, ˌstɪə.ri- (US) ˌster.i.ə'fɑː.nɪk, ˌstɪr-
stereophony ˌster.i'ɒf.ᵊn.i, ˌstɪə.ri'- (US) ˌster.i'ɑː.fᵊn-, ˌstɪr-
stereopticon ˌster.i'ɒp.tɪ.kən, ˌstɪə.ri'- (US) ˌster.i'ɑːp-, ˌstɪr-, -kɑːn **-s** -z
stereoscope 'ster.i.ə.skəʊp, 'stɪə.ri- (US) 'ster.i.ə.skoʊp, 'stɪr- **-s** -s
stereoscopic ˌster.i.ə'skɒp.ɪk, ˌstɪə.ri- (US) ˌster.i.ə'skɑː.pɪk, ˌstɪr- **-al** -ᵊl **-ally** -ᵊl.i, -li
stereoscopy ˌster.i'ɒs.kə.pi, ˌstɪə.ri'- (US) ˌster.i'ɑː.skə-, ˌstɪr-
stereotyp|e 'ster.i.əʊ.taɪp, 'stɪə.ri- (US) 'ster.i.ə-, 'stɪr- **-es** -s **-ing** -ɪŋ **-ed** -t
stereotypic|al ˌster.i.əʊ'tɪp.ɪ.k|ᵊl, ˌstɪə.ri- (US) ˌster.i.ə'-, ˌstɪr- **-ally** -ᵊl.i, -li
sterile 'ster.aɪl (US) -ᵊl
sterility stə'rɪl.ə.ti, ster'ɪl-, -ɪ.ti (US) stə'rɪl.ə.t̬i
sterilization, -isa- ˌster.ᵊl.aɪ'zeɪ.ʃᵊn, -ɪ.laɪ'-, -lɪ'- (US) -ᵊl.ɪ'- **-s** -z
sterilizle, -is|e 'ster.ᵊl.aɪz, -ɪ.laɪz (US) -ə.laɪz **-es** -ɪz **-ing** -ɪŋ **-ed** -d **-er/s** -əʳ/z (US) -ɚ/z
sterling (S) 'stɜː.lɪŋ (US) 'stɜːr-
stern (S) (*adj.*) stɜːn (US) stɜːrn **-er** -əʳ (US) -ɚ **-est** -ɪst, -əst **-ly** -li **-ness** -nəs, -nɪs
Sterne stɜːn (US) stɜːrn
stern|um 'stɜː.n|əm (US) 'stɜːr- **-ums** -əmz **-a** -ə
steroid 'stɪə.rɔɪd, 'ster.ɔɪd (US) 'ster-, 'stɪr- **-s** -z
stertorous 'stɜː.tᵊr.əs (US) 'stɜːr.t̬ɚ- **-ly** -li **-ness** -nəs, -nɪs
stet stet **-s** -s **-ting** -ɪŋ (US) 'stet̬.ɪŋ **-ted** -ɪd (US) 'stet̬.ɪd
stethoscope 'steθ.ə.skəʊp (US) -skoʊp **-s** -s
stethoscopic ˌsteθ.ə'skɒp.ɪk (US) -'skɑː.pɪk **-al** -ᵊl **-ally** -ᵊl.i, -li
stethoscopy steθ'ɒs.kə.pi (US) -'ɑː.skə-
Stetson® 'stet.sᵊn
Steve stiːv
stevedore 'stiː.və.dɔːʳ, -vɪ- (US) -və.dɔːr **-s** -z
Stevenage 'stiː.vᵊn.ɪdʒ
Steven 'stiː.vᵊn **-s** -z
Stevenson 'stiː.vᵊn.sᵊn
Stevenston 'stiː.vᵊn.stᵊn
Stevie 'stiː.vi
stew stjuː (US) stuː, stjuː **-s** -z **-ing** -ɪŋ **-ed** -d
steward (S) 'stjuː.əd, stjʊəd (US) 'stuː.ɚd, 'stjuː- **-s** -z **-ing** -ɪŋ **-ed** -ɪd
stewardess 'stjuː.ə.dɪs, 'stjʊə-, -dəs, -des; ˌstjuː.ə'des (US) 'stuː.ɚ.dɪs, 'stjuː- **-es** -ɪz
stewardship 'stjuː.əd.ʃɪp, 'stjʊəd- (US) 'stuː.ɚd-, 'stjuː-
Stewart stjʊət, 'stjuː.ət (US) 'stuː.ɚt, 'stjuː-, stʊrt
Stewarton 'stjʊə.tᵊn, 'stjuː.ə- (US) 'stuː.ɚ-, 'stjuː-, stʊr.tᵊn
Steyn staɪn
Steyne stiːn
Steyning 'sten.ɪŋ
St. Fagans sᵊn*t*'fæg.ᵊnz, sɪn*t*- (US) seɪnt'fæg-, -'feɪ.gᵊnz
St. Francis sᵊn*t*'frɑːn*t*.sɪs, sɪn*t*- (US) seɪnt'frænt-
stg. (*abbrev. for* **sterling**) 'stɜː.lɪŋ (US) 'stɜːr-
St. Gall sᵊn*t*'gæl, sɪn*t*-, -gɑːl, -gɔːl (US) seɪnt-
St. Gallen sᵊn*t*'gæl.ən, sɪn*t*- (US) seɪnt'gɑː.lən
St. George sᵊn*t*'dʒɔːdʒ, sɪn*t*- (US) seɪnt'dʒɔːrdʒ **-'s** -ɪz
St. Giles sᵊn*t*'dʒaɪlz, sɪn*t*- (US) seɪnt- **-'s** -ɪz
St. Godric sᵊn*t*'gɒd.rɪk, sɪn*t*- (US) seɪnt'gɑː.drɪk
St. Gotthard sᵊn*t*'gɒt.əd, sɪn*t*-, -ɑːd (US) seɪnt'gɑː.t̬ɚd
St. Helen sᵊnt'hel.ən, sɪnt-, -ɪn (US) seɪnt'hel.ən **-s** -z
St. Helena *Saint:* sᵊnt'hel.ə.nə, sɪnt-, '-ɪ- (US) ˌseɪnt.hə'liː-; seɪnt'hel.ə- *island:* ˌsent.*h*ɪ'liː.nə, ˌsɪnt-, sᵊnt-, -*h*ə'- (US) ˌseɪnt.hə'-; seɪnt'hel.ə-
St. Helier sᵊnt'hel.i.əʳ, sɪnt- (US) seɪnt'hel.jɚ **-s** -z
Stich stɪx *as if German:* ʃtiːx
stichomythia ˌstɪk.əʊ'mɪθ.i.ə (US) -ə'-, -oʊ'- **-s** -z
stick stɪk **-s** -s **-ing** -ɪŋ **stuck** stʌk '**stick** ˌ**insect** ; '**sticking** ˌ**plaster** ; '**stick** ˌ**shift** ; **get (**ˌ**hold of) the** ˌ**wrong** ˌ**end of the 'stick**
sticker 'stɪk.əʳ (US) -ɚ **-s** -z
stick-in-the-mud 'stɪk.ɪn.ðəˌmʌd **-s** -z
stickjaw 'stɪk.dʒɔː (US) -dʒɑː, -dʒɔː **-s** -z
stickleback 'stɪk.l̩.bæk **-s** -s
stickler 'stɪk.ləʳ, -l̩.əʳ (US) '-lɚ, -l̩.ɚ **-s** -z
stick-on 'stɪk.ɒn (US) -ɑːn
stickpin 'stɪk.pɪn
stick-up 'stɪk.ʌp **-s** -s
stick|y 'stɪk|.i **-ier** -i.əʳ (US) -i.ɚ **-iest** -i.ɪst, -i.əst **-ily** -ɪ.li, -ᵊl.i **-iness** -ɪ.nəs, -ɪ.nɪs
stickybeak 'stɪk.i.biːk **-s** -s
stiff stɪf **-er** -əʳ (US) -ɚ **-est** -ɪst, -əst **-ly** -li **-ness** -nəs, -nɪs ˌ**stiff** ˌ**upper 'lip**
stiffen 'stɪf.ᵊn **-s** -z **-ing** -ɪŋ, 'stɪf.nɪŋ **-ed** -d
Stiffkey 'stɪf.ki *old-fashioned local pronunciation:* 'stjuː.ki, 'stuː-
stiff-necked ˌstɪf'nekt (US) 'stɪf.nekt *stress shift:* ˌstiff-necked 'pride
stifl|e 'staɪ.fl̩ **-es** -z **-ing/ly** -ɪŋ/li, 'staɪ.flɪŋ/li **-ed** -d
Stiggins 'stɪg.ɪnz
stigma 'stɪg.mə **-s** -z **-tism** -tɪ.zᵊm
stigmata (*alternative plur. of* **stigmata**) stɪg'mɑː.tə (US) -t̬ə, -'mæt̬.ə
stigmatic stɪg'mæt.ɪk (US) -'mæt̬-
stigmatization, -isa- ˌstɪg.mə.taɪ'zeɪ.ʃᵊn, -tɪ'- (US) -t̬ɪ'-
stigmatiz|e, -is|e 'stɪg.mə.taɪz **-es** -ɪz **-ing** -ɪŋ **-ed** -d

stilbene 'stɪl.biːn
stilbestrol stɪl'biː.strəl, -'bes.trəl ⓊⓈ -'bes.trɔːl, -troʊl
stile staɪl **-s** -z
stiletto stɪ'let.əʊ ⓊⓈ -'leţ.oʊ **-(e)s** -z
still (S) stɪl **-s** -z **-er** -əʳ ⓊⓈ -ɚ/z **-est** -ɪst, -əst **-ness** -nəs, -nɪs **-ing** -ɪŋ **-ed** -d ˌ**still 'life** *stress shift:* ˌstill life 'painting
stillbirth 'stɪl.bɜːθ ⓊⓈ -bɜːrθ **-s** -s
stillborn ˌstɪl'bɔːn ⓊⓈ 'stɪl.bɔːrn *stress shift, British only:* ˌstillborn 'baby
Stillson 'stɪl.sᵊn **'Stillson ˌwrench®**
stilly 'stɪl.i
stilt stɪlt **-s** -s
stilted 'stɪl.tɪd ⓊⓈ -ţɪd **-ly** -li **-ness** -nəs, -nɪs
Stilton 'stɪl.tᵊn **-s** -z
Stimpson 'stɪmp.sᵊn
Stimson 'stɪm*p*.sᵊn
stimulant 'stɪm.jə.lənt, -jʊ- **-s** -s
stimu|late 'stɪm.jə|.leɪt, -jʊ- **-lates** -leɪts **-lating** -leɪ.tɪŋ ⓊⓈ -leɪ.ţɪŋ **-lated** -leɪ.tɪd ⓊⓈ -leɪ.ţɪd **-lator/s** -leɪ.təʳ/z ⓊⓈ -leɪ.ţɚ/z
stimulation ˌstɪm.jə'leɪ.ʃᵊn, -jʊ'- **-s** -z
stimulative 'stɪm.jə.lə.tɪv, -jʊ-, -leɪ- ⓊⓈ -leɪ.ţɪv
stimul|us 'stɪm.jə.l|əs, -jʊ- **-i** -aɪ, -iː
stim|y 'staɪ.m|i **-ies** -iz **-ying** -i.ɪŋ **-ied** -id
sting stɪŋ **-s** -z **-ing** -ɪŋ **stung** stʌŋ **stinger/s** 'stɪŋ.əʳ/z ⓊⓈ -ɚ/z **'stinging ˌnettle**
stingo 'stɪŋ.gəʊ ⓊⓈ -goʊ **-s** -z
stingray 'stɪŋ.reɪ **-s** -z
sting|y 'stɪn.dʒ|i **-ier** -i.əʳ ⓊⓈ -i.ɚ **-iest** -i.ɪst, -i.əst **-ily** -ɪ.li, -ᵊl.i **-iness** -ɪ.nəs, -ɪ.nɪs
stink stɪŋk **-s** -s **-ing** -ɪŋ **stank** stæŋk **stunk** stʌŋk
stink-bomb 'stɪŋk.bɒm ⓊⓈ -bɑːm **-s** -z
stinker 'stɪŋ.kəʳ ⓊⓈ -kɚ **-s** -z
stinkpot 'stɪŋk.pɒt ⓊⓈ -pɑːt **-s** -s
stint stɪnt **-s** -s **-ing** -ɪŋ ⓊⓈ 'stɪn.ţɪŋ **-ed** -ɪd ⓊⓈ 'stɪn.ţɪd
stipend 'staɪ.pend, -pənd **-s** -z
stipendiar|y staɪ'pen.di.ᵊr|.i, stɪ- ⓊⓈ staɪ'pen.di.er- **-ies** -iz
stippl|e 'stɪp.l̩ **-es** -z **-ing** -ɪŋ, 'stɪp.lɪŋ **-ed** -d **-er/s** -əʳ/z ⓊⓈ -ɚ/z
stipu|late 'stɪp.jə|.leɪt, -jʊ- **-lates** -leɪts **-lating** -leɪ.tɪŋ ⓊⓈ -leɪ.ţɪŋ **-lated** -leɪ.tɪd ⓊⓈ -leɪ.ţɪd
stipulation ˌstɪp.jə'leɪ.ʃᵊn, -jʊ'- **-s** -z
stipule 'stɪp.juːl **-s** -z
stir stɜːʳ ⓊⓈ stɜːr **-s** -z **-ring/ly** -ɪŋ/li **-red** -d **-rer/s** -əʳ/z ⓊⓈ -ɚ/z
stir|-fry ˌstɜː|'fraɪ ⓊⓈ 'stɜːr|.fraɪ **-fries** -'fraɪz ⓊⓈ -fraɪz **-frying** -'fraɪ.ɪŋ ⓊⓈ -ˌfraɪ.ɪŋ **-fried** -'fraɪd ⓊⓈ -fraɪd *stress shift, British only:* ˌstir-fried 'vegetables
Stirling 'stɜː.lɪŋ ⓊⓈ 'stɜːr- **-shire** -ʃəʳ, -ˌʃɪəʳ ⓊⓈ -ʃɚ, -ˌʃɪr
stirp|s stɜːp|s ⓊⓈ stɜːrp|s **-es** -iːz, -eɪz
stirrup 'stɪr.əp ⓊⓈ 'stɜːr-, 'stɪr- **-s** -s **'stirrup ˌpump**
stitch stɪtʃ **-es** -ɪz **-ing** -ɪŋ **-ed** -t
St. Ivel sᵊnt'aɪ.vᵊl, sɪnt- ⓊⓈ seɪnt-
St. Ives sᵊnt'aɪvz, sɪnt- ⓊⓈ seɪnt-
St. James sᵊn*t*'dʒeɪmz, sɪn*t*- ⓊⓈ seɪnt- **-'s** -ɪz
St. Joan sᵊn*t*'dʒəʊn, sɪn*t*- ⓊⓈ seɪnt'dʒoʊn
St. John *Saint, place:* sᵊn*t*'dʒɒn, sɪn*t*- ⓊⓈ seɪnt'dʒɑːn **-'s** -z *surname:* 'sɪn.dʒᵊn ⓊⓈ seɪnt'dʒɑːn **-'s** -z
St. Joseph sᵊn*t*'dʒəʊ.zɪf, sɪn*t*-, -zəf ⓊⓈ seɪnt'dʒoʊ.zəf, -səf
St. Kilda sᵊn*t*'kɪl.də, sɪn*t*- ⓊⓈ seɪnt-
St. Kitts sᵊn*t*'kɪts, sɪn*t*- ⓊⓈ seɪnt-
St. Kitts-Nevis sᵊn*t*ˌkɪts'niː.vɪs, sɪnt- ⓊⓈ seɪnt-
St. Laurent *Yves:* ˌsæ̃n.lɔː'rɑ̃ːŋ, -lə'- ⓊⓈ -lɔː'rɑːn *place in Canada:* ˌsæn.lɔː'rɒ̃ŋ, -lə'-, -'rɑːnt ⓊⓈ ˌsæ̃.lɔː'rɑːn, ˌsæn.lɔː'rent
St. Lawrence sᵊn*t*'lɒr.ᵊn*t*s, sɪn*t*- ⓊⓈ seɪnt'lɔːr- **St. ˌLawrence 'Seaway**
St. Leger *surname:* sᵊn*t*'ledʒ.əʳ, sɪnt-; 'sel.ɪn.dʒəʳ ⓊⓈ seɪnt'ledʒ.ɚ; 'sel.ɪn.dʒɚ
Note: Most people bearing this name (including the Irish families) pronounce /sᵊn*t*'ledʒ.əʳ ⓊⓈ seɪnt-/. But there are members of the Doncaster family who pronounce /'sel.ɪn.dʒəʳ ⓊⓈ -dʒɚ/.
St. Leger *race:* sᵊn*t*'ledʒ.əʳ, sɪnt- ⓊⓈ seɪnt'ledʒ.ɚ
St. Leonards sᵊn*t*'len.ədz, sɪnt- ⓊⓈ seɪnt'len.ɚdz *city in Quebec:* sæn'leɪ.əʊ.nɑːʳ, -oʊ.nɑːr
St. Levan sᵊn*t*'lev.ən, sɪnt- ⓊⓈ seɪnt-
St. Louis *city in US:* sᵊn*t*'luː.ɪs, sɪnt- ⓊⓈ seɪnt-, -i, *sometimes locally:* sænt- *places in Canada:* sᵊn*t*'luː.i, sɪn*t*-, -ɪs ⓊⓈ seɪnt-
St. Lucia sᵊn*t*'luː.ʃə, sɪnt-, -ʃi.ə, -si.ə ⓊⓈ seɪnt'luː.ʃi.ə, -si-, '-ʃə
St. Ludger sᵊn*t*'luː.dʒəʳ, sɪnt- ⓊⓈ seɪnt'luː.dʒɚ
St. Luke sᵊn*t*'luːk, sɪnt- ⓊⓈ seɪnt-
St. Malo sᵊn*t*'mɑː.ləʊ, sɪn*t*-, sæ̃n- *as if French:* ˌsæ̃n.mɑː'ləʊ ⓊⓈ ˌsæn.mɑː'loʊ
St. Margaret sᵊn*t*'mɑː.gᵊr.ɪt, sɪn*t*-, '-grɪt ⓊⓈ seɪnt'mɑːr.grət **-'s** -s
St. Mark sᵊn*t*'mɑːk, sɪn*t*- ⓊⓈ seɪnt'mɑːrk **-'s** -s
St. Martin sᵊn*t*'mɑː.tɪn, sɪn*t*- ⓊⓈ seɪnt'mɑːr.tᵊn **-'s** -z
St. Mary sᵊn*t*'meə.ri, sɪn*t*- ⓊⓈ seɪnt'mer.i **-'s** -z
St. Mary Axe sᵊn*t*ˌmeə.ri'æks, sɪn*t*- ⓊⓈ seɪntˌmer.i'-
Note: The old form /ˌsɪm.ᵊr.i'æks/ is used in Gilbert and Sullivan's opera 'The Sorcerer'.
St. Marylebone sᵊn*t*'mær.ᵊl.ə.bən, sɪn*t*-, -ɪ.lə- ⓊⓈ seɪnt'mer.ᵊl.ə.boʊn
St. Mary-le-Bow sᵊn*t*ˌmeə.ri.lə'bəʊ, sɪn*t*- ⓊⓈ seɪntˌmer.i.lə'boʊ
St. Matthew sᵊn*t*'mæθ.juː, sɪn*t*- ⓊⓈ seɪnt-
St. Mawes sᵊn*t*'mɔːz, sɪn*t*- ⓊⓈ seɪnt'mɑːz, -'mɔːz
St. Michael sᵊn*t*'maɪ.kᵊl, sɪn*t*- ⓊⓈ seɪnt- **-'s** -z
St. Moritz ˌsæn.mᵊr'ɪts, ˌsæm-; sᵊn*t*'mɒr.ɪts, sɪn*t*- ⓊⓈ ˌsæn.mə'rɪts, ˌseɪnt-, -mɔː'-
St. Neots sᵊn*t*'niː.əts, sɪn*t*-, -niːts ⓊⓈ seɪnt-
St. Nicholas sᵊn*t*'nɪk.ᵊl.əs, sɪn*t*-, '-ləs ⓊⓈ seɪnt-
stoat stəʊt ⓊⓈ stoʊt **-s** -s
Stobart 'stəʊ.bɑːt ⓊⓈ 'stoʊ.bɑːrt
stochastic stɒk'æs.tɪk, stə'kæs- ⓊⓈ stoʊ'kæs-, stə-
stock stɒk ⓊⓈ stɑːk **-s** -s **-ing** -ɪŋ **-ed** -t **'stock ˌcar**; **'stock ˌcube**; **'stock exˌchange**; **'stock ˌmarket**
stockad|e stɒk'eɪd ⓊⓈ stɑː'keɪd **-es** -z **-ing** -ɪŋ **-ed** -ɪd
stockbreed|er 'stɒkˌbriː.d|əʳ ⓊⓈ 'stɑːkˌbriː.d|ɚ **-ers** -əz ⓊⓈ -ɚz **-ing** -ɪŋ
Stockbridge 'stɒk.brɪdʒ ⓊⓈ 'stɑːk-
stockbrok|er 'stɒkˌbrəʊ.k|əʳ ⓊⓈ 'stɑːkˌbroʊ.k|ɚ **-ers** -əʳz ⓊⓈ -ɚz **-ing** -ɪŋ **'stockbroker ˌbelt**
stockfish 'stɒk.fɪʃ ⓊⓈ 'stɑːk-
Stockhausen 'stɒkˌhaʊ.zᵊn *as if German:* 'ʃtɒk- ⓊⓈ 'stɑːk-
stockholder 'stɒkˌhəʊl.dəʳ ⓊⓈ 'stɑːkˌhoʊl.dɚ **-s** -z
Stockholm 'stɒk.həʊm ⓊⓈ 'stɑːk.hoʊlm, -hoʊm
stockinet(te) ˌstɒk.ɪ'net ⓊⓈ ˌstɑː.kɪ'-
stocking 'stɒk.ɪŋ ⓊⓈ 'stɑː.kɪŋ **-s** -z **-ed** -d **'stocking ˌcap**; **'stocking ˌfiller**; **'stocking ˌstitch**; **in one's ˌstocking/ed 'feet**
stock-in-trade ˌstɒk.ɪn'treɪd ⓊⓈ ˌstɑːk-
stockist 'stɒk.ɪst ⓊⓈ 'stɑː.kɪst **-s** -s
stockjobb|er 'stɒkˌdʒɒb|.əʳ ⓊⓈ 'stɑːkˌdʒɑː|.bɚ **-ers** -əz ⓊⓈ -ɚz **-ing** -ɪŋ
stock|man (S) 'stɒk.mən ⓊⓈ 'stɑːk- **-men** -men, -mən
stockpil|e 'stɒk.paɪl ⓊⓈ 'stɑːk- **-es** -z **-ing** -ɪŋ **-ed** -d

Stockport 'stɒk.pɔːt (US) 'stɑːk.pɔːrt
stockpot 'stɒk.pɒt (US) 'stɑːk.pɑːt **-s** -s
stockroom 'stɒk.rʊm, -ruːm (US) 'stɑːk.ruːm, -rʊm **-s** -z
Stocksbridge 'stɒks.brɪdʒ (US) 'stɑːks-
stock-still ˌstɒk'stɪl (US) ˌstɑːk-
stocktaking 'stɒkˌteɪ.kɪŋ (US) 'stɑːk-
Stockton 'stɒk.tən (US) 'stɑːk-
Stockton-on-Tees ˌstɒk.tən.ɒn'tiːz (US) ˌstɑːk.tən.ɑːn'-
Stockwell 'stɒk.wel, -wəl (US) 'stɑːk-
stock|y 'stɒk|.i (US) 'stɑː.k|i **-ier** -i.əʳ (US) -i.ɚ **-iest** -i.ɪst, -i.əst **-iness** -ɪ.nəs, -ɪ.nɪs **-ily** -ɪ.li
Stoddard 'stɒd.əd, -ɑːd (US) 'stɑː.dɚd
Stoddart 'stɒd.ət, -ɑːt (US) 'stɑː.dɚt
stodg|e stɒdʒ (US) stɑːdʒ **-es** -ɪz **-ing** -ɪŋ **-ed** -d **-y** -i **-ier** -i.əʳ (US) -i.ɚ **-iest** -i.ɪst, -i.əst **-iness** -ɪ.nəs, -ɪ.nɪs
stoep stuːp **-s** -s
Stogumber *in Somerset:* stəʊ'gʌm.bəʳ; 'stɒg.əm- (US) stoʊ'gʌm.bɚ; 'stɑː.gəm- *character in Shaw's 'Saint Joan':* 'stɒg.əm.bəʳ (US) 'stɑː.gəm.bɚ, 'stɔː-
Stogursey stəʊ'gɜː.zi (US) stoʊ'gɜːr-
stoic (S) 'stəʊ.ɪk (US) 'stoʊ- **-s** -s **-al** -ᵊl **-ally** -ᵊl.i, -li
stoicism (S) 'stəʊ.ɪ.sɪ.zᵊm, '-ə- (US) 'stoʊ.ɪ-
stok|e (S) stəʊk (US) stoʊk **-es** -s **-ing** -ɪŋ **-ed** -t **-er/s** -əʳ/z (US) -ɚ/z
Stoke Courcy stəʊ'gɜː.zi (US) stoʊ'gɜːr-
Stoke d'Abernon ˌstəʊk'dæb.ᵊn.ən (US) ˌstoʊk'dæb.ɚ.nən
stokehold 'stəʊk.həʊld (US) 'stoʊk.hoʊld **-s** -z
stokehole 'stəʊk.həʊl (US) 'stoʊk.hoʊl **-s** -z
Stoke Mandeville ˌstəʊk'mæn.də.vɪl, '-dɪ- (US) ˌstoʊk-
Stoke on Trent ˌstəʊk.ɒn'trent (US) ˌstoʊk.ɑːn'-
Stoke Poges ˌstəʊk'pəʊ.dʒɪz (US) ˌstoʊk'poʊ-
stoker (S) 'stəʊ.kəʳ (US) 'stoʊ.kɚ **-s** -z
STOL stɒl, 'es.tɒl (US) stɑːl, 'es.tɑːl
St. Olaves, St. Olave's sᵊnt'ɒl.ɪvz, sɪnt-, -əvz (US) seɪnt'ɑː.lɪvz, -ləvz
stole (S) stəʊl (US) stoʊl **-s** -z
stol|e (*from* **steal**) stəʊl (US) stoʊl **-en** -ən
stolid 'stɒl.ɪd (US) 'stɑː.lɪd **-est** -ɪst, -əst **-ly** -li
stolidity stɒl'ɪd.ə.ti, stə'lɪd-, -ɪ.ti (US) stə'lɪd.ə.t̬i
Stoll stəʊl, stɒl (US) stoʊl, stɑːl
stollen 'stɒl.ən *as if German:* 'ʃtɒl- (US) 'stoʊ.lən *as if German:* 'ʃtoʊ- **-s** -z
stolon 'stəʊ.lɒn, -lən (US) 'stoʊ.lɑːn, -lən **-s** -z

stoma 'stəʊ.mə (US) 'stoʊ- **-s** -z **-ta** -tə
stomach 'stʌm.ək **-s** -s **-ing** -ɪŋ **-ed** -t **'stomach ˌpump**
stomachache 'stʌm.ək.eɪk **-s** -s
stomacher 'stʌm.ə.kəʳ (US) -kɚ **-s** -z
stomachic stəʊ'mæk.ɪk, stɒm'æk-; 'stʌm.ə.kɪk (US) stə'mæk.ɪk
stomati|tis ˌstəʊ.mə'taɪ|.tɪs, ˌstɒm.ə'- (US) ˌstoʊ.mə'taɪ|.t̬ɪs, ˌstɑː- **-tides** -tɪ.diːz **-tises** -tɪ.siːz, -tɪ.ziːz
stomatoscope stəʊ'mæt.ə.skəʊp, stɒm'æt- (US) stoʊ'mæt̬.ə.skoʊp, stɑː- **-s** -s
stomp stɒmp (US) stɑːmp **-s** -s **-ing** -ɪŋ **-ed** -t
ston|e (S) stəʊn (US) stoʊn **-es** -z **-ing** -ɪŋ **-ed** -d **-y** -i **'Stone ˌAge; kill ˌtwo ˌbirds with ˌone 'stone; leave ˌno ˌstone un'turned; a 'stone's ˌthrow, a ˌstone's 'throw**
stone-blind ˌstəʊn'blaɪnd, ˌstəʊm- (US) ˌstoʊn- **-ness** -nəs, -nɪs
stonechat 'stəʊn.tʃæt (US) 'stoʊn- **-s** -s
stone-cold ˌstəʊn'kəʊld, ˌstəʊŋ- (US) ˌstoʊn'koʊld *stress shift, see compound:* **ˌstone-cold 'sober**
stonecrop 'stəʊn.krɒp, 'stəʊŋ- (US) 'stoʊn.krɑːp **-s** -s
stonecutter 'stəʊnˌkʌt.əʳ, 'stəʊŋ- (US) 'stoʊnˌkʌt̬.ɚ **-s** -z
stone-dead ˌstəʊn'ded (US) ˌstoʊn-
stone-deaf ˌstəʊn'def (US) ˌstoʊn- **-ness** -nəs, -nɪs
stoneground ˌstəʊn'graʊnd, ˌstəʊŋ- (US) ˌstoʊn-
Stonehaven 'stəʊnˌheɪ.vᵊn (US) 'stoʊn-
Stonehenge ˌstəʊn'hendʒ (US) 'stoʊn.hendʒ
Stonehouse 'stəʊn.haʊs (US) 'stoʊn-
stonemason 'stəʊnˌmeɪ.sᵊn, 'stəʊm- (US) 'stoʊn- **-s** -z
stonewall (S) ˌstəʊn'wɔːl (US) 'stoʊn- **-s** -z **-ing** -ɪŋ **-ed** -d **-er/s** -əʳ/z (US) -ɚ/z
stoneware 'stəʊn.weəʳ (US) 'stoʊn.wer
stone-washed ˌstəʊn'wɒʃt (US) ˌstoʊn'wɑːʃt, '-- *stress shift, British only:* ˌstonewashed 'jeans
stonework 'stəʊn.wɜːk (US) 'stoʊn.wɜːrk
Stoney 'stəʊ.ni (US) 'stoʊ-
stonking 'stɒŋ.kɪŋ (US) 'stɑːŋ- **-ly** -li
Stonor 'stəʊ.nəʳ, 'stɒn.əʳ (US) 'stoʊ.nɚ, 'stɑː.nɚ
ston|y 'stəʊ.n|i (US) 'stoʊ- **-ier** -i.əʳ (US) -i.ɚ **-iest** -i.ɪst, -i.əst **-ily** -ɪ.li, -ᵊl.i **-iness** -ɪ.nəs, -ɪ.nɪs **ˌstony 'broke**
stony-hearted ˌstəʊ.ni'hɑː.tɪd (US) 'stoʊ.niˌhɑːr.t̬ɪd **-ness** -nəs, -nɪs
Stony Stratford ˌstəʊ.ni'stræt.fəd (US) ˌstoʊ.ni'stræt.fɚd
stood (*from* **stand**) stʊd
stoog|e stuːdʒ **-es** -ɪz **-ing** -ɪŋ **-ed** -d

stook stuːk, stʊk **-s** -s
stool stuːl **-s** -z **'stool ˌpigeon; ˌfall beˌtween two 'stools**
stoop stuːp **-s** -s **-ing** -ɪŋ **-ed** -t **-er/s** -əʳ/z (US) -ɚ/z
stop stɒp (US) stɑːp **-s** -s **-ping** -ɪŋ **-ped** -t **-per/s** -əʳ/z (US) -ɚ/z **'stop ˌvolley**
stopcock 'stɒp.kɒk (US) 'stɑːp.kɑːk **-s** -s
Stopes stəʊps (US) stoʊps
Stopford 'stɒp.fəd (US) 'stɑːp.fɚd
stopgap 'stɒp.gæp (US) 'stɑːp- **-s** -s
stop-go ˌstɒp'gəʊ (US) ˌstɑːp'goʊ
stoplight 'stɒp.laɪt (US) 'stɑːp- **-s** -s
stopover 'stɒpˌəʊ.vəʳ (US) 'stɑːpˌoʊ.vɚ **-s** -z
stoppag|e 'stɒp.ɪdʒ (US) 'stɑː.pɪdʒ **-es** -ɪz
Stoppard 'stɒp.ɑːd, -əd (US) 'stɑː.pɚd
stopper 'stɒp.əʳ (US) 'stɑː.pɚ **-s** -z **-ing** -ɪŋ **-ed** -d
stop-press ˌstɒp'pres (US) ˌstɑːp-
stopwatch 'stɒp.wɒtʃ (US) 'stɑːp.wɑːtʃ, -wɔːtʃ **-es** -ɪz
storage 'stɔː.rɪdʒ (US) 'stɔːr.ɪdʒ **'storage ˌheater**
stor|e stɔːʳ (US) stɔːr **-es** -z **-ing** -ɪŋ **-ed** -d **-able** -ə.bl̩ **'store ˌbrand; 'store deˌtective, ˌstore de'tective**
storefront 'stɔː.frʌnt (US) 'stɔːr- **-s** -s
storehou|se 'stɔː.haʊ|s (US) 'stɔːr- **-ses** -zɪz
storekeep|er 'stɔːˌkiː.p|əʳ (US) 'stɔːrˌkiː.p|ɚ **-ers** -əz (US) -ɚz **-ing** -ɪŋ
storeroom 'stɔː.rʊm, -ruːm (US) 'stɔːr.ruːm, -rʊm **-s** -z
storey (S) 'stɔː.ri (US) 'stɔːr.i **-s** -z **-ed** -d
storiated 'stɔː.ri.eɪ.tɪd (US) 'stɔːr.i.eɪ.t̬ɪd
stork stɔːk (US) stɔːrk **-s** -s
storm (S) stɔːm (US) stɔːrm **-s** -z **-ing** -ɪŋ **-ed** -d **'storm ˌcloud; 'storm ˌlantern; 'storm ˌpetrel; 'storm ˌtrooper; 'storm ˌwindow; a ˌstorm in a 'teacup**
stormbound 'stɔːm.baʊnd (US) 'stɔːrm-
Stormont 'stɔː.mɒnt, -mənt (US) 'stɔːr.mɑːnt, -mənt
Stormonth 'stɔː.mən*t*θ, -mʌn*t*θ (US) 'stɔːr-
stormproof 'stɔːm.pruːf (US) 'stɔːrm-
storm|y 'stɔː.m|i (US) 'stɔːr- **-ier** -i.əʳ (US) -i.ɚ **-iest** -i.ɪst, -i.əst **-ily** -ɪ.li, -ᵊl.i **-iness** -ɪ.nəs, -ɪ.nɪs
Stornoway 'stɔː.nə.weɪ (US) 'stɔːr-
Storr stɔːʳ (US) stɔːr **-s** -z
Storrington 'stɒr.ɪŋ.tən (US) 'stɔːr-
Stort stɔːt (US) stɔːrt

Stortford 'stɔːt.fəd, 'stɔː- ⓤⓢ 'stɔːrt.fɚd, 'stɔːr-
Storthing 'stɔː.tɪŋ ⓤⓢ 'stɔːr.t̬ɪŋ
stor|y (S) 'stɔː.r|i ⓤⓢ 'stɔːr|.i **-ies** -iz **-ied** -id
storyboard 'stɔː.ri.bɔːd ⓤⓢ 'stɔːr.i.bɔːrd **-s** -z
storybook 'stɔː.ri.bʊk ⓤⓢ 'stɔːr.i- **-s** -s
storytell|er 'stɔː.ri,tel|.əʳ ⓤⓢ 'stɔːr.i,tel|.ɚ **-ers** -əʳz ⓤⓢ -ɚz **-ing** -ɪŋ
St. Osyth sᵊnt'əʊ.zɪθ, sɪnt-, -sɪθ ⓤⓢ seɪnt'oʊ-
Stotfold 'stɒt.fəʊld ⓤⓢ 'stɑːt.foʊld
Stothard 'stɒð.əd ⓤⓢ 'stɑː.ðɚd
stotink|a stɒt'ɪŋ.k|ə ⓤⓢ stoʊ'tɪŋ- **-i** -iː
Stoughton *in West Sussex, Leicestershire and US:* 'stəʊ.tᵊn ⓤⓢ 'stoʊ- *in Somerset:* 'stɔː.tᵊn ⓤⓢ 'stɔː-, 'stɑː- *in Surrey:* 'staʊ.tᵊn *surname:* 'stɔː.tᵊn, 'staʊ-, 'stəʊ- ⓤⓢ 'stɔː-, 'stɑː-, 'staʊ-, 'stoʊ-
Note: /'stəʊ.tᵊn ⓤⓢ 'stoʊ-/ in **Hodder & Stoughton**, the publishers.
stoup stuːp **-s** -s
Stour *in Suffolk, Essex:* stʊəʳ ⓤⓢ stʊr *in Kent:* stʊəʳ, staʊəʳ ⓤⓢ stʊr, staʊɚ *in Hampshire:* staʊəʳ, stʊəʳ ⓤⓢ staʊɚ, stʊr *in Warwickshire, Hereford & Worcestershire and Oxfordshire:* staʊəʳ, stəʊəʳ ⓤⓢ staʊɚ, stoʊɚ *in Dorset:* staʊəʳ ⓤⓢ staʊɚ
Stourbridge *in West Midlands:* 'staʊə.brɪdʒ, 'stəʊə- ⓤⓢ 'staʊɚ-, 'stoʊɚ- *Common in Cambridge:* 'staʊə.brɪdʒ ⓤⓢ 'staʊɚ-
Stourhead 'stɔː.hed, 'staʊə- ⓤⓢ 'stɔːr-, 'staʊɚ-
Stourmouth 'staʊə.maʊθ, 'stʊə- ⓤⓢ 'staʊɚ-, 'stʊr-
Stourport 'staʊə.pɔːt, 'stʊə- ⓤⓢ 'staʊɚ.pɔːrt, 'stʊr-
Stourton *surname:* 'stɜː.tᵊn ⓤⓢ 'stɜːr- *in Hereford & Worcestershire:* 'stɔː.tᵊn ⓤⓢ 'stɔːr- *in Wiltshire:* 'stɜː.tᵊn, 'stɔː- ⓤⓢ 'stɜːr-, 'stɔːr-
stout (S) staʊt **-s** -s **-er** -əʳ ⓤⓢ 'staʊ.t̬ɚ **-est** -ɪst, -əst ⓤⓢ 'staʊ.t̬ɪst, -t̬əst **-ly** -li **-ness** -nəs, -nɪs
stout-hearted ,staʊt'hɑː.tɪd ⓤⓢ -'hɑːr.t̬ɪd **-ly** -li **-ness** -nəs, -nɪs
stoutish 'staʊ.tɪʃ ⓤⓢ -t̬ɪʃ
stove stəʊv ⓤⓢ stoʊv **-s** -z
stovepipe 'stəʊv.paɪp ⓤⓢ 'stoʊv- **-s** -s
stovetop 'stəʊv.tɒp ⓤⓢ 'stoʊv.tɑːp **-s** -s
stow (S) stəʊ ⓤⓢ stoʊ **-s** -z **-ing** -ɪŋ **-ed** -d **-age** -ɪdʒ
stowaway 'stəʊ.ə,weɪ ⓤⓢ 'stoʊ- **-s** -z
Stowe stəʊ ⓤⓢ stoʊ
Stowers staʊəz ⓤⓢ staʊɚz
Stowey 'stəʊ.i ⓤⓢ 'stoʊ-
Stowmarket 'stəʊ,mɑː.kɪt ⓤⓢ 'stoʊ,mɑːr-
Stow-on-the-Wold ,stəʊ.ɒn.ðə'wəʊld ⓤⓢ ,stoʊ.ɑːn.ðə'woʊld
St. Pancras sᵊn*t*'pæŋ.krəs, sɪn*t*-, sᵊm- ⓤⓢ seɪnt-, -'pæn-
St. Patrick sᵊn*t*'pæt.rɪk, sɪn*t*-, sᵊm- ⓤⓢ seɪnt- **St. 'Patrick's ,Day**
St. Paul sᵊn*t*'pɔːl, sɪn*t*-, sᵊm- ⓤⓢ seɪnt'pɑːl, -'pɔːl **-'s** -z
St. Peter sᵊn*t*'piː.təʳ, sɪn*t*-, sᵊm- ⓤⓢ seɪnt'piː.t̬ɚ **-'s** -z
St. Petersburg sᵊn*t*'piː.təz.bɜːg, sɪn*t*-, sᵊm- ⓤⓢ seɪnt'piː.t̬ɚz.bɜːrg
Strabane strə'bæn
strabismus strə'bɪz.məs, stræb'ɪz- ⓤⓢ strə'bɪz-
Strabo 'streɪ.bəʊ ⓤⓢ -boʊ
Strabolgi strə'bəʊ.gi ⓤⓢ -'boʊ-
Strachan strɔːn; 'stræk.ən ⓤⓢ strɑːn, strɔːn; 'stræk.ən
Strachey 'streɪ.tʃi ⓤⓢ -ki, -tʃi
Strad stræd **-s** -z
Strada® 'strɑː.də **-s** -z
straddl|e 'stræd.l̩ **-es** -z **-ing** -ɪŋ, 'stræd.lɪŋ **-ed** -d
Stradivari ,stræd.ɪ'vɑː.ri, -ə'- ⓤⓢ ,strɑː.di'vɑːr.i **-s** -z
Stradivarius ,stræd.ɪ'veə.ri.əs, -ə'-, -'vɑː- ⓤⓢ -ə'ver.i- **-es** -ɪz
straf|e strɑːf, streɪf ⓤⓢ streɪf **-s** -s **-ing/s** -ɪŋ/z **-ed** -t
Strafford 'stræf.əd ⓤⓢ -ɚd
straggl|e 'stræg.l̩ **-es** -z **-ing** -ɪŋ, 'stræg.lɪŋ **-ed** -d **-er/s** -əʳ/z, 'stræg.ləʳ/z ⓤⓢ '-l̩.ɚ/z, '-lɚ/z
straggl|y 'stræg.l̩|.i, '-l|i **-iness** -ɪ.nəs, -ɪ.nɪs
Strahan strɔːn, strɑːn
straight streɪt **-er** -əʳ ⓤⓢ 'streɪ.t̬ɚ **-est** -ɪst, -əst ⓤⓢ 'streɪ.t̬ɪst, -t̬əst **-ness** -nəs, -nɪs **,straight 'face** ; **,straight and 'narrow**
straightaway ,streɪt.ə'weɪ ⓤⓢ ,streɪt̬- **-s**
straightedg|e 'streɪt.edʒ ⓤⓢ 'streɪt̬- **-es** -ɪz
straighten 'streɪ.tᵊn **-s** -z **-ing** -ɪŋ, 'streɪt.nɪŋ **-ed** -d
straight-faced ,streɪt'feɪst **-ly** -'feɪ.sɪd.li *stress shift:* ,straight-faced 'speaker
straightforward ,streɪt'fɔː.wəd ⓤⓢ -'fɔːr.wɚd **-ly** -li **-ness** -nəs, -nɪs
straightjacket 'streɪt,dʒæk.ɪt **-s** -s **-ing** -ɪŋ **-ed** -ɪd
straightlaced ,streɪt'leɪst ⓤⓢ '-- **-ly** -'leɪ.sɪd.li **-ness** -nəs, -nɪs *stress shift, British only:* ,straightlaced 'teacher
straightway 'streɪt.weɪ
strain (S) streɪn **-s** -z **-ing** -ɪŋ **-ed** -d **-er/s** -əʳ/z ⓤⓢ -ɚ/z
strait (S) streɪt **-s** -s **-ened** -ᵊnd
straitjacket 'streɪt,dʒæk.ɪt **-s** -s **-ing** -ɪŋ **-ed** -ɪd
straitlaced ,streɪt'leɪst ⓤⓢ '-- **-ly** -'leɪ.sɪd.li **-ness** -nəs, -nɪs *stress shift, British only:* ,straitlaced 'teacher
Straker 'streɪ.kəʳ ⓤⓢ -kɚ
strand (S) strænd **-s** -z **-ing** -ɪŋ **-ed** -ɪd
strang|e (S) streɪndʒ **-er** -əʳ ⓤⓢ -ɚ **-est** -ɪst, -əst **-ly** -li **-ness** -nəs, -nɪs
stranger 'streɪn.dʒəʳ ⓤⓢ -dʒɚ **-s** -z
Strangeways 'streɪndʒ.weɪz
Strangford 'stræŋ.fəd ⓤⓢ -fɚd
strangl|e 'stræŋ.gl̩ **-es** -z **-ing** -ɪŋ, 'stræŋ.glɪŋ **-ed** -d **-er/s** -əʳ/z ⓤⓢ -ɚ/z
stranglehold 'stræŋ.gl̩.həʊld ⓤⓢ -hoʊld **-s** -z
strangu|late 'stræŋ.gjə|.leɪt, -gjʊ- **-lates** -leɪts **-lating** -leɪ.tɪŋ ⓤⓢ -leɪ.t̬ɪŋ **-lated** -leɪ.tɪd ⓤⓢ -leɪ.t̬ɪd
strangulation ,stræŋ.gjə'leɪ.ʃᵊn, -gjʊ'- **-s** -z
Strangways 'stræŋ.weɪz
Stranraer stræn'rɑːʳ, strən- ⓤⓢ -'rɑːr
strap stræp **-s** -s **-ping** -ɪŋ **-ped** -t **-per/s** -əʳ/z ⓤⓢ -ɚ/z **-py** -i
strap|hang 'stræp|.hæŋ **-hangs** -hæŋz **-hanging** -,hæŋ.ɪŋ **-hung** -hʌŋ **-hanger/s** -,hæŋ.əʳ/z ⓤⓢ -ɚ/z
strapless 'stræp.ləs, -lɪs
Strasb(o)urg 'stræz.bɜːg, -bʊəg, -bɔːg ⓤⓢ 'strɑːs.bʊrg, 'strɑːz-; 'stræs.bɜːrg
strata (*plur. of* **stratum**) 'strɑː.tə, 'streɪ- ⓤⓢ 'streɪ.t̬ə, 'stræt̬.ə
stratagem 'stræt.ə.dʒəm, '-ɪ-, -dʒɪm, -dʒem ⓤⓢ 'stræt̬.ə.dʒəm **-s** -z
strategic strə'tiː.dʒɪk, stræt'iː- ⓤⓢ strə'tiː- **-al** -ᵊl **-ally** -ᵊl.i, -li **Stra,tegic De'fence I,nitiative**
strategist 'stræt.ə.dʒɪst, '-ɪ- ⓤⓢ 'stræt̬.ə- **-s** -s
strateg|y 'stræt.ə.dʒ|i, '-ɪ- ⓤⓢ 'stræt̬.ə- **-ies** -iz
Stratford 'stræt.fəd ⓤⓢ -fɚd
Stratford-atte-Bowe ,stræt.fəd,æt.ɪ'bəʊ, -'bəʊ.i; -,æt.ə'bəʊ.ə ⓤⓢ -fɚd,æt̬.ə'boʊ
Stratford-upon-Avon ,stræt.fəd.ə.pɒn'eɪ.vᵊn ⓤⓢ -fɚd.ə.pɑːn'-, -vɑːn
strath stræθ **-s** -s
Strathaven 'streɪ.vᵊn
Strathavon stræθ'ɑːn
Strathclyde stræθ'klaɪd *stress shift:* ,Strathclyde 'campus
Strathcona stræθ'kəʊ.nə ⓤⓢ -'koʊ-
Strathearn stræθ'ɜːn ⓤⓢ -'ɜːrn
Strathmore stræθ'mɔːʳ ⓤⓢ -'mɔːr
strathspey (S) stræθ'speɪ **-s** -z
stratification ,stræt.ɪ.fɪ'keɪ.ʃᵊn, ,-ə- ⓤⓢ ,stræt̬.ə-

strati|fy ˈstræt.ɪ|.faɪ, ˈ-ə- ⓊⓈ ˈstræt̬.ə- **-fies** -faɪz **-fying** -faɪ.ɪŋ **-fied** -faɪd

stratocruiser ˈstræt.əˌkruː.zəʳ ⓊⓈ ˈstræt̬.əˌkruː.zɚ **-s** -z

Straton ˈstræt.ᵊn

stratosphere ˈstræt.əʊˌsfɪəʳ ⓊⓈ ˈstræt̬.ə.sfɪr **-s** -z

stratospheric ˌstræt.əʊˈsfer.ɪk ⓊⓈ ˌstræt̬.əˈsfɪr-, -ˈsfer-

Stratton ˈstræt.ᵊn

strat|um ˈstreɪ.t|əm, ˈstrɑː- ⓊⓈ ˈstreɪ.t̬|əm, ˈstræt̬|.əm **-a** -ə

stratus ˈstreɪ.təs, ˈstrɑː- ⓊⓈ ˈstreɪ.t̬əs, ˈstræt̬.əs

Straus(s) straʊs *as if German:* ʃtraʊs

Stravinsky strəˈvɪn*t*.ski

straw strɔː ⓊⓈ strɑː, strɔː **-s** -z **-y** -i **ˌstraw ˈpoll** ⓊⓈ **ˈstraw ˌpoll** ; **ˌstraw ˈvote** ⓊⓈ **ˈstraw ˌvote** ; **ˌclutch at ˈstraws** ; **the ˌstraw that ˌbreaks the ˌcamel's ˈback**

strawberr|y ˈstrɔː.bᵊr|.i, -br|i ⓊⓈ ˈstrɑːˌber|.i, ˈstrɔː- **-ies** -iz **ˌstrawberry ˈblonde** ; **ˈstrawberry ˌmark**

strawboard ˈstrɔː.bɔːd ⓊⓈ ˈstrɑː.bɔːrd, ˈstrɔː-

stray (S) streɪ **-s** -z **-ing** -ɪŋ **-ed** -d

streak striːk **-s** -s **-ing** -ɪŋ **-ed** -t

streak|y ˈstriː.k|i **-ier** -i.əʳ ⓊⓈ -i.ɚ **-iest** -i.ɪst, -i.əst **-iness** -ɪ.nəs, -ɪ.nɪs **ˌstreaky ˈbacon**

stream striːm **-s** -z **-ing** -ɪŋ **-ed** -d

streamer ˈstriː.məʳ ⓊⓈ -mɚ **-s** -z

streamlet ˈstriːm.lət, -lɪt ⓊⓈ -lɪt **-s** -s

streamlin|e ˈstriːm.laɪn **-es** -z **-ing** -ɪŋ **-ed** -d

stream-of-consciousness ˌstriːm.əvˈkɒn.*t*ʃəs.nəs, -nɪs ⓊⓈ -ˈkɑːn*t*.ʃəs-

Streatham ˈstret.əm ⓊⓈ ˈstret̬-

Streatley ˈstriːt.li

Streep striːp

street (S) striːt **-s** -s **ˈstreet ˌcred** ; **ˌstreet crediˈbility** ⓊⓈ **ˈstreet crediˌbility** ; **ˌstreet ˈtheatre/ˈtheater** ⓊⓈ **ˈstreet ˌtheatre/ˌtheater** ; **ˈstreet ˌvalue**

streetcar ˈstriːt.kɑːʳ ⓊⓈ -kɑːr **-s** -z

streetlight ˈstriːt.laɪt **-s** -s

streetwalk|er ˈstriːtˌwɔː.k|əʳ ⓊⓈ -ˌwɑː.k|ɚ, -ˌwɔː- **-ers** -əz ⓊⓈ -ɚz **-ing** -ɪŋ

streetwise ˈstriːt.waɪz

St. Regis sᵊntˈriː.dʒɪs, sɪnt- ⓊⓈ seɪnt-

Streisand ˈstraɪ.zænd, -sənd, -sænd

strength streŋ*k*θ **-s** -s

strengthen ˈstreŋ*k*.θᵊn **-s** -z **-ing** -ɪŋ, ˈstreŋ*k*θ.nɪŋ **-ed** -d **-er/s** -əʳ/z, ˈstreŋ*k*θ.nəʳ/z ⓊⓈ ˈstreŋ*k*.θᵊn.ɚ/z, ˈstreŋ*k*θ.nɚ/z

strenuous ˈstren.ju.əs **-ly** -li **-ness** -nəs, -nɪs

strep strep **ˌstrep ˈthroat**

strepto|coccus ˌstrep.təʊ|ˈkɒk.əs ⓊⓈ -tə|ˈkɑː.kəs **-cocci** -ˈkɒk.saɪ, -aɪ, -iː ⓊⓈ -ˈkɑːk.saɪ, -aɪ **-coccal** -ˈkɒk.ᵊl ⓊⓈ -ˈkɑː.kᵊl **-coccic** -ˈkɒk.ɪk ⓊⓈ -ˈkɑː.kɪk

streptomycin ˌstrep.təʊˈmaɪ.sɪn ⓊⓈ -təˈ-

stress stres **-es** -ɪz **-ing** -ɪŋ **-ed** -t

stressful ˈstres.fʊl, -fᵊl **-ly** -i **-ness** -nəs, -nɪs

stressless ˈstres.ləs, -lɪs **-ness** -nəs, -nɪs

stretch stretʃ **-es** -ɪz **-ing** -ɪŋ **-ed** -t **ˌstretch(ed) ˈlimo**

stretcher ˈstretʃ.əʳ ⓊⓈ -ɚ **-s** -z **-ing** -ɪŋ **-ed** -d

stretcher-bearer ˈstretʃ.əˌbeə.rəʳ ⓊⓈ -ɚˌber.ɚ **-s** -z

stretchmark ˈstretʃ.mɑːk ⓊⓈ -mɑːrk **-s** -s

stretch|y ˈstretʃ|.i **-ier** -i.əʳ ⓊⓈ -i.ɚ **-iest** -i.ɪst, -i.əst

Stretford ˈstret.fəd ⓊⓈ -fɚd

Strevens ˈstrev.ᵊnz

strew struː **-s** -z **-ing** -ɪŋ **-ed** -d **-n** -n

strewth struːθ

stri|a ˈstraɪ|.ə **-ae** -iː

stri|ate (*v.*) ˈstrɪ|.eɪt **-ates** -eɪts **-ating** -eɪ.tɪŋ ⓊⓈ -eɪ.t̬ɪŋ **-ated** -eɪ.tɪd ⓊⓈ -eɪ.t̬ɪd **striˌated ˈmuscle**

striation straɪˈeɪ.ʃᵊn **-s** -z

stricken (*from* **strike**) ˈstrɪk.ᵊn

Strickland ˈstrɪk.lənd

strict strɪkt **-er** -əʳ ⓊⓈ -ɚ **-est** -ɪst, -əst **-ly** -li **-ness** -nəs, -nɪs

stricture ˈstrɪk.tʃəʳ ⓊⓈ -tʃɚ **-s** -z

strid|e straɪd **-es** -z **-ing** -ɪŋ **strode** strəʊd ⓊⓈ stroʊd **stridden** ˈstrɪd.ᵊn

stridency ˈstraɪ.dᵊn*t*.si

strident ˈstraɪ.dᵊnt **-ly** -li

StrideRite® ˈstraɪd.raɪt

stridu|late ˈstrɪd.jə|.leɪt, -jʊ- ⓊⓈ ˈstrɪdʒ.ə-, ˈ-ʊ- **-lates** -leɪts **-lating** -leɪ.tɪŋ ⓊⓈ -leɪ.t̬ɪŋ **-lated** -leɪ.tɪd ⓊⓈ -leɪ.t̬ɪd **-lation/s** ˌ--ˈleɪ.ʃᵊn/z

strife straɪf

strigil ˈstrɪdʒ.ɪl **-s** -z

strik|e straɪk **-es** -s **-ing/ly** -ɪŋ/li **struck** strʌk **stricken** ˈstrɪk.ᵊn **striker/s** ˈstraɪ.kəʳ/z ⓊⓈ -kɚ/z **ˈstrike ˌpay** ; **ˌstrike while the ˌiron's ˈhot**

strikebound ˈstraɪk.baʊnd

strikebreak|er ˈstraɪkˌbreɪ.k|əʳ ⓊⓈ -k|ɚ **-ers** -əz ⓊⓈ -ɚz **-ing** -ɪŋ

strike-pay ˈstraɪk.peɪ

strim strɪm **-s** -z **-ming** -ɪŋ **-med** -d

Strimmer® ˈstrɪm.əʳ ⓊⓈ -ɚ

Strindberg ˈstrɪn*d*.bɜːg, ˈstrɪm- ⓊⓈ ˈstrɪn*d*.bɜːrg

string strɪŋ **-s** -z **-ing** -ɪŋ **-ed** -d **strung** strʌŋ **stringer/s** ˈstrɪŋ.əʳ/z ⓊⓈ -ɚ/z **ˌstring ˈbean** ; **ˌstring quarˈtet**

stringency ˈstrɪn.dʒən*t*.si

stringendo strɪnˈdʒen.dəʊ ⓊⓈ -doʊ

stringent ˈstrɪn.dʒənt **-ly** -li

stringer (S) ˈstrɪŋ.əʳ ⓊⓈ -ɚ

Stringfellow ˈstrɪŋˌfel.əʊ ⓊⓈ -oʊ

string-pull|ing ˈstrɪŋˌpʊl|.ɪŋ **-er/s** -əʳ/z ⓊⓈ -ɚ/z

string|y ˈstrɪŋ|.i **-ier** -i.əʳ ⓊⓈ -i.ɚ **-iest** -i.ɪst, -i.əst **-iness** -ɪ.nəs, -ɪ.nɪs

strip strɪp **-s** -s **-ping** -ɪŋ **-ped** -t **-per/s** -əʳ/z ⓊⓈ -ɚ/z **ˌstrip carˈtoon** ; **ˈstrip ˌclub** ; **ˈstrip ˌlight** ; **ˌstrip ˈpoker**

strip|e straɪp **-es** -s **-ing** -ɪŋ **-ed** -t **-(e)y** -i **-iness** -ɪ.nəs, -ɪ.nɪs

striplight ˈstrɪp.laɪt **-s** -s **-ing** -ɪŋ

stripling ˈstrɪp.lɪŋ **-s** -z

strippagram ˈstrɪp.ə.græm **-s** -z

strip-search ˌstrɪpˈsɜːtʃ, ˈ-- ⓊⓈ ˈstrɪp.sɜːrtʃ **-es** -ɪz **-ing** -ɪŋ **-ed** -t

stripteas|e ˈstrɪp.tiːz, ˌ-ˈ- **-er/s** -əʳ/z ⓊⓈ -ɚ/z

striv|e straɪv **-es** -z **-ing/s** -ɪŋ/z **strove** strəʊv ⓊⓈ stroʊv **striven** ˈstrɪv.ᵊn **striver/s** ˈstraɪ.vəʳ/z ⓊⓈ -vɚ/z

strobe strəʊb ⓊⓈ stroʊb **-s** -z **ˈstrobe ˌlight**

stroboscope ˈstrəʊ.bə.skəʊp, ˈstrɒb.ə- ⓊⓈ ˈstroʊ.bə.skoʊp, ˈstrɑː- **-s** -s

stroboscopic ˌstrəʊ.bəˈskɒp.ɪk, ˌstrɒb.əˈ- ⓊⓈ ˌstroʊ.bəˈskɑː.pɪk, ˌstrɑː-

stroboscopy strəʊˈbɒs.kə.pi, strɒbˈɒs- ⓊⓈ strəˈbɑː.skə-

strode (*from* **stride**) strəʊd ⓊⓈ stroʊd

stroganoff ˈstrɒg.ə.nɒf ⓊⓈ ˈstrɔː.gə.nɔːf, ˈstroʊ- **-s** -s

strok|e strəʊk ⓊⓈ stroʊk **-es** -s **-ing** -ɪŋ **-ed** -t

stroll strəʊl ⓊⓈ stroʊl **-s** -z **-ing** -ɪŋ **-ed** -d **-er/s** -əʳ/z ⓊⓈ -ɚ/z

Stromberg ˈstrɒm.bɜːg ⓊⓈ ˈstrɑːm.bɜːrg

Stromboli ˈstrɒm.bᵊl.i, -bʊ.li, -bəʊ-; strɒmˈbəʊ.li ⓊⓈ ˈstrɑːm.bə-, -ˈboʊ.li

Stromness ˈstrɒm.nes, ˈstrʌm- ⓊⓈ ˈstrɑːm-, ˈstrʌm-

St. Ronan sᵊntˈrəʊ.nən, sɪnt- ⓊⓈ seɪntˈroʊ-

strong (S) strɒŋ ⓊⓈ strɑːŋ, strɔːŋ **-er** -gəʳ ⓊⓈ -gɚ **-est** -gɪst, -gəst **-ly** -li **-ish** -ɪʃ **ˌstrong ˈlanguage** ; **ˈstrong ˌroom** ; **ˈstrong ˌpoint**

strong-arm ˈstrɒŋ.ɑːm ⓊⓈ ˈstrɑːŋ.ɑːrm, ˈstrɔːŋ- **-s** -z **-ing** -ɪŋ **-ed** -d

strongbox ˈstrɒŋ.bɒks ⓊⓈ ˈstrɑːŋ.bɑːks, ˈstrɔːŋ- **-es** -ɪz

stronghold 'strɒŋ.həʊld (US) 'strɑːŋ.hoʊld, 'strɔːŋ- **-s** -z
strong|man 'strɒŋ|.mæn **-men** -men
strong-minded ˌstrɒŋ'maɪn.dɪd (US) 'strɑːŋ-, 'strɔːŋ- **-ly** -li **-ness** -nəs, -nɪs *stress shift:* ˌstrong-minded 'person
strong-willed ˌstrɒŋ'wɪld **-ness** -nəs, -nɪs *stress shift:* ˌstrong-willed 'child
stronti|a 'strɒn.ti|.ə, -*t*ʃi-, '-*t*ʃ|ə, -tj|ə (US) 'strɑːn*t*.ʃi.|ə, '-ʃ|ə **-an** -ən **-um** -əm
Strood struːd
strop strɒp (US) strɑːp **-s** -s **-ping** -ɪŋ **-ped** -t
strophe 'strəʊ.fi, 'strɒf.i (US) 'stroʊ.fi **-s** -z
strophic 'strɒf.ɪk, 'strəʊ.fɪk (US) 'strɑː.fɪk, 'stroʊ-
stropp|y 'strɒp|.i (US) 'strɑː.p|i **-ier** -i.əʳ (US) -i.ɚ **-iest** -i.ɪst, -i.əst **-iness** -ɪ.nəs, -ɪ.nɪs
Stroud straʊd
Note: *As a surname, the pronunciation* /struːd/ *is sometimes heard.*
strove (*from* **strive**) strəʊv (US) stroʊv
strow strəʊ (US) stroʊ **-s** -z **-ing** -ɪŋ **-ed** -d **-n** -n
struck (*from* **strike**) strʌk
structural 'strʌk.tʃᵊr.ᵊl **-ly** -i ˌ**structural engi'neer**
structural|ism 'strʌk.tʃᵊr.ᵊl|.ɪ.zᵊm **-ist/s** -ɪst/s
structur|e 'strʌk.tʃəʳ (US) -tʃɚ **-es** -z **-ing** -ɪŋ **-ed** -d
strudel 'struː.dᵊl *as if German:* 'ʃtruː- **-s** -z
struggl|e 'strʌg.l̩ **-es** -z **-ing** -ɪŋ, 'strʌg.lɪŋ **-ed** -d **-er/s** -əʳ/z, 'strʌg.ləʳ/z (US) '-l̩.ɚ/z, '-lɚ/z
strum strʌm **-s** -z **-ming** -ɪŋ **-med** -d **-mer/s** -əʳ/z (US) -ɚ/z
strumpet 'strʌm.pɪt **-s** -s
strung (*from* **string**) strʌŋ ˌ**strung 'out**
strung-up ˌstrʌŋ'ʌp
strut strʌt **-s** -s **-ting** -ɪŋ (US) 'strʌt̬.ɪŋ **-ted** -ɪd (US) 'strʌt̬.ɪd
struth struːθ
Struthers 'strʌð.əz (US) -ɚz
Strutt strʌt
Struwwelpeter ˌstruː.əl'piː.təʳ, 'struː.əlˌpiː-; ˌstruːl'piː-, '-ˌ-- (US) 'struː.əlˌpiː.t̬ɚ
strychnine 'strɪk.niːn, -nɪn (US) -naɪn, -nɪn, -niːn
St. Salvator's sᵊn*t*.sæl'veɪ.təz, sɪnt- (US) seɪnt'sæl.və.tɔːrz
St. Simon sᵊn*t*'saɪ.mən, sɪn*t*- (US) seɪnt-
St. Swithin sᵊn*t*'swɪð.ɪn, sɪn*t*- (US) seɪnt-
St. Thomas sᵊn*t*'tɒm.əs, sɪn*t*- (US) seɪnt'tɑː.məs **-'s** -ɪz
St. Trinian's sᵊnt'trɪn.i.ənz
St. Tropez ˌsæ̃n.trəʊ'peɪ (US) ˌsæ̃n.trɔː'peɪ, -troʊ'-
Stuart stjʊət, 'stjuː.ət (US) 'stuː.ɚt, 'stjuː-, stʊrt **-s** -s
stub stʌb **-s** -z **-bing** -ɪŋ **-bed** -d
Stubbings 'stʌb.ɪŋz
Stubbington 'stʌb.ɪŋ.tən
stubbl|e 'stʌb.l̩ **-y** -i, 'stʌb.li
stubborn 'stʌb.ən (US) -ɚn **-er** -əʳ (US) -ɚ **-est** -ɪst, -əst **-ly** -li **-ness** -nəs, -nɪs
Stubbs stʌbz
stubb|y 'stʌb|.i **-ier** -i.əʳ (US) -i.ɚ **-iest** -i.ɪst, -i.əst **-iness** -ɪ.nəs, -ɪ.nɪs **-ies** -iz
stucco 'stʌk.əʊ (US) -oʊ **-(e)s** -z **-ing** -ɪŋ **-ed** -d
stuck (*from* **stick**) stʌk
stuck-up ˌstʌk'ʌp
Stucley 'stjuː.kli (US) 'stuː-, 'stjuː-
stud stʌd **-s** -z **-ding** -ɪŋ **-ded** -ɪd ˌ**stud 'poker**
studding-sail 'stʌd.ɪŋ.seɪl *nautical pronunciation:* 'stʌn*t*.sᵊl **-s** -z
Studebaker 'stjuː.dɪˌbeɪ.kəʳ (US) 'stuː.dəˌbeɪ.kɚ, 'stjuː-
student 'stjuː.dᵊnt (US) 'stuː-, 'stjuː- **-s** -s ˌ**student 'grant** ; ˌ**student 'loan** ; ˌ**student 'teacher** ; ˌ**student 'union**
studentship 'stjuː.dᵊnt.ʃɪp (US) 'stuː-, 'stjuː- **-s** -s
studio 'stjuː.di.əʊ (US) 'stuː.di.oʊ, 'stjuː- **-s** -z ˌ**studio 'flat** (US) '**studio** ˌ**flat**
studious 'stjuː.di.əs (US) 'stuː-, 'stjuː- **-ly** -li **-ness** -nəs, -nɪs
Studley 'stʌd.li
stud|y 'stʌd|.i **-ies** -iz **-ying** -i.ɪŋ **-ied** -id
stuff stʌf **-s** -s **-ing** -ɪŋ **-ed** -t ˌ**stuffed 'shirt**
stuffing 'stʌf.ɪŋ **-s** -z
stuff|y 'stʌf|.i **-ier** -i.əʳ (US) -i.ɚ **-iest** -i.ɪst, -i.əst **-iness** -ɪ.nəs, -ɪ.nɪs **-ily** -ɪ.li
stultification ˌstʌl.tɪ.fɪ'keɪ.ʃᵊn, -tə- (US) -t̬ə-
stulti|fy 'stʌl.tɪ|.faɪ, -tə- (US) -t̬ə- **-fies** -faɪz **-fying** -ˌfaɪ.ɪŋ **-fied** -faɪd
stum stʌm
stumbl|e 'stʌm.bl̩ **-es** -z **-ing** -ɪŋ, 'stʌm.blɪŋ **-ed** -d **-er/s** -əʳ/z, 'stʌm.bləʳ/z (US) '-bl̩.ɚ/z, '-blɚ/z '**stumbling** ˌ**block**
stumm ʃtʊm
stump stʌmp **-s** -s **-ing** -ɪŋ **-ed** -t **-y** -i **-ier** -i.əʳ (US) -i.ɚ **-iest** -i.ɪst, -i.st **-iness** -ɪ.nəs, -ɪ.nɪs
stun stʌn **-s** -z **-ning/ly** -ɪŋ/li **-ned** -d '**stun** ˌ**gun**
stung (*from* **sting**) stʌŋ
stunk (*from* **stink**) stʌŋk
stunner 'stʌn.əʳ (US) -ɚ **-s** -z
stunt stʌnt **-s** -s **-ing** -ɪŋ (US) 'stʌn.t̬ɪŋ **-ed** -ɪd (US) 'stʌn.t̬ɪd
stunt|man 'stʌnt|.mæn **-men** -men
stunt|woman 'stʌnt|ˌwʊm.ən **-women** -ˌwɪm.ɪn
stupa 'stuː.pə **-s** -z
stupe stjuːp (US) stuːp, stjuːp **-s** -s
stupefaction ˌstjuː.pɪ'fæk.ʃᵊn (US) ˌstuː.pə'-, ˌstjuː-
stupe|fy 'stjuː.pɪ|.faɪ (US) 'stuː.pə-, 'stjuː- **-fies** -faɪz **-fying/ly** -ˌfaɪ.ɪŋ **-fied** -faɪd
stupendous stjuː'pen.dəs (US) stuː-, stjuː- **-ly** -li **-ness** -nəs, -nɪs
stupid 'stjuː.pɪd (US) 'stuː-, 'stjuː- **-er** -əʳ (US) -ɚ **-est** -ɪst, -əst **-ly** -li **-ness** -nəs, -nɪs
stupidit|y stjuː'pɪd.ə.t|i, -ɪ.t|i (US) stuː'pɪd.ə.t̬|i, stjuː- **-ies** -iz
stupor 'stjuː.pəʳ (US) 'stuː.pɚ, 'stjuː-
sturd|y 'stɜː.d|i (US) 'stɜːr- **-ier** -i.əʳ (US) -i.ɚ **-iest** -i.ɪst, -i.əst **-ily** -ɪ.li, -ᵊl.i **-iness** -ɪ.nəs, -ɪ.nɪs
sturgeon (S) 'stɜː.dʒᵊn (US) 'stɜːr- **-s** -z
Sturminster 'stɜː.mɪn*t*.stəʳ (US) 'stɜːr.mɪn*t*.stɚ
Sturm und Drang ˌʃtʊəm.ʊn*t*'dræŋ, ˌstʊəm- (US) ˌʃtʊrm.ʊnt'drɑːŋ
Sturtevant 'stɜː.tɪ.vənt, -tə-, -vænt (US) 'stɜːr.t̬ə-
stutt|er 'stʌt|.əʳ (US) 'stʌt̬|.ɚ **-ers** -əz (US) -ɚz **-ering** -ᵊr.ɪŋ **-ered** -əd (US) -ɚd **-erer/s** -ᵊr.əʳ/z (US) -ɚ.ɚ/z
Stuttgart 'ʃtʊt.gɑːt, 'stʊt- (US) 'stʌt.gɑːrt, 'stʊt-, 'ʃtʊt-
Stuyvesant 'staɪ.vɪ.sənt, -və- (US) -və-
St. Valentine sᵊnt'væl.ᵊn.taɪn (US) seɪnt **St. 'Valentine's** ˌ**Day**
St. Vincent sᵊn*t*'vɪn*t*.sᵊnt, sɪn*t*- (US) seɪnt-
St. Vitus sᵊn*t*'vaɪ.təs, sɪn*t*- (US) seɪnt'vaɪ.t̬əs **-'s** -ɪz **St.** ˌ**Vitus's 'dance** (US) **St. 'Vitus's** ˌ**dance**
st|y st|aɪ **-ies** -aɪz
Styal staɪəl
stye staɪ **-s** -z
stygian (S) 'stɪdʒ.i.ən (US) -i.ən, '-ən
styl|e staɪl **-es** -z **-ing** -ɪŋ **-ed** -d
styleless 'staɪl.ləs, -lɪs **-ly** -li **-ness** -nəs, -nɪs
Styles staɪlz
stylet 'staɪ.lət, -lɪt (US) -lɪt **-s** -s
stylish 'staɪ.lɪʃ **-ly** -li **-ness** -nəs, -nɪs
stylist 'staɪ.lɪst **-s** -s
stylistic staɪ'lɪs.tɪk **-s** -s **-ally** -ᵊl.i, -li
stylite 'staɪ.laɪt **-s** -s
Stylites staɪ'laɪ.tiːz (US) -t̬iːz
stylization, -isa- ˌstaɪ.laɪ'zeɪ.ʃᵊn, -lɪ'- (US) -lɪ'-
styliz|e, -is|e 'staɪ.laɪz **-es** -ɪz **-ing** -ɪŋ **-ed** -d

stylograph ˈstaɪ.ləʊ.grɑːf, -græf US -lə.græf **-s** -s
stylographic ˌstaɪ.ləʊˈgræf.ɪk US -ləˈ-
styl|us ˈstaɪ.l|əs **-uses** -ə.sɪz **-i** -aɪ
stym|ie ˈstaɪ.m|i **-ies** -iz **-ying** -i.ɪŋ **-ied** -id
styptic ˈstɪp.tɪk ˌ**styptic** ˈ**pencil**
styrax ˈstaɪə.ræks US ˈstaɪ- **-es** -ɪz
Styrofoam® ˈstaə.rəʊ.fəʊm US -rə.foʊm
Styron ˈstaə.rən
Styx stɪks
suable ˈsuː.ə.bl̩, ˈsjuː- US ˈsuː-
Suak|im ˈsuː.ɑː.k|ɪm, ˈswɑː.k|ɪm US ˈswɑː- **-in** -ɪn
suasion ˈsweɪ.ʒən
sua sponte ˌsuː.ɑːˈspɒn.teɪ US ˌswɑːˈspɑːn.teɪ
suav|e swɑːv **-er** -əʳ US -ɚ **-est** -ɪst, -əst **-ely** -li **-eness** -nəs, -nɪs
suavity ˈswɑː.və.ti, ˈsweɪ-, ˈswæv.ə-, -ɪ.ti US ˈswɑː.və.t̬i, ˈswæv.ə-
sub- sʌb-
sub sʌb **-s** -z **-bing** -ɪŋ **-bed** -d
subacid sʌbˈæs.ɪd, ˌsʌb-
subacute ˌsʌb.əˈkjuːt
subalpine sʌbˈæl.paɪn, ˌsʌb- US -paɪn, -pɪn
subaltern ˈsʌb.əl.tən US səbˈɔːl.tɚn, -ˈɑːl- **-s** -z
subaqua sʌbˈæk.wə, ˌsʌb- US -ˈɑː.kwə, -ˈæk.wə
subarctic sʌbˈɑːk.tɪk, ˌsʌb- US -ˈɑːrk-
Subaru® ˌsuː.bəˈruː, ˈ--- US ˈsuː.bə.ruː **-s** -z
subatomic ˌsʌb.əˈtɒm.ɪk US -ˈtɑː.mɪk ˌ**subatomic** ˈ**particles**
sub-bass ˌsʌbˈbeɪs US ˈ-- **-es** -ɪz
Subbuteo® səˈbjuː.ti.əʊ, sʌbˈjuː-, -ˈuː- US sʌbˈjuː.t̬i.oʊ
subclass ˈsʌb.klɑːs US -klæs **-es** -ɪz
subclassification sʌbˌklæs.ɪ.fɪˈkeɪ.ʃən, ˌsʌb.klæs-, -ə- US ˌsʌb.klæs- **-s** -z
subclassi|fy sʌbˈklæs.ɪ|.faɪ, ˌsʌb-, ˈ-ə- US ˈ-ə- **-fies** -faɪz **-fying** -faɪ.ɪŋ **-fied** -faɪd
subclinical sʌbˈklɪn.ɪ.kəl, ˌsʌb-
subcommittee ˈsʌb.kəˌmɪt.i, ˌsʌb.kəˈmɪt.i US -ˌmɪt̬- **-s** -z
subcompact ˌsʌbˈkɒm.pækt US -ˈkɑːm- **-s** -s
subconscious sʌbˈkɒn.tʃəs, ˌsʌb- US -ˈkɑːnt.ʃəs **-ly** -li **-ness** -nəs, -nɪs
subcontinent sʌbˈkɒn.tɪ.nənt, ˌsʌb- US ˈsʌbˌkɑːn.tən.ənt, ˌsʌbˈkɑːn-
subcontinental ˌsʌb.kɒn.tɪˈnen.təl, -təˈ- US -kɑːn.t̬ənˈen.t̬əl **-ly** -i
subcontract (*v.*) ˌsʌb.kənˈtrækt US sʌbˈkɑːn.trækt **-s** -s **-ing** -ɪŋ **-ed** -ɪd **-or/s** -əʳ/z US -ɚ/z
subcontract (*n.*) ˈsʌbˌkɒn.trækt US -ˌkɑːn-, -ˈkɑːn- **-s** -s **-or/s**
subculture ˈsʌbˌkʌl.tʃəʳ US -tʃɚ **-s** -z
subcutaneous ˌsʌb.kjuːˈteɪ.ni.əs
subdean sʌbˈdiːn, ˌsʌb- **-s** -z
subdivid|e ˌsʌb.dɪˈvaɪd, -dəˈ-, ˈ--ˌ- **-es** -z **-ing** -ɪŋ **-ed** -ɪd
subdivision ˌsʌb.dɪˈvɪʒ.ən, -dəˈ-, ˈsʌb.dɪˌvɪʒ-, -dəˌ- US ˌsʌb.dɪˈvɪʒ.ən, ˈsʌb.dɪˌvɪʒ- **-s** -z
subdominant sʌbˈdɒm.ɪ.nənt, ˌsʌb- US -ˈdɑː.mə- **-s** -s
subdu|e səbˈdjuː US -ˈduː, -ˈdjuː **-es** -z **-ing** -ɪŋ **-ed** -d **-er/s** -əʳ/z US -ɚ/z **-able** -ə.bl̩
subed|it sʌbˈed|.ɪt, ˌsʌb- **-its** -ɪts **-iting** -ɪ.tɪŋ US -ɪ.t̬ɪŋ **-ited** -ɪ.tɪd US -ɪ.t̬ɪd
subeditor sʌbˈed.ɪ.təʳ, ˈsʌbˌed- US sʌbˈed.ɪ.t̬ɚ **-s** -z **-ship/s** -ʃɪp/s
subentr|y ˈsʌbˌen.tr|i, ˌ-ˈ-- **-ies** -iz
subfamil|y ˈsʌbˌfæm.əl|.i, -ɪ.l|i US -əl|.i **-ies** -iz
subfusc ˈsʌb.fʌsk, -ˈ-
subgroup ˈsʌb.gruːp **-s** -s
subhead sʌbˈhed, ˌsʌb- US ˈsʌb.hed **-s** -z
subheading ˈsʌbˌhed.ɪŋ, -ˈ-- US ˈsʌbˌhed- **-s** -z
subhuman sʌbˈhjuː.mən, ˌsʌb- **-s** -z
subito ˈsuː.bɪ.təʊ, ˈsʊb.ɪ- US -t̬oʊ
subjacency sʌbˈdʒeɪ.sənt.si, səb- US sʌb-
subjacent sʌbˈdʒeɪ.sənt, səb- US sʌb-
subject (*n. adj.*) ˈsʌb.dʒɪkt, -dʒekt **-s** -s ˈ**subject** ˌ**matter**
subject (*v.*) səbˈdʒekt, sʌb-; ˈsʌb.dʒekt, -dʒɪkt US səbˈdʒekt **-s** -s **-ing** -ɪŋ **-ed** -ɪd
subjection səbˈdʒek.ʃən
subjective səbˈdʒek.tɪv, sʌb- US səb- **-ly** -li **-ness** -nəs, -nɪs
subjectivism səbˈdʒek.tɪ.vɪ.zəm, sʌb- US səb-
subjectivity ˌsʌb.dʒekˈtɪv.ə.ti, -dʒɪk-, -ɪ.ti US -ə.t̬i
subjoin sʌbˈdʒɔɪn, ˌsʌb- US səb- **-s** -z **-ing** -ɪŋ **-ed** -d
sub judice ˌsʌbˈdʒuː.dɪ.si, ˌsʊb-, -də-, -seɪ; US ˌsʌbˈdʒuː.də.si
subju|gate ˈsʌb.dʒə|.geɪt, -dʒʊ- **-gates** -geɪts **-gating** -geɪ.tɪŋ US -geɪ.t̬ɪŋ **-gated** -geɪ.tɪd US -geɪ.t̬ɪd **-gator/s** -geɪ.təʳ/z US -geɪ.t̬ɚ/s
subjugation ˌsʌb.dʒəˈgeɪ.ʃən, -dʒʊˈ-
subjunct ˈsʌb.dʒʌŋ*k*t **-s** -s
subjunctive səbˈdʒʌŋ*k*.tɪv **-s** -z
subleas|e (*n.*) ˈsʌb.liːs **-s** -ɪz
subleas|e (*v.*) sʌbˈliːs, ˌsʌb- **-es** -ɪz **-ing** -ɪŋ **-ed** -t
sublessee ˌsʌb.lesˈiː **-s** -z
sublessor ˌsʌb.lesˈɔːʳ US -ˈɔːr; sʌbˈles.ɔːr **-s** -z
suble|t sʌbˈle|t, ˌsʌb- US sʌbˈle|t, ˌsʌb-, ˈ-- **-ts** -ts **-tting** -tɪŋ US -t̬ɪŋ
sublieutenanc|y ˌsʌb.lefˈten.ənt.s|i, -ləf- US -luː- **-ies** -iz
sublieutenant ˌsʌb.lefˈten.ənt, -ləfˈ- US -luːˈ- **-s** -s
sublimate (*n.*) ˈsʌb.lɪ.mət, -lə-, -mɪt, -meɪt US -meɪt, -mɪt **-s** -s
subli|mate (*v.*) ˈsʌb.lɪ|.meɪt, -lə- **-mates** -meɪts **-mating** -meɪ.tɪŋ US -meɪ.t̬ɪŋ **-mated** -meɪ.tɪd US -meɪ.t̬ɪd
sublimation ˌsʌb.lɪˈmeɪ.ʃən, -ləˈ-
sublim|e səˈblaɪm **-ely** -li **-eness** -nəs, -nɪs **-es** -z **-ing** -ɪŋ **-ed** -d
subliminal sʌbˈlɪm.ɪ.nəl, səˈblɪm-, -ən.əl US sʌbˈlɪm.ən- **-ly** -i
sublimity səˈblɪm.ə.ti, -ɪ.ti US -ə.t̬i
submachine gun ˌsʌb.məˈʃiːnˌgʌn, -ˈʃiːnˌ- US -ˈʃiːn.- **-s** -z
submarin|e ˌsʌb.mərˈiːn, ˈ--- US ˈsʌb.mə.riːn, ˌ--ˈ- **-es** -z **-ing** -ɪŋ **-ed** -d
submariner sʌbˈmær.ɪ.nəʳ, ˌsʌb-, -ən.əʳ US ˌsʌb.məˈriː.nɚ, ˈsʌb.məˌriː-; sʌbˈmer.ən.ɚ, -ˈmær- **-s** -z
submerg|e səbˈmɜːdʒ, sʌb- US -ˈmɜːrdʒ **-es** -ɪz **-ing** -ɪŋ **-ed** -d **-ence** -ən*t*s
submers|e səbˈmɜːs, sʌbˈ- US səbˈmɜːrs **-es** -ɪz **-ing** -ɪŋ **-ed** -t
submersible səbˈmɜː.sə.bl̩, sʌb-, -sɪ- US -ˈmɜːr.sə- **-s** -z
submersion səbˈmɜː.ʃən, sʌb- US -ˈmɜːr.ʒən, -ʃən **-s** -z
submission səbˈmɪʃ.ən **-s** -z
submissive səbˈmɪs.ɪv **-ly** -li **-ness** -nəs, -nɪs
sub|mit səb|ˈmɪt **-mits** -ˈmɪts **-mitting** -ˈmɪt.ɪŋ US -ˈmɪt̬.ɪŋ **-mitted** -ˈmɪt.ɪd US -ˈmɪt̬.ɪd
submultiple sʌbˈmʌl.tɪ.pl̩, ˌsʌb- US -t̬ə- **-s** -z
subnormal sʌbˈnɔː.məl, ˌsʌb- US -ˈnɔːr- **-ly** -i
subnormality ˌsʌb.nɔːˈmæl.ə.ti, -ɪ.ti US -nɔːr.mæl.ə.t̬i
subnuclear sʌbˈnjuː.kli.əʳ, ˌsʌb- US -ˈnuː.kli.ɚ, -ˈnjuː-
suboctave ˈsʌbˌɒk.tɪv US -ˌɑːk- **-s** -z
suborbital sʌbˈɔː.bɪ.təl, ˌsʌb- US -ˈɔːr.bə.t̬əl
subordinate (*n. adj.*) səˈbɔː.dən.ət, -dɪ.nət, -ˈbɔːd.nət, -nɪt US -ˈbɔːr.dən.ɪt **-s** -s **-ly** -li
subordin|ate (*v.*) səˈbɔː.dɪ.n|eɪt US -ˈbɔːr.dən|.eɪt **-ates** -eɪts **-ating** -eɪ.tɪŋ US -eɪ.t̬ɪŋ **-ated** -eɪ.tɪd US -eɪ.t̬ɪd
subordination səˌbɔː.dɪˈneɪ.ʃən US -ˌbɔːr.dənˈeɪ-

subordinative sə'bɔː.dɪ.nə.tɪv, -dᵊn.ə- Ⓤⓢ -'bɔːr.dᵊn.eɪ.t̬ɪv, -dɪ.nə-
suborn sə'bɔːn, sʌb'ɔːn Ⓤⓢ sə'bɔːrn -s -z -ing -ɪŋ -ed -d -er/s -əʳ/z Ⓤⓢ -ɚ/z
subornation ˌsʌb.ɔː'neɪ.ʃᵊn Ⓤⓢ -ɔːr'-
Subotica sə'bɒt.ɪ.tʃə, sʊ- Ⓤⓢ 'suː.bɔː.tiːt.sə, -bə-
subplot 'sʌb.plɒt Ⓤⓢ -plɑːt -s -s
subpoena səb'piː.nə, sʌb-, sə- Ⓤⓢ sə- -s -z -ing -ɪŋ -ed -d
subpostmaster ˌsʌb'pəʊst,mɑː.stəʳ Ⓤⓢ -'poʊst,mæs.tɚ -s -z
subpostmistress ˌsʌb'pəʊst,mɪs.trəs, -trɪs Ⓤⓢ -'poʊst- -es -ɪz
subpostoffice ˌsʌb'pəʊst,ɒf.ɪs Ⓤⓢ -'poʊst,ɑː.fɪs -s -ɪz
subprefect sʌb'priː.fekt, ˌsʌb- -s -s
subprogram ˌsʌb'prəʊ.græm Ⓤⓢ 'sʌb,proʊ-, -grəm -s -z
subrogation ˌsʌb.rəʊ'geɪ.ʃᵊn Ⓤⓢ -roʊ'-, -rə'-
subrogee ˌsʌb.rəʊ'giː Ⓤⓢ -roʊ'-, -rə'- -s -z
subrogor ˌsʌb.rəʊ'gɔːʳ Ⓤⓢ 'sʌb.rə.gɔːr -s -z
sub rosa ˌsʌb'rəʊ.zə, -zɑː Ⓤⓢ -'roʊ.zə
subroutine 'sʌb.ruː,tiːn -s -z
subscrib|e səb'skraɪb -es -z -ing -ɪŋ -ed -d -er/s -əʳ/z Ⓤⓢ -ɚ/z
subscript 'sʌb.skrɪpt
subscription səb'skrɪp.ʃᵊn -s -z
subsection 'sʌb,sek.ʃᵊn -s -z
subsequent 'sʌb.sɪ.kwənt, -sə- Ⓤⓢ -sɪ- -ly -li
subserv|e səb'sɜːv, sʌb- Ⓤⓢ səb'sɜːrv -es -z -ing -ɪŋ -ed -d
subservien|ce səb'sɜː.vi.ənt|s, sʌb- Ⓤⓢ səb'sɜːr- -cy -si
subservient səb'sɜː.vi.ənt, sʌb- Ⓤⓢ səb'sɜːr- -ly -li
subset 'sʌb.set -s -s
subsid|e səb'saɪd -es -z -ing -ɪŋ -ed -ɪd
subsidence səb'saɪ.dᵊnts; 'sʌb.sɪ.dᵊnts, -sə- -s -ɪz
subsidiarity səb,sɪd.i'ær.ə.ti, -ɪ.ti Ⓤⓢ -'er.ə.t̬i, -'ær-
subsidiar|y səb'sɪd.i.ᵊr|.i Ⓤⓢ -er-, -ɚ- -ies -iz -ily -ᵊl.i, -ɪ.li
subsidization ˌsʌb.sɪ.daɪ'zeɪ.ʃᵊn, -sə- Ⓤⓢ -dɪ'- -s -z
subsidiz|e, -is|e 'sʌb.sɪ.daɪz, -sə- Ⓤⓢ -sə- -es -ɪz -ing -ɪŋ -ed -d
subsid|y 'sʌb.sɪ.d|i, -sə- Ⓤⓢ -sə- -ies -iz
sub silentio Ⓤⓢ ˌsʌb.sɪ'len.ti.oʊ, -'lent.ʃi-
subsist səb'sɪst -s -s -ing -ɪŋ -ed -ɪd
subsistence səb'sɪs.tᵊnts **sub'sistence ˌlevel**
subsoil 'sʌb.sɔɪl -s -z
subsonic sʌb'sɒn.ɪk, ˌsʌb- Ⓤⓢ -'sɑː.nɪk
subspecies 'sʌb,spiː.ʃiːz, -ʃɪz, -siːz, -sɪz Ⓤⓢ -ʃiːz, -siːz
substanc|e 'sʌb.stᵊnts -es -ɪz -less -ləs, -lɪs
substandard sʌb'stæn.dəd, ˌsʌb- Ⓤⓢ -dɚd
substantial səb'stæn.tʃᵊl, -'stɑːn- Ⓤⓢ -'stænt.ʃᵊl -ly -i -ness -nəs, -nɪs
substantiality səb,stæn.tʃi'æl.ə.ti, -,stɑːn-, -ɪ.ti Ⓤⓢ -,stænt.ʃi'æl.ə.t̬i
substanti|ate səb'stæn.tʃi|.eɪt, -'stɑːn-; -'stænt.si-, -'stɑːnt- Ⓤⓢ -'stænt.ʃi- -ates -eɪts -ating -eɪ.tɪŋ Ⓤⓢ -eɪ.t̬ɪŋ -ated -eɪ.tɪd Ⓤⓢ -eɪ.t̬ɪd
substantiation səb,stæn.tʃi'eɪ.ʃᵊn, -,stɑːn-, -,stænt.si'-, -,stɑːnt- Ⓤⓢ -,stænt.ʃi'-
substantival ˌsʌb.stᵊn'taɪ.vᵊl
substantive (*n.*) 'sʌb.stᵊn.tɪv Ⓤⓢ -t̬ɪv -s -z
substantive (*adj.*) 'sʌb.stᵊn.tɪv; səb'stæn- Ⓤⓢ -t̬ɪv -s -z -ly -li -ness -nəs, -nɪs
Note: In British English, generally /səb'stæn.tɪv/when applied to rank, pay, etc.
substation 'sʌb,steɪ.ʃᵊn -s -z
substitutable 'sʌb.stɪ.tjuː.tə.bl̩, ˌsʌb.stɪ'tjuː- Ⓤⓢ 'sʌb.stə.tuː.t̬ə-, -tjuː-
substitu|te 'sʌb.stɪ.tjuː|t Ⓤⓢ -stə.tuː|t, -tjuː|t -tes -ts -ting -tɪŋ Ⓤⓢ -t̬ɪŋ -ted -tɪd Ⓤⓢ -t̬ɪd
substitution ˌsʌb.stɪ'tjuː.ʃᵊn Ⓤⓢ -stə'tuː-, -'tjuː- -s -z
substitutional ˌsʌb.stɪ'tjuː.ʃᵊn.ᵊl, -'tjuːʃ.nᵊl Ⓤⓢ -stə'tuː.ʃᵊn.ᵊl, -'tjuː- -ly -i
substitutive 'sʌb.stɪ.tjuː.tɪv Ⓤⓢ -stə.tuː.t̬ɪv, -tjuː-
substrate 'sʌb.streɪt -s -s
substratosphere sʌb'stræt.əʊ,sfɪəʳ, -'strɑː.təʊ- Ⓤⓢ -'stræt.ə.sfɪr -s -z
substrat|um sʌb'strɑː.t|əm, -'streɪ-, '-,-- Ⓤⓢ 'sʌb,streɪ.t̬|əm, -,stræt̬|.əm -a -ə
substructure 'sʌb,strʌk.tʃəʳ Ⓤⓢ -tʃɚ -s -z
subsum|e səb'sjuːm Ⓤⓢ -'suːm -es -z -ing -ɪŋ -ed -d
subsystem 'sʌb,sɪs.təm, -tɪm Ⓤⓢ -təm -s -z
subtangent sʌb'tæn.dʒᵊnt, ˌsʌb- -s -s
subtenancy sʌb'ten.ənt.si, ˌsʌb-, 'sʌb,ten- Ⓤⓢ sʌb'ten-, ˌsʌb-
subtenant sʌb'ten.ᵊnt, ˌsʌb-, '-,-- Ⓤⓢ 'sʌb,ten- -s -s
subtend səb'tend, sʌb- -s -z -ing -ɪŋ -ed -ɪd
subterfug|e 'sʌb.tə.fjuːdʒ Ⓤⓢ -tɚ- -es -ɪz
subterrane|an ˌsʌb.tᵊr'eɪ.ni|.ən Ⓤⓢ -tə'reɪ- -ous -əs
subtext 'sʌb.tekst -s -s
subtil(e) 'sʌt.ᵊl Ⓤⓢ 'sʌt̬.ᵊl; 'sʌb.tɪl
subtility sʌb'tɪl.ə.ti, -ɪ.ti Ⓤⓢ -ə.t̬i
subtiliz|e, -is|e 'sʌt.ᵊl.aɪz, -ɪ.laɪz Ⓤⓢ 'sʌt̬.ᵊl.aɪz, 'sʌb.tɪ.laɪz -es -ɪz -ing -ɪŋ -ed -d
subtilty 'sʌt.ᵊl.ti, -ɪl- Ⓤⓢ 'sʌt̬.ᵊl.t̬i, 'sʌb.tɪl-
subtitl|e 'sʌb,taɪ.tl̩, -'-- Ⓤⓢ 'sʌb,taɪ.t̬l̩ -es -z -ing -ɪŋ -ed -d
subtl|e 'sʌt.l̩ Ⓤⓢ 'sʌt̬- -er -əʳ, 'sʌt.ləʳ Ⓤⓢ 'sʌt̬.l̩.ɚ, 'sʌt.lɚ -est -ɪst, -əst, 'sʌt.lɪst, -ləst Ⓤⓢ 'sʌt̬.l̩.ɪst, -əst, 'sʌt.lɪst, -ləst -y -i -eness -nəs, -nɪs
subtlet|y 'sʌt.l̩.t|i Ⓤⓢ 'sʌt̬.l̩.t̬|i -ies -iz
subtopia sʌb'təʊ.pi.ə Ⓤⓢ -'toʊ-
subtotal 'sʌb,təʊ.tᵊl, -'--, ,-'-- Ⓤⓢ 'sʌb,toʊ.t̬ᵊl -s -s -(l)ing -ɪŋ -(l)ed -d
subtract səb'trækt -s -s -ing -ɪŋ -ed -ɪd
subtraction səb'træk.ʃᵊn -s -z
subtrahend 'sʌb.trə.hend -s -z
subtropic sʌb'trɒp.ɪk Ⓤⓢ -'trɑː.pɪk -s -s
subtropical sʌb'trɒp.ɪ.kᵊl, ˌsʌb- Ⓤⓢ -'trɑː.pɪ-
suburb 'sʌb.ɜːb Ⓤⓢ -ɜːrb -s -z
suburban sə'bɜː.bᵊn Ⓤⓢ -'bɜːr-
suburbanite sə'bɜː.bᵊn.aɪt Ⓤⓢ -'bɜːr- -s -s
suburbanization, -isa- sə,bɜː.bᵊn.aɪ'zeɪ.ʃᵊn Ⓤⓢ -,bɜːr-, -ɪ'-
suburbaniz|e, -is|e sə'bɜː.bᵊn.aɪz Ⓤⓢ -'bɜːr- -es -ɪz -ing -ɪŋ -ed -d
suburbia sə'bɜː.bi.ə Ⓤⓢ -'bɜːr-
subvariet|y 'sʌb.vᵊr,aɪ.ə.t|i Ⓤⓢ -və,raɪ.ə.t̬|i -ies -iz
subvention səb'ven.tʃᵊn, sʌb- Ⓤⓢ -'vent.ʃᵊn -s -z
subversion səb'vɜː.ʃᵊn, sʌb-, -ʒᵊn Ⓤⓢ -'vɜːr.ʒᵊn, -ʃᵊn
subversive səb'vɜː.sɪv, sʌb- Ⓤⓢ -'vɜːr- -ly -li -ness -nəs, -nɪs
sub|vert sʌb|'vɜːt, səb- Ⓤⓢ -'vɜːrt -verts -'vɜːts Ⓤⓢ -'vɜːrts -verting -'vɜː.tɪŋ Ⓤⓢ -'vɜːr.t̬ɪŋ -verted -'vɜː.tɪd Ⓤⓢ -'vɜːr.t̬ɪd
subway 'sʌb.weɪ -s -z
subzero sʌb'zɪə.rəʊ, ˌsʌb- Ⓤⓢ -'zɪr.oʊ, -'ziː.roʊ
succeed sək'siːd -s -z -ing -ɪŋ -ed -ɪd
succès de scandale sjuːk,seɪ.də,skɑ̃ːn'dɑːl *as if French:* sʊk-
success sək'ses -es -ɪz **suc'cess ˌstory**
successful sək'ses.fᵊl, -fʊl -ly -li -ness -nəs, -nɪs
succession sək'seʃ.ᵊn -s -z
successive sək'ses.ɪv -ly -li
successor sək'ses.əʳ Ⓤⓢ -ɚ -s -z

succinct sək'sɪŋkt, sʌk- **-ly** -li **-ness** -nəs, -nɪs
succ|or 'sʌk|.əʳ (US) -ɚ **-ors** -əz (US) -ɚz **-oring** -ᵊr.ɪŋ **-ored** -əd (US) -ɚd
succory 'sʌk.ᵊr.i
succotash 'sʌk.ə.tæʃ
Succoth 'sʌk.əs, 'sʊk-; sʊ'kɒt (US) 'sʊk.əs; 'suː.koːt
succ|our 'sʌk|.əʳ (US) -ɚ **-ours** -əz (US) -ɚz **-ouring** -ᵊr.ɪŋ **-oured** -əd (US) -ɚd
succub|a 'sʌk.jə.b|ə, -jʊ- **-ae** -iː
succub|us 'sʌk.jə.b|əs, -jʊ- **-i** -aɪ
succulence 'sʌk.jə.lənts, -jʊ-
succulent 'sʌk.jə.lənt, -jʊ- **-ly** -li
succumb sə'kʌm **-s** -z **-ing** -ɪŋ **-ed** -d
such *usual form:* sʌtʃ *occasional weak form:* sətʃ
such-and-such 'sʌtʃ.ᵊn.sʌtʃ
Suchard® 'suː.ʃɑːd, -ʃɑː (US) -ʃɑːrd
suchlike 'sʌtʃ.laɪk
suck sʌk **-s** -s **-ing** -ɪŋ **-ed** -t **'sucking ˌpig**
sucker 'sʌk.əʳ (US) -ɚ **-s** -z
suckl|e 'sʌk.l̩ **-es** -z **-ing** -ɪŋ, 'sʌk.lɪŋ **-ed** -d
suckling (S) 'sʌk.lɪŋ, '-l̩.ɪŋ **-s** -z
sucre *currency:* 'suː.kreɪ **-s** -z
Sucre *in Bolivia:* 'suː.kreɪ
sucrose 'suː.krəʊs, 'sjuː-, -krəʊz (US) 'suː.kroʊs
suction 'sʌk.ʃᵊn **'suction ˌpad**; **'suction ˌpump**
Sudan suː'dɑːn, sʊ-, -'dæn (US) suː'dæn
Sudanese ˌsuː.dᵊn'iːz
Sudanic suː'dæn.ɪk, sʊ- (US) suː-
sudarium sjuː'deə.ri.əm, suː- (US) suː'der.i- **-s** -z
sudatory 'sjuː.də.tᵊr.i, 'suː- (US) 'suː.də.toːr-
Sudbury 'sʌd.bᵊr.i, 'sʌb- (US) 'sʌd.ber-, -bɚ-
sudd sʌd
sudden 'sʌd.ᵊn **-est** -ɪst, -əst **-ly** -li **-ness** -nəs, -nɪs **ˌsudden 'death**
Sudetenland sʊ'deɪ.tᵊn.lænd (US) suː-
sudorific ˌsjuː.dᵊr'ɪf.ɪk, ˌsuː-, -dɒr'- (US) ˌsuː.də'rɪf- **-s** -s
suds sʌdz
suds|y 'sʌd.z|i **-ier** -i.əʳ (US) -i.ɚ **-iest** -i.ɪst, -i.əst **-iness** -ɪ.nəs, -ɪ.nɪs
su|e (S) suː, sjuː (US) suː **-es** -z **-ing** -ɪŋ **-ed** -d
suede sweɪd
su|et 'suː|.ɪt, 'sjuː- (US) 'suː- **-ety** -ɪ.ti (US) -ɪ.t̬i **ˌsuet 'pudding**
Suetonius swɪ'təʊ.ni.əs, swiː-, ˌsjuː.ɪ'-, ˌsuː-, -iː'- (US) swiː'toʊ-, swɪ-
Suez 'suː.ɪz, 'sjuː- (US) suː'ez, '-- **ˌSuez Ca'nal**
suff|er 'sʌf|.əʳ (US) -ɚ **-ers** -əz (US) -ɚz **-ering/s** -ᵊr.ɪŋ/z **-ered** -əd (US) -ɚd **-erer/s** -ᵊr.əʳ/z (US) -ɚ.ɚ/z **-erable** -ᵊr.ə.bl̩ **-erance** -ᵊr.ᵊnts
suffic|e sə'faɪs **-es** -ɪz **-ing** -ɪŋ **-ed** -t
sufficiency sə'fɪʃ.ᵊnt.si
sufficient sə'fɪʃ.ᵊnt **-ly** -li
suffix (*v.*) 'sʌf.ɪks; sə'fɪks, sʌf'ɪks (US) 'sʌf.ɪks; sə'fɪks **-es** -ɪz **-ing** -ɪŋ **-ed** -t
suffix (*n.*) 'sʌf.ɪks **-es** -ɪz
suffo|cate 'sʌf.ə|.keɪt **-cates** -keɪts **-cating/ly** -keɪ.tɪŋ/li (US) -keɪ.t̬ɪŋ/li **-cated** -keɪ.tɪd (US) -keɪ.t̬ɪd
suffocation ˌsʌf.ə'keɪ.ʃᵊn
Suffolk 'sʌf.ək
suffragan 'sʌf.rə.gən **-s** -z
suffrag|e 'sʌf.rɪdʒ **-es** -ɪz
suffragette ˌsʌf.rə'dʒet **-s** -s
suffragist 'sʌf.rə.dʒɪst **-s** -s
suffus|e sə'fjuːz, sʌf'juːz (US) sə'fjuːz **-es** -ɪz **-ing** -ɪŋ **-ed** -d
suffusion sə'fjuː.ʒᵊn, sʌf'juː- (US) sə'fjuː- **-s** -z
Suf|i 'suː.f|i **-is** -iz **-ism** -ɪ.zᵊm **-ic** -ɪk
sug|ar 'ʃʊg|.əʳ (US) -ɚ **-ars** -əz (US) -ɚz **-aring** -ᵊr.ɪŋ **-ared** -əd (US) -ɚd **'sugar ˌbeet**; **'sugar ˌdaddy**
sugarcane 'ʃʊg.ə.keɪn (US) '-ɚ- **-s** -z
sugarloa|f 'ʃʊg.ə.ləʊ|f (US) -ɚ.loʊ|f **-ves** -vz **ˌSugarloaf 'Mountain**
sugarplum 'ʃʊg.ə.plʌm (US) '-ɚ- **-s** -z
sugar|y 'ʃʊg.ᵊr|.i **-iest** -i.ɪst, -i.əst **-iness** -ɪ.nəs, -ɪ.nɪs
suggest sə'dʒest (US) səg-, sə- **-s** -s **-ing** -ɪŋ **-ed** -ɪd
suggestibility səˌdʒes.tə'bɪl.ə.ti, -tɪ'-, -ɪ.ti (US) -ə.t̬i
suggestible sə'dʒes.tə.bl̩, -tɪ- (US) səg'dʒes.tə-
suggestion sə'dʒes.tʃᵊn, -'dʒeʃ- (US) səg'dʒes- **-s** -z
suggestive sə'dʒes.tɪv (US) səg'dʒes- **-ly** -li **-ness** -nəs, -nɪs
suicidal ˌsuː.ɪ'saɪ.dᵊl, ˌsjuː- (US) ˌsuː.ə'- **-ly** -i
suicide 'suː.ɪ.saɪd, 'sjuː- (US) 'suː.ə- **-s** -z
sui generis ˌsjuː.iː'dʒen.ᵊr.ɪs, ˌsuː-, -aɪ'-, -'gen- (US) ˌsuː.iː'dʒen-, -aɪ'-
sui juris ˌsjuː.iː'dʒʊə.rɪs, ˌsuː-, -aɪ'-, -'dʒoː- (US) ˌsuː.iː'dʒʊr.ɪs, -aɪ'-
suit suːt, sjuːt (US) suːt **-s** -s **-ing/s** -ɪŋ/z (US) 'suː.t̬ɪŋ/z **-ed** -ɪd (US) 'suː.t̬ɪd
suitability ˌsuː.tə'bɪl.ə.ti, ˌsjuː-, -ɪ.ti (US) ˌsuː.t̬ə'bɪl.ə.t̬i
suitab|le 'suː.tə.b|l̩, 'sjuː- (US) 'suː.t̬ə- **-ly** -li **-leness** -l̩.nɪs, -nəs
suitcas|e 'suːt.keɪs, 'sjuːt- (US) 'suːt- **-es** -ɪz
suite swiːt **-s** -s
suitor 'suː.təʳ, 'sjuː- (US) 'suː.t̬ɚ **-s** -z
sukiyaki ˌsuː.ki'jæk.i (US) -'jɑː.ki, ˌsʊk.i'-
Sukkot(h) 'sʊk.ɒt
Sukkur 'sʊk.ʊə (US) 'sʊk.ʊr, -ɚ
Sulawesi ˌsuː.lə'weɪ.si, -læ'- (US) -lɑː'-
sulcal 'sʌl.kᵊl
sulcalization, -isa- ˌsʌl.kᵊl.aɪ'zeɪ.ʃᵊn, -lɪ'- (US) -lɪ'-
sulcaliz|e, -is|e 'sʌl.kᵊl.aɪz **-es** -ɪz **-ing** -ɪŋ **-ed** -d
sulcate 'sʌl.keɪt, -kɪt, -kət (US) -keɪt
Suleiman ˌsʊl.eɪ'mɑːn, ˌsuː.leɪ'-, -lɪ'-, '--- (US) 'suː.leɪ.mɑːn, -lə-
sulfanilamide ˌsʌl.fə'nɪl.ə.maɪd (US) -maɪd, -mɪd
sulfate 'sʌl.feɪt, -fɪt, -fət (US) -feɪt **-s** -s
sulf|ide 'sʌl.f|aɪd **-ides** -aɪdz **-ite/s** -aɪt/s
sulfonamide sʌl'fɒn.ə.maɪd (US) -'fɑː.nə-, -mɪd **-s** -z
sulfur 'sʌl.fəʳ (US) -fɚ
sulfureous sʌl'fjʊə.ri.əs, -'fjoː- (US) -'fjʊr.i-
sulfuretted 'sʌl.fjʊ.ret.ɪd, -fjʊə-, -fə- (US) -fjə.ret̬-, -fə-, -fjʊ-
sulfuric sʌl'fjʊə.rɪk, -'fjoː- (US) -'fjʊr.ɪk **sulˌfuric 'acid**
sulfurous 'sʌl.fᵊr.əs, -fjʊ.rəs (US) -fɚ-; sʌl'fjʊr.əs
sulfury 'sʌl.fᵊr.i
Suliman ˌsʊl.ɪ'mɑːn, '--- (US) 'suː.leɪ.mɑːn, -lə-
sulk sʌlk **-s** -s **-ing** -ɪŋ **-ed** -t **-y** -i **-ier** -i.əʳ (US) -i.ɚ **-iest** -i.ɪst, -i.əst **-ily** -ɪ.li, -ᵊl.i **-iness** -ɪ.nəs, -ɪ.nɪs
Sulla 'sʌl.ə, 'sʊl- (US) 'sʌl-
sullen 'sʌl.ən **-est** -ɪst, -əst **-ly** -li **-ness** -nəs, -nɪs
Sullivan 'sʌl.ɪ.vᵊn
Sullom Voe ˌsuː.ləm'vəʊ, ˌsʌl.əm'- (US) -'voʊ
sull|y (S) 'sʌl|.i **-ies** -iz **-ying** -i.ɪŋ **-ied** -id
sulphanilamide ˌsʌl.fə'nɪl.ə.maɪd (US) -maɪd, -mɪd
sulphate 'sʌl.feɪt, -fɪt, -fət (US) -feɪt **-s** -s
sulph|ide 'sʌl.f|aɪd **-ides** -aɪdz **-ite/s** -aɪt/s
sulphonamide sʌl'fɒn.ə.maɪd (US) -'fɑː.nə-, -mɪd **-s** -z
sulphur 'sʌl.fəʳ (US) -fɚ
sulphureous sʌl'fjʊə.ri.əs, -'fjoː- (US) -'fjʊr.i-
sulphuretted 'sʌl.fjʊ.ret.ɪd, -fjʊə-, -fə- (US) -fjə.ret̬-, -fə-, -fjʊ-
sulphuric sʌl'fjʊə.rɪk, -'fjoː- (US) -'fjʊr.ɪk **sulˌphuric 'acid**
sulphurous 'sʌl.fᵊr.əs, -fjʊ.rəs (US) -fɚ.əs; sʌl'fjʊr.əs
sulphury 'sʌl.fᵊr.i
sultan (S) 'sʌl.tᵊn **-s** -z
sultana *kind of raisin:* sᵊl'tɑː.nə, sʌl- (US) sʌl'tæn.ə, -'tɑː.nə **-s** -z

sultana (S) *sultan's wife, mother, etc.:* sʌlˈtɑː.nə, sʊl- (US) sʌlˈtæn.ə, -ˈtɑː.nə **-s** -z
sultanate ˈsʌl.tə.nət, -neɪt, -nɪt (US) -tᵊn.ɪt, -eɪt **-s** -s
sultr|y ˈsʌl.tr|i **-ier** -i.əʳ (US) -i.ɚ **-iest** -i.ɪst, -i.əst **-ily** -ᵊl.i, -ɪ.li **-iness** -ɪ.nəs, -ɪ.nɪs
Sulu ˈsuː.luː
sum sʌm **-s** -z **-ming** -ɪŋ **-med** -d ˌ**sum** ˈ**total**
sumac(h) ˈʃuː.mæk, ˈsuː-, ˈsjuː- (US) ˈsuː.mæk, ˈʃʊm.æk **-s** -s
Sumatr|a sʊˈmɑː.tr|ə, sjʊ- (US) suː- **-an/s** -ən/z
Sumburgh ˈsʌm.bᵊr.ə
Sumerian sʊˈmɪə.ri.ən, suː-, sjʊ-, sjuː-, -ˈmeə- (US) suːˈmɪr.i-, -ˈmer-
summa cum laude ˌsʊm.ɑː.kʊmˈlaʊ.deɪ (US) -əˌ-, -di; ˌsʌm.əˌkʌmˈlɔː.di
summariz|e, is|e ˈsʌm.ᵊr.aɪz (US) -ə.raɪz **-es** -ɪz **-ing** -ɪŋ **-ed** -d
summar|y ˈsʌm.ᵊr|.i **-ies** -iz **-ily** -ᵊl.i, -ɪ.li **-iness** -ɪ.nəs, -ɪ.nɪs
summat ˈsʌm.ət
summation sʌmˈeɪ.ʃᵊn, səˈmeɪ- (US) səˈmeɪ- **-s** -z
summer (S) ˈsʌm.əʳ (US) -ɚ **-s** -z **-ing** -ɪŋ **-ed** -d **-like** -laɪk ˌ**summer** ˈ**pudding**; ˈ**summer** ˌ**school**; ˈ**Summer** ˌ**Time**
Summerfield ˈsʌm.ə.fiːld (US) ˈ-ɚ- **-s** -z
summerhou|se ˈsʌm.ə.haʊ|s (US) ˈ-ɚ- **-ses** -zɪz
Summers ˈsʌm.əz (US) -ɚz
summertime ˈsʌm.ə.taɪm (US) ˈ-ɚ-
Summerville ˈsʌm.ə.vɪl (US) ˈ-ɚ-
summery ˈsʌm.ᵊr.i
summing-up ˌsʌm.ɪŋˈʌp **summings-up** ˌsʌm.ɪŋzˈ-
summit ˈsʌm.ɪt **-s** -s
summiteer ˌsʌm.ɪˈtɪəʳ (US) -tɪɚ **-s** -z
summon ˈsʌm.ən **-s** -z **-ing** -ɪŋ **-ed** -d **-er/s** -əʳ/z (US) -ɚ/z
summons ˈsʌm.ənz **-es** -ɪz **-ing** -ɪŋ **-ed** -d
Sumner ˈsʌm.nəʳ (US) -nɚ
sumo ˈsuː.məʊ (US) -moʊ ˈ**sumo** ˌ**wrestler**, ˌ**sumo** ˈ**wrestler**; ˌ**sumo** ˈ**wrestling** ˈ**sumo** ˌ**wrestling**
sump sʌmp **-s** -s
sumpter (S) ˈsʌm*p*.təʳ (US) -tɚ **-s** -z
sumptuary ˈsʌm*p*.tjʊə.ri, -tjʊ-, -tʃʊə-, -tʃʊ- (US) -tʃu.er.i
sumptuous ˈsʌm*p*.tʃu.əs, -tju- (US) -tʃu- **-ly** -li **-ness** -nəs, -nɪs
sun (S) sʌn **-s** -z **-ning** -ɪŋ **-ned** -d ˌ**Sun** ˈ**City**; ˈ**sun** ˌ**deck**; ˈ**sun** ˌ**hat**; ˈ**sun** ˌ**lounge**
Sun. (*abbrev. for* **Sunday**) ˈsʌn.deɪ, -di
sunbaked ˈsʌn.beɪkt, ˈsʌm- (US) ˈsʌn-
sunba|th ˈsʌn.bɑː|θ, ˈsʌm- (US) ˈsʌn.bæ|θ **-ths** -ðz
sunbath|e ˈsʌn.beɪð, ˈsʌm- (US) ˈsʌn- **-es** -z **-ing** -ɪŋ **-ed** -d **-er/s** -əʳ/z (US) -ɚ/z
sunbeam (S) ˈsʌn.biːm, ˈsʌm- (US) ˈsʌn- **-s** -z
sunbed ˈsʌn.bed, ˈsʌm- (US) ˈsʌn- **-s** -z
sun-belt ˈsʌn.belt, ˈsʌm- **-s** -s
sunblind ˈsʌn.blaɪnd, ˈsʌm- (US) ˈsʌn- **-s** -z
sunblock ˈsʌn.blɒk, ˈsʌm- (US) ˈsʌn.blɑːk **-s** -s
sun-bonnet ˈsʌnˌbɒn.ɪt, ˈsʌm- (US) ˈsʌnˌbɑː.nɪt **-s** -s
sunburn ˈsʌn.bɜːn, ˈsʌm- (US) ˈsʌn.bɜːrn **-s** -z **-ed** -d **-t** -t
sunburst ˈsʌn.bɜːst, ˈsʌm- (US) ˈsʌn.bɜːrst **-s** -s
Sunbury ˈsʌn.bᵊr.i, ˈsʌm- (US) ˈsʌn-, -beri
Sunda ˈsʌn.də
sundae ˈsʌn.deɪ (US) -di, -deɪ **-s** -z
Sundanese ˌsʌn.dəˈniːz
Sunday ˈsʌn.deɪ, -di **-s** -z ˌ**Sunday** ˈ**best**; ˈ**Sunday** ˌ**school**; **in a** ˌ**month of** ˈ**Sundays**
sund|er ˈsʌn.d|əʳ (US) -d|ɚ **-ers** -əz (US) -ɚz **-ering** -ᵊr.ɪŋ **-ered** -əd (US) -ɚd
Sunderland ˈsʌn.dᵊl.ənd (US) -dɚ.lənd
sundial ˈsʌn.daɪl **-s** -z
sundown ˈsʌn.daʊn
sundowner ˈsʌnˌdaʊ.nəʳ (US) -nɚ **-s** -z
sundrenched ˈsʌn.dren*t*ʃt
sundress ˈsʌn.dres **-es** -ɪz
sun-dried ˈsʌn.draɪd
sundr|y ˈsʌn.dr|i **-ies** -iz
sunfish ˈsʌn.fɪʃ
sunflower ˈsʌn.flaʊəʳ (US) -flaʊɚ **-s** -z ˈ**sunflower** ˌ**seed**
sung (*from* **sing**) sʌŋ
Sung sʊŋ, sʌŋ (US) sʊŋ
sunglasses ˈsʌnˌglɑː.sɪz, ˈsʌŋ- (US) ˈsʌnˌglæs.ɪs
sunk (*from* **sink**) sʌŋk
sunken (*from* **sink**) ˈsʌŋ.kən
sunkissed ˈsʌn.kɪst, ˈsʌŋ-
sunlamp ˈsʌn.læmp **-s** -s
sunless ˈsʌn.ləs, -lɪs
sun|light ˈsʌn|.laɪt **-lit** -lɪt
sunlounger ˈsʌnˌlaʊn.dʒəʳ (US) -dʒɚ **-s** -z
Sunn|i ˈsʊn|.i, ˈsʌn- (US) ˈsʊn- **-ite/s** -aɪt/s **-ism** -ɪ.zᵊm ˌ**Sunni** ˈ**Muslim**
Sunningdale ˈsʌn.ɪŋ.deɪl
sunn|y ˈsʌn|.i **-ier** -i.əʳ (US) -i.ɚ **-iest** -i.ɪst, -i.əst **-iness** -ɪ.nəs, -ɪ.nɪs ˌ**sunny-side** ˈ**up**
Sunnyside ˈsʌn.i.saɪd
sunproof ˈsʌn.pruːf, ˈsʌm- (US) ˈsʌn-
sunray ˈsʌn.reɪ **-s** -z
sunris|e ˈsʌn.raɪz **-es** -ɪz
sunroo|f ˈsʌn.ruː|f (US) -ruː|f, -rʊ|f **-fs** -fs **-ves** -vz
sunscreen ˈsʌn.skriːn **-s** -z **-ing** -ɪŋ
sunset ˈsʌn.set **-s** -s
sunshade ˈsʌn.ʃeɪd **-s** -z
sunshin|e ˈsʌn.ʃaɪn **-y** -i
sunspot ˈsʌn.spɒt (US) -spɑːt **-s** -s
sunstroke ˈsʌn.strəʊk (US) -stroʊk **-s** -s
suntan ˈsʌn.tæn **-s** -z **-ned** -d
suntrap ˈsʌn.træp **-s** -s
sunup ˈsʌn.ʌp **-s** -s
sun-worship ˈsʌnˌwɜː.ʃɪp (US) -ˌwɜːr- **-per/s** -əʳ/z (US) -ɚ/z
suo nomine ˌsuː.əʊˈnəʊ.mɪ.neɪ, ˌsjuː-, -ˈnɒm.ɪ- (US) ˌsuː.oʊˈnoʊ.mɪ-, -ˈnɑː-
sup sʌp **-s** -s **-ping** -ɪŋ **-ped** -t
super- ˈsuː.pəʳ-, ˈsjuː- (US) ˈsuː.pɚ-
super ˈsuː.pəʳ, ˈsjuː- (US) ˈsuː.pɚ **-s** -z
superab|le ˈsuː.pᵊr.ə.b|l̩, ˈsjuː- (US) ˈsuː- **-ly** -li **-leness** -l̩.nəs, -nɪs
superabundan|ce ˌsuː.pᵊr.əˈbʌn.dən|*t*s, ˌsjuː- (US) ˌsuː- **-t/ly** -t/li
superannu|ate ˌsuː.pᵊrˈæn.ju|.eɪt, ˌsjuː- (US) ˌsuː- **-ates** -eɪts **-ating** -eɪ.tɪŋ (US) -eɪ.t̬ɪŋ **-ated** -eɪ.tɪd (US) -eɪ.t̬ɪd
superannuation ˌsuː.pᵊrˌæn.juˈeɪ.ʃᵊn, ˌsjuː- (US) ˌsuː- **-s** -z
superb suːˈpɜːb, sjuː-, sʊ-, sjʊ- (US) səˈpɜːrb, sʊ-, suː- **-ly** -li **-ness** -nəs, -nɪs
superbug ˈsuː.pə.bʌg, ˈsjuː- (US) ˈsuː.pɚ- **-s** -z
supercargo ˈsuː.pəˌkɑː.gəʊ, ˈsjuː- (US) ˈsuː.pɚˌkɑːr.goʊ **-es** -z
supercharg|e ˈsuː.pə.tʃɑːdʒ, ˈsjuː- (US) ˈsuː.pɚ.tʃɑːrdʒ **-es** -ɪz **-ing** -ɪŋ **-ed** -d
supercharger ˈsuː.pəˌtʃɑː.dʒəʳ, ˈsjuː- (US) ˈsuː.pɚˌtʃɑːr.dʒɚ **-s** -z
superchip ˈsuː.pə.tʃɪp, ˈsjuː- (US) ˈsuː.pɚ- **-s** -s
supercilious ˌsuː.pəˈsɪl.i.əs, ˌsjuː- (US) ˌsuː.pɚˈ- **-ly** -li **-ness** -nəs, -nɪs
supercomputer ˈsuː.pə.kəmˌpjuː.təʳ, ˈsjuː- (US) ˈsuː.pɚ.kəmˌpjuː.t̬ɚ **-s** -z
superconductivity ˌsuː.pəˌkɒn.dʌkˈtɪv.ə.ti, ˌsjuː-, -dəkˈ-, -ɪ.ti (US) ˌsuː.pɚˌkɑːn.dʌkˈtɪv.ə.t̬i
superconduct|or ˈsuː.pə.kənˌdʌk.t|əʳ, ˈsjuː- (US) ˈsuː.pɚ.kənˌdʌk.t|ɚ **-ors** -əz (US) -ɚz **-ing** -ɪŋ
supercool ˌsuː.pəˈkuːl, ˌsjuː- (US) ˌsuː.pɚˈ- **-s** -z **-ing** -ɪŋ **-ed** -d
super-duper ˌsuː.pəˈduː.pəʳ, ˌsjuː- (US) ˌsuː.pɚˈduː.pɚ
superego ˌsuː.pᵊrˈiː.gəʊ, ˌsjuː-, -ˈeg.əʊ (US) ˌsuː.pɚˈiː.goʊ **-s** -z
supererogation ˌsuː.pᵊrˌer.əʊˈgeɪ.ʃᵊn, ˌsjuː- (US) ˌsuː.pɚˌer.əˈ-
supererogatory ˌsuː.pᵊr.erˈɒg.ə.tᵊr.i, ˌsjuː-, -ɪˈrɒg- (US) ˌsuː.pɚ.ɪˈrɑː.gə.tɔːr-

superfici|al ˌsuː.pəˈfɪʃ|.əl, ˌsjuː- ⓊⓈ ˌsuː.pɚˈ- **-ally** -əl.i **-alness** -əl.nəs, -nɪs
superficialit|y ˌsuː.pəˌfɪʃ.iˈæl.ə.t|i, ˌsjuː-, -ɪ.t|i ⓊⓈ ˌsuː.pɚˌfɪʃ.iˈæl.ə.t̬|i **-ies** -iz
superficies ˌsuː.pəˈfɪʃ.iːz, ˌsjuː-, -i.iːz ⓊⓈ ˌsuː.pɚˈfɪʃ.i.iːz, ˈ-iːz
superfine ˌsuː.pəˈfaɪn, ˌsjuː-, ˈ--- ⓊⓈ ˈsuː.pɚ.faɪn, ˌ--ˈ-
superfix ˈsuː.pə.fɪks, ˈsjuː- ⓊⓈ ˈsuː.pɚ-
superfluit|y ˌsuː.pəˈfluː.ə.t|i, ˌsjuː-, -ɪ.t|i ⓊⓈ ˌsuː.pɚˈfluː.ə.t̬|i **-ies** -iz
superfluous suːˈpɜː.flu.əs, sjuː-, sʊ-, sjʊ- ⓊⓈ -ˈpɝː- **-ly** -li **-ness** -nəs, -nɪs
superglottal ˌsuː.pəˈglɒt.əl, ˌsjuː- ⓊⓈ ˌsuː.pɚˈglɑː.t̬əl
Superglue® ˈsuː.pə.gluː, ˈsjuː- ⓊⓈ ˈsuː.pɚ-
supergrass ˈsuː.pə.grɑːs, ˈsjuː- ⓊⓈ ˈsuː.pɚ.græs **-es** -ɪz
supergravity ˌsuː.pəˈgræv.ə.ti, ˌsjuː-, -ɪ.ti ⓊⓈ ˌsuː.pɚˈgræv.ə.t̬i
supergun ˈsuː.pə.gʌn, ˈsjuː- ⓊⓈ ˈsuː.pɚ- **-s** -z
superheat (*v.*) ˌsuː.pəˈhiːt, ˌsjuː- ⓊⓈ ˌsuː.pɚˈ- **-s** -s **-ing** -ɪŋ **-ed** -ɪd **-er/s**
superheat (*n.*) ˈsuː.pə.hiːt, ˈsjuː- ⓊⓈ ˈsuː.pɚ-
superhero ˈsuː.pəˌhɪə.rəʊ, ˈsjuː-, ˌsuː.pəˈhɪə.rəʊ ⓊⓈ ˈsuː.pɚ- **-es** -z
superheterodyne ˌsuː.pəˈhet.ər.əʊ.daɪn, ˌsjuː- ⓊⓈ ˌsuː.pɚˈhet̬.ə.roʊ.daɪn **-s** -z
superhighway ˌsuː.pəˈhaɪ.weɪ, ˌsjuː-, ˈsuː.pəˌhaɪ.weɪ ⓊⓈ ˈsuː.pɚ- **-s** -z **ˌinformation ˈsuperˌhighway, ˌinformation ˌsuperˈhighway**
superhuman ˌsuː.pəˈhjuː.mən, ˌsjuː- ⓊⓈ ˌsuː.pɚˈ- **-ly** -li **-ness** -nəs, -nɪs
superimpos|e ˌsuː.pər.ɪmˈpəʊz, ˌsjuː- ⓊⓈ ˌsuː.pɚ.ɪmˈpoʊz **-es** -ɪz **-ing** -ɪŋ **-ed** -d
superintend ˌsuː.pər.ɪnˈtend, ˌsjuː- ⓊⓈ ˌsuː.pɚ- **-s** -z **-ing** -ɪŋ **-ed** -ɪd **-ence** -ənts
superintendenc|y ˌsuː.pər.ɪnˈten.dənt.s|i, ˌsjuː- ⓊⓈ ˌsuː.pɚ- **-ies** -iz
superintendent ˌsuː.pər.ɪnˈten.dənt, ˌsjuː- ⓊⓈ ˌsuː.pɚ- **-s** -s
superior (S) suːˈpɪə.ri.ər, sjuː-, sʊ-, sjʊ-, sə- ⓊⓈ səˈpɪr.i.ɚ, sʊ- **-s** -z
superiorit|y suːˌpɪə.riˈɒr.ə.t|i, sjuː-, sʊ-, sjʊ-, sə-, -ɪ.t|i ⓊⓈ səˌpɪr.iˈɔːr.ə.t̬|i, sʊ- **-ies** -iz
superlative suːˈpɜː.lə.tɪv, sjuː-, sʊ-, sjʊ- ⓊⓈ səˈpɝː.lə.t̬ɪv, sʊ-, suː- **-s** -z **-ly** -li **-ness** -nəs, -nɪs
super|man (S) ˈsuː.pə|.mæn, ˈsjuː- ⓊⓈ ˈsuː.pɚ- **-men** -men
supermarket ˈsuː.pəˌmɑː.kɪt, ˈsjuː- ⓊⓈ ˈsuː.pɚˌmɑːr- **-s** -s
supermodel ˈsuː.pəˌmɒd.əl, ˈsjuː- ⓊⓈ ˈsuː.pɚˌmɑː.dəl **-s** -z
supernal suːˈpɜː.nəl, sjuː-, sʊ-, sjʊ- ⓊⓈ səˈpɝː-, sʊ-, suː-
supernatural ˌsuː.pəˈnætʃ.ər.əl, ˌsjuː-, ˌsjʊ.pəˈ-, ˌsʊ-, -ʊ.rəl ⓊⓈ ˌsuː.pɚˈnætʃ.ɚ.əl **-ly** -i **-ness** -nəs, -nɪs
supernormal ˌsuː.pəˈnɔː.məl, ˌsjuː- ⓊⓈ ˌsuː.pɚˈnɔːr-
supernov|a ˌsuː.pəˈnəʊ.v|ə, ˌsjuː- ⓊⓈ ˌsuː.pɚˈnoʊ- **-ae** -iː **-as** -əz
supernumerar|y ˌsuː.pəˈnjuː.mər.ər|.i, ˌsjuː- ⓊⓈ ˌsuː.pɚˈnuː.mə.rer|.i, -ˈnjuː- **-ies** -iz
superoctave ˈsuː.pərˌɒk.tɪv, ˈsjuː- ⓊⓈ ˈsuː.pɚˌɑːk- **-s** -z
superordinate ˌsuː.pərˈɔː.dən.ət, ˌsjuː-, -dɪ.nət, -nɪt, -neɪt ⓊⓈ ˌsuː.pɚˈɔːr.dən.ɪt **-s** -s
superpos|e ˌsuː.pəˈpəʊz, ˌsjuː- ⓊⓈ ˌsuː.pɚˈpoʊz **-es** -ɪz **-ing** -ɪŋ **-ed** -d
superposition ˌsuː.pə.pəˈzɪʃ.ən, ˌsjuː- ⓊⓈ ˌsuː.pɚ- **-s** -z
superpower ˈsuː.pəˌpaʊər, ˈsjuː- ⓊⓈ ˈsuː.pɚˌpaʊɚ **-s** -z
superpriorit|y ˌsuː.pə.praɪˈɒr.ə.t|i, ˌsjuː-, -ɪ.t|i ⓊⓈ ˌsuː.pɚ.praɪˈɔːr.ə.t̬|i **-ies** -iz
superscrib|e ˌsuː.pəˈskraɪb, ˌsjuː-, ˈ--- ⓊⓈ ˈsuː.pɚ.skraɪb **-es** -z **-ing** -ɪŋ **-ed** -d
superscript ˈsuː.pə.skrɪpt, ˈsjuː- ⓊⓈ ˈsuː.pɚ-
superscription ˌsuː.pəˈskrɪp.ʃən, ˌsjuː- ⓊⓈ ˌsuː.pɚˈ- **-s** -z
supersed|e ˌsuː.pəˈsiːd, ˌsjuː- ⓊⓈ ˌsuː.pɚˈ- **-es** -z **-ing** -ɪŋ **-ed** -ɪd
supersession ˌsuː.pəˈseʃ.ən, ˌsjuː- ⓊⓈ ˌsuː.pɚˈ-
supersonic ˌsuː.pəˈsɒn.ɪk, ˌsjuː- ⓊⓈ ˌsuː.pɚˈsɑː.nɪk **-s** -z **-ally** -əl.i, -li
superstar ˈsuː.pə.stɑːr, ˈsjuː- ⓊⓈ ˈsuː.pɚ.stɑːr **-s** -z **-dom** -dəm
superstate ˈsuː.pə.steɪt, ˈsjuː- ⓊⓈ ˈsuː.pɚ- **-s** -s
superstition ˌsuː.pəˈstɪʃ.ən, ˌsjuː- ⓊⓈ ˌsuː.pɚˈ- **-s** -z
superstitious ˌsuː.pəˈstɪʃ.əs, ˌsjuː- ⓊⓈ ˌsuː.pɚˈ- **-ly** -li **-ness** -nəs, -nɪs
superstore ˈsuː.pə.stɔːr, ˈsjuː- ⓊⓈ ˈsuː.pɚ.stɔːr **-s** -z
superstring ˈsuː.pə.strɪŋ, ˈsjuː- ⓊⓈ ˈsuː.pɚ- **-s** -z
superstructure ˈsuː.pəˌstrʌk.tʃər, ˈsjuː- ⓊⓈ ˈsuː.pɚˌstrʌk.tʃɚ **-s** -z
supertanker ˈsuː.pəˌtæŋ.kər, ˈsjuː- ⓊⓈ ˈsuː.pɚˌtæŋ.kɚ **-s** -z
supertax ˈsuː.pə.tæks, ˈsjuː-, ˌ--ˈ- ⓊⓈ ˈsuː.pɚ.tæks **-es** -ɪz
supertitle ˈsuː.pəˌtaɪ.tl̩, ˈsjuː- ⓊⓈ ˈsuː.pɚ- **-s** -z
supertonic ˌsuː.pəˈtɒn.ɪk, ˌsjuː- ⓊⓈ ˌsuː.pɚˈtɑː.nɪk **-s** -s
superven|e ˌsuː.pəˈviːn, ˌsjuː- ⓊⓈ ˌsuː.pɚˈ- **-es** -z **-ing** -ɪŋ **-ed** -d
supervis|e ˈsuː.pə.vaɪz, ˈsjuː- ⓊⓈ ˈsuː.pɚ- **-es** -ɪz **-ing** -ɪŋ **-ed** -d
supervision ˌsuː.pəˈvɪʒ.ən, ˌsjuː- ⓊⓈ ˌsuː.pɚˈ- **-s** -z
supervisor ˈsuː.pə.vaɪ.zər, ˈsjuː- ⓊⓈ ˈsuː.pɚ.vaɪ.zɚ **-s** -z
supervisory ˌsuː.pəˈvaɪ.zər.i, ˌsjuː-, ˈsuː.pə.vaɪ-, ˈsjuː- ⓊⓈ ˌsuː.pɚˈvaɪ.zɚ-
super|woman ˈsuː.pə|ˌwʊm.ən, ˈsjuː- ⓊⓈ ˈsuː.pɚˌ- **-women** -ˌwɪm.ɪn
supine (*n.*) ˈsuː.paɪn, ˈsjuː- ⓊⓈ ˈsuː- **-s** -z
supine (*adj.*) ˈsuː.paɪn, ˈsjuː-, -ˈ- ⓊⓈ suːˈpaɪn, ˈ-- **-ly** -li **-ness** -nəs, -nɪs
supper ˈsʌp.ər ⓊⓈ -ɚ **-s** -z **-less** -ləs, -lɪs
sup|plant səˈ|plɑːnt ⓊⓈ -ˈplænt **-plants** -ˈplɑːnts ⓊⓈ -ˈplænts **-planting** -ˈplɑːn.tɪŋ ⓊⓈ -ˈplæn.t̬ɪŋ **-planted** -ˈplɑːn.tɪd ⓊⓈ -ˈplæn.t̬ɪd **-planter/s** -ˈplɑːn.tər/z ⓊⓈ -ˈplæn.t̬ɚ/z
supp|le ˈsʌp|.l̩ **-leness** -l̩.nəs, -nɪs **-ly** -li, -l̩.i
supplement (*n.*) ˈsʌp.lɪ.mənt, -lə- ⓊⓈ -lə- **-s** -s
supple|ment (*v.*) ˈsʌp.lɪ|.ment, -lə-, ˌ--ˈ- ⓊⓈ ˈsʌp.lə- **-ments** -ments **-menting** -men.tɪŋ ⓊⓈ -men.t̬ɪŋ **-mented** -men.tɪd ⓊⓈ -men.t̬ɪd
supplemental ˌsʌp.lɪˈmen.təl, -ləˈ- ⓊⓈ -ləˈmen.t̬əl
supplementary ˌsʌp.lɪˈmen.tər.i, -ləˈ-, ˈ-tri ⓊⓈ -ləˈmen.t̬ɚ.i *stress shift, see compound:* **ˌsupplementary ˈbenefit**
supplementation ˌsʌp.lɪ.menˈteɪ.ʃən, -lə- ⓊⓈ -lə-
suppliant ˈsʌp.li.ənt **-s** -s **-ly** -li
supplicant ˈsʌp.lɪ.kənt, -lə- ⓊⓈ -lə- **-s** -s
suppli|cate ˈsʌp.lɪ|.keɪt, -lə- ⓊⓈ -lə- **-cates** -keɪts **-cating/ly** -keɪ.tɪŋ/li ⓊⓈ -keɪ.t̬ɪŋ/li **-cated** -keɪ.tɪd ⓊⓈ -keɪ.t̬ɪd
supplication ˌsʌp.lɪˈkeɪ.ʃən, -ləˈ- ⓊⓈ -ləˈ- **-s** -z
supplicatory ˈsʌp.lɪ.kə.tər.i, -lə-, -keɪ- ⓊⓈ -lə.kə.tɔːr-
supplier səˈplaɪ.ər ⓊⓈ -ɚ **-s** -z
suppl|y səˈpl|aɪ **-ies** -aɪz **-ying** -aɪ.ɪŋ **-ied** -aɪd **supˌply and deˈmand ; supˈply ˌteacher**
supply-sid|e səˈplaɪ.saɪd **-er/s** -ər/z ⓊⓈ -ɚ/z
sup|port səˈ|pɔːt ⓊⓈ -ˈpɔːrt **-ports** -ˈpɔːts ⓊⓈ -ˈpɔːrts **-porting** -ˈpɔː.tɪŋ ⓊⓈ -ˈpɔːr.t̬ɪd **-ported** -ˈpɔː.tɪd

(US) -ˈpɔːr.t̬ɪd **-porter/s** -ˈpɔː.təʳ/z (US) -ˈpɔːr.t̬ɚ/z
supportab|le səˈpɔː.tə.b|l̩ (US) -ˈpɔːr.t̬ə- **-ly** -li
supportive səˈpɔː.tɪv (US) -ˈpɔːr.t̬ɪv
suppos|e səˈpəʊz (US) -ˈpoʊz **-es** -ɪz **-ing** -ɪŋ **-ed** -d
supposedly səˈpəʊ.zɪd.li (US) -ˈpoʊ-
supposition ˌsʌp.əˈzɪʃ.ᵊn **-s** -z
suppositional ˌsʌp.əˈzɪʃ.ᵊn.ᵊl, ˈ-nᵊl **-li** -i
supposititious səˌpɒz.ɪˈtɪʃ.əs, -əˈ- (US) -ˌpɑː.zəˈ- **-ly** -li **-ness** -nəs, -nɪs
suppositor|y səˈpɒz.ɪ.tᵊr|.i, ˈ-ə-, -tr|i (US) -ˈpɑː.zə.tɔːr|.i **-ies** -iz
suppress səˈpres **-es** -ɪz **-ing** -ɪŋ **-ed** -t **-or/s** -əʳ/z (US) -ɚ/z **-ible** -ə.bl̩, -ɪ.bl̩
suppressant səˈpres.ᵊnt **-s** -s
suppression səˈpreʃ.ᵊn **-s** -z
suppu|rate ˈsʌp.jə|.reɪt, -jʊ- **-rates** -reɪts **-rating** -reɪ.tɪŋ (US) -reɪ.t̬ɪŋ **-rated** -reɪ.tɪd (US) -reɪ.t̬ɪd
suppuration ˌsʌp.jᵊrˈeɪ.ʃᵊn, -jʊˈreɪ- (US) -jəˈreɪ-, -jʊˈ- **-s** -z
supra- ˈsuː.prə, ˈsjuː- (US) ˈsuː.prə-
supradental ˌsuː.prəˈden.tᵊl, ˌsjuː- (US) ˌsuː.prəˈden.t̬ᵊl
suprafix ˈsuː.prə.fɪks, ˈsjuː- (US) ˈsuː-
supranational ˌsuː.prəˈnæʃ.ᵊn.ᵊl, ˌsjuː-, ˈ-nᵊl (US) ˌsuː- **-ly** -li
suprarenal ˌsuː.prəˈriː.nᵊl, ˌsjuː-, ˈsuː.prəˌriː-, ˈsjuː- (US) ˌsuː.prəˈriː
suprasegmental ˌsuː.prə.segˈmen.tᵊl, ˌsjuː- (US) ˌsuː.prə.segˈmen.t̬ᵊl
supremacist suːˈprem.ə.sɪst, sjuː-, sʊ-, sjʊ- (US) səˈ-, sʊ-, suː- **-s** -s
supremac|y suːˈprem.ə.s|i, sjuː-, sʊ-, sjʊ- (US) sə-, sʊ-, suː- **-ies** -iz
supreme suːˈpriːm, sjuː-, sʊ-, sjʊ- (US) sə-, sʊ-, suː- **-ly** -li **-ness** -nəs, -nɪs **Suˌpreme ˈCourt** ; **Suˌpreme ˈSoviet**
supremo suːˈpriː.məʊ, sjuː-, sʊ-, sjʊ- (US) suːˈpriː.moʊ, sʊ-, sə- **-s** -z
supt (S) (*abbrev. for* **superintendent**) ˌsuː.pᵊr.ɪnˈten.dənt, ˌsjuː- (US) ˌsuː.pɚ-
sura ˈsʊə.rə (US) ˈsʊr.ə **-s** -z
surah ˈsjʊə.rə (US) ˈsʊr.ə
surat sʊˈræt, sjuː- (US) ˈsʊr.æt
Surat ˈsʊə.rət, ˈsuː-; sʊˈrɑːt, -ˈræt (US) ˈsʊr.ət; səˈræt
Surbiton ˈsɜː.bɪ.tᵊn (US) ˈsɜːr.bɪ.t̬ən
surceas|e (*v.*) sɜːˈsiːs (US) sɜːr- **-es** -ɪz **-ing** -ɪŋ **-ed** -t
surceas|e (*n.*) sɜːˈsiːs (US) sɜːr-, ˈ-- **-es** -ɪz
surcharg|e (*n.*) ˈsɜː.tʃɑːdʒ, ˌ-ˈ- (US) ˈsɜːr.tʃɑːrdʒ **-es** -ɪz
surcharg|e (*v.*) ˈsɜː.tʃɑːdʒ, ˌ-ˈ- (US) ˈsɜːr.tʃɑːrdʒ, -ˈ- **-es** -ɪz **-ing** -ɪŋ **-ed** -d
surcingle ˈsɜː.sɪŋ.gl̩ (US) ˈsɜːr- **-s** -z
surcoat ˈsɜː.kəʊt (US) ˈsɜːr.koʊt **-s** -s
surd sɜːd (US) sɜːrd **-s** -z **-ity** -ə.ti, -ɪ.ti (US) -ə.t̬i
sur|e ʃʊəʳ, ʃɔːʳ (US) ʃʊr **-er** -əʳ (US) -ɚ **-est** -ɪst, -əst **-ness** -nəs, -nɪs
surefire ˈʃɔːˌfaɪəʳ, ˈʃʊə- (US) ˈʃʊrˌfaɪɚ
surefooted ˌʃɔːˈfʊt.ɪd, ˌʃʊə- (US) ˈʃʊrˌfʊː.t̬ɪd **-ly** -li **-ness** -nəs, -nɪs
surely ˈʃɔː.li, ˈʃʊə- (US) ˈʃʊr-
suret|y ˈʃɔː.rə.t|i, ˈʃʊə- (US) ˈʃʊr.ə.t̬|i, ˈ-t̬|i **-ies** -iz **-yship/s** -i.ʃɪp/s
surf sɜːf (US) sɜːrf **-s** -s **-ing** -ɪŋ **-ed** -t
surfac|e ˈsɜː.fɪs, -fəs (US) ˈsɜːr- **-es** -ɪz **-ing** -ɪŋ **-ed** -t **ˈsurface ˌmail** ; **ˈsurface ˌstructure** ; **ˌsurface ˈtension** (US) **ˈsurface ˌtension**
surface-to-air ˌsɜː.fɪs.tuˈeəʳ (US) ˌsɜːr.fɪs.tuˈer *stress shift:* ˌsurface-to-air ˈmissile
surface-to-surface ˌsɜː.fɪs.təˈsɜː.fɪs (US) ˌsɜːr.fɪs.təˈsɜːr- *stress shift:* ˌsurface-to-surface ˈmissile
surfactant sɜːˈfæk.tənt (US) sɜːr- **-s** -s
surfboard ˈsɜːf.bɔːd (US) ˈsɜːrf.bɔːrd **-s** -z **-er/s** -əʳ/z (US) -ɚ/z
surfboat ˈsɜːf.bəʊt (US) ˈsɜːrf.boʊt **-s** -s
surfei|t ˈsɜː.fɪ|t, -ə|t (US) ˈsɜːr.fɪ|t **-ts** -ts **-ting** -tɪŋ (US) -t̬ɪŋ **-ted** -tɪd (US) -t̬ɪd
surfer ˈsɜː.fəʳ (US) ˈsɜːr.fɚ **-s** -z
surfing ˈsɜː.fɪŋ (US) ˈsɜːr-
surg|e sɜːdʒ (US) sɜːrdʒ **-es** -ɪz **-ing** -ɪŋ **-ed** -d
surgeon ˈsɜː.dʒᵊn (US) ˈsɜːr- **-s** -z
surger|y ˈsɜː.dʒᵊr|.i (US) ˈsɜːr- **-ies** -iz
surgic|al ˈsɜː.dʒɪ.k|ᵊl (US) ˈsɜːr- **-ally** -ᵊl.i, -li **ˌsurgical ˈspirit**
Suriname, Surinam ˌsʊə.rɪˈnæm, ˌsjʊə-, ˈ--- (US) ˌsʊr.ɪˈnɑːm; ˈsʊr.ɪ.næm
Surinamese ˌsʊə.rɪ.næmˈiːz, ˌsjʊə-
surl|y ˈsɜː.l|i (US) ˈsɜːr- **-ier** -i.əʳ (US) -i.ɚ **-iest** -i.ɪst, -i.əst **-ily** -ɪ.li, -ᵊl.i **-iness** -ɪ.nəs, -ɪ.nɪs
surmis|e (*n.*) ˈsɜː.maɪz; ˌ-ˈ-, sə- (US) sɚˈmaɪz; ˈsɜːr.maɪz **-es** -ɪz
surmis|e (*v.*) sɜːˈmaɪz, sə-; ˈsɜː.maɪz (US) sɚˈmaɪz **-es** -ɪz **-ing** -ɪŋ **-ed** -d
sur|mount sə|ˈmaʊnt, sɜː- (US) sɚ- **-mounts** -ˈmaʊnts **-mounting** -ˈmaʊn.tɪŋ (US) -ˈmaʊn.t̬ɪŋ **-mounted** -ˈmaʊn.tɪd (US) -ˈmaʊn.t̬ɪd **-mountable** -ˈmaʊn.tə.bl̩ (US) -ˈmaʊn.t̬ə.bl̩
surnam|e ˈsɜː.neɪm (US) ˈsɜːr- **-es** -z **-ing** -ɪŋ **-ed** -d
surpass səˈpɑːs, sɜː- (US) sɚˈpæs **-es** -ɪz **-ing/ly** -ɪŋ/li **-ed** -t **-able** -ə.bl̩
surplic|e ˈsɜː.plɪs, -pləs (US) ˈsɜːr- **-es** -ɪz **-ed** -t
surplus ˈsɜː.pləs (US) ˈsɜːr-, -plʌs **-es** -ɪz **-age** -ɪdʒ
surpris|e səˈpraɪz (US) sɚ- **-es** -ɪz **-ing/ly** -ɪŋ/li **-ed/ly** -ɪd/li, -d/li
surreal səˈrɪəl (US) səˈriː.əl, -ˈriːl
surreal|ism səˈrɪə.lɪ|.zᵊm (US) -ˈriː.ə-, -ˈriː.lɪ- **-ist/s** -ɪst/s
surrealistic səˌrɪəˈlɪs.tɪk (US) -ˌriː.əˈ-, -ˌriːˈ-
surrend|er sᵊrˈen.d|əʳ (US) səˈren.d|ɚ **-ers** -əz (US) -ɚz **-ering** -ᵊr.ɪŋ **-ered** -əd (US) -ɚd
surreptitious ˌsʌr.əpˈtɪʃ.əs, -ɪpˈ-, -epˈ- (US) ˌsɜːr.əpˈ- **-ly** -li **-ness** -nəs, -nɪs
Surrey, surrey ˈsʌr.i (US) ˈsɜːr-
surrogac|y ˈsʌr.ə.gə.s|i **-ies** -iz
surrogate ˈsʌr.ə.gɪt, -gət, -geɪt (US) ˈsɜːr.ə.gɪt, -geɪt **-s** -s **ˌsurrogate ˈmother**
surround səˈraʊnd **-s** -z **-ing/s** -ɪŋ/z **-ed** -ɪd **surˌround ˈsound**
sursum corda ˌsɜː.səmˈkɔː.də, -sʊmˈ- (US) ˌsɜːr.səmˈkɔːr-, -sʊmˈ-
surtax ˈsɜː.tæks (US) ˈsɜːr- **-es** -ɪz
Surtees ˈsɜː.tiːz (US) ˈsɜːr-
surtitl|e ˈsɜːˌtaɪ.tl̩ (US) ˈsɜːrˌtaɪ.t̬l̩ **-es** -z **-ing** -ɪŋ, -ˌtaɪt.lɪŋ **-ed** -d
Surtsey ˈsɜːt.si, -seɪ (US) ˈsɜːrt-
surveil səˈveɪ **-s** -z **-ing** -ɪŋ **-led** -d **-lant/s** -ənt/s
surveillance sɜːˈveɪ.lənts, sə- (US) sɚ-, -ˈveɪl.jənts
survey (*n.*) ˈsɜː.veɪ; ˌ-ˈ-, sə- (US) ˈsɜːr.veɪ **-s** -z
survey (*v.*) səˈveɪ, sɜː-; ˈsɜː.veɪ (US) sɚˈveɪ; ˈsɜːr.veɪ **-s** -z **-ing** -ɪŋ **-ed** -d
surveyor səˈveɪ.əʳ (US) sɚˈveɪ.ɚ **-s** -z
survival səˈvaɪ.vᵊl (US) sɚ- **-s** -z **surˌvival of the ˈfittest**
survivalist səˈvaɪ.vᵊl.ɪst (US) sɚ- **-s** -s
surviv|e səˈvaɪv (US) sɚ- **-es** -z **-ing** -ɪŋ **-ed** -d **-able** -ə.bl̩
survivor səˈvaɪ.vəʳ (US) sɚˈvaɪ.vɚ **-s** -z
Susan ˈsuː.zᵊn
Susanna(h) suːˈzæn.ə, sʊ-
susceptibilit|y səˌsep.təˈbɪl.ə.t|i, -tɪˈ-, -ɪ.t|i (US) -təˈbɪl.ə.t̬|i **-ies** -iz
susceptib|le səˈsep.tə.b|l̩, -tɪ- (US) -tə- **-ly** -li
susceptive səˈsep.tɪv
sushi ˈsuː.ʃi
Susie ˈsuː.zi
suspect (*n. adj.*) ˈsʌs.pekt **-s** -s
suspect (*v.*) səˈspekt **-s** -s **-ing** -ɪŋ **-ed** -ɪd
suspend səˈspend **-s** -z **-ing** -ɪŋ **-ed** -ɪd
suspender səˈspen.dəʳ (US) -dɚ **-s** -z **suˈspender ˌbelt**
suspens|e səˈspents **-ible** -ə.bl̩, -ɪ.bl̩
suspensibility səˌspent.sɪˈbɪl.ə.ti, -səˈ-, -ɪ.ti (US) -səˈbɪl.ə.t̬i
suspension səˈspen.tʃᵊn (US) -ˈspent.ʃᵊn **-s** -z **suˈspension ˌbridge**

suspens|ive sə'spent.sɪv **-ory** -ᵊr.i
suspicion sə'spɪʃ.ᵊn **-s** -z
suspicious sə'spɪʃ.əs **-ly** -li **-ness** -nəs, -nɪs
suss sʌs **-es** -ɪz **-ing** -ɪŋ **-ed** -t
Sussex 'sʌs.ɪks
Susskind 'sʊs.kɪnd (US) 'sʌs-
sustain sə'steɪn **-s** -z **-ing** -ɪŋ **-ed** -d **-er/s** -əʳ/z (US) -ɚ/z **-able** -ə.bl̩
sustainability səˌsteɪ.nə'bɪl.ə.ti, -ɪ.ti (US) -ə.ţi
sustenance 'sʌs.tɪ.nənts, -tᵊn.ənts (US) -tᵊn.ənts
sustentation ˌsʌs.ten'teɪ.ʃᵊn, -tən'-
susurr|ate 'suː.sᵊr|.eɪt, 'sjuː- (US) suː'sɜːr|.eɪt, sʊ-, sə- **-ates** -eɪts **-ating** -eɪ.tɪŋ (US) -eɪ.ţɪŋ **-ated** -eɪ.tɪd (US) -eɪ.ţɪd
susurration ˌsuː.sᵊr'eɪ.ʃᵊn, ˌsjuː- (US) ˌsuː.sə'reɪ- **-s** -z
Sutcliffe 'sʌt.klɪf
Sutherland 'sʌð.ᵊl.ənd (US) -ɚ.lənd
Sutlej 'sʌt.lɪdʒ, -ledʒ (US) -ledʒ
sutler 'sʌt.ləʳ (US) -lɚ **-s** -z
Sutro 'suː.trəʊ (US) -troʊ
suttee 'sʌt.iː, -'- (US) sə'tiː; 'sʌt.iː **-s** -z
Sutton 'sʌt.ᵊn
Sutton Coldfield ˌsʌt.ᵊn'kəʊld.fiːld (US) -'koʊld-
Sutton Hoo ˌsʌt.ᵊn'huː
sutur|e 'suː.tʃəʳ, 'sjuː-, -tjəʳ (US) 'suː.tʃɚ **-s** -z **-ing** -ɪŋ **-ed** -d
Suva 'suː.və
Suzanne suː'zæn, sʊ-
suzerain 'suː.zᵊr.eɪn, 'sjuː- (US) 'suː.zɚ.ɪn, -zə.raɪn **-s** -z
suzeraint|y 'suː.zᵊr.eɪn.t|i, 'sjuː-, -ᵊn- (US) 'suː.zɚ.ɪn-, -zə.raɪn- **-ies** -iz
Suzuki® sə'zuː.ki, sʊ- **-s** -z
Suzy 'suː.zi
svarabhakti ˌsvʌr.ə'bʌk.ti, ˌsvɑː.rə'-, -'bæk-, -tiː (US) ˌsvɑːr.ɑː'bɑːk-
svelt|e svelt, sfelt **-ely** -li **-eness** -nəs, -nɪs
Svengali sveŋ'gɑː.li, sfeŋ- (US) sven-, sfen- **-s** -z
Sverdlovsk sveəd'lɒvsk, -'lɒfsk; '--, -ləvsk, -ləfsk (US) sverd'lɔːfsk
SW (*abbrev. for* **southwest**) ˌes'dʌb.l̩.juː, saʊθ'west
swab swɒb (US) swɑːb **-s** -z **-bing** -ɪŋ **-bed** -d **-ber/s** -əʳ/z (US) -ɚ/z
Swabi|a 'sweɪ.bi|.ə **-an/s** -ən/z
swaddl|e 'swɒd.l̩ (US) 'swɑː.dl̩ **-es** -z **-ing** -ɪŋ, 'swɒd.lɪŋ (US) 'swɑːd- **-ed** -d **'swaddling ˌclothes**
Swadlincoat 'swɒd.lɪn.kəʊt, -lɪŋ- (US) 'swɑːd.lɪn.koʊt
Swadling 'swɒd.lɪŋ (US) 'swɑːd-
Swaffer 'swɒf.əʳ (US) 'swɑː.fɚ
Swaffham 'swɒf.əm (US) 'swɑː.fəm
swag swæg
swag|e sweɪdʒ **-es** -ɪz **-ing** -ɪŋ **-ed** -d
Swaggart 'swæg.ət (US) -ɚt
swagg|er 'swæg|.əʳ (US) -ɚ **-ers** -əz (US) -ɚz **-ering/ly** -ᵊr.ɪŋ/li **-ered** -əd (US) -ɚd **-erer/s** -ᵊr.əʳ/z (US) -ɚ.ɚ/z **'swagger ˌstick**
swag|man 'swæg|.mæn, -mən **-men** -men, -mən
Swahili swɑː'hiː.li, swə- (US) swɑː- **-s** -z
swain (S) sweɪn **-s** -z
swale (S) sweɪl
Swaledale 'sweɪl.deɪl
SWALK swɔːlk (US) swɑːk, swɔːk
swallow 'swɒl.əʊ (US) 'swɑː.loʊ **-s** -z **-ing** -ɪŋ **-ed** -d
swallowtail 'swɒl.əʊ.teɪl (US) 'swɑː.loʊ- **-s** -z **-ed** -d
swam (*from* **swim**) swæm
swami 'swɑː.mi **-(e)s** -z
swamp swɒmp (US) swɑːmp, swɔːmp **-s** -s **-ing** -ɪŋ **-ed** -t **-y** -i **-ier** -i.əʳ (US) -i.ɚ **-iest** -i.ɪst, -i.əst **-iness** -ɪ.nəs, -ɪ.nɪs
swampland 'swɒmp.lænd (US) 'swɑːmp- **-s** -z
swan (S) swɒn (US) swɑːn **-s** -z **-ning** -ɪŋ **-ned** -d **'swan ˌsong**
Swanage 'swɒn.ɪdʒ (US) 'swɑː.nɪdʒ
Swanee 'swɒn.i (US) 'swɑː.ni
swank swæŋk **-y** -i **-ier** -i.əʳ (US) -i.ɚ **-iest** -i.ɪst, -i.əst **-ily** -ɪ.li, -ᵊl.i **-iness** -ɪ.nəs, -ɪ.nɪs
Swanley 'swɒn.li (US) 'swɑːn-
Swann swɒn (US) swɑːn
swanner|y 'swɒn.ᵊr|.i (US) 'swɑː.nɚ- **-ies** -iz
Swanscombe 'swɒnz.kəm (US) 'swɑːnz-
swansdown 'swɒnz.daʊn (US) 'swɑːnz-
Swansea *in Wales:* 'swɒn.zi (US) 'swɑːn- *in Tasmania:* 'swɒnt.si, -siː (US) 'swɑːnt-
Swanson 'swɒnt.sən (US) 'swɑːnt-
swan-upp|ing 'swɒnˌʌp|.ɪŋ (US) 'swɑːn- **-er/s** -əʳ/z (US) -ɚ/z
Swanwick 'swɒn.ɪk (US) 'swɑː.nɪk
swap swɒp (US) swɑːp **-s** -s **-ping** -ɪŋ **-ped** -t **'swap ˌshop**
Swapo, SWAPO 'swɑː.pəʊ, 'swɒp.əʊ (US) 'swɑː.poʊ
sward swɔːd (US) swɔːrd **-s** -z
swarf swɔːf (US) swɔːrf
Swarfega® swɔː'fiː.gə (US) swɔːr-
swarm swɔːm (US) swɔːrm **-s** -z **-ing** -ɪŋ **-ed** -d
swart swɔːt (US) swɔːrt
swarth|y 'swɔː.ð|i (US) 'swɔːr-, -θ|i **-ier** -i.əʳ (US) -i.ɚ **-iest** -i.ɪst, -i.əst **-ily** -ɪ.li, -ᵊl.i **-iness** -ɪ.nəs, -ɪ.nɪs
swash swɒʃ (US) swɑːʃ **-es** -ɪz **-ing** -ɪŋ **-ed** -t
swashbuckl|er 'swɒʃˌbʌk.l̩|.əʳ, ˌ-l|əʳ (US) 'swɑːʃˌbʌk.l̩|.ɚ, ˌ-l|ɚ **-ers** -əz (US) -ɚz **-ing** -ɪŋ
swastika 'swɒs.tɪ.kə (US) 'swɑː.stɪ- **-s** -z
swat swɒt (US) swɑːt **-s** -s **-ting** -ɪŋ (US) 'swɑː.ţɪŋ **-ted** -ɪd (US) 'swɑː.ţɪd **-ter/s** -əʳ/z (US) 'swɑː.ţɚ/s
swatch® swɒtʃ (US) swɑːtʃ **-es** -ɪz
swa|th swɒ|θ, swɔː|θ (US) swɑː|θ, swɔː|θ **-ths** -θs, -ðz
swath|e sweɪð **-es** -z **-ing** -ɪŋ **-ed** -d
sway sweɪ **-s** -z **-ing** -ɪŋ **-ed** -d
Swazi 'swɑː.zi **-s** -z
Swaziland 'swɑː.zi.lænd
swear sweəʳ (US) swer **-s** -z **-ing** -ɪŋ **swore** swɔːʳ (US) swɔːr **sworn** swɔːn (US) swɔːrn
swearword 'sweə.wɜːd (US) 'swer.wɜːrd **-s** -z
sweat swet **-s** -s **-ing** -ɪŋ (US) 'sweţ.ɪŋ **-ed** -ɪd (US) 'sweţ.ɪd
sweatband 'swet.bænd **-s** -z
sweater 'swet.əʳ (US) 'sweţ.ɚ **-s** -z
sweatpants 'swet.pænts
sweatshirt 'swet.ʃɜːt (US) -ʃɜːrt **-s** -s
sweatshop 'swet.ʃɒp (US) -ʃɑːp **-s** -s
sweat|y 'swet|.i (US) 'sweţ- **-ier** -i.əʳ (US) -i.ɚ **-iest** -i.ɪst, -i.əst **-iness** -ɪ.nəs, -ɪ.nɪs
swede (S) swiːd **-s** -z
Sweden 'swiː.dᵊn
Swedenborg 'swiː.dᵊn.bɔːg, -dᵊm- (US) -dᵊn.bɔːrg
Swedenborgian ˌswiː.dᵊn'bɔː.dʒən, -dᵊm'-, -dʒi.ən, -gən, -gi.ən (US) -dᵊn'bɔːr.dʒi.ən, -gi- **-s** -z
Swedish 'swiː.dɪʃ **ˌSwedish 'massage** (US) **ˌSwedish mas'sage**
Sweeney 'swiː.ni
sweep swiːp **-s** -s **-ing/s** -ɪŋ **swept** swept **sweeper/s** 'swiː.pəʳ/z (US) -pɚ/z
sweepstake 'swiːp.steɪk **-s** -s
sweet (S) swiːt **-s** -s **-er** -əʳ (US) 'swiː.ţɚ **-est** -ɪst, -əst (US) 'swiː.ţɪst, -ţəst **-ly** -li **-ness** -nəs, -nɪs **ˌsweet 'nothings** ; **ˌsweet 'pea** ; **ˌsweet po'tato** (US) **'sweet poˌtato** ; **ˌsweet 'tooth** (US) **'sweet ˌtooth** ; **ˌsweet 'William** ; **ˌsweetness and 'light**
sweet-and-sour ˌswiːt.ᵊn'saʊəʳ (US) -'saʊɚ
sweetbread 'swiːt.bred **-s** -z
sweetbrier 'swiːt.braɪəʳ (US) -braɪɚ **-s** -z
sweetcorn 'swiːt.kɔːn (US) -kɔːrn
sweeten 'swiː.tᵊn **-s** -z **-ing** -ɪŋ, 'swiːt.nɪŋ **-ed** -d **-er/s** -əʳ/z, 'swiːt.nəʳ/z (US) 'swiː.tᵊn.ɚ/z, 'swiːt.nɚ/z
Sweetex® 'swiː.teks
sweetheart 'swiːt.hɑːt (US) -hɑːrt **-s** -s

sweetie ˈswiː.ti US -t̬i **-s** -z
sweeting (S) ˈswiː.tɪŋ US -t̬ɪŋ **-s** -z
sweetish ˈswiː.tɪʃ US -t̬ɪʃ
sweetmeal ˈswiːt.miːl
sweetmeat ˈswiːt.miːt **-s** -s
sweet-talk ˈswiːt.tɔːk US -tɑːk, -tɔːk **-s** -s **-ing** -ɪŋ **-ed** -t
sweet|y ˈswiː.t|i US -t̬|i **-ies** -iz
swell swel **-s** -z **-ing/s** -ɪŋ/z **-ed** -d **swollen** ˈswəʊ.lən US ˈswoʊ- ˌ**swelled** ˈ**head**
swelt|er ˈswel.t|əʳ US -t̬|ɚ **-ers** -əz US -ɚz **-ering/ly** -ᵊr.ɪŋ/li **-ered** -əd US -ɚd
swept (*from* **sweep**) swept
swerv|e swɜːv US swɝːv **-es** -z **-ing** -ɪŋ **-ed** -d
Swettenham ˈswet.ᵊn.əm
swift (S) swɪft **-s** -s **-er** -əʳ US -ɚ **-est** -ɪst, -əst **-ly** -li **-ness** -nəs, -nɪs
Swiftsure ˈswɪft.ʃɔːʳ, -ʃʊəʳ US -ʃʊr
swig swɪɡ **-s** -z **-ging** -ɪŋ **-ged** -d
swill swɪl **-s** -z **-ing** -ɪŋ **-ed** -d **-er/s** -əʳ/z US -ɚ/z
swim swɪm **-s** -z **-ming/ly** -ɪŋ/li **swam** swæm **swum** swʌm **swimmer/s** ˈswɪm.əʳ/z US -ɚ/z ˈ**swimming** ˌ**bath(s)** ; ˈ**swimming** ˌ**costume** ; ˈ**swimming** ˌ**pool**
swimsuit ˈswɪm.suːt, -sjuːt US -suːt **-s** -s
swimwear ˈswɪm.weəʳ US -wer
Swinbourne ˈswɪn.bɔːn, ˈswɪm- US ˈswɪn.bɔːrn
Swinburne ˈswɪn.bɜːn, ˈswɪm-, -bən US ˈswɪn.bɝːn, -bɚn
swindl|e ˈswɪn.dl̩ **-es** -z **-ing** -ɪŋ, ˈswɪnd.lɪŋ **-ed** -d **-er/s** -əʳ/z, ˈswɪnd.ləʳ/z US ˈswɪn.dl̩.ɚ/z, ˈswɪnd.lɚ/z
Swindon ˈswɪn.dən
swine swaɪn **-s** -z
swineherd ˈswaɪn.hɜːd US -hɝːd **-s** -z
swing swɪŋ **-s** -z **-ing** -ɪŋ **swung** swʌŋ **swinger/s** ˈswɪŋ.əʳ/z US -ɚ/z ˌ**swing** ˈ**door** ; ˌ**swings and** ˈ**roundabouts**
swingbridge swɪŋˈbrɪdʒ **-s** -ɪz
swingeing ˈswɪn.dʒɪŋ
swingl|e ˈswɪŋ.ɡl̩ **-es** -z **-ing** -ɪŋ, ˈswɪŋ.ɡlɪŋ **-ed** -d
swingometer swɪŋˈɒm.ɪ.təʳ, -ə.təʳ US ˈɑː.mə.t̬ɚ **-s** -z
swing-wing ˌswɪŋˈwɪŋ US ˈ-- *stress shift:* ˌswing-wing ˈplane
swinish ˈswaɪ.nɪʃ **-ly** -li **-ness** -nəs, -nɪs
Swinton ˈswɪn.tən US -tᵊn
swip|e swaɪp **-es** -s **-ing** -ɪŋ **-ed** -t **-er/s** -əʳ/z US -ɚ/z
swirl swɜːl US swɝːl **-s** -z **-ing** -ɪŋ **-ed** -d **-y** -i
swish swɪʃ **-es** -ɪz **-ing** -ɪŋ **-ed** -t
swish|y ˈswɪʃ|.i **-ier** -i.əʳ US -i.ɚ **-iest** -i.ɪst, -i.əst
Swiss swɪs ˌ**Swiss** ˈ**cheese** ; ˌ**Swiss** ˈ**cheese** ˌ**plant** ; ˌ**Swiss** ˈ**roll**
Swissair® swɪsˈeəʳ US -er
switch (S®) swɪtʃ **-es** -ɪz **-ing** -ɪŋ **-ed** -t
switchback ˈswɪtʃ.bæk **-s** -s
switchblade ˈswɪtʃ.bleɪd **-s** -z
switchboard ˈswɪtʃ.bɔːd US -bɔːrd **-s** -z
switchgear ˈswɪtʃ.ɡɪəʳ US -ɡɪr
Swithin ˈswɪð.ɪn, ˈswɪθ-
Switzerland ˈswɪt.sᵊl.ənd US -sɚ.lənd
swivel ˈswɪv.ᵊl **-s** -z **-(l)ing** -ɪŋ, ˈswɪv.lɪŋ **-(l)ed** -d ˌ**swivel** ˈ**chair**
swiz(z) swɪz **-es** -ɪz
swizzl|e ˈswɪz.l̩ **-es** -z **-ing** -ɪŋ, ˈswɪz.lɪŋ **-ed** -d **-er/s** -əʳ/z, ˈswɪz.ləʳ/z US ˈ-l̩.ɚ/z, ˈ-lɚ/z ˈ**swizzle** ˌ**stick**
swollen (*from* **swell**) ˈswəʊ.lən US ˈswoʊ- ˌ**swollen** ˈ**head**
swoon swuːn **-s** -z **-ing** -ɪŋ **-ed** -d
swoop swuːp **-s** -s **-ing** -ɪŋ **-ed** -t
swoosh swuːʃ, swʊʃ **-es** -ɪz **-ing** -ɪŋ **-ed** -t
swop swɒp US swɑːp **-s** -s **-ping** -ɪŋ **-ped** -t
sword sɔːd US sɔːrd **-s** -z ˈ**sword** ˌ**dance**
Sworder ˈsɔː.dəʳ US ˈsɔːr.dɚ
swordfish ˈsɔːd.fɪʃ US ˈsɔːrd-
swordplay ˈsɔːd.pleɪ US ˈsɔːrd-
swords|man ˈsɔːdz|.mən US ˈsɔːrdz- **-men** -mən **-manship** -mən.ʃɪp
swordstick ˈsɔːd.stɪk US ˈsɔːrd- **-s** -s
sword-swallower ˈsɔːdˌswɒl.əʊ.əʳ US ˈsɔːrdˌswɑː.loʊ.ɚ **-s** -z
swore (*from* **swear**) swɔːʳ US swɔːr
sworn (*from* **swear**) swɔːn US swɔːrn
swot swɒt US swɑːt **-s** -s **-ting** -ɪŋ US ˈswɑː.t̬ɪŋ **-ted** -ɪd US ˈswɑː.t̬ɪd **-ter/s** -əʳ/z US ˈswɑː.t̬ɚ/z
swum (*from* **swim**) swʌm
swung (*from* **swing**) swʌŋ
Sybaris ˈsɪb.ᵊr.ɪs; sɪˈbɑːr- US ˈsɪb.ɚ.ɪs
sybarite ˈsɪb.ᵊr.aɪt US -ə.raɪt **-s** -s
sybaritic ˌsɪb.ᵊrˈɪt.ɪk US -əˈrɪt̬- **-ally** -ᵊl.i, -li
Sybil ˈsɪb.ɪl, -ᵊl US -ᵊl
Note: As a feminine name, /ˈsɪb.ᵊl/ is more common in British English; the /-ɪl/ ending is more usual for the soothsayer.
sycamore (S) ˈsɪk.ə.mɔːʳ US -mɔːr **-s** -z
syc|e saɪs **-es** -ɪz
sycophancy ˈsɪk.ə.fᵊn*t*.si, ˈsaɪ.kə-, -ˈfæn*t*- US -fᵊn*t*-
sycophant ˈsɪk.ə.fænt, ˈsaɪ.kə-, -fənt US -fᵊnt **-s** -s
sycophantic ˌsɪk.əʊˈfæn.tɪk, ˌsaɪ.kəˈ- US -t̬ɪk
Sydenham ˈsɪd.ᵊn.əm, ˈ-nəm
Sydney ˈsɪd.ni
Sydneysider ˈsɪd.niˌsaɪ.dəʳ US -dɚ
syenite ˈsaɪ.ə.naɪt, ˈ-ɪ- US ˈ-ə-
Sykes saɪks
syllabar|y ˈsɪl.ə.bᵊr|.i US -ber- **-ies** -iz
syllabic sɪˈlæb.ɪk, sə- US sɪ- **-ally** -ᵊl.i, -li
syllabi|cate sɪˈlæb.ɪ|.keɪt, sə-, ˈ-ə- US sɪˈlæb.ə- **-cates** -keɪts **-cating** -keɪ.tɪŋ US -keɪ.t̬ɪŋ **-cated** -keɪ.tɪd US -keɪ.t̬ɪd
syllabication sɪˌlæb.ɪˈkeɪ.ʃᵊn, sə-, -əˈ- US sɪˌlæb.əˈ-
syllabicity ˌsɪl.əˈbɪs.ə.ti, -ɪ.ti US -ə.t̬i
syllabification sɪˌlæb.ɪ.fɪˈkeɪ.ʃᵊn, sə-, ˌ-ə- US sɪˌlæb.ə-
syllabi|fy sɪˈlæb.ɪ|.faɪ, sə-, ˈ-ə- US sɪˈlæb.ə- **-fies** -faɪz **-fying** -faɪ.ɪŋ **-fied** -faɪd
syllabism ˈsɪl.ə.bɪ.zᵊm
syllable ˈsɪl.ə.bl̩ **-s** -z
syllabub ˈsɪl.ə.bʌb
syllab|us ˈsɪl.ə.b|əs **-uses** -əs.ɪz **-i** -aɪ
syllep|sis sɪˈlep|.sɪs, sə- US sɪ- **-tic** -tɪk
syllogism ˈsɪl.ə.dʒɪ.zᵊm **-s** -z
syllogistic ˌsɪl.əˈdʒɪs.tɪk **-ally** -ᵊl.i, -li
syllogiz|e, -is|e ˈsɪl.ə.dʒaɪz **-es** -ɪz **-ing** -ɪŋ **-ed** -d
sylph sɪlf **-s** -s
sylphlike ˈsɪlf.laɪk
sylvan ˈsɪl.vən
Sylvester sɪlˈves.təʳ US -tɚ
Sylvia ˈsɪl.vi.ə
symbiont ˈsɪm.baɪ.ɒnt, -bi- US -bi-, -baɪ-, -ɑːnt **-s** -s
symbiosis ˌsɪm.baɪˈəʊ.sɪs, -biˈ- US -bi-, -baɪ-, -ˈoʊ-
symbiotic ˌsɪm.baɪˈɒt.ɪk, -biˈ- US -bi-, -baɪ-, -ˈɑː.t̬ɪk
symbol ˈsɪm.bᵊl **-s** -z
symbolic sɪmˈbɒl.ɪk US -ˈbɑː.lɪk **-al** -ᵊl **-ally** -ᵊl.i, -li
symbolism ˈsɪm.bᵊl.ɪ.zᵊm
symbolist ˈsɪm.bᵊl.ɪst **-s** -s
symbolization, -isa- ˌsɪm.bᵊl.aɪˈzeɪ.ʃᵊn, -ɪˈ- US -ɪˈ-
symboliz|e, -is|e ˈsɪm.bᵊl.aɪz US -bə.laɪz **-es** -ɪz **-ing** -ɪŋ **-ed** -d
Syme saɪm
Symington ˈsaɪ.mɪŋ.tən, ˈsɪm.ɪŋ-
symmetric sɪˈmet.rɪk, sə- US sɪ- **-al** -ᵊl **-ally** -ᵊl.i, -li **-alness** -ᵊl.nəs, -nɪs
symmetry ˈsɪm.ə.tri, ˈ-ɪ- US ˈ-ə-
Symond ˈsaɪ.mənd
Symonds ˈsaɪ.mən*dz*, ˈsɪm.ən*dz*
Symonds Yat ˌsɪm.ən*dz*ˈjæt
Symons ˈsaɪ.mənz, ˈsɪm.ənz
sympathetic ˌsɪm.pəˈθet.ɪk US -ˈθet̬- **-al** -ᵊl **-ally** -ᵊl.i, -li
sympathiz|e, is|e ˈsɪm.pə.θaɪz **-es** -ɪz **-ing** -ɪŋ **-ed** -d **-er/s** -əʳ/z US -ɚ/z

sympath|y ˈsɪm.pə.θ|i **-ies** -iz
symphonic sɪmˈfɒn.ɪk US -ˈfɑː.nɪk
symphon|y ˈsɪm*p*.fə.n|i **-ies** -iz **ˈsymphony ˌorchestra** US **ˌsymphony ˈorchestra**
symposi|um sɪmˈpəʊ.zi|.əm US -ˈpoʊ- **-ums** -əmz **-a** -ə
symptom ˈsɪm*p*.təm **-s** -z
symptomatic ˌsɪm*p*.təˈmæt.ɪk US -ˈmæt̬- **-ally** -ᵊl.i, -li
synaesthesia ˌsɪn.ɪsˈθiː.zi.ə, -iːsˈ-, -əsˈ-, -ʒə, -ʒi.ə US -ɪsˈθiː.ʒə, -ʒi.ə, -zi-
synagogue ˈsɪn.ə.gɒg US -gɑːg, -gɔːg **-s** -z
synaloepha ˌsɪn.ᵊlˈiː.fə US -əˈliː-
synapse ˈsaɪ.næps, ˈsɪn.æps; sɪˈnæps US ˈsɪn.æps; sɪˈnæps
synap|sis sɪˈnæp|.sɪs **-ses** -siːz **-tic/ally** -tɪk/.ᵊl.i, -tɪk/.li
sync(h) sɪŋk **-s** -s **-ing** -ɪŋ **-ed** -t
synchromesh ˈsɪŋ.krəʊ.meʃ, ˈsɪn-, ˌ--ˈ- US ˈsɪŋ.krə-, ˈsɪn-, -kroʊ- **-es** -ɪz
synchronic sɪŋˈkrɒn.ɪk, sɪn- US sɪnˈkrɑː.nɪk, sɪŋ-
synchronicity ˌsɪŋ.krəˈnɪs.ə.ti, ˌsɪn-, -krɒnˈɪs-, -ɪ.ti US -krəˈnɪs.ə.t̬i
synchronism ˈsɪŋ.krə.nɪ.zᵊm, ˈsɪn-
synchronistic ˌsɪŋ.krəˈnɪs.tɪk, ˌsɪn-
synchronization, -isa- ˌsɪŋ.krə.naɪˈzeɪ.ʃᵊn, ˌsɪn-, -nɪˈ- US -nɪˈ- **-s** -z
synchroniz|e, -is|e ˈsɪŋ.krə.naɪz, ˈsɪn- **-es** -ɪz **-ing** -ɪŋ **-ed** -d **ˌsynchronized ˈswimming**
synchronous ˈsɪŋ.krə.nəs, ˈsɪn- **-ly** -li **-ness** -nəs, -nɪs
synchrony ˈsɪŋ.krə.ni, ˈsɪn-
synchrotron ˈsɪŋ.krəʊ.trɒn, ˈsɪn- US -krə.trɑːn **-s** -z
synco|pate ˈsɪŋ.kə|.peɪt US ˈsɪŋ-, ˈsɪn- **-pates** -peɪts **-pating** -peɪ.tɪŋ US -peɪ.t̬ɪŋ **-pated** -peɪ.tɪd US -peɪ.t̬ɪd
syncopation ˌsɪn.kəˈpeɪ.ʃᵊn, ˌsɪŋ- US ˌsɪŋ-, ˌsɪn- **-s** -z
syncope ˈsɪŋ.kə.pi, ˈsɪn-
syncretic sɪŋˈkriː.tɪk, sɪn-, -ˈkret.ɪk US -ˈkret̬.ɪk
syncretism ˈsɪŋ.krɪ.tɪ.zᵊm, ˈsɪn- US -krə-
syndesis sɪnˈdiː.sɪs US ˈsɪn.də-; sɪnˈdiː-
syndetic sɪnˈdet.ɪk US -ˈdet̬-
syndic ˈsɪn.dɪk **-s** -s
syndical|ism ˈsɪn.dɪ.kᵊl|.ɪ.zᵊm **-ist/s** -ɪst/s
syndicate (*n.*) ˈsɪn.dɪ.kət, -kɪt US -də.kɪt **-s** -s
syndi|cate (*v.*) ˈsɪn.dɪ|.keɪt US -də- **-cates** -keɪts **-cating** -keɪ.tɪŋ US -keɪ.t̬ɪŋ **-cated** -keɪ.tɪd US -keɪ.t̬ɪd
syndication ˌsɪn.dɪˈkeɪ.ʃᵊn US -dəˈ-
syndrome ˈsɪn.drəʊm US -droʊm **-s** -z
syne saɪn
synecdoche sɪˈnek.də.ki
syneres|is sɪˈnɪə.rə.s|ɪs, -rɪ- US -ˈner.ə- **-es** -iːz
synergism ˈsɪn.ə.dʒɪ.zᵊm US ˈ-ɚ-
synergy ˈsɪn.ə.dʒi US ˈ-ɚ-
synesthesia ˌsɪn.ɪsˈθiː.zi.ə, -iːsˈ-, -əsˈ-, -ʒə, -ʒi.ə US -ɪsˈθiː.ʒə, -ʒi.ə, -zi-
Synge sɪŋ
synod ˈsɪn.əd, -ɒd US -əd **-s** -z **-al** -ᵊl
synodic sɪˈnɒd.ɪk US -ˈnɑː.dɪk **-al** -ᵊl **-ally** -ᵊl.i, -li
synonym ˈsɪn.ə.nɪm **-s** -z
synonymous sɪˈnɒn.ɪ.məs, ˈ-ə- US -ˈnɑː.nə- **-ly** -li
synonymy sɪˈnɒn.ɪ.mi, ˈ-ə- US -ˈnɑː.nə-
synops|is sɪˈnɒp.s|ɪs US -ˈnɑːp- **-es** -iːz
synoptic sɪˈnɒp.tɪk US -ˈnɑːp- **-s** -s **-al** -ᵊl **-ally** -ᵊl.i, -li
synovi|a saɪˈnəʊ.vi|.ə, sɪ- US sɪˈnoʊ- **-al** -ᵊl
synovitis ˌsaɪ.nəʊˈvaɪ.tɪs, ˌsɪn.əʊˈ- US ˌsaɪ.nəˈvaɪ.t̬ɪs, ˌsɪn.əˈ-
syntactic sɪnˈtæk.tɪk **-al** -ᵊl **-ally** -ᵊl.i, -li
syntagm ˈsɪn.tæm **-s** -z
syntagmatic ˌsɪn.tægˈmæt.ɪk US -ˈmæt̬-
syntax ˈsɪn.tæks **-es** -ɪz
synthes|is ˈsɪn*t*.θə.s|ɪs, -θɪ- US -θə- **-es** -iːz
synthesiz|e, -is|e ˈsɪn*t*.θə.saɪz, -θɪ- US -θə- **-es** -ɪz **-ing** -ɪŋ **-ed** -d **-er/s** -əʳ/z US -ɚ/z
synthetic sɪnˈθet.ɪk US -ˈθet̬- **-s** -s **-ally** -ᵊl.i, -li
syphilis ˈsɪf.ɪ.lɪs, -ᵊl.ɪs US -ᵊl.ɪs
syphilitic ˌsɪf.ɪˈlɪt.ɪk, -ᵊlˈɪt- US -əˈlɪt̬-
syphon ˈsaɪ.fᵊn **-s** -z **-ing** -ɪŋ **-ed** -d
Syracusan ˌsaɪə.rəˈkjuː.zᵊn, ˌsɪr.əˈ- US ˌsɪr.əˈ-
Syracuse *in classical history:* ˈsaɪə.rə.kjuːz US ˈsɪr.ə- *modern town in Sicily:* ˈsaɪə.rə.kjuːz, ˈsɪr.ə- US ˈsɪr.ə- *town in US:* ˈsɪr.ə.kjuːs, -kjuːz
Syri|a ˈsɪr.i|.ə **-an/s** -ən/z
Syriac ˈsɪr.i.æk
syringa sɪˈrɪŋ.gə **-s** -z
syring|e sɪˈrɪn*d*ʒ, sə-; ˈsɪr.ɪndʒ US səˈrɪndʒ; ˈsɪr.ɪndʒ **-es** -ɪz **-ing** -ɪŋ **-ed** -d
syrinx ˈsɪr.ɪŋks **-es** -ɪz
syrophoenician ˌsaɪə.rəʊ.fɪˈnɪʃ.ᵊn, -fiːˈ-, -ʃi.ən, -si.ən US ˌsaɪ.roʊ.fiːˈnɪʃ.ᵊn, -fɪˈ-
syr|tis (S) ˈsɜː|.tɪs US ˈsɜːr|.t̬ɪs **-tes** -tiːz
syrup ˈsɪr.əp US ˈsɪr-, ˈsɜːr- **-s** -s **-y** -i
systaltic sɪˈstæl.tɪk US -ˈstɑːl.t̬ɪk, -ˈstæl-
system ˈsɪs.təm, -tɪm US -təm **-s** -z **ˌsystems ˈanalyst**
systematic ˌsɪs.təˈmæt.ɪk, -tɪˈ- US -təˈmæt̬- **-ally** -ᵊl.i, -li
systematization, -isa- ˌsɪs.tə.mə.taɪˈzeɪ.ʃᵊn, -tɪ-, -tɪˈ- US -tə.mə.t̬ɪˈ-
systematiz|e, -is|e ˈsɪs.tə.mə.taɪz, -tɪ- US -tə- **-es** -ɪz **-ing** -ɪŋ **-ed** -d **-er/s** -əʳ/z US -ɚ/z
systemic sɪˈstem.ɪk, -ˈstiː.mɪk US -ˈstem.ɪk
systemiz|e ˈsɪs.tə.maɪz, -tɪ- US -tə- **-es** -ɪz **-ing** -ɪŋ **-ed** -d
systole ˈsɪs.tᵊl.i
systolic sɪˈstɒl.ɪk US -ˈɑː.lɪk
syzyg|y ˈsɪz.ɪ.dʒ|i, ˈ-ə- US ˈ-ə- **-ies** -iz
Szczecin ˈʃtʃet.ʃiːn
Szeged ˈseg.ed

T

t (T) tiː **-'s** -z
ta *Tonic Sol-fa name for diminished seventh from the tonic:* tɔː Ⓤⓢ tɑː **-s** -z
ta *syllable used in Tonic Sol-fa for counting time:* tɑː
ta *thank you:* tɑː
Note: This form is used in casual British English.
Taal tɑːl
tab tæb **-s** -z **-bing** -ɪŋ **-bed** -d
tabard 'tæb.ɑːd, -əd Ⓤⓢ -ɚd **-s** -z
Tabasco® tə'bæs.kəʊ Ⓤⓢ -koʊ
Tabatha 'tæb.ə.θə
tabbouleh tə'buː.lə, -li
tabb|y 'tæb|.i **-ies** -iz
tabernacle 'tæb.əˌnæk.l̩ Ⓤⓢ -ɚˌ- **-s** -z
Taberner tə'bɜː.nəʳ; 'tæb.ᵊn.əʳ Ⓤⓢ tə'bɝː.nɚ; 'tæb.ɚ.nɚ
tabes 'teɪ.biːz
Tabitha 'tæb.ɪ.θə, '-ə-
tabla 'tæb.lə Ⓤⓢ 'tɑː.blə, -blɑː **-s** -z
tablature 'tæb.lə.tʃəʳ, -lɪ-, -tjʊəʳ Ⓤⓢ -lə.tʃɚ **-s** -z
tabl|e (T) 'teɪ.bl̩ **-es** -z **-ing** -ɪŋ, 'teɪ.blɪŋ **-ed** -d **'table ˌlinen ; 'table ˌmanners ; 'table ˌtennis, ˌtable 'tennis ; 'table ˌwine ; ˌdrink someone ˌunder the 'table ; ˌturn the 'tables on ˌsomeone**
tableau 'tæb.ləʊ Ⓤⓢ -loʊ, -'- **-s** -z
tableaux (*alternative plur. of* **tableau**) 'tæb.ləʊ, -ləʊz Ⓤⓢ -loʊ, -loʊz, -'-
table|cloth 'teɪ.bl̩|.klɒθ Ⓤⓢ -klɑːθ **-cloths** -klɒθs, -klɒðz Ⓤⓢ -klɑːθs, -klɑːðz
table d'hôte ˌtɑː.bl̩'dəʊt, -blə'- Ⓤⓢ -bl̩'doʊt, ˌtæb.l̩'-
table-hop 'teɪ.bl̩.hɒp Ⓤⓢ -hɑːp **-s** -s **-ping** -ɪŋ **-ped** -t **-per/s** -əʳ/z Ⓤⓢ -ɚ/z
tableland 'teɪ.bl̩.lænd **-s** -z
tablemat 'teɪ.bl̩.mæt **-s** -s
tablespoon 'teɪ.bl̩.spuːn **-s** -z
tablespoonful 'teɪ.bl̩ˌspuːn.fʊl **-s** -z
tablespoonsful (*alternative plur. of* **tablespoonful**) 'teɪ.bl̩ˌspuːnz.fʊl
tablet 'tæb.lət, -lɪt Ⓤⓢ -lɪt **-s** -s **ˌtablets of 'stone**
table-turning 'teɪ.bl̩ˌtɜː.nɪŋ Ⓤⓢ -ˌtɝː-
tableware 'teɪ.bl̩.weəʳ Ⓤⓢ -wer
tabloid 'tæb.lɔɪd **-s** -z
taboo tə'buː, tæb'uː **-s** -z **-ing** -ɪŋ **-ed** -d
tabor 'teɪ.bəʳ, -bɔːʳ Ⓤⓢ -bɚ **-s** -z
Tabor 'teɪ.bɔːʳ, -bəʳ Ⓤⓢ -bɚ
tabo(u)ret 'tæb.ᵊr.ɪt, -et Ⓤⓢ ˌtæb.ə'ret, '--- **-s** -s
Tabriz tæb'riːz Ⓤⓢ tɑː'briːz, tə-
tabular 'tæb.jə.ləʳ, -jʊ- Ⓤⓢ -lɚ
tabula rasa ˌtæb.jə.lə'rɑː.sə, -jʊ-, -zə **tabulae rasae** ˌtæb.jə.liː'rɑː.siː, -jʊ-, -ziː
tabu|late 'tæb.jə|.leɪt, -jʊ- **-lates** -leɪts **-lating** -leɪ.tɪŋ Ⓤⓢ -leɪ.t̬ɪŋ **-lated** -leɪ.tɪd Ⓤⓢ -leɪ.t̬ɪd **-lator/s** -leɪ.təʳ/z Ⓤⓢ -leɪ.t̬ɚ/z
tabulation ˌtæb.jə'leɪ.ʃᵊn, -jʊ'- **-s** -z
tacet 'teɪ.set, 'tæs.et, -ɪt Ⓤⓢ 'teɪ.set, 'tæs.et; 'tɑː.ket
tach|e tɑːʃ, tæʃ Ⓤⓢ tætʃ **-es** -ɪz
tach|ism (T) 'tæʃ|.ɪ.zᵊm **-ist/s** -ɪst/s **-iste/s** -'iːst/s
tachograph 'tæk.əʊ.grɑːf, -græf Ⓤⓢ -ə.græf **-s** -s
tachometer tæk'ɒm.ɪ.təʳ, '-ə- Ⓤⓢ tæk'ɑː.mə.t̬ɚ, tə'kɑː- **-s** -z
tachycardia ˌtæk.ɪ'kɑː.di.ə Ⓤⓢ -'kɑːr-
tachygraph 'tæk.ɪ.grɑːf, -græf Ⓤⓢ -græf **-s** -s
tachygraph|y tæk'ɪ.grə.f|i, tə'kɪg- **-er/s** -əʳ/z Ⓤⓢ -ɚ/z
tacit 'tæs.ɪt **-ly** -li **-ness** -nəs, -nɪs
taciturn 'tæs.ɪ.tɜːn Ⓤⓢ -ə.tɝːn **-ly** -li
taciturnity ˌtæs.ɪ'tɜː.nə.ti, -nɪ- Ⓤⓢ -ə'tɝː.nə.t̬i
Tacitus 'tæs.ɪ.təs Ⓤⓢ -t̬əs
tack tæk **-s** -s **-ing** -ɪŋ **-ed** -t
tackl|e 'tæk.l̩ *nautical often:* 'teɪ.kl̩ **-es** -z **-ing** -ɪŋ, 'tæk.lɪŋ, 'teɪ.klɪŋ **-ed** -d **-er/s** -əʳ/z, 'tæk.ləʳ/z, 'teɪ.kləʳ/z Ⓤⓢ 'tæk.l̩.ɚ/z, 'teɪ.kl̩.ɚ/z, 'tæk.lɚ/z, 'teɪ.klɚ/z
tack|y 'tæk|.i **-ier** -i.əʳ Ⓤⓢ -i.ɚ **-iest** -i.ɪst, -i.əst **-ily** -ɪ.li, -ᵊl.i **-iness** -ɪ.nəs, -ɪ.nɪs
taco 'tɑː.kəʊ, 'tæk.əʊ Ⓤⓢ 'tɑː.koʊ **-s** -z
Tacoma tə'kəʊ.mə Ⓤⓢ -'koʊ-
tact tækt
tactful 'tækt.fᵊl, -fʊl **-ly** -i **-ness** -nəs, -nɪs
tactic 'tæk.tɪk **-s** -s **-al** -ᵊl **-ally** -ᵊl.i, -li
tactician tæk'tɪʃ.ᵊn **-s** -z
tactile 'tæk.taɪl Ⓤⓢ -tᵊl
tactless 'tækt.ləs, -lɪs **-ly** -li **-ness** -nəs, -nɪs
tactual 'tæk.tju.əl, -tʃu- Ⓤⓢ -tʃu- **-ly** -i
tad tæd **-s** -z
Tadcaster 'tædˌkæs.təʳ, -kə.stəʳ Ⓤⓢ -ˌkæs.tɚ
Tadema 'tæd.ɪ.mə, '-ə-
Tadley 'tæd.li
tadpole 'tæd.pəʊl Ⓤⓢ -poʊl **-s** -z
Tadworth 'tæd.wəθ, -wɜːθ Ⓤⓢ -wɚθ, -wɝːθ
Tadzhik 'tɑː.dʒiːk, -'- Ⓤⓢ ˌtɑː'dʒɪk, -'dʒiːk
Tadzhikistan tɑːˌdʒɪk.ɪ'stɑːn, -ˌdʒiː.kɪ'- Ⓤⓢ -'dʒɪk.ɪ.stæn, -'dʒiː.kɪ-, -stɑːn
Taegu ˌteɪ'guː Ⓤⓢ 'taɪ.guː, -'-
Tae Kwon Do ˌtaɪ'kwɒn.dəʊ, ˌteɪ-, ˌ--'- Ⓤⓢ ˌtaɪ.kwɑːn'doʊ, ˌ-'--
tael teɪl **-s** -z
ta'en (*dialectal for* **taken**) teɪn
Taff tæf
Taff-Ely ˌtæf'iː.li
taffeta 'tæf.ɪ.tə, '-ə- Ⓤⓢ -ɪ.t̬ə
taffrail 'tæf.reɪl, -rɪl, -rəl Ⓤⓢ -reɪl **-s** -z
Taff|y *Brit slang for Welsh:* 'tæf|.i **-ies** -iz
taffy *US for toffee:* 'tæf.i
Taft *surname* tæft, tɑːft Ⓤⓢ tæft *town in Iran:* tɑːft
tag tæg **-s** -z **-ging** -ɪŋ **-ged** -d **'tag ˌquestion**
Tagalog tə'gɑː.lɒg, -ləg Ⓤⓢ -lɑːg, -ləg
tagetes tædʒ'iː.tiːz
Taggart 'tæg.ət Ⓤⓢ -ɚt
tagliatelle ˌtæl.jə'tel.i Ⓤⓢ ˌtɑːl.jə'-
tagmeme 'tæg.miːm **-s** -z
tagmemic tæg'miː.mɪk **-s** -s
Tagore tə'gɔːʳ Ⓤⓢ -'gɔːr
Tagus 'teɪ.gəs
tahini tɑː'hiː.ni, tə- Ⓤⓢ tə-, tɑː-
Tahi|ti tɑː'hiː|.ti, tə- Ⓤⓢ tə'hiː|.t̬i **-tian/s** -ʃᵊn/z Ⓤⓢ -ʃᵊn/z, -t̬i.ənz
Tahoe 'tɑː.həʊ Ⓤⓢ -hoʊ
t'ai chi, tai chi ˌtaɪ'tʃiː, -'dʒiː Ⓤⓢ -'dʒiː, -'tʃiː
Taichung, T'ai-chung ˌtaɪ'tʃʊŋ
Taig taɪk, taɪx **-s** -s
taiga 'taɪ.gə, -gɑː Ⓤⓢ -gə
tail teɪl **-s** -z **-ing** -ɪŋ **-ed** -d **-less** -ləs, -lɪs **ˌtail 'end ; 'tail ˌpipe ; make ˌhead or 'tail of ; with one's ˌtail between one's 'legs**
tailback 'teɪl.bæk **-s** -s
tailboard 'teɪl.bɔːd Ⓤⓢ -bɔːrd **-s** -z
tailbone 'teɪl.bəʊn Ⓤⓢ -boʊn **-s** -z
tailcoat ˌteɪl'kəʊt, '-- Ⓤⓢ 'teɪl.koʊt **-s** -s
tail|gate 'teɪl|.geɪt **-gates** -geɪts **-gating** -geɪ.tɪŋ Ⓤⓢ -geɪ.t̬ɪŋ **-gated** -geɪ.tɪd Ⓤⓢ -geɪ.t̬ɪd **-gater/s** -ˌgeɪ.təʳ/z Ⓤⓢ -ˌgeɪ.t̬ɚ/z
taille taɪ Ⓤⓢ teɪl
tail|or 'teɪ.l|əʳ Ⓤⓢ -l|ɚ **-ors** -əz Ⓤⓢ -ɚz **-oring** -ᵊr.ɪŋ **-ored** -əd Ⓤⓢ -ɚd
tailor-made ˌteɪ.lə'meɪd Ⓤⓢ -lɚ'- **-s** -z *stress shift:* ˌtailor-made 'suit
tailpiec|e 'teɪl.piːs **-es** -ɪz
tailpipe 'teɪl.paɪp **-s** -s
tail-rhyme 'teɪl.raɪm
tailspin 'teɪl.spɪn **-s** -z
tailwind 'teɪl.wɪnd **-s** -z
Taine teɪn
taint teɪnt **-s** -s **-ing** -ɪŋ Ⓤⓢ 'teɪn.t̬ɪŋ **-ed** -ɪd Ⓤⓢ 'teɪn.t̬ɪd **-less** -ləs, -lɪs
taipan 'taɪ.pæn Ⓤⓢ '--, -'- **-s** -z
Taipei ˌtaɪ'peɪ
Taiping ˌtaɪ'pɪŋ
Tait teɪt

Taiwan ˌtaɪˈwɑːn, -ˈwæn ⓊⓈ -ˈwɑːn
Taiwanese ˌtaɪ.wəˈniːz, -wɑːˈ- ⓊⓈ -wəˈniːz, -ˈniːs
Ta'izz teɪˈiːz, tæ- ⓊⓈ tæˈɪz
Tajikistan tɑːˈdʒiː.kɪˌstɑːn, -ˌstæn
Taj Mahal ˌtɑːdʒ.məˈhɑːl
taka ˈtɑː.kɑː
tak|e teɪk **-es** -s **-ing** -ɪŋ **took** tʊk **taken** ˈteɪ.kᵊn **taker/s** ˈteɪ.kəʳ/z ⓊⓈ -kɚ/z ˌ**take a ˈwalk** ; ˌ**take a ˈhike**
takeaway ˈteɪk.ə.weɪ **-s** -z
take-home pay ˈteɪk.həʊmˌpeɪ, ˌ--ˈ- ⓊⓈ ˈteɪk.hoʊmˌpeɪ
take-it-or-leave-it ˌteɪk.ɪt.ɔːˈliːv.ɪt, -əˈ- ⓊⓈ -ɔːrˈ-, -ɚˈ-
take-off ˈteɪk.ɒf ⓊⓈ -ɑːf **-s** -s
takeout ˈteɪk.aʊt **-s** -s
takeover ˈteɪkˌəʊ.vəʳ ⓊⓈ -ˌoʊ.vɚ **-s** -z ˈ**takeover** ˌ**bid**
take-up ˈteɪk.ʌp **-s** -s
taking ˈteɪ.kɪŋ **-s** -z **-ly** -li **-ness** -nəs, -nɪs
tala ˈtɑː.lɑː
Talbot ˈtɔːl.bət, ˈtɒl- ⓊⓈ ˈtɔːl-, ˈtæl-
Note: Both pronunciations are current for **Port Talbot** in Wales.
talc tælk **-s** -s
Talcahuano ˌtæl.kəˈwɑː.nəʊ ⓊⓈ ˌtɑːl.kɑːˈwɑː.noʊ, ˌtæl.kəˈ-
talcum powder ˈtæl.kəmˌpaʊ.dəʳ ⓊⓈ -dɚ **-s** -z
tale teɪl **-s** -z
talebearer ˈteɪlˌbeə.rəʳ ⓊⓈ -ˌber.ɚ **-s** -z
tal|ent ˈtæl|.ənt **-ents** -ənts **-ented** -ən.tɪd ⓊⓈ -ən.t̬ɪd **-entless** -ənt.ləs, -lɪs ˈ**talent** ˌ**contest** ; ˈ**talent** ˌ**scout**
talent|-spot ˈtæl.ənt|.spɒt ⓊⓈ -spɑːt **-spots** -spɒts ⓊⓈ -spɑːts **-spotting** -ˌspɒt.ɪŋ ⓊⓈ -ˌspɑː.t̬ɪŋ **-spotted** -ˌspɒt.ɪd ⓊⓈ -ˌspɑː.t̬ɪd **-spotter/s** -ˌspɒt.əʳ/z ⓊⓈ -ˌspɑː.t̬ɚ/z
tales *law:* ˈteɪ.liːz ⓊⓈ ˈteɪ.liːz; teɪlz
tales|man ˈteɪ.liːz|.mən, ˈteɪlz-, -mæn ⓊⓈ ˈteɪlz-, ˈteɪl.iːz- **-men** -mən, -men
taletell|er ˈteɪlˌtel|.əʳ ⓊⓈ -ɚ **-er/s** -əʳ/z ⓊⓈ -ɚ/z **-ing** -ɪŋ
Talfourd ˈtæl.fəd ⓊⓈ -fɚd
Taliesin ˌtæl.iˈes.ɪn, ˌ-ˈjes- ⓊⓈ -iˈes.ɪn
talisman ˈtæl.ɪz.mən, -ɪs- **-s** -z
talismanic ˌtæl.ɪzˈmæn.ɪk, -ɪsˈ- **-ally** -ᵊl.i, -li
talk tɔːk ⓊⓈ tɔːk, tɑːk **-s** -s **-ing** -ɪŋ **-ed** -t **-er/s** -əʳ/z ⓊⓈ -ɚ/z ˌ**talking** ˈ**head** ; ˈ**talking** ˌ**point** ; ˈ**talk** ˌ**show** ; **(to)** ˌ**talk** ˈ**shop**
talkathon ˈtɔː.kə.θɒn ⓊⓈ -θɑːn, ˈtɑː- **-s** -z
talkative ˈtɔː.kə.tɪv ⓊⓈ -t̬ɪv, ˈtɑː- **-ly** -li **-ness** -nəs, -nɪs
talkback ˈtɔːk.bæk ⓊⓈ ˈtɔːk-, ˈtɑːk- **-s** -s
talkie ˈtɔː.ki ⓊⓈ ˈtɔː-, ˈtɑː- **-s** -z
talking-to ˈtɔː.kɪŋ.tuː ⓊⓈ ˈtɔː-, ˈtɑː- **-s** -z
tall tɔːl **-er** -əʳ ⓊⓈ -ɚ **-est** -ɪst, -əst **-ness** -nəs, -nɪs ˌ**tall** ˈ**story**
tallage ˈtæl.ɪdʒ
Tallahassee ˌtæl.əˈhæs.i
tallboy ˈtɔːl.bɔɪ **-s** -z
Talleyrand ˈtæl.i.rænd
Tallin(n) ˈtæl.ɪn, -ˈ-, -ˈiːn ⓊⓈ ˈtɑː.lɪn, ˈtæl.ɪn
Tallis ˈtæl.ɪs
tallish ˈtɔː.lɪʃ
tallow ˈtæl.əʊ ⓊⓈ -oʊ **-y** -i
Tallulah təˈluː.lə
tall|y ˈtæl|.i **-ies** -iz **-ying** -i.ɪŋ **-ied** -id
tally-ho ˌtæl.iˈhəʊ ⓊⓈ -ˈhoʊ **-s** -z
tally|man ˈtæl.i|.mən **-men** -mən, -men
Talman ˈtɔːl.mən
Talmud ˈtæl.mʊd, -məd, -mʌd ⓊⓈ ˈtɑːl.mʊd, ˈtæl-, -məd
talmudic (T) tælˈmʊd.ɪk, -ˈmʌd-, -ˈmjuː.dɪk ⓊⓈ tɑːlˈmʊd.ɪk, tæl- **-al** -ᵊl
talmud|ism (T) ˈtæl.mʊd|.ɪ.zᵊm, -məd-, -mʌd- **-ist/s** -ɪst/s
talon ˈtæl.ən **-s** -z
Tal-y-llyn ˌtæl.iˈ*h*lɪn, -əˈ-, -ˈθlɪn
tamable ˈteɪ.mə.bl̩
tamale *Mexican dish:* təˈmɑː.li, -leɪ
Tamale *in Ghana:* təˈmɑː.leɪ
Tamaqua təˈmɑː.kwə
Tamar *river in W. of England:* ˈteɪ.məʳ, -mɑːʳ ⓊⓈ -mɚ, -mɑːr
Tamar *biblical name:* ˈteɪ.mɑːʳ, -məʳ ⓊⓈ -mɑːr, -mɚ
Tamara təˈmɑː.rə, -ˈmær.ə; ˈtæm.ᵊr.ə ⓊⓈ təˈmɑːr.ə, -ˈmær-, -ˈmer-
tamarillo ˌtæm.ᵊrˈɪl.əʊ ⓊⓈ -əˈrɪl.oʊ **-s** -z
tamarin ˈtæm.ᵊr.ɪn ⓊⓈ -ɚ.ɪn, -ə.ræn **-s** -z
tamarind ˈtæm.ᵊr.ɪnd **-s** -z
tamarisk ˈtæm.ᵊr.ɪsk **-s** -s
tambala tæmˈbɑː.lə ⓊⓈ tɑːmˈbɑː.lɑː **-s** -z
tamber ˈtæm.bəʳ ⓊⓈ -bɚ **-s** -z
Tambo ˈtæm.bəʊ ⓊⓈ -boʊ
tambour ˈtæm.bʊəʳ, -bɔːʳ, -bəʳ ⓊⓈ -bʊr **-s** -z
tamboura tæmˈbʊə.rə, -ˈbɔː- ⓊⓈ tɑːmˈbʊr.ə **-s** -z
tambourine ˌtæm.bᵊrˈiːn ⓊⓈ -bəˈriːn **-s** -z
Tamburlaine ˈtæm.bə.leɪn ⓊⓈ -bɚ-
tam|e teɪm **-er/s** -əʳ/z ⓊⓈ -ɚ/z **-est** -ɪst, -əst **-ely** -li **-eness** -nəs, -nɪs **-es** -z **-ing** -ɪŋ **-ed** -d
tameable ˈteɪ.mə.bl̩
Tamerlane ˈtæm.ə.leɪn ⓊⓈ ˈ-ɚ-
Tameside ˈteɪm.saɪd
Tamil ˈtæm.ɪl, -ᵊl ⓊⓈ -ᵊl, ˈtɑː.mᵊl, ˈtʊm.ᵊl **-s** -z
Tamil Nadu ˌtæm.ɪlˈnɑː.duː, -ᵊl- ⓊⓈ -ᵊlˈnɑː.duː, ˌtɑː.mᵊlˈ-, ˌtʊm.ᵊlˈ-, -nɑːˈduː
Tammany ˈtæm.ᵊn.i
Tammerfors ˈtæm.ə.fɔːz ⓊⓈ -ɚ.fɔːrz
Tammuz ˈtæm.uːz, -ʊz ⓊⓈ ˈtɑː.mʊz
Tammy ˈtæm.i
Tamora ˈtæm.ᵊr.ə
tam-o'-shanter ˌtæm.əˈʃæn.təʳ ⓊⓈ ˈtæm.əˌʃæn.t̬ɚ **-s** -z
tamp tæmp **-s** -s **-ing** -ɪŋ **-ed** -t **-er/s** -əʳ/z ⓊⓈ -ɚ/z
Tampa ˈtæm.pə
Tampax® ˈtæm.pæks
tamp|er ˈtæm.p|əʳ ⓊⓈ -p|ɚ **-ers** -əz ⓊⓈ -ɚz **-ering** -ᵊr.ɪŋ **-ered** -əd ⓊⓈ -ɚd **-erer/s** -ə.rəʳ/z ⓊⓈ -ɚ.ɚ/z
Tampere ˈtæm.pᵊr.eɪ ⓊⓈ ˈtɑːm.pə.reɪ
tamper-evident ˌtæm.pᵊrˈev.ɪ.dᵊnt ⓊⓈ -pɚˈ-
tamper-proof ˈtæm.pə.pruːf ⓊⓈ -pɚ-
Tampico tæmˈpiː.kəʊ ⓊⓈ -koʊ, tɑːm-
tampon ˈtæm.pɒn ⓊⓈ -pɑːn **-s** -z
Tamsin ˈtæm.zɪn, -sɪn
Tamworth ˈtæm.wəθ, -wɜːθ ⓊⓈ -wɚθ, -wɜːrθ
tan tæn **-s** -z **-ning** -ɪŋ **-ned** -d **-ner/s** -əʳ/z ⓊⓈ -ɚ/z
Tancred ˈtæŋ.kred, -krɪd ⓊⓈ -krɪd
tandem ˈtæn.dəm, -dem ⓊⓈ -dəm **-s** -z
tandoori tænˈdʊə.ri, -ˈdɔː- ⓊⓈ tɑːnˈdʊr.i
Tandy ˈtæn.di
Tanfield ˈtæn.fiːld
tang tæŋ **-s** -z **-y** -i
Tang tæŋ ⓊⓈ tɑːŋ
Tanga ˈtæŋ.gə
Tanganyika ˌtæŋ.gəˈnjiː.kə, -gænˈjiː- ⓊⓈ -gəˈnjiː-
tangenc|y ˈtæn.dʒən*t*.s|i **-ies** -iz
tangent ˈtæn.dʒᵊnt **-s** -s
tangential tænˈdʒen.*t*ʃᵊl ⓊⓈ -ˈdʒen*t*.ʃᵊl **-ly** -i **-ness** -nəs, -nɪs
tangerine ˌtæn.dʒᵊrˈiːn, ˈ--- ⓊⓈ ˌtæn.dʒəˈriːn, ˈ--- **-s** -z
tangibility ˌtæn.dʒəˈbɪl.ə.ti, -dʒɪˈ-, -ɪ.ti ⓊⓈ -dʒəˈbɪl.ə.t̬i
tangib|le ˈtæn.dʒə.bl̩|, -dʒɪ- ⓊⓈ -dʒə- **-ly** -li **-leness** -l̩.nəs, -nɪs
Tangier tænˈdʒɪəʳ, ˈ-- ⓊⓈ tænˈdʒɪr **-s** -z
tangl|e ˈtæŋ.gl̩ **-es** -z **-ing** -ɪŋ, ˈtæŋ.glɪŋ **-ed** -d
Tanglewood ˈtæŋ.gl̩.wʊd
tangly ˈtæŋ.gli, ˈ-gl̩.i
tango ˈtæŋ.gəʊ ⓊⓈ -goʊ **-s** -z **-ing** -ɪŋ **-ed** -d
tang|y ˈtæŋ|.i **-ier** -i.əʳ ⓊⓈ -i.ɚ **-iest** -i.ɪst, -i.əst **-iness** -ɪ.nəs, -ɪ.nɪs
Tangye ˈtæŋ.gi
tanh θæn, tæn*t*ʃ
tank tæŋk **-s** -s **-age** -ɪdʒ **-er/s** -əʳ/z ⓊⓈ -ɚ/z ˈ**tank** ˌ**top** ; ˌ**tanked** ˈ**up**

tankard ˈtæŋ.kəd (US) -kɚd **-s** -z

tankful ˈtæŋk.fʊl **-s** -z

tanner (T) ˈtæn.əʳ (US) -ɚ **-s** -z

tanner|y ˈtæn.ᵊr|.i **-ies** -iz

Tannhäuser ˈtænˌhɔɪ.zəʳ (US) ˈtɑːnˌhɔɪ.zɚ, ˈtæn-

tann|ic ˈtæn|.ɪk **-in** -ɪn ˌ**tannic ˈacid**

Tannoy® ˈtæn.ɔɪ

Tanqueray ˈtæŋ.kᵊr.i, -eɪ (US) -kə.reɪ, -kɚ.i

tansy (T) ˈtæn.zi

tantalization, -isa- ˌtæn.tᵊl.aɪˈzeɪ.ʃᵊn, -ɪˈ- (US) -t̬ᵊl.ɪˈ- **-s** -z

tantaliz|e, -is|e ˈtæn.tᵊl.aɪz (US) -t̬ə.laɪz **-es** -ɪz **-ing/ly** -ɪŋ/li **-ed** -d **-er/s** -əʳ/z (US) -ɚ/z

tantalum ˈtæn.tᵊl.əm (US) -t̬ᵊl- **-s** -z

tantalus (T) ˈtæn.tᵊl.əs (US) -t̬ᵊl- **-es** -ɪz

tantamount ˈtæn.tə.maʊnt (US) -t̬ə-

tantiv|y tænˈtɪv|.i **-ies** -iz

tanto ˈtæn.təʊ (US) -toʊ

tantr|a (T) ˈtæn.tr|ə, ˈtʌn- (US) ˈtʌn-, ˈtɑːn-, ˈtæn- **-ic** -ɪk

tantrum ˈtæn.trəm **-s** -z

Tanya ˈtæn.jə, ˈtɑː.njə (US) ˈtɑː.njə, ˈtæn.jə

Tanzani|a ˌtæn.zəˈniː|.ə; tænˈzeɪ.ni- (US) ˌtæn.zəˈniː- **-an/s** -ən/z

Tao taʊ (US) daʊ, taʊ

Taoiseach ˈtiː.ʃək, -ʃəx (US) -ʃək

Tao|ism ˈtaʊ|.ɪ.zᵊm, ˈteɪ.əʊ- (US) ˈdaʊ|.ɪ-, ˈtaʊ- **-ist/s** -ɪst/s

tap tæp **-s** -s **-ping** -ɪŋ **-ped** -t **-per/s** -əʳ/z (US) -ɚ/z

tapas ˈtæp.æs, -əs ˈ**tapas** ˌ**bar**

tap-danc|e ˈtæpˌdɑːnts (US) -ˌdænts **-es** -ɪz **-ing** -ɪŋ **-ed** -t **-er/s** -əʳ/z (US) -ɚ/z

tap|e (T) teɪp **-es** -s **-ing** -ɪŋ **-ed** -t ˈ**tape** ˌ**deck**; ˈ**tape** ˌ**measure**; ˈ**tape re**ˌ**corder**

tap|er ˈteɪ.p|əʳ (US) -p|ɚ **-ers** -əz (US) -ɚz **-ering** -ᵊr.ɪŋ **-ered** -əd (US) -ɚd

tapestr|y ˈtæp.ɪ.str|i, ˈ-ə- (US) ˈ-ə- **-ies** -iz

tapeworm ˈteɪp.wɜːm (US) -wɝːm **-s** -z

tapioca ˌtæp.iˈəʊ.kə (US) -ˈoʊ-

tapir ˈteɪ.pəʳ, -pɪəʳ (US) -pɚ **-s** -z

tapis ˈtæp.iː, -pi (US) -i, -ɪs; tæpˈiː

Tapling ˈtæp.lɪŋ

Tappertit ˈtæp.ə.tɪt (US) ˈ-ɚ-

tappet ˈtæp.ɪt **-s** -s

taproom ˈtæp.rʊm, -ruːm (US) -ruːm, -rʊm **-s** -z

tap-root ˈtæp.ruːt **-s** -s

tapster ˈtæp.stəʳ (US) -stɚ **-s** -z

tar tɑːʳ (US) tɑːr **-s** -z **-ring** -ɪŋ **-red** -d

Tara *literary location, place in Ireland:* ˈtɑː.rə (US) ˈter.ə, ˈtær- *female name:* ˈtɑː.rə (US) ˈtɑːr.ə

taradiddle ˈtær.əˌdɪd.l̩ (US) ˈter-, ˈtær- **-s** -z

taramasalata, taramosalata ˌtær.ə.mə.səˈlɑː.tə (US) ˌtɑːr.ɑː.mɑː.sɑːˈlɑː.tɑː

tarantella ˌtær.ᵊnˈtel.ə (US) ˌter-, ˌtær- **-s** -z

Tarantino ˌtær.ᵊnˈtiː.nəʊ (US) ˌter.ᵊnˈtiː.noʊ, ˌtær-

Taranto təˈræn.təʊ; (US) -toʊ; ˈtɑːr.ɑːn-

tarantula təˈræn.tjə.lə, -tjʊ-, -tʃə- (US) -tʃə-, -tʃʊ-, -tjʊ-, -t̬ə- **-s** -z

Tarawa təˈrɑː.wə (US) təˈrɑː-; ˈtɑːr.ə-

taraxacum təˈræk.sə.kəm

Tarbuck ˈtɑː.bʌk (US) ˈtɑːr-

Tardis ˈtɑː.dɪs (US) ˈtɑːr- **-es** -ɪz

tard|y ˈtɑː.d|i (US) ˈtɑːr- **-ier** -i.əʳ (US) -i.ɚ **-iest** -i.ɪst, -i.əst **-ily** -ɪ.li, -ᵊl.i **-iness** -ɪ.nəs, -ɪ.nɪs

tare teəʳ (US) ter **-s** -z

tar|get ˈtɑː|.gɪt (US) ˈtɑːr- **-gets** -gɪts **-geting** -gɪ.tɪŋ (US) -gɪ.t̬ɪŋ **-geted** -gɪ.tɪd (US) -gɪ.t̬ɪd ˈ**target** ˌ**practice**

tariff ˈtær.ɪf (US) ˈter-, ˈtær- **-s** -s

Tariq ˈtær.ɪk, ˈtɑː.rɪk (US) ˈtɑːr.ɪk

Tarka ˈtɑː.kə (US) ˈtɑːr-

Tarkington ˈtɑː.kɪŋ.tən (US) ˈtɑːr-

Tarleton ˈtɑːl.tən, ˈtɑː.lə- (US) ˈtɑːrl.tən, ˈtɑːr.lə-

tarmac (T®) ˈtɑː.mæk (US) ˈtɑːr- **-s** -s **-king** -ɪŋ **-ked** -t

tarmacadam ˌtɑː.məˈkæd.əm (US) ˌtɑːr-

tarn tɑːn (US) tɑːrn **-s** -z

tarnation tɑːˈneɪ.ʃᵊn (US) tɑːr-

tarnish ˈtɑː.nɪʃ (US) ˈtɑːr- **-es** -ɪz **-ing** -ɪŋ **-ed** -t

tarot ˈtær.əʊ (US) -oʊ, -ət, ˈter-; təˈroʊ **-s** -z ˈ**tarot** ˌ**card** (US) **taˈrot** ˌ**card**

tarpaulin tɑːˈpɔː.lɪn (US) tɑːrˈpɑː-, -ˈpɔː-; ˈtɑːr.pə- **-s** -z

Tarpeian tɑːˈpiː.ən (US) tɑːr-

tarpon ˈtɑː.pɒn (US) ˈtɑːr.pən, -pɑːn **-s** -z

Tarquin ˈtɑː.kwɪn (US) ˈtɑːr- **-s** -z

Tarquini|us tɑːˈkwɪn.i|.əs (US) tɑːr- **-i** -aɪ, -iː

tarradiddle ˈtær.əˌdɪd.l̩ (US) ˈter-, ˈtær- **-s** -z

tarragon ˈtær.ə.gən (US) ˈter.ə.gɑːn, ˈtær-

Tarragona ˌtær.əˈgəʊ.nə (US) ˌter.əˈgoʊ-, ˌtær-, ˌtɑːr.ɑːˈ-

tarrah təˈrɑː; trɑː

Tarrant ˈtær.ᵊnt (US) ˈter-, ˈtær-

Tarring ˈtær.ɪŋ (US) ˈter-, ˈtær-

tarrock ˈtær.ək (US) ˈter-, ˈtær- **-s** -s

tarry *(adj.) tarred, like tar:* ˈtɑː.ri (US) ˈtɑːr.i

tarr|y *(v.) wait:* ˈtær|.i (US) ˈter-, ˈtær- **-ies** -iz **-ying** -i.ɪŋ **-ied** -id **-ier/s** -i.əʳ/z (US) -i.ɚ/z

Tarshish ˈtɑː.ʃɪʃ (US) ˈtɑːr-

tars|us (T) ˈtɑː.s|əs (US) ˈtɑːr- **-i** -aɪ

tart tɑːt (US) tɑːrt **-s** -s **-ly** -li **-ness** -nəs, -nɪs

tartan ˈtɑː.tᵊn (US) ˈtɑːr- **-s** -z

tartar, tartare (T) ˈtɑː.təʳ (US) ˈtɑːr.t̬ɚ **-s** -z ˌ**tartar** ˈ**sauce** (US) ˈ**tartar** ˌ**sauce**

tartaric tɑːˈtær.ɪk (US) tɑːr-, -ˈter-, -ˈtɑːr- **tar**ˌ**taric** ˈ**acid**

Tartar|us ˈtɑː.tᵊr|.əs (US) ˈtɑːr.t̬ɚ- **-y** -i

tartlet ˈtɑːt.lət, -lɪt (US) ˈtɑːrt.lət, -lɪt **-s** -s

tartrazine ˈtɑː.trə.ziːn, -zɪn (US) ˈtɑːr-

Tartu ˈtɑː.tu (US) ˈtɑːr-

Tartuffe tɑːˈtʊf, -ˈtuːf (US) tɑːr-

tart|y ˈtɑː.t|i (US) ˈtɑːr.t̬|i **-ier** -i.əʳ (US) -i.ɚ **-iest** -i.ɪst, -i.əst **-ily** -ɪ.li, -ᵊl.i **-iness** -ɪ.nəs, -ɪ.nɪs

Tarzan ˈtɑː.zᵊn, -zæn (US) ˈtɑːr-

Tasha ˈtæʃ.ə

Tashkent tæʃˈkent (US) tæʃ-, tɑːʃ-

Tashtego tæʃˈtiː.gəʊ (US) -goʊ

task tɑːsk (US) tæsk **-s** -s **-ing** -ɪŋ **-ed** -t ˈ**task** ˌ**force**

Tasker ˈtæs.kəʳ (US) -kɚ

taskmaster ˈtɑːskˌmɑː.stəʳ (US) ˈtæskˌmæs.tɚ **-s** -z

taskmistress ˈtɑːskˌmɪs.trəs, -trɪs (US) ˈtæskˌmɪs.trɪs **-es** -ɪz

Tasman ˈtæz.mən

Tasmani|a tæzˈmeɪ.ni|.ə, -nj|ə **-an/s** -ən/z

Tass, TASS tæs

tassel ˈtæs.ᵊl **-s** -z **-led** -d

tassie (T) ˈtæs.i

Tasso ˈtæs.əʊ (US) -oʊ

tast|e teɪst **-es** -s **-ing** -ɪŋ **-ed** -ɪd **-er/s** -əʳ/z (US) -ɚ/z ˈ**taste** ˌ**bud**; ˌ**give someone a** ˌ**taste of their** ˌ**own** ˈ**medicine**

tasteful ˈteɪs*t*.fᵊl, -fʊl **-ly** -i **-ness** -nəs, -nɪs

tasteless ˈteɪs*t*.ləs, -lɪs **-ly** -li **-ness** -nəs, -nɪs

tast|y ˈteɪ.st|i **-ier** -i.əʳ (US) -i.ɚ **-iest** -i.ɪst, -i.əst **-ily** -ɪ.li, -ᵊl.i **-iness** -ɪ.nəs, -ɪ.nɪs

tat tæt **-s** -s **-ting** -ɪŋ (US) ˈtæt̬.ɪŋ **-ted** -ɪd (US) ˈtæt̬.ɪd

ta-ta təˈtɑː, tætˈɑː (US) tɑːˈtɑː

tatami təˈtɑː.mi, tɑː-, tætˈɑː- (US) təˈtɑː- **-s** -z

Tatar ˈtɑː.təʳ (US) -t̬ɚ **-s** -z

Tate teɪt ˌ**Tate** ˈ**Gallery**

Tatham ˈteɪ.θᵊm, -ðəm; ˈtæt.əm

Tati ˈtæt.i, -ˈ- (US) tɑːˈtiː

Tatiana ˌtæt.iˈɑː.nə (US) ˌ-ˈjɑː.nə

tatler (T®) ˈtæt.ləʳ (US) -lɚ **-s** -z

Tatra ˈtɑː.trə, ˈtæt.rə (US) ˈtɑː.trə

tatter ˈtæt.əʳ (US) ˈtæt̬.ɚ **-s** -z **-ed** -d

tatterdemalion ˌtæt.ə.dəˈmeɪ.li.ən, -dɪˈ-, -ˈmæl.i- (US) ˌtæt̬.ɚ-

tattersall (T) 'tæt.ə.sɔːl, -sᵊl (US) 'tæţ.ɚ.sɔːl, -sɑːl **-s** -z
tattl|e 'tæt.l̩ (US) 'tæţ- **-es** -z **-ing** -ɪŋ, 'tæt.lɪŋ **-ed** -d **-er/s** -əʳ/z, 'tæt.ləʳ/z (US) '-l̩.ɚ/z, '-lɚ/z
tattletale 'tæt.l̩.teɪl (US) 'tæţ- **-s** -z
tattoo tæt'uː, tə'tuː (US) tæt'uː **-s** -z **-ing** -ɪŋ **-ed** -d **-er/s** -əʳ/z (US) -ɚ/z
tattooist tæt'uː.ɪst, tə'tuː- (US) tæt'uː- **-s** -s
tatt|y 'tæt|.i (US) 'tæţ- **-ier** -i.əʳ (US) -i.ɚ **-iest** -i.ɪst, -i.əst **-ily** -ɪ.li, -ᵊl.i **-iness** -ɪ.nəs, -ɪ.nɪs
Tatum 'teɪ.təm (US) -ţəm
tau taʊ, tɔː (US) taʊ, tɔː, tɑː
Tauchnitz 'taʊk.nɪts *as if German:* 'taʊx-
taught (*from* **teach**) tɔːt (US) tɑːt, tɔːt
taun|t tɔːn|t (US) tɑːn|t, tɔːn|t **-ts** -ts **-ting/ly** -tɪŋ/li (US) -ţɪŋ/li **-ted** -tɪd (US) -ţɪd **-ter/s** -təʳ/z (US) -ţɚ/z
Taunton 'tɔːn.tən, *locally:* 'tɑːn- (US) 'tɑːn-, 'tɔːn-
taupe təʊp (US) toʊp
Taupo 'taʊ.pəʊ (US) 'toʊ.poʊ
Taurean 'tɔː.ri.ən; tɔː'riː- (US) 'tɔːr.i- **-s** -z
Taurus 'tɔː.rəs (US) 'tɔːr.əs
taut tɔːt (US) tɑːt, tɔːt **-ly** -li **-ness** -nəs, -nɪs
tautologic ˌtɔː.tə'lɒdʒ.ɪk (US) ˌtɑː.ţə'lɑː.dʒɪ-, ˌtɔː- **-al** -ᵊl **-ally** -ᵊl.i, -li
tautologic|al ˌtɔː.tə'lɒdʒ.ɪk|.ᵊl (US) ˌtɑː.ţə'lɑː.dʒɪk-, ˌtɔː- **-ally** -ᵊl.i, -li
tautologism tɔː'tɒl.ə.dʒɪ.zᵊm (US) tɑː'tɑː.lə-, tɔː'- **-s** -z
tautologiz|e, -is|e tɔː'tɒl.ə.dʒaɪz (US) tɑː'tɑː.lə-, tɔː- **-es** -ɪz **-ing** -ɪŋ **-ed** -d
tautologous tɔː'tɒl.ə.gəs (US) tɑː'tɑː.lə-, tɔː-
tautolog|y tɔː'tɒl.ə.dʒ|i (US) tɑː'tɑː.lə-, tɔː- **-ies** -iz
Taverham 'teɪ.vᵊr.əm
tavern 'tæv.ᵊn (US) -ɚn **-s** -z **-er/s** -əʳ/z (US) -ɚ/z
taverna tə'vɜː.nə, ˌtæv'ɜː- (US) tɑː'vɜːr-, tə- **-s** -z
Tavistock 'tæv.ɪ.stɒk, '-ə- (US) -ə.stɑːk
taw tɔː (US) tɑː, tɔː **-s** -z **-ing** -ɪŋ **-ed** -d
tawdr|y 'tɔː.dr|i (US) 'tɑː-, 'tɔː- **-ier** -i.əʳ (US) -i.ɚ **-iest** -i.ɪst, -i.əst **-ily** -ᵊl.i, -ɪ.li **-iness** -ɪ.nəs, -ɪ.nɪs
Tawe 'taʊ.i, -eɪ
Tawell tɔːl; 'tɔː.əl (US) tɑːl, tɔːl, 'tɑː.əl, 'tɔː-
tawn|y 'tɔː.n|i (US) 'tɑː-, 'tɔː- **-ier** -i.əʳ (US) -i.ɚ **-iest** -i.ɪst, -i.əst **-iness** -ɪ.nəs, -ɪ.nɪs **ˌtawny 'owl, 'tawny ˌowl**
tax tæks **-es** -ɪz **-ing/ly** -ɪŋ/li **-ed** -t **-er/s** -əʳ/z (US) -ɚ/z **'tax eˌvasion ; 'tax ˌexile ; 'tax ˌhaven ; 'tax inˌspector ; 'tax ˌoffice ; 'tax reˌturn ; 'tax ˌyear**
taxability ˌtæk.sə'bɪl.ə.ti, -ɪ.ti (US) -ə.ţi
taxable 'tæk.sə.bl̩ **-ness** -nəs, -nɪs
taxation tæk'seɪ.ʃᵊn **-s** -z
tax-deductible ˌtæks.dɪ'dʌk.tə.bl̩, -də'- *stress shift:* ˌtax-deductible 'earnings
tax-deferred ˌtæks.dɪ'fɜːd (US) -'fɜːrd *stress shift:* ˌtax-deferred 'earnings
taxeme 'tæk.siːm
taxemic tæk'siː.mɪk
tax-exempt ˌtæks.ɪg'zempt, -eg'-; -ɪk'sempt, -ek'- (US) -ɪg'zempt, -eg'- *stress shift:* ˌtax-exempt 'earnings
tax-free ˌtæks'friː *stress shift:* ˌtax-free 'bonus
tax|i (*v.*) 'tæk.s|i **-i(e)s** -iz **-ying** -i.ɪŋ **-iing** -i.ɪŋ **-ied** -id **'taxi ˌrank ; 'taxi ˌstand**
taxicab 'tæk.si.kæb **-s** -z
taxidermic ˌtæk.sɪ'dɜː.mɪk (US) -'dɜːr-
taxidermist 'tæk.sɪ.dɜː.mɪst, ˌtæk.sɪ'dɜː-; tæk'sɪd.ə- (US) 'tæk.sɪ.dɜːr- **-s** -s
taxidermy 'tæk.sɪ.dɜː.mi (US) -dɜːr-
taximeter 'tæk.siˌmiː.təʳ (US) -ţɚ **-s** -z
tax|is (T) 'tæk.s|ɪs **-es** -iːz
taxiway 'tæk.si.weɪ **-s** -z
taxman 'tæks.mæn **-men** -men
taxonomic ˌtæk.sə'nɒm.ɪk (US) -'nɑː.mɪk **-ally** -ᵊl.i, -li
taxonom|y tæk'sɒn.ə.m|i (US) -'sɑː.nə- **-ist/s** -ɪst/s
taxpayer 'tæksˌpeɪ.əʳ (US) -ɚ **-s** -z
tay *syllable used in Tonic Sol-fa in counting time:* teɪ, te
Note: In the sequence 'tay fe' this may be pronounced /te/.
Tay teɪ
tayberr|y 'teɪ.bᵊr|.i, '-br|i, -ˌber|.i (US) -ˌber|.i **-ies** -iz
Taylor 'teɪ.ləʳ (US) -lɚ
Taylorian teɪ'lɔː.ri.ən (US) -'lɔːr.i-
Taymouth 'teɪ.maʊθ, -məθ
Tay-Sachs ˌteɪ'sæks (US) ˌ-'-, '-- ˌTay-'Sachs diˌsease
Tayside 'teɪ.saɪd
TB ˌtiː'biː
T-bar 'tiː.bɑːʳ (US) -bɑːr **-s** -z
Tbilisi tə.bɪ'liː.si; tə'bɪl.ɪ- (US) təˌbɪl.i'siː; ˌtʌb.ɪ'liː.si; tə'bɪl.i-
T-bone 'tiː.bəʊn (US) -boʊn **-s** -z **ˌT-bone 'steak**
tbs., tbsp. (*abbrev. for* **tablespoon, tablespoonful**) 'teɪ.bl̩.spuːn, 'teɪ.bl̩ˌspuːn.fʊl
Tchad tʃæd
Tchaikovsky tʃaɪ'kɒf.ski, -'kɒv- (US) -'kɔːf-, -'kɑːv-
Tcherkasy tʃɜː'kæs.i (US) tʃɜːr-
TCP® ˌtiː.siː'piː
te *Tonic Sol-fa name for leading note:* tiː **-s** -z
tea tiː **-s** -z **'tea ˌbag ; 'tea ˌbreak ; 'tea ˌchest ; 'tea ˌcosy ; 'tea ˌdance ; 'tea ˌlady ; 'tea ˌleaf ; 'tea ˌparty ; 'tea ˌset ; 'tea ˌshop ; 'tea ˌtowel ; 'tea ˌtray ; 'tea ˌtrolley ; 'tea ˌwagon ; not for ˌall the ˌtea in 'China**
teabread 'tiː.bred
tea-cadd|y 'tiːˌkæd|.i **-ies** -iz
teacake 'tiː.keɪk **-s** -s
teach tiːtʃ **-es** -ɪz **-ing/s** -ɪŋ/z **taught** tɔːt (US) tɑːt, tɔːt **'teaching ˌpractice**
teachability ˌtiː.tʃə'bɪl.ə.ti, -ɪ.ti (US) -ə.ţi
teachable 'tiː.tʃə.bl̩ **-ness** -nəs, -nɪs
teacher 'tiː.tʃəʳ (US) -tʃɚ **-s** -z **ˌteacher(s') 'training ˌcollege**
teach-in 'tiːtʃ.ɪn **-s** -z
tea|cloth 'tiː|.klɒθ (US) -klɑːθ **-cloths** -klɒθs, -klɒðz (US) -klɑːθs, -klɑːðz
teacup 'tiː.kʌp **-s** -s **-ful/s** -fʊl/z
Teague tiːg **-s** -z
teahou|se 'tiː.haʊ|s **-ses** -zɪz
teak tiːk
teal tiːl **-s** -z
team tiːm **-s** -z **-ing** -ɪŋ **-ed** -d **ˌteam 'spirit, 'team ˌspirit**
teammate 'tiːm.meɪt **-s** -s
teamster (T) 'tiːmp.stəʳ (US) -stɚ **-s** -z **ˌTeamsters' 'Union** (US) **'Teamsters' ˌUnion**
teamwork 'tiːm.wɜːk (US) -wɜːrk
teapot 'tiː.pɒt (US) -pɑːt **-s** -s
teapoy 'tiː.pɔɪ **-s** -z
tear (*n.*) *fluid from the eye:* tɪəʳ (US) tɪr **-s** -z **'tear ˌgas**
tear (*n. v.*) *pull apart, rush, a rent etc.:* teəʳ (US) ter **-s** -z **-ing** -ɪŋ **tore** tɔːʳ (US) tɔːr **torn** tɔːn (US) tɔːrn
tearaway 'teə.rə.weɪ (US) 'ter.ə- **-s** -z
teardrop 'tɪə.drɒp (US) 'tɪr.drɑːp **-s** -s
tearful 'tɪə.fᵊl, -fʊl (US) 'tɪr- **-ly** -i **-ness** -nəs, -nɪs
teargas 'tɪə.gæs (US) 'tɪr- **-es** -ɪz **-sing** -ɪŋ **-sed** -t
tearjerker 'tɪəˌdʒɜː.kəʳ (US) 'tɪrˌdʒɜːr.kɚ **-s** -z
tearless 'tɪə.ləs, -lɪs (US) 'tɪr- **-ly** -li **-ness** -nəs, -nɪs
tearoom 'tiː.rʊm, -ruːm (US) -ruːm, -rʊm **-s** -z
tearstained 'tɪə.steɪnd (US) 'tɪr-
tear|y 'tɪə.r|i (US) 'tɪr|.i **-ily** -ɪ.li
teas|e tiːz **-es** -ɪz **-ing/ly** -ɪŋ/li **-ed** -d **-er/s** -əʳ/z (US) -ɚ/z
teasel 'tiː.zᵊl **-s** -z **-(l)ing** -ɪŋ, 'tiːz.lɪŋ **-(l)ed** -d

Teasmade® 'tiː.meɪd
teaspoon 'tiː.spuːn **-s** -z
teaspoonful 'tiː.spuːn.fʊl **-s** -z
teaspoonsful (*alternative plur. of* **teaspoonful**) 'tiː.spuːnz.fʊl
tea-strainer 'tiːˌstreɪ.nəʳ (US) -nɚ **-s** -z
teat tiːt **-s** -s
tea-table 'tiːˌteɪ.bl̩ **-s** -z
teatime 'tiː.taɪm
tea-tree 'tiː.triː **-s** -z **'tea-tree ˌoil**
tea-urn 'tiː.ɜːn (US) -ɜːrn **-s** -z
teazel 'tiː.zᵊl **-s** -z
teazle (T) 'tiː.zᵊl **-s** -z
Tebay 'tiː.beɪ *locally:* -bi
tec tek **-s** -s
tech tek **-s** -s
technetium tek'niː.ʃi.əm, -si-, '-ʃəm (US) -ʃi.əm, '-ʃəm
technic|al 'tek.nɪ.k|ᵊl **-ally** -ᵊl.i, -li **-alness** -l̩.nəs, -nɪs **'technical ˌcollege**
technicalit|y ˌtek.nɪ'kæl.ə.t|i, -nə'-, -ɪ.t|i (US) -nə'kæl.ə.t̬|i **-ies** -iz
technician tek'nɪʃ.ᵊn **-s** -z
Technicolor® 'tek.nɪˌkʌl.əʳ (US) -ɚ
technicolo(u)r 'tek.nɪˌkʌl.əʳ (US) -ɚ **-ed** -d
technics (T®) 'tek.nɪks
technique tek'niːk **-s** -s
techno- tek.nəʊ-; tek'nɒ- (US) 'tek.noʊ-, -nə-; tek'nɑː-
Note: Prefix. This may carry primary or secondary stress on the first or second syllable, e.g. **technophobe** /'tek.nə.fəʊb (US) -foʊb/, **technophobia** /ˌtek.nə'fəʊ.bi.ə (US) -'foʊ-/, or on the second syllable, e.g. **technology** /tek'nɒl.ə.dʒi (US) tek'nɑː-/.
technocrat 'tek.nəʊ.kræt (US) -nə- **-s** -s
technocratic ˌtek.nəʊ'kræt.ɪk (US) -nə'kræt̬-
technological ˌtek.nə'lɒdʒ.ɪ.kᵊl (US) -'lɑː.dʒɪ-
technolog|y tek'nɒl.ə.dʒ|i (US) -'nɑː.lə- **-ist/s** -ɪst/s
technophobe 'tek.nəʊ.fəʊb (US) -nə.foʊb **-s** -z
technophob|ia ˌtek.nəʊ'fəʊ.b|i.ə (US) -nə'foʊ- **-ic** -ɪk
tech|y 'tetʃ|.i **-ier** -i.əʳ (US) -i.ɚ **-iest** -i.ɪst, -i.əst **-ily** -ɪ.li, -ᵊl.i **-iness** -ɪ.nəs, -ɪ.nɪs
Teck tek
tectonic tek'tɒn.ɪk (US) -'tɑː.nɪk **-s** -s **tecˌtonic 'plates**
ted (T) ted **-s** -z **-ding** -ɪŋ **-ded** -ɪd **-der/s** -əʳ/z (US) -ɚ/z
Teddington 'ted.ɪŋ.tən
tedd|y (T) 'ted|.i **-ies** -iz **'teddy ˌbear** ; **ˌTeddy Bear's 'Picnic** ; **'teddy ˌboy**
Te Deum ˌteɪ'deɪ.ʊm, ˌtiː'diː.əm; **-s** -z
tedious 'tiː.di.əs (US) -di.əs, -dʒəs **-ly** -li **-ness** -nəs, -nɪs
tedium 'tiː.di.əm
tee tiː **-s** -z **-ing** -ɪŋ **-d** -d
tee-hee ˌtiː'hiː **-s** -z
teem tiːm **-s** -z **-ing** -ɪŋ **-ed** -d
teen tiːn **-s** -z
teenage 'tiːn.eɪdʒ **-d** -d
teenager 'tiːnˌeɪ.dʒəʳ (US) -dʒɚ **-s** -z
teens|y 'tiːn.z|i **-ier** -i.əʳ (US) -i.ɚ **-iest** -i.ɪst, -i.əst
teensy-weensy ˌtiːn.zi'wiːn.zi, ˌtiːnt.si'wiːnt.si *stress shift:* ˌteensy-weensy 'house
teen|y 'tiː.n|i **-iest** -i.ɪst, -i.əst
teenybopper 'tiː.niˌbɒp.əʳ (US) -ˌbɑː.pɚ **-s** -z
teeny-weeny ˌtiː.ni'wiː.ni *stress shift:* ˌteeny-weeny 'house
teepee 'tiː.piː **-s** -z
Tees tiːz
Teesdale 'tiːz.deɪl
teeshirt 'tiː.ʃɜːt (US) -ʃɜːrt **-s** -s
tee-square 'tiː.skweəʳ, ˌ-'- (US) 'tiː.skwer **-s** -z
Teesside 'tiː.saɪd, 'tiːz-
teet|er 'tiː.t|əʳ (US) -t̬|ɚ **-ers** -əz (US) -ɚz **-ering** -ᵊr.ɪŋ **-ered** -əd (US) -ɚd
teeter-tott|er ˌtiː.tə'tɒt|.əʳ (US) -t̬ɚ'tɑː.t̬|ɚ **-ers** -əz (US) -ɚz **-ering** -ᵊr.ɪŋ **-ered** -əd (US) -ɚd
teeth (*plur. of* **tooth**) tiːθ **ˌgrit one's 'teeth** ; **ˌset someone's 'teeth on ˌedge**
teeth|e tiːð **-es** -z **-ing** -ɪŋ **-ed** -d **'teething ˌring** ; **'teething ˌtroubles**
teetotal ˌtiː'təʊ.tᵊl (US) -'toʊ.t̬ᵊl, 'ˌ-ˌ-- **-ism** -ɪ.zᵊm
teetotal(l)er ˌtiː'təʊ.tᵊl.əʳ, -'təʊt.ləʳ (US) -'toʊ.t̬ᵊl.ɚ, -'toʊt.lɚ, 'tiːˌtoʊ.t̬ᵊl.ɚ, -ˌtoʊt.lɚ **-s** -z
teetotum ˌtiː'təʊ.təm, '-ˌ--; ˌtiː.təʊ'tʌm (US) ˌtiː'toʊt̬.əm **-s** -z
TEFL 'tef.l̩
Teflon® 'tef.lɒn (US) -lɑːn
Tegucigalpa teɡˌuː.sɪ'ɡæl.pə (US) -sə'ɡæl.pɑː, -'ɡɑːl-
tegument 'teɡ.jʊ.mənt, -jə- **-s** -s
Tehran, Teheran teə'rɑːn, -'ræn; ˌte.hᵊr'ɑːn, ˌteɪ.ᵊr'-, -'æn (US) ter'ɑːn, tə'rɑːn, teə-, -'ræn
Tehuantepec tə'wɑːn.tə.pek (US) -t̬ə-
Teifi 'taɪ.vi
Teign tɪn, tiːn
Teignbridge 'tɪn.brɪdʒ, 'tiːn-, 'tɪm-, 'tiːm- (US) 'tɪn-, 'tiːn-
Teignmouth 'tɪn.məθ, 'tiːn-, 'tɪm-, 'tiːm- *locally also:* 'tɪŋ- (US) 'tɪn-, 'tiːn-
Teignton 'teɪn.tən (US) -tᵊn
Teiresias taɪə'riː.si.əs (US) taɪ-
Te Kanawa teɪ'kɑː.nə.wə, tɪ-
tel. (*abbrev. for* **telephone**) 'tel.ɪ.fəʊn (US) -ə.foʊn
telaesthesia ˌtel.əs'θiː.zi.ə, -ɪs'-, -iːs'-, -ʒi-, '-ʒə (US) ˌtel.əs'θiː.ʒə
telaesthetic ˌtel.əs'θet.ɪk, -ɪs'-, -iːs'- (US) -'θet̬- **-s** -s **-ally** -ᵊl.i, -li
telamon (T) 'tel.ə.mən, -mɒn (US) -mən, -mɑːn **-s** -z
TelAutograph® tel'ɔː.tə.ɡrɑːf, -ɡræf (US) -'ɑː.t̬ə.ɡræf, -'ɔː-
Tel Aviv ˌtel.ə'viːv, -æv'iːv, -'ɪv (US) -ə'viːv, -ɑː'-
tele- tel.ɪ-; tɪ'le-, tə- (US) 'tel.ə-; tɪ'le-, tə-, tel.ɪ-
Note: Prefix. This may carry primary or secondary stress on the first syllable, e.g. **telephone** /'tel.ɪ.fəʊn (US) 'tel.ə.foʊn/, **telegraphic** /ˌtel.ɪ'ɡræf.ɪk (US) -ə'-/, or on the second syllable, e.g. **telephony** /tə'lef.ə.ni/.
tele 'tel.i **-s** -z
telebanking 'tel.ɪˌbæŋ.kɪŋ
telecamera 'tel.ɪˌkæm.ᵊr.ə, ˌ-rə **-s** -z
telecast 'tel.ɪ.kɑːst (US) -kæst **-s** -s **-ing** -ɪŋ **-ed** -ɪd **-er/s** -əʳ/z (US) -ɚ/z
tele-cine ˌtel.ɪ'sɪn.i
telecom® 'tel.ɪ.kɒm (US) -kɑːm
telecommunication ˌtel.ɪ.kəˌmjuː.nɪ'keɪ.ʃᵊn, ˌ-ə-, -nə'- **-s** -z
telecommuting ˌtel.ɪ.kə'mjuː.tɪŋ (US) 'tel.ɪ.kəˌmjuː.t̬ɪŋ
teleconferenc|e ˌtel.ɪ'kɒn.fᵊr.ᵊnts (US) 'tel.ɪˌkɑːn- **-es** -ɪz
telefilm 'tel.ɪ.fɪlm (US) '-ə- **-s** -z
telegenic ˌtel.ɪ'dʒen.ɪk (US) -ə'-
telegram 'tel.ɪ.ɡræm **-s** -z **-ming** -ɪŋ **-med** -d
telegramese ˌtel.ɪ.ɡræm'iːz
telegraph 'tel.ɪ.ɡrɑːf, -ɡræf (US) -ɡræf **-s** -s **-ing** -ɪŋ **-ed** -t **'telegraph ˌpole** ; **'telegraph ˌwire**
telegrapher tɪ'leɡ.rə.fəʳ, tel'eɡ-, tə'leɡ- (US) tə'leɡ.rə.fɚ **-s** -z
telegraphese ˌtel.ɪ.ɡrɑː'fiːz, -ɡræf'iːz, -ɡrə'fiːz (US) -ɡræf'iːz, -ɡrə'fiːz
telegraphic ˌtel.ɪ'ɡræf.ɪk (US) -ə'- **-ally** -ᵊl.i, -li
telegraph|y tɪ'leɡ.rə.f|i, tel'eɡ-, tə'leɡ- (US) tə'leɡ- **-ist/s** -ɪst/s
teleki|nesis ˌtel.ɪ.kɪ'niː.sɪs, ˌ-ə-, -kaɪ'- (US) -kɪ'- **-netic** -'net.ɪk (US) -'net̬-
Telemachus tɪ'lem.ə.kəs, tel'em-, tə'lem- (US) tə'lem-
Telemann 'teɪ.lə.mæn (US) -mɑːn
telemark 'tel.ɪ.mɑːk, '-ə- (US) -ə.mɑːrk **-s** -s **-ing** -ɪŋ **-ed** -t
telemarketing ˌtel.ɪ'mɑː.kɪ.tɪŋ, -kə-, 'tel.ɪˌmɑː- (US) 'tel.əˌmɑːr.kə.t̬ɪŋ
Telemessag|e® 'tel.ɪˌmes.ɪdʒ **-es** -ɪz
telemet|er tə'lem.ɪ.t|əʳ, '-ə-; 'tel.ɪˌmiː- (US) 'tel.əˌmiː.t̬|ɚ; tə'lem.ə- **-ers** -əz (US) -ɚz **-ering** -ᵊr.ɪŋ **-ered** -əd (US) -ɚd

telemetric ˌtel.ɪˈmet.rɪk (US) -ə- **-ally** -ᵊl.i, -li
telemetry tɪˈlem.ɪ.tri, tə-, ˈ-ə- (US) təˈlem.ə-
teleological ˌtel.i.əˈlɒdʒ.ɪ.kᵊl, ˌtiː.li- (US) ˌtiː.li.əˈlɑː.dʒɪ-, ˌtel.i-
teleolog|y ˌtel.iˈɒl.ə.dʒ|i, ˌtiː.liˈ- (US) ˌtiː.liˈɑː.lə-, ˌtel.iˈ- **-ist/s** -ɪst/s
telepathic ˌtel.ɪˈpæθ.ɪk (US) -əˈ- **-ally** -ᵊl.i, -li
telepathiz|e, -is|e tɪˈlep.ə.θaɪz, telˈep-, təˈlep- (US) təˈlep- **-es** -ɪz **-ing** -ɪŋ **-ed** -d
telepath|y tɪˈlep.ə.θ|i, telˈep-, təˈlep- (US) təˈlep- **-ist/s** -ɪst/s
telephon|e ˈtel.ɪ.fəʊn (US) -ə.foʊn **-es** -z **-ing** -ɪŋ **-ed** -d **-er/s** -əʳ/z (US) -ɚ/z **ˈtelephone ˌbooth** ; **ˈtelephone ˌbook** ; **ˈtelephone ˌbox** ; **ˈtelephone ˌcall** ; **ˈtelephone diˌrectory** ; **ˈtelephone ˌnumber** ; **ˈtelephone ˌpole**
telephonic ˌtel.ɪˈfɒn.ɪk, -əˈ- (US) -əˈfɑː.nɪk **-ally** -ᵊl.i, -li
telephonist tɪˈlef.ᵊn.ɪst, telˈef-, təˈlef- (US) təˈlef- **-s** -s
telephony tɪˈlef.ᵊn.i, telˈef-, təˈlef- (US) təˈlef-
telephoto ˌtel.ɪˈfəʊ.təʊ (US) ˈtel.ə.foʊ.t̬oʊ **-s** -z *stress shift, see compound:* **ˌtelephoto ˈlens**
telephotography ˌtel.ɪ.fəˈtɒg.rə.fi (US) -ə.fəˈtɑː.grə-
teleprinter ˈtel.ɪˌprɪn.təʳ (US) -əˌprɪn.t̬ɚ **-s** -z
TelePrompTer® ˈtel.ɪˌprɒmp.təʳ (US) -əˌprɑːmp.tɚ **-s** -z
telerecord (*n.*) ˈtel.ɪˌrek.ɔːd (US) -ɚd **-s** -z
telerecord (*v.*) ˈtel.ɪ.rɪˌkɔːd, -rəˌ-, ˌtel.ɪ.rɪˈkɔːd, -rəˈ- (US) ˈtel.ɪ.rɪˌkɔːrd, -rə-, ˌtel.ɪ.rɪˈkɔːrd, -rəˈ- **-s** -z **-ing/s** -ɪŋ/z **-ed** -ɪd
telesales ˈtel.ɪ.seɪlz
telescop|e ˈtel.ɪ.skəʊp (US) -ə.skoʊp **-es** -s **-ing** -ɪŋ **-ed** -t
telescopic ˌtel.ɪˈskɒp.ɪk (US) -əˈskɑː.pɪk **-ally** -ᵊl.i, -li
telescreen ˈtel.ɪ.skriːn **-s** -z
teleshopping ˈtel.ɪˌʃɒp.ɪŋ, ˌtel.ɪˈʃɒp- (US) ˈtel.əˌʃɑː.pɪŋ
telesthesia ˌtel.əsˈθiː.zi.ə, -ɪsˈ-, -iːsˈ-, -ʒi-, ˈ-ʒə- (US) ˌtel.əsˈθiː.ʒə
telesthetic ˌtel.əsˈθet.ɪk, -ɪsˈ-, -iːsˈ- (US) -ˈθet̬- **-s** -s **-ally** -ᵊl.i, -li
Teletex® ˈtel.ɪ.teks
teletext ˈtel.ɪ.tekst (US) ˈ-ə- **-s** -s
telethon ˈtel.ɪ.θɒn (US) -ə.θɑːn **-s** -z
Teletype® ˈtel.ɪ.taɪp (US) ˈ-ə- **-s** -s
Teletypesetter® ˌtel.ɪˈtaɪpˌset.əʳ (US) -əˈtaɪpˌset̬.ɚ **-s** -z
televangel|ism ˌtel.ɪˈvæn.dʒə.l|ɪ.zᵊm, -dʒɪ- **-ist/s** -ɪst/s
teleview ˈtel.ɪ.vjuː (US) ˈ-ə- **-s** -z **-ing** -ɪŋ **-ed** -d **-er/s** -əʳ/z (US) -ɚ/z
televis|e ˈtel.ɪ.vaɪz (US) ˈ-ə- **-es** -ɪz **-ing** -ɪŋ **-ed** -d
television ˈtel.ɪ.vɪʒ.ᵊn, ˌtel.ɪˈvɪʒ- (US) ˈtel.ə.vɪʒ- **-s** -z **ˈtelevision ˌset, teleˈvision ˌset**
televisor ˈtel.ɪ.vaɪ.zəʳ (US) -ə.vaɪ.zɚ **-s** -z
televisual ˌtel.ɪˈvɪʒ.u.əl, -ˈvɪz.ju- (US) -əˈvɪʒ.u- **-ly** -i
telework|ing ˈtel.ɪˌwɜː.k|ɪŋ (US) -ˌwɜːr- **-er/s** -əʳ/z (US) -ɚ/z
telex ˈtel.eks **-es** -ɪz **-ing** -ɪŋ **-ed** -t
Telfer ˈtel.fəʳ (US) -fɚ
Telford ˈtel.fəd (US) -fɚd
telic ˈtel.ɪk (US) ˈtiː.lɪk, ˈtel.ɪk
tell (T) tel **-s** -z **-ing/ly** -ɪŋ/li **told** təʊld (US) toʊld
teller (T) ˈtel.əʳ (US) -ɚ **-s** -z
telling-off ˌtel.ɪŋˈɒf (US) -ˈɑːf **tellings-off** ˌtel.ɪŋzˈɒf (US) -ˈɑːf
telltale ˈtel.teɪl **-s** -z
tellurian telˈʊə.ri.ən, təˈlʊə-, tɪ-, -ˈljʊə- (US) telˈʊr.i-, təˈlʊr- **-s** -z
telluric telˈʊə.rɪk, təˈlʊə-, tɪ-, -ˈljʊə- (US) telˈʊr.ɪk, təˈlʊr-
tellurium telˈʊə.ri.əm, təˈlʊə-, tɪ-, -ˈljʊə- (US) telˈʊr.i-, təˈlʊr-
tell|y ˈtel|.i **-ies** -iz
Telstar® ˈtel.stɑːʳ (US) -stɑːr
Telugu ˈtel.ə.guː, ˈ-ʊ- (US) ˈ-ə- **-s**
temerity tɪˈmer.ə.ti, tə-, temˈer-, -ɪ.ti (US) təˈmer.ə.t̬i
temp temp **-s** -s **-ing** -ɪŋ **-ed** -t
Tempe ˈtem.pi
tempeh ˈtem.peɪ **-s** -z
temp|er ˈtem.p|əʳ (US) -p|ɚ **-ers** -əz (US) -ɚz **-ering** -ᵊr.ɪŋ **-ered** -əd (US) -ɚd **-erer/s** -ᵊr.əʳ/z (US) -ɚ.ɚ/z
tempera ˈtem.pᵊr.ə
temperable ˈtem.pᵊr.ə.bl̩, -prə.bl̩
temperament ˈtem.pᵊr.ə.mənt, -prə.mənt **-s** -s
temperamental ˌtem.pᵊr.əˈmen.tᵊl, -prəˈ- (US) -t̬ᵊl **-ly** -i
temperance ˈtem.pᵊr.ᵊnts, ˈ-prənts
temperate ˈtem.pᵊr.ət, ˈ-prət, -prɪt **-ly** -li **-ness** -nəs, -nɪs
temperature ˈtem.prə.tʃəʳ, -prɪ-, -pᵊr.ə-, -ɪ- (US) -pɚ.ə.tʃɚ, ˈ-prə-, -pɚ-, -pə- **-s** -z
-tempered -ˈtem.pəd (US) -pɚd **-ly** -li
Temperley ˈtem.pᵊl.i (US) -pɚ.li
tempest ˈtem.pɪst, -pəst **-s** -s
tempestuous temˈpes.tju.əs, -tʃu- (US) -tʃu-, -tʃə.wəs **-ly** -li **-ness** -nəs, -nɪs
Templar ˈtem.pləʳ, -plɑːʳ (US) -plɚ **-s** -z
template ˈtem.pleɪt, -plɪt (US) -plɪt **-s** -s
temple (T) ˈtem.pl̩ **-s** -z
templet ˈtem.plɪt, -plət (US) -plɪt **-s** -s
Templeton ˈtem.pl̩.tən (US) -tən
temp|o ˈtem.p|əʊ (US) -p|oʊ **-os** -əʊz (US) -oʊz **-i** -iː
temporal ˈtem.pᵊr.ᵊl **-ly** -i
temporality ˌtem.pᵊrˈæl.ə.ti, -ɪ.ti (US) -pəˈræl.ə.t̬i
temporar|y ˈtem.pᵊr.ᵊr|.i, -prᵊr- (US) -pə.rer|.i **-ies** -iz **-ily** -ᵊl.i, -ɪ.li **-iness** -ɪ.nəs, -ɪ.nɪs
temporization, -isa- ˌtem.pᵊr.aɪˈzeɪ.ʃᵊn, -ɪˈ- (US) -ɪˈ-
temporiz|e, -is|e ˈtem.pᵊr.aɪz (US) -pə.raɪz **-es** -ɪz **-ing/ly** -ɪŋ/li **-ed** -d **-er/s** -əʳ/z (US) -ɚ/z
tempt tempt **-s** -s **-ing** -ɪŋ **-ed** -ɪd **-er/s** -əʳ/z (US) -ɚ/z
temptation tempˈteɪ.ʃᵊn **-s** -z
tempting ˈtemp.tɪŋ **-ly** -li **-ness** -nəs, -nɪs
temptress ˈtemp.trəs, -trɪs (US) -trɪs **-es** -ɪz
tempura ˈtem.pᵊr.ə; temˈpʊə.rə (US) ˈtem.pʊ.rɑː; temˈpʊr.ə
tempus fugit ˌtem.pəsˈfjuː.dʒɪt, -pʊsˈ-, -gɪt (US) -pəsˈfjuː.dʒɪt
ten ten **-s** -z **ˌTen Comˈmandments**
tenability ˌten.əˈbɪl.ə.ti, -ɪ.ti (US) -ə.t̬i
tenable ˈten.ə.bl̩ **-ness** -nəs, -nɪs
tenacious tɪˈneɪ.ʃəs, tə-, tenˈeɪ- (US) təˈneɪ- **-ly** -li **-ness** -nəs, -nɪs
tenacity tɪˈnæs.ə.ti, tə-, tenˈæs-, -ɪ.ti (US) təˈnæs.ə.t̬i
tenanc|y ˈten.ənt.s|i **-ies** -iz
tenant ˈten.ənt **-s** -s
tenantry ˈten.ən.tri
Tenbury ˈten.bᵊr.i, ˈtem- (US) ˈten.ber-, -bɚ-
Tenby ˈten.bi, ˈtem- (US) ˈten-
tench tentʃ
tend tend **-s** -z **-ing** -ɪŋ **-ed** -ɪd
tendencious tenˈden.tʃəs (US) -ˈdent.ʃəs **-ly** -li **-ness** -nəs, -nɪs
tendenc|y ˈten.dənt.s|i **-ies** -iz
tendentious tenˈden.tʃəs (US) -ˈdent.ʃəs **-ly** -li **-ness** -nəs, -nɪs
tend|er ˈten.d|əʳ (US) -d|ɚ **-ers** -əz (US) -ɚz **-erer** -ᵊr.əʳ (US) -ɚ.ɚ **-erest** -ᵊr.ɪst, -əst **-erly** -ᵊl.i (US) -ɚ.li **-erness** -ə.nəs, -nɪs (US) -ɚ.nəs, -nɪs **-ering** -ᵊr.ɪŋ **-ered** -əd (US) -ɚd
tender|foot ˈten.də|.fʊt (US) -dɚ- **-foots** -s **-feet** -fiːt
tender-hearted ˌten.dəˈhɑː.tɪd, ˈten.dəˌhɑː- (US) ˈten.dɚˌhɑːr.t̬ɪd, ˌten.dɚˈhɑːr- **-ly** -li **-ness** -nəs, -nɪs *stress shift, British only:* ˌtender-hearted ˈperson
tenderization, -isa- ˌten.dᵊr.aɪˈzeɪ.ʃᵊn, -ɪˈ- (US) -ɪˈ-

tenderiz|e, -is|e 'ten.dər.aɪz (US) -də.raɪz **-es** -ɪz **-ing** -ɪŋ **-ed** -d **-er/s** -ər/z (US) -ɚ/z
tenderloin 'ten.dəl.ɔɪn (US) -dɚ.lɔɪn **-s** -z
tendinitis ˌten.dɪ'naɪ.tɪs, -də'-
tendon 'ten.dən **-s** -z
tendonitis ˌten.də'naɪ.tɪs (US) -t̬ɪs
tendril 'ten.drəl, -drɪl (US) -drəl **-s** -z
Tenebrae 'ten.ɪ.briː, '-ə-, -breɪ, -braɪ (US) -ə.breɪ, -briː
tenebrous 'ten.ɪ.brəs, '-ə- (US) '-ə-
tenement 'ten.ə.mənt, '-ɪ- (US) '-ə- **-s** -s
Tenerif(f)e ˌten.ər'iːf (US) -ə'riːf
tenet 'ten.ɪt **-s** -s
tenfold 'ten.fəʊld (US) -foʊld
ten-gallon hat ˌtenˌgæl.ən'hæt, ˌteŋ- (US) ˌten- **-s** -s
Tengu 'teŋ.gu **-s** -z
Teniers 'ten.i.əz, '-jəz (US) -i.ɚz, '-jɚz; tə'nɪrz
Tenison 'ten.ɪ.sən
Tenko 'teŋ.kəʊ (US) -koʊ
Tenn. (*abbrev. for* **Tennessee**) ˌten.ə'siː, -ɪ'- (US) ˌten.ɪ'siː *regionally:* 'ten.ɪ.si, -ə-
Tennant 'ten.ənt
tenner 'ten.ər (US) -ɚ **-s** -z
Tennessee ˌten.ə'siː, -ɪ'- (US) ˌten.ɪ'siː *regionally:* 'ten.ɪ.si, -ə-
Tenniel 'ten.i.əl, '-jəl
tennis 'ten.ɪs **'tennis ˌball ; 'tennis ˌcourt ; ˌtennis 'elbow ; 'tennis ˌracket**
Tennyson 'ten.ɪ.sən
tenon 'ten.ən **-s** -z
tenor 'ten.ər (US) -ɚ **-s** -z
tenour 'ten.ər (US) -ɚ
ten|pence 'ten|.pənts, 'tem- (US) 'ten- **-penny** -pən.i
tenpin 'ten.pɪn, 'tem- (US) 'ten- **-s** -z ˌ**tenpin 'bowling**
tenpins 'ten.pɪnz, 'tem- (US) 'ten-
tens|e tents **-es** -ɪz **-er** -ər (US) -ɚ **-est** -ɪst, -əst **-ely** -li **-eness** -nəs, -nɪs
tensile 'tent.saɪl (US) -sɪl, -saɪl
tension 'ten.tʃən (US) 'tent.ʃən **-s** -z
tensity 'tent.sə.ti, -sɪ- (US) -sə.t̬i
tensor 'tent.sər (US) -sɚ **-s** -z
tent tent **-s** -s **-ing** -ɪŋ (US) 'ten.t̬ɪŋ **-ed** -ɪd (US) 'ten.t̬ɪd
tentacle 'ten.tə.kl̩, -tɪ- (US) -t̬ə- **-s** -z
tentacular ten'tæk.jə.lər, -jʊ- (US) -lɚ
tentative 'ten.tə.tɪv (US) -t̬ə.t̬ɪv **-s** -z **-ly** -li
tenter 'ten.tər (US) -t̬ɚ **-s** -z
Tenterden 'ten.tə.dən (US) -t̬ɚ-
tenterhook 'ten.tə.hʊk (US) -t̬ɚ- **-s** -s
tenth tentθ **-s** -s **-ly** -li
tentpegging 'tentˌpeg.ɪŋ
Tentsmuir tents'mjʊər (US) -'mjʊr
tenu|is 'ten.ju|.ɪs **-es** -iːz, -eɪz
tenuity ten'juː.ə.ti, tə'njuː-, tɪ-, -ɪ.ti (US) tə'nuː.ə.t̬i, -'njuː-
tenuous 'ten.ju.əs **-ly** -li **-ness** -nəs, -nɪs
tenur|e 'ten.jər, -jʊər (US) -jɚ, -jʊr **-es** -z **-ed** -d
tepal 'tiː.pəl, 'tep.əl
tepee 'tiː.piː **-s** -z
tepid 'tep.ɪd **-est** -ɪst, -əst **-ly** -li **-ness** -nəs, -nɪs
tepidity tep'ɪd.ə.ti, -ɪ.ti (US) tə'pɪd.ə.t̬i
tequila tə'kiː.lə, tɪ- (US) tə- **-s** -z **teˌquila 'sunrise**
ter *three times:* tɜːr (US) tɜːr, ter
Ter *river in Essex:* tɑːr (US) tɑːr
teraph 'ter.əf **-im** -ɪm
terbium 'tɜː.bi.əm (US) 'tɜːr-
tercel *hawk:* 'tɜː.səl (US) 'tɜːr- **-s** -z
Tercel *car:* 'tɜː.sel (US) tɚ'sel
tercentenar|y ˌtɜː.sen'tiː.nər|.i, -'ten.ər-; tɜː'sen.tɪ.nər- (US) tɚ'sen.tən.er-; ˌtɜːr.sen'ten.ɚ- **-ies** -iz
tercentennial ˌtɜː.sen'ten.i.əl (US) ˌtɜːr-
tercet 'tɜː.sɪt, -set (US) 'tɜːr.sɪt; tɚ'set **-s** -s
terebene 'ter.ə.biːn, '-ɪ- (US) '-ə-
terebinth 'ter.ə.bɪntθ, '-ɪ- (US) '-ə- **-s** -s
Terence 'ter.ənts
Teresa tə'riː.zə, tɪ-, -'reɪ-, ter'iː- (US) tə'riː.sə, -zə, -'reɪ-
tergiver|sate 'tɜː.dʒɪ.vɜː|.seɪt, -və- (US) 'tɜːr.dʒɪ.vɚ- **-sates** -seɪts **-sating** -seɪ.tɪŋ (US) -seɪ.t̬ɪŋ **-sated** -seɪ.tɪd (US) -seɪ.t̬ɪd
tergiversation ˌtɜː.dʒɪ.vɜː'seɪ.ʃən, -və'- (US) ˌtɜːr.dʒɪ.vɚ-
teriyaki ˌter.i'æk.i (US) -'jɑː.ki
Terling 'tɑː.lɪŋ, 'tɜː- (US) 'tɑːr-, 'tɜːr-
term tɜːm (US) tɜːrm **-s** -z **-ly** -li
termagant (T) 'tɜː.mə.gənt (US) 'tɜːr- **-s** -s **-ly** -li
terminab|le 'tɜː.mɪ.nə.bl|̩, -mə- (US) 'tɜːr- **-ly** -li **-leness** -l̩.nəs, -nɪs
terminal 'tɜː.mɪ.nəl, -mə- (US) 'tɜːr- **-s** -z **-ly** -i
termi|nate 'tɜː.mɪ|.neɪt, -mə- (US) 'tɜːr- **-nates** -neɪts **-nating** -neɪ.tɪŋ (US) -neɪ.t̬ɪŋ **-nated** -neɪ.tɪd (US) -neɪ.t̬ɪd **-nator/s** -neɪ.tər/z (US) -neɪ.t̬ɚ/z
termination ˌtɜː.mɪ'neɪ.ʃən, -mə'- (US) ˌtɜːr- **-s** -z
terminative 'tɜː.mɪ.nə.tɪv, -mə-, -neɪ- (US) 'tɜːr.mɪ.neɪ.t̬ɪv, -mə- **-ly** -li
terminer 'tɜː.mɪ.nər, -mə- (US) 'tɜːr.mɪ.nɚ, -mə-
terminologic|al ˌtɜː.mɪ.nə'lɒdʒ.ɪ.k|əl, -mə- (US) ˌtɜːr.mɪ.nə'lɑː.dʒɪ-, -mə- **-ally** -əl.i, -li
terminolog|y ˌtɜː.mɪ'nɒl.ə.dʒ|i, -mə'- (US) ˌtɜːr.mɪ'nɑː.lə-, -mə'- **-ies** -iz
termin|us 'tɜː.mɪ.n|əs, -mə- (US) 'tɜːr- **-i** -aɪ **-uses** -ə.sɪz
termite 'tɜː.maɪt (US) 'tɜːr- **-s** -s
termtime 'tɜːm.taɪm (US) 'tɜːrm-
tern tɜːn (US) tɜːrn **-s** -z
ternary 'tɜː.nər.i (US) 'tɜːr-
Ternate tɜː'nɑː.ti (US) tɜːr'nɑː.teɪ
Terpsichore tɜːp'sɪk.ər.i (US) tɚp-
terpsichorean ˌtɜː.p.sɪ.kər'iː.ən, -kɒr'- (US) ˌtɜːrp.sɪ.kə'riː-; ˌtɜːrp.sɪ'kɔːr.i-
terra 'ter.ə
terrac|e 'ter.ɪs, -əs **-es** -ɪz **-ing** -ɪŋ **-ed** -t
terracotta ˌter.ə'kɒt.ə (US) -'kɑː.t̬ə
terra firma ˌter.ə'fɜː.mə (US) -'fɜːr-
terrain tə'reɪn, tɪ-, ter'eɪn; 'ter.eɪn (US) ter'eɪn, tə'reɪn; 'ter.eɪn **-s** -z
terra incognita ˌter.ə.ɪŋ'kɒg.nɪ.tə, -ɪn'-; -kɒg'niː.tə- (US) -ɪn'kɑːg.niː.t̬ə, -nɪ- **terrae incognitae** ˌter.i.ɪŋ'kɒg.nɪ.ti, -ɪn'-; -kɒg'niː.ti (US) -ɪn'kɑːg.niː.t̬i, -nɪ-
Terramycin® ˌter.ə'maɪ.sɪn
Terrance 'ter.ənts
terrapin 'ter.ə.pɪn **-s** -z
terrari|um tə'reə.ri|.əm, ter'eə-, tɪ'reə- (US) tə'rer.i- **-ums** -əmz **-a** -ə
terrazzo ter'æt.səʊ, tə'ræt-, tɪ- (US) tə'rɑːt.soʊ, ter'ɑːt-; tə'ræz.oʊ **-s** -z
Terrell 'ter.əl
Terrence 'ter.ənts
terrestrial tə'res.tri.əl, ter'es-, tɪ'res- (US) tə'res- **-s** -z **-ly** -i **-ness** -nəs, -nɪs
terret 'ter.ɪt **-s** -s
Terri 'ter.i
terrib|le 'ter.ə.bl|̩, '-ɪ- (US) '-ə- **-ly** -li **-leness** -l̩.nəs, -nɪs
terricolous tə'rɪk.əl.əs, ter'ɪk-, tɪ'rɪk- (US) ter'ɪk-, tə'rɪk-
terrier 'ter.i.ər (US) -ɚ **-s** -z
terrific tə'rɪf.ɪk, tɪ- (US) tə- **-ally** -əl.i, -li
terri|fy 'ter.ə|.faɪ, '-ɪ- (US) '-ə- **-fies** -faɪz **-fying** -faɪ.ɪŋ **-fied** -faɪd
terrine ter'iːn, tə'riːn; 'ter.iːn (US) ter'iːn **-s** -z
territorial ˌter.ɪ'tɔː.ri.əl, -ə'- (US) -ə'tɔːr.i- **-s** -z **-ly** -i *stress shift, see compounds:* ˌ**Territorial 'Army, Terriˌtorial 'Army ; terriˌtorial 'waters**
territorializ|e, -is|e ˌter.ɪ'tɔː.ri.əl.aɪz, -ə'- (US) -ə'tɔːr.i- **-es** -ɪz **-ing** -ɪŋ **-ed** -d
territor|y 'ter.ɪ.tər|.i, '-ə-, -tr|i (US) -ə.tɔːr|.i **-ies** -iz
terror 'ter.ər (US) -ɚ **-s** -z
terror|ism 'ter.ər|.ɪ.zəm **-ist/s** -ɪst/s
terrorization, -isa-, ˌter.ər.aɪ'zeɪ.ʃən, -ɪ'- (US) -ɪ'-
terroriz|e, -is|e 'ter.ər.aɪz (US) -ə.raɪz **-es** -ɪz **-ing** -ɪŋ **-ed** -d **-er/s** -ər/z (US) -ɚ/z
terror-stricken 'ter.əˌstrɪk.ən (US) -ɚˌ-
terror-struck 'ter.ə.strʌk (US) '-ɚ-

terr|y (T) 'ter|.i **-ies** -iz ˌterry 'nappy ; ˌterry 'towelling
ters|e tɜːs (US) tɜːrs **-er** -əʳ (US) -ɚ **-est** -ɪst, -əst **-ely** -li **-eness** -nəs, -nɪs
tertian 'tɜː.ʃᵊn, -ʃi.ən (US) 'tɜːr.ʃᵊn
tertiary 'tɜː.ʃᵊr.i, -ʃi.ᵊr- (US) 'tɜːr.ʃi.er-, -ʃɚ.i ˌtertiary edu'cation
tertium quid ˌtɜː.ti.əm'kwɪd, ˌ-ʃəm'-, -ʃi.əm'- (US) ˌtɜːr.ʃi.əm'-; ˌter.ti.ʊm'-
Tertius 'tɜː.ʃəs, -ʃi.əs, -ti-
Tertullian tɜː'tʌl.i.ən, '-jən (US) tɚ-
terylene (T®) 'ter.ə.liːn, '-ɪ- (US) '-ɪ-
terza rima ˌteət.sə'riː.mə, ˌtɜːt- (US) ˌtert-
Tesco® 'tes.kəʊ (US) -koʊ **-'s** -z
TESL 'tes.l̩
tesla (T) 'tes.lə
TESOL 'tiː.sɒl (US) -sɑːl; 'tes.ᵊl
Tess tes
Tessa, TESSA 'tes.ə
tessell|ate 'tes.ᵊl|.eɪt, -ɪ.l|eɪt (US) -ə.l|eɪt **-ates** -eɪts **-ating** -eɪ.tɪŋ (US) -eɪ.t̬ɪŋ **-ated** -eɪ.tɪd (US) -eɪ.t̬ɪd
tessellation ˌtes.ᵊl'eɪ.ʃᵊn, -ɪ'leɪ- (US) -ə'leɪ-
tessitura ˌtes.ɪ'tʊə.rə, -ə'-, -'tjʊə-, -'tɔː-, -'tjɔː- (US) -ɪ'tʊr.ə
test (T) test **-s** -s **-ing** -ɪŋ **-ed** -ɪd **-able** -ə.bl̩ **-er/s** -əʳ/z (US) -ɚ/z 'test ˌcard ; 'test ˌcase ; 'test ˌmatch
testace|an tes'teɪ.ʃ|ᵊn, -ʃi|.ən (US) '-ʃ|ən **-ous** -əs
testacy 'tes.tə.si
testament (T) 'tes.tə.mənt **-s** -s
testament|ary ˌtes.tə'men.t|ᵊr.i (US) -t̬ɚ- **-al** -ᵊl
testate 'tes.teɪt, -tɪt (US) -teɪt **-s** -s
testator tes'teɪ.təʳ (US) 'tes.teɪ.t̬ɚ, -'-- **-s** -z
testatri|x tes'teɪ.trɪ|ks **-ces** -siːz
test-bed 'test.bed **-s** -z
test-|drive 'test|.draɪv **-drives** -draɪvz **-driving** -ˌdraɪ.vɪŋ **-drove** -drəʊv (US) -droʊv **-driven** -ˌdrɪv.ᵊn
testes (*plur. of* **testis**) 'tes.tiːz
testicle 'tes.tɪ.kl̩, -tə- **-s** -z
testicular tes'tɪk.jə.ləʳ, -jʊ- (US) -lɚ
testification ˌtes.tɪ.fɪ'keɪ.ʃᵊn, -tə- **-s** -z
testi|fy 'tes.tɪ|.faɪ, -tə- **-fies** -faɪz **-fying** -faɪ.ɪŋ **-fied** -faɪd **-fier/s** -faɪ.əʳ/z (US) -faɪ.ɚ/z
testimonial ˌtes.tɪ'məʊ.ni.əl, -tə'- (US) -'moʊ- **-s** -z
testimonializ|e, -is|e ˌtes.tɪ'məʊ.ni.ᵊl.aɪz, -tə'- (US) -'moʊ.ni.ə.laɪz **-es** -ɪz **-ing** -ɪŋ **-ed** -d
testimon|y 'tes.tɪ.mə.n|i, -tə- (US) -moʊ.n|i **-ies** -iz
test|is 'tes.t|ɪs **-es** -iːz
Teston 'tiː.sᵊn
testosterone tes'tɒs.tᵊr.əʊn (US) -'tɑː.stə.roʊn
test-tube 'test.tjuːb, -tʃuːb (US) -tuːb, -tjuːb **-s** -z ˌtest-tube 'baby (US) 'test-tube ˌbaby
testud|o tes'tjuː.d|əʊ, -'tuː- (US) -'tuː.d|oʊ, -'tjuː- **-os** -əʊz (US) -oʊz **-ines** -dɪ.niːz, -neɪz (US) -dɪ.niːz
test|y 'tes.t|i **-ier** -i.əʳ (US) -i.ɚ **-iest** -i.ɪst, -i.əst **-ily** -ɪ.li, -ᵊl.i **-iness** -ɪ.nəs, -ɪ.nɪs
tetanus 'tet.ᵊn.əs
Tetbury 'tet.bᵊr.i (US) -ber-, -bɚ-
tetch|y 'tetʃ|.i **-ier** -i.əʳ (US) -i.ɚ **-iest** -i.ɪst, -i.əst **-ily** -ɪ.li, -ᵊl.i **-iness** -ɪ.nəs, -ɪ.nɪs
tête-à-tête ˌteɪt.ɑː'teɪt, ˌtet.ə'tet (US) ˌteɪt.ə'teɪt, ˌtet.ə'tet **-s** -s
teth|er 'teð.əʳ (US) -ɚ **-ers** -əz (US) -ɚz **-ering** -ᵊr.ɪŋ **-ered** -əd (US) -ɚd
Tetley 'tet.li
Tétouan tet'wɑːn (US) tet'wɑːn; 'teɪ.twɑːn
Tetovo tet'əʊ.vəʊ (US) -'oʊ.voʊ
tetrachord 'tet.rə.kɔːd (US) -kɔːrd **-s** -z
tetrad 'tet.ræd, -rəd (US) -ræd **-s** -z
tetragon 'tet.rə.gən (US) -gɑːn **-s** -z
tetrahedr|on ˌtet.rə'hiː.dr|ᵊn, -'hed.r|ᵊn (US) -'hiː- **-ons** -ᵊnz **-a** -ə **-al** -ᵊl
tetralog|y tet'ræl.ə.dʒ|i, tə'træl- (US) tet'rɑː.lə- **-ies** -iz
tetrameter tet'ræm.ɪ.təʳ, '-ə- (US) -ə.t̬ɚ **-s** -z
tetrarch 'tet.rɑːk (US) -rɑːrk **-s** -s **-y** -i **-ies** -iz
tetrasyllabic ˌtet.rə.sɪ'læb.ɪk, -sə'- (US) -sɪ'-
tetrasyllable 'tet.rəˌsɪl.ə.bl̩, ˌtet.rə'sɪl- **-s** -z
tetrathlon tet'ræθ.lɒn, tɪ'træθ-, tə-, -lən (US) tet'ræθ.lɑːn
Tettenhall 'tet.ᵊn.hɔːl
tetter 'tet.əʳ (US) 'tet̬.ɚ
Teucer 'tjuː.səʳ (US) 'tuː.sɚ, 'tjuː-
Teuton 'tjuː.tᵊn (US) 'tuː-, 'tjuː- **-s** -z
Teutonic tjuː'tɒn.ɪk (US) tuː'tɑː.nɪk, tjuː-
teutonization, -isa- ˌtjuː.tᵊn.aɪ'zeɪ.ʃᵊn, -ɪ'- (US) ˌtuː.tᵊn.ɪ'-, ˌtjuː-
teutoniz|e, -is|e 'tjuː.tᵊn.aɪz (US) 'tuː-, 'tjuː- **-es** -ɪz **-ing** -ɪŋ **-ed** -d
Teviot *river:* 'tiː.vi.ət *Lord:* 'tev.i.ət
Teviotdale 'tiː.vi.ət.deɪl
Tewfik 'tjuː.fɪk (US) 'tuː-, 'tjuː-
Tewkesbury 'tjuːks.bᵊr.i (US) 'tuːks.ber-, 'tjuːks-, -bɚ-
Tex. (*abbrev. for* **Texas**) 'tek.səs, -sæs (US) -səs
Texaco® 'tek.sə.kəʊ (US) -sɪ.koʊ, -sə-
Texan 'tek.sᵊn **-s** -z
Texas 'tek.səs, -sæs (US) -səs
Texel 'tek.sᵊl
Tex-Mex ˌteks'meks *stress shift:* ˌTex-Mex 'food
text tekst **-s** -s
textbook 'tekst.bʊk **-s** -s
textile 'tek.staɪl (US) -staɪl, -stɪl **-s** -z
textual 'teks.tju.əl (US) -tʃu- **-ly** -i
textur|e 'teks.tʃəʳ (US) -tʃɚ **-s** -z **-ing** -ɪŋ **-ed** -d
Tey teɪ
Teynham 'ten.əm, 'teɪ.nəm
Note: The former is appropriate for Baron Teynham.
-th -θ
Note: Suffix. Not a syllable in itself, and does not affect the word stress, e.g. **tenth** /tentθ/.
Thacker 'θæk.əʳ (US) -ɚ
Thackeray 'θæk.ᵊr.i, '-ri
Thackley 'θæk.li
Thaddeus 'θæd.i.əs; θæd'iː-
Thai taɪ **-s** -z
Thailand 'taɪ.lænd, -lənd
Thake θeɪk
thalam|us 'θæl.ə.m|əs **-i** -aɪ, -iː
thalassotherapy θəˌlæs.əʊ'θer.ə.pi, θælˌæs- (US) -ə'-
Thalben 'θæl.bən, 'θɔːl-
thaler 'tɑː.ləʳ (US) -lɚ **-s** -z
Thales 'θeɪ.liːz
Thali|a *of the three Graces:* θə'laɪ|.ə **-an** -ən *Greek Muse:* 'θæl.i.ə, '-jə (US) 'θeɪ.li.ə, 'θeɪl.jə
thalidomide θə'lɪd.ə.maɪd, θæl'ɪd- (US) θə'lɪd-
thallium 'θæl.i.əm
Thame teɪm
Thames *in England, Canada, New Zealand:* temz *in Connecticut:* θeɪmz, teɪmz, temz
than *strong form:* ðæn *weak forms:* ðᵊn, ðən, ðn̩
Note: Weak form word. The strong form /ðæn/ is rarely used; it is sometimes found in emphatic utterances such as 'The Queen, than whom no-one is richer...', but it normally has the weak pronunciation /ðən/, e.g. 'faster than sound', /ˌfɑː.stə.ðən'saʊnd/, or in rapid speech /ðn̩/, e.g. 'better than ever', /ˌbet.ə.ðn̩'ev.ə/.
Thanatos 'θæn.ə.tɒs (US) -tɑːs
thane (T) θeɪn **-s** -z
Thanet 'θæn.ɪt
thank θæŋk **-s** -s **-ing** -ɪŋ **-ed** -t **-er/s** -əʳ/z (US) -ɚ/z
thankful 'θæŋk.fᵊl, -fʊl **-ly** -i **-ness** -nəs, -nɪs

thankless 'θæŋ.kləs, -klɪs **-ly** -li **-ness** -nəs, -nɪs
thanksgiving (T) ˌθæŋks'gɪv.ɪŋ (US) ˌ-'--, '-ˌ-- **-s** -z **Thanks'giving ˌDay** (US) **Thanks'giving ˌDay, 'Thanksgiving ˌDay**
thankworth|y 'θæŋkˌwɜː.ð|i (US) -ˌwɜːr- **-iness** -ɪ.nəs, -ɪ.nɪs
thank-you 'θæŋk.ju **-s** -z
Note: Although the most common abbreviation for 'thank you' is 'thanks', the pronunciation /kjuː/ is also heard in British English, usually with high pitch, in casual speech. **'thank-you ˌletter**
Thant θænt
that (*adj., demonstr. pron., adv.*) ðæt
Note: Weak form word. When used demonstratively it is always pronounced with its strong form /ðæt/, e.g. 'that's final', 'I like **that** one'.
that (*relative pron.*) *strong form:* ðæt *weak form:* ðət *weak form:* ðt
Note: The strong form is seldom used, except in very deliberate speech or when the word is said in isolation.
that (*conj.*) *strong form:* ðæt *weak form:* ðət
Note: The strong form is rarely used.
thataway 'ðæt.əˌweɪ (US) 'ðæt̬-
thatch θætʃ **-es** -ɪz **-ing** -ɪŋ **-ed** -t **-er/s** -əʳ/z (US) -ɚ/z
Thatcham 'θætʃ.əm
Thatch|er 'θætʃ|.əʳ (US) -ɚ **-erism** -ᵊr.ɪ.zᵊm **-erite/s** -ᵊr.aɪt/s (US) -ə.raɪt/s
thaumaturg|e 'θɔː.mə.tɜːdʒ (US) -tɜːrdʒ, 'θɑː- **-es** -ɪz
thaumaturgic ˌθɔː.mə'tɜː.dʒɪk (US) -'tɜːr-, ˌθɑː-
thaumaturg|y 'θɔː.mə.tɜː.dʒ|i (US) -tɜːr-, 'θɑː- **-ist/s** -ɪst/s
thaw (T) θɔː (US) θɑː, θɔː **-s** -z **-ing** -ɪŋ **-ed** -d
the *strong form:* ðiː *weak form before vowels:* ði *weak form before consonants:* ðə
Note: Weak form word. The strong form /ðiː/ is used for emphasis, e.g. 'This is **the** place to eat' or contrast, e.g. 'It's not **a** solution, but **the** solution'. Weak forms are /ðə/ before consonants, e.g 'the cat' /ðə'kæt/ and /ði/ before vowels, e.g. 'the apple' /ði'æp.l̩/.
Thea θɪə, 'θiː.ə (US) 'θiː.ə
Theakston 'θiːk.stən **-'s** -z
theatre, theater 'θɪə.təʳ, 'θiː.ə-; θi'et.əʳ (US) 'θiː.ə.t̬ɚ **-s** -z
theatregoer, theatergoer 'θɪə.təˌgəʊ.əʳ, 'θiː.ə-; θi'et.əˌ- (US) 'θiː.ə.t̬ɚˌgoʊ.ɚ **-s** -z
theatreland, theaterland 'θɪə.tə.lænd, 'θiː.ə-; θi'et.ə- (US) 'θiː.ə.t̬ɚ-
theatric|al θi'æt.rɪ.k|ᵊl **-als** -ᵊlz **-ally** -ᵊl.i, -li **-alness** -ᵊl.nəs, -nɪs **-alism** -ᵊl.ɪ.zᵊm
theatricality θiˌæt.rɪ'kæl.ə.ti, -ɪ.ti (US) -ə.t̬i
theatrics θi'æt.rɪks
Thebaid 'θiː.beɪ.ɪd, -bi-
Theban 'θiː.bən **-s** -z
thebe 'tiː.beɪ
Thebes θiːbz
thee *normal form:* ðiː *occasional weak form:* ði
theft θeft **-s** -s
thegn θeɪn **-s** -z
their *normal form:* ðeəʳ (US) ðer *occasional weak form when a vowel follows:* ðᵊr (US) ðɚ
Note: The weak form is found in commonly-used phrases such as 'on their own' /ˌɒn.ðᵊr'əʊn (US) ˌɑːn.ðɚ'oʊn/.
theirs ðeəz (US) ðerz
the|ism 'θiː|.ɪ.zᵊm **-ist/s** -ɪst/s
theistic θiː'ɪs.tɪk **-al** -ᵊl
Thelma 'θel.mə
Thelwall 'θel.wɔːl
Thelwell 'θel.wəl, -wel
them *strong form:* ðem *weak forms:* ðəm, ðm̩ *occasional weak forms:* əm, ᵊm
Note: Weak form word. The strong form /ðem/ is used for contrast, e.g. 'them and us' or for emphasis, e.g. 'look at **them**'. The weak form is usually /ðəm/, e.g. 'leave them alone' /ˌliːv.ðəm.ə'ləʊn (US) -'loʊn/, or in rapid, casual speech /ðm/, e.g. 'run them out', /ˌrʌn.ðm'aʊt/.
thematic θɪ'mæt.ɪk, θiː- (US) θiː'mæt̬- **-ally** -ᵊl.i, -li
theme θiːm **-s** -z **'theme ˌpark**
Themistocles θɪ'mɪs.tə.kliːz, θem'ɪs-, θə'mɪs- (US) θə'mɪs-
themselves ðəm'selvz (US) ðəm-, ðem-
then ðen
thence ðen*t*s
thenceforth ˌðen*t*s'fɔːθ (US) -'fɔːrθ
thenceforward ˌðen*t*s'fɔː.wəd (US) -'fɔːr.wɚd
theo- θiː.əʊ-, θɪə-; θi'ɒ- (US) θi.oʊ-, -ə-, θi'ɑː-
Note: Prefix. This is most commonly stressed on the second syllable, e.g. **theology** /θi'ɒl.ə.dʒi (US) θi'ɑː-/, but in other words there is instead secondary stress on the first syllable, e.g. **theological** /ˌθiː.ə'lɒdʒ.ɪ.kl̩ (US) -'lɑːdʒ-/. This prefix is not present in 'theory' and related words.
Theo 'θiː.əʊ (US) -oʊ
Theobald 'θiː.ə.bɔːld, 'θɪə- *formerly:* 'θɪb.ᵊld, 'tɪb- (US) 'θiː.ə.bɔːld, -bɑːld; 'tɪb.ᵊld
Theobalds *in Hertfordshire:* 'θiː.ə.bɔːldz, 'θɪə- (US) 'θiː.ə-, -bɑːldz *road in London:* 'θiː.ə.bɔːldz, 'θɪə- *formerly:* 'tɪb.ᵊldz (US) 'θiː.ə.bɔːldz, -bɑːldz; 'tɪb.ᵊldz
theocrac|y θi'ɒk.rə.s|i (US) -'ɑː.krə- **-ies** -iz
theocratic ˌθiː.əʊ'kræt.ɪk, ˌθɪə'- (US) ˌθiː.ə'kræt̬- **-al** -ᵊl
Theocritus θi'ɒk.rɪ.təs (US) -'ɑː.krə.t̬əs
theodicy θi'ɒd.ɪ.si, '-ə- (US) -'ɑː.də-
theodolite θi'ɒd.ᵊl.aɪt (US) -'ɑː.də.laɪt **-s** -s
Theodora ˌθiː.ə'dɔː.rə, ˌθɪə'- (US) ˌθiː.ə'dɔːr.ə
Theodore 'θiː.ə.dɔːʳ, 'θɪə- (US) 'θiː.ə.dɔːr
Theodoric θi'ɒd.ᵊr.ɪk (US) -'ɑː.dɚ-
Theodosi|a ˌθiː.ə'dəʊ.si|.ə, ˌθɪə'- (US) ˌθiː.oʊ'doʊ.ʃi|.ə, -ə'-, '-ʃ|ə **-us** -əs
theologian ˌθiː.ə'ləʊ.dʒᵊn, ˌθɪə'-, -dʒi.ən (US) ˌθiː.ə'loʊ.dʒᵊn, -dʒi.ən **-s** -z
theologic ˌθiː.ə'lɒdʒ.ɪk, ˌθɪə'- (US) ˌθiː.ə'lɑː.dʒɪk **-al** -ᵊl **-ally** -ᵊl.i, -li
theologi|cal ˌθiː.ə'lɒdʒ.ɪ|.kᵊl, ˌθɪə'- (US) ˌθiː.ə'lɑː.dʒɪ- **-cally** -kᵊl.i, -kli
theologiz|e, -is|e θi'ɒl.ə.dʒaɪz (US) -'ɑː.lə- **-es** -ɪz **-ing** -ɪŋ **-ed** -d
theolog|y θi'ɒl.ə.dʒ|i (US) -'ɑː.lə- **-ist/s** -ɪst/s
Theophilus θi'ɒf.ɪ.ləs, -ᵊl.əs (US) -'ɑː.fᵊl-
Theophrastus ˌθiː.əʊ'fræs.təs, ˌθɪə'- (US) ˌθiː.oʊ'-, -ə'-
theorbo θi'ɔː.bəʊ (US) -'ɔːr.boʊ **-s** -z
theorem 'θɪə.rəm, -rem, -rɪm (US) 'θiː.ɚ.əm, 'θɪr.əm, -em **-s** -z
theoretic θɪə'ret.ɪk, ˌθiː.ə'- (US) ˌθiː.ə'ret̬- **-al** -ᵊl **-ally** -ᵊl.i, -li
theoreti|cal θɪə'ret.ɪ|.kᵊl, ˌθiː.ə'- (US) ˌθiː.ə'ret̬- **-cally** -kᵊl.i, -kli
theoretician ˌθɪə.rə'tɪʃ.ᵊn, ˌθiː.ə-, -rɪ'-, -ret'ɪʃ- (US) ˌθiː.ə.rə'tɪʃ-, ˌθɪr.ə'- **-s** -z
theorist 'θɪə.rɪst, 'θiː.ə- (US) 'θiː.ɚ.ɪst, 'θɪr.ɪst **-s** -s
theoriz|e, -is|e 'θɪə.raɪz, 'θiː.ə- (US) 'θiː.ə-, 'θɪr.aɪz **-es** -ɪz **-ing** -ɪŋ **-ed** -d **-er/s** -əʳ/z (US) -ɚ/z
theor|y 'θɪə.r|i, 'θiː.ə- (US) 'θiː.ə-, 'θɪr|.i **-ies** -iz
theosophic ˌθiː.ə'sɒf.ɪk, ˌθɪə'- (US) ˌθiː.ə'sɑː.fɪk **-al** -ᵊl **-ally** -ᵊl.i, -li
theosophiz|e, -is|e θi'ɒs.ə.faɪz (US) -'ɑː.sə- **-es** -ɪz **-ing** -ɪŋ **-ed** -d
theosoph|y θi'ɒs.ə.f|i (US) -'ɑː.sə- **-ist/s** -ɪst/s **-ism** -ɪ.zᵊm
Thera 'θɪə.rə (US) 'θɪr.ə
therapeutic ˌθer.ə'pjuː.tɪk (US) -t̬ɪk **-s** -s **-ally** -ᵊl.i, -li

therapeutist ˌθer.əˈpjuː.tɪst Ⓤⓢ -t̬ɪst **-s** -s
therap|y ˈθer.ə.p|i **-ist/s** -ɪst/s
Theravada ˌθer.əˈvɑː.də
there *strong form:* ðeəʳ Ⓤⓢ ðer *weak form:* ðəʳ Ⓤⓢ ðɚ *alternative weak form before vowels:* ðᵊr Ⓤⓢ ðɚ
Note: Weak form word. The weak forms occur only when 'there' is used existentially as in 'there is', 'there are', 'there was', 'there won't be', etc. The strong form /ðeəʳ Ⓤⓢ ðer/ is also used in such expressions, and is the normal pronunciation for 'there' as a place adverbial, e.g. 'there it is'.
thereabout ˈðeə.rə.baʊt, ˌ--ˈ- Ⓤⓢ ˈðer.ə.baʊt, ˌ--ˈ- **-s** -s
Note: The form /ˌðeəʳ.əˈbaʊts Ⓤⓢ ˌðer-/ is always used in the expression 'there or thereabouts'.
thereafter ˌðeəˈrɑːf.təʳ Ⓤⓢ ˌðerˈæf.tɚ
thereat ˌðeəˈræt Ⓤⓢ ˌðer-
thereby ˌðeəˈbaɪ Ⓤⓢ ˌðer-
there'd ðeəd Ⓤⓢ ðerd
therefor ˌðeəˈfɔːʳ Ⓤⓢ ˌðerˈfɔːr
therefore ˈðeə.fɔːʳ Ⓤⓢ ˈðer.fɔːr
therefrom ˌðeəˈfrɒm Ⓤⓢ ˌðerˈfrʌm, -ˈfrɑːm
therein ˌðeəˈrɪn Ⓤⓢ ˌðerˈɪn
thereinafter ˌðeə.rɪnˈɑːf.təʳ Ⓤⓢ ˌðer.ɪnˈæf.tɚ
thereinto ˌðeəˈrɪn.tuː Ⓤⓢ ˌðerˈɪn-
there'll ðeəl *weak form:* ðəl, ðl̩ Ⓤⓢ ðerl
Note: See note for 'there'.
thereof ˌðeəˈrɒv Ⓤⓢ ˌðerˈɑːv, -ˈʌv
thereon ˌðeəˈrɒn Ⓤⓢ ˌðerˈɑːn
there's (= there is, there has) *strong form:* ðeəz Ⓤⓢ ðerz *weak form:* ðəz Ⓤⓢ ðɚz
Note: See note for 'there'.
Theresa tɪˈriː.zə, tə- Ⓤⓢ təˈriː.sə, -zə
thereto ˌðeəˈtuː Ⓤⓢ ˌðer-
theretofore ˌðeə.tuːˈfɔːʳ Ⓤⓢ ˌðer.t̬əˈfɔːr, ˈ---
thereunder ˌðeəˈrʌn.dəʳ Ⓤⓢ ˌðerˈʌn.dɚ
thereunto ˌðeəˈrʌn.tuː, ˌ--ˈ- Ⓤⓢ ˌðerˈʌn.tuː, ˌ--ˈ-
thereupon ˌðeə.rəˈpɒn, ˈ--- Ⓤⓢ ˌðer.əˈpɑːn, ˈ---
there've *strong forms:* ˈðeəʳ.əv Ⓤⓢ ˈðer- *weak forms:* ðəʳ.əv, ðəv Ⓤⓢ ðɚ.əv
therewith ˌðeəˈwɪð, -ˈwɪθ Ⓤⓢ ˌðer-
therewithal ˌðeə.wɪðˈɔːl, -wɪθˈ- *when used as a noun:* ˈ--- Ⓤⓢ ˌðer-, ˈ---
therm θɜːm Ⓤⓢ θɝːm **-s** -z
thermal ˈθɜː.mᵊl Ⓤⓢ ˈθɝː- **-ly** -i
thermic ˈθɜː.mɪk Ⓤⓢ ˈθɝː- **-ally** -ᵊl.i, -li
Thermidor ˈθɜː.mɪ.dɔːʳ Ⓤⓢ ˈθɝː.mə.dɔːr
thermion ˈθɜː.mi.ən Ⓤⓢ ˈθɝː- **-s** -z
thermionic ˌθɜː.miˈɒn.ɪk Ⓤⓢ ˌθɝː.miˈɑː.nɪk **-s** -s
thermistor θɜːˈmɪs.təʳ Ⓤⓢ ˈθɝː.mɪ.stɚ, θɚˈmɪs.tɚ **-s** -z
Thermit® ˈθɜː.mɪt Ⓤⓢ ˈθɝː-
thermite ˈθɜː.maɪt Ⓤⓢ ˈθɝː-
thermo- θɜː.məʊ-; θəˈmɒ- Ⓤⓢ θɝː.moʊ-, -mə-, θɚˈmɑː-
Note: Prefix. There may be primary or secondary stress on the first syllable, e.g. **thermocouple** /ˈθɜː.məˌkʌp.l̩ Ⓤⓢ ˈθɝː.mə-/, **thermometric** /ˌθɜː.məʊˈmet.rɪk Ⓤⓢ ˌθɝː.moʊˈ-/, or on the second syllable, e.g. **thermometer** /θəˈmɒm.ɪ.tə Ⓤⓢ θɚˈmɑː.mə.t̬ɚ/.
thermocouple ˈθɜː.məʊˌkʌp.l̩ Ⓤⓢ ˈθɝː.moʊ-, -mə- **-s** -z
thermodynamic ˌθɜː.məʊ.daɪˈnæm.ɪk, -dɪˈ- Ⓤⓢ ˌθɝː.moʊ.daɪˈ-, -mə- **-s** -s **-ally** -ᵊl.i, -li
thermoelectric ˌθɜː.məʊ.ɪˈlek.trɪk, -əˈ- Ⓤⓢ ˌθɝː.moʊ- **-ally** -ᵊl.i, -li
thermoelectricity ˌθɜː.məʊ.ɪˌlekˈtrɪs.ə.ti, -əˌ-, -ˌiː.lekˈ-, -ˈtrɪz-, -ɪ.ti Ⓤⓢ ˌθɝː.moʊˌiː.lekˈtrɪs.ə.t̬i
thermograph ˈθɜː.məʊ.grɑːf, -græf Ⓤⓢ ˈθɝː.moʊ.græf, -mə- **-s** -s
thermometer θəˈmɒm.ɪ.təʳ, ˈ-ə- Ⓤⓢ θɚˈmɑː.mə.t̬ɚ **-s** -z
thermometric ˌθɜː.məʊˈmet.rɪk Ⓤⓢ ˌθɝː.moʊˈ-, -məˈ- **-al** -ᵊl **-ally** -ᵊl.i, -li
thermonuclear ˌθɜː.məʊˈnjuː.kli.əʳ Ⓤⓢ ˌθɝː.moʊˈnuː.kli.ɚ, -məˈ-, -ˈnjuː-
thermopile ˈθɜː.məʊ.paɪl Ⓤⓢ ˈθɝː.moʊ-, -mə- **-s** -z
thermoplastic ˌθɜː.məʊˈplæs.tɪk, -ˈplɑː.stɪk Ⓤⓢ ˌθɝː.moʊˈplæs.tɪk, -məˈ- **-s** -s
Thermopylae θɜːˈmɒp.ɪ.liː, θə-, -ᵊl.iː, -i, -aɪ Ⓤⓢ θɚˈmɑː.pə.liː
Thermos® ˈθɜː.mɒs, -məs Ⓤⓢ ˈθɝː.məs **-es** -ɪz ˈ**Thermos** ˌ**flask**
thermosetting ˈθɜː.məʊˌset.ɪŋ Ⓤⓢ ˈθɝː.moʊˌset̬-, -məˌ-
thermostat ˈθɜː.mə.stæt Ⓤⓢ ˈθɝː.mə- **-s** -s **-(t)ing** -ɪŋ **-(t)ed** -ɪd
thermostatic ˌθɜː.məˈstæt.ɪk Ⓤⓢ ˌθɝː.məˈstæt̬-
Theroux θəˈruː
Thersites θɜːˈsaɪ.tiːz, θə- Ⓤⓢ θɚˈsaɪ-
thesaur|us θɪˈsɔː.r|əs, θiː-, θə- Ⓤⓢ θɪˈsɔːr|.əs **-i** -aɪ **-uses** -ə.sɪz
these (*plur. of* **this**) ðiːz
Theseus *in Greek legend:* ˈθiː.sjuːs, -sjəs, -si.əs Ⓤⓢ -si.əs, -sjuːs *Shakespearian character, and as name of ship:* ˈθiː.sjəs, -si.əs
Thesiger ˈθes.ɪ.dʒəʳ Ⓤⓢ -dʒɚ
thes|is *dissertation:* ˈθiː.s|ɪs **-es** -iːz
thesis *metrical term:* ˈθes.ɪs, ˈθiː.sɪs Ⓤⓢ ˈθiː.sɪs
thespian (T) ˈθes.pi.ən **-s** -z
Thespis ˈθes.pɪs
Thessalonian ˌθes.ᵊlˈəʊ.ni.ən Ⓤⓢ -əˈloʊ- **-s** -z
Thessalonika ˌθes.ᵊlˈɒn.ɪ.kə Ⓤⓢ -əˈlɑː.nɪ-
Thessaly ˈθes.ᵊl.i
theta ˈθiː.tə Ⓤⓢ ˈθeɪ.t̬ə, ˈθiː- **-s** -z
Thetford ˈθet.fəd Ⓤⓢ -fɚd
Thetis *Greek:* ˈθet.ɪs Ⓤⓢ ˈθet̬- *otherwise:* ˈθiː.tɪs Ⓤⓢ -t̬ɪs
thews θjuːz
they ðeɪ
they'd ðeɪd
Theydon Bois ˌθeɪ.dᵊnˈbɔɪz
they'd've ˈðeɪ.dᵊv
they'll ðeɪl
they're ðeəʳ Ⓤⓢ ðer
they've ðeɪv
thiamin(e) ˈθaɪə.miːn, -mɪn Ⓤⓢ -mɪn, -miːn
thick θɪk **-er** -əʳ Ⓤⓢ -ɚ **-est** -ɪst, -əst **-ly** -li **-ness/es** -nəs/ɪz, -nɪs/ɪz **as** ˌ**thick as** ˈ**thieves ; as** ˌ**thick as** ˌ**two** ˌ**short** ˈ**planks ;** ˌ**give someone a** ˌ**thick** ˈ**ear ; through** ˌ**thick and** ˈ**thin**
thicken ˈθɪk.ᵊn **-s** -z **-ing** -ɪŋ, ˈθɪk.nɪŋ **-ed** -d **-er/s** -əʳ/z Ⓤⓢ -ɚ/z
thicket ˈθɪk.ɪt **-s** -s
thickhead ˈθɪk.hed **-s** -z
thickheaded ˌθɪkˈhed.ɪd Ⓤⓢ ˈ-ˌ--, ˌ-ˈ-- **-ness** -nəs, -nɪs *stress shift, British only:* ˌthickheaded ˈfool
thickish ˈθɪk.ɪʃ
thickset ˌθɪkˈset Ⓤⓢ ˈ--, ˌ-ˈ- *stress shift, British only:* ˌthickset ˈman
thick-skinned ˌθɪkˈskɪnd Ⓤⓢ ˈ--, ˌ-ˈ- *stress shift, British only:* ˌthick-skinned ˈman
thick-skulled ˌθɪkˈskʌld Ⓤⓢ ˈ--, ˌ-ˈ- *stress shift, British only:* ˌthick-skulled ˈidiot
thick-witted ˌθɪkˈwɪt.ɪd Ⓤⓢ ˈθɪkˌwɪt̬.ɪd, ˌ-ˈ-- *stress shift, British only:* ˌthick-witted ˈfool
thie|f θiː|f **-ves** -vz
Thiès tjez Ⓤⓢ tjes
thiev|e θiːv **-es** -z **-ing** -ɪŋ **-ed** -d **-ery** -ᵊr.i
thievish ˈθiː.vɪʃ **-ly** -li **-ness** -nəs, -nɪs
thigh θaɪ **-s** -z
thighbone ˈθaɪ.bəʊn Ⓤⓢ -boʊn **-s** -z
thill θɪl **-s** -z
thimble ˈθɪm.bl̩ **-s** -z **-ful/s** -fʊl/z
thimblerig ˈθɪm.bl̩.rɪg **-s** -z **-ging** -ɪŋ **-ged** -d
Thimbu ˈθɪm.buː
Thimphu ˈθɪm*p*.fuː

thin θɪn **-ner** -ər (US) -ɚ **-nest** -ɪst, -əst **-ly** -li **-ness** -nəs, -nɪs **-s** -z **-ning** -ɪŋ **-ned** -d **into ˌthin 'air**
thine ðaɪn
thing θɪŋ **-s** -z
thingamabob 'θɪŋ.ə.məˌbɒb (US) -ˌbɑːb **-s** -z
thingamajig 'θɪŋ.ə.məˌdʒɪg **-s** -z
thingam|y 'θɪŋ.ə.m|i **-ies** -iz
thingie 'θɪŋ.i **-s** -z
thingumabob 'θɪŋ.ə.məˌbɒb (US) -ˌbɑːb **-s** -z
thingumajig 'θɪŋ.ə.məˌdʒɪg **-s** -z
thingumm|y 'θɪŋ.ə.m|i **-ies** -iz
thing|y 'θɪŋ|.i **-ies** -iz
think θɪŋk **-s** -s **-ing/ly** -ɪŋ/li **thought** θɔːt (US) θɑːt, θɔːt **thinker/s** 'θɪŋ.kər/z (US) -kɚ/z **'think ˌtank**
thinkable 'θɪŋ.kə.bl̩
thinktank 'θɪŋkˌtæŋk **-s** -s
Thinn θɪn
thinnish 'θɪn.ɪʃ
thin-skinned ˌθɪn'skɪnd (US) '-- *stress shift, British only:* ˌthin-skinned 'person
third θɜːd (US) θɜːrd **-s** -z **-ly** -li **ˌthird 'class ; ˌthird di'mension ; ˌthird 'party ; ˌthird 'person ; ˌThird 'World ; ˌgive someone the ˌthird de'gree**
third-degree ˌθɜːd.dɪ'griː, -də'- (US) ˌθɜːrd- *stress shift, see compound:* **ˌthird-degree 'burn**
thirdhand ˌθɜːd'hænd (US) ˌθɜːrd- *stress shift:* ˌthirdhand 'gossip
third-ra|te ˌθɜːd'reɪ|t (US) ˌθɜːrd- **-ter/s** -tər/z (US) -t̬ɚ/z *stress shift:* ˌthird-rate 'drama
Thirsk θɜːsk (US) θɜːrsk
thirst θɜːst (US) θɜːrst **-s** -s **-ing** -ɪŋ **-ed** -ɪd
thirst|y 'θɜː.st|i (US) 'θɜːr- **-ier** -i.ər (US) -i.ɚ **-iest** -i.ɪst, -i.əst **-ily** -ɪ.li, -əl.i **-iness** -ɪ.nəs, -ɪ.nɪs
thirteen θɜː'tiːn (US) θɜːr- **-s** -z *stress shift:* ˌthirteen 'pounds
thirteenth θɜː'tiːntθ (US) θɜːr- **-s** -s *stress shift:* ˌthirteenth 'place
thirtieth 'θɜː.ti.əθ (US) 'θɜːr.t̬i- **-s** -s
thirt|y 'θɜː.t|i (US) 'θɜːr.t̬|i **-ies** -iz **'thirty ˌsomething ; ˌThirty ˌYears' 'War**
thirtyfold 'θɜː.ti.fəʊld (US) 'θɜːr.t̬i.foʊld
this ðɪs *occasional weak form:* ðəs
Note: Some speakers use a weak form /ðəs/ in 'this morning, afternoon, evening'. **ˌthis, ˌthat, and the 'other**
Thisbe 'θɪz.bi
Thiselton 'θɪs.l̩.tən
thistle 'θɪs.l̩ **-s** -z
thistledown 'θɪs.l̩.daʊn
thistly 'θɪs.l̩.i, '-li
thither 'ðɪð.ər (US) 'θɪð.ɚ, 'ðɪð- **-ward/s** -wəd/z (US) -wɚd/z
tho' ðəʊ (US) ðoʊ
Thoday 'θəʊ.deɪ (US) 'θoʊ-
thole θəʊl (US) θoʊl **-s** -z
Thom tɒm (US) tɑːm
Thomas 'tɒm.əs (US) 'tɑː.məs
Thomasin 'tɒm.ə.sɪn (US) 'tɑː.mə-
Thomond 'θəʊ.mənd (US) 'θoʊ-
Thompson 'tɒmp.sən (US) 'tɑːmp-
Thompstone 'tɒmp.stəʊn (US) 'tɑːmp.stoʊn
Thomson 'tɒmp.sən (US) 'tɑːmp-
-thon -θɒn, -θən (US) -θɑːn
Note: Suffix. Normally unstressed, e.g. /'mær.ə.θən (US) 'mer.ə.θɑːn/.
thong θɒŋ (US) θɑːŋ, θɔːŋ **-s** -z
Thor θɔːr (US) θɔːr
Thora 'θɔː.rə (US) 'θɔːr.ə
thoraces (*alternative plur. of* **thorax**) 'θɔː.rə.siːz
thoracic θɔː'ræs.ɪk, θɒr'æs-, θə'ræs- (US) θɔː'ræs-, θə-
thorax 'θɔː.ræks (US) 'θɔːr.æks **-es** -ɪz
Thorburn 'θɔː.bɜːn (US) 'θɔːr.bɚn
Thoreau θɔː'rəʊ, θə-; 'θɔː.rəʊ (US) θə'roʊ, θɔː-; 'θɔːr.oʊ
thorium 'θɔː.ri.əm (US) 'θɔːr.i-
thorn (T) θɔːn (US) θɔːrn **-s** -z **a ˌthorn in one's 'flesh/side**
Thornaby 'θɔː.nə.bi (US) 'θɔːr-
Thornbury 'θɔːn.bər.i, 'θɔːm- (US) 'θɔːrn.ber-, -bɚ-
thornbush 'θɔːn.bʊʃ, 'θɔːm- (US) 'θɔːrn- **-es** -ɪz
Thorndike 'θɔːn.daɪk (US) 'θɔːrn-
Thorne θɔːn (US) θɔːrn
Thorneycroft 'θɔː.nɪ.krɒft (US) 'θɔːr.nɪ.krɑːft
Thornhill 'θɔːn.hɪl (US) 'θɔːrn-
thornless 'θɔːn.ləs, -lɪs (US) 'θɔːrn-
Thornton 'θɔːn.tən (US) 'θɔːrn.tən
thorn|y 'θɔː.n|i (US) 'θɔːr- **-ier** -i.ər (US) -i.ɚ **-iest** -i.ɪst, -i.əst **-ily** -ɪ.li, -əl.i **-iness** -ɪ.nəs, -ɪ.nɪs
Thorold 'θɒr.əld, 'θʌr- (US) 'θɔːr-, 'θɜːr-
thorough 'θʌr.ə (US) 'θɜːr.oʊ, -ə **-ly** -li **-ness** -nəs, -nɪs
thoroughbass 'θʌr.ə.beɪs (US) 'θɜːr.oʊ-, '-ə-
thoroughbred 'θʌr.ə.bred (US) 'θɜːr.oʊ-, '-ə- **-s** -z
thoroughfare 'θʌr.ə.feər (US) 'θɜːr.oʊ.fer, '-ə- **-s** -z
thoroughgoing ˌθʌr.ə'gəʊ.ɪŋ (US) ˌθɜːr.oʊ'goʊ-, -ə'-
thorough-paced ˌθʌr.ə'peɪst (US) 'θɜːr.oʊ.peɪst, '-ə-
Thorowgood 'θʌr.ə.gʊd (US) 'θɜːr.oʊ-
Thorpe θɔːp (US) θɔːrp
Thorrowgood 'θʌr.ə.gʊd (US) 'θɜːr-
those (*plur. of* **that**) ðəʊz (US) ðoʊz
Thoth θəʊθ, təʊt, θɒθ (US) θoʊθ, toʊt
thou *you:* ðaʊ
thou (*abbrev. for* **thousand**) θaʊ
though ðəʊ (US) ðoʊ
thought (*from* **think**) θɔːt (US) θɑːt, θɔːt **-s** -s
thoughtful 'θɔːt.fəl, -fʊl (US) 'θɑːt-, 'θɔːt- **-ly** -i **-ness** -nəs, -nɪs
thoughtless 'θɔːt.ləs, -lɪs (US) 'θɑːt-, 'θɔːt- **-ly** -li **-ness** -nəs, -nɪs
thought-out ˌθɔːt'aʊt (US) ˌθɑːt̬-, ˌθɔːt̬-
thought-provoking 'θɔːt.prəˌvəʊ.kɪŋ (US) 'θɑːt.prəˌvoʊ-, 'θɔːt-
Thouless 'θaʊ.les, -lɪs
thous|and 'θaʊ.zənd **-ands** -əndz **ˌThousand ˌIsland 'dressing**
thousandfold 'θaʊ.zənd.fəʊld (US) -foʊld
thousandth 'θaʊ.zəndθ **-s** -s
Thrace θreɪs
Thracian 'θreɪ.ʃən, -ʃi.ən (US) '-ʃən **-s** -z
thrall θrɔːl (US) θrɔːl, θrɑːl **-s** -z **-ing** -ɪŋ **-ed** -d
thral(l)dom 'θrɔːl.dəm (US) 'θrɔːl-, 'θrɑːl-
thrash θræʃ **-es** -ɪz **-ing** -ɪŋ **-ed** -t **-er/s** -ər/z (US) -ɚ/z
thread θred **-s** -z **-ing** -ɪŋ **-ed** -ɪd
threadbare 'θred.beər (US) -ber
Threadneedle ˌθred'niː.dl̩, '-ˌ--
thread|y 'θred|.i **-iness** -ɪ.nəs, -ɪ.nɪs
threat θret **-s** -s
threaten 'θret.ən **-s** -z **-ing/ly** -ɪŋ/li, 'θret.nɪŋ/li **-ed** -d
three θriː **-s** -z **three R's** ˌθriː'ɑːz (US) -'ɑːrz
three-cornered ˌθriː'kɔː.nəd (US) -'kɔːr- *stress shift:* ˌthree-cornered 'hat
three-D, 3-D ˌθriː'diː *stress shift:* ˌthree-D 'glasses
three-day ˌθriː'deɪ **ˌthree-day e'vent ; ˌthree-day 'week**
three-decker ˌθriː'dek.ər (US) 'θriːˌdek.ɚ **-s** -z
three-dimensional ˌθriː.dɪ'men.tʃən.əl, -daɪ'-, -'mentʃ.nəl (US) -də'ment.ʃən.əl
threefold 'θriː.fəʊld (US) -foʊld
threeish 'θriː.ɪʃ
three-legged ˌθriː'legd, -'leg.ɪd (US) 'θriː.legd, -ˌleg.ɪd *stress shift:* ˌthree-legged 'stool **ˌthree-'legged ˌrace**
three-line ˌθriː'laɪn *stress shift, see compound:* **ˌthree-line 'whip**
three|pence 'θre|p.ənts, 'θrɪ|p-, 'θrʌ|p-, 'θrʊ|p- **-pences** -pənt.sɪz **-penny** -pən.i, -p.ni
Note: See note for **penny**.
three-piece ˌθriː'piːs *stress shift, see compound:* **ˌthree-piece 'suite**

three-ply 'θriː.plaɪ, ˌ-'-
three-point ˌθriː'pɔɪnt *stress shift, see compound:* **ˌthree-point 'turn**
three-quarter ˌθriː'kwɔː.təʳ ⓤⓢ -'kwɔːr.t̬ɚ **-s** -z *stress shift:* ˌthree-quarter 'length
three-ring ˌθriː'rɪŋ *stress shift, see compound:* **ˌthree-ring 'circus**
threescore ˌθriː'skɔːʳ ⓤⓢ 'θriː.skɔːr *stress shift:* ˌthreescore 'years **ˌthreescore ˌyears and 'ten**
threesome 'θriː.səm **-s** -z
three-star ˌθriː'stɑːʳ ⓤⓢ -'stɑːr *stress shift:* ˌthree-star ho'tel
threnod|y 'θren.ə.d|i, 'θriː.nə- ⓤⓢ 'θren.ə- **-ies** -iz
thresh θreʃ **-es** -ɪz **-ing** -ɪŋ **-ed** -t **-er/s** -əʳ/z ⓤⓢ -ɚ/z **'threshing maˌchine**
thresher (T®) 'θreʃ.əʳ ⓤⓢ -ɚ **-s** -z
threshold 'θreʃ.*h*əʊld ⓤⓢ -*h*oʊld **-s** -z
threw (*from* **throw**) θruː
thrice θraɪs
thrift θrɪft **'thrift ˌshop**
thriftless 'θrɪft.ləs, -lɪs **-ly** -li **-ness** -nəs, -nɪs
thrift|y 'θrɪf.t|i **-ier** -i.əʳ ⓤⓢ -i.ɚ **-iest** -i.ɪst, -i.əst **-ily** -ɪ.li, -ᵊl.i **-iness** -ɪ.nəs, -ɪ.nɪs
thrill θrɪl **-s** -z **-ing/ly** -ɪŋ/li **-ed** -d **-er/s** -əʳ/z ⓤⓢ -ɚ/z
Thring θrɪŋ
thrip θrɪp **-s** -s
thriv|e θraɪv **-es** -z **-ing** -ɪŋ **-ed** -d **throve** θrəʊv ⓤⓢ θroʊv **thriven** 'θrɪv.ᵊn
thro' θruː
throat θrəʊt ⓤⓢ θroʊt **-s** -s **-ed** -ɪd ⓤⓢ 'θroʊ.t̬ɪd
throat|y 'θrəʊ.t|i ⓤⓢ 'θroʊ.t̬|i **-ier** -i.əʳ ⓤⓢ -i.ɚ **-iest** -i.ɪst, -i.əst **-ily** -ɪ.li, -ᵊl.i **-iness** -ɪ.nəs, -ɪ.nɪs
throb θrɒb ⓤⓢ θrɑːb **-s** -z **-bing/ly** -ɪŋ/li **-bed** -d
throes θrəʊz ⓤⓢ θroʊz
Throgmorton θrɒg'mɔː.tᵊn, '--- ⓤⓢ θrɑːg'mɔːr-, θrɔːg-, '---
thrombin 'θrɒm.bɪn ⓤⓢ 'θrɑːm-
thrombos|is θrɒm'bəʊ.s|ɪs ⓤⓢ θrɑːm'boʊ- **-es** -iːz
thromb|us 'θrɒm.b|əs ⓤⓢ 'θrɑːm- **-i** -aɪ
thron|e θrəʊn ⓤⓢ θroʊn **-es** -z **-ing** -ɪŋ **-ed** -d
throng θrɒŋ ⓤⓢ θrɑːŋ, θrɔːŋ **-s** -z **-ing** -ɪŋ **-ed** -d
throstle 'θrɒs.l̩ ⓤⓢ 'θrɑː.sl̩ **-s** -z
throttl|e 'θrɒt.l̩ ⓤⓢ 'θrɑː.t̬l̩ **-es** -z **-ing** -ɪŋ, 'θrɒt.lɪŋ ⓤⓢ 'θrɑːt- **-ed** -d
through θruː **ˌthrough and 'through**
Througham 'θrʌf.əm
throughout θru'aʊt
throughput 'θruː.pʊt **-s** -s
throve (*from* **thrive**) θrəʊv ⓤⓢ θroʊv
throw θrəʊ ⓤⓢ θroʊ **-s** -z **-ing** -ɪŋ **threw** θruː **thrown** θrəʊn ⓤⓢ θroʊn **thrower/s** 'θrəʊ.əʳ/z ⓤⓢ 'θroʊ.ɚ/z
throwaway 'θrəʊ.ə.weɪ ⓤⓢ 'θroʊ- **-s**
throwback 'θrəʊ.bæk ⓤⓢ 'θroʊ- **-s** -s
thru θruː
thrum θrʌm **-s** -z **-ming** -ɪŋ **-med** -d
thrush θrʌʃ **-es** -ɪz
thrust θrʌst **-s** -s **-ing** -ɪŋ
thruway 'θruː.weɪ **-s** -z
Thucydides θjuː'sɪd.ɪ.diːz, θjʊ-, '-ə- ⓤⓢ θuː'sɪd.ə-
thud θʌd **-s** -z **-ding** -ɪŋ **-ded** -ɪd
thug θʌg **-s** -z
thuggery 'θʌg.ᵊr.i
thuggish 'θʌg.ɪʃ **-ly** -li **-ness** -nəs, -nɪs
thuja 'θuː.jə ⓤⓢ 'θuː-, 'θjuː- **-s** -z
Thule *Northernmost region of the world:* 'θjuː.liː, 'θuː-, -li; θuːl ⓤⓢ 'θuː.li, 'θjuː-, 'tuː-, 'tjuː- *Eskimo settlement:* 'tuː.li ⓤⓢ 'θuː-, 'θjuː-
thulium 'θuː.li.əm ⓤⓢ 'θuː-, 'θjuː-
thumb θʌm **-s** -z **-ing** -ɪŋ **-ed** -d **ˌthumb 'index**
thumbnail 'θʌm.neɪl **-s** -z **ˌthumbnail 'sketch**
thumbprint 'θʌm.prɪnt **-s** -s
thumbscrew 'θʌm.skruː **-s** -z
thumbs-down ˌθʌmz'daʊn
thumbstall 'θʌm.stɔːl ⓤⓢ -stɔːl, -stɑːl **-s** -z
thumbs-up ˌθʌmz'ʌp
thumbtack 'θʌm.tæk **-s** -s
Thummim 'θʌm.ɪm *in Jewish usage also:* 'θʊm-, tʊm-
thump θʌmp **-s** -s **-ing** -ɪŋ **-ed** -t **-er/s** -əʳ/z ⓤⓢ -ɚ/z
Thun tuːn
thund|er 'θʌn.d|əʳ ⓤⓢ -d|ɚ **-ers** -əz ⓤⓢ -ɚz **-ering/ly** -ᵊr.ɪŋ/li **-ered** -əd ⓤⓢ -ɚd **-erer/s** -ᵊr.əʳ/z ⓤⓢ -ɚ.ɚ/z
thunderbird (T) 'θʌn.də.bɜːd ⓤⓢ -dɚ.bɜːrd **-s** -z
thunderbolt 'θʌn.də.bəʊlt ⓤⓢ -dɚ.boʊlt **-s** -s
thunderclap 'θʌn.də.klæp ⓤⓢ -dɚ- **-s** -s
thundercloud 'θʌn.də.klaʊd ⓤⓢ -dɚ- **-s** -z
thunderfl|y 'θʌn.də.fl|aɪ ⓤⓢ -dɚ- **-ies** -aɪz
thunderhead 'θʌn.də.hed ⓤⓢ -dɚ- **-s** -z
thunderous 'θʌn.dᵊr.əs **-ly** -li
thunderstorm 'θʌn.də.stɔːm ⓤⓢ -dɚ.stɔːrm **-s** -z
thunderstruck 'θʌn.də.strʌk ⓤⓢ -dɚ-
thunder|y 'θʌn.dᵊr|.i **-iness** -ɪ.nəs, -ɪ.nɪs
Thur. (*abbrev. for* **Thursday**) 'θɜːz.deɪ, -di ⓤⓢ 'θɜːrz-
Note: This abbreviation may also be pronounced /θɜːʳ/ in British English.
Thurber 'θɜː.bəʳ ⓤⓢ 'θɜːr.bɚ
Thurcroft 'θɜː.krɒft ⓤⓢ 'θɜːr.krɑːft
thurible 'θjʊə.rɪ.bl̩, 'θjɔː-, -rə- ⓤⓢ 'θɜːr.ə-, 'θʊr-, 'θjʊr- **-s** -z
Thuringi|a θjʊə'rɪn.dʒi|.ə, tʊə-, -'rɪŋ.gi|.ə ⓤⓢ θʊ'rɪn.dʒi|.ə, θjʊ-, '-dʒ|ə **-an/s** -ən/z
Thurloe, Thurlow 'θɜː.ləʊ ⓤⓢ 'θɜːr.loʊ
Thurnscoe 'θɜːnz.kəʊ ⓤⓢ 'θɜːrnz.koʊ
Thuron tʊə'rɒn, tə- ⓤⓢ -'rɑːn
Thurs. (*abbrev. for* **Thursday**) 'θɜːz.deɪ, -di ⓤⓢ 'θɜːrz-
Note: This abbreviation may also be pronounced /θɜːz/in British English.
Thursday 'θɜːz.deɪ, -di ⓤⓢ 'θɜːrz- **-s** -z
Thurso 'θɜː.səʊ, -zəʊ ⓤⓢ 'θɜːr.soʊ, -zoʊ
Thurston 'θɜː.stᵊn ⓤⓢ 'θɜːr-
thus ðʌs
thwack θwæk **-s** -s **-ing** -ɪŋ **-ed** -t
Thwackum 'θwæk.əm
thwaite (T) θweɪt **-s** -s
thwart *of a boat:* θwɔːt ⓤⓢ θwɔːrt *in nautical usage also:* θɔːt ⓤⓢ θɔːrt **-s** -s
thwart (*v.*) θwɔːt ⓤⓢ θwɔːrt **-s** -s **-ing** -ɪŋ ⓤⓢ 'θwɔːr.t̬ɪŋ **-ed** -ɪd ⓤⓢ 'θwɔːr.t̬ɪd
thy ðaɪ
thyme taɪm **-s** -z
thymine 'θaɪ.miːn ⓤⓢ -miːn, -mɪn
thymol 'θaɪ.mɒl ⓤⓢ -mɔːl, -moʊl
thymus 'θaɪ.məs **-es** -ɪz
Thynne θɪn
thyroid 'θaɪ.rɔɪd **-s** -z **'thyroid ˌgland**
thyroxin θaɪ'rɒk.siːn, -sɪn ⓤⓢ -'rɑːk-
Thyrsis 'θɜː.sɪs ⓤⓢ 'θɜːr-
thyself ðaɪ'self
Tia Maria® ˌtiː.ə.mə'riː.ə
Tiananmen Square tiˌæn.ən.mɪn'skweəʳ, -men'- ⓤⓢ ˌtjɑː.nɑːn.mɪn'skwer; tiˌæn.ən-
Tianjin ˌtjen'dʒɪn
tiara ti'ɑː.rə ⓤⓢ -'er.ə, -'ær-, -'ɑːr- **-s** -z **-ed** -d
Tibbitts 'tɪb.ɪts
Tibbs tɪbz
Tiber 'taɪ.bəʳ ⓤⓢ -bɚ
Tiberias taɪ'bɪə.ri.æs, -əs ⓤⓢ -'bɪr.i.əs
Tiberius taɪ'bɪə.ri.əs ⓤⓢ -'bɪr.i-
Tibet tɪ'bet
Tibetan tɪ'bet.ᵊn **-s** -s
tibi|a 'tɪb.i|.ə, 'taɪ.bi- ⓤⓢ 'tɪb.i- **-ae** -iː **-as** -əz
Tibullus tɪ'bʌl.əs, -'bʊl-
tic tɪk **-s** -s
tic douloureux ˌtɪk.duː.lᵊr'ɜː ⓤⓢ -lʊ'ruː
tic|e taɪs **-es** -ɪz **-ing** -ɪŋ **-ed** -t
Ticehurst 'taɪs.hɜːst ⓤⓢ -hɜːrst
Tichborne 'tɪtʃ.bɔːn, -bən ⓤⓢ -bɔːrn, -bɚn
Ticino tɪ'tʃiː.nəʊ ⓤⓢ -noʊ

tick tɪk **-s** -s **-ing** -ɪŋ **-ed** -t **-er/s** -əʳ/z (US) -ɚ/z ˌ**ticking 'off**
tickertape 'tɪk.ə.teɪp (US) '-ɚ- ˌ**tickertape re'ception** ; **'tickertape ˌparade**
tick|et 'tɪk|.ɪt **-ets** -ɪts **-eting** -ɪ.tɪŋ (US) -ɪ.t̬ɪŋ **-eted** -ɪ.tɪd (US) -ɪ.t̬ɪd **'ticket ˌoffice**
tickety-boo ˌtɪk.ɪ.ti'buː, ˌ-ə- (US) -ə.t̬i'-
ticking 'tɪk.ɪŋ **-s** -z
ticking-off ˌtɪk.ɪŋ'ɒf (US) -'ɑːf **tickings-off** ˌtɪk.ɪŋz'ɒf (US) -'ɑːf
tickl|e 'tɪk.l̩ **-es** -z **-ing** -ɪŋ, 'tɪk.lɪŋ **-ed** -d **-er/s** -əʳ/z, 'tɪk.ləʳ/z (US) '-l̩.ɚ/z, '-lɚ/z
Tickler 'tɪk.ləʳ (US) -lɚ
ticklish 'tɪk.lɪʃ, '-l̩.ɪʃ **-ly** -li **-ness** -nəs, -nɪs
tickl|y 'tɪk.l̩|.i, '-l|i **-ier** -i.əʳ (US) -i.ɚ **-iest** -i.ɪst, -i.əst **-iness** -ɪ.nəs, -ɪ.nɪs
ticktacktoe ˌtɪkˌtæk'təʊ (US) -'toʊ
ticktock 'tɪk.tɒk (US) -tɑːk **-s** -s
tic-tac-toe ˌtɪkˌtæk'təʊ (US) -'toʊ
tidal 'taɪ.dəl **'tidal ˌwave**, ˌ**tidal 'wave**
tidbit 'tɪd.bɪt **-s** -s
tiddledywink 'tɪd.l̩.di.wɪŋk **-s** -s
tiddler 'tɪd.l̩.əʳ, '-ləʳ (US) '-lɚ, '-l̩.ɚ **-s** -z
Tiddles 'tɪd.l̩z
tiddl|y 'tɪd.l|i, '-l̩|.i **-ier** -i.əʳ (US) -i.ɚ **-iest** -i.ɪst, -i.əst **-iness** -ɪ.nəs, -ɪ.nɪs
tiddlywink 'tɪd.l̩.i.wɪŋk, '-li- (US) '-li-, '-l̩.i- **-s** -s
tid|e taɪd **-es** -z **-ing** -ɪŋ **-ed** -ɪd
tideland 'taɪd.lænd **-s** -z
tidemark 'taɪd.mɑːk (US) -mɑːrk **-s** -s
tidewater 'taɪdˌwɔː.təʳ (US) -ˌwɑː.t̬ɚ, -ˌwɔː-
tideway 'taɪd.weɪ
tidings 'taɪ.dɪŋz
Tidworth 'tɪd.wəθ, -wɜːθ (US) -wɚθ, -wɜːrθ
tid|y 'taɪ.d|i **-ies** -iz **-ier** -i.əʳ (US) -i.ɚ **-iest** -i.ɪst, -i.əst **-ily** -ɪ.li, -əl.i **-iness** -ɪ.nəs, -ɪ.nɪs **-ying** -i.ɪŋ **-ied** -id
tie taɪ **-s** -z **tying** 'taɪ.ɪŋ **tieing** 'taɪ.ɪŋ **tied** taɪd **'tie ˌbreak** ; ˌ**tied 'house**
tie-break 'taɪ.breɪk **-s** -s **-er/s** -əʳ/z (US) -ɚ/z
tie-dy|e 'taɪ.daɪ **-es** -z **-ing** -ɪŋ **-ed** -d
tie-in 'taɪ.ɪn **-s** -z
Tientsin ˌtjent'sɪn
tiepin 'taɪ.pɪn **-s** -z
Tiepolo ti'ep.əl.əʊ (US) -ə.loʊ
tier *one who ties:* 'taɪ.əʳ (US) -ɚ **-s** -z
tier *set of seats in theatre, etc.:* tɪəʳ (US) tɪr **-s** -z **-ed** -d
tierc|e *in music, fencing, cash:* tɪəs (US) tɪrs **-es** -ɪz
tierc|e *in cards:* tɜːs, tɪəs (US) tɪrs **-es** -ɪz
tiercel 'tɜː.səl, 'tɪə- (US) 'tɪr- **-s** -z
Tierra del Fuego tiˌer.ə.del'fweɪ.gəʊ, ˌtjer.ə-, -fu'eɪ- (US) tiˌer.ə.del'fweɪ.goʊ
tiff tɪf **-s** -s **-ing** -ɪŋ **-ed** -t
tiffany (T) 'tɪf.ən.i
tiffin (T) 'tɪf.ɪn **-s** -z
Tiflis 'tɪf.lɪs
tig tɪg **-s** -z
tig|e tiːʒ **-es** -ɪz
tiger 'taɪ.gəʳ (US) -gɚ **-s** -z **'tiger ˌlily** ; **'tiger ˌmoth**
tigerish 'taɪ.gər.ɪʃ **-ly** -li **-ness** -nəs, -nɪs
Tigger 'tɪg.əʳ (US) -ɚ
Tiggy-Winkle 'tɪg.iˌwɪŋ.kl̩
Tighe taɪ
tight taɪt **-er** -əʳ (US) 'taɪ.t̬ɚ **-est** -ɪst, -əst (US) 'taɪ.t̬ɪst, -t̬əst **-ly** -li **-ness** -nəs, -nɪs
tighten 'taɪ.tən **-s** -z **-ing** -ɪŋ, 'taɪt.nɪŋ **-ed** -d **-er/s** -əʳ/z, 'taɪt.nəʳ/z (US) 'taɪ.tən.ɚ/z, 'taɪt.nɚ/z
tightfisted ˌtaɪt'fɪs.tɪd (US) '-ˌ--, ˌ-'-- **-ly** -li **-ness** -nəs, -nɪs *stress shift, British only:* ˌtightfisted 'miser
tightknit ˌtaɪt'nɪt (US) '--, ˌ-'- *stress shift, British only:* ˌtightknit 'group
tight-lipped ˌtaɪt'lɪpt (US) '--, ˌ-'- *stress shift, British only:* ˌtight-lipped 'speaker
tightrope 'taɪt.rəʊp (US) -roʊp **'tightrope ˌwalker**
tights taɪts
tightwad 'taɪt.wɒd (US) 'wɑːd **-s** -z
Tiglath-pileser ˌtɪg.læθ.paɪ'liː.zəʳ, -pɪ'-, -pə'- (US) -zɚ
tigon 'taɪ.gən **-s** -z
Tigré 'tiː.greɪ
tigress 'taɪ.gres, -grɪs (US) -grɪs **-es** -ɪz
Tigris 'taɪ.grɪs
Tijuana tɪ'*h*wɑː.nə, ˌtiː.ə'- (US) ˌtiː.ə'wɑː-, tiː'*h*wɑː-
tike taɪk **-s** -s
tikka 'tɪk.ə, 'tiː.kə
tilbur|y (T) 'tɪl.bər|.i (US) -ber-, -bɚ- **-ies** -iz
tilde 'tɪl.də, -di, -deɪ; tɪld (US) 'tɪl.də **-s** -z
til|e taɪl **-es** -z **-ing** -ɪŋ **-ed** -d **-er/s** -əʳ/z (US) -ɚ/z
Tilehurst 'taɪl.hɜːst (US) -hɜːrst
till (T) tɪl **-s** -z **-ing** -ɪŋ **-ed** -d **-er/s** -əʳ/z (US) -ɚ/z **-able** -ə.bl̩ **-age** -ɪdʒ
tiller 'tɪl.əʳ (US) -ɚ **-s** -z
Tilley 'tɪl.i
Tillicoultry ˌtɪl.ɪ'kuː.tri, -ə'-
Tilling 'tɪl.ɪŋ **-s** -z
Tillotson 'tɪl.ət.sən
Tilly 'tɪl.i
tilt tɪlt **-s** -s **-ing** -ɪŋ (US) 'tɪl.t̬ɪŋ **-ed** -ɪd (US) 'tɪl.t̬ɪd **-er/s** -əʳ/z (US) 'tɪl.t̬ɚ/z
tilth tɪlθ
tilt-yard 'tɪlt.jɑːd (US) -jɑːrd **-s** -z
Tim tɪm
Timaeus taɪ'miː.əs, tɪ- (US) taɪ'-
timbal 'tɪm.bəl **-s** -z
timbale tæm'bɑːl; tɪm'-, 'tɪm.bəl, tɪm'bɑːl (US) 'tɪm.bəl; tɪm'bɑːl, tæm- **-s** -z
timb|er 'tɪm.b|əʳ (US) -b|ɚ **-ers** -əz (US) -ɚz **-ering** -ər.ɪŋ **-ered** -əd (US) -ɚd
Timberlake 'tɪm.bə.leɪk (US) -bɚ-
timberland (T®) 'tɪm.bə.lænd (US) -bɚ- **-s** -z
timberline 'tɪm.bə.laɪn (US) -bɚ-
timbre 'tæ̃m.brə, 'tæm-, -bəʳ; 'tɪm.bəʳ (US) 'tæm.bɚ, 'tɪm- **-s** -z
timbrel 'tɪm.brəl **-s** -z
Timbuktu, Timbuctoo ˌtɪm.bʌk'tuː, -bək'- (US) -bʌk'-
tim|e taɪm **-es** -z **-ing** -ɪŋ **-ed** -d **-er/s** -əʳ/z (US) -ɚ/z ˌ**time and a 'half** ; ˌ**time and 'motion** ; ˌ**time after 'time** ; **since ˌtime imme'morial** ; **'time ˌbomb** ; **'time ˌcapsule** ; ˌ**time 'off** ; **'time ˌswitch** ; **'time ˌwarp** ; **'time ˌzone** ; ˌ**fall on ˌhard 'times**
time-consuming 'taɪm.kənˌsjuː.mɪŋ, -ˌsuː- (US) -ˌsuː-
time-hono(u)red 'taɪmˌɒn.əd, ˌ-'-- (US) 'taɪmˌɑː.nɚd
timekeep|er 'taɪmˌkiː.p|əʳ (US) -p|ɚ **-ers** -əz (US) -ɚz **-ing** -ɪŋ
time-lapse 'taɪm.læps **-s** -ɪz ˌ**time-lapse pho'tography**
timeless 'taɪm.ləs, -lɪs **-ly** -li **-ness** -nəs, -nɪs
time-lock 'taɪm.lɒk (US) -lɑːk **-s** -s
timel|y 'taɪm.l|i **-ier** -i.əʳ (US) -i.ɚ **-iest** -i.ɪst, -i.əst **-iness** -ɪ.nəs, -ɪ.nɪs
timeous 'taɪ.məs
time-out ˌtaɪm'aʊt, '-- **time-outs** ˌtaɪm'aʊts, '-- **times-out** ˌtaɪmz'aʊt, '--
timepiec|e 'taɪm.piːs **-es** -ɪz
time-saving 'taɪmˌseɪ.vɪŋ
timescale 'taɪm.skeɪl
timeserv|er 'taɪmˌsɜː.v|əʳ (US) -ˌsɜːr.v|ɚ **-ers** -əz (US) -ɚz **-ing** -ɪŋ
timeshar|e 'taɪm.ʃeəʳ (US) -ʃer **-es** -z **-er/s** -əʳ/z (US) -ɚ/z **-ing** -ɪŋ
timesheet 'taɪm.ʃiːt **-s** -s
time-switch 'taɪm.swɪtʃ **-es** -ɪz
timetabl|e 'taɪmˌteɪ.bl̩ **-es** -z **-ing** -ɪŋ, -ˌteɪ.blɪŋ **-ed** -d
timework 'taɪm.wɜːk (US) -wɜːrk **-er/s** -əʳ/z (US) -ɚ/z
timeworn 'taɪm.wɔːn (US) -wɔːrn
Timex® 'taɪ.meks
timid 'tɪm.ɪd **-est** -ɪst, -əst **-ly** -li **-ness** -nəs, -nɪs
timidity tɪ'mɪd.ə.ti, -ɪ.ti (US) -ə.t̬i
Timisoara ˌtɪm.ɪ'ʃwɑː.rə (US) ˌtiː.miː'ʃwɑːr.ə

Timmins ˈtɪm.ɪnz
Timms tɪmz
Timon ˈtaɪ.mən, -mɒn ⓊⓈ -mən
Timor ˈtiː.mɔːʳ, ˈtaɪ- ⓊⓈ -mɔːr; tiːˈmɔːr
timorous ˈtɪm.ᵊr.əs **-ly** -li **-ness** -nəs, -nɪs
Timotheus tɪˈməʊ.θi.əs ⓊⓈ -ˈmoʊ-, taɪ-, -ˈmɑː-
Timothy ˈtɪm.ə.θi
timpan|i, timpan|y ˈtɪm.pə.n|i **-ist/s** -ɪst/s
Timpson ˈtɪmp.sᵊn
tin tɪn **-s** -z **-ning** -ɪŋ **-ned** -d ˌ**tin ˈcan** ; ˌ**tin ˈgod** ; ˈ**tin ˌopener** ; ˌ**tin ˌpan ˈalley**
Tina ˈtiː.nə
tinctorial tɪŋkˈtɔː.ri.əl ⓊⓈ -ˈtɔːr.i-
tinct|ure ˈtɪŋk.tʃ|əʳ ⓊⓈ -tʃ|ɚ **-ures** -əz ⓊⓈ -ɚz **-uring** -ᵊr.ɪŋ **-ured** -əd ⓊⓈ -ɚd
Tindal(l), Tindale ˈtɪn.dᵊl
tinder ˈtɪn.dəʳ ⓊⓈ -dɚ
tinderbox ˈtɪn.də.bɒks ⓊⓈ -dɚ.bɑːks **-es** -ɪz
tine taɪn **-s** -z
tinfoil ˈtɪn.fɔɪl, ˌ-ˈ- ⓊⓈ ˈtɪn.fɔɪl
ting tɪŋ
ting|e tɪndʒ **-es** -ɪz **-(e)ing** -ɪŋ **-ed** -d
Tingey ˈtɪŋ.gi
tingl|e ˈtɪŋ.gl̩ **-es** -z **-ing** -ɪŋ, ˈtɪŋ.glɪŋ **-ed** -d
tingly ˈtɪŋ.gli, ˈ-gl̩.i
tink|er ˈtɪŋ.k|əʳ ⓊⓈ -k|ɚ **-ers** -əz ⓊⓈ -ɚz **-ering** -ᵊr.ɪŋ **-ered** -əd ⓊⓈ -ɚd ˌ**tinker's ˈcuss** ; ˌ**tinker's ˈdamn**
Tinkerbell ˈtɪŋ.kə.bel ⓊⓈ -kɚ-
Tinkertoy® ˈtɪŋ.kə.tɔɪ ⓊⓈ -kɚ-
tinkl|e ˈtɪŋ.kl̩ **-es** -z **-ing/s** -ɪŋ/z, ˈtɪŋ.klɪŋ/z **-ed** -d
Tinnevelly tɪˈnev.ᵊl.i; ˌtɪn.ɪˈvel.i
tinnitus tɪˈnaɪ.təs, tə-; ˈtɪn.ɪ.təs, ˈ-ə- ⓊⓈ tɪˈnaɪ.t̬əs; ˈtɪn.ɪ-
tinn|y ˈtɪn|.i **-ies** -iz **-ier** -i.əʳ ⓊⓈ -i.ɚ **-iest** -i.ɪst, -i.əst **-ily** -ɪ.li, -ᵊl.i **-iness** -ɪ.nəs, -ɪ.nɪs
Tinos ˈtiː.nɒs ⓊⓈ -nɑːs
tinplate ˈtɪn.pleɪt, ˈtɪm-, ˌ-ˈ- ⓊⓈ ˈtɪn.pleɪt **-d** -ɪd
tin-pot ˈtɪn.pɒt, ˈtɪm- ⓊⓈ ˈtɪn.pɑːt ˌ**tin-pot dicˈtator**
tinsel ˈtɪnt.sᵊl **-ly** -i ˈ**tinsel ˌtown**
tint tɪnt **-s** -s **-ing** -ɪŋ ⓊⓈ ˈtɪn.t̬ɪŋ **-ed** -ɪd ⓊⓈ ˈtɪn.t̬ɪd **-er/s** -əʳ/z ⓊⓈ ˈtɪn.t̬ɚ/z
Tintagel tɪnˈtædʒ.ᵊl
Tintern ˈtɪn.tən, -tɜːn ⓊⓈ -tɚn, -tɜːrn
Tintin ˈtin.tɪn
tintinnabulation ˌtɪn.tɪˌnæb.jəˈleɪ.ʃᵊn, -jʊˈ- **-s** -z
tintinnabul|um ˌtɪn.tɪˈnæb.jə.l|əm, -jʊ- **-a** -ə **-ar** -əʳ ⓊⓈ -ɚ **-ary** -ᵊr.i **-ous** -əs
Tintoretto ˌtɪn.tᵊrˈet.əʊ, -tɒrˈ- ⓊⓈ -təˈret̬.oʊ **-s** -z
tin|y ˈtaɪ.n|i **-ier** -i.əʳ ⓊⓈ -i.ɚ **-iest** -i.ɪst, -i.əst **-iness** -ɪ.nəs, -ɪ.nɪs
-tion -ʃᵊn
Note: Suffix. Words containing **-tion** are normally stressed on the penultimate syllable, e.g. **fruition** /fruˈɪʃ.ᵊn/.
Tio Pepe® ˌtiː.əʊˈpep.eɪ, -i ⓊⓈ -oʊˈ-
-tious -ʃəs
Note: Suffix. Words containing **-tious** are normally stressed on the penultimate syllable, e.g. **propitious** /prəˈpɪʃ.əs/.
tip tɪp **-s** -s **-ping** -ɪŋ **-ped** -t **-per/s** -əʳ/z ⓊⓈ -ɚ/z
tipcat ˈtɪp.kæt
Tipo® ˈtiː.pəʊ ⓊⓈ -poʊ
tip-off ˈtɪp.ɒf ⓊⓈ -ɑːf **-s** -s
Tippell ˈtɪp.ᵊl
Tipperary ˌtɪp.ᵊrˈeə.ri ⓊⓈ -əˈrer.i
tippet ˈtɪp.ɪt **-s** -s
Tippett ˈtɪp.ɪt
Tipp-Ex® ˈtɪp.eks
Tippex ˈtɪp.eks **-es** -ɪz **-ing** -ɪŋ **-ed** -t
tippl|e ˈtɪp.l̩ **-es** -z **-ing** -ɪŋ, ˈtɪp.lɪŋ **-ed** -d **-er/s** -əʳ/z, ˈtɪp.ləʳ/z ⓊⓈ ˈ-l̩.ɚ/z, ˈ-lɚ/z
tip|staff ˈtɪp|.stɑːf ⓊⓈ -stæf **-staves** -steɪvz
tipster ˈtɪp.stəʳ ⓊⓈ -stɚ **-s** -z
tips|y ˈtɪp.s|i **-ier** -i.əʳ ⓊⓈ -i.ɚ **-iest** -i.ɪst, -i.əst **-ily** -ɪ.li, -ᵊl.i **-iness** -ɪ.nəs, -ɪ.nɪs
tipto|e ˈtɪp.təʊ ⓊⓈ -toʊ **-es** -z **-ing** -ɪŋ **-ed** -d
Tipton ˈtɪp.tᵊn
tiptop ˌtɪpˈtɒp ⓊⓈ ˈtɪp.tɑːp *stress shift:* ˌtiptop ˈshape
Tiptree ˈtɪp.triː
tirade taɪˈreɪd, tɪ-, -ˈrɑːd ⓊⓈ ˈtaɪ.reɪd, -ˈ- **-s** -z
tiramisu ˌtɪr.ə.mɪˈsuː ⓊⓈ -ˈmiː.suː
Tirana, Tiranë tɪˈrɑː.nə ⓊⓈ tɪ-, tiː-
tirass|e tɪˈræs **-es** -ɪz
tir|e taɪəʳ ⓊⓈ taɪɚ **-es** -z **-ing** -ɪŋ **-ed** -d
tired taɪəd ⓊⓈ taɪɚd **-ly** -li **-ness** -nəs, -nɪs
Tiree taɪˈriː
tireless ˈtaɪə.ləs, -lɪs ⓊⓈ ˈtaɪɚ- **-ly** -li **-ness** -nəs, -nɪs
Tiresias taɪəˈriː.si.æs, -ˈres.i-, -əs, ˈ-sjəs ⓊⓈ taɪˈriː.si.əs
tiresome ˈtaɪə.səm ⓊⓈ ˈtaɪɚ- **-ly** -li **-ness** -nəs, -nɪs
Tirney ˈtɜː.ni ⓊⓈ ˈtɜːr-
tiro ˈtaɪə.rəʊ ⓊⓈ ˈtaɪ.roʊ **-s** -z
Tirol tɪˈrəʊl; ˈtɪr.əʊl ⓊⓈ tɪˈroʊl, -ˈrɑːl; ˈtɪr.oʊl, ˈtaɪ.roʊl, -rɑːl
Tirolean ˌtɪr.əʊˈliː.ən ⓊⓈ tɪˈroʊ.li-, taɪ-; ˌtɪr.əˈliː-
Tirolese ˌtɪr.əʊˈliːz ⓊⓈ -əˈliːz, -ˈliːs
Tiruchchirappalli ˌtɪr.əˌtʃɪr.əˈpʌl.i; tɪˌruː.tʃɪˈrɑː.pᵊl- ⓊⓈ ˌtɪr.ə.tʃɪˈrɑː.pᵊl-; -ˌtʃɪr.əˈpuː.li, -ˈpʌl.i
'tis tɪz
tisane tɪˈzæn, tiː-, -ˈsæn ⓊⓈ tɪˈzæn **-s** -z
Tishbite ˈtɪʃ.baɪt **-s** -s
Tissaphernes ˌtɪs.əˈfɜː.niːz ⓊⓈ -ˈfɜːr-
Tissot ˈtiː.səʊ ⓊⓈ tiːˈsoʊ
tissue ˈtɪʃ.uː, ˈtɪs.juː ⓊⓈ ˈtɪʃ.uː **-s** -z ˈ**tissue ˌpaper**
tit tɪt **-s** -s ˌ**tit for ˈtat**
titan (T) ˈtaɪ.tᵊn **-s** -z
Titania tɪˈtɑː.njə, taɪ-, -ˈteɪ-, -ni.ə ⓊⓈ tɪˈteɪ.ni.ə, taɪ-, -ˈtɑː-
titanic (T) taɪˈtæn.ɪk, tɪ- **-ally** -ᵊl.i, -li
titanium tɪˈteɪ.ni.əm, taɪ- ⓊⓈ taɪ-, tɪ-
titbit ˈtɪt.bɪt **-s** -s
titch tɪtʃ
titch|y ˈtɪtʃ|.i **-ier** -i.əʳ ⓊⓈ -i.ɚ **-iest** -i.ɪst, -i.əst
tith|e taɪð **-es** -z **-ing** -ɪŋ **-ed** -d
tithing ˈtaɪ.ðɪŋ **-s** -z
Tithonus tɪˈθəʊ.nəs, taɪ- ⓊⓈ -ˈθoʊ-
Titian ˈtɪʃ.ᵊn, -i.ən ⓊⓈ -ᵊn **-s** -z
Titicaca ˌtɪt.ɪˈkɑː.kɑː, -kə ⓊⓈ ˌtɪt.ɪ-, ˌtiː.tɪˈ-
titill|ate ˈtɪt.ɪ.l|eɪt, -ᵊl|.eɪt ⓊⓈ -ᵊl|.eɪt **-ates** -eɪts **-ating** -eɪ.tɪŋ ⓊⓈ -eɪ.t̬ɪŋ **-ated** -eɪ.tɪd ⓊⓈ -eɪ.t̬ɪd
titillation ˌtɪt.ɪˈleɪ.ʃᵊn, -ᵊlˈeɪ- ⓊⓈ -ᵊlˈeɪ- **-s** -z
titi|vate ˈtɪt.ɪ|.veɪt, ˈ-ə- ⓊⓈ ˈtɪt̬.ə- **-vates** -veɪts **-vating** -veɪ.tɪŋ ⓊⓈ -veɪ.t̬ɪŋ **-vated** -veɪ.tɪd ⓊⓈ -veɪ.t̬ɪd
titivation ˌtɪt.ɪˈveɪ.ʃᵊn, -əˈ- ⓊⓈ ˌtɪt̬.əˈ- **-s** -z
title ˈtaɪ.tl̩ ⓊⓈ -t̬l̩ **-s** -z **-ing** -ɪŋ **-d** -d **-less** -ləs, -lɪs ˈ**title ˌdeed**
titleholder ˈtaɪ.tl̩ˌhəʊl.dəʳ ⓊⓈ -ˌhoʊl.dɚ **-s** -z
titling ˈtaɪt.lɪŋ, ˈtaɪ.tl̩.ɪŋ ⓊⓈ ˈtaɪt.lɪŋ, ˈtaɪ.t̬l̩.ɪŋ **-s** -z
Titmarsh ˈtɪt.mɑːʃ ⓊⓈ -mɑːrʃ
tit|mouse ˈtɪt|.maʊs **-mice** -maɪs
Tito ˈtiː.təʊ ⓊⓈ -t̬oʊ, -toʊ
Titograd ˈtiː.təʊ.græd ⓊⓈ -t̬oʊ-, -grɑːd
titration taɪˈtreɪ.ʃᵊn, tɪ- ⓊⓈ taɪ-
titt|er ˈtɪt|.əʳ ⓊⓈ ˈtɪt̬|.ɚ **-ers** -əz ⓊⓈ -ɚz **-ering** -ᵊr.ɪŋ **-ered** -əd ⓊⓈ -ɚd **-erer/s** -ᵊr.əʳ/z ⓊⓈ -ɚ.ɚ/z
tittle ˈtɪt.l̩ ⓊⓈ ˈtɪt̬- **-s** -z
tittle-tattle ˈtɪt.l̩ˌtæt.l̩ ⓊⓈ ˈtɪt̬.l̩ˌtæt̬-
titular ˈtɪt.jə.ləʳ, -jʊ- ⓊⓈ ˈtɪtʃ.ə.lɚ, ˈ-ʊ-, ˈtɪt.jə-, -jʊ- **-s** -z **-ly** -li
titular|y ˈtɪt.jə.lᵊr|.i, -jʊ- ⓊⓈ ˈtɪtʃ.ə.ler-, ˈ-ʊ-, ˈtɪt.jə-, -jʊ- **-ies** -iz
Titus ˈtaɪ.təs ⓊⓈ -t̬əs

Tiverton 'tɪv.ə.tᵊn (US) -ɚ.t̬ən
Tivoli 'tɪv.ᵊl.i
Tivy 'taɪ.vi
Tizard 'tɪz.əd (US) -ɚd
Tizer® 'taɪ.zəʳ (US) -zɚ
tizz tɪz **-es** -ɪz
tizz|y 'tɪz|.i **-ies** -iz
T-junction 'tiː,dʒʌŋk.ʃᵊn **-s** -z
Tlaxcala tlə'skɑː.lə, tlæs'kɑː- (US) tlɑː'skɑː.lə
Tlemcen tlem'sen
TM ,tiː'em
tmesis 'tmiː.sɪs, 'miː-; tə'miː- (US) tə'miː-, 'miː-
TN (*abbrev. for* **Tennessee**) ten.ə'siː, -ɪ'- (US) 'ten.ə.siː *regionally:* 'ten.ɪ.si, -ə-
TNT ,tiː.en'tiː
to (*adv.*) tuː
Note: This form of **to** is found in expressions such as 'to and fro'.
to (*prep.*) *strong form:* tuː *weak forms:* tʊ, tu, tə (US) tə, t̬ə, tu
Note: Weak form word. The strong form /tuː/ is used contrastively, e.g. 'the letter was **to** him, not **from** him', and sometimes in final position, e.g. 'I don't want to', though the /u/ vowel is more often used in this context. The weak form /tə/ is used before consonants, e.g. 'to cut' /tə'kʌt/, while the pronunciation /tu/ is used before vowels in British English, e.g. 'to eat' /tu'iːt/. In American English, the schwa form is usual before both vowels and consonants, so the latter is /tə'iːt/.
toad təʊd (US) toʊd **-s** -z
toadflax 'təʊd.flæks (US) 'toʊd-
toad-in-the-hole ,təʊd.ɪn.ðə'həʊl (US) ,toʊd.ɪn.ðə'hoʊl
toadstool 'təʊd.stuːl (US) 'toʊd- **-s** -z
toad|y 'təʊ.d|i (US) 'toʊ- **-ies** -iz **-ying** -i.ɪŋ **-ied** -id
Toal təʊl (US) toʊl
to-and-fro ,tuː.ənd'frəʊ (US) -'froʊ
toast təʊst (US) toʊst **-s** -s **-ing** -ɪŋ **-ed** -ɪd **-er/s** -əʳ/z (US) -ɚ/z **'toasting ,fork ; 'toast ,rack**
toastmaster 'təʊst,mɑː.stəʳ (US) 'toʊst,mæs.tɚ **-s** -z
tobacco tə'bæk.əʊ (US) -oʊ **-s** -z
tobacconist tə'bæk.ᵊn.ɪst **-s** -s
Tobagan təʊ'beɪ.gən (US) tə- **-s** -z
Tobago təʊ'beɪ.gəʊ (US) toʊ'beɪ.goʊ, tə-
Tobagonian ,təʊ.bə'gəʊ.ni.ən (US) ,toʊ.bə'goʊ- **-s** -z
to-be tə'biː
Tobermory ,təʊ.bə'mɔː.ri (US) ,toʊ.bɚ'mɔːr.i
Tobias təʊ'baɪ.əs (US) toʊ-, tə-
Tobin 'təʊ.bɪn (US) 'toʊ-
Tobit 'təʊ.bɪt (US) 'toʊ-
Toblerone® 'təʊ.blə.rəʊn (US) 'toʊ.blə.roʊn
toboggan tə'bɒg.ᵊn (US) -'bɑː.gᵊn **-s** -z **-ing** -ɪŋ **-ed** -d **-er/s** -əʳ/z (US) -ɚ/z
Tobruk tə'brʊk (US) tə-, toʊ-
tob|y (T) 'təʊ.b|i (US) 'toʊ- **-ies** -iz **'toby ,jug**
toccata tə'kɑː.tə, tɒk'ɑː- (US) tə'kɑː.t̬ə **-s** -z
Toc H ,tɒk'eɪtʃ (US) ,tɑːk-
Tocharian tɒk'eə.ri.ən, təʊ'keə-, -'kɑː- (US) toʊ'ker.i-, -'kær-, -'kɑːr-
Tocqueville 'tɒk.vɪl, 'təʊk- (US) 'toʊk-, 'tɑːk-
tocsin 'tɒk.sɪn (US) 'tɑːk- **-s** -z
tod (T) tɒd (US) tɑːd **-s** -z
today tə'deɪ, tʊ- (US) tə-, tʊ-, tu-
Todd tɒd (US) tɑːd
toddl|e 'tɒd.l̩ (US) 'tɑː.dl̩ **-es** -z **-ing** -ɪŋ, 'tɒd.lɪŋ (US) 'tɑːd- **-ed** -d **-er/s** -əʳ/z, 'tɒd.ləʳ/z (US) 'tɑːd.l̩.ɚ/z, '-lɚ/z
todd|y 'tɒd|.i (US) 'tɑː.d|i **-ies** -iz
Todhunter 'tɒd,hʌn.təʳ, -*h*ən.təʳ (US) 'tɑːd,hʌn.t̬ɚ, -*h*ən.t̬ɚ
Todmorden 'tɒd.mə.dən, -,mɒː.dᵊn (US) 'tɑːd.mɚ.dən, -,mɔːr.dᵊn
to-do tə'duː, tʊ- **-s** -z
toe təʊ (US) toʊ **-s** -z **-ing** -ɪŋ **-d** -d **'toe ,cap ; ,toe the 'line ; ,tread on someone's 'toes**
toea 'təʊ.ɑː (US) 'toʊ-
toehold 'təʊ.həʊld (US) 'toʊ.hoʊld **-s** -z
toenail 'təʊ.neɪl (US) 'toʊ- **-s** -z
toerag 'təʊ.ræg (US) 'toʊ- **-s** -z
toff tɒf (US) tɑːf **-s** -s
toffee 'tɒf.i (US) 'tɑː.fi **-s** -z **'toffee ,apple, ,toffee 'apple**
toffee-nosed 'tɒf.i.nəʊzd (US) 'tɑː.fi.noʊzd
toff|y 'tɒf|.i (US) 'tɑː.f|i **-ies** -iz
Tofts tɒfts (US) tɑːfts
tofu 'təʊ.fuː (US) 'toʊ-
tog tɒg (US) tɑːg, tɔːg **-s** -z **-ging** -ɪŋ **-ged** -d
toga 'təʊ.gə (US) 'toʊ- **-s** -z **-ed** -d
together tə'geð.əʳ (US) -ɚ **-ness** -nəs, -nɪs
toggery 'tɒg.ᵊr.i (US) 'tɑː.gɚ-, 'tɔː-
toggle 'tɒg.l̩ (US) 'tɑː.gl̩, 'tɔː- **-s** -z **-d** -d
Togo 'təʊ.gəʊ (US) 'toʊ.goʊ **-land** -lænd
Togolese ,təʊ.gəʊ'liːz (US) ,toʊ.goʊ'-, -'liːs *stress shift:* ,Togolese 'people
toil tɔɪl **-s** -z **-ing** -ɪŋ **-ed** -d **-er/s** -əʳ/z (US) -ɚ/z
toile twɑːl, twɔːl (US) twɑːl **-s** -z
toilet 'tɔɪ.lɪt, -lət **-s** -s **'toilet ,bag ; 'toilet ,paper ; 'toilet ,roll ; 'toilet ,training ; 'toilet ,water**
toiletr|y 'tɔɪ.lɪ.tr|i, -lə- **-ies** -iz
toilette twɑː'let **-s** -s
toilsome 'tɔɪl.səm **-ly** -li **-ness** -nəs, -nɪs
toilworn 'tɔɪl.wɔːn (US) -wɔːrn
to-ing and fro-ing ,tuː.ɪŋ.ənd'frəʊ.ɪŋ (US) -'froʊ- **to-ings and fro-ings** ,tuː.ɪŋz.ənd'frəʊ.ɪŋz (US) -'froʊ-
tokay (T) təʊ'keɪ, -'kaɪ, '--; tɒk'aɪ, -'eɪ (US) toʊ'keɪ
Tokelau 'təʊ.kə.laʊ, 'tɒk.ə- (US) 'toʊ.kə-
token 'təʊ.kᵊn (US) 'toʊ- **-s** -z **-ism** -ɪ.zᵊm
Tokharian tɒk'eə.ri.ən, təʊ'keə-, -'kɑː- (US) toʊ'ker.i-, -'kær-
Toklas 'tɒk.ləs, 'təʊk-, -læs (US) 'toʊk.ləs
Tokley 'təʊ.kli (US) 'toʊ-
Tokyo 'təʊ.ki.əʊ (US) 'toʊ.ki.oʊ
Toland 'təʊ.lənd (US) 'toʊ-
told (*from* **tell**) təʊld (US) toʊld
toledo *blade:* tə'liː.dəʊ, tɒl'iː- (US) tə'liː.doʊ **-s** -z
Toledo *in Spain:* tɒl'eɪ.dəʊ, tə'leɪ-, -'liː- (US) tə'liː.doʊ, -'leɪ- *in US:* tə'liː.dəʊ (US) -doʊ
tolerability ,tɒl.ᵊr.ə'bɪl.ə.ti, -ɪ.ti (US) ,tɑː.lɚ.ə'bɪl.ə.t̬i
tolerab|le 'tɒl.ᵊr.ə.b|l̩ (US) 'tɑː.lɚ- **-ly** -li **-leness** -l̩.nəs, -nɪs
tolerance 'tɒl.ᵊr.ᵊnts (US) 'tɑː.lɚ-
tolerant 'tɒl.ᵊr.ᵊnt (US) 'tɑː.lɚ- **-ly** -li
toler|ate 'tɒl.ᵊr|.eɪt (US) 'tɑː.lə.r|eɪt **-ates** -eɪts **-ating** -eɪ.tɪŋ (US) -eɪ.t̬ɪŋ **-ated** -eɪ.tɪd (US) -eɪ.t̬ɪd
toleration ,tɒl.ᵊr'eɪ.ʃᵊn (US) ,tɑː.lə'reɪ-
Tolkien 'tɒl.kiːn, -'- (US) 'toʊl.kiːn, 'tɑːl-
toll təʊl (US) toʊl **-s** -z **-ing** -ɪŋ **-ed** -d **-er/s** -əʳ/z (US) -ɚ/z **'toll ,bridge ; 'toll ,call**
toll|booth 'tɒl|.buːθ, 'təʊl-, -buːð (US) 'toʊl- **-booths** -buːθs, -buːðz
Tollemache 'tɒl.mæʃ, -mɑːʃ (US) 'tɑːl-
Tollesbury 'təʊlz.bᵊr.i (US) 'toʊlz.ber-, -bɚ-
Tolleshunt 'təʊlz.hʌnt (US) 'toʊlz-
Tolley 'tɒl.i (US) 'tɑː.li
toll-free ,təʊl'friː, ,toʊl- *stress shift:* ,toll-free 'call
tollgate 'təʊl.geɪt (US) 'toʊl- **-s** -s
tollhou|se 'təʊl.haʊ|s (US) 'toʊl- **-ses** -zɪz
Tolpuddle 'tɒl,pʌd.l̩ *locally also:* -,pɪd- (US) 'tɑːl-
Tolstoy 'tɒl.stɔɪ (US) 'tɑːl-, 'toʊl-
Toltec 'tɒl.tek (US) 'tɑːl-, 'toʊl- **-s** -s
tolu (T) tɒl'uː, təʊ'luː, -'ljuː (US) toʊ'luː
toluene 'tɒl.ju.iːn (US) 'tɑːl-
Tolworth 'tɒl.wəθ, -wɜːθ (US) 'tɑːl.wɚθ, -wɜːrθ
tom (T) tɒm (US) tɑːm **-s** -z **,Tom 'Collins ; ,Tom, ,Dick and 'Harry ; ,Tom and 'Jerry ; ,Tom 'Thumb**
tomahawk 'tɒm.ə.hɔːk (US) 'tɑː.mə.hɑːk, -hɔːk **-s** -s **-ing** -ɪŋ **-ed** -t

Tomalin 'tɒm.ᵊl.ɪn Ⓤⓢ 'tɑː.mᵊl-
toman təʊ'mɑːn Ⓤⓢ toʊ-, tə- **-s** -z
tomato tə'mɑː.təʊ Ⓤⓢ -'meɪ.t̬oʊ **-es** -z
tomb tuːm **-s** -z
tombola tɒm'bəʊ.lə Ⓤⓢ tɑːm'boʊ-, 'tɑːm.bᵊl.ə **-s** -z
tomboy 'tɒm.bɔɪ Ⓤⓢ 'tɑːm- **-s** -z
tombstone (T) 'tuːm.stəʊn Ⓤⓢ -stoʊn **-s** -z
tomcat 'tɒm.kæt Ⓤⓢ 'tɑːm- **-s** -s
tome təʊm Ⓤⓢ toʊm **-s** -z
Tomelty 'tʌm.ᵊl.ti Ⓤⓢ -t̬i
tomfool ˌtɒm'fuːl Ⓤⓢ ˌtɑːm- **-s** -z **-ery** -ᵊr.i Ⓤⓢ -ɚ.i
Tomintoul ˌtɒm.ɪn'taʊl, -ən'- Ⓤⓢ ˌtɑːm-
Tomkins 'tɒmp.kɪnz Ⓤⓢ 'tɑːmp-
Tomlinson 'tɒm.lɪn.sən Ⓤⓢ 'tɑːm-
tommy-gun 'tɒm.i.gʌn Ⓤⓢ 'tɑː.mi- **-s** -z
tomm|y, tomm|ie (T) 'tɒm|.i Ⓤⓢ 'tɑː.m|i **-ies** -iz **'tommy ˌgun**
tommyrot 'tɒm.i.rɒt, ˌ--'- Ⓤⓢ 'tɑː.mi.rɑːt
tomogram 'təʊ.mə.græm, 'tɒm.ə- Ⓤⓢ 'toʊ.mə- **-s** -z
tomography tə'mɒg.rə.fi Ⓤⓢ toʊ'mɑː.grə-, tə'-
tomorrow tə'mɒr.əʊ, tʊ- Ⓤⓢ -'mɑːr.oʊ **-s** -z **toˌmorrow after'noon ; toˌmorrow 'evening ; toˌmorrow 'morning ; toˌmorrow 'night**
Tompion 'tɒm.pi.ən Ⓤⓢ 'tɑːm-
Tompkins 'tɒmp.kɪnz Ⓤⓢ 'tɑːmp-
Tomsk tɒmpsk Ⓤⓢ tɑːmpsk
tomtit 'tɒm.tɪt, ˌ-'- Ⓤⓢ ˌtɑːm'tɪt, '-- **-s** -s
tom-tom 'tɒm.tɒm Ⓤⓢ 'tɑːm.tɑːm **-s** -z
ton *weight:* tʌn **-s** -z
ton *fashion:* tɔ̃ːŋ Ⓤⓢ tõʊn
tonal 'təʊ.nᵊl Ⓤⓢ 'toʊ-
tonalit|y təʊ'næl.ə.t|i, -ɪ.t|i Ⓤⓢ toʊ'næl.ə.t̬|i, tə- **-ies** -iz
Tonbridge 'tʌn.brɪdʒ, 'tʌm- Ⓤⓢ 'tʌn-
ton|e təʊn Ⓤⓢ toʊn **-es** -z **-ing** -ɪŋ **-ed** -d
tone-deaf ˌtəʊn'def Ⓤⓢ 'toʊn-, ˌ-'- **-ness** -nəs, -nɪs *stress shift, British only:* ˌtone-deaf 'person
toneless 'təʊn.ləs, -lɪs Ⓤⓢ 'toʊn- **-ly** -li **-ness** -nəs, -nɪs
tonematic ˌtəʊ.nɪ'mæt.ɪk Ⓤⓢ ˌtoʊ.nɪ'mæt̬.ɪk **-s** -s
toneme 'təʊ.niːm Ⓤⓢ 'toʊ- **-s** -z
tonemic təʊ'niː.mɪk Ⓤⓢ toʊ-, tə- **-s** -s
toner (T) 'təʊ.nəʳ Ⓤⓢ 'toʊ.nɚ **-s** -z
tonetic təʊ'net.ɪk Ⓤⓢ toʊ'net̬-, tə- **-s** -s
ton|ey 'təʊ.n|i Ⓤⓢ 'toʊ- **-ier** -i.əʳ Ⓤⓢ -i.ɚ **-iest** -i.ɪst, -i.əst

tonga *cart, medicinal bark:* 'tɒŋ.gə Ⓤⓢ 'tɑːŋ-, 'tɔːŋ- **-s** -z
Tong|a *Pacific islands:* 'tɒŋ|.ə, -g|ə Ⓤⓢ 'tɑːŋ-, 'tɔːŋ- **-an/s** -ᵊn/z
Tong|a *East Africa:* 'tɒŋ.g|ə Ⓤⓢ 'tɑːŋ-, 'tɔːŋ- **-as** -əz **-an** -ən
Tongking ˌtɒŋ'kɪŋ Ⓤⓢ ˌtɑːŋ-, ˌtɔːŋ-
tongs tɒŋz Ⓤⓢ tɑːŋz, tɔːŋz
tongu|e tʌŋ **-es** -z **-ing** -ɪŋ **-ed** -d **-eless** -ləs, -lɪs **ˌtongue and 'groove ; 'tongue ˌtwister ; ˌbite one's 'tongue**
tongue-in-cheek ˌtʌŋ.ɪn'tʃiːk *stress shift:* ˌtongue-in-cheek 'article
tongue-lashing 'tʌŋˌlæʃ.ɪŋ **-s** -z
tongue-tied 'tʌŋ.taɪd
Toni 'təʊ.ni Ⓤⓢ 'toʊ-
tonic 'tɒn.ɪk Ⓤⓢ 'tɑː.nɪk **-s** -s **-ally** -ᵊl.i, -li
tonicity təʊ'nɪs.ə.ti, -ɪ.ti Ⓤⓢ toʊ'nɪs.ə.t̬i, tə-
tonic-solfa, ˌtɒn.ɪk.sɒl'fɑː Ⓤⓢ ˌtɑː.nɪk.soʊl'fɑː, -sɑːl'-
tonight tə'naɪt
tonka bean 'tɒŋ.kə.biːn Ⓤⓢ 'tɑːŋ-, 'tɔːŋ- **-s** -z
Tonks tɒŋks Ⓤⓢ tɑːŋks, tɔːŋks
tonnag|e 'tʌn.ɪdʒ **-es** -ɪz
tonne tʌn **-s** -z
tonsil 'tɒnt.sᵊl, -sɪl Ⓤⓢ 'tɑːnt.sᵊl **-s** -z
tonsillectom|y ˌtɒnt.sᵊl'ek.tə.m|i, -sɪ'lek- Ⓤⓢ ˌtɑːnt.sə'lek- **-ies** -iz
tonsil(l)itis ˌtɒnt.sᵊl'aɪ.tɪs, -sɪ'laɪ- Ⓤⓢ ˌtɑːnt.sə'laɪ.t̬ɪs
tonsorial tɒn'sɔː.ri.əl Ⓤⓢ tɑːn'sɔːr.i-
tonsure 'tɒn.tʃəʳ, 'tɒnt.ʃʊəʳ, -ˌsjʊəʳ Ⓤⓢ 'tɑːnt.ʃɚ **-s** -z **-d** -d
tontine 'tɒn.tiːn, -taɪn; tɒn'tiːn Ⓤⓢ 'tɑːn.tiːn, -'-
Tonto 'tɒn.təʊ Ⓤⓢ 'tɑːn.t̬oʊ
ton-up ˌtʌn'ʌp *stress shift:* ˌton-up 'bike
ton|y (T) 'təʊ.n|i Ⓤⓢ 'toʊ- **-ier** -i.əʳ Ⓤⓢ -i.ɚ **-iest** -i.ɪst, -i.əst **'Tony AˌWard**
Tonya 'tɒn.jə Ⓤⓢ 'tɑːn-
Tonypandy ˌtɒn.i'pæn.di Ⓤⓢ ˌtɑː.ni'-
Tonyrefail ˌtɒn.i'rev.aɪl Ⓤⓢ ˌtɑː.ni'-
too tuː
toodle-oo ˌtuː.dl̩'uː
toodle-pip ˌtuː.dl̩'pɪp
took (*from* **take**) tʊk
Tooke tʊk
tool tuːl **-s** z **-ing** ɪŋ **-ed** -d
toolbox 'tuːl.bɒks Ⓤⓢ -bɑːks **-es** -ɪz
Toole tuːl
Tooley 'tuː.li
toolmaker 'tuːlˌmeɪ.kəʳ Ⓤⓢ -kɚ **-s** -z
toot tuːt **-s** -s **-ing** -ɪŋ Ⓤⓢ 'tuː.t̬ɪŋ **-ed** -ɪd Ⓤⓢ 'tuː.t̬ɪd **-er/s** -əʳ/z Ⓤⓢ 'tuː.t̬ɚ/z
tooth tuːθ **-s** -s **-ing** -ɪŋ **-ed** -t **teeth** tiːθ **'tooth ˌfairy ; 'tooth ˌpowder ; ˌtooth and 'nail ; ˌlong in the 'tooth**
toothache 'tuːθ.eɪk

toothbrush 'tuːθ.brʌʃ **-es** -ɪz **-ing** -ɪŋ
toothless 'tuːθ.ləs, -lɪs **-ly** -li **-ness** -nəs, -nɪs
toothpaste 'tuːθ.peɪst **-s** -s
toothpick 'tuːθ.pɪk **-s** -s
toothsome 'tuːθ.səm **-ly** -li **-ness** -nəs, -nɪs
tooth|y 'tuː.θ|i **-ier** -i.əʳ Ⓤⓢ -i.ɚ **-iest** -i.ɪst, -i.əst **-ily** -ɪ.li, -ᵊl.i **-iness** -ɪ.nəs, -ɪ.nɪs
Tooting 'tuː.tɪŋ Ⓤⓢ -t̬ɪŋ
tootl|e 'tuː.tl̩ Ⓤⓢ -t̬l̩ **-es** -z **-ing** -ɪŋ, 'tuːt.lɪŋ **-ed** -d
toots|y, toots|ie 'tʊt.s|i, 'tuːt- Ⓤⓢ 'tʊt- **-ies** -iz
Toowoomba tə'wʊm.bə, tʊ-
top tɒp Ⓤⓢ tɑːp **-s** -s **-ping** -ɪŋ **-ped** -t **ˌtop 'brass ; ˌtop 'dog ; ˌtop 'drawer ; ˌtop 'gear ; ˌtop 'hat** Ⓤⓢ **'top ˌhat ; ˌtop 'secret ; at the ˌtop of one's 'voice ; ˌoff the ˌtop of one's 'head ; on ˌtop of the 'world**
topaz 'təʊ.pæz Ⓤⓢ 'toʊ- **-es** -ɪz
top-class ˌtɒp'klɑːs Ⓤⓢ ˌtɑːp'klæs *stress shift:* ˌtop-class 'model
topcoat 'tɒp.kəʊt Ⓤⓢ 'tɑːp.koʊt **-s** -s
top-down ˌtɒp'daʊn Ⓤⓢ ˌtɑːp- *stress shift:* ˌtop-down 'processing
top-dress ˌtɒp'dres, '-- Ⓤⓢ 'tɑːp.dres **-es** -ɪz **-ing** -ɪŋ **-ed** -t
top|e təʊp Ⓤⓢ toʊp **-es** -s **-ing** -ɪŋ **-ed** -t **-er/s** -əʳ/z Ⓤⓢ -ɚ/z
topee 'təʊ.piː, -pi; toʊ'piː Ⓤⓢ toʊ'piː, '-- **-s** -z
Topeka təʊ'piː.kə Ⓤⓢ tə-
top-flight ˌtɒp'flaɪt Ⓤⓢ 'tɑːp.flaɪt, ˌ-'- *stress shift:* ˌtop-flight 'surgeon
topgallant ˌtɒp'gæl.ᵊnt Ⓤⓢ ˌtɑːp- *nautical pronunciation:* tə'gæl-
Topham 'tɒp.əm Ⓤⓢ 'tɑː.pəm
top-heav|y ˌtɒp'hev|.i Ⓤⓢ 'tɑːpˌhev- **-iness** -ɪ.nəs, -ɪ.nɪs *stress shift:* ˌtop-heavy 'cargo
Tophet(h) 'təʊ.fet Ⓤⓢ 'toʊ-
top-hole ˌtɒp'həʊl Ⓤⓢ ˌtɑːp'hoʊl
topi 'təʊ.piː, -pi; toʊ'piː Ⓤⓢ toʊ'piː, '-- **-s** -z
topiary 'təʊ.pjᵊr.i, -pi.ᵊr- Ⓤⓢ 'toʊ.pi.er-
topic 'tɒp.ɪk Ⓤⓢ 'tɑː.pɪk **-s** -s **-al** -ᵊl **-ally** -ᵊl.i, -li
topicalit|y ˌtɒp.ɪ'kæl.ə.t|i, -ɪ.t|i Ⓤⓢ ˌtɑː.pɪ'kæl.ə.t̬|i **-ies** -iz
topknot 'tɒp.nɒt Ⓤⓢ 'tɑːp.nɑːt **-s** -s
Toplady 'tɒpˌleɪ.di Ⓤⓢ 'tɑːp-
topless 'tɒp.ləs, -lɪs Ⓤⓢ 'tɑːp- **-ness** -nəs, -nɪs
top-level ˌtɒp'lev.ᵊl Ⓤⓢ 'tɑːpˌlev- *stress shift, British only:* ˌtop-level 'leak
topmast 'tɒp.mɑːst Ⓤⓢ 'tɑːp.mæst *nautical pronuciation:* -məst **-s** -s

topmost ˈtɒp.məʊst (US) ˈtɑːp-
top-notch ˌtɒpˈnɒtʃ (US) ˌtɑːpˈnɑːtʃ, ˌ-ˈ- *stress shift:* ˌtop-notch ˈperson
topographic ˌtɒp.əʊˈgræf.ɪk (US) ˌtɑː.pəˈ- **-al** -ᵊl **-ally** -ᵊl.i, -li
topograph|y tɒpˈɒg.rə.f|i, təˈpɒg- (US) təˈpɑː.grə- **-er/s** -əʳ/z (US) -ɚ/z
topologic|al ˌtɒp.ᵊlˈɒdʒ.ɪ.k|ᵊl (US) ˌtɑː.pəˈlɑː.dʒɪ- **-ally** -ᵊl.i, -li
topolog|y tɒpˈɒl.ə.dʒ|i, təˈpɒl- (US) təˈpɑː.lə- **-ies** -iz **-ist/s** -ɪst/s
toponymy tɒpˈɒn.ɪ.mi, təˈpɒn-, ˈ-ə- (US) təˈpɑː.nə-, toʊ-
top|os ˈtɒp|.ɒs (US) ˈtoʊ.poʊs, -ɑːs **-oi** -ɔɪ
topper ˈtɒp.əʳ (US) ˈtɑː.pɚ **-s** -z
topping (T) ˈtɒp.ɪŋ (US) ˈtɑː.pɪŋ **-s** -z **-ly** -li
toppl|e ˈtɒp.l̩ (US) ˈtɑː.pl̩ **-es** -z **-ing** -ɪŋ, ˈtɒp.lɪŋ (US) ˈtɑː.plɪŋ **-ed** -d
top-ranking ˌtɒpˈræŋ.kɪŋ (US) ˌtɑːp- *stress shift:* ˌtop-ranking ˈamateur
topsail ˈtɒp.seɪl (US) ˈtɑːp- *nautical pronunciation:* -sᵊl **-s** -z
Topsham ˈtɒp.səm (US) ˈtɑːp-
topside ˈtɒp.saɪd (US) ˈtɑːp-
topsoil ˈtɒp.sɔɪl (US) ˈtɑːp- **-s** -z
topspin ˈtɒp.spɪn (US) ˈtɑːp- **-s**
topsy-turv|y ˌtɒp.siˈtɜː.v|i (US) ˌtɑːp.siˈtɝː- **-ily** -ɪ.li, -ᵊl.i **-yness** -ɪ.nəs, -nɪs **-iness** -ɪ.nəs, -nɪs **-ydom** -ɪ.dəm
top-up ˈtɒp.ʌp, ˌ-ˈ- (US) ˈtɑːp.ʌp, ˌ-ˈ- **-s** -s
toque təʊk (US) toʊk **-s** -s
tor tɔːʳ (US) tɔːr **-s** -z
Torah ˈtɔː.rə *with some Jews:* ˈtəʊ.rɑː, ˌ-ˈ-, ˌtɔː- (US) ˈtɔːr.ə; tɔːrˈɑː; ˈtoʊ.rə
Torbay ˌtɔːˈbeɪ (US) ˌtɔːr- *stress shift:* ˌTorbay ˈguesthouse
torch tɔːtʃ (US) tɔːrtʃ **-es** -ɪz **-ing** -ɪŋ **-ed** -t ˈ**torch** ˌ**song**
torchlight ˈtɔːtʃ.laɪt (US) ˈtɔːrtʃ-
torchon ˈtɔː.ʃᵊn, -ʃɒn (US) ˈtɔːr.ʃɑːn
tore (*from* **tear**) tɔːʳ (US) tɔːr
toreador ˈtɒr.i.ə.dɔːʳ (US) ˈtɔːr.i.ə.dɔːr **-s** -z
Torfaen ˌtɔːˈvaɪn (US) ˌtɔːr-
torment (*n.*) ˈtɔː.ment (US) ˈtɔːr- **-s** -s
torment (*v.*) tɔːˈment (US) tɔːr-, ˈ-- **-ts** -ts **-ting/ly** -tɪŋ/li (US) -t̬ɪŋ/li **-ted** -tɪd (US) -t̬ɪd
tormentor, **tormenter** tɔːˈmen.təʳ (US) tɔːrˈmen.t̬ɚ, ˈ--- **-s** -z
torn (*from* **tear**) tɔːn (US) tɔːrn
tornado tɔːˈneɪ.dəʊ (US) tɔːrˈneɪ.doʊ **-(e)s** -z
Toronto təˈrɒn.təʊ (US) -ˈrɑːn.t̬oʊ
torpedo tɔːˈpiː.dəʊ (US) tɔːrˈpiː.doʊ **-es** -z **-ing** -ɪŋ **-ed** -d
Torpenhow ˈtɔː.pən.haʊ, trɪˈpen.ə *locally:* trə- (US) ˈtɔːr.pen.haʊ

torpid ˈtɔː.pɪd (US) ˈtɔːr- **-s** -z **-ly** -li **-ness** -nəs, -nɪs
torpidity tɔːˈpɪd.ə.ti, -ɪ.ti (US) tɔːrˈpɪd.ə.t̬i
Torpoint ˌtɔːˈpɔɪnt (US) ˌtɔːr-
torpor ˈtɔː.pəʳ (US) ˈtɔːr.pɚ
Torquay ˌtɔːˈkiː (US) ˌtɔːr- *stress shift:* ˌTorquay ˈguesthouse
torque tɔːk (US) tɔːrk **-s** -s
Torquemada ˌtɔː.kɪˈmɑː.də, -kemˈɑː-, -kwɪˈmɑː-, -kwemˈɑː- (US) ˌtɔːr.kəˈmɑː-, -kwəˈ-
torr tɔːʳ (US) tɔːr
Torrance ˈtɒr.ᵊnts (US) ˈtɔːr-
torrefaction ˌtɒr.ɪˈfæk.ʃᵊn, -əˈ- (US) ˌtɔːr.əˈ-
torre|fy ˈtɒr.ɪ|.faɪ, ˈ-ə- (US) ˈtɔːr.ə- **-fies** -faɪz **-fying** -faɪ.ɪŋ **-fied** -faɪd
Torremolinos ˌtɒr.ɪ.məˈliː.nɒs, ˌ-ə- (US) ˌtɔːr.ə.məˈliː.nɑːs, -əs
Torrens ˈtɒr.ᵊnz (US) ˈtɔːr-
torrent ˈtɒr.ᵊnt (US) ˈtɔːr- **-s** -s
torrential təˈren.tʃᵊl, tɒrˈen- (US) tɔːˈrent.ʃᵊl, tə- **-ly** -i
torrentiality təˌren.tʃiˈæl.ə.ti, tɒrˌen-, -ɪ.ti (US) tɔːˌrent.ʃiˈæl.ə.t̬i, tə-
Torres ˈtɒr.ɪs, ˈtɔː.rɪs, -rɪz (US) ˈtɔːr.ɪz, -ɪs
Torricelli ˌtɒr.ɪˈtʃel.i (US) ˌtɔːr.əˈ- **-an** -ən
torrid ˈtɒr.ɪd (US) ˈtɔːr.ɪd **-ly** -li **-ness** -nəs, -nɪs
Torridge ˈtɒr.ɪdʒ (US) ˈtɔːr-
Torrington ˈtɒr.ɪŋ.tən (US) ˈtɔːr-
torsion ˈtɔː.ʃᵊn (US) ˈtɔːr-
torso ˈtɔː.səʊ (US) ˈtɔːr.soʊ **-s** -z
tort tɔːt (US) tɔːrt **-s** -s
torte ˈtɔː.tə; tɔːt (US) tɔːrt; ˈtɔːr.tə **-s** -z
Tortelier tɔːˈtel.i.eɪ (US) tɔːr-
tortellini ˌtɔː.tᵊlˈiː.ni (US) ˌtɔːr.t̬əˈliː-
tortelloni ˌtɔː.tᵊlˈəʊ.ni (US) ˌtɔːr.t̬əˈloʊ-
tortfeasor ˌtɔːtˈfiː.zəʳ (US) ˌtɔːrtˈfiː.zɚ **-s** -z
tortilla tɔːˈtiː.ə, -jə; -ˈtɪl.ə (US) tɔːrˈtiː.jə **torˈtilla** ˌ**chip**
tortious ˈtɔː.ʃəs (US) ˈtɔːr- **-ly** -li
tortois|e ˈtɔː.təs (US) ˈtɔːr.t̬əs **-es** -ɪz
tortoiseshell ˈtɔː.təʃ.ʃel, -tə.ʃel (US) ˈtɔːr.t̬əs.ʃel
tortuosity ˌtɔː.tʃuˈɒs.ə.ti, -tjuˈ-, -ɪ.ti (US) ˌtɔːr.tʃuˈɑː.sə.t̬i
tortuous ˈtɔː.tʃu.əs, -tju- (US) ˈtɔːr.tʃu- **-ly** -li **-ness** -nəs, -nɪs
tort|ure ˈtɔː.tʃ|əʳ (US) ˈtɔːr.tʃ|ɚ **-ures** -əz (US) -ɚz **-uring/ly** -ᵊr.ɪŋ/li **-ured** -əd (US) -ɚd **-urer/s** -ᵊr.əʳ/z (US) -ɚ.ɚ/z ˈ**torture** ˌ**chamber**
torturous ˈtɔː.tʃᵊr.əs (US) ˈtɔːr- **-ly** -li **-ness** -nəs, -nɪs
tor|us ˈtɔː.r|əs (US) ˈtɔːr|.əs **-i** -aɪ
Torvill ˈtɔː.vɪl (US) ˈtɔːr-

tor|y (T) ˈtɔː.r|i (US) ˈtɔːr|.i **-ies** -iz **-yism** -i.ɪ.zᵊm ˈ**Tory** ˌ**party**
Toscanini ˌtɒs.kəˈniː.ni (US) ˌtɑː.skəˈ-
tosh tɒʃ (US) tɑːʃ
Toshiba® təˈʃiː.bə, tɒʃˈiː- (US) toʊˈʃiː.bə, tə-
toss tɒs (US) tɑːs **-es** -ɪz **-ing** -ɪŋ **-ed** -t **-er/s** -əʳ/z (US) -ɚ/z ˌ**argue the** ˈ**toss**
tosspot ˈtɒs.pɒt (US) ˈtɑːs.pɑːt **-s** -s
toss-up ˈtɒs.ʌp (US) ˈtɑːs- **-s** -s
tostad|a tɒsˈtɑː.d|ə (US) toʊˈstɑː- **-as** -əz **-o** -əʊ (US) -oʊ **-os** -əʊz (US) -oʊz
tot tɒt (US) tɑːt **-s** -s **-ting** -ɪŋ (US) ˈtɑː.t̬ɪŋ **-ted** -ɪd (US) ˈtɑː.t̬ɪd
total (T) ˈtəʊ.tᵊl (US) ˈtoʊ.t̬ᵊl **-s** -z **-ly** -i **-(l)ing** -ɪŋ, -ɪŋ **-(l)ed** -d ˌ**total** ˈ**recall**, ˌ**total reˈcall**
totalitarian təʊˌtæl.ɪˈteə.ri.ən, -əˈ-; ˌtəʊ.tæl- (US) toʊˌtæl.əˈter.i-, ˌtoʊ.tæl- **-ism** -ɪ.zᵊm
totalit|y təʊˈtæl.ə.t|i, -ɪ.t|i (US) toʊˈtæl.ə.t̬|i **-ies** -iz
totalizator, **-isa-** ˈtəʊ.tᵊl.aɪ.zeɪ.təʳ, -ɪ- (US) ˈtoʊ.t̬ᵊl.ɪ.zeɪ.t̬ɚ **-s** -z
totaliz|e, **-is|e** ˈtəʊ.tᵊl.aɪz (US) ˈtoʊ.t̬ə.laɪz **-es** -ɪz **-ing** -ɪŋ **-ed** -d **-er/s** -əʳ/z (US) -ɚ/z
tot|e təʊt (US) toʊt **-es** -s **-ing** -ɪŋ **-ed** -ɪd ˈ**tote** ˌ**bag**
totem ˈtəʊ.təm (US) ˈtoʊ.t̬əm **-s** -z **-ism** -ɪ.zᵊm ˈ**totem** ˌ**pole**
totemic təʊˈtem.ɪk (US) toʊ- **-ally** -ᵊl.i, -li
t'other, **tother** ˈtʌð.əʳ (US) -ɚ
Tothill ˈtɒt.hɪl (US) ˈtɑː.tɪl, ˈtɑːt.hɪl
Totnes ˈtɒt.nɪs, -nəs (US) ˈtɑːt-
Totten ˈtɒt.ᵊn (US) ˈtɑː.tᵊn
Tottenham ˈtɒt.ᵊn.əm, ˈ-nəm (US) ˈtɑː.tᵊn.əm ˌ**Tottenham Court** ˈ**Road**; ˌ**Tottenham** ˈ**Hotspur**
tott|er ˈtɒt|.əʳ (US) ˈtɑː.t̬|ɚ **-ers** -əz (US) -ɚz **-ering/ly** -ᵊr.ɪŋ/li **-ered** -əd (US) -ɚd **-erer/s** -ᵊr.əʳ/z (US) -ɚ.ɚ/z **-ery** -ᵊr.i
Totteridge ˈtɒt.ᵊr.ɪdʒ (US) ˈtɑː.t̬ɚ-
Tottington ˈtɒt.ɪŋ.tən (US) ˈtɑː.t̬ɪŋ-
Totton ˈtɒt.ᵊn (US) ˈtɑː.tᵊn
toucan ˈtuː.kæn, -kən (US) -kæn, -kɑːn, -kən; tuːˈkæn, -ˈkɑːn **-s** -z
touch tʌtʃ **-es** -ɪz **-ing** -ɪŋ **-ed** -t ˌ**touch and** ˈ**go**
touchable ˈtʌtʃ.ə.bl̩
touchdown ˈtʌtʃ.daʊn
touché ˈtuː.ʃeɪ, -ˈ- (US) tuːˈʃeɪ
touching ˈtʌtʃ.ɪŋ **-ly** -li **-ness** -nəs, -nɪs
touchline ˈtʌtʃ.laɪn **-s** -z
touchpaper ˈtʌtʃˌpeɪ.pəʳ (US) -pɚ
touchstone (T) ˈtʌtʃ.stəʊn (US) -stoʊn **-s** -z
touch-tone ˈtʌtʃ.təʊn (US) -toʊn
touch-typ|e ˈtʌtʃ.taɪp **-es** -s **-ing** -ɪŋ **-ed** -t **-ist/s** -ɪst/s

touchwood ˈtʌtʃ.wʊd

touch|y ˈtʌtʃ|.i **-ier** -i.əʳ (US) -i.ɚ **-iest** -i.ɪst, -i.əst **-ily** -ɪ.li, -ᵊl.i **-iness** -ɪ.nəs, -ɪ.nɪs

tough tʌf **-s** -s **-er** -əʳ (US) -ɚ **-est** -ɪst, -əst **-ly** -li **-ness** -nəs, -nɪs

toughen ˈtʌf.ᵊn **-s** -z **-ing** -ɪŋ, ˈtʌf.nɪŋ **-ed** -d

tough|ie, tough|y ˈtʌf|.i **-ies** -z

Toulon tuːˈlɔ̃ːŋ (US) -ˈlõʊn, -ˈlɑːn

Toulouse tuːˈluːz

Toulouse-Lautrec ˌtuː.luːz.ləʊˈtrek, tuːˌluːz- (US) tuːˌluːz.loʊˈ-, -ˌluːs-, -ləˈ-

toupée, toupee ˈtuː.peɪ, -ˈ- (US) tuːˈpeɪ **-s** -z

tour tʊəʳ, tɔːʳ (US) tʊr **-s** -z **-ing** -ɪŋ **-ed** -d **-er/s** -əʳ/z (US) -ɚ/z **ˈtour ˌoperator**

Touraine tʊˈreɪn (US) -ˈreɪn, -ˈren

tourbillion tʊəˈbɪl.i.ən, ˈ-jən (US) tʊrˈbɪl.jən **-s** -z

tour de force ˌtʊə.dəˈfɔːs, ˌtɔː- (US) ˌtʊr.dəˈfɔːrs **tours de force** ˌtʊəz-, ˌtɔːz- (US) ˌtʊrz-

Tour de France ˌtʊə.dəˈfrɑːnts, ˌtɔː- (US) ˌtʊr-

Tourette syndrome tʊəˈretˌsɪn.drəʊm, tɔː- (US) tʊˈretˌsɪn.droʊm

tourism ˈtʊə.rɪ.zᵊm, ˈtɔː- (US) ˈtʊr.ɪ-

tourist ˈtʊə.rɪst, ˈtɔː- (US) ˈtʊr.ɪst **-s** -s **ˈtourist atˌtraction** ; **ˈtourist ˌclass** ; **ˌtourist inforˈmation office**

touristic tʊəˈrɪs.tɪk, tɔː- (US) tʊˈrɪs- **-ally** -ᵊl.i, -li

touristy ˈtʊə.rɪ.sti, ˈtɔː- (US) ˈtʊr.ɪ-

tourmaline ˈtʊə.mə.liːn, ˈtɜː-, ˈtɔː-, -lɪn (US) ˈtʊr.mə.lɪn, -liːn

Tournai ˈtʊə.neɪ, -ˈ- (US) tʊrˈneɪ

tournament ˈtʊə.nə.mənt, ˈtɔː-, ˈtɜː- (US) ˈtɜːr-, ˈtʊr- **-s** -s

tournedos (*sing.*) ˈtʊə.nə.dəʊ, ˈtɔː-, ˈtɜː- (US) ˈtʊr.nə.doʊ, ˌ--ˈ- (*plur.*) -z

Tourneur ˈtɜː.nəʳ (US) ˈtɜːr.nɚ

tourney ˈtʊə.ni, ˈtɔː- (US) ˈtɜːr-, ˈtʊr- **-s** -z

tourniquet ˈtʊə.nɪ.keɪ, ˈtɔː-, ˈtɜː- (US) ˈtɜːr.nɪ.kɪt, ˈtʊr-, -ket **-s** -z

tournure ˈtʊə.njʊəʳ, ˈtɔː-, -ˈ- (US) ˈtɜːr.njʊr **-s** -z

Tours *French town:* tʊəʳ (US) tʊr *English musical composer:* tʊəz, tɔːz (US) tʊrz

tousl|e ˈtaʊ.zl̩ **-es** -z **-ing** -ɪŋ, ˈtaʊz.lɪŋ **-ed** -d

tout taʊt **-s** -s **-ing** -ɪŋ (US) ˈtaʊ.t̬ɪŋ **-ed** -ɪd (US) ˈtaʊ.t̬ɪd

Tout *in Belle Tout in East Sussex:* tuːt *surname:* taʊt

tout court ˌtuːˈkʊəʳ, -ˈkɔːʳ (US) -ˈkʊr

tout de suite ˌtuːtˈswiːt

Tovey ˈtəʊ.vi, ˈtʌv.i (US) ˈtoʊ.vi, ˈtʌv.i

tow (T) təʊ (US) toʊ **-s** -z **-ing** -ɪŋ **-ed** -d

towage ˈtəʊ.ɪdʒ (US) ˈtoʊ-

toward (*adj.*) ˈtəʊ.əd; tɔːd (US) tɔːrd; ˈtoʊ.ɚd **-ly** -li **-ness** -nəs, -nɪs

toward (*prep.*) təˈwɔːd, tʊ-; twɔːd, tɔːd (US) tɔːrd, twɔːrd; ˈtoʊ.ɚd; təˈwɔːrd **-s** -z

towaway ˈtəʊ.ə.weɪ (US) ˈtoʊ- **-s** -z

towbar ˈtəʊ.bɑːʳ (US) ˈtoʊ.bɑːr **-s** -z

Towcester ˈtəʊ.stəʳ (US) ˈtoʊ.stɚ

towel taʊəl **-s** -z **-(l)ing** -ɪŋ **-(l)ed** -d **ˌthrow in the ˈtowel**

towelette ˌtaʊəˈlet (US) ˌtaʊə- **-s** -s

tower (T) taʊəʳ (US) taʊɚ **-s** -z **-ing/ly** -ɪŋ **-ed** -d **ˈtower ˌblock** ; **ˌTower ˈHamlets** ; **ˌTower of ˈLondon** ; **ˌtower of ˈstrength**

towhead ˈtəʊ.hed (US) ˈtoʊ- **-s** -z **-ed** -ɪd

Towle təʊl (US) toʊl

Towler ˈtaʊ.ləʳ (US) -lɚ

town taʊn **-s** -z **ˌtown ˈcentre** ; **ˌtown ˈcrier** ; **ˌtown ˈhall** ; **ˈtown ˌhouse** ; **ˌtown ˈplanning** ; **ˌpaint the ˌtown ˈred**

Towne taʊn **-s** -z

townee taʊˈniː, ˈ-- **-s** -z

townie ˈtaʊ.ni **-s** -z

townscape ˈtaʊn.skeɪp **-s** -s

Townsend ˈtaʊn.zend

townsfolk ˈtaʊnz.fəʊk (US) -foʊk

Townshend ˈtaʊn.zend

township ˈtaʊn.ʃɪp **-s** -s

towns|man ˈtaʊnz|.mən **-men** -mən, -men

townspeople ˈtaʊnzˌpiː.pl̩

Townsville ˈtaʊnz.vɪl

towns|woman ˈtaʊnz|ˌwʊm.ən **-women** -ˌwɪm.ɪn

town|y ˈtaʊ.n|i **-ies** -iz

towpa|th ˈtəʊ.pɑː|θ (US) ˈtoʊ.pæ|θ **-ths** -ðz (US) -θs, -ðz

towrope ˈtəʊ.rəʊp (US) ˈtoʊ.roʊp **-s** -z

Towton ˈtaʊ.tᵊn

Towy ˈtaʊ.i

Towyn ˈtaʊ.ɪn

tox(a)emia tɒkˈsiː.mi.ə (US) tɑːk-

toxic ˈtɒk.sɪk (US) ˈtɑːk- **-al** -ᵊl **-ally** -ᵊl.i, -li **ˌtoxic ˈshock ˌsyndrome** ; **ˌtoxic ˈwaste**

toxicity tɒkˈsɪs.ə.ti, -ɪ.ti (US) tɑːkˈsɪs.ə.t̬i

toxicological ˌtɒk.sɪ.kᵊlˈɒdʒ.ɪ.kᵊl (US) ˌtɑːk.sɪ.kəˈlɑː.dʒɪ-

toxicolog|y ˌtɒk.sɪˈkɒl.ə.dʒ|i (US) ˌtɑːk.sɪˈkɑː.lə- **-ist/s** -ɪst/s

toxin ˈtɒk.sɪn (US) ˈtɑːk- **-s** -z

toxophilite tɒkˈsɒf.ɪ.laɪt, -ᵊl.aɪt (US) tɑːkˈsɑː.fə.laɪt **-s** -s

toxoplasmosis ˌtɒk.səʊ.plæzˈməʊ.sɪs (US) ˌtɑːk.soʊ.plæzˈmoʊ-

Toxteth ˈtɒk.steθ, -stəθ (US) ˈtɑːk-

toy tɔɪ **-s** -z **-ing** -ɪŋ **-ed** -d

Toya(h) ˈtɔɪ.ə

toyboy ˈtɔɪ.bɔɪ **-s** -z

Toye tɔɪ

Toynbee ˈtɔɪn.biː, ˈtɔɪm- (US) ˈtɔɪn-

Toyota® tɔɪˈəʊ.tə, tɔːˈjəʊ- (US) tɔɪˈjoʊ.t̬ə, -ˈoʊ-

toyshop ˈtɔɪ.ʃɒp (US) -ʃɑːp **-s** -s

Tozer ˈtəʊ.zəʳ (US) ˈtoʊ.zɚ

trac|e treɪs **-es** -ɪz **-ing** -ɪŋ **-ed** -t **-er/s** -əʳ/z (US) -ɚ/z **ˈtrace ˌelement** ; **ˈtracing ˌpaper**

traceab|le ˈtreɪ.sə.b|l̩ **-ly** -li **-leness** -l̩.nəs, -nɪs

tracer|y ˈtreɪ.sᵊr|.i **-ies** -iz

Tracey ˈtreɪ.si

trache|a trəˈkiː|.ə; ˈtreɪ.ki- (US) ˈtreɪ.ki- **-as** -əz **-ae** -iː

tracheal trəˈkiː.əl; ˈtreɪ.ki- (US) ˈtreɪ.ki-

tracheotomy ˌtræk.iˈɒt.ə.mi (US) ˌtreɪ.kiˈɑː.t̬ə-

trachoma trəˈkəʊ.mə, trækˈəʊ- (US) trəˈkoʊ-

Traci ˈtreɪ.si

tracing ˈtreɪ.sɪŋ **-s** -z

track træk **-s** -s **-ing** -ɪŋ **-ed** -t **-er/s** -əʳ/z (US) -ɚ/z **ˌtrack and ˈfield** ; **ˈtrack eˌvent** ; **ˈtrack ˌrecord, ˌtrack ˈrecord** (US) **ˈtrack ˌrecord** ; **keep ˈtrack of ˌsomeone/something** ; **ˌoff the ˌbeaten ˈtrack**

trackless ˈtræk.ləs, -lɪs

tracksuit ˈtræk.suːt, -sjuːt (US) -suːt **-s** -s **-ed** -ɪd

tract trækt **-s** -s

tractability ˌtræk.təˈbɪl.ə.ti, -ɪ.ti (US) -ə.t̬i

tractab|le ˈtræk.tə.b|l̩ **-ly** -li **-leness** -l̩.nəs, -nɪs

Tractarian trækˈteə.ri.ən (US) -ˈter.i- **-s** -z **-ism** -ɪ.zᵊm

tractate ˈtræk.teɪt **-s** -s

tractile ˈtræk.taɪl (US) -tɪl, -taɪl

traction ˈtræk.ʃᵊn **ˈtraction ˌengine**

tractor ˈtræk.təʳ (US) -tɚ **-s** -z

Tracy ˈtreɪ.si

trad træd **ˌtrad ˈjazz**

trad|e treɪd **-es** -z **-ing** -ɪŋ **-ed** -ɪd **-er/s** -əʳ/z (US) -ɚ/z **ˈtrade ˌbook** ; **ˌTrades Desˈcription ˌAct** ; **ˈtrading eˌstate** ; **ˈtrade ˌfair** ; **ˈtrade ˌgap** ; **ˈtrade ˌname** ; **ˈtrading ˌpost** ; **ˈtrade ˌprice** ; **ˈtrade ˌroute** ; **ˌtrade ˈsecret** ; **ˌtrade(s) ˈunion** (US) **ˈtrade(s) ˌunion** ; **ˈtrade ˌwind**

trade-in ˈtreɪd.ɪn **-s** -z

trademark ˈtreɪd.mɑːk (US) -mɑːrk **-s** -s **-ing** -ɪŋ **-ed** -t

trade-off ˈtreɪd.ɒf (US) -ɑːf **-s** -s

Tradescant trəˈdes.kənt

tradescantia ˌtræd.ɪˈskæn.ti.ə, ˌtreɪ.dɪˈ-, -desˈkæn-, -dəˈskæn- (US) ˌtræd.esˈkænt.ʃi.ə, ˈ-ʃə **-s** -z

tradesfolk 'treɪdz.fəʊk (US) -foʊk
trades|man 'treɪdz|.mən **-men** -mən
tradespeople 'treɪdzˌpiː.pl̩
tradition trə'dɪʃ.ən **-s** -z
traditional trə'dɪʃ.ən.əl, -'dɪʃ.nəl **-ly** -i
traditional|ism trə'dɪʃ.ən.əl|.ɪ.zəm, '-nəl- **-ist/s** -ɪst/s
traduc|e trə'djuːs, -'dʒuːs (US) -'duːs, -'djuːs **-es** -ɪz **-ing** -ɪŋ **-ed** -t **-er/s** -ər/z (US) -ɚ/z **-ement** -mənt
Trafalgar *in Spain:* trə'fæl.gər *archaic and poetical:* ˌtræf.əl'gɑːr (US) trə'fæl.gɚ
Trafalgar *Square:* trə'fæl.gər (US) -gɚ *Viscount:* trə'fæl.gər (US) -gɚ
Note: The present Lord Nelson pronounces the family name as /trə'fæl.gər (US) -gɚ/. Previous holders of the title pronounced /ˌtræf.əl'gɑːr (US) -'gɑːr/. *House near Salisbury:* ˌtræf.əl'gɑːr; trə'fæl.gər (US) ˌtræf.əl'gɑːr; trə'fæl.gɚ
traffic 'træf.ɪk **-s** -s **-king** -ɪŋ **-ked** -t **-ker/s** -ər/z (US) -ɚ/z **'traffic ˌcalming** ; **'traffic ˌcircle** ; **'traffic ˌjam** ; **'traffic ˌlight** ; **'traffic ˌwarden**
trafficator 'træf.ɪ.keɪ.tər (US) -t̬ɚ **-s** -z
Trafford 'træf.əd (US) -ɚd
tragacanth 'træg.ə.kænθ, 'trædʒ-, -sænθ (US) -kænθ
tragedian trə'dʒiː.di.ən **-s** -z
traged|y 'trædʒ.ə.d|i, '-ɪ- (US) '-ə- **-ies** -iz
Trager 'treɪ.gər (US) -gɚ
tragic 'trædʒ.ɪk **-al** -əl **-ally** -əl.i, -li
tragicomed|y ˌtrædʒ.ɪ'kɒm.ə.d|i, '-ɪ- (US) -'kɑː.mə- **-ies** -iz
tragicomic ˌtrædʒ.ɪ'kɒm.ɪk (US) -'kɑː.mɪk **-al** -əl **-ally** -əl.i, -li
tra|gus 'treɪ|.gəs **-gi** -gaɪ, -dʒaɪ (US) -dʒaɪ
Traherne trə'hɜːn (US) -'hɜːrn
trail treɪl **-s** -z **-ing** -ɪŋ **-ed** -d **-er/s** -ər/z (US) -ɚ/z
trailblaz|er 'treɪlˌbleɪ.z|ər (US) -z|ɚ **-ers** -əz (US) -ɚ/z **-ing** -ɪŋ
train treɪn **-s** -z **-ing/s** -ɪŋ/z **-ed** -d **-er/s** -ər/z (US) -ɚ/z **'training ˌcollege** ; **'training ˌcourse** ; **'train ˌset** ; **'training ˌshoe** ; **'train ˌspotter**
trainbearer 'treɪnˌbeə.rər, 'treɪm- (US) 'treɪnˌber.ɚ **-s** -z
trainee ˌtreɪ'niː **-s** -z **-ship/s** -ʃɪp/s
Trainor 'treɪ.nər (US) -nɚ
traips|e treɪps **-es** -ɪz **-ing** -ɪŋ **-ed** -t
trait treɪ, treɪt (US) treɪt **traits** treɪz, treɪts (US) treɪts
traitor 'treɪ.tər (US) -t̬ɚ **-s** -z
traitoress 'treɪ.tər.ɪs, -əs (US) -t̬ɚ- **-es** -ɪz
traitorous 'treɪ.tər.əs (US) -t̬ɚ- **-ly** -li **-ness** -nəs, -nɪs

Trajan 'treɪ.dʒən
trajector|y trə'dʒek.tər|.i, '-tr|i (US) -tɚ|.i **-ies** -iz
Tralee trə'liː
tram træm **-s** -z
tramcar 'træm.kɑːr (US) -kɑːr **-s** -z
tramline 'træm.laɪn **-s** -z
trammel 'træm.əl **-s** -z **-(l)ing** -ɪŋ **-(l)ed** -d
tramontane trə'mɒn.teɪn (US) trə'mɑːn-; træm'ɑːn-; ˌtræm.ɑːn'teɪn
tramp træmp **-s** -s **-ing** -ɪŋ **-ed** -t **-er/s** -ər/z (US) -ɚ/z
trampl|e 'træm.pl̩ **-es** -z **-ing** -ɪŋ, 'træm.plɪŋ **-ed** -d **-er/s** -ər/z, 'træm.plər/z (US) '-pl̩.ɚ/z, '-plɚ/z
trampolin|e 'træm.pəl.iːn, -ɪn; ˌtræm.pəl'iːn (US) 'træm.pə.liːn, -pəl.ɪn; ˌtræm.pə'liːn **-es** -z **-ing** -ɪŋ **-ist/s** -ɪst/s
tramway 'træm.weɪ **-s** -z
tranc|e trɑːnts (US) trænts **-es** -ɪz
tranch|e trɑːntʃ, trɔːntʃ, træntʃ (US) trɑːntʃ **-es** -ɪz
Tranent trə'nent
trann|y, trann|ie 'træn|.i **-ies** -iz
tranquil 'træŋ.kwɪl (US) 'træŋ-, 'træn- **-ly** -i **-ness** -nəs, -nɪs
tranquil(l)ity træŋ'kwɪl.ə.ti, -ɪ.ti (US) -ə.t̬i, træn-
tranquil(l)ization, -isa- ˌtræŋ.kwɪ.laɪ'zeɪ.ʃən, -kwə-, -lɪ'- (US) -kwə.lɪ'-, ˌtræn-
tranquil(l)iz|e, -is|e 'træŋ.kwɪ.laɪz, -kwə- (US) 'træŋ-, 'træn- **-es** -ɪz **-ing/ly** -ɪŋ/li **-ed** -d **-er/s** -ər/z (US) -ɚ/z
trans- trænts-, trɑːnts-, trænz-, trɑːnz- (US) trænts-, trænz-
Note: Prefix. May carry primary or secondary stress, or be unstressed; see individual entries.
transact træn'zækt, trɑːn-, -'sækt (US) træn- **-s** -s **-ing** -ɪŋ **-ed** -ɪd **-or/s** -ər/z (US) -ɚ/z
transaction træn'zæk.ʃən, trɑːn-, -'sæk- (US) træn- **-s** -z
transalpine træn'zæl.paɪn, trɑːn- (US) træn-
transatlantic ˌtræn.zət'læn.tɪk, ˌtrɑːn- (US) ˌtrænt.sæt'-, ˌtræn.zæt'- *stress shift:* ˌtransatlantic 'yacht
transcend træn'send, trɑːn- (US) træn- **-s** -z **-ing** -ɪŋ **-ed** -ɪd
transcenden|ce træn'sen.dənt|s, trɑːn- (US) træn- **-cy** -si
transcendent træn'sen.dənt, trɑːn- (US) træn- **-ly** -li
transcendental ˌtrænt.sen'den.təl, ˌtrɑːnt-, -sən'- (US) ˌtrænt.sen'den.t̬əl **-ly** -i ˌ**transcendental medi'tation**

transcendental|ism ˌtrænt.sen'den.təl|.ɪ.zəm, ˌtrɑːnt-, -sən'- (US) ˌtrænt.sen'den.t̬əl- **-ist/s** -ɪst/s
transcontinental ˌtrænsˌkɒn.tɪ'nen.təl, ˌtrɑːns-, -tə'- (US) ˌtræntsˌkɑːn.tən'en-, ˌtrænz-
transcrib|e træn'skraɪb, trɑːn- (US) træn- **-es** -z **-ing** -ɪŋ **-ed** -d **-er/s** -ər/z (US) -ɚ/z
transcript 'trænt.skrɪpt, 'trɑːnt- (US) 'trænt- **-s** -s
transcription træn'skrɪp.ʃən, trɑːn- (US) træn- **-s** -z
transducer trænz'djuː.sər, trɑːnz-, trænts-, trɑːnts- (US) trænts'duː.sɚ, trænz-, -'djuː- **-s** -z
transept 'trænt.sept, 'trɑːnt- (US) 'trænt- **-s** -s
transexual træn'sek.ʃʊəl, trɑːn-, -ʃu.əl, -sjʊəl, -sju.əl (US) træn'sek.ʃu.əl **-s** -z **-ism** -ɪ.zəm
transexuality trænˌsek.ʃu'æl.ɪ.ti, -sju-, -ə.ti (US) -ʃu'æl.ə.t̬i
transfer (*n.*) 'trænts.fɜːr, 'trɑːnts- (US) 'trænts.fɜːr **-s** -z
transfer (*v.*) trænts'fɜːr, trɑːnts- (US) trænts'fɜːr, '-- **-s** -z **-ring** -ɪŋ **-red** -d **-rer/s** -ər/z (US) -ɚ/z
transferability ˌtrænts.fər.ə'bɪl.ə.ti, ˌtrɑːnts-, -ɪ.ti; træntsˌfɜː.rə'-, trɑːnts- (US) træntsˌfɜːr.ə'bɪl.ə.t̬i
transferable trænts'fɜː.rə.bl̩, trɑːnts-; 'trænts.fər.ə-, 'trɑːnts- (US) trænts'fɜːr.ə-
transferee ˌtrænts.fɜː'riː, ˌtrɑːnts-, -fə'- (US) ˌtrænts.fə'riː **-s** -z
transferenc|e trænts'fɜː.rənts, trɑːnts-; 'trænts.fər.ənts, 'trɑːnts- (US) trænts'fɜːr-; 'trænts.fɚ- **-es** -ɪz
transfiguration (T) ˌtrænts.fɪ.gər'eɪ.ʃən, ˌtrɑːnts-, -fɪg.jər'eɪ-; træntsˌfɪg.ər'-, trɑːnts-, -jər'- (US) ˌtrænts.fɪg.jə'reɪ-, træntsˌfɪg-, -jʊ'- **-s** -z
transfig|ure trænts'fɪg|.ər, trɑːnts- (US) trænts'fɪg.j|ɚ **-ures** -əz (US) -ɚz **-uring** -ər.ɪŋ **-ured** -əd (US) -ɚd **-urement/s** -ə.mənt/s (US) -ɚ.mənt/s
transfinite trænts'faɪ.naɪt, trɑːnts- (US) trænts-
transfix trænts'fɪks, trɑːnts- (US) trænts- **-es** -ɪz **-ing** -ɪŋ **-ed** -t
transfixion trænts'fɪk.ʃən, trɑːnts- (US) trænts- **-s** -z
transform trænts'fɔːm, trɑːnts- (US) trænts'fɔːrm **-s** -z **-ing** -ɪŋ **-ed** -d **-er/s** -ər/z (US) -ɚ/z **-able** -ə.bl̩
transformation ˌtrænts.fə'meɪ.ʃən, ˌtrɑːnts-, -fɔː'- (US) ˌtrænts.fɚ'-, -fɔːr'- **-s** -z

transformational ˌtrænts.fəˈmeɪ.ʃᵊn.ᵊl, ˌtrɑːnts-, -ˈmeɪʃ.nᵊl (US) ˌtrænts.fɚˈ-, -fɔːrˈ- *stress shift, see compound:* ˌ**transformational ˈgrammar**

transfusable træntsˈfjuː.zə.bl̩, trɑːnts- (US) trænts-

transfus|e træntsˈfjuːz, trɑːnts- (US) trænts- **-es** -ɪz **-ing** -ɪŋ **-ed** -d **-er/s** -əʳ/z (US) -ɚ/z

transfusible træntsˈfjuː.zə.bl̩, trɑːnts-, -zɪ- (US) trænts-

transfusion træntsˈfjuː.ʒᵊn, trɑːnts- (US) trænts- **-s** -z

transgress trænzˈgres, trɑːnz-, trænts-, trɑːnts- (US) trænts-, trænz- **-es** -ɪz **-ing** -ɪŋ **-ed** -t **-or/s** -əʳ/z (US) -ɚ/z

transgression trænzˈgreʃ.ᵊn, trɑːnz-, trænts-, trɑːnts- (US) trænts-, trænz- **-s** -z

tranship træntsˈʃɪp, trɑːnts-, trænz-, trɑːnz-, træn-, trɑːn- (US) træn- **-s** -s **-ping** -ɪŋ **-ped** -t **-ment/s** -mənt/s

transhuman|ce træntsˈhjuː.mən|ts, trɑːnts- (US) trænts-, trænz- **-t** -t

transien|ce ˈtræn.zi.ənt|s, ˈtrɑːn-; ˈtrænt.si-, ˈtrɑːnt- (US) ˈtrænt.ʃᵊnt|s, -si.ənt|s; ˈtræn.ʒᵊnt|s, -zi.ənt|s **-cy** -si

transient ˈtræn.zi.ənt, ˈtrɑːn-; ˈtrænt.si.ənt, ˈtrɑːnt- (US) ˈtrænt.ʃᵊnt, -si.ənt; ˈtræn.ʒᵊnt, -zi.ənt **-ly** -li **-ness** -nəs, -nɪs

transilient trænˈsɪl.i.ənt, trɑːn-, -ˈzɪl-, ˈ-jənt (US) træn-

transistor trænˈzɪs.təʳ, trɑːn-, -ˈsɪs- (US) trænˈzɪs.tɚ, -ˈsɪs- **-s** -z **tranˌsistor ˈradio**, ˌ**transistor ˈradio**

transistoriz|e, -is|e trænˈzɪs.tᵊr.aɪz, trɑːn-, -ˈsɪs- (US) trænˈzɪs.tə.raɪz, -ˈsɪs- **-es** -ɪz **-ing** -ɪŋ **-ed** -d

transit ˈtrænt.sɪt, ˈtrɑːnt-; ˈtræn.zɪt, ˈtrɑːn- (US) ˈtrænt.sɪt; ˈtræn.zɪt **-s** -s ˈ**transit** ˌ**lounge**

transition trænˈzɪʃ.ᵊn, trɑːn-, trən-, -ˈsɪʒ- (US) trænˈzɪʃ-, -ˈsɪʃ-, -ˈsɪʒ- **-s** -z

transitional trænˈzɪʃ.ᵊn.əl, trɑːn-, trən-, -ˈsɪʒ-, ˈ-nᵊl (US) trænˈzɪʃ-, -ˈsɪʃ-, -ˈsɪʒ- **-li** -i

transitive ˈtrænt.sə.tɪv, ˈtrɑːnt-, -sɪ-; ˈtræn.zə-, ˈtrɑːn-, -zɪ- (US) ˈtrænt.sə.t̬ɪv; ˈtræn.zə- **-ly** -li **-ness** -nəs, -nɪs

transitivity ˌtrænt.səˈtɪv.ɪ.ti, ˌtrɑːnt-, -sɪˈ-; ˌtræn.zəˈ-, ˌtrɑːn-, -zɪˈ- (US) ˌtrænt.səˈtɪv.ə.t̬i; ˌtræn.zəˈ-

transitor|y ˈtrænt.sɪ.tᵊr|.i, ˈtrɑːnt-, -sə-; ˈtræn.zɪ-, ˈtrɑːn-, -zə- (US) ˈtrænt.sə.tɔːr-; ˈtræn.zə- **-ily** -ᵊl.i, -ɪ.li **-iness** -ɪ.nəs, -ɪ.nɪs

Transkei ˌtræntˈskaɪ, ˌtrɑːnt-; ˌtrænzˈkaɪ, ˌtrɑːnz- (US) trænˈskeɪ, -ˈskaɪ

transla|te trænzˈleɪ|t, trɑːnz-; træntˈsleɪ|t, trɑːnt- (US) trænˈsleɪ|t, ˈ--; trænzˈleɪ|t, ˈ-- **-tes** -ts **-ting** -tɪŋ (US) -t̬ɪŋ **-ted** -tɪd (US) -t̬ɪd **-tor/s** -təʳ/z (US) -t̬ɚ/z **-table** -tə.bl̩ (US) -t̬ə.bl̩

translation trænzˈleɪ.ʃᵊn, trɑːnz-; træntˈsleɪ-, trɑːnt- (US) trænˈsleɪ-; trænzˈleɪ- **-s** -z

translative trænzˈleɪ.tɪv, trɑːnz-; træntˈsleɪ-, trɑːnt- (US) trænˈsleɪ.t̬ɪv; trænzˈleɪ-

translatory trænzˈleɪ.tᵊr.i, trɑːnz-; træntˈsleɪ-, trɑːnt- (US) trænˈsleɪ.t̬ɚ-; trænzˈleɪ-

transliter|ate trænzˈlɪt.ᵊr|.eɪt, trɑːnz-; træntˈslɪt-, trɑːnt- (US) trænˈslɪt̬.ə.r|eɪt; trænzˈlɪt̬- **-ates** -eɪts **-ating** -eɪ.tɪŋ (US) -eɪ.t̬ɪŋ **-ated** -eɪ.tɪd (US) -eɪ.t̬ɪd **-ator/s** -eɪ.təʳ/z (US) -eɪ.t̬ɚ/z

transliteration ˌtrænz.lɪ.tᵊrˈeɪ.ʃᵊn, ˌtrɑːnz-; trænzˌlɪt.ᵊrˈ-, trɑːnz-; ˌtrænt.slɪ.tᵊr-, ˌtrɑːnt-; trænˌslɪt.ᵊrˈ-, trɑːn- (US) trænˌslɪt̬.əˈreɪ-; trænzˌlɪt̬- **-s** -z

translucenc|e trænzˈluː.sᵊnts, trɑːnz-, -ˈljuː-; trænˈsluː-, trɑːn-; trænsˈljuː-, trɑːns- (US) trænˈsluː-; trænzˈluː- **-y** -i

translucent trænzˈluː.sᵊnt, trɑːnz-, -ˈljuː-; trænˈsluː-, trɑːn-; trænsˈljuː-, trɑːns- (US) trænˈsluː-; trænzˈluː- **-ly** -li

transmigra|te ˌtrænz.maɪˈgreɪ|t, ˌtrɑːnz-; ˌtrænt.smaɪˈ-, ˌtrɑːnt- (US) ˌtræntˈsmaɪ.greɪ|t; ˌtrænzˈmaɪ- **-tes** -ts **-ting** -tɪŋ (US) -t̬ɪŋ **-ted** -tɪd (US) -t̬ɪd **-tor/s** -təʳ/z (US) -t̬ɚ/z

transmigration ˌtrænz.maɪˈgreɪ.ʃᵊn, ˌtrɑːnz-; ˌtrænt.smaɪˈ-, ˌtrɑːnt- (US) ˌtrænt.smaɪˈ-; ˌtrænz.maɪˈ- **-s** -z

transmigratory trænzˈmaɪ.grə.tᵊr.i, trɑːnz-; trænˈsmaɪ-, trɑːn- (US) trænˈsmaɪ.grə.tɔːr-; trænzˈmaɪ-

transmissibility trænzˌmɪs.əˈbɪl.ə.ti, trɑːnz-, -ɪˈ-, -ɪ.ti; trænˌsmɪs-, trɑːn-; ˌtrænz.mɪ.səˈ-, ˌtrɑːnz-, -sɪˈ-; ˌtrænt.smɪ-, ˌtrɑːnt- (US) ˌtrænt.smɪs.əˈbɪl.ə.t̬i; ˌtrænz.mɪs-

transmissible trænzˈmɪs.ə.bl̩, trɑːnz-, ˈ-ɪ-; trænˈsmɪs-, trɑːn- (US) trænˈsmɪs-; trænzˈmɪs-

transmission trænzˈmɪʃ.ᵊn, trɑːnz-; trænˈsmɪʃ-, trɑːn- (US) trænˈsmɪʃ-; trænzˈmɪʃ- **-s** -z

transmi|t trænzˈmɪ|t, trɑːnz-; trænˈsmɪ|t, trɑːn- (US) trænˈsmɪ|t; trænzˈmɪ|t **-ts** -ts **-tting** -tɪŋ (US) -t̬ɪŋ **-tted** -tɪd (US) -t̬ɪd **-tter/s** -təʳ/z (US) -t̬ɚ/z

transmittal trænzˈmɪt.ᵊl, trɑːnz-; trænˈsmɪt-, trɑːn- (US) trænˈsmɪt̬-; trænzˈmɪt̬- **-s** -z

transmittanc|e trænzˈmɪt.ᵊnts, trɑːnz-; trænˈsmɪt-, trɑːn- (US) trænˈsmɪt̬-; trænzˈmɪt̬- **-es** -ɪz

transmogrification ˌtrænz.mɒg.rɪ.fɪˈkeɪ.ʃᵊn, ˌtrɑːnz-, trænzˌmɒg-, trɑːnz-, -rə-; ˌtrænt.smɒg-, ˌtrɑːnt-, trænˌsmɒg-, trɑːn- (US) trænˌsmɑː.grə-; trænzˌmɑːg-

transmogri|fy trænzˈmɒg.rɪ|.faɪ, trɑːnz-, -rə-; trænˈsmɒg-, trɑːn- (US) trænˈsmɑː.grə-; trænzˈmɑː- **-fies** -faɪz **-fying** -faɪ.ɪŋ **-fied** -faɪd

transmutability trænzˌmjuː.təˈbɪl.ə.ti, trɑːnz-, trænts-, trɑːnts-, ˌtrænz.mjuː-, ˌtrɑːnz-, ˌtrænts-, ˌtrɑːnts-, -ɪ.ti (US) ˌtrænts.mjuː.t̬əˈbɪl.ə.t̬i, ˌtrænz-

transmutation ˌtrænz.mjuːˈteɪ.ʃᵊn, ˌtrɑːnz-, ˌtrænts-, ˌtrɑːnts-, -mjʊˈ- (US) ˌtrænts-, ˌtrænz- **-s** -z

trans|mute trænz|ˈmjuːt, trɑːnz-, trænts-, trɑːnts- (US) trænts-, trænz- **-mutes** -ˈmjuːts **-muting** -ˈmjuː.tɪŋ (US) -ˈmjuː.t̬ɪŋ **-muted** -ˈmjuː.tɪd (US) -ˈmjuː.t̬ɪd **-muter/s** -ˈmjuː.təʳ/z (US) -ˈmjuː.t̬ɚ/z **-mutable** -ˈmjuː.tə.bl̩ (US) -ˈmjuː.t̬ə.bl̩

transnational trænzˈnæʃ.ᵊn.ᵊl, trɑːnz-, ˈ-nᵊl; trænˈsnæʃ-, trɑːn- (US) trænˈsnæʃ-; trænzˈnæʃ-

transoceanic ˌtræn.zəʊ.ʃiˈæn.ɪk, -siˈ-; ˌtrænt.səʊ- (US) ˌtrænt.soʊ.ʃiˈ-; ˌtræn.zoʊ-

transom ˈtrænt.səm **-s** -z

transpacific ˌtrænt.spəˈsɪf.ɪk, ˌtrɑːnts-; ˌtrænz.pəˈ-, ˌtrɑːnz- (US) ˌtrænt.spə-, ˌtrænz-

transparenc|y trænˈspær.ᵊnt.s|i, trɑːn-, trən-, -ˈspeə.rᵊnt-; trænzˈpær.ᵊnt-, trɑːnz-, trənz-, -ˈpeə.rᵊnt- (US) trænˈsper.ᵊnt-, -ˈspær- **-ies** -iz

transparen|t træntˈspær.ᵊn|t, trɑːnt-, trənt-, -speə.rᵊn|t; trænzˈpær.ᵊn|t, trɑːnz-, trənz-, -ˈpeə.rᵊn|t (US) trænˈsper.ᵊn|t, -ˈspær- **-tly** -t.li **-tness** -t.nəs, -t.nɪs **-ce** -ts

transpiration ˌtrænt.spɪˈreɪ.ʃᵊn, ˌtrɑːnt-, -spəˈ- (US) ˌtrænt-

transpir|e trænˈspaɪəʳ, trɑːn- (US) trænˈspaɪɚ **-es** -z **-ing** -ɪŋ **-ed** -d

transplan|t (*v.*) træn'splɑːn|t, trɑːn- (US) træn'splæn|t; 'trænt.splæn|t **-ts** -ts **-ting** -tɪŋ (US) -t̬ɪŋ **-ted** -tɪd (US) -t̬ɪd **-table** -tə.bl̩ (US) -t̬ə.bl̩
transplant (*n.*) 'trænt.splɑːnt, 'trɑːn- (US) 'trænt.splænt **-s** -s
transplantation ˌtrænt.splɑːn'teɪ.ʃᵊn, ˌtrɑːnt- (US) ˌtrænt.splæn'- **-s** -z
transponder træn'spɒn.dəʳ, trɑːn- (US) træn'spɑːn.dɚ **-s** -z
transpontine trænt'spɒn.taɪn, trɑːnt-; trænz'pɒn-, trɑːnz- (US) træn'spɑːn.taɪn, -tɪn, -tiːn
transport (*n.*) 'trænt.spɔːt, 'trɑːnt- (US) 'trænt.spɔːrt **-s** -s **'transport ˌcafe**
transpor|t (*v.*) træn'spɔː|t, trɑːn- (US) træn'spɔːr|t, '-- **-ts** -ts **-ting** -tɪŋ (US) -t̬ɪŋ **-ted** -tɪd (US) -t̬ɪd **-table** -tə.bl̩ (US) -t̬ə.bl̩
transportability ˌtrænt.spɔː.tə'bɪl.ə.ti, ˌtrɑːnt-, trænˌspɔː-, trɑːn-, -ɪ.ti (US) trænˌspɔːr.t̬ə'bɪl.ə.t̬i
transportation ˌtrænt.spɔː'teɪ.ʃᵊn, ˌtrɑːnt-, -spə'- (US) ˌtrænt.spɚ'- **-s** -z
transporter træn'spɔː.təʳ, trɑːn- (US) træn'spɔːr.t̬ɚ **-s** -z
transpos|e træn'spəʊz, trɑːn- (US) træn'spoʊz **-es** -ɪz **-ing** -ɪŋ **-ed** -d **-er/s** -əʳ/z (US) -ɚ/z **-able** -ə.bl̩ **-al/s** -ᵊl/z
transposition ˌtrænt.spə'zɪʃ.ᵊn, ˌtrɑːnt- (US) ˌtrænt- **-s** -z
transputer træn'spjuː.təʳ, trɑːn-; trænz'pjuː-, trɑːnz- (US) træn'spjuː.t̬ɚ **-s** -z
transsexual træn'sek.ʃʊəl, trɑːn-, trænts-, trɑːnts-, -ʃu.əl, -sjʊəl, -sju.əl (US) træn'sek.ʃu.əl, trænts- **-s** -z **-ism** -ɪ.zᵊm
transsexuality trænˌsek.ʃu'æl.ɪ.ti, -sju-, -ə.ti (US) -ʃu'æl.ə.t̬i
transship trænts'ʃɪp, trɑːnts-, trænz-, trɑːnz-, træn-, trɑːn- (US) træns'ʃɪp **-s** -s **-ping** -ɪŋ **-ped** -t **-ment/s** -mənt/s
Trans-Siberian ˌtrænts.saɪ'bɪə.ri.ən, ˌtrɑːnts-, ˌtrænz-, ˌtrɑːnz- (US) ˌtrænts.saɪ'bɪr.i-, ˌtrænz-
transubstanti|ate ˌtrænt.səb'stæn.tʃi|.eɪt, ˌtrɑːnt-, -'stɑːn-; -'stænt.si-, -'stɑːnt- (US) ˌtrænt.səb'stænt.ʃi- **-ates** -eɪts **-ating** -eɪ.tɪŋ (US) -eɪ.t̬ɪŋ **-ated** -eɪ.tɪd (US) -eɪ.t̬ɪd
transubstantiation ˌtrænt.səbˌstæn.tʃi'eɪ.ʃᵊn, ˌtrɑːnt-, -ˌstɑːn-; -ˌstænts.i-, -ˌstɑːnt- (US) ˌtrænt.səbˌstænt.ʃi'- **-s** -z
Transvaal 'trænz.vɑːl, 'trɑːnz-, 'trænts-, 'trɑːnts-, ˌ-'- (US) ˌtrænts'vɑːl, ˌtrænz-
Transvaaler 'trænzˌvɑː.ləʳ, 'trɑːnz-, 'trænts-, 'trɑːnts-, ˌ-'-- (US) ˌtrænts'vɑː.lɚ, ˌtrænz- **-s** -z
transversal trænz'vɜː.sᵊl, trɑːnz-, trænts-, trɑːnts- (US) trænts'vɜːr-, trænz- **-s** -z
transverse trænz'vɜːs, trɑːnz-, trænts-, trɑːnts- (US) trænts'vɜːrs, trænz- **-ly** -li *stress shift:* ˌtransverse 'engine
transverse (*n.*) 'trænz.vɜːs, 'trɑːnz-, 'trænts-, 'trɑːnts-, ˌ-'- (US) 'trænts-, 'trænz-
transvestism trænz'ves.tɪ.zᵊm, trɑːnz-, trænts-, trɑːnts- (US) trænts-, trænz-
transvestite trænz'ves.taɪt, trɑːnz-, trænts-, trɑːnts- (US) trænts-, trænz- **-s** -s
Transylvani|a ˌtrænt.sɪl'veɪ.ni|.ə, ˌtrɑːnt-, -sᵊl'-, '-nj|ə (US) ˌtrænt- **-an/s** -ən
tranter (T) 'træn.təʳ (US) -t̬ɚ **-s** -z
trap træp **-s** -s **-ping/s** -ɪŋ/z **-ped** -t **-per/s** -əʳ/z (US) -ɚ/z
trapdoor ˌtræp'dɔːʳ (US) 'træp.dɔːr, ˌ-'- **-s** -z *stress shift, British only:* ˌtrapdoor 'spider
trapes treɪps **-es** -ɪz **-ing** -ɪŋ **-ed** -t
trapez|e trə'piːz (US) træp'iːz, trə'piːz **-es** -ɪz
trapezi|um trə'piː.zi|.əm **-ums** -əmz **-a** -ə
trapezoid 'træp.ɪ.zɔɪd **-s** -z
Trapp træp
trappings 'træp.ɪŋz
Trappist 'træp.ɪst **-s** -s
trapshoot|ing 'træpˌʃuː.t|ɪŋ **-er/s** -əʳ/z (US) -ɚ/z
Traquair trə'kweəʳ (US) -'kwer
trash træʃ **-es** -ɪz **-ing** -ɪŋ **-ed** -t
trashcan 'træʃ.kæn **-s** -z
trash|man 'træʃ|.mæn, -mən **-men** -men, -mən
trash|y 'træʃ|.i **-ier** -i.əʳ (US) -i.ɚ **-iest** -i.ɪst, -i.əst **-iness** -ɪ.nəs, -ɪ.nɪs
Trasimene 'træz.ɪ.miːn, '-ə- (US) 'trɑː.zɪ.miːn, -zə-
trattoria ˌtræt.ᵊr'iː.ə (US) ˌtrɑː.t̬ə'riː.ə, -tɔː'-; trɑː'tɔːr.i- **-s** -z
traum|a 'trɔː.m|ə, 'traʊ- (US) 'trɑː-, 'trɔː-, 'traʊ- **-as** -əz **-ata** -ə.tə (US) -ə.t̬ə
traumatic trɔː'mæt.ɪk, traʊ- (US) trɑː'mæt̬-, trɔː-, traʊ- **-ally** -ᵊl.i, -li
traumatism 'trɔː.mə.tɪ.zᵊm (US) 'trɑː-, 'trɔː- **-s** -z
traumatization, -isa- ˌtrɔː.mə.taɪ'zeɪ.ʃᵊn, ˌtraʊ-, -tɪ'- (US) ˌtrɑː.mə.t̬ɪ'-, ˌtrɔː-, ˌtraʊ-
traumatiz|e, -is|e 'trɔː.mə.taɪz, 'traʊ- (US) 'trɑː-, 'trɔː-, 'traʊ- **-es** -ɪz **-ing** -ɪŋ **-ed** -d
travail 'træv.eɪl; trə'veɪl (US) trə'veɪl; 'træv.eɪl **-s** -z **-ing** -ɪŋ **-ed** -d
Travancore ˌtræv.ᵊŋ'kɔːʳ (US) -'kɔːr
travel 'træv.ᵊl **-s** -z **-(l)ing** -ɪŋ, 'træv.lɪŋ **-(l)ed** -d **'travel ˌagency**; **'travel ˌagent**; **'travelling exˌpenses**; **ˌtravelling 'salesman**; **'travel ˌsickness**
travelator 'træv.ᵊl.eɪ.təʳ (US) -ə.leɪ.t̬ɚ **-s** -z
Travelcard 'træv.ᵊl.kɑːd (US) -kɑːrd
travel(l)er 'træv.ᵊl.əʳ, '-ləʳ (US) '-ᵊl.ɚ, '-lɚ **-s** -z **'travel(l)er's ˌcheque**
travelogue, travelog 'træv.ᵊl.ɒg (US) -ə.lɑːg, -lɔːg **-s** -z
Travers 'træv.əz (US) -ɚz
travers|e (*n. adj.*) 'træv.əs, -ɜːs; trə'vɜːs, træv'ɜːs (US) 'træv.ɚs, -ɜːrs; trə'vɜːrs, træv'ɜːrs **-es** -ɪz
travers|e (*v.*) trə'vɜːs, træv'ɜːs; 'træv.ɜːs (US) trə'vɜːrs, træv'ɜːrs; 'træv.ɚs **-es** -ɪz **-ing** -ɪŋ **-ed** -t
travest|y 'træv.ə.st|i, '-ɪ- (US) '-ɪ- **-ies** -iz **-ying** -i.ɪŋ **-ied** -id **ˌtravesty of 'justice**
Traviata ˌtræv.i'ɑː.tə (US) ˌtrɑː.vi'ɑː.t̬ə
Travis 'træv.ɪs
travolator 'træv.ᵊl.eɪ.təʳ (US) -t̬ɚ **-s** -z
Travolta trə'vəʊl.tə, -'vɒl- (US) -'voʊl.t̬ə
trawl trɔːl (US) trɑːl, trɔːl **-s** -z **-ing** -ɪŋ **-ed** -d
trawler 'trɔː.ləʳ (US) 'trɑː.lɚ, 'trɔː- **-s** -z
trawler|man 'trɔː.lə|.mən (US) 'trɑː.lɚ-, 'trɔː- **-men** -mən
tray treɪ **-s** -z
Traynor 'treɪ.nəʳ (US) -nɚ
treacherous 'tretʃ.ᵊr.əs **-ly** -li **-ness** -nəs, -nɪs
treacher|y 'tretʃ.ᵊr|.i **-ies** -iz
treacle 'triː.kl̩ **-s** -z ˌ**treacle 'tart**
treacl|y 'triː.kl̩|.i, '-kl|i **-iness** -ɪ.nəs, -ɪ.nɪs
tread tred **-s** -z **-ing** -ɪŋ **trod** trɒd (US) trɑːd **trodden** 'trɒd.ᵊn (US) 'trɑː.dᵊn **treader/s** 'tred.əʳ/z (US) -ɚ/z ˌ**tread on someone's 'toes**
treadle 'tred.l̩ **-s** -z
treadmill 'tred.mɪl **-s** -z
Treadwell 'tred.wel
treason 'triː.zᵊn **-s** -z
treasonab|le 'triː.zᵊn.ə.bl|̩, 'triːz.nə- **-ly** -li **-leness** -l̩.nəs, -nɪs
treasonous 'triː.zᵊn.əs, 'triːz.nəs
treas|ure 'treʒ|.əʳ (US) -ɚ **-ures** -əz (US) -ɚz **-uring** -ᵊr.ɪŋ **-ured** -əd (US) -ɚd **'treasure ˌhunt**; **'treasure ˌtrove**
treasure-hou|se 'treʒ.ə.haʊ|s (US) '-ɚ- **-ses** -zɪz
treasurer 'treʒ.ᵊr.əʳ (US) -ɚ **-s** -z
treasurership 'treʒ.ᵊr.ə.ʃɪp (US) -ɚ- **-s** -s
treasure-trove 'treʒ.ə.trəʊv (US) '-ɚ.troʊv

treasur|y (T) 'treʒ.ᵊr|.i **-ies** -iz
treat triːt **-s** -s **-ing** -ɪŋ (US) 'triː.t̬ɪŋ **-ed** -ɪd (US) 'triː.t̬ɪd
treatis|e 'triː.tɪz, -tɪs (US) -t̬ɪs **-es** -ɪz
treatment 'triːt.mənt **-s** -s
treat|y 'triː.t|i (US) -t̬|i **-ies** -iz
Trebizond 'treb.ɪ.zɒnd (US) -zɑːnd
trebl|e 'treb.l̩ **-es** -z **-y** -i, 'treb.li **-ing** -ɪŋ, 'treb.lɪŋ **-ed** -d
Treblinka trə'blɪŋ.kə, treb'lɪŋ- (US) trə'blɪŋ-; treb'liːŋ-
Trebor 'triː.bɔːʳ (US) -bɔːr
Tredegar trɪ'diː.gəʳ, trə- (US) -gɚ
tree (T) triː **-s** -z **-ing** -ɪŋ **-d** -d **'tree ˌfrog ; ˌTree of 'Knowledge ; 'tree ˌsurgeon ; ˌbark up the ˌwrong 'tree**
treecreeper 'triːˌkriː.pəʳ (US) -pɚ **-s** -z
treeless 'triː.ləs, -lɪs
treeline 'triː.laɪn
tree-lined 'triː.laɪnd
treetop 'triː.tɒp (US) -tɑːp **-s** -z
trefoil 'tref.ɔɪl, 'triː.fɔɪl, 'trɪf.ɔɪl (US) 'triː.fɔɪl, 'tref.ɔɪl **-s** -z
Trefor 'trev.əʳ (US) -ɚ
Trefusis trɪ'fjuː.sɪs, trə-
Tregear trɪ'gɪəʳ, trə- (US) -'gɪr
Treharne trɪ'hɑːn, trə-, -'hɜːn (US) -'hɑːrn, -'hɜːrn
Treharris trɪ'hær.ɪs, trə- (US) -'her-, -'hær-
Treherne trɪ'hɜːn, trə- (US) -'hɜːrn
trek trek **-s** -s **-king** -ɪŋ **-ked** -t **-ker/s** -əʳ/z (US) -ɚ/z
Trekkie 'trek.i **-s** -z
Trelawn(e)y trɪ'lɔː.ni, trə- (US) -'lɑː-, -'lɔː-
Treleaven trɪ'lev.ᵊn, trə-
trellis 'trel.ɪs **-es** -ɪz **-ed** -t
trelliswork 'trel.ɪs.wɜːk (US) -wɜːrk
Tremadoc trɪ'mæd.ək, trə-
Tremain, Tremayne trɪ'meɪn, trə-
trembl|e 'trem.bl̩ **-es** -z **-ing/ly** -ɪŋ/li, 'trem.blɪŋ/li **-ed** -d **-er/s** -əʳ/z, 'trem.bləʳ/z (US) '-l̩.ɚ/z, '-lɚ/z
trembl|y 'trem.bl|i, '-bl̩|.i **-ier** -i.əʳ (US) -i.ɚ **-iest** -i.ɪst, -i.əst **-iness** -ɪ.nəs, -ɪ.nɪs
tremendous trɪ'men.dəs, trə- **-ly** -li **-ness** -nəs, -nɪs
tremolo 'trem.ᵊl.əʊ (US) -ə.loʊ **-s** -z
tremor 'trem.əʳ (US) -ɚ **-s** -z
tremulant 'trem.jə.lənt, -jʊ- **-s** -s
tremulous 'trem.jə.ləs, -jʊ- **-ly** -li **-ness** -nəs, -nɪs
trench (T) trentʃ **-es** -ɪz **-ing** -ɪŋ **-ed** -t **-er/s** -əʳ/z (US) -ɚ/z **'trench ˌcoat ; ˌtrench 'foot ; ˌtrench 'warfare**
trenchancy 'tren.*t*ʃənt.si
trenchant 'tren.*t*ʃənt **-ly** -li
Trenchard 'tren.*t*ʃɑːd, -*t*ʃəd (US) -*t*ʃɑːrd, -*t*ʃɚd
trencher|man 'tren.*t*ʃə|.mən (US) -*t*ʃɚ- **-men** -mən
trend trend **-s** -z **-ing** -ɪŋ **-ed** -ɪd
trendsett|er 'trendˌset|.əʳ (US) -ˌset̬|.ɚ **-s** -əʳ/z (US) -ɚ/z **-ing** -ɪŋ
trend|y 'tren.d|i **-ies** -iz **-ier** -i.əʳ (US) -i.ɚ **-iest** -i.ɪst, -i.əst **-ily** -ɪ.li **-iness** -ɪ.nəs, -ɪ.nɪs
Trent trent
Trentham 'tren.təm
Trenton 'tren.tən (US) -tᵊn
trepan trɪ'pæn, trə- **-s** -z **-ning** -ɪŋ **-ned** -d
trepang trɪ'pæŋ, trə- **-s** -z
trephin|e trɪ'fiːn, tref'iːn, trə'fiːn, -'faɪn (US) trɪ'faɪn, triː-, -'fiːn **-es** -z **-ing** -ɪŋ **-ed** -d
trepidation ˌtrep.ɪ'deɪ.ʃᵊn, -ə'-
Tresilian trɪ'sɪl.i.ən, trə-, '-jən
trespass (*v.*) 'tres.pəs (US) -pæs, -pəs **-es** -ɪz **-ing** -ɪŋ **-ed** -t **-er/s** -əʳ/z (US) -ɚ/z
trespass (*n.*) 'tres.pəs **-es** -ɪz
tress tres **-es** -ɪz **-ed** -t
trestle 'tres.l̩ **-s** -z **ˌtrestle 'table, 'trestle ˌtable**
Trethowan trɪ'θəʊən, trə-, -'θaʊən, -'θɔː.ən (US) -'θoʊən, -'θaʊən, -'θɑː.ən, -'θɔː-
Trevelyan *in Cornwall:* trɪ'vɪl.jən, trə- (US) trɪ'vel-, -'vɪl- *in Northumbria:* trɪ'vel.jən, trə-
Treves triːvz
Trevethick trɪ'veθ.ɪk, trə-
Trevisa trɪ'viː.sə, trə-
Trevithick 'trev.ɪ.θɪk (US) -ə-
Trevor 'trev.əʳ (US) -ɚ
Trevor-Roper ˌtrev.ə'rəʊ.pəʳ (US) -ɚ'roʊ.pɚ
Trewin trɪ'wɪn, trə-
trews truːz
trey treɪ **-s** -z
tri- traɪ-, trɪ-, triː-
Note: Prefix. See individual entries for pronunciation and stressing.
triable 'traɪ.ə.bl̩ **-ness** -nəs, -nɪs
triad (T) 'traɪ.æd, -əd **-s** -z
triage 'triː.ɑːʒ; 'traɪ.ɪdʒ (US) 'triː.ɑːʒ
trial traɪəl **-s** -z **-(l)ing** -ɪŋ **-(l)ed** -d **ˌtrial and 'error ; ˌtrials and tribu'lations ; ˌtrial 'run**
trialogue 'traɪ.ə.lɒg (US) -lɑːg, -lɔːg **-s** -z
triangle 'traɪ.æŋ.gl̩ **-s** -z **-d** -d
triangular traɪ'æŋ.gjə.ləʳ, -gjʊ- (US) -lɚ **-ly** -li
triangularity traɪˌæŋ.gjə'lær.ə.ti, ˌtraɪ.æŋ-, -jʊ'-, -ɪ.ti (US) traɪˌæŋ.gjə'ler.ə.t̬i, -gjʊ'-, -'lær-
triangu|late traɪ'æŋ.gjə|.leɪt, -gjʊ- **-lates** -leɪts **-lating** -leɪ.tɪŋ (US) -leɪ.t̬ɪŋ **-lated** -leɪ.tɪd (US) -leɪ.t̬ɪd
triangulation traɪˌæŋ.gjə'leɪ.ʃᵊn, ˌtraɪ.æŋ-, -gjʊ'- (US) traɪˌæŋ-
Triangulum traɪ'æŋ.gjə.ləm, -gjʊ-
Triassic traɪ'æs.ɪk
triathlete traɪ'æθ.liːt **-s** -s
triathlon traɪ'æθ.lɒn, -lən (US) -lɑːn, -lən **-s** -z
triatomic ˌtraɪ.ə'tɒm.ɪk (US) -'tɑː.mɪk
tribadism 'trɪb.ə.dɪ.zᵊm, 'traɪ.bə-
tribal 'traɪ.bᵊl **-ly** -i **-ism** -ɪ.zᵊm
tribalistic ˌtraɪ.bᵊl'ɪs.tɪk (US) -bə'lɪs-
tribasic traɪ'beɪ.sɪk
tribe traɪb **-s** -z
tribes|man 'traɪbz|.mən **-men** -mən, -men **-woman** -ˌwʊm.ən **-women** -ˌwɪm.ɪn
tribespeople 'traɪbzˌpiː.pl̩
tribrach 'traɪ.bræk, 'trɪb.ræk **-s** -s
tribrachic traɪ'bræk.ɪk, trɪ-
tribulation ˌtrɪb.jə'leɪ.ʃᵊn, -jʊ'- **-s** -z
tribunal traɪ'bjuː.nᵊl, trɪ- **-s** -z
tribunate 'trɪb.jə.neɪt, -jʊ-, -nɪt, -nət (US) -nɪt, -neɪt **-s** -s
tribune (T) 'trɪb.juːn **-s** -z
tributar|y 'trɪb.jə.tᵊr|.i, -jʊ-, -tr|i (US) -ter|.i **-ies** -iz
tribute 'trɪb.juːt **-s** -s
trice traɪs
Tricel® 'traɪ.sel
triceps 'traɪ.seps **-es** -ɪz
trichin|a trɪ'kaɪ.n|ə, trə- **-ae** -iː **-as** -əz
Trichinopoly ˌtrɪtʃ.ɪ'nɒp.ᵊl.i, -ə'- (US) -'nɑː.pᵊl-
trichinosis ˌtrɪk.ɪ'nəʊ.sɪs, -ə'- (US) -ɪ'noʊ-
trichloride traɪ'klɔː.raɪd (US) -'klɔːr.aɪd **-s** -z
trichology trɪ'kɒl.ə.dʒ|i, trə- (US) -'kɑː.lə- **-ist/s** -ɪst/s
trichord 'traɪ.kɔːd (US) -kɔːrd **-s** -z
trichosis trɪ'kəʊ.sɪs, trə- (US) -'koʊ-
trichotomy trɪ'kɒt.ə.mi, trə- (US) -'kɑː.t̬ə-
Tricia 'trɪʃ.ə
Tricity® 'trɪs.ə.ti, -ɪ.ti (US) -ə.t̬i
trick trɪk **-s** -s **-ing** -ɪŋ **-ed** -t **-er/s** -əʳ/z (US) -ɚ/z **ˌtrick 'cyclist ; ˌtrick or 'treat**
tricker|y 'trɪk.ᵊr|.i **-ies** -iz
trickl|e 'trɪk.l̩ **-es** -z **-ing** -ɪŋ, 'trɪk.lɪŋ **-ed** -d **'trickle ˌcharger**
trickledown 'trɪk.l̩.daʊn
trickly 'trɪk.l̩.i, '-li
trickster 'trɪk.stəʳ (US) -stɚ **-s** -z
tricks|y 'trɪk.s|i **-ier** -i.əʳ (US) -i.ɚ **-iest** -i.ɪst, -i.əst **-iness** -ɪ.nəs, -ɪ.nɪs
trick|y 'trɪk|.i **-ier** -i.əʳ (US) -i.ɚ **-iest** -i.ɪst, -i.əst **-ily** -ɪ.li, -ᵊl.i **-iness** -ɪ.nəs, -ɪ.nɪs
tricolo(u)r 'trɪk.ᵊl.əʳ; 'traɪˌkʌl.əʳ (US) 'traɪˌkʌl.ɚ **-s** -z
tricorn(e) 'traɪ.kɔːn (US) -kɔːrn

tricot 'triː.kəʊ, 'trɪk.əʊ (US) 'triː.koʊ **-s** -z
tricycl|e 'traɪ.sɪ.kl̩, -sə- **-es** -z **-ing** -ɪŋ, -klɪŋ **-ed** -d
trident (T) 'traɪ.dᵊnt **-s** -s
Tridentine traɪ'den.taɪn, trɪ-, trə-, -tiːn (US) traɪ'den.taɪn, -tiːn, -tɪn
tried (*from* **try**) traɪd
triennial traɪ'en.i.əl, '-jəl **-ly** -i
trier 'traɪ.əʳ (US) -ɚ **-s** -z
Trier trɪəʳ (US) trɪr
trierarch 'traɪ.ᵊr.ɑːk (US) -ə.rɑːrk **-s** -s **-y** -i **-ies** -iz
tries (*from* **try**) traɪz
Trieste tri'est; -'es.teɪ
triffid (T) 'trɪf.ɪd **-s** -z
trifid 'traɪ.fɪd
trifl|e 'traɪ.fl̩ **-es** -z **-ing/ly** -ɪŋ/li, 'traɪ.flɪŋ/li **-ed** -d **-er/s** -əʳ/z, 'traɪ.fləʳ/z (US) '-fl̩.ɚ/z, '-flɚ/z
trifolium traɪ'fəʊ.li.əm (US) -'foʊ- **-s** -z
trifori|um traɪ'fɔː.ri|.əm (US) -'fɔːr.i- **-a** -ə
trig trɪg **-s** -z **-ging** -ɪŋ **-ged** -d
Trigg trɪg
trigg|er 'trɪg|.əʳ (US) -ɚ **-ers** -əz (US) -ɚz **-ering** -ᵊr.ɪŋ **-ered** -əd (US) -ɚd
trigger-happy 'trɪg.əˌhæp.i (US) -ɚˌ-
triglyph 'traɪ.glɪf, 'trɪg.lɪf (US) 'traɪ.glɪf **-s** -s
trigon 'traɪ.gən, -gɒn (US) -gɑːn **-s** -z
trigonometric ˌtrɪg.ə.nəʊ'met.rɪk (US) -nə'- **-al** -ᵊl **-ally** -ᵊl.i, -li
trigonometr|y ˌtrɪg.ə'nɒm.ɪ.tr|i, '-ə- (US) -'nɑː.mə- **-ies** -iz
trigraph 'traɪ.grɑːf, -græf (US) -græf **-s** -s
trihedral traɪ'hiː.drəl
trike traɪk **-s** -s
trilateral traɪ'læt.ᵊr.ᵊl, '-rᵊl (US) -'læt̬.ɚ.ᵊl, -'læt.rᵊl **-ly** -i **-ness** -nəs, -nɪs
trilb|y (T) 'trɪl.b|i **-ies** -iz
trilingual traɪ'lɪŋ.gwᵊl **-ly** -i
triliteral traɪ'lɪt.ᵊr.ᵊl, '-rᵊl (US) -'lɪt̬.ɚ.ᵊl, -'lɪt.rᵊl
trill trɪl **-s** -z **-ing** -ɪŋ **-ed** -d
Trilling 'trɪl.ɪŋ
trillion 'trɪl.jən, -i.ən (US) '-jən **-s** -z **-th/s** -*t*.θ/s
trilobite 'traɪ.ləʊ.baɪt (US) -loʊ-, -lə- **-s** -s
trilog|y 'trɪl.ə.dʒ|i **-ies** -iz
trim (T) trɪm **-mer/s** -əʳ/z (US) -ɚ/z **-mest** -ɪst, -əst **-ly** -li **-ness** -nəs, -nɪs **-s** -z **-ming/s** -ɪŋ/z **-med** -d
trimaran 'traɪ.mᵊr.æn, ˌ--'- (US) 'traɪ.mə.ræn **-s** -z
Trimble 'trɪm.bl̩
trimester trɪ'mes.təʳ, traɪ- (US) traɪ'mes.tɚ, '--- **-s** -z
trimestral trɪ'mes.trᵊl, traɪ- (US) traɪ-, '---
trimestrial trɪ'mes.tri.əl, traɪ- (US) traɪ-
trimeter 'trɪm.ɪ.təʳ, '-ə- (US) -ə.t̬ɚ **-s** -z
Trincomalee ˌtrɪŋ.kəʊ.mᵊl'iː (US) -koʊ.mə'liː
Trinculo 'trɪŋ.kjə.ləʊ, -kjʊ- (US) -loʊ
Trinder 'trɪn.dəʳ (US) -dɚ
trine (T) traɪn **-s** -z
Tring trɪŋ
Trinidad 'trɪn.ɪ.dæd, '-ə-, ˌ--'- (US) 'trɪn.ɪ.dæd ˌ**Trinidad and To'bago**
Trinidadian ˌtrɪn.ɪ'dæd.i.ən, -ə'-, -'deɪ.di- (US) -ɪ'dæd.i- **-s** -z
Trinitarian ˌtrɪn.ɪ'teə.ri.ən, -ə'- (US) -ɪ'ter.i- **-s** -z **-ism** -ɪ.zᵊm
trinitroglycerin(e) ˌtraɪ.naɪ.trəʊ'glɪs.ᵊr.ɪn, traɪˌnaɪ-, -iːn (US) traɪˌnaɪ.troʊ'glɪs.ɚ.ɪn
trinitrotoluene ˌtraɪ.naɪ.trəʊ'tɒl.ju.iːn, traɪˌnaɪ- (US) traɪˌnaɪ.troʊ'tɑːl-
trinit|y (T) 'trɪn.ə.t|i, -ɪ.t|i (US) -ə.t̬|i **-ies** -iz
trinket 'trɪŋ.kɪt, -kət **-s** -s
trinomial traɪ'nəʊ.mi.əl (US) -'noʊ- **-s** -z
trio 'triː.əʊ (US) -oʊ **-s** -z
triode 'traɪ.əʊd (US) -oʊd **-s** -z
triolet 'triː.əʊ.let, 'traɪ-, 'trɪə.let, -lɪt, -lət (US) 'triː.ə-, 'traɪ- **-s** -s
trioxide traɪ'ɒk.saɪd (US) -'ɑːk- **-s** -z
trip trɪp **-s** -s **-ping/ly** -ɪŋ/li **-ped** -t **-per/s** -əʳ/z (US) -ɚ/z **'trip** ˌ**wire**
tripartite ˌtraɪ'pɑː.taɪt (US) -'pɑːr- **-ly** -li *stress shift:* ˌtripartite 'talks
tripe traɪp
triphibi|ous traɪ'fɪb.i|.əs **-an/s** -ən/z
triphthong 'trɪf.θɒŋ, 'trɪp- (US) -θɑːŋ, -θɔːŋ **-s** -z
triphthongal trɪf'θɒŋ.gᵊl, trɪp- (US) -'θɑːŋ-, -'θɔːŋ- **-ly** -i
triplane 'traɪ.pleɪn **-s** -z
tripl|e 'trɪp.l̩ **-y** -i **-es** -z **-ing** -ɪŋ, 'trɪp.lɪŋ **-ed** -d **'triple** ˌ**jump** , ˌ**triple 'jump**
triplet 'trɪp.lət, -lɪt **-s** -s
triplex (T®) 'trɪp.leks **-es** -ɪz
triplicate (*adj.*) 'trɪp.lɪ.kət, -lə-, -kɪt (US) -kɪt
tripli|cate (*v.*) 'trɪp.lɪ|.keɪt, -lə- **-cates** -keɪts **-cating** -keɪ.tɪŋ (US) -keɪ.t̬ɪŋ **-cated** -keɪ.tɪd (US) -keɪ.t̬ɪd
triploid 'trɪp.lɔɪd **-s** -z **-y** -i
tripod 'traɪ.pɒd (US) -pɑːd **-s** -z
Tripoli, tripoli 'trɪp.ᵊl.i
Tripolitania ˌtrɪp.ᵊl.ɪ'teɪ.ni.ə, -ɒl-; trɪˌpɒl- (US) ˌtrɪp.ᵊl.ə'-; trɪˌpɑː.lə'-
tripos 'traɪ.pɒs (US) -pɑːs **-es** -ɪz
triptych 'trɪp.tɪk **-s** -s
tripwire 'trɪp.waɪəʳ (US) -waɪɚ **-s** -z
trireme 'traɪ.riːm **-s** -z
trisect traɪ'sekt **-s** -s **-ing** -ɪŋ **-ed** -ɪd **-or/s** -əʳ/z (US) -ɚ/z
trisection traɪ'sek.ʃᵊn **-s** -z
Trisha 'trɪʃ.ə
Tristan 'trɪs.tən, -tæn (US) -tən, -tæn, -tɑːn
Tristan da Cunha ˌtrɪs.tən.də'kuː.nə, -njə
Tristram 'trɪs.trəm, -træm (US) -trəm
trisyllabic ˌtraɪ.sɪ'læb.ɪk, -sə'- (US) -sɪ'- **-al** -ᵊl **-ally** -ᵊl.i, -li
trisyllable traɪ'sɪl.ə.bl̩ **-s** -z
trit|e traɪt **-er** -əʳ (US) 'traɪ.t̬ɚ **-est** -ɪst, -əst (US) 'traɪ.t̬ɪst, -t̬əst **-ely** -li **-eness** -nəs, -nɪs
tritium 'trɪt.i.əm, '-jəm (US) 'trɪt̬.i.əm, 'trɪʃ-
triton (T) *sea god, mollusc:* 'traɪ.tɒn, -tᵊn (US) -tᵊn *physics:* 'traɪ.tɒn, -tᵊn (US) -tɑːn **-s** -z
tritone 'traɪ.təʊn (US) -toʊn **-s** -z
triumph (T®) 'traɪ.əm*p*f, -ʌm*p*f **-s** -s **-ing** -ɪŋ **-ed** -t
triumphal traɪ'ʌm*p*.fᵊl **-ism** -ɪ.zᵊm
triumphant traɪ'ʌm*p*.fənt **-ly** -li
triumv|ir traɪ'ʌm.v|əʳ, tri-, -'ʊm-, -v|ɪəʳ, -v|ɜːʳ; 'traɪ.ʌm-, -əm- (US) traɪ'ʌm.v|ɪr, -v|ɚ **-irs** -əz, -ɪəz, -ɜːz (US) -ɪrz, -ɚz **-iri** -ɪˌriː, -ᵊr.iː, -aɪ (US) -ɪˌraɪ
triumvirate traɪ'ʌm.vɪ.rət, tri-, -vᵊr.ət, -ɪt (US) traɪ'ʌm.vɪ.rɪt, -vɚ.ɪt **-s** -s
triumviri traɪ'ʌm.vɪˌriː, tri-, -vᵊr.iː, -aɪ, 'traɪ.ʌm-, -əm- (US) traɪ'ʌm.vɪˌraɪ, -vɚ-
triune (T) 'traɪ.uːn (US) -juːn
trivalent traɪ'veɪ.lᵊnt; 'trɪv.ᵊl.ᵊnt (US) traɪ'veɪ.lᵊnt, ˌtraɪ-, '---
trivet 'trɪv.ɪt **-s** -s
trivia 'trɪv.i.ə
trivial 'trɪv.i.əl **-ly** -i **-ness** -nəs, -nɪs ˌ**Trivial Pur'suit®**
trivialit|y ˌtrɪv.i'æl.ə.t|i, -ɪ.t|i (US) -ə.t̬|i **-ies** -iz
trivializ|e, -is|e 'trɪv.i.ᵊl.aɪz, '-jᵊl- (US) -i.ᵊl- **-es** -ɪz **-ing** -ɪŋ **-ed** -d
trivi|um 'trɪv.i|.əm **-a** -ə
Trixie 'trɪk.si
trizonal traɪ'zəʊ.nᵊl (US) -'zoʊ-
Trizone 'traɪ.zəʊn (US) -zoʊn
Troad 'trəʊ.æd (US) 'troʊ-
Troas 'trəʊ.æs (US) 'troʊ-
Trocadero ˌtrɒk.ə'dɪə.rəʊ (US) ˌtrɑː.kə'der.oʊ, ˌtroʊ-
trochaic trəʊ'keɪ.ɪk, trɒk'eɪ- (US) troʊ'keɪ-
troch|e trəʊʃ (US) 'troʊ.ki **-es** -ɪz
trochee 'trəʊ.kiː, -ki (US) 'troʊ- **-s** -z
trod (*from* **tread**) trɒd (US) trɑːd **-den** -ᵊn
Troed-y-rhiw ˌtrɔɪd.ə.ri'uː

troglodyte 'trɒg.ləʊ.daɪt (US) 'trɑː.glə- **-s** -s
troika 'trɔɪ.kə **-s** -z
troilism 'trɔɪ.lɪ.zᵊm
Troilus 'trɔɪ.ləs, 'trəʊ.ɪ.ləs (US) 'trɔɪ.ləs, 'troʊ.ə-
Trojan 'trəʊ.dʒᵊn (US) 'troʊ- **-s** -z **ˌTrojan 'horse** ; **ˌTrojan 'War**
troll trəʊl, trɒl (US) troʊl **-s** -z **-ing** -ɪŋ **-ed** -d
trolley 'trɒl.i (US) 'trɑː.li **-s** -z
trolleybus 'trɒl.i.bʌs (US) 'trɑː.li- **-es** -ɪz
trollop 'trɒl.əp (US) 'trɑː.ləp **-s** -s
Trollope 'trɒl.əp (US) 'trɑː.ləp
Tromans 'trəʊ.mənz (US) 'troʊ-
trombone trɒm'bəʊn (US) trɑːm'boʊn, trəm-; 'trɑːm.boʊn **-s** -z
trombonist trɒm'bəʊ.nɪst (US) trɑːm'boʊ-, '--- **-s** -s
trompe l'œil ˌtrɒmp'lɔɪ *as if French:* ˌtrɔ̃ːmp'lɜː.i (US) ˌtrɔːmp'lɔɪ **-s** -z
Trondheim 'trɒnd.haɪm (US) 'trɑːn.heɪm
Troon truːn
troop truːp **-s** -s **-ing** -ɪŋ **-ed** -t **-er/s** -əʳ/z (US) -ɚ/z **'troop ˌcarrier**
trope trəʊp (US) troʊp **-s** -s
trophic 'trɒf.ɪk (US) 'trɑː.fɪk
troph|y 'trəʊ.f|i (US) 'troʊ- **-ies** -iz
tropic 'trɒp.ɪk (US) 'trɑː.pɪk **-s** -s **-al** -ᵊl **-ally** -ᵊl.i, -li **ˌtropic of 'Cancer** ; **ˌtropic of 'Capricorn**
tropism 'trəʊ.pɪ.zᵊm (US) 'troʊ- **-s** -z
tropistic trəʊ'pɪs.tɪk (US) troʊ-
troppo 'trɒp.əʊ (US) 'trɑː.poʊ
Trossachs 'trɒs.əks, -æks, -əxs (US) 'trɑː.səks, -sæks
trot (T) trɒt (US) trɑːt **-s** -s **-ting** -ɪŋ (US) 'trɑː.t̬ɪŋ **-ted** -ɪd (US) 'trɑː.t̬ɪd
troth trəʊθ, trɒθ (US) trɑːθ, trɔːθ, troʊθ
Trotsky 'trɒt.ski (US) 'trɑːt- **-ist/s** -ɪst/s **-ite/s** -aɪt/s **-ism** -ɪ.zᵊm
Trotskyite 'trɒt.ski.aɪt (US) 'trɑːt- **-s** -s
Trott trɒt (US) trɑːt
trotter (T) 'trɒt.əʳ (US) 'trɑː.t̬ɚ **-s** -z
Trottiscliffe 'trɒz.li, 'trɒs- (US) 'trɑːz-, 'trɑːs-
troubadour 'truː.bə.dɔːʳ, -dʊəʳ (US) -dɔːr **-s** -z
troubl|e 'trʌb.l̩ **-es** -z **-ing/ly** -ɪŋ/li, 'trʌb.lɪŋ/li **-ed** -d **-er/s** -əʳ/z, 'trʌb.ləʳ/z (US) '-l̩.ɚ/z, '-lɚ/z **ˌtrouble and 'strife** ; **'trouble ˌspot**
trouble-free ˌtrʌb.l̩'friː *stress shift:* ˌtrouble-free 'journey
troublemaker 'trʌb.l̩ˌmeɪ.kəʳ (US) -kɚ **-s** -z
troubleshoot|er 'trʌb.l̩ˌʃuː.t|əʳ (US) -t̬|ɚ **-ers** -əz (US) -ɚz **-ing** -ɪŋ
troublesome 'trʌb.l̩.səm **-ly** -li **-ness** -nəs, -nɪs
troublous 'trʌb.ləs **-ly** -li **-ness** -nəs, -nɪs
Troubridge 'truː.brɪdʒ
trough trɒf (US) trɑːf, trɔːf **-s** -s
Note: Some bakers pronounce /traʊ/.
Troughton 'traʊ.tᵊn, 'trɔː-
trounc|e traʊnts **-es** -ɪz **-ing/s** -ɪŋ/z **-ed** -t
Troup truːp
troup|e truːp **-es** -s **-er/s** -əʳ/z (US) -ɚ/z
trouper 'truː.pəʳ (US) -pɚ **-s** -z
trouser 'traʊ.zəʳ (US) -zɚ **'trouser ˌpress** ; **'trouser ˌsuit**
trousers 'traʊ.zəz (US) -zɚz
trousseau 'truː.səʊ, -'- (US) 'truː.soʊ, -'- **-s** -z **-x** -z
trout traʊt **-s** -s
trove trəʊv (US) troʊv
trover 'trəʊ.vəʳ (US) 'troʊ.vɚ
trow trəʊ, traʊ (US) troʊ
Trowbridge 'trəʊ.brɪdʒ (US) 'troʊ-
trowel traʊəl **-s** -z **-(l)ing** -ɪŋ **-(l)ed** -d
Trowell trəʊəl, traʊəl (US) troʊəl, traʊəl
troy (T) trɔɪ
truancy 'truː.ənt.si
truant 'truː.ənt **-s** -s
Trübner 'truːb.nəʳ (US) -nɚ
truc|e truːs **-es** -ɪz
trucial (T) 'truː.ʃᵊl (US) '-ʃᵊl
truck trʌk **-s** -s **-ing** -ɪŋ **-ed** -t **-age** -ɪdʒ **-er/s** -əʳ/z (US) -ɚ/z **'truck ˌstop**
truckl|e 'trʌk.l̩ **-es** -z **-ing** -ɪŋ, 'trʌk.lɪŋ **-ed** -d **'truckle ˌbed**
truckload 'trʌk.ləʊd (US) -loʊd **-s** -z
truculen|ce 'trʌk.jə.lᵊnt|s, -jʊ- **-cy** -si
truculent 'trʌk.jə.lᵊnt, -jʊ- **-ly** -li
Trudeau 'truː.dəʊ (US) truː'doʊ, '--
trudg|e trʌdʒ **-es** -ɪz **-ing** -ɪŋ **-ed** -d **-er/s** -əʳ/z (US) -ɚ/z
trudgen (T) 'trʌdʒ.ᵊn
Trudgill 'trʌd.gɪl
Trudy, **Trudi** 'truː.di
tru|e (T) truː **-er** -əʳ (US) -ɚ **-est** -ɪst, -əst **-ly** -li **-eness** -nəs, -nɪs
true-blue ˌtruː'bluː **-s** -z *stress shift:* ˌtrue-blue 'Tory
trueborn 'truː.bɔːn (US) -bɔːrn
Truefitt 'truː.fɪt
truehearted ˌtruː'hɑː.tɪd (US) 'truːˌhɑːr.t̬ɪd **-ness** -nəs, -nɪs *stress shift, British only:* ˌtruehearted 'person
true-life ˌtruː'laɪf *stress shift:* ˌtrue-life 'story
truelove 'truː.lʌv
Trueman 'truː.mən
Truffaut 'truː.fəʊ, 'trʊf.əʊ (US) truː'foʊ
truffle 'trʌf.l̩ **-s** -z **-d** -d
trug trʌg **-s** -z
truism 'truː.ɪ.zᵊm **-s** -z
Trujillo trʊ'hiː.jəʊ (US) truː'hiː.joʊ
Truk trʌk, trʊk
truly 'truː.li
Truman 'truː.mən
Trumbull 'trʌm.bʊl (US) -bʊl, -bᵊl
trump (T) trʌmp **-s** -s **-ing** -ɪŋ **-ed** -t **'trump ˌcard**, **ˌtrump 'card**
trumped-up ˌtrʌmpt'ʌp *stress shift:* ˌtrumped-up 'charges
Trumper 'trʌm.pəʳ (US) -pɚ
trumpery 'trʌm.pᵊr.i
trum|pet 'trʌm|.pɪt (US) -pət **-pets** -pɪts (US) -pəts **-peting/s** -pɪ.tɪŋ/z (US) -pə.t̬ɪŋ/z **-peted** -pɪ.tɪd (US) -pə.t̬ɪd **-peter/s** -pɪ.təʳ/z (US) -pə.t̬ɚ/z **ˌblow one's ˌown 'trumpet**
trunca|te trʌŋ'keɪ|t, '-- (US) 'trʌŋ.keɪ|t, 'trʌn- **-tes** -ts **-ting** -tɪŋ (US) -t̬ɪŋ **-ted** -tɪd (US) -t̬ɪd
truncation trʌŋ'keɪ.ʃᵊn (US) trʌŋ-, trʌn- **-s** -z
truncheon 'trʌn.tʃᵊn (US) 'trʌnt.ʃᵊn **-s** -z **-ing** -ɪŋ **-ed** -d
trundl|e 'trʌn.dl̩ **-es** -z **-ing** -ɪŋ, 'trʌnd.lɪŋ **-ed** -d **-er/s** -əʳ/z (US) -ɚ/z
trunk trʌŋk **-s** -s **-ful/s** -fʊl/z **'trunk ˌcall** ; **'trunk ˌroad**
trunnion 'trʌn.i.ən, '-jən (US) '-jən **-s** -z **-ed** -d
Truro 'trʊə.rəʊ (US) 'trʊr.oʊ
Truscott 'trʌs.kət (US) -kət, -kɑːt
Truslove 'trʌs.lʌv
truss trʌs **-es** -ɪz **-ing** -ɪŋ **-ed** -t
trust trʌst **-s** -s **-ing/ly** -ɪŋ/li **-ed** -ɪd **'trust ˌfund**
trustee trʌs'tiː **-s** -z
trusteeship trʌs'tiː.ʃɪp **-s** -s
trustful 'trʌst.fᵊl, -fʊl **-ly** -i **-ness** -nəs, -nɪs
Trusthouse Forte® ˌtrʌst.haʊs'fɔː.teɪ (US) -'fɔːr-
trustworth|y 'trʌstˌwɜː.ð|i (US) -ˌwɜːr- **-iness** -ɪ.nəs, -ɪ.nɪs
trust|y 'trʌs.t|i **-ier** -i.əʳ (US) -i.ɚ **-iest** -i.ɪst, -i.əst **-ily** -ɪ.li, -ᵊl.i **-iness** -ɪ.nəs, -ɪ.nɪs
tru|th truː|θ **-ths** -ðz, -θs **'truth ˌdrug**
truthful 'truːθ.fᵊl, -fʊl **-ly** -i **-ness** -nəs, -nɪs
tr|y tr|aɪ **-ies** -aɪz **-ying/ly** -aɪ.ɪŋ/li **-ied** -aɪd **-ier/s** -aɪ.əʳ/z (US) -aɪ.ɚ/z
Tryon traɪən
try-on 'traɪ.ɒn (US) -ɑːn **-s** -z
try-out 'traɪ.aʊt **-s** -s
trypanosome 'trɪp.ə.nəʊ.səʊm; trɪ'pæn.ə- (US) trɪ'pæn.ə.soʊm; 'trɪp.ə.noʊ- **-s** -z
trypanosomiasis ˌtrɪp.ə.nəʊ.səʊ'maɪ.ə.sɪs; trɪˌpæn.əʊ- (US) trɪˌpæn.ə.soʊ'-; ˌtrɪp.ə.noʊ-
trypsin 'trɪp.sɪn
trypsinogen trɪp'sɪn.ə.dʒᵊn (US) '-oʊ-
tryst trɪst **-s** -s **-ing** -ɪŋ **-ed** -ɪd
Trystan 'trɪs.tæn, -tən

tsar (T) zɑːʳ, tsɑːʳ US zɑːr, tsɑːr **-s** -z
tsarevitch, tsarevich (T) ˈzɑː.rə.vɪtʃ, ˈtsɑː-, -rɪ- US ˈzɑːr.ə-, ˈtsɑːr- **-es** -ɪz
tsarina (T) zɑːˈriː.nə, tsɑː- **-s** -z
tsarism ˈzɑː.rɪ.zᵊm, ˈtsɑː- US ˈzɑːr.ɪ-, ˈtsɑːr-
tsarist ˈzɑː.rɪst, ˈtsɑː- US ˈzɑːr.ɪst, ˈtsɑːr- **-s** -s
TSB® ˌtiː.esˈbiː
tsetse ˈtet.si, ˈtset- US ˈtset-, ˈtsiːt-, ˈtet-, ˈtiːt- **-s** -z **ˈtsetse ˌfly**
T-shirt ˈtiː.ʃɜːt US -ʃɜːrt **-s** -s
tsk (*interj.*) tɪsk
Note: This spelling represents the tongue click used (usually repeated) to indicate disapproval; it may be described as a voiceless affricated alveolar click, symbolized as [!ˢ]. The transcription given above is only used in mock disapproval. See also **tut**.
tsp (*abbrev. for* **teaspoonful**) ˈtiː.spuːn.fʊl
T-square ˈtiː.skweəʳ US -skwer **-s** -z
tsunam|i tsʊˈnɑː.m|i, sʊ-, -ˈnæm|.i US tsuːˈnɑː.m|i **-is** -iz **-ic** -ɪk
Tswana ˈtswɑː.nə, ˈswɑː- **-s** -z
TT ˌtiːˈtiː ˌ**TˈT ˌraces**
Tuamotu ˌtuː.əˈməʊ.tuː US -ˈmoʊ-
Tuareg ˈtwɑː.reg US ˈtwɑːr.eg **-s** -z
tub tʌb **-s** -z **-bing** -ɪŋ **-bed** -d
tuba ˈtjuː.bə, ˈtʃuː- US ˈtuː-, ˈtjuː- **-s** -z
tubb|y ˈtʌb|.i **-ier** -i.əʳ US -i.ɚ **-iest** -i.ɪst, -i.əst **-iness** -ɪ.nəs, -ɪ.nɪs
tube tjuːb, tʃuːb US tuːb, tjuːb **-s** -z
tubeless ˈtjuːb.ləs, ˈtʃuː-, -blɪs US ˈtuː-, ˈtjuː-
tuber ˈtjuː.bəʳ US ˈtuː.bɚ, ˈtjuː- **-s** -z
tubercle ˈtjuː.bə.kl̩, -bɜː- US ˈtuː.bɚ-, ˈtjuː- **-s** -z
tubercular tjuːˈbɜː.kjə.ləʳ, tjʊ-, -kjʊ- US tuːˈbɜːr.kjə.lɚ, tjuː-, tə-, -kjʊ-
tuberculin tjuːˈbɜː.kjə.lɪn, tjʊ-, -kjʊ- US tuːˈbɜːr-, tjuː-, tə-
tuberculization, -isa- tjuːˌbɜː.kjə.laɪˈzeɪ.ʃᵊn, tjʊ-, -kjʊ-, -lɪˈ- US tuːˌbɜːr.kjə.lɪˈ-, tjuː-, tə-, -kjʊ-
tuberculiz|e, -is|e tjuːˈbɜː.kjə.laɪz, tjʊ-, -kjʊ- US tuːˈbɜːr-, tjuː-, tə- **-es** -ɪz **-ing** -ɪŋ **-ed** -d
tuberculoid tjuːˈbɜː.kjə.lɔɪd, tjʊ-, -kjʊ- US tuːˈbɜːr-, tjuː-, tə-
tuberculosis tjuːˌbɜː.kjəˈləʊ.sɪs, tjʊ-, -kjʊ- US tuːˌbɜːr.kjəˈloʊ-, tjuː-, tə-, -kjʊ-
tuberculous tjuːˈbɜː.kjə.ləs, tjʊ-, -kjʊ- US tuːˈbɜːr-, tjuː-, tə-
tuberose (*n.*) ˈtjuː.bᵊr.əʊz US ˈtuː.broʊz, ˈtjuː-, -bə.roʊz
tuberose (*adj.*) ˈtjuː.bᵊr.əʊs US ˈtuː.bə.roʊs, ˈtjuː-
tuberous ˈtjuː.bᵊr.əs US ˈtuː-, ˈtjuː-
tubful ˈtʌb.fʊl **-s** -z
tubiform ˈtjuː.bɪ.fɔːm, ˈtʃuː- US ˈtuː.bɪ.fɔːrm, ˈtjuː-
tubing ˈtjuː.bɪŋ, ˈtʃuː- US ˈtuː-, ˈtjuː- **-s** -z
Tübingen ˈtuː.bɪŋ.ən, ˈtjuː-
tub-thump|ing ˈtʌbˌθʌm.p|ɪŋ **-er/s** -əʳ/z US -ɚ/z
Tubuai ˌtuː.buˈaɪ
tubular ˈtjuː.bjə.ləʳ, ˈtʃuː-, -bjʊ- US ˈtuː.bjə.lɚ, ˈtjuː-, -bjʊ-
tubule ˈtjuː.bjuːl, ˈtʃuː- US ˈtuː-, ˈtjuː- **-s** -z
TUC ˌtiː.juːˈsiː
tuck (T) tʌk **-s** -s **-ing** -ɪŋ **-ed** -t
tucker (T) ˈtʌk.əʳ US -ɚ **-s** -z
tuck-shop ˈtʌk.ʃɒp US -ʃɑːp **-s** -s
Tucson ˈtuː.sɒn US ˈtuː.sɑːn
Tudor ˈtjuː.dəʳ, ˈtʃuː- US ˈtuː.dɚ, ˈtjuː- **-s** -z
Tue. (*abbrev. for* **Tuesday**) ˈtjuːz.deɪ, ˈtʃuːz-, -di US ˈtuːz-, ˈtjuːz-
Note: This abbreviation may also be pronounced /tjuː/ in British English.
Tues. (*abbrev. for* **Tuesday**) ˈtjuːz.deɪ, ˈtʃuːz-, -di US ˈtuːz-, ˈtjuːz-
Note: This abbreviation may also be pronounced /tjuːz/ in British English.
Tuesday ˈtjuːz.deɪ, ˈtʃuːz-, -di US ˈtuːz-, ˈtjuːz- **-s** -z
tufa ˈtjuː.fə US ˈtuː-, ˈtjuː-
tuffet ˈtʌf.ɪt, -ət **-s** -s
Tufnell ˈtʌf.nᵊl ˌ**Tufnell ˈPark**
tuft tʌft **-s** -s **-ing** -ɪŋ **-ed** -ɪd
tuft|y ˈtʌf.t|i **-ier** -i.əʳ US -i.ɚ **-iest** -i.ɪst, -i.əst **-iness** -ɪ.nəs, -ɪ.nɪs
tug tʌg **-s** -z **-ging** -ɪŋ **-ged** -d **-ger/s** -əʳ/z US -ɚ/z
tugboat ˈtʌg.bəʊt US -boʊt **-s** -s
tug-of-love ˌtʌg.əvˈlʌv
tug-of-war ˌtʌg.əvˈwɔːʳ US -ˈwɔːr **-s** -z **tugs-of-war** ˌtʌgz.əvˈwɔːʳ US -ˈwɔːr
tugrik ˈtuː.griːk **-s** -s
Tuileries ˈtwiː.lᵊr.iː, -i US -iː, -i, -iz
tuition tjuˈɪʃ.ᵊn US tu-, tju- **-s** -z **-al** -ᵊl
Tuke tjuːk US tuːk, tjuːk
tulip ˈtjuː.lɪp, ˈtʃuː- US ˈtuː-, ˈtjuː- **-s** -s
Tull tʌl
tulle tjuːl US tuːl **-s** -z
Tulloch ˈtʌl.ək, -əx US -ək
Tulsa ˈtʌl.sə
Tulse tʌls
tum tʌm **-s** -z
tumbl|e ˈtʌm.bl̩ **-es** -z **-ing** -ɪŋ, -blɪŋ **-ed** -d **-er/s** -əʳ/z US -ɚ/z
tumbledown (T) ˈtʌm.bl̩.daʊn
tumble-drier, tumble-dryer ˌtʌm.bl̩ˈdraɪ.əʳ, ˈtʌm.bl̩ˌdraɪ- US -ɚ **-s** -z
tumble-dr|y ˌtʌm.bl̩ˈdr|aɪ, ˈ--- **-ies** -aɪz **-ying** -aɪ.ɪŋ **-ied** -aɪd
tumbler ˈtʌm.bləʳ, ˈ-bl̩.əʳ US ˈ-blɚ, ˈ-bl̩.ɚ **-s** -z **-ful/s** -fʊl/z
tumbleweed ˈtʌm.bl̩.wiːd
tumbrel ˈtʌm.brᵊl **-s** -z
tumbril ˈtʌm.brɪl, -brᵊl **-s** -z
tumefaction ˌtjuː.mɪˈfæk.ʃᵊn, -məˈ- US ˌtuː.məˈ-, ˌtjuː-
tume|fy ˈtjuː.mɪ|.faɪ, -mə- US ˈtuː.mə-, ˈtjuː- **-fies** -faɪz **-fying** -faɪ.ɪŋ **-fied** -faɪd
tumescen|t tjuːˈmes.ᵊn|t, tjʊ- US tuː-, tjuː- **-ce** -*t*s
tumid ˈtjuː.mɪd US ˈtuː-, ˈtjuː- **-ly** -li
tumidity tjuːˈmɪd.ə.ti, tjʊ-, -ɪ.ti US tuːˈmɪd.ə.t̬i, tjuː-
Tummel ˈtʌm.ᵊl
tumm|y ˈtʌm|.i **-ies** -iz **ˈtummy ˌache** ; **ˈtummy ˌbutton**
tumo(u)r ˈtjuː.məʳ, ˈtʃuː- US ˈtuː.mɚ, ˈtjuː- **-s** -z
tumo(u)rous ˈtjuː.mᵊr.əs, ˈtʃuː- US ˈtuː-, ˈtjuː-
tumult ˈtjuː.mʌlt, -məlt US ˈtuː-, ˈtjuː- **-s** -s
tumultuous tjuːˈmʌl.tju.əs, tjʊ- US tuːˈmʌl.tʃuː.əs, tjuː-, tə-, -tʃə.wəs **-ly** -li **-ness** -nəs, -nɪs
tumul|us ˈtjuː.mjə.l|əs, -mjə- US ˈtuː-, ˈtjuː- **-i** -aɪ
tun tʌn **-s** -z
tuna ˈtjuː.nə, ˈtuː- US ˈtuː-, ˈtjuː- **-s** -z **ˈtuna ˌfish**
Tunbridge ˈtʌn.brɪdʒ, ˈtʌm- US ˈtʌn- ˌ**Tunbridge ˈWells**
tundra ˈtʌn.drə **-s** -z
tun|e tjuːn, tʃuːn US tuːn, tjuːn **-es** -z **-ing** -ɪŋ **-ed** -d **-er/s** -əʳ/z US -ɚ/z **ˈtuning ˌfork** ; **ˈtuning ˌpeg** ; ˌ**change one's ˈtune**
tuneful ˈtjuːn.fᵊl, ˈtʃuːn-, -fʊl US ˈtuːn-, ˈtjuːn- **-ly** -i **-ness** -nəs, -nɪs
tuneless ˈtjuːn.ləs, ˈtʃuːn-, -lɪs US ˈtuːn-, ˈtjuːn- **-ly** -li **-ness** -nəs, -nɪs
tunesmith ˈtjuːn.smɪθ, ˈtʃuːn- US ˈtuːn-, ˈtjuːn- **-s** -s
tungsten ˈtʌŋ*k*.stən
tunic ˈtjuː.nɪk, ˈtʃuː- US ˈtuː-, ˈtjuː- **-s** -s
tunicle ˈtjuː.nɪ.kl̩ US ˈtuː-, ˈtjuː- **-s** -z
Tunis ˈtjuː.nɪs US ˈtuː-, ˈtjuː-
Tunisi|a tjuːˈnɪz.i|.ə, tjʊ-, -ˈnɪs- US tuːˈniː.ʒ|ə, tjuː-, -ˈnɪʒ|.ə, -ˈnɪʃ|.ə **-an/s** -ən/z
Tunnard ˈtʌn.əd US -ɚd
tunnel ˈtʌn.ᵊl **-s** -z **-(l)ing** -ɪŋ **-(l)ed** -d **-(l)er/s** -əʳ/z US -ɚ/z ˌ**tunnel ˈvision** ; ˌ**light at the ˌend of the ˈtunnel**
Tunnicliff(e) ˈtʌn.ɪ.klɪf
tunn|y ˈtʌn|.i **-ies** -iz
Tunstall ˈtʌn*t*.stᵊl, -stɔːl

Tuoh(e)y 'tuː.i, -hi
Tupman 'tʌp.mən
tuppenc|e 'tʌp.ᵊnts, -ᵊmps **-es** -ɪz
tuppenny 'tʌp.ᵊn.i, '-ni
tuppeny 'tʌp.ᵊn.i, '-ni
Tupperware® 'tʌp.ə.weəʳ (US) -ɚ.wer
tu quoque ˌtuː'kwəʊ.kwi, -'kwɒk.weɪ (US) ˌtuː'kwoʊ.kwi, ˌtjuː-, -kweɪ **-s** -z
Turandot 'tʊə.rən.dɒt, 'tjʊə-, -dəʊ (US) 'tʊr.ən.dɑːt, -doʊ
Turani|a tjʊə'reɪ.ni|.ə (US) tʊ'reɪ-, tjʊ-, -'rɑː- **-an/s** -ən/z
turban 'tɜː.bən (US) 'tɜːr- **-s** -z **-(n)ed** -d
turbid 'tɜː.bɪd (US) 'tɜːr- **-ly** -li **-ness** -nəs, -nɪs
turbidity tɜː'bɪd.ə.ti, -ɪ.ti (US) tɜːr'bɪd.ə.t̬i
turbine 'tɜː.baɪn, -bɪn (US) 'tɜːr.bɪn, -baɪn **-s** -z
turbo 'tɜː.bəʊ (US) 'tɜːr.boʊ **-s** -z
turbocharg|e 'tɜː.bəʊ.tʃɑːdʒ (US) 'tɜːr.boʊ.tʃɑːrdʒ **-es** -ɪz **-ing** -ɪŋ **-ed** -d **-er/s** -əʳ/z (US) -ɚ/z
turbofan 'tɜː.bəʊ.fæn (US) 'tɜːr.boʊ- **-s** -z
turbo-jet 'tɜː.bəʊ.dʒet, ˌ--'- (US) 'tɜːr.boʊ.dʒet **-s** -s
turbo-prop 'tɜː.bəʊ.prɒp, ˌ--'- (US) 'tɜːr.boʊ.prɑːp **-s** -s
turbot 'tɜː.bət (US) 'tɜːr- **-s** -s
turbulence 'tɜː.bjə.lənts, -jʊ- (US) 'tɜːr-
turbulent 'tɜː.bjə.lənt, -bjʊ- (US) 'tɜːr- **-ly** -li
Turco- 'tɜː.kəʊ- (US) 'tɜːr.koʊ-, -kə-
Turcoman 'tɜː.kəʊ.mən, -mæn, -mɑːn (US) 'tɜːr.koʊ.mən, -kə- **-s** -z
turd tɜːd (US) tɜːrd **-s** -z
tureen tə'riːn, tʊ-, tjʊ-, tjə- (US) tʊ-, tjʊ- **-s** -z
tur|f tɜː|f (US) tɜːr|f **-fs** -fs **-ves** -vz **-ing** -ɪŋ **-ed** -t **'turf acˌcountant**
turf (*v.*) tɜːf (US) tɜːrf **-s** -s **-ing** -ɪŋ **-ed** -t
Turgenev tɜː'geɪ.njev, tʊə-, -'gen.jev, -jef, -jɪf, -ev, -əv (US) tʊr'geɪ.nəf, tɜːr-, -gen-, -njef, -njev
turgescen|ce tɜː'dʒes.ᵊn|ts **-t** -t
turgid 'tɜː.dʒɪd (US) 'tɜːr- **-ly** -li **-ness** -nəs, -nɪs
turgidity tɜː'dʒɪd.ə.ti, -ɪ.ti (US) tɜːr'dʒɪd.ə.t̬i
turgor 'tɜː.gəʳ (US) 'tɜːr.gɚ
Turin tjʊə'rɪn (US) tʊ-, tjʊ- *stress shift, see compound:* **ˌTurin 'Shroud**
Turing 'tjʊə.rɪŋ (US) 'tʊr.ɪŋ, 'tjʊr-
Turk tɜːk (US) tɜːrk **-s** -s
Turkestan ˌtɜː.kɪ'stɑːn, -kə'-, -stæn (US) 'tɜːr.kɪ.stæn, -stɑːn
turkey (T) 'tɜː.ki (US) 'tɜːr- **-s** -z
turkey-cock 'tɜː.ki.kɒk (US) 'tɜːr.ki.kɑːk **-s** -s
Turki 'tɜː.kiː, -ki (US) 'tɜːr-
Turkic 'tɜː.kɪk (US) 'tɜːr-
Turkington 'tɜː.kɪŋ.tən (US) 'tɜːr-
Turkish 'tɜː.kɪʃ (US) 'tɜːr- **ˌTurkish 'bath ; ˌTurkish de'light**
Turkmenia tɜːk'miː.ni.ə (US) tɜːrk-
Turkmenistan tɜːkˌmen.ɪ'stɑːn, -'stæn (US) tɜːrk'men.ɪ.stæn, -stɑːn
Turko- 'tɜː.kəʊ- (US) 'tɜːr.koʊ-, -kə-
Turkoman 'tɜːk.əʊ.mən, -mæn, -mɑːn (US) 'tɜːr.koʊ.mən, -kə- **-s** -z
Turku 'tʊə.kuː, 'tɜː- (US) 'tʊr-
Turley 'tɜː.li (US) 'tɜːr-
turmeric 'tɜː.mᵊr.ɪk (US) 'tɜːr-
turmoil 'tɜː.mɔɪl (US) 'tɜːr-
turn tɜːn (US) tɜːrn **-s** -z **-ing** -ɪŋ **-ed** -d **-er/s** -əʳ/z (US) -ɚ/z **'turning ˌpoint ; ˌturn of 'phrase**
turnabout 'tɜː.nəˌbaʊt (US) 'tɜːrn- **-s** -s
turnaround 'tɜːn.ᵊr'aʊnd (US) 'tɜːrn.ɚ- **-s** -z
Turnbull 'tɜːn.bʊl, 'tɜːm- (US) 'tɜːrn-, -bᵊl
turncoat 'tɜːn.kəʊt, 'tɜːŋ- (US) 'tɜːrn.koʊt **-s** -s
turned-on ˌtɜːnd'ɒn (US) ˌtɜːrnd'ɑːn
turner (T) 'tɜː.nəʳ (US) 'tɜːr.nɚ **-s** -z
turnery 'tɜː.nᵊr.i (US) 'tɜːr-
Turnham 'tɜː.nəm (US) 'tɜːr-
Turnhouse 'tɜːn.haʊs (US) 'tɜːrn-
turning 'tɜː.nɪŋ (US) 'tɜːr- **-s** -z
turning-point 'tɜː.nɪŋ.pɔɪnt (US) 'tɜːr- **-s** -s
turnip 'tɜː.nɪp (US) 'tɜːr- **-s** -s
turnkey 'tɜːn.kiː, 'tɜːŋ- (US) 'tɜːrn- **-s** -z
turn-off 'tɜːn.ɒf (US) 'tɜːrn.ɑːf **-s** -s
turn-on 'tɜːn.ɒn (US) 'tɜːrn.ɑːn **-s** -z
turnout 'tɜːn.aʊt (US) 'tɜːrn- **-s** -s
turnover 'tɜːnˌəʊ.vəʳ (US) 'tɜːrnˌoʊ.vɚ **-s** -z
turnpike 'tɜːn.paɪk, 'tɜːm- (US) 'tɜːrn- **-s** -s
turnround 'tɜːn.raʊnd (US) 'tɜːrn- **-s** -z
turnstile 'tɜːn.staɪl (US) 'tɜːrn- **-s** -z
turnstone 'tɜːn.stəʊn (US) 'tɜːrn.stoʊn **-s** -z
turntable 'tɜːnˌteɪ.bl̩ (US) 'tɜːrn- **-s** -z
turn-up 'tɜːn.ʌp (US) 'tɜːrn- **-s** -s
turpentine 'tɜː.pᵊn.taɪn, -pᵊm- (US) 'tɜːr.pᵊn-
Turpin 'tɜː.pɪn (US) 'tɜːr-
turpitude 'tɜː.pɪ.tjuːd, -tʃuːd (US) 'tɜːr.pɪ.tuːd, -tjuːd
turps tɜːps (US) tɜːrps
turquois|e 'tɜː.kwɑːz, -kwɔɪz (US) 'tɜːr.kwɔɪz, -kɔɪz **-es** -ɪz
turre|t 'tʌr.ɪ|t, -ə|t (US) 'tɜːr.ɪ|t **-ts** -ts **-ted** -tɪd (US) -t̬ɪd
turtle 'tɜː.tl̩ (US) 'tɜːr.t̬l̩ **-s** -z
turtledove 'tɜː.tl̩.dʌv (US) 'tɜːr.t̬l̩- **-s** -z
turtleneck 'tɜː.tl̩.nek (US) 'tɜːr.t̬l̩- **-s** -s
Turton 'tɜː.tᵊn (US) 'tɜːr-
turves (*plur. of* **turf**) tɜːvz (US) tɜːrvz
Tuscan 'tʌs.kən **-s** -z
Tuscany 'tʌs.kə.ni
tush (*interj.*) tʌʃ
tush *tooth:* tʌʃ **-es** -ɪz
tush *buttocks:* tʊʃ **-es** -ɪz
tusk tʌsk **-s** -s **-ed** -t
tusker 'tʌs.kəʳ (US) -kɚ **-s** -z
tussah 'tʌs.ə
Tussaud *surname:* 'tuː.səʊ (US) tuː'soʊ
Tussaud's *exhibition:* tʊ'sɔːdz, tjʊ-, tə-, -'səʊdz, -'səʊz (US) tʊ'soʊz, tə-, -'sɑːd, -'sɔːd; 'tuː.soʊz
Tusser 'tʌs.əʳ (US) -ɚ
tussl|e 'tʌs.l̩ **-es** -z **-ing** -ɪŋ, 'tʌs.lɪŋ **-ed** -d **-er/s** -əʳ/z (US) -ɚ/z
tussock 'tʌs.ək **-s** -s **-y** -i
tussore 'tʌs.əʳ, -ɔːʳ (US) -ɚ
tut tʌt **-s** -s **-ting** -ɪŋ (US) 'tʌt̬.ɪŋ **-ted** -ɪd (US) 'tʌt̬.ɪd
tut (*interj.*) tʌt
Note: This spelling represents the tongue click used (usually repeated - see **tut-tut**) to indicate disapproval; it may be described as a voiceless affricated alveolar click, symbolised as [ǃˢ].
Tutankhamen, **Tutankhamon** ˌtuː.tᵊn'kɑː.mən, -təŋ-, -tæŋ-, -tɑːŋ-, -kɑː'muːn
Tutbury 'tʌt.bᵊr.i (US) -ber-, -bɚ-
tutee ˌtjuː'tiː, ˌtʃuː- (US) ˌtuː-, ˌtjuː- **-s** -z
tutelage 'tjuː.tɪ.lɪdʒ, -tᵊl.ɪdʒ (US) 'tuː.t̬ᵊl.ɪdʒ, 'tjuː-
tutelar 'tjuː.tᵊl.əʳ (US) 'tuː.t̬ᵊl.ɚ, 'tjuː-
tutelary 'tjuː.tᵊl.ᵊr.i (US) 'tuː.t̬ᵊl.er.i, 'tjuː-
Tutin 'tjuː.tɪn (US) 'tuː-, 'tjuː-
tut|or 'tjuː.t|əʳ, 'tʃuː- (US) 'tuː.t̬|ɚ, 'tjuː- **-ors** -əz (US) -ɚz **-oring** -ᵊr.ɪŋ **-ored** -əd (US) -ɚd **-orage** -ᵊr.ɪdʒ
tutorial tjuː'tɔː.ri.əl, tjʊ-, tʃuː-, tʃʊ- (US) tuː'tɔːr.i-, tjuː- **-s** -z **-ly** -i
tutorship 'tjuː.tə.ʃɪp, 'tʃuː- (US) 'tuː.t̬ɚ-, 'tjuː- **-s** -s
Tutsi 'tʊt.si **-s** -z
tutti 'tʊt.i, 'tuː.ti, -tiː (US) 'tuː.t̬i **-s** -z
tutti-frutti ˌtuː.ti'fruː.ti, ˌtʊt.i'-, -'frʊt.i (US) ˌtuː.t̬i'fruː.t̬i **-s** -z
Tuttle 'tʌt.l̩ (US) 'tʌt̬-
tut|-tut ˌtʌt|'tʌt **-tuts** -'tʌts **-tutting** -'tʌt.ɪŋ (US) -'tʌt̬.ɪŋ **-tutted** -'tʌt.ɪd (US) -'tʌt̬.ɪd
tutu (T) 'tuː.tuː **-s** -z
Tuvalu tuː'vɑː.luː; 'tuː.və- (US) ˌtuː.və'luː; tuː'vɑː.luː
tu-whit tu-whoo tʊˌ*h*wɪt.tʊ'*h*wuː, tə-, -tə'-
tux tʌks **-es** -ɪz
tuxedo (T) tʌk'siː.dəʊ (US) -doʊ **-(e)s** -z
Tuxford 'tʌks.fəd (US) -fɚd
Tuzla 'tʊz.lə, 'tuːz- (US) 'tuːz.lɑː

TV ˌtiːˈviː **-s** -z ˌ**TV ˈdinner** ; ˌ**TˈV ˌprogram(me)**
Twaddell ˈtwɒd.əl; twɒdˈel (US) twɑːˈdel; ˈtwɑː.dəl
twaddl|e ˈtwɒd.l̩ (US) ˈtwɑː.dl̩ **-es** -z **-ing** -ɪŋ, ˈtwɒd.lɪŋ (US) ˈtwɑːd- **-ed** -d **-er/s** -əʳ/z, ˈtwɒd.ləʳ/z (US) ˈtwɑː.dl̩.ɚ/z, ˈtwɑːd.lɚ/z **-y** -i, ˈtwɒd.li (US) ˈtwɑː.dl̩.i, ˈtwɑːd.li
twain (T) tweɪn
twang twæŋ **-s** -z **-ing** -ɪŋ **-ed** -d **-y** -i
Twank(e)y ˈtwæŋ.ki
ˈtwas *strong form:* twɒz (US) twɑːz *weak form:* twəz
twat twæt, twɒt (US) twɑːt **-s** -s
tweak twiːk **-s** -s **-ing** -ɪŋ **-ed** -t
twee twiː
tweed (T) twiːd **-s** -z
Tweeddale ˈtwiːd.deɪl
Tweedie ˈtwiː.di
tweedl|e ˈtwiː.dl̩ **-es** -z **-ing** -ɪŋ, ˈtwiːd.lɪŋ **-ed** -d
Tweedledee ˌtwiː.dl̩ˈdiː
Tweedledum ˌtwiː.dl̩ˈdʌm
Tweedmouth ˈtwiːd.məθ, -maʊθ
Tweedsmuir ˈtwiːdz.mjʊəʳ, -mjɔːʳ (US) -mjʊr, -mjʊɚ
tweed|y ˈtwiː.d|i **-ier** -i.əʳ (US) -i.ɚ **-iest** -i.ɪst, -i.əst **-iness** -ɪ.nəs, -ɪ.nɪs
ˈtween twiːn
tween|y ˈtwiː.n|i **-ies** -iz
tweet twiːt **-s** -s **-ing** -ɪŋ (US) ˈtwiː.t̬ɪŋ **-ed** -ɪd (US) ˈtwiː.t̬ɪd **-er/s** -əʳ/z (US) ˈtwiː.t̬ɚ/z
tweezers ˈtwiː.zəz (US) -zɚz
twelfth twelfθ **-s** -s **-ly** -li ˌ**Twelfth ˈNight** (US) ˈ**Twelfth** ˌ**Night**
twelve twelv **-s** -z
twelvemonth ˈtwelv.mʌn*t*θ **-s** -s
twelvish ˈtwel.vɪʃ
twentieth ˈtwen.ti.ɪθ, -əθ (US) -t̬i- **-s** -s
twent|y ˈtwen.t|i (US) -t̬|i **-ies** -iz ˌ**twenty-**ˌ**twenty ˈvision**
twenty-first ˌtwen.tiˈfɜːst (US) -t̬iˈfɜːrst *stress shift:* ˌtwenty-first ˈbirthday
twentyfold ˈtwen.ti.fəʊld (US) -t̬i.foʊld
Twentyman ˈtwen.ti.mən (US) -t̬i-
twenty-one ˌtwen.tiˈwʌn (US) -t̬iˈ- *stress shift:* ˌtwenty-one ˈyears
ˈtwere *strong form:* twɜːʳ (US) twɜːr *weak form:* twəʳ (US) twɚ
twerp twɜːp (US) twɜːrp **-s** -s
Twi twiː
twice twaɪs
twice-told twaɪsˈtəʊld (US) -ˈtoʊld *stress shift:* ˌtwice-told ˈtale
Twickenham ˈtwɪk.ən.əm, ˈ-nəm
twiddl|e ˈtwɪd.l̩ **-es** -z **-ing** -ɪŋ, ˈtwɪd.lɪŋ **-ed** -d ˌ**twiddle your ˈthumbs**

twiddl|y ˈtwɪd.l|i, -l̩|.i **-ier** -i.əʳ (US) -i.ɚ **-iest** -i.ɪst **iest** -i.əst
twig twɪg **-s** -z **-ging** -ɪŋ **-ged** -d
Twigg twɪg
twiggy (T) ˈtwɪg.i
twilight ˈtwaɪ.laɪt **-s** -s ˈ**twilight** ˌ**zone**
twilit ˈtwaɪ.lɪt
twill twɪl **-s** -z **-ing** -ɪŋ **-ed** -d **-y** -i
ˈtwill *normal form:* twɪl *occasional weak form:* twəl
twin twɪn **-s** -z **-ning** -ɪŋ **-ned** -d ˌ**twin ˈbed** ; ˈ**twin** ˌ**set**
twin|e twaɪn **-es** -z **-ing/ly** -ɪŋ/li **-ed** -d **-er/s** -əʳ/z (US) -ɚ/z
twing|e twɪndʒ **-es** -ɪz **-(e)ing** -ɪŋ **-ed** -d
Twingo ˈtwin.gəʊ, ˈtwɪŋ- (US) -goʊ
Twining ˈtwaɪ.nɪŋ **-s**
Twinkie® ˈtwɪŋ.ki **-s** -z
twinkl|e ˈtwɪŋ.kl̩ **-es** -z **-ing** -ɪŋ, ˈtwɪŋ.klɪŋ **-ed** -d **-er/s** -əʳ/z, ˈtwɪŋ.kləʳ/z (US) ˈ-kl.ɚ/z, ˈ-klɚ/z
Twinn twɪn
twinset ˈtwɪn.set **-s** -s
twin-track ˌtwɪnˈtræk *stress shift:* ˌtwin-track ˈrailway
twin-tub ˈtwɪn.tʌb **-s** -z
twirl twɜːl (US) twɜːrl **-s** -z **-ing** -ɪŋ **-ed** -d **-y** -i
twirp twɜːp (US) twɜːrp **-s** -s
twist (T) twɪst **-s** -s **-ing** -ɪŋ **-ed** -ɪd **-er/s** -əʳ/z (US) -ɚ/z
Twistington ˈtwɪs.tɪŋ.tən
twist|y ˈtwɪs.t|i **-ier** -i.əʳ (US) -i.ɚ **-iest** -i.ɪst, -i.əst **-iness** -ɪ.nəs, -ɪ.nɪs
twit twɪt **-s** -s **-ting/ly** -ɪŋ/li (US) ˈtwɪt̬.ɪŋ/li **-ted** -ɪd (US) ˈtwɪt̬.ɪd
twitch twɪtʃ **-es** -ɪz **-ing/s** -ɪŋ/z **-ed** -t **-er/s** -əʳ/z (US) -ɚ/z
twitch|y ˈtwɪtʃ|.i **-ier** -i.əʳ (US) -i.ɚ **-iest** -i.ɪst, -i.əst
twite twaɪt **-s** -s
twitt|er ˈtwɪt|.əʳ (US) ˈtwɪt̬|.ɚ **-ers** -əz (US) -ɚz **-ering** -ər.ɪŋ (US) -ɚ.ɪŋ **-ered** -əd (US) -ɚd **-ery** -ər.i (US) -ɚ.i
ˈtwixt twɪkst
two tuː **-s** -z **put** ˌ**two and** ˌ**two toˈgether**
two-bit tuːˈbɪt (US) ˈ-- *stress shift, British only:* ˌtwo-bit ˈliar
two-by-four ˌtuː.baɪˈfɔːʳ, -bəˈ-, -bɪˈ- (US) ˈtuː.baɪ.fɔːr, -bə-
two-dimensional ˌtuː.dɪˈmen.*t*ʃən.əl, -daɪˈ-, -ˈmen*t*ʃ.nəl (US) -dəˈ-, -dɪˈ-, -daɪˈ-
two-edged ˌtuːˈedʒd *stress shift:* ˌtwo-edged ˈsword
two-|faced ˌtuː|ˈfeɪst (US) ˈ-- **-facedly** -ˈfeɪ.sɪd.li; -ˈfeɪst.li (US) -feɪ.sɪd.li, -feɪst.li **-facedness** -ˈfeɪ.sɪd.nəs, -nɪs; -ˈfeɪst.nəs, -nɪs (US) -feɪ.sɪd.nəs, -nɪs; -feɪst.nəs, -nɪs *stress shift, British only:* ˌtwo-faced ˈliar

twofold ˈtuː.fəʊld (US) -foʊld
two-ish ˈtuː.ɪʃ
two-legged ˌtuːˈlegd; -ˈleg.ɪd (US) ˈtuː.legd; -ˌleg.ɪd *stress shift, British only:* ˌtwo-legged ˈcreature
twopenc|e ˈtʌp.ən*t*s, -əm*p*s **-es** -ɪz
Note: The British English pronunciation of **twopenny, twopence,** etc., date from the period before the introduction of decimal coinage in 1971. They remain in use to suggest a very small value (e.g. a twopenny-halfpenny bus ride).
twopenny ˈtʌp.ən.i, ˈ-ni
twopenny-halfpenny ˌtʌp.niˈheɪp.ni, ˌtʌp.ən.iˈheɪ.pən.i
twopennyworth ˌtuːˈpen.i.wɜːθ, ˈ-əθ; ˈtʌp.ən.i.wɜːθ, ˈ-ni-, -wəθ (US) -wɜːrθ, -wɚθ **-s** -s
two-piece ˈtuː.piːs
two-ply ˈtuː.plaɪ
two-seater ˌtuːˈsiː.təʳ (US) -t̬ɚ, ˈ-ˌ-- **-s** -z *stress shift:* ˌtwo-seater ˈsportscar
twosome ˈtuː.səm **-s** -z
two-step ˈtuː.step **-s** -s
two-stroke ˈtuː.strəʊk (US) -stroʊk
two-time ˌtuːˈtaɪm, ˈ-- (US) ˈ-- **-s** -z **-ing** -ɪŋ **-ed** -d **-er/s** -əʳ/z (US) -ɚ/z
two-tone ˌtuːˈtəʊn, ˈ-- (US) ˈtuː.toʊn **-d** -d
two-way ˌtuːˈweɪ (US) ˈ-- *stress shift, British only:* ˌtwo-way ˈmirror
Twyford ˈtwaɪ.fəd (US) -fɚd
TX (*abbrev. for* **Texas**) ˈtek.səs
Tybalt ˈtɪb.əlt
Tyburn ˈtaɪ.bɜːn (US) -bɜːrn
Tycho ˈtaɪ.kəʊ (US) -koʊ
tycoon taɪˈkuːn **-s** -z
Tydeus ˈtaɪ.djuːs, -djəs, -di.əs (US) ˈtaɪ.di.əs, ˈ-djəs
Tydfil ˈtɪd.vɪl
tyger ˈtaɪ.gəʳ (US) -gɚ
tying (*from* **tie**) ˈtaɪ.ɪŋ
tyke taɪk **-s** -s
Tyldesley ˈtɪldz.li
Tyler ˈtaɪ.ləʳ (US) -lɚ
tympan|i ˈtɪm.pə.n|i **-ist/s** -ɪst/s
tympanic tɪmˈpæn.ɪk
tympan|um ˈtɪm.pən|.əm **-ums** -əmz **-a** -ə
tympan|y ˈtɪm.pən|.i **-ies** -iz
Tynan ˈtaɪ.nən
Tyndale, Tyndall ˈtɪn.dəl
Tyndrum ˈtaɪn.drʌm
Tyne taɪn ˌ**Tyne and ˈWear**
Tynemouth ˈtaɪn.məθ, ˈtaɪm-, -maʊθ ; ˈtɪn.məθ, ˈtɪm- (US) ˈtaɪn-
Tynesid|e ˈtaɪn.saɪd **-er/s** -əʳ/z (US) -ɚ/z
Tynwald ˈtɪn.wəld
typ|e taɪp **-es** -s **-ing** -ɪŋ **-ed** -t ˈ**typing** ˌ**pool**

typecast 'taɪp.kɑːst (US) -kæst **-s** -s **-ing** -ɪŋ
Typee ˌtaɪ'piː
typefac|e 'taɪp.feɪs **-es** -ɪz
typefounder 'taɪpˌfaʊn.dəʳ (US) -dɚ **-s** -z
typefoundr|y 'taɪpˌfaʊn.dr|i **-ies** -iz
typescript 'taɪp.skrɪpt **-s** -s
type|set 'taɪp|.set **-sets** -sets **-setting** -ˌset.ɪŋ (US) -ˌseṱ.ɪŋ **-setter/s** -ˌset.əʳ/z (US) -ˌseṱ.ɚ/z
typesetter 'taɪpˌset.əʳ (US) -ˌseṱ.ɚ **-s** -z
type|write 'taɪp|.raɪt **-writes** -raɪts **-writing** -ˌraɪ.tɪŋ (US) -ˌraɪ.ṱɪŋ **-wrote** -rəʊt (US) -roʊt **-written** -ˌrɪt.ᵊn
typewriter 'taɪpˌraɪ.təʳ (US) -ṱɚ **-s** -z
typhoid 'taɪ.fɔɪd
typhonic taɪ'fɒn.ɪk (US) -'fɑː.nɪk
Typhoo® taɪ'fuː
typhoon taɪ'fuːn **-s** -z
typh|us 'taɪ.f|əs **-ous** -əs
typic|al 'tɪp.ɪ.k|ᵊl **-ally** -ᵊl.i, -li **-alness** -ᵊl.nəs, -nɪs
typicality ˌtɪp.ɪ'kæl.ə.ti, -ɪ.ti (US) -ə.ṱi
typi|fy 'tɪp.ɪ|.faɪ **-fies** -faɪz **-fying** -faɪ.ɪŋ **-fied** -faɪd
typist 'taɪ.pɪst **-s** -s
typo 'taɪ.pəʊ (US) -poʊ **-s** -z
typographic ˌtaɪ.pəʊ'græf.ɪk (US) -pə'-, -poʊ'- **-al** -ᵊl **-ally** -ᵊl.i, -li
typograph|y taɪ'pɒg.rə.f|i (US) -'pɑː.grə- **-er/s** -əʳ/z (US) -ɚ/z
typolog|y taɪ'pɒl.ə.dʒ|i (US) -'pɑː.lə- **-ies** -iz
tyrannic|al tɪ'ræn.ɪ.k|ᵊl, tə-, taɪ- (US) tə-, tɪ-, taɪ- **-ally** -ᵊl.i, -li **-alness** -ᵊl.nəs, -nɪs
tyrannicide tɪ'ræn.ɪ.saɪd, tə-, taɪ- (US) tə-, tɪ-, taɪ- **-s** -z
tyranniz|e, -is|e 'tɪr.ᵊn.aɪz **-es** -ɪz **-ing** -ɪŋ **-ed** -d
tyrannosaur tɪ'ræn.ə.sɔːʳ, tə-, taɪ- (US) tə'ræn.ə.sɔːr, tɪ-, taɪ- **-s** -z
tyrannosaurus tɪˌræn.ə'sɔː.rəs, tə-, taɪ- (US) təˌræn.ə'sɔːr.əs, tɪ-, taɪ- **-es** -ɪz **tyˌrannoˌsaurus 'rex**
tyrannous 'tɪr.ᵊn.əs **-ly** -li
tyrann|y 'tɪr.ᵊn|.i **-ies** -iz
tyrant 'taɪə.rənt (US) 'taɪ- **-s** -s
tyre (T) taɪəʳ (US) taɪɚ **-s** -z
Tyrian 'tɪr.i.ən **-s** -z
tyro 'taɪə.rəʊ (US) 'taɪ.roʊ **-s** -z
Tyrol tɪ'rəʊl, tə-; 'tɪr.ᵊl (US) tɪ'roʊl, taɪ-; 'tɪr.oʊl, -ɑːl
Tyrolean ˌtɪr.əʊ'liː.ən; tɪ'rəʊ.li-, tə- (US) tɪ'roʊ.li-, taɪ-; ˌtɪr.ə'liː-
Tyrolese ˌtɪr.əʊ'liːz (US) -ə'liːz, -'liːs
Tyrolienne tɪˌrəʊ.li'en, tə-; ˌtɪr.əʊ- (US) tɪ'roʊ.li.ən; ˌtɪr.ə'liː-, ˌtaɪ.rə'- **-s** -z
Tyrone *in Ireland:* tɪ'rəʊn, tə- (US) -'roʊn
Tyrone *person's name:* 'taɪə.rəʊn; taɪ'rəʊn, tɪ-, tə- (US) 'taɪ.roʊn, ˌ-'-
Tyrrell 'tɪr.ᵊl
Tyrrhenian tɪ'riː.ni.ən, tə- (US) tɪ-
Tyrtaeus tɜː'tiː.əs (US) tɜːr-
Tyrwhitt 'tɪr.ɪt
Tyser 'taɪ.zəʳ (US) -zɚ
Tyson 'taɪ.sᵊn
Tytler 'taɪt.ləʳ (US) -lɚ
Tyzack 'taɪ.zæk, 'tɪz.æk, -ək
tzar (T) zɑːʳ, tsɑːʳ (US) zɑːr, tsɑːr **-s** -z
tzarina (T) zɑː'riː.nə, tsɑː- **-s** -z
tzar|ism 'zɑː.r|ɪ.zᵊm, 'tsɑː- (US) 'zɑːr.ɪ-, 'tsɑːr- **-ist/s** -ɪst/s
tzetze 'tet.si, 'tset- (US) 'tset-, 'tsiːt-, 'tet-, 'tiːt- **-s** -z **'tzetze ˌfly**

U

u (U) juː **-'s** -z
UAE ˌjuː.eɪ'iː
UB40 ˌjuː.biː'fɔː.ti ⓊⓈ -'fɔːr.t̬i **-s** -z
Ubbelohde 'ʌb.əl.əʊd ⓊⓈ -oʊd
U-bend 'juː.bend **-s** -z
Übermensch 'uː.bə.mentʃ ⓊⓈ -bɚ- **-en** -ən
ubiquitarian (U) juːˌbɪk.wɪ'teə.ri.ən, ˌjuː.bɪ.kwɪ'- ⓊⓈ juːˌbɪk.wə'ter.i- **-s** -z
ubiquitous juː'bɪk.wɪ.təs ⓊⓈ -wə.t̬əs **-ly** -li **-ness** -nəs, -nɪs
ubiquity juː'bɪk.wə.ti, -wɪ- ⓊⓈ -wə.t̬i
U-boat 'juː.bəʊt ⓊⓈ -boʊt **-s** -s
Ubu Roi ˌuː.buː'rwɑː
UCAS 'juː.kæs
UCATT 'ʌk.ət, 'juː.kæt
UCCA 'ʌk.ə
Uccello uː'tʃel.əʊ ⓊⓈ -oʊ
Uckfield 'ʌk.fiːld
UDA ˌjuː.diː'eɪ
Udall 'juː.dəl ⓊⓈ -dɔːl, -dɑːl, -dəl
udder 'ʌd.əʳ ⓊⓈ -ɚ **-s** -z
Uddin 'ʌd.ɪn
Uddingston 'ʌd.ɪŋ.stən
UDI ˌjuː.diː'aɪ
Udolpho uː'dɒl.fəʊ, juː- ⓊⓈ -'dɑːl.foʊ
udometer juː'dɒm.ɪ.təʳ, '-ə- ⓊⓈ -'dɑː.mə.t̬ɚ **-s** -z
UDR ˌjuː.diː'ɑːʳ ⓊⓈ -'ɑːr
UEFA juː'eɪ.fə, -'iː-
Uffizi juː'fɪt.si, uː-, -'fiːt-
UFO ˌjuː.ef'əʊ ⓊⓈ -'oʊ **-(')s** -z
ufolog|y juː'fɒl.ə.dʒ|i ⓊⓈ -'fɑː.lə- **-ist/s** -ɪst/s
Ugand|a juː'gæn.d|ə, jʊ- ⓊⓈ juː-, uː- **-an/s** -ən/z
Ugaritic ˌuː.gər'ɪt.ɪk, ˌjuː- ⓊⓈ -gə'rɪt̬-
ugh ɯːx, ɯh, ʌx, uɸ, ʊh, ɜːh, ʌg
Note: Used to indicate disgust.
ugli 'ʌg.li **-s** -z **'ugli ˌfruit**
uglification ˌʌg.lɪ.fɪ'keɪ.ʃən, -lə-
ugli|fy 'ʌg.lɪ|.faɪ **-fies** -faɪz **-fying** -faɪ.ɪŋ **-fied** -faɪd
ugl|y 'ʌg.l|i **-ier** -i.əʳ ⓊⓈ -i.ɚ **-iest** -i.ɪst, -i.əst **-iness** -ɪ.nəs, -ɪ.nɪs **ˌugly 'duckling**
Ugrian 'uː.gri.ən, 'juː- **-s** -z
Ugric 'uː.grɪk, 'juː-
UHF ˌjuː.eɪtʃ'ef
uh-huh ʌ'hʌ, 'ʌ.hʌ
uhlan 'uː.lɑːn, 'juː-, -lən; uː'lɑːn, juː- **-s** -z
Uhland 'uː.lənd, -lænd, -lɑːnd ⓊⓈ -lɑːnt, -lɑːnd
UHT ˌjuː.eɪtʃ'tiː *stress shift, see compound:* **ˌUHT 'milk**
Uhu® 'juː.huː, 'uː-
uh-uh 'ʌʔˌʌʔ ⓊⓈ 'ʌ̃ʔˌʌ̃
Note: Used to indicate alarm or anxiety.
uhuru (U) uː'huː.ruː, -'hʊə-
Uig 'uː.ɪg, 'juː-
Uist 'juː.ɪst
uitlander (U) 'eɪtˌlæn.dəʳ, 'ɔɪt- ⓊⓈ 'ɔɪtˌlæn.dɚ, 'eɪt-, 'aɪt- **-s** -z
UK ˌjuː'keɪ *stress shift:* ˌUK 'citizen
ukas|e juː'keɪz, -'keɪs ⓊⓈ juː'keɪz, -'keɪs, '-- **-es** -ɪz
uke juːk **-s** -s
ukelele ˌjuː.kəl'eɪ.li ⓊⓈ -kə'leɪ- **-s** -z
Ukraine juː'kreɪn ⓊⓈ -'kreɪn, 'juː.kreɪn
ukulele ˌjuː.kəl'eɪ.li ⓊⓈ -kə'leɪ- **-s** -z
ulan 'uː.lɑːn, 'juː-, -lən; uː'lɑːn, juː- **-s** -z
Ulan Bator uːˌlɑːn'bɑː.tɔːʳ ⓊⓈ ˌuː.lɑːn'bɑː.tɔːr
Ulan-Ude uːˌlɑːn.uː'deɪ ⓊⓈ uːˌlɑːn.uː'deɪ, uː'lɑːn.uːˌdeɪ
ulcer 'ʌl.səʳ ⓊⓈ -sɚ **-s** -z
ulcer|ate 'ʌl.sər|.eɪt ⓊⓈ -sə.r|eɪt **-ates** -eɪts **-ating** -eɪ.tɪŋ ⓊⓈ -eɪ.t̬ɪŋ **-ated** -eɪ.tɪd ⓊⓈ -eɪ.t̬ɪd
ulceration ˌʌl.sər'eɪ.ʃən ⓊⓈ -sə'reɪ- **-s** -z
ulcerative 'ʌl.sər.ə.tɪv, -eɪ- ⓊⓈ -sə.reɪ.t̬ɪv, -sɚ.ə-
ulcerous 'ʌl.sər.əs
ulema 'uː.lɪ.mə, -lə-, -mɑː; ˌuː.lɪ'mɑː, -lə'- ⓊⓈ ˌuː.lə'mɑː, '--- **-s** -z
Ulfilas 'ʊl.fɪ.læs, -fə-, -ləs ⓊⓈ 'ʌl.fɪ.ləs
Ulgham 'ʌf.əm
ullage 'ʌl.ɪdʒ
Ullah 'ʌl.ə
Ullapool 'ʌl.ə.puːl
Ullman(n) 'ʊl.mən, 'ʌl- ⓊⓈ 'ʌl-, 'ʊl-
Ullswater 'ʌlzˌwɔː.təʳ ⓊⓈ -ˌwɑː.t̬ɚ, -ˌwɔː-
Ulm ʊlm
uln|a 'ʌl.n|ə **-as** -əz **-ae** -iː **-ar** -əʳ ⓊⓈ -ɚ
Ulrica 'ʊl.rɪkə, 'ʌl-
Ulrich 'ʊl.rɪk *as if German:* -rɪx ⓊⓈ 'ʌl-, 'ʊl-
Ulster, ulster 'ʌl.stəʳ ⓊⓈ -stɚ **-s** -z
Ulster|man 'ʌl.stə|.mən ⓊⓈ -stɚ- **-men** -mən
Ulster|woman 'ʌl.stə|ˌwʊm.ən ⓊⓈ -stɚ- **-women** -ˌwɪm.ɪn
ulterior ʌl'tɪə.ri.əʳ ⓊⓈ -'tɪr.i.ɚ **-ly** -li **ulˌterior 'motive**
ultima 'ʌl.tɪ.mə, -tə- ⓊⓈ -t̬ɪ- **ˌultima 'Thule**
ultimate 'ʌl.tɪ.mət, -tə-, -mət ⓊⓈ -t̬ə.mɪt **-ly** -li
ultimat|um ˌʌl.tɪ'meɪ.t|əm ⓊⓈ -t̬ə'meɪ.t̬|əm **-ums** -əmz **-a** -ə
ultimo 'ʌl.tɪ.məʊ, -tə- ⓊⓈ -t̬ɪ.moʊ
ultra- ʌl.trə-
Note: Prefix. Normally takes primary or secondary stress on the first syllable, e.g. **ultrasound** /'ʌl.trə.saʊnd/, **ultrasonic** /ˌʌl.trə'sɒn.ɪk ⓊⓈ -'sɑː.nɪk/.
ultra 'ʌl.trə **-s** -z
ultra-high frequenc|y ˌʌl.trəˌhaɪ'friː.kwənt.s|i **-ies** -iz
ultramarine ˌʌl.trə.mə'riːn *stress shift:* ˌultramarine 'blue
ultramodern ˌʌl.trə'mɒd.ən ⓊⓈ -'mɑː.dɚn **-ist/s** -ɪst/s *stress shift:* ˌultramodern 'styling
ultramontane ˌʌl.trə'mɒn.teɪn, -mɒn'teɪn ⓊⓈ -'mɑːn.teɪn, -mɑːn'teɪn
ultramontanism (U) ˌʌl.trə'mɒn.tə.nɪ.zəm, -tɪ-, -teɪ- ⓊⓈ -'mɑːn.tə-
ultrasonic ˌʌl.trə'sɒn.ɪk ⓊⓈ -'sɑː.nɪk **-s** -s **-ally** -əl.i, -li *stress shift:* ˌultrasonic 'scanner
ultrasound 'ʌl.trə.saʊnd
ultraviolet ˌʌl.trə'vaɪə.lət, -lɪt ⓊⓈ -lɪt *stress shift, see compound:* **ˌultraviolet 'light**
ultra vires ˌʌl.trə'vaɪə.riːz, ˌʊl.trɑː'vɪə.reɪz ⓊⓈ ˌʌl.trə'vaɪ.riːz
ululant 'juː.ljə.lənt, 'ʌl.jə-, -jʊ- ⓊⓈ 'juːl.juː.lənt, 'ʌl-, -jə-
ulu|late 'juː.ljə|.leɪt, 'ʌl.jə-, -jʊ- ⓊⓈ 'juːl.juː-, 'ʌl-, -jə- **-lates** -leɪts **-lating** -leɪ.tɪŋ ⓊⓈ -leɪ.t̬ɪŋ **-lated** -leɪ.tɪd ⓊⓈ -leɪ.t̬ɪd
ululation ˌjuː.ljə'leɪ.ʃən, ˌʌl.jə'-, -jʊ'- ⓊⓈ ˌjuːl.juː'-, ˌʌl-, -jə'- **-s** -z
Uluru uː'luː.ruː; ˌʊl.ə'ruː
Ulverston 'ʌl.və.stən ⓊⓈ -vɚ-
Ulyanovsk ʊl'jɑː.nɒfsk ⓊⓈ uːl'jɑː.nɔːfsk
Ulysses 'juː.lɪ.siːz; juː'lɪs.iːz ⓊⓈ juː'lɪs-
umbel 'ʌm.bəl, -bel **-s** -z
umbellifer ʌm'bel.ɪ.fəʳ ⓊⓈ -fɚ
umbelliferae ˌʌm.bəl'ɪf.ər.iː, -bel'- ⓊⓈ -bə'lɪf.ə.riː
umbelliferous ˌʌm.bəl'ɪf.ər.əs, -bel'- ⓊⓈ -bə'lɪf-
umber 'ʌm.bəʳ ⓊⓈ -bɚ **-s** -z
Umberto ʊm'beə.təʊ, -'bɜː- ⓊⓈ -'ber.toʊ
umbilical ʌm'bɪl.ɪ.kl̩, '-ə-, ˌʌm.bɪ'laɪ-, -bə'- ⓊⓈ ʌm'bɪl.ɪ-, '-ə- **umˌbilical 'cord, ˌumbiˌlical 'cord** ⓊⓈ **um'bilical ˌcord**
umbilic|us ʌm'bɪl.ɪ.k|əs, '-ə-; ˌʌm.bɪ'laɪ-, -bə'- **-uses** -ə.sɪz **-i** -aɪ
umbles 'ʌm.bl̩z
um|bo 'ʌm|.bəʊ ⓊⓈ -boʊ **-bos** -bəʊz ⓊⓈ -boʊz **-bones** -'bəʊ.neɪz ⓊⓈ -'boʊ-
umbr|a 'ʌm.br|ə **-as** -əz **-ae** -iː **-al** -əl

umbrage 'ʌm.brɪdʒ
umbrageous ʌm'breɪ.dʒəs **-ly** -li **-ness** -nəs, -nɪs
umbrated 'ʌm.breɪ.tɪd ⓤⓢ -t̬ɪd
umbration ʌm'breɪ.ʃᵊn **-s** -z
umbrella ʌm'brel.ə **-s** -z
Umbri|a 'ʌm.bri|.ə **-an/s** -ən/z
Umbro® 'ʌm.brəʊ ⓤⓢ -broʊ
unemployability ˌʌn.ɪmˌplɔɪ.ə'bɪl.ɪ.ti, -emˌ-, -ə.ti ⓤⓢ -ə.t̬i
Umfreville 'ʌm.frə.vɪl
umiak 'uː.mi.æk, -mjæk **-s** -s
umlaut 'ʊm.laʊt **-s** -s
umpirag|e 'ʌm.paɪ.ᵊr.ɪdʒ **-es** -ɪz
umpir|e 'ʌm.paɪəʳ ⓤⓢ -paɪɚ **-es** -z **-ing** -ɪŋ **-ed** -d
umpteen ʌmp'tiːn **-th** -θ *stress shift:* ˌumpteen 'times
un- ʌn-
Note: Prefix. It may be unstressed, usually when a stressed syllable follows it and it is a frequently-used word, e.g. **unable** /ʌn'eɪ.bl̩/. Otherwise it will have secondary stress, e.g. **unadvisable** /ˌʌn.əd'vaɪ.zə.bl̩/. This syllable frequently becomes the main stress in the word through stress-shift, e.g. **unattended** /ˌʌn.ə'ten.dɪd/, **unattended parking** /ˌʌn.ə.ten.dɪd'pɑː.kɪŋ ⓤⓢ -'pɑːr-/. There are so many such cases that individual examples are not given for each word.
'un ən **-s** -z
Note: Old-fashioned colloquial form for 'one', as in 'little' un'.
UN ˌjuː'en
Una 'juː.nə, 'uː-
unabash|ed ˌʌn.ə'bæʃ|t **-edly** -ɪd.li
unabated ˌʌn.ə'beɪ.tɪd ⓤⓢ -t̬ɪd **-ly** -li
unable ʌn'eɪ.bl̩, ˌʌn-
unabridged ˌʌn.ə'brɪdʒd
unaccented ˌʌn.ək'sen.tɪd, -æk'- ⓤⓢ ʌn'æk.sen.t̬ɪd
unaccepta|ble ˌʌn.ək'sep.tə|.bl̩, -æk'- **-bly** -bli
unacceptability ˌʌn.ək.sep.tə'bɪl.ə.ti, -ɪ.ti ⓤⓢ -ə.t̬i
unaccompanied ˌʌn.ə'kʌm.pə.nid, -'kʌmp.nid
unaccountability ˌʌn.əˌkaʊn.tə'bɪl.ɪ.ti, -ə.ti ⓤⓢ -t̬ə'bɪl.ə.t̬i
unaccountab|le ˌʌn.ə'kaʊn.tə.b|l̩ ⓤⓢ -t̬ə- **-ly** -li **-leness** -l̩.nəs, -nɪs
unaccounted ˌʌn.ə'kaʊn.tɪd ⓤⓢ -t̬ɪd ˌunac'counted ˌfor
unaccustomed ˌʌn.ə'kʌs.təmd **-ly** -li
unacknowledged ˌʌn.ək'nɒl.ɪdʒd ⓤⓢ -'nɑː.lɪdʒd
unacquainted ˌʌn.ə'kweɪn.tɪd ⓤⓢ -t̬ɪd
unadaptable ˌʌn.ə'dæp.tə.bl̩
unaddressed ˌʌn.ə'drest
unadopted ˌʌn.ə'dɒp.tɪd ⓤⓢ -'dɑːp-
unadorned ˌʌn.ə'dɔːnd ⓤⓢ -'dɔːrnd
unadulterated ˌʌn.ə'dʌl.tᵊr.eɪ.tɪd ⓤⓢ -t̬ə.reɪ.t̬ɪd
unadvised ˌʌn.əd'vaɪzd
unadvisedly ˌʌn.əd'vaɪ.zɪd.li
unaffected ˌʌn.ə'fek.tɪd **-ly** -li **-ness** -nəs, -nɪs
unaffectionate ˌʌn.ə'fek.ʃᵊn.ət **-ly** -li
unafraid ˌʌn.ə'freɪd
unaided ʌn'eɪ.dɪd, ˌʌn-
unalienab|le ʌn'eɪ.li.ə.nə.b|l̩, ˌʌn-, '-ljə- ⓤⓢ -li.ə-, -'eɪl.jə- **-ly** -li
unaligned ˌʌn.ə'laɪnd
unalloyed ˌʌn.ə'lɔɪd
unalterability ʌnˌɔːl.tᵊr.ə'bɪl.ɪ.ti, ˌʌn-, -ə.ti ⓤⓢ -ˌɑːl.t̬ɚ.ə'bɪl.ə.t̬i, -ˌɔːl-
unalterab|le ʌn'ɔːl.tᵊr.ə.b|l̩, ˌʌn- ⓤⓢ -'ɔːl.t̬ɚ-, -'ɑːl- **-ly** -li **-leness** -l̩.nəs ⓤⓢ -nɪs
unaltered ʌn'ɔːl.təd, ˌʌn- ⓤⓢ -t̬ɚd, -'ɑːl-
unambiguous ˌʌn.æm'bɪg.ju.əs **-ly** -li **-ness** -nəs, -nɪs
unambivalent ˌʌn.æm'bɪv.ᵊl.ənt **-ly** -ly
un-American ˌʌn.ə'mer.ɪ.kən
unanalysab|le ʌnˌæn.ᵊl'aɪ.zə.b|l̩, ˌʌn-, -'æn.ᵊl.aɪ- ⓤⓢ -ˌæn.ə'laɪ-, -'æn.ə.laɪ- **-ly** -li **-leness** -l̩.nəs, -nɪs
unanimity ˌjuː.nə'nɪm.ə.ti, -næn'ɪm-, -ɪ.ti ⓤⓢ -nə'nɪm.ə.t̬i
unanimous juː'næn.ɪ.məs, '-ə- ⓤⓢ '-ə- **-ly** -li **-ness** -nəs, -nɪs, -nəs
unannounced ˌʌn.ə'naʊn*t*st
unanswerability ʌnˌɑːn*t*.sᵊr.ə'bɪl.ɪ.ti, ˌʌn-, -ə.ti ⓤⓢ -ˌæn*t*.sɚ.ə'bɪl.ə.t̬i
unanswerab|le ʌn'ɑːn*t*.sᵊr.ə.b|l̩, ˌʌn- ⓤⓢ -'æn*t*- **-ly** -li
unanswered ʌn'ɑːn*t*.səd, ˌʌn- ⓤⓢ -'æn*t*.sɚd
unappealing ˌʌn.ə'piː.lɪŋ **-ly** -li
unappeasable ˌʌn.ə'piː.zə.bl̩
unappeased ˌʌn.ə'piːzd
unappetizing, -ising ʌn'æp.ɪ.taɪ.zɪŋ, ˌʌn-, '-ə- ⓤⓢ '-ə- **-ly** -li
unapplied ˌʌn.ə'plaɪd
unappreciated ˌʌn.ə'priː.ʃi.eɪ.tɪd ⓤⓢ -t̬ɪd
unappreciative ˌʌn.ə'priː.ʃi.ə.tɪv ⓤⓢ -t̬ɪv **-ly** -li
unapproachability ˌʌn.əˌprəʊ.tʃə'bɪl.ɪ.ti, -ə.ti ⓤⓢ -ˌproʊ.tʃə'bɪl.ə.t̬i
unapproachab|le ˌʌn.ə'prəʊ.tʃə.b|l̩ ⓤⓢ -'proʊ- **-ly** -bli **-leness** -bl̩.nəs, -nɪs
unappropriate ˌʌn.ə'prəʊ.pri.ət ⓤⓢ -'proʊ- **-ly** -li **-ness** -nəs, -nɪs
unappropriated ˌʌn.ə'prəʊ.pri.eɪ.tɪd ⓤⓢ -'proʊ.pri.eɪ.t̬ɪd
unapproved ˌʌn.ə'pruːvd
unapt ʌn'æpt **-ly** -li **-ness** -nəs, -nɪs
unarguab|le ʌn'ɑː.gju.ə.b|l̩ ⓤⓢ -'ɑːr- **-ly** -li **-leness** -l̩.nəs, -nɪs
unarm ʌn'ɑːm, ˌʌn- ⓤⓢ -'ɑːrm **-s** -z **-ing** -ɪŋ **-ed** -d ˌ**unarmed 'combat**
unarticulated ˌʌn.ɑː'tɪk.jə.leɪ.tɪd, -jʊ- ⓤⓢ -ɑːr'tɪk.jə.leɪ.t̬ɪd
unary 'juː.nᵊr.i
unasha|med ˌʌn.ə'ʃeɪ|md **-medly** -mɪd.li **-medness** -mɪd.nəs, -nɪs
unasked ʌn'ɑːskt, ˌʌn- ⓤⓢ -'æskt
unaspirated ʌn'æs.pᵊr.eɪ.tɪd, ˌʌn- ⓤⓢ -pə.reɪ.t̬ɪd
unassailability ˌʌn.əˌseɪ.lə'bɪl.ɪ.ti, -ə.ti ⓤⓢ -ə.t̬i
unassailab|le ˌʌn.ə'seɪ.lə.b|l̩ **-ly** -li **-leness** -l̩.nəs, -nɪs
unassertive ˌʌn.ə'sɜː.tɪv ⓤⓢ -'sɜːr.t̬ɪv **-ly** -li **-ness** -nəs, -nɪs
unassigned ˌʌn.ə'saɪnd
unassimilated ˌʌn.ə'sɪm.ᵊl.eɪ.tɪd, -ɪ.leɪ- ⓤⓢ -t̬ɪd
unassisted ˌʌn.ə'sɪs.tɪd
unassuageable ˌʌn.ə'sweɪ.dʒə.bl̩
unassuming ˌʌn.ə'sjuː.mɪŋ ⓤⓢ, -'suː- ⓤⓢ -'suː- **-ly** -li **-ness** -nəs, -nɪs
unattached ˌʌn.ə'tætʃt
unattainab|le ˌʌn.ə'teɪ.nə.b|l̩ **-ly** -li **-ness** -nəs, -nɪs
unattended ˌʌn.ə'ten.dɪd
unattested ˌʌn.ə'tes.tɪd
unattractive ˌʌn.ə'træk.tɪv **-ly** -li **-ness** -nəs, -nɪs
unauthenticated ˌʌn.ɔː'θen.tɪ.keɪ.tɪd ⓤⓢ -ɑː'θen.t̬ɪ.keɪ.t̬ɪd, -ɔː'-
unauthorized, -ised ʌn'ɔː.θᵊr.aɪzd, ˌʌn- ⓤⓢ -'ɑː.θə.raɪzd, -'ɔː-
unavailability ˌʌn.əˌveɪ.lə'bɪl.ɪ.ti, -ə.ti ⓤⓢ -ə.t̬i
unavailable ˌʌn.ə'veɪ.lə.bl̩
unavailing ˌʌn.ə'veɪ.lɪŋ **-ly** -li **-ness** -nəs, -nɪs
unavenged ˌʌn.ə'ven*d*ʒd
unavoidab|le ˌʌn.ə'vɔɪ.də.b|l̩ **-ly** -li
unaware ˌʌn.ə'weəʳ ⓤⓢ -'wer **-s** -z **-ly** -li **-ness** -nəs, -nɪs
unbalanc|e ʌn'bæl.ən*t*s, ˌʌn-, ʌm-, ˌʌm- ⓤⓢ ʌn-, ˌʌn- **-es** -ɪz **-ing** -ɪŋ **-ed** -t
unbaptized ˌʌn.bæp'taɪzd, ˌʌm- ⓤⓢ ʌn'bæp.taɪzd
unbar ʌn'bɑːʳ, ˌʌn-, ʌm-, ˌʌm- ⓤⓢ ʌn'bɑːr, ˌʌn- **-s** -z **-ring** -ɪŋ **-red** -d
unbearab|le ʌn'beə.rə.b|l̩, ˌʌn-, ʌm-, ˌʌm- ⓤⓢ ʌn'ber.ə-, -nəs, ˌʌn- **-ly** -li **-leness** -l̩.nəs, -nɪs
unbeatab|le ʌn'biː.tə.b|l̩, ˌʌn-, ʌm-, ˌʌm- ⓤⓢ ʌn'biː.t̬ə-, ˌʌn- **-ly** -ly
unbeaten ʌn'biː.tᵊn, ˌʌn-, ʌm-, ˌʌm- ⓤⓢ ʌn-, ˌʌn-
unbecoming ˌʌn.bɪ'kʌm.ɪŋ, ˌʌm-, -bə'- ⓤⓢ ˌʌn- **-ly** -li **-ness** -nəs, -nɪs

unbegotten ˌʌn.bɪˈgɒt.ən, ˌʌm-, -bəˈ- ⓤⓢ ˌʌn.bɪˈgɑː.tən, -bəˈ-
unbeknown ˌʌn.bɪˈnəʊn, ˌʌm-, -bəˈ- ⓤⓢ ˌʌn.bɪˈnoʊn, -bəˈ- **-st** -*t*st
unbelief ˌʌn.bɪˈliːf, ˌʌm-, -bəˈ- ⓤⓢ ˌʌn-
unbelievab|le ˌʌn.bɪˈliː.və.b|l̩, ˌʌm-, -bəˈ- ⓤⓢ ˌʌn- **-ly** -li
unbeliever ˌʌn.bɪˈliː.vəʳ, ˌʌm-, -bəˈ- ⓤⓢ ˌʌn.bɪˈliː.vɚ, -bəˈ- **-s** -z
unbelieving ˌʌn.bɪˈliː.vɪŋ, ˌʌm-, -bəˈ- ⓤⓢ ˌʌn- **-ly** -li
un|bend ʌnˈbend, ˌʌn-, ʌm-, ˌʌm- ⓤⓢ ʌn-, ˌʌn- **-bends** -ˈbendz **-bending** -ˈben.dɪŋ **-bended** -ˈben.dɪd **-bent** -ˈbent
unbeneficed ʌnˈben.ɪ.fɪst, ˌʌn-, ʌm-, ˌʌm- ⓤⓢ ʌn-, ˌʌn-
unbias(s)ed ʌnˈbaɪəst, ˌʌn-, ʌm-, ˌʌm- ⓤⓢ ʌn-, ˌʌn- **-ness** -nəs, -nɪs
unbidden ʌnˈbɪd.ən, ˌʌn-, ʌm-, ˌʌm- ⓤⓢ ʌn-, ˌʌn-
un|bind ʌn|ˈbaɪnd, ˌʌn-, ʌm-, ˌʌm- ⓤⓢ ʌn-, ˌʌn- **-binds** -ˈbaɪndz **-binding** -ˈbaɪn.dɪŋ **-bound** -ˈbaʊnd
unbleached ʌnˈbliːtʃt, ˌʌn-, ʌm-, ˌʌm- ⓤⓢ ʌn-, ˌʌn-
unblemished ʌnˈblem.ɪʃt, ˌʌn-, ʌm-, ˌʌm- ⓤⓢ ʌn-, ˌʌn-
unblinking ʌnˈblɪŋ.kɪŋ, ʌm- ⓤⓢ ʌn- **-ly** -li **-ness** -nəs, -nɪs
unblock ʌnˈblɒk, ʌm- ⓤⓢ ʌnˈblɑːk **-s** -s **-ing** -ɪŋ **-ed** -t **-er/s** -əʳ/z ⓤⓢ -ɚ/z
unblushing ʌnˈblʌʃ.ɪŋ, ˌʌn-, ʌm-, ˌʌm- ⓤⓢ ʌn-, ˌʌn- **-ly** -li
un|bolt ʌn|ˈbəʊlt, ˌʌn-, ʌm-, ˌʌm- ⓤⓢ ʌn|ˈboʊlt, ˌʌn- **-bolts** -ˈbəʊlts ⓤⓢ -ˈboʊlts **-bolting** -ˈbəʊl.tɪŋ ⓤⓢ -ˈboʊl.t̬ɪŋ **-bolted** -ˈbəʊl.tɪd ⓤⓢ -ˈboʊl.t̬ɪd
unborn ʌnˈbɔːn, ˈʌn-, ʌm-, ˌʌm- ⓤⓢ ʌnˈbɔːrn, ˌʌn- ˌ**unborn** ˈ**child**
unbosom ʌnˈbʊz.əm, ˌʌn-, ʌm-, ˌʌm- ⓤⓢ ʌn-, ˌʌn- **-s** -z **-ing** -ɪŋ **-ed** -d
unbound ʌnˈbaʊnd, ˌʌn-, ʌm-, ˌʌm- ⓤⓢ ʌn-, ˌʌn-
unbounded ʌnˈbaʊn.dɪd, ˌʌn-, ʌm-, ˌʌm- ⓤⓢ ʌn-, ˌʌn- **-ness** -nəs, -nɪs
unbowed ʌnˈbaʊd, ˌʌn-, ʌm-, ˌʌm- ⓤⓢ ʌn-, ˌʌn-
unbridled ʌnˈbraɪ.dl̩d, ˌʌn-, ʌm-, ˌʌm- ⓤⓢ ʌn-, ˌʌn-
unbroken ʌnˈbrəʊ.kən, ˌʌn-, ʌm-, ˌʌm- ⓤⓢ ʌnˈbroʊ-, ˌʌn-
unbuckl|e ʌnˈbʌk.l̩, ˌʌn-, ʌm-, ˌʌm- ⓤⓢ ʌn-, ˌʌn- **-es** -z **-ing** -ɪŋ, -ˈbʌk.lɪŋ **-ed** -d
unbuilt ʌnˈbɪlt, ʌm- ⓤⓢ ʌn-
unburden ʌnˈbɜː.dən, ˌʌn-, ʌm-, ˌʌm- ⓤⓢ ʌnˈbɜːr-, ˌʌn- **-s** -z **-ing** -ɪŋ **-ed** -d
unburied ʌnˈber.id, ˌʌn-, ʌm-, ˌʌm- ⓤⓢ ʌn-, ˌʌn-
unbusiness-like ʌnˈbɪz.nɪs.laɪk, -nəs-, ˌʌn-, ʌm-, ˌʌm- ⓤⓢ ʌn-, ˌʌn-
unbutton ʌnˈbʌt.ən, ˌʌn-, ʌm-, ˌʌm- ⓤⓢ ʌn-, ˌʌn- **-s** -z **-ing** -ɪŋ, -ˈbʌt.nɪŋ **-ed** -d
uncalculat|ed ʌnˈkæl.kjə.leɪ.t|ɪd, ʌŋ-, -kjʊ- ⓤⓢ ʌn- **-ing** -ɪŋ
uncalled-for ʌnˈkɔːld.fɔːʳ, ˌʌn-, ʌŋ-, ˌʌŋ- ⓤⓢ ʌnˈkɔːld.fɔːr, ˌʌn-, -ˈkɑːld-
uncann|y ʌnˈkæn|.i, ˌʌn-, ʌŋ-, ˌʌŋ- ⓤⓢ ʌn-, ˌʌn- **-ier** -i.əʳ ⓤⓢ -i.ɚ **-iest** -i.ɪst, -i.əst **-ily** -ɪ.li, -əl.i **-iness** -ɪ.nəs, -ɪ.nɪs
uncanonical ˌʌn.kəˈnɒn.ɪ.kəl, ˌʌŋ- ⓤⓢ ˌʌn.kəˈnɑː.nɪ-
uncap ʌnˈkæp, ˌʌn-, ʌŋ-, ˌʌŋ- ⓤⓢ ʌn-, ˌʌn- **-s** -s **-ping** -ɪŋ **-ped** -t
uncared-for ʌnˈkeəd.fɔːʳ, ˌʌn-, ʌŋ-, ˌʌŋ- ⓤⓢ ʌnˈkerd.fɔːr, ˌʌn-
uncaring ʌnˈkeə.rɪŋ, ʌŋ- ⓤⓢ ʌn- **-ly** -li **-ness** -nəs, -nɪs
Uncas ˈʌŋ.kəs
uncatalog(u)ed ʌnˈkæt.əl.ɒgd, ˌʌn-, ʌŋ-, ˌʌŋ- ⓤⓢ ʌnˈkæt̬.əl.ɑːgd, ˌʌn-, -ɔːgd
unceasing ʌnˈsiː.sɪŋ, ˌʌn- **-ly** -li **-ness** -nəs, -nɪs
uncensored ʌnˈsen*t*.səd, ˌʌn- ⓤⓢ -sɚd
unceremonious ʌnˌser.ɪˈməʊ.ni.əs, ˌʌn-, -əˈ- ⓤⓢ -ˈmoʊ- **-ly** -li **-ness** -nəs, -nɪs
uncertain ʌnˈsɜː.tən, ˌʌn- ⓤⓢ -ˈsɜːr- **-ly** -li
uncertaint|y ʌnˈsɜː.tən.t|i, ˌʌn- ⓤⓢ -ˈsɜːr.tən.t̬|i **-ies** -iz
unchain ʌnˈtʃeɪn, ˌʌn- **-s** -z **-ing** -ɪŋ **-ed** -d
unchallenged ʌnˈtʃæl.ɪndʒd, ˌʌn-, -əndʒd
unchangeability ʌnˌtʃeɪn.dʒəˈbɪl.ɪ.ti, ˌʌn-, -ə.ti ⓤⓢ -ə.t̬i
unchangeab|le ʌnˈtʃeɪn.dʒə.b|l̩, ˌʌn- **-ly** -bli **-leness** -l̩.nəs, -nɪs
unchanged ʌnˈtʃeɪndʒd, ˌʌn-
unchanging ʌnˈtʃeɪn.dʒɪŋ, ˌʌn-
uncharacteristic ˌʌn.kær.ək.təˈrɪs.tɪk, ʌnˈkær-, ˌʌŋ- ⓤⓢ ʌnˌker.ɪk.təˈrɪs.tɪk, -ˌkær- **-ally** -əl.i, -li
uncharged ʌnˈtʃɑːdʒd, ˌʌn- ⓤⓢ -ˈtʃɑːrdʒd
uncharitab|le ʌnˈtʃær.ɪ.tə.b|l̩, ˌʌn-, ˈ-ə- ⓤⓢ -ˈtʃer.ə.t̬ə-, -ˈtʃær- **-ly** -li **-leness** -l̩.nəs, -nɪs
uncharted ʌnˈtʃɑː.tɪd, ˌʌn- ⓤⓢ -ˈtʃɑːr.t̬ɪd **un**ˌ**charted** ˈ**waters**, ˌ**uncharted** ˈ**waters**
unchartered ʌnˈtʃɑː.təd, ˌʌn- ⓤⓢ -ˈtʃɑːr.t̬ɚd
unchaste ʌnˈtʃeɪst ⓤⓢ ˌʌn- **-ly** -li
unchastened ʌnˈtʃeɪ.sənd, ˌʌn-
unchecked ʌnˈtʃekt, ˌʌn-
unchivalrous ʌnˈʃɪv.əl.rəs **-ly** -li **-ness** -nəs, -nɪs
unchristian ʌnˈkrɪs.tʃən, ˌʌn-, ʌŋ-, ˌʌŋ-, -ˈkrɪʃ-, -ti.ən ⓤⓢ ʌnˈkrɪs-, ˌʌn-
uncial ˈʌn*t*.si.əl ⓤⓢ -ʃi-, ˈ-ʃəl **-s** -z
unciform ˈʌn*t*.sɪ.fɔːm ⓤⓢ -fɔːrm
uncinate ˈʌn.sɪ.nɪt, -neɪt, -nət
uncircumcised ʌnˈsɜː.kəm.saɪzd, ˌʌn- ⓤⓢ -ˈsɜːr-
uncircumcision ʌnˌsɜː.kəmˈsɪʒ.ən, ˌʌn- ⓤⓢ -ˌsɜːr-
uncivil ʌnˈsɪv.əl, -ɪl, ˌʌn- **-ly** -i
uncivilized, -ised, ʌnˈsɪv.əl.aɪzd, ˌʌn-, -ɪ.laɪzd
unclaimed ʌnˈkleɪmd, ˌʌn-, ʌŋ-, ˌʌŋ- ⓤⓢ ʌn-, ˌʌn-
unclamp ʌnˈklæmp, ʌŋ- ⓤⓢ ʌn- **-s** -s **-ing** -ɪŋ **-ed** -t
unclasp ʌnˈklɑːsp, ˌʌn-, ʌŋ-, ˌʌŋ- ⓤⓢ ʌnˈklæsp, ˌʌn- **-s** -s **-ing** -ɪŋ **-ed** -t
unclassified ʌnˈklæs.ɪ.faɪd, ˌʌn-, ʌŋ-, ˌʌŋ- ⓤⓢ ʌn-, ˌʌn-
uncle ˈʌŋ.kl̩ **-s** -z ˌ**Uncle** ˈ**Sam** ; ˌ**Uncle** ˈ**Tom**
unclean ʌnˈkliːn, ˌʌn-, ʌŋ-, ˌʌŋ- ⓤⓢ ʌn-, ˌʌn- **-ly** -li **-ness** -nəs, -nɪs
uncleanl|y ʌnˈklen.l|i, ˌʌn-, ʌŋ-, ˌʌŋ- ⓤⓢ ʌn-, ˌʌn- **-iness** -ɪ.nəs, -ɪ.nɪs
unclear ʌnˈklɪəʳ, ˌʌn-, ʌŋ-, ˌʌŋ- ⓤⓢ ʌnˈklɪr, ˌʌn-
unclench ʌnˈklen*t*ʃ, ˌʌn-, ʌŋ-, ˌʌŋ- ⓤⓢ ʌnˈklentʃ, ˌʌn- **-es** -ɪz **-ing** -ɪŋ **-ed** -t
unclog ʌnˈklɒg, ʌŋ- ⓤⓢ ʌnˈklɑːg, -ˈklɔːg **-s** -z **-ging** -ɪŋ **-ged** -d
unclos|e ʌnˈkləʊz, ˌʌn-, ʌŋ-, ˌʌŋ- ⓤⓢ ʌnˈkloʊz, ˌʌn- **-es** -ɪz **-ing** -ɪŋ **-ed** -d
unclothed ʌnˈkləʊðd, ˌʌn-, ʌŋ-, ˌʌŋ- ⓤⓢ ʌnˈkloʊðd, ˌʌn-
unclouded ʌnˈklaʊ.dɪd, ˌʌn-, ʌŋ-, ˌʌŋ- ⓤⓢ ʌn-, ˌʌn-
uncluttered ʌnˈklʌt.əd, ˌʌn-, ʌŋ-, ˌʌŋ- ⓤⓢ ʌnˈklʌt̬.ɚd, ˌʌn-
uncoil ʌnˈkɔɪl, ˌʌn-, ʌŋ-, ˌʌŋ- ⓤⓢ ʌn-, ˌʌn- **-s** -z **-ing** -ɪŋ **-ed** -d
uncollected ˌʌn.kəˈlek.tɪd, ˌʌŋ- ⓤⓢ ˌʌn-
uncolo(u)red ʌnˈkʌl.əd, ˌʌn-, ʌŋ-, ˌʌŋ- ⓤⓢ ʌnˈkʌl.ɚd, ˌʌn-
uncomfortab|le ʌnˈkʌmpf.tə.b|l̩, ˌʌn-, ʌŋ-, ˌʌŋ-, -ˈkʌm*p*.fə.tə- ⓤⓢ ʌnˈkʌm*p*.fɚ.t̬ə-, ˌʌn-, -ˈkʌmpf.tə- **-ly** -li **-leness** -l̩.nəs, -nɪs
uncommercial ˌʌn.kəˈmɜː.ʃəl, ˌʌŋ- ⓤⓢ ˌʌn.kəˈmɜːr-
uncommercialized, -ised ˌʌn.kəˈmɜː.ʃəl.aɪzd, ˌʌŋ- ⓤⓢ ˌʌn.kəˈmɜːr-
uncommitted ˌʌn.kəˈmɪt.ɪd, ˌʌŋ- ⓤⓢ ˌʌn.kəˈmɪt̬-
uncommon ʌnˈkɒm.ən, ˌʌn-, ʌŋ-, ˌʌŋ- ⓤⓢ ʌnˈkɑː.mən, ˌʌn- **-ly** -li **-ness** -nəs, -nɪs

uncommunicable ˌʌn.kəˈmjuː.nɪ.kə.bl̩, ˌʌŋ-, -nə- (US) ˌʌn-

uncommunicated ˌʌn.kəˈmjuː.nɪ.keɪ.tɪd, ˌʌŋ-, -nə- (US) ˌʌn.kəˈmjuː.nɪ.keɪ.t̬ɪd, -nə-

uncommunicative ˌʌn.kəˈmjuː.nɪ.kə.tɪv, ˌʌŋ-, -nə-, -keɪ- (US) ˌʌn.kəˈmjuː.nɪ.kə.t̬ɪv, -nə-, -keɪ- **-ness** -nəs, -nɪs

uncompetitive ˌʌn.kəmˈpet.ɪ.tɪv, ˌʌŋ-, ˈ-ə- (US) ˌʌn.kəmˈpet̬.ə.t̬ɪv **-ly** -li **-ness** -nəs, -nɪs

uncomplaining ˌʌn.kəmˈpleɪ.nɪŋ, ˌʌŋ- (US) ˌʌn- **-ly** -li

uncompleted ˌʌn.kəmˈpliː.tɪd, ˌʌŋ- (US) ˌʌn.kəmˈpliː.t̬ɪd

uncomplicated ˌʌnˈkɒm.plɪ.keɪ.tɪd, ˌʌŋ- (US) ʌnˈkɑːm.plɪ.keɪ.t̬ɪd

uncomplimentary ʌnˌkɒm.plɪˈmen.tᵊr.i, ˌʌn-, ʌŋ-, ˌʌŋ-, -pləˈ- (US) ʌnˌkɑːm.pləˈmen.t̬ɚ-, ˌʌn-

uncompounded ˌʌn.kəmˈpaʊn.dɪd, ˌʌŋ- (US) ˌʌn-

uncomprehending ˌʌn.kɒm.prɪˈhen.dɪŋ, ˌʌŋ- (US) ˌʌn.kɑːm- **-ly** -li

uncompromising ʌnˈkɒm.prə.maɪ.zɪŋ, ˌʌn-, ʌŋ-, ˌʌŋ- (US) ʌnˈkɑːm-, ˌʌn- **-ly** -li **-ness** -nəs, -nɪs

unconcealed ˌʌn.kənˈsiːld, ˌʌŋ- (US) ˌʌn-

unconcern ˌʌn.kənˈsɜːn, ˌʌŋ- (US) ˌʌn.kənˈsɝːrn **-ed** -d **-edly** -d.li, -ɪd.li **-edness** -d.nəs, -nɪs, -ɪd.nəs, -nɪs

unconditional ˌʌn.kənˈdɪʃ.ᵊn.ᵊl, ˌʌŋ-, ˈ-nᵊl (US) ˌʌn- **-ly** -i ˌ**unconditional ˈoffer**

unconditioned ˌʌn.kənˈdɪʃ.ᵊnd, ˌʌŋ- (US) ˌʌn-

unconfined ˌʌn.kənˈfaɪnd, ˌʌŋ- (US) ˌʌn-

unconfirmed ˌʌn.kənˈfɜːmd, ˌʌŋ- (US) ˌʌn.kənˈfɝːrmd

unconformit|y ˌʌn.kənˈfɔː.mə.t|i, ˌʌŋ-, -mɪ.t|i (US) ˌʌn.kənˈfɔːr.mə.t̬|i **-ies** -iz

uncongenial ˌʌn.kənˈdʒiː.ni.əl, ˌʌŋ- (US) ˌʌn-, -jəl

uncongeniality ˌʌn.kənˌdʒiː.niˈæl.ɪ.ti, ˌʌŋ-, -ə.ti (US) ˌʌn.kənˌdʒiː.niˈæl.ə.t̬i

unconnected ˌʌn.kəˈnek.tɪd, ˌʌŋ- (US) ˌʌn- **-ness** -nəs, -nɪs

unconquerab|le ʌnˈkɒŋ.kᵊr.ə.b|l̩, ˌʌn-, ʌŋ-, ˌʌŋ- (US) ʌnˈkɑːŋ-, ˌʌn- **-ly** -li

unconquered ʌnˈkɒŋ.kəd, ˌʌn-, ʌŋ-, ˌʌŋ- (US) ʌnˈkɑːŋ.kɚd, ˌʌn-

unconscionab|le ʌnˈkɒn.*t*ʃᵊn.ə.b|l̩, ˌʌn-, ʌŋ-, ˌʌŋ- (US) ʌnˈkɑːn-, ˌʌn- **-ly** -li **-leness** -l̩.nəs, -nɪs

unconscious ʌnˈkɒn.*t*ʃəs, ˌʌn-, ʌŋ-, ˌʌŋ- (US) ʌnˈkɑːn-, ˌʌn- **-ly** -li **-ness** -nəs, -nɪs

unconsecrated ʌnˈkɒn*t*.sɪ.kreɪ.tɪd, ˌʌn-, ʌŋ-, ˌʌŋ-, -sə- (US) ʌnˈkɑːn*t*.sə-, ˌʌn-

unconsidered ˌʌn.kənˈsɪd.əd, ˌʌŋ- (US) ˌʌn.kənˈsɪd.ɚd

unconstitutional ʌnˌkɒn*t*.stɪˈtjuː.ʃᵊn.ᵊl, ˌʌn-, ʌŋ-, ˌʌŋ-, -stəˈ-, -ˈtʃuː-, -ˈtjuːʃ.nᵊl, -ˈtʃuːʃ- (US) ʌnˌkɑːn*t*.stəˈtuː-, ˌʌn-, -ˈtjuː- **-ly** -i

unconstrain|ed ˌʌn.kənˈstreɪn|d, ˌʌŋ- (US) ˌʌn- **-edly** -d.li, -ɪd.li

uncontaminated ˌʌn.kənˈtæm.ɪ.neɪ.tɪd, ˌʌŋ-, ˈ-ə- (US) ˌʌn.kənˈtæm.ɪ.neɪ.t̬ɪd, ˈ-ə-

uncontestable ˌʌn.kənˈtes.tə.bl̩, ˌʌŋ- (US) ˌʌn-

uncontested ˌʌn.kənˈtes.tɪd, ˌʌŋ- (US) ˌʌn-

uncontradicted ʌnˌkɒn.trəˈdɪk.tɪd, ˌʌn-, ʌŋ-, ˌʌŋ- (US) ʌnˌkɑːn-, ˌʌn-

uncontrollab|le ˌʌn.kənˈtrəʊ.lə.b|l̩, ˌʌŋ- (US) ˌʌn.kənˈtroʊ- **-ly** -li **-leness** -l̩.nəs, -nɪs

uncontrolled ˌʌn.kənˈtrəʊld, ˌʌŋ- (US) ˌʌn.kənˈtroʊld

unconvention|al ˌʌn.kənˈven.*t*ʃᵊn|.ᵊl, ˌʌŋ-, -ˈven*t*ʃ.n|ᵊl (US) ˌʌn.kənˈven*t*.ʃᵊn|.ᵊl, -ˈven*t*ʃ.n|ᵊl **-ally** -ᵊl.i

unconventionalit|y ˌʌn.kənˌven.*t*ʃᵊnˈæl.ə.t|i, ˌʌŋ-, -ɪ.t|i (US) ˌʌn.kənˌven.*t*ʃᵊnˈæl.ə.t̬|i **-ies** -iz

unconverted ˌʌn.kənˈvɜː.tɪd, ˌʌŋ- (US) ˌʌn.kənˈvɝːr.t̬ɪd

unconvertible ˌʌn.kənˈvɜː.tə.bl̩, ˌʌŋ-, -tɪ- (US) ˌʌn.kənˈvɝːr.t̬ə-

unconvinced ˌʌn.kənˈvɪn*t*st, ˌʌŋ- (US) ˌʌn-

unconvincing ˌʌn.kənˈvɪn*t*.sɪŋ, ˌʌŋ- (US) ˌʌn- **-ly** -li

uncooked ʌnˈkʊkt, ˌʌn-, ʌŋ-, ˌʌŋ- (US) ʌn-, ˌʌn-

uncool ʌnˈkuːl, ˌʌn-, ʌŋ- (US) ʌn-, ˌʌn- **-ly** -li **-ness** -nəs, -nɪs

uncooperative ˌʌn.kəʊˈɒp.ᵊr.ə.tɪv, ˌʌŋ-, ˈ-rə- (US) ˌʌn.koʊˈɑː.pɚ.ə.t̬ɪv, ˈ-prə- **-ly** -li **-ness** -nəs, -nɪs

uncoordinated ˌʌn.kəʊˈɔː.dɪ.neɪ.tɪd, ˌʌŋ- (US) ˌʌn.koʊˈɔːr.dᵊn.eɪ.t̬ɪd

uncork ʌnˈkɔːk, ˌʌn-, ʌŋ-, ˌʌŋ- (US) ʌnˈkɔːrk, ˌʌn- **-s** -s **-ing** -ɪŋ **-ed** -t

uncorrected ˌʌn.kᵊrˈek.tɪd, ˌʌŋ- (US) ˌʌn.kəˈrek-

uncorroborated ˌʌn.kᵊrˈɒb.ᵊr.eɪ.tɪd, ˌʌŋ- (US) ˌʌn.kəˈrɑː.bə.reɪ.t̬ɪd

uncorrupt ˌʌn.kᵊrˈʌpt, ˌʌŋ- (US) ˌʌn.kəˈrʌpt **-ness** -nəs, -nəs, -nɪs

uncorrupted ˌʌn.kᵊrˈʌp.tɪd, ˌʌŋ- (US) ˌʌn.kəˈrʌp-

uncountable ʌnˈkaʊn.tə.bl̩, ˌʌn-, ʌŋ-, ˌʌŋ- (US) ʌnˈkaʊn.t̬ə-, ˌʌn- unˌ**countable ˈnoun**

uncounted ʌnˈkaʊn.tɪd, ˌʌn-, ʌŋ-, ˌʌŋ- (US) ʌnˈkaʊn.t̬ɪd, ˌʌn-

uncoupl|e ʌnˈkʌp.l̩, ˌʌn-, ʌŋ-, ˌʌŋ- (US) ʌn-, ˌʌn- **-es** -z **-ing** -ɪŋ, -ˈkʌp.lɪŋ **-ed** -d

uncouth ʌnˈkuːθ, ˌʌn-, ʌŋ-, ˌʌŋ- (US) ʌn-, ˌʌn- **-ly** -li **-ness** -nəs, -nɪs

uncov|er ʌnˈkʌv|.əʳ, ˌʌn-, ʌŋ-, ˌʌŋ- (US) ʌnˈkʌv|.ɚ, ˌʌn- **-ers** -əz (US) -ɚz **-ering** -ᵊr.ɪŋ **-ered** -əd (US) -ɚd

uncritic|al ʌnˈkrɪt.ɪ.k|ᵊl, ˌʌn-, ʌŋ-, ˌʌŋ- (US) ʌnˈkrɪt̬.ɪ-, ˌʌn- **-ally** -ᵊl.i, -li

uncrossed ʌnˈkrɒst, ˌʌn-, ʌŋ-, ˌʌŋ- (US) ʌnˈkrɑːst, ˌʌn-

uncrowned ʌnˈkraʊnd, ˌʌn-, ʌŋ-, ˌʌŋ- (US) ʌn-, ˌʌn- *stress shift, see compounds:* ˌ**uncrowned ˈking** ; ˌ**uncrowned ˈqueen**

uncrushable ʌnˈkrʌʃ.ə.bl̩, ˌʌn-, ʌŋ-, ˌʌŋ- (US) ʌn-, ˌʌn-

unction ˈʌŋk.ʃᵊn **-s** -z

unctuosity ˌʌŋk.tjuˈɒs.ə.ti, -tʃuˈ-, -ɪ.ti (US) -tʃuˈɑː.sə.t̬i

unctuous ˈʌŋk.tju.əs, -tʃu- (US) -tʃu-, ˈ-tʃəs **-ly** -li **-ness** -nəs, -nɪs

uncultivated ʌnˈkʌl.tɪ.veɪ.tɪd, ˌʌn-, ʌŋ-, ˌʌŋ-, -tə- (US) ʌnˈkʌl.t̬ə.veɪ.t̬ɪd, ˌʌn-

uncultured ʌnˈkʌl.tʃəd, ˌʌn-, ʌŋ-, ˌʌŋ- (US) ʌnˈkʌl.tʃɚd, ˌʌn-

uncurbed ʌnˈkɜːbd, ˌʌn-, ʌŋ-, ˌʌŋ- (US) ʌnˈkɝːrbd, ˌʌn-

uncurl ʌnˈkɜːl, ˌʌn-, ʌŋ-, ˌʌŋ- (US) ʌnˈkɝːrl, ˌʌn- **-s** -z **-ing** -ɪŋ **-ed** -d

uncut ʌnˈkʌt, ˌʌn-, ʌŋ-, ˌʌŋ- (US) ʌn-, ˌʌn-

undamaged ʌnˈdæm.ɪdʒd, ˌʌn-

undated *wavy:* ˈʌn.deɪ.tɪd (US) -t̬ɪd

undated *not dated:* ʌnˈdeɪ.tɪd, ˌʌn- (US) -t̬ɪd

undaunted ʌnˈdɔːn.tɪd, ˌʌn- (US) -ˈdɑːn.t̬ɪd, -ˈdɔːn- **-ly** -li **-ness** -nəs, -nɪs

undebated ˌʌn.dɪˈbeɪ.tɪd, -dəˈ- (US) -t̬ɪd

undeceiv|e ˌʌn.dɪˈsiːv, -dəˈ- **-es** -z **-ing** -ɪŋ **-ed** -d

undecided ˌʌn.dɪˈsaɪ.dɪd, -dəˈ- **-ly** -li **-ness** -nəs, -nɪs

undecipherab|le ˌʌn.dɪˈsaɪ.fᵊr.ə.b|l̩, -dəˈ- **-ly** -li

undecisive ˌʌn.dɪˈsaɪ.sɪv, -dəˈ-, -zɪv (US) -sɪv **-ly** -li **-ness** -nəs, -nɪs

undeclared ˌʌn.dɪˈkleəd, -dəˈ- (US) -ˈklerd

undefended ˌʌn.dɪˈfen.dɪd, -dəˈ-

undefiled ˌʌn.dɪˈfaɪld, -dəˈ-

undefinab|le ˌʌn.dɪˈfaɪ.nə.bl̩, -dəˈ- **-ly** -li
undefined ˌʌn.dɪˈfaɪnd, -dəˈ-
undelivered ˌʌn.dɪˈlɪv.əd, -dəˈ- (US) -ɚd
undemocratic ʌn.dem.əˈkræt.ɪk, ˌʌn- **-ally** -əl.i, -li
undemonstrative ˌʌn.dɪˈmɒnt.strə.tɪv, -dəˈ- (US) -ˈmɑːnt.strə.t̬ɪv **-ly** -li **-ness** -nəs, -nɪs
undeniab|le ˌʌn.dɪˈnaɪ.ə.bl̩, -dəˈ- **-ly** -li
undenominational ˌʌn.dɪˌnɒm.ɪˈneɪ.ʃən.əl, -dəˌ-, -əˈ-, -ˈneɪʃ.nəl (US) -ˌnɑː.mɪˈ-, -məˈ- **-ism** -ɪ.zəm
under- ʌn.dər- (US) ʌn.dɚ-
Note: Prefix. May receive primary stress, e.g. **undercarriage** /ˈʌn.dəˌkær.ɪdʒ (US) ˈʌn.dɚ-/, or secondary stress, e.g. **understand** /ˌʌn.dəˈstænd (US) -dɚˈ-/. Such secondary-stressed syllables may come to carry the strongest stress in the word through stress-shift, e.g. **understand** /ˌʌn.dəˈstænd (US) ˌʌn.dɚ-/, **understand problems** /ˌʌn.də.stændˈprɒb.ləmz (US) ˌʌn.dɚ.stændˈprɑː.bləmz/. Although /r/ is normally assigned to a following strong syllable in American English, when /ɚ/ is perceived to be morphemically linked to the preceding unit /r/ is retained as /ɚ/.
under ˈʌn.dər (US) -dɚ **-s** -z ˌ**under** ˈ**way**
underachiev|e ˌʌn.dər.əˈtʃiːv (US) -dɚ- **-es** -z **-ing** -ɪŋ **-ed** -d **-er/s** -ər/z (US) -ɚ/z **-ment/s** -mənt/s
underact ˌʌn.dərˈækt (US) -dɚˈ- **-s** -s **-ing** -ɪŋ **-ed** -ɪd
under-age ˌʌn.dərˈeɪdʒ (US) -dɚˈ- *stress shift:* ˌunder-age ˈdrinking
underarm ˈʌn.dər.ɑːm (US) -dɚ.ɑːrm
underbell|y ˈʌn.dəˌbel|.i (US) -dɚˌ- **-ies** -iz
underbid ˌʌn.dəˈbɪd (US) -dɚˈ- **-s** -z **-ding** -ɪŋ **-der/s** -ər/z (US) -ɚ/z
underbred ˌʌn.dəˈbred (US) -dɚˈ- *stress shift:* ˌunderbred ˈstock
underbrush ˈʌn.də.brʌʃ (US) -dɚ-
underbudgeted ˌʌn.dəˈbʌdʒ.ɪ.tɪd, ˈ-ə- (US) -dɚˈbʌdʒ.ɪ.t̬ɪd
under|buy ˌʌn.də|ˈbaɪ (US) -dɚˈ- **-buys** -ˈbaɪz **-buying** -ˈbaɪ.ɪŋ **-bought** -ˈbɔːt (US) -ˈbɑːt, -ˈbɔːt
undercapitaliz|e, -is|e ˌʌn.dəˈkæp.ɪ.təl.aɪz (US) -dɚˈ- **-es** -ɪz **-ing** -ɪŋ **-ed** -d
undercarriag|e ˈʌn.dəˌkær.ɪdʒ (US) -dɚˌker-, -ˌkær- **-es** -ɪz
undercharg|e (*n.*) ˈʌn.dəˌtʃɑːdʒ, ˌ--ˈ- (US) ˈʌn.dɚ.tʃɑːrdʒ **-es** -ɪz
undercharg|e (*v.*) ˌʌn.dəˈtʃɑːdʒ (US) -dɚˈtʃɑːrdʒ **-es** -ɪz **-ing** -ɪŋ **-ed** -d
underclass ˈʌn.də.klɑːs (US) -dɚ.klæs **-es** -ɪz
under-clerk ˈʌn.də.klɑːk (US) -dɚ.klɜːrk **-s** -s
underclothes ˈʌn.də.kləʊðz (US) -dɚ.kloʊðz, -kloʊz
underclothing ˈʌn.dəˌkləʊ.ðɪŋ (US) -dɚˌkloʊ-
undercoat ˈʌn.də.kəʊt (US) -dɚ.koʊt **-s** -s **-ing** -ɪŋ
undercook ˌʌn.dəˈkʊk (US) -dɚˈ- **-s** -s **-ing** -ɪŋ **-ed** -t
undercover ˌʌn.dəˈkʌv.ər (US) -dɚˈkʌv.ɚ *stress shift:* ˌundercover ˈagent
undercroft ˈʌn.də.krɒft (US) -dɚ.krɑːft **-s** -s
undercurrent ˈʌn.dəˌkʌr.ənt (US) -dɚˌkɜːr- **-s** -s
undercut (*n.*) ˈʌn.də.kʌt (US) -dɚ- **-s** -s
under|cut (*adj. v.*) ˌʌn.də|ˈkʌt (US) -dɚˈ- **-cuts** -ˈkʌts **-cutting** -ˈkʌt.ɪŋ (US) -ˈkʌt̬.ɪŋ
underdevelop|ed ˌʌn.də.dɪˈvel.əp|t, -dəˈ- (US) -dɚ- **-ment** -mənt *stress shift:* ˌunderdeveloped ˈbrain
under|do ˌʌn.də|ˈduː (US) -dɚˈ- **-does** -ˈdʌz **-doing** -ˈduː.ɪŋ **-did** -ˈdɪd **-done** -ˈdʌn
underdog ˈʌn.də.dɒg (US) -dɚ.dɑːg, -dɔːg **-s** -z
underdone ˌʌn.dəˈdʌn (US) -dɚˈ- *stress shift:* ˌunderdone ˈbeef
underdress ˌʌn.dəˈdres (US) -dɚˈ- **-es** -ɪz **-ing** -ɪŋ **-ed** -t
undereducated ˌʌn.dərˈedʒ.ʊ.keɪ.tɪd, -ˈed.jʊ- (US) -dɚˈedʒ.ʊ.keɪ.t̬ɪd, ˈ-ə-
undereducation ˌʌn.dər.edʒ.ʊˈkeɪ.ʃən, -ed.jʊ- (US) -dɚ.edʒ.ʊ-, -əˈ-
underemployed ˌʌn.dər.ɪmˈplɔɪd, -emˈ- (US) -dɚ- *stress shift:* ˌunderemployed ˈworkforce
underemployment ˌʌn.dər.ɪmˈplɔɪ.mənt (US) -dɚ-
underestimate (*n.*) ˌʌn.dərˈes.tɪ.mət, -tə-, -mɪt, -meɪt (US) -dɚˈes.tə.mɪt, -mət **-s** -s
underesti|mate (*v.*) ˌʌn.dərˈes.tɪ|.meɪt, -tə- (US) -dɚˈes.tə- **-mates** -meɪts **-mating** -meɪ.tɪŋ (US) -meɪ.t̬ɪŋ **-mated** -meɪ.tɪd (US) -meɪ.t̬ɪd
underestimation ˌʌn.dərˌes.tɪˈmeɪ.ʃən, -təˈ- (US) -dɚˌes.təˈ- **-s** -z
under-expos|e ˌʌn.dər.ɪkˈspəʊz, -ekˈ- (US) -dɚ.ɪkˈspoʊz, -ekˈ- **-es** -ɪz **-ing** -ɪŋ **-ed** -d
underexposure ˌʌn.dər.ɪkˈspəʊ.ʒər, -ekˈ- (US) -dɚ.ɪkˈspoʊ.ʒɚ, -ekˈ- **-s** -z
under-eye ˈʌn.dər.aɪ
under|feed ˌʌn.də|ˈfiːd (US) -dɚˈ- **-feeds** -ˈfiːdz **-feeding** -ˈfiː.dɪŋ **-fed** -ˈfed *stress shift:* ˌunderfed ˈchickens
underfelt ˈʌn.də.felt (US) -dɚ- **-s** -s
underfinanced ˌʌn.dəˈfaɪ.næntst (US) -dɚˈ-
underfloor ˌʌn.dəˈflɔːr (US) -dɚˈflɔːr *stress shift:* ˌunderfloor ˈheating
underfoot ˌʌn.dəˈfʊt (US) -dɚˈ-
underfund ˌʌn.dəˈfʌnd (US) -dɚˈ- **-s** -z **-ing** -ɪŋ **-ed** -ɪd
undergarment ˈʌn.dəˌgɑː.mənt (US) -dɚˌgɑːr- **-s** -s
under|go ˌʌn.də|ˈgəʊ (US) -dɚ|ˈgoʊ **-goes** -ˈgəʊz (US) -ˈgoʊz **-going** -ˈgəʊ.ɪŋ (US) -ˈgoʊ.ɪŋ **-went** -ˈwent **-gone** -ˈgɒn (US) -ˈgɑːn *stress shift:* ˌundergo ˈtreatment
undergrad ˈʌn.də.græd (US) -dɚ- **-s** -z
undergraduate ˌʌn.dəˈgrædʒ.u.ət, -ˈgræd.ju-, -ɪt (US) -dɚˈgrædʒ.u.ət, -ə.wət **-s** -s *stress shift:* ˌundergraduate ˈhumour
underground (U) (*n. adj.*) ˈʌn.də.graʊnd (US) -dɚ- **-er/s** -ər/z (US) -ɚ/z
underground (*adv.*) ˌʌn.dəˈgraʊnd (US) -dɚˈ-
undergrown ˌʌn.dəˈgrəʊn (US) -dɚˈgroʊn *stress shift:* ˌundergrown ˈtrees
undergrowth ˈʌn.də.grəʊθ (US) -dɚ.groʊθ
underhand ˌʌn.dəˈhænd (US) -dɚˈ- **-ed/ly** -ɪd/li **-edness** -ɪd.nəs, -nɪs *stress shift:* ˌunderhand ˈtrick
Underhill ˈʌn.də.hɪl (US) -dɚ-
underhung ˌʌn.dəˈhʌŋ (US) -dɚˈ- *stress shift:* ˌunderhung ˈaxle
underinsured ˌʌn.dər.ɪnˈʃʊəd, -ˈʃɔːd (US) -dɚ.ɪnˈʃʊrd
underlay (*n.*) ˈʌn.dəl.eɪ (US) -dɚ.leɪ **-s** -z
under|lay (*v.*) ˌʌn.də|ˈleɪ (US) -dɚˈ- **-lays** -ˈleɪz **-laying** -ˈleɪ.ɪŋ **-laid** -ˈleɪd
under|let ˌʌn.də|ˈlet (US) -dɚˈ- **-lets** -ˈlets **-letting** -ˈlet.ɪŋ (US) -ˈlet̬.ɪŋ
under|lie ˌʌn.də|ˈlaɪ (US) -dɚˈ- **-lies** -ˈlaɪz **-lying** -ˈlaɪ.ɪŋ **-lay** -ˈleɪ **-lain** -ˈleɪn
underline (*n.*) ˈʌn.dəl.aɪn (US) ˈʌn.dɚ.laɪn **-s** -z
underlin|e (*v.*) ˌʌn.dəˈlaɪn (US) -dɚˈ-, ˈ--- **-es** -z **-ing** -ɪŋ **-ed** -d
underling ˈʌn.dəl.ɪŋ (US) -dɚ.lɪŋ **-s** -z
underlip ˈʌn.dəl.ɪp (US) -dɚ.lɪp **-s** -s
underlying ˌʌn.dəˈlaɪ.ɪŋ (US) -dɚˈ- ˈʌn.dɚˌlaɪ.ɪŋ *stress shift, British only:* ˌunderlying ˈcause
underman ˌʌn.dəˈmæn (US) -dɚˈ- **-s** -z **-ning** -ɪŋ **-ned** -d *stress shift:* ˌundermanned ˈindustry
undermentioned ˌʌn.dəˈmen.tʃənd (US) -dɚˈ- *stress shift:* ˌundermentioned ˈclause

undermin|e ˌʌn.dəˈmaɪn (US) -dɚˈ-, ˈ--- **-es** -z **-ing** -ɪŋ **-ed** -d **-er/s** -ər/z (US) -ɚ/z *stress shift, British only:* ˌundermine ˈconfidence
undermost ˈʌn.də.məʊst (US) -dɚ.moʊst
underneath ˌʌn.dəˈniːθ (US) -dɚˈ- *stress shift:* ˌunderneath ˈeverything
undernourish ˌʌn.dəˈnʌr.ɪʃ (US) -dɚˈnɜːr- **-es** -ɪz **-ing** -ɪŋ **-ed** -t **-ment** -mənt
underpants ˈʌn.də.pænts (US) -dɚ-
underpass ˈʌn.də.pɑːs (US) -dɚ.pæs **-es** -ɪz
under|pay ˌʌn.dəˈpeɪ (US) -dɚˈ- **-pays** -ˈpeɪz **-paying** -ˈpeɪ.ɪŋ **-paid** -ˈpeɪd *stress shift:* ˌunderpaid ˈstaff
underpayment ˌʌn.dəˈpeɪ.mənt (US) -dɚˈ- **-s** -s
underpin ˌʌn.dəˈpɪn (US) -dɚˈ-, ˈ--- **-s** -z **-ning** -ɪŋ **-ned** -d
underpinning ˈʌn.dəˌpɪn.ɪŋ (US) -dɚˌ- **-s** -z
underplay ˌʌn.dəˈpleɪ (US) -dɚˈ-, ˈ--- **-s** -z **-ing** -ɪŋ **-ed** -d
underpopulated ˌʌn.dəˈpɒp.jə.leɪ.tɪd, -pjʊ- (US) -dɚˈpɑː.pjə-, -pjʊ-
underpri|ce ˌʌn.dəˈpraɪ|s (US) -dɚˈ- **-ces** -sɪz **-ced** -st **-cing** -sɪŋ
underprivileged ˌʌn.dəˈprɪv.əl.ɪdʒd, -vɪ.lɪdʒd (US) -dɚˈprɪv.əl.ɪdʒd, ˈ-lɪdʒd
underproduc|e ˌʌn.də.prəˈdjuːs, -ˈdʒuːs (US) -dɚ.prəˈduːs, -ˈdjuːs **-es** -ɪz **-ing** -ɪŋ **-ed** -t
underproduction ˌʌn.də.prəˈdʌk.ʃən (US) -dɚ-
underprop ˌʌn.dəˈprɒp (US) -dɚˈprɑːp **-s** -s **-ping** -ɪŋ **-ped** -t
under|rate ˌʌn.dəˈreɪt (US) -dɚˈ- **-rates** -ˈreɪts **-rating** -ˈreɪ.tɪŋ (US) -ˈreɪ.t̬ɪŋ **-rated** -ˈreɪ.tɪd (US) -ˈreɪ.t̬ɪd
underrepresentation ˌʌn.dəˌrep.rɪ.zenˈteɪ.ʃən (US) -dɚˌrep- **-s** -z
underrepresented ˌʌn.dəˌrep.rɪˈzen.tɪd, -rəˈ- (US) -dɚˌrep.rɪˈzen.t̬ɪd
underripe ˌʌn.dəˈraɪp (US) -dɚˈ- *stress shift:* ˌunderripe ˈfruit
under|run ˌʌn.dəˈrʌn (US) -dɚˈ- **-runs** -ˈrʌnz **-running** -ˈrʌn.ɪŋ **-ran** -ˈræn
underscor|e (*v.*) ˌʌn.dəˈskɔːr (US) -dɚˈskɔːr, ˈ--- **-es** -z **-ing** -ɪŋ **-ed** -d
underscore (*n.*) ˈʌn.də.skɔːr (US) -dɚ.skɔːr **-s** -z
undersea ˌʌn.dəˈsiː (US) -dɚˈ- **-s** -z *stress shift:* ˌundersea ˈcable
underseal ˈʌn.də.siːl (US) -dɚ- **-s** -z **-ing** -ɪŋ **-ed** -d
undersecretar|y ˌʌn.dəˈsek.rə.tər|.i, -rɪ-, -tr|i (US) -dɚˈsek.rə.ter- **-ies** -iz **-yship/s** -i.ʃɪp/s
under|sell ˌʌn.dəˈsel (US) -dɚˈ- **-sells** -ˈselz **-selling** -ˈsel.ɪŋ **-sold** -ˈsəʊld (US) -ˈsoʊld
undersexed ˌʌn.dəˈsekst (US) -dɚˈ-
Undershaft ˈʌn.də.ʃɑːft (US) -dɚ.ʃæft
undersheriff ˈʌn.dəˌʃer.ɪf (US) -dɚˌ- **-s** -s
undershirt ˈʌn.də.ʃɜːt (US) -dɚ.ʃɜːrt **-s** -s
under|shoot (*v.*) ˌʌn.dəˈʃuːt (US) -dɚˈ- **-shoots** -ˈʃuːts **-shooting** -ˈʃuː.tɪŋ (US) -ˈʃuː.t̬ɪŋ **-shot** -ˈʃɒt (US) -ˈʃɑːt
undershoot (*n.*) ˈʌn.də.ʃuːt, ˌ--ˈ- (US) ˈʌn.dɚ.ʃuːt, ˌ--ˈ- **-s** -s
undershorts ˈʌn.də.ʃɔːts (US) -dɚˈʃɔːrts
undershot (*adj.*) ˌʌn.dəˈʃɒt (US) -ˈʃɑːt *stress shift:* ˌundershot ˈwheel
undershot (*from* **undershoot**) ˌʌn.dəˈʃɒt (US) -dɚˈʃɑːt
underside ˈʌn.də.saɪd (US) -dɚ- **-s** -z
undersigned ˈʌn.də.saɪnd, ˌ--ˈ- (US) ˈʌn.dɚ.saɪnd
undersized ˌʌn.dəˈsaɪzd (US) ˈʌn.dɚ.saɪzd *stress shift, British only:* ˌundersized ˈbelt
underskirt ˈʌn.də.skɜːt (US) -dɚ.skɜːrt **-s** -s
underspend ˌʌn.dəˈspend (US) -dɚˈ- **-s** -z **-ing** -ɪŋ **underspent** ˌʌn.dəˈspent (US) -dɚˈ-
understaffed ˌʌn.dəˈstɑːft (US) -dɚˈstæft *stress shift:* ˌunderstaffed ˈschool
under|stand ˌʌn.dəˈstænd (US) -dɚˈ- **-stands** -ˈstændz **-standing** -ˈstæn.dɪŋ **-stood** -ˈstʊd
understandab|le ˌʌn.dəˈstæn.də.b|l̩ (US) -dɚˈ- **-ly** -li
under|state ˌʌn.dəˈsteɪt (US) -dɚˈ- **-states** -ˈsteɪts **-stating** -ˈsteɪ.tɪŋ (US) -ˈsteɪ.t̬ɪŋ **-stated** -ˈsteɪ.tɪd (US) -ˈsteɪ.t̬ɪd
understatement ˌʌn.dəˈsteɪt.mənt, ˈʌn.dəˌsteɪt- (US) ˌʌn.dɚˈsteɪt-, ˈʌn.dɚˌsteɪt- **-s** -s
understocked ˌʌn.dəˈstɒkt (US) -dɚˈstɑːkt *stress shift:* ˌunderstocked ˈshelves
understood (*from* **understand**) ˌʌn.dəˈstʊd (US) -dɚˈ- *stress shift:* ˌunderstood ˈplan
understrapper ˈʌn.dəˌstræp.ər (US) -dɚˌstræp.ɚ **-s** -z
understud|y ˈʌn.dəˌstʌd|.i (US) -dɚˌ- **-ies** -iz **-ying** -i.ɪŋ **-ied** -id
undersubscrib|e ˌʌn.də.səbˈskraɪb (US) -dɚ- **-es** -z **-ing** -ɪŋ **-ed** -d
under|take *agree or promise to do something:* ˌʌn.dəˈteɪk (US) -dɚˈ- **-takes** -ˈteɪks **-taking** -ˈteɪ.kɪŋ **-took** -ˈtʊk **-taken** -ˈteɪ.kən, -kəŋ (US) -kən
undertaker *person who agrees to do something:* ˌʌn.dəˈteɪ.kər (US) -dɚˈteɪ.kɚ **-s** -z *person who arranges funerals:* ˈʌn.dəˌteɪ.kər (US) -dɚˌteɪ.kɚ **-s** -z
undertaking *enterprise, promise:* ˌʌn.dəˈteɪ.kɪŋ, ˈʌn.dəˌteɪ- (US) ˌʌn.dɚˈteɪ-, ˈʌn.dɚˌteɪ- **-s** -z *arranging funerals:* ˈʌn.dəˌteɪ.kɪŋ (US) -dɚˌ-
under-the-counter ˌʌn.də.ðəˈkaʊn.tər (US) -dɚ.ðəˈkaʊn.t̬ɚ *stress shift:* ˌunder-the-counter ˈdeal
underthings ˈʌn.də.θɪŋz (US) -dɚ-
undertint ˈʌn.də.tɪnt (US) -dɚ- **-s** -s
undertone ˈʌn.də.təʊn (US) -dɚ.toʊn **-s** -z
undertook (*from* **undertake**) ˌʌn.dəˈtʊk (US) -dɚˈ-
undertow ˈʌn.də.təʊ (US) -dɚ.toʊ **-s** -z
underused ˌʌn.dəˈjuːzd (US) -dɚˈ- *stress shift:* ˌunderused ˈpath
underutiliz|e, -is|e ˌʌn.dəˈjuː.tɪ.laɪz, -təl.aɪz (US) -dɚˈjuː.t̬əl.aɪz **-es** -ɪz **-ing** -ɪŋ **-ed** -d
undervaluation ˌʌn.dəˌvæl.juˈeɪ.ʃən (US) -dɚˌ- **-s** -z
underval|ue ˌʌn.dəˈvæl|.juː (US) -dɚˈ- **-ues** -juːz **-uing** -juː.ɪŋ **-ued** -juːd *stress shift:* ˌundervalued ˈshares
underwater ˌʌn.dəˈwɔː.tər (US) -dɚˈwɑː.t̬ɚ, -ˈwɔː- *stress shift:* ˌunderwater ˈcamera
underwear ˈʌn.də.weər (US) -dɚ.wer
underweight ˌʌn.dəˈweɪt (US) -dɚˈ-, ˈ--- *stress shift:* ˌunderweight ˈbaggage
underwent (*from* **undergo**) ˌʌn.dəˈwent (US) -dɚˈ- *stress shift:* ˌunderwent ˈsurgery
underwhelm ˌʌn.dəˈ*h*welm (US) -dɚˈ- **-s** -z **-ing** -ɪŋ **-ed** -d
underwing ˈʌn.də.wɪŋ (US) -dɚ- **-s** -z
underwired ˌʌn.dəˈwaɪəd (US) -dɚˈwaɪɚd, ˈ--- *stress shift:* ˌunderwired ˈbra
underwood (U) ˈʌn.də.wʊd (US) -dɚ- **-s** -z
underworld (U) ˈʌn.də.wɜːld (US) -dɚ.wɜːrld
underwri|te ˌʌn.dərˈaɪ|t, ˈ--- (US) ˈʌn.dɚ.raɪ|t **-tes** -ts **-ting** -tɪŋ (US) -t̬ɪŋ **underwrote** ˌʌn.dərˈəʊt, ˈ--- (US) ˈʌn.dɚ.roʊt **underwritten** ˌʌn.dərˈɪt.ən, ˈʌn.dərˌɪt- (US) ˈʌn.dɚˌrɪt.ən
underwriter ˈʌn.dərˌaɪ.tər (US) -dɚˌraɪ.t̬ɚ **-s** -z
undescended ˌʌn.dɪˈsen.dɪd
undescribab|le ˌʌn.dɪˈskraɪ.bə.b|l̩, -dəˈ- **-ly** -li

undeserv|ed ˌʌn.dɪˈzɜːv|d, -dəˈ- ⓤⓢ -ˈzɜːrv|d **-edly** -ɪd.li **-edness** -ɪd.nəs, -nɪs
undeserving ˌʌn.dɪˈzɜː.vɪŋ, -dəˈ- ⓤⓢ -ˈzɜːr- **-ly** -li
undesigning ˌʌn.dɪˈzaɪ.nɪŋ
undesirability ˌʌn.dɪˌzaɪə.rəˈbɪl.ə.ti, -dəˌ-, -ɪ.ti ⓤⓢ -ˌzaɪ.rəˈbɪl.ə.t̬i
undesirab|le ˌʌn.dɪˈzaɪə.rə.b|l̩, -dəˈ- ⓤⓢ -ˈzaɪ- **-ly** -li **-leness** -l̩.nəs, -nɪs
undetected ˌʌn.dɪˈtek.tɪd, -dəˈ-
undeterminable ˌʌn.dɪˈtɜː.mɪ.nə.bl̩, -dəˈ-, -mə- ⓤⓢ -ˈtɜːr-
undeterminate ˌʌn.dɪˈtɜː.mɪ.nət, -dəˈ-, -mə-, -nɪt ⓤⓢ -ˈtɜːr- **-ly** -li **-ness** -nəs, -nɪs
undetermination ˌʌn.dɪˌtɜː.mɪˈneɪ.ʃən, -də-, -məˈ- ⓤⓢ -ˌtɜːr-
undetermined ˌʌn.dɪˈtɜː.mɪnd, -dəˈ- ⓤⓢ -ˈtɜːr-
undeterred ˌʌn.dɪˈtɜːd, -dəˈ- ⓤⓢ -ˈtɜːrd
undeveloped ˌʌn.dɪˈvel.əpt, -dəˈ-
undeviating ʌnˈdiː.vi.eɪ.tɪŋ, ˌʌn- ⓤⓢ -t̬ɪŋ **-ly** -li
undid (*from* **undo**) ʌnˈdɪd, ˌʌn-
undies ˈʌn.diz
undigested ˌʌn.daɪˈdʒes.tɪd, -dɪˈ-, -dəˈ-
undignified ʌnˈdɪg.nɪ.faɪd, ˌʌn-, -nə-
undiluted ˌʌn.daɪˈluː.tɪd, -dɪˈ-, -ˈljuː- ⓤⓢ -ˈluː.t̬ɪd
undiminished ˌʌn.dɪˈmɪn.ɪʃt, -dəˈ-
undimmed ʌnˈdɪmd, ˌʌn-
undine (U) ˈʌn.diːn; ʌnˈdiːn, ʊn- ⓤⓢ ʌnˈdiːn; ˈʌn.diːn, -daɪn **-s** -z
undiplomatic ˌʌn.dɪp.ləˈmæt.ɪk ⓤⓢ -ˈmæt̬- **-ally** -əl.i, -li
undiscerning ˌʌn.dɪˈsɜː.nɪŋ, -dəˈ-, -ˈzɜː- ⓤⓢ -ˈsɜːr-, -ˈzɜːr-
undischarged ˌʌn.dɪsˈtʃɑːdʒd ⓤⓢ -ˈtʃɑːrdʒd
undisciplined ʌnˈdɪs.ɪ.plɪnd, ˌʌn-, ˈ-ə-
undisclosed ˌʌn.dɪsˈkləʊzd ⓤⓢ -ˈkloʊzd
undiscouraged ˌʌn.dɪˈskʌr.ɪdʒd ⓤⓢ -ˈskɜːr-
undiscovered ˌʌn.dɪˈskʌv.əd ⓤⓢ -ɚd
undiscussed ˌʌn.dɪˈskʌst
undisguised ˌʌn.dɪsˈgaɪzd, -dɪzˈ-
undismayed ˌʌn.dɪˈsmeɪd, -dəˈ-
undisputed ˌʌn.dɪˈspjuː.tɪd, -dəˈ- ⓤⓢ -t̬ɪd
undissolved ˌʌn.dɪˈzɒlvd, -ˈsɒlvd ⓤⓢ -ˈzɑːlvd
undistinguishab|le ˌʌn.dɪˈstɪŋ.gwɪ.ʃə.b|l̩, -dəˈ- **-ly** -li **-leness** -l̩.nəs, -nɪs
undistinguished ˌʌn.dɪˈstɪŋ.gwɪʃt, -dəˈ-
undistracted ˌʌn.dɪˈstræk.tɪd, -dəˈ-
undisturbed ˌʌn.dɪˈstɜːbd, -dəˈ- ⓤⓢ -ˈstɜːrbd
undivided ˌʌn.dɪˈvaɪ.dɪd, -dəˈ- **-ly** -li **-ness** -nəs, -nɪs
un|do ʌn|ˈduː, ˌʌn- **-does** -ˈdʌz **-doing** -ˈduː.ɪŋ **-did** -ˈdɪd **-done** -ˈdʌn **-doer/s** -ˈduː.əʳ/z ⓤⓢ -ˈduː.ɚ/z
undock ʌnˈdɒk, ˌʌn- ⓤⓢ -ˈdɑːk **-s** -s **-ing** -ɪŋ **-ed** -t
undomesticated ˌʌn.dəˈmes.tɪ.keɪ.tɪd ⓤⓢ -t̬ɪd
undone (*from* **undo**) ʌnˈdʌn, ˌʌn-
undoubted ʌnˈdaʊ.tɪd, ˌʌn- ⓤⓢ -t̬ɪd **-ly** -li
undreamed, undreamt ʌnˈdriːmd, ˌʌnˈdrem*p*t **unˈdreamed ˌof**
undress ʌnˈdres, ˌʌn- **-es** -ɪz **-ing** -ɪŋ **-ed** -t
undrinkable ʌnˈdrɪŋ.kə.bl̩, ˌʌn-
undrunk ʌnˈdrʌŋk
undue ʌnˈdjuː, ˌʌn- ⓤⓢ -ˈduː, -ˈdjuː
undulant ˈʌn.djəl.ənt, -djʊ.lənt, -dʒəl.ənt, -dʒʊ.lənt ⓤⓢ -dʒəl.ənt, -djəl-
undu|late ˈʌn.djə|.leɪt, -djʊ-, -dʒə-, -dʒʊ- ⓤⓢ -dʒə-, -djə- **-lates** -leɪts **-lating/ly** -leɪ.tɪŋ/li ⓤⓢ -leɪ.t̬ɪŋ/li **-lated** -leɪ.tɪd ⓤⓢ -leɪ.t̬ɪd
undulation ˌʌn.djəˈleɪ.ʃən, -djʊˈ-, -dʒəˈ-, -dʒʊˈ- ⓤⓢ -dʒəˈ-, -djəˈ-, -dəˈ- **-s** -z
undulatory ˈʌn.djəl.ə.tər.i, -djʊ.lə-, -dʒəl.ə-, -dʒʊ.lə-, -tri; ˌʌn.djəˈleɪ.tər-, -djʊˈ- ⓤⓢ ˈʌn.dʒəl.ə.tɔːr.i, -djəl-, -dəl-
unduly ʌnˈdjuː.li, ˌʌn-, -ˈdʒuː- ⓤⓢ -ˈduː-, -ˈdjuː-
undutiful ʌnˈdjuː.tɪ.fəl, ˌʌn-, -ˈdʒuː-, -fʊl ⓤⓢ -ˈduː.t̬ɪ-, -ˈdjuː- **-ly** -i **-ness** -nəs, -nɪs
undying ʌnˈdaɪ.ɪŋ, ˌʌn- **-ly** -li
unearned ʌnˈɜːnd, ˌʌn- ⓤⓢ -ˈɜːrnd
unearth ʌnˈɜːθ, ˌʌn- ⓤⓢ -ˈɜːrθ **-s** -s **-ing** -ɪŋ **-ed** -t
unearthl|y ʌnˈɜːθ.l|i, ˌʌn- ⓤⓢ -ˈɜːrθ- **-iness** -ɪ.nəs, -ɪ.nɪs
unease ʌnˈiːz, ˌʌn-
uneas|y ʌnˈiː.z|i, ˌʌn- **-ier** -i.əʳ ⓤⓢ -i.ɚ **-iest** -i.ɪst, -i.əst **-ily** -ɪ.li, -əl.i **-iness** -ɪ.nəs, -ɪ.nɪs
uneatable ʌnˈiː.tə.bl̩, ˌʌn- ⓤⓢ -t̬ə- **-ness** -nəs, -nɪs
uneaten ʌnˈiː.tən, ˌʌn-
uneconomic ʌnˌiː.kəˈnɒm.ɪk, ˌʌn-, -ˌek.əˈ- ⓤⓢ -ˌek.əˈnɑː.mɪk, -ˌiː.kəˈ- **-al** -əl **-ally** -əl.i, -li
unedifying ʌnˈed.ɪ.faɪ.ɪŋ, ˌʌn-
unedited ʌnˈed.ɪ.tɪd ⓤⓢ -t̬ɪd
uneducated ʌnˈedʒ.ʊ.keɪ.tɪd, ˌʌn-, ˈ-ə-, -ˈed.jʊ-, -jə- ⓤⓢ -ˈedʒ.ʊ.keɪ.t̬ɪd, ˈ-ə-
unelected ˌʌn.ɪˈlek.tɪd
unembarrassed ˌʌn.ɪmˈbær.əst, -emˈ- ⓤⓢ -emˈber-, -ɪmˈ-, -ˈbær-
unemotional ˌʌn.ɪˈməʊ.ʃən.əl ⓤⓢ -ˈmoʊ- **-ly** -i
unemphatic ˌʌn.ɪmˈfæt.ɪk, -emˈ- ⓤⓢ -ˈfæt̬- **-ally** -əl.i, -li
unemployable ˌʌn.ɪmˈplɔɪ.ə.bl̩, -emˈ-
unemployed ˌʌn.ɪmˈplɔɪd, -emˈ-
unemployment ˌʌn.ɪmˈplɔɪ.mənt, -emˈ- **unemˈployment ˌbenefit, ˌunemployment ˈbenefit** ⓤⓢ **unemˈployment ˌbenefit**
unenclosed ˌʌn.ɪnˈkləʊzd, -ɪŋˈ-, -enˈ-, -eŋˈ- ⓤⓢ -ɪnˈkloʊzd, -enˈ-
unencumbered ˌʌn.ɪŋˈkʌm.bəd, -ɪnˈ-, -eŋˈ-, -enˈ- ⓤⓢ -ɪnˈkʌm.bɚd, -enˈ-
unending ʌnˈen.dɪŋ, ˌʌn- **-ly** -li
unendowed ˌʌn.ɪnˈdaʊd, -enˈ-
unendurab|le ˌʌn.ɪnˈdjʊə.rə.b|l̩, -enˈ-, -ˈdjɔː- ⓤⓢ -ˈdʊr.ə-, -ˈdjʊr-, -ˈdɜːr- **-ly** -li **-leness** -l̩.nəs, -nɪs
unenforceable ˌʌn.ɪnˈfɔː.sə.bl̩ ⓤⓢ -ˈfɔːr-
unengaged ˌʌn.ɪŋˈgeɪdʒd, -ɪnˈ-, -eŋˈ-, -enˈ- ⓤⓢ -ɪnˈ-, -enˈ-
un-English ˌʌnˈɪŋ.glɪʃ **-ness** -nəs, -nɪs
unenlightened ˌʌn.ɪnˈlaɪ.tənd, -enˈ-
unenterprising ʌnˈen.tə.praɪ.zɪŋ, ˌʌn- ⓤⓢ -t̬ɚ- **-ly** -li
unenthusiastic ˌʌn.ɪnˌθjuː.ziˈæs.tɪk, -enˌ- ⓤⓢ -ˌθuː-, -ˌθjuː- **-ally** -əl.i, -li
unenviab|le ʌnˈen.vi.ə.b|l̩, ˌʌn- **-ly** -li
unequal ʌnˈiː.kwəl, ˌʌn- **-s** -z **-ly** -i **-ness** -nəs, -nɪs **-(l)ed** -d
unequitab|le ʌnˈek.wɪ.tə.b|l̩, ˌʌn-, -wə- ⓤⓢ -t̬ə- **-ly** -li
unequivoc|al ˌʌn.ɪˈkwɪv.ə.k|əl **-ally** -əl.i, -li **-alness** -əl.nəs, -nɪs
unerring ʌnˈɜː.rɪŋ, ˌʌn- ⓤⓢ -ˈɜːr.ɪŋ, -ˈer- **-ly** -li **-ness** -nəs, -nɪs
unescapable ˌʌn.ɪˈskeɪ.pə.bl̩
UNESCO juːˈnes.kəʊ ⓤⓢ -koʊ
unessential ˌʌn.ɪˈsen.*t*ʃəl
unethic|al ʌnˈeθ.ɪ.k|əl **-ly** -əl.i, -li **-ness** -nəs, -nɪs
uneven ʌnˈiː.vən, ˌʌn- **-ly** -li **-ness** -nəs, -nɪs
uneventful ˌʌn.ɪˈvent.fəl, -fʊl **-ly** -i **-ness** -nəs, -nɪs
unexampled ˌʌn.ɪgˈzɑːm.pl̩d, -egˈ-, -ɪkˈsɑːm-, -ekˈ- ⓤⓢ -ɪgˈzæm-, -egˈ-
unexceptionab|le ˌʌn.ɪkˈsep.ʃən.ə.b|l̩, -ekˈ-, -ˈsepʃ.nə- **-ly** -li **-leness** -l̩.nəs ⓤⓢ -nɪs
unexceptional ˌʌn.ɪkˈsep.ʃən.əl, -ekˈ-, -ˈsepʃ.nəl **-ly** -i
unexhausted ˌʌn.ɪgˈzɔː.stɪd, -egˈ-, -ɪkˈsɔː-, -ekˈ- ⓤⓢ -ɪgˈzɑː-, -egˈ-, -ˈzɔː-
unexpected ˌʌn.ɪkˈspek.tɪd, -ekˈ- **-ly** -li **-ness** -nəs, -nɪs
unexpired ˌʌn.ɪkˈspaɪəd, -ekˈ- ⓤⓢ -ˈspaɪɚd
unexplained ˌʌn.ɪkˈspleɪnd, -ekˈ-

unexplored ˌʌn.ɪkˈsplɔːd, -ekˈ- Ⓤⓢ -ˈsplɔːrd
unexposed ˌʌn.ɪkˈspəʊzd, -ekˈ- Ⓤⓢ -ˈspoʊzd
unexpressib|le ˌʌn.ɪkˈspres.ə.b|l̩, -ekˈ-, ˈ-ɪ- **-ly** -li
unexpressive ˌʌn.ɪkˈspres.ɪv, -ekˈ-
unexpurgated ʌnˈek.spə.geɪ.tɪd, ˌʌn-, -spɜː- Ⓤⓢ -spɚ.geɪ.t̬ɪd
unfading ʌnˈfeɪ.dɪŋ, ˌʌn- **-ly** -li
unfailing ʌnˈfeɪ.lɪŋ, ˌʌn- **-ly** -li **-ness** -nəs, -nɪs
unfair ʌnˈfeəʳ, ˌʌn- Ⓤⓢ -ˈfer **-ly** -li **-ness** -nəs, -nɪs ˌ**unfair disˈmissal**
unfaithful ʌnˈfeɪθ.fəl, ˌʌn-, -fʊl **-ly** -i **-ness** -nəs, -nɪs
unfaltering ʌnˈfɔːl.tər.ɪŋ, ˌʌn-, -ˈfɒl- Ⓤⓢ -ˈfɑːl.t̬ɚ-, -ˈfɔːl- **-ly** -li
unfamiliar ˌʌn.fəˈmɪl.jəʳ, ˈ-i.əʳ Ⓤⓢ ˈ-jɚ **-ly** -li
unfamiliarity ˌʌn.fəˌmɪl.iˈær.ə.ti, -ɪ.ti Ⓤⓢ -ˈer.ə.t̬i, -ˈær-
unfashionab|le ʌnˈfæʃ.ən.ə.b|l̩, ˌʌn-, ˈ-nə- **-ly** -li
unfasten ʌnˈfɑː.sən, ˌʌn- Ⓤⓢ -ˈfæs- **-s** -z **-ing** -ɪŋ, -ˈfɑːs.nɪŋ Ⓤⓢ -ˈfæs.nɪŋ **-ed** -d
unfathomab|le ʌnˈfæð.ə.mə.b|l̩, ˌʌn- **-ly** -li **-leness** -l̩.nəs, -nɪs
unfathomed ʌnˈfæð.əmd, ˌʌn-
unfavo(u)rab|le ʌnˈfeɪ.vər.ə.b|l̩, ˌʌn-, -ˈfeɪv.rə- **-ly** -li **-leness** -l̩.nəs, -nɪs
unfavo(u)rite ʌnˈfeɪ.vər.ɪt, ˌʌn-, -ˈfeɪv.rɪt
unfazed ʌnˈfeɪzd
unfed ʌnˈfed, ˌʌn-
unfeeling ʌnˈfiː.lɪŋ, ˌʌn- **-ly** -li **-ness** -nəs, -nɪs
unfeigned ʌnˈfeɪnd, ˌʌn-
unfeigned|ly ʌnˈfeɪ.nɪd|.li, ˌʌn- **-ness** -nəs, -nɪs
unfelt ʌnˈfelt, ˌʌn-
unfermented ˌʌn.fəˈmen.tɪd, -fɜːˈ- Ⓤⓢ -fɚˈmen.t̬ɪd
unfertilized, -ised ʌnˈfɜː.təl.aɪzd, ˌʌn-, -tɪ.laɪzd Ⓤⓢ -ˈfɝː.t̬əl.aɪzd
unfett|er ʌnˈfet|.əʳ, ˌʌn- Ⓤⓢ -ˈfet̬|.ɚ **-ers** -əz Ⓤⓢ -ɚz **-ering** -ər.ɪŋ **-ed** -əd Ⓤⓢ -ɚd
unfettered ʌnˈfet.əd Ⓤⓢ -ˈfet̬.ɚd
unfilial ʌnˈfɪl.i.əl, ˌʌn- **-ly** -i
unfinished ʌnˈfɪn.ɪʃt, ˌʌn- ˌ**unfinished ˈbusiness, unˌfinished ˈbusiness**
unfit (*adj.*) ʌnˈfɪt **-ly** -li **-ness** -nəs, -nɪs
un|fit (*v.*) ʌn|ˈfɪt, ˌʌn- **-fits** -ˈfɪts **-fitting/ly** -ˈfɪt.ɪŋ/li Ⓤⓢ -ˈfɪt̬.ɪŋ/li **-fitted** -ˈfɪt.ɪd Ⓤⓢ -ˈfɪt̬.ɪd
unfix ʌnˈfɪks, ˌʌn- **-es** -ɪz **-ing** -ɪŋ **-ed** -t
unflagging ʌnˈflæg.ɪŋ, ˌʌn- **-ly** -li
unflappab|le ʌnˈflæp.ə.b|l̩, ˌʌn- **-ly** -li
unflattering ʌnˈflæt.ər.ɪŋ, ˌʌn- Ⓤⓢ -ˈflæt̬- **-ly** -li
unfledged ʌnˈfledʒd, ˌʌn-
unflinching ʌnˈflɪn.tʃɪŋ, ˌʌn- **-ly** -li **-ness** -nəs, -nɪs
unfold ʌnˈfəʊld, ˌʌn- Ⓤⓢ -ˈfoʊld **-s** -z **-ing** -ɪŋ **-ed** -ɪd
unforeseeable ˌʌn.fɔːˈsiː.ə.bl̩, -fəˈ- Ⓤⓢ -fɔːrˈ-, -fɚˈ-
unforeseen ˌʌn.fɔːˈsiːn, -fəˈ- Ⓤⓢ -fɔːrˈ-, -fɚˈ- ˌ**unforeseen ˈcircumstances**
unforgettab|le ˌʌn.fəˈget.ə.b|l̩ Ⓤⓢ -fɚˈget̬- **-ly** -li
unforgivable ˌʌn.fəˈgɪv.ə.bl̩ Ⓤⓢ -fɚˈ-
unforgiven ˌʌn.fəˈgɪv.ən Ⓤⓢ -fɚˈ-
unforgiving ˌʌn.fəˈgɪv.ɪŋ Ⓤⓢ -fɚˈ- **-ly** -li **-ness** -nəs, -nɪs
unforgotten ˌʌn.fəˈgɒt.ən Ⓤⓢ -fɚˈgɑː.tən
unformatted ʌnˈfɔː.mæt.ɪd Ⓤⓢ -ˈfɔːr.mæt̬-
unformed ʌnˈfɔːmd, ˌʌn- Ⓤⓢ -ˈfɔːrmd
unforthcoming ˌʌn.fɔːθˈkʌm.ɪŋ Ⓤⓢ -fɔːrθ-
unfortified ʌnˈfɔː.tɪ.faɪd, ˌʌn- Ⓤⓢ -ˈfɔːr.t̬ɪ-
unfortunate ʌnˈfɔː.tʃən.ət, ˌʌn-, -ɪt Ⓤⓢ -ˈfɔːr- **-ly** -li **-ness** -nəs, -nɪs
unfounded ʌnˈfaʊn.dɪd, ˌʌn-
unframed ʌnˈfreɪmd, ˌʌn-
un|freeze ʌn|ˈfriːz Ⓤⓢ ˌʌn- **-freezes** -ˈfriː.zɪz **-froze** -ˈfrəʊz Ⓤⓢ -ˈfroʊz **-frozen** -ˈfrəʊ.zən Ⓤⓢ -ˈfroʊ.zən
unfrequented ˌʌn.frɪˈkwen.tɪd Ⓤⓢ ʌnˈfriː.kwen.t̬ɪd, ˌʌn-
unfriend|ly ʌnˈfrend.|li, ˌʌn- **-liness** -lɪ.nəs, -lɪ.nɪs
unfrock ʌnˈfrɒk, ˌʌn- Ⓤⓢ -ˈfrɑːk **-s** -s **-ing** -ɪŋ **-ed** -t
unfruitful ʌnˈfruːt.fəl, ˌʌn-, -fʊl **-ly** -i **-ness** -nəs, -nɪs
unfulfilled ˌʌn.fʊlˈfɪld
unfurl ʌnˈfɜːl, ˌʌn- Ⓤⓢ -ˈfɝːl **-s** -z **-ing** -ɪŋ **-ed** -d
unfurnished ʌnˈfɜː.nɪʃt, ˌʌn- Ⓤⓢ -ˈfɝː-
ungainl|y ʌnˈgeɪn.l|i, ˌʌn-, ʌŋ-, ˌʌŋ- Ⓤⓢ ʌn-, ˌʌn- **-iest** -i.ɪst, -i.əst **-iness** -ɪ.nəs, -ɪ.nɪs
ungallant ʌnˈgæl.ənt, ˌʌn.gəˈlænt, ʌŋ-, ˌʌŋ- Ⓤⓢ ʌnˈgæl.ənt, ˌʌn.gəˈlænt, -ˈlɑːnt **-ly** -li
ungenerous ʌnˈdʒen.ər.əs, ˌʌn- **-ly** -li
ungentleman|ly ʌnˈdʒent.l̩.mən.l|i, ˌʌn- **-iness** -ɪ.nəs, -ɪ.nɪs
un-get-at-able ˌʌn.getˈæt.ə.bl̩, ˌʌŋ- Ⓤⓢ ˌʌn.get̬ˈæt̬-
ungird ʌnˈgɜːd, ˌʌn-, ʌŋ-, ˌʌŋ- Ⓤⓢ ʌnˈgɝːrd, ˌʌn- **-s** -z **-ing** -ɪŋ **-ed** -ɪd
unglazed ʌnˈgleɪzd, ˌʌn-, ʌŋ-, ˌʌŋ- Ⓤⓢ ʌn-, ˌʌn-
ungloved ʌnˈglʌvd, ˌʌn-, ʌŋ-, ˌʌŋ- Ⓤⓢ ʌn-, ˌʌn-
unglu|e ʌnˈgluː, ˌʌn-, ʌŋ-, ˌʌŋ- Ⓤⓢ ʌn-, ˌʌn- **-es** -z **-ing** -ɪŋ **-ed** -d
ungodl|y ʌnˈgɒd.l|i, ˌʌn-, ʌŋ-, ˌʌŋ- Ⓤⓢ ʌnˈgɑːd.l|i, ˌʌn- **-ier** -i.əʳ Ⓤⓢ -i.ɚ **-iest** -i.ɪst, -i.əst **-iness** -ɪ.nəs, -ɪ.nɪs
Ungoed ˈʌŋ.gɔɪd
ungotten ʌnˈgɒt.ən, ˌʌn-, ʌŋ-, ˌʌŋ- Ⓤⓢ ʌnˈgɑː.tən, ˌʌn-
ungovernab|le ʌnˈgʌv.ən.ə.b|l̩, ˌʌn-, ʌŋ-, ˌʌŋ-, ˈ-nə- Ⓤⓢ ʌnˈgʌv.ɚ.nə-, ˌʌn- **-ly** -li **-leness** -l̩.nəs Ⓤⓢ -nɪs
ungoverned ʌnˈgʌv.ənd, ˌʌn-, ʌŋ-, ˌʌŋ- Ⓤⓢ ʌnˈgʌv.ɚnd, ˌʌn-
ungraceful ʌnˈgreɪs.fəl, ˌʌn-, ʌŋ-, ˌʌŋ-, -fʊl Ⓤⓢ ʌn-, ˌʌn- **-ly** -i **-ness** -nəs, -nɪs
ungracious ʌnˈgreɪ.ʃəs, ˌʌn-, ʌŋ-, ˌʌŋ- Ⓤⓢ ʌn-, ˌʌn- **-ly** -li **-ness** -nəs, -nɪs
ungrammatic|al ˌʌn.grəˈmæt.ɪ.k|əl, ˌʌŋ- Ⓤⓢ ˌʌn.grəˈmæt̬- **-ally** -əl.i, -li
ungrateful ʌnˈgreɪt.fəl, ˌʌn-, ʌŋ-, ˌʌŋ-, -fʊl Ⓤⓢ ʌn-, ˌʌn- **-ly** -li **-ness** -nəs, -nɪs
ungrounded ʌnˈgraʊn.dɪd, ˌʌn-, ʌŋ-, ˌʌŋ- Ⓤⓢ ʌn-, ˌʌn-
ungrudging ʌnˈgrʌdʒ.ɪŋ, ˌʌn-, ʌŋ-, ˌʌŋ- Ⓤⓢ ʌn-, ˌʌn- **-ly** -li
unguarded ʌnˈgɑː.dɪd, ˌʌn-, ʌŋ-, ˌʌŋ- Ⓤⓢ ʌnˈgɑːr-, ˌʌn- **-ly** -li **-ness** -nəs, -nɪs
unguent ˈʌŋ.gwənt, -gju.ənt Ⓤⓢ -gwənt **-s** -s
unguided ʌnˈgaɪ.dɪd, ˌʌn-, ʌŋ-, ˌʌŋ- Ⓤⓢ ʌn-, ˌʌn-
ungul|a ˈʌŋ.gjə.l|ə, -gjʊ- **-ae** -iː
ungulate ˈʌŋ.gjə.leɪt, -gjʊ-, -lət, -lɪt Ⓤⓢ -lɪt, -leɪt **-s** -s
unhallowed ʌnˈhæl.əʊd, ˌʌn- Ⓤⓢ -oʊd
unhampered ʌnˈhæm.pəd, ˌʌn- Ⓤⓢ -pɚd
unhand ʌnˈhænd, ˌʌn- **-s** -z **-ing** -ɪŋ **-ed** -ɪd
unhandy ʌnˈhæn.di, ˌʌn-
unhapp|y ʌnˈhæp|.i, ˌʌn- **-ier** -i.əʳ Ⓤⓢ -i.ɚ **-iest** -i.ɪst, -i.əst **-ily** -ɪ.li, -əl.i **-iness** -ɪ.nɪs, -ɪ.nəs
unharmed ʌnˈhɑːmd, ˌʌn- Ⓤⓢ -ˈhɑːrmd
unharness ʌnˈhɑː.nɪs, ˌʌn- Ⓤⓢ -ˈhɑːr- **-es** -ɪz **-ing** -ɪŋ **-ed** -t
unhatched ʌnˈhætʃt, ˌʌn-
unhealth|y ʌnˈhel.θ|i, ˌʌn- **-ier** -i.əʳ Ⓤⓢ -i.ɚ **-iest** -i.ɪst, -i.əst **-ily** -ɪ.li, -əl.i **-iness** -ɪ.nəs, -ɪ.nɪs
unheard ʌnˈhɜːd, ˌʌn- Ⓤⓢ -ˈhɝːrd
unheard-of ʌnˈhɜːd,ɒv Ⓤⓢ -ˈhɝːrd,ɑːv, -əv
unheeded ʌnˈhiː.dɪd, ˌʌn-

unheeding ʌn'hiː.dɪŋ **-ly** -li
unhelpful ʌn'help.fʊl, -fəl **-ly** -i **-ness** -nəs, -nɪs
unhesitating ʌn'hez.ɪ.teɪ.tɪŋ, ˌʌn-, '-ə- (US) -t̬ɪŋ **-ly** -li
unhing|e ʌn'hɪndʒ, ˌʌn- **-es** -ɪz **-ing** -ɪŋ **-ed** -d
unhistoric ˌʌn.hɪ'stɒr.ɪk, -ɪ'- (US) -hɪ'stɔːr- **-al** -əl
unhitch ʌn'hɪtʃ, ˌʌn- **-es** -ɪz **-ing** -ɪŋ **-ed** -t
unhol|y ʌn'həʊ.l|i, ˌʌn- (US) -'hoʊ- **-iness** -ɪ.nəs, -ɪ.nɪs **unˌholy al'liance**
unhook ʌn'hʊk, ˌʌn- **-s** -s **-ing** -ɪŋ **-ed** -t
unhoped-for ʌn'həʊptˌfɔːr (US) -'hoʊptˌfɔːr
unhors|e ʌn'hɔːs, ˌʌn- (US) -'hɔːrs **-es** -ɪz **-ing** -ɪŋ **-ed** -t
unhous|e ʌn'haʊz, ˌʌn- **-es** -ɪz **-ing** -ɪŋ **-ed** -d
unhuman ʌn'hjuː.mən, ˌʌn-
unhung ʌn'hʌŋ, ˌʌn-
unhurried ʌn'hʌr.ɪd, ˌʌn- (US) -'hɜːr- **-ly** -li **-ness** -nəs, -nɪs
unhurt ʌn'hɜːt, ˌʌn- (US) -'hɜːrt
uni- juː.nɪ-, -ni-
Note: Prefix. Normally takes primary or secondary stress on the first syllable, e.g. **unify** /'juː.nɪ.faɪ (US) -nə-/, **unification** /ˌjuː.nɪ.fɪ'keɪ.ʃən (US) -nə-/.
uni 'juː.ni **-s** -z
Uniate 'juː.ni.ət, -ɪt, -eɪt (US) -ɪt, -eɪt **-s** -s
unicameral ˌjuː.nɪ'kæm.ər.əl
UNICEF 'juː.nɪ.sef
unicellular ˌjuː.nɪ'sel.jə.lər, -jʊ- (US) -jə.lɚ
unicorn 'juː.nɪ.kɔːn (US) -kɔːrn **-s** -z
unicycl|e 'juː.nɪˌsaɪ.kl̩ (US) -nə- **-es** -z **-ist/s** -ɪst/s
unidentified ˌʌn.aɪ'den.tɪ.faɪd (US) -t̬ə- ˌ**unidentified ˌflying 'object**
unidimensional ˌjuː.nɪ.daɪ'men.tʃən.əl, -dɪ'-, -də'- (US) -nə.də'ment.ʃə-, -dɪ'-, -daɪ-
unidiomatic ʌnˌɪd.i.əʊ'mæt.ɪk, ˌʌn- (US) -ə'mæt̬- **-ally** -əl.i, -li
unifiable 'juː.nɪ.faɪ.ə.bl̩ (US) -nə-
unification ˌjuː.nɪ.fɪ'keɪ.ʃən, -nə- (US) -nə- **-s** -z
uniform 'juː.nɪ.fɔːm, -nə- (US) -nə.fɔːrm **-s** -z **-ed** -d **-ly** -li **-ness** -nəs, -nɪs
uniformity ˌjuː.nɪ'fɔː.mə.ti, -nə'-, -mɪ- (US) -nə'fɔːr.mə.t̬i
uni|fy 'juː.nɪ|.faɪ, -nə- (US) -nə- **-fies** -faɪz **-fying** -faɪ.ɪŋ **-fied** -faɪd **-fier/s** -faɪ.ər/z (US) -faɪ.ɚ/z
Unigate® 'juː.nɪ.geɪt, -nə- (US) -nə-
unilateral ˌjuː.nɪ'læt.ər.əl (US) -nə'læt̬- **-ly** -i **-ism** -ɪ.zəm **-ist/s** -ɪst/s
Unilever® 'juː.nɪ.liː.vər (US) -nə.liː.vɚ
unimaginab|le ˌʌn.ɪ'mædʒ.ɪ.nə.b|l̩, -ən.ə- **-ly** -li **-leness** -l̩.nəs, -nɪs
unimaginative ˌʌn.ɪ'mædʒ.ɪ.nə.tɪv, -ən.ə- (US) -t̬ɪv **-ly** -li **-ness** -nəs, -nɪs
unimagined ˌʌn.ɪ'mædʒ.ɪnd, -ənd
unimpaired ˌʌn.ɪm'peəd (US) -'perd
unimpassioned ʌn.ɪm'pæʃ.ənd
unimpeachab|le ˌʌn.ɪm'piː.tʃə.b|l̩ **-ly** -li **-leness** -l̩.nəs, -nɪs
unimpeded ˌʌn.ɪm'piː.dɪd
unimportance ˌʌn.ɪm'pɔː.tənts (US) -'pɔːr-
unimportant ˌʌn.ɪm'pɔː.tənt (US) -'pɔːr- **-ly** -li
unimpressed ˌʌn.ɪm'prest
unimpressive ˌʌn.ɪm'pres.ɪv **-ly** -li
unimproved ʌn.ɪm'pruːvd
uninflated ˌʌn.ɪn'fleɪ.tɪd (US) -t̬ɪd
uninflected ˌʌn.ɪn'flek.tɪd
uninfluenced ʌn'ɪn.flu.əntst, ˌʌn-, -flʊəntst (US) -flu.əntst
uninformative ˌʌn.ɪn'fɔː.mə.tɪv (US) -'fɔːr.mə.t̬ɪv **-ly** -li
uninformed ˌʌn.ɪn'fɔːmd (US) -'fɔːrmd
uninhabitable ˌʌn.ɪn'hæb.ɪ.tə.bl̩, '-ə- (US) -t̬ə- **-ness** -nəs, -nɪs
uninhabited ˌʌn.ɪn'hæb.ɪ.tɪd, '-ə- (US) -t̬ɪd
uninhibited ˌʌn.ɪn'hɪb.ɪ.tɪd, '-ə- (US) -t̬ɪd **-ly** -li **-ness** -nəs, -nɪs
uninitiated ˌʌn.ɪ'nɪʃ.i.eɪ.tɪd (US) -t̬ɪd
uninjured ʌn'ɪn.dʒəd, ˌʌn- (US) -dʒɚd
uninspired ˌʌn.ɪn'spaɪəd (US) -'spaɪɚd
uninspiring ˌʌn.ɪn'spaɪə.rɪŋ (US) -'spaɪ- **-ly** -li
uninstructed ˌʌn.ɪn'strʌk.tɪd
uninsured ˌʌn.ɪn'ʃʊəd, -'ʃɔːd (US) -'ʃʊrd
unintelligent ˌʌn.ɪn'tel.ɪ.dʒənt, '-ə- **-ly** -li
unintelligibility ˌʌn.ɪnˌtel.ɪ.dʒə'bɪl.ə.ti, ˌ-ə-, -dʒɪ'-, -ɪ.ti (US) -ə.t̬i
unintelligib|le ˌʌn.ɪn'tel.ɪ.dʒə.b|l̩, '-ə-, -dʒɪ- **-ly** -li
unintentional ˌʌn.ɪn'ten.tʃən.əl, -'tentʃ.nəl **-ly** -i
uninterest|ed ʌn'ɪn.trə.st|ɪd, ˌʌn-, -trɪ-, -tres.t|ɪd, -tər.ə.st|ɪd, -ɪ-, -es.t|ɪd (US) -trɪ.st|ɪd, -trə-, -tres.t|ɪd, -tɚ.es-, -ə.st|ɪd **-ing** -ɪŋ
uninterrupted ʌnˌɪn.tər'ʌp.tɪd, ˌʌn- (US) -tə'rʌp- **-ly** -li
uninvited ˌʌn.ɪn'vaɪ.tɪd (US) -t̬ɪd
uninviting ʌn.ɪn'vaɪ.tɪŋ (US) -t̬ɪŋ **-ly** -li **-ness** -nəs, -nɪs
union (U) 'juː.njən, -ni.ən (US) '-njən **-s** -z ˌ**Union 'Jack**
union|ism (U) 'juː.njə.n|ɪ.zəm, -ni.ə- (US) -njə- **-ist/s** -ɪst/s
unionization, -isa- ˌjuː.njə.naɪ'zeɪ.ʃən, -ni.ə-, -ɪ'- (US) -njə.nɪ'-
unioniz|e, -is|e 'juː.njə.naɪz, -ni.ə- (US) -'njə- **-es** -ɪz **-ing** -ɪŋ **-ed** -d
unipartite ˌjuː.nɪ'pɑː.taɪt (US) -'pɑːr-
unique juː'niːk **-ly** -li **-ness** -nəs, -nɪs
Uniroyal® 'juː.nɪ.rɔɪəl
unisex 'juː.nɪ.seks (US) -nə-
unisexual ˌjuː.nɪ'sek.ʃʊəl, -sjʊəl (US) -nə'sek.ʃu.əl
unison 'juː.nɪ.sən, -nə-, -zən (US) -nə- **-s** -z
unissued ʌn'ɪʃ.uːd, ˌʌn-, -'ɪs.juːd (US) -'ɪʃ.uːd
unit 'juː.nɪt **-s** -s ˌ**unit 'trust**
UNITA juː'niː.tə (US) -t̬ə
unitable juː'naɪ.tə.bl̩ (US) -t̬ə-
unitarian (U) ˌjuː.nɪ'teə.ri.ən (US) -'ter.i- **-s** -z **-ism** -ɪ.zəm
unitary 'juː.nɪ.tər.i, -tri (US) -ter.i
u|nite juː|'naɪt, jʊ- **-nites** -'naɪts **-niting** -'naɪ.tɪŋ (US) -'naɪ.t̬ɪŋ **-nited/ly** -'naɪ.tɪd/li (US) -'naɪ.t̬ɪd/li **-niter/s** -'naɪ.tər/z (US) -'naɪ.t̬ɚ/z
United Arab Emirates juːˌnaɪ.tɪdˌær.əb'em.ɪ.rəts, jʊ-, -ər.əts, -ɪts, -eɪts (US) -t̬ɪdˌer.əb'em.ɚ.əts, -ˌær-; -ɪ'mɪr-
United Kingdom juːˌnaɪ.tɪd'kɪŋ.dəm, jʊ- (US) -t̬ɪd'-
United Nations juːˌnaɪ.tɪd'neɪ.ʃənz, jʊ- (US) -t̬ɪd'-
United Reformed Church juːˌnaɪ.tɪd.rɪ'fɔːmdˌtʃɜːtʃ, jʊ- (US) -t̬ɪd.rɪ'fɔːrmdˌtʃɜːrtʃ
United States juːˌnaɪ.tɪd'steɪts, jʊ- (US) -t̬ɪd'- **Uˌnited ˌStates of A'merica**
unit|y (U) 'juː.nə.t|i, -nɪ- (US) -nə.t̬|i **-ies** -iz
univalen|t ˌjuː.nɪ'veɪ.lən|t (US) -nə'-; juː'nɪv.əl.ən|t **-ce** -ts
univalve 'juː.nɪ.vælv (US) -nə- **-s** -z
universal ˌjuː.nɪ'vɜː.səl, -nə'- (US) -nə'vɜːr- **-s** -z **-ly** -i **-ness** -nəs, -nɪs **-ism** -ɪ.zəm **-ist/s** -ɪst/s *stress shift:* ˌuniversal 'joint
universality ˌjuː.nɪ.vɜː'sæl.ə.ti, -nə-, -ɪ.ti (US) -nə.vɜːr'sæl.ə.t̬i
universaliz|e, -is|e ˌjuː.nɪ'vɜː.səl.aɪz, -nə'- (US) -nə'vɜːr.sə.laɪz **-es** -ɪz **-ing** -ɪŋ **-ed** -d
univers|e 'juː.nɪ.vɜːs, -nə- (US) -nə.vɜːrs **-es** -ɪz
universit|y ˌjuː.nɪ'vɜː.sə.t|i, -nə'-, -sɪ- (US) -nə'vɜːr.sə.t̬|i **-ies** -iz *stress shift:* ˌuniversity 'grant
univocal ˌjuː.nɪ'vəʊ.kəl (US) -'nɪv.ə- **-s** -z
Unix®, UNIX 'juː.nɪks
unjust ʌn'dʒʌst, ˌʌn- **-ly** -li **-ness** -nəs, -nɪs

unjustifiab|le ʌnˌdʒʌs.tɪˈfaɪ.ə.bl̩, ˌʌn.dʒʌs-, ˌʌnˌdʒʌs-, -təˈ- ⓊⓈ ʌnˌdʒʌs.tɪˈfaɪ.ə.bl̩, ˌʌn-, -təˈ-, -ˈdʒʌs.tɪ.faɪ-, -tə- **-ly** -li **-leness** -l̩.nəs, -nɪs
unjustified ʌnˈdʒʌs.tɪ.faɪd, ˌʌn-, -tə- **-ly** -li
unkempt ʌnˈkempt, ˌʌn-, ʌŋ-, ˌʌŋ- ⓊⓈ ʌn-, ˌʌn-
unkept ʌnˈkept, ˌʌn-, ʌŋ-, ˌʌŋ- ⓊⓈ ʌn-, ˌʌn-
unkin|d ʌnˈkaɪn|d, ˌʌn-, ʌŋ-, ˌʌŋ- ⓊⓈ ʌn-, ˌʌn- **-der** -dəʳ ⓊⓈ -dɚ **-dest** -dɪst, -dəst **-dly** -d.li **-dness** -*d*.nɪs, -nəs
un|knot ʌn|ˈnɒt, ˌʌn- ⓊⓈ -ˈnɑːt **-knots** -ˈnɒts ⓊⓈ -ˈnɑːts **-knotting** -ˈnɒt.ɪŋ ⓊⓈ -ˈnɑː.t̬ɪŋ **-knotted** -ˈnɒt.ɪd ⓊⓈ -ˈnɑː.t̬ɪd
unknowable ʌnˈnəʊ.ə.bl̩, ˌʌn- ⓊⓈ -ˈnoʊ-
unknowing ʌnˈnəʊ.ɪŋ, ˌʌn- ⓊⓈ -ˈnoʊ- **-ly** -li **-ness** -nəs, -nɪs
unknown ʌnˈnəʊn, ˌʌn- ⓊⓈ -ˈnoʊn ˌ**Unknown ˈSoldier** ; ˌ**unknown ˈquantity**
unlac|e ʌnˈleɪs, ˌʌn- **-es** -ɪz **-ing** -ɪŋ **-ed** -t
unlad|e ʌnˈleɪd ⓊⓈ ˌʌn- **-es** -z **-ing** -ɪŋ **-ed** -ɪd **-en** -ᵊn
unladylike ʌnˈleɪ.di.laɪk, ˌʌn-
unlamented ˌʌn.ləˈmen.tɪd ⓊⓈ -t̬ɪd
unlash ʌnˈlæʃ ⓊⓈ ˌʌn- **-es** -ɪz **-ing** -ɪŋ **-ed** -t
unlatch ʌnˈlætʃ ⓊⓈ ˌʌn- **-es** -ɪz **-ing** -ɪŋ **-ed** -t
unlawful ʌnˈlɔː.fᵊl, ˌʌn-, -fʊl ⓊⓈ -ˈlɑː-, -ˈlɔː- **-ly** -i **-ness** -nəs, -nɪs
unleaded ʌnˈled.ɪd, ˌʌn- ˌ**unleaded ˈpetrol**, **unˌleaded ˈpetrol**
unlearn ʌnˈlɜːn, ˌʌn- ⓊⓈ -ˈlɜːrn **-s** -z **-ing** -ɪŋ **-ed** -t, -d **-t** -t
unlearned ʌnˈlɜː.nɪd, ˌʌn- ⓊⓈ -ˈlɜːr- **-ly** -li **-ness** -nəs, -nɪs
unleash ʌnˈliːʃ, ˌʌn- **-es** -ɪz **-ing** -ɪŋ **-ed** -t
unleavened ʌnˈlev.ᵊnd, ˌʌn- ˌ**unleavened ˈbread**, **unˌleavened ˈbread**
unled ʌnˈled, ˌʌn-
unless ənˈles, ʌn-
unlettered ʌnˈlet.əd, ˌʌn- ⓊⓈ -ˈlet̬.ɚd
unliberated ʌnˈlɪb.ᵊr.eɪ.tɪd, ˌʌn- ⓊⓈ -ə.reɪ.t̬ɪd
unlicensed ʌnˈlaɪ.sᵊn*t*st, ˌʌn-
unlike ʌnˈlaɪk, ˌʌn-
unlikel|y ʌnˈlaɪ.kl|i, ˌʌn- **-ihood** -ɪ.hʊd **-iness** -ɪ.nəs, -ɪ.nɪs
unlikeness ʌnˈlaɪk.nəs, ˌʌn-, -nɪs
unlimb|er ʌnˈlɪm.b|əʳ, ˌʌn- ⓊⓈ -b|ɚ **-ers** -əz ⓊⓈ -ɚz **-ering** -ᵊr.ɪŋ **-ered** -əd ⓊⓈ -ɚd
unlimited ʌnˈlɪm.ɪ.tɪd, ˌʌn- ⓊⓈ -t̬ɪd
unlink ʌnˈlɪŋk ⓊⓈ ˌʌn- **-s** -s **-ing** -ɪŋ **-ed** -t
unliquidated ʌnˈlɪk.wɪ.deɪ.tɪd, ˌʌn-, -wə- ⓊⓈ -wə.deɪ.t̬ɪd
unlisted ʌnˈlɪs.tɪd
unlit ʌnˈlɪt, ˌʌn-
unload ʌnˈləʊd, ˌʌn- ⓊⓈ -ˈloʊd **-s** -z **-ing** -ɪŋ **-ed** -ɪd **-er/s** -əʳ/z ⓊⓈ -ɚ/z
unlock ʌnˈlɒk, ˌʌn- ⓊⓈ -ˈlɑːk **-s** -s **-ing** -ɪŋ **-ed** -t
unlooked-for ʌnˈlʊktˌfɔːʳ, ˌʌn- ⓊⓈ -ˌfɔːr
unloos|e ʌnˈluːs, ˌʌn- **-es** -ɪz **-ing** -ɪŋ **-ed** -t
unloosen ʌnˈluː.sᵊn, ˌʌn- **-s** -z **-ing** -ɪŋ, -ˈluːs.nɪŋ **-ed** -d
unlovel|y ʌnˈlʌv.l|i, ˌʌn- **-iness** -ɪ.nəs, -ɪ.nɪs
unloving ʌnˈlʌv.ɪŋ, ˌʌn-
unluck|y ʌnˈlʌk|.i, ˌʌn- **-ier** -i.əʳ ⓊⓈ -i.ɚ **-iest** -i.ɪst, -i.əst **-ily** -ɪ.li, -ᵊl.i **-iness** -ɪ.nəs, -ɪ.nɪs
unmade ʌnˈmeɪd, ˌʌn-
un|make ʌn|ˈmeɪk, ˌʌn- **-makes** -ˈmeɪks **-making** -ˈmeɪ.kɪŋ **-made** -ˈmeɪd
unman ʌnˈmæn, ˌʌn- **-s** -z **-ning** -ɪŋ **-ned** -d
unmanageab|le ʌnˈmæn.ɪ.dʒə.b|l̩, ˌʌn-, ˈ-ə- **-ly** -li **-leness** -l̩.nəs, -nɪs
unmanl|y ʌnˈmæn.l|i, ˌʌn- **-iness** -ɪ.nəs, -ɪ.nɪs
unmannered ʌnˈmæn.əd ⓊⓈ -ɚd **-ly** -li
unmannerl|y ʌnˈmæn.ᵊl|l.i, ˌʌn- ⓊⓈ -ɚ.l|i **-iness** -ɪ.nəs, -ɪ.nɪs
unmarked ʌnˈmɑːkt, ˌʌn- ⓊⓈ -ˈmɑːrkt
unmarriageable ʌnˈmær.ɪ.dʒə.bl̩, ˌʌn- ⓊⓈ -ˈmer-, -ˈmær-
unmarried ʌnˈmær.ɪd, ˌʌn- ⓊⓈ -ˈmer-, -ˈmær-
unmask ʌnˈmɑːsk, ˌʌn- ⓊⓈ -ˈmæsk **-s** -s **-ing** -ɪŋ **-ed** -t
unmatched ʌnˈmætʃt, ˌʌn-
unmeaning ʌnˈmiː.nɪŋ, ˌʌn-
unmeaning|ly ʌnˈmiː.nɪŋ|.li, ˌʌn- **-ness** -nəs, -nɪs
unmeasurable ʌnˈmeʒ.ᵊr.ə.bl̩, ˌʌn-
unmeasured ʌnˈmeʒ.əd, ˌʌn- ⓊⓈ -ɚd
unmentionable ʌnˈmen.*t*ʃᵊn.ə.bl̩, ˌʌn-, -ˈmen*t*ʃ.nə- ⓊⓈ -ˈment.ʃᵊn.ə-, -ˈmen*t*ʃ.nə- **-s** -z **-ness** -nəs, -nɪs
unmentioned ʌnˈmen.*t*ʃᵊnd, ˌʌn- ⓊⓈ -ˈmen*t*.ʃᵊnd
unmerciful ʌnˈmɜː.sɪ.fᵊl, ˌʌn-, -sə-, -fʊl ⓊⓈ -ˈmɜːr- **-ly** -i **-ness** -nəs, -nɪs
unmerited ʌnˈmer.ɪ.tɪd, ˌʌn- ⓊⓈ -t̬ɪd
unmethodic|al ˌʌn.məˈθɒd.ɪ.k|ᵊl, -mɪˈ-, -meθˈɒd- ⓊⓈ -məˈθɑː.dɪ- **-ally** -ᵊl.i, -li
unmindful ʌnˈmaɪn*d*.fᵊl, ˌʌn-, -fʊl **-ly** -i **-ness** -nəs, -nɪs
unmissable ʌnˈmɪs.ə.bl̩
unmistakab|le ˌʌn.mɪˈsteɪ.kə.b|l̩ **-ly** -li **-leness** -l̩.nəs, -nɪs
unmitigated ʌnˈmɪt.ɪ.geɪ.tɪd, ˌʌn-, ˈ-ə- ⓊⓈ -ˈmɪt̬.ə.geɪ.t̬ɪd
unmixed ʌnˈmɪkst, ˌʌn-
unmodifiable ʌnˈmɒd.ɪ.faɪ.ə.bl̩, ˌʌn- ⓊⓈ -ˈmɑː.dɪ-
unmodified ʌnˈmɒd.ɪ.faɪd, ˌʌn- ⓊⓈ -ˈmɑː.dɪ-
unmolested ˌʌn.məʊˈles.tɪd ⓊⓈ -məˈ-
unmounted ʌnˈmaʊn.tɪd, ˌʌn- ⓊⓈ -t̬ɪd
unmourned ʌnˈmɔːnd, ˌʌn- ⓊⓈ -ˈmɔːrnd
unmov(e)able ʌnˈmuː.və.bl̩, ˌʌn-
unmoved ʌnˈmuːvd, ˌʌn-
unmuffl|e ʌnˈmʌf.l̩, ˌʌn- **-es** -z **-ing** -ɪŋ, -ˈmʌf.lɪŋ **-ed** -d
unmusic|al ʌnˈmjuː.zɪ.k|ᵊl, ˌʌn- **-ally** -ᵊl.i, -li
unmuzzl|e ʌnˈmʌz.l̩, ˌʌn- **-es** -z **-ing** -ˈmʌz.lɪŋ **-ed** -d
unnamed ʌnˈneɪmd, ˌʌn-
unnatural ʌnˈnætʃ.ᵊr.ᵊl, ˌʌn-, -ʊ.rᵊl ⓊⓈ -ɚ.əl, ˈ-rᵊl **-ly** -i **-ness** -nəs, -nɪs
unnavigable ʌnˈnæv.ɪ.gə.bl̩, ˌʌn-
unnecessarily ʌnˈnes.ə.sᵊr.ᵊl.i, ˌʌn-, ˈ-ɪ-, -ɪ.li; -ˌnes.əˈser-, -ɪˈ- ⓊⓈ -ˌnes.əˈser-; -ˈnes.ə.ser-
unnecessary ʌnˈnes.ə.sᵊr.i, ˌʌn-, ˈ-ɪ-, -ser- ⓊⓈ -ser-
unneighbo(u)rl|y ʌnˈneɪ.bᵊl|l.i, ˌʌn- ⓊⓈ -bɚ.l|i **-iness** -ɪ.nəs, -ɪ.nɪs
unnerv|e ʌnˈnɜːv, ˌʌn- ⓊⓈ -ˈnɜːrv **-es** -z **-ing/ly** -ɪŋ/li **-ed** -d
unnoticeab|le ʌnˈnəʊ.tɪ.sə.b|l̩, ˌʌn-, -tə- ⓊⓈ -ˈnoʊ.t̬ə- **-ly** -li
unnoticed ʌnˈnəʊ.tɪst, ˌʌn- ⓊⓈ -ˈnoʊ.t̬ɪst
unnumbered ʌnˈnʌm.bəd, ˌʌn- ⓊⓈ -bɚd
UNO ˈjuː.nəʊ ⓊⓈ -noʊ
uno (U) ˈuː.nəʊ, ˈjuː- ⓊⓈ -noʊ ˌ**Fiat ˈUno**
unobjectionab|le ˌʌn.əbˈdʒək.ʃᵊn.ə.b|l̩, -ˈdʒekʃ.nə- **-ly** -li
unobliging ˌʌn.əˈblaɪ.dʒɪŋ **-ly** -li
unobliterated ˌʌn.əˈblɪt.ᵊr.eɪ.tɪd ⓊⓈ -ˈblɪt̬.ə.reɪ.t̬ɪd
unobservant ˌʌn.əbˈzɜː.vᵊnt ⓊⓈ -ˈzɜːr- **-ly** -li
unobserv|ed ˌʌn.əbˈzɜːv|d ⓊⓈ -ˈzɜːrv|d **-edly** -ɪd.li
unobstructed ˌʌn.əbˈstrʌk.tɪd
unobtainable ˌʌn.əbˈteɪ.nə.bl̩
unobtrusive ˌʌn.əbˈtruː.sɪv ⓊⓈ -əbˈ- **-ly** -li **-ness** -nəs, -nɪs
unoccupied ʌnˈɒk.jə.paɪd, ˌʌn-, -jʊ- ⓊⓈ -ˈɑː.kjə-
unoffending ˌʌn.əˈfen.dɪŋ

unoffensive ˌʌn.əˈfent.sɪv
unofficial ˌʌn.əˈfɪʃ.ᵊl **-ly** -li
unopened ʌnˈəʊ.pᵊnd, ʌn- US -ˈoʊ-
unopposed ˌʌn.əˈpəʊzd US -ˈpoʊzd
unordained ˌʌn.ɔːˈdeɪnd US -ɔːrˈ-
unordered ʌnˈɔː.dəd, ˌʌn- US -ˈɔːr.dɚd
unorganized, -ise- ʌnˈɔː.gᵊn.aɪzd, ˌʌn- US -ˈɔːr-
unorthodox ʌnˈɔː.θə.dɒks, ˌʌn- US -ˈɔːr.θə.dɑːks **-ly** -li
unorthodoxy ʌnˈɔː.θə.dɒk.si, ˌʌn- US -ˈɔːr.θə.dɑːk-
unostentatious ʌnˌɒs.tenˈteɪ.ʃəs, ˌʌn-, -tənˈ- US -ˌɑː.stənˈ- **-ly** -li **-ness** -nəs, -nɪs
unowned ʌnˈəʊnd, ˌʌn- US -ˈoʊnd
unpack ʌnˈpæk, ˌʌn-, ʌm-, ˌʌm- US ʌn-, ˌʌn- **-s** -s **-ing** -ɪŋ **-ed** -t **-er/s** -əʳ/z US -ɚ/z
unpaid ʌnˈpeɪd, ˌʌn-, ʌm-, ˌʌm- US ʌn-, ˌʌn-
unpaired ʌnˈpeəd, ˌʌn-, ʌm-, ˌʌm- US ʌnˈperd, ˌʌn-
unpalatability ʌnˌpæl.ə.təˈbɪl.ɪ.ti, ˌʌn-, ʌm-, ˌʌm-, -ɪ-, -ə.ti US ʌnˌpæl.ə.t̬əˈbɪl.ə.t̬i, ˌʌn-
unpalatab|le ʌnˈpæl.ə.tə.b|l̩, ˌʌn-, ʌm-, ˌʌm-, ˈ-ɪ- US ʌnˈpæl.ə.t̬ə-, ˌʌn- **-leness** -l̩.nəs, -nɪs
unparalleled ʌnˈpær.ᵊl.eld, ˌʌn-, ʌm-, ˌʌm- US ʌnˈper-, ˌʌn-, -ˈpær-
unpardonab|le ʌnˈpɑː.dᵊn.ə.b|l̩, ˌʌn-, ʌm-, ˌʌm-, -ˈpɑːd.nə- US ʌnˈpɑːr.dᵊn.ə-, ˌʌn-, -ˈpɑːrd.nə- **-ly** -li **-leness** -l̩.nəs, -nɪs
unpardonab|ly ʌnˈpɑː.dᵊn.ə.b|li, ˌʌn-, ʌm-, ˌʌm-, -ˈpɑːd.nə- US ʌnˈpɑːr.dᵊn.ə-, ˌʌn-, -ˈpɑːrd.nə-
unparliamentary ʌnˌpɑː.ləˈmen.tᵊr.i, ˌʌn-, ʌm-, ˌʌm-, -lɪˈ-, -li.əˈ- US ʌnˌpɑːr.ləˈmen.t̬ɚ-, ˌʌn-, ˈ-tri
unpasteurized, -ised ʌnˈpæs.tʃᵊr.aɪzd, ˌʌn-, ʌm-, ˌʌm-, -ˈpɑːs-, -tjᵊr-, -tᵊr- US ʌnˈpæs.tʃə.raɪzd, ˌʌn-, -tə-
unpatriotic ʌnˌpæt.riˈɒt.ɪk, ˌʌn-, ʌm-, ˌʌm-, -ˌpeɪ.triˈ- US ʌnˌpeɪ.triˈɑː.t̬ɪk, ˌʌn- **-ally** -ᵊl.i, -li
unpaved ʌnˈpeɪvd, ˌʌn-, ʌm-, ˌʌm- US ʌn-, ˌʌn-
unpeeled ʌnˈpiːld, ˌʌn-, ʌm-, ˌʌm- US ʌn-, ˌʌn-
unperceiv|able ˌʌn.pəˈsiː.v|ə.bl̩, ˌʌm- US ˌʌn.pɚˈ- **-ed** -d
unperforated ʌnˈpɜː.fᵊr.eɪ.tɪd, ˌʌn-, ʌm-, ˌʌm- US ʌnˈpɜːr.fə.reɪ.t̬ɪd, ˌʌn-
unperformed ˌʌn.pəˈfɔːmd, ˌʌm- US ˌʌn.pɚˈfɔːrmd
unpersuadable ˌʌn.pəˈsweɪ.də.bl̩, ˌʌm- US ˌʌn.pɚˈ-
unpersuaded ˌʌn.pəˈsweɪ.dɪd, ˌʌm- US ˌʌn.pɚˈ-
unpersuasive ˌʌn.pəˈsweɪ.sɪv, ˌʌm-, -zɪv US ˌʌn.pɚˈ-
unperturbable ˌʌn.pəˈtɜː.bə.bl̩, ˌʌm- US ˌʌn.pɚˈtɜːr-
unperturbed ˌʌn.pəˈtɜːbd, ˌʌm- US ˌʌn.pɚˈtɜːrbd
unphilosophic|al ʌnˌfɪl.əˈsɒf.ɪ.k|ᵊl US -ˈsɑː.fɪ- **-ally** -ᵊl.i, -li **-alness** -ᵊl.nəs, -nɪs
unpick ʌnˈpɪk, ˌʌn-, ʌm-, ˌʌm- US ʌn-, ˌʌn- **-s** -s **-ing** -ɪŋ **-ed** -t
unpiloted ʌnˈpaɪ.lə.tɪd, ˌʌn-, ʌm-, ˌʌm- US ʌnˈpaɪ.lə.t̬ɪd, ˌʌn-
unpin ʌnˈpɪn, ˌʌn-, ʌm-, ˌʌm- US ʌn-, ˌʌn- **-s** -z **-ning** -ɪŋ **-ned** -d
unpitying ʌnˈpɪt.i.ɪŋ, ˌʌn-, ʌm-, ˌʌm- US ʌnˈpɪt̬.i-, ˌʌn- **-ly** -li
unplaced ʌnˈpleɪst, ˌʌn-, ʌm-, ˌʌm- US ʌn-, ˌʌn-
unplanned ʌnˈplænd, ˌʌn-, ʌm-, ˌʌm- US ʌn-, ˌʌn-
unplayable ʌnˈpleɪ.ə.bl̩, ˌʌn-, ʌm-, ˌʌm- US ʌn-, ˌʌn-
unpleasant ʌnˈplez.ᵊnt, ˌʌn-, ʌm-, ˌʌm- US ʌn-, ˌʌn- **-ly** -li **-ness** -nəs, -nɪs
unpleasing ʌnˈpliː.zɪŋ, ˌʌn-, ʌm-, ˌʌm- US ʌn-, ˌʌn- **-ly** -li **-ness** -nəs, -nɪs
unplug ʌnˈplʌg, ˌʌn-, ʌm-, ˌʌm- US ʌn-, ˌʌn- **-s** -z **-ging** -ɪŋ **-ged** -d
unplumbed ʌnˈplʌmd, ˌʌn-, ʌm-, ˌʌm- US ʌn-, ˌʌm-
unpoetic|al ˌʌn.pəʊˈet.ɪ.k|ᵊl, ˌʌm- US ˌʌn.poʊˈet̬- **-ally** -ᵊl.i, -li **-alness** -ᵊl.nəs, -nɪs
unpolished ʌnˈpɒl.ɪʃt, ˌʌn-, ʌm-, ˌʌm- US ʌnˈpɑː.lɪʃt, ˌʌn-
unpolitical ˌʌn.pəˈlɪt.ɪ.kᵊl, ˌʌm- US ˌʌn.pəˈlɪt̬-
unpolluted ˌʌn.pəˈluː.tɪd, ˌʌm-, -ˈljuː- US ˌʌn.pəˈluː.t̬ɪd
unpopular ʌnˈpɒp.jə.ləʳ, ˌʌn-, ʌm-, ˌʌm-, -jʊ- US ʌnˈpɑː.pjə.lɚ, ˌʌn-
unpopularity ʌnˌpɒp.jəˈlær.ə.ti, ˌʌn-, ʌm-, ˌʌm-, -jʊˈ-, -ɪ.ti US ʌnˌpɑː.pjəˈler.ə.t̬i, ˌʌn-, -pjʊˈ-, -ˈlær-
unpractic|al ʌnˈpræk.tɪ.k|ᵊl, ˌʌn-, ʌm-, ˌʌm- US ʌn-, ˌʌn- **-ally** -ᵊl.i, -li
unpracticality ʌnˌpræk.tɪˈkæl.ə.ti, ˌʌn-, ʌm-, ˌʌm-, -təˈ-, -ɪ.ti US ʌnˌpræk.təˈkæl.ə.t̬i, ˌʌn-
unpractised, -iced ʌnˈpræk.tɪst, ˌʌn-, ʌm-, ˌʌm- US ʌn-, ˌʌn-
unprecedented ʌnˈpres.ɪ.dᵊn.tɪd, ˌʌn-, ʌm-, ˌʌm-, -ˈpriː.sɪ-, -den- US ʌnˈpres.ə.den.t̬ɪd, ˌʌn-
unpredictability ˌʌn.prɪˌdɪk.təˈbɪl.ɪ.ti, ˌʌm-, -prə-, -ɪ.ti US ˌʌn.prɪˌdɪk.təˈbɪl.ə.t̬i, -ˌpriː-
unpredictab|le ˌʌn.prɪˈdɪk.tə.b|l̩, ˌʌm-, -prəˈ- US ˌʌn.prɪˈ-, -priːˈ- **-ly** -li
unprejudiced ʌnˈpredʒ.ə.dɪst, ˌʌn-, ʌm-, ˌʌm-, ˈ-ʊ- US ʌnˈpredʒ.ə-, ˌʌn-
unpremeditated ˌʌn.priːˈmed.ɪ.teɪ.tɪd, ˌʌm-, -prɪˈ-, ˈ-ə- US ˌʌn.priːˈmed.ɪ.teɪ.t̬ɪd
unpre|pared ˌʌn.prɪ|ˈpeəd, ˌʌm-, -prəˈ- US ˌʌn.prɪ|ˈperd, -priːˈ- **-paredly** -ˈpeə.rɪd.li, -ˈpeəd.li US -ˈper.ɪd.li, -ˈperd.li **-paredness** -ˈpeə.rɪd.nəs, -ˈpeəd.nəs, -nɪs US -ˈper.ɪd.nəs, -ˈperd.nəs, -nɪs
unprepossessing ʌnˌpriː.pəˈzes.ɪŋ, ˌʌn-, ʌm-, ˌʌm- US ʌn-, ˌʌn- **-ly** -li
unpresentable ˌʌn.prɪˈzen.tə.bl̩, ˌʌm-, -prəˈ- US ˌʌn.prɪˈzen.t̬ə-, -priːˈ-
unpresuming ˌʌn.prɪˈzjuː.mɪŋ, ˌʌm-, -prəˈ-, -ˈzuː- US ˌʌn.prɪˈzuː-, -priːˈ-, -ˈzjuː-
unpretending ˌʌn.prɪˈten.dɪŋ, ˌʌm-, -prəˈ- US ˌʌn.prɪˈten.dɪŋ, -priːˈ- **-ly** -li
unpretentious ˌʌn.prɪˈten.tʃəs, ˌʌm-, -prəˈ- US ˌʌn.prɪˈ-, -priːˈ- **-ly** -li **-ness** -nəs, -nɪs
unpreventable ˌʌn.prɪˈven.tə.bl̩, ˌʌm-, -prəˈ- US ˌʌn.prɪˈven.t̬ə-, -priːˈ-
unpriced ʌnˈpraɪst, ˌʌn-, ʌm-, ˌʌm- US ʌn-, ˌʌn-
unprincipled ʌnˈprɪnt.sə.pl̩d, ˌʌn-, ʌm-, ˌʌm-, -sɪ- US ʌn-, ˌʌn-
unprintable ʌnˈprɪn.tə.bl̩, ˌʌn-, ʌm-, ˌʌm- US ʌnˈprɪn.t̬ə-, ˌʌn-
unprinted ʌnˈprɪn.tɪd, ˌʌn-, ʌm-, ˌʌm- US ʌnˈprɪn.t̬ɪd, ˌʌn-
unproclaimed ˌʌn.prəʊˈkleɪmd, ˌʌm- US ˌʌn.proʊˈ-, -prəˈ-
unprocurable ˌʌn.prəˈkjʊə.rə.bl̩, ˌʌm-, -ˈkjɔː- US ˌʌn.prəˈkjʊr.ə-, -proʊˈ-
unproductive ˌʌn.prəˈdʌk.tɪv, ˌʌm- US ˌʌn- **-ly** -li **-ness** -nəs, -nɪs
unprofessional ˌʌn.prəˈfeʃ.ᵊn.ᵊl, ˌʌm-, -ˈfeʃ.nᵊl US ˌʌn- **-ly** -i **-ness** -nəs, -nɪs
unprofitab|le ʌnˈprɒf.ɪ.tə.b|l̩, ˌʌn-, ʌm-, ˌʌm-, ˈ-ə- US ʌnˈprɑː.fɪ.t̬ə-, ˌʌn- **-ly** -li **-leness** -l̩.nəs, -nɪs
Unprofor ˈʌn.prə.fɔːʳ, ˈʌm- US ˈʌn.prə.fɔːr
unprohibited ˌʌn.prəʊˈhɪb.ɪ.tɪd, ˌʌm-, ˈ-ə- US ˌʌn.proʊˈhɪb.ə.t̬ɪd, -prəˈ-
unpromising ʌnˈprɒm.ɪ.sɪŋ, ˌʌn-, ʌm-, ˌʌm-, ˈ-ə- US ʌnˈprɑː.mə-, ˌʌn- **-ly** -li
unprompted ʌnˈprɒmp.tɪd, ˌʌn-, ʌm-, ˌʌm- US ʌnˈprɑːmp-, ˌʌn-
unpronounceable ˌʌn.prəˈnaʊnt.sə.bl̩, ˌʌm- US ˌʌn-
unprop ʌnˈprɒp, ˌʌn-, ʌm-, ˌʌn- US ʌnˈprɑːp, ˌʌn- **-s** -s **-ping** -ɪŋ **-ped** -t
unpropitious ˌʌn.prəˈpɪʃ.əs, ˌʌm- US ˌʌn.prəˈ-, -proʊˈ- **-ly** -li **-ness** -nəs, -nɪs

unprotected ˌʌn.prəˈtek.tɪd, ˌʌm- US ˌʌn-
unproved ʌnˈpruːvd, ˌʌn-, ʌm-, ˌʌm- US ʌn-, ˌʌn-
unproven ʌnˈpruː.vᵊn, ˌʌn-, ʌm-, ˌʌm-, -ˈprəʊ- US ʌnˈpruː-, ˌʌn-
unprovided ˌʌn.prəˈvaɪ.dɪd, ˌʌm- US ˌʌn-
unprovok|ed ˌʌn.prəˈvəʊk|t, ˌʌm- US ˌʌn.prəˈvoʊk|t **-edly** -ɪd.li, -t.li
unpublished ʌnˈpʌb.lɪʃt, ˌʌn-, ʌm-, ˌʌm- US ʌn-, ˌʌn-
unpunctual ʌnˈpʌŋk.tʃu.əl, ˌʌn-, ʌm-, ˌʌm-, -tʃʊəl, -tju.əl, -tjʊəl US ʌnˈpʌŋk.tʃu.əl, ˌʌn- **-ly** -i
unpunctuality ʌnˌpʌŋk.tʃuˈæl.ə.ti, ˌʌn-, ʌm-, ˌʌm-, -tjuˈ-, -ɪ.ti US ʌnˌpʌŋk.tʃuˈæl.ə.t̬i, ˌʌn-
unpunished ʌnˈpʌn.ɪʃt, ˌʌn-, ʌm-, ˌʌm- US ʌn-, ˌʌn-
unputdownable ˌʌn.pʊtˈdaʊ.nə.bl̩, ˌʌm- US ˌʌn-
unqualified ʌnˈkwɒl.ɪ.faɪd, ˌʌn-, ʌŋ-, ˌʌŋ-, ˈ-ə- US ʌnˈkwɑː.lə-, ˌʌn-
unquenchable ʌnˈkwen.tʃə.bl̩, ˌʌn-, ʌŋ-, ˌʌŋ- US ʌn-, ˌʌn-
unquestionab|le ʌnˈkwes.tʃə.nə.b|l̩, ˌʌn-, ʌŋ-, ˌʌŋ-, -ˈkweʃ- US ʌnˈkwes.tʃə-, ˌʌn-, -tjə- **-ly** -li **-leness** -l̩.nəs, -nɪs
unquestioned ʌnˈkwes.tʃənd, ˌʌn-, ʌŋ-, ˌʌŋ-, -ˈkweʃ- US ʌnˈkwes.tʃənd, ˌʌn-, -tjənd
unquestioning ʌnˈkwes.tʃə.nɪŋ, ˌʌn-, ʌŋ-, ˌʌŋ-, -ˈkweʃ- US ʌnˈkwes.tʃə-, ˌʌn-, -tjə- **-ly** -li
unquiet ʌnˈkwaɪət, ʌŋ- **-ly** -li **-ness** -nəs, -nɪs
unquote ʌnˈkwəʊt, ˌʌn-, ʌŋ-, ˌʌŋ- US ʌnˈkwoʊt, ˌʌn-
unravel ʌnˈræv.ᵊl, ˌʌn- **-s** -z **-(l)ing** -ɪŋ, -ˈræv.lɪŋ **-(l)ed** -d **-(l)er/s** -əʳ/z, -ɚ/z US -ˈræv.lɚ/z, -lɚ/z
unread ʌnˈred, ˌʌn-
unreadable ʌnˈriː.də.bl̩, ˌʌn- **-ness** -nəs, -nɪs
unread|y ʌnˈred|.i, ˌʌn- **-ily** -ɪ.li, -ᵊl.i **-iness** -ɪ.nəs, -ɪ.nɪs
unreal ʌnˈrɪəl, ˌʌn- US -ˈriːl, -ˈriː.əl
unrealistic ˌʌn.rɪəˈlɪs.tɪk US -ri.əˈ- **-ally** -ᵊl.i, -li
unrealit|y ˌʌn.riˈæl.ə.t|i, -ɪ.t|i US -ə.t̬|i **-ies** -iz
unreason ʌnˈriː.zᵊn, ˌʌn-
unreasonab|le ʌnˈriː.zᵊn.ə.b|l̩, ˌʌn-, -ˈriːz.nə- **-ly** -li **-leness** -l̩.nəs, -nɪs
unreasoning ʌnˈriː.zᵊn.ɪŋ, ˌʌn-, -ˈriːz.nɪŋ
unreceived ˌʌn.rɪˈsiːvd, -rəˈ- US -rɪˈ-
unreciprocated ˌʌn.rɪˈsɪp.rə.keɪ.tɪd, -rəˈ- US -rɪˈsɪp.rə.keɪ.t̬ɪd
unreckoned ʌnˈrek.ᵊnd, ˌʌn-
unreclaimed ˌʌn.rɪˈkleɪmd
unrecognizable, -isa- ʌnˈrek.əg.naɪ.zə.bl̩, ˌʌn-, ˌʌn.rek.əgˈnaɪ- US ˌʌn.rek.əgˈnaɪ-, ʌnˈrek.əg.naɪ-, ˌʌn-
unrecognized, -ised ʌnˈrek.əg.naɪzd, ˌʌn-
unreconcilable ʌnˈrek.ᵊn.saɪ.lə.bl̩, ˌʌn-, ˌʌn.rek.ᵊnˈsaɪ-
unreconciled ʌnˈrek.ᵊn.saɪld, ˌʌn-
unreconstructed ˌʌn.riː.kənˈstrʌk.tɪd
unrecorded ˌʌn.rɪˈkɔː.dɪd, -rəˈ- US -rɪˈkɔːr-
unrecounted ˌʌn.rɪˈkaʊn.tɪd, -rəˈ- US -rɪˈkaʊn.t̬ɪd
unredeemable ˌʌn.rɪˈdiː.mə.bl̩, -rəˈ- US -rɪˈ-
unredeemed ˌʌn.rɪˈdiːmd, -rəˈ- US -rɪˈ-
unrefined ˌʌn.rɪˈfaɪnd, -rəˈ- US -rɪˈ-
unreflecting ˌʌn.rɪˈflek.tɪŋ, -rəˈ- US -rɪˈ-
unreformed ˌʌn.rɪˈfɔːmd, -rəˈ- US -rɪˈfɔːrmd
unrefuted ˌʌn.rɪˈfjuː.tɪd, -rəˈ- US -rɪˈfjuː.t̬ɪd
unregenerate ˌʌn.rɪˈdʒen.ᵊr.ət, -rəˈ-, -ɪt US -rəˈdʒen.ɚ.ɪt
unregistered ʌnˈredʒ.ɪ.stəd, ˌʌn- US -stɚd
unrehearsed ˌʌn.rɪˈhɜːst, -rəˈ- US -rɪˈhɜːrst
unrelated ˌʌn.rɪˈleɪ.tɪd, -rəˈ- US -rɪˈleɪ.t̬ɪd
unrelaxed ˌʌn.rɪˈlækst, -rəˈ- US -rɪˈ-
unrelenting ˌʌn.rɪˈlen.tɪŋ, -rəˈ- US -rɪˈlen.t̬ɪŋ **-ly** -li **-ness** -nəs, -nɪs
unreliability ˌʌn.rɪ.laɪ.əˈbɪl.ɪ.ti, -rə-, -ə.ti US -rɪ.laɪ.əˈbɪl.ə.t̬i
unreliab|le ˌʌn.rɪˈlaɪ.ə.b|l̩, -rəˈ- US -rɪˈ- **-ly** -li **-leness** -l̩.nəs, -nɪs
unreliev|ed ˌʌn.rɪˈliːv|d, -rəˈ- US -rɪˈ- **-edly** -ɪd.li
unremembered ˌʌn.rɪˈmem.bəd, -rəˈ- US -rɪˈmem.bɚd
unremitting ˌʌn.rɪˈmɪt.ɪŋ, -rəˈ- US -rɪˈmɪt̬- **-ly** -li **-ness** -nəs, -nɪs
unremonstrative ˌʌn.rɪˈmɒnt.strə.tɪv, -rəˈ- US -rɪˈmɑːnt.strə.t̬ɪv
unremovable ˌʌn.rɪˈmuː.və.bl̩, -rəˈ- US -rɪˈ-
unremunerative ˌʌn.rɪˈmjuː.nᵊr.ə.tɪv, -rəˈ- US -rɪˈmjuː.nɚ.ə.t̬ɪv, -nə.reɪ-
unrepaired ˌʌn.rɪˈpeəd US -ˈperd
unrepeatable ˌʌn.rɪˈpiː.tə.bl̩, -rəˈ- US -rɪˈpiː.t̬ə-
unrepentant ˌʌn.rɪˈpen.tənt, -rəˈ- US -rɪˈpen.tᵊnt
unreplaceable ˌʌn.rɪˈpleɪs.ə.bl̩
unreported ˌʌn.rɪˈpɔː.tɪd, -rəˈ- US -rɪˈpɔːr.t̬ɪd
unrepresentative ˌʌn.rep.rɪˈzen.tə.tɪv US -t̬ə.t̬ɪv
unrepresented ˌʌn.rep.rɪˈzen.tɪd US -t̬ɪd
unrequested ˌʌn.rɪˈkwes.tɪd, -rəˈ- US -rɪˈ-
unrequited ˌʌn.rɪˈkwaɪ.tɪd, -rəˈ- US -rɪˈkwaɪ.t̬ɪd *stress shift:* ˌ**unrequited** ˈ**love**
unreserv|ed ˌʌn.rɪˈzɜːv|d, -rəˈ- US -rɪˈzɜːrv|d **-edly** -ɪd.li **-edness** -ɪd.nəs, -nɪs
unresisting ˌʌn.rɪˈzɪs.tɪŋ, -rəˈ- US -rɪˈ- **-ly** -li
unresolved ˌʌn.rɪˈzɒlvd, -rəˈ- US -rɪˈzɑːlvd
unresponsive ˌʌn.rɪˈspɒnt.sɪv, -rəˈ- US -rɪˈspɑːnt- **-ly** -li **-ness** -nəs, -nɪs
unrest ʌnˈrest, ˌʌn- US ʌnˈrest, ˌʌn-, ˈ--
unrestful ʌnˈrest.fᵊl, ˌʌn-, -fʊl **-ly** -i **-ness** -nəs, -nɪs
unresting ʌnˈres.tɪŋ, ˌʌn-
unrestored ˌʌn.rɪˈstɔːd, -rəˈ- US -rɪˈstɔːrd
unrestrain|ed ˌʌn.rɪˈstreɪn|d, -rəˈ- US -rɪˈ- **-edly** -ɪd.li
unrestraint ˌʌn.rɪˈstreɪnt
unrestricted ˌʌn.rɪˈstrɪk.tɪd, -rəˈ- US -rɪˈ-
unretentive ˌʌn.rɪˈten.tɪv, -rəˈ- US -rɪˈten.t̬ɪv
unreveal|ed ˌʌn.rɪˈviːl|d, -rəˈ- US -rɪˈ- **-ing** -ɪŋ
unrevoked ˌʌn.rɪˈvəʊkt, -rəˈ- US -rɪˈvoʊkt
unrewarded ˌʌn.rɪˈwɔː.dɪd, -rəˈ- US -rɪˈwɔːr-
unriddl|e ʌnˈrɪd.l̩ **-es** -z **-ing** -ɪŋ **-ed** -d
unrighteous ʌnˈraɪ.tʃəs, -ti.əs US -tʃəs **-ly** -li **-ness** -nəs, -nɪs
unrightful ʌnˈraɪt.fᵊl, ˌʌn-, -fʊl **-ly** -i **-ness** -nəs, -nɪs
unripe ʌnˈraɪp, ˌʌn- **-ness** -nəs, -nɪs
unripeness ʌnˈraɪp.nəs, ˌʌn-, -nəs
unrivalled ʌnˈraɪ.vᵊld, ˌʌn-
unrob|e ʌnˈrəʊb, ˌʌn- US -ˈroʊb **-es** -z **-ing** -ɪŋ **-ed** -d
unroll ʌnˈrəʊl, ˌʌn- US -ˈroʊl **-s** -z **-ing** -ɪŋ **-ed** -d
unromantic ˌʌn.rəʊˈmæn.tɪk US -roʊˈmæn.t̬ɪk, -rəˈ- **-ally** -ᵊl.i, -li
unrounded ʌnˈraʊn.dɪd, ˌʌn-
unruffled ʌnˈrʌf.l̩d, ˌʌn-
unrul|y ʌnˈruː.l|i, ˌʌn- **-ier** -i.əʳ US -i.ɚ **-iest** -i.ɪst, -i.əst **-iness** -ɪ.nəs, -ɪ.nɪs
unsaddl|e ʌnˈsæd.l̩, ˌʌn- **-es** -z **-ing** -ɪŋ, -ˈsæd.lɪŋ **-ed** -d
unsafe ʌnˈseɪf, ˌʌn- **-ly** -li **-ness** -nəs, -nɪs
unsaid ʌnˈsed, ˌʌn-
unsal(e)able ʌnˈseɪ.lə.bl̩, ˌʌn-
unsalted ʌnˈsɔːl.tɪd, ˌʌn-, -ˈsɒl- US -ˈsɔːl.t̬ɪd, -sɑː-

unsanctified ʌn'sæŋk.tɪ.faɪd, ˌʌn-
unsanitary ʌn'sæn.ɪ.tᵊr.i, ˌʌn-, '-ə-, -tri ⓊⓈ -'sæn.ə.ter.i
unsatisfactor|y ʌnˌsæt.ɪs'fæk.tᵊr|.i, ˌʌn.sæt-, ˌʌnˌsæt- ⓊⓈ ʌnˌsæṭ-, ˌʌn- **-ily** -ᵊl.i, -ɪ.li **-iness** -ɪ.nəs, -ɪ.nɪs
unsatisf|ied ʌn'sæt.ɪs.f|aɪd, ˌʌn- ⓊⓈ -'sæṭ- **-ying** -aɪ.ɪŋ
unsaturated ʌn'sætʃ.ᵊr.eɪ.tɪd, ˌʌn-, -tʃʊ.reɪ-, -tjᵊr.eɪ, -tjʊ.reɪ- ⓊⓈ -'sætʃ.ə.reɪ.ṭɪd **unˌsaturated 'fat**
unsavo(u)r|y ʌn'seɪ.vᵊr|.i, ˌʌn- **-iness** -ɪ.nəs, -ɪ.nɪs
un|say ʌn|'seɪ, ˌʌn- **-says** -'sez **-saying** -'seɪ.ɪŋ **-said** -'sed **-sayable** -'seɪ.ə.bl̩
unscathed ʌn'skeɪðd, ˌʌn-
unscented ʌn'sen.tɪd, ˌʌn- ⓊⓈ -ṭɪd
unscheduled ʌn'ʃed.juːld, ˌʌn-, -'ʃedʒ.uːld, -'sked.juːld, -'skedʒ.uːld, -ᵊld ⓊⓈ -'skedʒ.ʊld, -uːld, -u.əld
unscholarly ʌn'skɒl.ə.li, ˌʌn- ⓊⓈ -'skɑː.lɚ-
unschooled ʌn'skuːld, ˌʌn-
unscientific ˌʌn.saɪən'tɪf.ɪk **-ally** -ᵊl.i, -li
unscrambl|e ʌn'skræm.bl̩, ˌʌn- **-es** -z **-ing** -ɪŋ, -'skræm.blɪŋ **-ed** -d
unscrew ʌn'skruː, ˌʌn- **-s** -z **-ing** -ɪŋ **-ed** -d
unscripted ʌn'skrɪp.tɪd, ˌʌn-
unscriptural ʌn'skrɪp.tʃᵊr.ᵊl, ˌʌn-, -tʃʊ.rᵊl ⓊⓈ -tʃɚ.ᵊl **-ly** -i
unscrupulous ʌn'skruː.pjə.ləs, ˌʌn-, -pjʊ- ⓊⓈ -pjə- **-ly** -li **-ness** -nəs, -nɪs
unseal ʌn'siːl, ˌʌn- **-s** -z **-ing** -ɪŋ **-ed** -d
unseasonab|le ʌn'siː.zᵊn.ə.b|l̩, ˌʌn-, -'siːz.nə- **-ly** -li **-leness** -l̩.nəs, -nɪs
unseasoned ʌn'siː.zᵊnd, ˌʌn-
un|seat ʌn|'siːt, ˌʌn- **-seats** -'siːts **-seating** -'siː.tɪŋ ⓊⓈ -'siː.ṭɪŋ **-seated** -'siː.tɪd ⓊⓈ -'siː.ṭɪd
unseaworth|y ʌn'siːˌwɜː.ð|i, ˌʌn- ⓊⓈ -ˌwɜːr- **-iness** -ɪ.nəs, -ɪ.nɪs
unsectarian ˌʌn.sek'teə.ri.ən ⓊⓈ -'ter.i-
unsecured ˌʌn.sɪ'kjʊəd, -sə'-, -'kjɔːd ⓊⓈ -'kjʊrd
unseeded ʌn'siː.dɪd, ˌʌn-
unseeing ʌn'siː.ɪŋ, ˌʌn- **-ly** -li
unseeml|y ʌn'siːm.l|i ⓊⓈ ˌʌn- **-iness** -ɪ.nəs, -ɪ.nɪs
unseen ʌn'siːn, ˌʌn-
unselfconscious ˌʌn.self'kɒn.tʃəs ⓊⓈ -'kɑːn- **-ly** -li **-ness** -nəs, -nɪs
unselfish ʌn'sel.fɪʃ, ˌʌn- **-ly** -li **-ness** -nəs, -nɪs
unsensational ˌʌn.sen'seɪ.ʃᵊn.ᵊl, -sᵊn'-, -'seɪʃ.nᵊl
unsensitive ʌn'sent.sə.tɪv, ˌʌn-, -sɪ- ⓊⓈ -sə.ṭɪv **-ly** -li **-ness** -nəs, -nɪs
unsentimental ˌʌn.sen.tɪ'men.tᵊl ⓊⓈ -ṭᵊl **-ly** -i
unserviceable ʌn'sɜː.vɪ.sə.bl̩, ˌʌn- ⓊⓈ -'sɜːr-
unsettl|e ʌn'set.l̩, ˌʌn- ⓊⓈ -'seṭ- **-es** -z **-ing/ly** -ɪŋ/li, -'set.lɪŋ/li **-ness** -nəs, -nɪs
unsettled ʌn'set.l̩d ⓊⓈ -'seṭ-
unsevered ʌn'sev.əd, ˌʌn- ⓊⓈ -ɚd
unshackl|e ʌn'ʃæk.l̩, ˌʌn- **-es** -z **-ing** -ɪŋ, -'ʃæk.lɪŋ **-ed** -d
unshak(e)able ʌn'ʃeɪ.kə.bl̩, ˌʌn-
unshaken ʌn'ʃeɪ.kᵊn, ˌʌn-
unshapely ʌn'ʃeɪ.pli, ˌʌn-
unshaven ʌn'ʃeɪ.vᵊn, ˌʌn-
unsheath|e ʌn'ʃiːð, ˌʌn- **-es** -z **-ing** -ɪŋ **-ed** -d
unship ʌn'ʃɪp, ˌʌn- **-s** -s **-ping** -ɪŋ **-ped** -t
unshockability ˌʌn.ʃɒk.ə'bɪl.ɪ.ti, -ˌʃɒk-, -ə.ti ⓊⓈ -ʃɑː.kə'bɪl.ə.ṭi, -ˌʃɑː-
unshockable ʌn'ʃɒk.ə.bl̩, ˌʌn- ⓊⓈ -'ʃɑː.kə-
unshod ʌn'ʃɒd, ˌʌn- ⓊⓈ -'ʃɑːd
unshorn ʌn'ʃɔːn, ˌʌn- ⓊⓈ -'ʃɔːrn
unshrinkable ʌn'ʃrɪŋ.kə.bl̩, ˌʌn-
unshrinking ʌn'ʃrɪŋ.kɪŋ, ˌʌn- **-ly** -li
unsighted ʌn'saɪ.tɪd, ˌʌn- ⓊⓈ -ṭɪd
unsightl|y ʌn'saɪt.l|i, ˌʌn- **-ier** -i.əʳ ⓊⓈ -i.ɚ **-iest** -i.ɪst, -i.əst **-iness** -ɪ.nəs, -ɪ.nɪs
unsigned ʌn'saɪnd, ˌʌn-
unskilful ʌn'skɪl.fᵊl, ˌʌn-, -fʊl **-ly** -i
unskilled ʌn'skɪld, ˌʌn- **ˌunskilled 'worker**
unslaked ʌn'sleɪkt, ˌʌn-
unsliced ʌn'slaɪst
unsociability ˌʌn.səʊ.ʃə'bɪl.ɪ.ti, -ˌsəʊ-, -ə.ti ⓊⓈ -soʊ.ʃə'bɪl.ə.ṭi, -ˌsoʊ-
unsociab|le ʌn'səʊ.ʃə.b|l̩, ˌʌn- ⓊⓈ -'soʊ- **-ly** -li **-leness** -l̩.nəs, -nɪs
unsocial ʌn'səʊ.ʃᵊl, ˌʌn- ⓊⓈ -'soʊ- **-ly** -i **ˌunsocial 'hours, unˌsocial 'hours**
unsold ʌn'səʊld, ˌʌn- ⓊⓈ -'soʊld
unsold|er ʌn'səʊl.d|əʳ, ˌʌn-, -'sɒl- ⓊⓈ -'sɑː.d|ɚ **-ers** -əz ⓊⓈ -ɚz **-ering** -ᵊr.ɪŋ **-ered** -əd ⓊⓈ -ɚd
unsolicited ˌʌn.sə'lɪs.ɪ.tɪd ⓊⓈ -ṭɪd
unsolved ʌn'sɒlvd, ˌʌn- ⓊⓈ -'sɑːlvd, -'sɔːlvd
unsophisticated ˌʌn.sə'fɪs.tɪ.keɪ.tɪd, -tə- ⓊⓈ -tə.keɪ.ṭɪd **-ly** -li **-ness** -nəs, -nɪs
unsophistication ˌʌn.səˌfɪs.tɪ'keɪ.ʃᵊn, -tə'-
unsorted ʌn'sɔː.tɪd, ˌʌn- ⓊⓈ -'sɔːr.ṭɪd
unsought ʌn'sɔːt, ˌʌn- ⓊⓈ -'sɑːt, -'sɔːt
unsound ʌn'saʊnd, ˌʌn- **-ly** -li **-ness** -nəs, -nɪs
unsparing ʌn'speə.rɪŋ, ˌʌn- ⓊⓈ -'sper.ɪŋ **-ly** -li **-ness** -nəs, -nɪs
unspeakab|le ʌn'spiː.kə.b|l̩, ˌʌn- **-ly** -li
unspecified ʌn'spes.ɪ.faɪd, ˌʌn-, -'ə-
unspent ʌn'spent, ˌʌn-
unspoiled ʌn'spɔɪlt, ˌʌn-, -'spɔɪld ⓊⓈ -'spɔɪld
unspoilt ʌn'spɔɪlt, ˌʌn-
unspoken ʌn'spəʊ.kᵊn, ˌʌn- ⓊⓈ -'spoʊ-
unsporting ʌn'spɔː.tɪŋ, ˌʌn- ⓊⓈ -'spɔːr.ṭɪŋ **-ly** -li **-ness** -nəs, -nɪs
unsportsmanlike ʌn'spɔːts.mən.laɪk, ˌʌn- ⓊⓈ -'spɔːrts-
unspotted ʌn'spɒt.ɪd, ˌʌn- ⓊⓈ -'spɑː.ṭɪd
Unst ʌnᵗst
unstable ʌn'steɪ.bl̩, ˌʌn- **-ness** -nəs, -nɪs
unstack ʌn'stæk, ˌʌn- **-s** -s **-ing** -ɪŋ **-ed** -t
unstamped ʌn'stæmᵖt, ˌʌn-
unstarched ʌn'stɑːtʃt, ˌʌn- ⓊⓈ -'stɑːrtʃt
unstated ʌn'steɪ.tɪd ⓊⓈ -ṭɪd
unstatesmanlike ʌn'steɪts.mən.laɪk, ˌʌn-
unsteadfast ʌn'sted.fɑːst, ˌʌn-, -fəst ⓊⓈ -fæst, -fəst **-ly** -li **-ness** -nəs, -nɪs
unstead|y ʌn'sted|.i, ˌʌn- **-ier** -i.əʳ ⓊⓈ -i.ɚ **-iest** -i.ɪst, -i.əst **-ily** -ɪ.li, -ᵊl.i **-iness** -ɪ.nəs, -ɪ.nɪs
unstick ʌn'stɪk, ˌʌn- **-s** -s **-ing** -ɪŋ **unstuck** ʌn'stʌk, ˌʌn-
unstinted ʌn'stɪn.tɪd, ˌʌn- ⓊⓈ -ṭɪd
unstinting ʌn'stɪn.tɪŋ, ˌʌn- ⓊⓈ -ṭɪŋ **-ly** -li
unstitch ʌn'stɪtʃ, ˌʌn- **-es** -ɪz **-ing** -ɪŋ **-ed** -t
unstop ʌn'stɒp, ˌʌn- ⓊⓈ -'stɑːp **-s** -s **-ping** -ɪŋ **-ped** -t
unstoppab|le ʌn'stɒp.ə.b|l̩, ˌʌn- ⓊⓈ -'stɑː.pə- **-ly** -li
unstrap ʌn'stræp, ˌʌn- **-s** -s **-ping** -ɪŋ **-ped** -t
unstressed ʌn'strest, ˌʌn-
unstructured ʌn'strʌk.tʃəd ⓊⓈ -tʃɚd
unstrung ʌn'strʌŋ, ˌʌn-
unstuck (*from* **unstick**) ʌn'stʌk, ˌʌn- **ˌcome un'stuck**
unstudied ʌn'stʌd.ɪd, ˌʌn-
unstylish ʌn'staɪ.lɪʃ, ˌʌn- **-ly** -li
unsubmissive ˌʌn.səb'mɪs.ɪv **-ly** -li **-ness** -nəs, -nɪs
unsubstantial ˌʌn.səb'stæn.ᵗʃᵊl, -'stɑːn- ⓊⓈ -'stænᵗ.ʃᵊl **-ly** -i
unsubstantiality ˌʌn.səbˌstæn.ᵗʃi'æl.ə.ti, -ˌstɑːn-, -ɪ.ti ⓊⓈ -ˌstænᵗ.ʃi'æl.ə.ṭi
unsubstantiated ˌʌn.səb'stæn.ᵗʃi.eɪ.tɪd, -'stɑːn- ⓊⓈ -'stænᵗ.ʃi.eɪ.ṭɪd
unsuccess ˌʌn.sək'ses, '--- ⓊⓈ ˌʌn.sək'ses

unsuccessful ˌʌn.sək'ses.fᵊl, -fʊl **-ly** -i **-ness** -nəs, -nɪs
unsuitability ˌʌn.suː.tə'bɪl.ə.ti, -sjuː-, ʌnˌsuː-, -ˌsjuː-, -ɪ.ti (US) ˌʌn.suː.t̬ə'bɪl.ə.t̬i, ʌnˌsuː-
unsuitab|le ʌn'suː.tə.b|l̩, ˌʌn-, -'sjuː- (US) -'suː.t̬ə- **-ly** -li **-leness** -l̩.nəs, -nɪs
unsuited ʌn'suː.tɪd, ˌʌn-, -'sjuː- (US) -'suː.t̬ɪd
unsullied ʌn'sʌl.ɪd, ˌʌn-
unsung ʌn'sʌŋ, ˌʌn-
unsupportab|le ˌʌn.sə'pɔː.tə.b|l̩ (US) -'pɔːr.t̬ə- **-ly** -li **-leness** -l̩.nəs, -nɪs
unsupported ˌʌn.sə'pɔː.tɪd (US) -'pɔːr.t̬ɪd
unsure ʌn'ʃʊəʳ, ˌʌn-, -ʃɔːʳ (US) -'ʃʊr
unsurmountab|le ˌʌn.sə'maʊn.tə.b|l̩ (US) -sɚ'maʊn.t̬ə- **-ly** -li
unsurpassable ˌʌn.sə'pɑː.sə.bl̩ (US) -sɚ'pæs.ə-
unsurpassed ˌʌn.sə'pɑːst (US) -sɚ'pæst
unsurprising ʌn.sə'praɪ.zɪŋ (US) -sɚ- **-ly** -li
unsusceptibility ˌʌn.səˌsep.tə'bɪl.ə.ti, -tɪ'-, -ɪ.ti (US) -ə.t̬i
unsusceptible ˌʌn.sə'sep.tə.bl̩, -tɪ-
unsuspected ˌʌn.sə'spek.tɪd
unsuspecting ˌʌn.sə'spek.tɪŋ **-ly** -li **-ness** -nəs, -nɪs
unsuspicious ˌʌn.sə'spɪʃ.əs **-ly** -li **-ness** -nəs, -nɪs
unsweetened ʌn'swiː.tᵊnd, ˌʌn-
unswerving ʌn'swɜː.vɪŋ, ˌʌn- (US) -'swɜːr- **-ly** -li
unsymmetric ˌʌn.sɪ'met.rɪk, -sə'- **-al** -ᵊl **-ally** -ᵊl.i, -li
unsymmetry ʌn'sɪm.ɪ.tri, ˌʌn-, '-ə-
unsympathetic ˌʌn.sɪm.pə'θet.ɪk, -ˌsɪm- (US) -'θet̬- **-ally** -ᵊl.i, -li
unsystematic ˌʌn.sɪ.stə'mæt.ɪk, -ˌsɪs.tə'-, -tɪ'- (US) -stə'mæt̬- **-al** -ᵊl **-ally** -ᵊl.i, -li
untainted ʌn'teɪn.tɪd, ˌʌn- (US) -t̬ɪd
untamable, untameable ʌn'teɪ.mə.bl̩, ˌʌn-
untangl|e ʌn'tæŋ.gl̩, ˌʌn- **-es** -z **-ing** -ɪŋ, -'tæŋ.glɪŋ **-ed** -d
untapped ʌn'tæpt, ˌʌn-
untarnished ʌn'tɑː.nɪʃt, ˌʌn- (US) -'tɑːr-
untaught ʌn'tɔːt, ˌʌn- (US) -'tɑːt, -'tɔːt
untaxed ʌn'tækst, ˌʌn-
unteachable ʌn'tiː.tʃə.bl̩, ˌʌn-
untempered ʌn'tem.pəd, ˌʌn- (US) -pɚd
untenability ˌʌn.ten.ə'bɪl.ɪ.ti, -ˌten-, -ə.ti (US) -ə.t̬i
untenable ʌn'ten.ə.bl̩, ˌʌn-
untenanted ʌn'ten.ən.tɪd, ˌʌn- (US) -t̬ɪd
unthankful ʌn'θæŋk.fᵊl, ˌʌn-, -fʊl **-ly** -i **-ness** -nəs, -nɪs
unthinka|ble ʌn'θɪŋ.kə|.bl̩, ˌʌn- **-bly** -bli
unthinking ʌn'θɪŋ.kɪŋ, ˌʌn- **-ly** -li
unthought ʌn'θɔːt (US) -'θɑːt, -'θɔːt
unˈthought of
unthoughtful ʌn'θɔːt.fᵊl, ˌʌn-, -fʊl (US) -'θɑːt-, -'θɔːt- **-ly** -i **-ness** -nəs, -nɪs
unthread ʌn'θred, ˌʌn- **-s** -z **-ing** -ɪŋ **-ed** -ɪd
untid|y ʌn'taɪ.d|i, ˌʌn- **-ier** -i.əʳ (US) -i.ɚ **-iest** -i.ɪst, -i.əst **-ily** -ɪ.li, -ᵊl.i **-iness** -ɪ.nəs, -ɪ.nɪs **-ies** -iz **-ying** -i.ɪŋ **-ied** -id
un|tie ʌn|'taɪ, ˌʌn- **-ties** -'taɪz **-tying** -'taɪ.ɪŋ **-tied** -'taɪd
until ᵊn'tɪl, ʌn'tɪl
Note: There is an occasional weak form /'ʌn.tɪl, -tᵊl/ in stress-shift environments (e.g. ˌuntil 'death), but this is rare.
untimel|y ʌn'taɪm.l|i, ˌʌn- **-iness** -ɪ.nəs, -ɪ.nɪs
untinged ʌn'tɪndʒd, ˌʌn-
untiring ʌn'taɪə.rɪŋ, ˌʌn- (US) -'taɪ- **-ly** -li **-ness** -nəs, -nɪs
untitled ʌn'taɪ.tl̩d, ˌʌn- (US) -t̬l̩d
unto 'ʌn.tuː, -tu, -tə (US) -tuː, -t̬ə, -tu
untold ʌn'təʊld, ˌʌn- (US) -'toʊld
untouchability ʌnˌtʌtʃ.ə'bɪl.ə.ti, ˌʌn-, -ɪ.ti (US) -ə.t̬i
untouchable ʌn'tʌtʃ.ə.bl̩, ˌʌn- **-s** -z
untouched ʌn'tʌtʃt, ˌʌn-
untoward ˌʌn.tə'wɔːd, -tʊ'-; -'təʊəd (US) -'tɔːrd, tə'wɔːrd **-ly** -li **-ness** -nəs, -nɪs
untraceable ʌn'treɪ.sə.bl̩, ˌʌn-
untrained ʌn'treɪnd, ˌʌn-
untrammel(l)ed ʌn'træm.ᵊld, ˌʌn-
untransferable ˌʌn.træn*t*s'fɜː.rə.bl̩, -trɑːn*t*s'-, ʌn'træn*t*s.fɜː-, -'trɑːn*t*s- (US) ˌʌn.træn*t*s'fɜːr.ə-, ʌn'træn*t*s.fɚ-
untranslat|able ˌʌn.træn*t*'sleɪ.t|ə.bl̩, -trɑːn*t*'-, -trᵊn'-; -trænz'leɪ-, -trɑːnz'-, -trᵊnz'- (US) -træn'sleɪ.t̬|ə-, -trænz'leɪ- **-ed** -ɪd
untried ʌn'traɪd, ˌʌn-
untrimmed ʌn'trɪmd, ˌʌn-
untrodden ʌn'trɒd.ᵊn, ˌʌn- (US) -'trɑː.dᵊn
untroubled ʌn'trʌb.l̩d, ˌʌn-
untrue ʌn'truː, ˌʌn- **-ness** -nəs, -nɪs
untruly ʌn'truː.li, ˌʌn-
untrustworth|y ʌn'trʌstˌwɜː.ð|i, ˌʌn- (US) -ˌwɜːr- **-ily** -ɪ.li, -ᵊl.i **-iness** -ɪ.nəs, -ɪ.nɪs
untru|th ʌn'truː|θ, ˌʌn- **-ths** -ðz, -θs
untruthful ʌn'truːθ.fᵊl, ˌʌn-, -fʊl **-ly** -i **-ness** -nəs, -nɪs
untuck ʌn'tʌk, ˌʌn- **-s** -s **-ing** -ɪŋ **-ed** -t
unturned ʌn'tɜːnd, ˌʌn- (US) -'tɜːrnd
ˌleave no ˌstone un'turned, leave ˌno ˌstone un'turned
untutored ʌn'tjuː.təd, ˌʌn- (US) -'tuː.t̬ɚd, -'tjuː-
untwist ʌn'twɪst, ˌʌn- **-s** -s **-ing** -ɪŋ **-ed** -ɪd
unused *not made use of:* ʌn'juːzd, ˌʌn-
unused *not accustomed:* ʌn'juːst, ˌʌn-
unusual ʌn'juː.ʒᵊl, ˌʌn-, -ʒu.əl (US) -ʒu.əl, -'juːʒ.*w*əl **-ly** -i **-ness** -nəs, -nɪs
unutterab|le ʌn'ʌt.ᵊr.ə.b|l̩, ˌʌn- (US) -'ʌt̬- **-ly** -li **-leness** -l̩.nəs, -nɪs
unvariable ʌn'veə.ri.ə.bl̩, ˌʌn- (US) -'ver.i-
unvaried ʌn'veə.rid, ˌʌn- (US) -'ver.id, -'vær-
unvarnished ʌn'vɑː.nɪʃt, ˌʌn- (US) -'vɑːr-
unvarying ʌn'veə.ri.ɪŋ, ˌʌn- (US) -'ver.i-, -'vaer.i-
unveil ʌn'veɪl, ˌʌn- **-s** -z **-ing** -ɪŋ **-ed** -d
unventilated ʌn'ven.tɪ.leɪ.tɪd, ˌʌn-, -tə- (US) -t̬ə.leɪ.t̬ɪd
unversed ʌn'vɜːst, ˌʌn- (US) -'vɜːrst
unvoiced ʌn'vɔɪst, ˌʌn-
unwaged ʌn'weɪdʒd, ˌʌn-
unwanted ʌn'wɒn.tɪd, ˌʌn- (US) -'wɑːn.t̬ɪd
unwarlike ʌn'wɔː.laɪk, ˌʌn- (US) -'wɔːr-
unwarmed ʌn'wɔːmd, ˌʌn- (US) -'wɔːrmd
unwarned ʌn'wɔːnd, ˌʌn- (US) -'wɔːrnd
unwarrantab|le ʌn'wɒr.ᵊn.tə.b|l̩, ˌʌn- (US) -'wɔːr.ᵊn.t̬ə-, -'wɑːr- **-ly** -li **-leness** -l̩.nəs, -nɪs
unwarranted ʌn'wɒr.ᵊn.tɪd, ˌʌn- (US) -'wɔːr.ᵊn.t̬ɪd, -'wɑːr-
unwar|y ʌn'weə.r|i, ˌʌn- (US) -'wer|.i **-ily** -ɪ.li, -ᵊl.i **-iness** -ɪ.nəs, -ɪ.nɪs
unwashed ʌn'wɒʃt, ˌʌn- (US) -'wɑːʃt, -'wɔːʃt
unwavering ʌn'weɪ.vᵊr.ɪŋ, ˌʌn- **-ly** -li
unwearable ʌn'weə.rə.bl̩, ˌʌn- (US) -'wer.ə-
unwearied ʌn'wɪə.rid, ˌʌn- (US) -'wɪr.id
unwearying ʌn'wɪə.ri.ɪŋ, ˌʌn- (US) -'wɪr.i-
unwed ʌn'wed, ˌʌn-
unwelcome ʌn'wel.kəm, ˌʌn-
unwell ʌn'wel, ˌʌn-
unwholesome ʌn'həʊl.səm, ˌʌn- (US) -'hoʊl- **-ly** -li **-ness** -nəs, -nɪs
unwield|y ʌn'wiːl.d|i, ˌʌn- **-ier** -i.əʳ (US) -i.ɚ **-iest** -i.ɪst, -i.əst **-ily** -ɪ.li, -ᵊl.i **-iness** -ɪ.nəs, -ɪ.nɪs
unwilling ʌn'wɪl.ɪŋ, ˌʌn- **-ly** -li **-ness** -nəs, -nɪs
Unwin 'ʌn.wɪn
unwind ʌn'waɪnd, ˌʌn- **-s** -z **-ing** -ɪŋ
unwound ʌn'waʊnd, ˌʌn-
unwise ʌn'waɪz, ˌʌn- **-ly** -li
unwish ʌn'wɪʃ **-es** -ɪz **-ing** -ɪŋ **-ed** -t
un'wished ˌfor

unwitting ʌn'wɪt.ɪŋ, ˌʌn- US -'wɪt̬- **-ly** -li

unwomanl|y ʌn'wʊm.ən.l|i, ˌʌn- **-iness** -ɪ.nəs, -ɪ.nɪs

unwonted ʌn'wəʊn.tɪd, ˌʌn- US -'wɔːn.t̬ɪd, -'woʊn-, -'wɑːn-, -'wʌn- **-ly** -li **-ness** -nəs, -nɪs

unworkable ʌn'wɜː.kə.bl̩, ˌʌn- US -'wɝː-

unworkmanlike ʌn'wɜːk.mən.laɪk, ˌʌn- US -'wɝːk-

unworldl|y ʌn'wɜːld.l|i, ˌʌn- US -'wɝːrld- **-iness** -ɪ.nəs, -ɪ.nɪs

unworn ʌn'wɔːn, ˌʌn- US -'wɔːrn

unworth|y ʌn'wɜː.ð|i, ˌʌn- US -'wɝːr- **-ily** -ɪ.li, -ᵊl.i **-iness** -ɪ.nəs, -ɪ.nɪs

unwound (*from* **unwind**) ʌn'waʊnd, ˌʌn-

unwounded ʌn'wuːn.dɪd, ˌʌn-

unwrap ʌn'ræp, ˌʌn- **-s** -s **-ping** -ɪŋ **-ped** -t

unwritten ʌn'rɪt.ᵊn, ˌʌn- **ˌunwritten ˌconsti'tution ; ˌunwritten 'law ; ˌunwritten 'rule**

unwrought ʌn'rɔːt, ˌʌn- US -'rɑːt, -'rɔːt

unyielding ʌn'jiːl.dɪŋ, ˌʌn- **-ly** -li **-ness** -nəs, -nɪs

unyok|e ʌn'jəʊk, ˌʌn- US -'joʊk **-es** -s **-ing** -ɪŋ **-ed** -t

unzip ʌn'zɪp, ˌʌn- **-s** -s **-ping** -ɪŋ **-ped** -t

up- ʌp-

Note: Prefix. It is normally unstressed or receives secondary stress. It may carry the strongest stress in stress shift cases.

up ʌp **-s** -s **-ping** -ɪŋ **-ped** -t

up-and-coming ˌʌp.ᵊŋ'kʌm.ɪŋ, -ᵊnd- US -ᵊnd- *stress shift:* ˌup-and-coming 'leader

up-and-down ˌʌp.ᵊnd'daʊn *stress shift:* ˌup-and-down 'motion

up-and-up ˌʌp.ᵊnd'ʌp

Upanishad ʊ'pʌn.ɪ.ʃəd, jʊ-, -'pæn-, -ʃæd US uː'pæn.ɪ.ʃæd, juː-, -'pɑː.nɪ-, -ʃɑːd **-s** -z

upas 'juː.pəs **-es** -ɪz

upbeat (*adj.*) ʌp'biːt US '-- *stress shift, British only:* ˌupbeat 'ending

upbeat (*n.*) 'ʌp.biːt **-s** -s

upbraid ʌp'breɪd, ˌʌp- **-s** -z **-ing** -ɪŋ **-ed** -ɪd

upbringing 'ʌpˌbrɪŋ.ɪŋ

upcast 'ʌp.kɑːst US -kæst **-s** -s

upchuck 'ʌp.tʃʌk **-s** -s **-ing** -ɪŋ **-ed** -t

upcoming 'ʌpˌkʌm.ɪŋ, -'-- US 'ʌpˌkʌm-

Upcott 'ʌp.kət, -kɒt US -kət, -kɑːt

up-countr|y (*n. adj.*) ˌʌp'kʌn.tr|i US '--- **-ies** -iz *stress shift, British only:* ˌup-country 'farm

up-country (*adv.*) ʌp'kʌn.tri

update (*n.*) 'ʌp.deɪt **-s** -s

up|date (*v.*) ʌp|'deɪt, ˌʌp- **-dates** -'deɪts **-dating** -'deɪ.tɪŋ US -'deɪ.t̬ɪŋ **-dated** -'deɪ.tɪd US -'deɪ.t̬ɪd

Updike 'ʌp.daɪk

upend ʌp'end, ˌʌp- **-s** -z **-ing** -ɪŋ **-ed** -ɪd

up-front ʌp'frʌnt, ˌʌp- *stress shift:* ˌup-front 'payment

upgrad|e (*v.*) ʌp'greɪd, ˌʌp- **-es** -z **-ing** -ɪŋ **-ed** -ɪd

upgrade (*n.*) 'ʌp.greɪd **-s** -z

Upham 'ʌp.əm

upheaval ʌp'hiː.vᵊl **-s** -z

upheav|e ʌp'hiːv **-es** -z **-ing** -ɪŋ **-ed** -d

upheld (*from* **uphold**) ʌp'held

uphill ʌp'hɪl, ˌʌp- *stress shift:* ˌuphill 'struggle

uphold ʌp'həʊld US -'hoʊld **-holds** -'həʊldz US -'hoʊldz **-holding** -'həʊl.dɪŋ US -'hoʊl.dɪŋ **upheld** ʌp'held **upholder/s** ʌp'həʊl.dəʳ/z US -'hoʊl.dɚ/z

upholst|er ʌp'həʊl.st|əʳ, əp- US ʌp'hoʊl.st|ɚ **-ers** -əz US -ɚz **-ering** -ᵊr.ɪŋ **-ered** -əd US -ɚd **-erer/s** -ᵊr.əʳ/z US -ɚ.ɚ/z **-ery** -ᵊr.i

Upjohn 'ʌp.dʒɒn US -dʒɑːn

upkeep 'ʌp.kiːp

upland 'ʌp.lənd US -lənd, -lænd **-s** -z **-er/s** -əʳ/z US -ɚ/z

uplift (*n.*) 'ʌp.lɪft

uplift (*v.*) ʌp'lɪft, ˌʌp- **-s** -s **-ing** -ɪŋ **-ed** -ɪd

uplifting ʌp'lɪf.tɪŋ, ˌʌp- *stress shift:* ˌuplifting 'day

uplighter 'ʌpˌlaɪ.təʳ US -t̬ɚ **-s** -z

up-market ˌʌp'mɑː.kɪt US 'ʌpˌmɑːr- *stress shift, British only:* ˌup-market 'shop

Upminster 'ʌpˌmɪnt.stəʳ US -stɚ

upmost 'ʌp.məʊst US -moʊst

upon *strong form:* ə'pɒn US -'pɑːn *occasional weak form:* ə.pən

upper 'ʌp.əʳ US -ɚ **-s** -z **ˌupper 'class ; ˌupper 'crust ; ˌUpper 'House ; ˌstiff upper 'lip ; have the ˌupper 'hand**

upper-case ˌʌp.ə'keɪs US -ɚ'- *stress shift, see compound:* **ˌupper-case 'letters**

uppercut 'ʌp.ə.kʌt US '-ɚ- **-s** -s

Uppermill 'ʌp.ə.mɪl US '-ɚ-

uppermost 'ʌp.ə.məʊst US -ɚ.moʊst

Uppingham 'ʌp.ɪŋ.əm

uppish 'ʌp.ɪʃ **-ly** -li **-ness** -nəs, -nɪs

uppity 'ʌp.ɪ.ti US -t̬i **-ness** -nəs, -nɪs

Uppsala ʊp'sɑː.lə, ʌp-, '---; 'ʌp.sᵊl.ə, 'ʊp-, -sɑː.lɑː US ʌp'sɑː.lɑː, ʊp-; 'ʌp.sᵊl.ə

uprais|e ʌp'reɪz, ˌʌp- **-es** -ɪz **-ing** -ɪŋ **-ed** -d

uprear ʌp'rɪəʳ, ˌʌp- US -'rɪr **-s** -z **-ing** -ɪŋ **-ed** -d

Uprichard juː'prɪtʃ.ɑːd, -əd; ʌp'rɪtʃ.əd US juː'prɪtʃ.ɑːrd, -ɚd; ʌp'rɪtʃ.ɚd

upright 'ʌp.raɪt **-s** -s **-ly** -li **-ness** -nəs, -nɪs

uprising 'ʌpˌraɪ.zɪŋ, -'--, ˌ-'-- US 'ʌpˌraɪ- **-s** -z

upriver ˌʌp'rɪv.əʳ US -ɚ

uproar 'ʌp.rɔːʳ US -rɔːr **-s** -z

uproarious ʌp'rɔː.ri.əs US -'rɔːr.i- **-ly** -li **-ness** -nəs, -nɪs

up|root ʌp|'ruːt, ˌʌp- **-roots** -'ruːts **-rooting** -'ruː.tɪŋ US -'ruː.t̬ɪŋ **-rooted** -'ruː.tɪd US -'ruː.t̬ɪd **-rooter/s** -'ruː.təʳ/z US -'ruː.t̬ɚ/z

upsadaisy ˌʌps.ə'deɪ.zi, ˌʊps-

Upsala ʊp'sɑː.lə, ʌp-, '---; 'ʌp.sᵊl.ə, 'ʊp-, -sɑː.lɑː US ʌp'sɑː.lɑː, ʊp-; 'ʌp.sᵊl.ə

upscale ˌʌp'skeɪl

upset (*n.*) 'ʌp.set **-s** -s

upset (*adj.*) ʌp'set, ˌʌp- *stress shift, see compound:* **ˌupset 'stomach**

up|set (*v.*) ʌp|'set, ˌʌp- **-sets** -'sets **-setting** -'set.ɪŋ US -'set̬.ɪŋ

upshot 'ʌp.ʃɒt US -ʃɑːt

upside 'ʌp.saɪd **-s** -z **ˌupside 'down**

upsilon juːp'saɪ.lən, ʊp-, ʌp-, -lɒn; 'juːp.sɪl.ən, 'ʌp-, -ɒn US 'ʌp.sə.lɑːn, 'uːp- **-s** -z

upstag|e (*v.*) ʌp'steɪdʒ, ˌʌp- **-es** -ɪz **-ing** -ɪŋ **-ed** -d

upstage ʌp'steɪdʒ, ˌʌp- US 'ʌp.steɪdʒ *stress shift, British only:* ˌupstage 'speech

upstairs ʌp'steəz, ˌʌp- US -'sterz *stress shift:* ˌupstairs 'window

upstanding ʌp'stæn.dɪŋ, ˌʌp- **-ness** -nəs, -nɪs *stress shift:* ˌupstanding 'soldier

upstart 'ʌp.stɑːt US -stɑːrt **-s** -s

upstate ˌʌp'steɪt US 'ʌp-, -'- *stress shift, British only:* ˌupstate 'town

upstream ʌp'striːm, ˌʌp- *stress shift:* ˌupstream 'journey

upstretched ʌp'stretʃt, ˌʌp- *stress shift:* ˌupstretched 'hands

upstroke 'ʌp.strəʊk US -stroʊk **-s** -s

upsurg|e 'ʌp.sɜːdʒ US -sɝːrdʒ **-es** -ɪz

upswept ʌp'swept, ˌʌp- *stress shift:* ˌupswept 'wings

upswing (*n.*) 'ʌp.swɪŋ **-s** -z

upswing (*v.*) ʌp'swɪŋ, ˌʌp- **-s** -z **-ing** -ɪŋ **upswung** ʌp'swʌŋ, ˌʌp-

uptake 'ʌp.teɪk **-s** -s

up-tempo ˌʌp'tem.pəʊ US -poʊ

upthrust 'ʌp.θrʌst **-s** -s

uptight ʌp'taɪt, ˌʌp- **-ness** -nəs, -nɪs *stress shift:* ˌuptight 'person

up|tilt ʌp|'tɪlt, ˌʌp- **-tilts** -'tɪlts **-tilting** -'tɪl.tɪŋ US -'tɪl.t̬ɪŋ **-tilted** -'tɪl.tɪd US -'tɪl.t̬ɪd

up-to-date ˌʌp.təˈdeɪt **-ness** -nəs, -nɪs *stress shift:* ˌup-to-date ˈmethod
Upton ˈʌp.tən
up-to-the-minute ˌʌp.tə.ðəˈmɪn.ɪt, -tʊ- *stress shift:* ˌup-to-the-minute ˈstyling
uptown ʌpˈtaʊn, ˌʌp- (US) ˈʌp.taʊn, ˌ-ˈ- *stress shift, British only:* ˌuptown ˈhouse
upturn (*v.*) ʌpˈtɜːn (US) -ˈtɜːrn **-s** -z **-ing** -ɪŋ **-ed** -d
upturn (*n.*) ˈʌp.tɜːn (US) -tɜːrn **-s** -z
upturned ʌpˈtɜːnd, ˌʌp- (US) -ˈtɜːrnd *stress shift:* ˌupturned ˈboat
upward ˈʌp.wəd (US) -wɚd **-ly** -li **-s** -z ˌ**upwardly** ˈ**mobile**
upwind ʌpˈwɪnd
Ur ɜːʳ, ʊəʳ (US) ɜːr, ʊr
uraemia jʊəˈriː.mi.ə, jə-, jɔː- (US) juːˈriː-, jʊ-
Ural ˈjʊə.rəl, ˈjɔː- (US) ˈjʊr.əl **-s** ˌ**Ural** ˈ**Mountains**
uralite ˈjʊə.rəl.aɪt, ˈjɔː- (US) ˈjʊr.ə.laɪt
Urani|a jʊəˈreɪ.ni|.ə, jə-, jɔː- (US) jʊ- **-an** -ən
uranium jʊəˈreɪ.ni.əm, jə-, jɔː- (US) jʊ-, jə-
Uranus ˈjʊə.rən.əs, ˈjɔː-; jʊəˈreɪ.nəs, jə- (US) ˈjʊr.ən.əs; juːˈreɪ.nəs
urate ˈjʊə.reɪt, ˈjɔː-, -rɪt (US) ˈjʊr.eɪt **-s** -s
urban (U) ˈɜː.bən (US) ˈɜːr- **-ite/s** -aɪt/s ˌ**urban gueˈrrilla**
Urbana ɜːˈbæn.ə, -ˈbɑː.nə (US) ɜːrˈbæn.ə
urbane ɜːˈbeɪn (US) ɜːr- **-ly** -li **-ness** -nəs, -nɪs
urban|ism ˈɜː.bən|.ɪ.zəm (US) ˈɜːr- **-ist/s** -ɪst/s
urbanistic ˌɜː.bənˈɪs.tɪk (US) ˌɜːr- **-ally** -əl.i, -li
urbanity ɜːˈbæn.ə.ti, -ɪ.ti (US) ɜːrˈbæn.ə.t̬i
urbanization, -isa- ˌɜː.bən.aɪˈzeɪ.ʃən, -ɪˈ- (US) ˌɜːr.bən.ɪˈ-
urbaniz|e, -is|e ˈɜː.bən.aɪz (US) ˈɜːr- **-es** -ɪz **-ing** -ɪŋ **-ed** -d
Urbervilles ˈɜː.bə.vɪlz (US) ˈɜːr-
urchin ˈɜː.tʃɪn (US) ˈɜːr- **-s** -z
Urdu ˈʊə.duː, ˈɜː-, ˌ-ˈ- (US) ˈʊr.duː, ˈɜːr-
Ure jʊəʳ (US) jʊr
-ure -əʳ (US) -ɚ
Note: Suffix. In words containing **-ure** where the stem is free, **-ure** does not normally affect the stress pattern of the word, e.g. **proceed** /prəʊˈsiːd (US) prə-/, **procedure** /prəʊˈsiː.dʒəʳ (US) prəˈsiː.dʒɚ/. Where the stem is bound, the word is normally stressed on the penultimate or antepenultimate syllable, e.g. **furniture** /ˈfɜː.nɪ.tʃəʳ (US) ˈfɜːr.nɪ.tʃɚ/. Exceptions exist; see individual entries.
ure|a jʊəˈriː|.ə; ˈjʊə.ri-, ˈjɔː- (US) jʊˈriː-; ˈjʊr.i- **-al** -əl
ureter jʊəˈriː.təʳ; ˈjʊə.rɪ-, -rə- (US) jʊˈriː.t̬ɚ **-s** -z
ureth|ra jʊəˈriː.θ|rə (US) jʊ- **-rae** -riː **-ras** -rəz
urethritis ˌjʊə.rəˈθraɪ.tɪs, ˌjɔː-, -rɪˈ- (US) ˌjʊr.əˈθraɪ.t̬ɪs
uretic jʊəˈret.ɪk, jə- (US) jʊˈret̬.ɪk **-s** -s
urg|e ɜːdʒ (US) ɜːrdʒ **-es** -ɪz **-ing** -ɪŋ **-ed** -d **-er/s** -əʳ/z (US) -ɚ/z
urgency ˈɜː.dʒənt.si (US) ˈɜːr-
urgent ˈɜː.dʒənt (US) ˈɜːr- **-ly** -li
Uriah jʊəˈraɪə, jə- (US) jʊ-
uric ˈjʊə.rɪk, ˈjɔː- (US) ˈjʊr.ɪk
Uriel ˈjʊə.ri.əl, ˈjɔː- (US) ˈjʊr.i-
Urim ˈjʊə.rɪm, ˈjɔː-, ˈʊə- (US) ˈjʊr.ɪm
urinal jʊəˈraɪ.nəl, jə-; ˈjʊə.rɪ.nəl, ˈjɔː-, -rən.əl; (US) ˈjʊr.ən.əl **-s** -z
urinary ˈjʊə.rɪ.nər.i, ˈjɔː-, -rən.ər- (US) ˈjʊr.ə.ner.i
urin|ate ˈjʊə.rɪ.n|eɪt, ˈjɔː-, -rən|.eɪt (US) ˈjʊr.ə.n|eɪt **-ates** -eɪts **-ating** -eɪ.tɪŋ (US) -eɪ.t̬ɪŋ **-ated** -eɪ.tɪd (US) -eɪ.t̬ɪd
urination ˌjʊə.rɪˈneɪ.ʃən, ˌjɔː-, -rənˈeɪ- (US) ˌjʊr.əˈneɪ-
urine ˈjʊə.rɪn, ˈjɔː- (US) ˈjʊr.ɪn **-s** -z
uriniferous ˌjʊə.rɪˈnɪf.ər.əs, ˌjɔː-, -rənˈɪf- (US) ˌjʊr.əˈnɪf-
urinogenital ˌjʊə.rɪ.nəʊˈdʒen.ɪ.təl, ˌjɔː-, ˈ-ə- (US) ˌjʊr.ə.noʊˈdʒen.ə.t̬əl
Urmia ˈɜː.mi.ə, ˈʊə- (US) ˈʊr-
Urmston ˈɜːm.stən (US) ˈɜːrm-
urn ɜːn (US) ɜːrn **-s** -z
uro- ˌjʊə.rəʊ-, ˌjɔː- (US) ˌjʊr.oʊ-, ˌ-ə-
urolog|y jʊəˈrɒl.ə.dʒ|i (US) jʊrˈɑː- **-ist/s** -ɪst/s
Urquhart ˈɜː.kət (US) ˈɜːr.kɚt, -kɑːrt
Ursa ˈɜː.sə (US) ˈɜːr- ˌ**Ursa** ˈ**Major** ; ˌ**Ursa** ˈ**Minor**
ursine ˈɜː.saɪn (US) ˈɜːr-, -sɪn
Ursula ˈɜː.sjə.lə, -sjʊ-, -ʃə-, -ʃʊ- (US) ˈɜːr.sə.lə
Ursuline ˈɜː.sjə.laɪn, -sjʊ-, -ʃə-, -ʃʊ-, -lɪn (US) ˈɜːr.sə.lɪn, -laɪn **-s** -z
urticaria ˌɜː.tɪˈkeə.ri.ə (US) ˌɜːr.t̬ɪˈker.i-
Uruguay ˈjʊə.rə.gwaɪ, ˈʊr.ə-, ˈ-ʊ-, -gweɪ (US) ˈjʊr.ə.gweɪ, ˈʊr-, ˈuː.ruː-, -gwaɪ
Uruguayan ˌjʊə.rəˈgwaɪ.ən, ˌʊr.əˈ-, -ʊˈ-, -ˈgweɪ- (US) ˌjʊr.əˈgweɪ-, ˌʊr-, ˌuː.ruː-, -ˈgwaɪ- **-s** -z
urus ˈjʊə.rəs, ˈjɔː- (US) ˈjʊr.əs
us *strong form:* ʌs *weak forms:* əs, s
Note: Weak form word. The strong form is used mainly for contrast, e.g. 'a them and us attitude', or for emphasis, e.g. 'This land belongs to **us**'. The weak form is used when unstressed, and can occur in final position, e.g. 'They joined us' /ðeɪˈdʒɔɪnd.əs/.
US ˌjuːˈes
USA ˌjuː.esˈeɪ
usability ˌjuː.zəˈbɪl.ə.ti, -ɪ.ti (US) -ə.t̬i
usable ˈjuː.zə.bl̩
USAF ˌjuː.es.eɪˈef
usag|e ˈjuː.sɪdʒ, -zɪdʒ **-es** -ɪz
usanc|e ˈjuː.zənts **-es** -ɪz
USDAW ˈʌs.dɔː, ˈʌz- (US) -dɑː, -dɔː
use (*n.*) juːs **uses** ˈjuː.sɪz
us|e (*v.*) *make use of:* juːz **-es** -ɪz **-ing** -ɪŋ **-ed** -d **-er/s** -əʳ/z (US) -ɚ/z
useab|le ˈjuː.zə.bl|̩ **-ly** -li **-leness** -l̩.nəs, -nɪs
used (*from* **use** *v.*) juːzd
used (*adj.*) *accustomed:* juːst, juːzd
used (*v.*) *was or were accustomed; when followed by* **to**: juːst *when not followed by* **to**: juːst, juːzd
usedn't *when followed by* **to**: ˈjuː.sənt *when not followed by* **to**: ˈjuː.sənt
Note: This form is rare in present-day English, especially in American English.
useful ˈjuːs.fəl, -fʊl **-ly** -i **-ness** -nəs, -nɪs
useless ˈjuː.sləs, -slɪs **-ly** -li **-ness** -nəs, -nɪs
usen't *when followed by* **to**: ˈjuː.sənt *when not followed by* **to**: ˈjuː.sənt
Note: See note for 'usedn't'.
user-friendl|y ˌjuː.zəˈfrend.l|i (US) -zɚˈ- **-iness** -ɪ.nəs, -ɪ.nɪs *stress shift:* ˌuser-friendly ˈproduct
uses (*plur. of* **use** *n.*) ˈjuː.sɪz
uses (*from* **use** *v.*) ˈjuː.zɪz
Ushant ˈʌʃ.ənt
Ushaw ˈʌʃ.ə, -ɔː (US) -ə, -ɑː, -ɔː
ush|er (U) ˈʌʃ|.əʳ (US) -ɚ **-ers** -əz (US) -ɚz **-ering** -ər.ɪŋ **-ered** -əd (US) -ɚd
usherette ˌʌʃ.ərˈet **-s** -s
Usk ʌsk
USN ˌjuː.esˈen
usquebaugh ˈʌs.kwɪ.bɔː, -kwə- (US) -bɑː, -bɔː **-s** -z
Ussher ˈʌʃ.əʳ (US) -ɚ
USSR ˌjuː.es.esˈɑːʳ (US) -ˈɑːr
Ustinov ˈjuː.stɪ.nɒf, ˈuː-, -stə-, -nɒv (US) -nɑːf, -nɔːf, -nɑːv
usu. (*abbrev. for* **usual/ly**) ˈjuː.ʒəl/i, -ʒu.əl- (US) -ʒu.əl-, ˈjuːʒ.wəl-
usual ˈjuː.ʒəl, -ʒu.əl (US) -ʒu.əl, ˈjuːʒ.wəl **-ly** -i **-ness** -nəs, -nɪs
usufruct ˈjuː.sjʊ.frʌkt, -zjʊ- (US) -zʊ-, -sʊ-, -zə-, -sə- **-s** -s
usurer ˈjuː.ʒər.əʳ (US) -ɚ **-s** -z
usurious juːˈzjʊə.ri.əs, -ˈʒʊə-, -ˈzjɔː- (US) juːˈʒʊr.i- **-ly** -li **-ness** -nəs, -nɪs

usurp juː'zɜːp, -'sɜːp ⓊⓈ -'sɜːrp, -'zɜːrp **-s** -s **-ing** -ɪŋ **-ed** -t **-er/s** -ər/z ⓊⓈ -ɚ/z
usurpation ˌjuː.zɜː'peɪ.ʃən, -sɜː'- ⓊⓈ -sɚ'-, -zɚ'- **-s** -z
usury 'juː.ʒər.i ⓊⓈ -ʒɚ.i
Ut. (*abbrev. for* **Utah**) 'juː.tɑː ⓊⓈ -tɔː, -tɑː
Utah 'juː.tɑː ⓊⓈ -tɔː, -tɑː
Ute juːt **-s** -s
utensil juː'tent.səl, -sɪl ⓊⓈ -səl **-s** -z
uteri (*alternative plur. of* **uterus**) 'juː.tər.aɪ ⓊⓈ -t̬ə.raɪ
uterine 'juː.tər.aɪn ⓊⓈ -t̬ɚ.ɪn, -t̬ə.raɪn
uterus 'juː.tər.əs ⓊⓈ -t̬ɚ- **-es** -ɪz
Uther 'juː.θər ⓊⓈ -θɚ
Utica 'juː.tɪ.kə ⓊⓈ -t̬ɪ-
utilitarian ˌjuː.tɪ.lɪ'teə.ri.ən, -lə'-; juːˌtɪl.ɪ'-, -ə'- ⓊⓈ juːˌtɪl.ə'ter.i- **-s** -z **-ism** -ɪ.zəm
utilit|y juː'tɪl.ə.t|i, -ɪ.t|i ⓊⓈ -ə.t̬|i **-ies** -iz
utilization, -isa- ˌjuː.təl.aɪ'zeɪ.ʃən, -tɪ.laɪ'-, -lɪ'- ⓊⓈ -t̬əl.ɪ'-
utiliz|e, -is|e 'juː.tɪ.laɪz, -təl.aɪz ⓊⓈ -t̬əl.aɪz **-es** -ɪz **-ing** -ɪŋ **-ed** -d **-er/s** -ər/z ⓊⓈ -ɚ/z **-able** -ə.bl̩
utmost 'ʌt.məʊst, -məst ⓊⓈ -moʊst
utopi|a (U) juː'təʊ.pi|.ə ⓊⓈ -'toʊ- **-an/s** -ən/z
utopianism (U) juː'təʊ.pi.ə.nɪ.zəm ⓊⓈ -'toʊ-
Utrecht 'juː.trekt, -trext, -'- ⓊⓈ 'juː.trekt
utricle 'juː.trɪ.kl̩ **-s** -z
Utrillo juː'trɪl.əʊ, uː- ⓊⓈ -oʊ
Utsira uːt'sɪə.rə ⓊⓈ -'sɪr.ə
Uttar Pradesh ˌʊt.ə.prə'deʃ, -'deɪʃ ⓊⓈ ˌuː.t̬ɚ-
utt|er 'ʌt|.ər ⓊⓈ 'ʌt̬|.ɚ **-erly** -əl.i ⓊⓈ -ɚ.li **-erness** -ə.nəs, -nɪs ⓊⓈ -ɚ- **-ers** -əz ⓊⓈ -ɚz **-ering** -ər.ɪŋ **-ered** -əd ⓊⓈ -ɚd **-erer/s** -ər.ər/z ⓊⓈ -ɚ.ɚ/z **-erable** -ər.ə.bl̩
utteranc|e 'ʌt.ər.ənts ⓊⓈ 'ʌt̬- **-es** -ɪz
uttermost 'ʌt.ə.məʊst ⓊⓈ 'ʌt̬.ɚ.moʊst
Uttley 'ʌt.li
Uttoxeter juː'tɒk.sɪ.tər, ʌt'ɒk-, 'ʌk.sɪ- ⓊⓈ juː'tɑːk.sɪ.t̬ɚ, ʌt̬'ɑːk-, 'ʌk.sɪ-
Note: The common pronunciation is /juː'tɒk.sɪ.tər ⓊⓈ -'tɑːk.sɪ.t̬ɚ/ or /ʌt'ɒk.sɪ.tər ⓊⓈ -'ɑːk.sɪ.t̬ɚ/. The former is more frequent, and is the pronunciation of most outsiders.
U-turn 'juː.tɜːn, ˌjuː'tɜːn ⓊⓈ 'juː.tɜːrn, ˌ-'- **-s** -z
UV ˌjuː'viː *stress shift, see compound:* ˌ**UV 'light**
uvul|a 'juː.vjə.l|ə, -vjʊ- **-as** -z **-ae** -i
uvular 'juː.vjə.lər, -vjʊ- ⓊⓈ -lɚ
Uxbridge 'ʌks.brɪdʒ
uxorial ʌk'sɔː.ri.əl ⓊⓈ -'sɔːr.i-; ʌg'zɔːr-
uxorious ʌk'sɔː.ri.əs ⓊⓈ -'sɔːr.i-; ʌg'zɔːr- **-ly** -li **-ness** -nəs, -nɪs
Uzbek 'ʊz.bek, 'ʌz- **-s** -s
Uzbekistan ʊzˌbek.ɪ'stɑːn, ʌz- ⓊⓈ -'stæn, -'stɑːn **-i/s** -i/z
Uzi® 'uː.zi

V

v (V) viː **-'s** -z **'v ˌsign**
v. *versus:* viː, 'vɜː.səs (US) viː, 'vɜːr- *vide:* viː, siː, 'viːd.eɪ, 'vaɪ.di (US) 'viː.deɪ
Va. (*abbrev. for* **Virginia**) və'dʒɪn.jə, vɜː-, -i.ə; ˌviː'eɪ (US) vɚ'dʒɪn.jə; ˌviː'eɪ
Vaal vɑːl
vac væk **-s** -s
vacanc|y 'veɪ.kənt.s|i **-ies** -iz
vacant 'veɪ.kənt **-ly** -li ˌ**vacant 'lot**
vaca|te və'keɪ|t, veɪ- (US) 'veɪ.keɪ|t, -'- **-tes** -ts **-ting** -tɪŋ (US) -t̬ɪŋ **-ted** -tɪd (US) -t̬ɪd
vacation və'keɪ.ʃən (US) veɪ-, və- **-s** -z **-er/s** -ər/z (US) -ɚ/z **-ist/s** -ɪst/s
vaccin|ate 'væk.sɪ.n|eɪt, -sən|.eɪt (US) -sə.n|eɪt **-ates** -eɪts **-ating** -eɪ.tɪŋ (US) -eɪ.t̬ɪŋ **-ated** -eɪ.tɪd (US) -eɪ.t̬ɪd **-ator/s** -eɪ.tər/z (US) -eɪ.t̬ɚ/z
vaccination ˌvæk.sɪ'neɪ.ʃən, -sən'eɪ- (US) -sə'neɪ- **-s** -z
vaccine 'væk.siːn, -sɪn (US) væk'siːn, '-- **-s** -z
Vachel(l) 'veɪ.tʃəl
Vacher 'væʃ.ər, 'veɪ.tʃər (US) 'væʃ.ɚ, 'veɪ.tʃɚ
vacill|ate 'væs.əl|.eɪt, -sɪ.l|eɪt (US) -ə.l|eɪt **-ates** -eɪts **-ating/ly** -eɪ.tɪŋ/li (US) -eɪ.t̬ɪŋ/li **-ated** -eɪ.tɪd (US) -eɪ.t̬ɪd **-ator/s** -eɪ.tər/z (US) -eɪ.t̬ɚ/z
vacillation ˌvæs.əl'eɪ.ʃən, -ɪ'leɪ- (US) -ə'leɪ- **-s** -z
Václav 'væt.slæv (US) 'vɑːt.slɑːf
vacuity væk'juː.ə.ti, və'kjuː-, -ɪ.ti (US) -ə.t̬i
vacuolar ˌvæk.ju'əʊ.lər (US) 'væk.ju.wə.lɚ; ˌvæk.ju'oʊ-, -lɑːr
vacuole 'væk.ju.əʊl (US) -oʊl **-s** -z
vacuous 'væk.ju.əs **-ly** -li **-ness** -nəs, -nɪs
vacuum 'væk.juːm, -jʊm, -jʊəm (US) -juːm, -ju.əm, -jʊm, -jəm **-s** -z **-ing** -ɪŋ **-ed** -d **'vacuum ˌcleaner**; **'vacuum ˌflask**; **'vacuum ˌpump**
vacuum-packed ˌvæk.juːm'pækt, -jʊm'-, -jʊəm'- (US) -ju.əm'-, -juːm'-, -jʊm'-, -jəm'-, '---
vade-mecum ˌvɑː.deɪ'meɪ.kəm, -kʊm; ˌveɪ.di'miː.kəm, -kʌm (US) ˌveɪ.di'miː.kəm, ˌvɑː-, -'meɪ- **-s** -z
Vaduz vɑː'duːts
vagabond 'væg.ə.bɒnd, -bənd (US) -bɑːnd **-s** -z **-ish** -ɪʃ **-ism** -ɪ.zəm
vagabondage 'væg.əˌbɒn.dɪdʒ (US) -ˌbɑːn-
vagar|y 'veɪ.gər|.i; və'geə.r|i (US) 'veɪ.gɚ|.i; və'ger|.i **-ies** -iz
vagina və'dʒaɪ.nə **-s** -z
vaginal və'dʒaɪ.nəl; 'vædʒ.ɪ-, -ən.əl (US) 'vædʒ.ən.əl **-ly** -i
vaginismus ˌvædʒ.ɪ'nɪz.məs, -ə'-, -'nɪs- (US) -ə'nɪz-
vagrancy 'veɪ.grənt.si
vagrant 'veɪ.grənt **-s** -s
vagu|e veɪg **-er** -ər (US) -ɚ **-est** -ɪst, -əst **-ely** -li **-eness** -nəs, -nɪs
vail (V) veɪl **-s** -z **-ing** -ɪŋ **-ed** -d
Vaile veɪl
vain veɪn **-er** -ər (US) -ɚ **-est** -ɪst, -əst **-ly** -li **-ness** -nəs, -nɪs
vainglorious ˌveɪn'glɔː.ri.əs, ˌveɪŋ'- (US) ˌveɪn'glɔːr.i- **-ly** -li **-ness** -nəs, -nɪs
vainglory ˌveɪn'glɔː.ri, ˌveɪŋ- (US) 'veɪnˌglɔːr.i, ˌ-'--
Vaishnav|a 'veʃ.nə.v|ɑː **-ism** -ɪ.zəm
Val væl
Valais 'væl.eɪ
valanc|e 'væl.ənts (US) 'væl-, 'veɪ.lənts **-es** -ɪz **-ed** -t
Valdez væl'diːz
vale (V) *valley:* veɪl **-s** -z
vale *latin word meaning "goodbye":* 'vɑː.leɪ, 'veɪ.li, 'væl.eɪ (US) 'veɪ.li, 'vɑː.leɪ
valediction ˌvæl.ɪ'dɪk.ʃən, -ə'- (US) ˌvæl.ə'dɪk.ʃən **-s** -z
valedictorian ˌvæl.ɪ.dɪk'tɔː.ri.ən, ˌ-ə- (US) ˌvæl.ə.dɪk'tɔːr.i- **-s** -z
valedictor|y ˌvæl.ɪ'dɪk.tər|.i, -ə'- (US) ˌvæl.ə'dɪk.tɚ- **-ies** -iz
valence 'veɪ.lənts
Valencia və'lent.ʃi.ə, -si-, '-ʃə
Valenciennes ˌvæl.ən.si'en, -ɑ̃ːn-, -ɑːnt-, -'sjen (US) -si'enz, -'sjenz; vəˌlent.si'enz, -ˌlɑːnt-
valenc|y 'veɪ.lənt.s|i **-ies** -iz
valentine (V) *person or card:* 'væl.ən.taɪn **-s** -z **'Valentine's ˌcard**; **'Valentine's ˌDay**
Valentine *first name* 'væl.ən.taɪn, -tɪn (US) -taɪn
Valentinian ˌvæl.ən'tɪn.i.ən
Valentino ˌvæl.ən'tiː.nəʊ (US) -noʊ
valerian (V) və'lɪə.ri.ən, -'leə- (US) -'lɪr.i- **-s** -z
Valerie, Valery 'væl.ər.i
Valerius və'lɪə.ri.əs, -'leə- (US) -'lɪr.i-
Valéry 'væl.eə.riː, ˌvæl.eə'riː (US) ˌvæl.ə'riː, ˌvɑː.leɪ'iː
valet 'væl.eɪ, -ɪt, -ət, -i (US) 'væl.ɪt; və'leɪ, væl'eɪ; 'væl.eɪ **valets** 'væl.eɪz, -ɪts, -əts, -iz (US) 'væl.ɪts; və'leɪz, væl'eɪz; 'væl.eɪz **valeting** 'væl.eɪ.ɪŋ, -ɪ.tɪŋ, -ə.tɪŋ, -i.ɪŋ (US) 'væl.ɪ.t̬ɪŋ; və'leɪ.ɪŋ, væl'eɪ.ɪŋ; 'væl.eɪ.ɪŋ **valeted** 'væl.eɪd, -ɪ.tɪd, -ə.tɪd, '-id (US) 'væl.ɪ.t̬ɪd; və'leɪd, væl'eɪd; 'væl.eɪd **'valet ˌparking**
valetudinarian ˌvæl.ɪ.tjuː.dɪ'neə.ri.ən, ˌ-ə-, -tʃuː- (US) -əˌtuː.də'ner.i-, -ˌtjuː- **-s** -z **-ism** -ɪ.zəm
Valhalla væl'hæl.ə (US) væl'hæl-, vɑːl'hɑː.lə
valiant 'væl.i.ənt, '-jənt (US) '-jənt **-ly** -li **-ness** -nəs, -nɪs
valid 'væl.ɪd **-ly** -li **-ness** -nəs, -nɪs
vali|date 'væl.ɪ|.deɪt, '-ə- (US) '-ə- **-dates** -deɪts **-dating** -deɪ.tɪŋ (US) -deɪ.t̬ɪŋ **-dated** -deɪ.tɪd (US) -deɪ.t̬ɪd
validation ˌvæl.ɪ'deɪ.ʃən, -ə'- (US) -ə'- **-s** -z
validit|y və'lɪd.ə.t|i, væl'ɪd-, -ɪ.t|i (US) və'lɪd.ə.t̬|i **-ies** -iz
valis|e və'liːz, væl'iːz, -'iːs (US) və'liːs, -'liːz **-es** -ɪz
Valium® 'væl.i.əm (US) '-i.əm, '-jəm **-s** -z
Valkyrie væl'kɪə.ri, 'væl.kər.i, -kɪ.ri (US) væl'kɪr.i, 'væl.kɚ.i, -kɪ.ri **-s** -z
Valladolid ˌvæl.ə.dəʊ'lɪd, -dɒl'ɪd *as if Spanish:* ˌvaɪ.ɑː.dɒl'iːd (US) -doʊ'lɪd
Valletta və'let.ə (US) vɑː'let.ɑː
valley 'væl.i **-s** -z
Valois 'væl.wɑː (US) vɑːl'wɑː; 'væl.wɑː
valor 'væl.ər (US) -ɚ
valorization, -isa- ˌvæl.ər.aɪ'zeɪ.ʃən, -ɪ'- (US) -ɪ'- **-s** -z
valoriz|e, -is|e 'væl.ər.aɪz (US) -ə.raɪz **-es** -ɪz **-ing** -ɪŋ **-ed** -d
valorous 'væl.ər.əs **-ly** -li **-ness** -nəs, -nɪs
valour 'væl.ər (US) -ɚ
Valparaiso ˌvæl.pər'aɪ.zəʊ, -'eɪ- (US) -pə'raɪ.zoʊ, -'reɪ-
Valpolicella ˌvæl.pɒl.ɪ'tʃel.ə (US) ˌvɑːl.poʊ.lɪ-
vals|e vɑːls, væls, vɔːls (US) vɑːls, vʌls **-es** -ɪz
valuab|le 'væl.ju.ə.b|l̩, -jə.b|l̩, -jʊ- **-les** -l̩z **-ly** -li **-leness** -l̩.nəs, -nɪs
valuat|e 'væl.ju.eɪt **-es** -s **-ing** -ɪŋ **-ed** -ɪd
valuation ˌvæl.ju'eɪ.ʃən **-s** -z
valu|e 'væl.juː **-es** -z **-ing** -ɪŋ **-ed** -d **-er/s** -ər/z (US) -ɚ/z **'value ˌjudgment**; ˌ**family 'values**
value-added ˌvæl.juː'æd.ɪd ˌ**value-ˌadded 'tax**, ˌ**value-'added tax**
valueless 'væl.juː.ləs, -jʊ-, -lɪs
valve vælv **-s** -z
valvular 'væl.vjə.lər, -vjʊ- (US) -vjə.lɚ
valvule 'væl.vjuːl **-s** -z

vamoos|e və'muːs, væm'uːs
(US) væm'uːs, və'muːs **-es** -ɪz **-ing** -ɪŋ
-ed -t
vamp væmp **-s** -s **-ing** -ɪŋ **-ed** -t
vampire 'væm.paɪəʳ (US) -paɪɚ **-s** -z
'vampire ˌbat
vampirism 'væm.paɪə.rɪ.zᵊm (US) -paɪ-, -pɪ-
vampish 'væm.pɪʃ **-ly** -li **-ness** -nəs, -nɪs
van (V) væn **-s** -z
vanadium və'neɪ.di.əm
Van Allen væn'æl.ən **Van ˌAllen 'belt**
(US) **Van 'Allen ˌbelt**
Vanbrugh 'væn.brə, 'væm-
(US) 'væn.bruː
Note: **Sir John Vanbrugh**, the seventeenth-century dramatist and architect, is also sometimes referred to as /'væn.bruː/ in British English.
Vance vænts, vɑːnts (US) vænts
Vancouver væn'kuː.vəʳ, væŋ-
(US) væn'kuː.vɚ
V and A, V & A (*abbrev. for* **Victoria and Albert Museum**) ˌviː.ənd'eɪ
vandal (V) 'væn.dᵊl **-s** -z
vandalism 'væn.dᵊl.ɪ.zᵊm
vandaliz|e, -is|e 'væn.dᵊl.aɪz **-es** -ɪz
-ing -ɪŋ **-ed** -d
Van de Graaff generator
ˌvæn.dəˌgrɑːf'dʒen.ᵊ.reɪ.təʳ
(US) -t̬ɚ, -ˌgræf'- **-s** -z
Vanderbilt 'væn.də.bɪlt (US) -dɚ-
Vanderbyl 'væn.də.bɪl (US) -dɚ-
Vandermeer ˌvæn.də'mɪəʳ (US) -dɚ'mɪr
van der Post ˌvæn.də'pɒst
(US) -dɚ'pɑːst
Van Diemen væn'diː.mən
Vandyke, Van Dyck væn'daɪk *stress shift, see compound:* **ˌVandyke 'brown** ; **ˌVandyke 'collar**
vane (V) veɪn **-s** -z **-d** -d
Vanessa və'nes.ə
Van Eyck væn'aɪk **-s** -s
Vange vændʒ
Van Gogh væn'gɒf, væŋ-, -'gɒk, -'gɒx
(US) væn'goʊ, -'gɔːx
vanguard 'væn.gɑːd, 'væŋ-
(US) 'væn.gɑːrd **-s** -z
Van Helsing væn'hel.sɪŋ (US) væn-, vɑːn-
vanilla və'nɪl.ə **va'nilla ˌpod**
vanish 'væn.ɪʃ **-es** -ɪz **-ing** -ɪŋ **-ed** -t
'vanishing ˌcream ; **'vanishing ˌpoint**
Vanitory® 'væn.ɪ.tᵊr.i **'Vanitory ˌunit**
vanit|y 'væn.ə.t|i, -ɪ.t|i (US) -ə.t̬|i
-ies -iz **'vanity ˌcase** ; **ˌVanity 'Fair** ;
'vanity ˌplates ; **'vanity ˌtable**
vanquish 'væŋ.kwɪʃ (US) 'væŋ-, 'væn-
-es -ɪz **-ing** -ɪŋ **-ed** -t **-er/s** -əʳ/z
(US) -ɚ/z **-able** -ə.bl̩
Vansittart væn'sɪt.ət, -ɑːt (US) -'sɪt̬.ɚt

van Straubenzee ˌvæn.strɔː'ben.zi
(US) -strɑː'-, -strɔː'-
vantag|e 'vɑːn.tɪdʒ (US) 'væn.t̬ɪdʒ
-es -ɪz **'vantage ˌpoint**
Vanuatu ˌvæn.u'ɑː.tuː, -'æt.uː
(US) væn'wɑː.tuː
Van Vechten væn'vek.tən
Vanya 'vɑː.njə, 'væn.jə (US) 'vɑː.njə
vapid 'væp.ɪd **-ly** -li **-ness** -nəs, -nɪs
vapidity væp'ɪd.ə.ti, və'pɪd-, -ɪ.ti
(US) væp'ɪd.ə.t̬i
vap|or 'veɪ.p|əʳ (US) -p|ɚ **-ors** -əz
(US) -ɚz **-ory** -ᵊr.i **'vapor ˌtrail**
vaporett|o ˌvæp.ᵊr'et|.əʊ
(US) -pə'ret̬|.oʊ **-os** -əʊz (US) -oʊz **-i** -i
vaporization, -isa- ˌveɪ.pᵊr.aɪ'zeɪ.ʃᵊn, -ɪ'- (US) -ɪ'- **-s** -z
vaporiz|e, -is|e 'veɪ.pᵊr.aɪz
(US) -pə.raɪz **-es** -ɪz **-ing** -ɪŋ **-ed** -d **-er/s** -əʳ/z (US) -ɚ/z
vaporosity ˌveɪ.pᵊr'ɒs.ə.ti, -ɪ.ti
(US) -pə'rɑː.sə.t̬i
vaporous 'veɪ.pᵊr.əs **-ly** -li **-ness** -nəs, -nɪs
vap|our 'veɪ.p|əʳ (US) -p|ɚ **-ours** -əz
(US) -ɚz **-oury** -ᵊr.i **'vapour ˌtrail**
Varah 'vɑː.rə (US) 'vɑːr.ə
Varden 'vɑː.dᵊn (US) 'vɑːr-
varec 'vær.ek, -ɪk (US) 'ver-, 'vær-
variability ˌveə.ri.ə'bɪl.ə.ti, -ɪ.ti
(US) ˌver.i.ə'bɪl.ə.t̬i, ˌvær-
variab|le 'veə.ri.ə.b|l̩ (US) 'ver.i-, 'vær-
-les -l̩z **-ly** -li **-leness** -l̩.nəs, -nɪs
variance 'veə.ri.ənts (US) 'ver.i-, 'vær-
variant 'veə.ri.ənt (US) 'ver.i-, 'vær-
-s -s
variate 'veə.ri.ət, -ɪt (US) 'ver.i.ɪt, 'vær- **-s** -s
variation ˌveə.ri'eɪ.ʃᵊn (US) ˌver.i'-, ˌvær- **-s** -z
varicella ˌvær.ɪ'sel.ə (US) ˌver-, ˌvær-, -ə-
varices (*plur. of* **varix**) 'vær.ɪ.siːz, 'veə.rɪ- (US) 'ver.ə.siːz, 'vær-
varicose 'vær.ɪ.kəʊs (US) 'ver.ə.koʊs, 'vær- **ˌvaricose 'veins**
varicosity ˌvær.ɪ'kɒs.ə.ti, -ɪ.ti
(US) ˌver.ɪ'kɑː.sə.t̬i, ˌvær-
varied 'veə.rɪd (US) 'ver.ɪd, 'vær- **-ly** -li
varie|gate 'veə.rɪ|.geɪt, -ri.ə-
(US) 'ver.i.ə-, 'vær- **-gates** -geɪts
-gating -geɪ.tɪŋ (US) -geɪ.t̬ɪŋ **-gated** -geɪ.tɪd (US) -geɪ.t̬ɪd **-gator/s** -geɪ.təʳ/z (US) -geɪ.t̬ɚ/z
variegation ˌveə.rɪ'geɪ.ʃᵊn, -ri.ə'-
(US) ˌver.i.ə'-, ˌvær- **-s** -z
varietal və'raɪə.tᵊl (US) -t̬ᵊl
variet|y və'raɪə.t|i (US) -t̬|i **-ies** -iz
va'riety ˌshow ; **va'riety ˌstore**
variform 'veə.rɪ.fɔːm
(US) 'ver.ə.fɔːrm, 'vær-
Varig® 'vær.ɪg (US) 'ver-, 'vær-

variola və'raɪ.ə.lə
variole 'veə.ri.əʊl (US) 'ver.i.oʊl, 'vær- **-s** -z
variorum ˌveə.ri'ɔː.rəm, ˌvær-
(US) ˌver.i'ɔːr.əm, ˌvær-
various 'veə.ri.əs (US) 'ver.i-, 'vær-
-ly -li **-ness** -nəs, -nɪs
variphone 'veə.rɪ.fəʊn
(US) 'ver.ɪ.foʊn, 'vær- **-s** -z
varix 'veə.rɪks (US) 'ver.ɪks, 'vær-
varices 'vær.ɪ.siːz, 'veə.rɪ-
(US) 'vær.ə-, 'ver-
varlet 'vɑː.lət, -lɪt (US) 'vɑːr- **-s** -s
Varley 'vɑː.li (US) 'vɑːr-
varmint 'vɑː.mɪnt (US) 'vɑːr- **-s** -s
Varna 'vɑː.nə (US) 'vɑːr-
Varney 'vɑː.ni (US) 'vɑːr-
varnish 'vɑː.nɪʃ (US) 'vɑːr- **-es** -ɪz
-ing -ɪŋ **-ed** -t **-er/s** -əʳ/z (US) -ɚ/z
Varro 'vær.əʊ (US) -oʊ, 'ver-
varsit|y 'vɑː.sə.t|i, -ɪ.t|i
(US) 'vɑːr.sə.t̬|i **-ies** -iz
Varuna vær'uː.nə (US) vʌr-, vɑː'ruː-
var|y 'veə.r|i (US) 'ver|.i, 'vær- **-ies** -iz
-ying/ly -i.ɪŋ/li **-ied** -id
Vasari və'sɑː.ri (US) vɑː'sɑːr.i
Vasco da Gama ˌvæs.kəʊ.də'gɑː.mə, -dɑː'- (US) ˌvɑː.skoʊ-, -'gæm.ə
vascular 'væs.kjə.ləʳ, -kjʊ- (US) -kjə.lɚ
vascularity ˌvæs.kjə'lær.ə.ti, -kjʊ'-, -ɪ.ti (US) -kjə'ler.ə.t̬i, -'lær-
vascul|um 'væs.kjə.l|əm, -kjʊ-
(US) -kjə- **-a** -ə
vas deferens ˌvæs'def.ə.renz, ˌvæz-
(US) ˌvæs'def.ə.renz
vas|e vɑːz (US) veɪs, veɪz, vɑːz **-es** -ɪz
vasectom|y və'sek.tə.m|i, væs'ek-
-ies -ɪz
Vaseline® 'væs.ᵊl.iːn, -ɪ.liːn, ˌ--'-
(US) 'væs.ə.liːn, ˌ--'-
Vashti 'væʃ.ti (US) 'vɑːʃ.ti, -taɪ
vasoconstriction
ˌveɪ.zəʊ.kən'strɪk.ʃᵊn, ˌvæs.əʊ-
(US) ˌvæs.oʊ-, ˌveɪ.zoʊ-
vasoconstrictor ˌveɪ.zəʊ.kən'strɪk.təʳ, ˌvæs.əʊ- (US) ˌvæs.oʊ-, ˌveɪ.zoʊ-
-s -z
vasodilation ˌveɪ.zəʊ.daɪ'leɪ.ʃᵊn, ˌvæs.əʊ- (US) ˌvæs.oʊ-, ˌveɪ.zoʊ-
vasodilator ˌveɪ.zəʊ.daɪ'leɪ.təʳ, ˌvæs.əʊ- (US) ˌvæs.oʊ'daɪ.leɪ.t̬ɚ, ˌveɪ.zoʊ-, -də'-; -daɪ'leɪ- **-s** -z
vasomotor ˌveɪ.zəʊ'məʊ.təʳ, ˌvæs.əʊ-
(US) ˌvæs.oʊ'moʊ.t̬ɚ, ˌveɪ.zoʊ'-
vassal 'væs.ᵊl **-s** -z
vassalage 'væs.ᵊl.ɪdʒ
vast vɑːst (US) væst **-er** -əʳ (US) -ɚ **-est** -ɪst, -əst **-ly** -li **-ness/es** -nəs/ɪz, -nɪs/ɪz
Västerås ˌves.tə'rɔːs
vat væt **-s** -s **-ting** -ɪŋ (US) 'væt̬.ɪŋ
-ted -ɪd (US) 'væt̬.ɪd

VAT ˌviː.eɪˈtiː, væt **-able** ˈvæt.ə.bl̩
Vathek ˈvæθ.ek, ˈvɑː.θek
vatic ˈvæt.ɪk ⓊⓈ ˈvæt̬-
Vatican ˈvæt.ɪ.kən ⓊⓈ ˈvæt̬- ˌ**Vatican** ˈ**City**
vatici|nate vəˈtɪs.ɪ|.neɪt, vætˈɪs- ⓊⓈ ˈ-ə- **-nates** -neɪts **-nating** -neɪ.tɪŋ ⓊⓈ -neɪ.t̬ɪŋ **-nated** -neɪ.tɪd ⓊⓈ -neɪ.t̬ɪd
vaticination ˌvæt.ɪ.sɪˈneɪ.ʃᵊn, ˌ-ə-; vəˌtɪs.ɪˈ-, vætˌɪs- ⓊⓈ ˌvæt̬.ə.səˈ-; vəˌtɪs-, vætˌɪs- **-s** -z
vatu ˈvɑː.tuː **-s** -z
Vaucluse vəʊˈkluːz ⓊⓈ voʊ-
Vaud vəʊ ⓊⓈ voʊ
vaudeville ˈvɔː.də.vɪl, ˈvəʊ-; ˈvɔːd.vɪl, -vᵊl ⓊⓈ ˈvɑːd.vɪl, ˈvɔːd-, ˈvoʊd-, ˈvɑː.də-, ˈvɔː-, ˈvoʊ- **-s** -z
vaudevillian ˌvɔː.dəˈvɪl.i.ən, ˌvəʊ-, ˌvɔːdˈvɪl- ⓊⓈ ˌvɑːdˈvɪl-, ˌvɔːd-, ˌvoʊd-, ˌvɑː.dəˈ-, ˌvɔː-, ˌvoʊ- **-s** -z
Vaudin ˈvəʊ.dɪn ⓊⓈ ˈvoʊ-
Vaudois (*sing.*) ˈvəʊ.dwɑː, -ˈ-, -dwɔː ⓊⓈ voʊˈdwɑː (*plur.*) -z
Vaughan vɔːn ⓊⓈ vɑːn, vɔːn
Vaughan Williams ˌvɔːnˈwɪl.jəmz, -i.əmz ⓊⓈ ˌvɑːnˈ-, ˌvɔːnˈ-
Vaughn vɔːn ⓊⓈ vɑːn, vɔːn
vault vɔːlt, vɒlt ⓊⓈ vɑːlt, vɔːlt **-s** -s **-ing/s** -ɪŋ/z ⓊⓈ ˈvɑːl.t̬ɪŋz, ˈvɔːl- **-ed** -ɪd ⓊⓈ ˈvɑːl.t̬ɪd, ˈvɔːl- **-er/s** -əʳ/z ⓊⓈ ˈvɑːl.t̬ɚ/z, -ˈvɔːl- ˈ**vaulting** ˌ**horse**
vaunt vɔːnt ⓊⓈ vɑːnt, vɔːnt **-s** -s **-ing/ly** -ɪŋ/li ⓊⓈ ˈvɑːn.t̬ɪŋ/li, ˈvɔːn- **-ed** -ɪd ⓊⓈ ˈvɑːn.t̬ɪd, ˈvɔːn- **-er/s** -əʳ/z ⓊⓈ ˈvɑːn.t̬ɚ/z, ˈvɔːn-
Vaux *English surname:* vɔːz, vɒks, vɔːks, vəʊks ⓊⓈ vɔːks, vɑːks *in de Vaux:* vəʊ ⓊⓈ voʊ
Note: **Brougham and Vaux** is ˈbrʊm.ənˈvɔːks
Vauxhall® ˈvɒk.sɔːl, ˈvɒks.hɔːl, -ˈ- ⓊⓈ ˈvɑːks.hɔːl, ˈvɔːks-
vavaso(u)r (V) ˈvæv.ə.sʊəʳ, -sɔːʳ ⓊⓈ -sɔːr **-s** -z
VAX® væks
VC ˌviːˈsiː **-s** -z
VCR ˌviː.siːˈɑːʳ ⓊⓈ -ˈɑːr **-s** -z
VD ˌviːˈdiː
VDT ˌviː.diːˈtiː **-s** -z
VDU, vdu ˌviː.diːˈjuː **-s** -z
-'ve (= have) -v, -əv
veal viːl **-y** -i
Veblen ˈveb.lən
vector (*n.*) ˈvek.təʳ, -tɔːʳ ⓊⓈ -tɚ **-s** -z
vect|or (*v.*) ˈvek.t|əʳ ⓊⓈ -t|ɚ **-ors** -əz ⓊⓈ -ɚz **-oring** -ᵊr.ɪŋ **-ored** -əd ⓊⓈ -ɚd
vectorial vekˈtɔː.ri.əl ⓊⓈ -ˈtɔːr.i-
Veda ˈveɪ.də, ˈviː- **-s** -z
Vedanta vedˈɑːn.tə, vɪˈdɑːn-, və-, -ˈdæn- ⓊⓈ vɪˈdɑːn-, -ˈdæn-
V-E Day ˌviːˈiː.deɪ
vedette vɪˈdet, və-, vedˈet ⓊⓈ və- **-s** -s
Vedic ˈveɪ.dɪk, ˈviː-
veep (V) viːp
veer vɪəʳ ⓊⓈ vɪr **-s** -z **-ing/ly** -ɪŋ/li **-ed** -d
veg vedʒ ˌ**meat and two** ˈ**veg**
Vega *star:* ˈviː.gə ⓊⓈ ˈviː-, ˈveɪ- *Spanish dramatist:* ˈveɪ.gə
vegan ˈviː.gən **-s** -z **-ism** -ɪzᵊm
Vegas ˈveɪ.gəs
vegeburger ˈvedʒ.iˌbɜː.gəʳ ⓊⓈ -ˌbɜːr.gɚ **-s** -z
Vegemite® ˈvedʒ.i.maɪt, ˈ-ə-
vegetable ˈvedʒ.tə.bl̩, ˈ-ə.tə-, ˈ-ɪ- ⓊⓈ ˈvedʒ.tə-, -ə.t̬ə- **-s** -z
vegetal ˈvedʒ.ɪ.tᵊl, ˈ-ə- ⓊⓈ ˈ-ə-
vegetarian ˌvedʒ.ɪˈteə.ri.ən, -əˈ- ⓊⓈ -əˈter.i- **-s** -z **-ism** -ɪ.zᵊm
vege|tate ˈvedʒ.ɪ|.teɪt, ˈ-ə- ⓊⓈ ˈ-ə- **-tates** -teɪts **-tating** -teɪ.tɪŋ ⓊⓈ -teɪ.t̬ɪŋ **-tated** -teɪ.tɪd ⓊⓈ -teɪ.t̬ɪd
vegetation ˌvedʒ.ɪˈteɪ.ʃᵊn, -əˈ- ⓊⓈ -əˈ- **-s** -z
vegetative ˈvedʒ.ɪ.tə.tɪv, ˈ-ə-, -teɪ- ⓊⓈ -ə.teɪ.t̬ɪv **-ly** -li
veggie ˈvedʒ.i **-s** -z
veggieburger ˈvedʒ.iˌbɜː.gəʳ ⓊⓈ ˌbɜːr.gɚ **-s** -z
vegg|y ˈvedʒ|.i **-ies** -iz
vehemence ˈviː.ə.mənts, ˈ-ɪ-, -hɪ-, -hə-, ˈvɪə.mənts ⓊⓈ ˈviː.ə-, -hə-
vehement ˈviː.ə.mənt, ˈ-ɪ-, -hɪ-, -hə-, ˈvɪə.mənt ⓊⓈ ˈviː.ə-, -hə- **-ly** -li
vehicle ˈvɪə.kl̩, ˈviː.ɪ- ⓊⓈ ˈviː.ə-, -hɪ- **-s** -z
vehicular viˈɪk.jə.ləʳ, vɪˈhɪk-, və-, -jʊ- ⓊⓈ viːˈhɪk.jə.lɚ, -jʊ-
veil veɪl **-s** -z **-ing/s** -ɪŋ/z **-ed** -d
Veil viːl ⓊⓈ veɪ, viːl
vein veɪn **-s** -z **-ed** -d **-less** -ləs, -lɪs
vein|y ˈveɪ.n|i **-ier** -i.əʳ ⓊⓈ -i.ɚ **-iest** -i.ɪst, -i.əst
Veitch viːtʃ
velar ˈviː.ləʳ ⓊⓈ -lɚ **-s** -z
velaric viːˈlær.ɪk, vɪ- ⓊⓈ -ˈler-, -ˈlær-
velarization, -isa- ˌviː.lᵊr.aɪˈzeɪ.ʃᵊn, -ɪˈ- ⓊⓈ -ɪˈ- **-s** -z
velariz|e, -is|e ˈviː.lᵊr.aɪz ⓊⓈ -lə.raɪz **-es** -ɪz **-ing** -ɪŋ **-ed** -d
Velasquez, Velazquez vɪˈlæs.kwɪz, velˈæs-, -kɪz, -kez, -kwɪθ ⓊⓈ vəˈlɑː.skes, -ˈlæs.kes, -kwez
Velcro® ˈvel.krəʊ ⓊⓈ -kroʊ
veldt, veld (V) velt ⓊⓈ velt, felt
velic ˈviː.lɪk
velleity velˈiː.ə.ti, vəˈliː-, -ɪ.ti ⓊⓈ vəˈliː-
vellum ˈvel.əm **-s** -z
veloce vɪˈləʊ.tʃeɪ, velˈəʊ-, vəˈləʊ- ⓊⓈ veɪˈloʊ.tʃeɪ
velocipede vɪˈlɒs.ɪ.piːd, və-, ˈ-ə- ⓊⓈ vəˈlɑː.sə- **-s** -z
velocit|y vɪˈlɒs.ə.t|i, və-, -ɪ.t|i ⓊⓈ vəˈlɑː.sə.t̬|i **-ies** -iz
velodrome ˈvel.ə.drəʊm, ˈviː.ləʊ- ⓊⓈ ˈvel.ə.droʊm **-s** -z
velour vəˈlʊəʳ ⓊⓈ -ˈlʊr **-s** -z
velouté vəˈluː.teɪ **-s** -z
vel|um ˈviː.l|əm **-a** -ə
velvet ˈvel.vɪt, -vət **-s** -s
velveteen ˌvel.vɪˈtiːn, -vəˈ-, ˈ--- **-s** -z
velvet|y ˈvel.vɪ.t|i, -və- ⓊⓈ -və.t̬|i **-iness** -ɪ.nəs, -nɪs
Venables ˈven.ə.bl̩z
vena cava ˌviː.nəˈkeɪ.və, -ˈkɑː- ⓊⓈ -ˈkeɪ- **venae cavae** -niːˈkeɪ.viː, -ˈkɑː- ⓊⓈ -ˈkeɪ-
venal ˈviː.nᵊl ⓊⓈ **-ly** -i
venality viːˈnæl.ə.ti, vɪ-, -ɪ.ti ⓊⓈ vɪˈnæl.ə.t̬i
venation viːˈneɪ.ʃᵊn
vend vend **-s** -z **-ing** -ɪŋ **-ed** -ɪd **-er/s** -əʳ/z ⓊⓈ -ɚ/z ˈ**vending ma**ˌ**chine**
Venda ˈven.də
vendee venˈdiː **-s** -z
vendetta venˈdet.ə ⓊⓈ -ˈdet̬- **-s** -z
vendor ˈven.dɔːʳ, -dəʳ ⓊⓈ -dɚ, -dɔːr **-s** -z
veneer vəˈnɪəʳ, vɪ- ⓊⓈ -ˈnɪr **-s** -z **-ing** -ɪŋ **-ed** -d
venerab|le ˈven.ᵊr.ə.b|l̩ **-ly** -li **-ness** -l̩.nəs, -nɪs
vener|ate ˈven.ᵊr|.eɪt ⓊⓈ -ə.r|eɪt **-ates** -eɪts **-ating** -eɪ.tɪŋ ⓊⓈ -eɪ.t̬ɪŋ **-ated** -eɪ.tɪd ⓊⓈ -eɪ.t̬ɪd **-ator/s** -eɪ.təʳ/z ⓊⓈ -eɪ.t̬ɚ/z
veneration ˌven.ᵊrˈeɪ.ʃᵊn ⓊⓈ -əˈreɪ-
venereal vəˈnɪə.ri.əl, vɪ- ⓊⓈ vəˈnɪr.i- **ve**ˈ**nereal di**ˌ**sease**
venery ˈven.ᵊr.i
Venetia vəˈniː.ʃi.ə, vɪ-, ˈ-ʃə
Venetian, venetian vəˈniː.ʃᵊn, vɪ- ⓊⓈ ˈ-ʃᵊn **-s** -z **ve**ˌ**netian** ˈ**blind**
Venezuel|a ˌven.ɪˈzweɪ.l|ə, -ezˈweɪ-, -əˈzweɪ- ⓊⓈ -əˈzweɪ-, -ˈzwiː- **-an/s** -ən/z
veng|e vendʒ **-es** -ɪz **-ing** -ɪŋ **-ed** -d
vengeance ˈven.dʒᵊnts
vengeful ˈvendʒ.fᵊl, -fʊl **-ly** -i **-ness** -nəs ⓊⓈ -nɪs
veni, vidi, vici ˌveɪ.niːˌviː.diːˈviː.kiː, ˌweɪ.niːˌwiː.diːˈwiː.kiː
venial ˈviː.ni.əl, ˈ-njəl **-ly** -i **-ness** -nəs, -nɪs ˌ**venial** ˈ**sin**
veniality ˌviː.niˈæl.ə.ti, -ɪ.ti ⓊⓈ -ə.t̬i
Venice ˈven.ɪs
venire vəˈnɪə.riː ⓊⓈ -ˈnaɪ-, -ˈnɪr.iː
venison ˈven.ɪ.sᵊn, ˈ-ə-, -zᵊn
Venite vɪˈnaɪ.ti, venˈaɪ-, -ˈniː- ⓊⓈ vəˈniː- **-s** -z
Venn ven ˈ**Venn** ˌ**diagram**, ˌ**Venn** ˈ**diagram**

Venner 'ven.ər (US) -ɚ
venom 'ven.əm **-s** -z **-ed** -d
venomous 'ven.ə.məs **-ly** -li **-ness** -nəs, -nɪs
venous 'viː.nəs **-ly** -li
vent vent **-s** -s **-ing** -ɪŋ (US) 'ven.t̬ɪŋ **-ed** -ɪd (US) 'ven.t̬ɪd
Vent-Axia® ˌvent'æk.si.ə
ventil|ate 'ven.tɪ.l|eɪt, -təl|.eɪt (US) -t̬ə.l|eɪt **-ates** -eɪts **-ating** -eɪ.tɪŋ (US) -eɪ.t̬ɪŋ **-ated** -eɪ.tɪd (US) -eɪ.t̬ɪd
ventilation ˌven.tɪ'leɪ.ʃən, -təl'eɪ- (US) -t̬ə'leɪ-
ventilator 'ven.tɪ.leɪ.tər, -təl.eɪ- (US) -t̬ə.leɪ.t̬ɚ **-s** -z
Ventnor 'vent.nər (US) -nɚ
Ventolin® 'ven.təʊ.lɪn, -təl.ɪn (US) -t̬əl.ɪn, -toʊ.lɪn
ventral 'ven.trəl **-ly** -i
ventricle 'ven.trɪ.kl̩ **-s** -z
ventricular ven'trɪk.jə.lər, -jʊ- (US) -jə.lɚ
ventriloquial ˌven.trɪ'ləʊ.kwi.əl, -trə'- (US) -trə'loʊ- **-ly** -i
ventriloquism ven'trɪl.ə.kwɪ.zəm
ventriloquist ven'trɪl.ə.kwɪst **-s** -s
ventriloquiz|e, -is|e ven'trɪl.ə.kwaɪz **-es** -ɪz **-ing** -ɪŋ **-ed** -d
ventriloquy ven'trɪl.ə.kwi
vent|ure 'ven.tʃ|ər (US) -tʃ|ɚ **-ures** -əz (US) -ɚz **-uring** -ər.ɪŋ **-ured** -əd (US) -ɚd **-urer/s** -ər.ər/z (US) -ɚ.ɚ/z ˌ**venture 'capital** (US) '**venture** ˌ**capital**; '**Venture** ˌ**Scout**
venturesome 'ven.tʃə.səm (US) -tʃɚ- **-ly** -li **-ness** -nəs, -nɪs
venturi ven'tjʊə.ri, -'tʃʊə- (US) -'tʊr.i **-s** -z
venturous 'ven.tʃər.əs **-ly** -li **-ness** -nəs, -nɪs
venue 'ven.juː **-s** -z
venul|ar 'ven.jʊ.l|ər, -jə- (US) -juː.l|ɚ, 'viː.njuː-, -njə- **-ose** -əʊs (US) -oʊs
venule 'ven.juːl (US) 'ven.juːl, 'viː.njuːl **-s** -z
Venus 'viː.nəs **-es** -ɪz ˌ**Venus' 'flytrap**
Venusian vɪ'njuː.si.ən, və-, -zi.ən (US) vɪ'nuː.ʃən, -ʒən, -zi.ən **-s** -z
Vera 'vɪə.rə (US) 'vɪr.ə
veracious və'reɪ.ʃəs, vɪ-, ver'eɪ- (US) və'reɪ- **-ly** -li **-ness** -nəs, -nɪs
veracity və'ræs.ə.ti, vɪ-, ver'æs-, -ɪ.ti (US) və'ræs.ə.t̬i
Veracruz ˌvɪə.rə'kruːz, ˌver.ə'-, ˌveə.rə'- (US) ˌver.ə'-
veranda(h) və'ræn.də **-s** -z
verb vɜːb (US) vɜːrb **-s** -z
verbal 'vɜː.bəl (US) 'vɜːr- **-ly** -i
verbal|ism 'vɜː.bəl|.ɪ.zəm (US) 'vɜːr- **-ist/s** -ɪst/s
verbalization ˌvɜː.bəl.aɪ'zeɪ.ʃən, -ɪ'- (US) ˌvɜːr.bəl.ɪ'-
verbaliz|e, -is|e 'vɜː.bəl.aɪz (US) 'vɜːr.bə.laɪz **-es** -ɪz **-ing** -ɪŋ **-ed** -d
verbatim vɜː'beɪ.tɪm, və- (US) vɚ'beɪ.t̬ɪm, -t̬əm
verbena vɜː'biː.nə, və- (US) vɚ- **-s** -z
verbiage 'vɜː.bi.ɪdʒ (US) 'vɜːr-
verbose vɜː'bəʊs, və- (US) vɚ'boʊs **-ly** -li **-ness** -nəs, -nɪs
verbosity vɜː'bɒs.ə.ti, və-, -ɪ.ti (US) vɚ'bɑː.sə.t̬i
verboten vɜː'bəʊ.tən *as if German:* fə'- (US) vɚ'boʊ-
Vercingetorix ˌvɜː.sɪn'dʒet.ə.rɪks, -sən'-, -'get- (US) ˌvɜːr.sɪn'dʒet̬.ɚ.ɪks, -'get̬-
verdancy 'vɜː.dənt.si (US) 'vɜːr-
verdant 'vɜː.dənt (US) 'vɜːr- **-ly** -li
Verde vɜːd (US) vɜːrd
Verdi 'veə.diː, -di (US) 'ver- **-an** -ən
verdict 'vɜː.dɪkt (US) 'vɜːr- **-s** -s
verdigris 'vɜː.dɪ.grɪs, -griːs (US) 'vɜːr.dɪ.griːs, -grɪs, -griː
Verdun vɜː'dʌn, '-- (US) ver'dʌn, 'vɜːr-
verdure 'vɜː.djər, -dʒər, -djʊər (US) 'vɜːr.dʒɚ
Vere vɪər (US) vɪr
verg|e vɜːdʒ (US) vɜːrdʒ **-es** -ɪz **-ing** -ɪŋ **-ed** -d
verger 'vɜː.dʒər (US) 'vɜːr.dʒɚ **-s** -z
Vergil 'vɜː.dʒɪl (US) 'vɜːr- **-s** -z
Vergilian vɜː'dʒɪl.i.ən, və- (US) vɜːr-, '-jən
verifiable 'ver.ɪ.faɪ.ə.bl̩, '-ə-, ˌver.ɪ'faɪ-, -ə'- (US) 'ver.ə.faɪ-
verification ˌver.ɪ.fɪ'keɪ.ʃən, ˌ-ə- (US) ˌ-ə- **-s** -z
veri|fy 'ver.ɪ|.faɪ, '-ə- (US) '-ə- **-fies** -faɪz **-fying** -faɪ.ɪŋ **-fied** -faɪd **-fier/s** -faɪ.ər/z (US) -faɪ.ɚ/z
verily 'ver.əl.i, -ɪ.li
verisimilitude ˌver.ɪ.sɪ'mɪl.ɪ.tjuːd, ˌ-ə-, -sə'- (US) -ə.sə'mɪl.ə.tuːd, -tjuːd
verismo və'rɪz.moʊ
veritab|le 'ver.ɪ.tə.b|l̩ (US) -ə.t̬ə- **-ly** -li
verit|y (V) 'ver.ə.t|i, -ɪ.t|i (US) -ə.t̬|i **-ies** -iz
verjuice 'vɜː.dʒuːs (US) 'vɜːr-
Verlaine veə'len, vɜː- (US) vɚ'leɪn, -'len
Vermeer və'mɪər, vɜː-, -'meər (US) vɚ'mɪr **-s** -z
vermeil 'vɜː.meɪl, -mɪl (US) 'vɜːr.mɪl; vɚ'meɪl
vermicelli ˌvɜː.mɪ'tʃel.i, -'sel- (US) ˌvɜːr.mə'tʃel-, -'sel-
vermicide 'vɜː.mɪ.saɪd (US) 'vɜːr.mə- **-s** -z
vermicular vɜː'mɪk.jə.lər, -jʊ- (US) vɚ'mɪk.jə.lɚ
vermiform 'vɜː.mɪ.fɔːm (US) 'vɜːr.mə.fɔːrm ˌ**vermiform ap'pendix**
vermil(l)ion və'mɪl.jən, vɜː-, -i.ən (US) vɚ'mɪl.jən **-s** -z
vermin 'vɜː.mɪn (US) 'vɜːr- **-ous** -əs
Vermont və'mɒnt, vɜː- (US) vɚ'mɑːnt
vermouth 'vɜː.məθ, -muːθ; vɜː'muːθ, və- (US) vɚ'muːθ **-s** -s
vernacular və'næk.jə.lər, vɜː-, -jʊ- (US) vɚ'næk.jə.lɚ **-s** -z **-ly** -li
vernal 'vɜː.nəl (US) 'vɜːr- **-ly** -i ˌ**vernal 'equinox**
Verne vɜːn, veən (US) vɜːrn
Verner *English surname:* 'vɜː.nər (US) 'vɜːr.nɚ *Danish grammarian:* 'vɜː.nər, 'veə- (US) 'vɜːr.nɚ, 'ver-
Verney 'vɜː.ni (US) 'vɜːr-
vernier 'vɜː.ni.ər (US) 'vɜːr.ni.ɚ **-s** -z
Vernon 'vɜː.nən (US) 'vɜːr-
Verona və'rəʊ.nə, vɪ-, ver'əʊ- (US) və'roʊ-
Veronal® 'ver.ə.nəl
Veronese *artist:* ˌver.əʊ'neɪ.zeɪ (US) -ə'neɪ.si, -zi
Veronese *(person) from Verona:* ˌver.ə'niːz, -əʊ'- (US) -ə'niːz
veronica (V) və'rɒn.ɪ.kə, vɪ-, ver'ɒn- (US) və'rɑː.nɪ- **-s** -z
Verrazano ˌver.ə'zɑː.nəʊ (US) -noʊ *stress shift, see compound:* ˌ**Verrazano 'Narrows**
verru|ca və'ruː|.kə, vɪ-, ver'uː- (US) və'ruː- **-cas** -kəz **-cae** -kiː, -kaɪ
verrucose və'ruː.kəʊs, vɪ-, ver'uː- (US) 'ver.uː.koʊs, -jə-
Versailles *in France:* veə'saɪ, vɜː- (US) vɜːr'saɪ-, ver- *in US:* vɜː'seɪlz (US) vɜːr-
versant 'vɜː.sənt (US) 'vɜːr- **-s** -s
versatile 'vɜː.sə.taɪl (US) 'vɜːr.sə.t̬əl **-ly** -li **-ness** -nəs, -nɪs
versatility ˌvɜː.sə'tɪl.ə.ti, -ɪ.ti (US) ˌvɜːr.sə'tɪl.ə.t̬i
vers de société ˌveə.dəˌsɒs.jeɪ'teɪ (US) ˌver.dɪ.soʊ'siː.eɪ.teɪ; -dəˌsɑː.sjeɪ'teɪ
vers|e vɜːs (US) vɜːrs **-es** -ɪz **-ed** -t
versicle 'vɜː.sɪ.kl̩ (US) 'vɜːr- **-s** -z
versification ˌvɜː.sɪ.fɪ'keɪ.ʃən, -sə- (US) ˌvɜːr.sə-
versificator 'vɜː.sɪ.fɪ.keɪ.tər, -sə- (US) 'vɜːr.sə.fɪ.keɪ.t̬ɚ **-s** -z
versi|fy 'vɜː.sɪ|.faɪ, -sə- (US) 'vɜːr.sə- **-fies** -faɪz **-fying** -faɪ.ɪŋ **-fied** -faɪd **-fier/s** -faɪ.ər/z (US) -faɪ.ɚ/z
version 'vɜː.ʃən, -ʒən (US) 'vɜːr.ʒən, -ʃən **-s** -z
verso 'vɜː.səʊ (US) 'vɜːr.soʊ **-s** -z
versus 'vɜː.səs (US) 'vɜːr-
vert (V) vɜːt (US) vɜːrt **-s** -s
vertebr|a 'vɜː.tɪ.br|ə, -tə- (US) 'vɜːr.t̬ə- **-ae** -iː, -aɪ, -eɪ **-as** -əz
vertebral 'vɜː.tɪ.brəl, -tə- (US) 'vɜːr.t̬ə- **-ly** -i ˌ**vertebral 'column**

vertebrata ˌvɜː.tɪˈbrɑː.tə, -təˈ-, -ˈbreɪ- (US) -ˈbreɪ.t̬ə, -ˈbrɑː-

vertebrate ˈvɜː.tɪ.breɪt, -tə-, -brət, -brɪt (US) ˈvɝː.t̬ə.brɪt, -breɪt **-s** -s

ver|tex ˈvɜː|.teks (US) ˈvɝː- **-tices** -tɪ.siːz (US) -t̬ɪ- **-texes** -tek.sɪz

vertic|al ˈvɜː.tɪ.k|ᵊl, -tə- (US) ˈvɝː.t̬ə- **-ally** -ᵊl.i, -li **-alness** -ᵊl.nəs, -nɪs

vertiginous vɜːˈtɪdʒ.ɪ.nəs, ˈ-ə- (US) vɚˈtɪdʒ.ə- **-ly** -li

vertigo ˈvɜː.tɪ.ɡəʊ, -tə- (US) ˈvɝː.t̬ə.ɡoʊ

Verulam ˈver.ʊ.ləm (US) -juː-

Verulamium ˌver.ʊˈleɪ.mi.əm (US) -juːˈ-

vervain ˈvɜː.veɪn (US) ˈvɝː-

verve vɜːv (US) vɝːv

Verwood ˈvɜː.wʊd (US) ˈvɝː-

very (*adj. adv.*) ˈver.i

Very *surname:* ˈvɪə.ri, ˈver.i (US) ˈvɪr.i, ˈver-

Vesalius vesˈeɪ.li.əs

Vesey ˈviː.zi

vesi|ca ˈves.ɪ|.kə; vɪˈsaɪ|.kə, və- (US) vɪˈsaɪ-, -ˈsiː- **-cae** -kiː

vesicle ˈves.ɪ.kl̩ **-s** -z

vesicular vɪˈsɪk.jə.ləʳ, və- (US) -lɚ

vesiculate vɪˈsɪk.jə.leɪt, vəˈ-

Vespa® ˈves.pə

Vespasian vesˈpeɪ.zi.ən, -ʒi-, ˈ-ʒᵊn (US) ˈ-ʒᵊn, -ʒi.ən

vesper (V) ˈves.pəʳ (US) -pɚ **-s** -z

vespertine ˈves.pə.taɪn (US) -pɚ.tɪn, -taɪn

Vespucci vesˈpuː.tʃi

vessel ˈves.ᵊl **-s** -z

vest vest **-s** -s **-ing** -ɪŋ **-ed** -ɪd ˌ**vested** ˈ**interest**

vesta (V) ˈves.tə **-s** -z

vestal ˈves.tᵊl **-s** -z ˌ**vestal** ˈ**virgin**

vestiar|y ˈvest.jə.r|i **-ies** -iz

vestibular vesˈtɪb.jə.ləʳ, -jʊ- (US) -jə.lɚ

vestibule ˈves.tɪ.bjuːl (US) -tə- **-s** -z **-d** -d

vestig|e ˈves.tɪdʒ **-es** -ɪz

vestigial vesˈtɪdʒ.i.əl, ˈ-əl **-ly** -i

vestiture ˈves.tɪ.tʃəʳ (US) -tʃɚ

vestment ˈves*t*.mənt **-s** -s

vest-pocket ˌvestˈpɒk.ɪt (US) -ˈpɑː.kɪt, ˈ-ˌ--

Vestris ˈves.trɪs

vestr|y ˈves.tr|i **-ies** -iz

vesture ˈves.tʃəʳ, -tjəʳ (US) -tʃɚ **-s** -z

vesuvian (V) vɪˈsuː.vi.ən, və-, -ˈsjuː- (US) vəˈsuː- **-s** -z **-ite** -aɪt

Vesuvius vɪˈsuː.vi.əs, və-, -ˈsjuː- (US) vəˈsuː-

vet vet **-s** -s **-ting** -ɪŋ (US) ˈvet̬.ɪŋ **-ted** -ɪd (US) ˈvet̬.ɪd

vetch vetʃ **-es** -ɪz

veteran ˈvet.ᵊr.ᵊn, -rən (US) ˈvet̬.ɚ.ᵊn; ˈvet.rən **-s** -z ˈ**Veterans** ˌ**Day**

veterinarian ˌvet.ᵊr.ɪˈneə.ri.ən, ˌ-rəˈ- (US) -ˈner.i- **-s** -z

veterinar|y ˈvet.ᵊr.ɪ.nᵊr|.i, ˈ-rə.nᵊr- (US) -ner- **-ies** -iz ˈ**veterinary** ˌ**surgeon**

veto ˈviː.təʊ (US) -t̬oʊ **-es** -z **-ing** -ɪŋ **-ed** -d **-er/s** -əʳ/z (US) -ɚ/z

Vevey ˈvev.eɪ, -i (US) vəˈveɪ

vex veks **-es** -ɪz **-ing** -ɪŋ **-ed** -t ˌ**vexed** ˈ**question**

vexation vekˈseɪ.ʃᵊn **-s** -z

vexatious vekˈseɪ.ʃəs **-ly** -li **-ness** -nəs, -nɪs

vgc ˌviː.dʒiːˈsiː

VHF ˌviː.eɪtʃˈef

via vaɪə (US) vaɪə, ˈviː.ə

viability ˌvaɪ.əˈbɪl.ə.ti, -ɪ.ti (US) -ə.t̬i

viab|le ˈvaɪ.ə.b|l̩ **-ly** -li

via dolorosa, ˌviː.əˌdɒl.əˈrəʊ.sə (US) -ˌdɑː.ləˈroʊ-, -ˌdoʊ-

viaduct ˈvaɪə.dʌkt **-s** -s

vial vaɪəl (US) ˈvaɪ.əl; vaɪl **-s** -z

viand ˈvaɪ.ənd **-s** -z

viatic|um vaɪˈæt.ɪ.k|əm, vi- (US) vaɪˈæt̬- **-ums** -əmz **-a** -ə

vibes vaɪbz

vibrancy ˈvaɪ.brən*t*.si

vibrant ˈvaɪ.brənt **-ly** -li

vibraphone ˈvaɪ.brə.fəʊn (US) -foʊn **-s** -z

vibra|te vaɪˈbreɪ|t (US) ˈ-- **-tes** -ts **-ting** -tɪŋ (US) -t̬ɪŋ **-ted** -tɪd (US) -t̬ɪd

vibration vaɪˈbreɪ.ʃᵊn **-s** -z

vibrational vaɪˈbreɪ.ʃᵊn.ᵊl, -ˈbreɪʃ.nᵊl

vibrative vaɪˈbreɪ.tɪv (US) ˈvaɪ.brə.t̬ɪv

vibrato vɪˈbrɑː.təʊ (US) -t̬oʊ **-s** -z

vibrator vaɪˈbreɪ.təʳ (US) ˈvaɪ.breɪ.t̬ɚ **-s** -z

vibratory ˈvaɪ.brə.tᵊr.i; vaɪˈbreɪ- (US) ˈvaɪ.brə.tɔːr-

viburnum vaɪˈbɜː.nəm (US) -ˈbɝː- **-s** -z

vic (V) vɪk **-s** -s

vicar ˈvɪk.əʳ (US) -ɚ **-s** -z

vicarag|e ˈvɪk.ᵊr.ɪdʒ **-es** -ɪz

vicarial vɪˈkeə.ri.əl, vaɪ-, və- (US) -ˈker.i-, -ˈkær-

vicarious vɪˈkeə.ri.əs, vaɪ-, və- (US) -ˈker.i-, -ˈkær- **-ly** -li **-ness** -nəs, -nɪs

vice- ˌvaɪs-

Note: Prefix. This usually receives secondary stress. It may carry the strongest stress in the word in stress shift cases.

vic|e (*n.*) vaɪs **-es** -ɪz ˈ**vice** ˌ**squad**

vice (*prep.*) ˈvaɪ.si, -sə (US) -sə, -si

vice-admiral ˌvaɪsˈæd.mᵊr.ᵊl, -mɪ.rᵊl **-s** -z *stress shift:* ˌvice-admiral's ˈflag

vice-chair|man ˌvaɪsˈtʃeə|.mən (US) -ˈtʃer- **-men** -mən *stress shift:* ˌvice-chairman's ˈprivilege

vice-chancellor ˌvaɪsˈtʃɑːn*t*.sᵊl.əʳ (US) -ˈtʃænt- **-s** -z *stress shift:* ˌvice-chancellor's ˈsecretary

vice-consul ˌvaɪsˈkɒn*t*.sᵊl (US) -ˈkɑːn*t*- **-s** -z *stress shift:* ˌvice-consul's ˈpost

vice-consulate ˌvaɪsˈkɒn*t*.sjə.lət, -sjʊ-, -lɪt (US) -ˈkɑːn*t*.sə.lət **-s** -s

vicegerent ˌvaɪsˈdʒer.ᵊnt, -ˈdʒɪə.rᵊnt (US) -ˈdʒɪr.ᵊnt **-s** -s

vice-presidenc|y ˌvaɪsˈprez.ɪ.dᵊn*t*.s|i **-ies** -iz

vice-president ˌvaɪsˈprez.ɪ.dᵊnt **-s** -s *stress shift:* ˌvice-president's ˈvote

vice-presidential ˌvaɪs.prez.ɪˈden*t*.ʃᵊl

vice-principal ˌvaɪsˈprɪn*t*.sə.pᵊl, -sɪ.pᵊl **-s** -z *stress shift:* ˌvice-principal's ˈoffice

viceregal ˌvaɪsˈriː.ɡᵊl *stress shift:* ˌviceregal ˈprivilege

vicereine ˌvaɪsˈreɪn, ˈ-- (US) ˈvaɪs.reɪn **-s** -z

viceroy ˈvaɪs.rɔɪ **-s** -z

viceroyalt|y ˌvaɪsˈrɔɪ.əl.t|i (US) -t̬|i **-ies** -iz

viceroyship ˈvaɪs.rɔɪ.ʃɪp **-s** -s

vice versa ˌvaɪ.siˈvɜː.sə, -səˈ-, ˌvaɪsˈ- (US) ˌvaɪ.səˈvɝː-, ˌvaɪsˈ-

Vichy ˈviː.ʃiː, -ʃi, ˈvɪʃ.iː, -i

vichyssoise ˌviː.ʃiˈswɑːz, ˌvɪʃ.iˈ-

vicinage ˈvɪs.ɪ.nɪdʒ, ˈ-ə- (US) ˈ-ə-

vicinity vɪˈsɪn.ə.ti, və-, vaɪ-, -ɪ.ti (US) vəˈsɪn.ə.t̬i

vicious ˈvɪʃ.əs **-ly** -li **-ness** -nəs, -nɪs ˌ**vicious** ˈ**circle**

vicissitude vɪˈsɪs.ɪ.tjuːd, və-, vaɪs-, ˈ-ə- (US) vɪˈsɪs.ə.tuːd, -tjuːd **-s** -z

Vick® vɪk

Vickers ˈvɪk.əz (US) -ɚz

Vickery ˈvɪk.ᵊr.i

Vicki, Vicky ˈvɪk.i

victim ˈvɪk.tɪm, -təm **-s** -z **-less** -ləs, -lɪs

victimization, -isa- ˌvɪk.tɪ.maɪˈzeɪ.ʃᵊn, -tə-, -mɪˈ- (US) -tə.mɪˈ-

victimiz|e, -is|e ˈvɪk.tɪ.maɪz, -tə- (US) -tə- **-es** -ɪz **-ing** -ɪŋ **-ed** -d **-er/s** -əʳ/z (US) -ɚ/z

victor (V) ˈvɪk.təʳ (US) -tɚ **-s** -z

Victoria, victoria vɪkˈtɔː.ri.ə (US) -ˈtɔːr.i- **-s** -z **Vic**ˌ**toria** ˈ**Cross** ; **Vic**ˈ**toria** ˌ**Day** ; **Vic**ˌ**toria** ˈ**Falls** ; **Vic**ˌ**toria** ˈ**sandwich**

Victorian, victorian vɪkˈtɔː.ri.ən (US) -ˈtɔːr.i- **-s** -z **Vic**ˌ**torian** ˈ**values**

Victoriana ˌvɪk.tɔː.riˈɑː.nə, vɪkˌtɔː- (US) vɪkˌtɔːr.iˈæn.ə

victorious vɪkˈtɔː.ri.əs (US) -ˈtɔːr.i- **-ly** -li **-ness** -nəs, -nɪs

victor ludorum ˌvɪk.təˌluːˈdɔː.rəm (US) -tɚ.luːˈdɔːr.əm **victores ludorum** vɪkˌtɔː.reɪsˌ- (US) -ˌtɔːr.eɪs-

victor|y ˈvɪk.tᵊr|.i, ˈ-tr|i **-ies** -iz

Victory-V® ˌvɪk.tᵊr.iˈviː

victual ˈvɪt.ᵊl (US) ˈvɪt̬- **-s** -z **-(l)ing** -ɪŋ **-(l)ed** -d **-(l)er/s** -əʳ/z (US) -ɚ/z

vicuña, **vicuna** vɪ'kjuː.nə, vaɪ-, və-, -'kuː-, -'kuː.njə (US) vaɪ'kjuː.nə, vɪ-, -'kuː-, -'kuː.njə
Vidal vɪ'dɑːl, və-, -'dæl; 'vaɪ.dəl (US) vɪ'dæl, -'dɑːl
Note: The author Gore Vidal is normally /vɪ'dɑːl/; Vidal Sassoon is normally /vɪ'dæl/.
vide 'vaɪ.diː, -di; 'vɪd.eɪ (US) 'vaɪ.diː, -di; 'viː.deɪ, 'wiː-
videlicet vɪ'diː.lɪ.set, vaɪ-, və-; -'deɪ.lɪ.ket (US) vɪ'del.ə.sɪt, wɪ-
video 'vɪd.i.əʊ (US) -oʊ **-s** -z **-ing** -ɪŋ **-ed** -d **'video ar,cade ; 'video ,camera ; 'video ,game ; ,video 'nasty ; 'video rec,order**
videocassette ,vɪd.i.əʊ.kə'set, -kæs'et (US) -oʊ.kə'set **-s** -s **,video-cas'sette rec,order**
videoconferenc|e ,vɪd.i.əʊ'kɒn.fər.ənts (US) 'vɪd.i.oʊ,kɑːn.fɚ-, -frəns **-es** -ɪz **-ing** -ɪŋ
videodisc 'vɪd.i.əʊ.dɪsk (US) -oʊ- **-s** -s
videofit 'vɪd.i.əʊ.fɪt (US) -oʊ **-s** -s
video-link 'vɪd.i.əʊ.lɪŋk (US) -oʊ- **-s** -s **-ing** -ɪŋ **-ed** -t
Videophone® 'vɪd.i.əʊ.fəʊn (US) -oʊ.foʊn
videorecorder 'vɪd.i.əʊ.rɪ,kɔː.dər (US) -oʊ.rɪ,kɔːr.dɚ **-s** -z
videorecording 'vɪd.i.əʊ.rɪ,kɔː.dɪŋ, -rə,- (US) -oʊ.rɪ,kɔːr-, -rə,- **-s** -z
videotap|e 'vɪd.i.əʊ.teɪp (US) -oʊ- **-es** -s **-ing** -ɪŋ **-ed** -t
videotext 'vɪd.i.əʊ.tekst (US) -oʊ- **-s** -s
vie vaɪ **vies** vaɪz **vying** 'vaɪ.ɪŋ **vied** vaɪd
Vienna vi'en.ə
Viennese ,vɪə'niːz (US) ,viː.ə'-
Vientiane ,vjen'tjɑːn
Vietcong, **Viet Cong** ,vjet'kɒŋ (US) ,viː.et'kɑːŋ, -'kɔːŋ; vi,et'-; ,vjet'- *stress shift:* ,Vietcong 'fighters
Vietminh ,vjet'mɪn (US) ,viː.et'-; vi,et'-; ,vjet'-
Vietnam, **Viet Nam** ,vjet'næm, -'nɑːm (US) ,viː.et'nɑːm, -ət'-, -'næm; vɪ,et'-; ,vjet'- *stress shift:* ,Vietnam 'war
Vietnamese ,vjet.nə'miːz (US) vi,et-; ,vjet-, ,viː.ət- *stress shift:* ,Vietnamese 'people
view vjuː **-s** -z **-ing** -ɪŋ **-ed** -d **-er/s** -ər/z (US) -ɚ/z **-able** -ə.bl̩ **-less** -ləs, -lɪs
viewfinder 'vjuː,faɪn.dər (US) -dɚ **-s** -z
Viewpark 'vjuː.pɑːk (US) -pɑːrk
viewpoint 'vjuː.pɔɪnt **-s** -s
Vigar 'vaɪ.gər (US) -gɚ
Vigers 'vaɪ.gəz (US) -gɚz
vigil 'vɪdʒ.ɪl, -əl (US) -əl **-s** -z
vigilance 'vɪdʒ.ɪ.ləns, -əl.ənts
vigilant 'vɪdʒ.ɪ.lənt, -əl.ənt **-ly** -li
vigilant|e ,vɪdʒ.ɪ'læn.t|i, -ə'- (US) -t̬|i **-es** -iz **-ism** -ɪ.zəm
vig|nette vɪ|'njet, -'net (US) -'njet **-nettes** -'njets, -'nets (US) -'njets **-netting** -'njet.ɪŋ, -'net- (US) -'njet̬.ɪŋ **-netted** -'njet.ɪd, -'net- (US) -'njet̬.ɪd **-nettist/s** -'njet.ɪst/s (US) -'njet̬.ɪst/s
Vignoles 'viː.njəʊlz, 'vɪn.jəʊlz, -jəʊl, -jɒlz; vɪ'njɒlz, -'njəʊlz (US) viː'njoʊl, -'njoʊlz, '--
Vigo 'viː.gəʊ, 'vaɪ- (US) 'viː.goʊ
vigor 'vɪg.ər (US) -ɚ
vigorous 'vɪg.ər.əs **-ly** -li **-ness** -nəs, -nɪs
vigour 'vɪg.ər (US) -ɚ
viking (V) 'vaɪ.kɪŋ **-s** -z
Vila 'viː.lə
vil|e vaɪl **-er** -ər (US) -ɚ **-est** -ɪst, -əst **-ely** -li **-eness** -nəs, -nɪs
vilification ,vɪl.ɪ.fɪ'keɪ.ʃən, ,-ə- (US) ,-ə-
vili|fy 'vɪl.ɪ|.faɪ, '-ə- (US) '-ə- **-fies** -faɪz **-fying** -faɪ.ɪŋ **-fied** -faɪd **-fier/s** -faɪ.ər/z (US) -faɪ.ɚ/z
villa (V) *house:* 'vɪl.ə **-s** -z
Villa *foreign name:* 'viː.ə
villag|e 'vɪl.ɪdʒ **-es** -ɪz
villager 'vɪl.ɪ.dʒər, '-ə- (US) -ə.dʒɚ **-s** -z
villain 'vɪl.ən *in historical sense also:* -ɪn, -eɪn (US) -ən **-s** -z
villainage 'vɪl.ɪ.nɪdʒ, '-ə- (US) '-ə-
villainess ,vɪl.ə'nes **-es** -ɪz
villainous 'vɪl.ə.nəs **-ly** -li **-ness** -nəs, -nɪs
villain|y 'vɪl.ə.n|i **-ies** -iz
Villa-Lobos ,viː.ə'ləʊ.bɒs, ,viː.lə- (US) ,viː.lə'loʊ.bəs, -boʊs
villanelle ,vɪl.ə'nel **-s** -z
-ville -vɪl, -viːl (US) -vɪl, -vəl
villein 'vɪl.ɪn, -eɪn (US) -ən **-s** -z **-age** -ɪdʒ
villenage 'vɪl.ə.nɪdʒ, -ɪ-
Villette vɪ'let
Villiers 'vɪl.əz, -jəz, -i.əz (US) '-ɚz, -jɚz
Villon 'vɪl.ən *as if French:* viː'jɔ̃ːŋ (US) viː'joʊn
vill|us 'vɪl|.əs **-i** -aɪ
Vilna 'vɪl.nə
Vilnius 'vɪl.ni.əs (US) -ʊs, -əs
vim (V®) vɪm
Vimto® 'vɪmp.təʊ (US) -toʊ
vin(s) væ̃ŋ, væn
Viña del Mar ,viː.njə.del'mɑːr (US) -'mɑːr
vinaigrette ,vɪn.ɪ'gret, -eɪ'- (US) -ə'- **-s** -s
Vince vɪnts
Vincennes *in France:* væ̃n'sen, væn- (US) væn- *in Indiana:* vɪn'senz
Vincent 'vɪnt.sənt
Vinci 'vɪn.tʃiː, -tʃi
vincul|um 'vɪŋ.kjə.l|əm, -kjʊ- (US) -kjə- **-a** -ə **-ums** -əmz
vindaloo ,vɪn.dəl'uː (US) -də'luː **-s** -z
vin(s) de pays ,væ̃n.də.peɪ'iː, ,væn-
vindicability ,vɪn.dɪ.kə'bɪl.ə.ti, -ɪ.ti (US) -ə.t̬i
vindicable 'vɪn.dɪ.kə.bl̩
vindi|cate 'vɪn.dɪ|.keɪt (US) -də- **-cates** -keɪts **-cating** -keɪ.tɪŋ (US) -keɪ.t̬ɪŋ **-cated** -keɪ.tɪd (US) -keɪ.t̬ɪd **-cator/s** -keɪ.tər/z (US) -keɪ.t̬ɚ/z
vindication ,vɪn.dɪ'keɪ.ʃən (US) -də'-
vindicative 'vɪn.dɪ.kə.tɪv, -keɪ-; vɪn'dɪk.ə- (US) vɪn'dɪk.ə.t̬ɪv; 'vɪn.dɪ.keɪ-
vindictive vɪn'dɪk.tɪv **-ly** -li **-ness** -nəs, -nɪs
vine vaɪn **-s** -z
vineg|ar 'vɪn.ɪ.g|ər, '-ə- (US) -ə.g|ɚ **-ars** -əz (US) -ɚz **-ary** -ər.i
viner|y 'vaɪ.nər|.i **-ies** -iz
Viney 'vaɪ.ni
vineyard 'vɪn.jəd, -jɑːd (US) -jɚd **-s** -z
vingt-et-un ,væ̃n.teɪ'ɜ̃ːŋ, ,væn-, -'ɜːn (US) ,væn.teɪ'ɜːn
viniculture 'vɪn.ɪ,kʌl.tʃər, ,vɪn.ɪ'kʌl- (US) 'vɪn.ɪ,kʌl.tʃɚ
viniculturist ,vɪn.ɪ'kʌl.tʃər.ɪst, 'vɪn.ɪ,kʌl- (US) ,vɪn.ɪ'kʌl- **-s** -s
vino 'viː.nəʊ (US) -noʊ
vin(s) ordinaire(s) ,væ̃n,ɔː.dɪ'neər, ,væn- (US) ,væ̃n,ɔːr.dən'er
vinous 'vaɪ.nəs
vintag|e 'vɪn.tɪdʒ (US) -t̬ɪdʒ **-es** -ɪz **,vintage 'year**
Vinter 'vɪn.tər (US) -t̬ɚ
vintner 'vɪnt.nər (US) -nɚ **-s** -z
viny 'vaɪ.ni
vinyl 'vaɪ.nəl, -nɪl (US) -nəl
viol vaɪəl, vaɪl, vɪəl (US) vaɪəl **-s** -z
viola *flower:* 'vaɪə.lə, 'vaɪ.əʊ-, 'viː.ə-, -əʊ-; vaɪ'əʊ-, vi'- (US) 'viː.ə.lə; vaɪ'oʊ- **-s** -z
viola *musical instrument:* vi'əʊ.lə (US) vi'oʊ- **-s** -z
Viola *female name:* 'vaɪə.lə, 'vaɪ.əʊ-, 'viː.ə.lə; vi'əʊ-, vaɪ- (US) vaɪ'oʊ.lə, vi-; viː.ə-
violable 'vaɪə.lə.bl̩
viola da gamba vi,əʊ.lə.də'gæm.bə (US) -,oʊ.lə.də'gɑːm- **-s** -z **viole da gamba** vi,əʊ.leɪ- (US) -,oʊ-
viola d'amore vi,əʊ.lə.dæm'ɔː.reɪ (US) -,oʊ.lə.dɑː'mɔːr.eɪ **viole d'amore** vi,əʊ.leɪ- (US) -,oʊ-
vio|late (*v.*) 'vaɪə|.leɪt, 'vaɪ.əʊ- (US) 'vaɪə- **-lates** -leɪts **-lating** -leɪ.tɪŋ (US) -leɪ.t̬ɪŋ **-lated** -leɪ.tɪd (US) -leɪ.t̬ɪd **-lator/s** -leɪ.tər/z (US) -leɪ.t̬ɚ/z
violate (*adj.*) 'vaɪə.lɪt, 'vaɪ.əʊ- (US) 'vaɪə-
violation ,vaɪə'leɪ.ʃən, ,vaɪ.əʊ'- (US) ,vaɪə'- **-s** -z
violence 'vaɪə.lənts

violent 'vaɪə.lᵊnt **-ly** -li
violet (V) 'vaɪə.lət, -lɪt US -lɪt **-s** -s
violin ˌvaɪə'lɪn **-s** -z
violinist vaɪə'lɪn.ɪst, ˌvaɪə- **-s** -s
violist *viola player:* vi'əʊ.lɪst US -'oʊ- **-s** -s *viol player:* 'vaɪə.lɪst **-s** -s
violoncellist ˌvaɪə.lən'tʃel.ɪst, ˌvɪə.lən'-, -lɪn'- US ˌviː.ə.lɑːn'-, ˌvaɪə.lɑːn'- **-s** -s
violoncello ˌvaɪə.lən'tʃel.əʊ, ˌvɪə.lən'-, -lɪn'- US ˌviː.ə.lɑːn'tʃel.oʊ, ˌvaɪə.lɑːn'- **-s** -z
violone 'vaɪə.ləʊn, 'vɪə-, ˌvɪə'ləʊ.neɪ US ˌviː.ə'loʊ- **-s** -z
VIP ˌviː.aɪ'piː **-s** -z
vip|er 'vaɪ.p|əʳ US -p|ɚ **-ers** -əz US -ɚz **-erish** -ᵊr.ɪʃ **-erous** -ᵊr.əs
virago (V) vɪ'rɑː.gəʊ, -'reɪ- US və'rɑː.goʊ, -'reɪ-; 'vɪr.ə- **-(e)s** -z
viral 'vaɪə.rᵊl US 'vaɪ-
vires 'vaɪə.riːz US 'vaɪ-
Virgil 'vɜː.dʒɪl US 'vɜːr.dʒᵊl **-s** -z
Virgilian vɜː'dʒɪl.i.ən, və- US vɜːr-, '-jən
virgin (V®) 'vɜː.dʒɪn US 'vɜːr- **-s** -z ˌ**virgin 'birth**; **'Virgin ˌIslands** US ˌ**Virgin 'Islands**; ˌ**Virgin 'Mary**
virginal 'vɜː.dʒɪ.nᵊl, -dʒᵊn.ᵊl US 'vɜːr- **-s** -z **-ly** -li
Virgini|a, virgini|a və'dʒɪn.j|ə, vɜː-, -i|.ə US vɚ- **-as** -əz **-an/s** -ən/z virˌ**ginia 'creeper**
virginity və'dʒɪn.ə.ti, vɜː-, -ɪ.ti US vɚ'dʒɪn.ə.t̬i
Virgo *constellation:* 'vɜː.gəʊ, 'vɪə- US 'vɜːr.goʊ **-s** -z
Virgoan vɜː'gəʊ.ən US vɜːr'goʊ- **-s** -z
virgule 'vɜː.gjuːl US 'vɜːr- **-s** -z
viridescen|t ˌvɪr.ɪ'des.ᵊn|t US -ə'- **-ce** -*t*s
viridian vɪ'rɪd.i.ən, və- US və-
virile 'vɪr.aɪl US -ᵊl, -aɪl
virility vɪ'rɪl.ə.ti, və-, -ɪ.ti US və'rɪl.ə.t̬i
virolog|y vaɪə'rɒl.ə.dʒ|i US vaɪ'rɑː.lə- **-ist/s** -ɪst/s
virtu vɜː'tuː US vɚ-; 'vɜːr.tuː
virtual 'vɜː.tʃu.əl, -tju-, '-tʃʊəl, -tjʊəl US 'vɜːr.tʃu- **-ly** -i ˌ**virtual re'ality**
virtue 'vɜː.tjuː, -tʃuː US 'vɜːr.tʃuː **-s** -z
virtuosity ˌvɜː.tju'ɒs.ə.ti, -tʃu'-, -ɪ.ti US ˌvɜːr.tʃu'ɑː.sə.t̬i
virtuos|o ˌvɜː.tju'əʊ.s|əʊ, -tʃu'-, -z|əʊ US ˌvɜːr.tʃu'oʊ.s|oʊ **-os** -əʊz US -oʊz **-i** -i
virtuous 'vɜː.tʃu.əs, -tju- US 'vɜːr.tʃu- **-ly** -li **-ness** -nəs, -nɪs
virulence 'vɪr.ʊ.lᵊnts, '-ə-, -jʊ-, -jə- US -jə-, '-ə-, -jʊ-
virulent 'vɪr.ʊ.lᵊnt, '-ə-, -jʊ-, -jə- US -jə-, '-ə-, -jʊ- **-ly** -li
virus 'vaɪə.rəs US 'vaɪ- **-es** -ɪz
vis vɪs
visa (V®) 'viː.zə US -zə, -sə **-s** -z **-ing** -ɪŋ **-ed** -d
visag|e 'vɪz.ɪdʒ **-es** -ɪz
visagiste ˌvɪz.ɑː'ʒiːst **-s** -s
vis-à-vis ˌviːz.ɑː'viː, ˌvɪz-, -ə'-, -æ'- US ˌviːz.ə'viː
viscera 'vɪs.ᵊr|.ə
visceral 'vɪs.ᵊr.ᵊl **-ly** -i
viscid 'vɪs.ɪd
viscidity vɪ'sɪd.ə.ti, -ɪ.ti US -ə.t̬i
Visconti vɪ'skɒn.ti US -'skɑːn-
viscose 'vɪs.kəʊs, -kəʊz US -koʊs, -koʊz
viscosity vɪ'skɒs.ə.ti, -ɪ.ti US -'skɑː.sə.t̬i
vis|count 'vaɪ|.kaʊnt **-counts** -kaʊnts **-county** -kaʊn.ti US -kaʊn.t̬i **-counties** -kaʊn.tiz US -kaʊn.t̬iz
viscountc|y 'vaɪ.kaʊnt.s|i **-ies** -iz
viscountess ˌvaɪ.kaʊn'tes; 'vaɪ.kaʊn.tɪs, -təs US 'vaɪ.kaʊn.t̬ɪs **-es** -ɪz
viscous 'vɪs.kəs **-ness** -nəs, -nɪs
visé 'viː.zeɪ US 'viː.zeɪ, -'- **-s** -z **-ing** -ɪŋ **-d** -d
vis|e vaɪs **-es** -ɪz **-ing** -ɪŋ **-ed** -t
Vishnu 'vɪʃ.nuː
visibility ˌvɪz.ə'bɪl.ə.ti, -ɪ'-, -ɪ.ti US -ə'bɪl.ə.t̬i
visib|le 'vɪz.ə.b|l̩, '-ɪ- US '-ə- **-ly** -li **-leness** -l̩.nəs, -nɪs
Visigoth 'vɪz.ɪ.gɒθ, 'vɪs- US -ə.gɑːθ **-s** -s
Visigothic ˌvɪz.ɪ'gɒθ.ɪk, ˌvɪs- US -ə'gɑː.θɪk
vision 'vɪʒ.ᵊn **-s** -z
visional 'vɪʒ.ᵊn.ᵊl, '-nᵊl US 'vɪʒ.ᵊn.ᵊl **-ly** -i
visionar|y 'vɪʒ.ᵊn.ᵊr|.i, -ᵊn.r|i US -ᵊn.er|.i **-ies** -iz
vis|it 'vɪz|.ɪt **-its** -ɪts **-iting** -ɪ.tɪŋ US -ɪ.t̬ɪŋ **-ited** -ɪ.tɪd US -ɪ.t̬ɪd **'visiting ˌcard**; ˌ**visiting pro'fessor**
visitant 'vɪz.ɪ.tᵊnt US -t̬ənt **-s** -s
visitation ˌvɪz.ɪ'teɪ.ʃᵊn US -ə'- **-s** -z
visitor 'vɪz.ɪ.təʳ US -t̬ɚ **-s** -z **'visitors' ˌbook**
vis major ˌvɪs'meɪ.dʒəʳ US -dʒɚ
visor 'vaɪ.zəʳ US -zɚ **-s** -z
vista 'vɪs.tə **-s** -z
Vistula 'vɪs.tjʊ.lə US -tʃuː-
visual 'vɪʒ.u.əl, 'vɪz.ju- US 'vɪʒ.u- **-s** -z **-ly** -i ˌ**visual 'aid**; ˌ**visual di'splay ˌunit**
visualization, -isa- ˌvɪʒ.u.ᵊl.aɪ'zeɪ.ʃᵊn, ˌvɪz.ju-, -ɪ'- US ˌvɪʒ.u.ᵊl.ɪ'-
visualiz|e, -is|e 'vɪʒ.u.ᵊl.aɪz, 'vɪz.ju- US 'vɪʒ.u.ə.laɪz **-es** -ɪz **-ing** -ɪŋ **-ed** -d **-er/s** -əʳ/z US -ɚ/z
vita *glass:* 'vaɪ.tə US -t̬ə *aqua:* 'viː.tə US -t̬ə
Vita 'viː.tə US -t̬ə
vitae *curriculum:* 'viː.taɪ, 'vaɪ.tiː US 'vaɪ.t̬iː, 'viː-, -taɪ
vital 'vaɪ.tᵊl US -t̬ᵊl **-ly** -i ˌ**vital 'signs** US **'vital ˌsigns**; ˌ**vital sta'tistics**
Vitalite® 'vaɪ.tə.laɪt
vitality vaɪ'tæl.ə.ti, -ɪ.ti US -ə.t̬i
vitalization, -isa- ˌvaɪ.tᵊl.aɪ'zeɪ.ʃᵊn US -tᵊl.ɪ'-
vitaliz|e, -is|e 'vaɪ.tᵊl.aɪz US -t̬ə.laɪz **-es** -ɪz **-ing** -ɪŋ **-ed** -d
vitals 'vaɪ.tᵊlz US -t̬ᵊlz
vitamin 'vɪt.ə.mɪn, 'vaɪ- US 'vaɪ.t̬ə- **-s** -z ˌ**vitamin 'C**
VitBe® 'vɪt.biː
vitellus vɪ'tel.əs US vɪ-, vaɪ-
Vitez 'viː.tez
viti|ate 'vɪʃ.i|.eɪt **-ates** -eɪts **-ating** -eɪ.tɪŋ US -eɪ.t̬ɪŋ **-ated** -eɪ.tɪd US -eɪ.t̬ɪd **-ator/s** -eɪ.təʳ/z US -eɪ.t̬ɚ/z
vitiation ˌvɪʃ.i'eɪ.ʃᵊn
viticulture 'vɪt.ɪˌkʌl.tʃəʳ, 'vaɪ- US -t̬əˌkʌl.tʃɚ
vitiligo ˌvɪt.ɪ'laɪ.gəʊ US ˌvɪt̬.ɪ'laɪ.goʊ
vitreous 'vɪt.ri.əs **-ness** -nəs, -nɪs
vitrescen|t vɪ'tres.ᵊn|t **-ce** -*t*s
vitric 'vɪt.rɪk
vitrifaction ˌvɪt.rɪ'fæk.ʃᵊn US -rə'-
vitrification ˌvɪt.rɪ.fɪ'keɪ.ʃᵊn, -rə- US -rə-
vitri|fy 'vɪt.rɪ|.faɪ US -trə- **-fies** -faɪz **-fying** -faɪ.ɪŋ **-fied** -faɪd **-fiable** -faɪ.ə.bl̩
vitriol 'vɪt.ri.əl, -ɒl US -əl, -ɔːl
vitriolic ˌvɪt.ri'ɒl.ɪk US -'ɑː.lɪk **-ally** -ᵊl.i, -li
vitro 'viː.trəʊ US -troʊ
Vitruvius vɪ'truː.vi.əs
vittles 'vɪt.l̩z US 'vɪt̬-
Vittoria vɪ'tɔː.ri.ə US -'tɔːr.i-
vituper|ate vɪ'tjuː.pᵊr|.eɪt, vaɪ- US vaɪ'tuː.pə.r|eɪt, vɪ-, -'tjuː- **-ates** -eɪts **-ating** -eɪ.tɪŋ US -eɪ.t̬ɪŋ **-ated** -eɪ.tɪd US -eɪ.t̬ɪd **-ator/s** -eɪ.təʳ/z US -eɪ.t̬ɚ/z
vituperation vɪˌtjuː.pᵊr'eɪ.ʃᵊn, vaɪ- US vaɪˌtuː.pə'reɪ-, vɪ-, -ˌtjuː- **-s** -z
vituperative vɪ'tjuː.pᵊr.ə.tɪv, vaɪ-, -eɪ- US vaɪ'tuː.pɚ.ə.t̬ɪv, vɪ-, -'tjuː-, -pə.reɪ- **-ly** -li
vituperatory vɪ'tjuː.pᵊr.ə.tᵊr.i, vaɪ- US vaɪ'tuː.pɚ.ə.tɔːr-, -tjuː-, -prə.tɔːr-
Vitus 'vaɪ.təs US -t̬əs
viva *long live:* 'viː.və
viva *examination:* 'vaɪ.və US 'vaɪ.və, 'viː- **-s** -z ˌ**viva 'voce**
Viva® 'viː.və
vivace vɪ'vɑː.tʃeɪ US -tʃeɪ **-s** -z

vivacious vɪ'veɪ.ʃəs, vaɪ- **-ly** -li **-ness** -nəs, -nɪs

vivacity vɪ'væs.ə.ti, vaɪ-, -ɪ.ti US -ə.t̬i

Vivaldi vɪ'væl.di US -'vɑːl-

vivari|um vaɪ'veə.ri|.əm, vɪ- US vaɪ'ver.i- **-ums** -əmz **-a** -ə

vivat 'vaɪ.væt, 'viː-

vive viːv

Vivian 'vɪv.i.ən

vivid 'vɪv.ɪd **-ly** -li **-ness** -nəs, -nɪs

Vivien 'vɪv.i.ən

Vivienne 'vɪv.i.ən, ˌvɪv.i'en

vivification ˌvɪv.ɪ.fɪ'keɪ.ʃᵊn US ˌ-ə-

vivi|fy 'vɪv.ɪ|.faɪ US '-ə- **-fies** -faɪz **-fying** -faɪ.ɪŋ **-fied** -faɪd

viviparity ˌvɪv.ɪ'pær.ə.ti, -ɪ.ti US -ə'per.ə.t̬i, -'pær-

viviparous vɪ'vɪp.ᵊr.əs, vaɪ- US vaɪ- **-ly** -li **-ness** -nəs, -nɪs

vivisect ˌvɪv.ɪ'sekt, '--- US 'vɪv.ə.sekt **-s** -s **-ing** -ɪŋ **-ed** -ɪd **-or/s** -əʳ/z US -ɚ/z

vivisection ˌvɪv.ɪ'sek.ʃᵊn US -ə'-, 'vɪv.ə.sek-

vivisectionist ˌvɪv.ɪ'sek.ʃᵊn.ɪst US -ə'- **-s** -s

vixen 'vɪk.sᵊn **-s** -z

vixenish 'vɪk.sᵊn.ɪʃ

Viyella® vaɪ'el.ə

viz. vɪz; vɪ'diː.lɪ.set, vaɪ-; vɪ'deɪ.lɪ.ket US vɪz; vɪ'del.ɪ.set, wɪ-

Note: Many people in reading aloud substitute **namely** (/'neɪm.li/) for this word.

Vizetelly ˌvɪz.ɪ'tel.i

vizier vɪ'zɪəʳ, 'vɪz.ɪəʳ; US vɪ'zɪr; 'vɪz.jɚ **-s** -z

vizor 'vaɪ.zəʳ US -zɚ **-s** -z

VJ-Day ˌviː'dʒeɪ.deɪ

Vladimir 'vlæd.ɪ.mɪəʳ, -məʳ, vlæd'iː.mɪəʳ US -ə.mɪr

Vladivostok ˌvlæd.ɪ'vɒs.tɒk US -'vɑː.stɑːk

V-neck ˌviː'nek US '-- **-s** -s **-ed** -t

vocab 'vəʊ.kæb US 'voʊ-

vocable 'vəʊ.kə.bl̩ US 'voʊ- **-s** -z

vocabular|y vəʊ'kæb.jə.lᵊr|.i, -jʊ- US voʊ'kæb.jə.ler-, -jʊ- **-ies** -iz

vocal 'vəʊ.kᵊl US 'voʊ- **-s** -z **-ly** -i ˌ**vocal 'cords** US '**vocal** ˌ**cords**

vocalic vəʊ'kæl.ɪk US voʊ-

vocalism 'vəʊ.kᵊl.ɪ.zᵊm US 'voʊ-

vocalist 'vəʊ.kᵊl.ɪst US 'voʊ- **-s** -s

vocality vəʊ'kæl.ə.ti, -ɪ.ti US voʊ'kæl.ə.t̬i

vocalization, -isa- ˌvəʊ.kᵊl.aɪ'zeɪ.ʃᵊn, -ɪ'- US ˌvoʊ.kᵊl.ɪ'- **-s** -z

vocaliz|e, -is|e 'vəʊ.kᵊl.aɪz US 'voʊ.kə.laɪz **-es** -ɪz **-ing** -ɪŋ **-ed** -d **-er/s** -əʳ/z US -ɚ/z

vocation vəʊ'keɪ.ʃᵊn US voʊ- **-s** -z

vocational vəʊ'keɪ.ʃᵊn.ᵊl, -'keɪʃ.nᵊl US voʊ- **-ly** -i

vocational|ism vəʊ'keɪ.ʃᵊn.ᵊl|.ɪ.zᵊm, -'keɪʃ.nᵊl- US voʊ- **-ist/s** -ɪst/s

vocative 'vɒk.ə.tɪv US 'vɑː.kə.t̬ɪv **-s** -z

voce (*in* **viva voce**) 'vəʊ.si, -tʃi, -tʃeɪ US 'voʊ.siː (*in* **sotto voce**) 'vəʊ.tʃi US 'voʊ.tʃi, -tʃeɪ

vocifer|ate vəʊ'sɪf.ᵊr|.eɪt US voʊ'sɪf.ə.r|eɪt **-ates** -eɪts **-ating** -eɪ.tɪŋ US -eɪ.t̬ɪŋ **-ated** -eɪ.tɪd US -eɪ.t̬ɪd **-ator/s** -eɪ.təʳ/z US -eɪ.t̬ɚ/z

vociferation vəʊˌsɪf.ə'reɪ.ʃᵊn US voʊ- **-s** -z

vociferous vəʊ'sɪf.ᵊr.əs US voʊ- **-ly** -li **-ness** -nəs, -nɪs

vocoid 'vəʊ.kɔɪd US 'voʊ- **-s** -z

Vodafone®, Vodaphone 'vəʊ.də.fəʊn US 'voʊ.də.foʊn

vodka 'vɒd.kə US 'vɑːd- **-s** -z

Vogt *English surname:* vəʊkt US voʊkt

vogue (**V®**) vəʊg US voʊg

voic|e vɔɪs **-es** -ɪz **-ing** -ɪŋ **-ed** -t ˌ**Voice of A'merica**; '**voice** ˌ**box**

voiceless 'vɔɪ.sləs, -slɪs **-ly** -li **-ness** -nəs, -nɪs

voice-over 'vɔɪsˌəʊ.vəʳ US -ˌoʊ.vɚ **-s** -z

voiceprint 'vɔɪs.prɪnt **-s** -s

void vɔɪd **-s** -z **-ing** -ɪŋ **-ed** -ɪd **-able** -ə.bl̩ **-ance** -ᵊn*t*s **-ness** -nəs, -nɪs

voilà vwæl'ɑː, vwɒl-, vwɑː'lɑː US vwɑː'lɑː

voile vɔɪl

voir dire ˌvwɑː'dɪəʳ US ˌvwɑːr'dɪr

vol vɒl US vɑːl

volant 'vəʊ.lənt US 'voʊ-

Volapük 'vɒl.ə.puːk, 'vəʊl-, -pʊk, ˌ--'- US 'voʊ.lɑː-, 'vɑː-

volatile (*adj.*) 'vɒl.ə.taɪl US 'vɑː.lə.t̬ᵊl **-ness** -nəs, -nɪs

volatile (*in* **sal volatile**) vəʊ'læt.ə.li, vɒl'æt- US voʊ'læt.li

volatility ˌvɒl.ə'tɪl.ə.ti, -ɪ.ti US ˌvɑː.lə'tɪl.ə.t̬i

volatilization, -isa- vɒlˌæt.ɪ.laɪ'zeɪ.ʃᵊn, vəʊˌlæt-, -ᵊl.aɪ'-, -ɪ'-; ˌvɒl.ə.tɪ.laɪ'-, -tᵊl.aɪ'-, -ɪ'- US ˌvɑː.lə.t̬ᵊl.ɪ'-

volatiliz|e, -is|e vɒl'æt.ɪ.laɪz, vəʊ'læt-, -ᵊl.aɪz; 'vɒl.ə.tɪ.laɪz, -tᵊl.aɪz US 'vɑː.lə.tə.laɪz **-es** -ɪz **-ing** -ɪŋ **-ed** -d

vol-au-vent 'vɒl.əʊ.vɑ̃ː*ŋ*, ˌ--'- US ˌvɔː.loʊ'vɑ̃ː*n*, ˌvoʊ- **-s** -z

volcanic vɒl'kæn.ɪk US vɑːl- **-ally** -ᵊl.i, -li

volcanicity ˌvɒl.kə'nɪs.ə.ti, -ɪ.ti US ˌvɑːl.kə'nɪs.ə.t̬i

volcanism 'vɒl.kə.nɪ.zᵊm US 'vɑːl-

volcano vɒl'keɪ.nəʊ US vɑːl'keɪ.noʊ **-(e)s** -z

volcanology ˌvɒl.kə'nɒl.ə.dʒi US ˌvɑːl.kə'nɑː.lə-

vole vəʊl US voʊl **-s** -z

volenti non fit injuria vɒlˌen.tiːˌnəʊn.fɪt.ɪn'jʊə.ri.ə, -'jɔː- US voʊˌlen.ti.nɑːnˌfɪt.ɪn'dʒʊr.i.ə

volet 'vɒl.eɪ US 'voʊ.leɪ, -'- **-s** -z

Volga 'vɒl.gə US 'vɑːl-, 'voʊl-

Volgograd 'vɒl.gəʊ.græd US 'vɑːl.gə-, 'voʊl-

volition vəʊ'lɪʃ.ᵊn US voʊ-, və- **-al** -ᵊl

volitive 'vɒl.ɪ.tɪv, '-ə- US 'vɑː.lə.t̬ɪv

volks|lied 'fɒlks|.liːd, 'vɒlks- *as if German:* -liːt US 'fɔːlks|.liːt **-lieder** -ˌliː.dəʳ US -ˌliː.dɚ

volkstaat 'fɒlk.ʃtɑːt US 'fɔːlk- **-s** -s

Volkswagen® 'fɒlksˌvɑː.gən, 'vɒlks- US 'fɔːlks-, 'vɔːlks-, 'voʊks-, -ˌwɑː-, -ˌwæg.ᵊn **-s** -z

volley 'vɒl.i US 'vɑː.li **-s** -z **-ing** -ɪŋ **-ed** -d **-er/s** -əʳ/z US -ɚ/z

volleyball 'vɒl.i.bɔːl US 'vɑː.li-

Volos 'vɒl.ɒs US 'vɔː.lɑːs

volplan|e 'vɒl.pleɪn US 'vɑːl- **-es** -z **-ing** -ɪŋ **-ed** -d

Volpone vɒl'pəʊ.neɪ, -ni US vɑːl'poʊ-

Volsci 'vɒl.skiː, -saɪ US 'vɑːl.saɪ, -skiː

Volscian 'vɒl.ski.ən, -ʃi-, -si- US 'vɑːl.ʃᵊn, -ski.ən

Volstead 'vɒl.sted US 'vɑːl-

Volsung 'vɒl.sʊŋ US 'vɑːl-

volt *electric unit:* vəʊlt, vɒlt US voʊlt **-s** -s

volt *movement of horse, movement in fencing:* vɒlt US voʊlt, vɑːlt, vɔːlt **-s** -s

Volta (**V**) *physicist:* 'vɒl.tə, 'vəʊl- US 'voʊl.t̬ə

Volta *lake and river:* 'vɒl.tə US 'vɑːl.t̬ə, 'vɔːl-, 'voʊl-

volta *dance:* 'vɒl.tə US 'vɑːl- **-s** -z

voltag|e 'vəʊl.tɪdʒ, 'vɒl- US 'voʊl.t̬ɪdʒ **-es** -ɪz

voltaic vɒl'teɪ.ɪk US vɑːl-, voʊl-

Voltaire vɒl'teəʳ, '-- US voʊl'ter, vɑːl-

voltameter vɒl'tæm.ɪ.təʳ, vəʊl-, '-ə- US voʊl'tæm.ə.t̬ɚ, vɑːl- **-s** -z

volte 'vɒl.teɪ, -ti US vɑːlt, voʊlt **-s** -z

volte-fac|e ˌvɒlt'fɑːs, -'fæs US ˌvɑːlt'fɑːs **-es** -ɪz

voltmeter 'vəʊltˌmiː.təʳ, 'vɒlt- US 'voʊltˌmiː.t̬ɚ **-s** -z

volubility ˌvɒl.jə'bɪl.ə.ti, -jʊ'-, -ɪ.ti US ˌvɑːl.jə'bɪl.ə.t̬i, -jʊ'-

volub|le 'vɒl.jə.b|l̩, -jʊ- US 'vɑːl- **-ly** -li **-leness** -l̩.nəs, -nɪs

volume 'vɒl.juːm, -jʊm, -jəm US 'vɑːl.juːm, -jəm **-s** -z

volumeter vɒl'juː.mɪ.təʳ, və'ljuː-, -'luː-, -mə- US 'vɑːl.jʊˌmiː.t̬ɚ **-s** -z

volumetric ˌvɒl.jəˈmet.rɪk, -jʊˈ- Ⓤⓢ ˌvɑːl- **-al** -əl **-ally** -əl.i, -li
voluminous vəˈluː.mɪ.nəs, vɒlˈuː-, -ˈjuː-, -mə- Ⓤⓢ vəˈluː.mə- **-ly** -li **-ness** -nəs, -nɪs
voluntar|y ˈvɒl.ən.tər|.i, -tr|i Ⓤⓢ ˈvɑː.lən.ter|.i **-ies** -iz **-ily** -əl.i, -ɪ.li, ˌvɒl.ənˈteə.rəl.i, -ˈtær-, -ɪ.li **-iness** -ɪ.nəs, -ɪ.nɪs
volunteer ˌvɒl.ənˈtɪəʳ Ⓤⓢ ˌvɑː.lənˈtɪr **-s** -z **-ing** -ɪŋ **-ed** -d
voluptuar|y vəˈlʌp.tjʊə.r|i, -tʃʊə- Ⓤⓢ -tʃu.er|.i **-ies** -iz
voluptuous vəˈlʌp.tʃu.əs, -tju.əs Ⓤⓢ -tʃu- **-ly** -li **-ness** -nəs, -nɪs
volu|te vəʊˈluː|t, vɒlˈuː|t, -ˈjuː|t Ⓤⓢ vəˈluː|t **-tes** -ts **-ted** -tɪd Ⓤⓢ -t̬ɪd
volution vəʊˈluː.ʃən, vɒlˈuː-, -ˈjuː- Ⓤⓢ vəˈluː- **-s** -z
Volvo® ˈvɒl.vəʊ Ⓤⓢ ˈvɑːl.voʊ **-s** -z
vom|it ˈvɒm|.ɪt Ⓤⓢ ˈvɑː.m|ɪt **-its** -ɪts **-iting** -ɪ.tɪŋ Ⓤⓢ -ɪ.t̬ɪŋ **-ited** -ɪ.tɪd Ⓤⓢ -ɪ.t̬ɪd
vomitor|y ˈvɒm.ɪ.tər|.i, -tr|i Ⓤⓢ ˈvɑː.mə.tɔːr|.i **-ies** -iz
von (V) vɒn, fɒn Ⓤⓢ vɑːn, fɑːn
Vonnegut ˈvɒn.ɪ.gət Ⓤⓢ ˈvɑː.nə-
voodoo ˈvuː.duː **-s** -z **-ing** -ɪŋ **-ed** -d **-ist/s** -ɪst/s **-ism** -ɪ.zəm
Vooght vuːt
voracious vəˈreɪ.ʃəs, vɔː-, vɒrˈeɪ- Ⓤⓢ vɔːˈreɪ-, və- **-ly** -li **-ness** -nəs, -nɪs
voracity vəˈræs.ə.ti, vɔː-, vɒrˈæs-, -ɪ.ti Ⓤⓢ vɔːˈræs.ə.t̬i, və-
Vorster ˈfɔː.stəʳ Ⓤⓢ ˈfɔːr.stɚ
vort|ex ˈvɔː.t|eks Ⓤⓢ ˈvɔːr- **-ices** -ɪ.siːz **-exes** -ek.sɪz
vortic|al ˈvɔː.tɪ.k|əl Ⓤⓢ ˈvɔːr.t̬ɪ- **-ally** -əl.i, -li
vortices (*plur. of* **vortex**) ˈvɔː.tɪ.siːz Ⓤⓢ ˈvɔːr.t̬ɪ-
vortic|ism (V) ˈvɔː.tɪ.s|ɪ.zəm Ⓤⓢ ˈvɔːr.t̬ɪ- **-ist/s** -ɪst/s
Vortigern ˈvɔː.tɪ.gɜːn, -gən Ⓤⓢ ˈvɔːr.t̬ɪ.gɜːrn
Vosges vəʊʒ Ⓤⓢ voʊʒ
Voss vɒs Ⓤⓢ vɑːs
votaress ˈvəʊ.tər.es, -ɪs Ⓤⓢ ˈvoʊ.t̬ɚ.əs, ˈ-trəs **-es** -ɪz
votar|y ˈvəʊ.tər|.i Ⓤⓢ ˈvoʊ.t̬ɚ- **-ies** -iz **-ist/s** -ɪst/s
vot|e vəʊt Ⓤⓢ voʊt **-es** -s **-ing** -ɪŋ Ⓤⓢ ˈvoʊ.t̬ɪŋ **-ed** -ɪd Ⓤⓢ ˈvoʊ.t̬ɪd **-er/s** -əʳ/z Ⓤⓢ ˈvoʊ.t̬ɚ/z ˌ**vote of (**ˌ**no) ˈconfidence** ; ˌ**vote of ˈthanks** ; ˌ**vote with one's ˈfeet**
voteless ˈvəʊt.ləs, -lɪs Ⓤⓢ ˈvoʊt-
votive ˈvəʊ.tɪv Ⓤⓢ ˈvoʊ.t̬ɪv **-ly** -li **-ness** -nəs, -nɪs
vouch vaʊtʃ **-es** -ɪz **-ing** -ɪŋ **-ed** -t
voucher ˈvaʊ.tʃəʳ Ⓤⓢ -tʃɚ **-s** -z ˈ**voucher** ˌ**system**
vouchsaf|e ˌvaʊtʃˈseɪf, ˈ-- **-es** -s **-ing** -ɪŋ **-ed** -t
Vouvray ˈvuː.vreɪ Ⓤⓢ -ˈ-
vow vaʊ **-s** -z **-ing** -ɪŋ **-ed** -d
vowel vaʊəl **-s** -z **-(l)ing** -ɪŋ **-(l)ed** -d
Vowles vəʊlz, vaʊlz Ⓤⓢ voʊlz, vaʊlz
vox (V) vɒks Ⓤⓢ vɑːks
vox humana ˌvɒks.hjuːˈmɑː.nə Ⓤⓢ ˌvɑːks-, -ˈmeɪ- **-s** -z
vox pop ˌvɒksˈpɒp Ⓤⓢ ˌvɑːksˈpɑːp
vox populi ˌvɒksˈpɒp.jʊ.liː, -jə- Ⓤⓢ ˌvɑːksˈpɑː.pjuː.laɪ, -liː
voyag|e ˈvɔɪ.ɪdʒ **-es** -ɪz **-ing** -ɪŋ **-ed** -d
voyager ˈvɔɪ.ɪ.dʒəʳ, ˈvɔɪ.ə- Ⓤⓢ ˈvɔɪ.ɪ.dʒɚ **-s** -z
voyeur vwɑːˈjɜːʳ, vɔɪˈɜːʳ Ⓤⓢ vɔɪˈjɜːr, vwɑː- **-s** -z
voyeurism vwɑːˈjɜː.rɪ.zəm, vɔɪˈɜː-, ˈvwɑː.jɜː-, ˈvɔɪ.ɜː- Ⓤⓢ vɔɪˈjɜːr.ɪ-, vwɑː-; ˈvɔɪ.jɚ.ɪ-
voyeuristic ˌvɔɪ.əˈrɪ.stɪk, ˌvwɑː.jɜːˈ- Ⓤⓢ ˌvɔɪ.jəˈ-, ˌvwɑː- **-ally** -əl.i, li
VP ˌviːˈpiː **-s** -z
vroom vruːm, vrʊm
vs. ˈvɜː.səs Ⓤⓢ ˈvɜːr-
VSO ˌviː.esˈəʊ Ⓤⓢ -ˈoʊ
V/STOL ˈviːˌstɒl Ⓤⓢ -ˌstɑːl
Vt. (*abbrev. for* **Vermont**) vəˈmɒnt, vɜː- Ⓤⓢ vɚˈmɑːnt
VTOL ˈviː.tɒl Ⓤⓢ -tɑːl
Vuillard ˈvuː.jɑː, -ˈ-
Vuitton® ˈvjuː.ɪ.tɔ̃ːŋ, ˈvwiː.tɒn Ⓤⓢ vwiːˈtɔ̃ːn
Vukovar ˈvʊk.ə.vəʳ, -vɑːʳ Ⓤⓢ -vɚ
Vulcan ˈvʌl.kən **-s** -z
vulcanite ˈvʌl.kə.naɪt
vulcanization, -isa- ˌvʌl.kə.naɪˈzeɪ.ʃən, -nɪˈ- Ⓤⓢ -nɪˈ-
vulcaniz|e, -is|e ˈvʌl.kə.naɪz **-es** -ɪz **-ing** -ɪŋ **-ed** -d
vulgar (V) ˈvʌl.gəʳ Ⓤⓢ -gɚ **-ly** -li ˌ**Vulgar ˈLatin**
vulgarian vʌlˈgeə.ri.ən Ⓤⓢ -ˈger.i- **-s** -z
vulgarism ˈvʌl.gər.ɪ.zəm **-s** -z
vulgarit|y vʌlˈgær.ə.t|i, -ɪ.t|i Ⓤⓢ -ˈger.ə.t̬|i, -ˈgær- **-ies** -iz
vulgarization, -isa- ˌvʌl.gər.aɪˈzeɪ.ʃən, -ɪˈ- Ⓤⓢ -ɪˈ-
vulgariz|e, -is|e ˈvʌl.gər.aɪz Ⓤⓢ -gə.raɪz **-es** -ɪz **-ing** -ɪŋ **-ed** -d **-er/s** -əʳ/z Ⓤⓢ -ɚ/z
vulgate (V) ˈvʌl.geɪt, -gɪt, -gət Ⓤⓢ -geɪt, -gɪt
Vulliamy ˈvʌl.jə.mi
vulnerability ˌvʌl.nər.əˈbɪl.ə.ti, ˌvʌn.ər-, ˌvʌn.rəˈ-, -ɪ.ti Ⓤⓢ ˌvʌl.nɚ.əˈbɪl.ə.t̬i
vulnerab|le ˈvʌl.nər.ə.b|l̩, ˈvʌn.ər-, ˈvʌn.rə.b|l̩ Ⓤⓢ ˈvʌl.nɚ.ə- **-ly** -li **-leness** -l̩.nəs, -nɪs
Vulpecula vʌlˈpek.jə.lə, -jʊ-
vulpine ˈvʌl.paɪn Ⓤⓢ -paɪn, -pɪn
vulture ˈvʌl.tʃəʳ Ⓤⓢ -tʃɚ **-s** -z
vulturine ˈvʌl.tʃər.aɪn, -tʃʊ.raɪn, -tjər.aɪn, -tjʊ.raɪn Ⓤⓢ -tʃə.raɪn, -rɪn
vulturous ˈvʌl.tʃər.əs, -tʃʊ.rəs, -tjər.əs, -tjʊ.rəs Ⓤⓢ -tʃɚ.əs
vulv|a ˈvʌl.v|ə **-as** -əz **-ae** -iː
VW ˌviːˈdʌb.l̩.ju, -juː Ⓤⓢ -juː, -jə **-s** -z
Vye vaɪ
vying (*from* **vie**) ˈvaɪ.ɪŋ

W

w (W) ˈdʌb.l̩.juː, -ju (US) -juː, -jə -ˈs -z
W (*abbrev. for* **west**) west
Waaf, WAAF wæf **-s** -s
Wabash ˈwɔː.bæʃ (US) ˈwɔː-, ˈwɑː-
Wace weɪs
wacko ˈwæk.əʊ (US) -oʊ **-s** -z
wack|y ˈwæk|.i **-ier** -i.əʳ (US) -i.ɚ **-iest** -i.ɪst, -i.əst **-ily** -ɪ.li, -əl.i **-iness** -ɪ.nəs, -ɪ.nɪs
Waco ˈweɪ.kəʊ (US) -koʊ
wad wɒd (US) wɑːd **-s** -z **-ding** -ɪŋ **-ded** -ɪd
Waddell wɒdˈel, ˈwɒd.əl (US) wɑːˈdel, ˈwɑː.dəl
wadding ˈwɒd.ɪŋ (US) ˈwɑː.dɪŋ
Waddington ˈwɒd.ɪŋ.tən (US) ˈwɑː.dɪŋ-
waddl|e ˈwɒd.l̩ (US) ˈwɑː.dl̩ **-es** -z **-ing** -ɪŋ, -lɪŋ, ˈwɒd.lɪŋ (US) ˈwɑːd- **-ed** -d **-er/s** ˈwɒd.ləʳ/z (US) ˈwɑː.dl̩.ɚ/z, ˈwɑːd.lɚ/z
wadd|y (W) ˈwɒd|.i (US) ˈwɑː.dli **-ies** -iz
wad|e (W) weɪd **-es** -z **-ing** -ɪŋ **-ed** -ɪd
Wadebridge ˈweɪd.brɪdʒ
Wade-Giles ˌweɪdˈdʒaɪlz
wader ˈweɪ.dəʳ (US) -dɚ **-s** -z
Wadey ˈweɪ.di
wadg|e wɒdʒ (US) wɑːdʒ **-es** -ɪz
Wadham ˈwɒd.əm (US) ˈwɑː.dəm
Wadhurst ˈwɒd.hɜːst (US) ˈwɑːd.hɜːrst
wadi ˈwɒd.i, ˈwæd-, ˈwɑː.di (US) ˈwɑː.di **-s** -z
Wadi Halfa ˌwɒd.iˈhæl.fə, ˌwæd-, ˌwɑː.diˈ- (US) ˌwɑː.diˈhɑːl.fə
Wadman ˈwɒd.mən (US) ˈwɑːd-
Wad Medani ˌwɑːd.məˈdɑː.ni
Wadsworth ˈwɒdz.wəθ, -wɜːθ (US) ˈwɑːdz.wɚθ, -wɜːrθ
WAF, Waf wæf **-s** -s
Wafd wɒft, wæft, wɑːft (US) wɑːft
waf|er ˈweɪ.f|əʳ (US) -f|ɚ **-ers** -əz (US) -ɚz **-ery** -ər.i
wafer-thin ˌweɪ.fəˈθɪn (US) -fɚˈ- *stress shift:* ˌwafer-thin ˈmints
waffl|e ˈwɒf.l̩ (US) ˈwɑː.fl̩ **-es** -z **-ing** -ɪŋ, ˈwɒf.lɪŋ (US) ˈwɑːf- **-ed** -d **-er/s** -əʳ/z, ˈwɒf.ləʳ/z (US) ˈwɑː.fl̩.ɚ/z, ˈwɑːf.lɚ/z **-y** -i, ˈwɒf.li (US) ˈwɑː.fl̩.i, ˈwɑːf.li
waffle-iron ˈwɒf.l̩ˌaɪən (US) ˈwɑː.fl̩ˌaɪɚn **-s** -z
waft wɒft, wɑːft (US) wɑːft, wæft **-s** -s **-ing** -ɪŋ **-ed** -ɪd
wag wæg **-s** -z **-ging** -ɪŋ **-ged** -d
wag|e weɪdʒ **-es** -ɪz **-ing** -ɪŋ **-ed** -d **ˈwage ˌpacket**
wage-earner ˈweɪdʒˌɜː.nəʳ (US) -ˌɜːr.nɚ **-s** -z
wag|er ˈweɪ.dʒ|əʳ (US) -dʒ|ɚ **-ers** -əz (US) -ɚz **-ering** -ər.ɪŋ **-ered** -əd (US) -ɚd **-erer/s** -ər.əʳ/z (US) -ɚ.ɚ/z
wageworker ˈweɪdʒˌwɜː.kəʳ (US) -ˌwɜːr.kɚ **-s** -z
waggish ˈwæg.ɪʃ **-ly** -li **-ness** -nəs, -nɪs
waggl|e ˈwæg.l̩ **-es** -z **-ing** -ɪŋ, ˈwæg.lɪŋ **-ed** -d
waggon ˈwæg.ən **-s** -z
waggoner ˈwæg.ən.əʳ (US) -ɚ **-s** -z
waggonette ˌwæg.əˈnet **-s** -s
Waghorn ˈwæg.hɔːn (US) -hɔːrn
Wagnall ˈwæg.nəl
Wagner *English name:* ˈwæg.nəʳ (US) -nɚ *German composer:* ˈvɑːg.nəʳ (US) -nɚ
Wagnerian vɑːgˈnɪə.ri.ən (US) -ˈnɪr.i-, -ˈner- **-s** -z
wagon ˈwæg.ən **-s** -z
wagoner ˈwæg.ə.nəʳ (US) -nɚ **-s** -z
wagonette ˌwæg.əˈnet **-s** -s
wagon-lit ˌvæg.ɔ̃ːnˈliː, ˌvɑːg-, -gɒnˈ-, ˈ--- (US) ˌvɑː.gɔ̃ːnˈliː **-s** -z
Wagstaff ˈwæg.stɑːf (US) -stæf
wagtail ˈwæg.teɪl **-s** -z
Wah(h)abi wəˈhɑː.bi, wɑː- **-s** -z
waif weɪf **-s** -s
Waikiki ˌwaɪ.kiˈkiː, ˈ---
wail weɪl **-s** -z **-ing/ly** -ɪŋ/li **-ed** -d
wain (W) weɪn **-s** -z
Wain(e) weɪn
Wainfleet ˈweɪn.fliːt
wainsco|t ˈweɪn.skə|t, ˈwen-, -skɒ|t (US) ˈweɪn.skə|t, -skɑː|t, -skoʊ|t **-ts** -ts **-t(t)ing** -tɪŋ (US) -t̬ɪŋ **-t(t)ed** -tɪd (US) -t̬ɪd
Wainwright ˈweɪn.raɪt
waist weɪst **-s** -s **-ed** -ɪd
waistband ˈweɪst.bænd **-s** -z
waistcoat ˈweɪst.kəʊt *old-fashioned:* ˈwes.kət, -kɪt (US) ˈwes.kət, ˈweɪst.koʊt **-s** -s
waist-deep ˌweɪstˈdiːp *stress shift:* ˌwaist-deep ˈwater
waist-high ˌweɪstˈhaɪ *stress shift:* ˌwaist-high ˈwater
waistline ˈweɪst.laɪn **-s** -z
wait weɪt **-s** -s **-ing** -ɪŋ (US) ˈweɪ.t̬ɪŋ **-ed** -ɪd (US) ˈweɪ.t̬ɪd **ˈwaiting ˌlist**
Waite weɪt
waiter ˈweɪ.təʳ (US) -t̬ɚ **-s** -z
waiting-room ˈweɪ.tɪŋ.rʊm, -ruːm (US) -t̬ɪŋ.ruːm, -rʊm **-s** -z
wait|person ˈweɪt|ˌpɜː.sən (US) -ˌpɜːr- **-people** -ˌpiː.pl̩
waitress ˈweɪ.trəs, -trɪs (US) -trɪs **-es** -ɪz
Waitrose® ˈweɪ.trəʊz (US) -troʊz
waiv|e weɪv **-es** -z **-ing** -ɪŋ **-ed** -d
waiver ˈweɪ.vəʳ (US) -vɚ **-s** -z
Wajda ˈvaɪ.də
wak|e weɪk **-es** -s **-ing** -ɪŋ **-ed** -t **woke** wəʊk (US) woʊk **woken** ˈwəʊ.kən (US) ˈwoʊ-
Wakefield ˈweɪk.fiːld
wakeful ˈweɪk.fəl, -fʊl **-ly** -i **-ness** -nəs, -nɪs
Wakehurst ˈweɪk.hɜːst (US) -hɜːrst
Wakeling ˈweɪ.klɪŋ
Wakeman ˈweɪk.mən
waken ˈweɪ.kən **-s** -z **-ing** -ɪŋ, ˈweɪk.nɪŋ **-ed** -d
wakey wakey ˌweɪ.kiˈweɪ.ki
Wakley ˈweɪ.kli
Wakonda wəˈkɒn.də (US) wɑːˈkɑːn-
Wal wɒl, wɔːl (US) wɑːl
Walachi|a wɒlˈeɪ.ki|.ə, wəˈleɪ- (US) wɑːˈleɪ-, wə- **-an/s** -ən/z
Walberswick ˈwɔːl.bəz.wɪk, ˈwɒl- (US) ˈwɔːl.bɚz-, ˈwɑːl-
Walbrook ˈwɔːl.brʊk, ˈwɒl- (US) ˈwɔːl-, ˈwɑːl-
Walcott ˈwɔːl.kət, ˈwɒl-, -kɒt (US) ˈwɔːl.kət, ˈwɑːl-, -kɑːt
Waldeck ˈwɔːl.dek, ˈwɒl- (US) ˈwɔːl-, ˈvɑːl-
Waldegrave ˈwɔːl.greɪv, ˈwɒl-, -də.greɪv (US) ˈwɔːl-, ˈwɑːl-
Note: Earl Waldegrave is /ˈwɔːl.greɪv, ˈwɒl- (US) ˈwɔːl-, ˈwɑːl-/; the politician William Waldegrave is /ˈwɔːl.də.greɪv, ˈwɒl- (US) ˈwɔːl-, ˈwɑːl-/.
Waldemar ˈvæl.də.mɑːʳ, ˈvɑːl-, ˈwɔːl-, -dɪ- (US) ˈvɑːl.də.mɑːr
Walden ˈwɔːl.dən, ˈwɒl- (US) ˈwɔːl-, ˈwɑːl-
Waldheim ˈvɑːld.haɪm *as if German:* ˈvælt- (US) ˈwɑːld- *as if German:* ˈvɑːlt-
Waldhere ˈwɑːlˌheə.rə (US) ˈwɔːldˌher.ə, ˈwɑːld-
Waldo ˈwɔːl.dəʊ, ˈwɒl- (US) ˈwɔːl.doʊ, ˈwɑːl-
Waldock ˈwɔːl.dɒk, ˈwɒl- (US) ˈwɔːl.dɑːk, ˈwɑːl-
Waldorf ˈwɔːl.dɔːf, ˈwɒl- (US) ˈwɔːl.dɔːrf, ˈwɑːl- **ˌWaldorf ˈsalad**
Waldron ˈwɔːl.drən, ˈwɒl- (US) ˈwɔːl-, ˈwɑːl-
Waldstein *American name:* ˈwɔːld.staɪn, ˈwɒld- (US) ˈwɔːld-, ˈwɑːld- *German name, Beethoven sonata:* ˈvæld.staɪn, ˈvɑːld-, ˈvɔːld-, ˈvɒld-, ˈwɔːld-, ˈwɒld-, -ʃtaɪn (US) ˈvɑːlt.ʃtaɪn, ˈvɑːld-
wale weɪl **-s** -z
waler (W) ˈweɪ.ləʳ (US) -lɚ **-s** -z
Waleran *Baron:* ˈwɔːl.rən, ˈwɒl- (US) ˈwɔːl-, ˈwɑːl- *buildings in Borough High Street, London:* ˈwɒl.ər.ən (US) ˈwɑː.lɚ-, ˈwɔː-

Wales weɪlz
Walesa vɑːˈwen*t*.sə, væˈ- (US) wɑːˈlen*t*.sə; vɑːˈwen*t*.sɑː
Waley ˈweɪ.li
Walfish ˈwɔːl.fɪʃ, ˈwɒl- (US) ˈwɔːl-, ˈwɑːl-
Walford ˈwɔːl.fəd, ˈwɒl- (US) ˈwɔːl.fɚd, ˈwɑːl-
Walhalla vælˈhæl.ə (US) wɑːlˈhɑː.lə; wælˈhæl.ə, væl-
Walham ˈwɒl.əm (US) ˈwɑː.ləm
walk wɔːk (US) wɑːk, wɔːk **-s** -s **-ing** -ɪŋ **-ed** -t **-er/s** -əʳ/z (US) -ɚ/z **ˈwalking ˌstick**
walkabout ˈwɔː.kəˌbaʊt (US) ˈwɑː-, ˈwɔː- **-s** -s
walkaway ˈwɔː.kə.weɪ (US) ˈwɑː-, ˈwɔː-
Walkden ˈwɔːk.dən (US) ˈwɑːk-, ˈwɔːk-
Walker ˈwɔː.kəʳ (US) ˈwɑː.kɚ, ˈwɔː-
Walkern ˈwɔːl.kən, -kɜːn (US) ˈwɔːl.kɚn, ˈwɑːl-, -kɜːrn
walkies ˈwɔː.kiz (US) ˈwɑː-, ˈwɔː-
walkie-talkie ˌwɔː.kiˈtɔː.ki (US) ˌwɑː.kiˈtɑː-, ˌwɔː-, -ˈtɔː- **-s** -z
walk-in ˈwɔːk.ɪn (US) ˈwɑːk-, ˈwɔːk-
Walkman® ˈwɔːk.mən (US) ˈwɑːk-, ˈwɔːk- **-s** -z
walk-on ˈwɔːk.ɒn (US) ˈwɑːk.ɑːn, ˈwɔːk- **-s** -z
walk-out ˈwɔːk.aʊt (US) ˈwɑːk-, ˈwɔːk- **-s** -s
walkover ˈwɔːkˌəʊ.vəʳ (US) ˈwɑːkˌoʊ.vɚ, ˈwɔːk- **-s** -z
walkway ˈwɔːk.weɪ (US) ˈwɑːk-, ˈwɔːk- **-s** -z
Walkyrie vælˈkɪə.ri; ˈvæl.kᵊr.i, -kɪ.ri (US) wɑːlˈkɪr.i; ˈwɑːl.kɚ-, ˈvɑːl- **-s** -z
walky-talk|y ˌwɔː.kiˈtɔː.k|i (US) ˌwɑː.kiˈtɑː-, ˌwɔː-, -ˈtɔː- **-ies** -iz
wall (W) wɔːl (US) wɔːl, wɑːl **-s** -z **-ing** -ɪŋ **-ed** -d **ˈWall ˌStreet** ; **ˌWall Street ˈJournal** ; **ˌbang one's ˌhead against a ˌbrick ˈwall**
wallab|y (W) ˈwɒl.ə.b|i (US) ˈwɑː.lə- **-ies** -iz
Wallace ˈwɒl.ɪs, -əs (US) ˈwɑː.lɪs, -ləs
Wallach ˈwɒl.ək (US) ˈwɑː.lək **-s** -s
Wallachi|a wɒlˈeɪ.ki|.ə, wəˈleɪ- (US) wɑːˈleɪ- **-an/s** -an/z
walla(h) ˈwɒl.ə (US) ˈwɑː.lɑː **-s** -z
Wallasey ˈwɒl.ə.si (US) ˈwɑː.lə-
wallboard ˈwɔːl.bɔːd (US) ˈwɔːl.bɔːrd, ˈwɑːl-
wallchart ˈwɔːl.tʃɑːt (US) -tʃɑːrt, ˈwɑːl- **-s** -s
Waller ˈwɒl.əʳ (US) ˈwɑː.lɚ
wallet ˈwɒl.ɪt (US) ˈwɑː.lɪt **-s** -s
wall-eye ˈwɔːl.aɪ (US) ˈwɔːl-, ˈwɑːl- **-s** -z **-d** -d
wallflower ˈwɔːl.flaʊəʳ (US) -flaʊɚ, ˈwɑːl- **-s** -z
Wallingford ˈwɒl.ɪŋ.fəd (US) ˈwɑː.lɪŋ.fɚd
Wallington ˈwɒl.ɪŋ.tən (US) ˈwɑː.lɪŋ-
Wallis ˈwɒl.ɪs (US) ˈwɑː.lɪs
Wallonia wəˈləʊ.ni.ə (US) wɑːˈloʊ-
Walloon wɒlˈuːn, wəˈluːn (US) wɑːˈluːn **-s** -z
wallop ˈwɒl.əp (US) ˈwɑː.ləp **-s** -s **-ing/s** -ɪŋ/z **-ed** -t
wallow ˈwɒl.əʊ (US) ˈwɑː.loʊ **-s** -z **-ing** -ɪŋ **-ed** -d **-er/s** -əʳ/z (US) -ɚ/z
wallpap|er ˈwɔːlˌpeɪ.p|əʳ (US) -p|ɚ, ˈwɑːl- **-ers** -əz (US) -ɚz **-ering** -ᵊr.ɪŋ **-ered** -əd (US) -ɚd
Wallsend ˈwɔːl.zend (US) ˈwɔːl-, ˈwɑːl-
wall-to-wall ˌwɔːl.təˈwɔːl, -tuˈ- (US) -t̬əˈ-, ˌwɑːl-, -ˈwɑːl
Wallwork ˈwɔːl.wɜːk, ˈwɒl- (US) ˈwɔːl.wɜːrk, ˈwɑːl-
wall|y (W) ˈwɒl|.i (US) ˈwɑː.l|i **-ies** -iz
Wal-Mart ˈwɒl.mɑːt (US) ˈwɔːl.mɑːrt, ˈwɑːl-
Walmer ˈwɔːl.məʳ, ˈwɒl- (US) ˈwɔːl.mɚ, ˈwɑːl-
Walm(e)sley ˈwɔːmz.li (US) ˈwɑːmz-, ˈwɔːmz-
Walmisley ˈwɔːmz.li (US) ˈwɑːmz-, ˈwɔːmz-
Walney ˈwɔːl.ni, ˈwɒl- (US) ˈwɔːl-, ˈwɑːl-
walnut ˈwɔːl.nʌt, -nət (US) ˈwɔːl-, ˈwɑːl- **-s** -s
Walpole ˈwɔːl.pəʊl, ˈwɒl- (US) ˈwɔːl.poʊl, ˈwɑːl-
Walpurgis vælˈpʊə.gɪs, vɑːl-, -ˈpɜː- (US) vɑːlˈpʊr.gɪs
walrus ˈwɔːl.rəs, ˈwɒl-, -rʌs (US) ˈwɔːl.rəs, ˈwɑːl- **-es** -ɪz
Walsall ˈwɔːl.sɔːl, ˈwɒl-, -sᵊl (US) ˈwɔːl.sɔːl, ˈwɑːl-, -sɑːl
Walsh wɒlʃ, wɔːlʃ (US) wɔːlʃ, wɑːlʃ
Walsham ˈwɔːl.ʃəm *locally:* -səm (US) ˈwɔːl-, ˈwɑːl-
Walsingham *surname:* ˈwɔːl.sɪŋ.əm, ˈwɒl- (US) ˈwɔːl-, ˈwɑːl- *place:* ˈwɔːl.zɪŋ.əm, ˈwɒl-, -sɪŋ- (US) ˈwɔːl-, ˈwɑːl-
Walt wɒlt, wɔːlt (US) wɔːlt, wɑːlt
Walter *English name:* ˈwɒl.təʳ, ˈwɔːl- (US) ˈwɔːl.t̬ɚ, ˈwɑːl- *German name:* ˈvɑːl.təʳ (US) -t̬ɚ
Walter Mitty ˌwɒl.təˈmɪt.i, ˌwɔːl- (US) ˌwɔːl.t̬ɚˈmɪt̬-, ˌwɑːl-
Walters ˈwɒl.təz, ˈwɔːl- (US) ˈwɔːl.t̬ɚz, ˈwɑːl-
Waltham *Great and Little, in Essex:* ˈwɔːl.təm, ˈwɒl- (US) ˈwɔːl-, ˈwɑːl-
Note: Some new residents pronounce /-θəm/. *other places:* ˈwɔːl.θəm, ˈwɒl- (US) ˈwɔːl-, ˈwɑːl- **ˌWaltham ˈForest**
Walthamstow ˈwɒl.θəm.stəʊ, ˈwɔːl- (US) ˈwɔːl.θəm.stoʊ, ˈwɑːl-
Walther ˈvɑːl.təʳ (US) -t̬ɚ
Walton ˈwɒl.tᵊn, ˈwɔːl- (US) ˈwɔːl-, ˈwɑːl-
Walton-on-the-Naze ˌwɒl.tᵊnˌɒn.ðəˈneɪz, ˌwɔːl- (US) ˌwɔːl.tᵊnˌɑːn-, ˌwɑːl-
waltz wɒls, wɔːls, wɒlts, wɔːlts (US) wɔːlts, wɑːlts **-es** -ɪz **-ing** -ɪŋ **-ed** -t **-er/s** -əʳ/z (US) -ɚ/z
Walworth ˈwɒl.wəθ, ˈwɔːl-, -wɜːθ (US) ˈwɔːl.wɜːrθ, ˈwɑːl-, -wɚθ
wampum ˈwɒm.pəm (US) ˈwɑːm-, ˈwɔːm- **-s** -z
WAN wæn
wan wɒn (US) wɑːn **-ner** -əʳ (US) -ɚ **-nest** -ɪst, -əst **-ly** -li **-ness** -nəs, -nɪs
Wanamaker ˈwɒn.ə.meɪ.kəʳ (US) ˈwɑː.nə.meɪ.kɚ
wand (W) wɒnd (US) wɑːnd **-s** -z
Wanda ˈwɒn.də (US) ˈwɑːn-
wand|er ˈwɒn.d|əʳ (US) ˈwɑːn.d|ɚ **-ers** -əz (US) -ɚz **-ering/s** -ᵊr.ɪŋ/z **-ered** -əd (US) -ɚd **-erer/s** -ᵊr.əʳ/z (US) -ɚ.ɚ/z
wanderlust ˈwɒn.də.lʌst, ˈvɑːn.də.lʊst (US) ˈwɑːn.dɚ.lʌst
Wandle ˈwɒn.dḷ (US) ˈwɑːn-
Wandsworth ˈwɒn*d*z.wəθ (US) ˈwɑːn*d*z.wɚθ
wan|e weɪn **-es** -z **-ing** -ɪŋ **-ed** -d
Wang® wæŋ
Wanganui *in New Zealand:* ˌwɒŋ.əˈnuː.i, ˌwɒn.gə- (US) ˌwɔːŋ.gə-, ˌwɑːn-
Note: The first is the form always used by those of Polynesian descent.
wangl|e ˈwæŋ.gḷ **-es** -z **-ing** -ɪŋ (US) ˈwæŋ.glɪŋ **-ed** -d
wank wæŋk **-s** -s **-ing** -ɪŋ **-ed** -t
wanker ˈwæŋ.kəʳ (US) -kɚ **-s** -z
Wann wɒn (US) wɑːn
wanna ˈwɒn.ə (US) ˈwɑː.nə
wannabe(e) ˈwɒn.ə.bi, -biː (US) ˈwɑː.nə- **-s** -z
Wansbeck ˈwɒnz.bek (US) ˈwɑːnz-
Wanstall ˈwɒn.stɔːl (US) ˈwɑːn.stɑːl, -stɔːl
Wanstead ˈwɒn*t*.sted, -stɪd (US) ˈwɑːn*t*-
wan|t wɒn|t (US) wɑːn|t, wɔːn|t, wʌn|t **-ts** -ts **-ting** -tɪŋ (US) -t̬ɪŋ **-ted** -tɪd (US) -t̬ɪd
Wantage ˈwɒn.tɪdʒ (US) ˈwɑːn.t̬ɪdʒ
wanton ˈwɒn.tən (US) ˈwɑːn.tᵊn **-ly** -li **-ness** -nəs, -nɪs
wapentake ˈwæp.ən.teɪk, ˈwɒp- (US) ˈwɑː.pən-, ˈwæp.ən- **-s** -s
wapiti ˈwɒp.ɪ.ti (US) ˈwɑː.pə.t̬i **-s** -z
Wapping ˈwɒp.ɪŋ (US) ˈwɑː.pɪŋ
Wappinger ˈwɒp.ɪn.dʒəʳ (US) ˈwɑː.pɪn.dʒɚ
war wɔːʳ (US) wɔːr **-s** -z **-ring** -ɪŋ **-red** -d **ˈwar ˌcrime** ; **ˈwar ˌdance** ; **ˈwar**

ˌgame ; ˈwar meˌmorial ; ˌwar of ˈnerves ; ˈwar ˌpaint ; ˈwar ˌwidow
Warbeck ˈwɔː.bek (US) ˈwɔːr-
warbl|e ˈwɔː.bḷ (US) ˈwɔːr- **-es** -z **-ing** -ɪŋ, ˈ-blɪŋ (US) ˈwɔːr.bḷ.ɪŋ, ˈ-blɪŋ **-ed** -d
warbler ˈwɔː.bləʳ, -bḷ.əʳ (US) ˈwɔːr.blɚ, -bḷ.ɚ **-s** -z
Warburg ˈwɔː.bɜːg (US) ˈwɔːr.bɜːrg
Warburton ˈwɔː.bə.tᵊn, -bɜː- (US) ˈwɔːr.bɚ-, -bɜːr-
war-cr|y ˈwɔː.kr|aɪ (US) ˈwɔːr- **-ies** -aɪz
ward (W) wɔːd (US) wɔːrd **-s** -z **-ing** -ɪŋ **-ed** -ɪd
-ward -wəd (US) -wɚd
Note: Suffix. Normally unstressed, e.g. **homeward** /ˈhəʊm.wəd (US) ˈhoʊm.wɚd/.
warden (W) ˈwɔː.dᵊn (US) ˈwɔːr- **-s** -z
warder (W) ˈwɔː.dəʳ (US) ˈwɔːr.dɚ **-s** -z
Wardlaw ˈwɔːd.lɔː (US) ˈwɔːrd.lɑː, -lɔː
Wardle ˈwɔː.dḷ (US) ˈwɔːr-
Wardour ˈwɔː.dəʳ (US) ˈwɔːr.dɚ
wardress *fem. warder:* ˈwɔː.drɪs, -drəs (US) ˈwɔːr.drɪs **-es** -ɪz
war-dress *war costume:* ˈwɔː.dres (US) ˈwɔːr- **-es** -ɪz
wardrobe ˈwɔː.drəʊb (US) ˈwɔːr.droʊb **-s** -z
wardroom ˈwɔːd.rʊm, -ruːm (US) ˈwɔːrd.ruːm, -rʊm **-s** -z
-wards -wədz (US) -wɚdz
Note: See note for **-ward**.
wardship ˈwɔːd.ʃɪp (US) ˈwɔːrd- **-s** -s
ware (W) weəʳ (US) wer **-s** -z
-ware -weəʳ (US) -wer
Note: Suffix. Normally unstressed, e.g. **tableware** /ˈteɪ.bḷ.weəʳ (US) -wer/.
Wareham ˈweə.rəm (US) ˈwer.əm
warehou|se (*n.*) ˈweə.haʊ|s (US) ˈwer- **-ses** -zɪz
warehou|se (*v.*) ˈweə.haʊ|z, -haʊ|s (US) ˈwer- **-ses** -zɪz, -sɪz **-sing** -zɪŋ, -sɪŋ **-sed** -zd, -st
warehouse|man ˈweə.haʊs|.mən (US) ˈwer- **-men** -mən
warfare ˈwɔː.feəʳ (US) ˈwɔːr.fer
warfarin ˈwɔː.fᵊr.ɪn (US) ˈwɔːr-
Wargrave ˈwɔː.greɪv (US) ˈwɔːr-
Warham ˈwɔː.rəm (US) ˈwɔːr.əm
warhead ˈwɔː.hed (US) ˈwɔːr- **-s** -z
Warhol ˈwɔː.həʊl (US) ˈwɔːr.hɔːl, -hoʊl
warhors|e ˈwɔː.hɔːs (US) ˈwɔːr.hɔːrs **-es** -ɪz
Waring ˈweə.rɪŋ (US) ˈwer.ɪŋ
warlike ˈwɔː.laɪk (US) ˈwɔːr-
Warlingham ˈwɔː.lɪŋ.əm (US) ˈwɔːr-
warlock (W) ˈwɔː.lɒk (US) ˈwɔːr- **-s** -s
warlord ˈwɔː.lɔːd (US) ˈwɔːr.lɔːrd **-s** -z
warm wɔːm (US) wɔːrm **-er** -əʳ (US) -ɚ **-est** -ɪst, -əst **-ly** -li **-ness** -nəs, -nɪs **-s** -z **-ing** -ɪŋ **-ed** -d
warm-blooded ˌwɔːmˈblʌd.ɪd (US) ˌwɔːrm- **-ness** -nəs, -nɪs *stress shift:* ˌwarm-blooded ˈanimal
warmer ˈwɔː.məʳ (US) ˈwɔːr.mɚ **-s** -z
warm-hearted ˌwɔːmˈhɑː.tɪd (US) ˌwɔːrmˈhɑːr.t̬ɪd **-ly** -li **-ness** -nəs, -nɪs *stress shift:* ˌwarm-hearted ˈperson
warming-pan ˈwɔː.mɪŋ.pæn (US) ˈwɔːr- **-s** -z
Warmington ˈwɔː.mɪŋ.tən (US) ˈwɔːr-
Warminster ˈwɔː.mɪn*t*.stəʳ (US) ˈwɔːr.mɪn*t*.stɚ
war-mong|er ˈwɔːˌmʌŋ.g|əʳ (US) ˈwɑːrˌmʌŋ.g|ɚ, ˈwɔːr-, -ˌmɑːŋ- **-ers** -əz (US) -ɚz **-ering** -ᵊr.ɪŋ
warmth wɔːm*p*θ (US) wɔːrm*p*θ
warn wɔːn (US) wɔːrn **-s** -z **-ing/ly** -ɪŋ/li **-ed** -d
Warne wɔːn (US) wɔːrn
Warner ˈwɔː.nəʳ (US) ˈwɔːr.nɚ
warning ˈwɔː.nɪŋ (US) ˈwɔːr- **-s** -z
Warnock ˈwɔː.nɒk (US) ˈwɔːr.nɑːk
warp wɔːp (US) wɔːrp **-s** -s **-ing** -ɪŋ **-ed** -t
warpath ˈwɔː.pɑːθ (US) ˈwɔːr.pæθ
warr|ant ˈwɒr|.ᵊnt (US) ˈwɔːr-, ˈwɑːr- **-ants** -ᵊnts **-anting** -ᵊn.tɪŋ (US) -ᵊn.t̬ɪŋ **-anted** -ᵊn.tɪd (US) -ᵊn.t̬ɪd **-anter/s** -ᵊn.təʳ/z (US) -ᵊn.t̬ɚ/z ˈ**warrant** ˌ**officer**
warrantab|le ˈwɒr.ᵊn.tə.bl| (US) ˈwɔːr.ᵊn.t̬ə-, ˈwɑːr- **-ly** -li **-leness** -ḷ.nəs, -nɪs
warrantee ˌwɒr.ᵊnˈtiː (US) ˌwɔːr-, ˌwɑːr- **-s** -z
warrantor ˈwɒr.ᵊn.tɔːʳ, -təʳ, ˌwɒr.ᵊnˈtɔːʳ (US) ˈwɔːr.ᵊn.tɔːr, ˈwɑːr-, -t̬ɚ **-s** -z
warrant|y ˈwɒr.ᵊn.t|i (US) ˈwɔːr.ᵊn.t̬|i, ˈwɑːr- **-ies** -iz
Warre wɔːʳ (US) wɔːr
warren (W) ˈwɒr.ᵊn, -ɪn (US) ˈwɔːr.ᵊn, ˈwɑːr- **-s** -z
Warrender ˈwɒr.ən.dəʳ, -ɪn- (US) ˈwɔːr.ən.dɚ, ˈwɑːr-, -ɪn-
Warrenpoint ˈwɒr.ən.pɔɪnt, -əm- (US) ˈwɔːr.ən-, ˈwɑːr-
Warrington ˈwɒr.ɪŋ.tən (US) ˈwɔːr-, ˈwɑːr-
warrior (W) ˈwɒr.i.əʳ (US) ˈwɔːr.jɚ, ˈwɑːr-, -i.ɚ **-s** -z
Warrnambool ˈwɔː.nəm.buːl (US) ˈwɔːr-
Warsaw ˈwɔː.sɔː (US) ˈwɔːr.sɑː, -sɔː ˌ**Warsaw** ˈ**Pact**
warship ˈwɔː.ʃɪp (US) ˈwɔːr- **-s** -s
Warsop ˈwɔː.səp (US) ˈwɔːr-
Warspite ˈwɔː.spaɪt (US) ˈwɔːr-
wart wɔːt (US) wɔːrt **-s** -s **-y** -i (US) ˈwɔːr.t̬i
warthog ˈwɔːt.hɒg (US) ˈwɔːrt.hɑːg, -hɔːg **-s** -z
wartime ˈwɔː.taɪm (US) ˈwɔːr-
Warton ˈwɔː.tᵊn (US) ˈwɔːr-
war-weary ˈwɔːˌwɪə.ri (US) ˈwɔːrˌwɪr.i
Warwick *in Britain:* ˈwɒr.ɪk (US) ˈwɔːr.ɪk, ˈwɑːr- **-shire** -ʃəʳ, -ˌʃɪəʳ (US) -ʃɚ, -ˌʃɪr *in US:* ˈwɔː.wɪk (US) ˈwɔːr-
war-worn ˈwɔː.wɔːn (US) ˈwɔːr.wɔːrn
war|y ˈweə.r|i (US) ˈwer|.i **-ier** -i.əʳ (US) -i.ɚ **-iest** -i.ɪst, -i.əst **-ily** -ᵊl.i, -ɪ.li **-iness** -ɪ.nəs, -ɪ.nɪs
was (*from* **be**) *strong forms:* wɒz (US) wɑːz, wʌz *weak forms:* wəz, wz
Note: Weak form word. The strong forms are used in contrastive contexts (e.g. 'I don't know whether it **was** or it **wasn't**), and for emphasis (e.g. '**I was** right!'). The strong form is also usual in final position (e.g. 'That's where it was'). The weak forms are used elsewhere; the form /wz/ is found only in rapid, casual speech.
Wasbrough ˈwɒz.brə (US) ˈwɑːz-
wash (W) wɒʃ (US) wɑːʃ, wɔːʃ **-es** -ɪz **-ing** -ɪŋ **-ed** -t **-able** -ə.bḷ ˌ**wash and** ˈ**wear**
Wash. (*abbrev. for* **Washington**) ˈwɒʃ.ɪŋ.tən (US) ˈwɑː.ʃɪŋ-, ˈwɔː-
washbasin ˈwɒʃˌbeɪ.sᵊn (US) ˈwɑːʃ-, ˈwɔːʃ- **-s** -z
washboard ˈwɒʃ.bɔːd (US) ˈwɑːʃ.bɔːrd, ˈwɔːʃ- **-s** -z
washbowl ˈwɒʃ.bəʊl (US) ˈwɑːʃ.boʊl, ˈwɔːʃ- **-s** -z
wash|cloth ˈwɒʃ|.klɒθ (US) ˈwɑːʃ|.klɑːθ, ˈwɔːʃ- **-cloths** -klɒθs, -klɒðz (US) -klɑːθs, -klɑːðz
washday ˈwɒʃ.deɪ (US) ˈwɑːʃ-, ˈwɔːʃ- **-s** -z
washed-out ˌwɒʃtˈaʊt (US) ˌwɑːʃt-, ˌwɔːʃt- *stress shift:* ˌwashed-out ˈcolour
washed-up ˌwɒʃtˈʌp (US) ˌwɑːʃt-, ˌwɔːʃt- *stress shift:* ˌwashed-up ˈwriter
washer ˈwɒʃ.əʳ (US) ˈwɑː.ʃɚ, ˈwɔː- **-s** -z
washer-dryer ˌwɒʃ.əˈdraɪ.əʳ (US) ˌwɑː.ʃɚˈdraɪ.ɚ, ˌwɔː- **-s** -z
washer-up ˌwɒʃ.əʳˈʌp (US) ˌwɑː.ʃɚ-, ˌwɔː- **washers-up** ˌwɒʃ.əzˈ- (US) ˌwɑː.ʃɚzˈ-, ˌwɔː-
washer|woman ˈwɒʃ.əˌwʊm.ən (US) ˈwɑː.ʃɚ-, ˈwɔː- **-women** -ˌwɪm.ɪn
wash-hou|se ˈwɒʃ.haʊ|s (US) ˈwɑːʃ-, ˈwɔːʃ- **-ses** -zɪz
washing ˈwɒʃ.ɪŋ (US) ˈwɑː.ʃɪŋ, ˈwɔː- ˈ**washing maˌchine** ; ˈ**washing** ˌ**powder**
Washingborough ˈwɒʃ.ɪŋˌbʌr.ə (US) ˈwɑː.ʃɪŋ.bɚ.oʊ, ˈwɔː-
Washington ˈwɒʃ.ɪŋ.tən (US) ˈwɑː.ʃɪŋ-, ˈwɔː- ˌ**Washington** ˌ**D'C** ; ˌ**Washington** ˈ**State**

Washingtonian ˌwɒʃ.ɪŋˈtəʊ.ni.ən Ⓤ ˌwɑː.ʃɪŋˈtoʊ-, ˌwɔː- **-s** -z
washing-up ˌwɒʃ.ɪŋˈʌp Ⓤ ˌwɑː.ʃɪŋˈ-, ˌwɔː-
washout ˈwɒʃ.aʊt Ⓤ ˈwɑːʃ-, ˈwɔːʃ- **-s** -s
washrag ˈwɒʃ.ræg Ⓤ ˈwɑːʃ-, ˈwɔːʃ- **-s** -z
washroom ˈwɒʃ.rʊm, -ruːm Ⓤ ˈwɑːʃ.ruːm, ˈwɔːʃ-, -rʊm **-s** -z
washstand ˈwɒʃ.stænd Ⓤ ˈwɑːʃ-, ˈwɔːʃ- **-s** -z
wash-tub ˈwɒʃ.tʌb Ⓤ ˈwɑːʃ-, ˈwɔːʃ- **-s** -z
wash|y ˈwɒʃ|.i Ⓤ ˈwɑː.ʃ|i, ˈwɔː- **-ier** -i.əʳ Ⓤ -i.ɚ **-iest** -i.ɪst, -i.əst **-iness** -ɪ.nəs, -ɪ.nɪs
wasn't ˈwɒz.ᵊnt Ⓤ ˈwɑː.zᵊnt, ˈwʌz-
wasp, WASP (W) wɒsp Ⓤ wɑːsp **-s** -s
waspish ˈwɒs.pɪʃ Ⓤ ˈwɑː.spɪʃ **-ly** -li **-ness** -nəs, -nɪs
wassail ˈwɒs.eɪl, ˈwæs-, -ᵊl Ⓤ ˈwɑː.sᵊl, ˈwæs.ᵊl, -eɪl; wɑːˈseɪl **-s** -z
wassailing ˈwɒs.ᵊl.ɪŋ, ˈwæs-, -eɪ.lɪŋ Ⓤ ˈwɑː.sᵊl.ɪŋ, ˈwæs.ᵊl-, -eɪ.lɪŋ; wɑːˈseɪ.lɪŋ
Wassell ˈwæs.ᵊl
Wasson ˈwɒs.ᵊn Ⓤ ˈwɑː.sᵊn
wast *(from* **be**) *strong forms:* wɒst Ⓤ wɑːst *weak form:* wəst
Wast wɒst Ⓤ wɑːst
wast|e weɪst **-es** -s **-ing** -ɪŋ **-ed** -ɪd **-er/s** -əʳ/z Ⓤ -ɚ/z **-age** -ɪdʒ ˈ**waste** ˌ**product,** ˌ**waste** ˈ**product**
wastebasket ˈweɪs*t*ˌbɑː.skɪt Ⓤ -ˌbæs.kət **-s** -s
wasteful ˈweɪs*t*.fᵊl, -fʊl **-ly** -i **-ness** -nəs, -nɪs
wasteland ˈweɪs*t*.lænd **-s** -z
wastepaper ˌweɪs*t*ˈpeɪ.pəʳ, ˈ-ˌ-- Ⓤ ˈweɪs*t*ˌpeɪ.pɚ **waste**ˈ**paper** ˌ**basket,** ˈ**wastepaper** ˌ**basket**; **waste**ˈ**paper** ˌ**bin**
wastepipe ˈweɪs*t*.paɪp **-s** -s
wastrel ˈweɪ.strᵊl **-s** -z
Wastwater ˈwɒstˌwɔː.təʳ Ⓤ ˈwɑːstˌwɑː.t̬ɚ, -ˌwɔː-
Wat wɒt Ⓤ wɑːt
watch wɒtʃ Ⓤ wɑːtʃ, wɔːtʃ **-es** -ɪz **-ing** -ɪŋ **-ed** -t **-er/s** -əʳ/z Ⓤ -ɚ/z
watchable ˈwɒtʃ.ə.bl̩ Ⓤ ˈwɑː.tʃə-, ˈwɔː-
watchamacallit ˈwɒtʃ.ə.məˌkɔːl.ɪt Ⓤ ˈwɑː.tʃə-, ˈwɔː-, -ˌkɑːl- **-s** -s
watch-cas|e ˈwɒtʃ.keɪs Ⓤ ˈwɑːtʃ-, ˈwɔːtʃ- **-es** -ɪz
watchdog ˈwɒtʃ.dɒg Ⓤ ˈwɑːtʃ.dɑːg, ˈwɔːtʃ-, -dɔːg **-s** -z
Watchet ˈwɒtʃ.ɪt Ⓤ ˈwɑː.tʃɪt, ˈwɔː-
watchful ˈwɒtʃ.fᵊl, -fʊl Ⓤ ˈwɑːtʃ-, ˈwɔːtʃ- **-ly** -i **-ness** -nəs, -nɪs
watchmak|er ˈwɒtʃˌmeɪ.k|əʳ Ⓤ ˈwɑːtʃˌmeɪ.k|ɚ, ˈwɔːtʃ- **-ers** -əz Ⓤ -ɚz **-ing** -ɪŋ
watch|man ˈwɒtʃ|.mən Ⓤ ˈwɑːtʃ-, ˈwɔːtʃ- **-men** -mən, -men
watchstrap ˈwɒtʃ.stræp Ⓤ ˈwɑːtʃ-, ˈwɔːtʃ- **-s** -s
watchtower (W) ˈwɒtʃ.taʊəʳ Ⓤ ˈwɑːtʃ.taʊɚ, ˈwɔːtʃ- **-s** -z
watchword ˈwɒtʃ.wɜːd Ⓤ ˈwɑːtʃ.wɜːrd, ˈwɔːtʃ- **-s** -z
wat|er ˈwɔː.t|əʳ Ⓤ ˈwɑː.t̬|ɚ, ˈwɔː- **-ers** -əz Ⓤ -ɚz **-ering** -ᵊr.ɪŋ **-ered** -əd Ⓤ -ɚd ˈ**water** ˌ**bed**; ˈ**water** ˌ**beetle**; ˈ**water** ˌ**bottle**; ˈ**water** ˌ**buffalo**; ˌ**water** ˈ**buffalo** Ⓤ ˈ**water** ˌ**buffalo**; ˈ**water** ˌ**cannon**; ˌ**water** ˈ**chestnut** Ⓤ ˈ**water** ˌ**chestnut**; ˈ**water** ˌ**closet**; ˈ**water** ˌ**ice**; ˈ**water** ˌ**main**; ˈ**water** ˌ**meadow**; ˈ**water** ˌ**mill**; ˈ**water** **sup**ˌ**ply**; ˈ**water** ˌ**table**; ˈ**water** ˌ**tower**; ˌ**keep one's** ˌ**head above** ˈ**water**; ˌ**pour cold** ˈ**water on**; **like** ˌ**water off a** ˌ**duck's** ˈ**back** Ⓤ **like** ˌ**water off a** ˈ**duck's** ˌ**back**; ˌ**water** ˌ**under the** ˈ**bridge**
water-borne ˈwɔː.tə.bɔːn Ⓤ ˈwɑː.t̬ɚ.bɔːrn, ˈwɔː-
waterbuck ˈwɔː.tə.bʌk Ⓤ ˈwɑː.t̬ɚ-, ˈwɔː-
Waterbur|y ˈwɔː.tə.bᵊr|.i Ⓤ ˈwɑː.t̬ɚˌber-, ˈwɔː-, -bɚ- **-ies** -iz
water-chute ˈwɔː.tə.ʃuːt Ⓤ ˈwɑː.t̬ɚ-, ˈwɔː- **-s** -s
watercolo(u)r ˈwɔː.təˌkʌl.əʳ Ⓤ ˈwɑː.t̬ɚˌkʌl.ɚ, ˈwɔː- **-s** -z
watercolo(u)rist ˈwɔː.təˌkʌl.ᵊr.ɪst Ⓤ ˈwɑː.t̬ɚ-, ˈwɔː- **-s** -s
water-cooled ˌwɔː.təˈkuːld Ⓤ ˈwɑː.t̬ɚ.kuːld, ˈwɔː- *stress shift, British only:* ˌwater-cooled ˈengines
watercours|e ˈwɔː.tə.kɔːs Ⓤ ˈwɑː.t̬ɚ.kɔːrs, ˈwɔː- **-es** -ɪz
watercress ˈwɔː.tə.kres Ⓤ ˈwɑː.t̬ɚ-, ˈwɔː-
water-divin|ing ˈwɔː.tə.dɪˌvaɪ.n|ɪŋ, -də,- Ⓤ ˈwɑː.t̬ɚ-, ˈwɔː- **-er/s** -əʳ/z Ⓤ -ɚ/z
watered-down ˌwɔː.tədˈdaʊn Ⓤ ˌwɑː.t̬ɚdˈ-, ˌwɔː- *stress shift:* ˌwatered-down ˈrum
waterfall ˈwɔː.tə.fɔːl Ⓤ ˈwɑː.t̬ɚ.fɔːl, ˈwɔː-, -fɑːl **-s** -z
water-finder ˈwɔː.təˌfaɪn.dəʳ Ⓤ ˈwɑː.t̬ɚˌfaɪn.dɚ, ˈwɔː- **-s** -z
Waterford ˈwɔː.tə.fəd Ⓤ ˈwɑː.t̬ɚ.fɚd, ˈwɔː-
waterfowl ˈwɔː.tə.faʊl Ⓤ ˈwɑː.t̬ɚ-, ˈwɔː- **-s** -z **-er/s** -əʳ/z Ⓤ -ɚ/z
waterfront ˈwɔː.tə.frʌnt Ⓤ ˈwɑː.t̬ɚ-, ˈwɔː- **-s** -s
Watergate ˈwɔː.tə.geɪt Ⓤ ˈwɑː.t̬ɚ-, ˈwɔː-
waterhole ˈwɔː.tə.həʊl Ⓤ ˈwɑː.t̬ɚ.hoʊl, ˈwɔː- **-s** -z
Waterhouse ˈwɔː.tə.haʊs Ⓤ ˈwɑː.t̬ɚ-, ˈwɔː-
wateriness ˈwɔː.tᵊr.ɪ.nəs, -nəs Ⓤ ˈwɑː.t̬ɚ-, ˈwɔː-
watering-can ˈwɔː.tᵊr.ɪŋ.kæn Ⓤ ˈwɑː.t̬ɚ-, ˈwɔː- **-s** -z
watering-hole ˈwɔː.tᵊr.ɪŋ.həʊl Ⓤ ˈwɑː.t̬ɚ.ɪŋ.hoʊl, ˈwɔː- **-s** -z
watering-plac|e ˈwɔː.tᵊr.ɪŋ.pleɪs Ⓤ ˈwɑː.t̬ɚ-, ˈwɔː- **-es** -ɪz
waterless ˈwɔː.tᵊl.əs, -lɪs Ⓤ ˈwɑː.t̬ɚ.ləs, ˈwɔː-
water-level ˈwɔː.təˌlev.ᵊl Ⓤ ˈwɑː.t̬ɚ-, ˈwɔː- **-s** -z
water-lil|y ˈwɔː.təˌlɪl|.i Ⓤ ˈwɑː.t̬ɚ-, ˈwɔː- **-ies** -iz
water-line ˈwɔː.tə.laɪn Ⓤ ˈwɑː.t̬ɚ-, ˈwɔː- **-s** -z
waterlog ˈwɔː.tə.lɒg Ⓤ ˈwɑː.t̬ɚ.lɑːg, ˈwɔː-, -lɔːg **-s** -z **-ging** -ɪŋ **-ged** -d
waterlogged ˈwɔː.tə.lɒgd Ⓤ ˈwɑː.t̬ɚ.lɑːgd, ˈwɔː-, -lɔːgd
waterloo (W) ˌwɔː.təˈluː Ⓤ ˈwɑː.t̬ɚ-, ˈwɔː-, ˌ--ˈ- **-s** -z *stress shift, British only:* ˌWaterloo ˈBridge
Waterlooville ˌwɔː.təˈluː.vɪl, ˌwɔː.tᵊl.uːˈvɪl Ⓤ ˌwɑː.t̬ɚ.luːˈ-, ˌwɔː-, ˈwɑː.t̬ɚ.luː.vɪl
water|man (W) ˈwɔː.tə|.mən Ⓤ ˈwɑː.t̬ɚ-, ˈwɔː- **-men** -mən, -men
watermark ˈwɔː.tə.mɑːk Ⓤ ˈwɑː.t̬ɚ.mɑːrk, ˈwɔː- **-s** -s **-ing** -ɪŋ **-ed** -t
watermelon ˈwɔː.təˌmel.ən Ⓤ ˈwɑː.t̬ɚ-, ˈwɔː- **-s** -z
watermill ˈwɔː.tə.mɪl Ⓤ ˈwɑː.t̬ɚ-, ˈwɔː- **-s** -z
water-nymph ˈwɔː.tə.nɪm*p*f Ⓤ ˈwɑː.t̬ɚ-, ˈwɔː- **-s** -s
waterpolo ˈwɔː.təˌpəʊ.ləʊ Ⓤ ˈwɑː.t̬ɚˌpoʊ.loʊ, ˈwɔː-
waterproof ˈwɔː.tə.pruːf Ⓤ ˈwɑː.t̬ɚ-, ˈwɔː- **-s** -s **-ing** -ɪŋ **-ed** -t
water-resistant ˈwɔː.tə.rɪˌzɪs.tənt, -rə- Ⓤ ˈwɑː.t̬ɚ-, ˈwɔː-
Waters ˈwɔː.təz Ⓤ ˈwɑː.t̬ɚz, ˈwɔː-
watershed ˈwɔː.tə.ʃed Ⓤ ˈwɑː.t̬ɚ-, ˈwɔː- **-s** -z
Watership ˈwɔː.tə.ʃɪp Ⓤ ˈwɑː.t̬ɚ-, ˈwɔː-
watersid|e ˈwɔː.tə.saɪd Ⓤ ˈwɑː.t̬ɚ-, ˈwɔː- **-er/s** -əʳ/z Ⓤ -ɚ/z
water-ski ˈwɔː.tə.skiː Ⓤ ˈwɑː.t̬ɚ-, ˈwɔː- **-s** -z **-ing** -ɪŋ **-ed** -d **-er/s** -əʳ/z Ⓤ -ɚ/z
waterspout ˈwɔː.tə.spaʊt Ⓤ ˈwɑː.t̬ɚ-, ˈwɔː- **-s** -s

watertight ˈwɔː.tə.taɪt (US) ˈwɑː.t̬ɚ-, ˈwɔː-
waterway ˈwɔː.tə.weɪ (US) ˈwɑː.t̬ɚ-, ˈwɔː- **-s** -z
waterwheel ˈwɔː.tə.*h*wiːl (US) ˈwɑː.t̬ɚ-, ˈwɔː- **-s** -z
waterwings ˈwɔː.tə.wɪŋz (US) ˈwɑː.tɚ-, ˈwɔː-
waterworks ˈwɔː.tə.wɜːks (US) ˈwɑː.t̬ɚ.wɜːrks, ˈwɔː-
water|y ˈwɔː.tᵊr|.i, -tr|i (US) ˈwɑː.t̬ɚ|.i, ˈwɔː- **-iness** -ɪ.nəs, -ɪ.nɪs
Watford ˈwɒt.fəd (US) ˈwɑːt.fɚd
Wath upon Dearne ˌwɒθ.əˌpɒnˈdɜːn, ˌwæθ- (US) ˌwɑːθ.əˌpɑːnˈdɜːrn, ˌwæθ-
Watkin ˈwɒt.kɪn (US) ˈwɑːt- **-s** -z
Watling ˈwɒt.lɪŋ (US) ˈwɑːt-
Watson ˈwɒt.sᵊn (US) ˈwɑːt-
watt (W) wɒt (US) wɑːt **-s** -s
wattag|e ˈwɒt.ɪdʒ (US) ˈwɑː.t̬ɪdʒ **-es** -ɪz
Watteau ˈwɒt.əʊ (US) wɑːˈtoʊ
Watters ˈwɔː.təz, ˈwɒt.əz (US) ˈwɑː.t̬ɚz, ˈwɔː-
Watterson ˈwɔː.tə.sᵊn, ˈwɒt.ə- (US) ˈwɑː.t̬ɚ-, ˈwɔː-
wattle ˈwɒt.l̩ (US) ˈwɑː.t̬l̩ **-s** -z **-d** -d
wattmeter ˈwɒtˌmiː.təʳ (US) ˈwɑːtˌmiː.t̬ɚ **-s** -z
Watton ˈwɒt.ᵊn (US) ˈwɑː.tᵊn
Wauchope ˈwɔː.kəp, ˈwɒx.əp (US) ˈwɑː.kəp, ˈwɔː-
Waugh wɔː, wɒx, wɒf, wɑːf (US) wɑː, wɔː
Note: /wɔː (US) wɑː, wɔː/ are the appropriate pronunciations for authors Auberon and Evelyn Waugh.
wav|e weɪv **-es** -z **-ing** -ɪŋ **-ed** -d **-eless** -ləs, -lɪs
waveband ˈweɪv.bænd **-s** -z
waveform ˈweɪv.fɔːm (US) -fɔːrm **-s** -z
wavelength ˈweɪv.leŋ*k*θ **-s** -s
wavelet ˈweɪv.lət, -lɪt **-s** -s
Wavell ˈweɪ.vᵊl
Waveney ˈweɪv.ni
wav|er ˈweɪ.v|əʳ (US) -v|ɚ **-ers** -əz (US) -ɚz **-ering/ly** -ᵊr.ɪŋ/li **-ered** -əd (US) -ɚd **-erer/s** -ᵊr.əʳ/z (US) -ɚ.ɚ/z
Waverley ˈweɪ.vᵊl.i (US) -vɚ.li
wav|y ˈweɪ.v|i **-ier** -i.əʳ (US) -i.ɚ **-iest** -i.ɪst, -i.əst **-ily** -ɪ.li, -ᵊl.i **-iness** -ɪ.nəs, -ɪ.nɪs
wax wæks **-es** -ɪz **-ing** -ɪŋ **-ed** -t **-en** -ᵊn
waxwing ˈwæks.wɪŋ **-s** -z
waxwork ˈwæks.wɜːk (US) -wɜːrk **-s** -s
wax|y ˈwæk.s|i **-ier** -i.əʳ (US) -i.ɚ **-iest** -i.ɪst, -i.əst **-iness** -ɪ.nəs, -ɪ.nɪs
way (W) weɪ **-s** -z ˌ**right of 'way** (US) '**right of ˌway**; ˌ**ways and 'means**
waybill ˈweɪ.bɪl **-s** -z
wayfar|er ˈweɪˌfeə.r|əʳ (US) -ˌfer|.ɚ **-ers** -əz (US) -ɚz **-ing** -ɪŋ
Wayland ˈweɪ.lənd
way|lay ˌweɪ|ˈleɪ (US) ˈweɪ|.leɪ, -ˈ- **-lays** -ˈleɪz (US) -leɪz, -ˈleɪz **-laying** -ˈleɪ.ɪŋ (US) -ˌleɪ.ɪŋ, -ˈleɪ.ɪŋ **-laid** -ˈleɪd (US) -leɪd, -ˈleɪd **-layer/s** -ˈleɪ.əʳ/z (US) -ˌleɪ.ɚ/z, -ˈleɪ.ɚ/z
Wayman ˈweɪ.mən
Wayne weɪn
Waynflete ˈweɪn.fliːt
way-out *unusual and daring:* ˌweɪˈaʊt *stress shift:* ˌway-out 'clothes
way out *exit:* ˌweɪˈaʊt
-ways -weɪz, -wɪz
Note: Suffix. Normally unsrtressed, e.g. **lengthways** /ˈleŋ*k*θ.weɪz/.
wayside ˈweɪ.saɪd ˌ**fall by the 'wayside**
wayward ˈweɪ.wəd (US) -wɚd **-ly** -li **-ness** -nəs, -nɪs
wazzock ˈwæz.ək **-s** -s
WC ˌdʌb.l̩.juːˈsiː, -jʊ- (US) -juːˈ-, -jəˈ- **-s** -z
we *strong form:* wiː *weak form:* wi
Note: Weak form word. The strong form is used contrastively (e.g. 'We, not they, will win it') or for emphasis (e.g. '**We** are the winners'). It is also used in final position (e.g. 'So are we'). The weak form is used elsewhere.
weak wiːk **-er** -əʳ (US) -ɚ **-est** -ɪst, -əst **-ly** -li ˌ**weak at the 'knees**
weaken ˈwiː.kᵊn **-s** -z **-ing** -ɪŋ, ˈwiːk.nɪŋ **-ed** -d
weak-kneed ˌwiːkˈniːd (US) ˈwiːk.niːd *stress shift, British only:* ˌweak-kneed 'coward
weakling ˈwiː.klɪŋ **-s** -z
weak-minded ˌwiːkˈmaɪn.dɪd **-ness** -nəs, -nɪs *stress shift:* ˌweak-minded 'person
weakness ˈwiːk.nəs, -nɪs **-es** -ɪz
weal wiːl **-s** -z
weald (W) wiːld **-s** -z
wealden (W) ˈwiːl.dᵊn
Wealdstone ˈwiːld.stəʊn (US) -stoʊn
wealth welθ
wealth|y ˈwel.θ|i **-ier** -i.əʳ (US) -i.ɚ **-iest** -i.ɪst, -i.əst **-ily** -ɪ.li, -ᵊl.i **-iness** -ɪ.nəs, -ɪ.nɪs
wean *child or baby:* weɪn **-s** -z
wean *withdraw mother's milk:* wiːn **-s** -z **-ing** -ɪŋ **-ed** -d
weaner ˈwiː.nəʳ (US) -nɚ **-s** -z
weanling ˈwiːn.lɪŋ **-s** -z
weapon ˈwep.ən **-s** -z **-less** -ləs, -lɪs **-ry** -ri
wear (*v.*) weəʳ (US) wer **-s** -z **-ing** -ɪŋ **wore** wɔːʳ (US) wɔːr **worn** wɔːn (US) wɔːrn **wearer/s** ˈweə.rəʳ/z (US) ˈwer.ɚ/z ˌ**wear and 'tear**
Wear *river:* wɪəʳ (US) wɪr
wearability ˌweə.rəˈbɪl.ə.ti, -ɪ.ti (US) ˌwer.əˈbɪl.ə.t̬i
wearable ˈweə.rə.bl̩ (US) ˈwer.ə-
Wearing ˈweə.rɪŋ (US) ˈwer.ɪŋ
wearisome ˈwɪə.rɪ.sᵊm (US) ˈwɪr.ɪ- **-ly** -li **-ness** -nəs, -nɪs
Wearmouth ˈwɪə.məθ, -maʊθ (US) ˈwɪr-
Wearn wɜːn (US) wɜːrn
wear|y ˈwɪə.r|i (US) ˈwɪr|.i **-ier** -i.əʳ (US) -i.ɚ **-iest** -i.ɪst, -i.əst **-ily** -ᵊl.i, -ɪ.li **-iness** -ɪ.nəs, -ɪ.nɪs **-ies** -iz **-ying** -i.ɪŋ **-ied** -id
weasel ˈwiː.zᵊl **-s** -z
weaselly ˈwiː.zᵊl.i, ˈwiːz.li
weath|er ˈweð|.əʳ (US) -ɚ **-ers** -əz (US) -ɚz **-ering** -ᵊr.ɪŋ **-ered** -əd (US) -ɚd '**weather ˌforecast**; **make ˌheavy 'weather of ˌsomething**
weather-beaten ˈweð.əˌbiː.tᵊn (US) -ɚˌ-
weatherboard ˈweð.ə.bɔːd (US) -ɚ.bɔːrd **-s** -z **-ing** -ɪŋ
weather-bound ˈweð.ə.baʊnd (US) ˈ-ɚ-
weathercock ˈweð.ə.kɒk (US) -ɚ.kɑːk **-s** -s
weather-eye ˈweð.əʳ.aɪ, ˌ--ˈ- (US) ˈweð.ɚ.aɪ **-s** -z ˌ**keep a 'weather-eye open for something**
weather-glass ˈweð.ə.glɑːs (US) -ɚ.glæs **-es** -ɪz
Weatherhead ˈweð.ə.hed (US) ˈ-ɚ-
weatherly (W) ˈweð.ᵊl.i (US) -ɚ.li
weather|man ˈweð.ə|.mæn (US) ˈ-ɚ- **-men** -men
weatherproof ˈweð.ə.pruːf (US) ˈ-ɚ-
weathership ˈweð.ə.ʃɪp (US) ˈ-ɚ- **-s** -s
weathervane ˈweð.ə.veɪn (US) ˈ-ɚ- **-s** -z
weather-wise ˈweð.ə.waɪz (US) ˈ-ɚ-
weather-worn ˈweð.ə.wɔːn (US) -ɚ.wɔːrn
Weatly ˈwiːt.li
weav|e wiːv **-es** -z **-ing** -ɪŋ **-ed** -d **wove** wəʊv (US) woʊv **woven** ˈwəʊ.vᵊn (US) ˈwoʊ-
weaver (W) ˈwiː.vəʳ (US) -vɚ **-s** -z
Weaverham ˈwiː.və.hæm, -vᵊr.əm (US) -vɚ.hæm, -əm
web web **-s** -z
Webb(e) web
webbed webd ˌ**webbed 'feet**
Webber ˈweb.əʳ (US) -ɚ
webb|ing ˈweb|.ɪŋ **-y** -i
Weber *English name:* ˈweb.əʳ, ˈweɪ.bəʳ, ˈwiː- (US) ˈweb.ɚ, ˈweɪ.bɚ, ˈwiː- *German composer:* ˈveɪ.bəʳ (US) -bɚ
Webern ˈveɪ.bɜːn (US) -bɚn
webfooted ˌwebˈfʊt.ɪd, ˈwebˌfʊt̬.ɪd *stress shift, British only:* ˌwebfooted 'bird
Webster ˈweb.stəʳ (US) -stɚ **-s** -z
we'd (= **we had, we would**) *strong form:* wiːd *weak form:* wid
Note: Weak form word. The weak form is used when the word is unstressed (e.g.

'We'd be silly to do it' /wid.bi'sɪl.i.tə,duː.ɪt/).
wed wed **-s** -z **-ing** -ɪŋ **-ded** -ɪd
Wed. (*abbrev. for* **Wednesday**) 'wenz.deɪ, 'wed.ᵊnz-, -di ⓊⓈ 'wenz.deɪ, -di
Note: This abbreviation may also be pronounced /wed/ in British English.
Weddell *surname:* wə'del, 'wed.ᵊl *Sea:* 'wed.ᵊl
Wedderburn 'wed.ə.bɜːn ⓊⓈ -ɚ.bɜːrn
wedding 'wed.ɪŋ **'wedding ,breakfast** ; **'wedding ,cake** ; **'wedding ,day** ; **'wedding ,dress** ; **'wedding ,march** ; **'wedding ,ring**
Wedekind 'veɪ.də.kɪnd, -kɪnt ⓊⓈ -kɪnt, -kɪnd
wedg|e wedʒ **-es** -ɪz **-ing** -ɪŋ **-ed** -d **-ewise** -waɪz
wedge-shaped 'wedʒ.ʃeɪpt
Wedg(e)wood 'wedʒ.wʊd
wedlock 'wed.lɒk ⓊⓈ -lɑːk
Wednesbury 'wenz.bᵊr.i *locally also:* 'wedʒ- ⓊⓈ 'wenz.bɚ-
Wednesday 'wenz.deɪ, 'wed.nz-, -di ⓊⓈ 'wenz.deɪ, -di **-s** -z
Wednesfield 'wenz.fiːld *locally also:* 'wedʒ- ⓊⓈ 'wenz-
Weds. (*abbrev. for* **Wednesday**) 'wenz.deɪ, 'wed.nz-, -di ⓊⓈ 'wenz.deɪ, -di
Note: This abbreviation may also be pronounced /wedz/ in British English.
wee wiː
weed wiːd **-s** -z **-ing** -ɪŋ **-ed** -ɪd
weedkiller 'wiːd,kɪl.əʳ ⓊⓈ -ɚ **-s** -z
Weedon 'wiː.dᵊn
weed|y 'wiː.d|i **-ier** -i.əʳ ⓊⓈ -i.ɚ **-iest** -i.ɪst, -i.əst **-iness** -ɪ.nəs, -ɪ.nɪs
week wiːk **-s** -s
weekday 'wiːk.deɪ **-s** -z
weekend ,wiːk'end, '-- ⓊⓈ 'wiːk.end **-s** -z *stress shift, British only:* ,weekend 'traffic
weekender ,wiːk'en.dəʳ ⓊⓈ 'wiːk.,en.dɚ **-s** -z
Weekes wiːks
Weekl(e)y 'wiː.kli
weekl|y (*n. adv.*) 'wiː.kl|i **-ies** -iz
weeknight 'wiːk.naɪt **-s** -s
Weeks wiːks
Weelkes wiːlks
ween wiːn **-s** -z **-ing** -ɪŋ **-ed** -d
ween|y 'wiː.n|i **-ies** -iz **-ier** -i.əʳ ⓊⓈ -i.ɚ **-iest** -i.ɪst, -i.əst
weenybopper 'wiː.ni,bɒp.əʳ ⓊⓈ -,bɑː.pɚ **-s** -z
weep wiːp **-s** -s **-ing** -ɪŋ **wept** wept
weeper 'wiː.pəʳ ⓊⓈ -pɚ **-s** -z
weepie 'wiː.pi **-s** -z
weep|y 'wiː.p|i **-ier** -i.əʳ ⓊⓈ -i.ɚ **-iest** -i.ɪst, -i.əst **-ily** -ɪ.li, -ᵊl.i **-iness** -ɪ.nəs, -ɪ.nɪs
Weetabix® 'wiː.tə.bɪks
weever 'wiː.vəʳ ⓊⓈ -vɚ **-s** -z
weevil 'wiː.vᵊl, -vɪl ⓊⓈ -vᵊl **-s** -z
wee-wee 'wiː.wiː **-s** -z **-ing** -ɪŋ **-d** -d
weft weft
Weidenfeld 'vaɪ.dᵊn.felt, 'waɪ-
Weigall 'waɪ.gɔːl
weigela waɪ'dʒiː.lə, -'giː- ⓊⓈ waɪ'giː-, -'jiː-; 'waɪ.gə- **-s** -z
weigelia waɪ'dʒiː.li.ə, -'giː- ⓊⓈ waɪ'giː- **-s** -z
weigh weɪ **-s** -z **-ing** -ɪŋ **-ed** -d **-able** -ə.bl̩
weighbridg|e 'weɪ.brɪdʒ **-es** -ɪz
weight weɪt **-s** -s **-ing** -ɪŋ ⓊⓈ 'weɪ.t̬ɪŋ **-ed** -ɪd ⓊⓈ 'weɪ.t̬ɪd **'weight ,training**
weightless 'weɪt.ləs, -lɪs **-ly** -li **-ness** -nəs, -nɪs
weightlift|ing 'weɪt,lɪf.t|ɪŋ **-er/s** -əʳ/z ⓊⓈ -ɚ/z
Weighton *in Market Weighton, Humberside* 'wiː.tᵊn
WeightWatchers® 'weɪt,wɒtʃ.əz ⓊⓈ -,wɑː.tʃɚz
weightwatch|ing 'weɪt,wɒtʃ|.ɪŋ ⓊⓈ -,wɑː.tʃ|ɪŋ **-er/s** -əʳ/z ⓊⓈ -ɚ/z
weight|y 'weɪ.t|i ⓊⓈ -t̬|i **-ier** -i.əʳ ⓊⓈ -i.ɚ **-iest** -i.ɪst, -i.əst **-ily** -ɪ.li, -ᵊl.i **-iness** -ɪ.nəs, -ɪ.nɪs
Weill *English surname:* wiːl, vaɪl *German composer:* vaɪl
Weimar 'vaɪ.mɑːʳ ⓊⓈ -mɑːr
Weinberger 'waɪn,bɜː.gəʳ, 'waɪm- ⓊⓈ 'waɪn,bɜːr.gɚ
weir (W) wɪəʳ ⓊⓈ wɪr **-s** -z
weird wɪəd ⓊⓈ wɪrd **-er** -əʳ ⓊⓈ -ɚ **-est** -ɪst, -əst **-ly** -li **-ness** -nəs, -nɪs
weirdo 'wɪə.dəʊ ⓊⓈ 'wɪr.doʊ **-s** -z
Weiss vaɪs
Weisshorn 'vaɪs.hɔːn ⓊⓈ -hɔːrn
Weissmuller 'vaɪs,mʊl.əʳ, 'waɪs- ⓊⓈ 'waɪs,mʌl.ɚ
Weland 'weɪ.lənd, 'wiː-
Welbeck 'wel.bek
Welby 'wel.bi
welch (W) (*v. adj.*) weltʃ **-es** -ɪz **-ing** -ɪŋ **-ed** -t **-er/s** -əʳ/z ⓊⓈ -ɚ/z
Welcombe 'wel.kəm
welcom|e 'wel.kəm **-es** -z **-ing** -ɪŋ **-ed** -d
weld weld **-s** -z **-ing** -ɪŋ **-ed** -ɪd **-er/s** -əʳ/z ⓊⓈ -ɚ/z
Weldon 'wel.dᵊn
welfare 'wel.feəʳ ⓊⓈ -fer **,welfare 'state** ⓊⓈ **'welfare ,state**
Welford 'wel.fəd ⓊⓈ -fɚd
welkin 'wel.kɪn
we'll (**= we will, we shall**) *strong form:* wiːl *weak form:* wil
Note: Weak form word. The weak form is used when the word is unstressed (e.g. 'We'll write today' /wil,raɪt.tə'deɪ/).
well wel **-s** -z **-ing** -ɪŋ **-ed** -d **-ness** -nəs, -nɪs
well-advised ,wel.əd'vaɪzd *stress shift:* ,well-advised 'action
Welland 'wel.ənd
well-appointed ,wel.ə'pɔɪn.tɪd ⓊⓈ -t̬ɪd *stress shift:* ,well-appointed 'office
well-balanced ,wel'bæl.əntst *stress shift:* ,well-balanced 'diet
well-behaved ,wel.bɪ'heɪvd, -bə'- *stress shift:* ,well-behaved 'dog
well-being 'wel,biː.ɪŋ, ,-'--
well-born ,wel'bɔːn ⓊⓈ -'bɔːrn *stress shift:* ,well-born 'lady
well-bred ,wel'bred *stress shift:* ,well-bred 'child
well-built ,wel'bɪlt *stress shift:* ,well-built 'person
Wellby 'wel.bi
well-chosen ,wel'tʃəʊ.zᵊn ⓊⓈ -'tʃoʊ- *stress shift:* ,well-chosen 'words
Wellcome 'wel.kəm
well-conducted ,wel.kən'dʌk.tɪd *stress shift:* ,well-conducted 'scheme
well-connected ,wel.kə'nek.tɪd *stress shift:* ,well-connected 'person
well-cooked ,wel'kʊkt *stress shift:* ,well-cooked 'food
well-disposed ,wel.dɪ'spəʊzd ⓊⓈ -'spoʊzd *stress shift:* ,well-disposed 'manner
well-do|er 'wel,duː|.əʳ, ,-'-- ⓊⓈ 'wel,duː|.ɚ **-ers** -əz ⓊⓈ -ɚz **-ing** -ɪŋ
Welldon 'wel.dᵊn
well-done ,wel'dʌn *stress shift:* ,well-done 'food
well-earned ,wel'ɜːnd ⓊⓈ -'ɜːrnd *stress shift:* ,well-earned 'rest
Weller 'wel.əʳ ⓊⓈ -ɚ
Welles welz
Wellesley 'welz.li
well-fed ,wel'fed *stress shift:* ,well-fed 'cat
well-formed ,wel'fɔːmd ⓊⓈ -'fɔːrmd *stress shift:* ,well-formed 'sentence
well-found ,wel'faʊnd *stress shift:* ,well-found 'ship
well-groomed ,wel'gruːmd *stress shift:* ,well-groomed 'man
well-grounded ,wel'graʊn.dɪd *stress shift:* ,well-grounded 'argument
well-heeled ,wel'hiːld *stress shift:* ,well-heeled 'owner
wellie 'wel.i **-s** -z
well-informed ,wel.ɪn'fɔːmd ⓊⓈ -'fɔːrmd *stress shift:* ,well-informed 'journalist

Welling 'wel.ɪŋ
Wellingborough 'wel.ɪŋ.bᵊr.ə
(US) -bɚ.oʊ
wellington (W) 'wel.ɪŋ.tən **-s** -z
ˌwellington 'boot (US) **'wellington ˌboot**
wellingtonia ˌwel.ɪŋ'təʊ.ni.ə
(US) -'toʊ- **-s** -z
well-intentioned ˌwel.ɪn'ten.tʃᵊnd *stress shift:* ˌwell-intentioned 'action
well-judged ˌwel'dʒʌdʒd *stress shift:* ˌwell-judged 'shot
well-known ˌwel'nəʊn (US) -'noʊn *stress shift:* ˌwell-known 'writer
well-made ˌwel'meɪd *stress shift:* ˌwell-made 'product
well-meaning ˌwel'miː.nɪŋ *stress shift:* ˌwell-meaning 'action
well-meant ˌwel'ment *stress shift:* ˌwell-meant 'gesture
well-nigh ˌwel'naɪ *stress shift:* ˌwell-nigh im'possible
well-off ˌwel'ɒf (US) -'ɑːf *stress shift:* ˌwell-off 'person
well-ordered ˌwel'ɔː.dəd
(US) -'ɔːr.dɚd *stress shift:* ˌwell-ordered 'household
well-proportioned ˌwel.prə'pɔː.ʃᵊnd
(US) -'pɔːr- *stress shift:* ˌwell-proportioned 'room
well-read ˌwel'red *stress shift:* ˌwell-read 'person
well-rounded ˌwel'raʊn.dɪd *stress shift:* ˌwell-rounded 'character
Wells welz
well-spoken ˌwel'spəʊ.kᵊn (US) -'spoʊ- *stress shift:* ˌwell-spoken 'person
wellspring 'wel.sprɪŋ **-s** -z
well-thumbed ˌwel'θʌmd *stress shift:* ˌwell-thumbed 'book
well-timed ˌwel'taɪmd *stress shift:* ˌwell-timed 'action
well-to-do ˌwel.tə'duː *stress shift:* ˌwell-to-do 'person
well-versed ˌwel'vɜːst (US) -'vɜːrst *stress shift:* ˌwell-versed 'teacher
well-wisher 'welˌwɪʃ.əʳ, ˌ-'--
(US) 'welˌwɪʃ.ɚ **-s** -z
well-worn ˌwel'wɔːn (US) -'wɔːrn *stress shift:* ˌwell-worn 'phrase
well|y 'wel|.i **-ies** -iz
welsh (W) welʃ **-es** -ɪz **-ing** -ɪŋ **-ed** -t **-er/s** -əʳ/z (US) -ɚ/z **ˌWelsh 'dresser**; **ˌWelsh 'Nationalists**; **ˌWelsh 'rarebit**
Welsh|man 'welʃ|.mən **-men** -mən
Welshpool 'welʃ.puːl, ˌ-'-
Welsh|woman 'welʃ|ˌwʊm.ən **-women** -ˌwɪm.ɪn
welt welt **-s** -s **-ing** -ɪŋ (US) 'wel.t̬ɪŋ **-ed** -ɪd (US) 'wel.t̬ɪd
weltanschauung (W) 'velt.ænˌʃaʊ.ʊŋ
(US) -ɑːnˌ-

welt|er 'wel.t|əʳ (US) -t̬|ɚ **-ers** -əz
(US) -ɚz **-ering** -ᵊr.ɪŋ **-ered** -əd (US) -ɚd
welterweight 'wel.tə.weɪt (US) -t̬ɚ- **-s** -s
weltschmerz (W) 'velt.ʃmeəts
(US) -ʃmerts
Welty 'wel.ti (US) -t̬i
Welwyn 'wel.ɪn **ˌWelwyn ˌGarden 'City**
Wembley 'wem.bli
Wemyss wiːmz
wen wen **-s** -z
Wenceslas 'wen.sɪ.sləs, -sə-, -slæs
(US) -sɪ.slɑːs, -slɔːs
wench wentʃ **-es** -ɪz
wend wend **-s** -z **-ing** -ɪŋ **-ed** -ɪd
Wend wend, vend **-s** -z **-ic** -ɪk **-ish** -ɪʃ
Wendell 'wen.dᵊl
Wendover 'wen.dəʊ.vəʳ (US) -doʊ.vɚ
Wendy 'wen.di **'Wendy ˌhouse**
Wengen 'veŋ.ən
Wengern Alp ˌveŋ.ən'ælp (US) -ɚn'-
Wenham 'wen.əm
Wenlock 'wen.lɒk (US) -lɑːk **ˌWenlock 'Edge**
Wensleydale 'wenz.lɪ.deɪl
went (*from* **go**) went
Wentworth 'went.wəθ, -wɜːθ
(US) -wɚθ, -wɜːrθ
wept (*from* **weep**) wept
we're (= **we are**) wɪəʳ (US) wɪr
were (*from* **be**) *strong forms:* wɜːʳ
(US) wɜːr *weak forms:* wəʳ (US) wɚ
Note: Weak form word. The strong form is used for emphasis (e.g. 'You **were** a long time') and for contrast (e.g. 'what they were and what they might have been'). The strong form is also usual in final position (e.g. 'We didn't know where we were'). The weak form is used elsewhere.
weren't wɜːnt (US) wɜːrnt
werewol|f 'weə.wʊl|f, 'wɪə-, 'wɜː-
(US) 'wer-, 'wɪr-, 'wɜːr- **-ves** -vz
Werner 'wɜː.nəʳ *as if German:* 'veə-
(US) 'wɜːr.nɚ *as if German:* 'vɜːr-
wert (*from* **be**) *strong forms:* wɜːt
(US) wɜːrt *weak forms:* wət (US) wɚt
Note: Archaic form; see information at **were**.
Weser *German river:* 'veɪ.zəʳ (US) -zɚ
Note: /'wiː.zəʳ (US) -zɚ/ is necessary for rhyme in Browning's 'Pied Piper', but this pronunciation is exceptional.
Wesker 'wes.kəʳ (US) -kɚ
Wesley 'wez.li, 'wes- (US) 'wes-, 'wez-
Note: Most people bearing the name **Wesley** pronounce /'wes.li/, but in Britain the pronunciation is commonly /'wez.li/.
Wesleyan 'wez.li.ən, 'wes- (US) 'wes-, 'wez- **-s** -z **-ism** -ɪ.zᵊm

Note: /'wes-/ appears to be the more usual pronunciation among Wesleyans; with those who are not Wesleyans /'wez-/ is probably the commoner form in British English. There exists also an old-fashioned pronunciation /wes'liː.ən/.
Wessex 'wes.ɪks
west (W) west **ˌWest 'Bank** *stress shift:* ˌWest Bank 'settlement; **ˌWest 'Coast** *stress shift:* ˌWest Coast 'singer; **'West ˌCountry**; **ˌWest 'End** *stress shift:* ˌWest End 'play; **ˌWest 'Indian**; **ˌWest 'Indies**; **ˌWest 'Point** (US) **'West ˌPoint**; **ˌWest ˌSide 'Story** (US) **'West Side ˌStory**; **ˌWest Vir'ginia**
westbound 'west.baʊnd
Westbourne 'west.bɔːn, -bən
(US) -bɔːrn, -bɚn
West Bridgford ˌwest'brɪdʒ.fəd
(US) -fɚd
Westbrook 'west.brʊk
Westbury 'west.bᵊr.i
Westcott 'west.kət
Westergate 'wes.tə.geɪt (US) -tɚ-
Westerham 'wes.tᵊr.əm
westering 'wes.tᵊr.ɪŋ
westerl|y 'wes.tᵊl|.i (US) -tɚ.l|i **-ies** -iz
western (W) 'wes.tən (US) -tɚn **-s** -z **-er/s** -əʳ/z (US) -ɚ/z **-most** -məʊst
(US) -moʊst **ˌWestern Aus'tralia**; **'Western ˌIsles**, **ˌWestern 'Isles**
westernization, -isa-
ˌwes.tᵊn.aɪ'zeɪ.ʃᵊn, -ɪ'- (US) -tɚ.nɪ'-
westerniz|e, -is|e 'wes.tən.aɪz
(US) -tɚ.naɪz **-es** -ɪz **-ing** -ɪŋ **-ed** -d
Westfield 'west.fiːld
Westgate 'west.geɪt, -gɪt
Westhill 'west.hɪl
Westhoughton ˌwest'hɔː.tᵊn
(US) -'hɑː-, -'hɔː-
Westinghouse 'wes.tɪŋ.haʊs
Westlake 'west.leɪk
Westland® 'west.lənd
Westly 'west.li
Westmeath ˌwest'miːð
West Mersea ˌwest'mɜː.zi (US) -'mɜːr-
Westminster west'mɪnt.stəʳ, '---
(US) west'mɪnt.stɚ, '--- **ˌWestminster 'Abbey**
Westmor(e)land 'west.mᵊl.ənd
(US) -mɔːr.lənd
west-northwest ˌwest.nɔːθ'west
(US) -nɔːrθ'- *nautical pronunciation:* -nɔː'- (US) -nɔːr'-
Weston 'wes.tən
Weston-super-Mare
ˌwes.tənˌsuː.pə'meəʳ, -ˌsjuː-; -'suː.pə.meəʳ, -'sjuː-
(US) -ˌsuː.pɚ'mer, -'suː.pɚ.mer
Westphali|a ˌwest'feɪ.li|.ə, '-lj|ə
(US) '-li|.ə, -'feɪl.j|ə **-an/s** -ən/z

Westray 'wes.treɪ
west-southwest ˌwest.saʊθ'west
nautical pronunciation: -saʊ'-
westward 'wes*t*.wəd (US) -wɚd **-s** -z **-ly** -li
Westward Ho! ˌwes*t*.wəd'həʊ (US) -wɚd'hoʊ
Westwood 'wes*t*.wʊd
wet wet **-ter** -əʳ (US) 'weţ.ɚ **-test** -ɪst, -əst (US) 'weţ.ɪst, -əst **-s** -s **-ting** -ɪŋ (US) 'weţ.ɪŋ **-ted** -ɪd (US) 'weţ.ɪd **-ly** -li **-ness** -nəs, -nɪs ˌ**wet 'blanket**; '**wet ˌsuit**; **(still)** ˌ**wet behind the 'ears**
wetback 'wet.bæk **-s** -s
wether 'weð.əʳ (US) -ɚ **-s** -z
Wetherby 'weð.ə.bi (US) '-ɚ-
wetland 'wet.lənd (US) -lænd **-s** -z
wet-look 'wet.lʊk
wet-nurs|e 'wet.nɜːs (US) -nɜːrs **-es** -ɪz
we've (= we have) *strong form:* wiːv *weak form:* wiv
Note: Weak form word. The weak form is usually found when the word is unstressed, but the strong form may also be used in this situation.
Wexford 'weks.fəd (US) -fɚd
Wey weɪ
Weybridge 'weɪ.brɪdʒ
Weyman 'weɪ.mən
Weymouth 'weɪ.məθ
whack *h*wæk **-s** -s **-ing/s** -ɪŋ/z **-ed** -t **-er/s** -əʳ/z (US) -ɚ/z
whacko '*h*wæk.əʊ (US) -oʊ
whack|y '*h*wæk|.i **-ier** -i.əʳ (US) -i.ɚ **-iest** -i.ɪst, -i.əst **-ily** -ɪ.li, -əl.i
whal|e (W) *h*weɪl **-es** -z **-ing** -ɪŋ **-er/s** -əʳ/z (US) -ɚ/z ˌ**have a 'whale of a ˌtime**
whalebone '*h*weɪl.bəʊn (US) -boʊn
whale-oil '*h*weɪl.ɔɪl
Whaley '*h*weɪ.li
Whalley *surname:* '*h*weɪ.li, '*h*wɔː-, '*h*wɒl.i (US) '*h*weɪ.li, '*h*wɑː.li *abbey near Blackburn:* '*h*wɔː.li (US) '*h*wɑː-
wham *h*wæm **-s** -z **-ming** -ɪŋ **-med** -d
whammo '*h*wæm.əʊ (US) -oʊ
whamm|y '*h*wæm|.i **-ies** -iz
whamo '*h*wæm.əʊ (US) -oʊ
whang *h*wæŋ **-s** -z **-ing** -ɪŋ **-ed** -d
whangee ˌ*h*wæŋ'giː, -'iː (US) -'iː
whar|f *h*wɔː|f (US) *h*wɔːr|f **-ves** -vz **-fs** -fs
wharfage '*h*wɔː.fɪdʒ (US) '*h*wɔːr-
Wharfedale '*h*wɔːf.deɪl (US) '*h*wɔːrf-
wharfinger '*h*wɔː.fɪn.dʒəʳ (US) '*h*wɔːr.fɪn.dʒɚ **-s** -z
Wharton '*h*wɔː.tən (US) '*h*wɔːr-
what *h*wɒt (US) *h*wʌt, *h*wɑːt
what-d'you-call-it '*h*wɒt.djʊˌkɔː.lɪt, -djəˌ-, -dʒʊˌ-, -dʒəˌ- (US) '*h*wʌţ.i.jəˌkɔː-, '*h*wʌtʃ.əˌ-, -ˌkɑː-
what-d'you-ma-call-it '*h*wɒt.djʊ.məˌkɔː.lɪt, -djə-, -dʒʊ-, -dʒə- (US) '*h*wʌţ.i.jə.məˌkɔː-, -*h*wʌtʃ.ə-, -kɑː-
whate'er *h*wɒt'eəʳ (US) *h*wʌt'er, *h*wɑːt-
Whateley '*h*weɪt.li
whatever *h*wɒt'ev.əʳ, (US) *h*wʌt'ev.ɚ, *h*wɑːt-
Whatley '*h*wɒt.li (US) '*h*wɑːt-
Whatman '*h*wɒt.mən (US) '*h*wɑːt-
Whatmough '*h*wɒt.məʊ (US) '*h*wɑːt.moʊ
whatnot '*h*wɒt.nɒt (US) '*h*wʌt.nɑːt, '*h*wɑːt- **-s** -s
what's-her-name '*h*wɒt.sən.eɪm (US) '*h*wʌt.sɚ.neɪm, '*h*wɑːt-
what's-his-name '*h*wɒt.sɪz.neɪm (US) '*h*wʌt-, '*h*wɑːt-
whatsit '*h*wɒt.sɪt (US) '*h*wʌt- **-s** -s
whatsoe'er ˌ*h*wɒt.səʊ'eəʳ (US) ˌ*h*wʌt.soʊ'er, ˌ*h*wɑːt-
whatsoever ˌ*h*wɒt.səʊ'ev.əʳ (US) ˌ*h*wʌt.soʊ'ev.ɚ, ˌ*h*wɑːt-
wheal *h*wiːl **-s** -z
wheat *h*wiːt **-en** -ən
wheatgerm '*h*wiːt.dʒɜːm (US) -dʒɜːrm
Wheathampstead '*h*wiː.təm*p*.sted, '*h*wet.əm*p*-
Wheatley '*h*wiːt.li
wheatmeal '*h*wiːt.miːl
Wheaton '*h*wiː.tən
Wheatstone '*h*wiːt.stən, -stəʊn (US) -stoʊn, -stən
wheedl|e '*h*wiː.dl̩ **-es** -z **-ing** -ɪŋ, '*h*wiːd.lɪŋ **-ed** -d **-er/s** -əʳ/z, '*h*wiːd.ləʳ/z (US) '*h*wiː.dl̩.əʳ/z, '*h*wiːd.lɚ/z
wheel *h*wiːl **-s** -z **-ing** -ɪŋ **-ed** -d '**wheel ˌclamp**
wheelbarrow '*h*wiːlˌbær.əʊ (US) -ˌber.oʊ, -ˌbær- **-s** -z
wheelbas|e '*h*wiːl.beɪs **-es** -ɪz
wheelchair '*h*wiːl.tʃeəʳ (US) -tʃer **-s** -z
wheeler (W) '*h*wiː.ləʳ (US) -lɚ **-s** -z
wheeler-dealer ˌ*h*wiː.lə'diː.ləʳ (US) -lɚ'diː.lɚ **-s** -z
wheelhou|se '*h*wiːl.haʊ|s **-ses** -zɪz
wheelie '*h*wiː.li **-s** -z '**wheelie ˌbin**
Wheelock '*h*wiː.lək
wheelwright, wheelright (W) '*h*wiːl.raɪt **-s** -s
Wheen '*h*wiːn
wheez|e *h*wiːz **-es** -ɪz **-ing** -ɪŋ **-ed** -d **-y** -i **-ier** -i.əʳ (US) -i.ɚ **-iest** -i.ɪst, -i.əst **-iness** -ɪ.nəs, -ɪ.nɪs
Whelan '*h*wiː.lən
whelk welk (US) *h*welk **-s** -s
whelm *h*welm **-s** -z **-ing** -ɪŋ **-ed** -d
whelp *h*welp **-s** -s **-ing** -ɪŋ **-ed** -t
when *h*wen
whence *h*wen*t*s
whene'er *h*wen'eəʳ (US) -'er
whenever *h*wen'ev.əʳ, *h*wən'- (US) -ɚ
whensoever ˌ*h*wen.səʊ'ev.əʳ (US) -soʊ'ev.ɚ
where *h*weəʳ (US) *h*wer
whereabout ˌ*h*weə.rə'baʊt (US) '*h*wer.əˌ-
whereabouts *(n.)* '*h*weə.rə.baʊts (US) '*h*wer.ə-
whereabouts *interrogation:* ˌ*h*weə.rə'baʊts (US) ˌ*h*wer.ə'-
whereas *h*weə'ræz, *h*wər- (US) *h*wer'æz, *h*wɚ-
whereat *h*weə'ræt, *h*wər- (US) *h*wer'æt, *h*wɚ-
whereby *h*weə'baɪ (US) *h*wer-
where'er *h*weə'reəʳ, *h*wə- (US) *h*wer'er, *h*wɚ-
wherefore '*h*weə.fɔːʳ (US) '*h*wer.fɔːr **-s** -z
wherein *h*weə'rɪn (US) *h*wer'ɪn
whereof *h*weə'rɒv (US) *h*wer'ɑːv
whereon *h*weə'rɒn (US) *h*wer'ɑːn
wheresoe'er ˌ*h*weə.səʊ'eəʳ (US) ˌ*h*wer.soʊ'er
wheresoever ˌ*h*weə.səʊ'ev.əʳ (US) ˌ*h*wer.soʊ'ev.ɚ
whereto *h*weə'tuː (US) *h*wer-
whereunder *h*weə'rʌn.dəʳ (US) *h*wer'ʌn.dɚ
whereunto ˌ*h*weə.rʌn'tuː (US) ˌ*h*wer.ʌn'-
whereupon ˌ*h*weə.rə'pɒn, '--ˌ- (US) '*h*wer.əˌpɑːn
wherever *h*weə'rev.əʳ, *h*wər- (US) *h*wer'ev.ɚ, *h*wɚ-
wherewith *h*weə'wɪθ, -'wɪð (US) *h*wer-
wherewithal *(n.)* '*h*weə.wɪ.ðɔːl (US) '*h*wer-, -θɔːl, -ðɑːl, -θɑːl
wherewithal *(adv.)* ˌ*h*weə.wɪ'ðɔːl, '--- (US) '*h*wer.wɪ.ðɔːl, -θɔːl, -ðɑːl, -θɑːl
Whernside '*h*wɜːn.saɪd (US) '*h*wɜːrn-
wherr|y '*h*wer|.i **-ies** -iz
whet *h*wet **-s** -s **-ting** -ɪŋ (US) '*h*weţ.ɪŋ **-ted** -ɪd (US) '*h*weţ.ɪd
whether '*h*weð.əʳ (US) -ɚ
whetstone (W) '*h*wet.stəʊn (US) -stoʊn **-s** -z
whew ɸ̥u̥, fjuː
Note: This is an attempt at a symbolic representation of an interjection used to indicate that the speaker is either surprised, or suffering from the heat. The sound is related to a whistle (falling or rising-falling pitch), but in speech is more usually a whispered sound. The pronunciation /fjuː/ is an alternative based on the spelling.
Whewell 'hjuː.əl, -el, -ɪl; hjʊəl (US) 'hjuː.əl
whey *h*weɪ
which *h*wɪtʃ
whichever *h*wɪ'tʃev.əʳ (US) -ɚ

whick|er (W) ˈ*h*wɪk|.əʳ ⓊⓈ -ɚ **-ers** -əz ⓊⓈ -ɚz **-ering** -ᵊr.ɪŋ **-ered** -əd ⓊⓈ -ɚd
Whickham ˈ*h*wɪk.əm
whiff *h*wɪf **-s** -s **-ing** -ɪŋ **-ed** -t
Whiffen ˈ*h*wɪf.ɪn, -ən
Whig *h*wɪg **-s** -z
Whigg|ery ˈ*h*wɪg|.ᵊr.i **-ism** -ɪ.zᵊm
Whiggish ˈ*h*wɪg.ɪʃ
Whigham ˈ*h*wɪg.əm
whil|e ˈ*h*waɪl **-es** -z **-ing** -ɪŋ **-ed** -d
whilst *h*waɪlst
whim *h*wɪm **-s** -z
whimbrel ˈ*h*wɪm.brᵊl **-s** -z
whimp|er ˈ*h*wɪm.p|əʳ ⓊⓈ -p|ɚ **-ers** -əz ⓊⓈ -ɚz **-ering/ly** -ᵊr.ɪŋ/li **-ered** -əd ⓊⓈ -ɚd
whimsic|al ˈ*h*wɪm.zɪ.k|ᵊl, -sɪ- ⓊⓈ -zɪ- **-ally** -ᵊl.i, -li **-alness** -ᵊl.nəs, -nɪs
whimsicality ˌ*h*wɪm.zɪˈkæl.ə.ti, -sɪˈ-, -ɪ.ti ⓊⓈ -zɪˈkæl.ə.t̬i
whims|y ˈ*h*wɪm.z|i **-ies** -iz
whin *h*wɪn **-s** -z
whinchat ˈ*h*wɪn.tʃæt **-s** -s
whin|e *h*waɪn **-es** -z **-ing/ly** -ɪŋ/li **-ed** -d **-er/s** -əʳ/z ⓊⓈ -ɚ/z
whing|e *h*wɪndʒ **-es** -ɪz **-(e)ing** -ɪŋ **-ed** -d **-er/s** -əʳ/z ⓊⓈ -ɚ/z
whinn|y ˈ*h*wɪn|.i **-ies** -iz **-ying** -i.ɪŋ **-ied** -id
whin|y ˈ*h*waɪ.n|i **-ier** -i.əʳ ⓊⓈ -i.ɚ **-iest** -i.ɪst, -i.əst **-iness** -ɪ.nəs, -ɪ.nɪs
whip *h*wɪp **-s** -s **-ping/s** -ɪŋ/z **-ped** -t **have the ˌwhip ˈhand**
whipcord ˈ*h*wɪp.kɔːd ⓊⓈ -kɔːrd
whiplash ˈ*h*wɪp.læʃ
whipp|er-in ˌ*h*wɪp|.əʳˈɪn ⓊⓈ -ɚˈ- **-ers-in** -əzˈɪn ⓊⓈ -ɚzˈ-
whippersnapper ˈ*h*wɪp.əˌsnæp.əʳ ⓊⓈ -ɚˌsnæp.ɚ **-s** -z
whippet ˈ*h*wɪp.ɪt **-s** -s
whipping-boy ˈ*h*wɪp.ɪŋ.bɔɪ **-s** -z
Whippingham ˈ*h*wɪp.ɪŋ.əm
Whipple ˈ*h*wɪp.l̩
whippoorwill ˈ*h*wɪp.ə.wɪl, -ʊə-, -pʊə-, -pɔː- ⓊⓈ ˈ-ɚ- **-s** -z
whip-round ˈ*h*wɪp.raʊnd **-s** -z
whipsaw ˈ*h*wɪp.sɔː ⓊⓈ -sɑː, -sɔː **-s** -z
Whipsnade ˈ*h*wɪp.sneɪd
whir *h*wɜːʳ ⓊⓈ *h*wɜːr **-s** -z **-ring/s** -ɪŋ/z **-red** -d
whirl *h*wɜːl ⓊⓈ *h*wɜːrl **-s** -z **-ing** -ɪŋ **-ed** -d
whirligig ˈ*h*wɜː.lɪ.gɪg ⓊⓈ ˈ*h*wɜːr- **-s** -z
whirlpool ˈ*h*wɜːl.puːl ⓊⓈ ˈ*h*wɜːrl- **-s** -z
whirlwind ˈ*h*wɜːl.wɪnd ⓊⓈ ˈ*h*wɜːrl- **-s** -z
whirlybird ˈ*h*wɜː.lɪ.bɜːd ⓊⓈ ˈ*h*wɜːr.lɪ.bɜːrd **-s** -z
whirr *h*wɜːʳ ⓊⓈ *h*wɜːr **-s** -z **-ing/s** -ɪŋ/z **-ed** -d
whisk *h*wɪsk **-s** -s **-ing** -ɪŋ **-ed** -t
Whiskas® ˈ*h*wɪs.kəz
whisker ˈ*h*wɪs.kəʳ ⓊⓈ -kɚ **-s** -z **-ed** -d
whiskey ˈ*h*wɪs.ki **-s** -z
whisk|y ˈ*h*wɪs.k|i **-ies** -iz
whisp|er ˈ*h*wɪs.p|əʳ ⓊⓈ -p|ɚ **-ers** -əz ⓊⓈ -ɚz **-ering/s** -ᵊr.ɪŋ/z **-ered** -əd ⓊⓈ -ɚd **-erer/s** -ᵊr.əʳ/z ⓊⓈ -ɚ.ɚ/z
whist *h*wɪst ˈ**whist** ˌ**drive**
whistl|e ˈ*h*wɪs.l̩ **-es** -z **-ing** -ɪŋ, ˈ*h*wɪs.lɪŋ **-ed** -d ˌ**blow the** ˈ**whistle** ˌ**on**
whistle-blower ˈ*h*wɪs.l̩ˌbləʊ.əʳ ⓊⓈ -ˌbloʊ.ɚ **-s** -z
whistler (W) ˈ*h*wɪs.ləʳ, -l̩.əʳ ⓊⓈ ˈ-lɚ, -l̩.ɚ **-s** -z
whistle-stop ˈ*h*wɪs.l̩.stɒp ⓊⓈ -stɑːp **-s** -s **-ping** -ɪŋ **-ped** -t ˌ**whistle-stop** ˈ**tour**
whit (W) *h*wɪt
Whitaker ˈ*h*wɪt.ə.kəʳ, ˈ-ɪ- ⓊⓈ *h*wɪt̬.ə.kɚ
Whitbread ˈ*h*wɪt.bred
Whitburn ˈ*h*wɪt.bɜːn ⓊⓈ -bɜːrn
Whitby ˈ*h*wɪt.bi
Whitchurch ˈ*h*wɪt.tʃɜːtʃ ⓊⓈ -tʃɜːrtʃ
Whitcombe ˈ*h*wɪt.kəm
Whitcut ˈ*h*wɪt.kʌt
whit|e (W) *h*waɪt **-es** -s **-er** -əʳ ⓊⓈ ˈ*h*waɪ.t̬ɚ **-est** -ɪst, -əst ⓊⓈ ˈ*h*waɪ.t̬ɪst, -t̬əst **-ely** -li **-eness** -nəs, -nɪs **-ing** -ɪŋ ⓊⓈ ˈ*h*waɪ.t̬ɪŋ **-ed** -ɪd ⓊⓈ ˈ*h*waɪ.t̬ɪd ˌ**white** ˈ**elephant** ; ˌ**white** ˈ**flag** ; ˈ**white** ˌ**goods** ; ˈ**White** ˌ**House** ; ˌ**white** ˈ**knight** ; ˌ**white** ˈ**lie** ; ˈ**white** ˌ**man** ; ˌ**white** ˈ**paper** ⓊⓈ ˈ**white** ˌ**paper** ; ˌ**white** ˈ**sauce** ⓊⓈ ˈ**white** ˌ**sauce** ; ˌ**white** ˈ**trash** ; ˌ**white** ˈ**wedding** ; ˌ**white as a** ˈ**sheet**
whitebait ˈ*h*waɪt.beɪt
whitebeard ˈ*h*waɪt.bɪəd ⓊⓈ -bɪrd **-s** -z **-ed** -ɪd
whiteboard ˈ*h*waɪt.bɔːd ⓊⓈ -bɔːrd **-s** -z
whitecap ˈ*h*waɪt.kæp **-s** -s
Whitechapel ˈ*h*waɪtˌtʃæp.ᵊl
white-collar ˌ*h*waɪtˈkɒl.əʳ ⓊⓈ -ˈkɑː.lɚ *stress shift:* ˌwhite-collar ˈworker
Whitefield ˈ*h*waɪt.fiːld, ˈ*h*wɪt-
whitefl|y ˈ*h*waɪt.fl|aɪ **-ies** -aɪz
Whitefriars ˈ*h*waɪt.fraɪəz, ˌ-ˈ- ⓊⓈ ˈ*h*waɪt.fraɪɚz, ˌ-ˈ-
Whitehall ˈ*h*waɪt.hɔːl, ˌ-ˈ- ⓊⓈ ˈ*h*waɪt.hɔːl, -hɑːl
Whitehaven ˈ*h*waɪtˌheɪ.vᵊn
whitehead (W) ˈ*h*waɪt.hed **-s** -z
Whitehorn ˈ*h*waɪt.hɔːn ⓊⓈ -hɔːrn
Whitehorse ˈ*h*waɪt.hɔːs ⓊⓈ -hɔːrs
white-hot ˌ*h*waɪtˈhɒt ⓊⓈ -ˈhɑːt *stress shift:* ˌwhite-hot ˈmetal
Whitehouse ˈ*h*waɪt.haʊs
Whitelaw ˈ*h*waɪt.lɔː ⓊⓈ -lɑː, -lɔː
Whiteley ˈ*h*waɪt.li
white-livered ˈ*h*waɪtˌlɪv.əd, ˌ-ˈ-- ⓊⓈ -ɚd
whiten ˈ*h*waɪ.tᵊn **-s** -z **-ing** -ɪŋ, ˈ*h*waɪt.nɪŋ **-ed** -d
whitener ˈ*h*waɪt.nəʳ, ˈ*h*waɪ.tᵊn.əʳ ⓊⓈ ˈ*h*waɪt.nɚ, ˈ*h*waɪ.tᵊn.ɚ **-s** -z
whiteout ˈ*h*waɪt.aʊt **-s** -s
Whiteside ˈ*h*waɪt.saɪd
whitethorn ˈ*h*waɪt.θɔːn ⓊⓈ -θɔːrn **-s** -z
whitethroat ˈ*h*waɪt.θrəʊt ⓊⓈ -θroʊt **-s** -s
whitewash ˈ*h*waɪt.wɒʃ ⓊⓈ -wɑːʃ **-es** -ɪz **-ing** -ɪŋ **-ed** -t **-er/s** -əʳ/z ⓊⓈ -ɚ/z
whitewater (W) ˈ*h*waɪt.wɔː.təʳ ⓊⓈ -wɑː.t̬ɚ, -wɔː- ˌ**whitewater** ˈ**rafting**
whitewood ˈ*h*waɪt.wʊd
whitey ˈ*h*waɪ.ti ⓊⓈ -t̬i
Whitfield ˈ*h*wɪt.fiːld
Whitgift ˈ*h*wɪt.gɪft
whither ˈ*h*wɪð.əʳ ⓊⓈ -ɚ
whithersoever ˌ*h*wɪð.ə.səʊˈev.əʳ ⓊⓈ -ɚ.soʊˈev.ɚ
whiting (W) ˈ*h*waɪ.tɪŋ ⓊⓈ -t̬ɪŋ **-s** -z
whitish ˈ*h*waɪ.tɪʃ ⓊⓈ -t̬ɪʃ
Whitlam ˈ*h*wɪt.ləm
Whitley ˈ*h*wɪt.li
whitlow ˈ*h*wɪt.ləʊ ⓊⓈ -loʊ **-s** -z
Whitman ˈ*h*wɪt.mən
Whitmarsh ˈ*h*wɪt.mɑːʃ ⓊⓈ -mɑːrʃ
Whitmore ˈ*h*wɪt.mɔːʳ ⓊⓈ -mɔːr
Whitney ˈ*h*wɪt.ni
Whitstable ˈ*h*wɪt.stə.bl̩
Whitstone ˈ*h*wɪt.stəʊn, -stᵊn ⓊⓈ -stoʊn, -stᵊn
Whitsun ˈ*h*wɪt.sᵊn
Whitsunday ˌ*h*wɪtˈsʌn.deɪ, -di; -sᵊnˈdeɪ **-s** -z
Whitsuntide ˈ*h*wɪt.sᵊn.taɪd **-s** -z
Whittaker ˈ*h*wɪt.ə.kəʳ, ˈ-ɪ- ⓊⓈ ˈ*h*wɪt̬.ə.kɚ
Whittall ˈ*h*wɪt.ᵊl, -ɔːl ⓊⓈ ˈ*h*wɪt̬-
Whittier ˈ*h*wɪt.i.əʳ ⓊⓈ ˈ*h*wɪt̬.i.ɚ
Whittingeham(e) ˈ*h*wɪt.ɪn.dʒəm ⓊⓈ ˈ*h*wɪt̬-
Whittington ˈ*h*wɪt.ɪŋ.tən ⓊⓈ ˈ*h*wɪt̬-
whittl|e (W) ˈ*h*wɪt.l̩ ⓊⓈ ˈ*h*wɪt̬- **-es** -z **-ing** -ɪŋ, ˈ*h*wɪt.lɪŋ **-ed** -d
Whittlesey ˈ*h*wɪt.l̩.si ⓊⓈ ˈ*h*wɪt̬-
Whitworth ˈ*h*wɪt.wəθ, -wɜːθ ⓊⓈ -wɚθ, -wɜːrθ
whit|y ˈ*h*waɪ.t|i ⓊⓈ -t̬|i **-iness** -ɪ.nəs, -ɪ.nɪs
whiz, **whiz|z** *h*wɪz **-zes** -ɪz **-zing** -ɪŋ **-zed** -d ˌ**gee** ˈ**whiz(z)** ; ˈ**whiz(z)** ˌ**kid**
whiz(z)-bang ˈ*h*wɪz.bæŋ **-s** -z
who *strong form:* huː *weak form:* hu
Note: Weak form word. The weak form is only found in unstressed syllables, and the /h/ is frequently not pronounced.

The strong form is also found in unstressed syllables. ˌ**Who's 'Who**
WHO ˌdʌb.l̩.juːˌeɪtʃ'əʊ ⓤⓢ ˌdʌb.l̩.juːˌeɪtʃ'oʊ, -jəˌ-
whoa *h*wəʊ ⓤⓢ *h*woʊ
who'd huːd
whodun(n)it ˌhuː'dʌn.ɪt **-s** -s
whoe'er huː'eəʳ, hu- ⓤⓢ -'er
whoever huː'ev.əʳ, hu- ⓤⓢ -ɚ
whole həʊl ⓤⓢ hoʊl **-ness** -nəs, -nɪs **go the** ˌ**whole 'hog**
wholefood 'həʊl.fuːd ⓤⓢ 'hoʊl- **-s** -z
wholegrain 'həʊl.greɪn ⓤⓢ 'hoʊl-
whole-hearted ˌhəʊl'hɑː.tɪd ⓤⓢ ˌhoʊl'hɑːr.t̬ɪd **-ly** -li **-ness** -nəs, -nɪs *stress shift:* ˌwhole-hearted 'effort
wholemeal 'həʊl.miːl ⓤⓢ 'hoʊl-
wholesale 'həʊl.seɪl ⓤⓢ 'hoʊl-
wholesaler 'həʊlˌseɪ.ləʳ ⓤⓢ 'hoʊlˌseɪ.lɚ **-s** -z
wholesom|e 'həʊl.səm ⓤⓢ 'hoʊl- **-est** -ɪst, -əst **-ely** -li **-eness** -nəs, -nɪs
wholewheat 'həʊl.*h*wiːt ⓤⓢ ˌhoʊl'*h*wiːt
wholism 'həʊ.lɪ.zəm ⓤⓢ 'hoʊ-
wholistic həʊ'lɪs.tɪk ⓤⓢ hoʊ-
who'll huːl
wholly 'həʊl.li, 'həʊ- ⓤⓢ 'hoʊl.li, 'hoʊ-
whom huːm
whomever ˌhuː'mev.əʳ, hʊ'-
whomsoever ˌhuːm.səʊ'ev.əʳ, ˌhʊm- ⓤⓢ -soʊ'ev.ɚ
whoop *h*wuːp, huːp **-s** -s **-ing** -ɪŋ **-ed** -t
whoopee (*n.*) '*h*wʊp.i ⓤⓢ '*h*wuː.pi '**whoopee** ˌ**cushion** (*interj.*) *h*wʊ'piː
Whoopi '*h*wʊp.i ⓤⓢ '*h*wʊp.i, '*h*wuː.pi
whooping-cough 'huː.pɪŋ.kɒf ⓤⓢ -kɑːf, 'hʊp.ɪŋ-, 'wuː.pɪŋ-, 'wʊp.ɪŋ-
whoops *h*wʊps ⓤⓢ *h*wʊps, *h*wuːps
whoops-a-daisy '*h*wʊps.əˌdeɪ.zi ⓤⓢ '*h*wʊps-, '*h*wuːps-
whoosh *h*wʊʃ ⓤⓢ *h*wʊʃ, *h*wuːʃ **-es** -ɪz **-ing** -ɪŋ **-ed** -t
whop *h*wɒp ⓤⓢ *h*wɑːp **-s** -s **-ping/s** -ɪŋ/z **-ped** -t
whopper '*h*wɒp.əʳ ⓤⓢ '*h*wɑː.pɚ **-s** -z
whopping '*h*wɒp.ɪŋ ⓤⓢ '*h*wɑː.pɪŋ
whor|e hɔːʳ ⓤⓢ hɔːr **-es** -z **-ing** -ɪŋ **-ed** -d
whoredom 'hɔː.dəm ⓤⓢ 'hɔːr-
whorehou|se 'hɔː.hau|s ⓤⓢ 'hɔːr- **-ses** -zɪz
whoreson 'hɔː.sən ⓤⓢ 'hɔːr- **-s** -z
Whorf *h*wɔːf ⓤⓢ *h*wɔːrf
whorish 'hɔː.rɪʃ ⓤⓢ 'hɔːr.ɪʃ
whorl *h*wɜːl ⓤⓢ *h*wɜːrl, *h*wɔːrl **-s** -z **-ed** -d
whortle '*h*wɜː.tl̩ ⓤⓢ '*h*wɜːr.t̬l̩ **-s** -z
whortleberr|y '*h*wɜː.tl̩ˌber|.i, -bər- ⓤⓢ '*h*wɜːr.t̬l̩ˌber- **-ies** -iz
who's huːz
whose huːz
whoso 'huː.səʊ ⓤⓢ -soʊ
whosoever ˌhuː.səʊ'ev.əʳ ⓤⓢ -soʊ'ev.ɚ
who've huːv
why *h*waɪ **-s** -z
Whybrow '*h*waɪ.braʊ
Whyle '*h*waɪ.li
why'll *h*waɪl
Whymper '*h*wɪm.pəʳ ⓤⓢ -pɚ
why're '*h*waɪ.əʳ ⓤⓢ -ɚ
why's *h*waɪz
Whyte *h*waɪt
Whytt *h*waɪt
why've *h*waɪv, '*h*waɪ.əv
WI ˌdʌb.l̩.juː'aɪ
Wichita 'wɪtʃ.ɪ.tɔː, '-ə- ⓤⓢ -ə.tɔː, -tɑː
wick (W) wɪk **-s** -s
wicked 'wɪk.ɪd **-est** -ɪst, -əst **-ly** -li **-ness/es** -nəs/ɪz, -nɪs/ɪz
Wicken 'wɪk.ən
Wickens 'wɪk.ɪnz
wicker (W) 'wɪk.əʳ ⓤⓢ -ɚ
wickerwork 'wɪk.ə.wɜːk ⓤⓢ -ɚ.wɜːrk
wicket 'wɪk.ɪt **-s** -s '**wicket** ˌ**gate**
wicket-keeper 'wɪk.ɪtˌkiː.pəʳ ⓤⓢ -pɚ **-s** -z
Wickford 'wɪk.fəd ⓤⓢ -fɚd
Wickham 'wɪk.əm
Wickliffe 'wɪk.lɪf
Wicklow 'wɪk.ləʊ ⓤⓢ -loʊ
Widdecombe, Widdicombe 'wɪd.ɪ.kəm
Widdowson 'wɪd.əʊ.sən ⓤⓢ -oʊ-, '-ə-
wid|e waɪd **-es** -z **-er** -əʳ ⓤⓢ -ɚ **-est** -ɪst, -əst **-ely** -li **-eness** -nəs, -nɪs '**wide** ˌ**boy**
wide-angle ˌwaɪd'æŋ.gl̩ *stress shift:* ˌwide-angle 'lens
wide-awake (*adj.*) ˌwaɪd.ə'weɪk
Widecombe 'wɪd.ɪ.kəm
wide-eyed ˌwaɪd'aɪd ⓤⓢ '-- *stress shift, British only:* ˌwide-eyed 'stare
Widemouth 'wɪd.məθ
widen 'waɪ.dən **-s** -z **-ing** -ɪŋ, 'waɪd.nɪŋ **-ed** -d
Wideopen 'waɪdˌəʊ.pən ⓤⓢ -ˌoʊ-
widespread 'waɪd.spred
widgeon 'wɪdʒ.ən, -ɪn **-s** -z
widget 'wɪdʒ.ɪt **-s** -s
widish 'waɪ.dɪʃ
Widmerpool 'wɪd.mə.puːl ⓤⓢ -mɚ-
Widnes 'wɪd.nəs, -nɪs
widow 'wɪd.əʊ ⓤⓢ -oʊ **-s** -z **-ed** -d
widower 'wɪd.əʊ.əʳ ⓤⓢ -oʊ.ɚ **-s** -z
widowhood 'wɪd.əʊ.hʊd ⓤⓢ -oʊ-
Widsith 'wɪd.sɪθ
width wɪtθ, wɪdθ **-s** -s
wield wiːld **-s** -z **-ing** -ɪŋ **-ed** -ɪd
Wiener schnitzel ˌviː.nə'ʃnɪt.səl ⓤⓢ 'viː.nɚˌʃnɪt- **-s** -z
Wiesbaden 'viːsˌbɑː.dən, 'viːz-, ˌ-'-- ⓤⓢ 'viːsˌbɑː-
Wiesenthal 'wiː.zən.tɑːl, 'viː- ⓤⓢ 'wiː.zən.tɑːl, 'viː-, -θɔːl
wi|fe waɪf **-ves** -vz
wife|hood 'waɪf|.hʊd **-less** -ləs, -lɪs
wifelike 'waɪf.laɪk
wifely 'waɪ.fli
wife-swapping 'waɪfˌswɒp.ɪŋ ⓤⓢ -ˌswɑː.pɪŋ
Wiffen 'wɪf.ɪn
Wiffle ball® 'wɪf.l̩ˌbɔːl ⓤⓢ -ˌbɑːl, -ˌbɔːl
wig wɪg **-s** -z **-ging** -ɪŋ **-ged** -d
Wigan 'wɪg.ən
wigeon 'wɪdʒ.ən, -ɪn **-s** -z
Wiggin 'wɪg.ɪn **-s** -z
wigging 'wɪg.ɪŋ **-s** -z
wiggl|e 'wɪg.l̩ **-es** -z **-ing** -ɪŋ, 'wɪg.lɪŋ **-ed** -d
Wigglesworth 'wɪg.l̩z.wəθ, -wɜːθ ⓤⓢ -wɚθ, -wɜːrθ
wiggly 'wɪg.l̩.i, 'wɪg.li
wight (W) waɪt **-s** -s
Wigley 'wɪg.li
Wigmore 'wɪg.mɔːʳ ⓤⓢ -mɔːr
Wigram 'wɪg.rəm
Wigston 'wɪg.stən
Wigton 'wɪg.tən
Wigtown 'wɪg.taʊn, -tən
Wigtownshire 'wɪg.tən.ʃəʳ, -ˌʃɪəʳ ⓤⓢ -ʃɚ, -ˌʃɪr
wigwam 'wɪg.wæm ⓤⓢ -wɑːm **-s** -z
Wilberforce 'wɪl.bə.fɔːs ⓤⓢ -bɚ.fɔːrs
Wilbraham *surname:* 'wɪl.brə.hæm, '-brəm, '-bri.əm ⓤⓢ '-brə.hæm, '-brəm ***Great and Little in Cambridgeshire:*** 'wɪl.brəm, -brə.hæm
Wilbur 'wɪl.bəʳ ⓤⓢ -bɚ
Wilbye 'wɪl.bi
wilco 'wɪl.kəʊ ⓤⓢ -koʊ
Wilcox 'wɪl.kɒks ⓤⓢ -kɑːks
wild (W) waɪld **-s** -z **-er** -əʳ ⓤⓢ -ɚ **-est** -ɪst, -əst **-ly** -li **-ness** -nəs, -nɪs '**wild** ˌ**card** ; '**wild** ˌ**child** ; ˌ**Wild 'West** ; ˌ**sow one's** ˌ**wild 'oats**
wild|cat 'waɪld|.kæt **-cats** -kæts **-catting** -ˌkæt.ɪŋ ⓤⓢ -ˌkæt̬.ɪŋ **-catted** -ˌkæt.ɪd ⓤⓢ -ˌkæt̬.ɪd **-catter/s** -ˌkæt.əʳ/z ⓤⓢ -ˌkæt̬.ɚ/z ˌ**wildcat 'strike**
Wilde waɪld
wildebeest 'wɪl.dɪ.biːst, 'vɪl-, -də- ⓤⓢ -də- **-s** -s
Wilder 'waɪl.dəʳ ⓤⓢ -dɚ
wilderness 'wɪl.də.nəs, -nɪs ⓤⓢ -dɚ- **-es** -ɪz
Wilderspin 'wɪl.də.spɪn ⓤⓢ -dɚ-
Wildfell 'waɪld.fel
wildfire 'waɪld.faɪəʳ ⓤⓢ -faɪɚ
wildfowl 'waɪld.faʊl **-ing** -ɪŋ **-er/s** -əʳ/z ⓤⓢ -ɚ/z

wild-goose chase ˌwaɪld'guːsˌtʃeɪs
wilding (W) 'waɪl.dɪŋ **-s** -z
wildlife 'waɪld.laɪf **'wildlife ˌpark**
wil|e (W) waɪl **-es** -z **-ing** -ɪŋ **-ed** -d
Wiley 'waɪ.li
Wilfred, Wilfrid 'wɪl.frɪd, -frəd Ⓤⓢ 'wɪl-
wilful 'wɪl.fᵊl, -fʊl **-ly** -i **-ness** -nəs, -nɪs
Wilhelmina ˌwɪl.hel'miː.nə, -ə'-
Wilkerson 'wɪl.kə.sᵊn Ⓤⓢ -kɚ-
Wilkes wɪlks
Wilkie 'wɪl.ki
Wilkin 'wɪl.kɪn
Wilkins 'wɪl.kɪnz
Wilkinson 'wɪl.kɪn.sᵊn
Wilks wɪlks
will (W) (*n.*) wɪl **-s** -z
will (*transitive v.*) wɪl **-s** -z **-ing** -ɪŋ **-ed** -d
will (*auxil. v.*) *strong form:* wɪl *weak forms:* wᵊl, ᵊl
Note: Weak form word. The strong form is used for emphasis (e.g. 'I **will** do it') and contrast (e.g. 'I don't know if I will or not'). It is also the usual form of 'will' in final position (e.g. 'I think they both will'). Elsewhere the weak form (often spelt in contracted form as **'ll**) is used.
Willard 'wɪl.ɑːd, -əd Ⓤⓢ -ɚd
Willcocks, -cox 'wɪl.kɒks Ⓤⓢ -kɑːks
Willenhall 'wɪl.ən.hɔːl
Willes wɪlz
Willesden 'wɪlz.dᵊn
Willett 'wɪl.ɪt **-s** -s
willful 'wɪl.fᵊl, -fʊl **-ly** -i **-ness** -nəs, -nɪs
William 'wɪl.jəm, -i.əm Ⓤⓢ '-jəm **-s** -z **-son** -sᵊn
willie (W) 'wɪl.i **-s** -z
willing (W) 'wɪl.ɪŋ **-ly** -li **-ness** -nəs, -nɪs
Willingdon 'wɪl.ɪŋ.dən
Willington 'wɪl.ɪŋ.tən
Willis 'wɪl.ɪs
Willmott 'wɪl.mɒt, -mət Ⓤⓢ -mɑːt, -mət
will-o'-the-wisp ˌwɪl.ə.ðə'wɪsp, 'wɪl.ə.ðə.wɪsp Ⓤⓢ ˌwɪl.ə.ðə'wɪsp **-s** -s
Willoughby 'wɪl.ə.bi
willow 'wɪl.əʊ Ⓤⓢ -oʊ **-s** -z **-ing** -ɪŋ **-ed** -d
willowherb 'wɪl.əʊ.hɜːb Ⓤⓢ -oʊ.*h*ɜːrb
willow-pattern 'wɪl.əʊˌpæt.ᵊn Ⓤⓢ -oʊˌpæt̬.ᵊn
willowy 'wɪl.əʊ.i Ⓤⓢ -oʊ-
willpower 'wɪl.paʊəʳ Ⓤⓢ -paʊɚ **-s** -z
Wills wɪlz
Willson 'wɪl.sᵊn
Willsteed 'wɪl.stiːd
will|y (W) 'wɪl|.i **-ies** -iz
willy-nilly ˌwɪl.i'nɪl.i
Wilma 'wɪl.mə
Wilmcote 'wɪlm.kəʊt Ⓤⓢ -koʊt, -kət
Wilmington 'wɪl.mɪŋ.tən
Wilmot(t) 'wɪl.mɒt, -mət Ⓤⓢ -mɑːt, -mət
Wilmslow 'wɪlmz.ləʊ *locally:* 'wɪmz.ləʊ Ⓤⓢ 'wɪlmz.loʊ
Wilna 'vɪl.nə
Wilno 'wɪl.nəʊ Ⓤⓢ -noʊ
Wilsden 'wɪlz.dᵊn
Wilshire 'wɪl.ʃəʳ, -ˌʃɪəʳ Ⓤⓢ -ʃɚ, -ˌʃɪr
Wilson 'wɪl.sᵊn
wilt (*from* **will,** *auxil. v.*) *normal form:* wɪlt *occasional weak form:* ᵊlt
Note: This archaic form is rarely used.
wilt wɪlt **-s** -s **-ing** -ɪŋ Ⓤⓢ 'wɪl.t̬ɪŋ **-ed** -ɪd Ⓤⓢ 'wɪl.t̬ɪd
Wilton 'wɪl.tən Ⓤⓢ -tən, -tᵊn **-s** -z
Wilts. (*abbrev. for* **Wiltshire**) wɪlts
Wiltshire 'wɪlt.ʃəʳ, -ˌʃɪəʳ Ⓤⓢ -ʃɚ, -ˌʃɪr
wil|y 'waɪ.l|i **-ier** -i.əʳ Ⓤⓢ -i.ɚ **-iest** -i.ɪst, -i.əst **-iness** -ɪ.nəs, -ɪ.nɪs
wimble 'wɪm.bl̩ **-s** -z
Wimbledon 'wɪm.bl̩.dᵊn ˌ**Wimbledon 'Common**
Wimborne 'wɪm.bɔːn Ⓤⓢ -bɔːrn
Wimms wɪmz
wimp wɪmp **-s** -s **-y** -i
WIMP wɪmp
Wimpey 'wɪm.pi
wimpish 'wɪm.pɪʃ **-ly** -li **-ness** -nəs, -nɪs
wimple 'wɪm.pl̩ **-s** -z
Wimpole 'wɪm.pəʊl Ⓤⓢ -poʊl
Wimpy® 'wɪm.pi **-bar/s** -bɑːʳ/z Ⓤⓢ -bɑːr/z
Wimsey 'wɪm.zi
win wɪn **-s** -z **-ning** -ɪŋ **won** wʌn **winner/s** 'wɪn.əʳ/z Ⓤⓢ -ɚ/z
Winalot® 'wɪn.ə.lɒt Ⓤⓢ -lɑːt
Wincanton wɪŋ'kæn.tən, wɪn- Ⓤⓢ wɪn'kæn.tᵊn
winc|e wɪn*t*s **-es** -ɪz **-ing** -ɪŋ **-ed** -t
wincey 'wɪn*t*.si
winceyette ˌwɪn*t*.si'et
winch wɪn*t*ʃ **-es** -ɪz
Winchelsea 'wɪn.*t*ʃᵊl.si
Winchester 'wɪn.tʃɪ.stəʳ, -tʃə- Ⓤⓢ -tʃes.tɚ, -tʃə.stɚ
Winchfield 'wɪn*t*ʃ.fiːld
Winchilsea 'wɪn.*t*ʃᵊl.si
Winchmore 'wɪn*t*ʃ.mɔːʳ Ⓤⓢ -mɔːr
wind (*n.*) *air blowing:* wɪnd **-s** -z **'wind ˌtunnel ; take the ˌwind out of someone's 'sails**
wind (*v.*) *go round, roll round:* waɪnd **-s** -z **-ing** -ɪŋ **wound** waʊnd **-er/s** -əʳ/z Ⓤⓢ -ɚ/z
wind (*v.*) *blow horn:* waɪnd Ⓤⓢ waɪnd, wɪnd **-s** -z **-ing** -ɪŋ **-ed** -ɪd
wind (*v.*) *detect by scent, make unable to breathe:* wɪnd **-s** -z **-ing** -ɪŋ **-ed** -ɪd
windage 'wɪn.dɪdʒ
windbag 'wɪn*d*.bæg **-s** -z
windblown 'wɪn*d*.bləʊn Ⓤⓢ -bloʊn
windbreak 'wɪn*d*.breɪk **-s** -s **-er/s** -əʳ/z Ⓤⓢ -ɚ/z
windburn 'wɪn*d*.bɜːn Ⓤⓢ -bɜːrn **-ed** -t, -d **-t** -t
windcheater 'wɪn*d*ˌtʃiː.təʳ Ⓤⓢ -t̬ɚ **-s** -z
wind-chest 'wɪn*d*.tʃest **-s** -s
windchill 'wɪn*d*.tʃɪl
wind-cone 'wɪn*d*.kəʊn Ⓤⓢ -koʊn **-s** -z
Windermere 'wɪn.də.mɪəʳ Ⓤⓢ -dɚ.mɪr
windfall 'wɪn*d*.fɔːl Ⓤⓢ -fɔːl, -fɑːl **-s** -z
Windham 'wɪn.dəm
Windhoek 'wɪnd.hʊk, 'wɪnt-, 'vɪnt- Ⓤⓢ 'vɪnt-
windhover 'wɪndˌhɒv.əʳ Ⓤⓢ -ˌhʌv.ɚ, -ˌhɑː.vɚ **-s** -z
winding *in furnaces:* 'wɪn.dɪŋ
winding (*n. adj.*) 'waɪn.dɪŋ **-s** -z **-ly** -li
winding-sheet 'waɪn.dɪŋ.ʃiːt **-s** -s
winding-up ˌwaɪn.dɪŋ'ʌp
wind-instrument 'wɪndˌɪn.strə.mənt, -strʊ- **-s** -s
windjammer 'wɪn*d*ˌdʒæm.əʳ Ⓤⓢ -ɚ **-s** -z
windlass 'wɪnd.ləs **-es** -ɪz
Windley 'wɪnd.li
windmill 'wɪn*d*.mɪl **-s** -z
Windolene® 'wɪn.dəʊ.liːn Ⓤⓢ -doʊ-, -də-
window 'wɪn.dəʊ Ⓤⓢ -doʊ **-s** -z **'window ˌbox ; 'window ˌcleaner ; 'window ˌdressing ; 'window ˌseat**
windowpane 'wɪn.dəʊ.peɪn Ⓤⓢ -doʊ- **-s** -z
window-shop 'wɪn.dəʊ.ʃɒp Ⓤⓢ -doʊ.ʃɑːp **-s** -s **-ing** -ɪŋ **-ed** -t
windowsill 'wɪn.dəʊ.sɪl Ⓤⓢ -doʊ- **-s** -z
windpipe 'wɪn*d*.paɪp **-s** -s
windproof 'wɪn*d*.pruːf
windrow 'wɪn.drəʊ Ⓤⓢ -droʊ **-s** -z
Windrush 'wɪn.drʌʃ
Windscale 'wɪn*d*.skeɪl
windscreen 'wɪn*d*.skriːn **-s** -z **'windscreen ˌwiper**
windshield 'wɪn*d*.ʃiːld **-s** -z **'windshield ˌwiper**
windsock 'wɪn*d*.sɒk Ⓤⓢ -sɑːk **-s** -s
Windsor 'wɪn*d*.zəʳ Ⓤⓢ -zɚ ˌ**Windsor 'Castle ; ˌDuke of 'Windsor ; ˌDuchess of 'Windsor**
windstorm 'wɪnd.stɔːm Ⓤⓢ -stɔːrm **-s** -z
windsurf 'wɪn*d*.sɜːf Ⓤⓢ -sɜːrf **-s** -s **-ing** -ɪŋ **-ed** -t **-er/s** -əʳ/z Ⓤⓢ -ɚ/z
windswept 'wɪn*d*.swept
wind-up 'waɪnd.ʌp **-s** -s
Windus 'wɪn.dəs
windward (W) 'wɪn*d*.wəd Ⓤⓢ -wɚd
wind|y 'wɪn.d|i **-ier** -i.əʳ Ⓤⓢ -i.ɚ **-iest**

-i.ɪst, -i.əst **-ily** -ɪ.li, -əl.i **-iness** -ɪ.nəs, -ɪ.nɪs ˌ**Windy** ˈ**City**
wine waɪn **-s** -z ˈ**wine** ˌ**bar**; ˈ**wine** ˌ**bottle**; ˈ**wine** ˌ**cellar**; ˌ**wine** ˈ**vinegar**
winebibber ˈwaɪnˌbɪb.əʳ (US) -ɚ **-s** -z
wineglass ˈwaɪn.glɑːs (US) -glæs **-es** -ɪz
winer|y ˈwaɪ.nər|.i **-ies** -iz
winey ˈwaɪ.ni
Winfrey ˈwɪn.fri
wing (W) wɪŋ **-s** -z **-ing** -ɪŋ **-ed** -d ˈ**wing** ˌ**nut**; ˌ**clip someone's** ˈ**wings**
Wingate ˈwɪn.geɪt, ˈwɪŋ-, -gɪt (US) ˈwɪn-
wing-commander ˌwɪŋ.kəˈmɑːn.dəʳ (US) ˈwɪŋ.kəˌmæn.dɚ **-s** -z *stress shift, British only:* ˌwing-commander ˈSmith
winged wɪŋd
-winger -ˈwɪŋ.əʳ (US) -ɚ **-s** -z
Note: Suffix. Normally carries primary stress as shown, e.g. **left-winger** /ˌleftˈwɪŋ.əʳ (US) -ɚ/.
winger ˈwɪŋ.əʳ (US) -ɚ **-s** -z
Wingerworth ˈwɪŋ.ə.wəθ, -wɜːθ (US) -ɚ.wɚθ, -wɜːrθ
Wingfield ˈwɪŋ.fiːld
wingspan ˈwɪŋ.spæn
Winifred ˈwɪn.ɪ.frɪd (US) ˈ-ə-
wink (W) wɪŋk **-s** -s **-ing** -ɪŋ **-ed** -t **-er/s** -əʳ/z (US) -ɚ/z
Winkfield ˈwɪŋk.fiːld
Winkie ˈwɪŋ.ki
winkle (W) ˈwɪŋ.kl̩ **-s** -z
winkle-picker ˈwɪŋ.kl̩ˌpɪk.əʳ (US) -ɚ **-s** -z
winner ˈwɪn.əʳ (US) -ɚ **-s** -z
Winnie ˈwɪn.i
Winnie-the-Pooh ˌwɪn.i.ðəˈpuː
winning (W) ˈwɪn.ɪŋ **-s** -z **-ly** -li
winning-post ˈwɪn.ɪŋ.pəʊst (US) -poʊst **-s** -s
Winnipeg ˈwɪn.ɪ.peg
winnow ˈwɪn.əʊ (US) -oʊ **-s** -z **-ing** -ɪŋ **-ed** -d **-er/s** -əʳ/z (US) -ɚ/z
wino ˈwaɪ.nəʊ (US) -noʊ **-s** -z
Winona wɪˈnəʊ.nə (US) -ˈnoʊ-
Winsford ˈwɪnz.fəd, ˈwɪns- (US) -fɚd
Winslow ˈwɪnz.ləʊ (US) -loʊ
winsome ˈwɪn.səm **-ly** -li **-ness** -nəs, -nɪs
Winstanley *in Greater Manchester:* ˈwɪnt.stən.li; wɪnˈstæn- *surname:* wɪnˈstæn.li; ˈwɪnt.stən-
Winston ˈwɪnt.stən
Winstone ˈwɪnt.stəʊn, -stən (US) -stoʊn, -stən
wint|er (W) ˈwɪn.t|əʳ (US) -t̬|ɚ **-ers** -əz (US) -ɚz **-ering** -ər.ɪŋ **-ered** -əd (US) -ɚd ˌ**winter** ˈ**sports**; ˌ**Winter O**ˈ**lympics**
Winterbourne ˈwɪn.tə.bɔːn (US) -t̬ɚ.bɔːrn
Winters ˈwɪn.təz (US) -tɚz
Winterthur ˈvɪn.tə.tʊəʳ (US) -t̬ɚ.tʊr
wintertime ˈwɪn.tə.taɪm (US) -t̬ɚ-
Winterton ˈwɪn.tə.tən (US) -t̬ɚ.tən
Winthrop ˈwɪn.θrɒp, ˈwɪnt.θrəp (US) ˈwɪnt.θrəp
Winton ˈwɪn.tən (US) -tən
Wintour ˈwɪn.təʳ (US) -t̬ɚ
wintr|y ˈwɪn.tr|i **-iness** -ɪ.nəs (US) -ɪ.nɪs
Winwick ˈwɪn.ɪk
Winwood ˈwɪn.wʊd
winy ˈwaɪ.ni
wip|e waɪp **-es** -s **-ing** -ɪŋ **-ed** -t **-er/s** -əʳ/z (US) -ɚ/z ˌ**wiped** ˈ**out**
wipeout ˈwaɪp.aʊt **-s** -s
wir|e waɪəʳ (US) waɪɚ **-es** -z **-ing** -ɪŋ **-ed** -d
wire-cutter ˈwaɪəˌkʌt.əʳ (US) ˈwaɪɚˌkʌt̬.ɚ **-s** -z
wire|draw ˈwaɪə|.drɔː (US) ˈwaɪɚ|.drɑː, -drɔː **-draws** -drɔːz (US) -drɑːz, -drɔːz **-drawing** -ˌdrɔː.ɪŋ (US) -ˌdrɑː.ɪŋ, -ˌdrɔː- **-drew** -druː **-drawn** -drɔːn (US) -drɑːn, -drɔːn **-drawer/s** -ˌdrɔː.əʳ/z (US) -ˌdrɑː.ɚ/z, -ˌdrɔː-
wire-haired ˈwaɪə.heəd (US) ˈwaɪɚ.herd
wireless ˈwaɪə.ləs, -lɪs (US) ˈwaɪɚ- **-es** -ɪz
wire-tapping ˈwaɪəˌtæp.ɪŋ (US) ˈwaɪɚ-
wireworm ˈwaɪə.wɜːm (US) ˈwaɪɚ.wɜːrm **-s** -z
wiring ˈwaɪə.rɪŋ (US) ˈwaɪɚ.ɪŋ
Wirksworth ˈwɜːk.swəθ, -swɜːθ (US) ˈwɜːrk.swɚθ, -swɜːrθ
Wirral ˈwɪr.əl
wir|y ˈwaɪə.r|i (US) ˈwaɪɚ|.i **-ier** -i.əʳ (US) -i.ɚ **-iest** -i.ɪst, -i.əst **-iness** -ɪ.nəs, -ɪ.nɪs
Wis. (*abbrev. for* **Wisconsin**) wɪˈskɒnt.sɪn (US) -ˈskɑːnt.sən
Wisbech ˈwɪz.biːtʃ *locally:* -bɪtʃ
Wisbey ˈwɪz.bi
Wisconsin wɪˈskɒnt.sɪn (US) -ˈskɑːnt.sən
Wisden ˈwɪz.dən
wisdom ˈwɪz.dəm ˈ**wisdom** ˌ**tooth**
wis|e (W) waɪz **-er** -əʳ (US) -ɚ **-est** -ɪst, -əst **-ely** -li **-eness** -nəs, -nɪs ˈ**wise** ˌ**guy**; ˌ**three** ˌ**wise** ˈ**men**
wiseacre ˈwaɪzˌeɪ.kəʳ (US) -kɚ **-s** -z
wisecrack ˈwaɪz.kræk **-s** -s
Wiseman ˈwaɪz.mən
wish wɪʃ **-es** -ɪz **-ing** -ɪŋ **-ed** -t **-er/s** -əʳ/z (US) -ɚ/z
Wishart ˈwɪʃ.ət (US) -ɚt
Wishaw ˈwɪʃ.ɔː (US) -ɑː, -ɔː
wishbone ˈwɪʃ.bəʊn (US) -boʊn **-s** -z
wishful ˈwɪʃ.fəl, -fʊl **-ly** -i **-ness** -nəs, -nɪs ˌ**wishful** ˈ**thinking**
wishing-well ˈwɪʃ.ɪŋ.wel **-s** -z
wish-wash ˈwɪʃ.wɒʃ (US) -wɑːʃ, -wɔːʃ
wishy-washy ˈwɪʃ.iˌwɒʃ.i, ˌwɪʃ.iˈwɒʃ- (US) ˈwɪʃ.iˌwɑː.ʃi, -ˌwɔː-
wisp wɪsp **-s** -s
wisp|y ˈwɪs.p|i **-ier** -i.əʳ (US) -i.ɚ **-iest** -i.ɪst, -i.əst **-ily** -ɪ.li, -əl.i **-iness** -ɪ.nəs, -ɪ.nɪs
wist wɪst
Wistar ˈwɪs.təʳ (US) -tɚ
wistaria wɪˈsteə.ri.ə, -ˈstɪə- (US) -ˈster.i-, -ˈstɪr- **-s** -z
Wister ˈwɪs.təʳ (US) -tɚ
wisteria wɪˈstɪə.ri.ə, -ˈsteə- (US) -ˈstɪr.i-, -ˈster- **-s** -z
wistful ˈwɪst.fəl, -fʊl **-ly** -i **-ness** -nəs, -nɪs
wit wɪt **-s** -s
witch wɪtʃ **-es** -ɪz **-ing/ly** -ɪŋ/li **-ed** -t
witchcraft ˈwɪtʃ.krɑːft (US) -kræft
witchdoctor ˈwɪtʃˌdɒk.təʳ (US) -ˌdɑːk.tɚ **-s** -z
witcher|y ˈwɪtʃ.ər|.i **-ies** -iz
witch-hazel ˈwɪtʃˌheɪ.zəl, ˌ-ˈ-- (US) ˈwɪtʃˌheɪ- **-s** -z
witch-hunt ˈwɪtʃ.hʌnt **-s** -s **-er/s** -əʳ/z (US) -ɚ/z
witching ˈwɪtʃ.ɪŋ ˈ**witching** ˌ**hour**
witenagemot(e) ˌwɪt.ɪ.nə.gɪˈməʊt, -ən.ə-, -gəˈ- (US) ˌwɪt.ən.ə.gəˈmoʊt
with wɪð, wɪθ
Note: The pronunciation /wɪθ/ is most frequently found when followed by a voiceless consonant (e.g. 'with care' /wɪθˈkeə (US) -ˈker/).
withal wɪˈðɔːl (US) wɪˈðɔːl, -ˈðɑːl
Witham ˈwɪð.əm *town in Essex:* ˈwɪt.əm (US) ˈwɪt̬-
withdraw wɪðˈdrɔː, wɪθ- (US) -ˈdrɑː, -ˈdrɔː **-s** -z **-ing** -ɪŋ **withdrew** wɪðˈdruː, wɪθ- **withdrawn** wɪðˈdrɔːn, wɪθ- (US) -ˈdrɑːn, -ˈdrɔːn
withdrawal wɪðˈdrɔː.əl, wɪθ- (US) -ˈdrɑː-, -ˈdrɔː- **-s** -z **with**ˈ**drawal** ˌ**method**; **with**ˈ**drawal** ˌ**symptoms**
withe wɪθ, wɪð, waɪð **-s** -s, -z
with|er (W) ˈwɪð|.əʳ (US) -ɚ **-ers** -əz (US) -ɚz **-ering/ly** -ər.ɪŋ/li **-ered** -əd (US) -ɚd
Withernsea ˈwɪð.ən.siː (US) -ɚn-
withers (W) (*n.*) ˈwɪð.əz (US) -ɚz
Witherspoon ˈwɪð.ə.spuːn (US) ˈ-ɚ-
with|hold wɪθ|ˈhəʊld, wɪð- (US) -ˈhoʊld **-holds** -ˈhəʊldz (US) -ˈhoʊldz **-holding** -ˈhəʊl.dɪŋ (US) -ˈhoʊl.dɪŋ **-held** -ˈheld **-holden** -ˈhəʊl.dən (US) -ˈhoʊl.dən **-holder/s** -ˈhəʊl.dəʳ/z (US) -ˈhoʊl.dɚ/z
within wɪˈðɪn; ˈwɪð.ɪn (US) wɪˈðɪn, -ˈθɪn
with-it ˈwɪð.ɪt (US) ˈwɪð-, ˈwɪθ-
withless ˈwɪt.ləs, -lɪs **-ly** -li **-ness** -nəs, -nɪs
without wɪˈðaʊt; ˈwɪð.aʊt (US) wɪˈðaʊt, -ˈθaʊt

withstand wɪðˈstænd, wɪθ- (US) wɪθ-, wɪð- **-s** -z **-ing** -ɪŋ **withstood** wɪðˈstʊd, wɪθ- (US) wɪθ-, wɪð-
with|y ˈwɪð|.i (US) ˈwɪð-, ˈwɪθ- **-ies** -iz
witless ˈwɪt.ləs, -lɪs **-ly** -li **-ness** -nəs, -nɪs
Witley ˈwɪt.li
witness (*n. v.*) ˈwɪt.nəs, -nɪs **-es** -ɪz **-ing** -ɪŋ **-ed** -t ˈ**witness ˌbox**
witney (W) ˈwɪt.ni
-witted -ˈwɪt.ɪd, -ˌwɪt.ɪd (US) -ˌwɪt̬.ɪd
Note: Suffix. May take either primary or secondary stress in British English, unless it is used attributively, in which case it always takes secondary stress, e.g. **quick-witted** /ˌkwɪkˈwɪt.ɪd/, ˌquick-witted ˈfox. Normally takes only secondary stress in American English.
Wittenberg ˈvɪt.ən.bɜːg, -beəg *old-fashioned:* ˈwɪt.ən.bɜːg (US) ˈwɪt.ən.bɜːrg, ˈvɪt-
witter ˈwɪt.əʳ (US) ˈwɪt̬- **-s** -z **-ing** -ɪŋ **-ed** -d **-er/s** -əʳ/z (US) -ɚ/z
Wittgenstein ˈvɪt.gən.ʃtaɪn, -staɪn
witticism ˈwɪt.ɪ.sɪ.zəm (US) ˈwɪt̬.ə- **-s** -z
wittingly ˈwɪt.ɪŋ.li (US) ˈwɪt̬-
witt|y ˈwɪt|.i (US) ˈwɪt̬- **-ier** -i.əʳ (US) -i.ɚ **-iest** -i.ɪst, -i.əst **-ily** -ɪ.li, -əl.i **-iness** -ɪ.nəs, -ɪ.nɪs
Witwatersrand wɪtˈwɔː.təz.rænd, -rɑːnd, -rɑːnt; ˈwɪtˌwɔː-, ˈvɪtˌvɑː.təz.rɒnt (US) wɪtˈwɔː.t̬ɚz.rænd, -ˈwɑː-
Wiveliscombe ˈwɪv.əl.ɪ.skəm, ˌwɪv.əˈlɪs.kəm *locally also:* ˈwɪl.skəm
Wivelsfield ˈwɪv.əlz.fiːld
Wivenhoe ˈwɪv.ən.həʊ (US) -hoʊ
wivern ˈwaɪ.vən, -vɜːn (US) -vɚn, -vɜːrn **-s** -z
wives (*plur. of* **wife**) waɪvz
wizard ˈwɪz.əd (US) -ɚd **-s** -z **-ry** -ri
wizen ˈwɪz.ən **-ed** -d
wk (*abbrev. for* **week**) wiːk
WNW (*abbrev. for* **west-northwest**) ˌwest.nɔːθˈwest (US) -nɔːrθˈ- *nautical pronunciation:* -nɔːˈ- (US) -nɔːrˈ-
wo wəʊ (US) woʊ
woad wəʊd (US) woʊd
wobbl|e ˈwɒb.l̩ (US) ˈwɑː.bl̩ **-es** -z **-ing** -ɪŋ, ˈwɒb.lɪŋ (US) ˈwɑː.blɪŋ **-ed** -d **-er/s** -əʳ/z (US) ˈwɒb.ləʳ/z, ˈwɑː.bl̩.əʳ/z (US) ˈwɑː.blɚ/z
wobbl|y ˈwɒb.l̩|.i, ˈ-l|i (US) ˈwɑː.bl̩|.i, ˈ-bl|i **-iness** -ɪ.nəs, -ɪ.nɪs
Wobegon ˈwəʊ.bɪ.gɒn (US) ˈwoʊ.bɪ.gɑːn
Woburn *Abbey:* ˈwuː.bɜːn, -bən (US) -bɜːrn, -bɚn *street and square in London:* ˈwəʊ.bən, -bɜːn (US) ˈwoʊ.bɚn, -bɜːrn *village:* ˈwəʊ.bən, ˈwuː- (US) ˈwoʊ.bɚn, ˈwuː-
Wodehouse ˈwʊd.haʊs
Woden ˈwəʊ.dən (US) ˈwoʊ-
wodge wɒdʒ (US) wɑːdʒ **-s** -ɪz
woe wəʊ (US) woʊ **-s** -z
woebegone ˈwəʊ.bɪ.gɒn (US) ˈwoʊ.bɪ.gɑːn
woeful ˈwəʊ.fəl, -fʊl (US) ˈwoʊ- **-ly** -i **-ness** -nəs, -nɪs
Woffington ˈwɒf.ɪŋ.tən (US) ˈwɑː.fɪŋ-
wog wɒg (US) wɑːg, wɔːg **-s** -z
Wogan ˈwəʊ.gən (US) ˈwoʊ-
wok wɒk (US) wɑːk **-s** -s
woke (*from* **wake**) wəʊk (US) woʊk
woken (*from* **wake**) ˈwəʊ.kən (US) ˈwoʊ-
Woking ˈwəʊ.kɪŋ (US) ˈwoʊ-
Wokingham ˈwəʊ.kɪŋ.əm (US) ˈwoʊ-
Wolborough ˈwɒl.bər.ə (US) ˈwɑːl.bɚ.oʊ
Wolcot(t) ˈwʊl.kət (US) ˈwʊl-, ˈwɔːl-
wold wəʊld (US) woʊld **-s** -z
Woldingham ˈwəʊl.dɪŋ.əm (US) ˈwoʊl-
Woledge ˈwʊl.ɪdʒ
wol|f (W) (*n.*) wʊl|f **-ves** -vz **a ˌwolf in ˌsheep's ˈclothing ; keep the ˌwolf from, the ˈdoor, keep the ˈwolf from the ˌdoor**
wolf (*v.*) wʊlf **-s** -s **-ing** -ɪŋ **-ed** -t
wolf-cub ˈwʊlf.kʌb **-s** -z
Wolfe wʊlf
Wolfenden ˈwʊl.fən.dən
Wolff wʊlf, vɒlf (US) wʊlf, vɔːlf
Wolfgang ˈwʊlf.gæŋ
wolfhound ˈwʊlf.haʊnd **-s** -z
wolfish ˈwʊl.fɪʃ **-ly** -li **-ness** -nəs, -nɪs
wolfram (W) ˈwʊl.frəm **-ite** -aɪt
wolf-whistl|e ˈwʊlfˌ*h*wɪs.l̩ **-es** -z **-ing** -ɪŋ, -ˌ*h*wɪs.lɪŋ **-ed** -d
Wollard ˈwʊl.ɑːd (US) -ɑːrd, -ɚd
Wollaston ˈwʊl.ə.stən
Wollaton ˈwʊl.ə.tən (US) -tən
Wollongong ˈwʊl.ən.gɒŋ, -əŋ- (US) -ən.gɑːŋ
Wollstonecraft ˈwʊl.stən.krɑːft (US) -kræft, -krɑːft
Wolmer ˈwʊl.məʳ (US) -mɚ
Wolseley® ˈwʊlz.li
Wolsey ˈwʊl.zi
Wolsingham ˈwɒl.sɪŋ.əm (US) ˈwɑːl-
Wolstenholme ˈwʊl.stən.həʊm (US) -hoʊm
Wolverhampton ˈwʊl.vəˌhæm*p*.tən, ˌwʊl.vəˈhæm*p*- (US) ˈwʊl.vɚˌhæm*p*-
wolverine ˈwʊl.vər.iːn (US) ˌwʊl.vəˈriːn, ˈ--- **-s** -z
Wolverton ˈwʊl.və.tən (US) -vɚ-
wolves (*plur. of* **wolf**) wʊlvz
woman ˈwʊm.ən **women** ˈwɪm.ɪn ˌ**woman of the ˈworld**
woman-hat|er ˈwʊm.ənˌheɪ.t|əʳ (US) -t̬|ɚ **-ers** -əz (US) -ɚz **-ing** -ɪŋ
womanhood ˈwʊm.ən.hʊd
womanish ˈwʊm.ə.nɪʃ **-ly** -li **-ness** -nəs, -nɪs
womanist ˈwʊm.ə.nɪst **-s** -s
womaniz|e, -is|e ˈwʊm.ə.naɪz **-es** -ɪz **-ing** -ɪŋ **-ed** -d **-er/s** -əʳ/z (US) -ɚ/z
womankind ˌwʊm.ənˈkaɪnd, -əŋˈ-, ˈ--- (US) ˈwʊm.ən.kaɪnd
womanlike ˈwʊm.ən.laɪk
womanl|y ˈwʊm.ən.l|i **-iness** -ɪ.nəs, -ɪ.nɪs
womb wuːm **-s** -z
wombat ˈwɒm.bæt (US) ˈwɑːm- **-s** -s
Womble ˈwɒm.bl̩, ˈwʌm- (US) ˈwɑː.m-
Wombourne ˈwɒm.bɔːn (US) ˈwɑːm.bɔːrn
Wombwell *place in South Yorkshire:* ˈwʊm.wel, -wəl *surname:* ˈwʊm.wəl, ˈwʌm-, ˈwɒm- (US) ˈwʊm-, ˈwʌm-, ˈwɑːm-
women (*plur. of* **woman**) ˈwɪm.ɪn ˌ**Women's ˈInstitute ; ˌwomen's ˈlib ; ˈwomen's ˌmovement ; ˈwomen's ˌroom**
womenfolk ˈwɪm.ɪn.fəʊk (US) -foʊk
womenkind ˌwɪm.ɪnˈkaɪnd, -ɪŋˈ-, ˈ--- (US) ˈwɪm.ɪn.kaɪnd
won (*from* **win**) wʌn
won *Korean money:* wɒn (US) wɑːn
wond|er (W) ˈwʌn.d|əʳ (US) -d|ɚ **-ers** -əz (US) -ɚz **-ering/ly** -ər.ɪŋ/li **-ered** -əd (US) -ɚd **-erer/s** -ər.əʳ/z (US) -ɚ.ɚ/z
wonder|ful ˈwʌn.də.l.fəl, -fʊl (US) -dɚ- **-fully** -fəl.i, -fʊl-, -fli **-fulness** -fəl.nəs, -fʊl-, -nɪs
wonderland (W) ˈwʌn.dəl.ænd (US) -dɚ.lænd ˌ**Alice in ˈWonderland**
wonderment ˈwʌn.də.mənt (US) -dɚ-
wondrous ˈwʌn.drəs **-ly** -li **-ness** -nəs, -nɪs
wonk ˈwɒŋk (US) ˈwɑːŋk **-s** -s
wonk|y ˈwɒŋ.k|i (US) ˈwɑːŋ-, ˈwɔːŋ- **-ier** -i.əʳ (US) -i.ɚ **-iest** -i.ɪst, -i.əst **-ily** -ɪ.li, -əl.i **-iness** -ɪ.nəs, -ɪ.nɪs
Wonsan ˌwɒnˈsæn (US) ˌwɑːnˈsɑːn, ˌwʌn-
won|t (*n. adj.*) wəʊn|t (US) wɔːn|t, wɑːn|t, woʊn|t, wʌn|t **-ted** -tɪd (US) -t̬ɪd
won't wəʊnt (US) woʊnt
wonton ˌwɒnˈtɒn (US) ˈwɑːn.tɑːn
woo wuː **-s** -z **-ing** -ɪŋ **-ed** -d **-er/s** -əʳ/z (US) -ɚ/z
wood (W) wʊd **-s** -z **-ed** -ɪd **not see the ˌwood for the ˈtrees**
Woodall ˈwʊd.ɔːl (US) -ɔːl, -ɑːl
Woodard ˈwʊd.ɑːd (US) -ɚd
woodbine (W) ˈwʊd.baɪn **-s** -z
woodblock ˈwʊd.blɒk (US) -blɑːk **-s** -s
Woodbridge ˈwʊd.brɪdʒ
Woodbury ˈwʊd.bər.i (US) -ber-, -bɚ-
wood-carv|er ˈwʊdˌkɑː.v|əʳ

(US) -ˌkɑːr.v|ɚ **-ers** -ɚz (US) -ɚz **-ing/s** -ɪŋ/z
woodchuck ˈwʊd.tʃʌk **-s** -s
woodcock (W) ˈwʊd.kɒk (US) -kɑːk **-s** -s
woodcut ˈwʊd.kʌt **-s** -s
woodcutter ˈwʊdˌkʌt.əʳ (US) -ˌkʌt̬.ɚ **-s** -z
wooden ˈwʊd.ᵊn **-ly** -li **-ness** -nəs, -nɪs
wooden-headed ˌwʊd.ᵊnˈhed.ɪd *stress shift:* ˌwooden-headed ˈperson
Woodfield ˈwʊd.fiːld
Woodford(e) ˈwʊd.fəd (US) -fɚd
Woodhouse ˈwʊd.haʊs
woodland ˈwʊd.lənd **-s** -z
Woodley ˈwʊd.li
wood-|louse ˈwʊd|.laʊs **-lice** -laɪs
wood|man (W) ˈwʊd|.mən **-men** -mən
wood-nymph ˈwʊd.nɪmpf **-s** -s
woodpecker ˈwʊdˌpek.əʳ (US) -ɚ **-s** -z
wood-pigeon ˈwʊdˌpɪdʒ.ən, -ɪn **-s** -z
Woodroffe ˈwʊd.rɒf, -rʌf (US) -rɑːf, -rʌf
Woodrow ˈwʊd.rəʊ (US) -roʊ
woodruff (W) ˈwʊd.rʌf **-s** -s
Woods wʊdz
woodshed ˈwʊd.ʃed **-s** -z **-ing** -ɪŋ **-ed** -ɪd
Woodside ˌwʊdˈsaɪd, ˈ-- (US) ˈwʊd.saɪd
woodsman ˈwʊdz.mən
Woodstock ˈwʊd.stɒk (US) -stɑːk
Woodward ˈwʊd.wəd (US) -wɚd
woodwind ˈwʊd.wɪnd **-s** -z
woodwork ˈwʊd.wɜːk (US) -wɜːrk **-ing** -ɪŋ
woodworm ˈwʊd.wɜːm (US) -wɜːrm
wood|y (W) ˈwʊd|.i **-ier** -i.əʳ (US) -i.ɚ **-iest** -i.ɪst, -i.əst **-iness** -ɪ.nəs, -ɪ.nɪs
woof *weaving:* wuːf (US) wuːf, wʊf **-s** -s
Woof *surname:* wʊf
woof *dog's bark:* wʊf **-s** -s
woofer ˈwʊf.əʳ (US) -ɚ **-s** -z
woofter ˈwʊf.təʳ (US) -tɚ **-s** -z
Wookey ˈwʊk.i
wool wʊl **-s** -z
Woolacombe ˈwʊl.ə.kəm
Wooldridge ˈwʊl.drɪdʒ
woolen ˈwʊl.ən **-s** -z
Wooler ˈwʊl.əʳ (US) -ɚ
Woolf wʊlf
Woolfardisworthy *near Bideford, Devon:* ˈwʊl.zᵊr.i, ˈwʊl.fɑː.dɪˌswɜː.ði (US) ˈwʊl.zɚ.i, ˈwʊl.fɑːr.dɪ.swɜːr.ði *near Crediton, Devon:* ˈwʊl.fɑː.dɪˌswɜː.ði (US) -fɑːr.dɪˌswɜːr-
Woolford ˈwʊl.fəd (US) -fɚd
wool-gathering ˈwʊlˌgæð.ᵊr.ɪŋ
Woollard ˈwʊl.ɑːd (US) -ɚd
woollen ˈwʊl.ən **-s** -z
Woolley ˈwʊl.i
wooll|y ˈwʊl|.i **-ies** -iz **-ier** -i.əʳ (US) -i.ɚ **-iest** -i.ɪst, -i.əst **-iness** -ɪ.nəs, -ɪ.nɪs
woolly-headed ˌwʊl.iˈhed.ɪd (US) ˈwʊl.iˌhed- *stress shift, British only:* ˌwoolly-headed ˈperson
Woolner ˈwʊl.nəʳ (US) -nɚ
Woolnough ˈwʊl.nəʊ (US) -noʊ
woolpack ˈwʊl.pæk **-s** -s
woolsack ˈwʊl.sæk **-s** -s
Woolsey ˈwʊl.zi
Woolwich ˈwʊl.ɪdʒ, -ɪtʃ
Woolworth ˈwʊl.wəθ, -wɜːθ (US) -wɚθ, -wɜːrθ **-'s** -s
wool|y ˈwʊl|.i **-ier** -i.əʳ (US) -i.ɚ **-iest** -i.ɪst, -i.əst **-iness** -ɪ.nəs, -ɪ.nɪs
Woomera ˈwʊm.ᵊr.ə, ˈwuː.mᵊr-
Woorstead ˈwʊs.tɪd, -təd (US) ˈwʊs-, ˈwɜːr-
Woosley ˈwuːz.li
Woosnam ˈwuːz.nəm
Wooster ˈwʊs.təʳ (US) -tɚ
Woot(t)on ˈwʊt.ᵊn
wooz|y ˈwuː.z|i **-ier** -i.əʳ (US) -i.ɚ **-iest** -i.ɪst, -i.əst **-ily** -ɪ.li, -ᵊl.i **-iness** -ɪ.nəs, -ɪ.nɪs
wop wɒp (US) wɑːp **-s** -s
Worboys ˈwɔː.bɔɪz (US) ˈwɔːr-
Worcester ˈwʊs.təʳ (US) -tɚ **-shire** -ʃəʳ, -ˌʃɪəʳ (US) -ʃɚ, -ˌʃɪr ˌ**Worcester** ˈ**sauce**
Worcs. (*abbrev. for* **Worcestershire**) ˈwʊs.tə.ʃəʳ, -ˌʃɪəʳ (US) -tɚ.ʃɚ, -ˌʃɪr
word wɜːd (US) wɜːrd **-s** -z **-ing/s** -ɪŋ/z **-ed** -ɪd **-less** -ləs, -lɪs ˈ**word** ˌ**order**; ˈ**word** ˌ**processor**, ˌ**word** ˈ**processor** ˌ**eat one's** ˈ**words**; **get a** ˌ**word in** ˈ**edgewise**; **put** ˌ**words in(to) someone's** ˈ**mouth** (US) **put** ˈ**words in(to) someone's** ˌ**mouth**
wordbook ˈwɜːd.bʊk (US) ˈwɜːrd- **-s** -s
Worde wɔːd (US) wɔːrd
word-formation ˈwɜːd.fɔːˌmeɪ.ʃᵊn (US) ˈwɜːrd.fɔːrˌ-
word-for-word ˌwɜːd.fəˈwɜːd (US) ˌwɜːrd.fɚˈwɜːrd
wordless ˈwɜːd.ləs, -lɪs (US) ˈwɜːrd- **-ly** -li **-ness** -nəs, -nɪs
word-of-mouth ˌwɜːd.əvˈmaʊθ (US) ˌwɜːrd-
word-perfect ˌwɜːdˈpɜː.fɪkt, -fekt (US) ˌwɜːrdˈpɜːr.fɪkt
wordplay ˈwɜːd.pleɪ (US) ˈwɜːrd- **-s** -z
word processing ˈwɜːdˌprəʊ.ses.ɪŋ, ˌ-ˈ--- (US) ˈwɜːrdˌprɑː-, -ˌproʊ-
wordsmith ˈwɜːd.smɪθ (US) ˈwɜːrd- **-s** -s
Wordsworth ˈwɜːdz.wəθ, -wɜːθ (US) ˈwɜːrdz.wɚθ, -wɜːrθ
Wordsworthian ˌwɜːdzˈwɜː.θi.ən (US) ˌwɜːrdzˈwɜːr-
word|y ˈwɜː.d|i (US) ˈwɜːr- **-ier** -i.əʳ (US) -i.ɚ **-iest** -i.ɪst, -i.əst **-ily** -ɪ.li, -ᵊl.i **-iness** -ɪ.nəs, -ɪ.nɪs
wore (*from* **wear**) wɔːʳ (US) wɔːr
work wɜːk (US) wɜːrk **-s** -s **-ing/s** -ɪŋ/z **-ed** -t **-er/s** -əʳ/z (US) -ɚ/z ˌ**working** ˈ**day** (US) ˈ**working** ˌ**day**; ˌ**working** ˈ**knowledge** (US) ˈ**working** ˌ**knowledge**; ˌ**work of** ˈ**art**; ˌ**working** ˈ**order** (US) ˈ**working** ˌ**order**
workable ˈwɜː.kə.bl̩ (US) ˈwɜːr- **-ness** -nəs, -nɪs
workaday ˈwɜː.kə.deɪ (US) ˈwɜːr-
workaholic ˌwɜː.kəˈhɒl.ɪk (US) ˌwɜːr.kəˈhɑː.lɪk **-s** -s
workaholism ˈwɜː.kə.hɒl.ɪ.zᵊm (US) ˈwɜːr.kə.hɑː.lɪ-
workbag ˈwɜːk.bæg (US) ˈwɜːrk- **-s** -z
workbasket ˈwɜːkˌbɑː.skɪt (US) ˈwɜːrkˌbæs.kɪt **-s** -s
workbench ˈwɜːk.bentʃ (US) ˈwɜːrk- **-es** -ɪz
workbook ˈwɜːk.bʊk (US) ˈwɜːrk- **-s** -s
workbox ˈwɜːk.bɒks (US) ˈwɜːrk.bɑːks **-es** -ɪz
workday ˈwɜːk.deɪ (US) ˈwɜːrk- **-s** -z
worker ˈwɜː.kəʳ (US) ˈwɜːr.kɚ **-s** -z
workforc|e ˈwɜːk.fɔːs (US) ˈwɜːrk.fɔːrs **-es** -ɪz
workhors|e ˈwɜːk.hɔːs (US) ˈwɜːrk.hɔːrs **-es** -ɪz
workhou|se ˈwɜːk.haʊ|s (US) ˈwɜːrk- **-ses** -zɪz
working-class (*adj.*) ˌwɜː.kɪŋˈklɑːs (US) ˈwɜːr.kɪŋˌklæs *stress shift, British only:* ˌworking-class ˈorigins
working class (*n.*) ˌwɜː.kɪŋˈklɑːs (US) ˈwɜːr.kɪŋˌklæs **-es** -ɪz
Workington ˈwɜː.kɪŋ.tən (US) ˈwɜːr-
workload ˈwɜːk.ləʊd (US) ˈwɜːrk.loʊd **-s** -z
work|man (W) ˈwɜːk|.mən (US) ˈwɜːrk- **-men** -mən
workman|like ˈwɜːk.mən|.laɪk (US) ˈwɜːrk- **-ly** -li
workmanship ˈwɜːk.mən.ʃɪp (US) ˈwɜːrk-
workmate ˈwɜːk.meɪt (US) ˈwɜːrk- **-s** -s
workout ˈwɜːk.aʊt (US) ˈwɜːrk- **-s** -s
workpeople ˈwɜːkˌpiː.pl̩ (US) ˈwɜːrk-
workplac|e ˈwɜːk.pleɪs (US) ˈwɜːrk- **-es** -ɪz
workroom ˈwɜːk.rʊm, -ruːm (US) ˈwɜːrk.ruːm, -rʊm **-s** -z
workshop ˈwɜːk.ʃɒp (US) ˈwɜːrk.ʃɑːp **-s** -s
work-shy ˈwɜːk.ʃaɪ (US) ˈwɜːrk-
Worksop ˈwɜːk.sɒp, -səp (US) ˈwɜːrk.sɑːp, -səp
workstation ˈwɜːkˌsteɪ.ʃᵊn (US) ˈwɜːrk- **-s** -s
worktable ˈwɜːkˌteɪ.bl̩ (US) ˈwɜːrk- **-s** -z
worktop ˈwɜːk.tɒp (US) ˈwɜːrk.tɑːp **-s** -s
work-to-rule ˌwɜːk.təˈruːl (US) ˌwɜːrk- **-s** -z

world wɜːld (US) wɜːrld **-s** -z ˌ**World ˈCup** ; ˌ**World ˈSeries** ; ˌ**World ˈService** ; ˌ**world ˈwar** ; ˌ**World ˌWar ˈI** ; ˌ**World ˌWar ˈII** ; ˌ**World Wide ˈWeb** ; ˌ**out of this ˈworld**
world-class ˌwɜːldˈklɑːs (US) ˈwɜːrld.klæs, ˌ-ˈ- *stress shift, British only:* ˌworld-class ˈsportsman
world-famous ˌwɜːldˈfeɪ.məs (US) ˈwɜːrldˌfeɪ-, ˌ-ˈ-- *stress shift, British only:* ˌworld-famous ˈactor
worldling ˈwɜːld.lɪŋ (US) ˈwɜːrld- **-s** -z
worldl|y ˈwɜːld.l|i (US) ˈwɜːrld- **-ier** -i.əʳ (US) -i.ɚ **-iest** -i.ɪst, -i.əst **-iness** -ɪ.nəs, -ɪ.nɪs
worldly-wise ˌwɜːld.liˈwaɪz (US) ˈwɜːrld.liˌwaɪz, ˌ--ˈ- *stress shift, British only:* ˌworldly-wise ˈperson
worldview ˈwɜːld.vjuː, ˌ-ˈ- (US) ˈwɜːrld- **-s** -z
world-wear|y ˌwɜːldˈwɪə.r|i, ˈ-ˌ-- (US) ˈwɜːrldˌwɪr|.i **-ier** -i.əʳ (US) -i.ɚ **-iest** -i.ɪst, -i.əst **-ily** -ɪ.li, -əl.i **-iness** -ɪ.nəs, -ɪ.nɪs *stress shift, British only:* ˌworld-weary ˈattitude
worldwide ˌwɜːldˈwaɪd (US) ˈwɜːrld.waɪd, ˌ-ˈ- *stress shift, British only:* ˌworldwide ˈcoverage
worm wɜːm (US) wɜːrm **-s** -z **-ing** -ɪŋ **-ed** -d
WORM wɜːm (US) wɜːrm
wormcast ˈwɜːm.kɑːst (US) ˈwɜːrm.kæst **-s** -s
worm-eaten ˈwɜːmˌiː.tən (US) ˈwɜːrm-
wormhole ˈwɜːm.həʊl (US) ˈwɜːrm.hoʊl **-s** -z
Worms vɔːmz, wɜːmz (US) wɜːrmz, vɔːrmz
wormwood (W) ˈwɜːm.wʊd (US) ˈwɜːrm- ˌ**Wormwood ˈScrubs**
worm|y ˈwɜː.m|i (US) ˈwɜːr- **-iness** -ɪ.nəs, -ɪ.nɪs
worn (*from* **wear**) wɔːn (US) wɔːrn
worn-out ˌwɔːnˈaʊt (US) ˌwɔːrn- *stress shift:* ˌworn-out ˈshoes
Worple ˈwɔː.pl̩ (US) ˈwɔːr-
Worplesdon ˈwɔː.pl̩z.dən (US) ˈwɔːr-
Worrall ˈwʌr.əl, ˈwɒr- (US) ˈwɔːr-, ˈwɜːr-
worrisome ˈwʌr.ɪ.səm (US) ˈwɜːr.i- **-ly** -li
worr|y ˈwʌr|.i (US) ˈwɜːr- **-ies** -iz **-ying/ly** -i.ɪŋ/li **-ied** -id **-ier/s** -i.əʳ/z (US) -i.ɚ/z ˈ**worry** ˌ**beads**
worrywart ˈwʌr.i.wɔːt (US) ˈwɜːr.i.wɔːrt **-s** -s
Worsborough ˈwɜːz.bər.ə (US) ˈwɜːrz.bɚ.oʊ, -ə
worse wɜːs (US) wɜːrs
worsen ˈwɜː.sən (US) ˈwɜːr- **-s** -z **-ing** -ɪŋ, ˈwɜːs.nɪŋ (US) ˈwɜːrs- **-ed** -d
worse-off ˌwɜːsˈɒf (US) ˌwɜːrsˈɑːf *stress shift:* ˌworse-off ˈcircumstances
Worsfold ˈwɜːs.fəʊld, ˈwɔːz- (US) ˈwɜːrs.foʊld, ˈwɔːrz-
worship (W) ˈwɜː.ʃɪp (US) ˈwɜːr- **-s** -s **-(p)ing** -ɪŋ **-(p)ed** -t **-(p)er/s** -əʳ/z (US) -ɚ/z
worshipful ˈwɜː.ʃɪp.fəl, -fʊl (US) ˈwɜːr- **-ly** -i **-ness** -nəs, -nɪs
Worsley *surname:* ˈwɜː.sli, ˈwɜːz.li (US) ˈwɜːr.sli, ˈwɜːrz.li *place near Manchester:* ˈwɜː.sli (US) ˈwɜːr-
worst wɜːst (US) wɜːrst **-s** -s **-ing** -ɪŋ **-ed** -ɪd
worst-case ˌwɜːstˈkeɪs (US) ˌwɜːrs*t*- *stress shift:* ˌworst-case sceˈnario
Worstead ˈwʊs.tɪd, -təd (US) ˈwʊs-, ˈwɜːr.stɪd, -stəd
worsted *yarn, cloth:* ˈwʊs.tɪd, -təd (US) ˈwʊs-, ˈwɜːr.stɪd, -stəd
worsted (*from* **worst**) ˈwɜː.stɪd (US) ˈwɜːr-
Worsthorne ˈwɜːs.θɔːn (US) ˈwɜːrs.θɔːrn
Worswick ˈwɜː.sɪk (US) ˈwɜːr-
wort wɜːt (US) wɜːrt, wɔːrt **-s** -s
worth (W) wɜːθ (US) wɜːrθ
Worthing ˈwɜː.ðɪŋ (US) ˈwɜːr- **-ton** -tən
worthless ˈwɜːθ.ləs, -lɪs (US) ˈwɜːrθ- **-ly** -li **-ness** -nəs, -nɪs
worthwhile ˌwɜːθˈ*h*waɪl (US) ˌwɜːrθ- *stress shift:* ˌworthwhile ˈprogress
worth|y ˈwɜː.ð|i (US) ˈwɜːr- **-ies** -iz **-ier** -i.əʳ (US) -i.ɚ **-iest** -i.ɪst, -i.əst **-ily** -ɪ.li (US) -əl.i **-iness** -ɪ.nəs, -ɪ.nɪs
Wortley ˈwɜːt.li (US) ˈwɜːrt-
wot wɒt (US) wɑːt
Wotan wəʊ.tæn, ˈvəʊ- (US) ˈvoʊ.tɑːn
wotcha ˈwɒtʃ.ə (US) ˈwɑː.tʃə
wotcher ˈwɒt.ʃəʳ (US) ˈwɑː.tʃɚ
Wotherspoon ˈwɒð.ə.spuːn (US) ˈwɑː.ðɚ-
Wotton ˈwɒt.ən, ˈwʊt- (US) ˈwɑː.tən, ˈwʊt.ən
Note: The place in Buckinghamshire is pronounced /ˈwʊt.ən/.
would (*from* **will**) *strong form:* wʊd *weak forms:* wəd, əd, d
Note: Weak form word. The strong form is used contrastively (e.g. 'I don't know if he would or he wouldn't') and emphatically (e.g. 'I certainly **would**'). The strong form is always used in final position, even when unstressed (e.g. 'I **knew** she would'). The weak forms are used elsewhere. The forms /əd/ and /d/ are usually represented in spelling as 'd (e.g 'John'd do it' /ˈdʒɒn.əd,duː.ɪt (US) ˈdʒɑːn- /; 'I'd do it' /ˈaɪd,duː.ɪt/).
would-be ˈwʊd.bi
wouldn't ˈwʊd.ənt
wouldst wʊdst
wound (*n. v.*) wuːnd **-s** -z **-ing** -ɪŋ **-ed** -ɪd
wound (*from* **wind,** *v.*) waʊnd
wov|e (*from* **weave**) wəʊv (US) woʊv **-en** -ən
wow waʊ **-s** -z **-ing** -ɪŋ **-ed** -d
wowser ˈwaʊ.zəʳ (US) -zɚ **-s** -z
Wozzeck ˈvɒt.sek (US) ˈvɑːt.sek
WP ˌdʌb.l̩.juːˈpiː
WPC ˌdʌb.l̩.juːˌpiːˈsiː, -jʊˌ- (US) -juːˌ-, -jəˌ- **-s** -z *stress shift:* ˌWPC ˈSmith
WRAC ræk, ˌdʌb.l̩.juːˌɑːʳˌeɪˈsiː, -ju- (US) ræk, -juːˌɑːr-, -jəˌ-
wrack ræk **-s** -s **-ing** -ɪŋ **-ed** -t
WRAF ræf; ˌdʌb.l̩.juːˌɑːʳ.eɪˈef (US) ræf; ˌdʌb.l̩.juːˌɑːr.eɪˈef
wraith reɪθ **-s** -s
wrangl|e ˈræŋ.gl̩ **-es** -z **-ing** -ɪŋ, ˈ-glɪŋ **-ed** -d **-er/s** -əʳ/z, ˈ-gləʳ/z (US) ˈ-gl̩.ɚ/z, ˈ-glɚ/z
wrangler (W®) ˈræŋ.gləʳ (US) -glɚ **-s** -z
wrap ræp **-s** -s **-ping/s** -ɪŋ/z **-ped** -t
wraparound ˈræp.ə.raʊnd **-s** -z
wrapper ˈræp.əʳ (US) -ɚ **-s** -z
wrapround ˈræp.raʊnd
wrass|e ræs **-es** -ɪz
wrath rɒθ, rɔːθ (US) ræθ, rɑːθ
Wrath *Cape:* rɔːθ, rɑːθ, ræθ (US) ræθ, rɑːθ
wrathful ˈrɒθ.fəl, ˈrɔːθ-, -fʊl (US) ˈræθ-, ˈrɑːθ- **-ly** -i **-ness** -nəs, -nɪs
Wratislaw ˈræt.ɪ.slɔː (US) ˈræt̬.ɪ.slɑː, -slɔː
Wraxall ˈræk.sɔːl
Wray reɪ
wreak riːk **-s** -s **-ing** -ɪŋ **-ed** -t
wrea|th riː|θ **-ths** -ðz, -θs
wreath|e riːð **-es** -z **-ing** -ɪŋ **-ed** -d
Wreay reɪ *locally:* rɪə
wreck rek **-s** -s **-ing** -ɪŋ **-ed** -t **-er/s** -əʳ/z (US) -ɚ/z
wreckag|e ˈrek.ɪdʒ **-es** -ɪz
Wrekin ˈriː.kɪn
wren (W) ren **-s** -z
wrench ren*t*ʃ **-es** -ɪz **-ing** -ɪŋ **-ed** -t
Wrenn ren
wrest rest **-s** -s **-ing** -ɪŋ **-ed** -ɪd
wrestl|e ˈres.l̩ **-es** -z **-ing** -ɪŋ, ˈres.lɪŋ **-ed** -d **-er/s** -əʳ/z, ˈres.ləʳ/z (US) ˈres.l̩.ɚ/z, ˈres.lɚ/z
wretch retʃ **-es** -ɪz
wretched ˈretʃ.ɪd **-ly** -li **-ness** -nəs, -nɪs
Wrexham ˈrek.səm
wriggl|e ˈrɪg.l̩ **-es** -z **-ing** -ɪŋ, ˈrɪg.lɪŋ **-ed** -d **-er/s** -əʳ/z, ˈrɪg.ləʳ/z (US) ˈrɪg.l̩.ɚ/z, ˈrɪg.lɚ/z
wright (W) raɪt **-s** -s
Wrigley ˈrɪg.li
wring rɪŋ **-s** -z **-ing** -ɪŋ **-er/s** -əʳ/z (US) -ɚ/z **wrung** rʌŋ
wringing-wet ˌrɪŋ.ɪŋˈwet *stress shift:* ˌwringing-wet ˈcloth

wrinkl|e 'rɪŋ.kl̩ **-es** -z **-ing** -ɪŋ, 'rɪŋ.klɪŋ **-ed** -d
wrinkl|y 'rɪŋ.kl|i **-ies** -iz
Wriothesley 'raɪəθ.sli
wrist rɪst **-s** -s
wristband 'rɪst.bænd **-s** -z
wristlet 'rɪs*t*.lɪt, -lət **-s** -s
wristwatch 'rɪs*t*.wɒtʃ ⓤⓢ -wɑːtʃ **-es** -ɪz
wristy 'rɪs.ti
writ rɪt **-s** -s
writ (= **written**) rɪt
writ|e raɪt **-es** -s **-ing/s** -ɪŋ/z ⓤⓢ 'raɪ.t̬ɪŋ/z **wrote** rəʊt ⓤⓢ roʊt **written** 'rɪt.ᵊn **writer/s** 'raɪ.təʳ/z ⓤⓢ 'raɪ.t̬ɚ/z ˌ**writer's** '**cramp**
writh|e raɪð **-es** -z **-ing** -ɪŋ **-ed** -d
writing 'raɪ.tɪŋ ⓤⓢ -t̬ɪŋ **-s** -z **see the** ˌ**writing on the** '**wall**
writing-cas|e 'raɪ.tɪŋ.keɪs ⓤⓢ -t̬ɪŋ- **-es** -ɪz
writing-paper 'raɪ.tɪŋˌpeɪ.pəʳ ⓤⓢ -t̬ɪŋˌpeɪ.pɚ
written-off ˌrɪt.ᵊn'ɒf ⓤⓢ -'ɑːf
Writtle 'rɪt.l̩ ⓤⓢ 'rɪt̬-
WRNS (*abbrev. for* **Women's Royal Navy Service**) renz; ˌdʌb.l̩.juːˌɑːʳ.en'es ⓤⓢ renz; ˌdʌb.l̩.juːˌɑːr.en'es
Wroclaw 'vrɒt.slɑːf, -slæf, -swɑːf ⓤⓢ 'vrɑːt.slɑːf
wrong (W) rɒŋ ⓤⓢ rɑːŋ, rɔːŋ **-s** -z **-ly** -li **-ness** -nəs, -nɪs **-ing** -ɪŋ **-ed** -d
wrong-doer 'rɒŋˌduː.əʳ, ˌ-'-- ⓤⓢ 'rɑːŋˌduː.ɚ, 'rɔːŋ- **-s** -z
wrong-doing 'rɒŋˌduː.ɪŋ, ˌ-'-- ⓤⓢ 'rɑːŋˌduː-, 'rɔːŋ-
wrong|-foot ˌrɒŋ|'fʊt ⓤⓢ ˌrɑːŋ-, ˌrɔːŋ- **-foots** -'fʊts **-footing** -'fʊt.ɪŋ ⓤⓢ -'fʊt̬.ɪŋ **-footed** -'fʊt.ɪd ⓤⓢ -'fʊt̬.ɪd
wrongful 'rɒŋ.fᵊl, -fʊl ⓤⓢ 'rɑːŋ-, 'rɔːŋ- **-ly** -i **-ness** -nəs, -nɪs
wrongheaded ˌrɒŋ'hed.ɪd ⓤⓢ ˌrɑːŋ-, ˌrɔːŋ-, '-ˌ-- **-ly** -li **-ness** -nəs, -nɪs
wrote (*from* **write**) rəʊt ⓤⓢ roʊt
wroth rəʊθ, rɔːθ, rɒθ ⓤⓢ rɔːθ, rɑːθ
Wrotham 'ruː.təm ⓤⓢ -t̬əm
Wrottesley 'rɒt.sli ⓤⓢ 'rɑːt-
wrought rɔːt ⓤⓢ rɑːt, rɔːt
wrought-iron ˌrɔːt'aɪən ⓤⓢ ˌrɑːt'aɪɚn, ˌrɔːt- *stress shift:* ˌwrought-iron 'gate
Wroughton 'rɔː.tᵊn ⓤⓢ 'rɑː-, 'rɔː-
Wroxham 'rɒk.səm ⓤⓢ 'rɑːk-
wrung (*from* **wring**) rʌŋ
W.R.V.S. ˌdʌb.l̩.juːˌɑːˌviː'es, -jʊˌ- ⓤⓢ -juːˌɑːrˌ-, -jəˌ-
wry raɪ **wrier, wryer** 'raɪ.əʳ ⓤⓢ -ɚ **wriest, wryest** 'raɪ.ɪst, -əst **wryly** 'raɪ.li **wryness** 'raɪ.nəs, -nɪs
wryneck 'raɪ.nek **-s** -s
Wrythe raɪð
WSW (*abbrev. for* **west southwest**) ˌwest.saʊθ'west *nautical pronunciation:* -saʊ'-
wt (*abbrev. for* **weight**) weɪt
Wuhan ˌwuː'hæn ⓤⓢ -'hɑːn
Wulf wʊlf
Wulfila 'wʊl.fɪ.lə
Wulfstan 'wʊlf.stən ⓤⓢ -stæn, -stɑːn
wunder|kind 'wʊn.də|.kɪnd, 'vʊn- ⓤⓢ -dɚ|.kɪnt, 'wʌn- **-kinder** -ˌkɪn.dəʳ ⓤⓢ -ˌkɪn.dɚ
Wurlitzer 'wɜː.lɪt.səʳ, -lət- ⓤⓢ 'wɜːr.lət.sɚ **-s** -z
Württemberg 'vɜː.təm.beəg; 'wɜː.təm.bɜːg ⓤⓢ 'wɜːr.t̬əm.bɜːrg; 'vɜːr.təm.berk
Würzburg 'vɜːts.beəg; 'wɜːts.bɜːg ⓤⓢ 'wɜːrts.bɜːrg; 'vɜːrts.burk
wuss wʊs
Wuthering 'wʌð.ᵊr.ɪŋ ˌ**Wuthering** '**Heights**
W.Va. (*abbrev. for* **West Virginia**) ˌwest.və'dʒɪn.jə, -vɜː'-, -i.ə ⓤⓢ -vɚ'-
WVS ˌdʌb.l̩.juːˌviː'es, -jʊˌ- ⓤⓢ -juːˌ-, -jəˌ-
Wyandotte 'waɪən.dɒt ⓤⓢ -dɑːt **-s** -s
Wyat(t) waɪət
Wych waɪtʃ, wɪtʃ
Wycherley 'wɪtʃ.ᵊl.i ⓤⓢ -ɚ.li
wych-hazel 'wɪtʃˌheɪ.zᵊl, ˌ-'-- ⓤⓢ 'wɪtʃˌheɪ- **-s** -z
Wycliffe, Wyclif 'wɪk.lɪf
Wycliffite 'wɪk.lɪ.faɪt **-s** -s
Wycombe 'wɪk.əm
Wye waɪ
Wygram 'waɪ.grəm
Wykeham 'wɪk.əm **-ist/s** -ɪst/s
Wyld(e) waɪld
Wyl(l)ie 'waɪ.li
Wyman 'waɪ.mən
Wymondham *in Norfolk:* 'wɪm.ən.dəm *locally:* 'wɪn.dəm *in Leicestershire:* 'waɪ.mən.dəm
Wyndham 'wɪn.dəm
Wynn(e) wɪn
Wynyard 'wɪn.jəd, -jɑːd ⓤⓢ -jɚd, -jɑːrd
Wyo. (*abbrev. for* **Wyoming**) waɪ'əʊ.mɪŋ ⓤⓢ -'oʊ-
Wyoming waɪ'əʊ.mɪŋ ⓤⓢ -'oʊ-
WYSIWYG 'wɪz.i.wɪg
Wyss waɪs
Wystan 'wɪs.tən
Wytch Farm ˌwɪtʃ'fɑːm ⓤⓢ -'fɑːrm
Wytham 'waɪ.təm ⓤⓢ -t̬əm
Wythenshawe 'wɪð.ᵊn.ʃɔː ⓤⓢ -ʃɑː, -ʃɔː
wyvern (W) 'waɪ.vən, -vɜːn ⓤⓢ -vɚn, -vɜːrn **-s** -z

X

x (**X**) eks **-'s** -ɪz
Xanadu ˈzæn.ə.duː, ˌ--ˈ- Ⓤⓢ ˈzæn.ə.duː, -djuː, ˌ--ˈ-
Xanthe ˈzænt.θi
Xanthipp|e zæntˈθɪp|.i, zænˈtɪp- Ⓤⓢ zænˈtɪp- **-us** -əs
Xanthus ˈzænt.θəs
Xantia® ˈzæn.ti.ə Ⓤⓢ zænˈtiː-
Xavier ˈzæv.i.əʳ, -eɪ, ˈzeɪ.vi.əʳ, ˈ-vjəʳ Ⓤⓢ ˈzeɪ.vjɚ, ˈzæv.jɚ, -i.ɚ
X-certificate ˌeks.səˈtɪf.ɪ.kət, -sɜːˈ-, ˈ-ə-, -kɪt Ⓤⓢ -sɚˈ- **-s** -s
xebec ˈziː.bek **-s** -s
Xenia ˈzen.i.ə, ˈksen-, ˈziː.ni-, ˈksiː-, ˈ-njə Ⓤⓢ ˈziː.njə, ˈ-ni.ə
xeno- zen.əʊ-, ziː.nəʊ-; zɪˈnɒ- Ⓤⓢ zen.oʊ-, ziː.noʊ-, -nə-; zɪˈnɑː-
Note: Prefix. Normally either takes primary or secondary stress on the first syllable, e.g. **xenophobe** /ˈzen.əʊ.fəʊb Ⓤⓢ -ə.foʊb/, **xenophobia** /ˌzen.əʊˈfəʊ.bi.ə Ⓤⓢ -əˈfoʊ-/, or primary stress on the second syllable, e.g. **xenogamy** /zɪˈnɒg.ə.mi Ⓤⓢ -ˈnɑː.gə-/.
xenogamy zɪˈnɒg.ə.mi Ⓤⓢ -ˈnɑː.gə-
xenon ˈziː.nɒn Ⓤⓢ -nɑːn, ˈzen.ɑːn
xenophobe ˈzen.əʊ.fəʊb Ⓤⓢ -ə.foʊb, ˈziː.nə-, -noʊ- **-s** -z
xenophobia ˌzen.əʊˈfəʊ.bi.ə Ⓤⓢ -əˈfoʊ-, ˌziː.nəˈ-, -noʊˈ-
xenophobic ˌzen.əʊˈfəʊ.bɪk Ⓤⓢ -əˈfoʊ-, ˌziː.nə-, -noʊ- *stress shift:* ˌxenophobic ˈsentiment
Xenophon ˈzen.ə.fᵊn Ⓤⓢ -fən, -fɑːn
xerography zɪəˈrɒg.rə.fi, zerˈɒg- Ⓤⓢ zɪˈrɑː.grə
xerox (**X®**) (*n. v.*) ˈzɪə.rɒks Ⓤⓢ ˈzɪr.ɑːks, ˈziː.rɑːks **-es** -ɪz **-ing** -ɪŋ **-ed** -t
Xerxes ˈzɜːk.siːz Ⓤⓢ ˈzɜːrk-
Xhosa ˈkɔː.sə, ˈkəʊ-, -zə Ⓤⓢ ˈkoʊ.sɑː, -zɑː
xi saɪ, ksaɪ Ⓤⓢ zaɪ, saɪ **-'s** -z
Xmas ˈkrɪst.məs, ˈeks.məs Ⓤⓢ ˈkrɪs-
X-rated ˈeksˌreɪ.tɪd Ⓤⓢ -t̬ɪd
X-ray ˈeks.reɪ, ˌ-ˈ- Ⓤⓢ ˈek.sreɪ **-s** -z **-ing** -ɪŋ **-ed** -d
xu suː
xylem ˈzaɪ.ləm, -lem Ⓤⓢ ˈzaɪ-
xylene ˈzaɪ.liːn
xylograph ˈzaɪ.ləʊ.grɑːf, -græf Ⓤⓢ -loʊ.græf, -lə- **-s** -s
xylograph|y zaɪˈlɒg.rə.f|i Ⓤⓢ -ˈlɑː.grə- **-er/s** -əʳ/z Ⓤⓢ -ɚ/z
xylonite ˈzaɪ.lə.naɪt
xylophone ˈzaɪ.lə.fəʊn Ⓤⓢ -foʊn **-s** -z
xylose ˈzaɪ.ləʊs, -ləʊz Ⓤⓢ -loʊs
xyster ˈzɪs.təʳ Ⓤⓢ -tɚ

Y

y (Y) waɪ **-'s** -z
yacht jɒt (US) jɑːt **-s** -s **-ing** -ɪŋ (US) 'jɑː.t̬ɪŋ **-ed** -ɪd (US) 'jɑː.t̬ɪd
yachts|man 'jɒts|.mən (US) 'jɑːts- **-men** -mən **-woman** -ˌwʊm.ən **-women** -ˌwɪm.ɪn
yack jæk **-s** -s
yah jɑː
yahoo (Y) *(interj.)* jə'huː, jɑː- **-s** -z *(n.)* 'jɑː.huː (US) 'jɑː-, 'jeɪ-
Note: The pronunciation for the noun is also suitable for the characters in Swift's **Gulliver's Travels**.
Yahveh 'jɑː.veɪ, -və, jɑː'veɪ (US) 'jɑː.veɪ
Yahweh 'jɑː.weɪ
yak jæk **-s** -s
yakka 'jæk.ə
Yakutsk jæk'ʊtsk, jɑː'kʊtsk, jə- (US) jɑː-
yakuza 'jæk.ʊ.zɑː (US) 'jɑː.kʊ- **-s** -z
Yalding *surname:* 'jæl.dɪŋ *place name:* 'jɔːl.dɪŋ (US) 'jɑːl-, 'jɔːl-
Yale jeɪl
y'all jɑːl
Yalta 'jæl.tə, 'jɔːl-, 'jɒl- (US) 'jɑːl.t̬ə, 'jɔːl-, -tə
yam jæm **-s** -z
Yamaha 'jæm.ə.hɑː, -hə (US) 'jɑː.mə-
Yamamoto ˌjæm.ə'məʊ.təʊ (US) ˌjɑː.mə'moʊ.t̬oʊ, -toʊ
yamm|er 'jæm|.əʳ (US) -ɚ **-ers** -əz (US) -ɚz **-ering** -ᵊr.ɪŋ **-ed** -əd (US) -ɚd
yang jæŋ (US) jæŋ, jɑːŋ
Yangtze, **Yangtse**, **Yangzi** 'jæŋ*k*t.si (US) 'jæŋ*k*t-, 'jɑːŋ*k*t-
yank (Y) jæŋk **-s** -s **-ing** -ɪŋ **-ed** -t
Yankee 'jæŋ.ki **-s** -z
Yaoundé jɑː'ʊn.deɪ, -'uːn- (US) ˌjɑː.ʊn'deɪ
yap jæp **-s** -s **-ping** -ɪŋ **-ped** -t
Yap jæp (US) jɑːp, jæp
yard jɑːd (US) jɑːrd **-s** -z **'yard ˌsale**
yardage 'jɑː.dɪdʒ (US) 'jɑːr- **-s** -ɪz
yardarm 'jɑːd.ɑːm (US) 'jɑːrd.ɑːrm **-s** -z
yardbird 'jɑːd.bɜːd (US) 'jɑːrd.bɜːrd **-s** -z
Yardley 'jɑːd.li (US) 'jɑːrd-
yardstick 'jɑːd.stɪk (US) 'jɑːrd- **-s** -s
Yare *in Norfolk:* jeəʳ (US) jer *in the Isle of Wight:* jɑːʳ (US) jɑːr
Yarm jɑːm (US) jɑːrm
yarmelke 'jʌm.ʊl.kə, 'jɑː.mʊl-, -mᵊl- (US) 'jɑːr.məl-, 'jɑː- **-s** -z
Yarmouth 'jɑː.məθ (US) 'jɑːr-
yarmulke, yarmulka 'jʌm.ʊl.kə, 'jɑː.mʊl-, -mᵊl- (US) 'jɑːr.məl-, 'jɑː- **-s** -z
yarn jɑːn (US) jɑːrn **-s** -z **-ing** -ɪŋ **-ed** -d
Yaroslavl ˌjær.əʊ'slɑː.vᵊl (US) ˌjɑːr.oʊ'slɑː.vᵊl, -ə'-
yarrow (Y) 'jær.əʊ (US) 'jer.oʊ, 'jær-
yashmak 'jæʃ.mæk (US) 'jɑːʃ.mɑːk, 'jæʃ.mæk **-s** -s
Yasmin 'jæz.mɪn
Yasser 'jæs.əʳ (US) -ɚ, 'jɑː.sɚ
yataghan 'jæt.ə.gən (US) -gæn, -gən **-s** -z
Yate jeɪt **-s** -s
Yately 'jeɪt.li
Yatman 'jæt.mən
Yatton 'jæt.ᵊn
yaw jɔː (US) jɑː, jɔː **-s** -z **-ing** -ɪŋ **-ed** -d
Yaweh 'jɑː.weɪ
yawl jɔːl (US) jɑːl, jɔːl **-s** -z
yawn jɔːn (US) jɑːn, jɔːn **-s** -z **-ing/ly** -ɪŋ/li **-ed** -d
yaws jɔːz (US) jɑːz, jɔːz
Yaxley 'jæk.sli
yclept ɪ'klept (US) i-
yd *(abbrev. for* **yard***) singular:* jɑːd (US) jɑːrd *plural:* jɑːdz (US) jɑːrdz
ye *you. Normal form:* jiː *occasional weak form:* ji
Note: The weak form is rarely used, and only in imitation of archaic or dialect sayings such as 'Sit ye down' /ˌsɪt.ji'daʊn/.
ye *the:* jiː
Note: As a pronunciation of the definite article, this is rarely used except in joking. It is a mistake resulting from reading the Old English letter "thorn" (which represented 'th' sounds) as a 'y', which it resembles.
yea jeɪ
Yeading 'jed.ɪŋ
Yeadon 'jiː.dᵊn
yeah jeə (US) jeə, jæə
Note: Aside from the examples given for American English, there are many possibilities here, another being /jɑː/.
Yeames jiːmz
yean jiːn **-s** -z **-ing** -ɪŋ **-ed** -d
year jɪəʳ, jɜːʳ (US) jɪr **-s** -z **-ly** -li **ˌyear in (and) ˌyear 'out**
yearbook 'jɪə.bʊk, 'jɜː- (US) 'jɪr- **-s** -s
yearling 'jɪə.lɪŋ, 'jɜː- (US) 'jɪr- **-s** -z
yearlong ˌjɪə'lɒŋ, ˌjɜː- (US) 'jɪr.lɑːŋ, -lɔːŋ, ˌ-'- *stress shift, British only:* ˌyearlong 'truce
yearn jɜːn (US) jɜːrn **-s** -z **-ing/s** -ɪŋ/z **-ed** -d
yeast jiːst **-y** -i **-iness** -ɪ.nəs, -ɪ.nɪs
Yeates jeɪts
Yeatman 'jiːt.mən, 'jeɪt-, 'jet-
Yeats jeɪts
Yeddo 'jed.əʊ (US) -oʊ
Yehudi je'huː.di, jɪ-, jə-
yell (Y) jel **-s** -z **-ing** -ɪŋ **-ed** -d
yellow 'jel.əʊ (US) -oʊ **-s** -z **-ing** -ɪŋ **-ed** -d **-y** -i **ˌyellow 'fever** ; **ˌyellow 'line** ; **ˌYellow 'Pages** (US) **'Yellow ˌPages**; **ˌyellow 'peril**; **ˌyellow ˌbrick 'road**
yellowhammer 'jel.əʊˌhæm.əʳ (US) -oʊˌhæm.ɚ **-s** -z
yellowish 'jel.əʊ.ɪʃ (US) -oʊ- **-ness** -nəs, -nɪs
yellowjacket 'jel.əʊˌdʒæk.ɪt (US) -oʊ- **-s** -s
Yellowknife 'jel.əʊ.naɪf (US) -oʊ-
yellowness 'jel.əʊ.nəs, -nɪs (US) -oʊ-
Yellowstone 'jel.əʊ.stəʊn, -stən (US) -oʊ.stoʊn
yelp jelp **-s** -s **-ing** -ɪŋ **-ed** -t
Yeltsin 'jelt.sɪn
Yemen 'jem.ən, -en (US) -ən, 'jeɪ.mən **-i** -i **-is** -iz
Yemenite 'jem.ən.aɪt (US) 'jem-, 'jeɪ.mən- **-s** -s
yen jen **-s** -z
Yeo jəʊ (US) joʊ
Yeoburgh 'jɑː.bᵊr.ə
yeo|man 'jəʊ|.mən (US) 'joʊ- **-men** -mən **-manly** -mən.li
yeomanry 'jəʊ.mən.ri (US) 'joʊ-
Yeomans 'jəʊ.mənz (US) 'joʊ-
Yeovil 'jəʊ.vɪl (US) 'joʊ-
yep jep
yer jeə, jɜː (US) je
Note: This is a written or spoken informal form of **yes** in British English. The **r** in the spelling is not pronounced in American English forms and is not linking in British English.
Yerby 'jɜː.bi (US) 'jɜːr-
Yerevan ˌjer.ə'vɑːn
Yerkes 'jɜː.kiːz (US) 'jɜːr-
yes jes
yes|-man 'jes|.mæn **-men** -men
yesterday 'jes.tə.deɪ, ˌ--'-, -di (US) -tɚ-
yesteryear 'jes.tə.jɪəʳ, ˌ--'- (US) -tɚ.jɪr
yet jet
Yetholm 'jet.əm (US) 'jet̬-
yeti 'jet.i (US) 'jet̬- **-s** -z
Yevtushenko ˌjev.tʊ'ʃeŋ.kəʊ, -tuː'- (US) -koʊ
yew juː **-s** -z
Y-Front® 'waɪ.frʌnt **-s** -s
Yg(g)drasil 'ɪg.drə.sɪl, ɪg'dræs.ᵊl (US) 'ɪg.drə.sɪl
yid jɪd
Yiddish 'jɪd.ɪʃ
yield jiːld **-s** -z **-ing/ly** -ɪŋ/li **-ed** -ɪd
yin jɪn
yippee jɪ'piː (US) 'jɪp.iː
Yitzhak 'jɪt.saːk, -sæk
ylang-ylang ˌiː.læŋ.iː'læŋ (US) -lɑːŋ'iː.lɑːŋ

YMCA ˌwaɪ.em.siːˈeɪ
Ynys Mon ˌʌn.ɪsˈmɔːn
yo jəʊ ⓊⓈ joʊ
yob jɒb ⓊⓈ jɑːb **-s** -z
yobbish ˈjɒb.ɪʃ ⓊⓈ ˈjɑː.bɪʃ **-ly** -li **-ness** -nəs, -nɪs
yobbo ˈjɒb.əʊ ⓊⓈ ˈjɑː.boʊ **-s** -z
yod jɒd ⓊⓈ jɑːd **-s** -z
yodel ˈjəʊ.dəl ⓊⓈ ˈjoʊ- **-s** -z **-(l)ing** -ɪŋ, ˈjəʊd.lɪŋ ⓊⓈ ˈjoʊd- **-(l)ed** -d **-ler/s** -əʳ/z ⓊⓈ -ɚ/z
yog|a ˈjəʊ.g|ə ⓊⓈ ˈjoʊ- **-ic** -ɪk
yogh(o)urt ˈjɒg.ət, ˈjəʊ.gət, -gɜːt ⓊⓈ ˈjoʊ.gɚt
yog|i ˈjəʊ.g|i ⓊⓈ ˈjoʊ- **-is** -iz **-ism** -ɪ.zəm ˌ**Yogi** ˈ**Bear**, ˈ**Yogi** ˌ**Bear**
yogic ˈjəʊ.gɪk ⓊⓈ ˈjoʊ-
yogurt ˈjɒg.ət, ˈjəʊ.gət, -gɜːt ⓊⓈ ˈjoʊ.gɚt **-s** -s
Yohji ˈjəʊ.dʒi, ˈjɒdʒ.i ⓊⓈ ˈjoʊ.dʒi
yoicks jɔɪks
yok|e jəʊk ⓊⓈ joʊk **-es** -s **-ing** -ɪŋ **-ed** -t
yokel ˈjəʊ.kəl ⓊⓈ ˈjoʊ- **-s** -z
Yokohama ˌjəʊ.kəʊˈhɑː.mə ⓊⓈ ˌjoʊ.kəˈ-
Yolanda, Yolande jəʊˈlæn.də ⓊⓈ joʊˈlɑːn-, -ˈlæn-
yolk jəʊk ⓊⓈ joʊk **-s** -s **-y** -i
Yom Kippur ˌjɒm.kɪˈpʊəʳ; -ˈkɪp.əʳ ⓊⓈ ˌjɑːm'kɪp.ɚ, ˌjɔːm-; -kɪˈpʊr
yomp jɒmp ⓊⓈ jɑːmp **-s** -s **-ing** -ɪŋ **-ed** -t **-er/s** -əʳ/z ⓊⓈ -ɚ/z
yon jɒn ⓊⓈ jɑːn
yond jɒnd ⓊⓈ jɑːnd
yonder ˈjɒn.dəʳ ⓊⓈ ˈjɑːn.dɚ
Yonge jʌŋ
Yonkers ˈjɒŋ.kəz ⓊⓈ ˈjɑːŋ.kɚz, ˈjɔːŋ-
yonks jɒŋks ⓊⓈ jɑːŋks, jɔːŋks
Yorba Linda ˌjɔː.bəˈlɪn.də ⓊⓈ ˌjɔːr-
yore jɔːʳ ⓊⓈ jɔːr
Yorick ˈjɒr.ɪk ⓊⓈ ˈjɔːr-
York jɔːk ⓊⓈ jɔːrk
Yorke jɔːk ⓊⓈ jɔːrk
yorker ˈjɔː.kəʳ ⓊⓈ ˈjɔːr.kɚ **-s** -z
Yorkist ˈjɔː.kɪst ⓊⓈ ˈjɔːr- **-s** -s
Yorks. (*abbrev. for* **Yorkshire**) jɔːks ⓊⓈ jɔːrks
Yorkshire ˈjɔːk.ʃəʳ, -ˌʃɪəʳ ⓊⓈ ˈjɔːrk.ʃɚ, -ˌʃɪr ˌ**Yorkshire** ˈ**pudding** ; ˌ**Yorkshire** ˈ**terrier**
Yorkshire|man ˈjɔːk.ʃə.|mən ⓊⓈ ˈjɔːrk.ʃɚ- **-men** -mən, -men **-woman** -ˌwʊm.ən **-women** -ˌwɪm.ɪn
Yorktown ˈjɔːk.taʊn ⓊⓈ ˈjɔːrk-
Yoruba ˈjɒr.ʊ.bə, ˈjəʊ.rʊ- ⓊⓈ ˈjɔːr.ə.bə, ˈjoʊ.rə-, -ruː-, -bɑː
Yosemite jəʊˈsem.ɪ.ti ⓊⓈ joʊˈsem.ə.ţi **Yo**ˌ**semite** ˌ**National** ˈ**Park** ; **Yo**ˌ**semite** ˈ**Sam**
Yossarian jɒsˈeə.ri.ən ⓊⓈ joʊˈser.i-, -ˈsɑːr-
Yost jəʊst ⓊⓈ joʊst **-s** -s
you *strong form:* juː *weak forms:* ju, jə
Note: Weak form word. The strong form is used contrastively (e.g. 'Will it be you, or me?') or emphatically (e.g. 'It was **you** that broke it'). Elsewhere the weak forms are used: in British English, /ju/ is the form found before vowels and in final position (e.g. 'You ought' /juˈɔːt ⓊⓈ -ɑːt/; 'Thank you' /ˈθæŋk.ju/), while /jə/ is only used before consonants (e.g. 'if you can' /ɪf.jəˈkæn/); in American English, /jə/ predominates in both environments. The strong form is also found in unstressed syllables. Sometimes when 'you' is weakly stressed and is preceded by a word normally ending in /d/, the two words are joined closely together as if they formed a single word with the affricate sound /dʒ/ linking the two parts. Thus 'did you' is often pronounced /ˈdɪdʒ.u/, and 'behind you' /bɪˈhaɪn.dʒu/. Similarly when the preceding word normally ends in /t/ (e.g. 'hurt you') it is sometimes pronounced /ˈhɜː.tʃu ⓊⓈ ˈhɜːr-/ and 'don't you know' as /ˌdəʊn.tʃəˈnəʊ ⓊⓈ ˌdoʊn.tʃəˈnoʊ/.
you-all juˈɔːl ⓊⓈ juˈɔːl, jɔːl, jɑːl
Youens ˈjuː.ɪnz
Youghal *near Cork:* jɔːl *on Lake Derg:* ˈjɒk.əl, ˈjɒx- ⓊⓈ ˈjɑː.kəl
Youmans ˈjuː.mənz
young (Y) jʌŋ **-er** -gəʳ ⓊⓈ -gɚ **-est** -gɪst, -gəst
Younger ˈjʌŋ.əʳ, -gəʳ ⓊⓈ -gɚ, -ɚ
Younghusband ˈjʌŋˌhʌz.bənd
youngish ˈjʌŋ.ɪʃ, -gɪʃ
Youngman ˈjʌŋ.mən
youngster ˈjʌŋ*k*.stəʳ ⓊⓈ -stɚ **-s** -z
younker ˈjʌŋ.kəʳ ⓊⓈ -kɚ **-s** -z
your *normal forms:* jɔːʳ, jʊəʳ ⓊⓈ jʊr, jɔːr *occasional weak forms:* jəʳ ⓊⓈ jɚ
Note: Weak form word. The strong form /jʊə ⓊⓈ jʊr/ or /jɔː ⓊⓈ jɔːr/ is usually used for emphasis (e.g. 'It's **your** fault') or contrast (e.g. 'with **your** looks and **my** brains'). This pronunciation is quite common also in weakly stressed positions in careful speech. In British English, the weak form is /jə/ before consonants (e.g. 'take your time' /ˌteɪk.jəˈtaɪm/) and /jər/ before vowels (e.g. 'on your own' /ɒn.jərˈəʊn/); in American English, /jɚ/ is used in both cases.
you're (= **you are**) *strong forms:* jɔːʳ, jʊəʳ ⓊⓈ jʊr, jɔːr *occasional weak forms:* jəʳ ⓊⓈ jɚ
Note: The use of strong and weak forms follows that of **your**.
yours jɔːz, jʊəz ⓊⓈ jʊrz, jɔːrz
yoursel|f jɔːˈsel|f, jʊə-, jə- ⓊⓈ jʊr-, jɔːr-, jɚ- **-ves** -vz
you|th juː|θ **-ths** -ðz ˈ**youth** ˌ**club** ; ˈ**youth** ˌ**hostel** ; ˌ**youth** ˈ**training** ˌ**scheme**
youthful ˈjuːθ.fəl, -fʊl **-ly** -i **-ness** -nəs, -nɪs
you've (= **you have**) *normal form:* juːv *occasional weak forms:* jʊv, jəv
yowl jaʊl
yo-yo ˈjəʊ.jəʊ ⓊⓈ ˈjoʊ.joʊ **-s** -z **-ing** -ɪŋ **-ed** -d
Ypres *in Belgium:* ˈiː.prə, ˈiː.pəz *sometimes facetiously:* ˈaɪ.pəz, ˈwaɪ.pəz ⓊⓈ ˈiː.prə
Ypres *tower at Rye:* ˈiː.prə, ˈiː.preɪ, ˈwaɪ.pəz ⓊⓈ ˈiː.prə
Note: The 'Ypres Castle', a public house near by, is called locally the /ˈwaɪ.pəz/.
Yser ˈiː.zəʳ ⓊⓈ -zɚ, -zer
Ysolde ɪˈzɒl.də ⓊⓈ -ˈzoʊl-
Ystradgynlais ˌʌs.trædˈgʌn.laɪs, -trəd'-
Ystwyth ˈʌs.twɪθ
Ythan ˈaɪ.θən
YTS ˌwaɪ.tiːˈes
ytterbium ɪˈtɜː.bi.əm ⓊⓈ -ˈtɜːr-
yttrium ˈɪt.ri.əm
Yucatan ˌjuː.kəˈtɑːn, ˌjʊk.əˈ-, -ˈtæn ⓊⓈ ˌjuː.kəˈtæn, -ˈtɑːn
yucca ˈjʌk.ə **-s** -z
yuck jʌk **-y** -i **-ier** -i.əʳ ⓊⓈ -i.ɚ **-iest** -i.ɪst, -i.əst
Yugoslav ˈjuː.gəʊ.slɑːv, ˌ--ˈ- ⓊⓈ ˈjuː.goʊ.slɑːv, -gə- **-s** -z
Yugoslavi|a ˌjuː.gəʊˈslɑː.vi|.ə ⓊⓈ -goʊˈ- **-an** -ən
Yuill ˈjuː.ɪl
yuk jʌk **-ky** -i
Yukon ˈjuː.kɒn ⓊⓈ -kɑːn
yule (Y) juːl ˈ**yule** ˌ**log**
yuletide (Y) ˈjuːl.taɪd
yumm|y ˈjʌm|.i **-ier** -i.əʳ ⓊⓈ -i.ɚ **-iest** -i.ɪst, -i.əst
Yum-Yum ˌjʌmˈjʌm
Yunnan jʊˈnæn
yuppie ˈjʌp.i **-s** -z
yupp|y, yupp|ie ˈjʌp|.i **-ies** -iz
yurt jɜːt, jʊət ⓊⓈ jʊrt, jɜːrt **-s** -s
Yussuf ˈjʊs.ʊf, -əf
Yves iːv
Yvette ɪˈvet, iːˈ- ⓊⓈ iː-
Yvonne ɪˈvɒn, iːˈ- ⓊⓈ iːˈvɑːn
Ywain ɪˈweɪn, iːˈ-
YWCA ˌwaɪˌdʌb.l̩.juː.siːˈeɪ, -ju- ⓊⓈ -juː-, -jə-

Z

z (Z) zed US ziː **-'s** -z
zabaglione ˌzæb.ᵊl'jəʊ.ni, -neɪ, -æl'- US ˌzɑː.bᵊl'joʊ-, -bɑːl'-, -neɪ
Zacchaeus zæk'iː.əs, zə'kiː-
Zachariah ˌzæk.ᵊr'aɪ.ə US -ə'raɪ-
Zacharias ˌzæk.ᵊr'aɪ.əs, -æs US -ə'raɪ-
Zachary 'zæk.ᵊr.i
Zadar 'zæd.ɑːʳ US 'zɑː.dɑːr
Zadok 'zeɪ.dɒk US -dɑːk
Zagreb 'zɑː.greb, 'zæg.reb; zɑː'greb US 'zɑː.greb
zaire zaɪ'ɪəʳ, zɑː- US -'ɪr
Zaïr|e, Zair|e zaɪ'ɪəʳ, zɑː- US -'ɪr **-ean** -i.ən
Zambezi, Zambesi zæm'biː.zi
Zambi|a 'zæm.bi|.ə **-an** -ən
Zamboni® zæm'bəʊ.ni US -'boʊ-
Zamenhof 'zɑː.mᵊn.hɒf US -hɑːf
Zangwill 'zæŋ.gwɪl US -gwɪl, -wɪl
zan|y 'zeɪ.n|i **-ies** -iz **-ier** -i.əʳ US -i.ɚ **-iest** -i.ɪst, -i.əst
Zanzibar 'zæn.zɪ.bɑːʳ, ˌ--'- US -zə.bɑːr
zap zæp **-s** -s **-ping** -ɪŋ **-ped** -t **-per/s** -əʳ/z US -ɚ/z
Zaporozhye ˌzæp.ə'rəʊ.ʒeɪ, -ɔː'- US ˌzɑː.pə'roʊ.ʒə
Zapotek 'zæp.ə.tek, 'zɑː.pə-, ˌ--'- US 'zɑː.pə.tek, 'sɑː- **-s** -s
Zappa 'zæp.ə
zapp|y 'zæp|.i **-ier** -i.əʳ US -i.ɚ **-iest** -i.ɪst, -əst
Zaragoza ˌsær.ə'gɒs.ə *as if Spanish:* ˌθær.ə'gɒθ.ə US ˌzær.ə'goʊ.zə, ˌzer-
Zarathustra ˌzær.ə'θuː.strə, ˌzɑː.rə'- US ˌzer.ə'-, ˌzær-
zareba zə'riː.bə **-s** -z
Zaria 'zɑː.ri.ə US 'zɑːr.i-
Zarqa 'zɑː.kə US 'zɑːr-
Zatopek 'zæt.ə.pek US 'zæţ-
zeal ziːl
Zealand 'ziː.lənd **-er/s** -əʳ/z US -ɚ/z
zealot 'zel.ət **-s** -s **-ry** -ri
zealous 'zel.əs **-ly** -li **-ness** -nəs, -nɪs
Zebedee 'zeb.ɪ.diː, '-ə- US '-ə-
zebra 'zeb.rə, 'ziː.brə US 'ziː.brə **-s** -z ˌ**zebra 'crossing**
zebu 'ziː.buː, -bjuː US -bjuː, -buː **-s** -z
Zebulon, Zebulun 'zeb.jʊ.lən; zeb'juː-, zə'bjuː- US 'zeb.jʊ-, -lɑːn
Zechariah ˌzek.ə'raɪ.ə
zed zed **-s** -z
Zedekiah ˌzed.ɪ'kaɪ.ə, -ə'- US -ə'-
Zeebrugge ziː'brʊg.ə, zeɪ-, '--- US 'ziː.brʊg-
Zeeland 'ziː.lənd, 'zeɪ- US 'ziː-
Zeffirelli ˌzef.ə'rel.i, -ɪ'-
Zeiss zaɪs *as German:* tsaɪs **-es** -ɪz
zeitgeist 'tsaɪt.gaɪst, 'zaɪt-
Zelazny zel'æz.ni US zə'lɑːz.ni
Zelda 'zel.də
Zeller 'zel.əʳ US -ɚ
Zelotes ziː'ləʊ.tiːz, zɪ-, zə- US -'loʊ-
zemindar 'zem.ɪn.dɑːʳ US -dɑːr; zə'miːn- **-s** -z
zemstvo 'zemst.vəʊ US -voʊ **-s** -z
Zen zen
Zena 'ziː.nə
zenana zen'ɑː.nə, zɪ'nɑː- US zen'ɑː- **-s** -z
Zenawi zen'ɑː.wi
Zend zend
Zenda 'zen.də
zenica 'zen.ɪ.kə, 'zen.ɪt.sə
zenith 'zen.ɪθ US 'ziː.nɪθ **-s** -s
Zeno 'ziː.nəʊ US -noʊ
Zenobia zɪ'nəʊ.bi.ə, zen'əʊ- US zə'noʊ-
Zenocrate 'zen.əʊ.kræt US -oʊ-
Zepa 'ʒep.ə
Zephaniah ˌzef.ə'naɪ.ə
zephyr (Z) 'zef.əʳ US -ɚ **-s** -z
Zephyrus 'zef.ᵊr.əs
zeppelin (Z) 'zep.ᵊl.ɪn US '-lɪn, 'zep.ə.lɪn **-s** -z
Zermatt 'zɜː.mæt US 'zɜːr.mɑːt, -'-
zero 'zɪə.rəʊ US 'zɪr.oʊ, 'ziː.roʊ **-(e)s** -z **'zero ˌhour**
Zerubbabel zɪ'rʌb.ə.bᵊl, zə-; *in Jewish usage also:* zɪ'ruːˌbɑː-, zə- US zə'rʌb.ə-
zest zest **-ful/ly** fᵊl/i, fʊl/i
zest|y 'zes.t|i **-ier** -i.əʳ US -i.ɚ **-iest** -i.ɪst, -i.əst
zeta 'ziː.tə US 'zeɪ.ţə, 'ziː- **-s** -z
Zetland 'zet.lənd
zeugma 'zjuːg.mə, 'zuːg- US 'zuːg- **-s** -z
Zeus zjuːs US zuːs
Zhirinovsky ˌʒɪr.ɪ'nɒf.ski US -'nɑːf-
Zhivago ʒɪ'vɑː.gəʊ, ʒə- US -goʊ
Zhou ʒuː US dʒoʊ
ziggurat 'zɪg.ə.ræt, '-ʊ- **-s** -s
zigzag 'zɪg.zæg **-s** -z **-ging** -ɪŋ **-ged** -d
zilch zɪltʃ
zillion 'zɪl.jən, -i.ən US '-jən **-s** -z
Zimbabwe zɪm'bɑːb.weɪ, -'bæb-, -wi US -'bɑːb-
Zimbabwean zɪm'bɑːb.wi.ən, -'bæb-, -weɪ- US -'bɑːb- **-s** -z
Zimmer® 'zɪm.əʳ US -ɚ **'Zimmer ˌframe**
Zimmerman 'zɪm.ə.mən US '-ɚ-
zinc zɪŋk **-s** -s **-king** -ɪŋ **-ked** -t **-ky** -i
zinco 'zɪŋ.kəʊ US -koʊ **-s** -z
zincograph 'zɪŋ.kəʊ.grɑːf, -græf US -koʊ.græf, -kə- **-s** -s
zinfandel (Z) 'zɪn.fən.del, ˌ--'- US 'zɪn.fən.del
zing zɪŋ **-s** -z **-ing** -ɪŋ **-ed** -d **-y** -i
zingar|o (Z) 'zɪŋ.gᵊr|.əʊ US -gə.r|oʊ **-i** -iː
zinnia 'zɪn.i.ə **-s** -z
Zion za.ən **-ism** -ɪ.zᵊm **-ist/s** -ɪst/s
zip zɪp **-s** -s **-ping** -ɪŋ **-ped** -t **'zip ˌcode**; ˌ**zip 'fastener**
zipper 'zɪp.əʳ US -ɚ **-s** -z
Zipporah zɪ'pɔː.rə, 'zɪp.ᵊr.ə US 'zɪp.ɚ.ə
zipp|y 'zɪp|.i **-ier** -i.əʳ US -i.ɚ **-iest** -i.ɪst, -i.əst
zircon 'zɜː.kɒn US 'zɜːr.kɑːn
zirconia zɜː'kəʊ.ni.ə, zə- US zɚ'koʊ-
zirconium zɜː'kəʊ.ni.əm, zə- US zɚ'koʊ-
zit zɪt **-s** -s
zither 'zɪð.əʳ, 'zɪθ- US 'zɪθ.ɚ, 'zɪð- **-s** -z
zloty 'zlɒt.i *as if Polish:* 'zwɒt- US 'zlɔː.ţi, 'zlɑː- **-s** -z
Zoar 'zəʊ.ɑːʳ, zəʊəʳ US 'zoʊ.ɑːr, zoʊɚ
zodiac 'zəʊ.di.æk US 'zoʊ-
zodiacal zəʊ'daɪ.ə.kᵊl US zoʊ-
Zoe, Zoë 'zəʊ.i US 'zoʊ-
Zog zɒg US zɔːg, zɑːg
-zoic -'zəʊ.ɪk US -'zoʊ.ɪk
Zola 'zəʊ.lə US 'zoʊ-; zoʊ'lɑː
zollverein 'tsɒl.fᵊr.aɪn, 'zɒl.vᵊr- US 'tsɔːl.fə.raɪn **-s** -z
zombie 'zɒm.bi US 'zɑːm- **-s** -z
zonal 'zəʊ.nᵊl US 'zoʊ- **-ly** -i
zon|e zəʊn US zoʊn **-es** -z **-ing** -ɪŋ **-ed** -d **-eless** -ləs, -lɪs
zonked zɒŋkt US zɑːŋkt, zɔːŋkt
zoo- zəʊ.əʊ-, zuː.əʊ-; zəʊ'ɒ-, zu'ɒ- US zoʊ.oʊ-, zuː.oʊ-, -ə-; zoʊ'ɑː-, zu'ɑː-

Note: Prefix. Normally either takes primary or secondary stress on the first syllable, e.g. **zoophyte** /'zəʊ.ə.faɪt US 'zoʊ-/, **zoomorphic** /ˌzəʊ.ə'mɔː.fɪk US ˌzoʊ.ə'mɔːr-/, or primary stress on the second syllable, e.g. **zoology** /zu'ɒl.ə.dʒi US zoʊ'ɑː.lə-/.

zoo zuː **-s** -z
zoochemi|stry ˌzəʊ.əʊ'kem.ɪ|.stri US ˌzoʊ.ə'- **-cal** -kᵊl
zoograph|er zəʊ'ɒg.rə.f|əʳ US zoʊ'ɑː.grə.f|ɚ **-ers** -əz US -ɚz **-y** -i
zooks zuːks US zuːks, zʊks
zoolite 'zəʊ.əʊ.laɪt US 'zoʊ.oʊ.laɪt, '-ə- **-s** -s
zoologic|al ˌzəʊ.əʊ'lɒdʒ.ɪ.k|ᵊl, ˌzuː.ə'- US ˌzoʊ.ə'lɑː.dʒɪ- **-ally** -ᵊl.i, -li zooˌlogical 'gardens
zoologist zu'ɒl.ə.dʒɪst, zəʊ- US zoʊ'ɑːlə-, zu- **-s** -s
zoolog|y zu'ɒl.ə.dʒ|i, zəʊ- US zoʊ'ɑː.lə-, zu- **-ist/s** -ɪst/s
zoom zuːm **-s** -z **-ing** -ɪŋ **-ed** -d **'zoom ˌlens**

zoomorphic ˌzəʊ.əˈmɔː.fɪk
 (US) ˌzoʊ.əˈmɔːr-
-zo|on -ˈzəʊ|.ɒn (US) -ˈzoʊ|.ɑːn, -ən **-a** -ə
Note: Suffix. Normally carries primary stress as shown, e.g. **protozoon** /ˌprəʊ.təʊˈzəʊ.ɒn (US) ˌproʊ.t̬oʊˈzoʊ.ɑːn/.
zoophyte ˈzəʊ.ə.faɪt (US) ˈzoʊ.ə- **-s** -s
zooplankton ˌzəʊ.əʊˈplæŋk.tən, -tɒn
 (US) ˌzoʊ.əˈplæŋk.tən **-s** -z
zoot zuːt **-s** -s **ˈzoot ˌsuit**
zoril ˈzɒr.ɪl (US) ˈzɔːr- **-s** -z
Zoroaster ˌzɒr.əʊˈæs.təʳ, ˈzɒr.əʊ.æs-
 (US) ˈzɔːr.oʊ.æs.tɚ
Zoroastrian ˌzɒr.əʊˈæs.tri.ən
 (US) ˌzɔːr.oʊˈ- **-s** -z **-ism** -ɪ.zᵊm
Zorro ˈzɒr.əʊ (US) ˈzɔːr.oʊ
zouave (**Z**) zuˈɑːv; zwɑːv; ˈzuː.ɑːv
 (US) zuˈɑːv, zwɑːv **-s** -z
Zouch(e) zuːʃ
zounds zuːndz, zaʊndz (US) zaʊndz
Zsa Zsa ˈʒɑː.ʒɑː
zucchini zʊˈkiː.ni (US) zuː- **-s** -z
Zugspitze ˈzʊg.ʃpɪt.sə *as if German:* ˈtsuːk-
Zuider Zee ˌzaɪ.dəˈziː, -ˈzeɪ (US) -dɚˈziː
Zuleika zuːˈleɪ.kə, zʊ-, -ˈlaɪ-
Zulu ˈzuː.luː **-s** -z
Zululand ˈzuː.luː.lænd
Zuñi, Zuni ˈzʊn.ji (US) ˈzuː.ni, -nji
zuppa inglese ˌzʊp.ɑː.ɪŋˈgleɪ.zeɪ, -zi
 (US) ˌzuː.pə.ɪnˈgleɪ.zeɪ, ˌtsuː-, -ɪŋˈ-
Zürich ˈzjʊə.rɪk, ˈzʊə- *as if German:* ˈtsjʊə- (US) ˈzʊr.ɪk
Zutphen ˈzʌt.fən
Zwelithini ˌzwel.ɪˈθiː.ni
zwieback ˈzwiː.bæk, -bɑːk
 (US) ˈzwaɪ.bæk, ˈzwiː-, ˈswiː-, ˈswaɪ-, -bɑːk **-s** -s
zygoma zaɪˈgəʊ.mə, zɪ- (US) -ˈgoʊ- **-ta** -tə (US) -t̬ə
zygote ˈzaɪ.gəʊt, ˈzɪg.əʊt
 (US) ˈzaɪ.goʊt, ˈzɪg.oʊt **-s** -s
zymosis zaɪˈməʊ.sɪs, zɪ- (US) -ˈmoʊ-
zymotic zaɪˈmɒt.ɪk, zɪ- (US) -ˈmɑː.t̬ɪk
zzz zː
Note: This is rarely pronounced, but is used in comic strips to represent sleeping, or, more specifically, snoring. The suggested pronunciation derives from the spelling.